HISTORICAL
BIOGRAPHICAL
DICTIONARIES
MASTER INDEX

The Gale Biographical Index Series

HISTORICAL BIOGRAPHICAL DICTIONARIES MASTER INDEX

A consolidated index to biographical information concerning historical personages in over 35 of the principal retrospective biographical dictionaries.

Edited by Barbara McNeil and Miranda C. Herbert

FIRST EDITION

Gale Biographical Index Series
Number 7

Gale Research Company • Book Tower • Detroit, Michigan
1980

Editors: Barbara McNeil, Miranda C. Herbert

Editorial Associates: Patricia Faletti, John Krol

Editorial Assistants: Doris Goulart, Ann Blake, Dorothy Cotter,
Terry Lafaro, Sue Lynch, Paula Morgan, Barbara Ann Mulholland,
Mildred Piccini, Jean Portfolio, Joyce Stone, Sharon Wagner, Barbara Zippo

Proofreaders: Barbara Brandenburg, Toni Grow, Kathleen Mailloux

Editorial Consultant: Dennis LaBeau

Production Director: Michaeline Nowinski

Production Assistants: Eutropia Henderson, Nancy Nagy

Cover Design: Art Chartow

Computerized photocompostion by
Computer Composition Corporation,
Madison Heights, Michigan

Library of Congress Cataloging in Publication Data

Main entry under title:

Historical biographical dictionaries master index.

(Gale biographical index series ; no. 7)
Bibliography: p. vii
1. United States--Biography--Indexes. I. McNeil,
Barbara. II. Herbert, Miranda C.
Z5305.U5H57 [CT215] 920'.073'016   80-10719
ISBN 0-8103-1089-9

Introduction

Historical Biographical Dictionaries Master Index enables the user to locate easily citations to biographical information from more than 304,000 entries in over 35 historical sources. In function, but not in content, it is a counterpart to Gale's *Biographical Dictionaries Master Index* (1976) and *Supplement* (1979), *Author Biographies Master Index* (1978), *Theatre, Film and Television Biographies Master Index* (1979), and other titles in the Gale Biographical Index Series.

HBDMI informs the user which edition of which publication to consult, or almost as helpful, it reveals that there is no listing for a given individual in the publications indexed. In cases where *HBDMI* has multiple listings for the same person, the user is able to choose the source which is most convenient for him, or to locate multiple sketches to compare.

The emphasis of the works indexed—and hence of *HBDMI*—is on deceased persons who were prominent in the United States. However, some general sources have been included, so not all persons cited are deceased nor are they all from the United States. All names in an indexed work are listed in *HBDMI*, whether Americans or not, whether living or deceased. Thus, there is no need to consult the sources themselves if the desired name is not shown in *HBDMI*.

How to Read a Citation

Each citation gives the person's name, followed by the years of birth and/or death. If there is no year of birth, the death date is preceded by a lower case *d*. The codes for the books indexed follow the dates:

> **Cook**, Mehitabel Jones 1809- *New YHSD*
> **Hamilton**, Frank Hastings 1813-1886 *ApCAB, DcAmB, NatCAB 9,*
> *TwCBDA, WhAm H*
> **Tallerday**, Howard G d1946 WhAm 2

A list of the works indexed in *HBDMI* and the codes used to refer to them is printed on the endsheets as well as in the *Bibliographic Key* which follows this introduction.

HBDMI is a Unique Reference Work

HBDMI is the first attempt in recent times to offer an index to some of the standard sources relating to historical personages. Each source indexed includes at least a moderate amount of biographical, critical or career-related information on these persons, and most include a substantial amount.

The books indexed in *HBDMI* are readily available and widely held in most reference collections. Included are general works on outstanding Americans: *Appleton's Cyclopaedia of American Biography, The National Cyclopaedia of American Biography, The Dictionary of American Biography,* and *Who was Who in America*. Also included are sources on specific occupations and groups such as works on women: *Notable American Women, American Women (Woman of the Century);* works on scientists: *Dictionary of Scientific Biography;* works on artists: *Britannica Encyclopedia of American Art;* and works on politicians: *Biographical Directory of the American Congress*. Several of the works indexed have a universal time span: *Webster's American Biographies* and *Who's Who in Military History*.

Editorial Practices

HBDMI follows the standard alphabetizing rules used by the Library of Congress with the exception of *Mac* and *Mc*, which are interfiled alphabetically. Not all sources use this method of alphabetizing, so the user is advised to be aware that the alphabetic position of the citation in the source book may not be the same as in *HBDMI*.

Searchers should look under all possible variant listings for a name, especially in the case of names with prefixes or suffixes, Spanish names which may be listed in sources under either part of the surname, or names transliterated from non-Roman alphabets.

In a very few cases, extremely long names have been shortened slightly because of typesetting limitations.

For example: *Lafayette, Marie Jean Paul Joseph Roche Yves Gilbert du Montier, Marquis de* has been shortened to: *Lafayette, M J P Y DuMontier, Marquis De*. It is believed that such editing will not affect the usefulness of the individual entries.

To simplify the listings and to help the user, some missing names and dates have been supplied when it appeared certain that the same person was referred to by the variant citations. Years of birth and death are cited as found in the source works. If a source has indicated that the dates may not be accurate, the questionable date(s) are followed by a question mark. Thus ca. 1802 becomes 1802?, as does 1802-3. If a given individual's name or dates differ from publication to publication, citations in *HBDMI* have retained those discrepancies:

> **Adams,** Stephen d1857 *ApCAB, BiAUS*
> **Adams,** Stephen 1804-1857 *NatCAB 3, TwCBDA*
> **Adams,** Stephen 1807-1857 *BiDrAC, WhAm H, WhAmP*
>
> **Adet,** Pierre Auguste 1763-1832 *ApCAB*
> **Adet,** Pierre-Auguste 1763-1834 *DcScB*
> **Adet,** Pierre Augustus 1763-1832? *Drake*

Despite the variations in dates, it is clear that the same people are referred to in the above citations. The fact of such variations can be of importance to anyone attempting to determine biographical details about the individuals.

All cross references appearing in the source publications have been cited in *HBDMI*. In addition, the editors have included cross references when they feel the information in the publications is not sufficient to lead the user from one name to the other.

Suggestions Are Welcome

Future editions of *HBDMI* are planned. Additional sources will be added as their availability and usefulness become known. The editors welcome suggestions and comments from users.

Bibliographic Key to Publication Codes
for Use in Locating Sources

Code   ***Book Indexed***

AmBi   *American Biographies.* By Wheeler Preston. New York: Harper & Brothers Publishers, 1940. Reprinted, Detroit: Gale Research Company, 1974.

AmWom   *American Women;* a revised edition of *Woman of the Century,* fifteen hundred biographies with over 1400 portraits; a comprehensive encyclopedia of the lives and achievements of American women during the nineteenth century. Two volumes. Edited by Frances E. Willard and Mary A. Livermore. New York: Mast, Crowell & Kirkpatrick, 1897. Reprinted, Detroit: Gale Research Company, 1973.

ApCAB   *Appleton's Cyclopaedia of American Biography.* Six volumes. Edited by James Grant Wilson and John Fiske. New York: D. Appleton and Company, 1888-1889. Reprinted, Detroit: Gale Research Company, 1968.

ApCAB Sup   *Appleton's Cyclopaedia of American Biography.* Volume seven, Supplement. Edited by James Grant Wilson. New York: D. Appleton and Company, 1901. Reprinted, Detroit: Gale Research Company, 1968.

ApCAB X   *A Supplement to Appleton's Cyclopaedia of American Biography.* Six volumes. Originally published as *The Cyclopaedia of American Biography, Supplementary Edition.* Edited by L.E. Dearborn. New York: The Press Association Compilers, Inc., 1918-1931. Reprinted, Detroit: Gale Research Company, 1976.

AsBiEn   *Asimov's Biographical Encyclopedia of Science and Technology;* the lives and achievements of 1195 great scientists from ancient times to the present chronologically arranged. New revised edition. By Isaac Asimov. New York: Avon, 1976.

BiAUS   *Biographical Annals of the Civil Government of the United States, During its First Century;* from original and official sources. By Charles Lanman. Washington: James Anglim, Publisher, 1876. Reprinted, Detroit: Gale Research Company, 1976.

     An Additional Facts *section, indicated in this index by the code* Sup, *begins on page 633.*

BiCAW   *The Biographical Cyclopaedia of American Women.* Two volumes. Volume 1: Compiled under the supervision of Mabel Ward Cameron. New York: The Halvord Publishing Company, Inc., 1924. Volume 2: Compiled under the supervision of Erma Conkling Lee. New York: The Franklin W. Lee Publishing Corporation, 1925. Both volumes reprinted, Detroit: Gale Research Company, 1974.

     Use the index at the end of volume 2 to locate biographies.

BiDAmEd   *Biographical Dictionary of American Educators.* Three volumes. Edited by John F. Ohles. Westport, Connecticut: Greenwood Press, 1978.

BiDConf   *Biographical Dictionary of the Confederacy.* By John L. Wakelyn. Westport, Connecticut: Greenwood Press, 1977.

BiDrAC   *Biographical Directory of the American Congress 1774-1971;* the Continental Congress (September 5, 1774, to October 21, 1788) and the Congress of the United States (From the first through the ninety-first Congress March 4,

1789, to January 3, 1971, inclusive). Washington: United States Government Printing Office, 1971.

Biographies begin page 487.

BiDrUSE
Ref
E
176
.B575

Biographical Directory of the United States Executive Branch 1774-1971. Edited by Robert Sobel. Westport, Connecticut: Greenwood Publishing Company, 1971.

BiHiMed
R
134
.T55
Main

A Biographical History of Medicine; excerpts and essays on the men and their work. By John H. Talbott, M.D. New York: Grune & Stratton, 1970.

Use the Name Index *beginning page 1193 to locate biographies.*

BnEnAmA
Ref
6505
.B73

The Britannica Encyclopedia of American Art. Chicago: Encyclopaedia Britannica Educational Corporation, 1973.

DcAmB
Ref
E
176
.D56

Dictionary of American Biography. Edited under the auspices of the American Council of Learned Societies. 20 volumes (A-Z). New York: Charles Scribner's Sons, 1928-1936.

DcAmB S1	Supplement 1, 1944.
DcAmB S2	Supplement 2, 1958.
DcAmB S3	Supplement 3, 1973.
DcAmB S4	Supplement 4, 1974.
DcAmB S5	Supplement 5, 1977.

DcAmLiB
720
.B5
Lib.Sci.

Dictionary of American Library Biography. Edited by Bohdan S. Wynar. Littleton, Colorado: Libraries Unlimited, Inc., 1978.

DcAmReB
BL
72
.B68
Ref
also
MVC

Dictionary of American Religious Biography. By Henry Warner Bowden. Westport, Connecticut: Greenwood Press, 1977.

DcScB
Ref.
Q
141
.D5

Dictionary of Scientific Biography. 14 volumes. Edited by Charles Coulston Gillispie. New York: Charles Scribner's Sons, 1970-1976.

DcScB Sup	Volume 15, Supplement 1, 1978.

Drake

Drake, Francis S. *Dictionary of American Biography including Men of the Time;* containing nearly ten thousand notices of persons of both sexes, of native and foreign birth, who have been remarkable, or prominently connected with the arts, sciences, literature, politics, or history, of the American continent. Giving also the pronunciation of many of the foreign and peculiar American names, a key to the assumed names of writers, and a Supplement. Boston: James R. Osgood and Company, 1872. Reprinted, Detroit: Gale Research Company, 1974.

The Supplement, *indicated in this index by the code* Sup, *begins on page 1015.*

EncAAH
Ref
S
441
.S36

Encyclopedia of American Agricultural History. By Edward L. Schapsmeier and Frederick H. Schapsmeier. Westport, Connecticut: Greenwood Press, 1975.

EncAB
Ref
CT
213
.G37

Encyclopedia of American Biography. Edited by John A. Garraty. New York: Harper & Row, Publishers, 1974.

IlBEAAW
N
6214.5
U6
S25
Main

The Illustrated Biographical Encyclopedia of Artists of the American West. By Peggy and Harold Samuels. Garden City: Doubleday & Company, Inc., 1976.

McGEWB
CT
103
.M27
Main

The McGraw-Hill Encyclopedia of World Biography; an international reference work in twelve volumes including an index. New York: McGraw-Hill Book Company, 1973.

NatCAB

The National Cyclopaedia of American Biography. 57 volumes. New York and Clifton, New Jersey: James T. White & Company, 1892-1977. Volumes 1-50 reprinted, Ann Arbor: University Microfilms, 1967-1971.

Volume number follows source book code. Use the index in back of each volume to locate biographies.

NewYHSD   *The New-York Historical Society's Dictionary of Artists in America 1564-1860.* By George C. Groce and David H. Wallace. New Haven and London: Yale University Press, 1957.

NotAW   *Notable American Women 1607-1950;* a biographical dictionary. Three volumes. Edited by Edward T. James. Cambridge, Massachusetts: The Belknap Press of Harvard University Press, 1971.

REnAW   *The Reader's Encyclopedia of the American West.* Edited by Howard R. Lamar. New York: Thomas Y. Crowell Company, 1977.

TwCBDA   *The Twentieth Century Biographical Dictionary of Notable Americans;* brief biographies of authors, administrators, clergymen, commanders, editors, engineers, jurists, merchants, officials, philanthropists, scientists, statesmen, and others who are making American history. Ten volumes. Edited by Rossiter Johnson. Boston: The Biographical Society, 1904. Reprinted, Detroit: Gale Research Company, 1968.

WebAB   *Webster's American Biographies.* Edited by Charles Van Doren. Springfield, Massachusetts: G. & C. Merriam Company, 1974.

WebAMB   *Webster's American Military Biographies.* Springfield, Massachusetts: G. & C. Merriam Company, 1978.

WhAm H   *Who was Who in America, Historical Volume, 1607-1896.* Revised edition, 1967. Chicago: Marquis Who's Who, Incorporated, 1967.

   The Addendum, *indicated in this index by the code* A, *begins on page 677.*

WhAm 1   *Who was Who in America, Volume I, 1897-1942;* a component volume of Who's Who in American History. Chicago: The A.N. Marquis Company, 1943.

   The Corrigenda, *indicated in this index by the code* C, *begins on page x.*

WhAm 2   *Who was Who in America, Volume II, 1943-1950;* a companion biographical reference work to Who's Who in America. Chicago: The A.N. Marquis Company, 1963.

   The Addendum *and* Corrigenda, *indicated in this index by the codes* A *and* C *respectively, begin on pages 14 and 5.*

WhAm 3   *Who was Who in America, Volume III, 1951-1960;* a component of Who's Who in American History. Chicago: Marquis Who's Who, Inc., 1974.

   The Addendum, *indicated in this index by the code* A, *begins on page 952.*

WhAm 4   *Who was Who in America with World Notables, Volume IV, 1961-1968;* a component volume of Who's Who in American History. Chicago: Marquis Who's Who, Inc., 1968.

   The Addendum, *indicated in this index by the code* A, *begins on page 1049.*

WhAm 5   *Who was Who in America with World Notables, Volume V, 1969-1973.* Chicago: Marquis Who's Who, Inc., 1973.

WhAm 6   *Who was Who in America with World Notables, Volume VI, 1974-1976.* Chicago: Marquis Who's Who, Inc., 1976.

WhAmP   *Who was Who in American Politics;* a biographical dictionary of over 4,000 men and women who contributed to the United States political scene from colonial days up to and including the immediate past. By Don and Inez Morris. New York: Hawthorn Books, Inc., Publishers, 1974.

WhWW-II   *Who was Who in World War II.* Edited by John Keegan. London: Arms and Armour Press, 1978.

WhoColR   *Who's Who of the Colored Race;* a general biographical dictionary of men and women of African descent. Volume 1, 1915. Edited by Frank Lincoln Mather. Chicago, 1915. Reprinted, Detroit: Gale Research Company, 1976.

   The Addenda, *indicated in this index by the code* A, *begins on page xxvi.*

WhoMilH   *Who's Who in Military History;* from 1453 to the present day. By John Keegan and Andrew Wheatcroft. New York: William Morrow & Co. Inc., 1976.

WomWWA
14   *Woman's Who's Who of America;* a biographical dictionary of contemporary women of the United States and Canada. 1914-1915. Edited by John William Leonard. New York: The American Commonwealth Company, 1914. Reprinted, Detroit: Gale Research Company, 1976.

The Addenda and Corrections *and* Deaths during Printing *sections, indicated in this index by the code* a, *begin on page 29.*

A

Aalders, Catherine Ann Olding Hebb 1931-1972 *WhAm 6*
Aalto, Hugo Alvar Henrik 1898- *McGEWB*
Aamand *NewYHSD*
Aamond *NewYHSD*
Aandahl, Fred George 1897-1966 *BiDrAC, WhAm 4, WhAmP*
Aaron, Charles Dettie 1866-1906 *WhAm 5, WhAm 6*
Aaron, Ely Mayer 1896-1975 *WhAm 6*
Aaron, Henry Louis 1934- *WebAB*
Aaron, Herman 1862-1939 *NatCAB 30*
Aaron, Marcus 1869-1954 *NatCAB 46, WhAm 3*
Aaron, Samuel 1800-1865 *ApCAB*
Aasgaard, Johan Arnd 1876- *WhAm 6*
Abad, Diego Jose 1727-1779 *ApCAB*
Abad Y Queipo, Manuel 1775?-1824? *ApCAB*
Abadiano, Diego Jose 1727-1779 *ApCAB*
Abadie, Eugene H 1814?-1874 *ApCAB*
Abailard, Pierre 1079-1142 *DcScB*
Abano, Pietro D' 1257-1315? *DcScB*
Abarbanell, Jacob Ralph 1852-1922 *WhAm 1*
Abarbanell, Lina 1880- *WhAm 6*
Abascal, Jose Fernando 1743-1821 *ApCAB, Drake*
Abasola, Mariano 1780-1811 *Drake*
Abasolo, Mariano 1780?-1811 *ApCAB*
Abba Arika 175?-247? *McGEWB*
Abbadie, Antoine Thomson D' 1810- *ApCAB*
Abbadie, D' 1710?-1765 *ApCAB*
Abbadie, M D' d1765 *Drake*
Abbas I 1571-1629 *McGEWB, WhoMilH*
Abbas, Ferhat 1899- *McGEWB*
Abbas Ibn Firnas d274 *DcScB*
Abbas Ibn Said Al-Jawhari, Al- *DcScB*
Abbate, Paolo *ApCAB X*
Abbatt, Agnes Dean 1847-1917 *AmWom, NatCAB 8, WhAm 1, WomWWA 14*
Abbatt, William 1851-1935 *WhAm 1*
Abbe, Adelaide Eaton 1860- *WomWWA 14*
Abbe, Charles Minott 1898-1963 *WhAm 4*
Abbe, Cleveland 1838-1916 *AmBi, ApCAB, ApCAB X, AsBiEn, DcAmB, DcScB, NatCAB 8, TwCBDA, WebAB, WhAm 1*
Abbe, Cleveland, Jr. 1872-1934 *ApCAB X, NatCAB 26, TwCBDA, WhAm 1*
Abbe, Elisabeth Frances 1866- *WomWWA 14*
Abbe, Ernst 1840-1905 *DcScB*
Abbe, Robert 1851-1928 *ApCAB X, NatCAB 21, WhAm 1*
Abbe, Truman 1873-1955 *ApCAB X, NatCAB 44, WhAm 4*
Abbell, Maxwell 1902-1957 *NatCAB 43, WhAm 3*
Abbett, Leon 1836-1894 *ApCAB Sup, ApCAB X, DcAmB, NatCAB 1, TwCBDA, WhAm H, WhAmP*
Abbett, Merle J 1885-1956 *WhAm 3*
Abbeville, Claude D' d1632 *ApCAB, Drake*
Abbey, Edward Norman 1882- *ApCAB X*

Abbey, Edwin Austin 1852-1911 *AmBi, ApCAB, ApCAB X, BnEnAmA, DcAmB, NatCAB 15, TwCBDA, WebAB, WhAm 1*
Abbey, Glenn Allan 1898-1962 *WhAm 4*
Abbey, Henry 1842-1911 *ApCAB, DcAmB, NatCAB 7, TwCBDA, WhAm 1*
Abbey, Henry Eugene 1846-1896 *ApCAB X, DcAmB, TwCBDA, WhAm H*
Abbey, Henry Eugene 1848-1896 *NatCAB 7*
Abbey, Mary Gertrude Mead *WomWWA 14*
Abbey, Richard 1805- *ApCAB*
Abbiati, F Alexander 1904-1952 *NatCAB 45, WhAm 3*
Abbink, John 1890-1958 *WhAm 3*
Abbitt, John Willis 1886-1955 *NatCAB 42*
Abbitt, Watkins Moorman 1908- *BiDrAC*
Abbondandolo, Renzo 1900-1970 *NatCAB 57*
Abbot, Abiel 1765-1859 *ApCAB, Drake*
Abbot, Abiel 1770-1828 *ApCAB, Drake, NatCAB 7, WhAm H*
Abbot, Abiel Jacob 1850-1921 *NatCAB 18*
Abbot, Alexander Crever 1860- *TwCBDA*
Abbot, Alice Balch 1867- *WhAm 4, WomWWA 14*
Abbot, Amos 1786-1868 *TwCBDA*
Abbot, Benjamin 1762-1849 *ApCAB, BiDAmEd, DcAmB, Drake, NatCAB 10, WhAm H*
Abbot, Charles Greeley 1872-1973 *ApCAB X, WhAm 6*
Abbot, Charles Wheaton 1829-1907 *WhAm 1*
Abbot, Charles Wheaton 1860-1923 *NatCAB 20*
Abbot, E Stanley 1863-1957 *NatCAB 47*
Abbot, Edwin Hale 1834-1927 *WhAm 1*
Abbot, Etheldred *WomWWA 14*
Abbot, Everett Vergnies 1862-1925 *NatCAB 20, WhAm 2A*
Abbot, Ezra 1819-1884 *AmBi, ApCAB, DcAmB, DcAmLiB, NatCAB 4, TwCBDA, WhAm H*
Abbot, Francis Ellingwood 1836-1903 *AmBi, ApCAB, DcAmB, DcAmReB, NatCAB 7, NatCAB 24, WebAB, WhAm 1*
Abbot, Frank Prentice 1853-1918 *NatCAB 18*
Abbot, Frederic Vaughan 1858-1928 *WhAm 1*
Abbot, Gorham Dummer 1807-1874 *DcAmB, NatCAB 10, WhAm H*
Abbot, Helen Munro 1877- *WomWWA 14*
Abbot, Helene Black 1883- *WomWWA 14*
Abbot, Henry Larcom 1831-1927 *ApCAB, DcAmB, NatCAB 11, TwCBDA, WebAMB*
Abbot, Henry Larcon 1821-1927 *WhAm 1*
Abbot, Hull 1702-1774 *Drake*
Abbot, Joel 1766-1826 *ApCAB, BiAUS, NatCAB 13, TwCBDA*
Abbot, Joel 1793-1855 *ApCAB, DcAmB, NatCAB 9, TwCBDA, WhAm H*
Abbot, John 1759-1843 *TwCBDA*
Abbot, John Emery 1793-1819 *Drake*

Abbot, Joseph Hale 1802-1873 *ApCAB*
Abbot, Samuel 1732-1812 *ApCAB, Drake, NatCAB 5, TwCBDA*
Abbot, Samuel 1786-1839 *ApCAB, Drake*
Abbot, Stephen 1878-1961 *NatCAB 49*
Abbot, Theophilus Capen 1826-1892 *NatCAB 9*
Abbot, Willis John 1863-1934 *DcAmB S1, NatCAB 11, NatCAB 32, TwCBDA, WhAm 1*
Abbott, Aimee 1876- *WomWWA 14*
Abbott, Alexander Crever 1860-1935 *WhAm 1*
Abbott, Allan 1876-1956 *NatCAB 45, WhAm 3*
Abbott, Amos 1786-1868 *BiAUS, BiDrAC, WhAm H*
Abbott, Arletta Maria *WomWWA 14*
Abbott, Arthur James 1885-1963 *WhAm 4*
Abbott, Arthur Preston 1861-1934 *NatCAB 27*
Abbott, Arthur Vaughan 1854-1906 *WhAm 1*
Abbott, Augustus Levi 1858-1934 *WhAm 1*
Abbott, Austin 1831-1896 *AmBi, ApCAB, DcAmB, Drake, NatCAB 2, TwCBDA, WhAm H*
Abbott, Benjamin 1732-1796 *ApCAB, DcAmB, WhAm H*
Abbott, Benjamin Vaughan 1830-1890 *AmBi, ApCAB, DcAmB, Drake, NatCAB 5, TwCBDA, WhAm H*
Abbott, Berenice 1898- *BnEnAmA*
Abbott, Bud 1898-1974 *WhAm 6*
Abbott, Byrdine Akers 1866-1936 *NatCAB 30, WhAm 1*
Abbott, Charles Carroll 1870-1943 *NatCAB 33*
Abbott, Charles Conrad 1843-1919 *AmBi, ApCAB, DcAmB, NatCAB 10, TwCBDA, WhAm 1*
Abbott, Charles David 1900-1961 *WhAm 4*
Abbott, Charles Edward, Jr. 1898-1962 *NatCAB 50*
Abbott, Charles Frederick 1876-1933 *ApCAB X, NatCAB 24, WhAm 1*
Abbott, Christopher J 1889-1954 *WhAm 3*
Abbott, Clifton Smith 1871-1945 *NatCAB 34*
Abbott, Clinton Gilbert 1881-1946 *WhAm 2A*
Abbott, Cornelius James 1889-1971 *NatCAB 56*
Abbott, Cornelius Webster 1855-1932 *NatCAB 24*
Abbott, David 1765-1822 *NatCAB 6, TwCBDA*
Abbott, Donald Putnam 1884-1936 *NatCAB 48*
Abbott, E Farrington 1882-1952 *NatCAB 40*
Abbott, Ebenezer Augustus, Jr. 1890- *WhoColR*
Abbott, Edith 1876-1957 *WhAm 3, WomWWA 14*
Abbott, Edville Gerhardt 1871-1938 *NatCAB 17, WhAm 1*
Abbott, Edward 1841-1908 *ApCAB, DcAmB, NatCAB 8, TwCBDA, WhAm 1*
Abbott, Edward Farrington 1882-1952 *WhAm 3*
Abbott, Edward Prince d1967 *WhAm 4*
Abbott, Edwin Milton 1877-1940 *NatCAB 45,*

WhAm 1

Abbott, Elizabeth M Griffin *WomWWA 14*

Abbott, Elizabeth Robinson 1852- *AmWom*

Abbott, Emma 1850-1891 *AmBi, AmWom, ApCAB Sup, ApCAB X, DcAmB, NotAW, TwCBDA, WhAm H*

Abbott, Ernest Hamlin 1870-1931 *WhAm 1*

Abbott, Frances Matilda 1857-1939 *WhAm 1, WomWWA 14*

Abbott, Frank 1836-1897 *DcAmB, NatCAB 2, WhAm H*

Abbott, Frank Danford 1853-1944 *WhAm 2A*

Abbott, Frank Frost 1860-1924 *AmBi, DcAmB, NatCAB 19, WhAm 1*

Abbott, Frank Wayland 1841-1901 *NatCAB 21*

Abbott, Fred Hull 1866- *WhAm 4*

Abbott, Frederick H 1872-1932 *WhAm 1*

Abbott, Frederick Wallace 1861-1919 *NatCAB 18, WhAm 1*

Abbott, Freeland Knight 1919-1971 *WhAm 5*

Abbott, Gardner 1878-1948 *NatCAB 46*

Abbott, George Alonzo 1874- *WhAm 5*

Abbott, George Birch 1850-1908 *WhAm 1*

Abbott, George Kenneth 1890-1943 *NatCAB 35*

Abbott, Gordon 1863-1937 *NatCAB 28, WhAm 1*

Abbott, Gorham Dummer 1807-1874 *ApCAB, BiDAmEd, TwCBDA*

Abbott, Grace 1878-1939 *ApCAB X, DcAmB S2, EncAB, NatCAB 29, NotAW, WebAB, WhAm 1, WhAmP, WomWWA 14*

Abbott, Helen Griswold 1859- *WomWWA 14*

Abbott, Henry Pryor Almon 1881-1945 *WhAm 2*

Abbott, Herbert Vaughan 1865-1929 *NatCAB 34, WhAm 1*

Abbott, Horace 1806-1887 *ApCAB, DcAmB, WhAm H*

Abbott, Horatio Johnson 1876-1936 *WhAm 1*

Abbott, Howard Strickland 1863-1944 *ApCAB X, NatCAB 33, WhAm 2*

Abbott, Howard Strickland 1864-1944 *NatCAB 16*

Abbott, Inez Louise 1869- *WomWWA 14*

Abbott, Ira Anson 1845-1921 *NatCAB 18, WhAm 1*

Abbott, Jacob d1847 *Drake*

Abbott, Jacob 1803-1879 *AmBi, ApCAB, BiDAmEd, DcAmB, Drake, NatCAB 6, TwCBDA, WhAm H*

Abbott, James Francis 1876-1926 *WhAm 1*

Abbott, Jane Drake 1881- *WhAm 6*

Abbott, Jo 1840-1908 *BiDrAC, TwCBDA, WhAm 1*

Abbott, Joel 1776-1826 *BiDrAC, WhAm H*

Abbott, John *ApCAB, Drake*

Abbott, John 1869-1943 *NatCAB 32*

Abbott, John Blackler 1883-1963 *NatCAB 50*

Abbott, John C 1825- *BiAUS*

Abbott, John Edward 1845- *TwCBDA*

Abbott, John Hammill 1848- *TwCBDA*

Abbott, John Jay 1871-1942 *WhAm 2*

Abbott, John Joseph Caldwell 1811- *ApCAB*

Abbott, John Stephens Cabot 1805-1877 *ApCAB, NatCAB 6, TwCBDA*

Abbott, John Stevens Cabot 1805-1877 *AmBi, DcAmB, Drake, WhAm H*

Abbott, John True 1850- *NatCAB 13*

Abbott, Joseph Carter 1825-1881 *BiDrAC, DcAmB, WhAmP*

Abbott, Joseph Carter 1825-1882 *ApCAB, NatCAB 5, TwCBDA, WhAm H*

Abbott, Joseph Florence 1888-1961 *WhAm 4*

Abbott, Josiah Gardner 1814-1891 *BiDrAC, NatCAB 8, NatCAB 29, TwCBDA, WhAm H*

Abbott, Josiah Gardner 1815-1891 *ApCAB Sup*

Abbott, Keene d1941 *WhAm 2A*

Abbott, Lawrence Fraser 1859-1933 *WhAm 1*

Abbott, Leon Martin 1867-1932 *WhAm 1*

Abbott, Leonard Dalton 1878-1953 *WhAm 3*

Abbott, Luther Jewett 1871-1914 *WhAm 1*

Abbott, Lyman 1835-1922 *AmBi, ApCAB, DcAmB, DcAmReB, Drake, McGEWB, NatCAB 1, TwCBDA, WebAB, WhAm 1, WhAmP*

Abbott, Mabel Avery *WomWWA 14*

Abbott, Mabelle Foster 1888- *WomWWA 14*

Abbott, Mary Perkins 1857-1904 *WhAm 1*

Abbott, Mather Almon 1874-1934 *NatCAB 24, WhAm 1*

Abbott, Nathan 1854-1941 *WhAm 1*

Abbott, Nehemiah 1804-1877 *BiDrAC, WhAm H*

Abbott, Nehemiah 1806-1877 *BiAUS*

Abbott, Othman Ali 1842- *NatCAB 17*

Abbott, Paul 1898-1971 *WhAm 5*

Abbott, Robert Duane 1892-1954 *NatCAB 43*

Abbott, Robert Osborne 1824-1867 *ApCAB, TwCBDA*

Abbott, Robert Sengstacke 1868-1940 *DcAmB S2, WebAB*

Abbott, Robert Sengstacke 1870-1940 *WhAm 2*

Abbott, Russell Bigelow 1823-1917 *NatCAB 29, TwCBDA, WhAm 4*

Abbott, Samuel Appleton Brown 1846-1931 *TwCBDA*

Abbott, Samuel Appleton Browne 1846-1931 *NatCAB 32, WhAm 1*

Abbott, Samuel Warren 1837-1904 *DcAmB, NatCAB 20, TwCBDA, WhAm 1*

Abbott, Theodore Jacob 1872-1951 *NatCAB 39, WhAm 3*

Abbott, W Herbert 1866-1928 *WhAm 1*

Abbott, W Lewis 1889-1949 *WhAm 2*

Abbott, Waldo Lovejoy 1836-1926 *ApCAB X*

Abbott, Wallace Calvin 1857-1921 *NatCAB 24, WhAm 1*

Abbott, Walter Russell 1886-1941 *NatCAB 30*

Abbott, Wilbur Cortez 1869-1947 *WhAm 2A*

Abbott, William *WhAm H*

Abbott, William Hawkins 1819-1901 *DcAmB, WhAm H*

Abbott, William Lamont 1861- *WhAm 5*

Abbott, William Louis 1860-1936 *NatCAB 27*

Abbott, William Martin 1872-1941 *WhAm 1, WhAm 2*

Abbott, William Rufus 1869-1950 *NatCAB 17, WhAm 2A*

Abbott, William Tabor 1868-1922 *NatCAB 14, WhAm 1*

Abbott, Winifred Buck 1872- *WomWWA 14*

Abbott, Yarnall 1870-1938 *NatCAB 38*

Abboud, Ibrahim 1900- *McGEWB*

Abd Al-Malik 646-705 *McGEWB*

Abd Al-Mumin 1094?-1163 *McGEWB*

Abd Al-Rahman I 731-788 *McGEWB*

Abd Al-Rahman III 891-961 *McGEWB*

Abd El-Kader 1807-1883 *WhoMilH*

Abd El-Kadir 1807-1883 *McGEWB*

Abd El-Krim, Mahommed Ibn 1882-1963 *WhoMilH*

Abd El-Krim El-Khatabi, Mohamed Ben 1882?-1963 *McGEWB*

Abduh Ibn Hasan Khayr Allah, Muhammad 1849-1905 *McGEWB*

Abdu'l-Baha 1844-1921 *DcAmReB*

Abdul-Hamid II 1842-1918 *McGEWB*

Abdul-Huda, Tawfiq Pasha *WhAm 3*

Abdul-Ilah Hashimi 1913-1958 *WhAm 3*

Abdul Rahman, Prince Tuanka d1960 *WhAm 3A*

Abdullah, Achmed 1881-1945 *WhAm 2*

Abdullah, Ibn Al Hussein 1882-1951 *WhAm 3*

Abdullah Ibn Husein 1882-1951 *McGEWB*

Abdullah Ibn Yasin d1059 *McGEWB*

Abdy, Rowena Meeks 1887-1945 *IIBEAAW*

Abeel, Albert Jay 1859-1928 *NatCAB 21*

Abeel, David d1840 *Drake*

Abeel, David 1804-1846 *ApCAB, DcAmB, Drake, TwCBDA, WhAm H*

Abeel, Essie O 1887-1968 *WhAm 5*

Abeel, George 1839- *NatCAB 14*

Abeel, Gustavus 1801-1887 *TwCBDA*

Abeel, John Nelson 1769-1812 *Drake*

Abegg, Carl Julius 1891-1973 *WhAm 6*

Abegg, Richard 1869-1910 *AsBiEn*

Abel, Annie Heloise 1873-1947 *NotAW, WomWWA 14*

Abel, Annie Heloise *see also* Abel-Henderson, Annie Heloise

Abel, Frederic Laurence 1857- *WhAm 4*

Abel, Sir Frederick Augustus 1827-1902 *AsBiEn*

Abel, Hazel Hempel 1888-1966 *BiDrAC*

Abel, Henry C *NewYHSD*

Abel, John A 1886-1955 *WhAm 3*

Abel, John Jacob 1857-1938 *AmBi, DcAmB S2, DcScB, NatCAB 28, WhAm 1*

Abel, Mary Hinman 1850- *WomWWA 14*

Abel, Niels Henrik 1802-1829 *AsBiEn, DcScB*

Abel, Othenio 1875-1946 *DcScB*

Abel-Henderson, Annie Heloise 1873-1947 *DcAmB S4*

Abel-Henderson, Annie Heloise *see also* Abel, Annie Heloise

Abelard, Peter 1079-1142 *DcScB, McGEWB*

Abele, Homer E 1916- *BiDrAC*

Abeles, Edward S 1869-1919 *WhAm 1*

Abeles, Julian Theodore 1892-1973 *WhAm 5*

Abell, Arunah S 1806-1888 *NatCAB 3, TwCBDA*

Abell, Arunah Shepardson 1806-1888 *ApCAB Sup*

Abell, Arunah Shepherdson 1806-1888 *AmBi, DcAmB, NatCAB 21, WebAB, WhAm H*

Abell, Burt 1864-1947 *NatCAB 36*

Abell, Charles Shepherdson 1876-1953 *NatCAB 42*

Abell, Edwin Franklin 1840-1904 *NatCAB 21, WhAm 1*

Abell, Harry Clinton 1871-1938 *NatCAB 32, WhAm 1, WhAm 2*

Abell, Irvin 1876-1949 *NatCAB 40, WhAm 2*

Abell, Nathan Douglas 1874-1958 *NatCAB 46*

Abell, Robert Ephraim 1887-1963 *NatCAB 51*

Abell, Theodore Curtis 1891-1960 *WhAm 4*

Abell, Walter William 1872-1941 *NatCAB 30*

Abells, Harry Delmont 1872-1958 *WhAm 3*

Abelmann, Henry William 1880-1957 *NatCAB 45*

Abels, Henry 1867-1962 *NatCAB 51*

Abelson, Philip Hauge 1913- *AsBiEn*

Abenare *DcScB*

Abend, Hallett Edward 1884-1955 *WhAm 3*

Abendroth, William Henry 1895-1970 *WhAm 5*

Abenguefith *DcScB*

Abercrombie, Daniel Webster 1853-1935 *WhAm 2*

Abercrombie, David Thomas *ApCAB X*

Abercrombie, Fred Clapp 1882-1945 *NatCAB 35*

Abercrombie, James 1706-1781 *ApCAB, Drake, NatCAB 1*

Abercrombie, James 1732-1775 *Drake, NatCAB 1*

Abercrombie, James 1758-1841 *ApCAB, Drake*

Abercrombie, James 1795-1861 *BiAUS, BiDrAC, WhAm H*

Abercrombie, John Joseph 1802-1877 *ApCAB, Drake, TwCBDA*

Abercrombie, John William 1866-1940 *BiDAmEd, BiDrAC, NatCAB 12, WhAm 1*

Abercrombie, Richard Mason 1822-1884 *TwCBDA*

Abercrombie, Thomas Franklin 1879- *WhAm 6*

Abercromby, James 1706-1781 *AmBi, DcAmB, WhAm H*

Abercromby, Sir Ralph 1734-1801 *WhoMilH*

Abercromby, Sir Robert 1740-1827 *ApCAB, Drake, WhoMilH*

Aberdeen, George H Gordon, Earl Of 1784-1860 *McGEWB*

Aberdeen, Sir John Campbell Hamilton G 1847- *ApCAB Sup*

Aberhart, William 1878-1943 *McGEWB*

Aberly, John 1867- *WhAm 5*

Abern, Oscar G 1903-1954 *WhAm 3*

Abernathy *see also* Abernethy

Abernathy, Alonzo 1836-1915 *WhAm 1*

Abernathy, Charles Laban 1872-1955 *WhAmP*

Abernathy, Chess, Jr. 1912-1969 *WhAm 5*

Abernathy, George 1807-1877 *WhAmP*

Abernathy, Harry Thomas 1865- *WhAm 5*

Abernathy, Milton Aubrey 1892-1955 *WhAm 3*

Abernethie, Thomas d1796? *NewYHSD*

Abernethy *see also* Abernathy

Abernethy, Alonzo 1836- *TwCBDA*

Abernethy, Arthur Talmage 1872- *TwCBDA, WhAm 5*

Abernethy, Charles Laban 1872-1955 *BiDrAC, WhAm 3*

Abernethy, Ernest Henry 1899-1964
NatCAB 51
Abernethy, George 1807-1877 DcAmB,
NatCAB 8, WhAm H
Abernethy, Heustis Barnett 1872-1944
NatCAB 33
Abernethy, John 1764-1831 BiHiMed
Abernethy, Robert Labon 1822-1894 TwCBDA
Abernethy, Robert Swepston 1874-1952
WhAm 3
Abernethy, Thomas Gerstle 1903- BiDrAC
Abernethy, Thomas Perkins 1890- EncAAH
Abernethy, Wilbur Murrah 1910-1975 WhAm 6
Abernethy, William Ellis 1860-1936 TwCBDA,
WhAm 3
Abernethy, William Shattuck 1872- WhAm 5
Abert, Byron D L 1841- NatCAB 1
Abert, Charles E 1855- NatCAB 1
Abert, George 1817-1890 NatCAB 1
Abert, George A 1840- NatCAB 1
Abert, James William 1820-1871 ApCAB,
IlBEAAW, NatCAB 4, NewYHSD,
WhAm H
Abert, John B 1848- NatCAB 1
Abert, John James 1788-1863 ApCAB,
DcAmB S1, NatCAB 4, WebAMB,
WhAm H
Abert, John James 1791-1863 Drake
Abert, Silvanus Thayer 1828-1903 ApCAB,
WhAm 1
Abert, William Stone 1845-1921 WhAm 1
Abert, William Stretch 1836-1867 ApCAB,
Drake, NatCAB 4
Abetti, Antonio 1846-1928 DcScB
Abeyta, Narciso Platero 1918- IlBEAAW
Abhedananda, Swami 1866- WhAm 4
Abich, Otto Hermann Wilhelm 1806-1886
DcScB
Abington, George Sexton 1861- WhoColR
Abner, David 1860- WhoColR
Abney, Joel Richard 1895-1959 NatCAB 44
Abney, John Sidney 1921-1961 NatCAB 48
Abney, Mary Lloyd Pendleton WomWWA 14
Abney, William DeWiveleslie 1843-1920 DcScB
Aboaly DcScB
Aborn, Carlton Nisbet 1874-1946 NatCAB 37
Aborn, Milton 1864-1933 DcAmB S1,
WhAm 1
Abott, Bessie Pickens d1919 WhAm 1
Aboville, Francois Marie, Comte D' 1730-1817
ApCAB
Aboville, Francois Marie, Count D' 1730-1819
Drake
Abrahall, Frances Helen WomWWA 14
Abraham DcScB
Abraham Ben Jacob DcScB
Abraham Ben Meir Ibn Ezra DcScB
Abraham Judaeus DcScB
Abraham, Abraham 1843-1911 ApCAB X,
NatCAB 25, WhAm 1
Abraham, Frances Smith WomWWA 14
Abraham, Herbert 1883-1967 WhAm 4
Abraham, Max 1875-1922 DcScB
Abraham, Solomon NewYHSD
Abraham Bar Hiyya Ha-Nasi DcScB
Abrahams, Edmund Hezekial 1881-1945
NatCAB 34
Abrahams, Henry 1855-1923 WhAm 1
Abrahams, Israel 1858-1925 McGEWB
Abrahams, John Vanneman 1867-1940
NatCAB 42
Abrahams, Joseph B 1884-1969 NatCAB 54
Abrahams, Simeon 1809-1867 ApCAB
Abrahams, Woodward 1814- NatCAB 3
Abrahamson, Laurentius G 1856-1946 WhAm 2
Abram, Phil Leslie 1896-1955 NatCAB 41
Abramowitz, William Lewis 1914-1972
NatCAB 57
Abrams, Albert 1863-1924 ApCAB X, DcAmB,
NatCAB 19, WhAm 1
Abrams, Allen 1889-1968 NatCAB 54
Abrams, Benjamin d1967 WhAm 4
Abrams, Charles 1902-1970 NatCAB 56,
WhAm 5
Abrams, Creighton Williams, Jr. 1914-1974
WebAMB, WhAm 6
Abrams, Duff Andrew 1880- WhAm 6
Abrams, Harold Joseph 1909-1963 NatCAB 50

Abrams, Hiram 1878- NatCAB 17
Abrams, Leroy 1874- WhAm 5
Abrams, Lucien 1870-1941 NatCAB 30
Abrams, Peter 1889-1963 NatCAB 48
Abrams, Stanley L 1899-1954 WhAm 3
Abrams, William Henry 1843-1926 NatCAB 21
Abramse, Eliza 1776-1865 NewYHSD
Abravanel, Isaac BenJudah 1437-1508
McGEWB
Abreu, Aleixo De 1568-1630 DcScB
Abruzzo, Matthew T 1889-1971 WhAm 5
Abt, Arthur Frederick 1898-1974 WhAm 6
Abt, Edgar Leo 1897-1948 NatCAB 36
Abt, Henry Edward 1904-1962 NatCAB 50,
WhAm 4
Abt, Isaac Arthur 1867-1955 DcAmB S5,
WhAm 3
Abu Bakr 573?-634 McGEWB
Abu Bakr M Ibn Al-H Al-Karaji, Al-Hasib
DcScB
Abu Hamid Al-Gharnati 1080-1169 DcScB
Abu Jafar Al-Khazin DcScB
Abu Kamil Shuja Ibn Aslam M Ibn Shuja
850?-930? DcScB
Abu-L-Ala Al-Maarri 973-1058 McGEWB
Abu Mashar Al-Balkhi, Jafar Ibn Muhammad
787-886 DcScB
Abu Nasr Al-Farabi DcScB
Abu Nuwas 756?-813 McGEWB
Abu Ubayd Al-Bakri DcScB
Abu'l-Barakat Al-Baghdadi, Hibat Al-Lah
1080?-1164? DcScB
Abu'l-Fida Ismail Ibn Ayyub, Imad Al-Din
1273-1331 DcScB
Abul Hassan WhoMilH
Abu'l-Rayhan M Ibn Ahmad Al-Biruni DcScB
Abu'l-Shukr, Ibn DcScB
Abu'l-Wafa Al-Buzjani, Muhammad Al-Abbas
940-997? DcScB
Acamapictli I d1389 ApCAB
Acamapixtle I d1389 Drake
Acaxitli, Francisco DeSandoval ApCAB Sup
Accau, Michel DcAmB, WhAm H
Accault, Michael ApCAB
Accault, Michel AmBi
Accum, Friedrich Christian 1769-1838 DcScB
Acer, Victor 1893-1964 WhAm 4
Achard, Franz Karl 1753-1821 DcScB
Acharius, Erik 1757-1819 DcScB
Achebe, Chinua 1930- McGEWB
Achelis, Bertha Franziska 1855- WomWWA 14
Achelis, Fritz 1843-1924 NatCAB 22
Achelis, Johnfritz 1890-1965 NatCAB 51
Acher, Howard Mossman 1889-1957
NatCAB 49, WhAm 3
Acheson, Albert Robert 1882-1941 WhAm 1
Acheson, Alexander Mahon 1858- WhAm 4
Acheson, Alexander W 1842-1934 WhAm 1
Acheson, Alexander Wilson 1809-1890
TwCBDA
Acheson, Barclay 1887-1957 WhAm 3
Acheson, Dean Gooderham 1893-1971 BiDrUSE,
EncAB, McGEWB, NatCAB 56, WebAB,
WhAm 5
Acheson, Edward Campion 1858-1934
NatCAB 26, WhAm 1
Acheson, Edward Campion 1902-1966 WhAm 4
Acheson, Edward Goodrich 1856-1931 AmBi,
AsBiEn, DcAmB S1, NatCAB 13,
NatCAB 14, NatCAB 23, WhAm 1
Acheson, Edward Goodrich, Jr. 1887-1962
NatCAB 50
Acheson, Ernest Francis 1855-1917 BiDrAC,
TwCBDA, WhAm 1, WhAmP
Acheson, Henry NewYHSD
Acheson, John Carey 1870-1937 NatCAB 28,
WhAm 1
Acheson, Marcus Wilson 1828-1906 ApCAB X,
NatCAB 10, TwCBDA, WhAm 1
Acheson, Marcus Wilson, Jr. 1873-1943
WhAm 2
Acheson, Mary Virginia Berry 1873- WhAm 5
Acheson, Sarah C 1844- AmWom
Acheson, William McCarthy 1878-1930
WhAm 1
Achey, Mary E IlBEAAW
Achillini, Alessandro 1463-1512 DcScB
Achor, Harold Edward 1907-1967 NatCAB 54,
WhAm 4

Achorn, Edgar Oakes 1859-1931 ApCAB X,
WhAm 1, WhAm 1C
Achron, Isidor 1892-1948 WhAm 2
Achron, Joseph 1886-1943 WhAm 2
Acikalin, Cevat 1898-1970 WhAm 5
Acken, Henry S, Jr. 1899-1970 WhAm 5
Acker, Charles Ernest 1868-1920 AmBi,
DcAmB, NatCAB 13, WhAm 1
Acker, David D 1822-1888 NatCAB 1
Acker, Ephraim Leister 1827-1903 BiAUS,
BiDrAC, WhAmP
Acker, George Gerald 1914-1974 WhAm 6
Acker, George Nicholas 1852-1923 WhAm 1
Acker, Margaret Kate WomWWA 14
Acker, Mary Clarke WomWWA 14
Ackerly, Jennie WomWWA 14
Ackerly, Orville Burnell 1842-1923 NatCAB 21
Ackerman, Amos T 1819- BiAUS
Ackerman, Carl Frederick 1873- WhAm 5
Ackerman, Carl William 1890-1970 WhAm 5
Ackerman, Charles Nelson 1871-1955
NatCAB 44
Ackerman, David D 1872-1936 NatCAB 27
Ackerman, Edward Augustus 1911-1973
WhAm 5
Ackerman, Emil 1840- NewYHSD
Ackerman, Ernest Robinson 1863-1931 BiDrAC,
WhAm 1, WhAmP
Ackerman, Ethel Serviss 1874- WomWWA 14
Ackerman, Fred W 1894-1972 WhAm 5
Ackerman, Frederick Lee 1878-1950 WhAm 2A
Ackerman, Irene 1869- WomWWA 14
Ackerman, James 1813?- NewYHSD
Ackerman, James Franklin 1864- ApCAB X
Ackerman, John Henry 1854-1921 WhAm 1
Ackerman, Lloyd Stuart 1882-1968 NatCAB 54
Ackerman, Nathan Ward 1908-1971
NatCAB 56, WhAm 5
Ackerman, Ralph Henry 1892-1957 WhAm 3
Ackerman, Robert NewYHSD
Ackerman, Robert B 1886-1958 WhAm 3
Ackerman, Samuel NewYHSD
Ackerman, William Cooper 1908-1974 WhAm 6
Ackermann, Carl 1858-1943 WhAm 2
Ackermann, Jessie A 1860- AmWom
Ackers NewYHSD
Ackers, Deane Emmett 1893-1966 WhAm 4
Ackerson, James Lee 1881-1931 WhAm 1
Ackert, Charles H 1856-1927 WhAm 1
Ackert, Helena VanVliet WomWWA 14
Ackland, Lady Christina H Caroline Fox
1750-1815 Drake
Acklen, Joseph Hayes 1850-1938 BiDrAC,
NatCAB 30, WhAmP
Ackley, Charles Breck 1878-1964 WhAm 4
Ackley, David Bartine 1876-1959 NatCAB 48
Acklin, Arthur Ashton 1893-1975 WhAm 6
Acland, Christina Harriet Caroline Fox
1750-1815 ApCAB
Aco, Michel AmBi, DcAmB, WhAm H
Acolhua I ApCAB
Acolhua II ApCAB
Acosta, Bertram Blanchard 1895-1954
DcAmB S5
Acosta, Cecilio 1831-1880 ApCAB
Acosta, Cristobal 1525?-1594? DcScB
Acosta, Joaquin 1799-1852 ApCAB, Drake
Acosta, Jose De 1539-1600 ApCAB, DcScB
Acosta, Joseph D' 1539-1600 Drake
Acosta, Manuel Gregorio 1921- IlBEAAW
Acosta, Santos 1830- ApCAB
Acosta Garcia, Julio 1872-1954 WhAm 3
Acquavella, A Lawrence 1906- WhAm 5
Acree, Solomon Farley 1875-1957 WhAm 3
Acrelius, Israel 1714-1800 AmBi, ApCAB,
DcAmB, Drake, WhAm H
Acret, George Edward 1886- WhAm 3
Actedius, Petrus DcScB
Acton, Baron John Emerich Edward Dalberg
1834-1902 McGEWB
Acton, Thomas Coxon 1823-1898 ApCAB Sup,
NatCAB 1, TwCBDA
Acualmetzli 1520-1542 ApCAB
Acuff, Herbert 1886-1951 NatCAB 46,
WhAm 3
Acuff, Samuel David 1861-1924 NatCAB 6
Acuna, Christopher D' 1597-1675 Drake
Acuna, Cristobal De 1597-1676? ApCAB

Acuna, Juan d1774 *ApCAB*
Acuna, Manuel 1849-1873 *ApCAB*
Acyuta Pisarati 1550?-1621 *DcScB*
Adachi, Hatazo 1890-1947 *WhWW-II*
Adair, Bethenia Owens *NotAW*
Adair, Edgar Harvey 1896-1964 *NatCAB 56*
Adair, Edwin Ross 1907- *BiDrAC*
Adair, Fred Lyman 1877- *WhAm 5*
Adair, George Washington 1823- *NatCAB 2*
Adair, George William 1848- *WhAm 4*
Adair, Harry David 1892-1960 *NatCAB 50*
Adair, Henry Porterfield 1883-1955 *WhAm 3*
Adair, Hugh Rogers 1889-1971 *WhAm 5*
Adair, Jackson Leroy 1887-1956 *BiDrAC,*
NatCAB 44, WhAm 3, WhAmP
Adair, James 1709?-1783? *AmBi, ApCAB,*
DcAmB, Drake, NatCAB 4, WhAm H
Adair, John 1757-1840 *AmBi, BiDrAC,*
DcAmB, NatCAB 13, WhAm H,
WhAmP
Adair, John 1758-1840 *BiAUS*
Adair, John 1758-1850 *NatCAB 2*
Adair, John 1759-1840 *ApCAB, Drake,*
TwCBDA
Adair, John Alfred McDowell 1864-1938
BiDrAC, WhAm 1, WhAmP
Adair, Marion Hopkinson 1904-1965
NatCAB 51
Adair, William P 1828?-1880 *ApCAB,*
TwCBDA
Adaire, Nannie *WomWWA 14*
Adam Of Bodenstein 1528-1577 *DcScB*
Adam, Charles Darwin 1856-1938 *WhAm 2*
Adam, Fred Blattner 1869-1944 *NatCAB 53*
Adam, Graeme Mercer 1839- *ApCAB*
Adam, James 1730-1794 *McGEWB*
Adam, James Noble 1842-1912 *WhAm 1*
Adam, John Douglas 1866- *WhAm 4*
Adam, Paul James 1909-1969 *WhAm 5*
Adam, Robert 1728-1792 *McGEWB*
Adam, William 1846- *IIBEAAW*
Adami, Charles John 1877-1955 *NatCAB 41*
Adamic, Louis 1899-1951 *DcAmB S5,*
WhAm 3
Adamowski, Joseph 1862-1930 *WhAm 1,*
WhAm 1C
Adamowski, Timothee 1857-1943 *NatCAB 32*
Adams, A Pratt 1880-1943 *NatCAB 33*
Adams, Abby Merrill *WomWWA 14*
Adams, Abigail Brown Brooks 1808-1889
BiCAW
Adams, Abigail Smith 1744-1818 *AmBi,*
AmWom, ApCAB, BiCAW, DcAmB,
Drake, NatCAB 2, NotAW, TwCBDA,
WebAB, WhAm H, WhAmP
Adams, Abijah 1754?-1816 *DcAmB, WhAm H*
Adams, Adam Athos 1886-1952 *NatCAB 42*
Adams, Adeline Valentine Pond d1948
WhAm 2
Adams, Albert Sheldon 1879-1926 *NatCAB 20*
Adams, Alice 1930- *BnEnAmA*
Adams, Alice Dana 1864- *WomWWA 14*
Adams, Allen Willson 1848- *NatCAB 3*
Adams, Alton Dermont 1864-1943 *NatCAB 32*
Adams, Alva 1850-1922 *ApCAB X, DcAmB,*
NatCAB 6, TwCBDA, WhAm 1,
WhAmP
Adams, Alva Blanchard 1875-1941 *ApCAB X,*
BiDrAC, WhAm 1, WhAm 2, WhAmP
Adams, Alvin 1804-1877 *ApCAB, DcAmB,*
NatCAB 7, TwCBDA, WhAm H
Adams, Amos 1728-1775 *ApCAB, Drake*
Adams, Amos Francis 1842-1911 *NatCAB 16*
Adams, Andrew 1736-1797 *ApCAB, BiDrAC,*
DcAmB, Drake, TwCBDA, WhAm H,
WhAmP
Adams, Andrew 1736-1799 *BiAUS,*
NatCAB 11
Adams, Andrew Addison 1864-1936 *WhAm 1*
Adams, Andrew Napoleon 1830- *TwCBDA*
Adams, Andy 1859-1935 *DcAmB S1, EncAAH,*
REnAW, WebAB, WhAm 2
Adams, Annette Abbott 1877-1956 *BiCAW,*
NatCAB 43, WhAm 3A
Adams, Ansel Easton 1902- *BnEnAmA,*
WebAB
Adams, Arthur 1881-1943 *WhAm 2*
Adams, Arthur 1881-1960 *WhAm 4*

Adams, Arthur Barto 1887-1959 *WhAm 4*
Adams, Arthur Frank 1881-1958 *NatCAB 44,*
WhAm 3
Adams, Arthur Lincoln 1864-1913 *WhAm 1*
Adams, Asael Edward 1866-1930 *WhAm 1*
Adams, Austin 1826-1890 *NatCAB 12,*
TwCBDA
Adams, Avery C 1897-1963 *WhAm 4*
Adams, Benjamin 1764-1837 *BiAUS, BiDrAC,*
TwCBDA, WhAm H, WhAmP
Adams, Benjamin 1765-1837 *ApCAB, Drake,*
NatCAB 11
Adams, Benjamin Cullen 1880-1959 *WhAm 3*
Adams, Bertram Martin 1879- *WhAm 6*
Adams, Blanche Spalding Griffin 1874-
WomWWA 14
Adams, Bristow 1875-1957 *WhAm 3*
Adams, Brockman 1927- *BiDrAC*
Adams, Brooks 1848-1927 *AmBi, ApCAB,*
ApCAB X, DcAmB, EncAB, NatCAB 10,
TwCBDA, WebAB, WhAm 1
Adams, C H 1824-1902 *BiAUS*
Adams, C H *see also* Adams, Charles Henry
Adams, Calvin Charles 1925-1973 *WhAm 6*
Adams, Cassily 1843-1921 *IIBEAAW*
Adams, Cedric M 1902-1961 *WhAm 4*
Adams, Chancey 1861-1943 *NatCAB 32*
Adams, Charles *NewYHSD*
Adams, Charles 1785-1861 *ApCAB, Drake*
Adams, Charles 1845-1895 *DcAmB,*
NatCAB 13, WhAm H, WhAmP
Adams, Charles 1847-1924 *WhAm 1*
Adams, Charles Albertus 1872- *WhAm 5*
Adams, Charles Baker 1814-1853 *ApCAB,*
DcAmB, Drake, NatCAB 8, WhAm H
Adams, Charles Bayley 1887-1961 *NatCAB 49,*
WhAm 4
Adams, Charles Christopher 1873-1955
ApCAB X, NatCAB 46, WhAm 3
Adams, Charles Clarence 1883-1948 *WhAm 2*
Adams, Charles Closson 1858-1938 *NatCAB 14,*
WhAm 2
Adams, Charles Coffin 1810-1888 *ApCAB Sup*
Adams, Charles Darwin 1856-1938 *NatCAB 29,*
WhAm 4
Adams, Charles E 1859-1933 *WhAm 1*
Adams, Charles Edward 1881-1957 *WhAm 3*
Adams, Charles F 1876-1946 *WhAm 2*
Adams, Charles Fellen 1842-1918 *WhAm 1*
Adams, Charles Follen 1842-1918 *AmBi,*
ApCAB, DcAmB, NatCAB 1, TwCBDA
Adams, Charles Francis 1807-1886 *AmBi,*
ApCAB, ApCAB X, BiAUS, BiDrAC,
DcAmB, Drake, EncAB, McGEWB,
NatCAB 8, TwCBDA, WebAB,
WhAm H, WhAmP
Adams, Charles Francis 1862-1943 *WhAm 2*
Adams, Charles Francis 1866-1954 *BiDrUSE,*
DcAmB S5, NatCAB 53, WhAm 3
Adams, Charles Francis, Jr. 1835-1915 *ApCAB,*
ApCAB X, DcAmB, EncAB, NatCAB 8,
REnAW, TwCBDA, WebAB, WhAm 1,
WhAmP
Adams, Charles Francis, Jr. 1836-1915 *AmBi*
Adams, Charles Franklin 1859-1936
NatCAB 27
Adams, Charles Frederick 1877-1950
NatCAB 50
Adams, Charles Henry 1824-1902 *BiDrAC,*
NatCAB 5, WhAmP
Adams, Charles Henry 1859- *WhAm 4*
Adams, Charles Henry *see also* Adams, C H
Adams, Charles Josiah 1850- *WhAm 4*
Adams, Charles Kendall 1835-1902 *AmBi,*
ApCAB, BiDAmEd, DcAmB, NatCAB 4,
TwCBDA, WhAm 1
Adams, Charles Partridge 1858-1942 *IIBEAAW,*
WhAm 2
Adams, Charles Perkins 1876-1950 *NatCAB 38*
Adams, Charles R 1834-1900 *DcAmB,*
WhAm H
Adams, Charles Remington 1881-1938 *WhAm 1*
Adams, Charles Robert 1883-1948 *NatCAB 36*
Adams, Charles Ross 1894-1960 *NatCAB 50*
Adams, Charles Ryan 1874-1948 *WhAm 2*
Adams, Charles W 1817-1878 *TwCBDA*
Adams, Chauncey Corbin 1872- *WhAm 5*
Adams, Christopher *NewYHSD*

Adams, Clair Stark 1862-1940 *WhAm 1*
Adams, Clarence Henry 1879-1944 *NatCAB 32,*
WhAm 2
Adams, Clarence Raymond 1898-1965 *WhAm 4*
Adams, Claris 1891-1960 *WhAm 4*
Adams, Claude Mitchell 1895-1958 *WhAm 3*
Adams, Comfort Avery 1868-1958 *ApCAB X,*
WhAm 3
Adams, Cuyler 1852-1932 *ApCAB X,*
WhAm 1
Adams, Cyrus Cornelius 1849-1928 *AmBi,*
DcAmB S1, NatCAB 42, WhAm 1
Adams, Cyrus Hall 1849-1923 *NatCAB 14,*
NatCAB 22
Adams, Cyrus Hall 1881-1968 *NatCAB 54*
Adams, Daniel 1773-1864 *ApCAB, BiDAmEd,*
DcAmB, Drake, NatCAB 20, WhAm H
Adams, Daniel Weisiger 1821-1872 *BiDConf*
Adams, Daniel Weissiger 1820-1872 *DcAmB,*
WhAm H
Adams, David 1766-1847 *ApCAB Sup*
Adams, David Ernest 1891-1952 *NatCAB 39*
Adams, Dickens Stanley 1886-1951 *NatCAB 39*
Adams, Donald Alison 1881- *WhAm 6*
Adams, Dorothy 1908-1970 *WhAm 5*
Adams, Dudley W 1831-1897 *DcAmB,*
EncAAH, WhAm H, WhAmP
Adams, Dunlap *NewYHSD*
Adams, Earl Frederick 1900-1956 *WhAm 3*
Adams, Ebenezer 1765-1841 *BiDAmEd,*
DcAmB, Drake, NatCAB 9, WhAm H
Adams, Edith Almy *WomWWA 14*
Adams, Edson 1824- *NatCAB 12*
Adams, Edson Francis 1860-1946 *NatCAB 39*
Adams, Edward Dean 1846-1931 *DcAmB S1,*
NatCAB 10, WhAm 1
Adams, Edward Francis 1839-1929 *WhAm 1*
Adams, Edward LeGrand 1851-1928 *WhAm 1,*
WhAm 4
Adams, Edward Richmond 1892-1972 *WhAm 5*
Adams, Edward Roscoe 1860-1915 *NatCAB 17*
Adams, Edward Thomas 1860-1939 *NatCAB 43*
Adams, Edwin 1834-1877 *ApCAB, DcAmB,*
Drake, NatCAB 5, WhAm H
Adams, Edwin Augustus 1837-1927 *WhAm 1*
Adams, Edwin Plimpton 1878-1956 *WhAm 3*
Adams, Elbridge Lapham 1866- *ApCAB X*
Adams, Eldridge Stevens 1891-1957
NatCAB 45
Adams, Eliphalet 1677-1753 *ApCAB, DcAmB,*
Drake, WhAm H
Adams, Elizabeth Kemper 1872-1948 *WhAm 3,*
WomWWA 14
Adams, Elizabeth Starbuck 1873-
WomWWA 14
Adams, Elmer Bragg 1842-1916 *NatCAB 5,*
TwCBDA, WhAm 1
Adams, Elmer Ellsworth 1861-1950 *NatCAB 44,*
WhAm 3
Adams, Emma L *WomWWA 14*
Adams, Emma Lily Arabella Parsons
WomWWA 14
Adams, Emma Saul 1844- *WomWWA 14*
Adams, Ephraim Douglass 1865-1930
DcAmB S1, NatCAB 22, WhAm 1
Adams, Ernest Germain 1874-1954 *NatCAB 45,*
WhAm 5
Adams, Eugene Taylor 1906-1971 *NatCAB 56,*
WhAm 5
Adams, Eva Argene 1874- *WomWWA 14*
Adams, Eva B 1908- *REnAW*
Adams, Evangeline Smith 1868-1932 *BiCAW,*
NatCAB 25, WomWWA 14
Adams, Evelyn Parkes 1865- *WomWWA 14*
Adams, Ezra Eastman 1813-1871 *ApCAB,*
NatCAB 6
Adams, F W 1787-1859 *ApCAB*
Adams, Florence Adelaide Fowle 1863-
AmWom
Adams, Frances E Lofthus 1861-
WomWWA 14
Adams, Frances Smith 1907-1964 *WhAm 4*
Adams, Francis Alexandre 1874- *WhAm 5*
Adams, Frank 1856-1927 *NatCAB 33*
Adams, Frank 1875- *WhAm 5*
Adams, Frank Dawson 1859-1942 *DcScB*
Adams, Frank Durward 1876-1962 *WhAm 4*
Adams, Frank Hicks 1886-1958 *WhAm 3*

Adams, Frank Mears 1881-1952 *NatCAB 41*

Adams, Frank Ramsay 1883-1963 *WhAm 4*

Adams, Frank Yale 1867-1919 *NatCAB 29, WhAm 4*

Adams, Franklin George 1824-1899 *NatCAB 6, TwCBDA, WhAm 1*

Adams, Franklin Oliver 1881- *WhAm 6*

Adams, Franklin Pierce 1868-1940 *WhAm 1*

Adams, Franklin Pierce 1881-1960 *WebAB, WhAm 3A*

Adams, Fred Ray 1884-1955 *NatCAB 42*

Adams, Fred Winslow 1866-1945 *WhAm 2*

Adams, Frederic 1840-1923 *NatCAB 41, WhAm 1*

Adams, Frederick Baldwin 1878-1961 *WhAm 4*

Adams, Frederick Blanchard 1875-1938 *NatCAB 28*

Adams, Frederick James 1879-1945 *NatCAB 49*

Adams, Frederick Upham 1859-1921 *AmBi, DcAmB, NatCAB 14, WhAm 1*

Adams, Frederick W 1786-1858 *NatCAB 9, WhAm H*

Adams, George *BiAUS*

Adams, George Bethune 1845-1911 *WhAm 1*

Adams, George Burrett 1870-1943 *NatCAB 40*

Adams, George Burton 1851-1925 *AmBi, DcAmB, NatCAB 14, WhAm 1*

Adams, George Dana 1863-1939 *NatCAB 31*

Adams, George E 1814-1885 *NewYHSD*

Adams, George Edward 1874-1966 *WhAm 4, WhAm 5*

Adams, George Everett 1840-1917 *BiDrAC, NatCAB 14, NatCAB 19, TwCBDA, WhAm 1, WhAmP*

Adams, George Francis 1863-1937 *WhAm 1*

Adams, George Herbert 1851-1911 *NatCAB 17, WhAm 1*

Adams, George Heyl 1885-1949 *WhAm 2*

Adams, George Irving 1870-1932 *WhAm 1*

Adams, George Madison 1837-1920 *BiAUS, BiDrAC, TwCBDA, WhAmP*

Adams, George Matthew 1878-1962 *NatCAB 47, WhAm 4*

Adams, George Moulton 1824-1906 *WhAm 1*

Adams, George Sheldon 1876- *WhAm 5*

Adams, George Wendell d1953 *WhAm 3*

Adams, George William 1838-1886 *NatCAB 15*

Adams, Grace Smith *WomWWA 14*

Adams, Granger 1852-1928 *WhAm 1*

Adams, Green 1812-1884 *BiAUS, BiDrAC, WhAm H, WhAmP*

Adams, Hampton 1897-1965 *NatCAB 52, WhAm 4*

Adams, Hank 1943- *REnAW*

Adams, Hannah 1755-1831 *AmBi, DcAmB, Drake, NotAW, TwCBDA, WhAm H*

Adams, Hannah 1755-1832 *AmWom, ApCAB, NatCAB 5*

Adams, Harold Plank 1912-1974 *WhAm 6*

Adams, Harriet Chalmers 1875-1937 *ApCAB X, NotAW, WhAm 1, WomWWA 14*

Adams, Harry Alden 1870-1941 *NatCAB 32*

Adams, Harry Milo 1867-1932 *NatCAB 24, WhAm 1*

Adams, Harry Wilfred 1879-1956 *NatCAB 52*

Adams, Henry 1838-1918 *ApCAB, NatCAB 11, TwCBDA, WhAm HA, WhAm 1, WhAm 4A, WhAmP*

Adams, Henry A, Jr. 1833-1878 *ApCAB, TwCBDA*

Adams, Henry Austin 1861-1931 *WhAm 1*

Adams, Henry Brooks 1838-1918 *AmBi, BiDAmEd, DcAmB, EncAB, McGEWB, WebAB*

Adams, Henry Carter 1851-1921 *AmBi, DcAmB, EncAB, TwCBDA, WhAm 1*

Adams, Henry Carter 1852-1921 *NatCAB 12*

Adams, Henry Cullen 1850-1906 *AmBi, BiDrAC, DcAmB, EncAAH, NatCAB 20, WhAmP*

Adams, Henry Cullen 1850-1907 *WhAm 1*

Adams, Henry Foster 1882-1973 *WhAm 5*

Adams, Henry Heberling 1845-1907 *WhAm 1*

Adams, Henry Herschel 1844-1906 *NatCAB 2, WhAm 1*

Adams, Henry Joseph 1816-1870 *NatCAB 13*

Adams, Henry Llewellyn 1875-1947 *NatCAB 38*

Adams, Henry Martyn 1844-1909 *WhAm 1*

Adams, Henry Sewall 1864-1927 *ApCAB X, NatCAB 21*

Adams, Herbert 1858-1945 *ApCAB X, BnEnAmA, NatCAB 13, TwCBDA, WhAm 2*

Adams, Herbert Baxter 1850-1901 *AmBi, ApCAB, BiDAmEd, DcAmB, EncAB, McGEWB, NatCAB 8, TwCBDA, WebAB, WhAm 1, WhAmP*

Adams, Herbert H 1876- *WhAm 5*

Adams, Herbert Samuel 1858-1945 *DcAmB S3*

Adams, Isaac 1802-1883 *AmBi, DcAmB, WhAm H*

Adams, Isaac 1803-1883 *ApCAB, Drake, NatCAB 9, TwCBDA*

Adams, Mrs. J G *NewYHSD*

Adams, J Hampton 1875-1935 *NatCAB 37*

Adams, J Hampton *see also* Adams, John Hampton

Adams, James Alonzo 1842-1925 *WhAm 1*

Adams, James Barton 1843- *NatCAB 13, WhAm 3*

Adams, James Dexter 1848-1922 *WhAm 1*

Adams, James Fairchild 1892-1971 *NatCAB 56*

Adams, James Forster Alleyne 1844- *WhAm 4*

Adams, James Hopkins 1811?-1861 *ApCAB, BiAUS, Drake, TwCBDA*

Adams, James Hopkins 1812-1861 *AmBi, DcAmB, NatCAB 12, WhAm H, WhAmP*

Adams, James McKee 1886-1945 *WhAm 3*

Adams, James Meade 1862- *WhAm 4*

Adams, James Pickwell 1895-1969 *NatCAB 54*

Adams, James Randolph 1898-1956 *WhAm 3*

Adams, James Truslow 1878-1949 *DcAmB S4, NatCAB 36, WebAB, WhAm 2*

Adams, Jane Kelley 1852- *AmWom*

Adams, Jasper 1793-1841 *ApCAB, DcAmB, Drake, NatCAB 12, TwCBDA, WhAm H*

Adams, Jed Cobb 1876-1935 *WhAm 1*

Adams, Jedidiah Howe 1866-1919 *WhAm 3*

Adams, Jennie Belle 1870- *WomWWA 14*

Adams, Jennie Kelly 1852- *ApCAB X*

Adams, Jesse Earl 1888-1945 *NatCAB 40, WhAm 2*

Adams, Jewett W 1835-1904 *NatCAB 11*

Adams, Jewett W 1835-1920 *WhAm 1*

Adams, John 1704-1740 *ApCAB, Drake, NatCAB 7, WhAm H*

Adams, John 1735-1826 *AmBi, ApCAB, BiAUS, BiDrAC, BiDrUSE, DcAmB, Drake, EncAAH, EncAB, McGEWB, NatCAB 2, TwCBDA, WebAB, WhAm H, WhAmP*

Adams, John 1772-1863 *ApCAB, DcAmB, NatCAB 10, TwCBDA, WhAm H*

Adams, John 1778-1854 *BiAUS, BiDrAC, WhAm H, WhAmP*

Adams, John 1796-1886 *ApCAB*

Adams, John 1825-1864 *ApCAB, BiDConf, DcAmB, Drake, NatCAB 4, TwCBDA, WhAm H*

Adams, John Alexander *NewYHSD*

Adams, John Coleman 1849-1922 *AmBi, DcAmB, NatCAB 11, TwCBDA, WhAm 1*

Adams, John Couch 1819-1892 *AsBiEn, DcScB, McGEWB*

Adams, John Davis 1860-1942 *WhAm 2*

Adams, John Duncan 1879- *WhAm 6*

Adams, John Emery 1899-1970 *NatCAB 55, WhAm 5*

Adams, John Frederick 1790-1881 *ApCAB, NatCAB 6, TwCBDA*

Adams, John Gregory Bishop 1841-1900 *NatCAB 4, TwCBDA, WhAm 1*

Adams, John Hampton 1875-1935 *WhAm 1*

Adams, John Hampton *see also* Adams, J Hampton

Adams, John Haslup 1871-1927 *WhAm 1*

Adams, John James 1895-1968 *NatCAB 54*

Adams, John Jay 1860-1926 *WhAm 1*

Adams, John Joseph 1848-1919 *BiDrAC, WhAmP*

Adams, John Lanson 1860-1914 *NatCAB 17*

Adams, John Milton 1819- *NatCAB 1*

Adams, John Ottis 1851-1927 *NatCAB 21, WhAm 1*

Adams, John Quincy 1767-1848 *AmBi, ApCAB, BiAUS, BiDrAC, BiDrUSE, DcAmB, Drake, EncAAH, EncAB, McGEWB, NatCAB 5, REnAW, TwCBDA, WebAB, WhAm H, WhAmP*

Adams, John Quincy 1833-1894 *ApCAB, NatCAB 11, TwCBDA*

Adams, John Quincy 1848- *WhAm 4*

Adams, John Quincy 1878-1927 *NatCAB 21*

Adams, John R 1802-1866 *NatCAB 6*

Adams, John Snyder 1907-1966 *WhAm 4*

Adams, John Stokes 1864-1954 *WhAm 3*

Adams, John Taylor 1862-1939 *ApCAB X, WhAm 1*

Adams, John Taylor 1863-1939 *NatCAB 30*

Adams, John Taylor 1873-1942 *WhAm 2*

Adams, John Trevor 1891-1962 *NatCAB 49*

Adams, John Wesley 1832-1915 *NatCAB 19*

Adams, John William 1862-1926 *WhAm 1*

Adams, John Wolcott 1874-1925 *WhAm 1*

Adams, Jonathan 1798-1872 *NatCAB 6*

Adams, Joseph 1689-1783 *NewYHSD*

Adams, Joseph Alexander 1803-1875 *ApCAB Sup*

Adams, Joseph Alexander 1803-1880 *DcAmB, NewYHSD, WhAm H*

Adams, Joseph Henry 1867- *ApCAB X*

Adams, Joseph Quincy 1881-1946 *DcAmB S4, NatCAB 39, WhAm 2*

Adams, Juliette Aurelia Graves 1858- *WomWWA 14*

Adams, Julius W 1840-1865 *ApCAB*

Adams, Julius Walker 1812-1899 *ApCAB, NatCAB 9, TwCBDA, WhAm 1*

Adams, Karl Langdon 1888-1948 *NatCAB 39, WhAm 2*

Adams, Kathryn Newell 1876- *WomWWA 14*

Adams, Kenneth Miller 1897-1966 *IIBEAAW, WhAm 4*

Adams, Kenneth Stanley 1899-1975 *WhAm 6*

Adams, L Sherman 1887-1959 *NatCAB 47, WhAm 3*

Adams, Leverett Allen 1877- *WhAm 5*

Adams, Lewis Mulford 1881-1967 *WhAm 4*

Adams, Lewis Whitaker 1904-1971 *WhAm 5*

Adams, Lida Stokes 1862- *WomWWA 14*

Adams, Louisa Catherine Johnson 1775-1852 *AmBi, BiCAW, NatCAB 5, NotAW*

Adams, Louise Catherine Johnson 1775-1852 *AmWom*

Adams, Loula Rhyne 1866- *WomWWA 14*

Adams, Lucien 1856- *WhoColR*

Adams, Lucy Frances *WomWWA 14*

Adams, Luther Bentley 1876- *WhAm 5*

Adams, M B *NewYHSD*

Adams, M Ray 1892-1966 *WhAm 4*

Adams, Mabel Ellery 1865- *WomWWA 14*

Adams, Maldon Browning 1869- *WhAm 5*

Adams, Manley Urial 1845-1920 *ApCAB X*

Adams, Margaret Catharine Zillafro 1869- *WomWWA 14*

Adams, Marian Hooper 1843-1885 *NotAW*

Adams, Mark Hancock 1912-1956 *NatCAB 48*

Adams, Mary Dean *WomWWA 14*

Adams, Mary King Humphrey *WomWWA 14*

Adams, Mary Mathews 1840-1902 *AmWom, WhAm 1*

Adams, Matthew d1749 *Drake*

Adams, Maude 1872-1953 *ApCAB X, DcAmB S5, NatCAB 13, TwCBDA, WebAB, WhAm 3, WomWWA 14*

Adams, Maxwell 1869-1939 *WhAm 1*

Adams, Melvin Ohio 1850-1920 *WhAm 1*

Adams, Miller 1894-1975 *WhAm 6*

Adams, Milton Butler 1845- *WhAm 4*

Adams, Milward 1857-1923 *NatCAB 6, WhAm 1*

Adams, Morgan 1886-1951 *WhAm 3*

Adams, Moses Samuel 1882- *WhoColR*

Adams, Myron 1841-1895 *TwCBDA*

Adams, Myron Eugene 1876-1930 *WhAm 1*

Adams, Myron Winslow 1860-1939 *NatCAB 32, WhAm 1*

Adams, Nathan 1869- *WhAm 5*

Adams, Nathaniel 1756-1829 *Drake*

Adams, Nehemiah 1806-1878 *ApCAB, DcAmB, Drake, NatCAB 2, WhAm H*

Adams, Nicholson Barney 1895-1970 *WhAm 5*
Adams, Ninette Forehand 1871- *WomWWA 14*
Adams, Numa Pompilius Garfield 1885-1940 *WhAm 2*
Adams, Oliver Stephen 1844-1924 *WhAm 1*
Adams, Oscar Fay 1855-1919 *ApCAB X, NatCAB 10, NatCAB 19, WhAm 1*
Adams, Oscar Sherman 1874-1962 *WhAm 4*
Adams, Otto Vincent 1884-1971 *WhAm 5*
Adams, Parmenio 1776-1832 *BiAUS, BiDrAC, WhAm H*
Adams, Peter Chardon Brooks 1848-1927 *McGEWB*
Adams, Philip 1881- *WhAm 6*
Adams, Porter Hartwell 1894-1945 *NatCAB 34, WhAm 2*
Adams, R R d1953 *WhAm 3*
Adams, Ralph Hudson 1908-1965 *NatCAB 52*
Adams, Ralph Snyder 1894-1933 *WhAm 1*
Adams, Ramon F 1889- *REnAW*
Adams, Randolph Greenfield 1892-1951 *DcAmB S5, DcAmLiB, NatCAB 42, WhAm 3*
Adams, Raymond Fletcher 1900-1955 *WhAm 3*
Adams, Raymond Franklin 1881-1956 *NatCAB 47*
Adams, Robert 1791-1875 *BiHiMed*
Adams, Robert 1846-1906 *DcAmB*
Adams, Robert, Jr. 1849-1906 *BiDrAC, NatCAB 12, TwCBDA, WhAm 1, WhAmP*
Adams, Robert Brooks 1887-1956 *WhAm 3*
Adams, Robert Huntington 1792-1830 *ApCAB, BiAUS, BiDrAC, NatCAB 3*
Adams, Robert Huntington 1792-1832 *WhAm H*
Adams, Robert J 1902-1967 *WhAm 4*
Adams, Robert McCormick 1890-1955 *NatCAB 48*
Adams, Robert Morton 1900-1972 *WhAm 5*
Adams, Robert Newton 1835- *WhAm 4*
Adams, Robert Simeon 1897-1950 *WhAm 3*
Adams, Roger 1889-1971 *DcScB Sup, NatCAB 57, WebAB, WhAm 5*
Adams, Romanzo 1868-1942 *BiDAmEd, WhAm 2*
Adams, Roy Elder 1881-1956 *NatCAB 47*
Adams, Russell Vroom 1888-1965 *NatCAB 51*
Adams, S Jarvis 1837-1918 *NatCAB 24*
Adams, Sallie Harp 1873- *WomWWA 14*
Adams, Samuel 1722-1803 *AmBi, ApCAB, BiAUS, BiDrAC, DcAmB, Drake, EncAB, McGEWB, NatCAB 1, TwCBDA, WebAB, WhAm H, WhAmP*
Adams, Samuel 1805-1850 *BiAUS, NatCAB 10*
Adams, Samuel 1823-1867 *ApCAB, NatCAB 9*
Adams, Samuel 1871-1935 *WhAm 1*
Adams, Samuel 1876-1927 *WhAm 1*
Adams, Samuel Barnard 1853-1938 *WhAm 1*
Adams, Samuel Hopkins 1871-1958 *NatCAB 14, NatCAB 49, WebAB, WhAm 3*
Adams, Samuel Shugert 1853-1928 *WhAm 1*
Adams, Sarah Jennie Kelley *WomWWA 14*
Adams, Seth 1807-1873 *ApCAB, Drake*
Adams, Sherman 1899- *BiDrAC*
Adams, Sherman Walcott 1836-1898 *TwCBDA*
Adams, Silas 1839-1896 *BiDrAC, WhAm H*
Adams, Spencer 1871- *NatCAB 18*
Adams, Stephen d1857 *ApCAB, BiAUS*
Adams, Stephen 1804-1857 *NatCAB 3, TwCBDA*
Adams, Stephen 1807-1857 *BiDrAC, WhAm H, WhAmP*
Adams, Susan Louise 1882- *WomWWA 14*
Adams, Suzanne 1873- *TwCBDA, WhAm 5*
Adams, Suzanne 1874- *NatCAB 13*
Adams, Theodore Louis 1858-1917 *NatCAB 17*
Adams, Thomas 1730?-1788 *BiAUS, BiDrAC, NatCAB 7, TwCBDA, WhAm H*
Adams, Thomas 1876-1949 *NatCAB 38*
Adams, Thomas, Jr. 1846-1926 *NatCAB 21*
Adams, Thomas Sewall 1873-1933 *DcAmB S1, NatCAB 25, WhAm 1*
Adams, Thomas W *NewYHSD*
Adams, Thurston Madison 1909-1961 *WhAm 4*

Adams, Virginia Claiborne 1853- *WomWWA 14*
Adams, Walter Anderson 1900-1959 *NatCAB 48*
Adams, Walter Sydney 1876-1956 *ApCAB X, AsBiEn, DcScB, WebAB, WhAm 3*
Adams, Warren Austin 1861-1944 *WhAm 2*
Adams, Washington Irving Lincoln 1865-1946 *NatCAB 10, WhAm 2*
Adams, Wayman 1883-1959 *NatCAB 49, WhAm 3*
Adams, Weston Woollard 1904-1973 *WhAm 6*
Adams, Wilbur Louis 1884-1937 *BiDrAC, WhAm 1*
Adams, William 1807-1880 *AmBi, ApCAB, DcAmB, Drake, NatCAB 7, TwCBDA, WhAm H*
Adams, William 1813-1897 *ApCAB, TwCBDA*
Adams, William, II 1922-1973 *WhAm 5*
Adams, William A 1853-1902 *WhAm 1*
Adams, William Alexander 1870-1934 *NatCAB 30*
Adams, William Althorpe 1797-1878 *NewYHSD*
Adams, William B *NewYHSD*
Adams, William Edward 1866-1946 *WhAm 3A*
Adams, William Elias 1902-1973 *WhAm 6*
Adams, William Forbes 1833-1920 *ApCAB, NatCAB 12, TwCBDA, WhAm 1*
Adams, William Grant 1867-1911 *WhAm 1*
Adams, William H *NewYHSD*
Adams, William Henry 1841-1903 *WhAm 1*
Adams, William Herbert 1861-1954 *NatCAB 42, WhAm 3*
Adams, William Jackson 1860-1934 *NatCAB 40, NatCAB 47, WhAm 1*
Adams, William Lysander 1821-1906 *DcAmB, REnAW, WhAmP*
Adams, William Milton 1905-1957 *WhAm 3*
Adams, William Montgomery 1904-1965 *NatCAB 52, WhAm 4*
Adams, William Ray 1888-1940 *NatCAB 31*
Adams, William Taylor 1822-1897 *AmBi, ApCAB, DcAmB, Drake, NatCAB 1, TwCBDA, WebAB, WhAm H*
Adams, William Wirt 1819-1888 *BiDConf, DcAmB, WhAm H, WhAmP*
Adams, Willis A 1854-1932 *IIBEAAW*
Adams, Winborn d1777 *Drake*
Adams, Winifred Brady 1871- *WomWWA 14*
Adams, Winston Davis 1883-1929 *WhAm 1*
Adams, Zabdiel 1739-1801 *Drake*
Adams, Zabdiel Boylston 1875-1940 *NatCAB 35*
Adamson, Alfred 1836-1915 *WhAm 1*
Adamson, Charles 1859-1931 *WhAm 1*
Adamson, Ernie 1894-1971 *NatCAB 57*
Adamson, George Purseglove 1864-1933 *NatCAB 26*
Adamson, J E 1884-1961 *WhAm 4*
Adamson, Robert 1871-1935 *WhAm 2*
Adamson, Tilden *ApCAB X*
Adamson, William Augustus 1883-1956 *NatCAB 43*
Adamson, William Charles 1854-1929 *BiDrAC, NatCAB 18, TwCBDA, WhAm 1, WhAmP*
Adank, J L 1907-1970 *WhAm 5*
Adanson, Michel 1727-1806 *DcScB*
Adcock, Clarence Lionel 1895-1967 *NatCAB 54, WhAm 4*
Adcock, Edmund David 1877-1951 *WhAm 3*
Addabbo, Joseph Patrick 1925- *BiDrAC*
Addams, Charles Samuel 1912- *WebAB*
Addams, Clifford Isaac 1876-1942 *WhAm 2*
Addams, George Stanton 1869-1933 *NatCAB 24*
Addams, Jane 1860-1935 *AmBi, ApCAB X, DcAmB S1, EncAB, McGEWB, NatCAB 13, NatCAB 27, NotAW, WebAB, WhAm 1, WhAmP, WomWWA 14*
Addams, William 1777-1858 *BiAUS, BiDrAC, WhAm H*
Addelsterren, Mrs. L E *NewYHSD*
Addeman, Joshua Melancthon 1840-1930 *WhAm 1*
Addenbrook, J Arthur 1881-1949 *NatCAB 38*
Adderley, Julian Edwin 1928-1975 *WhAm 6*

Addicks, Frank F 1892-1954 *WhAm 3*
Addicks, George B 1854-1910 *TwCBDA, WhAm 1*
Addicks, John Edward 1841-1919 *WhAm 1*
Addicks, John Edward O'Sullivan 1841-1919 *DcAmB*
Addicks, John Edward Sullivan 1841-1919 *WhAmP*
Addicks, Lawrence 1878- *ApCAB X, WhAm 6*
Addington, Isaac 1645-1715 *Drake, NatCAB 4*
Addington, Keene Harwood 1874-1922 *WhAm 1*
Addington, Sarah 1891-1940 *WhAm 1*
Addis, Thomas 1881-1949 *WhAm 2*
Addison, Alexander 1759-1807 *Drake*
Addison, Daniel Dulany 1863-1936 *NatCAB 13, NatCAB 27, TwCBDA, WhAm 1*
Addison, James Thayer 1887-1953 *NatCAB 41, WhAm 3*
Addison, Joseph 1672-1719 *McGEWB*
Addison, Julia DeWolf 1866- *ApCAB X, WhAm 4, WomWWA 14*
Addison, Kate R 1863- *WomWWA 14*
Addison, Margaret Eleanor Theodora 1868- *WomWWA 14*
Addison, Thomas 1793-1860 *AsBiEn, BiHiMed, McGEWB*
Addison, Thomas 1793-1890 *DcScB*
Addison, Walter Dulany 1769-1848 *TwCBDA*
Addison, William H F 1880-1963 *WhAm 4*
Additon, Forrest 1879-1958 *NatCAB 47*
Addonizio, Hugh Joseph 1914- *BiDrAC, WhAmP*
Addums, Mozis 1828-1883 *AmBi*
Addy, James *NewYHSD*
Ade, George 1866-1944 *ApCAB X, DcAmB S3, NatCAB 11, TwCBDA, WebAB, WhAm 2*
Adee, Alvey Augustus 1842-1924 *DcAmB, NatCAB 12, TwCBDA, WhAm 1, WhAmP*
Adee, George Augustus 1847-1908 *NatCAB 24*
Adee, George Townsend 1874-1948 *NatCAB 41*
Adelard Of Bath 1090?-1150? *AsBiEn, DcScB*
Adelson, Abraham Nathan 1884-1949 *NatCAB 37*
Adelung, Ernst 1824- *NewYHSD*
Adems, Dunlap *NewYHSD*
Adenauer, Konrad 1876-1967 *McGEWB, WhAm 4*
Adenaw, Charlotte Milnor Gillet 1880- *WomWWA 14*
Aderhold, Arthur Chairrier 1881- *WhAm 6*
Aderhold, Omer Clyde 1899-1969 *BiDAmEd, WhAm 5*
Aders, Oral Madison 1901-1974 *WhAm 6*
Adet, Pierre Auguste 1763-1832 *ApCAB*
Adet, Pierre-Auguste 1763-1834 *DcScB*
Adet, Pierre Augustus 1763-1832? *Drake*
Adgate, Andrew d1793 *DcAmB, WhAm H*
Adgate, Asa 1767-1832 *BiAUS, BiDrAC, WhAm H*
Adgate, Frederick Whitney 1868-1934 *WhAm 1*
Adger, John Bailey 1879-1957 *NatCAB 47*
Adger, Julian Francis 1876- *WhoColR*
Adie, David Craig 1888-1943 *DcAmB S3, WhAm 2*
Adkin, Thomas Franklin 1871-1924 *NatCAB 20*
Adkins, Charles 1863-1941 *BiDrAC, WhAm 1, WhAmP*
Adkins, Curtis D 1897-1956 *WhAm 3*
Adkins, Galen Horatio 1908-1966 *WhAm 4*
Adkins, Homer Burton 1892-1949 *DcAmB S4, WhAm 3*
Adkins, Homer Martin 1890-1964 *WhAm 4*
Adkins, Jesse Corcoran 1879-1955 *NatCAB 44, WhAm 3*
Adkins, John Scudder d1931 *WhAm 1, WhAm 1C*
Adkins, Leonard Dawson 1893-1967 *WhAm 4*
Adkins, Mary Ewart *WomWWA 14*
Adkins, William H 1862- *WhAm 4*
Adkinson, Mary Osburn 1843- *AmWom*
Adlam, T Napier 1888-1952 *NatCAB 41*
Adler, Albert Stanley 1860-1924 *NatCAB 22*
Adler, Alfred 1870-1937 *AsBiEn, McGEWB, WhAm HA, WhAm 4*

Adler, Arthur Henry 1893-1948 *NatCAB 38*
Adler, Betty 1919-1973 *WhAm 6*
Adler, Buddy 1908-1960 *NatCAB 47,*
WhAm 4
Adler, Clarence 1886-1969 *WhAm 5*
Adler, Cyrus 1863-1940 *AmBi, ApCAB Sup,*
ApCAB X, BiDAmEd, DcAmB S2,
DcAmLiB, DcAmReB, NatCAB 11,
NatCAB 41, TwCBDA, WebAB,
WhAm 1
Adler, Dankmar 1844-1900 *BnEnAmA,*
NatCAB 11, WebAB, WhAm 1
Adler, David 1883-1949 *WhAm 3*
Adler, Elmer 1884-1962 *WhAm 4*
Adler, Emanuel Philip 1872-1949 *WhAm 2*
Adler, F Charles 1889-1959 *WhAm 3*
Adler, Felix 1851-1933 *AmBi, ApCAB,*
ApCAB X, BiDAmEd, DcAmB S1,
DcAmReB, McGEWB, NatCAB 1,
NatCAB 23, TwCBDA, WebAB,
WhAm 1, WhAmP
Adler, Frederick Henry Herbert 1885-1959
WhAm 4
Adler, Frederick Max 1869-1946 *NatCAB 33*
Adler, Freyda Nacque d1970 *WhAm 5*
Adler, George J 1821-1868 *ApCAB, DcAmB,*
Drake, TwCBDA, WhAm H
Adler, Harry Clay 1865-1940 *NatCAB 29*
Adler, Helen Goldmark 1859- *BiCAW,*
WomWWA 14
Adler, Herman Morris 1876-1935 *NatCAB 26,*
WhAm 1, WhAm 1C
Adler, Isaac 1849- *NatCAB 11, WhAm 4*
Adler, Joel B 1934-1973 *WhAm 6*
Adler, Julius Ochs 1892-1955 *WhAm 3*
Adler, Leopold 1861- *WhAm 5*
Adler, Liebmann 1812-1892 *NatCAB 11*
Adler, Max 1866-1952 *WhAm 3*
Adler, Mortimer Jerome 1902- *WebAB*
Adler, Samuel 1809-1891 *DcAmB,*
NatCAB 11, TwCBDA, WhAm H
Adler, Sara 1858-1953 *DcAmB S5*
Adler, Simon Louis 1867-1934 *WhAm 1,*
WhAm 1C
Adlerblum, Nima H 1886-1974 *WhAm 6*
Adley, Michael Louis 1901-1970 *NatCAB 56*
Adlum, John 1759-1836 *AmBi, DcAmB,*
WhAm H
Adney, Edwin Tappan 1868-1950 *IlBEAAW,*
WhAm 3
Adoian, Vosdanig Manoog *WebAB*
Adolph, William Henry 1890-1958 *NatCAB 44*
Adolphe, Albert Jean 1865- *WhAm 1*
Adoue, Jean Baptiste, Jr. 1884-1956 *WhAm 3*
Adrain, Garnett B -1878 *BiAUS*
Adrain, Garnett B 1816-1878 *ApCAB*
Adrain, Garnett Bowditch 1815-1878 *BiDrAC,*
WhAm H
Adrain, Robert 1775-1843 *ApCAB, DcAmB,*
DcScB, Drake, NatCAB 1, WhAm H
Adrain, Robert 1853- *NatCAB 5*
Adreon, Edward Lawrence 1847-1913
NatCAB 17
Adriaanson, Adriaan *DcScB*
Adrian, Baron Edgar Douglas 1889- *McGEWB*
Adrian, G 1903-1958 *WhAm 3*
Adrian, Matthew Bernard 1886-1957
NatCAB 43
Adrian, William Lawrence 1883-1972 *WhAm 5*
Adriance, John Sabin 1861- *WhAm 4*
Adriance, William Allen 1864-1926 *NatCAB 25*
Adsit, Allen Clark 1837- *NatCAB 7*
Adsit, Charles George 1874-1935 *NatCAB 28*
Adsit, Henry 1880-1935 *NatCAB 31*
Adsit, Nancy H 1825- *AmWom*
Adson, Alfred Washington 1887-1951 *WhAm 3*
Adt, Howard Ellsworth 1862-1923 *NatCAB 25*
Ady, Dora Belle 1862- *WomWWA 14*
Ady, George 1842-1919 *NatCAB 18*
Aebersold, Paul C 1910-1967 *WhAm 4*
Aegidius *DcScB*
Aelfric 955-1012? *McGEWB*
Aepinus, Franz Ulrich Theodosius 1724-1802
DcScB
Aeschylus 524BC-456BC *McGEWB*
Aesculapius *BiHiMed*
Aetatis Sue Limner *BnEnAmA*
Aetius Of Amida *DcScB*

Affel, Herman Andrew 1893-1972 *WhAm 6*
Affelder, William L 1879-1963 *WhAm 4*
Affeldt, George August 1888-1952 *NatCAB 44*
Affick, William H *NewYHSD*
Affleck, Benjamin Franklin 1869-1944 *WhAm 2*
Affleck, James Gelston 1892-1972 *WhAm 5*
Affleck, Thomas 1812-1861 *EncAAH*
Affleck, Thomas 1812-1868 *DcAmB*
Affonso I 1460?-1545 *McGEWB*
Afinogenov, Aleksandr Nikolaevich 1904-1941
McGEWB
Aflah, Ibn *DcScB*
Africa, John Simpson 1832-1900 *NatCAB 8,*
WhAm 1
Africa, Walter Greenland 1863-1925
NatCAB 20
Aga Khan I 1800-1881 *McGEWB*
Aga Khan III 1877-1957 *McGEWB*
Aga Khan, Aga Sultan Mohamad Shah
1877-1957 *WhAm 3*
Agan, Frank Walter 1869-1934 *NatCAB 34*
Agar, John Giraud 1856-1935 *NatCAB 3,*
WhAm 1
Agar, William Macdonough 1894-1972
WhAm 5
Agard, Isaac Merritt 1854-1925 *NatCAB 20*
Agardh, Carl Adolph 1785-1859 *DcScB*
Agardh, Jacob Georg 1813-1901 *DcScB*
Agassiz, Alexander 1835-1910 *AmBi, ApCAB,*
ApCAB X, DcAmB, DcScB, NatCAB 3,
TwCBDA, WebAB, WhAm 1
Agassiz, Elizabeth Cabot Cary 1822- *BiCAW*
Agassiz, Elizabeth Cabot Cary 1822-1901
BiDAmEd
Agassiz, Elizabeth Cabot Cary 1822-1907 *AmBi,*
AmWom, DcAmB, NatCAB 12, NotAW,
WhAm 1
Agassiz, George Russell 1862-1951 *NatCAB 37,*
WhAm 3
Agassiz, Jean Louis Rodolphe 1807-1873
AsBiEn, BiDAmEd, DcAmB, DcScB,
EncAAH, EncAB, McGEWB, NatCAB 2,
WhAm H
Agassiz, Jean Louis Rudolphe 1807-1873
ApCAB, TwCBDA
Agassiz, Louis 1807-1873 *AmBi, WebAB*
Agassiz, Louis John Rudolph 1807-1873 *Drake*
Agassiz, Rodolphe Louis 1871-1933 *WhAm 1*
Agate, Alfred T 1812-1846 *DcAmB, IlBEAAW,*
NewYHSD, WhAm H
Agate, Frederick Styles 1803-1844 *DcAmB,*
WhAm H
Agate, Frederick Styles 1807-1844 *Drake,*
NewYHSD
Agate, Miss H *NewYHSD*
Agathinus, Claudius *DcScB*
Agee, Alva 1858-1943 *WhAm 2*
Agee, Fannie Heaslip Lea *WomWWA 14*
Agee, James 1909-1955 *DcAmB S5, EncAAH,*
NatCAB 42, WebAB, WhAm HA,
WhAm 4
Ager, Waldemar 1869-1941 *WhAm 1*
Agersborg, H P K 1881-1960 *WhAm 4*
Agesilaus II 444?BC-360BC *McGEWB*
Ageton, Arthur Ainslie 1900-1971 *WhAm 5*
Agg, Thomas Radford 1878-1947 *WhAm 2*
Aggeler, William Tell 1866-1937 *WhAm 1*
Agger, Eugene Ewald 1879-1966 *WhAm 4*
Aggrey, James Emman Kwegyir 1875-1927
DcAmB S1, WhAmP, WhoColR
Agha Mohammad Khan 1742?-1797 *McGEWB*
Agis IV 262?BC-241BC *McGEWB*
Agnel, Hyacinth R d1871 *Drake*
Agnelli, Joseph B 1902-1972 *WhAm 5*
Agnesi, Maria Gaetana 1718-1799 *DcScB*
Agnew, Alexander McLeod 1818-1891
NatCAB 1
Agnew, Andrew Davison 1867-1951 *WhAm 3*
Agnew, Benjamin Lashells 1833- *WhAm 4*
Agnew, Cornelius Rea 1830-1888 *ApCAB,*
DcAmB, NatCAB 8, TwCBDA,
WhAm H
Agnew, Daniel 1809-1902 *ApCAB X,*
NatCAB 4, TwCBDA, WhAm 1
Agnew, David Hayes 1818-1892 *AmBi,*
ApCAB Sup, ApCAB X, BiDAmEd,
DcAmB, NatCAB 8, TwCBDA, WebAB,
WhAm H

Agnew, Eliza 1807-1883 *DcAmB, WhAm H*
Agnew, George Bliss 1868-1941 *NatCAB 30*
Agnew, George Harvey 1895-1971 *WhAm 5*
Agnew, Hobart McVickar 1893-1965
NatCAB 51
Agnew, Hugh Elmer 1875-1955 *WhAm 3*
Agnew, James d1777 *ApCAB, Drake*
Agnew, James Howard 1884-1954 *NatCAB 45*
Agnew, Janet Margaret 1903-1975 *WhAm 6*
Agnew, Paul Gough 1881-1954 *NatCAB 40,*
WhAm 3
Agnew, Peter Lawrence 1901-1969 *WhAm 5*
Agnew, Spiro Theodore 1918- *BiDrAC,*
BiDrUSE, EncAB, WebAB, WhAmP
Agnew, Walter D 1873- *WhAm 5*
Agnew, William Henry 1881-1931 *NatCAB 25,*
WhAm 1
Agnew, William John Clarke 1891-1955
NatCAB 45, WhAm 3
Agnon, Shmuel Yosef Halevi 1888-1970
WhAm 5
Agnon, Shmuel Yoseph 1888-1970 *McGEWB*
Agnus, Felix 1839-1925 *ApCAB Sup,*
ApCAB X, DcAmB, NatCAB 1,
TwCBDA, WhAm 1, WhAmP
Agoos, Solomon 1880-1953 *NatCAB 42,*
WhAm 3
Agostini, Peter 1913- *BnEnAmA*
Agostino DiDuccio 1418-1481? *McGEWB*
Agramonte, Aristides 1869-1931 *WhAm 1*
Agramonte, Ignacio 1841-1873 *ApCAB*
Agramonte Y Simoni, Aristides 1868-1931
DcAmB S1
Agricola, Georgius 1494-1555 *AsBiEn, DcScB,*
McGEWB
Agricola, Otto 1865-1939 *NatCAB 32*
Agrippa, Heinrich Cornelius 1486-1535? *DcScB*
Agry, Warren C 1889-1958 *WhAm 3*
Aguado, Pedro *ApCAB, ApCAB Sup*
Ague, John Barge 1859-1926 *NatCAB 20*
Aguero, Joaquin De 1816-1851 *ApCAB*
Agueynaba I d1510 *ApCAB*
Agueynaba II *ApCAB*
Aguilar, Maria 1695-1756 *ApCAB*
Aguilar, Roberto Trigueros 1888-1959 *WhAm 3*
Aguilon, Francois D' 1546-1617 *DcScB*
Aguinaldo, Emilio 1869-1964 *McGEWB,*
WhAm HA, WhAm 4
Aguinaldo Y Famy, Emilio 1872- *ApCAB Sup*
Aguirre, Jose Maria 1778-1852 *ApCAB*
Aguirre, Lope De *ApCAB, Drake*
Agur, Hezekiah *NewYHSD*
Ahad Haam 1856-1927 *McGEWB*
Ahalt, Arthur M 1907-1958 *WhAm 3*
Ahearn, Margaret Howitt *WomWWA 14*
Ahern, Andrew 1827?- *NewYHSD*
Ahern, Eugene Leslie 1895-1960 *WhAm 3A*
Ahern, James *WebAB*
Ahern, Leo James 1886-1973 *WhAm 6*
Ahern, Martin 1817?- *NewYHSD*
Ahern, Mary Eileen 1860-1938 *BiDAmEd,*
DcAmLiB, NotAW, WhAm 1,
WomWWA 14
Ahern, Michael Joseph 1877-1951 *WhAm 3*
Ahidjo, Ahmadou 1924- *McGEWB*
Ahl, Henry Hammond 1869- *WhAm 5*
Ahl, John A 1815- *BiAUS*
Ahl, John Alexander 1813-1882 *BiDrAC,*
WhAm H
Ahl, Orville Walter 1901-1964 *WhAm 4*
Ahlbrand, Albert Henry 1872-1946 *NatCAB 39*
Ahlday, Josephine Ford 1849- *WomWWA 14*
Ahlen, Anton L 1876-1949 *NatCAB 38*
Ahlport, Brodie E 1898-1968 *WhAm 5*
Ahlquist, Miriam Sweet 1910-1972 *WhAm 6*
Ahlquist, Robert Wilhelm 1898-1966 *WhAm 4*
Ahlqvist, Harald 1876-1938 *NatCAB 30*
Ahmad, King Of Yemen 1891-1962 *WhAm 4*
Ahmad Ibn Ibrahim Al-Uqlidisi *DcScB*
Ahmad Ibn Muhammad Ibn Abd A Al-Sizji
DcScB
Ahmad Ibn Muhammad Ibn Al-Banna *DcScB*
Ahmad Ibn Musa Ibn Shakir *DcScB*
Ahmad Ibn Yusuf d912? *DcScB*
Ahmad Ibn Yusuf Al-Tifashi *DcScB*
Ahmanson, Howard Fieldstead 1906-1968
WhAm 5
Ahmose *AsBiEn*

Ahonen, Arvey Augustinus 1898-1955
  NatCAB 43

Ahrens, Edward Hamblin 1884-1947 WhAm 2

Ahrens, Henry Adolf 1873-1951 NatCAB 41

Ahrens, Hermann NewYHSD

Ahrens, Mary A 1836- AmWom, WhAm 4,
  WomWWA 14

Ahrens, Theodore 1859-1938 NatCAB 18,
  WhAm 1

Ahuitzol Drake

Ahuizotl d1502 ApCAB

Ahumada, Miguel 1844- ApCAB Sup

Ahumada Y Villalon, Agustin De d1760 ApCAB

Aid, George Charles 1872-1938 WhAm 1

Aida, Yasuaki 1747-1817 DcScB

Aiello, Gaetan Rudolph 1895-1973 WhAm 6

Aigeltinger, Arthur 1883-1941 NatCAB 32

Aigler, Ralph William 1885-1964 WhAm 4

Aiken, Alfred Lawrence 1870-1946 NatCAB 35,
  WhAm 2

Aiken, Carolyn Jones WomWWA 14

Aiken, Charles Augustus 1827-1892 ApCAB,
  DcAmB, NatCAB 7, TwCBDA,
  WhAm H

Aiken, Charles Avery 1872-1965 WhAm 4

Aiken, Charles Francis 1863-1925 NatCAB 20,
  WhAm 1

Aiken, Charles Sedgwick 1863-1911 WhAm 1

Aiken, Conrad Potter 1889-1973 ApCAB X,
  WebAB, WhAm 6

Aiken, David Wyatt 1828-1887 BiDrAC,
  DcAmB, NatCAB 20, WhAm H,
  WhAmP

Aiken, E Clarence 1856- WhAm 4

Aiken, Edith Kenney WomWWA 14

Aiken, Ednah 1872- WhAm 5

Aiken, Frank Eugene 1840-1910 WhAm 1

Aiken, Gayle 1859- WhAm 4

Aiken, George David 1892- BiDrAC

Aiken, George L 1830-1876 DcAmB,
  WhAm H

Aiken, Howard Hathaway 1900-1973 WhAm 5

Aiken, John 1797-1867 NatCAB 6

Aiken, John Adams 1850-1927 WhAm 1

Aiken, Paul C 1910-1974 WhAm 6

Aiken, Robert Leon 1903-1970 WhAm 5

Aiken, Walter Scott 1892-1953 NatCAB 41

Aiken, William 1806-1887 ApCAB, BiAUS,
  BiDrAC, DcAmB, Drake, NatCAB 12,
  TwCBDA, WhAm H, WhAmP

Aiken, William Appleton 1833-1929 WhAm 1

Aiken, William Appleton 1907-1957
  NatCAB 46

Aiken, William Hamblen 1916-1974 WhAm 6

Aiken, William Martin 1855-1908 WhAm 1

Aiken, Wyatt 1863-1923 BiDrAC, WhAm 2,
  WhAmP

Aikens, Amanda L 1833-1892 AmWom

Aikens, Andrew Jackson 1830-1909 ApCAB X,
  DcAmB, NatCAB 1, WhAm 1

Aikens, Berton Allen, Jr. 1903-1965 NatCAB 53

Aikens, Charles Thomas 1862-1927 WhAm 1

Aikin, James Cornelius 1840- NatCAB 14

Aikin, Wilford Merton 1882-1965 WhAm 4

Aikins, Herbert Austin 1867-1946 NatCAB 36,
  WhAm 4

Aikins, James Cox 1823- ApCAB

Aikman, Alexander 1755-1838 ApCAB, Drake

Aikman, Granville P 1858-1923 NatCAB 20

Aikman, Hugh 1790-1867 NatCAB 4

Aikman, Walter M NewYHSD

Aikman, Walter Monteith 1857-1939 WhAm 2

Aikman, William 1824-1909 NatCAB 9,
  TwCBDA, WhAm 1

Ailes, John William, III 1907-1974 WhAm 6

Ailes, Milton Everett 1867-1925 ApCAB X,
  WhAm 1

Ailgeltinger, Arthur 1883-1941 NatCAB 31

Aillebout, Louis D' d1660 ApCAB, Drake

Ailly, Pierre D' 1350-1420 DcScB, McGEWB

Ailshie, James Franklin 1868-1947 NatCAB 14,
  NatCAB 18, WhAm 2

Ailshie, Margaret Cobb 1886-1959 WhAm 3

Ailshie, Robert 1908-1947 WhAm 2

Aime, Valcour 1798-1867 DcAmB, EncAAH,
  NatCAB 21, WhAm H

Aimee, Sister WebAB

Aimes, Hubert Hilary Suffren 1876- WhAm 5

Ainey, William David Blakeslee 1864-1932
  BiDrAC

Ainey, William David Blakeslee 1864-1933
  WhAm 1

Ainey, William Henry 1834-1907 NatCAB 37

Ainslie, George 1838-1913 BiDrAC, WhAm 1

Ainslie, George 1868-1931 WhAm 2

Ainslie, Hew 1792-1878 ApCAB, DcAmB,
  Drake, NatCAB 8, WhAm H

Ainslie, James Stuart 1856- WhAm 4

Ainslie, Peter 1867-1934 DcAmB S1,
  WhAm 1

Ainsworth, Dorothy Sears 1894-1976 BiDAmEd

Ainsworth, Edward Maddin 1902-1968
  WhAm 5

Ainsworth, Frank Beverridge 1841- NatCAB 5

Ainsworth, Frank Kenley 1856-1929 WhAm 2

Ainsworth, Fred Crayton 1852-1934 WhAm 1

Ainsworth, Frederick Crayton 1852-1934
  ApCAB Sup, DcAmB S1, TwCBDA,
  WebAMB, WhAmP

Ainsworth, Harry 1862-1930 NatCAB 38

Ainsworth, Henry Albijence 1833-1914
  NatCAB 27

Ainsworth, Herman Reeve 1841-1914
  NatCAB 17

Ainsworth, James Edward 1830-1909
  NatCAB 20

Ainsworth, John Churchill 1870-1943
  NatCAB 33, WhAm 2

Ainsworth, John Commigers 1822-1893
  NatCAB 20, NatCAB 25

Ainsworth, Laban 1757-1858 ApCAB, Drake

Ainsworth, Lucien Lester 1831-1902 BiAUS,
  BiDrAC

Ainsworth, Sarah Frances Anderson 1849-
  WomWWA 14

Ainsworth, Walden L 1886-1960 WhAm 4,
  WhWW-II

Ainsworth, William Louis 1892-1956
  NatCAB 54

Ainsworth, William Newman 1872-1942
  NatCAB 38, NatCAB 47, WhAm 2

Aird, Alexander N 1903-1958 WhAm 3

Aird, John William 1863-1953 NatCAB 41

Airey, Charles Theodore 1866-1930 WhAm 1

Airey, John 1885-1962 NatCAB 52, WhAm 4

Airey, Joseph Alexander 1872-1949 NatCAB 38

Airey, Richard 1868- WhAm 4

Airhart, John C 1916-1972 WhAm 5

Airy, Sir George Biddell 1801-1892 AsBiEn,
  DcScB

Airy, John NewYHSD

Aishton, Richard Henry 1860-1946 WhAm 2

Aitchison, Clyde Bruce 1875-1962 NatCAB 47,
  WhAm 4

Aitchison, John Young 1868-1926 WhAm 1

Aitchison, Paul Floyd 1891-1956 NatCAB 47

Aitchison, Robert J 1891-1961 WhAm 4

Aitken, David D 1854-1930 WhAm 4

Aitken, David Demerest 1853-1930 BiDrAC

Aitken, David Demorest 1853-1930 NatCAB 21

Aitken, James NewYHSD

Aitken, Jane 1764-1832 NotAW

Aitken, Peter 1858- WhAm 4

Aitken, Robert 1734-1802 ApCAB, DcAmB,
  Drake, NewYHSD, WhAm H

Aitken, Robert Grant 1864-1951 ApCAB X,
  DcAmB S5, DcScB, NatCAB 42,
  WhAm 3

Aitken, Robert Ingersoll 1878-1949 ApCAB X,
  NatCAB 15, WhAm 2

Aitkenhead, William 1872-1949 NatCAB 41

Aitkin, Thomas NewYHSD

Aiton, William 1731-1793 DcScB

Aiton, William Townsend 1766-1849 DcScB

Ajima, Naonobu 1732?-1798 DcScB

Akar, John J 1927-1975 WhAm 6

Akbar 1542-1605 WhoMilH

Akbar, Jalal-Ud-Din Mohammed 1542-1605
  McGEWB

Ake, Russell Everett 1908-1962 WhAm 4

Aked, Charles Frederic 1864-1941 WhAm 1

Akelaitis, Andrew John 1904-1955 NatCAB 44

Akeley, Carl Ethan 1864-1926 AmBi, DcAmB,
  NatCAB 26, WebAB, WhAm 1,
  WhAm 1C

Akeley, Healy Cady 1836-1912 WhAm 1

Akeley, Lewis Ellsworth 1861- WhAm 4

Akeley, Mary L Jobe 1966 WhAm 4

Akerberg, Herbert Vestner 1897-1964 WhAm 4

Akerly, Samuel 1785-1845 ApCAB, Drake

Akerman, Alexander 1869-1948 WhAm 2

Akerman, Amos Tappan 1819-1880 ApCAB,
  Drake

Akerman, Amos Tappan 1821-1880 BiDrUSE,
  DcAmB, NatCAB 9, WhAm H, WhAmP

Akerman, Amos Tappan 1823-1880 NatCAB 4,
  TwCBDA

Akerman, John D 1897-1972 WhAm 5

Akerman, Joseph 1872-1943 NatCAB 33

Akers, Benjamin Paul 1825-1861 AmBi,
  ApCAB, DcAmB, Drake, NewYHSD,
  TwCBDA, WhAm H

Akers, Charles 1835?-1906 NewYHSD

Akers, Elizabeth Chase 1832-1911 DcAmB,
  NotAW, WhAm 1

Akers, George Washington 1893-1964
  NatCAB 51

Akers, Lewis Robeson 1881- WhAm 6

Akers, Milburn Peter 1900-1970 NatCAB 55,
  WhAm 5

Akers, Oscar Perry 1872- WhAm 5

Akers, Paul 1825-1861 NatCAB 6

Akers, Sheldon Buckingham 1898-1973
  WhAm 6

Akers, Thomas Peter 1828-1877 BiAUS,
  BiDrAC, WhAm H

Akerson, George Edward 1888-1937
  NatCAB 29

Akerson, George Edward 1889-1937 WhAm 1

Akharaj Varadhara, Phya 1861- WhAm 4

Akhmatova, Anna 1889-1966 McGEWB

Akiba BenJoseph 050?-135? McGEWB

Akin, Mrs. James NewYHSD

Akin, James 1773?-1846 NewYHSD

Akin, John 1912-1962 WhAm 4

Akin, Louis B 1868-1913 IIBEAAW

Akin, Margaret Catherine Rouse 1913-1972
  WhAm 6

Akin, Otis Franklin 1872-1949 NatCAB 38

Akin, Spencer Ball 1889-1973 WhAm 6

Akin, Theron 1855-1933 BiDrAC, WhAm 1

Akin, Thomas Beamish 1809- ApCAB

Akin, Thomas Russell 1867-1945 NatCAB 35,
  WhAm 2

Akin, Warren 1811-1877 BiDConf

Akins, John 1827?- NewYHSD

Akins, Zoe 1886-1958 ApCAB X, WhAm 3,
  WomWWA 14

Ako, Michel DcAmB

Ala, Hussein d1964 WhAm 4

Ala-Ud-Din d1316 McGEWB

Alabaster, Francis Asbury 1866-1946 WhAm 3

Alain De Lille d1203 DcScB

Alaman, Lucas 1792-1853 ApCAB, Drake,
  McGEWB

Alaminos, Antonio ApCAB

Alanson, Bertram Edward 1877-1958 WhAm 3

Alarcon, Hernando WhAm H

Alarcon, Hernando D' ApCAB

Alarcon, Hernando De AmBi, DcAmB, Drake

Alarcon, Pedro Antonio De 1833-1891
  McGEWB

Alarcon Y Mendoza, Juan Ruiz D' 1580?-1639
  ApCAB

Alarcon Y Mendoza, Juan Ruiz De 1581?-1639
  McGEWB

Alarcon Y Mendoza, Juan Ruiz De 1600?-1639
  Drake

Alaric 370?-410 McGEWB

Alaungpaya 1715-1760 McGEWB

Alba, Fernando A DeToledo, Duke Of 1507-1582
  McGEWB

Alba, Fernando A DeToledo, Duke Of see also
  Alva, Fernando

Alba, Fernando D' ApCAB

Alba, Peter F 1835-1915 NatCAB 17

Albach, George H 1892-1961 WhAm 4

Alban NewYHSD

Albani, Madame 1851-1930 WhAm 3

Albani, Emma 1851-1930 AmWom

Albani, Emma 1852-1930 WhAm HA,
  WhAm 4

Albani, Marie Emma LaJeunesse 1851-1930
  ApCAB, TwCBDA

Albarda, Horatius 1904-1965 *WhAm 4*
Albategni *DcScB*
Albategnius 858?-929 *AsBiEn*
Albaugh, George Sylvanus 1871- *ApCAB X,*
WhAm 5
Albaugh, John W 1837-1909 *NatCAB 2,*
WhAm 1
Albaugh, Walter Hugh 1890-1942 *BiDrAC*
Albear, Francisco 1816- *ApCAB*
Albee, Edward Franklin 1857-1930 *ApCAB X,*
DcAmB S1, NatCAB 22, WhAm 1
Albee, Edward Franklin 1928- *EncAB, WebAB*
Albee, Ernest 1865-1927 *AmBi, DcAmB,*
WhAm 1
Albee, Fred Houdlett 1876-1945 *ApCAB X,*
NatCAB 15, WhAm 2
Albee, Helen Rickey 1864- *WomWWA 14*
Albee, John 1833-1915 *NatCAB 4,*
NatCAB 15, WhAm 1
Albee, Maria Hawes *WomWWA 14*
Albee, Percy F 1883-1959 *WhAm 3*
Albemarle, Duke Of 1608-1670 *ApCAB*
Alber, David O 1909-1968 *WhAm 5*
Alber, Louis John 1879-1962 *WhAm 4*
Alberdi, Juan Bautista 1810-1884 *McGEWB*
Albers, Anni 1899- *BnEnAmA*
Albers, George 1872- *WhAm 5*
Albers, Henri 1867- *WhAm 4*
Albers, Homer 1863-1947 *NatCAB 35,*
WhAm 2
Albers, Josef 1888- *BnEnAmA, WebAB*
Albers, Joseph H 1891-1966 *WhAm 4*
Albers, Minnie Martin 1865- *WomWWA 14*
Albers, William Henry 1880-1954 *NatCAB 43,*
WhAm 3
Albert 1819-1861 *McGEWB*
Albert I 1875-1934 *McGEWB, WhoMilH*
Albert Of Bollstadt *DcScB*
Albert I Of Monaco 1848-1922 *DcScB*
Albert Of Saxony 1316?-1390 *DcScB*
Albert, A Adrian 1905-1972 *WhAm 5*
Albert, Allen Diehl 1874- *WhAm 5*
Albert, Allen Diehl, Jr. 1902- *WhAm 5*
Albert, Aristides Elphonso Peter 1853-
ApCAB Sup, WhAm 4
Albert, Calvin Dodge 1876- *WhAm 5*
Albert, Carl Bert 1908- *BiDrAC, WebAB*
Albert, Charles Allen 1877-1951 *NatCAB 40*
Albert, Charles Stanley 1847-1912 *WhAm 1*
Albert, Charles Sumner 1858-1923 *WhAm 1*
Albert, Clifford Edmund 1872-1960 *WhAm 4*
Albert, Elma Gates 1866- *WhAm 3*
Albert, Ernest 1857-1946 *NatCAB 36,*
WhAm 2
Albert, Grace *WomWWA 14*
Albert, Henry 1878-1930 *WhAm 1*
Albert, Isaac 1888-1966 *NatCAB 52*
Albert, John James 1789-1863 *REnAW*
Albert, John S 1834-1880 *NatCAB 9*
Albert, John S 1835-1880 *ApCAB*
Albert, Brother Sylvester 1918-1962 *WhAm 4*
Albert, William Julian 1816-1879 *BiAUS,*
BiDrAC, WhAm H
Albert, William Stone 1845- *NatCAB 4*
Alberti, Friedrich August Von 1795-1878 *DcScB*
Alberti, Leon Battista 1404-1472 *McGEWB*
Alberti, Leone Battista 1404-1472 *AsBiEn,*
DcScB
Alberti, Salomon 1540-1600 *DcScB*
Albertina, Sister *NotAW*
Alberts, Joseph Ortan 1907-1967 *WhAm 4*
Albertson, Abraham Horace 1872-1964
NatCAB 51, WhAm 4
Albertson, Charles Carroll 1865-1959 *WhAm 3*
Albertson, Dean 1920- *EncAAH*
Albertson, Frederick William 1892-1961
NatCAB 53
Albertson, George Roger 1886-1931 *WhAm 1,*
WhAm 1C
Albertson, J Mark 1891-1963 *WhAm 4*
Albertson, James Herbert 1925-1967
NatCAB 54, WhAm 4
Albertson, Lucy Durfee Clark 1865-
WomWWA 14
Albertson, Nathaniel 1800-1863 *BiAUS,*
BiDrAC, WhAm H
Albertson, Ralph 1866-1951 *NatCAB 15,*
WhAm 3

Albertus Magnus, Saint 1193?-1280 *AsBiEn,*
McGEWB
Albertus Magnus, Saint 1200?-1280 *DcScB*
Alberty, Harold 1890-1971 *WhAm 5*
Alberty, Harold Bernard 1890-1971 *BiDAmEd*
Albery, Bronson James 1881-1971 *WhAm 5*
Albery, Faxon Franklin Duane 1848- *WhAm 4*
Albig, John William 1899-1963 *WhAm 4*
Albin, John Henry 1843- *NatCAB 14*
Albing, Otto Frederick 1840-1905 *WhAm 1*
Albinus, Bernard 1653-1721 *DcScB Sup*
Albinus, Bernard Siegfried 1697-1770
DcScB Sup
Albinus, Bernhard Siegfried 1697-1770 *BiHiMed*
Albinus, Christiaan Bernard 1698?-1752
DcScB Sup
Albinus, Frederik Bernard 1715-1778
DcScB Sup
Albion, James Francis 1860- *WhAm 4*
Albray, Raymonde Adair 1880-1968
NatCAB 54
Albrecht, Archduke 1817-1895 *WhoMilH*
Albrecht, Albert August 1853-1936 *NatCAB 46*
Albrecht, Carl Theodor 1843-1915 *DcScB*
Albrecht, Charles Frederick 1857-1921
NatCAB 6
Albrecht, George Moritz 1884-1956 *NatCAB 43*
Albrecht, Gilmon Frederick 1904-1955
NatCAB 46
Albrecht, Jennie Butler *WomWWA 14*
Albrecht, Sebastian 1876- *ApCAB X*
Albrecht, Walter William Frederick 1885-1961
NatCAB 48
Albren, Edward Joseph 1919-1972 *WhAm 6*
Albright, Adam Emory 1862-1957 *WhAm 3*
Albright, Andrew 1831- *ApCAB Sup,*
NatCAB 4
Albright, Charles 1830-1880 *BiAUS, BiDrAC,*
WhAm H
Albright, Charles Clinton 1879- *WhAm 6*
Albright, Charles Edgar 1867-1946 *NatCAB 17,*
NatCAB 35, WhAm 2
Albright, Charles Jefferson 1816-1883 *BiAUS,*
BiDrAC, WhAm H
Albright, Daniel K *NewYHSD*
Albright, Edward 1873-1937 *WhAm 1*
Albright, Edwin 1838-1902 *WhAm 1*
Albright, Eliza Downing 1847- *AmWom*
Albright, Evelyn Mary 1880- *WomWWA 14*
Albright, Floyd Thron 1897- *IIBEAAW*
Albright, Frank Herman 1865-1940 *WhAm 1*
Albright, Fuller 1900-1969 *WhAm 5*
Albright, Guy Harry 1876- *WhAm 5*
Albright, Hermann Oliver 1876-1944 *IIBEAAW*
Albright, Horace Marden 1890- *EncAAH*
Albright, Ivan LeLorraine 1897- *BnEnAmA,*
WebAB
Albright, Jacob 1759-1808 *ApCAB, DcAmB,*
DcAmReB, NatCAB 11, TwCBDA,
WebAB, WhAm H
Albright, Jacob 1769-1808 *AmBi*
Albright, Jacob Dissinger 1870-1926
NatCAB 20, WhAm 5
Albright, John Joseph 1848-1931 *NatCAB 51,*
WhAm 1
Albright, Percy R 1866-1936 *WhAm 1*
Albright, Raymond Wolf 1901-1965 *WhAm 4*
Albright, Robert Choate 1903-1973 *WhAm 6*
Albright, Susan Gertrude Fuller *WomWWA 14*
Albright, W Edward 1873-1937 *NatCAB 35*
Albright, William *NewYHSD*
Albright, William Foxwell 1891-1971 *EncAB,*
NatCAB 56, WebAB, WhAm 5
Albright, William Haines 1875-1942
NatCAB 32
Albrizio, Humbert 1901-1970 *WhAm 5*
Albro, Addis 1855-1911 *WhAm 1*
Albro, Mrs. Curtis Sanford 1893-1950 *WhAm 3*
Albro, John 1824?- *NewYHSD*
Albro, Lewis Colt 1876-1924 *DcAmB*
Albumasar *DcScB*
Albuquerque, Afonso De 1460?-1515 *McGEWB*
Albutt, Sir Thomas Clifford 1836-1925 *BiHiMed*
Alcabitius *DcScB*
Alcala, Galiano Dionisio 1762-1805 *ApCAB*
Alcantara, Francisco Linares 1830-1879 *ApCAB*
Alcedo, Antonio *ApCAB*
Alciatore, Roy Louis 1902-1972 *WhAm 5*

Alcibar, Jose *ApCAB*
Alcibiades 450?BC-404BC *McGEWB*
Alcmaeon 500?BC- *AsBiEn*
Alcmaeon Of Crotona 535?BC- *DcScB*
Alcocer, Vidal 1801-1860 *ApCAB*
Alcock, Nathaniel Graham 1881-1953
NatCAB 47, WhAm 3
Alcorn, Douglas Earle 1906-1968 *WhAm 5*
Alcorn, Hugh Mead 1872-1955 *WhAm 3*
Alcorn, James Lusk 1816-1894 *ApCAB,*
BiAUS, BiDConf, BiDrAC, DcAmB,
McGEWB, NatCAB 13, TwCBDA,
WhAm H, WhAmP
Alcorn, Roy Anvil 1925-1973 *WhAm 6*
Alcott, Amos Bronson 1799-1888 *AmBi,*
ApCAB, BiDAmEd, DcAmB, Drake,
McGEWB, NatCAB 2, TwCBDA,
WebAB, WhAm H
Alcott, Carroll Duard 1901-1965 *WhAm 4*
Alcott, Louisa May 1832-1888 *AmBi, AmWom,*
ApCAB, DcAmB, EncAB, McGEWB,
NatCAB 1, NotAW, TwCBDA, WebAB,
WhAm H
Alcott, May 1840-1879 *AmWom, ApCAB,*
NewYHSD, TwCBDA
Alcott, Ralph Waldo Emerson 1850-1928
NatCAB 21
Alcott, William Alexander 1798-1859 *ApCAB,*
Drake, NatCAB 12, TwCBDA
Alcott, William Andrus 1798-1859 *AmBi,*
BiDAmEd, DcAmB, WhAm H
Alcuin Of York 730?-804 *McGEWB*
Alcuin Of York 735?-804 *AsBiEn, DcScB*
Alda, Frances 1883-1952 *ApCAB X,*
NatCAB 39
Aldag, Charles M 1872-1927 *NatCAB 20*
Aldama, Ignacio d1811 *ApCAB*
Aldana, Ramon 1832-1882 *ApCAB*
Aldeen, Gedor Wilhelm 1886-1962 *NatCAB 52*
Alden, Bertram F 1873-1939 *WhAm 1*
Alden, Bradford R 1800-1870 *ApCAB*
Alden, Bradford R 1810-1870 *TwCBDA*
Alden, Carlos Coolidge 1866-1956 *WhAm 4*
Alden, Carroll Storrs 1876- *WhAm 5*
Alden, Charles Henry 1836- *WhAm 4*
Alden, Charles Henry 1867-1951 *WhAm 3*
Alden, Cynthia May Westover 1861-1931
BiCAW, NatCAB 22, WhAm 1
Alden, Cynthia May Westover 1862-1931
ApCAB X, DcAmB S1, NatCAB 14,
WomWWA 14
Alden, Ebenezer 1788-1881 *ApCAB, DcAmB,*
Drake, NatCAB 19, TwCBDA, WhAm H
Alden, Edmund Kimball 1825-1896 *NatCAB 9,*
TwCBDA
Alden, Edward S 1888-1953 *WhAm 3*
Alden, Eliot 1874-1946 *NatCAB 34*
Alden, Emily Gillmore 1834- *AmWom*
Alden, Ezra Hyde 1866-1945 *WhAm 2*
Alden, George Henry 1866- *WhAm 4*
Alden, George Ira 1843-1926 *NatCAB 20*
Alden, Harold Lee 1890-1964 *NatCAB 52*
Alden, Henry Mills 1836-1919 *AmBi, ApCAB,*
ApCAB X, DcAmB, NatCAB 1,
TwCBDA, WhAm 1
Alden, Herbert Watson 1870-1950 *NatCAB 45,*
WhAm 3
Alden, Ichabod 1739-1778 *ApCAB, DcAmB,*
Drake, WebAMB, WhAm H
Alden, Isabella Macdonald 1841-1930 *AmWom,*
ApCAB, ApCAB Sup, DcAmB S1,
NotAW, TwCBDA, WhAm 1
Alden, Isabella Macdonald 1842-1930
NatCAB 10
Alden, Isabelle Macdonald 1841-1930
WomWWA 14
Alden, James 1810-1877 *AmBi, ApCAB,*
DcAmB, Drake, NatCAB 24, NewYHSD,
TwCBDA, WebAMB, WhAm H
Alden, James Madison 1834-1922 *IIBEAAW,*
NewYHSD
Alden, John 1599?-1687 *AmBi, ApCAB,*
DcAmB, Drake, NatCAB 10, TwCBDA,
WebAB, WhAm H
Alden, John 1860-1934 *NatCAB 24, WhAm 1*
Alden, John Berry 1847-1924 *ApCAB X,*
WhAm 1
Alden, John Ferris 1852-1917 *DcAmB*

Alden, Joseph 1807-1885 *ApCAB, BiDAmEd, DcAmB, Drake, NatCAB 5, TwCBDA, WhAm H*

Alden, Lucy Morris Chaffee 1836- *AmWom*

Alden, Priscilla Mullens 1604?-1680 *AmBi*

Alden, Priscilla Mullins 1602?-1680 *NotAW*

Alden, Raymond Macdonald 1873-1924 *AmBi, DcAmB, NatCAB 20, WhAm 1*

Alden, Roger 1748-1836 *Drake*

Alden, Roger 1754-1836 *ApCAB*

Alden, Timothy 1771-1839 *ApCAB, DcAmB, Drake, TwCBDA, WhAm H*

Alden, Timothy 1781-1839 *NatCAB 13*

Alden, Timothy 1819-1858 *ApCAB, Drake*

Alden, Timothy 1823-1858 *NatCAB 12, TwCBDA*

Alden, William C *NewYHSD*

Alden, William Clinton 1871-1959 *WhAm 4*

Alden, William Livingston 1837-1908 *ApCAB, DcAmB, NatCAB 6, TwCBDA, WhAm 1*

Alden, William Livingstone 1837-1908 *ApCAB Sup*

Alden, William Tracy 1866- *WhAm 3*

Alder, Byron 1883-1951 *WhAm 3*

Alder, Eugene C *ApCAB X*

Alder, Kurt 1902-1958 *AsBiEn, DcScB, WhAm 3*

Alderdice, George Frederick 1876-1934 *NatCAB 28*

Alderdyce, William Wesley 1871-1959 *NatCAB 50*

Alderfer, Clayton Harley 1870-1964 *NatCAB 50*

Alderman, Edward Sinclair 1861- *TwCBDA, WhAm 4*

Alderman, Edwin Anderson 1861-1931 *BiDAmEd, DcAmB S1, NatCAB 13, NatCAB 23, TwCBDA, WhAm 1*

Alderman, Frank 1879- *WhAm 6*

Alderman, Grover Henry 1886-1930 *WhAm 1*

Alderman, Rhenas Hoffard 1881- *WhAm 6*

Aldermann, Lewis R 1872- *WhAm 5*

Alderotti, Taddeo 1223-1295? *DcScB*

Alderson, John Duffy 1854-1910 *BiDrAC*

Alderson, Victor Clifton 1862-1946 *ApCAB X, TwCBDA, WhAm 2*

Alderson, Victor Clifton 1863-1946 *NatCAB 12*

Alderson, Wroe 1898-1965 *WhAm 4*

Alderton, William *NewYHSD*

Aldinger, Albert Henry 1877-1942 *NatCAB 31*

Aldington, Hilda Doolittle 1886-1961 *NatCAB 46*

Aldington, Richard 1892-1962 *WhAm 4*

Aldini, Giovanni 1762-1834 *DcScB*

Aldis, Arthur Taylor 1861-1933 *NatCAB 31, WhAm 1*

Aldis, Asa 1770?-1847 *NatCAB 4*

Aldis, Dorothy Keeley 1897-1966 *WhAm 4*

Aldis, Graham 1895-1966 *NatCAB 52, WhAm 4*

Aldis, Mary Reynolds 1872-1949 *WhAm 2*

Aldis, Owen Franklin 1852-1925 *NatCAB 44*

Aldis, Owen Franklin 1853-1925 *NatCAB 11*

Aldred, John Edward d1945 *WhAm 2*

Aldredge, Amanda Ira *WhoColR*

Aldredge, Sawnie Robertson 1890-1949 *NatCAB 38*

Aldrey Y Montolio, Pedro De 1864-1936 *WhAm 1*

Aldrich, Alonzo 1858-1931 *NatCAB 25*

Aldrich, Anne Reeve 1866-1892 *AmWom, NatCAB 4, WhAm H*

Aldrich, Annette Howland 1859- *WomWWA 14*

Aldrich, Mrs. Arthur *WomWWA 14*

Aldrich, Auretta Roys 1829- *WhAm 4, WomWWA 14*

Aldrich, Bess Streeter 1881-1954 *DcAmB S5, NatCAB 46, WhAm 3*

Aldrich, Charles 1828-1908 *ApCAB Sup, NatCAB 9, TwCBDA, WhAm 1*

Aldrich, Charles Anderson 1888-1949 *DcAmB S4, WhAm 2*

Aldrich, Charles Henry 1850-1929 *NatCAB 13*

Aldrich, Charles John 1861-1908 *WhAm 1*

Aldrich, Charles Spaulding 1871- *WhAm 6*

Aldrich, Chester Hardy 1862-1924 *NatCAB 25, WhAm 1*

Aldrich, Chester Holmes 1871-1940 *ApCAB X, DcAmB S2, NatCAB 33, WhAm 1*

Aldrich, Chilson Darragh 1876-1948 *WhAm 2*

Aldrich, Cyrus 1808-1871 *BiAUS, BiDrAC, WhAm H*

Aldrich, Darragh d1967 *WhAm 4*

Aldrich, Donald Bradshaw 1892-1961 *WhAm 4*

Aldrich, Edgar 1848-1921 *DcAmB, NatCAB 19, TwCBDA, WhAm 1*

Aldrich, Edward Burgess 1871-1957 *WhAm 3*

Aldrich, Flora L 1859- *AmWom*

Aldrich, Fred Abbott 1861-1957 *NatCAB 48*

Aldrich, George Ames 1872-1941 *NatCAB 31, WhAm 1*

Aldrich, Henry Clay 1857-1922 *WhAm 1, WhAm 1C*

Aldrich, Herbert Lincoln 1860- *WhAm 4*

Aldrich, James 1810-1856 *ApCAB, Drake*

Aldrich, James 1810-1866 *NatCAB 9, WhAm H*

Aldrich, James 1850-1910 *NatCAB 3, NatCAB 26*

Aldrich, James Franklin 1853-1933 *BiDrAC, WhAmP*

Aldrich, James Thomas 1819-1875 *NatCAB 12*

Aldrich, John Gladding 1864-1952 *WhAm 3, WhAm 5*

Aldrich, John Merton 1866-1934 *ApCAB X, NatCAB 46, WhAm 1*

Aldrich, Josephine Cables 1843- *AmWom, NatCAB 5*

Aldrich, Julia Carter 1834- *AmWom*

Aldrich, Kildroy Philip 1877- *WhAm 5*

Aldrich, Leander Jefferson 1851- *TwCBDA, WhAm 4*

Aldrich, Louis 1843-1901 *DcAmB, NatCAB 13, WhAm H*

Aldrich, Louise Banister 1880- *WhAm 6, WomWWA 14*

Aldrich, Loyal Blaine 1884-1965 *WhAm 4*

Aldrich, Lynn Ellis 1890-1974 *WhAm 6*

Aldrich, Margaret Chester 1870- *WomWWA 14*

Aldrich, Mary Jane 1833-1909 *AmWom, WhAm 1*

Aldrich, Mildred 1853-1928 *WhAm 1*

Aldrich, Morton Arnold 1874- *WhAm 3*

Aldrich, Nelson Wilmarth 1841-1915 *AmBi, ApCAB, ApCAB X, BiDrAC, DcAmB, EncAAH, EncAB, McGEWB, NatCAB 10, NatCAB 25, TwCBDA, WebAB, WhAm 1, WhAmP*

Aldrich, Orlando Wesley 1840- *ApCAB X, NatCAB 12, WhAm 4*

Aldrich, Perley Dunn 1863-1933 *WhAm 1*

Aldrich, Raymond Elbert 1888-1947 *NatCAB 34*

Aldrich, Richard 1863-1937 *AmBi, DcAmB S2, NatCAB 33, WhAm 1, WhAm 1C*

Aldrich, Richard Steere 1883-1941 *NatCAB 30*

Aldrich, Richard Steere 1884-1941 *BiDrAC, WhAm 1, WhAmP*

Aldrich, Samuel Nelson 1839-1908 *WhAm 1*

Aldrich, Sherwood 1868-1927 *WhAm 1*

Aldrich, Spencer 1854-1936 *NatCAB 38*

Aldrich, Susanna Valentine 1828- *AmWom*

Aldrich, Thomas Bailey 1836-1907 *AmBi, ApCAB, ApCAB X, DcAmB, Drake, NatCAB 1, WebAB, WhAm 1*

Aldrich, Thomas Bailey 1837-1907 *TwCBDA*

Aldrich, Truman Heminway 1848-1932 *BiDrAC, WhAm 1, WhAmP*

Aldrich, William 1820-1885 *BiDrAC, WhAm H, WhAmP*

Aldrich, William Farrington 1815-1878 *NatCAB 8*

Aldrich, William Farrington 1853-1925 *BiDrAC, NatCAB 5, TwCBDA, WhAm 1, WhAmP*

Aldrich, William Sleeper 1863- *WhAm 4*

Aldrich, William Truman 1880-1966 *NatCAB 53, WhAm 4*

Aldrich, Winthrop Williams 1885-1974 *WhAm 6*

Aldridge, Clayson Wheeler 1899-1944 *WhAm 2*

Aldridge, Frances Ellen Wooten *WomWWA 14*

Aldridge, George Washington 1856- *WhAm 4*

Aldridge, Ira Frederick d1867 *ApCAB*

Aldridge, Ira Frederick 1804?-1867 *Drake, WebAB*

Aldridge, Ira Frederick 1805?-1867 *WhAm H*

Aldridge, Ira Frederick 1807-1867 *DcAmB*

Aldridge, Walter Hull 1867-1959 *NatCAB 43, WhAm 3*

Aldrovandi, Ulisse 1522-1605 *DcScB*

Aldunate, Don Santiago d1918 *WhAm 1*

Aldworth, Mr. *NewYHSD*

Alegre, Francisco J 1729-1788 *ApCAB*

Aleijadinho, O 1738-1814 *McGEWB*

Alekseev, Mikhail Vasilievich 1857-1918 *WhoMilH*

Aleman, Mateo 1547-1615? *McGEWB*

Aleman, Miguel 1902- *McGEWB*

Alemany, Jose Sadoc 1814-1888 *DcAmB, WhAm H*

Alemany, Joseph Sadoc 1814-1888 *ApCAB, Drake, NatCAB 12, REnAW, TwCBDA*

Alembert, Jean LeRond D' 1717-1783 *DcScB, McGEWB*

Alenca, Jose Martiniano D' 1829-1877 *ApCAB*

Alencastre, Stephen Peter 1876-1940 *WhAm 2*

Alencastre Norona Y Silva, Fernando *ApCAB*

Alerding, Herman Joseph 1845-1924 *NatCAB 13, WhAm 1*

Aleshire, Arthur William 1900-1940 *BiDrAC, WhAm 1, WhAmP*

Aleshire, Edward 1907-1965 *WhAm 4*

Aleshire, James Buchanan 1856-1925 *WhAm 1*

Alessandri, Arturo 1868-1950 *McGEWB*

Alessandri, Jorge 1896- *McGEWB*

Alessandri-Palma, Arturo 1868- *WhAm 5*

Alessandroni, Walter Edwin 1914-1966 *WhAm 4*

Alexander *NewYHSD*

Alexander I 1777-1825 *McGEWB*

Alexander II 1818-1881 *McGEWB*

Alexander III 1845-1894 *McGEWB*

Alexander VI 1431-1503 *McGEWB*

Alexander Nevsky 1219?-1263 *McGEWB*

Alexander Of Aphrodisias *DcScB*

Alexander Of Myndos *DcScB*

Alexander Of Tralles *DcScB*

Alexander Of Tunis 1891-1967 *McGEWB*

Alexander Of Tunis see also Alexander, Sir Harold

Alexander Of Yugoslavia 1888-1934 *McGEWB*

Alexander The Great 356BC-323BC *McGEWB*

Alexander, Abel Cidney 1861-1940 *NatCAB 34*

Alexander, Abraham d1786 *Drake*

Alexander, Abraham 1717-1786 *DcAmB, WhAm H, WhAmP*

Alexander, Abraham 1718-1776 *TwCBDA*

Alexander, Abraham 1718-1786 *ApCAB*

Alexander, Adam 1772-1851 *WhAm H*

Alexander, Adam Rankin *BiAUS, BiDrAC, WhAm H*

Alexander, Albert Victor 1885-1965 *WhAm 4*

Alexander, Archer 1810?-1879 *ApCAB, NatCAB 12, TwCBDA*

Alexander, Archibald 1772-1851 *AmBi, ApCAB, DcAmB, DcAmReB, Drake, NatCAB 2, TwCBDA*

Alexander, Archie Alphonse 1888-1958 *NatCAB 49*

Alexander, Archie Alphonso 1888-1958 *WhoColR*

Alexander, Armstead Milton 1834-1892 *BiDrAC, WhAm H*

Alexander, Arthur Allen 1870-1949 *NatCAB 39*

Alexander, Ashton 1769-1855 *NatCAB 32*

Alexander, Barton Stone 1819-1878 *ApCAB, DcAmB, Drake, NatCAB 4, WhAm H*

Alexander, Ben 1894-1944 *WhAm 2*

Alexander, Caleb 1755-1828 *ApCAB, Drake*

Alexander, Carter 1881-1965 *WhAm 4*

Alexander, Charles 1868- *WhoColR*

Alexander, Charles 1897-1962 *WhAm 5*

Alexander, Charles 1935- *EncAAH*

Alexander, Charles Beatty 1849-1927 *ApCAB X, NatCAB 15, WhAm 1*

Alexander, Charles McCallon 1867-1920 *WhAm 1*

Alexander, Charles Tripler 1833-1918 *NatCAB 26, WhAm 1*

Alexander, Charlton 1884-1935 *WhAm 1*
Alexander, Chester *ApCAB X*
Alexander, Christine 1893-1975 *WhAm 6*
Alexander, Clyde C 1892-1965 *WhAm 4*
Alexander, Clyde H 1881- *WhAm 6*
Alexander, Cosmo 1724?-1772 *NewYHSD,*
WhAm 1
Alexander, Cosmos 1724?-1772 *BnEnAmA*
Alexander, DeAlva Stanwood 1845-1925 *AmBi,*
DcAmB, WhAm 1
Alexander, DeAlva Stanwood 1846-1925
BiDrAC, NatCAB 20, TwCBDA, WhAmP
Alexander, Donald 1891-1959 *WhAm 3*
Alexander, Douglas 1864-1949 *WhAm 2*
Alexander, Eben 1851- *NatCAB 12, TwCBDA,*
WhAm 1
Alexander, Edmund Brooke 1800?-1888
NatCAB 4
Alexander, Edmund Brooke 1802?-1888 *ApCAB,*
Drake, TwCBDA
Alexander, Edward Albert 1873-1948
NatCAB 35, WhAm 2
Alexander, Edward Porter 1835-1910 *BiDConf,*
DcAmB, NatCAB 8, TwCBDA,
WebAMB, WhAm 1
Alexander, Emma Cleora Thornton
WomWWA 14
Alexander, Emory Graham 1880-1930
NatCAB 36
Alexander, Ethel Vivian 1888- *WhoColR*
Alexander, Evan Shelby 1767?-1809 *BiAUS,*
BiDrAC, WhAm H
Alexander, Frances Gordon Paddock *BiCAW*
Alexander, Francesca 1837-1917 *NewYHSD,*
NotAW, WhAm 1
Alexander, Francis 1800- *ApCAB*
Alexander, Francis 1800-1880 *BnEnAmA,*
NewYHSD
Alexander, Francis 1800-1881? *DcAmB,*
WhAm H
Alexander, Franz 1891-1964 *NatCAB 52,*
WhAm 4
Alexander, Fred Barber 1853-1939 *NatCAB 30*
Alexander, Frederick 1870- *WhAm 5*
Alexander, Frederick Hall 1884-1966
NatCAB 52
Alexander, George 1814- *ApCAB*
Alexander, George 1843-1930 *NatCAB 23,*
TwCBDA, WhAm 1
Alexander, George Forrest 1882-1948
NatCAB 39, WhAm 2
Alexander, Georgia 1868- *WomWWA 14*
Alexander, Grace Caroline 1872- *WhAm 5,*
WomWWA 14
Alexander, Gross 1852-1915 *DcAmB,*
NatCAB 21, WhAm 1
Alexander, Grover Cleveland 1887-1950
DcAmB S4
Alexander, Sir Harold 1891-1969 *WhWW-II,*
WhoMilH
Alexander, Sir Harold *see also* Alexander Of
Tunis
Alexander, Harold David 1874- *WhAm 5*
Alexander, Harriet L 1882- *WomWWA 14*
Alexander, Harry 1871-1932 *NatCAB 23*
Alexander, Hartley Burr 1873-1939 *ApCAB X,*
BiDAmEd, DcAmB S2, NatCAB 46,
WhAm 1
Alexander, Hattie Caroline Beringer
WomWWA 14
Alexander, Hattie Elizabeth 1901-1968
WhAm 5
Alexander, Henry Clay 1902-1969 *WhAm 5*
Alexander, Henry Martyn d1899 *WhAm 1*
Alexander, Henry Martyn 1869-1952
NatCAB 55, WhAm 3
Alexander, Henry P 1802-1867 *BiAUS*
Alexander, Henry Porteous 1801-1867 *BiDrAC,*
WhAm H
Alexander, Herbert G B 1860-1928 *WhAm 1*
Alexander, Hooper 1858- *WhAm 1*
Alexander, Hubbard Foster 1879-1952
NatCAB 17, WhAm 3
Alexander, Hugh Quincy 1911- *BiDrAC*
Alexander, J B *NewYHSD*
Alexander, James d1756 *Drake*
Alexander, James 1690?-1756 *ApCAB*
Alexander, James 1691-1756 *DcAmB,*

WhAm H
Alexander, James, Jr. 1789-1846 *BiAUS,*
BiDrAC, WhAm H
Alexander, James F 1824-1901 *WhAm 1*
Alexander, James Henry 1837-1919 *NatCAB 26*
Alexander, James Patterson 1883-1948
NatCAB 51, WhAm 2
Alexander, James Strange 1865-1932 *ApCAB X,*
NatCAB 24, WhAm 1
Alexander, James Waddel 1804-1859 *ApCAB,*
NatCAB 6, TwCBDA, WhAm H
Alexander, James Waddell 1804-1859 *Drake*
Alexander, James Waddell 1839-1915
ApCAB Sup, NatCAB 15, WhAm 1
Alexander, James Waddell, II 1888-1971
WhAm 5
Alexander, Jane Grace 1848- *AmWom*
Alexander, Jerome 1876-1959 *NatCAB 52,*
WhAm 3
Alexander, John 1777-1848 *BiAUS, BiDrAC,*
WhAm H
Alexander, John 1891-1954 *WhAm 3*
Alexander, John Brevard 1834- *WhAm 4*
Alexander, John E 1894-1963 *WhAm 4*
Alexander, John Edmiston 1815- *NatCAB 7*
Alexander, John Grant 1893- *BiDrAC*
Alexander, John Henry 1812-1867 *ApCAB,*
DcAmB, Drake, NatCAB 9, TwCBDA,
WhAm H
Alexander, John L 1878-1932 *WhAm 1*
Alexander, John Macmillan 1891-1957
WhAm 3
Alexander, John Romich 1849-1940 *WhAm 3*
Alexander, John White 1856-1915 *AmBi,*
ApCAB X, BnEnAmA, DcAmB,
NatCAB 11, WhAm 1
Alexander, Joseph Addison 1809-1860 *AmBi,*
ApCAB, DcAmB, Drake, NatCAB 1,
TwCBDA, WhAm H
Alexander, Joseph Eli 1874- *NatCAB 17*
Alexander, Joshua Willis 1852-1936 *BiDrAC,*
BiDrUSE, NatCAB 27, WhAm 1,
WhAmP
Alexander, Julian 1889-1933 *NatCAB 23*
Alexander, Julian Power 1887-1953 *WhAm 3*
Alexander, Julius 1885-1964 *NatCAB 55*
Alexander, Lawrence Dade 1878-1939
NatCAB 30
Alexander, Leigh 1883-1948 *WhAm 2*
Alexander, Lester Fisher 1879-1954 *WhAm 3*
Alexander, Lucien Hugh 1866-1926 *NatCAB 28*
Alexander, M Moss d1959 *WhAm 3*
Alexander, Magnus Washington 1870-1932
NatCAB 23, WhAm 1
Alexander, Maitland 1867-1940 *WhAm 1*
Alexander, Mark 1792-1883 *BiAUS, BiDrAC,*
WhAm H, WhAmP
Alexander, Mary Corlinda Batcheller
WomWWA 14
Alexander, Mary Spratt Provoost 1693-1760
NotAW
Alexander, Matilda 1842- *NatCAB 4*
Alexander, Michael 1807?- *NewYHSD*
Alexander, Minnie 1877- *WhAm 5*
Alexander, Moses 1853-1932 *NatCAB 23,*
WhAm 1
Alexander, Nathaniel 1756-1808 *ApCAB,*
BiAUS, BiDrAC, Drake, NatCAB 4,
WhAm H, WhAmP
Alexander, Oakey Logan 1878-1950 *WhAm 2A*
Alexander, Orline St. John 1866-
WomWWA 14
Alexander, Osa Franklyn 1900-1957
NatCAB 47
Alexander, Paul W 1888-1967 *WhAm 4*
Alexander, Peter *NewYHSD*
Alexander, Peter Wellington 1824-1886 *BiDConf*
Alexander, Ralph Irwin 1890-1965 *NatCAB 52*
Alexander, Raymond Pace 1898-1974 *WhAm 6*
Alexander, Rob Roy 1878-1966 *ApCAB X,*
NatCAB 52
Alexander, Robert 1740?-1805 *ApCAB Sup,*
BiAUS, BiDrAC, WhAm H
Alexander, Robert 1846- *NatCAB 10*
Alexander, Robert 1863-1941 *ApCAB X,*
WhAm 1
Alexander, Robert Carter 1857-1899 *NatCAB 6,*
WhAm 1

Alexander, Robert Clark 1886-1954 *NatCAB 46*
Alexander, Roy Heber 1891-1965 *NatCAB 56*
Alexander, Samuel 1859-1938 *McGEWB*
Alexander, Samuel Davies 1819-1894 *ApCAB,*
DcAmB, TwCBDA, WhAm H
Alexander, Samuel Nathan 1910-1967
NatCAB 54, WhAm 5
Alexander, Samuel Thomas 1836-1904
NatCAB 36
Alexander, Stephen 1806-1883 *AmBi, ApCAB,*
DcAmB, Drake, NatCAB 11, TwCBDA,
WhAm H
Alexander, Suydenham B 1840-1921 *WhAm 4*
Alexander, Sydenham Benoni 1840-1921
BiDrAC, NatCAB 33, WhAmP
Alexander, Taliaferro 1846- *WhAm 1*
Alexander, Taliaferro 1847- *NatCAB 10*
Alexander, Thomas 1774-1820 *ApCAB*
Alexander, Thomas 1887-1972 *WhAm 5*
Alexander, Thomas 1908-1966 *NatCAB 53*
Alexander, Truman Hudson 1891-1941
WhAm 2
Alexander, Vance Jackson 1884-1967
NatCAB 52, WhAm 4
Alexander, Virginia *WomWWA 14*
Alexander, Wallace McKinney 1869-1939
WhAm 1
Alexander, Walter Gilbert 1880- *WhoColR*
Alexander, Walter R 1889-1954 *WhAm 3*
Alexander, Wellington Grenville 1856-
NatCAB 7
Alexander, Wilford S 1878-1959 *WhAm 3*
Alexander, Will Winton 1884- *WhAm 3*
Alexander, William *Drake*
Alexander, Sir William 1580-1640 *ApCAB,*
Drake
Alexander, William 1726-1783 *AmBi, ApCAB,*
DcAmB, Drake, NatCAB 1, TwCBDA,
WebAMB, WhAm H, WhAmP
Alexander, William 1831-1906 *NatCAB 5,*
TwCBDA, WhAm 1
Alexander, Sir William 1874-1954 *WhAm 3*
Alexander, William Albert 1875-1943 *WhAm 2*
Alexander, William Anthony 1837-1914
NatCAB 33
Alexander, William Cooper 1806-1874
TwCBDA
Alexander, William Cowper 1806-1874 *ApCAB,*
NatCAB 13
Alexander, William DeWitt 1833-1913 *DcAmB,*
WhAm 1
Alexander, William Gay 1867-1949 *NatCAB 37*
Alexander, William Henry 1867- *WhAm 5*
Alexander, William Leidy 1842-1915 *WhAm 1*
Alexander, William Marvin 1877-1940
NatCAB 30
Alexander, William McFaddin 1860?-1944
WhAm 3
Alexander, William Valentine *WhAm 5*
Alexander, William Vollie, Jr. 1934- *BiDrAC*
Alexanderson, Ernst Frederik Werner 1878-1975
WebAB, WhAm 6
Alexanderson, Frederik Werner 1878-1975
ApCAB X
Alexis Mikhailovich Romanov 1629-1676
McGEWB
Alexis Of Piedmont *DcScB*
Alexis, Algert Daniel 1897-1967 *NatCAB 53,*
WhAm 4A
Alexis, Joseph Anthony 1894-1955 *NatCAB 42*
Alexius I, Comnenus 1048?-1118 *McGEWB*
Alexy, Janko 1894- *WhAm 5*
Aley, Robert Judson 1863-1935 *ApCAB X,*
NatCAB 15, WhAm 1
Alfano, Vincenzo 1854- *WhAm 1*
Alfaro, Colon Eloy 1891-1957 *WhAm 3*
Alfaro, Jose Eloy 1842-1912 *McGEWB*
Alfaro, Prudencio 1860?- *ApCAB Sup*
Alfaro, Ricardo Joaquin 1882-1971 *WhAm 5*
Alfaro, Victor Ricardo 1907-1974 *WhAm 6*
Alfieri, Conte Vittorio 1749-1803 *McGEWB*
Alfonce, Jean 1482?-1557? *AmBi, DcAmB,*
WhAm H
Alfonse 1500?- *ApCAB Sup*
Alfonso III 1210-1279 *McGEWB*
Alfonso VI 1040-1109 *McGEWB*
Alfonso X 1221-1284 *McGEWB*
Alfonso XIII 1886-1941 *McGEWB*

Alfonso El Sabio 1221-1284 *DcScB*
Alfonso I, Henriques 1109?-1185 *McGEWB*
Alfonso X Of Castile 1221-1284 *AsBiEn*
Alford, Alonzo 1837-1916 *NatCAB 16*
Alford, Fred Fergus 1899-1964 *NatCAB 52*
Alford, John 1686-1761 *Drake*
Alford, Julius Caesar 1799-1863 *BiAUS,*
  BiDrAC, WhAm H
Alford, Leon Pratt 1877-1942 *DcAmB S3,*
  WhAm 1, WhAm 2
Alford, Mrs. Neil d1957 *WhAm 3*
Alford, Ora Wadsworth 1871- *WomWWA 14*
Alford, Theodore Crandall 1885-1947
  NatCAB 40, WhAm 2
Alford, Thomas Dale 1916- *BiDrAC, WhAmP*
Alford, Walter Hulbert 1876-1930 *NatCAB 28*
Alford, William Hays 1866- *WhAm 4*
Alfraganus *DcScB*
Alfred The Great 849-899 *McGEWB*
Alfred The Great 849-900 *AsBiEn*
Alfred, Frank H 1866- *WhAm 4*
Alfredson, Bernard Victor 1908-1968
  NatCAB 54, WhAm 5
Alfriend, Edward Morrisson 1843- *WhAm 4*
Alfriend, Thomas Lee 1843-1901 *NatCAB 8*
Algeo, Sara MacCormack 1876- *WomWWA 14*
Alger, Bruce Reynolds 1918- *BiDrAC,*
  WhAmP
Alger, Cyrus 1781-1856 *ApCAB, DcAmB,*
  TwCBDA, WebAB, WhAm H
Alger, Cyrus 1782-1856 *Drake, NatCAB 6*
Alger, Frederick M, Jr. 1907-1967 *WhAm 4*
Alger, Frederick Moulton 1876-1933
  NatCAB 24
Alger, George William 1872-1967 *NatCAB 53,*
  WhAm 4
Alger, Horatio 1832-1899 *DcAmB, McGEWB,*
  NatCAB 11, WebAB
Alger, Horatio 1834-1899 *AmBi, ApCAB,*
  Drake, EncAB, TwCBDA, WhAm 1
Alger, John Lincoln 1864- *WhAm 4*
Alger, Philip Rounseville 1859-1912 *NatCAB 15,*
  WhAm 1
Alger, Mrs. Russell A *AmWom*
Alger, Russell Alexander 1836- *ApCAB,*
  TwCBDA
Alger, Russell Alexander 1836-1905 *BiDrUSE*
Alger, Russell Alexander 1836-1907 *AmBi,*
  BiDrAC, DcAmB, NatCAB 5, WhAm 1,
  WhAmP
Alger, William Rounseville 1822-1905 *ApCAB,*
  DcAmB, Drake, NatCAB 6, TwCBDA,
  WhAm 1
Algire, Glenn Horner 1907-1958 *NatCAB 47*
Algoe, Margaret Tracy 1867- *WomWWA 14*
Alhadeff, Nessim David 1884-1950 *NatCAB 40*
Alhazen 965?-1038 *AsBiEn*
Alhazen 965-1040? *DcScB*
Ali 600?-661 *McGEWB*
Ali, Sunni d1492 *McGEWB*
Ali, Anwar 1913-1974 *WhAm 6*
Ali, Ben *NewYHSD*
Ali, Mohammed 1909-1963 *WhAm 4*
Ali, Muhammad 1942- *EncAB, WebAB*
Ali Arslan 1741-1822 *WhoMilH*
Ali Khan, Liaquat 1895-1951 *WhAm 3*
Alibert, Jean Louis 1768-1837 *BiHiMed*
Alig, Clarence Schirmer 1887-1941 *NatCAB 30*
Alinsky, Saul David 1909-1972 *WebAB,*
  WhAm 5
Alison, Francis 1705-1779 *BiDAmEd, DcAmB,*
  Drake, NatCAB 1, WhAm H
Alker, Alphonse Henry 1851-1913 *NatCAB 24*
Alker, Carroll Booth 1893-1946 *NatCAB 47*
Alker, Edward Paul 1887-1938 *NatCAB 29*
Alker, Henry 1820-1886 *NatCAB 8*
Alker, Henry Alphonse 1886-1951 *NatCAB 40*
Alker, James Ward 1883-1931 *NatCAB 24*
Alker, Paul Brady 1861-1912 *NatCAB 16*
Alkindus *DcScB*
Allaire, James Peter 1785-1858 *DcAmB,*
  NatCAB 24, WhAm H
Allaire, William Herbert 1858-1933 *WhAm 1*
Allal Al-Fassi, Mohamed 1910- *McGEWB*
Allan, Alexander MacMillan 1859-1930
  NatCAB 23
Allan, Chilton 1786-1858 *BiDrAC, TwCBDA,*
  WhAm H

Allan, Denison Maurice 1897-1974 *WhAm 6*
Allan, George William 1822- *ApCAB*
Allan, Sir Hugh 1810-1882 *ApCAB*
Allan, J McGregor *NewYHSD*
Allan, John 1746-1805 *ApCAB, DcAmB,*
  Drake, WhAmP
Allan, John 1747-1805 *WhAm H*
Allan, John 1777-1863 *ApCAB, NatCAB 10*
Allan, John J 1887-1960 *WhAm 4*
Allan, Sarah Campbell 1861- *WomWWA 14*
Allanson, John 1800-1859 *NewYHSD*
Allard, John S 1897-1967 *WhAm 4A*
Allardice, Robert Edgar 1862-1928 *WhAm 1*
Allardice, Samuel d1798 *NewYHSD*
Allbright, William 1795?- *NewYHSD*
Allbright, William Broughton 1856-1939
  NatCAB 33
Allbutt, Sir Thomas Clifford 1836-1925 *AsBiEn*
Allcock, Thomas 1814-1891 *TwCBDA*
Allderdice, Norman 1894-1961 *NatCAB 48,*
  WhAm 4
Allderdice, Taylor 1863-1934 *NatCAB 32*
Alldredge, Eugene Perry 1875-1953 *WhAm 3*
Alldredge, J Haden 1887-1962 *WhAm 4*
Allebach, Leroy 1880-1943 *NatCAB 36*
Allebaugh, Carl Franklin 1896-1970
  NatCAB 57
Allee, James Francis 1857-1938 *NatCAB 13*
Allee, James Frank 1857-1938 *BiDrAC,*
  WhAm 1
Allee, Marjorie Hill 1890-1945 *WhAm 2,*
  WhAm 2C
Allee, Warder Clyde 1885-1955 *NatCAB 42,*
  WhAm 3
Allefonsce, Jean 1482?-1557? *AmBi, DcAmB,*
  WhAm H
Allegri, Joseph *NewYHSD*
Alleman, Gellert 1871-1946 *WhAm 2*
Alleman, Herbert Christian 1868-1953 *WhAm 3*
Allemang, Herbert John 1902-1962 *NatCAB 48,*
  WhAm 4
Allen, Miss *NewYHSD*
Allen, Abel Leighton 1850-1927 *WhAm 1*
Allen, Ada Mary Eaton *WomWWA 14*
Allen, Addison 1865- *WhAm 4*
Allen, Alexander John 1900-1968 *WhAm 5*
Allen, Alexander Joseph 1887-1956 *NatCAB 46*
Allen, Alexander Viets Griswold 1841-1908
  ApCAB, DcAmB, NatCAB 10, TwCBDA,
  WhAm 1
Allen, Alfred 1866-1947 *WhAm 2*
Allen, Alfred Gaither 1867-1932 *BiDrAC,*
  WhAm 1
Allen, Alfred James 1859- *WhoColR*
Allen, Alfred Reginald 1876-1918 *WhAm 1*
Allen, Alice Ranney 1862- *WomWWA 14*
Allen, Amos Lawrence 1837-1911 *BiDrAC,*
  WhAm 1, WhAmP
Allen, Andrew 1740-1825 *ApCAB, BiAUS,*
  BiDrAC, DcAmB, TwCBDA, WhAm H,
  WhAmP
Allen, Andrew A 1855- *NatCAB 12*
Allen, Andrew Aniel 1857- *WhAm 4*
Allen, Andrew Hussey 1855-1921 *WhAm 1*
Allen, Andrew Jackson 1776-1853 *WhAm H*
Allen, Andrew Woodard 1881-1960 *NatCAB 48*
Allen, Andrews 1870-1931 *WhAm 1*
Allen, Annie King Blair *WomWWA 14*
Allen, Annie Winsor 1865- *WomWWA 14*
Allen, Anthony Benezet 1802-1892 *DcAmB,*
  EncAAH, WhAm H
Allen, Arch Turner 1875-1934 *BiDAmEd,*
  NatCAB 26, WhAm 1
Allen, Arthur Augustus 1885-1964 *WhAm 4*
Allen, Arthur Francis 1867-1949 *WhAm 2*
Allen, Arthur Moulton 1876-1950 *WhAm 3*
Allen, Arthur Potter 1892-1955 *NatCAB 44*
Allen, Arthur Watts 1879-1966 *NatCAB 53,*
  WhAm 4
Allen, Arthur Wilburn 1887-1958 *WhAm 3*
Allen, Asa Leonard 1891-1969 *BiDrAC,*
  WhAmP
Allen, Augustus Chapman 1864- *NatCAB 9*
Allen, Austin Oscar 1892-1970 *WhAm 5*
Allen, Bartholomew Manlove 1889-1951
  NatCAB 41
Allen, Benjamin *NewYHSD*
Allen, Benjamin 1789-1829 *ApCAB, Drake,*

  TwCBDA
Allen, Benjamin 1848-1924 *WhAm 1*
Allen, Benjamin 1896-1958 *WhAm 3*
Allen, Benjamin Franklin 1872- *WhAm 5,*
  WhoColR
Allen, Benjamin Leach 1874-1939 *WhAm 1*
Allen, Bennet Mills 1877-1963 *WhAm 4*
Allen, Beverly Sprague 1881-1934 *WhAm 1*
Allen, Calvin Francis 1851-1948 *TwCBDA,*
  WhAm 2
Allen, Carlos Eben 1873-1945 *WhAm 3*
Allen, Charles 1797-1869 *ApCAB, BiAUS,*
  BiDrAC, Drake, NatCAB 9, TwCBDA,
  WhAm H, WhAmP
Allen, Charles 1827-1913 *DcAmB, TwCBDA,*
  WhAm 1
Allen, Charles Chester 1880-1942 *NatCAB 33*
Allen, Charles Claflin 1855-1927 *WhAm 1*
Allen, Charles Claflin 1893-1974 *WhAm 6*
Allen, Charles Curtis 1886-1950 *WhAm 3*
Allen, Charles Dexter 1865-1926 *TwCBDA,*
  WhAm 1
Allen, Charles Edward 1891-1935 *WhAm 1*
Allen, Charles Elmer 1872-1954 *NatCAB 42,*
  WhAm 3
Allen, Charles Emery 1863- *WhoColR*
Allen, Charles Everett 1886-1954 *NatCAB 44*
Allen, Charles Frederick 1816-1899 *NatCAB 14,*
  TwCBDA
Allen, Charles Herbert 1848-1934 *ApCAB Sup,*
  BiDrAC, NatCAB 25, TwCBDA,
  WhAm 1, WhAmP
Allen, Charles Julius 1840-1915 *WhAm 1*
Allen, Charles Linnaeus 1849-1916 *NatCAB 8*
Allen, Charles Lucius 1858-1940 *WhAm 1*
Allen, Charles Metcalf 1871-1950 *NatCAB 37,*
  WhAm 3
Allen, Charles Morse 1859-1942 *WhAm 2*
Allen, Charles Ricketson 1862-1938 *BiDAmEd,*
  WhAm 2
Allen, Charles Warrenne 1854- *WhAm 1*
Allen, Charles Wesley 1872-1923 *NatCAB 20*
Allen, Chester Arthur 1893-1961 *WhAm 4*
Allen, Chilton 1786-1858 *BiAUS*
Allen, Christopher 1838?- *NewYHSD*
Allen, Clarence Emir 1852-1932 *BiDrAC,*
  NatCAB 27, WhAmP
Allen, Claxton Edmonds 1881- *WhAm 3*
Allen, Clay 1875- *WhAm 5*
Allen, Clinton L 1893-1960 *WhAm 4*
Allen, Cora Williams *WomWWA 14*
Allen, Courtney 1896-1969 *WhAm 5*
Allen, Crombie d1946 *WhAm 2*
Allen, D Emery 1876-1958 *NatCAB 47*
Allen, David Oliver 1799-1863 *DcAmB,*
  WhAm H
Allen, David Oliver 1800-1863 *ApCAB,*
  NatCAB 6
Allen, David Oliver 1804-1863 *Drake*
Allen, Devere 1891-1955 *WhAm 3*
Allen, Don 1901-1959 *NatCAB 43*
Allen, Don B 1889-1966 *WhAm 4*
Allen, Don Cameron 1903-1972 *NatCAB 56,*
  WhAm 5
Allen, Don Thomas 1898-1962 *NatCAB 49*
Allen, Dudley Peter 1852-1915 *NatCAB 14,*
  NatCAB 16, WhAm 1
Allen, Duff S 1895-1958 *WhAm 3*
Allen, E Ross 1911-1962 *NatCAB 49*
Allen, Ebenezer d1805 *Drake*
Allen, Ebenezer 1743-1806 *ApCAB,*
  NatCAB 6, TwCBDA
Allen, Edgar 1892-1943 *DcAmB S3, DcScB,*
  WhAm 2
Allen, Edgar Fiske 1862-1937 *NatCAB 31*
Allen, Edgar VanNuys 1900-1961 *NatCAB 50,*
  WhAm 4
Allen, Edmund Thompson 1836-1913 *WhAm 1*
Allen, Edward Archibald 1843- *WhAm 4*
Allen, Edward Bartlett 1888-1964 *WhAm 4*
Allen, Edward Beecher 1862-1935 *NatCAB 27*
Allen, Edward Bingham 1878-1956 *NatCAB 46*
Allen, Edward Chauncey 1823-1887 *NatCAB 2*
Allen, Edward Ellis 1861-1950 *BiDAmEd,*
  DcAmB S4, WhAm 3
Allen, Edward Jay 1830-1915 *NatCAB 30*
Allen, Edward Joseph Evarts 1871-1943
  NatCAB 32

Allen, Edward Mortimer 1881-1965 *WhAm 4*
Allen, Edward Normand 1891-1972 *NatCAB 57, WhAm 5*
Allen, Edward P 1839- *TwCBDA*
Allen, Edward Patrick 1852-1926 *TwCBDA*
Allen, Edward Patrick 1853-1926 *ApCAB Sup, NatCAB 13, WhAm 1*
Allen, Edward Payson 1839-1909 *BiDrAC, WhAmP*
Allen, Edward Pennington 1883-1949 *NatCAB 38*
Allen, Edward Tyson 1875-1942 *DcAmB S3, NatCAB 18, WhAm 3*
Allen, Edwin Brown 1898-1974 *WhAm 6*
Allen, Edwin Madison d1947 *WhAm 2*
Allen, Edwin West 1864-1929 *WhAm 1*
Allen, Eldreth Gordon 1871-1955 *NatCAB 43*
Allen, Eleanor Whitney 1882- *BiCAW, WomWWA 14*
Allen, Eleanora Isabel 1864- *WomWWA 14*
Allen, Eliot Dinsmore 1918-1971 *WhAm 5*
Allen, Elisabeth Walbridge Cleveland *WomWWA 14*
Allen, Elisha Hunt 1804-1883 *ApCAB, ApCAB X, BiAUS, BiDrAC, DcAmB, NatCAB 9, NatCAB 27, TwCBDA, WhAm H, WhAmP*
Allen, Elizabeth *WomWWA 14*
Allen, Elizabeth Anne Chase Akers 1832-1911 *AmWom, ApCAB, DcAmB, NatCAB 6, NotAW, TwCBDA*
Allen, Emma Potter 1870- *WomWWA 14*
Allen, Ephraim W 1780?-1846 *Drake*
Allen, Erastus Smith 1889-1963 *NatCAB 52*
Allen, Eric William 1879-1944 *WhAm 2*
Allen, Ernest Bourner d1931 *WhAm 1*
Allen, Esther Lavilla 1834- *AmWom*
Allen, Esther Saville 1837- *AmWom*
Allen, Ethan 1737-1789 *AmBi, ApCAB, DcAmB, Drake, REnAW, TwCBDA, WhAmP*
Allen, Ethan 1738-1789 *DcAmReB, McGEWB, NatCAB 1, WebAB, WebAMB, WhAm H, WhoMilH*
Allen, Ethan 1832-1911 *WhAm 1*
Allen, Eugene Thomas 1864-1964 *WhAm 4*
Allen, Ezra Griffen 1885-1952 *WhAm 3*
Allen, Ezra T *NewYHSD*
Allen, Florence Eliza 1876- *WomWWA 14*
Allen, Florence Ellinwood 1884-1966 *NatCAB 52, WhAm 4*
Allen, Frances 1784-1819 *WhAm H*
Allen, Frances 1854- *WomWWA 14*
Allen, Francis Henry 1866-1953 *WhAm 4*
Allen, Francis Richmond 1843-1931 *NatCAB 32, WhAm 1, WhAm 1C*
Allen, Frank 1863-1947 *NatCAB 40, WhAm 2*
Allen, Frank Berry 1887-1945 *NatCAB 36*
Allen, Frank Bigelow 1900-1957 *WhAm 3*
Allen, Frank Gates 1858-1940 *NatCAB 46*
Allen, Frank Gilman 1874-1950 *NatCAB 46, WhAm 3*
Allen, Frank Philip, Jr. 1881-1943 *WhAm 2*
Allen, Frank Waller 1878- *WhAm 6*
Allen, Fred 1894-1956 *WebAB, WhAm 3*
Allen, Fred Hovey 1845-1926 *NatCAB 8, WhAm 1*
Allen, Fred William, Jr. 1901-1973 *WhAm 6*
Allen, Frederic DeForest 1844-1897 *DcAmB, WhAm H*
Allen, Frederic Sturges 1861-1920 *WhAm 1*
Allen, Frederic Winthrop 1877-1933 *NatCAB 30, WhAm 1*
Allen, Frederick Baylies 1840- *WhAm 1*
Allen, Frederick DeForest 1844-1897 *NatCAB 12*
Allen, Frederick Henry 1909-1965 *WhAm 4*
Allen, Frederick Hobbes 1858-1937 *ApCAB X, NatCAB 9, NatCAB 18, NatCAB 27, WhAm 1*
Allen, Frederick Innes 1859-1938 *NatCAB 5, WhAm 1*
Allen, Frederick James 1864-1927 *WhAm 1*
Allen, Frederick Lathrop 1863-1938 *NatCAB 29*
Allen, Frederick Lewis 1890-1954 *DcAmB S5, NatCAB 46, WebAB, WhAm 3*
Allen, Frederick Madison 1879-1964 *ApCAB X,*

NatCAB 50, WhAm 6
Allen, Freeman 1870-1930 *NatCAB 38*
Allen, Freeman Harlow 1862-1942 *WhAm 2*
Allen, G *NewYHSD*
Allen, Gardner Weld 1856-1944 *NatCAB 33, WhAm 2*
Allen, George *NewYHSD*
Allen, George 1808-1876 *AmBi, ApCAB, DcAmB, NatCAB 9, WhAm H*
Allen, George 1847-1921 *NatCAB 43*
Allen, George A, Jr. 1868-1932 *WhAm 1*
Allen, George Edward 1896-1973 *WhAm 5*
Allen, George Garland 1874-1960 *NatCAB 47, WhAm 4*
Allen, George Henry 1876-1950 *WhAm 3*
Allen, George Murdoch 1853- *NatCAB 5*
Allen, George Venable 1903-1970 *WhAm 5*
Allen, George Walton Holker 1889-1973 *NatCAB 16, WhAm 6*
Allen, George Washington 1844-1928 *NatCAB 24, WhAm H*
Allen, George Wesley 1854- *WhoColR*
Allen, George Whiting 1854-1922 *WhAm 1*
Allen, Gertrude *WomWWA 14*
Allen, Glover Morrill 1879-1942 *DcAmB S3, NatCAB 31, WhAm 2*
Allen, Gordon 1877- *WhAm 5*
Allen, Gordon Forrest 1908-1973 *WhAm 6*
Allen, Gracie 1906-1964 *WhAm 4*
Allen, Grant 1848-1899 *ApCAB, WhAm 1*
Allen, Gretchen Brooks Stevens 1892- *WomWWA 14*
Allen, Grosvenor Noyes 1874-1954 *WhAm 3*
Allen, Guy Fletcher 1877-1951 *NatCAB 40, WhAm 5*
Allen, Hamilton Ford 1867- *WhAm 4*
Allen, Hans 1861- *WhAm 4*
Allen, Harold 1877-1939 *NatCAB 36*
Allen, Harris Campbell 1876- *WhAm 5*
Allen, Harrison 1841-1897 *ApCAB, DcAmB, NatCAB 9, TwCBDA, WhAm H*
Allen, Harry 1882-1957 *NatCAB 48*
Allen, Harry Kyes 1885-1950 *NatCAB 38*
Allen, Harry Nathaniel 1876-1965 *NatCAB 51*
Allen, Heman 1740-1778 *TwCBDA*
Allen, Heman 1776-1844 *BiAUS*
Allen, Heman 1777-1844 *BiDrAC, WhAm H*
Allen, Heman 1779-1852 *ApCAB, BiAUS, BiDrAC, Drake, NatCAB 11, TwCBDA, WhAm H*
Allen, Henry 1748-1784 *ApCAB, Drake, NatCAB 7*
Allen, Henry, Jr. 1908-1967 *WhAm 4*
Allen, Henry Butler 1887-1962 *WhAm 4*
Allen, Henry Crosby 1872-1942 *BiDrAC, NatCAB 32, WhAm 5*
Allen, Henry Dixon 1854-1924 *BiDrAC, WhAm 4*
Allen, Henry Justin 1868-1950 *BiDrAC, DcAmB S4, NatCAB 40, WhAm 2, WhAmP*
Allen, Henry Tureman 1859-1930 *AmBi, ApCAB X, DcAmB S1, NatCAB 44, REnAW, WebAMB, WhAm 1*
Allen, Henry Watkins 1820-1866 *ApCAB, DcAmB, Drake, NatCAB 10, WebAB, WebAMB, WhAm H, WhAmP*
Allen, Henry Watkins 1820-1867 *BiDConf, TwCBDA*
Allen, Hervey 1889-1949 *DcAmB S4, NatCAB 37, WhAm 2*
Allen, Homer Bryan 1891-1958 *NatCAB 47*
Allen, Hope Emily 1883-1960 *WhAm 4*
Allen, Horace Eugene 1890-1972 *WhAm 5*
Allen, Horace Newton 1858-1932 *NatCAB 28, TwCBDA, WhAm 1*
Allen, Horatio 1802-1889 *NatCAB 8, TwCBDA, WebAB*
Allen, Horatio 1802-1890 *AmBi*
Allen, Horatio 1802-1899 *DcAmB, WhAm H*
Allen, Howard Cameron 1896-1967 *WhAm 4*
Allen, Hubert A 1872-1942 *WhAm 2*
Allen, Hugh Earl 1892-1945 *NatCAB 33*
Allen, Ida Bailey d1973 *WhAm 6*
Allen, Ira 1751-1814 *AmBi, ApCAB, DcAmB, Drake, NatCAB 4, TwCBDA, WhAm H, WhAmP*
Allen, Ira Wilder 1827- *TwCBDA*

Allen, Ira Wilder 1865-1935 *WhAm 1*
Allen, Isaac 1741-1806 *ApCAB, Drake*
Allen, J Ernest 1880-1949 *NatCAB 37*
Allen, J Wilford 1865-1948 *NatCAB 36*
Allen, James 1632-1710 *Drake*
Allen, James 1692-1747 *ApCAB, Drake*
Allen, James 1739-1808 *Drake*
Allen, James 1824-1897 *NatCAB 9*
Allen, James 1849-1933 *WhAm 1*
Allen, James Brown 1927- *EncAAH*
Allen, James Browning 1912- *BiDrAC*
Allen, James C 1823- *BiAUS*
Allen, James Cameron 1822-1912 *BiDrAC, TwCBDA*
Allen, James E 1894-1964 *WhAm 4*
Allen, James Edward 1876-1950 *NatCAB 36, WhAm 2A*
Allen, James Edward, Jr. 1911-1971 *BiDAmEd, NatCAB 57, WhAm 5*
Allen, James H 1810?- *NewYHSD*
Allen, James Henry 1880-1950 *NatCAB 40, WhAm 3*
Allen, James Lane 1849-1925 *AmBi, DcAmB, NatCAB 8, TwCBDA, WhAm 1*
Allen, James Monroe 1844-1913 *NatCAB 27*
Allen, James Turney 1873-1949 *WhAm 2*
Allen, Jean Malven 1901-1972 *WhAm 6*
Allen, Jeremiah Mervin 1833-1903 *DcAmB, NatCAB 5, WhAm H*
Allen, Jerome 1830-1894 *TwCBDA*
Allen, Joel Asaph 1838-1921 *AmBi, ApCAB, DcAmB, NatCAB 3, TwCBDA, WhAm 1*
Allen, Joel Knott 1755-1825 *NewYHSD*
Allen, John *NewYHSD*
Allen, John 1763-1812 *BiAUS, BiDrAC, NatCAB 2, WhAm H*
Allen, John 1772-1813 *ApCAB, Drake*
Allen, John 1772-1814 *NatCAB 6*
Allen, John 1810-1892 *DcAmB, NatCAB 2, WebAB, WhAm H*
Allen, John 1860- *NewYHSD*
Allen, John Alpheus 1863- *WhAm 6*
Allen, John Beard 1845-1903 *BiDrAC, NatCAB 1, NatCAB 11, TwCBDA, WhAm 1, WhAmP*
Allen, John C *NewYHSD*
Allen, Sir John Campbell 1817-1898 *ApCAB Sup*
Allen, John Clayton 1860-1939 *BiDrAC, WhAm 3, WhAmP*
Allen, John D 1851-1947 *IIBEAAW*
Allen, John Denby 1887-1964 *WhAm 4*
Allen, John Eliot 1873-1945 *WhAm 2*
Allen, John F 1829-1900 *DcAmB, WhAm H*
Allen, John Henry 1836-1890? *TwCBDA*
Allen, John Herbert 1860-1939 *NatCAB 29*
Allen, John Howard 1866-1953 *NatCAB 41*
Allen, John James 1797-1871 *BiAUS, BiDrAC, DcAmB, NatCAB 7, WhAm H*
Allen, John Johnson 1842- *WhAm 4*
Allen, John Joseph, Jr. 1899- *BiDrAC, WhAmP*
Allen, John Kermott 1858- *WhAm 4*
Allen, John M 1847- *TwCBDA*
Allen, John Mills 1846-1917 *BiDrAC, NatCAB 17, WhAm 1, WhAmP*
Allen, John N *NewYHSD*
Allen, John Rex 1900-1969 *WhAm 5*
Allen, John Robert 1851- *WhAm 4*
Allen, John Robins 1869-1920 *NatCAB 19*
Allen, John Rowan 1856-1937 *NatCAB 32*
Allen, John Stevenson 1857- *WhAm 4*
Allen, John Wesley 1855- *WhAm 4*
Allen, John Weston 1872-1941 *WhAm 2*
Allen, John Weston 1872-1942 *WhAm 1*
Allen, John William 1802-1887 *BiAUS, BiDrAC, NatCAB 11, WhAm H*
Allen, John William 1848-1918 *NatCAB 18*
Allen, Joseph *NewYHSD*
Allen, Joseph 1749-1827 *ApCAB, BiAUS, BiDrAC, Drake, WhAm H*
Allen, Joseph 1790-1873 *ApCAB, Drake*
Allen, Joseph Dana 1865-1965 *WhAm 4*
Allen, Joseph Henry 1820-1898 *ApCAB, DcAmB, NatCAB 9, NatCAB 28, TwCBDA, WhAm H*
Allen, Joseph Holmes 1870- *WhAm 5*

Allen, Joseph Shepherd 1849-1916 *NatCAB 18*
Allen, Judson 1797-1880 *BiAUS, BiDrAC, WhAm H*
Allen, Julian 1900-1967 *WhAm 4*
Allen, Junius 1898-1962 *NatCAB 47, WhAm 4*
Allen, Kelcey 1875-1951 *DcAmB S5*
Allen, Kenneth 1857-1930 *WhAm 1*
Allen, L *NewYHSD*
Allen, Laurence Edmund 1908-1975 *WhAm 6*
Allen, Leo Elwood 1898-1973 *BiDrAC, WhAm 5, WhAmP*
Allen, Leon Menard 1863-1936 *NatCAB 39, WhAm 1*
Allen, Leroy 1878-1947 *WhAm 2*
Allen, Levi *WhAmP*
Allen, Lewis Falley 1800-1890 *DcAmB, WhAm H*
Allen, Lewis George 1891-1948 *WhAm 2*
Allen, Lewis Mines 1874-1949 *NatCAB 38*
Allen, Lloyd Raymond 1878-1956 *NatCAB 45*
Allen, Louis J 1840-1905 *WhAm 1*
Allen, Lucy Ellis d1943 *WhAm 2, WomWWA 14*
Allen, Lulu Pearl Jeffers *WomWWA 14*
Allen, Luther 1780-1821 *NewYHSD*
Allen, Luther 1846- *ApCAB X*
Allen, Lydia Jeannette McMillan 1853- *WomWWA 14*
Allen, Lyman Whitney 1854-1930 *NatCAB 12, WhAm 1*
Allen, M Marshall 1862- *WhAm 3*
Allen, Mabel Stanley Calef *WomWWA 14*
Allen, Madison Crencha 1890-1968 *NatCAB 55*
Allen, Margaret Pinckney Jackson *WomWWA 14*
Allen, Maria W *NewYHSD*
Allen, Marie 1815?- *NewYHSD*
Allen, Marion Boyd 1862- *BiCAW, WhAm 5*
Allen, Martha Elizabeth Moore 1849- *WomWWA 14*
Allen, Martha Meir 1854-1926 *WhAm 1, WomWWA 14*
Allen, Mary 1858- *WomWWA 14*
Allen, Mary Adele *WomWWA 14, WomWWA 14a*
Allen, Mary Dayton 1884- *WomWWA 14*
Allen, Mary Findlay 1881- *WomWWA 14*
Allen, Mary Jane 1841- *WomWWA 14*
Allen, Mary Montague Ferry 1853- *WomWWA 14*
Allen, Mary Wood 1841- *AmWom*
Allen, Maryland d1927 *WhAm 1*
Allen, Maud *WomWWA 14*
Allen, Milton Irving 1905-1967 *WhAm 4*
Allen, Miranda May 1870- *WomWWA 14*
Allen, Mollie MacClaughry *WomWWA 14*
Allen, Moses 1748-1779 *ApCAB, Drake, NatCAB 4*
Allen, N B 1892-1946 *WhAm 2*
Allen, Nathan 1813-1889 *ApCAB, DcAmB, TwCBDA, WhAm H*
Allen, Nathan H 1848-1925 *DcAmB*
Allen, Nathaniel 1780-1832 *BiAUS, BiDrAC, WhAm H*
Allen, Nathaniel Topliff 1823-1903 *NatCAB 20*
Allen, Nathaniel Topliffe 1823-1903 *BiDAmEd*
Allen, Nellie Burnham 1864- *WhAm 5*
Allen, Nelly Sherman Byers 1864- *WomWWA 14a*
Allen, Olney Carpenter 1880-1957 *NatCAB 44*
Allen, Orville 1842?- *NewYHSD*
Allen, Oscar Dana 1836- *ApCAB*
Allen, Oscar DeRoy 1833-1927 *NatCAB 22*
Allen, Oscar Kelly 1882-1936 *NatCAB 28*
Allen, Paul 1775-1826 *ApCAB, DcAmB, Drake, NatCAB 5, WhAm H*
Allen, Paul Hastings 1883-1952 *NatCAB 42*
Allen, Paul S 1905-1960 *WhAm 4*
Allen, Perle Even 1881-1956 *NatCAB 45*
Allen, Perry S 1854-1930 *NatCAB 27, WhAm 1*
Allen, Peter 1787-1864 *NatCAB 16*
Allen, Philip 1785-1865 *ApCAB, BiAUS, BiDrAC, DcAmB, Drake, NatCAB 9, TwCBDA, WhAm H, WhAmP*
Allen, Philip Loring 1878-1908 *WhAm 1*
Allen, Philip Ray 1873-1962 *NatCAB 51,*

WhAm 4
Allen, Philip Schuyler 1871-1937 *WhAm 1*
Allen, Phineas 1776-1860 *Drake*
Allen, Ralph 1913-1966 *WhAm 4*
Allen, Ralph Clayton 1883-1967 *NatCAB 53, WhAm 4*
Allen, Ray 1860-1938 *WhAm 1*
Allen, Richard 1741-1832 *NatCAB 7*
Allen, Richard 1760-1831 *AmBi, ApCAB, DcAmB, DcAmReB, EncAB, McGEWB, NatCAB 13, WebAB, WhAm H*
Allen, Richard C *BiAUS*
Allen, Richard Day 1887-1945 *WhAm 2*
Allen, Richard Frazer 1890-1957 *WhAm 3*
Allen, Richard Lamb 1803-1869 *ApCAB, DcAmB, Drake, TwCBDA, WhAm H*
Allen, Richard N 1827-1890 *NatCAB 9*
Allen, Richmond *NewYHSD*
Allen, Riley Harris 1884-1966 *WhAm 4*
Allen, Robert d1864 *BiAUS*
Allen, Robert 1777-1844 *ApCAB, Drake, TwCBDA*
Allen, Robert 1777-1864 *NatCAB 3*
Allen, Robert 1778-1844 *BiDrAC, WhAm H*
Allen, Robert 1794-1859 *BiAUS, BiDrAC, WhAm H*
Allen, Robert 1812-1886 *DcAmB, WhAm H*
Allen, Robert 1815-1886 *ApCAB, NatCAB 4, TwCBDA*
Allen, Robert 1836- *Drake*
Allen, Robert Edward Lee 1865-1951 *BiDrAC, WhAm 4*
Allen, Robert Emmet 1890-1955 *WhAm 3*
Allen, Robert Gray 1902-1963 *BiDrAC, WhAm 4*
Allen, Robert H 1870-1949 *WhAm 2*
Allen, Robert I 1898-1963 *WhAm 4*
Allen, Robert McDowell 1878- *WhAm 6*
Allen, Robert Porter 1905-1963 *WhAm 4*
Allen, Roderick Random 1894-1970 *WhAm 5*
Allen, Rolland Craten 1881-1948 *NatCAB 36, WhAm 2*
Allen, Russell Morton 1897-1967 *WhAm 4A*
Allen, Ruth Homer 1877- *WomWWA 14*
Allen, Samuel 1636-1705 *ApCAB, Drake, NatCAB 13, TwCBDA*
Allen, Samuel Clesson 1772-1842 *BiAUS, BiDrAC, Drake, WhAm H*
Allen, Samuel Edward 1858-1926 *WhAm 1*
Allen, Samuel G 1870-1956 *WhAm 3*
Allen, Samuel James McIntosh 1877- *WhAm 5*
Allen, Samuel Leeds 1841-1918 *NatCAB 17*
Allen, Samuel Louis 1808-1895 *NatCAB 9*
Allen, Sarah Lockhart 1793-1877 *NewYHSD*
Allen, Sherman 1875-1938 *WhAm 2*
Allen, Sidney J d1958 *WhAm 3*
Allen, Solomon 1751-1821 *ApCAB, Drake, NatCAB 4, TwCBDA*
Allen, Stephen 1767-1852 *NatCAB 4*
Allen, Stephen 1772?- *NatCAB 3*
Allen, Stephen Haley 1847-1931 *NatCAB 27, WhAm 1*
Allen, Steve 1921- *WebAB*
Allen, Sturges 1850-1929 *WhAm 3*
Allen, Terry DeLaMesa 1888-1969 *WebAMB*
Allen, Thomas *NewYHSD*
Allen, Thomas 1608-1673 *Drake*
Allen, Thomas 1743-1810 *ApCAB, Drake*
Allen, Thomas 1813-1882 *BiAUS Sup, BiDrAC, DcAmB, NatCAB 21, TwCBDA, WhAm H*
Allen, Thomas 1849-1924 *IlBEAAW, NatCAB 5, NatCAB 24, TwCBDA, WhAm 1*
Allen, Thomas 1887-1965 *NatCAB 51*
Allen, Thomas Grant 1863- *WhAm 4*
Allen, Thomas Hampton 1810- *NatCAB 5*
Allen, Thomas M 1797-1871 *DcAmB, WhAm H*
Allen, Thomas Stinson 1865-1945 *NatCAB 35, WhAm 2*
Allen, Thomas Woodruff 1855-1929 *NatCAB 22*
Allen, Timothy Field 1837-1902 *ApCAB, DcAmB, NatCAB 7, TwCBDA, WhAm 1*
Allen, Valentine R *NewYHSD*
Allen, Victor Maxon 1870-1916 *NatCAB 17*

Allen, Viola Emily 1867-1948 *DcAmB S4, NatCAB 34, NotAW, WhAm 2, WomWWA 14*
Allen, Viola Emily 1868-1948 *NatCAB 13*
Allen, W Lloyd 1888-1971 *NatCAB 56*
Allen, Walter 1840-1907 *WhAm 1*
Allen, Walter Barth 1892-1951 *WhAm 3*
Allen, Walter Cleveland 1877-1945 *WhAm 2*
Allen, Wellesca Pollock 1871- *WomWWA 14*
Allen, Wilbur Price 1879- *NatCAB 17*
Allen, Will Dean 1874-1946 *NatCAB 35*
Allen, William *NewYHSD*
Allen, William d1780 *Drake*
Allen, William 1704-1780 *AmBi, DcAmB, WhAm H*
Allen, William 1710-1780 *ApCAB, NatCAB 5, TwCBDA*
Allen, William 1784-1868 *ApCAB, DcAmB, Drake, NatCAB 1, TwCBDA, WhAm H*
Allen, William 1803-1879 *BiDrAC, DcAmB, WhAm H, WhAmP*
Allen, William 1806-1879 *ApCAB, BiAUS, NatCAB 3*
Allen, William 1807-1879 *TwCBDA*
Allen, William 1810-1891 *TwCBDA*
Allen, William 1822-1891 *TwCBDA*
Allen, William 1827-1881 *BiAUS, BiDrAC, WhAm H*
Allen, William 1870-1967 *NatCAB 54*
Allen, William B 1834?- *NewYHSD*
Allen, William C *NewYHSD*
Allen, William Fitch 1875-1951 *WhAm 3*
Allen, William Francis 1830-1889 *ApCAB, DcAmB, NatCAB 6, TwCBDA, WhAm H*
Allen, William Franklin 1883-1946 *BiDrAC*
Allen, William Frederick 1846-1915 *ApCAB X, DcAmB, NatCAB 14, NatCAB 23, TwCBDA, WhAm 1*
Allen, William Frederick 1856- *WhoColR*
Allen, William G *NewYHSD*
Allen, William Henry 1784-1813 *ApCAB, DcAmB, Drake, NatCAB 8, WebAMB, WhAm H*
Allen, William Henry 1808-1882 *ApCAB, DcAmB, NatCAB 7, TwCBDA, WhAm H*
Allen, William Herbert 1853-1943 *NatCAB 32, WhAm 2*
Allen, William Herschel 1885-1955 *NatCAB 44*
Allen, William Howard 1790-1822 *ApCAB, Drake, NatCAB 6*
Allen, William Humphries 1856-1929 *NatCAB 22*
Allen, William Joshua 1828-1900 *BiAUS, TwCBDA, WhAm 1*
Allen, William Joshua 1829-1901 *BiDrAC, DcAmB, NatCAB 20, WhAmP*
Allen, William Judson 1878-1963 *NatCAB 50*
Allen, William Lafayette 1857-1949 *NatCAB 37*
Allen, William Orville 1873-1929 *WhAm 1*
Allen, William Porter 1858-1930 *NatCAB 24*
Allen, William Ray 1885-1955 *WhAm 3*
Allen, William Reynolds 1860-1921 *WhAm 1*
Allen, William Seward 1885-1955 *NatCAB 42*
Allen, William Sims 1888-1951 *NatCAB 38, WhAm 3*
Allen, William Temple 1855- *NatCAB 3*
Allen, William Vincent 1847-1924 *ApCAB Sup, BiDrAC, DcAmB, NatCAB 5, REnAW, TwCBDA, WhAm 1, WhAmP*
Allen, William Wirt 1835-1894 *BiDConf, NatCAB 19*
Allen, Willis 1806-1859 *BiAUS, BiDrAC, WhAm H*
Allen, Willis Boyd 1855-1938 *NatCAB 10, TwCBDA, WhAm 1*
Allen, Wilmar Mason 1894-1956 *NatCAB 46, WhAm 3*
Allen, Wyeth 1893-1973 *WhAm 5*
Allen, Young John 1836-1907 *DcAmB, NatCAB 21*
Allen, Zachariah 1795-1882 *AmBi, ApCAB, DcAmB, NatCAB 8, TwCBDA, WhAm H*
Allenby, Edmund Henry Hynman 1861-1936 *McGEWB, WhoMilH*

Allende, Ignacio 1779-1811 *ApCAB*
Allende, J d1811 *Drake*
Allender, Clarence Lacelle 1876-1947
   NatCAB 38
Allendoerfer, Carl Barnett 1911-1974 *WhAm 6*
Allendoerfer, Carl W 1880-1955 *WhAm 3*
Allenson, Hazel Sandiford 1902-1973 *WhAm 6*
Aller, Howard Lewis 1883-1954 *WhAm 3*
Allerdice *NewYHSD*
Allerton, Ellen Palmer 1835- *AmWom*
Allerton, Isaac 1583?-1659 *ApCAB, Drake,*
   NatCAB 6, TwCBDA
Allerton, Isaac 1586?-1659 *AmBi, DcAmB,*
   WhAm H
Allerton, Samuel Walters 1828-1914 *ApCAB X*
Allerton, Samuel Waters 1828-1914 *DcAmB,*
   EncAAH, NatCAB 17, WhAm 1
Allerup, Paul Richard 1912-1974 *WhAm 6*
Alley, Cal 1915-1970 *NatCAB 57*
Alley, Calvin Lane 1915-1970 *WhAm 5*
Alley, Charles Edwin 1912-1971 *WhAm 5*
Alley, James Pinckney 1885-1934 *WhAm 1*
Alley, John Bassett 1817-1896 *BiAUS, BiDrAC,*
   WhAm H
Alley, John Buffum 1817-1896 *TwCBDA*
Alley, Rayford W 1890-1965 *WhAm 4*
Alleyn, Charles 1817-1890 *ApCAB Sup*
Alleyn, Richard 1836-1883 *ApCAB Sup*
Allez, George Clare 1897-1950 *WhAm 3*
Allgood, Dwight Maurice 1903-1967 *WhAm 5*
Allgood, Miles Clayton 1878- *BiDrAC,*
   WhAm 6
Alliaco, Petrus De *DcScB*
Allibone, Samuel Austin 1816-1889 *AmBi,*
   ApCAB, DcAmB, Drake, NatCAB 6,
   TwCBDA, WhAm H
Allin, Arthur 1869-1903 *WhAm 1*
Allin, Benjamin Casey 1886-1960 *NatCAB 46*
Allin, Bushrod Warren 1899-1968 *WhAm 5*
Allin, Cephas Daniel 1875-1927 *WhAm 1*
Allin, Eugenia *WomWWA 14*
Allin, George Litchfield 1875- *WhAm 5*
Allin, George R 1880- *WhAm 6*
Allin, Heloise M Litchfield 1854-
   WomWWA 14
Allin, John 1596-1671 *ApCAB, Drake*
Allin, Josephine Turner 1877- *WomWWA 14*
Allin, Roger 1848-1936 *NatCAB 38, TwCBDA,*
   WhAm 1
Alline, Henry 1748-1784 *DcAmB, WhAm H*
Alline, Mary Clapp *WomWWA 14*
Alling, Arthur Nathaniel 1862-1949 *WhAm 2*
Alling, Asa Alling 1862-1900 *WhAm 1*
Alling, E Roy 1888-1948 *NatCAB 36*
Alling, Harold Lattimore 1888-1960 *WhAm 4*
Alling, John Wesley 1841-1927 *NatCAB 27,*
   WhAm 1
Alling, Joseph Tilden 1855-1937 *WhAm 1*
Alling, Paul Humiston 1896-1949 *NatCAB 35,*
   WhAm 2
Allington, Homer C 1898-1960 *WhAm 4*
Allinson, Anne Crosby Emery 1871-1932
   DcAmB S1, WhAm 1
Allinson, Annie Crosby Emery 1871-1932
   WomWWA 14
Allinson, David 1774-1858 *ApCAB Sup*
Allinson, Francis Greenleaf 1856-1931
   DcAmB S1, NatCAB 23, WhAm 1
Allinson, Samuel 1808-1883 *ApCAB Sup*
Alliot, Hector 1862-1919 *WhAm 1*
Allis, Annie Gibson *BiCAW*
Allis, Charles 1853-1918 *NatCAB 18*
Allis, Edward Phelps 1824-1889 *DcAmB,*
   EncAAH, NatCAB 7, WhAm H
Allis, Edward Phelps, Jr. 1851-1947 *NatCAB 39,*
   WhAm 4
Allis, Fannie Augusta 1863- *WomWWA 14*
Allis, James Ashton 1881- *WhAm 6*
Allis, Lizzie May *WomWWA 14*
Allis, Louis 1866-1950 *WhAm 3*
Allis, Mary Elizabeth *WomWWA 14*
Allis, Oscar Huntington 1836-1921 *NatCAB 24,*
   WhAm 1
Allis, Oswald Thompson 1880-1973 *WhAm 5*
Allis, Wallace Steele 1859-1935 *NatCAB 26*
Allis, William Watson 1849-1918 *NatCAB 18*
Allison, Burgess 1753-1827 *ApCAB, TwCBDA*
Allison, Claude Willis 1884-1952 *NatCAB 40*

Allison, Clay 1840-1887 *REnAW*
Allison, Fred 1882-1974 *WhAm 6*
Allison, Guy William 1885- *WhoColR*
Allison, Henry 1840-1917 *NatCAB 32*
Allison, Henry Willard 1846-1913 *NatCAB 16*
Allison, Isaac 1876-1942 *NatCAB 35*
Allison, James 1838-1916 *NatCAB 17*
Allison, James, Jr. 1772-1854 *BiAUS, BiDrAC,*
   WhAm H
Allison, James Boyd 1901-1964 *WhAm 4*
Allison, James Edward 1870-1955 *NatCAB 45,*
   WhAm 5
Allison, James Ekin 1865-1926 *NatCAB 21*
Allison, James Nicholls 1848-1918 *NatCAB 18,*
   WhAm 1
Allison, John 1812- *BiAUS*
Allison, John 1812-1873 *TwCBDA*
Allison, John 1812-1878 *BiDrAC, WhAm H,*
   WhAmP
Allison, John Maudgridge Snowden 1888-1944
   WhAm 2
Allison, John McIntosh 1856- *WhoColR*
Allison, John Phillip 1910-1967 *NatCAB 53,*
   WhAm 4
Allison, Joseph 1819-1896 *TwCBDA*
Allison, Joseph B 1837?- *NewYHSD*
Allison, Marjorie 1887-1961 *NatCAB 49*
Allison, Nathaniel 1876-1931 *WhAm 1*
Allison, Nathaniel 1876-1932 *DcAmB S1,*
   NatCAB 26
Allison, Noah Dwight 1899-1971 *WhAm 5*
Allison, Patrick 1740-1802 *Drake*
Allison, Richard 1757-1816 *DcAmB S1,*
   WhAm H
Allison, Robert 1777-1840 *BiAUS, BiDrAC,*
   WhAm H
Allison, Robert Burns 1916-1974 *WhAm 6*
Allison, Samuel King 1900-1965 *WhAm 4*
Allison, William Boyd 1829-1908 *AmBi,*
   ApCAB, BiAUS, BiDrAC, DcAmB,
   EncAAH, EncAB, NatCAB 1, TwCBDA,
   WebAB, WhAm 1, WhAmP
Allison, William Henry 1870-1941 *NatCAB 31,*
   WhAm 1, WhAm 1C, WhAm 2
Allison, William Merle 1880- *IIBEAAW*
Allman, David Bacharach 1891-1971
   NatCAB 55, WhAm 5
Allman, Francis Charles 1909-1968 *NatCAB 54*
Allman, Justin Paul 1873- *WhAm 5*
Allman, Leslie Coover 1891- *WhAm 4*
Allmendinger, David Frederick 1848-1916
   NatCAB 17
Allmond, Marcus Blakey 1851- *NatCAB 13,*
   WhAm 4
Alloez, Claude Jean 1622-1689 *DcAmB*
Allonville, J E D' *DcScB*
Allott, Gordon Llewellyn 1907- *BiDrAC*
Allouez, Claude *Drake*
Allouez, Claude Jean 1620-1690 *ApCAB*
Allouez, Claude Jean 1622-1689 *AmBi,*
   DcAmB, WebAB, WhAm H
Alloway, J Lionel 1900-1954 *NatCAB 48*
Alloway, Mary Louise Tuttle 1858-
   WomWWA 14
Allport, Fayette Ward 1893-1958 *WhAm 3*
Allport, Frank 1857-1935 *WhAm 1*
Allport, Gordon Willard 1897-1967 *BiDAmEd,*
   WebAB, WhAm 4, WhAm 5
Allred, Berten Wendell 1904- *REnAW*
Allred, James V 1899-1959 *WhAm 3*
Allsopp, Clinton Bonfield 1887-1962 *WhAm 4*
Allsopp, Frederick William 1867-1946 *WhAm 2*
Allston see also Alston
Allston, James Henderson 1862- *WhoColR*
Allston, Joseph 1778-1816 *ApCAB, BiAUS,*
   Drake, TwCBDA
Allston, Philip J 1860- *WhoColR*
Allston, Robert Francis Withers 1801-1864
   AmBi, ApCAB, BiAUS, DcAmB, Drake,
   NatCAB 12, TwCBDA, WebAB,
   WhAm H, WhAmP
Allston, Theodosia Burr 1783-1812? *TwCBDA*
Allston, Washington 1779-1843 *AmBi, ApCAB,*
   BnEnAmA, DcAmB, Drake, McGEWB,
   NatCAB 5, NewYHSD, TwCBDA,
   WebAB, WhAm H
Allston, William 1757-1839 *ApCAB, Drake,*
   TwCBDA

Allstrum, Esther *WomWWA 14*
Allton, James Miller 1895-1974 *WhAm 6*
Allwardt, Henry Augustus 1840-1910 *WhAm 1*
Allwell, William *NewYHSD*
Allwood, John *NewYHSD*
Allwork, Eleanor Bloom 1911-1968 *WhAm 5*
Allyn, Arden Lacey 1887-1962 *WhAm 4*
Allyn, Arthur Cecil 1887-1960 *WhAm 4*
Allyn, Eunice Eloisae Gibbs *AmWom*
Allyn, Harriet May 1883-1957 *BiDAmEd*
Allyn, Harriett May 1883-1957 *WhAm 3*
Allyn, John 1767-1833 *ApCAB, NatCAB 6*
Allyn, John 1843- *ApCAB X*
Allyn, Joseph P *BiAUS*
Allyn, Robert 1817-1894 *BiDAmEd, DcAmB,*
   TwCBDA, WhAm H
Allyn, Robert Starr 1875-1956 *NatCAB 46*
Allyn, Stanley Charles 1891-1970 *WhAm 5*
Alma-Gro, Diego 1463?-1538 *Drake*
Almack, John Conrad 1883-1953 *BiDAmEd,*
   NatCAB 42, WhAm 3
Almagro, Diego 1463?-1538 *ApCAB*
Almagro, Diego 1520-1542 *ApCAB*
Almagro, Diego De 1474?-1538 *McGEWB*
Almaine, George D *NewYHSD*
Almand, Claude Marion 1915-1957 *WhAm 3*
Almert, Harold 1876- *WhAm 5*
Almirall, Raymond Francis 1869-1939
   NatCAB 29
Almoguera, Juan De 1605-1676 *ApCAB*
Almon, Edward Berton 1860-1933 *BiDrAC,*
   WhAm 1, WhAmP
Almon, John 1737-1805 *ApCAB*
Almon, John 1738-1805 *Drake*
Almon, William Johnson 1816- *ApCAB Sup*
Almond, Edward Mallory 1892- *WebAMB*
Almond, James Edward 1889-1960 *WhAm 3A*
Almond, James Lindsay, Jr. 1898- *BiDrAC,*
   WhAmP
Almond, Nina 1882-1964 *WhAm 4*
Almonte, Juan Nepomuceno 1804-1869 *ApCAB,*
   Drake
Alms, Julius John 1907-1964 *NatCAB 50*
Alms, William Henry 1842-1920 *NatCAB 27*
Almstedt, Hermann Benjamin 1872- *WhAm 5*
Almy, Amy Celesta 1875- *WomWWA 14*
Almy, Frederic 1858-1935 *WhAm 1*
Almy, Helen Cabot 1856- *WomWWA 14*
Almy, John Jay 1814-1895 *ApCAB, Drake,*
   TwCBDA
Almy, John Jay 1815-1895 *DcAmB, NatCAB 4,*
   WhAm H
Almy, Oscar 1818?- *NewYHSD*
Almy, Robert Forbes 1901-1969 *WhAm 5*
Almy, William 1601-1676? *NatCAB 9*
Almy, William 1761-1836 *ApCAB, Drake,*
   TwCBDA
Aloe, Louis Patrick 1867-1929 *NatCAB 27*
Aloes, Claude Jean 1622-1689 *DcAmB*
Alofsen, Solomon 1808-1876 *ApCAB*
Alonso, Amado 1896-1952 *WhAm 3*
Alp Arslan 1026?-1072 *McGEWB*
Alpaugh, Norman Walton 1885-1954
   NatCAB 43
Alperin, Louis Israel 1891-1956 *NatCAB 44*
Alpers, William Charles 1851-1917 *NatCAB 22,*
   WhAm 1
Alpetragius *DcScB*
Alpharabius *DcScB*
Alphonce, Jean 1482?-1557? *AmBi, DcAmB*
Alphonsa, Mother 1851-1926 *AmBi, DcAmB,*
   WhAm HA, WhAm 4
Alphonsa, Mother Mary *NotAW*
Alpini, Prospero 1553-1616 *DcScB*
Alpini, Prospero 1553-1617 *AsBiEn*
Alpuche, Wenceslas 1804-1841 *ApCAB*
Alpuche E Infante, Jose Maria 1780- *ApCAB*
Alrich, Emma B 1845- *AmWom*
Alrich, Herbert Ware 1872-1938 *NatCAB 28*
Alrichs, Peter d1697 *NatCAB 16*
Alricks, Hermanus 1804-1874 *ApCAB*
Alsberg, Carl Lucas 1877-1940 *NatCAB 30,*
   WhAm 1
Alsberg, Julius 1878-1972 *NatCAB 57*
Alschuler, Alfred Samuel 1876-1940
   NatCAB 31, WhAm 1
Alschuler, Benjamin Philip 1876- *WhAm 5*
Alschuler, Samuel 1859-1939 *NatCAB 29,*

WhAm 1

Alshuch, Martin 1832?- *NewYHSD*

Alsina, Adolfo 1829- *ApCAB*

Alsop, George 1638-1666 *ApCAB, DcAmB, Drake, NatCAB 8, WhAm H*

Alsop, John 1724-1794 *ApCAB, BiAUS, BiDrAC, Drake, NatCAB 1, TwCBDA, WhAm H*

Alsop, John 1776-1841 *ApCAB*

Alsop, Joseph Wright 1876-1953 *WhAm 3*

Alsop, Reese Fell 1837- *WhAm 4*

Alsop, Richard 1761-1815 *AmBi, ApCAB, DcAmB, Drake, NatCAB 4, WhAm H*

Alsop, Stewart Johonnot Oliver 1914-1974 *WhAm 6*

Alsop, William Kite 1872-1936 *NatCAB 26*

Alspaugh, John Wesley 1882-1955 *NatCAB 44*

Alsted, Johann Heinrich 1588-1638 *DcScB*

Alston see also Allston

Alston, Alice Manolia 1890- *WhoColR*

Alston, Angus Sorensen 1914-1975 *WhAm 6*

Alston, Caesar Jony 1855- *WhoColR*

Alston, Caroline Lamar DuBignon 1876- *WomWWA 14*

Alston, Charles Henry 1873- *WhoColR A*

Alston, George L 1887-1964 *WhAm 4*

Alston, Joseph 1778-1816 *NatCAB 12*

Alston, Joseph 1779-1816 *DcAmB, WhAm H*

Alston, Lemuel James 1760-1836 *BiAUS, BiDrAC, TwCBDA, WhAm H*

Alston, Nellie V Landry 1875- *WhoColR*

Alston, Philip Henry 1880- *WhAm 6*

Alston, Philip Whitmel *Drake*

Alston, Robert Cotten 1873-1938 *WhAm 1*

Alston, Samuel Fitts 1859-1922 *NatCAB 22*

Alston, Theodosia Burr 1783-1813 *AmBi, DcAmB, NotAW*

Alston, William 1757-1839 *NatCAB 6*

Alston, William Jeffreys 1800-1876 *BiAUS, BiDrAC, WhAm H*

Alston, Willis 1769-1837 *ApCAB, BiAUS, BiDrAC, Drake, NatCAB 2, TwCBDA, WhAm H, WhAmP*

Alston, Willis, Jr. *ApCAB*

Alstork, John Wesley 1852-1920 *WhAm 1, WhoColR*

Alt, Gustav Adolf Friedrich Wilhelm 1851- *NatCAB 5*

Alt, Howard Lang 1900-1972 *WhAm 5*

Altamira Y Crevea, Rafael 1866-1951 *McGEWB*

Altamirano, Ignacio M *ApCAB*

Altdorfer, Albrecht 1480?-1538 *McGEWB*

Alte, Visconde De *WhAm 3*

Alter, David 1807-1881 *DcAmB, WebAB, WhAm H*

Alter, Dinsmore 1888-1968 *NatCAB 54, WhAm 5*

Alter, Franklin 1831-1916 *NatCAB 32*

Alter, George Elias 1868-1940 *NatCAB 32, WhAm 1*

Alter, Isaac Read 1881-1958 *NatCAB 48*

Alter, Lucien Weaver Scott 1892-1966 *NatCAB 51, WhAm 4*

Alter, Nicholas Mark 1892-1970 *NatCAB 54, WhAm 5*

Alter, Wilbur McClure 1879- *WhAm 6*

Alter, William 1897-1957 *NatCAB 46*

Alterman, Zipora Stephania Balaban 1925-1974 *WhAm 6*

Altgeld, John Peter 1847-1902 *AmBi, ApCAB Sup, DcAmB, EncAB, McGEWB, NatCAB 11, WebAB, WhAm 1, WhAmP*

Altgeld, John Peter 1848-1902 *TwCBDA*

Altglass, Max Mayer 1895-1952 *WhAm 3*

Altham, George J 1863- *TwCBDA*

Altham, John d1641 *ApCAB*

Altham, John 1589-1640 *DcAmB, DcAmReB, WhAm H*

Althaus, Edward 1849- *WhAm 4*

Althauser, Norman Ray 1896-1962 *WhAm 4*

Althauser, Norman Roy 1896-1962 *NatCAB 49*

Altheimer, Benjamin 1850-1938 *NatCAB 29*

Alther, Joseph G 1892-1976 *WhAm 6*

Altherr, Alfred 1911-1972 *WhAm 5*

Althoff, Henry 1873-1947 *NatCAB 15, WhAm 2*

Althouse, Harry Witman 1867- *WhAm 1*

Althouse, Howell Halberstadt 1869- *WhAm 5*

Althouse, Paul Marcks 1916-1972 *WhAm 5*

Althouse, Paul Shearer 1889-1954 *WhAm 3*

Althouse, William Lawrence Peter 1867-1955 *NatCAB 42*

Altmaier, Clinton John 1882-1950 *WhAm 3*

Altman, Benjamin 1840-1913 *AmBi, ApCAB X, DcAmB, NatCAB 15, WebAB, WhAm HA, WhAm 4*

Altman, David 1911-1971 *NatCAB 56*

Altman, Harold 1912-1961 *NatCAB 49*

Altman, Henry 1854-1911 *NatCAB 6*

Altman, Julian Allen 1911-1974 *WhAm 6*

Altman, Oscar Louis 1909-1968 *WhAm 5*

Altmann, Franz 1901-1968 *NatCAB 54*

Altmeyer, Arthur Joseph 1891-1972 *WhAm 5*

Alton, Alfred Edward 1874-1940 *NatCAB 30, WhAm 5*

Alton, Charles DeLancey 1845- *WhAm 4*

Altrocchi, Julia Cooley 1893-1972 *WhAm 6*

Altrocchi, Rudolph 1882-1953 *WhAm 3*

Altschul, Frank Joseph 1899-1971 *NatCAB 56*

Altschuler, Modest 1873- *ApCAB X, WhAm 5*

Altsheler, Joseph Alexander 1862-1919 *DcAmB, TwCBDA, WhAm 1*

Altsheler, Joseph Alexander 1863-1919 *NatCAB 11*

Altstaetter, Frederick William *ApCAB X*

Altstaetter, Rebecca Barnard Raoul 1878- *WomWWA 14*

Altube, Pedro 1827-1916 *REnAW*

Altvater, H Hugh 1897-1952 *WhAm 3*

Alva, Fernando A DeToledo, Duque De 1508-1583 *WhoMilH*

Alva, Fernando A DeToledo, Duque De see also Alba, Fernando

Alvarado, Alonzo D' d1553 *ApCAB*

Alvarado, Alonzo De *Drake*

Alvarado, Henry Victor 1857-1932 *NatCAB 26*

Alvarado, Jean Bautista 1809-1882 *TwCBDA*

Alvarado, Juan Bautista 1809-1882 *AmBi, ApCAB, DcAmB, WhAm H*

Alvarado, Pedro De 1485?-1541 *AmBi, ApCAB, Drake*

Alvaredo, Pedro De 1485?-1541 *WhoMilH*

Alvarenga, Manoel Ignacio DaSilva *ApCAB*

Alvarez, Alejandro 1868- *WhAm 5*

Alvarez, Bernardo D' 1514-1584 *ApCAB*

Alvarez, Bernardo De 1514-1584 *Drake*

Alvarez, Diego D' 1750?-1824 *ApCAB*

Alvarez, Juan 1780-1867 *McGEWB*

Alvarez, Juan 1790?-1867 *ApCAB, Drake*

Alvarez, Luis Walter 1911- *AsBiEn, WebAB*

Alvarez, Manuel 1794-1856 *REnAW*

Alvaro, Francisco *ApCAB*

Alvensleben, Gustav Von 1803-1881 *WhoMilH*

Alvensleben, Konstantin Von 1809-1882 *WhoMilH*

Alverson, Claude B 1878-1922 *NatCAB 19, WhAm 1*

Alves, Henry F 1894-1969 *WhAm 5*

Alvey, Richard Henry 1826-1906 *DcAmB, NatCAB 12, TwCBDA, WhAm 1, WhAmP*

Alvich, Joseph Paul 1900-1965 *NatCAB 51*

Alvinczy, Josef Freiherr Von 1735-1810 *WhoMilH*

Alvord, Benjamin 1813-1884 *ApCAB, DcAmB, Drake, NatCAB 4, TwCBDA, WhAm H*

Alvord, Benjamin 1860-1927 *WhAm 1*

Alvord, Clarence Walworth 1868-1928 *AmBi, REnAW, WhAm 1*

Alvord, Clarence Walworth 1868-1929 *DcAmB, EncAAH*

Alvord, Corydon A 1812-1874 *ApCAB*

Alvord, Corydon Alexis 1813-1874 *DcAmB, WhAm H*

Alvord, Elijah Smead, Jr. 1866-1946 *NatCAB 35*

Alvord, Ellsworth Chapman 1895-1964 *WhAm 4*

Alvord, Henry Elijah 1844-1904 *AmBi, ApCAB, BiDAmEd, DcAmB, NatCAB 22, TwCBDA, WhAm 1*

Alvord, Idress Head *WhAm 5*

Alvord, James Church 1808-1839 *BiAUS, BiDrAC, WhAm H*

Alvord, James Church 1865- *WhAm 4*

Alvord, John F *ApCAB X*

Alvord, John Watson 1861-1943 *NatCAB 16, NatCAB 33, WhAm 2*

Alvord, Katharine Sprague 1871- *WhAm 5, WomWWA 14*

Alvord, Lucy Fairbanks 1868- *WomWWA 14*

Alvord, Thomas Gold 1810-1897 *ApCAB, NatCAB 2, TwCBDA*

Alvord, William 1833- *NatCAB 12*

Alward, Herbert Vaughan 1880- *WhAm 6*

Alward, Vaughn Lee 1873-1938 *NatCAB 29*

Alway, Frederick James 1874- *WhAm 5*

Alwood, Olin Good 1870- *WhAm 3*

Alwood, William Bradford 1859-1946 *WhAm 2*

Alworth, Royal D d1967 *WhAm 4*

Alwyne, Horace 1891-1974 *WhAm 6*

Aly Khan, Shah 1911-1960 *WhAm 4*

Alzate Y Ramirez, Jose Antonio d1795? *Drake*

Alzate Y Ramirez, Jose Antonio 1729-1790 *ApCAB*

Alzate Y Ramirez, Jose Antonio 1738-1799 *DcScB*

Alzheimer, Alois 1864-1915 *BiHiMed*

Amadas, Philip 1550-1618 *AmBi, DcAmB*

Amadas, Phillip *WhAm H*

Amadeus, Mother Mary 1846-1917 *AmBi*

Amado, Jorge 1912- *McGEWB*

Amagat, Emile Hilaire 1841-1915 *AsBiEn, DcScB*

Amans, Jacques 1801-1888 *NewYHSD*

Amat, Thaddeus 1810-1878 *WhAm H*

Amat, Thaddeus 1811-1878 *NatCAB 12, TwCBDA*

Amateis, Louis 1855-1913 *DcAmB, WhAm HA, WhAm 4*

Amato, Pasquale 1879-1942 *WhAm 2*

Amatus Lusitanus *DcScB*

Ambartzumian, Victor Amazaspovich 1908- *AsBiEn*

Ambauen, Andrew Joseph 1847- *NatCAB 7, TwCBDA, WhAm 4*

Ambedkar, Bhimrao Ramji 1891-1956 *McGEWB*

Amberc, Richard Hiller 1912-1967 *WhAm 4*

Amberg, Emil 1868-1948 *NatCAB 36, WhAm 2*

Amberg, Harold Vincent 1886-1961 *NatCAB 46, WhAm 4*

Amberg, Julius Houseman 1890-1951 *NatCAB 39, WhAm 3*

Amberg, Rudolph Herman 1893-1952 *NatCAB 39*

Amberg, Samuel 1874- *WhAm 5*

Amberg, William Adam 1847-1918 *NatCAB 14, NatCAB 39*

Ambler, Benjamin Mason 1850- *WhAm 1*

Ambler, Charles Henry 1876-1957 *NatCAB 42, WhAm 3*

Ambler, Chase P 1865- *WhAm 4*

Ambler, Frank Rhoades 1890-1965 *NatCAB 52, WhAm 4*

Ambler, Henry Smith 1877-1939 *NatCAB 29*

Ambler, Jacob A 1829-1906 *BiAUS, BiDrAC, WhAmP*

Ambler, James Markham Marshall 1848-1881 *ApCAB Sup, DcAmB, WhAm H*

Ambler, James Murray 1854- *WhAm 4*

Ambler, Mason Gaither 1876-1947 *WhAm 2*

Ambler, Sara Ellmaker 1866- *WhAm 4, WomWWA 14*

Ambler, William E 1845- *ApCAB X, NatCAB 1*

Ambrogi, Lawrence Paul 1902-1960 *NatCAB 49*

Ambrose, Saint 339-397 *McGEWB*

Ambrose, Arthur Warren 1889-1952 *WhAm 3*

Ambrose, Henry Frizzell 1884-1965 *NatCAB 51*

Ambrose, John Wolfe 1838-1899 *NatCAB 24*

Ambrose, Paul 1868- *WhAm 5*

Ambrose, Warren Delaware 1889-1947 *NatCAB 36*

Ambrose, Wiley Vance 1881-1939 *NatCAB 41*

Ambrose, William Alfred 1887-1960 *NatCAB 48*

Ambrose, William Clement 1888-1962 *NatCAB 50*

Ambrosio, Vittorio 1879-1950 *WhWW-II*

Ambruster, Howard Watson 1878-1961 *WhAm 4*

Ambruster, Watson 1842-1904 *WhAm 1*
Amburn, Jessie Eoline Bowles 1875-
WomWWA 14
Amdur, Isadore 1910-1970 *WhAm 5*
Amee, Mrs. John 1868- *WomWWA 14*
Ameghino, Florentino 1854?-1911 *DcScB*
Ameli, Howard Wilmurt 1881- *WhAm 6*
Amelia *WhAm H*
Amelung, Johann Friedrich 1741-1798
BnEnAmA
Amen, Harlan Page 1853-1913 *NatCAB 10,*
WhAm 1
Amen, John Harlan 1898-1960 *WhAm 3A*
Amench *NewYHSD*
Amend, Bernhard Gottwald d1917 *WhAm 3*
Amend, Carl Gustave 1887-1949 *NatCAB 43*
Amend, Edward Bernard 1858-1914 *WhAm 1*
Amend, Otto Paul 1858-1936 *NatCAB 43*
Amendt, Philip *NewYHSD*
Amenemhet I *McGEWB*
Amenhotep III *McGEWB*
Ament, James Eli 1863-1936 *NatCAB 27,*
WhAm 1, WhAm 1C
Ament, William Scott 1851-1909 *DcAmB*
Amerige, Annette Jackson *ApCAB X*
Amerige, Edward Russell 1857-1915 *ApCAB X*
Amerige, George Henry 1855- *ApCAB X*
Amerigo Vespucci 1451-1512 *ApCAB X*
Ameringer, Oscar 1870-1943 *DcAmB S3*
Amerman, James Lyman 1882-1968
NatCAB 55
Amerman, Lemuel 1846-1897 *BiDrAC,*
NatCAB 9, WhAm H
Amerman, Ralph Alonzo 1884-1941 *WhAm 1*
Amery, Leopold 1873-1955 *WhWW-II*
Ames, Adelbert 1835-1933 *ApCAB, BiAUS,*
BiDrAC, DcAmB S1, Drake, McGEWB,
NatCAB 13, TwCBDA, WhAmP
Ames, Adelbert, Jr. 1880-1955 *NatCAB 44,*
WhAm 3
Ames, Alexander *NewYHSD*
Ames, Blanche Ames 1878-1969 *NatCAB 53,*
WomWWA 14
Ames, Butler 1871-1954 *BiDrAC, NatCAB 53,*
WhAm 3, WhAmP
Ames, Charles Bismark 1870-1935 *WhAm 1*
Ames, Charles Gordon 1828-1912 *DcAmB,*
NatCAB 14, NatCAB 23, TwCBDA,
WhAm 1
Ames, Charles Lesley 1884-1969 *NatCAB 55*
Ames, Charles Wilberforce 1855-1921
NatCAB 14, NatCAB 27, WhAm 1
Ames, Daniel *NewYHSD*
Ames, Daniel F *NewYHSD*
Ames, Edgar 1868-1944 *WhAm 2*
Ames, Edward B 1806- *Drake*
Ames, Edward Elbridge 1881-1952 *NatCAB 41,*
WhAm 3
Ames, Edward Gardner *ApCAB X*
Ames, Edward Raymond 1806-1879 *ApCAB,*
NatCAB 3, TwCBDA, WhAm H
Ames, Edward Raymond 1806-1897 *DcAmB*
Ames, Edward Scribner 1870-1958 *DcAmReB,*
WhAm 3
Ames, Edwin Ayres *ApCAB X*
Ames, Edwin Gardner 1856-1935 *NatCAB 27*
Ames, Eleanor Kirk 1831-1908 *WhAm 1*
Ames, Eleanor M 1830- *AmWom*
Ames, Ezra 1768-1836 *BnEnAmA, DcAmB,*
IlBEAAW, NatCAB 22, NewYHSD,
WhAm H
Ames, Fanny Baker 1840-1931 *AmWom,*
NotAW
Ames, Fisher 1758-1808 *AmBi, ApCAB,*
BiAUS, BiDrAC, DcAmB, Drake,
McGEWB, NatCAB 2, TwCBDA,
WebAB, WhAm H, WhAmP
Ames, Fisher 1838- *WhAm 4*
Ames, Frederick Lothrop 1835-1893 *AmBi,*
DcAmB, NatCAB 14, TwCBDA,
WhAm H
Ames, Frederick Lothrop 1873-1921 *ApCAB X*
Ames, Frederick Lothrop 1876-1921
NatCAB 19
Ames, Herman Vandenburg 1865-1935
DcAmB S1, WhAm 1
Ames, Hobart 1865-1945 *WhAm 2*
Ames, James Barr 1846-1910 *AmBi, BiDAmEd,*

DcAmB, NatCAB 13, NatCAB 18,
TwCBDA, WhAm HA, WhAm 1,
WhAm 4
Ames, James Tyler 1810-1883 *DcAmB,*
NatCAB 25, WhAm H
Ames, James Webb 1864- *WhoColR*
Ames, Jesse H 1875-1957 *WhAm 3*
Ames, John Griffith 1834-1910 *WhAm 1*
Ames, John Griffith 1872-1945 *WhAm 3*
Ames, John Hubbard 1838-1908 *NatCAB 17*
Ames, John Lincoln 1863- *WhAm 4*
Ames, John Ormsbee 1872-1936 *WhAm 1*
Ames, John Worthington 1871-1954
NatCAB 51
Ames, Joseph Alexander 1816-1872 *ApCAB,*
DcAmB, Drake, NatCAB 7, NewYHSD,
TwCBDA, WhAm H
Ames, Joseph Bushnell 1878-1928 *WhAm 1*
Ames, Joseph Sweetman 1864-1943 *ApCAB X,*
DcAmB S3, DcScB, TwCBDA, WhAm 2
Ames, Julia A 1861-1891 *AmWom, TwCBDA*
Ames, Julius Rubens 1801-1850 *NewYHSD*
Ames, Knowlton Lyman d1931 *WhAm 1*
Ames, Knowlton Lyman, Jr. 1893-1965
NatCAB 53
Ames, Lawrence Marion 1900-1966 *NatCAB 52*
Ames, Lewis Darwin 1869- *WhAm 5*
Ames, Louis Annin 1866-1952 *NatCAB 15,*
WhAm 3
Ames, Lucia True 1856- *AmWom*
Ames, Maria 1836?- *NewYHSD*
Ames, Mary Clemmer d1884 *AmWom*
Ames, Mary Clemmer 1831-1884 *DcAmB,*
NotAW
Ames, Mary Clemmer 1839-1884 *ApCAB,*
NatCAB 7
Ames, Mary Clemmer 1840-1884 *TwCBDA*
Ames, Mary Lesley d1929 *WhAm 1,*
WomWWA 14
Ames, Nathan Peabody 1803-1847 *ApCAB,*
DcAmB, Drake, NatCAB 25, TwCBDA,
WhAm H
Ames, Nathaniel d1835 *Drake*
Ames, Nathaniel 1708-1764 *AmBi, ApCAB,*
DcAmB, Drake, NatCAB 8, WhAm H
Ames, Norman Bruce 1896-1960 *WhAm 4*
Ames, Oakes 1804-1873 *AmBi, ApCAB,*
BiAUS, BiDrAC, DcAmB, NatCAB 2,
REnAW, TwCBDA, WebAB, WhAm H,
WhAmP
Ames, Oakes 1874-1950 *DcAmB S4,*
NatCAB 53, WhAm 3
Ames, Oakes Angier 1829-1899 *NatCAB 2,*
TwCBDA
Ames, Oliver 1779-1863 *DcAmB, NatCAB 14,*
TwCBDA, WhAm H
Ames, Oliver 1807-1877 *ApCAB, DcAmB,*
NatCAB 4, TwCBDA, WhAm H
Ames, Oliver 1831-1895 *DcAmB, NatCAB 1,*
TwCBDA, WhAm H, WhAmP
Ames, Oliver 1864-1929 *NatCAB 28,*
WhAm 1
Ames, Robert Parker Marr 1856- *WhAm 4*
Ames, Samuel 1806-1865 *ApCAB, BiAUS,*
DcAmB, NatCAB 10, TwCBDA,
WhAm H
Ames, Sarah Fisher 1817-1901 *NewYHSD*
Ames, Seth 1805-1881 *ApCAB Sup*
Ames, Susie M 1888-1969 *WhAm 5*
Ames, Wardwell 1846-1910 *NatCAB 17*
Ames, William 1576-1633 *DcScB*
Ames, William 1842-1914 *NatCAB 36,*
WhAm 1
Ames, William Lafayette 1857-1951 *WhAm 3*
Ames, William Rolfe 1870-1936 *NatCAB 28*
Ames, William Van Bergen 1858-1922
ApCAB X
Ames, Winthrop 1870-1937 *DcAmB S2*
Ames, Winthrop 1871-1937 *NatCAB 15,*
WhAm 1
Amesse, John William 1874-1949 *NatCAB 39*
Amet, Edward Hill 1860-1948 *NatCAB 36*
Amey, Harry Burton 1868-1949 *WhAm 3*
Amey, Henry 1831?- *NewYHSD*
Amezaga, Juan Jose 1882-1956 *WhAm 3*
Amherst, J H 1776-1851 *ApCAB*
Amherst, Jeffery 1717-1797 *ApCAB, DcAmB,*
McGEWB, NatCAB 1, WhAm H,

WhAmP
Amherst, Jeffrey 1717-1797 *AmBi, Drake,*
WhoMilH
Ami, Henry M 1858- *ApCAB*
Amici, Giovan Battista 1786-1868 *DcScB*
Amick, Erwin Hamer, Jr. 1910-1970 *WhAm 5*
Amick, Robert Wesley 1879-1970? *IlBEAAW*
Amidas, Philip 1550-1618 *AmBi, ApCAB,*
Drake
Amidon, Beulah 1895-1958 *WhAm 3*
Amidon, Beulah McHenry 1866-
WomWWA 14
Amidon, Charles Fremont 1856-1937
DcAmB S2, NatCAB 27, REnAW,
WhAm 1, WhAmP
Amidon, Royal Wells 1854-1938 *NatCAB 29*
Amidon, Samuel Barker 1863-1925 *WhAm 1*
Amies, Olive Pond *AmWom*
Amiger, William Thomas 1870-1929 *WhAm 1,*
WhoColR
Amlie, Thomas Ryum 1897- *BiDrAC, WhAmP*
Amling, Herbert Arnold 1894-1968 *NatCAB 56*
Ammann, Othmar Hermann 1879-1965
NatCAB 52, WhAm 4
Ammar, Abbas Moustafa 1907-1974 *WhAm 6*
Ammen, Daniel 1819-1898 *DcAmB, Drake,*
WhAm H
Ammen, Daniel 1820-1898 *ApCAB, NatCAB 4,*
TwCBDA
Ammen, Jacob 1807-1894 *DcAmB, WhAm H*
Ammen, Jacob 1808-1894 *ApCAB, Drake,*
NatCAB 4, TwCBDA
Ammen, Samuel Zenas 1843- *WhAm 4*
Ammidown, Edward Holmes 1820- *NatCAB 3*
Ammidown, Edward Holmes 1830- *WhAm 4*
Ammon, Edith Darlington *WomWWA 14*
Ammon, John Henry 1840-1904 *NatCAB 28*
Ammonius, Son Of Hermias d526? *DcScB*
Ammons, Elias Milton 1860-1925 *ApCAB X,*
DcAmB, NatCAB 15, NatCAB 34,
WhAm 1, WhAmP
Ammons, Eugene 1925-1974 *WhAm 6*
Ammons, Teller 1895-1972 *WhAm 5*
Amonson, Louis Sverre 1869-1913 *NatCAB 17*
Amontons, Guillaume 1663-1705 *AsBiEn,*
DcScB
Amorsolo, Fernando 1892- *McGEWB*
Amory, Arthur 1841-1911 *NatCAB 12,*
WhAm 1
Amory, Charles Bean 1841-1919 *ApCAB X*
Amory, Charles Walter 1842-1913 *NatCAB 15,*
WhAm 1
Amory, Estelle Mendell 1845- *AmWom*
Amory, Harcourt 1894-1969 *WhAm 5*
Amory, John James 1856-1930 *NatCAB 14,*
WhAm 1
Amory, Robert 1842-1910 *ApCAB, TwCBDA,*
WhAm 1
Amory, Robert 1885-1972 *WhAm 5*
Amory, Thomas 1682-1728 *AmBi, DcAmB,*
WhAm H
Amory, Thomas Coffin 1810-1889 *ApCAB*
Amory, Thomas Coffin 1812-1889 *TwCBDA*
Amory, Thomas J C 1830?-1864 *ApCAB,*
NatCAB 4, TwCBDA
Amory, William 1869-1954 *NatCAB 40,*
WhAm 3
Amos *McGEWB*
Amos 'n' Andy *WebAB*
Amos, Ernest Clarence 1872-1962 *NatCAB 51*
Amos, Frank Rezin 1890-1961 *NatCAB 50,*
WhAm 4
Amos, Isaiah H 1844-1915 *NatCAB 17*
Amos, James Oliver 1833-1918 *NatCAB 19*
Amos, Roy 1891-1967 *NatCAB 53*
Amos, Thyrsa Wealhtheow 1879-1941 *WhAm 1*
Amos, William Frederick 1869-1956
NatCAB 42, WhAm 5
Amoss, David Alfred 1857-1915 *NatCAB 17*
Amoss, Harold Lindsay 1886-1956 *NatCAB 43,*
WhAm 3
Amoss, Walter James 1899-1968 *NatCAB 54*
Ampere, Andre Marie 1775-1836 *AsBiEn,*
DcScB, McGEWB
Ampudia, Pedro De *ApCAB, Drake*
Amram, Beulah Brylawski 1881-
WomWWA 14
Amrine, William Frederick 1875- *WhAm 5*

Amsbary, Frank C, Jr. 1900-1960 *WhAm 4*
Amsbary, Wallace Bruce 1867- *WhAm 3*
Amsler, Henry Moore 1896-1975 *WhAm 6*
Amsler, Jakob 1823-1912 *DcScB*
Amstead, William 1831?- *NewYHSD*
Amster, Nathan Leonard 1869-1939 *WhAm 1*
Amstuz, John O 1893-1964 *WhAm 4*
Amtman, Leo 1904-1964 *NatCAB 51*
Amunategui, Gergorio Victor 1830-
　　ApCAB Sup
Amunategui, Miguel Luis 1828-1888
　　ApCAB Sup
Amundsen, Roald Engelbregt Gravning
　　1872-1928 *AsBiEn, McGEWB*
Amundson, John A 1856- *NatCAB 5*
Amweg, Frederick James 1856-1933
　　NatCAB 16, WhAm 1, WhAm 1C
Amyot, Louis Joseph Adjutor 1884-1968
　　WhAm 5
An, Lu-Shan 703-757 *McGEWB*
Anacaona *ApCAB*
Anagnos, Julia Romana Howe 1844-1886
　　WhAm H
Anagnos, Michael 1837-1906 *BiDAmEd,*
　　DcAmB, NatCAB 13, WhAm HA,
　　WhAm 4
Anami, Korechika 1887-1945 *WhWW-II*
Anan BenDavid *McGEWB*
Anaritius *DcScB*
Anasco, Juan De *ApCAB*
Anast, James Louis 1918-1964 *WhAm 4*
Anastassy d1966 *WhAm 5*
Anathan, Simon Joseph 1879-1959 *NatCAB 45*
Anatolius Of Alexandria *DcScB*
Anaxagoras 500?BC-428?BC *AsBiEn, DcScB,*
　　McGEWB
Anaxilaus Of Larissa *DcScB*
Anaximander 610?BC-546?BC *AsBiEn, DcScB,*
　　McGEWB
Anaximenes 570?BC-500?BC *AsBiEn,*
　　McGEWB
Anaximenes Of Miletus 570?BC-500?BC *DcScB*
Anaya, Pedro Maria *ApCAB*
Anburey, Thomas *Drake*
Ancel, Paul Albert 1873-1961 *DcScB*
Anceney, Charles L 1863- *WhAm 1*
Ancerl, Karel 1908-1973 *WhAm 6*
Anchieta, Jose De 1533-1597 *ApCAB, Drake*
Anchieta, Jose De 1534-1597 *McGEWB*
Ancona, Sydenham Elnathan 1824-1913 *BiAUS,*
　　BiDrAC
Ancora, Pietro *NewYHSD*
Andagoya, Pascual De d1548 *ApCAB*
Anderegg, Frederick 1852-1922 *WhAm 1*
Anderes, Robert L 1902-1958 *WhAm 3*
Anderledy, Anthony Maria 1819-1892 *WhAm H*
Anderman, William 1892-1966 *WhAm 4*
Andernach, Gunther *DcScB*
Anders, Howard Schultz 1866-1954 *NatCAB 43*
Anders, James Meschter 1854-1936 *ApCAB X,*
　　NatCAB 17, NatCAB 27, WhAm 1
Anders, John Daniel 1771-1847 *ApCAB,*
　　NatCAB 5, WhAm H
Anders, Paul R 1894-1966 *WhAm 4*
Anders, Thomas Jefferson 1838-1910
　　NatCAB 13, TwCBDA, WhAm 1
Anders, William Alison 1933- *WebAMB*
Anders, Wladyslaw 1892-1970 *WhWW-II,*
　　WhoMilH
Andersen, Albert M 1898-1959 *WhAm 3*
Andersen, Andreas Storrs 1908-1974 *WhAm 6*
Andersen, Arthur Edward 1885-1947
　　NatCAB 17, NatCAB 35, WhAm 2
Andersen, Arthur Olaf 1880-1958 *NatCAB 48,*
　　WhAm 3
Andersen, Bjorn 1897-1971 *WhAm 5*
Andersen, Charles Martin 1871-1956
　　NatCAB 43
Andersen, Christian Schmidt 1879-1931
　　WhAm 1
Andersen, Hans Christian 1805-1875 *McGEWB*
Andersen, Hendrik Christian 1872-1940
　　WhAm 1, WhAm 2
Andersen, Herman Carl 1897- *BiDrAC*
Andersen, James Roy 1904-1945 *WhAm 2*
Andersen, John Dibos 1910-1962 *WhAm 4*
Andersen, Joyce Marilyn Off 1923-1969
　　WhAm 5

Anderson, Abraham Archibald 1846-1940
　　NatCAB 29
Anderson, Abraham Archibald 1847-1940
　　NatCAB 14, WhAm 1, WhAm 2
Anderson, Ada Woodruff 1860- *ApCAB X,*
　　WhAm 4, WomWWA 14
Anderson, Adna 1827-1889 *NatCAB 33*
Anderson, Alan Ross 1925-1973 *WhAm 6*
Anderson, Albert 1859-1932 *WhAm 1*
Anderson, Albert 1876-1948 *WhAm 2*
Anderson, Albert Barnes 1857-1938 *WhAm 1*
Anderson, Albert Raney 1837-1898 *BiDrAC*
Anderson, Alden 1867-1944 *NatCAB 16,*
　　WhAm 2
Anderson, Alexander 1774-1870 *Drake*
Anderson, Alexander 1775-1870 *AmBi, ApCAB,*
　　BnEnAmA, DcAmB, NatCAB 6,
　　NewYHSD, TwCBDA, WhAm H
Anderson, Alexander Outlaw 1794-1869 *ApCAB,*
　　BiAUS, BiDrAC, NatCAB 11, WhAm H,
　　WhAmP
Anderson, Alexander Pierce 1862-1943
　　WhAm 2
Anderson, Alexandra Koesis 1864-
　　WomWWA 14
Anderson, Alfred Leonard 1900-1964
　　NatCAB 51
Anderson, Alvin George 1911-1975 *WhAm 6*
Anderson, Amabel A 1883-1936 *WhAm 1*
Anderson, Amos Carey 1897-1972 *WhAm 5*
Anderson, Andrew *NewYHSD*
Anderson, Andrew Freeman 1866-1936
　　WhAm 1
Anderson, Andrew Runni 1876-1936 *WhAm 3*
Anderson, Andrew Work 1864- *WhAm 2*
Anderson, Ann *NewYHSD*
Anderson, Anton Bennett 1888-1974 *WhAm 6*
Anderson, Arch W 1877-1946 *WhAm 2*
Anderson, Archibald Watson 1905-1965
　　BiDAmEd, NatCAB 51, WhAm 4
Anderson, Archie Albert 1903-1963 *NatCAB 50*
Anderson, Arthur Julius 1889-1964 *WhAm 4*
Anderson, Arthur Marvin 1880-1966
　　NatCAB 54, WhAm 4
Anderson, Arvid Robert 1890- *ApCAB X*
Anderson, Asher 1846-1925 *WhAm 1*
Anderson, Austin Flint 1889-1955 *NatCAB 43*
Anderson, Axel Gordon 1904-1974 *WhAm 6*
Anderson, Axel Henry 1894-1966 *WhAm 4*
Anderson, Belle Bingley *WomWWA 14*
Anderson, Benjamin McAlester, Jr. 1886-1949
　　ApCAB X, DcAmB S4, WhAm 2
Anderson, Carl Carey 1877-1912 *BiDrAC,*
　　WhAm 1
Anderson, Carl David 1905- *AsBiEn,*
　　McGEWB, WebAB
Anderson, Carl Harold 1926-1974 *WhAm 6*
Anderson, Carl Magnus 1905-1972 *WhAm 5*
Anderson, Carl Thomas 1865-1948 *WhAm 2*
Anderson, Carlotta Adele 1876-1956 *WhAm 3,*
　　WomWWA 14
Anderson, Chandler Parsons 1866-1936
　　WhAm 1
Anderson, Chapman Levy 1845-1924 *BiDrAC,*
　　WhAmP
Anderson, Charles 1814-1895 *BiAUS,*
　　TwCBDA
Anderson, Charles Albert 1889-1962 *WhAm 4*
Anderson, Charles Arthur 1899- *BiDrAC*
Anderson, Charles E *BiAUS*
Anderson, Charles Hardin 1907-1971 *WhAm 5*
Anderson, Charles Harry 1879- *WhoColR*
Anderson, Charles Joseph 1880- *WhAm 6*
Anderson, Charles Lee 1903-1958 *NatCAB 47*
Anderson, Charles Loftus Grant 1863- *WhAm 5*
Anderson, Charles Marley 1845-1908 *BiDrAC*
Anderson, Charles Orlin 1861-1941 *NatCAB 36*
Anderson, Charles Palmerston 1863-1930
　　TwCBDA
Anderson, Charles Palmerston 1864-1930
　　NatCAB 4, WhAm 1
Anderson, Charles William 1866- *WhoColR*
Anderson, Chester A *WhoColR*
Anderson, Clarence William 1891- *IlBEAAW*
Anderson, Clifford 1833-1899 *BiDConf,*
　　NatCAB 3
Anderson, Clifford LeConte 1862-1933
　　ApCAB X, NatCAB 10, WhAm 1

Anderson, Clinton Presba 1895-1975 *BiDrAC,*
　　BiDrUSE, EncAAH, WhAm 6
Anderson, David 1814-1885 *ApCAB Sup*
Anderson, David Allen 1874- *WhAm 5*
Anderson, David Lawrence 1850-1911 *DcAmB,*
　　NatCAB 23
Anderson, Dennis Henry 1868- *WhoColR*
Anderson, Dice Robins 1880-1942 *WhAm 2*
Anderson, Dillon 1906-1974 *WhAm 6*
Anderson, Donald Brown 1904-1956 *WhAm 3*
Anderson, Douglas Smith 1871-1954 *WhAm 3*
Anderson, Dwight 1882-1953 *NatCAB 45,*
　　WhAm 3
Anderson, Dwight 1896-1962 *WhAm 4*
Anderson, E Ruth 1879- *WomWWA 14*
Anderson, Earl W 1897-1965 *WhAm 4*
Anderson, Edgar 1897-1969 *WhAm 5*
Anderson, Edgar Lee 1868-1941 *NatCAB 31*
Anderson, Edward 1833-1916 *WhAm 1*
Anderson, Edward 1864-1937 *NatCAB 30*
Anderson, Edward Alexander 1855-1920
　　NatCAB 45
Anderson, Edward Delmar 1902-1956 *WhAm 3*
Anderson, Edward Lee 1913-1969 *WhAm 5*
Anderson, Edward Lowell 1842-1916 *WhAm 1*
Anderson, Edward Wharton 1903- *WhAm 2*
Anderson, Edwin Alexander 1860-1933
　　WhAm 1
Anderson, Edwin Hatfield 1861-1947
　　DcAmB S4, DcAmLiB, TwCBDA,
　　WhAm 2
Anderson, Elam Jonathan 1890-1944
　　NatCAB 32, WhAm 2
Anderson, Elbert Ellery 1833-1903 *TwCBDA,*
　　WhAm 1
Anderson, Elbridge R 1864-1944 *WhAm 2*
Anderson, Elda Emma 1899-1961 *NatCAB 50*
Anderson, Eleanor Eudora 1877-
　　WomWWA 14
Anderson, Elizabeth Milbank 1850-1921 *AmBi,*
　　DcAmB, NatCAB 23, NotAW
Anderson, Elizabeth Preston 1861- *BiCAW,*
　　WhAm 4, WomWWA 14
Anderson, Elmer Theodore 1888-1943
　　NatCAB 32
Anderson, Elsie Grace *WhAm 5*
Anderson, Emmeline *NewYHSD*
Anderson, Ernest 1881-1954 *NatCAB 43,*
　　WhAm 3
Anderson, Ernest Masson 1877-1960 *DcScB*
Anderson, Esther L *WhAm 5*
Anderson, Eva Greenslit d1972 *WhAm 6*
Anderson, Florence Gray 1890- *WhoColR*
Anderson, Florence Stewart *WomWWA 14*
Anderson, Frank 1876-1956 *WhAm 3*
Anderson, Frank Bartow 1863-1935 *WhAm 1*
Anderson, Frank Leonard 1935- *WhAm 1*
Anderson, Frank Maley 1871-1961 *WhAm 6*
Anderson, Frank Maloy 1871-1961 *NatCAB 48*
Anderson, Frederick Irving 1877-1947 *WhAm 2*
Anderson, Frederick Lewis 1905-1969
　　NatCAB 56, WhAm 5
Anderson, Frederick Lincoln 1862- *WhAm 4*
Anderson, Frederick Paul 1867-1934 *WhAm 1*
Anderson, Galusha 1832-1918 *ApCAB,*
　　DcAmB, NatCAB 1, NatCAB 11,
　　TwCBDA, WhAm 1, WhAmP
Anderson, George A 1885-1970 *WhAm 5*
Anderson, George Alburtus 1853-1896 *BiDrAC,*
　　WhAm H
Anderson, George B 1830-1862 *TwCBDA*
Anderson, George B 1831-1862 *ApCAB, Drake,*
　　NatCAB 4
Anderson, George Edward 1897-1972 *WhAm 5*
Anderson, George Everett 1869-1940
　　NatCAB 34, WhAm 1
Anderson, George Kerr 1868-1943 *NatCAB 36*
Anderson, George Laverne 1905-1971 *WhAm 6*
Anderson, George Lucius 1849-1934 *WhAm 1,*
　　WhAm 1C
Anderson, George Minor 1873-1958 *WhAm 3*
Anderson, George Smith 1849-1915 *WhAm 1*
Anderson, George Thomas 1824-1901 *BiDConf,*
　　DcAmB, NatCAB 13, WhAm H
Anderson, George Washington 1832-1902
　　BiAUS, BiDrAC, WhAmP
Anderson, George Weston 1861-1938 *WhAm 1*
Anderson, George Whelan, Jr. 1906- *WebAMB*

Anderson, George Wood 1873- *WhAm 5*
Anderson, Glenn Malcolm 1913- *BiDrAC*
Anderson, Gordon Earle 1896-1963 *NatCAB 50*
Anderson, Grace Lee *WomWWA 14*
Anderson, H T 1811-1872 *ApCAB*
Anderson, H T *see also* Anderson, Henry
   Tompkins
Anderson, Harold 1894-1968 *NatCAB 54,*
   WhAm 5
Anderson, Harold Durbin 1887-1950 *WhAm 3*
Anderson, Harold MacDonald 1876-1940
   WhAm 1
Anderson, Harold Spurrier 1891-1941
   NatCAB 30
Anderson, Harold V 1890-1965 *WhAm 4*
Anderson, Harry Bennett 1879-1935 *WhAm 1*
Anderson, Harry Reuben 1844-1918 *WhAm 1*
Anderson, Harry William 1891-1959 *WhAm 3*
Anderson, Helen Elona *WomWWA 14*
Anderson, Helen Natalie Johnson d1965
   WhAm 4
Anderson, Henrietta E 1859- *WomWWA 14*
Anderson, Henry Burrall 1863-1938 *NatCAB 29*
Anderson, Henry Clay 1872-1939 *NatCAB 32,*
   WhAm 1
Anderson, Henry Hill 1827-1896 *NatCAB 24,*
   WhAm H
Anderson, Henry Hill 1893-1945 *NatCAB 34*
Anderson, Henry James 1798-1875 *Drake*
Anderson, Henry James 1799-1875 *ApCAB,*
   NatCAB 6, TwCBDA, WhAm H
Anderson, Henry Tompkins 1812-1872 *DcAmB,*
   NatCAB 22, WhAm H
Anderson, Henry Tompkins *see also* Anderson, H
   T
Anderson, Henry Watkins 1870-1954
   NatCAB 44, WhAm 3
Anderson, Henry William 1885-1940 *WhAm 1*
Anderson, Howard B 1902-1962 *WhAm 4*
Anderson, Hugh *NewYHSD*
Anderson, Hugh 1839-1911 *NatCAB 32*
Anderson, Hugh Johnston 1801-1881 *BiAUS,*
   BiDrAC, Drake, NatCAB 6, WhAm H
Anderson, Isaac 1760-1838 *ApCAB Sup,*
   BiAUS, BiDrAC, WhAm H
Anderson, Isaac 1780-1857 *ApCAB, Drake*
Anderson, Isabel Weld Perkins 1876-1948
   BiCAW, NatCAB 40, WhAm 2
Anderson, J *NewYHSD*
Anderson, J Aubrey 1882-1946 *NatCAB 44*
Anderson, J B *NewYHSD*
Anderson, J Hartley 1868-1915 *NatCAB 16*
Anderson, J Hartley *see also* Anderson, James
   Hartley
Anderson, J P *BiAUS*
Anderson, J P *see also* Anderson, James Patton
Anderson, Jacob Nelson 1867- *WhAm 4*
Anderson, Jacob S d1857 *NewYHSD*
Anderson, James d1820 *Drake*
Anderson, James 1678-1740 *Drake*
Anderson, James 1784-1861 *NatCAB 17*
Anderson, James 1798-1886 *NatCAB 24*
Anderson, James Archibald 1857- *ApCAB X*
Anderson, James Arthur 1857- *WhAm 4*
Anderson, James Aylor 1892-1964 *NatCAB 50*
Anderson, James Cuyler 1920-1969 *WhAm 5*
Anderson, James Hartley 1868-1915 *ApCAB X*
Anderson, James Hartley *see also* Anderson, J
   Hartley
Anderson, James Harvey 1848- *WhoColR*
Anderson, James Henry 1868- *WhoColR*
Anderson, James Howard 1875- *WhAm 5*
Anderson, James Kerr 1891-1950 *NatCAB 41*
Anderson, James M *NewYHSD*
Anderson, James Nesbitt 1864-1945 *WhAm 2*
Anderson, James Patton *Drake*
Anderson, James Patton 1820?-1873 *ApCAB,*
   NatCAB 4
Anderson, James Patton 1822-1872 *BiDConf,*
   BiDrAC, DcAmB, TwCBDA
Anderson, James Patton 1822-1873 *WhAm H*
Anderson, James Patton *see also* Anderson, J P
Anderson, James R *WhAm H*
Anderson, James Thomas 1866-1949
   NatCAB 38
Anderson, James Thomas 1883-1958
   NatCAB 48
Anderson, James Vernie 1889-1951 *NatCAB 41*

Anderson, James Wayman 1863- *WhoColR*
Anderson, James Wright 1831- *TwCBDA*
Anderson, Jefferson Charles 1868- *WhoColR*
Anderson, Jefferson Randolph 1861-1950
   ApCAB X, NatCAB 16, NatCAB 39,
   WhAm 5
Anderson, Jessie Isabel Calhoun *WomWWA 14*
Anderson, John 1792-1853 *BiAUS, BiDrAC,*
   Drake, WhAm H
Anderson, John 1836-1910 *NatCAB 10,*
   WhAm 1
Anderson, John 1837-1909 *REnAW*
Anderson, John 1857-1940 *ApCAB X,*
   NatCAB 30
Anderson, Sir John 1882-1958 *WhWW-II*
Anderson, John 1888-1957 *WhAm 3*
Anderson, John 1891-1953 *WhAm 3*
Anderson, John 1896-1943 *WhAm 2*
Anderson, John Albert 1914-1967 *NatCAB 53,*
   WhAm 4
Anderson, John Alexander 1834-1892 *BiDrAC,*
   DcAmB, NatCAB 8, TwCBDA,
   WhAm H, WhAmP
Anderson, John August 1876-1959 *WhAm 3*
Anderson, John Bayard 1922- *BiDrAC*
Anderson, John Benjamin 1869-1952 *WhAm 3*
Anderson, John Crawford 1863- *NatCAB 18,*
   WhAm 1
Anderson, John Edward 1879-1947 *WhAm 2*
Anderson, John Edward 1893-1966 *NatCAB 52,*
   WhAm 4
Anderson, John Fleming, Jr. 1840- *NatCAB 7*
Anderson, John Fletz 1873-1958 *NatCAB 47,*
   WhAm 3
Anderson, John Francis 1848-1927 *WhAm 1*
Anderson, John George 1866-1943 *WhAm 2*
Anderson, John Henry 1810?- *ApCAB*
Anderson, John Jacob 1821-1906 *ApCAB,*
   BiDAmEd, TwCBDA, WhAm 1
Anderson, John Murray d1954 *WhAm 3*
Anderson, John Quincy 1916-1975 *WhAm 6*
Anderson, John W 1899-1976 *WhAm 6*
Anderson, John W Carver *NewYHSD*
Anderson, John Wallace 1802-1830 *Drake*
Anderson, John Wendell 1867-1945 *NatCAB 34*
Anderson, John Will 1883-1967 *WhAm 4*
Anderson, John William 1871-1954 *NatCAB 41,*
   WhAm 5
Anderson, John Zuinglius 1904- *BiDrAC,*
   WhAmP
Anderson, Joseph 1757-1837 *ApCAB, BiAUS,*
   BiDrAC, DcAmB, Drake, NatCAB 2,
   TwCBDA, WhAm H, WhAmP
Anderson, Joseph 1836-1916 *NatCAB 7,*
   TwCBDA, WhAm 1
Anderson, Joseph Gaudentius 1865-1927
   NatCAB 15, WhAm 1
Anderson, Joseph Halstead 1800-1870 *BiAUS,*
   BiDrAC, WhAm H
Anderson, Joseph McNair 1807-1861 *BiAUS*
Anderson, Joseph Morgan 1872-1927
   NatCAB 23
Anderson, Joseph Reid 1813-1892 *ApCAB Sup,*
   BiDConf, DcAmB, NatCAB 12,
   TwCBDA, WebAB, WebAMB, WhAm H
Anderson, Joseph Starr 1884-1959 *WhAm 3*
Anderson, Joseph Wilson 1877-1957
   NatCAB 47
Anderson, Josiah McNair 1807-1861 *BiDrAC,*
   WhAm H
Anderson, Julian Piper 1896-1956 *NatCAB 43*
Anderson, Karl 1874-1956 *WhAm 3*
Anderson, Karl Leopold 1905-1968 *WhAm 5*
Anderson, Sir Kenneth 1891-1959 *WhWW-II*
Anderson, Larz 1803-1878 *ApCAB*
Anderson, Larz 1866-1937 *ApCAB X,*
   NatCAB 15, NatCAB 28, WhAm 1
Anderson, Lee 1896-1972 *WhAm 5*
Anderson, Lee William 1926-1973 *WhAm 6*
Anderson, Leroy 1908-1975 *WhAm 6*
Anderson, Leroy Dean 1877-1961 *WhAm 4*
Anderson, LeRoy Hagen 1906- *BiDrAC*
Anderson, Lewis Flint 1866-1932 *WhAm 1*
Anderson, Lily Strickland *WomWWA 14*
Anderson, Lizzie Pershing 1852- *WomWWA 14*
Anderson, Lloyd Douglas Hesley 1896-1964
   NatCAB 50
Anderson, Louis Bernard 1871- *WhoColR*

Anderson, Louis Francis 1861-1950 *WhAm 3*
Anderson, Lucian 1824-1898 *BiDrAC*
Anderson, Lucien 1824-1898 *BiAUS*
Anderson, Margaret 1893?-1973 *WebAB*
Anderson, Margaret Pauline 1870-
   WomWWA 14
Anderson, Margaret Steele *WomWWA 14*
Anderson, Margarethe Urdahl *WomWWA 14*
Anderson, Marian 1902- *EncAB, McGEWB,*
   WebAB
Anderson, Martin 1882-1966 *WhAm 4*
Anderson, Martin Brewer 1815-1890 *ApCAB,*
   BiDAmEd, DcAmB, NatCAB 12,
   TwCBDA, WhAm H
Anderson, Mary 1859-1940 *AmWom, ApCAB,*
   DcAmB S2, NatCAB 1, NotAW,
   TwCBDA, WhAm HA, WhAm 4
Anderson, Mary 1872-1964 *WhAm 4, WhAmP*
Anderson, Mary Josephine *WomWWA 14*
Anderson, Mary Mortlock 1916-1969 *WhAm 5*
Anderson, Mary Slater 1856- *WomWWA 14*
Anderson, Maxwell 1888-1959 *EncAB,*
   McGEWB, WebAB, WhAm 3
Anderson, Melville Best 1851-1933 *TwCBDA,*
   WhAm 1
Anderson, Merle Hampton 1873- *WhAm 5*
Anderson, Neal Larkin 1865-1931 *WhAm 1*
Anderson, Nelson Paul 1899-1957 *WhAm 3*
Anderson, Newton Mitchell 1858- *WhAm 4*
Anderson, Nicholas Longworth 1838-1892
   TwCBDA
Anderson, Nils 1882-1965 *NatCAB 52,*
   WhAm 4
Anderson, Olof 1869-1931 *NatCAB 33*
Anderson, Ophelia Brown 1813-1852 *ApCAB,*
   Drake
Anderson, Oscar 1873-1953 *NatCAB 43*
Anderson, Oscar Edward 1918- *EncAAH*
Anderson, Oscar V 1903-1972 *WhAm 5*
Anderson, Oskar Johann Viktor 1887-1960
   DcScB
Anderson, P *NewYHSD*
Anderson, Paul Lewis 1880-1956 *WhAm 3*
Anderson, Paul N 1898-1968 *WhAm 5*
Anderson, Paul Vernon 1874- *WhAm 5*
Anderson, Paul Yewell 1893-1938 *DcAmB S2,*
   WhAm 1
Anderson, Peirce 1870-1924 *NatCAB 32,*
   WhAm 1
Anderson, Peter *NewYHSD*
Anderson, Peter Augustus 1891-1968
   NatCAB 57
Anderson, Peyton Everett 1861- *WhoColR*
Anderson, Peyton Fortine 1890- *WhoColR*
Anderson, Peyton Tooke 1873-1944 *NatCAB 33*
Anderson, Ralph J 1888-1962 *WhAm 4*
Anderson, Rasmus Bjorn 1846-1936 *AmBi,*
   ApCAB, NatCAB 9, TwCBDA, WebAB,
   WhAm 1
Anderson, Raymond T 1895-1962 *WhAm 4*
Anderson, Reuben Bennett 1894-1947
   NatCAB 35
Anderson, Richard d1835 *Drake*
Anderson, Richard Clough 1750-1826 *ApCAB,*
   DcAmB, NatCAB 6, TwCBDA,
   WhAm H
Anderson, Richard Clough, Jr. 1788-1826
   ApCAB, BiAUS, BiDrAC, DcAmB, Drake,
   NatCAB 6, TwCBDA, WhAm H,
   WhAmP
Anderson, Richard Henry 1821-1879 *NatCAB 4*
Anderson, Richard Henry 1822?-1879 *Drake*
Anderson, Richard Heron 1821-1879 *AmBi,*
   BiDConf, DcAmB, WebAMB, WhAm H,
   WhoMilH
Anderson, Richard Herron 1821-1879 *ApCAB,*
   TwCBDA
Anderson, Richard James 1901-1971 *WhAm 5*
Anderson, Rinard W 1855-1928 *NatCAB 22*
Anderson, Robbins Battell 1877-1968
   NatCAB 54
Anderson, Robert 1805-1871 *AmBi, ApCAB,*
   DcAmB, Drake, NatCAB 4, TwCBDA,
   WebAMB, WhAm H
Anderson, Robert Bernard 1910- *BiDrUSE*
Anderson, Robert Campbell 1864-1955
   WhAm 3
Anderson, Robert Earle 1881-1967 *NatCAB 54,*

WhAm 4

Anderson, Robert Edward, Jr. 1906-1969 *WhAm 5*

Anderson, Robert Gordon 1881-1950 *ApCAB X, NatCAB 38, WhAm 3*

Anderson, Robert Hargis 1890-1964 *Drake, WhAm 4*

Anderson, Robert Houstoun 1835-1888 *ApCAB, BiDConf, NatCAB 4, TwCBDA*

Anderson, Robert VanVleck 1884-1949 *WhAm 2*

Anderson, Roger 1891-1971 *NatCAB 57*

Anderson, Rose 1865- *WhAm 4*

Anderson, Roy Nels 1902-1973 *WhAm 6*

Anderson, Rudolph John 1879-1961 *WhAm 4*

Anderson, Rudolph Martin 1876-1961 *WhAm 4*

Anderson, Rufus 1765-1814 *Drake*

Anderson, Rufus 1796-1880 *ApCAB, Drake, NatCAB 11, NatCAB 24, TwCBDA, WhAm H*

Anderson, Samuel d1836 *Drake*

Anderson, Samuel 1773-1850 *BiDrAC, WhAm H*

Anderson, Samuel 1774-1850 *BiAUS*

Anderson, Samuel 1839-1881 *ApCAB Sup*

Anderson, Samuel Wagner 1898-1962 *NatCAB 49, WhAm 4*

Anderson, Sherwood 1876-1941 *ApCAB X, DcAmB S3, McGEWB, WebAB, WhAm 1*

Anderson, Sherwood 1877-1941 *NatCAB 36*

Anderson, Simeon H 1802-1840 *BiAUS, BiDrAC, WhAm H*

Anderson, Sophie *NewYHSD, WhAm H*

Anderson, Stonewall 1864-1928 *WhAm 1*

Anderson, Swan Friteaf 1879-1963 *NatCAB 52*

Anderson, Sydney 1881-1948 *BiDrAC, WhAm 2, WhAmP*

Anderson, Thomas 1819-1874 *DcScB*

Anderson, Thomas Davis 1853-1928 *WhAm 1*

Anderson, Thomas H 1848-1916 *NatCAB 12, WhAm 1*

Anderson, Thomas Joel, Jr. 1898-1967 *WhAm 4*

Anderson, Thomas Lilbourne 1808-1885 *BiAUS, BiDrAC, WhAm H*

Anderson, Thomas MacArthur 1836-1917 *TwCBDA*

Anderson, Thomas McArthur 1836-1917 *ApCAB Sup, NatCAB 4, WebAMB, WhAm H*

Anderson, Trent Gloster 1890-1960 *NatCAB 48*

Anderson, Troyer Steele 1900-1948 *WhAm 2*

Anderson, Victor E 1902-1962 *WhAm 4*

Anderson, Victor Emanuel 1883-1948 *WhAm 2*

Anderson, Victor Vance 1879-1960 *WhAm 4*

Anderson, Walker 1801-1857 *NatCAB 12*

Anderson, Walter *NewYHSD*

Anderson, Walter d1886? *WhAm H*

Anderson, Walter Alexander 1903-1964 *WhAm 4*

Anderson, Walter L 1880-1963 *NatCAB 51*

Anderson, Walter W *NewYHSD*

Anderson, Walter Williams 1879- *WhAm 6*

Anderson, Wells Foster 1902-1958 *WhAm 3*

Anderson, Wendell W 1901-1959 *WhAm 3*

Anderson, William 1759?-1829 *Drake*

Anderson, William 1762-1829 *BiDrAC, DcAmB, WhAm H*

Anderson, William 1763-1829 *ApCAB, BiAUS, NatCAB 4*

Anderson, William 1818?- *NewYHSD*

Anderson, William 1834?- *NewYHSD*

Anderson, William 1888-1975 *WhAm 6*

Anderson, William A d1930 *WhAm 1*

Anderson, William Allison 1870-1944 *NatCAB 33, WhAm 2*

Anderson, William Andrew 1873-1954 *NatCAB 42, WhAm 3*

Anderson, William Beverly 1899-1970 *WhAm 5*

Anderson, William Black 1830-1901 *BiAUS, BiDrAC*

Anderson, William Brennan 1868-1940 *WhAm 1*

Anderson, William C 1860-1940 *WhAm 1*

Anderson, Mrs. William C 1879- *WomWWA 14*

Anderson, William Clayton 1826-1861 *BiAUS, BiDrAC, WhAm H*

Anderson, William Coleman 1853-1902 *BiDrAC*

Anderson, William D 1873-1957 *WhAm 3*

Anderson, William Downs 1874- *WhAm 5*

Anderson, William Dozier 1862-1952 *NatCAB 42, WhAm 5*

Anderson, William E 1791-1841 *BiAUS*

Anderson, William Franklin 1860-1944 *NatCAB 14, WhAm 2*

Anderson, William Franklin 1869-1944 *ApCAB X*

Anderson, William Gilbert 1860-1947 *BiDAmEd, NatCAB 36, WhAm 2*

Anderson, William Hamilton 1874-1959 *WhAm 3*

Anderson, William Harry 1905-1972 *WhAm 5*

Anderson, William Henry 1862-1940 *WhAm 1*

Anderson, William Henry 1866-1940 *ApCAB X*

Anderson, William Joseph, Jr. 1908-1965 *WhAm 4*

Anderson, William Ketcham 1888-1947 *WhAm 2*

Anderson, William Louis 1868- *WhoColR*

Anderson, William Madison 1889-1935 *WhAm 1*

Anderson, William Otto 1920-1964 *WhAm 4*

Anderson, William Pelby 1793-1850 *ApCAB*

Anderson, William Pope 1874-1951 *NatCAB 42*

Anderson, William Robert 1921- *BiDrAC*

Anderson, William T 1863- *WhoColR*

Anderson, William Thomas 1871-1945 *NatCAB 33, WhAm 2*

Anderson, William Thompson 1861- *WhAm 4*

Anderson, William Wallace *WhAm H*

Anderson, Winfield Scott *NewYHSD*

Anderson, Winslow d1917 *WhAm 1*

Anderson, Winslow Samuel 1898-1948 *WhAm 2*

Anderson-Gilman, Wilma *WomWWA 14*

Andersson, Alfred Oscar 1874-1950 *WhAm 3*

Anderton, Elizabeth Palmer *WomWWA 14*

Anderton, G 1825?-1890? *NewYHSD*

Anderton, John Howard 1880-1962 *NatCAB 50*

Anderton, Stephen Philbin 1874-1947 *WhAm 2*

Andoyer, Henri 1862-1929 *DcScB*

Andrada, Jose Bonifacio De 1763-1838 *McGEWB*

Andrada E Sylva, Bonifacio Jose De 1765-1838 *Drake*

Andrada E Sylva, Bonifacio Joze D' 1765-1838 *ApCAB*

Andrade, Cipriano 1840-1911 *WhAm 1*

Andrade, Ignacio 1839- *ApCAB Sup*

Andrade, Jose 1838- *ApCAB Sup*

Andrae, George Henry Joseph 1893-1961 *NatCAB 50*

Andral, Gabriel 1797-1876 *BiHiMed*

Andrassy, Count Julius 1823-1890 *McGEWB*

Andrau, Evert Willem Karel 1900-1951 *NatCAB 40*

Andre, Carl 1935- *BnEnAmA*

Andre, Charles Louis Francois 1842-1912 *DcScB*

Andre, Floyd 1909-1972 *WhAm 5*

Andre, John 1751-1780 *AmBi, ApCAB, Drake, NatCAB 1, NewYHSD, TwCBDA, WhAm H*

Andre, Louis 1623?-1715 *DcAmB*

Andre, Louis 1631?-1715 *WhAm H*

Andre, Noble 1910-1960 *NatCAB 47*

Andrea DelCastagno 1421-1457 *McGEWB*

Andrea DelSarto 1486-1530 *McGEWB*

Andrea Pisano 1290?-1348 *McGEWB*

Andrea, Frank A D 1888-1965 *NatCAB 52*

Andrea, Frank A D 1889-1965 *WhAm 4*

Andreae, Johann Valentin 1586-1654 *DcScB*

Andreasen, Milian Lauritz 1876- *WhAm 5*

Andreassen, Anders *WebAB*

Andree, Karl Theodor 1808- *ApCAB*

Andree, Salomon August 1854-1897 *McGEWB*

Andreen, Gustav Albert 1864-1940 *WhAm 1*

Andrei, Giovanni 1770-1824 *NewYHSD*

Andreis, Andrew James F Bartholomew De 1778-1820 *DcAmB*

Andreozzi, Louis George 1909-1962 *NatCAB 49*

Andres, Charles John 1913- *IlBEAAW*

Andresen, Albert Frederick Ruger 1885-1961 *WhAm 4*

Andresen, August Herman 1890-1958 *BiDrAC, WhAm 3, WhAmP*

Andress, James Mace 1881-1942 *WhAm 1,*

Andress, Robert Joseph 1910-1966 *WhAm 4*

Andressohn, John Carl 1884-1966 *NatCAB 53*

Andretta, S A 1898-1965 *WhAm 4*

Andretti, Mario Gabriel 1940- *WebAB*

Andrew, Abram Piatt, Jr. 1873-1936 *ApCAB X, BiDrAC, DcAmB S2, NatCAB 14, NatCAB 15, WhAm 1*

Andrew, Abram Platt, Jr. 1873-1936 *WhAmP*

Andrew, Benjamin 1730-1799? *BiDrAC*

Andrew, Edwin Lee 1894-1973 *WhAm 6*

Andrew, Fred Delmar 1856-1944 *NatCAB 35*

Andrew, Hardage L 1889-1955 *WhAm 3*

Andrew, Harriet White Fisher 1865-1939 *BiCAW, WhAm 1*

Andrew, Henry Hersey 1858-1934 *WhAm 1*

Andrew, James Osgood 1794-1871 *ApCAB, DcAmB, DcAmReB, Drake, NatCAB 1, TwCBDA, WhAm H*

Andrew, James Timothy 1857-1917 *NatCAB 18*

Andrew, John 1815-1875 *NewYHSD*

Andrew, John 1879-1947 *NatCAB 37*

Andrew, John Albion 1813-1867 *TwCBDA*

Andrew, John Albion 1813-1867 *AmBi, ApCAB, BiAUS, DcAmB, Drake, McGEWB, NatCAB 1, WebAB, WhAm H, WhAmP*

Andrew, John Forrester 1850-1895 *BiDrAC, WhAm H*

Andrew, Joseph Atkins 1885-1967 *NatCAB 54, WhAm 5*

Andrew, Laurence Clyde 1893-1961 *NatCAB 55*

Andrew, Norman Corbin 1903-1958 *NatCAB 47*

Andrew, Samuel 1656-1738 *DcAmB, NatCAB 1, WhAm H*

Andrewes, Sir William 1899-1974 *WhAm 6*

Andrews *NewYHSD*

Andrews, A V 1863-1935 *NatCAB 27*

Andrews, Addison Fletcher 1857-1924 *WhAm 1*

Andrews, Adolphus 1879-1948 *NatCAB 48, WhAm 2*

Andrews, Albert Anson 1882- *WhoColR*

Andrews, Alexander Boyd 1841-1915 *DcAmB, NatCAB 2, WhAm 1*

Andrews, Alexander Boyd 1873-1946 *WhAm 2*

Andrews, Alexander Speer 1875- *WhAm 5*

Andrews, Alfred Hinsdale 1836- *NatCAB 14*

Andrews, Alice A *AmWom*

Andrews, Allen S d1898 *TwCBDA*

Andrews, Ambrose *NewYHSD, WhAm H*

Andrews, Andrew Irving 1895-1966 *NatCAB 52*

Andrews, Annie M 1835- *ApCAB*

Andrews, Annulet 1866-1943 *WhAm 2*

Andrews, Arthur Glenn 1909- *BiDrAC*

Andrews, Arthur Leonard 1855-1938 *WhAm 1*

Andrews, Arthur Lynn 1871-1945 *NatCAB 37*

Andrews, Avery DeLano 1864-1959 *ApCAB X, WhAm 3*

Andrews, Bert 1901-1953 *DcAmB S5, WhAm 3*

Andrews, Bret Lattin 1871-1925 *NatCAB 22*

Andrews, C C 1829-1922 *BiAUS*

Andrews, C C *see also* Andrews, Christopher Columbus

Andrews, Champe Seabury 1875- *NatCAB 14*

Andrews, Charles 1814-1852 *BiAUS, BiDrAC, WhAm H*

Andrews, Charles 1827-1918 *DcAmB, NatCAB 12, TwCBDA, WhAm 1*

Andrews, Charles 1841?- *NewYHSD*

Andrews, Charles Bartlett 1834-1902 *TwCBDA, WhAm 1*

Andrews, Charles Bartlett 1836-1902 *DcAmB, NatCAB 10*

Andrews, Charles Cecil 1896-1967 *NatCAB 53, WhAm 4*

Andrews, Charles D *NewYHSD*

Andrews, Charles Edgar, Jr. 1881-1958 *WhAm 3*

Andrews, Charles Henry 1866-1931 *WhAm 2*

Andrews, Charles McLean 1863-1943 *BiDAmEd, DcAmB S3, McGEWB, NatCAB 13, WebAB, WhAm 2*

Andrews, Charles Oscar 1877-1946 *BiDrAC, NatCAB 33, WhAm 2, WhAmP*

Andrews, Charles Oscar, Jr. 1910-1969 *WhAm 5*

Andrews, Charles Sidney 1843-1916
NatCAB 17
Andrews, Charlton 1878- *WhAm 6*
Andrews, Chauncey Humason 1823-1894
NatCAB 27
Andrews, Chauncey Hummason 1823-1893
DcAmB, WhAm H
Andrews, Chauncey Hunn 1823-1893
NatCAB 14
Andrews, Christopher Columbus 1829- *ApCAB,*
NatCAB 11, TwCBDA
Andrews, Christopher Columbus 1829-1922
AmBi, DcAmB
Andrews, Christopher Columbus 1829-1923
WhAm 1
Andrews, Christopher Columbus *see also*
Andrews, C C
Andrews, Clarence Edward 1883-1932 *WhAm 1,*
WhAm 1C
Andrews, Clarence L 1862- *WhAm 5*
Andrews, Clarence Ladelle 1882-1962
NatCAB 48
Andrews, Clayton Farrington 1891-1964
NatCAB 50, WhAm 4
Andrews, Clement Walker 1858-1930 *DcAmLiB,*
NatCAB 14, TwCBDA, WhAm 1
Andrews, Constant Abram 1844- *NatCAB 14*
Andrews, Daniel Marshall 1853-1917 *WhAm 1*
Andrews, David *NewYHSD*
Andrews, DeLano 1894-1958 *NatCAB 48*
Andrews, Donald Cochrane 1902-1952
NatCAB 39
Andrews, Donald Hatch 1898-1973 *WhAm 6*
Andrews, Ebenezer Baldwin 1821-1880 *ApCAB*
Andrews, Edmund 1824-1904 *ApCAB,*
TwCBDA, WhAm 1
Andrews, Edmund 1892-1941 *NatCAB 32*
Andrews, Edward Gayer 1825-1907 *ApCAB,*
DcAmB, NatCAB 12, TwCBDA,
WhAm 1
Andrews, Edward Palmer 1874-1954
NatCAB 44
Andrews, Edward Wyllys 1856-1927 *WhAm 1*
Andrews, Elihu Benjamin 1844- *ApCAB Sup*
Andrews, Eliphalet Frazer 1835-1915
NatCAB 8, NewYHSD
Andrews, Eliphalet Frazer 1835-1932 *WhAm 3*
Andrews, Elisha 1768-1840 *ApCAB*
Andrews, Elisha Benjamin 1844-1917 *AmBi,*
ApCAB X, BiDAmEd, DcAmB,
NatCAB 1, NatCAB 8, TwCBDA,
WhAm 1
Andrews, Eliza Frances 1840-1931 *BiDAmEd,*
NatCAB 6, NotAW, WhAm 1,
WomWWA 14
Andrews, Eliza Frances 1847-1931 *AmWom*
Andrews, Elizabeth M *WomWWA 14*
Andrews, Elizabeth Moffett 1849-
WomWWA 14
Andrews, Elmer Frank 1890-1964 *WhAm 4*
Andrews, Emanuel *NewYHSD*
Andrews, Emily Russell 1890-1973 *NatCAB 57*
Andrews, Emma Dixon 1853- *WomWWA 14*
Andrews, Emory Cobb 1878-1932 *NatCAB 23*
Andrews, Ethan Allen 1787-1858 *AmBi,*
ApCAB, Drake, NatCAB 13
Andrews, Ethan Allen 1797-1858 *BiDAmEd*
Andrews, Ethan Allen 1859- *WhAm 4*
Andrews, Ethel Montgomery 1879-
WomWWA 14
Andrews, Eugene Plumb 1866-1957 *NatCAB 47,*
WhAm 4
Andrews, Evangeline Walker 1870-1962
WhAm 4, WomWWA 14
Andrews, F *NewYHSD*
Andrews, Fannie Fern Phillips 1867-1950
BiCAW, NotAW, WhAm 3,
WomWWA 14
Andrews, Frank 1864-1936 *NatCAB 27,*
WhAm 1
Andrews, Frank L 1892-1966 *WhAm 4*
Andrews, Frank Maxwell 1884-1943 *DcAmB S3,*
NatCAB 32, WebAB, WebAMB,
WhAm 2
Andrews, Frank Mills 1867-1948 *NatCAB 42,*
WhAm 2
Andrews, Frank Taylor 1858-1940 *WhAm 1*
Andrews, Fred Lowry 1873-1967 *NatCAB 55*

Andrews, Garnett 1837-1903 *DcAmB,*
NatCAB 4, WebAMB, WhAm 1
Andrews, Garnett 1870-1946 *NatCAB 35,*
WhAm 2
Andrews, George *NewYHSD*
Andrews, George 1826- *NatCAB 5*
Andrews, George 1850-1928 *NatCAB 22,*
WhAm 1
Andrews, George Emory 1854-1934 *NatCAB 26*
Andrews, George Henry 1816-1898 *IlBEAAW*
Andrews, George Leonard 1827-1899 *Drake*
Andrews, George Leonard 1828-1899 *ApCAB,*
DcAmB, NatCAB 5, NatCAB 16,
TwCBDA, WhAm H, WhAm 1
Andrews, George Lippitt 1828-1920 *WhAm 1*
Andrews, George Pierce 1835-1902 *DcAmB,*
WhAm 1
Andrews, George Rex 1808-1873 *BiAUS,*
BiDrAC, WhAm H
Andrews, George Rex 1874-1933 *NatCAB 31*
Andrews, George Whitefield 1833- *TwCBDA*
Andrews, George Whitfield 1861-1932 *WhAm 1*
Andrews, George William 1906-1971 *BiDrAC,*
WhAm 5
Andrews, Georgina I S *WomWWA 14*
Andrews, Grace *WomWWA 14*
Andrews, Grace 1869- *WomWWA 14*
Andrews, Gwendolen Foulke 1863- *WhAm 4,*
WomWWA 14
Andrews, Harold Augustus 1889-1958
NatCAB 47
Andrews, Harold MacLean 1890-1968
NatCAB 55
Andrews, Harry Eugene 1861-1926 *WhAm 1*
Andrews, Helen Frances *WomWWA 14*
Andrews, Helen Slade 1870- *WomWWA 14*
Andrews, Herbert Lee 1844-1906 *NatCAB 14*
Andrews, Herbert Marston 1851-1929 *WhAm 1*
Andrews, Hiram Bertrand 1867- *WhAm 4*
Andrews, Horace 1861-1939 *NatCAB 30*
Andrews, Horace Ellsworth 1863-1918 *WhAm 1*
Andrews, Irene Osgood 1877- *WhAm 5*
Andrews, Irene Osgood 1879- *WomWWA 14*
Andrews, Israel DeWolf 1813?-1871
BiAUS Sup, DcAmB S1, WhAm H
Andrews, Israel Ward 1815-1888 *DcAmB,*
TwCBDA, WhAm H
Andrews, J Warren 1860-1932 *WhAm 1*
Andrews, James DeWitt 1856-1928 *WhAm 1*
Andrews, James Harper 1870-1956 *NatCAB 46*
Andrews, James Henry Millar 1876-1948
NatCAB 43
Andrews, James J 1829?-1862 *NatCAB 9,*
WebAMB
Andrews, James Oliver 1851-1922 *NatCAB 19*
Andrews, James Parkhill 1854-1936 *WhAm 2*
Andrews, Jane 1833-1887 *BiDAmEd, NotAW*
Andrews, Jesse 1874-1961 *WhAm 4*
Andrews, John 1746-1813 *ApCAB, DcAmB,*
Drake, NatCAB 1, TwCBDA, WhAm H
Andrews, John 1894-1950 *WhAm 3*
Andrews, John Bertram 1880-1943 *DcAmB S3,*
WhAm 1
Andrews, John Newman 1838-1903 *WhAm 1*
Andrews, John Tuttle 1803-1894 *BiAUS,*
BiDrAC, WhAm H
Andrews, John Williams 1898-1975 *WhAm 6*
Andrews, Johnnie 1907-1957 *NatCAB 43*
Andrews, Joseph 1805?-1873 *AmBi, DcAmB,*
NewYHSD, WhAm H
Andrews, Joseph 1806-1873 *ApCAB, Drake,*
NatCAB 11, TwCBDA
Andrews, Joshua P 1800?- *NewYHSD*
Andrews, Judith Walker 1826- *AmWom*
Andrews, Judson Boardman 1834-1894
TwCBDA
Andrews, Julia Lincoln Ray 1867- *WhAm 4*
Andrews, Justin 1819-1894 *TwCBDA*
Andrews, Justin Meredith 1902-1967
NatCAB 54, WhAm 4A
Andrews, Landaff Watson 1803-1887 *BiAUS,*
BiDrAC, WhAm H
Andrews, Launcelot Winchester 1856-1938
NatCAB 46, WhAm 1, WhAm 1C
Andrews, Lee 1900-1962 *NatCAB 49*
Andrews, Leila Edna 1876- *WhAm 5*
Andrews, Leland Stanford 1898-1969 *WhAm 5*
Andrews, Lewis Whiting 1869- *WhAm 4*

Andrews, Lincoln Clark 1867-1950 *NatCAB 39,*
WhAm 3
Andrews, Loren 1819-1861 *ApCAB*
Andrews, Lorenzo Frank 1828-1915 *NatCAB 16*
Andrews, Lorin 1819-1861 *BiDAmEd, DcAmB,*
NatCAB 7, WhAm H
Andrews, Loring 1768-1805 *Drake,*
NatCAB 20
Andrews, Lorrin 1795-1868 *AmBi, ApCAB,*
BiDAmEd, DcAmB, NatCAB 9,
TwCBDA, WhAm H
Andrews, Lorrin 1872- *ApCAB X*
Andrews, Marie Louise 1849-1891 *AmWom*
Andrews, Marie Scherer 1914-1973 *NatCAB 57,*
WhAm 6
Andrews, Marietta Minnigerode 1869-1931
WhAm 1
Andrews, Marilla 1864- *WomWWA 14*
Andrews, Mark 1926- *BiDrAC*
Andrews, Marshall 1899-1973 *WhAm 6*
Andrews, Martin Register 1842-1913 *WhAm 1*
Andrews, Mary Canfield *WomWWA 14*
Andrews, Mary Elizabeth *WomWWA 14*
Andrews, Mary Garard 1852- *AmWom*
Andrews, Mary Raymond Shipman 1860-1936
NotAW, WhAm 1
Andrews, Matthew Page 1879-1947 *WhAm 2*
Andrews, Matthew Thomas 1869-1939 *WhAm 1*
Andrews, Mira McCoy *WomWWA 14*
Andrews, Nellie Greenwood 1864-
WomWWA 14
Andrews, Newton Lloyd 1841-1918 *NatCAB 5,*
TwCBDA, WhAm 1
Andrews, Paul Shipman 1887-1967 *WhAm 4*
Andrews, Philip 1866-1945 *WhAm 2*
Andrews, R Snowden 1830-1903 *NatCAB 28*
Andrews, Robert d1856? *NewYHSD*
Andrews, Robert Christie 1914-1966 *WhAm 4*
Andrews, Robert Day 1857- *WhAm 1*
Andrews, Robert Macon 1870- *WhAm 5*
Andrews, Robert Marshall 1881-1962
NatCAB 52
Andrews, Robert Robbins 1844-1921 *WhAm 1*
Andrews, Roger Mercein 1874-1943 *WhAm 3*
Andrews, Roland Franklyn d1930 *WhAm 1*
Andrews, Rollin Garard 1892-1957 *NatCAB 47*
Andrews, Roy Chapman 1884-1960 *ApCAB X,*
AsBiEn, McGEWB, NatCAB 44, WebAB,
WhAm 3A
Andrews, Samuel G 1799-1863 *BiAUS*
Andrews, Samuel George 1796-1863 *BiDrAC,*
WhAm H
Andrews, Samuel James 1817-1906 *ApCAB,*
DcAmB, TwCBDA, WhAm 1
Andrews, Schofield 1889-1973 *WhAm 5*
Andrews, Sherlock James 1801-1880 *ApCAB,*
BiAUS, BiDrAC, DcAmB, NatCAB 6,
WhAm H, WhAmP
Andrews, Sidney 1835-1880 *DcAmB,*
WhAm H
Andrews, Sidney Francis 1857-1933 *WhAm 1*
Andrews, Sophia Maxwell Dolson 1829-
WomWWA 14
Andrews, Steffan 1914- *WhAm 3*
Andrews, Stephen Pearl 1812-1886 *AmBi,*
ApCAB, DcAmB, Drake, NatCAB 6,
TwCBDA, WebAB, WhAm H
Andrews, T D *NewYHSD*
Andrews, T Wingate 1882-1937 *WhAm 1*
Andrews, Thomas 1813-1885 *AsBiEn, DcScB*
Andrews, Thomas Galphin 1882-1942 *WhAm 2*
Andrews, Thomas Gaylord 1915-1967
NatCAB 54, WhAm 4
Andrews, Timothy Patrick 1794-1868 *ApCAB,*
Drake, NatCAB 4, WhAm H
Andrews, Timothy Patrick 1795-1868 *TwCBDA*
Andrews, Upson Austin 1851-1905 *NatCAB 32*
Andrews, Vernon Daniel 1890-1937 *WhAm 1*
Andrews, W Earle 1899-1965 *WhAm 4*
Andrews, Walter Gresham 1889-1949 *BiDrAC,*
NatCAB 39, WhAm 2
Andrews, Walter Pemberton 1865-1935
NatCAB 26, WhAm 1
Andrews, Wilfred Leslie 1898-1954 *NatCAB 41,*
WhAm 3
Andrews, William Draper 1818- *ApCAB,*
Drake, NatCAB 13, TwCBDA
Andrews, William Ezekiel 1854-1942 *BiDrAC,*

WhAm 5, WhAmP

Andrews, William Given 1835-1912 *WhAm 1*

Andrews, William Henry 1846-1919 *BiDrAC, WhAm P*

Andrews, William Henry 1860-1923 *NatCAB 21*

Andrews, William Johnston 1871-1942 *NatCAB 34*

Andrews, William Loring 1837-1920 *AmBi, DcAmB, NatCAB 13, WhAm 1*

Andrews, William Noble 1876-1937 *BiDrAC, WhAm 1*

Andrews, William Page 1848-1916 *WhAm 1*

Andrews, William Shankland 1858-1936 *WhAm 1*

Andrews, William Symes 1847-1929 *WhAm 1*

Andrews, William Taylor 1861-1933 *NatCAB 29*

Andrews, William Trent 1864- *WhoColR*

Andrews, William Watson 1810-1897 *DcAmB, NatCAB 21, WhAm H*

Andric, Ivo 1892-1975 *WhAm 6*

Andries, Raymond Carl 1883-1963 *NatCAB 50*

Andrieu, Adolph *NewYHSD*

Andrieu, C *NewYHSD*

Andrieu, Mathuren Arthur d1896 *NewYHSD, WhAm H*

Andrist, Charles Martin 1868-1924 *NatCAB 6*

Andronov, Aleksandr Aleksandrovich 1901-1952 *DcScB Sup*

Andros, Charles Henry 1885-1959 *NatCAB 47*

Andros, Sir Edmund 1637-1714 *AmBi, ApCAB, DcAmB, Drake, EncAB, McGEWB, NatCAB 6, TwCBDA, WebAB, WhAm H*

Andros, Milton 1823- *NatCAB 9*

Andros, R S S d1868 *ApCAB, Drake*

Andros, Thomas 1759-1845 *ApCAB, Drake*

Andrus, Alpheus Newell 1843-1919 *NatCAB 18*

Andrus, Clift d1968 *WhAm 5*

Andrus, Elizabeth M Alexander 1860- *WomWWA 14*

Andrus, John Emory 1841-1934 *BiDrAC, NatCAB 30, WhAm 1*

Andrus, Reuben 1829-1887 *NatCAB 7*

Andrusov, Nikolai Ivanovich 1861-1924 *DcScB*

Andruss, E VanArsdale 1839-1910 *WhAm 1*

Andruss, Helen J 1866- *WomWWA 14*

Andy, John Baptist *NewYHSD*

Anelli, Francisco 1805?- *NewYHSD*

Anet, L *NewYHSD*

Anfinsen, Christian Boehmer 1916- *WebAB*

Anfuso, Victor L'Episcopo 1905-1966 *BiDrAC, WhAm 4, WhAmP*

Angas, W Mack 1892-1960 *WhAm 4*

Ange, Francis d1767 *Drake*

Angel, Benjamin Franklin 1815-1894 *ApCAB, BiAUS, DcAmB, NatCAB 10, TwCBDA, WhAm H*

Angel, Franz 1887- *WhAm 6*

Angel, John 1881-1960 *WhAm 4*

Angel, William G 1790-1858 *BiAUS, BiDrAC, WhAm H*

Angela, Mother 1824-1887 *AmBi, DcAmB, NotAW, WhAm H*

Angelain, Antoine *NewYHSD*

Angelesco, Constantin 1869-1948 *WhAm 2*

Angeli, Pier 1933-1971 *WhAm 5*

Angeli, Stefano Degli 1623-1697 *DcScB*

Angelico, Fra 1400?-1455 *McGEWB*

Angelini, Arabella 1863- *AmWom*

Angell, Alexis Caswell 1857-1932 *WhAm 1*

Angell, Earl Jerome 1883-1936 *NatCAB 28*

Angell, Emmett Dunn 1879- *WhAm 6*

Angell, Ernest 1889-1973 *WhAm 5*

Angell, Fanny Cary Cooley 1857- *WomWWA 14*

Angell, Frank 1857-1939 *WhAm 1*

Angell, George Thorndike 1823-1909 *AmBi, DcAmB, NatCAB 7, TwCBDA, WhAm 1*

Angell, Helen Jeffries 1868- *WomWWA 14*

Angell, Henry Clay 1829-1911 *ApCAB, NatCAB 11, WhAm 1*

Angell, Homer Daniel 1875-1968 *BiDrAC, NatCAB 56, WhAmP*

Angell, Israel d1832 *Drake*

Angell, Israel 1740-1832 *DcAmB, WhAm H*

Angell, Israel 1741-1832 *ApCAB*

Angell, James Burrill 1829-1916 *AmBi, ApCAB, ApCAB X, BiDAmEd, DcAmB, EncAB, NatCAB 1, TwCBDA, WebAB, WhAm 1, WhAmP*

Angell, James Rowland 1869-1949 *BiDAmEd, DcAmB S4, NatCAB 14, NatCAB 40, WhAm 2*

Angell, Joseph Kinnicut 1794-1857 *ApCAB, Drake, TwCBDA*

Angell, Joseph Kinnicutt 1794-1857 *DcAmB, NatCAB 9, WhAm H*

Angell, Lisbeth Gertrude 1870- *WhAm 5, WomWWA 14*

Angell, Martin Fuller 1878-1930 *WhAm 1*

Angell, Mary Eleanor 1868- *WomWWA 14*

Angell, Montgomery B 1889-1959 *WhAm 3*

Angell, Sir Norman 1872-1967 *WhAm 4*

Angell, Norman 1874-1967 *WhAm 5*

Angell, Pauline Knickerbocker 1886- *WomWWA 14*

Angell, Robert Henderson 1868-1933 *WhAm 1*

Angell, Thomas Lemuel 1837-1923 *NatCAB 20*

Angell, Walter Foster 1858-1936 *WhAm 1*

Angell, William Gorham 1811-1870 *DcAmB, NatCAB 2, WhAm H*

Angell, William Robert 1877-1950 *WhAm 2A*

Angellotti, Frank Marion 1861-1932 *NatCAB 18, NatCAB 23, WhAm 1, WhAm 1C*

Angelo, Gaspar 1905-1971 *NatCAB 56*

Angelus, Johannes 1453?-1512 *DcScB*

Anger, Sister Mary Alacoque 1892-1969 *WhAm 5*

Angers, Real 1823-1860 *ApCAB, Drake*

Angert, Eugene Henry 1877-1929 *WhAm 1*

Angevine, Jay B 1890-1969 *WhAm 5*

Anghiera, Pietro Martire D' 1455-1526 *ApCAB*

Anghiera, Pietro Martiro De 1455-1526 *Drake*

Angier, Donald H 1900-1949 *NatCAB 45*

Angier, Elizabeth 1851- *WomWWA 14*

Angier, Nedom L 1814-1892 *NatCAB 2*

Angier, Roswell Parker 1874-1946 *NatCAB 36, WhAm 2*

Angier, Walter Eugene 1863-1928 *NatCAB 21, WhAm 1*

Angland, Emmett Cyril 1909-1970 *WhAm 5*

Angle, Edward Hartley 1855-1930 *NatCAB 22, WhAm 1*

Angle, Edward John 1864-1940 *NatCAB 31, WhAm 1*

Angle, George Keyser 1865- *WhAm 5*

Angle, Glenn D 1891-1966 *WhAm 5*

Angle, Helen Goldthorpe Williams *WomWWA 14*

Angle, Jay Warren 1867-1929 *WhAm 3*

Angle, Johnson Boone 1892-1946 *NatCAB 35*

Angle, Paul McClelland 1900-1975 *EncAAH, WhAm 6*

Angle, Wesley Motley 1882-1960 *WhAm 4*

Angleman, Sydney Winfield 1902-1971 *WhAm 5*

Anglin, Margaret 1876- *BiCAW, WhAm 5*

Anglin, Timothy Warren 1822- *ApCAB*

Anglin-Hull, Mary Margaret 1876- *WomWWA 14*

Angly, Edward 1898-1950 *WhAm 3*

Ango, Jean 1480?-1551 *ApCAB Sup*

Angood, Sidney Bernard 1897-1967 *WhAm 5*

Angrave, George Raymond 1896-1957 *NatCAB 46*

Angstman, Charlotte Smith 1859- *WomWWA 14*

Angstrom, Anders Jonas 1814-1874 *AsBiEn, DcScB*

Anguillara, Luigi 1512?-1570 *DcScB*

Angulo, Pedro De 1500-1562 *ApCAB*

Angulo Y Heredia, Antonio 1837- *ApCAB*

Angus, Joseph 1816- *ApCAB*

Angus, Samuel 1784-1840 *ApCAB, Drake, TwCBDA*

Anheuser, Eberhard 1880-1963 *WhAm 4*

Anisfeld, Boris 1879-1973 *WhAm 6*

Anjaria, Jashwantrai Jayantilal 1908-1970 *WhAm 5*

Ankcorn, Charles M d1955 *WhAm 3*

Ankeney, John Sites 1870-1946 *WhAm 2*

Ankeny, John D'Art 1879-1942 *NatCAB 36,*

WhAm 2

Ankeny, Levi 1844-1921 *ApCAB X, BiDrAC, NatCAB 30, WhAm 1, WhAmP*

Ann, Mother *WebAB*

Anna Comnena 1083-1148 *McGEWB*

Anna Ivanovna 1693-1740 *McGEWB*

Annadown, Ruth Vivian 1910-1967 *WhAm 5*

Annan, Anna Bright Green *WomWWA 14*

Annand, Percy Nicol 1898-1950 *NatCAB 40, WhAm 3*

Annand, William 1808- *ApCAB*

Anne 1665-1714 *McGEWB*

Anneke, Mathilde Franziska Giesler 1817-1884 *DcAmB, NatCAB 4, NotAW*

Annenberg, Moses Louis 1878-1942 *DcAmB S3*

Anness, Samuel *NewYHSD*

Annibale, George Oliver 1829?-1887 *NewYHSD*

Annin, Phineas F *NewYHSD*

Annin, William B *NewYHSD*

Annunzio, Frank 1915- *BiDrAC*

Annus, Bernard *NewYHSD*

Anokhin, Petr Kusmich 1898-1974 *WhAm 6*

Anokye, Okomfo *McGEWB*

Anouilh, Jean 1910- *McGEWB*

Ansbacher, Adolph Benedict 1832-1917 *NatCAB 23*

Ansberry, Timothy Thomas 1871-1943 *BiDrAC, WhAm 2, WhAmP*

Anschutz, Karl 1813-1870 *ApCAB, Drake*

Anschutz, Karl 1815-1870 *WhAm H*

Anschutz, Richard 1852-1937 *DcScB*

Ansel, Martin Frederick 1850- *NatCAB 14, WhAm 4*

Ansell, Burr Tracy 1906-1955 *NatCAB 47*

Ansell, Samuel Tilden 1875-1954 *ApCAB X, NatCAB 47, WhAm 5*

Anselm, Saint 1033-1109 *McGEWB*

Anselme, Jacques Bernard Modeste D' 1740-1812 *Drake*

Anselme, Jacques Bernard Modeste D' 1740-1814 *ApCAB*

Ansermet, Ernest Alexandre 1883-1969 *WhAm 5*

Anshen, S Robert 1910-1964 *WhAm 5*

Anshen, Siegfried Robert 1910-1964 *NatCAB 53*

Anshutz, Edward Pollock 1846-1918 *WhAm 1*

Anshutz, Thomas Pollock 1851-1912 *BnEnAmA, DcAmB, NatCAB 15, WhAm 1*

Ansley, Clarke Fisher 1869-1939 *AmBi, NatCAB 29, WhAm 1*

Ansley, Elizabeth *WomWWA 14*

Anslinger, Harry Jacob 1892-1975 *WhAm 6*

Anslow, Gladys Amelia 1892-1969 *WhAm 5*

Anslow, W Parker, Jr. 1912-1966 *WhAm 4*

Anson, Adrian Constantine 1851-1922 *WebAB*

Anson, Adrian Constantine 1852-1922 *DcAmB, WhAm HA, WhAm 4*

Anson, Edward Hiram 1902-1959 *NatCAB 44*

Anson, Baron George 1697-1762 *WhoMilH*

Anson, Mae Harris *WomWWA 14*

Anson, William *NewYHSD*

Anson, William 1872-1926 *NatCAB 28*

Ansorge, Charles 1817-1866 *ApCAB, Drake, NatCAB 5*

Ansorge, Martin Charles 1882-1967 *BiDrAC, WhAm 4*

Anspach, Brooke Melancthon 1876-1951 *NatCAB 38, WhAm 5*

Anspach, Frederick Rinehart 1815-1867 *ApCAB*

Anspach, L A *Drake*

Anspach, William Earl 1891-1966 *NatCAB 52*

Anspacher, Kathryn Kidder *WomWWA 14*

Anspacher, Louis Kaufman 1878-1947 *NatCAB 34, WhAm 2*

Ansprenger, Aloys George 1905-1972 *WhAm 6*

Anstadt, Henry 1869- *WhAm 1*

Ansted, Harry Bidwell 1893-1955 *WhAm 3*

Anstice, Henry 1841-1922 *WhAm 1*

Antek, Samuel 1908-1958 *NatCAB 43*

Antes, Henry 1701-1755 *ApCAB, DcAmB, WhAm H*

Antes, John 1740-1811 *WhAm H*

Antes, Philip Frederick 1730-1801 *ApCAB*

Antheil, George 1900-1959 *NatCAB 45, WhAm 3*

Anthelme, Voituret 1618?-1683 *DcScB*

Anthemius Of Tralles *DcScB*

Anthoine, Francois Paul 1860-1944 *WhoMilH*
Anthoine, Isaiah Gilman 1846-1927 *NatCAB 22*
Anthon, Charles 1797-1867 *AmBi, ApCAB, BiDAmEd, DcAmB, Drake, NatCAB 6, TwCBDA, WhAm H*
Anthon, Charles Edward 1822-1883 *ApCAB, WhAm H*
Anthon, Charles Edward 1823-1883 *DcAmB*
Anthon, George Christian 1820-1877 *ApCAB*
Anthon, Henry 1795-1861 *ApCAB, Drake, NatCAB 9, TwCBDA*
Anthon, John 1784-1863 *ApCAB, DcAmB, Drake, NatCAB 12, TwCBDA, WhAm H*
Anthon, William Henry 1827-1875 *ApCAB*
Anthony, Saint 250?-356 *McGEWB*
Anthony, Sister 1814-1897 *AmBi, DcAmB, WhAm H*
Anthony, Alfred Williams 1860-1939 *WhAm 1*
Anthony, Alice *WomWWA 14*
Anthony, Andrew Varick Stout 1835-1906 *AmBi, ApCAB, DcAmB, NewYHSD, TwCBDA*
Anthony, Andrew Varick Stout 1838-1906 *WhAm 1*
Anthony, Ann 1886-1962 *WhAm 4*
Anthony, Arthur Cox 1866-1931 *WhAm 3*
Anthony, Benjamin Harris 1863-1932 *WhAm 1*
Anthony, Brayman William 1854- *WhAm 4*
Anthony, Daniel Read 1824-1904 *NatCAB 6, TwCBDA, WhAm 1*
Anthony, Daniel Read, Jr. 1870-1931 *ApCAB X, BiDrAC, NatCAB 36, WhAm 1, WhAmP*
Anthony, David 1786-1867 *TwCBDA*
Anthony, Donald Elliot 1899-1974 *WhAm 6*
Anthony, Earle Charles 1880-1961 *NatCAB 53, WhAm 4*
Anthony, Edmund 1808-1876 *TwCBDA*
Anthony, Edward 1895-1971 *WhAm 5*
Anthony, Ernest Lee 1888-1966 *WhAm 4*
Anthony, Gardner Chace 1856-1937 *WhAm 1*
Anthony, George Tobey 1824-1896 *DcAmB, NatCAB 8, TwCBDA, WhAm H, WhAmP*
Anthony, Henry Bowen 1815-1884 *AmBi, ApCAB, BiAUS, BiDrAC, DcAmB, Drake, NatCAB 9, TwCBDA, WhAm H, WhAmP*
Anthony, Isham Henry 1868- *WhoColR*
Anthony, John Gould 1804-1877 *ApCAB, DcAmB, NatCAB 10, TwCBDA, WhAm H*
Anthony, Joseph Biles 1795-1851 *BiAUS, BiDrAC, WhAm H*
Anthony, Katharine Susan 1877-1965 *WhAm 4, WhAm 5, WomWWA 14*
Anthony, Lovick Pierce 1877- *WhAm 5*
Anthony, Luther B 1876-1955 *WhAm 3*
Anthony, Mary Borden 1863- *WomWWA 14*
Anthony, Norman 1889-1968 *WhAm 5*
Anthony, Robert Lincoln 1866- *WhoColR*
Anthony, Robert Warren 1880-1960 *NatCAB 48*
Anthony, S Reed 1863-1914 *NatCAB 15*
Anthony, Sarkis Jabour 1910-1956 *NatCAB 46*
Anthony, Susan Brownell 1820-1906 *AmBi, AmWom, ApCAB, DcAmB, Drake, EncAB, McGEWB, NatCAB 4, NotAW, TwCBDA, WebAB, WhAm 1, WhAmP*
Anthony, Susanna 1726-1791 *ApCAB, Drake*
Anthony, William Arnold 1835-1908 *ApCAB, DcAmB S1, NatCAB 11, TwCBDA, WhAm 1*
Antigone Of Carystus *DcScB*
Antigonus I 382BC-301BC *McGEWB*
Antin, Mary 1881-1949 *DcAmB S4, NatCAB 39, NotAW, WebAB, WhAm 6*
Antiochus III 241BC-187BC *McGEWB*
Antiochus IV 215?BC-163BC *McGEWB*
Antiphon *DcScB*
Antisdale, Louis Marlin 1869-1923 *WhAm 1*
Antisdel, Clarence Baumes 1863-1943 *WhAm 2*
Antisell, Thomas 1817-1893 *NatCAB 19*
Antisthenes 450?BC-360BC *McGEWB*
Antognilli, David *NewYHSD*
Antoine, Pere 1748-1829 *DcAmB, WhAm H*
Antoine, Josephine Louise 1907-1971 *WhAm 5*
Anton, Mark 1892-1972 *WhAm 5*

Anton, Roberta Charlotte Weiss 1929- *WhAm 6*
Antonakos, Stephen 1926- *BnEnAmA*
Antonelli, Juan d1616 *ApCAB*
Antonello DaMessina 1430?-1479 *McGEWB*
Antonescu, Ion 1882-1946 *WhWW-II*
Antonia, Sister 1873-1944 *WhAm 2*
Antonia, Amanda *NewYHSD*
Antoniadi, Eugene M 1870-1944 *DcScB*
Antoniewicz, Wlodzimierz 1893-1973 *WhAm 6*
Antonio DeSedilla 1730-1829 *ApCAB*
Antonio, Joseph 1846- *TwCBDA*
Antonioni, Michelangelo 1912- *McGEWB*
Antonov, Alexei I 1896-1962 *WhWW-II*
Antony, Edwin LeRoy 1852-1913 *BiDrAC, TwCBDA*
Antony, Mark 082?BC-030BC *McGEWB*
Antrim, Doron Kemp 1889-1960 *WhAm 4*
Antrim, Ernest Irving 1869-1953 *WhAm 3*
Antrim, Eugene Marion 1874-1953 *WhAm 3*
Antrim, Max Buswell 1895-1965 *NatCAB 52*
Antrim, Minna Thomas 1856- *WhAm 4*
Antrim, Minna Thomas 1859- *WomWWA 14*
Antrim, William *REnAW*
Antrobus, John 1837-1907 *NewYHSD, WhAm HA, WhAm 4*
Antz, G *NewYHSD*
Anuchin, Dmitrii Nikolaevich 1843-1923 *DcScB*
Anundsen, Brynild 1844-1913 *WhAm 1*
Anuszkiewicz, Richard 1930- *BnEnAmA*
Anville, Jean-Baptiste Bourguignon D' 1697-1782 *DcScB*
Anville, N DeLaRochefoucauld, Duke D' 1700?-1746 *Drake*
Anyon, James *NewYHSD*
Anza, Juan Bautista De 1735-1788 *AmBi, DcAmB, McGEWB, REnAW, WebAB, WhAm H*
Anzoategui, Jose Antonio 1789-1819 *ApCAB*
Aoki, Siuzo, Viscount 1844- *WhAm 4*
Aosta, Amadeo, Duke Of 1898-1942 *WhWW-II*
Apathy, Stephan 1863-1922 *DcScB*
Apelles *McGEWB*
Apelt, Ernst Friedrich 1812-1859 *DcScB*
Apes, William *Drake*
Apes, William 1798- *DcAmB, WhAm H*
Apes, William 1800?- *ApCAB*
Apfel, Arthur Henry 1865-1935 *NatCAB 26*
Apfel, Henry 1838- *NewYHSD*
Apgar, Austin Craig 1838-1908 *WhAm 1*
Apgar, Ellis A 1836-1905 *BiDAmEd*
Apgar, Virginia 1909-1974 *WhAm 6*
Apgar, W Holt 1861-1936 *NatCAB 39*
Apian, Peter 1495-1552 *DcScB*
Apicella, John Phillips 1920-1966 *NatCAB 53*
Apithy, Sourou Migan 1913- *McGEWB*
Aplin, Henry Harrison 1841-1910 *BiDrAC, WhAm 4*
Aplington, Kate Adele 1859- *WomWWA 14*
Apmeyer, Charles Ascin 1866-1923 *NatCAB 26*
Apodaca, Juan Ruiz 1770?-1835 *ApCAB*
Apollinaire, Guillaume 1880-1918 *McGEWB*
Apollodorus *McGEWB*
Apollonius Of Perga 261?BC-190?BC *AsBiEn, DcScB, McGEWB*
Apostle To The Indians *WebAB*
App, Frank 1886-1967 *WhAm 4*
Appel, Daniel Frederick 1857-1929 *WhAm 1*
Appel, Emma Scribner MacKay 1876- *NatCAB 18*
Appel, George Frederick Baer 1903-1970 *NatCAB 56, WhAm 5*
Appel, John Wilberforce, Jr. 1887-1942 *WhAm 2*
Appel, Joseph Herbert 1873-1949 *NatCAB 18, WhAm 2*
Appel, Leon Howard 1921-1974 *WhAm 6*
Appel, Monte 1887-1970 *WhAm 5*
Appel, Sidney J 1908-1964 *NatCAB 51*
Appel, Theodore 1823-1907 *ApCAB, TwCBDA, WhAm 1*
Appel, Theodore Burton 1871-1937 *WhAm 1*
Appel, William Nevin 1862-1937 *NatCAB 46*
Appelbaum, Solomon Jacob 1881-1945 *NatCAB 38*
Appell, Louis Jacob 1894-1951 *NatCAB 40*
Appell, Paul 1855-1930 *DcScB*
Appelt, Frank R 1885-1939 *NatCAB 31,*

WhAm 1
Appenzellar, Paul 1875- *WhAm 3*
Appenzeller, Alice Rebecca 1885-1950 *WhAm 3*
Appenzeller, Henry Gerhard 1858-1902 *DcAmB, WhAm H*
Appenzeller, Henry Gerhart 1858-1902 *NatCAB 23*
Apperman, Isaac 1896-1952 *NatCAB 45*
Apperson, Elmer 1861-1920 *NatCAB 24*
Appert, Nicolas 1752-1841 *AsBiEn*
Applbaum, Karl 1910-1974 *WhAm 6*
Apple, Andrew Thomas Geiger 1858-1918 *WhAm 1*
Apple, Billy 1935- *BnEnAmA*
Apple, Henry Harbaugh 1869-1943 *NatCAB 14, NatCAB 32, WhAm 2*
Apple, Joseph Henry 1865-1948 *TwCBDA, WhAm 2*
Apple, Thomas Gilmore 1829-1898 *ApCAB, BiDAmEd, DcAmB, NatCAB 12, TwCBDA, WhAm H*
Applebee, Constance M K *WomWWA 14*
Appleby, Alice Montague 1859- *WomWWA 14*
Appleby, Frank 1864-1924 *WhAm 1*
Appleby, John Francis 1840-1917 *DcAmB, EncAAH, NatCAB 11, WebAB*
Appleby, Stewart Hoffman 1890-1964 *BiDrAC*
Appleby, Theodore Frank 1864-1924 *BiDrAC, WhAmP*
Appleby, Thomas Henry Montague Villiers 1843- *WhAm 4*
Appleby, Troy Wilson 1874-1947 *WhAm 2*
Appleby, William Remsen 1865-1941 *WhAm 1*
Applegate, Frank G 1882-1931 *WhAm 1*
Applegate, Frank G 1882-1934? *IIBEAAW*
Applegate, H W d1930 *WhAm 1*
Applegate, Irvamae Vincent 1920-1973 *WhAm 6*
Applegate, Jesse 1811-1888 *AmBi, DcAmB, McGEWB, NatCAB 20, REnAW, WebAB, WhAm H, WhAmP*
Applegate, John Stilwell 1837-1916 *ApCAB X, NatCAB 15, WhAm 1*
Applegate, Mina W *WomWWA 14*
Applegate, Paul Ray 1878-1962 *WhAm 4*
Appleman, Charles Orville 1878-1964 *WhAm 4*
Appleman, Leighton Francis 1874-1968 *NatCAB 55*
Appleseed, Johnny 1774-1845 *WebAB*
Appleseed, Johnny 1775-1847 *NatCAB 11, WhAm H*
Appleton, Allen Lansing 1880-1944 *NatCAB 33*
Appleton, Benjamin Ward 1864-1927 *NatCAB 39*
Appleton, Charles Lanier 1886-1921 *NatCAB 20*
Appleton, Charles William 1874-1945 *NatCAB 47, WhAm 2*
Appleton, Daniel 1785-1849 *AmBi, ApCAB, DcAmB, Drake, NatCAB 2, TwCBDA, WhAm H*
Appleton, Daniel 1852-1929 *WhAm 1*
Appleton, Daniel Fuller 1826- *NatCAB 11*
Appleton, Daniel Sidney 1824-1890 *NatCAB 2, TwCBDA*
Appleton, Sir Edward Victor 1892-1965 *AsBiEn, DcScB, WhAm 4*
Appleton, Floyd 1871-1952 *WhAm 3*
Appleton, Francis Henry 1847-1939 *NatCAB 12, TwCBDA, WhAm 1*
Appleton, Francis Randall 1854-1929 *ApCAB X, WhAm 1*
Appleton, Francis Randall, Jr. 1885-1974 *WhAm 6*
Appleton, George Swett 1821-1878 *NatCAB 2, TwCBDA*
Appleton, George Washington 1805-1831 *NewYHSD*
Appleton, James 1785-1862 *DcAmB, TwCBDA, WhAm H*
Appleton, James 1786-1862 *ApCAB, NatCAB 11*
Appleton, Jesse 1772-1819 *ApCAB, DcAmB, Drake, NatCAB 1, TwCBDA, WhAm H*
Appleton, John 1804-1891 *ApCAB Sup, BiAUS, DcAmB, Drake, NatCAB 11, TwCBDA, WhAm H, WhAmP*
Appleton, John 1815-1864 *ApCAB, BiAUS,*

BiDrAC, DcAmB, Drake, NatCAB 12, WhAm H, WhAmP

Appleton, John 1815-1894 *TwCBDA*

Appleton, John Adams 1817-1881 *NatCAB 2, TwCBDA*

Appleton, John Adams 1891-1966 *WhAm 4*

Appleton, John Francis 1839-1871 *ApCAB Sup*

Appleton, John Howard 1844-1930 *ApCAB, TwCBDA, WhAm 1*

Appleton, John James 1789?-1864 *ApCAB*

Appleton, John James 1789-1865 *TwCBDA*

Appleton, John James 1792-1864 *BiAUS, Drake, NatCAB 13*

Appleton, Julius Henry 1840-1904 *NatCAB 32*

Appleton, L Estelle 1858-1937 *WhAm 1, WomWWA 14*

Appleton, Nathan 1779-1861 *AmBi, ApCAB, BiAUS, BiDrAC, DcAmB, Drake, McGEWB, NatCAB 11, TwCBDA, WhAm H, WhAmP*

Appleton, Nathaniel 1693-1784 *ApCAB, Drake, NatCAB 7*

Appleton, Nathaniel Walker 1755-1795 *DcAmB, WhAm H*

Appleton, Samuel 1766-1853 *ApCAB, DcAmB, Drake, NatCAB 5, TwCBDA, WhAm H*

Appleton, Samuel Etherington 1834-1909 *NatCAB 14*

Appleton, Thomas Gold 1812-1884 *AmBi, ApCAB, DcAmB, NatCAB 8, NewYHSD, TwCBDA, WhAm H*

Appleton, Victor 1862-1930 *WebAB*

Appleton, William 1786-1862 *ApCAB, BiAUS, BiDrAC, Drake, NatCAB 5, TwCBDA, WhAm H*

Appleton, William Channing 1897-1972 *WhAm 5*

Appleton, William Henry 1814-1899 *DcAmB, NatCAB 2, TwCBDA, WhAm H, WhAm 1*

Appleton, William Hyde 1842-1926 *NatCAB 28, TwCBDA, WhAm 3*

Appleton, William Sumner 1840- *TwCBDA*

Appleton, William Sumner 1874-1947 *DcAmB S4, WhAm 2*

Appleton, William Worthen 1845-1924 *DcAmB, WhAm 1*

Appleyard, Geoffrey 1916-1943 *WhWW-II*

Appling, Daniel 1787-1817 *ApCAB, Drake*

Apraxin, Count Fedor Matyeevich 1661-1728 *WhoMilH*

Apsley, Lewis Dewart 1852-1925 *BiDrAC, NatCAB 20*

Apt, Frederick Gazlay 1889-1958 *NatCAB 50*

Apted, D Bradford 1902-1968 *NatCAB 54*

Aptheker, Herbert 1915- *EncAAH*

Apthorp, East 1733-1816 *Drake*

Apthorp, William Foster 1848-1913 *DcAmB, NatCAB 21, TwCBDA, WhAm 4*

Aquinas, Thomas, Saint 1225?-1274 *AsBiEn, DcScB*

Aracena, Dominick 1810-1874 *ApCAB*

Arado, Charles C 1897- *NatCAB 18*

Arago, Dominique Francois Jean 1786-1853 *AsBiEn, DcScB*

Arago, Jean 1788-1836 *ApCAB*

Aragon, Louis 1897- *McGEWB*

Araki, Eikichi 1891-1959 *WhAm 3*

Aramburu, Pedro Eugenio 1903-1970 *WhAm 5*

Araneta, Gregorio 1869- *WhAm 1*

Arango, Rafael De 1788-1850 *ApCAB*

Arango Y Escandon, Alejandro 1821- *ApCAB*

Arango Y Parreno, Francisco De 1765-1837 *ApCAB*

Aranha, Osvaldo 1894-1960 *McGEWB*

Aranna, Oswaldo 1894-1960 *WhAm 3*

Arant, Herschel Whitfield 1887-1941 *WhAm 1*

Aranzazu, Juan DeDios d1845 *ApCAB*

Aranzio, Giulio Cesare 1529?-1589 *DcScB*

Aratus 271BC-213BC *McGEWB*

Aratus Of Soli 310?BC-239?BC *DcScB*

Araujo Y Rio, Jose *ApCAB*

Arbeely, Abraham Joseph 1852- *WhAm 4*

Arber, Agnes Robertson 1879-1960 *DcScB*

Arbessier, F *NewYHSD*

Arbogast, Louis Francois Antoine 1759-1803 *DcScB*

Arboleda, Julio d1872 *ApCAB*

Arbos, Philippe 1882-1956 *DcScB*

Arbuckle, Charles Nathaniel 1879-1955 *WhAm 3*

Arbuckle, Howard Bell 1870-1945 *WhAm 2*

Arbuckle, John d1912 *WhAm 1*

Arbuckle, John 1838-1912 *NatCAB 15*

Arbuckle, John 1839-1912 *ApCAB X, DcAmB*

Arbuckle, John D 1868- *WhAm 4*

Arbuckle, John Milton 1865- *WhoColR*

Arbuckle, Maclyn 1866-1931 *WhAm 1*

Arbuckle, Matthew 1775-1851 *TwCBDA*

Arbuckle, Matthew 1776-1851 *ApCAB, Drake*

Arbuckle, Matthew 1828-1883 *WhAm H*

Arbuckle, Millard Fillmore 1883-1954 *NatCAB 43*

Arbuckle, Roscoe Conkling 1887-1933 *WhAm 1*

Arbuckle, W Chantler 1890-1948 *NatCAB 47*

Arbus, Diane 1923-1971 *BnEnAmA, WhAm 5*

Arbuthnot, Charles Criswell 1876-1963 *WhAm 4, WhAm 5*

Arbuthnot, John 1667-1735 *BiHiMed, DcScB*

Arbuthnot, Marriot 1711?-1794 *AmBi, ApCAB, Drake*

Arbuthnot, May Hill 1884-1969 *BiDAmEd, DcAmLiB, WhAm 5*

Arbuthnot, Thomas Shaw 1871-1956 *NatCAB 46, WhAm 5*

Arbuthnot, Wilson S 1865-1938 *WhAm 1*

Arcaro, George Edward 1916- *WebAB*

Arcaya, Pedro Manuel 1874- *WhAm 5*

Arce, Francisco 1822-1878 *ApCAB*

Arce, Jose 1881- *WhAm 5*

Arce, Manuel 1725-1785 *ApCAB*

Arce, Manuel Jose *Drake*

Archambault, A Margaretta d1956 *WhAm 3*

Archbald, Harry Ruthven 1872-1951 *NatCAB 39*

Archbald, James, VI 1866-1937 *WhAm 1*

Archbald, Robert Wodrow 1848-1926 *WhAm 1*

Archbold, George 1848- *ApCAB*

Archbold, John Dustin 1848-1916 *ApCAB X, DcAmB, NatCAB 21, WhAm 1*

Archbold, John Foster 1877-1930 *NatCAB 25*

Archdale, John 1642?-1717? *ApCAB, DcAmB, Drake, NatCAB 12, TwCBDA, WhAm H*

Archer, Allen Thurman 1889-1959 *NatCAB 50, WhAm 4*

Archer, Belle 1860-1900 *WhAm 1*

Archer, Branch Tanner 1790-1856 *ApCAB, DcAmB, Drake, NatCAB 6, TwCBDA, WhAm H, WhAmP*

Archer, Clifford Paul 1893-1968 *WhAm 5*

Archer, Franklin Morse 1873-1950 *WhAm 2A*

Archer, Frederic 1838-1901 *DcAmB, WhAm 1*

Archer, Gabriel 1570?-1609? *NatCAB 8*

Archer, George Frost 1871-1953 *NatCAB 40*

Archer, Gleason Leonard 1880-1966 *ApCAB X, BiDAmEd, NatCAB 16, WhAm 4*

Archer, Harry 1886-1960 *NatCAB 48*

Archer, Henry Hayes 1860- *NatCAB 6*

Archer, James *NewYHSD*

Archer, James 1800?- *NewYHSD*

Archer, James Jay 1817-1864 *BiDConf, DcAmB, WhAm H*

Archer, John *NewYHSD*

Archer, John 1741-1810 *ApCAB, BiAUS, BiDrAC, DcAmB, Drake, NatCAB 22, WhAm H, WhAmP*

Archer, John Abner 1885-1943 *NatCAB 33*

Archer, John Clark 1881-1957 *WhAm 3*

Archer, Julian Lawrence 1898-1963 *WhAm 4*

Archer, Peter 1873-1962 *WhAm 4*

Archer, Ralph Curtis 1892-1957 *WhAm 3*

Archer, Robert Harris 1882-1948 *NatCAB 37*

Archer, Samuel 1771-1839 *DcAmB*

Archer, Samuel B 1790-1825 *ApCAB, Drake*

Archer, Samuel Howard 1870- *WhoColR*

Archer, Sarah F Fisher *WomWWA 14*

Archer, Shreve MacLaren 1888-1947 *WhAm 2*

Archer, Shreve McLaren 1888-1947 *NatCAB 36*

Archer, Stephenson 1786-1848 *Drake*

Archer, Stevenson 1786-1848 *ApCAB, BiAUS, BiDrAC, DcAmB, NatCAB 7, WhAm H, WhAmP*

Archer, Stevenson 1827-1898 *BiAUS, BiDrAC, TwCBDA, WhAm H, WhAmP*

Archer, Thomas Porter 1885-1949 *NatCAB 37,*

WhAm 2

Archer, William Segar 1789-1855 *ApCAB, BiAUS, BiDrAC, DcAmB, Drake, NatCAB 11, TwCBDA, WhAm H, WhAmP*

Archer, William Thomson 1875-1958 *NatCAB 49*

Archiac, E-J-Adolphe D DeS, Vicomte D' 1802-1868 *DcScB*

Archibald, Sir Adams George 1814- *ApCAB*

Archibald, Andrew Webster 1851-1926 *WhAm 1*

Archibald, Edith Jessie 1854- *AmWom*

Archibald, Frank C 1857-1935 *WhAm 1*

Archibald, Mrs. George *WhAm 1*

Archibald, George D 1820- *NatCAB 2*

Archibald, H Teller 1879-1936 *NatCAB 31*

Archibald, James Francis Jewell 1871- *WhAm 5*

Archibald, Mabel Evangeline *WomWWA 14*

Archibald, Maynard Brown 1891-1956 *WhAm 3*

Archibald, Raymond Clare 1875-1955 *NatCAB 46, WhAm 3*

Archibald, Thomas Dickson 1813- *ApCAB*

Archibald, William 1892-1950 *NatCAB 38*

Archigenes 054?- *DcScB*

Archimedes 287?BC-212BC *AsBiEn, DcScB, McGEWB*

Archinard, Paul Emile 1859- *NatCAB 9*

Archipenko, Alexander 1887-1964 *McGEWB, WhAm 4*

Archytas Of Tarentum *DcScB*

Arciszeffski, Christopher 1600?-1668 *Drake*

Arcos, Jose Brunetti G DeLosC, Duke Of 1839- *ApCAB Sup*

Arcos Y Moreno, Alonso *ApCAB*

Arctowska, Adrian Jane 1875- *WhAm 5*

Arctowski, Henryk 1871-1958 *WhAm 3*

Arden, Agnes Ann Eagleson *WomWWA 14*

Arden, Edwin Hunter Pendleton 1864-1918 *DcAmB, NatCAB 20, WhAm 1*

Arden, Elizabeth 1884-1966 *WebAB*

Arden, Elizabeth 1891-1966 *WhAm 4*

Ardenond *NewYHSD*

Arderne, John 1306?-1380? *BiHiMed*

Ardery, William Breckenridge 1887-1967 *WhAm 4*

Ardison, Robert Joseph 1911-1965 *WhAm 4*

Ardrien, James 1815?- *NewYHSD*

Arduino, Giovanni 1714-1795 *DcScB*

Arechaga, Juan De *ApCAB*

Aref, Abdul Salam *WhAm 5*

Arenales, Jose 1790?- *ApCAB*

Arenales Catalan, Emilio 1922-1969 *WhAm 5*

Arenberg, Albert Lee 1891-1969 *WhAm 5*

Arend, Harry O 1903-1966 *WhAm 4*

Arendell, Falconer Benjamin 1856-1916 *NatCAB 16*

Arends, Katharine 1871- *WomWWA 14*

Arends, Leslie Cornelius 1895- *BiDrAC*

Arendt, Hannah 1906-1975 *WebAB, WhAm 6*

Arendt, Morton 1877- *WhAm 5*

Arens, Egmont 1889-1966 *WhAm 4*

Arens, Franz Xavier 1856-1932 *NatCAB 11, WhAm 1*

Arens, Henry Martin 1873-1963 *BiDrAC, WhAm 5*

Arens, Richard 1913-1969 *WhAm 5*

Arensberg, Walter Conrad 1878-1954 *DcAmB S5, WhAm 3*

Arents, Albert 1840-1914 *ApCAB, DcAmB, TwCBDA, WhAm 4*

Arents, George 1875-1961 *WhAm 4*

Arentz, Frederic C H 1862- *WhAm 4*

Arentz, Samuel Shaw 1879-1934 *BiDrAC, WhAmP*

Aretaeus Of Cappadocia *BiHiMed, DcScB*

Arevalo, Juan Jose 1904- *McGEWB*

Arey, Gordon Coates 1901-1948 *NatCAB 40*

Arey, Harriet Ellen Grannis 1819- *ApCAB, Drake*

Arey, Harriett Ellen Grannis 1819- *AmWom*

Arey, Hawthorne 1905-1972 *NatCAB 56, WhAm 5*

Arey, Melvin Franklin 1844-1931 *WhAm 1*

Arfvedson, Johann August 1792-1841 *DcScB Sup*

Argall, Philip 1854-1922 *DcAmB, WhAm 1*

Argall, Sir Samuel 1572?-1626 *AmBi*

Argall, Sir Samuel 1572-1639 *ApCAB, Drake, TwCBDA, WhAm H*
Argall, Samuel 1580?-1626? *NatCAB 13*
Arganbright, Ned Arlo 1893-1961 *NatCAB 49*
Argand, Emile 1879-1940 *DcScB*
Argand, Jean Robert 1768-1822 *DcScB*
Argelander, Friedrich Wilhelm August 1799-1875 *AsBiEn, DcScB*
Argenson, Pierre DeVoyer, Viscount D' 1626-1709? *ApCAB, Drake*
Argenville, Antoine-Joseph Dezallier D' 1680-1765 *DcScB*
Argetsinger, J C 1883-1955 *WhAm 3*
Argo, Ella Butler *WomWWA 14*
Argoli, Andrea 1570?-1657 *DcScB*
Argondelis, Nicholas Anthony 1903-1967 *NatCAB 51*
Argue, Hiram Septemus 1879-1944 *NatCAB 35*
Arguello, Concepcion 1790-1857 *ApCAB*
Arguello, Jose Dario *WhAm H*
Arguello, Leonardo 1875-1947 *WhAm 2*
Arguello, Luis Antonio 1784-1830 *ApCAB, TwCBDA, WhAm H*
Argyle, William Robertson 1891-1964 *NatCAB 50, WhAm 4*
Argyll, Archibald Campbell, Marquis Of 1607-1661 *WhoMilH*
Arias, Francisco Gabino d1808? *ApCAB, Drake*
Arias DeBenavides, Pedro *ApCAB*
Arillaga, Basilio Manuel 1785?-1867 *ApCAB, Drake*
Ariosto, Ludovico 1474-1533 *McGEWB*
Arismendi, Juan Bautista 1786- *ApCAB, Drake*
Arista, Mariano 1802-1855 *AmBi, ApCAB, Drake*
Aristaeus *DcScB*
Aristarchus 320?BC-250?BC *AsBiEn*
Aristarchus Of Samos 310?BC-230BC *DcScB, McGEWB*
Aristizabal, Gabriel De 1743-1805 *ApCAB*
Aristophanes 450?BC-385?BC *McGEWB*
Aristotle 384BC-322BC *AsBiEn, DcScB, McGEWB*
Aristoxenus 375?BC-360BC *DcScB*
Aristyllus *DcScB*
Arius d336? *McGEWB*
Arjona, Jaime Homero 1906-1967 *NatCAB 54, WhAm 4*
Arkadiev, Vladimir Konstantinovich 1884-1953 *DcScB*
Arkell, Bartlett 1862-1946 *NatCAB 35, WhAm 2*
Arkell, James *NatCAB 1*
Arkell, William Clark 1887-1962 *NatCAB 48, WhAm 4*
Arkell, William J 1856-1930 *NatCAB 26, WhAm 1*
Arkell, William Joscelyn 1904-1958 *DcScB*
Arkins, John 1842- *NatCAB 1*
Arkush, Ralph Montgomery 1887-1965 *WhAm 4*
Arkwright, George Alfred 1888-1972 *NatCAB 57, WhAm 5*
Arkwright, Preston Stanley 1871-1947 *WhAm 2*
Arkwright, Sir Richard 1732-1792 *AsBiEn, McGEWB*
Arlen, Harold 1905- *WebAB*
Arlen, Michael 1895-1956 *WhAm 3*
Arliss, George 1868-1946 *ApCAB X, DcAmB S4, WhAm 2*
Arluck, Hyman *WebAB*
Armacost, Richard Ralph 1914-1959 *NatCAB 49*
Armand, Charles Trefin 1751-1793 *ApCAB*
Armand, Charles Tufin, Marquis DeLaR 1756-1793 *Drake*
Armand, G *NewYHSD*
Armand, Polermo 1842?- *NewYHSD*
Armando, John *NewYHSD*
Armas, Carlos Castillo 1914-1957 *WhAm 3*
Armat, Thomas 1866-1948 *NatCAB 50*
Armbrecht, William Henry 1874-1941 *WhAm 2*
Armbrister, Victor Stradley 1902-1962 *NatCAB 49, WhAm 4*
Armbruster, Adolph Henry 1895-1951 *WhAm 3*
Armbruster, Anthony *NewYHSD*
Armbruster, Sara Dary 1862- *AmWom*

Armendariz, Lope Diaz De *ApCAB*
Armes, Ethel Marie *WomWWA 14*
Armes, George Arthur 1872-1955 *NatCAB 52*
Armes, Henry Beard 1874-1962 *NatCAB 52*
Armes, Marie Theodosia 1864- *WomWWA 14*
Armes, William Dallam 1860- *WhAm 4*
Armfield, Lucille 1873- *WomWWA 14*
Armfield, Robert Franklin 1829-1898 *BiDrAC*
Armijo, Manuel 1792?-1853 *REnAW*
Armin, Emil 1883- *IIBEAAW*
Arminio, Joseph John 1912-1962 *NatCAB 50*
Arminius, Jacobus 1560-1609 *McGEWB*
Armistead, D Branch 1905-1962 *NatCAB 50*
Armistead, George 1780-1818 *AmBi, ApCAB, DcAmB, Drake, NatCAB 13, TwCBDA, WebAMB, WhAm H*
Armistead, George, Jr. 1902-1960 *NatCAB 50*
Armistead, Henry Beauford 1833-1914 *NatCAB 8, WhAm 3*
Armistead, Henry Marshall 1874-1958 *WhAm 3*
Armistead, Henry Watson 1868- *WhoColR*
Armistead, Jesse Warren 1899- *WhAm 3*
Armistead, Lewis Addison 1816-1863 *BiDConf*
Armistead, Lewis Addison 1817-1863 *AmBi, ApCAB, DcAmB, Drake, NatCAB 5, TwCBDA, WebAMB, WhAm H*
Armistead, Walker Keith 1785?-1845 *ApCAB, TwCBDA*
Armistead, Walter Keith 1785?-1845 *Drake, NatCAB 5*
Armitage, A Donnally 1872-1953 *NatCAB 42*
Armitage, Albert T 1893-1968 *WhAm 5*
Armitage, Joseph Bradley 1881-1957 *NatCAB 43*
Armitage, Merle 1893-1975 *WhAm 6*
Armitage, Paul 1873-1949 *WhAm 2*
Armitage, Thomas 1819-1896 *ApCAB, NatCAB 9, TwCBDA*
Armitage, William Edmond 1830-1873 *ApCAB, NatCAB 11, TwCBDA*
Armor, Charles Lee *BiAUS*
Armor, Mary Elizabeth Harris 1863- *WhAm 4*
Armor, Samuel *NewYHSD*
Armour, A Watson 1882-1953 *WhAm 3*
Armour, Allison Vincent 1863-1941 *WhAm 1*
Armour, Andrew Watson 1829-1892 *NatCAB 7*
Armour, Bernard R d1949 *WhAm 2*
Armour, Herman Ossian 1837-1901 *NatCAB 7, WhAm 1*
Armour, J Ogden 1863-1927 *ApCAB X, NatCAB 23, WhAm 1*
Armour, Laurance Hearne 1888-1952 *NatCAB 47, WhAm 3*
Armour, Lester 1895-1970 *NatCAB 56, WhAm 5*
Armour, Philip Danforth 1832-1901 *AmBi, ApCAB Sup, ApCAB X, DcAmB, EncAAH, McGEWB, NatCAB 7, TwCBDA, WebAB, WhAm 1*
Armour, Philip Danforth 1893-1958 *WhAm 3*
Armour, Simeon Brooks 1828- *NatCAB 7*
Arms, Frank Thornton 1866-1948 *WhAm 2*
Arms, John Taylor 1887-1953 *NatCAB 42*
Arms, John Taylor 1887-1954 *WhAm 3*
Arms, Leo Murray 1893-1972 *NatCAB 57*
Arms, Samuel Dwight 1891-1961 *WhAm 4*
Arms, Thomas Seelye 1893-1970 *WhAm 5*
Armsby, George Newell 1876-1942 *NatCAB 31, WhAm 2*
Armsby, Henry Prentiss 1853-1921 *AmBi, DcAmB, EncAAH, NatCAB 22, WhAm 1*
Armsby, James H 1809-1875 *ApCAB*
Armstead *NewYHSD*
Armstead, George Brooks 1883-1950 *WhAm 3*
Armstead, Henry Howell 1872-1940 *WhAm 1, WhAm 1C*
Armstrong, A Joseph 1873-1954 *NatCAB 46, WhAm 3*
Armstrong, Addison Cooke 1884-1944 *NatCAB 33*
Armstrong, Agnes Maria *WomWWA 14*
Armstrong, Alexander 1877-1939 *WhAm 1*
Armstrong, Andrew Campbell 1860-1935 *WhAm 1*
Armstrong, Anne Wetzell 1872-1958 *WhAm 3*
Armstrong, Arthur 1798-1851 *NewYHSD*
Armstrong, Arthur Henry 1866-1938 *WhAm 1*

Armstrong, Barbara Nachtrieb 1890-1976 *WhAm 6*
Armstrong, C Dudley 1888-1954 *WhAm 3*
Armstrong, Charles 1886-1967 *WhAm 4A*
Armstrong, Charles Clyde 1890-1949 *NatCAB 39*
Armstrong, Charles Dickey 1861-1935 *NatCAB 25, WhAm 1*
Armstrong, Charles Dorsey 1917-1962 *NatCAB 51*
Armstrong, Charles Wallace 1889-1968 *NatCAB 55, WhAm 5*
Armstrong, Charlotte 1905-1969 *WhAm 5*
Armstrong, Christopher *NewYHSD*
Armstrong, Clairette Papin 1886- *WomWWA 14*
Armstrong, Clare Hibbs 1894-1969 *WhAm 5*
Armstrong, Clyde Allman 1898-1975 *WhAm 6*
Armstrong, Dallas Warren 1872- *WhAm 5*
Armstrong, Daniel Louis 1900-1971 *EncAB*
Armstrong, David Hartley 1812-1893 *ApCAB, BiDrAC, NatCAB 5, TwCBDA, WhAm H*
Armstrong, David Maitland 1836-1918 *AmBi, DcAmB, NatCAB 19, NewYHSD, WhAm 1*
Armstrong, David Maitland 1837?-1918 *ApCAB, ApCAB Sup, TwCBDA*
Armstrong, David William 1885-1963 *WhAm 4*
Armstrong, Della M *WomWWA 14*
Armstrong, DeWitt Clinton 1867-1914 *NatCAB 17*
Armstrong, DeWitt Clinton 1868-1914 *WhAm 1*
Armstrong, Donald Budd 1886-1968 *ApCAB X, WhAm 5*
Armstrong, E Royce 1873-1939 *NatCAB 29*
Armstrong, Edward Ambler 1858-1932 *WhAm 1*
Armstrong, Edward Cooke 1871-1944 *DcAmB S3, WhAm 2*
Armstrong, Edward Frankland 1878-1945 *DcScB*
Armstrong, Edward Pickering 1865-1942 *NatCAB 33*
Armstrong, Edwin Howard 1890-1954 *AsBiEn, DcAmB S5, DcScB, McGEWB, WebAB, WhAm 3*
Armstrong, Edwin James 1861-1925 *NatCAB 20*
Armstrong, Eliza Dickson 1845- *WomWWA 14*
Armstrong, Eugene Lawson 1896-1950 *NatCAB 38*
Armstrong, Frances Louisa 1842- *WomWWA 14*
Armstrong, Frank 1871-1954 *NatCAB 43*
Armstrong, Frank 1874-1947 *NatCAB 36*
Armstrong, Frank Alton, Jr. 1902-1969 *WhAm 5*
Armstrong, Frank Crawford 1835-1909 *BiDConf, DcAmB, WhAm 1*
Armstrong, Frank Hall 1877-1955 *NatCAB 44*
Armstrong, Frank Hough 1853-1920 *ApCAB X, NatCAB 19*
Armstrong, Gayle Geard 1900-1950 *NatCAB 44, WhAm 3*
Armstrong, George Buchanan 1822-1871 *DcAmB, NatCAB 46, WhAm H*
Armstrong, George Dod 1813-1899 *DcAmB, WhAm H*
Armstrong, George Dodd 1813-1899 *ApCAB, NatCAB 19, WhAm 1*
Armstrong, George Simpson 1886-1962 *WhAm 4*
Armstrong, George W, Jr. 1900-1965 *WhAm 4*
Armstrong, George Washington 1836-1901 *DcAmB, NatCAB 2, TwCBDA, WhAm H*
Armstrong, George Washington 1866-1954 *NatCAB 47*
Armstrong, George William, Jr. 1857-1932 *WhAm 1, WhAm 1C*
Armstrong, Gertrude Virginia Ludden *WomWWA 14*
Armstrong, Grace Leonard *WomWWA 14*
Armstrong, H C 1904-1971 *WhAm 5*
Armstrong, Hamilton Fish 1893-1973 *WhAm 5*
Armstrong, Harris 1899-1973 *WhAm 6*
Armstrong, Harry Worthington 1879-1951 *NatCAB 40*

Armstrong, Helen Maitland 1869-1948 *BiCAW,*
WhAm 2
Armstrong, Henry B 1791-1884 *ApCAB*
Armstrong, Henry Edward 1848-1937 *DcScB*
Armstrong, Henry Worthington 1879-1951
DcAmB S5
Armstrong, Herbert Deuel 1907-1973 *WhAm 6*
Armstrong, Homer Volk 1882-1940 *NatCAB 36*
Armstrong, Horace White 1882-1947
NatCAB 38
Armstrong, Houston Churchwell 1875-
WhAm 5
Armstrong, Hugh Collins 1904-1971
NatCAB 57
Armstrong, J Evan 1883-1959 *WhAm 4*
Armstrong, J P Taylor 1882-1962 *WhAm 4*
Armstrong, J Tarbottom 1848-1933 *NatCAB 24*
Armstrong, Mrs. James *NewYHSD*
Armstrong, James d1795 *ApCAB*
Armstrong, James 1748-1828 *BiDrAC,*
WhAm H
Armstrong, James 1794-1868 *ApCAB, Drake,*
TwCBDA
Armstrong, James 1821- *ApCAB*
Armstrong, James 1834-1917 *WhAm 1*
Armstrong, James Edward 1915-1968 *WhAm 5*
Armstrong, James F 1816-1873 *Drake*
Armstrong, James F 1817-1873 *ApCAB,*
NatCAB 4, TwCBDA
Armstrong, James Francis 1750-1816 *Drake*
Armstrong, James Reverdy 1876- *WhAm 5*
Armstrong, John d1795 *BiAUS, Drake*
Armstrong, John 1717-1795 *BiDrAC, DcAmB,*
WebAMB, WhAm H, WhAmP
Armstrong, John 1725-1795 *ApCAB,*
NatCAB 14, TwCBDA
Armstrong, John 1755-1816 *DcAmB, WebAB,*
WebAMB, WhAm H
Armstrong, John 1755-1843 *BiAUS, BiDrAC*
Armstrong, John 1758-1843 *AmBi, ApCAB,*
BiDrUSE, DcAmB, Drake, NatCAB 1,
TwCBDA, WebAB, WebAMB, WhAm H,
WhAmP
Armstrong, John Harold 1896-1952 *NatCAB 39*
Armstrong, John Irvine 1872-1924 *WhAm 1*
Armstrong, John Nelson 1870-1944 *WhAm 2*
Armstrong, John Samuel 1857-1917
NatCAB 17
Armstrong, Joseph Gillespie, III 1901-1964
WhAm 4
Armstrong, Joseph Morgan 1867-1955
NatCAB 45
Armstrong, Leroy 1854-1927 *WhAm 1*
Armstrong, Lewis Robert 1860-1915
NatCAB 17
Armstrong, Lilian Harden 1903-1971 *WhAm 5*
Armstrong, Louis Daniel 1900-1971 *McGEWB,*
WebAB, WhAm 5
Armstrong, Lyndon King 1859-1942 *WhAm 2,*
WhAm 4
Armstrong, M K 1832-1906 *IIBEAAW*
Armstrong, Margaret 1867-1944 *WhAm 2*
Armstrong, Marion 1886- *WomWWA 14*
Armstrong, Mary Alice 1864- *WomWWA 14*
Armstrong, Maurice Whitman 1905-1967
WhAm 5
Armstrong, Moses Kimball 1832-1906 *ApCAB,*
BiAUS, BiDrAC, REnAW, TwCBDA,
WhAm 3, WhAmP
Armstrong, Neil Alden 1930- *AsBiEn,*
McGEWB, WebAB, WebAMB
Armstrong, Orland Kay 1893- *BiDrAC*
Armstrong, Paul 1869-1915 *DcAmB,*
NatCAB 18, WhAm 1
Armstrong, Paul Galloway 1890-1958 *WhAm 3*
Armstrong, Philander Banister 1847-
NatCAB 1, WhAm 4
Armstrong, Reuben Hanson 1854- *WhoColR*
Armstrong, Richard d1823? *ApCAB, Drake*
Armstrong, Richard 1805-1860 *ApCAB,*
BiDAmEd, Drake, TwCBDA
Armstrong, Richard H 1903-1959 *WhAm 3*
Armstrong, Robert 1790-1854 *ApCAB, BiAUS,*
Drake, TwCBDA
Armstrong, Robert 1792-1854 *DcAmB,*
WhAm H
Armstrong, Robert 1885-1946 *NatCAB 34*

Armstrong, Robert Allen 1860-1936
NatCAB 27, WhAm 1
Armstrong, Robert Burns 1873-1946 *WhAm 2*
Armstrong, Robert Hayden 1869- *WhAm 5*
Armstrong, Robert Helms 1900-1961 *WhAm 4*
Armstrong, Robert John d1957 *WhAm 3*
Armstrong, Ruth Alice 1850- *AmWom*
Armstrong, S T 1784-1850 *BiAUS*
Armstrong, Samuel Chapman 1839-1893 *AmBi,*
ApCAB Sup, BiDAmEd, DcAmB,
DcAmReB, McGEWB, NatCAB 1,
NatCAB 38, TwCBDA, WebAB,
WhAm H
Armstrong, Samuel Treat 1859-1944 *WhAm 2*
Armstrong, Samuel Turell 1784-1850 *ApCAB,*
DcAmB, NatCAB 6, TwCBDA,
WhAm H
Armstrong, Sarah B 1857- *AmWom*
Armstrong, Sydney *WomWWA 14*
Armstrong, T Edmund Gardiner 1880-1939
NatCAB 30
Armstrong, Theodore 1844- *NatCAB 10*
Armstrong, Thomas *NewYHSD*
Armstrong, Thomas, Jr. 1857-1937 *WhAm 1*
Armstrong, Thomas Morrell 1889-1959
NatCAB 48
Armstrong, Walter Preston 1884-1949
NatCAB 47, WhAm 2A
Armstrong, Wesley Earl 1899- *BiDAmEd*
Armstrong, William d1942 *WhAm 2*
Armstrong, William 1782-1865 *BiAUS,*
BiDrAC, WhAm H
Armstrong, William Coulson 1859-1923
NatCAB 20, WhAm 1
Armstrong, William G 1823-1890 *NewYHSD*
Armstrong, William Gilbert 1906-1966
WhAm 5
Armstrong, William Henry 1902-1960
NatCAB 47
Armstrong, William Hepburn 1824-1919 *BiAUS,*
BiDrAC
Armstrong, William Jackson 1841- *WhAm 4*
Armstrong, William Jessup 1796-1846 *ApCAB,*
Drake
Armstrong, William Morris 1797-1861 *Drake*
Armstrong, William Park 1874-1944 *WhAm 2*
Armstrong, William W 1822-1914 *IIBEAAW*
Armstrong, William Wallace 1833-1905
NatCAB 24
Armstrong, William Winnie 1864-1944
NatCAB 33
Armstrong, William Wright 1865-1932
WhAm 1
Armstrong, Zella *WomWWA 14*
Armstrong-Hopkins, George Franklin 1855-
WhAm 4
Armstrong-Hopkins, Saleni 1855- *WhAm 4*
Arn, Elmer Raymond 1886-1951 *WhAm 3*
Arn, William Godfrey 1877- *WhAm 5*
Arnal, Leon E 1880-1963 *WhAm 4*
Arnald Of Villanova 1240?-1311 *DcScB*
Arnald Of Villanova *see also* Arnold Of Villanova
Arnauld, Antoine 1612-1694 *DcScB*
Arndt, C O 1899-1966 *WhAm 4*
Arndt, Elmer Jacob Frederick 1908-1969
NatCAB 56, WhAm 5
Arndt, Karl M 1901-1956 *WhAm 3*
Arndt, Robert Norton Downs 1904-1975
WhAm 6
Arndt, Walter Tallmadge 1873-1932
NatCAB 23, WhAm 1, WhAm 1C
Arndt, William Frederick 1880-1957 *WhAm 3*
Arne, Thomas Augustine 1710-1778 *McGEWB*
Arneberg, John Gyro 1874-1958 *NatCAB 49*
Arneill, James Rae 1869-1950 *WhAm 3*
Arnell, Samuel Mayes 1833-1903 *BiAUS,*
BiDrAC
Arner, George Byron Louis 1883-1952
NatCAB 40
Arnesen, Sigurd J 1887-1966 *WhAm 4*
Arneson, Ben 1883-1958 *WhAm 3*
Arneson, Robert 1930- *BnEnAmA*
Arnett, Alex Mathews 1888-1945 *NatCAB 36,*
WhAm 2
Arnett, Benjamin William 1838-1906
NatCAB 3, WhAm 1
Arnett, Charles Henry 1858- *WhoColR*
Arnett, Clare Newton 1884-1933 *WhAm 1*

Arnett, Eugene 1875-1938 *NatCAB 29*
Arnett, Leslie 1889-1972 *NatCAB 57*
Arnett, Trevor 1870-1955 *WhAm 3*
Arnette, D W 1882-1957 *WhAm 4*
Arney, C E, Jr. 1891-1956 *WhAm 3*
Arnheim, Ralph Leroy 1891-1974 *WhAm 6*
Arnholtz, Arthur 1901-1973 *WhAm 6*
Arnim, Achim Von 1781-1831 *McGEWB*
Arnim, Hans Georg Von 1581-1641 *WhoMilH*
Arnim, Jurgen Von 1889- *WhWW-II*
Arnn, Charles Edward 1897-1955 *WhAm 3*
Arno, Peter 1904-1968 *WebAB, WhAm 4A*
Arnold Of Brescia 1100?-1155 *McGEWB*
Arnold Of Villanova 1235?-1311 *AsBiEn*
Arnold Of Villanova *see also* Arnald Of Villanova
Arnold, A Sherley 1892- *WhoColR*
Arnold, Aaron 1794-1876 *ApCAB*
Arnold, Abby Noyes *WomWWA 14*
Arnold, Abraham B 1820- *TwCBDA*
Arnold, Abraham Kerns 1837-1901 *ApCAB Sup,*
NatCAB 40, WhAm 1
Arnold, Albert Nicholas 1814-1883 *ApCAB,*
TwCBDA
Arnold, Alfred Colburn 1863- *WhAm 4*
Arnold, Alma Cusian 1871- *ApCAB X,*
WhAm 5, WomWWA 14
Arnold, Almon Al 1887-1955 *WhAm 3*
Arnold, Anna E *WomWWA 14*
Arnold, Arthur 1884-1962 *WhAm 4*
Arnold, Arthur Z 1898-1965 *WhAm 4*
Arnold, Asa 1788-1855? *NatCAB 13*
Arnold, Augusta Foote 1844-1903 *WhAm 1*
Arnold, Aza 1788-1865 *DcAmB, WhAm H*
Arnold, Ben 1892-1955 *WhAm 3*
Arnold, Benedict 1615-1678 *ApCAB, Drake,*
NatCAB 10, TwCBDA
Arnold, Benedict 1741-1801 *AmBi, ApCAB,*
DcAmB, Drake, EncAB, McGEWB,
NatCAB 1, TwCBDA, WebAB,
WebAMB, WhAm H, WhoMilH
Arnold, Benedict 1780-1849 *BiAUS, BiDrAC,*
WhAm H
Arnold, Benjamin Walworth 1865-1932
NatCAB 25
Arnold, Benjamin William, Jr. 1870- *WhAm 5*
Arnold, Bernard *NewYHSD*
Arnold, Bion Joseph 1861-1942 *ApCAB X,*
NatCAB 13, NatCAB 14, WhAm 1,
WhAm 2
Arnold, Birch *WhAm 4*
Arnold, Carl Franklin 1896-1941 *WhAm 2*
Arnold, Carl Raymond 1891-1964 *NatCAB 52,*
WhAm 4
Arnold, Charles 1879- *WhAm 6*
Arnold, Charles Elwood 1876-1947 *NatCAB 50*
Arnold, Charles William Henry 1860-1933
NatCAB 30
Arnold, Constantine Peter 1860- *WhAm 3*
Arnold, Conway Hillyer 1848-1917 *NatCAB 17,*
WhAm 1
Arnold, Cornelia Eliza MacMullan 1869-1945
NatCAB 33
Arnold, Earl Caspar 1884-1949 *WhAm 3*
Arnold, Edith Sarah 1876- *WomWWA 14*
Arnold, Edmund Samuel Foster 1820- *WhAm 1*
Arnold, Edward *NewYHSD*
Arnold, Edward 1890-1956 *NatCAB 45,*
WhAm 3
Arnold, Edwin Gustaf 1905-1960 *WhAm 4*
Arnold, Eliza Almy Peckham 1823- *WhAm 4*
Arnold, Elizabeth Maclay Tittle 1864-
WomWWA 14
Arnold, Ellen M *WomWWA 14*
Arnold, Ernst Hermann 1865-1929 *NatCAB 26,*
WhAm 1
Arnold, Eugene Hamilton 1849-1940
NatCAB 43
Arnold, Everett Denison 1859-1924 *NatCAB 31*
Arnold, Felix 1879- *WhAm 1, WhAm 5*
Arnold, Francis A, Jr. 1910-1967 *WhAm 5*
Arnold, Francis Joseph 1872-1950 *WhAm 3*
Arnold, Frank Atkinson 1867-1958 *WhAm 3*
Arnold, Frank Russell 1871- *WhAm 5*
Arnold, Frazer 1887-1970 *NatCAB 56*
Arnold, Gene Ray 1913-1965 *NatCAB 50*
Arnold, George *NewYHSD*
Arnold, George 1834-1865 *ApCAB, DcAmB,*
Drake, NatCAB 9, TwCBDA, WhAm H

Arnold, George G *NewYHSD*
Arnold, George Stanleigh 1881-1942 *WhAm 1,*
WhAm 2
Arnold, Grace Louise Russell *WomWWA 14*
Arnold, Harold DeForest 1883-1933 *DcAmB S1,*
DcScB, NatCAB 25, WhAm 1
Arnold, Harriet Pritchard 1858- *AmWom*
Arnold, Harry Wayne 1902-1963 *WhAm 4*
Arnold, Hazen S 1901-1953 *WhAm 3*
Arnold, Henry Harley 1886-1950 *DcAmB S4,*
McGEWB, NatCAB 45, WebAB,
WebAMB, WhAm 2, WhWW-II,
WhoMilH
Arnold, Henry J 1887-1959 *NatCAB 48,*
WhAm 3
Arnold, Horace David 1862-1935 *WhAm 2*
Arnold, Howard Payson 1831-1910 *WhAm 1*
Arnold, Isaac Newton 1813-1884 *NatCAB 11*
Arnold, Isaac Newton 1815-1884 *AmBi,*
ApCAB, BiAUS, BiDrAC, DcAmB,
Drake, TwCBDA, WhAm H, WhAmP
Arnold, J 1827?- *NewYHSD*
Arnold, J J G *NewYHSD*
Arnold, James E 1895-1971 *WhAm 5*
Arnold, James Loring 1868-1935 *WhAm 1*
Arnold, James M d1898 *NatCAB 5*
Arnold, James Newell 1844- *WhAm 4*
Arnold, Sir James Robertson 1780-1854 *ApCAB,*
Drake
Arnold, John, Jr. 1831-1886 *WhAm H*
Arnold, John A 1890-1973 *WhAm 6*
Arnold, John Anderson 1907-1963 *NatCAB 50,*
WhAm 4
Arnold, John Carlisle 1887-1958 *NatCAB 48,*
WhAm 3
Arnold, John Hampton 1921-1972 *NatCAB 57,*
WhAm 6
Arnold, John Himes 1839- *WhAm 4*
Arnold, John Jacob 1870-1933 *WhAm 1*
Arnold, John James Trumbull *NewYHSD*
Arnold, John Knowlton 1834-1909 *NewYHSD*
Arnold, Jonathan 1741-1793 *BiDrAC, DcAmB,*
NatCAB 13, WhAm H, WhAmP
Arnold, Jonathan 1741-1798 *ApCAB, BiAUS,*
Drake, TwCBDA
Arnold, Joseph Addison 1857- *WhAm 4*
Arnold, Joseph Leon 1903-1953 *NatCAB 42*
Arnold, Josiah Lyndon 1768-1796 *Drake*
Arnold, Julean 1876- *WhAm 5*
Arnold, Julia Isabel *WomWWA 14*
Arnold, Julian Biddulph 1862- *WhAm 4*
Arnold, Kate Lewis 1887- *WomWWA 14*
Arnold, Lauren Briggs 1814-1888 *DcAmB,*
TwCBDA, WhAm H
Arnold, Laurence Fletcher 1891-1966 *BiDrAC,*
NatCAB 54, WhAm 4
Arnold, Lemuel Hastings 1792-1852 *ApCAB,*
BiAUS, BiDrAC, Drake, NatCAB 9,
TwCBDA, WhAm H, WhAmP
Arnold, Leslie Philip 1894-1961 *WhAm 4*
Arnold, Lewis G 1815-1871 *ApCAB,*
NatCAB 4, TwCBDA
Arnold, Lewis G 1816?-1871 *Drake*
Arnold, Lewis Golding 1817-1871 *DcAmB,*
WhAm H
Arnold, Lloyd 1888-1963 *NatCAB 51,*
WhAm 4
Arnold, Lois J 1904-1972 *WhAm 5*
Arnold, Louis George 1886-1965 *NatCAB 51*
Arnold, Lowry 1870-1933 *NatCAB 25*
Arnold, Lynn John 1864-1920 *WhAm 1*
Arnold, Margaret 1760-1804 *AmBi*
Arnold, Margaret Shippen 1751?-1834
NatCAB 7
Arnold, Marshall 1845-1913 *BiDrAC, WhAmP*
Arnold, Matthew 1822-1888 *McGEWB*
Arnold, Maurice 1865- *WhAm 4*
Arnold, Morris Allen 1866-1946 *NatCAB 35,*
WhAm 2
Arnold, Nason Henry 1847-1884 *NatCAB 16*
Arnold, Nathaniel Dowdy 1859-1928
NatCAB 23
Arnold, Newton Darling 1843-1916 *WhAm 1*
Arnold, Oliver 1726-1770 *NatCAB 9*
Arnold, Olney 1861-1916 *WhAm 1*
Arnold, Olney 1862-1917 *NatCAB 30*
Arnold, Orson Murray 1844-1923 *NatCAB 19*
Arnold, Oswald James 1873-1949 *NatCAB 42,*

Arnold, Peleg d1820 *BiAUS, Drake*
Arnold, Peleg 1751-1820 *BiDrAC, WhAm H,*
WhAmP
Arnold, Peleg 1752-1820 *ApCAB, NatCAB 4,*
TwCBDA
Arnold, Philip Sheridan 1891-1967 *NatCAB 53*
Arnold, Ralph 1875- *ApCAB X, WhAm 6*
Arnold, Remmie Leroy 1894-1971 *WhAm 5*
Arnold, Reuben 1833-1914 *NatCAB 7,*
NatCAB 16
Arnold, Reuben Rose 1868-1960 *WhAm 4*
Arnold, Richard 1828-1882 *ApCAB, DcAmB,*
Drake, NatCAB 4, TwCBDA, WhAm H
Arnold, Richard 1845- *TwCBDA, WhAm 4*
Arnold, Richard Dennis 1808-1876 *DcAmB,*
NatCAB 22, WhAm H, WhAmP
Arnold, Samuel 1806-1869 *BiAUS, BiDrAC,*
WhAm H
Arnold, Samuel 1838?-1906 *DcAmB*
Arnold, Samuel George 1806-1891 *NatCAB 9*
Arnold, Samuel Greene 1821-1880 *AmBi,*
ApCAB, BiAUS, BiDrAC, DcAmB,
Drake, NatCAB 13, TwCBDA, WhAm H,
WhAmP
Arnold, Samuel Tomlinson 1892-1956
NatCAB 46, WhAm 3
Arnold, Samuel Washington 1879-1961 *BiDrAC*
Arnold, Sarah Louise d1943 *WhAm 2,*
WomWWA 14
Arnold, Thomas 1795-1842 *McGEWB*
Arnold, Thomas Dickens 1798-1870 *ApCAB,*
BiAUS, BiDrAC, TwCBDA, WhAm H,
WhAmP
Arnold, Thomas Jackson 1845-1933 *WhAm 1*
Arnold, Thurman Wesley 1891-1969 *McGEWB,*
NatCAB 55, WebAB, WhAm 5
Arnold, Waldo Robert 1896-1946 *WhAm 2*
Arnold, Walter P 1902-1965 *WhAm 4*
Arnold, Warren Otis 1839-1910 *BiDrAC,*
TwCBDA
Arnold, Welcome 1745-1798 *NatCAB 9*
Arnold, William C d1955 *WhAm 3*
Arnold, William Campbell 1860-1925
NatCAB 20
Arnold, William Carlile 1851-1906 *BiDrAC*
Arnold, William Carlisle 1851-1906 *TwCBDA*
Arnold, William F 1898-1959 *WhAm 3*
Arnold, William Hendrick 1861-1946 *WhAm 2*
Arnold, William Joseph 1906-1966 *WhAm 4*
Arnold, William Richard 1881-1965 *WhAm 4*
Arnold, William Rosenzweig 1872-1929
WhAm 1
Arnold, William Searls 1811- *NatCAB 16*
Arnold, William Wright 1877-1957 *BiDrAC,*
WhAm 3, WhAmP
Arnold, Winifred 1874- *WhAm 5,*
WomWWA 14
Arnoldson, Sigrid *WhAm 5*
Arnolfo DiCambio 1245?-1302 *McGEWB*
Arnolt, Frederick M 1886-1960 *NatCAB 49*
Arnot, David H *NewYHSD*
Arnot, John 1793-1873 *NatCAB 8*
Arnot, John 1831-1911 *BiDrAC, NatCAB 8*
Arnot, Philip Howard 1894-1974 *NatCAB 57*
Arnote, Walter James 1905-1965 *WhAm 5*
Arnoux, Campbell 1895-1966 *NatCAB 54*
Arnoux, William Henry 1831-1907 *WhAm 1*
Arnstein, Albert 1856- *WhAm 4*
Arnstein, Henry 1886-1935 *WhAm 1*
Arnstein, Karl 1887-1974 *WhAm 6*
Arnstein, Margaret G 1904-1972 *WhAm 5*
Arny, Clara Maude Brown 1888-1966 *BiDAmEd*
Arny, Henry Vinecome 1868-1943 *NatCAB 33,*
WhAm 2
Aromatari, Giuseppe Degli 1587-1660 *DcScB*
Aron, Albert William 1886-1945 *WhAm 2*
Aronhold, Siegfried Heinrich 1819-1884 *DcScB*
Aronoff, Jacob Broches 1896-1952 *NatCAB 42*
Aronovici, Carol 1881-1957 *NatCAB 45,*
WhAm 6
Aronowitz, Leon 1893-1969 *WhAm 5*
Aronson, Albert Y 1886-1957 *WhAm 4*
Aronson, David Klapp 1893-1957 *NatCAB 44*
Aronson, Jacob 1887-1951 *WhAm 3*
Aronson, Maurice 1869- *WhAm 5*
Aronson, Robert Louis 1907-1969 *WhAm 5*
Aronson, Rudolph 1856-1919 *WhAm 1*

Aronstam, Noah Ephraim 1872-1957 *WhAm 3*
Arosemena, Carlos C 1869-1946 *WhAm 2*
Arosemena, Justo 1817- *ApCAB*
Arouet, Francois-Marie *DcScB*
Arp, Bill *EncAAH, WebAB*
Arp, Jean 1887-1966 *McGEWB, WhAm 4*
Arpa Y Perea, Jose 1868?- *IlBEAAW*
Arpin, Paul 1811-1865 *ApCAB, Drake*
Arps, Bruno Frederick 1890-1965 *NatCAB 51*
Arps, George Frederick 1874-1939 *WhAm 1*
Arrascaeta, Enrique De 1819- *ApCAB*
Arrasmith, John W 1850- *WhAm 4*
Arrate, Jose Felix De 1697-1766 *ApCAB*
Arrel, George Francis 1840-1923 *NatCAB 19,*
WhAm 1
Arrest, Heinrich Louis D' 1822-1875 *DcScB*
Arrhenius, Svante August 1859-1927 *AsBiEn,*
DcScB, McGEWB
Arriaga, Pablo Jose 1562- *ApCAB*
Arricitiva, Juan *WhAm H*
Arrighi, Antonio Andrea 1835- *WhAm 4*
Arrillaga, Jose Joaquin 1750-1814 *ApCAB*
Arrington, Alfred W 1810-1867 *ApCAB,*
BiAUS, DcAmB, Drake, TwCBDA,
WhAm H
Arrington, Archibald Hunter 1809-1872
BiDConf, BiDrAC, WhAm H
Arrington, H Archibald 1809-1872 *BiAUS*
Arrington, John White, Jr. 1890-1956
NatCAB 46
Arrington, Kenneth Barton 1908-1970 *WhAm 5*
Arrington, Leonard James 1917- *EncAAH,*
REnAW
Arrington, Richard Olney 1897-1963
NatCAB 50, WhAm 4
Arrington, Roscoe Conklin 1881-1952
NatCAB 41
Arriola, Fortunato 1827-1872 *IlBEAAW,*
NewYHSD
Arrow, Kenneth Joseph 1921- *WebAB*
Arrowood, Charles Flinn 1887-1951 *NatCAB 40,*
WhAm 3
Arrowsmith, Harold Noel 1886-1955
NatCAB 47
Arrowsmith, Leighton Macdonald 1887-1961
NatCAB 50
Arrowsmith, Robert 1860-1928 *NatCAB 24,*
WhAm 1
Arrowsmith, Thomas VanBrackle 1866-1946
NatCAB 35
Arroyo DelRio, Carlos d1969 *WhAm 5*
Arrue DeMiranda, Luz 1852- *ApCAB*
Arscott, A E 1889-1951 *WhAm 3*
Arsonval, Arsene D' 1851-1940 *DcScB*
Artaguette *ApCAB*
Arteaga, Jose Maria 1830-1865 *ApCAB*
Arteaga, Sebastian De *ApCAB*
Artedi, Peter 1705-1735 *DcScB*
Arter, Charles Kingsley 1875- *WhAm 5*
Arter, Frank Asbury 1841-1928 *ApCAB X,*
WhAm 4
Arter, Jared Mawrice 1850- *WhoColR*
Arters, John Manley 1877-1943 *WhAm 3*
Arthur, Alfred 1844-1918 *NatCAB 12,*
WhAm 1
Arthur, Alfred Franklin 1876-1938 *WhAm 1*
Arthur, Chester Alan 1829-1886 *EncAB,*
WebAB
Arthur, Chester Alan 1830-1886 *AmBi,*
ApCAB, BiDrAC, BiDrUSE, DcAmB,
EncAAH, McGEWB, NatCAB 4,
TwCBDA, WhAm H, WhAmP
Arthur, Chester Alan, II 1864-1937 *NatCAB 28*
Arthur, Clara B 1859- *WomWWA 14*
Arthur, Clara Blanche 1858- *NatCAB 17*
Arthur, Mrs. Daniel V *WomWWA 14*
Arthur, Ellen Lewis Herndon 1837-1880 *NotAW*
Arthur, Franklin Kilnore, Jr. 1910-1974
WhAm 6
Arthur, Gabriel *REnAW*
Arthur, Sir George 1784-1854 *ApCAB, Drake*
Arthur, Harold John 1904-1971 *NatCAB 57,*
WhAm 5
Arthur, Helen 1879- *WomWWA 14*
Arthur, James 1842-1930 *NatCAB 31*
Arthur, James B McKee 1886-1963 *WhAm 4*
Arthur, John H V *NewYHSD*

Arthur, John Morris 1893-1975 *WhAm 6*
Arthur, Joseph Charles 1850-1942 *DcAmB S3,*
  NatCAB 12, WhAm 2
Arthur, Julia 1869-1950 *ApCAB X,*
  NatCAB 10, NotAW, WhAm 5
Arthur, Paul Harrison 1894-1962 *WhAm 4*
Arthur, Peter M 1831-1903 *DcAmB, TwCBDA,*
  WhAm 1
Arthur, Thomas 1860-1925 *NatCAB 20,*
  WhAm 1
Arthur, Timothy Shay 1809-1885 *AmBi,*
  ApCAB, DcAmB, Drake, NatCAB 8,
  TwCBDA, WebAB, WhAm H
Arthur, W C 1885-1967 *WhAm 5*
Arthur, W H *NewYHSD*
Arthur, William 1796-1875 *ApCAB*
Arthur, William 1797-1875 *DcAmB, WhAm H*
Arthur, William Evans 1825-1897 *BiAUS,*
  BiDrAC, WhAm H
Arthur, William Hemple 1856-1936 *WhAm 1*
Arthur, William Reed 1876- *WhAm 6*
Arthurs, Biddle 1866-1938 *NatCAB 31*
Arthurs, Stanley Massey 1877-1950 *IIBEAAW,*
  WhAm 3
Arthurs, Walter Clifford 1864-1928 *NatCAB 22*
Artigas, Jose 1755-1851 *ApCAB*
Artigas, Jose 1760?-1825 *Drake*
Artigas, Jose Gervasio 1764-1850 *McGEWB*
Artin, Emil 1898-1962 *DcScB, WhAm 4*
Artis, Dillard 1868- *WhoColR*
Artman, Enos Reeser 1838-1912 *NatCAB 18*
Artois, Mister *NewYHSD*
Artom, Camilio 1893-1970 *WhAm 5*
Artom, Camillo 1893-1970 *NatCAB 55*
Artom, Eugenio 1896-1975 *WhAm 6*
Artsimovich, Lev Andreevich 1909-1973
  DcScB Sup
Artzybasheff, Boris 1899-1965 *WhAm 4*
Arundell, Charles Rogers 1885-1968
  NatCAB 54, WhAm 5
Arvelo, Rafael 1814-1870? *ApCAB*
Arvin, Newton 1900-1963 *WhAm 4*
Arvine, Earlliss Porter 1846-1914 *WhAm 1*
Ary, Henry 1802?-1859 *NewYHSD, WhAm H*
Ary, Lester Clyde 1893-1962 *NatCAB 50*
Aryabhata I 476- *DcScB*
Aryabhata II *DcScB*
Arzachel *DcScB*
Arzao, Antonio Rodriguez *ApCAB*
Arzt, Franz Joseph 1843-1923 *NatCAB 21*
Arzt, Philip Garfield 1881-1960 *NatCAB 48*
Asada, Goryu 1734-1799 *DcScB*
Asah, Spencer 1907?-1954 *IIBEAAW*
Asakawa, Kwan-Ichi 1873-1948 *WhAm 2*
Asam, Cosmas Damian 1686-1739 *McGEWB*
Asam, Egid Quirin 1692-1750 *McGEWB*
Asboth, Alexander Sandor 1811-1868 *ApCAB,*
  BiAUS, DcAmB, Drake, NatCAB 4,
  TwCBDA, WhAm H
Asbury, Dorsey Frost 1877-1936 *NatCAB 27*
Asbury, Francis 1745-1816 *AmBi, ApCAB,*
  DcAmB, DcAmReB, Drake, McGEWB,
  NatCAB 6, TwCBDA, WebAB,
  WhAm H
Asbury, Herbert 1891-1963 *WhAm 4*
Asbury, Wilbur Francis 1911-1972 *WhAm 6*
Ascension, Antonio DeLa 1560-1623
  ApCAB Sup
Asch, Morris Joseph 1833-1902 *DcAmB,*
  WhAm H
Asch, Nathan 1902-1964 *WhAm 4*
Asch, Shalom 1880-1957 *McGEWB*
Asch, Sholem 1880-1957 *NatCAB 48,*
  WhAm 3
Ascham, John Bayne 1873-1950 *WhAm 3*
Ascher, Abraham Harry 1906-1973 *WhAm 6*
Ascher, Hans Albert 1895-1972 *WhAm 5*
Aschman, Frederick Theodor 1918-1971
  NatCAB 57
Aschner, Bernard 1883-1960 *NatCAB 49*
Aschoff, Ludwig 1866-1942 *BiHiMed*
Asclepiades 130?BC-040?BC *DcScB*
Asdale, William James *WhAm 5*
Aselli, Gaspare 1581-1625 *DcScB*
Aselli, Gaspare 1581-1626 *BiHiMed*
Aseltine, Walter Morley 1886-1971 *WhAm 5*
Asgill, Sir Charles 1762-1823 *ApCAB, Drake*
Ash, Charles 1857-1954 *NatCAB 43*

Ash, Josephine Wharton *WomWWA 14*
Ash, Louis Russell 1873-1930 *WhAm 1*
Ash, Michael Woolston 1789-1858 *BiAUS,*
  BiDrAC, WhAmP
Ash, Nichael Woolston 1789-1858 *WhAm H*
Ash, Percy 1865-1933 *WhAm 1*
Ashari, Abu Al-Hasan Ali, Al- 873?-935
  McGEWB
Ashbaugh, Delphine Dodge 1868-
  WomWWA 14
Ashbridge, Samuel H 1849-1906 *WhAm 1*
Ashbrook, Ernest Shepardson 1879-1956
  WhAm 3
Ashbrook, John Milan 1928- *BiDrAC*
Ashbrook, M Forest 1896-1968 *WhAm 5*
Ashbrook, William Albert 1867-1940 *BiDrAC,*
  WhAm 1, WhAmP
Ashburn, George W d1868 *ApCAB,*
  NatCAB 4, TwCBDA
Ashburn, Percy Moreau 1872-1940 *WhAm 1*
Ashburn, Thomas Quinn 1874-1941 *NatCAB 30,*
  WhAm 1
Ashburner, Charles Albert 1854-1889 *ApCAB,*
  DcAmB, NatCAB 11, TwCBDA,
  WhAm H
Ashburner, Charles Edward 1870-1932 *WebAB*
Ashburner, William 1831-1888 *ApCAB Sup*
Ashburton, Baron 1774-1848 *WhAm H*
Ashburton, Lord Alexander Baring 1774-1848
  ApCAB, Drake
Ashby, Darrel Leroy 1938- *EncAAH*
Ashby, George Franklin 1885-1950 *WhAm 3*
Ashby, Samuel 1868-1943 *NatCAB 32,*
  WhAm 2
Ashby, Thomas Almond 1848-1916 *NatCAB 33,*
  WhAm 4
Ashby, Thompson Eldridge 1883-1953
  NatCAB 41
Ashby, Turner 1824-1862 *ApCAB, Drake,*
  NatCAB 4
Ashby, Turner 1828-1862 *BiDConf, DcAmB,*
  TwCBDA, WhAm H, WhoMilH
Ashby, Winifred Mayer 1879- *WhAm 6*
Ashcraft, Lee 1871-1953 *WhAm 3*
Ashcraft, Leon Thomas 1866-1945 *WhAm 2*
Ashcraft, Mary Cosby Lewis 1878-
  WomWWA 14
Ashcraft, Raymond Moore 1876-1946
  NatCAB 41
Ashcraft, Thomas 1786-1866 *BiDConf*
Ashcroft, Harriet Elizabeth *WomWWA 14*
Ashcroft, Thomas Calvin 1866-1935
  NatCAB 33
Ashdown, Cecil S 1875- *ApCAB X*
Ashe, Arthur Robert, Jr. 1943- *WebAB*
Ashe, Bowman Foster 1885-1952 *NatCAB 41,*
  WhAm 3
Ashe, Edmund Marion 1870- *WhAm 5*
Ashe, Edward Joseph 1889-1968 *WhAm 5*
Ashe, George B 1891-1971 *WhAm 5*
Ashe, John 1720?-1781 *AmBi, ApCAB,*
  DcAmB, NatCAB 6, TwCBDA,
  WebAMB, WhAm H, WhAmP
Ashe, John 1721-1781 *Drake*
Ashe, John Baptista 1748-1802 *ApCAB,*
  BiDrAC, DcAmB, WhAm H, WhAmP
Ashe, John Baptista 1810-1857 *BiAUS,*
  BiDrAC, DcAmB, WhAm H, WhAmP
Ashe, John Baptiste 1748-1802 *BiAUS, Drake,*
  TwCBDA
Ashe, Ragon 1889-1947 *NatCAB 37*
Ashe, Robert Sherman 1868-1946 *NatCAB 36*
Ashe, Samuel 1725-1813 *ApCAB, BiAUS,*
  DcAmB, Drake, NatCAB 4, TwCBDA,
  WhAm H, WhAmP
Ashe, Samuel 1763-1834 *Drake*
Ashe, Samuel A'Court 1840-1938 *NatCAB 28,*
  TwCBDA, WhAm 1
Ashe, Thomas *ApCAB, Drake*
Ashe, Thomas 1770-1835 *ApCAB, Drake*
Ashe, Thomas Samuel 1812-1887 *BiAUS,*
  BiDConf, BiDrAC, DcAmB, NatCAB 7,
  WhAm H, WhAmP
Ashe, William A *NewYHSD*
Ashe, William Francis, Jr. 1909-1966 *WhAm 4*
Ashe, William S d1864 *BiAUS*
Ashe, William Sheppard 1813-1862 *BiDConf*
Ashe, William Shepperd 1813-1862 *BiDrAC,*

WhAmP
Ashe, William Shepperd 1814-1862 *DcAmB,*
  WhAm H
Ashely, James Mitchell 1824-1896 *BiAUS*
Ashely, Ossian Doolittle 1821-1904 *WhAm 1*
Ashenfelter, Nettie Bennett 1852-
  WomWWA 14
Asher, Joseph Mayor 1872-1909 *DcAmB*
Asher, Louis Eller 1877-1948 *NatCAB 38*
Asher, Walter Simpson 1872-1946 *NatCAB 34*
Asherman, Edward Goodwin 1913-1969
  NatCAB 55
Ashford, Bailey Kelly 1873-1934 *DcAmB S1,*
  WebAMB, WhAm 1
Ashford, Charles Hall 1902-1967 *NatCAB 55*
Ashford, Emma Louise 1850-1930 *WhAm 1*
Ashford, Hallie Quillian 1879- *WomWWA 14*
Ashford, Mahlon 1881- *WhAm 3*
Ashhurst, Astley Paston Cooper 1876-1932
  NatCAB 33, WhAm 1, WhAm 1C
Ashhurst, John 1839-1900 *ApCAB Sup,*
  DcAmB, TwCBDA, WhAm 1
Ashhurst, John 1865-1932 *WhAm 1*
Ashhurst, Richard Lewis 1838-1911 *WhAm 1*
Ashhurst, Sarah Wayne 1874- *WomWWA 14*
Ashikaga, Takauji 1305-1358 *McGEWB*
Ashkenaz, David Morton 1908-1964
  NatCAB 51
Ashley, Barnes Freeman 1833- *WhAm 4*
Ashley, Charles Sumner 1858-1941 *NatCAB 40,*
  WhAm 1
Ashley, Chester 1790-1848 *ApCAB, BiAUS,*
  BiDrAC, NatCAB 7, TwCBDA,
  WhAm H
Ashley, Clarence Degrand 1851-1916
  NatCAB 7, WhAm 1
Ashley, Clifford Warren 1881-1947 *ApCAB X,*
  NatCAB 37, WhAm 2
Ashley, Daniel W 1894-1947 *WhAm 2*
Ashley, Delos Rodeyn 1828-1873 *BiAUS,*
  BiDrAC, WhAm H
Ashley, Douglas Vanneman 1881-1928
  NatCAB 22
Ashley, Edward 1854-1931 *WhAm 1*
Ashley, Edward Everett 1883-1958 *NatCAB 48*
Ashley, Frank Merwin 1867-1942 *NatCAB 32*
Ashley, Frederick William 1863-1943 *WhAm 3*
Ashley, George Hall 1866-1951 *WhAm 3*
Ashley, Henry 1778-1829 *BiAUS, BiDrAC,*
  WhAm H
Ashley, Herbert Henry 1843-1923 *NatCAB 19*
Ashley, James Mitchell 1822-1896 *NatCAB 11*
Ashley, James Mitchell 1824-1896 *AmBi,*
  BiDrAC, DcAmB, WhAm H, WhAmP
Ashley, James Monroe 1824-1896 *ApCAB,*
  TwCBDA
Ashley, Jessie d1919 *BiCAW, WomWWA 14*
Ashley, John d1799 *Drake*
Ashley, John Pritchard 1862- *NatCAB 13,*
  TwCBDA, WhAm 1
Ashley, Jonathan 1713-1787 *Drake*
Ashley, Maurice C 1863- *WhAm 4*
Ashley, Ossian Doolittle 1821-1904 *NatCAB 7*
Ashley, Roscoe Lewis 1872-1965 *WhAm 4*
Ashley, Samuel Stanford 1819-1887 *BiDAmEd*
Ashley, Schuyler 1897-1927 *NatCAB 21*
Ashley, Solomon *NewYHSD*
Ashley, Susan Riley 1840- *WomWWA 14*
Ashley, Thomas William Ludlow 1923- *BiDrAC*
Ashley, William Henry 1778-1838 *AmBi,*
  ApCAB, BiAUS, BiDrAC, DcAmB,
  Drake, EncAB, McGEWB, REnAW,
  TwCBDA, WebAB, WhAm H, WhAmP
Ashman, James Ernest 1902-1973 *WhAm 6*
Ashmead, Henry Graham 1838- *NatCAB 4*
Ashmead, Isaac 1790-1870 *ApCAB, DcAmB,*
  Drake, WhAm H
Ashmead, William Harris 1855-1908 *AmBi,*
  DcAmB, NatCAB 20, WhAm 1
Ashmole, Elias 1617-1692 *DcScB*
Ashmore, Frank Leon 1925-1973 *WhAm 6*
Ashmore, John Durant 1819-1871 *BiAUS,*
  BiDrAC, WhAm H
Ashmore, Otis 1853- *WhAm 4*
Ashmore, Robert Thomas 1904- *BiDrAC,*
  WhAmP
Ashmore, Sidney Gillespie 1852-1911 *WhAm 1*
Ashmore, William 1824-1909 *DcAmB,*

NatCAB 25, WhAm HA

Ashmore, William 1851- *WhAm 4*

Ashmun, Eli Porter d1819 *BiAUS*

Ashmun, Eli Porter 1770-1819 *ApCAB, BiDrAC, Drake, TwCBDA, WhAm H, WhAmP*

Ashmun, Eli Porter 1771-1819 *NatCAB 11*

Ashmun, George 1804-1870 *ApCAB, BiAUS, BiDrAC, DcAmB, Drake, NatCAB 6, TwCBDA, WhAm H, WhAmP*

Ashmun, George Coates 1841-1929 *WhAm 1*

Ashmun, Jehudi 1794-1828 *AmBi, ApCAB, DcAmB, Drake, McGEWB, NatCAB 6, TwCBDA, WebAB, WhAm H*

Ashmun, John Hooker 1800-1833 *ApCAB, Drake*

Ashmun, Margaret Eliza d1940 *WhAm 1, WhAm 1C*

Ashton, Albert A 1908-1975 *WhAm 6*

Ashton, Auto *NewYHSD*

Ashton, Dorothy Laing 1888-1958 *NatCAB 49*

Ashton, Eve 1898-1962 *WhAm 4*

Ashton, Frederick Turner 1884-1959 *NatCAB 48*

Ashton, Henry Rusling 1898-1970 *WhAm 5*

Ashton, John 1742-1814? *WhAm H*

Ashton, John 1880-1952 *WhAm 4*

Ashton, John William 1900-1971 *WhAm 5*

Ashton, Joseph Huberly 1836-1907 *BiAUS*

Ashton, Joseph Hubley 1836-1907 *WhAm 1*

Ashton, Leonard Capron 1887-1956 *NatCAB 49*

Ashton, Raymond J d1973 *WhAm 6*

Ashton, Thomas B *NewYHSD*

Ashton, Thomas George 1866-1933 *NatCAB 24*

Ashton, William 1860- *WhAm 4*

Ashton, William Easterly 1859-1933 *WhAm 1, WhAm 1C*

Ashton, William H *NewYHSD*

Ashton, Winifred d1965 *WhAm 4*

Ashurbanipal d630?BC *McGEWB*

Ashurst, Henry Fountain 1874-1962 *BiDrAC, NatCAB 15, WhAm 4, WhAmP*

Ashway, Jerry Nicholas 1901-1973 *NatCAB 57*

Ashway, Benjamin Harrison 1888-1952 *NatCAB 46*

Ashworth, Hattie Tiller 1904-1970 *WhAm 5*

Ashworth, John H 1879-1942 *WhAm 2*

Ashworth, Robert Archibald 1871-1959 *WhAm 3*

Ashworth, Walter C 1868- *WhAm 4*

Asiel, Nelson Irving 1886-1965 *NatCAB 51*

Asimov, Isaac 1920- *AsBiEn, WebAB*

Askam, John Charles 1894-1957 *NatCAB 44*

Askenstedt, Fritz Conrad 1865-1943 *WhAm 2*

Askew, Elisabeth *WomWWA 14*

Askew, Ralph Kirk, Jr. 1903-1974 *WhAm 6*

Askew, Sarah Byrd d1942 *WhAm 2*

Askew, Sarah Byrd 1863-1942 *DcAmLiB*

Askew, Sarah Byrd 1877-1942 *NotAW*

Askew, Thyrza Simonton 1879- *WhAm 3*

Askey, Edwin Vincent 1895-1974 *WhAm 6*

Askin, Robert J 1898-1961 *WhAm 4*

Askren, William David 1885-1964 *WhAm 4*

Askwig, Jenny Keogh 1866- *WomWWA 14*

Asman, Bernard 1872-1969 *NatCAB 56*

Asmar, Alice 1929- *IlBEAAW*

Asoka *McGEWB*

Aspegren, John 1876-1924 *ApCAB X, WhAm 1*

Aspell, R C *NewYHSD*

Asper, Joel Funk 1822-1872 *ApCAB, BiAUS, BiDrAC, WhAm H*

Aspinall, Joseph d1939 *WhAm 1*

Aspinall, Richard 1881- *WhAm 6*

Aspinall, Wayne Norviel 1896- *BiDrAC*

Aspinwall, Alicia Stuart *WomWWA 14*

Aspinwall, Clarence Aikin 1874-1964 *WhAm 4*

Aspinwall, Glenn William 1898-1970 *WhAm 5*

Aspinwall, Horatio G *NewYHSD*

Aspinwall, J Lawrence 1854- *WhAm 4*

Aspinwall, Lloyd 1830-1886 *ApCAB*

Aspinwall, Thomas 1784-1876 *Drake*

Aspinwall, Thomas 1786-1876 *ApCAB*

Aspinwall, Thomas 1853-1918 *WhAm 1*

Aspinwall, William 1743-1823 *ApCAB, DcAmB, Drake, NatCAB 11, WhAm H*

Aspinwall, William Billings 1874-1955 *NatCAB 44, WhAm 3*

Aspinwall, William Henry 1807-1875 *AmBi, ApCAB, DcAmB, NatCAB 8, TwCBDA, WhAm H*

Aspirol, Manuel De 1836- *ApCAB Sup*

Asplund, Eric Gunnar 1885-1945 *McGEWB*

Asplund, Julia Duncan Brown 1875- *WomWWA 14*

Asplund, Rupert Franz 1875-1952 *WhAm 3*

Asplundh, Carl Hjalmar 1903-1967 *NatCAB 55*

Asplundh, E T 1888-1975 *WhAm 6*

Asquith, Anthony 1902-1968 *WhAm 5*

Asquith, Herbert Henry, Earl Of Oxford 1852-1928 *McGEWB*

Assalti, Pietro 1680-1728 *DcScB*

Asserson, Henry Raymond 1867-1936 *NatCAB 28*

Asserson, Peter Christian 1839-1906 *NatCAB 28*

Assing, Norman *REnAW*

Assmann, Franz August 1853-1936 *NatCAB 38*

Assmuth, Joseph 1871-1954 *WhAm 3*

Assum, Arthur Louis 1917-1970 *WhAm 6*

Ast, Adolph 1890-1928 *ApCAB X*

Astaire, Fred 1899- *WebAB*

Astaurov, Boris Lvovich 1904-1974 *WhAm 6*

Astbury, William Thomas 1898-1961 *DcScB*

Astie, Jean Frederic 1822- *ApCAB Sup*

Astley, G Mason 1882-1954 *NatCAB 42*

Aston, Anthony 1701-1730 *WhAm H*

Aston, Francis William 1877-1945 *AsBiEn, DcScB, McGEWB*

Aston, James 1876-1962 *WhAm 4*

Aston, Ralph 1841-1904 *WhAm 1*

Aston, Richard Douglas 1901-1973 *WhAm 5*

Aston, Mrs. Samuel 1873- *WomWWA 14*

Astor, Viscountess d1964 *WhAm 4*

Astor, Caroline Webster Schermerhorn 1830-1908 *NotAW*

Astor, Charlotte Augusta 1825-1887 *ApCAB Sup*

Astor, John Jacob 1763-1848 *AmBi, ApCAB, DcAmB, Drake, EncAB, McGEWB, NatCAB 8, REnAW, TwCBDA, WebAB, WhAm H*

Astor, John Jacob 1822-1890 *AmBi, ApCAB Sup, DcAmB, NatCAB 8, TwCBDA, WhAm H, WhAmP*

Astor, John Jacob 1864-1912 *AmBi, ApCAB Sup, DcAmB, NatCAB 8, TwCBDA, WhAm 1*

Astor, William 1829-1892 *NatCAB 8*

Astor, William 1830-1892 *TwCBDA*

Astor, William Backhouse 1792-1875 *AmBi, ApCAB, DcAmB, NatCAB 8, TwCBDA, WhAm H*

Astor, William Vincent 1891-1959 *NatCAB 47, WhAm 3, WhAmP*

Astor, William Waldorf 1848-1919 *AmBi, ApCAB, DcAmB, NatCAB 8, TwCBDA, WhAm 1*

Astor Of Hever, Baron 1886-1971 *WhAm 5*

Astrop, Robert Collins 1891-1948 *NatCAB 37*

Astruc, Jean 1684-1766 *BiHiMed, DcScB*

Asturias, Miguel Angel 1899-1974 *McGEWB, WhAm 6*

Aswell, Edward C 1900-1958 *WhAm 3*

Aswell, James Benjamin 1869-1931 *BiDAmEd, BiDrAC, WhAm 1, WhAmP*

Atahualpa 1502-1533 *ApCAB, Drake, McGEWB, WhoMilH*

Ataturk 1881-1938 *WhoMilH*

Ataturk, Ghazi Mustapha Kemal 1881-1938 *McGEWB*

Atcheson, George, Jr. 1896-1947 *NatCAB 36, WhAm 2*

Atcheson, John Franklin 1854-1915 *NatCAB 17*

Atchison, David Rice 1807-1886 *AmBi, ApCAB, BiAUS, BiDrAC, DcAmB, Drake, EncAAH, McGEWB, NatCAB 10, REnAW, TwCBDA, WebAB, WhAm H, WhAmP*

Atchison, Thomas Cunningham 1855-1940 *WhAm 1*

Atchley, James Franklin 1880-1968 *NatCAB 54*

Atempanectl *ApCAB*

Aten, Fred N 1885-1951 *WhAm 3*

Aten, Mae E Greene *WomWWA 14*

Aten, William Banta 1885-1965 *NatCAB 51*

Atencio, Gilbert Benjamin 1930- *IlBEAAW*

Atha, Henry George 1902-1953 *NatCAB 45*

Athanasius, Saint 296?-373 *McGEWB*

Athearn, Fred Goodrich 1874-1956 *WhAm 3*

Athearn, Robert Greenleaf 1914- *EncAAH, REnAW*

Athearn, Walter Scott 1872-1934 *NatCAB 27, WhAm 1*

Athenaeus Of Attalia *DcScB*

Athenagoras, His All Holiness 1896-1972 *WhAm 5*

Atherton, Caroline Ober Stone 1863- *WomWWA 14*

Atherton, Charles Gordon 1804-1853 *ApCAB, BiAUS, BiDrAC, DcAmB, Drake, NatCAB 10, TwCBDA, WhAm H, WhAmP*

Atherton, Charles Humphrey 1773-1853 *ApCAB, BiAUS, BiDrAC, Drake, NatCAB 11, WhAm H*

Atherton, Edwin Newton 1896-1944 *WhAm 2*

Atherton, Ella Blaylock 1860- *WomWWA 14*

Atherton, Ezra *NewYHSD*

Atherton, Frank Cooke 1877-1945 *NatCAB 37, WhAm 2*

Atherton, Frederic 1865-1936 *NatCAB 28*

Atherton, George Washington 1837-1906 *BiDAmEd, DcAmB, NatCAB 20, TwCBDA, WhAm 1*

Atherton, Gertrude Franklin *TwCBDA, WomWWA 14*

Atherton, Gertrude Franklin 1850?- *ApCAB Sup*

Atherton, Gertrude Franklin 1857-1948 *DcAmB S4, NatCAB 36, NotAW, REnAW, WhAm 2*

Atherton, Gertrude Franklin 1859-1948 *ApCAB X, NatCAB 10*

Atherton, Gibson 1831-1887 *BiDrAC, WhAm H*

Atherton, Henry Francis 1883-1949 *WhAm 2*

Atherton, Humphrey d1661 *ApCAB, Drake*

Atherton, J William 1891-1967 *NatCAB 53*

Atherton, John C 1900-1952 *WhAm 3*

Atherton, Joseph Ballard 1837-1903 *NatCAB 17*

Atherton, Joseph Ballard 1910-1962 *WhAm 4*

Atherton, Joshua 1737-1809 *ApCAB, DcAmB, Drake, NatCAB 3, WhAm H, WhAmP*

Atherton, LeBaron 1863- *ApCAB X*

Atherton, Lewis E 1905- *EncAAH, REnAW*

Atherton, Louis Morse 1878-1950 *NatCAB 38, WhAm 3*

Atherton, Mary Alderson Chandler 1849- *NatCAB 18*

Atherton, Melanie 1857- *WomWWA 14*

Atherton, Percy Lee 1871-1944 *NatCAB 17, NatCAB 33, WhAm 2*

Atherton, Ray 1883-1960 *WhAm 3A*

Atherton, Walter 1863-1945 *NatCAB 33*

Athey, George Washington 1898-1959 *NatCAB 48*

Athlone, Godard VanReede, Earl Of 1644-1703 *WhoMilH*

Atkenson, Peter *NewYHSD*

Atkeson, Clarence Lee Conner 1899-1975 *WhAm 6*

Atkeson, Floyd Warnick 1893-1958 *WhAm 3*

Atkeson, Thomas Clark 1852-1935 *WhAm 1*

Atkeson, William Oscar 1854-1931 *BiDrAC*

Atkeson, William Oscar 1854-1932 *WhAm 2*

Atkielski, Roman R 1898-1969 *WhAm 5*

Atkin, Edmund 1707-1761 *REnAW*

Atkin, Isaac Cubitt Raymond 1892-1957 *WhAm 3*

Atkin, James 1832?- *NewYHSD*

Atkin, Mildred Tommy 1903-1969 *NatCAB 53*

Atkins, A Raymond 1898-1968 *NatCAB 54*

Atkins, Albert Henry d1951 *WhAm 3*

Atkins, Mrs. Albert L 1865- *WomWWA 14*

Atkins, Arthur d1966 *WhAm 4*

Atkins, Arthur Kennedy 1881- *WhAm 6*

Atkins, Charles Duke 1876-1964 *WhAm 4*

Atkins, Edwin Farnsworth 1850-1926 *ApCAB X, NatCAB 16, WhAm 1*

Atkins, Elias Cornelius 1833-1901 *NatCAB 13, NatCAB 16*

Atkins, Gaius Glenn 1868-1956 *NatCAB 45*

Atkins, George Tyng 1878-1945 *WhAm 2*
Atkins, George Washington Ely 1850-
 NatCAB 14, *WhAm 4*
Atkins, Harry T 1849-1919 *WhAm 1*
Atkins, Harry Thomas 1910-1970 *WhAm 5*
Atkins, Henry *ApCAB*
Atkins, Henry Cornelius 1868-1944 *NatCAB 33*
Atkins, Henry Hornby 1939- *WhAm 5*
Atkins, Henry Skillman 1867-1918 *NatCAB 18*
Atkins, James 1850-1923 *NatCAB 14,*
 WhAm 1
Atkins, Jearum *DcAmB,* *WhAm H*
Atkins, John DeWitt Clinton 1825-1908 *BiAUS,*
 BiDConf, BiDrAC, WhAm 1, WhAmP
Atkins, Joseph Alexander 1879- *WhAm 6*
Atkins, Joseph Preston 1909-1974 *WhAm 6*
Atkins, Louise Allen d1953 *WhAm 3*
Atkins, Mary 1819-1882 *NotAW*
Atkins, Richard Lovell 1834-1928 *NatCAB 21*
Atkins, S G *WhoColR*
Atkins, Smith Dykins 1836-1913 *WhAm 1*
Atkins, Thomas *NewYHSD*
Atkins, Thomas V Dolivia 1877- *WhoColR*
Atkins, Willard Earl 1892-1971 *WhAm 5*
Atkinson, Mister *NewYHSD*
Atkinson, Albert Algernon 1867- *WhAm 5*
Atkinson, Albert Weist 1861-1929 *NatCAB 30*
Atkinson, Alfred 1879-1958 *BiDAmEd,*
 NatCAB 48
Atkinson, Alice Minerva *WomWWA 14*
Atkinson, Archibald 1792-1872 *BiAUS,*
 BiDrAC, WhAm H
Atkinson, Arthur Kimmins 1891-1964
 NatCAB 53, WhAm 4
Atkinson, Benjamin Searcy 1870-1948 *WhAm 3*
Atkinson, Brooks 1894- *WebAB*
Atkinson, Byron A 1854- *NatCAB 3*
Atkinson, Charles Edwin 1884-1960 *WhAm 4*
Atkinson, Charles R *WhAm 5*
Atkinson, Christopher Joseph 1858-1935
 WhAm 1
Atkinson, Donald Taylor 1874-1959 *NatCAB 48,*
 WhAm 3
Atkinson, Dorothy Bridgman 1890-
 WomWWA 14
Atkinson, Edward 1827-1905 *AmBi, ApCAB,*
 ApCAB Sup, DcAmB, EncAB,
 NatCAB 9, NatCAB 28, TwCBDA,
 WhAm 1
Atkinson, Edward Williams 1859-1940
 NatCAB 29
Atkinson, Eleanor d1942 *WhAm 2,*
 WomWWA 14
Atkinson, Elizabeth Bispham Page
 WomWWA 14
Atkinson, Florence Lewis *WomWWA 14*
Atkinson, Fred Washington 1865-1941
 NatCAB 34, WhAm 4
Atkinson, Frederick Grant 1864-1940
 NatCAB 30
Atkinson, Frederick Melville 1914-1961
 NatCAB 49
Atkinson, Geoffroy 1892-1960 *NatCAB 46*
Atkinson, Geoffroy 1892-1961 *WhAm 4*
Atkinson, George Francis 1854-1918 *ApCAB X,*
 DcAmB, NatCAB 13, WhAm 1
Atkinson, George Henry 1819-1889 *BiDAmEd,*
 DcAmB, NatCAB 6, WhAm H
Atkinson, George Wesley 1845-1925 *ApCAB X,*
 BiDrAC, DcAmB, NatCAB 12, TwCBDA,
 WhAm 1, WhAmP
Atkinson, Guy F 1875-1968 *WhAm 5*
Atkinson, Harry Hunt 1881-1968 *WhAm 5*
Atkinson, Henry 1782-1842 *ApCAB, DcAmB,*
 Drake, NatCAB 11, REnAW, WebAB,
 WebAMB, WhAm H
Atkinson, Henry Aaron 1845-1914 *NatCAB 16*
Atkinson, Henry Avery 1877-1960 *NatCAB 44,*
 WhAm 3
Atkinson, Henry M 1838- *BiAUS, NatCAB 12*
Atkinson, Henry Morrell 1862-1939 *NatCAB 5,*
 WhAm 1
Atkinson, Herbert Spencer 1887-1952 *WhAm 3*
Atkinson, Herschel C 1903-1966 *WhAm 4*
Atkinson, Isaac Edmondson 1846- *WhAm 1*
Atkinson, J Robert 1887-1964 *WhAm 4*
Atkinson, John 1835-1897 *ApCAB, DcAmB,*
 TwCBDA, WhAm H

Atkinson, John Bradshaw 1894-1965 *WhAm 4*
Atkinson, John Mayo Pleasants 1817-1883
 NatCAB 2
Atkinson, Joseph Story 1904-1968 *WhAm 5*
Atkinson, Justin Brooks *WebAB*
Atkinson, Louis Evans 1841-1910 *BiDrAC,*
 TwCBDA, WhAm 1, WhAmP
Atkinson, Mary B 1830?- *NewYHSD*
Atkinson, R M *NewYHSD*
Atkinson, Ralph 1871- *WhAm 2*
Atkinson, Ralph Waldo 1887-1961 *WhAm 4*
Atkinson, Richard Merrill 1894-1947 *BiDrAC,*
 WhAmP
Atkinson, Robert J *BiAUS*
Atkinson, Samuel Carter 1864-1942
 NatCAB 40, WhAm 2
Atkinson, Theodore 1697-1779 *BiAUS, Drake,*
 NatCAB 11
Atkinson, Theodore, Jr. 1737-1769 *Drake*
Atkinson, Thomas 1807-1881 *ApCAB, DcAmB,*
 NatCAB 6, TwCBDA, WhAm H
Atkinson, Thomas Edgar 1895-1960 *WhAm 4*
Atkinson, Thomas Wilson 1867-1933
 NatCAB 24, WhAm 1
Atkinson, Wade Hampton 1866-1942
 NatCAB 31
Atkinson, William Biddle 1832-1909 *DcAmB,*
 WhAm 4
Atkinson, William Brockliss 1918-1961
 WhAm 4
Atkinson, William Brockliss 1918-1962
 NatCAB 50
Atkinson, William DeBoice 1862-1945
 NatCAB 35
Atkinson, William E 1880-1940 *WhAm 1*
Atkinson, William Elrie 1852-1935 *NatCAB 5,*
 WhAm 1
Atkinson, William King 1764-1820 *Drake*
Atkinson, William Parsons 1820-1890 *TwCBDA*
Atkinson, William Sackston 1864- *WhAm 1*
Atkinson, William Walker 1862-1932 *WhAm 1*
Atkinson, William Yates 1854-1899 *DcAmB,*
 NatCAB 13, WhAm H, WhAmP
Atkinson, William Yates 1855-1899
 ApCAB Sup, ApCAB X, WhAm 1
Atkinson, William Yates 1856-1899 *TwCBDA*
Atkinson, William Yates 1887-1953 *WhAm 3*
Atkinson, Wilmer 1840-1920 *AmBi, DcAmB,*
 NatCAB 18, WhAm 1
Atlas, Charles 1894-1972 *WebAB*
Atlas, Lawrence Newman 1906-1958
 NatCAB 47
Atlass, H Leslie 1894-1960 *WhAm 4*
Atlee, Clement Richard Atlee, Earl 1883-1967
 McGEWB
Atlee, John Light 1799-1885 *ApCAB, DcAmB,*
 NatCAB 11, WhAm H
Atlee, John Light 1875-1950 *WhAm 3*
Atlee, Samuel John 1738-1786 *BiAUS, Drake*
Atlee, Samuel John 1739-1786 *ApCAB Sup,*
 BiDrAC, TwCBDA, WhAm H
Atlee, Washington Lemuel 1808-1878 *ApCAB,*
 DcAmB, Drake, NatCAB 11, TwCBDA,
 WhAm H
Atlee, William Augustus 1735-1793 *NatCAB 16*
Atondo Y Antillon, Isidoro *ApCAB, Drake*
Atoy *REnAW*
Atran, Frank Zelman 1885-1952 *NatCAB 39*
Atta-Culla-Culla *ApCAB*
Attar, Farid Ed-Din 1140?-1234? *McGEWB*
Attaway, Douglas 1878-1957 *NatCAB 47*
Attebery, Olin Moody 1887-1954 *WhAm 3*
Atterbury, Anson Phelps 1854-1931 *WhAm 1*
Atterbury, Grosvenor 1869-1956 *BnEnAmA,*
 WhAm 3
Atterbury, John Turner 1847-1912 *NatCAB 31*
Atterbury, William Wallace 1866-1935
 ApCAB X, DcAmB S1, NatCAB 26,
 WhAm 1
Atteridge, Harold Richard 1886-1938 *WhAm 1,*
 WhAm 2
Atteridge, James Leo 1886-1958 *NatCAB 51*
Attila d453 *McGEWB*
Attlee, Earl 1883-1967 *WhAm 4*
Attlee, Clement 1883-1967 *WhWW-II*
Attridge, Richard 1908-1964 *WhAm 4*
Attucks, Crispus 1723?-1770 *ApCAB, DcAmB,*
 Drake, TwCBDA, WebAB, WebAMB,

WhAm H
Attwill, Henry Converse 1872-1936 *WhAm 1*
Attwood, Miss E H *NewYHSD*
Attwood, Frederic 1883-1969 *WhAm 5*
Attwood, J Kenneth 1889-1958 *NatCAB 47*
Attwood, Julius 1824-1901 *NatCAB 2*
Attwood, Stephen S 1897-1965 *WhAm 4*
Attwood, William d1709? *NatCAB 12*
Attwood, William Elijah 1864-1950 *NatCAB 46*
Atwater, A Russell 1889-1933 *NatCAB 30*
Atwater, Adeline Lobdell 1887- *WomWWA 14*
Atwater, Amzi 1776-1851 *NatCAB 6,*
 TwCBDA
Atwater, Caleb 1778-1867 *ApCAB, DcAmB,*
 Drake, NatCAB 22, TwCBDA, WhAm H,
 WhAmP
Atwater, Caroline Swift 1857- *WomWWA 14*
Atwater, David Hay 1898-1944 *NatCAB 33,*
 WhAm 2
Atwater, Edward Perrin 1902-1967 *WhAm 5*
Atwater, Edward Storrs 1853-1922 *NatCAB 35*
Atwater, Francis 1858-1935 *WhAm 1*
Atwater, Fred 1870-1933 *NatCAB 25*
Atwater, George Parkin 1874-1932 *WhAm 1*
Atwater, Helen Woodard 1876-1947
 NatCAB 46, NotAW, WhAm 2,
 WomWWA 14
Atwater, Henry 1843-1921 *NatCAB 6*
Atwater, Henry Greene 1879-1950 *NatCAB 40,*
 WhAm 3
Atwater, James Robert 1872-1957 *NatCAB 43*
Atwater, Jeremiah 1773-1858 *NatCAB 12*
Atwater, Jeremiah 1774-1858 *Drake*
Atwater, John Wilbur 1840-1910 *BiDrAC,*
 WhAm 4, WhAmP
Atwater, Lyman Hotchkiss 1813-1883 *ApCAB,*
 BiDAmEd, DcAmB, NatCAB 12,
 TwCBDA, WhAm H
Atwater, Mary Meigs 1878-1956 *WhAm 3*
Atwater, Reginald Myers 1892-1957 *WhAm 3*
Atwater, Richard Mead 1844-1922 *WhAm 1*
Atwater, Wilbur Olin 1844-1907 *AmBi,*
 ApCAB, BiDAmEd, DcAmB, DcScB,
 EncAAH, NatCAB 6, TwCBDA, WebAB,
 WhAm 1
Atwater, William Cutler 1861-1940 *NatCAB 28,*
 WhAm 1
Atwell, Charles Beach 1855-1937 *WhAm 1*
Atwell, William Hawley 1869-1961 *WhAm 4*
Atwill, Douglass Henry 1881-1960 *WhAm 4*
Atwill, Edward Robert 1840-1911 *ApCAB Sup,*
 NatCAB 12, TwCBDA, WhAm 1
Atwill, Lionel 1885-1946 *WhAm 2*
Atwill, William 1883- *WhAm 1*
Atwood, A Wilson 1877-1964 *NatCAB 51*
Atwood, Albert William 1879-1975 *WhAm 6*
Atwood, Arthur Raymond 1891-1954
 NatCAB 48, WhAm 3
Atwood, Charles Bowler 1849-1895 *DcAmB,*
 NatCAB 22, TwCBDA, WhAm H
Atwood, Charles Edwin 1861-1930 *TwCBDA,*
 WhAm 1
Atwood, Clarence Leon 1859-1925 *NatCAB 44*
Atwood, David 1815-1889 *BiDrAC, DcAmB,*
 WhAm H, WhAmP
Atwood, Edward Leland 1872- *WhAm 5*
Atwood, Edwin Byron 1842-1909 *WhAm 1*
Atwood, Ellis Dexter 1889-1950 *NatCAB 40*
Atwood, Elmer Bugg 1874-1957 *NatCAB 54,*
 WhAm 3
Atwood, Ethel 1870- *AmWom*
Atwood, Eugene 1846-1926 *ApCAB X,*
 NatCAB 20
Atwood, Euna Clum 1856- *WomWWA 14*
Atwood, Felix 1908-1974 *WhAm 6*
Atwood, Frank Ely 1878-1943 *WhAm 2*
Atwood, Fred Holmes 1863-1921 *NatCAB 19*
Atwood, Frederick Edwin 1875-1948
 NatCAB 37
Atwood, George 1745-1807 *DcScB*
Atwood, George Edward 1851- *WhAm 4*
Atwood, Gertrude Pearson 1875-
 WomWWA 14
Atwood, Harrison 1886-1956 *NatCAB 45,*
 WhAm 3
Atwood, Harrison Henry 1863-1954 *BiDrAC,*
 WhAmP
Atwood, Harry 1870-1930 *NatCAB 25,*

Atwood *WhAm 1*

Atwood, Henry 1892-1950 *WhAm 3*

Atwood, Hinckley Gardner 1871-1941 *WhAm 2*

Atwood, Isaac Morgan 1838-1917 *ApCAB Sup, NatCAB 10, TwCBDA, WhAm 1*

Atwood, J *NewYHSD*

Atwood, J Arthur 1864-1949 *WhAm 2*

Atwood, James Thomas 1881-1961 *NatCAB 50*

Atwood, Jesse 1802?-1854? *NewYHSD, WhAm H*

Atwood, John Cowan 1863-1939 *NatCAB 29*

Atwood, John Harrison 1860-1934 *NatCAB 18, WhAm 1*

Atwood, John M 1818?- *NewYHSD*

Atwood, John Murray 1869-1951 *NatCAB 41, WhAm 3*

Atwood, Julius Walter 1857-1945 *NatCAB 33, WhAm 2*

Atwood, Lemuel True 1852-1909 *WhAm 1*

Atwood, Lewis John 1827-1909 *DcAmB*

Atwood, Louis K *WhoColR*

Atwood, Luther 1826-1868 *NatCAB 13*

Atwood, Mary Elizabeth *WomWWA 14*

Atwood, Maud Smith 1879- *WomWWA 14*

Atwood, Millard V 1886-1941 *WhAm 1, WhAm 2*

Atwood, Oscar 1842-1909 *WhAm 1*

Atwood, Philip Trowbridge 1908-1955 *NatCAB 43*

Atwood, Robert 1892- *IIBEAAW*

Atwood, Roy Franklin 1899-1963 *WhAm 4*

Atwood, Wallace Walter 1872-1949 *BiDAmEd, DcAmB S4, NatCAB 37, WhAm 2*

Atwood, William 1830-1884 *NatCAB 13*

Atwood, William C *NewYHSD*

Atwood, William F *NewYHSD*

Atzerodt, George A 1832?-1865 *DcAmB*

Aub, Jacob *NewYHSD*

Aub, Joseph Charles 1890-1973 *WhAm 6*

Aubanel *NewYHSD*

Aube *NewYHSD*

Auber, Pierre Alexandre 1784-1843 *ApCAB*

Auber, Virginia Felicia 1825- *ApCAB*

Auberg, John *NewYHSD*

Aubert, Charles J *NewYHSD*

Aubert, Lloyd Lees 1898-1972 *WhAm 5*

Aubert, Marion Bragg *BiCAW*

Aubert, Mrs. Paul *NewYHSD*

Aubert DeGaspe, Philippe 1786-1871 *McGEWB*

Aubert Dubayet, Jean Baptiste Annibale 1759-1797 *Drake*

Aubert Dupetit-Thouars, L M *DcScB*

Auberteuil, Hillard D' *Drake*

Aubery, Jean 1810-1893 *NewYHSD*

Aubineau, Lewis *NewYHSD*

Aubrey, D' d1770 *ApCAB*

Aubrey, Edwin Ewart 1896-1956 *NatCAB 42, WhAm 3*

Aubrey, Henry George 1906-1970 *WhAm 5*

Aubrey, James Thomas 1888-1962 *WhAm 4*

Aubrey, John Edmond 1870- *WhAm 5*

Aubrey, Lady Letitia *ApCAB*

Aubrey, Thomas d1814 *Drake*

Aubrey, William 1853- *WhAm 1*

Aubry *NewYHSD*

Aubry, Captain d1770 *Drake*

Aubry, Adolphe *NewYHSD*

Aubry, Auguste Eugene 1819- *ApCAB Sup*

Aubuisson DeVoisins, Jean-Francois D' 1769-1841 *DcScB*

Auch, John F 1858- *WhAm 4*

Auchiah, James 1906- *IIBEAAW*

Auchincloss, Charles Crooke 1881-1961 *NatCAB 50, WhAm 4*

Auchincloss, Gordon 1886-1943 *WhAm 2*

Auchincloss, Hugh Dudley 1858-1913 *NatCAB 37*

Auchincloss, James Coats 1885- *BiDrAC, WhAmP*

Auchincloss, John Winthrop d1938 *WhAm 1*

Auchincloss, William Stuart 1842-1928 *WhAm 1*

Auchinleck, Sir Claude 1884- *WhWW-II, WhoMilH*

Auchmuty, Richard Tylden 1831-1893 *DcAmB, NatCAB 9, TwCBDA, WhAm H*

Auchmuty, Robert d1750 *ApCAB, DcAmB, Drake, TwCBDA, WhAm H*

Auchmuty, Robert d1788 *ApCAB, DcAmB, Drake, WhAm H*

Auchmuty, Samuel 1722-1777 *ApCAB, DcAmB, Drake, NatCAB 9, WhAm H*

Auchmuty, Sir Samuel 1756-1822 *AmBi*

Auchmuty, Sir Samuel 1758-1822 *ApCAB, Drake*

Auchter, Eugene Curtis 1889-1952 *WhAm 3*

Aucock, Arthur Morgan 1861- *WhAm 5*

Aud, Guy 1887-1959 *NatCAB 46, WhAm 4*

Audebert, William A *NewYHSD*

Auden, Wystan Hugh 1907-1973 *McGEWB, WebAB, WhAm 6*

Audenreid, Charles Young 1863-1930 *ApCAB X*

Audenried, Charles Young 1863-1930 *NatCAB 44*

Audenried, Joseph Crain 1839-1880 *ApCAB, NatCAB 4, TwCBDA*

Audibert, Louis 1818?- *NewYHSD*

Audin *NewYHSD*

Audin, Jr. *NewYHSD*

Audouin, Jean Victor 1797-1841 *DcScB*

Audrieth, Ludwig Frederick 1901-1967 *WhAm 4*

Audsley, George Ashdown 1838-1925 *DcAmB, NatCAB 24, WhAm 4*

Audubon, John James 1780-1851 *ApCAB, Drake, NatCAB 6, TwCBDA*

Audubon, John James 1785-1851 *AmBi, AsBiEn, BnEnAmA, DcAmB, DcScB, EncAAH, EncAB, IIBEAAW, McGEWB, NewYHSD, REnAW, WebAB, WhAm H*

Audubon, John Woodhouse 1812-1862 *IIBEAAW, NewYHSD, WhAm H*

Audubon, Victor Gifford 1809-1860 *NewYHSD, WhAm H*

Audy, Jack Ralph 1914-1974 *WhAm 6*

Audy, Roy *NewYHSD*

Auel, Carl Bennett 1870-1937 *NatCAB 28*

Auenbrugger, Joseph Leopold 1722-1809 *BiHiMed, DcScB*

Auer, Clara Meltzer 1874- *WomWWA 14*

Auer, Harry Anton 1878- *WhAm 6*

Auer, John 1875-1948 *DcAmB S4, NatCAB 37, WhAm 2*

Auer, John Frederick 1884-1961 *NatCAB 48*

Auer, John Gottlieb 1832-1874 *ApCAB, NatCAB 5, TwCBDA*

Auer, Joseph Lawrence 1898-1963 *WhAm 4*

Auer, Karl, Baron Von Welsbach 1858-1929 *AsBiEn*

Auer, Leopold 1845-1930 *NatCAB 22, WhAm 1*

Auerbach, Beatrice Fox 1887-1968 *WhAm 5*

Auerbach, Erich 1892-1957 *WhAm 3*

Auerbach, Frank Ludwig 1910-1964 *WhAm 4*

Auerbach, Henry Abram 1866-1948 *NatCAB 36*

Auerbach, Herbert S 1882-1945 *WhAm 2*

Auerbach, Joseph S d1944 *WhAm 2*

Auerbach, Leopold 1828-1897 *BiHiMed*

Auerbach-Levy, William 1889-1964 *NatCAB 51, WhAm 4*

Auf DerHeide, Oscar Louis 1874-1945 *BiDrAC, WhAm 2, WhAmP*

Auge, Emily Geary Whitten 1874-1934 *NatCAB 26*

Augenstein, Leroy George 1928-1969 *WhAm 5*

Auger *NewYHSD*

Auger, Charles L 1860-1939 *WhAm 1*

Augereau, Pierre Francois Charles 1757-1816 *WhoMilH*

Augero, Francesco *NewYHSD*

Aughinbaugh, William Edmund 1871-1940 *WhAm 1*

Augsbury, Mary Ellis *WomWWA 14*

Augspurger, Owen Beal 1913-1969 *WhAm 5*

Augur, Christopher Colon 1821-1898 *ApCAB, Drake, NatCAB 4, TwCBDA*

Augur, Christopher Columbus 1821-1898 *DcAmB, WhAm H*

Augur, Hezekiah 1791-1858 *ApCAB, BnEnAmA, DcAmB, Drake, NatCAB 8, NewYHSD, TwCBDA, WhAm H*

Augur, Jacob Arnold 1849-1909 *ApCAB, WhAm 1*

August, Harry Wirt 1899-1970 *WhAm 5*

August, John *WebAB*

August, William P 1842?- *NewYHSD*

Augustine Of Canterbury, Saint d606? *McGEWB*

Augustine Of Hippo, Saint 354-430 *DcScB*

Augustine, Saint 354-430 *McGEWB*

Augustine, Harry Hamill 1892-1959 *NatCAB 48, WhAm 4*

Augustine, William Franklin 1885-1947 *WhAm 2*

Augustus 063BC-014AD *McGEWB*

Augustus II 1670-1733 *McGEWB*

Augustus II, Frederick 1670-1733 *WhoMilH*

Augustus, Albert Anthony 1860-1927 *NatCAB 21*

Augustus, Ellsworth Hunt 1897-1964 *NatCAB 57, WhAm 4*

Augustus, John 1785-1859 *ApCAB, DcAmB, Drake, NatCAB 6, TwCBDA, WhAm H*

Augustyn, Godfrey William 1872-1944 *WhAm 2*

Aul *NewYHSD*

Aulard, Francois Victor Alphonse 1849-1928 *McGEWB*

Auld, David 1844-1927 *NatCAB 24*

Auld, George Percival 1881-1962 *NatCAB 49, WhAm 4*

Auld, John Maxwell 1855- *WhAm 4*

Auld, Robert Campbell 1857- *NatCAB 15*

Auld, Wilberforce *NewYHSD*

Aulick, John H 1789-1873 *ApCAB, BiAUS, Drake, NatCAB 13, TwCBDA*

Aull, John Weston 1866-1955 *NatCAB 47*

Aulnay DeCharnise *ApCAB*

Ault, Bromwell 1899-1973 *WhAm 5*

Ault, George Christian 1891-1948 *IIBEAAW, NatCAB 40*

Ault, James Percy 1881-1929 *WhAm 1*

Ault, Lee Addison 1851-1930 *NatCAB 28*

Ault, Nelson Allen 1915-1963 *WhAm 4*

Ault, Otto Thurman 1892-1954 *WhAm 3*

Aultman, Dwight Edward 1872-1929 *WhAm 1*

Aumale, Henri E P L D'Orleans, Duc D' 1822-1897 *WhoMilH*

Auman, Orrin W 1873-1951 *WhAm 3*

Auman, Russell Frank 1899-1972 *WhAm 5*

Auman, William 1838-1920 *WhAm 1*

Aung San 1915-1947 *McGEWB*

Aung San, U 1915-1947 *WhWW-II*

Aunt Fanny *NotAW*

Aurand, Samuel Herbert 1854- *WhAm 4*

Aurangzeb 1618-1707 *McGEWB*

Auray, Mister *NewYHSD*

Aurelio, Antonio, I 1830?- *ApCAB*

Aurell, Alvin Karl 1896-1961 *WhAm 4*

Aurell, George Emanuel 1905-1970 *WhAm 5*

Auringer, Horace Edward 1889-1961 *NatCAB 50*

Auringer, Obadiah Cyrus 1849-1937 *TwCBDA, WhAm 1*

Auringer, Obediah Cyrus 1849-1937 *NatCAB 7*

Auriol, Vincent 1884-1966 *WhAm 4*

Aury, Louis De 1780?- *ApCAB*

Aury, Luis De *Drake*

Ause, Orval Hope 1909-1974 *WhAm 6*

Ausley, Charles Saxon 1907-1972 *WhAm 6*

Austell, Adelaide Roberts 1905-1975 *WhAm 6*

Austell, Alfred 1814-1881 *DcAmB, NatCAB 1, WhAm H*

Austen, Alice 1866-1952 *DcAmB S5*

Austen, Benjamin 1752-1820 *WhAm H*

Austen, Ellen Munroe 1855- *WomWWA 14*

Austen, Jane 1775-1817 *McGEWB*

Austen, Peter Townsend 1852-1907 *ApCAB, DcAmB, NatCAB 13, WhAm 1*

Austen, R *NewYHSD*

Austen, Ralph A C *DcScB*

Austerlitz, Fred *WebAB*

Austill, Jeremiah 1795-1879 *NatCAB 11*

Austin, A Eugene 1868-1948 *NatCAB 37*

Austin, Albert Elmer 1877-1942 *BiDrAC, WhAm 1, WhAm 2, WhAmP*

Austin, Alexander *NewYHSD*

Austin, Amanda Petronella 1856-1917 *IIBEAAW*

Austin, Archibald 1772-1837 *BiAUS, BiDrAC, WhAm H*

Austin, Aubrey Ernest 1880-1949 *NatCAB 37*

Austin, Benjamin 1752-1820 *ApCAB, DcAmB, Drake, NatCAB 12, TwCBDA, WhAmP*

Austin, Benjamin Fish 1850- *ApCAB Sup,
WhAm 4*
Austin, Calvin d1936 *WhAm 1*
Austin, Caroline Sprague 1863- *WomWWA 14*
Austin, Charles Burgess 1879- *WhAm 6*
Austin, Charles Percy 1883-1948 *IlBEAAW*
Austin, Charles Taylor 1873-1960 *NatCAB 48*
Austin, Chellis Asahel 1876-1929 *NatCAB 22*
Austin, Clyde Bernard 1891-1966 *NatCAB 53,
WhAm 4*
Austin, Coe Finch 1831-1880 *ApCAB*
Austin, Cyrus Brooks 1851-1924 *WhAm 1*
Austin, David 1759-1831 *DcAmB, WhAm H*
Austin, David 1760-1831 *ApCAB, Drake*
Austin, DeWitt Ray 1892-1956 *NatCAB 45*
Austin, Dwight Bertram 1898-1955 *NatCAB 44,
WhAm 3*
Austin, Edward Thompson 1897-1975 *WhAm 6*
Austin, Ennis Raymond 1863-1951 *NatCAB 47,
WhAm 3*
Austin, Eugene Kelly 1872- *ApCAB X*
Austin, Eugene Munger 1910-1962 *WhAm 4*
Austin, Francis Marion 1862-1922 *WhAm 1*
Austin, Frank *WebAB*
Austin, Fred Thaddeus 1866-1938 *WhAm 1*
Austin, Frederick Carleton 1853-1931
ApCAB X, WhAm 1
Austin, George Curtis 1863- *NatCAB 7,
WhAm 4*
Austin, Harold Raymond 1883-1970
NatCAB 56
Austin, Harriet Bunker 1844- *AmWom*
Austin, Helen Vickroy 1829- *AmWom*
Austin, Henry 1804-1891 *BnEnAmA, DcAmB,
NatCAB 22, WhAm H*
Austin, Henry 1858- *WhAm 4*
Austin, Herbert 1874-1949 *NatCAB 40*
Austin, Herbert Douglas 1876- *WhAm 5*
Austin, Horace 1831- *BiAUS, BiAUS Sup,
NatCAB 10*
Austin, Howard 1851- *WhAm 4*
Austin, Howard Albert, Jr. 1915-1971 *WhAm 5*
Austin, Isabella McHugh d1915 *WhAm 1*
Austin, James Harold 1883-1952 *WhAm 3*
Austin, James Trecothic 1784-1870 *ApCAB,
Drake*
Austin, James Trecothick 1784-1870 *DcAmB,
NatCAB 22, WhAm H, WhAmP*
Austin, Jane Goodwin 1831-1894 *AmWom,
ApCAB Sup, DcAmB, NatCAB 6,
TwCBDA, WhAm H*
Austin, John Corneby Wilson 1870- *WhAm 5*
Austin, John Langshaw 1911-1960 *McGEWB,
WhAm 4*
Austin, John Mather 1805- *Drake*
Austin, John Osborne 1849-1918 *WhAm 1*
Austin, John Turnell 1869-1948 *NatCAB 18,
NatCAB 39, WhAm 5*
Austin, Jonathan Loring 1748-1826 *ApCAB,
DcAmB, Drake, NatCAB 7, TwCBDA,
WhAm H, WhAmP*
Austin, Jonathan Williams 1751-1778 *ApCAB,
Drake*
Austin, Laura Osborne *WomWWA 14*
Austin, Leonard S 1846-1929 *WhAm 1*
Austin, Lloyd Lewis 1904-1968 *NatCAB 53,
WhAm 5*
Austin, Louis Winslow 1867-1932 *AmBi,
DcScB, NatCAB 24, WhAm 1*
Austin, Mary Hunter 1866-1934 *REnAW*
Austin, Mary Hunter 1868-1934 *AmBi,
BiCAW, DcAmB S1, NotAW, WebAB,
WhAm 1, WomWWA 14*
Austin, Moses 1761-1821 *AmBi, ApCAB,
DcAmB, Drake, NatCAB 5, REnAW,
WhAm H, WhAmP*
Austin, Oscar Phelps 1847-1933 *ApCAB X,
NatCAB 24, WhAm 1*
Austin, Richard Loper 1859-1948 *WhAm 2*
Austin, Richard Wilson 1857-1919 *BiDrAC,
NatCAB 11, WhAm 1*
Austin, Samuel 1760-1830 *ApCAB, DcAmB,
Drake, NatCAB 2, TwCBDA, WhAm H*
Austin, Samuel 1850-1936 *NatCAB 46*
Austin, Samuel Yates 1877-1958 *NatCAB 53*
Austin, Stephen Fuller 1793-1836 *AmBi,
ApCAB, DcAmB, Drake, EncAAH,*

*EncAB, McGEWB, NatCAB 6, REnAW,
TwCBDA, WebAB, WhAm H, WhAmP*
Austin, Thomas 1848-1922 *NatCAB 19*
Austin, Walter 1864-1929 *NatCAB 26*
Austin, Walter Warner 1880-1951 *NatCAB 41*
Austin, Warren Robinson 1877-1962 *BiDrAC,
WhAmP*
Austin, Warren Robinson 1877-1963 *WhAm 4*
Austin, Wilbert John 1876-1940 *NatCAB 31,
WhAm 1*
Austin, William 1778-1841 *ApCAB, DcAmB,
Drake, NatCAB 4, WhAm H*
Austin, William Lacy 1872-1958 *WhAm 3*
Austin, William Lane 1871-1949 *NatCAB 38,
NatCAB 47, WhAm 2*
Austin, William Liseter 1852-1932 *NatCAB 22,
WhAm 1*
Austin-Ball, Thomas 1872- *WhAm 5*
Austrian, Alfred S 1870-1932 *WhAm 1*
Austrian, Carl Joseph 1892-1970 *WhAm 5*
Austrian, Charles Robert 1885-1956 *WhAm 3*
Austrins, Emilija Pone 1908-1973 *WhAm 6*
Auten, Henry Franklin 1861-1918 *NatCAB 18*
Auten, James Ernest 1883-1947 *WhAm 2*
Auten, Nellie Mason 1875- *WomWWA 14*
Auten, Theodore Augustus 1870- *WhoColR*
Autenrieth, Charles *NewYHSD*
Autenrieth, Ludwig 1832?- *NewYHSD*
Authier, George Francis 1876- *WhAm 5*
Autichamp, Antoine J DeB, Comte D' 1744-1822
Drake
Autio, Rudy 1926- *BnEnAmA*
Autolycus Of Pitane *DcScB*
Autry, Gene *REnAW*
Auvergne, William Of *DcScB*
Auwers, Arthur Julius G Friedrich Von
1838-1915 *DcScB*
Auwers, Karl Friedrich Von 1863-1939 *DcScB*
Auzout, Adrien 1622-1691 *DcScB*
Avalos Y Figuera, Diego De *Drake*
Avancena, Ramon *WhAm 5*
Avann, Ella R Brockway 1853- *AmWom*
Avary, Myrta Lockett *WomWWA 14*
Avaugour, Pierre DuBois, Baron D' d1664 *Drake*
Avebury, Baron *DcScB*
Avedon, Richard 1923- *BnEnAmA*
Aveledo, Agustin 1836- *ApCAB*
Avellaneda, Gertrudis Gomez De 1816-1864
ApCAB
Avellaneda, Nicolas 1836- *ApCAB*
Avellanus, Arcadius 1851-1935 *WhAm 1*
Avempace *DcScB*
Avenare *DcScB*
Avendano, Andres 1650?-1720? *ApCAB Sup*
Avent, Joseph Emory 1878-1958 *NatCAB 46,
WhAm 3*
Averbach, Albert 1902-1975 *WhAm 6*
Averbuck, Samuel Harris 1901-1963
NatCAB 52
Averell, William Woods 1832-1900 *AmBi,
ApCAB, DcAmB, NatCAB 4, TwCBDA,
WebAMB, WhAm H*
Averett, Thomas Hamlet 1800-1855 *BiAUS,
BiDrAC, WhAm H*
Averhill, John Thomas 1825-1889 *ApCAB,
BiAUS*
Averill *NewYHSD*
Averill, Blanche M 1872- *WomWWA 14*
Averill, Edith Alice Sherman *WomWWA 14*
Averill, George G 1869-1954 *WhAm 3*
Averill, Glenn Mark 1868-1940 *WhAm 1*
Averill, Heman Otis 1856-1923 *NatCAB 27*
Averill, James Kent 1904-1944 *NatCAB 36*
Averill, John H *WhAm 5*
Averill, John Thomas 1825-1889 *BiDrAC,
WhAm H*
Averill, Mary Martin *WomWWA 14*
Averill, Walter Albert 1900-1967 *NatCAB 54*
Averill, William W 1830- *Drake*
Averitt, George Alfred 1895-1969 *WhAm 5*
Averitt, Ransom Stringfield 1901-1970
NatCAB 55
Averroes 1126-1198 *AsBiEn, DcScB,
McGEWB*
Avers, Henry Godfrey 1886-1947 *WhAm 2*
Avery, Albert Everett 1858-1939 *NatCAB 29*
Avery, Alphonso Calhoun 1835-1913
NatCAB 42, TwCBDA, WhAm 4

Avery, Alphonso Calhoun 1837-1913 *NatCAB 3*
Avery, Benjamin P 1829-1875 *ApCAB, BiAUS*
Avery, Benjamin Parke 1828-1875 *DcAmB,
NatCAB 1, WhAm H, WhAmP*
Avery, Brainard 1873-1947 *NatCAB 35*
Avery, Catharine Hitchcock Tilden 1844-
AmWom
Avery, Catherine Hitchcock Tilden 1844-
WhAm 1, WomWWA 14
Avery, Charles Hammond 1854-1927
NatCAB 37
Avery, Christopher Lester 1872-1956 *WhAm 3*
Avery, Clara Arlette 1850- *ApCAB X,
WomWWA 14*
Avery, Clarence Renshaw 1893-1953
NatCAB 42
Avery, Clarence Willard 1882-1949 *WhAm 2*
Avery, Coleman 1880-1938 *NatCAB 46,
WhAm 1*
Avery, Courtney Chandus 1861-1946
NatCAB 40
Avery, Cyrus Stevens 1871- *WhAm 5*
Avery, Daniel 1766-1842 *BiAUS, BiDrAC,
WhAm H*
Avery, Delos 1883-1966 *WhAm 4*
Avery, Elisabeth McElroy 1873- *WomWWA 14*
Avery, Elroy McKendree 1844-1935
*ApCAB Sup, ApCAB X, BiDAmEd,
NatCAB 5, NatCAB 26, WhAm 1*
Avery, Elroy McKendrel 1844-1935 *TwCBDA*
Avery, Ephraim K 1799?-1869 *Drake*
Avery, George C 1852-1911 *WhAm 1*
Avery, George True 1880-1944 *WhAm 2*
Avery, George Whitefield 1836-1893 *TwCBDA*
Avery, Henry Ogden 1852-1890 *NatCAB 1,
WhAm H*
Avery, Herbert Spaulding 1883-1968
NatCAB 54
Avery, Isaac Wheeler 1837-1887 *TwCBDA*
Avery, Isaac Wheeler 1837-1897 *DcAmB,
NatCAB 3, WhAm H, WhAm 1*
Avery, Issac Wheeler 1837-1897 *WhAmP*
Avery, John *NewYHSD*
Avery, John 1824-1914 *BiDrAC, TwCBDA,
WhAm HA, WhAm 1, WhAm 1C,
WhAm 4*
Avery, John 1837-1887 *DcAmB, WhAm H*
Avery, John 1902-1951 *NatCAB 39*
Avery, John Campbell 1851-1921 *NatCAB 8*
Avery, John Moses 1876- *WhoColR*
Avery, Johnston 1901-1970 *WhAm 5*
Avery, Martha Gallison Moore 1851-1929
NotAW
Avery, Maurice Wescott 1896-1973 *NatCAB 57*
Avery, Milton 1893-1965 *BnEnAmA, WhAm 4*
Avery, Moses Nathan 1855-1942 *WhAm 2*
Avery, Myron Haliburton 1899-1952
NatCAB 41
Avery, Nathan Prentice 1869-1947 *NatCAB 35,
WhAm 2*
Avery, Oswald Theodore 1877-1955 *AsBiEn,
DcAmB S5, DcScB, NatCAB 44,
WhAm 3*
Avery, Rachel Foster 1858-1919 *AmWom,
NotAW, WhAm 4, WomWWA 14, WhAm 1*
Avery, Ray Dudley 1886-1958 *NatCAB 46*
Avery, Ray Longfellow 1884-1965 *NatCAB 51*
Avery, Robert 1839-1912 *WhAm 1*
Avery, Rosa Miller 1830-1894 *AmWom,
NatCAB 6*
Avery, Samuel 1865-1936 *NatCAB 14,
WhAm 1*
Avery, Samuel Putnam 1822-1904 *AmBi,
DcAmB, NatCAB 1, NewYHSD,
TwCBDA, WhAm 1*
Avery, Sewell Lee 1873-1960 *NatCAB 49,
WhAm 4*
Avery, Stephen Morehouse 1893-1948
NatCAB 37
Avery, Susan Look 1817-1915 *WhAm 1,
WomWWA 14*
Avery, Thomas Burt 1910-1964 *WhAm 4*
Avery, Waightstill 1745-1821 *ApCAB*
Avery, Waitstill 1745-1821 *Drake, NatCAB 6,
TwCBDA*
Avery, William *NewYHSD*
Avery, William Henry 1911- *BiDrAC*
Avery, William T 1819-1880 *BiAUS*

Avery, William Tecumsah 1819-1880 *BiDrAC*

Avery, William Tecumseh 1819-1880 *WhAm H*

Avery, William Waightstill 1816-1864 *BiDConf, NatCAB 7, WhAm H*

Avery, William Waigstill 1816-1864 *DcAmB, WhAmP*

Avery, Willis Frank 1881-1971 *WhAm 6*

Aves, Dreda d1942 *WhAm 2*

Aves, Henry Damerel 1853-1936 *WhAm 1*

Aves, Wesley 1905-1970 *NatCAB 54*

Avey, Albert Edwin 1886-1963 *NatCAB 50*

Avezac, Auguste Genevieve Valentin D' 1777-1851 *ApCAB, Drake*

Avezac, Jean Pierre Valentin 1756-1803 *ApCAB*

Avezac, Pierre V Dominique Julian D' 1769-1831 *ApCAB, Drake*

Avezzana, Giuseppe 1797- *ApCAB*

Avezzana, Joseph 1797- *Drake*

Avicenna 980?-1037 *AsBiEn, BiHiMed, DcScB, McGEWB*

Avignon *NewYHSD*

Avignone, Antonio 1814?- *NewYHSD*

Avila Camacho, Manuel 1897-1955 *McGEWB*

Avildsen, Clarence 1898-1964 *WhAm 4*

Aviles, Pedro Menendez De 1523-1574 *ApCAB*

Avinoam, Reuben 1905-1974 *WhAm 6*

Avinoff, Audrey 1884-1949 *WhAm 2*

Avirett, John Williams 1863-1914 *NatCAB 16*

Aviritt, May Amelia Goodwin *WomWWA 14*

Avis, John Boyd 1875-1944 *WhAm 2*

Avis, Samuel Brashear 1872-1924 *BiDrAC, WhAm 1, WhAm 1C*

Avitabile, Salvatore 1873-1957 *WhAm 3*

Avnet, Lester Francis 1912-1970 *WhAm 5*

Avnsoe, Thorkild 1884-1958 *WhAm 3*

Avogadro, Amedeo, Count Of Quaregna 1776-1856 *AsBiEn, DcScB, McGEWB*

Avram, Mois Herban 1880-1971 *ApCAB X, NatCAB 18, NatCAB 55, WhAm 6*

Awa Tsireh 1895?-1955 *IIBEAAW*

Awl, William Maclay 1799-1876 *DcAmB, NatCAB 22, WhAm H*

Awolowo, Obagemi 1909- *McGEWB*

Awwam Abu Zakariyya Yahya Ibn M, Ibn Al- *DcScB*

Axayacatl d1477 *ApCAB*

Axe, Emerson Wirt 1895-1964 *WhAm 4*

Axe, Ruth Houghton 1901-1967 *WhAm 4*

Axel, Hans 1755-1810 *WhAm H*

Axelrad, Sidney 1913-1976 *WhAm 6*

Axelrod, Haim Izchak 1925-1971 *WhAm 5*

Axelrod, Julius 1912- *WebAB*

Axelrod, Leonard Richardson 1927-1975 *WhAm 6*

Axelson, Charles Frederic 1881-1971 *WhAm 5*

Axicoat *ApCAB*

Axline, George Andrew 1871-1919 *BiDAmEd, NatCAB 19, WhAm 1*

Axline, Samuel Preston 1849-1916 *NatCAB 17*

Axopil *ApCAB*

Axson, Stockton 1867-1935 *NatCAB 46, WhAm 1*

Axtell, Decatur 1848-1922 *NatCAB 20, WhAm 1*

Axtell, Delos 1855-1919 *NatCAB 18*

Axtell, Edwin Rodarmel 1866-1899 *WhAm 1*

Axtell, Frances Cleveland 1866- *WhAm 4*

Axtell, Harold Lucius 1876-1955 *WhAm 3*

Axtell, John Thomas 1856-1937 *NatCAB 36, WhAm 1*

Axtell, Samuel Beach 1809-1891 *TwCBDA*

Axtell, Samuel Beach 1819-1891 *BiAUS, BiDrAC, DcAmB, WhAm H, WhAmP*

Axtell, William 1720-1795 *Drake*

Axtelle, George Edward 1893-1974 *BiDAmEd, WhAm 6*

Axton, Edwin Dymond 1874-1961 *NatCAB 48*

Axton, John Thomas 1870-1934 *WhAm 1, WhAm 1C*

Axton, Woodford Fitch 1872-1935 *NatCAB 26*

Axworthy, H Harold 1892-1941 *NatCAB 30*

Ayala, Gabriel *ApCAB Sup*

Ayala, Juan Bautista De *ApCAB*

Ayala, Juan Manuel De *AmBi, DcAmB, WhAm H*

Ayars, George W 1897-1970 *WhAm 5*

Aycock, Charles Brantley 1859-1912 *BiDAmEd, DcAmB, NatCAB 13, WhAm 1, WhAmP*

Aycock, Martha Magan 1881- *WomWWA 14*

Aycrigg, John Bancker 1798-1856 *BiAUS, BiDrAC, WhAm H*

Aycrigg, William Anderson 1859-1936 *NatCAB 26*

Aydelott, James Howard 1883-1966 *WhAm 4*

Aydelotte, Dora 1878-1968 *WhAm 5*

Aydelotte, Frank 1880-1956 *BiDAmEd, NatCAB 43, WhAm 3*

Aydlett, Edwin Ferebee 1857-1930 *WhAm 1*

Ayer, Anna Perkins Chandler 1873- *WomWWA 14*

Ayer, Benjamin Franklin 1825-1903 *NatCAB 9, WhAm 1*

Ayer, Charles 1841?- *NewYHSD*

Ayer, Charles Fanning 1865-1956 *NatCAB 46, WhAm 3*

Ayer, Charles Frederick 1863-1961 *NatCAB 50, WhAm 5*

Ayer, Charles James 1858-1927 *NatCAB 23, NatCAB 24*

Ayer, Clarence Walter 1862-1913 *WhAm 1*

Ayer, Edward Everett 1841-1927 *DcAmB, NatCAB 20, WhAm 1*

Ayer, Emma Burbank *WomWWA 14*

Ayer, Francis Wayland 1848-1923 *AmBi, DcAmB, NatCAB 20, WebAB, WhAm 1*

Ayer, Franklin Deming 1832- *WhAm 4*

Ayer, Fred Carleton 1880- *WhAm 6*

Ayer, Fred Wellington 1855-1936 *NatCAB 27*

Ayer, Frederic Eugene 1876- *WhAm 5*

Ayer, Frederick 1822-1918 *NatCAB 15, TwCBDA, WhAm 1*

Ayer, Frederick Fanning 1851-1924 *NatCAB 21, WhAm 1*

Ayer, Hannah Gilbert Palfrey 1881- *WomWWA 14*

Ayer, Harriet Hubbard 1849-1903 *NatCAB 43, NotAW*

Ayer, Harriet Hubbard 1852-1903 *AmWom*

Ayer, Harriet Hubbard 1854-1903 *WhAm 1*

Ayer, James Bourne 1882-1963 *NatCAB 57, WhAm 4*

Ayer, James Cook 1818-1878 *ApCAB, DcAmB, NatCAB 26, WhAm H*

Ayer, James Cook 1862- *ApCAB X*

Ayer, Janet Hopkins 1854- *WomWWA 14*

Ayer, John 1883-1961 *WhAm 4*

Ayer, Joseph Cullen 1866-1944 *WhAm 2*

Ayer, L *NewYHSD*

Ayer, Leslie James 1879-1949 *NatCAB 38*

Ayer, Lewis Malone, Jr. 1821-1895 *BiDConf*

Ayer, Margaret Hubbard 1879- *WomWWA 14*

Ayer, Mary Allette *WomWWA 14*

Ayer, May Hancock 1873- *WomWWA 14*

Ayer, Nathaniel Farwell 1879- *WhAm 6*

Ayer, Peter 1760-1857 *Drake*

Ayer, Richard Small 1829-1896 *BiAUS, BiDrAC, WhAm H, WhAmP*

Ayer, Winslow B 1860- *WhAm 4*

Ayers, Allan Farrell 1880-1963 *WhAm 4*

Ayers, Charles *NewYHSD*

Ayers, Charles Pierson 1861-1933 *NatCAB 44*

Ayers, Clarence Edwin 1891-1972 *WhAm 5*

Ayers, Edward Everett 1865- *WhAm 4*

Ayers, Edward Mathews 1863-1942 *NatCAB 37*

Ayers, Franklin Egbert 1859-1918 *NatCAB 17*

Ayers, Fred Wesley 1884-1966 *WhAm 4*

Ayers, Harry Mell 1885-1964 *NatCAB 56, WhAm 4*

Ayers, Henrietta P *WomWWA 14*

Ayers, Howard 1861-1933 *NatCAB 18, TwCBDA, WhAm 1*

Ayers, Joseph Burton 1881- *WhAm 6*

Ayers, Lemuel 1915-1955 *NatCAB 41, WhAm 3*

Ayers, Mary Frances *WomWWA 14*

Ayers, Mary Lizzie 1877- *WhoColR*

Ayers, Roy Elmer 1882-1955 *BiDrAC, NatCAB 44, WhAm 3, WhAmP*

Ayers, Rufus Adolphus 1849- *WhAm 4*

Ayers, William Judson 1875- *WhoColR*

Ayers, William P 1905-1974 *WhAm 6*

Ayerza, Abel 1861-1918 *BiHiMed*

Ayeta, Francisco De *Drake, WhAm H*

Ayler, Albert 1936-1970 *WhAm 5*

Aylesworth, Barton Orville 1860-1933 *NatCAB 11, TwCBDA, WhAm 1*

Aylesworth, Merlin Hall 1886-1952 *NatCAB 46, WhAm 3*

Aylesworth, Ray Wallace 1893-1950 *NatCAB 39*

Ayling, Charles Lincoln 1875-1970 *WhAm 5*

Ayllon, Lucas Vasquez De 1475?-1526 *AmBi, DcAmB, Drake*

Ayllon, Lucas Vasquez De 1780?-1813 *WhAm H*

Ayllon, Lucas Vazquez De d1526 *ApCAB*

Aylmer, Mathew Whitworth 1775-1850 *ApCAB*

Aylmer, Matthew Whitworth 1775-1850 *Drake*

Aylsworth, Leon Emmons 1869- *WhAm 5*

Aylsworth, Nicholas John 1843- *WhAm 4*

Aylsworth, William Prince 1844- *TwCBDA, WhAm 1*

Aylwin, John Cushing 1780?-1813 *DcAmB, WhAm H*

Ayme, Francis *NewYHSD*

Ayme, Louis Henri 1855-1912 *WhAm 1*

Ayme, Marcel 1902-1967 *WhAm 4A*

Aynesworth, Kenneth Hazen 1873-1944 *WhAm 2*

Ayolas, Juan De d1538 *ApCAB, Drake*

Ayr, John F *NewYHSD*

Ayres, Albert Douglass 1874-1944 *WhAm 2*

Ayres, Alice Stanley Taylor 1866- *WomWWA 14*

Ayres, Anna C Marston 1862- *WomWWA 14*

Ayres, Anne 1816-1896 *DcAmB, NotAW, WhAm H*

Ayres, Atlee Bernard 1874- *WhAm 5*

Ayres, Brown 1856-1919 *DcAmB, NatCAB 18, WhAm 1*

Ayres, Burt Wilmot 1895- *WhAm 5*

Ayres, Clarence L *NewYHSD*

Ayres, Daniel 1824-1892 *TwCBDA*

Ayres, Edward 1857-1919 *WhAm 1*

Ayres, Eugene Edmond 1859-1920 *WhAm 1*

Ayres, Francis Oliver 1862-1941 *NatCAB 31*

Ayres, Frank C 1886- *WhAm 3*

Ayres, Franklin Herman 1865- *WhAm 4*

Ayres, George Frederic 1865-1913 *WhAm 1*

Ayres, Harry Morgan 1881-1948 *NatCAB 36, WhAm 2*

Ayres, Helen 1869- *WomWWA 14*

Ayres, Herbert Franklin 1906-1964 *NatCAB 52*

Ayres, Joseph Gerrish 1839-1922 *WhAm 1*

Ayres, Leonard Porter 1879-1946 *BiDAmEd, DcAmB S4, NatCAB 45, WhAm 2*

Ayres, Louis 1874-1947 *WhAm 2*

Ayres, Milan Church 1850- *WhAm 1*

Ayres, Milan Valentine 1875- *WhAm 5*

Ayres, Patti 1876-1921 *NatCAB 19*

Ayres, Philip Wheelock 1861- *WhAm 5*

Ayres, Quincy Claude 1891-1963 *NatCAB 50, WhAm 4*

Ayres, Romeyn Beck 1825-1888 *ApCAB, DcAmB, Drake, NatCAB 4, TwCBDA, WhAm H*

Ayres, Samuel Gardiner 1865-1942 *TwCBDA, WhAm 2*

Ayres, Samuel Loring Percival 1835-1917 *WhAm 1*

Ayres, Stephen Cooper 1840-1921 *WhAm 1*

Ayres, Steven Beckwith 1861-1929 *BiDrAC, WhAm 1, WhAmP*

Ayres, Thomas A 1820?-1858 *IIBEAAW, NewYHSD, WhAm H*

Ayres, William Augustus 1867-1952 *BiDrAC, DcAmB S5, NatCAB 40, WhAm 3, WhAmP*

Ayres, William Hanes 1916- *BiDrAC*

Ayub Khan, Mohammed 1907-1974 *McGEWB, WhAm 6*

Azad, Abul Kalam Maulana *WhAm 5*

Azana, Manuel 1880-1940 *McGEWB*

Azanza, Miguel Jose 1750?- *ApCAB*

Azara, Felix De 1742-1821 *DcScB*

Azara, Felix De 1746-1811 *ApCAB, Drake*

Azara, Felix De 1746-1821 *McGEWB*

Azarias, Brother 1847-1893 *BiDAmEd, DcAmB, WhAm H*

Azcarate Y Florez, Pablo De 1890-1971 *WhAm 5*

Azevedo, Antonio Araujo De 1784-1817 *ApCAB*

Azevedo, Ignacius 1527-1570 *ApCAB*

Azevedo, Philadelpho 1894-1951 *WhAm 3*

Azevedo Coutinho, Jose Joaquim DaCunha
  1742-1821 *Drake*
Azevedo Coutinho, Joze Joaquim DaCunha
  1742-1821 *ApCAB*
Azevedo Y Zuniga, Gaspard De d1606 *Drake*
Azhari, Sayyid Ismail, Al- 1898-1969 *McGEWB*
Azikiwe, Nnamdi 1904- *McGEWB*
Azpilcueta, Juan 1515- *ApCAB*
Azuela, Mariano 1873-1952 *McGEWB,*
  WhAm 5
Azuola, Eduardo 1892-1950 *WhAm 3*

B

B G S *NewYHSD*
B L T *WebAB*
Ba Maw 1893- *McGEWB*
Ba Maw, U 1893- *WhWW-II*
Baab, Otto J 1896-1958 *WhAm 3*
Baackes, Frank 1863- *NatCAB 15*
Baade, Walter 1893-1960 *AsBiEn, WebAB, WhAm 4*
Baade, Wilhelm Heinrich Walter 1893-1960 *DcScB*
Baal Shem Tov 1700?-1760? *McGEWB*
Baar, Arnold R 1891-1954 *WhAm 3*
Baare, Frederick 1823-1910 *NatCAB 15*
Baars, Henry Gerhardt Sophus 1844-1909 *NatCAB 16*
Baars, Theo 1876-1941 *NatCAB 48*
Babasinian, V S 1876-1939 *WhAm 1*
Babb, Alta Woody 1867- *WomWWA 14*
Babb, Charles Wilkes 1863-1956 *NatCAB 49*
Babb, Clement Edwin 1821-1906 *WhAm 1*
Babb, Cyrus Cates 1867-1937 *WhAm 1*
Babb, Deborah Bertha White *WomWWA 14*
Babb, James Elisha 1864-1934 *NatCAB 26, WhAm 1*
Babb, James Tinkham 1899-1968 *NatCAB 54, WhAm 5*
Babb, Maurice Jefferies 1870-1945 *NatCAB 34*
Babb, Max Wellington 1874-1943 *NatCAB 32, WhAm 2*
Babb, Robert 1839?- *NewYHSD*
Babb, Washington Irving 1844-1925 *WhAm 1*
Babbage, Charles 1791-1871 *McGEWB*
Babbage, Charles 1792-1871 *AsBiEn, DcScB*
Babbidge, Harold Joseph 1888-1926 *NatCAB 6*
Babbitt, Benjamin Talbot 1809-1889 *DcAmB, NatCAB 8, WhAm H*
Babbitt, Charles Albert 1851-1911 *NatCAB 19*
Babbitt, Charles James 1865-1956 *REnAW, WhAm 4*
Babbitt, Clinton 1831-1907 *BiDrAC*
Babbitt, David H 1858-1929 *REnAW*
Babbitt, Edward J 1868-1943 *REnAW*
Babbitt, Edwin B 1802?-1881 *ApCAB, NatCAB 5*
Babbitt, Edwin Burr 1862-1939 *NatCAB 30, WhAm 1*
Babbitt, Edwin Dwight 1828- *WhAm 4*
Babbitt, Elijah 1795-1887 *BiDrAC, WhAm H, WhAmP*
Babbitt, Elijah 1796-1887 *BiAUS*
Babbitt, Eugene Howard 1859- *WhAm 4*
Babbitt, Frank Cole 1867-1935 *NatCAB 25, WhAm 1*
Babbitt, George 1860-1920 *REnAW*
Babbitt, George Franklin 1848- *WhAm 4*
Babbitt, Irving 1865-1933 *AmBi, BiDAmEd, DcAmB S1, EncAB, NatCAB 23, WebAB, WhAm 1*
Babbitt, Isaac 1799-1862 *AmBi, ApCAB, DcAmB, Drake, NatCAB 13, TwCBDA, WebAB, WhAm H*
Babbitt, James Edward 1902-1944 *NatCAB 43*
Babbitt, John Edward 1872-1936 *NatCAB 30*
Babbitt, Juliette M d1930 *WhAm 3, WomWWA 14*
Babbitt, Kurnal R 1864-1920 *WhAm 1*
Babbitt, Lawrence Sprague 1839-1903 *TwCBDA, WhAm 1*
Babbitt, Mary Brigham King *WomWWA 14*
Babbitt, Mary Edith Tarbox *WomWWA 14*
Babbitt, Milton Byron 1916- *McGEWB, WebAB*
Babbitt, William 1863-1930 *REnAW*
Babbott, Frank Lusk 1854-1933 *NatCAB 25,*

WhAm 1
Babbott, Frank Lusk 1891-1970 *NatCAB 55*
Babbs, Arthur Vergil 1864- *WhAm 4*
Babbs, Charles Frederick 1903-1973 *WhAm 6*
Babcock, Albert 1848-1930 *NatCAB 25, WhAm 4*
Babcock, Alfred 1805-1871 *BiAUS, BiDrAC, WhAm H*
Babcock, Allen d1969 *WhAm 5*
Babcock, Amory L *NewYHSD*
Babcock, Bernie 1868- *WhAm 5*
Babcock, Birnie 1868- *WomWWA 14*
Babcock, Birton E 1870-1941 *WhAm 1*
Babcock, Charles 1829-1913 *TwCBDA, WhAm 1*
Babcock, Charles A 1833-1876 *ApCAB*
Babcock, Charles Henry *WhAm 1*
Babcock, Charles Henry 1899-1967 *WhAm 4A, WhAm 5*
Babcock, Christopher Avery 1757-1780 *ApCAB Sup*
Babcock, Courtlandt Guynet 1839-1896 *NatCAB 19*
Babcock, Dean 1888- *IIBEAAW*
Babcock, Earle Brownell 1881-1935 *WhAm 1*
Babcock, Earle Jay 1865-1925 *NatCAB 25, WhAm 1*
Babcock, Edward Vose 1864-1948 *WhAm 2A*
Babcock, Elisha d1821 *Drake*
Babcock, Elnora Monroe 1852- *AmWom*
Babcock, Emma Whitcomb 1849- *AmWom*
Babcock, Ernest Brown 1877-1954 *WhAm 3*
Babcock, George DeAlbert 1875-1942 *NatCAB 31*
Babcock, George Henry 1852-1916 *NatCAB 17*
Babcock, George Herman 1832-1893 *DcAmB, NatCAB 5, WhAm H*
Babcock, Guilford Carlile 1874-1945 *NatCAB 39*
Babcock, Hannah Almy 1855- *NatCAB 16*
Babcock, Harold Delos 1882-1968 *WhAm 5*
Babcock, Harold Lester 1886-1953 *NatCAB 40*
Babcock, Harriet d1952 *WhAm 3*
Babcock, Harry Allan 1891-1960 *WhAm 4*
Babcock, Havilah 1837-1905 *NatCAB 12, NatCAB 40*
Babcock, Havilah 1898-1964 *WhAm 4*
Babcock, Helen Louise B 1867- *AmWom*
Babcock, Henry 1736-1800 *ApCAB, Drake, NatCAB 8*
Babcock, Howard Edward 1889-1950 *DcAmB S4, WhAm 3*
Babcock, Ida Dobson 1870- *IIBEAAW*
Babcock, Irving Brown 1891-1964 *WhAm 4*
Babcock, James Chester 1908-1974 *WhAm 6*
Babcock, James F 1809-1874 *ApCAB*
Babcock, James Francis 1844-1897 *ApCAB, DcAmB, NatCAB 10, TwCBDA, WhAm H*
Babcock, James Wood 1856-1922 *DcAmB*
Babcock, James Woods 1856-1922 *NatCAB 22, WhAm 1*
Babcock, John Breckinridge 1843-1909 *WhAm 1*
Babcock, John Pease 1860- *WhAm 4*
Babcock, Joseph Weeks 1850-1909 *BiDrAC, DcAmB, TwCBDA, WhAm 1, WhAmP*
Babcock, Josephine 1882- *WomWWA 14*
Babcock, Joshua 1707-1783 *NatCAB 4*
Babcock, Kendric Charles 1864-1932 *NatCAB 25, WhAm 1*
Babcock, Leander 1811-1864 *BiAUS, BiDrAC, WhAm H*
Babcock, Louis Locke 1868- *WhAm 5*

Babcock, Maltbie Davenport 1858-1901 *DcAmB, NatCAB 14, WhAm H*
Babcock, Maud May 1867- *WomWWA 14*
Babcock, Morey Seth 1871-1947 *NatCAB 35*
Babcock, Nathan 1824-1902 *NatCAB 16*
Babcock, O E 1835-1884 *BiAUS Sup*
Babcock, Orville E 1835-1884 *ApCAB, DcAmB, NatCAB 4, TwCBDA, WebAMB, WhAm H, WhAmP*
Babcock, Orville Elias 1835-1894 *NatCAB 16*
Babcock, Richard Earle 1889-1957 *WhAm 3*
Babcock, Richard Fayerweather 1887-1954 *NatCAB 41*
Babcock, Robert Hall 1851-1930 *ApCAB X, NatCAB 18, WhAm 1*
Babcock, Robert Weston 1893-1963 *WhAm 4*
Babcock, Robert Witbeck 1895-1965 *NatCAB 53*
Babcock, Rufus 1798-1875 *ApCAB, DcAmReB, Drake, NatCAB 8, TwCBDA*
Babcock, S B *NatCAB 1*
Babcock, Samuel Denison 1822-1902 *NatCAB 12, WhAm 1*
Babcock, Samuel Gavitt 1851-1942 *WhAm 2*
Babcock, Sarah Perkins Johnson *WomWWA 14*
Babcock, Stephen Moulton 1843-1931 *AmBi, DcAmB S1, DcScB, EncAAH, McGEWB, NatCAB 22, WebAB, WhAm 1*
Babcock, Warren LaVerne 1873-1942 *NatCAB 32, WhAm 2*
Babcock, Washington Irving 1858-1917 *DcAmB, WhAm 1*
Babcock, William 1785-1838 *BiAUS, BiDrAC, WhAm H*
Babcock, William Augustus 1851-1913 *NatCAB 16*
Babcock, William Henry 1849-1922 *NatCAB 20, WhAm 1*
Babcock, William P 1826-1899 *NewYHSD*
Babcock, William Waterman 1903-1966 *WhAm 4*
Babcock, William Wayne 1872- *ApCAB X, WhAm 5*
Babcock, Winnifred Eaton 1879- *WhAm 6, WomWWA 14*
Babel, Isaac Emmanuelovich 1894-1941 *McGEWB*
Baber, Ambrose *BiAUS*
Baber, George W 1898-1970 *WhAm 5*
Baber, Ray Erwin 1891-1960 *WhAm 4*
Babeuf, Francois Noel 1760-1797 *McGEWB*
Babin, Anna Bullion 1878- *WomWWA 14*
Babin, Hosea John 1842- *WhAm 5*
Babin, Victor 1908-1972 *WhAm 5*
Babinet, Jacques 1794-1872 *AsBiEn, DcScB*
Babington, Charles Cardale 1808-1895 *DcScB*
Babington, William 1756-1833 *DcScB*
Babinski, Joseph 1857-1932 *BiHiMed*
Babize, August Charles 1862- *NatCAB 18*
Babka, John Joseph 1884-1937 *BiDrAC, WhAmP*
Babler, Bernard Joseph 1914-1974 *WhAm 6*
Babler, Jacob Leonard 1870-1945 *NatCAB 33*
Babler, Jacob Leonard 1872-1945 *ApCAB X, WhAm 2*
Babson, Caroline Wheeler 1856- *WomWWA 14*
Babson, Helen Corliss *WomWWA 14*
Babson, Henry Blake 1875-1970 *NatCAB 55*
Babson, Herman 1871-1925 *WhAm 1*
Babson, Joseph Edward 1830-1875 *NatCAB 19*
Babson, Paul Talbot 1894-1972 *WhAm 5*
Babson, R *NewYHSD*

Babson, Robert E *NewYHSD*

Babson, Roger Ward 1875-1967 *NatCAB 53,*
WebAB, WhAm 4

Babst, Earl D 1870-1967 *NatCAB 54,*
WhAm 4

Babtiste, Gertrude Tifft 1875- *WomWWA 14*

Babur 1483-1530 *WhoMilH*

Babur, Zahir-Ud-Din Muhammed 1483-1530
McGEWB

Baby, Francois d1864 *ApCAB*

Baby, Louis Francois George 1834- *ApCAB*

Baby Doe *REnAW*

Baca, Elfego 1865-1945 *REnAW*

Baca, Luis 1826-1855 *ApCAB*

Baccaloni, Salvatore 1900-1969 *WhAm 5*

Baccelli, Guido 1830-1916 *DcScB*

Bacchus, Thomas Walley 1862-1944
NatCAB 36

Bach, Aleksei Nikolaevich 1857-1946 *DcScB*

Bach, Carl Philipp Emanuel 1714-1788
McGEWB

Bach, Ernest Norman 1891-1966 *NatCAB 52*

Bach, George William 1877-1954 *NatCAB 41*

Bach, Harry 1922-1974 *WhAm 6*

Bach, Johann Christian 1735-1782 *McGEWB*

Bach, Johann Sebastian 1685-1750 *McGEWB*

Bach, Oscar Bruno 1884- *WhAm 3*

Bach, Ralph Edward 1903-1973 *WhAm 5*

Bach, Richard F d1968 *WhAm 4A*

Bach, Theodore Franklin 1900-1962
NatCAB 50

Bach, Thomas Cumming 1854- *WhAm 4*

Bacharach, Burt 1929- *WebAB*

Bacharach, Eric William 1883-1965 *WhAm 5*

Bacharach, Isaac 1870-1956 *BiDrAC,*
WhAm 3, WhAmP

Bache, Alexander Dallas 1806-1867 *AmBi,*
ApCAB, BiAUS, BiDAmEd, DcAmB,
DcScB, Drake, McGEWB, NatCAB 3,
TwCBDA, WebAB, WhAm H

Bache, Benjamin Franklin 1769-1798 *AmBi,*
ApCAB, DcAmB, Drake, NatCAB 19,
TwCBDA, WebAB, WhAm H, WhAmP

Bache, Benjamin Franklin 1801-1881 *ApCAB,*
TwCBDA

Bache, Dallas d1902 *WhAm 1*

Bache, Emily Hinds 1880- *WomWWA 14*

Bache, Franklin 1792-1864 *AmBi, ApCAB,*
DcAmB, Drake, NatCAB 5, TwCBDA

Bache, Franklin 1797-1864 *WhAm H*

Bache, George M 1840- *NatCAB 13*

Bache, George Mifflin 1810?-1846 *Drake*

Bache, Harold L 1894-1968 *WhAm 5*

Bache, Hartman 1797?-1872 *ApCAB, Drake,*
TwCBDA

Bache, Henrietta Ellicott 1842- *WomWWA 14*

Bache, Henry W 1839-1878 *ApCAB*

Bache, Jules Semon 1861-1944 *DcAmB S3,*
NatCAB 14, NatCAB 34, WhAm 2

Bache, Leopold Semon 1865-1927 *NatCAB 21,*
WhAm 1

Bache, Louise Franklin d1948 *WhAm 2*

Bache, Margaret Hartman 1875-
WomWWA 14

Bache, Nannie Greenway Trigg *WomWWA 14*

Bache, Rene 1861- *WhAm 4*

Bache, Richard 1737-1811 *AmBi, ApCAB,*
DcAmB, Drake, NatCAB 7, TwCBDA,
WhAm H, WhAmP

Bache, Sarah 1744-1808 *ApCAB, Drake,*
NatCAB 7, TwCBDA

Bache, Sarah Franklin 1743-1808 *NotAW*

Bache, Theophylact 1734?-1807 *ApCAB,*
DcAmB, NatCAB 1

Bache, Theophylact 1735-1807 *WhAm H*

Bache, William 1771-1845 *NewYHSD,*
WhAm H

Bache-Wiig, Jens 1880- *WhAm 6*

Bachelard, Gaston 1884-1962 *DcScB*

Bachelder, John 1817-1906 *AmBi, DcAmB,*
NatCAB 12

Bachelder, John Badger 1825-1894 *NewYHSD,*
WhAm H

Bachelder, Nahum Josiah 1854-1934
NatCAB 13, WhAm 1

Bachelier, Louis 1870-1946 *DcScB*

Bacheller, Addison Irving 1859-1950
NatCAB 12

Bacheller, Irving 1859-1950 *ApCAB X,*
DcAmB S4, NatCAB 40, WhAm 2A

Bacheller, Joseph Henry 1869-1939 *WhAm 1*

Bachem, Albert 1888-1957 *WhAm 3*

Bacher, Otto Henry 1856-1909 *DcAmB,*
NatCAB 21, WhAm 1

Bachert, Max *ApCAB X*

Bachet DeMeziriac, Claude-Gaspar 1581-1638
DcScB

Bachhuber, Louis Martin 1870-1927
NatCAB 22

Bachi, Pietro 1787-1853 *ApCAB, Drake*

Bachiller Y Morales, Antonio 1812- *ApCAB*

Bachke, Halvard Huitfeldt 1873-1948 *WhAm 3*

Bachman, A Johnson 1882-1955 *NatCAB 50*

Bachman, Absalom Pierre 1861- *WhAm 4*

Bachman, Allan Earnshaw 1908-1970 *WhAm 5*

Bachman, C *NewYHSD*

Bachman, Dora Sandoe 1869- *WomWWA 14*

Bachman, Frank Puterbaugh 1871-1934
WhAm 1

Bachman, Henry 1838?- *NewYHSD*

Bachman, Henry T 1835-1896 *NatCAB 5*

Bachman, Ingeborg 1926-1974 *WhAm 6*

Bachman, John *NewYHSD*

Bachman, John 1790-1874 *AmBi, ApCAB,*
DcAmB, Drake, TwCBDA, WhAm H

Bachman, Jonathan Waverley 1837-1924
NatCAB 20

Bachman, Jonathan Waverly 1837-1924
WhAm 1

Bachman, Maria Martin *NotAW*

Bachman, Max 1862- *TwCBDA*

Bachman, Nathan 1832-1914 *WhAm 1*

Bachman, Nathan Lynn 1878-1937 *BiDrAC,*
NatCAB 33, WhAm 1, WhAmP

Bachman, Paul Stanton 1901-1957 *WhAm 3*

Bachman, Reuben Knecht 1834-1911 *BiDrAC*

Bachman, Robert Abraham 1872- *WhAm 5*

Bachman, Solomon 1827- *NatCAB 3*

Bachmann, Augustus Quirinus 1652-1723 *DcScB*

Bachmann, Carl George 1890- *BiDrAC,*
WhAmP

Bachmann, Louis 1872-1947 *NatCAB 36*

Bachmann, Max 1862- *IlBEAAW*

Bachmann, Paul Gustav Heinrich 1837-1920
DcScB

Bachmann, Raphael Otto 1921-1972 *WhAm 5*

Bachmann, Werner Emmanuel 1901-1951
DcAmB S5, WhAm 3

Bachmeyer, Arthur Charles 1886-1953
NatCAB 46, WhAm 3

Bachour, Rafic Jibrail 1901-1973 *WhAm 6*

Bachrach, Benjamin Charles *ApCAB X*

Bachrach, Grace Baer 1884-1962 *NatCAB 47*

Bachrach, Louis Fabian 1881-1963 *WhAm 4*

Bachrach, Walter Keyser 1888-1963 *WhAm 4*

Bacigalupi, James Augustus 1882-1950
NatCAB 39, WhAm 3

Bacigalupi, John Jerome 1867-1943 *NatCAB 40*

Bacigalupi, Tadini 1881-1962 *WhAm 4*

Back, Ernest Adna 1880-1959 *NatCAB 47,*
WhAm 6

Back, Ernst E A 1881-1959 *DcScB*

Back, Sir George 1796-1878 *ApCAB, Drake*

Back, George Irving 1894-1972 *WhAm 5*

Back, Joe W 1899- *IlBEAAW*

Backer, George 1903-1974 *WhAm 6*

Backer, Marcus 1896-1966 *NatCAB 53*

Backer, Otto Henry 1856-1909 *AmBi*

Backer, Samuel 1906-1957 *NatCAB 46*

Backes, John H 1863-1935 *WhAm 1*

Backhaus, Wilhelm 1884-1969 *WhAm 5*

Backlin, Axel Frederick 1863-1929 *NatCAB 22*

Backlund, Jons Oskar 1846-1916 *DcScB*

Backman, Kenneth B 1895-1960 *WhAm 4*

Backofen, Charles 1801?- *NewYHSD*

Backstrand, Clifford J 1897-1968 *WhAm 5*

Backus, Annie Amelia *WomWWA 14*

Backus, August Charles 1877-1952 *WhAm 3*

Backus, Azel 1765-1816 *DcAmB, Drake,*
NatCAB 7, TwCBDA, WhAm H

Backus, Azel 1765-1817 *ApCAB*

Backus, Carrie Haskins 1860- *WomWWA 14*

Backus, Charles 1749-1803 *ApCAB, Drake,*
NatCAB 12

Backus, Charles 1831-1880 *NatCAB 12*

Backus, Charles Chapman 1816-1899 *TwCBDA*

Backus, Edward Wellington 1860-1934
NatCAB 36, WhAm 1

Backus, Edwin Burdette 1888-1955 *WhAm 3*

Backus, Electus d1813 *ApCAB, Drake*

Backus, Electus 1804-1862 *ApCAB*

Backus, Emma S *WomWWA 14*

Backus, Franklin Thomas 1813-1870 *ApCAB,*
Drake, NatCAB 13, TwCBDA

Backus, Harriet Ivins *WomWWA 14*

Backus, Henry Clinton 1848-1908 *NatCAB 6*

Backus, Henry T *BiAUS*

Backus, Isaac 1724-1806 *AmBi, ApCAB,*
DcAmB, DcAmReB, Drake, McGEWB,
NatCAB 7, TwCBDA, WebAB,
WhAm H

Backus, James 1764-1816 *TwCBDA*

Backus, Louise Burton Laidlaw 1906-1973
NatCAB 57, WhAm 6

Backus, Manson Franklin 1853-1935
NatCAB 11, WhAm 1

Backus, Samuel Woolsey 1844- *WhAm 4*

Backus, Standish 1875-1943 *WhAm 2*

Backus, Susan Emily Foote *WomWWA 14*

Backus, Truman Jay 1842-1908 *DcAmB,*
NatCAB 5, TwCBDA, WhAm 1

Backus, William Woodbridge 1803-1892
TwCBDA

Backus, Wilson Marvin 1865-1945 *WhAm 2*

Bacoats, John Alvin 1892-1965 *NatCAB 52,*
WhAm 4

Bacon, A Barry 1870-1936 *NatCAB 36*

Bacon, Albert Williamson 1841-1922 *ApCAB X,*
WhAm 1

Bacon, Albion Fellows 1865-1933 *ApCAB X,*
NatCAB 15, NatCAB 34, NotAW,
WhAm 1, WomWWA 14

Bacon, Alexander Samuel 1853-1920 *WhAm 1*

Bacon, Alice Mabel 1858-1918 *AmBi, DcAmB,*
NotAW, WhAm 1, WomWWA 14

Bacon, Augustus Octavius 1839-1914
ApCAB Sup, BiDrAC, DcAmB,
NatCAB 12, TwCBDA, WhAm 1,
WhAmP

Bacon, Benjamin Wisner 1860-1932 *DcAmB S1,*
NatCAB 23, WhAm 1

Bacon, Caroline Tilden 1873-1931 *NatCAB 22,*
WomWWA 14

Bacon, Charles Harrison 1877-1955 *NatCAB 47*

Bacon, Charles Sumner 1856-1947 *WhAm 2*

Bacon, Charls Beattie 1887-1953 *NatCAB 42*

Bacon, Clara Latimer 1866-1948 *WhAm 2*

Bacon, Corinne *WomWWA 14*

Bacon, Daniel 1862-1934 *NatCAB 24*

Bacon, David 1771-1817 *ApCAB, DcAmB,*
WhAm H

Bacon, David Francis 1813-1866 *ApCAB,*
Drake

Bacon, David W 1814-1874 *ApCAB*

Bacon, David William 1813-1874 *NatCAB 10,*
TwCBDA, WhAm H

Bacon, Delia Salter 1811-1859 *AmBi, ApCAB,*
DcAmB, NatCAB 1, NotAW, TwCBDA,
WebAB, WhAm H

Bacon, Dolores 1870- *WomWWA 14*

Bacon, E F *NewYHSD*

Bacon, Edgar Mayhew 1855-1935 *WhAm 1*

Bacon, Edmund 1776-1826 *ApCAB, TwCBDA*

Bacon, Edward Alsted 1897-1968 *NatCAB 54*

Bacon, Edward Payson 1834-1916 *DcAmB,*
NatCAB 2, TwCBDA, WhAm 1

Bacon, Edward Rathbone 1846-1915 *WhAm 1*

Bacon, Edward Rathbone 1847-1915 *NatCAB 4*

Bacon, Edwin Munroe 1844-1916 *ApCAB,*
DcAmB, NatCAB 13, TwCBDA,
WhAm 1, WhAm 2

Bacon, Elizabeth Daken 1844- *WomWWA 14*

Bacon, Ellis Williams 1874-1961 *NatCAB 48*

Bacon, Ezekiel 1776-1870 *ApCAB, BiAUS,*
BiDrAC, Drake, NatCAB 5, TwCBDA,
WhAm H, WhAmP

Bacon, Francis d1912 *WhAm 1*

Bacon, Sir Francis 1561-1626 *AsBiEn, DcScB,*
McGEWB

Bacon, Francis 1831-1905 *NatCAB 2*

Bacon, Francis 1909- *McGEWB*

Bacon, Francis Leonard 1889-1958 *NatCAB 48,*
WhAm 3

Bacon, Francis McNiel 1835-1912 *NatCAB 17*

Bacon, Francis R 1888-1965 *WhAm 4*
Bacon, Frank *IIBEAAW*
Bacon, Frank 1864-1922 *AmBi, DcAmB, NatCAB 20, WhAm 1*
Bacon, Frank Rogers 1872-1949 *WhAm 2*
Bacon, Frederic William 1874-1951 *NatCAB 41*
Bacon, Frederick Hampden 1849-1928 *NatCAB 6*
Bacon, Gaspar Griswold 1886-1947 *WhAm 2*
Bacon, George *NewYHSD*
Bacon, George Albert 1869-1945 *NatCAB 35*
Bacon, George Allen 1830- *NatCAB 5*
Bacon, George Andrew 1847-1930 *WhAm 1*
Bacon, George Morgan 1872- *WhAm 5*
Bacon, George P 1866-1941 *WhAm 1*
Bacon, George Wood 1869-1953 *NatCAB 44, WhAm 3*
Bacon, Georgeanna Muirson Woolsey *NotAW*
Bacon, Gorham 1855-1940 *NatCAB 29*
Bacon, Helen Hazard 1862- *WomWWA 14*
Bacon, Henry 1813-1856 *Drake*
Bacon, Henry 1839-1912 *NewYHSD*
Bacon, Henry 1840-1912 *ApCAB, Drake*
Bacon, Henry 1846-1915 *BiDrAC, WhAmP*
Bacon, Henry 1866-1924 *AmBi, ApCAB X, DcAmB, NatCAB 20, WhAm 1*
Bacon, Henry Selden 1872-1954 *NatCAB 45*
Bacon, Irving R 1875-1962 *IIBEAAW*
Bacon, James Terrell 1826- *NatCAB 3*
Bacon, Joel Smith 1801-1869 *Drake*
Bacon, Joel Smith 1802-1869 *NatCAB 3*
Bacon, John 1737-1820 *BiAUS, Drake*
Bacon, John 1738-1820 *BiDrAC, DcAmB, NatCAB 22, WhAm H, WhAmP*
Bacon, John E *NewYHSD*
Bacon, John Edmund 1830-1897 *NatCAB 12*
Bacon, John Edmund 1832-1897 *ApCAB*
Bacon, John Harwood 1875- *WhAm 5*
Bacon, John Mosby 1844-1913 *ApCAB Sup, WhAm 1*
Bacon, John Watson 1827-1907 *NatCAB 6, WhAm 1*
Bacon, Josephine Dodge Daskam 1876- *ApCAB X, WhAm 5, WomWWA 14*
Bacon, Leon Brooks 1870- *NatCAB 18*
Bacon, Leonard 1802-1881 *AmBi, ApCAB, DcAmB, DcAmReB, Drake, NatCAB 1, TwCBDA, WhAm H, WhAmP*
Bacon, Leonard 1887-1954 *DcAmB S5, NatCAB 49, WhAm 3*
Bacon, Leonard Woolsey 1830-1907 *ApCAB, DcAmB, NatCAB 12, TwCBDA, WhAm 1*
Bacon, Lester Campbell 1901-1959 *NatCAB 45*
Bacon, Louis *NewYHSD*
Bacon, Mark Reeves 1852-1941 *BiDrAC*
Bacon, Mary Ann 1787?- *NewYHSD*
Bacon, Mary Elizabeth 1898-1974 *WhAm 6*
Bacon, Mary Schell Hoke 1870- *WhAm 5*
Bacon, Nathaniel 1620-1692 *NatCAB 13*
Bacon, Nathaniel 1630?-1676 *TwCBDA*
Bacon, Nathaniel 1630?-1677 *ApCAB*
Bacon, Nathaniel 1646?-1676 *Drake*
Bacon, Nathaniel 1647-1676 *AmBi, DcAmB, EncAAH, EncAB, McGEWB, NatCAB 5, REnAW, WebAB, WebAMB, WhAm H*
Bacon, Nathaniel Terry 1858-1926 *NatCAB 32*
Bacon, Peggy 1895- *BnEnAmA*
Bacon, Rachel Haines 1880- *WomWWA 14*
Bacon, Raymond Foss 1880-1954 *NatCAB 46, WhAm 3*
Bacon, Rebecca Taylor *ApCAB*
Bacon, Robert 1860-1919 *AmBi, ApCAB X, BiDrUSE, DcAmB, NatCAB 14, WhAm 1*
Bacon, Robert Law 1884-1938 *WhAmP*
Bacon, Robert Low 1884-1938 *BiDrAC, NatCAB 29, WhAm 1*
Bacon, Robert Stillwell 1907-1973 *WhAm 5*
Bacon, Roger 1214?-1294 *BiHiMed, McGEWB*
Bacon, Roger 1219?-1292? *DcScB*
Bacon, Roger 1220?-1292? *AsBiEn*
Bacon, Samuel 1781-1820 *ApCAB, Drake, TwCBDA*
Bacon, Selden 1861-1946 *WhAm 2*
Bacon, Sherman Joseph 1812- *NatCAB 3*
Bacon, Theodore *ApCAB*

Bacon, Thomas 1700?-1768 *DcAmB, Drake, WhAm H*
Bacon, Thomas Scott 1825- *NatCAB 5*
Bacon, Walter W 1880-1962 *WhAm 4*
Bacon, Willard Michael 1860-1947 *NatCAB 36*
Bacon, William Johnson 1803-1889 *BiDrAC, WhAm H, WhAmP*
Bacon, William Stevens 1877-1955 *WhAm 3*
Bacon, William Thompson 1814-1881 *ApCAB, Drake*
Bacone, Almon C 1830- *NatCAB 3*
Bacote, Samuel William 1866- *WhoColR*
Badawi Pasha, Abdel Hamid 1887-1965 *WhAm 4*
Bade, William Frederic 1871-1936 *DcAmB S2, NatCAB 27, WhAm 1*
Bade, William Frederick 1871-1936 *AmBi*
Badeau, Adam 1831-1895 *ApCAB, DcAmB, Drake, NatCAB 6, TwCBDA, WhAm H, WhAmP*
Badeau, Isaac *NewYHSD*
Badeau, Jonathan F *NewYHSD*
Badeau, Marie 1883- *WomWWA 14*
Baden-Powell, Robert Stephenson Smyth 1857-1941 *WhoMilH*
Badenberger, Henry 1899-1961 *WhAm 4*
Badenhausen, John Phillips 1876-1954 *NatCAB 41*
Bader, Sir Douglas 1910- *WhWW-II*
Bader, Jesse Moren 1886-1963 *WhAm 4*
Bader, Ralph Hedrick 1888-1939 *WhAm 1*
Bader, Richard George 1920-1974 *WhAm 6*
Badger, Algernon Sidney 1839- *NatCAB 10*
Badger, Charles Johnston 1853-1932 *DcAmB S1, WhAm 1*
Badger, DeWitt Clinton 1858-1926 *BiDrAC, WhAm 4, WhAmP*
Badger, Erastus Beethoven 1886-1964 *NatCAB 54*
Badger, George Edmund 1795-1866 *ApCAB, BiAUS, BiDrAC, BiDrUSE, DcAmB, Drake, NatCAB 3, TwCBDA, WhAm H, WhAmP*
Badger, George Henry 1859- *WhAm 4*
Badger, James W *NewYHSD*
Badger, John C 1822?- *NewYHSD*
Badger, Jonathan *NewYHSD*
Badger, Joseph 1708-1765 *AmBi, BnEnAmA, DcAmB, NewYHSD, WhAm H*
Badger, Joseph 1722-1803 *ApCAB, Drake, TwCBDA*
Badger, Joseph 1757-1846 *ApCAB, DcAmB, Drake, NatCAB 6, WhAm H*
Badger, Joseph 1792-1852 *ApCAB, TwCBDA*
Badger, Joseph W *NewYHSD*
Badger, Luther 1785-1869 *BiAUS, BiDrAC, Drake, WhAm H*
Badger, Mrs. Milton *NewYHSD*
Badger, Milton 1800-1873 *ApCAB, NatCAB 6*
Badger, Oscar Charles 1823-1899 *ApCAB, DcAmB, NatCAB 5, TwCBDA, WhAm 1*
Badger, Oscar Charles 1890-1958 *WhAm 3*
Badger, Philip Owen 1891-1973 *WhAm 5*
Badger, S *NewYHSD*
Badger, S W *NewYHSD*
Badger, Sherwin Campbell 1901-1972 *NatCAB 56*
Badger, Stephen 1726-1803 *Drake*
Badger, Thomas 1792-1868 *NewYHSD*
Badger, Thomas H *NewYHSD*
Badger, Walter Irving 1859-1926 *WhAm 1*
Badger, Walter Lucius 1886-1958 *NatCAB 47, WhAm 3*
Badger, William *NewYHSD*
Badger, William 1779-1852 *ApCAB, BiAUS, Drake, NatCAB 11, TwCBDA*
Badger, William Earl 1879-1926 *NatCAB 20*
Badger, William Otis, Jr. 1879- *NatCAB 17*
Badgerow, Gordon Ralph 1846-1916 *NatCAB 17*
Badgley, Maxwell Forrest 1898-1969 *WhAm 5*
Badgley, Sidney Rose 1850- *WhAm 1*
Badi Al-Zaman Al-Jazari *DcScB*
Badin, Stephen Theodore 1768-1853 *ApCAB, DcAmB, REnAW, TwCBDA, WebAB, WhAm H*
Bading, Gerhard Adolph 1870-1946 *NatCAB 34,*

**WhAm 2*
Badlam *NewYHSD*
Badlam, Ezra 1746-1788 *ApCAB, TwCBDA*
Badlam, Stephen 1748-1815 *ApCAB, TwCBDA*
Badlam, Stephen 1751-1815 *Drake*
Badley, Brenton Thoburn 1876-1949 *WhAm 2*
Badoglio, Pietro 1871-1956 *McGEWB, WhWW-II, WhoMilH*
Badt, Milton Benjamin 1884-1966 *NatCAB 54, WhAm 4*
Baehr, Carl Adolph 1885-1959 *WhAm 4*
Baehr, Max Joseph 1858-1934 *WhAm 1*
Baehr, William Alfred 1873-1943 *WhAm 2*
Baehr, William Frederick Otto 1899-1972 *WhAm 5*
Baekeland, Celine d1957 *WhAm 3*
Baekeland, George 1895-1966 *NatCAB 52, WhAm 4*
Baekeland, Leo Hendrik 1863-1944 *ApCAB X, AsBiEn, DcAmB S3, DcScB, McGEWB, NatCAB 15, NatCAB 32, WebAB, WhAm 2*
Baena, Antonio Ladislao Monteiro d1851? *ApCAB*
Baena, Antonio Ladislaus Monteiro d1851? *Drake*
Baensch, Emil 1857- *WhAm 3*
Baensch, Willy E 1893-1972 *WhAm 5*
Baepler, Walter A 1893-1958 *WhAm 3*
Baer *NewYHSD*
Baer, Arthur 1886-1969 *WebAB*
Baer, Arthur A 1896-1975 *WhAm 6*
Baer, George, Jr. 1763-1834 *BiAUS, BiDrAC, WhAm H, WhAmP*
Baer, George Frederick 1842-1914 *AmBi, DcAmB, EncAB, NatCAB 14, WebAB, WhAm 1*
Baer, George James 1911-1966 *NatCAB 54*
Baer, Jean Hitchcock 1918-1974 *WhAm 6*
Baer, John M 1886-1969 *WhAm 5*
Baer, John Miller 1886-1970 *BiDrAC*
Baer, John Willis 1861-1931 *TwCBDA, WhAm 1*
Baer, Joseph Augustus 1878- *WhAm 6*
Baer, Joseph Jay 1888-1965 *NatCAB 53*
Baer, Joseph Louis 1880-1954 *NatCAB 42, WhAm 3*
Baer, Karl Ernst Von 1792-1876 *AsBiEn, DcScB, McGEWB*
Baer, Libbie C *WomWWA 14*
Baer, Libbie C 1846- *WhAm 4*
Baer, Libbie C Riley 1849- *AmWom*
Baer, Sidney R 1891-1956 *WhAm 3*
Baer, Townsend W 1903-1974 *WhAm 6*
Baer, Walter Hilmar 1902-1968 *NatCAB 54*
Baer, William Bush 1902-1958 *WhAm 3*
Baer, William Jacob 1860-1941 *NatCAB 5, WhAm 1*
Baer, William Stevenson 1872-1931 *DcAmB S1, NatCAB 28*
Baerer, Henry 1837-1908 *NatCAB 12, NewYHSD*
Baerle, Gaspard Van 1584-1648 *ApCAB*
Baermann, Carl 1839-1913 *DcAmB*
Baermann, Walter Peter 1903-1972 *NatCAB 57*
Baerresen, Harald William 1846- *NatCAB 12*
Baerwald, Paul 1871- *WhAm 5*
Baetjer, Edwin George 1868-1945 *NatCAB 34, WhAm 2*
Baetjer, Frederick Henry 1874-1933 *DcAmB S1, NatCAB 25, WhAm 1*
Baeyer, Adolf Johann F Wilhelm Von 1835-1917 *DcScB*
Baeyer, Johann Friedrich W Adolf Von 1835-1917 *AsBiEn, McGEWB*
Baez, Buenaventura d1884 *ApCAB*
Baez, Buenaventura 1812-1884 *McGEWB*
Baez, Buenaventura 1820-1884 *Drake*
Baez, Cecilio 1862- *WhAm 4*
Baez, Joan 1941- *WebAB*
Baeza, Marco A 1923-1965 *WhAm 4*
Baffin, William 1584?-1622 *ApCAB, AsBiEn, Drake, McGEWB*
Baganz, Crawford Norbert 1905-1955 *NatCAB 44*
Bagar, Robert 1899-1957 *WhAm 3*
Bagby, Albert Morris 1859-1941 *NatCAB 33,*

WhAm 1

Bagby, Arthur Pendleton 1794-1858 *ApCAB,*
BiAUS, BiDrAC, DcAmB, Drake,
TwCBDA, WhAm H, WhAmP
Bagby, Arthur Pendleton 1796-1858
NatCAB 10
Bagby, George Franklin 1865- *WhAm 4*
Bagby, George Poindexter 1879-1934 *WhAm 1*
Bagby, George William 1828-1883 *AmBi,*
ApCAB, BiDConf, DcAmB, NatCAB 7,
NatCAB 24, WhAm H
Bagby, John Courts 1819-1896 *BiAUS,*
BiDrAC, WhAm H
Bagby, John Hampden Chamberlayne 1867-1934
NatCAB 24, WhAm 1
Bagby, William Buck 1855- *WhAm 4*
Bagdatopoulos, William Spencer 1888-1965
WhAm 5
Bagehot, Walter 1826-1877 *McGEWB*
Bagett, A *NewYHSD*
Bagg, Clara B 1861- *AmWom*
Bagg, Henry Howard 1852-1928 *IIBEAAW*
Bagg, Lyman Hotchkiss 1846-1911 *WhAm 1*
Bagg, Rufus Mather 1869- *WhAm 5*
Bagger, Henry Horneman 1893-1967 *WhAm 4*
Baggett, Alice 1840?- *AmWom*
Baggett, Samuel Graves 1894-1964 *NatCAB 51,*
WhAm 4
Baggs, Arthur Eugene 1886-1947 *NatCAB 35,*
WhAm 2
Baggs, Mae Lacy d1922 *WhAm 1*
Baggs, William Calhoun 1922-1969 *WhAm 5*
Baghdadi, Abu Mansur Abd Al-Qahir, Al- d1037
DcScB Sup
Bagioli, Antonio 1795-1871 *ApCAB*
Bagley, Blanche Pentecost 1858- *AmWom*
Bagley, Charles, Jr. 1882-1957 *NatCAB 45*
Bagley, Charles Benedict 1887-1946
NatCAB 36
Bagley, Charles Leland 1873- *WhAm 5*
Bagley, Clarence Booth 1843-1932 *WhAm 1*
Bagley, David Worth 1883-1960 *WhAm 4*
Bagley, Emmet Mellynn 1877-1939 *NatCAB 39*
Bagley, Florence MacLean Winger 1874-
WomWWA 14
Bagley, George Augustus 1826-1915 *BiAUS,*
BiDrAC
Bagley, George Colt 1851- *NatCAB 15*
Bagley, Isabelle Tipton *WomWWA 14*
Bagley, James M 1837-1910 *IIBEAAW*
Bagley, James Warren 1881-1947 *NatCAB 37*
Bagley, John Holroyd, Jr. 1832-1902 *BiDrAC*
Bagley, John Judson 1832-1881 *ApCAB,*
BiAUS, NatCAB 5, TwCBDA
Bagley, John Newbury 1860-1929 *NatCAB 23*
Bagley, Paul Frederick 1869-1931 *NatCAB 37*
Bagley, Sarah G *NotAW*
Bagley, William Chandler 1874-1946 *BiDAmEd,*
DcAmB S4, NatCAB 35, WebAB,
WhAm 2
Bagley, Willis Gaylord Clark 1873-1943
WhAm 2
Bagley, Worth 1874-1898 *ApCAB Sup,*
TwCBDA
Baglivi, Georgius 1668-1707 *DcScB*
Bagnall, Francis Asbury 1866-1950 *NatCAB 39*
Bagnall, Robert Wellington 1883- *WhoColR*
Bagnell, Robert 1865-1946 *WhAm 2*
Bagot, Sir Charles 1781-1843 *ApCAB, Drake,*
WhAm H
Bagramyan, Ivan 1897- *WhWW-II*
Bagration, Prince Petr Ivanovitch 1765-1812
WhoMilH
Bagstad, Anna Emilia 1876- *WhAm 5*
Bagster-Collins, Elijah William 1873- *WhAm 5*
Bagwell, Paul D 1913-1973 *WhAm 6*
Bahan, William Henry 1881-1949 *NatCAB 39*
Bahin, Louis Joseph *NewYHSD*
Bahl, William Edgar 1889-1958 *WhAm 3*
Bahler, Clyde 1900-1963 *NatCAB 56*
Bahn, Chester Bert 1893-1962 *WhAm 4*
Bahnson, Agnew Hunter 1886-1966 *NatCAB 53,*
WhAm 4
Bahnson, George Frederic 1805-1869
NatCAB 11
Bahnson, George Frederick 1805-1869 *ApCAB*
Bahr, Abel William 1877-1959 *NatCAB 48*
Bahr, C O *NewYHSD*

Bahr, Emory J 1903-1964 *WhAm 4*
Bahr, Walter Julien d1971 *WhAm 6*
Bahrenburg, Carrie Thomas Alexander 1860-
WomWWA 14
Bahrenburg, Louis P H 1873-1940 *WhAm 1*
Baier, Johann Jacob 1677-1735 *DcScB*
Baier, Victor 1861-1921 *NatCAB 12,*
WhAm 1
Baikie, William Balfour 1825-1864 *McGEWB*
Bail, Frank Wooster 1891-1964 *NatCAB 51*
Bail, Louis *NewYHSD*
Bailak Al-Qabajaqi *DcScB*
Bailey, A *NewYHSD*
Bailey, Adella Browne 1860- *WomWWA 14*
Bailey, Adolph 1822?- *NewYHSD*
Bailey, Agnes McGiffert *WomWWA 14*
Bailey, Albert Edward 1871- *WhAm 5*
Bailey, Alexander Hamilton 1817-1874 *BiAUS,*
BiDrAC, WhAm H
Bailey, Alfred 1823- *NewYHSD*
Bailey, Alfred Halsey 1869-1948 *WhAm 3*
Bailey, Alfred Miller 1879-1943 *NatCAB 35*
Bailey, Alice VanB Foos *WomWWA 14*
Bailey, Alice Ward 1857- *WhAm 4,*
WomWWA 14
Bailey, Almeria Adgate 1864- *WomWWA 14*
Bailey, Ann 1725?-1825 *AmWom, ApCAB*
Bailey, Ann 1742-1825 *AmBi, DcAmB,*
WhAm H
Bailey, Anna Leland *WomWWA 14*
Bailey, Anna Peabody 1866- *WomWWA 14*
Bailey, Anna Warner 1758-1850 *AmWom,*
ApCAB
Bailey, Anna Warner 1758-1851 *DcAmB,*
WebAMB, WhAm H
Bailey, Arnold Brown 1903-1967 *NatCAB 53*
Bailey, Arthur Low 1867-1940 *WhAm 1,*
WhAm 1C
Bailey, Arthur Scott 1877- *WhAm 5*
Bailey, B Herman 1901-1962 *NatCAB 49*
Bailey, Benjamin *NewYHSD*
Bailey, Benjamin Franklin 1860-1944
NatCAB 35
Bailey, Benjamin Franklin 1875-1944 *WhAm 2*
Bailey, Bert Heald 1875-1917 *WhAm 1*
Bailey, Bertha 1866-1935 *WhAm 1,*
WomWWA 14
Bailey, Calvin Weston 1861- *WhAm 5*
Bailey, Carl Edward 1894-1948 *WhAm 2*
Bailey, Carolyn Sherwin 1876- *WomWWA 14*
Bailey, Cassius Mercer 1876-1935 *WhAm 1*
Bailey, Charles Franklin 1863-1949 *NatCAB 17,*
WhAm 4
Bailey, Charles Henry 1831-1915 *NatCAB 31*
Bailey, Charles Justin 1859-1946 *WhAm 2*
Bailey, Charles Langdon 1909-1970 *WhAm 5*
Bailey, Charles Olin 1860-1928 *WhAm 1*
Bailey, Charles Reuben 1863- *WhAm 1*
Bailey, Charles William 1884-1959 *NatCAB 49,*
WhAm 4
Bailey, Clarence Mitchell 1841-1920 *WhAm 1*
Bailey, Cleveland Monroe 1886-1965 *BiDrAC,*
WhAmP
Bailey, Daniel Hanford 1834- *NatCAB 17*
Bailey, David Jackson 1812-1897 *BiAUS,*
BiDrAC, WhAm H, WhAmP
Bailey, Dewey Crossman 1882-1932
NatCAB 26
Bailey, Dudley Perkins 1843- *NatCAB 15*
Bailey, E Prentiss 1834-1913 *NatCAB 16*
Bailey, Ebenezer 1795-1839 *ApCAB,*
BiDAmEd, DcAmB, Drake, NatCAB 4,
WhAm H
Bailey, Edgar Henry Summerfield 1848-1933
WhAm 1
Bailey, Edith Lawrence Black 1870-
WomWWA 14
Bailey, Edward 1861-1938 *WhAm 1*
Bailey, Edward Battersby 1881-1965 *DcScB*
Bailey, Edward Latta 1872-1934 *NatCAB 25*
Bailey, Edward Monroe 1879-1948 *NatCAB 36,*
WhAm 2
Bailey, Edward Walter *WhoColR*
Bailey, Edward William 1843-1920 *NatCAB 40*
Bailey, Edwin Noyes 1849-1923 *NatCAB 21*
Bailey, Edwin Warren Marble 1863-1940
NatCAB 33
Bailey, Eli Stillman 1851-1926 *WhAm 1*

Bailey, Elijah Prentiss 1834-1913 *WhAm 1*
Bailey, Eliza Randall Simmons 1861-1939
NatCAB 29, WomWWA 14
Bailey, Ellene Alice *AmWom*
Bailey, Ervin George 1880- *WhAm 6*
Bailey, Everett Hoskins 1850-1938 *WhAm 1*
Bailey, Ezra Brewster 1841-1920 *NatCAB 6*
Bailey, F Lee 1933- *WebAB*
Bailey, Florence Augusta Merriam 1863-1948
BiCAW, DcAmB S4, NatCAB 13,
NotAW, WhAm 2, WomWWA 14
Bailey, Florence Kate *WomWWA 14*
Bailey, Francis 1735?-1815 *DcAmB,*
NewYHSD, WhAm H
Bailey, Francisco 1817?- *NewYHSD*
Bailey, Frank 1865-1953 *NatCAB 43,*
WhAm 3
Bailey, Frank Harvey 1851-1921 *DcAmB,*
WhAm 1
Bailey, Frank Moye 1876-1958 *WhAm 4*
Bailey, Frank Raymond 1877-1949 *NatCAB 38*
Bailey, Frank William 1900-1965 *NatCAB 52*
Bailey, Frazer Anderson 1888-1960 *NatCAB 47*
Bailey, Fred Oliver 1901-1964 *WhAm 4*
Bailey, Frederick Augustus Washington
1817?-1895 *WebAB*
Bailey, Frederick Randolph 1871-1923 *WhAm 1*
Bailey, Gamaliel 1807-1859 *AmBi, ApCAB,*
DcAmB, Drake, McGEWB, NatCAB 2,
TwCBDA, WebAB, WhAm H, WhAmP
Bailey, George Carter 1870-1949 *NatCAB 40*
Bailey, George Davis 1890-1966 *WhAm 4*
Bailey, George M *NewYHSD*
Bailey, George Milroy 1862- *NatCAB 5*
Bailey, George Washington 1840-1916 *WhAm 1*
Bailey, George Whitman 1848-1927
NatCAB 21
Bailey, George Wicks 1856-1909 *WhAm 1*
Bailey, Gilbert Ellis 1852-1924 *NatCAB 22,*
WhAm 1
Bailey, Gilbert Stephen 1822-1891 *ApCAB,*
NatCAB 22
Bailey, Goldsmith Fox 1823-1862 *BiAUS,*
BiDrAC, WhAm H
Bailey, Guilford Dudley 1834-1862 *ApCAB,*
NatCAB 4, TwCBDA
Bailey, Guy Winfred 1876-1940 *WhAm 1*
Bailey, Hannah Johnston 1839-1923 *AmWom,*
NatCAB 10, NotAW, WhAm 1,
WomWWA 14
Bailey, Harold Harris 1878- *WhAm 6*
Bailey, Harold Wood 1901-1974 *WhAm 6*
Bailey, Harry Louis 1877-1962 *WhAm 4*
Bailey, Henry Lloyd 1874-1961 *NatCAB 49*
Bailey, Henry Turner 1864-1931 *BiDAmEd*
Bailey, Henry Turner 1865-1931 *NatCAB 23,*
WhAm 1
Bailey, Herbert Dexter 1862-1918 *NatCAB 20*
Bailey, Hollis Russell 1852-1934 *WhAm 1*
Bailey, Hugh Coleman 1929- *EncAAH*
Bailey, Irving Widmer 1884-1967 *WhAm 4A*
Bailey, Isaac 1883- *WhoColR*
Bailey, Ivon Arthur 1900-1963 *WhAm 4*
Bailey, Jacob 1728-1816 *ApCAB, Drake,*
NatCAB 8
Bailey, Jacob 1731-1808 *ApCAB, Drake*
Bailey, Jacob 1731-1818 *DcAmB, WhAm H*
Bailey, Jacob 1738-1816 *NatCAB 1*
Bailey, Jacob Whitman 1811-1857 *ApCAB,*
DcAmB, Drake, NatCAB 10, TwCBDA,
WhAm H
Bailey, James *NewYHSD*
Bailey, James Anthony 1847-1906 *DcAmB,*
NatCAB 24, TwCBDA, WhAm 1
Bailey, James Edmund 1822-1885 *ApCAB,*
BiDrAC, NatCAB 12, TwCBDA,
WhAm H
Bailey, James Garfield 1882-1929 *WhAm 1*
Bailey, James John 1873-1930 *NatCAB 22*
Bailey, James McConnell 1873-1941
NatCAB 32
Bailey, James Montgomery 1841-1894 *AmBi,*
ApCAB, DcAmB, NatCAB 6, TwCBDA,
WhAm H
Bailey, James Robinson 1868-1941 *NatCAB 31*
Bailey, James Roosevelt *NatCAB 2*
Bailey, James Stanton 1817- *NatCAB 3*
Bailey, Jennings 1867-1963 *WhAm 4*

Bailey, Jeremiah 1773-1853 *BiAUS, BiDrAC, WhAm H*
Bailey, Jessie Emerson 1880- *WhAm 6*
Bailey, Jessie Emerson 1886- *WomWWA 14*
Bailey, John 1730-1810 *ApCAB, Drake*
Bailey, John 1786-1835 *BiAUS, BiDrAC, WhAm H*
Bailey, John Hays 1900-1968 *WhAm 5*
Bailey, John L 1795- *BiAUS*
Bailey, John Moran 1904-1975 *WhAm 6*
Bailey, John Mosher 1838-1902 *WhAm 1*
Bailey, John Mosher 1838-1916 *BiDrAC, WhAm H*
Bailey, John Ora 1880-1959 *WhAm 3*
Bailey, John Tyley 1868- *NatCAB 17*
Bailey, John Wendell 1895-1967 *NatCAB 52, WhAm 4A*
Bailey, John William 1859-1929 *NatCAB 22*
Bailey, Joseph d1867 *Drake*
Bailey, Joseph 1810-1885 *BiDrAC, WhAm H, WhAmP*
Bailey, Joseph 1825-1867 *DcAmB, WebAMB, WhAm H*
Bailey, Joseph 1827-1867 *ApCAB, NatCAB 5, TwCBDA*
Bailey, Joseph Alexis 1825-1883 *ApCAB, Drake*
Bailey, Joseph Mead 1833-1895 *ApCAB, NatCAB 13*
Bailey, Joseph Roosevelt 1814- *Drake*
Bailey, Joseph T 1806-1854 *WhAm H*
Bailey, Joseph Weldon 1862-1929 *BiDrAC, WhAmP*
Bailey, Joseph Weldon 1863-1929 *DcAmB S1, NatCAB 13, TwCBDA, WhAm 1*
Bailey, Joseph Weldon, III 1892-1943 *NatCAB 35*
Bailey, Joseph Weldon, Jr. 1892-1943 *BiDrAC, WhAm 2, WhAmP*
Bailey, Josiah William 1873-1946 *BiDrAC, DcAmB S4, NatCAB 36, WhAm 2, WhAmP*
Bailey, Kiah 1770-1857 *Drake*
Bailey, Leonard Henry 1880-1962 *NatCAB 50, WhAm 4*
Bailey, Lepha Eliza 1845- *AmWom*
Bailey, Lewis W 1880- *WhAm 6*
Bailey, Liberty Hyde 1858-1954 *ApCAB X, BiDAmEd, DcAmB S5, DcScB, EncAAH, NatCAB 10, NatCAB 43, TwCBDA, WebAB, WhAm 3*
Bailey, Loring Woart 1839-1925 *ApCAB, DcScB, NatCAB 13*
Bailey, Louis Jonathan 1881-1962 *WhAm 4*
Bailey, Lydia R 1779-1869 *DcAmB, WhAm H*
Bailey, Margaret Emerson d1949 *WhAm 3A*
Bailey, Margaret Jewett 1812?-1882 *REnAW*
Bailey, Mark 1891-1947? *NatCAB 34*
Bailey, Mark, Jr. 1867- *NatCAB 12, WhAm 4*
Bailey, Mercer Silas 1841-1926 *WhAm 1*
Bailey, Mervyn J 1894-1955 *WhAm 3*
Bailey, Mildred 1907-1951 *DcAmB S5*
Bailey, Milus Kendrick 1891-1964 *WhAm 4*
Bailey, Minnie Keith 1869- *WomWWA 14*
Bailey, Mortimer Grimball, Jr. 1870-1927 *NatCAB 21*
Bailey, Morton 1895-1957 *WhAm 3*
Bailey, Morton Shelley 1855-1922 *WhAm 1*
Bailey, N Herbert 1880-1958 *NatCAB 47*
Bailey, Neill Alexander 1861- *WhoColR*
Bailey, Pearce 1865-1922 *NatCAB 24, WhAm 4*
Bailey, Percival 1892-1973 *WhAm 6*
Bailey, Ralph Edward 1888-1967 *WhAm 4*
Bailey, Ralph Emerson 1878-1948 *BiDrAC, WhAm 6*
Bailey, Ralph Waldo 1873-1953 *NatCAB 42*
Bailey, Ray W 1887-1951 *WhAm 3*
Bailey, Robert Lieutenant 1885- *WhoColR*
Bailey, Rufus William 1793-1863 *ApCAB, BiDAmEd, DcAmB, Drake, TwCBDA, WhAm H*
Bailey, Samuel Robinson 1894-1951 *NatCAB 40*
Bailey, Sara Lord 1856- *AmWom*
Bailey, Silas 1809-1874 *NatCAB 1, TwCBDA*
Bailey, Silas 1812?-1874 *ApCAB*

Bailey, Simon Whitehead 1877-1956 *NatCAB 48*
Bailey, Solon Irving 1854-1931 *AmBi, ApCAB X, DcAmB S1, DcScB, NatCAB 28, WhAm 1*
Bailey, Steele 1845- *WhAm 4*
Bailey, Taber Davis 1874-1938 *NatCAB 27*
Bailey, Temple 188-?-1953 *DcAmB S5, WhAm 3*
Bailey, Theodore Mead 1888-1949 *NatCAB 40, WhAm 3*
Bailey, Theodorus 1752-1828 *BiAUS, Drake*
Bailey, Theodorus 1758-1828 *ApCAB, BiDrAC, NatCAB 13, WhAm H*
Bailey, Theodorus 1803-1877 *Drake*
Bailey, Theodorus 1805-1877 *AmBi, ApCAB, DcAmB, NatCAB 2, TwCBDA, WebAMB, WhAm H*
Bailey, Thomas David 1897-1974 *BiDAmEd*
Bailey, Thomas Lowry 1888-1946 *NatCAB 35, WhAm 2*
Bailey, Thomas Pearce 1867-1949 *WhAm 2*
Bailey, Thomas Sargent 1875-1941 *NatCAB 37*
Bailey, Thomas Williamson 1826- *ApCAB Sup*
Bailey, Tillinghast 1823?- *NewYHSD*
Bailey, Vernon 1864-1942 *WhAm 2*
Bailey, Vernon Howe 1874-1953 *WhAm 3*
Bailey, Walter C *NewYHSD*
Bailey, Walter Thomas 1882- *WhoColR*
Bailey, Warren Worth 1855-1928 *BiDrAC, NatCAB 41, WhAm 1*
Bailey, Wesley 1808-1889 *TwCBDA*
Bailey, William 1833- *NatCAB 13*
Bailey, William 1879-1957 *NatCAB 47*
Bailey, William A 1827?- *NewYHSD*
Bailey, William Arthur 1884-1968 *WhAm 5*
Bailey, William Bacon 1873-1952 *WhAm 3*
Bailey, William D 1868-1929 *NatCAB 22*
Bailey, William H 1831- *TwCBDA*
Bailey, William Whitman 1843-1914 *ApCAB, NatCAB 10, NatCAB 29, TwCBDA, WhAm 1, WhAm 4*
Bailey, Willis Joshua 1854-1932 *BiDrAC, NatCAB 13, WhAm 1, WhAmP*
Bailey And Matthewson *NewYHSD*
Bailhache, Preston Heath 1835-1919 *WhAm 1*
Bailie, Earle 1890-1940 *WhAm 1*
Bailie, James *NewYHSD*
Bailie, Virginia 1867-1906 *WhAm 1*
Bailie, William 1866- *WhAm 4*
Bailie, William Lamdin 1843-1912 *WhAm 1*
Baillairge, Charles P Florent 1827- *ApCAB Sup*
Baillairge, George Frederick 1824- *ApCAB*
Baillargeon, C F 1798-1870 *Drake*
Baillargeon, Cebert 1889-1964 *WhAm 4*
Baillargeon, Charles Francis 1798-1870 *ApCAB*
Baillargeon, Pierre 1812- *ApCAB*
Baillie, Archie Fraser 1887-1954 *WhAm 3*
Baillie, David Gemmell, Jr. 1894-1971 *NatCAB 55*
Baillie, Frank Seymour 1869-1951 *NatCAB 42*
Baillie, Hugh 1890-1966 *WhAm 4*
Baillie, James S *NewYHSD*
Baillie, John 1886-1960 *WhAm 4*
Baillie, Matthew 1761-1823 *BiHiMed, DcScB*
Baillie, Thomas Gilbert 1881-1969 *NatCAB 55*
Baillot, Edouard Paul 1861- *WhAm 4*
Baillou, Guillaume De 1538?-1616 *BiHiMed, DcScB*
Bailly, A *NewYHSD*
Bailly, Alexis J *NewYHSD*
Bailly, Jean-Sylvain 1736-1793 *DcScB*
Bailly, Joseph Alexis 1825-1883 *AmBi, DcAmB, NewYHSD, WhAm H*
Bailly-Blanchard, Arthur 1855-1925 *WhAm 1*
Bailor, Edwin Maurice 1890-1970 *WhAm 5*
Bailwitz, Alexander 1878-1959 *NatCAB 44*
Baily, A *NewYHSD*
Baily, Alfred William 1857- *WhAm 4*
Baily, Belle C 1858- *WomWWA 14*
Baily, Elisha Ingram 1824-1908 *WhAm 1*
Baily, Francis 1774-1844 *AsBiEn, DcScB*
Baily, Harold James 1887-1964 *NatCAB 52, WhAm 4*
Baily, Joel J 1826-1903 *NatCAB 13*
Baily, John 1644-1697 *ApCAB, Drake*
Baily, Joseph 1810- *BiAUS*
Baily, Joshua L 1826-1916 *WhAm 1*

Baily, Julius T *NewYHSD*
Baily, William A *NewYHSD*
Bain, Alexander 1818-1903 *DcScB*
Bain, Charles Wesley 1864-1915 *WhAm 1*
Bain, Edgar Collins 1891-1971 *WhAm 5*
Bain, Edward 1823-1898 *NatCAB 31*
Bain, Ferdinand Randall 1861-1945 *ApCAB X, WhAm 2*
Bain, Fred B d1968 *WhAm 5*
Bain, George Grantham 1865- *WhAm 4*
Bain, George Luke Scobie 1836-1891 *DcAmB, NatCAB 4, WhAm H*
Bain, George Washington 1840-1927 *WhAm 1*
Bain, Gertrude Benchley *WomWWA 14*
Bain, H Foster 1871-1948 *NatCAB 36*
Bain, H Foster 1872-1948 *WhAm 2*
Bain, Jarvis Johnson 1880- *WhAm 6*
Bain, Lydia Katherine Smith 1862- *WomWWA 14*
Bain, Robert Edward Mather 1858-1932 *WhAm 1*
Bainborough, William *NewYHSD*
Bainbridge, Alexander Gilbert 1885-1936 *WhAm 1*
Bainbridge, Henry *NewYHSD*
Bainbridge, Henry 1803-1857 *ApCAB, Drake*
Bainbridge, Lucy Elizabeth Seaman 1842-1928 *NatCAB 23, WhAm 1*
Bainbridge, William 1774-1833 *AmBi, ApCAB, DcAmB, Drake, NatCAB 8, TwCBDA, WebAB, WebAMB, WhAm H*
Bainbridge, William Seaman 1870-1947 *NatCAB 37, WhAm 2*
Bainbriggs, Philip *NewYHSD*
Baine, A C 1810-1863 *Drake*
Bainer, John David 1887-1965 *NatCAB 52*
Baines, Allen Mackenzie 1853- *ApCAB*
Baines, Edward Richards 1887-1969 *WhAm 5*
Baines-Miller, Minnie Willis *WhAm 5, WomWWA 14*
Bains, Thomas Mellor 1877-1958 *NatCAB 47*
Bainter, Fay Okell 1893-1968 *WhAm 5*
Baird, Absalom 1824-1905 *AmBi, ApCAB, DcAmB, Drake, NatCAB 12, TwCBDA, WhAm 1*
Baird, Andrew D 1839-1923 *WhAm 1*
Baird, Andrew McClung 1896-1967 *WhAm 4*
Baird, Bruce 1892-1960 *NatCAB 48, WhAm 4*
Baird, Cameron 1905-1960 *WhAm 4*
Baird, Charles 1853-1940 *NatCAB 39*
Baird, Charles Washington 1828-1887 *ApCAB, DcAmB, NatCAB 8, TwCBDA, WhAm H*
Baird, Cora 1912-1967 *WhAm 5*
Baird, David 1839-1927 *BiDrAC, NatCAB 20, WhAm 1*
Baird, David, Jr. 1881-1955 *BiDrAC, WhAm 3*
Baird, David W E 1898-1974 *WhAm 6*
Baird, Dudley 1877-1939 *NatCAB 31*
Baird, E Thompson *NatCAB 7*
Baird, Edward Carey 1836-1874 *ApCAB Sup*
Baird, Edward Rouzie 1909-1974 *WhAm 6*
Baird, Ellen Richardson 1849- *WomWWA 14*
Baird, Frank Burkett 1852-1939 *NatCAB 31, WhAm 1*
Baird, George 1895-1962 *NatCAB 51*
Baird, George Washington 1843-1930 *NatCAB 1, WhAm 1*
Baird, George William 1839-1906 *WhAm 1*
Baird, Hattie E 1854- *WomWWA 14*
Baird, Henry Carey 1825- *ApCAB, NatCAB 5*
Baird, Henry Carey 1825-1901 *TwCBDA*
Baird, Henry Carey 1825-1912 *AmBi, DcAmB, WhAm 1*
Baird, Henry Martin 1823- *TwCBDA*
Baird, Henry Martyn 1832-1906 *AmBi, ApCAB, DcAmB, NatCAB 8, WhAm 1*
Baird, Henry Samuel 1800-1875 *ApCAB Sup, TwCBDA*
Baird, Henry W 1881-1963 *WhAm 4*
Baird, James 1873-1953 *NatCAB 42, WhAm 3*
Baird, Jean Katherine 1872-1918 *WhAm 1, WomWWA 14*
Baird, Jennette Fergus *WomWWA 14*
Baird, John 1820-1891 *TwCBDA*
Baird, John Faris 1851- *NatCAB 2*

Baird, John Grier 1859-1927 *NatCAB 21*
Baird, John L 1857- *WhAm 4*
Baird, John Wallace 1869-1919 *NatCAB 22*
Baird, John Wallace 1873-1919 *WhAm 1*
Baird, Joseph Edward 1865-1942 *BiDrAC,*
 WhAm 2, WhAmP
Baird, Julian William 1859-1911 *WhAm 1*
Baird, Lee Oren 1881-1943 *NatCAB 32*
Baird, Louise 1910-1968 *WhAm 5*
Baird, Lucius Olmsted 1863-1948 *WhAm 2*
Baird, Lucy 1871- *WomWWA 14*
Baird, Matthew 1817-1877 *DcAmB,*
 NatCAB 6, WhAm H
Baird, Phil C 1863-1923 *WhAm 1*
Baird, Raleigh William 1870-1941 *WhAm 1*
Baird, Richard F 1884-1951 *WhAm 3*
Baird, Richard Loper 1850-1921 *NatCAB 19*
Baird, Robert 1798-1863 *ApCAB, DcAmB,*
 DcAmReB, Drake, NatCAB 8, TwCBDA,
 WhAm H
Baird, Robert W 1883-1969 *WhAm 5*
Baird, Samuel John 1817-1893 *ApCAB,*
 DcAmB, WhAm H
Baird, Samuel Thomas 1861-1899 *BiDrAC,*
 TwCBDA, WhAmP
Baird, Spencer Fullerton 1823-1887 *AmBi,*
 ApCAB, BiAUS, DcAmB, DcScB, Drake,
 EncAAH, NatCAB 3, TwCBDA, WebAB,
 WhAm H
Baird, Thomas H 1787-1866 *WhAm H*
Baird, Thomas James 1794-1842 *ApCAB Sup*
Baird, William Jesse 1890-1951 *WhAm 3*
Baird, William Raimond 1858-1917 *WhAm 1*
Baird, William Smyllie 1873-1936 *NatCAB 41*
Baird, William Torrey 1855-1941 *NatCAB 31*
Baire, Rene Louis 1874-1932 *DcScB*
Bairuni, Al- *DcScB*
Baitar, Ibn Al- *DcScB*
Baiter, Richard Englis 1913- *WhAm 5*
Baits, Vera Burridge 1892-1963 *WhAm 4*
Baity, George Perry 1862- *WhAm 4*
Baity, Herman Glenn 1895-1975 *WhAm 6*
Baity, James L 1871- *WhAm 5*
Baity, Roscoe Flake 1898-1951 *NatCAB 40*
Baizley, Rudolph Roger 1848-1918 *NatCAB 44*
Bajja, Abu Bakr Muhammad Al-Saigh, Ibn
 d1138? *DcScB*
Bajpai, Sir Girja Shankar 1891-1954 *WhAm 3*
Bakeman, Caroline *WomWWA 14*
Bakenhus, Reuben Edwin 1873-1967
 NatCAB 55, WhAm 4A
Baker, Abijah Richardson 1805-1876 *ApCAB,*
 NatCAB 14, TwCBDA, WhAm H
Baker, Aimee Cevilla 1870- *WomWWA 14*
Baker, Albert 1851-1942 *NatCAB 35,*
 WhAm 2
Baker, Albert C 1845-1921 *WhAm 1*
Baker, Albert Rufus 1858-1911 *WhAm 1*
Baker, Alfred 1811-1896 *NatCAB 2*
Baker, Alfred Brittin 1836-1938 *WhAm 1*
Baker, Alfred E *NewYHSD*
Baker, Alfred Landon 1859-1927 *NatCAB 14,*
 WhAm 1
Baker, Alfred Zantzinger 1870- *WhAm 5*
Baker, Alpheus 1825-1891 *NatCAB 4*
Baker, Alpheus 1828-1891 *BiDConf*
Baker, Alton Fletcher 1894-1961 *WhAm 4*
Baker, Alvin H 1808?- *NewYHSD*
Baker, Anderson Yancey 1876-1930
 NatCAB 22
Baker, Annie Cunningham 1871-
 WomWWA 14
Baker, Anthony George 1849- *WhAm 4*
Baker, Archibald Eachern 1862-1934 *WhAm 1*
Baker, Archibald Earle 1895-1951 *NatCAB 40*
Baker, Arthur Garfield 1880-1956 *NatCAB 43*
Baker, Arthur Josiah Mountford 1881-1953
 WhAm 3
Baker, Arthur Latham 1853-1934 *WhAm 1*
Baker, Arthur Mulford 1880-1941 *WhAm 1*
Baker, Asa George 1866-1940 *WhAm 1*
Baker, Asher Carter 1850-1926 *WhAm 1*
Baker, Benedict J d1948 *WhAm 2*
Baker, Benjamin A 1818-1890 *DcAmB*
Baker, Benjamin Everett 1855- *NatCAB 14*
Baker, Benjamin Franklin 1811-1889 *AmBi,*
 ApCAB, BiDAmEd, DcAmB, NatCAB 7,
 TwCBDA, WhAm H

Baker, Benjamin Webb 1841-1909 *TwCBDA,*
 WhAm 1
Baker, Bernard Nadal 1854-1918 *WhAm 1*
Baker, Bertha Kunz d1943 *WhAm 2,*
 WhAm 5, WomWWA 14
Baker, Blanche Hutchinson 1876-
 WomWWA 14
Baker, Bryant 1881-1970 *WhAm 5*
Baker, Burke 1887-1964 *NatCAB 53*
Baker, Caleb 1762-1849 *BiAUS, BiDrAC,*
 WhAm H
Baker, Caroline Isabel *WomWWA 14*
Baker, Charles *NewYHSD*
Baker, Charles Fuller 1872-1927 *NatCAB 21,*
 WhAm 1
Baker, Charles Grosh 1875-1955 *NatCAB 48*
Baker, Charles Henry 1793-1872 *WhAm H*
Baker, Charles Hinckley 1864- *WhAm 1*
Baker, Charles Joseph 1821-1894 *TwCBDA*
Baker, Charles Samuel 1855- *WhAm 4*
Baker, Charles Simeon 1839-1902 *BiDrAC,*
 TwCBDA, WhAmP
Baker, Charles Whiting 1865-1941 *NatCAB 16,*
 WhAm 1
Baker, Charles William 1862-1938 *NatCAB 28,*
 WhAm 1
Baker, Charlotte Alice 1833-1909 *BiCAW*
Baker, Charlotte LeBreton Johnson 1855-
 AmWom, WomWWA 14
Baker, Charlotte Sanford 1859-1932
 NatCAB 28
Baker, Chauncey Brooke 1860-1936 *WhAm 1*
Baker, Chester Alonzo 1873-1952 *NatCAB 40*
Baker, Claude Milem 1892-1962 *WhAm 4*
Baker, Conrad 1817-1885 *BiAUS, NatCAB 13*
Baker, Cora Warman 1867- *WhAm 5*
Baker, Cornelia 1855-1930 *WhAm 1,*
 WomWWA 14
Baker, Crosby Fred 1887-1954 *WhAm 3*
Baker, Daniel 1775?-1836 *ApCAB, Drake*
Baker, Daniel 1791-1857 *ApCAB, DcAmB,*
 Drake, WhAm H
Baker, Daniel 1858-1921 *NatCAB 32*
Baker, Daniel, Jr. 1890-1956 *NatCAB 45*
Baker, Daniel Clifton, Jr. 1908-1974 *WhAm 6*
Baker, Darius 1845-1926 *NatCAB 32,*
 WhAm 1
Baker, David 1861- *WhAm 4*
Baker, David 1881- *WhoColR*
Baker, David Dudrow 1897-1950 *WhAm 3*
Baker, David Floyd 1919-1970 *WhAm 5*
Baker, David Jewett 1792-1869 *ApCAB,*
 BiAUS, BiDrAC, Drake, NatCAB 11,
 WhAm H
Baker, David Jewett 1834- *NatCAB 12*
Baker, David Jewett 1865-1926 *NatCAB 21*
Baker, Davis 1884-1933 *NatCAB 36*
Baker, Donald Cameron 1888-1950 *NatCAB 46*
Baker, Donald Vinton 1915-1963 *NatCAB 51*
Baker, Dorothy 1907-1968 *WhAm 5*
Baker, E Reece 1884-1950 *NatCAB 38*
Baker, Earl Dewey 1898-1970 *WhAm 5*
Baker, Earle A 1884-1958 *WhAm 3*
Baker, Edgar Campbell 1895-1973 *WhAm 6*
Baker, Edgar Robey 1920-1969 *WhAm 5*
Baker, Edna Dean 1883-1956 *BiDAmEd,*
 NatCAB 43, WhAm 3
Baker, Edward D 1811-1861 *BiAUS*
Baker, Edward David 1896-1918 *NatCAB 24*
Baker, Edward Dickenson 1811-1861 *ApCAB,*
 NatCAB 2, TwCBDA
Baker, Edward Dickinson 1811-1861 *AmBi,*
 BiDrAC, DcAmB, Drake, WebAMB,
 WhAm H, WhAmP
Baker, Edward John 1868-1959 *NatCAB 47*
Baker, Edwin George 1885-1961 *WhAm 4*
Baker, Edwin Myron 1893-1943 *NatCAB 32*
Baker, Elbert H 1854-1933 *WhAm 1*
Baker, Elbert Hall, Jr. 1889-1962 *NatCAB 50*
Baker, Eleanor Robinson *WomWWA 14*
Baker, Elisha Avery 1872-1933 *NatCAB 26*
Baker, Elizabeth Bradford Faulkner 1886-1973
 WhAm 5
Baker, Elizabeth Gowdy d1927 *BiCAW,*
 WhAm 1, WomWWA 14
Baker, Ellen Gillette 1850- *WomWWA 14*
Baker, Ellis Crain 1889-1949 *WhAm 2*
Baker, Emerson Woods 1882-1934 *NatCAB 25*

Baker, Emilie Kip *WhAm 5*
Baker, Emma C Andrews 1851- *WomWWA 14*
Baker, Emma Sophia *WomWWA 14*
Baker, Eric Wilfred 1899-1973 *WhAm 6*
Baker, Ernest Hamlin 1889-1975 *WhAm 6*
Baker, Everett Moore 1901-1950 *WhAm 3*
Baker, Ezra *BiAUS, BiDrAC, WhAm H*
Baker, Ezra Flavius 1869- *WhAm 5*
Baker, Ezra Henry 1859- *WhAm 4*
Baker, F Cecil 1889-1961 *NatCAB 50*
Baker, Francis Aloysius 1820-1865 *NatCAB 4*
Baker, Francis Asbury 1820-1865 *WhAm H*
Baker, Francis Elisha 1860-1924 *NatCAB 22,*
 WhAm 1
Baker, Frank 1840-1916 *ApCAB X,*
 NatCAB 17, WhAm 1
Baker, Frank 1841-1918 *DcAmB, NatCAB 19,*
 WhAm 1
Baker, Frank Collins 1867-1942 *WhAm 2*
Baker, Frank Elmer 1877-1961 *NatCAB 45,*
 WhAm 5
Baker, Frank Kline 1866- *WhAm 4*
Baker, Frank Smith 1879-1960 *NatCAB 53,*
 WhAm 4
Baker, Franklin, Jr. 1872-1946 *NatCAB 33,*
 WhAm 5
Baker, Franklin Thomas 1864-1949 *WhAm 2*
Baker, Fred Austin 1874-1942 *NatCAB 31*
Baker, Frederick Cecil 1889-1961 *WhAm 4*
Baker, Frederick Storrs 1890-1965 *WhAm 4*
Baker, Frederick VanVliet 1876- *WhAm 5*
Baker, Sir George 1722-1809 *BiHiMed*
Baker, George 1837-1924 *NatCAB 17*
Baker, George 1877?-1965 *WebAB*
Baker, George 1915-1975 *WebAB, WebAMB,*
 WhAm 6
Baker, George Augustus 1760- *NewYHSD*
Baker, George Augustus 1821-1880 *ApCAB,*
 DcAmB, NatCAB 5, NewYHSD,
 TwCBDA, WhAm H
Baker, George Augustus 1849- *ApCAB,*
 WhAm 4
Baker, George Barr 1870-1948 *WhAm 2*
Baker, George Bernard 1834- *ApCAB*
Baker, George Bramwell 1866-1937 *NatCAB 18,*
 WhAm 1
Baker, George Claude, Jr. 1904-1974 *WhAm 6*
Baker, George Danielson 1840-1903 *WhAm 1*
Baker, George Fisher 1840-1931 *AmBi,*
 DcAmB S1, NatCAB 23, WebAB,
 WhAm 1
Baker, George Fisher 1878-1937 *NatCAB 43,*
 WhAm 1
Baker, George Hall 1850-1911 *NatCAB 6,*
 WhAm 1
Baker, George Holbrook 1827-1906 *IlBEAAW,*
 NewYHSD, WhAm HA, WhAm 4
Baker, George J *NewYHSD*
Baker, George L 1868- *WhAm 4*
Baker, George Merrick 1878- *WhAm 6*
Baker, George Pierce 1866-1935 *AmBi,*
 BiDAmEd, DcAmB S1, NatCAB 25,
 WebAB, WhAm 1
Baker, George Randolph 1871-1941 *WhAm 1,*
 WhAm 2
Baker, George Theodore 1900-1963 *WhAm 4*
Baker, George Titus 1857-1940 *WhAm 1*
Baker, George Washington 1845-1909
 NatCAB 27
Baker, George Wells 1834-1896 *NatCAB 21*
Baker, Gladden Whetstone 1898-1974 *WhAm 6*
Baker, Gordon Harrington 1878-1963
 NatCAB 50, WhAm 4
Baker, Grafton *BiAUS*
Baker, H Ray 1911- *IlBEAAW*
Baker, Harold Bruss 1909-1969 *WhAm 5*
Baker, Harold Dainforth 1884-1949
 NatCAB 43
Baker, Harold Griffith 1899-1956 *WhAm 3*
Baker, Harriet Newell Woods 1815-1893
 TwCBDA
Baker, Harriette Newell Woods 1815-1893
 AmWom, ApCAB, NatCAB 14, WhAm H
Baker, Harry B 1895-1956 *WhAm 3*
Baker, Harvey Almy 1881-1951 *WhAm 3*
Baker, Harvey Humphrey 1869-1915 *DcAmB,*
 NatCAB 21, WhAm 1
Baker, Helen Bartlett *WomWWA 14*

Baker, Henry 1698-1774 *DcScB*
Baker, Henry Albert 1848- *NatCAB 15*
Baker, Henry Brooks 1837- *ApCAB,*
NatCAB 12
Baker, Henry Dunster 1873-1939 *WhAm 1*
Baker, Henry Felt 1797-1857 *Drake*
Baker, Henry M 1810-1874 *NewYHSD*
Baker, Henry Moore 1841-1912 *BiDrAC,*
NatCAB 18, WhAm 1, WhAm 4
Baker, Herbert 1866-1939 *WhAm 1*
Baker, Herbert Abram 1881-1940 *WhAm 1*
Baker, Herbert Leslie 1859-1919 *NatCAB 8*
Baker, Herbert Madison 1879- *WhAm 6*
Baker, Herbert Smith 1866-1934 *NatCAB 39*
Baker, Hettie Gray 1881- *WomWWA 14*
Baker, Hollis 1888-1966 *WhAm 4*
Baker, Holmes Davenport 1880-1950 *WhAm 3*
Baker, Horace *WhAm 5*
Baker, Horace 1833-1918 *NewYHSD*
Baker, Horace Forbes 1878-1950 *WhAm 3*
Baker, Howard Henry 1902-1964 *BiDrAC,*
WhAm 4, WhAmP
Baker, Howard Henry, Jr. 1925- *BiDrAC*
Baker, Hugh Benton 1882-1964 *WhAm 4*
Baker, Hugh Jacob 1882-1938 *NatCAB 30*
Baker, Hugh Jacob, Jr. 1910-1968 *NatCAB 57*
Baker, Hugh Potter 1878-1950 *DcAmB S4,*
NatCAB 39, WhAm 3
Baker, I H *NewYHSD*
Baker, I Wayles d1867 *BiAUS*
Baker, Ida Wikoff 1859- *AmWom*
Baker, Ira Osborn 1853-1925 *WhAm 1*
Baker, Irene Bailey 1901- *BiDrAC*
Baker, Isaac C *NewYHSD*
Baker, Isaac D 1819-1850 *TwCBDA*
Baker, Isaac Post 1855-1938 *WhAm 1*
Baker, J F *NewYHSD*
Baker, J Thompson 1847-1919 *WhAm 1*
Baker, J Whitney 1883-1949 *NatCAB 38*
Baker, Jacob 1895-1967 *NatCAB 54*
Baker, Jacob Thompson 1847-1919 *BiDrAC*
Baker, James *NewYHSD*
Baker, James 1818-1898 *DcAmB, REnAW,*
WhAm H
Baker, James 1830- *ApCAB Sup*
Baker, James Addison 1857-1941 *WhAm 1*
Baker, James Andrew 1910-1975 *WhAm 6*
Baker, James Barnes 1864-1918 *WhAm 1*
Baker, James Beckworth 1847-1918 *NatCAB 18*
Baker, James Chamberlain 1879- *WhAm 6*
Baker, James Heaton 1829-1913 *ApCAB,*
BiAUS, DcAmB, NatCAB 4, WhAm 1,
WhAmP
Baker, James Hutchins 1848-1925 *BiDAmEd,*
DcAmB, NatCAB 6, TwCBDA,
WhAm 1
Baker, James Marion 1861-1940 *NatCAB 34,*
WhAm 1
Baker, James McNair 1821-1892 *NatCAB 5*
Baker, James McNair 1822-1892 *BiDConf*
Baker, James Norment 1876-1941 *NatCAB 31,*
WhAm 2
Baker, Jehu 1822- *BiAUS*
Baker, Jehu 1822-1901 *NatCAB 12*
Baker, Jehu 1822-1903 *BiDrAC, DcAmB S1,*
TwCBDA, WhAm 1, WhAmP
Baker, Joanna 1862- *AmWom*
Baker, John *NewYHSD*
Baker, John d1823 *BiAUS, BiDrAC,*
WhAm H
Baker, John Clark 1884-1967 *NatCAB 55*
Baker, John Daniel 1864- *WhAm 4*
Baker, John Earl 1880-1957 *WhAm 3*
Baker, John Edgar 1860-1941 *NatCAB 32*
Baker, John Gilbert 1834-1920 *DcScB*
Baker, John H 1833-1915 *BiAUS*
Baker, John Harris 1832-1915 *BiDrAC,*
WhAm 1, WhAmP
Baker, John Hopkinson 1894-1973 *NatCAB 57,*
WhAm 6
Baker, John S *NewYHSD*
Baker, John S 1861- *ApCAB X*
Baker, John Stewart 1893-1966 *WhAm 4*
Baker, John Townsend 1860-1935 *NatCAB 26*
Baker, Joseph Dill 1854-1938 *NatCAB 44,*
WhAm 1
Baker, Joseph E *NewYHSD*
Baker, Joseph Richardson 1872-1946 *WhAm 2*

Baker, Josephine 1906-1975 *WebAB, WhAm 6*
Baker, Josephine Turck d1942 *WhAm 2,*
WomWWA 14
Baker, Joshua 1799-1886 *NatCAB 10*
Baker, Julia Wetherill 1858- *WomWWA 14*
Baker, Julia Wetherill 1859- *WhAm 4*
Baker, Julie Wetherill 1859- *AmWom*
Baker, Karle Wilson 1878-1960 *WhAm 4*
Baker, Katherine 1876-1919 *BiCAW*
Baker, Lafayette C 1824-1868 *Drake*
Baker, LaFayette Curry 1826-1868 *ApCAB,*
DcAmB, NatCAB 5, TwCBDA,
WhAm H
Baker, Laurence Simmons 1830-1907 *BiDConf,*
DcAmB
Baker, Lawrence Simons 1830-1907 *WhAm 1*
Baker, Lennie VanHolland 1851-
WomWWA 14
Baker, Leonard Theodore 1868-1955
NatCAB 48, WhAm 3
Baker, Lewis 1832-1899 *ApCAB X,*
NatCAB 1, TwCBDA, WhAm H
Baker, Loran Ellis 1831- *ApCAB Sup*
Baker, Lorenzo Dow 1840-1908 *DcAmB,*
NatCAB 14
Baker, Louise Regina *WomWWA 14*
Baker, Louise S 1846- *AmWom*
Baker, Lucien 1846-1907 *ApCAB Sup,*
BiDrAC, NatCAB 12, TwCBDA,
WhAm 1, WhAmP
Baker, Lucius K 1855-1929 *WhAm 1*
Baker, Luther Elijah 1865- *NatCAB 5*
Baker, Luther Henry 1872-1944 *NatCAB 33*
Baker, M A *NewYHSD*
Baker, Mabel Kimball 1871- *WomWWA 14*
Baker, Mandlebert Wendell 1875-1939
NatCAB 29
Baker, Marcus 1849-1903 *ApCAB, DcAmB,*
NatCAB 11, TwCBDA, WhAm 1
Baker, Marian Una Strong *WomWWA 14*
Baker, Marjorie Montgomery Ward d1959
WhAm 3
Baker, Martha Sue 1871-1911 *NatCAB 15*
Baker, Martha Susan d1911 *WhAm 1*
Baker, Mary Francis 1876- *WhAm 5*
Baker, Milo Stannard 1828-1894 *NatCAB 31*
Baker, Morton 1913-1972 *WhAm 6*
Baker, Moses Nelson 1864- *WhAm 4*
Baker, Murray M 1872-1964 *WhAm 4,*
WhAm 5
Baker, Naaman Rimmon 1868- *WhAm 4*
Baker, Nathan F 1822?- *NewYHSD*
Baker, Nathaniel Bradley 1818-1876 *ApCAB,*
NatCAB 11, TwCBDA
Baker, Newman Freese 1898-1941 *WhAm 1*
Baker, Newton Diehl 1871-1937 *AmBi,*
ApCAB X, BiDrUSE, DcAmB S2,
EncAB, McGEWB, NatCAB 27, WebAB,
WhAm 1, WhAmP
Baker, Norma Jean *WebAB*
Baker, Oliver Edwin 1883-1949 *DcAmB S4,*
NatCAB 37, WhAm 2
Baker, Orlando Harrison 1830-1913 *WhAm 1*
Baker, Oscar William 1879- *WhoColR*
Baker, Osman Cleander 1812-1871 *Drake*
Baker, Osmon Cleander 1812-1871 *ApCAB,*
DcAmB, TwCBDA, WhAm H
Baker, Osmond Cleander 1812-1871 *NatCAB 5*
Baker, Osmyn 1800-1875 *BiAUS, BiDrAC,*
WhAm H
Baker, Page M 1840-1910 *NatCAB 13,*
WhAm 1
Baker, Peter Carpenter 1822-1889 *ApCAB Sup,*
DcAmB, TwCBDA, WhAm H
Baker, Phil 1898-1963 *WhAm 4*
Baker, Philip Hawk 1885- *ApCAB X*
Baker, Philip Pontius 1846-1920 *NatCAB 5,*
NatCAB 38
Baker, Purley Albert 1858-1924 *NatCAB 14,*
WhAm 1
Baker, Ralph Jackson 1888-1966 *WhAm 4*
Baker, Ray Stannard 1870-1946 *ApCAB X,*
DcAmB S4, EncAB, McGEWB,
NatCAB 14, NatCAB 49, WebAB,
WhAm 2
Baker, Raymond Thomas 1877-1935
NatCAB 27, WhAm 1
Baker, Remember 1737-1775 *DcAmB,*

WhAm H
Baker, Remember 1740?-1775 *ApCAB, Drake,*
TwCBDA
Baker, Rhodes Semmes 1874-1940 *NatCAB 33*
Baker, Robert 1862-1943 *BiDrAC, WhAm 4*
Baker, Robert Breckenridge 1867- *NatCAB 14*
Baker, Robert Harper 1892-1956 *NatCAB 45*
Baker, Robert Homes 1858-1935 *WhAm 1*
Baker, Robert Peter 1886-1940 *NatCAB 34*
Baker, Roland Morris 1865- *WhAm 4*
Baker, Roy Newsom 1906-1968 *WhAm 5*
Baker, S Josephine 1873-1945 *NatCAB 36,*
WhAm 2, WomWWA 14
Baker, Sam Rice 1909-1965 *NatCAB 51*
Baker, Samuel Aaron 1874-1933 *BiDAmEd,*
NatCAB 27, WhAm 1
Baker, Samuel F *NewYHSD*
Baker, Samuel Garland 1902-1974 *WhAm 6*
Baker, Sir Samuel White 1821-1893 *McGEWB*
Baker, Sara Josephine 1873-1945 *DcAmB S3,*
NotAW
Baker, Sarah Pfeil 1882- *WomWWA 14*
Baker, Sarah Schoonmaker 1824-1906 *WhAm 1*
Baker, Scipio Eugene 1860-1921 *NatCAB 6*
Baker, Simon Strousse 1866-1932 *NatCAB 24,*
WhAm 1
Baker, Smith 1836-1917 *NatCAB 18,*
WhAm 1
Baker, Stephen 1819-1875 *BiAUS, BiDrAC,*
WhAm H
Baker, Stephen 1859-1946 *WhAm 2*
Baker, Stephen Dayton 1868-1944 *NatCAB 35*
Baker, Stetson 1906-1956 *NatCAB 46*
Baker, Tarkington 1878-1924 *WhAm 1*
Baker, Thomas Rakestraw 1837-1930
NatCAB 22, WhAm 1
Baker, Thomas Stockham 1871-1939 *WhAm 1*
Baker, Virginia 1859- *WhAm 4,*
WomWWA 14
Baker, W Browne 1900-1968 *NatCAB 55,*
WhAm 5
Baker, Walter Browne 1900-1968 *WhAm 6*
Baker, Walter Charles 1868-1955 *NatCAB 42*
Baker, Walter Cummings 1893-1971 *WhAm 5*
Baker, Walter Darell 1874-1941 *NatCAB 41*
Baker, Walter Hays 1876-1949 *NatCAB 39*
Baker, Walter Hudson 1879- *WhAm 2*
Baker, Walter Ransom Gail 1892-1960
NatCAB 48, WhAm 4
Baker, Wilder Dupuy 1890-1975 *WhAm 6*
Baker, William 1831-1910 *BiDrAC, TwCBDA*
Baker, William Benjamin 1840-1911 *BiDrAC,*
TwCBDA, WhAm 1
Baker, William Bliss 1859- *ApCAB, TwCBDA*
Baker, William Clyde, Jr. 1904-1966
NatCAB 53, WhAm 4
Baker, William D *NewYHSD*
Baker, William Edgar 1856-1921 *NatCAB 19,*
WhAm 1
Baker, William Gideon, Jr. 1874-1948 *WhAm 2*
Baker, William H 1825-1875 *ApCAB,*
NewYHSD, TwCBDA
Baker, William Henry 1827-1911 *BiAUS,*
BiDrAC
Baker, William Henry 1845-1914 *NatCAB 15*
Baker, William Henry 1855-1918 *NatCAB 14,*
WhAm 1
Baker, William Henry 1899- *IIBEAAW*
Baker, William Jay *NewYHSD*
Baker, William Jesse 1894-1958 *NatCAB 48,*
WhAm 3
Baker, William L 1860-1939 *WhAm 1*
Baker, Sir William Morrant 1839-1896
BiHiMed
Baker, William Mumford 1825-1883 *ApCAB,*
DcAmB, NatCAB 8, TwCBDA,
WhAm H
Baker, William Nowers 1911-1960 *NatCAB 50*
Baker, William Paul 1890-1951 *NatCAB 40*
Baker, William Pimm 1870-1930 *WhAm 1*
Baker, William Reginald, Jr. 1898-1975
WhAm 6
Baker, William Roberts 1861-1937 *NatCAB 32*
Baker, William Spohn 1824-1897 *ApCAB Sup,*
TwCBDA
Baker, William Taylor 1841-1903 *NatCAB 10,*
WhAm 1

Baker, William Thomas Henderson 1871-1956
NatCAB 50
Baker, William W 1861- *WhAm 4*
Baketel, H Sheridan 1872-1955 *NatCAB 42,*
WhAm 3
Baketel, Oliver Sherman 1849-1937 *WhAm 1*
Bakewell, Benjamin 1767-1844 *NatCAB 22*
Bakewell, Charles Montague 1867-1957 *BiDrAC,*
NatCAB 45, WhAm 3
Bakewell, Claude Ignatius 1912- *BiDrAC*
Bakewell, Donald Campbell 1887- *WhAm 3*
Bakewell, Paul 1858- *WhAm 4*
Bakewell, Robert 1768-1843 *DcScB*
Bakewell, Robert 1790?- *NewYHSD*
Bakewell, William 1823-1900 *NatCAB 14*
Bakh, Aleksei Nikolaevich *DcScB*
Bakhmeteff, Boris Alexander 1880-1951
WhAm 3
Bakhmeteff, George d1928 *WhAm 1*
Bakhshi, Chulam Mohammad 1907-1972
WhAm 5
Bakke, E Wight 1903-1971 *NatCAB 56,*
WhAm 5
Bakken, Clarence John 1902-1967 *WhAm 5*
Bakken, Herman Ernst 1892-1964 *WhAm 4*
Bakkum, Glenn A d1972 *WhAm 5*
Baklanoff, Georges 1882-1938 *WhAm 1*
Bakos, Jozef G 1891- *IIBEAAW*
Bakri, Abu Ubayd A Al-Aziz Muhammad, Al-
1010?-1094 *DcScB*
Bakst, Henry Jacob 1906-1972 *NatCAB 57,*
WhAm 5
Bakunin, Mikhail Aleksandrovich 1814-1876
McGEWB
Bakwin, Harry 1894-1973 *WhAm 6*
Balaban, Abraham Joseph 1889-1962 *WhAm 4*
Balaban, Barney 1887-1971 *WhAm 5*
Balaban, Emanuel 1895-1973 *WhAm 5*
Balaban, John 1894-1957 *WhAm 3*
Balaguer, Joaquin 1907- *McGEWB*
Balakian, Diran 1877-1939 *NatCAB 41*
Balanchine, George 1904- *EncAB, McGEWB,*
WebAB
Balandin, Aleksey Aleksandrovich 1898-1967
DcScB
Balard, Antoine Jerome 1802-1876 *AsBiEn,*
DcScB
Balassone, Francis Salvatore 1915-1972
WhAm 6
Balatka, Christian F 1861- *NatCAB 13*
Balatka, Hans 1827-1899 *WhAm H*
Balatka, Hans 1836-1899 *ApCAB X,*
NatCAB 10
Balbach, Edward, Jr. 1839-1910 *DcAmB,*
NatCAB 7, NatCAB 17, WhAm 4
Balbach, Edward, Sr. 1804-1890 *NatCAB 7*
Balbach, Julia Anna 1852- *NatCAB 17,*
WomWWA 14
Balbiani, Edouard-Gerard 1823-1899 *DcScB*
Balbo, Italo 1896-1940 *WhWW-II*
Balboa, Miguel Cavello *Drake*
Balboa, Vasco Nunez De 1475?-1517 *ApCAB,*
Drake, NatCAB 5, WhAm H
Balboa, Vasco Nunez De 1475?-1519 *McGEWB*
Balbuena, Bernardo De 1568-1627 *ApCAB,*
Drake
Balbus *DcScB*
Balcarres, Alexander Lindsay, Earl Of 1752-1825
ApCAB, Drake
Balch, Alfred *BiAUS*
Balch, Allan Christopher 1864-1943 *WhAm 2*
Balch, Edwin Swift 1856-1927 *WhAm 1*
Balch, Emily Greene 1867-1961 *WebAB,*
WhAm 4, WomWWA 14
Balch, Ernest Berkeley 1860- *WhAm 4*
Balch, Eugene *NewYHSD*
Balch, Eugenia Hargous Macfarlane
WomWWA 14
Balch, Frank 1880-1937 *NatCAB 27*
Balch, Franklin Greene 1864-1958 *WhAm 3*
Balch, George Beall 1821-1908 *ApCAB,*
DcAmB, Drake, NatCAB 5, TwCBDA,
WhAm 1
Balch, John Adrian 1876-1951 *NatCAB 39*
Balch, Leland, Jr. *NewYHSD*
Balch, Marion Casares *WomWWA 14*
Balch, Thomas 1821-1876 *TwCBDA*
Balch, Thomas Willing 1866-1927 *DcAmB,*

WhAm 1
Balch, Vistus 1799-1884 *NewYHSD*
Balch, William 1704-1792 *Drake*
Balch, William Monroe 1871-1941 *WhAm 2*
Balch, William Ralston 1852-1923 *NatCAB 19*
Balchen, Bernt 1899-1973 *WebAMB, WhAm 6*
Balck, Hermann 1893- *WhWW-II, WhoMilH*
Balcom, Homer Gage 1870-1938 *NatCAB 35*
Balcom, Lowell Leroy 1887-1938 *NatCAB 28*
Balcom, Max Fenton 1888-1966 *NatCAB 52,*
WhAm 4
Bald, J Dorsey 1826?-1878? *NewYHSD,*
WhAm H
Bald, Robert 1793?-1856? *NewYHSD*
Bald, Robert Cecil 1901-1965 *WhAm 4*
Bald, Robert L 1826?-1853? *NewYHSD*
Baldanzi, George 1907-1972 *WhAm 5*
Baldensperger, Fernand 1871- *WhAm 5*
Balderston, John Lloyd 1889-1954 *NatCAB 43,*
WhAm 3
Balderston, Lydia Ray *WhAm 5*
Baldes, Edward James 1898-1975 *WhAm 6*
Baldes, Raymond Charles 1895-1968 *WhAm 5*
Baldi, Bernardino 1553-1617 *DcScB*
Balding, Martha Joab *WomWWA 14*
Baldinger, Albert Henry 1876- *WhAm 5*
Baldinger, Lawrence H 1907-1970 *WhAm 5*
Baldock, Robert Hugh 1889-1968 *NatCAB 54*
Baldomir, Alfredo 1884-1948 *WhAm 2*
Baldridge, Cyrus Leroy 1889- *IIBEAAW*
Baldridge, H Clarence 1868-1947 *WhAm 2*
Baldridge, Harry Alexander 1880-1952
NatCAB 40
Baldridge, Howard Hammond 1864-1928
WhAm 1
Baldridge, Kenneth Ferguson 1886-1971
WhAm 5
Baldridge, Thomas Jackson 1872-1964 *WhAm 4*
Baldrige, Howard Malcolm 1894- *BiDrAC*
Baldwin I 1058?-1118 *McGEWB*
Baldwin, Abel Seymour 1811- *NatCAB 5,*
WhAm 4
Baldwin, Abraham 1754-1807 *AmBi, ApCAB,*
BiAUS, BiDrAC, DcAmB, Drake,
NatCAB 9, TwCBDA, WhAm H,
WhAmP
Baldwin, Abram Martin 1860-1931 *WhAm 1*
Baldwin, Adele Clagett 1885- *WomWWA 14*
Baldwin, Albertus Hutchinson 1865- *WhAm 4*
Baldwin, Alexander Richards 1874-1956
WhAm 3
Baldwin, Alexander W 1835-1869 *BiAUS,*
NatCAB 13
Baldwin, Alfred Carleton 1872-1957
NatCAB 46
Baldwin, Alice Mary 1879-1960 *WhAm 4,*
WomWWA 14
Baldwin, Almon *NewYHSD*
Baldwin, Archibald Stuart 1861-1922 *WhAm 1*
Baldwin, Arthur Charles 1875-1960 *WhAm 3*
Baldwin, Arthur Douglas 1876-1955
NatCAB 46, WhAm 5
Baldwin, Arthur J 1868-1939 *WhAm 1*
Baldwin, Asa Columbus 1887-1942 *WhAm 2*
Baldwin, Asa Fred 1906-1966 *WhAm 4*
Baldwin, Ashbel 1757-1846 *ApCAB, Drake,*
TwCBDA
Baldwin, Auburn Lewis 1915-1962 *NatCAB 48*
Baldwin, Augustus Carpenter 1817-1903 *BiAUS,*
BiDrAC, NatCAB 9, TwCBDA
Baldwin, Benjamin 1913- *BnEnAmA*
Baldwin, Benjamin James 1856-1932 *WhAm 1,*
WhAm 2
Baldwin, Bird Thomas 1875-1928 *WhAm 1*
Baldwin, Caleb 1824-1876 *BiAUS,*
NatCAB 13
Baldwin, Calvin Benham 1902-1975 *WhAm 6*
Baldwin, Charles Candee 1834-1895
NatCAB 21
Baldwin, Charles H 1822-1888 *ApCAB, Drake,*
NatCAB 4, TwCBDA
Baldwin, Charles Jacobs 1841- *WhAm 4*
Baldwin, Charles Sears 1867-1935 *WhAm 1*
Baldwin, Christopher Columbus 1830?-1897
NatCAB 12
Baldwin, Clara Frances 1871- *WomWWA 14*
Baldwin, Clara Waters *WomWWA 14*
Baldwin, Clarke Edward 1872-1932 *WhAm 3*

Baldwin, Clifford Park 1889- *IIBEAAW*
Baldwin, Cuthbert Slocomb 1891-1969
NatCAB 57
Baldwin, Daniel Pratt 1837-1908 *WhAm 1*
Baldwin, Edward Chauncey 1869-1940
NatCAB 32
Baldwin, Edward Chauncey 1870-1940
WhAm 5
Baldwin, Edward J *WhAm H*
Baldwin, Edward Robinson 1864-1947
DcAmB S4, NatCAB 34, WhAm 2
Baldwin, Elbert Francis 1857-1927 *NatCAB 33,*
WhAm 1
Baldwin, Elias Jackson 1828-1909 *NatCAB 22*
Baldwin, Elihu Whittlesey 1789-1840 *AmBi,*
DcAmB, Drake, WhAm H
Baldwin, Enos *NewYHSD*
Baldwin, Ephraim Francis 1837-1916
NatCAB 32
Baldwin, Esther E 1840- *AmWom*
Baldwin, Eugene Francis 1840- *NatCAB 16*
Baldwin, Evelyn Briggs 1862-1933 *ApCAB X,*
DcAmB S1, WhAm 1
Baldwin, F Spencer 1870-1934 *WhAm 1*
Baldwin, Francis Everett 1856- *WhAm 3*
Baldwin, Francis Joseph 1874-1963 *NatCAB 48*
Baldwin, Francis Marsh 1885-1951 *WhAm 3*
Baldwin, Frank 1869-1934 *NatCAB 25*
Baldwin, Frank A 1891-1951 *WhAm 3*
Baldwin, Frank Conger 1869-1945 *WhAm 2*
Baldwin, Frank Dwight 1842-1923 *ApCAB X,*
NatCAB 14, WhAm 1
Baldwin, Frank F 1878-1960 *WhAm 4*
Baldwin, Frank Stephen 1838-1925 *DcAmB,*
NatCAB 16
Baldwin, Frederick John 1867- *NatCAB 17*
Baldwin, G Daniel 1876-1946 *NatCAB 36*
Baldwin, Geoffrey P 1892-1951 *WhAm 3*
Baldwin, George Augustus 1874-1964
NatCAB 52
Baldwin, George Benjamin 1876-1951
NatCAB 45
Baldwin, George C 1818?-1879? *NewYHSD*
Baldwin, George Colfax 1817-1899 *ApCAB,*
WhAm 1
Baldwin, George D *NewYHSD*
Baldwin, George Decatur 1884-1957
NatCAB 47
Baldwin, George Johnson 1856-1927
NatCAB 27, WhAm 1
Baldwin, George Porter 1874-1932 *NatCAB 25*
Baldwin, George Rumford 1798-1888
NatCAB 10
Baldwin, George VanNest 1838- *NatCAB 1*
Baldwin, Hadley 1867-1949 *WhAm 3*
Baldwin, Harmon Allen 1869-1936 *WhAm 1*
Baldwin, Harry Streett 1894-1952 *BiDrAC,*
WhAm 3, WhAmP
Baldwin, Helen 1865-1946 *NatCAB 36,*
WomWWA 14
Baldwin, Henry 1779-1844 *BiAUS, Drake*
Baldwin, Henry 1780-1844 *ApCAB, BiDrAC,*
DcAmB, NatCAB 2, TwCBDA, WebAB,
WhAm H, WhAmP
Baldwin, Henry 1832-1905 *WhAm 1*
Baldwin, Henry Alexander 1871-1946 *BiDrAC,*
WhAm 2, WhAmP
Baldwin, Henry DeForest 1862-1947 *WhAm 2*
Baldwin, Henry E 1815-1855 *NatCAB 19*
Baldwin, Henry Perrine 1842-1911 *DcAmB S1,*
NatCAB 40
Baldwin, Henry Perrine 1903-1963 *WhAm 4*
Baldwin, Henry Porter 1814-1892 *ApCAB,*
BiAUS, BiDrAC, DcAmB, Drake,
NatCAB 5, TwCBDA, WhAm H,
WhAmP
Baldwin, Herbert Belcher 1864-1939
NatCAB 29
Baldwin, Heston I 1860-1933 *NatCAB 23*
Baldwin, Howard Charles 1891-1963
NatCAB 52, WhAm 4
Baldwin, Howard Milton 1889-1941
NatCAB 31
Baldwin, Hunter Vallerd 1869-1945 *NatCAB 35*
Baldwin, J G *NewYHSD*
Baldwin, J G d1864 *BiAUS*
Baldwin, J G see also Baldwin, Joseph Glover
Baldwin, J L *NewYHSD*

Baldwin, James *NewYHSD*
Baldwin, James 1841-1925 *BiDAmEd, NatCAB 14, TwCBDA, WhAm 1*
Baldwin, James Arthur 1924- *EncAB, McGEWB, WebAB*
Baldwin, James Fairchild 1850-1936 *WhAm 1*
Baldwin, James Fosdick 1871- *WhAm 5*
Baldwin, James Fowle 1782-1862 *ApCAB, NatCAB 10*
Baldwin, James Fowler 1818-1891 *WhAm H*
Baldwin, James Hewitt 1876- *WhAm 5*
Baldwin, James Mark 1861-1934 *AmBi, ApCAB X, BiDAmEd, DcAmB S1, NatCAB 10, NatCAB 25, TwCBDA, WhAm 1*
Baldwin, Jane North 1876- *WhAm 5, WomWWA 14*
Baldwin, Jeduthan 1732-1788 *ApCAB, Drake*
Baldwin, Jesse A 1854-1921 *WhAm 1*
Baldwin, John 1772-1850 *BiAUS, BiDrAC, WhAm H*
Baldwin, John 1799-1884 *DcAmB, NatCAB 21, WhAm H*
Baldwin, John Brown 1820-1873 *BiDConf, DcAmB, NatCAB 19, WhAm H*
Baldwin, John Denison 1809-1883 *ApCAB, BiDrAC, DcAmB, NatCAB 6, TwCBDA, WhAmP*
Baldwin, John Denison 1810-1883 *BiAUS, Drake, WhAm H*
Baldwin, John Finley, Jr. 1915-1966 *BiDrAC, NatCAB 53, WhAm 4, WhAmP*
Baldwin, John Harvey 1844-1925 *NatCAB 20*
Baldwin, John Thomas, Jr. 1910-1974 *WhAm 6*
Baldwin, Joseph 1827-1899 *BiDAmEd, DcAmB*
Baldwin, Joseph Clark 1838- *NatCAB 14*
Baldwin, Joseph Clark 1897-1957 *BiDrAC, WhAm 3, WhAmP*
Baldwin, Joseph Clark, Jr. 1871-1937 *NatCAB 14, NatCAB 37, WhAm 1*
Baldwin, Joseph Glover 1815-1864 *AmBi, ApCAB, DcAmB, Drake, WhAm H*
Baldwin, Joseph Glover, *see also* Baldwin, J G
Baldwin, Kate M Shoemaker 1858- *WomWWA 14*
Baldwin, Laverne 1899-1968 *WhAm 5*
Baldwin, Lawrence Alexander 1909-1946 *NatCAB 48*
Baldwin, LeRoy Wilbur 1865-1939 *WhAm 1*
Baldwin, Lewis Warrington 1875-1946 *WhAm 2*
Baldwin, Loammi 1740-1807 *AmBi*
Baldwin, Loammi 1744?-1807 *DcAmB*
Baldwin, Loammi 1745-1807 *ApCAB, Drake, NatCAB 10, TwCBDA, WebAB, WhAm H*
Baldwin, Loammi, Jr. 1780-1838 *ApCAB, DcAmB, NatCAB 10, WebAB, WhAm H*
Baldwin, Maitland 1918-1970 *WhAm 5*
Baldwin, Manuel Liston 1862- *WhoColR*
Baldwin, Maria Louise 1856-1922 *BiDAmEd, NotAW*
Baldwin, Marshall Whithed 1903-1975 *WhAm 6*
Baldwin, Martin 1891-1968 *WhAm 5*
Baldwin, Martin Mortimer 1873-1955 *WhAm 3*
Baldwin, Matthias William 1795-1866 *AmBi, ApCAB, DcAmB, Drake, NatCAB 9, WebAB, WhAm H*
Baldwin, Maurice Scollard 1836- *ApCAB Sup*
Baldwin, Melvin Riley 1838-1901 *BiDrAC*
Baldwin, Minor Coe 1856-1950 *WhAm 3*
Baldwin, Myra Rush 1865- *WomWWA 14*
Baldwin, Neilson Abeel 1839- *WhAm 1*
Baldwin, Nellie Elizabeth 1865- *WhAm 4, WomWWA 14*
Baldwin, Noyes 1826-1893 *WhAm H*
Baldwin, Oliver Hazard Perry 1904-1972 *WhAm 5*
Baldwin, Onias Barber 1882-1964 *NatCAB 51*
Baldwin, Ralph Lyman 1872- *WhAm 5*
Baldwin, Raymond Earl 1893- *BiDrAC*
Baldwin, Raymond Peacock 1894-1971 *WhAm 5*
Baldwin, Robert 1804-1858 *ApCAB, McGEWB*
Baldwin, Robert James 1917-1973 *WhAm 5*
Baldwin, Roderick 1833- *NatCAB 1*
Baldwin, Roger Sherman 1793-1863 *AmBi,*

ApCAB, BiAUS, BiDrAC, DcAmB, Drake, NatCAB 10, TwCBDA, WhAm H, WhAmP
Baldwin, Roger Sherman 1873-1949 *WhAm 2*
Baldwin, Roland Dennis 1896-1951 *WhAm 3*
Baldwin, Ruth Standish 1865- *WomWWA 14*
Baldwin, Samuel Alexander 1885-1950 *NatCAB 48*
Baldwin, Samuel Atkinson 1862-1949 *NatCAB 37, WhAm 4*
Baldwin, Samuel Prentiss 1868-1938 *NatCAB 45, WhAm 1*
Baldwin, Seth Weaver 1880-1930 *NatCAB 31*
Baldwin, Sherman 1897-1969 *NatCAB 54, WhAm 5*
Baldwin, Simeon 1761-1851 *BiAUS, BiDrAC, DcAmB, Drake, TwCBDA, WhAm H, WhAmP*
Baldwin, Simeon Eben 1840-1927 *AmBi, ApCAB X, DcAmB, NatCAB 10, NatCAB 21, TwCBDA, WhAm 1, WhAmP*
Baldwin, Stanley Baldwin, Earl 1867-1947 *McGEWB*
Baldwin, Sylvanus 1787?- *WhAm H*
Baldwin, Theodore Anderson 1839-1925 *WhAm 1*
Baldwin, Theoron 1801-1870 *ApCAB*
Baldwin, Theron 1801-1870 *BiDAmEd, DcAmB, NatCAB 6, TwCBDA, WhAm H*
Baldwin, Thomas 1753-1825 *ApCAB, Drake, NatCAB 5*
Baldwin, Thomas Scott 1856-1923 *NatCAB 34*
Baldwin, Thomas Scott 1860-1923 *WhAm 1*
Baldwin, Walter Isaac 1885-1926 *NatCAB 50*
Baldwin, Ward 1856-1920 *NatCAB 19*
Baldwin, Wesley Manning 1879-1975 *WhAm 6*
Baldwin, Wilbur McIntosh 1875-1938 *WhAm 1*
Baldwin, William *NewYHSD*
Baldwin, William 1779-1819 *DcAmB, NatCAB 10, WhAm H*
Baldwin, William 1808?- *NewYHSD*
Baldwin, William Alpheus 1859- *WhAm 3*
Baldwin, William Ayer 1876-1945 *WhAm 2*
Baldwin, William Delavan 1856-1930 *NatCAB 15*
Baldwin, William Delevan 1856-1930 *NatCAB 23, WhAm 1*
Baldwin, William Dwight 1873-1943 *NatCAB 40*
Baldwin, William Edward 1888-1967 *WhAm 4A, WhAm 5*
Baldwin, William H 1826- *TwCBDA*
Baldwin, William Henry 1851-1923 *WhAm 1*
Baldwin, William Henry 1860-1930 *NatCAB 26*
Baldwin, William Henry, Jr. 1863-1905 *ApCAB X, DcAmB, NatCAB 24, WhAm 1*
Baldwin, William James St. John 1844-1924 *ApCAB X, WhAm 1*
Baldwin, William Lester 1894-1964 *NatCAB 51, WhAm 4*
Baldwin, William M 1862- *NatCAB 14*
Baldwin, William Owen 1818-1886 *NatCAB 12*
Baldwin, William Wright 1845-1936 *WhAm 2*
Baldy, Christopher 1885-1959 *WhAm 4*
Baldy, Edward Vincent 1861-1929 *WhAm 1, WhAm 1C*
Baldy, John Montgomery 1860-1934 *NatCAB 14, WhAm 2*
Baldy, Peter 1789-1880 *NatCAB 8*
Bale, James *NewYHSD*
Bale, Louis *NewYHSD*
Balenciaga, Cristobal 1895-1972 *WhAm 5*
Balentine, Mary Pollok Nimmo *WomWWA 14*
Bales, Emery Ray 1882-1948 *NatCAB 36*
Bales, James Anthony 1889-1961 *WhAm 4*
Bales, Walter John 1864-1947 *NatCAB 36*
Balestier, Charles Wolcott 1861-1891 *DcAmB, TwCBDA, WhAm H*
Balestier, Joseph *BiAUS*
Balestier, Wolcott 1861- *ApCAB*
Balewa, Alhaji Abubaker Tafawa 1912-1966 *WhAm 4*
Balfour, Arthur James Balfour, Earl Of 1848-1930 *McGEWB*
Balfour, Donald Church 1882-1963 *WhAm 4*

Balfour, Francis Maitland 1851-1882 *AsBiEn, DcScB*
Balfour, Isaac Bayley 1853-1922 *DcScB*
Balfour, John Hutton 1808-1884 *DcScB*
Balfour, Nisbet 1743-1823 *ApCAB, Drake*
Balfour, Walter 1776-1852 *ApCAB*
Balfour, Walter 1777-1852 *Drake*
Balfour, William 1758-1811 *ApCAB*
Balfour Of Burleigh, Lord 1883-1967 *WhAm 4A*
Baliani, Giovanni Battista 1582-1666 *DcScB*
Balignant *NewYHSD*
Baline, Israel 1888- *WebAB*
Balink, Henry C 1882-1963 *IIBEAAW*
Balis, C *NewYHSD*
Balk, Robert 1899-1955 *WhAm 3*
Balke, Clarence William 1880-1948 *NatCAB 37, WhAm 2*
Balken, Edward Duff 1874-1960 *WhAm 4*
Balkhi, Al- *DcScB*
Ball, Albert 1835-1927 *AmBi, DcAmB*
Ball, Alice Worthington d1929 *WhAm 1, WomWWA 14*
Ball, Alonzo Brayton 1840-1908 *WhAm 1*
Ball, Ancell Harrison 1872-1943 *NatCAB 32*
Ball, Bertha Crosley *WomWWA 14*
Ball, Caroline Peddle 1869-1938 *WhAm 2, WomWWA 14*
Ball, Charles Backus 1854-1928 *WhAm 1*
Ball, Charles Henry 1861-1928 *NatCAB 22*
Ball, Charles Thomas 1866- *WhAm 4*
Ball, David Clifton 1857-1951 *ApCAB X, NatCAB 39*
Ball, David Haines 1869-1940 *NatCAB 29*
Ball, Dyer 1796-1866 *ApCAB, Drake*
Ball, Ebenezer Burgess 1817-1903 *NatCAB 6*
Ball, Edmund Burke 1855-1925 *NatCAB 20*
Ball, Edward 1811-1872 *BiAUS, BiDrAC, WhAm H, WhAmP*
Ball, Elmer Darwin 1870-1943 *NatCAB 18, WhAm 2*
Ball, Ephraim 1812-1872 *ApCAB, DcAmB, Drake, NatCAB 11, TwCBDA, WhAm H*
Ball, Ethan Frank 1892-1967 *NatCAB 54*
Ball, Eustace Hale 1881-1931 *NatCAB 24*
Ball, Ezra H 1824?- *NewYHSD*
Ball, F Carlton 1911- *BnEnAmA*
Ball, Farlin Q 1838-1917 *WhAm 1*
Ball, Fay Hill 1867-1947 *NatCAB 40*
Ball, Francis Kingsley 1863-1940 *NatCAB 18, WhAm 2*
Ball, Frank Clayton 1857-1943 *DcAmB S3, WhAm 2*
Ball, Frank Harvey 1847- *WhAm 4*
Ball, Franklin *NewYHSD*
Ball, Fred Samuel 1866-1942 *WhAm 2*
Ball, Frederick Joseph 1903-1965 *WhAm 4*
Ball, Frederick Stephen 1907-1958 *NatCAB 50*
Ball, George Alexander 1862-1955 *DcAmB S5, WhAm 3*
Ball, George Harvey 1819-1907 *WhAm 1*
Ball, Gordon Reginald 1897-1959 *WhAm 3*
Ball, Helen Elizabeth Voellmig d1974 *WhAm 6*
Ball, Henry Price 1868-1941 *NatCAB 30, WhAm 2*
Ball, Henry Seymour 1830-1916 *NatCAB 16*
Ball, Herman Frederick 1867-1955 *NatCAB 46, WhAm 5*
Ball, Hugh Swinton d1838 *NewYHSD*
Ball, Ida M 1858- *WomWWA 14*
Ball, Isabel Worrell 1855- *AmWom, WomWWA 14*
Ball, James Moores 1863-1929 *NatCAB 21, WhAm 1, WhAm 1C*
Ball, John Chester 1861-1922 *NatCAB 19*
Ball, John Dryer 1896-1951 *NatCAB 41*
Ball, John Rice 1881-1953 *NatCAB 42, WhAm 3*
Ball, Joseph Hurst 1905- *BiDrAC, WhAmP*
Ball, L Heisler 1861-1933 *NatCAB 29, WhAm 1*
Ball, Lewis Heisler 1861- *ApCAB X, NatCAB 13*
Ball, Lewis Heisler 1861-1932 *BiDrAC, WhAmP*
Ball, Liberty P *NewYHSD*
Ball, Louise Charlotte 1887-1946 *WhAm 2*
Ball, Lucille 1911- *WebAB*
Ball, Luther 1827?- *NewYHSD*

Ball, Margaret *NewYHSD*
Ball, Martha Violet 1811- *AmWom*
Ball, Max Waite 1885-1954 *NatCAB 44,*
  WhAm 3
Ball, Michael Valentine 1868-1945 *WhAm 2*
Ball, Minnie Warner 1865- *WomWWA 14*
Ball, Nellie Boeck 1867- *WomWWA 14*
Ball, Norman Critchfield 1873-1932
  NatCAB 23
Ball, Norman T 1905-1971 *WhAm 5*
Ball, Oscar Melville 1868-1942 *WhAm 2*
Ball, Otho Fisher 1875-1953 *WhAm 3*
Ball, Philip DeCatesby 1864-1933 *NatCAB 24*
Ball, Raymond Nathaniel 1891-1966
  NatCAB 53, WhAm 4
Ball, Robert Bruce 1878- *WhAm 6*
Ball, Robert Lee *WhAm 5*
Ball, S *NewYHSD*
Ball, Samuel Ephrem 1870-1956 *NatCAB 42*
Ball, Sophia *NewYHSD*
Ball, Spencer Fairfax 1856-1917 *NatCAB 17*
Ball, Sydney Hobart 1877-1949 *NatCAB 40,*
  WhAm 2
Ball, Sylvia Ernestine 1883- *WomWWA 14*
Ball, Thomas 1819-1911 *AmBi, ApCAB,*
  ApCAB X, BnEnAmA, DcAmB, Drake,
  NatCAB 5, NewYHSD, TwCBDA,
  WhAm 1
Ball, Thomas 1836-1917 *NatCAB 39*
Ball, Thomas Henry 1859-1944 *BiDrAC,*
  TwCBDA, WhAm 2, WhAmP
Ball, Thomas Raymond 1896-1943 *BiDrAC,*
  NatCAB 35, WhAm 2
Ball, Thomas Watson 1863-1934 *NatCAB 26*
Ball, W *NewYHSD*
Ball, Webster Clay 1847-1922 *NatCAB 42*
Ball, Wilbur Laing 1874-1941 *NatCAB 31*
Ball, William, Jr. 1794?-1813 *NewYHSD*
Ball, William Charles 1852-1921 *NatCAB 19*
Ball, William David 1885-1971 *WhAm 5*
Ball, William Lee 1781-1824 *BiAUS, BiDrAC,*
  WhAm H
Ball, William Sherman 1871- *WhAm 5*
Ball, William Watts 1868- *WhAm 5*
Ball, Willis Manville 1859-1947 *WhAm 2*
Balla, Giacomo 1871-1958 *McGEWB*
Ballagh, James Curtis d1944 *WhAm 2*
Ballagh, Josephine Jackson *WomWWA 14*
Ballaine, Francis Knight 1906-1964 *WhAm 4*
Ballance, Harriet N *WomWWA 14*
Ballantine, Alexander Thompson 1835-1901
  NatCAB 7
Ballantine, Arthur Atwood 1883-1960 *WhAm 4*
Ballantine, Edward 1886-1971 *WhAm 5*
Ballantine, Henry Winthrop 1880-1951
  NatCAB 41, WhAm 3
Ballantine, Joseph William 1888-1973 *WhAm 5*
Ballantine, Stuart 1897-1944 *WhAm 2*
Ballantine, William Gay 1848-1937 *NatCAB 2,*
  NatCAB 27, TwCBDA, WhAm 1
Ballantyne, John 1900-1949 *NatCAB 39,*
  WhAm 2
Ballard, Aaron Edward 1820-1919 *WhAm 1*
Ballard, Addison 1822-1914 *NatCAB 3,*
  TwCBDA, WhAm 1
Ballard, Anna 1828- *WomWWA 14*
Ballard, Bland Williams 1759-1853 *DcAmB,*
  WhAm H, WhAmP
Ballard, Bland Williams 1761-1853 *ApCAB,*
  Drake, NatCAB 5, TwCBDA
Ballard, Byron LeRoy 1890-1952 *NatCAB 41*
Ballard, Charles Duane 1874-1942 *NatCAB 32*
Ballard, Charles William 1887-1963
  NatCAB 51, WhAm 4
Ballard, Claudius 1890- *WhoColR*
Ballard, Edna Wheeler 1886-1971 *DcAmReB*
Ballard, Edward 1805-1870 *Drake*
Ballard, Edward Lathrop 1870-1937 *WhAm 1*
Ballard, Ellis Ames 1861-1938 *WhAm 1*
Ballard, Ernest Schwefel 1885-1952 *WhAm 3*
Ballard, Frances Anne Keay 1878-
  WomWWA 14
Ballard, Frank Llewellyn 1891-1971
  NatCAB 56
Ballard, Frederic Lyman 1888-1952 *WhAm 4*
Ballard, George *NewYHSD*
Ballard, Guy Warren 1878-1939 *DcAmReB*
Ballard, Harlan Hoge 1853-1934 *ApCAB,*

NatCAB 9, *TwCBDA, WhAm 1*
Ballard, Henry E 1785-1855 *ApCAB, Drake*
Ballard, James Franklin 1851-1931 *NatCAB 25,*
  WhAm 1
Ballard, Lloyd Vernor 1887-1969 *NatCAB 54*
Ballard, Mary Canfield 1852- *AmWom*
Ballard, Nathaniel Harrison 1866- *WhAm 3*
Ballard, Otis A *NewYHSD*
Ballard, Russell Henry 1875-1932 *WhAm 1*
Ballard, Sam M 1902-1963 *WhAm 4*
Ballard, Samuel Thruston 1855-1926
  NatCAB 20, WhAm 1
Ballard, Sumner 1865-1941 *NatCAB 34,*
  WhAm 1
Ballard, W C, Jr. 1888-1953 *WhAm 3*
Ballard, William Henry, Sr. 1862- *WhoColR*
Ballard, William Stevens 1915-1970
  NatCAB 55
Ballenger, Edgar Garrison 1877- *NatCAB 15,*
  WhAm 5
Ballenger, George Walter 1860-1938 *WhAm 1*
Ballenger, Howard C 1886-1965 *WhAm 4*
Ballenger, William Lincoln 1861-1915 *WhAm 1*
Ballenger, William Sylvester 1866-1951
  NatCAB 40, WhAm 3
Ballentine, George Andrew 1899-1968 *WhAm 5*
Ballentine, James Arthur 1871-1949
  NatCAB 40
Ballentine, John Goff 1825-1915 *BiDrAC*
Ballentine, John Jennings 1896-1970
  NatCAB 55, WhAm 5
Ballentine, Lynton Yates 1899-1964 *NatCAB 51*
Baller, Stuart Taylor 1903-1975 *WhAm 6*
Ballevian, Adolfo d1874 *ApCAB*
Balliet, Letson 1873- *NatCAB 12*
Balliet, Thomas Minard 1852-1942 *BiDAmEd,*
  NatCAB 31, WhAm 2
Ballin, Hugo d1956 *WhAm 3*
Ballin, J *NewYHSD*
Ballin, Max 1869-1934 *WhAm 1*
Balling, Henry James 1900-1968 *NatCAB 54*
Balling, Ole Peter Hansen 1823-1906
  NewYHSD
Ballinger, Charles L 1899-1974 *WhAm 6*
Ballinger, Harold Lawrence 1904-1964
  NatCAB 51
Ballinger, John H 1879- *WhAm 6*
Ballinger, Richard Achilles 1858-1922 *AmBi,*
  BiDrUSE, DcAmB, NatCAB 11,
  NatCAB 14, WhAm 1, WhAmP
Ballinger, Robert Irving 1892-1974 *WhAm 6*
Ballinger, William Pitt 1825-1888 *ApCAB Sup*
Ballivian, Jose 1805-1852 *McGEWB*
Ballmann, Martin 1863-1931 *WhAm 1*
Ballmer, Robert Sidney 1904-1964 *NatCAB 51*
Balloch, Edward Arthur 1857-1948 *WhAm 2*
Ballonius *DcScB*
Ballot, Christoph Buys *DcScB*
Ballou, Adin 1803-1890 *AmBi, DcAmB,*
  EncAAH, NatCAB 7, WebAB,
  WhAm H
Ballou, Barton Allan 1835-1922 *NatCAB 19*
Ballou, Bertha 1891- *IIBEAAW*
Ballou, Charles Clarendon 1862-1928 *WebAMB,*
  WhAm 1
Ballou, Daniel Ross 1837-1923 *NatCAB 25*
Ballou, Edward Richardson 1871-1926
  NatCAB 25
Ballou, Ella Maria 1852- *AmWom*
Ballou, Frank Washington 1879-1955 *WhAm 3*
Ballou, Frederic Allen 1866-1943 *NatCAB 35*
Ballou, Frederick Allan 1869-1949 *NatCAB 47*
Ballou, Frederick Allan, Jr. 1893-1964
  NatCAB 53
Ballou, Giddings Hyde 1820-1886 *NewYHSD*
Ballou, Hosea 1771-1852 *AmBi, ApCAB,*
  DcAmB, DcAmReB, Drake, NatCAB 5,
  TwCBDA, WebAB, WhAm H
Ballou, Hosea, II 1796-1861 *AmBi, ApCAB,*
  DcAmB, Drake, NatCAB 6, TwCBDA,
  WhAm H
Ballou, Hosea Starr 1857-1943 *WhAm 2*
Ballou, John Benjamin 1874-1957 *NatCAB 46*
Ballou, John Henry 1853- *WhoColR*
Ballou, Latimer Whipple 1812-1900 *ApCAB,*
  BiAUS, BiDrAC, NatCAB 4, TwCBDA
Ballou, Latimer Whipple 1818-1900 *WhAmP*
Ballou, Levi Herbert 1883-1958 *WhAm 3*

Ballou, Mathurin Murray 1820-1895 *TwCBDA*
Ballou, Maturin M 1822-1895 *Drake*
Ballou, Maturin Murray 1820-1895 *ApCAB,*
  DcAmB, NatCAB 7, WhAm H
Ballou, Moses 1811-1879 *ApCAB, TwCBDA*
Ballou, Sidney Miller 1870-1929 *NatCAB 21,*
  WhAm 1
Ballou, Susan Ann 1844- *WomWWA 14*
Ballou, William Hosea 1857-1937 *WhAm 2*
Balluff, Bernard Fraser 1916-1963 *NatCAB 50*
Bally, Louis Henry 1897-1963 *WhAm 5*
Balmaceda, Jose Manuel 1840-1891 *ApCAB,*
  McGEWB
Balmanno, Charles Gorden 1864-1916 *WhAm 1*
Balmanno, Mrs. Robert *NewYHSD*
Balmaseda, Francisco J 1833- *ApCAB*
Balmer, Edwin 1883-1959 *WhAm 3*
Balmer, Frank Everett 1883-1954 *WhAm 3*
Balmer, Helen Pratt *WomWWA 14*
Balmer, Johann Jakob 1825-1898 *AsBiEn,*
  DcScB
Balmer, Thomas 1888-1959 *WhAm 3*
Balmes, Francisco Javier *ApCAB*
Balough, Charles 1883-1966 *NatCAB 52,*
  WhAm 4
Balsam, Aldo R 1903-1963 *WhAm 4*
Balser, Arthur Conrad 1875-1949 *NatCAB 38*
Balsinger, William Ernest 1881-1953
  NatCAB 41
Balsley, Alfred Harcourt 1828- *NatCAB 2*
Balta, Jose d1872 *ApCAB*
Balter, Morris 1896-1971 *NatCAB 57*
Baltes, Peter Joseph 1820-1886 *WhAm H*
Baltes, Peter Joseph 1827-1886 *ApCAB,*
  NatCAB 12, TwCBDA
Baltimore, Baron *WebAB, WhAm H*
Baltimore, Lord *Drake, WhAm H*
Baltimore, Lords *AmBi, ApCAB*
Baltimore, Charles Calvert, Lord 1629-1715
  DcAmB
Baltimore, George Calvert, Lord 1580?-1632
  DcAmB
Baltimore, Sir George Calvert, Lord 1582-1632
  TwCBDA
Baltz, William Nicolas 1860-1943 *BiDrAC,*
  WhAm 4, WhAmP
Baltzell, Maude Day 1892-1966 *WhAm 4*
Baltzell, Robert C 1879-1950 *WhAm 3*
Baltzell, Thomas d1866 *NatCAB 12*
Baltzell, Winton James 1864-1928 *WhAm 1*
Baltzly, Oliver Daniel 1871- *WhAm 5*
Baluffi, Gaetano 1798-1866 *ApCAB*
Balutis, Bronius Kasimir 1879- *WhAm 6*
Balz, Albert George Adam 1887-1957
  NatCAB 46, WhAm 3
Balz, Arcada Stark 1883-1973 *NatCAB 57*
Balzac, Honore De 1799-1850 *McGEWB*
Balzar, Frederick Bennett 1880-1934
  NatCAB 27
Balzar, Fredrick Bennett 1880-1934 *WhAm 1*
Bamba, Amadou 1850-1927 *McGEWB*
Bamberger, Edgar Sutro 1883-1952 *NatCAB 40*
Bamberger, Ernest 1877-1958 *WhAm 3*
Bamberger, Eugen 1857-1932 *DcScB*
Bamberger, Julian Maas 1889-1967 *NatCAB 54*
Bamberger, Louis 1855-1944 *DcAmB S3,*
  NatCAB 33, WhAm 2
Bamberger, Ralph 1871- *WhAm 5*
Bamberger, Simon 1847-1926 *NatCAB 20,*
  WhAm 1
Bamborough, William 1792-1860 *NewYHSD,*
  WhAm H
Bamboschek, Giuseppe 1890-1969 *WhAm 5*
Bamford, Mary Ellen 1857- *WhAm 5,*
  WomWWA 14
Banach, Stefan 1892-1945 *DcScB*
Banachiewicz, Thaddeus 1882-1954 *DcScB*
Banay, Ralph Steven 1896-1970 *WhAm 5*
Bancker, Mary Clark *WomWWA 14*
Bancker, Mary E C 1860- *AmWom*
Bancker, Mary Whitaker *WomWWA 14*
Bancroft, Aaron 1755-1839 *ApCAB, DcAmB,*
  Drake, NatCAB 4, WhAm H
Bancroft, Albert Stokes 1890-1972 *IIBEAAW*
Bancroft, Cecil Franklin Patch 1839-1901
  BiDAmEd, DcAmB, NatCAB 10,
  NatCAB 24, TwCBDA, WhAm 1

Bancroft, Cecil Kittredge 1868-1932
NatCAB 25
Bancroft, Charles Foster 1873-1948 *NatCAB 36*
Bancroft, Charles Grey 1867-1955 *WhAm 3*
Bancroft, Charles Parker 1852-1923
NatCAB 20, *WhAm 1*
Bancroft, Edgar Addison 1857-1925 *DcAmB,*
NatCAB 14, *WhAm 1,* *WhAmP*
Bancroft, Edward 1744-1820 *ApCAB,* *Drake,*
TwCBDA
Bancroft, Edward 1744-1821 *AmBi,* *DcAmB,*
WebAB, *WhAm H*
Bancroft, Eleanor Stow 1874- *WomWWA 14*
Bancroft, Emma Cooper *WomWWA 14*
Bancroft, Everett Clair 1894-1971 *NatCAB 56*
Bancroft, Francis Sydney 1881-1957 *WhAm 3*
Bancroft, Frederic 1860-1945 *DcAmB S3,*
NatCAB 10, *TwCBDA,* *WhAm 2*
Bancroft, George 1800-1891 *AmBi,* *ApCAB,*
BiAUS, *BiDrUSE,* *DcAmB,* *Drake,*
EncAAH, *EncAB,* *McGEWB,* *NatCAB 3,*
TwCBDA, *WebAB,* *WhAm H,* *WhAmP*
Bancroft, Howland 1886-1964 *WhAm 4*
Bancroft, Hubert Howe 1832-1918 *AmBi,*
ApCAB, *DcAmB,* *EncAAH,* *McGEWB,*
NatCAB 5, *REnAW,* *TwCBDA,* *WebAB,*
WhAm 1
Bancroft, Hugh 1879-1933 *NatCAB 33,*
WhAm 1
Bancroft, J Sellers 1843-1919 *WhAm 1*
Bancroft, Jane Marie *NotAW*
Bancroft, Jane Wallis Waldron 1877-1949
NatCAB 38
Bancroft, Jessie Hubbell 1867-1952 *BiDAmEd,*
WhAm 4, *WomWWA 14*
Bancroft, John 1856-1933 *NatCAB 25*
Bancroft, Joseph 1803-1874 *NatCAB 33*
Bancroft, Joseph 1875-1936 *NatCAB 27,*
WhAm 1
Bancroft, Levi Horace 1861-1948 *WhAm 3*
Bancroft, Lucius Whiting 1827- *NatCAB 5*
Bancroft, Margaret Healy *WomWWA 14*
Bancroft, Milton H 1866-1947 *WhAm 2*
Bancroft, Philip 1881- *WhAm 6*
Bancroft, Samuel 1840-1915 *NatCAB 15,*
NatCAB 31
Bancroft, Thomas Moore 1902-1970 *WhAm 5*
Bancroft, Wilder Dwight 1867-1953 *DcAmB S5,*
DcScB, *NatCAB 14,* *NatCAB 42,*
WhAm 3
Bancroft, William Amos 1855-1922 *NatCAB 9,*
WhAm 1
Bancroft, William Hazard 1840-1915
NatCAB 17, *WhAm 1*
Bancroft, William Henry 1860-1932 *IlBEAAW*
Bancroft, William Poole 1835-1928 *NatCAB 22,*
WhAm 1
Band, Charles Shaw 1885-1969 *WhAm 5*
Banda, Hastings Kamuzu 1905- *McGEWB*
Bandaranaike, Solomon West Ridgeway Dias
1899-1959 *WhAm 4*
Bandelier, Adolph Francis Alphonse 1840-1914
AmBi, *ApCAB,* *DcAmB,* *REnAW,*
WebAB, *WhAm 1*
Bandelier, Adolphe Francis Alphonse 1840-1914
NatCAB 26
Bandholtz, Harry Hill 1864-1925 *ApCAB X,*
NatCAB 19, *WhAm 1*
Bandini, Juan 1800-1859 *ApCAB*
Bandler, Clarence Garfield 1880-1957
NatCAB 46, *WhAm 3*
Bandmann, Daniel Edward 1840-1905
ApCAB X, *WhAm 1*
Bandstra, Bert Andrew 1922- *BiDrAC*
Bandy, Burl Judson 1888-1948 *NatCAB 38*
Bandy, Mark Chance 1900-1963 *NatCAB 51*
Bandy, Mary Albertson 1874- *WomWWA 14*
Bandy, Orville Lee 1917-1973 *WhAm 6*
Bane, Abner Clarke *ApCAB X*
Bane, Clinton Eugene 1894-1956 *NatCAB 47*
Bane, John Curry 1861- *NatCAB 18*
Bane, Juliet Lita 1887-1957 *NatCAB 43,*
WhAm 3
Banerjee, Surendranath 1848-1925 *McGEWB*
Banes, Charles H 1831- *NatCAB 4*
Banfield, Richard Wallace 1911-1963 *WhAm 4*
Banfield, Thomas Harry 1885-1950 *NatCAB 40,*
WhAm 3

Bang, Bernhard 1848-1932 *BiHiMed*
Bang, Mary Phillips 1849- *WomWWA 14*
Bangham, Ralph Vandervort 1895-1966
WhAm 4
Bangs, Edith *BiCAW*
Bangs, Francis A 1836?- *NewYHSD*
Bangs, Francis C 1837- *ApCAB*
Bangs, Francis Nehemiah 1828-1885 *ApCAB,*
DcAmB, *NatCAB 11,* *WhAm H,*
WhAmP
Bangs, Francis Reginald 1869-1939 *WhAm 1*
Bangs, Frank C 1833-1908 *DcAmB*
Bangs, George Archer 1867-1955 *ApCAB X,*
WhAm 3
Bangs, Isaac Sparrow 1831-1903 *WhAm 1*
Bangs, J Edward 1853- *NatCAB 16*
Bangs, J Edward 1857- *WhAm 4*
Bangs, John Kendrick 1862-1922 *AmBi,*
ApCAB Sup, *ApCAB X,* *DcAmB,*
NatCAB 9, *TwCBDA,* *WhAm 1*
Bangs, L Bolton 1842-1914 *WhAm 1*
Bangs, Nathan 1778-1862 *AmBi,* *ApCAB,*
DcAmB, *DcAmReB,* *Drake,* *NatCAB 9,*
TwCBDA, *WhAm H*
Bangs, Outram 1863-1932 *WhAm 1,*
WhAm 1C
Bangs, Tracy Rollin 1862-1936 *ApCAB X,*
WhAm 1
Bangsberg, Harry Frederick 1928-1967
WhAm 4
Banister, Alan Boyd 1905-1963 *NatCAB 55*
Banister, John d1787 *ApCAB,* *Drake,*
NatCAB 7
Banister, John 1650-1692 *ApCAB,* *DcAmB,*
DcScB, *WhAm H*
Banister, John 1650-1693 *Drake*
Banister, John 1734-1788 *BiAUS,* *BiDrAC,*
DcAmB, *WhAm H,* *WhAmP*
Banister, John Monro 1854-1929 *NatCAB 23*
Banister, Marion Glass d1951 *WhAm 3*
Banister, William Brodnax 1861- *WhAm 4*
Banister, Zilpah Polly Grant 1794-1874
BiDAmEd, *DcAmB,* *NotAW,* *WhAm H*
Bankard, Henry Nicholas 1834-1903 *NatCAB 2*
Banker, Elmer Fisk 1871-1939 *NatCAB 30*
Banker, Hezekiah 1860- *NewYHSD*
Banker, Howard James 1866- *ApCAB X*
Banker, Howard James 1866-1940 *NatCAB 30*
Banker, Howard James 1866-1943 *WhAm 2*
Banker, Walter 1881- *WhAm 6*
Bankhardt, Valentine 1841-1922 *NatCAB 38*
Bankhead, Henry Clay 1828-1894 *ApCAB Sup*
Bankhead, Henry McAuley 1876- *WhAm 5*
Bankhead, James 1783-1856 *ApCAB,* *Drake,*
TwCBDA
Bankhead, John Hollis 1842-1920 *ApCAB X,*
BiDrAC, *DcAmB,* *NatCAB 14,* *TwCBDA,*
WhAm 1, *WhAmP*
Bankhead, John Hollis 1872-1946 *BiDrAC,*
DcAmB S4, *EncAAH,* *NatCAB 43,*
WhAm 2, *WhAmP*
Bankhead, John Pine 1821-1867 *ApCAB,*
NatCAB 5, *TwCBDA*
Bankhead, Tallulah Brockman 1903-1968
WebAB, *WhAm 5*
Bankhead, Walter Will 1897- *BiDrAC*
Bankhead, William Brockman 1874-1940
BiDrAC, *DcAmB S2,* *WebAB,* *WhAm 1,*
WhAmP
Banks, A A 1890-1954 *WhAm 3*
Banks, Alexander French 1861-1948 *WhAm 2*
Banks, Alexander Robinson 1850- *WhAm 4*
Banks, Alexander Scott 1884-1949 *NatCAB 45*
Banks, Alida Priscilla 1887- *WhoColR*
Banks, Aloysius Burton 1868- *WhAm 4*
Banks, Charles 1873- *WhoColR*
Banks, Charles Edward 1854-1931 *DcAmB S1*
Banks, Charles Eugene 1852-1932 *NatCAB 14,*
WhAm 1
Banks, Charlotte Mooney 1847- *WomWWA 14*
Banks, David 1786-1871 *ApCAB*
Banks, David 1796-1871 *TwCBDA*
Banks, David 1827- *NatCAB 12*
Banks, Edgar James 1866-1945 *ApCAB X,*
WhAm 2
Banks, Elizabeth d1938 *WhAm 1,*
WomWWA 14
Banks, Emanuel S 1900-1956 *WhAm 3*

Banks, Florence S Woolley 1853-
WomWWA 14
Banks, Frank Arthur 1883-1957 *WhAm 3*
Banks, Gardner d1871 *ApCAB*
Banks, George B 1888-1965 *WhAm 4*
Banks, Harry Pickands 1884- *WhAm 3*
Banks, James *NewYHSD*
Banks, James Jones 1861- *WhAm 3*
Banks, James Lenox 1890-1946 *NatCAB 44*
Banks, Jeff 1904-1957 *NatCAB 49*
Banks, John 1793-1864 *BiAUS,* *BiDrAC,*
Drake, *WhAm H,* *WhAmP*
Banks, John Henry 1861-1934 *WhAm 1*
Banks, John Wallace 1867-1958 *WhAm 3*
Banks, Sir Joseph 1743-1820 *AsBiEn,* *DcScB,*
McGEWB
Banks, Linn 1784-1842 *BiAUS,* *BiDrAC,*
TwCBDA, *WhAm H,* *WhAmP*
Banks, Louis Albert 1855-1933 *NatCAB 13,*
WhAm 1
Banks, Mary Ross 1846- *AmWom*
Banks, Maud *ApCAB*
Banks, Nathan 1868-1953 *NatCAB 40,*
WhAm 3
Banks, Nathanial Prentiss 1816-1894 *WhAm H*
Banks, Nathaniel P 1816-1894 *BiAUS*
Banks, Nathaniel Prentice 1816-1894 *BiDrAC,*
NatCAB 4
Banks, Nathaniel Prentiss 1816-1894 *AmBi,*
ApCAB, *DcAmB,* *Drake,* *TwCBDA,*
WebAB, *WebAMB,* *WhAmP,* *WhoMilH*
Banks, Noble Calhoun 1872-1943 *NatCAB 35*
Banks, Sarah Gertrude 1839- *NatCAB 18*
Banks, Stanley Day 1898-1963 *NatCAB 49*
Banks, Theodore H 1866-1933 *WhAm 1*
Banks, Theodore Howard 1895-1969
NatCAB 55
Banks, William Henry 1874-1958 *NatCAB 47*
Banks, William Nathaniel 1884-1965 *WhAm 4*
Banks, William Webb 1862- *WhoColR*
Bankson, Virgil Lee 1908-1962 *WhAm 4*
Bann, Charles 1826?- *NewYHSD*
Banna Al Marrakushi, Ibn Al- 1256-1321 *DcScB*
Bannan, Theresa 1868- *WomWWA 14*
Bannard, Darby 1931- *BnEnAmA*
Bannard, Otto Tremont 1854-1929 *ApCAB X,*
WhAm 1
Banneker, Benjamin 1731-1806 *ApCAB,* *Drake,*
EncAB, *McGEWB,* *NatCAB 5,* *WebAB,*
WhAm H, *WhAmP*
Banner, John 1910-1973 *WhAm 5*
Banner, Peter *DcAmB,* *WhAm H*
Bannerman, Arthur Marling 1900-1976
WhAm 6
Bannerman, Francis 1851-1918 *ApCAB X,*
NatCAB 19
Bannerman, James *NewYHSD*
Bannerman, John *NewYHSD*
Bannerman, John B *NewYHSD*
Bannerman, William W *NewYHSD*
Bannick, Christian John 1887-1957 *NatCAB 43*
Bannin, Michael Eugene 1846- *NatCAB 14*
Banning, Carrie B Carpenter 1857-
WomWWA 14
Banning, Ephraim 1849-1907 *WhAm 1*
Banning, Henry B 1834- *BiAUS*
Banning, Henry Blackstone 1836-1881 *BiDrAC,*
NatCAB 16, *WhAm H,* *WhAmP*
Banning, Kendall 1879-1944 *WhAm 2*
Banning, Margaret Culkin *BiCAW*
Banning, Pierson Worrall 1879-1927 *ApCAB X,*
NatCAB 20, *WhAm 1*
Banning, Sarah Jane 1854- *WomWWA 14*
Banning, William J 1810-1856 *NewYHSD*
Banning, William Lowber 1814-1893
NatCAB 16
Banning, William Lowber 1899-1950
NatCAB 38
Banning, William Vaughn 1906-1972 *WhAm 6*
Bannister, E M 1833-1901 *ApCAB*
Bannister, Edward M 1833-1901 *NewYHSD,*
WhAm 4
Bannister, Edwin 1823?- *NewYHSD*
Bannister, Harry Ray 1894-1967 *WhAm 4*
Bannister, Henry Martyn 1844- *WhAm 4*
Bannister, James 1821-1901 *NewYHSD*
Bannister, Lucius Ward 1871-1958 *WhAm 3*

Bannister, Nathaniel Harrington 1813-1847
DcAmB, NatCAB 22, WhAm H

Bannister, Robert James 1878-1967 *NatCAB 54,
WhAm 6*

Bannon, Henry Towne 1867-1950 *BiDrAC,
WhAm 3, WhAmP*

Bannon, John Francis 1905- *EncAAH,
REnAW*

Bannon, John Joseph, Jr. 1896-1973 *WhAm 6*

Bannon, William Henry 1880-1963 *NatCAB 52*

Bannow, Rudolph F 1897-1962 *WhAm 4*

Banon, E Magawly 1868-1944 *NatCAB 32*

Banon, Edward M *ApCAB X*

Banoni *NewYHSD*

Banov, Leon 1888-1971 *WhAm 6*

Banta, Arthur Mangun 1877-1946 *NatCAB 35,
WhAm 2*

Banta, Charles Woodbury 1877-1922
NatCAB 19

Banta, Melissa Elizabeth Riddle 1834- *AmWom*

Banta, N Moore 1867-1932 *WhAm 1*

Banta, Parke Monroe 1891-1970 *BiDrAC,
WhAm 5, WhAmP*

Banta, Philip Raymond 1899-1965 *NatCAB 51*

Banta, Theodore M *NewYHSD*

Banta, Weart *NewYHSD*

Bantel, Edward Christian Henry 1873-
WhAm 5

Banti, Guido 1852-1925 *BiHiMed, DcScB*

Banting, Frederick Grant 1891-1941 *AsBiEn,
BiHiMed, DcScB, McGEWB*

Banton, Conwell 1875- *WhoColR*

Banton, J *NewYHSD*

Banton, T S *NewYHSD*

Banu Musa *DcScB*

Banvard, John 1815-1891 *AmBi, DcAmB,
IlBEAAW, NatCAB 5, NewYHSD,
WhAm H*

Banvard, John 1820?-1891 *ApCAB*

Banvard, John 1821-1891 *TwCBDA*

Banvard, Joseph 1810-1887 *ApCAB, DcAmB,
TwCBDA, WhAm H*

Banzhaf, Henry Leo 1865-1951 *WhAm 3*

Bao Dai 1913- *McGEWB, WhWW-II*

Bapst, John 1815-1887 *BiDAmEd, DcAmB,
WhAm H*

Bapst, Robert Thomas 1880-1959 *WhAm 3*

Bar *NewYHSD*

Bar Kochba, Simeon d135 *McGEWB*

Bara, Theda 1885-1955 *DcAmB S5*

Bara, Theda 1890-1955 *WebAB, WhAm 3*

Barabin, Joseph Hercules 1874- *WhoColR*

Barach, Frederica Pisek 1904- *WhAm 3*

Barach, Joseph Hayem 1883-1954 *NatCAB 43,
WhAm 3*

Barach, Louis Victor 1885-1955 *NatCAB 43*

Barack, Louis Barry 1910-1967 *WhAm 5*

Baraga, Frederic 1797-1868 *AmBi, DcAmB,
Drake, NatCAB 12, REnAW*

Baraga, Frederick 1797-1868 *ApCAB,
TwCBDA*

Baraguay D'Hilliers, Achille 1795-1878
WhoMilH

Baragwanath, John Gordon 1888-1965 *WhAm 4*

Baraka, Imamu Amiri 1934- *McGEWB,
WebAB*

Barakat, Mohammad Zaki Taha Ibrahim
1914-1974 *WhAm 6*

Baralt, Rafael Maria 1810- *ApCAB*

Baranda, Joaquin 1840- *ApCAB Sup*

Baranda, Pedro Sainz De 1787-1845 *ApCAB*

Baranoff, Alexander Andrevitch 1746-1819
ApCAB

Baranov, Aleksandr Andreevich 1747-1819
REnAW

Baranov, Aleksandr Andreievich 1747-1819
McGEWB

Baranov, Aleksandr Andreyevich 1746-1819
AmBi

Baranov, Alexander Andreevich 1746-1819
DcAmB

Baranov, Alexander Andrevich 1746-1819
WhAm H

Baranov, Alexandre Andre Vith d1819 *Drake*

Barany, Robert 1876-1936 *BiHiMed, DcScB*

Baranzano, Giovanni Antonio 1590-1622 *DcScB*

Baratieri, Oreste 1841-1901 *WhoMilH*

Baraza, Frederic 1797-1868 *WhAm H*

Barba, Alvaro Alonso 1569-1640? *DcScB*

Barba, Charles Elmer 1877- *WhAm 5*

Barba, Pedro *ApCAB*

Barbacena, Fesberto Caldeira Brant 1772-1841
ApCAB

Barbarossa 1483-1546 *WhoMilH*

Barbaud, Auguste *NewYHSD*

Barbaud, J J A *NewYHSD*

Barbe, Marbois *Drake*

Barbe, Waitman 1864-1925 *NatCAB 20,
WhAm 1*

Barbee, David Rankin 1874-1958 *WhAm 3*

Barbee, Herbert 1848- *NatCAB 18*

Barbee, Hugh Arthur 1874- *WhAm 5*

Barbee, James Thomas 1838- *WhAm 4*

Barbee, T R *NewYHSD*

Barbee, William J 1816-1892 *ApCAB,
TwCBDA*

Barbee, William Randolph 1818-1868
NatCAB 18, NewYHSD, WhAm H

Barbelin, Felix Joseph 1808-1869 *WhAm H*

Barber *NewYHSD*

Barber, Albert Gilman 1857- *NatCAB 17*

Barber, Alice *NotAW*

Barber, Alice Sherman *WomWWA 14*

Barber, Amos Walker 1861- *NatCAB 11*

Barber, Amzi Lorenzo 1843-1909 *DcAmB,
NatCAB 3, WhAm 1*

Barber, Calvin Fremyre 1859-1934 *NatCAB 25*

Barber, Charles Edward 1840-1917 *NatCAB 16*

Barber, Charles Newell 1884-1958 *WhAm 3*

Barber, Charles Russel 1855-1935 *NatCAB 30*

Barber, Charles Williams 1872-1943 *WhAm 2*

Barber, D Fletcher 1855-1946 *NatCAB 36*

Barber, Daniel 1756-1834 *WhAm H*

Barber, Donn 1871-1925 *DcAmB, NatCAB 14,
NatCAB 25, WhAm 1*

Barber, Dorman Bruister 1900-1965
NatCAB 56

Barber, Edmund L *NewYHSD*

Barber, Edward John 1887-1953 *NatCAB 42,
WhAm 3*

Barber, Edwin AtLee 1851-1916 *DcAmB,
NatCAB 22, WhAm 1*

Barber, Elsie Yandell *BiCAW*

Barber, Francis 1751-1783 *AmBi, ApCAB,
DcAmB, Drake, NatCAB 1, TwCBDA,
WhAm H*

Barber, Francis M 1845- *TwCBDA*

Barber, Frank Elliott 1878-1954 *NatCAB 45*

Barber, George 1804-1879 *NatCAB 24*

Barber, George Edward 1859-1940 *NatCAB 30*

Barber, George Garfield 1883-1943 *NatCAB 32,
WhAm 2*

Barber, George Holcomb 1864-1926 *WhAm 1*

Barber, Gershom Morse 1823-1892 *NatCAB 2,
WhAm 4*

Barber, Grove Ettinger 1843-1931 *NatCAB 17,
NatCAB 27*

Barber, H 1875- *WhAm 5*

Barber, Harry Haughey 1878-1948 *NatCAB 38*

Barber, Henry A, Jr. 1896-1956 *WhAm 3*

Barber, Henry Hervey 1835- *WhAm 4*

Barber, Henry Hiram 1852-1919 *NatCAB 17*

Barber, Herbert 1847-1915 *NatCAB 35*

Barber, Herbert Goodell 1870-1947 *WhAm 3*

Barber, Hiram, Jr. 1835-1924 *BiDrAC*

Barber, Isaac Ambrose 1852-1909 *BiDrAC*

Barber, Isaac Henry 1829-1896 *NatCAB 9*

Barber, J Allen 1809-1881 *BiAUS*

Barber, J DeVere 1871-1945 *NatCAB 33*

Barber, J Max 1878- *WhoColR*

Barber, James 1825?- *NewYHSD*

Barber, James Morgan 1866-1949 *NatCAB 38*

Barber, James Wells 1852-1928 *NatCAB 31*

Barber, Jason Alonzo 1855-1938 *NatCAB 42*

Barber, Joel Allen 1809-1881 *BiDrAC,
WhAm H*

Barber, John 1898-1965 *NatCAB 52*

Barber, John Jay 1840- *ApCAB, NewYHSD,
TwCBDA*

Barber, John Norton 1870-1933 *NatCAB 30*

Barber, John Warner 1798-1885 *AmBi,
ApCAB, DcAmB, Drake, NatCAB 3,
NewYHSD, TwCBDA, WhAm H*

Barber, Jonathan 1784-1864 *Drake*

Barber, Laird Howard 1848-1928 *BiDrAC*

Barber, Levi 1777-1833 *BiAUS, BiDrAC,*

Barber, Mary Augustine 1789-1860 *AmWom,
ApCAB*

Barber, Mary I d1963 *WhAm 4*

Barber, Mary Saxton 1848- *WomWWA 14*

Barber, Milton Augustus 1869-1938 *WhAm 1*

Barber, Moses Jesse 1851-1947 *NatCAB 39*

Barber, Muriel Virginia 1904-1971 *NatCAB 57,
WhAm 6*

Barber, Noyes 1781-1844 *BiDrAC, TwCBDA,
WhAm H, WhAmP*

Barber, Noyes 1781-1845 *BiAUS*

Barber, Ohio Columbus 1841-1920 *ApCAB X,
DcAmB, NatCAB 2, NatCAB 34,
WhAm 1*

Barber, Orion Metcalf 1857-1930 *WhAm 1*

Barber, Raymond Jenness 1884-1955 *WhAm 3*

Barber, Samuel 1910- *McGEWB, WebAB*

Barber, Sidman I 1898-1971 *WhAm 5*

Barber, Virgil 1782-1847 *WhAm H*

Barber, Wilford Whitaker 1892-1965
NatCAB 52

Barber, William *NewYHSD*

Barber, William 1807-1879 *NewYHSD*

Barber, William A 1869-1950 *WhAm 2A*

Barber, William Harley 1878-1973 *WhAm 6*

Barber, William Henry 1864- *WhAm 4*

Barbey, Daniel Edward 1889-1969 *WebAMB,
WhAm 5*

Barbey, John Edward 1890-1956 *WhAm 3*

Barbier *NewYHSD*

Barbier, Joseph-Emile 1839-1889 *DcScB*

Barbier-Walbonne, Jacques Luc 1769-1860
NewYHSD

Barbieri, Leonardo *NewYHSD*

Barbirolli, Sir John 1899-1970 *WhAm 5*

Barborka, Clifford Joseph 1894-1971 *WhAm 5*

Barbosa, Ruy 1849-1923 *McGEWB*

Barbosa-Bacellar, Antonio 1600?-1663
ApCAB Sup

Barbosa-Machado, Diogo 1682-1770
ApCAB Sup

Barbosa-Machado, Ignacio 1682-1770
ApCAB Sup

Barbot, Blanche Hermine 1842- *AmWom*

Barbot, Louis J *WhAm H*

Barbour, Amy Louise *WomWWA 14*

Barbour, Anna Maynard d1941 *WhAm 1,
WomWWA 14*

Barbour, Anne Violet 1884- *WomWWA 14*

Barbour, Clarence Augustus 1867-1937
DcAmB S2, NatCAB 27, WhAm 1

Barbour, Elizabeth Graeme *WomWWA 14*

Barbour, Erwin Hinckley 1856- *NatCAB 14*

Barbour, Erwin Hinckley *WhAm 5*

Barbour, F *NewYHSD*

Barbour, Florence Newell 1866-1946
NatCAB 37

Barbour, Francis Edward 1870-1948
NatCAB 36

Barbour, Frank Alexander 1870-1947 *WhAm 3*

Barbour, George Harrison 1843-1921
NatCAB 5, WhAm 1

Barbour, George Harrison 1846-1921
NatCAB 18

Barbour, Henry Ellsworth 1877-1945 *BiDrAC,
WhAm 2, WhAmP*

Barbour, Henry Gray 1885-1943 *DcScB*

Barbour, Henry Gray 1886-1943 *DcAmB S3,
WhAm 2*

Barbour, Henry Merlin 1848- *WhAm 4*

Barbour, James 1775-1842 *AmBi, ApCAB,
BiAUS, BiDrAC, BiDrUSE, DcAmB,
Drake, NatCAB 5, TwCBDA, WhAm H,
WhAmP*

Barbour, James Joseph 1869- *WhAm 5*

Barbour, John Carlyle 1895-1962 *WhAm 4*

Barbour, John Humphrey 1854-1900 *WhAm 1*

Barbour, John Merrett 1807-1881 *ApCAB*

Barbour, John S 1810-1855 *BiAUS*

Barbour, John S 1866-1952 *WhAm 3*

Barbour, John Strode 1790-1855 *ApCAB,
BiDrAC, Drake, NatCAB 12, WhAm H,
WhAmP*

Barbour, John Strode, Jr. 1820-1892 *BiDrAC,
DcAmB, NatCAB 12, TwCBDA,
WhAm H, WhAmP*

Barbour, Levi Lewis 1840-1925 *NatCAB 21*

Barbour, Lola Diehl 1864- *WhAm 4*
Barbour, Louise 1882- *WomWWA 14*
Barbour, Lucien 1811-1880 *ApCAB,*
ApCAB Sup, BiAUS, BiDrAC,
NatCAB 11, WhAm H
Barbour, Lucius Albert 1846- *NatCAB 5*
Barbour, Oliver Lorenzo 1811-1889 *AmBi,*
ApCAB, DcAmB, WhAm H
Barbour, Orville Everett 1893-1956 *NatCAB 43*
Barbour, Percy E 1875-1943 *WhAm 2*
Barbour, Philip Foster 1867-1944 *NatCAB 38,*
WhAm 2
Barbour, Philip Norbourne 1817-1846 *TwCBDA*
Barbour, Philip P 1779-1841 *BiAUS*
Barbour, Philip Pendleton 1783-1841 *AmBi,*
ApCAB, BiDrAC, DcAmB, Drake,
NatCAB 2, TwCBDA, WebAB,
WhAm H, WhAmP
Barbour, Ralph Henry 1870-1944 *NatCAB 33,*
WhAm 2
Barbour, Thomas 1884-1946 *DcAmB S4,*
WhAm 2
Barbour, Thomas Seymour 1853-1915 *WhAm 1*
Barbour, W Warren 1888-1943 *WhAm 2*
Barbour, William d1917 *WhAm 1*
Barbour, William 1847-1917 *NatCAB 15*
Barbour, William 1857-1917 *ApCAB X*
Barbour, William Rinehart 1884-1962 *WhAm 4*
Barbour, William Tefft 1877-1955 *WhAm 3*
Barbour, William Warren 1888-1943 *BiDrAC,*
NatCAB 32
Barboza, Mary 1845-1890 *NatCAB 5*
Barca, Francisco 1831-1883 *ApCAB*
Barcella, Ernest Lawrence 1910-1974 *WhAm 6*
Barcena, Alfonso d1598 *Drake*
Barcena, Alfonso De 1666-1723 *ApCAB*
Barcena, Mariano DeLa 1853- *ApCAB*
Barchfeld, Andrew Jackson 1863-1922 *BiDrAC,*
WhAm 1, WhAmP
Barchus, Eliza R 1857-1959 *IIBEAAW*
Barchusen, Johann Conrad 1666-1723 *DcScB*
Barcia, Andrea Gonzalez De d1743 *Drake*
Barcia, Andres Gonzalez De d1743 *ApCAB*
Barck, Carl 1857-1943 *NatCAB 34*
Barck, Carl 1859-1943 *WhAm 4*
Barclay, Albert Hampton 1911-1958
NatCAB 46
Barclay, Bertram Donald 1898-1953 *WhAm 3*
Barclay, Charles Frederick 1844-1914 *BiDrAC,*
WhAm 1, WhAmP
Barclay, Charles James 1843-1909 *WhAm 1*
Barclay, David 1823-1889 *BiAUS, BiDrAC,*
WhAm H
Barclay, George A d1964 *WhAm 4*
Barclay, Henry 1734-1764 *Drake*
Barclay, Henry Anthony 1844-1905 *ApCAB X*
Barclay, J T 1807- *Drake*
Barclay, James Edward 1848- *WhAm 4*
Barclay, John 1758-1826 *DcScB*
Barclay, John Charles 1856-1934 *NatCAB 14,*
NatCAB 26
Barclay, John Peter 1893-1954 *NatCAB 45*
Barclay, McClelland 1891-1943 *NatCAB 34,*
WhAm 2
Barclay, McKee 1869- *WhAm 5*
Barclay, Portia Lomax 1890- *WomWWA 14*
Barclay, R H d1837 *Drake*
Barclay, Robert 1648-1690 *ApCAB*
Barclay, Robert 1857-1927 *NatCAB 6,*
WhAm 4
Barclay, Robert H d1837 *ApCAB*
Barclay, Shepard 1847- *NatCAB 12,*
WhAm 1
Barclay, Thomas 1753-1830 *AmBi, ApCAB,*
DcAmB, WhAm H
Barclay, Wade Crawford 1874- *WhAm 5*
Barclay, William Franklin 1842- *NatCAB 7,*
WhAm 4
Barclay, William Kenedy *NewYHSD*
Barclay, William Kennedy, Jr. 1896-1954
WhAm 3
Barclay, Wright *ApCAB X*
Barclay DeTolly, Prince M Bogdanovich
1761-1818 *WhoMilH*
Barco Centenera, Martin *ApCAB*
Barcroft, Joseph 1872-1947 *BiHiMed, DcScB*
Barcus, Betty Belle *WomWWA 14*
Barcus, Emma Mason *WhoColR*

Barcus, James Samuel 1865- *WhAm 5*
Barcus, John M 1860-1928 *WhAm 1*
Barcus, Norman 1905-1970 *WhAm 5*
Barcus, Robert Barclay 1878- *WhoColR*
Bard, A T 1889-1959 *WhAm 3*
Bard, Albert Sprague 1866- *WhAm 4*
Bard, Cephas L d1902 *WhAm 1*
Bard, Charles 1827-1921 *ApCAB X,*
NatCAB 20
Bard, David 1744-1815 *BiAUS, BiDrAC,*
WhAm H, WhAmP
Bard, Guy Kurtz 1895-1953 *WhAm 3*
Bard, Harry Erwin 1867-1955 *WhAm 3*
Bard, James 1815-1897 *BnEnAmA,*
NewYHSD
Bard, John 1716-1799 *AmBi, ApCAB,*
DcAmB, Drake, WebAB, WhAm H
Bard, John 1815-1856 *BnEnAmA, NewYHSD*
Bard, John 1819- *ApCAB*
Bard, Ralph A 1884-1975 *WhAm 6*
Bard, Roy Emerson 1888-1959 *WhAm 3*
Bard, Samuel 1742-1821 *AmBi, ApCAB,*
BiDAmEd, BiHiMed, DcAmB, Drake,
NatCAB 8, TwCBDA, WebAB,
WhAm H
Bard, Sara Foresman d1971 *WhAm 5*
Bard, Thomas Robert 1841-1915 *BiDrAC,*
NatCAB 12, TwCBDA, WhAm 1
Bard, William 1777-1853 *ApCAB*
Bard, William 1778-1853 *DcAmB, WebAB,*
WhAm H
Bardach, Paul 1884-1955 *NatCAB 44*
Bardeen, Charles Russell 1871-1935 *WhAm 1*
Bardeen, Charles Valdo 1850-1903 *NatCAB 17,*
WhAm 1
Bardeen, Charles William 1847-1924 *BiDAmEd,*
DcAmB, WhAm 1
Bardeen, John 1908- *AsBiEn, WebAB*
Bardel, William 1846-1926 *WhAm 1*
Barden, Frank Edwin 1917-1966 *NatCAB 54*
Barden, Graham Arthur 1896-1967 *BiDrAC,*
WhAm 4, WhAmP
Barden, Richard Holcomb 1895-1964
NatCAB 50
Barden, Roderick Dudley 1900-1975 *WhAm 6*
Barden, William Jones 1870-1956 *NatCAB 43*
Bardet *NewYHSD*
Bardgett, Edward Russell 1875- *WhAm 5*
Bardo, August John 1917-1972 *WhAm 6*
Bardo, Clinton Lloyd 1867-1937 *WhAm 1*
Bardon, Thomas 1848-1923 *NatCAB 17,*
WhAm 1
Bardon, Thomas 1889-1964 *NatCAB 52,*
WhAm 4
Bardsen, Ivor 1300?-1350? *ApCAB Sup*
Bardwell, Darwin Long 1860-1915 *NatCAB 16*
Bardwell, Rodney Jewett 1870-1950
NatCAB 51, WhAm 3
Bardwell, Willis Arthur 1840- *TwCBDA*
Bardwell, Winfield William 1872-1946 *WhAm 2*
Barefoot, Graham Ballard 1900-1967
NatCAB 54
Bareis, Grace M *WomWWA 14*
Barela, Casimiro 1847-1920 *REnAW*
Barelet *NewYHSD*
Barents, Willem d1597 *McGEWB*
Bargar, Allen Elwood 1889-1959 *NatCAB 47*
Barge, Benjamin Franklin 1834-1926
NatCAB 21
Barger, Floyd 1906-1975 *WhAm 6*
Barger, George 1878-1939 *DcScB Sup*
Barger, James Hafford 1894-1956 *NatCAB 48*
Barger, Milton Sanford 1875-1925 *WhAm 1*
Barger, Samuel F 1832-1914 *NatCAB 2,*
WhAm 4
Bargeron, Carlisle d1965 *WhAm 4*
Barham, Charles 1867- *WhAm 3*
Barham, Frank Forrest 1879-1953 *ApCAB X,*
WhAm 3
Barham, John A 1844-1926 *WhAm 4*
Barham, John All 1843-1926 *BiDrAC*
Barhite, Jared *ApCAB X*
Barhydt, Theodore Wells 1835- *NatCAB 2*
Barincou, J *NewYHSD*
Baring, Alexander 1774-1848 *WhAm H*
Baring, Maurice 1874- *WhAm 5*
Baring, Walter Stephan 1911-1975 *BiDrAC,*
WhAm 6

Barinsou, F *NewYHSD*
Barja, Cesar 1890-1951 *WhAm 3*
Bark, John Daly 1775?-1808 *WhAm H*
Barkan, Adolf 1845-1935 *WhAm 1*
Barkan, Adolph 1845-1935 *NatCAB 48*
Barkan, Hans 1882-1960 *NatCAB 47*
Barkan, Otto 1887-1958 *NatCAB 48,*
WhAm 3
Barkdull, Charles J d1953 *WhAm 3*
Barkdull, Howard L 1887-1962 *WhAm 4*
Barkenburg, John *NewYHSD*
Barkenbus, Charles 1894-1959 *NatCAB 50*
Barker, Abraham Andrews 1816-1898 *BiAUS,*
BiDrAC
Barker, Albert Smith 1843-1916 *AmBi,*
ApCAB Sup, DcAmB, NatCAB 30,
TwCBDA, WhAm 1
Barker, Albert Winslow 1874-1947 *NatCAB 35,*
WhAm 2
Barker, B Devereux 1878- *WhAm 6*
Barker, Benjamin Fordyce 1818-1891 *AmBi,*
DcAmB, WhAm H
Barker, Burt Brown 1873-1969 *NatCAB 55,*
WhAm 6
Barker, Charles F 1875- *IIBEAAW*
Barker, Charles Whitney Tillinghast 1882-1938
WhAm 1
Barker, Clare Wright 1895-1960 *WhAm 4*
Barker, David 1868-1967 *WhAm 4*
Barker, David, Jr. 1797-1834 *BiAUS, BiDrAC,*
WhAm H
Barker, David R 1806-1881 *NewYHSD,*
WhAm H
Barker, Miss E J *NewYHSD*
Barker, E Nellie 1879- *WomWWA 14*
Barker, Edgar Earl 1884-1948 *NatCAB 40*
Barker, Edward *NewYHSD*
Barker, Eliza Harris Lawton *WomWWA 14*
Barker, Ellen Blackmar *WhAm 5,*
WomWWA 14
Barker, Ellen Blackmer 1859- *ApCAB Sup*
Barker, Ellen Frye 1873- *WomWWA 14*
Barker, Elsa d1954 *WhAm 3*
Barker, Emma DeLand Dinsmoor 1851-
WomWWA 14
Barker, Ernest Franklin 1886-1970 *WhAm 5*
Barker, Fordyce 1818-1891 *NatCAB 4*
Barker, Fordyce 1819-1891 *ApCAB, TwCBDA*
Barker, Forrest Edson 1853-1914 *NatCAB 16*
Barker, Frances Crosby Buffington
WomWWA 14, WomWWA 14a
Barker, Frank Philip Kendrick 1884-1956
NatCAB 44
Barker, Franklin Davis 1877-1936 *NatCAB 27,*
WhAm 1
Barker, Frederick William 1864-1948 *WhAm 2*
Barker, George 1823-1903 *WhAm 1*
Barker, George 1882-1965 *IIBEAAW,*
NatCAB 51
Barker, George Frederic 1835-1910 *ApCAB*
Barker, George Frederick 1835-1910 *DcAmB,*
NatCAB 4, TwCBDA, WhAm 1
Barker, Harold Richard 1881-1965 *WhAm 4*
Barker, Harry 1881- *WhAm 6*
Barker, Harry Colburn 1870-1941 *NatCAB 30*
Barker, Helen Morton 1834-1910 *WhAm 1*
Barker, Henry Ames 1866-1929 *NatCAB 21*
Barker, Henry Ames 1868-1929 *WhAm 1*
Barker, Henry Stites 1850-1928 *NatCAB 31,*
WhAm 1
Barker, Howard Hines 1848-1910 *WhAm 1*
Barker, J J *NewYHSD*
Barker, Jacob 1779-1871 *AmBi, ApCAB,*
DcAmB, Drake, NatCAB 11, TwCBDA,
WhAm H
Barker, James L 1880- *WhAm 6*
Barker, James Madison 1839-1905 *NatCAB 14,*
WhAm 1
Barker, James Madison 1886-1974 *WhAm 6*
Barker, James Nelson 1784-1858 *AmBi,*
ApCAB, DcAmB, Drake, NatCAB 12,
WhAm H
Barker, James William 1815-1869 *ApCAB,*
DcAmB, WhAm H, WhAmP
Barker, Jeremiah 1752-1835 *DcAmB,*
WhAm H
Barker, John d1860 *Drake*
Barker, John 1878-1957 *NatCAB 53*

Barker, John, Jr. 1906-1970 *NatCAB 56,*
WhAm 5
Barker, John Henry 1844-1910 *ApCAB X,*
NatCAB 29
Barker, John Jesse *NewYHSD*
Barker, John Marshall 1849- *WhAm 1*
Barker, John Tull d1958 *WhAm 3*
Barker, Joseph *NewYHSD*
Barker, Joseph 1751-1815 *BiAUS, BiDrAC,*
WhAm H
Barker, Joseph Warren 1891-1975 *WhAm 6*
Barker, Josiah 1763-1847 *ApCAB, DcAmB,*
NatCAB 22, WhAm H
Barker, LeBaron R, Jr. 1904-1973 *WhAm 6*
Barker, LeBaron Russell 1874-1949 *NatCAB 38*
Barker, Lewellys Franklin 1867-1943
NatCAB 32, WhAm 2
Barker, Lillian Marion d1968 *WhAm 5*
Barker, M *NewYHSD*
Barker, Miss M A *NewYHSD*
Barker, M Herbert 1899-1947 *WhAm 2*
Barker, Marion Herbert 1899-1947 *NatCAB 37*
Barker, Nellie Florence 1862- *WomWWA 14*
Barker, Nelson W 1899-1968 *WhAm 5*
Barker, Olin George Andrews 1872-1941
NatCAB 34
Barker, Olive Ruth 1885- *IlBEAAW*
Barker, Philip Lincoln 1860-1927 *NatCAB 21*
Barker, Prelate Demick 1835- *WhAm 4*
Barker, Ralph Hollenback 1912-1969 *WhAm 5*
Barker, Ralph Malcolm 1875-1952 *WhAm 3*
Barker, Reginald Charles 1881-1937 *WhAm 1,*
WhAm 5
Barker, Reginald J *ApCAB X*
Barker, Samuel Haydock 1872- *WhAm 5*
Barker, Theodore Gaillard 1832- *WhAm 4*
Barker, W Halsey 1907-1949 *NatCAB 37*
Barker, Walter R 1890-1959 *WhAm 3*
Barker, Wendell Phillips 1884-1941 *WhAm 1*
Barker, Wharton 1846-1921 *ApCAB Sup,*
ApCAB X, DcAmB, NatCAB 1,
TwCBDA, WhAm 1, WhAmP
Barker, William *NewYHSD*
Barker, William Edward 1895-1957 *NatCAB 46*
Barker, William Grant 1865-1963 *NatCAB 50*
Barker, William J *NewYHSD*
Barker, William Morris 1854-1901 *ApCAB Sup,*
NatCAB 13, TwCBDA, WhAm 1
Barkhausen, Heinrich Georg 1881-1956 *AsBiEn,*
DcScB
Barkhausen, Johann Conrad *DcScB*
Barkhorn, Henry Charles 1885-1949
NatCAB 38, WhAm 2
Barkla, Charles Glover 1877-1944 *AsBiEn,*
DcScB
Barkley, Alben William 1877-1956 *BiDrAC,*
BiDrUSE, NatCAB 42, WebAB,
WhAm 3, WhAmP
Barkley, Henry L 1858-1915 *WhAm 1*
Barkley, James Morrison 1846-1922 *WhAm 1*
Barkley, Jane Rucker 1911-1964 *WhAm 4*
Barkley, Keitt Carson 1880-1955 *NatCAB 43*
Barkley, Rufus Calvin 1901-1959 *NatCAB 49*
Barkley, William Elliot 1863-1944 *WhAm 2*
Barksdale, Alfred Dickinson 1892-1972
WhAm 5
Barksdale, C Bruce 1894-1966 *NatCAB 52*
Barksdale, Elisha 1881-1957 *NatCAB 46*
Barksdale, Ethelbert 1824-1893 *BiDConf,*
BiDrAC, WhAm H, WhAmP
Barksdale, Ethelbert Courtland 1905-1974
WhAm 6
Barksdale, Hamilton Macfarland 1861-1918
NatCAB 22
Barksdale, John Woodson 1876- *WhAm 5*
Barksdale, Joseph Downs 1874-1944 *WhAm 2*
Barksdale, William 1821-1863 *ApCAB, BiAUS,*
BiDConf, BiDrAC, DcAmB, Drake,
NatCAB 4, TwCBDA, WhAm H,
WhAmP
Barlach, Ernst 1870-1938 *McGEWB*
Barley, Rex 1913-1971 *WhAm 5*
Barlow, Alpha Winifred *WomWWA 14*
Barlow, Arthur 1550?-1620? *ApCAB*
Barlow, Arthur J 1893-1949 *WhAm 2*
Barlow, Bradley 1814-1889 *BiDrAC,*
WhAm H
Barlow, Charles 1820-1880 *NatCAB 14*

Barlow, Charles Averill 1858-1927 *BiDrAC,*
WhAmP
Barlow, Charlotte Emily 1855- *WomWWA 14*
Barlow, Claude Heman 1876-1969 *WhAm 5*
Barlow, DeWitt Dukes 1880-1945 *NatCAB 34,*
WhAm 2
Barlow, Edward 1832?- *NewYHSD*
Barlow, Elbert Spicer 1878-1948 *NatCAB 37*
Barlow, Elmer Elbert 1887-1948 *WhAm 2*
Barlow, Ernest Andrew 1900-1963 *NatCAB 50*
Barlow, Francis Channing 1834-1896 *AmBi,*
ApCAB, DcAmB, Drake, NatCAB 8,
TwCBDA, WebAMB, WhAm H,
WhAmP
Barlow, Fred, Jr. 1902-1954 *WhAm 3*
Barlow, Harry Elmore 1880-1935 *WhAm 3*
Barlow, Henry N 1824-1884 *NewYHSD*
Barlow, Howard 1892-1972 *WhAm 5*
Barlow, Joel 1754-1812 *AmBi, ApCAB,*
DcAmB, EncAB, McGEWB, NatCAB 3,
TwCBDA, WebAB, WhAm H, WhAmP
Barlow, Joel 1755-1812 *BiAUS, Drake*
Barlow, John 1872-1944 *WhAm 2*
Barlow, John Quincy 1861-1949 *NatCAB 37,*
WhAm 4
Barlow, John Whitney 1838-1914 *DcAmB,*
WebAMB, WhAm 1
Barlow, Kate Brown *WomWWA 14*
Barlow, Maximillan A J 1885-1960 *WhAm 4*
Barlow, Milton Theodore 1844-1930 *WhAm 1*
Barlow, Peter 1776-1862 *DcScB*
Barlow, Samuel Kimbrough *WhAm H*
Barlow, Samuel Latham Mitchell 1826-1889
ApCAB, TwCBDA
Barlow, Samuel Latham Mitchill 1826-1889
DcAmB, TwCBDA
Barlow, Stephen 1779-1845 *BiAUS, BiDrAC,*
WhAm H
Barlow, T Noble 1861- *WhAm 4*
Barlow, Thomas Harris 1789-1865 *ApCAB,*
TwCBDA
Barlow, W Jarvis 1868-1937 *NatCAB 36,*
WhAm 1
Barlow, William 1845-1934 *DcScB*
Barlow, William Edward 1870-1938 *WhAm 1*
Barlow, William Harvey 1910-1969 *WhAm 5*
Barmm, Charles Henry 1827-1895 *NatCAB 7*
Barmm, Frank Herman 1864- *NatCAB 7*
Barnabas, Brother 1865-1929 *WhAm 1*
Barnabee, Henry Clay 1833-1917 *DcAmB,*
NatCAB 8, WhAm 1
Barnacle, Clarke Horace 1906-1962 *NatCAB 50*
Barnard, Charles 1838-1920 *ApCAB, DcAmB,*
NatCAB 13, TwCBDA, WhAm 1
Barnard, Charles Francis 1808-1884 *DcAmB,*
NatCAB 8, WhAm H
Barnard, Charles Inman 1850-1942 *WhAm 2*
Barnard, Chester Irving 1886-1961 *NatCAB 46,*
WhAm 4
Barnard, Christiaan Neethling 1922- *AsBiEn*
Barnard, Daniel Dewey 1796-1861 *DcAmB*
Barnard, Daniel Dewey 1797-1861 *ApCAB,*
BiAUS, BiDrAC, Drake, NatCAB 10,
TwCBDA, WhAm H, WhAmP
Barnard, Edward Chester 1863-1921 *NatCAB 6,*
WhAm 1
Barnard, Edward Emerson 1857-1923 *AmBi,*
ApCAB, AsBiEn, DcAmB, DcScB,
McGEWB, NatCAB 7, TwCBDA,
WebAB, WhAm 1
Barnard, Ernest Sargent 1874-1931 *WhAm 1*
Barnard, Frederick Augustus Porter 1809-1889
AmBi, ApCAB, BiDAmEd, DcAmB,
Drake, McGEWB, NatCAB 6, TwCBDA,
WebAB, WhAm H
Barnard, George Grey 1863-1938 *AmBi,*
ApCAB Sup, ApCAB X, BnEnAmA,
DcAmB S2, WebAB, WhAm 1
Barnard, George Murphey 1881-1949
NatCAB 36, WhAm 2
Barnard, George N 1819-1902 *BnEnAmA*
Barnard, Hannah Jenkins 1754?-1825 *NotAW*
Barnard, Harrison Bernard 1872-1952 *WhAm 3*
Barnard, Harry Eliot 1892-1973 *WhAm 6*
Barnard, Harry Everett 1874-1946 *WhAm 2*
Barnard, Henry 1811-1900 *AmBi, ApCAB,*
BiAUS, BiDAmEd, DcAmB, Drake,
EncAB, McGEWB, NatCAB 1,

TwCBDA, WebAB, WhAm H
Barnard, Henry S 1818?- *NewYHSD*
Barnard, Isaac D 1789-1834 *TwCBDA*
Barnard, Isaac Dutton 1791-1834 *ApCAB,*
BiAUS, BiDrAC, Drake, NatCAB 7,
WhAm H
Barnard, J Augustus 1871-1958 *NatCAB 47*
Barnard, J Lynn 1867-1941 *WhAm 2*
Barnard, James 1820?- *NewYHSD*
Barnard, Job 1844- *WhAm 4*
Barnard, John 1681-1770 *ApCAB, DcAmB,*
Drake, NatCAB 7, TwCBDA, WhAm H
Barnard, John Gross 1815-1882 *AmBi, ApCAB,*
DcAmB, NatCAB 4, TwCBDA,
WhAm H
Barnard, Jonathan G 1815- *Drake*
Barnard, Joseph Folger 1823-1904 *WhAm 1*
Barnard, Kate 1874-1930 *REnAW*
Barnard, Kate 1875-1930 *NotAW*
Barnard, Kate 1878-1930 *WhAm 6*
Barnard, Kate 1879?-1930 *NatCAB 15*
Barnard, Marie Ellene 1867- *NatCAB 10*
Barnard, Marion Harvie 1875- *WomWWA 14*
Barnard, S *NewYHSD*
Barnard, Therina Townsend 1875-
WomWWA 14
Barnard, Thomas 1716-1776 *NatCAB 7*
Barnard, William *NewYHSD*
Barnard, William Nichols 1875-1947
NatCAB 35, WhAm 2
Barnard, William Oscar 1852-1939 *BiDrAC,*
WhAm 3
Barnard, William S 1809?- *NewYHSD*
Barnard, William Stebbins 1849- *ApCAB*
Barnard, William Stebbins 1849-1887
NatCAB 12
Barnard, William Stebbins 1849-1888 *TwCBDA*
Barnason, Charles Frederick 1886-1949
WhAm 2
Barnds, William Paul 1904-1973 *WhAm 5*
Barndt, Milton A 1859- *WhAm 4*
Barnes *NewYHSD*
Barnes, Abraham *NatCAB 13*
Barnes, Alanson H *BiAUS*
Barnes, Albert 1789-1870 *DcAmReB*
Barnes, Albert 1798-1870 *AmBi, ApCAB,*
DcAmB, Drake, NatCAB 7, TwCBDA,
WhAm H
Barnes, Albert 1839?- *NewYHSD*
Barnes, Albert Coombs 1872-1951 *DcAmB S5*
Barnes, Albert Rice 1851-1925 *NatCAB 6*
Barnes, Alfred Cutler 1842-1904 *NatCAB 4*
Barnes, Alfred Edward 1892-1960 *WhAm 4*
Barnes, Alfred Smith 1817-1888 *ApCAB Sup,*
NatCAB 4, TwCBDA
Barnes, Alfred Victor 1870-1944 *NatCAB 34,*
WhAm 2
Barnes, Amos 1828-1906 *NatCAB 3,*
WhAm 1
Barnes, Amos Warren 1867-1953 *NatCAB 42*
Barnes, Anna Maria 1857- *WomWWA 14*
Barnes, Annie Maria 1857- *AmWom,*
WhAm 4
Barnes, Arthur Hart 1904-1957 *NatCAB 47*
Barnes, Asa David Clifford 1877- *WhoColR*
Barnes, Benjamin F 1868-1909 *WhAm 1*
Barnes, Cassius McDonald 1845-1925
NatCAB 24, TwCBDA, WhAm 6
Barnes, Catharine Weed 1851- *AmWom,*
NatCAB 3
Barnes, Charles Albert 1855-1913 *WhAm 3*
Barnes, Charles Benjamin 1868- *WhAm 5*
Barnes, Charles P 1869-1952 *WhAm 3*
Barnes, Charles Reid 1858-1910 *AmBi,*
DcAmB, NatCAB 13, TwCBDA,
WhAm 1
Barnes, Charlotte Mary Sanford 1818-1863
DcAmB, WhAm H
Barnes, Clarence Alfred 1882-1970 *WhAm 5*
Barnes, Clifford Webster 1864-1944
NatCAB 45, TwCBDA, WhAm 2
Barnes, Daniel H 1785-1818 *Drake*
Barnes, Daniel Henry 1785-1828 *ApCAB,*
TwCBDA
Barnes, David Leonard *BiAUS*
Barnes, David Leonard 1858-1896 *TwCBDA*
Barnes, Demas 1827-1888 *ApCAB, BiAUS,*
BiDrAC, WhAm H

Barnes, Dewey Loyd 1898-1966 *WhAm 4*
Barnes, Donald C 1880- *WhAm 6*
Barnes, Donald Lee, Jr. 1917-1975 *WhAm 6*
Barnes, Earl 1861-1935 *BiDAmEd, WhAm 1*
Barnes, Earl Brandon 1881-1966 *WhAm 4, WhAm 4A*
Barnes, Edward Larrabee 1915- *BnEnAmA*
Barnes, Elias 1882-1962 *NatCAB 49*
Barnes, Elmer Clark 1870-1921 *NatCAB 19*
Barnes, Eric Wollencott 1907-1962 *WhAm 4*
Barnes, Ethan Allen 1862-1923 *NatCAB 6*
Barnes, Floyd Morgan 1877-1957 *WhAm 3*
Barnes, Frances Julia 1846- *AmWom, TwCBDA, WhAm 4, WomWWA 14*
Barnes, Francis George 1866-1910 *WhAm 1*
Barnes, Frank Haslehurst 1872- *WhAm 5*
Barnes, Frank Lister 1872-1943 *NatCAB 38*
Barnes, Fred Asa 1876-1950 *NatCAB 40, WhAm 3*
Barnes, Frederick Joseph 1863-1948 *NatCAB 36*
Barnes, Fuller Forbes 1887-1955 *NatCAB 49, WhAm 3*
Barnes, George Anthony 1909-1965 *WhAm 4*
Barnes, George Edward 1871- *WhAm 5*
Barnes, George Emerson 1882-1948 *WhAm 2*
Barnes, George Mortimer 1851-1916 *NatCAB 18*
Barnes, George O 1878-1944 *WhAm 2*
Barnes, George Thomas 1833-1901 *BiDrAC, NatCAB 2, TwCBDA, WhAmP*
Barnes, Gertrude Jameson 1865- *WomWWA 14*
Barnes, Gilbert Hobbs 1889-1945 *WhAm 2*
Barnes, Gladeon Marcus 1887-1961 *WhAm 4*
Barnes, H Edgar 1884-1940 *NatCAB 30*
Barnes, Harlan Ward 1883-1947 *WhAm 2*
Barnes, Harold Arthur 1887-1953 *WhAm 3*
Barnes, Harold Reade 1895-1972 *NatCAB 56*
Barnes, Harry Clarke 1889-1966 *NatCAB 52*
Barnes, Harry Elmer 1889-1968 *BiDAmEd, NatCAB 54*
Barnes, Harry George 1898-1966 *WhAm 4*
Barnes, Harry Lee 1877-1934 *NatCAB 27*
Barnes, Helen Florence 1863-1953 *WhAm 3*
Barnes, Helen Florence 1867-1953 *BiCAW*
Barnes, Henry A 1906-1968 *WhAm 5*
Barnes, Henry Burr 1845-1911 *WhAm 1*
Barnes, Henry Whitmer 1832-1914 *WhAm 1*
Barnes, Hiram Putnam 1857- *WhAm 4*
Barnes, Howard 1904-1968 *WhAm 5*
Barnes, Howel Henry, Jr. 1875- *WhAm 6*
Barnes, Irving Franklin 1872-1958 *WhAm 3*
Barnes, James d1869 *Drake*
Barnes, James 1801-1869 *DcAmB, WhAm H*
Barnes, James 1806-1869 *TwCBDA*
Barnes, James 1807-1869 *NatCAB 4*
Barnes, James 1809?-1869 *ApCAB*
Barnes, James 1866-1936 *ApCAB Sup, NatCAB 14, TwCBDA, WhAm 1*
Barnes, James I 1872-1956 *NatCAB 43*
Barnes, James Martin 1899-1958 *BiDrAC, WhAm 3, WhAmP*
Barnes, James Phillips 1881- *WhAm 6*
Barnes, Jasper Converse 1861-1931 *WhAm 1*
Barnes, Jay Preston 1869-1943 *NatCAB 31*
Barnes, Jeremiah 1844- *WhoColR*
Barnes, Mrs. John *WhAm H*
Barnes, John 1859-1919 *ApCAB X, WhAm 1*
Barnes, John Beaumont 1846-1921 *NatCAB 18, WhAm 1*
Barnes, John Bryson 1876-1956 *WhAm 3*
Barnes, John George Moroni 1860-1932 *NatCAB 24*
Barnes, John Hampton 1860-1952 *WhAm 3*
Barnes, John Peter 1881-1959 *WhAm 3*
Barnes, John Potts 1902-1970 *WhAm 5*
Barnes, John Wilcox 1902-1964 *WhAm 4*
Barnes, Joseph Fels 1907-1970 *WhAm 5*
Barnes, Joseph K 1817-1883 *ApCAB, DcAmB, NatCAB 4, TwCBDA, WhAm H*
Barnes, Julius Howland 1873-1959 *NatCAB 53, WhAm 3*
Barnes, Lemuel Call 1854-1938 *NatCAB 28, WhAm 1*
Barnes, Leon Simeon 1894-1959 *NatCAB 49*
Barnes, Lewis Chesley 1885-1958 *NatCAB 50*
Barnes, Lyman Eddy 1855-1904 *BiDrAC*

Barnes, Margaret Ayer 1886-1967 *WhAm 4, WomWWA 14*
Barnes, Margaret Campbell 1891-1962 *WhAm 4*
Barnes, Mark Hopkins 1895-1967 *NatCAB 53*
Barnes, Mary Clark 1851- *WhAm 2*
Barnes, Mary Downing Sheldon 1850-1898 *AmWom, BiDAmEd, DcAmB, NotAW, WhAm H*
Barnes, Matthew Rackham 1880-1951 *IlBEAAW*
Barnes, Maynard Bertram 1897-1970 *WhAm 5*
Barnes, Morgan 1870-1963 *WhAm 4*
Barnes, Mortimer Grant 1867-1930 *NatCAB 22, WhAm 1*
Barnes, Nathan 1914-1975 *WhAm 6*
Barnes, Nathaniel Waring 1884- *WhAm 3*
Barnes, Oliver Weldon 1823-1908 *NatCAB 12, WhAm 1*
Barnes, Parker Thayer 1874- *WhAm 5*
Barnes, Parry 1892-1950 *WhAm 3*
Barnes, Penelope Birch *NewYHSD*
Barnes, Phineas 1842- *ApCAB*
Barnes, Phinehas 1811-1871 *ApCAB, TwCBDA*
Barnes, Ralph W 1899-1940 *WhAm 1*
Barnes, Raymond F 1877-1949 *WhAm 1*
Barnes, Raymond Joseph 1897-1969 *WhAm 5*
Barnes, Robert Christopher 1856- *WhoColR*
Barnes, Robert Lenox 1886-1944 *NatCAB 34*
Barnes, Roswell Parkhurst 1901-1949 *WhAm 2*
Barnes, Sarah Short *WomWWA 14*
Barnes, Stephen Goodyear 1853-1931 *NatCAB 24, WhAm 1*
Barnes, Stuart Knowlton 1907-1968 *WhAm 4A, WhAm 5*
Barnes, Thomas Robert 1862-1941 *WhAm 1*
Barnes, Thurlow Weed 1853-1918 *ApCAB, TwCBDA, WhAm 1*
Barnes, Will Croft 1858-1936 *WhAm 1*
Barnes, William 1824-1913 *NatCAB 1, WhAm 1*
Barnes, William 1860-1930 *WhAm 1*
Barnes, William 1866-1930 *WhAm 1*
Barnes, William H 1843-1904 *WhAm 1*
Barnes, William Henry 1829-1918 *WhAm 1*
Barnes, William James 1892-1964 *NatCAB 51*
Barnes, William Preston 1866-1944 *WhAm 2*
Barnes, Willis Lambert 1840-1922 *NatCAB 20*
Barnet, Herbert L d1970 *WhAm 5*
Barnet, W A *NewYHSD*
Barnet, William Armand *NewYHSD*
Barnett *NewYHSD*
Barnett, Augustus Edward 1867- *WhAm 4*
Barnett, Bion Hall 1857-1958 *WhAm 3*
Barnett, Charles Eldridge 1866-1959 *NatCAB 47, WhAm 4*
Barnett, Charles Mitchell 1870-1940 *NatCAB 30*
Barnett, Claribel Ruth 1872-1951 *WhAm 3, WomWWA 14*
Barnett, Claude Albert 1889-1967 *NatCAB 54, WhAm 4, WhAm 5*
Barnett, Edward Hammet 1840- *NatCAB 2*
Barnett, Eugene Epperson 1888-1970 *NatCAB 55, WhAm 5*
Barnett, Evelyn Scott Snead d1921 *WhAm 1, WomWWA 14*
Barnett, Frank Willis 1865-1941 *WhAm 2*
Barnett, George 1859-1930 *NatCAB 32, WebAMB, WhAm 1*
Barnett, George DeForest 1884-1955 *NatCAB 45*
Barnett, George Ernest 1873-1938 *DcAmB S2, WhAm 5*
Barnett, Harold Montgomery 1903-1956 *NatCAB 45*
Barnett, Harry 1888-1952 *WhAm 3*
Barnett, Herbert Phillip 1910-1972 *WhAm 5*
Barnett, Ida B Wells 1864-1931 *NotAW, WhAmP, WhoColR*
Barnett, Isa 1924- *IlBEAAW*
Barnett, J Mercer 1882-1936 *NatCAB 27*
Barnett, James 1821-1911 *NatCAB 2, WhAm 1*
Barnett, James Foote 1869- *WhAm 5*
Barnett, James Miller 1878-1951 *NatCAB 40*

Barnett, John T 1869-1942 *WhAm 2*
Barnett, Joseph W 1902-1974 *WhAm 6*
Barnett, Lelia Jefferson Harvie 1873- *WomWWA 14*
Barnett, Lelia Sinclair Montague *WomWWA 14*
Barnett, Otto Raymond 1868-1945 *WhAm 2*
Barnett, R J 1874- *WhAm 5*
Barnett, Samuel 1824-1895 *NatCAB 2*
Barnett, Samuel Jackson 1873- *WhAm 5*
Barnett, Stanley Pugh 1892-1969 *WhAm 5*
Barnett, Stephen Trent 1871- *WhAm 5*
Barnett, Tom P 1870-1929 *WhAm 1*
Barnett, William *BiAUS*
Barnett, William 1761-1832 *BiDrAC*
Barnett, William 1761-1834 *WhAm H*
Barnette, William Jay 1847- *WhAm 3*
Barney, Alice Pike d1931 *WhAm 1*
Barney, Austin Dunham 1896-1971 *WhAm 5*
Barney, Charles Neal 1875-1949 *WhAm 3*
Barney, Charles Tracy 1851-1907 *NatCAB 34, WhAm 1*
Barney, Edgar Starr 1861-1938 *WhAm 1*
Barney, Everett Hosmer 1835- *NatCAB 3*
Barney, George Deverell 1865- *NatCAB 12*
Barney, Hiram 1811-1895 *TwCBDA*
Barney, John d1856 *ApCAB*
Barney, John 1785-1857 *BiAUS, BiDrAC, WhAm H*
Barney, Joshua 1759-1818 *AmBi, ApCAB, DcAmB, Drake, NatCAB 4, TwCBDA, WebAB, WebAMB, WhAm H*
Barney, Margaret Higginson 1881- *WomWWA 14*
Barney, Nathan 1819-1902 *NatCAB 12*
Barney, Samuel Stebbins 1846-1919 *BiDrAC, NatCAB 28, TwCBDA, WhAm 1, WhAmP*
Barney, Sarah L W 1857- *WomWWA 14*
Barney, Susan Hammond *AmWom*
Barney, William Joshua 1884-1954 *WhAm 3*
Barnhardt, George Columbus 1868-1930 *NatCAB 22, WhAm 1*
Barnhardt, Jesse Homer 1873-1945 *WhAm 2*
Barnhart, Frank Pierce 1873-1961 *NatCAB 48*
Barnhart, Henry A 1858-1934 *BiDrAC, WhAm 1, WhAmP*
Barnhart, John D 1895-1967 *WhAm 5*
Barnhart, John Hendley 1871-1949 *NatCAB 38*
Barnhart, Thomas Frederick 1902-1955 *NatCAB 43, WhAm 3*
Barnhart, William Gray 1880-1921 *WhAm 1*
Barnhill, James Uriah 1853- *NatCAB 13*
Barnhill, John Finch 1865-1943 *NatCAB 31, WhAm 2*
Barnhill, John Henry 1903-1973 *WhAm 6*
Barnhill, Leonard Ellsworth 1889- *WhoColR*
Barnhorn, Clement J *WhAm 1*
Barnhouse, Donald Grey 1895-1960 *WhAm 4*
Barnickel, William Sidney 1878-1923 *WhAm 1*
Barnitz, Albert 1835- *WhAm 4*
Barnitz, Charles Augustus 1780-1850 *BiAUS, BiDrAC, WhAm H*
Barnouw, Adriaan Jacob 1877-1968 *IlBEAAW, WhAm 5*
Barnowe, Theodore Joseph 1917-1971 *WhAm 5*
Barns, Merl Angell 1906-1959 *NatCAB 50*
Barns, William 1795-1865 *ApCAB*
Barns, William Eddy 1853-1915 *WhAm 1*
Barnsback, Roy Smith 1874-1957 *NatCAB 48*
Barnsdall, Theodore Newton 1851-1917 *NatCAB 35*
Barnston, George 1800-1883 *ApCAB Sup*
Barnston, Henry 1868-1949 *NatCAB 39*
Barnum, Charlotte Cynthia 1860-1934 *WhAm 1, WomWWA 14*
Barnum, Dana Dwight 1872-1947 *WhAm 2*
Barnum, Frances Courtenay Baylor 1848-1920 *DcAmB*
Barnum, Gertrude 1866-1948 *NotAW, WhAm 3A*
Barnum, Hedrick Ware 1879-1936 *WhAm 1*
Barnum, Henry A 1833-1892 *ApCAB, DcAmB, NatCAB 4, TwCBDA, WhAm H*
Barnum, Henry Samuel 1837-1915 *WhAm 1*
Barnum, Herman Norton 1826-1910 *WhAm 1*
Barnum, Jerome Dewitt 1888-1965 *NatCAB 51, WhAm 4*

Barnum, Leslie Pease 1846-1915 *NatCAB 16*
Barnum, Malvern-Hill 1863-1942 *WhAm 2*
Barnum, Mary G 1869- *WomWWA 14*
Barnum, Phineas Taylor 1810-1891 *AmBi,*
ApCAB, DcAmB, Drake, EncAB,
McGEWB, NatCAB 3, REnAW,
TwCBDA, WebAB, WhAm H
Barnum, Samuel Weed 1820-1891 *NatCAB 10,*
WhAm H
Barnum, William Henry 1818-1889 *ApCAB,*
BiAUS, BiDrAC, NatCAB 12, TwCBDA,
WhAm H, WhAmP
Barnum, William Henry 1882-1963 *NatCAB 52*
Barnum, William Milo 1856-1926 *ApCAB X,*
NatCAB 20, WhAm 1
Barnum, Zenas 1810-1865 *ApCAB*
Barnum, Zenus 1810-1865 *DcAmB,*
NatCAB 22, WhAm H
Barnwell, Charles Heyward 1868-1961 *WhAm 4*
Barnwell, Henry Stephen 1881- *WhAm 6*
Barnwell, John 1671?-1724 *ApCAB, DcAmB,*
WhAm H
Barnwell, John Blair 1895-1966 *WhAm 4*
Barnwell, Joseph Walker 1846-1930
NatCAB 35
Barnwell, Middleton Stuart 1882-1957 *WhAm 3*
Barnwell, R Sim, Jr. 1918-1972 *NatCAB 57*
Barnwell, Robert d1814 *BiAUS*
Barnwell, Robert 1761-1814 *BiDrAC,*
WhAm H, WhAmP
Barnwell, Robert 1762-1814 *ApCAB*
Barnwell, Robert Woodward 1801-1882 *ApCAB,*
BiAUS, BiDConf, BiDrAC, DcAmB,
Drake, NatCAB 11, TwCBDA, WhAm H,
WhAmP
Barnwell, Robert Woodward 1849-1902
NatCAB 13, TwCBDA, WhAm 1
Baroch, Charles Thomas 1901-1970 *NatCAB 55*
Barocius, Franciscus 1537-1604 *DcScB*
Baroja Y Nessi, Pio 1872-1956 *McGEWB*
Barolet, *NewYHSD*
Baron, Clemire *NewYHSD*
Baron, Edgar 1910-1957 *NatCAB 46*
Baron, Herman 1892-1961 *NatCAB 47,*
WhAm 4
Baron, Joseph Louis 1894-1960 *WhAm 4*
Baron, Salo Wittmayer 1895- *McGEWB*
Baronto, Louis *NewYHSD*
Barr, Albert James 1851-1912 *NatCAB 5,*
NatCAB 30, WhAm 1
Barr, Alfred Hamilton 1868-1935 *WhAm 1*
Barr, Alton Parker 1903-1960 *WhAm 4*
Barr, Amelia E 1832- *AmWom*
Barr, Amelia Edith *WomWWA 14*
Barr, Amelia Edith 1831- *ApCAB, NatCAB 4,*
TwCBDA
Barr, Amelia Edith 1831-1918 *ApCAB X,*
WhAm 1
Barr, Amelia Edith Huddleston 1831-1919
DcAmB, NotAW
Barr, Annie Leonora 1876- *WomWWA 14*
Barr, Arthur A 1877-1950 *NatCAB 41*
Barr, Arvil Sylvester 1892-1962 *BiDAmEd,*
WhAm 4
Barr, Charles 1864-1911 *DcAmB, WhAm HA,*
WhAm 4
Barr, Charles Elisha 1860- *NatCAB 5,*
WhAm 4
Barr, Clara L 1851- *WomWWA 14*
Barr, David Goodwin 1895-1970 *WhAm 5*
Barr, Edward 1845- *NatCAB 9*
Barr, Frank d1914 *WhAm 1*
Barr, Frank Stringfellow 1897- *BiDAmEd*
Barr, George Andre 1873-1945 *NatCAB 37*
Barr, George Andrew 1873-1945 *WhAm 2*
Barr, Granville Walter 1860- *NatCAB 13,*
WhAm 3
Barr, James Adam 1863- *WhAm 4*
Barr, James M 1855- *WhAm 4*
Barr, John 1892-1957 *NatCAB 46*
Barr, John Henry 1861-1937 *NatCAB 27,*
WhAm 1
Barr, John Watson 1826-1907 *NatCAB 10,*
WhAm 1
Barr, Joseph Seaton 1901-1964 *WhAm 5*
Barr, Joseph Walker 1918- *BiDrAC*
Barr, Joseph Wilson 1875-1955 *NatCAB 43*

Barr, Katharine Louise Kennedy 1863-
WomWWA 14
Barr, Lloyd Stanley 1889-1970 *NatCAB 56*
Barr, Lyman 1896-1968 *WhAm 5*
Barr, Norman Burton 1868-1943 *NatCAB 32,*
WhAm 4
Barr, Paul E 1892-1953 *IIBEAAW*
Barr, Richard Alexander 1871- *WhAm 3*
Barr, Robert 1850-1912 *ApCAB Sup,*
WhAm 2
Barr, Roy Evan 1883-1974 *WhAm 6*
Barr, Samuel Davis 1826- *NatCAB 5,*
WhAm 3
Barr, Samuel Fleming 1829-1919 *BiDrAC,*
WhAm 3
Barr, Thomas Carson 1858- *NatCAB 4*
Barr, Thomas Francis 1837-1916 *NatCAB 28,*
TwCBDA, WhAm 1
Barr, Thomas Jefferson 1812-1881 *BiAUS,*
BiDrAC, WhAm H, WhAmP
Barr, Thomas T 1833- *WhAm 4*
Barr, William 1827-1908 *NatCAB 14*
Barr, William 1867-1933 *IIBEAAW*
Barr, William Alexander 1856-1923 *WhAm 1*
Barr, William Andrew 1896-1963 *NatCAB 52,*
WhAm 4
Barr, William Francis 1865-1937 *WhAm 1*
Barrac *NewYHSD*
Barradall, Edward 1704-1743 *DcAmB,*
WhAm H
Barradas, Isidro *ApCAB*
Barragan, Miguel 1789-1835 *ApCAB*
Barralet, John James 1747?-1815 *NewYHSD,*
WhAm H
Barralett *NewYHSD*
Barrande, Joachim 1799-1883 *DcScB*
Barrangon, Lucy Eloise Lord 1876-
WomWWA 14
Barras, Charles M 1826-1873 *ApCAB*
Barras, Harry Watson 1868-1936 *WhAm 1*
Barras, Count Louis De d1800? *ApCAB,*
Drake
Barras, Paul F J N, Vicomte De 1755-1829
McGEWB
Barratt, Henry *NewYHSD*
Barratt, Norris Stanley 1862-1924 *WhAm 1*
Barratt, Thomas E 1814?- *NewYHSD*
Barraza, Jose L 1787-1843 *ApCAB*
Barre *NewYHSD*
Barre, Antoine Joseph Lefevre DeLa 1625?-1688
ApCAB, Drake
Barre, Isaac 1726-1802 *ApCAB, Drake*
Barre DeSaint Venant *DcScB*
Barreda, Gabino 1820-1881 *ApCAB*
Barrell, Daniel Alden 1877-1928 *NatCAB 22*
Barrell, Joseph 1869-1919 *DcAmB, DcScB,*
WhAm 1
Barrell, Walter Lewis 1866-1927 *NatCAB 21*
Barrere, Claude 1906-1966 *WhAm 4*
Barrere, Georges 1876-1944 *DcAmB S3,*
WhAm 2
Barrere, Granville 1829-1889 *BiAUS, BiDrAC,*
WhAm H
Barrere, Nelson 1808-1883 *BiAUS, BiDrAC,*
WhAm H
Barres, Auguste Maurice 1862-1923 *McGEWB*
Barreswil, Charles-Louis 1817-1870 *DcScB*
Barret, Anthony *NewYHSD*
Barret, Gladys Hermione Gittings 1888-
WomWWA 14
Barret, John Richard 1825-1903 *BiDrAC*
Barret, Thomas Charles 1860- *NatCAB 9*
Barrett, Albert Moore 1871-1936 *DcAmB S2,*
NatCAB 38, WhAm 1
Barrett, Alexander 1833?- *NewYHSD*
Barrett, Alva Pearl 1878- *WhAm 6*
Barrett, Arthur Gilbert 1873-1946 *NatCAB 36*
Barrett, Benjamin Fisk 1808-1892 *ApCAB*
Barrett, Benjamin Fiske 1808-1892 *DcAmB,*
WhAm H
Barrett, Channing Whitney 1866-1958 *WhAm 3*
Barrett, Charles D 1885-1943 *WhAm 2*
Barrett, Charles F 1861- *WhAm 4*
Barrett, Charles Joseph 1900-1963 *NatCAB 51,*
WhAm 4
Barrett, Charles Raymond 1874- *WhAm 5*
Barrett, Charles Simon 1866-1935 *DcAmB S1,*

EncAAH, WhAm 1
Barrett, Clifford Leslie 1894-1971 *WhAm 5*
Barrett, Daisy Adelaide 1872- *WomWWA 14*
Barrett, Darwin Sherwood, Jr. 1891-1943
NatCAB 31, WhAm 2
Barrett, Don Carlos 1868-1943 *WhAm 2*
Barrett, Dulin Adelbert 1875-1959 *NatCAB 47*
Barrett, E Murray 1910-1959 *NatCAB 49*
Barrett, Edward 1828-1880 *ApCAB, TwCBDA*
Barrett, Edward 1828-1881 *NatCAB 5*
Barrett, Edward Francis 1888-1958 *NatCAB 48,*
WhAm 3
Barrett, Edward Peer 1920-1967 *NatCAB 53*
Barrett, Edward Ware 1866-1922 *NatCAB 39,*
WhAm 1
Barrett, Ella Teresa 1867- *WomWWA 14*
Barrett, Francis Grover 1892-1971 *NatCAB 57*
Barrett, Frank Aloysius 1892-1962 *BiDrAC,*
WhAm 4, WhAmP
Barrett, Fred Dennett 1906-1970 *WhAm 5*
Barrett, Frederick Richard 1868-1946
NatCAB 34
Barrett, George Carter 1838-1906 *TwCBDA,*
WhAm 1
Barrett, George Hooker 1794-1860 *ApCAB,*
NatCAB 4
Barrett, George Horton 1794-1860 *DcAmB,*
WhAm H
Barrett, Harold W 1868- *WhoColR*
Barrett, Harrison D 1863- *WhAm 1*
Barrett, Harry McWhirter 1869-1940 *WhAm 1*
Barrett, Henry Robertson 1869-1940
NatCAB 29
Barrett, Isaac Baker 1849-1916 *NatCAB 17*
Barrett, J Lawrence 1880-1958 *NatCAB 44*
Barrett, J Richard *BiAUS*
Barrett, James Richard 1863- *WhoColR*
Barrett, Janie Porter 1865-1948 *BiDAmEd,*
DcAmB S4, NotAW
Barrett, Jay Amos 1865- *WhAm 4*
Barrett, Jesse W 1884- *WhAm 3*
Barrett, John 1866-1938 *ApCAB X,*
DcAmB S2, NatCAB 10, NatCAB 44,
TwCBDA, WhAm 1, WhAmP
Barrett, John Erigena 1849- *NatCAB 4*
Barrett, John Ignatius 1884-1944 *WhAm 2*
Barrett, John Patrick 1837- *TwCBDA,*
WhAm 4
Barrett, Joseph Hartwell 1824-1907 *BiAUS,*
NatCAB 13, WhAm 1
Barrett, Kate Harwood Waller 1857-1925
NotAW
Barrett, Kate Waller 1858-1925 *DcAmB,*
WhAm 1
Barrett, Kate Waller 1859-1925 *WomWWA 14*
Barrett, Lawrence 1838-1891 *AmBi, ApCAB,*
DcAmB, NatCAB 1, TwCBDA,
WhAm H
Barrett, Lawrence Lorus 1897-1973 *IIBEAAW*
Barrett, Leonard Andrew 1874-1945 *WhAm 2*
Barrett, Lillian Foster 1884-1963 *WhAm 4*
Barrett, Linton Lomas 1904-1972 *WhAm 5*
Barrett, Mary Franklin 1879- *WomWWA 14*
Barrett, Michael Thomas 1881-1940
NatCAB 30, WhAm 1
Barrett, O Slack 1893-1953 *NatCAB 44*
Barrett, Oliver Rogers 1873-1950 *WhAm 2A*
Barrett, Oscar Fitzallen 1860-1935 *WhAm 1*
Barrett, Otis Warren 1872-1950 *WhAm 3*
Barrett, Ralph Lester 1892-1962 *NatCAB 50*
Barrett, Raymond F 1904-1968 *WhAm 5*
Barrett, Raymond Lathrop 1894-1954
NatCAB 45
Barrett, Reginald 1861-1940 *WhAm 1*
Barrett, Reginald 1912-1966 *WhAm 4*
Barrett, Richard Carroll 1907-1962 *NatCAB 51*
Barrett, Richard Cornelius 1858- *WhAm 4*
Barrett, Richard Warren 1872-1946 *WhAm 2*
Barrett, Robert Edward 1881-1945 *NatCAB 46*
Barrett, Robert South 1877-1959 *WhAm 3*
Barrett, Rollin Hayes 1891-1965 *NatCAB 51*
Barrett, Sampson Kirby 1886-1948 *NatCAB 50*
Barrett, Samuel Alfred 1879-1965 *WhAm 4*
Barrett, Stephen Melvil 1865- *WhAm 4*
Barrett, Storrs Barrows 1864-1937 *NatCAB 28*
Barrett, Thomas 1829- *NatCAB 9*
Barrett, Thomas Weeks 1902-1947 *NatCAB 36*
Barrett, W Franklin 1900-1967 *WhAm 4*

Barrett, Wilbert Hamilton 1858- *WhAm 3*
Barrett, William A 1896- *BiDrAC*
Barrett, William E 1850-1906 *WhAm 1*
Barrett, William Emerson 1858-1906 *BiDrAC, NatCAB 14, TwCBDA, WhAmP*
Barrett, William Felton d1955 *WhAm 3*
Barrett, William Hale 1866-1941 *NatCAB 45, WhAm 1*
Barrett, William Henry 1881- *WhAm 6*
Barrett, William Henry Ambrose 1887- *WhoColR*
Barrett, William Hunter 1877-1955 *NatCAB 47*
Barrett, William M 1858-1937 *WhAm 1*
Barrett, Wilson 1848-1904 *WhAm 1*
Barrette, Antonio 1899-1968 *WhAm 5*
Barrette, John Davenport 1862-1934 *WhAm 1*
Barretto, Laurence Brevoort 1890-1971 *NatCAB 57*
Barretto, Laurence Brevoort 1890-1972 *WhAm 5*
Barrie, Sir James Matthew 1860-1937 *McGEWB*
Barrientos, Rene Ortuno d1969 *WhAm 5*
Barrier, Charles Wesley 1889-1967 *NatCAB 53*
Barrier, Joseph Henry 1890-1970 *WhAm 5*
Barriere, Hippolite *WhAm H*
Barriger, John Walker 1832-1906 *ApCAB, WhAm 1*
Barriger, William Lillard 1897-1976 *WhAm 6*
Barringer, Benjamin Stockwell 1877-1953 *NatCAB 50*
Barringer, Daniel Laurens 1781-1852 *TwCBDA*
Barringer, Daniel Laurens 1788-1852 *BiAUS, BiDrAC, WhAm H, WhAmP*
Barringer, Daniel Moreau d1873 *BiAUS*
Barringer, Daniel Moreau 1806-1873 *BiDrAC, DcAmB, TwCBDA, WhAm H, WhAmP*
Barringer, Daniel Moreau 1807?-1873 *ApCAB, Drake, NatCAB 11*
Barringer, Daniel Moreau 1860-1929 *AsBiEn, NatCAB 22, WhAm 1*
Barringer, Edwin C 1892-1965 *WhAm 4*
Barringer, Emily Dunning 1876-1961 *BiCAW, NatCAB 50, WomWWA 14*
Barringer, Lewin Bennett 1906-1943 *NatCAB 31*
Barringer, Paul Brandon 1857-1941 *NatCAB 13, WhAm 1*
Barringer, Paul Brandon, Jr. 1887-1973 *NatCAB 57, WhAm 5*
Barringer, Rufus 1821-1895 *ApCAB Sup, BiDConf, DcAmB, NatCAB 8, TwCBDA, WhAm H*
Barringer, Victor Clay 1827-1896 *NatCAB 13, TwCBDA*
Barringer, Victor Clay 1891-1971 *NatCAB 56*
Barrionuevo, Francisco De *ApCAB*
Barrios, Gerardo d1865 *ApCAB*
Barrios, Justo Rufino 1835-1885 *ApCAB, McGEWB*
Barritt, Frances Fuller 1826- *ApCAB, Drake*
Barritt, William 1822?- *NewYHSD*
Barroeta *NewYHSD*
Barroeta Y Angel, Pedro Antonio 1700?-1775 *ApCAB*
Barrois, Charles 1851-1939 *DcScB*
Barron, Bernard Sidney 1895-1959 *NatCAB 43*
Barron, Carter Tate 1905-1950 *WhAm 3*
Barron, Clarence Walker 1855-1928 *AmBi, ApCAB X, DcAmB S1, NatCAB 21, WebAB, WhAm 1*
Barron, E S Guzman 1898-1957 *WhAm 3*
Barron, Elbert Macby 1903-1969 *WhAm 5*
Barron, Elwyn Alfred d1929 *WhAm 1*
Barron, Ernest R 1844- *NatCAB 3, WhAm 4*
Barron, George Davis 1860-1947 *NatCAB 36, WhAm 2*
Barron, H D *BiAUS*
Barron, Jacob Thomas 1884-1950 *NatCAB 38*
Barron, James 1768-1851 *DcAmB, Drake, WebAB, WebAMB, WhAm H*
Barron, James 1769-1851 *AmBi, ApCAB, NatCAB 5, TwCBDA*
Barron, James Leslie 1890-1947 *NatCAB 37*
Barron, James T *ApCAB X*
Barron, Jane Carson 1879- *WomWWA 14*
Barron, John W 1826?- *NewYHSD*
Barron, Joseph Day 1833- *WhAm 4*

Barron, Leonard 1868-1938 *WhAm 1*
Barron, Mark 1905-1960 *WhAm 4*
Barron, Mary Butler 1873- *WomWWA 14*
Barron, Minerva Crowell Rogers 1902-1972 *WhAm 6*
Barron, Robert E 1873-1940 *WhAm 1*
Barron, Robert J *ApCAB X*
Barron, Samuel d1888 *Drake*
Barron, Samuel 1763?-1810 *ApCAB, TwCBDA*
Barron, Samuel 1765-1810 *Drake, NatCAB 4*
Barron, Samuel 1802?-1888 *ApCAB, NatCAB 4, TwCBDA*
Barron, Samuel 1809-1888 *BiDConf, DcAmB, WebAMB, WhAm H*
Barron, Walter J 1846- *NatCAB 3*
Barron, William Andros, Jr. 1892-1964 *NatCAB 51, WhAm 4*
Barros Arana, Diego 1830- *ApCAB Sup*
Barrow, Alexander 1801-1846 *ApCAB, BiAUS, BiDrAC, NatCAB 7, TwCBDA, WhAm H*
Barrow, Clyde *REnAW*
Barrow, David 1753-1819 *NatCAB 4*
Barrow, David 1858- *WhAm 4*
Barrow, David Crenshaw 1852-1929 *NatCAB 15, WhAm 1*
Barrow, Edward Grant 1868-1953 *DcAmB S5*
Barrow, Elizabeth N 1869- *WhAm 5, WomWWA 14*
Barrow, Frances Elizabeth 1822-1894 *AmWom, ApCAB, NatCAB 4, TwCBDA, WhAm H*
Barrow, Henry Yeaman 1885-1962 *NatCAB 49*
Barrow, Isaac 1630-1677 *DcScB*
Barrow, J L *NewYHSD*
Barrow, John Dobson 1823-1907 *NewYHSD*
Barrow, John V *ApCAB X*
Barrow, Joseph Louis 1914- *WebAB*
Barrow, Middleton Pope 1839-1903 *BiDrAC*
Barrow, Pope 1839-1903 *NatCAB 9, WhAm 1*
Barrow, Thomas *NewYHSD*
Barrow, Washington d1866 *BiAUS*
Barrow, Washington 1807-1866 *BiDrAC*
Barrow, Washington 1817-1866 *ApCAB, DcAmB, Drake, NatCAB 13, WhAm H*
Barrow, William Edward 1879-1957 *NatCAB 49*
Barrow, William Hulbert 1886-1950 *NatCAB 39*
Barrows, Albert Armington 1877-1944 *NatCAB 33*
Barrows, Alice Prentice 1877-1954 *BiDAmEd, DcAmB S5*
Barrows, Alice Prentice 1878-1954 *WomWWA 14*
Barrows, Anna 1864-1948 *BiDAmEd, WhAm 3, WomWWA 14*
Barrows, Arthur Stanhope 1884-1963 *WhAm 4*
Barrows, Bella S *NotAW*
Barrows, Charles Clifford 1857-1916 *ApCAB X, NatCAB 3, NatCAB 36, WhAm 1*
Barrows, Charles Henry 1853-1918 *WhAm 1*
Barrows, Chester Willard 1872-1931 *NatCAB 38, WhAm 1*
Barrows, David Nye 1887-1965 *NatCAB 51*
Barrows, David Prescott 1873-1954 *ApCAB X, DcAmB S5, NatCAB 52, WhAm 5*
Barrows, Edwin Armington 1869-1948 *WhAm 2*
Barrows, Elijah Porter 1807-1888 *NatCAB 10*
Barrows, Elijah Porter 1817-1888 *ApCAB*
Barrows, Eulalie A *WomWWA 14*
Barrows, Frank Elisha 1888-1962 *NatCAB 49*
Barrows, Harlan Hiram 1877-1960 *NatCAB 45, WhAm 4*
Barrows, Harold Kilbrith 1873-1954 *WhAm 3*
Barrows, Isabel Chapin 1845-1913 *WhAm 1, WomWWA 14, WomWWA 14a*
Barrows, John Chester 1909-1963 *WhAm 4*
Barrows, John Henry 1847-1902 *ApCAB Sup, DcAmB, NatCAB 8, TwCBDA, WhAm 1*
Barrows, John Otis 1833-1918 *WhAm 1*
Barrows, Katharine Isabel Hayes Chapin 1845-1913 *NotAW*
Barrows, Lewis Orin 1893-1967 *WhAm 4*
Barrows, Mary *WomWWA 14*

Barrows, Mary Livermore Norris 1877- *WomWWA 14*
Barrows, Morton 1856-1936 *NatCAB 39, WhAm 4*
Barrows, Nat A 1905-1949 *WhAm 2*
Barrows, Nathaniel Haven 1877-1952 *NatCAB 39, WhAm 3*
Barrows, Raymond H 1899-1958 *WhAm 3*
Barrows, Samuel June 1845-1909 *BiDrAC, DcAmB, TwCBDA, WhAm 1, WhAmP*
Barrows, Stanley Hill 1883-1949 *NatCAB 42, WhAm 2*
Barrows, Thomas Nichols 1900-1962 *WhAm 4*
Barrows, Walter Manning 1846-1899 *ApCAB Sup*
Barrows, Wayne Groves 1880- *WhAm 6*
Barrows, Willard 1806-1868 *ApCAB*
Barrows, William 1815-1891 *TwCBDA*
Barrows, William Morton 1883-1946 *WhAm 2*
Barrows, William Stanley 1861-1940 *WhAm 1*
Barrs, Burton 1889-1959 *NatCAB 47*
Barrundia, Jose Francisco 1779-1854 *Drake*
Barrundia, Jose Francisco 1780?-1854 *ApCAB*
Barrus, Clara 1864-1931 *WhAm 1, WomWWA 14*
Barrus, George Hale 1854-1929 *WhAm 1*
Barry, Alexander Grant 1892-1952 *BiDrAC*
Barry, Charles 1820?- *NewYHSD*
Barry, Charles A 1830-1892 *NewYHSD*
Barry, Charles Copeland 1848-1911 *NatCAB 16*
Barry, Charles Hart 1857-1918 *NatCAB 18*
Barry, Daniel 1824?- *NewYHSD*
Barry, David J *NewYHSD*
Barry, David Sheldon 1859-1936 *WhAm 1*
Barry, Edward Buttevant 1849-1938 *WhAm 1*
Barry, Emily S 1845- *WomWWA 14*
Barry, Etheldred Breeze 1870- *WhAm 5*
Barry, Flora Elizabeth 1836- *AmWom*
Barry, Frederick George 1845-1909 *BiDrAC*
Barry, Frederick Lehrle 1897-1960 *WhAm 4*
Barry, Henry W d1875 *ApCAB, BiAUS*
Barry, Henry W 1835?-1875 *NatCAB 4, TwCBDA*
Barry, Henry W 1840-1875 *BiDrAC, WhAm H*
Barry, Herbert 1867-1947 *WhAm 2*
Barry, James Henry 1855-1927 *NatCAB 21*
Barry, James Henry 1856-1927 *WhAm 1*
Barry, John d1859 *Drake*
Barry, John 1745-1803 *AmBi, ApCAB, DcAmB, Drake, McGEWB, NatCAB 4, TwCBDA, WebAB, WebAMB, WhAm H*
Barry, John 1790-1859 *WhAm H*
Barry, John 1799?-1859 *ApCAB, NatCAB 12, TwCBDA*
Barry, John Daniel 1866-1942 *WhAm 2*
Barry, John Gerald 1884-1963 *NatCAB 51*
Barry, John H d1955 *WhAm 3*
Barry, John Reasoner 1914-1962 *NatCAB 49*
Barry, John Stetson 1819-1872 *ApCAB*
Barry, John Stewart 1802-1870 *ApCAB, BiAUS, DcAmB, Drake, NatCAB 5, TwCBDA, WhAm H, WhAmP*
Barry, Joseph Gayle Hurd 1858-1931 *ApCAB X, WhAm 1*
Barry, Leland Clifford 1901-1963 *WhAm 4*
Barry, Leonora Marie Kearney 1849-1930 *NotAW, WebAB*
Barry, Lily Emily Frances *WomWWA 14*
Barry, Maggie Wilkins Hill 1865- *WhAm 4, WomWWA 14*
Barry, Martin 1802-1855 *DcScB*
Barry, Maurice Joseph 1880- *WhAm 6*
Barry, Patrick 1816-1890 *AmBi, ApCAB, DcAmB, NatCAB 13, WhAm H*
Barry, Patrick 1868-1940 *WhAm 1*
Barry, Peter 1912-1973 *WhAm 5*
Barry, Philip James Quinn 1896-1949 *DcAmB S4, NatCAB 37, WhAm 2*
Barry, Robert Raymond 1915- *BiDrAC*
Barry, Susan E 1826- *AmWom*
Barry, Theodore *NewYHSD*
Barry, Thomas Henry 1855-1919 *NatCAB 21, WhAm 1*
Barry, Thomas J 1834?- *NewYHSD*
Barry, Timothy *NewYHSD*
Barry, Walter R d1963 *WhAm 4*

Barry, William 1805-1885 *ApCAB, TwCBDA*
Barry, William Bernard 1902-1946 *BiDrAC, WhAm 2, WhAmP*
Barry, William Farquhar 1818-1879 *AmBi, ApCAB, DcAmB, Drake, NatCAB 5, TwCBDA, WhAm H*
Barry, William Taylor 1780-1835 *BiAUS*
Barry, William Taylor 1784-1835 *BiDrAC, Drake, WhAmP*
Barry, William Taylor 1785-1835 *AmBi, ApCAB, BiDrUSE, DcAmB, NatCAB 5, TwCBDA, WhAm H*
Barry, William Taylor Sullivan 1821-1868 *ApCAB, BiAUS, BiDConf, BiDrAC, DcAmB, Drake, TwCBDA, WhAm H*
Barry-Lake, Mrs. 1849-1930 *WebAB*
Barrymore, Ethel 1879-1959 *ApCAB X, McGEWB, WebAB, WhAm 3, WomWWA 14*
Barrymore, Georgiana Emma Drew 1854-1893 *NotAW*
Barrymore, Georgiana Emma Drew 1856-1893 *ApCAB Sup, DcAmB, WhAm H*
Barrymore, John 1882-1942 *DcAmB S3, EncAB, McGEWB, WebAB, WhAm 2*
Barrymore, Lionel 1878-1954 *DcAmB S5, McGEWB, WebAB, WhAm 3*
Barrymore, Maurice 1847-1905 *AmBi, ApCAB Sup, DcAmB, WebAB, WhAm 1*
Barrymore, William d1847 *ApCAB*
Barsanti, Olinto Mark 1917-1973 *WhAm 5*
Barse, Dane 1901-1960 *NatCAB 54*
Barse, George Randolph, Jr. 1861-1938 *IIBEAAW, NatCAB 28, TwCBDA, WhAm 1*
Barsham, J W *NewYHSD*
Barsky, Joseph Mitchell 1892-1948 *NatCAB 38*
Barsotte, Francisco *NewYHSD*
Barsotti, Charles 1850-1927 *AmBi, DcAmB*
Barss, John Edmund 1871- *WhAm 5*
Barston, John L 1832- *TwCBDA*
Barstow, Amos Chafee 1813- *NatCAB 3*
Barstow, Clara Gerrish 1879- *WomWWA 14*
Barstow, Edith d1960 *WhAm 3*
Barstow, Edwin Ormond 1879-1967 *WhAm 5*
Barstow, Edwin Ormond 1880-1967 *NatCAB 53*
Barstow, Frank Quarles 1846-1909 *NatCAB 24*
Barstow, Frank Quarles 1847-1909 *WhAm 1*
Barstow, Gamaliel Henry 1784-1865 *BiAUS, BiDrAC, WhAm H*
Barstow, George Eames 1849-1924 *NatCAB 18, WhAm 1*
Barstow, George Eames 1875-1939 *NatCAB 31*
Barstow, Gideon 1783-1852 *BiAUS, BiDrAC, WhAm H*
Barstow, John Lester 1832-1913 *NatCAB 8, WhAm 1*
Barstow, Robbins Wolcott 1890-1962 *WhAm 4*
Barstow, Miss S M *NewYHSD*
Barstow, William A d1865 *Drake*
Barstow, William A 1811-1865 *ApCAB, BiAUS*
Barstow, William Augustus 1813-1865 *DcAmB, NatCAB 12, TwCBDA, WhAm H, WhAmP*
Barstow, William Augustus 1877-1922 *NatCAB 24*
Barstow, William Slocum 1866-1942 *NatCAB 32, WhAm 2*
Barstow, Wilson 1830-1869 *ApCAB*
Barstow, Zedekiah Smith 1790-1873 *ApCAB*
Bart, Jean 1650-1702 *WhoMilH*
Bartch, George Washington 1849-1927 *NatCAB 13, NatCAB 20, WhAm 1*
Bartel, William Edwin 1903-1958 *WhAm 3*
Bartell, Floyd Earl 1883-1961 *NatCAB 49, WhAm 4*
Bartell, Sarah *NewYHSD*
Bartelle, D W C *NewYHSD*
Bartello *NewYHSD*
Bartelme, Mary Margaret 1869-1954 *NatCAB 47, WomWWA 14*
Bartels, Julius 1899-1964 *DcScB*
Bartels, Louisa M *NewYHSD*
Bartels, Vernon C 1905-1957 *WhAm 3*
Bartelt, Edward F 1895-1958 *WhAm 3*
Barth, Carl Georg Lange 1860-1939 *DcAmB S2, NatCAB 34, WhAm 1*

Barth, Charles H 1858-1926 *WhAm 1*
Barth, Charles H, Jr. 1903-1943 *WhAm 2*
Barth, Frederick 1804?- *NewYHSD*
Barth, George Bittman 1897-1969 *WhAm 5*
Barth, Heinrich 1821-1865 *McGEWB*
Barth, Irvin Victor 1877-1931 *NatCAB 27*
Barth, John Simmons 1930- *WebAB*
Barth, Karl 1886-1968 *McGEWB, WhAm 5*
Barth, Moritz 1834-1919 *NatCAB 19*
Barth, Rudolph F 1836?- *NewYHSD*
Barth, Theodore H 1891-1967 *WhAm 4A*
Barth, Theodore Nott 1898-1961 *WhAm 4*
Barth, Valentine *NewYHSD*
Barth, William George 1908-1967 *WhAm 4*
Barthberger, Charles 1823-1896 *WhAm H*
Barthe, J G *Drake*
Barthel, Oliver Edward 1877-1969 *NatCAB 16, NatCAB 55, WhAm 5*
Barthel, Otto Frederick 1876-1941 *NatCAB 30*
Barthelmess, Richard d1963 *WhAm 4*
Barthez, Paul-Joseph 1734-1806 *DcScB*
Barthman, Henry Charles 1868-1941 *NatCAB 31*
Barthold, Robert M 1879- *WhAm 6*
Bartholdi, Frederic Auguste 1834- *ApCAB, TwCBDA*
Bartholdt, Richard 1853-1932 *NatCAB 7, TwCBDA*
Bartholdt, Richard 1855-1932 *AmBi, BiDrAC, DcAmB S1, NatCAB 25, WhAm 1, WhAmP*
Bartholf, John Charles Palmer 1891-1969 *WhAm 5*
Bartholin, Caspar 1585-1629 *DcScB*
Bartholin, Casper, I 1585-1629 *BiHiMed*
Bartholin, Casper, II 1655-1738 *BiHiMed*
Bartholin, Erasmus 1625-1698 *AsBiEn, DcScB*
Bartholin, Thomas 1616-1680 *BiHiMed, DcScB*
Bartholomay, Anthony Francis 1919-1975 *WhAm 6*
Bartholomew, Abram Glenni 1878-1936 *WhAm 1*
Bartholomew, Albert Lloyd 1841-1918 *NatCAB 17*
Bartholomew, Allen R 1855-1933 *WhAm 1*
Bartholomew, Charles L 1869-1949 *WhAm 2*
Bartholomew, Edward Fry 1846-1946 *WhAm 2*
Bartholomew, Edward Sheffield 1822-1858 *AmBi, ApCAB, ApCAB X, DcAmB, Drake, NatCAB 8, NewYHSD, WhAm H*
Bartholomew, Elam 1852-1934 *NatCAB 26*
Bartholomew, Ethel Hague 1866- *WomWWA 14*
Bartholomew, George Kellam 1835-1917 *NatCAB 16, WhAm 4*
Bartholomew, Harry Ives 1873-1956 *NatCAB 46*
Bartholomew, J M 1843-1901 *WhAm 1*
Bartholomew, Joseph Milton 1843-1901 *NatCAB 13*
Bartholomew, Miles Marshall 1844- *NatCAB 3*
Bartholomew, Morey Cutler 1883-1948 *NatCAB 37*
Bartholomew, Pliny Webster 1840-1931 *NatCAB 18, WhAm 1*
Bartholomew, Rudolph Artillus 1886-1969 *NatCAB 55, WhAm 5*
Bartholomew, Tracy 1884-1951 *WhAm 3*
Bartholomew, Truman C 1809-1867 *NewYHSD, WhAm H*
Bartholomew, William Fayette 1871- *ApCAB X*
Bartholomew, William Henry 1840-1927 *WhAm 2*
Bartholomew, William Nelson 1822-1907 *BiDAmEd*
Bartholomew, William Newton 1822-1898 *IIBEAAW, NewYHSD, WhAm H*
Bartholow, Otho Ford 1869-1951 *NatCAB 41*
Bartholow, Roberts 1831-1904 *ApCAB, DcAmB, NatCAB 22, WhAm 1*
Bartine, Horace Franklin 1848-1918 *BiDrAC, TwCBDA, WhAm 4, WhAmP*
Bartky, Adolph John 1899-1974 *WhAm 6*
Bartky, Walter 1901-1958 *WhAm 3*
Bartle, H Roe d1974 *WhAm 6*
Bartleman, Richard Milne 1863- *WhAm 4*
Bartleson, John *WhAm H*

Bartlet, William 1748-1841 *DcAmB, NatCAB 10, TwCBDA, WhAm H*
Bartlet, William *see also* Bartlett, William
Bartlet, William Stoodley 1809- *Drake*
Bartlett, Adolphus Clay 1844-1922 *NatCAB 31, WhAm 1*
Bartlett, Albert LeRoy 1852-1934 *WhAm 1*
Bartlett, Alden Eugene 1872- *WhAm 5*
Bartlett, Adolphus Clay 1844-1922 *ApCAB X*
Bartlett, Alice Elinor 1848- *WhAm 4*
Bartlett, Alice Elinor 1849- *WomWWA 14*
Bartlett, Alice Eloise 1848- *AmWom*
Bartlett, Alice Hunt 1870- *WhAm 5*
Bartlett, Allan Charles 1897-1970 *WhAm 5*
Bartlett, Amanda S *WomWWA 14*
Bartlett, Arthur Charles 1901-1964 *WhAm 4*
Bartlett, Asa *BiAUS*
Bartlett, Bailey 1750-1830 *BiAUS, BiDrAC, WhAm H, WhAmP*
Bartlett, Boyd Wheeler 1897-1965 *NatCAB 53, WhAm 4*
Bartlett, Caroline Julia 1858- *AmWom, NotAW*
Bartlett, Sir Charles John 1889-1955 *WhAm 3*
Bartlett, Charles Joseph 1864-1956 *NatCAB 51*
Bartlett, Charles Lafayette 1853-1938 *BiDrAC, TwCBDA, WhAm 1, WhAmP*
Bartlett, Charles Ward 1850-1910 *WhAm 1*
Bartlett, Charles William 1845- *WhAm 4*
Bartlett, Clarence 1858-1935 *NatCAB 3, NatCAB 45, WhAm 4*
Bartlett, Claude Jay 1891-1941 *NatCAB 31*
Bartlett, Craig Scott 1897-1963 *WhAm 4*
Bartlett, Dana 1878-1957 *IIBEAAW*
Bartlett, Dana Webster 1860- *WhAm 4*
Bartlett, David 1855-1913 *NatCAB 18*
Bartlett, David L 1816- *NatCAB 1*
Bartlett, Dora Tripp 1879- *WomWWA 14*
Bartlett, Edgar Elliott 1856-1929 *WhAm 1*
Bartlett, Edmund Morgan 1849- *WhAm 4*
Bartlett, Edward Everett, Jr. 1885-1961 *NatCAB 55, WhAm 4*
Bartlett, Edward Lewis 1904-1968 *BiDrAC, NatCAB 54, WhAm 5*
Bartlett, Edward Louis 1904-1968 *WhAmP*
Bartlett, Edward Payson 1884-1965 *NatCAB 54*
Bartlett, Edward Randolph 1889-1952 *WhAm 3*
Bartlett, Edward Theodore 1841-1910 *WhAm 1*
Bartlett, Edwin Ichabod 1883-1954 *NatCAB 41*
Bartlett, Edwin Julius 1851-1932 *ApCAB, WhAm 1*
Bartlett, Edwin Rice 1883-1957 *NatCAB 48, WhAm 3*
Bartlett, Edwin Wilcox 1839-1913 *NatCAB 16*
Bartlett, Elisha 1804-1855 *AmBi, DcAmB, Drake, NatCAB 12, WhAm H*
Bartlett, Elisha 1805-1855 *ApCAB, TwCBDA*
Bartlett, Sir Ellis Ashmead 1849- *ApCAB, ApCAB Sup*
Bartlett, Frank Leslie 1852- *WhAm 4*
Bartlett, Frank W 1856- *WhAm 4*
Bartlett, Franklin 1847-1909 *BiDrAC, WhAm 1*
Bartlett, Sir Frederic Charles 1886-1969 *McGEWB*
Bartlett, Frederic Clay 1873-1953 *NatCAB 43, WhAm 3*
Bartlett, Frederic Huntington 1872-1948 *NatCAB 37, WhAm 2*
Bartlett, Frederic Pearson 1909-1970 *WhAm 5*
Bartlett, Frederick Bethune 1882-1941 *WhAm 1*
Bartlett, Frederick Orin 1876- *WhAm 5*
Bartlett, Genevieve Kinne 1866- *WomWWA 14*
Bartlett, George Arthur 1869-1951 *BiDrAC, WhAm 5, WhAmP*
Bartlett, George Griffiths 1872- *WhAm 5*
Bartlett, George True 1856-1949 *NatCAB 39, WhAm 2*
Bartlett, Gray 1885-1951 *IIBEAAW*
Bartlett, Harley Harris 1886-1960 *WhAm 4*
Bartlett, Harold Terry 1887-1955 *NatCAB 42*
Bartlett, Harriet Tuttle 1860- *WomWWA 14*
Bartlett, Helen *WomWWA 14*
Bartlett, Herschel 1841-1923 *NatCAB 6*
Bartlett, Homer Lyman 1830-1905 *NatCAB 2, WhAm 4*
Bartlett, Homer Newton 1845-1920 *DcAmB, WhAm 4*

Bartlett, Homer Newton 1846-1920 *ApCAB X,*
NatCAB 7, TwCBDA
Bartlett, Ichabod 1786-1853 *ApCAB, BiAUS,*
BiDrAC, DcAmB, Drake, NatCAB 10,
TwCBDA, WhAm H, WhAmP
Bartlett, J Kemp 1863-1948 *NatCAB 45*
Bartlett, Jane Wetherell *WomWWA 14*
Bartlett, Jason Robbins *NewYHSD*
Bartlett, John 1820-1905 *AmBi, ApCAB,*
DcAmB, NatCAB 11, TwCBDA, WebAB,
WhAm 1
Bartlett, John Frank 1902-1969 *WhAm 5*
Bartlett, John Henry 1869-1952 *NatCAB 40,*
WhAm 3
Bartlett, John Pomeroy 1858-1948 *WhAm 2*
Bartlett, John Russell 1805-1886 *AmBi,*
ApCAB, BiAUS, DcAmB, Drake,
IlBEAAW, NatCAB 9, NewYHSD,
REnAW, TwCBDA, WebAB, WhAm H,
WhAmP
Bartlett, John Russell 1843-1904 *ApCAB,*
TwCBDA, WhAm 1
Bartlett, John S 1845-1925 *WhAm 1*
Bartlett, John Sherren 1790-1863 *ApCAB,*
DcAmB, Drake, NatCAB 22, WhAm H
Bartlett, John Thomas 1892-1947 *WhAm 2*
Bartlett, John W 1891-1961 *WhAm 4*
Bartlett, Joseph 1762-1827 *ApCAB, DcAmB,*
Drake, NatCAB 13, WhAm H
Bartlett, Joseph Gardner 1872-1927 *WhAm 1*
Bartlett, Joseph Jackson d1893 *BiAUS*
Bartlett, Joseph Jackson 1820?-1893 *ApCAB,*
NatCAB 4
Bartlett, Joseph Jackson 1834-1893 *TwCBDA*
Bartlett, Joseph Warren 1876-1960 *WhAm 4*
Bartlett, Josiah 1727-1795 *BiAUS*
Bartlett, Josiah 1729-1795 *AmBi, ApCAB,*
BiDrAC, DcAmB, Drake, NatCAB 11,
TwCBDA, WhAm H, WhAmP
Bartlett, Josiah, Jr. 1768-1838 *BiAUS, BiDrAC,*
WhAm H, WhAmP
Bartlett, Lillie Harral 1875- *WomWWA 14*
Bartlett, Louis 1872- *WhAm 5*
Bartlett, Lynn Mahlon 1904-1970 *WhAm 5*
Bartlett, Maitland 1869-1944 *WhAm 2*
Bartlett, Margaret Abbott 1892-1949 *WhAm 3*
Bartlett, Martin Firth 1864-1918 *NatCAB 18*
Bartlett, Maud Whitehead 1865- *AmWom*
Bartlett, Murray 1871-1949 *NatCAB 38,*
WhAm 2
Bartlett, Neil 1932- *AsBiEn*
Bartlett, Paul Dana 1891-1964 *NatCAB 51,*
WhAm 4
Bartlett, Paul Wayland 1865-1925 *AmBi,*
ApCAB X, BnEnAmA, DcAmB,
IlBEAAW, NatCAB 12, NatCAB 30,
TwCBDA, WhAm 1
Bartlett, Percy 1871-1951 *NatCAB 38*
Bartlett, Peter Mason 1820-1901 *TwCBDA*
Bartlett, Philip Golden 1859- *ApCAB X*
Bartlett, Ralph Jackson 1889-1958 *NatCAB 43*
Bartlett, Raymond Seeley 1880-1961
NatCAB 49
Bartlett, Richard Adams 1920- *EncAAH*
Bartlett, Robert Abram 1875-1946 *ApCAB X,*
NatCAB 41, WebAB, WhAm 2
Bartlett, Rolla Willis 1869- *ApCAB X*
Bartlett, Ruhl Jacob 1897- *EncAAH*
Bartlett, Samuel Colcord 1817-1898 *AmBi,*
ApCAB, DcAmB, NatCAB 9, TwCBDA,
WhAm H
Bartlett, Sidney 1799-1889 *NatCAB 11*
Bartlett, Thomas, Jr. 1808-1876 *BiAUS,*
BiDrAC, WhAm H, WhAmP
Bartlett, Truman Howe 1835-1923 *NewYHSD*
Bartlett, Truman Howe 1836-1923 *TwCBDA*
Bartlett, Vashti R *WomWWA 14*
Bartlett, Wallace Moore 1878- *WomWWA 14*
Bartlett, Walter Manny 1862- *WhAm 5*
Bartlett, Washington 1824-1887 *NatCAB 4*
Bartlett, Washington Allen 1820?-1871 *ApCAB,*
NatCAB 13
Bartlett, Willard 1846-1925 *NatCAB 15,*
WhAm 1
Bartlett, Willard 1868-1950 *NatCAB 42*
Bartlett, William 1748-1841 *ApCAB, Drake*
Bartlett, William *see also* Bartlet, William
Bartlett, William Francis 1840-1876 *ApCAB,*

Drake Sup, NatCAB 4, TwCBDA
Bartlett, William H 1827-1867 *BiAUS*
Bartlett, William H C 1804-1893 *Drake*
Bartlett, William Henry d1904 *WhAm 1*
Bartlett, William Henry 1809-1854 *NewYHSD,*
WhAm H
Bartlett, William Holmes Chambers 1804-1893
DcAmB S1
Bartlett, William Holms Chambers 1804-1893
TwCBDA
Bartlett, William Holms Chambers 1809-1893
ApCAB
Bartlett, William L A Burdett-Coutts 1851-
ApCAB
Bartlett, William Lehman Ashmead 1851-
ApCAB Sup
Bartlett, William Pitt Greenwood 1837-1865
ApCAB
Bartlett, William Stoodley 1809- *Drake*
Bartlette, Mrs. *NewYHSD*
Bartley, Donald 1897-1968 *WhAm 5*
Bartley, Elias Hudson 1849-1937 *ApCAB,*
NatCAB 8, TwCBDA, WhAm 1
Bartley, Mordecai 1783-1870 *ApCAB, BiAUS,*
BiDrAC, DcAmB, Drake, NatCAB 3,
TwCBDA, WhAm H, WhAmP
Bartley, S Potter 1890-1952 *NatCAB 41*
Bartley, Thomas Welles 1812- *BiAUS,*
NatCAB 7
Bartlow, John Davis 1887-1954 *NatCAB 42*
Bartman, Russell C 1897-1975 *WhAm 6*
Bartney, John *NewYHSD*
Bartok, Bela 1881-1945 *McGEWB,*
WhAm HA, WhAm 4
Bartol, Cyrus Augustus 1813- *ApCAB, Drake*
Bartol, Cyrus Augustus 1813-1900 *AmBi,*
DcAmB, TwCBDA, WhAm H, WhAm 1
Bartol, Cyrus Augustus 1813-1901 *NatCAB 4*
Bartol, George 1857-1936 *NatCAB 27*
Bartol, George E 1858-1917 *WhAm 1*
Bartol, James Lawrence 1813-1887 *NatCAB 7*
Bartol, John Washburn 1864-1950 *NatCAB 39,*
WhAm 5
Bartol, William Cyrus 1847-1940 *WhAm 1*
Bartolache, Jose Ignacio 1739-1790 *ApCAB*
Bartolarchi, Sebastian *NewYHSD*
Bartoli, Daniello 1608-1685 *DcScB*
Bartoli, F *NewYHSD*
Bartoli, J *IlBEAAW*
Bartoll, Samuel 1765?-1835 *NewYHSD*
Bartoll, William Thompson 1817-1859?
NewYHSD
Bartolotti, Gian Giacomo 1470?-1530? *DcScB*
Barton, Andrew *WhAm H*
Barton, Arthur James 1867-1942 *WhAm 2*
Barton, Bayard Winston 1880-1920 *NatCAB 18*
Barton, Benjamin Smith 1766-1815 *AmBi,*
ApCAB, BiDAmEd, DcAmB, DcScB,
Drake, NatCAB 8, WhAm H
Barton, Bolling Walker 1881-1942 *NatCAB 32*
Barton, Bruce 1886-1967 *BiDrAC, EncAB,*
WebAB, WhAm 4, WhAmP
Barton, Mrs. Caleb D *NewYHSD*
Barton, Carlyle 1885-1962 *WhAm 4*
Barton, Charles C d1851 *NewYHSD*
Barton, Charles Harmon 1871-1930 *WhAm 1*
Barton, Charles Raymond 1891-1943
NatCAB 31
Barton, Charles Sumner 1857-1914 *ApCAB X*
Barton, Charles William 1887-1956 *WhAm 3*
Barton, Clara 1821-1912 *AmBi, DcAmB,*
DcAmReB, EncAB, McGEWB,
NatCAB 15, NotAW, WebAB, WebAMB,
WhAm 1
Barton, Clara 1826-1912 *NatCAB 3*
Barton, Clara 1830?-1912 *AmWom, ApCAB*
Barton, Clarissa Harlowe 1821-1912 *TwCBDA*
Barton, David d1837 *BiAUS*
Barton, David 1783-1837 *BiDrAC, DcAmB S1,*
REnAW, WhAm H, WhAmP
Barton, David 1785?-1837 *ApCAB, NatCAB 7,*
TwCBDA
Barton, Donald Clinton 1889-1939 *NatCAB 40,*
WhAm 1
Barton, Edgar F *NewYHSD*
Barton, Sir Edmund 1849-1920 *McGEWB*
Barton, Edmund Mills 1838- *TwCBDA,*
WhAm 4

Barton, Enos Melancthon 1842-1916
NatCAB 14, NatCAB 30, WhAm 1
Barton, Francis Brown 1886-1971 *WhAm 5*
Barton, George 1866-1940 *WhAm 1*
Barton, George Aaron 1859-1942 *DcAmB S3,*
WhAm 2
Barton, George Hunt 1852-1933 *WhAm 1*
Barton, George Preston 1851-1925 *ApCAB X*
Barton, Guy Conger 1839- *NatCAB 13*
Barton, Herbert Jewett 1853-1933 *NatCAB 25*
Barton, James d1848 *WhAm H*
Barton, James Casper 1885-1956 *NatCAB 43*
Barton, James Levi 1855-1936 *DcAmB S2,*
NatCAB 27, WhAm 1
Barton, James Moore 1846-1926 *WhAm 1*
Barton, James Pierce 1817-1891 *NewYHSD*
Barton, John Kennedy 1853-1921 *WhAm 1*
Barton, John Pembroke 1845- *WhoColR*
Barton, John Rhea 1794-1871 *DcAmB,*
NatCAB 22, WhAm H
Barton, John Wynne 1892-1936 *WhAm 1*
Barton, Joseph Wesley 1881- *WhAm 6*
Barton, L H *NewYHSD*
Barton, Lela Viola 1901-1967 *WhAm 5*
Barton, Levi Elder 1870- *WhAm 5*
Barton, Loren Roberta 1893- *IlBEAAW*
Barton, M *NewYHSD*
Barton, Nathan Bowen 1853-1917 *NatCAB 17*
Barton, Olive Roberts 1880-1957 *WhAm 3*
Barton, Peter *NewYHSD*
Barton, Philip Price 1865- *WhAm 4*
Barton, Ralph 1891-1931 *WhAm 1*
Barton, Ralph Martin 1875-1941 *WhAm 2*
Barton, Randolph 1844- *WhAm 4*
Barton, Richard Walker 1800-1859 *BiAUS,*
BiDrAC, WhAm H
Barton, Robert McKinney 1851-1928 *WhAm 1*
Barton, Robert Thomas 1842-1917 *DcAmB,*
NatCAB 7, WhAm 1
Barton, Rose Mayard *WomWWA 14*
Barton, Samuel *NewYHSD*
Barton, Samuel 1785-1858 *BiAUS, BiDrAC,*
WhAm H
Barton, Samuel Marx 1859-1926 *WhAm 1*
Barton, Seth 1795-1850 *BiAUS, NatCAB 13*
Barton, Seth Maxwell 1829-1900 *DcAmB*
Barton, Silas Reynolds 1872-1915 *WhAm 1*
Barton, Silas Reynolds 1872-1916 *BiDrAC*
Barton, Stephen Emory 1848- *WhAm 4*
Barton, Thomas 1730-1780 *ApCAB, TwCBDA*
Barton, Thomas Harry 1881-1960 *WhAm 4*
Barton, Thomas Pennant 1803-1869 *ApCAB,*
DcAmB, NatCAB 14, WhAm H
Barton, Wilfred Mason 1871-1930 *WhAm 1*
Barton, William 1747-1831 *Drake*
Barton, William 1748-1831 *AmBi, ApCAB,*
DcAmB, NatCAB 1, TwCBDA,
WebAMB, WhAm H
Barton, William Edward 1868-1955 *BiDrAC,*
WhAm 5
Barton, William Eleazar 1861-1930 *ApCAB X,*
DcAmB S1, NatCAB 17, NatCAB 42,
WhAm 1
Barton, William Henry, Jr. 1893-1944 *WhAm 2*
Barton, William P C d1855 *Drake*
Barton, William Paul Crillon 1786-1856 *AmBi,*
ApCAB, DcAmB, NatCAB 13,.
NewYHSD, TwCBDA, WhAm H
Bartow, Bernard 1849-1920 *NatCAB 21*
Bartow, Charles K 1889-1957 *WhAm 3*
Bartow, Edward 1870-1958 *NatCAB 46,*
WhAm 3
Bartow, Francis Dwight 1881-1945 *WhAm 2*
Bartow, Francis Stebbins 1816-1861 *BiDConf,*
Drake
Bartow, Harry Edwards 1877- *WhAm 5*
Bartram, John 1699-1777 *AmBi, ApCAB,*
DcAmB, DcScB, Drake, EncAAH,
McGEWB, NatCAB 7, NewYHSD,
REnAW, TwCBDA, WebAB, WhAm H
Bartram, William 1739-1823 *AmBi, ApCAB,*
DcAmB, DcScB, Drake, McGEWB,
NatCAB 7, NewYHSD, TwCBDA,
WebAB, WhAm H
Bartran, William Henry 1874-1950 *NatCAB 40*
Bartsch, Edward 1895-1966 *WhAm 4*
Bartsch, Paul 1871-1960 *WhAm 4*

Bartter, Frances Crosby Buffington
WomWWA 14a

Baruch, Bernard Mannes 1870-1965 *ApCAB X,*
EncAAH, EncAB, McGEWB, WebAB,
WhAm 4, WhAmP, WhWW-II

Baruch, Dorothy Walter 1899-1962 *WhAm 4*

Baruch, Emanuel DeMarnay 1870-1935
WhAm 1

Baruch, Harry Nathan 1874-1927 *ApCAB X*

Baruch, Herman Benjamin 1872-1953
NatCAB 39, WhAm 3

Baruch, Simon 1840-1921 *AmBi, ApCAB X,*
DcAmB, NatCAB 18, WhAm 1

Baruch, Sydney Norton 1895-1959 *WhAm 3*

Baruh, Joseph Y 1868-1960 *WhAm 4*

Barus, Annie G 1855- *WomWWA 14*

Barus, Annie Howes *WhAm 5*

Barus, Carl 1856-1935 *AmBi, ApCAB Sup,*
DcAmB S1, DcScB, NatCAB 13,
NatCAB 26, TwCBDA, WhAm 1

Baruth, Ralph Howard 1888-1947 *WhAm 2*

Barwell-Walker, Francis John 1881- *WhAm 6*

Barwig, Charles 1837-1912 *BiDrAC*

Barwise, Joseph Hudson 1868-1941 *NatCAB 33*

Barwise, Seth William 1900-1965 *NatCAB 52*

Bary, Heinrich Anton De *DcScB*

Barzini, Luigi 1874- *WhAm 5*

Barzun, Jacques Martin 1907- *WebAB*

Barzynski, Joseph E 1884-1972 *WhAm 5*

Barzynski, Vincent 1838-1899 *DcAmB,*
WhAm H

Basaldella, Mirko 1910- *WhAm 5*

Basch, Antonin 1896-1971 *WhAm 5*

Bascom, Andrew J *NewYHSD*

Bascom, Elva Lucile 1870- *WomWWA 14*

Bascom, Emma Curtiss 1828- *AmWom*

Bascom, Florence 1862-1945 *BiCAW,*
DcAmB S3, NotAW, WhAm 2,
WomWWA 14

Bascom, Henry Bidleman 1796-1850 *AmBi,*
ApCAB, DcAmB, Drake, NatCAB 4,
TwCBDA, WhAm H

Bascom, Henry Clay 1844-1896 *NatCAB 12*

Bascom, John 1827-1911 *AmBi, ApCAB,*
BiDAmEd, DcAmB, NatCAB 8,
TwCBDA, WhAm 1

Bascom, Ruth Henshaw Miles 1772-1848
BnEnAmA, NewYHSD

Bascom, Wyman Samuel 1885-1966
NatCAB 54

Basdevant, Jules 1877-1968 *WhAm 5*

Basdevant, Pierre Jules 1914-1968 *WhAm 4A*

Base, Daniel 1869-1926 *WhAm 1*

Basedow, Johann Bernhard 1724-1790
McGEWB

Basedow, Karl Adolph Von 1799-1854 *BiHiMed*

Basehore, Samuel Elmer 1875-1962 *NatCAB 50*

Bash, Appleton 1862- *NatCAB 8*

Bash, Bertha Runkle *WomWWA 14*

Bash, Louis Hermann 1872-1952 *NatCAB 40,*
WhAm 3

Basham, Frederick *NewYHSD*

Bashev, Ivan Hristov 1916-1972 *WhAm 5*

Bashford, Coles 1816-1878 *ApCAB, BiAUS,*
BiDrAC, DcAmB, NatCAB 12, TwCBDA,
WhAm H, WhAmP

Bashford, Herbert 1871-1928 *NatCAB 26,*
WhAm 1

Bashford, James Whitford 1849-1919 *AmBi,*
DcAmB, NatCAB 4, TwCBDA,
WhAm 1

Bashford, Jane Field 1853- *WomWWA 14*

Bashir, Antony 1898-1966 *WhAm 4*

Basho, Matsuo 1644-1694 *McGEWB*

Bashore, Harry William 1880-1973 *WhAm 5*

Bashore, Harvey Brown 1864-1934 *WhAm 1*

Basie, William 1904- *WebAB*

Basil I 812?-886 *McGEWB*

Basil II 958?-1025 *McGEWB*

Basil The Great, Saint 329-379 *McGEWB*

Basil Valentine *DcScB*

Basil, George Chester 1902-1954 *NatCAB 46*

Basile, Anthony Robert 1918-1973 *WhAm 6*

Basilio DeGama, Jose 1740-1795? *Drake*

Basing, Charles 1865- *WhAm 4*

Basinger, Clair Eugene 1921-1971 *NatCAB 56*

Basinger, William S 1873-1948 *WhAm 3*

Baskervill, Charles Read 1872-1935 *WhAm 1*

Baskervill, William Malone 1850-1899
TwCBDA

Baskervill, William Malone 1888-1953 *WhAm 3*

Baskerville, Charles 1870-1922 *DcAmB,*
NatCAB 13, WhAm 1

Baskerville, H Coleman 1905-1969 *NatCAB 55*

Baskerville, Harry Herbert 1880-1949
NatCAB 38

Baskett, James Newton 1849-1925 *NatCAB 13,*
WhAm 1

Baskette, Gideon Hicks 1845-1927 *NatCAB 8,*
TwCBDA, WhAm 1

Baskin, Charles Llewellyn 1882-1959
NatCAB 48

Baskin, Eldridge 1873-1957 *NatCAB 45*

Baskin, Leonard 1922- *BnEnAmA, WebAB*

Baskin, Morris Jacob 1895-1953 *NatCAB 42*

Baskin, Robert N *WhAm 5*

Basov, Nikolai Gennadievich 1922- *AsBiEn*

Basquin, Olin Hanson 1869-1946 *WhAm 2*

Basralian, Joseph Bedros 1901-1972
NatCAB 57

Bass, Albert Theodore 1870-1928 *NatCAB 22*

Bass, Charles Cassedy 1875- *WhAm 5*

Bass, Charlotta A 1890- *WhAmP*

Bass, Clare Reynolds 1879- *WomWWA 14*

Bass, Edgar Wales 1843-1918 *WhAm 1*

Bass, Edward *NewYHSD*

Bass, Edward 1726-1803 *ApCAB, DcAmB,*
Drake, NatCAB 6, TwCBDA, WhAm H

Bass, Edward 1760?-1847 *NewYHSD*

Bass, Elizabeth d1950 *WhAm 3*

Bass, Elizabeth 1876-1956 *NatCAB 45*

Bass, Frederic Herbert 1875-1954 *WhAm 3*

Bass, George Arthur 1864- *WhAm 4,*
WhAm 5

Bass, Harry W *WhoColR*

Bass, Ivan Ernest 1877-1967 *WhAm 4*

Bass, John Foster 1866-1931 *NatCAB 23,*
WhAm 1

Bass, John Henry 1835-1922 *NatCAB 20*

Bass, John Meredith 1845-1908 *WhAm 1*

Bass, Joseph Parker 1835-1919 *WhAm 1*

Bass, Leo 1878-1951 *WhAm 3*

Bass, Lyman Kidder 1836-1889 *BiAUS,*
BiDrAC, WhAm H

Bass, Lyman Metcalfe d1955 *WhAm 3*

Bass, Nathan 1808-1890 *BiDConf*

Bass, Perkins 1827-1899 *NatCAB 20*

Bass, Perkins 1912- *BiDrAC, WhAmP*

Bass, Ray Spurgeon 1895-1954 *WhAm 3*

Bass, Ray Spurgeon 1895-1955 *NatCAB 46*

Bass, Robert Perkins 1873-1960 *WhAm 4*

Bass, Ross 1918- *BiDrAC*

Bass, Sam 1851-1878 *DcAmB, REnAW,*
WebAB, WhAm H

Bass, Ula Leffentz 1868- *WomWWA 14*

Bass, Ula LeHentz 1868- *WhAm 4*

Bass, William Capers 1831-1894 *DcAmB,*
NatCAB 5, WhAm H

Bassani, Francesco 1853-1916 *DcScB*

Basse, Jeremiah d1725 *DcAmB, WhAm H*

Basset, William Rupert 1883-1953 *WhAm 3*

Bassett, Adelaide Florence 1845- *WhAm 4,*
WomWWA 14

Bassett, Allan Lee 1827-1892 *NatCAB 5*

Bassett, Austin Bradley 1859-1916 *WhAm 1*

Bassett, Burwell 1764-1841 *BiAUS, BiDrAC,*
WhAm H, WhAmP

Bassett, Carrol Phillips 1863-1952 *NatCAB 5*

Bassett, Carroll Phillips 1863-1952 *WhAm 3*

Bassett, Charles A, II 1931-1966 *WhAm 4*

Bassett, Charles Franklin 1862-1916
NatCAB 25

Bassett, Charles Nebeker 1880-1944 *WhAm 2*

Bassett, E D *BiAUS*

Bassett, Ebenezer Don Carlos 1833-1908
ApCAB, NatCAB 13, WhAm 1

Bassett, Edward Murray 1863-1948 *BiDrAC,*
DcAmB S4, NatCAB 44, WhAm 2

Bassett, Florence Shust Knoll 1917- *BnEnAmA*

Bassett, George Jarvis 1869-1954 *WhAm 3*

Bassett, Harry Hoxie 1875-1926 *NatCAB 50*

Bassett, Harry Winfred 1875- *WhAm 5*

Bassett, Helen Chase 1873- *WomWWA 14*

Bassett, Homer Franklin 1826-1902 *NatCAB 6,*
TwCBDA

Bassett, Iona H 1829?- *NewYHSD*

Bassett, J D, Jr. d1966 *WhAm 4*

Bassett, James 1834-1906 *AmBi, ApCAB,*
DcAmB, TwCBDA

Bassett, John 1886-1958 *WhAm 3*

Bassett, John David, Sr. 1866-1965 *WhAm 4*

Bassett, John Samuel 1830-1912 *NatCAB 16*

Bassett, John Spencer 1867-1928 *AmBi,*
DcAmB, NatCAB 41, WhAm 1

Bassett, Karolyn Wells 1892- *BiCAW*

Bassett, Lee Emerson 1872- *WhAm 5*

Bassett, Louis D 1904-1972 *WhAm 6*

Bassett, Neal 1871-1947 *WhAm 5*

Bassett, Norman Earle 1869-1931 *WhAm 1*

Bassett, Reveau Mott 1897- *IIBEAAW*

Bassett, Richard 1745-1815 *ApCAB, BiAUS,*
BiDrAC, DcAmB, Drake, NatCAB 11,
TwCBDA, WhAm H, WhAmP

Bassett, Royal, III 1900-1966 *WhAm 4*

Bassett, Samuel Eliot 1873-1936 *NatCAB 28,*
WhAm 1

Bassett, Samuel Hopkins 1897-1962
NatCAB 49

Bassett, Sara Ware 1872- *BiCAW, WhAm 5*

Bassett, Thomas J 1848- *WhAm 4*

Bassett, W H *NewYHSD*

Bassett, W M d1960 *WhAm 4*

Bassett, William 1656-1721 *NatCAB 19*

Bassett, William Austin 1876-1929 *WhAm 1*

Bassett, William Hastings 1868-1934
DcAmB S1, NatCAB 26, WhAm 1

Bassette, Roy Donald 1883-1965 *NatCAB 51*

Bassford, Homer S 1870-1938 *WhAm 1*

Bassford, Horace Richardson 1889-1952
WhAm 3

Bassi, Agostino Maria 1773-1856 *DcScB*

Bassi, Amadeo 1876- *WhAm 5*

Bassie, Adele *NewYHSD*

Bassill, John E 1896-1959 *WhAm 3*

Bassini, Carlo 1812-1870 *ApCAB, Drake*

Bassini, Edoardo 1844-1924 *BiHiMed*

Bassler, Anthony 1874-1959 *WhAm 3*

Bassler, Ray Smith 1878-1961 *NatCAB 49,*
WhAm 6

Bassler, Raymond Smith 1878-1961 *DcScB*

Basso, Hamilton 1904-1964 *WhAm 4*

Basso, Sebastian *DcScB*

Bastedo, Paul Henry 1887-1951 *NatCAB 39,*
WhAm 3

Basterot *NewYHSD*

Bastian, Henry Charlton 1837-1915 *DcScB*

Bastian, John 1832?- *NewYHSD*

Bastian, Robert Owen 1917-1970 *WhAm 5*

Bastian, Walter Maximillian 1891-1975
WhAm 6

Bastianini, Ettore d1967 *WhAm 4*

Bastico, Ettore *WhWW-II*

Bastidas, Rodriguez De 1460?- *ApCAB*

Bastide, John Henry 1710- *ApCAB*

Bastin, Edson Sewell *NatCAB 5*

Bastin, Edson Sunderland 1878-1953 *WhAm 3*

Bastin, Frank Joseph 1872-1937 *NatCAB 35*

Bastress, Edgar Ralph 1891-1931 *NatCAB 23*

Bastrup, Louis 1856-1914 *NatCAB 16*

Basye, Arthur Herbert 1884-1958 *NatCAB 48*

Basyn, Thomas 1898-1962 *WhAm 4*

Bataillon, Jean Eugene 1864-1953 *DcScB*

Batchelder *NewYHSD*

Batchelder, Alice Lizzie *WomWWA 14*

Batchelder, Ann 1881-1955 *WhAm 3*

Batchelder, Charles Clarence 1867-1946
WhAm 2

Batchelder, Charles Foster 1856-1954 *WhAm 3*

Batchelder, Edward Trumbull 1906-1950
WhAm 3

Batchelder, Ernest Allen 1876- *WhAm 5*

Batchelder, Francis 1847-1926 *NatCAB 23*

Batchelder, Frank Charles 1857-1931 *WhAm 1,*
WhAm 1C

Batchelder, Frank Roe 1869-1947 *NatCAB 34*

Batchelder, Horton 1880-1956 *NatCAB 45*

Batchelder, John Putnam 1784-1868 *ApCAB,*
DcAmB, NatCAB 9, WhAm H

Batchelder, Loren Harrison 1846- *WhAm 4*

Batchelder, Mark Daniel 1868-1935
NatCAB 31

Batchelder, Nathaniel Horton 1880-1956
WhAm 3

Batchelder, Richard N 1832-1901 *TwCBDA,*

WhAm 1

Batchelder, Roger 1897-1947 *WhAm 2*

Batchelder, Samuel 1784-1879 *ApCAB, DcAmB, Drake, NatCAB 5, TwCBDA, WhAm H*

Batchelder, Wallace 1875-1919 *WhAm 1*

Batchell, Charles Willard 1892-1965 *NatCAB 52*

Batcheller, Birney Clark 1865-1950 *NatCAB 38*

Batcheller, Frederick S 1837-1889 *NewYHSD*

Batcheller, George Clinton 1834-1915 *NatCAB 4, WhAm 1*

Batcheller, George Sherman 1836-1908 *NatCAB 4*

Batcheller, George Sherman 1837-1908 *DcAmB, WhAm 1, WhAmP*

Batcheller, Hiland Garfield 1885-1961 *WhAm 4*

Batcheller, Tryphosa Bates d1952 *BiCAW, WhAm 3*

Batchelor, George 1836-1923 *DcAmB, WhAm 1*

Batchelor, Horace 1887-1963 *WhAm 4*

Batchelor, James Madison 1870- *WhAm 5*

Batchelor, Joseph B 1825- *TwCBDA*

Batchman, John M 1874- *WhoColR*

Batdorf, Grant David 1874-1954 *WhAm 3*

Bate, Florence E *WomWWA 14*

Bate, Henry *DcScB*

Bate, Henry Clay 1839-1917 *NatCAB 2*

Bate, John W 1857- *WhoColR*

Bate, R Alexander 1871-1956 *NatCAB 46*

Bate, William Bremage 1826-1905 *ApCAB Sup, TwCBDA*

Bate, William Brimage 1826-1905 *AmBi, BiDConf, BiDrAC, DcAmB, WhAm 1, WhAmP*

Bate, William Brimage 1830-1905 *NatCAB 7*

Bateham, Josephine A Penfield Cushman 1829-1901 *AmWom, NotAW*

Bateholts, Clinton L 1880-1943 *NatCAB 33*

Bateman, Alan Mara 1889-1971 *WhAm 5*

Bateman, Charles E *NewYHSD*

Bateman, Charles Heisler 1861-1934 *WhAm 1*

Bateman, Clifford Harris 1890-1957 *NatCAB 43*

Bateman, E Allen 1895-1960 *WhAm 4*

Bateman, Ellen *WebAB*

Bateman, Ephraim d1829 *BiAUS*

Bateman, Ephraim 1770-1829 *ApCAB, Drake, NatCAB 12, TwCBDA*

Bateman, Ephraim 1780-1829 *BiDrAC, WhAm H, WhAmP*

Bateman, Frank 1842-1924 *NatCAB 20*

Bateman, George Cecil 1882-1963 *WhAm 4*

Bateman, George F d1948 *WhAm 2*

Bateman, George Monroe 1897-1972 *NatCAB 56, WhAm 5*

Bateman, Harry 1882-1946 *DcAmB S4, DcScB, WhAm 2*

Bateman, Herbert D 1877-1956 *WhAm 3*

Bateman, Hezekiah Linthicum 1812-1875 *AmBi, WebAB*

Bateman, Isabel 1854- *AmWom*

Bateman, J Fremont 1897-1952 *NatCAB 42*

Bateman, John 1877-1955 *WhAm 3*

Bateman, John Henry 1892-1953 *NatCAB 42, WhAm 3*

Bateman, Kate Josephine d1917 *WebAB*

Bateman, Kate Josephine 1842-1917 *AmWom, ApCAB, Drake, NatCAB 10, NotAW, TwCBDA*

Bateman, Kate Josephine 1843-1917 *AmBi, DcAmB*

Bateman, Newton 1822-1897 *AmBi, ApCAB, BiDAmEd, DcAmB, NatCAB 27, TwCBDA, WhAm H*

Bateman, Robert Johnston 1879-1943 *WhAm 2*

Bateman, Sidney Frances Cowell 1823-1881 *DcAmB, NotAW, WebAB, WhAm H*

Bateman, Thomas 1778-1821 *BiHiMed*

Bateman, Warner Mifflin 1827-1897 *NatCAB 19*

Bateman, William *NewYHSD*

Baten, Anderson Edith 1855- *WhAm 1*

Baten, Anderson Monroe 1888-1943 *WhAm 2*

Bates *NewYHSD*

Bates, Albert Carlos 1865- *WhAm 5*

Bates, Albert H 1869-1952 *WhAm 3*

Bates, Alexander Berry 1842-1917 *WhAm 1*

Bates, Alfred Elliott 1840-1909 *ApCAB Sup, NatCAB 13, TwCBDA, WhAm 1*

Bates, Alva Lillistone 1888-1958 *NatCAB 43*

Bates, Arlo 1850-1918 *AmBi, ApCAB, DcAmB, NatCAB 8, TwCBDA, WhAm 1*

Bates, Arthur Laban 1859-1934 *ApCAB X, BiDrAC, WhAm 1, WhAmP*

Bates, Barnabas 1785-1853 *ApCAB, DcAmB, Drake, TwCBDA, WhAm H*

Bates, Barton 1824-1891 *NatCAB 12*

Bates, Benjamin E 1808-1878 *NatCAB 21*

Bates, Blanche 1873-1941 *DcAmB S3, NotAW, WhAm 1, WhAm 2, WomWWA 14*

Bates, Charles Austin 1866- *NatCAB 15, WhAm 4*

Bates, Charles Woodson 1864-1928 *NatCAB 21*

Bates, Charlotte Fisk 1838-1916 *NatCAB 13*

Bates, Charlotte Fiske 1838-1916 *AmWom, ApCAB, TwCBDA, WhAm 1, WomWWA 14*

Bates, Clara Doty 1838-1895 *AmWom*

Bates, Clara Nettie 1876- *WomWWA 14*

Bates, Clement 1845-1931 *NatCAB 23, WhAm 1, WhAm 1C*

Bates, Clinton Owen 1858- *WhAm 4*

Bates, Creed Fulton 1848-1928 *NatCAB 23*

Bates, Daisy Mae 1861-1951 *McGEWB*

Bates, Daniel Moore 1821-1879 *DcAmB, NatCAB 13, WhAm H, WhAmP*

Bates, Daniel Moore 1876-1953 *NatCAB 40*

Bates, David 1810?-1870 *ApCAB, NatCAB 4*

Bates, David Stanhope 1777-1839 *ApCAB, NatCAB 18, TwCBDA, WhAm H*

Bates, Dewey 1851- *ApCAB*

Bates, Eda Tibbles 1868-1950 *NatCAB 37*

Bates, Edith Talcott *WomWWA 14*

Bates, Edward 1793-1869 *AmBi, ApCAB, BiAUS, BiDrAC, BiDrUSE, DcAmB, Drake, NatCAB 2, REnAW, TwCBDA, WebAB, WhAm H, WhAmP*

Bates, Emer D 1885-1962 *NatCAB 49, WhAm 4*

Bates, Emily Rusling 1884- *WomWWA 14*

Bates, Emma *WomWWA 14*

Bates, Emma Frances Duncan 1845-1929 *BiCAW, WhAm 1, WomWWA 14*

Bates, Ernest Sutherland 1879-1939 *AmBi, WhAm 1*

Bates, Frederick 1777-1825 *ApCAB, BiAUS, DcAmB, NatCAB 12, WhAm H, WhAmP*

Bates, Frederick 1877-1958 *WhAm 3*

Bates, George Andrew 1847-1925 *WhAm 1*

Bates, George Dennis 1866-1932 *WhAm 1*

Bates, George Handy 1845-1916 *DcAmB, WhAm HA, WhAm 4, WhAmP*

Bates, George Harold 1877-1965 *NatCAB 52*

Bates, George Joseph 1891-1949 *BiDrAC, NatCAB 39, WhAm 2, WhAmP*

Bates, George W 1851- *WhAm 1*

Bates, George Williams 1848- *WhAm 1*

Bates, H Boswell 1870-1931 *NatCAB 18*

Bates, Harriet Hegar 1921-1974 *WhAm 6*

Bates, Harriet Leonora Vose 1856-1886 *NatCAB 8, WhAm H*

Bates, Harry C 1882-1969 *WhAm 5*

Bates, Harry Cole 1891-1948 *WhAm 2*

Bates, Helen Page 1860- *WomWWA 14*

Bates, Henry Clay 1843-1909 *WhAm 1*

Bates, Henry Liberty 1853-1949 *NatCAB 43, WhAm 4*

Bates, Henry Moore 1869-1949 *WhAm 2*

Bates, Henry Walter 1825-1892 *ApCAB, DcScB, McGEWB*

Bates, Herbert 1868-1929 *NatCAB 21, WhAm 1*

Bates, Herbert Ernest 1905-1974 *WhAm 6*

Bates, Isaac Chapman 1779-1845 *BiDrAC, WhAm H, WhAmP*

Bates, Isaac Chapman 1780-1845 *ApCAB, BiAUS, Drake, NatCAB 3, TwCBDA*

Bates, Isaac Chapman 1817-1875 *ApCAB*

Bates, J Herbert 1884-1963 *NatCAB 50*

Bates, J Woodson 1788-1846 *BiAUS*

Bates, James 1789-1882 *BiAUS, BiDrAC, DcAmB, NatCAB 21, WhAm H*

Bates, James L 1880-1962 *WhAm 4*

Bates, James Woodson 1788-1846 *BiAUS, BiDrAC, WhAm H*

Bates, Jefferson Blakely 1896-1966 *NatCAB 53, WhAm 4*

Bates, John· *WhAm H*

Bates, John Coalter 1842-1919 *DcAmB, NatCAB 14, TwCBDA, WebAMB, WhAm 1*

Bates, John Lewis 1859- *NatCAB 10, TwCBDA, WhAm 2*

Bates, Joseph Baxter 1841-1917 *NatCAB 25*

Bates, Joseph Bengal 1893-1965 *BiDrAC, WhAmP*

Bates, Josephine White *WhAm 5*

Bates, Joshua 1776-1854 *ApCAB, Drake, NatCAB 12*

Bates, Joshua 1788-1864 *ApCAB, DcAmB, Drake, NatCAB 5, TwCBDA, WhAm H*

Bates, Joshua H 1817?- *ApCAB*

Bates, Juanita Breckenridge 1860- *WomWWA 14*

Bates, Katharine Lee 1859-1929 *AmBi, AmWom, BiDAmEd, NatCAB 9, NatCAB 42, NotAW, TwCBDA, WebAB, WhAm 1*

Bates, Katherine Lee 1859-1929 *DcAmB S1, WomWWA 14*

Bates, Lewis Elon 1910-1972 *WhAm 6*

Bates, Lindon Wallace 1858-1924 *NatCAB 15, WhAm 1*

Bates, Lindon Wallace, Jr. 1883-1915 *ApCAB X, WhAm 1*

Bates, Louise 1857- *WomWWA 14*

Bates, Margaret Holmes 1844- *AmWom, WomWWA 14*

Bates, Margret Holmes 1844- *NatCAB 10, WhAm 4*

Bates, Marston 1906-1974 *WhAm 6*

Bates, Martha Frances Sutphen 1857- *WomWWA 14*

Bates, Martin Waltham 1786-1869 *NatCAB 13*

Bates, Martin Waltham 1787-1869 *ApCAB, BiAUS, BiDrAC, TwCBDA*

Bates, Mary Elizabeth 1861- *NatCAB 18, WhAm 4, WomWWA 14*

Bates, Mary Russell 1872- *WomWWA 14*

Bates, Miner Lee 1869-1930 *WhAm 1*

Bates, Onward 1850-1936 *DcAmB S2, NatCAB 15, WhAm 1*

Bates, Oric 1883-1918 *WhAm 1*

Bates, Phaon Hilborn 1879- *WhAm 6*

Bates, Putnam Asbury 1875- *WhAm 5*

Bates, Richard Waller 1892-1973 *WhAm 6*

Bates, Robert Peck 1872-1944 *NatCAB 33*

Bates, Roxie Ellen 1855- *WomWWA 14*

Bates, Samuel Lewis 1865-1932 *NatCAB 47*

Bates, Samuel Penniman 1827-1902 *ApCAB, DcAmB, TwCBDA, WhAm 1*

Bates, Sanford 1884-1972 *WhAm 5*

Bates, Sarah Glazier 1846- *WomWWA 14*

Bates, Theodora *WomWWA 14*

Bates, Theodore Cornelius 1843-1912 *WhAm 1*

Bates, Theodore Lewis 1901-1972 *WhAm 5*

Bates, Vyrl Raymond 1903-1971 *WhAm 5*

Bates, Walter 1760-1842 *DcAmB, WhAm H*

Bates, Walter Irving 1873-1934 *WhAm 1*

Bates, William A 1853-1922 *NatCAB 19*

Bates, William Albert 1895-1964 *WhAm 4*

Bates, William Henry 1917-1969 *BiDrAC, WhAm 5, WhAmP*

Bates, William Horatio 1841-1918 *NatCAB 17*

Bates, William Horatio 1860-1931 *NatCAB 24*

Bates, William Nickerson 1867-1949 *WhAm 2*

Bates, William Oscar 1852-1924 *WhAm 1*

Bates, William Rufus 1845-1921 *NatCAB 19*

Bates, William Wallace 1827-1912 *NatCAB 1, WhAm 1*

Bateson, William 1861-1926 *AsBiEn, DcScB*

Bath, Albert Alcus 1876- *WhAm 5*

Bather, Francis Arthur 1863-1934 *DcScB*

Bather, George 1826?- *NewYHSD*

Bathier, Madame *NewYHSD*

Bathon, Wingrove 1876- *WhAm 5*

Bathrick, Ellsworth Raymond 1863-1917 *NatCAB 17, WhAm 1*

Bathrick, Elsworth Raymond 1863-1917 *BiDrAC*

Batista, Fulgencio 1901-1973 *WhAm 5*
Batista Y Zaldivar, Fulgencio 1901-1973
  McGEWB
Batjer, Lawrence Paul 1907-1967 *WhAm 5*
Batlle, Lorenzo 1812- *ApCAB*
Batlle Berres, Luis d1964 *WhAm 4*
Batlle Y Ordonez, Jose 1856-1929 *McGEWB*
Batman, Levi Gordon 1869- *WhAm 5*
Baton, Edgar F 1832?- *NewYHSD*
Baton, Henry C 1834?- *NewYHSD*
Batson, David William 1854- *WhAm 4*
Batson, Felix Ives 1819-1871 *BiDConf*
Batson, Melvina Hobson 1826-1853 *NewYHSD*
Batson, William Howard 1881-1954 *WhAm 3*
Batt, William Loren 1885-1965 *WhAm 4*
Battaglia, Dominic Thomas 1908-1963
  NatCAB 50
Battani, Abu Allah Muhammad Al-Sabi, Al-
  DcScB
Battee, John O *NewYHSD*
Battell, Joseph 1839-1915 *WhAm 1*
Battell, Robbins 1819-1895 *NatCAB 14*
Battelle, Gordon 1814-1862 *ApCAB, TwCBDA*
Battelle, John Gordon 1845-1918 *NatCAB 17*
Battels, Mary Miller 1860- *WomWWA 14*
Battels, Sarah M E 1839- *NatCAB 1,*
  WhAm 1
Batten, Charles Edward 1910-1963 *WhAm 4*
Batten, Harry Albert 1897-1966 *NatCAB 54,*
  WhAm 4
Batten, John Mullin 1837- *NatCAB 5*
Batten, Joseph Minton 1893-1954 *WhAm 3*
Batten, Loring Woart 1859-1946 *WhAm 3*
Batten, Percy Haight 1877-1960 *WhAm 4*
Batten, Samuel Zane 1859-1925 *WhAm 1*
Battenfeld, Jesse Raymond 1888-1947
  NatCAB 38
Battenhouse, Henry Martin 1885-1960
  NatCAB 51, WhAm 4
Batter, Carl John 1894-1963 *NatCAB 50*
Batterman, Henry 1849-1912 *NatCAB 47*
Batterman, Henry Lewis 1876-1961 *NatCAB 47*
Battershall, Fletcher Williams 1866- *WhAm 4*
Battershall, Jesse Park 1851-1891 *ApCAB,*
  TwCBDA
Battershall, Walton Wesley 1840-1920
  NatCAB 12, TwCBDA, WhAm 1
Batterson, Hermon Griswold 1827-1903
  ApCAB Sup, NatCAB 9, WhAm 1
Batterson, James *NewYHSD*
Batterson, James Goodwin 1823-1901
  ApCAB Sup, DcAmB, NatCAB 6,
  WhAm 1
Batterton, J *NewYHSD*
Battese, Stanley 1936- *IlBEAAW*
Battey, Emily Verdery 1828- *AmWom*
Battey, Robert 1828-1895 *AmBi, ApCAB,*
  DcAmB, NatCAB 9, TwCBDA,
  WhAm H
Battey, Sumter Beauregard *NatCAB 2*
Battier *NewYHSD*
Battin, Charles Reginald 1880-1950 *WhAm 3*
Battin, Charles Thomas 1887-1964 *WhAm 4*
Battin, James Franklin 1925- *BiDrAC*
Battin, John T 1805?- *NewYHSD*
Battin, Sylvester Strong 1829-1904 *NatCAB 13*
Battin, T *NewYHSD*
Battle, Archibald John 1826-1907 *BiDAmEd,*
  NatCAB 6, TwCBDA, WhAm 1
Battle, Augustus Allen *WhoColR*
Battle, Burrell Bunn 1838-1917 *DcAmB,*
  WhAmP
Battle, Burrill Bunn 1838-1917 *NatCAB 6,*
  WhAm 1
Battle, Charles T 1888- *WhoColR*
Battle, Cullen Andrews 1829-1905 *BiDConf,*
  DcAmB, NatCAB 12, WhAm 1, WhAmP
Battle, George Gordon 1868-1949 *NatCAB 15,*
  WhAm 2
Battle, Henry Wilson 1856- *NatCAB 12,*
  WhAm 5
Battle, Herbert Bemerton 1862-1929 *WhAm 1*
Battle, Hyman Llewellyn 1896-1973 *WhAm 5*
Battle, Jacob 1852-1916 *NatCAB 34*
Battle, John Stewart 1890-1972 *NatCAB 56,*
  WhAm 5
Battle, John Thomas Johnson 1859-1940
  WhAm 1

Battle, Kemp Davis 1888-1973 *WhAm 6*
Battle, Kemp Plummer 1831-1919 *DcAmB,*
  NatCAB 13, TwCBDA, WhAm 1
Battle, Kemp Plummer 1859-1922 *WhAm 1*
Battle, Laurie Calvin 1912- *BiDrAC*
Battle, Lorenzo 1812- *Drake*
Battle, Milan *NewYHSD*
Battle, Richard Henry 1835-1912 *NatCAB 38,*
  WhAm 1
Battle, S Westray 1854-1927 *NatCAB 27,*
  WhAm 1
Battle, Samuel Jesse 1883- *WhoColR*
Battle, Thomas Hall 1860-1936 *WhAm 1*
Battle, Wallace Aaron 1872- *WhoColR*
Battle, William Horn 1802-1879 *ApCAB,*
  BiAUS, DcAmB, NatCAB 11, TwCBDA,
  WhAm H, WhAmP
Battle, William James 1870-1955 *WhAm 3*
Battleway, James *NewYHSD*
Battley, Joseph F 1896-1970 *WhAm 5*
Batton *NewYHSD*
Batts, Arthur Alanson 1884-1953 *WhAm 3*
Batts, Robert Lynn 1864-1935 *DcAmB S1,*
  WhAm 1
Batts, William Oscar 1880- *WhAm 6*
Battuta, Ibn 1304-1368? *DcScB*
Batu Khan d1255 *McGEWB*
Batum, William Henry 1876- *WhoColR*
Baturone, Jose *NewYHSD*
Batz, A De *NewYHSD*
Bauchman, Edward *NewYHSD*
Baucom, George Urias, Jr. 1887-1963
  NatCAB 50
Baucum, A W 1910-1972 *WhAm 5*
Baudelaire, Charles Pierre 1821-1867 *McGEWB*
Bauder, Ezra 1824- *NatCAB 1*
Bauder, Reginald I 1901-1966 *WhAm 4*
Baudier, Alexander *NewYHSD*
Baudoin, Michael 1692-1768 *WhAm H*
Baudrimont, Alexandre Edouard 1806-1880
  DcScB
Bauer, Augustus 1827-1894 *WhAm H*
Bauer, Benjamin F 1864- *WhAm 4*
Bauer, Charles Christian 1881-1947 *WhAm 2*
Bauer, Charles Edward 1902-1953 *NatCAB 43*
Bauer, Edmond 1880-1963 *DcScB*
Bauer, Elizabeth Kelley 1920- *EncAAH*
Bauer, Eugene Casper 1891-1973 *WhAm 6*
Bauer, Ferdinand Lucas 1760-1826 *DcScB*
Bauer, Franz Andreas 1758-1840 *DcScB*
Bauer, Franz Karl 1917-1976 *WhAm 6*
Bauer, Frederick *NewYHSD*
Bauer, Frederick Robert 1888-1951 *NatCAB 41*
Bauer, Georg *DcScB*
Bauer, George Neander 1872-1952 *NatCAB 41,*
  WhAm 5
Bauer, H G 1903-1969 *WhAm 5*
Bauer, Harold Victor 1873-1951 *DcAmB S5,*
  WhAm 3
Bauer, Johannes Henrik 1890-1961 *WhAm 4*
Bauer, John Edward 1906-1967 *NatCAB 54*
Bauer, Leland Mason 1904-1970 *WhAm 5*
Bauer, Louis 1814- *NatCAB 5*
Bauer, Louis Agricola 1865-1932 *AmBi,*
  ApCAB X, DcAmB S1, DcScB,
  NatCAB 14, NatCAB 23, WhAm 1
Bauer, Louis Hopewell 1888-1964 *WhAm 4*
Bauer, Marion Eugenie 1887-1955 *NatCAB 43,*
  WhAm 3
Bauer, Norman 1915-1960 *NatCAB 48*
Bauer, Ralph S 1867-1941 *WhAm 1*
Bauer, Ralph Stanley 1883-1950 *WhAm 3*
Bauer, Walter 1898-1963 *WhAm 4*
Bauer, William Charles 1873-1962 *NatCAB 52,*
  WhAm 5
Bauer, William Hans d1956 *WhAm 3*
Bauer, William Waldo 1892-1967 *NatCAB 53,*
  NatCAB 54, WhAm 4A
Bauerle, Charles B *NewYHSD*
Baugh, Daniel 1836-1921 *NatCAB 19*
Baugh, Philander Valentine 1882- *WhoColR*
Baugh, Samuel Adrian 1914- *WebAB*
Baugher, A Charles 1893-1962 *WhAm 4*
Baugher, Henry L 1803?-1868 *Drake*
Baugher, Henry L 1805?-1868 *ApCAB,*
  TwCBDA
Baugher, Henry Louis 1804-1868 *DcAmB,*
  WhAm H

Baugher, Norman J 1917-1968 *WhAm 5*
Baughman, Howard Elsworth 1892-1961
  NatCAB 49
Baughman, L Victor d1906 *WhAm 1*
Baughman, Lyle Lynden 1899-1960 *WhAm 4*
Baughman, Roland 1902-1967 *WhAm 4*
Baughn, Otis James 1877-1948 *NatCAB 39*
Bauhin, Gaspard 1560-1624 *DcScB*
Bauhin, Jean 1541-1613 *DcScB*
Baukhage, Hilmar Robert 1889-1976 *WhAm 6*
Bault *NewYHSD*
Bauly, William *NewYHSD*
Baum, Dwight James 1886-1939 *NatCAB 29,*
  WhAm 1
Baum, Ellis Conrad 1895-1961 *WhAm 4*
Baum, Frank George 1870-1932 *ApCAB X,*
  WhAm 1
Baum, Friedrich d1777 *ApCAB*
Baum, Harry 1882-1959 *WhAm 3*
Baum, Harry Lester 1887-1951 *NatCAB 40*
Baum, Henry Mason 1848- *WhAm 4*
Baum, Isidor 1892-1966 *WhAm 4*
Baum, James Edwin 1887-1955 *NatCAB 57*
Baum, L Frank 1856-1919 *NatCAB 18,*
  WhAm 1
Baum, Lyman Frank 1856-1919 *AmBi,*
  ApCAB X, DcAmB, EncAAH, WebAB
Baum, M Louise *WomWWA 14*
Baum, Mary Helen 1920-1975 *WhAm 6*
Baum, Morton J 1897-1963 *WhAm 4*
Baum, Paull Franklin 1886-1964 *WhAm 4*
Baum, Vicki 1888-1960 *NatCAB 52, WhAm 4*
Baum, Walter Emerson 1884-1956 *NatCAB 45,*
  WhAm 3
Baum, William Miller, Jr. 1858- *WhAm 1*
Bauman, Edward 1828-1889 *WhAm H*
Bauman, Val Samuel 1909-1960 *WhAm 4*
Baumann, Albert 1881- *WhoColR*
Baumann, Albert Vogt 1891-1956 *NatCAB 44*
Baumann, Annie Rose Greene 1869-
  WomWWA 14
Baumann, Eugen 1846-1896 *AsBiEn*
Baumann, Frances Osgood 1875-
  WomWWA 14
Baumann, Frederick Llewellyn 1889-1967
  NatCAB 54
Baumann, Gustave 1881-1971 *IlBEAAW,*
  WhAm 6
Baumann, Rudolf 1910-1971 *WhAm 5*
Baumberger, James Percy 1892-1973 *WhAm 6*
Baume, Antoine 1728-1804 *DcScB*
Baume, Frederick d1777 *Drake*
Baume, James Simpson 1857-1919 *WhAm 1*
Baumeister, John 1849-1900 *NatCAB 12*
Baumer, Bertha d1951 *WhAm 3*
Baumes, Caleb Howard 1863-1937 *AmBi,*
  WhAm 1
Baumgardner, Evelyn Julia Groves d1973
  WhAm 6
Baumgardt, B R 1862-1935 *WhAm 1*
Baumgarten, Gustav 1837-1910 *NatCAB 12,*
  WhAm 1
Baumgarten, Gustavus E 1837-1910 *NewYHSD*
Baumgarten, Joseph 1890-1960 *NatCAB 47*
Baumgarten, Julius 1835?- *NewYHSD*
Baumgarten, William 1845-1906 *NatCAB 11*
Baumgartner, Apollinaris d1970 *WhAm 5*
Baumgartner, Helen Morgan 1877-
  WomWWA 14
Baumgartner, Josephine Mae d1973 *WhAm 6*
Baumgartner, N A *NewYHSD*
Baumgartner, Warren William 1894-1963
  WhAm 4
Baumgartner, William Jacob 1871- *WhAm 5*
Baumgras, Peter 1827-1904 *NatCAB 10,*
  NewYHSD
Baumhart, Albert David, Jr. 1908- *BiDrAC*
Baumhauer, Edouard Henri Von 1820-1885
  DcScB
Baumhauer, Heinrich Adolf 1848-1926 *DcScB*
Baumhofer, Walter Martin 1904- *IlBEAAW*
Baunach, Charles *NewYHSD*
Baur, Bertha 1862-1940 *NatCAB 31,*
  WhAm 1
Baur, Bertha E d1940 *WhAm 3*
Baur, Bertha E d1967 *WhAm 4A*
Baur, Clara d1912 *NatCAB 26, WhAm 1*
Baur, Ferdinand Christian 1792-1860 *McGEWB*

Baur, George A *NewYHSD*

Baur, Theodore 1835- *IlBEAAW*

Bausa, Felipe 1760?-1833 *ApCAB*

Bausch, Edward 1854-1944 *DcAmB S3,
WhAm 2*

Bausch, John Jacob 1830-1926 *WhAm 1*

Bausch, William 1861-1944 *WhAm 2*

Bauslin, David Henry 1854-1922 *WhAm 1*

Bausman, Benjamin 1824-1909 *DcAmB,
WhAm 1*

Bausman, Frederick 1861-1931 *WhAm 1*

Bausman, John Watts Baer 1855-1940
NatCAB 38, WhAm 1

Bausmon, Benjamin 1824- *TwCBDA*

Bautista, Jose *ApCAB*

Bautista, Juan 1555-1612? *ApCAB*

Bautz, Robert August 1867-1933 *NatCAB 26*

Bautze, Frank Augustus 1915-1966 *NatCAB 52*

Bauvais, A *BiAUS*

Bawden, Sir Frederick Charles 1908- *AsBiEn*

Bawden, John 1827- *NatCAB 3*

Bawden, Samuel Day 1868-1946 *WhAm 2*

Bawden, Sarah Elizabeth *WomWWA 14*

Bawden, William Thomas 1875-1960 *BiDAmEd,
WhAm 5*

Baxendale, Esther Minerva 1846- *WhAm 4*

Baxeres, Jose DeAlzugaray 1865-1937
NatCAB 27

Baxley, Henry Willis 1803-1876 *DcAmB,
WhAm H*

Baxley, William Ward 1903-1959 *NatCAB 48*

Baxter, Algernon Sidney 1819-1897
ApCAB Sup

Baxter, Annie White 1864- *AmWom,
TwCBDA*

Baxter, Arthur Reyburn 1876-1957 *NatCAB 47*

Baxter, Batsell 1886-1956 *WhAm 3*

Baxter, Blanche Weber *WomWWA 14*

Baxter, Bruce Richard 1892-1947 *NatCAB 38,
WhAm 2*

Baxter, Charles 1813-1847 *NatCAB 9*

Baxter, Charles Minturn 1862-1941
NatCAB 30

Baxter, Chauncey Buel 1888-1957 *NatCAB 46*

Baxter, Clarence Hughson 1858- *WhAm 1*

Baxter, DeWitt C 1829?- *NewYHSD*

Baxter, Dow Vawter 1898-1965 *NatCAB 53*

Baxter, Dow Vawter 1898-1966 *WhAm 4*

Baxter, Earl Hayes 1892-1971 *NatCAB 57,
WhAm 5*

Baxter, Edgar *NewYHSD*

Baxter, Edmund Dillabunty 1838-1910
WhAm 1

Baxter, Edmund Francis 1900-1967 *WhAm 4A*

Baxter, Elijah 1848-1939 *NatCAB 29*

Baxter, Elisha 1827-1899 *ApCAB, BiAUS,
DcAmB, NatCAB 10, TwCBDA,
WhAm H, WhAmP*

Baxter, Florus Randall 1857-1944 *NatCAB 34*

Baxter, George Addison 1771-1841 *Drake,
NatCAB 2*

Baxter, George Edwin 1874-1966 *WhAm 4,
WhAm 5*

Baxter, George Owen 1892-1944 *WebAB*

Baxter, George Simpson 1879-1955 *NatCAB 47*

Baxter, George Strong 1845-1928 *WhAm 1*

Baxter, George White 1855-1929 *NatCAB 23*

Baxter, Gregory Paul 1876-1953 *NatCAB 52,
WhAm 5*

Baxter, H R 1901-1964 *WhAm 4*

Baxter, Henry 1821-1873 *ApCAB, BiAUS,
DcAmB, NatCAB 4, TwCBDA,
WhAm H*

Baxter, Howard Wentworth 1896-1957
NatCAB 46

Baxter, Irving Franklin 1863- *WhAm 1*

Baxter, James Phinney 1831-1921 *AmBi,
ApCAB Sup, NatCAB 9, TwCBDA,
WhAm 1*

Baxter, James Phinney, III 1893-1975 *WhAm 6*

Baxter, Jedediah Hyde 1837-1890 *NatCAB 4*

Baxter, Jere 1852-1904 *WhAm 1*

Baxter, John d1866 *ApCAB*

Baxter, John 1819-1886 *DcAmB, NatCAB 11,
TwCBDA, WhAm H*

Baxter, John Babington Macaulay 1868-1946
WhAm 2

Baxter, John Brown 1876-1940 *NatCAB 39*

Baxter, John Crichton 1877-1933 *NatCAB 24*

Baxter, Lionel David MacKenzie 1889-
WhAm 3

Baxter, Lydia 1809-1874 *ApCAB, TwCBDA*

Baxter, Marion Babcock 1850- *AmWom,
TwCBDA*

Baxter, Martha Wheeler *WomWWA 14*

Baxter, Milton Seneca Stephen 1856-1938
NatCAB 30

Baxter, Nathaniel, Jr. 1844-1913 *NatCAB 15*

Baxter, Norman Washington 1891-1952
WhAm 3

Baxter, Percival Proctor 1876-1969 *WhAm 5*

Baxter, Portus 1806-1868 *BiAUS, BiDrAC,
WhAm H, WhAmP*

Baxter, Richard 1615-1691 *McGEWB*

Baxter, Sylvester 1850-1927 *WhAm 1*

Baxter, W H *NewYHSD*

Baxter, Warner 1889-1951 *NatCAB 39*

Baxter, Warner 1891-1951 *WhAm 3*

Baxter, William 1820-1880 *DcAmB, WhAm H*

Baxter, William 1823?-1880 *ApCAB*

Baxter, William Fales 1868-1938 *NatCAB 28*

Baxter, William Henry 1889-1970 *NatCAB 40*

Baxter, William Joseph 1899-1970 *WhAm 5*

Baxter, William M 1850- *NatCAB 3*

Bay, Charles Ulrick 1888-1955 *WhAm 3*

Bay, Elihu Hall 1754-1838 *Drake*

Bay, Jens Christian 1871-1962 *DcAmLiB,
NatCAB 50, WhAm 4*

Bay, Robert Parke 1884-1940 *NatCAB 29*

Bay, William Frederick 1872-1950 *NatCAB 40*

Bay, William VanNess 1818-1894 *BiAUS,
BiDrAC, WhAm H*

Bayard, Edwin Stanton 1867- *WhAm 3*

Bayard, Fairfax 1874- *WhAm 5*

Bayard, George Dashiell 1835-1862 *ApCAB,
Drake, NatCAB 9, TwCBDA*

Bayard, James A 1767-1815 *BiAUS*

Bayard, James Asheton 1767-1815 *AmBi,
ApCAB, BiDrAC, NatCAB 7, TwCBDA,
WhAm H, WhAmP*

Bayard, James Asheton 1799-1880 *ApCAB,
BiAUS, BiDrAC, DcAmB, NatCAB 13,
TwCBDA, WhAm H, WhAmP*

Bayard, James Ashton 1767-1815 *DcAmB,
Drake*

Bayard, John Bubenheim 1738-1807 *ApCAB,
BiAUS, BiDrAC, DcAmB, Drake,
NatCAB 1, TwCBDA, WhAm H,
WhAmP*

Bayard, Nicholas 1644-1707 *ApCAB, DcAmB,
TwCBDA, WhAm H*

Bayard, Orlena Hunting 1870- *WomWWA 14*

Bayard, Richard Henry 1796-1868 *ApCAB,
BiAUS, BiDrAC, DcAmB, NatCAB 4,
TwCBDA, WhAm H, WhAmP*

Bayard, Samuel 1765-1840 *Drake*

Bayard, Samuel 1767-1840 *ApCAB, DcAmB,
TwCBDA, WhAm H*

Bayard, Thomas Francis 1828-1898 *AmBi,
ApCAB, ApCAB X, BiAUS, BiDrAC,
BiDrUSE, DcAmB, EncAB, TwCBDA,
WebAB, WhAm H, WhAmP*

Bayard, Thomas Francis 1829-1898 *NatCAB 2*

Bayard, Thomas Francis 1868-1942 *ApCAB X,
BiDrAC, NatCAB 31, WhAm 2,
WhAmP*

Bayard, William *BiAUS*

Bayard, William 1729-1804 *ApCAB*

Bayard, William 1761-1826 *DcAmB,
WhAm H*

Bayard, William 1764?-1826 *NatCAB 1*

Bayazid II 1481-1512 *WhoMilH*

Baydur, Huseyin Ragip 1891-1955 *WhAm 3*

Bayen, Pierre 1725-1798 *DcScB*

Bayer, Adele Parmentier 1814-1892 *NotAW*

Bayer, Alfred Joseph 1876-1945 *NatCAB 36*

Bayer, Edwin Stanton 1870-1928 *NatCAB 31*

Bayer, Jane *NewYHSD*

Bayer, Johann 1572-1625 *AsBiEn, DcScB*

Bayer, Justin *NewYHSD*

Bayer, Lloyd Felch 1893-1958 *WhAm 3*

Bayerlein, Fritz *WhWW-II*

Bayes, Nora 1880?-1928 *NotAW, WebAB*

Bayes, Thomas 1702-1761 *DcScB*

Bayfield, Henry Wolsey 1795-1885 *ApCAB,
Drake, REnAW*

Bayh, Birch Evan 1928- *BiDrAC*

Baylak Al-Qibjaqi *DcScB*

Baylat *NewYHSD*

Bayle, Gaspard-Laurent 1744-1816 *BiHiMed*

Bayle, Pierre 1647-1706 *McGEWB*

Bayles, Edwin Atkinson 1875- *WhAm 5*

Bayles, George James 1869-1914 *WhAm 1*

Bayles, James 1853-1924 *ApCAB X*

Bayles, James Copper 1845-1913 *ApCAB,
DcAmB, NatCAB 13, TwCBDA,
WhAm 4*

Bayles, Lewis Condict 1872-1946 *NatCAB 35*

Bayles, Theodore Floyd 1871-1952 *WhAm 3*

Bayless, Herman Armstrong 1882-1968
NatCAB 55

Bayless, William Henry *NewYHSD*

Bayless, William Silver 1883-1935 *WhAm 1*

Bayley, E Covell 1899-1969 *NatCAB 55*

Bayley, Edward Bancroft 1864-1936 *WhAm 1*

Bayley, Edwin Fisher 1845-1920 *ApCAB X,
NatCAB 19*

Bayley, Francis Reed 1877- *WhAm 5*

Bayley, Frank Tappan 1846-1917 *WhAm 1*

Bayley, James Roosevelt 1814-1877 *ApCAB,
DcAmB, DcAmReB, NatCAB 1,
TwCBDA, WhAm H*

Bayley, Matthias d1789? *Drake*

Bayley, Richard 1745-1801 *AmBi, ApCAB,
BiHiMed, DcAmB, Drake, NatCAB 8,
WebAB, WhAm H*

Bayley, Richard 1745-1811 *TwCBDA*

Bayley, Robert Hebard 1906-1969 *NatCAB 55*

Bayley, Thomas *BiAUS*

Bayley, Thomas M 1775-1834 *BiAUS*

Bayley, Warner Baldwin 1845-1928 *WhAm 1*

Bayley, William *NewYHSD*

Bayley, William Shirley 1861-1943 *WhAm 3*

Baylies, Edmund Lincoln 1857-1932 *ApCAB X,
NatCAB 18, NatCAB 34, WhAm 1*

Baylies, Edwin 1840- *WhAm 4*

Baylies, Francis 1783-1852 *ApCAB, BiAUS,
DcAmB, Drake, NatCAB 11, TwCBDA*

Baylies, Francis 1784-1852 *BiDrAC, WhAm H,
WhAmP*

Baylies, Frederick Wheaton 1871-1918
NatCAB 18

Baylies, Nicholas 1772-1847 *ApCAB, Drake*

Baylies, Walter Cabot 1862-1936 *WhAm 1*

Baylies, William 1743-1826 *ApCAB, BiAUS,
Drake, TwCBDA*

Baylies, William 1776-1865 *BiAUS, BiDrAC,
WhAm H, WhAmP*

Baylis, Charles T 1869- *WhAm 5*

Baylis, John Robert 1885-1963 *NatCAB 51*

Baylis, Richard *NewYHSD*

Baylis, Robert Nelson 1867-1942 *WhAm 2*

Bayliss, Alfred 1847-1911 *WhAm 1*

Bayliss, Clara Kern 1848- *WhAm 4,
WomWWA 14*

Bayliss, Leonard Ernest 1900-1964 *DcScB*

Bayliss, Major William 1848-1919 *NatCAB 12,
WhAm 1*

Bayliss, Sir William Maddock 1860-1924
AsBiEn, DcScB

Baylor, Adelaide Steele d1935 *WhAm 1*

Baylor, Frances Courtenay 1848-1920 *AmWom,
ApCAB, ApCAB Sup, DcAmB,
NatCAB 1, TwCBDA, WhAm HA,
WhAm 4*

Baylor, George 1752-1784 *ApCAB, DcAmB,
Drake, TwCBDA, WhAm H*

Baylor, Harry Dietrich 1880-1950 *NatCAB 39*

Baylor, James Bowen 1849-1924 *WhAm 1*

Baylor, John Robert 1822-1894 *BiDConf,
REnAW*

Baylor, John Roy d1926 *WhAm 3*

Baylor, R E B *BiAUS*

Baylor, Robert Emmet Bledsoe 1793-1873 *AmBi,
DcAmB*

Baylor, Robert Emmett Bledsoe 1793-1873
WhAm H

Baylor, Robert Emmett Bledsoe 1793-1874
ApCAB, BiDrAC, TwCBDA, WhAmP

Baylor, William Henry 1865- *WhAm 5*

Bayly, Thomas 1775-1829 *BiDrAC, WhAm H*

Bayly, Thomas Henry 1810-1856 *BiAUS,
BiDrAC, DcAmB, Drake, WhAm H,
WhAmP*

Bayly, Thomas Monteagle 1775-1834 *BiDrAC, WhAm H, WhAmP*
Bayma, Joseph 1816-1892 *DcAmB, NatCAB 17, WhAm H*
Baynam, William 1749-1814 *ApCAB*
Baynard, Samuel Harrison 1851-1925 *NatCAB 31*
Bayne, Eliza *NewYHSD*
Bayne, Herbert Andrew 1846-1886 *ApCAB*
Bayne, Howard 1878-1958 *WhAm 3*
Bayne, Howard Randolph 1851-1933 *WhAm 1*
Bayne, Hugh Aiken 1870-1954 *WhAm 3*
Bayne, J Breckinridge 1880-1964 *NatCAB 51*
Bayne, John 1806-1859 *ApCAB*
Bayne, John Woart 1846-1905 *NatCAB 21*
Bayne, Reed Taft 1885-1954 *WhAm 3*
Bayne, Samuel Gamble 1844-1924 *WhAm 1*
Bayne, Stephen Fielding, Jr. 1908-1974 *WhAm 6*
Bayne, Thomas McKee 1836-1894 *BiDrAC, WhAm H, WhAmP*
Bayne, Walter McPherson 1795-1859 *NewYHSD*
Bayne, William 1841-1922 *NatCAB 20*
Bayne, William 1890-1955 *WhAm 3*
Bayne-Jones, Stanhope 1888-1970 *NatCAB 55, WhAm 5*
Baynes, Edward d1829 *ApCAB*
Baynes, Ernest Harold 1868-1925 *WhAm 1*
Baynes, John 1842-1903 *WhAm 1*
Baynham, William 1749-1814 *DcAmB, WhAm H*
Bayol, Edgar Sansom 1907-1970 *WhAm 5*
Bayrd, Frank Arthur 1873-1940 *NatCAB 30*
Bays, Alfred William 1876-1957 *NatCAB 47, WhAm 3*
Baysinger, Stuart Lee 1869-1953 *NatCAB 44*
Baytar Al-Malaqi, Diya Al-Din, Ibn Al-1190?-1248 *DcScB*
Bayuk, Samuel 1870-1954 *WhAm 3*
Bazaine, Achille 1811-1888 *WhoMilH*
Bazaine, Francois Achille 1811-1888 *ApCAB*
Bazavoff, Serge Bazil 1886-1958 *NatCAB 43*
Bazeley, William Alliston Ley *ApCAB X*
Bazett, Henry Cuthbert 1885-1950 *DcAmB S4, WhAm 3*
Bazin, John A 1796-1847 *ApCAB*
Bazin, John Stephen 1796-1848 *NatCAB 12, TwCBDA, WhAm H*
Baziotes, William 1912-1963 *BnEnAmA, WhAm 4*
Bazley, Halsey Rapson 1896-1952 *NatCAB 39*
Bazna, Elyesa Cicero *WhWW-II*
Bea, Cardinal Augustin 1881-1968 *WhAm 5*
Bea, Cardinal Augustinus 1881-1968 *McGEWB*
Beach, Abraham 1740-1828 *ApCAB, Drake*
Beach, Albert Isaac 1883-1939 *WhAm 1*
Beach, Alfred B 1821- *NatCAB 9*
Beach, Alfred Ely 1826-1896 *DcAmB, NatCAB 8, TwCBDA, WebAB, WhAm H*
Beach, Allen Samuel 1864-1960 *NatCAB 48*
Beach, Amy Marcy Cheney 1867-1944 *ApCAB X, DcAmB S3, NatCAB 7, NotAW, WhAm 2, WomWWA 14*
Beach, Arthur Grandville 1870-1934 *WhAm 1*
Beach, Charles Coffing 1856-1948 *NatCAB 39*
Beach, Charles Fisk 1827-1908 *WhAm 1*
Beach, Charles Fisk 1854-1934 *NatCAB 1, WhAm 1*
Beach, Charles Lewis 1866-1933 *NatCAB 40, WhAm 1*
Beach, Chester 1881-1956 *NatCAB 42, WhAm 3*
Beach, Clifton Bailey 1845-1902 *BiDrAC*
Beach, Daniel 1830-1913 *NatCAB 7, WhAm 1*
Beach, Daniel Magee 1873-1948 *WhAm 2*
Beach, David Nelson 1848-1926 *WhAm 1*
Beach, Earl Edward 1909-1974 *WhAm 6*
Beach, Edward Latimer 1867- *WhAm 4*
Beach, Edward Latimer 1918- *WebAMB*
Beach, Edward Woodbridge 1895-1968 *NatCAB 55*
Beach, Francis Asbury 1866- *WhAm 4*
Beach, Frederick Converse 1848-1918 *DcAmB, NatCAB 17, WebAB, WhAm 1*
Beach, George Corwin, Jr. 1888-1948 *WhAm 2*

Beach, George Raimes 1873-1970 *NatCAB 56*
Beach, Mrs. H H A 1867-1944 *AmWom, DcAmB S3, NatCAB 15, TwCBDA*
Beach, H Prescott 1871-1943 *WhAm 2*
Beach, Harlan Page 1854-1933 *AmBi, DcAmB S1, NatCAB 14, WhAm 1*
Beach, Harrison L 1863-1928 *WhAm 1*
Beach, Henry Harris Aubrey 1843-1910 *ApCAB, NatCAB 15, WhAm 1*
Beach, Herman Kissam 1881-1941 *NatCAB 31*
Beach, J Watson 1823-1887 *NatCAB 26*
Beach, John Kimberly 1855-1938 *WhAm 1*
Beach, John Newton 1837- *NatCAB 3, WhAm 4*
Beach, John W 1825- *NatCAB 9*
Beach, Joseph Warren 1880-1957 *NatCAB 47, WhAm 3*
Beach, King D d1957 *WhAm 3*
Beach, Lansing Hoskins 1860-1945 *WhAm 2*
Beach, Laura Jennie 1864- *WomWWA 14*
Beach, Lewis 1835-1886 *BiDrAC, WhAm H*
Beach, Lucy Ward 1855- *WomWWA 14*
Beach, Mabel Creglow 1874- *WomWWA 14*
Beach, Miles 1840-1902 *WhAm 1*
Beach, Moses Sperry 1822-1892 *DcAmB, NatCAB 13, WebAB, WhAm H*
Beach, Moses Yale 1800-1868 *AmBi, ApCAB, DcAmB, Drake, McGEWB, NatCAB 1, TwCBDA, WebAB, WhAm H*
Beach, R Clyde 1867- *WhAm 3*
Beach, Reuel Williams 1884-1964 *NatCAB 51*
Beach, Rex Ellingwood 1877-1949 *DcAmB S4, NatCAB 14, WhAm 2*
Beach, Ross 1890-1961 *NatCAB 56*
Beach, S Judd 1879-1953 *NatCAB 40, WhAm 3*
Beach, Samuel Henry, Jr. 1897-1953 *NatCAB 42*
Beach, Seth Curtis 1837- *WhAm 4*
Beach, Spencer Ambrose 1860-1923 *WhAm 1*
Beach, Stanley Yale 1877- *WhAm 5*
Beach, Sylvester Woodbridge 1852-1940 *NatCAB 33, WhAm 1*
Beach, Sylvia Woodbridge 1887-1962 *NatCAB 47*
Beach, Walter Greenwood 1868-1948 *NatCAB 43, WhAm 2*
Beach, William Augustus 1809-1884 *ApCAB, DcAmB, TwCBDA, WhAm H*
Beach, William Austin 1842- *NatCAB 5*
Beach, William Dorrance 1856-1932 *NatCAB 24, WhAm 1*
Beach, William Harrison 1835- *WhAm 4*
Beach, William Mulholland 1859-1930 *WhAm 1, WhAm 2*
Beach, Wooster 1794-1868 *DcAmB, NatCAB 23, WhAm H*
Beacham, Joseph, Jr. 1874-1958 *WhAm 3*
Beachley, Charles E 1892-1955 *WhAm 3*
Beachley, Ralph Gregory 1895-1969 *WhAm 5*
Beacom, Thomas H 1899-1962 *NatCAB 50, WhAm 3, WhAm 4*
Beadell, Henry 1862-1947 *NatCAB 37*
Beadenkopf, Charles Glen 1881-1941 *NatCAB 31*
Beadle, Chauncey Delos 1866-1950 *WhAm 3*
Beadle, Erastus Flavel 1821-1894 *DcAmB S1, NatCAB 19, REnAW, WebAB, WhAm H*
Beadle, George Wells 1903- *AsBiEn, McGEWB, WebAB*
Beadle, John Hanson 1840-1897 *NatCAB 18*
Beadle, William Henry Harrison 1838-1915 *AmBi, ApCAB, BiDAmEd, DcAmB, NatCAB 17, REnAW, TwCBDA, WhAm 1*
Beadles, Jesse Asa 1878-1953 *NatCAB 48*
Beadles, Nicholas Nunnemacher 1885-1934 *NatCAB 25*
Beahan, Bessie DeWitt 1854- *WomWWA 14*
Beahan, Willard 1854-1928 *WhAm 1*
Beahm, William McKinley 1896-1964 *WhAm 4*
Beaird, Pat 1899-1963 *NatCAB 50, WhAm 4*
Beake, Harold Carnes 1895-1971 *WhAm 5*
Beakes, Crosby Jordan 1876-1948 *WhAm 2*
Beakes, Samuel Willard 1861-1927 *BiDrAC, WhAm 1, WhAmP*
Beakman, Daniel Frederick 1760?-1869 *ApCAB*

Beal, Abraham 1803?-1872 *ApCAB*
Beal, Alvin Casey 1872-1929 *WhAm 1*
Beal, Carl Hugh 1889-1946 *NatCAB 35*
Beal, Edwin George 1876-1951 *NatCAB 50*
Beal, Foster Ellenborough Lascelles 1840-1916 *ApCAB, WhAm 1*
Beal, Francis Leavitt 1864- *WhAm 4*
Beal, George Denton 1887-1972 *WhAm 5*
Beal, George Lafayette 1825-1896 *ApCAB, TwCBDA*
Beal, Gerald F 1895-1971 *WhAm 5*
Beal, Gifford Reynolds 1879-1956 *WhAm 3*
Beal, Harry 1885-1944 *WhAm 2*
Beal, Helen Clark 1860- *WomWWA 14*
Beal, Henry C 1891-1959 *WhAm 3*
Beal, Henry J 1886-1953 *NatCAB 43*
Beal, James H 1869-1922 *ApCAB X*
Beal, James Hartley 1861-1945 *ApCAB X, TwCBDA, WhAm 2*
Beal, John M 1888-1957 *WhAm 3*
Beal, Junius Emery 1860-1942 *WhAm 2*
Beal, Mary Louise Barnes 1844- *WhAm 4, WomWWA 14*
Beal, Merrill 1898- *EncAAH*
Beal, Reynolds 1867-1951 *WhAm 3*
Beal, Royal 1899-1969 *NatCAB 55, WhAm 5*
Beal, Thaddeus Reynolds 1870-1932 *NatCAB 25*
Beal, Thomas Andrew 1874- *WhAm 2*
Beal, Thomas Prince 1849-1923 *WhAm 1*
Beal, Walter Henry 1867-1946 *WhAm 2*
Beal, William James 1833-1924 *AmBi, ApCAB, DcAmB, NatCAB 11, TwCBDA, WhAm 1*
Beale, Arthur Stanley 1881-1938 *WhAm 1*
Beale, Bertha Fitzgerald 1877- *WomWWA 14*
Beale, Carrie Phelan *WomWWA 14*
Beale, Charles Hallock 1854-1939 *WhAm 2*
Beale, Charles Lewis 1824-1900 *BiAUS, BiDrAC*
Beale, Charles Willing 1845- *WhAm 4*
Beale, Edward Fitzgerald 1822-1893 *AmBi, ApCAB, DcAmB, NatCAB 11, REnAW, TwCBDA, WhAm H*
Beale, Frank D 1890-1968 *WhAm 5*
Beale, G D *NewYHSD*
Beale, George William 1842-1921 *WhAm 3*
Beale, Horace Alexander 1870-1927 *NatCAB 25*
Beale, James Madison Hite 1786-1866 *BiAUS, BiDrAC, WhAm H*
Beale, John Forbes 1850-1923 *ApCAB X*
Beale, Joseph 1814-1889 *TwCBDA*
Beale, Joseph Grant 1839-1915 *BiDrAC, WhAm 4*
Beale, Joseph Henry 1861-1943 *DcAmB S3, WhAm 2*
Beale, Leonard Tillinghast 1881-1966 *NatCAB 52, WhAm 4*
Beale, Lionel Smith 1828-1906 *DcScB*
Beale, Maria Parker Taylor 1849- *WhAm 4, WomWWA 14*
Beale, R L T 1819-1893 *BiAUS*
Beale, Richard L T 1819-1893 *ApCAB*
Beale, Richard Lee Turberville 1819-1893 *BiDrAC, DcAmB, WhAm H*
Beale, Richard Lee Turbeville 1819-1893 *BiDConf*
Beale, Robert Cecil 1877-1952 *NatCAB 44*
Beale, Samuel Marsden, Jr. 1876-1965 *NatCAB 53*
Beale, Stephen 1903-1958 *WhAm 3*
Beale, Truxtun 1856-1936 *NatCAB 13, NatCAB 27, WhAm 1*
Beale, William Gerrish 1854-1923 *NatCAB 20, WhAm 1*
Beale And Craven *NewYHSD*
Bealer, Alexander Winkler 1860-1921 *WhAm 3*
Bealer, Howard Kennedy 1899-1959 *WhAm 4*
Beales, Cyrus William 1877-1927 *BiDrAC, WhAm 1*
Beales, Leverne 1875- *WhAm 5*
Beall, Benjamin Lloyd 1800?-1863 *ApCAB, Drake, NatCAB 5, TwCBDA*
Beall, Elias James 1835- *WhAm 4*
Beall, Forest Wade 1910-1967 *WhAm 5*
Beall, Frank Forrest 1877-1939 *NatCAB 29*
Beall, Jack 1866-1929 *NatCAB 43, WhAm 1*

Beall, Jack 1898-1963 *WhAm 4*
Beall, James Andrew 1866-1929 *BiDrAC, WhAmP*
Beall, James Glenn 1894-1971 *BiDrAC, WhAm 5, WhAmP*
Beall, James Henry, Jr. 1896-1956 *NatCAB 44*
Beall, John Glenn, Jr. 1927- *BiDrAC*
Beall, John Yates 1833?-1865 *NatCAB 4*
Beall, John Yates 1835-1865 *DcAmB, WhAm H*
Beall, John Young 1835-1865 *ApCAB, TwCBDA*
Beall, Mary Stevens d1917 *WhAm 1*
Beall, Nannie Lewis *WomWWA 14*
Beall, Reasin 1769-1843 *BiDrAC, WhAm H*
Beall, Reazin d1843 *Drake*
Beall, Reazin 1769-1843 *NatCAB 11*
Beall, Reazin 1770-1843 *ApCAB*
Beall, Rezin d1843 *BiAUS*
Beall, Samuel Wooton 1807-1868 *TwCBDA*
Beall, Samuel Wootton 1807-1868 *ApCAB, DcAmB, WhAm H, WhAmP*
Beall, William Dent 1755-1829 *ApCAB, Drake*
Beals, Anna Maria Bourne *WomWWA 14*
Beals, Carrie *NewYHSD*
Beals, Charles Edward 1869-1931 *WhAm 1*
Beals, David Thomas 1889-1963 *NatCAB 47, WhAm 4*
Beals, Edward Alden 1855-1931 *NatCAB 24, WhAm 1*
Beals, Frank Abram 1879-1945 *NatCAB 35*
Beals, Frank Lee 1881-1972 *WhAm 5*
Beals, Jessie Tarbox 1870- *WomWWA 14*
Beals, John David 1868-1928 *NatCAB 22*
Beals, Katharine McMillan *WomWWA 14*
Beals, Othilia Gertrude *WomWWA 14*
Beals, Ralph Albert 1899-1954 *DcAmB S5, DcAmLiB, NatCAB 40, WhAm 3*
Beals, Robert Diggs 1914-1971 *WhAm 5*
Beals, Rose Fairbank *WomWWA 14*
Beals, Walter Burges 1876-1960 *WhAm 4*
Beam, Augustus Godfrey 1882- *WhoColR*
Beam, Francis H 1900-1965 *WhAm 4*
Beam, Harry Peter 1892-1968 *BiDrAC, WhAm 4A, WhAmP*
Beam, Jacob Newton 1869-1954 *NatCAB 42*
Beam, Walter Irvin 1885-1957 *WhAm 3*
Beam, William H *ApCAB X*
Beaman *NewYHSD*
Beaman, Alexander Gaylord Emmons 1885-1943 *WhAm 2*
Beaman, Bartlett 1891-1947 *WhAm 2*
Beaman, Charles Cotesworth 1840-1900 *DcAmB, NatCAB 15, WhAm 1*
Beaman, Fernando Cortez 1814-1882 *BiAUS, BiDrAC, WhAm H, WhAmP*
Beaman, George William 1837-1917 *WhAm 1*
Beaman, Jane Witter Stetson *WomWWA 14*
Beaman, Joseph N 1868- *WhoColR*
Beaman, Middleton 1877-1951 *NatCAB 41*
Beaman, Nathaniel 1859-1921 *NatCAB 6*
Beaman, Robert Prentis 1891-1953 *NatCAB 49, WhAm 3*
Beaman, William Major 1867- *WhAm 4*
Beament, Thomas Harold 1898- *IlBEAAW*
Beamer, Elmer A 1881-1941 *WhAm 1*
Beamer, George Noah 1904-1974 *WhAm 6*
Beamer, John Valentine 1896-1964 *BiDrAC, NatCAB 51, WhAm 4, WhAmP*
Beamish, Richard Joseph 1867-1945 *NatCAB 34*
Beamish, Richard Joseph 1869-1945 *WhAm 2*
Beams, Argyl Jackson 1891-1961 *NatCAB 52*
Beamsley, Foster Gilman 1890-1960 *WhAm 3*
Bean, Arthur John 1883-1931 *WhAm 1*
Bean, Ashton Garrett 1871-1935 *NatCAB 27*
Bean, Barton A 1860- *WhAm 4*
Bean, Benning Moulton 1782-1866 *BiAUS, BiDrAC, WhAm H, WhAmP*
Bean, Charles Homer 1870- *WhAm 5*
Bean, Curtis Coe 1828-1904 *BiDrAC*
Bean, Edwin Curtis 1854-1926 *NatCAB 20*
Bean, Ellis P 1783-1846 *NatCAB 21*
Bean, Ernest F 1882-1961 *NatCAB 49*
Bean, Francis Atherton 1878-1955 *WhAm 3*
Bean, George W 1875-1950 *WhAm 4*
Bean, Harold Cedric 1889-1930 *NatCAB 22*
Bean, Henry J 1853-1941 *WhAm 1*

Bean, Holly Marshall 1837- *WhAm 4*
Bean, Irving M 1838- *NatCAB 1*
Bean, L L 1872-1967 *WhAm 4*
Bean, Mary 1869- *WomWWA 14*
Bean, Mary T 1818?-1875? *NatCAB 4*
Bean, Morris Monroe 1905-1970 *NatCAB 56*
Bean, Nehemiah S 1818-1896 *TwCBDA*
Bean, R Bennett 1874-1944 *WhAm 2*
Bean, Richard Menefee 1879-1947 *NatCAB 37, WhAm 6*
Bean, Robert Sharp 1854-1931 *NatCAB 13, NatCAB 22, WhAm 1*
Bean, Roy 1825?-1903 *REnAW, WebAB*
Bean, Tarleton Hoffman 1846-1916 *AmBi, ApCAB Sup, DcAmB, TwCBDA, WhAm 1*
Bean, Tarleton Hoffmann 1846-1916 *NatCAB 24*
Bean, Theodora *WomWWA 14*
Bean, William *ApCAB*
Bean, William 1891-1974 *WhAm 6*
Bean, William Hill 1867-1925 *NatCAB 31*
Bean, William Smith 1890- *WhAm 2*
Beanblossom, Moody Lewis 1885-1923 *WhAm 1*
Beane, Fred Emery 1853- *WhAm 1*
Beane, John G 1864- *WhAm 4*
Beane, Mary Ellen Smith 1870- *WomWWA 14*
Beane, Walter Henry 1893-1954 *NatCAB 48*
Bear, Charles Henry 1885-1949 *NatCAB 39*
Bear, Donald 1905-1952 *NatCAB 42*
Bear, Firman Edward 1884-1968 *WhAm 5*
Bear, Harry 1890-1950 *WhAm 3*
Bear, Joseph 1889-1948 *NatCAB 38*
Bear, Joseph Alnslle 1878-1955 *WhAm 3*
Bear, Olive May 1870- *WomWWA 14*
Bear, Samuel, Jr. 1853-1916 *NatCAB 16*
Bearce, Henry Walter 1881-1968 *WhAm 5*
Bearce, Ralph King 1875- *WhAm 5*
Beard, Adelia Belle d1920 *WhAm 1, WomWWA 14*
Beard, Andrew 1849- *NatCAB 4*
Beard, Augustus Field 1833-1934 *WhAm 1*
Beard, Charles Austin 1874-1948 *BiDAmEd, DcAmB S4, EncAAH, EncAB, McGEWB, WebAB, WhAm 2, WhAm 2C*
Beard, Charles Heady 1855-1916 *WhAm 1*
Beard, Cyrus 1850-1920 *NatCAB 17, WhAm 1*
Beard, Daniel Carter 1850-1941 *ApCAB, DcAmB S3, EncAAH, IlBEAAW, NatCAB 5, NatCAB 33, TwCBDA, WebAB, WhAm 1*
Beard, Edward E 1850-1924 *WhAm 1*
Beard, Frank *ApCAB*
Beard, Frederica *WomWWA 14*
Beard, George *NewYHSD*
Beard, George 1855-1944 *IlBEAAW*
Beard, George Miller 1839-1883 *AmBi, ApCAB, DcAmB, NatCAB 8, TwCBDA, WhAm H*
Beard, Gerald Hamilton 1862-1921 *WhAm 1*
Beard, Harriet Elizabeth *WomWWA 14*
Beard, Harry *ApCAB*
Beard, Harry Elmer 1897-1963 *NatCAB 49*
Beard, James Carter 1837-1913 *ApCAB, DcAmB, IlBEAAW, NewYHSD, WhAm 1*
Beard, James Henry 1812-1893 *AmBi, BnEnAmA, DcAmB, IlBEAAW, NatCAB 5, NewYHSD, TwCBDA, WhAm H*
Beard, James Henry 1814-1893 *ApCAB*
Beard, James Henry 1815-1893 *Drake*
Beard, James Randolph 1903-1959 *WhAm 3*
Beard, James Thom 1855-1941 *WhAm 1, WhAm 2*
Beard, John Grover 1888-1946 *NatCAB 34, WhAm 2*
Beard, John Jacob 1876-1955 *NatCAB 43*
Beard, Joseph Howard 1883-1950 *WhAm 3*
Beard, Lina d1933 *WhAm 1, WomWWA 14*
Beard, Mary 1876-1946 *DcAmB S4, NatCAB 35, WhAm 2*
Beard, Mary Ritter 1876-1958 *WhAm 3, WomWWA 14*
Beard, Oliver Thomas 1832- *WhAm 4*
Beard, Reuben Alview 1851-1941 *WhAm 2*
Beard, Richard 1799-1880 *ApCAB, DcAmB,*

NatCAB 21, TwCBDA, WhAm H
Beard, Stanley Drew 1884-1970 *NatCAB 55*
Beard, Thomas Francis 1842-1905 *AmBi, DcAmB, IlBEAAW, NatCAB 13, WhAm 1*
Beard, Vida Fleming *WomWWA 14*
Beard, William Dwight 1837-1910 *NatCAB 13, WhAm 1*
Beard, William Holbrook 1824-1900 *AmBi, BnEnAmA, DcAmB, Drake, IlBEAAW, NewYHSD*
Beard, William Holbrook 1825-1900 *ApCAB, NatCAB 11, TwCBDA, WhAm 1*
Beard, Wolcott LeClear 1867- *WhAm 4*
Beardall, John Reginald 1887-1967 *WhAm 4*
Bearden, Romare Howard 1914- *McGEWB*
Beardshear, William Miller 1850-1902 *DcAmB, NatCAB 12, WhAm 1*
Beardslee, Clark Smith 1850-1914 *WhAm 1*
Beardslee, Guy Roosevelt 1856-1939 *NatCAB 29*
Beardslee, John Walter, Jr. 1879-1962 *NatCAB 49, WhAm 4*
Beardslee, Lester Anthony 1835-1903 *ApCAB Sup*
Beardslee, Lester Anthony 1836-1903 *NatCAB 13, TwCBDA, WhAm 1*
Beardsley, Alonzo G 1820- *NatCAB 3*
Beardsley, Arthur 1843- *ApCAB, NatCAB 10, TwCBDA*
Beardsley, Aubrey Vincent 1872-1898 *McGEWB*
Beardsley, Charles Alexander 1882-1963 *WhAm 4*
Beardsley, Charles Sumner 1874-1962 *WhAm 4*
Beardsley, Eben Edwards 1808-1891 *ApCAB, DcAmB, TwCBDA, WhAm H*
Beardsley, Emily Call Griffith 1851- *WomWWA 14*
Beardsley, Frank Allen 1892-1955 *NatCAB 45*
Beardsley, Frank Grenville 1870-1954 *WhAm 3*
Beardsley, Glover 1881-1961 *WhAm 4*
Beardsley, Grenville 1898-1960 *NatCAB 47, WhAm 4*
Beardsley, Guy Erastus 1874-1960 *NatCAB 48, WhAm 5*
Beardsley, Harry M 1893- *WhAm 3*
Beardsley, Henry Mahan 1858-1938 *WhAm 1*
Beardsley, James Wallace 1860-1944 *WhAm 2*
Beardsley, Jefferson *IlBEAAW, NewYHSD*
Beardsley, John 1730-1810 *ApCAB*
Beardsley, John 1876-1946 *NatCAB 35*
Beardsley, Leon William Smith 1878-1927 *NatCAB 22*
Beardsley, Levi 1785-1857 *ApCAB, TwCBDA*
Beardsley, Morris Beach 1849-1923 *NatCAB 3, NatCAB 26*
Beardsley, Nelson 1807- *NatCAB 3*
Beardsley, Samuel 1790-1860 *ApCAB, BiAUS, BiDrAC, DcAmB, Drake, NatCAB 4, TwCBDA, WhAm H, WhAmP*
Beardsley, Samuel Arthur 1856-1932 *NatCAB 18, NatCAB 37, WhAm 1*
Beardsley, Samuel Fayerweather 1874-1940 *NatCAB 30*
Beardsley, Samuel Raymond 1814-1863 *ApCAB*
Beardsley, Thomas Hopper 1882-1962 *NatCAB 49*
Beardsley, William Agur 1865-1946 *WhAm 2*
Beardsley, William H 1852-1925 *ApCAB X, WhAm 1*
Beardsley, William S 1901-1954 *WhAm 3*
Beardsley Limner, The *BnEnAmA*
Beardwood, Joseph Thomas, Jr. 1896-1970 *WhAm 5*
Beardwood, Matthew 1872- *WhAm 1*
Bearns, James Sterling 1816-1913 *NatCAB 17*
Bearor, Robert Amie 1922-1970 *NatCAB 56*
Bearsdley, Arthur Lehman 1869-1944 *WhAm 2*
Bearss, Hiram Iddings 1875-1938 *NatCAB 29*
Beary, Donald Bradford 1888-1966 *WhAm 4*
Beaseley, Nathaniel 1751-1835 *ApCAB*
Beasley, Frederic 1777-1845 *NatCAB 1*
Beasley, Frederick 1777-1845 *ApCAB, DcAmB, Drake, TwCBDA, WhAm H*
Beasley, Jean Tallman 1921-1973 *WhAm 6*
Beasley, John 1860- *WhAm 1*
Beasley, Marie Wilson 1862?- *AmWom*

Beasley, Mercer 1815-1897 *DcAmB,*
NatCAB 13, WhAm H
Beasley, Nathaniel d1835 *Drake*
Beasley, Oscar Hill 1893-1967 *NatCAB 53*
Beasley, Rex Webb 1892-1961 *WhAm 4*
Beasley, Ronald Storey 1900-1969 *WhAm 5*
Beasley, Rowland Fowler 1871-1953 *WhAm 3*
Beasley, Victoria Louise Dowling 1888-1956
NatCAB 45
Beasom, William Henry 1861-1944 *NatCAB 38*
Beastall *NewYHSD*
Beates, Henry, Jr. 1857-1926 *NatCAB 11,*
WhAm 1
Beath, Robert Burns 1839-1914 *NatCAB 13,*
WhAm 1
Beatien Yazz 1928- *IlBEAAW*
Beatley, Clara Bancroft 1858-1923 *WhAm 1,*
WomWWA 14
Beatman, Joseph William 1901-1965
NatCAB 51
Beaton, David 1848-1920 *WhAm 1*
Beaton, Kenneth Carrol 1871- *WhAm 5*
Beaton, Lindsay Eugene 1911-1967 *WhAm 4*
Beaton, Ralph Hastings 1876-1943 *WhAm 2*
Beatrice, Sister *NotAW*
Beatson, Andrew Kay 1854-1914 *NatCAB 16*
Beatson, Helena *NewYHSD*
Beattie, Charlton Reid 1869-1925 *WhAm 1*
Beattie, Edward William 1874-1944
NatCAB 46
Beattie, Eva Townsend 1853- *WomWWA 14*
Beattie, Fountain Fox 1878- *WhAm 6*
Beattie, Francis Robert 1848-1906 *DcAmB,*
NatCAB 21, WhAm 1
Beattie, George William 1859-1949 *NatCAB 39*
Beattie, Hamlin 1835-1914 *NatCAB 2*
Beattie, J Isabella Macklin *WomWWA 14*
Beattie, James A 1845- *TwCBDA, WhAm 4*
Beattie, John Walter 1885-1962 *WhAm 4*
Beattie, R Leslie 1891-1953 *WhAm 3*
Beattie, Robert 1870-1956 *NatCAB 45*
Beattie, Robert Brewster 1875-1946 *WhAm 2*
Beattie, Ronald Hanna 1903-1974 *WhAm 6*
Beattie, William Henry 1877-1949 *NatCAB 39*
Beatty, Adam 1777-1858 *DcAmB, NatCAB 20,*
NatCAB 21, WhAm H
Beatty, Alfred Chester 1875-1968 *WhAm 4A,*
WhAm 5
Beatty, Alfred Chester 1876-1968 *NatCAB 14*
Beatty, Anne Meem Peachy *WomWWA 14*
Beatty, Arthur 1869-1943 *WhAm 2*
Beatty, Bessie 1886-1947 *WhAm 2*
Beatty, Charles Clinton 1715?-1772 *ApCAB,*
DcAmB, Drake, TwCBDA, WhAm H
Beatty, Clara Smith *WhAm 5*
Beatty, Cora B Hamnett 1860- *WomWWA 14*
Beatty, David 1871-1936 *WhoMilH*
Beatty, Edith Graves 1878- *WomWWA 14*
Beatty, Sir Edward 1877-1943 *WhAm 2*
Beatty, Erkuries 1759-1823 *ApCAB*
Beatty, Frank Edmund 1853-1926 *WhAm 1*
Beatty, Henry Oscar 1812-1892 *NatCAB 12*
Beatty, Henry Russell 1906-1972 *NatCAB 56,*
WhAm 5
Beatty, Hugh Gibson 1880-1971 *WhAm 5*
Beatty, James Helmick 1836-1927 *NatCAB 21,*
WhAm 5
Beatty, James Laughead 1893-1968 *WhAm 5*
Beatty, Jerome 1886-1967 *WhAm 4*
Beatty, John 1749-1826 *ApCAB, BiAUS,*
BiDrAC, DcAmB, Drake, TwCBDA,
WhAm H, WhAmP
Beatty, John 1828-1914 *ApCAB, BiAUS,*
BiDrAC, DcAmB, Drake Sup,
NatCAB 11, NatCAB 16, TwCBDA,
WhAm 1, WhAmP
Beatty, John Wesley 1851-1924 *ApCAB X,*
NatCAB 14, NatCAB 28, WhAm 1
Beatty, John William 1869-1941 *IlBEAAW*
Beatty, Martin *BiAUS*
Beatty, Martin see also Beaty, Martin
Beatty, Morgan 1902-1975 *WhAm 6*
Beatty, Nellie Griswold 1862- *WomWWA 14*
Beatty, Norman Madrid 1902-1948 *NatCAB 36*
Beatty, Ormond 1815-1890 *TwCBDA*
Beatty, Paul Cousart 1918-1973 *WhAm 6*
Beatty, Richmond Croom 1905-1961 *WhAm 4*
Beatty, Robert Muir 1850- *NatCAB 7*

Beatty, Ross James 1854-1950 *NatCAB 38*
Beatty, Samuel 1820-1885 *ApCAB, TwCBDA*
Beatty, Troy 1866-1922 *NatCAB 20,*
WhAm 1
Beatty, Willard Walcott 1891-1961 *WhAm 4*
Beatty, William 1787-1851 *BiAUS, BiDrAC,*
WhAm H
Beatty, William Henry 1838-1914 *DcAmB,*
NatCAB 12, WhAm 1
Beatty, William Henry 1886-1931 *NatCAB 22*
Beatty, William Irons 1846-1926 *NatCAB 22*
Beattys, George Davis 1862-1945 *WhAm 2*
Beaty, Amos Leonidas 1870-1939 *DcAmB S2,*
WhAm 1
Beaty, James 1798- *ApCAB Sup*
Beaty, James 1831- *ApCAB Sup*
Beaty, John Owen 1890-1961 *NatCAB 47,*
WhAm 4
Beaty, John Yocum 1884- *WhAm 3*
Beaty, Julian Bonar 1880- *WhAm 6*
Beaty, Martin *BiDrAC, WhAm H*
Beaty, Martin see also Beatty, Martin
Beaty, Richard A D 1888-1951 *WhAm 3*
Beau, John Anthony *NewYHSD*
Beau Jonathan *WhAm H*
Beaubien, Carlos 1800-1864 *REnAW*
Beaubien, DeGaspe 1881- *WhAm 6*
Beauce *NewYHSD*
Beauchamp, Edwin 1916-1964 *WhAm 4*
Beauchamp, Emerson d1971 *WhAm 5*
Beauchamp, Frances E *WomWWA 14*
Beauchamp, James K 1859- *WhAm 4*
Beauchamp, Lou Jenks 1851-1920 *WhAm 1*
Beauchamp, Mary Elizabeth 1825- *AmWom*
Beauchamp, Virginia Carter Halstead 1841-
WomWWA 14
Beauchamp, William 1772-1824 *ApCAB,*
DcAmB, TwCBDA, WhAm H
Beauchamp, William Benjamin 1869-1931
NatCAB 23, WhAm 1
Beauchamp, William Martin 1830-1925 *DcAmB,*
NatCAB 20, WhAm 1
Beaucourt, Francois *NewYHSD*
Beaudette, F R 1897-1957 *WhAm 3*
Beaudette, Fred 1897-1957 *NatCAB 44*
Beaudiekamp, B S *NewYHSD*
Beaudoin, L Rene 1912-1970 *WhAm 5*
Beaudry, Louis Napoleon 1833- *ApCAB Sup*
Beaugrand, Honore 1848- *ApCAB*
Beaugrand, Jean 1595?-1640? *DcScB*
Beaugureau *NewYHSD*
Beaugureau, Francis Henry 1920- *IlBEAAW*
Beaugureau, P H, Jr. *NewYHSD*
Beauharnais, Alex, Viscount 1760-1794 *Drake*
Beauharnais, Alexandre De 1760-1794 *ApCAB*
Beauharnais, Charles, Marquis De 1670?-1749
Drake
Beauharnais, Charles DeLaBoische De
1670?-1749 *ApCAB*
Beaujeu, Hyacinthe Marie L De 1711-1755
ApCAB, Drake
Beaujolais, Louis Charles D'Orleans 1779-1808
NewYHSD, WhAm H
Beaujour, Louis Felix De 1765-1836 *ApCAB,*
Drake
Beaulaurier, Leo James 1912- *IlBEAAW*
Beaulieu, Emile F *NewYHSD*
Beaulieu, Jean Pierre De 1725-1819 *WhoMilH*
Beaumarchais, Pierre August Caron De
1732-1799 *McGEWB*
Beaumarchais, Pierre Augustin Caron De
1732-1799 *ApCAB, Drake*
Beaumont, Andre Alden 1900-1974 *WhAm 6*
Beaumont, Andrew 1790-1853 *BiAUS, BiDrAC,*
WhAm H
Beaumont, Arthur Bishop 1887-1961
NatCAB 49
Beaumont, Betty Bentley 1828- *AmWom*
Beaumont, Campbell Eben 1883-1954 *WhAm 3*
Beaumont, Carrie R 1868- *WomWWA 14*
Beaumont, Mrs. Charles *NewYHSD*
Beaumont, Charles *NewYHSD*
Beaumont, Charles Herbert 1893-1948
NatCAB 37
Beaumont, Edmond Eckhart 1892-1968
WhAm 5
Beaumont, Elie De *DcScB*
Beaumont, Francis 1584?-1616 *McGEWB*

Beaumont, Gustave A DeLaBonniere De
1802-1866 *AmBi*
Beaumont, John Colt 1821-1882 *DcAmB,*
WhAm H
Beaumont, John Colt 1878-1942 *WhAm 2*
Beaumont, John G 1821-1882 *ApCAB,*
NatCAB 9, TwCBDA
Beaumont, John P *NewYHSD*
Beaumont, Lilian Adele 1880- *WhAm 1*
Beaumont, William 1785-1853 *AmBi, AsBiEn,*
BiHiMed, DcAmB, DcScB, Drake,
EncAB, McGEWB, NatCAB 18, REnAW,
WebAB, WebAMB, WebAB, WhAm H
Beaumont, William 1796-1853 *ApCAB*
Beaumont DeLaBonniere, Gustave A De
1802-1866 *ApCAB, Drake*
Beaupoil DeSaint Aulaire *NewYHSD*
Beaupre, Arthur Matthias 1850?-1919
NatCAB 5
Beaupre, Arthur Matthias 1853-1919 *AmBi,*
DcAmB, NatCAB 14, WhAm 1
Beauregard, Augustin Toutant 1885-1951
WhAm 3
Beauregard, Donald 1884-1914 *IlBEAAW*
Beauregard, Elie *WhAm 3*
Beauregard, Marie Antoinette 1868-1940
WhAm 1
Beauregard, Peter Gustavus Toutant 1817-1893
Drake
Beauregard, Pierre Gustave Toutant 1815-1893
WhAm H
Beauregard, Pierre Gustave Toutant 1818-1893
AmBi, ApCAB, BiDConf, DcAmB,
EncAB, McGEWB, NatCAB 4,
TwCBDA, WebAB, WebAMB, WhoMilH
Beaurepaire-Rohan, Henry De 1818?- *ApCAB*
Beausoleil, Cleophas 1845- *ApCAB Sup*
Beausoleil, Joseph Maxime *ApCAB Sup*
Beauvais, Armand *NatCAB 10*
Beaux, Cecilia d1942 *WhAm 2,*
WomWWA 14
Beaux, Cecilia 1855-1942 *DcAmB S3,*
NatCAB 40, NotAW
Beaux, Cecilia 1863-1942 *BnEnAmA,*
NatCAB 11
Beaven, Albert William 1882-1943 *WhAm 2*
Beaven, J C 1895-1951 *WhAm 3*
Beaven, Thomas 1851- *TwCBDA*
Beaven, Thomas Daniel 1849- *ApCAB Sup,*
NatCAB 5, WhAm 4
Beaver, Fred 1911- *IlBEAAW*
Beaver, Frederick Phillip 1845-1936 *NatCAB 26*
Beaver, George Washington 1825-1900
NatCAB 25
Beaver, Guy Moody 1895-1952 *NatCAB 44*
Beaver, Harry C 1876-1947 *WhAm 2*
Beaver, James Addams 1837-1914 *ApCAB,*
ApCAB X, DcAmB, NatCAB 2,
TwCBDA, WhAm 1, WhAmP
Beaver, Mollie E 1846- *WomWWA 14*
Beaver, Sandy 1883-1969 *WhAm 5*
Beaver, William Carl 1896-1970 *NatCAB 56*
Beaverbrook, Lord 1879-1964 *WhAm 4*
Beaverbrook, Maxwell Aitken, Lord 1879-1964
WhWW-II
Beavers, Genevieve W 1883- *WomWWA 14*
Beavers, Thomas N d1965 *WhAm 4*
Beazell, William Preston 1877-1946 *WhAm 2*
Beazley, George Grimes, Jr. 1914-1973
WhAm 6
Beban, George 1873-1928 *WhAm 1*
Bebb, Charles Herbert 1856-1942 *NatCAB 32,*
WhAm 2
Bebb, William 1802-1873 *BiAUS, NatCAB 3*
Bebek, Tibor Jalsoviczky 1894-1960
NatCAB 50
Beberman, Max 1925-1971 *BiDAmEd,*
WhAm 5
Bebian, Roch Ambroise Auguste 1789-1834
ApCAB
Bebie, Henry 1824?-1888 *NewYHSD*
Bebie, Jules 1877-1956 *NatCAB 44*
Bebie, W *NewYHSD*
Beccari, Nello 1883-1957 *DcScB*
Beccaria, Cesare Bonesana, Marchese Di
1738-1794 *McGEWB*
Beccaria, Giambatista 1716-1781 *DcScB*
Becerra, Diego d1533 *ApCAB*

Becerra, Francisco *ApCAB*

Bech, Georg 1875-1951 *WhAm 3*

Bech, Johan Peter 1878-1945 *NatCAB 37*

Bech, Joseph 1887-1975 *WhAm 6*

Bechamp, Pierre Jacques Antoine 1816-1908
DcScB Sup

Bechdolt, Frederick Ritchie 1874-1950
NatCAB 41, WhAm 3

Becher, Arthur E 1877- *IIBEAAW*

Becher, Clarence 1840?- *NewYHSD*

Becher, George T 1817?- *NewYHSD*

Becher, Johann Joachim 1635-1682 *AsBiEn,
DcScB*

Bechet, F L *NewYHSD*

Bechet, Paul Esnard 1881- *WhAm 6*

Bechet, Sidney 1897-1959 *EncAB, WhAm 3,
WhAm 4*

Bechhoefer, Charles 1864-1932 *NatCAB 23*

Bechill, Fred Henry 1910-1960 *NatCAB 50*

Bechler, Christian 1828?- *NewYHSD*

Bechler, John Christian 1784-1857 *ApCAB,
NatCAB 4*

Bechman, William George 1883-1966
NatCAB 53

Bechman, William George 1884-1966 *WhAm 4*

Becht, J George 1865-1925 *WhAm 1*

Bechtel, David B *NewYHSD*

Bechtel, Edward Ambrose 1867- *WhAm 5*

Bechtel, Edwin DeTurck 1880-1957 *NatCAB 42,
WhAm 3*

Bechtel, George 1840-1889 *NatCAB 3*

Bechtel, George Martin 1868-1952 *NatCAB 43,
WhAm 3*

Bechtel, Warren A 1872-1933 *NatCAB 24*

Bechtner, Paul 1882-1961 *NatCAB 50*

Beck, Adam L 1862-1939 *NatCAB 29,
WhAm 1*

Beck, Allen Frank 1883-1955 *NatCAB 45*

Beck, Brooks 1918-1969 *WhAm 5*

Beck, C H *NewYHSD*

Beck, Carl 1856-1911 *DcAmB, NatCAB 10,
NatCAB 30, WhAm 1*

Beck, Carl 1859-1911 *AmBi*

Beck, Carl 1864- *WhAm 4*

Beck, Carol H d1908 *WhAm 1*

Beck, Charles 1798-1866 *ApCAB, BiDAmEd,
DcAmB, Drake, WhAm H*

Beck, Charles E 1867-1948 *NatCAB 41*

Beck, Christian John 1877-1949 *NatCAB 36*

Beck, Clara A 1860- *WomWWA 14*

Beck, Claude Schaeffer 1894-1971 *WhAm 5*

Beck, D Elden 1906-1967 *WhAm 4*

Beck, Earl 1895-1954 *NatCAB 44*

Beck, Edward Adam 1885-1925 *WhAm 1*

Beck, Edward Scott 1868-1942 *NatCAB 31,
WhAm 2*

Beck, Ellis William 1892-1964 *NatCAB 51*

Beck, Emil George 1866- *NatCAB 17*

Beck, Erasmus Williams 1833-1898 *BiAUS,
BiDrAC*

Beck, Mrs. George *NewYHSD*

Beck, George 1748?-1812 *NewYHSD,
WhAm H*

Beck, George 1749-1812 *ApCAB, Drake*

Beck, George Jacob *NewYHSD*

Beck, Gilbert Monroe 1899-1953 *NatCAB 42*

Beck, Harvey Grant 1870-1951 *NatCAB 39*

Beck, Herbert Huebener 1875-1960 *NatCAB 49*

Beck, Herbert Wardle d1954 *WhAm 3*

Beck, Horace Palmer 1872-1936 *NatCAB 27*

Beck, Ira Addison 1878-1947 *NatCAB 36*

Beck, Irma Wanda 1881- *WomWWA 14*

Beck, J Augustus 1831-1918? *NewYHSD*

Beck, James Burnie 1822-1890 *ApCAB,
BiAUS, BiAUS Sup, BiDrAC,
NatCAB 3, TwCBDA, WhAm H,
WhAmP*

Beck, James Montgomery 1861-1936 *BiDrAC,
DcAmB S2, NatCAB 27, WhAm 1,
WhAmP*

Beck, Jean-Baptiste 1881-1943 *WhAm 2*

Beck, Jennie Florence 1848- *WomWWA 14*

Beck, Johann Heinrich 1856-1924 *DcAmB,
NatCAB 24, WhAm 1, WhAm 1C*

Beck, John Broadhead 1794-1851 *TwCBDA*

Beck, John Brodhead 1794-1851 *AmBi,
ApCAB, DcAmB, Drake, NatCAB 20*

Beck, Joseph David 1866-1936 *BiDrAC,*

NatCAB 28, WhAm 1, WhAmP

Beck, Joseph Marcus 1823-1893 *NatCAB 12*

Beck, Leonora 1862- *AmWom*

Beck, Lewis Caleb 1798-1853 *AmBi, ApCAB,
DcAmB, Drake, NatCAB 5, WhAm H*

Beck, Ludwig August Theodor 1880-1944
McGEWB, WhWW-II

Beck, Marcus Wayland 1860-1943 *NatCAB 32,
WhAm 2*

Beck, Martin 1867-1940 *DcAmB S2,
WhAm HA, WhAm 4*

Beck, Mary d1833 *NewYHSD, WhAm H*

Beck, Paul 1760?-1844 *ApCAB, Drake*

Beck, Rachel Wyatt Elizabeth Tongate
WomWWA 14

Beck, Robert McCandlass, Jr. 1879-1970
WhAm 5

Beck, Robert William 1896-1968 *NatCAB 55*

Beck, Ruth Everett *WomWWA 14a*

Beck, Samuel M 1827?- *NewYHSD*

Beck, Theoderic Romeyn 1791-1855 *NatCAB 9*

Beck, Theodoric Romeyn 1791-1855 *AmBi,
ApCAB, Drake, TwCBDA*

Beck, Theodric Romeyn 1791-1855 *DcAmB,
WhAm H*

Beck, Thomas Hambly 1881-1951 *WhAm 3*

Beck, Victor Emanuel 1894-1963 *WhAm 4*

Beck, Walter 1864-1954 *WhAm 4*

Beck, William 1869-1925 *WhAm 1*

Beck, William A 1883-1967 *WhAm 4*

Beck, William E 1832-1892 *NatCAB 5*

Beck, William Henry 1842-1911 *WhAm 1*

Beck, William Hopkins 1892-1957 *NatCAB 45,
WhAm 3*

Beck, William Stephen 1862-1939 *NatCAB 29*

Becke, Friedrich Johann Karl 1855-1931 *DcScB*

Becker, Abraham G 1857-1925 *NatCAB 23*

Becker, Alfred LeRoy 1878-1948 *NatCAB 17,
WhAm 2*

Becker, Arthur Charles 1895-1976 *WhAm 6*

Becker, Arthur Dow 1878-1947 *WhAm 2*

Becker, August H 1840-1903? *IIBEAAW,
NewYHSD*

Becker, Benjamin Vogel 1871-1955 *ApCAB X,
WhAm 3*

Becker, Carl Lotus 1873-1945 *BiDAmEd,
DcAmB S3, McGEWB, NatCAB 33,
WebAB, WhAm 2*

Becker, Charles E 1896-1968 *WhAm 5*

Becker, Charles Morris 1868-1927 *NatCAB 21*

Becker, Charles W 1896-1971 *WhAm 5*

Becker, Edmund 1861-1923 *NatCAB 21*

Becker, Elery Ronald 1896-1962 *WhAm 4*

Becker, Elizabeth H 1913-1970 *WhAm 5*

Becker, F Otto 1854-1945 *IIBEAAW*

Becker, Florence Hague d1971 *WhAm 5*

Becker, Folke 1891-1962 *NatCAB 50*

Becker, Folke *see also* Becker, Nils Folke

Becker, Frank John 1899- *BiDrAC, WhAmP*

Becker, Fred Harry 1885-1954 *NatCAB 44*

Becker, Frederic Harry 1885-1954 *WhAm 3*

Becker, Frederick W 1888- *IIBEAAW*

Becker, George Ferdinand 1847-1919 *AmBi,
ApCAB, DcAmB, DcScB, NatCAB 20,
TwCBDA, WebAB, WhAm 1*

Becker, Gustav Louis 1861-1959 *NatCAB 15*

Becker, Gustave Louis 1861-1959 *WhAm 3*

Becker, Harry J 1909-1975 *WhAm 6*

Becker, Henry Augustus 1870-1939 *NatCAB 29*

Becker, Henry Clinton 1877-1962 *NatCAB 51*

Becker, Howard 1899-1960 *WhAm 4*

Becker, Isidor Schultz 1897-1963 *WhAm 4*

Becker, James Herman 1894-1970 *NatCAB 55,
WhAm 5*

Becker, Joseph 1841-1910 *IIBEAAW, REnAW*

Becker, Joseph 1887-1966 *NatCAB 53,
WhAm 4*

Becker, Lawrence 1869- *WhAm 5*

Becker, Louis 1864-1919 *NatCAB 18*

Becker, Max Joseph 1828-1896 *NatCAB 12*

Becker, May Lamberton 1873-1958 *WhAm 3*

Becker, Neal Dow 1883-1955 *WhAm 3*

Becker, Nils Folke 1891-1962 *WhAm 4*

Becker, Nils Folke *see also* Becker, Folke

Becker, Owen Chauncey 1875-1954 *WhAm 3*

Becker, P L d1960 *WhAm 4*

Becker, Raymond Herman 1903-1975 *WhAm 6*

Becker, Robert 1890-1962 *WhAm 4*

Becker, Sherburn Merrill 1876-1949
NatCAB 38, WhAm 5

Becker, Thomas A 1831-1899 *NatCAB 12*

Becker, Thomas A 1832-1899 *ApCAB,
TwCBDA, WhAm 1*

Becker, Tracy Chatfield 1855- *WhAm 4*

Becker, Victor Hugo, Jr. 1877-1933 *NatCAB 25*

Becker, Washington 1847-1929 *NatCAB 10,
NatCAB 22, WhAm 1*

Becker, William Dee d1943 *WhAm 2*

Beckers, William Gerard 1874-1948 *ApCAB X,
WhAm 2*

Becket, Evro McDonald 1886-1960 *NatCAB 47*

Becket, Frederick Mark 1875-1942 *DcAmB S3,
WhAm 2*

Becket, Thomas, Saint 1128?-1170 *McGEWB*

Becket, Welton David 1902-1969 *WhAm 5*

Beckett, A Grant 1899-1966 *NatCAB 51*

Beckett, Charles E *NewYHSD*

Beckett, Frederick Arthur 1861-1918
NatCAB 42

Beckett, Guy Hamilton 1893-1965 *NatCAB 51*

Beckett, Percy Gordon 1882-1973 *WhAm 5*

Beckett, Peter Gordon Stewart 1922-1974
WhAm 6

Beckett, R Capel 1886-1954 *NatCAB 43*

Beckett, Richard Capel 1845-1921 *NatCAB 43*

Beckett, Richard Creighton 1893-1948 *WhAm 3*

Beckett, Samuel 1906- *McGEWB*

Beckett, Thomas Gervus, Jr. 1911-1956
WhAm 3

Beckett, Wesley Wilbur 1857-1936 *NatCAB 13,
WhAm 1*

Beckett, William Wesley 1857- *WhAm 4*

Beckett, Wymond Joe 1860-1944 *NatCAB 33*

Beckford, Fred Alexander 1882-1945
NatCAB 35

Beckford, William 1709-1770 *ApCAB*

Beckh, Frederick 1814?- *NewYHSD*

Beckh, H V A V *NewYHSD*

Beckham, Clifford Myron 1915-1971 *WhAm 5*

Beckham, John Crepps Wickliffe 1869-1940
*BiDrAC, NatCAB 13, TwCBDA,
WhAm 1, WhAmP*

Beckhart, Benjamin Haggott 1897-1975
WhAm 6

Beckington, Alice 1868-1942 *WhAm 1,
WomWWA 14*

Beckjord, Walter Clarence 1888-1965
NatCAB 51, WhAm 4

Beckler, William Alexander *WhAm 5*

Beckley, John *BiAUS*

Beckley, John James 1757-1807 *DcAmLiB*

Beckley, John Newton 1848- *NatCAB 5*

Beckley, Quitman F 1891-1963 *WhAm 4*

Beckley, Zoe d1961 *WhAm 4*

Beckman, Francis Joseph 1875-1948
NatCAB 35, WhAm 2

Beckman, Frederick William 1873-1957
WhAm 3

Beckman, Henry Frederick 1876- *WhAm 5*

Beckman, Joseph Henry 1913-1963 *NatCAB 50*

Beckman, L J *WhAm 5*

Beckman, Nellie Sims *WomWWA 14*

Beckman, Nils Arvid Teodor 1902-1972
WhAm 5

Beckman, P E 1899-1959 *WhAm 4*

Beckman, Theodore N 1895-1973 *WhAm 5*

Beckman, Vincent Henry 1879-1951 *WhAm 3*

Beckman, William Henry 1872-1956
NatCAB 49

Beckman And Brothers *NewYHSD*

Beckmann, Ernst Otto 1853-1923 *DcScB*

Beckmann, Johann 1739-1811 *DcScB*

Beckmann, Max 1884-1950 *IIBEAAW,
McGEWB, WhAm 4*

Becknell, William 1790?-1865 *AmBi, REnAW*

Becknell, William 1796?-1865 *DcAmB,
WebAB, WhAm H*

Becknell, William 1797?-1865 *McGEWB*

Beckner, Lucien 1872- *WhAm 5*

Beckner, Marie Warren 1875- *WomWWA 14*

Beckner, William Morgan 1841-1910 *BiDrAC*

Beckway, Harvey George 1898-1972 *WhAm 6*

Beckwith, Amos 1825-1894 *TwCBDA*

Beckwith, Amos 1830?-1894 *ApCAB*

Beckwith, Arthur 1860-1930? *IIBEAAW*

Beckwith, Charles Dyer 1838-1921 *BiDrAC*

Beckwith, Charles Minnigerode 1851-1928
NatCAB 13, WhAm 1
Beckwith, Clarence Augustine 1849-1931
DcAmB S1, WhAm 1
Beckwith, Clarence George 1902-1971
NatCAB 57
Beckwith, Cora Jipson 1875- *WomWWA 14*
Beckwith, Edmund Ruffin 1890-1949
NatCAB 37
Beckwith, Edward Anson 1879- *WhAm 6*
Beckwith, Edward Griffin 1818-1881 *ApCAB,*
TwCBDA
Beckwith, Edward Pierrepont 1877-1966
NatCAB 52
Beckwith, Emma 1849- *AmWom,*
WomWWA 14
Beckwith, Frank Clarence 1870-1954
NatCAB 41
Beckwith, Frederick Downey 1926-1971
WhAm 6
Beckwith, Sir George 1753-1823 *ApCAB,*
Drake
Beckwith, George C 1800-1870 *ApCAB, Drake*
Beckwith, Henry *NewYHSD*
Beckwith, Isbon Thaddeus 1843-1936 *WhAm 2*
Beckwith, James Carroll 1852-1917 *AmBi,*
ApCAB, ApCAB X, DcAmB, NatCAB 7,
TwCBDA, WhAm 1
Beckwith, Jane Elizabeth Warfield 1876-
WomWWA 14
Beckwith, John *NewYHSD*
Beckwith, John Watrous 1831-1890 *NatCAB 6*
Beckwith, John Watrus 1831-1890 *ApCAB,*
TwCBDA
Beckwith, Kate Reynolds 1865- *WomWWA 14*
Beckwith, Paul Edmond 1848-1907 *WhAm 1*
Beckwith, Theodore Day 1879-1946 *WhAm 2*
Beckworth, Lindley Gary 1913- *BiDrAC,*
WhAmP
Beckwourth, James P 1798-1867? *DcAmB,*
TwCBDA, WhAm H
Beckwourth, James P 1800-1867 *ApCAB*
Beckwourth, Jim 1800?-1866? *REnAW*
Becnel, Lezin Armant 1861-1923 *NatCAB 32*
Becquer, Gustavo Adolfo Dominguez 1836-1870
McGEWB
Becquerel, Alexandre-Edmond 1820-1891
DcScB
Becquerel, Antoine-Cesar 1788-1878 *DcScB*
Becquerel, Antoine Henri 1852-1908 *AsBiEn,*
DcScB, McGEWB
Becquerel, Paul 1879-1955 *DcScB*
Becton, Joseph D 1865-1931 *WhAm 1*
Bedard, Pierre 1763-1827 *ApCAB, Drake*
Bedard, Pierre 1895-1970 *WhAm 5, WhAm 6*
Bedaux, Charles Eugene 1886-1944 *DcAmB S3,*
WhAm 2
Beddall, Edward Fitch 1839- *WhAm 4*
Beddoe, John 1826-1911 *DcScB*
Beddoe, Robert Earl 1882-1952 *NatCAB 41*
Beddoes, Thomas 1760-1808 *DcScB*
Beddow, Elizabeth Russell *WomWWA 14*
Beddows, Charles Roland 1895-1972 *WhAm 5*
Bede 673-735 *AsBiEn*
Bede, Saint 672?-735 *McGEWB*
Bede, The Venerable 672?-735 *DcScB*
Bede, James Adam 1856-1942 *BiDrAC,*
WhAm 2, WhAmP
Bedel, John 1822-1875 *ApCAB, TwCBDA*
Bedel, Timothy d1787 *Drake, NatCAB 14*
Bedel, Timothy 1730?-1787 *NatCAB 17*
Bedel, Timothy 1740?-1787 *ApCAB*
Bedell, Arthur J 1879- *WhAm 6*
Bedell, Cornelia Frances 1876- *WomWWA 14*
Bedell, Frederick 1868-1958 *ApCAB X,*
NatCAB 51, WhAm 4
Bedell, Gregory Thurston 1817-1892 *ApCAB,*
Drake Sup, NatCAB 7, TwCBDA,
WhAm H
Bedell, Gregory Townsend 1793-1834 *ApCAB,*
Drake, NatCAB 11, TwCBDA
Bedell, Gregory Townshend 1793-1834
WhAm H
Bedell, Mary Crehore 1870- *WomWWA 14*
Bedell Smith, Walter 1895-1961 *WhWW-II*
Bedenkapp, Glen Ray 1890-1966 *NatCAB 52*
Bedford, Alfred Cotton 1862-1925 *NatCAB 23*
Bedford, Alfred Cotton 1864-1925 *WhAm 1*

Bedford, Bruce 1876-1962 *NatCAB 49*
Bedford, Edward Thomas 1849-1931 *ApCAB X,*
NatCAB 14, NatCAB 22, WhAm 1
Bedford, Frederick Henry 1854-1931
NatCAB 23
Bedford, Frederick Henry, Jr. 1891-1952
NatCAB 41, WhAm 3
Bedford, Frederick Thomas 1877-1963
NatCAB 50, WhAm 4
Bedford, Gunning d1797 *BiAUS, Drake*
Bedford, Gunning 1730?-1797 *ApCAB,*
TwCBDA
Bedford, Gunning 1742-1797 *BiDrAC, DcAmB,*
NatCAB 11, WhAm H, WhAmP
Bedford, Gunning, Jr. 1747-1812 *AmBi,*
ApCAB, BiAUS, BiDrAC, DcAmB,
Drake, NatCAB 2, TwCBDA, WhAm H,
WhAmP
Bedford, Gunning S 1806-1870 *AmBi, ApCAB,*
Drake, NatCAB 9, TwCBDA, WhAm H
Bedford, Henry Clark 1875- *WhAm 5*
Bedford, Henry Moore d1880 *ApCAB*
Bedford, Homer F 1880- *WhAm 6*
Bedford, Lou Singletary 1837- *AmWom*
Bedford, Paul 1875-1967 *WhAm 5*
Bedford, Scott Elias William 1876- *WhAm 5*
Bedford-Jones, Henry James O'Brien 1887-1949
NatCAB 37, WhAm 2
Bedichek, Roy 1878-1959 *REnAW*
Bedinger, George Michael d1830? *BiAUS,*
Drake
Bedinger, George Michael 1750?-1830? *ApCAB,*
TwCBDA
Bedinger, George Michael 1756-1843 *BiDrAC,*
DcAmB, NatCAB 21, WhAm H,
WhAmP
Bedinger, Henry d1858 *BiAUS, NatCAB 11*
Bedinger, Henry 1810-1858 *ApCAB, Drake,*
TwCBDA
Bedinger, Henry 1812-1858 *BiDrAC,*
WhAm H, WhAmP
Bedinger, Maria Voorhees *WomWWA 14*
Bedle, Althea Fitz Randolph 1842-
WomWWA 14
Bedle, Joseph D 1831-1894 *ApCAB*
Bedle, Joseph Dorset 1831-1894 *BiAUS*
Bedle, Joseph Dorsett 1821-1894 *NatCAB 5,*
WhAm H
Bedle, Joseph Dorsett 1831-1894 *TwCBDA*
Bedlow, Henry 1821- *NatCAB 7*
Bedon, Peter d1561 *ApCAB*
Bedsole, Joseph Linyer 1881- *WhAm 6*
Bedwell, Thomas *NewYHSD*
Bee, Barnard E 1823-1861 *NatCAB 7*
Bee, Barnard E 1825?-1861 *Drake*
Bee, Barnard Elliott 1824-1861 *DcAmB,*
WebAB, WebAMB, WhAm H
Bee, Bernard E 1823?-1861 *ApCAB, TwCBDA*
Bee, Carlos 1867-1932 *BiDrAC*
Bee, Hamilton Prioleau 1822-1897 *ApCAB Sup,*
BiDConf, DcAmB, WhAm H
Bee, Henry Jubilee 1810?- *ApCAB*
Bee, Thomas d1812 *BiAUS, Drake*
Bee, Thomas 1725-1812 *BiDrAC, WhAm H,*
WhAmP
Bee, Thomas 1729-1812 *ApCAB*
Beebe, Alice Geissler 1874- *WomWWA 14*
Beebe, Bezaleel 1741-1824 *ApCAB, Drake,*
TwCBDA
Beebe, Brooks Ford 1850- *WhAm 1*
Beebe, Charles William 1877-1962 *AsBiEn,*
WebAB
Beebe, Ebenezer d1812 *ApCAB*
Beebe, Evanore Olds 1858- *WomWWA 14*
Beebe, Frederick Sessions 1914-1973 *WhAm 5*
Beebe, George Monroe 1836-1927 *BiAUS,*
BiDrAC, NatCAB 20, WhAmP
Beebe, James Albert 1878-1934 *NatCAB 26,*
WhAm 1, WhAm 1C
Beebe, James Lyndon 1889-1966 *NatCAB 53,*
WhAm 4
Beebe, Junius 1854-1934 *NatCAB 25*
Beebe, Katherine 1860-1943 *WhAm 3*
Beebe, Kenneth John 1889-1970 *WhAm 5*
Beebe, Lewis C 1891-1951 *WhAm 3*
Beebe, Lucius 1810-1884 *NatCAB 25*
Beebe, Lucius Morris 1902-1966 *NatCAB 55,*
WebAB, WhAm 4

Beebe, Milton Earl 1840- *NatCAB 3*
Beebe, Minnie Mason *WomWWA 14*
Beebe, Murray Charles 1876-1943 *WhAm 2*
Beebe, Philip S 1888-1960 *WhAm 4*
Beebe, Raymond Nelson 1890-1971 *WhAm 5*
Beebe, Royden Eugene, Jr. 1908-1959 *WhAm 3*
Beebe, William 1851-1917 *WhAm 1*
Beebe, William 1877-1962 *NatCAB 47,*
WebAB, WhAm 4
Beebee, Alexander MacWhorter 1820-1897
NatCAB 27
Beeber, Dimner 1854-1930 *NatCAB 11,*
WhAm 1
Beeby, Nell Viola 1896-1957 *NatCAB 45*
Beech, Raymond Henry 1907-1962 *NatCAB 50*
Beech, Walter Herschel 1891-1950 *NatCAB 39,*
WhAm 3
Beecham, Sir Thomas 1879-1961 *WhAm 4*
Beeche, Octavio 1866- *WhAm 4*
Beecher, Amariah Dwight 1839- *NewYHSD,*
WhAm H
Beecher, Catharine Esther 1800-1878 *AmBi,*
BiDAmEd, DcAmB, Drake, NatCAB 3,
NotAW, WebAB, WhAm H, WhAmP
Beecher, Catherine Esther 1800-1878 *AmWom,*
ApCAB, TwCBDA
Beecher, Charles 1810-1900 *Drake*
Beecher, Charles 1815-1900 *ApCAB, DcAmB,*
NatCAB 3, TwCBDA, WhAm 1
Beecher, Charles Emerson 1856-1904 *AmBi,*
DcAmB, NatCAB 13, TwCBDA,
WhAm 1
Beecher, Edward 1803-1895 *ApCAB, DcAmB,*
DcAmReB, NatCAB 3, TwCBDA,
WebAB, WhAm H
Beecher, Edward 1804-1895 *Drake*
Beecher, Eunice White Bullard 1812-1897
ApCAB, NatCAB 3, TwCBDA, WhAm H
Beecher, Frederick Henry 1841-1868 *ApCAB,*
NatCAB 13, TwCBDA, WebAMB
Beecher, George 1809-1843 *ApCAB,*
NatCAB 3
Beecher, George Allen 1868- *WhAm 5*
Beecher, Hattie Foster 1854- *WomWWA 14*
Beecher, Henry Ward 1813-1887 *AmBi,*
ApCAB, DcAmB, DcAmReB, Drake,
EncAB, McGEWB, NatCAB 3,
TwCBDA, WebAB, WhAm H, WhAmP
Beecher, Isabel Garghill 1872- *WomWWA 14*
Beecher, James Chaplin 1828-1886 *ApCAB,*
NatCAB 3, TwCBDA
Beecher, Laban S 1805?- *NewYHSD,*
WhAm H
Beecher, Lyman 1775-1863 *AmBi, ApCAB,*
DcAmB, DcAmReB, Drake, McGEWB,
NatCAB 3, TwCBDA, WebAB,
WhAm H, WhAmP
Beecher, Martha A *WomWWA 14*
Beecher, Philemon 1775-1839 *BiAUS, BiDrAC,*
WhAm H, WhAmP
Beecher, Philip 1835?- *NewYHSD*
Beecher, Roxana 1775- *NewYHSD*
Beecher, Thomas Kennicutt 1824-1900
TwCBDA
Beecher, Thomas Kinnicut 1824-1900 *ApCAB,*
DcAmB, NatCAB 3, WhAm 1
Beecher, William Constantine 1849-1928
NatCAB 31
Beecher, William Henry 1802-1889 *ApCAB,*
NatCAB 3, TwCBDA
Beecher, Willis Judson 1838-1912 *NatCAB 8,*
NatCAB 16, TwCBDA, WhAm 1
Beechey, Frederic William 1796-1856 *Drake*
Beechey, Frederick William 1796-1856 *ApCAB*
Beechler, Glenn Curtis 1881-1954 *WhAm 3*
Beechwood, Floyd F 1889-1965 *NatCAB 51*
Beeckman, Eleanor Thomas 1878-1920 *BiCAW*
Beeckman, Isaac 1588-1637 *DcScB*
Beeckman, R Livingston 1866-1935 *NatCAB 52,*
WhAm 1
Beecroft, John William Richard 1902-1966
WhAm 4
Beede, Frank Herbert 1859-1932 *WhAm 1*
Beede, Herbert Gould 1870-1943 *WhAm 2*
Beede, Joshua William 1871-1940 *WhAm 1*
Beede, Victor Augustus 1886-1957 *NatCAB 47*
Beedy, Carroll Linwood 1880-1947 *WhAm 2*
Beedy, Carroll Lynwood 1880-1947 *BiDrAC,*

WhAmP
Beegle, Frederick N 1863-1923 *NatCAB 19*
Beehan *NewYHSD*
Beehler, William Henry 1848-1915 *WhAm 1*
Beek, Alice D Engley 1867-1951 *WhAm 3*
Beekey, Cyrus Ezra 1906-1974 *WhAm 6*
Beekman, Benjamin B 1863- *NatCAB 17*
Beekman, Charles Keller 1868-1941
NatCAB 14, NatCAB 30
Beekman, Cornelius C 1828-1915 *NatCAB 17*
Beekman, Dow 1863-1945 *NatCAB 34*
Beekman, Fenwick 1882-1962 *WhAm 4*
Beekman, Frederick Warren 1871-1964
NatCAB 51, WhAm 5
Beekman, Gerardus d1728? *ApCAB,*
NatCAB 10
Beekman, Gerardus 1653-1723 *TwCBDA*
Beekman, Henry Rutgers 1845-1900
NatCAB 12, WhAm 4
Beekman, James William 1815-1877 *ApCAB,*
NatCAB 12, TwCBDA
Beekman, John K *WhAm H*
Beekman, Thomas 1824- *BiAUS, BiDrAC,*
WhAm H
Beekman, William Bedlow 1842-1898
NatCAB 33
Beeks, William Tecumseh Sherman 1866-1928
NatCAB 21
Beeler, Charles H *NewYHSD*
Beeler, Helen Marion 1907- *WhAm 6*
Beeler, Irving Neff 1883-1936 *NatCAB 33*
Beeler, Joe 1931- *IIBEAAW*
Beeler, John A 1867-1945 *WhAm 2*
Beeler, Roy Hood 1882-1954 *WhAm 3*
Beeley, Arthur Lewton 1890-1973 *WhAm 6*
Beem, Emma B 1860- *WomWWA 14*
Beeman, Joseph Henry 1833-1909 *BiDrAC*
Beemer, Allen Dayton 1843-1909 *NatCAB 17*
Beer, Dorcas Grizzel *WomWWA 14*
Beer, George Louis 1872-1920 *AmBi, DcAmB,*
NatCAB 19, WhAm 1, WhAmP
Beer, Katherine J *WomWWA 14*
Beer, Mary Elizabeth *WomWWA 14*
Beer, Thomas 1889-1940 *DcAmB S2,*
WhAm 1
Beer, Wilhelm 1797-1850 *AsBiEn, DcScB*
Beer, William 1849-1927 *DcAmB, DcAmLiB,*
NatCAB 12, WhAm 1
Beerbohm, Sir Max 1872-1956 *WhAm 3*
Beermann, Ralph Frederick 1912- *BiDrAC*
Beers, Alfred Bishop 1845-1920 *NatCAB 20,*
WhAm 1
Beers, Barnet William 1896-1971 *WhAm 5*
Beers, Clifford Whittingham 1876-1943
DcAmB S3, NatCAB 34, WebAB,
WhAm 1
Beers, Cyrus 1786-1850 *BiAUS, BiDrAC,*
WhAm H
Beers, Edward McMath 1877-1932 *BiDrAC,*
WhAmP
Beers, Ethel Lynn 1827-1879 *AmBi, ApCAB,*
DcAmB, WhAm H
Beers, Ethelinda Eliot 1827-1879 *TwCBDA*
Beers, Ethelinda Elliot 1827-1879 *NatCAB 8*
Beers, Frederick 1880-1955 *WhAm 3*
Beers, Frederick 1880-1956 *NatCAB 42*
Beers, George Emerson 1865-1947 *NatCAB 39,*
WhAm 2
Beers, Henry Augustin 1847-1926 *AmBi,*
ApCAB, DcAmB, NatCAB 7,
NatCAB 44, TwCBDA, WhAm 1
Beers, Julie Hart *NewYHSD*
Beers, Keturah G *WomWWA 14a*
Beers, Lila Eliza 1867- *WomWWA 14*
Beers, Lucius Hart 1859-1948 *WhAm 2*
Beers, N P *NewYHSD*
Beers, Nathan Thomas 1874-1950 *NatCAB 41*
Beers, Reid Lafeal 1908-1962 *NatCAB 50*
Beers, William George 1846- *ApCAB Sup*
Beers, William Harmon 1881-1949 *WhAm 2*
Beers, William Henry 1823-1893 *NatCAB 33*
Beers, William Henry 1877-1946 *NatCAB 40*
Beery, Noah *IIBEAAW*
Beery, Roy F, Jr. 1917-1964 *NatCAB 51*
Beery, Wallace 1886-1949 *WebAB, WhAm 2*
Beery, Wallace Fitzgerald 1885-1949
DcAmB S4
Beese, Charles William 1891-1958 *NatCAB 52,*

WhAm 3
Beese, H *NewYHSD*
Beesley, Eugene Nevin 1909-1976 *WhAm 6*
Beeson, Charles Henry 1870-1949 *DcAmB S4,*
WhAm 2
Beeson, Henry White 1791-1863 *BiAUS,*
BiDrAC, WhAm H
Beeson, Jasper Luther 1867-1943 *WhAm 2*
Beeson, Malcolm Alfred 1879- *WhAm 6*
Beest, Albert Van 1820-1860 *ApCAB,*
NewYHSD, WhAm H
Beet, Cornelius De 1772?- *NewYHSD*
Beethoven, Ludwig Van 1770-1827 *McGEWB*
Beetle, David Harold 1908-1972 *WhAm 5*
Beets, Henry 1869-1947 *WhAm 2*
Beeuwkes, Adelia Marie 1910-1966 *NatCAB 52,*
WhAm 4
Beevor, Charles Edward 1854-1908 *DcScB*
Beffa, Harvey Arthur 1900-1975 *WhAm 6*
Beffel, Olive Baker *WomWWA 14*
Begay, Apie *IIBEAAW*
Begay, Harrison 1917- *IIBEAAW*
Begbie, Sir Matthew Baillie 1819-1894
ApCAB Sup
Begeman, Louis 1865-1958 *NatCAB 49,*
WhAm 3
Begg, Alexander Swanson 1881-1940 *WhAm 1*
Begg, Colin Luke 1873-1941 *NatCAB 31*
Begg, James Thomas 1877-1963 *BiDrAC,*
WhAm 5
Begg, John Alfred 1903-1974 *WhAm 6*
Begg, Robert Burns Haldane 1880- *WhAm 6*
Beggs, Daniel Richardson 1876-1955
NatCAB 45
Beggs, Frederic 1875-1941 *NatCAB 34*
Beggs, George Erle 1883-1939 *NatCAB 39,*
WhAm 1
Beggs, Gertrude Harper 1874- *WhAm 5,*
WomWWA 14
Beggs, John Irvin 1847-1925 *NatCAB 20*
Beggs, Lyall T 1899-1973 *WhAm 6*
Beghin, Henri 1876-1969 *DcScB*
Beghtol, Maxwell Vance 1886-1956 *NatCAB 48*
Begich, Nicholas Joseph 1932-1972 *WhAm 5*
Begien, Ralph Norman 1875-1944 *WhAm 2*
Begin, Louis-Nazaire 1840- *ApCAB Sup*
Begle, Grace Griffith 1878- *WomWWA 14*
Begley, Ed 1901-1970 *WhAm 5*
Begley, John Patrick 1894-1974 *WhAm 6*
Begoden, Achilles 1816?-1899 *NewYHSD*
Begole, George Davis 1877- *WhAm 5*
Begole, Josiah Williams 1815-1896 *BiAUS,*
BiDrAC, NatCAB 5, TwCBDA,
WhAm H, WhAmP
Beguelin, Henry Eugene 1840- *NatCAB 1*
Beguin, Jean 1550?-1620? *DcScB*
Beguyer DeChancourtois, Alexandre-Emile
1820-1886 *AsBiEn, DcScB*
Behaim, Martin 1459?-1506 *ApCAB*
Behaim, Martin 1459-1507 *DcScB*
Behan, Bessie 1872- *AmWom*
Behan, Brendan Francis 1923-1964 *WhAm 4*
Behan, Helen Peters 1904-1974 *WhAm 6*
Behan, Joseph C 1873-1949 *WhAm 3*
Behan, Katie Walker 1847- *NatCAB 14*
Behan, Richard Joseph 1879- *WhAm 6*
Behan, Thomas *NewYHSD*
Behan, Warren Palmer 1871-1952 *WhAm 3*
Behan, William James 1840-1928 *DcAmB,*
NatCAB 14, WhAm 1, WhAmP
Beharrell, Sir George 1873-1959 *WhAm 3*
Behel, Aquila Olin 1857-1914 *NatCAB 16*
Behem, Martin 1430?-1506 *Drake*
Behle, Augustus Calvin 1871-1951 *NatCAB 51*
Behm, Walter Henry John 1890-1951 *WhAm 3*
Behn, Hernand 1880-1933 *NatCAB 53,*
WhAm 1
Behn, Sosthenes 1882-1957 *NatCAB 53,*
WhAm 3
Behncke, David L d1953 *WhAm 3*
Behne, Gustavus Adolphus 1828-1895
NewYHSD
Behner, Albert Jacob 1888-1928 *WhAm 1*
Behounek, Frantisek 1898-1973 *WhAm 6*
Behre, Gerhard Frederick 1892-1952
NatCAB 42
Behrend, Anton Friedrich Robert 1856-1926
DcScB Sup

Behrend, Bernard Arthur 1875-1932 *DcAmB S1,*
NatCAB 35, WhAm 1
Behrend, Ernst Richard 1869-1940 *NatCAB 31,*
WhAm 1, WhAm 2
Behrend, Genevieve A 1881- *WhAm 6*
Behrend, Otto Frederick 1872-1957 *NatCAB 46*
Behrend, Rudolph Bernhard 1877-1958
NatCAB 43
Behrends, Adolphus Julius Frederick 1839-1900
DcAmB, NatCAB 8, TwCBDA, WhAm 1
Behrendt, Leo Aloys 1896-1959 *NatCAB 52*
Behrendt, Walter Curt 1884-1945 *DcAmB S3,*
WhAm 2
Behrens, Charles August 1885-1950 *WhAm 3*
Behrens, Charles Frederick 1896-1974 *WhAm 6*
Behrens, H Frederick 1870-1935 *WhAm 1*
Behrens, Henry 1815-1895 *DcAmB, WhAm H*
Behrens, Herman Albert 1883-1945 *NatCAB 34,*
WhAm 2
Behrens, James 1824- *ApCAB*
Behrens, L *NewYHSD*
Behrens, Peter 1868-1940 *McGEWB*
Behrens, William John 1860-1940 *NatCAB 31*
Behrens, William Wohlsen 1898-1965 *WhAm 4*
Behrensmeyer, Charles Frederick 1908-1960
NatCAB 48
Behring, Emil Adolf Von 1854-1917 *AsBiEn*
Behring, Emil Adolph Von 1854-1917 *McGEWB*
Behring, Emil Von 1854-1917 *DcScB*
Behring, Vitus 1680-1741 *Drake*
Behringer, Albert Christian 1885-1954
NatCAB 41
Behrman, Martin 1864-1926 *NatCAB 14,*
WhAm 1
Behrman, Samuel Nathaniel 1893-1973
WhAm 6
Behymer, Arthur Livingstone 1869- *WhAm 5*
Behymer, Francis Albert 1870-1956 *WhAm 3*
Behymer, Lynden Ellsworth 1862-1947
WhAm 2
Behzad d1530? *McGEWB*
Beich, Otto Gerken 1892-1964 *NatCAB 51*
Beich, Paul Frank 1864-1937 *NatCAB 34*
Beich, Paul Marion 1916-1968 *NatCAB 54*
Beiderbecke, Leon Bismarck 1903-1931 *WebAB*
Beiderbecke, Leon Bix 1903-1931 *WhAm HA,*
WhAm 4
Beidler, Jacob Atlee 1852-1912 *BiDrAC,*
WhAm 4, WhAmP
Beier, Walter Charles 1891-1962 *NatCAB 49*
Beigel, John *NewYHSD*
Beijerinck, Martinus Willem 1851-1931 *AsBiEn,*
BiHiMed, DcScB Sup
Beik, Arthur Kennedy 1882-1949 *NatCAB 38*
Beil, Charles A *IIBEAAW*
Beilfuss, Albert William 1854-1914 *NatCAB 16*
Beilharz, Edwin Alanson 1907- *EncAAH*
Beilstein, Edward Henry 1913-1973 *WhAm 6*
Beilstein, Friedrich Konrad 1838-1906 *AsBiEn*
Beilstein, Konrad Friedrich 1838-1906 *DcScB*
Beilstein, Laura Lee 1887- *WomWWA 14*
Beinecke, Edwin John 1886-1970 *ApCAB X,*
NatCAB 57, WhAm 5
Beinecke, Frederick William 1887-1971
NatCAB 56, WhAm 5
Beinecke, Richard Sperry 1917-1966 *WhAm 4*
Beinecke, Walter 1888-1958 *WhAm 3*
Beinfield, Henry Harold 1892-1971 *NatCAB 55*
Beirn, Martin Joseph, Jr. 1877-1944
NatCAB 33
Beirne, Andrew 1771-1845 *BiDrAC, WhAm H,*
WhAmP
Beirne, Joseph Anthony 1911-1974 *WhAm 6*
Beisler, Simon Lawrence 1900-1973 *NatCAB 57*
Beissel, Johann Conrad 1690-1768 *AmBi,*
ApCAB, DcAmB, DcAmReB, McGEWB,
NatCAB 7, WebAB, WhAm H
Beiter, Alfred Florian 1894- *BiDrAC*
Beitler, Abraham Merklee 1853-1935
NatCAB 29
Beitler, Harold Bornemann 1880- *WhAm 6*
Beitoldi, J *NewYHSD*
Bek, William Godfrey 1873-1948 *WhAm 2*
Bekesy, Georg Von 1899-1972 *AsBiEn, WebAB*
Beketov, Nikolai Nikolaevich 1827-1911 *DcScB*
Bekhterev, Vladimir Mikhailovich 1857-1927
DcScB
Bekins, Melvin 1896-1966 *WhAm 4*

Bekker, Leander J De 1872-1931 *WhAm 1*
Bel, George Sam 1872-1939 *NatCAB 30*
Bel Geddes, Norman 1893-1958 *BnEnAmA,*
  WebAB
Belaiew, Nicholas Timothy 1878-1955 *DcScB*
Belanger, F J *NewYHSD*
Belanger, John W 1901-1968 *WhAm 5*
Belanger, Solomon d1863 *ApCAB*
Belasco, David 1853-1931 *DcAmB S1, EncAB,*
  McGEWB, WebAB
Belasco, David 1854-1931 *AmBi, WhAm 1*
Belasco, David 1858-1931 *ApCAB Sup,*
  ApCAB X, TwCBDA
Belasco, David 1859-1931 *NatCAB 14*
Belaume, J *NewYHSD*
Belaunde, Victor Andres 1883-1966 *WhAm 4*
Belaval, Jose S 1879- *WhAm 6*
Belcher, Andrew *ApCAB*
Belcher, Cynthia Holmes 1827- *AmWom*
Belcher, Sir Edward 1799-1877 *ApCAB, Drake*
Belcher, Edwin Newton, Jr. 1913-1971 *WhAm 5*
Belcher, Frank Garrettson 1905-1959
  NatCAB 47, WhAm 3
Belcher, Frank J, Jr. 1878-1952 *NatCAB 42,*
  WhAm 3
Belcher, George E 1850-1924 *ApCAB X*
Belcher, Hilda 1881-1963 *WhAm 4,*
  WomWWA 14
Belcher, Hiram 1790-1857 *BiAUS, BiDrAC,*
  WhAm H, WhAmP
Belcher, James Elmer 1885-1972 *WhAm 5*
Belcher, Jonathan 1681?-1757 *AmBi, ApCAB,*
  DcAmB, TwCBDA, WhAmP
Belcher, Jonathan 1682-1757 *Drake,*
  NatCAB 6, WebAB, WhAm H
Belcher, Jonathan 1710-1776 *ApCAB, Drake*
Belcher, Joseph 1794-1859 *ApCAB, Drake*
Belcher, Nathan 1813-1891 *BiAUS, BiDrAC,*
  WhAm H
Belcher, Page Henry 1899- *BiDrAC*
Belcher, Supply 1751-1836 *WhAm H*
Belcher, Wallace Edward 1879-1959
  NatCAB 47, WhAm 6
Belcher, Warren Joseph 1868-1943 *NatCAB 33*
Belcourt, George Antoine 1803-1874 *DcAmB,*
  WhAm H
Belden, Albert Clinton 1845-1890 *NatCAB 3*
Belden, Augustus A 1837-1921 *NatCAB 19*
Belden, Charles Dwight 1845-1919 *WhAm 1*
Belden, Charles Francis Dorr 1870-1931
  DcAmLiB, NatCAB 23, WhAm 1
Belden, Ellsworth Burnett 1866-1939
  NatCAB 37, WhAm 1
Belden, Frank Annis 1880-1944 *NatCAB 32*
Belden, George O 1797-1833 *BiAUS*
Belden, George Ogilvie 1797-1833 *BiDrAC*
Belden, George Oglivie 1797-1833 *WhAm H*
Belden, Henry Marvin 1865- *WhAm 4*
Belden, James Jerome 1825-1904 *ApCAB Sup,*
  BiDrAC, TwCBDA, WhAm 1, WhAmP
Belden, Jessie VanZile 1857-1910 *WhAm 1*
Belden, Joseph Congdon 1876-1939 *NatCAB 39*
Belden, Josiah 1815-1892 *ApCAB, DcAmB,*
  WhAm H, WhAmP
Belden, Paul Blake 1882-1970 *NatCAB 57*
Belden, Webster Whitall 1892-1930 *NatCAB 23*
Belden, William Burlingame 1902- *WhAm 5*
Belding, Alvah Norton 1838-1925 *ApCAB X,*
  NatCAB 18, WhAm 1
Belding, Anson Wood 1881-1970 *NatCAB 55,*
  WhAm 6
Belding, David Lawrence 1884-1970 *WhAm 5*
Belding, Don 1898-1969 *WhAm 5*
Belding, Frederick Norton 1887-1945 *WhAm 2*
Belding, Milo Merrick 1833-1917 *NatCAB 1,*
  WhAm 1
Belding, Milo Merrick, Jr. 1865-1931 *ApCAB X,*
  WhAm 1
Beldock, George J 1904-1970 *WhAm 5*
Belehetzi d1524 *ApCAB*
Belew, David Owen 1885-1964 *NatCAB 51*
Beley, Maximilian 1821?- *NewYHSD*
Belfield, Ada Marshall 1872- *WomWWA 14*
Belfield, Anne Wallace Miller 1848-
  WomWWA 14
Belfield, Elizabeth Mills 1875- *WomWWA 14*
Belfield, Henry Holmes 1837-1912 *BiDAmEd,*
  NatCAB 20, WhAm 1

Belfield, William Thomas 1856-1929 *WhAm 1*
Belford, James Burns 1837-1910 *BiAUS,*
  BiDrAC, WhAm 1, WhAmP
Belford, John L 1861-1951 *WhAm 3*
Belford, Joseph McCrum 1852-1917 *BiDrAC*
Belfour, C Stanton 1906-1969 *WhAm 5*
Belgrano, Frank N, Jr. 1895-1959 *WhAm 3*
Belgrano, Manuel 1770-1820 *ApCAB, Drake,*
  McGEWB
Belidor, Bernard Forest De 1697?-1761 *DcScB*
Belin, Ferdinand Lammet 1881- *WhAm 6*
Belin, G D'Andelot 1888-1954 *WhAm 3*
Belinsky, Vissarion Grigorievich 1811-1848
  McGEWB
Belisarius 506?-565 *McGEWB*
Belisle, Hector Louis 1873-1950 *WhAm 3*
Belk, Henry 1898-1972 *WhAm 5*
Belk, William Henry 1862-1952 *WhAm 3*
Belknap, Charles 1880-1954 *NatCAB 44,*
  WhAm 4
Belknap, Charles Eugene 1846-1929 *BiDrAC,*
  TwCBDA
Belknap, Charles H 1842- *NatCAB 12*
Belknap, Daniel 1771-1815 *WhAm H*
Belknap, Edwin Star *WhAm 1*
Belknap, George Eugene 1832-1903 *AmBi,*
  ApCAB, DcAmB, NatCAB 4,
  NatCAB 42, TwCBDA, WhAm 1
Belknap, George Myron 1919-1970 *NatCAB 56*
Belknap, Henry Wyckoff 1860- *WhAm 4*
Belknap, Hugh Reid 1860-1901 *BiDrAC*
Belknap, Jeremy 1744-1798 *AmBi, ApCAB,*
  DcAmB, Drake, EncAAH, NatCAB 7,
  TwCBDA, WhAm H
Belknap, Morris Burke 1856-1910 *WhAm 1*
Belknap, Paul Edward 1910-1975 *WhAm 6*
Belknap, Raymond Harvey 1907-1966
  NatCAB 52, WhAm 4
Belknap, Reginald Rowan 1871-1959 *WhAm 3*
Belknap, Robert Lenox 1848-1896 *NatCAB 30*
Belknap, William Burke 1885-1965 *NatCAB 51*
Belknap, William Ethelbert 1867-1942
  NatCAB 31
Belknap, William Goldsmith 1794-1851 *ApCAB,*
  Drake
Belknap, William Richardson 1849-1914
  NatCAB 16, WhAm 1
Belknap, William Worth 1829-1890 *AmBi,*
  ApCAB, BiDrUSE, DcAmB, NatCAB 4,
  TwCBDA, WhAm H, WhAmP
Belknap, William Worth 1831-1890 *BiAUS,*
  BiAUS Sup, Drake
Belknap, Zedekiah 1781-1858 *NewYHSD*
Bell, Agnes Isabel Taylor *WomWWA 14*
Bell, Agrippa Nelson 1820-1911 *NatCAB 8,*
  TwCBDA, WhAm 1
Bell, Albert Cunningham 1873-1957
  NatCAB 45
Bell, Albert Mortimer 1885-1946 *NatCAB 36*
Bell, Alexander Graham 1847-1922 *AmBi,*
  ApCAB, ApCAB X, AsBiEn, BiDAmEd,
  DcAmB, DcScB, EncAB, McGEWB,
  NatCAB 6, TwCBDA, WebAB, WhAm 1
Bell, Alexander Melville 1819-1905 *AmBi,*
  ApCAB, DcAmB, NatCAB 9, TwCBDA,
  WhAm 1
Bell, Alfred Lee Loomis 1890-1974 *WhAm 6*
Bell, Alphonzo 1914- *BiDrAC*
Bell, Alphonzo Edward 1875-1947 *NatCAB 36,*
  WhAm 2
Bell, Andrew 1753-1832 *McGEWB*
Bell, Anna Adams 1849- *WomWWA 14*
Bell, Archie 1877- *WhAm 5*
Bell, Bennett D 1851- *WhAm 4*
Bell, Bernard Iddings 1886-1958 *DcAmReB,*
  NatCAB 43, WhAm 3
Bell, Bert 1894-1959 *WhAm 3*
Bell, Brian 1890-1942 *WhAm 2*
Bell, Bryan 1878-1945 *NatCAB 35*
Bell, Caroline Horton 1840- *AmWom*
Bell, Carolyn E 1850- *WomWWA 14*
Bell, Casper Wister 1819-1898 *BiDConf*
Bell, Sir Charles 1774-1842 *BiHiMed, DcScB*
Bell, Charles H 1798-1875 *ApCAB, Drake,*
  NatCAB 2, TwCBDA
Bell, Charles Henry 1823-1893 *ApCAB,*
  BiDrAC, DcAmB, NatCAB 11, TwCBDA,
  WhAm H, WhAmP

Bell, Charles James 1845-1909 *NatCAB 13,*
  WhAm 1
Bell, Charles James 1858-1929 *WhAm 1*
Bell, Charles Jasper 1885- *BiDrAC, WhAmP*
Bell, Charles John 1858-1929 *NatCAB 21*
Bell, Charles Keith 1853-1913 *BiDrAC,*
  TwCBDA, WhAmP
Bell, Charles S 1880-1965 *WhAm 2, WhAm 4*
Bell, Charles Upham 1843-1922 *ApCAB X,*
  NatCAB 18
Bell, Charles Webster 1857-1927 *BiDrAC,*
  WhAm 2
Bell, Clark 1832-1918 *AmBi, ApCAB,*
  DcAmB, TwCBDA, WhAm 1
Bell, Clarke 1832-1918 *NatCAB 13*
Bell, Daniel Wafena 1891-1971 *NatCAB 56,*
  WhAm 5
Bell, Digby 1849-1917 *WhAm 1*
Bell, Dixon Tucker 1896-1955 *NatCAB 54*
Bell, Earl Hoyt 1903-1963 *WhAm 4*
Bell, Edward 1882-1924 *WhAm 1*
Bell, Edward August 1861-1953 *NatCAB 7,*
  NatCAB 44, WhAm 3
Bell, Edward Bryce 1896-1968 *NatCAB 55*
Bell, Edward Price 1869-1943 *WhAm 2*
Bell, Edward Theodore 1843-1921 *WhAm 1*
Bell, Elexious Thompson 1880-1963 *NatCAB 52*
Bell, Ellen Chesbro *WomWWA 14*
Bell, Emily Ruth Harris *WomWWA 14*
Bell, Enoch Frye 1874-1945 *NatCAB 34,*
  WhAm 2
Bell, Eric Temple 1883-1960 *DcScB,*
  NatCAB 54, WhAm 4
Bell, Ernest R 1889-1973 *NatCAB 57*
Bell, Eudorus N *DcAmReB*
Bell, Forrest Gunn 1891-1960 *NatCAB 50*
Bell, Francis Robert 1888-1958 *NatCAB 46*
Bell, Frank Breckenridge 1876-1949 *WhAm 2*
Bell, Frank Frederick 1855- *NatCAB 5*
Bell, Frederic Somers 1859-1938 *DcAmB S2,*
  WhAm 1, WhAm 2
Bell, Gail Shepard *WomWWA 14*
Bell, George 1828-1907 *WhAm 1*
Bell, George 1832?- *ApCAB*
Bell, George, Jr. 1859-1926 *NatCAB 25,*
  WhAm 1
Bell, George Alfred 1878-1956 *WhAm 3*
Bell, George Fisher 1877-1941 *WhAm 1*
Bell, George Godfrey 1867-1948 *NatCAB 36*
Bell, Bishop George Kennedy Allen 1883-1958
  WhAm 3, WhWW-II
Bell, George L 1888-1958 *WhAm 3*
Bell, George Maxwell 1911-1972 *WhAm 5*
Bell, George William 1873-1920 *NatCAB 19*
Bell, Graham Bernat 1923-1968 *WhAm 5*
Bell, Harmon 1855-1929 *WhAm 1*
Bell, Helene S Taylor 1835- *WhAm 1,*
  WomWWA 14
Bell, Henry Gough 1880- *WhAm 6*
Bell, Henry Haywood 1808?-1868 *ApCAB,*
  DcAmB, Drake, NatCAB 2, TwCBDA,
  WhAm H
Bell, Herbert Clifford Francis 1881-1966
  WhAm 4
Bell, Hill McClelland 1860-1927 *NatCAB 20,*
  WhAm 1
Bell, Hillary 1857-1903 *WhAm 1*
Bell, Hiram 1808-1855 *BiAUS, BiDrAC,*
  WhAm H
Bell, Hiram Parks 1827-1907 *ApCAB, BiAUS,*
  BiDConf, BiDrAC, TwCBDA, WhAm 1,
  WhAmP
Bell, Howard James, Jr. 1914-1948 *WhAm 2*
Bell, Hugh McKee 1902-1967 *WhAm 5*
Bell, Idris 1879-1967 *WhAm 5*
Bell, Isaac 1814-1897 *ApCAB Sup*
Bell, Isaac 1846-1889 *DcAmB, NatCAB 7,*
  WhAm H
Bell, Isaac Bonaparte 1849-1919 *NatCAB 19*
Bell, J Carleton 1872-1946 *WhAm 2*
Bell, Jack L 1904-1975 *WhAm 6*
Bell, Jacob 1792-1852 *DcAmB, NatCAB 24,*
  WhAm H
Bell, James *NewYHSD*
Bell, James 1804-1857 *ApCAB, BiAUS,*
  BiDrAC, Drake, NatCAB 7, TwCBDA,
  WhAm H
Bell, James Ford 1879-1961 *WhAm 4*

Bell, James Franklin 1856-1919 *DcAmB S1,*
NatCAB 14, NatCAB 22, WebAMB,
WhAm 1
Bell, James Madison 1826-1902 *DcAmB,*
WhAm H
Bell, James Martin 1796-1849 *BiAUS, BiDrAC,*
WhAm H
Bell, James Montgomery 1837-1919
NatCAB 19, WhAm 1
Bell, James Munsie 1880-1934 *WhAm 1*
Bell, James Stroud 1847-1915 *DcAmB,*
NatCAB 15, WhAm 1
Bell, James Warsaw 1869- *WhAm 5*
Bell, James Washington 1890-1966 *NatCAB 53,*
WhAm 4
Bell, Jesse Spencer 1906-1967 *WhAm 4*
Bell, John d1836 *Drake*
Bell, John 1763-1820 *BiHiMed*
Bell, John 1765-1836 *NatCAB 11*
Bell, John 1766-1836 *BiAUS*
Bell, John 1796-1869 *BiAUS, BiDrAC,*
WebAB, WhAm H
Bell, John 1796-1872 *ApCAB*
Bell, John 1797-1869 *AmBi, ApCAB, BiAUS,*
BiDrAC, BiDrUSE, DcAmB, Drake,
NatCAB 3, TwCBDA, WhAm H,
WhAmP
Bell, John 1800-1830 *ApCAB*
Bell, John C *NewYHSD*
Bell, John Calhoun 1851-1933 *BiDrAC,*
TwCBDA, WhAm 1, WhAmP
Bell, John Cromwell 1861-1935 *WhAm 1*
Bell, John Cromwell, Jr. 1892-1974 *WhAm 6*
Bell, John Gibbs 1894-1949 *NatCAB 38,*
WhAm 3
Bell, John Hendren 1883-1934 *NatCAB 25*
Bell, John Junior 1910-1963 *BiDrAC*
Bell, John Lewis 1913- *WhAm 5*
Bell, John W 1853- *WhAm 4*
Bell, Joseph A 1904-1968 *WhAm 5*
Bell, Joseph B 1900- *WhAm 3*
Bell, Joseph Clark 1892-1960 *WhAm 4*
Bell, Joseph Milligan 1876- *WhAm 5*
Bell, Joshua Fry 1811-1870 *BiAUS, BiDrAC,*
NatCAB 13, WhAm H
Bell, Kenneth C 1895-1956 *WhAm 3*
Bell, L Nelson 1894-1973 *WhAm 6*
Bell, Laird 1883-1965 *NatCAB 51, WhAm 4*
Bell, Larry 1939- *BnEnAmA*
Bell, Laura Joyce 1858-1904 *WhAm 1*
Bell, Lawrence Dale 1894-1956 *WhAm 3*
Bell, Lilian 1865-1929 *WhAm 1,*
WomWWA 14
Bell, Lillian 1865-1929 *NatCAB 14*
Bell, Louis 1836-1865 *ApCAB*
Bell, Louis 1837-1865 *TwCBDA*
Bell, Louis 1861-1923 *WhAm 1*
Bell, Louis 1864-1923 *DcAmB*
Bell, Louis V 1853-1925 *ApCAB X*
Bell, Luther Vose 1806-1862 *ApCAB, DcAmB,*
Drake, NatCAB 22, WhAm H, WhAmP
Bell, Mabel Gardiner *WomWWA 14*
Bell, Major Townsend 1897-1969 *WhAm 5*
Bell, Marcus Lafayette 1880-1945 *WhAm 2*
Bell, Marshall Odom 1902-1961 *NatCAB 49*
Bell, Mary Adelaide Fuller 1863- *WhAm 4,*
WomWWA 14
Bell, Merle 1880-1936 *NatCAB 38*
Bell, Miller Stephens 1874- *WhAm 2*
Bell, Neil 1887-1964 *WhAm 4*
Bell, Nicholas Montgomery 1842- *WhAm 4*
Bell, Nicholas Montgomery 1846- *NatCAB 12*
Bell, Orelia Key 1864- *AmWom*
Bell, Ovid 1875-1953 *WhAm 3*
Bell, Peter H d1898 *BiAUS*
Bell, Peter Hansborough 1808-1898 *DcAmB*
Bell, Peter Hansborough 1810-1898 *WhAm H*
Bell, Peter Hansborough 1812-1898 *NatCAB 9*
Bell, Peter Hansbrough d1898 *Drake*
Bell, Peter Hansbrough 1810-1898 *BiDrAC,*
WhAmP
Bell, Peter Hansbrough 1820?-1898 *TwCBDA*
Bell, Rae Floyd 1887-1968 *WhAm 5*
Bell, Raley Husted 1869-1931 *WhAm 1*
Bell, Reason Chesnutt 1880- *WhAm 6*
Bell, Rex 1903-1962 *WhAm 4*
Bell, Robert 1732?-1784 *DcAmB, WhAm H*
Bell, Robert 1841-1917 *ApCAB, DcScB*

Bell, Robert Benjamin 1872- *WhoColR*
Bell, Robert Cook 1880-1964 *WhAm 4*
Bell, Robert Edward 1918-1973 *WhAm 6*
Bell, Robert Kirk 1906-1966 *NatCAB 53*
Bell, Robert Norman 1864-1935 *NatCAB 37,*
WhAm 4
Bell, Roscoe Rutherford 1858- *WhAm 1*
Bell, Samuel 1770-1850 *ApCAB, BiAUS,*
BiDrAC, DcAmB, Drake, NatCAB 11,
TwCBDA, WhAm H, WhAmP
Bell, Samuel Dana 1798-1868 *ApCAB, Drake,*
NatCAB 12
Bell, Samuel Newell 1829-1889 *ApCAB,*
BiAUS, BiDrAC, WhAm H
Bell, Samuel Paris 1870-1949 *WhAm 4*
Bell, Solomon *WhAm H*
Bell, Stoughton 1874- *WhAm 6*
Bell, Susan Kite Alsop *WomWWA 14*
Bell, Theodore Arlington 1872-1922 *BiDrAC,*
WhAm 1
Bell, Theodore S 1807-1884 *NatCAB 6*
Bell, Thomas *NewYHSD*
Bell, Thomas Montgomery 1861-1941 *BiDrAC,*
WhAm 1, WhAmP
Bell, Thomas Sloan *IlBEAAW*
Bell, Thomas Sloan 1800-1861 *NatCAB 17*
Bell, Ulric 1891-1960 *NatCAB 45, WhAm 3*
Bell, Vereen McNeill 1911-1944 *NatCAB 39*
Bell, Wilbur Cosby 1881-1933 *WhAm 1*
Bell, Will Otto 1876-1944 *NatCAB 33*
Bell, William Abraham 1841-1921 *IlBEAAW,*
NatCAB 24
Bell, William Allen 1833-1906 *NatCAB 12,*
WhAm 3
Bell, William Augustus 1882-1961 *WhAm 4,*
WhoColR
Bell, William Bonar 1877-1949 *WhAm 2*
Bell, William Brown 1879-1950 *NatCAB 46,*
WhAm 3
Bell, William Constantine 1890-1966 *WhAm 5*
Bell, William Dixon 1865-1951 *NatCAB 54*
Bell, William H 1883-1961 *WhAm 4*
Bell, William Hemphill 1834-1906 *ApCAB Sup,*
TwCBDA, WhAm 1
Bell, William Melvin 1860-1933 *WhAm 1*
Bell, William Park 1886-1953 *NatCAB 42*
Bell, William Roe 1859- *WhAm 1*
Bell, William Temple 1843- *NatCAB 16*
Bell, William Yancy 1887-1962 *WhAm 4*
Bell-Smith, Frederic Marlett 1846-1923
IlBEAAW
Bell-Smith, Frederick Marlett 1846-1923
ApCAB
Bellah, Mildred Marie d1975 *WhAm 6*
Bellaire, Robert Thomas 1914-1945 *WhAm 2*
Bellamah, Jeanne Lees d1970 *WhAm 5*
Bellamann, Henry 1882-1945 *WhAm 2*
Bellamann, Katherine d1956 *WhAm 3*
Bellamy, Blanche Wilder 1850- *WomWWA 14*
Bellamy, Blanche Wilder 1852- *WhAm 4*
Bellamy, Charles Joseph 1852-1910 *WhAm 1*
Bellamy, David 1888-1960 *NatCAB 46*
Bellamy, Edward 1850-1898 *AmBi,*
ApCAB Sup, DcAmB, EncAB, McGEWB,
NatCAB 1, TwCBDA, WebAB,
WhAm H, WhAmP
Bellamy, Elizabeth Whitfield Croom 1837-1900
DcAmB, NatCAB 12, WhAm H
Bellamy, Emily Whitfield Croom 1839-1900
AmWom, ApCAB
Bellamy, Emmett Hargrove 1891-1952
NatCAB 41
Bellamy, F Wilder 1887-1955 *NatCAB 46,*
WhAm 3
Bellamy, Francis 1855-1931 *NatCAB 47,*
WhAm HA, WhAm 4
Bellamy, Francis Rufus 1886-1972 *WhAm 5*
Bellamy, George Albert 1872-1960 *NatCAB 49*
Bellamy, Gladys Carmen 1904-1973 *WhAm 6*
Bellamy, John *ApCAB*
Bellamy, John Dillard 1854-1942 *BiDrAC,*
WhAm 2, WhAmP
Bellamy, John Haley 1836-1914 *NewYHSD*
Bellamy, Joseph 1719-1790 *ApCAB, DcAmB,*
DcAmReB, Drake, NatCAB 7, TwCBDA,
WhAm H
Bellamy, Leslie Burgess 1909-1962 *WhAm 4*
Bellamy, Marsden 1878-1968 *NatCAB 55*

Bellamy, Mary Godat *WomWWA 14*
Bellamy, Paul 1884-1956 *WhAm 3*
Bellamy, Raymond 1885-1970 *WhAm 5*
Bellamy, William 1846- *WhAm 4*
Bellanca, Dorothy Jacobs 1894-1946 *DcAmB S4,*
NotAW
Bellanca, Frank Merlo 1882-1962 *NatCAB 52*
Bellanca, Giuseppe Mario 1886-1960
NatCAB 52
Bellanca, Giuseppe Mario 1886-1960 *WhAm 4*
Bellani, Angelo 1776-1852 *DcScB*
Bellar, Charles John 1885-1947 *NatCAB 35*
Bellard, Maxim 1830?- *NewYHSD*
Bellardi, Luigi 1818-1889 *DcScB*
Bellarmine, Robert 1542-1621 *DcScB,*
McGEWB
Bellatti, C Robert 1886-1953 *WhAm 3*
Bellatty, Charles E 1877- *WhAm 5*
Bellavitis, Giusto 1803-1880 *DcScB*
Bellaw, Americus Wellington 1842- *NatCAB 5*
Belle Isle, Charles L Fouquet, Duc De 1684-1761
WhoMilH
Belleau, Hercules E 1888-1964 *NatCAB 51*
Bellegarde, Henri, Comte De 1756-1845
WhoMilH
Bellemere, Fred 1888-1963 *NatCAB 50*
Bellenot, Charles *NewYHSD*
Beller, Augustus G 1830- *NewYHSD*
Bellerose, Joseph Hyacinthe 1820- *ApCAB*
Belleval, Pierre Richer De 1564?-1632 *DcScB*
Bellew, Frank Henry Temple 1828-1888 *DcAmB,*
NewYHSD, WhAm H
Bellew, Frank W P 1862-1894 *TwCBDA*
Bellew, Kyrle 1857-1911 *WhAm 1*
Bellezza, Russell G 1897-1958 *WhAm 3*
Bellezza, Vincenzo 1888-1964 *WhAm 4*
Belli, Amato 1836?- *NewYHSD*
Belli, Dominica 1835?- *NewYHSD*
Belli, Michael *NewYHSD*
Bellinger, Charles Byron 1839-1905 *TwCBDA,*
WhAm 1
Bellinger, Frank Earl 1874-1951 *NatCAB 41*
Bellinger, Herman Carl 1867-1941 *NatCAB 37*
Bellinger, John Bellinger 1862-1931 *WhAm 1*
Bellinger, Joseph 1773-1830 *BiAUS, BiDrAC,*
WhAm H
Bellinger, Martha Fletcher 1870- *WhAm 5,*
WomWWA 14
Bellinger, Patrick Neison Lynch 1885-1962
WebAMB
Bellinger, Patrick Niesen Lynch 1885-1962
WhAm 4
Bellinger, William Whaley 1863-1943 *WhAm 2*
Bellingham, Richard 1592?-1672 *AmBi,*
ApCAB, DcAmB, Drake, NatCAB 5,
TwCBDA, WhAm H, WhAmP
Bellingrath, Mary Nesbitt Elmore 1876-1955
NatCAB 47
Bellingrath, Walter Duncan 1869-1955
NatCAB 45
Bellingrath, William Albert 1868-1937
NatCAB 27
Bellingshausen, Fabian Von *DcScB*
Bellini, Giovanni 1435?-1516 *McGEWB*
Bellini, Lorenzo 1643-1704 *DcScB*
Bellini, Vincenzo 1801-1835 *McGEWB*
Bellinsgauzen, Faddei F 1779-1852 *DcScB*
Bellis, Leon Robert 1910-1972 *WhAm 5*
Bellman, Edwin d1900? *NewYHSD*
Bellman, Lawrence Stevens 1876- *WhAm 5*
Bellman, Russell 1896-1974 *WhAm 6*
Bellmare, Raphael 1821- *ApCAB*
Bellmon, Henry Louis 1921- *BiDrAC*
Bello, Alhaji Sir Ahmadu 1909-1966 *McGEWB*
Bello, Andres 1780-1865 *ApCAB*
Bello Y Lopez, Andres 1781-1865 *McGEWB*
Belloc, Hilaire 1870-1953 *WhAm 3*
Belloc, Joseph Hilaire Pierre 1870-1953
McGEWB
Bellomont, Richard Coote, Earl Of 1636-1701
AmBi, ApCAB, DcAmB, Drake,
TwCBDA, WhAm H
Bellot, Joseph Rene 1826-1853 *ApCAB*
Bellow, Saul 1915- *EncAB, McGEWB,*
WebAB
Bellows, Albert Fitch 1829-1883 *AmBi,*
ApCAB, DcAmB, NatCAB 7, NewYHSD,
TwCBDA, WhAm H

Bellows, Arthur Benjamin 1868-1920 *ApCAB X*
Bellows, Benjamin 1740-1802 *ApCAB,*
TwCBDA
Bellows, Francis Leroy 1859-1913 *NatCAB 17*
Bellows, George Wesley 1882-1925 *AmBi,*
ApCAB X, BnEnAmA, DcAmB, EncAB,
IIBEAAW, McGEWB, NatCAB 20,
WebAB, WhAm 1
Bellows, Henry Adams 1803-1873 *ApCAB,*
BiAUS, NatCAB 12, TwCBDA
Bellows, Henry Adams 1885-1939 *WhAm 1*
Bellows, Henry Whitney 1814-1882 *AmBi,*
ApCAB, DcAmB, Drake, McGEWB,
NatCAB 3, TwCBDA, WhAm H
Bellows, Howard Perry 1852-1934 *NatCAB 26,*
WhAm 1
Bellows, Ida I Perry 1859- *WomWWA 14*
Bellows, Johnson McClure 1870-1949 *WhAm 2*
Bellows, Robert Peabody 1877-1957 *WhAm 3*
Bellows, Warren S 1868- *ApCAB X*
Belluschi, Pietro 1899- *BnEnAmA*
Belmont, Alva E Smith Vanderbilt 1853-1933
DcAmB S1, NotAW, WebAB, WhAm 4,
WhAmP, WomWWA 14
Belmont, Alva E Smith Vanderbilt *see also*
Belmont, Mrs. O H P
Belmont, August 1813-1890 *EncAB*
Belmont, August 1816-1890 *AmBi, ApCAB,*
BiAUS, DcAmB, NatCAB 11, TwCBDA,
WebAB, WhAm H, WhAmP
Belmont, August 1853-1924 *ApCAB Sup,*
ApCAB X, NatCAB 11, NatCAB 37,
WhAm 1
Belmont, August, Jr. 1882- *NatCAB 4*
Belmont, Eleanor Elsie Robson *WomWWA 14*
Belmont, Francis Vachon De d1732 *ApCAB,*
Drake
Belmont, Morgan 1892- *WhAm 3*
Belmont, Mrs. O H P 1853-1933 *WhAm 1*
Belmont, Mrs. O H P *see also* Belmont, Alva E
Smith Vanderbilt
Belmont, Oliver Hazard Perry 1858-1908
ApCAB Sup, BiDrAC, WhAm 1, WhAmP
Belmont, Perry 1850-1947 *WhAm 2*
Belmont, Perry 1851-1947 *ApCAB, ApCAB X,*
BiDrAC, NatCAB 11, TwCBDA,
WhAmP
Belnap, Lamonte Judson 1877- *WhAm 6*
Belo, Alfred H 1873-1906 *WhAm 1*
Belo, Alfred Horatio 1839-1901 *DcAmB,*
NatCAB 1, TwCBDA, WhAm 1
Belon, Pierre 1517-1564 *AsBiEn, DcScB*
Belopolsky, Aristarkh Apollonovich 1854-1934
DcScB
Belsaw, Edward Thomas *WhoColR*
Belser, James Edwin 1805-1859 *BiAUS,*
BiDrAC, WhAm H
Belser, Susan Mishler 1862- *WomWWA 14*
Belsterling, Charles Starne 1874-1959 *WhAm 3*
Belt, Benjamin Carleton 1889-1962 *WhAm 4*
Belt, Harry H 1883-1950 *WhAm 3*
Belt, Herbert F 1858- *WhoColR*
Belt, Orrien Carrolton 1877-1961 *NatCAB 48*
Belt, William Bradley Tyler 1871- *WhAm 5*
Belter, John Henry 1804-1863 *BnEnAmA*
Belting, Arthur Whitaker 1878-1941
NatCAB 31
Belton, Francis S 1790?-1861 *ApCAB, Drake*
Beltrami, Eugenio 1835-1899 *DcScB*
Beltrami, Giacomo Constantino 1779-1855
ApCAB
Beltran, Basil Raphael 1889-1949 *NatCAB 37*
Beltran, Orlando Alfredo 1906-1957
NatCAB 47
Beltran DeSanta Rosa, Pedro *ApCAB*
Beltz, William Ray 1936-1973 *WhAm 6*
Beltzhoover, Frank Eckels 1841-1923 *BiDrAC,*
WhAmP
Belucan, C 1822?- *NewYHSD*
Belviso, Thomas Henry 1898-1967 *WhAm 4*
Belyayev, Pavel Ivanovich 1925-1970 *WhAm 5*
Belyea, Brynn William 1899-1946 *NatCAB 36*
Belz, Mrs. Henry 1913-1974 *WhAm 6*
Belzons, Jean *NewYHSD*
Beman, Allen C *NewYHSD*
Beman, Nathan Sidney Smith 1785-1871
DcAmB, NatCAB 5, TwCBDA, WhAm H

Beman, Nathaniel Sydney Smith 1785-1871
ApCAB
Beman, Solon Spencer 1853-1914 *NatCAB 14,*
WhAm 1
Beman, Wooster Woodruff 1850-1922 *TwCBDA,*
WhAm 1
Bembo, Pietro 1470-1547 *McGEWB*
Bemelmans, Ludwig 1898-1962 *NatCAB 48,*
WhAm 4
Bement, Alburto 1862- *WhAm 4*
Bement, Alon 1876-1954 *NatCAB 41,*
WhAm 3
Bement, Caleb N 1790-1868 *DcAmB,*
WhAm H
Bement, Clarence Edwin 1856-1935 *WhAm 1*
Bement, Clarence Sweet 1843-1923 *DcAmB*
Bement, George *NewYHSD*
Bement, Howard 1875-1936 *WhAm 1*
Bement, Ruth Ware 1887- *WomWWA 14*
Bemis *NewYHSD*
Bemis, Albert Farwell 1870-1936 *WhAm 1*
Bemis, Edward Webster 1860-1930 *ApCAB X,*
TwCBDA, WhAm 1
Bemis, George 1816-1878 *DcAmB, WhAm H*
Bemis, George Pickering 1838- *NatCAB 11*
Bemis, Harold Edward 1883-1931 *DcAmB S1,*
NatCAB 24
Bemis, Harold Medberry 1884-1970 *WhAm 5*
Bemis, Horace Erastus 1868-1914 *NatCAB 17*
Bemis, Judson Stephen 1867- *WhAm 1*
Bemis, Merrick 1820- *NatCAB 12*
Bemis, Samuel Flag 1891-1973 *WhAm 6*
Bemis, Samuel Flagg 1891-1973 *WebAB*
Bemis, Thomas Frederick 1925-1974 *WhAm 6*
Bemis, William Otis 1819-1883 *IIBEAAW*
Bemiss, John Harrison 1856-1897 *NatCAB 9*
Bemiss, Samuel Merrifield 1821- *ApCAB,*
NatCAB 9
Bemiss, Samuel Merrifield 1894-1966 *WhAm 4*
Ben, Ali *NewYHSD*
Ben-Gurion, David 1886-1973 *WhAm 6*
Ben-Gurion, David 1886-1974 *WhWW-II*
Ben-Zvi, Izhak 1884-1963 *WhAm 4*
Benade, Andrew 1769-1859 *ApCAB,*
NatCAB 5
Benade, James Arthur 1823-1853 *NewYHSD,*
WhAm H
Benalcazar, Sebastian De d1550 *ApCAB*
Benalcazar, Sebastian De d1551 *McGEWB*
Benard, Henri Jean Emile 1844- *WhAm 4*
Benavente Benavides, Bartolome d1652 *ApCAB*
Benavente Y Martinez, Jacinto 1866-1954
McGEWB
Benavides, Alfonso *ApCAB*
Benavides, Alonso De 1580?- *Drake, REnAW*
Benavides, Alonzo De 1580?- *DcAmB, WebAB*
Benavides Y DeLaCueva, Diego 1600?-1666
ApCAB
BenBella, Ahmed 1918- *McGEWB*
Benbridge, Mrs. Henry *NewYHSD*
Benbridge, Henry 1743-1812 *BnEnAmA,*
NewYHSD
Benbridge, Henry 1744-1812 *DcAmB,*
WhAm H
Benbrook, Edward Antony 1892-1967 *WhAm 4*
Benchley, Robert Charles 1889-1945 *DcAmB S3,*
NatCAB 33, WebAB, WhAm 2
Benchoff, Howard Johnston 1876-1958
WhAm 3
Benchoff, Robert J 1909-1968 *WhAm 5*
Benckenstein, Leonard Julius 1894-1967
WhAm 4
Benda, Harry Jindrich 1919-1971 *WhAm 5*
Benda, Wladyslaw Theodor 1873-1948
IIBEAAW, WhAm 2
Bendann, David *NewYHSD*
Bendelari, Arthur Enrico 1879- *WhAm 6*
Bendelari, George 1851-1927 *WhAm 1*
Bender, Albert Maurice 1866-1941 *WhAm 1*
Bender, Bill 1920- *IIBEAAW*
Bender, Charles Albert 1883-1954 *DcAmB S5*
Bender, Eric J 1902-1966 *WhAm 4*
Bender, Frederick *NewYHSD*
Bender, George Harrison 1896-1961 *BiDrAC,*
WhAm 4, WhAmP
Bender, Harold H 1882-1951 *WhAm 3*
Bender, Ida Catherine 1858-1916 *NatCAB 21*
Bender, Jack I d1966 *WhAm 5*

Bender, John Frederick 1879- *WhAm 6*
Bender, Leonard Franklin 1893-1943
NatCAB 32
Bender, Melvin T 1877- *WhAm 5*
Bender, Prosper 1844- *WhAm 4*
Bender, Robert Jacob 1890-1936 *NatCAB 28*
Bender, W Ralph G 1906-1968 *NatCAB 55*
Bender, Walter 1891- *WhAm 5*
Bender, Wilbur H 1860-1927 *WhAm 1*
Bender, Wilbur Joseph 1903-1969 *NatCAB 57,*
WhAm 5
Bendere, Edward Charles 1880-1951
NatCAB 38
Bendes, Jacob Harry 1889-1963 *NatCAB 51*
Bendiner, Alfred 1899-1964 *WhAm 4*
Bendire, Charles E *WhAm H*
Bendix, Ella Crosby d1969 *WhAm 5*
Bendix, John E 1818-1877 *ApCAB, TwCBDA*
Bendix, Max 1866-1945 *WhAm 2*
Bendix, Vincent 1881-1945 *DcAmB S3*
Bendix, Vincent 1882-1945 *WebAB, WhAm 2*
Bendix, William d1964 *WhAm 4*
Bendixen, Peter Alfred 1882-1934 *NatCAB 33*
Bendixsen, Aage 1887-1950 *NatCAB 38*
Benecke, Adelbert Oswald 1855- *WhAm 4*
Benecke, Thomas *NewYHSD*
Benedek, Ludwig August Ritter Von 1804-1881
WhoMilH
Beneden, Edouard Van 1846-1910 *AsBiEn,*
DcScB
Beneden, Pierre-Joseph Van 1809-1894 *DcScB*
Benedetti, Alessandro 1450?-1512 *DcScB*
Benedetti, Giovanni Battista 1530-1590 *DcScB*
Benedicks, Carl Axel Fredrik 1875-1958 *DcScB*
Benedict XV 1854-1922 *McGEWB*
Benedict, Saint 480?-547 *McGEWB*
Benedict, A L 1865- *WhAm 4*
Benedict, Abner R 1830?-1867 *ApCAB*
Benedict, Abner Raleigh 1839-1867 *TwCBDA*
Benedict, Alfred Barnum 1856-1933
NatCAB 25, WhAm 1
Benedict, Alice M 1863- *WomWWA 14*
Benedict, Andrew Bell 1885-1953 *NatCAB 42,*
WhAm 3
Benedict, Anne Kendrick 1851- *WhAm 4,*
WomWWA 14
Benedict, Asa Gardiner 1848- *NatCAB 7,*
WhAm 4
Benedict, C Harry 1876-1963 *NatCAB 52,*
WhAm 5
Benedict, Charles Brewster 1828-1901 *BiDrAC*
Benedict, Charles Coleman 1869-1951
NatCAB 38
Benedict, Charles L *BiAUS*
Benedict, Cleveland Keith 1864- *WhAm 4*
Benedict, Cooper Procter 1907-1968 *WhAm 5*
Benedict, Crystal Eastman 1881- *NotAW,*
WhAm 6
Benedict, Curtis Thaddeus 1837- *NatCAB 3*
Benedict, David 1778-1874 *Drake*
Benedict, David 1779-1874 *ApCAB, DcAmB,*
NatCAB 9, TwCBDA, WhAm H
Benedict, Elias Cornelius 1834- *WhAm 4*
Benedict, Emma Lee 1857- *AmWom*
Benedict, Erastus Cornelius 1800-1880 *ApCAB,*
BiDAmEd, DcAmB, Drake, NatCAB 5,
TwCBDA, WhAm H
Benedict, Francis Gano 1870-1957 *DcScB,*
WhAm 3
Benedict, Frank Lee 1834-1910 *WhAm 1*
Benedict, George Grenville 1826-1907 *ApCAB,*
WhAm 1
Benedict, George Grenville 1827-1907 *TwCBDA*
Benedict, George Wyllys 1796-1871 *ApCAB,*
TwCBDA
Benedict, George Wyllys 1872- *WhAm 5*
Benedict, Harris Miller 1873-1928 *NatCAB 38,*
WhAm 1
Benedict, Harry Yandell 1869-1937 *WhAm 1*
Benedict, Henry Harper 1844-1935 *ApCAB X,*
WhAm 1
Benedict, Henry Stanley 1878-1930 *BiDrAC*
Benedict, James Everard 1854-1940 *WhAm 2*
Benedict, Jay Leland 1882-1953 *NatCAB 42,*
WhAm 3
Benedict, Kirby *BiAUS*
Benedict, Lewis 1817-1864 *ApCAB, Drake,*
NatCAB 5, TwCBDA

Benedict, Lorenzo 1861-1932 *NatCAB 23,*
WhAm 1
Benedict, Lydia Carrie LeFavor *WomWWA 14*
Benedict, Marie A Potter *WomWWA 14*
Benedict, Mary Kendrick 1874- *WomWWA 14*
Benedict, Micaiah 1801-1881 *ApCAB X*
Benedict, Ralph C 1883-1965 *WhAm 4*
Benedict, Robert Dewey 1828-1911 *WhAm 1*
Benedict, Russell 1859-1936 *WhAm 1*
Benedict, Ruth Fulton 1887-1948 *BiDAmEd,*
DcAmB S4, EncAAH, EncAB, McGEWB,
NatCAB 36, NotAW, WebAB, WhAm 2
Benedict, Samuel Durlin 1871- *WhAm 5*
Benedict, Samuel Ravaud 1882-1936 *WhAm 1*
Benedict, Seelye 1848-1929 *ApCAB X*
Benedict, Stanley Rossiter 1884-1936
DcAmB S2, WhAm 1
Benedict, Susan Rose 1873- *WomWWA 14*
Benedict, Wayland Richardson 1848-1915
WhAm 1
Benedict, Wayne LeClaire 1906-1971
NatCAB 56, WhAm 5
Benedict, William Leonard 1860-1935 *WhAm 1*
Benedict, William Sommer 1843- *NatCAB 9*
Benediktsson, Bjarni 1908-1970 *WhAm 5*
Benedum, Michael Late 1869-1959 *WhAm 3*
Beneker, Gerrit Albertus 1882-1934 *WhAm 1*
Benes, Edouard 1884-1948 *WhWW-II*
Benes, Eduard 1884-1948 *McGEWB,*
WhAm 2
Benesch, Alfred Abraham 1879- *WhAm 6*
Benet, Christie 1879-1951 *BiDrAC,*
NatCAB 40, WhAm 3
Benet, Laurence Vincent 1863-1948 *WhAm 2*
Benet, Stephen Vincent 1827-1895 *ApCAB,*
Drake, NatCAB 30, TwCBDA
Benet, Stephen Vincent 1898-1943 *ApCAB X,*
DcAmB S3, EncAAH, McGEWB,
NatCAB 33, WebAB, WhAm 2
Benet, Walker 1857- *WhAm 4*
Benet, William Rose 1886-1950 *ApCAB X,*
DcAmB S4, NatCAB 37, WebAB,
WhAm 3
Beneworth, James C *NewYHSD*
Benezet, Anthony 1713-1784 *AmBi, ApCAB,*
BiDAmEd, DcAmB, DcAmReB, Drake,
McGEWB, NatCAB 5, TwCBDA,
WhAm H
Benezet, Louis Paul 1878-1961 *WhAm 4*
Bengough, Elisa Armstrong *WhAm 1*
Bengough, Richard *NewYHSD*
Bengs, Hilding Arvid 1904-1958 *NatCAB 44*
Bengston, Norman Elliott 1901-1961
NatCAB 47
Bengtson, Nels August 1879- *WhAm 6*
BenGurion, David 1886- *McGEWB*
Benham, Allen Rogers 1879- *WhAm 6*
Benham, Andrew Ellicott Kennedy 1832-1905
ApCAB Sup, NatCAB 5, TwCBDA,
WhAm 1
Benham, DeWitt Miles 1862- *NatCAB 7*
Benham, Fred Robert 1904-1954 *NatCAB 44*
Benham, Guy Everett 1880-1969 *NatCAB 56*
Benham, Henry Washington 1813-1884 *DcAmB,*
WhAm H
Benham, Henry Washington 1816?-1884 *Drake,*
TwCBDA
Benham, Henry Washington 1817-1884 *ApCAB,*
NatCAB 4
Benham, Ida Whipple 1849- *AmWom*
Benham, John Samuel 1863-1935 *BiDrAC,*
WhAm 4
Benham, Robert T 1745?-1809 *NatCAB 6*
Benham, Silas N 1840-1921 *ApCAB X*
Benington, Arthur 1865-1923 *WhAm 1*
Benington, George Arthur 1893-1964 *WhAm 4*
Benioff, Hugo 1899-1968 *NatCAB 54,*
WhAm 4A, WhAm 5
Benito, F *NewYHSD*
Benito, Marcos *ApCAB*
Benitz, William Logan 1872- *WhAm 3*
Benivieni, Antonio 1443-1502 *DcScB*
Benjamin, A Cornelius 1897-1968 *WhAm 5*
Benjamin, Alfred Hanson 1870-1925
NatCAB 20
Benjamin, Anna Northend 1874-1902 *WhAm 1*
Benjamin, Anna Smeed 1834- *AmWom*
Benjamin, Asher 1773-1845 *BnEnAmA,*

DcAmB, McGEWB, WebAB, WhAm H
Benjamin, Carolyn Gilbert *WomWWA 14*
Benjamin, Charles Henry 1856-1937 *WhAm 1*
Benjamin, David Joel 1917-1967 *WhAm 4*
Benjamin, David Marcellus 1834-1892
NatCAB 16
Benjamin, Dowling 1849- *NatCAB 5,*
WhAm 4
Benjamin, Emanuel Victor 1870-1934
NatCAB 33
Benjamin, Eugene S 1862-1941 *WhAm 1*
Benjamin, Fanny Nichols 1844- *WomWWA 14*
Benjamin, George 1799-1864 *ApCAB*
Benjamin, George Hillard 1852-1927 *DcAmB,*
NatCAB 17, NatCAB 29, WhAm 1
Benjamin, George Powell 1850-1921
NatCAB 32
Benjamin, Gilbert Giddings 1874-1941 *WhAm 2*
Benjamin, Hamilton Fish 1877-1938
NatCAB 29
Benjamin, Harold Raymond Wayne 1893-1969
BiDAmEd
Benjamin, Jack Ansel 1887-1961 *NatCAB 49*
Benjamin, John Forbes 1817-1877 *ApCAB,*
BiAUS, BiDrAC, TwCBDA, WhAm H,
WhAmP
Benjamin, Judah Peter 1812- *Drake*
Benjamin, Judah Philip 1811-1884 *AmBi,*
ApCAB, BiAUS, BiDConf, BiDrAC,
DcAmB, McGEWB, NatCAB 4, REnAW,
TwCBDA, WebAB, WhAm H, WhAmP
Benjamin, Louis 1883- *WhAm 1*
Benjamin, Lucile Joullin *IIBEAAW*
Benjamin, M *NewYHSD*
Benjamin, Marcus 1857-1932 *NatCAB 10,*
NatCAB 40, WhAm 1
Benjamin, Mary Gladding Wheeler 1814-1871
ApCAB
Benjamin, Nathan 1811-1855 *ApCAB, DcAmB,*
TwCBDA, WhAm H
Benjamin, Park 1809-1864 *AmBi, ApCAB,*
DcAmB, Drake, NatCAB 7, TwCBDA,
WhAm H
Benjamin, Park 1849-1922 *AmBi, ApCAB,*
DcAmB, TwCBDA, WhAm 1
Benjamin, Raphael 1846-1906 *NatCAB 10,*
WhAm 1
Benjamin, Raymond 1872-1952 *NatCAB 41,*
WhAm 3
Benjamin, Reuben Moore 1833-1917 *NatCAB 8,*
WhAm 1
Benjamin, Robert Morris 1896-1966
NatCAB 52, WhAm 4
Benjamin, Roy Abraham 1887-1963
NatCAB 52
Benjamin, Samuel G W 1837-1914 *NatCAB 7*
Benjamin, Samuel Green Wheeler 1837-1914
ApCAB X, NewYHSD
Benjamin, Samuel Greene Wheeler 1837-1914
AmBi, ApCAB, DcAmB, TwCBDA,
WhAm 1, WhAmP
Benjamin, Samuel Nicoll 1839-1886 *ApCAB,*
TwCBDA
Benjamin, William Evarts 1859-1940
NatCAB 35
Benkard, J Philip 1872-1929 *NatCAB 26*
Benken, Eugene Edwin 1889-1974 *WhAm 6*
Benkert, Ambrose William 1888-1962
NatCAB 49
Benmosche, M 1883-1952 *WhAm 3*
Benn, Gottfried 1886-1956 *McGEWB*
Bennard, George 1873- *WhAm 5*
Benne, Kenneth Dean 1908- *BiDAmEd*
Benner, Edward Hopkins 1878-1964
NatCAB 52
Benner, George Jacob 1859-1930 *BiDrAC*
Benner, Henry C *NewYHSD*
Benner, Philip 1762-1832 *ApCAB, DcAmB,*
TwCBDA, WhAm H
Benner, Philip 1763-1832 *Drake*
Benner, Raymond Calvin 1877-1950
NatCAB 39, WhAm 5
Benner, Samuel Armstrong 1871-1921
ApCAB X
Benner, Walter Meredith 1907-1967 *WhAm 5*
Benner, Winthrop Webster 1881-1950
NatCAB 39, WhAm 3
Benners, Augustus 1872- *WhAm 5*

Benneson, Cora Agnes 1851-1919 *NatCAB 17,*
WhAm 1
Bennet, A A 1825-1890 *WhAm H*
Bennet, Augustus Witschief 1897- *BiDrAC*
Bennet, Benjamin 1762-1840 *BiAUS*
Bennet, Benjamin 1764-1840 *BiDrAC,*
WhAm H
Bennet, David 1615-1719 *Drake*
Bennet, Gertrude Witschief *WomWWA 14*
Bennet, Hiram Pitt 1826-1914 *BiDrAC,*
WhAmP
Bennet, John Bradbury 1865-1930 *NatCAB 22*
Bennet, Orlando 1818-1880 *ApCAB*
Bennet, Richard *ApCAB, TwCBDA*
Bennet, Robert Ames 1870-1954 *WhAm 3*
Bennet, Sanford Fillmore 1836-1898 *DcAmB,*
WhAm H
Bennet, Thomas *BiAUS*
Bennet, Walter Mills 1861-1938 *WhAm 1*
Bennet, William Stiles 1870-1962 *BiDrAC,*
WhAm 4, WhAmP
Bennett, Adelaide George 1848- *AmWom*
Bennett, Albert Arnold 1888-1971 *WhAm 5*
Bennett, Albert Dwight 1858- *WhAm 4*
Bennett, Alden Joseph 1847-1919 *NatCAB 19*
Bennett, Alfred Allen 1850- *WhAm 4*
Bennett, Alfred S 1854-1925 *WhAm 1*
Bennett, Alice 1851-1925 *AmWom, NotAW,*
TwCBDA
Bennett, Ambrose Allen 1882- *WhoColR*
Bennett, Andrew Carl d1972 *WhAm 2,*
WhAm 5
Bennett, Archibald Synica 1877-1957 *WhAm 3*
Bennett, Arthur Ellsworth 1865- *WhAm 2,*
WhAm 5
Bennett, Arthur James 1866-1940 *NatCAB 39*
Bennett, Arthur King 1881-1966 *NatCAB 53*
Bennett, Arthur Lawton 1898-1974 *WhAm 6*
Bennett, Belle Harris 1852-1922 *NotAW,*
WhAm 1, WomWWA 14
Bennett, Burton Ellsworth 1863- *WhAm 1*
Bennett, Caleb Prew 1758-1836 *BiAUS,*
DcAmB, Drake, NatCAB 11, WhAm H,
WhAmP
Bennett, Caswell 1836-1894 *NatCAB 12*
Bennett, Charles Alpheus 1864-1942 *BiDAmEd,*
NatCAB 33
Bennett, Charles Andrew Armstrong 1885-1930
WhAm 1
Bennett, Charles Day 1857-1930 *NatCAB 34*
Bennett, Charles Edward 1910- *BiDrAC*
Bennett, Charles Edwin 1858-1921 *AmBi,*
BiDAmEd, DcAmB, WhAm 1
Bennett, Charles Ernest 1882-1945 *NatCAB 35*
Bennett, Charles Goodwin 1863-1914 *BiDrAC,*
WhAm 1, WhAmP
Bennett, Charles Henry 1863-1956 *WhAm 3*
Bennett, Charles Washington 1833-1906
WhAm 1
Bennett, Charles Wesley 1828- *ApCAB*
Bennett, Charles Wilbur 1870- *WhAm 5*
Bennett, Clarence Franklin 1872-1950
NatCAB 39, WhAm 5
Bennett, Claude E 1879-1952 *NatCAB 44*
Bennett, Claude Henry 1877-1953 *NatCAB 42*
Bennett, Claude Nathaniel 1866-1926 *WhAm 1*
Bennett, Constance 1914-1965 *WhAm 4*
Bennett, Corwin Ruthven 1897-1950
NatCAB 38
Bennett, Daniel S 1829?- *NewYHSD*
Bennett, David Smith 1811-1894 *BiAUS,*
BiDrAC, WhAm H
Bennett, DeRobigne Mortimer 1818-1882
ApCAB, DcAmB, WhAm H
Bennett, Donald 1910- *WhWW-II*
Bennett, Donald Menzies 1897-1971 *WhAm 5*
Bennett, Earl Willard 1880-1973 *WhAm 6*
Bennett, Edmund Hatch 1824-1898 *DcAmB,*
NatCAB 11, TwCBDA, WhAm H
Bennett, Edward 1876-1951 *NatCAB 39,*
WhAm 3
Bennett, Edward Brown 1842-1927 *WhAm 1*
Bennett, Edward Herbert 1874-1954
NatCAB 44, WebAB, WhAm 3
Bennett, Elbert G 1888-1950 *WhAm 3*
Bennett, Ella Collins *WomWWA 14*
Bennett, Ella May 1855- *AmWom*
Bennett, Ellen J F *WomWWA 14*

Bennett, Emerson 1822-1905 *ApCAB, DcAmB, TwCBDA, WhAm 1*

Bennett, Enoch Arnold 1867-1931 *McGEWB*

Bennett, Ethelwyn Foote 1875- *WomWWA 14*

Bennett, Eugene Dunlap d1968 *WhAm 5*

Bennett, Floyd 1890-1928 *AmBi, DcAmB, NatCAB 29, WebAB, WebAMB*

Bennett, Frank Marion 1857-1924 *NatCAB 20, WhAm 3*

Bennett, Frank Woodrow 1904-1960 *WhAm 4*

Bennett, Fred Smith 1867-1930 *NatCAB 23*

Bennett, George Allen 1904-1958 *WhAm 3*

Bennett, George Kettner 1904-1975 *WhAm 6*

Bennett, George Slocum 1842-1910 *NatCAB 15*

Bennett, Granville Gaylord 1833-1910 *BiDrAC, WhAm 1, WhAmP*

Bennett, H S 1807-1891 *BiAUS*

Bennett, Harriet 1871- *WhAm 5*

Bennett, Hendley Stone 1807-1891 *BiDrAC, WhAm H*

Bennett, Henry 1808-1868 *BiAUS, BiDrAC, WhAm H, WhAmP*

Bennett, Henry Eastman 1873-1941 *NatCAB 36, WhAm 2*

Bennett, Henry Garland 1886-1951 *DcAmB S5, WhAm 3*

Bennett, Henry Gordon 1887-1962 *WhWW-II*

Bennett, Henry Holcomb 1863-1924 *WhAm 1*

Bennett, Henry Stanley 1838-1895 *TwCBDA*

Bennett, Henry Wells Newell 1873-1966 *NatCAB 53*

Bennett, Henry William 1858-1936 *WhAm 1*

Bennett, Hiram P 1826- *BiAUS*

Bennett, Horace Wilson 1862-1941 *NatCAB 31, WhAm 2*

Bennett, Howard Franklin 1911-1974 *WhAm 6*

Bennett, Hugh Hammond 1881-1960 *EncAAH, WhAm 4*

Bennett, Ida Elizabeth Dandridge 1860-1925 *WhAm 1, WomWWA 14*

Bennett, Ira Elbert 1868-1957 *WhAm 3*

Bennett, Irving T 1900-1955 *WhAm 3*

Bennett, James A T 1833?- *NewYHSD*

Bennett, James Eugene 1889-1964 *NatCAB 50, WhAm 4*

Bennett, James Gordon 1795-1872 *AmBi, ApCAB, DcAmB, EncAB, McGEWB, NatCAB 7, TwCBDA, WebAB, WhAm H, WhAmP*

Bennett, James Gordon 1800?-1872 *Drake*

Bennett, James Gordon 1841-1918 *AmBi, ApCAB, DcAmB, EncAB, McGEWB, NatCAB 7, TwCBDA, WebAB, WhAm 1*

Bennett, James Haynes 1909-1956 *NatCAB 47*

Bennett, James Levi 1849-1918 *NatCAB 8*

Bennett, James Murrell 1904-1973 *WhAm 6*

Bennett, James O'Donnell 1870-1940 *NatCAB 30, WhAm 1*

Bennett, James William, Jr. 1920-1972 *WhAm 5*

Bennett, Jesse Lee 1885-1931 *WhAm 1*

Bennett, John 1865-1956 *NatCAB 43, WhAm 3*

Bennett, John Bonifas 1904-1964 *BiDrAC, NatCAB 50, WhAmP*

Bennett, John Bonifas 1905-1964 *WhAm 4*

Bennett, John Coleman 1902- *McGEWB*

Bennett, John Emory 1833-1893 *NatCAB 5, NatCAB 14*

Bennett, John Foster 1865-1938 *NatCAB 52, WhAm 1*

Bennett, John George 1891-1957 *WhAm 3*

Bennett, John Griffith 1846-1912 *NatCAB 16*

Bennett, John Harrington 1845-1920 *NatCAB 18*

Bennett, John Hughes 1812-1875 *BiHiMed*

Bennett, John James 1894-1967 *WhAm 4*

Bennett, John Newton 1867-1948 *WhAm 3*

Bennett, John William 1865- *WhAm 4*

Bennett, Johnstone d1906 *WhAm 1*

Bennett, Joseph 1840- *NatCAB 12*

Bennett, Joseph Augustus 1852-1921 *NatCAB 19*

Bennett, Joseph Bentley 1859-1923 *BiDrAC, WhAm 3, WhAmP*

Bennett, Josiah Kendall 1831-1874 *NatCAB 8*

Bennett, Lawrence 1888-1970 *NatCAB 56, WhAm 4*

Bennett, Lester 1893-1959 *NatCAB 48*

Bennett, Logan Johnson 1907-1957 *NatCAB 47*

Bennett, Louis 1828-1897 *AmBi, WhAm H*

Bennett, Louis 1849-1918 *NatCAB 22*

Bennett, Louis L 1886-1949 *WhAm 2*

Bennett, Louis Winston 1889-1958 *WhAm 3*

Bennett, M Katharine Jones 1864-1950 *WhAm 3, WomWWA 14*

Bennett, Maillard 1904-1975 *WhAm 6*

Bennett, Margaret Chesney *WomWWA 14*

Bennett, Marion Horton 1895-1958 *NatCAB 49*

Bennett, Marion Tinsley 1914-1964 *BiDrAC, WhAmP*

Bennett, Martin 1838-1899 *NatCAB 32*

Bennett, Mary Katharine Jones 1864-1950 *NotAW*

Bennett, May Friend 1863- *WhAm 4*

Bennett, Melba Berry 1901-1968 *NatCAB 54*

Bennett, Melba Berry 1901-1970 *WhAm 5*

Bennett, Merrill Kelley 1897-1969 *NatCAB 55*

Bennett, Michael John 1905- *WhAm 2*

Bennett, Mills 1882-1950 *NatCAB 42*

Bennett, Milo Lyman 1790-1868 *ApCAB, BiAUS, Drake, TwCBDA*

Bennett, Nathaniel 1818-1886 *DcAmB, WhAm H*

Bennett, Philip Allen 1881-1942 *BiDrAC, NatCAB 40, WhAm 2, WhAmP*

Bennett, Ralph Culver 1878-1959 *WhAm 3*

Bennett, Rawson 1905-1968 *WhAm 5*

Bennett, Raymond Franklin 1875-1949 *NatCAB 38*

Bennett, Richard *NatCAB 7*

Bennett, Richard 1870-1944 *DcAmB S3*

Bennett, Richard 1872-1944 *NatCAB 33, WhAm 2*

Bennett, Richard Bedford 1870-1947 *McGEWB*

Bennett, Richard Heber 1866- *WhAm 4*

Bennett, Richard Rodney 1936- *McGEWB*

Bennett, Risden Tyler 1840-1913 *BiDrAC, WhAmP*

Bennett, Robert L 1912- *REnAW*

Bennett, Robert Root 1865-1933 *NatCAB 24, WhAm 1*

Bennett, Samuel Crocker 1858-1925 *WhAm 1*

Bennett, Sanford Fillmore 1836-1898 *NatCAB 7*

Bennett, Sarah Davis 1842- *WomWWA 14*

Bennett, Smith 1859-1935 *NatCAB 35*

Bennett, Stephen Alexander 1881- *WhoColR*

Bennett, Thomas *NatCAB 12*

Bennett, Thomas Gray 1845-1930 *WhAm 1*

Bennett, Thomas Warren 1831-1893 *ApCAB, BiAUS, BiDrAC, WhAm H, WhAmP*

Bennett, Victor Wilson 1895-1955 *WhAm 3*

Bennett, W R 1875-1971 *WhAm 5*

Bennett, Wallace Foster 1898- *BiDrAC*

Bennett, Walter Harper 1869-1963 *WhAm 4*

Bennett, Wendell C 1905-1953 *WhAm 3*

Bennett, William James 1787-1844 *NewYHSD, WhAm H*

Bennett, William Lyon 1848- *WhAm 4*

Bennett, William Rainey 1869- *WhAm 5*

Bennett, William Wirt 1869-1932 *WhAm 1*

Bennett, William Zebina 1856-1938 *ApCAB, WhAm 1*

Bennett, Winchester 1877-1953 *NatCAB 48*

Bennette, Howard 1890-1935 *NatCAB 26*

Bennetts, James Mitchell 1860-1929 *WhAm 1*

Benney, Edith Neil *WomWWA 14*

Bennigsen, Count Levin August 1745-1826 *WhoMilH*

Benning, Bernhard 1902-1974 *WhAm 6*

Benning, Henry A 1882-1960 *WhAm 4*

Benning, Henry Lewis 1814-1875 *ApCAB Sup, BiDConf, DcAmB, WebAMB, WhAm H, WhAmP*

Benninghoven, Rhein 1902-1966 *NatCAB 53*

Bennington, Wesley Henry 1861-1928 *NatCAB 21*

Bennion, Adam Samuel 1886-1958 *WhAm 3*

Bennion, Milton 1870-1953 *BiDAmEd, WhAm 5*

Bennion, Samuel Otis 1874- *WhAm 5*

Bennion, Vernal Rowland 1908-1964 *NatCAB 51*

Bennitt, George Stephen 1849-1915 *WhAm 1*

Bennitt, Rudolf 1898-1950 *WhAm 3*

Benns, F Lee 1889-1967 *NatCAB 54*

Benny, Allan 1867-1942 *BiDrAC, WhAm 2*

Benny, Jack 1894-1974 *WebAB, WhAm 6*

Benoist, Mary Hunt 1865- *WomWWA 14*

Benoit, Constant Alexandre 1884-1951 *NatCAB 40*

Benoit, Justin-Mirande Rene 1844-1922 *DcScB*

Benoit-Levy, Jean 1888-1959 *WhAm 3*

Benoliel, Solomon D 1874-1932 *WhAm 1*

Benoni *NewYHSD*

Benrimo, Joseph Henry McAlpin 1871-1942 *WhAm 1*

Benrimo, Thomas Duncan 1887-1958 *IlBEAAW*

Bensadon, J *NewYHSD*

Bensel, Francis Scott 1905-1973 *WhAm 6*

Bensel, James Berry 1856-1886 *ApCAB, NatCAB 4, WhAm H*

Bensel, John Anderson 1863-1922 *NatCAB 11, WhAm 1*

Bensell, George Frederick 1837-1879 *IlBEAAW, NewYHSD*

Bensinger, Arthur Blackburn 1880-1935 *NatCAB 26*

Bensinger, Benjamin Edward 1868-1935 *WhAm 1*

Bensinger, C G d1963 *WhAm 4*

Bensinger, Moses 1839-1904 *NatCAB 14*

Bensley, Robert Russell 1867-1956 *DcScB, WhAm 3*

Benson, Aaron Shaw 1837-1917 *NatCAB 18*

Benson, Adolph Burnett 1881-1962 *NatCAB 49*

Benson, Alden Richardson 1860-1927 *NatCAB 20*

Benson, Alfred Washburn 1843-1916 *BiDrAC, NatCAB 2, NatCAB 21, WhAm 1*

Benson, Allan Louis 1871-1940 *NatCAB 35, WhAm 1*

Benson, Arthur Wight 1887-1946 *NatCAB 35*

Benson, Benjamin W *NewYHSD*

Benson, Blackwood Ketcham 1845- *WhAm 4*

Benson, C Beverley 1895-1957 *NatCAB 46*

Benson, Carl 1820-1874 *AmBi, WhAm H*

Benson, Carville Dickinson 1872-1929 *BiDrAC, WhAm 1, WhAmP*

Benson, Charles Emile 1881-1963 *NatCAB 50, WhAm 4*

Benson, Clara Cynthia 1875- *WomWWA 14*

Benson, Egbert 1746-1833 *AmBi, ApCAB, BiAUS, BiDrAC, DcAmB, Drake, NatCAB 3, TwCBDA, WhAm H, WhAmP*

Benson, Einar William 1901- *WhAm 4*

Benson, Elizabeth English d1972 *WhAm 6*

Benson, Elmer Austin 1895- *BiDrAC, WhAmP*

Benson, Emanuel Mervyn 1904-1971 *WhAm 5*

Benson, Emil Joseph 1890-1964 *NatCAB 50*

Benson, Eugene 1837-1908 *ApCAB, TwCBDA, WhAm 4*

Benson, Eugene 1839-1908 *DcAmB, NewYHSD*

Benson, Ezra Taft 1899- *BiDrUSE, EncAAH*

Benson, F Murray 1895-1963 *NatCAB 51*

Benson, Frank Weston 1862-1951 *BnEnAmA, DcAmB S5, NatCAB 13, NatCAB 41, WhAm 3*

Benson, Frank Williamson 1858-1911 *NatCAB 14, WhAm 1*

Benson, Franklin Thomas 1862-1929 *WhAm 1*

Benson, George A 1889-1959 *WhAm 3*

Benson, George Edward 1875- *WhAm 5*

Benson, Guy Alfred 1885-1949 *NatCAB 39*

Benson, Henry C 1815- *ApCAB*

Benson, Henry Kreitzer 1877-1954 *NatCAB 44, WhAm 4*

Benson, Henry Lamdin 1854-1921 *WhAm 1*

Benson, Henry Perkins 1866- *WhAm 5*

Benson, James Rea *ApCAB*

Benson, John *NewYHSD*

Benson, John 1872-1962 *WhAm 4*

Benson, John Howard 1901-1956 *NatCAB 44*

Benson, John Joseph 1896-1967 *WhAm 4*

Benson, John Meade 1872- *WhoColR*

Benson, John Thomas 1873- *NatCAB 18*

Benson, Joseph *NewYHSD*

Benson, Joseph Phillip 1879-1955 *NatCAB 44*

Benson, Louis FitzGerald 1855-1930 *WhAm 1*

Benson, Oscar Herman 1875-1951 *DcAmB S5, WhAm 3*

Benson, Philip Adolphus 1881-1946 *WhAm 2*

Benson, Ramsey 1866- *WhAm 4*

Benson, Rebecca Elizabeth Hamilton 1875-
  WomWWA 14
Benson, Reuel A 1878-1956 WhAm 3
Benson, Richard Dale 1841- WhAm 4
Benson, Robert Dix 1861-1931 ApCAB X,
  WhAm 1
Benson, Robert Louis 1880-1957 NatCAB 46,
  WhAm 6
Benson, Sally 1900-1972 WhAm 5
Benson, Samuel Page 1804-1876 BiAUS,
  BiDrAC, WhAm H, WhAmP
Benson, Simon 1852-1942 NatCAB 33,
  WhAm 4
Benson, Stuart 1877-1949 WhAm 2
Benson, Wilbur Earle 1921-1971 WhAm 5
Benson, William Shepherd 1855-1932 AmBi,
  DcAmB S1, NatCAB 23, WebAMB,
  WhAm 1
Benson, William Sumner 1864-1942
  NatCAB 35
Benswanger, William Edward 1892-1972
  NatCAB 57, WhAm 5
Bent, Charles 1799-1847 AmBi, DcAmB,
  NatCAB 19, REnAW, WebAB,
  WhAm H, WhAmP
Bent, Charles Dexter 1850-1923 NatCAB 19
Bent, Erling Sundt 1894-1955 WhAm 3
Bent, Ernest Fairman 1882-1959 NatCAB 47
Bent, Fenwick W 1865-1930 ApCAB X
Bent, George 1814-1847 REnAW
Bent, George Payne 1854- NatCAB 18
Bent, H Stanley 1873-1953 NatCAB 40
Bent, H Stanley, Jr. 1914-1953 NatCAB 40
Bent, Henry NewYHSD
Bent, Josiah 1771-1836 DcAmB, WhAm H
Bent, Myron Hammond 1865- WhAm 1
Bent, Quincy 1879-1955 NatCAB 45,
  WhAm 3
Bent, Robert 1816-1841 REnAW
Bent, Samuel Arthur 1841-1912 WhAm 1
Bent, Silas 1768-1827 BiAUS, NatCAB 12
Bent, Silas 1820-1887 DcAmB, WhAm H
Bent, Silas 1882-1945 DcAmB S3,
  NatCAB 34, WhAm 2
Bent, William 1809-1869 DcAmB, NatCAB 19,
  REnAW, WebAB, WhAm H
Bente, Frederick 1858-1930 WhAm 1
Benteen, Frederick W 1834-1898 REnAW
Benthall, Michael Pickersgill 1919-1974
  WhAm 6
Bentham, George 1800-1884 DcScB
Bentham, Jeremy 1748-1832 McGEWB
Benthin, Howard Arthur 1907-1968 WhAm 5
Bentley, Alvin Morell 1918-1969 BiDrAC,
  NatCAB 54, WhAm 5, WhAmP
Bentley, Arthur 1876-1946 WhAm 2
Bentley, Arthur Fisher 1870-1957 EncAB,
  McGEWB, WhAm 3
Bentley, Augusta Zug BiCAW
Bentley, Calvin Pardee 1883-1964 WhAm 4
Bentley, Charles Edwin 1859-1929 WhAm 1
Bentley, Charles Eugene 1841-1905
  ApCAB Sup, WhAm 1
Bentley, Charles Harvey 1869-1922 ApCAB X,
  NatCAB 35, WhAm 1
Bentley, Charles Staughton 1846- WhAm 4
Bentley, Clara Augusta WomWWA 14
Bentley, Cyril Edmund 1893-1957 WhAm 3
Bentley, Daniel Van 1887-1957 NatCAB 49
Bentley, Edwin 1824-1917 NatCAB 6,
  WhAm 4
Bentley, Ellida Pattison 1856- WomWWA 14
Bentley, Franklin Romine 1869- NatCAB 16
Bentley, Gideon 1751-1858 Drake
Bentley, Gordon Mansir 1875-1954 WhAm 3
Bentley, Harry Clark 1877- WhAm 5
Bentley, Henry 1880-1938 NatCAB 28,
  WhAm 1, WhAm 1C
Bentley, Henry Wilbur 1838-1907 BiDrAC
Bentley, Herbert 1884-1931 NatCAB 26
Bentley, Irene d1940 WhAm 1
Bentley, James Knowlton 1846-1928
  NatCAB 23
Bentley, Jerome Harold 1881-1961 WhAm 4
Bentley, John 1879-1930 NatCAB 24
Bentley, John A 1836- NatCAB 13
Bentley, John Edward 1887-1965 WhAm 4
Bentley, Julian 1908-1968 WhAm 4A

Bentley, Luette P 1841- WomWWA 14
Bentley, Mabel E Davison WomWWA 14
Bentley, Madison 1870-1955 NatCAB 45,
  WhAm 3
Bentley, Neil Isaac 1881-1955 NatCAB 45
Bentley, Percy Jardine 1898-1962 WhAm 4
Bentley, Raymond 1889-1940 NatCAB 30
Bentley, Richard 1894-1970 WhAm 5
Bentley, Robert Irving 1864-1932 WhAm 1
Bentley, Thomas Wallace 1861-1932
  NatCAB 24
Bentley, Walter E 1864- WhAm 4
Bentley, William 1759-1819 AmBi, DcAmB,
  Drake, WhAm H
Bentley, William Burdelle 1866-1945 WhAm 3
Bentley, William Frederick 1859-1936 WhAm 1
Bentley, Wilson Alwyn 1865-1931 DcAmB S1,
  NatCAB 23, WhAm 1
Benton, Allen Richardson 1822-1914 DcAmB,
  NatCAB 8
Benton, Alva Hartley 1886-1945 WhAm 2
Benton, Angelo Ames 1837- WhAm 1
Benton, Arthur Burnette 1858-1927 ApCAB X,
  WhAm 1
Benton, Cassius Richmond 1862-1922
  NatCAB 21
Benton, Charles Swan 1810-1882 BiAUS,
  BiDrAC, WhAm H
Benton, Charles William 1852-1913 WhAm 1
Benton, Dwight 1834- NewYHSD
Benton, Edward Walden WhoColR
Benton, Elbert Jay 1871-1946 WhAm 2
Benton, Elma Hixson 1874-1942 WhAm 2
Benton, Frank 1852- WhAm 4
Benton, George Alden 1848-1921 WhAm 1
Benton, Guy Porter 1865-1927 TwCBDA
Benton, Guy Potter 1865-1927 NatCAB 15,
  WhAm 1
Benton, Herbert E 1849-1898 NatCAB 6
Benton, Jacob 1814-1892 BiDrAC, WhAm H
Benton, Jacob 1819-1892 ApCAB, BiAUS
Benton, James Gilchrist 1820-1881 ApCAB,
  DcAmB, IlBEAAW, NatCAB 4,
  TwCBDA, WebAMB, WhAm H
Benton, James Webb 1892-1947 WhAm 2
Benton, Jay Rogers 1885-1953 WhAm 3
Benton, Jeannette Scott 1862- WomWWA 14
Benton, Joel 1832-1911 ApCAB, DcAmB,
  NatCAB 8, WhAm 1
Benton, John Edwin 1875-1948 NatCAB 37,
  WhAm 2
Benton, John Keith 1896-1956 WhAm 3
Benton, John Robert 1876-1930 NatCAB 22,
  WhAm 1
Benton, Josiah Henry 1843-1917 DcAmB,
  WhAm 1
Benton, Lemuel 1754-1818 BiDrAC, WhAm H,
  WhAmP
Benton, Louisa Dow 1831- AmWom
Benton, Maecenas Eason 1848-1924 BiDrAC,
  WhAmP
Benton, Maecenas Eason 1849-1924 TwCBDA,
  WhAm 4
Benton, Margaret Peake d1975 WhAm 6
Benton, Mary Lathrop 1864-1955 WhAm 3,
  WomWWA 14
Benton, Mary P S NewYHSD
Benton, Nathaniel S 1792-1869 ApCAB,
  TwCBDA
Benton, Rita 1881- WhAm 6
Benton, Samuel BiAUS
Benton, Stephen Olin 1849-1915 WhAm 1
Benton, Thomas Hart 1782-1858 AmBi,
  ApCAB, BiAUS, BiDrAC, DcAmB,
  Drake, EncAAH, EncAB, McGEWB,
  NatCAB 4, REnAW, TwCBDA, WebAB,
  WhAm H, WhAmP
Benton, Thomas Hart 1816-1879 BiDAmEd,
  DcAmB, WhAm H
Benton, Thomas Hart 1889-1975 BnEnAmA,
  EncAAH, EncAB, IlBEAAW, McGEWB,
  WebAB, WhAm 6
Benton, William 1900-1973 BiDrAC, WebAB,
  WhAm 5, WhAmP
Benton, William Plummer 1828-1867 ApCAB
Bentonelli, Joseph 1898-1975 WhAm 6
Bentsen, Lloyd Millard, Jr. 1921- BiDrAC
Bentsur, Shmuel 1906-1973 WhAm 6

Benway, Mabel Reed WomWWA 14
Benyaurd, William H H 1841-1900 WhAm 1
BenYehuda, Eliezer 1858-1922 McGEWB
Benz, Alexander Otto 1880- WhAm 6
Benz, Francis E 1899-1954 WhAm 3
Benz, Harry Edward 1899-1963 WhAm 4
Benz, Margaret Gilbert 1899-1967 WhAm 5
Benze, C Theodore 1865-1936 WhAm 1
Benzel, Charles Frederick, Sr. 1905- WhAm 5
Benzenberg, George Henry 1847-1925
  NatCAB 14, WhAm 1
Benzenberg, Johann Friedrich 1777-1846 DcScB
Benziger, August 1867-1955 NatCAB 44,
  WhAm 3
Benziger, Gertrude Lytton 1875-
  WomWWA 14
Benzinger, Frederic 1858- WhAm 4
Benzoni, Girolamo 1520?- ApCAB
Beranger, Clara d1956 WhAm 3
Berard, Arthur Allen 1893-1971 NatCAB 56
Berard, Augusta Blanche 1824- ApCAB
Berard, Claudius 1786-1848 ApCAB
Berard, Jacques Etienne 1789-1869 DcScB
Berard, Joseph Frederic 1789-1828 DcScB
Berardino, Michael 1894-1957 NatCAB 48
Berch, Samuel Harry 1888-1951 NatCAB 40,
  WhAm 3
Berchtold, Count Leopold Von 1863-1942
  McGEWB
Berckel, Peter I Van d1800 Drake
Berckmans, Bruce 1901-1968 NatCAB 54,
  WhAm 5
Bercoli, Aug 1832?- NewYHSD
Bercovici, Konrad 1882-1961 NatCAB 46,
  WhAm 4
Bercovici, Naomi LeBrescu 1883-1957
  NatCAB 46
Berdan, Hiram 1823?-1893 ApCAB Sup,
  TwCBDA
Berdan, John 1903-1958 NatCAB 49,
  WhAm 3
Berdanier, Paul Frederick 1879-1961 WhAm 4
Berdell, Charles Prescott, Jr. 1886-1972
  NatCAB 57
Berdell, Theodore 1888-1950 NatCAB 38
Berdie, Ralph Freimuth 1916-1974 WhAm 6
Berdine, Harold Sloop 1901-1966 NatCAB 53
Berdyaev, Nicholas Alexandrovich 1874-1948
  McGEWB
Berdyaev, Nickolai Alexandrovich 1874-1948
  WhAm 4
Berendsen, John Christian 1873-1956
  NatCAB 44
Berendsohn, Sigmond 1831?- NewYHSD
Berendt, Karl Hermann 1817-1878 ApCAB Sup
Berengario DaCarpi, Giacomo 1460?-1530?
  DcScB
Berenger, Victor Henry 1867-1952 WhAm 3
Berens, Conrad 1859-1923 NatCAB 26
Berens, Conrad 1889-1963 NatCAB 50,
  WhAm 4
Berenson, Bernard 1865-1959 EncAB,
  NatCAB 48, WebAB, WhAm 3
Berenson, Lawrence 1891-1970 NatCAB 55
Berenson, Senda 1868-1954 DcAmB S5
Beresford, Charles William DeLaPoer 1846-1919
  WhoMilH
Beresford, Harry 1867-1944 WhAm 2
Beresford, Percival 1874-1943 NatCAB 32
Beresford, Richard 1755-1803 BiAUS, BiDrAC,
  WhAm H
Beretta, John King 1861-1948 NatCAB 37,
  WhAm 2
Berezowsky, Nicolai 1900-1953 WhAm 3
Berg, A T NewYHSD
Berg, Alban 1885-1935 McGEWB, WhAm 4
Berg, Albert Ashton 1872-1950 WhAm 3
Berg, Carl 1897-1964 NatCAB 50
Berg, Charles I 1856-1926 WhAm 1
Berg, Clara DeLissa 1876- WomWWA 14
Berg, Douglas Spearman 1924-1968 WhAm 5
Berg, Ernst Julius 1871-1941 NatCAB 35,
  WhAm 1
Berg, George Olaf 1875-1935 WhAm 1
Berg, Gertrude 1899-1966 NatCAB 52,
  WhAm 4
Berg, Helen McGregor Morse 1830-
  WomWWA 14

Berg, Herman Casper *ApCAB*
Berg, Irving Husted 1878-1941 *NatCAB 31,*
  WhAm 1
Berg, J Frederic 1871-1958 *WhAm 3*
Berg, John Daniel 1882-1949 *WhAm 2*
Berg, Joseph Frederic 1812-1871 *DcAmB,*
  WhAm H
Berg, Joseph Frederick 1812-1871 *ApCAB,*
  NatCAB 21, TwCBDA
Berg, Kaj 1899-1972 *WhAm 5*
Berg, Lev Simonovich 1876-1950 *DcScB*
Berg, Lillie *AmWom*
Berg, Louis 1901-1972 *WhAm 5*
Berg, Per Torsten 1853- *NatCAB 14*
Berg, Royal Howard 1895-1965 *WhAm 4*
Berg, Walter Gilman 1858-1908 *WhAm 1*
Berg, William Henry 1882-1940 *WhAm 1*
Bergan, Gerald T 1892-1972 *WhAm 5*
Berge, Edward 1876-1924 *WhAm 1*
Berge, Fritjof Emil 1868-1956 *NatCAB 47*
Berge, Irenee 1870-1926 *WhAm 1*
Berge, Wendell 1903-1955 *WhAm 3*
Bergel, Egon Ernest 1894-1969 *WhAm 5*
Bergemann, Gustav Ernst 1862- *WhAm 5*
Bergen, Caroline McPhail 1859- *WomWWA 14*
Bergen, Charles 1805?- *NewYHSD*
Bergen, Christopher Augustus 1841-1905
  BiDrAC
Bergen, Cornelia M 1837- *AmWom*
Bergen, Edgar John 1903- *WebAB*
Bergen, Fanny Dickerson 1846- *ApCAB,*
  WhAm 4, WomWWA 14
Bergen, Helen Corinne 1868- *AmWom*
Bergen, James J 1847-1923 *WhAm 1*
Bergen, John Adrian 1886-1942 *NatCAB 31*
Bergen, John Tallmadge 1860-1948 *WhAm 2*
Bergen, John Teunis 1786-1855 *BiAUS,*
  BiDrAC, WhAm H, WhAmP
Bergen, Joseph Young 1851- *ApCAB,*
  WhAm 4
Bergen, Paul David 1860-1915 *NatCAB 16*
Bergen, Peter G *NewYHSD*
Bergen, Ralph David 1895-1967 *NatCAB 54*
Bergen, Teunis Garret 1806-1881 *BiAUS,*
  BiDrAC, WhAm H
Bergen, Tunis G 1847-1929 *WhAm 1*
Bergen, Tunis Garret 1848- *NatCAB 12*
Bergen, VanBrunt 1841-1917 *WhAm 1*
Bergendahl, Emil Henry 1921-1971 *NatCAB 56*
Bergener, Gustav Julius 1867-1926 *NatCAB 20*
Bergengren, Anna Farquhar 1865- *NatCAB 14,*
  WomWWA 14
Bergengren, Leslie Merritt 1880-
  WomWWA 14
Bergengren, Roy Frederick 1879-1955
  NatCAB 44, WhAm 3
Bergenstal, Delbert Mauritz 1917-1959
  NatCAB 48
Bergenthal, Alice Dacy 1876- *WomWWA 14*
Berger, Adolph 1882-1961 *WhAm 4*
Berger, Alexander 1857-1940 *NatCAB 29*
Berger, Anita Louise Fremault d1970 *WhAm 6*
Berger, Anton *NewYHSD*
Berger, Arthur Schoene 1903-1960 *NatCAB 47*
Berger, Augustin 1861- *WhAm 4*
Berger, C A 1901-1966 *WhAm 4*
Berger, Calvin Michael 1870-1929 *WhAm 1*
Berger, Charles F *NewYHSD*
Berger, Charles L 1870-1948 *WhAm 2*
Berger, Christian Louis 1842-1922 *NatCAB 19*
Berger, Daniel 1832-1920 *DcAmB*
Berger, Edmund Henry 1903-1961 *NatCAB 49*
Berger, Edward Henry 1893-1952 *NatCAB 46*
Berger, Frederick Gardiner Bart 1893-1919
  ApCAB X
Berger, George Bart 1869-1939 *WhAm 1*
Berger, George William 1880- *WhAm 6*
Berger, Hans 1873-1941 *AsBiEn, DcScB*
Berger, Henry *NewYHSD*
Berger, Johann Gottfried 1659-1736 *DcScB*
Berger, John Milton 1883-1943 *NatCAB 34*
Berger, Josef 1903-1971 *NatCAB 57*
Berger, Knute 1890-1949 *NatCAB 41*
Berger, Louis Herman 1879-1965 *NatCAB 54*
Berger, Lowe 1896-1959 *WhAm 4*
Berger, Maurice Wibert 1906-1968 *WhAm 5*
Berger, Meta 1873- *WomWWA 14*
Berger, Meyer 1898-1959 *NatCAB 46,*

Berger, Samuel Alexander 1882-1972
  NatCAB 56
Berger, Victor L 1860-1929 *NatCAB 22,*
  WhAm 1
Berger, Victor Louis 1860-1929 *AmBi,*
  DcAmB S1, EncAB, McGEWB, WebAB
Berger, Victor Luitpold 1860-1929 *BiDrAC,*
  WhAmP
Berger, Vilhelm 1867- *WhAm 1*
Berger, William Henry 1841-1934 *NatCAB 27*
Bergerman, Melbourne 1900-1973 *WhAm 6*
Bergey, David Hendricks 1860-1937
  NatCAB 28, WhAm 1
Bergfeld, J D 1873- *WomWWA 14*
Bergh, Albert Ellery 1861- *WhAm 4*
Bergh, Arthur d1962 *WhAm 4*
Bergh, Christian 1763-1843 *DcAmB,*
  WhAm H
Bergh, Henry 1811-1888 *AmBi, DcAmB,*
  WebAB, WhAm H
Bergh, Henry 1820-1888 *TwCBDA*
Bergh, Henry 1823-1888 *ApCAB, NatCAB 3*
Bergh, Lillie D'Angelo *WhAm 5*
Bergh, Louis DeCoppet 1856-1913 *WhAm 1*
Bergh, Louis O 1885-1955 *WhAm 3*
Berghaus, Albert *IIBEAAW*
Berghausen, Alfred 1882-1959 *NatCAB 48*
Berghausen, Oscar 1879-1959 *NatCAB 50*
Bergherm, Charles Russell 1908-1966 *WhAm 4*
Berghoff, Gustav August 1863-1940
  NatCAB 31
Berghoff, Robert S 1889-1965 *WhAm 4*
Bergholz, Leo Allen 1857- *WhAm 4*
Bergida, Jerome Jacob 1907-1974 *WhAm 6*
Bergin, Alfred 1866-1944 *WhAm 2*
Bergin, Charles Kniese 1904-1964 *WhAm 4*
Bergin, Darby 1826- *ApCAB*
Bergin, John William 1872-1947 *WhAm 2*
Bergius, Friedrich Karl Rudolf 1884-1949
  AsBiEn, DcScB
Bergland, John McFarland 1879- *WhAm 6*
Bergler, Edmund 1899-1961 *WhAm 4*
Berglund, Abraham 1875-1942 *WhAm 2*
Berglund, Alfred 1871-1961 *NatCAB 53*
Berglund, Everett Rudolph 1915-1971 *WhAm 6*
Bergman, Ingmar 1918- *McGEWB*
Bergman, Ingram 1899-1962 *NatCAB 50*
Bergman, Justin 1880-1960 *NatCAB 48*
Bergman, Torbern Olof 1735-1784 *AsBiEn,*
  DcScB
Bergman, Walter James 1904-1972 *WhAm 5*
Bergmann, Carl 1821-1876 *AmBi, ApCAB,*
  DcAmB, WhAm H
Bergmann, Charles 1821-1876 *NatCAB 5*
Bergmann, Max 1886-1944 *DcAmB S3,*
  DcScB Sup
Bergmann, Werner 1904-1959 *NatCAB 48,*
  WhAm 3
Bergner, Charles William 1854-1903 *ApCAB X*
Bergosa Y Jordan, Antonio *ApCAB*
Bergquist, J Victor 1877-1935 *WhAm 1*
Bergquist, Stanard Gustaf 1892-1956 *WhAm 3*
Bergren, Edgar 1903- *WebAB*
Bergsaker, Anders Johannessen 1877-1951
  WhAm 3
Bergson, Henri 1859-1941 *DcScB, McGEWB,*
  WhAm HA, WhAm 4A
Bergson, Henri 1859-1943 *WhAm 2*
Bergstrom, George Edwin 1876- *NatCAB 16,*
  WhAm 5
Bergstrom, John Nelson 1874-1951 *NatCAB 40*
Bergtold, William Henry 1865-1936 *WhAm 1*
Bergvall, Jakob Ludvig 1876-1945 *NatCAB 33*
Beria, Lavrenty 1899-1954 *WhWW-II*
Beria, Lavrenty Pavlovich 1899-1953 *McGEWB*
Berigard, Claude Guillermet De 1578?-1663?
  DcScB
Bering, Frank West 1877-1965 *NatCAB 53,*
  WhAm 4
Bering, Joshua 1834?- *NewYHSD*
Bering, Vitus 1680-1741 *ApCAB, WhAm H*
Bering, Vitus 1681-1741 *DcScB, McGEWB*
Beringer, George M 1860-1928 *WhAm 1*
Beringer, Johann Bartholomaeus Adam
  1667?-1738 *DcScB*
Beringer, Lester Eastwood 1891-1958
  NatCAB 48

Beringer, Milton S 1893-1967 *WhAm 4*
Berio, Luciano 1925- *McGEWB*
Beristain, Joaquin 1817-1839 *ApCAB*
Beristain, Mariano 1756-1817 *ApCAB*
Beritashvili, Ivane 1884-1974 *WhAm 6*
Berkan, Otto 1834-1906 *NewYHSD*
Berkander, George Frederick 1879-1937
  NatCAB 34
Berke, Ernest 1921- *IIBEAAW*
Berke, Mark 1914- *WhAm 6*
Berkebile, Orris N 1898-1961 *NatCAB 50*
Berkeley, Busby 1895-1976 *WebAB, WhAm 6*
Berkeley, Lady Frances 1634- *NotAW*
Berkeley, George 1684-1753 *ApCAB, Drake,*
  NatCAB 6, TwCBDA
Berkeley, George 1685-1753 *DcScB, McGEWB*
Berkeley, James Percival 1879- *WhAm 6*
Berkeley, John d1622 *ApCAB, DcAmB,*
  WhAm H
Berkeley, Miles Joseph 1803-1889 *DcScB*
Berkeley, Norborne 1718?-1770 *AmBi, DcAmB,*
  NatCAB 13, WhAm H
Berkeley, Norborne 1891-1964 *WhAm 4*
Berkeley, Randolph Carter 1875-1960
  NatCAB 50, WhAm 3
Berkeley, Stanley d1909 *IIBEAAW*
Berkeley, Sir William 1606-1677 *AmBi,*
  DcAmB, EncAB, McGEWB, WebAB,
  WhAmP
Berkeley, Sir William 1608-1677 *NatCAB 13,*
  WhAm H
Berkeley, Sir William 1610?-1677 *ApCAB,*
  Drake
Berkeley, William Nathaniel 1868- *WhAm 1*
Berkenmeyer, John 1730-1791 *Drake*
Berkenmeyer, Wilhelm Christoph 1686-1751
  DcAmB, WhAm H
Berkey, Charles Peter 1867-1955 *NatCAB 46,*
  WhAm 3
Berkey, Peter 1885-1959 *WhAm 3*
Berkey, Robert Peter 1912-1962 *NatCAB 50*
Berkheiser, Elven James 1887-1958 *NatCAB 43*
Berkhofer, Robert Frederick 1931- *EncAAH*
Berkley, Claude Wellington 1890-1957
  WhAm 4
Berkley, George Carleton 1870-1948
  NatCAB 37
Berkley, Henry Johns 1860-1940 *NatCAB 30,*
  WhAm 1
Berkman, Alexander 1870-1936 *DcAmB S2,*
  WhAm HA, WhAm 4
Berkman, Anton Hilmer 1897-1973 *WhAm 6*
Berkman, David Mayo 1886-1958 *NatCAB 47*
Berkner, Lloyd Viel 1906-1967 *WhAm 4A*
Berkowitz, Abram 1892-1973 *WhAm 5*
Berkowitz, E Bertram 1889-1966 *NatCAB 52*
Berkowitz, Henry 1857-1924 *ApCAB Sup,*
  DcAmB, DcAmReB, NatCAB 20,
  NatCAB 22, WhAm 1
Berkowitz, Mortimer 1887-1966 *NatCAB 53,*
  WhAm 4
Berkowitz, Walter J 1892-1966 *WhAm 4*
Berkson, Maurice 1880- *WhAm 6*
Berkson, Seymour 1905-1959 *WhAm 3*
Berkstresser, Celia Smith 1854- *WomWWA 14*
Berky, Oswin Weller 1875-1949 *NatCAB 37*
Berl, Ernst 1877-1946 *WhAm 2*
Berl, Eugene Ennalls 1889-1954 *NatCAB 44,*
  WhAm 3
Berla, Julian Emerson 1902-1976 *WhAm 6*
Berlack, Harris 1898-1968 *WhAm 5*
Berlage, Hendrik Petrus 1856-1968 *WhAm 5*
Berle, Adolf Augustus 1865-1960 *WhAm 4*
Berle, Adolf Augustus 1895-1971 *EncAB,*
  McGEWB, NatCAB 56, WhAm 5
Berle, Adolph Augustus 1895-1971 *WebAB*
Berle, Milton 1908- *WebAB*
Berlin, Alfred Franklin 1848-1925 *WhAm 1*
Berlin, Bernard Simonson 1883-1947
  NatCAB 39
Berlin, Harold Robert 1896-1965 *WhAm 4*
Berlin, Irving 1888- *EncAB, McGEWB,*
  WebAB
Berlin, John Cook 1859-1952 *NatCAB 43*
Berlin, Theodore H 1917-1962 *WhAm 4*
Berlin, William Markle 1880-1962 *BiDrAC*
Berliner, Abraham 1913-1966 *NatCAB 53*
Berliner, Emile 1851-1929 *AmBi, ApCAB,*

AsBiEn, DcAmB S1, NatCAB 10,
NatCAB 21, WebAB, WhAm 1
Berliner, Henry Adler 1895-1970 NatCAB 56,
WhAm 5
Berlinger, Milton 1908- WebAB
Berlioz, Louis Hector 1803-1869 McGEWB
Berman, Benjamin Frank 1903-1966 WhAm 4
Berman, Eugene 1899-1972 BnEnAmA,
WhAm 5
Berman, Harry 1902-1944 NatCAB 33
Berman, Louis 1893-1946 NatCAB 39,
WhAm 2
Berman, Morris 1891-1945 WhAm 2
Berman, Oscar 1876-1951 WhAm 3
Berman, Philip Grossman 1900-1968 WhAm 5
Bermann, Isidor Samuel Leopold 1845-
WhAm 4
Bermejo, Bartolome McGEWB
Bermingham, Arthur Thomas 1884-1969
WhAm 5
Bermingham, Edward John 1887-1958
NatCAB 43
Bermingham, John 1875-1941 NatCAB 31
Bermingham, Thomas Costello 1850-1914
NatCAB 16
Bermudez, Edouard Edmond 1832-1892 DcAmB
Bermudez, Edouard Edmund 1832-1892
WhAm H
Bermudez, Edward Edmond 1832-1892
NatCAB 5
Bermudez, Jose Manuel 1760?-1830 ApCAB
Bermudez, Juan ApCAB
Bermudez, Remigo Morales 1836-1894
ApCAB Sup
Bern, Paul 1889-1932 WhAm 1
Bernadotte, Count Folke 1895-1948 WhWW-II
Bernadotte, Jean Baptiste Jules 1763-1844
WhoMilH
Bernadotte Folke, Count 1895-1948 WhAm 2
Bernadou, John Baptiste 1858-1908 NatCAB 9,
WhAm 1
Bernal, Calixto 1804- ApCAB
Bernal, John Desmond 1901-1971 DcScB Sup
Bernam, Andrew 1830?- NewYHSD
Bernanos, Georges 1888-1948 McGEWB
Bernard NewYHSD
Bernard Of Chartres d1130? DcScB
Bernard Of Clairvaux, Saint 1090-1153
McGEWB
Bernard Of LeTreille 1240?-1292 DcScB
Bernard Of Trevisan DcScB
Bernard Of Verdun DcScB
Bernard Silvestre DcScB
Bernard, Arnold 1815?- NewYHSD
Bernard, Bayle 1807-1875 DcAmB
Bernard, Claude 1813-1878 AsBiEn, BiHiMed,
DcScB, McGEWB
Bernard, E 1830?- NewYHSD
Bernard, Frances Fenton 1880-1953 WhAm 3
Bernard, Sir Francis 1712-1779 AmBi, DcAmB,
WhAm H, WhAmP
Bernard, Sir Francis 1714-1779 ApCAB, Drake,
NatCAB 5, TwCBDA
Bernard, Francisco NewYHSD
Bernard, Frank Basil 1886-1970 WhAm 5
Bernard, George 1881-1951 NatCAB 38
Bernard, Germain 1873-1954 NatCAB 44
Bernard, Hugh Robertson WhAm 5
Bernard, John 1744-1809 ApCAB
Bernard, John 1756-1828 ApCAB, DcAmB,
NatCAB 21, WhAm H
Bernard, John 1756-1829 Drake
Bernard, John Toussaint 1893- BiDrAC
Bernard, Joseph Alphonsus 1881- WhAm 6
Bernard, Lawrence Joseph 1905-1968 WhAm 5
Bernard, Lloyd Duckworth 1900-1962
NatCAB 50
Bernard, Luther Lee 1881-1951 BiDAmEd,
NatCAB 39, WhAm 3
Bernard, Merrill 1892-1951 WhAm 3
Bernard, Noel 1874-1911 DcScB
Bernard, Sam 1863-1927 WhAm 1
Bernard, Simon 1779-1836 ApCAB
Bernard, Simon 1779-1839 AmBi, DcAmB,
Drake, NatCAB 24, WebAMB,
WhAm H
Bernard, Thomas 1746-1818 ApCAB
Bernard, Victor Ferdinand 1845- WhAm 4

Bernard, William Bayle 1807-1875 ApCAB,
DcAmB, WhAm H
Bernard DuHautcilly, Auguste NewYHSD
Bernardet NewYHSD
Bernardin, Joseph Mariotte 1868- WhAm 4
Bernardina, Mother NotAW
Bernardino, Fray ApCAB
Bernardy, Amy Allemand 1880- WhAm 6
Bernatowicz, Albert John 1920-1971 WhAm 5
Bernays, Augustus Charles 1854-1907 ApCAB,
DcAmB, NatCAB 6, TwCBDA,
WhAm 1
Bernays, Murray C 1894-1970 NatCAB 54
Bernays, Thekla Marie WomWWA 14
Bernbaum, Ernest 1879-1958 WhAm 3
Berne, Eric Lennard 1910-1970 WhAm 5
Berne-Allen, Allan 1902-1969 WhAm 5
Bernecker, Edward M 1892-1955 WhAm 3
Bernegau, Carl Maria 1866-1948 NatCAB 38
Berneker, Louis Frederick 1876- WhAm 1
Berner, Harry M 1896-1954 WhAm 3
Bernet, Albert 1868-1918 NatCAB 17
Bernet, John Joseph 1868-1935 DcAmB S1,
WhAm 1
Bernet Kempers, Karel Phillipus 1897-1974
WhAm 6
Bernett, Louis 1831?- NewYHSD
Bernhard, Duke Of Saxe-Weimar 1604-1639
WhoMilH
Bernhard, Prince Of The Netherlands 1911-
WhWW-II
Bernhard, Alva Douglas 1886- WhAm 3
Bernhard, Dorothy Lehman 1903-1969 WhAm 5
Bernhard, Joseph 1889- WhAm 3
Bernhard, Richard J 1893-1961 WhAm 4
Bernhard, William 1897-1970 WhAm 5
Bernhardt, Sarah 1845-1923 WhAm 1
Bernhardt, Wilhelm d1909 WhAm 1
Bernheim, Bertram Moses 1880-1958 WhAm 3
Bernheim, Gotthardt Dellmann 1827-
NatCAB 9
Bernheim, Hippolyte 1840-1919 DcScB
Bernheim, Oscar Frederick 1868- WhAm 4
Bernheimer, Adolph 1833- NatCAB 3
Bernheimer, Adolph L ApCAB X
Bernheimer, Charles L 1864-1944 ApCAB X,
NatCAB 15, WhAm 2
Bernheimer, Charles Seligman 1868- WhAm 5
Bernheimer, Simon E 1849- NatCAB 3
Bernhisel, John Milton 1799-1881 BiAUS,
BiDrAC, REnAW, WhAm H, WhAmP
Bernie, Ben 1893-1943 WhAm 2
Bernier, Paul 1906-1964 WhAm 4
Bernier, Thomas Alfred 1845- ApCAB Sup
Berninghaus, Julius Charles 1905- IIBEAAW
Berninghaus, Oscar Edmund 1874-1952
IIBEAAW, REnAW, WhAm 3
Bernini, Gian Lorenzo 1598-1680 McGEWB
Berno, Jack Charles 1920-1973 WhAm 6
Bernoulli, Daniel 1700-1782 AsBiEn, DcScB,
McGEWB
Bernoulli, Jakob, I 1654-1705 DcScB
Bernoulli, Jakob, II 1759-1789 DcScB
Bernoulli, Johann, I 1667-1748 DcScB
Bernoulli, Johann, II 1710-1790 DcScB
Bernoulli, Johann, III 1744-1807 DcScB
Bernoulli, Nikolaus, I 1687-1759 DcScB
Bernoulli, Nikolaus, II 1695-1726 DcScB
Bernstein, Aline WhAm 3
Bernstein, Aline 1880-1955 NatCAB 47
Bernstein, Aline 1882-1955 DcAmB S5
Bernstein, Arnold 1888-1971 NatCAB 56
Bernstein, Benjamin Abram 1881-1964
NatCAB 51
Bernstein, Charles 1872-1942 WhAm 2
Bernstein, David d1945 WhAm 2
Bernstein, Eduard 1850-1932 McGEWB
Bernstein, Felix 1878-1956 DcScB
Bernstein, Herman 1876-1935 DcAmB S1,
WhAm 1, WhAmP
Bernstein, Jacob Lawrence 1902-1970 WhAm 5
Bernstein, Julius 1839-1917 DcScB Sup
Bernstein, Leonard 1918- EncAB, McGEWB,
WebAB
Bernstein, Lotte Kirschner 1897-1971
NatCAB 57
Bernstein, Louis 1878-1962 WhAm 4
Bernstein, Louis 1882-1922 WhAm 1

Bernstein, Sergey Natanovich 1880-1968 DcScB,
DcScB Sup
Bernstorff, Count Johann 1862-1939 WhAm 1
Bernstrom, Victor d1907 WhAm 1
Bernthal, Theodore George 1904-1968
NatCAB 54
Bernthal, Walter George 1902-1962 NatCAB 48
Bernthsen, Heinrich August 1855-1931 DcScB
Berol, Alfred C 1892-1974 WhAm 6
Berolzheimer, Edwin Michael 1887-1949
WhAm 2
Beroujon, Claude WhAm H
Berra, Lawrence Peter 1925- WebAB
Berredo, Bernardo Pereira De 1680-1748
ApCAB Sup
Berres, Albert Julius 1873- WhAm 5
Berresford, Arthur William 1872-1941 WhAm 1
Berreth, Herbert Raymond 1931-1972 WhAm 6
Berrey, Rhodes Clay 1911-1973 WhAm 6
Berrey, Ruth Robertson 1906-1973 WhAm 6
Berri, William 1848-1917 WhAm 1
Berrian, Hobart BiAUS
Berrian, William 1787-1862 ApCAB, Drake,
TwCBDA
Berrien, Cornelius Roach 1873-1944
NatCAB 34, WhAm 5
Berrien, F Kenneth 1909-1971 NatCAB 56
Berrien, Frank Dunn 1877-1951 NatCAB 39,
WhAm 3
Berrien, John M 1802-1883 ApCAB
Berrien, John Macpherson 1781-1856 ApCAB,
BiDrAC, BiDrUSE, DcAmB, Drake,
NatCAB 5, TwCBDA, WhAm H,
WhAmP
Berrien, John Macpherson 1802-1883 TwCBDA
Berrien, John McPherson 1781-1856 BiAUS
Berrigan, John Joseph 1864-1929 NatCAB 21
Berrigan, Thomas Joseph 1904-1970 WhAm 5
Berrisford, Paul Dee 1884-1941 NatCAB 33
Berruguete, Alonso 1486?-1561 McGEWB
Berry, A Moore 1849- NatCAB 6
Berry, Abraham J 1799-1865 ApCAB,
TwCBDA
Berry, Adaline Hohf 1859- AmWom
Berry, Albert Edgar 1878-1929 WhAm 1
Berry, Albert Gleaves 1848-1938 WhAm 1
Berry, Albert Seaton 1836-1908 BiDrAC,
WhAm 1, WhAmP
Berry, Campbell Polson 1834-1901 BiDrAC,
WhAmP
Berry, Cecil Ralph 1895-1968 NatCAB 55,
WhAm 5
Berry, Charles Edward Anderson 1926- WebAB
Berry, Charles Fred 1865-1929 ApCAB X
Berry, Charles Harold 1889-1965 NatCAB 52,
WhAm 4
Berry, Charles Scott 1875- WhAm 6
Berry, Charles White 1871-1941 NatCAB 37,
WhAm 3
Berry, Clarence Jesse 1867-1930 NatCAB 27
Berry, Edward Atkinson 1847-1934 NatCAB 27
Berry, Edward Robie 1879-1934 NatCAB 26
Berry, Edward Wilber 1875-1945 DcAmB S3,
NatCAB 33, WhAm 2
Berry, Edward Willard 1900-1968 WhAm 5
Berry, Elizabeth Robbins WomWWA 14
Berry, Ellis Yarnal 1902- BiDrAC
Berry, Frank 1904-1969 WhAm 5
Berry, Frank Allen 1885-1965 WhAm 4
Berry, Fred 1878-1955 NatCAB 47
Berry, Frederick Aymond 1881-1955
NatCAB 45
Berry, George Leonard 1882-1948 BiDrAC,
DcAmB S4, NatCAB 36, WhAm 2,
WhAmP
Berry, George Ricker 1865-1945 WhAm 2
Berry, George Titus 1865-1956 WhAm 3
Berry, Gilbert Milo 1862-1931 WhAm 1
Berry, Gordon 1880-1953 NatCAB 42
Berry, Gordon Lockwood 1884-1932
NatCAB 23, WhAm 1
Berry, Grace Ella 1870- WomWWA 14
Berry, Harold Haile 1883-1961 WhAm 4
Berry, Harold Lee 1877-1962 WhAm 4
Berry, Harriet Morehead 1877-1940 NotAW
Berry, Hiram George 1824-1863 ApCAB,
Drake, TwCBDA
Berry, Hiram Gregory 1824-1863 DcAmB,

NatCAB 4, WhAm H
Berry, Howard 1886-1958 *WhAm 3*
Berry, James Berthold 1880- *WhAm 6*
Berry, James Dufur 1878-1941 *NatCAB 43*
Berry, James Edward 1881-1966 *WhAm 4*
Berry, James Henderson 1841-1913
  ApCAB Sup, BiDrAC, DcAmB,
  NatCAB 1, NatCAB 10, TwCBDA,
  WhAm 1, WhAmP
Berry, James M 1841-1913 *ApCAB X*
Berry, Jennie Iowa Peet 1866- *WomWWA 14*
Berry, Joel Halbert 1888-1952 *NatCAB 41*
Berry, John 1833-1879 *BiAUS, BiDrAC,*
  WhAm H
Berry, John Cutting 1847-1936 *NatCAB 27,*
  WhAm 4
Berry, Joseph Flintoft 1856-1931 *NatCAB 13,*
  WhAm 1
Berry, Joseph Francis 1880- *WhAm 6*
Berry, Joseph Hooper 1839-1917 *NatCAB 18*
Berry, Josephine Thorndike *WomWWA 14*
Berry, Kearie Lee 1893-1965 *WhAm 4*
Berry, Lillian Gay 1872- *WhAm 5*
Berry, Lucien Grant 1863-1937 *NatCAB 28*
Berry, Lucien W 1815-1858 *NatCAB 7*
Berry, Lucy Haldane 1887- *WomWWA 14*
Berry, Mark Perrin Lowrey 1878- *WhAm 6*
Berry, Martha McChesney 1866-1942
  BiDAmEd, DcAmB S3, NotAW, WhAm 2,
  WomWWA 14
Berry, Martia L Davis 1844- *AmWom*
Berry, Mervin Albert 1940-1971 *WhAm 6*
Berry, Nathaniel Springer 1796-1894 *ApCAB,*
  BiAUS, DcAmB, NatCAB 11, TwCBDA,
  WhAm H, WhAmP
Berry, Nixon T 1905-1975 *WhAm 6*
Berry, Noah, Jr. 1916- *IlBEAAW*
Berry, Raymond Harry 1891-1959 *NatCAB 48*
Berry, Raymond Hirst 1897-1971 *WhAm 5*
Berry, Robert Mallory 1846-1929 *NatCAB 21,*
  WhAm 1
Berry, Robert W 1902-1960 *WhAm 4*
Berry, Sarah Nichols Page *NewYHSD*
Berry, Thomas d1951 *WhAm 3*
Berry, Thomas 1829-1916 *NatCAB 24*
Berry, Tiernan Brien 1859-1912 *NatCAB 31*
Berry, Tom 1879-1951 *NatCAB 41*
Berry, Walter VanRensselaer 1859-1927
  NatCAB 22, WhAm 1
Berry, Ward Leonard 1911-1967 *WhAm 4*
Berry, Wilbur Fisk 1851- *WhAm 4*
Berry, William Eugene 1879-1960 *NatCAB 48*
Berry, William Franklin 1844-1914 *WhAm 1*
Berry, William H 1852- *WhAm 4*
Berry, William H 1908-1972 *WhAm 5*
Berry, William James Courtnald 1847-
  TwCBDA
Berryhill, James Guest 1852- *NatCAB 17*
Berryhill, Virginia Joynes *WomWWA 14*
Berryman, Clifford Kennedy 1869-1949
  DcAmB S4, NatCAB 39, WhAm 2
Berryman, James Thomas 1902-1971 *WhAm 5*
Berryman, Jerome Woods 1870- *WhAm 1*
Berryman, John 1914-1970 *WebAB, WhAm 5*
Berryman, John Brondgeest 1862-1945
  NatCAB 34, WhAm 2
Berryman, W A 1892-1952 *WhAm 3*
Bersell, Petrus Olof Immanuel 1882-1967
  WhAm 5
Berson, I P *NewYHSD*
Bersted, Alfred 1898-1972 *NatCAB 56,*
  WhAm 5
Bert, Mabel 1862- *AmWom*
Bert, Paul 1833-1886 *AsBiEn, BiHiMed,*
  DcScB
Bertalanffy, Ludwig Von 1901-1972 *WhAm 6*
Bertch, George Edwin 1870-1920 *NatCAB 19*
Berthaut, Tony *NewYHSD*
Berthelot, Henri Mathias 1861-1931 *WhoMilH*
Berthelot, Pierre Eugene Marcelin 1827-1907
  AsBiEn
Berthelot, Pierre Eugene Marcellin 1827-1907
  DcScB
Berthelot DeLaBoileverie, Lily Kendall
  WomWWA 14
Berthier, Louis Alexander 1753-1815 *Drake*
Berthier, Louis Alexandre 1753-1815 *ApCAB,*
  WhoMilH

Berthier, Pierre 1782-1861 *DcScB*
Berthold, Arnold Adolphe 1803-1861 *DcScB*
Bertholf, Ellsworth Price 1866-1921 *NatCAB 18,*
  WhAm 1
Berthollet, Claude Louis 1748-1822 *AsBiEn,*
  DcScB, McGEWB
Bertholon, Pierre 1741-1800 *DcScB*
Berthot, Armand Guy 1878-1951 *NatCAB 48*
Berthrong, Donald John 1922- *EncAAH,*
  REnAW
Berti, Gasparo 1600?-1643 *DcScB*
Bertillon, Alphonse 1853-1914 *McGEWB*
Bertin, Louis-Emile 1840-1924 *DcScB*
Bertine, Edwin Kellogg 1898-1960 *NatCAB 47*
Bertini, Amedeo August 1881-1931 *NatCAB 23*
Bertini, Eugenio 1846-1933 *DcScB*
Bertola, Mariana 1868- *WomWWA 14*
Bertolet, William S 1875- *WhAm 5*
Berton, C 1824?- *NewYHSD*
Bertram, Helen 1869- *WhAm 5,*
  WomWWA 14
Bertram, James 1872-1934 *DcAmLiB,*
  WhAm 1
Bertram, John 1796-1882 *DcAmB, WhAm H*
Bertram, William *NewYHSD*
Bertrand, Charles-Eugene 1851-1917 *DcScB*
Bertrand, Ernest 1888-1958 *WhAm 3*
Bertrand, Gabriel 1867-1962 *DcScB*
Bertrand, Joseph Louis Francois 1822-1900
  DcScB
Bertrand, Marcel-Alexandre 1847-1907 *DcScB*
Bertrand, Saint Louis 1526-1581 *ApCAB*
Bertrandias, Victor Emile 1893-1961 *WhAm 4*
Bertron, Samuel Reading 1865-1938 *WhAm 1*
Bertron, Samuel Reading 1881-1953
  NatCAB 44, WhAm 3
Bertsch, Charles Harley 1879-1961 *NatCAB 49*
Bertsch, Howard 1909-1969 *WhAm 5*
Berwald, William 1864- *WhAm 4*
Berwanger, Eugene Harley 1929- *EncAAH*
Berwick, James, Duke Of 1670-1734 *WhoMilH*
Berwick, William Edward Hodgson 1888-1944
  DcScB
Berwin, Franklin 1881- *WhAm 6*
Berwind, Edward Julius 1848-1936 *ApCAB X,*
  DcAmB S2, WhAm 1
Beryl, Louis 1909-1969 *NatCAB 53*
Berzarin, Nikolai 1904-1945 *WhWW-II*
Berzelius, Jons Jacob 1779-1848 *BiHiMed,*
  DcScB, McGEWB
Berzelius, Jons Jakob 1779-1848 *AsBiEn*
Besancon, Justin J *NewYHSD*
Besant, Annie Wood 1847-1933 *DcAmReB,*
  McGEWB
Beseler, Fred Charles 1896-1972 *NatCAB 57*
Besemer, Howard Burhans 1869-1918 *WhAm 1*
Besessen, Mrs. Henry J 1881- *WomWWA 14*
Beshlin, Earl Hanley 1870-1971 *BiDrAC,*
  WhAm 5
Beshoar, Michael 1833-1907 *NatCAB 2*
Besler, William George 1864-1942 *NatCAB 31,*
  WhAm 2
Besley, Fred Wilson 1872- *WhAm 5*
Besley, Frederic Atwood 1868-1944 *NatCAB 33,*
  WhAm 2
Besosa, Harry Felipe 1881- *WhAm 6*
Bess, Demaree Caughey 1893-1962 *WhAm 4*
Bess, Elmer Allen 1869- *WhAm 5*
Bessau, Oscar *NewYHSD*
Besse, Arthur Lyman 1887-1951 *DcAmB S5,*
  NatCAB 39, WhAm 3
Besse, Lyman Waterman 1854-1930
  NatCAB 41
Bessel, Friedrich Wilhelm 1784-1846 *AsBiEn,*
  DcScB, McGEWB
Bessels, Emil 1847- *ApCAB*
Bessemer, Sir Henry 1813-1898 *AsBiEn,*
  DcScB Sup, McGEWB
Bessesen, Alfred Nicholas 1870-1947
  NatCAB 36
Bessey, Charles Edwin 1845-1915 *AmBi,*
  ApCAB, ApCAB Sup, BiDAmEd,
  DcAmB, DcScB, NatCAB 8, REnAW,
  TwCBDA, WhAm 1
Bessey, Earle Emerson 1871-1931 *NatCAB 23*
Bessey, Ernst Athearn 1877-1957 *WhAm 3*
Bessieres, Jean Baptiste 1768-1813 *WhoMilH*
Besson, Harlan 1887-1949 *WhAm 2*

Besson, Linford Shepherd 1888-1948
  NatCAB 37
Besson, Samuel Austin 1853- *NatCAB 5*
Besson, Waldemar Max 1929-1971 *WhAm 5*
Bessunger, Morris 1818-1916 *NatCAB 17*
Best, Alfred M 1876-1958 *WhAm 3*
Best, Arthur W 1865?- *IlBEAAW*
Best, Charles Herbert 1899- *AsBiEn,*
  McGEWB
Best, Clarence Leo 1878-1951 *NatCAB 40,*
  WhAm 3
Best, Daniel 1838-1923 *NatCAB 40*
Best, Edward S 1826-1865 *NewYHSD*
Best, Ernest Maurice 1880-1963 *WhAm 4*
Best, Eva 1851- *AmWom*
Best, Frederick Charles 1874-1945 *NatCAB 35*
Best, George Newton 1846-1926 *WhAm 1*
Best, Gertrude Delprat 1869-1947 *NatCAB 41,*
  WhAm 2
Best, Harry 1880-1971 *WhAm 5*
Best, Harry Cassie 1863-1936 *IlBEAAW*
Best, Henry Riley 1872-1934 *WhAm 1*
Best, Howard Richard 1894-1958 *WhAm 3*
Best, James Irvin 1902-1966 *WhAm 4*
Best, James MacLeod 1903-1970 *WhAm 5*
Best, John Garvin 1921-1970 *NatCAB 56,*
  WhAm 5
Best, Marjorie Ayres 1874- *NatCAB 16,*
  WomWWA 14
Best, McOcal 1902-1955 *NatCAB 46*
Best, Nolan Rice 1871-1930 *WhAm 1,*
  WhAm 1C
Best, Philip 1814-1869 *NatCAB 3*
Best, Willard Lowery 1897-1970 *NatCAB 56*
Best, William *NewYHSD*
Best, William d1955 *WhAm 3*
Best, William E St. Clair 1885- *WhoColR*
Best, William Hall 1877-1960 *NatCAB 49,*
  WhAm 4
Best, William Henry 1885-1942 *NatCAB 31*
Best, William Newton 1860-1922 *NatCAB 21*
Best, William Parker 1864-1938 *WhAm 1*
Bestic, John Brereton 1915-1969 *WhAm 5*
Beston, Henry 1888-1968 *NatCAB 55,*
  WhAm 5
Bestor, Arthur 1920- *EncAAH*
Bestor, Arthur Eugene 1879-1944 *BiDAmEd,*
  DcAmB S3, NatCAB 33, WhAm 2
Bestor, Paul 1882-1962 *NatCAB 49, WhAm 4*
Bestrom, Leonard L 1904-1969 *WhAm 5*
Beswick, Samuel 1855-1921 *NatCAB 19*
Beswick, William Frederick 1904-1971
  NatCAB 56
Betancourt, Agustin 1620-1700 *ApCAB*
Betancourt, Jose Ramon 1823- *ApCAB*
Betancourt, Romulo 1908- *McGEWB*
Betancourt Y Molina, Augustin De 1758-1824
  DcScB
Betanzos, Domingo De d1549 *ApCAB*
Betanzos, Pedro d1570 *ApCAB*
Betelle, James O 1879- *WhAm 6*
Beteta, Gregorio 1500?-1562 *ApCAB*
Beteta, Ramon 1901-1965 *WhAm 4*
Beth, Hilary Raymond 1919-1962 *WhAm 4*
Bethe, Hans Albrecht 1906- *AsBiEn,*
  McGEWB, WebAB
Bethea, Andrew Jackson 1879-1945 *NatCAB 33*
Bethea, Jack 1892-1928 *WhAm 1, WhAm 1C*
Bethea, Oscar Walter 1878- *WhAm 6*
Bethea, Solomon Hicks d1909 *WhAm 1*
Bethel, George Emmett 1894-1935 *WhAm 1*
Bethel, John P 1904-1958 *WhAm 3*
Bethel, Lawrence Lee 1906-1965 *NatCAB 52,*
  WhAm 4
Bethel, Mary Wright Thomas *WomWWA 14*
Bethell, Frank Hartsuff 1903-1959 *NatCAB 47,*
  WhAm 3
Bethell, Frank Hopkins 1870- *WhAm 5*
Bethell, Union Noble 1859-1933 *NatCAB 15,*
  NatCAB 23, WhAm 1
Bethencourt, Manuel *NewYHSD*
Bethencourt, Pedro 1619-1667 *ApCAB*
Bethisy, Jules Jacques E, Vicomte De 1747-1816
  Drake
Bethisy, Jules Jaques Eleonore 1747-1816
  ApCAB
Bethke, William 1885-1966 *WhAm 4*

Bethmann Hollweg, Theobald Von 1856-1921 *McGEWB*
Bethune, Alexander Neil 1800-1879 *ApCAB*
Bethune, Charles James Stewart 1838- *ApCAB*
Bethune, George Washington 1805-1862 *ApCAB, DcAmB, Drake, NatCAB 8, TwCBDA, WhAm H*
Bethune, James 1840-1884 *ApCAB*
Bethune, Joanna Graham 1770-1860 *BiDAmEd, NotAW*
Bethune, Lauchlin 1785-1874 *BiDrAC, WhAm H*
Bethune, Laughlin *BiAUS*
Bethune, Louise Blanchard 1856-1913 *AmWom, NatCAB 12, NotAW, WhAm 1, WomWWA 14*
Bethune, Marion 1816-1895 *BiDrAC, WhAm H*
Bethune, Mary McLeod 1875-1955 *BiDAmEd, DcAmB S5, DcAmReB, EncAB, McGEWB, NatCAB 49, WebAB, WhAm 3, WhAmP, WhoColR*
Bethune, Robert Armour 1855- *NatCAB 12*
Beti, Mongo 1932- *McGEWB*
Bettcher, Carl Welch 1887-1968 *NatCAB 54*
Bettelheim, Bruno 1903- *BiDAmEd, McGEWB, WebAB*
Bettelheim, Edwin Sumner, Jr. 1887-1959 *NatCAB 49, WhAm 3*
Betten, Cornelius 1877- *WhAm 5*
Betten, Francis Salesius 1863-1942 *WhAm 2*
Bettendorf, Edwin Joseph 1889-1954 *NatCAB 45*
Bettendorf, Joseph William 1864-1933 *ApCAB X, NatCAB 23, WhAm 1*
Bettendorf, William Peter 1857-1910 *ApCAB X, DcAmB, NatCAB 21, WhAm HA, WhAm 4*
Betteridge, Walter Robert 1863-1916 *WhAm 1*
Betters, Paul Vernon 1906-1956 *NatCAB 45, WhAm 3*
Bettersworth, John Knox 1909- *EncAAH*
Bettes, Torrey James 1888-1949 *NatCAB 39*
Bettes, William E 1838?- *NewYHSD*
Betti, Enrico 1823-1892 *DcScB*
Betti, Ugo 1892-1953 *McGEWB, WhAm 4*
Bettinger, Albert 1854-1922 *NatCAB 19*
Bettis, Mary Alice Smith *WomWWA 14*
Bettles, Alfred John 1856- *NatCAB 17*
Bettman, Adalbert Goodman 1883-1964 *NatCAB 50*
Bettman, Alfred 1873-1945 *DcAmB S3, WhAm 2*
Bettman, Gilbert 1881-1942 *NatCAB 31, WhAm 2*
Bettmann, Bernhard 1834-1915 *WhAm 1*
Betton, Silas 1768-1822 *BiAUS, BiDrAC, WhAm H, WhAmP*
Betts, Albert Deems 1882-1958 *WhAm 4*
Betts, Anna Whelan *WomWWA 14*
Betts, B Frank 1845-1909 *NatCAB 3, WhAm 1*
Betts, Beverley Robinson 1827- *ApCAB*
Betts, Charles Henry 1863-1929 *NatCAB 21, WhAm 1*
Betts, Craven Langstroth 1853-1941 *NatCAB 38, WhAm 1*
Betts, Edgar Hayes 1877-1951 *WhAm 3*
Betts, Edward C 1890-1946 *WhAm 2*
Betts, Edwin C 1856-1917 *IIBEAAW*
Betts, Emmett Albert 1903- *BiDAmEd*
Betts, Frederic Henry 1843-1905 *NatCAB 2, WhAm 1*
Betts, Frederick A 1858- *WhAm 4*
Betts, Frederick William 1858-1932 *WhAm 1*
Betts, George Frederic 1827-1898 *NatCAB 22*
Betts, George Herbert 1868-1934 *BiDAmEd, NatCAB 30, WhAm 1*
Betts, George Whitefield, Jr. 1871-1959 *WhAm 3*
Betts, Harold Harrington 1881- *IIBEAAW*
Betts, Jackson Edward 1904- *BiDrAC*
Betts, James A 1853-1928 *WhAm 1*
Betts, James Alfred 1875-1951 *NatCAB 41*
Betts, Louis 1873-1961 *NatCAB 47, WhAm 4*
Betts, Mary N 1860- *WomWWA 14*
Betts, Philander, III 1868-1945 *WhAm 2*
Betts, Rome Abel 1903-1973 *WhAm 6*

Betts, Samuel Rossiter 1776-1868 *NatCAB 22*
Betts, Samuel Rossiter 1786-1868 *AmBi, DcAmB, NatCAB 11*
Betts, Samuel Rossiter 1787-1868 *ApCAB, BiAUS, BiDrAC, Drake, TwCBDA, WhAm H*
Betts, Thaddeus 1789-1840 *ApCAB, BiAUS, BiDrAC, Drake, NatCAB 4, WhAm H*
Betts, William 1802-1884 *ApCAB*
Betts, William James 1847- *WhAm 4*
Betts, Wyllys Rosseter 1875-1932 *NatCAB 23*
Betty, Frank F 1880- *WhAm 6*
Betz, Herman 1891-1960 *NatCAB 48*
Betz, Robert Milton 1911-1969 *WhAm 5*
Beudant, Francois-Sulpice 1787-1850 *DcScB*
Beugler, Edwin James 1869- *WhAm 5*
Beukema, Herman 1891-1960 *WhAm 4*
Beunan, Thomas Francis 1853- *TwCBDA*
Beurling, George 1922-1948 *WhWW-II*
Beury, Charles Christian 1863-1923 *NatCAB 26*
Beury, Charles Ezra 1879-1953 *NatCAB 42, WhAm 3*
Beutel, Albert Phillip 1892-1972 *WhAm 5*
Beutenmuller, William 1864-1934 *WhAm 1*
Beutner, Reinhard Heinrich 1885-1964 *NatCAB 51*
Beutner, Victor 1870- *NatCAB 12*
Bevan, Arthur Dean 1861-1943 *DcAmB S3, NatCAB 31, WhAm 2*
Bevan, Charles Frederick *WhAm 5*
Bevan, Frank Samuel 1886-1960 *NatCAB 48*
Bevan, Laurence A 1890-1963 *WhAm 4*
Bevan, Lynne J 1881-1952 *WhAm 3*
Bevan, Ralph Hervey 1881- *WhAm 6*
Bevan, Thomas Horatio 1887-1938 *NatCAB 38, WhAm 1*
Bevan, Wilson Lloyd 1866-1935 *WhAm 1*
Bevanda, Matt Jacob 1888-1958 *NatCAB 50*
Bevans, James Lung 1869-1944 *NatCAB 32*
Beven, John Lansing 1887-1945 *WhAm 2*
Beveridge, Albert Jeremiah 1862-1927 *AmBi, ApCAB Sup, ApCAB X, BiDrAC, DcAmB, EncAB, NatCAB 13, TwCBDA, WebAB, WhAm 1, WhAmP*
Beveridge, Andrew Bennie 1915-1972 *WhAm 5*
Beveridge, Frank Stanley 1879-1956 *NatCAB 45, WhAm 3*
Beveridge, Hugh Raymond 1899-1961 *WhAm 4*
Beveridge, James Wallace 1879-1926 *NatCAB 20*
Beveridge, John *ApCAB, Drake, NatCAB 7*
Beveridge, John Harrie 1869-1932 *WhAm 1*
Beveridge, John Lourie 1824-1910 *ApCAB, BiAUS, BiDrAC, NatCAB 11, TwCBDA, WhAm 1, WhAmP*
Beveridge, Kuhne 1877- *WhAm 5*
Beveridge, William Henry 1879-1963 *McGEWB, WhAm 4, WhWW-II*
Beverley, Robert d1716 *Drake*
Beverley, Robert 1673?-1722 *AmBi, DcAmB, EncAB, McGEWB, WhAmP*
Beverly, Robert 1670?-1735 *NatCAB 7*
Beverly, Robert 1673?-1722 *WhAm H*
Beverly, Robert 1675?-1716 *ApCAB*
Bevier, Isabel 1860-1942 *BiDAmEd, DcAmB S3, NotAW, WhAm 2, WomWWA 14*
Bevier, Louis 1857-1925 *WhAm 1*
Bevill, Tom 1921- *BiDrAC*
Bevin, Abner Avery 1843-1922 *NatCAB 20*
Bevin, Ernest 1881-1951 *McGEWB, WhAm 3, WhWW-II*
Bevins, Elmer Russell 1881-1950 *NatCAB 45*
Bevis, Howard Landis 1885-1968 *NatCAB 54, WhAm 5*
Bewer, Julius August 1877-1953 *WhAm 3*
Bewley, Anthony 1804-1860 *ApCAB, DcAmB, WhAm H, WhAmP*
Bewley, Edwin Elmore 1881-1946 *WhAm 2*
Bewley, Luther Boone 1876- *WhAm 5*
Bewley, William 1878-1953 *NatCAB 44*
Bexell, John Andrew 1867-1938 *NatCAB 29, WhAm 2*
Bexon, Gabriel-Leopold-Charles-Ame 1747-1784 *DcScB*
Beye, Howard Lombard 1886-1936 *WhAm 1*
Beye, William 1881-1941 *WhAm 1*

Beyea, Herbert Writer 1895-1972 *WhAm 5*
Beyer, David Stewart 1880-1937 *NatCAB 27*
Beyer, Edward 1820-1865 *NewYHSD*
Beyer, Frederick *NewYHSD*
Beyer, Frederick Charles 1858- *WhAm 4*
Beyer, George 1844- *NatCAB 16*
Beyer, George Eugene 1861- *WhAm 4*
Beyer, Gustav 1840- *WhAm 4*
Beyer, Henry Gustav 1850-1918 *NatCAB 14, WhAm 1*
Beyer, Otto Sternoff 1886-1948 *WhAm 2*
Beyer, Samuel Walker 1865-1931 *NatCAB 40, WhAm 1*
Beyer, Walter Frederic 1890-1950 *NatCAB 39*
Beyers, Henry Wendell 1870-1936 *WhAm 1*
Beyl, John Lewis 1863- *WhAm 4*
Beymer, William Gilmore 1881- *WhAm 6*
Beyrich, Heinrich Ernst 1815-1896 *DcScB*
Bezanson, Osborne 1888-1961 *WhAm 4*
Bezanson, Philip Thomas 1916-1975 *WhAm 6*
Beze, M *NewYHSD*
Bezi, Cheri *NewYHSD*
Beziat, Andre 1870-1924 *WhAm 1*
Beziat DeBordes, Kate Mills Bradley *WomWWA 14*
Bezold, Albert Von 1836-1868 *DcScB*
Bezout, Etienne 1739-1783 *DcScB*
Bhabha, Homi Jehangir 1909-1966 *DcScB Sup, McGEWB, WhAm 4*
Bhaskara I *DcScB*
Bhaskara II 1115- *DcScB*
Bhave, Vinoba 1895- *McGEWB*
Biaggi, Mario 1917- *BiDrAC*
Biaggio Pelicani *DcScB*
Bialik, Hayyim Nahman 1873-1934 *McGEWB*
Bialobrzeski, Czeslaw 1878-1953 *DcScB*
Bianchi, Angelo Ralph 1873-1966 *NatCAB 53*
Bianchi, John Anthony 1902-1969 *NatCAB 55*
Bianchi, Julio Domingo 1879-1958 *WhAm 3*
Bianchi, Luigi 1856-1928 *DcScB*
Bianchi, Martha Gilbert Dickinson d1943 *WhAm 2, WomWWA 14*
Bianchi-Bandinelli, Ranuccio 1900-1975 *WhAm 6*
Bianco, Margery Williams 1881-1944 *NotAW, WhAm 6*
Biard, Peter 1565-1622 *ApCAB, Drake*
Biard, Pierre 1567?-1622 *AmBi, DcAmB, WhAm H*
Bias, Clothilde Gaujot 1883- *WomWWA 14*
Bias, John Henry 1877- *WhoColR*
Bias, Randolph 1875-1958 *WhAm 3*
Bibaud, Francois Marie Uncas Maximilien 1824- *ApCAB*
Bibaud, Michel 1782-1857 *ApCAB, Drake*
Bibb, George M 1771-1859 *TwCBDA*
Bibb, George M 1772-1859 *ApCAB, BiAUS, Drake, NatCAB 6*
Bibb, George Mortimer 1776-1859 *BiDrUSE, DcAmB, WhAmP*
Bibb, George Motier 1772-1859 *WhAm H*
Bibb, George Motier 1776-1859 *BiDrAC*
Bibb, Merwyn R 1876- *WhoColR*
Bibb, Thomas 1784-1838 *BiAUS, NatCAB 10*
Bibb, William Wyatt d1820 *BiAUS*
Bibb, William Wyatt 1780-1820 *ApCAB, BiDrAC, Drake, TwCBDA, WhAmP*
Bibb, William Wyatt 1781-1820 *AmBi, DcAmB, NatCAB 10, WhAm H*
Bibbins, Arthur Barneveld 1860-1936 *NatCAB 29*
Bibbins, Ruthelda Bernard Mary *WomWWA 14*
Bibbs, Edmund 1866- *WhoColR*
Bibby, James Harry 1897-1970 *WhAm 5*
Bibby, William *NewYHSD*
Biberman, Herbert J 1900-1971 *WhAm 5*
Biberoy, L S d1855 *NewYHSD*
Bibighaus, Thomas M 1816-1853 *BiAUS*
Bibighaus, Thomas Marshal 1817-1853 *BiDrAC, WhAm H*
Bible, Alan Harvey 1909- *BiDrAC*
Bible, Frank William d1937 *WhAm 1*
Bible, George Albert 1878-1950 *WhAm 3*
Bibo, Irving 1889-1962 *NatCAB 50*
Bicha, Karel Denis 1937- *EncAAH*
Bichat, Marie Francois Xavier 1771-1802 *AsBiEn, BiHiMed, DcScB, McGEWB*

Bichowsky, F Russell 1889-1951 *NatCAB 39*
Bickel, Alexander Mordecai 1924-1974
WhAm 6
Bickel, Karl August 1882-1972 *WhAm 5*
Bickel, Luke Washington 1866-1917 *DcAmB*
Bickel, Shlomo 1896-1969 *WhAm 5*
Bickelhaupt, Carroll Owen 1888-1954
NatCAB 45, WhAm 3
Bickelhaupt, George Bernard 1875- *WhAm 5*
Bickelhaupt, William George 1865-1936
NatCAB 27
Bicker, Walter 1796-1886 *ApCAB*
Bickerdyke, Mary Ann Ball 1817-1901 *AmWom,
DcAmB, NatCAB 21, NotAW, WebAMB,
WhAm H*
Bickerton, Alexander William 1842-1929 *DcScB*
Bicket, James Pratt 1876-1937 *WhAm 1*
Bickett, Fanny Neal Yarborough 1870-1942
WhAm 3
Bickett, Thomas Walter 1869-1921 *DcAmB,
NatCAB 25, WhAm 1, WhAmP*
Bickford, John Hanson 1860-1932 *NatCAB 25*
Bickford, Samuel Longley 1885-1959
NatCAB 49
Bickford, Thomas 1853-1917 *WhAm 1*
Bickford, Walter Mansur 1852- *ApCAB X,
WhAm 1*
Bickham, Mrs. *NewYHSD*
Bickham, Warren Stone 1861-1936 *WhAm 1*
Bicking, Ada Elizabeth d1953 *WhAm 3*
Bickle, Edward William 1890-1961 *WhAm 4*
Bickley, Francis Daniel Tull 1855-1927
NatCAB 20
Bickley, George Harvey 1868-1924 *WhAm 1*
Bickley, George Howard 1880-1938 *NatCAB 45*
Bickley, Howard Lee 1871-1947 *NatCAB 35,
WhAm 2*
Bickmore, Albert Smith 1839-1914 *AmBi,
ApCAB, DcAmB, NatCAB 8, WhAm 1*
Bicknell, Albion Harris 1837-1915 *NewYHSD*
Bicknell, Bennet 1781-1841 *BiDrAC,
WhAm H*
Bicknell, Bennet 1803-1863 *BiAUS*
Bicknell, Ernest Percy 1862-1935 *NatCAB 25,
WhAm 1*
Bicknell, Eugene Pintard 1859-1925
NatCAB 21
Bicknell, Evelyn Montague 1857- *TwCBDA*
Bicknell, Frank Alfred 1866-1943 *WhAm 2*
Bicknell, Frank Martin 1854-1916 *WhAm 1*
Bicknell, Frederick Thompson 1842-1915
ApCAB X, NatCAB 16
Bicknell, George Augustus 1815-1891 *BiDrAC,
WhAm H*
Bicknell, George Augustus 1846-1925 *WhAm 1*
Bicknell, Joshua 1759-1837 *NatCAB 8*
Bicknell, Lewis Williams 1885-1953 *WhAm 3*
Bicknell, Thomas Williams 1834-1925 *ApCAB,
BiDAmEd, NatCAB 1, TwCBDA,
WhAm 1*
Bicknell, Warren 1868-1941 *ApCAB X,
NatCAB 31*
Bicknell, Warren, Jr. 1902-1975 *WhAm 6*
Bicknell, Warren Moses 1868-1941 *WhAm 1*
Bicknell, William Harry Warren 1860-
WhAm 4
Bicks, Alexander 1901-1963 *WhAm 4*
Bicksler, W Scott 1861- *WhAm 1*
Bidaga 1866?-1954 *DcAmB S5*
Bidder, Friedrich Heinrich 1810-1894 *DcScB*
Biddinger, Noble Lycester 1909-1971
NatCAB 56, WhAm 5
Biddle, Alexander 1819-1899 *ApCAB Sup*
Biddle, Alexander 1893-1973 *WhAm 5*
Biddle, Alexander Williams 1856-1916
NatCAB 42
Biddle, Andrew Porter 1862-1944 *WhAm 2*
Biddle, Anthony Joseph Drexel 1874-1948
NatCAB 7, WhAm 2
Biddle, Anthony Joseph Drexel 1896-1961
WhAm 4
Biddle, Anthony Joseph Drexel 1897-1961
NatCAB 53
Biddle, Arney Sylvenus 1848-1914 *WhAm 1*
Biddle, Arthur 1853-1897 *NatCAB 30*
Biddle, Chapman 1822-1880 *ApCAB Sup*
Biddle, Charles John 1819-1873 *ApCAB,
BiAUS, BiDrAC, Drake, NatCAB 11,*

NatCAB 25, TwCBDA, WhAm H
Biddle, Charles John 1890-1972 *NatCAB 57*
Biddle, Charles John 1890-1973 *WhAm 5*
Biddle, Clement 1740-1814 *AmBi, ApCAB,
DcAmB, Drake, NatCAB 14, TwCBDA,
WhAm H*
Biddle, Clement Cornell 1784-1855 *ApCAB,
NatCAB 5, TwCBDA*
Biddle, Clement Miller 1838-1902 *NatCAB 22*
Biddle, Clement Miller 1876-1959 *NatCAB 47,
WhAm 5*
Biddle, Craig 1823- *ApCAB Sup, TwCBDA*
Biddle, Edward 1738-1779 *BiDrAC,
NatCAB 13, WhAm H, WhAmP*
Biddle, Edward 1739-1779 *ApCAB, BiAUS,
Drake, TwCBDA*
Biddle, Edward William 1852-1931 *WhAm 1*
Biddle, Francis 1886-1968 *BiDrUSE,
NatCAB 54, WhAm 5, WhWW-II*
Biddle, George 1885-1973 *BnEnAmA,
IIBEAAW, WhAm 6*
Biddle, Gertrude Bosler 1857- *WomWWA 14*
Biddle, Henry Chalmers 1869-1935 *WhAm 1*
Biddle, Horace P 1811-1900 *DcAmB,
NatCAB 11, TwCBDA, WhAm 1*
Biddle, Horace P 1818?- *ApCAB, Drake*
Biddle, J Wilmer 1861-1927 *NatCAB 32*
Biddle, James 1783-1848 *AmBi, ApCAB,
BiAUS, DcAmB, Drake, NatCAB 6,
TwCBDA, WebAB, WebAMB, WhAm H*
Biddle, James 1832-1910 *WhAm 1*
Biddle, James Garrett 1868-1947 *NatCAB 50*
Biddle, James Stokes 1818-1900 *ApCAB Sup,
WhAm 1*
Biddle, James Wilmer 1861-1927 *ApCAB X*
Biddle, John d1859 *BiAUS*
Biddle, John 1789-1859 *ApCAB*
Biddle, John 1792-1859 *BiDrAC, WhAm H,
WhAmP*
Biddle, John 1859-1936 *NatCAB 26, WhAm 1*
Biddle, Joseph Franklin 1871-1936 *BiDrAC*
Biddle, Mary Duke 1887-1960 *NatCAB 49*
Biddle, Nicholas 1750-1778 *AmBi, ApCAB,
DcAmB, Drake, NatCAB 5, TwCBDA,
WebAMB, WhAm H*
Biddle, Nicholas 1786-1844 *AmBi, ApCAB,
BiAUS, DcAmB, Drake, EncAB,
McGEWB, NatCAB 6, TwCBDA,
WebAB, WhAm H, WhAmP*
Biddle, Nicholas 1879-1923 *WhAm 1*
Biddle, Richard 1796-1847 *ApCAB, BiAUS,
BiDrAC, Drake, NatCAB 11, WhAm H,
WhAmP*
Biddle, Robert 1867-1935 *NatCAB 28*
Biddle, Robert Stone d1857? *NewYHSD*
Biddle, Sydney Geoffrey 1889-1954 *NatCAB 48*
Biddle, Thomas d1875 *BiAUS, NatCAB 12*
Biddle, Thomas 1790-1831 *ApCAB, Drake,
NatCAB 7, TwCBDA*
Biddle, Ward Gray 1891-1946 *WhAm 2*
Biddle, William Baxter 1856-1923 *NatCAB 6,
WhAm 1*
Biddle, William Canby 1864-1942 *NatCAB 32*
Biddle, William Phillips 1853-1923 *WebAMB,
WhAm 1*
Bidelspacher, Charles Franklin 1876-1959
NatCAB 50
Bidlack, Benjamin Alden 1804-1849 *BiAUS,
BiDrAC, DcAmB, NatCAB 13,
WhAm H, WhAmP*
Bidloo, Govard 1649-1713 *DcScB Sup*
Bidwell, Alfred Morrell 1888-1947 *NatCAB 38*
Bidwell, Annie Ellicott Kennedy 1839- *WhAm 1,
WomWWA 14*
Bidwell, Barnabas 1763-1833 *BiAUS, BiDrAC,
DcAmB, NatCAB 20, WhAm H,
WhAmP*
Bidwell, Charles Clarence 1881-1967 *WhAm 4*
Bidwell, Daniel D 1816?-1864 *ApCAB, Drake,
TwCBDA*
Bidwell, Daniel Doane 1866-1937 *WhAm 1*
Bidwell, Edwin Curtis 1821-1905 *WhAm 1*
Bidwell, George Rogers 1858- *WhAm 4*
Bidwell, John 1819-1900 *ApCAB, BiAUS,
BiDrAC, DcAmB, McGEWB, NatCAB 3,
REnAW, TwCBDA, WebAB, WhAm H,
WhAmP*
Bidwell, Marshal S 1798-1872 *ApCAB*

Bidwell, Marshall Spring 1799-1872 *DcAmB,
WhAm H*
Bidwell, Marshall Spring 1893-1966 *WhAm 4*
Bidwell, Mary W *NewYHSD*
Bidwell, Percy Wells 1888-1970 *NatCAB 55,
WhAm 5*
Bidwell, Raymond Austin 1876-1954
NatCAB 41
Bidwell, Thomas *NewYHSD*
Bidwell, Walter Hilliard 1798-1881 *ApCAB,
DcAmB, TwCBDA, WhAm H*
Biebel, Franklin Matthews 1908-1966 *WhAm 4*
Bieber, Charles L 1901-1965 *WhAm 4*
Bieber, Ralph Paul 1894- *REnAW*
Bieber, Sidney 1874- *WhAm 5*
Bieberbach, Walter Daniels 1881-1959
NatCAB 48
Biederbick, Henry 1859-1916 *WhAm 1*
Biedermann, August Julius 1825- *WhAm 4*
Biederwolf, William Edward 1867-1939
WhAm 1
Biedma, Luis Hernandez De *ApCAB, Drake*
Biefeld, Paul Alfred 1867-1943 *NatCAB 39,
WhAm 4*
Bieghler, Alice Miller *WomWWA 14*
Biegler, Philip Sheridan 1880-1948 *WhAm 2*
Biel *IIBEAAW*
Biela, Wilhelm Von 1782-1856 *AsBiEn, DcScB*
Bielaski, Alexander Bruce 1883-1964 *WhAm 4*
Bielefeldt, Oscar 1896-1966 *NatCAB 52*
Biemiller, Andrew John 1906- *BiDrAC*
Bien, Julius 1826-1909 *DcAmB, NatCAB 28,
NewYHSD, WhAm 1*
Bien, Morris 1859-1932 *WhAm 1*
Bien, Sylvan 1892-1959 *NatCAB 47*
Bienayme, Irenee-Jules 1796-1878 *DcScB Sup*
Bienewitz, Peter *DcScB*
Bienpica Y Sotomayor, Salvador 1730-1802
ApCAB
Bienstock, David Paul 1943-1973 *WhAm 6*
Bienville, Sieur De *WhAm H*
Bienville, Jean B Lemoine, Sieur De 1680-1768
Drake
Bienville, Jean B LeMoyne, Sieur De *TwCBDA*
Bienville, Jean B LeMoyne, Sieur De 1680-1765
ApCAB
Bienville, Jean B LeMoyne, Sieur De 1680-1767
DcAmB
Bienville, Jean B LeMoyne, Sieur De 1680-1768
AmBi, McGEWB, REnAW, WebAB
Bierbaum, Christopher Henry 1864-1947
WhAm 2
Bierbower, Austin d1913 *WhAm 1*
Bierce, Ambrose 1842-1914 *ApCAB Sup,
NatCAB 14, REnAW, WhAm 4*
Bierce, Ambrose Gwinnett 1842-1914? *AmBi,
DcAmB, McGEWB, WhAm HA*
Bierce, Ambrose Gwinnett 1842-1914? *EncAB,
WebAB*
Bierce, Sarah Elizabeth 1838- *AmWom*
Bierd, William Grant 1864-1944 *WhAm 2*
Bierer, Andrew Gordon Curtin, Jr. 1899-1956
WhAm 3
Bierer, Andrew Gregg Curtin 1862-1951
NatCAB 39, WhAm 3
Bierhals, Otto 1879- *IIBEAAW*
Bieri, Bernhard Henry 1889-1971 *WhAm 5*
Bierly, Glenn Leedy 1898-1953 *NatCAB 44*
Bierman, E Benjamin 1839- *TwCBDA*
Bierman, Everett Carlyle 1903-1965
NatCAB 51
Biermann, Frederick Elliott 1884-1968 *BiDrAC*
Bierne, Andrew *BiAUS*
Bierring, Walter Lawrence 1868-1961 *WhAm 4*
Biers, Howard 1904-1967 *WhAm 4*
Bierstadt, Albert 1829-1902 *Drake*
Bierstadt, Albert 1830-1902 *AmBi, ApCAB,
BnEnAmA, DcAmB, EncAAH, EncAB,
IIBEAAW, McGEWB, NatCAB 11,
NewYHSD, REnAW, TwCBDA, WebAB,
WhAm 1*
Bierstadt, Anne Morton Turner *WomWWA 14*
Bierstadt, Oscar A *ApCAB X*
Biery, James Soloman 1839-1904 *BiAUS,
BiDrAC*
Biery, Paul Hiram 1903-1962 *NatCAB 51*
Biesecker, Frederick Winters 1858-1936
WhAm 1

Biester, Anthony 1840-1917 *NewYHSD*
Biester, Edward George, Jr. 1931- *BiDrAC*
Biesterfeld, Chester Henry 1888-1951
NatCAB 39, WhAm 3
Biesterfeld, J H *DcScB*
Bifelt *NewYHSD*
Biffle, Leslie L 1889-1966 *WhAm 4*
Big Bow, Woodrow Wilson 1914- *IlBEAAW*
Bigalke, Albert Alexander 1880-1958
NatCAB 44
Bigby, John Summerfield 1832-1898 *BiAUS,*
BiDrAC
Bigeard, Marcel Maurice 1916- *WhoMilH*
Bigelow, Abijah 1775-1860 *BiAUS, BiDrAC,*
WhAm H, WhAmP
Bigelow, Albert Francis 1880- *WhAm 6*
Bigelow, Alice Houghton 1875- *WomWWA 14*
Bigelow, Archibald Pierce 1868-1942 *WhAm 3*
Bigelow, Asa 1779-1850 *NatCAB 5*
Bigelow, Belle G 1851- *AmWom*
Bigelow, Bessie P 1861- *WomWWA 14*
Bigelow, Bruce Macmillan 1903-1954 *WhAm 3*
Bigelow, Carolyn Lois Clark *WomWWA 14*
Bigelow, Charles Carleton 1897-1954
NatCAB 46, WhAm 3
Bigelow, Charles Emerson 1851-1939
NatCAB 28
Bigelow, Charles Wesley 1861-1942 *NatCAB 31*
Bigelow, Daniel Folger 1823-1910 *NatCAB 6,*
NewYHSD, WhAm HA, WhAm 4
Bigelow, Edith Evelyn 1861- *WhAm 4*
Bigelow, Edward Alexander 1885-1966
NatCAB 51
Bigelow, Edward Fuller 1860-1938 *NatCAB 29,*
WhAm 1
Bigelow, Edward Manning 1850-1918
NatCAB 20
Bigelow, Ella Augusta 1849- *AmWom*
Bigelow, Emerson 1896-1966 *NatCAB 53*
Bigelow, Erastus Brigham 1814-1879 *ApCAB,*
DcAmB, Drake, NatCAB 3, TwCBDA,
WebAB, WhAm H
Bigelow, Florence 1864-1945 *WhAm 3,*
WomWWA 14
Bigelow, Florence Rawn *WomWWA 14*
Bigelow, Francis Hill 1859-1933 *WhAm 1*
Bigelow, Frank Barna 1869- *TwCBDA*
Bigelow, Frank Hagar 1851-1924 *ApCAB Sup,*
DcAmB, NatCAB 10, TwCBDA,
WhAm 1
Bigelow, Frank Hoffnagel 1873-1937 *WhAm 1*
Bigelow, Fred Andrew 1868-1941 *NatCAB 30*
Bigelow, Frederic Russell 1870-1946
NatCAB 49, WhAm 2
Bigelow, Frederick Nolton 1885-1924
NatCAB 20
Bigelow, Frederick Southgate 1871-1954
WhAm 3
Bigelow, George Alexander 1853-1942
NatCAB 33
Bigelow, George Hoyt 1890-1934 *NatCAB 25,*
WhAm 1
Bigelow, George Tyler 1810-1878 *Drake,*
NatCAB 7
Bigelow, George Willis 1832-1928 *NatCAB 21*
Bigelow, Gertrude 1872- *WomWWA 14*
Bigelow, Harriet Williams 1870-1934 *WhAm 1,*
WomWWA 14
Bigelow, Harry Augustus 1874-1950 *BiDAmEd,*
DcAmB S4, WhAm 2
Bigelow, Henry Bryant 1879-1967 *WhAm 4A*
Bigelow, Henry Forbes 1867-1929 *WhAm 1*
Bigelow, Henry Jacob 1818-1890 *AmBi,*
BiHiMed, DcAmB, NatCAB 7,
WhAm H
Bigelow, Herbert Seely 1870-1951 *BiDrAC,*
WhAm 3, WhAmP
Bigelow, Hobart B 1834-1891 *NatCAB 10,*
TwCBDA
Bigelow, Jacob 1786-1879 *AmBi, WebAB*
Bigelow, Jacob 1787-1879 *ApCAB, DcAmB,*
Drake, NatCAB 4, TwCBDA, WhAm H
Bigelow, Mrs. James W *NewYHSD*
Bigelow, James W *NewYHSD*
Bigelow, John 1817-1911 *AmBi, ApCAB,*
BiAUS, DcAmB, Drake, McGEWB,
NatCAB 7, NatCAB 26, TwCBDA,
WebAB, WhAm 1, WhAmP

Bigelow, John 1854-1936 *ApCAB, NatCAB 35,*
WhAm 1
Bigelow, John Milton 1846- *WhAm 4*
Bigelow, John Milton 1847- *NatCAB 4*
Bigelow, John Ogden 1883-1975 *WhAm 6*
Bigelow, Leslie Lawson 1880-1943 *NatCAB 32*
Bigelow, Lettie Salina 1849- *AmWom,*
NatCAB 6
Bigelow, Lewis 1783?-1838 *ApCAB, BiAUS*
Bigelow, Lewis 1785-1838 *BiDrAC, Drake,*
NatCAB 11, WhAm H
Bigelow, Marshall Train 1822-1902 *WhAm 1*
Bigelow, Mary Helena 1862- *WomWWA 14*
Bigelow, Mason Huntington 1888-1971
WhAm 5
Bigelow, Maurice Alpheus 1872-1955
NatCAB 15, NatCAB 44, WhAm 3
Bigelow, Melville Madison 1846-1921 *AmBi,*
ApCAB, DcAmB, NatCAB 11,
NatCAB 28, TwCBDA, WhAm 1
Bigelow, Nelson Pendleton 1862-1925
NatCAB 21
Bigelow, Ogden 1899-1971 *NatCAB 56*
Bigelow, Poultney 1855-1954 *ApCAB,*
ApCAB X, NatCAB 9, NatCAB 54,
TwCBDA, WebAB, WhAm 3
Bigelow, Prescott 1884-1937 *WhAm 1*
Bigelow, Robert Mansfield 1906-1970 *WhAm 5*
Bigelow, Robert Payne 1863-1955 *NatCAB 46,*
WhAm 3
Bigelow, S Lawrence 1870-1947 *WhAm 2*
Bigelow, Samuel *NewYHSD*
Bigelow, Samuel Augustus 1838-1913
NatCAB 32
Bigelow, Sophia B *NewYHSD*
Bigelow, Timothy 1739-1790 *ApCAB, Drake,*
NatCAB 5, TwCBDA
Bigelow, Timothy 1767-1821 *ApCAB,*
TwCBDA
Bigelow, Timothy 1767-1829 *NatCAB 5*
Bigelow, Walter King *ApCAB X*
Bigelow, Willard Dell 1866-1939 *NatCAB 38,*
WhAm 1
Bigelow, William Frederick 1879-1966 *WhAm 4*
Bigelow, William Sturgis 1850-1926 *DcAmB,*
NatCAB 20, WhAm 1
Biggar, Frank 1917-1974 *WhAm 6*
Biggar, Hamilton Fisk 1839-1926 *WhAm 1*
Biggar, Oliver Mowat 1876-1948 *WhAm 2*
Biggart, Mabelle 1861- *AmWom*
Bigge, John Thomas 1780-1843 *McGEWB*
Bigger, Finley *BiAUS*
Bigger, Frederick d1963 *WhAm 4*
Bigger, Isaac Alexander 1893-1955 *WhAm 3*
Bigger, Robert Rush 1867- *WhAm 4*
Bigger, Samuel 1800?-1845 *BiAUS, Drake*
Bigger, Samuel 1802-1846 *NatCAB 13*
Biggers, Earl Derr 1884-1933 *DcAmB S1,*
WhAm 1
Biggers, George Clinton 1893-1963 *NatCAB 52,*
WhAm 4
Biggers, John David 1888-1973 *WhAm 6*
Biggin, Frederic Child 1869-1943 *WhAm 2*
Biggins, Henry *NewYHSD*
Biggs, Albert Welburne 1871-1914 *WhAm 1*
Biggs, Asa 1811-1878 *ApCAB, BiAUS,*
BiDrAC, DcAmB, NatCAB 11, TwCBDA,
WhAm H, WhAmP
Biggs, Benjamin Thomas 1821-1893 *BiAUS,*
BiDrAC, NatCAB 11, TwCBDA,
WhAm H, WhAm 1, WhAmP
Biggs, Burton Beecher 1898-1967 *NatCAB 57*
Biggs, Clyde Hunter 1893-1952 *NatCAB 39*
Biggs, David Clifton 1866-1931 *WhAm 1*
Biggs, Edward Asbury 1866-1939 *NatCAB 29*
Biggs, Hermann Michael 1859-1923 *AmBi,*
DcAmB, McGEWB, NatCAB 19,
WhAm 1
Biggs, J Crawford 1872-1960 *WhAm 3*
Biggs, J Rozier 1882-1952 *NatCAB 40*
Biggs, John David 1888-1954 *NatCAB 47*
Biggs, Kate Britt 1899-1972 *WhAm 6*
Biggs, Marion 1823-1910 *BiDrAC*
Biggs, Montgomery Herman 1870-1948
NatCAB 38
Biggs, Walter d1968 *WhAm 4A*
Biggs, William Henry 1842- *NatCAB 7*
Biggs, William Richardson 1901-1974 *WhAm 6*

Bigham, John Alvin 1881- *WhoColR*
Bigham, Madge Alford 1874- *WhAm 5*
Bigham, Truman C 1896-1952 *WhAm 3*
Biglan, Albert Manley 1902-1964 *NatCAB 55*
Bigler, David 1806-1875 *ApCAB, NatCAB 5,*
TwCBDA
Bigler, Henry William 1815-1900 *WhAm H*
Bigler, John 1804-1871 *ApCAB, Drake Sup*
NatCAB 4, TwCBDA
Bigler, John 1805-1871 *DcAmB, WhAm H,*
WhAmP
Bigler, John Adolph 1896-1963 *NatCAB 50,*
WhAm 4
Bigler, Regina Marie 1860- *WhAm 4*
Bigler, William 1814-1880 *ApCAB, BiAUS,*
BiDrAC, DcAmB, Drake, NatCAB 2,
TwCBDA, WhAm H, WhAmP
Bigler, William H 1840-1904 *NatCAB 3,*
WhAm 1
Biglow, Hosea *WebAB*
Biglow, Lucius Horatio 1833- *WhAm 4*
Biglow, William 1773-1844 *ApCAB, Drake*
Bignell, Effie Molt 1855- *WhAm 4,*
WomWWA 14
Bigot, Alphonse 1828?-1873? *NewYHSD*
Bigot, Francis *NewYHSD*
Bigot, Toussaint Francois 1794?-1869
NewYHSD
Bigot, William Valentine 1838-1908 *NatCAB 6*
Bigourdan, Camille Guillaume 1851-1932 *DcScB*
Bijlaard, Paul Peter 1898-1967 *NatCAB 53*
Bijur, Nathan 1862-1930 *NatCAB 32,*
WhAm 1
Bikle, Henry Wolf 1877-1942 *WhAm 1*
Bikle, Lucy Leffingwell Cable *WomWWA 14*
Bikle, Philip Melanchthon 1844-1934 *WhAm 1*
Bikram, Tribhubana Bir 1906-1955 *WhAm 3*
Bilbo, Theodore Gilmore 1877-1947 *BiDrAC,*
DcAmB S4, WebAB, WhAm 2, WhAmP
Bilby, George N 1868-1939 *WhAm 1*
Bilder, Nathaniel 1881- *WhAm 6*
Bildersee, Adele 1883-1971 *WhAm 5*
Biles, George Phineas 1857-1920 *WhAm 1*
Biles, William d1710? *NatCAB 16*
Bilfeldt, John Joseph 1793-1849? *NewYHSD*
Bilfield *NewYHSD*
Bilgram, Hugo 1847-1932 *WhAm 1,*
WhAm 1C
Bilhartz, Harrell Louis 1922-1968 *NatCAB 54*
Bilharz, Oscar Carl Maximillian 1863-1923
NatCAB 21
Bilharz, Theodor 1825-1862 *DcScB*
Bill, Alfred Hoyt 1879-1964 *WhAm 4*
Bill, Charles Alfred 1871-1942 *NatCAB 34*
Bill, Charles Gurdon 1870-1952 *NatCAB 46*
Bill, E Gordon 1884-1947 *WhAm 2*
Bill, Edward Lyman 1862-1916 *NatCAB 12,*
WhAm 1
Bill, Harry Leon 1881- *WhAm 6*
Bill, Harry Satterlee 1876-1946 *NatCAB 36*
Bill, John G 1904-1959 *WhAm 3*
Bill, Ledyard 1836- *WhAm 1*
Bill, Nathan D 1855- *WhAm 4*
Bill, Raymond 1896-1957 *WhAm 3*
Billado, Francis William 1907-1966 *WhAm 4*
Billany, Harry Hilton 1860- *WhAm 4*
Biller, George, Jr. 1874-1915 *NatCAB 20,*
WhAm 1
Billhardt, Fred A 1908-1968 *WhAm 5*
Billikopf, Jacob 1883-1950 *DcAmB S4,*
WhAm 3
Billing, Gustav Albert 1840-1890 *NatCAB 23*
Billinghurst, Benson Dillon 1869-1935 *WhAm 1*
Billinghurst, Charles 1818-1865 *BiAUS,*
BiDrAC, WhAm H
Billinghurst, Christopher Colon 1845-1921
NatCAB 19
Billings, A *NewYHSD*
Billings, Albert Merritt 1814-1897 *ApCAB X,*
NatCAB 9
Billings, Anna Hunt 1861- *WomWWA 14,*
WomWWA 14a
Billings, Asa White Kenney 1876-1949
DcAmB S4
Billings, Charles Ethan 1835-1920 *DcAmB,*
NatCAB 5, WhAm 4
Billings, Cornelius Kingsley Garrison 1861-1937
WhAm 1

Billings, E *New YHSD*
Billings, Edmund 1868-1929 *WhAm 1*
Billings, Edward C *BiAUS Sup*
Billings, Edward Everett 1855- *WhAm 4*
Billings, Edwin T 1824-1893 *New YHSD*
Billings, Elkanah 1820-1876 *ApCAB, DcScB, Drake*
Billings, Frank 1854-1932 *AmBi, DcAmB S1, NatCAB 23, WhAm 1*
Billings, Frank 1855- *NatCAB 12*
Billings, Frank Seaver 1845- *WhAm 4*
Billings, Franklin Swift 1862-1935 *WhAm 1*
Billings, Frederic Church 1864- *WhAm 5*
Billings, Frederic Tremaine 1873-1933 *NatCAB 24*
Billings, Frederick 1823-1890 *ApCAB X, DcAmB, NatCAB 14, NatCAB 25, TwCBDA, WebAB, WhAm H*
Billings, Frederick Horatio 1869- *WhAm 5*
Billings, George Eddy 1851-1929 *NatCAB 29*
Billings, George Herric 1845-1913 *TwCBDA*
Billings, George Herrick 1845-1913 *ApCAB, NatCAB 11, WhAm 1*
Billings, Gilbert Miggens 1890-1970 *NatCAB 55*
Billings, Hammatt 1816-1874 *ApCAB, New YHSD*
Billings, Harley DeHart 1868-1940 *NatCAB 31*
Billings, J Harland 1888-1971 *WhAm 5*
Billings, John Shaw 1838-1913 *AmBi, ApCAB, BiHiMed, DcAmB, DcAmLiB, EncAB, NatCAB 4, TwCBDA, WebAB*
Billings, John Shaw 1839-1913 *WhAm 1*
Billings, John Shaw 1898-1975 *WhAm 6*
Billings, Joseph *New YHSD*
Billings, Joseph 1758?- *ApCAB, Drake*
Billings, Josh *AmBi, ApCAB, DcAmB, EncAAH, TwCBDA, WebAB, WhAm H*
Billings, Luther Guiteau 1842-1920 *WhAm 1*
Billings, Moses 1809-1884 *New YHSD*
Billings, Richardson *New YHSD*
Billings, Stephen Ellsworth 1909-1972 *WhAm 5*
Billings, Thomas Henry 1881- *WhAm 6*
Billings, W Chester 1872-1939 *NatCAB 30, WhAm 1*
Billings, William 1746-1800 *AmBi, ApCAB, DcAmB, Drake, EncAB, McGEWB, NatCAB 5, TwCBDA, WebAB, WhAm H*
Billingsley, Allen Loren 1890-1954 *NatCAB 51, WhAm 3*
Billingsley, Charles Edward 1872- *NatCAB 13*
Billingsley, Paul 1887-1962 *WhAm 4*
Billingsley, Sherman 1900-1966 *WhAm 4*
Billingsley, William Newton 1853- *WhAm 4*
Billington, Monroe 1928- *EncAAH*
Billington, Ray Allen 1903- *EncAAH, REnAW*
Billman, Carl 1913-1974 *WhAm 6*
Billman, Howard 1854-1928 *NatCAB 24*
Billmeyer, Alexander 1841-1924 *BiDrAC*
Billner, Karl Paul 1887-1965 *WhAm 4*
Billner, Karl Pauli 1882-1965 *NatCAB 52*
Billock, George D 1909-1973 *WhAm 6*
Billopp, Christopher 1737-1827 *ApCAB*
Billotte, Gaston Herve Gustave 1875-1940 *WhWW-II*
Billow, Clayton Oscar 1860-1945 *WhAm 2*
Billroth, Christian Albert Theodor 1829-1894 *DcScB*
Billroth, Theodor 1829-1894 *BiHiMed*
Bills, Hubert Leo 1897-1962 *WhAm 4*
Billson, William Weldon 1847-1923 *WhAm 1*
Billups, Henry Lee 1863- *WhoColR*
Billups, Richard Alphonzo 1878- *WhAm 6*
Billy The Kid 1859-1881 *DcAmB, McGEWB, REnAW, WebAB, WhAm H*
Billy, Jacques De 1602-1679 *DcScB*
Bilmanis, Alfred 1887-1948 *WhAm 2*
Bilmer, Colby *New YHSD*
Bilotti, Anton d1963 *WhAm 4*
Biltz, John Fredric 1936-1973 *WhAm 6*
Biltz, Norman Henry 1902-1973 *REnAW, WhAm 6*
Bimeler, Joseph Michael 1778?-1853 *AmBi, DcAmB, NatCAB 13, WhAm H*
Bimson, Lloyd A 1920-1967 *WhAm 4*
Bin Ishak, Inche Yusoff d1970 *WhAm 5*
Bin-Nun, Dov 1910-1968 *WhAm 5*

Binch, Wilfred Reese 1896-1967 *WhAm 5*
Binckley, John M *BiAUS*
Binder, Carroll 1896-1956 *WhAm 3*
Binder, Rudolph Michael 1865-1950 *WhAm 3*
Binderup, Charles Gustav 1873-1950 *BiDrAC, WhAm 3, WhAmP*
Binding, Solomon Gotlip *New YHSD*
Bine, Rene 1882-1956 *NatCAB 45*
Bines, Thomas d1826 *BiAUS, BiDrAC, WhAm H*
Binet, Alfred 1857-1911 *AsBiEn, DcScB, McGEWB*
Binford, Florence Clark 1854- *WomWWA 14*
Binford, Frank Leslie 1886-1954 *NatCAB 44*
Binford, Henry Connard 1874- *WhoColR*
Binford, Jessica Florence *WomWWA 14*
Binford, Jessie Florence 1876-1966 *WhAm 4*
Binford, Lloyd Tilghman 1866-1956 *WhAm 3*
Binford, Peter Alvin 1876-1959 *NatCAB 51*
Binford, Raymond 1876-1951 *NatCAB 42, WhAm 5*
Binford, Thomas Howell 1896-1973 *WhAm 6*
Bing, Alexander Maximillian 1878-1959 *NatCAB 48*
Bing, Alexander Simon 1905-1969 *NatCAB 55*
Binga, Anthony J 1843- *WhoColR*
Binga, Jesse 1865-1950 *DcAmB S4*
Bingay, Malcolm Wallace 1884-1953 *DcAmB S5, WhAm 3*
Bingham, Albert Young d1973 *WhAm 6*
Bingham, Amelia 1869-1927 *BiCAW, DcAmB, NatCAB 21, WhAm 1, WomWWA 14*
Bingham, Anne Louisa d1848 *ApCAB*
Bingham, Anne Willing 1764-1801 *ApCAB, DcAmB, NotAW, WhAm H*
Bingham, Arthur Walker 1873-1928 *ApCAB X*
Bingham, Arthur Walter 1872-1943 *NatCAB 33*
Bingham, Caleb 1757-1817 *AmBi, DcAmB, Drake, NatCAB 8, WhAm H*
Bingham, Caleb 1757-1819 *BiDAmEd*
Bingham, Carl Geary 1880-1959 *NatCAB 47*
Bingham, Charles Tracy 1866-1946 *NatCAB 35*
Bingham, Charles William 1846-1929 *NatCAB 35*
Bingham, David Judson 1831-1909 *WhAm 1*
Bingham, Edmund Franklin 1828- *ApCAB Sup*
Bingham, Edward Franklin 1828-1907 *NatCAB 11, WhAm 4*
Bingham, Eugene Cook 1878-1945 *WhAm 2*
Bingham, Florence Cornell 1886-1963 *WhAm 4*
Bingham, Frederick Conant 1877-1944 *NatCAB 35*
Bingham, George Caleb 1811-1879 *BnEnAmA, DcAmB, EncAAH, EncAB, IlBEAAW, McGEWB, New YHSD, REnAW, WebAB, WhAm H, WhAmP*
Bingham, George Hutchins 1864-1949 *NatCAB 46, WhAm 5*
Bingham, Gonzalez Sidney 1857- *WhAm 4*
Bingham, Guy Morse 1872- *WhAm 5*
Bingham, Harold Clyde 1888-1964 *NatCAB 51*
Bingham, Harry 1821-1900 *DcAmB, NatCAB 13, TwCBDA, WhAm H, WhAmP*
Bingham, Henry Harrison 1841-1912 *ApCAB Sup, BiDrAC, TwCBDA, WhAm 1, WhAmP*
Bingham, Herbert Mackay 1901-1960 *WhAm 4*
Bingham, Hiram 1789-1869 *AmBi, ApCAB, DcAmB, DcAmReB, New YHSD, WhAm H*
Bingham, Hiram 1831-1908 *AmBi, DcAmB, NatCAB 14, TwCBDA, WhAm 1*
Bingham, Hiram 1875-1956 *ApCAB X, BiDrAC, WhAm 3, WhAmP*
Bingham, Jennie M 1859- *AmWom*
Bingham, Joel Foote 1827-1914 *NatCAB 2, WhAm 1*
Bingham, John A 1815- *ApCAB, BiAUS, Drake*
Bingham, John A 1815-1900 *TwCBDA*
Bingham, John Arende 1815- *NatCAB 9*
Bingham, John Armor 1815-1885 *WhAmP*
Bingham, John Armor 1815-1900 *AmBi, BiDrAC, DcAmB, WhAm H*
Bingham, John H *New YHSD*
Bingham, Jonathan Brewster 1914- *BiDrAC*
Bingham, Joseph Walter 1878-1973 *WhAm 6*

Bingham, Judson David 1831-1895 *ApCAB, TwCBDA*
Bingham, Kinsley Scott 1808-1859 *WhAm H*
Bingham, Kinsley Scott 1808-1861 *ApCAB, BiAUS, BiDrAC, Drake, NatCAB 5, TwCBDA, WhAmP*
Bingham, Lena Maud 1870- *WomWWA 14*
Bingham, Lucille Rutherford *WomWWA 14*
Bingham, Luther *New YHSD*
Bingham, Maria Matilda *ApCAB*
Bingham, Mary Homer *WomWWA 14*
Bingham, Mary Lily Kenan 1867-1917 *NatCAB 38*
Bingham, Millard Fillmore 1847-1921 *NatCAB 19*
Bingham, Millicent Todd 1880-1968 *WhAm 5*
Bingham, Norman Williams 1872-1958 *NatCAB 57, WhAm 3*
Bingham, Ralph 1870-1925 *WhAm 1*
Bingham, Robert 1838-1927 *WhAm 1*
Bingham, Robert Fry 1891-1947 *NatCAB 45, WhAm 2*
Bingham, Robert Worth 1871-1937 *AmBi, DcAmB S2, NatCAB 29, WhAm 1, WhAmP*
Bingham, Samuel *New YHSD*
Bingham, Stillman 1873-1933 *WhAm 1*
Bingham, Theodore Alfred 1858-1934 *WhAm 1*
Bingham, Theodore Clifton 1925-1973 *WhAm 6*
Bingham, Thomas T *New YHSD*
Bingham, Walter VanDyke 1880-1952 *DcAmB S5, NatCAB 39, WhAm 3*
Bingham, Wheelock Hayward 1907-1972 *WhAm 5*
Bingham, William *New YHSD*
Bingham, William d1804 *BiAUS*
Bingham, William 1751-1804 *ApCAB, Drake*
Bingham, William 1752-1804 *BiDrAC, DcAmB, NatCAB 2, TwCBDA, WhAm H, WhAmP*
Bingham, William 1835-1873 *ApCAB, DcAmB, WhAm H*
Bingham, William 1879-1955 *NatCAB 55, WhAm 3*
Bingham, William J 1889-1971 *WhAm 5*
Bingham, William Theodore 1861-1929 *WhAm 1*
Bingley, George 1813?- *New YHSD*
Bingley, Joseph 1805?- *New YHSD*
Bingley, Thomas *New YHSD*
Bining, Arthur Cecil 1893-1957 *WhAm 3*
Bininger, W B *New YHSD*
Binken, Jacobus 1623-1677 *ApCAB Sup*
Binkley, Almond M 1900-1970 *WhAm 5*
Binkley, Christian Kreider 1870-1938 *NatCAB 29, WhAm 5*
Binkley, John Thomas, III 1914-1960 *NatCAB 47*
Binkley, Robert Cedric 1897-1940 *DcAmB S2, NatCAB 31, WhAm 1*
Binkley, Wilfred Ellsworth 1883-1965 *WhAm 4*
Binkley, William Campbell 1889-1970 *WhAm 5*
Binney, Amos 1803-1847 *ApCAB, DcAmB, Drake, NatCAB 7, TwCBDA, WhAm H*
Binney, Arthur 1865-1924 *WhAm 1*
Binney, Barnabas 1751-1787 *NatCAB 10*
Binney, Charles Chauncey 1855-1913 *WhAm 1*
Binney, Edwin 1866-1934 *ApCAB X, NatCAB 25, WhAm 1*
Binney, Henry Prentice 1863-1940 *NatCAB 30*
Binney, Hibbert 1819- *ApCAB, Drake*
Binney, Horace 1780-1875 *AmBi, ApCAB, BiAUS, BiDrAC, DcAmB, Drake, NatCAB 10, TwCBDA, WebAB, WhAm H*
Binney, Horace, Jr. 1809-1870 *ApCAB, NatCAB 10*
Binney, James *BiAUS*
Binney, John 1844-1913 *TwCBDA, WhAm 1*
Binney, Joseph Getchell 1807-1877 *NatCAB 3*
Binnicker, Richard Johnson 1874- *WhAm 5*
Binnie, John Fairbairn 1863- *WhAm 4*
Binnion, Randall 1878- *WhAm 1*
Binns, Archie 1899-1971 *WhAm 5*
Binns, Charles Fergus 1852-1934 *AmBi*
Binns, Charles Fergus 1857-1934 *NatCAB 25, WhAm 1*
Binns, H Stanley 1890-1948 *NatCAB 36*

Binns, Jack 1884-1959 *WhAm 3*
Binns, John 1772-1860 *ApCAB, DcAmB, Drake, WhAm H, WhAmP*
Binns, John Alexander 1761-1813 *AmBi, DcAmB, EncAAH, WhAm H*
Binns, John Robinson 1884-1959 *NatCAB 48*
Binns, Walter Pope 1895-1966 *WhAm 4*
Binon, J B *NewYHSD*
Binsse, Louis Francis DePaul 1774-1844 *NewYHSD, WhAm H*
Binsted, Norman Spencer 1890-1961 *WhAm 4*
Binswanger, Samuel Emanuel 1895-1960 *NatCAB 45*
Binyon, Robert Laurence 1869-1943 *WhAm 2*
Binzen, Frederick William 1890-1961 *NatCAB 49*
Bioletti, Frederic Theodore 1865- *WhAm 4*
Bion, Nicolas 1652?-1733 *DcScB*
Bioren, John 1772-1835 *NatCAB 20*
Bioren, John Seymour 1863-1951 *NatCAB 40*
Biossat, Bruce d1974 *WhAm 6*
Biot, Jean-Baptiste 1774-1862 *AsBiEn, DcScB*
Biow, Milton H 1892-1976 *WhAm 6*
Bippus, Rupert Frederick 1890-1951 *WhAm 3*
Birch *NewYHSD*
Birch, Alexander Clitherall 1878- *WhAm 6*
Birch, B *NewYHSD*
Birch, David Robert 1876- *WhAm 5*
Birch, Frank Victor 1894-1973 *WhAm 6*
Birch, George *NewYHSD*
Birch, J *NewYHSD*
Birch, Raymond Russell 1881-1959 *NatCAB 47, WhAm 6*
Birch, Reginald Bathurst 1856-1943 *DcAmB S3, NatCAB 11, WhAm 2*
Birch, Stephen 1872-1940 *NatCAB 41, WhAm 1*
Birch, Stephen 1873-1940 *NatCAB 15*
Birch, T Bruce 1866-1937 *WhAm 1*
Birch, Thomas 1779?-1851 *AmBi, ApCAB, BnEnAmA, DcAmB, Drake, NatCAB 12, NewYHSD, WhAm H*
Birch, Thomas Howard 1875-1929 *ApCAB X, NatCAB 22, WhAm 1*
Birch, William Fred 1870-1946 *BiDrAC*
Birch, William Russell 1755-1834 *DcAmB, NewYHSD, WhAm H*
Birchall, Frederick Thomas 1868-1955 *DcAmB S5*
Birchard, Clarence C 1867- *WhAm 4*
Birchard, Glen Robbins 1914-1967 *WhAm 4*
Birchard, Matthew 1804-1876 *NatCAB 4, NatCAB 15*
Birchim, Dorcas 1923- *IlBEAAW*
Birchmore, Harrison Agnew 1907-1968 *NatCAB 54*
Birckhead, Hugh 1876-1929 *WhAm 1*
Birckhead, Oliver W d1962 *WhAm 4*
Bird, Abraham Calvin 1843- *WhAm 4*
Bird, Albert G 1800?- *NewYHSD*
Bird, Anna Child 1856- *BiCAW, WhAm 4, WomWWA 14*
Bird, Anna Pennock *WhAm 5*
Bird, Arthur 1856-1923 *AmBi, DcAmB, NatCAB 9, WhAm 3*
Bird, Arthur Snell 1895-1958 *NatCAB 43*
Bird, Charles 1838-1920 *WhAm 1*
Bird, Charles 1893-1957 *WhAm 3*
Bird, Charles Sumner 1855-1927 *NatCAB 22, WhAm 1*
Bird, Constant Mayer 1870-1920 *NatCAB 6*
Bird, Eugene Hunt 1893-1960 *WhAm 4*
Bird, Francis Wesley 1882-1964 *NatCAB 53*
Bird, Francis William 1881-1918 *NatCAB 22*
Bird, Frederic Mayer 1838-1908 *AmBi, DcAmB, NatCAB 11, WhAm 1*
Bird, Frederick *NewYHSD*
Bird, Frederick Mayer 1838-1908 *ApCAB*
Bird, George Emerson 1847-1926 *NatCAB 20, WhAm 1*
Bird, George Kurtz 1876-1930 *ApCAB X, NatCAB 25*
Bird, Golding 1814-1854 *BiHiMed*
Bird, Harriet Williams 1863- *WomWWA 14*
Bird, Hobart Stanley 1873-1960 *WhAm 4*
Bird, Horatio G 1824?- *NewYHSD*
Bird, James Philip 1866-1933 *NatCAB 25*
Bird, James Pyper 1871-1947 *WhAm 3*

Bird, John *NewYHSD*
Bird, John 1709-1776 *DcScB*
Bird, John 1768-1806 *BiAUS, BiDrAC, WhAm H*
Bird, John Blymyer 1870-1925 *NatCAB 31*
Bird, John Everett 1861-1928 *NatCAB 22, WhAm 1*
Bird, John Taylor 1829-1911 *BiAUS, BiDrAC, WhAmP*
Bird, Maria Elvy 1845- *WomWWA 14*
Bird, Paul Percy 1877- *WhAm 5*
Bird, Philip Smead 1886-1948 *WhAm 2*
Bird, Reginald William 1872-1959 *WhAm 3*
Bird, Remsen DuBois 1888-1971 *WhAm 5*
Bird, Richard Ely 1878-1955 *BiDrAC, WhAm 6*
Bird, Robert Boone 1904-1970 *NatCAB 57*
Bird, Robert Montgomery 1803-1854 *ApCAB, Drake, NatCAB 7*
Bird, Robert Montgomery 1805-1854 *TwCBDA*
Bird, Robert Montgomery 1806-1854 *AmBi, DcAmB, McGEWB, WhAm H*
Bird, Robert Montgomery 1867-1938 *NatCAB 38, WhAm 1*
Bird, Samuel 1874-1951 *NatCAB 38*
Bird, W Edwin 1886-1956 *NatCAB 42*
Bird, Wallace Samuel 1917-1971 *WhAm 5*
Bird, William Warren 1846-1926 *ApCAB X*
Bird, Winfield Austin Scott 1855- *WhAm 4*
Bird Woman 1787?-1812 *DcAmB*
Birdsall, Anna Palmyra *WomWWA 14*
Birdsall, Ausburn d1903 *BiAUS, BiDrAC*
Birdsall, Benjamin Pixley 1858-1917 *BiDrAC, WhAm 1*
Birdsall, Carl A 1892-1956 *WhAm 3*
Birdsall, Gregg Custis 1883-1952 *NatCAB 41*
Birdsall, James 1783-1856 *BiAUS, BiDrAC, WhAm H*
Birdsall, Katharine Newbold 1877- *WomWWA 14*
Birdsall, Samuel 1791-1872 *BiAUS, BiDrAC, WhAm H*
Birdsall, Virginia Field *WomWWA 14*
Birdsall, William Edwin 1903-1954 *NatCAB 41*
Birdsall, William Randall 1852- *ApCAB*
Birdsall, William Wilfred 1854-1909 *NatCAB 6, NatCAB 13, TwCBDA, WhAm 1*
Birdsell, John Comly 1815-1894 *NatCAB 11*
Birdseye, Clarence 1886-1956 *WhAm 3*
Birdseye, Claude Hale 1878-1941 *NatCAB 33, WhAm 1*
Birdseye, Miriam 1878- *WomWWA 14*
Birdseye, Nathan 1714-1818 *Drake*
Birdseye, Victory 1782-1853 *BiAUS, BiDrAC, WhAm H, WhAmP*
Birdsong, Henry Walter 1883-1944 *NatCAB 33*
Birdwell, Alton William 1870-1954 *WhAm 3*
Birdzell, Luther Earle 1880- *WhAm 6*
Birely, Charles 1854-1942 *NatCAB 33*
Birge, Edward Asahel 1851-1950 *ApCAB, DcAmB S4, DcScB, NatCAB 12, TwCBDA, WhAm 3*
Birge, Edward Asahiel 1851-1950 *BiDAmEd*
Birge, Edward Bailey 1868-1952 *BiDAmEd, WhAm 3*
Birge, Henry Warner d1888 *Drake Sup*
Birge, Henry Warner 1825-1888 *DcAmB, WhAm H*
Birge, Henry Warner 1830?-1888 *ApCAB, TwCBDA*
Birge, Julius 1909-1958 *WhAm 3*
Birge, Julius Charles 1839-1923 *NatCAB 19*
Biringuccio, Vannoccio 1480-1539? *DcScB, McGEWB*
Birk, Newman Peter 1906-1966 *WhAm 4*
Birk, W Otto 1891-1973 *NatCAB 57*
Birkbeck, Morris d1825 *ApCAB, Drake*
Birkbeck, Morris 1763-1825 *NatCAB 11*
Birkbeck, Morris 1764-1825 *AmBi, DcAmB, WhAm H*
Birke, William D 1911-1963 *WhAm 4*
Birkenmayer, Wilson Clayton 1876-1954 *NatCAB 42*
Birkenmeyer, Carl Bruce 1909-1970 *WhAm 5*
Birkenstock, Carl Frederick 1897-1958 *NatCAB 47*
Birkhead, Claude Vivian 1880-1950 *WhAm 3*
Birkhead, Leon Milton 1885-1954 *WhAm 3*

Birkhimer, William Edward 1848-1914 *WhAm 1*
Birkhoff, George, Jr. 1852-1914 *NatCAB 34*
Birkhoff, George David 1884-1944 *BiDAmEd, DcAmB S3, DcScB, WebAB, WhAm 2*
Birkholz, Eugenie S 1853- *AmWom*
Birkinbine, John 1844-1915 *NatCAB 12, WhAm 1*
Birkmire, William Harvey 1860-1924 *WhAm 1*
Birks, Julia Miles 1874- *WomWWA 14*
Birmingham, Henry Patrick 1854-1932 *WhAm 1*
Birmingham, James Bishop 1888-1952 *NatCAB 47*
Birmingham, John 1816?-1884 *DcScB*
Birnbaum, Martin 1878-1970 *WhAm 5*
Birnbaum, Nathan 1907-1975 *WhAm 6*
Birney, Alice Josephine McLellan 1858-1907 *NotAW*
Birney, Arthur Alexis 1852-1916 *NatCAB 21, WhAm 1*
Birney, David Bell 1825-1864 *AmBi, ApCAB, DcAmB, Drake, NatCAB 4, TwCBDA, WhAm H*
Birney, Dion d1864 *ApCAB*
Birney, Dion Scott 1889-1965 *NatCAB 51*
Birney, Fitzhugh d1864 *ApCAB*
Birney, Hoffman 1891-1958 *WhAm 3*
Birney, James 1817-1888 *ApCAB, DcAmB, NatCAB 12, TwCBDA, WhAm H, WhAmP*
Birney, James Gillespie 1792-1857 *AmBi, ApCAB, DcAmB, Drake, EncAAH, EncAB, McGEWB, NatCAB 2, TwCBDA, WebAB, WhAm H, WhAmP*
Birney, Lauress J 1871-1937 *WhAm 1*
Birney, William 1819-1907 *AmBi, ApCAB, DcAmB, NatCAB 28, TwCBDA, WhAm 1*
Birney, William Verplanck 1858-1909 *WhAm 1*
Birnie, Douglas Putnam 1856-1937 *NatCAB 45*
Birnie, Rogers 1851-1939 *NatCAB 33, WhAm 2*
Birnie, Upton, Jr. 1877-1957 *WhAm 3*
Birnkrant, Michael Charles 1900-1966 *NatCAB 53, WhAm 4*
Biron, Armand Louis, Duc De 1747-1793 *WhoMilH*
Birren, Joseph P 1864-1933 *WhAm 1*
Birt, William Radcliff 1804-1881 *DcScB*
Birtley, Robert Lewis 1893-1955 *WhAm 3*
Birtwell, Charles Wesley 1860-1932 *WhAm 1*
Biruni, Abu Rayhan, Al- 973-1050? *McGEWB*
Biruni, Abu Rayhan M Ibn Ahmad, Al- 973-1050? *DcScB*
Bisbee, Eldon 1866-1952 *NatCAB 39, WhAm 1*
Bisbee, Elmer 1883-1950 *NatCAB 38*
Bisbee, Ezra *NewYHSD*
Bisbee, Frederick Adelbert 1855-1923 *WhAm 1*
Bisbee, Genevieve *WomWWA 14*
Bisbee, Horatio 1839-1916 *BiDrAC, NatCAB 5, NatCAB 31, WhAm 4*
Bisbee, John *NewYHSD*
Bisbee, Joseph Bartlett 1853-1926 *NatCAB 31, WhAm 4*
Bisbee, Marvin Davis 1845-1913 *NatCAB 9, TwCBDA, WhAm 1*
Bisbee, Spaulding 1890-1958 *WhAm 3*
Bisbee, William Henry 1840-1942 *WhAm 2*
Bisbing, Henry Singlewood 1849-1933 *IlBEAAW, NatCAB 5, WhAm 1*
Biscaccianti, Eliza 1825- *ApCAB, Drake*
Bisch, Louis Edward 1885-1963 *NatCAB 47, WhAm 5*
Bischebou *NewYHSD*
Bischof, Carl Gustav Christoph 1792-1870 *DcScB*
Bischoff, Elmer 1916- *BnEnAmA*
Bischoff, Ernst 1864-1935 *NatCAB 39*
Bischoff, Eugene Henry 1880-1954 *IlBEAAW*
Bischoff, Frederick Christopher 1771-1834 *NewYHSD*
Bischoff, Gottlieb Wilhelm 1797-1854 *DcScB*
Bischoff, Henry, Jr. 1852-1913 *WhAm 1*
Bischoff, Theodor Ludwig Wilhelm 1807-1882 *DcScB*
Biscoe, Alvin B 1900-1967 *WhAm 4*

Biscoe, Ellen B *TwCBDA*
Biscoe, Howard Morton 1869-1951 *WhAm 3*
Biscoe, Thomas Dwight 1840-1930 *WhAm 3*
Biscoe, Walter Stanley 1853-1933 *DcAmLiB*
Bisdorf, Peter J *NewYHSD*
Bisey, Sunker Abaji 1867-1935 *WhAm 1*
Bisgyer, Maurice 1897-1973 *WhAm 6*
Bishaboy *NewYHSD*
Bishboy *NewYHSD*
Bishop *NewYHSD*
Bishop, Abraham 1763-1844 *DcAmB, Drake, WhAm H*
Bishop, Albert Webb 1832-1901 *NatCAB 26*
Bishop, Alice Lyman 1872- *WomWWA 14*
Bishop, Ancil Hiram 1891-1956 *NatCAB 42*
Bishop, Angelica *NewYHSD*
Bishop, Anna 1814-1884 *AmWom, ApCAB, NatCAB 3*
Bishop, Anna 1816-1884 *Drake*
Bishop, Anna Riviere 1810-1884 *NotAW*
Bishop, Anne 1814-1884 *TwCBDA*
Bishop, Annette *NewYHSD*
Bishop, Arthur Garnett 1875-1948 *NatCAB 49*
Bishop, Arthur Giles 1851-1944 *NatCAB 34, WhAm 2*
Bishop, Arthur Vaughan 1883-1955 *WhAm 3*
Bishop, Avard Longley 1875-1932 *NatCAB 22, WhAm 1*
Bishop, Bernice Pauahi 1831-1884 *NotAW*
Bishop, Bruce Clay 1919-1968 *WhAm 5*
Bishop, Carlton Thomas 1882-1957 *NatCAB 45*
Bishop, Cecil William 1890-1971 *BiDrAC*
Bishop, Charles Alvord 1854-1908 *NatCAB 12, WhAm 1*
Bishop, Charles McTyeire 1862-1949 *WhAm 2*
Bishop, Charles Pleasant 1854-1941 *NatCAB 34*
Bishop, Charles R 1835-1862 *NatCAB 14*
Bishop, Charles Reed 1822-1915 *DcAmB S1, WhAm HA, WhAm 4*
Bishop, Clarence Morton 1878-1969 *NatCAB 54*
Bishop, Curtis Vance 1894-1966 *WhAm 4*
Bishop, Daniel Sanborn 1900-1959 *WhAm 3*
Bishop, David Horace 1870- *WhAm 5*
Bishop, Eben Faxon 1863-1943 *NatCAB 40, WhAm 2*
Bishop, Edwin Whitney 1869-1942 *WhAm 2*
Bishop, Elias B 1869-1934 *WhAm 1*
Bishop, Elizabeth Loraine *WomWWA 14*
Bishop, Ella Matilda Clark 1856-1926 *NatCAB 21*
Bishop, Emily Montague 1858- *WhAm 1, WomWWA 14*
Bishop, Emily Mulkin 1858- *AmWom*
Bishop, Ernest Simons 1876-1927 *WhAm 1*
Bishop, Eugene Lindsay 1886-1951 *NatCAB 38, WhAm 3*
Bishop, Everett L 1892-1963 *WhAm 4*
Bishop, F Warner 1887-1947 *NatCAB 39*
Bishop, Farnham 1886-1930 *WhAm 1*
Bishop, Frederic Lendall d1948 *WhAm 2*
Bishop, George *ApCAB, Drake*
Bishop, George Lee 1870- *WhAm 5*
Bishop, George Sayles 1836-1914 *WhAm 1*
Bishop, George Taylor 1864-1940 *NatCAB 40, WhAm 1*
Bishop, Harriet E 1817-1883 *NotAW*
Bishop, Harriet E 1818-1883 *BiDAmEd*
Bishop, Harriette Anna 1845- *WomWWA 14*
Bishop, Harry Gore 1874-1934 *NatCAB 26, WhAm 1*
Bishop, Heber Reginald 1840-1902 *NatCAB 22, WhAm 1*
Bishop, Helen Louise 1872- *WomWWA 14*
Bishop, Henry Alfred 1860-1934 *NatCAB 30, WhAm 1*
Bishop, Horace Alonzo 1849-1914 *NatCAB 16*
Bishop, Hubert Keeney 1870- *WhAm 5*
Bishop, Hutchens C *WhoColR*
Bishop, Inez Shannon 1892-1974 *WhAm 6*
Bishop, Irving Prescott 1849- *WhAm 4*
Bishop, Isabel 1902- *BnEnAmA*
Bishop, James 1816-1895 *BiAUS, BiDrAC, WhAm H*
Bishop, James 1870-1924 *WhAm 1*
Bishop, James Robert Thoburn 1896-1956 *WhAm 3*
Bishop, Joel Prentiss 1814-1901 *ApCAB,*

DcAmB, Drake, WhAm H
Bishop, John Asa 1856- *NatCAB 8*
Bishop, John Peale 1892-1944 *DcAmB S3, WhAm 2*
Bishop, John Remsen 1860-1934 *BiDAmEd, NatCAB 7, WhAm 4*
Bishop, Joseph Bucklin 1847-1928 *TwCBDA, WhAm 1*
Bishop, Judson Wade 1831- *ApCAB Sup, WhAm 4*
Bishop, Mrs. L Brackett 1861- *WhAm 4*
Bishop, Levi 1815-1881 *ApCAB*
Bishop, Louis Faugeres 1864-1941 *ApCAB X, WhAm 1*
Bishop, Mary Agnes Dalrymple 1857- *AmWom, BiCAW*
Bishop, Morris Gilbert 1893-1973 *WhAm 6*
Bishop, Nathan 1808-1880 *DcAmB, WhAm H*
Bishop, Nelle Smith 1877- *WomWWA 14*
Bishop, Oakley Maurice 1887-1931 *NatCAB 24*
Bishop, Percy Poe 1877-1967 *WhAm 4*
Bishop, Phanuel 1739-1812 *BiAUS, BiDrAC, WhAm H, WhAmP*
Bishop, R Spencer 1886-1946 *NatCAB 36*
Bishop, Richard Edgar 1892-1973 *NatCAB 57*
Bishop, Richard Moore 1812-1893 *ApCAB Sup, NatCAB 3, TwCBDA*
Bishop, Robert H 1903-1965 *WhAm 4*
Bishop, Robert Hamilton 1771-1855 *WhAm H*
Bishop, Robert Hamilton 1777-1855 *ApCAB, BiDAmEd, DcAmB S1, Drake, TwCBDA*
Bishop, Robert Hamilton, Jr. 1879-1955 *NatCAB 44*
Bishop, Robert Nicholas Charles Bochsa 1789- *ApCAB*
Bishop, Robert Roberts 1834-1909 *DcAmB*
Bishop, Roswell Peter 1843-1920 *BiDrAC, TwCBDA, WhAm 4, WhAmP*
Bishop, Samuel A 1874- *WhAm 5*
Bishop, Samuel Henry 1864-1914 *WhAm 1*
Bishop, Samuel Rogers 1871-1963 *NatCAB 50*
Bishop, Sereno Edwards 1827-1909 *WhAm 1*
Bishop, Seth Scott 1852-1923 *DcAmB, NatCAB 21, WhAm 1*
Bishop, Sherman Chauncey 1887-1951 *NatCAB 40*
Bishop, Susan Washburne *WomWWA 14*
Bishop, Thomas *NewYHSD*
Bishop, Thomas 1753?-1840? *NewYHSD*
Bishop, Walter Palmer 1850-1917 *NatCAB 17*
Bishop, William Avery 1894-1956 *WhoMilH*
Bishop, William Darius 1827-1904 *ApCAB, BiAUS, BiDrAC, DcAmB, NatCAB 11, NatCAB 30, TwCBDA, WhAm 1*
Bishop, William Henry 1803-1873 *ApCAB*
Bishop, William Henry 1847-1928 *ApCAB, NatCAB 8, WhAm 1*
Bishop, William Samuel 1865-1944 *WhAm 2*
Bishop, William Warner 1871-1955 *DcAmLiB, WhAm 3*
Bishopbois, August 1814?- *NewYHSD*
Bishopp, Fred Corry 1884-1970 *NatCAB 55, WhAm 5*
Bisland, Elizabeth 1863- *AmWom*
Bismarck, Otto Eduard Leopold Von 1815-1898 *McGEWB*
Bispham, Caroline Russell *WomWWA 14*
Bispham, Clarence Wyatt 1865-1929 *NatCAB 23*
Bispham, David Scull 1857-1921 *AmBi, ApCAB X, DcAmB, NatCAB 11, WhAm 1*
Bispham, George Tucker 1838-1906 *ApCAB Sup, NatCAB 19, TwCBDA, WhAm 1*
Bispham, Henry Collins 1841-1882 *ApCAB, TwCBDA*
Bissell, Albert West 1891-1949 *NatCAB 39*
Bissell, Alpheus 1801- *NatCAB 7*
Bissell, Arthur Douglas 1844-1926 *WhAm 1*
Bissell, Bertha Abby Nichols 1870- *WomWWA 14*
Bissell, Charles Spencer 1893-1969 *WhAm 5*
Bissell, Clark 1782-1857 *ApCAB, BiAUS, Drake, NatCAB 10, TwCBDA*
Bissell, Clayton Lawrence 1896-1972 *WhAm 5*
Bissell, Daniel d1833 *ApCAB, Drake*
Bissell, David Shields 1859-1935 *NatCAB 26*

Bissell, Dougal 1864-1935 *ApCAB X, NatCAB 36, WhAm 1*
Bissell, E Perot d1944 *WhAm 2*
Bissell, Edward Cone 1832-1894 *ApCAB Sup*
Bissell, Edwin Cone 1832-1894 *DcAmB, NatCAB 21, TwCBDA, WhAm H*
Bissell, Emily Perkins 1861-1948 *NatCAB 38, NotAW*
Bissell, Evelyn L 1836-1905 *NatCAB 8*
Bissell, Evelyn L 1839-1905 *TwCBDA*
Bissell, French Rayburn 1861-1933 *WhAm 1*
Bissell, George Edwin 1839-1920 *AmBi, BnEnAmA, DcAmB, NatCAB 8, NewYHSD, WhAm 1*
Bissell, George Henry 1821-1884 *DcAmB, NatCAB 25, WebAB, WhAm H*
Bissell, George Welton 1866- *WhAm 4*
Bissell, Herbert Porter 1856-1919 *NatCAB 5, NatCAB 22, WhAm 1*
Bissell, Hezekiah d1928 *WhAm 1*
Bissell, Hillary Rarden 1912-1975 *WhAm 6*
Bissell, Howard 1878-1937 *WhAm 1*
Bissell, John Henry 1846- *WhAm 1*
Bissell, John William 1843- *TwCBDA, WhAm 4*
Bissell, Joseph Bidleman 1859- *NatCAB 16*
Bissell, Josiah Wolcott 1818- *ApCAB*
Bissell, Julia 1862-1928 *NatCAB 21*
Bissell, Marie Truesdale 1879- *WomWWA 14*
Bissell, Mary Taylor *WhAm 5, WomWWA 14*
Bissell, Melville Reuben 1843-1889 *NatCAB 7*
Bissell, Melville Reuben 1882-1972 *NatCAB 56*
Bissell, Pelham St. George 1887-1943 *ApCAB X, NatCAB 32, WhAm 2*
Bissell, Richard Mervin 1862-1941 *NatCAB 30, WhAm 1*
Bissell, Simon B 1808-1883 *ApCAB, Drake*
Bissell, Walter Henry 1858-1933 *NatCAB 30, WhAm 1*
Bissell, William Grosvenor 1870-1919 *WhAm 1*
Bissell, William H 1811-1860 *ApCAB, BiAUS, Drake*
Bissell, William Harrison 1811-1860 *BiDrAC, WhAmP*
Bissell, William Henry 1811-1860 *DcAmB, NatCAB 11, TwCBDA, WhAm H*
Bissell, William Henry Augustus 1814-1893 *ApCAB, NatCAB 11, TwCBDA*
Bissell, Wilson Shannon 1847-1903 *ApCAB Sup, BiDrUSE, DcAmB, NatCAB 13, TwCBDA, WhAm 1*
Bisselle, Hulbert T 1900-1959 *WhAm 4*
Bisset, Andrew G 1893-1976 *WhAm 6*
Bisset, George 1899-1976 *WhAm 6*
Bissett, Clark Prescott 1875-1932 *WhAm 1*
Bisshopp, Cecil 1783-1813 *ApCAB Sup*
Bisshopp, Kenneth Edward 1909-1975 *WhAm 6*
Bissier, Julius 1893-1965 *WhAm 4*
Bissikummer, Charles Hills 1867- *WhAm 4*
Bissman, Carl August 1893-1951 *NatCAB 38*
Bissonnette, T Hume 1885-1951 *WhAm 3*
Bissot, Francois Marie 1700-1736 *WhAm H*
Bissot, Jean Baptiste 1668-1719 *WhAm H*
Bissy *NewYHSD*
Bissy, A *NewYHSD*
Bisterfeld, Johann Heinrich 1605?-1655 *DcScB*
Bistline, Francis M 1896-1969 *WhAm 5*
Bisttram, Emil James 1895-1976 *IlBEAAW*
Bitner, Harry Murray 1883-1960 *NatCAB 45, WhAm 4*
Bitruji, Nur Al-Din Abu Ishaq, Al- 1150?-1200 *McGEWB*
Bitruji Al-Ishbili, Abu Ishaq, Al- *DcScB, DcScB Sup*
Bittenbender, Ada Matilda Cole 1848-1925 *AmWom, NotAW*
Bittenbender, Glace Edward 1912-1957 *NatCAB 46*
Bitter, Francis 1902-1967 *WhAm 4*
Bitter, Karl Theodore Francis 1867-1915 *AmBi, ApCAB X, BnEnAmA, DcAmB, NatCAB 5, NatCAB 24, TwCBDA, WebAB, WhAm 1*
Bitters, Neziah Wright 1840?-1882? *NewYHSD*
Bitting, William Coleman 1857-1931 *WhAm 1*
Bittinger, Charles 1879- *WhAm 6*
Bittinger, John Lawrence 1833-1911 *NatCAB 1,*

WhAm 1

Bittinger, Lucy Forney 1859- *WhAm 4,
WomWWA 14*
Bittle, David Frederick 1811-1876 *NatCAB 10*
Bittner, John Joseph 1904-1961 *AsBiEn,
WhAm 4*
Bittner, VanAmberg 1885-1949 *NatCAB 37*
Bittner, VanAmburg 1885-1949 *WhAm 2*
Bitzer, George William 1872-1944 *DcAmB S3*
Bixby, Ammi Leander 1856-1934 *NatCAB 13,
WhAm 1*
Bixby, Anna Pierce Hobbs 1808?-1869
WhAm H
Bixby, Augustus Rufus 1832- *WhAm 4*
Bixby, Edson Kingman 1887-1940 *WhAm 1*
Bixby, Fred Hathaway 1875-1952 *NatCAB 41*
Bixby, Harold McMillan 1890-1965 *WhAm 4*
Bixby, Horace Ezra 1826-1912 *DcAmB,
REnAW, WhAm HA, WhAm 4*
Bixby, James Thompson 1843-1921 *DcAmB,
NatCAB 11, WhAm 1*
Bixby, Joel Heatwole 1888-1940 *NatCAB 30*
Bixby, John Munson 1800-1876 *ApCAB,
TwCBDA*
Bixby, Jotham W *ApCAB X*
Bixby, Kenneth Roberts 1891-1969 *WhAm 5*
Bixby, Maritje V P *WomWWA 14*
Bixby, Moses Homan 1827-1901 *TwCBDA*
Bixby, Robert F *ApCAB*
Bixby, Samuel Merrill 1833-1912 *ApCAB X,
NatCAB 5*
Bixby, Tams 1855-1921 *NatCAB 19*
Bixby, Tams 1855-1922 *WhAm 1*
Bixby, Walter Edwin 1896-1972 *WhAm 6*
Bixby, Willard Goldthwaite *ApCAB X*
Bixby, William Herbert 1849-1928 *AmBi,
NatCAB 21, WhAm 1*
Bixby, William Keeney 1857-1931 *NatCAB 12,
NatCAB 28, WhAm 1*
Bixer, Edmond P 1899-1972 *WhAm 5*
Bixler, Albert George 1857-1943 *NatCAB 32*
Bixler, Edward Clinton 1877- *WhAm 5*
Bixler, Harris Jacob 1870-1941 *BiDrAC,
WhAmP*
Bixler, J Louis 1879-1951 *NatCAB 40*
Bixler, James Wilson 1861-1943 *WhAm 2*
Bize, Louis A 1871- *WhAm 5*
Bizet, Georges 1838-1875 *McGEWB*
Bizzell, James Adrian 1876-1944 *NatCAB 34,
WhAm 2*
Bizzell, William Bennett 1876-1944 *NatCAB 40,
WhAm 2*
Bizzozero, Giulio Cesare 1846-1901 *DcScB*
Bjerknes, Carl Anton 1825-1903 *DcScB*
Bjerknes, Jacob Aall Bonnevie 1897-1975
AsBiEn, WhAm 6
Bjerknes, Vilhelm Frimann Koren 1862-1951
DcScB
Bjerregaard, Carl Henrik Andreas 1845-1922
DcAmB
Bjerregaard, Carl Henry Andrew 1845-1922
NatCAB 13, TwCBDA, WhAm 1
Bjerrum, Niels Janniksen 1879-1958 *DcScB*
Bjoerling, Jussi 1911-1960 *WhAm 4*
Bjork, David Knuth 1891-1962 *NatCAB 50,
WhAm 4*
Bjork, Eskil Iver 1896-1975 *WhAm 6*
Bjorklund, Lorence F *IlBEAAW*
Bjorkman, Edwin 1866-1951 *WhAm 3*
Bjorkman, Frances Maule 1879- *WomWWA 14*
Bjornson, Bjorn Gudmundar 1898-1969
NatCAB 55
Bjornson, Bjornstjerne 1832-1910 *McGEWB*
Bjornsson, Sveinn 1881-1952 *WhAm 3*
Bjornstad, Alfred William 1874-1934
NatCAB 25, WhAm 1
Bjurman, Andrew 1876-1943 *IlBEAAW*
Blabon, Edwin Littlefield 1873-1934
NatCAB 26
Blabon, Joseph Ward 1858-1933 *WhAm 1*
Blacher, Boris 1903-1975 *WhAm 6*
Blachly, Charles Dallas 1878-1949 *NatCAB 38*
Blachly, Clarence Dan 1881- *WhAm 6*
Blachly, Frederick Frank 1880-1975 *WhAm 6*
Black, Miss *NewYHSD*
Black, Adam Herbert 1873-1959 *NatCAB 44*
Black, Albert Gain 1896-1966 *WhAm 4*
Black, Alexander 1859-1940 *WhAm 1*

Black, Alfred Lawrence 1858-1927 *WhAm 1*
Black, Arthur Davenport 1870-1937 *WhAm 1*
Black, Barron Foster 1893-1974 *WhAm 6*
Black, Belinda Miles Bogardus 1874-
WomWWA 14
Black, Benjamin Warren 1887-1945
NatCAB 35, WhAm 2
Black, Carl E 1862- *WhAm 4*
Black, Carlyle H 1887-1973 *WhAm 6*
Black, Charles Clarke 1858-1947 *NatCAB 37,
WhAm 2*
Black, Charles E 1896-1954 *WhAm 3*
Black, Charles Frederick 1884-1950
NatCAB 38
Black, Charles Gilbert 1868-1944 *NatCAB 33*
Black, Charles Newbold 1867-1935 *NatCAB 26*
Black, Chauncey Forward d1904 *ApCAB,
WhAm 1*
Black, Clinton R, Jr. 1894-1963 *WhAm 4*
Black, Clyde Wigbert 1873- *WhoColR*
Black, David William 1869-1921 *NatCAB 19*
Black, Davidson 1884-1934 *DcScB*
Black, Dugald 1906-1964 *NatCAB 50,
WhAm 4*
Black, E Charlton 1861-1927 *NatCAB 41,
WhAm 1*
Black, Edward Junius 1806-1846 *BiAUS,
BiDrAC, WhAm H, WhAmP*
Black, Eli M d1975 *WhAm 6*
Black, Ernest Bateman 1882-1949 *NatCAB 37,
WhAm 2*
Black, Etta Roe 1862- *WomWWA 14*
Black, Eugene 1879-1975 *BiDrAC, WhAm 6*
Black, Eugene Robert 1873-1934 *DcAmB S1,
NatCAB 28, WhAm 1*
Black, Fannie DeGrasse 1856- *AmWom,
WomWWA 14*
Black, Florence Atwood *WomWWA 14*
Black, Forrest Revere 1894-1943 *WhAm 2*
Black, Francis Marion 1836-1902 *NatCAB 13*
Black, Frank Blymyer 1865-1937 *NatCAB 28,
WhAm 1*
Black, Frank Sweet 1853-1913 *TwCBDA*
Black, Frank Swett 1853-1913 *ApCAB Sup,
ApCAB X, BiDrAC, DcAmB,
NatCAB 13, NatCAB 16, WhAm 1,
WhAmP*
Black, Garland C 1894- *WhAm 3*
Black, George Douglas 1858-1932 *NatCAB 26*
Black, George H 1871-1949 *NatCAB 37*
Black, George Harold 1873-1952 *NatCAB 41,
WhAm 3*
Black, George Robison 1835-1886 *BiDrAC,
NatCAB 16, WhAm H*
Black, Greene Vardiman 1836-1915 *AmBi,
DcAmB, NatCAB 13, WebAB, WhAm 1*
Black, Harold Alfred 1895-1970 *WhAm 5*
Black, Harry Alfred 1866-1935 *WhAm 1*
Black, Harry Crawford 1845-1921 *NatCAB 6*
Black, Harry S 1863-1929 *ApCAB X,
WhAm 1*
Black, Henry 1783-1841 *BiAUS, BiDrAC,
WhAm H*
Black, Henry Campbell 1860-1927 *WhAm 1*
Black, Howard 1896-1967 *WhAm 4A*
Black, Hugh 1868-1953 *WhAm 3*
Black, Hugh Ratchford 1856-1933 *NatCAB 35*
Black, Hugh Snoddy 1892-1950 *NatCAB 40,
WhAm 3*
Black, Hugo LaFayette 1886-1971 *BiDrAC,
EncAB, McGEWB, WebAB, WhAm 5,
WhAmP*
Black, James 1787?-1867 *DcScB*
Black, James 1793-1872 *BiAUS, BiDrAC,
WhAm H, WhAmP*
Black, James 1814?- *NewYHSD*
Black, James 1823- *ApCAB*
Black, James 1823-1893 *AmBi, DcAmB,
NatCAB 19, WhAm H, WhAmP*
Black, James 1823-1894 *TwCBDA*
Black, James 1857-1919 *NatCAB 17*
Black, James Augustus 1793-1848 *BiAUS,
BiDrAC, WhAm H, WhAmP*
Black, James Bailey 1887-1965 *NatCAB 51*
Black, James Byers 1890-1965 *WhAm 4*
Black, James Conquest Cross 1842-1928
BiDrAC, WhAm 1, WhAmP
Black, James Dixon 1849-1938 *NatCAB 31,*

Black, James Harvey 1884-1958 *NatCAB 46*
Black, James Harvey 1884-1959 *WhAm 3*
Black, James Rush 1827- *ApCAB, TwCBDA*
Black, James Stanislaus 1874-1947 *NatCAB 38*
Black, James Walter 1870-1923 *NatCAB 20*
Black, James William 1866-1934 *TwCBDA,
WhAm 1*
Black, Jennie Prince 1869- *WomWWA 14*
Black, Jenny O d1951 *WhAm 3*
Black, Jeremiah Sullivan 1810-1883 *AmBi,
ApCAB, BiAUS, BiDrUSE, DcAmB,
Drake, NatCAB 5, TwCBDA, WebAB,
WhAm H, WhAmP*
Black, John d1854 *BiAUS, BiDrAC,
NatCAB 11, WhAm H*
Black, John 1792-1873 *ApCAB, BiAUS*
Black, John 1818-1882 *ApCAB Sup*
Black, John Alexander 1903-1958 *NatCAB 43*
Black, John Charles 1839-1915 *ApCAB X,
BiDrAC, DcAmB, NatCAB 12, TwCBDA,
WhAm 1, WhAmP*
Black, John Clarke 1837-1917 *WhAm 1*
Black, John Donald 1872-1959 *NatCAB 49,
WhAm 3*
Black, John Donald 1883-1960 *WhAm 4*
Black, John Janvier 1837- *WhAm 1*
Black, Joseph 1728-1799 *AsBiEn, BiHiMed,
DcScB, McGEWB*
Black, Laverne Nelson 1887-1938 *IlBEAAW*
Black, Lee Jackson 1870-1934 *NatCAB 25*
Black, Leon Harold 1918-1974 *WhAm 6*
Black, Lewis Cass 1844-1919 *NatCAB 19*
Black, Lloyd Llewellyn 1889-1950 *NatCAB 39,
WhAm 3*
Black, Loring Milton, Jr. 1886-1956 *BiDrAC,
WhAmP*
Black, Madeleine Elmer *WhAm 5*
Black, Madeline *WomWWA 14*
Black, Malcolm Stuart 1894-1960 *WhAm 4*
Black, Marian Watkins 1905-1975 *WhAm 6*
Black, Mary 1842?- *NewYHSD*
Black, Mary Fleming 1848- *AmWom*
Black, Mary Grace Witherbee 1852-
WomWWA 14
Black, Melville 1866- *WhAm 5*
Black, Mignonette Bird Johnson *WomWWA 14*
Black, Nellie Peters 1851- *WomWWA 14*
Black, Newton Henry 1874- *WhAm 5*
Black, Newton Wade 1912-1974 *WhAm 6*
Black, Norman David 1887-1944 *NatCAB 41,
WhAm 2*
Black, Norman David, Jr. 1913-1969 *WhAm 5*
Black, Ralph Peters 1881-1960 *NatCAB 47*
Black, Robert Fager 1889-1975 *WhAm 6*
Black, Robert Howell 1918-1960 *WhAm 4*
Black, Robert Lounsbury 1881-1954
NatCAB 43, WhAm 3
Black, Robert Sommerville 1892-1957
NatCAB 47
Black, Ruby Aurora 1896-1957 *WhAm 3*
Black, Ryland Melville 1867- *WhAm 4*
Black, S Bruce 1892-1968 *NatCAB 55,
WhAm 5*
Black, Samuel Charles 1869-1921 *NatCAB 23,
WhAm 1*
Black, Samuel Duncan 1883- *WhAm 3*
Black, Samuel Luccock 1859- *WhAm 4*
Black, Samuel W *BiAUS*
Black, Sarah Hearst 1846- *AmWom*
Black, Susan Geiger 1843- *WomWWA 14*
Black, Thurston W 1810?- *NewYHSD*
Black, Valentine Lorentz 1864-1938
NatCAB 29
Black, Van-Lear 1875-1930 *WhAm 1*
Black, Walter 1859-1923 *NatCAB 6*
Black, Walter Joseph 1893-1958 *NatCAB 44,
WhAm 3*
Black, William 1760-1834 *ApCAB*
Black, William 1876-1930 *WhAm 1*
Black, William Alexander 1894-1956
NatCAB 46
Black, William H H *NewYHSD*
Black, William Harman 1868- *WhAm 5*
Black, William Henry 1854-1930 *NatCAB 25,
TwCBDA, WhAm 1*
Black, William Joseph 1864- *WhAm 4*
Black, William Murray 1855-1933 *DcAmB S1,*

NatCAB 44, WhAm 1

Black, William Thurston *NewYHSD*

Black, William Wesley 1859- *WhAm 2*

Black, Winifred 1869-1936 *WhAm 1, WomWWA 14*

Black, Winifred Sweet 1863-1936 *NotAW*

Black, Witherbee 1879-1959 *WhAm 3*

Black Bart 1830-1917? *REnAW*

Black Beaver 1808-1880 *NatCAB 19*

Black Elk 1863-1950 *REnAW*

Black Hawk 1767-1838 *AmBi, ApCAB, DcAmB, Drake, EncAAH, McGEWB, NatCAB 9, REnAW, TwCBDA, WebAB, WebAMB, WhAm H*

Black Kettle 1803?-1868 *NatCAB 19, WhAm H*

Blackall, Christopher Rubey 1830-1924 *WhAm 1*

Blackall, Clarence Howard 1857- *ApCAB X, NatCAB 18*

Blackall, Clarence Howard 1857-1941 *WhAm 1*

Blackall, Clarence Howard 1857-1942 *WhAm 2*

Blackall, Emily Lucas 1832-1892 *AmWom*

Blackall, Frederick Steele 1865-1928 *WhAm 1*

Blackall, Frederick Steele, Jr. 1896-1963 *WhAm 4*

Blackall, Robert Murray 1889-1963 *NatCAB 49*

Blackard, James Washington 1857-1938 *WhAm 1*

Blackbeard *WhAm H*

Blackburn, Alexander 1844-1921 *WhAm 1*

Blackburn, Armour Jennings 1903-1970 *WhAm 5*

Blackburn, Benjamin Bentley 1927- *BiDrAC*

Blackburn, Bryan Martin 1884-1955 *NatCAB 46*

Blackburn, Daniel Asa 1864- *NatCAB 10*

Blackburn, Edmond Spencer 1868-1912 *BiDrAC*

Blackburn, Edmund Spencer 1868-1912 *WhAm 4*

Blackburn, Fletcher Jordan 1884-1959 *NatCAB 44*

Blackburn, Frederick George 1892-1972 *WhAm 5*

Blackburn, George Andrew 1861-1918 *WhAm 1*

Blackburn, George Stebbins 1901- *WhAm 4*

Blackburn, Gideon 1772-1838 *ApCAB, DcAmB, DcAmReB, Drake, NatCAB 13, TwCBDA, WhAm H*

Blackburn, J C S 1838-1918 *BiAUS*

Blackburn, Jasper 1869-1944 *NatCAB 46*

Blackburn, John Hail 1880-1931 *NatCAB 41*

Blackburn, John Henry 1876-1951 *WhAm 3*

Blackburn, John Simpson 1907-1964 *WhAm 4*

Blackburn, Joseph 1700?-1760 *AmBi, BnEnAmA, DcAmB, NewYHSD, WhAm H*

Blackburn, Joseph Clay Stiles 1838-1918 *ApCAB X, BiDrAC, NatCAB 1, WhAmP*

Blackburn, Joseph Clay Styles 1838-1918 *ApCAB, DcAmB, TwCBDA, WhAm 1*

Blackburn, Joseph E 1860- *WhAm 4*

Blackburn, K Wilde 1906-1954 *WhAm 3*

Blackburn, Luke Pryor 1816-1887 *DcAmB, NatCAB 13, WhAm H, WhAmP*

Blackburn, Merrill Mason 1876-1957 *WhAm 3*

Blackburn, Oliver A *ApCAB X*

Blackburn, Robert E Lee 1870-1935 *BiDrAC, WhAm 1*

Blackburn, Samuel 1758-1835 *TwCBDA*

Blackburn, Walter Evans 1907-1974 *WhAm 6*

Blackburn, William 1814-1867 *ApCAB*

Blackburn, William J 1868-1944 *NatCAB 35*

Blackburn, William J 1872- *WhAm 2*

Blackburn, William Jasper 1820-1899 *ApCAB, BiAUS, BiDrAC, TwCBDA, WhAm 1, WhAmP*

Blackburn, William Maxwell 1828- *ApCAB, NatCAB 9*

Blackburn, William Maxwell 1828-1898 *BiDAmEd, DcAmB*

Blackburn, William Maxwell 1828-1900 *TwCBDA, WhAm 1*

Blackburn, William Wallace 1859-1931 *NatCAB 24, WhAm 4*

Blackburn, Willis Clifford 1903-1967 *WhAm 5*

Blackburne, Mary Frances 1874- *WhAm 5*

Blacker, Daniel James 1873- *WhAm 5*

Blacker, Robert Roe 1845-1931 *NatCAB 25*

Blackerby, Philip Earle 1881-1948 *WhAm 2*

Blackett, Hill 1892-1967 *NatCAB 57*

Blackett, Patrick Maynard Stuart 1897-1974 *AsBiEn, WhAm 6*

Blackfan, Kenneth Daniel 1883-1941 *DcAmB S3, NatCAB 32, WhAm 1*

Blackford, Charles Minor 1833-1903 *DcAmB, NatCAB 19*

Blackford, Eugene Gilbert 1839-1904 *ApCAB, NatCAB 3, TwCBDA, WhAm 1*

Blackford, Eugene Gilbert 1886-1964 *NatCAB 51*

Blackford, Isaac Newton 1786-1859 *ApCAB, BiAUS, Drake, NatCAB 11*

Blackford, John Minor 1886-1945 *NatCAB 38*

Blackford, Katherine M H 1875- *WhAm 5*

Blackford, Launcelot Minor 1837-1914 *WhAm 1*

Blackford, Staige D 1898-1949 *WhAm 2*

Blackford, William Matthews 1801-1864 *BiAUS, NatCAB 34*

Blackham, George Edmund 1846-1928 *NatCAB 13, WhAm 1*

Blackhoof d1831 *Drake*

Blackington, Ada J 1867- *WomWWA 14*

Blackistone, Nathaniel *NatCAB 7*

Blackledge, William d1828 *BiAUS, BiDrAC, WhAm H*

Blackledge, William Salter 1793-1857 *BiAUS, BiDrAC, WhAm H*

Blacklidge, Luella Larmore 1864- *WomWWA 14*

Blackman, Carrie Horton 1856- *WomWWA 14*

Blackman, Edward Bernard 1916-1970 *WhAm 5*

Blackman, Frederick Frost 1866-1947 *DcScB*

Blackman, George Curtis 1819-1871 *ApCAB*

Blackman, Learner 1781?-1815 *ApCAB*

Blackman, Lee Rush 1881-1942 *NatCAB 33*

Blackman, Maulsby Willett 1876-1943 *NatCAB 32*

Blackman, Olive J 1864- *WomWWA 14*

Blackman, William Fremont 1855-1932 *NatCAB 23, WhAm 1*

Blackman, William Waldo 1856-1943 *WhAm 2*

Blackmar, Abel Edward 1852-1931 *WhAm 1*

Blackmar, Charles Maxwell 1884-1962 *WhAm 4*

Blackmar, Esbon 1805-1857 *BiAUS, BiDrAC, WhAm H*

Blackmar, Frank Wilson 1854-1931 *AmBi, NatCAB 9, TwCBDA, WhAm 1*

Blackmar, Wilmon Whilldin 1841- *NatCAB 10*

Blackmarr, Frank Hamlin 1871- *WhAm 5*

Blackmer, Anna Maye 1872- *WomWWA 14*

Blackmer, Henry M 1869- *WhAm 5*

Blackmer, Lucian Richmond 1848-1914 *NatCAB 16*

Blackmer, Percy Richmond 1888-1944 *NatCAB 37*

Blackmer, Samuel Howard 1902-1951 *WhAm 3*

Blackmer, Sydney 1898-1973 *WhAm 6*

Blackmon, Fred Leonard 1873-1921 *BiDrAC, WhAmP*

Blackmon, Frederick Leonard 1873-1921 *WhAm 1*

Blackmore, Emil A 1917-1967 *WhAm 4*

Blackmore, George Augustus 1884-1948 *WhAm 2*

Blackmore, Henry Spencer 1868- *WhAm 4*

Blackmore, Simon Augustine 1849-1926 *WhAm 1*

Blackmun, Harry Andrew 1908- *WebAB*

Blackmur, Richard Palmer 1904-1965 *WhAm 4*

Blacknall, George B 1860- *WhoColR A*

Blackney, William Wallace 1876-1963 *BiDrAC, WhAm 4, WhAmP*

Blackorby, Edward 1911- *EncAAH*

Blackowl, Archie 1911- *IlBEAAW*

Blackshear, Edward Levocscer 1863- *WhoColR*

Blackstock, Ira Burton 1866-1931 *WhAm 1*

Blackstock, Leo Guy 1899-1972 *NatCAB 57*

Blackstone, A E 1886-1951 *WhAm 3*

Blackstone, Basil Brown Gordon 1892-1949 *NatCAB 38*

Blackstone, George Vandergrift 1860-1910 *NatCAB 29*

Blackstone, Harriet *WomWWA 14*

Blackstone, Richard 1843-1922 *WhAm 1*

Blackstone, Timothy B 1829-1900 *WhAm 1*

Blackstone, Timothy Bailey 1829-1900 *ApCAB Sup*

Blackstone, Timothy Beach 1829-1900 *NatCAB 14, WhAm H*

Blackstone, William d1675 *ApCAB, Drake*

Blackstone, William 1590?-1675 *TwCBDA*

Blackstone, William 1595-1675 *AmBi, DcAmB, NatCAB 8, WhAm H*

Blackstone, Sir William 1723-1780 *McGEWB*

Blackstone, William Morse 1888-1934 *NatCAB 29*

Blackton, James Stuart 1875-1941 *DcAmB S3, WhAm 1*

Blackwelder, Bascom 1884-1961 *NatCAB 49*

Blackwelder, Charles Davis 1895-1965 *WhAm 4*

Blackwelder, Elliot 1880- *WhAm 6*

Blackwelder, Gertrude Boughton 1853- *WomWWA 14*

Blackwelder, Paul 1878- *WhAm 6*

Blackwell, Alice Stone 1857-1950 *AmWom, DcAmB S4, NotAW, WhAm 2A, WhAmP, WomWWA 14*

Blackwell, Annie Walker 1862- *WhoColR*

Blackwell, Antoinette Louisa Brown 1825-1921 *AmBi, AmWom, ApCAB, DcAmB, NatCAB 9, NatCAB 29, NotAW, TwCBDA, WebAB, WhAm 1, WhAmP, WomWWA 14*

Blackwell, Ashby Carlyle 1896-1975 *WhAm 6*

Blackwell, Elizabeth 1821-1910 *AmBi, AmWom, ApCAB, BiHiMed, DcAmB, Drake, EncAB, McGEWB, NatCAB 9, NotAW, TwCBDA, WebAB, WhAm 1*

Blackwell, Emily 1826-1910 *AmWom, NatCAB 9, NotAW, WhAm 1, WhAm 1C*

Blackwell, George Lincoln 1861- *WhAm 4, WhoColR*

Blackwell, Henry Brown 1825-1909 *AmBi, DcAmB, WhAmP*

Blackwell, Henry Browne 1825-1909 *NatCAB 20*

Blackwell, Hubert Charles Hansard d1955 *WhAm 3*

Blackwell, James Shannon 1844-1923 *NatCAB 8, WhAm 4*

Blackwell, John 1688- *NatCAB 18*

Blackwell, Julius W *BiAUS, BiDrAC, WhAm H*

Blackwell, Lucy Stone *AmBi, DcAmB, NotAW, TwCBDA*

Blackwell, Mary B 1924-1973 *WhAm 6*

Blackwell, Otto Bernard 1884-1970 *WhAm 5*

Blackwell, Paul Julian 1882- *WhoColR*

Blackwell, Robert Emory 1854-1938 *NatCAB 33, WhAm 1*

Blackwell, S Ellen *NewYHSD*

Blackwell, Sarah Ellen 1828- *AmWom, NatCAB 9*

Blackwell, Thomas Joseph 1896-1964 *NatCAB 53, WhAm 4*

Blackwell, Thomas Winfield 1884-1943 *NatCAB 35*

Blackwood, Alexander Leslie 1862- *WhAm 1*

Blackwood, Andrew Watterson 1882-1966 *NatCAB 52, WhAm 4*

Blackwood, Ibra Charles 1878-1936 *NatCAB 28, WhAm 1*

Blackwood, Norman Jerome 1866-1938 *NatCAB 29, WhAm 1*

Blackwood, Oswald Hance 1888-1953 *NatCAB 40 WhAm 3*

Blackwood, William G *BiAUS*

Blada, V *NewYHSD*

Bladen, Ronald 1918- *BnEnAmA*

Bladen, Thomas 1698-1780 *ApCAB, NatCAB 7*

Bladen, William 1673-1718? *DcAmB, WhAm H*

Blades, Mary *NewYHSD*

Blades, William Benjamin 1854-1920 *NatCAB 31*

Blaess, August F 1871- *WhAm 5*
Blaeu, Willem Janszoon 1571-1638 *DcScB*
Blaffer, Robert Lee 1876-1942 *NatCAB 31,*
WhAm 2
Blagden, Augustus Silliman 1879-1960
WhAm 4
Blagden, Sir Charles 1748-1820 *BiHiMed,*
DcScB
Blagonrarov, Anatoli Arkadyevich 1894-1975
WhAm 6
Blahd, Mose Emmett 1883-1940 *WhAm 1*
Blaikie, William 1843-1904 *ApCAB, DcAmB,*
TwCBDA, WhAm 1
Blain, Alexander William 1885-1958
NatCAB 46, WhAm 4
Blain, Hugh Mercer, Sr. 1874- *WhAm 5*
Blain, Thomas James 1861-1931 *NatCAB 25*
Blaine, Anita McCormick 1866-1954
DcAmB S5, NatCAB 44
Blaine, Mrs. Emmons 1866-1954 *WhAm 3*
Blaine, Harriet Gertrude 1861- *WomWWA 14*
Blaine, Helen Louise Townsend 1920-1972
WhAm 5
Blaine, James Gillespie 1830-1893 *AmBi,*
ApCAB, BiAUS, BiDrAC, BiDrUSE,
DcAmB, Drake, EncAB, McGEWB,
NatCAB 1, TwCBDA, WebAB,
WhAm H, WhAmP
Blaine, James Gillespie 1888-1969 *WhAm 5*
Blaine, John James 1875-1934 *BiDrAC,*
DcAmB S1, NatCAB 26, WhAm 1,
WhAmP
Blainville, Henri Marie Ducrotay De 1777-1850
DcScB
Blair *NewYHSD*
Blair, Adeline Cleveland 1863- *WomWWA 14*
Blair, Albert 1840- *NatCAB 17*
Blair, Albion Zelophehad 1861- *WhAm 4*
Blair, Algernon 1873-1952 *WhAm 3*
Blair, Andrew 1896-1948 *NatCAB 38*
Blair, Andrew Alexander 1846-1932 *ApCAB*
Blair, Andrew Alexander 1848-1932
NatCAB 25, WhAm 1
Blair, Apolline Madison 1860- *WhAm 4,*
WomWWA 14
Blair, Arless Arland 1891-1955 *NatCAB 42*
Blair, Austin 1818-1894 *ApCAB, BiAUS,*
BiDrAC, DcAmB, Drake, NatCAB 5,
TwCBDA, WhAm H, WhAmP
Blair, Barnard 1801-1880 *BiAUS*
Blair, Bernard 1801-1880 *BiDrAC, WhAm H*
Blair, C Ledyard 1867-1949 *NatCAB 50,*
WhAm 4
Blair, Charles Austin 1854-1912 *NatCAB 15,*
WhAm 1
Blair, Charlotte 1861-1917 *NatCAB 23*
Blair, Chauncey Justus 1845-1916 *NatCAB 21,*
WhAm 1
Blair, Cowgill 1889-1966 *WhAm 4*
Blair, Daniel Augustus 1898-1960 *NatCAB 50*
Blair, David Ellmore 1874-1954 *WhAm 3*
Blair, David Hunt 1868-1944 *NatCAB 33,*
WhAm 2
Blair, DeWitt Clinton 1833-1915 *NatCAB 31*
Blair, Donald McKensie 1883-1963 *NatCAB 50*
Blair, Edna Sheldon 1875- *WomWWA 14*
Blair, Edward Holden 1879-1944 *NatCAB 37*
Blair, Edwin Foster 1901-1970 *WhAm 5*
Blair, Eliza Nelson d1907 *WhAm 1*
Blair, Ellen A Dayton 1827- *AmWom*
Blair, Emily Newell 1877-1951 *DcAmB S5,*
WhAm 3, WomWWA 14
Blair, Emma Helen d1911 *WhAm 1*
Blair, Eugenie *WhAm 5*
Blair, Floyd Gilbert 1891-1965 *WhAm 4*
Blair, Francis Grant 1864-1942 *WhAm 1,*
WhAm 2
Blair, Francis Preston 1791-1876 *AmBi,*
ApCAB, BiAUS, DcAmB, Drake, EncAB,
McGEWB, NatCAB 4, TwCBDA,
WebAB, WhAm H, WhAmP
Blair, Francis Preston, Jr. 1821-1875 *AmBi,*
ApCAB, BiAUS, BiDrAC, DcAmB,
Drake, NatCAB 4, REnAW, TwCBDA,
WebAB, WhAm H, WhAmP
Blair, Frank Warrenner 1870-1950 *WhAm 3*
Blair, Frederic Howes 1887-1953 *WhAm 3*
Blair, Harry Wallace 1877-1964 *WhAm 4*

Blair, Henry Alexander 1900-1971 *NatCAB 57,*
WhAm 5
Blair, Henry Augustus 1852-1932 *NatCAB 14,*
WhAm 1
Blair, Henry Patterson 1867-1948 *WhAm 2*
Blair, Henry William 1834-1920 *ApCAB,*
BiDrAC, DcAmB, NatCAB 1, TwCBDA,
WhAm 1, WhAmP
Blair, Herbert Francis 1875- *WhAm 5*
Blair, Hugh McLeod 1853-1923 *WhAm 1*
Blair, Jack F 1931-1970 *WhAm 5*
Blair, Jacob Beeson 1821-1901 *BiAUS,*
BiAUS Sup, BiDrAC, NatCAB 12,
WhAmP
Blair, James 1655-1743 *AmBi, DcAmB,*
DcAmReB, McGEWB, NatCAB 3,
WebAB, WhAm H
Blair, James 1656-1743 *ApCAB, BiDAmEd,*
TwCBDA
Blair, James 1660?-1743 *Drake*
Blair, James 1790?-1834 *BiAUS, BiDrAC,*
WhAm H, WhAmP
Blair, James 1807- *NatCAB 4*
Blair, James A, Jr. 1880-1934 *WhAm 1*
Blair, James Carroll 1877-1953 *NatCAB 41,*
WhAm 3
Blair, James Gorrall 1825-1904 *BiDrAC*
Blair, James Lawrence 1854-1904 *WhAm 1*
Blair, James T, Jr. 1902-1962 *WhAm 4*
Blair, James Thomas 1871-1944 *WhAm 2*
Blair, John *IIBEAAW*
Blair, John 1687-1771 *DcAmB, WhAm H*
Blair, John 1689-1771 *ApCAB, Drake,*
NatCAB 13, TwCBDA
Blair, John 1720-1771 *ApCAB*
Blair, John 1732-1800 *ApCAB, BiAUS,*
DcAmB, Drake, NatCAB 1, TwCBDA,
WebAB, WhAm H
Blair, John 1790-1863 *BiAUS, BiDrAC,*
WhAm H, WhAmP
Blair, John Durbarrow 1759-1823 *ApCAB*
Blair, John Halsey 1865-1934 *WhAm 1*
Blair, John Inslee 1802-1899 *NatCAB 7*
Blair, John Insley 1802-1899 *AmBi, ApCAB,*
DcAmB, TwCBDA, WhAm 1
Blair, John Leo 1888-1962 *WhAm 4*
Blair, Joseph Cullen 1871-1940 *WhAm 1*
Blair, Joseph Paxton 1859-1942 *NatCAB 10,*
NatCAB 31, WhAm 2
Blair, Julian MacFarlane 1892-1961
NatCAB 48
Blair, Margaret Josephine 1863- *WhAm 4,*
WomWWA 14
Blair, Margaretta E 1844- *WomWWA 14*
Blair, Marion 1824-1901 *NewYHSD*
Blair, Mary Jesup 1826- *WomWWA 14*
Blair, Montgomery 1813-1883 *AmBi, ApCAB,*
BiAUS, BiDrUSE, DcAmB, Drake,
NatCAB 2, NatCAB 44, TwCBDA,
WebAB, WhAm H, WhAmP
Blair, Patrick d1728 *DcScB*
Blair, Paxton 1892-1974 *WhAm 6*
Blair, Salome Annette 1856- *WomWWA 14*
Blair, Samuel 1712-1751 *ApCAB, DcAmB,*
Drake, WhAm H
Blair, Samuel 1741-1818 *ApCAB, Drake,*
NatCAB 9
Blair, Samuel Steel 1821-1890 *BiAUS,*
BiDrAC, WhAm H
Blair, Thomas Jackson 1891-1963 *NatCAB 52*
Blair, Vilray Papin 1871-1955 *WhAm 3*
Blair, Vivian Beatrice Losse *WomWWA 14*
Blair, Walter 1835-1909 *ApCAB X,*
NatCAB 9, NatCAB 16
Blair, Walter 1856?-1930 *REnAW*
Blair, Walter Dabney 1877-1953 *NatCAB 50,*
WhAm 3
Blair, Watson Franklin 1854-1928 *WhAm 1*
Blair, William 1818- *NatCAB 7*
Blair, William Allen 1859-1948 *WhAm 2*
Blair, William Reed 1875-1949 *WhAm 2*
Blair, William Reid 1875-1949 *NatCAB 36*
Blair, William Richards 1874-1962 *NatCAB 53,*
WhAm 6
Blair, William Wightman 1866-1957
NatCAB 49, WhAm 3
Blair, Woodbury 1852-1933 *NatCAB 25*

Blair-Smith, Robert McPhail 1906-1968
NatCAB 53, WhAm 5
Blais, Andre Albert 1842- *ApCAB Sup*
Blaisdell, Albert Franklin 1847-1927
ApCAB Sup, WhAm 1
Blaisdell, Anthony Houghtaling 1848-1905
WhAm 1
Blaisdell, Daisy Luana 1866- *WomWWA 14*
Blaisdell, Daniel d1832 *BiAUS*
Blaisdell, Daniel 1762-1833 *BiDrAC,*
WhAm H, WhAmP
Blaisdell, Gideon Moores 1918-1971 *WhAm 5*
Blaisdell, H G *BiAUS*
Blaisdell, Harold Alfred 1897-1964 *NatCAB 51*
Blaisdell, James Arnold 1867-1957 *WhAm 3*
Blaisdell, James J 1827-1896 *TwCBDA*
Blaisdell, Mary Frances 1874- *WomWWA 14*
Blaisdell, Thomas Charles 1867-1948 *WhAm 2*
Blaisdell, Warren Carl 1911-1970 *WhAm 5*
Blaise *DcScB*
Blake, A Harold 1896-1951 *NatCAB 41,*
WhAm 3
Blake, Alice R Jordan 1864- *AmWom*
Blake, Anson Stiles 1870-1959 *NatCAB 49*
Blake, Arthur Welland 1840-1893 *NatCAB 23*
Blake, B Gary 1905-1968 *NatCAB 54*
Blake, Blanche Morgan 1866- *WomWWA 14*
Blake, Bruce 1881-1957 *NatCAB 43*
Blake, Caroline Placide *ApCAB*
Blake, Charles Frederic 1834-1881 *NatCAB 8*
Blake, Charles S 1860-1931 *WhAm 1*
Blake, Chauncey Etheridge 1881- *WhAm 2*
Blake, Clarence John 1843-1919 *ApCAB,*
TwCBDA, WhAm 1
Blake, Claude Wallace 1885-1957 *NatCAB 47*
Blake, Clinton Hamlin 1883-1947 *WhAm 2*
Blake, E W *NewYHSD*
Blake, E Wilson 1866-1947 *NatCAB 36*
Blake, Ebenezer Nelson 1831-1921 *NatCAB 19*
Blake, Edgar 1869-1943 *NatCAB 35,*
WhAm 2
Blake, Edgar, Jr. d1947 *WhAm 2*
Blake, Edward 1833- *ApCAB*
Blake, Edward Everett 1875-1947 *WhAm 2*
Blake, Edwin Mortimer 1868-1955 *NatCAB 42*
Blake, Eli Judson 1879-1935 *NatCAB 33*
Blake, Eli Whitney 1795-1886 *AmBi, ApCAB,*
DcAmB, NatCAB 9, WhAm H
Blake, Eli Whitney 1836-1895 *ApCAB,*
TwCBDA
Blake, Emily Calvin *WhAm 3*
Blake, Eugene Maurice 1882-1969 *NatCAB 54*
Blake, Euphenia Vale 1825- *AmWom*
Blake, Eva M *WomWWA 14*
Blake, Francis 1850-1913 *DcAmB,*
NatCAB 13, NatCAB 22, TwCBDA,
WhAm 1
Blake, Francis Gilman 1887-1952 *DcAmB S5,*
WhAm 3
Blake, Frederic Columbus 1877- *WhAm 5*
Blake, George A H 1812-1884 *ApCAB, Drake*
Blake, George Fordyce 1819- *NatCAB 11,*
NatCAB 12
Blake, George H 1884-1971 *WhAm 5*
Blake, George Smith 1803-1871 *ApCAB,*
Drake, NatCAB 13, TwCBDA
Blake, Harold Hamilton 1873- *WhAm 5*
Blake, Harrison Gray Otis 1818-1876 *BiAUS,*
BiDrAC, WhAm H, WhAmP
Blake, Henry Nichols 1838-1933 *BiAUS,*
NatCAB 13, WhAm 1
Blake, Henry Seavey 1888-1956 *NatCAB 45,*
WhAm 3
Blake, Henry Taylor 1828-1922 *NatCAB 22*
Blake, Henry William 1865-1929 *NatCAB 22,*
WhAm 1
Blake, Homer Crane 1822-1880 *ApCAB,*
DcAmB, NatCAB 4, TwCBDA,
WhAm H
Blake, Ira Green 1832-1904 *NatCAB 13*
Blake, James Henry 1845- *WhAm 4*
Blake, James Vila 1842-1925 *NatCAB 20,*
WhAm 1
Blake, John, Jr. 1762-1826 *BiAUS, BiDrAC,*
WhAm H, WhAmP
Blake, John B 1802- *BiAUS*
Blake, John Charles 1873- *WhAm 5*
Blake, John George 1837-1918 *WhAm 1*

Blake, John Lauris 1788-1857 *ApCAB, DcAmB, Drake, NatCAB 21, TwCBDA, WhAm H*
Blake, John Lauris 1831-1899 *BiDrAC*
Blake, John Philip 1867-1954 *NatCAB 43*
Blake, John Walter 1858- *WhAm 4*
Blake, Joseph 1620?-1700? *ApCAB, BiAUS, Drake, NatCAB 12*
Blake, Joseph Augustus 1864-1937 *ApCAB X, WhAm 1*
Blake, Katharine Aldrich *WomWWA 14*
Blake, Katherine Alexander Duer 1879-1930 *WhAm 1*
Blake, Katherine D Umsted 1858- *WomWWA 14*
Blake, Leslie Appleton *WomWWA 14*
Blake, Lillie Devereaux 1835-1913 *AmBi*
Blake, Lillie Devereux 1833-1913 *NotAW*
Blake, Lillie Devereux 1835-1913 *AmWom, ApCAB, DcAmB, NatCAB 11, TwCBDA, WhAm 1, WomWWA 14, WomWWA 14a*
Blake, Lucien Ira 1853-1916 *NatCAB 18*
Blake, Lucien Ira 1854-1916 *WhAm 1*
Blake, Lucien Ira 1856-1916 *TwCBDA*
Blake, Lucius S 1816-1894 *NatCAB 10*
Blake, Luther Lee d1953 *WhAm 3*
Blake, Lyman Reed 1835-1883 *DcAmB, WhAm H*
Blake, Lynn Stanford 1889-1959 *WhAm 4*
Blake, Mabelle B 1880- *WomWWA 14*
Blake, Marshall Bronson 1814-1894 *NatCAB 19*
Blake, Mary Elizabeth McGrath 1840-1907 *AmWom, DcAmB, NatCAB 11, WhAm 1*
Blake, Mary Jane Safford *NotAW*
Blake, Mary Katharine Evans 1859- *WhAm 4, WomWWA 14*
Blake, Maxwell 1877-1959 *WhAm 3*
Blake, Monroe Williams 1900-1955 *WhAm 3*
Blake, Mortimer 1813-1884 *TwCBDA*
Blake, Ralph Mason 1889-1950 *WhAm 3*
Blake, Robert 1599-1657 *WhoMilH*
Blake, Robert Edwin 1885-1962 *NatCAB 50*
Blake, Robert Pierpont 1886-1950 *WhAm 3*
Blake, Samuel Hume 1835- *ApCAB*
Blake, Sidney Fay 1892-1959 *WhAm 4*
Blake, Sue Avis 1875- *WomWWA 14*
Blake, T Whitney 1866-1919 *NatCAB 19*
Blake, Thatcher 1809- *NatCAB 11*
Blake, Theodore Evernghim 1869-1949 *WhAm 2*
Blake, Thomas Holdsworth 1792-1849 *ApCAB, BiAUS, BiDrAC, WhAm H*
Blake, Tiffany 1870-1943 *WhAm 2*
Blake, Walter 1848-1915 *NatCAB 17*
Blake, Warren Everett 1900-1966 *WhAm 4*
Blake, William 1757-1827 *McGEWB*
Blake, William Henry 1872-1951 *NatCAB 41*
Blake, William Hume 1809-1870 *ApCAB, Drake*
Blake, William John 1894-1956 *NatCAB 46*
Blake, William Phipps 1825-1910 *DcAmB, IlBEAAW, NewYHSD*
Blake, William Phipps 1826-1910 *ApCAB, NatCAB 10, NatCAB 25, TwCBDA, WhAm 1*
Blake, William Rufus 1805-1863 *ApCAB, DcAmB, Drake, NatCAB 4, WhAm H*
Blake, William W *NewYHSD*
Blakeley, George Henry 1865-1942 *DcAmB S3, WhAm 2*
Blakeley, Harold Whittle 1893-1966 *NatCAB 52*
Blakeley, John Treat 1777-1857 *NatCAB 22*
Blakeley, Johnston 1781-1814 *ApCAB, Drake, NatCAB 5, TwCBDA*
Blakeley, William A 1898- *WhAmP*
Blakelock, David Hazen 1895-1975 *WhAm 6*
Blakelock, Ralph Albert 1847-1919 *AmBi, ApCAB, ApCAB X, BnEnAmA, DcAmB, IlBEAAW, McGEWB, NatCAB 15, WebAB, WhAm 1*
Blakely, Bertha Eliza 1870- *WhAm 5*
Blakely, Charles Adams 1879-1950 *NatCAB 42, WhAm 6*
Blakely, Delora Edith Wilkins 1864- *WomWWA 14*

Blakely, Edward Bradford 1878- *WhAm 6*
Blakely, Elbert Follett 1875-1957 *NatCAB 46*
Blakely, George 1870- *WhAm 5*
Blakely, Gilbert Sykes 1865-1925 *NatCAB 20*
Blakely, John Russell Young 1872-1942 *WhAm 2*
Blakely, Johnston 1781-1814 *AmBi, DcAmB, WebAMB, WhAm H*
Blakely, LaMotte Marcus 1895-1941 *NatCAB 30*
Blakely, Stephens Laurie 1878-1959 *NatCAB 47*
Blakeman, Edward William 1880- *WhAm 6*
Blakeman, Thomas Greenleaf 1887-1953 *NatCAB 48*
Blakemore, Arthur Hendley 1897-1970 *WhAm 5*
Blakemore, Lizzie McFarland 1851- *WomWWA 14*
Blakeney, Albert Alexander 1850-1924 *BiDrAC, WhAm 1*
Blakeney, William John 1851-1925 *NatCAB 20*
Blaker, Adelaide Marion Cornell 1878- *WomWWA 14*
Blaker, Eliza Ann Cooper 1854-1926 *BiDAmEd, NotAW*
Blaker, Ernest 1870-1947 *NatCAB 36*
Blakeslee, Adeline Graves 1873- *WomWWA 14*
Blakeslee, Albert Francis 1874-1954 *AsBiEn, NatCAB 42, WhAm 3*
Blakeslee, Arthur Lyman 1891-1961 *NatCAB 49, WhAm 4*
Blakeslee, Charles Gray 1884-1954 *NatCAB 44*
Blakeslee, Clarence 1863-1954 *WhAm 4*
Blakeslee, Dennis A 1856-1933 *WhAm 1*
Blakeslee, Donald 1915- *WhWW-II*
Blakeslee, Edwin Mitchell 1901-1962 *WhAm 4*
Blakeslee, Erastus 1838-1908 *DcAmB, WhAm 1*
Blakeslee, Francis Durbin 1846-1942 *WhAm 2*
Blakeslee, Fred Gilbert 1868-1942 *WhAm 2*
Blakeslee, George Hubbard 1871-1954 *NatCAB 53, WhAm 3*
Blakeslee, Harvey Dwight, Jr. 1877-1949 *NatCAB 37*
Blakeslee, Howard Walter 1880-1952 *DcAmB S5, WhAm 3*
Blakeslee, James Irwin 1870-1926 *NatCAB 21*
Blakeslee, Raymond Ives 1875-1941 *WhAm 1*
Blakeslee, Victor Franklin 1898-1947 *NatCAB 40*
Blakey, Roy Gillispie 1880-1967 *WhAm 5*
Blakly, William Arvis 1898-1976 *BiDrAC, WhAm 6*
Blakslee, James I 1870- *WhAm 5*
Blakslee, James I 1815- *NatCAB 5*
Blalock, Alfred 1899-1964 *WebAB, WhAm 4*
Blalock, Jesse Marion 1898-1970 *WhAm 5*
Blalock, Myron Geer 1891-1950 *WhAm 3*
Blalock, Nelson Gales 1836-1913 *DcAmB*
Blalock, U Benton 1873- *WhAm 5*
Blamer, Dewitt 1872- *WhAm 5*
Blamey, Sir Thomas 1884-1951 *WhWW-II*
Blanc, Alberto-Carlo 1906-1960 *DcScB*
Blanc, Anthony *NewYHSD*
Blanc, Anthony 1792-1860 *ApCAB, Drake, NatCAB 7, TwCBDA*
Blanc, Antoine 1792-1860 *DcAmB, WhAm H*
Blanc, Louis 1811-1882 *McGEWB*
Blanc, Vincent Le 1554-1640 *ApCAB, Drake*
Blanch, Arnold 1896-1968 *WhAm 5*
Blanch, Norman 1896-1950 *NatCAB 40*
Blanchan, Neltje *NotAW*
Blanchard, Albert Gallatin 1810-1891 *ApCAB, NatCAB 4, TwCBDA*
Blanchard, Alonzo *NewYHSD*
Blanchard, Amy Ella 1856-1926 *WhAm 1, WomWWA 14*
Blanchard, Arthur Alphonzo 1876-1956 *NatCAB 44, WhAm 4*
Blanchard, Arthur Hall 1881-1963 *NatCAB 51*
Blanchard, Arthur Horace 1877- *WhAm 5*
Blanchard, Charles *NewYHSD*
Blanchard, Charles Albert 1848-1925 *NatCAB 26, TwCBDA, WhAm 1*
Blanchard, Charles Elton 1868-1945 *NatCAB 33*
Blanchard, Clarence John 1863- *WhAm 4*

Blanchard, Eliza H *NewYHSD*
Blanchard, Elizabeth d1891 *NewYHSD*
Blanchard, Elizabeth Miller 1865- *WomWWA 14*
Blanchard, Ethel West 1874- *WomWWA 14*
Blanchard, Ferdinand Quincy 1876- *WhAm 5*
Blanchard, Frances S Carothers *WomWWA 14*
Blanchard, Frank LeRoy 1858-1936 *ApCAB X, WhAm 1*
Blanchard, Frederic Thomas 1878-1947 *WhAm 2*
Blanchard, George Roberts 1841-1900 *WhAm 1*
Blanchard, George Washington 1884-1964 *BiDrAC, NatCAB 50*
Blanchard, Grace d1944 *WhAm 2*
Blanchard, Harold Hooper 1891-1971 *NatCAB 56, WhAm 5*
Blanchard, Harold Mercer 1895-1960 *NatCAB 48, WhAm 4*
Blanchard, Helen Augusta *AmWom*
Blanchard, Henry 1833-1918 *WhAm 1*
Blanchard, Henry Franklin 1885-1926 *NatCAB 20*
Blanchard, Herbert Wheeler 1863-1930 *NatCAB 28*
Blanchard, Irene M 1876- *WomWWA 14*
Blanchard, James Armstrong 1845-1916 *NatCAB 2, WhAm 1*
Blanchard, Jean Pierre Francois 1753-1809 *AsBiEn*
Blanchard, John 1787-1849 *BiAUS, BiDrAC, WhAm H*
Blanchard, Jonathan 1738-1788 *BiAUS, BiDrAC, WhAm H, WhAmP*
Blanchard, Jonathan 1811-1892 *DcAmB, NatCAB 21, WhAm H*
Blanchard, Joseph 1704-1758 *ApCAB*
Blanchard, Joseph 1705-1758 *Drake*
Blanchard, Joshua P 1782-1868 *ApCAB*
Blanchard, Justus Wardwell 1811-1877 *ApCAB*
Blanchard, Lafayette Randall 1889-1970 *WhAm 5*
Blanchard, Lucy Mansfield 1869-1927 *WhAm 1*
Blanchard, Mary Miles 1867- *WomWWA 14*
Blanchard, Maurice Leland 1891-1959 *NatCAB 48*
Blanchard, Murray 1874- *WhAm 5*
Blanchard, Nathan Weston 1831-1917 *WhAm 1*
Blanchard, Newton Crain 1849-1922 *BiDrAC, DcAmB, NatCAB 4, TwCBDA, WhAm 1, WhAmP*
Blanchard, Noah Farwell 1821-1881 *NatCAB 5*
Blanchard, Ozro Seth 1876-1956 *WhAm 3*
Blanchard, Ralph Harris 1895-1972 *NatCAB 56, WhAm 5*
Blanchard, Ralph Harrub 1890-1973 *WhAm 6*
Blanchard, Randall Howard 1872-1930 *NatCAB 23*
Blanchard, Raoul 1877-1965 *DcScB, WhAm 5*
Blanchard, Rufus 1821-1904 *WhAm 1*
Blanchard, Samuel Stillman 1835-1901 *NatCAB 8*
Blanchard, Thomas *NewYHSD*
Blanchard, Thomas 1788-1864 *AmBi, ApCAB, DcAmB, Drake, NatCAB 6, TwCBDA, WebAB, WhAm H*
Blanchard, Washington 1808- *NewYHSD*
Blanchard, William H 1916-1966 *WhAm 4*
Blanchard, William Martin 1874-1942 *NatCAB 38, WhAm 2*
Blanchelande, Philibert F Roussel De 1735-1793 *ApCAB, Drake*
Blanchet, Augustin Magliore Alexander 1797-1887 *TwCBDA*
Blanchet, Augustine Magloire Alexander 1797-1887 *ApCAB, NatCAB 13*
Blanchet, Clement Theophilus 1845- *WhAm 4*
Blanchet, Emilio 1829- *ApCAB*
Blanchet, Francis Herbert 1795-1883 *NatCAB 13*
Blanchet, Francis Norbert 1795-1883 *ApCAB, TwCBDA*
Blanchet, Francois 1777-1830 *ApCAB Sup*
Blanchet, Francois Norbert 1795-1883 *DcAmB, REnAW, WhAm H*
Blanchet, John Baptiste 1856- *WhAm 3*
Blanchet, Joseph Goderick 1829- *ApCAB*
Blanchett *NewYHSD*

Blanchfield, Florence A 1884-1971 *WebAMB*
Blanck, Frederick Conrad 1881-1965 *NatCAB 51*
Blanck, Jacob Nathaniel 1906-1974 *WhAm 6*
Blanck, Jurian, Jr. 1645?-1714 *BnEnAmA*
Blancke, Leo Mulford 1894-1966 *WhAm 4*
Blancke, William Henry 1855-1951 *WhAm 3*
Blancke, Wilton Wallace 1884-1949 *NatCAB 35*
Blancke, Wilton Wendell 1908-1971 *WhAm 5*
Blanco, Jose Felix 1782-1872 *ApCAB Sup*
Blanco, Jose G 1917-1971 *WhAm 6*
Blanco, Nunez Vela *ApCAB*
Blanco-Fombona, Rufino 1874- *WhAm 5*
Bland, Ballard *BiAUS*
Bland, Charles Clelland 1837-1918 *NatCAB 17*
Bland, Harry MacNeill 1885-1960 *NatCAB 48*
Bland, Henry Meade 1863- *WhAm 1*
Bland, James A 1854-1911 *WebAB*
Bland, John Randolph 1851-1923 *WhAm 1*
Bland, Oscar Edward 1877-1951 *BiDrAC, WhAm 3, WhAmP*
Bland, Pascal Brooke 1875-1940 *WhAm 1*
Bland, Richard d1790 *BiAUS*
Bland, Richard 1708-1776 *Drake*
Bland, Richard 1710-1776 *ApCAB, BiDrAC, DcAmB, WhAm H, WhAmP*
Bland, Richard 1710-1778 *NatCAB 7, TwCBDA*
Bland, Richard Howard 1880-1959 *WhAm 3*
Bland, Richard Parks 1835-1899 *AmBi, ApCAB, BiAUS, BiDrAC, DcAmB, EncAAH, NatCAB 10, REnAW, TwCBDA, WhAm 1, WhAmP*
Bland, Schuyler Otis 1872-1950 *BiDrAC, WhAm 2A, WhAmP*
Bland, Theoderic 1742-1790 *NatCAB 7*
Bland, Theoderic 1742-1790 *ApCAB, BiAUS, Drake, TwCBDA*
Bland, Theoderic 1777-1846 *BiAUS, Drake*
Bland, Theodorick 1742-1790 *AmBi, BiDrAC, DcAmB, WhAm H, WhAmP*
Bland, Thomas 1809-1885 *DcAmB, WhAm H*
Bland, William Thomas 1861-1928 *BiDrAC, NatCAB 22, WhAm 1*
Blanda, George Frederick 1927- *WebAB*
Blanden, Charles Granger 1857-1933 *WhAm 1*
Blandford, John Bennett, Jr. 1897-1972 *WhAm 5*
Blandford, Mark Hardin 1826-1902 *BiDConf*
Blandin, Charles Kenneth 1872-1958 *WhAm 3*
Blanding, Albert Hazen 1876-1970 *WhAm 5*
Blanding, Don 1894-1957 *NatCAB 46, WhAm 3*
Blanding, Sarah Gibson 1898- *WebAB*
Blandy, Charles 1847- *NatCAB 9*
Blandy, William Henry Purnell 1890-1954 *DcAmB S5, WhAm 3*
Blaney, Dwight 1865-1944 *WhAm 2*
Blaney, Henry R 1855- *WhAm 4*
Blaney, Isabella Williams d1933 *WhAm 1*
Blaney, William Osgood 1841-1910 *WhAm 1*
Blank, Abe H 1879- *WhAm 6*
Blanke, Cyrus Frederick 1861- *NatCAB 12*
Blankenbuehler, John H 1901-1964 *WhAm 4*
Blankenburg, Lucretia Longshore 1845-1937 *NotAW, WhAm 2, WomWWA 14*
Blankenburg, Rudolph 1843-1918 *DcAmB, NatCAB 17, WhAm 1, WhAmP*
Blankenhorn, David 1886- *ApCAB X*
Blankenhorn, Marion Arthur 1885-1957 *NatCAB 47, WhAm 3*
Blankenship, Georgiana Mitchell 1860- *WomWWA 14*
Blankinship, Leslie Charles 1909-1973 *WhAm 6*
Blanks, Robert Franklin 1900-1958 *WhAm 3*
Blann, John Edward 1905-1973 *WhAm 6*
Blanning, Edwin Joseph 1872-1929 *NatCAB 22*
Blanqui, Louis Auguste 1805-1881 *McGEWB*
Blanshard, Frances Bradshaw 1895-1966 *NatCAB 54*
Blanton, Annie Webb 1870-1945 *BiDAmEd, WhAm 2*
Blanton, John Diell 1859-1933 *WhAm 1*
Blanton, Joseph Philip 1849-1909 *NatCAB 27*
Blanton, Joseph Philip 1898- *WhAm 4*
Blanton, Leonard Ray 1930- *BiDrAC*
Blanton, Lindsay Hughes 1832-1914 *WhAm 1*

Blanton, Lindsay Hughes 1834-1914 *NatCAB 5, TwCBDA*
Blanton, Smiley 1882-1966 *WhAm 4*
Blanton, Thomas Lindsay 1872-1957 *BiDrAC, WhAm 3, WhAmP*
Blanton, Wayne Warren 1921-1967 *NatCAB 54*
Blanton, Wyndham Bolling 1890-1960 *WhAm 4*
Blaquiere, Peter Boyle De 1784-1860 *Drake*
Blasar, Jeanette *WomWWA 14*
Blaschke, Wilhelm Johann Eugen 1885-1962 *DcScB*
Blasco, Nunez 1490- *ApCAB*
Blasdel, Henry Goode 1825-1900 *DcAmB, NatCAB 11, WhAm H, WhAmP*
Blash, Andrew Adams 1902-1970 *NatCAB 56*
Blash, Rudolph F d1956 *WhAm 3*
Blashfield, Albert Dodd 1860-1920 *WhAm 1*
Blashfield, Edwin Howland 1848-1936 *AmBi, ApCAB, ApCAB X, BnEnAmA, DcAmB S2, NatCAB 9, NatCAB 27, TwCBDA, WhAm 1*
Blashfield, Evangeline Wilbour 1858-1915 *BiCAW*
Blasius Of Parma 1345?-1416 *DcScB*
Blasko, John Joseph 1912-1968 *NatCAB 54*
Blaskowitz, Johannes Von 1883-1948 *WhWW-II*
Blass, Robert 1867- *NatCAB 14*
Blatch, Harriot Eaton Stanton 1856-1940 *BiCAW, DcAmB S2, NotAW, WhAm 1, WhAmP*
Blatch, Harriot Stanton 1856-1940 *WomWWA 14*
Blatchford, Charles Hammond 1874-1953 *NatCAB 40, WhAm 3*
Blatchford, Eliphalet Wickes 1826-1914 *NatCAB 33, WhAm 1*
Blatchford, Richard Milford 1798-1875 *ApCAB, BiAUS, DcAmB, WhAm H*
Blatchford, Richard Milford 1859-1934 *NatCAB 25, WhAm 1*
Blatchford, Samuel 1767-1828 *ApCAB Sup, NatCAB 20*
Blatchford, Samuel 1820-1893 *ApCAB, BiAUS, DcAmB, NatCAB 1, TwCBDA, WebAB, WhAm H*
Blatchford, Thomas Wyndeatt 1794-1866 *ApCAB Sup*
Blatchley, Willis Stanley 1859-1940 *WhAm 1*
Blatherwick, Alex Arthur 1881-1952 *NatCAB 41*
Blatherwick, Norman Robert 1887-1961 *NatCAB 46*
Blatherwick, Wilfred Francis 1890-1960 *NatCAB 48*
Blathwayt, William 1649?-1717 *ApCAB*
Blatnik, John Anton 1911- *BiDrAC*
Blatt, Maurice Lamm 1879-1944 *NatCAB 33*
Blatt, William M 1876- *WhAm 5*
Blatteis, Simon Risefeld 1876-1968 *WhAm 5*
Blattenberger, Raymond 1892-1971 *WhAm 5*
Blattmachr, George Gustav 1908-1972 *NatCAB 57*
Blau, Max Friedrich 1864-1923 *WhAm 1*
Blauch, Lloyd E 1889-1974 *WhAm 6*
Blauel, Charles *NewYHSD*
Blauer, William Edward 1879-1957 *NatCAB 46, WhAm 3*
Blaustein, David 1866-1912 *DcAmB*
Blaustein, Jacob 1892-1970 *WhAm 5*
Blaustein, Louis 1869-1937 *WhAm 1*
Blauteau, E *NewYHSD*
Blauvelt, Augustus 1832-1900 *ApCAB, TwCBDA*
Blauvelt, Bradford 1906-1969 *WhAm 5*
Blauvelt, Charles F 1824-1900 *NewYHSD, WhAm 1*
Blauvelt, George Alanson 1866-1924 *NatCAB 20*
Blauvelt, Hiram B Demarest 1897-1957 *NatCAB 47*
Blauvelt, James Gillmor 1871-1946 *NatCAB 34*
Blauvelt, Lillian Evans 1873-1947 *NatCAB 12, WomWWA 14*
Blauvelt, Lillian Evans 1874-1947 *WhAm 2*
Blauvelt, Martin Post 1865-1923 *WhAm 1*
Blauvelt, Mary Taylor 1868- *WomWWA 14*
Blauvelt, Mary Taylor 1869- *WhAm 5*
Blauw, Willem *DcScB*

Blavatsky, Helena Petrovna Hahn 1831-1891 *AmBi, DcAmB, DcAmReB, NatCAB 15, NotAW, TwCBDA, WhAm H*
Blavatsky, Helene Petrovna 1820-1891 *AmWom*
Blavatsky, Helene Petrovna 1831?-1891 *ApCAB*
Blaxter, Henry Vaughan 1882-1948 *WhAm 2*
Blaylock, Louis 1849-1932 *WhAm 1*
Blayney, John McClusky 1841-1909 *WhAm 1*
Blayney, Lindsey 1874-1971 *WhAm 6*
Blayney, T Lindsey 1874-1971 *WhAm 5*
Blayney, William Nassau Walker 1859-1936 *NatCAB 27*
Blazer, Paul Garrett 1890-1966 *WhAm 4*
Blazer, Rexford Sydney 1907-1974 *NatCAB 57, WhAm 6*
Blazhko, Sergei Nikolaevich 1870-1956 *DcScB*
Bleach, Herny Augustus 1872- *WhoColR*
Bleakley, Ben Joseph 1894-1969 *NatCAB 57*
Bleakley, Cara Rogers *WomWWA 14*
Bleakley, Orrin Dubbs 1854-1927 *BiDrAC*
Bleakley, William Francis 1883-1969 *WhAm 5*
Bleakley, William James 1849-1908 *NatCAB 43*
Blease, Coleman Livingston 1868-1942 *ApCAB X, BiDrAC, DcAmB S3, NatCAB 15, WhAm 1, WhAm 2, WhAmP*
Blech, Miss C *NewYHSD*
Bleckley, Logan Edwin 1827-1907 *DcAmB, NatCAB 2, TwCBDA, WhAm 1*
Bleckley, Olle Evans *WomWWA 14*
Bleckwenn, William Jefferson 1895-1965 *NatCAB 51, WhAm 4*
Bledsoe, Albert Taylor 1809-1877 *ApCAB, BiDConf, DcAmB, Drake, McGEWB, NatCAB 8, TwCBDA, WhAm H, WhAmP*
Bledsoe, Benjamin Franklin 1874-1938 *ApCAB X, WhAm 1*
Bledsoe, Jesse 1776-1836 *BiDrAC, WhAm H*
Bledsoe, Jesse 1776-1837 *ApCAB, BiAUS, Drake, NatCAB 11, TwCBDA*
Bledsoe, Murff Franklin 1879-1929 *NatCAB 23*
Bledsoe, Samuel Thomas 1868-1939 *NatCAB 29, WhAm 1*
Bledsoe, Thomas Braden 1885-1959 *NatCAB 47*
Bledsoe, Walter Arthur 1875-1950 *NatCAB 36*
Bleecker, Ann Eliza 1752-1783 *ApCAB, DcAmB, Drake, NatCAB 8, NotAW, TwCBDA, WhAm H*
Bleecker, Anthony 1770-1827 *ApCAB, TwCBDA*
Bleecker, Harmanus 1779-1849 *ApCAB, BiDrAC, NatCAB 11, TwCBDA, WhAm H, WhAmP*
Bleecker, Hermanus 1779-1849 *BiAUS, Drake*
Bleecker, John R *NewYHSD*
Bleecker, John VanBenthuysen 1847-1922 *WhAm 1*
Bleecker, Richard Wade 1821-1875 *ApCAB*
Blegen, Carl William 1887-1971 *WhAm 5*
Bleich, Clements Harry 1911-1972 *WhAm 5*
Bleicher, Clarence E 1890-1952 *WhAm 3*
Bleicher, Hugo 1899- *WhWW-II*
Bleile, Albert Martin 1856-1933 *NatCAB 24*
Bleininger, Albert Victor 1873-1946 *NatCAB 39, WhAm 2*
Bleistein, George 1861- *NatCAB 1*
Blenac, Charles De *ApCAB*
Blender, Dorothea Klotz 1908-1972 *WhAm 5*
Blenderman, Helen Clara Riedel 1881- *WomWWA 14*
Blendinger, Fred Lawrence 1867-1929 *ApCAB X, WhAm 1*
Blener, James 1834?- *NewYHSD*
Blenk, James Hubert 1856-1917 *DcAmB, NatCAB 14, WhAm 1*
Blenker, Lewis 1812-1863 *Drake*
Blenker, Louis 1812-1863 *ApCAB, TwCBDA*
Blenkinsop, Peter 1818-1896 *WhAm H*
Blenner, Carle John 1862-1952 *WhAm 3*
Blennerhassett, Adeline Agnew *ApCAB*
Blennerhassett, Harman 1764?-1831 *ApCAB, NatCAB 13, TwCBDA*
Blennerhassett, Harman 1765-1831 *AmBi, DcAmB, WhAm H, WhAmP*
Blennerhassett, Herman 1767-1831 *Drake*
Blesh, Abraham Lincoln 1866-1934 *WhAm 1*

Blesse, Frederick Arthur 1888-1954 *WhAm 3*
Blessed, Clarence Dewey 1898-1970
NatCAB 55
Blessing, Edgar M 1876- *WhAm 5*
Blessing, George Frederick 1875-1921 *WhAm 1*
Blessing, Lewis Greene 1873-1964 *WhAm 4*
Blessing, Riley Andrew 1875- *WhAm 5*
Blethen, Alden Joseph 1846-1915 *NatCAB 17,*
WhAm 1
Blethen, Clarance Brettun 1879-1941
NatCAB 38
Blethen, Clarence Brettun 1879-1941 *WhAm 2*
Blethen, Frank Alden 1904-1967 *WhAm 5*
Blethen, William Kingsley 1913-1967 *WhAm 4*
Bleuler, Eugen 1857-1939 *McGEWB*
Blewer, Clarence Frederick 1907-1968 *WhAm 5*
Blewett, Ben 1856-1917 *WhAm 1*
Blewett, Benjamin T 1820-1914 *NatCAB 6*
Blewett, Jean 1872- *WomWWA 14*
Blewett, William E, Jr. 1894-1965 *WhAm 4*
Bley, Caroline Averill 1858- *WomWWA 14*
Bleyer, Herman 1850-1924 *WhAm 3*
Bleyer, J Mount 1859- *WhAm 4*
Bleyer, Willard Grosvenor 1873-1935 *BiDAmEd,*
DcAmB S1, WhAm 1
Blichfeldt, Emil Harry 1874- *WhAm 5*
Blichfeldt, Eva Potter 1875- *WomWWA 14*
Blichfeldt, Hans Frederick 1873-1945 *DcScB*
Blichfeldt, Hans Frederik 1873-1945 *DcAmB S3,*
WhAm 2
Blickensderfer, Herman 1897-1965 *NatCAB 53*
Blickensderfer, Joseph Patrick 1894-1960
WhAm 4
Blickensderfer, Robert 1841- *WhAm 4*
Blicker, George 1833?- *NewYHSD*
Bliem, Milton Jacob 1860- *WhAm 4*
Bligh, James Dominic 1895-1967 *NatCAB 54*
Bligh, Julia Morum 1855- *WomWWA 14*
Bligh, William 1754-1817 *McGEWB*
Blight, Reynold E 1879-1951 *WhAm 3*
Blim, Miles G 1898-1972 *WhAm 6*
Blinn, Charles Payson, Jr. 1879- *WhAm 6*
Blinn, Holbrook 1872-1928 *DcAmB,*
NatCAB 21, WhAm 1
Blinn, Oscar Samuel 1888-1958 *NatCAB 47*
Blinn, Randolph 1887-1943 *WhAm 2*
Blish, George William 1837-1906 *NatCAB 2*
Blish, H A *NewYHSD*
Bliss, Aaron Thomas 1837-1906 *BiDrAC,*
DcAmB, NatCAB 13, TwCBDA,
WhAm 1, WhAmP
Bliss, Alexander 1827-1896 *ApCAB Sup*
Bliss, Andrew Richard, Jr. 1887-1941
NatCAB 31
Bliss, Andrew Richard, Jr. 1889-1941 *WhAm 1*
Bliss, Anna Elvira *NotAW*
Bliss, Archibald M 1837-1923 *BiAUS*
Bliss, Archibald Meserole 1838-1923 *BiDrAC,*
WhAmP
Bliss, Arthur 1891-1975 *WhAm 6*
Bliss, Charles Bemis 1868- *WhAm 4*
Bliss, Collins Pechin 1866-1946 *WhAm 2*
Bliss, Cornelius Newton 1833-1911 *AmBi,*
ApCAB Sup, ApCAB X, BiDrUSE,
DcAmB, NatCAB 11, TwCBDA,
WhAm 1, WhAmP
Bliss, Cornelius Newton 1874-1949 *DcAmB S4,*
WhAm 2
Bliss, D Spencer d1950 *WhAm 3*
Bliss, Daniel 1740-1806 *ApCAB*
Bliss, Daniel 1823-1916 *AmBi, ApCAB,*
DcAmB, NatCAB 19, WhAm 1
Bliss, Delos 1841- *NatCAB 10*
Bliss, Don Alfonso 1854- *WhAm 4*
Bliss, Don C 1868- *WhAm 4*
Bliss, Donald Everett 1903-1951 *NatCAB 40*
Bliss, Edgar Sumner 1867-1942 *NatCAB 32*
Bliss, Edwin Elisha 1817-1892 *DcAmB,*
WhAm H
Bliss, Edwin Munsell 1848-1919 *DcAmB,*
WhAm 1
Bliss, Eleanora Emma *WomWWA 14*
Bliss, Eleanora Frances 1883- *WomWWA 14*
Bliss, Eliakim Raymond 1846-1923 *WhAm 1*
Bliss, Eliphalet Williams 1836-1903 *DcAmB,*
NatCAB 15, WhAm 1
Bliss, Elizabeth Bancroft 1868- *WomWWA 14*
Bliss, Elmer Jared 1867-1945 *WhAm 2*

Bliss, Eugene Frederick 1836- *WhAm 4*
Bliss, Frederick Jones 1859-1937 *DcAmB S2,*
WhAm 4
Bliss, George 1793-1873 *ApCAB, TwCBDA*
Bliss, George 1813-1868 *BiAUS, BiDrAC,*
WhAm H, WhAmP
Bliss, George 1816-1896 *DcAmB, NatCAB 8,*
WhAm H
Bliss, George 1830-1897 *DcAmB, TwCBDA,*
WhAm H, WhAmP
Bliss, George Laurence 1896- *WhAm 5*
Bliss, George Ripley 1816-1893 *NatCAB 19*
Bliss, George Yemens 1864-1924 *NatCAB 25,*
WhAm 1
Bliss, Gilbert Ames 1876-1951 *DcAmB S5,*
WhAm 3
Bliss, Gilbert Ames 1876-1961 *DcScB*
Bliss, Harding 1911-1971 *WhAm 5*
Bliss, Harold Nelson 1886-1956 *NatCAB 46*
Bliss, Harry Hayner 1871-1937 *WhAm 1*
Bliss, Henry Evelyn 1870-1955 *DcAmLiB,*
WhAm 5
Bliss, Horace G *NewYHSD*
Bliss, Howard Sweetser 1860-1920 *DcAmB,*
NatCAB 19, WhAm 1
Bliss, J Herbert 1893-1945 *NatCAB 35*
Bliss, James Harris 1889-1952 *WhAm 3*
Bliss, John Carlton 1868-1924 *WhAm 3*
Bliss, John Murray 1771-1834 *ApCAB*
Bliss, Jonathan 1742-1822 *ApCAB, DcAmB,*
WhAm H
Bliss, Justin Ashley 1816-1901 *NatCAB 25*
Bliss, Laura Adella *WomWWA 14*
Bliss, Lizzie Plummer 1864-1931 *NotAW*
Bliss, Louis Denton 1871- *WhAm 5*
Bliss, Louis G 1907-1972 *WhAm 5*
Bliss, Malcolm Andrews 1863-1934 *WhAm 1*
Bliss, Mary H 1867- *WomWWA 14*
Bliss, Mildred 1879- *WhAm 6*
Bliss, Paul Southworth 1889-1940 *WhAm 1*
Bliss, Philemon 1813-1889 *BiDrAC,*
NatCAB 29, TwCBDA, WhAmP
Bliss, Philemon 1814-1889 *BiAUS, DcAmB,*
WhAm H
Bliss, Philip Elijah 1885-1939 *WhAm 1*
Bliss, Philip Paul 1838-1876 *AmBi, ApCAB,*
DcAmB, NatCAB 8, TwCBDA
Bliss, Phillip Paul 1838-1876 *WhAm H*
Bliss, Porter Cornelius 1838-1885 *AmBi,*
ApCAB, DcAmB, TwCBDA, WhAm H
Bliss, Ralph Kenneth 1880-1972 *WhAm 6*
Bliss, Raymond Whitcomb 1888-1965
NatCAB 52, WhAm 4
Bliss, Richard 1842- *TwCBDA*
Bliss, Robert Pratt 1861- *WhAm 4*
Bliss, Robert Woods 1875-1962 *ApCAB X,*
NatCAB 49, WhAm 4
Bliss, Ruth Shorkley 1885- *WomWWA 14*
Bliss, Sydney Rushton 1878-1939 *NatCAB 45*
Bliss, Tasker Howard 1853-1930 *AmBi,*
ApCAB X, DcAmB S1, NatCAB 21,
WebAB, WebAMB, WhAm 1
Bliss, Walter Phelps 1870-1924 *NatCAB 20,*
WhAm 1
Bliss, William 1834-1907 *WhAm 1*
Bliss, William Carpenter 1874- *WhAm 5*
Bliss, William Dwight Porter 1856-1926 *DcAmB,*
DcAmReB, NatCAB 20, WhAm 1
Bliss, William Henry 1844-1932 *NatCAB 27,*
WhAm 1
Bliss, William J 1915-1973 *WhAm 5*
Bliss, William Julian Albert 1867-1940
WhAm 1
Bliss, William Lancer 1876- *WhAm 6*
Bliss, William Root 1825-1906 *WhAm 1*
Bliss, William Wallace Smith 1815-1853
ApCAB, Drake
Bliss, Zenas Randall 1835-1900 *TwCBDA*
Bliss, Zenas Work 1867-1957 *WhAm 3*
Bliss, Zenos Randall 1835-1900 *ApCAB Sup*
Blissett, Francis 1773?-1848 *Drake*
Blisterfeld, J H *DcScB*
Blitch, Iris Faircloth 1912- *BiDrAC, WhAmP*
Blitz, Anne Dudley 1881-1951 *WhAm 3*
Blitz, Antonio 1810-1877 *ApCAB, DcAmB,*
WhAm H
Blitzstein, Marc 1905-1964 *NatCAB 52,*

WebAB, WhAm 4
Bliven, Miss M A *NewYHSD*
Blixen-Finecke, Karen Christentze 1885-1962
WhAm 4
Blixen-Finecke, Karen Christentze *see also*
Dinesen, Isak
Blizard, Everitt Pinnell 1916-1966 *NatCAB 56*
Blizzard, Reese d1940 *WhAm 4*
Blizzard, Warren Lale 1888-1954 *REnAW,*
WhAm 3
Bloch, Adolph 1873-1948 *NatCAB 37*
Bloch, Albert 1882-1961 *WhAm 4*
Bloch, Alexander 1881- *WhAm 1*
Bloch, Bernard 1907-1965 *WhAm 4*
Bloch, Charles Julian 1893-1974 *WhAm 6*
Bloch, Claude Charles 1878-1967 *NatCAB 53,*
WhAm 4A
Bloch, Ernest 1880-1959 *McGEWB,*
NatCAB 44, WebAB, WhAm 3
Bloch, Felix 1905- *AsBiEn, WebAB*
Bloch, Henry 1883-1970 *NatCAB 55*
Bloch, Herbert Aaron 1904-1965 *NatCAB 51,*
WhAm 4
Bloch, Ivan 1836-1902 *WhoMilH*
Bloch, Jesse A d1951 *WhAm 3*
Bloch, Julius 1888-1966 *WhAm 4*
Bloch, Konrad Emil 1912- *AsBiEn, WebAB*
Bloch, Louis 1875-1951 *NatCAB 39, WhAm 3*
Bloch, Marc 1886-1944 *McGEWB*
Bloch, Max Emanuel 1874-1943 *NatCAB 32*
Bloch, Monroe Percy 1894-1970 *WhAm 5*
Bloch, Oscar Edgeworth 1871-1951 *NatCAB 40*
Bloch, Robert Gustav 1894-1975 *WhAm 6*
Block, Adriaen *AmBi, ApCAB, DcAmB,*
NatCAB 10, WhAm H
Block, Alexander 1881-1953 *NatCAB 43*
Block, Anita C 1882- *WomWWA 14*
Block, Edward 1902-1961 *NatCAB 51,*
WhAm 4
Block, Elizabeth Orme *WomWWA 14*
Block, H 1835?- *NewYHSD*
Block, Herbert Lawrence 1909- *EncAB,*
WebAB
Block, Herman 1891-1951 *NatCAB 44*
Block, J Horace 1897-1961 *NatCAB 46*
Block, John 1879-1969 *NatCAB 54*
Block, Julius Herrman 1860-1915 *NatCAB 16*
Block, Karl Morgan 1886-1958 *NatCAB 45,*
WhAm 3
Block, Laurens *NewYHSD*
Block, Leopold E 1869-1952 *WhAm 3*
Block, Louis James 1851-1927 *WhAm 1*
Block, Melvin A 1908-1963 *NatCAB 52,*
WhAm 4
Block, Paul 1877-1941 *DcAmB S3, WhAm 1*
Block, Philip Dee 1871-1942 *WhAm 2*
Block, Ralph 1889-1974 *WhAm 6*
Block, Rudolph 1870-1940 *WhAm 1*
Block, S John 1880-1955 *NatCAB 41*
Block, Samuel Westheimer 1911-1970 *WhAm 5*
Block, Siegfried 1882-1955 *NatCAB 44*
Block, Virginia Lee 1902-1970 *NatCAB 56*
Blocker, Dan 1929-1972 *WhAm 5*
Blocker, Daniel James 1873-1957 *WhAm 3*
Blocker, William Preston 1892-1947 *WhAm 2*
Blocklinger, Gottfried 1847-1930 *WhAm 1*
Blocksom, Augustus Perry 1854-1931 *WhAm 1*
Blocksom, Berget Henri 1875-1951 *NatCAB 45*
Blodget, Lorin 1823-1901 *ApCAB, DcAmB,*
NatCAB 4, TwCBDA, WhAm 1
Blodget, Samuel *NewYHSD*
Blodget, Samuel 1724-1807 *ApCAB, DcAmB,*
Drake, NatCAB 13
Blodget, Samuel 1757-1814 *DcAmB*
Blodget, Samuel *see also* Blodgett, Samuel
Blodgett, Benjamin Coleman 1838-1925
NatCAB 20
Blodgett, Benjamin Colman 1838-1925 *DcAmB,*
WhAm 4
Blodgett, Charles Erastus 1861-1929
NatCAB 24
Blodgett, Constantine 1802-1879 *NatCAB 9*
Blodgett, Daisy Albertine Peck 1862-1947
BiCAW, NatCAB 37
Blodgett, Delos Abiel 1825-1908 *NatCAB 6*
Blodgett, Edward Everett 1865- *ApCAB X*
Blodgett, Edward Wilkinson 1857-1933
NatCAB 29

Blodgett, Foster 1826-1877 *ApCAB*
Blodgett, Francis Branch 1875- *WhAm 5*
Blodgett, Frank Dickinson 1871- *WhAm 5*
Blodgett, Henry Williams 1821-1905
ApCAB Sup, *BiAUS*, *DcAmB*, *NatCAB 6*,
WhAm 1
Blodgett, Hugh Carlton 1896-1972 *WhAm 5*
Blodgett, Isaac N 1838-1905 *NatCAB 12*,
WhAm 1
Blodgett, John Taggard 1859-1912 *WhAm 1*
Blodgett, John Wood 1860-1951 *DcAmB S5*,
NatCAB 38, *WhAm 3*
Blodgett, Katharine Frances 1880-
WomWWA 14
Blodgett, Mabel Louise Fuller 1869-1959
WhAm 3, *WomWWA 14*
Blodgett, Minnie Cumnock *WomWWA 14*
Blodgett, Rufus 1834-1910 *ApCAB Sup*,
BiDrAC, *NatCAB 1*, *TwCBDA*,
WhAm 1, *WhAmP*
Blodgett, Samuel 1724-1807 *WhAm H*
Blodgett, Samuel 1757-1814 *WhAm H*
Blodgett, Samuel see also Blodget, Samuel
Blodgett, Thomas Harper 1877-1964 *WhAm 4*
Blodgett, Thurston P 1899-1971 *WhAm 5*
Blodgett, Wells Howard 1839-1929 *NatCAB 12*,
WhAm 1
Bloede, Gertrude 1845-1905 *AmWom*, *DcAmB*,
NatCAB 10, *WhAm 1*
Bloede, Marie 1821-1870 *ApCAB*
Bloede, Victor Gustav 1849-1937 *NatCAB 27*
Bloede, Victor Gustave 1849-1937 *WhAm 1*
Bloedel, Julius Harold 1864-1957 *NatCAB 46*,
WhAm 5
Bloedorn, Charles Frederick William 1880-1971
NatCAB 57
Bloedorn, Fernando Germane 1913-1975
WhAm 6
Bloembergen, Nicolaas 1920- *AsBiEn*
Blois, Marsden Scott 1891-1964 *WhAm 4*
Blok, Aleksandr Aleksandrovich 1880-1921
McGEWB
Blom, Frans 1893-1963 *WhAm 4*
Blomberg, Werner Von 1878-1943 *WhWW-II*,
WhoMilH
Blomgren, Carl August 1865- *WhAm 4*
Blommaert, Samuel 1590?-1670? *ApCAB*
Blomquist, Edwin Oscar 1894-1965 *WhAm 4*
Blomquist, Hugo Leander 1888-1964
NatCAB 52, *WhAm 4*
Blomstrand, Christian Wilhelm 1826-1897
DcScB
Blon, E Van *NewYHSD*
Blonde, Adolph 1812?- *NewYHSD*
Blonde, Geston 1839?- *NewYHSD*
Blondel, Andre Eugene 1863-1938 *DcScB*
Blondel, Jacob D 1817-1877 *NewYHSD*,
WhAm H
Blondel, Nicolas-Francois d1686 *DcScB*
Blondin, Emile Gravelet 1830?- *ApCAB*
Blondin, M 1830?- *Drake*
Blondlot, Rene-Prosper 1849-1930 *DcScB*
Blondner, Aline Reese *AmWom*
Blood, Aretas 1816-1898 *NatCAB 7*
Blood, Benjamin Paul 1832-1919 *DcAmB*
Blood, Bryant Harmon 1865-1946 *NatCAB 36*
Blood, Charles H 1866- *WhAm 4*
Blood, Henry Ames 1838- *WhAm 1*
Blood, Henry Hooper 1872-1942 *NatCAB 38*,
WhAm 2
Blood, John H *NewYHSD*
Blood, Robert McCutchins 1883-1950 *WhAm 3*
Blood, Robert Oscar 1887-1975 *WhAm 6*
Blood, William Henry, Jr. 1866-1933
NatCAB 26, *WhAm 1*
Bloodgood, Clare Sutton 1870-1907 *WhAm 1*
Bloodgood, Delavan 1831-1902 *ApCAB*,
NatCAB 4, *TwCBDA*, *WhAm 1*
Bloodgood, Joseph Colt 1867-1935 *DcAmB S1*,
NatCAB 26, *WhAm 1*
Bloodgood, Simeon DeWitt 1799-1866 *ApCAB*
Bloodgood, Wheeler Peckham 1871-1930
WhAm 1
Bloodgood, William Denton 1864-1940
NatCAB 31
Bloodworth, Andrew Dunn Franklin 1894-1955
WhAm 3

Bloodworth, Francis Douglas 1842-1920
NatCAB 18
Bloodworth, Timothy 1736-1814 *ApCAB*,
BiAUS, *BiDrAC*, *DcAmB*, *Drake*,
NatCAB 5, *WhAm H*, *WhAmP*
Bloodworth, Timothy 1736-1815 *TwCBDA*
Bloom, Bessie Luella Kutcher 1880-
WomWWA 14
Bloom, Charles James 1886-1947 *WhAm 2*
Bloom, Edgar Selden 1874-1955 *WhAm 3*
Bloom, Isaac 1716?-1803 *BiAUS*, *BiDrAC*
Bloom, Issac 1716?-1803 *WhAm H*
Bloom, John Porter 1924- *REnAW*
Bloom, Lansing Bartlett 1880-1946 *REnAW*
Bloom, Melvin Harold 1925-1974 *WhAm 6*
Bloom, Nathan Peixotto 1890-1968 *NatCAB 54*
Bloom, Sidney 1907-1965 *NatCAB 54*
Bloom, Sol 1870-1949 *BiDrAC*, *DcAmB S4*,
NatCAB 38, *WhAm 2*, *WhAmP*
Bloom, William 1899-1972 *NatCAB 57*
Bloom, William Knighton 1866-1934 *WhAm 1*
Bloomberg, Maxwell Hillel 1899-1968 *WhAm 5*
Bloome, Robert *NewYHSD*
Bloomer, Amelia Jenks 1818-1894 *AmBi*,
AmWom, *ApCAB*, *DcAmB*, *McGEWB*,
NatCAB 8, *NotAW*, *TwCBDA*, *WebAB*,
WhAm H, *WhAmP*
Bloomer, Edgar Nelson 1896-1952 *NatCAB 45*,
WhAm 4
Bloomer, Edward *NewYHSD*
Bloomer, Gaylord Talmage 1895-1953
NatCAB 44
Bloomer, Millard J 1870- *WhAm 5*
Bloomer, Millard J, Jr. 1899-1974 *WhAm 6*
Bloomer, Philip Arthur 1876-1950 *NatCAB 39*
Bloomfield, Arthur Collier 1873- *WhAm 5*
Bloomfield, Arthur Leonard 1888-1962
NatCAB 50
Bloomfield, Charles Cunningham 1843-
NatCAB 17
Bloomfield, Daniel 1890-1963 *NatCAB 52*,
WhAm 4
Bloomfield, James Henry 1888-1963
NatCAB 50
Bloomfield, Joseph d1823 *ApCAB*, *BiAUS*,
Drake
Bloomfield, Joseph 1753-1823 *BiDrAC*,
DcAmB, *WhAm H*, *WhAmP*
Bloomfield, Joseph 1755?-1823 *NatCAB 5*,
TwCBDA
Bloomfield, Leonard 1887-1949 *BiDAmEd*,
DcAmB S4, *McGEWB*, *WebAB*,
WhAm 2
Bloomfield, Maurice 1855-1928 *AmBi*,
ApCAB X, *DcAmB*, *NatCAB 10*,
NatCAB 38, *WhAm 1*
Bloomfield, Meyer 1878-1938 *DcAmB S2*,
WhAm 1
Bloomfield, Sir Thomas 1744-1822 *ApCAB Sup*
Bloomfield-Moore, Clara Sophia Jessup *NotAW*
Bloomfield-Zeisler, Fannie 1863-1927 *DcAmB*,
NotAW
Bloomgarden, Solomon 1870-1927 *DcAmB*
Bloomgarden, Solomon 1871-1927 *AmBi*
Bloomingdale, Charles 1868-1942 *WhAm 2*
Bloomingdale, Emanuel Watson 1852-1928
WhAm 1
Bloomingdale, Joseph Benjamin 1842-1904
NatCAB 2
Bloomingdale, Joseph Bernard 1842-1904
NatCAB 30
Bloomingdale, Samuel Joseph 1873-1968
WhAm 5
Bloomstein, Elizabeth Lee 1859-
WomWWA 14
Bloomstein, Max, Jr. 1906-1960 *WhAm 4*
Bloor, Alfred Janson d1917 *WhAm 1*
Bloor, Ella Reeve 1862-1951 *DcAmB S5*
Bloor, Walter Ray 1877-1966 *WhAm 4*
Bloss, Benjamin Gorham 1819-1895 *NatCAB 8*
Bloss, James Ramsdell 1881-1951 *WhAm 3*
Bloss, Michael *NewYHSD*
Bloss, William Clough 1795-1863 *NatCAB 12*
Blosser, Clarence 1874-1924 *NatCAB 20*
Blosser, Emanuel 1877-1953 *NatCAB 42*
Blossom, Dudley Stuart 1879-1938 *NatCAB 28*
Blossom, Francis 1870- *WhAm 5*
Blossom, George W, Jr. 1890-1960 *WhAm 4*

Blossom, Harold Hill 1879-1935 *WhAm 1*
Blossom, Henry Martyn, Jr. 1866-1919
WhAm 1
Blossom, Robert Alden 1923-1971 *WhAm 6*
Blossom, Thomas d1633 *ApCAB*
Blot, Pierre 1818?-1874 *ApCAB*
Blough, Earl 1876-1971 *WhAm 5*
Blough, Elijah Robert 1878- *WhAm 6*
Blough, Sanford P 1920-1969 *WhAm 5*
Blount, Alma 1866- *WomWWA 14*
Blount, Anna Ellsworth 1872- *WomWWA 14*
Blount, George Dexter 1881- *WhAm 6*
Blount, George Wesley *WhoColR*
Blount, Henry Fitch 1829-1915 *ApCAB X*,
WhAm 4
Blount, James Henderson 1837-1903 *BiAUS*,
BiDrAC, *DcAmB*, *NatCAB 13*, *WhAmP*
Blount, James Henderson 1869-1918 *WhAm 1*
Blount, James Polk 1849-1928 *NatCAB 23*
Blount, Marie Ross 1881- *WomWWA 14*
Blount, Roy A 1913-1974 *WhAm 6*
Blount, Thomas d1812 *BiAUS*, *TwCBDA*
Blount, Thomas 1759-1812 *BiDrAC*, *DcAmB*,
WhAm H, *WhAmP*
Blount, Thomas 1760-1812 *ApCAB*, *Drake*,
NatCAB 2
Blount, William d1810 *BiAUS*
Blount, William 1744-1800 *ApCAB*, *Drake*
Blount, William 1749-1800 *AmBi*, *BiDrAC*,
DcAmB, *EncAAH*, *NatCAB 7*, *REnAW*,
TwCBDA, *WebAB*, *WhAm H*, *WhAmP*
Blount, William Alexander 1851-1921
ApCAB X, *NatCAB 9*, *WhAm 1*
Blount, William Grainger 1784-1827 *BiAUS*,
BiDrAC, *WhAm H*, *WhAmP*
Blount, Willie d1835 *BiAUS*, *Drake*
Blount, Willie 1767-1835 *ApCAB*, *TwCBDA*
Blount, Willie 1768-1835 *DcAmB*, *NatCAB 7*,
WhAm H, *WhAmP*
Blount, Winton Malcolm 1921- *BiDrUSE*
Blow, Allmand M 1891-1948 *WhAm 2*
Blow, Alziere Kennerly 1866- *WomWWA 14*
Blow, George Preston 1860-1922 *NatCAB 29*
Blow, Henry Taylor 1817-1875 *ApCAB*,
BiAUS, *BiDrAC*, *DcAmB*, *Drake Sup*,
NatCAB 4, *TwCBDA*, *WhAm H*,
WhAmP
Blow, Susan Elizabeth 1843-1916 *AmBi*,
BiDAmEd, *DcAmB*, *NotAW*
Blowers, Sampson Salter 1742-1842 *DcAmB*,
Drake, *WhAm H*
Blowers, Sampson Salters 1742-1842 *ApCAB*
Bloxham, William Dunnington 1835-1911
DcAmB, *NatCAB 11*, *TwCBDA*,
WhAm 1, *WhAmP*
BLT *WebAB*
Blu, Elmer Francis 1882-1961 *NatCAB 49*
Blucher, Franz 1896-1959 *WhAm 3*
Blucher, Gebhard Leberecht Von 1742-1819
McGEWB
Blucher, Gebhard Liberecht Von 1742-1819
WhoMilH
Blucher, Joseph 1810?- *NewYHSD*
Blucher, Xavier *NewYHSD*
Blue, Burdette 1886-1943 *NatCAB 33*,
WhAm 2
Blue, Frederick Omar 1872- *WhAm 5*
Blue, John, Jr. 1901-1968 *NatCAB 55*
Blue, John Howard 1877- *WhAm 5*
Blue, Richard Whiting 1841-1907 *BiDrAC*
Blue, Rupert 1867-1948 *NatCAB 15*,
NatCAB 40
Blue, Rupert 1868-1948 *WhAm 2*
Blue, Thomas Fountain 1866-1935 *DcAmLiB*,
WhoColR
Blue, Victor 1865-1928 *ApCAB Sup*, *DcAmB*,
NatCAB 15, *WhAm 1*
Blue Eagle, Acee 1907-1959 *IIBEAAW*,
REnAW
Bluemel, Charles Sidney 1884-1960 *NatCAB 52*
Bluemner, Oscar Florians 1867-1938 *DcAmB S2*
Bluett, John Joseph 1905-1965 *WhAm 4*
Bluford, Ferdinand Douglas 1882-1955
NatCAB 47, *WhAm 3*
Bluford, John Henry 1876- *WhoColR*
Blugerman, Lee N 1899-1972 *WhAm 5*
Blum, Albert 1869-1940 *NatCAB 31*
Blum, Charlotte 1882- *WomWWA 14*

Blum, Daniel 1900-1965 *WhAm 4*
Blum, Edward Charles 1863-1946 *WhAm 2*
Blum, Elias 1881- *WhAm 6*
Blum, Harry d1971 *WhAm 5*
Blum, Harry H d1966 *WhAm 4*
Blum, Herman 1885-1973 *NatCAB 57*
Blum, Jerome S 1884- *IlBEAAW*
Blum, Leon 1872-1950 *McGEWB, WhAm 2A, WhWW-II*
Blum, Richard Leon 1872-1950 *NatCAB 40*
Blum, Robert 1911-1965 *WhAm 4*
Blum, Robert D *NewYHSD*
Blum, Robert Frederic 1857-1903 *ApCAB X*
Blum, Robert Frederick 1857-1903 *AmBi, DcAmB, NatCAB 10, TwCBDA, WhAm 1*
Blum, Samuel J 1849- *WhAm 3*
Blum, Theodor 1883-1962 *NatCAB 49*
Blum, William 1881-1972 *WhAm 5*
Blumberg, Henry 1902-1958 *NatCAB 47*
Blumberg, Hyman 1885-1968 *WhAm 5*
Blumberg, Leo 1894-1971 *NatCAB 56*
Blumberg, Nathan J d1960 *WhAm 4*
Blume, Clinton Willis 1898-1973 *WhAm 6*
Blume, Fred H 1875- *WhAm 5*
Blume, John Calvin 1892-1965 *NatCAB 52*
Blume, Louis Frederick 1882-1946 *NatCAB 35*
Blume, Peter 1906- *BnEnAmA*
Blumenau, Lili *BnEnAmA*
Blumenbach, Johann Friedrich 1752-1840 *DcScB*
Blumenberg, John Herman 1886-1953 *NatCAB 41*
Blumenberg, Marc A 1851-1913 *WhAm 1*
Blumenfeld, Ralph David 1864- *WhAm 4*
Blumenfield, Samuel M 1901-1972 *WhAm 5*
Blumenschein, Ernest Leonard 1874-1960 *IlBEAAW, REnAW, WhAm 4*
Blumenschein, Helen Greene 1909- *IlBEAAW*
Blumenschein, Mary Shepard Greene 1869?-1958 *IlBEAAW, WhAm 3, WomWWA 14*
Blumenschein, William Leonard 1849-1916 *WhAm 1*
Blumenschine, Leonard G 1894- *WhAm 5*
Blumenstock, David Irving 1913-1963 *NatCAB 50*
Blumenthal, George 1858-1941 *NatCAB 30, WhAm 1*
Blumenthal, Gustave Adolph 1867- *WhAm 1*
Blumenthal, Sidney 1863-1948 *WhAm 2*
Blumentritt, Gunther 1892- *WhWW-II*
Blumer, G Alder 1857-1940 *WhAm 1*
Blumer, George 1872-1962 *NatCAB 49, WhAm 4*
Blumeyer, Arthur Adolphus 1886-1959 *WhAm 3*
Blumka, Leopold 1897-1973 *NatCAB 57*
Blumner, Frederick *NewYHSD*
Blun, Henry 1873-1939 *WhAm 1*
Blundell, James 1790-1877 *BiHiMed*
Blundon, Ada C Pollock 1863- *WomWWA 14*
Blunt, Edmund *NewYHSD*
Blunt, Edmund 1799-1866 *ApCAB, Drake, TwCBDA*
Blunt, Edmund March 1770-1862 *ApCAB, DcAmB, Drake, TwCBDA, WhAm H*
Blunt, George William 1802-1878 *AmBi, ApCAB, DcAmB, NatCAB 21, WhAm H*
Blunt, Hugh Francis 1877- *WhAm 5*
Blunt, James Gillpatrick 1826-1881 *AmBi, ApCAB, DcAmB, Drake, NatCAB 9, TwCBDA, WhAm H*
Blunt, James H 1837-1903 *TwCBDA*
Blunt, John Ellsworth 1828-1923 *WhAm 1*
Blunt, John S 1798-1835 *NewYHSD, WhAm H*
Blunt, Joseph 1792-1860 *ApCAB, Drake*
Blunt, Joseph S *NewYHSD*
Blunt, Katharine 1876-1954 *BiDAmEd, WhAm 3, WomWWA 14*
Blunt, Matthew M 1830-1907 *WhAm 1*
Blunt, Olive M 1859- *WomWWA 14*
Blunt, Simon F *NewYHSD*
Blunt, Stanhope English 1850-1926 *NatCAB 20, WhAm 1*
Blustein, Abraham 1885-1966 *NatCAB 53*
Blustein, Herman 1916-1970 *WhAm 6*
Blutau, Theodore Carl 1898-1954 *NatCAB 41*
Bly, Eleanor Schooley 1907-1969 *WhAm 5*

Bly, John Marius 1885-1947 *WhAm 2*
Bly, Myron Tuthill 1854-1933 *NatCAB 24*
Bly, Nellie *DcAmB, NotAW*
Bly, Nelly *WebAB, WhAm HA, WhAm 4*
Bly, Robert Stewart 1893-1958 *WhAm 3*
Blyde, Lewis J N 1889-1970 *WhAm 5*
Blyden, Edward Wilmot 1832-1912 *ApCAB, McGEWB*
Blyden, Larry 1925-1975 *WhAm 6*
Blydenburg, S *NewYHSD*
Blydenburgh, Charles Edward 1854-1921 *WhAm 1*
Blye, Birdice *WomWWA 14*
Blye, Birdie 1870?- *AmWom*
Blyley, Katherine Gillette d1961 *WhAm 4*
Blymyer, William Hervey 1865-1939 *NatCAB 28*
Blynn, Lloyd Ross 1875- *WhAm 5*
Blyth, Benjamin *NewYHSD*
Blyth, Charles Reginald 1883-1959 *NatCAB 51, WhAm 3*
Blyth, Edward 1810-1873 *DcScB*
Blyth, Lester Wilbert 1872-1936 *NatCAB 39*
Blyth, Samuel d1795 *NewYHSD*
Blythe, David Gilmore 1815-1865 *BnEnAmA*
Blythe, David Gilmour 1815-1865 *NewYHSD, WhAm H*
Blythe, Herbert 1847-1905 *AmBi, DcAmB, WebAB*
Blythe, James 1765-1842 *ApCAB, NatCAB 2, NatCAB 4, TwCBDA*
Blythe, Joseph Lee 1890-1949 *NatCAB 38, WhAm 3*
Blythe, Joseph William 1850-1909 *WhAm 1*
Blythe, Lucien Hoguet 1880-1913 *NatCAB 16*
Blythe, Samuel 1784-1814 *ApCAB*
Blythe, Samuel George 1868-1947 *WhAm 2*
Blythe, Vernon 1887-1918 *WebAB*
Blythin, Edward 1884-1958 *WhAm 3*
Blythin, Robert 1914-1966 *WhAm 4*
Blyukher, Vasilii Konstantinovich 1889-1938 *WhoMilH*
Boak, Arthur Edward Romilly 1888-1962 *NatCAB 49, WhAm 4*
Boak, Mabel *WomWWA 14*
Boak, Thomas Isaac Slack 1890-1969 *NatCAB 54*
Boal, James McC 1800?-1862 *NewYHSD*
Boal, Pierre DeLagarde 1895-1966 *WhAm 4*
Board, Cornelius d1745 *NatCAB 25*
Board, William Louis 1876- *WhoColR*
Boardley, B *NewYHSD*
Boardley, Peale *NewYHSD*
Boardley, Thomas 1813?- *NewYHSD*
Boardley, William *NewYHSD*
Boardman, Albert Barnes 1853-1933 *WhAm 1*
Boardman, Anne Calef 1881- *WomWWA 14*
Boardman, Charles d1879 *TwCBDA*
Boardman, Charles Willis 1885-1959 *WhAm 3*
Boardman, David Sherman 1768-1864 *ApCAB, BiAUS*
Boardman, Elijah 1760-1823 *ApCAB, BiAUS, BiDrAC, NatCAB 4, WhAm H*
Boardman, Mrs. G A *NewYHSD*
Boardman, George Dana 1801-1831 *ApCAB, Drake, TwCBDA*
Boardman, George Dana 1828-1903 *ApCAB, NatCAB 12, TwCBDA, WhAm 1*
Boardman, George Henry 1902-1969 *WhAm 5*
Boardman, George Nye 1825-1915 *NatCAB 6, WhAm 1*
Boardman, Harold Sherburne 1874- *WhAm 5*
Boardman, Harry Clow 1887-1956 *NatCAB 45, WhAm 3*
Boardman, Harry L 1866- *WhAm 4*
Boardman, Henry Augustus 1808-1880 *ApCAB, Drake, NatCAB 13, WhAm H*
Boardman, Henry Bradford 1869-1940 *NatCAB 32, WhAm 1*
Boardman, J Griffith 1904-1960 *NatCAB 50*
Boardman, Mabel Thorp 1860-1946 *BiCAW, DcAmB S4, NotAW, WhAm 2, WomWWA 14*
Boardman, Paul Lawrence 1906-1974 *WhAm 6*
Boardman, Samuel Hort 1866-1923 *NatCAB 23*
Boardman, Samuel Lane 1836-1914 *WhAm 1*
Boardman, Samuel Ward 1830-1917 *NatCAB 26, TwCBDA, WhAm 1*

Boardman, Sarah Hall *NotAW*
Boardman, Thomas Danforth 1784-1873 *AmBi, DcAmB, WhAm H*
Boardman, Thomas Danforth 1870-1946 *NatCAB 35*
Boardman, Waldo Elias 1851-1922 *NatCAB 14, WhAm 1*
Boardman, William Bradford 1871-1961 *WhAm 4*
Boardman, William G 1815?- *NewYHSD*
Boardman, William H *NewYHSD*
Boardman, William Henry 1846-1914 *WhAm 1*
Boardman, William Whiting 1794-1871 *BiAUS, BiDrAC, WhAm H*
Boarman, Aleck 1839-1916 *WhAm 3*
Boarman, Alexander 1839-1916 *BiDrAC*
Boarman, Charles d1879 *ApCAB*
Boarts, Robert Marsh 1904-1960 *NatCAB 48, WhAm 4*
Boas, Emil Leopold 1854-1912 *DcAmB, NatCAB 10, WhAm 1*
Boas, Ernst Philip 1891-1955 *WhAm 3*
Boas, Franz 1858-1942 *ApCAB X, BiDAmEd, DcAmB S3, DcScB, EncAB, McGEWB, NatCAB 12, REnAW, WebAB, WhAm 2*
Boas, Harriet Betty *WomWWA 14*
Boas, Ralph Philip 1887-1945 *NatCAB 35*
Boatner, Charles Jahleal 1849-1903 *BiDrAC, TwCBDA, WhAmP*
Boatner, Victor Vincent 1881-1950 *WhAm 2A*
Boatright, Byron B 1900-1957 *WhAm 3*
Boatright, Mody Coggin 1896-1970 *REnAW, WhAm 5*
Boatright, William Louis 1876-1938 *WhAm 1*
Boatsman, Deark Mennen 1848-1921 *NatCAB 19*
Boatwright, Frederic William 1868-1951 *NatCAB 46, WhAm 3*
Boatwright, Frederick William 1868-1951 *NatCAB 11*
Boatwright, Gertrude Floyd Harris *WhAm 5*
Boaz, Hiram Abiff 1866-1962 *WhAm 4, WhAm 5*
Bobadilla, Francisco d1502 *ApCAB*
Bobb, Byron Arthur 1870- *WhAm 5*
Bobb, Clyde S 1876-1957 *WhAm 3*
Bobb, Earl Victor 1874-1939 *WhAm 3*
Bobbett, Albert 1824?-1888? *NewYHSD*
Bobbett, Alfred *NewYHSD*
Bobbink, Lambertus Christian 1866-1950 *NatCAB 40*
Bobbitt, Franklin 1876-1956 *WhAm 3*
Bobbitt, John Franklin 1876-1956 *BiDAmEd*
Bobbitt, Joseph Matthew 1908-1975 *WhAm 6*
Bobbitt, Mary Lavinia Reed 1914-1972 *WhAm 6*
Bobbs, William Conrad 1861-1926 *WhAm 1*
Bober, Sam Henry 1891-1973 *WhAm 5*
Bobillier, Etienne 1798-1840 *DcScB*
Bocage, Andre 1892-1953 *BiHiMed*
Boccaccio, Giovanni 1313-1375 *McGEWB*
Boccioni, Umberto 1882-1916 *McGEWB*
Bochart DeSaron, Jean-Baptiste-Gaspard 1730-1794 *DcScB*
Bocher, Maxime 1867-1918 *DcAmB, DcScB, NatCAB 18, WhAm 1*
Bochler *NewYHSD*
Bock, Fedor Von 1880-1945 *WhoMilH*
Bock, Fedor Von 1885-1945 *WhWW-II*
Bock, Harold Pattendon 1901-1972 *WhAm 5*
Bock, Jerome 1498-1554 *DcScB*
Bock, Otto 1881-1942 *WhAm 2*
Bock, Stella Nathan 1885- *WomWWA 14a*
Bockee, Abraham 1783-1865 *BiAUS*
Bockee, Abraham 1784-1865 *BiDrAC, WhAm H, WhAmP*
Bockhoff, William Frederick 1861-1928 *NatCAB 30*
Bocklin, Arnold 1827-1901 *McGEWB*
Bockman, Marcus Olaus 1849-1942 *WhAm 2*
Bockoven, William Alonzo 1894-1947 *NatCAB 46*
Bockus, Charles E 1868-1940 *WhAm 1*
Bocock, Clarence Edgar 1876-1932 *WhAm 1*
Bocock, John Holmes 1890-1958 *WhAm 3*
Bocock, Thomas S 1815-1891 *ApCAB, BiAUS, TwCBDA, WhAm H*
Bocock, Thomas Salem 1815-1891 *NatCAB 11*

Bocock, Thomas Stanhope 1815-1891 *BiDrAC*, *WhAmP*
Bocock, Thomas Stanley 1815-1891 *BiDConf*, *DcAmB*
Bocock, Willis Henry 1865- *WhAm 4*
Bocqueraz, Leon Edward 1871- *WhAm 6*
Bodach, Robert Martin 1902-1957 *NatCAB 45*
Bodansky, Meyer 1896-1941 *WhAm 1*
Bodanzky, Artur 1877-1939 *DcAmB S2*, *NatCAB 29*, *WhAm 1*
Bodde, John R 1872- *WhAm 5*
Boddie, John Thomas 1864-1931 *NatCAB 23*
Boddington, Ernest Fearby 1873- *WhAm 5*
Boddis, George 1866- *WhAm 4*
Boddy, E Manchester 1891-1967 *WhAm 4*
Boddy, James Mamaduke 1866- *WhoColR*
Boddy, William Henry 1886- *WhAm 1*
Bode, Boyd Henry 1873-1953 *BiDAmEd*, *DcAmB S5*, *WhAm 3*
Bode, Frederick 1856-1934 *NatCAB 26*, *WhAm 1*
Bode, J Carl 1901-1955 *NatCAB 43*
Bode, Johann Elert 1747-1826 *AsBiEn*, *DcScB*
Bodecker, Carl Friedrich Wilhelm 1846-1912 *NatCAB 8*, *NatCAB 28*, *WhAm 4*
Bodecker, Charles Francis 1880-1965 *NatCAB 55*
Bodega Y Quadra, Juan Francisco d1794 *ApCAB*
Bodell, David Eugene 1933-1968 *WhAm 5*
Bodell, Joseph James 1881-1950 *WhAm 3*
Boden, Andrew d1835 *BiAUS*, *BiDrAC*, *WhAm H*
Boden, Edward *NewYHSD*
Boden, Reynold Blomerley 1893-1965 *WhAm 4*
Bodenhamer, Osee Lee 1892-1933 *WhAm 1*
Bodenheim, Maxwell 1892-1954 *DcAmB S5*
Bodenheim, Maxwell 1893-1954 *WebAB*
Bodenheim, Maxwell 1895-1954 *WhAm 3*
Bodenheimer, Fritz Simon 1897-1959 *DcScB*
Bodenstab, William Henry 1870-1962 *NatCAB 51*
Bodenstein, Adam Of *DcScB*
Bodenstein, Max 1871-1942 *DcScB Sup*
Bodenwein, Theodore 1864-1939 *WhAm 1*
Boder, Bartlett 1885-1967 *WhAm 5*
Boder, David Pablo 1886-1961 *WhAm 4*
Bodfish, John Dunning Whitney 1878-1956 *NatCAB 44*
Bodfish, Joshua P 1839- *TwCBDA*
Bodfish, Morton 1902-1966 *NatCAB 52*, *WhAm 4*
Bodfish, William P *IlBEAAW*
Bodin, Jean 1529?-1596 *McGEWB*
Bodin, Louis *NewYHSD*
Bodine, A Aubrey 1906-1970 *WhAm 5*
Bodine, Alfred VanSant 1894-1966 *NatCAB 54*, *WhAm 4*
Bodine, James Morrison 1831-1915 *WhAm 1*
Bodine, Joseph Hall 1894-1954 *NatCAB 46*
Bodine, Joseph Hall 1895-1954 *WhAm 3*
Bodine, Joseph Lamb 1883-1950 *WhAm 3*
Bodine, Marc Williams 1899-1971 *NatCAB 57*
Bodine, Robert Nall 1837-1914 *BiDrAC*
Bodine, Roy L 1883-1974 *WhAm 6*
Bodine, S Laurence 1864-1937 *NatCAB 27*
Bodine, Samuel Louis 1899-1958 *WhAm 3*
Bodine, Samuel Taylor 1854-1932 *NatCAB 14*, *NatCAB 23*, *WhAm 1*
Bodine, William Budd 1841-1907 *NatCAB 7*, *NatCAB 23*
Bodine, William Budd 1869-1955 *WhAm 3*
Bodine, William Warden 1887-1959 *NatCAB 51*, *WhAm 3*
Bodington, George 1799-1882 *BiHiMed*
Bodisco, Waldemar De d1878 *ApCAB*
Bodkin, Henry Grattan 1886-1972 *NatCAB 57*
Bodle, Charles d1836 *BiAUS*
Bodle, Charles 1787-1835 *BiDrAC*, *WhAm H*
Bodley, Rachel Littler 1831-1888 *AmWom*, *ApCAB Sup*, *BiDAmEd*, *NotAW*
Bodley, Temple 1852-1940 *WhAm 1*
Bodman, Edward Whitney 1879-1956 *NatCAB 45*
Bodman, Ernest James 1875-1958 *WhAm 3*
Bodman, Henry Edward 1874-1963 *WhAm 4*
Bodman, Ida M *WomWWA 14*
Bodman, Rose Maria *WomWWA 14*

Bodmer, Carl 1809-1893 *REnAW*
Bodmer, Karl 1805-1893 *ApCAB*
Bodmer, Karl 1809-1893 *BnEnAmA*, *IlBEAAW*, *NewYHSD*, *REnAW*, *WhAm H*
Bodmer, Walter 1903-1973 *WhAm 6*
Bodstein, Herman *NewYHSD*
Bodwell, Joseph Robinson 1818-1887 *ApCAB*, *NatCAB 6*, *TwCBDA*
Body, Charles William Edmund 1851-1912 *WhAm 1*
Body, Ralph C 1903-1973 *WhAm 6*
Boe, Franz DeLa *DcScB*
Boe, Lars Wilhelm 1875-1942 *NatCAB 44*, *WhAm 2*
Boeck, Caesar Peter Moeller 1845-1917 *BiHiMed*
Boecklin, Roland 1900-1972 *WhAm 5*
Boeger, Louis Francis 1866-1943 *NatCAB 36*
Boegner, Marc 1881-1970 *WhAm 5*
Boehler, John E 1811?- *NewYHSD*
Boehler, Peter 1712-1774 *NatCAB 9*, *TwCBDA*
Boehler, Peter 1712-1775 *AmBi*, *ApCAB*, *DcAmB*, *WhAm H*
Boehm, Edward Marshall 1912-1969 *WhAm 5*
Boehm, Henry 1775-1875 *AmBi*, *ApCAB*, *DcAmB*, *TwCBDA*, *WhAm H*
Boehm, John Philip 1683-1749 *DcAmB*, *DcAmReB*, *WhAm H*
Boehm, Martin 1725-1812 *AmBi*, *DcAmB*, *NatCAB 21*, *WhAm H*
Boehme, Ernest Adolph 1848- *WhAm 4*
Boehme, Jacob 1575-1624 *DcScB*, *McGEWB*
Boehmer, Max 1847-1913 *WhAm 1*
Boehmore, Francis 1828?- *NewYHSD*
Boehne, John William 1856-1946 *BiDrAC*, *WhAmP*
Boehne, John William, Jr. 1895-1973 *BiDrAC*, *NatCAB 57*, *WhAmP*
Boeing, William Edward 1881-1956 *WhAm 3*
Boelcke, Oswald 1891-1916 *WhoMilH*
Boelen, Jacob 1654?-1729 *DcAmB*, *WhAm H*
Boell, William *NewYHSD*
Boelte, Maria *NotAW*
Boelter, Llewellyn Michael Kraus 1898-1966 *NatCAB 53*, *WhAm 4*
Boen, Haldor Erickson 1851-1912 *BiDrAC*, *WhAmP*
Boerhaave, Hermann 1668-1738 *AsBiEn*, *BiHiMed*, *DcScB*, *McGEWB*
Boericke, Edith Gertrude Schoff *WomWWA 14*
Boericke, Garth Wilkinson 1893-1968 *WhAm 5*
Boericke, Helene *WomWWA 14*
Boericke, Johanna Magdaline 1868- *WomWWA 14*
Boernstein, Henry 1805- *ApCAB*, *Drake*
Boernstein, Ralph A 1893-1969 *WhAm 5*
Boerum, Simeon *NewYHSD*
Boerum, Simon 1724-1775 *ApCAB*, *BiAUS*, *BiDrAC*, *WhAm H*
Boeschenstein, Charles 1862-1952 *WhAm 3*
Boeschenstein, Harold 1896-1972 *WhAm 5*
Boese, Henry *NewYHSD*
Boesel, Frank Tilden 1876- *WhAm 6*
Boesser, H 1820?- *NewYHSD*
Boethius, Anicius Manlius Severinus 480?-524? *AsBiEn*, *DcScB*
Boethius, Anicius Manlius Severinus 480?-525? *McGEWB*
Boetius DeBoodt, Anselmus *DcScB*
Boettcher, Charles 1852-1948 *WhAm 2*
Boettcher, Charles, II 1901-1943 *WhAm 4*
Boettcher, Claude Kedzie 1875-1957 *WhAm 3*
Boettcher, Henry Rudolph 1866-1945 *NatCAB 34*
Boettger, Adolph *NewYHSD*
Boettger, Henry William 1844-1913 *NatCAB 15*
Boettger, Rudolph Christian Von *DcScB*
Boettger, Theodore 1876-1975 *WhAm 6*
Boetticher, Otto 1816?- *NewYHSD*
Boetticher, William Henry 1860-1946 *NatCAB 34*
Boettiger, John 1900-1950 *WhAm 3*
Boeye, John Franklin 1867- *WhAm 4*

Boeynaems, Libert Hubert John Louis 1857-1926 *WhAm 3*
Boffrand, Gabriel Germain 1667-1754 *McGEWB*
Bofill, Antoine *IlBEAAW*
Bofinger, D T *WhAm 2*
Bogan, C Warren 1909-1972 *NatCAB 57*
Bogan, Louise 1897-1970 *WhAm 5*
Bogan, R A L 1896-1962 *WhAm 4*
Bogan, William Joseph 1870-1936 *WhAm 1*
Bogardus, Abraham 1822- *ApCAB*
Bogardus, Abram *NewYHSD*
Bogardus, Annetje Jansen 1600?-1663 *ApCAB*, *NatCAB 9*
Bogardus, Emory Stephen 1882-1973 *WhAm 6*
Bogardus, Estella Mae *WomWWA 14*
Bogardus, Everardus d1647 *ApCAB*
Bogardus, Everardus 1600?-1647 *NatCAB 9*
Bogardus, Everardus 1607-1647 *AmBi*, *DcAmB*, *WhAm H*
Bogardus, James 1800-1874 *AmBi*, *ApCAB*, *BnEnAmA*, *DcAmB*, *Drake*, *NatCAB 8*, *NewYHSD*, *WhAm H*
Bogardus, Mrs. James 1804-1878 *NewYHSD*
Bogardus, John D *NewYHSD*
Bogardus, Robert 1771-1841 *ApCAB*, *Drake*
Bogardus, Mrs. William *NewYHSD*
Bogardus, William *NewYHSD*
Bogart, Elizabeth 1806?- *ApCAB*, *Drake*
Bogart, Ernest Ludlow 1870-1958 *ApCAB X*, *NatCAB 53*, *WhAm 3*
Bogart, Humphrey DeForest 1899-1957 *McGEWB*, *NatCAB 45*, *WebAB*, *WhAm 3*
Bogart, John 1836-1920 *DcAmB*, *WhAm 1*
Bogart, Joseph Hegeman 1846-1926 *NatCAB 20*
Bogart, Paul Nebeker 1878-1961 *WhAm 4*
Bogart, Robert M *NewYHSD*
Bogart, Thomas Napoleon 1867-1922 *NatCAB 20*
Bogart, Walter Thompson 1906-1968 *NatCAB 56*, *WhAm 5*
Bogart, William Henry 1810-1888 *ApCAB*, *NatCAB 4*, *WhAm H*
Bogarte, Martin Eugene 1855- *WhAm 1*
Bogatay, Paul 1905-1972 *NatCAB 57*
Bogdanov, Aleksandr Aleksandrovich 1873-1928 *DcScB Sup*
Bogdanovich, Borislav 1900-1970 *IlBEAAW*
Bogen, Emil 1896-1962 *NatCAB 51*, *WhAm 4*
Bogen, Jules Irwin 1903-1963 *WhAm 4*
Boger, Cyrus Maxwell 1861- *NatCAB 17*
Boger, Glen Alvin 1891-1968 *WhAm 5*
Boger, Robert Forrester 1900-1968 *WhAm 5*
Bogert, Beverley 1868-1959 *NatCAB 50*
Bogert, Charles *NewYHSD*
Bogert, David *NewYHSD*
Bogert, Edward Strong 1836-1911 *WhAm 1*
Bogert, George Henry 1864-1944 *NatCAB 33*, *WhAm 2*
Bogert, J Augustus *NewYHSD*
Bogert, John Lawrence 1858- *NatCAB 16*
Bogert, Marston Taylor 1868-1954 *NatCAB 14*, *NatCAB 42*, *WhAm 3*
Bogert, Walter Lawrence 1864- *NatCAB 16*, *WhAm 5*
Bogert, William Benezet 1860-1948 *NatCAB 37*
Boggess, Arthur Clinton 1874- *WhAm 5*
Boggiano, James Edison 1889-1961 *NatCAB 47*
Boggs, Carroll Curtis 1843- *NatCAB 12*, *WhAm 1*
Boggs, Charles Stewart 1811-1888 *TwCBDA*
Boggs, Charles Stuart 1810-1888 *Drake*
Boggs, Charles Stuart 1811-1888 *ApCAB*, *DcAmB*, *NatCAB 2*, *WhAm H*
Boggs, Christina Marie *WomWWA 14*
Boggs, Earl Huffner 1905-1972 *WhAm 5*
Boggs, Edwin Palmer 1847-1910 *NatCAB 6*
Boggs, Frank Cranstoun 1874- *WhAm 5*
Boggs, Frank M 1855-1926 *WhAm 1*
Boggs, Gilbert Hillhouse 1875-1941 *WhAm 1*
Boggs, Hale 1914-1972 *NatCAB 57*
Boggs, James Caleb 1909- *BiDrAC*
Boggs, L W *BiAUS*
Boggs, L W 1798-1861 *ApCAB*
Boggs, Lilburn W 1798-1861 *NatCAB 12*
Boggs, Lillburn W 1792-1860 *AmBi*, *DcAmB*,

Bollman, Eric 1769-1821 *ApCAB, Drake*
Bollman, Justus Erich 1769-1821 *DcAmB, WhAm H*
Bollman, Wendell 1814- *NatCAB 11*
Bollum, Hiram Leonard 1890-1958 *NatCAB 49*
Bolm, Adolph Rudolphovitch 1884-1951 *DcAmB S5*
Bolmar, Jean Claude Antoine Bownin De 1797-1861 *NatCAB 10*
Bolos Of Mendes *DcScB*
Bolotov, Andrei Timofeevich 1738-1833 *DcScB*
Bolotov, Ivan Il'ich 1761-1799 *WhAm H*
Bolotowsky, Ilya 1907- *BnEnAmA*
Bolstad, Milo Myrum 1915-1974 *WhAm 6*
Bolster, John Aloysius 1894-1952 *NatCAB 41*
Bolster, Stanley Marshall 1874- *WhAm 5*
Bolster, Wilfred 1866-1947 *WhAm 2*
Bolster, William Wheeler 1823- *WhAm 4*
Bolt, Richard Arthur 1880-1959 *NatCAB 48, WhAm 4*
Bolte, William John 1907-1967 *WhAm 4*
Bolter, Andrew 1820-1901 *NatCAB 24*
Bolter, Joseph Charles 1859-1932 *NatCAB 24*
Bolthoff, Henry 1837-1925 *NatCAB 20*
Bolton, Abby 1827-1849 *NewYHSD, WhAm H*
Bolton, Adelaide 1830- *NewYHSD*
Bolton, Adelbert Elwin 1852-1921 *NatCAB 19*
Bolton, Benjamin Meade 1857-1929 *WhAm 1*
Bolton, Channing Moore 1843-1889 *NatCAB 2*
Bolton, Charles Edward 1841-1901 *NatCAB 1, TwCBDA, WhAm 1*
Bolton, Charles Knowles 1867-1950 *DcAmLiB, NatCAB 1, TwCBDA, WhAm 3*
Bolton, Chester Castle 1882-1939 *BiDrAC, NatCAB 34, WhAm 1, WhAmP*
Bolton, Elmer Keiser 1886-1968 *WhAm 5*
Bolton, Ethel Stanwood 1873-1954 *WhAm 3, WomWWA 14*
Bolton, Frances Payne 1885- *BiDrAC, WhAmP*
Bolton, Frank Leonard 1885-1954 *NatCAB 41*
Bolton, Frederick Elmer 1866- *WhAm 5*
Bolton, George McLeod 1902-1962 *NatCAB 49*
Bolton, Hale William 1885-1920? *IIBEAAW*
Bolton, Henry Carrington 1843-1903 *ApCAB, DcAmB, NatCAB 10, TwCBDA, WhAm 1*
Bolton, Herbert Eugene 1870-1953 *DcAmB S5, EncAAH, NatCAB 51, REnAW, WhAm 5*
Bolton, J Gray 1847-1931 *WhAm 1*
Bolton, James 1812-1869 *NatCAB 2*
Bolton, John 1818-1898 *NewYHSD, WhAm H*
Bolton, Margaret 1873-1943 *WhAm 3*
Bolton, Newell Castle 1888-1947 *NatCAB 37*
Bolton, Oliver Payne 1917- *BiDrAC, WhAmP*
Bolton, Paul H 1898-1959 *WhAm 4*
Bolton, Reginald Pelham 1856-1942 *NatCAB 13, WhAm 2*
Bolton, Sarah Knowles 1840?-1916 *ApCAB*
Bolton, Sarah Knowles 1841-1916 *AmBi, AmWom, DcAmB, NatCAB 1, TwCBDA, WhAm 1, WomWWA 14*
Bolton, Sarah Tittle Barrett 1812-1893 *AmWom*
Bolton, Sarah Tittle Barrett 1814-1893 *DcAmB, NotAW, WhAm H*
Bolton, Sarah Tittle Barrett 1815-1893 *ApCAB, NatCAB 10*
Bolton, Thaddeus Lincoln 1865-1948 *NatCAB 36, WhAm 2*
Bolton, Whitney 1900-1966 *WhAm 5*
Bolton, William Compton d1849 *Drake*
Bolton, William Jay 1816-1884 *NewYHSD, WhAm H*
Bolton, William Jordan 1833-1906 *WhAm 1*
Bolton, William P 1885-1964 *BiDrAC*
Bolton, William Worden 1900-1966 *NatCAB 51*
Boltwood, Bertram Borden 1870-1927 *AmBi, AsBiEn, DcAmB, DcScB, NatCAB 15, WhAm 1*
Boltwood, Charles Wright 1867-1945 *NatCAB 35*
Boltwood, Edward 1870-1924 *WhAm 1*
Boltzius, Johann Martin 1703-1765 *DcAmB, WhAm H*
Boltzmann, Ludwig Edward 1844-1906 *AsBiEn, DcScB, McGEWB*

Bolyai, Farkas 1775-1856 *DcScB*
Bolyai, Janos 1802-1860 *AsBiEn, DcScB*
Bolza, Oskar 1857-1942 *DcAmB S3, DcScB, WhAm 4*
Bolzano, Bernard 1781-1848 *DcScB*
Bomann, George Atkins 1864-1963 *NatCAB 50, WhAm 5*
Bomar, Edward Earle 1897-1953 *WhAm 3*
Bomar, Fleming Brown 1914-1967 *NatCAB 53*
Bomar, Paul Vernon 1863-1932 *NatCAB 23, WhAm 1*
Bombaugh, Charles Carroll 1828- *NatCAB 7*
Bombelli, Rafael 1526-1572 *DcScB*
Bomberger, Christian Martin 1884-1950 *NatCAB 42*
Bomberger, John Henry Augustus 1817-1890 *ApCAB, DcAmB, TwCBDA, WhAm H*
Bomberger, Louden Lane 1875-1958 *WhAm 4*
Bomeisler, Louis Edwin 1862-1941 *NatCAB 44*
Bomford, George 1780-1848 *ApCAB, Drake, NatCAB 7, TwCBDA, WebAMB*
Bomford, George 1782-1848 *AmBi, DcAmB, WhAm H*
Bomford, James V 1811-1892 *ApCAB, Drake, TwCBDA*
Bompas, William Carpenter 1834- *ApCAB Sup*
Bompiani, Sophia VanMatre 1835- *WhAm 4*
Bomze, Henry Daniel 1906-1974 *WhAm 6*
Bona Parte *NewYHSD*
Bonaccolto, Girolamo 1899-1973 *WhAm 6*
Bonacum, Thomas 1847-1911 *ApCAB Sup, NatCAB 12, TwCBDA, WhAm 1*
Bonanni, Filippo *DcScB*
Bonanni, Pietro 1789-1821 *NewYHSD*
Bonaparte, Charles Joseph 1851-1921 *AmBi, ApCAB, ApCAB X, BiDrUSE, DcAmB, NatCAB 13, NatCAB 14, WebAB, WhAm 1, WhAmP*
Bonaparte, Charles Lucien 1803-1857 *WhAm H*
Bonaparte, Charles Lucien *see also* Bonaparte, Lucien Jules
Bonaparte, Charles Lucien Jules Laurence 1803-1857 *Drake*
Bonaparte, Charles Lucien Jules Laurent 1803-1857 *ApCAB*
Bonaparte, Charlotte Julie 1802-1839 *NewYHSD, WhAm H*
Bonaparte, Elisabeth Patterson 1785-1879 *NotAW*
Bonaparte, Elizabeth Patterson 1785-1879 *AmBi, AmWom, ApCAB, DcAmB, TwCBDA, WebAB, WhAm H*
Bonaparte, Jerome 1784-1860 *AmBi, ApCAB*
Bonaparte, Jerome Napoleon 1805-1870 *ApCAB, Drake, TwCBDA*
Bonaparte, Jerome Napoleon 1830-1893 *DcAmB, WhAm H*
Bonaparte, Jerome Napoleon 1832-1893 *ApCAB, TwCBDA*
Bonaparte, Joseph 1768-1844 *ApCAB, McGEWB*
Bonaparte, Louis 1778-1846 *McGEWB*
Bonaparte, Louis Napoleon 1808-1873 *WhAm H*
Bonaparte, Lucien Jules Laurent 1803-1857 *DcScB*
Bonaparte, Lucien Jules Laurent *see also* Bonaparte, Charles
Bonaparte, Napoleon 1769-1821 *WhAm H*
Bonar, Thomas *NewYHSD*
Bonar, William *NewYHSD*
Bonard, Louis 1809-1871 *ApCAB, DcAmB, WhAm H*
Bonaschi, Alberto Cinzio 1869-1948 *WhAm 3*
Bonaventura, Federigo 1555-1602 *DcScB*
Bonaventure, Saint 1217-1274 *McGEWB*
Bonbright, Daniel 1831-1912 *NatCAB 25, TwCBDA, WhAm 1*
Bonbright, Irving Wayland 1871-1941 *NatCAB 49*
Bonbright, William Prescott 1859- *WhAm 4*
Boncher, Hector Peter 1904-1973 *WhAm 6*
Bonci, Alessandro 1870- *WhAm 5*
Boncompagni, Baldassarre 1821-1894 *DcScB*
Bond, A Russell 1876-1937 *WhAm 1*
Bond, Ahva J C 1875- *WhAm 5*
Bond, Albert Richmond 1874-1944 *WhAm 2*
Bond, Bernard Q 1879-1934 *WhAm 1*

Bond, Beverly Waugh, Jr. 1878- *WhAm 6*
Bond, Carrie Jacobs 1862-1946 *DcAmB S4, NotAW, WhAm 2*
Bond, Carrie Jacobs 1863-1946 *BiCAW, WomWWA 14*
Bond, Carroll Taney 1873-1943 *WhAm 2*
Bond, Charles Grosvenor 1877- *BiDrAC, WhAm 5*
Bond, Charles Otis 1870-1921 *NatCAB 19*
Bond, Charles Sumner 1856-1958 *WhAm 3*
Bond, Charles V *NewYHSD*
Bond, Drew 1876- *WhAm 5*
Bond, Earl Danford 1879- *WhAm 6*
Bond, Edward Austin 1849-1929 *NatCAB 12, WhAm 1*
Bond, Edward Johnson 1888-1941 *WhAm 1*
Bond, Edwin E 1904-1966 *WhAm 4*
Bond, Elizabeth Powell 1841-1926 *AmBi, AmWom, DcAmB, NatCAB 6, WhAm 3, WomWWA 14*
Bond, Ford 1904-1962 *WhAm 4*
Bond, Francis Augustus 1838-1923 *NatCAB 19*
Bond, Frank 1856-1940 *WhAm 1*
Bond, Frank Austin 1889-1960 *NatCAB 46*
Bond, Frank Stuart 1830-1912 *WhAm 1*
Bond, George Edward 1866-1923 *NatCAB 6*
Bond, George Hopkins 1873-1954 *WhAm 3*
Bond, George Hopkins, Jr. 1909-1973 *WhAm 6*
Bond, George Meade 1852-1935 *WhAm 1*
Bond, George Phillips 1825-1865 *AmBi, ApCAB, AsBiEn, DcAmB, DcScB, Drake, NatCAB 5, TwCBDA, WebAB, WhAm H*
Bond, Henry *NewYHSD*
Bond, Henry 1790-1859 *ApCAB, Drake, TwCBDA*
Bond, Henry 1856-1925 *WhAm 1*
Bond, Henry Herrick 1847-1881 *NatCAB 2*
Bond, Henry Herrick 1881-1962 *NatCAB 47*
Bond, Henry Whitelaw 1848-1919 *NatCAB 25, WhAm 1*
Bond, Holdsworth Wheeler 1867- *NatCAB 12, WhAm 4*
Bond, Hugh L 1828-1893 *ApCAB, BiAUS*
Bond, Hugh Lennox 1828-1893 *DcAmB, TwCBDA, WhAmP*
Bond, Hugh Lennox, Jr. 1858-1922 *WhAm 1*
Bond, Hugh Lenox 1828-1893 *NatCAB 11, WhAm H*
Bond, Isabella Bacon *WomWWA 14*
Bond, James Leslie 1877- *WhAm 5*
Bond, John R S 1822-1872 *ApCAB*
Bond, Joseph 1852-1902 *NatCAB 21*
Bond, Julian 1940- *WebAB*
Bond, Lester Legrand 1829-1903 *NatCAB 9, WhAm 1*
Bond, Mabel Cornish 1867- *BiCAW, WomWWA 14*
Bond, Maria *NewYHSD*
Bond, Marshall S P *NewYHSD*
Bond, Nelson L 1903-1974 *WhAm 6*
Bond, Octavia Zollicoffer 1846- *WomWWA 14*
Bond, Oliver James 1865-1933 *WhAm 1*
Bond, Paul Stanley 1879-1955 *NatCAB 44*
Bond, Perry A 1878- *WhAm 6*
Bond, Phineas 1717-1773 *NatCAB 13*
Bond, Reford 1877-1954 *NatCAB 40, WhAm 3*
Bond, Richard *WhAm H*
Bond, Robert *NewYHSD*
Bond, Shadrach 1773-1832 *DcAmB, Drake, NatCAB 11, TwCBDA, WhAm H*
Bond, Shadrack 1773-1832 *ApCAB, BiAUS, BiDrAC, WhAmP*
Bond, Sirus Orestes 1877-1959 *WhAm 3*
Bond, Thomas 1712-1784 *AmBi, ApCAB, DcAmB, NatCAB 13, WebAB, WhAm H*
Bond, Thomas 1713-1784 *EncAB*
Bond, Thomas Burke 1889-1971 *WhAm 6*
Bond, Thomas Emerson 1782-1856 *ApCAB, Drake, NatCAB 11*
Bond, Thomas Emerson 1813-1872 *ApCAB*
Bond, Thomas Emerson 1876-1949 *WhAm 2*
Bond, Walter Huntington 1878- *NatCAB 18, WhAm 6*
Bond, Willard Faroe 1876- *WhAm 5*

Bond, William Bennett 1815- *ApCAB*
Bond, William Cranch 1789-1859 *AmBi, ApCAB, AsBiEn, DcAmB, DcScB, Drake, NatCAB 8, TwCBDA, WebAB, WhAm H*
Bond, William Key 1792-1864 *BiAUS, BiDrAC, WhAm H, WhAmP*
Bond, William Scott 1876-1952 *WhAm 3*
Bond, Young Hance 1846- *WhAm 4*
Bondar, H Kelliher 1908-1957 *NatCAB 43*
Bondet *NewYHSD*
Bondi, Jonas 1804-1874 *ApCAB*
Bonds, Archibald 1876- *WhAm 5*
Bonds, Margaret 1913-1972 *WhAm 6*
Bondurant, Alexander Lee 1865-1937 *WhAm 1*
Bondurant, Eugene Dubose 1862- *WhAm 5*
Bondurant, William Walton d1959 *WhAm 4*
Bondy, Jeanne Hale 1913-1969 *NatCAB 54*
Bondy, William 1871-1964 *WhAm 4*
Bone, Alfred Rufus, Jr. 1907-1972 *WhAm 5*
Bone, Herman David 1878-1966 *NatCAB 53*
Bone, Homer Truett 1883-1970 *BiDrAC, WhAm 5, WhAmP*
Bone, Merle 1885-1950 *NatCAB 39*
Bone, Myron Rundle 1891-1964 *NatCAB 51*
Bone, Scott Cardelle 1860-1936 *NatCAB 26, WhAm 1*
Bone, Winstead Paine 1861-1942 *WhAm 2*
Boneau *NewYHSD*
Bonebrake, P I 1836- *NatCAB 5*
Bonebrake, Peter Oren 1864- *WhAm 4*
Bonehill, Ralph *WhAm 1*
Bonell, Benjamin Walter 1867- *WhAm 5*
Boner, Halbert Evans 1884-1946 *NatCAB 35*
Boner, John Henry 1845-1903 *DcAmB, NatCAB 2, TwCBDA, WhAm 1*
Bones, Marietta M 1842- *AmWom*
Bonesteel, Charles Hartwell 1885-1964 *NatCAB 51, WhAm 4*
Bonesteel, Verne C 1890-1965 *WhAm 4*
Bonet, Theophile 1620-1689 *BiHiMed*
Boney, John *NewYHSD*
Boney, Leslie Norwood 1880-1964 *NatCAB 51*
Bonfanti, Marie 1847-1921 *NotAW*
Bonfield, George R 1802-1898 *NewYHSD, WhAm H*
Bonfield, William VanDeVelde *NewYHSD*
Bonfig, Henry Carl 1896-1962 *WhAm 4*
Bonfils, Charles Alden 1871-1955 *NatCAB 45*
Bonfils, Frederick Gilmer 1860-1933 *DcAmB S1, NatCAB 27, WebAB, WhAm HA, WhAm 4*
Bonfils, Frederick Walker 1894-1958 *NatCAB 49*
Bonfils, Helen Gertrude 1889-1972 *NatCAB 56, WhAm 5*
Bonfils, Winifred Sweet Black *NotAW*
Bong, Richard Ira 1920-1945 *NatCAB 34, WebAMB, WhWW-II*
Bonga, George 1802?- *REnAW*
Bonggren, Olof Jakob 1854- *WhAm 4*
Bongiorno, Henry Dominic 1904-1967 *NatCAB 54*
Bonham, B F *NatCAB 5*
Bonham, Dwight Turney 1899-1969 *NatCAB 54*
Bonham, Eleanor Milton 1881- *WomWWA 14*
Bonham, Horace 1835-1892 *NewYHSD*
Bonham, Kenneth Arlington 1903-1972 *WhAm 5*
Bonham, Mildred A 1840- *AmWom*
Bonham, Milledge Lipscomb 1854-1943 *NatCAB 32, WhAm 2*
Bonham, Milledge Louis, Jr. 1880-1941 *WhAm 1*
Bonham, Milledge Luke d1890 *BiAUS*
Bonham, Milledge Luke 1813-1890 *BiDConf, BiDrAC, DcAmB, NatCAB 12, WhAm H, WhAmP*
Bonham, Milledge Luke 1815-1890 *ApCAB, Drake, NatCAB 4, TwCBDA*
Bonham, Walter Melville 1876-1940 *NatCAB 30*
Bonheur, Marie Rosa 1822-1899 *IIBEAAW*
Bonhoeffer, Dietrich 1906-1945 *McGEWB*
Bonhoffer, Dietrich 1906-1945 *WhWW-II*
Boniface VII 1235?-1303 *McGEWB*
Boniface, Saint 672?-754 *McGEWB*
Boniface, Mother Mary 1899-1966 *WhAm 4*

Bonifacio, Andres 1863-1897 *McGEWB*
Bonifield, Charles Lybrand 1863-1932 *NatCAB 24, WhAm 1*
Bonilla, Policarpo 1858- *ApCAB Sup*
Bonillas, Ygnacio 1858-1944 *WhAm 2*
Bonin, Edward John 1904- *BiDrAC*
Bonine, Charles Edward 1874-1948 *NatCAB 37*
Bonington, Richard Parkes 1802-1828 *McGEWB*
Bonnar, James Millar 1878-1952 *NatCAB 42*
Bonnar, John Duncan 1852-1936 *NatCAB 27, WhAm 1*
Bonnard, Pierre 1867-1947 *McGEWB*
Bonneau, Alfred 1862-1920 *NatCAB 18*
Bonnell, Edwin 1836-1912 *NatCAB 15*
Bonnell, Henry Houston 1859-1926 *WhAm 1*
Bonnell, John Mitchell 1820-1871 *BiDAmEd, NatCAB 5*
Bonnell, William *NewYHSD*
Bonnelycke, Emil 1876-1936 *NatCAB 28*
Bonner, A W *NewYHSD*
Bonner, Albert Sydney 1891-1945 *NatCAB 34, WhAm 2*
Bonner, Arthur 1869-1952 *WhAm 3*
Bonner, Benjamin Franklin 1869-1944 *NatCAB 33*
Bonner, Campbell 1876- *WhAm 5*
Bonner, Charles 1896-1965 *WhAm 4*
Bonner, David Findley 1842- *WhAm 3*
Bonner, David Mahlon 1916-1964 *WhAm 4*
Bonner, Emmett Peyton 1918-1975 *WhAm 6*
Bonner, Francis A 1885-1953 *WhAm 3*
Bonner, Frederick Douglass 1878- *WhoColR*
Bonner, Genevieve Vollmer 1879- *WomWWA 14*
Bonner, Geraldine 1870-1930 *WhAm 1, WomWWA 14*
Bonner, Griffith 1885-1936 *WhAm 1*
Bonner, Herbert Covington 1891-1965 *BiDrAC, WhAm 4, WhAmP*
Bonner, Hugh d1908 *WhAm 1*
Bonner, James Bernard d1931 *WhAm 1*
Bonner, John 1643?-1725? *DcAmB*
Bonner, John 1643?-1726 *WhAm H*
Bonner, John 1828-1899 *NatCAB 12*
Bonner, John Joseph 1890-1945 *WhAm 2*
Bonner, John Woodrow 1902-1970 *WhAm 5*
Bonner, Joseph Claybaugh 1855- *WhAm 4*
Bonner, Mary Anita 1885-1935 *IIBEAAW*
Bonner, Mary Davenport 1866- *WomWWA 14*
Bonner, Mary Graham d1974 *WhAm 6*
Bonner, Paul Hyde 1893-1968 *WhAm 5*
Bonner, Robert 1820?-1899 *Drake*
Bonner, Robert 1824-1899 *AmBi, ApCAB, DcAmB, NatCAB 10, TwCBDA, WebAB, WhAm 1*
Bonner, Robert Johnson 1868-1946 *WhAm 2*
Bonner, Sherwood *ApCAB, NotAW, WhAm H*
Bonner, Tom Wilkerson 1910-1961 *WhAm 4*
Bonner, Walter Danie 1878-1956 *NatCAB 44, WhAm 3*
Bonner, Wilkerson Austin 1855-1916 *NatCAB 18*
Bonnet, Charles 1720-1793 *AsBiEn, DcScB*
Bonnet, Frank Henry 1886-1962 *WhAm 4*
Bonnet, Leon Durand 1868-1936 *NatCAB 34*
Bonnet, Pierre-Ossian 1819-1892 *DcScB*
Bonneville, Benjamin L E d1878 *TwCBDA*
Bonneville, Benjamin L E 1793-1878 *NatCAB 12*
Bonneville, Benjamin L E 1795?-1878 *ApCAB*
Bonneville, Benjamin Louis Eulalie De 1796-1878 *AmBi, DcAmB, Drake, REnAW, WebAB, WebAMB, WhAm H*
Bonneville, C De 1710?-1780? *ApCAB, Drake*
Bonney, Charles Carroll 1831-1903 *ApCAB Sup, DcAmB, NatCAB 28, TwCBDA, WhAm 1*
Bonney, Edward 1807-1864 *ApCAB Sup*
Bonney, Mary Lucinda 1816-1900 *BiDAmEd, NotAW*
Bonney, Sherman Grant 1864-1942 *WhAm 2*
Bonney, Thomas George 1833-1923 *DcScB*
Bonney, Wilbert Lowth 1872- *WhAm 5*
Bonney, William H 1859-1881 *DcAmB, REnAW, WebAB, WhAm H*
Bonnheim, Albert 1854-1916 *WhAm 1*

Bonnie And Clyde *REnAW*
Bonnier, Gaston 1853-1922 *DcScB*
Bonnifield, M S 1833- *NatCAB 12*
Bonnin, Gertrude Simmons 1876-1938 *NotAW*
Bonniwell, Eugene Cleophas 1872-1964 *NatCAB 50*
Bonno, Pierre *NewYHSD*
Bonnycastle, Charles 1792-1840 *ApCAB, Drake, NatCAB 13*
Bonnycastle, Sir Richard Henry 1791-1848 *ApCAB, Drake*
Bonnyman, Alexander 1868-1953 *WhAm 3*
Bonomo, Alfred J 1890-1955 *WhAm 3*
Bonomo, Giovan Cosimo 1666-1696 *DcScB*
Bonpland, Aime 1773-1858 *ApCAB, Drake*
Bonsack, Walter 1901-1963 *NatCAB 51*
Bonsal, Alonzo Felten 1895-1966 *NatCAB 51*
Bonsal, Stephen 1865-1951 *DcAmB S5, NatCAB 14, WhAm 3*
Bonsall, Amos 1830-1915 *WhAm 1*
Bonsall, Edward Horne 1859-1933 *NatCAB 10, WhAm 1*
Bonsall, Elisabeth F *WomWWA 14*
Bonsall, Elizabeth Hubbard 1890-1937 *WhAm 1*
Bonsall, Henry Lummis 1834- *NatCAB 4*
Bonsall, Mary W *WomWWA 14*
Bonsall, William Hartshorn 1846-1905 *WhAm 1*
Bonser, Frederick Gordon 1875-1931 *BiDAmEd, WhAm 1*
Bonser, Thomas A 1860-1935 *WhAm 1*
Bonsib, Roy Samuel 1886-1955 *NatCAB 44*
Bonstelle, Jessie d1932 *WomWWA 14*
Bonstelle, Jessie 1871-1932 *NatCAB 25, NotAW*
Bonstelle, Jessie 1872-1932 *DcAmB S1*
Bonte, A P *NewYHSD*
Bonte, George Willard 1873-1946 *WhAm 2*
Bontecou, Daniel 1851-1924 *NatCAB 6, NatCAB 21, WhAm 1*
Bontecou, Frederic Holdrege 1893-1959 *NatCAB 50*
Bontecou, Lee 1931- *BnEnAmA*
Bontecou, Reed Brockway 1824-1907 *TwCBDA, WhAm 1*
Bontempo, Joseph Felix 1898-1969 *NatCAB 55*
Bontemps, Arna Wendell 1902-1973 *DcAmLiB, WhAm 5*
Bontius, Jacobus 1592-1631 *BiHiMed*
Bonvalot, Pierre Gabriel Edouard 1853-1933 *McGEWB*
Bonvicino, Costanzo Benedetto 1739-1812 *DcScB*
Bonville, Charles 1836?- *NewYHSD*
Bonvin, Ludwig 1850-1939 *WhAm 1*
Bonvouloir, M De *ApCAB*
Bonwell, E *IIBEAAW*
Bonwill, William Gibson Arlington 1833-1899 *DcAmB, NatCAB 5, WhAm 1*
Bonynge, Paul 1876-1937 *NatCAB 30*
Bonynge, Robert William 1863-1939 *BiDrAC, WhAm 1, WhAmP*
Bonzano, Adolphus 1830-1913 *DcAmB, NatCAB 16*
Bonzano, John 1867-1927 *WhAm 1*
Bonzano, Maximilian Ferdinand 1858-1920 *NatCAB 19*
Boocock, Cornelius Brett 1898-1973 *WhAm 6*
Boocock, Philip Milledoler Brett 1905-1975 *WhAm 6*
Boodell, Thomas J 1906-1972 *WhAm 5*
Boodin, John Elof 1869- *WhAm 3*
Boodt, Anselmus Boetius De 1550?-1632 *DcScB*
Boody, Azariah 1815-1885 *BiAUS, BiDrAC, WhAm H*
Boody, Bertha M 1877-1943 *WhAm 3*
Boody, Charles Augustus 1870-1926 *ApCAB X, NatCAB 36*
Boody, David Augustus 1837-1930 *ApCAB X, BiDrAC, NatCAB 10, NatCAB 24, WhAm 1, WhAmP*
Boody, Edgar 1874-1962 *NatCAB 46*
Boog, Carle Michel 1877- *WhAm 5*
Boogher, Elbert Willis Griffin 1880- *WhAm 6*
Boogher, Jesse L 1833- *NatCAB 9*
Booher, Charles Ferris 1848-1921 *BiDrAC, WhAm 1, WhAmP*

Book, Dorothy L 1903-1955 *WhAm 3*
Book, George Milton 1845-1921 *WhAm 1*
Book, James Burgess 1843-1916 *ApCAB X,*
NatCAB 18
Book, John William 1850- *NatCAB 7*
Book, William Frederick 1873-1940 *WhAm 1*
Book, William Henry 1863-1946 *WhAm 2*
Booker, Edith Hill 1868- *WomWWA 14*
Booker, George Edward 1872-1951 *WhAm 3*
Booker, George William 1821-1883 *ApCAB,*
BiAUS, BiDrAC, NatCAB 4, WhAm H
Booker, Joseph Albert 1859-1926 *TwCBDA,*
WhAm 1, WhoColR
Booker, Joseph Robert 1893-1960 *NatCAB 50*
Booker, William David 1844-1921 *WhAm 1*
Bookhout, Edward *NewYHSD*
Bookstaver, Henry Weller 1835-1907 *WhAm 1*
Bookwalter, Alfed Guitner 1873-1939 *WhAm 1*
Bookwalter, Charles A 1860- *WhAm 4*
Bookwalter, John W 1837- *WhAm 4*
Bookwalter, Lewis 1846-1935 *NatCAB 26,*
TwCBDA, WhAm 4
Boole, Ella Alexander 1858-1952 *DcAmB S5,*
NatCAB 38, WhAm 3, WomWWA 14
Boole, George 1815-1864 *AsBiEn, DcScB,*
McGEWB
Boole, William H 1827-1896 *TwCBDA*
Boomer, George Boardman 1832-1863 *ApCAB,*
Drake, TwCBDA
Boomer, George Ellsworth 1862- *WhAm 4*
Boomer, George Owens 1888-1972 *NatCAB 57*
Boomer, Lucius Messenger 1878-1947
NatCAB 36, WhAm 2
Boomer, Robert DeForest 1891-1966 *WhAm 4*
Boomhour, J Gregory 1873-1966 *WhAm 4*
Boomsliter, Alice Ella Colgan *WomWWA 14*
Boon, Henry George 1892-1952 *WhAm 3*
Boon, John Daniel 1874-1952 *NatCAB 41*
Boon, Ratliff 1781-1844 *BiAUS, BiDrAC,*
NatCAB 13, WhAm H, WhAmP
Boone, A R 1831-1886 *BiAUS*
Boone, Andrew Rechmond 1831-1886 *BiDrAC,*
WhAm H, WhAmP
Boone, Arthur Upshaw 1860- *WhAm 5*
Boone, Charles Henry Mantelle 1870- *WhoColR*
Boone, Charles Theodore 1838- *WhAm 1*
Boone, Daniel 1734-1820 *AmBi, DcAmB,*
EncAAH, EncAB, McGEWB, REnAW,
WebAB, WhAmP
Boone, Daniel 1735-1820 *ApCAB, Drake,*
NatCAB 3, TwCBDA, WhAm H
Boone, Daniel 1879-1944 *WhAm 2*
Boone, Enoch 1777-1862 *ApCAB*
Boone, Henry Burnham 1872- *WhAm 5*
Boone, James Louden 1891-1961 *NatCAB 49*
Boone, Joel Thompson 1889-1974 *WebAMB,*
WhAm 6
Boone, John Alfred 1906-1970 *NatCAB 57*
Boone, John Lee 1843- *WhAm 1*
Boone, Joseph Prince 1880-1964 *WhAm 4*
Boone, Richard Gause 1849-1923 *NatCAB 20,*
WhAm 1
Boone, Rodney Emerson 1882-1943 *NatCAB 36*
Boone, Thomas *ApCAB, NatCAB 12,*
TwCBDA, WhAm H
Boone, William F *BiAUS*
Boone, William Jones 1811-1864 *ApCAB,*
Drake, NatCAB 5, TwCBDA
Boone, William Jones 1846-1891 *NatCAB 5,*
TwCBDA
Boone, William Jones 1847-1891 *ApCAB*
Boone, William Judson 1860-1936 *NatCAB 29,*
REnAW, WhAm 1
Boone, William Kennedy 1868-1947
NatCAB 43
Boone, William Robinson 1879-1951
NatCAB 42
Booraem, J Francis 1869-1947 *NatCAB 36*
Booraem, John VanVorst 1838-1923 *WhAm 1*
Booraem, Robert Elmer 1856-1918 *WhAm 1*
Boord, Cecil Ernest 1884-1969 *WhAm 5*
Boorman, James 1783-1866 *ApCAB, DcAmB,*
TwCBDA, WhAm H
Boorman, Kitchell Monckton 1887-1946
NatCAB 35
Boorstin, Daniel Joseph 1914- *EncAAH*
Boos, Ludwig Charles 1903-1959 *WhAm 3*
Boos, William Frederick 1870- *WhAm 6*

Boot, Adrien 1580?-1650? *ApCAB Sup*
Boot, John Fletcher 1796?-1853 *ApCAB*
Boote, Charles William 1874-1960 *NatCAB 46*
Boote, Ward E 1899-1965 *WhAm 4*
Booth, Ada Pearl Dunlap 1884- *NatCAB 17*
Booth, Agnes d1910 *NatCAB 1*
Booth, Agnes 1841?-1910 *NotAW*
Booth, Agnes 1843-1910 *AmWom*
Booth, Agnes 1846-1910 *DcAmB, WhAm 1*
Booth, Ballington 1857-1940 *DcAmB S2,*
NatCAB 14, TwCBDA
Booth, Ballington 1859-1940 *WhAm 1,*
WhAm 2
Booth, Benjamin *ApCAB*
Booth, Bradford Allen 1909-1968 *WhAm 5*
Booth, Carlos Charles 1861-1928 *NatCAB 23*
Booth, Charles 1840-1916 *McGEWB*
Booth, Charles Arthur 1876- *WhAm 5*
Booth, Charles Brandon 1887- *WhAm 6*
Booth, Charles Gordon 1896-1949 *NatCAB 37,*
WhAm 2
Booth, Christopher Henry Hudson 1865-1939
NatCAB 37, WhAm 1
Booth, Clarence Moore 1876- *WhAm 5*
Booth, Edwin 1833-1893 *AmBi, ApCAB,*
Drake, McGEWB, NatCAB 3
Booth, Edwin Prince 1898-1969 *WhAm 5*
Booth, Edwin Shaw 1905-1967 *NatCAB 54*
Booth, Edwin Thomas 1833-1893 *DcAmB,*
TwCBDA, WebAB, WhAm H
Booth, Elizabeth Knox *BiCAW*
Booth, Ellen Warren Scripps 1863-1948 *NotAW*
Booth, Emma Scarr 1835- *AmWom*
Booth, Eugene Samuel 1850-1931 *NatCAB 23*
Booth, Evangeline Cory 1865-1950 *ApCAB X,*
BiCAW, DcAmB S4, DcAmReB, NotAW,
WhAm 3, WomWWA 14
Booth, Ewing E 1870-1949 *WhAm 2*
Booth, Fenton Whitlock 1869-1947 *NatCAB 40,*
WhAm 2
Booth, Frank Walworth 1855- *WhAm 4*
Booth, Franklin 1874- *WhAm 5*
Booth, George 1841- *NatCAB 7*
Booth, George Francis 1870-1955 *WhAm 3*
Booth, George Gough 1864-1949 *ApCAB X,*
WhAm 2
Booth, George N *NewYHSD*
Booth, Harold Simmons 1891-1950 *WhAm 3*
Booth, Henry 1895-1969 *NatCAB 57*
Booth, Henry Kendall 1876-1942 *WhAm 2*
Booth, Henry Matthias 1843-1899 *NatCAB 19,*
TwCBDA, WhAm 1
Booth, Henry Prosper 1836-1909 *NatCAB 16*
Booth, Hiram Evans 1860-1940 *WhAm 1*
Booth, Isaac Walter 1883-1970 *WhAm 5*
Booth, James d1855 *BiAUS*
Booth, James 1753-1828 *NatCAB 4*
Booth, James Curtis 1810-1888 *ApCAB,*
DcAmB, Drake, NatCAB 13, TwCBDA,
WhAm H
Booth, John Barker 1792-1869 *NatCAB 18*
Booth, John Henry 1880-1960 *WhAm 4*
Booth, John Wilkes 1838-1865 *AmBi, DcAmB,*
EncAB, McGEWB, NatCAB 3,
TwCBDA, WebAB, WhAm H, WhAmP
Booth, John Wilkes 1839-1865 *Drake*
Booth, Joseph 1851-1932 *McGEWB*
Booth, Junius Brutus 1796-1852 *AmBi, ApCAB,*
DcAmB, Drake, NatCAB 3, TwCBDA,
WebAB, WhAm H
Booth, Lionel Earl 1892-1964 *NatCAB 51*
Booth, Lionel Lussky 1907-1969 *NatCAB 55*
Booth, Louis Wineera 1911-1974 *WhAm 6*
Booth, Mary Allard 1843-1922 *WomWWA 14*
Booth, Mary Ann Allard 1843-1922 *NatCAB 15,*
WhAm 1
Booth, Mary H C 1831-1865 *ApCAB, Drake*
Booth, Mary Louise 1831-1889 *AmBi,*
AmWom, ApCAB, DcAmB, Drake,
NatCAB 7, NotAW, TwCBDA,
WhAm H
Booth, Maud Ballington Charlesworth 1865-1948
NatCAB 14, NatCAB 38, NotAW,
WhAm 2, WomWWA 14
Booth, Newell Snow 1903-1968 *WhAm 5*
Booth, Newton 1825-1892 *ApCAB, BiAUS,*
BiDrAC, DcAmB, NatCAB 4, TwCBDA,
WhAm H, WhAmP

Booth, Ralph Douglas 1899-1960 *WhAm 4*
Booth, Ralph Harman 1873-1931 *WhAm 1*
Booth, Rejoyce Ballance Collins 1876-
WomWWA 14
Booth, Robert Asbury 1858-1944 *NatCAB 35,*
WhAm 2
Booth, Robert Highman 1905-1972 *NatCAB 56,*
WhAm 5
Booth, Robert Plues 1900-1967 *WhAm 4*
Booth, Robert Russell 1830-1905 *WhAm 1*
Booth, Samuel Babcock 1883-1935 *WhAm 1*
Booth, Samuel Colton 1812-1895 *NatCAB 15*
Booth, T Dwight *NewYHSD*
Booth, Thomas Butler 1872-1940 *WhAm 1*
Booth, Vincent Ravi 1876-1950 *NatCAB 39*
Booth, Walter 1791-1870 *BiAUS, BiDrAC,*
WhAm H
Booth, Wilbur Franklin 1861- *WhAm 4*
Booth, William 1829-1912 *McGEWB*
Booth, William A 1805-1895 *NatCAB 10*
Booth, William Edward 1920-1973 *WhAm 6*
Booth, William Stone 1864-1926 *ApCAB X,*
NatCAB 20, WhAm 1
Booth, Willis H d1958 *WhAm 3*
Booth-Tucker, Emma Moss 1860-1903
ApCAB Sup, DcAmB, NotAW, WhAm 1
Booth-Tucker, Frederick St. G DeLautear
1853-1929 *ApCAB Sup, WhAm 1*
Boothby, Alonzo 1840-1902 *NatCAB 14*
Boothby, Everett J 1893-1973 *WhAm 6*
Boothby, Frederick Eleazer *ApCAB X*
Boothby, Walter Meredith 1880-1953
NatCAB 45, WhAm 3
Boothe, Gardner Lloyd 1872- *WhAm 5*
Boothe, Viva Belle 1893-1964 *NatCAB 51*
Boothman, Melvin Morella 1846-1904 *BiDrAC,*
WhAmP
Boothman, Melvin Morelli 1846-1904 *TwCBDA*
Boothroyd, Samuel Latimer 1874- *WhAm 5*
Boots, Ralph Henderson 1891-1968 *NatCAB 54*
Boott, Elizabeth *ApCAB*
Boott, Kirk 1790-1837 *ApCAB Sup, DcAmB,*
WhAm H
Booz, Edwin George 1887-1951 *NatCAB 40,*
WhAm 3
Booze, William Samuel 1862-1933 *BiDrAC*
Bope, Henry P 1858- *WhAm 4*
Boppe, Carl Hermann 1842-1899 *NatCAB 22*
Boqueta DeWoiseri, J L *NewYHSD*
Boqutea, I L *NewYHSD*
Bor-Komorowski, Tadeusz 1895-1966
WhWW-II
Boraas, Julius 1871-1952 *WhAm 3*
Borach, Fannie 1891-1951 *WebAB*
Borah, Leo Arthur 1889-1959 *WhAm 4*
Borah, Wayne G 1891-1966 *NatCAB 53,*
WhAm 4
Borah, William Edgar 1865-1940 *AmBi,*
ApCAB X, BiDrAC, DcAmB S2,
EncAAH, EncAB, McGEWB,
NatCAB 14, REnAW, WebAB, WhAm 1,
WhAmP
Borber, William 1885-1958 *WhAm 3*
Borch, Gaston 1871- *WhAm 5*
Borch, Oluf *DcScB*
Borchard, Edwin 1884-1951 *NatCAB 39,*
WhAm 3
Borchard, Miss H *NewYHSD*
Borchardt, Albert Hugo 1886-1962 *WhAm 4*
Borchardt, Alvin Lee 1905-1962 *NatCAB 50*
Borchardt, Carl Wilhelm 1817-1880 *DcScB*
Borchardt, Selma Munter d1968 *WhAm 5*
Borchers, Charles Martin 1869-1946 *BiDrAC,*
WhAm 5, WhAmP
Borda, Jean Charles 1733-1799 *ApCAB,*
DcScB, Drake
Bordeaux, LePecq Andree 1910-1973 *WhAm 6*
Bordeaux, Thomas 1852-1934 *NatCAB 26*
Borden, Bertram Harold 1868- *WhAm 4*
Borden, C Seymour 1880- *WhAm 3*
Borden, Cecil Alexander 1887-1949 *NatCAB 39*
Borden, Daniel Carey 1889-1964 *WhAm 4*
Borden, Daniel LeRay 1887-1969 *WhAm 5*
Borden, Edwin Howard *WhoColR*
Borden, Enoch R 1823-1870 *ApCAB*
Borden, Fanny *WomWWA 14*
Borden, Frank Kornegay 1857-1941 *NatCAB 35*
Borden, Gail 1801-1874 *AmBi, ApCAB,*

ApCAB X, AsBiEn, DcAmB, EncAAH,
McGEWB, NatCAB 7, TwCBDA,
WebAB, WhAm H
Borden, George Pennington 1844-1925 *WhAm 1*
Borden, Howard Seymour 1876- *WhAm 5*
Borden, James Wallace 1810- *BiAUS,*
NatCAB 12
Borden, John 1884-1961 *NatCAB 50,*
WhAm 4
Borden, John Gail 1844-1891 *ApCAB X*
Borden, Joseph 1719-1791 *BiAUS,*
NatCAB 13
Borden, Lewis Mercer 1879-1935 *NatCAB 26*
Borden, Lizzie Andrew 1860-1927 *DcAmB S1,*
NotAW, WebAB, WhAm HA, WhAm 4
Borden, Lucie Elizabeth *WomWWA 14*
Borden, Mary 1886-1968 *WhAm 5*
Borden, Matthew Chaloner Durfee 1842-
NatCAB 11
Borden, Nathaniel Briggs 1801-1865 *BiAUS,*
BiDrAC, TwCBDA, WhAm H, WhAmP
Borden, Richard 1795-1874 *DcAmB,*
NatCAB 10, WhAm H
Borden, Sir Robert Laird 1854-1937 *McGEWB*
Borden, Sam Wheatley 1899-1974 *WhAm 6*
Borden, Sarah Hildreth Ames *WomWWA 14*
Borden, Simeon 1798-1856 *ApCAB, DcAmB,*
Drake, NatCAB 24, TwCBDA, WhAm H
Borden, Spencer 1872-1957 *NatCAB 47,*
WhAm 3
Borden, Thomas James 1832-1902 *NatCAB 29*
Borden, Walter Eugene 1894-1960 *NatCAB 51*
Borden, William 1850-1896 *NatCAB 14*
Borden, William Alanson 1853-1931 *WhAm 1*
Borden, William Cline 1858-1934 *WhAm 2*
Borden, William Silvers 1893-1971 *WhAm 5*
Borders, Joseph H 1858- *WhAm 4*
Borders, M W 1867- *WhAm 4*
Bordet, Jules 1870-1961 *AsBiEn, DcScB,*
WhAm 4
Bordeu, Theophile De 1722-1776 *DcScB*
Bordewich, Henry 1844-1912 *WhAm 1*
Bordley, John Beale 1727-1804 *ApCAB,*
DcAmB, Drake, EncAAH, NewYHSD,
WhAm H
Bordley, John Beale 1800-1882 *NewYHSD,*
WhAm H
Bordley, Margaret C 1822?- *NewYHSD*
Bordman, H Clyde 1892-1957 *NatCAB 46*
Bordner, Harvey Albert 1872- *WhAm 5*
Bordone DellaScala, Giulio *DcScB*
Bordwell, Walter 1855-1926 *NatCAB 16,*
WhAm 1
Bore, Jean Etienne 1741-1820 *DcAmB,*
WhAm H
Borein, Edward 1873-1945 *REnAW*
Borein, John Edward 1872-1945 *IIBEAAW*
Boreing, Vincent 1839-1903 *BiDrAC,*
TwCBDA, WhAm 1
Borel, Emile 1871-1956 *DcScB*
Borel, Pierre 1620?-1671 *DcScB*
Borella, Victor 1906-1975 *WhAm 6*
Borelli, Giovanni Alfonso 1608-1679 *AsBiEn,*
DcScB
Borelli, Giovanni Alphonso 1608-1679 *BiHiMed*
Boreman, Arthur Inghram 1823-1896 *BiDrAC*
Boreman, Arthur Ingraham 1823-1896 *ApCAB,*
NatCAB 12, TwCBDA
Boreman, Arthur Ingram 1823-1896 *AmBi,*
DcAmB, WhAm H, WhAmP
Boreman, Jacob E 1831- *BiAUS*
Boreman, Jacob Smith 1831- *WhAm 4*
Boren, Cecil Addison, Jr. 1903-1960
NatCAB 49
Boren, James 1921- *IIBEAAW*
Boren, Lyle H 1909- *BiDrAC, WhAmP*
Boren, Samuel Hampson 1811-1881 *NatCAB 6*
Borg, Alvin Andrew 1904-1973 *WhAm 6*
Borg, Carl Oscar 1879-1946 *WhAm 2*
Borg, Carl Oscar 1879-1947 *IIBEAAW,*
NatCAB 39
Borg, Donald Gowen 1906-1975 *NatCAB 57,*
WhAm 6
Borg, George William 1887-1960 *WhAm 3*
Borg, Lawrence 1890-1954 *NatCAB 42*
Borg, Madeleine 1879- *BiCAW*
Borg, Myron Irving 1876-1931 *NatCAB 26*
Borg, Sidney Cecil 1874-1934 *ApCAB X,*

NatCAB 25
Borgella, Jerome-Maximilien 1773-1842 *ApCAB*
Borger, Edward M 1901-1953 *WhAm 3*
Borger, Hugh Donald 1905- *WhAm 5*
Borgerhoff, Elbert Benton Op'Teynde 1908-1968
WhAm 5
Borgerhoff, Joseph Leopold 1868- *WhAm 4*
Borges, Jorge Luis 1899- *McGEWB*
Borgese, G A 1882-1952 *WhAm 3*
Borgess, Caspar Henry 1824-1890 *TwCBDA,*
WhAm H
Borgess, Caspar Henry 1826-1890 *ApCAB,*
NatCAB 13
Borgfeldt, Georg 1833- *NatCAB 5*
Borghese, Prince Valerio 1912- *WhWW-II*
Borghoff, John Aloysius 1895-1957 *NatCAB 48*
Borgia, Cesare 1475-1507 *McGEWB*
Borglum, Emma Vignal 1868- *WomWWA 14*
Borglum, Gutzon 1867-1941 *BnEnAmA,*
NatCAB 14, NatCAB 30, WebAB
Borglum, Gutzon 1871-1941 *WhAm 1*
Borglum, James Lincoln DeLaMothe 1912-
IIBEAAW
Borglum, John Gutzon DeLaMothe 1867-1941
ApCAB X, DcAmB S3, IIBEAAW,
McGEWB
Borglum, Lucie Mothe 1866- *WomWWA 14*
Borglum, Mary Williams Montgomery 1874-
WomWWA 14
Borglum, Solon Hannibal 1868-1922 *BnEnAmA,*
DcAmB, IIBEAAW, NatCAB 13,
REnAW, WhAm 1
Borgman, Albert Stephens 1890-1954
NatCAB 48, WhAm 3
Borgman, John 1834?- *NewYHSD*
Borgmeyer, Charles Louis 1859-1918
NatCAB 19
Borgmeyer, Ernest d1974 *WhAm 6*
Borgognoni Of Lucca, Theodoric 1205?-1298
DcScB
Borgquist, Erasmus Swan 1887-1974 *WhAm 6*
Borhegyi, Stephan Francis De 1921-1969
WhAm 5
Bori, Lucrezia 1887-1960 *NatCAB 44,*
WhAm 4
Borie, Adolph Edward 1809-1880 *ApCAB,*
BiAUS, BiDrUSE, DcAmB, NatCAB 4,
TwCBDA, WhAm H
Borie, Adolphe 1877-1934 *DcAmB S1,*
NatCAB 31, WhAm 1
Borie, Charles Louis 1870-1943 *WhAm 2*
Borie, Edith Pettit *WomWWA 14*
Borin, Jacob 1894-1957 *NatCAB 47*
Boring, Alice Middleton 1883- *WomWWA 14*
Boring, Edwin Garrigues 1886-1968 *BiDAmEd,*
WebAB, WhAm 5
Boring, Florence Kimball 1867- *WomWWA 14*
Boring, William Alciphron 1858-1937
NatCAB 27
Boring, William Alciphron 1859-1937
DcAmB S2, NatCAB 14, WhAm 1
Boris III, King Of Bulgaria 1894-1943
WhWW-II
Borja, Ana 1635?-1706 *ApCAB*
Borja Y Aragon, Francisco 1582-1658 *ApCAB*
Borkland, G Walter 1900-1961 *NatCAB 50*
Borland *NewYHSD*
Borland, Andrew Allen 1878- *WhAm 6*
Borland, Charles, Jr. 1786-1852 *BiAUS,*
BiDrAC, WhAm H
Borland, Chauncey Blair 1878-1972 *WhAm 5*
Borland, John Jay 1837-1891 *NatCAB 14*
Borland, Maud Rives 1886- *WomWWA 14*
Borland, Solon d1864 *ApCAB, BiAUS, Drake,*
TwCBDA
Borland, Solon 1808-1864 *AmBi, BiDrAC,*
DcAmB, REnAW, WhAm H
Borland, Solon 1811-1864 *NatCAB 4*
Borland, Walter Siverly 1878-1959 *NatCAB 48*
Borland, Wilfred P 1860- *WhAm 4*
Borland, William Patterson 1867-1919 *BiDrAC,*
WhAm 1
Borlaug, Norman Ernest 1914- *EncAB,*
WebAB
Borman, Abraham *WhAm 6*
Borman, Frank 1928- *WebAMB*
Bormann, Martin 1900-1945? *WhWW-II*
Born, Ignaz Edler Von 1742-1791 *DcScB*

Born, Max 1882-1970 *AsBiEn, DcScB Sup,*
McGEWB, WhAm 5
Born, Wolfgang 1893-1949 *NatCAB 37*
Borne, John E 1852-1910 *WhAm 1*
Borneman, F W *NewYHSD*
Bornet, J *NewYHSD*
Bornholdt, Wallace John 1907-1974 *WhAm 6*
Bornman, John 1835-1926 *NatCAB 20*
Bornschein, Franz Carl 1879-1948 *NatCAB 37*
Bornstein, Sol d1967 *WhAm 4*
Bornstein, Yetta Libby Frieden d1968 *WhAm 5*
Borodin, Aleksandr Porfirevich 1833-1887
DcScB, McGEWB
Boroevic VonBojna, Svetozar 1856-1920
WhoMilH
Boroff, David 1917-1963 *NatCAB 51*
Boroff, George 1913-1968 *NatCAB 54*
Borovsky, Maxwell Philip 1896-1964 *WhAm 4*
Borowski, Felix 1872-1956 *NatCAB 42,*
WhAm 3
Borowsky, F Gordon 1906-1961 *NatCAB 49*
Borre, Prudhomme De *ApCAB*
Borrel, Jean *DcScB*
Borrell, James Harold 1890-1939 *NatCAB 29*
Borrell, Philip *NewYHSD*
Borrero, Eusebio 1793-1856 *ApCAB*
Borrette, Olive E 1862- *WomWWA 14*
Borri 1512-1592 *DcScB Sup*
Borrichius, Olaus 1626-1690 *DcScB*
Borries, Bodo Von 1905-1956 *DcScB*
Borrius, Hieronymus 1512-1592 *DcScB Sup*
Borro, Girolamo 1512-1592 *DcScB Sup*
Borromeo, Charles, Saint 1538-1584 *McGEWB*
Borromini, Francesco 1599-1667 *McGEWB*
Borron, J H *NewYHSD*
Borst, Guernsey J 1877-1955 *WhAm 3*
Borst, Henry Vroman 1857-1925 *WhAm 1*
Borst, Peter I 1797-1848 *BiAUS, BiDrAC,*
WhAm H
Borst, Sara Cone Bryant 1873- *WomWWA 14*
Borst, Victor Dow 1880-1961 *NatCAB 45*
Borsum, Louis 1854-1942 *NatCAB 31*
Borthwick *NewYHSD*
Borthwick, Harry Alfred 1898-1974 *WhAm 6*
Borthwick, Harry Robinson 1896-1963
NatCAB 48
Borthwick, John David 1825-1900? *IIBEAAW,*
NewYHSD, WhAm H
Bortkiewicz, Ladislaus Josephowitsch 1868-1931
DcScB
Bortman, Mark 1896-1967 *WhAm 4*
Bortolotti, Ettore 1866-1947 *DcScB*
Borton, Elon G 1889-1974 *WhAm 6*
Borton, Francis 1862-1929 *NatCAB 22*
Borton, Fred Ellsworth 1877-1948 *NatCAB 38*
Borton, Stockton 1852-1907 *NatCAB 18*
Bortz, Edward Leroy 1896-1970 *WhAm 5*
Borunda, Jose Ignacio 1740?-1800?
ApCAB Sup
Bory DeSaint-Vincent, Jean B G Marie
1778-1846 *DcScB*
Borzage, Frank 1895-1962 *WhAm 4*
Borzilleri, Charles Randolph 1873-1942
NatCAB 33
Bosanquet, Bernard 1848-1923 *McGEWB*
Bosbyshell, Oliver Christian 1839- *TwCBDA*
Bosc, Louis Augustin Guillaume 1759-1828
DcScB
Boscawen, Edward 1711-1761 *ApCAB, Drake*
Bosch, Albert Henry 1908- *BiDrAC*
Bosch, Carl 1874-1940 *DcScB*
Bosch, Herbert Michael 1907-1962 *NatCAB 50,*
WhAm 4
Bosch, Hieronymus 1453-1516 *McGEWB*
Bosch, Juan 1909- *McGEWB*
Bosch, Karl 1874-1940 *AsBiEn*
Boschen, Frederick Wegener 1876-1942
WhAm 2
Bose, Emil 1868-1927 *WhAm 1*
Bose, Georg Matthias 1710-1761 *DcScB*
Bose, Jagadis Chandra 1858-1937 *McGEWB*
Bose, Jagadis Chunder 1858-1937 *DcScB*
Bose, Jagadischandra 1858-1937 *DcScB Sup*
Bose, Satyendranath 1894-1974 *DcScB Sup*
Bose, Subhas Chandra 1897-1945 *McGEWB,*
WhWW-II, WhoMilH
Bosetti, Joseph 1886-1954 *WhAm 3*
Bosher, Kate Lee Langley 1865-1932 *WhAm 1,*

Bosher, Lewis Crenshaw 1860-1920 *WhAm 1*
Bosin, Francis Blackbear 1921- *IIBEAAW*
Boskovic, Rudjer J 1711-1787 *DcScB*
Boskowitz, George W 1856-1917 *WhAm 1*
Boslaugh, Paul E 1881-1964 *WhAm 4*
Bosley, Frederick Andrew 1881-1942
 NatCAB 33, WhAm 2
Bosley, Harold Augustus 1907-1975 *WhAm 6*
Bosley, William Bradford 1865- *WhAm 5*
Bosman, David 1864-1919 *WhAm 1*
Bosomworth, Thomas *ApCAB*
Boson, Adolphe *NewYHSD*
Bosone, Reva Zilpha Beck *BiDrAC, WhAmP*
Bosquet, Pierre Joseph Francois 1810-1861
 WhoMilH
Bosqui, Edward 1832-1917 *NewYHSD*
Boss, Andrew 1867-1947 *WhAm 2*
Boss, Benjamin 1880-1970 *WhAm 5*
Boss, E H *NewYHSD*
Boss, Henry M 1875- *WhAm 5*
Boss, Homer 1882-1956 *IIBEAAW*
Boss, John Linscom, Jr. 1780-1819 *BiAUS,
 BiDrAC, WhAm H*
Boss, Lewis 1846-1912 *DcAmB, DcScB,
 NatCAB 13, WhAm 1*
Boss, Louis Joseph 1917-1975 *WhAm 6*
Boss, Philip *NewYHSD*
Boss, William 1869- *WhAm 4*
Bossa, Harold Vincent 1900-1961 *NatCAB 49*
Bossange, Edward Raymond 1871-1947
 WhAm 2
Bossard, Guido 1860-1936 *WhAm 1*
Bossard, James Herbert Siward 1888-1960
 WhAm 3
Bossart, Karel Jan 1904-1975 *WhAm 6*
Bosse, Abraham 1602-1676 *DcScB*
Bossidy, John Collins 1860-1928 *WhAm 1*
Bossier, Peter E d1844 *BiAUS*
Bossier, Pierre Evariste John Baptiste 1797-1844
 BiDrAC, WhAm H
Bossom, Alfred Charles 1881-1965 *ApCAB X,
 WhAm 4*
Bosson, Edward Palfray 1864-1942 *NatCAB 32*
Bossu, F 1725?- *ApCAB, Drake*
Bossuet *NewYHSD*
Bossuet, Jacques Benigne 1627-1704 *McGEWB*
Bossut, Charles 1730-1814 *DcScB*
Bost, Ralph Walton 1901-1951 *WhAm 3*
Bostock, Edward Crary 1884-1960 *WhAm 4*
Bostock, John 1773-1846 *BiHiMed, DcScB*
Boston, Charles Anderson 1863-1935
 DcAmB S1, NatCAB 16, WhAm 1
Boston, Joseph H *WhAm 3*
Boston, L Napoleon 1871-1931 *WhAm 1*
Boston, L Napoleon 1872-1931 *NatCAB 26*
Bostrom, Wollmar Filip 1878-1956 *WhAm 3*
Bostwick, Arthur Elmore 1860-1942 *DcAmB S3,
 DcAmLiB, NatCAB 14, TwCBDA,
 WhAm 2*
Bostwick, Charles Dibble 1870-1937 *WhAm 1*
Bostwick, Charles Francis 1866-1923 *WhAm 1*
Bostwick, Clara Lena *WomWWA 14*
Bostwick, David 1721-1763 *ApCAB, Drake*
Bostwick, Delazon Swift 1893-1968 *NatCAB 54*
Bostwick, Donald Lloyd 1916-1960 *NatCAB 48*
Bostwick, Frank Matteson 1857-1945 *WhAm 2*
Bostwick, Harry Rice 1870-1931 *WhAm 1*
Bostwick, Helen Celia Ford 1848-1920 *BiCAW*
Bostwick, Helen Louise 1826- *ApCAB, Drake*
Bostwick, Lucius Allyn 1869-1940 *NatCAB 37,
 WhAm 1*
Bostwick, Roy Grier 1883-1947 *WhAm 2*
Bostwick, William L 1837- *NatCAB 4*
Bostwick, William Moreau, Jr. 1872-1932
 NatCAB 42
Boswell, Charles Martin 1859- *WhAm 1*
Boswell, Clay Carlton 1893-1973 *WhAm 6*
Boswell, Grover Cleveland d1953 *WhAm 3*
Boswell, Helen Varick 1869- *WomWWA 14*
Boswell, Ira Mathews 1866-1950 *WhAm 2A*
Boswell, James 1740-1795 *McGEWB*
Boswell, Peyton, Jr. 1904-1950 *WhAm 3*
Bosworth, Arthur Harding 1886-1949
 NatCAB 51, WhAm 3
Bosworth, Benjamin Drake 1865-1925
 NatCAB 20
Bosworth, Benjamin Miller 1848-1899 *WhAm 1*

Bosworth, Charles Ankeney 1853-1931
 NatCAB 26
Bosworth, Charles Wilder 1871- *WhAm 5*
Bosworth, Edward Increase 1861-1927 *DcAmB,
 WhAm 1, WhAm 1C*
Bosworth, Edwin Carpenter 1890-1971
 NatCAB 56, WhAm 5
Bosworth, Francke Huntington 1843-1925 *AmBi,
 DcAmB*
Bosworth, Francke Huntington, Jr. 1875-1949
 WhAm 2
Bosworth, Hobart VanZandt 1867-1943
 ApCAB X, WhAm 2
Bosworth, Karl A 1909-1970 *NatCAB 55*
Bosworth, Robert Graham 1888-1954 *WhAm 3*
Bosworth, Robert Joseph 1898-1967
 NatCAB 53
Bosworth, Sala 1805-1890 *NewYHSD*
Bosworth, Welles 1869-1966 *WhAm 4*
Botallo, Leonardo 1519?-1587? *DcScB*
Botein, Bernard 1900-1974 *NatCAB 57,
 WhAm 6*
Boteler, Alexander Robinson 1815-1892 *BiAUS,
 BiDConf, BiDrAC, DcAmB, TwCBDA,
 WhAm H*
Boteler, Henry 1817- *NewYHSD*
Botetourt, Baron *WhAm H*
Botetourt, Norbonne Berkeley, Baron De
 1734?-1770 *Drake*
Botetourt, Norborne Berkeley 1717?-1770
 ApCAB, TwCBDA
Botetourt, Norborne Berkeley, Baron De
 1718?-1770 *AmBi, DcAmB*
Botha, Louis 1862-1919 *McGEWB, WhoMilH*
Bothe, Albert Edward 1891-1955 *NatCAB 48*
Bothe, Frederick Augustus 1897-1963
 NatCAB 50
Bothe, Walther Wilhelm Georg Franz 1891-1957
 AsBiEn, DcScB, McGEWB, WhAm 3
Bothne, Gisle 1860-1934 *WhAm 1*
Boticher *NewYHSD*
Botke, Cornelis 1887-1954 *NatCAB 44*
Botke, Cornelius 1887-1954 *IIBEAAW*
Botke, Jessie Arms 1883-1971 *IIBEAAW,
 WhAm 6*
Botkin, Alexander Campbell 1842-1905
 WhAm 1
Botkin, Benjamin Albert 1901-1975 *WhAm 6*
Botkin, Harold Mitchell 1906-1970 *WhAm 5*
Botkin, Jeremiah Dunham 1849-1921 *BiDrAC,
 NatCAB 19, WhAm 1*
Botsford, Amos Edwin 1804- *ApCAB*
Botsford, Della Eliza Whiting 1884-
 WomWWA 14
Botsford, Elmer Francis 1861-1930 *NatCAB 11,
 WhAm 1*
Botsford, Florence Hudson *WhAm 5*
Botsford, George Willis 1862-1917 *ApCAB X,
 DcAmB, WhAm 1*
Botsford, Mary Rawson *WomWWA 14*
Botsford, Sarah Elizabeth Goodwin 1876-
 WomWWA 14
Botsford, Stephen Blakeslee 1919-1967
 WhAm 4A
Botsford, William 1763-1864 *ApCAB*
Botsford, William 1773-1864 *Drake*
Botsford, William Finn 1851-1912 *NatCAB 16*
Bott, Emil *NewYHSD*
Bott, Herbert Joseph 1896-1966 *WhAm 4*
Botta, Anne Charlotte Lynch d1891 *Drake*
Botta, Anne Charlotte Lynch 1815-1891 *AmBi,
 DcAmB, NotAW, TwCBDA, WhAm H*
Botta, Anne Charlotte Lynch 1820-1891
 AmWom, ApCAB, NatCAB 7
Botta, Carlo Giuseppe Guglielmo 1766-1837
 ApCAB, Drake
Botta, Vincenzo 1818-1894 *ApCAB, DcAmB,
 NatCAB 7, TwCBDA, WhAm H*
Bottazzi, Filippo 1867-1941 *DcScB*
Bottcher, John A *NewYHSD*
Bottenhorn, Irwin Alexander Hamilton
 1883-1942 *NatCAB 31*
Bottger, Rudolph Christian 1806-1881 *DcScB*
Botthof, Walter E 1888-1971 *WhAm 5*
Botticelli, Sandro 1444-1510 *McGEWB*
Botticher *NewYHSD*
Bottiger *NewYHSD*
Bottineau, Pierre 1817?-1895 *DcAmB,*

WhAm H
Botting, J Irving 1887-1956 *NatCAB 43*
Bottles, Joseph 1825?- *NewYHSD*
Bottolfsen, C A 1891-1964 *WhAm 4*
Bottom, Raymond Blanton 1893-1953 *WhAm 3*
Bottome, Harry Howard 1870-1963 *WhAm 4*
Bottome, Margaret McDonald 1827-1906
 *DcAmB, NatCAB 13, TwCBDA,
 WhAm 1*
Bottome, Phyllis 1884-1963 *WhAm 4*
Bottomley, Allen W T 1873-1933 *WhAm 1*
Bottomley, John Taylor 1869-1925 *NatCAB 20,
 WhAm 1*
Bottomley, Thomas 1805-1894 *TwCBDA*
Bottomley, William Lawrence 1883-1951
 NatCAB 39, WhAm 3
Bottomly, Raymond Victor, Sr. 1885-1961
 WhAm 4
Bottoms, George Washington 1848-1924
 NatCAB 28
Botts, Charles Tyler 1809-1884 *DcAmB,
 WhAm H*
Botts, Clarence Milton 1881- *WhAm 6*
Botts, George 1829?- *NewYHSD*
Botts, Hugh Pearce 1903-1964 *WhAm 4*
Botts, John Minor 1802-1869 *AmBi, ApCAB,
 BiAUS, BiAUS Sup, BiDrAC, DcAmB,
 Drake, NatCAB 8, TwCBDA, WhAm H*
Bottsford, Leslie Lee 1887-1956 *NatCAB 45*
Bottum, Elias Huntington 1850-1925
 NatCAB 20
Bottum, Joseph H 1903- *BiDrAC*
Bottume, George F 1828- *NewYHSD*
Boturini-Benaducci, Lorenzo d1760?
 ApCAB Sup
Bouattoura, Tewfik 1936-1970 *WhAm 5*
Boucek, Charles Frank 1875-1948 *NatCAB 36*
Bouchard, Adolph *NewYHSD*
Bouchard, James 1823-1889 *REnAW*
Bouche *NewYHSD*
Boucher, Anthony 1911-1968 *WhAm 5*
Boucher, Carl Opdycke 1904-1975 *WhAm 6*
Boucher, Charles T 1809-1884 *ApCAB*
Boucher, Chauncey Samuel 1886-1955
 NatCAB 46, WhAm 3
Boucher, Chauncey Watson 1851-1934
 WhAm 1
Boucher, Francois 1703-1770 *McGEWB*
Boucher, Horace Edward 1873-1935 *DcAmB S1,
 WhAm HA, WhAm 4*
Boucher, Jonathan 1737?-1804 *AmBi, DcAmB*
Boucher, Jonathan 1738-1804 *ApCAB, Drake,
 EncAB, NatCAB 9, TwCBDA, WhAm H*
Boucher, Pierre 1622-1717 *ApCAB, Drake*
Boucher DeCrevecoeur DePerthes, J 1788-1868
 AsBiEn, DcScB, DcScB Sup
Boucherville, Charles Eugene Boucher De 1820-
 ApCAB
Boucherville, George Boucher De 1812- *ApCAB*
Bouchet, Edward Alexander 1852- *WhoColR*
Bouchette, Joseph 1774-1841 *ApCAB, Drake*
Boucicault, Dion 1820-1890 *DcAmB,
 McGEWB, WebAB, WhAm H*
Boucicault, Dion 1822-1890 *ApCAB, TwCBDA*
Boucicault, Dion G 1859-1929 *WhAm 1*
Boucicault, Dionysius Lardner 1822-1890
 NatCAB 2
Boucicault, Ruth Baldwin Holt *WhAm 5*
Bouck, Francis Eugene 1873-1941 *NatCAB 36,
 WhAm 1*
Bouck, Gabriel 1828-1904 *BiDrAC*
Bouck, Joseph 1788-1858 *BiAUS, BiDrAC,
 WhAm H*
Bouck, William C 1786-1859 *ApCAB, BiAUS,
 DcAmB, Drake, NatCAB 3, TwCBDA,
 WhAm H*
Bouck, Zeh 1901-1946 *WhAm 2*
Boucke, Ewald Augustus 1871- *WhAm 5*
Boucke, O Fred 1881-1935 *WhAm 1*
Boude, Thomas 1752-1822 *BiAUS, BiDrAC,
 WhAm H*
Boudeman, Dallas 1846- *WhAm 4*
Boudeman, Robert Meier 1917-1974 *WhAm 6*
Bouden *NewYHSD*
Bouden, John Edward 1865-1930 *NatCAB 24*
Boudet, Miss *NewYHSD*
Boudet, Dominic W d1845 *NewYHSD,
 WhAm H*

Boudet, Nicholas Vincent *NewYHSD, WhAm H*
Boudet, William *NewYHSD*
Boudier, J J *NewYHSD*
Boudin, Louis Boudinoff 1874-1952 *DcAmB S5, WhAm 3*
Boudinot, Elias 1740-1821 *AmBi, ApCAB, BiAUS, BiDrAC, BiDrUSE, DcAmB, Drake, NatCAB 2, TwCBDA, WhAm H, WhAmP*
Boudinot, Elias 1802?-1839 *DcAmReB, NatCAB 19*
Boudinot, Elias 1803?-1839 *DcAmB, REnAW, WhAm H*
Boudinot, Elias Cornelius 1835-1890 *ApCAB Sup, BiDConf, DcAmB, NatCAB 19, TwCBDA, WhAm H*
Boudinot, Jane J *WhAm 5*
Boudinot, Truman Everett 1895-1945 *NatCAB 34, WhAm 2*
Boudit *NewYHSD*
Boudon *NewYHSD*
Boudon, David *NewYHSD*
Boue, Ami 1794-1881 *DcScB*
Bouelles, Charles De *DcScB*
Bouey, Forrest Lee 1870- *WhoColR*
Boufflers, Louis Francois, Duc De 1644-1711 *WhoMilH*
Bougainville, Louis Antoine De 1729-1811 *ApCAB, DcScB, Drake, McGEWB*
Boughan, Andrew Bartholomew 1871- *NatCAB 17*
Boughner, LaRue 1879-1944 *NatCAB 33*
Boughner, Leroy John 1880- *WhAm 6*
Boughner, Martha *WomWWA 14*
Boughton, Alice 1866- *WomWWA 14*
Boughton, Alice C 1885- *WomWWA 14*
Boughton, Caroline Greenbank 1854- *AmWom*
Boughton, George Henry 1833-1905 *NatCAB 15, NewYHSD, TwCBDA, WhAm H*
Boughton, George Henry 1834-1905 *WhAm 1*
Boughton, George Henry 1836-1905 *ApCAB*
Boughton, Guy Cluxton 1877-1950 *NatCAB 39*
Boughton, Lethe Hawes 1872- *WomWWA 14*
Boughton, Martha Arnold d1928 *WhAm 1, WomWWA 14*
Boughton, Willis 1854-1942 *ApCAB X, WhAm 2*
Bougrade, Peter 1845- *TwCBDA*
Bouguer, Pierre 1698-1758 *AsBiEn, DcScB*
Bouguereau, Elizabeth Jane Gardner 1837-1922 *NewYHSD, WhAm 4*
Bouguereau, P H, Jr. *NewYHSD*
Bouillaud, Jean Baptiste 1796-1881 *BiHiMed*
Bouille, Francis C Amour, Marquis De 1739-1800 *ApCAB, Drake*
Bouiller, Jule 1841?- *NewYHSD*
Bouilles, Charles De *DcScB*
Bouillon, Lincoln 1900-1966 *WhAm 5*
Bouin, Pol Andre 1870-1962 *DcScB*
Boulanger, Georges Ernest 1837-1891 *WhoMilH*
Boulbon, Gaston Raoulx, Comte De 1817-1854 *ApCAB, Drake*
Bouldin, James Wood 1792-1854 *BiAUS, BiDrAC, WhAm H, WhAmP*
Bouldin, Thomas Tyler 1781-1834 *BiAUS, BiDrAC, WhAm H, WhAmP*
Bouldin, Virgil 1866- *WhAm 5*
Boule, Marcellin 1861-1942 *DcScB*
Boulet, Alex 1818?- *NewYHSD*
Boulez, Pierre 1925- *McGEWB*
Bouligney, Dominique 1773-1833 *BiAUS, TwCBDA*
Bouligney, John Edmund 1824-1864 *BiAUS*
Bouligney, John Edward 1824-1864 *TwCBDA*
Bouligny, Charles Joseph Dominique 1773-1833 *BiDrAC, WhAmP*
Bouligny, Dominique 1771?-1833 *DcAmB, WhAm H*
Bouligny, Dominique 1773-1833 *ApCAB, NatCAB 11*
Bouligny, John Edward 1824-1864 *ApCAB, BiDrAC, WhAm H, WhAmP*
Boullanger, Nicolas-Antoine 1722-1759 *DcScB*
Boulliau, Ismael 1605-1694 *DcScB*
Boult, William Thomas 1886-1943 *WhAm 2*
Boulter, Howard Thornton 1907-1953 *WhAm 3*

Boulter, Thornton d1953 *WhAm 3*
Boulton, Charles Arkoll 1841-1899 *ApCAB Sup*
Boulton, Frances Schroeder 1874- *WomWWA 14*
Boulton, G d1833? *NewYHSD*
Boulton, George 1834-1916 *NatCAB 26*
Boulton, Payne Augustin 1864- *WhAm 4*
Boulware, Judson Powell 1890-1947 *NatCAB 39*
Boulware, William *BiAUS*
Bouma, Clarence 1891-1962 *NatCAB 50*
Boumediene, Houari 1932- *McGEWB*
Bound, Franklin 1829-1910 *BiDrAC*
Boundey, Burton Shepard 1879-1962 *IlBEAAW*
Bounell, Emery Guy 1871-1948 *NatCAB 41*
Bounetheau, Mrs. H B *NewYHSD*
Bounetheau, Henry Breintnall 1797-1877 *NewYHSD*
Bounetheau, Henry Brintell 1797-1877 *WhAm H*
Bounetheau, Henry Brintnell 1797-1877 *DcAmB*
Bounetheau, Mrs. J C *NewYHSD*
Bouquet *NewYHSD*
Bouquet, Henry 1719-1765 *AmBi, DcAmB, REnAW, WebAMB, WhAm H, WhoMilH*
Bouquet, Henry 1719-1766 *ApCAB, Drake, NatCAB 20*
Bouquet, Jean-Claude 1819-1885 *DcScB*
Bouquillon, Thomas Joseph 1840-1902 *DcAmB, WhAm 1*
Bour, Edmond 1832-1866 *DcScB*
Bour, John Martin 1863-1922 *NatCAB 35*
Bourassa, Joseph-Henri-Napoleon 1868-1952 *McGEWB*
Bourbaki, Charles Denis Sauter 1816-1897 *WhoMilH*
Bourbaki, Nicolas *DcScB*
Bourbon, Charles, Duc De 1490-1527 *WhoMilH*
Bourdelin, Claude 1621?-1699 *DcScB*
Bourdelot, Pierre Michon 1610-1685 *DcScB*
Bourdier, Lillian Blanche 1907-1973 *WhAm 6*
Bourdon, David *NewYHSD*
Bourdon, Eugene 1808-1884 *DcScB*
Bourgade, Peter 1845-1908 *ApCAB, NatCAB 12, WhAm 1*
Bourgard, Caroline B *WomWWA 14*
Bourgeois, Francis *NewYHSD*
Bourgeois, Leon 1851-1925 *McGEWB*
Bourgeois, Lewis Irving 1896-1956 *NatCAB 47*
Bourgeois, Lionel John, Sr. 1890-1956 *WhAm 4*
Bourgeois, Louise 1911- *BnEnAmA*
Bourgeois, Sister Margaret 1620-1700 *ApCAB*
Bourgeoys, Marguerite 1620-1700 *McGEWB*
Bourges, Arthur 1877- *WhoColR*
Bourget, Ignatius 1799-1885 *ApCAB*
Bourgmont, Etienne Venyard, Sieur De 1680?-1730? *DcAmB, WhAm H*
Bourgoin, Joseph *NewYHSD*
Bourgoine, Joseph John d1955 *WhAm 3*
Bourguet, Louis 1678-1742 *DcScB Sup*
Bourguiba, Habib 1903- *McGEWB*
Bourinot, John George 1837- *ApCAB*
Bourke, John Gregory 1846-1896 *ApCAB Sup, DcAmB, NatCAB 13, REnAW, WhAm H*
Bourke, Thomas *NewYHSD*
Bourke-White, Margaret 1906-1971 *WebAB, WhAm 5*
Bourlamarque, M De d1764 *ApCAB, Drake*
Bourland, Albert Pike 1861-1927 *WhAm 1*
Bourland, Benjamin Parsons 1870-1943 *NatCAB 32, WhAm 2*
Bourland, Caroline Brown 1871- *WhAm 5, WomWWA 14*
Bourlier, Alfred J B *NewYHSD*
Bourn, Augustus Osborn 1834-1925 *NatCAB 9, TwCBDA, WhAm 1*
Bourn, Benjamin 1755-1808 *BiDrAC, WhAmP*
Bourn, William Bowers 1857-1936 *NatCAB 28*
Bourne, Annie Thomson Nettleton *WomWWA 14*
Bourne, Benjamin 1755-1808 *ApCAB, BiAUS, DcAmB, Drake, NatCAB 12, TwCBDA, WhAm H*
Bourne, Edward Emerson 1797-1873 *ApCAB, TwCBDA*
Bourne, Edward Gaylord 1860-1908 *DcAmB, NatCAB 10, TwCBDA, WhAm 1*

Bourne, Emma 1846- *AmWom*
Bourne, Frank Augustus 1871-1936 *WhAm 1*
Bourne, Frederick Gilbert d1919 *WhAm 1*
Bourne, George 1760?-1845 *ApCAB*
Bourne, George 1780-1845 *ApCAB Sup, DcAmB, WhAm H*
Bourne, Henry Eldridge 1862-1946 *WhAm 2*
Bourne, Jonathan 1811-1889 *NatCAB 19*
Bourne, Jonathan, Jr. 1855-1940 *BiDrAC, DcAmB S2, NatCAB 30, WhAm 1, WhAmP*
Bourne, Mary Joy *WomWWA 14*
Bourne, Nehemiah 1611?-1691 *ApCAB, DcAmB, WhAm H*
Bourne, Randolph Silliman 1886-1918 *AmBi, DcAmB, EncAB, McGEWB, WebAB, WhAm 1*
Bourne, Richard d1682 *ApCAB, NatCAB 12, TwCBDA*
Bourne, Richard d1685? *Drake*
Bourne, Shearjashub 1720-1781 *NatCAB 12*
Bourne, Shearjashub 1746-1806 *BiDrAC, WhAm H, WhAmP*
Bourne, Shearjasub d1806 *BiAUS*
Bournon, Jacques-Louis, Comte De 1751-1825 *DcScB*
Bourns, Edward 1801-1871 *NatCAB 18*
Bourque, Norbert Odeon 1879-1946 *NatCAB 37*
Bourquin, Charles F 1800?- *NewYHSD*
Bourquin, Frederick 1808- *NewYHSD*
Bourquin, George McClellan 1863-1958 *ApCAB X, WhAm 3*
Bourskaya, Ina 1888-1955 *WhAm 3*
Bouscaren, Louis Frederic Gustave 1840-1904 *WhAm 1*
Bouscaren, Louis H G 1882-1966 *WhAm 4*
Bousfield, John Hodson Alfred 1877-1937 *NatCAB 31*
Bousfield, Midian Othello 1885-1948 *WhAm 2, WhoColR*
Boush, Clifford Joseph 1854-1936 *NatCAB 44, WhAm 1*
Boussinesq, Joseph Valentin 1842-1929 *DcScB*
Boussingault, Jean Baptiste J Dieudonne 1802-1887 *ApCAB, AsBiEn, DcScB*
Boutell, Arnold 1869-1947 *NatCAB 34*
Boutell, Henry Sherman 1856- *TwCBDA*
Boutell, Henry Sherman 1856-1916 *WhAmP*
Boutell, Henry Sherman 1856-1926 *BiDrAC, DcAmB, NatCAB 21, WhAm 1*
Boutelle, Charles Addison 1839-1901 *BiDrAC, DcAmB, TwCBDA, WhAm 1, WhAmP*
Boutelle, Clarence Miles 1851- *NatCAB 11*
Boutelle, DeWitt Clinton 1820-1884 *ApCAB, IlBEAAW, NewYHSD, TwCBDA, WhAm H*
Boutelle, Richard Schley 1898-1962 *WhAm 4*
Bouton, Archibald Lewis 1872-1941 *NatCAB 32, WhAm 2*
Bouton, Burrett Beebe 1903-1965 *WhAm 4*
Bouton, Charles Leonard 1869-1922 *NatCAB 30, WhAm 1*
Bouton, Edward 1834-1921 *NatCAB 19*
Bouton, Edward Henry 1858- *WhAm 4*
Bouton, Emily St. John *AmWom, WhAm 5, WomWWA 14*
Bouton, G B *NewYHSD*
Bouton, Harry Remington 1879-1946 *NatCAB 34*
Bouton, Jean B *NewYHSD*
Bouton, John Bell 1830-1902 *ApCAB, DcAmB, Drake, TwCBDA, WhAm H*
Bouton, Nathaniel d1878 *Drake*
Bouton, Nathaniel 1797-1878 *ApCAB*
Bouton, Nathaniel 1799-1878 *DcAmB, NatCAB 20, TwCBDA, WhAm H*
Bouton, Rosa 1860- *WhAm 4*
Bouton, Rosa 1869- *WomWWA 14*
Bouton, S Miles 1876- *WhAm 5*
Boutroux, Pierre Leon 1880-1922 *DcScB*
Bouts, Dirk 1415?-1475 *McGEWB*
Boutte, Matthew Virgil *WhoColR*
Boutwell, George S 1818-1905 *BiAUS*
Boutwell, George Sewall 1818-1905 *AmBi, ApCAB, BiDrUSE, DcAmB, Drake, NatCAB 1, NatCAB 4, TwCBDA, WebAB, WhAm 1*
Boutwell, George Sewel 1818-1905 *BiDrAC,*

WhAmP

Boutwell, Georgiana A 1843- *WomWWA 14*

Boutwell, John Mason 1874-1968 *NatCAB 54, WhAm 5*

Boutwell, Paul Winslow 1888-1971 *WhAm 5*

Boutwell, William Rowe 1860- *WhAm 4*

Bouvard, Alexis 1767-1843 *DcScB*

Bouve, Clement L 1878-1944 *WhAm 2*

Bouve, Elisha W *NewYHSD*

Bouve, Ephraim 1817-1897 *NewYHSD*

Bouve, Pauline Carrington d1928 *WhAm 1, WomWWA 14*

Bouve, Thomas Tracy 1815-1896 *ApCAB, NatCAB 7*

Bouve, Walter Lincoln 1849-1944 *NatCAB 34*

Bouvelles, Charles 1470?-1553? *DcScB*

Bouvet, Jeanne Marie 1864- *WhAm 4, WomWWA 14*

Bouvet, Marie Marguerite 1865-1915 *DcAmB, WhAm 1, WomWWA 14*

Bouvier, John 1787-1851 *AmBi, ApCAB, DcAmB, Drake, NatCAB 16, TwCBDA, WhAm H*

Bouvier, John Vernou 1891-1957 *NatCAB 47*

Bouvier, Maurice 1862- *WhAm 5*

Bovadilla, Don Francois De d1502 *Drake*

Bovaird, Emma Griffith *WomWWA 14*

Bovard, Charles Lincoln 1860-1930 *ApCAB X, WhAm 1*

Bovard, Freeman Daily 1851-1920 *WhAm 1*

Bovard, George Finley 1856-1932 *NatCAB 29, WhAm 1*

Bovard, John Freeman 1881- *WhAm 6*

Bovard, Marion McKinley 1847-1891 *NatCAB 23, NatCAB 29*

Bovard, Oliver Kirby 1872-1945 *DcAmB S3, NatCAB 35*

Bovard, Warren Bradley 1885-1930 *WhAm 1*

Bovard, William Sherman 1864-1936 *WhAm 1*

Bovee, Christian Nestell 1820-1904 *ApCAB, NatCAB 16, WhAm 1*

Bovee, I A *IlBEAAW*

Bovee, John Wesley 1861-1927 *NatCAB 22, WhAm 1*

Bovee, Marvin Henry 1827-1888 *ApCAB Sup*

Bovee, Matthias Jacob 1793-1872 *BiAUS, BiDrAC, WhAm H*

Bovell, John Vance 1799-1835 *NatCAB 7*

Bovell, Thomas W *NewYHSD*

Bovenizer, George Wallace 1879-1961 *NatCAB 48, WhAm 4*

Boveri, Theodor 1862-1915 *DcScB*

Boves, Jose Tomas d1814 *ApCAB*

Boves, Joseph Thomas d1814 *Drake*

Bovet, Daniele 1907- *AsBiEn*

Bovett, Ami 1818?- *NewYHSD*

Bovey, Charles Cranton 1864-1955 *WhAm 3*

Bovie, William T 1882-1958 *NatCAB 44, WhAm 3*

Bovillus *DcScB*

Boving, Adam Giede 1869- *WhAm 5*

Boving, Charles B 1871- *WhAm 5*

Bow, Charles Clinton 1858-1915 *NatCAB 16*

Bow, Clara 1905-1965 *WebAB*

Bow, Frank Townsend 1901-1972 *BiDrAC, WhAm 5*

Bow, Jonathan Gaines 1847- *WhAm 4*

Bow, Warren E 1891-1945 *WhAm 2*

Bow-Lec d1859 *Drake*

Bowa, Peter *NewYHSD*

Bowater, Sir Eric Vansittart 1895-1962 *WhAm 4*

Bowden, Aberdeen Orlando 1881-1946 *WhAm 2*

Bowden, Angie Burt 1862- *WomWWA 14*

Bowden, Charles Leonard 1865-1941 *NatCAB 33*

Bowden, Frederick Prescott 1868-1933 *NatCAB 25*

Bowden, Garfield Arthur 1880- *WhAm 2*

Bowden, George Edwin 1852-1908 *BiDrAC, WhAm 4*

Bowden, John 1751-1817 *ApCAB, DcAmB, Drake, NatCAB 6, TwCBDA, WhAm H*

Bowden, Laurens Reeve 1879-1948 *WhAm 2*

Bowden, Lemuel J 1812-1864 *BiAUS*

Bowden, Lemuel Jackson 1815-1864 *ApCAB, BiDrAC, NatCAB 4, TwCBDA, WhAm H*

Bowden, Paul Webster 1913-1967 *NatCAB 54*

Bowdish, Nelson S 1831-1916 *NewYHSD*

Bowditch, Charles Pickering 1842-1921 *DcAmB, NatCAB 20, WhAm 1*

Bowditch, Ernest William 1850-1918 *NatCAB 29*

Bowditch, Harold 1883-1964 *NatCAB 52*

Bowditch, Henry Ingersoll 1802-1892 *AmBi*

Bowditch, Henry Ingersoll 1808-1892 *ApCAB, DcAmB, McGEWB, NatCAB 8, TwCBDA, WhAm H*

Bowditch, Henry Pickering 1840-1911 *AmBi, ApCAB, BiDAmEd, BiHiMed, DcAmB, DcScB, NatCAB 12, TwCBDA, WhAm 1*

Bowditch, Manfred 1890-1960 *NatCAB 44*

Bowditch, Nathaniel 1773-1838 *AmBi, ApCAB, DcAmB, DcScB, Drake, EncAB, McGEWB, NatCAB 6, TwCBDA, WebAB, WhAm H*

Bowditch, Nathaniel Ingersoll 1805-1861 *ApCAB, Drake, TwCBDA*

Bowditch, Richard Lyon 1900-1959 *NatCAB 49, WhAm 3*

Bowditch, Sylvia Church Scudder *WomWWA 14*

Bowditch, Vincent Yardley 1852-1929 *WhAm 1*

Bowdle, Stanley Eyre 1868-1919 *BiDrAC, NatCAB 24, WhAm 4*

Bowdoin, George Edward 1898-1959 *NatCAB 47, WhAm 3*

Bowdoin, George Sullivan 1833-1913 *NatCAB 16, WhAm 1*

Bowdoin, James 1726-1790 *AmBi, DcAmB, McGEWB, TwCBDA, WebAB, WhAm H, WhAmP*

Bowdoin, James 1727-1790 *ApCAB, BiAUS, Drake, NatCAB 2*

Bowdoin, James 1752-1811 *ApCAB, DcAmB, Drake, NatCAB 1, WhAm H, WhAmP*

Bowdoin, Temple *ApCAB X*

Bowdoin, William Goodrich 1860- *WhAm 4*

Bowdon, Franklin Welsh 1817-1857 *BiAUS, BiDrAC, WhAm H*

Bowe, Augustine J 1892-1966 *WhAm 4*

Bowe, Edward 1873-1938 *NatCAB 34*

Bowe, Frederick Otto 1878-1943 *NatCAB 32*

Bowell, Mackenzie 1823- *ApCAB*

Bowen, Abel 1790-1850 *DcAmB, NatCAB 21, NewYHSD, WhAm H*

Bowen, Albert E 1876-1953 *WhAm 3*

Bowen, Anna Cara Cornelia *WomWWA 14*

Bowen, Annie Beauregard *WomWWA 14*

Bowen, Arthur John 1873- *WhAm 5*

Bowen, Asa Bosworth 1942- *WhAm 3*

Bowen, Benjamin Lester 1860-1920 *WhAm 1*

Bowen, Catherine Drinker 1897-1973 *WhAm 6*

Bowen, Charles C 1839?- *NewYHSD*

Bowen, Christopher Columbus 1832-1880 *BiAUS, BiDrAC, WhAm H*

Bowen, Clarence Winthrop 1852-1935 *ApCAB Sup, ApCAB X, NatCAB 27, TwCBDA, WhAm 1*

Bowen, Clayton Raymond 1877-1934 *WhAm 1*

Bowen, Cornelia 1870- *WhoColR*

Bowen, Crate Dwiggins 1871-1959 *NatCAB 49*

Bowen, Daniel 1760?-1856 *NewYHSD, WhAm H*

Bowen, Earl 1899-1965 *WhAm 4*

Bowen, Edgar Woodbury 1886-1935 *NatCAB 33*

Bowen, Edwin Winfield 1866-1953 *NatCAB 41, WhAm 3*

Bowen, Eli 1824-1886 *ApCAB*

Bowen, Elizabeth Dorothea Cole 1899-1973 *McGEWB, WhAm 5*

Bowen, Ezra 1891-1945 *WhAm 2*

Bowen, Francis 1811-1890 *AmBi, ApCAB, DcAmB, Drake, NatCAB 11, TwCBDA, WhAm H*

Bowen, George 1816-1888 *ApCAB Sup, DcAmB, WhAm H*

Bowen, George P *NewYHSD*

Bowen, George Thomas 1803-1828 *ApCAB, NatCAB 12, TwCBDA*

Bowen, George W 1821?- *NewYHSD*

Bowen, H M *NewYHSD*

Bowen, Harold Gardiner 1883-1965 *NatCAB 51, WhAm 4*

Bowen, Harry d1942 *WhAm 2*

Bowen, Henry 1841-1915 *BiDrAC*

Bowen, Henry Chandler 1813-1896 *AmBi, ApCAB Sup, DcAmB, NatCAB 1, TwCBDA, WhAm H*

Bowen, Henry James 1853- *ApCAB X*

Bowen, Herbert Wolcott 1856-1927 *ApCAB Sup, ApCAB X, DcAmB, NatCAB 13, NatCAB 20, TwCBDA, WhAm 1*

Bowen, Ira Sprague 1898-1973 *WhAm 5*

Bowen, Ivan 1886-1959 *WhAm 3*

Bowen, Jabez 1739-1815 *NatCAB 8*

Bowen, James 1808-1886 *ApCAB, TwCBDA*

Bowen, John *NewYHSD*

Bowen, John C d1954 *WhAm 3*

Bowen, John Campbell 1872- *WhAm 5*

Bowen, John Eliot 1858-1890 *ApCAB Sup, NatCAB 6*

Bowen, John Henry 1780-1822 *BiAUS, BiDrAC, WhAm H*

Bowen, John S 1829-1863 *ApCAB, Drake, NatCAB 12, TwCBDA*

Bowen, John Stevens 1830-1863 *BiDConf*

Bowen, John T 1801?-1856? *NewYHSD*

Bowen, John Templeton 1857-1940 *WhAm 1*

Bowen, John Wesley Edward 1855- *NatCAB 14, WhoColR*

Bowen, John Wesley Edward 1889-1962 *WhAm 4*

Bowen, Joseph Abraham 1832-1914 *NatCAB 17*

Bowen, Joseph Henry 1905-1961 *NatCAB 49, WhAm 4*

Bowen, Lavinia 1820?- *NewYHSD*

Bowen, Lem Warner 1857- *WhAm 1*

Bowen, Louise DeKoven 1859-1953 *BiCAW, DcAmB S5, WhAm 3, WomWWA 14*

Bowen, Marcellus 1846-1916 *WhAm 1*

Bowen, Margaret Barber 1874- *WomWWA 14*

Bowen, Mary M 1849- *WomWWA 14*

Bowen, Nathaniel 1779-1839 *ApCAB, Drake, NatCAB 12, TwCBDA*

Bowen, Norman Levi 1887-1956 *DcScB, WebAB, WhAm 3*

Bowen, Oliver d1800 *ApCAB, Drake*

Bowen, Rees Tate 1809-1879 *BiAUS, BiDrAC, WhAm H*

Bowen, Reuben Dean 1859-1939 *WhAm 1*

Bowen, Richard Lebaron 1878- *WhAm 6*

Bowen, Sayles Jenks 1813-1896 *TwCBDA*

Bowen, Temple 1898-1960 *NatCAB 48*

Bowen, Thomas d1790 *NewYHSD*

Bowen, Thomas M 1835-1906 *ApCAB, NatCAB 12, TwCBDA, WhAm 1*

Bowen, Thomas Mead 1835-1906 *BiDrAC, WhAmP*

Bowen, Thomas Meade 1835-1906 *DcAmB*

Bowen, Truman Neal 1900-1956 *NatCAB 51*

Bowen, Wilbur Pardon 1864-1928 *BiDAmEd, WhAm 1*

Bowen, William 1877-1937 *WhAm 1*

Bowen, William Abraham 1856-1921 *WhAm 1*

Bowen, William Alfred 1853-1919 *NatCAB 47*

Bowen, William Miller 1862-1937 *NatCAB 39, WhAm 1*

Bowen, William Spencer 1886-1959 *NatCAB 47*

Bowen, Willis Elliott 1871-1944 *NatCAB 34*

Bower, Albert Gordon 1890-1960 *NatCAB 47*

Bower, Alexander 1875-1952 *WhAm 3*

Bower, Andrew Park 1869-1949 *NatCAB 38*

Bower, Bertha Muzzy 1871-1940 *WhAm 1*

Bower, Emma E *WomWWA 14*

Bower, Ferdinand Augustus 1883-1971 *NatCAB 57*

Bower, Frederick Orpen 1855-1948 *DcScB*

Bower, George Hoyle 1864- *WhAm 4*

Bower, George Rosengarten 1866-1919 *NatCAB 26*

Bower, Gustavus B *BiAUS*

Bower, Gustavus Miller 1790-1864 *BiDrAC, WhAm H*

Bower, John *NewYHSD*

Bower, Joseph Augustus 1880- *WhAm 6*

Bower, Joseph Edward 1849-1925 *NatCAB 21*

Bower, Lucy Scott 1864-1934 *WhAm 1*

Bower, Olive Stanley 1871- *WomWWA 14*

Bower, Raymond G 1895-1962 *WhAm 4*

Bower, William *NewYHSD*

Bower, William Horton 1850-1910 *BiDrAC*
Bowerman, George Franklin 1868-1960
 DcAmLiB, NatCAB 14, WhAm 4
Bowerman, Guy Emerson 1866-1940 *WhAm 2*
Bowerman, Helen Cox 1878- *WomWWA 14*
Bowers, Alphonzo Benjamin 1830-1926
 NatCAB 12, WhAm 1
Bowers, Claude Gernade 1878-1958 *EncAB,
 McGEWB, NatCAB 44, WhAm 3*
Bowers, Mrs. D P 1830-1895 *AmWom*
Bowers, Don DeLargy 1902-1957 *NatCAB 47*
Bowers, Eaton Jackson 1865-1939 *BiDrAC,
 WhAm 4, WhAmP*
Bowers, Edgar 1866- *WhAm 4*
Bowers, Edison Louis 1898-1971 *WhAm 5*
Bowers, Edward 1822?- *NewYHSD*
Bowers, Edward Augustus 1857- *WhAm 4*
Bowers, Edward C 1809-1893 *TwCBDA*
Bowers, Edward Charles 1881-1947 *NatCAB 36*
Bowers, Elizabeth Crocker 1830-1895 *ApCAB,
 DcAmB, TwCBDA, WhAm H*
Bowers, Elsworth 1879- *WhAm 6*
Bowers, Frederick Mengel 1882-1964
 NatCAB 51
Bowers, George Henry 1866-1943 *NatCAB 38*
Bowers, George Meade 1863-1925 *BiDrAC,
 NatCAB 13, WhAm 1, WhAmP*
Bowers, George Walter 1878-1943 *NatCAB 35*
Bowers, Henry Francis 1837-1911 *WhAm 1*
Bowers, Henry Smith 1878- *WhAm 6*
Bowers, Herbert Edmund 1868-1910 *WhAm 1*
Bowers, John Hugh 1875-1923 *WhAm 1*
Bowers, John Myer 1772-1846 *BiAUS,
 BiDrAC, WhAm H*
Bowers, John Myer 1849-1918 *NatCAB 24*
Bowers, LaMont Montgomery 1847-1941
 NatCAB 31, WhAm 1
Bowers, Larkin Bruce 1877- *WhAm 1*
Bowers, Lillian Estella Shepard *WomWWA 14*
Bowers, Lloyd Wheaton 1859-1910 *DcAmB,
 NatCAB 14, NatCAB 22, WhAm 1*
Bowers, Paul Eugene 1886-1938 *NatCAB 27*
Bowers, Robert Graves 1869- *WhAm 5*
Bowers, Robert Hood 1877-1941 *NatCAB 35,
 WhAm 1*
Bowers, Rose Alexander *WomWWA 14*
Bowers, Spotswood Dandridge 1876-1939
 NatCAB 31
Bowers, Stephen 1832- *TwCBDA*
Bowers, Theodore Shelton 1832-1866 *ApCAB,
 DcAmB, TwCBDA, WhAm H*
Bowers, Thomas Wilson 1888-1950 *WhAm 2A*
Bowers, Walter Abraham 1898- *WhAm 6*
Bowers, William Gray 1879-1945 *WhAm 2*
Bowers, William Wallace 1834-1917 *BiDrAC,
 WhAmP*
Bowersoch, Justin D 1842- *TwCBDA*
Bowersock, Donald Curtis 1899-1954 *WhAm 3*
Bowersock, Justin DeWitt 1842-1922 *BiDrAC,
 NatCAB 44, WhAm 1, WhAmP*
Bowersock, Justin Dewitt 1871-1955
 NatCAB 44
Bowersox, Charles Alexander 1846-
 NatCAB 17
Bowery, Thomas *NewYHSD*
Bowes, Charles E *NewYHSD*
Bowes, Edward J 1874-1946 *DcAmB S4,
 WhAm 2*
Bowes, Frank B 1862-1939 *WhAm 1*
Bowes, Joseph *NewYHSD*
Bowes, Joseph 1885-1965 *WhAm 4*
Bowes, Robert Malcolm 1884-1945 *NatCAB 34*
Bowes, Theodore Faus 1904-1967 *NatCAB 53,
 WhAm 4, WhAm 5*
Bowie, A Gwynn 1896-1957 *NatCAB 44*
Bowie, Alfred William 1878-1934 *NatCAB 25*
Bowie, Clifford Pinckney 1879-1952 *WhAm 3*
Bowie, Edward Hall 1874-1943 *WhAm 2*
Bowie, James 1790?-1836 *ApCAB, TwCBDA*
Bowie, James 1795-1836 *NatCAB 4, REnAW*
Bowie, James 1796-1836 *DcAmB, WebAB,
 WebAMB, WhAm H*
Bowie, James 1799-1836 *AmBi*
Bowie, James Park 1853-1919 *NatCAB 18*
Bowie, Oden 1826-1894 *BiAUS, DcAmB,
 NatCAB 3, TwCBDA, WhAm H*
Bowie, Richard I 1807- *BiAUS*
Bowie, Richard Johns 1807-1881 *DcAmB,*

WhAm H
Bowie, Richard Johns 1807-1888 *BiDrAC,
 WhAmP*
Bowie, Richard Jones 1807-1881 *NatCAB 13*
Bowie, Robert d1818 *BiAUS, Drake*
Bowie, Robert 1749-1818 *NatCAB 9*
Bowie, Robert 1750?-1818 *ApCAB, DcAmB,
 TwCBDA, WhAm H, WhAmP*
Bowie, Sydney Johnston 1865-1928 *BiDrAC,
 WhAm 1, WhAmP*
Bowie, Thomas Fielder 1808-1869 *BiAUS,
 BiDrAC, WhAm H, WhAmP*
Bowie, Virginia Berkley 1880- *WomWWA 14*
Bowie, Walter 1748-1810 *BiAUS, BiDrAC,
 WhAm H*
Bowie, Walter Russell 1882-1969 *WhAm 5*
Bowie, William 1872-1940 *ApCAB X,
 DcAmB S2, DcScB, NatCAB 30,
 WhAm 1*
Bowie, William 1900-1966 *NatCAB 52*
Bowker, Frank Clarence 1872-1953 *NatCAB 42*
Bowker, Horace 1877-1954 *WhAm 3*
Bowker, Marion Esther 1885- *WomWWA 14*
Bowker, Richard Rogers 1848-1933 *ApCAB X,
 DcAmB S1, DcAmLiB, NatCAB 12,
 NatCAB 24, WebAB, WhAm 1*
Bowker, Richard Rogers 1848-1935 *AmBi*
Bowker, William Rushton 1872-1949
 NatCAB 38
Bowlby, Harry Laity 1874- *WhAm 6*
Bowlby, Helene Boileau 1866- *WomWWA 14*
Bowlby, Joel Morgan 1887- *WhAm 3*
Bowlen, John James d1959 *WhAm 4*
Bowler, Edmond Wesley 1892-1963 *WhAm 4*
Bowler, James Bernard 1875-1957 *BiDrAC,
 WhAm 3, WhAmP*
Bowler, John Pollard 1895-1974 *WhAm 6*
Bowler, John William 1865-1938 *WhAm 1*
Bowler, Joshua Soule 1847- *NewYHSD*
Bowler, Metcalf d1789 *BiAUS, NatCAB 4*
Bowler, Metcalf 1726-1789 *DcAmB, WhAm H*
Bowler, Metcalf 1730?-1789 *ApCAB*
Bowler, Sophia A *NewYHSD*
Bowler, William Howard 1871-1951 *WhAm 3*
Bowlers, Samuel 1826-1878 *ApCAB*
Bowles, Ada Chastina 1836- *AmWom,
 WomWWA 14*
Bowles, Benjamin Franklin 1869- *WhoColR*
Bowles, Charles 1884-1957 *WhAm 3*
Bowles, Charles Phillips 1906-1966 *WhAm 4*
Bowles, Chester Bliss 1901- *BiDrAC*
Bowles, Elliott A 1913-1957 *WhAm 3*
Bowles, Ernest Acheson 1880-1960 *NatCAB 46*
Bowles, Eva DelVakia 1875-1943 *NotAW*
Bowles, Francis Tiffany 1858-1927 *NatCAB 20,
 WhAm 1*
Bowles, Frank Hamilton 1907-1975 *WhAm 6*
Bowles, Frank Herbert 1880-1952 *NatCAB 41*
Bowles, George Hall 1860-1940 *NatCAB 30*
Bowles, George W 1882- *WhoColR*
Bowles, Gilbert 1869- *WhAm 5*
Bowles, Harry Hollowell 1884-1948 *NatCAB 39*
Bowles, Henry Leland 1866-1932 *BiDrAC,
 NatCAB 28, WhAm 1*
Bowles, Joshua *NewYHSD*
Bowles, Oliver 1877-1958 *WhAm 3*
Bowles, Phillip Ernest 1859-1926 *WhAm 1*
Bowles, Pinckney Downie 1835-1910 *WhAm 1*
Bowles, Samuel 1797-1851 *DcAmB,
 NatCAB 1, WebAB, WhAm H*
Bowles, Samuel 1826-1878 *AmBi, DcAmB,
 Drake, EncAB, McGEWB, NatCAB 1,
 TwCBDA, WebAB, WhAm H*
Bowles, Samuel 1851-1915 *ApCAB Sup,
 ApCAB X, DcAmB, NatCAB 1,
 TwCBDA, WhAm 1*
Bowles, Sherman Hoar d1952 *WhAm 3*
Bowles, Thomas Henry 1854- *NatCAB 2*
Bowles, William Augustus 1763-1805 *ApCAB,
 DcAmB, Drake, NatCAB 9, WhAm H*
Bowley, Albert Jesse 1875-1945 *NatCAB 34,
 WhAm 2*
Bowley, Arthur Lyon 1869- *WhAm 5*
Bowley, Charles G 1815?- *NewYHSD*
Bowlin, James Butler 1804- *ApCAB, BiAUS*
Bowlin, James Butler 1804-1874 *BiDrAC,
 WhAm H, WhAmP*
Bowlin, James Butler 1804-1894 *NatCAB 5,*

TwCBDA
Bowlin, William Ray 1881- *WhAm 6*
Bowling, Alonzo Jesse 1879- *WhoColR*
Bowling, Edgar Simeon 1875-1950 *NatCAB 38,
 WhAm 3*
Bowling, William Bismarck 1870-1946 *BiDrAC,
 WhAm 2, WhAmP*
Bowling, William Kirkman 1808-1885
 NatCAB 12
Bowlware, William 1805-1870 *NatCAB 12*
Bowman, A Smith 1868-1952 *NatCAB 42*
Bowman, Albert Chase 1875-1937 *NatCAB 34,
 WhAm 1*
Bowman, Alexander 1823?- *NewYHSD*
Bowman, Alexander Hamilton 1803-1865
 ApCAB, NatCAB 5, TwCBDA
Bowman, Alpheus Henry 1842-1926
 NatCAB 20, WhAm 1
Bowman, Betty Hill 1876- *WomWWA 14*
Bowman, Charles Calvin 1852-1941 *ApCAB X,
 BiDrAC, WhAm 1*
Bowman, Charles Grimes 1848-1918 *WhAm 1*
Bowman, Charles Henry 1873- *WhAm 5*
Bowman, Charles Roosevelt 1900-1968
 NatCAB 56
Bowman, Clellan Asbury 1861-1937 *WhAm 1*
Bowman, Clinton Alexander 1870-1945
 NatCAB 36
Bowman, Crete Dillon 1906-1968 *WhAm 5*
Bowman, Ed 1886-1961 *REnAW*
Bowman, Eda C 1877- *WomWWA 14*
Bowman, Edward J 1871-1935 *WhAm 1*
Bowman, Edward Morris 1848-1913 *AmBi,
 NatCAB 5, TwCBDA, WhAm 1*
Bowman, Elsa *WomWWA 14*
Bowman, Francis C 1877-1963 *NatCAB 51*
Bowman, Francis Caswell 1831-1884 *ApCAB,
 TwCBDA*
Bowman, Francis Favill 1872-1952 *NatCAB 41*
Bowman, Frank Llewellyn 1879-1936 *BiDrAC,
 WhAm 1, WhAmP*
Bowman, Frank Otto 1896- *WhAm 3*
Bowman, George B 1812-1888 *TwCBDA*
Bowman, George Ernest 1860-1941 *WhAm 1*
Bowman, George Lucas 1880-1922 *NatCAB 19*
Bowman, George Lynn 1874-1957 *WhAm 3*
Bowman, George T 1869-1951 *WhAm 3*
Bowman, George W *BiAUS*
Bowman, Gus Karl, Jr. 1928-1974 *WhAm 6*
Bowman, Harold Leonard 1889-1961 *WhAm 4*
Bowman, Harold Martin 1876-1949 *WhAm 2*
Bowman, Harry Lake 1889-1965 *WhAm 4*
Bowman, Harry Samuel 1880- *WhAm 6*
Bowman, Howard H M 1886- *WhAm 5*
Bowman, Ida Wright 1880- *WomWWA 14*
Bowman, Isaiah 1878-1950 *BiDAmEd,
 DcAmB S4, DcScB, McGEWB,
 NatCAB 40, WhAm 2A*
Bowman, Jacob Andrew 1862-1951 *NatCAB 42*
Bowman, James 1793-1842 *NewYHSD,
 WhAm H*
Bowman, James Clinton 1903-1971 *WhAm 5*
Bowman, James Cloyd 1880-1961 *WhAm 4*
Bowman, James Thomas 1854-1950 *NatCAB 38*
Bowman, Jennie 1877- *WomWWA 14*
Bowman, John Brady 1865-1936 *WhAm 1*
Bowman, John Bryan 1824-1891 *BiDAmEd,
 DcAmB, NatCAB 4, WhAm H*
Bowman, John Calvin 1849- *WhAm 1*
Bowman, John Edmond 1896-1965 *NatCAB 56*
Bowman, John Fife 1880- *WhAm 6*
Bowman, John Gabbert 1877-1962 *WhAm 4*
Bowman, John McEntee 1875-1931 *NatCAB 17,
 WhAm 1*
Bowman, John Ridgway 1910-1962 *NatCAB 55,
 WhAm 4*
Bowman, Joseph Merrell, Jr. 1931-1972
 WhAm 5
Bowman, Karl Murdock 1888-1973 *WhAm 5*
Bowman, Lloyd David 1896-1962 *WhAm 4*
Bowman, Luella Wait 1888- *WomWWA 14*
Bowman, Mabel E 1872- *WomWWA 14*
Bowman, Milo Jesse 1874-1948 *WhAm 3*
Bowman, Robert A 1855-1935 *WhAm 1*
Bowman, Robert Jay 1891-1958 *WhAm 3*
Bowman, Roland Claude 1870- *WhAm 1*
Bowman, Rufus David 1899- *WhAm 3*
Bowman, Samuel 1800-1861 *ApCAB, Drake,*

NatCAB 3, TwCBDA
Bowman, Samuel Henry 1853-1915 *NatCAB 17*
Bowman, Samuel Henry, Jr. 1887-1941
  NatCAB 30, WhAm 1
Bowman, Selwyn Zadock 1840-1928 *BiDrAC*
Bowman, Shadrach Laycock 1829-1906
  NatCAB 19
Bowman, Thomas 1817-1914 *ApCAB, DcAmB,*
  NatCAB 7, TwCBDA, WhAm 1
Bowman, Thomas 1836-1923 *NatCAB 19,*
  WhAm 1
Bowman, Thomas 1848-1917 *BiDrAC*
Bowman, Sir William 1816-1892 *BiHiMed,*
  DcScB
Bowman, Wirt George 1874-1949 *NatCAB 39*
Bown, Ralph 1891-1971 *NatCAB 56,*
  WhAm 5
Bowne, A *NewYHSD*
Bowne, Borden Parker 1847-1910 *AmBi,*
  ApCAB, DcAmB, DcAmReB,
  NatCAB 11, TwCBDA, WhAm 1
Bowne, J C *NewYHSD*
Bowne, John 1627?-1695 *DcAmB*
Bowne, John 1628-1695 *WhAm H*
Bowne, Obadiah 1822-1874 *BiAUS, BiDrAC,*
  WhAm H
Bowne, Samuel Smith 1800-1865 *BiAUS,*
  BiDrAC, WhAm H
Bowne, Walter *NatCAB 3*
Bowne, William Rainear 1878- *WhAm 6*
Bownocker, John Adams 1865-1928 *WhAm 1*
Bowra, Cecil Maurice 1898-1971 *WhAm 5*
Bowring, Eva Kelly 1892- *BiDrAC*
Bowron, Arthur John, Jr. 1907-1961 *WhAm 4*
Bowron, Fletcher 1887-1968 *WhAm 5*
Bowron, James 1844-1928 *NatCAB 24,*
  WhAm 1
Bowron, Robert Freeman 1909-1965
  NatCAB 51
Bowser, David Bustille 1820-1900 *NewYHSD*
Bowser, Edward Albert 1837-1910 *NatCAB 19,*
  WhAm 1
Bowser, Edward Albert 1845- *ApCAB Sup*
Bowsfield, Colvin C d1940 *WhAm 1*
Bowyer, John Marshall 1853-1912 *WhAm 1*
Bowyer, John Wilson 1901-1968 *WhAm 5*
Bowyer, Leonard L 1887-1942 *NatCAB 32*
Bowyer, Michael H *NewYHSD*
Bowyer, Walter Elijah 1873-1939 *NatCAB 29*
Box, Henry W 1836- *NatCAB 2*
Box, John Calvin 1871-1941 *BiDrAC,*
  WhAm 5, WhAmP
Boxer, Harold Horton 1907- *WhAm 6*
Boxley, Calvin Peyton 1901-1966 *WhAm 5*
Boxley, William Wise 1861-1940 *NatCAB 30*
Boyajian, Setrak Krikor 1884-1970 *WhAm 5*
Boyajohn, Haig Milton 1884-1956 *NatCAB 44*
Boyce, Addisone Schipper 1881-
  WomWWA 14
Boyce, Charles Meredith 1920-1969 *WhAm 5*
Boyce, Charles Prevost 1895-1955 *WhAm 3*
Boyce, Fred Comstock 1869-1953 *NatCAB 45*
Boyce, Fred Grayson, Jr. 1877-1960 *WhAm 4*
Boyce, Frederick Grayson, Jr. 1877-1960
  NatCAB 48
Boyce, Henry d1874 *BiAUS*
Boyce, Heyward E 1882-1950 *WhAm 3*
Boyce, James 1860-1910 *WhAm 1*
Boyce, James Petigru 1827-1888 *ApCAB,*
  DcAmB, NatCAB 21, TwCBDA,
  WhAm H
Boyce, John 1810-1864 *WhAm H*
Boyce, John Shaw 1889-1971 *NatCAB 57*
Boyce, Sir Leslie 1895-1955 *WhAm 3*
Boyce, Paul Llewellyn 1887-1941 *NatCAB 30*
Boyce, William A 1881- *WhAm 6*
Boyce, William D 1860-1923 *WhAm 2*
Boyce, William Henry 1855-1942 *BiDrAC,*
  WhAm 1
Boyce, William W 1819-1890 *BiAUS*
Boyce, William Waters 1818-1890 *BiDConf,*
  BiDrAC, WhAm H, WhAmP
Boyd, Adam 1738-1803 *NatCAB 7*
Boyd, Adam 1746-1835 *BiAUS, BiDrAC,*
  WhAm H, WhAmP
Boyd, Alan Stephenson 1922- *BiDrUSE*
Boyd, Alexander 1764-1857 *BiAUS, BiDrAC,*
  WhAm H

Boyd, Alfred 1872- *WhAm 5*
Boyd, Alfred Waller 1868-1930 *NatCAB 41*
Boyd, Andrew Hunter 1849-1925 *NatCAB 15,*
  WhAm 1
Boyd, Andrew Hunter Holmes 1814-1865
  ApCAB
Boyd, Anne Morris 1884-1974 *DcAmLiB*
Boyd, Augusto Samuel 1879-1957 *WhAm 3*
Boyd, Belle 1843-1900 *AmBi, NatCAB 23,*
  WhAm H
Boyd, Belle 1844-1900 *DcAmB, NotAW,*
  WebAMB
Boyd, Benjamin E *NewYHSD*
Boyd, Bernard Henry 1910-1975 *WhAm 6*
Boyd, Blanton M 1873-1947 *NatCAB 36*
Boyd, Charles Arthur 1878- *WhAm 6*
Boyd, Charles Morgan 1875-1958 *WhAm 3*
Boyd, Charles Samuel 1871-1952 *NatCAB 42*
Boyd, Charles Wesley 1865- *WhoColR*
Boyd, Colin Macnicol 1835- *WhAm 4*
Boyd, Cora Dunham 1860- *WomWWA 14*
Boyd, D Hartin 1880-1944 *NatCAB 33*
Boyd, D Knickerbacker 1872-1944 *WhAm 2*
Boyd, Darrell Sully 1889-1971 *WhAm 5*
Boyd, David 1833-1908 *NatCAB 8*
Boyd, David French 1834-1899 *BiDAmEd,*
  DcAmB, NatCAB 13, WhAm 1
Boyd, David Ross 1853-1936 *ApCAB X,*
  BiDAmEd, NatCAB 27, WhAm 1
Boyd, Donald Lewis 1899-1964 *WhAm 4*
Boyd, Edwin Forrest 1889-1971 *WhAm 5*
Boyd, Elizabeth Clarke *WomWWA 14*
Boyd, Ellen Wright 1833- *WhAm 4*
Boyd, Emma Louise Garrett 1876-
  WomWWA 14
Boyd, Ernest 1887-1946 *WhAm 2*
Boyd, Everett Marion 1894-1957 *WhAm 3*
Boyd, Fiske 1895-1975 *WhAm 6*
Boyd, Francis Evans 1887-1954 *NatCAB 41*
Boyd, Francis R 1881- *WhAm 6*
Boyd, George Adams 1898-1972 *WhAm 5*
Boyd, George H 1891-1965 *WhAm 4*
Boyd, George Washington 1848-1917
  NatCAB 17, WhAm 1
Boyd, Harriet Ann *DcAmB S3*
Boyd, Harry Alexander 1874-1958 *NatCAB 46*
Boyd, Harry Burton 1882-1959 *WhAm 3A*
Boyd, Harry Haycock 1861-1939 *NatCAB 29*
Boyd, Harry Hutcheson 1869- *WhAm 5*
Boyd, Henry Allen *WhoColR*
Boyd, Henry W, Jr. 1908-1958 *WhAm 3*
Boyd, Herbert Drummond 1869-1948
  NatCAB 37
Boyd, Homer Leon 1885-1965 *NatCAB 51*
Boyd, Isaac Snedecor 1843- *NatCAB 6*
Boyd, James 1858-1929 *WhAm 1*
Boyd, James 1888-1944 *DcAmB S3,*
  NatCAB 35, WhAm 2
Boyd, James Churchill 1871- *WhAm 5*
Boyd, James E 1834-1906 *NatCAB 1,*
  NatCAB 12, TwCBDA, WhAm 1
Boyd, James Edmund 1845- *WhAm 1*
Boyd, James Ellsworth 1863-1950 *NatCAB 40,*
  WhAm 3
Boyd, James Harrington 1862-1946 *WhAm 2*
Boyd, James Oscar 1874-1947 *WhAm 2*
Boyd, James P 1836-1910 *WhAm 1*
Boyd, James R 1804-1890 *ApCAB, TwCBDA*
Boyd, John *NewYHSD*
Boyd, John A 1837- *ApCAB*
Boyd, John Frank 1853-1945 *BiDrAC,*
  WhAm 3
Boyd, John Franklin 1853-1945 *NatCAB 41*
Boyd, John Hardgrove 1861-1922 *WhAm 1*
Boyd, John Huggins 1799-1868 *BiAUS,*
  BiDrAC, WhAm H
Boyd, John Parker 1764-1830 *AmBi, ApCAB,*
  DcAmB, Drake, NatCAB 10, TwCBDA,
  WhAm H
Boyd, Joseph Milton 1862- *WhAm 4*
Boyd, Kate Parker 1836- *AmWom*
Boyd, Kenneth Bray 1901-1955 *NatCAB 45*
Boyd, Linn 1800-1859 *AmBi, ApCAB, BiAUS,*
  BiDrAC, Drake, NatCAB 11, TwCBDA,
  WhAmP
Boyd, Linnaes Comer 1864-1921 *NatCAB 19*
Boyd, Louis Miller 1898-1965 *NatCAB 51*
Boyd, Louise Arner 1887-1972 *WhAm 5*

Boyd, Louise Esther Vickroy 1827- *AmWom*
Boyd, Lynn 1800-1859 *DcAmB, WebAB,*
  WhAm H
Boyd, Mary Brown Sumner 1876- *WhAm 5*
Boyd, Morton 1899-1963 *NatCAB 51*
Boyd, Paul Prentice 1877- *WhAm 5*
Boyd, Ralph E 1900-1971 *WhAm 5*
Boyd, Ralph Gates 1901-1972 *WhAm 5*
Boyd, Richard Henry 1843-1922 *DcAmB,*
  WhoColR
Boyd, Robert 1870- *WhAm 5*
Boyd, Robert James 1860- *WhoColR*
Boyd, Romaine 1873-1949 *NatCAB 41*
Boyd, Samuel 1836?- *NewYHSD*
Boyd, Sempronius Hamilton 1828-1894 *ApCAB,*
  BiAUS, BiDrAC, NatCAB 12, TwCBDA,
  WhAm H, WhAmP
Boyd, Theodore C *NewYHSD*
Boyd, Thomas Alexander 1830-1897 *BiDrAC,*
  WhAm H
Boyd, Thomas Alexander 1898-1935 *DcAmB S1,*
  NatCAB 26, WhAm 1
Boyd, Thomas C *NewYHSD*
Boyd, Thomas Duckett 1854-1932 *BiDAmEd,*
  DcAmB S1, NatCAB 13, TwCBDA,
  WhAm 4
Boyd, Thomas M 1860-1932 *NatCAB 24,*
  WhAm 1, WhAm 1C
Boyd, Walter Harrington 1894-1962
  NatCAB 50
Boyd, William 1864-1937 *NatCAB 49*
Boyd, William 1882-1947 *WhAm 2*
Boyd, William 1895-1972 *WhAm 5*
Boyd, William Clouser 1903- *AsBiEn*
Boyd, William Howard 1864-1947 *NatCAB 44,*
  WhAm 2
Boyd, William James 1887-1943 *NatCAB 32*
Boyd, William Kenneth 1879-1938 *DcAmB S2,*
  NatCAB 28, WhAm 1
Boyd, William Robert 1864-1950 *WhAm 3,*
  WhAm 4
Boyd, William Rufus, Jr. 1885-1959 *WhAm 3*
Boyd, William Sprott 1879-1958 *WhAm 3*
Boyd, William Waddell 1862-1944 *WhAm 2*
Boyd, William Warren 1881-1949 *NatCAB 46*
Boyd, William Young 1884-1932 *WhAm 1*
Boyd-Carpenter 1881- *WhAm 6*
Boyden, Albert 1871-1951 *WhAm 3*
Boyden, Albert Augustus 1875-1925 *WhAm 1*
Boyden, Albert Gardner 1827-1915 *BiDAmEd,*
  NatCAB 14, WhAm 1
Boyden, Archibald Henderson 1847-1929
  NatCAB 28
Boyden, Arthur Clarke 1852-1933 *NatCAB 25,*
  WhAm 1
Boyden, Elbridge 1819-1896 *WhAm H*
Boyden, Frank Learoyd 1879-1972 *BiDAmEd,*
  WhAm 5
Boyden, Guy Lee 1885-1958 *NatCAB 50,*
  WhAm 3
Boyden, John Allen 1862- *WhoColR*
Boyden, Nathaniel 1796-1873 *BiAUS, BiDrAC,*
  NatCAB 7, WhAm H
Boyden, Roland William 1863-1931 *AmBi,*
  DcAmB S1, NatCAB 23, WhAm 1
Boyden, Seth 1788-1870 *AmBi, ApCAB,*
  DcAmB, Drake, NatCAB 11, TwCBDA,
  WebAB, WhAm H
Boyden, Uriah Atherton 1804-1879 *ApCAB,*
  DcAmB, NatCAB 11, TwCBDA, WebAB,
  WhAm H
Boyden, William Cowper 1864-1929 *WhAm 1*
Boyden, William Cowper 1894-1965 *WhAm 4*
Boye, Martin Hans 1812-1909 *DcAmB,*
  WhAm 1
Boye, Walter Fred 1894-1960 *NatCAB 50*
Boyer, Alden Scott 1887-1953 *NatCAB 42*
Boyer, Arthur Truman 1874-1954 *NatCAB 43*
Boyer, Benjamin Markley 1823-1887 *BiAUS,*
  BiDrAC, WhAm H
Boyer, C Valentine 1880-1954 *NatCAB 43,*
  WhAm 4
Boyer, Charles Clinton 1860-1932 *WhAm 3*
Boyer, Charles Henry 1869- *WhoColR*
Boyer, Charles Shimer 1869-1936 *NatCAB 34*
Boyer, Charles Sumner 1856-1928 *NatCAB 21*
Boyer, Emanuel Roth 1857-1900 *WhAm 1*
Boyer, Francis 1893-1972 *NatCAB 57,*

WhAm 5

Boyer, Ida Porter 1859- *WomWWA 14*

Boyer, Jean Pierre 1776-1850 *ApCAB, Drake, McGEWB*

Boyer, John F 1907-1973 *WhAm 6*

Boyer, Joseph 1848-1930 *WhAm 1*

Boyer, Lewis Leonard 1886-1944 *BiDrAC*

Boyer, Lewis Leonard 1886-1949 *WhAm 3*

Boyer, Michael *NewYHSD*

Boyer, Pearce Fowler 1887-1949 *NatCAB 37, WhAm 3*

Boyer, Willis Boothe 1915-1974 *WhAm 6*

Boyer, Winifred B 1883- *WomWWA 14*

Boyers, E *NewYHSD*

Boyes, Kurwin Robert 1896-1956 *WhAm 3*

Boyesen, Hjalmar Hjorth 1848-1895 *AmBi, ApCAB, DcAmB, NatCAB 1, TwCBDA, WhAm H*

Boyington, Gregory 1912- *WebAMB*

Boyken, A William 1892-1965 *NatCAB 51*

Boykin, Caroline Morris *WomWWA 14*

Boykin, Charles Valk 1878-1936 *NatCAB 28*

Boykin, Frank William 1885-1969 *BiDrAC, WhAm 5, WhAmP*

Boykin, Garland Lester 1900-1966 *WhAm 4*

Boykin, James Chambers 1866-1929 *WhAm 1*

Boykin, Richard Manning 1878-1950 *NatCAB 38, WhAm 6*

Boykin, Samuel Francis 1874-1953 *WhAm 3*

Boylan, Grace Duffie d1935 *WhAm 1, WomWWA 14*

Boylan, John J 1889-1953 *WhAm 3*

Boylan, John Joseph 1878-1938 *BiDrAC, WhAm 1, WhAmP*

Boylan, John Patrick 1875-1960 *WhAm 4*

Boylan, Murtha Joseph 1874-1954 *WhAm 3*

Boylan, Richard Joseph 1886-1966 *WhAm 4*

Boylan, Robert P 1891-1960 *WhAm 4*

Boylan, Rose Marion 1872- *WomWWA 14*

Boylan, William Aloysius 1869-1940 *NatCAB 36, WhAm 1*

Boyland, George Halsted 1845- *ApCAB*

Boyle, Albert Clarence, Jr. 1880- *WhAm 6*

Boyle, Albert Julius 1910-1967 *NatCAB 54*

Boyle, Andrew Joseph 1906-1975 *WhAm 6*

Boyle, Caleb *NewYHSD*

Boyle, Charles Augustus 1907-1959 *BiDrAC, WhAm 3*

Boyle, Charles Edmund 1836-1888 *BiDrAC, WhAm H*

Boyle, Emmet Derby 1879-1926 *NatCAB 21, WhAm 1*

Boyle, Ferdinand Thomas Lee 1820-1906 *IlBEAAW, NewYHSD, WhAm HA, WhAm 4*

Boyle, Gertrude 1878-1937 *NatCAB 34*

Boyle, Harold Lauren 1888-1952 *NatCAB 42*

Boyle, Harold Vincent 1911-1974 *WhAm 6*

Boyle, Harry Joseph 1888-1953 *NatCAB 42*

Boyle, Henry 1849-1918 *NatCAB 19*

Boyle, Hugh Charles 1873-1950 *NatCAB 40, WhAm 3*

Boyle, James *NewYHSD*

Boyle, James 1853-1939 *WhAm 1*

Boyle, James A *NewYHSD*

Boyle, James Ernest 1873-1938 *WhAm 1*

Boyle, Jeremiah Tilford 1818-1871 *ApCAB, DcAmB, NatCAB 12, TwCBDA, WhAm H*

Boyle, John 1774-1834 *ApCAB, BiAUS, BiDrAC, Drake, NatCAB 11*

Boyle, John 1774-1835 *AmBi, DcAmB, WhAm H*

Boyle, John 1855-1936 *WhAm 1*

Boyle, John Alexander 1816-1863 *ApCAB*

Boyle, John C 1815?- *NewYHSD*

Boyle, John J 1851-1917 *AmBi, ApCAB X, BnEnAmA, DcAmB, IlBEAAW, NatCAB 13, WhAm 1*

Boyle, John W *BiAUS*

Boyle, Joseph 1812-1872 *NatCAB 7*

Boyle, Junius J 1802?-1870 *ApCAB*

Boyle, Leo Martin 1899-1969 *WhAm 5*

Boyle, M *NewYHSD*

Boyle, Mrs. M C *NewYHSD*

Boyle, Margaret E Cottman *WomWWA 14*

Boyle, Murat 1883-1930 *WhAm 1*

Boyle, R John 1874-1948 *NatCAB 37*

Boyle, Robert 1627-1691 *AsBiEn, BiHiMed, DcScB, McGEWB*

Boyle, Samuel Alexander, Jr. 1875-1924 *NatCAB 23*

Boyle, Thomas 1776?-1825? *AmBi, DcAmB, WhAm H*

Boyle, Thomas 1827?- *NewYHSD*

Boyle, Thomas Newton 1839-1911 *WhAm 1*

Boyle, Virginia Frazer 1863-1938 *BiCAW, NatCAB 13, WhAm 1, WomWWA 14*

Boyle, W H Wray 1857- *WhAm 4*

Boyle, Walter Fabien 1875-1956 *WhAm 3*

Boyle, Wilbur Fisk 1840-1911 *WhAm 1*

Boyle, William *NewYHSD*

Boyle, William Campbell 1855-1933 *NatCAB 25*

Boyle, William Fisk 1840-1911 *NatCAB 12*

Boyle, William Marshall, Jr. 1902-1961 *WhAm 4*

Boylen, Matthew James 1907-1970 *WhAm 5*

Boyles, Aubrey 1878- *WhAm 6*

Boyles, Charles Dickinson 1865-1936 *NatCAB 34*

Boyles, Emerson Richard 1881-1960 *NatCAB 48, WhAm 6*

Boylon, Francis Oscar 1912-1970 *WhAm 5*

Boylston, Nicholas 1716-1771 *ApCAB, Drake*

Boylston, Ward Nicholas 1749-1828 *ApCAB*

Boylston, Zabdiel 1679-1766 *AmBi, DcAmB, McGEWB, WebAB, WhAm H*

Boylston, Zabdiel 1680-1766 *ApCAB, Drake*

Boylston, Zabdiel 1680-1776 *TwCBDA*

Boylston, Zabdiel 1684-1766 *NatCAB 7*

Boynton, Arthur Jefferson 1876-1961 *NatCAB 51*

Boynton, Arthur Jerome 1870-1928 *NatCAB 21, WhAm 1*

Boynton, Ben Lynn 1909-1975 *WhAm 6*

Boynton, Catharine 1875- *BiCAW*

Boynton, Charles Albert 1867- *WhAm 5*

Boynton, Charles Augustus 1836-1915 *WhAm 1*

Boynton, Charles Brandon 1806-1883 *ApCAB, DcAmB, TwCBDA, WhAm H*

Boynton, Charles Homer *WhAm 5*

Boynton, Charles Hudson 1868-1935 *WhAm 1*

Boynton, Charles Theodore 1858-1923 *WhAm 1*

Boynton, Edward C 1846- *Drake*

Boynton, Edward Carlisle 1824-1893 *DcAmB, NatCAB 21, TwCBDA, WhAm H*

Boynton, Edward Carlisle 1825?-1893 *ApCAB*

Boynton, Edward Young 1895-1966 *NatCAB 53, WhAm 4*

Boynton, Frances Nichols 1868- *WomWWA 14*

Boynton, Frank David 1863-1930 *WhAm 1*

Boynton, George Mills 1837-1908 *WhAm 1*

Boynton, George Rufus d1945 *WhAm 2*

Boynton, George W d1884 *NewYHSD*

Boynton, George W 1842-1911 *NatCAB 15*

Boynton, Helen Augusta Mason *BiCAW*

Boynton, Henry VanNess 1835-1905 *ApCAB, TwCBDA, WhAm 1*

Boynton, Henry Walcott 1869- *WhAm 5*

Boynton, James Stoddard 1833-1902 *NatCAB 1, TwCBDA, WhAm 1*

Boynton, John Farnham 1811-1890 *NatCAB 4*

Boynton, Melbourne Parker 1867-1942 *ApCAB X, WhAm 2*

Boynton, Morrison Russell 1887-1953 *WhAm 3*

Boynton, Nathan Smith 1837- *WhAm 1*

Boynton, Nathaniel Augustus 1823-1900 *NatCAB 12*

Boynton, Nehemiah 1856-1933 *WhAm 1*

Boynton, Paul L 1898-1958 *WhAm 3*

Boynton, Percy Holmes 1875-1946 *BiDAmEd, NatCAB 35, WhAm 2*

Boynton, Perry Sanborn, Jr. 1909-1965 *NatCAB 51*

Boynton, Ray Scepter 1883-1951 *IlBEAAW*

Boynton, Richard Wilson 1870-1961 *WhAm 4*

Boynton, Samuel Smith 1837- *TwCBDA*

Boynton, Thomas Jefferson 1856-1945 *WhAm 2*

Boynton, Washington Wallace 1833- *NatCAB 12*

Boynton, William Parker 1878-1951 *NatCAB 39*

Boynton, William Pingry 1867-1955 *WhAm 3*

Boyer, William Charles Theodore 1869-1940 *NatCAB 29*

Boys, Charles Vernon 1855-1944 *DcScB Sup*

Boysen, J Lassen 1871-1959 *NatCAB 47*

Boysen Jensen, Peter 1883-1959 *WhAm 4*

Boyt, Elmer Woodard 1876-1958 *NatCAB 48*

Boyton, Neil 1884-1956 *WhAm 3*

Boyton, Paul 1848- *ApCAB, TwCBDA*

Bozell, Harold Veatch 1886-1972 *WhAm 5*

Bozell, Leo B 1886-1946 *WhAm 2*

Bozeman, John M 1835-1867 *AmBi, DcAmB, WebAB, WhAm H*

Bozeman, John M 1837-1867 *McGEWB*

Bozeman, Nathan 1825-1905 *DcAmB, NatCAB 21, TwCBDA*

Bozic, John Herbert 1901-1970 *NatCAB 56*

Bozman, John Leeds 1757-1823 *ApCAB, DcAmB, Drake, NatCAB 20, TwCBDA, WhAm H*

Bozyan, H Frank 1899-1965 *NatCAB 51*

Braan, Edward 1839?- *NewYHSD*

Braasch, William Frederick 1878-1975 *WhAm 6*

Brabham, Thomas Watson 1893-1961 *NatCAB 50*

Braboy, Joseph Albert 1846- *WhoColR*

Brabson, Reese Bowen 1817-1863 *BiAUS, BiDrAC, WhAm H*

Braby, Henry *NewYHSD*

Brace, Charles Loring 1826-1890 *AmBi, ApCAB, DcAmB, Drake, NatCAB 10, TwCBDA, WebAB, WhAm H*

Brace, Charles Loring 1855-1938 *DcAmB S2, NatCAB 31, WhAm 1*

Brace, DeWitt Bristol 1859-1905 *DcAmB, DcScB, WhAm 1*

Brace, Donald Clifford 1881-1955 *DcAmB S5, WhAm 3*

Brace, John Pierce 1793-1872 *ApCAB, DcAmB, TwCBDA, WhAm H*

Brace, Jonathan 1754-1837 *BiAUS, BiDrAC, NatCAB 12, WhAm H*

Brace, Julia 1806-1884 *AmBi*

Brace, Julia 1807-1884 *ApCAB*

Brace, Maria Porter 1852- *AmWom*

Brace, Robert Neill 1861-1938 *NatCAB 29*

Brace, Theodore 1835- *NatCAB 13, WhAm 4*

Bracelen, Charles Michael 1878-1942 *WhAm 2*

Brach, Edwin J d1965 *WhAm 4*

Brach, Emil J 1859-1947 *WhAm 2*

Brach, Frank Vincent 1891-1970 *NatCAB 55, WhAm 5*

Bracher, William 1828?- *NewYHSD*

Brachet, Albert 1869-1930 *DcScB*

Brachvogel, Udo 1835-1913 *DcAmB*

Bracken, Brendan 1901-1958 *WhWW-II*

Bracken, Clio Hinton d1925 *WhAm 1, WomWWA 14*

Bracken, Edward P d1937 *WhAm 1*

Bracken, Henry Martyn 1854-1938 *WhAm 1*

Bracken, John d1818 *ApCAB, Drake, NatCAB 3*

Bracken, John 1883-1969 *WhAm 5*

Bracken, Opal *WomWWA 14*

Bracken, Stanley 1890-1966 *WhAm 4*

Brackenridge, A *NewYHSD*

Brackenridge, Alexander 1893-1964 *WhAm 4*

Brackenridge, Eleanor *WomWWA 14*

Brackenridge, Henry Marie 1786-1871 *AmBi, ApCAB, BiAUS, BiDrAC, DcAmB, Drake, NatCAB 9, WhAm H, WhAmP*

Brackenridge, Henry Morgan 1856-1927 *NatCAB 21*

Brackenridge, Hugh Henry 1748-1816 *AmBi, ApCAB, DcAmB, Drake, NatCAB 8, REnAW, TwCBDA, WebAB, WhAm H, WhAmP*

Brackenridge, Hugh Henry 1749-1816 *McGEWB*

Brackenridge, William Algernon d1929 *WhAm 1*

Brackenridge, William D 1810-1893 *DcAmB, WhAm H*

Bracker, Milton 1909-1964 *WhAm 4*

Bracket, Dexter 1851-1915 *WhAm 1*

Brackett, Albert Gallatin 1829-1896 *ApCAB, TwCBDA*

Brackett, Anna Callender 1836-1911 *AmBi, BiDAmEd, DcAmB, NatCAB 21, NotAW, WhAm 1*

Brackett, Anthony d1689 *ApCAB, Drake*
Brackett, Antoinette Newell 1875-
   WomWWA 14
Brackett, Byron Briggs 1865-1937 *WhAm 1*
Brackett, Charles Albert 1850-1927 *WhAm 1*
Brackett, Charles Henri 1855-1927 *NatCAB 36*
Brackett, Christopher C *NewYHSD*
Brackett, Cyrus Fogg 1833-1915 *WhAm 1*
Brackett, E E 1876- *WhAm 5*
Brackett, Edgar Trumann 1853- *NatCAB 14*
Brackett, Edward Augustus 1818-1908 *AmBi,*
   BnEnAmA, DcAmB, NatCAB 13,
   NewYHSD
Brackett, Edward Augustus 1819-1908 *ApCAB,*
   TwCBDA
Brackett, Edward Sumner 1875-1951
   NatCAB 41
Brackett, Edwin E 1819- *Drake*
Brackett, Elliott Gray 1860-1942 *WhAm 2*
Brackett, F Ernest 1874-1938 *NatCAB 30*
Brackett, Frank Parkhurst 1865- *WhAm 5*
Brackett, Gustavus Benson 1827-1915 *WhAm 1*
Brackett, Miss H V *NewYHSD*
Brackett, Haven Darling 1876- *WhAm 5*
Brackett, Henry Gallatin 1829-1896 *Drake*
Brackett, J Raymond 1854-1922 *WhAm 1*
Brackett, Jeffrey Richardson 1860-1949
   BiDAmEd, DcAmB S4, NatCAB 38,
   WhAm 4
Brackett, John Charles 1918-1967 *NatCAB 54*
Brackett, John Quincy Adams 1842-1918
   NatCAB 1, TwCBDA, WhAm 1
Brackett, Joshua 1733-1802 *ApCAB, Drake,*
   TwCBDA
Brackett, Lavinia Maxwell Prescott 1844-
   WomWWA 14
Brackett, Ledru Joshua 1873- *WhAm 5*
Brackett, Richard Newman 1863- *WhAm 4*
Brackett, Sewall Carroll 1868-1952 *NatCAB 41*
Brackett, Walter M 1823-1919 *AmBi, ApCAB,*
   Drake, NewYHSD, TwCBDA, WhAm 1
Brackett, William Oliver 1901-1945 *WhAm 2*
Brackett, William Savage 1898-1959
   NatCAB 47
Brackin, Henry Bryan 1897-1971 *NatCAB 56*
Brackman, John *NewYHSD*
Braconnot, Henri 1780-1855 *DcScB*
Braconnot, Henri 1781-1855 *AsBiEn*
Bracq, Jean Charlemagne 1853-1934 *WhAm 1*
Bradbury, Albert Williams 1840- *WhAm 1*
Bradbury, Charles Leighton 1895-1956
   NatCAB 54
Bradbury, Clifford Clarence 1880-1963
   NatCAB 48
Bradbury, Edward *NewYHSD*
Bradbury, George 1770-1823 *BiAUS, BiDrAC,*
   WhAm H
Bradbury, Howard William 1892-1964 *WhAm 4*
Bradbury, James Ware 1802-1901 *BiDrAC,*
   DcAmB, TwCBDA, WhAm H, WhAmP
Bradbury, James Ware 1803-1901 *NatCAB 4*
Bradbury, James Ware 1805-1901 *ApCAB,*
   BiAUS
Bradbury, John 1768-1823 *REnAW*
Bradbury, Joseph Perry 1838-1915 *NatCAB 5,*
   NatCAB 24, WhAm 1
Bradbury, Margaret Jones 1835-
   WomWWA 14
Bradbury, Ora Clare 1890-1969 *NatCAB 57*
Bradbury, Ray Douglas 1920- *WebAB*
Bradbury, Robert Hart 1870-1949 *WhAm 2*
Bradbury, Samuel 1883-1947 *NatCAB 34,*
   WhAm 2
Bradbury, Theophilus 1739-1803 *ApCAB,*
   BiAUS, BiDrAC, DcAmB, Drake,
   NatCAB 2, TwCBDA, WhAm H
Bradbury, Thomas 1610-1695 *Drake*
Bradbury, William 1901-1964 *WhAm 4*
Bradbury, William Batchelder 1816-1868 *AmBi,*
   ApCAB, BiDAmEd, DcAmB, Drake,
   NatCAB 5, TwCBDA, WhAm H
Bradbury, William Frothingham 1829-1914
   ApCAB, TwCBDA, WhAm 1
Bradbury, Woodman 1866-1935 *WhAm 1*
Braddan, William S 1871- *WhoColR*
Braddock, Edward 1695-1755 *AmBi, ApCAB,*
   DcAmB, Drake, McGEWB, NatCAB 2,
   TwCBDA, WhAm H

Braddock, John Sellers 1844-1920 *NatCAB 19*
Braddock, Robert Louis 1911-1970 *WhAm 5*
Brademas, John 1927- *BiDrAC*
Braden, Anna Madge *AmWom*
Braden, Arthur 1881- *WhAm 6*
Braden, George Walter 1879- *WhAm 6*
Braden, J Noble 1892-1957 *WhAm 3*
Braden, James Andrew 1872-1954 *WhAm 3*
Braden, John 1826-1900 *TwCBDA, WhAm 1*
Braden, Spencer 1901-1969 *NatCAB 55*
Braden, William 1871-1942 *WhAm 2*
Bradfield, George Herndon 1880- *WhAm 6*
Bradfield, William D 1866- *WhAm 4*
Bradford *NewYHSD*
Bradford, Albert Sumner 1860-1933
   NatCAB 52
Bradford, Alden 1765-1843 *AmBi, ApCAB,*
   DcAmB, Drake, NatCAB 8, TwCBDA
Bradford, Alex Warfield 1815-1867 *Drake*
Bradford, Alexander Blackburn 1799-1873
   BiDConf
Bradford, Alexander Warfield 1815-1867
   ApCAB, DcAmB, TwCBDA, WhAm H
Bradford, Allen 1765-1843 *WhAm H*
Bradford, Allen Alexander 1815-1888 *BiAUS,*
   BiDrAC, NatCAB 13, WhAm H
Bradford, Amory Howe 1846-1911 *DcAmB,*
   NatCAB 7, TwCBDA, WhAm 1
Bradford, Andrew Sowles 1686-1742 *AmBi,*
   ApCAB, DcAmB, Drake, NatCAB 19,
   TwCBDA, WhAm H
Bradford, Augustus W d1881 *BiAUS*
Bradford, Augustus W 1805?-1881 *ApCAB,*
   TwCBDA
Bradford, Augustus Williamson 1806-1881
   AmBi, DcAmB, NatCAB 9, WhAm H,
   WhAmP
Bradford, Charles 1862-1917 *WhAm 1*
Bradford, Charles Cozad 1884-1953
   NatCAB 42
Bradford, Cornelia Foster 1847-1935 *NotAW*
Bradford, Cornelia Smith d1755 *NotAW*
Bradford, Edward Anthony 1851-1928
   ApCAB X, WhAm 1
Bradford, Edward Green 1819-1884 *BiAUS,*
   DcAmB, WhAm H
Bradford, Edward Green 1848-1928 *WhAm 1*
Bradford, Edward Hickling 1848-1926
   BiDAmEd, DcAmB, WhAm 1
Bradford, Ernest Smith 1877-1965 *NatCAB 52,*
   WhAm 4
Bradford, Ernest Wilder 1862- *NatCAB 16*
Bradford, Francis Scott 1898-1961 *NatCAB 46,*
   WhAm 4
Bradford, Gamaliel 1731-1807 *ApCAB, Drake*
Bradford, Gamaliel 1831-1911 *ApCAB,*
   DcAmB, NatCAB 19, TwCBDA,
   WhAm 1
Bradford, Gamaliel 1863-1932 *AmBi,*
   DcAmB S1, NatCAB 23, WhAm 1
Bradford, George Henry 1871-1945 *WhAm 2*
Bradford, George Partridge 1807-1890
   NatCAB 7
Bradford, Gerard 1887-1955 *WhAm 3*
Bradford, Harry E 1878- *WhAm 6*
Bradford, Henry *NewYHSD*
Bradford, Henry Colmore 1885-1956
   NatCAB 47
Bradford, Herbert Alfred 1884-1947
   NatCAB 36
Bradford, James Henry 1836-1913 *NatCAB 6*
Bradford, John 1749-1830 *AmBi, ApCAB Sup,*
   DcAmB, NatCAB 1, TwCBDA,
   WhAm H
Bradford, John Ewing 1866-1936 *WhAm 1*
Bradford, Joseph 1843-1886 *ApCAB, DcAmB,*
   TwCBDA, WhAm H
Bradford, Joseph M 1824-1872 *ApCAB,*
   TwCBDA
Bradford, Joseph Nelson 1860-1943 *WhAm 3*
Bradford, Joshua Taylor 1818-1871 *DcScB*
Bradford, Karl Slaughter 1889-1972 *WhAm 5*
Bradford, Lindsay 1892-1959 *NatCAB 44,*
   WhAm 3
Bradford, Lodowick H 1815?- *NewYHSD*
Bradford, Mary Carroll Craig 1856-1938
   AmWom

Bradford, Mary Carroll Craig 1862-1938
   BiDAmEd
Bradford, Mary Davison *WomWWA 14*
Bradford, Roark Whitney Wickliffe 1896-1948
   DcAmB S4, WhAm 2
Bradford, Robert 1750-1823 *ApCAB*
Bradford, Robert D 1903-1973 *WhAm 5*
Bradford, Robert Henry 1871-1931 *NatCAB 23*
Bradford, Royal Bird 1844-1914 *ApCAB Sup,*
   WhAm 1
Bradford, Saxton 1907-1966 *WhAm 4*
Bradford, Stella Stevens *WomWWA 14*
Bradford, Taul 1835-1883 *BiAUS, BiDrAC,*
   WhAm H
Bradford, Thomas 1745-1838 *ApCAB, DcAmB,*
   Drake, TwCBDA, WhAm H
Bradford, Thomas Lindsley 1847-1918
   NatCAB 3, WhAm 1
Bradford, Vincent Loockerman 1808-1884
   TwCBDA
Bradford, William 1588-1657 *ApCAB, Drake,*
   NatCAB 7, TwCBDA
Bradford, William 1589?-1657 *AmBi, DcAmB,*
   WhAm H
Bradford, William 1590-1657 *DcAmReB,*
   EncAAH, EncAB, McGEWB, WebAB,
   WhAmP
Bradford, William 1624-1704 *Drake*
Bradford, William 1658-1752 *ApCAB,*
   TwCBDA
Bradford, William 1659-1752 *Drake*
Bradford, William 1663-1752 *AmBi, DcAmB,*
   McGEWB, WhAm H, WhAmP
Bradford, William 1719-1791 *ApCAB, Drake,*
   TwCBDA
Bradford, William 1721?-1791 *DcAmB,*
   WhAmP
Bradford, William 1722-1791 *AmBi,*
   McGEWB, WhAm H
Bradford, William 1729-1808 *ApCAB, BiAUS,*
   BiDrAC, Drake, NatCAB 2, TwCBDA,
   WhAm H
Bradford, William 1755-1795 *ApCAB, BiAUS,*
   BiDrUSE, DcAmB, Drake, NatCAB 1,
   WhAm H
Bradford, William 1823-1892 *AmBi,*
   BnEnAmA, DcAmB, Drake, NewYHSD,
   WhAm H
Bradford, William 1824-1892 *TwCBDA*
Bradford, William 1827-1892 *ApCAB*
Bradford, William Brooks 1896-1965 *WhAm 4*
Bradfute, George Archibald 1893-1965
   NatCAB 51
Bradfute, Oscar Edwin 1862-1929 *WhAm 1*
Bradish, Alvah 1806-1901 *NewYHSD,*
   WhAm H
Bradish, Luther 1783-1863 *ApCAB, DcAmB,*
   Drake, NatCAB 3, TwCBDA, WhAm H
Bradlaugh, Charles 1833-1891 *McGEWB*
Bradlee, Arthur Tisdale 1867-1925 *WhAm 1*
Bradlee, Caleb Davis 1831-1897 *ApCAB,*
   Drake, NatCAB 4, TwCBDA, WhAm H
Bradlee, Edith Gerry Keene 1874-
   WomWWA 14
Bradlee, Henry G 1871-1947 *WhAm 2*
Bradlee, Nathaniel Jeremiah 1829-1888
   NatCAB 30, WhAm H
Bradley, A Ballard 1887-1954 *NatCAB 43*
Bradley, Abraham, Jr. *BiAUS*
Bradley, Alexander Stuart 1838- *WhAm 4*
Bradley, Alfred Eugene 1864-1922 *NatCAB 19,*
   WhAm 1
Bradley, Alice 1875-1946 *ApCAB X,*
   WhAm 2
Bradley, Alice Deering 1856- *WomWWA 14*
Bradley, Alva 1814-1885 *REnAW*
Bradley, Alva 1884- *WhAm 3*
Bradley, Amy Morris 1823-1904 *AmWom,*
   BiDAmEd, NotAW
Bradley, Andrew Coyle 1844-1902 *WhAm 1*
Bradley, Ann Weaver 1834- *AmWom*
Bradley, Benjamin Edgar 1869-1926
   NatCAB 20
Bradley, Benjamin Franklin 1825-1897 *BiDConf*
Bradley, Bernard James 1867-1936 *WhAm 1*
Bradley, Burke William 1904-1970 *NatCAB 55*
Bradley, Carolyn Gertrude d1954 *WhAm 3*
Bradley, Charles 1857-1938 *WhAm 1*

Bradley, Charles Burnet 1883-1960 *WhAm 4*
Bradley, Charles Clark 1879-1939 *WhAm 1*
Bradley, Charles Edward 1874-1960
NatCAB 50
Bradley, Charles Harvey 1899-1972 *WhAm 5*
Bradley, Charles Henry 1860-1921 *WhAm 1*
Bradley, Charles Henry 1860-1922 *DcAmB*
Bradley, Charles Leininger 1885-1943
NatCAB 33, WhAm 2
Bradley, Charles Schenck 1853-1929
NatCAB 15, WhAm 1
Bradley, Charles Smith 1819-1888 *ApCAB Sup,
NatCAB 13*
Bradley, Charles Trueworth 1818-1893
NatCAB 2
Bradley, Charles William 1807-1865 *DcAmB,
WhAm H*
Bradley, Cornelius Beach 1843-1936 *WhAm 3*
Bradley, Dan Freeman 1857-1939 *WhAm 1*
Bradley, David 1811-1899 *NatCAB 11*
Bradley, Denis Mary 1846-1903 *ApCAB,
DcAmB, NatCAB 12, TwCBDA,
WhAm 1*
Bradley, Dolly Holland *WomWWA 14*
Bradley, Dorothy Winchester 1909-1975
WhAm 6
Bradley, Dwight 1889-1957 *WhAm 3*
Bradley, Edward 1808-1847 *BiAUS, BiDrAC,
WhAm H*
Bradley, Edward Elias 1845-1917 *NatCAB 17*
Bradley, Edward Elias 1845-1938 *WhAm 1*
Bradley, Edward Lounsberry 1861- *WhAm 1*
Bradley, Edwin Colton 1833-1913 *NatCAB 25*
Bradley, Elizabeth Ganse 1891-1966 *WhAm 4*
Bradley, Emma Louise *WomWWA 14*
Bradley, Follett 1890-1952 *NatCAB 39,
WhAm 4*
Bradley, Francis 1880-1961 *WhAm 4*
Bradley, Francis Herbert 1846-1924 *McGEWB*
Bradley, Frank Howe 1838-1879 *DcAmB,
WhAm H*
Bradley, Frederick Truman 1860-1940
NatCAB 29
Bradley, Frederick VanNess 1898-1947 *BiDrAC,
WhAm 2, WhAmP*
Bradley, Frederick Worthen 1863-1933
DcAmB S1, NatCAB 28, WhAm 1
Bradley, Frederick Worthen 1904-1959
NatCAB 48
Bradley, George Beckwith 1825-1916 *WhAm 1*
Bradley, George Edgar 1924-1975 *WhAm 6*
Bradley, George Lothrop 1846-1906
NatCAB 14
Bradley, Glenn Danford 1884-1930 *WhAm 1*
Bradley, Guy M 1870-1905 *WhAm H*
Bradley, H W *NewYHSD*
Bradley, Harold Cornelius 1878- *WhAm 6*
Bradley, Harry 1869-1938 *NatCAB 29*
Bradley, Harry Lynde 1885-1965 *NatCAB 53,
WhAm 4*
Bradley, Henry D 1893-1973 *WhAm 6*
Bradley, Henry Stiles 1869- *WhAm 5*
Bradley, Herbert Edwin 1874-1961 *WhAm 4,
WhAm 5*
Bradley, I J H *NewYHSD*
Bradley, Irwin Charles 1884-1949 *NatCAB 38*
Bradley, Isaac Samuel 1853- *TwCBDA*
Bradley, J Kenneth 1903-1969 *WhAm 5*
Bradley, James *BiAUS*
Bradley, James 1693-1762 *AsBiEn, DcScB,
McGEWB*
Bradley, James 1858-1925 *NatCAB 20*
Bradley, James L 1891-1957 *WhAm 3*
Bradley, Jay D 1881-1951 *WhAm 3*
Bradley, Jennie E 1848- *WomWWA 14*
Bradley, Jerry Payson 1848- *ApCAB X*
Bradley, John *NewYHSD*
Bradley, John Davis 1910-1959 *NatCAB 53,
WhAm 4*
Bradley, John Dorr 1864-1928 *NatCAB 32*
Bradley, John Edwin 1839-1912 *DcAmB,
NatCAB 21, WhAm 1*
Bradley, John Edwin 1845-1912 *TwCBDA*
Bradley, John Hodgdon 1898-1962 *NatCAB 50,
WhAm 4*
Bradley, John Jewsbury 1869-1948 *WhAm 2*
Bradley, John Robins 1881- *WhAm 6*
Bradley, John Stone 1842-1926 *NatCAB 21*

Bradley, John William 1893-1959 *NatCAB 49*
Bradley, Jonathan Dorr 1803-1862 *NatCAB 8*
Bradley, Joseph Gardner 1881-1971 *ApCAB X,
NatCAB 56, WhAm 6*
Bradley, Joseph Harley 1844- *NatCAB 11*
Bradley, Joseph P 1813-1892 *ApCAB, BiAUS,
DcAmB, Drake Sup, NatCAB 1,
TwCBDA, WebAB, WhAm H*
Bradley, Joseph Sladen 1900-1961 *WhAm 4*
Bradley, Kenneth McPherson 1872-1954
WhAm 3
Bradley, Laura May Thompson d1970 *WhAm 5*
Bradley, Lee Carrington 1871-1942 *NatCAB 31,
WhAm 2*
Bradley, Leo Fabian 1881-1928 *NatCAB 22*
Bradley, Lewis *NewYHSD*
Bradley, Lewis Rice 1805-1879 *BiAUS,
NatCAB 11, REnAW*
Bradley, Liela Griswold 1862- *WomWWA 14*
Bradley, Lucas *WhAm H*
Bradley, Luke Calloway 1875-1944 *NatCAB 34,
WhAm 2*
Bradley, Luther Prentice 1822-1910 *ApCAB,
TwCBDA, WhAm 1*
Bradley, Lydia Moss 1816-1908 *DcAmB,
WhAm 1*
Bradley, Lyman 1807-1888 *ApCAB Sup*
Bradley, Lynde 1878-1942 *NatCAB 31*
Bradley, Manson James 1887-1946 *NatCAB 35*
Bradley, Marian Hawley *WomWWA 14*
Bradley, Mark Edward 1878- *WhAm 6*
Bradley, Mark Spaulding 1868-1933
NatCAB 26
Bradley, Michael Joseph 1897- *BiDrAC*
Bradley, Milton 1836-1911 *DcAmB,
NatCAB 11, WebAB, WhAm 1*
Bradley, Morris Alva 1859-1926 *NatCAB 33*
Bradley, Nathan Ball 1831-1906 *BiAUS,
BiDrAC*
Bradley, Newell Charles 1876-1957 *NatCAB 49*
Bradley, Omar Nelson 1893- *EncAB,
McGEWB, WebAB, WebAMB,
WhWW-II*
Bradley, Otis Treat 1895-1950 *NatCAB 41,
WhAm 3*
Bradley, Peter Butler 1850-1933 *NatCAB 25,
WhAm 1*
Bradley, Philip Read 1875-1948 *WhAm 2*
Bradley, Phineas *BiAUS*
Bradley, Relins 1831?- *NewYHSD*
Bradley, Richard d1732 *DcScB*
Bradley, Richards Merry 1861-1943
NatCAB 45
Bradley, Robert L 1866-1943 *WhAm 2*
Bradley, Robert McAfee 1807- *NatCAB 7*
Bradley, Robert Stow 1855-1945 *NatCAB 37,
WhAm 3*
Bradley, Samuel Stewart 1869-1947 *WhAm 2*
Bradley, Stephen Roe 1754-1830 *BiAUS*
Bradley, Stephen Row 1754-1830 *AmBi,
ApCAB, BiDrAC, DcAmB, Drake,
NatCAB 2, TwCBDA, WhAm H,
WhAmP*
Bradley, Stephen Rowe 1868-1941 *NatCAB 35*
Bradley, Susan Hinckley *BiCAW*
Bradley, Theodore James 1874-1936 *WhAm 1*
Bradley, Thomas 1838?- *NewYHSD*
Bradley, Thomas Eddy Dunham 1861-1943
NatCAB 33
Bradley, Thomas Joseph 1870-1901 *BiDrAC,
WhAm 5*
Bradley, Thomas Wilson 1844-1920 *BiDrAC,
WhAm 1, WhAmP*
Bradley, Walter Parke 1862- *WhAm 5*
Bradley, Warren Ives 1847-1868 *ApCAB,
NatCAB 4, TwCBDA, WhAm H*
Bradley, Will 1868-1962 *NatCAB 51,
WhAm 4*
Bradley, William Aspenwall 1878-1939
WhAm 1
Bradley, William Clark 1863-1947 *NatCAB 34,
WhAm 2*
Bradley, William Czar 1782-1867 *BiAUS,
BiDrAC, DcAmB, Drake, TwCBDA,
WhAm H, WhAmP*
Bradley, William Czar 1783-1867 *ApCAB,
NatCAB 2*
Bradley, William H 1802-1825 *Drake*

Bradley, William Harrison 1848-1929 *WhAm 1*
Bradley, William Horace 1883-1956
NatCAB 45
Bradley, William Lambert 1825-1894
NatCAB 24
Bradley, William O'Connell 1847-1914 *BiDrAC,
DcAmB, NatCAB 13, TwCBDA,
WhAm 1, WhAmP*
Bradley, Willis Winter 1884-1954 *BiDrAC,
WhAm 3*
Bradley, Wilmot Valentine 1863-1929
NatCAB 22
Bradman, Frederic Leison 1879- *WhAm 6*
Bradner, Edith Mitchel 1870- *WomWWA 14*
Bradner, Lester 1867-1929 *WhAm 1*
Bradshaw, Charles Sullivan 1871-1953 *WhAm 3*
Bradshaw, DeEmmett 1869-1960 *NatCAB 46,
WhAm 5*
Bradshaw, Elizabeth Mahan 1874-
WomWWA 14
Bradshaw, Frederick Joseph, Jr. 1904- *WhAm 5*
Bradshaw, Howard Holt 1904-1969 *NatCAB 56*
Bradshaw, Jean Paul 1906-1970 *WhAm 5*
Bradshaw, John H *NewYHSD*
Bradshaw, John Hammond 1860-1943
NatCAB 31, WhAm 2
Bradshaw, Leslie Havergal d1950 *WhAm 3*
Bradshaw, Michael 1903-1971 *WhAm 5*
Bradshaw, Preston John 1883-1953 *NatCAB 41*
Bradshaw, Robert Wallace 1900-1967 *WhAm 4*
Bradshaw, Samuel Carey 1809-1872 *BiAUS,
BiDrAC, WhAm H*
Bradshaw, Sidney Ernest 1869-1938 *WhAm 1*
Bradshaw, William Francis 1878-1930 *WhAm 1*
Bradshaw, William L 1896-1964 *WhAm 4*
Bradsher, Earl L 1879-1974 *WhAm 6*
Bradstreet, Alvah Judson 1862- *NatCAB 17*
Bradstreet, Anne Dudley 1612?-1672 *AmBi,
ApCAB, DcAmB, Drake, McGEWB,
NatCAB 7, NotAW, TwCBDA, WebAB,
WhAm H*
Bradstreet, John 1711?-1774 *AmBi, ApCAB,
DcAmB, Drake, TwCBDA, WebAMB,
WhAm H*
Bradstreet, Simon 1603-1697 *AmBi, ApCAB,
DcAmB, Drake, NatCAB 7, TwCBDA,
WhAm H*
Bradstreet, Simon 1671-1741 *ApCAB, Drake*
Bradstreet, Simon 1709-1771 *ApCAB*
Bradstreet, Thomas Dudley 1841-1915
NatCAB 17
Bradt, Charles Edwin 1863-1922 *WhAm 1*
Bradt, Peter Edward, III 1907-1968 *WhAm 5*
Bradt, Warren Lansing 1867-1939 *NatCAB 29*
Bradwardine, Thomas 1290?-1349 *DcScB*
Bradwell, James Bolesworth 1828-1907 *DcAmB,
TwCBDA, WhAm 1*
Bradwell, Myra Colby 1831-1894 *AmWom,
DcAmB, NatCAB 2, NotAW, TwCBDA,
WhAm H, WhAmP*
Bradwood, John 1824?- *NewYHSD*
Bradwood, Thomas W 1814?- *NewYHSD*
Brady *NewYHSD*
Brady, A Spates, Jr. 1904-1964 *NatCAB 50*
Brady, Alice 1892-1939 *AmBi, DcAmB S2,
NotAW, WebAB, WhAm 1*
Brady, Anthony Nicholas 1841-1913
NatCAB 16
Brady, Anthony Nicholas 1843-1913 *ApCAB X,
DcAmB, WhAm 1*
Brady, Charles Neave 1849-1938 *NatCAB 33*
Brady, Cyrus Townsend 1861-1920 *AmBi,
DcAmB, NatCAB 10, WhAm 1*
Brady, Francis M 1896-1969 *WhAm 5*
Brady, Francis X 1857-1911 *WhAm 1*
Brady, Hugh 1768-1851 *ApCAB, Drake,
TwCBDA*
Brady, James *NewYHSD*
Brady, James 1839?- *NewYHSD*
Brady, James Boyd 1845- *WhAm 4*
Brady, James Buchanan 1856-1917 *AmBi,
NatCAB 19, WebAB, WhAm HA,
WhAm 4*
Brady, James Cox 1882-1927 *WhAm 1*
Brady, James Cox 1907-1971 *WhAm 5*
Brady, James Dennis 1843-1900 *BiDrAC*
Brady, James H 1862-1918 *WhAm 1*
Brady, James Harry 1925-1974 *WhAm 6*

Brady, James Henry 1862-1918 *BiDrAC,*
NatCAB 15
Brady, James Hezekiah 1862-1918 *NatCAB 30*
Brady, James Topham 1815-1869 *ApCAB,*
DcAmB, Drake, NatCAB 3, WhAm H
Brady, Jasper E d1870 *BiAUS*
Brady, Jasper Ewing 1797-1893 *BiDrAC,*
WhAm H
Brady, John 1840-1910 *ApCAB Sup,*
TwCBDA
Brady, John 1842-1910 *WhAm 1*
Brady, John Everett 1860-1941 *WhAm 3*
Brady, John Green 1848-1918 *ApCAB X,*
DcAmB S1, NatCAB 42, REnAW,
WhAm 1, WhAmP
Brady, John Green 1849-1918 *NatCAB 12,*
TwCBDA
Brady, John J 1853-1916 *WhAm 1*
Brady, John Joseph 1868-1950 *NatCAB 38*
Brady, John Leeford 1866-1933 *WhAm 1*
Brady, John R 1821-1891 *NatCAB 3*
Brady, John R 1821-1893 *TwCBDA*
Brady, Joseph Caldwell 1851-1932 *NatCAB 33*
Brady, Jules Longmore 1908-1961 *WhAm 4*
Brady, Lionel Francis 1880-1963 *WhAm 4*
Brady, Mathew B 1823-1896 *AmBi, BnEnAmA,*
DcAmB, EncAB, McGEWB, NewYHSD
Brady, Matthew B 1823-1896 *TwCBDA,*
WebAB, WhAm H
Brady, Matthew Francis 1893-1959 *WhAm 4*
Brady, Nicholas Frederic 1878-1930 *WhAm 1*
Brady, Patrick Joseph 1891-1953 *NatCAB 41*
Brady, Paul T 1856-1928 *ApCAB X*
Brady, Robert Alexander 1901-1963 *WhAm 4*
Brady, Susie Frances Brown 1856-
WomWWA 14
Brady, Thomas, Jr. 1870-1944 *WhAm 2*
Brady, Thomas Allan 1902-1964 *WhAm 4*
Brady, Thomas Francis 1915-1972 *WhAm 5*
Brady, Thomas Jefferson 1839-1904 *WhAm 1*
Brady, Thomas Pickens 1903-1973 *WhAm 5*
Brady, William 1880-1972 *WhAm 5*
Brady, William Aloysius 1863-1950 *DcAmB S4,*
WebAB, WhAm 2
Brady, William Gage, Jr. 1887-1966 *WhAm 4*
Brady, William Otterwell Ignatius 1899-1961
WhAm 4
Brady, William Sobieski 1853-1923 *NatCAB 31*
Brady, Wyatt Tate 1870-1925 *NatCAB 20*
Braekeleer *NewYHSD*
Braeunlich, Sophia 1854-1898 *NatCAB 9*
Braeunlich, Sophia 1860-1898 *AmWom*
Braga, Bernardo 1875-1960 *WhAm 4*
Bragaw, Isaac 1857-1920 *NatCAB 18*
Bragdon, Charles Cushman 1847-1932
NatCAB 18, TwCBDA, WhAm 1
Bragdon, Claude Fayette 1866-1946 *DcAmB S4,*
WhAm 2
Bragdon, Edmund Erastus Eastman 1812-1862
ApCAB
Bragdon, Horace Elwood 1868-1935
NatCAB 31
Bragdon, John Stewart 1893-1964 *WhAm 4*
Bragdon, Joseph Henry 1887-1930 *NatCAB 21*
Bragdon, Merritt Caldwell 1850-1927
NatCAB 22
Bragdon, Merritt Caldwell 1892-1958
NatCAB 48, WhAm 3
Bragdon, Olive Hurd 1858-1915 *WhAm 1*
Bragdon, Oliver Hurd 1858-1915
WomWWA 14
Bragg, Braxton 1815?-1876 *Drake*
Bragg, Braxton 1817-1876 *AmBi, ApCAB,*
BiDConf, DcAmB, NatCAB 11,
TwCBDA, WebAB, WebAMB, WhAm H,
WhoMilH
Bragg, Edward Milton 1874-1960 *NatCAB 45,*
WhAm 5
Bragg, Edward Stuyvesant 1827-1912 *AmBi,*
ApCAB, BiDrAC, DcAmB, NatCAB 5,
NatCAB 10, TwCBDA, WhAm 1,
WhAmP
Bragg, George Freeman, Jr. 1863-1940
WhAm 3, WhoColR
Bragg, George T 1897-1964 *WhAm 4*
Bragg, John 1806-1878 *BiAUS, BiDrAC,*
WhAm H
Bragg, Jubie Barton 1876- *WhoColR*

Bragg, Sir Lawrence 1890-1971 *WhAm 5*
Bragg, Leslie Raymond 1873-1950 *NatCAB 40*
Bragg, Thomas 1810-1872 *AmBi, ApCAB,*
BiAUS, BiDConf, BiDrAC, DcAmB,
Drake, NatCAB 4, TwCBDA, WhAm H,
WhAmP
Bragg, Walter L 1838-1891 *TwCBDA*
Bragg, Sir William Henry 1862-1942 *AsBiEn,*
DcScB, McGEWB
Bragg, Sir William Lawrence 1890-1971 *AsBiEn,*
DcScB Sup
Braginton, Mary Victoria 1901-1973 *WhAm 6*
Braham, Chester Mark 1888-1969 *NatCAB 54*
Brahany, Thomas W 1876-1964 *WhAm 4*
Brahe, Tycho 1546-1601 *AsBiEn, DcScB,*
McGEWB
Braheney, Bernard F 1892-1954 *WhAm 3*
Brahm, John *NewYHSD*
Brahmadeva *DcScB*
Brahmagupta 598?-660? *AsBiEn*
Brahmagupta 598-665? *DcScB*
Brahms, Johannes 1833-1897 *McGEWB*
Braid, Andrew 1846- *WhAm 4*
Braid, James 1795-1860 *AsBiEn*
Braidwood, Thomas W *NewYHSD*
Braikenridge, William 1700?-1762 *DcScB*
Brain, Belle Marvel 1859-1933 *WhAm 1,*
WomWWA 14
Brain, Roy 1894-1972 *NatCAB 57*
Brain, Walter Russell 1895-1966 *WhAm 4*
Brainerd, Clifford Wayne 1893-1966
NatCAB 51
Brainard, Clinton Tyler 1865-1935 *WhAm 1*
Brainard, Daniel 1812-1866 *AmBi, ApCAB,*
DcAmB, NatCAB 20, WhAm H
Brainard, David Legg 1856-1946 *ApCAB,*
NatCAB 3, TwCBDA
Brainard, David Legge 1856-1946 *WhAm 2*
Brainard, Dyar Throop d1863 *ApCAB*
Brainard, James Jacob 1878-1953 *NatCAB 49*
Brainard, Jehu *NewYHSD*
Brainard, John 1830- *NatCAB 2*
Brainard, John Gardiner Calkins 1796-1828
ApCAB, DcAmB, NatCAB 8, TwCBDA,
WhAm H
Brainard, Kate J 1835- *AmWom*
Brainard, Morgan Bulkeley 1879-1957 *WhAm 3*
Brainard, Morgan Bulkeley, Jr. 1906-1960
WhAm 4, WhAm 5
Brainard, Newton Case 1880-1964 *NatCAB 52,*
WhAm 6
Brainard, Owen 1865-1919 *NatCAB 15,*
WhAm 1
Braine, Clinton Elgin, Jr. 1894- *WhAm 3*
Braine, Daniel Lawrence 1829-1898 *ApCAB,*
NatCAB 5, TwCBDA
Braine, Elizabeth Musgrove 1868-
WomWWA 14
Braine, Robert D 1861- *WhAm 4*
Brainerd, Miss *NewYHSD*
Brainerd, Arthur Alanson 1891-1966
NatCAB 53, WhAm 4
Brainerd, Cephas 1831-1910 *TwCBDA,*
WhAm 1
Brainerd, Chauncey Corey 1874-1922 *WhAm 1*
Brainerd, David 1718-1747 *AmBi, ApCAB,*
DcAmB, DcAmReB, Drake, NatCAB 2,
TwCBDA, WhAm H
Brainerd, Eleanor Hoyt 1868-1942 *WhAm 2*
Brainerd, Eleanor Hoyt 1869-1942
WomWWA 14
Brainerd, Erastus 1855-1922 *ApCAB X,*
DcAmB, NatCAB 19, REnAW, WhAm 1
Brainerd, Ezra 1844-1924 *AmBi, DcAmB,*
NatCAB 12, TwCBDA, WhAm 1
Brainerd, Ezra, Jr. 1878-1963 *NatCAB 49,*
WhAm 6
Brainerd, Frank 1854-1916 *WhAm 1*
Brainerd, Frank A 1870-1930 *NatCAB 23*
Brainerd, George Walton 1909-1956
NatCAB 46
Brainerd, Henry Dean, Sr. 1914-1969 *WhAm 5*
Brainerd, Henry Green 1852-1928 *ApCAB X,*
WhAm 1
Brainerd, Henry Warren Paine 1839-1915
NatCAB 16
Brainerd, John 1720-1781 *ApCAB, DcAmB,*
TwCBDA, WhAm H

Brainerd, John Gardiner Calkins 1796-1828
Drake
Brainerd, Lawrence 1794-1870 *ApCAB,*
BiAUS, BiDrAC, DcAmB, NatCAB 8,
WhAm H
Brainerd, Samuel Myron 1842-1898 *BiDrAC*
Brainerd, Thomas 1804-1866 *ApCAB, DcAmB,*
Drake, TwCBDA, WhAm H
Brainerd, Warren Coe 1910-1961 *NatCAB 51*
Braislin, Edward 1846-1915 *WhAm 1*
Braislin, Mary Raymond 1860- *WomWWA 14*
Braislin, William Coughlin 1865-1948
NatCAB 37, WhAm 2
Braisted, William Clarence 1864-1941
NatCAB 30, WhAm 1
Braithwaite, John Alexander 1877- *WhoColR*
Braithwaite, William Stanley Beaumont
1878-1962 *WhAm 4, WhoColR*
Braitmayer, Otto Ernest 1873-1940 *WhAm 1*
Brakeley, George Archibald 1884-1961
WhAm 4
Brakeman, Roy Edgar 1880-1957 *NatCAB 46*
Brakensiek, Clifton Mack 1909-1974 *WhAm 6*
Braley, Berton 1882-1966 *WhAm 4*
Braley, Henry King 1850-1929 *WhAm 1*
Braley, Love A Webb 1850- *WomWWA 14*
Bralley, Francis Marion 1867-1924 *BiDAmEd,*
WhAm 1
Bralliar, Floyd Burton 1875-1951 *WhAm 3*
Brally, James 1822?- *NewYHSD*
Bram, Joseph 1904-1974 *WhAm 6*
Braman, Benjamin 1831-1889 *ApCAB,*
TwCBDA
Braman, Dwight 1861-1929 *NatCAB 25,*
WhAm 1
Braman, Ella Frances 1850- *AmWom*
Braman, Packer 1873-1965 *NatCAB 57*
Bramante, Donato 1444-1514 *McGEWB*
Bramble, Anna Dripps 1885- *WomWWA 14*
Bramble, David Denman 1839-1910 *NatCAB 22*
Bramble, R Blaine 1903-1970 *NatCAB 57*
Bramblett, Ernest King 1901-1966 *BiDrAC*
Brameld, Theodore Burghard Hurt 1904-
BiDAmEd
Bramer, Benjamin 1588?-1652 *DcScB*
Bramer, Samuel Eugene 1885- *WhAm 2*
Bramhall, Edith Clementine 1874-1965
WhAm 4, WomWWA 14
Bramhall, Florence Adelaide 1864-
WomWWA 14
Bramhall, Howard Wellington 1895-1962
WhAm 4
Bramham, William Gibbons 1874-1947
WhAm 2
Bramkamp, John Milton 1867- *WhAm 5*
Bramlett, James E 1932- *IlBEAAW*
Bramlette, Thomas E 1817-1875 *ApCAB,*
BiAUS, DcAmB, NatCAB 13, TwCBDA,
WhAm H, WhAmP
Bramley, James Raymond 1885-1970
NatCAB 57
Bramley, Matthew Frederick 1868- *ApCAB X*
Brammer, George Edward 1886-1948 *WhAm 2*
Brammer, Joseph 1833-1904 *NewYHSD*
Brammer, Robert d1853 *NewYHSD*
Bramson *NewYHSD*
Bramson, Leo 1902-1975 *WhAm 6*
Bramuglia, Juan Atillo 1925-1962 *WhAm 4*
Branch, Alpheus 1843-1893 *NatCAB 4*
Branch, Anna Hempstead 1875-1937 *NotAW,*
WhAm 1, WomWWA 14
Branch, Anthony Martin 1823-1867 *BiDConf*
Branch, Anthony Martin 1824-1867 *NatCAB 8*
Branch, Ben 1884-1952 *NatCAB 41*
Branch, Charles Henry Hardin 1875- *WhAm 1*
Branch, Charles James 1834- *ApCAB*
Branch, Clement Tazewell, Jr. 1869- *WhoColR*
Branch, E Douglas 1905-1945 *REnAW*
Branch, Emmett Forest 1874-1932 *NatCAB 23*
Branch, Ernest A 1888-1958 *WhAm 3*
Branch, Ernest William 1863-1936 *WhAm 1*
Branch, George Lay 1875-1956 *NatCAB 47*
Branch, Harllee 1879-1967 *WhAm 4*
Branch, Harold Francis 1894-1966 *WhAm 4*
Branch, Houston 1905-1968 *WhAm 5*
Branch, Irving Lewis 1912-1966 *WhAm 4*
Branch, James Ransom 1863- *WhAm 4*
Branch, John 1782-1863 *ApCAB, BiAUS,*

BiDrAC, BiDrUSE, DcAmB, Drake,
NatCAB 5, TwCBDA, WhAm H,
WhAmP
Branch, John B 1851-1933 *WhAm 1*
Branch, John Kerr 1865-1930 *NatCAB 44*
Branch, John Patteson 1830-1915 *WhAm 1*
Branch, Joseph Gerald 1866- *WhAm 4*
Branch, Lawrence O'Brien 1820-1862 *ApCAB,*
BiAUS, Drake, NatCAB 4, TwCBDA
Branch, Lawrence O'Bryan 1820-1862 *BiDrAC,*
DcAmB, WhAm H, WhAmP
Branch, Mary Elizabeth 1880- *WhoColR*
Branch, Mary Lillian 1864- *WomWWA 14a*
Branch, Mary Lydia Bolles 1840-1922 *ApCAB,*
NatCAB 21, TwCBDA, WhAm 1,
WomWWA 14
Branch, Oliver Ernesto 1847-1916 *NatCAB 17,*
WhAm 1
Branch, Oliver Winslow 1879-1956 *NatCAB 42,*
WhAm 6
Branch, William Augustus Blount 1847-1910
BiDrAC, WhAmP
Branciforte, Miguel DeLaGrua Talamanca
ApCAB
Brancusi, Constantin 1876-1957 *McGEWB,*
WhAm 3
Brand, A Arnold 1892-1959 *NatCAB 54*
Brand, Albert Rich 1889-1940 *NatCAB 35*
Brand, Alfred 1884-1947 *NatCAB 38*
Brand, Carl Widlar 1880-1942 *NatCAB 31*
Brand, Charles 1871-1966 *BiDrAC, WhAm 4*
Brand, Charles 1879-1949 *EncAAH*
Brand, Charles Hillyer 1861-1933 *BiDrAC,*
WhAm 1, WhAmP
Brand, Charles John 1879-1949 *WhAm 2*
Brand, Charles L 1887-1953 *WhAm 3*
Brand, Edward Alexander 1879- *WhAm 6*
Brand, Edward Parish 1854-1924 *WhAm 1*
Brand, H Russell 1879-1950 *NatCAB 41*
Brand, Harrison, Jr. 1891- *WhAm 5*
Brand, Hennig 1630?- *AsBiEn*
Brand, James Tenney 1886-1964 *WhAm 4*
Brand, John W B d1939 *WhAm 1*
Brand, Louis 1885-1971 *WhAm 5*
Brand, Max 1892-1944 *DcAmB S3, REnAW,*
WebAB
Brand, Oscar James 1857-1928 *NatCAB 23*
Brand, Robert Henry 1878-1963 *WhAm 4*
Brand, Rudolf 1851-1916 *NatCAB 38*
Brand, William Henry 1892-1957 *WhAm 3*
Brande, Dorothea 1893-1948 *NatCAB 39,*
WhAm 2
Brande, William Thomas 1788-1866 *DcScB*
Brandeberry, John Benjamin 1893-1953
WhAm 3
Brandebury, L G *BiAUS*
Brandegee, Augustus 1828-1904 *BiAUS,*
BiDrAC, WhAmP
Brandegee, Frank Bosworth 1864-1924
ApCAB X, BiDrAC, DcAmB, NatCAB 13,
WhAm 1, WhAmP
Brandegee, Mary Katharine Layne Curran
1844-1920 *NotAW*
Brandegee, Robert Bolling 1849-1922
NatCAB 20
Brandegee, Townshend Stith 1843-1925 *DcAmB,*
NatCAB 23
Brandeis, Erich d1954 *WhAm 3*
Brandeis, Frederic 1835-1899 *WhAm H*
Brandeis, Frederick 1835-1899 *NatCAB 7,*
WhAm 1
Brandeis, Lewis Dembitz 1856-1941 *ApCAB X*
Brandeis, Louis Dembitz 1856-1941 *DcAmB S3,*
EncAB, McGEWB, NatCAB 14,
NatCAB 36, WebAB, WhAm 1
Brandeis, Paul 1911-1963 *NatCAB 48*
Brandel, S W d1955 *WhAm 3*
Brandelle, Gustaf Albert 1861-1936 *WhAm 1*
Branden, Paul Maerker 1888-1942 *WhAm 2*
Brandenburg, Earnest Silas 1915-1961 *WhAm 4*
Brandenburg, Edwin Charles 1865-1935
NatCAB 27, WhAm 1, WhAm 1C
Brandenburg, Frederick Harmon 1854-
WhAm 1
Brandenburg, Frederick Sarles 1888-1959
NatCAB 48
Brandenburg, George Clinton 1878-1934
WhAm 1

Brandenburg, Mort d1973 *WhAm 6*
Brandenburg, Samuel J 1880- *WhAm 6*
Brandenburg, William Aaron 1869-1940
BiDAmEd, NatCAB 35, WhAm 1
Brandenburg, William Aaron, Jr. 1910-1975
WhAm 6
Brandes *NewYHSD*
Brandes, Elmer Walker 1891-1964 *WhAm 4*
Brandes, Heinrich Wilhelm 1777-1834 *DcScB*
Brandes, Julius 1851- *NatCAB 18*
Brandhorst, Otto William 1889-1974 *WhAm 6*
Brandi, Hermann Theodor 1908-1973 *WhAm 6*
Brandjord, Iver Martinson 1873-1950 *WhAm 3*
Brando, Marlon 1924- *WebAB*
Brandon, Channing Webster 1858-1944
ApCAB X, NatCAB 34
Brandon, Edgar Ewing 1865-1957 *NatCAB 48,*
WhAm 3
Brandon, Edmund John 1894-1946 *WhAm 2*
Brandon, George C *BiAUS*
Brandon, Gerard Chittocque 1788-1850 *DcAmB,*
NatCAB 13, WhAm H, WhAmP
Brandon, Harry Palmer 1880-1947 *NatCAB 36*
Brandon, Jesse DeWitt 1891- *WhAm 3*
Brandon, Morris 1862-1940 *WhAm 1*
Brandon, Rodney Howe 1881- *WhAm 6*
Brandon, Samuel George Frederick 1907-
WhAm 5
Brandon, William Henry 1894-1960
NatCAB 49
Brandon, William Woodward 1868-1934
WhAm 1
Brandreth, Benjamin 1807-1880 *ApCAB*
Brandreth, William 1842- *NatCAB 2*
Brandriff, George Kennedy 1890-1936
IIBEAAW
Brandt, Allen Demmy 1908-1971 *NatCAB 57,*
WhAm 5
Brandt, Arthur John 1888-1944 *NatCAB 34*
Brandt, Carl Gunard 1897-1969 *NatCAB 54,*
WhAm 5
Brandt, Carl Ludwig 1831-1905 *ApCAB,*
IIBEAAW, NatCAB 8, NewYHSD,
TwCBDA, WhAm H, WhAm 3
Brandt, Erdmann Neumiester 1893-1966
WhAm 4
Brandt, Georg 1694-1768 *AsBiEn, DcScB*
Brandt, George Louis 1892-1971 *WhAm 5*
Brandt, Harry 1897-1972 *WhAm 5*
Brandt, Harry Nathaniel 1898-1972
NatCAB 57
Brandt, Herbert 1884-1955 *NatCAB 45*
Brandt, Herman Carl George 1850-1920
WhAm 1
Brandt, Herman Francis 1895-1955 *NatCAB 42*
Brandt, Joe 1882-1939 *NatCAB 28*
Brandt, Johann Friedrich 1802-1879 *DcScB*
Brandt, John 1885-1953 *WhAm 3*
Brandt, John Francis 1900-1966 *NatCAB 53*
Brandt, John Lincoln 1860-1946 *WhAm 2*
Brandt, Joseph 1742?-1807 *Drake*
Brandt, Joseph Granger 1880-1933 *WhAm 1*
Brandt, Karl 1899-1975 *WhAm 6*
Brandt, Mary Largent 1898-1962 *NatCAB 46*
Brandt, Nils 1824- *WhAm 4*
Brandt, Olaf Elias 1862- *WhAm 1*
Brandt, Raymond Peter 1896-1974 *WhAm 6*
Brandt, William Earle 1891-1963 *WhAm 4*
Brandt, Willy 1913- *McGEWB*
Branford, William Victor 1907-1964
NatCAB 51
Brangwyn, Sir Frank 1867-1956 *WhAm 3*
Branham, Harris Miller 1863-1938 *NatCAB 36*
Branham, Sara Elizabeth 1888- *WhAm 4*
Branham, Vernon Charles 1889-1951
NatCAB 39
Branham, William Charles 1867-1920 *WhAm 1*
Braniff, Thomas Elmer 1883-1954 *DcAmB S5,*
WhAm 3
Branigin, Elba Lloyd, Jr. 1909-1970 *NatCAB 54*
Branigin, Roger Douglas 1902-1975 *WhAm 6*
Branion, John Marshall 1892-1965 *NatCAB 51*
Brann, Donald W 1895-1945 *WhAm 2*
Brann, Henry Athanasius 1837-1921
ApCAB Sup, WhAm 1
Brann, Louis Jefferson 1875-1948 *NatCAB 35*
Brann, Louis Jefferson 1876-1948 *WhAm 2*
Brann, William Cowper 1855-1898 *DcAmB S1,*

WhAm H
Brannan, Charles Franklin 1903- *BiDrUSE,*
EncAAH
Brannan, John Milton 1819-1892 *AmBi,*
ApCAB, DcAmB, NatCAB 4, TwCBDA,
WhAm H
Brannan, John Milton 1820?-1892 *Drake*
Brannan, John Winters 1853-1936 *WhAm 1*
Brannan, Joseph Doddridge 1848-1930 *WhAm 1*
Brannan, Samuel 1819-1889 *AmBi, ApCAB,*
DcAmB, REnAW, TwCBDA, WebAB,
WhAm H, WhAmP
Brannan, Sophie Marston *WomWWA 14*
Brannan, William Forrest 1893-1956
NatCAB 45, WhAm 3
Brannan, William Penn 1825-1866 *ApCAB,*
Drake, NewYHSD
Brannen, Burton Alexander 1899-1967 *WhAm 4*
Brannen, John Franklin 1853-1927 *NatCAB 21*
Branner, John Casper 1850-1922 *AmBi,*
DcAmB, NatCAB 13, NatCAB 24,
TwCBDA, WhAm 1
Branner, Martin Michael 1888-1970
NatCAB 55, WhAm 5
Branner, Robert 1927-1973 *WhAm 6*
Branner, Susan Dow Kennedy *WomWWA 14*
Brannigan, Gladys 1882- *WhAm 2*
Brannon, Henry 1837-1914 *DcAmB, WhAm 1*
Brannon, Melvin Amos 1865-1950 *NatCAB 38,*
WhAm 2A
Brannon, Peter Alexander 1882-1967 *WhAm 4*
Brannon, William W 1853- *WhAm 4*
Brannt, William Theodore 1844- *WhAm 4*
Brano, Joseph *NewYHSD*
Branom, Mendel Everett 1889-1963 *WhAm 4*
Bransby, Carlos 1848-1923 *NatCAB 17,*
WhAm 1
Branscomb, John W 1905-1959 *WhAm 3*
Branscomb, Lewis Capers 1865-1930 *WhAm 1*
Branscombe, Gena 1881- *WhAm 6*
Bransford, Clifton Wood 1858-1933 *WhAm 1*
Bransford, John Francis 1846-1911 *NatCAB 16*
Branshaw, Charles E 1895-1949 *WhAm 3*
Bransom, John Paul 1885- *IIBEAAW*
Branson, Anna Mary 1883- *WomWWA 14*
Branson, Edwin Bayer 1877-1950 *WhAm 3*
Branson, Eugene Cunningham 1861-1933
WhAm 1
Branson, Frederick Page 1880- *WhAm 6*
Branson, John William 1888-1957 *WhAm 3*
Branson, Joseph Holmes 1866-1947 *NatCAB 36*
Branson, Taylor 1881-1969 *WhAm 5*
Branson, William Henry 1887-1961 *WhAm 4*
Branstetter, Winnie E 1879- *WomWWA 14*
Branstrom, William Jeremiah 1885-1964
NatCAB 55, WhAm 4
Brant, A Earl 1889-1967 *NatCAB 54*
Brant, Catherine Brant Johns 1800-1867
ApCAB
Brant, Edward 1845-1916 *NatCAB 16*
Brant, Gerald Clark 1880- *WhAm 6*
Brant, Jabez Anderson 1845- *NatCAB 16*
Brant, John 1794-1832 *ApCAB*
Brant, Joseph 1740?-1807 *NatCAB 9*
Brant, Joseph 1742-1807 *AmBi, ApCAB,*
DcAmB, EncAAH, McGEWB, REnAW,
TwCBDA, WebAB, WebAMB, WhAm H
Brant, Mary 1736?-1796 *NotAW*
Brant, Minnie Clothier *WomWWA 14,*
WomWWA 14a
Brant, Sebastian 1457-1521 *McGEWB*
Brantingham, Charles Simonson 1862-
WhAm 4
Brantley, Theodore 1851-1922 *DcAmB*
Brantley, William Gordon 1860-1934 *BiDrAC,*
TwCBDA, WhAm 1, WhAmP
Brantly, Theodore 1851-1922 *NatCAB 12,*
WhAm 1
Brantly, Theodore Lee 1892-1961 *WhAm 4*
Brantly, William Theophilus 1787-1845
TwCBDA
Brantly, William Theophilus 1852- *WhAm 4*
Branton, James Rodney 1906-1967 *WhAm 5*
Brantz, Lewis *NewYHSD*
Branyon, Robert 1930- *EncAAH*
Branzell, Karin 1897-1974 *WhAm 6*
Braque, Georges 1882-1963 *WhAm 4*
Braque, Georges 1882-1967 *McGEWB*

Bras, Harry Leonard 1862-1940 *WhAm 1*
Brasch, Frederick Edward 1875- *WhAm 6*
Brasco, Frank James 1932- *BiDrAC*
Brase, Hagbard 1877-1953 *WhAm 3*
Brasey, S B 1852- *WhoColR*
Brashear, John Alfred 1840-1920 *ApCAB X,*
DcAmB, DcScB, NatCAB 4, WhAm HA,
WhAm 1, WhAm 4
Brashear, Peter Cominges 1867-1943 *WhAm 2*
Brashears, Edwin Lawrence 1899-1973
WhAm 6
Brashears, James Russell 1858-1917
NatCAB 17
Brasher, Abraham 1734-1782 *ApCAB*
Brasher, John H 1827?-1869? *NewYHSD*
Brasher, Rex 1869-1960 *WhAm 3*
Brashman, Nikolai Dmitrievich 1796-1866
DcScB
Braskamp, Bernard 1887-1966 *WhAm 4*
Braslau, Sophie 1888-1935 *NotAW*
Braslau, Sophie 1892-1935 *DcAmB S1,*
WhAm 1
Brasol, Boris 1885-1963 *WhAm 4*
Brassert, Charles Alexander 1903-1959
NatCAB 46
Brassert, Herman Alexander 1875- *WhAm 5*
Brasseur DeBourbourg, Charles Etienne
1814-1874 *ApCAB*
Brasted, Alva Jennings 1876- *WhAm 5*
Brasted, Fred d1937 *WhAm 1*
Brastow, Lewis Orsmond 1834-1912 *NatCAB 8,*
TwCBDA, WhAm 1
Braswell, James Craig 1868-1951 *WhAm 4*
Braswell, John Thomas 1884-1945 *NatCAB 34*
Braswell, William Edward 1875- *WhoColR*
Bratenahl, George Carl Fitch 1862-1939
WhAm 1
Bratney, John Frederick 1880- *WhAm 6*
Bratt, Adolph *NewYHSD*
Bratt, Elmer Clark 1901-1970 *NatCAB 57,*
WhAm 6
Bratt, John 1842-1918 *REnAW*
Brattain, Walter Houser 1902- *AsBiEn,*
WebAB
Brattle, Thomas 1657-1713 *ApCAB*
Brattle, Thomas 1658-1713 *DcAmB, WebAB,*
WhAm H
Brattle, William 1662-1716? *DcAmB*
Brattle, William 1662-1717 *ApCAB,*
BiDAmEd, WhAm H
Brattle, William 1702?-1776 *ApCAB, Drake,*
TwCBDA
Bratton, Franklin *NewYHSD*
Bratton, John 1831-1898 *BiDConf, BiDrAC,*
DcAmB, NatCAB 21, WhAm H
Bratton, John Walter 1867-1947 *NatCAB 53,*
WhAm 4
Bratton, Leslie Emmett 1885-1959 *WhAm 3*
Bratton, Martha d1816 *ApCAB*
Bratton, Robert Franklin 1845-1894 *BiDrAC,*
WhAm H
Bratton, Sam Gilbert 1888-1963 *BiDrAC,*
WhAm 4
Bratton, Samuel Tilden 1878-1940 *WhAm 1*
Bratton, Theodore DuBose 1862-1944
NatCAB 12, WhAm 2
Bratton, Walter Andrew 1874-1943 *NatCAB 32,*
WhAm 2
Brau, Charles Frederick 1911-1973 *WhAm 6*
Braucher, Frank 1884-1968 *WhAm 5*
Braucher, Howard S 1881-1949 *WhAm 2*
Braucher, Pela Fay 1905-1966 *NatCAB 52*
Brauchitsch, Walter Von 1881-1948 *WhWW-II,*
WhoMilH
Braude, Jacob Morton 1896-1970 *WhAm 5*
Braudy, Harold Isaac 1890-1962 *NatCAB 52*
Brauer, Alfred 1895-1965 *WhAm 4*
Brauer, George R 1871-1935 *WhAm 1*
Brauer, John Charles 1905-1971 *WhAm 5*
Brauer, Kinley Jules 1935- *EncAAH*
Brauff, Herbert D 1890-1955 *WhAm 3*
Braumuller, Luetta Elmina 1856- *AmWom*
Braun, Alexander Carl Heinrich 1805-1877
DcScB
Braun, Antoine Nicholas 1815-1885
ApCAB Sup
Braun, Arthur E 1876- *WhAm 6*
Braun, Carl Franklin 1884-1954 *NatCAB 41,*

WhAm 3
Braun, Eva 1912-1945 *WhWW-II*
Braun, Ferdinand 1850-1918 *DcScB*
Braun, Frank John 1876-1951 *NatCAB 40*
Braun, Frederick William 1858- *ApCAB X*
Braun, John *NewYHSD*
Braun, John F d1939 *WhAm 1*
Braun, Karl Ferdinand 1850-1918 *AsBiEn*
Braun, L *NewYHSD*
Braun, Maurice 1877-1941 *IIBEAAW,*
WhAm 2
Braun, Robert 1872-1953 *WhAm 3*
Braun, Samuel John 1856-1938 *NatCAB 27*
Braun, Werner 1914-1972 *WhAm 5*
Braun, Wernher Von 1912-1977 *AsBiEn,*
WebAB, WebAMB, WhWW-II,
WhoMilH
Braune, Gustave Maurice 1872-1931 *WhAm 1*
Brauner, Bohuslav 1855-1935 *DcScB*
Brauner, Julius Frederick 1909-1974 *WhAm 6*
Brauner, Olaf Martinius 1869-1947 *NatCAB 36,*
WhAm 2
Braunlin, Edgar Louis 1890-1968 *NatCAB 54*
Braunmuhl, Anton Von 1853-1908 *DcScB*
Brauns, Walter Stewart 1887-1955 *NatCAB 45*
Braunschweiger, Walter J 1894-1974 *WhAm 6*
Braunstein, Benjamin 1892-1972 *NatCAB 55*
Brause, Edward 1908-1967 *WhAm 4*
Brautegam, Anthony Lewis 1891-1961
NatCAB 49
Bravais, Auguste 1811-1863 *DcScB*
Braver, Sol David 1920-1970 *NatCAB 56*
Braverman, Harold 1913-1971 *NatCAB 55*
Bravo, Nicolas 1790-1854 *ApCAB*
Bravo, Nicolas 1792?-1854 *Drake*
Brawley, Benjamin Griffith 1882-1939 *AmBi,*
BiDAmEd, NatCAB 37, WhAm 1,
WhoColR
Brawley, Frank 1875-1962 *WhAm 4*
Brawley, William H 1841-1911 *NatCAB 11,*
TwCBDA, WhAm 3
Brawley, William Hiram 1841-1916 *DcAmB*
Brawley, William Huggins 1841-1916 *BiDrAC*
Brawner, John Waggaman 1873-1929
NatCAB 22
Brawner, Luther Clifton 1915-1965 *NatCAB 51*
Braxton, A Caperton 1862-1914 *WhAm 1*
Braxton, Carter 1736-1797 *AmBi, ApCAB,*
BiAUS, BiDrAC, DcAmB, Drake,
NatCAB 7, TwCBDA, WhAm H,
WhAmP
Braxton, Elliott Muse 1823-1891 *BiAUS,*
BiDrAC, WhAm H
Bray, Andrew Watson 1855- *NatCAB 7*
Bray, Charles I 1882- *WhAm 3*
Bray, Charles Washington 1850-1922
NatCAB 19
Bray, Ella Williams 1866- *WomWWA 14*
Bray, Frank Chapin 1866-1949 *WhAm 2*
Bray, Harold Bryan 1896-1969 *WhAm 5*
Bray, Henry Truro 1846-1922 *WhAm 1*
Bray, James Albert 1870- *WhoColR*
Bray, Job F 1805?- *NewYHSD*
Bray, John Leighton 1890-1952 *WhAm 3*
Bray, John P 1859-1917 *WhAm 1*
Bray, Joseph W *NewYHSD*
Bray, Patrick Albert 1883-1953 *WhAm 4*
Bray, Paul Henry 1868- *WhoColR*
Bray, Robert Stuart 1915-1974 *WhAm 6*
Bray, Stephen 1878- *WhAm 6*
Bray, Thomas 1656-1729? *DcAmB*
Bray, Thomas 1656-1730 *AmBi, ApCAB,*
DcAmReB, TwCBDA, WhAm H
Bray, Thomas 1658-1730 *DcAmLiB*
Bray, Thomas Joseph 1867-1933 *NatCAB 25,*
WhAm 1
Bray, William Crowell 1879-1946 *NatCAB 35,*
WhAm 2
Bray, William Edward 1882-1959 *NatCAB 47*
Bray, William Gilmer 1903- *BiDrAC*
Bray, William L 1865-1953 *WhAm 3*
Brayman, Mason 1813-1895 *AmBi, ApCAB,*
DcAmB, NatCAB 21, TwCBDA,
WhAm H
Braymer, Daniel Harvey 1883-1932 *WhAm 1*
Braymer, Lawrence 1901-1965 *NatCAB 53*
Brayton, Aaron Martin 1872-1949 *NatCAB 38,*
WhAm 2

Brayton, Alembert Winthrop 1848-1926
WhAm 1
Brayton, Charles Ray 1840-1910 *DcAmB,*
NatCAB 16, WhAm 1, WhAmP
Brayton, George Arnold 1803-1880 *NatCAB 5*
Brayton, George Bailey 1829- *Drake Sup*
Brayton, Harry Jay 1880-1939 *NatCAB 29*
Brayton, Israel 1874- *WhAm 5*
Brayton, John Richard 1899-1967 *NatCAB 53*
Brayton, Samuel Nelson 1839- *ApCAB*
Brayton, Sarah H *WomWWA 14*
Brayton, William Daniel 1815-1887 *BiAUS,*
BiDrAC, WhAm H
Brazeau, Theodore Walter 1873- *WhAm 5*
Brazee, Carolina A Potter *WomWWA 14*
Brazelton, James Henry Augustus 1875-
WhoColR
Brazelton, William Buchanan 1857-1934
WhAm 1
Brazer, Clarence Wilson 1880-1956 *WhAm 3*
Brazer, John 1789-1846 *DcAmB, WhAm H*
Brazier, J Sidney 1886- *WhoColR*
Brazier, John Virgil 1897-1957 *NatCAB 50*
Brazier, Marion Howard 1850- *WhAm 1,*
WomWWA 14
Brazier, William Steele 1839-1922 *NatCAB 32*
Brazza, Pierre Paul F C Savorgnan De 1852-1905
McGEWB
Breadon, Sam 1876-1949 *WhAm 2*
Bready, Charles J *WhAm 5*
Brean, Herbert 1907-1973 *WhAm 6*
Brearley, David 1741-1790 *NatCAB 2*
Brearley, David 1745-1790 *ApCAB, TwCBDA,*
WhAm H
Brearley, Harrington Cooper 1893-1960
NatCAB 46
Brearley, Harry Chase 1870- *WhAm 6*
Brearley, Joseph *ApCAB*
Brearley, William Henry 1846-1909 *WhAm 1*
Brearly, David 1745-1790 *BiAUS, DcAmB,*
Drake
Breasted, James Henry 1865-1935 *AmBi,*
BiDAmEd, DcAmB S1, McGEWB,
NatCAB 29, WebAB, WhAm 1
Breathitt, James 1852- *WhAm 4*
Breathitt, John 1786-1834 *ApCAB, BiAUS,*
Drake, NatCAB 13, TwCBDA
Breaux, Joseph Arsenne 1838-1926 *DcAmB,*
NatCAB 13, WhAm 1
Breaux, S Locke 1860-1933 *NatCAB 26*
Breazeale, Phanon 1858-1934 *TwCBDA*
Breazeale, Phanor 1858-1934 *BiDrAC,*
WhAm 3
Brebeuf, Jean De 1593-1649 *ApCAB, Drake,*
McGEWB, TwCBDA
Brebner, John Bartlet 1895-1957 *WhAm 3*
Brebner, Robert 1888-1957 *NatCAB 43*
Brechemin, Lewis *NewYHSD*
Brecht, Bertolt Eugen Friedrich 1898-1956
McGEWB, WhAm HA, WhAm 4
Brecht, Robert Paul 1899-1970 *NatCAB 55,*
WhAm 5
Breck, Alphonse *NewYHSD*
Breck, Daniel d1845 *ApCAB*
Breck, Daniel 1788-1871 *ApCAB, BiAUS,*
BiDrAC, Drake, NatCAB 11, TwCBDA,
WhAm H
Breck, Daniel 1861-1938 *NatCAB 29*
Breck, Edward 1861-1929 *WhAm 1*
Breck, George William 1863-1920 *DcAmB,*
NatCAB 25, WhAm 1
Breck, James Lloyd 1818-1876 *AmBi, ApCAB,*
DcAmB, DcAmReB, TwCBDA,
WhAm H
Breck, John Henry 1877-1965 *NatCAB 52,*
WhAm 4
Breck, Joseph 1885-1933 *NatCAB 25,*
WhAm 1
Breck, Robert d1731 *ApCAB*
Breck, Robert 1713-1784 *ApCAB, Drake*
Breck, Samuel 1771-1862 *ApCAB, BiAUS,*
BiDrAC, DcAmB, Drake, WhAm H
Breck, Samuel 1834-1918 *ApCAB, NatCAB 4,*
TwCBDA, WhAm 1
Brecken, Frederick DeSt. Croix 1828- *ApCAB*
Breckenridge *see also* Breckinridge
Breckenridge, Clifton Rodes 1846-1932
WhAm 1

Breckenridge, Hugh Henry 1870-1937
  NatCAB 29, WhAm 1
Breckenridge, James 1763-1833 *DcAmB,*
  WhAm H
Breckenridge, James 1763-1846 *ApCAB,*
  BiAUS
Breckenridge, James Douglas d1849 *WhAm H*
Breckenridge, James Miller 1880-1961
  NatCAB 48, WhAm 4
Breckenridge, Jefferson 1800-1871 *WhAm H*
Breckenridge, John 1760-1806 *ApCAB,*
  NatCAB 3, WhAm H
Breckenridge, John 1797-1841 *ApCAB,*
  WhAm H
Breckenridge, John C 1858- *WhAm 4*
Breckenridge, John Cabell 1821-1875 *WhAm H*
Breckenridge, Joseph Cabell 1842- *ApCAB*
Breckenridge, Lester Paige 1858-1940 *WhAm 3*
Breckenridge, Ralph W 1860-1913 *WhAm 1*
Breckenridge, Robert Jefferson 1800-1871
  ApCAB, NatCAB 9
Breckenridge, William Campbell Preston
  1837-1904 *ApCAB*
Breckens, Josephine White *WomWWA 14*
Breckinridge *see also* Breckenridge
Breckinridge, Aida DeAcosta d1962 *WhAm 4*
Breckinridge, Clifton Rhodes 1846-1932
  ApCAB Sup
Breckinridge, Clifton Rodes 1846-1932 *BiDrAC,*
  NatCAB 8, TwCBDA, WhAmP
Breckinridge, Desha 1867-1935 *DcAmB S1,*
  NatCAB 29, WhAm 1
Breckinridge, Henry 1886-1960 *NatCAB 44,*
  WhAm 4
Breckinridge, James 1763-1833 *BiDrAC,*
  WhAmP
Breckinridge, James 1763-1846 *Drake,*
  TwCBDA
Breckinridge, James Carson 1877-1942
  WhAm 2
Breckinridge, James Douglas d1849 *BiAUS,*
  BiDrAC
Breckinridge, John 1760-1806 *AmBi, BiAUS,*
  BiDrAC, BiDrUSE, DcAmB, Drake,
  TwCBDA, WhAmP
Breckinridge, John 1797-1841 *AmBi, DcAmB,*
  Drake, NatCAB 22, TwCBDA
Breckinridge, John Cabell 1821-1875 *AmBi,*
  ApCAB, BiAUS, BiDConf, BiDrAC,
  BiDrUSE, DcAmB, Drake, EncAB,
  NatCAB 5, TwCBDA, WebAB,
  WebAMB, WhAmP, WhoMilH
Breckinridge, John Cabell 1870-1941
  NatCAB 32
Breckinridge, Joseph Cabell 1842-1920
  NatCAB 9, TwCBDA, WhAm 1
Breckinridge, Madeline McDowell 1872-1920
  NatCAB 29, NotAW, WhAm 1
Breckinridge, Mary 1881-1965 *WhAm 4*
Breckinridge, Mary Grace 1867-
  WomWWA 14
Breckinridge, Robert Jefferson 1800-1871 *AmBi,*
  BiDAmEd, DcAmB, Drake, TwCBDA
Breckinridge, Robert Jefferson 1834- *BiDConf*
Breckinridge, Samuel Miller 1828-1891
  TwCBDA
Breckinridge, Scott Dudley 1882-1941
  NatCAB 31
Breckinridge, Sophonisba Preston 1866-1948
  BiDAmEd, DcAmB S4, EncAB,
  NatCAB 37, NotAW, WhAm 2,
  WomWWA 14
Breckinridge, William Campbell Preston
  1837-1904 *BiDrAC, DcAmB, NatCAB 2,*
  NatCAB 29, TwCBDA, WhAm 1,
  WhAmP
Breckinridge, William Lewis 1803-1876
  TwCBDA
Breckinridge, William Lewis 1857-1929
  WhAm 1
Breckons, Robert W 1866-1918 *WhAm 1*
Bredikhin, Fedor Aleksandrovich 1831-1904
  DcScB
Bredin, James 1831- *NatCAB 4*
Bredin, R Sloan 1881-1933 *WhAm 1*
Bredlau, Ernest August 1890-1961 *NatCAB 49*
Bredon, Simon 1300?-1372? *DcScB*
Bree, Herbert 1828- *ApCAB*

Bree, William Andrew 1882-1951 *NatCAB 42*
Breece, George Elmer 1865-1942 *NatCAB 31*
Breece, John Tingle 1872-1946 *NatCAB 37*
Breed, Alice Ives 1853- *AmWom*
Breed, Charles Blaney 1875-1958 *WhAm 3*
Breed, Charles Henry 1876-1950 *NatCAB 40,*
  WhAm 3
Breed, David Riddle 1848-1931 *TwCBDA,*
  WhAm 1
Breed, Dwight Payson 1851-1925 *WhAm 1*
Breed, Ebenezer 1766-1839 *DcAmB, WhAm H*
Breed, Frances DeForest Martin 1882-
  WomWWA 14
Breed, James McVickar 1880-1963 *NatCAB 49*
Breed, Mary Bidwell 1870- *WhAm 6,*
  WomWWA 14
Breed, Persis Mary *WomWWA 14*
Breed, Richard Edwards 1866-1926 *NatCAB 35,*
  WhAm 1
Breed, Robert Huntington 1879-1946
  NatCAB 37
Breed, Robert Stanley 1877-1956 *WhAm 3*
Breed, William Constable 1871-1951
  NatCAB 41, WhAm 3
Breed, William Constable, Jr. 1904-1973
  WhAm 6
Breed, William James 1833-1908 *NatCAB 24*
Breed, William Pratt 1816-1889 *ApCAB Sup,*
  TwCBDA
Breeden, Harvey Oscar 1857- *WhAm 4*
Breeding, Glenn Edward 1911-1968 *WhAm 5*
Breeding, James Floyd 1901- *BiDrAC,*
  WhAmP
Breen, Aloysius Andrew 1867-1960 *WhAm 3*
Breen, Edward G 1908- *BiDrAC*
Breen, Henry Hegart 1805- *ApCAB*
Breen, Joseph Ignatius 1890-1965 *WhAm 4*
Breen, Patrick d1868 *ApCAB, DcAmB,*
  WhAm H
Breen, Robert A 1905-1959 *WhAm 3*
Breen, William John, Jr. 1904-1971 *WhAm 5*
Breen, William P 1859-1930 *WhAm 1*
Breene, Frank Thomas 1866-1931 *NatCAB 23,*
  WhAm 1
Breer, Robert 1926- *BnEnAmA*
Brees, Herbert Jay 1877- *WhAm 5*
Breese, Burtis Burr 1867-1939 *NatCAB 38,*
  WhAm 1
Breese, Edmund 1871-1936 *WhAm 1*
Breese, Kidder Randolph 1831-1881 *ApCAB,*
  DcAmB, NatCAB 13, TwCBDA
Breese, Randolph Kidder 1831-1881 *WhAm H*
Breese, Samuel Livingston 1794-1870 *ApCAB,*
  Drake, NatCAB 4, TwCBDA
Breese, Sidney 1800-1878 *AmBi, ApCAB,*
  BiAUS, BiDrAC, DcAmB, Drake,
  NatCAB 8, TwCBDA, WhAm H,
  WhAmP
Breese, William Llywelyn 1864-1954 *WhAm 3*
Breese, Zona Gale *NotAW*
Brefeld, Julius Oscar 1839-1925 *DcScB*
Brefichl *NewYHSD*
Breg, W Roy 1888-1954 *WhAm 3*
Bregstein, S Joseph 1899-1972 *NatCAB 56*
Breguet, Louis Francois Clement 1804-1883
  DcScB
Bregy, Francis Amedee 1846-1922 *WhAm 1*
Bregy, Katherine Marie Cornelia d1967
  WhAm 4, WomWWA 14
Brehan, Marquise De *NewYHSD, WhAm H*
Brehm, Cloide Everett 1889-1971 *NatCAB 55,*
  WhAm 5
Brehm, Henry Anthony 1867-1945 *NatCAB 34*
Brehm, John S 1874-1946 *WhAm 2*
Brehm, Marie Caroline 1859-1926 *WhAm 1,*
  WomWWA 14
Brehm, Walter Ellsworth 1892- *BiDrAC*
Breidenbaugh, Edward Swoyer 1849-1926
  ApCAB, TwCBDA, WhAm 1
Breidenthal, John W 1857-1910 *WhAm 1*
Breidenthal, John W 1911-1972 *WhAm 5*
Breidenthal, Maurice L 1888-1965 *WhAm 4*
Breidenthal, Maurice Lauren, Jr. 1916-1971
  WhAm 5
Breidenthal, Willard J 1884-1960 *WhAm 4*
Breil, Joseph Carl 1870-1926 *NatCAB 20,*
  WhAm 1
Breisach, Paul 1896-1952 *WhAm 3*

Breisacher, Leo 1866- *WhAm 4*
Breisky, John Victor 1899-1960 *NatCAB 49*
Breislak, Scipione 1750-1826 *DcScB*
Breitag, Otto William 1884-1949 *NatCAB 38*
Breitenbach, Edward Victor 1896-1974
  WhAm 6
Breitenbach, Oscar Carl 1878-1929 *NatCAB 22*
Breithaupt, Johann Friedrich August 1791-1873
  DcScB
Breithaupt, Louis Orville 1890-1960 *WhAm 4*
Breithut, Frederick Ernest 1880- *WhAm 6*
Breitung, Charles Adelbert 1892-1958 *WhAm 3*
Breitung, Charlotte Kaufman *BiCAW*
Breitung, Edward 1831-1887 *ApCAB X,*
  BiDrAC, WhAm H
Breitung, Edward Nicklas 1871-1924
  NatCAB 20, WhAm 1
Breitwieser, Joseph Valentine 1884-1950
  WhAm 3
Breivis, John James 1904-1952 *NatCAB 39*
Brelsford, Charles Henry 1853- *WhAm 4*
Brelsford, Millard 1873-1946 *WhAm 2*
Brem, Marion Wolcott Winkler *WomWWA 14*
Brem, Walter Vernon 1875-1937 *ApCAB X,*
  WhAm 1
Bremer, Adolf 1869-1939 *WhAm 1*
Bremer, Alexander Helgo Waldemar 1850-
  NatCAB 10
Bremer, Edward George 1897-1965 *NatCAB 51*
Bremer, Fredrika 1801-1865 *Drake*
Bremer, George A 1891-1956 *WhAm 3*
Bremer, Gerald John 1904-1965 *NatCAB 53*
Bremer, John Lewis 1874-1959 *WhAm 3*
Bremer, Otto 1867- *WhAm 3*
Bremer, Samuel Parker 1872-1925 *NatCAB 20*
Bremiker, Carl 1804-1877 *DcScB*
Bremner, George Hampton 1861-1927 *WhAm 1*
Bremner, Robert Gunn 1874-1914 *BiDrAC*
Bremner, William Hepburn 1869-1934
  NatCAB 36, WhAm 1
Brenan, Joseph 1829-1857 *ApCAB*
Brendel, Otto Johannes 1901-1973 *WhAm 6*
Brendel, Otto Rudolf Martin 1862-1939 *DcScB*
Brendler, Charles 1898-1965 *WhAm 4*
Brendlinger, Margaret Robinson 1873-
  WhAm 5, WomWWA 14
Brendon, Saint *ApCAB*
Breneiser, Stanley Grotevent 1890- *IIBEAAW*
Breneman, Abram Adam 1847-1928 *AmBi,*
  ApCAB, WhAm 1
Breneman, Paul Bruce 1870-1952 *NatCAB 44*
Brengle, Francis 1807-1846 *BiAUS, BiDrAC,*
  WhAm H
Brengle, Henry Gaw 1866-1943 *NatCAB 32,*
  WhAm 2
Brenizer, Addison Gorgas 1839-1918
  NatCAB 39
Brenke, William Charles 1874- *WhAm 5*
Brennan, Alfred Laurens 1853-1921 *AmBi,*
  DcAmB, WhAm 4
Brennan, Andrew James 1877-1956 *NatCAB 42,*
  WhAm 3
Brennan, Edward James 1871-1954 *WhAm 3*
Brennan, Francis Eugene 1874-1934
  NatCAB 25
Brennan, Frederick Hazlitt 1901-1962 *WhAm 4*
Brennan, George E d1928 *WhAm 1*
Brennan, George M 1895-1950 *WhAm 3*
Brennan, Gerald Leo 1896-1966 *WhAm 4*
Brennan, James 1802?- *NewYHSD*
Brennan, James Dowd 1881-1932 *WhAm 1*
Brennan, John *NewYHSD*
Brennan, John Francis 1893-1958 *WhAm 3*
Brennan, John Vincent 1872-1971 *NatCAB 57*
Brennan, Martin Adlai 1879-1941 *BiDrAC,*
  WhAm 1
Brennan, Martin S 1845-1927 *WhAm 2*
Brennan, Robert 1881- *WhAm 6*
Brennan, Robert Emery 1879-1969 *NatCAB 56*
Brennan, Thomas 1838-1889 *NatCAB 6*
Brennan, Thomas Francis 1853- *ApCAB Sup,*
  WhAm 4
Brennan, Thomas P 1860-1928 *ApCAB X*
Brennan, Vincent Morrison 1890-1959 *BiDrAC*
Brennan, Walter Andrew 1894-1974 *WhAm 6*
Brennan, William Henry 1897-1963 *WhAm 4*
Brennan, William Joseph, Jr. 1906- *WebAB*
Brennecke, Cornelius G 1906-1954 *WhAm 3*

Brennecke, Ernest 1896-1969 *NatCAB 54,*
WhAm 5
Brennecke, Henry 1892-1962 *WhAm 4*
Brennemann, Joseph 1872-1944 *DcAmB S3,*
WhAm 2
Brennen, William James 1850- *NatCAB 7*
Brenner, Carl Christian 1838-1888 *ApCAB Sup,*
IIBEAAW
Brenner, Harris 1850-1940 *NatCAB 36*
Brenner, John Lewis 1832-1906 *BiDrAC,*
WhAm 4
Brenner, Mortimer 1889-1969 *WhAm 5*
Brenner, Otto 1907-1972 *WhAm 5*
Brenner, Ruth Marie 1913-1973 *WhAm 6*
Brenner, Victor David 1871-1924 *AmBi,*
DcAmB, WhAm 1
Brenon, Herbert 1880-1958 *WhAm 3*
Brent, Charles Henry 1862-1929 *DcAmB S1,*
NatCAB 14, NatCAB 26, TwCBDA,
WhAm 1
Brent, Charles Maurice 1904-1959 *NatCAB 47*
Brent, Frank Pierce 1852- *WhAm 4*
Brent, Henry *NewYHSD*
Brent, Henry Johnson 1811-1880 *ApCAB,*
NatCAB 13, NewYHSD, WhAm H
Brent, Joseph Lancaster 1826-1905 *ApCAB Sup,*
WhAm 1
Brent, Margaret 1600?-1661 *BiCAW*
Brent, Margaret 1600-1670? *DcAmB,*
WhAm H, WhAmP
Brent, Margaret 1600?-1671? *AmBi, WebAB*
Brent, Margaret 1601?-1671? *NotAW*
Brent, Meade Stith 1881- *WhAm 6*
Brent, Richard d1814 *ApCAB, BiAUS*
Brent, Richard 1757-1814 *BiDrAC, WhAm H,*
WhAmP
Brent, Richard 1760?-1814 *NatCAB 7*
Brent, Theodore 1874-1953 *NatCAB 46,*
WhAm 3
Brent, Thomas Ludwell Lee 1784- *BiAUS,*
NatCAB 12
Brent, William, Jr. 1783-1848 *BiAUS,*
NatCAB 5
Brent, William Leigh 1784-1848 *BiAUS,*
BiDrAC, WhAm H
Brentano, Arthur 1858-1944 *WhAm 2*
Brentano, Clemens 1778-1842 *McGEWB*
Brentano, Franz Clemens 1838-1917 *McGEWB*
Brentano, Lorenz 1813-1891 *DcAmB,*
WhAm H
Brentano, Lorenzo 1813-1891 *ApCAB,*
BiDrAC, TwCBDA
Brentano, Lowell 1895-1950 *WhAm 3*
Brentano, Theodore 1854-1940 *ApCAB X,*
NatCAB 30, WhAm 1
Brenton, Charles Richmond d1924 *WhAm 1*
Brenton, Clyde Edward 1868-1938 *NatCAB 28,*
WhAm 1
Brenton, Cranston 1874-1937 *WhAm 1*
Brenton, Jahleel 1729-1802 *Drake*
Brenton, Jahleel 1770-1844 *ApCAB*
Brenton, Samuel 1810-1857 *ApCAB, BiAUS,*
BiDrAC, NatCAB 4, WhAm H
Brenton, William d1674 *ApCAB, Drake,*
NatCAB 10, TwCBDA
Brenton, Woodward Harold 1899-1968
NatCAB 55, WhAm 5
Brents, Thomas Hurley 1840-1916 *BiDrAC,*
WhAmP
Breobey *NewYHSD*
Brereton, John *DcAmB*
Brereton, Lewis Hyde 1890-1967 *WebAMB,*
WhAm 4A, WhWW-II
Bres, Edward Sedley 1888-1967 *NatCAB 54,*
WhAm 5
Breschard *WhAm H*
Breschet, Gilbert 1783-1845 *DcScB*
Bresky, Otto 1889-1974 *WhAm 6*
Breslaw *NewYHSD*
Breslich, Arthur Louis 1873-1924 *WhAm 1*
Breslich, Ernst Rudolph 1874- *WhAm 5*
Breslin, James H d1906 *WhAm 1*
Bresnahan, Maurice Vincent 1853-1930
ApCAB X
Bresnahan, Thomas F 1892-1971 *WhAm 5*
Bresnahan, William H d1947 *WhAm 2*
Bressani, Francesco Giuseppe 1612-1672
ApCAB

Bressi, Vincent 1887-1953 *NatCAB 40*
Bressler, Edwin Herman 1912-1966 *NatCAB 53*
Bressler, Max 1902-1966 *NatCAB 52*
Bressler, Raymond G, Jr. 1911-1968 *WhAm 4A*
Bressler, Raymond George 1887-1948
NatCAB 42, WhAm 2
Bressler, Robert E 1889-1962 *NatCAB 51*
Brestell, Rudolph Emile 1873- *WhAm 5*
Bret, Jean Jacques 1781-1819 *DcScB*
Bretherton, Sidney Elliott 1854-1929 *WhAm 1*
Brethorst, Alice Beatrice 1879- *WhAm 6*
Breton, Andre 1896-1966 *McGEWB, WhAm 4*
Breton, Raymond 1609-1679 *ApCAB*
Breton, Ruth 1902- *WhAm 4*
Breton, W L *NewYHSD*
Bretonneau, Pierre 1778-1862 *BiHiMed, DcScB*
Brett, Agnes Baldwin 1876-1955 *WhAm 3*
Brett, Alden Chase 1889-1970 *WhAm 5*
Brett, Alphonse *NewYHSD*
Brett, Axel 1886-1950 *WhAm 3*
Brett, Dorothy Eugenie 1883- *IIBEAAW*
Brett, Ellis 1840-1915 *NatCAB 17*
Brett, George Everett 1845-1915 *NatCAB 16*
Brett, George Platt 1858-1936 *DcAmB S2,*
NatCAB 42, WhAm 1
Brett, Homer 1877- *WhAm 5*
Brett, Lloyd M 1856-1927 *WhAm 1*
Brett, Margaret Strong *WomWWA 14*
Brett, Philip Milledoler 1871-1960 *WhAm 4*
Brett, Rutherford 1867- *WhAm 3*
Brett, Sereno Elmer 1891-1952 *NatCAB 44,*
WhAm 3
Brett, William Howard 1846-1918 *AmBi,*
DcAmB, DcAmLiB, NatCAB 6,
WhAm 1
Brett, William Pierce 1852- *WhAm 4*
Brettauer, Joseph 1863-1941 *NatCAB 33*
Brette, Professor *NewYHSD*
Bretz, John Lewis 1852-1920 *BiDrAC*
Bretz, Julian Pleasant 1876-1951 *WhAm 3*
Breuchaud, Jules 1857-1934 *NatCAB 29*
Breuer, Bessie 1893-1975 *WhAm 6*
Breuer, Carl A 1911-1974 *WhAm 6*
Breuer, Henry Joseph 1860-1932 *IIBEAAW,*
WhAm 4
Breuer, Josef 1842-1925 *DcScB*
Breuer, Louis Henry 1879-1964 *WhAm 4*
Breuer, Marcel 1902- *BnEnAmA, McGEWB*
Breuer, William Hayes 1876-1948 *NatCAB 35*
Breugger, Christian 1822-1895 *NewYHSD*
Breuil, Elizabeth Donner VanDerVeer 1876-
WomWWA 14
Breuil, Henri Edouard Prosper 1877-1961 *DcScB,*
McGEWB
Breul, H *NewYHSD*
Breunig, Joseph *NewYHSD*
Breuninger, Fred Mark 1885-1962 *NatCAB 50*
Breuninger, Lewis Talmage 1893-1974 *WhAm 6*
Brevard, Ephraim 1750?-1783? *ApCAB, Drake,*
TwCBDA
Brevard, James *BiAUS*
Brevard, Joseph 1766-1821 *BiDrAC, WhAm H*
Brevitt, Jessie *WomWWA 14*
Brevoort, Henry 1791-1874 *ApCAB*
Brevoort, James Carson 1818-1887 *ApCAB,*
NatCAB 9, TwCBDA, WhAm H
Brevoort, James Fenwick 1832-1918 *TwCBDA*
Brevoort, James Renwick 1832-1918 *AmBi,*
ApCAB, DcAmB, NewYHSD, WhAm 1
Brewbaker, Cassie Leta 1904-1970 *WhAm 6*
Brewbaker, Charles Warren 1869- *WhAm 5*
Brewer, Abraham T 1841-1933 *WhAm 1*
Brewer, Amy Waller 1884- *WomWWA 14*
Brewer, Annette Fitch *WomWWA 14*
Brewer, Arthur Allen, Jr. 1912-1969 *WhAm 6*
Brewer, Arthur Kendall 1862-1947 *NatCAB 38*
Brewer, Basil 1884-1975 *WhAm 6*
Brewer, Charles 1804-1885 *DcAmB, WhAm H*
Brewer, Charles Edward 1866-1941 *NatCAB 30,*
WhAm 1
Brewer, Charles Snow 1870-1934 *NatCAB 25,*
WhAm 1
Brewer, Clara Tagg d1934 *WhAm 1*
Brewer, D Chauncey 1861-1932 *WhAm 1*
Brewer, David Josiah 1837-1910 *AmBi,*
ApCAB, DcAmB, NatCAB 1, TwCBDA,
WebAB, WhAm 1

Brewer, Earl LeRoy 1869-1942 *NatCAB 15,*
NatCAB 44, WhAm 2
Brewer, Edward Vere 1887-1967 *WhAm 6*
Brewer, Elizabeth Hale 1847- *WomWWA 14*
Brewer, Estelle Hempstead Manning 1882-
WomWWA 14
Brewer, F Thrall 1906-1973 *WhAm 6*
Brewer, Francis Beattie 1820-1892 *BiDrAC,*
WhAm H
Brewer, Frank Grover 1892-1957 *NatCAB 47*
Brewer, Franklin Nourse 1864-1935 *WhAm 1*
Brewer, Gardner 1806-1874 *ApCAB*
Brewer, George Emerson 1861-1939 *ApCAB X,*
NatCAB 32, WhAm 1
Brewer, George St. P 1814-1852 *NewYHSD,*
WhAm H
Brewer, Grace D 1881- *WomWWA 14*
Brewer, Hugh Graham 1888-1967 *WhAm 4*
Brewer, James Arthur 1886-1957 *WhAm 3*
Brewer, James Franklin 1899-1963 *NatCAB 51*
Brewer, James Rawlings 1840- *TwCBDA*
Brewer, John Bruce 1846- *WhAm 4*
Brewer, John Hart 1844-1900 *BiDrAC*
Brewer, John Hyatt 1856-1931 *NatCAB 15,*
TwCBDA, WhAm 1
Brewer, John Marks 1877-1950 *WhAm 3*
Brewer, John S 1824?- *NewYHSD*
Brewer, Jonathan 1726-1784 *Drake*
Brewer, Josiah 1796-1872 *ApCAB, NatCAB 2,*
TwCBDA
Brewer, Laurana Richards 1808-1843
NewYHSD
Brewer, Leigh Richmond 1839-1916 *ApCAB,*
NatCAB 11, TwCBDA, WhAm 1
Brewer, Leighton 1896-1969 *NatCAB 55*
Brewer, Leo 1889-1965 *WhAm 4*
Brewer, Luther Albertus 1858-1933 *WhAm 1*
Brewer, Mark Spencer 1837-1901 *BiDrAC,*
DcAmB, NatCAB 8, TwCBDA,
WhAm 1, WhAmP
Brewer, Mary Grey Morgan 1875-
WomWWA 14
Brewer, Nicholas Richard 1857-1949 *IIBEAAW,*
NatCAB 12, NatCAB 44, WhAm 2
Brewer, Oby T 1893-1971 *WhAm 5*
Brewer, Robert DuBois 1881-1949 *WhAm 2*
Brewer, Robert Paine 1876-1933 *WhAm 1*
Brewer, Samuel d1781? *Drake*
Brewer, Susan *TwCBDA*
Brewer, Thomas Mayo 1814-1880 *ApCAB,*
DcAmB, NatCAB 22, TwCBDA,
WhAm H
Brewer, William A, Jr. 1835- *WhAm 4*
Brewer, William Henry 1828-1910 *ApCAB,*
DcAmB, EncAAH, NatCAB 13,
WhAm 1
Brewer, Willis 1844-1912 *BiDrAC, WhAm 5*
Brewerton, George Douglas 1820?-1901 *ApCAB,*
NewYHSD, TwCBDA
Brewerton, George Douglas 1827?-1901
IIBEAAW
Brewerton, Henry 1801-1879 *ApCAB, Drake,*
NatCAB 5, TwCBDA
Brewster *NewYHSD*
Brewster, Albert Vincent 1881-1956 *WhAm 3*
Brewster, Andre Walker 1862-1942 *WhAm 2*
Brewster, Anna Richards 1870- *WomWWA 14*
Brewster, Austin Kiney 1845-1927 *NatCAB 22*
Brewster, Benjamin 1828-1897 *NatCAB 22*
Brewster, Benjamin 1860-1941 *NatCAB 44,*
WhAm 1
Brewster, Benjamin Harris 1816-1888 *AmBi,*
ApCAB, BiDrUSE, DcAmB, TwCBDA,
WhAm H
Brewster, Benjamin Harris 1900-1961
NatCAB 50, WhAm 4
Brewster, Benjamin Harris, Jr. 1872-1941
WhAm 1
Brewster, Benjamin Harrison 1816-1888
NatCAB 4
Brewster, Charles Warren 1802-1868 *Drake,*
TwCBDA
Brewster, Charles Warren 1812-1868 *ApCAB*
Brewster, Chauncey Bunce 1848-1941
ApCAB Sup, NatCAB 7, TwCBDA,
WhAm 1
Brewster, Cora Belle 1859- *AmWom*
Brewster, Daniel Baugh 1923- *BiDrAC*

Brewster, Sir David 1781-1868 *AsBiEn, DcScB*
Brewster, David Lukens 1887-1945 *WhAm 2*
Brewster, David P 1801-1876 *BiAUS,*
BiAUS Sup, BiDrAC, WhAm H
Brewster, Edmund *NewYHSD*
Brewster, Edward Lester 1842-1911 *WhAm 1*
Brewster, Edwin Tenney 1866-1960 *WhAm 3*
Brewster, Elisha Franklin 1850-1918
NatCAB 36
Brewster, Elisha Hume 1871-1946 *WhAm 2*
Brewster, Emilie C 1877- *WomWWA 14*
Brewster, Ethel Hampson 1886-1947 *WhAm 2*
Brewster, Eugene Valentine 1871-1939
WhAm 1
Brewster, Few 1889-1957 *WhAm 3*
Brewster, Flora A 1852- *AmWom*
Brewster, Frances Stanton 1860- *WhAm 4,*
WomWWA 14
Brewster, Frederick Carroll 1825-1898
ApCAB Sup, DcAmB, NatCAB 3,
WhAm H
Brewster, Frederick Foster 1872-1958
NatCAB 57
Brewster, G D *NewYHSD*
Brewster, George M 1866-1930 *ApCAB X*
Brewster, George Thomas 1862-1943 *WhAm 2*
Brewster, George Washington Wales 1866-1939
WhAm 1
Brewster, Harold Pond 1859-1925 *NatCAB 20*
Brewster, Henry 1824-1887 *NatCAB 13*
Brewster, Henry Colvin 1845-1928 *BiDrAC,*
NatCAB 4, TwCBDA, WhAm 1
Brewster, Henry Milton 1841-1915 *NatCAB 16*
Brewster, Henry Pomeroy 1831- *NatCAB 13*
Brewster, James 1788-1866 *ApCAB, DcAmB,*
NatCAB 13, TwCBDA, WhAm H
Brewster, James Henry 1845- *NatCAB 16*
Brewster, James Henry 1856-1920 *WhAm 1*
Brewster, James Henry, Jr. 1882-1959 *WhAm 3*
Brewster, John, Jr. 1766-1846 *BnEnAmA,*
NewYHSD
Brewster, John McLaughlin 1899-1972
NatCAB 56
Brewster, Kingman, Jr. 1919- *EncAB*
Brewster, Lyman Dennison 1832-1904
NatCAB 6
Brewster, Margaret Powell 1872-
WomWWA 14
Brewster, Mary Jones 1862- *WomWWA 14*
Brewster, Mary Southgate 1877-
WomWWA 14
Brewster, O Byron 1886-1953 *NatCAB 43*
Brewster, Osmyn 1797-1889 *DcAmB,*
TwCBDA, WhAm H
Brewster, R R 1876-1946 *WhAm 2*
Brewster, Ralph Owen 1888-1961 *BiDrAC,*
WhAm 4
Brewster, Raymond 1906-1972 *WhAm 5*
Brewster, Sardius Mason 1870-1936 *WhAm 1*
Brewster, Walter Stanton 1872- *WhAm 3*
Brewster, William 1560?-1644 *ApCAB,*
DcAmReB, NatCAB 7, TwCBDA
Brewster, William 1566?-1644 *Drake,*
McGEWB
Brewster, William 1567-1644 *AmBi, DcAmB,*
WebAB, WhAm H, WhAmP
Brewster, William 1851-1919 *AmBi, ApCAB,*
DcAmB, NatCAB 12, NatCAB 22,
TwCBDA, WhAm 1
Brewster, William 1866-1949 *NatCAB 13,*
NatCAB 38
Brewster, William 1915-1966 *NatCAB 52*
Brewster, William Nesbitt 1862-1916 *WhAm 1*
Brewster, William R d1869 *ApCAB*
Brewster, William Roe 1896-1965 *WhAm 4*
Brewster, William Russell 1893-1973
NatCAB 57
Brewster, William Tenney 1869-1961 *WhAm 4*
Breyer, Frank Gottlob 1886-1966 *NatCAB 53*
Breyer, Henry W, Jr. 1904-1972 *WhAm 5*
Breyfogel, Sylvanus Charles 1851-1934
WhAm 1
Breyfogle, Caroline May *WomWWA 14*
Breyfogle, Edwin Willis 1885-1961 *NatCAB 49*
Breyman, William *NewYHSD*
Breymann, Eugene Stark 1861-1934
NatCAB 25
Brezhnev, Leonid Ilich 1906- *McGEWB*

Brezing, Herman 1877-1945 *WhAm 2*
Brialmont, Henri Alexis 1821-1903 *WhoMilH*
Brian, Donald 1875-1948 *NatCAB 36,*
WhAm 2
Brian, Julius *NewYHSD*
Brianchon, Charles-Julien 1783-1864 *DcScB*
Briand, Aristide 1862-1932 *McGEWB*
Brice, Albert G 1831- *NatCAB 11*
Brice, Benjamin W 1809-1892 *ApCAB,*
TwCBDA
Brice, Calvin Stewart 1845-1898 *ApCAB Sup,*
BiDrAC, DcAmB, NatCAB 2,
NatCAB 27, TwCBDA, WhAm H
Brice, Carrie Elizabeth 1890- *WhoColR*
Brice, Charles Rufus 1870-1963 *WhAm 4*
Brice, Fannie 1891-1951 *WebAB*
Brice, Fanny 1891-1951 *DcAmB S5, WhAm 3*
Brice, George Frederick 1881-1952 *NatCAB 41*
Brice, John A 1876-1946 *NatCAB 34,*
WhAm 2
Brice, John Jones 1842- *NatCAB 5*
Brice, R B *WhoColR*
Brice, Robert Lewis 1921-1968 *NatCAB 54*
Briceno, Alonso *ApCAB*
Briceno, Antonio Nicolas d1813 *ApCAB*
Bricher, Alfred Thompson 1837-1908 *ApCAB,*
BnEnAmA, NewYHSD, WhAm 3
Bricher, Alfred Thompson 1839-1908
NatCAB 13, TwCBDA
Bricher, Henry 1817?- *NewYHSD*
Brick, Abraham Lincoln 1860-1908 *BiDrAC,*
TwCBDA, WhAm 1, WhAmP
Brick, Alyea M 1895-1959 *WhAm 4*
Brick, Harry 1909-1967 *NatCAB 53*
Brick, Nicholas William 1861-1934 *WhAm 1*
Brickell, Henry Herschel 1889-1952 *DcAmB S5,*
WhAm 3
Brickell, John *NatCAB 7*
Brickell, Robert Coman 1824-1900 *DcAmB,*
NatCAB 7, WhAm 1
Brickell, William David 1852- *NatCAB 1,*
TwCBDA, WhAm 4
Bricken, Carl Ernest 1898-1971 *NatCAB 57,*
WhAm 5
Bricker, Edwin Dyson 1875-1967 *WhAm 4*
Bricker, Garland Armor 1881-1962 *NatCAB 49,*
WhAm 6
Bricker, John William 1893- *BiDrAC*
Bricker, Luther Otterbein 1874-1942 *WhAm 2*
Bricker, Mead L 1885-1964 *WhAm 4*
Bricker, Owen Peterson 1862-1965 *NatCAB 51*
Brickett, Edward Montgomery 1898-1961
NatCAB 49
Brickett, James 1737-1818 *ApCAB, Drake*
Brickett, John Charles 1860-1920 *ApCAB X*
Brickey, W J *NewYHSD*
Brickley, Bartholomew A 1883-1959 *WhAm 3*
Brickman, William Wolfgang 1913- *BiDAmEd*
Brickner, Barnett Robert 1892-1958
NatCAB 44, WhAm 3
Brickner, George H 1834-1904 *BiDrAC*
Brickner, Richard Max 1896-1959 *NatCAB 48*
Brickner, Walter M 1875-1930 *NatCAB 25,*
WhAm 1, WhAm 1C
Bride, William Witthaft 1881-1935 *WhAm 1*
Bridge, Ann 1889-1974 *WhAm 6*
Bridge, Arthur Franklin 1891-1958 *NatCAB 47*
Bridge, Gerard 1873- *WhAm 5*
Bridge, Horatio 1806-1893 *ApCAB, Drake,*
NatCAB 4, TwCBDA
Bridge, James Howard 1856-1939 *WhAm 1*
Bridge, Norman 1844-1925 *NatCAB 22,*
WhAm 1
Bridge, Samuel James 1809-1893 *TwCBDA*
Bridge, Ulysses Solomon Anglemyer 1867-1951
NatCAB 39
Bridgeforth, George Ruffin 1873- *WhoColR*
Bridgeman, Frederick Arthur 1847- *ApCAB X*
Bridgeman, Frederick Arthur *see also* Bridgman,
Frederick Arthur
Bridgens, Charles *NewYHSD*
Bridgens, Henry *NewYHSD*
Bridgens, Robert *NewYHSD*
Bridgens, William Henry *NewYHSD*
Bridger, James 1804-1881 *AmBi, DcAmB,*
EncAAH, McGEWB, NatCAB 13,
REnAW, WebAB, WhAm H
Bridger, James Albert 1900-1969 *NatCAB 57*

Bridger, Virginia Lawrence 1872-
WomWWA 14
Bridgers, Harvey Clifton 1885-1965 *NatCAB 51*
Bridgers, Robert Rufus 1819-1888 *BiDConf,*
DcAmB, NatCAB 7, WhAm H
Bridges, Calvin Blackman 1889-1938
DcAMB S2, DcScB, NatCAB 30,
WhAm 1
Bridges, Charles *BnEnAmA, NewYHSD*
Bridges, Charles Higbee 1873-1948 *NatCAB 44,*
WhAm 2
Bridges, Charles Scott 1903-1961 *NatCAB 49,*
WhAm 4
Bridges, E W *NewYHSD*
Bridges, Earl *NewYHSD*
Bridges, Edson Lowell 1874-1934 *WhAm 1*
Bridges, Eliza Wadsworth *WomWWA 14*
Bridges, Fidelia 1834-1923 *NotAW,*
WomWWA 14
Bridges, Fidelia 1835-1923 *ApCAB,*
NewYHSD, TwCBDA, WhAm 1
Bridges, George Washington 1821-1873 *ApCAB,*
TwCBDA
Bridges, George Washington 1825-1873 *BiAUS,*
BiDrAC, WhAm H
Bridges, H Francis G 1902-1947 *WhAm 2*
Bridges, Harry Renton 1901- *EncAB, REnAW,*
WebAB
Bridges, Henry Styles 1898-1961 *BiDrAC,*
WhAmP
Bridges, Horace James 1880-1955 *ApCAB X,*
WhAm 3
Bridges, James Robertson 1852-1930 *WhAm 1*
Bridges, Jesse B 1862-1927 *WhAm 1*
Bridges, Milton Arlanden 1894-1939 *WhAm 1*
Bridges, Robert d1656 *ApCAB, DcAmB,*
NatCAB 24, WhAm H
Bridges, Robert 1806-1882 *DcAmB,*
NatCAB 5, TwCBDA, WhAm H
Bridges, Robert 1858-1941 *WhAm 1*
Bridges, Ronald 1905-1959 *WhAm 4*
Bridges, S Russell d1960 *WhAm 4*
Bridges, Samuel Augustus 1802-1884 *BiAUS,*
BiDrAC, WhAm H, WhAmP
Bridges, Styles 1898-1961 *WhAm 4*
Bridges, Thomas Henry 1892- *WhAm 4*
Bridges, Thomas Reed 1896-1943 *WhAm 2*
Bridges, Wellington E *NewYHSD*
Bridges, Willson Orton 1856- *WhAm 4*
Bridgman, Donald Winchester 1886-1953
NatCAB 42
Bridgman, Elijah Coleman 1801-1861 *AmBi,*
DcAmB, WhAm H
Bridgman, Eliza Jane Gillet 1805-1871 *NotAW*
Bridgman, Ethel Young Comstock
WomWWA 14
Bridgman, Frederic Arthur 1847- *TwCBDA*
Bridgman, Frederic Arthur 1847-1927 *AmBi,*
DcAmB
Bridgman, Frederic Arthur 1847-1928 *WhAm 1*
Bridgman, Frederick Arthur 1847- *ApCAB,*
NatCAB 2
Bridgman, Frederick Arthur *see also* Bridgeman,
Frederick Arthur
Bridgman, George Henry 1841-1931
NatCAB 23, TwCBDA, WhAm 4
Bridgman, George Herbert 1853- *NatCAB 13,*
TwCBDA, WhAm 4
Bridgman, Grenville Temple 1881-1952
NatCAB 40, WhAm 3
Bridgman, Helen Bartlett *WhAm 5*
Bridgman, Herbert Lawrence 1844-1924 *AmBi,*
DcAmB, NatCAB 22, WhAm 1
Bridgman, Howard Allen 1860-1929 *WhAm 1*
Bridgman, Laura Dewey 1829-1889 *AmBi,*
AmWom, ApCAB, DcAmB, Drake,
NatCAB 2, NotAW, TwCBDA, WebAB,
WhAm H
Bridgman, Lewis Jesse 1857-1931 *WhAm 1*
Bridgman, Mary Elliott 1854- *WomWWA 14*
Bridgman, Olga Louise 1886-1974 *WhAm 6*
Bridgman, Percy Williams 1882-1961 *AsBiEn,*
DcScB, McGEWB, NatCAB 48, WebAB,
WhAm 4
Bridgman, Raymond Landon 1848-1925
WhAm 1
Bridgman, Statira Preble McDonald
WomWWA 14

Bridgwater, William 1908-1966 *WhAm 4*
Bridport, George *NewYHSD*
Bridport, Hugh 1794-1868? *NewYHSD,*
  WhAm H
Briefs, Goetz A 1889-1974 *WhAm 6*
Brien, Joseph 1841?- *NewYHSD*
Brien, William Given 1831- *WhAm 4*
Brier, Ernest 1879-1950 *WhAm 3*
Brier, Frank Lewis 1878-1957 *NatCAB 49*
Brier, Royce 1894-1975 *WhAm 6*
Brier, Warren Judson 1850-1929 *WhAm 1*
Brierley, John Rattcliffe 1886-1961 *NatCAB 49*
Brierley, Josiah Richards 1885-1967
  NatCAB 53
Brierley, Wilfrid Gordon 1885-1970 *WhAm 5*
Brierly, James Leslie 1881- *WhAm 6*
Brierton, John 1572-1619? *DcAmB, WhAm H*
Briesen, Arthur Von 1843-1920 *WhAm 1*
Brietzke, June Oneson 1917-1974 *WhAm 6*
Brigance, William Norwood 1896-1960
  BiDAmEd, NatCAB 47, WhAm 3
Briggs, Amos 1795-1874 *ApCAB*
Briggs, Ansel 1806-1881 *BiAUS, NatCAB 11*
Briggs, Arthur Hyslop 1858-1934 *WhAm 1*
Briggs, Asa Gilbert 1862-1945 *WhAm 2*
Briggs, Austin Eugene 1908-1973 *WhAm 6*
Briggs, Caleb 1812-1884 *ApCAB*
Briggs, Charles 1837-1923 *NatCAB 16,*
  WhAm 1
Briggs, Charles Augustus 1841-1913 *AmBi,*
  ApCAB, DcAmB, DcAmReB, NatCAB 7,
  TwCBDA, WhAm 1
Briggs, Charles Edward 1833-1894 *NatCAB 8*
Briggs, Charles Frederick 1804-1877 *AmBi,*
  ApCAB, DcAmB, Drake, NatCAB 9,
  TwCBDA, WhAm H
Briggs, Charles S 1851- *WhAm 4*
Briggs, Clare A 1875-1930 *ApCAB X,*
  DcAmB S1, NatCAB 23, WhAm 1
Briggs, Clay Stone 1876-1933 *BiDrAC,*
  WhAm 1, WhAmP
Briggs, Corona Hibbard 1849- *WhAm 4*
Briggs, Cyril V 1888- *WhoColR*
Briggs, Daisy-Marquis *WomWWA 14*
Briggs, Edward Cornelius 1856-1926 *WhAm 1*
Briggs, Elizabeth Darling 1888-1953 *WhAm 3*
Briggs, Ellis O 1899-1976 *WhAm 6*
Briggs, Emily Pomona Edson 1830-1910 *NotAW*
Briggs, Florence Lucy Chase 1862-
  WomWWA 14
Briggs, Frank Alonzo 1872-1958 *WhAm 3*
Briggs, Frank Arlington 1858-1898 *NatCAB 13*
Briggs, Frank Herschel 1865-1919 *NatCAB 18*
Briggs, Frank Obadiah 1851-1913 *ApCAB X,*
  BiDrAC, NatCAB 14, NatCAB 29,
  WhAm 1, WhAmP
Briggs, Frank Parks 1894- *BiDrAC*
Briggs, Frank Richmond 1874- *WhAm 5*
Briggs, Frederic Melancthon 1857- *WhAm 3*
Briggs, George 1805-1869 *BiAUS, BiDrAC,*
  WhAm H
Briggs, George Ernest 1873- *WhAm 5*
Briggs, George Isaac 1886-1944 *WhAm 2*
Briggs, George Nathaniel 1874-1952 *WhAm 3*
Briggs, George Nixon 1796-1851 *Drake*
Briggs, George Nixon 1796-1861 *ApCAB,*
  BiAUS, BiDrAC, DcAmB, NatCAB 1,
  TwCBDA, WhAm H, WhAmP
Briggs, George Waverley 1883-1957 *WhAm 3*
Briggs, George Weston 1874-1966 *WhAm 4*
Briggs, Gordon Dobson 1912-1954 *WhAm 3*
Briggs, Harold Edward 1896- *EncAAH,*
  REnAW
Briggs, Harry Tallmadge 1874-1957
  NatCAB 42
Briggs, Henry 1561-1630 *AsBiEn, DcScB*
Briggs, Henry Birdice Richmond 1881-1936
  WhAm 1
Briggs, Henry Harrison 1871-1931 *WhAm 1*
Briggs, Henry Shaw 1824- *ApCAB*
Briggs, J Emmons 1869-1942 *WhAm 1*
Briggs, James Frankland 1827-1905 *BiDrAC*
Briggs, John DeQuedville 1885-1965
  NatCAB 57, WhAm 4
Briggs, John Ely 1890-1952 *WhAm 3*
Briggs, Joseph William 1813-1872 *ApCAB,*
  TwCBDA
Briggs, L A *NewYHSD*

Briggs, Lavina B 1847- *WomWWA 14*
Briggs, LeBaron Russell 1855-1934 *AmBi,*
  DcAmB S1, NatCAB 7, TwCBDA,
  WhAm 1
Briggs, LeRoy Hewitt 1883-1953 *NatCAB 43*
Briggs, Lida May *WomWWA 14*
Briggs, Lloyd Vernon 1863-1941 *DcAmB S3,*
  NatCAB 42, WhAm 1
Briggs, Lucia Russell 1887-1960 *WhAm 3*
Briggs, Lyman James 1874-1963 *NatCAB 53,*
  WhAm 4
Briggs, Mary Blatchley 1846- *AmWom*
Briggs, R W *NewYHSD*
Briggs, Raymond Westcott 1878- *WhAm 6*
Briggs, Robert Aldrich 1912-1962 *WhAm 4*
Briggs, Roswell Emmons 1846- *WhAm 4*
Briggs, Stephen Albro 1911-1965 *WhAm 4*
Briggs, Thomas Arnold 1857-1928 *NatCAB 24*
Briggs, Thomas Henry 1847-1928 *NatCAB 23*
Briggs, Thomas Henry 1877-1971 *BiDAmEd,*
  WhAm 5
Briggs, Thomas Roland 1887-1952 *WhAm 3*
Briggs, Waldo 1854- *NatCAB 12*
Briggs, Walter 1859-1950 *NatCAB 38*
Briggs, Walter Owen 1877-1952 *NatCAB 51,*
  WhAm 3
Briggs, Walter Owen, Jr. 1912-1970 *WhAm 5*
Briggs, Ward Daniel 1892-1956 *NatCAB 45*
Briggs, Warren Richard 1850-1933 *WhAm 2*
Briggs, William Ellery 1853-1931 *NatCAB 55*
Briggs, William Harlowe 1876-1952 *WhAm 3*
Briggs, William Thompson 1829-1894
  NatCAB 12
Briggs, William Thompson 1881-1948
  NatCAB 37
Briggs, Willis Grandy 1875-1954 *NatCAB 44*
Brigham, Albert Perry 1855-1932 *AmBi,*
  BiDAmEd, DcAmB S1, NatCAB 17,
  NatCAB 24, WhAm 1
Brigham, Amariah 1798-1849 *ApCAB, DcAmB,*
  Drake, NatCAB 10, TwCBDA, WhAm H
Brigham, Arthur Amber 1856- *WhAm 4*
Brigham, C Frank 1867-1930 *NatCAB 35*
Brigham, Caleb Lewis 1858-1927 *NatCAB 21*
Brigham, Carl Campbell 1890-1943 *WhAm 2*
Brigham, Charles David 1819-1894 *NatCAB 9*
Brigham, Charles Henry 1820-1879 *ApCAB*
Brigham, Clarence Saunders 1877-1963
  DcAmLiB, WhAm 4
Brigham, Claude Ernest 1878- *WhAm 6*
Brigham, Clifford 1857-1910 *NatCAB 26*
Brigham, Elbert Sidney 1877-1962 *BiDrAC,*
  WhAm 4
Brigham, Elijah 1751-1816 *BiAUS, BiDrAC,*
  WhAm H
Brigham, F *NewYHSD*
Brigham, Gertrude Richardson d1971 *WhAm 5*
Brigham, Harold Frederick 1897-1971 *WhAm 5*
Brigham, Henry Randolph 1880-1964
  NatCAB 51, WhAm 4
Brigham, James Watkins 1892-1965
  NatCAB 53
Brigham, Johnson 1846-1936 *ApCAB X,*
  NatCAB 14, WhAm 1
Brigham, Joseph Henry 1838-1904 *DcAmB,*
  WhAm 1
Brigham, L Ward 1865- *WhAm 4*
Brigham, Lewis Alanson 1889-1963 *NatCAB 49*
Brigham, Lewis Alexander 1831-1885 *BiDrAC,*
  WhAm H
Brigham, Mary Ann 1824-1889 *NatCAB 4*
Brigham, Mary Ann 1829-1889 *DcAmB,*
  WhAm H
Brigham, Nat Maynard 1856-1915 *WhAm 1*
Brigham, Paul d1824 *Drake*
Brigham, Paul 1745-1824 *ApCAB*
Brigham, Paul 1746-1824 *NatCAB 8*
Brigham, Richard Douglas 1892-1957 *WhAm 3*
Brigham, Sarah Jeannette 1835-1929 *WhAm 1*
Brigham, William Erastus 1865- *WhAm 1*
Brigham, William H *NewYHSD*
Brigham, William Tufts 1841-1926 *NatCAB 16,*
  WhAm 1
Bright, Alfred Harris 1850- *WhAm 1*
Bright, Cora C 1860- *WomWWA 14*
Bright, David Edward 1907-1965 *WhAm 4*
Bright, Edward 1808-1894 *DcAmB, TwCBDA,*
  WhAm H

Bright, Emily Haskell *WomWWA 14*
Bright, Florence Zetilla 1868- *WomWWA 14*
Bright, Graham 1876-1961 *NatCAB 49*
Bright, Harry Aaron 1890-1961 *NatCAB 49*
Bright, J Russell 1908-1973 *NatCAB 57*
Bright, J S 1878- *WhAm 6*
Bright, James Wilson 1852-1926 *DcAmB,*
  NatCAB 20, WhAm 1
Bright, Jesse David 1812-1875 *ApCAB, BiAUS,*
  BiDrAC, DcAmB, Drake, NatCAB 3,
  TwCBDA, WhAm H, WhAmP
Bright, John 1811-1889 *McGEWB*
Bright, John 1848-1948 *WhAm 2*
Bright, John Douglas 1917-1972 *NatCAB 57*
Bright, John Morgan 1817-1911 *BiAUS,*
  BiDrAC, WhAmP
Bright, Jonathan Brown 1800-1879 *ApCAB,*
  Drake, TwCBDA
Bright, Lida Thomas *WhoColR*
Bright, Louis Victor 1863-1933 *WhAm 1*
Bright, Marion M 1873- *WomWWA 14*
Bright, Marshal Huntington 1834-1907 *ApCAB,*
  NatCAB 3, TwCBDA, WhAm 1
Bright, O Percy 1863-1938 *NatCAB 28*
Bright, Philip Vaughan 1879-1949 *NatCAB 40*
Bright, Richard 1789-1858 *BiHiMed, DcScB,*
  McGEWB
Bright, Robert Southall 1872-1943 *NatCAB 36*
Bright, Ruth Bean 1865- *WhoColR*
Bright Eyes 1854-1903 *AmBi, DcAmB,*
  NotAW, WhAm H
Brightly, Francis Frederick 1845- *ApCAB Sup*
Brightly, Frank Frederick 1845- *WhAm 4*
Brightly, Frederick Charles 1812-1888
  ApCAB Sup, DcAmB, NatCAB 5,
  WhAm H
Brightly, Henry 1822?- *NewYHSD*
Brightly, Henry A 1791?- *NewYHSD*
Brightly, Joseph H 1818?- *NewYHSD*
Brightman, Alvin Collins 1878-1932 *WhAm 1*
Brightman, Edgar Sheffield 1884-1953
  DcAmB S5, DcAmReB, NatCAB 41,
  WhAm 3
Brightman, Horace Irving 1872-1940 *WhAm 1,*
  WhAm 2
Brigman, Bennett Mattingly 1881-1938
  WhAm 1
Brignoli, Pasquale 1824-1884 *ApCAB,*
  TwCBDA
Brignoli, Pasqualino 1832- *Drake*
Briles, Charles Walter 1873- *WhAm 5*
Brill, Abraham Arden 1874-1948 *DcAmB S4,*
  WhAm 2
Brill, Alexander Wilhelm Von 1842-1935 *DcScB*
Brill, Alfred Polland 1882-1951 *NatCAB 41*
Brill, George MacKenzie 1866-1959
  NatCAB 47, WhAm 5
Brill, George Reiter 1867-1918 *WhAm 1*
Brill, Harvey Clayton 1881-1972 *NatCAB 57,*
  WhAm 5
Brill, Hascal Russel 1846-1922 *WhAm 3*
Brill, John Lewis 1902-1971 *NatCAB 57*
Brill, Joseph Eugene 1903-1975 *WhAm 6*
Brill, Nathan Edwin 1859-1925 *AmBi, DcAmB*
Brill, Nathan Edwin 1860-1925 *NatCAB 20,*
  WhAm 1
Brill, William Hascal 1871-1923 *WhAm 1*
Brillat-Savarin, Anthelme 1755-1826 *ApCAB*
Brillhart, David H d1956 *WhAm 3*
Brillouin, Marcel Louis 1854-1948 *DcScB*
Brim, Kenneth Milliken 1898-1974 *WhAm 6*
Brimberg, Samuel Nathan 1885-1963
  NatCAB 48
Brimhall, George Henry 1852-1932 *WhAm 1*
Brimson, William George 1845-1930 *WhAm 1*
Brincke, William Draper 1798-1862 *WhAm H*
Brinckerhoff, Arthur Freeman 1880-1959
  ApCAB X, WhAm 4
Brinckerhoff, Elbert Adrain 1838-1913
  NatCAB 15
Brinckerhoff, Henrietta Collins 1844-
  WomWWA 14
Brinckerhoff, Henry Morton 1868-1949
  NatCAB 50, WhAm 2
Brinckle, William Draper 1798-1862 *DcAmB*
Brind, Charles Albert, Jr. 1897-1970
  NatCAB 57, WhAm 5
Brind, Sir Patrick 1892-1963 *WhAm 4*

Brindis, Claudio J 1852- *ApCAB*
Brindle, Harry Robert 1908-1971 *NatCAB 56*
Brindley, John Edwin 1878- *WhAm 6*
Brindley, Paul 1896-1954 *WhAm 3*
Brine, Mary Dow *WomWWA 14*
Brinell, Johan August 1849-1925 *DcScB*
Brines, Osborne Allen 1894-1960 *NatCAB 49*
Briney, Paul Wallace 1906-1973 *WhAm 6*
Briney, Russell 1900-1966 *WhAm 4*
Bring, Erland Samuel 1736-1798 *DcScB*
Bringham, David 1794-1888 *ApCAB Sup*
Bringhard, Mike *NewYHSD*
Bringhurst, Robert Porter 1855-1925 *WhAm 1*
Brininstool, Earl Alonzo 1870-1957 *WhAm 3*
Brink, Charles Bernard 1910-1974 *WhAm 6*
Brink, Francis G 1893-1952 *WhAm 3*
Brink, Frederick 1883-1968 *NatCAB 54*
Brink, Gilbert Nicholas 1872-1936 *WhAm 1*
Brink, Louise *WomWWA 14*
Brinken, Carl Ernest 1898-1971 *WhAm 5*
Brinker, Howard Rasmus 1893-1965 *WhAm 4*
Brinker, Jean Beatrice Weber 1869-
 WomWWA 14
Brinker, Josiah Henry 1851-1920 *WhAm 1*
Brinkerhoff, Clara M 1828- *AmWom*
Brinkerhoff, Henry Roelif 1787-1844 *BiDrAC,*
 WhAm H
Brinkerhoff, Henry Roelif 1788-1844 *BiAUS*
Brinkerhoff, Jacob 1810-1880 *ApCAB, BiAUS,*
 BiDrAC, DcAmB, NatCAB 13,
 WhAm H, WhAmP
Brinkerhoff, Robert Moore 1880-1958 *WhAm 3*
Brinkerhoff, Roeliff 1828-1911 *DcAmB,*
 NatCAB 2, TwCBDA, WhAm 1
Brinkerhoff, William 1843- *NatCAB 2*
Brinkley, Jack Thomas 1930- *BiDrAC*
Brinkley, John 1763-1835 *DcScB*
Brinkley, John Richard 1885-1942 *DcAmB S3*
Brinkley, Nell 1886-1944 *NatCAB 33*
Brinkman, Mary A 1845- *AmWom, TwCBDA*
Brinkman, Oscar H 1893-1969 *WhAm 5*
Brinkman, William Augustus 1868-1936
 WhAm 1
Brinkmann, Reginald Roy 1898-1954
 NatCAB 41
Brinley, Charles A 1847- *ApCAB, WhAm 4*
Brinley, Charles Edward 1878-1963 *NatCAB 50,*
 WhAm 6
Brinley, Daniel Putnam 1879-1963 *IIBEAAW,*
 WhAm 4
Brinley, Edward 1860-1917 *ApCAB X*
Brinley, Francis 1800- *ApCAB, Drake*
Brinley, George 1817-1875 *ApCAB, TwCBDA*
Brinley, Godfrey Malbone 1864-1939
 NatCAB 40
Brinley, Henry DeNyse 1880-1957 *NatCAB 44*
Brinley, Kathrine Gordon Sanger 1879-1966
 WhAm 4
Brinser, Harry Lerch 1876-1945 *WhAm 2*
Brinsmade, Ada Gibson Colton 1864-
 WomWWA 14
Brinsmade, Chapin 1885-1928 *NatCAB 22*
Brinsmade, James Beebee 1884-1936
 NatCAB 22
Brinsmade, John Chapin 1852-1930 *NatCAB 22,*
 WhAm 1
Brinsmade, Mary Gold Gunn *WomWWA 14*
Brinsmade, Robert Bruce 1873-1936 *WhAm 1*
Brinsmade, Thomas Clark 1802-1868
 ApCAB Sup, NatCAB 20
Brinsmade, William Barrett 1865- *WhAm 4*
Brinson, Robert Laurie 1891-1962 *NatCAB 49*
Brinson, Samuel Mitchell 1870-1922 *BiDrAC,*
 WhAm 1
Brinson, William David 1880-1950 *NatCAB 38*
Brinstad, Charles William 1864-1942 *WhAm 2*
Brinton, Bradford 1880-1936 *NatCAB 28*
Brinton, Christian 1870-1942 *NatCAB 41,*
 WhAm 2
Brinton, Clarence C 1877-1962 *NatCAB 49*
Brinton, Daniel Garrison 1837- *ApCAB*
Brinton, Daniel Garrison 1837-1899 *DcAmB,*
 NatCAB 9, TwCBDA, WebAB, WhAm 1
Brinton, Daniel Garrison 1837-1909 *AmBi*
Brinton, Emma Southwick 1834- *AmWom*
Brinton, Howard T 1897-1966 *WhAm 4*
Brinton, Jasper Yeates 1878-1973 *WhAm 6*
Brinton, John Hill 1832-1907 *DcAmB,*

NatCAB 37, *WhAm 1*
Brinton, Joseph Painter 1835-1915 *NatCAB 17*
Brinton, Paul Henry Mallet-Prevost 1882-1966
 WhAm 4
Brinton, Walter 1863-1951 *NatCAB 40*
Brinton, Willard Cope 1880-1957 *WhAm 3*
Brinton, William Bryant 1850-1937 *NatCAB 28*
Brion, Luis 1782-1821 *ApCAB*
Brion, Peter Louis 1782-1821 *Drake*
Brioschi, Francesco 1824-1897 *DcScB*
Briot, Charles Auguste 1817-1882 *DcScB*
Brisacher, Emil Eli 1896-1951 *NatCAB 39*
Brisbane, Abbott Hall d1861 *ApCAB, Drake,*
 TwCBDA
Brisbane, Albert 1809-1890 *AmBi, DcAmB,*
 McGEWB, NatCAB 4, WebAB,
 WhAm H
Brisbane, Arthur 1864-1936 *AmBi, ApCAB X,*
 DcAmB S2, NatCAB 14, NatCAB 27,
 WebAB, WhAm 1
Brisbane, Margaret Hunt 1858- *AmWom*
Brisbane, Thomas 1773-1860 *DcScB*
Brisbane, William H 1803-1878 *ApCAB*
Brisbin, Clarence Franklin 1871- *WhAm 5*
Brisbin, James A 1837-1892 *NatCAB 4*
Brisbin, James S 1837-1892 *TwCBDA,*
 WhAm H
Brisbin, James S 1838?- *ApCAB*
Brisbin, John 1818-1880 *BiDrAC, WhAm H*
Brisbine, Annie M'Iver 1866- *WhAm 4*
Brisco, Norris Arthur 1875-1944 *WhAm 2*
Briscoe, A H *NewYHSD*
Briscoe, Birdsall Parmenas 1876-1971 *WhAm 5*
Briscoe, Daniel 1825?-1883 *NewYHSD*
Briscoe, Franklin Dulin 1844- *NatCAB 10*
Briscoe, Herman T 1893-1960 *WhAm 4*
Briscoe, John Parran 1853-1925 *WhAm 1*
Briscoe, Margaret Sutton *WomWWA 14*
Briscoe, Robert Pearce 1897-1968 *WhAm 5*
Briscoe, Robert Thomas 1882-1970 *NatCAB 55*
Briskin, Samuel Jacob 1897-1968 *WhAm 5*
Brissenden, Paul Frederick 1885-1974 *WhAm 6*
Brisset, Eugene *NewYHSD*
Brisson, Barnabe 1777-1828 *DcScB*
Brisson, Mathurin-Jacques 1723-1806 *DcScB*
Brissot DeOuarville, Jean Pierre 1754-1793
 Drake
Brissot DeWarville, Jean Pierre 1754-1793
 ApCAB
Brist, George Louis 1878- *WhAm 6*
Bristed, Charles Astor 1820-1874 *AmBi,*
 ApCAB, DcAmB, Drake, NatCAB 6,
 TwCBDA, WhAm H
Bristed, John 1778-1855 *ApCAB, DcAmB,*
 Drake, NatCAB 7, TwCBDA, WhAm H
Brister, Charles James *WhAm 3*
Brister, John Willard 1867-1939 *WhAm 1*
Bristley, Frank Dick 1867- *ApCAB X*
Bristol, Arthur Edward 1887-1954 *NatCAB 41,*
 WhAm 3
Bristol, Arthur LeRoy 1886-1942 *WhAm 2*
Bristol, Augusta Cooper 1835-1910 *AmWom,*
 ApCAB, TwCBDA, WhAm 1
Bristol, Charles Lawrence 1859-1931
 NatCAB 25, TwCBDA, WhAm 1
Bristol, Edward Newell 1860-1946 *NatCAB 35,*
 WhAm 2
Bristol, Frank Milton 1851-1932 *NatCAB 25,*
 WhAm 1
Bristol, Franklin Benjamin 1861-1904
 NatCAB 26
Bristol, George Prentiss 1856-1927 *WhAm 1*
Bristol, Grace Whitman 1863- *WomWWA 14*
Bristol, Helen Augusta Flack *WomWWA 14*
Bristol, Helen Finlay Waltz 1843-
 WomWWA 14
Bristol, Henry P 1889-1959 *WhAm 3*
Bristol, Herbert Greene 1894-1951 *NatCAB 41*
Bristol, James Edward 1853-1928 *ApCAB X*
Bristol, John Bunyan 1824-1909 *Drake*
Bristol, John Bunyan 1826-1909 *AmBi,*
 ApCAB, DcAmB, NewYHSD, TwCBDA,
 WhAm 1
Bristol, John Isaac Devoe 1845-1932 *NatCAB 3,*
 WhAm 1
Bristol, Lawrence 1893-1946 *NatCAB 34*
Bristol, Lee Hastings 1892-1962 *WhAm 4*
Bristol, Leverett Dale 1880-1957 *NatCAB 45,*

WhAm 3
Bristol, Mark Lambert 1868-1939 *DcAmB S2,*
 NatCAB 34, WebAMB, WhAm 1
Bristol, Theodore Louis 1870- *WhAm 5*
Bristol, Warren *BiAUS, BiAUS Sup*
Bristol, William 1779-1836 *BiAUS*
Bristol, William Henry 1859-1930 *DcAmB S1,*
 NatCAB 26, WhAm 1
Bristol, William McLaren 1860-1935
 NatCAB 36
Bristow, Algernon Thomas 1851-1913 *WhAm 1*
Bristow, Allen Samuel Hardy 1870-1943
 NatCAB 32
Bristow, Benjamin Helm 1832-1896 *AmBi,*
 ApCAB, BiAUS, BiDrUSE, DcAmB,
 McGEWB, NatCAB 4, TwCBDA,
 WebAB, WhAm H, WhAmP
Bristow, Francis Marion 1804-1864 *BiAUS,*
 BiDrAC, WhAm H
Bristow, George Frederick 1825-1898 *AmBi,*
 ApCAB, DcAmB, NatCAB 23, WhAm H,
 WhAm 4
Bristow, George Washington 1894-1961
 NatCAB 50, WhAm 4
Bristow, Henry 1840-1906 *BiDrAC*
Bristow, Joseph Little 1861-1944 *BiDrAC,*
 DcAmB S3, NatCAB 14, WhAm 2,
 WhAmP
Bristow, Louis Judson 1876- *WhAm 5*
Bristow, Myon Edison 1879-1955 *NatCAB 46*
Britan, Halbert Hains 1874-1945 *WhAm 3*
Brite, Lucas Charles 1860-1941 *NatCAB 31*
Brito Freire, Francisco d1692 *ApCAB*
Brito Freyre, Francisco De 1620?-1692
 ApCAB Sup
Britt, Albert 1874-1969 *NatCAB 57*
Britt, James Jefferson 1861-1939 *BiDrAC,*
 WhAm 1
Britt, Peter 1819- *NewYHSD*
Britt, Walter Stratton 1877-1938 *WhAm 1*
Britt, William W 1820?- *NewYHSD*
Brittain, Carlo Bonaparte 1867-1920 *WhAm 1*
Brittain, Charles Mercer 1873-1943 *WhAm 2*
Brittain, Frank Smith 1862-1929 *WhAm 1*
Brittain, Gertrude Fuller *WomWWA 14*
Brittain, Joseph Isaiah 1857-1930 *NatCAB 22*
Brittain, Joseph Isaiah 1858-1930 *WhAm 1*
Brittain, Marion Luther 1865-1953 *BiDAmEd*
Brittain, Marion Luther 1866-1953 *WhAm 3*
Brittan, Belle *WhAm H*
Brittan, Nathan 1808-1872 *ApCAB,*
 NatCAB 5, TwCBDA
Britten, Benjamin 1913- *McGEWB*
Britten, Edwin Franklin, Jr. 1885-1966 *WhAm 4*
Britten, Flora Phelps Harley 1864- *WhAm 4,*
 WomWWA 14
Britten, Fred Albert 1871-1946 *WhAm 2*
Britten, Fred Ernest 1860- *WhAm 4*
Britten, Frederick Albert 1871-1946 *BiDrAC,*
 WhAmP
Britten, James 1846-1924 *DcScB*
Britten, Stephen Toghill 1862-1934 *NatCAB 25*
Brittin, Abraham 1841-1932 *NatCAB 26*
Brittin, Lewis Hotchkiss 1877- *WhAm 5*
Brittingham, Ellen Brooks Bradbury
 WomWWA 14
Brittingham, Thomas Evans 1860-1924
 WhAm 1
Brittingham, Thomas Evans, Jr. 1899-1960
 NatCAB 48, WhAm 4
Britton, Alexander Thompson 1835-1899
 NatCAB 1, TwCBDA, WhAm 1
Britton, Edgar Clay 1891-1962 *NatCAB 52,*
 WhAm 4
Britton, Edward Elms 1864-1925 *WhAm 1*
Britton, Elizabeth Gertrude Knight 1858-1934
 NatCAB 25, NotAW, WhAm 1,
 WomWWA 14
Britton, Frank Hamilton 1850-1916 *ApCAB X,*
 NatCAB 19, WhAm 1
Britton, Frederick O 1910-1960 *WhAm 4*
Britton, George Emerson 1859-1949
 NatCAB 39
Britton, Harry Albert 1881-1959 *NatCAB 48*
Britton, Ida Freeman 1848- *WomWWA 14*
Britton, Isaac W *NewYHSD*
Britton, John *NewYHSD*
Britton, John Alexander 1855-1923 *WhAm 1*

Britton, Joseph 1825-1901 *NewYHSD*
Britton, Josephine 1882- *WomWWA 14*
Britton, Mason 1882-1974 *WhAm 6*
Britton, Nathaniel Lord 1858-1934 *ApCAB*
Britton, Nathaniel Lord 1859-1934 *AmBi, DcAmB S1, DcScB, NatCAB 12, NatCAB 25, WhAm 1*
Britton, Roy Frank 1881-1940 *ApCAB X, NatCAB 30*
Britton, William John 1872-1943 *NatCAB 33*
Britton, Wilton Everett 1868-1939 *AmBi, WhAm 1*
Brizzolara, Ralph Dominic 1895-1972 *WhAm 5*
Broad, Charlie Dunbar 1887- *McGEWB*
Broad, George Birney 1871-1961 *NatCAB 50*
Broadbent, James Thomas 1875- *WhAm 5*
Broadbent, Samuel 1759-1828 *NewYHSD*
Broadbent, William H 1835-1907 *BiHiMed*
Broaddus, Andrew 1770-1848 *ApCAB*
Broaddus, Bower 1888-1949 *NatCAB 39, WhAm 3*
Broaddus, Lucy Frances Duncan *WomWWA 14*
Broadfoot, Eleanor *NotAW*
Broadfoot, Grover L 1892-1962 *WhAm 4*
Broadhead, Garland Carr 1827-1912 *ApCAB, DcAmB, NatCAB 13, TwCBDA, WhAm 1*
Broadhead, James Overton 1819-1898 *BiDrAC, DcAmB, NatCAB 5, TwCBDA, WhAm H*
Broadhead, John C *BiAUS*
Broadhead, Stella Florine 1859- *WomWWA 14*
Broadhead, William 1819-1910 *NatCAB 23*
Broadhurst, Edward T 1879-1955 *WhAm 3*
Broadhurst, Edwin Borden 1915-1965 *NatCAB 53, WhAm 4*
Broadhurst, George H 1866-1952 *WhAm 3*
Broadhurst, Jean 1873-1954 *WhAm 3*
Broadus, John Albert 1827-1895 *ApCAB, DcAmB, DcAmReB, NatCAB 18, TwCBDA, WhAm H*
Broadwater, Charles Arthur 1840-1892 *NatCAB 45, REnAW*
Broadwater, Charles Chumasero 1875-1954 *NatCAB 45*
Broadwater, J A B 1895-1957 *WhAm 3*
Broadway, Augustine W 1854-1932 *NatCAB 4, NatCAB 24*
Broady, Jefferson Hunsaker 1844-1908 *NatCAB 45*
Broar, Benjamin 1850- *NewYHSD*
Brobst *NewYHSD*
Brobst, Samuel R Kistler 1822- *ApCAB*
Brobst, Sue E *WomWWA 14a*
Broca, Pierre Paul 1824-1880 *AsBiEn, BiHiMed, DcScB*
Brocard, A *NewYHSD*
Brocard, Pierre Rene Jean-Baptiste Henri 1845-1922 *DcScB*
Brocchi, Giovanni Battista 1772-1826 *DcScB*
Broch, Hermann Joseph 1886-1951 *WhAm 4*
Brochant DeVilliers, Andre-Jean-F-Marie 1772-1840 *DcScB*
Brochus, Perry E *BiAUS*
Brocius, Curly Bill d1882? *REnAW*
Brock, Arthur 1850-1909 *NatCAB 25*
Brock, Charles Robert 1865-1928 *NatCAB 18, NatCAB 24, WhAm 1*
Brock, Charles William Penn 1836-1916 *WhAm 1*
Brock, Clifford Edward 1893- *WhAm 3*
Brock, Elbert Hill 1865-1941 *NatCAB 32*
Brock, Elizabeth Tyler 1839- *WomWWA 14*
Brock, Elmer Leslie 1880-1949 *WhAm 4*
Brock, Evan Coleman 1881-1935 *NatCAB 27*
Brock, George William 1864-1941 *WhAm 2*
Brock, Henry Gibson 1886-1940 *NatCAB 31*
Brock, Henry Irving 1876- *WhAm 5*
Brock, Horace 1854-1917 *NatCAB 27*
Brock, Sir Isaac 1769-1812 *AmBi, ApCAB, Drake, McGEWB*
Brock, James Ellison 1862- *WhAm 4*
Brock, Larry 1906-1968 *WhAm 5*
Brock, Lawrence 1906-1968 *BiDrAC*
Brock, Loring Stewart 1911-1969 *NatCAB 55*
Brock, Loring Stewart 1911-1971 *WhAm 5*
Brock, Lynmar 1905-1964 *NatCAB 50*

Brock, Robert Alonzo 1839-1914 *WhAm 1*
Brock, Sidney G 1837- *NatCAB 1, TwCBDA*
Brock, Sidney Gorham 1836- *WhAm 4*
Brock, Thomas Sleeper 1874- *WhAm 5*
Brock, William Emerson 1872-1950 *BiDrAC, NatCAB 39, WhAm 3*
Brock, William Emerson, III 1930- *BiDrAC*
Brockenborough, William 1778-1838 *ApCAB, Drake*
Brockenbrough, J W 1806-1877 *BiAUS*
Brockenbrough, John White 1806-1877 *BiDConf*
Brockenbrough, William 1778-1838 *NatCAB 19*
Brockenbrough, William H 1813?-1850 *ApCAB, BiAUS*
Brockenbrough, William Henry 1812-1850 *BiDrAC, WhAm H*
Brockett, Andrew Jackson 1836-1912 *NatCAB 17*
Brockett, Linus Pierpont 1820-1893 *ApCAB, DcAmB, TwCBDA, WhAm H*
Brockhagen, Carl Homer 1877-1941 *NatCAB 31, WhAm 2*
Brockie, Arthur H 1875-1946 *WhAm 2*
Brocklesby, John 1811-1889 *ApCAB, NatCAB 12, TwCBDA, WhAm H*
Brockman, Fletcher Sims 1867-1944 *WhAm 2*
Brockmann, Harry Lyndon 1890-1971 *NatCAB 56*
Brockmeyer, Henry C 1828-1906 *DcAmB*
Brockson, Franklin 1865-1942 *BiDrAC, WhAm 1C, WhAm 4*
Brockway, Albert Leverett 1864-1933 *WhAm 1*
Brockway, Alcinda Beman 1872- *WomWWA 14*
Brockway, Ezra Smith 1891-1948 *NatCAB 36*
Brockway, Fred John 1860-1901 *WhAm 1*
Brockway, George A 1863- *WhAm 5*
Brockway, Hobart Mortimer, Jr. 1920-1973 *WhAm 6*
Brockway, Howard 1870-1951 *NatCAB 13, WhAm 3*
Brockway, John Hall 1801-1870 *ApCAB, BiAUS, BiDrAC, WhAm H*
Brockway, Zebulon Reed 1827-1920 *AmBi, DcAmB, NatCAB 19, WhAm 1*
Brockway, Zenas R 1827- *TwCBDA*
Broda, Frederick Martin 1895-1974 *WhAm 6*
Brodbeck, Andrew R 1860-1937 *BiDrAC, WhAm 1*
Brode, Charles Geiger 1909-1962 *WhAm 4*
Brode, Howard Stidham 1866- *WhAm 4*
Brode, Wallace Reed 1900-1974 *WhAm 6*
Brodeau, Anna Maria 1775-1865 *NewYHSD*
Brodek, Charles Adrian 1872-1944 *WhAm 2*
Brodel, Max 1870-1941 *DcAmB S3, DcScB Sup*
Brodel, Ruth Huntington 1877- *WomWWA 14*
Broder, Edward William 1881-1943 *NatCAB 32*
Broderick, Bonaventure Finnbarr 1868-1943 *WhAm 2*
Broderick, Carroll Joseph 1905-1972 *WhAm 5*
Broderick, Case 1839-1920 *BiDrAC, TwCBDA, WhAm 3, WhAmP*
Broderick, David Colbreth 1818-1859 *BiAUS, Drake*
Broderick, David Colbreth 1820-1859 *AmBi, ApCAB, BiDrAC, DcAmB, NatCAB 4, REnAW, TwCBDA, WhAm H, WhAmP*
Broderick, Henry 1880- *WhAm 6*
Broderick, John James 1846-1919 *NatCAB 18*
Broderick, John P 1904-1973 *WhAm 6*
Broderick, John T 1866- *WhAm 4*
Broderick, Joseph A 1881-1959 *WhAm 3*
Broderick, Michael Henry 1866-1934 *NatCAB 26*
Broderick, William Stephen 1878-1962 *WhAm 4*
Broders, Albert Compton 1885-1964 *WhAm 4*
Brodesser, Roman Adolph 1890-1964 *WhAm 4*
Brodeur, Clarence Arthur 1865-1923 *WhAm 1*
Brodhay, O Chester 1874-1954 *NatCAB 41*
Brodhead, Daniel 1736-1809 *AmBi, ApCAB, DcAmB, TwCBDA, WhAm H*
Brodhead, David 1736-1809 *Drake*
Brodhead, Edward H 1809-1890 *NatCAB 2*
Brodhead, Frank Martin 1882-1951 *NatCAB 39*
Brodhead, George Livingston 1869- *WhAm 5*
Brodhead, George Milton 1857- *WhAm 4*

Brodhead, Jacob 1782-1855 *ApCAB, Drake, NatCAB 13*
Brodhead, John 1770-1838 *ApCAB, BiAUS, BiDrAC, Drake, WhAm H*
Brodhead, John Curtis 1780-1859 *BiDrAC, WhAm H*
Brodhead, John M *ApCAB, BiAUS*
Brodhead, John Romeyn 1814-1873 *ApCAB, DcAmB, Drake, NatCAB 12, TwCBDA, WhAm H*
Brodhead, Joseph Davis 1859-1920 *BiDrAC, WhAm 1*
Brodhead, Richard 1811-1863 *ApCAB, BiAUS, BiDrAC, NatCAB 4, TwCBDA, WhAm H, WhAmP*
Brodhead, Robert Packer 1860-1922 *NatCAB 19*
Brodhead, Thornton F 1822-1862 *ApCAB*
Brodie, Alexander Lewis 1888-1952 *NatCAB 39*
Brodie, Alexander Oswald 1849-1918 *NatCAB 26, REnAW, WhAm 1*
Brodie, Allan Gibson 1897-1976 *WhAm 6*
Brodie, Andrew Melrose 1858- *WhAm 4*
Brodie, Sir Benjamin Collins 1783-1862 *BiHiMed, DcScB*
Brodie, Benjamin Collins, Jr. 1817-1880 *DcScB*
Brodie, Donald M 1890-1974 *WhAm 6*
Brodie, Edward Everett 1876-1939 *NatCAB 43, WhAm 1*
Brodie, Ethel Mary 1878- *WomWWA 14*
Brodie, Gandy 1924-1975 *WhAm 6*
Brodie, Israel B 1884-1965 *WhAm 4*
Brodie, William 1823-1900 *NatCAB 12*
Brodnax, William Henry 1786-1834 *NatCAB 19*
Brodney, Spencer 1883-1973 *WhAm 6*
Brodrick, Lynn Rosegrant 1892-1958 *WhAm 3*
Brodrick, Richard Godfrey 1871-1929 *WhAm 1*
Brodsky, Nathan 1916-1975 *WhAm 6*
Brodsky, Paul 1900-1970 *WhAm 5*
Brody, Clark Louis 1879-1961 *WhAm 4*
Brody, Daniel Anthony 1915-1975 *WhAm 6*
Brody, Joseph Isaac 1889-1963 *WhAm 4*
Brody, Samuel 1890-1956 *WhAm 3*
Broedel, Max 1870-1941 *WhAm 1, WhAm 2*
Broek, Jan Otto Marius 1904-1974 *WhAm 6*
Broek, John Yonker 1880-1963 *WhAm 4*
Broekman, David Hendrines 1899-1958 *WhAm 3*
Broening, William Frederick 1870-1953 *WhAm 3*
Brogan, Sir Denis William 1900-1974 *WhAm 6*
Brogan, Francis Albert 1860- *WhAm 5*
Brogan, James M 1869- *WhAm 5*
Brogan, John Habbick 1870-1944 *NatCAB 33*
Brogan, Thomas J d1965 *WhAm 4*
Brogden, Curtis H *BiAUS*
Brogden, Curtis H 1815?-1901 *ApCAB*
Brogden, Curtis Hooks 1816-1901 *BiDrAC, NatCAB 4, TwCBDA*
Brogden, Wilfred John 1912-1973 *WhAm 6*
Brogden, Willis James 1877-1935 *WhAm 1*
Brogger, Waldemar Christopher 1851-1940 *DcScB*
Broggi, Frank Scannell 1908-1971 *NatCAB 55*
Broghamer, George P 1909-1973 *WhAm 6*
Broglie, Duc De 1875-1960 *WhAm 4*
Broglie, Prince Claude Victor Marie De 1757-1794 *ApCAB, Drake*
Broglie, Louis-Cesar-Victor-Maurice De 1875-1960 *DcScB*
Broglie, Louis Victor Pierre Raymond, De 1892- *McGEWB*
Broglie, Victor Francois, Duc De 1718-1804 *WhoMilH*
Broido, Lucy Kaufmann 1900-1969 *NatCAB 55*
Broidy, Edward William 1886-1950 *WhAm 3*
Broili, Ferdinand 1874-1946 *DcScB*
Brokamp, Frank William 1899-1966 *WhAm 4*
Brokaw, Charles Livingston 1866-1936 *WhAm 1*
Brokaw, Howard Crosby 1875-1960 *WhAm 3*
Brokaw, Isaac Vail 1835-1913 *NatCAB 15*
Broke, Sir Philip Bowes Vere 1776-1841 *ApCAB, Drake*
Brokenshire, Charles Digory 1885-1954 *WhAm 3*
Brokenshire, Norman 1898-1965 *WhAm 4*

Brokenshire, William Samuel, Jr. 1899-1963 *WhAm 4*

Brokmeyer, Henry C 1828-1906 *DcAmB, WhAm HA, WhAm 4*

Bromberg, Frederick George 1837-1930 *BiAUS, BiDrAC, NatCAB 21, TwCBDA, WhAm 1*

Bromberg, Louie Nathaniel 1884-1952 *NatCAB 42*

Bromell, Magnus Von 1679-1731 *DcScB*

Bromer, Edward Sheppard 1869-1948 *WhAm 3*

Bromer, Ralph Shepherd 1886-1957 *WhAm 3*

Bromfield, Davenport 1882-1954 *NatCAB 42*

Bromfield, John 1779-1849 *ApCAB, DcAmB, Drake, NatCAB 6, TwCBDA, WhAm H*

Bromfield, John Davenport 1887-1955 *NatCAB 42*

Bromfield, Louis 1896-1956 *WebAB, WhAm 3*

Bromilow, Frank 1916-1975 *WhAm 6*

Bromley, Charles Dunham 1899-1968 *WhAm 5*

Bromley, Emmet Arthur 1858-1922 *NatCAB 6*

Bromley, Isaac Hill 1833-1898 *ApCAB, DcAmB, NatCAB 12*

Bromley, Joseph Henry 1881-1947 *NatCAB 50*

Bromley, Stanley Willard 1899-1954 *NatCAB 44*

Bromley, Valentine Walter 1848-1877 *IlBEAAW*

Bromme, Traugott 1802-1865 *ApCAB*

Bromstead, Henry 1806?- *NewYHSD*

Bromwell, Charles Summers 1869-1915 *WhAm 1*

Bromwell, Elizabeth Henrietta *IlBEAAW*

Bromwell, Henrietta Elizabeth *WomWWA 14*

Bromwell, Henry Pelham Holmes 1823-1903 *BiAUS, BiDrAC*

Bromwell, Jacob Henry 1847-1924 *TwCBDA, WhAm 4*

Bromwell, Jacob Henry 1848-1924 *BiDrAC, WhAmP*

Bromwell, James Edward 1920- *BiDrAC*

Bromwich, Thomas John I'Anson 1875-1929 *DcScB*

Bronaugh, Earl C, Jr. 1866- *ApCAB X*

Brondel, John B 1842-1903 *ApCAB, WhAm 1*

Brondel, John Baptist 1842-1903 *DcAmB, NatCAB 13*

Brondel, John Baptiste 1842-1903 *TwCBDA*

Bronfenbrenner, Jacques Jacob 1883-1953 *NatCAB 45, WhAm 3*

Bronfman, Samuel 1891-1971 *NatCAB 56, WhAm 5*

Brongniart, Adolphe-Theodore 1801-1876 *DcScB*

Brongniart, Alexandre 1770-1847 *DcScB*

Bronk, Detlev Wulf 1897-1975 *WebAB, WhAm 6*

Bronk, Isabelle d1943 *WhAm 2, WomWWA 14*

Bronk, Margaret Marcellus *WomWWA 14*

Bronk, Mitchell 1862-1950 *WhAm 3*

Bronlem, Isaac Hill 1833-1898 *WhAm H*

Bronn, Heinrich Georg 1800-1862 *DcScB*

Bronner, Augusta Fox 1881- *WhAm 6*

Bronner, Edmond D 1859-1930 *WhAm 1*

Bronner, Harry 1868-1940 *WhAm 1*

Bronowski, Jacob 1908-1974 *WhAm 6*

Bronson, Amey Talbot Taintor *WomWWA 14*

Bronson, Bennet 1887-1950 *WhAm 3*

Bronson, Carl 1871-1947 *NatCAB 36*

Bronson, Charles Eli 1857- *WhAm 4*

Bronson, Clarence Whittlesey 1880-1969 *NatCAB 55*

Bronson, D *NewYHSD*

Bronson, David 1800-1863 *BiAUS, BiDrAC, WhAm H*

Bronson, Dillon 1863-1943 *NatCAB 5, NatCAB 33, WhAm 2*

Bronson, Elliott Birdsey 1858- *NatCAB 6*

Bronson, Elsie Marion Straffin 1882- *WomWWA 14*

Bronson, Francis Woolsey 1901-1966 *NatCAB 53, WhAm 4*

Bronson, Greene Carrier 1789-1863 *ApCAB, Drake, NatCAB 3, TwCBDA*

Bronson, Harrison Arthur 1873-1947 *NatCAB 35, WhAm 2*

Bronson, Henry 1804-1893 *DcAmB, NatCAB 22, WhAm H*

Bronson, Henry Martyn 1836-1912 *NatCAB 39*

Bronson, Irlo Overstreet 1900-1973 *NatCAB 57*

Bronson, Isaac Hopkins 1802-1855 *ApCAB, BiAUS, BiDrAC, Drake, WhAm H*

Bronson, Ruth Muskrat 1897- *REnAW*

Bronson, Samuel Lathrop 1834-1917 *NatCAB 33, WhAm 1*

Bronson, Sherlock Anson 1807-1890 *NatCAB 7*

Bronson, Silas d1867 *ApCAB*

Bronson, Solon Cary 1855-1931 *WhAm 1*

Bronson, Thomas Bertrand 1857-1948 *WhAm 3*

Bronson, Walter Cochrane 1862-1928 *DcAmB, NatCAB 22, WhAm 1*

Bronson, William Howard 1912-1972 *NatCAB 57, WhAm 5*

Bronson, William Sherlock 1864- *WhAm 4*

Bronsted, Johannes Nicolaus 1879-1947 *AsBiEn, DcScB*

Bronte, Charlotte 1816-1855 *McGEWB*

Bronte, Emily 1818-1848 *McGEWB*

Bronzino 1503-1572 *McGEWB*

Broocks, Moses Lycurgus 1864-1908 *BiDrAC*

Brook, Alexander 1898- *BnEnAmA*

Brook, Charles Henry 1883-1957 *WhAm 4*

Brook, Clive 1891-1974 *WhAm 6*

Brook, Edith May *WomWWA 14*

Brooke, Sir Alan 1883-1963 *WhWW-II, WhoMilH*

Brooke, Avonia Stanhope Jones 1839-1867 *ApCAB*

Brooke, Ben C 1872- *WhAm 5*

Brooke, Charles Frederick Tucker 1883-1946 *DcAmB S4, NatCAB 36*

Brooke, D Tucker 1852-1915 *NatCAB 16*

Brooke, Edward William 1919- *BiDrAC*

Brooke, Flavius Lionel 1858-1912 *NatCAB 17, WhAm 1*

Brooke, Francis J 1763-1851 *ApCAB, BiAUS, Drake*

Brooke, Francis J 1802- *ApCAB*

Brooke, Francis Key 1852-1918 *ApCAB Sup, NatCAB 7, TwCBDA, WhAm 1*

Brooke, Francis Mark 1836-1882 *NatCAB 5*

Brooke, Francis Taliaferro 1763-1851 *DcAmB, NatCAB 7, TwCBDA, WhAm H*

Brooke, Franklin Ellsworth 1866- *WhAm 4*

Brooke, George Mercer d1851 *ApCAB, Drake*

Brooke, H St. George Tucker 1844-1914 *NatCAB 36*

Brooke, H St. George Tucker *see also* Brooke, St. George Tucker

Brooke, Homer 1842-1927 *NatCAB 20*

Brooke, Irving Emerson 1880-1968 *NatCAB 55*

Brooke, Sir James 1803-1868 *McGEWB*

Brooke, James J 1879- *WhAm 6*

Brooke, John Mercer 1826-1904 *BiDConf*

Brooke, John Mercer 1826-1906 *AmBi, DcAmB, NatCAB 22, WebAMB, WhAm 1*

Brooke, John Rutter 1838-1926 *ApCAB, ApCAB Sup, DcAmB, NatCAB 9, TwCBDA, WhAm 1*

Brooke, Mary Myrtle 1872- *WhAm 5*

Brooke, Richard Norris 1847-1920 *WhAm 1*

Brooke, Robert 1751-1799 *BiAUS, NatCAB 5*

Brooke, Robert Edward 1872-1942 *NatCAB 40*

Brooke, Rupert 1887-1915 *McGEWB*

Brooke, St. George Tucker 1844-1914 *WhAm 1*

Brooke, St. George Tucker *see also* Brooke, H St. George Tucker

Brooke, Thomas Preston 1859- *WhAm 4*

Brooke, Tucker 1883-1946 *WhAm 2*

Brooke, Walker 1813-1869 *ApCAB, BiDConf, BiDrAC, NatCAB 11*

Brooke, Walter *BiAUS*

Brooke, Walter 1813-1869 *WhAm H*

Brooke, William Ellsworth 1870-1963 *WhAm 4, WhAm 5*

Brooke-Popham, Sir Robert 1878-1953 *WhWW-II*

Brooke-Rawle, William 1843-1915 *NatCAB 10, TwCBDA, WhAm 1*

Brookeborough, Viscount 1888-1973 *WhAm 6*

Brooker, Charles Frederick 1847-1926 *ApCAB X, DcAmB, NatCAB 18, WhAm 1*

Brooker, John William 1899-1952 *WhAm 3*

Brooker, Lester Francis 1886-1965 *NatCAB 52*

Brookes, James Hall 1830- *NatCAB 5*

Brookes, John St. Clair, Jr. 1888-1959 *WhAm 4*

Brookes, Samuel Marsden 1816-1892 *IlBEAAW, NewYHSD, WhAm H*

Brookfield, William 1844- *NatCAB 3*

Brookhart, Smith Wildman 1869-1944 *ApCAB X, BiDrAC, DcAmB S3, EncAAH, WhAm 2*

Brookings, David Jenness 1842-1930 *NatCAB 23*

Brookings, Marian Kinney 1883- *WomWWA 14*

Brookings, Robert Somers 1850-1932 *AmBi, ApCAB X, DcAmB S1, NatCAB 7, NatCAB 33, WebAB, WhAm 1*

Brookings, W W *BiAUS*

Brookings, Walter DuBois 1873-1950 *WhAm 3, WhAm 4*

Brookings, Wilmot W 1830- *TwCBDA*

Brookins, Homer DeWitton 1855-1938 *WhAm 3*

Brookover, Charles 1870-1922 *NatCAB 20*

Brooks *NewYHSD*

Brooks, Alden Finney 1840- *NewYHSD*

Brooks, Alfred Hulse 1871-1924 *AmBi, DcAmB, DcScB, NatCAB 22, WhAm 1*

Brooks, Alfred Mansfield 1870- *WhAm 5*

Brooks, Allerton Frank 1890-1955 *WhAm 3*

Brooks, Alonzo Beecher 1873-1944 *WhAm 4*

Brooks, Amy *WomWWA 14*

Brooks, Anita Comfort *WomWWA 14*

Brooks, Annie Laurie 1857- *WomWWA 14*

Brooks, Annie Mabel *WomWWA 14*

Brooks, Anson Strong 1852-1937 *WhAm 1*

Brooks, Arbie Leroy 1889-1951 *WhAm 3*

Brooks, Arthur 1845-1895 *NatCAB 8, TwCBDA, WhAm H*

Brooks, Arthur Alford 1879-1947 *WhAm 2*

Brooks, Arthur Thomas 1881-1947 *WhAm 2*

Brooks, Arthur Wolfort 1889-1948 *WhAm 2*

Brooks, Basil Emory 1884-1940 *NatCAB 51*

Brooks, Belvidere 1859- *NatCAB 14*

Brooks, Benjamin Talbott 1885-1962 *WhAm 4*

Brooks, Bessie Estelle 1872- *WomWWA 14*

Brooks, Bryant Butler 1861-1944 *NatCAB 13, WhAm 2*

Brooks, Byron Alden 1845-1911 *DcAmB, NatCAB 3*

Brooks, Caroline Shawk 1840- *ApCAB, NewYHSD, TwCBDA*

Brooks, Charles 1795-1872 *ApCAB, BiDAmEd, DcAmB, Drake, NatCAB 12, TwCBDA, WhAm H*

Brooks, Charles Alvin 1871-1931 *WhAm 1*

Brooks, Charles Ames 1883-1931 *NatCAB 23*

Brooks, Charles Edward 1879-1936 *WhAm 1*

Brooks, Charles F 1891-1958 *WhAm 3*

Brooks, Charles Hayward 1859- *WhAm 5*

Brooks, Charles J 1861-1917 *ApCAB X*

Brooks, Charles Stephen 1878-1934 *NatCAB 41, WhAm 1*

Brooks, Charles Timothy 1813-1883 *ApCAB, DcAmB, Drake, NatCAB 8, TwCBDA, WhAm H*

Brooks, Charles Wayland 1897-1957 *BiDrAC, NatCAB 42, WhAm 3*

Brooks, Chauncey 1794-1880 *NatCAB 18*

Brooks, Christopher Parkinson 1866-1909 *WhAm 1*

Brooks, Clarence Richard 1901-1970 *WhAm 5*

Brooks, David 1736-1838 *BiAUS*

Brooks, David 1756-1838 *ApCAB, BiDrAC, Drake, NatCAB 2, TwCBDA, WhAm H*

Brooks, Edward 1831-1912 *ApCAB, BiDAmEd, NatCAB 2, TwCBDA, WhAm 1*

Brooks, Edward Fuller 1848-1916 *NatCAB 18*

Brooks, Edward Jewett 1850- *NatCAB 7*

Brooks, Edward Little 1883-1942 *NatCAB 32*

Brooks, Edward Schroeder 1867-1957 *BiDrAC, WhAm 4*

Brooks, Edward Toole 1828?- *ApCAB*

Brooks, Edward Ulysses Anderson 1872- *WhoColR*

Brooks, Edwin Bruce 1868-1933 *BiDrAC, WhAm 4*

Brooks, Elbridge Streeter 1846-1902 *DcAmB, NatCAB 7, TwCBDA, WhAm 1*

Brooks, Eleazer 1727-1806 *ApCAB, Drake*

Brooks, Erastus 1815-1886 *ApCAB, DcAmB, Drake, NatCAB 6, TwCBDA, WhAm H*
Brooks, Ethel Frances Fifield *WomWWA 14*
Brooks, Eugene Clyde 1871-1947 *BiDAmEd, NatCAB 36, WhAm 2*
Brooks, Eugene Clyde, Jr. 1903-1970 *NatCAB 56*
Brooks, Florence 1860-1948 *NatCAB 37*
Brooks, Florence 1868- *WhAm 4*
Brooks, Francis Marion 1866-1946 *NatCAB 38*
Brooks, Francis R 1867-1898 *NatCAB 7*
Brooks, Frank Hilliard 1868-1931 *WhAm 1*
Brooks, Frank Wilks 1864- *WhAm 4*
Brooks, Franklin Eli 1860-1916 *BiDrAC, WhAm 1*
Brooks, Fred Emerson 1850-1923 *WhAm 1*
Brooks, Frederick A 1895-1967 *WhAm 5*
Brooks, Frona Marie *WomWWA 14*
Brooks, George Grant 1870-1941 *NatCAB 30*
Brooks, George Merrick 1824-1893 *BiAUS, BiDrAC, WhAm H*
Brooks, George Sage 1882-1950 *NatCAB 41*
Brooks, George Sprague 1895-1961 *WhAm 4*
Brooks, George Washington 1821-1882 *BiAUS, DcAmB, NatCAB 8, WhAm H*
Brooks, George Wesley 1880- *WhoColR*
Brooks, George William 1862-1952 *NatCAB 47*
Brooks, Geraldine 1875- *WhAm 5, WomWWA 14*
Brooks, Gwendolyn 1917- *EncAB, WebAB*
Brooks, Harlow 1871-1936 *ApCAB X, NatCAB 27, WhAm 1*
Brooks, Harry Sayer 1852-1924 *NatCAB 5, WhAm 3*
Brooks, Henry Gilbert 1875-1944 *NatCAB 34*
Brooks, Henry Luesing 1905-1971 *WhAm 5*
Brooks, Henry S d1910 *WhAm 1*
Brooks, Henry Turner 1861- *WhAm 4*
Brooks, Herbert Barton 1869-1962 *NatCAB 50*
Brooks, Herbert Lee 1887-1963 *NatCAB 48*
Brooks, Herbert Thomas 1882-1959 *NatCAB 47*
Brooks, Horace 1814-1890 *ApCAB, Drake, TwCBDA*
Brooks, Ida Joe 1853- *AmWom*
Brooks, Ida Josephine *WomWWA 14*
Brooks, Jabez 1823-1910 *WhAm 1*
Brooks, Jack Bascom 1922- *BiDrAC*
Brooks, James 1810-1873 *ApCAB, BiAUS, BiDrAC, DcAmB, Drake, NatCAB 6, TwCBDA, WhAm H, WhAmP*
Brooks, James 1906- *BnEnAmA*
Brooks, James Byron 1839-1914 *WhAm 1*
Brooks, James Coffinberry 1875-1966 *NatCAB 52*
Brooks, James Gordon 1801-1841 *ApCAB, DcAmB, Drake, NatCAB 13, TwCBDA, WhAm H*
Brooks, James Gordon Carter 1837-1914 *ApCAB X, NatCAB 16*
Brooks, James Wilton 1854-1916 *TwCBDA, WhAm 1*
Brooks, Jennie 1853- *WomWWA 14*
Brooks, Jesse Wendell 1858-1920 *WhAm 1*
Brooks, John 1752-1825 *AmBi, ApCAB, BiAUS, DcAmB, Drake, NatCAB 1, TwCBDA, WhAm H*
Brooks, John 1814-1893 *TwCBDA*
Brooks, John B 1891-1975 *WhAm 6*
Brooks, John Gaunt 1913-1971 *NatCAB 54, WhAm 5*
Brooks, John Graham 1846-1938 *DcAmB S2, NatCAB 13, NatCAB 28, WhAm 1*
Brooks, John Pascal 1861- *WhAm 4*
Brooks, Joseph 1821-1877 *ApCAB, TwCBDA*
Brooks, Joseph Hudson 1845-1914 *WhAm 3*
Brooks, Joshua Loring 1868-1949 *WhAm 2*
Brooks, Joshua Twing 1884-1956 *BiDrAC*
Brooks, Juanita 1898- *REnAW*
Brooks, Julia M Clark *WomWWA 14*
Brooks, Kendall 1821-1898 *ApCAB, TwCBDA*
Brooks, Laurance Waddill 1900-1971 *WhAm 5*
Brooks, Laverne W 1875- *WhAm 5*
Brooks, Lawrence Bickford 1901-1954 *NatCAB 42*
Brooks, Leon Richard 1912-1967 *WhAm 4*
Brooks, Leroy 1881-1963 *NatCAB 56*
Brooks, LeRoy 1892-1953 *NatCAB 42*

Brooks, Lewis 1793-1877 *ApCAB, TwCBDA*
Brooks, Louis J 1853- *NatCAB 9*
Brooks, Louise Dudley Davis *WomWWA 14*
Brooks, Luella Jane 1853- *WomWWA 14*
Brooks, M Sears *AmWom*
Brooks, Maria 1845?-1913 *NatCAB 8*
Brooks, Maria Gowen 1794?-1845 *AmBi, DcAmB, NotAW, WhAm H*
Brooks, Maria Gowen 1795?-1845 *ApCAB, Drake, NatCAB 8, TwCBDA*
Brooks, Mary Naomi Willard 1864- *WhAm 3, WomWWA 14*
Brooks, Mary TenEyck Oakley *WomWWA 14*
Brooks, Micah 1775-1857 *BiAUS, BiDrAC, WhAm H*
Brooks, Morgan 1861-1947 *NatCAB 36, WhAm 2*
Brooks, Nathan Covington 1809-1898 *NatCAB 4*
Brooks, Nathan Covington 1819-1898 *ApCAB, Drake, TwCBDA*
Brooks, Ned 1901-1969 *WhAm 5*
Brooks, Neil 1906-1969 *WhAm 5*
Brooks, Newton *NewYHSD*
Brooks, Noah *NewYHSD*
Brooks, Noah 1830-1903 *AmBi, ApCAB, DcAmB, NatCAB 7, TwCBDA, WhAm 1*
Brooks, Olin L 1894-1963 *WhAm 4*
Brooks, Overton 1897-1961 *BiDrAC, WhAm 4, WhAmP*
Brooks, Paul David 1904-1958 *WhAm 3*
Brooks, Percival Willis 1867-1959 *NatCAB 48*
Brooks, Peter Anthony 1893-1948 *WhAm 2*
Brooks, Peter Chardon 1767-1849 *ApCAB, DcAmB, Drake, NatCAB 5, TwCBDA, WhAm H*
Brooks, Phillips 1835-1893 *AmBi, ApCAB, ApCAB X, DcAmB, DcAmReB, Drake, McGEWB, NatCAB 2, TwCBDA, WebAB, WhAm H*
Brooks, Phillips 1921-1975 *WhAm 6*
Brooks, Phillips Moore 1908-1967 *WhAm 5*
Brooks, Preston Smith 1819-1857 *AmBi, ApCAB, BiAUS, BiDrAC, DcAmB, Drake, TwCBDA, WhAm H, WhAmP*
Brooks, Ralph Gilmour 1898-1960 *WhAm 4*
Brooks, Raymond Cummings 1869-1944 *NatCAB 32, WhAm 2*
Brooks, Raymond Ernest 1883-1960 *NatCAB 48*
Brooks, Reuben Benjamin 1860- *WhoColR*
Brooks, Richard Edwin 1865-1919 *DcAmB, NatCAB 22, WhAm 1*
Brooks, Robert Blemker 1889-1960 *WhAm 4*
Brooks, Robert Clarkson 1874-1941 *NatCAB 33, WhAm 1*
Brooks, Robert M 1877-1945 *WhAm 2*
Brooks, Robert Nathaniel 1888-1953 *WhAm 3*
Brooks, Robert Preston 1881-1961 *NatCAB 53, WhAm 6*
Brooks, Rodney Joseph 1895-1952 *WhAm 3*
Brooks, Roelif Hasbrouck 1875- *WhAm 6*
Brooks, Samuel *NewYHSD*
Brooks, Samuel Palmer 1863-1931 *NatCAB 24, WhAm 1*
Brooks, Sarah Catherine 1856- *WomWWA 14*
Brooks, Sarah Warner d1906 *WhAm 1*
Brooks, Sidney 1892-1944 *NatCAB 38*
Brooks, Stewart 1867-1942 *WhAm 2*
Brooks, Stratton Duluth 1869-1949 *BiDAmEd, NatCAB 18, WhAm 2*
Brooks, Summer Cushing 1888-1948 *WhAm 3*
Brooks, Thomas Benton 1836-1900 *ApCAB, DcAmB, NatCAB 3, NatCAB 45, TwCBDA, WhAm 1*
Brooks, Thomas Cook 1859-1930 *NatCAB 24*
Brooks, Thomas Hope 1846-1919 *NatCAB 18*
Brooks, Thomas L *WhoColR*
Brooks, VanWyck 1886-1963 *WebAB, WhAm 4*
Brooks, Victor Lee 1870-1925 *NatCAB 20, WhAm 1*
Brooks, Walter Henderson 1861- *WhoColR*
Brooks, Walter Rollin 1886-1958 *NatCAB 47, WhAm 3*
Brooks, Warren Ainsworth 1915-1957 *NatCAB 47*

Brooks, Wendell Stanton 1886-1961 *WhAm 4*
Brooks, William Benthall 1832-1910 *WhAm 1*
Brooks, William E 1875- *WhAm 5*
Brooks, William F 1902-1975 *WhAm 6*
Brooks, William Francis 1865-1925 *ApCAB X*
Brooks, William Frederick 1863-1928 *NatCAB 21*
Brooks, William Frederick 1872-1950 *NatCAB 39*
Brooks, William Henry 1859- *WhoColR*
Brooks, William Keith 1848-1908 *AmBi, ApCAB, DcAmB, DcScB, NatCAB 23, TwCBDA, WhAm 1*
Brooks, William L 1849-1874 *REnAW*
Brooks, William McLin 1815-1894 *NatCAB 19*
Brooks, William Miron 1835-1924 *NatCAB 32*
Brooks, William Myron 1835-1924 *TwCBDA, WhAm 1*
Brooks, William Penn 1851-1938 *WhAm 1*
Brooks, William Robert 1844-1921 *AmBi, ApCAB Sup, DcAmB, DcScB, NatCAB 5, TwCBDA, WhAm 1*
Brooks, William T H 1815?-1870 *Drake*
Brooks, William Thomas Harbaugh 1821-1870 *ApCAB, DcAmB, NatCAB 12, TwCBDA, WhAm H*
Brooks, Winfield Sears 1902-1963 *WhAm 4*
Brooks-Aten, Florence 1875- *ApCAB X*
Brooksher, William Riley 1894-1971 *WhAm 6*
Brookshire, Elijah Voorhees 1856-1936 *BiDrAC, WhAm 1*
Broom, Jacob 1752-1810 *ApCAB, Drake, NatCAB 3*
Broom, Jacob 1808-1864 *ApCAB, BiAUS, BiDrAC, WhAm H*
Broom, James Madison d1850 *Drake*
Broom, James Madison 1776-1850 *BiDrAC, WhAm H*
Broom, James Madison 1778-1850 *ApCAB*
Broom, Robert 1866-1951 *DcScB*
Broomall, Anna Elizabeth 1847-1931 *NatCAB 24, NotAW*
Broomall, John Martin 1816-1894 *BiAUS, BiDrAC, WhAm H*
Broome, B C *IIBEAAW*
Broome, Edwin Cornelius 1874-1950 *NatCAB 43, WhAm 3*
Broome, Harvey 1902-1968 *WhAm 4A, WhAm 5*
Broome, Isaac 1835-1922 *NewYHSD, WhAm 1*
Broome, James E 1808-1883 *BiAUS, NatCAB 11*
Broome, James M *BiAUS*
Broome, John 1738-1810 *ApCAB, Drake, NatCAB 1*
Broome, John L 1824-1898 *ApCAB, NatCAB 5, TwCBDA*
Broome, LLIAM Robert 1844-1921 *AmBi, ApCAB Sup, DcAmB, DcScB, NatCAB 5, TwCBDA, WhAm 1*
Brooks, William T H 1815?-1870 *Drake*
Brooks, William lewis Henry 1849- *NatCAB 5*
Broome, Robert Edwin 1898-1966 *WhAm 4*
Broomell, Grace Browne 1873- *WomWWA 14*
Broomell, I Norman 1858-1941 *WhAm 1*
Broomfield, Archibald 1875-1952 *NatCAB 45*
Broomfield, John Calvin 1872-1950 *WhAm 2*
Broomfield, William S 1922- *BiDrAC*
Broonzy, William Lee Conley 1893-1958 *WhAm 4A*
Brophy, C Gerald 1898-1956 *WhAm 3*
Brophy, Daniel Francis 1899-1960 *WhAm 4*
Brophy, Ellen Amelia 1871- *WhAm 1*
Brophy, George R 1775-1880 *ApCAB*
Brophy, John Charles 1901- *BiDrAC*
Brophy, Thomas D'Arcy 1893-1967 *WhAm 4*
Brophy, Truman William 1848-1928 *DcAmB, NatCAB 12, WhAm 1*
Brophy, William Henry 1863-1922 *NatCAB 52, WhAm 1*
Brorein, Carl D 1895- *WhAm 6*
Brorein, William Gebhard 1861-1937 *NatCAB 32, WhAm 1*
Bros, Baron Antoine Jean 1771-1835 *McGEWB*
Broscius, Joannes *DcScB*
Brose, Louis D 1859-1931 *WhAm 1*
Brosius, Marriott 1843-1901 *BiDrAC, NatCAB 7, TwCBDA, WhAm 1, WhAmP*

Brosman, Paul William 1899-1955 *WhAm 3*
Brosmith, William 1854-1937 *WhAm 1*
Brosnahan, Patrick Edward 1876- *WhAm 5*
Brosnahan, Timothy 1856-1915 *TwCBDA,*
WhAm 1
Bross, Ernest 1860-1923 *NatCAB 19,*
WhAm 1
Bross, Robert S 1831?- *NewYHSD*
Bross, Samuel *NewYHSD*
Bross, William 1813- *ApCAB*
Bross, William 1813-1889 *TwCBDA*
Bross, William 1813-1890 *DcAmB,*
NatCAB 23, WhAm H
Brossart, Ferdinand 1849- *NatCAB 15,*
WhAm 4
Brosseau, Alfred J d1936 *WhAm 1*
Brossman, Charles 1877-1937 *NatCAB 28*
Brossolette, Pierre 1903-1944 *WhWW-II*
Brother, Doran Palmer d1965 *WhAm 4*
Brotherhead *NewYHSD*
Brothers, Frank Joseph 1889-1945 *NatCAB 34*
Brothers, George Raleigh 1887-1957
NatCAB 43
Brothers, Ridgway Hulin 1907-1961
NatCAB 50
Brotherton, Alice Willams d1930 *AmWom*
Brotherton, Alice William d1930
WomWWA 14
Brotherton, Alice Williams d1930 *WhAm 1*
Brotze, Rudolph 1820?- *NewYHSD*
Brotzman, Donald Glenn 1922- *BiDrAC*
Broudy, Harry Samuel 1905- *BiDAmEd*
Brough, Charles Henry 1813-1849 *ApCAB*
Brough, Charles Hillman 1876-1935 *DcAmB S1,*
NatCAB 42, WhAmP
Brough, John 1811-1865 *AmBi, ApCAB,*
BiAUS, DcAmB, Drake, NatCAB 3,
TwCBDA, WhAm H
Brough, William 1826- *WhAm 4*
Brougham, J *NewYHSD*
Brougham, John 1810-1880 *AmBi, ApCAB,*
DcAmB, NatCAB 9, TwCBDA,
WhAm H
Brougham, John 1814-1880 *Drake*
Brougher, J Whitcomb 1870-1967 *WhAm 4A,*
WhAm 5
Broughton, Carrie Loungee 1879- *WhAm 6*
Broughton, Charles Elmer 1873-1956 *WhAm 3*
Broughton, Charles Frederic 1878- *WhAm 6*
Broughton, Joseph Melville, Jr. 1888-1949
BiDrAC, NatCAB 37, WhAm 2, WhAmP
Broughton, Leonard Gaston 1864-1936
WhAm 1
Broughton, Leslie Nathan 1877- *WhAm 5*
Broughton, Levin Bowland 1886-1943 *WhAm 2*
Broughton, Thomas d1737 *NatCAB 12*
Broughton, Thomas d1738 *ApCAB, Drake*
Broughton, Thomas d1858 *BiAUS*
Broughton, William Robert 1762-1821 *ApCAB,*
Drake
Broughton, William S 1874-1951 *WhAm 3*
Brouillet, John 1813-1884 *REnAW*
Brouillette, T Gilbert 1906-1970 *WhAm 5*
Broullire, John Merlin 1917-1972 *WhAm 5*
Broun, Heywood 1888-1939 *AmBi, ApCAB X,*
DcAmB S2, NatCAB 30, WebAB,
WhAm 1
Broun, William LeRoy 1827-1902 *NatCAB 19,*
TwCBDA, WhAm 1
Brouncker, William 1620-1684 *DcScB*
Brounoff, Platon 1863-1924 *WhAm 1*
Brous, Cecil Else 1890-1945 *NatCAB 35*
Brouse, Charles Emery 1873-1947 *NatCAB 36*
Brouse, Edwin Walter 1879-1963 *WhAm 4*
Brouse, Eugene Raymond 1910-1971
NatCAB 56
Brouse, William Henry 1824- *ApCAB*
Broussais, Francois Joseph Victor 1772-1838
BiHiMed, DcScB
Broussard, Edwin Sidney 1874-1934 *ApCAB X,*
BiDrAC, NatCAB 44, WhAm 1,
WhAmP
Broussard, James Francis 1881-1942 *WhAm 2*
Broussard, Robert Foligny 1864-1918 *BiDrAC,*
NatCAB 15, TwCBDA, WhAm 1,
WhAmP
Brousseau, Jean Baptist 1841- *ApCAB*
Brousseau, Kate 1862-1938 *WhAm 1,*
WomWWA 14

Broussonet, Pierre-Auguste-Marie 1761-1807
DcScB
Brouwer, Adriaen 1605?-1638 *McGEWB*
Brouwer, Dirk 1902-1966 *DcScB, WhAm 4*
Brouwer, Luitzen Egbertus Jan 1881-1966
DcScB, WhAm 4
Brouwer, Stephen John 1876-1946 *NatCAB 35*
Broward, Napoleon Bonaparte 1857-1910
ApCAB X, DcAmB, NatCAB 14,
NatCAB 45, WhAm 1
Browder, Basil David 1899-1960 *WhAm 3A*
Browder, Earl Russell 1891-1973 *EncAB,*
McGEWB, WebAB, WhAm 5, WhAmP
Brower, Alfred Smith 1892-1968 *WhAm 5*
Brower, Daniel 1916-1974 *WhAm 6*
Brower, Daniel Roberts 1839-1908 *NatCAB 9,*
WhAm 1
Brower, Egmont Giles 1885-1918 *NatCAB 24*
Brower, Francis M 1823?- *NewYHSD*
Brower, George Ellsworth 1875-1961
NatCAB 49
Brower, Harriette Moore 1869-1928 *WhAm 1*
Brower, Jacob Vradenberg 1844-1905 *DcAmB,*
WhAm 1
Brower, John Morehead 1845-1913 *BiDrAC*
Brower, Josephine V *WomWWA 14*
Brower, Reuben Arthur 1908-1975 *WhAm 6*
Brower, Walter Scott 1888-1962 *WhAm 4*
Brower, Ward 1873- *ApCAB X*
Brower, William Leverich 1846-1940 *WhAm 1*
Browere, Albertis DelOrient 1814-1887
IIBEAAW
Browere, Albertus D O 1814-1887 *NewYHSD,*
WhAm H
Browere, John Henri Isaac 1790-1834
NewYHSD
Browere, John Henri Isaac 1792-1834
BnEnAmA, DcAmB, WhAm H
Brown, A Luther d1955 *WhAm 3*
Brown, A Page 1859-1896 *WhAm H*
Brown, A Watson 1879-1959 *NatCAB 51*
Brown, Aaron 1872- *WhoColR*
Brown, Aaron Switzer 1913-1969 *NatCAB 55,*
WhAm 5
Brown, Aaron V 1795-1859 *BiAUS, NatCAB 7*
Brown, Aaron Vail 1795-1859 *Drake,*
NatCAB 5
Brown, Aaron Venable 1795-1859 *AmBi,*
ApCAB, BiDrAC, BiDrUSE, DcAmB,
TwCBDA, WhAm H, WhAmP
Brown, Abbie Farwell 1871-1927 *NotAW,*
WhAm 1, WomWWA 14
Brown, Abby Mason *NewYHSD*
Brown, Abram English 1849-1909 *WhAm 1*
Brown, Adam 1826- *ApCAB*
Brown, Addison 1830-1913 *ApCAB Sup,*
DcAmB, TwCBDA, WhAm 1
Brown, Adelaide 1868- *WomWWA 14*
Brown, Adelaide Spenser 1860- *WomWWA 14*
Brown, Adelbert Erastus 1839-1916 *NatCAB 17*
Brown, Agnes *ApCAB*
Brown, Agnes Hewlett 1875- *WomWWA 14*
Brown, Alanson David 1847-1913 *NatCAB 12,*
NatCAB 25, WhAm 1
Brown, Albert Edmund 1874- *WhAm 5*
Brown, Albert Frederic 1862- *WhAm 4*
Brown, Albert Gallatin 1813-1880 *ApCAB,*
BiAUS, BiDConf, BiDrAC, DcAmB,
Drake, NatCAB 13, REnAW, TwCBDA,
WhAm H, WhAmP
Brown, Albert Louis 1899-1963 *NatCAB 50*
Brown, Albert Oscar 1852-1937 *WhAm 1*
Brown, Albert Sidney *WhAm 5*
Brown, Alexander 1764-1834 *AmBi, ApCAB,*
DcAmB, McGEWB, NatCAB 1,
WhAm H
Brown, Alexander 1843-1906 *AmBi, DcAmB,*
NatCAB 19, WhAm 1
Brown, Alexander 1858-1949 *NatCAB 1,*
TwCBDA, WhAm 2
Brown, Alexander Crum 1838-1922 *DcScB*
Brown, Alexander Cushing 1885-1964
NatCAB 51, WhAm 4
Brown, Alexander Ephraim 1852-1911 *DcAmB,*
NatCAB 33, WhAm 1
Brown, Alexander Timothy 1854-1929
NatCAB 14, NatCAB 35
Brown, Alfred Hodgdon 1871-1936 *NatCAB 27,*

WhAm 5
Brown, Alfred Seely 1906-1968 *WhAm 5*
Brown, Alice *NewYHSD*
Brown, Alice 1856-1948 *NotAW*
Brown, Alice 1857-1948 *NatCAB 15,*
TwCBDA, WhAm 2
Brown, Alice 1887- *WomWWA 14*
Brown, Alice Barlow 1869- *WomWWA 14*
Brown, Alice Cooke 1913-1974 *WhAm 6*
Brown, Alice Crawford *WomWWA 14*
Brown, Alice Margaret 1865- *WomWWA 14*
Brown, Alice VanVechten 1862-1949 *BiDAmEd,*
NotAW, WhAm 2, WomWWA 14
Brown, Allan Danvers 1843-1904 *NatCAB 18,*
TwCBDA
Brown, Alvin 1893-1972 *WhAm 5*
Brown, Amanda Elizabeth 1837-1918 *WhAm 1*
Brown, Ames 1892-1947 *NatCAB 36,*
WhAm 2
Brown, Ames Thorndike 1890-1961 *WhAm 4*
Brown, Amos Peaslee 1864-1917 *WhAm 1*
Brown, Andrew 1744?-1797 *ApCAB, Drake*
Brown, Ann Mary Marothy 1900-1968 *WhAm 5*
Brown, Anna C 1875- *WomWWA 14*
Brown, Anna Smith 1866- *WomWWA 14*
Brown, Anson 1800-1840 *BiAUS, BiDrAC,*
WhAm H
Brown, Anson Lee 1893-1954 *NatCAB 47*
Brown, Antoinette L 1825-1921 *AmBi, ApCAB,*
DcAmB, Drake, NotAW
Brown, Archer 1851-1904 *NatCAB 15*
Brown, Archer 1857-1904 *WhAm 1*
Brown, Archer Hitchcock 1882-1929
NatCAB 22
Brown, Archibald Manning 1881-1956
NatCAB 45, WhAm 3
Brown, Archie Lee 1884-1953 *NatCAB 42*
Brown, Arlo Ayres 1883-1961 *WhAm 4*
Brown, Armstead 1875-1951 *NatCAB 39,*
WhAm 4
Brown, Arthur *NewYHSD*
Brown, Arthur 1843-1906 *BiDrAC,*
NatCAB 13, TwCBDA, WhAm 1
Brown, Arthur, Jr. 1874-1957 *NatCAB 44,*
WhAm 3
Brown, Arthur Charles Lewis 1869-1946
WhAm 2
Brown, Arthur Edward 1876-1940 *WhAm 1*
Brown, Arthur Erwin 1850-1910 *WhAm 1*
Brown, Arthur Francis 1890-1969 *NatCAB 57*
Brown, Arthur Judson 1856-1963 *NatCAB 48,*
WhAm 4
Brown, Arthur Lewis 1854-1928 *TwCBDA,*
WhAm 1
Brown, Arthur McKimmon 1867- *WhoColR*
Brown, Arthur Morton 1877-1949 *WhAm 3*
Brown, Arthur Newton 1857- *TwCBDA*
Brown, Arthur Voorhees 1863-1949 *NatCAB 37,*
WhAm 2
Brown, Arthur William 1881-1960 *WhAm 4*
Brown, Arthur Winton 1873-1958 *NatCAB 46,*
WhAm 3
Brown, Ashmun 1872-1948 *WhAm 2*
Brown, B Gratz 1826-1885 *BiAUS, Drake,*
NatCAB 20
Brown, B Gratz *see also* Brown, Benjamin Gratz
Brown, Bailey LeFevre 1903-1971 *NatCAB 56*
Brown, Barnum 1873-1963 *NatCAB 51,*
WhAm 4
Brown, Bartholomew 1772-1854 *ApCAB,*
Drake, TwCBDA
Brown, Baxter Lamont 1864- *WhAm 3*
Brown, Bedford 1791-1871 *NatCAB 9*
Brown, Bedford 1792-1870 *DcAmB*
Brown, Bedford 1795-1870 *ApCAB, BiAUS,*
BiDrAC, TwCBDA, WhAm H, WhAmP
Brown, Bedford 1825- *NatCAB 5*
Brown, Benjamin *NewYHSD*
Brown, Benjamin 1756-1831 *BiAUS, BiDrAC,*
WhAm H
Brown, Benjamin Arthur 1891-1963
NatCAB 50
Brown, Benjamin Beuhring 1893-1949
NatCAB 38, WhAm 2
Brown, Benjamin Chambers 1865-1942
IIBEAAW, WhAm 1
Brown, Benjamin Franklin 1849-1922
NatCAB 19

Brown, Benjamin Gratz 1826-1885 *AmBi,*
ApCAB, BiDrAC, DcAmB, McGEWB,
NatCAB 12, TwCBDA, WebAB,
WhAm H, WhAmP
Brown, Benjamin Gratz *see also* Brown, B Gratz
Brown, Benjamin H *NewYHSD*
Brown, Benjamin Henry Inness 1879-1957
WhAm 3
Brown, Bernard 1908-1951 *WhAm 3*
Brown, Bertha Millard 1870- *WomWWA 14*
Brown, Bolton 1864-1936 *NatCAB 27,*
WhAm 1
Brown, Brian 1881- *WhAm 6*
Brown, Buckminster 1819-1891 *ApCAB,*
NatCAB 17, TwCBDA
Brown, Buford Mason 1909-1966 *WhAm 4*
Brown, Burdette Boardman 1871- *WhAm 5*
Brown, C Foster, Jr. 1917-1965 *NatCAB 52,*
WhAm 4
Brown, Calvin Luther 1854-1923 *NatCAB 18,*
WhAm 1
Brown, Calvin Scott 1859- *WhoColR*
Brown, Calvin Smith 1866-1945 *WhAm 2*
Brown, Carleton 1869-1941 *DcAmB S3,*
NatCAB 31, WhAm 1
Brown, Caroline *WomWWA 14*
Brown, Carrie Pfeiffer 1886- *WomWWA 14*
Brown, Carroll Neide 1869-1938 *AmBi*
Brown, Catharine 1800?-1823 *ApCAB, Drake*
Brown, Caxton 1879-1952 *WhAm 3*
Brown, Cecil Kenneth 1900-1957 *WhAm 3*
Brown, Chad 1600?-1665? *ApCAB, Drake,*
NatCAB 11, TwCBDA
Brown, Chad *see also* Browne, Chad
Brown, Chadd 1600?-1665? *TwCBDA*
Brown, Charles 1797-1883 *BiAUS, BiDrAC,*
WhAm H
Brown, Charles 1825?- *NewYHSD*
Brown, Charles Albert 1858-1938 *NatCAB 28*
Brown, Charles Allen 1872-1939 *WhAm 1*
Brown, Charles Alonzo 1882-1955 *NatCAB 45*
Brown, Charles Augustus 1873-1929 *ApCAB X,*
NatCAB 23
Brown, Charles Brockden 1771-1810 *AmBi,*
ApCAB, DcAmB, Drake, McGEWB,
NatCAB 7, TwCBDA, WebAB,
WhAm H
Brown, Charles Carroll 1856-1949 *WhAm 2*
Brown, Charles Edward 1866-1945 *NatCAB 34*
Brown, Charles Edward 1872-1946 *WhAm 2*
Brown, Charles Edward, Jr. 1894-1949
NatCAB 44
Brown, Charles Elwood 1834-1904 *BiDrAC*
Brown, Charles F *NewYHSD*
Brown, Charles Francis 1844-1929 *WhAm 1*
Brown, Charles Frederick 1856-1944
NatCAB 33
Brown, Charles H 1858-1933 *WhAm 1*
Brown, Charles Harrison 1920- *BiDrAC*
Brown, Charles Harry 1917-1966 *NatCAB 53*
Brown, Charles Harvey 1875-1960 *DcAmLiB,*
NatCAB 46, WhAm 3
Brown, Charles Henry 1865- *NatCAB 8*
Brown, Charles Ira 1861-1917 *WhAm 1*
Brown, Charles Irwin 1853-1899 *WhAm 1*
Brown, Charles Kenneth 1893-1944 *NatCAB 33*
Brown, Charles Leonard 1899-1959 *NatCAB 47,*
WhAm 3
Brown, Charles McDonald 1892-1945
NatCAB 35
Brown, Charles Reynolds 1862-1950 *DcAmB S4,*
NatCAB 39, WhAm 3
Brown, Charles Rufus 1849-1914 *DcAmB,*
WhAm 1
Brown, Charles Seamans 1885-1953
NatCAB 44
Brown, Charles Sumner 1860-1926 *WhAm 1*
Brown, Charles Walter 1866-1934 *WhAm 1*
Brown, Charles William 1858-1928 *ApCAB X,*
WhAm 1
Brown, Charles Wilson 1874- *WhAm 5*
Brown, Charlotte Amanda Blake 1846-1904
NotAW
Brown, Charlotte Emerson 1838-1895 *AmWom,*
DcAmB, WhAm H
Brown, Charlotte Harding 1873-1951 *WhAm 3,*
WomWWA 14
Brown, Charlotte Hawkins 1883-1961 *BiDAmEd,*

WhoColR
Brown, Christian Henry 1857- *WhAm 1*
Brown, Clara Maud *BiDAmEd*
Brown, Clarence Archie 1860-1917 *NatCAB 17*
Brown, Clarence J 1893-1965 *BiDrAC*
Brown, Clarence J 1895-1965 *WhAm 4*
Brown, Clarence J, Jr. 1927- *BiDrAC*
Brown, Clarence Montgomery 1868-1958
NatCAB 52, WhAm 3
Brown, Clarence William 1902-1971
NatCAB 57
Brown, Clark d1817 *Drake*
Brown, Claude *NewYHSD*
Brown, Claude Oliver 1891-1954 *NatCAB 41*
Brown, Cleon Whitemarch 1884- *WhoColR*
Brown, Clyde 1873-1932 *WhAm 1*
Brown, Colvin W 1888-1952 *WhAm 3*
Brown, Corinne Stubbs 1849- *AmWom*
Brown, Cornelia B Officer 1876-
WomWWA 14
Brown, Cornelia E *WomWWA 14*
Brown, Crawford F *NewYHSD*
Brown, Curtis 1866-1945 *WhAm 2*
Brown, Cyrus Jay 1875- *WhAm 5*
Brown, Cyrus Perrin 1868-1945 *WhAm 3*
Brown, D J 1882-1955 *WhAm 3*
Brown, Daniel Russell 1848-1919 *ApCAB X,*
NatCAB 9, TwCBDA, WhAm 1
Brown, David *NewYHSD*
Brown, David d1873 *ApCAB*
Brown, David 1806?-1829 *ApCAB, Drake*
Brown, David 1830?- *NewYHSD*
Brown, David Abraham 1875- *WhAm 5*
Brown, David Chester 1863-1943 *WhAm 2*
Brown, David L *NewYHSD*
Brown, David Paul 1795-1872 *ApCAB, DcAmB,*
Drake, NatCAB 3, TwCBDA, WhAm H
Brown, Dee 1908- *REnAW*
Brown, Demarchus Clariton 1857-1926
NatCAB 18, WhAm 1
Brown, Demetra Kenneth 1877- *WomWWA 14*
Brown, Demetra Vaka d1946 *WhAm 2*
Brown, Dewees E 1898-1959 *NatCAB 50*
Brown, Dickson Queen 1873- *NatCAB 14*
Brown, Don 1899- *IlBEAAW*
Brown, Donald C d1954 *WhAm 3*
Brown, Donald Lamont 1890-1940 *WhAm 1*
Brown, Donald Lee 1900-1966 *WhAm 4*
Brown, Donaldson 1885-1965 *WhAm 4*
Brown, Dorothy Woodhead 1899- *IlBEAAW*
Brown, Downing P 1887-1954 *WhAm 3*
Brown, Dudley B W 1908-1975 *WhAm 6*
Brown, Dyer Date Stanley 1819-1887
NatCAB 4
Brown, Earl Theodore 1890-1959 *WhAm 3*
Brown, Earle Godfrey 1887-1962 *WhAm 4*
Brown, Ebenezer 1795-1889 *DcAmB,*
WhAm H
Brown, Edgar 1871- *WhAm 5*
Brown, Edith 1874- *WhAm 5*
Brown, Edmund *NewYHSD*
Brown, Edna Adelaide 1875-1944 *WhAm 2*
Brown, Edward 1814-1895 *TwCBDA*
Brown, Edward 1835?- *NewYHSD*
Brown, Edward Eagle 1885-1959 *NatCAB 47,*
WhAm 3
Brown, Edward Fisher 1889-1973 *WhAm 6*
Brown, Edward G 1877- *WhoColR*
Brown, Edward Hall 1861- *WhoColR*
Brown, Edward Killoran 1905-1951 *WhAm 3*
Brown, Edward Lee 1864- *WhAm 4*
Brown, Edward Miles 1854- *WhAm 4*
Brown, Edward Milton 1869-1936 *NatCAB 29*
Brown, Edward Nonphlet 1862-1956
NatCAB 18
Brown, Edward Norphlet 1862-1956
NatCAB 42, WhAm 3
Brown, Edward Osgood 1847-1923 *WhAm 1*
Brown, Edward Scott 1876-1942 *WhAm 2*
Brown, Edward Vail Lapham 1876- *WhAm 5*
Brown, Edwin Franklin 1862- *NatCAB 14*
Brown, Edwin H 1851-1930 *ApCAB X*
Brown, Edwin Hacker 1875-1930 *NatCAB 24,*
WhAm 1
Brown, Edwin Merriman 1855-1935
NatCAB 26
Brown, Edwin Perkins 1868-1934 *ApCAB X,*
WhAm 1

Brown, Edwin Pierce 1903-1972 *WhAm 5*
Brown, Edwin Putnam 1869-1934 *WhAm 1*
Brown, Edwy Rolfe 1868-1942 *NatCAB 33,*
WhAm 1
Brown, Egbert Benson 1816- *ApCAB,*
TwCBDA
Brown, Elena Rhodes *WomWWA 14*
Brown, Eli Huston, Jr. 1875-1945 *WhAm 2*
Brown, Elias 1793-1857 *BiAUS, BiDrAC,*
WhAm H
Brown, Elijah Alexander 1857-1926 *NatCAB 21*
Brown, Eliphalet M, Jr. 1816-1886 *NewYHSD,*
WhAm H
Brown, Elisha Rhodes 1847-1922 *ApCAB X*
Brown, Elizabeth Leiper 1880- *WomWWA 14*
Brown, Elizabeth Stow 1860- *WomWWA 14*
Brown, Ellen W Babcock 1851- *WomWWA 14*
Brown, Elliot Chipman 1882-1946 *NatCAB 35*
Brown, Elliott Foss 1916-1959 *NatCAB 47*
Brown, Elliott Wilber 1859-1941 *WhAm 1*
Brown, Elmer d1968 *WhAm 5*
Brown, Elmer Ellsworth 1861-1934 *AmBi,*
BiDAmEd, DcAmB S1, NatCAB 14,
NatCAB 28, WhAm 1
Brown, Elon Rouse 1857- *WhAm 4*
Brown, Elzear Joseph 1900-1968 *WhAm 5*
Brown, Emilie Ward 1886- *WomWWA 14*
Brown, Emily Lynch *BiCAW*
Brown, Emma Elizabeth 1847- *AmWom,*
WhAm 4, WomWWA 14
Brown, Emma Kate 1865- *WomWWA 14*
Brown, Enoch 1892-1960 *WhAm 4*
Brown, Ephraim *NewYHSD*
Brown, Eric Gore d1964 *WhAm 4*
Brown, Ernest G 1896-1974 *WhAm 6*
Brown, Ernest S 1903-1965 *BiDrAC*
Brown, Ernest William 1866-1938 *DcAmB S2,*
DcScB, NatCAB 15, WhAm 1
Brown, Estelle Aubrey d1958 *WhAm 3*
Brown, Ethan Allen 1766-1852 *DcAmB,*
NatCAB 3, WhAm H
Brown, Ethan Allen 1776-1852 *ApCAB,*
BiAUS, BiDrAC, Drake, TwCBDA,
WhAmP
Brown, Ethel Pennewill *WomWWA 14*
Brown, Eva Robert Ingersoll 1863-1928
ApCAB X, WomWWA 14
Brown, Everett Chase 1863-1937 *NatCAB 28,*
WhAm 1
Brown, Everett J 1876-1947 *WhAm 2*
Brown, F H *NewYHSD*
Brown, Fanny Burton Hurd *WomWWA 14*
Brown, Fay 1881- *WhAm 6*
Brown, Fayette 1823-1910 *DcAmB,*
NatCAB 16, WhAm 1
Brown, Fayette 1881-1953 *WhAm 3*
Brown, Fletcher 1850-1912 *TwCBDA,*
WhAm 3
Brown, Florence M *WomWWA 14*
Brown, Floy Clare 1860- *WomWWA 14*
Brown, Foster Vincent 1852-1937 *BiDrAC*
Brown, Foster Vincent 1854-1937 *TwCBDA,*
WhAm 4
Brown, Frances Guion 1866- *WomWWA 14*
Brown, Francis 1784-1820 *ApCAB, DcAmB,*
NatCAB 9, WhAm H
Brown, Francis 1849-1916 *AmBi, ApCAB Sup,*
DcAmB, NatCAB 14, NatCAB 42,
TwCBDA, WhAm 1
Brown, Francis Cabell 1902-1966 *NatCAB 53,*
WhAm 4
Brown, Francis Henry 1835-1917 *WhAm 1*
Brown, Francis James 1894-1959 *WhAm 1*
Brown, Francis Shunk 1858-1940 *WhAm 1*
Brown, Francis Wiley 1884-1955 *NatCAB 43*
Brown, Frank 1846-1920 *NatCAB 9,*
TwCBDA, WhAm 1
Brown, Frank Chilton 1890-1955 *WhAm 3*
Brown, Frank Chouteau 1876-1947 *WhAm 2*
Brown, Frank Clyde 1870-1943 *WhAm 2*
Brown, Frank Collins 1875- *WomWWA 14*
Brown, Frank E 1882-1959 *WhAm 3*
Brown, Frank Herbert 1854-1928 *NatCAB 23*
Brown, Frank Hite 1910-1965 *NatCAB 53*
Brown, Frank James 1868- *WhoColR*
Brown, Frank Lampson 1860-1918 *NatCAB 18*
Brown, Frank Llewellyn 1862-1922 *WhAm 1*
Brown, Frank Xavier 1914-1968 *WhAm 5*

Brown, Franklin Quimby 1862-1955
NatCAB 44, WhAm 3
Brown, Franklin Reed 1885-1970 *NatCAB 56*
Brown, Franklin Stewart 1909-1970 *WhAm 5*
Brown, Fred 1902-1974 *WhAm 6*
Brown, Fred Comings 1884-1955 *NatCAB 43,
WhAm 4*
Brown, Fred Herbert 1879-1955 *BiDrAC,
WhAm 3, WhAmP*
Brown, Frederic Alden 1851- *NatCAB 5*
Brown, Frederic Kenyon 1882-1935 *WhAm 1*
Brown, Frederic L 1878- *WhAm 6*
Brown, Frederic Tilden 1853-1910 *DcAmB*
Brown, Frederick Anson 1867-1939 *WhAm 1*
Brown, Frederick Harvey 1842-1911
NatCAB 13
Brown, Frederick Harvey 1843-1911 *WhAm 1*
Brown, Frederick Ronald 1890- *WhAm 6*
Brown, Frederick Walworth 1875- *WhAm 5*
Brown, Frederick William 1872-1947 *WhAm 4*
Brown, Frederick Winfield 1908-1970 *WhAm 5*
Brown, Fredric 1906-1972 *WhAm 5*
Brown, G *NewYHSD*
Brown, G B *NewYHSD*
Brown, Garry Eldridge 1923- *BiDrAC*
Brown, George *BiAUS, NewYHSD*
Brown, George 1787-1859 *ApCAB, DcAmB,
NatCAB 1, WhAm H*
Brown, George 1818-1880 *ApCAB, McGEWB*
Brown, George 1823-1892 *DcAmB, WhAm H*
Brown, George 1835-1913 *ApCAB, TwCBDA,
WhAm H*
Brown, George 1850- *NewYHSD*
Brown, George Artemas 1858- *NatCAB 16*
Brown, George Edward, Jr. 1920- *BiDrAC*
Brown, George Francis 1843-1910 *WhAm 1*
Brown, George Garvin 1846-1917 *NatCAB 17*
Brown, George Garvin 1912-1969 *NatCAB 54,
WhAm 5*
Brown, George Granger 1896-1957 *NatCAB 43,
WhAm 3*
Brown, George H 1850-1936 *WhAm 1*
Brown, George Henry 1877- *WhoColR*
Brown, George Houston 1810-1865 *BiAUS,
BiDrAC, WhAm H*
Brown, George Lincoln 1869-1950 *WhAm 1*
Brown, George Loring 1814-1889 *AmBi,
ApCAB, BnEnAmA, Drake, NatCAB 7,
NewYHSD, TwCBDA, WhAm H*
Brown, George M 1864- *WhAm 1*
Brown, George Marion 1865-1942 *WhAm 2*
Brown, George Newland 1859- *WhAm 4*
Brown, George Pliny 1836-1910 *DcAmB,
WhAm 1*
Brown, George Ransom 1840-1916 *NatCAB 17*
Brown, George Rothwell d1960 *WhAm 4*
Brown, George Rowland, III 1867- *WhAm 5*
Brown, George S 1834-1890 *NatCAB 1*
Brown, George Samson 1865-1943 *WhAm 2*
Brown, George Scratchley 1918- *WebAMB*
Brown, George Stewart 1871-1934 *WhAm 2*
Brown, George Stewart 1871-1941 *WhAm 1*
Brown, George Stewart 1906-1957 *WhAm 3*
Brown, George Tilden 1848-1934 *NatCAB 24,
WhAm 4*
Brown, George VanIngen 1862-1948 *ApCAB X,
WhAm 2*
Brown, George W 1859-1906 *WhAm 1*
Brown, George Warren 1853-1921 *NatCAB 7,
NatCAB 12, NatCAB 26, WhAm 1*
Brown, George Washington 1841-1928
ApCAB X, NatCAB 15, WhAm 1
Brown, George William 1812-1890 *ApCAB Sup,
DcAmB, WhAm H, WhAmP*
Brown, George William 1815-1890 *TwCBDA*
Brown, George William 1888-1947 *WhAm 2*
Brown, George Woodford 1868- *WhAm 5*
Brown, Gertrude Foster 1867- *WhAm 4,
WomWWA 14*
Brown, Gideon Washington 1877- *WhoColR*
Brown, Gilmor d1960 *WhAm 3*
Brown, Glen David 1891-1957 *WhAm 3*
Brown, Glenn 1854-1932 *WhAm 1*
Brown, Godwin Moore 1869-1944 *NatCAB 34*
Brown, Goold 1791-1857 *ApCAB, BiDAmEd,
DcAmB, Drake, NatCAB 8, TwCBDA,
WhAm H*
Brown, Grace Mann 1859- *WhAm 4,*

WomWWA 14
Brown, Grafton T *NewYHSD*
Brown, Grafton Tyler 1841-1918 *IlBEAAW*
Brown, Grant Gratz 1875- *WhoColR*
Brown, Greeley Amos 1890-1945 *NatCAB 35*
Brown, Grover Charles 1883-1956 *NatCAB 43*
Brown, Guy Carlton 1885-1931 *NatCAB 24*
Brown, H Beattie 1862-1937 *NatCAB 28*
Brown, H E *NewYHSD*
Brown, H Harris 1864-1948 *IlBEAAW*
Brown, H I *NewYHSD*
Brown, H Martin 1850- *ApCAB X*
Brown, Hallie Quinn 1850-1949 *BiDAmEd,
NotAW, WhoColR*
Brown, Harold 1863-1900 *NatCAB 37*
Brown, Harold Eugene 1917-1972 *WhAm 6*
Brown, Harold Haven 1869-1932 *WhAm 1*
Brown, Harriet A 1844- *AmWom*
Brown, Harriet Chedie Connor 1872-
WomWWA 14
Brown, Harriet Johnson 1869- *WomWWA 14*
Brown, Harrison B 1831-1915 *NewYHSD*
Brown, Harry Abed 1877-1957 *NatCAB 47*
Brown, Harry Alvin 1879-1949 *NatCAB 38,
WhAm 6*
Brown, Harry B 1876-1962 *WhAm 4*
Brown, Harry Elmer 1872-1944 *NatCAB 36*
Brown, Harry Fletcher 1867-1944 *WhAm 2*
Brown, Harry Gunnison 1880-1975 *WhAm 6*
Brown, Harry James 1908- *EncAAH*
Brown, Harry Joe 1893-1972 *WhAm 5*
Brown, Harry Merrill 1914-1948 *NatCAB 39*
Brown, Harry Philip 1887-1951 *NatCAB 39*
Brown, Harry Sanford 1881-1950 *WhAm 2A*
Brown, Harvey 1795-1874 *ApCAB, Drake,
TwCBDA*
Brown, Harvey H, Jr. 1892- *WhAm 3*
Brown, Hattie 1861- *WomWWA 14*
Brown, Helen Dawes 1857-1941 *WhAm 1,
WomWWA 14*
Brown, Helen Gager 1878- *WomWWA 14*
Brown, Helen Gilman 1867-1942 *WhAm 2*
Brown, Helen Gilman Noyes 1868- *BiCAW*
Brown, Helen Hayes 1900- *WebAB*
Brown, Henry Armitt 1844-1879 *ApCAB,
TwCBDA*
Brown, Henry B *NewYHSD*
Brown, Henry B 1831-1860 *ApCAB*
Brown, Henry B 1847-1917 *WhAm 1*
Brown, Henry Bascom 1833-1916 *WhAm 1*
Brown, Henry Billings 1836-1913 *ApCAB,
DcAmB, NatCAB 1, TwCBDA, WebAB,
WhAm 1*
Brown, Henry Box 1831-1915 *IlBEAAW*
Brown, Henry Collins 1863-1961 *WhAm 4*
Brown, Henry Cordis 1820-1906 *DcAmB*
Brown, Henry Cordis 1820-1909 *NatCAB 16*
Brown, Henry Currier 1849-1927 *NatCAB 22*
Brown, Henry Daniels 1910-1970 *NatCAB 56,
WhAm 5*
Brown, Henry Francis 1837-1912 *NatCAB 16*
Brown, Henry Harrison 1840-1918 *WhAm 1*
Brown, Henry James 1811-1855 *NewYHSD*
Brown, Henry Kirke 1814-1886 *AmBi, ApCAB,
BiAUS, BnEnAmA, DcAmB, Drake,
NatCAB 1, NewYHSD, TwCBDA,
WhAm H*
Brown, Henry Martin 1850-1926 *NatCAB 12,
WhAm 1*
Brown, Henry Matthias 1867- *WhAm 5*
Brown, Henry Newton 1857-1884 *REnAW*
Brown, Henry Paul, Jr. 1888-1955 *NatCAB 43*
Brown, Henry S 1793-1834 *NatCAB 4*
Brown, Henry Seabury 1891-1966 *NatCAB 51*
Brown, Henry Seymour 1865-1966 *WhAm 4*
Brown, Herbert Daniel 1870-1963 *WhAm 4,
WhAm 5*
Brown, Herbert J 1861-1945 *WhAm 2*
Brown, Herbert Rutherford 1877-1954
NatCAB 41
Brown, Herman 1892-1962 *WhAm 4*
Brown, Hilton Ultimus 1859-1958 *NatCAB 18,
WhAm 3*
Brown, Hiram Chellis 1844- *WhAm 4*
Brown, Hiram Staunton 1882-1950 *WhAm 3*
Brown, Holcombe James 1879-1951 *WhAm 3*
Brown, Homer Caffee 1893-1950 *WhAm 3*

Brown, Horace 1876-1949 *NatCAB 37*
Brown, Horace Manchester 1857-1929 *WhAm 1*
Brown, Horatio Alford 1881-1943 *NatCAB 36*
Brown, Howard Benner 1903-1960 *WhAm 4*
Brown, Howard Junior 1924-1975 *WhAm 6*
Brown, Howard Nicholson 1849-1932 *WhAm 1*
Brown, Howell Chambers 1880-1954 *IlBEAAW*
Brown, Hugh Auchincloss d1975 *WhAm 6*
Brown, Hugh B 1883-1975 *WhAm 6*
Brown, Hugh Elmer 1881-1952 *NatCAB 41,
WhAm 3*
Brown, Hugh Henry 1872- *WhAm 1*
Brown, Hugh Stewart 1896-1961 *NatCAB 52,
WhAm 4*
Brown, Hulda Holmes Bergen 1851-
WomWWA 14
Brown, Inez *WomWWA 14*
Brown, Irving 1822-1897 *WebAB*
Brown, Isaac Brownell 1848- *NatCAB 14*
Brown, Isaac Eddy 1849-1917 *WhAm 1*
Brown, Isaac VanArsdale 1784-1861 *ApCAB,
DcAmB, TwCBDA, WhAm H*
Brown, Israel 1873-1928 *NatCAB 22*
Brown, Ivor John Carnegie 1891-1974 *WhAm 6*
Brown, J *BnEnAmA, NewYHSD*
Brown, J Appleton 1844-1902 *ApCAB,
TwCBDA, WhAm 1*
Brown, J Appleton *see also* Brown, John Appleton
Brown, J Earle 1877-1944 *NatCAB 35*
Brown, J Romaine 1833-1924 *NatCAB 24*
Brown, J Sinclair 1880-1965 *NatCAB 51*
Brown, Jacob Hay 1849-1930 *NatCAB 38,
WhAm 1*
Brown, Jacob Jennings 1775-1828 *AmBi,
ApCAB, BiAUS, DcAmB, Drake,
NatCAB 5, TwCBDA, WebAB,
WebAMB, WhAm H*
Brown, James 1666-1732 *ApCAB, TwCBDA*
Brown, James 1698-1739 *ApCAB, TwCBDA*
Brown, James 1766-1835 *ApCAB, BiAUS,
DcAmB, Drake, NatCAB 4, TwCBDA,
WhAm H, WhAmP*
Brown, James 1776-1835 *BiDrAC*
Brown, James 1791-1877 *ApCAB, DcAmB,
WhAm H*
Brown, James 1800-1855 *ApCAB, DcAmB,
NatCAB 5, TwCBDA, WhAm H*
Brown, James 1820?- *NewYHSD*
Brown, James 1858-1936 *WhAm 1*
Brown, James 1863-1935 *NatCAB 31,
WhAm 1*
Brown, James 1933- *WebAB*
Brown, James Allen 1821-1882 *ApCAB Sup*
Brown, James B 1872-1940 *WhAm 1*
Brown, James Barrett 1899-1971 *NatCAB 57,
WhAm 5*
Brown, James Cauldwell 1815-1862 *ApCAB,
TwCBDA*
Brown, James Dorsey, Jr. 1906-1958 *WhAm 3*
Brown, James Dowling 1902-1960 *NatCAB 49*
Brown, James Edgar 1865- *NatCAB 16*
Brown, James Elwyn 1873-1932 *NatCAB 25*
Brown, James Elwyn, Jr. 1902-1964 *WhAm 4*
Brown, James F 1890-1948 *WhAm 3*
Brown, James Frederick 1852-1921 *NatCAB 19,
WhAm 1*
Brown, James Greenlief 1880-1954 *NatCAB 44,
WhAm 3*
Brown, James Harvey 1836- *NatCAB 3*
Brown, James Henry 1859- *WhAm 4*
Brown, James Muncaster 1820-1890 *NatCAB 8*
Brown, James R 1863-1931 *WhAm 1*
Brown, James Salisbury 1802-1879 *DcAmB,
NatCAB 11, WhAm H*
Brown, James Sidney 1820-1893 *TwCBDA*
Brown, James Spencer 1863-1934 *NatCAB 26*
Brown, James Sproat 1824-1878 *BiAUS,
BiDrAC, WhAm H*
Brown, James Stanley 1863-1939 *WhAm 1*
Brown, James Thomas 1871-1957 *WhAm 3*
Brown, James W *NewYHSD*
Brown, James W 1838?- *NewYHSD*
Brown, James W 1844-1909 *ApCAB X,
BiDrAC*
Brown, James Walter 1872- *WhoColR*
Brown, James Wright 1873-1959 *WhAm 3*
Brown, James Wright, Jr. 1902-1970 *WhAm 5*
Brown, Jason Brevoort 1839-1898 *BiDrAC,*

TwCBDA, WhAmP

Brown, Jeanette Ferris 1867- *WomWWA 14*

Brown, Jennie R 1862- *WomWWA 14*

Brown, Jeremiah 1776-1848 *BiAUS*

Brown, Jeremiah 1785-1858 *BiDrAC, WhAm H*

Brown, Jerome Hofmayer 1893-1957 *NatCAB 45*

Brown, Jessica Christian 1875- *WomWWA 14*

Brown, Joe Evan 1892-1973 *WhAm 5*

Brown, Joel Bascom 1872- *WhAm 5*

Brown, John *NewYHSD*

Brown, John d1815 *BiAUS, BiDrAC, WhAm H*

Brown, John 1630?-1706? *ApCAB, TwCBDA*

Brown, John 1735-1788 *BiHiMed*

Brown, John 1736-1803 *ApCAB, ApCAB X, BiAUS, BiDrAC, DcAmB, Drake, TwCBDA, WhAm H*

Brown, John 1736-1828 *NatCAB 8*

Brown, John 1744-1780 *AmBi, ApCAB, DcAmB, Drake, NatCAB 1, TwCBDA, WhAm H*

Brown, John 1757-1837 *ApCAB, BiAUS, BiDrAC, DcAmB, Drake, NatCAB 6, TwCBDA, WhAm H, WhAmP*

Brown, John 1763-1842 *ApCAB, NatCAB 9, TwCBDA*

Brown, John 1771-1850 *ApCAB*

Brown, John 1772-1845 *BiAUS, BiDrAC, WhAm H*

Brown, John 1791-1884 *ApCAB, NatCAB 6, TwCBDA*

Brown, John 1800-1859 *AmBi, ApCAB, DcAmB, Drake, EncAAH, EncAB, McGEWB, NatCAB 2, REnAW, TwCBDA, WebAB, WhAm H, WhAmP*

Brown, John 1810-1882 *BiHiMed*

Brown, John 1837?- *NewYHSD*

Brown, John 1839?- *NewYHSD*

Brown, John Albert 1885-1944 *NatCAB 33, WhAm 2*

Brown, John Alexander 1788-1872 *ApCAB, DcAmB, NatCAB 5, WhAm H*

Brown, John Aloysius 1876- *NatCAB 14*

Brown, John Appleton 1844-1902 *AmBi, DcAmB*

Brown, John Appleton *see also* Brown, J Appleton

Brown, John B 1807-1867 *ApCAB*

Brown, John Barker 1857-1923 *ApCAB X, NatCAB 38*

Brown, John Bernis 1893-1969 *WhAm 5*

Brown, John Brewer 1836-1898 *BiDrAC*

Brown, John C 1860-1915 *WhAm 1*

Brown, John Calvin 1827-1889 *ApCAB, BiAUS, BiDConf, DcAmB, NatCAB 7, TwCBDA, WhAm H*

Brown, John Carter 1797-1874 *AmBi, ApCAB, DcAmB, NatCAB 11, TwCBDA, WhAm H*

Brown, John Crosby 1838-1909 *NatCAB 15, WhAm 1*

Brown, John Edwin 1864-1966 *NatCAB 53*

Brown, John Edwin, Jr. 1903-1958 *NatCAB 44*

Brown, John Elward 1879-1957 *WhAm 3*

Brown, John Franklin 1865-1940 *WhAm 1*

Brown, John George 1831-1913 *AmBi, ApCAB, DcAmB, NatCAB 10, NewYHSD, TwCBDA, WhAm 1*

Brown, John Gordon 1827- *ApCAB*

Brown, John Griest 1879-1941 *WhAm 2*

Brown, John Hamilton 1837- *NatCAB 4, WhAm 4*

Brown, John Hamilton 1898-1947 *NatCAB 34*

Brown, John Hammond 1877-1955 *WhAm 3*

Brown, John Henry 1818-1891 *NewYHSD, WhAm H*

Brown, John Henry 1820- *NatCAB 4, TwCBDA*

Brown, John Henry 1859- *WhoColR*

Brown, John Henry Hobart 1831-1888 *ApCAB, NatCAB 12, TwCBDA*

Brown, John Herbert, Jr. 1891-1963 *WhAm 4*

Brown, John Howard 1840-1917 *NatCAB 34, TwCBDA, WhAm 1*

Brown, John Jackson 1820-1891 *NatCAB 2, TwCBDA*

Brown, John Jacob 1873-1946 *WhAm 2*

Brown, John K 1832- *TwCBDA*

Brown, John Mackenzie 1878-1955 *WhAm 3*

Brown, John Marshall 1838-1907 *WhAm 1*

Brown, John Mason *REnAW*

Brown, John Mason 1837-1890 *TwCBDA*

Brown, John Mifflin 1817-1893 *DcAmB, NatCAB 5, WhAm H*

Brown, John Newton 1803-1868 *ApCAB, DcAmB, Drake, WhAm H*

Brown, John Nicholas 1861-1900 *TwCBDA*

Brown, John Pinkney 1842-1915 *WhAm 1*

Brown, John Porter 1814-1872 *ApCAB, DcAmB, TwCBDA, WhAm H*

Brown, John R 1836?- *NewYHSD*

Brown, John Richard 1870-1926 *WhAm 1*

Brown, John Robert 1842-1927 *BiDrAC*

Brown, John Scruggs 1857-1934 *NatCAB 36*

Brown, John Sidney 1833-1913 *NatCAB 7, NatCAB 15*

Brown, John Sullivan 1825- *Drake*

Brown, John Thompson 1882-1953 *NatCAB 39, WhAm 3*

Brown, John Vallance 1868-1926 *WhAm 1*

Brown, John W 1796-1875 *BiDrAC, WhAm H*

Brown, John W 1797?-1875 *BiAUS*

Brown, John W 1814-1849 *Drake*

Brown, John Wesley 1837-1900 *NatCAB 8*

Brown, John Wing 1852-1914 *NatCAB 16*

Brown, John Young 1835-1904 *BiAUS, BiDrAC, DcAmB, NatCAB 1, NatCAB 13, TwCBDA, WhAm 1, WhAmP*

Brown, John Young 1865-1919 *WhAm 1*

Brown, John Young 1900- *BiDrAC*

Brown, Jonas Bond 1795-1835 *NatCAB 20*

Brown, Joseph 1733-1785 *ApCAB, DcAmB, NatCAB 8, TwCBDA, WhAm H*

Brown, Joseph 1773-1862 *NatCAB 4*

Brown, Joseph 1880- *WhAm 6*

Brown, Joseph Alleine 1874- *WhAm 5*

Brown, Joseph Brownlee 1824-1888 *TwCBDA*

Brown, Joseph Clement 1845-1928 *NatCAB 21*

Brown, Joseph Clifton 1879-1945 *WhAm 2*

Brown, Joseph Eckford 1905-1958 *WhAm 3*

Brown, Joseph Edgar 1880-1939 *BiDrAC*

Brown, Joseph Emerson 1821-1894 *AmBi, ApCAB, BiAUS, BiDConf, BiDrAC, DcAmB, McGEWB, NatCAB 1, TwCBDA, WhAm H, WhAmP*

Brown, Joseph Gill 1854-1927 *WhAm 1*

Brown, Joseph Grant 1869-1967 *NatCAB 54*

Brown, Joseph Henry 1810-1886 *ApCAB Sup*

Brown, Joseph Mackey 1851-1931 *WhAm 1*

Brown, Joseph Mackey 1851-1932 *NatCAB 33*

Brown, Joseph Newton 1832-1921 *NatCAB 19*

Brown, Joseph Real 1892-1961 *WhAm 4*

Brown, Joseph Rogers 1810-1876 *AmBi, DcAmB, NatCAB 10, WhAm H*

Brown, Joseph Willard 1839- *TwCBDA*

Brown, Josephine English 1855- *WomWWA 14*

Brown, Josie Mayer 1875- *WomWWA 14*

Brown, Julius L 1848-1910 *NatCAB 1, WhAm 1*

Brown, Junius Calvin 1886-1968 *WhAm 5*

Brown, Junius Flag 1828- *NatCAB 7*

Brown, Justus Morris 1840-1912 *WhAm 1*

Brown, Kate Louise 1857-1921 *WhAm 1, WomWWA 14*

Brown, Katharine Holland 1876-1931 *NatCAB 29, WhAm 1, WomWWA 14*

Brown, Kenneth 1868- *WhAm 4*

Brown, Kenneth Rent 1896-1958 *NatCAB 46, WhAm 3*

Brown, Larue 1883-1969 *WhAm 5*

Brown, Lathrop 1883-1959 *ApCAB X, BiDrAC, WhAm 3*

Brown, Laura Amanda 1852- *WomWWA 14*

Brown, Laurence *NewYHSD*

Brown, Lawrason 1871-1937 *DcAmB S2, NatCAB 28, WhAm 1*

Brown, Lawrence Palmer 1887-1949 *NatCAB 37*

Brown, Lee David 1921-1971 *NatCAB 56*

Brown, Lee Lowell 1879- *WhoColR*

Brown, Lee Nathan 1869-1948 *NatCAB 37*

Brown, Leigh A 1887-1959 *WhAm 3*

Brown, LeRoy Decatur 1848-1898 *BiDAmEd, NatCAB 24*

Brown, Leroy Sunderland 1852-1940 *NatCAB 29*

Brown, Leslie Warnick 1862-1941 *NatCAB 42*

Brown, Levant Frederick 1849- *WhAm 4*

Brown, Lew 1893-1958 *NatCAB 43*

Brown, Lew 1894-1958 *WhAm 3*

Brown, Lewis H 1894-1951 *WhAm 3*

Brown, Lewis Jenks 1855- *WhoColR*

Brown, Lewis John 1891-1940 *NatCAB 30*

Brown, Lloyd Arnold 1907-1966 *WhAm 4*

Brown, Lloyd Davidson 1892-1950 *WhAm 3*

Brown, Lloyd Thornton 1880-1961 *NatCAB 50*

Brown, Louis Myron 1896-1969 *NatCAB 55, WhAm 5*

Brown, Louise Fargo d1955 *WhAm 3*

Brown, Lucius 1846-1924 *WhAm 1*

Brown, Lucius Polk 1867-1935 *WhAm 1*

Brown, Lucy Hall d1907 *WhAm 1*

Brown, Luman Spencer 1855-1937 *NatCAB 27*

Brown, Lyndon Osmond 1902-1966 *WhAm 4*

Brown, Lytle 1872-1951 *WhAm 3*

Brown, M, Jr. *NewYHSD*

Brown, M Belle 1850- *AmWom, WhAm 5*

Brown, M E D *NewYHSD*

Brown, M Earle 1886-1936 *NatCAB 27*

Brown, Miss M P *NewYHSD*

Brown, Mack Clinton 1856- *WhoColR*

Brown, Manuel Nicholas 1910-1972 *WhAm 5*

Brown, Margaret Lesley Bush 1857- *WomWWA 14*

Brown, Margaret Wise 1910-1952 *DcAmB S5, WhAm 3*

Brown, Marguerite Manierre 1879- *WomWWA 14*

Brown, Marguerite Mullin 1874- *WomWWA 14*

Brown, Marianna 1852- *WomWWA 14*

Brown, Marianna Catharine *WomWWA 14*

Brown, Marion Martin 1884-1949 *NatCAB 43*

Brown, Mark Anthony 1889-1968 *NatCAB 54, WhAm 5*

Brown, Mark W 1876-1929 *NatCAB 22*

Brown, Marshall 1852- *WhAm 4*

Brown, Marshall Stewart 1870-1948 *NatCAB 36, WhAm 2*

Brown, Martha McClellan 1838-1916 *AmWom, NatCAB 27, NotAW, WhAm 1*

Brown, Martin Bartholomew 1838-1893 *NatCAB 8*

Brown, Martin S 1805?- *NewYHSD*

Brown, Mary Ann *NewYHSD*

Brown, Mary Mitchell 1866- *WomWWA 14*

Brown, Mary Willcox *NotAW*

Brown, Mason 1799-1867 *ApCAB, BiAUS, Drake*

Brown, Mather 1761-1831 *BnEnAmA, DcAmB, NewYHSD, WhAm H*

Brown, Matthew 1776-1853 *ApCAB, Drake, NatCAB 4, TwCBDA*

Brown, Maudelle Tanner 1885- *WhoColR*

Brown, Maxine McFadden 1917-1969 *WhAm 5*

Brown, May Belleville 1867-1936 *WhAm 1*

Brown, Melville Cox 1838-1928 *NatCAB 38*

Brown, Mena DeWitt *WomWWA 14*

Brown, Merton Leopold 1915-1968 *NatCAB 53*

Brown, Milton 1804-1883 *BiAUS, BiDrAC, WhAm H, WhAmP*

Brown, Milton Wilbert 1873- *WhAm 5*

Brown, Montreville Jay 1884-1971 *NatCAB 57, WhAm 6*

Brown, Moreau Roberts 1853-1914 *NatCAB 16*

Brown, Morgan W *BiAUS*

Brown, Morris 1770-1849 *DcAmB, WhAm H*

Brown, Mortimer Jay 1882-1945 *NatCAB 34*

Brown, Moses 1738-1836 *AmBi, ApCAB, DcAmB, EncAB, McGEWB, NatCAB 2, TwCBDA, WhAm H*

Brown, Moses 1742-1804 *ApCAB, Drake, TwCBDA*

Brown, Moses 1742-1827 *DcAmB, WhAm H*

Brown, Moses True 1827-1900 *WhAm 1*

Brown, Mysterious *NewYHSD*

Brown, Nancy *NotAW*

Brown, Nathan *NewYHSD*

Brown, Nathan W 1819-1893 *ApCAB, NatCAB 4, TwCBDA*

Brown, Nathaniel Smith 1872-1943 *WhAm 2*

Brown, Neal 1856-1917 *WhAm 1*

Brown, Neil S 1810-1886 *ApCAB, BiAUS, NatCAB 7*
Brown, Neill Smith 1810-1886 *DcAmB, WhAm H*
Brown, Nicholas 1729-1791 *ApCAB, ApCAB X, DcAmB, NatCAB 8, TwCBDA, WhAm H*
Brown, Nicholas 1769-1841 *AmBi, ApCAB, ApCAB X, DcAmB, Drake, NatCAB 1, NatCAB 8, TwCBDA, WhAm H*
Brown, Norris 1863-1960 *ApCAB X, BiDrAC, NatCAB 14, NatCAB 52, WhAmP*
Brown, Norriw 1863-1960 *WhAm 3*
Brown, Obadiah 1770-1822 *TwCBDA*
Brown, Obadiah 1771-1822 *ApCAB, DcAmB, WhAm H*
Brown, Obadiah Bruen 1829- *NatCAB 12*
Brown, Olive Marie McIntosh 1883- *BiCAW, WomWWA 14*
Brown, Oliver Huff 1852- *NatCAB 3*
Brown, Olympia 1835-1926 *AmBi, AmWom, ApCAB, DcAmB, NatCAB 20, NotAW, TwCBDA, WebAB, WhAm 1, WhAmP*
Brown, Ophelia S 1871- *WomWWA 14*
Brown, Orlando *BiAUS*
Brown, Orville Harry 1875-1943 *NatCAB 32, WhAm 2*
Brown, Orvon Graff 1863-1934 *NatCAB 1, NatCAB 27, WhAm 4*
Brown, Orvon Groff 1863-1934 *TwCBDA*
Brown, Oswald Eugene 1861-1939 *WhAm 1*
Brown, Owen Clarence 1871-1947 *NatCAB 36, WhAm 5*
Brown, Owen Neill 1867-1925 *ApCAB X*
Brown, Owsley 1879-1952 *NatCAB 41, WhAm 3*
Brown, Parke 1883-1943 *NatCAB 32, WhAm 2*
Brown, Patrick 1720?-1790 *Drake*
Brown, Paul *NewYHSD*
Brown, Paul 1848- *NatCAB 12*
Brown, Paul 1864- *NatCAB 10*
Brown, Paul 1880-1961 *BiDrAC, WhAm 4, WhAmP*
Brown, Paul 1893-1958 *IIBEAAW*
Brown, Paul Goodwin 1871-1950 *WhAm 2A*
Brown, Paul Winthrop 1870-1937 *WhAm 1*
Brown, Percy 1875-1950 *DcAmB S4, WhAm 3*
Brown, Percy Arthur 1883-1962 *NatCAB 52, WhAm 4*
Brown, Percy Edgar 1885-1937 *WhAm 1*
Brown, Percy W 1887-1958 *WhAm 3*
Brown, Peter 1784-1863 *ApCAB*
Brown, Philip E 1856-1915 *WhAm 1*
Brown, Philip Greely 1855-1934 *WhAm 1*
Brown, Philip King 1869-1940 *WhAm 1, WhAm 2*
Brown, Philip Marshall 1875-1966 *WhAm 4*
Brown, Philip Sheridan, Jr. 1866- *NatCAB 16*
Brown, Phoebe Hinsdale 1783-1861 *ApCAB, DcAmB, Drake, NatCAB 11, WhAm H*
Brown, Prentiss Marsh 1889-1973 *BiDrAC, WhAm 6*
Brown, Preston 1872-1948 *NatCAB 46, WhAm 2*
Brown, R Lewis 1892- *WhAm 2*
Brown, Ralph Bradbury 1905-1949 *NatCAB 38*
Brown, Ralph Hall 1898-1948 *DcAmB S4, WhAm 2*
Brown, Ralph Randall 1858-1928 *NatCAB 30*
Brown, Rawdon 1803-1883 *ApCAB*
Brown, Ray 1865-1944 *WhAm 2*
Brown, Ray Andrews 1890-1970 *WhAm 5*
Brown, Ray Everett 1913-1974 *WhAm 6*
Brown, Ray Francis 1897-1964 *NatCAB 52*
Brown, Ray Hyer 1889- *WomWWA 14*
Brown, Raymond Dwight 1886-1959 *NatCAB 47, WhAm 3*
Brown, Raymond Russell 1897-1955 *NatCAB 49*
Brown, Rexwald 1878-1940 *WhAm 1*
Brown, Reynolds Driver 1869- *WhAm 5*
Brown, Rezeau Blanchard 1872-1952 *NatCAB 49, WhAm 3*
Brown, Richard 1773-1818 *ApCAB, Drake*
Brown, Richard Evan 1881- *WhAm 6*
Brown, Richard Hunt 1862-1918 *NatCAB 18*

Brown, Robert d1823 *BiAUS*
Brown, Robert 1744-1823 *BiDrAC, WhAm H, WhAmP*
Brown, Robert 1745-1823 *ApCAB, Drake, NatCAB 1, TwCBDA*
Brown, Robert 1773-1858 *AsBiEn, DcScB*
Brown, Robert 1812?-1832 *NewYHSD*
Brown, Robert Abner 1868-1936 *WhAm 1*
Brown, Robert Alexander 1859-1937 *WhAm 1*
Brown, Robert Arthur, Jr. 1914-1972 *WhAm 5*
Brown, Robert Burns 1844-1916 *NatCAB 14, WhAm 1*
Brown, Robert Campbell *NatCAB 4*
Brown, Robert Carlton 1886-1959 *NatCAB 47*
Brown, Robert Elliott 1873-1938 *WhAm 1*
Brown, Robert Elmer, Sr. 1874- *WhoColR*
Brown, Robert Frederick 1896-1971 *WhAm 5*
Brown, Robert K 1893-1944 *WhAm 2*
Brown, Robert Marshall 1870- *WhAm 6*
Brown, Robert Osgood 1890-1949 *NatCAB 37*
Brown, Robert Rankins 1869-1937 *NatCAB 47, WhAm 1*
Brown, Robert Sater 1900-1944 *WhAm 2*
Brown, Robert Sirrelle 1873-1938 *WhoColR*
Brown, Robert Turnbull 1821-1878 *NatCAB 17*
Brown, Robert Woodrow 1912-1974 *WhAm 6*
Brown, Robert Young 1905-1964 *WhAm 4*
Brown, Rockwood 1887-1956 *NatCAB 47*
Brown, Rollo Walter 1880-1956 *WhAm 3*
Brown, Rome G 1862-1926 *WhAm 1*
Brown, Roscoe Conklin 1884- *WhoColR*
Brown, Roscoe Conkling Ensign 1867-1946 *NatCAB 34, WhAm 2*
Brown, Roy 1879-1956 *NatCAB 46, WhAm 3*
Brown, Roy Howard 1878- *WhAm 6*
Brown, Roy Wilcox 1874-1959 *NatCAB 49*
Brown, Rufus Everson 1854- *WhAm 4*
Brown, Ruth Mowry 1867- *WhAm 4, WomWWA 14*
Brown, S Leroy 1881- *WhAm 6*
Brown, Sally Eugenia *WomWWA 14*
Brown, Samuel 1769-1830 *ApCAB, DcAmB, Drake, NatCAB 4, TwCBDA, WhAm H*
Brown, Samuel Alburtus 1874-1952 *WhAm 3*
Brown, Samuel Augustine 1848-1918 *NatCAB 18*
Brown, Samuel Bernard 1855-1922 *NatCAB 46*
Brown, Samuel E d1860 *NewYHSD*
Brown, Samuel Gilman 1813-1885 *ApCAB, DcAmB, Drake, NatCAB 7, TwCBDA, WhAm H*
Brown, Samuel Horton, Jr. 1878-1940 *NatCAB 30, WhAm 1*
Brown, Samuel Joe 1875- *WhoColR*
Brown, Samuel Peters 1816-1898 *NatCAB 15*
Brown, Samuel Queen 1835-1909 *NatCAB 15*
Brown, Samuel R 1775-1817 *ApCAB, Drake*
Brown, Samuel Robbins 1810-1880 *AmBi, ApCAB, DcAmB, NatCAB 8, TwCBDA, WhAm H*
Brown, Samuel Smith 1842-1905 *NatCAB 6*
Brown, Sanford Miller 1855-1938 *WhAm 1*
Brown, Sanford Stella DeLand *WomWWA 14*
Brown, Sanger 1852-1928 *WhAm 1*
Brown, Selden Stanley 1855-1940 *WhAm 1*
Brown, Seth W 1841-1923 *BiDrAC, NatCAB 6*
Brown, Seth W 1843-1923 *WhAm 4*
Brown, Sevellon Ledyard 1886-1956 *WhAm 3*
Brown, Simon 1802-1873 *DcAmB, NatCAB 22, WhAm H*
Brown, Solyman 1790- *Drake*
Brown, Solyman 1790-1865? *ApCAB*
Brown, Solyman 1790-1876 *AmBi, DcAmB, NewYHSD, TwCBDA, WhAm H*
Brown, Staley 1801-1877 *ApCAB*
Brown, Stanley Doty 1885-1967 *WhAm 4A*
Brown, Stanley L 1911- *WhAm 4*
Brown, Sterling Nelson 1858- *WhoColR*
Brown, Stimson Joseph 1854- *NatCAB 13, WhAm 1*
Brown, Sue M 1877- *WhoColR*
Brown, Sydney Barlow 1884-1957 *NatCAB 46, WhAm 3*
Brown, Mrs. Sydney E 1867- *WomWWA 14*
Brown, Sydney MacGillvary 1895-1952 *WhAm 3*
Brown, Sylvanus 1747-1824 *DcAmB,*

NatCAB 24, WhAm H
Brown, T Harold 1888-1961 *NatCAB 49*
Brown, T Wistar 1826-1916 *NatCAB 28*
Brown, Tarleton 1754-1846 *ApCAB*
Brown, Thaddeus Harold 1887- *WhAm 1*
Brown, Thatcher M 1876-1954 *WhAm 3*
Brown, Theodore Henry 1888-1973 *WhAm 6*
Brown, Theophilus 1879- *WhAm 6*
Brown, Theophilus B d1834 *NewYHSD*
Brown, Theron 1832-1914 *WhAm 1*
Brown, Theron Adelbert 1896-1964 *WhAm 4*
Brown, Thomas *NewYHSD*
Brown, Thomas d1828 *ApCAB, Drake*
Brown, Thomas 1740- *ApCAB*
Brown, Thomas 1785-1867 *BiAUS, NatCAB 11*
Brown, Thomas 1819-1867 *ApCAB, TwCBDA*
Brown, Thomas Allston 1836- *WhAm 4*
Brown, Thomas Coleman 1864-1914 *NatCAB 16*
Brown, Thomas Cook 1891-1966 *WhAm 4*
Brown, Thomas Edwin 1841- *WhAm 4*
Brown, Thomas F 1883-1962 *WhAm 4*
Brown, Thomas Jefferson 1836-1915 *NatCAB 18, WhAm 1*
Brown, Thomas Joshua 1855-1932 *NatCAB 28*
Brown, Thomas Kenneth 1898-1951 *NatCAB 41*
Brown, Thomas McKee 1841-1898 *NatCAB 11*
Brown, Thomas Richardson 1872-1950 *NatCAB 39, WhAm 3*
Brown, Thomas Storrow 1803- *ApCAB*
Brown, Thomas Wooldridge 1828- *NatCAB 10*
Brown, Thompson S 1807-1855 *ApCAB, NatCAB 4, TwCBDA*
Brown, Thurlow Weed d1866 *ApCAB*
Brown, Titus 1786-1849 *BiAUS, BiDrAC, WhAm H*
Brown, Uriah *NewYHSD*
Brown, Vandyke *WhAm H*
Brown, Varina Davis *WomWWA 14*
Brown, Volney Malott 1899-1966 *NatCAB 54*
Brown, Volney Mason 1876- *WhAm 6*
Brown, W *NewYHSD*
Brown, W David 1865- *WhoColR*
Brown, W Harry 1856-1921 *ApCAB X, NatCAB 27*
Brown, W Kennedy 1834-1915 *NatCAB 27, WhAm 1*
Brown, W L Lyons 1906-1973 *WhAm 5*
Brown, W Robinson 1875-1955 *NatCAB 44*
Brown, W Roderick 1895-1965 *NatCAB 50*
Brown, Wade Hampton 1878-1942 *WhAm 2*
Brown, Wade R 1866- *WhAm 4*
Brown, Waldron Post d1915 *WhAm 1*
Brown, Wallace Elias 1868-1939 *NatCAB 30, WhAm 1*
Brown, Wallace Winthrop 1899-1965 *WhAm 4*
Brown, Walston Hill 1842-1928 *ApCAB X*
Brown, Walter d1879 *NewYHSD*
Brown, Walter 1872- *WhoColR*
Brown, Walter Eugene 1887-1954 *NatCAB 44*
Brown, Walter Fletcher 1880-1951 *NatCAB 42*
Brown, Walter Folger 1869-1961 *BiDrUSE, WhAm 4, WhAm 5*
Brown, Walter Franklin 1891-1959 *WhAm 3*
Brown, Walter Henry 1876-1962 *NatCAB 49*
Brown, Walter John 1900-1972 *NatCAB 57*
Brown, Walter L 1893-1972 *WhAm 6*
Brown, Walter Lewis 1861-1931 *DcAmLiB, NatCAB 24, WhAm 1*
Brown, Warner 1882-1956 *NatCAB 48*
Brown, Warren Wilmer 1880-1946 *NatCAB 35*
Brown, Warwick Thomas 1890-1960 *WhAm 4*
Brown, Webster Everett 1851-1929 *BiDrAC, WhAm 4, WhAmP*
Brown, Wendell 1902-1965 *NatCAB 51*
Brown, Wendell Phillips 1866-1951 *NatCAB 39*
Brown, Wendell Stimpson 1889-1969 *NatCAB 55*
Brown, Wilbur Vincent 1860-1928 *WhAm 1*
Brown, Willard Dayton 1874- *WhAm 5*
Brown, Willard Stanbury 1868-1940 *NatCAB 30*
Brown, William *NewYHSD*
Brown, William d1809 *Drake*
Brown, William 1752-1792 *DcAmB, WhAm H*
Brown, William 1779-1833 *ApCAB, BiAUS,*

Brown, William 1784-1864 *ApCAB*
Brown, William 1835- *ApCAB*
Brown, William 1840-1909 *WhAm 1*
Brown, William Adams 1865-1943 *DcAmB S3, DcAmReB, WhAm 2*
Brown, William Adams, Jr. 1894-1957 *NatCAB 43, WhAm 3*
Brown, William Ambrose 1878-1965 *NatCAB 51*
Brown, William Atwell, Jr. 1908-1970 *WhAm 5*
Brown, William Averell 1885-1953 *WhAm 3*
Brown, William C d1964 *WhAm 4*
Brown, William Cabell 1861-1927 *NatCAB 25, WhAm 1*
Brown, William Carey 1854-1939 *WhAm 1*
Brown, William Carlos 1853-1924 *DcAmB, NatCAB 14, WhAm 1*
Brown, William Channing 1868- *WhAm 5*
Brown, William Cyril 1842-1917 *NatCAB 17*
Brown, William Edward d1937 *WhAm 1*
Brown, William Edward 1884-1960 *NatCAB 47*
Brown, William Faulkner d1881 *ApCAB*
Brown, William G *NewYHSD*
Brown, William G 1801-1884 *BiAUS*
Brown, William G 1874-1957 *NatCAB 47*
Brown, William Garl, Jr. 1823-1894 *IIBEAAW, NewYHSD, WhAm H*
Brown, William Garrott 1868-1913 *AmBi, DcAmB, EncAAH, NatCAB 22, WhAm 1*
Brown, William Gay 1800-1884 *BiDrAC, WhAm H, WhAmP*
Brown, William Gay, Jr. 1856-1916 *BiDrAC, WhAm 1, WhAmP*
Brown, William George 1853-1920 *WhAm 1*
Brown, William H *NewYHSD*
Brown, William Harrison 1848-1917 *ApCAB X, NatCAB 17*
Brown, William Harvey 1862-1913 *AmBi*
Brown, William Henry 1808-1883 *NatCAB 20, NewYHSD, WhAm H*
Brown, William Henry 1815-1875 *ApCAB*
Brown, William Henry 1836-1910 *DcAmB, NatCAB 44, WhAm 1*
Brown, William Henry 1859-1947 *NatCAB 35*
Brown, William Henry 1862-1937 *NatCAB 27*
Brown, William Henry 1884-1939 *NatCAB 40, WhAm 1*
Brown, William Hill d1793 *Drake*
Brown, William Hill 1765-1793 *DcAmB S1, WhAm H*
Brown, William Hill 1766-1793 *ApCAB*
Brown, William Horace 1855-1917 *NatCAB 18, WhAm 1*
Brown, William Hughey 1815-1875 *DcAmB, WhAm H*
Brown, William John 1805-1857 *BiAUS, BiDrAC, NatCAB 11, TwCBDA, WhAm H, WhAmP*
Brown, William K *NewYHSD*
Brown, William Launcelot 1873-1942 *NatCAB 35*
Brown, William Lee d1906 *WhAm 1*
Brown, William Lee 1888-1958 *NatCAB 48*
Brown, William Liston 1842-1929 *NatCAB 14, NatCAB 35, WhAm 1*
Brown, William M *NewYHSD*
Brown, William Mason 1828-1898 *NewYHSD*
Brown, William McKean 1850-1915 *NatCAB 16*
Brown, William Montgomery 1855-1937 *NatCAB 7, TwCBDA, WhAm 1*
Brown, William Norman 1892-1975 *WhAm 6*
Brown, William Oswell 1876-1956 *NatCAB 42, WhAm 3*
Brown, William Paul *NewYHSD*
Brown, William Perry 1847-1923 *WhAm 2*
Brown, William Perry 1860-1914 *NatCAB 15*
Brown, William Ripley 1840-1916 *BiAUS, BiDrAC*
Brown, William Thayer 1895-1953 *WhAm 3*
Brown, William Thurston 1861- *WhAm 4*
Brown, William Wallace 1836-1926 *BiDrAC, TwCBDA, WhAm 1, WhAmP*
Brown, William Wells 1815-1884 *EncAB, McGEWB*
Brown, William Wells 1816?-1884 *DcAmB,*

BiDrAC, Drake, WhAm H

WhAm H, WhAmP
Brown, Wilson 1882-1957 *NatCAB 49, WhAm 3*
Brown, Winfred Ainslie 1882-1958 *NatCAB 48*
Brown, Wolstan Richmond 1860- *NatCAB 5*
Brown, Wrisley 1883-1943 *NatCAB 31, WhAm 2*
Brown, Wylie 1877-1960 *WhAm 4*
Brown, Zaidee 1875- *WhAm 5*
Brown-Sequard, Charles-Edouard 1817-1894 *BiHiMed, DcScB, TwCBDA*
Brown-Sequard, Charles Edouard 1818-1894 *ApCAB*
Brown-Turner, Mae F 1846- *WomWWA 14*
Browne, Albert Gallatin 1835-1891 *NatCAB 19, TwCBDA*
Browne, Aldis Birdsey 1857-1914 *WhAm 1*
Browne, Alexander Cecil 1880- *WhoColR*
Browne, Alfred David 1879- *WhAm 6*
Browne, Arthur Lee 1867-1933 *NatCAB 25*
Browne, Arthur Wesley 1877-1945 *WhAm 2*
Browne, B Bernard 1842-1922 *ApCAB*
Browne, Belmore 1880-1954 *IIBEAAW, NatCAB 43, WhAm 3*
Browne, Benjamin Frederick 1793-1873 *DcAmB, WhAm H*
Browne, Bennet Bernard 1842-1922 *NatCAB 19, TwCBDA, WhAm 1*
Browne, Beverly F 1880- *WhAm 6*
Browne, Byron 1907-1961 *NatCAB 45, WhAm 4*
Browne, Causten 1828-1909 *NatCAB 10, WhAm 1*
Browne, Chad 1600?-1665? *ApCAB X*
Browne, Chad *see also* Brown, Chad
Browne, Charles 1875-1947 *BiDrAC, WhAm 2*
Browne, Charles Albert 1842-1907 *NatCAB 29*
Browne, Charles Albert 1870-1947 *DcAmB S4, NatCAB 35, WhAm 2*
Browne, Charles Farrar 1834-1867 *AmBi, ApCAB, DcAmB, Drake, EncAAH, NatCAB 1, TwCBDA, WebAB, WhAm H*
Browne, Charles Francis 1859-1920 *IIBEAAW, NatCAB 16, WhAm 1*
Browne, Daniel Jay 1804-1851 *DcAmB, WhAm H*
Browne, Daniel Jay 1804-1870? *EncAAH*
Browne, David Henry 1864-1917 *NatCAB 23*
Browne, Duncan Hodge 1879- *WhAm 3*
Browne, Edward Everts 1868-1945 *BiDrAC, NatCAB 34, WhAm 2, WhAmP*
Browne, Edward Tankard 1894-1959 *WhAm 3*
Browne, Ellen VanVolkenburg 1882- *WomWWA 14*
Browne, Ethel Nicholson 1885- *WomWWA 14*
Browne, Francis Fisher 1843-1913 *AmBi, ApCAB, DcAmB, NatCAB 10, TwCBDA, WhAm 1*
Browne, Frank Atwood 1881-1957 *NatCAB 47*
Browne, Frederick William 1875-1960 *WhAm 4*
Browne, George 1883-1912 *ApCAB X*
Browne, George Elmer 1871-1946 *WhAm 2*
Browne, George Henry 1857-1931 *NatCAB 38, WhAm 1*
Browne, George Huntington 1811-1885 *BiDrAC, WhAm H*
Browne, George Huntington 1818-1885 *BiAUS, NatCAB 13*
Browne, George Israel 1866-1930 *WhAm 3*
Browne, George Waldo 1851-1930 *NatCAB 12, WhAm 1, WhAm 1C*
Browne, Grace Greenwood 1869- *WomWWA 14*
Browne, Harry C 1878- *WhAm 3*
Browne, Herbert Janvrin 1861-1936 *NatCAB 27*
Browne, Herbert Wheildon Cotton 1860-1946 *DcAmB S4, WhAm H*
Browne, Hester Singer 1887- *WomWWA 14*
Browne, Irving 1835-1899 *ApCAB, DcAmB, NatCAB 11, TwCBDA, WhAm H*
Browne, Jefferson Beale 1857-1937 *WhAm 1*
Browne, Jennie Nicholson 1876- *WomWWA 14*
Browne, John d1662 *DcAmB, WhAm H*
Browne, John Dean 1836-1913 *NatCAB 17*
Browne, John Jay 1843-1912 *ApCAB X*
Browne, John Lewis 1866-1933 *WhAm 1*

Browne, John Mills 1831-1894 *ApCAB Sup, NatCAB 14*
Browne, John Ross 1817-1875 *ApCAB, BiAUS, Drake, TwCBDA, WhAm H*
Browne, John Ross 1821-1875 *DcAmB, IIBEAAW, NatCAB 8, REnAW*
Browne, Junius Henri 1833-1902 *ApCAB Sup, DcAmB, NatCAB 13, TwCBDA, WhAm H*
Browne, Lewis 1897-1949 *WhAm 2*
Browne, Lewis Allen 1876-1937 *WhAm 1*
Browne, Louis Edgar 1891-1951 *WhAm 3*
Browne, Margaret Fitzhugh 1884-1972 *NatCAB 57, WhAm 5*
Browne, Maria J B *ApCAB*
Browne, Mary Catherine 1886- *WomWWA 14*
Browne, Mary Frank 1835- *AmWom*
Browne, Mary Nicholson 1879- *WomWWA 14*
Browne, Matilda 1869- *WomWWA 14*
Browne, Maurice 1881-1954 *WhAm 3*
Browne, Michael Calistus 1851-1928 *NatCAB 22*
Browne, Milton Wilder 1860-1934 *NatCAB 27*
Browne, Nina Eliza 1860- *ApCAB X, WhAm 4, WomWWA 14*
Browne, O E *NewYHSD*
Browne, Orva M 1878- *WomWWA 14*
Browne, Page 1892-1970 *WhAm 5*
Browne, Porter Emerson 1879-1934 *NatCAB 31, WhAm 1*
Browne, Ralph Cowan 1880-1960 *NatCAB 46, WhAm 3*
Browne, Rhodes 1865-1936 *WhAm 1*
Browne, Robert Bell 1894-1959 *WhAm 3*
Browne, Robert Benson, Jr. 1894-1965 *NatCAB 51*
Browne, Robert H 1835- *WhAm 4*
Browne, Robert Tecumtha 1882- *WhoColR*
Browne, Roger J 1906-1974 *WhAm 6*
Browne, Rollin 1895-1970 *WhAm 6*
Browne, Rose Lane 1859- *WomWWA 14*
Browne, Samuel J 1788-1872 *ApCAB*
Browne, Sara H *ApCAB*
Browne, Sarah Alice 1855- *WomWWA 14*
Browne, Theodore Crowninshield 1892-1973 *NatCAB 57*
Browne, Sir Thomas 1605-1682 *BiHiMed, DcScB, McGEWB*
Browne, Thomas 1775-1825 *AmBi, ApCAB, DcAmB, Drake, WhAm H*
Browne, Thomas Haynes Bayly 1844-1892 *TwCBDA*
Browne, Thomas Henry Bayly 1844-1892 *BiDrAC, WhAm H*
Browne, Thomas McLelland 1829-1891 *BiDrAC, TwCBDA, WhAm H, WhAmP*
Browne, Waldo Ralph 1876-1954 *WhAm 3*
Browne, William 1737-1802 *ApCAB, DcAmB, Drake, WhAm H*
Browne, William Hand 1828-1912 *ApCAB, BiDAmEd, DcAmB, NatCAB 11, TwCBDA, WhAm 1*
Browne, William Hardcastle 1840-1906 *WhAm 1*
Browne, William Montague 1827-1883 *BiDConf*
Browne, William R *NewYHSD*
Browne, Wilson Northrop 1805-1857 *ApCAB Sup*
Brownell, Atherton 1866-1924 *WhAm 1*
Brownell, Baker 1887-1965 *NatCAB 51, WhAm 4*
Brownell, Charles DeWolf 1822-1909 *NewYHSD*
Brownell, Clarence Ludlow 1864-1927 *WhAm 1*
Brownell, Eleanor Olivia 1876-1968 *WhAm 5, WomWWA 14*
Brownell, Emery Albert 1902-1961 *WhAm 4*
Brownell, Francis Herbert 1867-1954 *NatCAB 43, WhAm 3*
Brownell, George Francis 1861-1934 *NatCAB 24, WhAm 1*
Brownell, George Griffin 1869-1931 *WhAm 1*
Brownell, George Loomis 1854-1944 *NatCAB 36*
Brownell, Harry Franklin 1882-1940 *WhAm 1*
Brownell, Harry Gault 1866- *WhAm 4*
Brownell, Helen M Davis 1836- *AmWom*
Brownell, Henry Howard 1820-1872 *ApCAB,*

DcAmB, NatCAB 5, TwCBDA,
WhAm H
Brownell, Herbert 1862-1936 *BiDAmEd,*
NatCAB 26
Brownell, Herbert, Jr. 1904- *BiDrUSE*
Brownell, Jane Louise 1860- *WhAm 4,*
WomWWA 14
Brownell, Kenneth C 1903-1958 *WhAm 3*
Brownell, Lucy Pearce 1871- *WomWWA 14*
Brownell, Silas B 1830- *WhAm 4*
Brownell, Thomas Church 1779-1865 *ApCAB,*
BiDAmEd, DcAmB, Drake, NatCAB 3,
TwCBDA, WhAm H
Brownell, Walter Abner 1838-1904 *NatCAB 2,*
TwCBDA, WhAm 1
Brownell, William Arthur 1895-1977 *BiDAmEd*
Brownell, William Crary 1851-1928 *AmBi,*
ApCAB X, DcAmB, NatCAB 15,
NatCAB 22, WhAm 1
Brownell, William V *NewYHSD*
Browning, Arthur Montcalm 1908-1974
WhAm 6
Browning, Charles Clifton 1861- *WhAm 1*
Browning, Charles Henry d1926 *WhAm 1*
Browning, Eliza Gordon 1856-1927 *NatCAB 6,*
TwCBDA, WhAm 5, WomWWA 14
Browning, Elizabeth Barrett 1806-1861
McGEWB
Browning, Elizabeth Sophia Bradley 1871-
WomWWA 14
Browning, Frederick Boy 1896-1966 *WhWW-II*
Browning, George Landon 1867-1947
NatCAB 36, WhAm 2
Browning, Gordon 1889- *BiDrAC*
Browning, Grace 1904-1951 *WhAm 3*
Browning, Mrs. H *NewYHSD*
Browning, J Hull 1841-1914 *NatCAB 1*
Browning, John Hull 1842-1914 *WhAm 1*
Browning, John Moses 1855-1926 *AmBi,*
DcAmB, NatCAB 20, REnAW, WebAB,
WebAMB, WhAm 1
Browning, Matthew Sandefur 1859-1923
WhAm 1
Browning, McPherson d1953 *WhAm 3*
Browning, Miles 1897-1954 *WhAm 3*
Browning, Orville Hickman d1881 *BiAUS*
Browning, Orville Hickman 1806-1881 *AmBi,*
BiDrAC, BiDrUSE, DcAmB, WhAm H,
WhAmP
Browning, Orville Hickman 1810-1881 *ApCAB,*
Drake, NatCAB 2, TwCBDA
Browning, Perry 1898-1970 *NatCAB 56*
Browning, Philip Embury 1866-1937
NatCAB 28, WhAm 1
Browning, Ralph Rushton d1963 *WhAm 4*
Browning, Robert 1812-1889 *McGEWB*
Browning, Robert Turner 1905-1969 *WhAm 5*
Browning, Sarah Perry *WomWWA 14*
Browning, Webster E 1869-1942 *WhAm 2*
Browning, William 1855-1941 *WhAm 1*
Browning, William Hull 1865-1947 *NatCAB 38,*
WhAm 4
Browning, William John 1850-1920 *BiDrAC,*
WhAm 1, WhAmP
Browning, William Stacy 1877-1944
NatCAB 34
Brownlee, Frederick Leslie 1883-1962 *WhAm 4*
Brownlee, Hugh Ria 1870- *ApCAB X*
Brownlee, James F 1891-1960 *WhAm 4*
Brownlee, James Leaman 1863- *WhAm 4*
Brownlee, Joseph Templeton 1862-1943
NatCAB 32
Brownlee, William Alva 1897-1950 *NatCAB 39*
Brownlee, William Craig 1783-1860
NatCAB 11
Brownlee, William Craig 1784-1860 *ApCAB,*
DcAmB, WhAm H
Brownlow, John Bell 1839-1922 *NatCAB 20*
Brownlow, Louis 1879-1963 *NatCAB 47,*
WhAm 4
Brownlow, Walter Preston 1851-1910 *BiDrAC,*
TwCBDA, WhAm 1, WhAmP
Brownlow, William Gannaway 1805-1877 *AmBi,*
ApCAB, BiAUS, BiDrAC, DcAmB,
Drake, McGEWB, NatCAB 7, TwCBDA,
WebAB, WhAm H, WhAmP
Brownrigg, Albert Edward 1872-1933
NatCAB 24

Brownrigg, Dorothy Ruth Akin 1914-1971
WhAm 6
Brownrigg, Richard Thomas 1831-1863
TwCBDA
Brownrigg, William 1711-1800 *DcScB*
Brownscombe, Jennie Augusta 1850-1936
AmWom, NatCAB 16, NotAW, WhAm 1,
WomWWA 14
Brownson, Carleton Lewis 1866-1948 *WhAm 2*
Brownson, Charles Bruce 1914- *BiDrAC*
Brownson, Henry Francis 1835-1913
NatCAB 16, TwCBDA, WhAm 4
Brownson, James Irwin 1856-1938 *NatCAB 29,*
WhAm 1
Brownson, Josephine VanDyke 1880-1942
BiDAmEd, NotAW
Brownson, Lemuel 1806?- *NewYHSD*
Brownson, Marcus Acheson 1859-1938
WhAm 1
Brownson, Mary Wilson *WhAm 5,*
WomWWA 14
Brownson, Nathan d1796 *ApCAB, BiAUS,*
Drake
Brownson, Nathan 1740?-1796 *NatCAB 2,*
TwCBDA
Brownson, Nathan 1742-1796 *BiDrAC,*
WhAm H
Brownson, Orestes Augustus 1803-1876 *AmBi,*
ApCAB, DcAmB, DcAmReB, Drake,
McGEWB, NatCAB 7, TwCBDA,
WebAB, WhAm H
Brownson, Truman Gaylord 1851- *TwCBDA,*
WhAm 4
Brownson, Willard Herbert 1845-1935
ApCAB X, DcAmB S1, NatCAB 25,
WhAm 1
Brownson, William M *NewYHSD*
Broy, Charles Clinton 1887-1943 *WhAm 2*
Broyde, Isaac 1867- *WhAm 4*
Broyhill, James Thomas 1927- *BiDrAC*
Broyhill, Joel Thomas 1919- *BiDrAC*
Broyles, Joseph Warren 1901-1945 *WhAm 2*
Brozek, Jan 1585-1652 *DcScB*
Brubacher, Abram Royer 1870-1939 *BiDAmEd,*
NatCAB 30, WhAm 1
Brubacher, John Seiler 1898- *BiDAmEd*
Bruback, Theodore 1851-1904 *NatCAB 7,*
WhAm 1
Brubaker, Albert Philson 1852- *WhAm 4*
Brubaker, Howard 1882-1957 *WhAm 3*
Brubeck, David Warren 1920- *WebAB*
Bruccini, Nicolao *NewYHSD*
Bruce, Ada Bromilow 1881- *WomWWA 14*
Bruce, Ailsa Mellon 1901-1969 *NatCAB 55*
Bruce, Alexander Campbell 1835- *NatCAB 3,*
WhAm 4
Bruce, Andrew d1792 *Drake*
Bruce, Andrew Alexander 1866-1934
DcAmB S1, NatCAB 28, WhAm 1
Bruce, Andrew Davis 1894-1969 *WhAm 5*
Bruce, Archibald 1777-1818 *ApCAB, DcAmB,*
Drake, NatCAB 9, TwCBDA, WhAm H
Bruce, Blanche Kelso 1841-1898 *AmBi,*
ApCAB, BiAUS, BiDrAC, DcAmB,
EncAB, McGEWB, NatCAB 11,
TwCBDA, WebAB, WhAm H, WhAmP
Bruce, Catherine Wolfe 1816-1900 *NotAW*
Bruce, Charles Arthur 1883-1966 *WhAm 4*
Bruce, Charles Eli 1851- *NatCAB 5*
Bruce, Charles Morelle 1853-1938 *WhAm 1*
Bruce, David 1855-1931 *DcScB, McGEWB*
Bruce, Donald Cogley 1921-1969 *BiDrAC,*
WhAm 5
Bruce, Dwight Hall 1834- *NatCAB 5*
Bruce, Dwight Hall 1834-1908 *WhAm 1*
Bruce, Dwight Hall 1834-1909 *NatCAB 24*
Bruce, Edward Bright 1879-1943 *DcAmB S3,*
WhAm 2
Bruce, Edward Caledon *NewYHSD*
Bruce, Eli Metcalfe 1828-1866 *BiDConf*
Bruce, Eugene Sewell 1860-1920 *WhAm 1*
Bruce, Frank M, Sr. 1885-1949 *WhAm 2*
Bruce, Frank M, Sr. 1885-1953 *WhAm 3*
Bruce, Sir Frederick William Adolphus
1814-1867 *ApCAB, Drake*
Bruce, George 1781-1866 *ApCAB, DcAmB,*
Drake, NatCAB 11, TwCBDA, WhAm H
Bruce, Grace Adelle *WomWWA 14*

Bruce, Gustav Marius 1879- *WhAm 6*
Bruce, H Duane 1883-1961 *WhAm 4*
Bruce, Harold Lawton 1887-1934 *NatCAB 29,*
WhAm 1
Bruce, Helm 1860-1927 *NatCAB 21,*
WhAm 1
Bruce, Henry 1798- *ApCAB*
Bruce, Henry Addington Bayley 1874-
NatCAB 14, WhAm 5
Bruce, Henry Jensen 1885-1952 *NatCAB 41*
Bruce, Henry William 1897-1945 *WhAm 2*
Bruce, Horatio Washington 1830-1903 *BiDConf*
NatCAB 11, WhAm 1
Bruce, Howard 1879-1961 *WhAm 4*
Bruce, Jackson Martin 1902-1964 *WhAm 4*
Bruce, Jacob Baldwin 1885-1963 *NatCAB 50*
Bruce, James 1730-1794 *DcScB, McGEWB*
Bruce, James Deacon 1872-1946 *NatCAB 36,*
WhAm 2
Bruce, James Douglas 1862-1923 *NatCAB 18,*
NatCAB 21, WhAm 1
Bruce, James Latimer 1880- *WhAm 6*
Bruce, John 1832-1901 *WhAm 1*
Bruce, John Edgar 1899-1958 *WhAm 3*
Bruce, John Edward 1856- *WhAm 4,*
WhoColR
Bruce, John Eldridge 1856-1924 *WhAm 1*
Bruce, Joseph A *NewYHSD*
Bruce, Kathleen 1885-1950 *NatCAB 42*
Bruce, Kenneth 1876- *NatCAB 14*
Bruce, Lenny 1926-1966 *WhAm 6*
Bruce, Logan Lithgow 1928- *WhAm 5*
Bruce, Louis R 1906- *REnAW*
Bruce, Matthew Linn 1860-1936 *WhAm 1*
Bruce, Nathanial C 1869- *WhoColR*
Bruce, Patrick Henry 1881-1937 *BnEnAmA*
Bruce, Philip Alexander 1856-1933 *DcAmB S1,*
NatCAB 18, NatCAB 42, WhAm 1
Bruce, Phineas 1762-1809 *BiAUS, BiDrAC,*
WhAm H
Bruce, Robert 1778-1846 *DcAmB, WhAm H*
Bruce, Robert Aldridge 1904-1966 *NatCAB 53*
Bruce, Robert Glenn 1885-1945 *WhAm 2*
Bruce, Robert J 1754-1826 *NewYHSD*
Bruce, Roscoe Conklin 1879- *WhoColR*
Bruce, Roscoe Conkling 1879- *WhAm 6*
Bruce, Sanders Dewees 1825-1902 *NatCAB 6*
Bruce, Saunders Dewees 1825-1902 *WhAm 1*
Bruce, Stanley, Viscount Of Melbourne
1883-1967 *McGEWB, WhWW-II*
Bruce, Wallace 1844-1914 *ApCAB,*
NatCAB 14, TwCBDA, WhAm 1
Bruce, William Cabell 1860-1946 *ApCAB X,*
BiDrAC, DcAmB S4, NatCAB 18,
NatCAB 35, WhAm 2, WhAmP
Bruce, William George 1856-1949 *WhAm 2*
Bruce, William Herschel 1856-1943 *BiDAmEd,*
WhAm 2
Bruce, William Mansfield, Jr. 1878-1929
NatCAB 22
Bruce, William Paterson 1858-1920 *WhAm 1*
Bruce, William Stebbing 1819-1896 *NatCAB 11*
Bruce Of Melbourne, Viscount 1883-1967
WhAm 4A
Bruchesi, Louis Paul Napoleon 1855-
ApCAB Sup
Bruchon, Gertrude Jones *WomWWA 14*
Brucke, Ernst Wilhelm Von 1819-1892 *DcScB*
Brucker, Ferdinand 1858-1904 *BiDrAC*
Brucker, Henry 1874-1949 *NatCAB 37*
Brucker, Joseph 1849- *WhAm 4*
Brucker, Wilber Marion 1894-1968 *NatCAB 55,*
WhAm 5
Bruckner, Aloys L 1901-1965 *WhAm 4*
Bruckner, Henry 1871-1942 *BiDrAC,*
NewYHSD, WhAm 1, WhAmP
Bruckner, Jacob Herbert 1905-1970 *WhAm 5*
Bruckner, Joseph Anton 1824-1896 *McGEWB*
Bruder, Charles 1811?- *NewYHSD*
Brudno, Ezra Selig 1878- *WhAm 6*
Brueckmann, John George 1841-1927
NatCAB 22
Brueckmann, John George 1904-1966 *WhAm 4*
Brueckner, Harold Hugo 1907-1957
NatCAB 47
Brueckner, Leo John 1890-1967 *BiDAmEd,*
WhAm 4A

Bruegel, Pieter, The Elder 1525?-1569 *McGEWB*

Brueggeman, Bessie Parker 1878- *WhAm 1*

Bruegger, John 1860- *WhAm 4*

Bruen, John C *NewYHSD*

Bruen, Matthias 1793-1829 *ApCAB, Drake, TwCBDA*

Bruen, Robert C *NewYHSD*

Bruening, Bertha M 1882- *WomWWA 14*

Bruening, Edward *NewYHSD*

Bruening, Edward H 1881- *WhAm 6*

Bruening, Heinrich 1885-1970 *WhAm 5*

Bruening, Joseph *NewYHSD*

Bruening, William Ferdinand 1905-1966 *WhAm 4*

Bruer, Ernest Adrian 1882-1954 *NatCAB 47*

Bruere, Gustave Ernst 1869-1950 *NatCAB 39*

Bruere, Henry 1882-1958 *WhAm 3*

Bruere, Martha Bensley *WomWWA 14*

Bruere, Robert Walter 1876- *WhAm 5*

Brues, Charles Thomas 1879-1955 *WhAm 3*

Bruestle, George Matthew 1871-1939 *WhAm 1*

Brueys D'Aigailliers, Francois Paul 1753-1798 *WhoMilH*

Bruff, J *NewYHSD*

Bruff, Joseph Goldsborough 1804-1889 *IlBEAAW, NewYHSD, WhAm H*

Bruff, Lawrence Laurenson 1851-1911 *WhAm 1*

Bruff, W *NewYHSD*

Bruggman, Charles 1889-1967 *WhAm 4A*

Brugh, Benjamin Franklin 1889-1951 *NatCAB 41*

Brugler, Charles Edward 1865-1935 *NatCAB 25*

Bruguiere, Francis 1880-1945 *BnEnAmA*

Bruhl *NewYHSD*

Bruhl, Gustav 1826-1903 *DcAmB, WhAm H*

Bruhl, Gustavus 1826-1903 *ApCAB*

Bruhn, Carl 1869- *WhAm 5*

Bruhn, Wilhelm L 1900-1960 *WhAm 3A, WhAm 4*

Bruhns, Karl Christian 1830-1881 *DcScB*

Bruin, Peter Bryan *BiAUS*

Bruins, John H 1896-1954 *WhAm 3*

Bruix, Eustache 1759-1805 *ApCAB Sup*

Brule, Etienne 1592?-1632 *DcAmB, WebAB, WhAm H*

Brule, Etienne 1592?-1633 *McGEWB*

Bruls *NewYHSD*

Brum, Charles 1815?- *NewYHSD*

Brumagim, Robert Smith 1907-1974 *WhAm 6*

Brumbaugh, Catherine Elliott 1868- *WomWWA 14*

Brumbaugh, Clement Laird 1863-1921 *BiDrAC, WhAm 1, WhAmP*

Brumbaugh, David Emmert 1894- *BiDrAC*

Brumbaugh, Gaius Marcus 1862- *WhAm 5*

Brumbaugh, I Harvey 1870-1937 *WhAm 1*

Brumbaugh, Martin Grove 1862-1930 *BiDAmEd, NatCAB 15, WhAm 1, WhAm 1C*

Brumbaugh, Roy Talmage 1890-1957 *WhAm 3*

Brumby, Frank Hardeman 1874- *WhAm 5*

Brumby, Richard Trapier 1804-1875 *DcAmB, WhAm H*

Brumby, Thomas Mason 1855-1899 *ApCAB Sup, WhAm 1*

Brumidi, Constantino 1805-1880 *DcAmB, NewYHSD, WhAm H*

Brumley, Benjamin Basil 1875- *WhAm 5*

Brumley, Daniel Joseph 1865-1959 *NatCAB 47, WhAm 4*

Brumley, Oscar Victor 1876-1945 *NatCAB 33, WhAm 2*

Brumm, Charles Napoleon 1838-1917 *BiDrAC, TwCBDA, WhAm 3, WhAmP*

Brumm, George Franklin 1878-1934 *WhAm 1*

Brumm, George Franklin 1880-1934 *BiDrAC, WhAmP*

Brumm, John Lewis 1878-1958 *WhAm 3*

Brummitt, Dan Brearley 1867-1939 *WhAm 1*

Brummitt, Dennis G 1881-1935 *WhAm 1*

Brumpt, Emile 1877-1951 *DcScB*

Brun, Constantin 1860-1945 *WhAm 2*

Brunauer, Esther Caukin 1901-1959 *WhAm 3*

Bruncken, Ernest 1865- *WhAm 4*

Brunckhorst, Marie 1853- *WomWWA 14*

Brundage, Albert Harrison 1862-1936 *WhAm 1*

Brundage, Avery 1887-1975 *WebAB, WhAm 6*

Brundage, Charles Edwin 1895-1972 *WhAm 5*

Brundage, Ebenezer F *NewYHSD*

Brundage, Edward Fosgate 1878-1967 *NatCAB 54*

Brundage, Edward Jackson 1869-1934 *WhAm 1*

Brundage, Olive Mann 1876- *WomWWA 14*

Brundage, William Milton 1857-1921 *NatCAB 12, WhAm 1*

Brundidge, Oscar Dean 1886-1956 *WhAm 3*

Brundidge, Stephen, Jr. 1857-1938 *BiDrAC, TwCBDA, WhAm 4, WhAmP*

Brundige, William *NewYHSD*

Brundred, Benjamin F 1849-1914 *NatCAB 39*

Brundred, William James 1882-1957 *NatCAB 45*

Brune, Adolf Gerhard 1870-1935 *WhAm 1*

Brune, Frederick William 1894-1972 *NatCAB 57, WhAm 5*

Brune, Guillaume Marie Anne 1763-1815 *WhoMilH*

Brunel, Alfred 1818- *ApCAB*

Brunel, Isambard Kingdom 1806-1859 *McGEWB*

Brunel, Sir Mark Isambard 1769-1849 *ApCAB*

Brunelleschi, Filippo 1377-1446 *DcScB, McGEWB*

Bruner, Abram Breneman 1891-1957 *NatCAB 46*

Bruner, Elizabeth Cutting Cooley *WomWWA 14*

Bruner, Henry Lane 1861-1945 *NatCAB 34, WhAm 2*

Bruner, Herbert Bascom 1892-1974 *WhAm 6*

Bruner, James Dowden 1864- *WhAm 4*

Bruner, Lawrence 1856-1937 *NatCAB 13, WhAm 1*

Bruner, Raymond Alphonse 1900-1970 *WhAm 5*

Bruner, Roland Edward 1860- *NatCAB 17*

Bruner, Weston 1867- *WhAm 4*

Bruner, William Evans 1866-1964 *NatCAB 51, WhAm 5*

Brunet, Robert Leonard 1885-1932 *NatCAB 23*

Brunet, Walter Minson 1887-1947 *NatCAB 34*

Brunetti, Joseph John 1912-1968 *NatCAB 55*

Brunfels, Otto 1489?-1534 *DcScB*

Brunhes, Jean 1869-1930 *DcScB*

Brunia, William Frans 1893-1968 *WhAm 5*

Bruning, Henry Dietrich 1875-1955 *NatCAB 44*

Bruning, Walter Henry 1904-1974 *WhAm 6*

Brunis, Georg 1902-1974 *WhAm 6*

Brunk, Clifford Franklin 1891-1961 *NatCAB 49*

Brunk, Gregory 1894-1965 *NatCAB 51*

Brunker, Albert Ridgely 1883-1959 *WhAm 3*

Brunner, Arnold William 1857-1925 *DcAmB, WhAm 1*

Brunner, David B 1835-1903 *BiDrAC, TwCBDA, WhAm 1*

Brunner, Edmund DeSchweinitz 1889-1973 *NatCAB 57, WhAm 6*

Brunner, Henry George 1884-1964 *WhAm 4*

Brunner, John 1866-1936 *WhAm 1*

Brunner, John Hamilton 1825- *NatCAB 12, TwCBDA, WhAm 4*

Brunner, John William 1880- *WhoColR*

Brunner, Nicholaus Joseph 1795-1859 *WhAm H*

Brunner, William Frank 1887-1965 *BiDrAC, WhAm 4, WhAmP*

Brunnow, Franz Friedrich Ernst 1821-1891 *NatCAB 13*

Brunnow, Rudolph Ernest 1858-1917 *WhAm 1*

Bruno, Francis Ernest 1914-1971 *NatCAB 56*

Bruno, Frank J 1874-1955 *WhAm 3*

Bruno, Giordano 1548-1600 *AsBiEn, DcScB, McGEWB*

Bruno, Samuel Joseph 1899-1953 *NatCAB 39*

Brunot, Felix R 1820-1898 *ApCAB, TwCBDA*

Brunot, Harney Felix 1860- *WhAm 4*

Bruns, Friedrich 1878- *WhAm 6*

Bruns, Henry Dickson 1859-1933 *WhAm 1*

Bruns, Henry Frederick 1889-1947 *WhAm 2*

Bruns, Thomas 1830?- *NewYHSD*

Bruns, Thomas Nelson Carter 1902-1966 *WhAm 4*

Brunschvicg, Leon 1869-1944 *DcScB*

Brunschwig, Alexander 1901-1969 *WhAm 5*

Brunschwig, Hieronymus 1450?-1512? *DcScB*

Brunschwig, Roger E 1891-1972 *WhAm 5*

Brunsdale, Clarence Norman 1891- *BiDrAC, WhAmP*

Brunson, James Edwin 1888-1961 *WhAm 4*

Brunson, May Augusta 1909-1970 *WhAm 5*

Brunstetter, Max Russell 1902-1972 *NatCAB 57*

Brunswick, Hyman *NewYHSD*

Brunswick, Karl W Ferdinand, Duke Of 1735-1806 *WhoMilH*

Brunswick, Mark 1902-1971 *WhAm 5*

Brunswick, Ruth Jane Mack 1897-1946 *DcAmB S4, NotAW*

Brunswick, Thomas M *NewYHSD*

Brunswig, Lucien Napoleon 1854-1943 *WhAm 2*

Brunton, Ann *NotAW*

Brunton, David William 1849-1927 *DcAmB, NatCAB 14, NatCAB 23, WhAm 1*

Brunton, Richard d1832 *NewYHSD*

Brunton, Sir Thomas Lauder 1844-1916 *BiHiMed, DcScB*

Bruorton, Oscar Lucas 1885-1950 *NatCAB 40*

Brush, Abbott Purdy 1884-1951 *NatCAB 39*

Brush, Alanson Partridge 1878-1952 *NatCAB 40*

Brush, Alexander 1824-1892 *NatCAB 3*

Brush, Alvin G 1896-1965 *WhAm 4*

Brush, Charles Benjamin 1848-1897 *NatCAB 9, TwCBDA*

Brush, Charles Eliphalet 1855- *NatCAB 11*

Brush, Charles Francis 1849-1929 *AmBi, ApCAB, DcAmB S1, NatCAB 4, NatCAB 21, TwCBDA, WhAm 1*

Brush, Charles Francis, Jr. 1893-1927 *NatCAB 20*

Brush, Charlotte T *NewYHSD*

Brush, Daniel Harmon 1813-1890 *NatCAB 11*

Brush, Daniel Harmon 1848-1920 *WhAm 1*

Brush, Edward Fletcher 1847-1927 *NatCAB 27*

Brush, Edward Nathaniel 1852-1933 *DcAmB S1, NatCAB 24, WhAm 1*

Brush, Florence 1908-1964 *WhAm 4*

Brush, Frank Spencer 1857-1940 *WhAm 1*

Brush, Frederic 1871- *WhAm 5*

Brush, George DeForest 1855-1941 *BnEnAmA, DcAmB S3, IlBEAAW, NatCAB 13, TwCBDA, WhAm 1*

Brush, George Jarvis 1831-1912 *ApCAB, DcAmB, NatCAB 10, NatCAB 28, TwCBDA, WhAm 1*

Brush, George Washington 1842-1927 *WhAm 1*

Brush, Harlan Willis 1865-1942 *NatCAB 35*

Brush, Henry 1778-1855 *BiAUS, BiDrAC, WhAm H*

Brush, Henry Raymond 1878-1941 *WhAm 1*

Brush, Howard Grafton 1903-1971 *WhAm 5*

Brush, Jacob Henry 1833- *WhAm 1*

Brush, Jesse 1830- *TwCBDA*

Brush, John Tomlinson 1845-1912 *NatCAB 15*

Brush, John Y 1826?- *NewYHSD*

Brush, Katharine 1900-1952 *NatCAB 43, WhAm 3*

Brush, Louis Herbert 1872-1948 *NatCAB 36, WhAm 2*

Brush, Matthew Chauncey 1877-1940 *WhAm 1*

Brush, Murray Peabody 1872- *WhAm 5*

Brush, Rodman *NewYHSD*

Brush, Sophia E *NewYHSD*

Brush, William *NewYHSD*

Brush, William Whitlock 1874-1962 *NatCAB 49, WhAm 5*

Brushingham, John Patrick 1854-1927 *NatCAB 14*

Brushingham, John Patrick 1855-1927 *WhAm 1*

Brushman, Charles 1825?- *NewYHSD*

Brusie, Charles Frederick 1864- *WhAm 4*

Brusilov, Alexei Alexeevich 1853-1926 *WhoMilH*

Bruske, August Friedrich 1847- *TwCBDA*

Bruske, Augustus Fredrich 1847- *WhAm 4*

Brusletten, Christian L 1853-1925 *NatCAB 20*

Brust, Peter 1869-1946 *WhAm 2*

Bruster, Edmund *NewYHSD*

Brute, Simon Gabriel 1779-1839 *ApCAB, NatCAB 12, TwCBDA*

Brute DeRemur, Simon William Gabriel 1779-1839 *DcAmB, DcAmReB, WhAm H*

Bruton, John Fletcher 1861-1946 *NatCAB 36, WhAm 5*

Bruton, Margaret 1894- *IIBEAAW*
Brutus, Marcus Junius 085?BC-042BC
McGEWB
Bruyas, Jacques *Drake*
Bruyas, Jaques *ApCAB*
Bruyn, Andrew DeWitt 1790-1838 *BiAUS,*
BiDrAC, WhAm H
Bruyn, Charles DeWitt d1959 *WhAm 3*
Bruyn, Charles DeWitt 1878-1957 *NatCAB 49*
Bryan, Adolphus Jerome 1900-1951 *WhAm 3*
Bryan, Anna E 1858-1901 *BiDAmEd, NotAW*
Bryan, Beauregard 1862- *WhAm 4*
Bryan, Benjamin Chambers 1858-1930
WhAm 1
Bryan, Charles 1828?- *NewYHSD*
Bryan, Charles Page 1855-1918 *NatCAB 12*
Bryan, Charles Page 1856-1918 *ApCAB Sup,*
TwCBDA, WhAm 1
Bryan, Charles Walter 1863-1927 *NatCAB 21*
Bryan, Charles Walter, Jr. 1890-1966
NatCAB 51, WhAm 4
Bryan, Charles Wayland 1867-1945 *ApCAB X,*
DcAmB S3, WhAm 2
Bryan, Claude S 1908-1951 *WhAm 3*
Bryan, Daniel Bunyan 1886-1963 *WhAm 4*
Bryan, Edward B *NewYHSD*
Bryan, Edward Payson 1847-1910 *NatCAB 11,*
WhAm 1
Bryan, Ella Howard 1872- *NatCAB 13,*
WomWWA 14
Bryan, Elmer Burritt 1865-1934 *NatCAB 14,*
WhAm 1
Bryan, Enoch Albert 1855-1941 *BiDAmEd,*
NatCAB 35, WhAm 1, WhAm 2
Bryan, Ernest Rowlett 1906-1954 *WhAm 3*
Bryan, Felix Angus *WhoColR*
Bryan, Frances Wickham 1890- *WomWWA 14*
Bryan, Frank 1890-1960 *NatCAB 48*
Bryan, Frederick Carlos 1858- *WhAm 1*
Bryan, George 1731-1791 *ApCAB, BiAUS,*
DcAmB, Drake, TwCBDA, WhAm H,
WhAmP
Bryan, George 1778-1791 *NatCAB 2*
Bryan, George 1860-1930 *WhAm 1*
Bryan, George S *BiAUS*
Bryan, George Sands 1879-1943 *NatCAB 32,*
WhAm 2
Bryan, Goode 1811-1885 *BiDConf*
Bryan, Gray MacWhorter 1891-1958
NatCAB 47
Bryan, Guy Morrison 1821-1901 *BiAUS,*
BiDrAC, WhAmP
Bryan, Guy Morrison 1871-1935 *WhAm 1*
Bryan, Hamilton Vose 1890-1944 *NatCAB 45*
Bryan, Henry Francis 1865-1944 *WhAm 3*
Bryan, Henry H d1835 *BiAUS, BiDrAC,*
WhAm H
Bryan, Henry Lewis 1853-1934 *WhAm 1*
Bryan, Henry Ravenscroft 1836- *WhAm 4*
Bryan, J Leslie 1886-1955 *NatCAB 42*
Bryan, J St. George 1879-1945 *NatCAB 34*
Bryan, James Wesley 1874-1956 *BiDrAC,*
WhAm 3
Bryan, James William 1882-1952 *NatCAB 40,*
WhAm 3
Bryan, John A *BiAUS, NatCAB 11*
Bryan, John Heritage 1798-1870 *BiAUS,*
BiDrAC, WhAm H
Bryan, John Pendleton Kennedy 1852-
NatCAB 11, WhAm 1
Bryan, John Stewart 1871-1944 *DcAmB S3,*
NatCAB 34, WhAm 2
Bryan, Jonathan 1708-1788 *ApCAB Sup*
Bryan, Joseph 1773-1812 *ApCAB Sup, BiAUS,*
BiDrAC, WhAm H
Bryan, Joseph 1845-1908 *NatCAB 31*
Bryan, Joseph Hammond 1856-1935
NatCAB 27, WhAm 4
Bryan, Joseph Hunter *BiAUS, BiDrAC,*
WhAm H
Bryan, Joseph Roberts 1864-1922 *WhAm 1*
Bryan, Julien 1899-1974 *WhAm 6*
Bryan, Kirk 1888-1950 *DcAmB S4, DcScB,*
WhAm 3
Bryan, L R, Jr. 1892-1959 *WhAm 3*
Bryan, Lewis Randolph 1858-1938 *WhAm 1*
Bryan, Louis Allen 1908-1966 *WhAm 4*
Bryan, Malcolm Honore 1902-1967 *NatCAB 53,*

WhAm 4
Bryan, Mary Baird 1861- *WomWWA 14*
Bryan, Mary Edwards 1838?-1913 *NotAW*
Bryan, Mary Edwards 1842-1913 *DcAmB,*
NatCAB 8
Bryan, Mary Edwards 1844-1913 *WhAm 1*
Bryan, Mary Edwards 1846-1913 *AmWom,*
ApCAB, TwCBDA
Bryan, Mary Elizabeth 1846- *WomWWA 14*
Bryan, Nathan 1748-1798 *BiAUS, BiDrAC,*
WhAm H
Bryan, Nathan Philemon 1872-1935 *BiDrAC,*
WhAm 1, WhAmP
Bryan, O N 1881- *WhAm 6*
Bryan, Oscar Eugene 1873-1933 *WhAm 1*
Bryan, R Marion *WomWWA 14*
Bryan, Ralph 1892-1965 *WhAm 4*
Bryan, Robert Coalter 1873-1941 *NatCAB 31,*
WhAm 1
Bryan, Samuel 1859-1924 *NatCAB 6*
Bryan, Sheldon Martin 1916-1968 *WhAm 5*
Bryan, Shepard 1871- *WhAm 6*
Bryan, Thomas Barbour 1828-1906 *ApCAB Sup,*
DcAmB, NatCAB 3, TwCBDA,
WhAm 1
Bryan, Thomas Jefferson 1800?-1870 *ApCAB*
Bryan, Thomas Pinckney 1882-1920
NatCAB 31
Bryan, Thomas Smith 1856-1923 *NatCAB 20*
Bryan, W S Plumer 1856-1925 *WhAm 1*
Bryan, Wilber Peck 1874-1932 *NatCAB 25*
Bryan, William Alanson 1875-1942 *WhAm 2*
Bryan, William Burnett 1905-1968 *NatCAB 56*
Bryan, William Edward 1876- *IIBEAAW*
Bryan, William James 1876-1908 *BiDrAC,*
NatCAB 14, WhAm 1
Bryan, William Jennings 1860-1925 *AmBi,*
ApCAB Sup, BiDrAC, BiDrUSE,
DcAmB, DcAmReB, EncAAH, EncAB,
McGEWB, NatCAB 9, NatCAB 19,
REnAW, TwCBDA, WebAB, WhAm 1,
WhAmP
Bryan, Mrs. William Jennings 1861-1930
WhAm 1
Bryan, William Juel, Jr. 1896-1956 *NatCAB 43*
Bryan, William Lowe 1860-1955 *BiDAmEd,*
NatCAB 13, WhAm 3
Bryan, William Shepard, Jr. 1859-1914
WhAm 1
Bryan, William Wright 1908-1958 *NatCAB 48*
Bryan, Winfred Francis 1872- *WhAm 5*
Bryan, Worcester Allen 1873-1940 *WhAm 1*
Bryan-Jones, Noel D d1974 *WhAm 6*
Bryans, Henry Bussell 1886-1973 *WhAm 5*
Bryans, William Alexander, III 1899-1960
WhAm 4
Bryans, William Remington 1884-1974
WhAm 6
Bryant, Alice G 1862- *ApCAB X*
Bryant, Alonzo William 1874- *WhoColR*
Bryant, Amasa Bancroft 1869-1933 *NatCAB 32*
Bryant, Anna Burnham *WhAm 5*
Bryant, Anna Groff *WomWWA 14*
Bryant, Anna M Dorr *WomWWA 14*
Bryant, Arthur Peyton 1868-1935 *WhAm 1*
Bryant, Chal Page 1880-1953 *NatCAB 40*
Bryant, Columbus Binkley 1899-1959
NatCAB 47
Bryant, Cushing 1797-1863 *NatCAB 3*
Bryant, Daniel Pennington 1908-1976 *WhAm 6*
Bryant, David E 1849-1910 *TwCBDA,*
WhAm 1
Bryant, DeWitt Clinton 1849- *WhAm 4*
Bryant, Donald H 1919-1975 *WhAm 6*
Bryant, Dorothy Wilberforce Lyon 1868-
WomWWA 14
Bryant, Edgar Reeve 1866-1917 *WhAm 1*
Bryant, Edward Francis 1861-1928 *NatCAB 22*
Bryant, Edwin 1805-1869 *ApCAB*
Bryant, Edwin Eustace 1835-1903 *TwCBDA,*
WhAm 1
Bryant, Eliot Hinman 1896-1955 *NatCAB 46,*
WhAm 3
Bryant, Elwyn Richard 1876-1942 *NatCAB 32*
Bryant, Emmons 1910-1974 *WhAm 6*
Bryant, Ernest Albert 1869-1933 *WhAm 1*
Bryant, Eugene 1902-1969 *NatCAB 55,*
WhAm 5

Bryant, Floyd Sherman 1894-1965 *NatCAB 52,*
WhAm 4
Bryant, Frank Adolph 1883-1953 *NatCAB 49*
Bryant, Frank Augustus 1851-1921 *NatCAB 11,*
WhAm 1
Bryant, Frederick Howard 1877-1945
NatCAB 35, WhAm 2
Bryant, George Archie 1889-1963 *WhAm 4*
Bryant, Gridley 1789-1867 *ApCAB, DcAmB,*
TwCBDA, WhAm H
Bryant, Gridley 1790-1868 *NatCAB 11*
Bryant, Harold Edward 1894-1950 *IIBEAAW*
Bryant, Henry 1812-1881 *NewYHSD,*
WhAm H
Bryant, Henry Clay, Jr. *WhoColR*
Bryant, Henry Edward Cowan 1873- *WhAm 5*
Bryant, Henry Grier 1859-1932 *NatCAB 25,*
WhAm 1
Bryant, Howard Butler 1892-1963 *NatCAB 51*
Bryant, Ira T 1877- *WhoColR*
Bryant, James Ryan 1891-1968 *NatCAB 54*
Bryant, Joel 1813-1868 *ApCAB*
Bryant, John Arthur 1880-1938 *NatCAB 31*
Bryant, John Collins 1821-1901 *BiDAmEd,*
NatCAB 18
Bryant, John H 1840-1906 *NatCAB 3,*
WhAm 1
Bryant, John Howard 1807-1902 *ApCAB,*
DcAmB, WhAm 1
Bryant, John Thomas 1864-1947 *NatCAB 37*
Bryant, Joseph Decatur 1845-1914 *BiDAmEd,*
DcAmB, NatCAB 14, NatCAB 23,
WhAm 1
Bryant, Julian *NewYHSD*
Bryant, Lane 1879-1951 *NatCAB 47*
Bryant, Leland Arthur 1890-1954 *NatCAB 42*
Bryant, Lorinda Munson 1855-1933 *WhAm 1,*
WomWWA 14
Bryant, Louise Stevens 1885-1956 *WhAm 3,*
WomWWA 14
Bryant, Martha Lyman 1860- *WomWWA 14*
Bryant, Mildred *WhoColR*
Bryant, Nathaniel C 1823-1874 *NatCAB 3*
Bryant, Ralph Clement 1877-1939 *BiDAmEd,*
DcAmB S2, NatCAB 28, WhAm 1
Bryant, Randolph 1893-1951 *WhAm 3*
Bryant, Samuel Hollinger 1905-1972 *WhAm 6*
Bryant, Samuel Wood 1877-1938 *WhAm 1*
Bryant, Sara Cone 1873- *WhAm 5,*
WomWWA 14
Bryant, Shirley E MacManus 1868-
WomWWA 14
Bryant, Solomon 1695-1775 *ApCAB*
Bryant, Thomas Wallace 1859-1934
NatCAB 32, WhAm 1
Bryant, Victor Silas 1867-1920 *WhAm 1*
Bryant, Waldo Calvin 1863-1930 *WhAm 1*
Bryant, Will *IIBEAAW*
Bryant, William Cullen 1794-1878 *AmBi,*
ApCAB, DcAmB, Drake, EncAAH,
EncAB, McGEWB, NatCAB 4,
TwCBDA, WebAB, WhAm H
Bryant, William Cullen 1849-1905 *TwCBDA,*
WhAm 1
Bryant, William McKendree 1843- *NatCAB 5,*
TwCBDA, WhAm 1
Bryant, William Perkins 1806-1860 *ApCAB,*
BiAUS, NatCAB 12
Bryant, William Sohier 1861- *NatCAB 15,*
WhAm 3
Bryce, Edwin Clinton 1884-1957 *NatCAB 44*
Bryce, George 1844- *ApCAB*
Bryce, James Viscount 1838-1922 *McGEWB,*
WhAm 1
Bryce, James Wares 1880-1949 *NatCAB 38*
Bryce, Lloyd 1851-1917 *ApCAB X, DcAmB,*
NatCAB 1, TwCBDA, WhAm 1
Bryce, Lloyd Stephens 1850-1917 *BiDrAC*
Bryce, Robert Alexander 1881- *WhAm 4*
Bryce, Ronald *WhAm 1*
Bryce, Wilson Bartlett 1908- *WhAm 6*
Bryde, Archibald M *BiAUS*
Bryden, Lucy Annette 1875- *WomWWA 14*
Bryden, William 1880-1972 *WhAm 5*
Brydges, Charles John 1826- *ApCAB*
Brymner, Douglas 1823- *ApCAB*
Bryn, Helmer Halvorsen 1865-1933 *WhAm 3*
Brynan, John 1828?- *NewYHSD*

Bryson Of Heraclea *DcScB*
Bryson, Andrew 1822-1892 *ApCAB, Drake, TwCBDA*
Bryson, Charles Lee 1868-1949 *WhAm 2*
Bryson, Charles William *WhAm 1*
Bryson, Edward A *NewYHSD*
Bryson, Gladys 1894-1952 *WhAm 3*
Bryson, James 1889-1961 *NatCAB 49*
Bryson, John Alexander 1907-1967 *NatCAB 54*
Bryson, John Paul 1846-1903 *NatCAB 5, WhAm 1*
Bryson, Joseph Montgomery 1867-1938 *WhAm 2*
Bryson, Joseph Raleigh 1893-1953 *BiDrAC, WhAm 3, WhAmP*
Bryson, Lyman Lloyd 1888-1959 *BiDAmEd, NatCAB 45, WhAm 3*
Bryson, Olive Flora 1875- *WhAm 5*
Bryson, Robert Hamilton 1864- *WhAm 4*
Bryson, Robert Hassey 1875-1938 *WhAm 1*
Brytte, Walter *DcScB*
Buache, Philippe 1700-1773 *DcScB*
Buat, Joseph *NewYHSD*
Bubb, Frank William 1892-1961 *NatCAB 50*
Bubb, Harry Clay 1856-1939 *NatCAB 29*
Bubb, Henry Clay 1856-1939 *WhAm 4*
Bubb, John Wilson 1843-1922 *WhAm 1*
Buber, Martin 1878-1965 *McGEWB, WhAm 4*
Buberi, Caspar 1834-1899 *NewYHSD*
Buberl, Caspar 1832-1899 *NatCAB 11*
Buberl, Caspar 1834-1899 *NewYHSD*
Bubert, Caspar 1830-1899 *ApCAB Sup*
Bubriski, Stanley William 1921-1965 *NatCAB 52*
Bucareli Y Ursua, Antonio Maria De d1779 *ApCAB*
Bucciarelli, John Anthony 1905-1968 *NatCAB 56*
Buch, Joseph Godfrey 1881-1945 *WhAm 2*
Buch, Leopold Von 1774-1853 *DcScB*
Buchan, David 1780-1837 *ApCAB*
Buchanan, Andrew 1734-1785 *ApCAB Sup*
Buchanan, Andrew 1780-1848 *BiAUS, BiDrAC, WhAm H*
Buchanan, Andrew Hays 1828-1914 *WhAm 1*
Buchanan, Anna F 1858- *WomWWA 14*
Buchanan, Arthur Stillingfleet 1856-1919 *NatCAB 18, WhAm 1*
Buchanan, Benjamin Franklin 1859-1932 *NatCAB 48, WhAm 1*
Buchanan, Charles Andrew 1860- *WhoColR*
Buchanan, Daniel Houston 1883-1959 *WhAm 3*
Buchanan, David H 1907-1972 *WhAm 5*
Buchanan, Edward Young 1811-1895 *TwCBDA*
Buchanan, Ella d1951 *WhAm 3*
Buchanan, Frank 1862-1930 *BiDrAC, WhAm 1*
Buchanan, Frank 1902-1951 *BiDrAC, WhAm 3, WhAmP*
Buchanan, Franklin 1800-1874 *AmBi, ApCAB, BiDConf, DcAmB, Drake, NatCAB 4, TwCBDA, WebAB, WebAMB, WhAm H, WhoMilH*
Buchanan, George 1698?-1750 *ApCAB Sup*
Buchanan, George 1763-1808 *ApCAB Sup*
Buchanan, George Edward 1869-1939 *WhAm 1*
Buchanan, George McAfee 1838-1926 *NatCAB 21*
Buchanan, George Sidney 1902-1967 *WhAm 4A*
Buchanan, Helen Davis 1890- *WomWWA 14*
Buchanan, Herbert Earle 1881-1974 *WhAm 6*
Buchanan, Hugh 1823-1890 *BiDrAC, WhAm H*
Buchanan, Isaac 1810-1883 *ApCAB, Drake*
Buchanan, Isabella Reid 1857- *WomWWA 14*
Buchanan, James d1851 *Drake*
Buchanan, James 1791-1868 *AmBi, ApCAB, BiAUS, BiDrAC, BiDrUSE, DcAmB, Drake, EncAAH, EncAB, McGEWB, NatCAB 5, TwCBDA, WebAB, WhAm H, WhAmP*
Buchanan, James 1839-1900 *BiDrAC, TwCBDA*
Buchanan, James Anderson 1843-1926 *NatCAB 41, WhAm 1*
Buchanan, James Isaac 1853-1931 *WhAm 1, WhAm 1C*
Buchanan, James L d1955 *WhAm 3*

Buchanan, James M 1803-1876 *ApCAB Sup, BiAUS, NatCAB 7*
Buchanan, James Paul 1867-1937 *BiDrAC, WhAm 1, WhAmP*
Buchanan, James Shannon 1864-1930 *NatCAB 35, WhAm 1*
Buchanan, James William 1888-1952 *WhAm 3*
Buchanan, John 1772-1844 *DcAmB, NatCAB 10, WhAm H*
Buchanan, John Alexander 1843-1921 *BiDrAC, TwCBDA, WhAm 1*
Buchanan, John Grier, Jr. 1917-1970 *NatCAB 56*
Buchanan, John Hall, Jr. 1928- *BiDrAC*
Buchanan, John Jenkins 1855-1937 *NatCAB 27, WhAm 1*
Buchanan, John Lee 1831-1922 *NatCAB 29, WhAm 4*
Buchanan, John Lee 1884-1939 *NatCAB 29*
Buchanan, John P 1847-1930 *NatCAB 7, TwCBDA, WhAm 3*
Buchanan, John Ripley 1891-1951 *NatCAB 41*
Buchanan, John Young 1844-1925 *DcScB*
Buchanan, Joseph 1785-1829 *ApCAB Sup, DcAmB, WhAm H*
Buchanan, Joseph Ray 1851-1924 *DcAmB, WhAm 1, WhAm 4*
Buchanan, Joseph Rhodes 1814-1899 *ApCAB, TwCBDA*
Buchanan, Joseph Rodes 1814-1899 *DcAmB, NatCAB 10, WhAm 1*
Buchanan, Kenneth 1892-1967 *WhAm 4*
Buchanan, Kenneth B 1895-1956 *WhAm 3*
Buchanan, Leonard Brown 1873-1955 *WhAm 3*
Buchanan, Malcolm Griswold 1881-1942 *WhAm 1*
Buchanan, McKean 1823-1872 *ApCAB, NatCAB 11*
Buchanan, Norman Sharpe 1905-1958 *WhAm 3*
Buchanan, Oswald C 1896-1966 *WhAm 4*
Buchanan, Richard Twells 1870-1928 *NatCAB 22*
Buchanan, Roberdeau 1839-1916 *WhAm 1*
Buchanan, Robert Christie 1810?-1878 *ApCAB, Drake, NatCAB 4, TwCBDA*
Buchanan, Robert Christie 1811-1878 *DcAmB, WhAm H*
Buchanan, Sarah d1831 *ApCAB*
Buchanan, Scott 1895-1968 *WhAm 5*
Buchanan, T Drysdale 1876-1940 *WhAm 1*
Buchanan, Thomas 1744-1815 *DcAmB, WhAm H*
Buchanan, Thomas C 1895-1958 *WhAm 3*
Buchanan, Thomas Elie 1899-1960 *NatCAB 52*
Buchanan, Thomas McKean 1837-1862 *ApCAB*
Buchanan, Thompson 1877-1937 *WhAm 1*
Buchanan, Vera Daerr 1902-1955 *BiDrAC, WhAm 3, WhAmP*
Buchanan, Virginia Ellen 1866- *ApCAB*
Buchanan, W C 1888-1968 *WhAm 5*
Buchanan, Walter Duncan 1859-1934 *WhAm 1*
Buchanan, Walter Solomon 1882- *WhoColR*
Buchanan, William *WhoColR*
Buchanan, William 1748-1824 *ApCAB Sup*
Buchanan, William 1853- *NatCAB 7*
Buchanan, William Asbury 1876-1954 *WhAm 3*
Buchanan, William Insco 1852-1909 *AmBi, DcAmB, NatCAB 2, TwCBDA*
Buchanan, William Insco 1853-1909 *WhAm 1*
Buchannan, Andrew *NewYHSD*
Buchbinder, Jacob Richter 1887-1947 *NatCAB 36, WhAm 3*
Buchen, Walther 1886-1961 *NatCAB 48, WhAm 4*
Bucher, August Johannes 1862-1937 *WhAm 1*
Bucher, John C 1792-1851 *BiAUS*
Bucher, John Calvin 1865-1945 *WhAm 2*
Bucher, John Conrad 1730-1780 *DcAmB, WhAm H*
Bucher, John Conrad 1792-1851 *BiDrAC, WhAm H*
Bucher, John Emery 1872- *WhAm 5*
Bucher, Robert Leon 1895-1952 *NatCAB 40*
Bucher, Walter Herman 1888-1965 *WhAm 4*
Bucher, Walter Herman 1889-1965 *DcScB*
Bucher, William Henry 1874-1934 *WhAm 1*
Bucherer, Alfred Heinrich 1863-1927 *DcScB*
Buchesne, T *NewYHSD*

Buchholz, Heinrich Ewald 1879-1955 *WhAm 3*
Buchholz, John Theodore 1888-1951 *WhAm 3*
Buchholz, Ludwig Wilhelm 1855-1935 *WhAm 1*
Buchholz, William 1877- *WhAm 1*
Buchholzer, Julius Johannes 1892-1960 *NatCAB 49*
Buchman, Frank Nathan Daniel 1878-1961 *DcAmReB, WebAB, WhAm 4*
Buchner, Eduard 1860-1917 *AsBiEn, DcScB*
Buchner, Edward Franklin 1868-1929 *WhAm 1*
Buchner, Friedrich Karl Christian Ludwig 1824-1899 *DcScB*
Buchner, Hans Ernst Angass 1850-1902 *AsBiEn*
Bucholaer, H *NewYHSD*
Bucholz, Christian Friedrich 1770-1818 *DcScB*
Buchser, Frank 1828-1890 *IlBEAAW, WhAm H*
Buchsieb, Emil George 1881-1956 *NatCAB 44*
Buchta, J William 1895-1966 *WhAm 4*
Buchtel, Henry Augustus 1847-1924 *NatCAB 14, NatCAB 36, TwCBDA, WhAm 1*
Buchtel, John Richards 1820-1892 *DcAmB, NatCAB 2, WhAm H*
Buchtel, John Richards 1822-1893 *TwCBDA*
Buchwalter, Mary Knox 1862- *WomWWA 14*
Buchweiler, S *NewYHSD*
Buck, Albert Henry 1842-1922 *DcAmB, NatCAB 9, WhAm 1*
Buck, Alfred Eliab 1832-1902 *BiAUS, BiDrAC, NatCAB 1, TwCBDA, WhAm 1*
Buck, Augustus Walker 1866-1924 *NatCAB 6*
Buck, Beaumont Bonaparte 1860-1950 *WhAm 3*
Buck, Benjamin F 1865-1922 *WhAm 1*
Buck, C Douglass 1890-1965 *WhAm 4*
Buck, Carl Darling 1866-1955 *WhAm 3*
Buck, Carl E 1891-1953 *WhAm 3*
Buck, Cassius M 1859- *WhAm 4*
Buck, Charles Francis 1841-1918 *BiDrAC, NatCAB 11*
Buck, Charles Henry 1889-1971 *WhAm 6*
Buck, Charles Neville 1879- *WhAm 6*
Buck, Charles William 1849-1930 *NatCAB 12, WhAm 1*
Buck, Clarence Frank 1870-1944 *WhAm 2*
Buck, Clayton Douglass 1890-1965 *BiDrAC*
Buck, Daniel d1817 *BiAUS*
Buck, Daniel 1753-1816 *BiDrAC, DcAmB, WhAm H*
Buck, Daniel 1760?-1817 *NatCAB 8*
Buck, Daniel 1857-1905 *WhAm 1*
Buck, Daniel Azro Ashley 1789-1841 *BiAUS, BiDrAC, WhAm H*
Buck, Dudley 1830-1909 *TwCBDA*
Buck, Dudley 1839-1909 *AmBi, ApCAB, DcAmB, NatCAB 7, WhAm 1*
Buck, Ellsworth Brewer 1892-1970 *BiDrAC, WhAm 5*
Buck, Ernest Ferguson 1881- *WhAm 6*
Buck, Florence 1860-1925 *WhAm 1, WomWWA 14*
Buck, Foster 1904- *WhAm 5*
Buck, Frank 1882-1950 *NatCAB 40*
Buck, Frank 1884-1950 *WebAB, WhAm 2A*
Buck, Frank Henry 1859-1916 *NatCAB 17, WhAm 1*
Buck, Frank Henry 1887-1942 *BiDrAC, WhAm 2, WhAmP*
Buck, Franklyn Howard 1884-1950 *DcAmB S4*
Buck, Fred 1858-1938 *NatCAB 27*
Buck, George Burton, Jr. 1917-1968 *NatCAB 55*
Buck, George Machan d1919 *WhAm 1*
Buck, George Sturges 1875-1931 *WhAm 1*
Buck, Gertrude 1871-1922 *WhAm 1, WomWWA 14*
Buck, Gordon Mountjoy 1875-1970 *NatCAB 55*
Buck, Gurdon 1807-1877 *ApCAB, DcAmB, NatCAB 11, TwCBDA, WhAm H*
Buck, Harold Winthrop 1873-1958 *NatCAB 43, WhAm 3*
Buck, Harry Lambert 1911-1972 *WhAm 5*
Buck, Henriette 1864- *AmWom*
Buck, Henry William 1906-1960 *WhAm 4*
Buck, Jirah Dewey 1838- *WhAm 1*
Buck, John Halsey 1869-1957 *NatCAB 49*
Buck, John Lossing 1890-1975 *WhAm 6*
Buck, John Ransom 1835-1917 *BiDrAC*

Buck, John Ransom 1836-1917 *WhAm 4*
Buck, Leffert Lefferts 1837-1909 *DcAmB,*
NatCAB 10, WhAm 1
Buck, Leonard William 1891-1953 *NatCAB 43*
Buck, Lillie West Brown *NotAW,*
WomWWA 14
Buck, Mary K 1849- *AmWom*
Buck, Nelson Leroy 1882-1956 *NatCAB 46*
Buck, Norman Sydney 1892-1964 *WhAm 4*
Buck, Oscar MacMillan 1885-1941 *WhAm 1*
Buck, Pearl Sydenstricker 1892-1973 *McGEWB,*
WebAB, WhAm 5
Buck, Peter Henry 1880-1951 *WhAm 3*
Buck, Philip Earl 1897-1947 *WhAm 2*
Buck, Philo Melvin 1846-1924 *DcAmB,*
NatCAB 22, WhAm 1
Buck, Philo Melvin, Jr. 1877-1950 *WhAm 3*
Buck, Raymond Elliott 1894-1971 *WhAm 5*
Buck, Richard Sutton 1864-1951 *NatCAB 46,*
WhAm 3
Buck, Roswell Riley 1826-1904 *NatCAB 22*
Buck, Samuel Henry 1841- *NatCAB 12*
Buck, Samuel Jay 1835-1918 *WhAm 1*
Buck, Seaver Burton 1869-1950 *NatCAB 39*
Buck, Solon Justus 1884-1962 *EncAAH,*
NatCAB 49, WhAm 4
Buck, Waldo Emerson 1856-1945 *NatCAB 34*
Buck, Walter Albert 1895-1955 *WhAm 3*
Buck, Walter E d1966 *WhAm 5*
Buck, Walter Hooper 1878-1962 *WhAm 4*
Buck, William Bradford 1874- *WhAm 6*
Buck, William Joseph 1825- *ApCAB Sup*
Buckalew, Charles H 1821-1899 *WhAm 1*
Buckalew, Charles Rollin 1821-1899 *ApCAB,*
BiAUS, BiDrAC, DcAmB, NatCAB 11,
TwCBDA, WhAmP
Buckbee, Anna 1855- *WhAm 4,*
WomWWA 14
Buckbee, Jennie Palmer 1833- *WomWWA 14*
Buckbee, John Theodore 1871-1936 *BiDrAC,*
WhAm 1, WhAmP
Bucke, Richard Maurice 1837- *ApCAB*
Buckel, Cloe Annette 1833-1912 *NotAW*
Buckeley, Peter 1583-1659 *WhAm H*
Buckendale, L Ray 1892-1952 *WhAm 3*
Buckham, James 1858-1908 *NatCAB 15,*
WhAm 1
Buckham, John Wright 1864-1945 *WhAm 2*
Buckham, Matthew Henry 1832-1910 *BiDAmEd,*
NatCAB 2, TwCBDA, WhAm 1
Buckhout, Isaac Craig 1830-1874 *DcAmB,*
WhAm H
Buckhout, Isaac Craig 1831-1874 *ApCAB,*
TwCBDA
Buckingham, Benjamin Horr 1848-1906
NatCAB 34
Buckingham, Burdette Ross 1876- *WhAm 5*
Buckingham, Catharinus Putnam 1808-1888
ApCAB, NatCAB 13, TwCBDA
Buckingham, Charles Luman 1852-1909
NatCAB 2, WhAm 1
Buckingham, Charles Luman, Jr. 1890-1918
NatCAB 24
Buckingham, David Eastburn 1870- *WhAm 5*
Buckingham, Edgar 1867-1940 *DcScB,*
NatCAB 29, WhAm 1
Buckingham, Edward Marshall 1848-1916
NatCAB 20
Buckingham, Edward Taylor 1874- *WhAm 5*
Buckingham, Edwin d1833 *ApCAB*
Buckingham, George Tracy 1864-1940
ApCAB X, NatCAB 17, WhAm 1
Buckingham, George Villiers, Duke Of 1592-1628
McGEWB
Buckingham, George Villiers, Duke Of 1628-1687
McGEWB
Buckingham, James Silk 1784-1855 *Drake*
Buckingham, James Silk 1786-1855 *ApCAB*
Buckingham, John Duncan 1855- *NatCAB 9*
Buckingham, Joseph Tinker 1779-1861 *ApCAB,*
DcAmB, Drake, NatCAB 7, NatCAB 29,
TwCBDA, WhAm H
Buckingham, Lucius Henry 1829-1885
NatCAB 29
Buckingham, Naomi Jennette Carpenter 1879-
WomWWA 14
Buckingham, Nellie B Hibbard 1860-
WomWWA 14

Buckingham, Norman Stanley 1881-1940
NatCAB 30, WhAm 1
Buckingham, Samuel Giles 1812-1898 *TwCBDA*
Buckingham, Theophilus Nash 1880- *WhAm 6*
Buckingham, Walter, Jr. 1924-1967 *WhAm 4*
Buckingham, William Alfred 1804-1875 *ApCAB,*
BiAUS, BiDrAC, DcAmB, Drake,
NatCAB 10, TwCBDA, WhAm H,
WhAmP
Buckland, Albert William James 1900-1960
WhAm 3
Buckland, Charles Clark 1899-1968 *WhAm 5*
Buckland, Cyrus 1799-1891 *ApCAB, DcAmB,*
Drake Sup, NatCAB 11, TwCBDA,
WhAm H
Buckland, Edward Grant 1866-1953 *WhAm 3*
Buckland, Ralph Pomeroy 1812-1892 *ApCAB,*
BiAUS, BiDrAC, DcAmB, NatCAB 11,
TwCBDA, WhAm H
Buckland, William 1734-1774 *BnEnAmA,*
WhAm H
Buckland, William 1784-1856 *DcScB*
Buckle, Henry Thomas 1821-1862 *McGEWB*
Buckle, John Franklin 1920-1969 *WhAm 5*
Buckler, Richard Thompson 1865-1950 *BiDrAC,*
WhAm 3, WhAmP
Buckler, Thomas Hepburn 1812-1901 *DcAmB,*
WhAm H
Buckler, William Hepburn 1867-1952 *WhAm 3*
Buckley, Albert Coulson 1873-1939 *WhAm 1*
Buckley, B Lord 1871-1932 *NatCAB 25*
Buckley, Bartholomew William 1877-1959
NatCAB 48
Buckley, Charles Anthony 1890-1967 *BiDrAC,*
WhAm 4, WhAmP
Buckley, Charles Waldron 1835-1906 *BiAUS,*
BiDrAC, NatCAB 13
Buckley, Charlotte Carter 1858- *WomWWA 14*
Buckley, Edmund 1855- *WhAm 4*
Buckley, Edward 1842-1927 *NatCAB 6,*
NatCAB 23
Buckley, Edwin M d1949 *WhAm 3*
Buckley, Ernest Robertson 1872-1912
NatCAB 19, WhAm 1
Buckley, George Wright 1850- *WhAm 4*
Buckley, Harry D 1889-1955 *WhAm 3*
Buckley, Homer John 1879-1960 *NatCAB 49,*
WhAm 6
Buckley, Isabella *NewYHSD*
Buckley, James Clayton 1909-1969 *NatCAB 54*
Buckley, James Monroe 1836-1920 *AmBi,*
ApCAB, ApCAB X, DcAmB,
NatCAB 12, TwCBDA, WhAm 1
Buckley, James Richard 1870-1945 *BiDrAC,*
WhAm 5
Buckley, James V 1892-1954 *WhAm 3*
Buckley, James Vincent 1894-1954 *BiDrAC*
Buckley, Jere D 1898-1962 *WhAm 4*
Buckley, John Peter 1873-1942 *NatCAB 33,*
WhAm 2
Buckley, Julian Gerard 1866-1935 *NatCAB 26*
Buckley, Leo Jerome 1899-1956 *WhAm 3*
Buckley, May 1875- *WhAm 5,*
WomWWA 14
Buckley, Michael John 1880-1960 *NatCAB 47*
Buckley, Oliver Ellsworth 1887-1959
NatCAB 53, WhAm 3
Buckley, Samuel Botsford 1809-1883 *DcAmB,*
WhAm H
Buckley, Samuel Botsford 1809-1884 *ApCAB,*
NatCAB 5, TwCBDA
Buckley, Tim 1947-1975 *WhAm 6*
Buckley, William Frank 1881-1958 *NatCAB 43*
Buckley, William Frank, Jr. 1925- *WebAB*
Bucklin, Bradley A 1824-1915 *NewYHSD*
Bucklin, Edward C d1934 *WhAm 1*
Bucklin, George Augustus 1875- *WhAm 5*
Bucklin, James C 1801-1880 *WhAm H*
Bucklin, James W 1856-1919 *WhAm 1*
Bucklin, Walter Stanley 1880-1965 *WhAm 4*
Buckman, Clarence Bennett 1851-1917 *BiDrAC,*
WhAm 3
Buckman, George Rex 1853- *NatCAB 15*
Buckman, Harry Oliver 1883-1964 *WhAm 4*
Buckman, Henry *NewYHSD*
Buckman, Henry Holland, II 1886-1968
WhAm 5
Buckman, John *NewYHSD*

Buckmaster, Bertrand Eugene 1875-1948
NatCAB 37
Buckmaster, Leland Stanford 1894-1967
WhAm 4
Buckmaster, Maurice 1910- *WhWW-II*
Buckminster, Joseph 1751-1812 *ApCAB, Drake,*
NatCAB 11, TwCBDA
Buckminster, Joseph Stevens 1784-1812 *ApCAB,*
DcAmB, Drake, NatCAB 7, TwCBDA,
WhAm H
Buckminster, William 1736-1786 *ApCAB,*
Drake
Buckminster, William J 1813-1878 *ApCAB*
Bucknam, Charles Calvin 1871-1954
NatCAB 46
Bucknam, Ransford D 1869-1915 *WhAm 1*
Bucknell, Howard, Jr. 1899-1971 *WhAm 5*
Bucknell, William 1811-1890 *DcAmB,*
WhAm H
Buckner, Albert Gallatin 1899- *WhAm 4*
Buckner, Alexander 1785-1833 *ApCAB,*
BiAUS, BiDrAC, NatCAB 4, WhAm H
Buckner, Anderson Duncan 1862-1918
NatCAB 17
Buckner, Aylett Hawes d1844 *BiAUS*
Buckner, Aylett Hawes 1816-1894 *BiDrAC,*
WhAm H, WhAmP
Buckner, Aylett Hawes 1817-1864 *NatCAB 13*
Buckner, Aylette 1806-1869 *BiDrAC,*
WhAm H
Buckner, Aylitt *BiAUS*
Buckner, Chester Arthur 1885-1958 *WhAm 3*
Buckner, David Ernest 1894-1956 *WhAm 3*
Buckner, E C 1897-1964 *WhAm 4*
Buckner, Edmund Garnett 1850-1920
NatCAB 25
Buckner, Emory Roy 1877-1941 *ApCAB X,*
DcAmB S3, WhAm 1
Buckner, George Washington 1855- *WhAm 4,*
WhoColR
Buckner, Henry *NewYHSD*
Buckner, Mortimer Norton 1873-1942 *WhAm 2*
Buckner, Richard Aylett 1763-1847 *BiAUS,*
BiDrAC, WhAm H
Buckner, Simon Bolivar 1823-1914 *AmBi,*
ApCAB, BiDConf, DcAmB, NatCAB 13,
NatCAB 16, TwCBDA, WebAB,
WebAMB, WhAm 1, WhoMilH
Buckner, Simon Bolivar 1824?-1914 *Drake*
Buckner, Simon Bolivar, Jr. 1886-1945
DcAmB S3, NatCAB 37, WebAB,
WebAMB, WhAm 2, WhWW-II
Buckner, Thaddeus Gaston 1888-1941
NatCAB 33
Buckner, Thomas Aylette 1865-1942 *WhAm 2*
Buckner, Walker 1871-1939 *WhAm 1*
Buckner, Walter Coleman 1883-1953 *WhAm 3*
Buckner, William Alexander 1872-1954
NatCAB 46
Bucknor, Helen Lewis 1838- *AmWom*
Bucks, William Henry 1848- *WhAm 4*
Buckstaff, Florence Tyng Griswold
WomWWA 14
Buckstone, John B 1802-1879 *WhAm H*
Buckwalter, Clifton Prizer 1880-1950
NatCAB 41
Buckwalter, Tracy Vero 1880-1948 *NatCAB 38,*
WhAm 2
Bucky, Gustav 1880-1963 *WhAm 4*
Bucky, Philip Barnett 1899-1957 *WhAm 3*
Bucove, Bernard 1912-1973 *WhAm 6*
Bucquet, Jean-Baptiste Michel 1746-1780 *DcScB*
Buda, Joseph 1917-1962 *WhAm 5*
Budan DeBoislaurent, Ferdinand F Desire
DcScB
Budd, Britton Ihrie 1871-1965 *ApCAB X,*
WhAm 4
Budd, Charles Arms 1831-1877 *TwCBDA*
Budd, Charles Henry 1822-1880 *ApCAB*
Budd, Charles Henry 1848-1929 *WhAm 3*
Budd, Charles Jay 1859-1926 *WhAm 1*
Budd, Edward Gowen 1870-1946 *DcAmB S4,*
NatCAB 36, WhAm 2
Budd, Edward Gowen, Jr. 1902-1971
NatCAB 57, WhAm 5
Budd, Henry 1849- *ApCAB Sup, WhAm 4*
Budd, James Herbert 1851-1908 *BiDrAC,*
NatCAB 4, TwCBDA, WhAmP

Budd, James Herbert 1853-1908 *WhAm 1*
Budd, Joseph Lancaster 1835-1904 *DcAmB, EncAAH*
Budd, Nathan P 1911-1971 *WhAm 5*
Budd, Ralph 1879-1962 *REnAW, WhAm 4*
Budd, William 1811-1880 *BiHiMed, DcScB*
Buddenhagen, Emerense Walters 1875- *WomWWA 14*
Buddha 560?BC-480BC *McGEWB*
Buddington, Jonathan *NewYHSD*
Buddington, Sidney Ozias 1823-1888 *ApCAB Sup*
Budds, Henry Harold 1903-1954 *NatCAB 43*
Buddy, Charles F 1887-1966 *WhAm 4*
Buddy, William M 1839?- *NewYHSD*
Bude, Guillaume 1467-1540 *McGEWB*
Budenny, Semen Mikhailovich 1883-1973 *WhoMilH*
Budenny, Semyon 1883-1973 *WhWW-II*
Budenz, Louis Francis 1891-1972 *WhAm 5*
Buder, Gustavus Adolphus 1871-1954 *NatCAB 43, WhAm 3*
Buder, Oscar Edward 1876-1965 *NatCAB 50*
Budge, Alfred 1868-1951 *WhAm 3*
Budge, David Clare 1873-1947 *WhAm 2*
Budge, Don 1915- *WebAB*
Budge, Hamer Harold 1910- *BiDrAC*
Budge, Ross A 1910-1950 *WhAm 3*
Budge, Thomas B 1878-1946 *NatCAB 48*
Budge, Walter Lyttleton 1906-1961 *WhAm 4*
Budge, William 1828-1919 *REnAW*
Budgett, Sidney Payne 1862- *WhAm 4*
Budie, Andrew 1837?- *NewYHSD*
Budina, Adolph Otto 1891-1975 *WhAm 6*
Budinger, John Michael 1900-1966 *NatCAB 53, WhAm 4*
Budington, Robert Allyn 1872-1954 *WhAm 3*
Budington, William Ives 1815-1879 *ApCAB, NatCAB 10*
Budlong, Frederick Grandy 1881-1953 *NatCAB 40, NatCAB 47, WhAm 3*
Budlong, Jessie Valentine *WomWWA 14*
Budlong, Minnie Franklin Clarke 1863- *WomWWA 14*
Budner, Erwin Milton 1903-1958 *NatCAB 44*
Budrow, Lester Rusk 1877- *WhAm 5*
Buechner *NewYHSD*
Buehler, Albert Carl 1897-1971 *WhAm 5*
Buehler, Alfred Grether 1900-1970 *NatCAB 56, WhAm 5*
Buehler, Amelia R Keller 1871- *WomWWA 14*
Buehler, Carl 1865-1932 *NatCAB 40*
Buehler, Henry Andrew 1876-1944 *NatCAB 37, WhAm 2*
Buehler, Huber Gray 1864-1924 *DcAmB, WhAm 1*
Buehler, John Henry 1889-1960 *NatCAB 48*
Buehler, William Emmett 1869-1938 *WhAm 1*
Buehler, William George 1837-1919 *WhAm 1*
Buehner, Carl William 1898-1974 *WhAm 6*
Buehr, Karl Albert d1952 *WhAm 3*
Buehrer, Theophil Frederic 1891-1974 *WhAm 6*
Buehring, Paul Henry 1880-1958 *WhAm 3*
Buehrle, Robert Koch 1840- *NatCAB 5*
Buehrman, Peter A 1895-1964 *WhAm 4*
Buek, Gustave Herman 1850-1927 *WhAm 1*
Buel, Alexander H d1853 *BiAUS*
Buel, Alexander Woodruff 1813-1868 *BiAUS, BiDrAC, WhAm H*
Buel, Clarence Clough 1850-1933 *NatCAB 26, TwCBDA, WhAm 1*
Buel, Elizabeth Cynthia Barney 1868-1943 *NatCAB 32, WomWWA 14*
Buel, Henry Wadhams 1820-1893 *NatCAB 28*
Buel, James William 1849-1920 *NatCAB 7, WhAm 1*
Buel, Jesse 1778-1839 *AmBi, ApCAB, DcAmB, EncAAH, McGEWB, NatCAB 11, WhAm H*
Buel, John Laidlaw 1861-1937 *NatCAB 28*
Buel, Samuel 1815-1891 *ApCAB Sup*
Buel, Samuel 1815-1892 *TwCBDA*
Buel, Walker Showers 1890-1957 *WhAm 3*
Buell, Abel 1741?-1822 *DcAmB, NewYHSD*
Buell, Abel 1742-1822 *AmBi, WebAB, WhAm H*
Buell, Abel 1750?-1825? *ApCAB, Drake, TwCBDA*

Buell, Alexander Hamilton 1801-1853 *BiDrAC, WhAm H*
Buell, Augustus C 1847-1904 *WhAm 1*
Buell, Caroline Brown 1843-1927 *AmWom, WhAm 1, WomWWA 14*
Buell, Charles Clinton 1866-1920 *NatCAB 23*
Buell, Charles Edward 1841-1903 *WhAm 1*
Buell, Charles W *NewYHSD*
Buell, Colin Sherman 1861-1938 *NatCAB 28*
Buell, Don Carlos 1818-1898 *AmBi, ApCAB, DcAmB, Drake, NatCAB 4, TwCBDA, WebAB, WebAMB, WhAm H, WhoMilH*
Buell, Dora Phelps *WomWWA 14*
Buell, Edward Armadale 1844-1921 *NatCAB 33*
Buell, Irene Cleveland 1874- *WomWWA 14*
Buell, Jacob Dockstader 1827- *ApCAB*
Buell, Jennie 1863- *WomWWA 14*
Buell, Jesse 1778-1839 *Drake*
Buell, Marcus Darius 1851-1933 *TwCBDA, WhAm 1*
Buell, Martha Merry 1864- *WomWWA 14*
Buell, Murray F 1905-1975 *WhAm 6*
Buell, Raymond Leslie 1896-1946 *NatCAB 34, WhAm 2*
Buell, Richard Hooker 1842- *ApCAB, TwCBDA*
Buell, Robert Carlin, Jr. 1911-1970 *WhAm 5*
Buell, Robert Lewis 1898-1966 *WhAm 4*
Buell, Rufus F 1813-1866 *ApCAB*
Buell, Walter Hull 1858-1944 *NatCAB 33*
Buenger, Edgar Walter 1897-1957 *NatCAB 47*
Buenger, Theodore 1860-1943 *WhAm 2*
Buensod, Alfred Charles 1886-1957 *NatCAB 44*
Buenting, Otto Wilhelm 1873-1940 *NatCAB 30*
Buenting, Otto Wilhelm 1873-1941 *WhAm 1*
Buerg, Johann Tobias *DcScB*
Buerger, Mary Bowles 1869- *WomWWA 14*
Buescher, Ferdinand August 1861-1937 *NatCAB 28*
Buesching, Charles Henry 1889-1962 *NatCAB 52, WhAm 4*
Buesser, Frederick Gustavus 1881-1950 *NatCAB 39, WhAm 3*
Buetow, Herbert Paul 1898-1972 *NatCAB 57, WhAm 5*
Buff, Conrad 1886- *IIBEAAW*
Buff, George Louis 1839-1923 *ApCAB X, NatCAB 20*
Buffalo Bill 1846-1917 *AmBi, DcAmB, EncAAH, McGEWB, REnAW, WebAB, WebAMB*
Buffalo Child Long Lance d1932 *WhAm 1*
Buffett, Howard Homan 1903-1964 *BiDrAC, WhAm 4*
Buffington, Adaline Allston *WomWWA 14*
Buffington, Adelbert Rinaldo 1837-1922 *ApCAB, ApCAB Sup, NatCAB 5, TwCBDA, WhAm 1*
Buffington, Arthur Howland 1887-1945 *NatCAB 34*
Buffington, Eugene Jackson 1863-1937 *NatCAB 32, WhAm 1*
Buffington, George 1898-1961 *NatCAB 50*
Buffington, James 1817-1875 *WhAm H*
Buffington, Joseph 1803-1872 *BiAUS, BiDrAC, WhAm H*
Buffington, Joseph 1855-1947 *NatCAB 33, WhAm 2*
Buffington, Leroy Sunderland 1847-1931 *BnEnAmA, NatCAB 22*
Buffington, Merrill 1900-1966 *WhAm 4*
Buffington, Wiley Ross 1875-1950 *NatCAB 39*
Buffinton, Harold Samuel Robinson 1887-1964 *NatCAB 50*
Buffinton, James 1817-1875 *BiAUS, BiDrAC, TwCBDA*
Buffon, Georges Louis Leclerc, Comte De 1707-1788 *AsBiEn, DcScB, McGEWB*
Bufford, James A *NewYHSD*
Bufford, John H *NewYHSD*
Bufford, John H d1871? *WhAm H*
Buffum, Arnold 1782-1859 *DcAmB, NatCAB 2, TwCBDA, WhAm H*
Buffum, Burt C 1868- *WhAm 4*
Buffum, Douglas Labaree 1878-1961 *WhAm 4*
Buffum, Edward Gould 1820?-1867 *ApCAB, Drake, TwCBDA*
Buffum, George Tower 1846-1926 *NatCAB 17,*

WhAm 1
Buffum, Harry 1895-1968 *NatCAB 54*
Buffum, Hugh Straight 1877-1959 *WhAm 3*
Buffum, Joseph, Jr. 1784-1874 *BiAUS, BiDrAC, WhAm H*
Buffum, Robert Earle 1879-1932 *NatCAB 29, WhAm 1*
Buffum, William Potter 1858- *NatCAB 17*
Buford, Abraham 1749-1833 *ApCAB, DcAmB, Drake, TwCBDA, WebAMB, WhAm H*
Buford, Abraham 1820?-1864 *ApCAB, NatCAB 13, TwCBDA*
Buford, Abraham 1820-1884 *DcAmB, WhAm H*
Buford, Charles Homer 1886-1960 *WhAm 4*
Buford, Elizabeth Burgess 1860- *WhAm 4, WomWWA 14*
Buford, John 1825-1863 *ApCAB, Drake, NatCAB 4*
Buford, John 1826-1863 *AmBi, DcAmB, TwCBDA, WebAMB, WhAm H*
Buford, Lawrence B 1879- *WhAm 6*
Buford, Napoleon Bonaparte 1807-1883 *ApCAB, DcAmB, Drake, NatCAB 4, TwCBDA, WhAm H*
Buford, Rivers Henderson 1878- *WhAm 6*
Bugaev, Nicolay Vasilievich 1837-1903 *DcScB Sup*
Bugan, Thomas Gregory 1896-1955 *NatCAB 44*
Bugan, Thomas Gregory 1898-1955 *WhAm 3*
Bugbee, Benjamin C 1879- *WhAm 3*
Bugbee, Harold Dow 1900-1963 *IIBEAAW*
Bugbee, Henry Greenwood 1881-1945 *NatCAB 35, WhAm 2*
Bugbee, Lester Gladstone 1869-1902 *WhAm 1*
Bugbee, Lucius Halen 1830- *ApCAB*
Bugbee, Lucius Hatfield 1874-1948 *WhAm 2*
Bugbee, Marion L 1871- *WomWWA 14*
Bugbee, Percy Isaac 1858-1935 *WhAm 3*
Bugbee, Perley Rufus 1865-1935 *NatCAB 31*
Bugbee, Ralph X 1884-1948 *NatCAB 42*
Bugbee, Raymond Gilbert 1882-1946 *NatCAB 35*
Bugeaud DeLaPiconnerie, Thomas Robert 1784-1849 *McGEWB, WhoMilH*
Bugee, John Arthur 1885-1928 *NatCAB 21*
Bugg, Benjamin Lamar 1869- *WhAm 5*
Bugg, James Lucknis, Jr. 1920- *EncAAH*
Bugg, Leila Hardin *WomWWA 14*
Bugg, Lelia Hardin *WhAm 5*
Bugg, Robert Malone 1805-1887 *BiAUS, BiDrAC, WhAm H*
Bugge, Reidar 1879-1960 *NatCAB 51*
Bugge, Sven Brun 1878-1949 *NatCAB 43, WhAm 2*
Buggelli, Blanche Swett 1870- *WhAm 5*
Bugniazet, G M d1960 *WhAm 3A*
Buhl, Arthur Hiram 1878-1935 *NatCAB 26, WhAm 1*
Buhl, Frank Henry 1848-1918 *NatCAB 24*
Buhl, Henry, Jr. 1848-1927 *NatCAB 25*
Buhl, Lawrence D d1956 *WhAm 3*
Buhl, Theodore DeLong 1844-1907 *NatCAB 18*
Buhl, Willis Edward 1875-1916 *NatCAB 36*
Buhle, Nicholas A *NewYHSD*
Buhler, Charlotte d1974 *WhAm 6*
Buhler, F *IIBEAAW*
Buhler, Gaspar *NewYHSD*
Buhr, Joseph Frank 1877-1951 *NatCAB 41*
Buhrer, Marguerite Paterson 1868- *WomWWA 14*
Buick, David Dunbar 1854-1929 *NatCAB 34*
Buick, James McNair 1867-1929 *WhAm 1*
Buie, Louis Arthur, Sr. 1890-1975 *WhAm 6*
Buie, Webster Millsaps 1880-1930 *NatCAB 23*
Buies, Arthur 1840- *ApCAB Sup*
Buikstra, Cyrus Renzo 1897-1955 *NatCAB 42*
Buil, Bernardo d1520 *ApCAB*
Buisseret S DeB, Count Conrad De 1865- *WhAm 4*
Buist, Archibald Johnston 1872-1943 *WhAm 2*
Buist, George 1770-1808 *ApCAB*
Buist, George Alexander 1877-1934 *NatCAB 25, WhAm 1*
Buist, George L 1888-1967 *WhAm 4*
Buist, George Lamb 1838-1907 *WhAm 1*
Buist, George Lamb 1872-1951 *NatCAB 40*
Buist, Harold J 1897-1957 *WhAm 3*

Buist, Henry 1829-1887 *NatCAB 2, TwCBDA*
Buist, Henry 1863-1946 *WhAm 2*
Buist, John Robinson 1834-1905 *NatCAB 8*
Buist, John Somers 1839-1910 *WhAm 1*
Bujac, Alfred *NewYHSD*
Buker, Henry 1873-1941 *NatCAB 31*
Bukhari, Muhammad Ibn Ismail, Al- 810-870 *McGEWB*
Bukharin, Nikolai Ivanovich 1858-1938 *McGEWB*
Bukofzer, Manfred F 1910-1955 *WhAm 3*
Bukowski, Peter Ivan 1894-1956 *WhAm 3*
Buley, Roscoe Carlyle 1893-1968 *REnAW, WhAm 5*
Bulfinch, Charles 1763-1844 *AmBi, ApCAB, BiAUS, BnEnAmA, DcAmB, Drake, EncAB, McGEWB, NatCAB 13, NewYHSD, TwCBDA, WebAB, WhAm H*
Bulfinch, Stephen Greenleaf 1809-1870 *ApCAB, Drake, TwCBDA*
Bulfinch, Thomas 1796-1867 *AmBi, ApCAB, DcAmB, Drake, WebAB, WhAm H*
Bulgakov, Leo 1888-1948 *NatCAB 35*
Bulgakov, Michael Afanasievich 1891-1940 *WhAm 4A*
Bulgakov, Mikhail Afanasievich 1891-1940 *McGEWB*
Bulganin, Nikolai Aleksandrovich 1895-1975 *WhAm 6*
Bulganin, Nikolay 1895-1975 *WhWW-II*
Bulger, Thomas J 1844?- *NewYHSD*
Bulkeley, Alpheus Tompkins 1851-1931 *NatCAB 24*
Bulkeley, Edwin 1817-1881 *NatCAB 16*
Bulkeley, Eliphalet Adams 1803-1872 *ApCAB*
Bulkeley, Harry Clough 1878-1948 *WhAm 2*
Bulkeley, John Duncan 1911- *WebAMB*
Bulkeley, Morgan Gardiner 1838-1922 *ApCAB, TwCBDA*
Bulkeley, Morgan Gardner 1837-1922 *BiDrAC, DcAmB, NatCAB 10, WhAm 1, WhAmP*
Bulkeley, Peter 1582?-1658? *DcAmB*
Bulkeley, Peter 1582-1659 *TwCBDA*
Bulkeley, Peter 1583-1659 *ApCAB, WebAB*
Bulkeley, William Eliphalet Adams 1868-1950 *NatCAB 39, WhAm 3*
Bulkeley, William Henry 1840- *TwCBDA*
Bulkley, Charles Henry Augustus 1818-1892 *TwCBDA*
Bulkley, Edwin 1818-1881 *NatCAB 4*
Bulkley, Edwin Muhlenberg 1862-1949 *NatCAB 38*
Bulkley, Frank 1857-1928 *WhAm 1*
Bulkley, George Grant d1940 *WhAm 1*
Bulkley, Harry Conant 1870-1943 *WhAm 2*
Bulkley, Henry Daggett 1803-1872 *ApCAB, TwCBDA*
Bulkley, Henry Daggett 1804-1872 *NatCAB 25*
Bulkley, John Williams 1802-1888 *BiDAmEd, DcAmB, NatCAB 13, WhAm H*
Bulkley, Jonathan Ogden 1898-1967 *NatCAB 53*
Bulkley, L Duncan 1845-1928 *NatCAB 12, NatCAB 13*
Bulkley, Lucius Duncan 1845-1928 *AmBi, ApCAB X, DcAmB, NatCAB 25, WhAm 1*
Bulkley, Mary Ezit *WomWWA 14*
Bulkley, Morgan Gardner 1838- *NatCAB 1*
Bulkley, Peter 1583-1659 *Drake*
Bulkley, Peter 1585-1659 *NatCAB 7*
Bulkley, Robert Johns 1880-1965 *BiDrAC, WhAm 4*
Bull *NewYHSD*
Bull, Alexander Thompson 1827- *NatCAB 5*
Bull, Alfred Castleman 1893-1967 *WhAm 5*
Bull, Archibald Hilton 1847-1920 *ApCAB X, NatCAB 32*
Bull, C Sanford 1871-1955 *NatCAB 43*
Bull, Carroll Gideon 1884-1931 *NatCAB 31, WhAm 1*
Bull, Charles Cornelius 1855- *ApCAB X*
Bull, Charles Livingston 1874-1932 *IIBEAAW, WhAm 1*
Bull, Charles Stedman 1846-1912 *ApCAB X, NatCAB 9, WhAm 1*
Bull, Cornelia Wilcox 1880- *WomWWA 14*

Bull, Dorothy 1887-1934 *WhAm 1*
Bull, E Myron 1904-1953 *WhAm 3*
Bull, Elizabeth A *WomWWA 14*
Bull, Ephraim Wales 1806-1895 *DcAmB, WhAm H*
Bull, Ernest Miller 1875-1943 *NatCAB 32, WhAm 2*
Bull, Frank Kellogg 1857-1927 *NatCAB 18, WhAm 1*
Bull, George Henry 1885-1943 *NatCAB 33*
Bull, George Mairs 1873- *WhAm 5*
Bull, Henry 1600?-1694 *NatCAB 10*
Bull, Henry 1609-1693 *ApCAB, Drake*
Bull, Henry 1610-1694 *TwCBDA*
Bull, Henry 1687-1771 *NatCAB 9*
Bull, James Henry 1852-1932 *NatCAB 41, WhAm 1*
Bull, John *NewYHSD*
Bull, John 1740?-1802 *BiDrAC, WhAm H*
Bull, John 1803-1863 *BiAUS, BiDrAC, WhAm H*
Bull, Ludlow Seguine 1886-1954 *NatCAB 42, WhAm 3*
Bull, Martin 1744-1825 *NewYHSD*
Bull, Mary Louisa 1863- *WomWWA 14*
Bull, Melville 1854-1909 *BiDrAC, TwCBDA, WhAm 1*
Bull, Ole Bornemann 1810-1880 *ApCAB, Drake, NatCAB 4, TwCBDA*
Bull, Richard Harrison 1817-1892 *NatCAB 9, TwCBDA*
Bull, Richard Sutton 1891-1939 *NatCAB 29*
Bull, Sally Franklin Wainwright 1882- *WomWWA 14*
Bull, Sara Chapman 1850-1911 *WhAm 1*
Bull, Sarah C Thorpe *AmWom*
Bull, Sitting 1837-1890 *NatCAB 13*
Bull, Stephen 1822-1913 *NatCAB 10, NatCAB 18*
Bull, Storm 1856-1907 *WhAm 1*
Bull, William 1683-1755 *DcAmB, NatCAB 12, WhAm H*
Bull, William 1710-1791 *ApCAB, DcAmB, NatCAB 12, WhAm H*
Bull, William 1714-1791 *Drake*
Bull, William Lanman 1844-1914 *WhAm 1*
Bull, William Lanman 1881-1912 *NatCAB 20*
Bull, William Rutledge 1880- *WhAm 6*
Bull, William Tillinghast 1849-1909 *AmBi, ApCAB X, DcAmB, NatCAB 9, TwCBDA, WhAm 1*
Bulla, Charles Dehaven d1932 *WhAm 1*
Bulla, Robert Nelson 1850-1935 *WhAm 1*
Bulla, Robert Nelson 1852-1935 *NatCAB 13*
Bullard, A *NewYHSD*
Bullard, Arthur 1879-1929 *NatCAB 21, WhAm 1*
Bullard, Asa 1804-1888 *ApCAB, TwCBDA*
Bullard, Bernice Frost 1854-1917 *NatCAB 18*
Bullard, Carrie *WomWWA 14*
Bullard, Charles *NewYHSD*
Bullard, Daniel R 1894-1972 *WhAm 5*
Bullard, Dudley Brewster 1869-1941 *NatCAB 31*
Bullard, Edward Clarke 1896-1973 *WhAm 5*
Bullard, Edward Payson 1841-1906 *NatCAB 31*
Bullard, Edward Payson, Jr. 1872-1953 *WhAm 3*
Bullard, Ernest Luther 1859-1931 *NatCAB 38, WhAm 1*
Bullard, F Lauriston 1866-1952 *WhAm 3*
Bullard, Frank Dearborn 1860-1936 *NatCAB 13, WhAm 1*
Bullard, Frederic Field 1864-1904 *NatCAB 13, WhAm 1*
Bullard, George Clough 1916-1966 *NatCAB 55*
Bullard, H Hays 1883-1954 *NatCAB 43*
Bullard, Henry Adams 1781-1851 *ApCAB, BiAUS, TwCBDA*
Bullard, Henry Adams 1788-1851 *BiDrAC, DcAmB, Drake, WhAm H*
Bullard, Herbert Spencer 1865-1945 *NatCAB 33*
Bullard, James Atkins 1887-1959 *WhAm 3*
Bullard, John Thornton 1864-1927 *NatCAB 31*
Bullard, Massena 1850- *NatCAB 11*
Bullard, Otis A 1816-1853 *NewYHSD, WhAm H*

Bullard, Ralph Hadley 1895-1961 *NatCAB 49, WhAm 4*
Bullard, Robert Felton 1908-1969 *WhAm 5*
Bullard, Robert Lee 1861-1947 *DcAmB S4, WebAMB, WhAm 2*
Bullard, Stanley Hale 1877-1931 *NatCAB 31, WhAm 1*
Bullard, Talbot 1815-1863 *ApCAB*
Bullard, W Irving d1948 *WhAm 2*
Bullard, William Hannum Grubb 1866-1927 *AmBi, DcAmB, WebAMB, WhAm 1*
Bullard, William Norton 1853-1931 *NatCAB 26, WhAm 1*
Bullard, William Potter 1861-1942 *NatCAB 32*
Bullen, Percy Sutherland 1868- *WhAm 5*
Bullen, Roy 1877-1930 *NatCAB 24*
Bullen, Mrs. William *NewYHSD*
Bullene, Egbert Frank 1895-1958 *WhAm 3*
Buller, Arthur Henry Reginald 1874-1944 *DcScB*
Buller, Sir Redvers Henry 1839-1908 *WhoMilH*
Bullet, Charles *NewYHSD*
Bullialdus, Ismael *DcScB*
Bulliet, Clarence Joseph 1883-1952 *WhAm 3*
Bullington, John P 1899-1948 *WhAm 2*
Bullington, Josiah Thomas 1875-1968 *NatCAB 54*
Bullions, Peter 1791-1864 *ApCAB, Drake, TwCBDA*
Bullis, Harry Amos 1890-1963 *NatCAB 50, WhAm 4*
Bullis, Jeannette 1876- *WomWWA 14*
Bullis, John Lapham 1841-1911 *WhAm 1*
Bullis, Spencer Seth 1849-1928 *NatCAB 35*
Bullitt, A Scott 1877-1932 *NatCAB 28*
Bullitt, Alexander Scott 1761-1816 *ApCAB, BiAUS, Drake, NatCAB 11, TwCBDA, WhAm H*
Bullitt, Alexander Scott 1762-1816 *DcAmB*
Bullitt, George *BiAUS*
Bullitt, Henry Massie 1817-1880 *DcAmB, WhAm H*
Bullitt, James Bell, Jr. 1906-1957 *NatCAB 49*
Bullitt, John Christian 1824-1902 *NatCAB 1, NatCAB 22, TwCBDA, WhAm 1*
Bullitt, John Christian, Jr. 1871-1925 *NatCAB 22*
Bullitt, Joshua Fry 1821-1897 *NatCAB 13*
Bullitt, Joshua Fry 1856- *NatCAB 18*
Bullitt, Margaret Emmons *WomWWA 14*
Bullitt, Scott 1880-1932 *WhAm 1*
Bullitt, Thomas Walker 1838-1910 *NatCAB 13, WhAm 1*
Bullitt, William Christian 1856-1914 *NatCAB 15*
Bullitt, William Christian 1891-1967 *WhAm 4*
Bullitt, William Marshall 1873-1957 *WhAm 3*
Bulloch, Archibald 1729?-1777 *DcAmB, WhAm H*
Bulloch, Archibald 1730?-1777 *ApCAB, BiDrAC, NatCAB 1, TwCBDA, WhAmP*
Bulloch, Archibald see also Bullock, Archibald
Bulloch, James Dunwody 1823-1901 *AmBi, DcAmB, WebAMB*
Bulloch, James Dunwoody 1823-1901 *BiDConf*
Bulloch, James Dunwoody see also Bullock, James Dunwoody
Bulloch, James R *BiAUS*
Bulloch, Joseph Gaston Baillie 1852- *WhAm 4*
Bulloch, William 1868-1941 *DcScB*
Bulloch, William Bellinger 1776-1852 *ApCAB, BiAUS, NatCAB 4, TwCBDA*
Bulloch, William Bellinger 1777-1852 *BiDrAC, WhAm H*
Bulloch, William Gaston 1815-1885 *ApCAB Sup*
Bullock, A George 1847-1926 *WhAm 1*
Bullock, Alexander Hamilton 1816-1882 *ApCAB, BiAUS, Drake, NatCAB 1, TwCBDA, WhAm H*
Bullock, Alexander Hamilton 1874-1962 *WhAm 4*
Bullock, Archibald d1777 *BiAUS, Drake*
Bullock, Archibald see also Bulloch, Archibald
Bullock, Calvin 1867-1944 *WhAm 2*
Bullock, Carl Curtis 1868-1934 *NatCAB 26*
Bullock, Chandler 1872- *WhAm 5*
Bullock, Charles 1826-1900 *NatCAB 5*

Bullock, Charles Harmon 1875- *WhoColR*
Bullock, Charles Jesse 1869-1941 *WhAm 1*
Bullock, Florence Gertrude 1875-
 WomWWA 14
Bullock, Harry Elmer 1884-1948 *WhAm 3*
Bullock, Helen Louise 1836- *AmWom*
Bullock, Helena M C 1872- *WomWWA 14*
Bullock, James Dunwoody 1823-1901 *WhAm H*
Bullock, James Dunwoody *see also* Bulloch,
 James Dunwoody
Bullock, James Edward 1844-1915 *NatCAB 17*
Bullock, Jonathan Russell 1815-1899 *ApCAB*,
 TwCBDA
Bullock, Mary Ann 1838-1918 *NatCAB 19*
Bullock, Matthew Washington 1881- *WhoColR*
Bullock, Miles Wayne 1844- *NatCAB 17*
Bullock, Motier Acklin 1851-1924 *WhAm 1*
Bullock, Robert 1828-1905 *BiDrAC*, *TwCBDA*
Bullock, Rockwood Hoar 1881-1958
 NatCAB 48
Bullock, Rufus Brown 1834-1907 *ApCAB*,
 BiAUS, *DcAmB*, *NatCAB 1*, *TwCBDA*,
 WhAmP
Bullock, Stephen 1735-1816 *BiAUS*, *BiDrAC*,
 NatCAB 2, *WhAm H*
Bullock, Theodore 1889-1953 *WhAm 3*
Bullock, Thomas Seaman 1853- *NatCAB 3*,
 WhAm 4
Bullock, William *Drake*
Bullock, William A 1813-1867 *AmBi*, *ApCAB*,
 DcAmB, *WhAm H*
Bullock, William Dexter 1850-1923 *NatCAB 20*
Bullock, Wingfield d1821 *BiAUS*, *BiDrAC*,
 WhAm H
Bullock, Wynn 1902- *BnEnAmA*
Bullowa, Emilie M 1869-1942 *NatCAB 31*
Bullowa, Jesse G M 1879-1943 *WhAm 2*
Bulluck, Ernest Southerland 1888-1944
 NatCAB 40
Bullus, Oscar 1800-1871 *ApCAB*, *TwCBDA*
Bulman, John Noel Thompson 1900-1971
 WhAm 5
Bulman, Olivier Meredith Boone 1902-1974
 WhAm 6
Bulnes, Manuel 1799-1866 *ApCAB Sup*,
 WhoMilH
Bulova, Arde 1889-1958 *NatCAB 49*,
 WhAm 3
Bulow, Dietrich Adam H Freiherr Von 1757-1807
 WhoMilH
Bulow, William John 1869-1960 *BiDrAC*,
 NatCAB 46, *WhAm 3*, *WhAmP*
Bulson, Florence J 1858- *WomWWA 14*
Bultmann, Rudolf Karl 1884- *McGEWB*
Bulwer, William Henry Lytton Earle 1801-1872
 ApCAB, *TwCBDA*
Bulwinkle, Alfred Lee 1883-1950 *BiDrAC*,
 NatCAB 41, *WhAm 3*, *WhAmP*
Bumby, John Harold 1900-1974 *WhAm 6*
Bumgardner, Helen Ayers 1929-1972 *WhAm 6*
Bumgarner, Ray Quincy 1902-1972 *WhAm 5*
Bump, Charles Weathers 1872-1908 *WhAm 1*
Bump, Milan Raynard 1881-1925 *ApCAB X*,
 WhAm 1
Bump, Orlando Franklin 1841-1881 *TwCBDA*
Bumpass, James 1867- *WhoColR*
Bumpous, E T 1892-1966 *WhAm 4*
Bumpus, Hermon Carey 1862- *NatCAB 13*
Bumpus, Hermon Carey 1862-1942 *NatCAB 32*
Bumpus, Hermon Carey 1862-1943 *WhAm 2*
Bumpus, Marie Louise *WomWWA 14*
Bumstead, Anna Hoit 1848- *WomWWA 14*
Bumstead, Charles W 1873- *WhAm 5*
Bumstead, Eudora Stone 1860- *AmWom*
Bumstead, Freeman Josiah 1826-1879 *ApCAB*,
 DcAmB, *Drake*, *TwCBDA*, *WhAm H*
Bumstead, Henry Andrews 1870-1920 *DcAmB*,
 NatCAB 15, *NatCAB 21*, *WhAm 1*
Bumstead, Horace 1841-1919 *DcAmB*,
 NatCAB 5, *NatCAB 26*, *TwCBDA*,
 WhAm 1
Bunau-Varilla, Philippe Jean 1859-1940
 McGEWB
Bunce, Allen Hamilton 1889-1965 *NatCAB 52*,
 WhAm 4
Bunce, Arthur C 1901-1953 *WhAm 3*
Bunce, Edgar F 1887-1974 *WhAm 6*
Bunce, Francis Marvin 1836-1901 *TwCBDA*,

WhAm 1
Bunce, Gedney 1840-1916 *NatCAB 18*
Bunce, J Oscar 1867- *WhAm 4*
Bunce, Jonathan Brace 1832-1912 *NatCAB 29*
Bunce, Oliver Bell 1825-1890 *WhAm H*
Bunce, Oliver Bell 1828-1890 *AmBi*, *ApCAB*,
 DcAmB, *NatCAB 2*, *TwCBDA*
Bunce, William Gedney 1840-1916 *AmBi*,
 DcAmB, *NatCAB 15*, *NewYHSD*,
 WhAm 1
Bunce, William Gedney 1842-1916 *ApCAB*,
 TwCBDA
Bunch, Samuel 1786-1849 *ApCAB*, *BiAUS*,
 BiDrAC, *Drake*, *WhAm H*
Bunche, Ralph Johnson 1904-1971 *EncAB*,
 McGEWB, *NatCAB 57*, *WebAB*,
 WhAm 5
Buncher, Henry *NewYHSD*
Buncombe, Edward d1777 *ApCAB*
Buncombe, Richard d1777 *Drake*
Bundel, Charles Michael 1875-1941 *WhAm 1*
Bundesen, Herman Niels 1882-1960 *WhAm 4*
Bundlie, Gerhard Julius 1889-1966 *NatCAB 57*,
 WhAm 4
Bundy, Edwin S 1889-1963 *WhAm 4*
Bundy, Eugene Halleck 1846-1917 *NatCAB 17*
Bundy, Harvey Hollister 1888-1963 *NatCAB 50*,
 WhAm 4
Bundy, Hezekiah Sanford 1817-1895 *BiAUS*,
 BiDrAC, *WhAm H*, *WhAmP*
Bundy, Horace 1814-1883 *NewYHSD*
Bundy, James F 1862- *WhoColR*
Bundy, John Elwood 1853-1933 *WhAm 1*
Bundy, Jonas Mills 1835-1891 *DcAmB*,
 NatCAB 1, *TwCBDA*, *WhAm H*
Bundy, McGeorge 1919- *EncAB*
Bundy, Omar 1861-1940 *NatCAB 29*,
 WebAMB, *WhAm 1*
Bundy, Richard C *WhoColR*
Bundy, Solomon 1823-1889 *BiDrAC*,
 WhAm H
Bundy, William Edgar 1866-1903 *WhAm 1*
Bungay, George Washington 1826-1892
 ApCAB Sup
Bunge, Gustav Von 1844-1920 *DcScB*
Bunge, Helen Lathrop 1906-1970 *WhAm 5*
Bunge, Sarah Emily Wheeler *WomWWA 14*
Bunim, Joseph Jay 1906-1964 *NatCAB 52*,
 WhAm 4
Bunin, Ivan Alekseevich 1870-1953 *McGEWB*,
 WhAm 3
Bunker, Alonzo 1837-1912 *WhAm 1*
Bunker, Annie Jerina Ellers *WomWWA 14*
Bunker, Arthur H 1895-1964 *WhAm 4*
Bunker, Berkeley Lloyd 1906- *BiDrAC*
Bunker, Charles C 1880- *WhAm 6*
Bunker, Charles Waite Orville 1882-1958
 WhAm 3
Bunker, Daisy Davenport Bryan 1879-
 WomWWA 14
Bunker, Elizabeth Johnson 1855-
 WomWWA 14
Bunker, Frank Forest 1873-1944 *WhAm 2*
Bunker, George Raymond 1845-1927
 NatCAB 26
Bunker, Harry Surfus 1900-1966 *WhAm 4*
Bunker, Marie Rowland *WomWWA 14*
Bunker, Paul Delmont 1881-1943 *NatCAB 33*
Bunkley, Joel William 1887-1967 *WhAm 4A*
Bunkley, Joel William, Jr. 1916-1971 *WhAm 5*
Bunn, Benjamin Hickman 1844-1907 *BiDrAC*,
 TwCBDA
Bunn, Charles Wilson 1855-1941 *NatCAB 33*,
 WhAm 1
Bunn, Charles Wilson 1893-1964 *ApCAB X*,
 WhAm 4
Bunn, Clinton Orrin 1877-1924 *WhAm 1*
Bunn, Edward Bernard 1896-1972 *WhAm 5*
Bunn, Edward Schaible 1906-1969 *WhAm 5*
Bunn, George Lincoln 1865-1918 *WhAm 1*
Bunn, Henry Gaston 1838-1908 *NatCAB 9*,
 WhAm 1
Bunn, Henry Walter 1874-1935 *NatCAB 26*
Bunn, Howard Stolpp 1899-1964 *WhAm 4*
Bunn, Jacob 1864-1926 *WhAm 1*
Bunn, Paul Axtell 1914-1970 *NatCAB 55*,
 WhAm 5
Bunn, Romanzo 1829-1909 *NatCAB 26*,

WhAm 1
Bunn, William Hall 1889-1961 *NatCAB 52*,
 WhAm 4
Bunnell, Charles Ernest 1878-1956 *BiDAmEd*,
 WhAm 3
Bunnell, Charles Ragland 1897-1968 *IIBEAAW*,
 NatCAB 54
Bunnell, Edward Horace 1882-1953 *WhAm 3*
Bunnell, Frank Charles *BiDrAC*
Bunnell, Sterling 1882-1957 *NatCAB 46*
Bunnell, Sterling Haight 1871- *WhAm 5*
Bunner, Henry Cuyler 1855-1896 *AmBi*,
 ApCAB Sup, *DcAmB*, *NatCAB 7*,
 TwCBDA, *WhAm H*
Bunner, Rudolph 1779-1837 *BiAUS*, *BiDrAC*,
 WhAm H
Bunse, Augustus *NewYHSD*
Bunsen, Robert Wilhelm Eberhard 1811-1899
 AsBiEn, *DcScB*, *McGEWB*
Bunshaft, Gordon 1909- *BnEnAmA*
Bunten, Alonzo *NewYHSD*
Buntin, Thomas Eugene 1896-1958 *NatCAB 48*
Bunting, Charles Edmund 1886-1956
 NatCAB 48
Bunting, Charles Henry 1875- *WhAm 5*
Bunting, Christopher William 1837- *ApCAB*
Bunting, Florence M 1879- *WomWWA 14*
Bunting, George Avery 1870-1960 *WhAm 3*
Bunting, Guy J 1881-1937 *WhAm 1*
Bunting, Henry Stanhope 1869-1948
 NatCAB 37
Bunting, Martha 1861- *WhAm 4*,
 WomWWA 14
Bunting, Morgan 1863-1929 *NatCAB 21*
Bunting, Russell Welford 1881-1962 *WhAm 4*
Bunting, Thomas Lathrop 1844-1898 *BiDrAC*
Buntline, Ned 1823-1886 *AmBi*, *WebAB*,
 WhAm H
Bunts, Frank Emory 1861-1928 *NatCAB 21*,
 WhAm 1
Bunuel, Luis 1900- *McGEWB*
Bunyakovsky, Viktor Yakovlevich 1804-1889
 DcScB Sup
Bunyan, John 1628-1688 *McGEWB*
Bunzell, Herbert Horace 1887-1964 *WhAm 4*
Bunzl, Carrie Elizabeth Goble 1865-
 WomWWA 14
Buonamici, Francesco d1603 *DcScB*
Buonanni, Filippo 1638-1725 *DcScB*
Buono, Paolo Del 1625-1659 *DcScB*
Buonvicino, Costanzo Benedetto *DcScB*
Buot, Jacques d1675? *DcScB*
Buquor, Adolph Paschal 1893-1971 *NatCAB 56*
Burali-Forti, Cesare 1861-1931 *DcScB*
Burba, Edwin Hess 1912-1970 *WhAm 5*
Burba, George Francis 1865-1920 *WhAm 1*
Burbage, William Henry 1854- *WhAm 4*
Burbank *NewYHSD*
Burbank, Alfred Post 1846-1894 *NatCAB 6*
Burbank, Caleb *NewYHSD*
Burbank, Elbridge Ayar 1858-1949 *REnAW*
Burbank, Elbridge Ayer 1858-1949 *IIBEAAW*,
 NatCAB 11, *WhAm 2*
Burbank, Harold Hitchings 1887-1951 *WhAm 3*
Burbank, J Maze *NewYHSD*
Burbank, James Brattle 1838-1928 *WhAm 1*
Burbank, Luther 1849-1926 *AmBi*, *ApCAB X*,
 AsBiEn, *DcAmB*, *EncAAH*, *EncAB*,
 McGEWB, *NatCAB 11*, *NatCAB 33*,
 WebAB, *WhAm 1*
Burbank, Mortimer Lincoln 1878-1956
 WhAm 3
Burbank, Robert Abraham 1872-1959
 NatCAB 47
Burbank, Sidney 1807-1882 *ApCAB*, *Drake*,
 TwCBDA
Burbank, T L 1814?- *NewYHSD*
Burbank, Wilbur Swett 1898-1975 *WhAm 6*
Burbeck, Henry 1754-1848 *ApCAB*, *Drake*,
 NatCAB 1, *TwCBDA*
Burberry, Martha Dashiell 1865-
 WomWWA 14
Burbidge, Earl LeRoy 1906-1962 *NatCAB 50*
Burbidge, Frederick 1864- *WhAm 4*
Burbidge, Sir Richard Grant Woodman
 1897-1966 *WhAm 4*
Burbridge, George Wheelock 1847- *ApCAB*
Burbridge, Stephen Gano 1831-1894 *ApCAB*,

DcAmB, NatCAB 11, TwCBDA,
WhAm H
Burch, Albert 1867-1943 *NatCAB 35,*
WhAm 5
Burch, Angelus Teague 1895-1967 *WhAm 4*
Burch, Bernard Owen 1900-1966 *NatCAB 53*
Burch, Charles Bell 1891-1959 *WhAm 3*
Burch, Charles Newell 1868-1938 *NatCAB 28,*
WhAm 1
Burch, Charles Sumner 1855-1920 *NatCAB 19,*
WhAm 1
Burch, Edward Parris 1870-1945 *WhAm 2*
Burch, Edward Parris 1906-1963 *NatCAB 51*
Burch, Ernest Ward 1875-1933 *WhAm 1*
Burch, Frank Earl 1876-1957 *WhAm 3*
Burch, George Bosworth 1902-1973 *WhAm 6*
Burch, Guy Irving 1899-1951 *WhAm 3*
Burch, H Wendel 1908-1970 *WhAm 5*
Burch, Henry Reed 1876- *WhAm 5*
Burch, James Merrill, Jr. 1887-1969
NatCAB 54
Burch, John Chilton 1826-1885 *BiDrAC,*
WhAm H
Burch, Lowell Ross 1887-1962 *NatCAB 50,*
WhAm 4
Burch, Lucius Edward 1874-1959 *WhAm 4*
Burch, Lucius Edward 1874-1960 *NatCAB 51*
Burch, Milton Gardner 1888-1952 *NatCAB 44*
Burch, Newnan Burgess 1887-1958 *NatCAB 47*
Burch, Newton Dexter 1871-1931 *WhAm 1*
Burch, Rousseau Angelus 1862- *WhAm 4*
Burch, Thomas *NewYHSD*
Burch, Thomas Granville 1869-1951 *BiDrAC,*
NatCAB 39, WhAm 3, WhAmP
Burch, William Arthur 1864- *NatCAB 16*
Burcham, Charles Austin 1859-1913 *NatCAB 8*
Burcham, James Taylor 1873-1924 *NatCAB 21*
Burcham, Thomas Andrew 1882-1965
NatCAB 51
Burchard, Alice Webb 1875- *WomWWA 14*
Burchard, Edward Lawyer 1867-1944
NatCAB 34, WhAm 4
Burchard, Edwin Day 1886-1970 *NatCAB 56*
Burchard, Ernest Francis 1875- *WhAm 5*
Burchard, Henry McNeil *ApCAB X*
Burchard, Horatio Chapin 1825-1908 *BiAUS,*
BiDrAC, NatCAB 13, WhAm 1,
WhAmP
Burchard, John Ely 1898-1975 *WhAm 6*
Burchard, Matthew *BiAUS*
Burchard, Samuel Dickerson 1812-1891
TwCBDA
Burchard, Samuel Dickinson 1812-1891 *ApCAB,*
DcAmB, NatCAB 11, WhAm H
Burchard, Samuel Dickinson 1836-1901 *BiAUS,*
BiDrAC
Burchard, Thomas Herring 1850-1896 *TwCBDA*
Burchenal, Elizabeth 1877-1959 *BiDAmEd*
Burchett, George Jerome 1847- *WhAm 4*
Burchfield, Albert Horne 1871-1942
NatCAB 38, WhAm 2
Burchfield, Albert Horne, Jr. 1903-1961
NatCAB 49, WhAm 4
Burchfield, Albert Pressly 1844-1910
NatCAB 38
Burchfield, Charles Ephraim 1893-1967
BnEnAmA, McGEWB, WebAB, WhAm 4
Burchfield, George Winston 1894-1957
NatCAB 50
Burchill, Thomas F 1882-1955 *WhAm 3*
Burchill, Thomas Francis 1882-1960 *BiDrAC*
Burchkhardt, Charles Jacob 1891-1974
WhAm 6
Burckhalter, Charles 1849-1923 *WhAm 1*
Burckhalter, Frank Lucien 1879-1936 *WhAm 1*
Burckhardt, Jacob Christoph 1818-1897
McGEWB
Burckhardt, Johann Ludwig 1784-1817
McGEWB
Burd, Eliza Howard *NewYHSD*
Burd, George 1793-1844 *BiAUS, BiDrAC,*
WhAm H
Burd, George Eli 1857-1924 *WhAm 1*
Burdach, Karl Friedrich 1776-1847 *DcScB*
Burdell, William Frederick 1857-1945 *WhAm 2*
Burden, Harry P 1890-1972 *WhAm 5*
Burden, Henry 1791-1871 *ApCAB, ApCAB X,*
DcAmB, Drake, NatCAB 2, TwCBDA,

WhAm H
Burden, Isaac Townsend 1838-1913 *NatCAB 15*
Burden, James Abercrombie 1833-1906 *ApCAB,*
ApCAB X, NatCAB 1, TwCBDA,
WhAm 1
Burden, James Abercrombie 1871-1932
ApCAB X, NatCAB 24, WhAm 1
Burden, Kinsey 1775-1859 *ApCAB Sup*
Burden, Oliver D 1873-1947 *WhAm 2*
Burden, Oscar R 1885-1960 *NatCAB 49*
Burdenko, Nicolai Nilovich 1876-1964 *DcScB*
Burdett, Charles Albert 1858-1922 *NatCAB 22*
Burdett, Elizabeth Terry White *WomWWA 14*
Burdett, Everett Watson 1854-1925 *NatCAB 34,*
WhAm 4
Burdett, Fred Hartshorn 1861-1935 *WhAm 1*
Burdett, George Albert 1856- *WhAm 4*
Burdett, Herbert C 1855-1891 *WhAm H*
Burdett, Samuel Swinfin 1836-1914 *BiAUS,*
BiDrAC, NatCAB 5, WhAm 1
Burdett, William Carter 1884-1944 *WhAm 2*
Burdett-Coutts *ApCAB Sup*
Burdette, Clara Bradley 1855- *WhAm 5,*
WomWWA 14
Burdette, Franklin L 1911-1975 *WhAm 6*
Burdette, Robert Jones 1844-1914 *AmBi,*
ApCAB, DcAmB, NatCAB 1,
NatCAB 24, TwCBDA, WhAm 1
Burdge, Franklin 1835- *WhAm 1*
Burdge, Howard Griffith 1873-1957 *WhAm 3*
Burdick, Alfred Stephen 1867-1933 *NatCAB 24,*
WhAm 1
Burdick, Charles Baker 1874-1955 *WhAm 3*
Burdick, Charles Kellogg 1883-1940
NatCAB 29, WhAm 1, WhAm 2
Burdick, Charles Williams 1860-1927 *WhAm 1*
Burdick, Clark 1868-1948 *BiDrAC, WhAm 2,*
WhAmP
Burdick, Clinton DeWitt 1863-1933 *WhAm 1*
Burdick, Donald Langworthy 1900-1967
WhAm 5
Burdick, Eugene L 1918-1965 *WhAm 4*
Burdick, Francis Marion 1845-1920 *DcAmB,*
NatCAB 12, NatCAB 26, WhAm 1
Burdick, Gordon Granger 1864-1956
NatCAB 47
Burdick, Harold Ormond 1897-1974 *WhAm 6*
Burdick, Irving Elisha 1876-1944 *NatCAB 33*
Burdick, James Manley 1864-1935 *NatCAB 29*
Burdick, Joel Wakeman 1853-1925 *ApCAB X,*
NatCAB 25, WhAm 1
Burdick, Julian 1878-1929 *NatCAB 31*
Burdick, Quentin Northrop 1908- *BiDrAC,*
EncAAH
Burdick, Reginald Houghton 1884-1953
NatCAB 41
Burdick, Theodore Weld 1836-1898 *BiDrAC*
Burdick, Usher Lloyd 1879-1960 *BiDrAC,*
REnAW, WhAm 4, WhAmP
Burdick, Willard DeLure 1863-1948 *WhAm 3*
Burdick, William Livesey 1860-1946
NatCAB 35, WhAm 2
Burdon-Sanderson, Sir John Scott 1828-1905
BiHiMed, DcScB
Burdorf, Fred G 1886-1962 *NatCAB 50*
Bureau, E A 1886-1954 *WhAm 3*
Bureau, Jacques Olivier 1820- *ApCAB*
Bures, Charles Edwin 1910-1974 *WhAm 6*
Burfield, George 1805?- *NewYHSD*
Burford, Archie Dean 1892- *WhAm 2*
Burford, Bernard Boyd 1912-1966 *WhAm 4*
Burford, Cyrus Edgar 1876-1972 *WhAm 5*
Burford, John *NewYHSD*
Burford, John Henry 1852-1922 *NatCAB 14,*
WhAm 1
Burg, Alfred William 1880-1956 *WhAm 3*
Burg, Copeland 1889-1961 *NatCAB 47*
Burg, Johann Tobias 1766-1834 *DcScB*
Burg, Louis 1820?- *NewYHSD*
Burgan, Isaac Medford 1848- *WhoColR*
Burgan, John 1913-1951 *WhAm 3*
Burgart, Laverda Adelia 1883- *WomWWA 14*
Burgdorff, Ferdinand 1881?- *IIBEAAW*
Burge, Edward Seymour 1909-1963 *NatCAB 50*
Burge, Flippen D 1894-1946 *WhAm 2*
Burge, J H Hobart 1823-1901 *WhAm 1*
Burgee, Clyde Elmore 1894-1970 *WhAm 5*
Burgee, Joseph Zeno 1897-1956 *WhAm 3*

Burgeni, Alfred Adolph 1903-1970 *NatCAB 55*
Burger, Charles F *NewYHSD*
Burger, Herman Carel 1893-1965 *DcScB*
Burger, John D 1887-1943 *WhAm 2*
Burger, Kathryn Reynolds d1958 *WhAm 3*
Burger, Louis 1821-1871 *ApCAB*
Burger, Owen Francis 1885-1928 *WhAm 1*
Burger, Robert *NewYHSD*
Burger, Walter Theodore 1905-1969
NatCAB 55
Burger, Warren Earl 1907- *WebAB*
Burger, William Henry 1874-1962 *WhAm 4,*
WhAm 5
Burgersdijk, Frank 1590-1635 *DcScB*
Burges, Bartholomew *NewYHSD*
Burges, Dempsey 1751-1800 *BiDrAC,*
WhAm H
Burges, Richard Fenner 1873-1945 *NatCAB 17,*
NatCAB 35, WhAm 2
Burges, Tristam 1770-1853 *ApCAB, BiAUS,*
BiDrAC, Drake, NatCAB 8, TwCBDA,
WhAm H, WhAmP
Burges, William Henry 1867-1946 *NatCAB 37,*
WhAm 2
Burgess, Abel Monroe 1866- *WhoColR*
Burgess, Albert 1856- *WhoColR*
Burgess, Albert Franklin 1873-1953 *NatCAB 43,*
WhAm 3
Burgess, Alexander 1819-1901 *ApCAB,*
DcAmB, NatCAB 11, TwCBDA,
WhAm 1
Burgess, Alexander Mackinnon 1850- *ApCAB*
Burgess, Charles Frederick 1873-1945
NatCAB 14, NatCAB 34, WhAm 2
Burgess, Charles McFetridge 1896-1972
WhAm 5
Burgess, Cora Louise Turney 1910-1962
WhAm 4
Burgess, Dempsey *BiAUS*
Burgess, Ebenezer 1790-1870 *ApCAB, Drake*
Burgess, Ebenezer 1805-1870 *ApCAB*
Burgess, Edward 1848-1891 *ApCAB, DcAmB,*
NatCAB 1, WhAm H
Burgess, Edward Sandford 1855-1928
NatCAB 21, WhAm 1
Burgess, Elizabeth Chamberlain 1877-1949
WhAm 2
Burgess, Ellis Beaver 1869-1947 *WhAm 2*
Burgess, Ernest Watson 1886-1966 *WhAm 4*
Burgess, Frances Elinor 1857- *WomWWA 14*
Burgess, Frank Gelett 1866-1951 *DcAmB S5*
Burgess, Frank H 1875-1939 *WhAm 1*
Burgess, Frederick 1853-1925 *NatCAB 13,*
TwCBDA, WhAm 1
Burgess, Gaven D 1835-1910 *WhAm 1*
Burgess, Gavon D 1834-1910 *NatCAB 12*
Burgess, Gelett 1866-1951 *NatCAB 14,*
WebAB, WhAm 3
Burgess, George 1809-1866 *ApCAB, DcAmB,*
Drake, NatCAB 4, TwCBDA, WhAm H
Burgess, George 1831-1905 *NewYHSD*
Burgess, George Farmer 1861-1919 *BiDrAC,*
WhAm 1, WhAmP
Burgess, George Heckman 1874-1957
NatCAB 48, WhAm 3
Burgess, George Henry 1831?-1905 *IIBEAAW*
Burgess, George Kimball 1874-1932 *AmBi,*
DcAmB S1, NatCAB 24, WhAm 1
Burgess, Harry 1872-1933 *WhAm 1*
Burgess, Ida Josephine *WhAm 1,*
WomWWA 14
Burgess, J Stewart 1883-1949 *NatCAB 39*
Burgess, John Albert 1876- *WhAm 5*
Burgess, John William 1844-1931 *AmBi,*
ApCAB, BiDAmEd, DcAmB S1,
NatCAB 13, NatCAB 23, TwCBDA,
WhAm 1
Burgess, Kenneth Farwell 1887-1965 *WhAm 4*
Burgess, May Ayres 1888-1953 *WhAm 3*
Burgess, Neil 1851-1910 *DcAmB, NatCAB 2*
Burgess, Paul Steere 1885-1968 *NatCAB 56*
Burgess, Perry 1886-1962 *WhAm 4*
Burgess, Philip 1876- *WhAm 5*
Burgess, Rembert Bennett 1894-1962 *WhAm 4*
Burgess, Robert Wilbur 1887-1969 *WhAm 5*
Burgess, Rosamond Tudor 1878-
WomWWA 14
Burgess, Roy Howard, Jr. 1910-1954 *WhAm 3*

Burgess, Ruth Payne Jewett d1934 *WhAm 1,*
WomWWA 14
Burgess, Mrs. Samuel Rostron *WhAm 5*
Burgess, Theodore Chalon 1859-1925 *BiDAmEd,*
NatCAB 20, WhAm 1
Burgess, Theodore Herbert 1882-1961
NatCAB 47, WhAm 4
Burgess, Theodore Phillips 1864-1917
NatCAB 17
Burgess, Thomas M 1903-1960 *WhAm 4*
Burgess, Thornton Waldo 1874-1965 *WhAm 4*
Burgess, W Starling 1878-1947 *DcAmB S4,*
NatCAB 37, WhAm 2
Burgess, William 1843-1922 *WhAm 1*
Burgess, William 1857-1929 *NatCAB 13,*
WhAm 1
Burgett, John M H 1850- *NatCAB 9*
Burgevine, Henry Andrea 1836-1863
NatCAB 22
Burgevine, Henry Andrea 1836-1865 *DcAmB,*
WhAm H
Burghalter, Daniel 1867-1947 *WhAm 2*
Burgham, Edwin Oliver 1889-1969 *NatCAB 57*
Burgher, Clarence Livingston 1866-1954
NatCAB 41
Burgi, Joost 1552-1632 *DcScB*
Burgin, Henry T 1882-1958 *WhAm 3*
Burgin, Samuel H C 1871- *WhAm 5*
Burgin, William Garner 1892-1970 *WhAm 5*
Burgin, William Olin 1877-1946 *BiDrAC,*
WhAm 2, WhAmP
Burgis, William *BnEnAmA, DcAmB,*
NewYHSD, WhAm H
Burgiss, William Wesley 1863- *WhAm 3*
Burgoa, Francisco 1605?-1681 *ApCAB*
Burgoyne, Ina Forrest Davis *WomWWA 14*
Burgoyne, John 1722-1792 *AmBi, WhAm H,*
WhoMilH
Burgoyne, John 1723-1792 *ApCAB, McGEWB*
Burgoyne, John 1730-1792 *Drake*
Burgoyne, Sir John Fox 1782-1871 *ApCAB*
Burgum, John 1826-1907 *NewYHSD*
Burgunder, B Bernei 1891-1948 *NatCAB 38*
Burgwin, George Collinson 1851-1925
NatCAB 21
Burhans, Daniel 1762-1853 *ApCAB Sup*
Burhop, William Henry 1889-1963 *WhAm 4*
Burianek, John, Jr. 1871- *NatCAB 16*
Buridan, Jean 1295?-1358? *DcScB*
Buridan, Jean 1300?-1385? *AsBiEn*
Burine *NewYHSD*
Burk, Addison Briggs 1847-1912 *NatCAB 28*
Burk, Frederic Lister 1862-1924 *BiDAmEd,*
DcAmB, WhAm 1
Burk, Henry 1850-1903 *BiDrAC*
Burk, Henry 1850-1905 *WhAm 1*
Burk, Jesse Young 1840-1904 *ApCAB X,*
WhAm 1
Burk, John Daly 1775?-1808 *ApCAB, DcAmB,*
NatCAB 19
Burk, John Junius 1800-1866 *ApCAB*
Burk, John Naglee 1891-1967 *NatCAB 53*
Burk, Joseph Edwill 1893-1946 *WhAm 2*
Burk, Martha Cannary 1852?-1903 *NotAW*
Burk, William Herbert 1867-1933 *ApCAB X,*
NatCAB 24, WhAm 1
Burk, William W 1878-1948 *NatCAB 37*
Burkam, Elzey Gallatin 1872-1940 *NatCAB 32*
Burkard, Oscar Rudolph 1877-1950 *NatCAB 39*
Burkart, Joseph Aloysius 1874-1942
NatCAB 33
Burke, Aedanus 1743-1802 *ApCAB, BiDrAC,*
DcAmB, Drake, NatCAB 13, WhAm H,
WhAmP
Burke, Alexander 1842-1914 *NatCAB 16*
Burke, Alfred Lee 1903-1967 *NatCAB 53*
Burke, Andrew H 1850- *NatCAB 1, TwCBDA,*
WhAm 4
Burke, Annie J Ferguson *WomWWA 14*
Burke, Arleigh Albert 1901- *WebAMB,*
WhWW-II
Burke, Arthur Devries 1893-1950 *WhAm 3*
Burke, Asenath Danforth Spalding 1856-
WomWWA 14
Burke, B Ellen 1850- *WhAm 4*
Burke, Billie 1886-1970 *WhAm 5,*
WomWWA 14
Burke, Carleton Francis 1882-1962 *NatCAB 49*

Burke, Charles H 1850- *NatCAB 1*
Burke, Charles Henry 1861-1944 *BiDrAC,*
NatCAB 33, NatCAB 43, TwCBDA,
WhAm 2, WhAmP
Burke, Charles Saint Thomas 1822-1854
NatCAB 8
Burke, Charles St. Thomas 1822-1854 *DcAmB,*
WhAm H
Burke, Cyril Joseph 1895-1956 *NatCAB 42*
Burke, Daniel 1873-1970 *WhAm 5*
Burke, Daniel Webster 1841-1911 *WhAm 1*
Burke, Edanus *BiAUS*
Burke, Edmund 1729-1797 *McGEWB,*
WhAm H
Burke, Edmund 1730-1797 *ApCAB, Drake*
Burke, Edmund 1809-1882 *ApCAB, BiAUS,*
BiDrAC, Drake, NatCAB 7, TwCBDA,
WhAm H, WhAmP
Burke, Edmund 1876-1970 *WhAm 5*
Burke, Edmund Jefferson 1870-1942
NatCAB 40
Burke, Edmund Stevenson, Jr. 1879-1962
NatCAB 49
Burke, Edmund Whitney 1850-1918 *WhAm 1*
Burke, Edward M 1893-1967 *WhAm 4A*
Burke, Edward Raymond 1880-1968 *BiDrAC,*
NatCAB 54, WhAm 5
Burke, Edward Timothy 1870-1935 *WhAm 1*
Burke, Ellen Coolidge 1901-1975 *WhAm 6*
Burke, Eugene Paul 1883-1961 *WhAm 4*
Burke, F Edward 1865-1942 *NatCAB 33*
Burke, Frank Welsh 1920- *BiDrAC*
Burke, G *NewYHSD*
Burke, George Alexander 1864-1938
NatCAB 28
Burke, George James 1885-1950 *NatCAB 39,*
WhAm 3
Burke, Haslett Platt 1874-1957 *WhAm 3*
Burke, J Herbert 1913- *BiDrAC*
Burke, James Anthony 1910- *BiDrAC*
Burke, James Francis 1867-1932 *BiDrAC,*
NatCAB 7, WhAm 1, WhAmP
Burke, James Owen 1906-1963 *WhAm 4*
Burke, Jeremiah 1843?- *NewYHSD*
Burke, Jeremiah Edmund 1867-1931 *WhAm 1*
Burke, John 1859-1937 *ApCAB X,*
NatCAB 14, REnAW, WhAm 1
Burke, John Daly d1808 *Drake*
Burke, John Edmund 1852- *ApCAB, WhAm 4*
Burke, John G 1846-1896 *DcAmB*
Burke, John Harley 1894-1951 *BiDrAC*
Burke, John Joseph 1875-1936 *DcAmB S2,*
DcAmReB, WhAm 1
Burke, John Masterson 1812-1909 *NatCAB 20*
Burke, John P 1862- *WhAm 4*
Burke, John Stephen 1889-1962 *WhAm 4*
Burke, John William 1826-1898 *NatCAB 2*
Burke, John Woolfolk 1884-1959 *WhAm 3*
Burke, Johnny 1908-1964 *NatCAB 52*
Burke, Joseph A d1962 *WhAm 4*
Burke, Joseph Henry 1876-1940 *WhAm 1*
Burke, Kathleen *BiCAW*
Burke, Kendall Edwards 1893-1943 *WhAm 2*
Burke, Madeleina Forrest *WomWWA 14*
Burke, Marion *WomWWA 14*
Burke, Martha Jane Canary 1852-1903 *AmBi,*
WebAB
Burke, Maurice Francis 1845-1923 *ApCAB Sup,*
NatCAB 12, TwCBDA, WhAm 1
Burke, Michael Edmund 1863-1918 *BiDrAC,*
WhAm 3, WhAmP
Burke, Milo Darwin 1841- *WhAm 4*
Burke, Myra Webster 1847- *WomWWA 14*
Burke, N Charles 1854- *WhAm 4*
Burke, Patrick H 1851-1957 *WhAm 3*
Burke, Raymond Hugh 1881-1954 *BiDrAC,*
WhAm 6
Burke, Robert Belle 1868-1944 *NatCAB 33,*
WhAm 4
Burke, Robert Emmet 1847-1901 *BiDrAC,*
WhAm 1
Burke, Robert O'Hara 1820-1861 *McGEWB*
Burke, Russell Ely 1875-1948 *NatCAB 48,*
NatCAB 49
Burke, Stephen Patrick 1897-1945 *WhAm 2*
Burke, Stevenson 1824-1904 *ApCAB X,*
NatCAB 9, WhAm 1
Burke, Stevenson 1826-1904 *ApCAB, DcAmB*

Burke, Thomas 1747?-1783 *ApCAB, BiAUS,*
BiDrAC, DcAmB, Drake, NatCAB 4,
NatCAB 7, TwCBDA, WhAm H,
WhAmP
Burke, Thomas 1848-1925 *WhAm 1*
Burke, Thomas 1849-1925 *DcAmB,*
NatCAB 11, NatCAB 21, REnAW
Burke, Thomas A 1898-1971 *BiDrAC,*
WhAm 5
Burke, Thomas Henry 1904-1959 *BiDrAC,*
WhAm 3
Burke, Thomas Joseph 1896-1966 *WhAm 4*
Burke, Thomas Martin Aloysius 1840-1915
ApCAB Sup, NatCAB 12, TwCBDA,
WhAm 1
Burke, Timothy Farrar 1855- *WhAm 4*
Burke, Victor 1882-1958 *WhAm 3*
Burke, Vincent John 1919-1973 *WhAm 6*
Burke, Wallace Raymond 1912-1969
NatCAB 55
Burke, Webster H 1881-1958 *WhAm 3*
Burke, William d1787 *Drake*
Burke, William Joseph 1862-1925 *BiDrAC,*
WhAm 1, WhAmP
Burket, Harlan Fessenden 1860- *WhAm 3*
Burket, Jacob F 1837-1906 *NatCAB 4,*
WhAm 1
Burket, John Fremont 1856-1921 *NatCAB 19*
Burkett, Charles William 1873-1962 *WhAm 4,*
WhAm 5
Burkett, Elmer Jacob 1867-1935 *ApCAB X,*
BiDrAC, NatCAB 13, TwCBDA,
WhAm 1
Burkett, Elmer Joacob 1867-1935 *WhAmP*
Burkett, Hugh Mason 1874- *WhoColR*
Burkett, John William Newton 1854-
NatCAB 9
Burkhalter, Edward Read 1844-1923 *WhAm 1*
Burkhalter, Everett Glen 1897-1975 *WhAm 6*
Burkhalter, Everett Glenn 1897-1975 *BiDrAC*
Burkhalter, Frank Elisha 1880- *WhAm 6*
Burkhalter, John Thomas 1873- *WhAm 5*
Burkhalter, Robert Proseus 1873- *NatCAB 18*
Burkhardt, Christian 1834-1931 *NatCAB 41*
Burkhardt, Ethyline Durrant 1884-
WomWWA 14
Burkhardt, George John 1909-1969 *NatCAB 54*
Burkhardt, Richard Peter 1845- *NatCAB 11*
Burkhardt, Samuel, Jr. 1865-1929 *WhAm 1*
Burkhardt, Wilbur Neil 1889- *WhAm 1*
Burkhart, Harvey Jacob 1861-1946 *WhAm 2*
Burkhart, Harvey Jacob 1864-1946 *NatCAB 12,*
NatCAB 39
Burkhart, Roy Abram 1895-1962 *WhAm 4*
Burkhart, Samuel Ellsworth 1914-1974
WhAm 6
Burkhart, Summers 1859-1932 *WhAm 1*
Burkhead, Liryum Skidmore 1824-1887
NatCAB 7
Burkhead, Margaret Bristow 1905-1975
WhAm 6
Burkholder, Charles Augustus 1886-1956
NatCAB 44
Burkholder, Charles Harvey 1876-1962
WhAm 4
Burkholder, Charles Irvine 1872- *WhAm 5*
Burkholder, Mabel Grace 1881- *WomWWA 14*
Burkholder, Paul Rufus 1903-1972 *WhAm 5*
Burkitt, Garrett 1893-1959 *NatCAB 44*
Burkle, George Henry 1904-1958 *NatCAB 48*
Burkley, Francis Joseph 1857-1940 *NatCAB 51*
Burklin, Robert Reyburn 1890-1960 *WhAm 4*
Burklund, Carl Edwin 1897-1964 *WhAm 4*
Burks, James Hampton 1873- *WhoColR*
Burks, Jesse Desmaux 1868- *WhAm 4*
Burks, Martin Parks 1851-1928 *WhAm 1*
Burleigh, Celia 1825-1875 *ApCAB*
Burleigh, Charles Calistus 1810-1878 *ApCAB,*
DcAmB, NatCAB 2, WhAm H
Burleigh, Clarence 1853-1923 *WhAm 1*
Burleigh, Clarence Blendon 1864-1910
NatCAB 14, WhAm 1
Burleigh, Edwin Chick 1843-1916 *ApCAB X,*
BiDrAC, NatCAB 1, TwCBDA,
WhAm 1, WhAmP
Burleigh, George Shepard 1821-1903
ApCAB Sup, DcAmB, NatCAB 8,
WhAm 1

Burleigh, George William 1870-1940 *WhAm 1*
Burleigh, Gertrude Florence *WomWWA 14*
Burleigh, Harry Thacker 1866-1949 *WebAB, WhAm 2*
Burleigh, Henry Gordon 1832-1900 *BiDrAC*
Burleigh, Henry Gordon 1833-1900 *NatCAB 2*
Burleigh, Henry Thacker 1866-1949 *DcAmB S4*
Burleigh, John Holmes 1822-1877 *BiAUS, BiDrAC, WhAm H*
Burleigh, Manferd 1900-1964 *NatCAB 51*
Burleigh, May Halsey Miller 1865- *WhAm 4, WomWWA 14*
Burleigh, Nathaniel George 1889-1970 *WhAm 5*
Burleigh, Sydney Richmond 1853-1931 *WhAm 1*
Burleigh, Walter Atwood 1820-1896 *BiAUS, BiDrAC, NatCAB 7, REnAW, TwCBDA, WhAm H*
Burleigh, William 1785-1827 *BiAUS, BiDrAC, WhAm H*
Burleigh, William Henry 1812-1871 *ApCAB, DcAmB, Drake, NatCAB 2, TwCBDA, WhAm H*
Burleson, Albert Sidney 1863-1937 *AmBi, BiDrAC, BiDrUSE, DcAmB S2, NatCAB 28, WhAm 1, WhAmP*
Burleson, Edward 1798-1851 *AmBi, DcAmB, WhAm H*
Burleson, Edward 1798-1852 *NatCAB 18*
Burleson, Hugh Latimer 1865-1933 *DcAmB S1, NatCAB 44, WhAm 1*
Burleson, Omar Truman 1906- *BiDrAC*
Burleson, Rufus Clarence 1823-1901 *DcAmB, NatCAB 3, TwCBDA*
Burleson, Rufus Columbus 1823-1901 *WhAm 1*
Burlew, Ebert Keiser 1885-1945 *WhAm 2*
Burlew, Roy 1883-1958 *NatCAB 48*
Burley, Benjamin Thomas 1874-1956 *NatCAB 43*
Burley, Bennett G *ApCAB*
Burley, Clarence Augustus 1849-1928 *WhAm 1*
Burley, Mack Primus 1880- *WhoColR*
Burley, Walter 1275?-1345? *DcScB*
Burlin, Harry Paul 1886-1969 *IIBEAAW*
Burlin, Natalie Curtis 1875-1921 *AmBi, DcAmB, EncAAH, NotAW, WhAm 1*
Burlin, Paul 1886-1969 *WhAm 5*
Burlin, Richard *NewYHSD*
Burling, Albert E 1891-1960 *WhAm 4*
Burling, Edward 1819-1892 *WhAm H*
Burling, Edward Burnham 1870-1966 *WhAm 5*
Burling, Gilbert 1843-1875 *ApCAB*
Burling, Temple 1896-1975 *WhAm 6*
Burlingame, Anson 1820-1870 *AmBi, ApCAB, BiDrAC, DcAmB, McGEWB, NatCAB 8, TwCBDA, WebAB, WhAm H, WhAmP*
Burlingame, Anson 1822-1870 *BiAUS, Drake*
Burlingame, Byers Alexander 1900-1970 *NatCAB 56*
Burlingame, Clarence Charles 1885-1950 *ApCAB X, WhAm 3*
Burlingame, Edward Livermore 1848-1922 *AmBi, ApCAB, DcAmB, NatCAB 8, TwCBDA, WhAm 1*
Burlingame, Emeline S 1836- *AmWom*
Burlingame, Eugene Watson 1876-1932 *WhAm 1*
Burlingame, Frederic Anson 1873-1939 *NatCAB 31*
Burlingame, Gordon Matthew 1903-1970 *NatCAB 55*
Burlingame, Harriet Grace Boyd 1852- *WomWWA 14*
Burlingame, Henry Allen 1846-1926 *NatCAB 21*
Burlingame, Leonas Lancelot 1876- *WhAm 5*
Burlingame, Leroy J 1896-1961 *WhAm 4*
Burlingame, Lillian M *BiCAW, WomWWA 14*
Burlingame, Luther Day 1865-1932 *NatCAB 23, WhAm 1*
Burlingame, Merrill G 1901- *REnAW*
Burlingame, Roger 1889-1967 *WhAm 4*
Burlingham, Aaron Hale 1822-1905 *WhAm 1*
Burlingham, Charles C 1858-1959 *WhAm 3*
Burlingham, Louis Herbert 1880-1946 *WhAm 2*
Burlison, Bill Dean 1933- *BiDrAC*

Burlison, William Leonidas 1882-1958 *NatCAB 46*
Burliuk, David Davidovich 1882-1967 *WhAm 4*
Burma, John Harmon 1874-1938 *WhAm 1*
Burman, Russell *NewYHSD*
Burmeister, Hermann 1807- *ApCAB*
Burmeister, Richard 1860- *WhAm 4*
Burn, Belle Sumner Angier 1870- *WhAm 5*
Burnam, Anthony Rollins 1846-1919 *NatCAB 12, WhAm 1*
Burnam, Curtis Field 1877-1947 *NatCAB 38, WhAm 2*
Burnam, John Miller 1864-1921 *DcAmB, WhAm 1*
Burnap, Daniel *NewYHSD*
Burnap, George Washington 1802-1859 *ApCAB, DcAmB, Drake, NatCAB 11, WhAm H*
Burnap, Willard Lathrop 1874-1951 *NatCAB 41*
Burnard, William S *NewYHSD*
Burne-Jones, Sir Edward Coley 1833-1898 *McGEWB*
Burnell, Barker 1798-1843 *BiAUS*
Burnell, Barker 1798-1844 *BiDrAC, WhAm H*
Burnell, Edward John 1888-1949 *WhAm 3*
Burnell, Edward John, Jr. 1912-1964 *WhAm 4*
Burnell, George Edwin 1863- *NatCAB 16*
Burnell, Max Ronald 1893-1959 *WhAm 3*
Burner, Willis Judson 1870-1957 *NatCAB 47*
Burnes, Alonzo D 1864- *WhAm 4*
Burnes, Daniel Dee 1851-1899 *BiDrAC*
Burnes, E P *NewYHSD*
Burnes, James Nelson 1827-1889 *BiDrAC, WhAm H*
Burnet, Dana 1888-1962 *NatCAB 51, WhAm 4*
Burnet, David Gouverneur 1788-1870 *AmBi, DcAmB, NatCAB 5, REnAW, TwCBDA, WhAm H, WhAmP*
Burnet, David Gouverneur 1789-1870 *ApCAB*
Burnet, Duncan 1876- *WhAm 5*
Burnet, Sir Frank Macfarlane 1899- *AsBiEn, McGEWB*
Burnet, Gilbert 1643-1715 *McGEWB*
Burnet, Jacob 1770-1853 *ApCAB, BiAUS, BiDrAC, DcAmB, Drake, NatCAB 11, TwCBDA, WhAm H, WhAmP*
Burnet, John M *NewYHSD*
Burnet, Mary Quick 1863- *WomWWA 14*
Burnet, Robert 1762-1854 *NatCAB 1*
Burnet, Robert 1823- *ApCAB*
Burnet, Thomas 1635?-1715 *DcScB*
Burnet, W Everit 1875-1954 *WhAm 3*
Burnet, William 1688-1728 *ApCAB*
Burnet, William 1688-1729 *AmBi, DcAmB, NatCAB 7, TwCBDA, WhAm H*
Burnet, William 1730-1791 *AmBi, ApCAB, BiDrAC, DcAmB, NatCAB 11, WhAm H, WhAmP*
Burnet, William Bromwell 1854-1909 *NatCAB 25*
Burnett, Albert Glenn 1856-1923 *NatCAB 6*
Burnett, Charles 1877-1939 *NatCAB 29, WhAm 1*
Burnett, Charles Henry 1842-1902 *ApCAB X, DcAmB, NatCAB 25, WhAm H*
Burnett, Charles Henry 1867-1954 *NatCAB 45*
Burnett, Charles Hoyt 1913-1967 *WhAm 5*
Burnett, Charles Hugh, Jr. 1902-1967 *WhAm 5*
Burnett, Charles Theodore 1873-1946 *NatCAB 35, WhAm 2*
Burnett, Cordas Chris 1917-1975 *WhAm 6*
Burnett, Cynthia S 1840- *AmWom*
Burnett, David G 1789-1870 *Drake*
Burnett, Edgar Albert 1865-1941 *NatCAB 39, WhAm 1*
Burnett, Edmund Cody 1864-1949 *WhAm 2*
Burnett, Edward 1849-1925 *BiDrAC*
Burnett, Edwin Clark 1854- *NatCAB 5, WhAm 1*
Burnett, Frances Eliza Hodgson 1849-1924 *AmBi, AmWom, ApCAB, ApCAB X, DcAmB, NatCAB 1, NatCAB 20, NotAW, TwCBDA, WhAm 1, WomWWA 14*
Burnett, Frank C 1842- *BiAUS*
Burnett, George Henry 1853-1927 *WhAm 1*

Burnett, George Jackson 1874- *WhAm 5*
Burnett, Harry 1850-1927 *NatCAB 26*
Burnett, Henry Clay 1825-1866 *ApCAB, BiAUS*
Burnett, Henry Cornelius 1825-1866 *BiDConf, BiDrAC, WhAm H, WhAmP*
Burnett, Henry Lawrence 1838-1916 *DcAmB, NatCAB 14, WhAm 1*
Burnett, Jesse McGarrity 1870- *WhAm 5*
Burnett, John Lawson 1854-1919 *ApCAB X, BiDrAC, TwCBDA, WhAm 1, WhAmP*
Burnett, John Torrey 1868- *WhAm 1*
Burnett, Joseph 1820-1894 *DcAmB, NatCAB 26, WhAm H*
Burnett, Joseph Herndon 1848- *WhAm 4*
Burnett, Junius Battish 1892- *WhoColR*
Burnett, Katherine D *WomWWA 14*
Burnett, Leo 1891-1971 *WhAm 5, WhAm 6*
Burnett, Paul Moreton 1867-1944 *WhAm 2*
Burnett, Peter Hardeman 1807-1895 *ApCAB, BiAUS, DcAmB, NatCAB 4, TwCBDA, WhAm H, WhAmP*
Burnett, Robert Carter 1896-1948 *NatCAB 39*
Burnett, Robert M d1929 *WhAm 1*
Burnett, Rogers Levering 1856- *WhAm 4*
Burnett, Samuel Burk 1849-1922 *NatCAB 32, REnAW*
Burnett, Swan Moses 1847-1906 *DcAmB, NatCAB 1, WhAm 1*
Burnett, Theodore Legrand 1829-1917 *BiDConf*
Burnett, Waldo Irving 1828-1854 *ApCAB, Drake, TwCBDA*
Burnett, Mrs. Walter D *NewYHSD*
Burnett, Ward Benjamin 1811-1884 *ApCAB, TwCBDA*
Burnett, Welbore Stewart 1874-1950 *NatCAB 51*
Burnett, Whit 1899-1973 *WhAm 5*
Burnett, Wilbur Emory 1854-1914 *NatCAB 16*
Burnett, William 1688-1729 *Drake*
Burnett, William 1730-1791 *BiAUS, Drake*
Burnette, Wells Dewey 1915-1974 *WhAm 6*
Burney, Fanny 1752-1840 *McGEWB*
Burney, Minnie Melton 1860- *WomWWA 14*
Burney, William Evans 1893-1969 *BiDrAC*
Burnham *NewYHSD*
Burnham, Alfred Avery 1819-1879 *BiAUS, BiDrAC, WhAm H*
Burnham, Athel Campbell 1880-1930 *NatCAB 24*
Burnham, Benjamin Franklin 1830-1898 *ApCAB Sup, NatCAB 9*
Burnham, Bertha H 1866- *AmWom*
Burnham, Charles Edwin 1860- *WhAm 4*
Burnham, Clara Louise 1854-1927 *AmWom, DcAmB, NatCAB 9, NatCAB 21, WhAm 1, WomWWA 14*
Burnham, Claude George 1879-1928 *WhAm 1*
Burnham, Curtis F 1820- *BiAUS*
Burnham, Daniel Hudson 1846-1912 *AmBi, ApCAB Sup, BnEnAmA, DcAmB, EncAB, McGEWB, NatCAB 9, TwCBDA, WebAB, WhAm 1*
Burnham, Daniel Hudson 1886-1961 *WhAm 4*
Burnham, E Lewis 1883-1969 *WhAm 5*
Burnham, Edward 1848-1924 *NatCAB 22*
Burnham, Edward Goodwin 1827- *NatCAB 12*
Burnham, Frederic 1881-1942 *NatCAB 32*
Burnham, Frederic Lynden 1871-1911 *WhAm 1*
Burnham, Frederick A 1851- *NatCAB 5*
Burnham, Frederick E 1906-1970 *WhAm 5*
Burnham, Frederick Russell 1861-1947 *ApCAB X, DcAmB S4, NatCAB 36, WebAMB, WhAm 2*
Burnham, Frederick William 1871- *WhAm 5*
Burnham, George 1868-1939 *BiDrAC, NatCAB 30, WhAm 1*
Burnham, George, Jr. 1849-1924 *WhAm 1*
Burnham, Gordon Webster 1803-1885 *ApCAB*
Burnham, Gordon Webster 1870-1950 *NatCAB 40*
Burnham, Henry Eben 1844-1917 *BiDrAC, NatCAB 13, NatCAB 30, TwCBDA, WhAm 1, WhAmP*
Burnham, Hiram d1864 *ApCAB, Drake*
Burnham, Horace Blois 1824-1894 *ApCAB Sup*
Burnham, Hosea Ballou 1829-1920 *NatCAB 19*
Burnham, Hubert 1882-1968 *WhAm 5*

Burnham, James C 1820?-1866 *ApCAB*
Burnham, John 1878- *NatCAB 18*
Burnham, John Bird 1869-1939 *WhAm 1*
Burnham, Jonathan Levi 1818-1891 *NatCAB 16*
Burnham, Josephine May *WomWWA 14*
Burnham, Laura Hunter 1855- *WomWWA 14*
Burnham, LeRoy 1891-1968 *NatCAB 55*
Burnham, Margaret Sherman 1850-
WomWWA 14
Burnham, Michael 1839-1905 *NatCAB 7,*
TwCBDA, WhAm 1
Burnham, Preston James 1913-1968 *NatCAB 54*
Burnham, Ralph W *WhAm 1*
Burnham, Roger Noble 1876-1962 *WhAm 4*
Burnham, Royal Edwin 1876-1953 *NatCAB 42*
Burnham, Samuel 1833-1873 *ApCAB*
Burnham, Sherburne Wesley 1838-1921
ApCAB Sup, DcAmB, DcScB,
NatCAB 11, WhAm 1
Burnham, Sherburne Wesley 1840-1921
TwCBDA
Burnham, Silas Henry 1848-1933 *WhAm 1*
Burnham, Smith 1866-1947 *WhAm 2*
Burnham, Sylvester 1842-1935 *NatCAB 27,*
WhAm 1
Burnham, T H O P *NewYHSD*
Burnham, Theodore Frelinghuysen 1845-
TwCBDA
Burnham, Thomas Mickell 1818-1866
NewYHSD
Burnham, Thomas Oliver Hazard Perry
1813-1891 *TwCBDA*
Burnham, Thomas Winston 1844-1920
NatCAB 19
Burnham, W Franklin 1874- *ApCAB X*
Burnham, Walter Henry 1886-1968 *WhAm 5*
Burnham, William 1846-1918 *NatCAB 26*
Burnham, William Addison 1847-1923
NatCAB 33
Burnham, William Henry 1855-1941 *BiDAmEd,*
DcAmB S3, WhAm 1
Burnham, William Power 1860-1930 *WhAm 1*
Burnight, Ralph Fletcher 1897-1973 *WhAm 6*
Burnite, Caroline 1875- *WhAm 5*
Burnquist, Joseph Alfred Arner 1879-1961
NatCAB 49, WhAm 4
Burns, Alexander 1834- *ApCAB*
Burns, Allen Tibbals 1876-1953 *WhAm 3*
Burns, Andrew J 1873-1958 *WhAm 3*
Burns, Anna Letitia *WhAm 5*
Burns, Anthony 1830?-1862 *ApCAB,*
TwCBDA
Burns, Anthony 1834-1862 *AmBi, DcAmB,*
McGEWB, WhAm H
Burns, Arthur Frank 1904- *WebAB*
Burns, Bob 1890-1956 *NatCAB 42, WhAm 3*
Burns, Charles Marquadant, Jr. 1834?-
NewYHSD
Burns, Charles Wesley 1874-1938 *NatCAB 40,*
WhAm 1
Burns, Clyde Edwin 1909-1962 *WhAm 4*
Burns, Cornelius F d1938 *WhAm 1*
Burns, Cornelius John 1919-1971 *NatCAB 56*
Burns, Daniel Monroe 1845-1927 *NatCAB 26,*
WhAm 4
Burns, David 1902-1971 *WhAm 5*
Burns, Dennis Francis 1889-1957 *WhAm 3*
Burns, Donald Bruce 1921-1975 *WhAm 6*
Burns, Edward H 1891-1955 *WhAm 3*
Burns, Edward John 1895-1954 *NatCAB 43*
Burns, Edward McNall 1897-1972 *WhAm 5*
Burns, Elmer Ellsworth 1868-1956 *WhAm 3*
Burns, Fannie Kay 1866- *WhoColR*
Burns, Francis 1809-1863 *ApCAB,*
NatCAB 13, TwCBDA
Burns, Francis Highlands 1873-1935 *WhAm 1*
Burns, Frank 1885-1945 *WhAm 2*
Burns, George *NewYHSD*
Burns, George Plumer 1871-1953 *WhAm 3*
Burns, George Washington 1848-1913
NatCAB 16
Burns, George Washington 1889-1944
NatCAB 34
Burns, Hendry Stuart Mackenzie 1900-1971
WhAm 5
Burns, Henry B 1900-1965 *WhAm 4*
Burns, Herbert Deschamps 1878-1960
WhAm 3A

Burns, Howard Fletcher 1888-1968 *WhAm 5*
Burns, James 1810?- *NewYHSD*
Burns, James Albert *WhoColR*
Burns, James Aloysius 1867-1940 *BiDAmEd,*
NatCAB 38, NatCAB 47, WhAm 1
Burns, James Austin 1840-1902 *ApCAB,*
NatCAB 4, TwCBDA, WhAm 1
Burns, James Henry 1885-1972 *NatCAB 57*
Burns, James J 1838-1911 *WhAm 1*
Burns, John Anthony 1909-1975 *BiDrAC,*
WhAm 6
Burns, John Arthur 1882-1961 *NatCAB 50*
Burns, John Horne 1916-1953 *WhAm 4*
Burns, John Joseph 1901-1957 *WhAm 3*
Burns, John Lawrence 1793-1872 *ApCAB,*
NatCAB 2, TwCBDA
Burns, Joseph 1800-1875 *BiAUS, BiDrAC,*
WhAm H
Burns, Judson Craighead 1870-1943
NatCAB 32
Burns, Kevin 1881-1958 *WhAm 3*
Burns, Lee 1872-1957 *WhAm 3*
Burns, Louis Henry 1878-1928 *NatCAB 18,*
WhAm 1
Burns, Louisa *WomWWA 14*
Burns, Lucy *WomWWA 14*
Burns, Luke Francis 1881-1956 *NatCAB 43*
Burns, Margaret Broad 1873- *WomWWA 14*
Burns, Matthew D 1897-1965 *WhAm 4*
Burns, Matthew James 1887-1967 *WhAm 4A*
Burns, Melvin P 1866-1930 *WhAm 1*
Burns, Michael Anthony 1884-1938 *WhAm 1*
Burns, Murray Edwin 1898-1971 *WhAm 6*
Burns, Nellie Marie 1850- *AmWom*
Burns, Otway 1775-1850 *AmBi, DcAmB,*
NatCAB 24, WhAm H
Burns, Owen McIntosh 1892-1952 *WhAm 3*
Burns, P P 1884-1957 *WhAm 3*
Burns, Ralph Arthur 1897-1975 *WhAm 6*
Burns, Robert 1759-1796 *McGEWB*
Burns, Robert 1792-1866 *BiAUS, BiDrAC,*
WhAm H
Burns, Robert 1798-1869 *ApCAB*
Burns, Robert Easton 1805-1863 *ApCAB*
Burns, Robert Edward 1909-1971 *WhAm 5*
Burns, Robert Emmett 1895-1969 *WhAm 5*
Burns, Robert Ferrier 1826- *ApCAB*
Burns, Robert Francis 1883-1950 *NatCAB 39*
Burns, Robert Whitney 1908-1964 *WhAm 4*
Burns, Rush Leslie 1877-1944 *NatCAB 42*
Burns, Stewart Morrow 1896-1952 *NatCAB 39*
Burns, Thomas Stephen 1890-1952 *NatCAB 40*
Burns, Tom 1836-1890 *REnAW*
Burns, Walter John 1855-1947 *NatCAB 38*
Burns, Walter Noble 1872-1932 *WhAm 1*
Burns, Wilber Newton 1879-1956 *NatCAB 46*
Burns, William Adams 1875-1951 *NatCAB 39*
Burns, William Henry 1840-1916 *WhAm 1*
Burns, William John 1861-1932 *ApCAB X,*
DcAmB S1, NatCAB 15, NatCAB 24,
WhAm 1
Burns, William Wallace 1825-1892 *ApCAB,*
NatCAB 12
Burns, William Wallace 1827?-1892 *Drake*
Burnside, Ambrose Everett 1824-1881 *AmBi,*
ApCAB, BiAUS, BiDrAC, DcAmB,
Drake, NatCAB 4, NatCAB 9, TwCBDA,
WebAB, WebAMB, WhAm H, WhAmP,
WhoMilH
Burnside, John 1800?-1881 *ApCAB*
Burnside, Maurice Gwinn 1902- *BiDrAC*
Burnside, Thomas d1827 *BiAUS*
Burnside, Thomas 1782-1851 *BiDrAC,*
NatCAB 16, WhAm H
Burnside, William 1852-1927 *DcScB*
Burnyeat, John 1631-1690 *ApCAB, Drake*
Burnz, Eliza Boardman 1823-1903 *AmWom,*
BiDAmEd, NatCAB 6
Burpeau, William Purdy 1901-1964 *NatCAB 51*
Burpee, Charles Winslow 1859- *WhAm 4*
Burpee, David 1893- *NatCAB 16*
Burpee, Frank Watts 1865-1939 *NatCAB 29*
Burpee, George William 1883-1967 *WhAm 4A*
Burpee, Isaac 1825-1885 *ApCAB*
Burpee, Lucien Francis 1855-1924 *NatCAB 18,*
WhAm 1
Burpee, Myra Blanche Walker *WomWWA 14*

Burpee, Washington Atlee 1858-1915
NatCAB 6, WhAm 1
Burpee, William Partridge 1846- *WhAm 4*
Burque, Henri Alphonse 1879-1947 *WhAm 2*
Burr *NewYHSD*
Burr, Aaron 1715?-1757 *DcAmB*
Burr, Aaron 1716-1757 *ApCAB, Drake,*
NatCAB 5, TwCBDA, WhAm H
Burr, Aaron 1756-1836 *AmBi, ApCAB,*
BiAUS, BiDrAC, BiDrUSE, DcAmB,
Drake, EncAAH, EncAB, McGEWB,
NatCAB 3, TwCBDA, WebAB,
WhAm H, WhAmP
Burr, Albert George 1829-1882 *BiAUS,*
BiDrAC, WhAm H
Burr, Alexander George 1871-1951 *WhAm 3*
Burr, Alfred Edmund 1815-1900 *DcAmB,*
NatCAB 2, WhAm H
Burr, Allston 1866-1949 *WhAm 2*
Burr, Anna Robeson 1873-1941 *WhAm 1,*
WomWWA 14
Burr, Augustus *NewYHSD*
Burr, Borden 1876-1952 *WhAm 3*
Burr, C B 1856-1931 *WhAm 1*
Burr, Carlos Calvin 1846-1927 *NatCAB 28*
Burr, Charles Walts 1861-1944 *NatCAB 33,*
WhAm 3
Burr, Christopher *NewYHSD*
Burr, Edward 1859-1952 *WhAm 3*
Burr, Eliza J *NewYHSD*
Burr, Enoch Fitch 1818-1907 *ApCAB, DcAmB,*
NatCAB 22, TwCBDA, WhAm 1
Burr, Eugene Wyllys 1875-1961 *WhAm 4*
Burr, Frank A 1843-1894 *TwCBDA*
Burr, Freeman Foster 1877-1956 *NatCAB 43,*
WhAm 5
Burr, George Elbert 1859-1939 *IIBEAAW,*
WhAm 1
Burr, George Howard d1939 *WhAm 1*
Burr, George Hutchison 1867- *WhAm 4*
Burr, George L 1889-1971 *WhAm 5*
Burr, George Lincoln 1857-1938 *DcAmB S2,*
NatCAB 4, TwCBDA, WhAm 1
Burr, George Washington 1865-1923
NatCAB 20, WhAm 1
Burr, Hanford Montrose 1864- *WhAm 4*
Burr, Harold S 1889-1973 *WhAm 5*
Burr, Helen Louise 1870- *WomWWA 14*
Burr, Henry Turner 1874- *WhAm 5*
Burr, Hippolyte *NewYHSD*
Burr, Hudson C d1949 *WhAm 3*
Burr, I Tucker 1858- *WhAm 4*
Burr, J H Ten-Eyck 1856-1927 *NatCAB 24*
Burr, Joseph Arthur 1850-1915 *WhAm 1*
Burr, Karl Edward 1877-1945 *NatCAB 37,*
WhAm 2
Burr, Mrs. L E *NewYHSD*
Burr, Leonard U *NewYHSD*
Burr, Leslie L 1881-1964 *WhAm 4*
Burr, Marjorie *WomWWA 14*
Burr, Nelson Beardsley 1871-1928 *WhAm 1*
Burr, Osmer Sherwood 1849- *NatCAB 3*
Burr, Peter 1668-1724 *NatCAB 13*
Burr, Theodora Dudley 1867- *WomWWA 14*
Burr, Theodosia 1783-1813 *AmBi, ApCAB,*
DcAmB, NotAW, TwCBDA, WhAm H
Burr, Thomas Shepard 1865-1928 *NatCAB 21*
Burr, Willard, Jr. 1852-1915 *NatCAB 15*
Burr, William Henry *NewYHSD*
Burr, William Henry 1819-1908 *WhAm 1*
Burr, William Hubert 1851-1934 *AmBi,*
ApCAB Sup, ApCAB X, DcAmB S1,
NatCAB 9, NatCAB 42, WhAm 1
Burr, William P 1856-1930 *WhAm 1*
Burr, William Wesley 1880-1963 *WhAm 4*
Burr, Willie Olcott 1843-1921 *NatCAB 19*
Burr, Winthrop 1861-1929 *NatCAB 40*
Burrage, Albert Cameron 1859-1931
NatCAB 12, WhAm 1
Burrage, Champlin 1874-1951 *NatCAB 38,*
WhAm 5
Burrage, Charles Dana 1857-1926 *WhAm 1*
Burrage, Dwight Grafton 1873- *WhAm 5*
Burrage, Edith May *WomWWA 14*
Burrage, Guy Hamilton 1867-1954 *WhAm 3*
Burrage, Harriet Greene Dyer 1879-
WomWWA 14
Burrage, Henry Sweetser 1837-1926 *DcAmB,*

TwCBDA, WhAm 1
Burrage, Henry Sweetzer 1827- *ApCAB Sup*
Burrage, Robert Lowell 1857-1911 *NatCAB 15*
Burrage, Walter Lincoln 1860-1935 *DcAmB S1,*
WhAm 1
Burrall, John Booth 1880-1920 *NatCAB 33*
Burrall, Jonathan 1753-1834 *ApCAB*
Burrall, William Porter 1806-1874 *ApCAB,*
DcAmB, TwCBDA, WhAm H
Burrau, Carl Jensen 1867-1944 *DcScB*
Burrell *NewYHSD*
Burrell, A M *NewYHSD*
Burrell, Caroline Benedict *WomWWA 14*
Burrell, Clara DeForest 1849- *WomWWA 14*
Burrell, David DeForest 1876- *WhAm 5*
Burrell, David Hamlin 1841-1919 *NatCAB 19*
Burrell, David James 1844-1926 *DcAmB,*
NatCAB 12, TwCBDA, WhAm 1
Burrell, Edward Parker 1871-1937 *WhAm 1*
Burrell, Frederick Augustus Muhlenberg
1858-1931 *ApCAB X, NatCAB 14,*
WhAm 1
Burrell, George Arthur 1882-1957 *NatCAB 46,*
WhAm 3
Burrell, George W 1871- *WhAm 5*
Burrell, H Cayford 1903-1953 *WhAm 3*
Burrell, Herbert Leslie 1856-1910 *NatCAB 14,*
WhAm 1
Burrell, J M *BiAUS*
Burrell, John Angus 1890-1957 *WhAm 3*
Burrell, Jonathan 1753-1834 *Drake*
Burrell, Joseph Dunn 1858-1930 *WhAm 1*
Burrell, Orlando 1826-1922 *BiDrAC*
Burrell, Tempe Garfield 1870- *WomWWA 14*
Burrell, William Chisolm 1865-1943
NatCAB 44
Burress, Walter March 1893-1950 *NatCAB 40*
Burrett, Claude Adelbert 1878-1941 *WhAm 1*
Burri, Alberto 1915- *McGEWB*
Burridge, Charles *NewYHSD*
Burridge, Lee Spear 1861-1915 *NatCAB 16*
Burridge, Thomas H *NewYHSD*
Burridge, William H *NewYHSD*
Burriel, Andres Marcos 1719-1762 *ApCAB*
Burrill, Alexander Mansfield 1807-1869 *ApCAB,*
DcAmB, Drake, WhAm H
Burrill, Edward *NewYHSD*
Burrill, Harvey D 1868-1938 *WhAm 1*
Burrill, James 1772-1820 *ApCAB, BiDrAC,*
DcAmB, Drake, NatCAB 11, TwCBDA,
WhAm H
Burrill, John Q 1841?- *NewYHSD*
Burrill, R *NewYHSD*
Burrill, Stanley Stinton 1902-1957 *WhAm 3*
Burrill, Thomas Jonathan 1839-1916 *AmBi,*
ApCAB, DcAmB, EncAAH, NatCAB 12,
NatCAB 18, TwCBDA, WhAm 1
Burrington, George d1734 *ApCAB*
Burrington, George 1680-1759 *DcAmB, Drake,*
WhAm H
Burrington, George 1685?-1759? *NatCAB 11*
Burrington, Howard Rice 1836- *WhAm 4*
Burris, Benjamin Jackson 1882-1927 *WhAm 1*
Burris, Benjamin Jackson 1882-1928
NatCAB 21
Burris, Evan Weisiger 1895-1949 *NatCAB 38*
Burris, Quincy Guy 1901-1971 *WhAm 5*
Burris, Thomas Frederick 1899-1968
NatCAB 54
Burris, William Paxton 1863-1946 *WhAm 2*
Burritt, Bailey Barton 1878-1954 *WhAm 3*
Burritt, Eldon Grant 1868- *WhAm 1*
Burritt, Elihu 1810-1879 *AmBi, ApCAB,*
DcAmB, McGEWB, NatCAB 6,
TwCBDA, WebAB, WhAm H
Burritt, Elihu 1811-1879 *Drake*
Burritt, Henry W 1892-1961 *WhAm 4*
Burritt, James 1772-1820 *BiAUS*
Burritt, William Alonzo 1853-1916 *NatCAB 17*
Burrough, Edmund Weidmann 1890-1962
NatCAB 46
Burrough, Edmund Weldmann 1890-1962
WhAm 4
Burrough, Mary Anna *WomWWA 14*
Burroughs, Alan 1897-1965 *NatCAB 56*
Burroughs, Ambrose Hammet 1859-1929
ApCAB X, NatCAB 25
Burroughs, Bryson 1869-1934 *DcAmB S1,*

WhAm 1
Burroughs, Charles 1787-1868 *ApCAB, Drake*
Burroughs, Charles Franklin 1871-1960
WhAm 4
Burroughs, Edgar Rice 1875-1950 *ApCAB X,*
DcAmB S4, WebAB, WhAm 2A
Burroughs, Edith Woodman 1871-1916
NatCAB 19, WhAm 1, WomWWA 14
Burroughs, Edna McCoy 1877- *WomWWA 14*
Burroughs, Edward Butler 1863- *WhoColR*
Burroughs, George 1650-1692 *ApCAB, Drake*
Burroughs, George 1874-1959 *NatCAB 44*
Burroughs, George Stockton 1855-1901
ApCAB Sup, WhAm 1
Burroughs, George W 1889-1950 *WhAm 3*
Burroughs, Harry Ernest 1890-1946 *WhAm 2*
Burroughs, J Edward, Jr. 1899-1962
NatCAB 49
Burroughs, John 1837-1921 *AmBi, ApCAB,*
ApCAB X, DcAmB, EncAAH, McGEWB,
NatCAB 1, TwCBDA, WebAB, WhAm 1
Burroughs, John Curtis 1817-1892 *DcAmB*
Burroughs, John Curtis 1818-1892 *ApCAB,*
NatCAB 11, TwCBDA, WhAm H
Burroughs, Jonothan Edington 1876-1966
NatCAB 53, WhAm 4
Burroughs, Julian 1878-1954 *NatCAB 41*
Burroughs, Marie 1866- *NatCAB 13,*
WhAm 4, WomWWA 14
Burroughs, Nannie Helen 1879- *WhoColR*
Burroughs, Prince Emmanuel 1871-1948
WhAm 2
Burroughs, Sarah A *NewYHSD*
Burroughs, Sherman Everett 1870-1923 *BiDrAC,*
NatCAB 24, WhAm 1
Burroughs, Silas Mainville 1810-1860 *BiAUS,*
BiDrAC, WhAm H
Burroughs, Stephen 1765-1840 *ApCAB, Drake*
Burroughs, W Dwight 1871- *WhAm 5*
Burroughs, William Seward 1855-1898
DcAmB S1, WebAB, WhAm H
Burroughs, William Seward 1857-1898
NatCAB 27
Burroughs, William Seward 1914- *WebAB*
Burrow, James Randall 1894-1941 *NatCAB 32,*
WhAm 1
Burrow, Joel Randall 1853-1931 *WhAm 1*
Burrow, Trigant 1875-1950 *DcAmB S4,*
NatCAB 39, WhAm 3
Burrowes, Alexander J 1853-1927 *WhAm 1*
Burrowes, Alonzo Moore 1887-1953 *WhAm 3*
Burrowes, Arthur Victor 1893-1968 *WhAm 5*
Burrowes, Edward Thomas 1852-1918 *DcAmB,*
WhAm 1
Burrowes, George 1811-1894 *ApCAB,*
TwCBDA
Burrowes, Katharine d1939 *WhAm 1,*
WomWWA 14
Burrowes, Peter Edward 1844- *WhAm 1*
Burrowes, Thomas 1904-1974 *WhAm 6*
Burrowes, Thomas Henry 1805-1871 *BiDAmEd,*
DcAmB, NatCAB 25, TwCBDA,
WhAm H
Burrowes, Verlista Shaul *WomWWA 14*
Burrows, Andrew Arthur 1883-1949
NatCAB 39
Burrows, Charles William 1849-1932 *WhAm 1*
Burrows, Daniel 1766-1858 *BiAUS, BiDrAC,*
WhAm H
Burrows, Daniel Chapel 1898-1971 *WhAm 5*
Burrows, Edwin Grant 1891-1958 *NatCAB 47*
Burrows, Frances Peck *WomWWA 14*
Burrows, Frederick Nelson 1856- *WhAm 4*
Burrows, George Lord 1836-1921 *NatCAB 37*
Burrows, Harry Oliver 1891-1956 *NatCAB 43*
Burrows, Henry *NewYHSD*
Burrows, Joseph Henry 1840-1914 *BiDrAC*
Burrows, Julius Caesar 1837-1915 *ApCAB Sup,*
ApCAB X, BiAUS, BiDrAC, DcAmB,
NatCAB 12, TwCBDA, WhAm 1,
WhAmP
Burrows, Lansing 1843-1919 *NatCAB 2,*
WhAm 1
Burrows, Lawton Arthur 1908-1969 *NatCAB 56*
Burrows, Lorenzo 1805-1885 *BiAUS, BiDrAC,*
WhAm H
Burrows, Marion Cowan *WomWWA 14*
Burrows, Mark 1868-1960 *WhAm 4*

Burrows, Montrose Thomas 1884-1947
WhAm 2
Burrows, Robert Jay 1882-1947 *NatCAB 37,*
WhAm 2
Burrows, Warren Booth 1877-1952 *NatCAB 41,*
WhAm 3
Burrows, William *WhoColR*
Burrows, William 1785-1813 *AmBi, ApCAB,*
DcAmB, Drake, NatCAB 7, TwCBDA,
WebAMB, WhAm H
Burrows, William Russell 1872-1955 *WhAm 3*
Burrows, William Ward 1758-1805 *WebAMB*
Burrus, James Dallas *WhoColR*
Burrus, John Houston 1849- *NatCAB 1,*
TwCBDA
Burrus, John Perry 1872-1933 *NatCAB 28,*
WhAm 1
Burrus, John Tilden 1876-1936 *NatCAB 28*
Burrus, John Tilden 1876-1938 *WhAm 1*
Burrus, Preston Robert *WhoColR*
Burruss, Julian Ashby 1874-1947 *NatCAB 43*
Burruss, Julian Ashby 1876-1947 *WhAm 2*
Burry, George W 1900-1963 *WhAm 4*
Burry, Louis *NewYHSD*
Burry, William 1851-1935 *WhAm 1*
Burse, Walter Morrill 1898-1970 *WhAm 5*
Bursley, Herbert Sidney 1896-1961 *WhAm 4*
Bursley, Joseph Aldrich 1877-1950 *WhAm 3*
Burson, Elbert Eugene 1872-1924 *NatCAB 6*
Burson, William Worth 1832-1913 *ApCAB X,*
DcAmB
Burson, Wilson Worth 1864- *ApCAB X*
Bursum, Holm Olaf 1867-1953 *ApCAB X,*
BiDrAC, WhAm 5
Bursum, Holm Olaf 1869-1953 *REnAW*
Burt, Alonzo 1849-1929 *WhAm 1*
Burt, Andrew Sheridan 1839-1915 *NatCAB 16,*
WhAm 1
Burt, Armistead 1802-1883 *ApCAB, BiAUS,*
BiDrAC, NatCAB 12, TwCBDA,
WhAm H, WhAmP
Burt, Austin 1870- *WhAm 5*
Burt, Benjamin 1729-1805 *BnEnAmA*
Burt, Charles Kennedy 1823-1892 *NatCAB 12,*
NewYHSD, WhAm H
Burt, Charles Morrison 1862- *WhAm 4*
Burt, Clayton Raymond 1874-1957 *WhAm 3*
Burt, David Allan 1876-1948 *NatCAB 41,*
WhAm 2
Burt, Edward Angus 1859-1939 *WhAm 1*
Burt, Francis 1809-1854 *BiAUS*
Burt, Frank Henry 1862- *WhAm 4*
Burt, Frank Henry 1863-1942 *WhAm 2*
Burt, Frederic Percy 1861- *WhAm 4*
Burt, George Haskell 1857- *WhAm 4*
Burt, Glenn Brigham, Jr. 1922-1972 *WhAm 6*
Burt, Grinnell 1822-1901 *NatCAB 6*
Burt, Helen Tyler *WomWWA 14*
Burt, Henry Jackson 1873-1928 *WhAm 1*
Burt, Horace Greeley 1849-1913 *WhAm 1*
Burt, James *NewYHSD*
Burt, John 1693-1746 *BnEnAmA*
Burt, John 1814-1886 *DcAmB, WhAm H*
Burt, John Otis 1835-1894 *TwCBDA*
Burt, Joseph Bell 1895- *WhAm 5*
Burt, Laura 1881- *WomWWA 14*
Burt, Marie Haines *IlBEAAW*
Burt, Mary Elizabeth 1850-1918 *DcAmB,*
WhAm 1, WomWWA 14
Burt, Mary Towne *AmWom*
Burt, Mazwell Struthers 1882-1954 *ApCAB X*
Burt, Nathaniel Clark 1825-1874 *ApCAB,*
TwCBDA
Burt, Robert Tecumseh 1873- *WhoColR*
Burt, Samuel 1724-1754 *BnEnAmA*
Burt, Silas Wright 1830-1912 *WhAm 1*
Burt, Stanley Gano 1870-1950 *NatCAB 37*
Burt, Stephen Smith 1850-1932 *TwCBDA,*
WhAm 1
Burt, Struthers 1882-1954 *WhAm 3*
Burt, Thomas Gregory 1867-1941 *WhAm 1*
Burt, William 1726-1751 *BnEnAmA*
Burt, William 1852-1936 *NatCAB 13,*
NatCAB 26, WhAm 1
Burt, William Austin 1792-1858 *AmBi,*
ApCAB, DcAmB, Drake, NatCAB 5,
NatCAB 18, TwCBDA, WebAB,
WhAm H

Burtin, Nicholas Victor 1828- *ApCAB Sup*
Burtin, Will 1908-1973 *WhAm 5*
Burtis, Aaron Longstreet 1880-1957 *NatCAB 43*
Burtis, Arthur 1841-1908 *WhAm 1*
Burtis, Mary E 1836- *WomWWA 14*
Burtness, Olger Burton 1884-1960 *BiDrAC, WhAm 4, WhAmP*
Burton, Miss A M H *NewYHSD*
Burton, Alfred Edgar 1857-1935 *NatCAB 45, WhAm 1*
Burton, Alice 1857- *WomWWA 14*
Burton, Allan A *BiAUS*
Burton, Allen A *NatCAB 5*
Burton, Andrew Mizell 1879-1966 *WhAm 4*
Burton, Asa 1752-1836 *ApCAB, DcAmB, Drake, WhAm H*
Burton, Charles *NewYHSD*
Burton, Charles Emerson 1869-1940 *WhAm 1*
Burton, Charles Germman 1846-1926 *BiDrAC, NatCAB 14, WhAm 1*
Burton, Charles Luther 1876-1961 *WhAm 4*
Burton, Charles Pierce 1862- *WhAm 4*
Burton, Charles Smith 1852-1936 *NatCAB 27*
Burton, Charles W *NewYHSD*
Burton, Charles Wesley 1884- *WhoColR*
Burton, Clarence Godber 1886- *BiDrAC*
Burton, Clarence Monroe 1853-1932 *ApCAB Sup, DcAmB S1, NatCAB 14, WhAm 1*
Burton, Edgar Gordon 1903-1968 *WhAm 5*
Burton, Edward Francis 1899-1962 *WhAm 4*
Burton, Ernest DeWitt 1856-1925 *AmBi, DcAmB, NatCAB 11, NatCAB 29, WhAm 1*
Burton, Frederick Russell 1861-1909 *AmBi, DcAmB, NatCAB 7, WhAm 1*
Burton, George Albert 1892-1958 *NatCAB 43*
Burton, George Dexter 1855-1918 *NatCAB 12, WhAm 1*
Burton, George Hall 1843-1917 *WhAm 1*
Burton, George Samuel 1879- *WhoColR*
Burton, George Smith 1850- *NatCAB 16*
Burton, George William 1818- *ApCAB Sup*
Burton, George William 1858- *WhAm 4*
Burton, George William 1880-1964 *NatCAB 52*
Burton, Harold Hitz 1888-1964 *BiDrAC, NatCAB 53, WebAB, WhAm 4*
Burton, Harry Edward 1878-1948 *WhAm 2*
Burton, Harry Edwin 1868-1944 *WhAm 2*
Burton, Hazen James 1847-1934 *NatCAB 17, WhAm 1*
Burton, Henry Fairfield 1851-1918 *NatCAB 12, WhAm 1*
Burton, Henry S 1818-1869 *ApCAB, Drake, TwCBDA*
Burton, Hiram Rodney 1841-1927 *BiDrAC, NatCAB 39*
Burton, Hiram Rodney 1842-1927 *WhAm 3*
Burton, Hutchings Gordon 1784-1836 *WhAm H*
Burton, Hutchings Gordon 1785?-1836 *NatCAB 4*
Burton, Hutchins Gordon d1836 *BiAUS, Drake*
Burton, Hutchins Gordon 1774?-1836 *DcAmB*
Burton, Hutchins Gordon 1782-1836 *BiDrAC*
Burton, James 1871- *WhAm 1*
Burton, James H *BiDConf*
Burton, James R *NewYHSD*
Burton, Jean d1952 *WhAm 3*
Burton, John E 1847- *NatCAB 3*
Burton, Jonathan Prescott 1876- *ApCAB X*
Burton, Joseph Ralph 1850-1923 *BiDrAC*
Burton, Joseph Ralph 1851-1923 *NatCAB 13, TwCBDA, WhAm 1*
Burton, Laurence Junior 1926- *BiDrAC*
Burton, Laurence V 1889-1970 *WhAm 5*
Burton, Lewis William 1852-1940 *ApCAB Sup, NatCAB 13, NatCAB 30, TwCBDA, WhAm 1*
Burton, Louis Albert 1894-1953 *NatCAB 40*
Burton, Marian Williams Perrin 1869- *WomWWA 14*
Burton, Marion LeRoy 1874-1925 *DcAmB, NatCAB 14, WhAm 1*
Burton, Martin 1818-1908 *NatCAB 10*
Burton, Myron Garfield 1880-1923 *WhAm 1*
Burton, Napier Christie 1759-1835 *ApCAB, Drake*

Burton, Nathan *NewYHSD*
Burton, Nathaniel Judson 1824-1887 *DcAmB, WhAm H*
Burton, Oliver Milton 1877- *NatCAB 15, WhAm 3*
Burton, Olly David 1868-1957 *NatCAB 47*
Burton, Phillip 1926- *BiDrAC*
Burton, Pierce 1834-1916 *ApCAB X*
Burton, Ralph d1768 *ApCAB, Drake*
Burton, Richard Eugene 1859-1940 *NatCAB 11*
Burton, Richard Eugene 1861-1940 *DcAmB S2, WhAm 1*
Burton, Sir Richard Francis 1821-1890 *McGEWB*
Burton, Robert 1577-1640 *McGEWB*
Burton, Robert 1747-1825 *ApCAB, BiAUS, BiDrAC, Drake, WhAm H*
Burton, Robert Allen 1878- *WhAm 5*
Burton, Robert Mitchell 1864-1925 *NatCAB 35, WhAm 1*
Burton, Spence 1881- *WhAm 6*
Burton, Theodore Elijah 1851-1929 *ApCAB X, BiDrAC, DcAmB S1, NatCAB 14, NatCAB 21, TwCBDA, WhAm 1, WhAmP*
Burton, Virgil Lee 1901-1967 *WhAm 5*
Burton, Warren 1800-1866 *ApCAB, BiDAmEd, DcAmB, Drake, NatCAB 7, WhAm H*
Burton, William 1789-1866 *BiAUS, DcAmB, NatCAB 11, WhAm H*
Burton, William Evans 1802-1860 *Drake*
Burton, William Evans 1804-1860 *AmBi, ApCAB, DcAmB, NatCAB 2, TwCBDA, WhAm H*
Burton, William Henry 1890-1964 *BiDAmEd, WhAm 4*
Burton, William Meriam 1865-1954 *NatCAB 41*
Burton-Opitz, Russell 1875-1954 *WhAm 3*
Burts, Charles Elford 1867- *WhAm 1*
Burtsell, Bertram Ward 1881-1945 *NatCAB 36*
Burtsell, Richard Lalor 1840- *TwCBDA*
Burtt, Joe Beatty 1862- *NatCAB 16*
Burtt, John 1789-1866 *ApCAB, TwCBDA*
Burtt, Wilson Bryant 1875-1957 *WhAm 3*
Burum, Peter Grove 1839-1900 *NatCAB 2*
Burwash, Henry J 1854-1917 *NatCAB 17*
Burwash, John 1842- *ApCAB Sup*
Burwash, Nathaniel 1839- *ApCAB Sup*
Burwell, Armistead 1839-1913 *WhAm 1*
Burwell, Arthur Warner 1867-1946 *WhAm 2*
Burwell, Benjamin Franklin 1866-1916 *NatCAB 17, WhAm 1*
Burwell, Charles Sidney 1893-1967 *NatCAB 53, WhAm 4A*
Burwell, Ethel Irene *WomWWA 14*
Burwell, John T, Jr. 1912-1971 *WhAm 5*
Burwell, Lewis 1710-1752 *NatCAB 13*
Burwell, William A 1780-1821 *BiAUS*
Burwell, William Armistead 1780-1821 *ApCAB Sup*
Burwell, William Armisted 1780-1821 *BiDrAC, WhAm H, WhAmP*
Burwell, William MacCreery 1809-1888 *ApCAB Sup*
Burwell, William Russell 1894-1971 *WhAm 5*
Burwell, William Turnbull 1846-1910 *WhAm 1*
Bury, John Jacob *NewYHSD*
Bury, William Coutts Keppel 1832- *ApCAB*
Busbee, Charles Manly 1845-1909 *TwCBDA, WhAm 1*
Busbee, Charles Manly 1893-1970 *WhAm 5*
Busbee, Fabius Haywood 1848-1908 *TwCBDA, WhAm 1*
Busbee, Jacques 1870- *WhAm 5*
Busbey, Fred Ernst 1895-1966 *BiDrAC, WhAm 4*
Busbey, Hamilton 1840-1924 *WhAm 1*
Busbey, Katharine Olive Graves 1872- *WomWWA 14*
Busbey, Katherine Olive Graves 1872- *WhAm 5*
Busbey, L White 1852-1925 *WhAm 1*
Busby, Charles A *NewYHSD*
Busby, George Henry 1794-1869 *BiAUS, BiDrAC, WhAm H*
Busby, Leonard Asbury 1869-1930 *WhAm 1*
Busby, Orel 1889-1965 *NatCAB 55, WhAm 4*
Busby, Thomas Jefferson 1884-1964 *BiDrAC*

Buscaglia, Christy James 1906-1953 *NatCAB 46*
Busch, Adolf Georg Wilhelm 1891-1952 *WhAm 3*
Busch, Adolphus 1839-1913 *DcAmB S1, WebAB, WhAm 1*
Busch, Adolphus 1842-1913 *NatCAB 12*
Busch, Adolphus, III 1891-1946 *WhAm 2*
Busch, August Anheuser 1865-1934 *NatCAB 38*
Busch, August Ludwig 1804-1855 *DcScB*
Busch, Carl 1862- *NatCAB 4*
Busch, Ernest 1885- *WhWW-II*
Busch, Francis Xavier 1879- *WhAm 6*
Busch, Fritz 1890-1951 *WhAm 3*
Busch, H A 1896-1966 *WhAm 4*
Busch, Henry Miller 1894-1970 *WhAm 5*
Busch, Joseph Francis 1866-1953 *NatCAB 15, WhAm 3*
Busch, Joseph Peter 1926-1975 *WhAm 6*
Busch, Julius Theodore 1821-1858 *NewYHSD*
Busch, Oliver Roy 1886- *WhoColR*
Buschemeyer, John Henry 1869-1935 *WhAm 1, WhAm 1C*
Buschman, S L d1945 *WhAm 2*
Busey, Mary Elizabeth 1854- *WomWWA 14*
Busey, Paul Graham 1881-1950 *WhAm 3*
Busey, Samuel Clagett 1828-1901 *WhAm 1*
Busey, Samuel Thompson 1835- *TwCBDA*
Busey, Samuel Thompson 1835-1909 *BiDrAC*
Busey, Samuel Thompson 1835-1910 *WhAm 3*
Bush, Albert Peyton 1876-1938 *WhAm 1*
Bush, Alvin Ray 1893-1959 *BiDrAC, NatCAB 48, WhAm 3*
Bush, Archibald Granville 1887-1966 *WhAm 4*
Bush, Archibald Granville 1889-1966 *NatCAB 52*
Bush, Arthur William 1871-1950 *NatCAB 40*
Bush, Asahel 1824-1913 *REnAW, WhAm 1*
Bush, Benjamin Franklin 1860-1927 *NatCAB 23, WhAm 1*
Bush, Benjamin Jay 1883-1957 *WhAm 3*
Bush, Bertha E 1866- *WomWWA 14*
Bush, Charles G 1842-1909 *WhAm 1*
Bush, Earl J 1891-1965 *WhAm 4*
Bush, Edward A 1839-1918 *NatCAB 6*
Bush, Emma Danforth 1881- *WomWWA 14*
Bush, Emma Louise *WomWWA 14, WomWWA 14a*
Bush, Florence Lilian 1865- *WhAm 4*
Bush, Florence Lillian 1865- *WomWWA 14*
Bush, Fred Charles 1892-1959 *NatCAB 50*
Bush, George d1794? *Drake*
Bush, George 1796-1859 *ApCAB, DcAmB, Drake, NatCAB 6, TwCBDA, WhAm H*
Bush, George Herbert Walker 1924- *BiDrAC*
Bush, George Washington 1791-1867 *REnAW*
Bush, Gordon Kenner 1903-1965 *NatCAB 51, WhAm 4*
Bush, Henry Tatnall 1880-1945 *WhAm 2*
Bush, Ira Benton 1876- *WhAm 1*
Bush, Irving Ter 1869-1948 *NatCAB 14, NatCAB 37, WhAm 2*
Bush, James Miles 1808-1875 *NatCAB 13*
Bush, Jennie Burchfield 1858- *AmWom*
Bush, John A 1882-1961 *WhAm 4*
Bush, John Curtis 1845- *NatCAB 11*
Bush, John E 1858- *WhoColR*
Bush, John Merchant 1878-1942 *NatCAB 31*
Bush, Joseph Henry 1793-1965 *NatCAB 6, NewYHSD*
Bush, Katharine Jeannette 1855-1937 *WhAm 1, WomWWA 14*
Bush, Leonard T 1891- *WhAm 3*
Bush, Lewis Potter 1812- *NatCAB 12*
Bush, Lincoln 1860-1940 *DcAmB S2, NatCAB 33, WhAm 1*
Bush, Loue Pollock 1865- *WomWWA 14*
Bush, Margaret Whiteley 1852- *WomWWA 14*
Bush, Morris Williams 1880-1932 *NatCAB 23*
Bush, Norton 1834-1894 *ApCAB, IlBEAAW, NatCAB 12, NewYHSD, TwCBDA*
Bush, Philip *NewYHSD*
Bush, Philip Lee 1875-1954 *NatCAB 43*
Bush, Prescott Sheldon 1895-1972 *BiDrAC, NatCAB 57, WhAm 5*
Bush, Robert Ray 1920-1971 *WhAm 5*
Bush, Robert Ray 1920-1972 *NatCAB 56*
Bush, Royal Robert 1877-1952 *WhAm 4*

Bush, Rufus Ter 1840-1890 *NatCAB 1,*
NatCAB 14, NatCAB 37
Bush, Samuel Prescott 1863-1948 *NatCAB 40*
Bush, Stephen 1818-1896 *NatCAB 2*
Bush, Thomas Frederic 1875-1940 *NatCAB 31*
Bush, Thomas Greene 1847- *WhAm 1*
Bush, Vannevar 1890-1974 *AsBiEn, EncAB,*
WebAB, WebAMB, WhAm 6, WhWW-II
Bush, W Leslie 1906-1966 *NatCAB 53*
Bush, Wendell T 1866-1941 *WhAm 1*
Bush, William Henry 1828-1901 *NatCAB 14*
Bush, William Herbert *WhoColR A*
Bush, William Lincoln 1861- *NatCAB 14*
Bush-Brown, Henry Kirke 1857-1935 *BnEnAmA,*
DcAmB S1, IIBEAAW, NatCAB 10,
WhAm 1
Bushby, Asa 1834-1897 *NewYHSD*
Bushby, Wilkie 1897-1971 *WhAm 5*
Bushee, Frederick Alexander 1872- *WhAm 5*
Bushee, James 1805-1888 *BiDAmEd*
Bushell, William Goodwin 1886-1961
NatCAB 48
Busher, Charles *NewYHSD*
Busher, George Dewey 1898-1973 *WhAm 6*
Bushfield, Harlan John 1882-1948 *BiDrAC,*
NatCAB 39, WhAm 2, WhAmP
Bushfield, Vera Cahalan 1889- *BiDrAC*
Bushman, Francis Xavier 1883-1966 *WebAB,*
WhAm 4
Bushnell, Allen Ralph 1833-1909 *BiDrAC*
Bushnell, Asa Smith 1834-1904 *DcAmB,*
NatCAB 8, TwCBDA, WhAm 1
Bushnell, Asa Smith 1900-1975 *WhAm 6*
Bushnell, Charles Ira 1826-1883 *ApCAB*
Bushnell, Charles Joseph 1875-1950 *WhAm 3*
Bushnell, David 1742?-1824 *ApCAB, DcAmB,*
NatCAB 9, WebAB, WebAMB,
WhAm H
Bushnell, David 1742?-1826 *TwCBDA*
Bushnell, David 1754?-1824 *Drake*
Bushnell, David I, Jr. 1875- *WhAm 5*
Bushnell, E L *NewYHSD*
Bushnell, Edward 1865-1944 *NatCAB 36,*
WhAm 2
Bushnell, Florence Ellsworth 1866-
WomWWA 14
Bushnell, George Edward 1887-1965
NatCAB 52, WhAm 4
Bushnell, George Ensign 1853-1924 *DcAmB,*
WhAm 1
Bushnell, Henry Allen 1855- *WhAm 4*
Bushnell, Henry Davis 1875- *WhAm 5*
Bushnell, Herbert Martin 1893- *WhAm 2*
Bushnell, Horace 1802-1876 *AmBi, ApCAB,*
DcAmB, DcAmReB, Drake, McGEWB,
NatCAB 8, TwCBDA, WebAB,
WhAm H
Bushnell, John Edward 1858-1945 *NatCAB 39,*
WhAm 4
Bushnell, Kate 1856- *AmWom*
Bushnell, Leland David 1880- *WhAm 6*
Bushnell, Madeline Vaughan 1871- *WhAm 5*
Bushnell, Nehemiah 1813-1873 *NatCAB 16*
Bushnell, Robert Tyng 1896-1949 *NatCAB 39,*
WhAm 2
Bushnell, Samuel Clarke 1852-1930 *NatCAB 22*
Bushnell, William 1800- *ApCAB*
Bushnell, William H 1823- *NatCAB 1*
Bushnell, Winthrop Grant 1864-1921 *WhAm 1*
Bushong, Isaac Newton 1855-1932 *NatCAB 35*
Bushong, Robert Grey 1883-1951 *BiDrAC,*
WhAm 3
Bushwry, Francis *NewYHSD*
Bushyhead, Jesse d1844 *ApCAB, BiAUS,*
Drake
Busia, Kofi Abrefa 1914- *McGEWB*
Busicco, Philip Salvatore 1901-1953
NatCAB 42
Busick, Adrien Fowler 1879-1969 *WhAm 5*
Busiel, Charles Albert 1842-1901 *NatCAB 11,*
TwCBDA, WhAm 1
Busk, George 1807-1886 *DcScB*
Buskin, Martin 1930-1976 *WhAm 6*
Buskirk, Hays Hardesty 1893-1948 *NatCAB 36*
Buskirk, John A *NewYHSD*
Busoni, Ferruccio Benvenuto 1866-1924
McGEWB
Buss, C G *NewYHSD*

Busse, Fred Adolph 1866-1914 *NatCAB 15*
Busse, Herman *NewYHSD*
Busselle, Harriet Murray 1880- *WomWWA 14*
Busser, Ralph Cox 1875-1955 *WhAm 3*
Bussert, Anne Elizabeth *WomWWA 14*
Bussewitz, Maxillian Alfred 1867-1942
WhAm 2
Bussey, Benjamin 1757-1842 *ApCAB, Drake,*
NatCAB 4, TwCBDA
Bussey, Cyrus 1833-1915 *ApCAB, DcAmB,*
NatCAB 1, TwCBDA, WhAm 1
Bussey, Gertrude Carman 1888-1961
NatCAB 49, WhAm 4
Bussey, William Henry 1879-1962 *NatCAB 51,*
WhAm 6
Bussing, Abraham 1828-1905 *NatCAB 16*
Bussing, John Stuyvesant 1838-1916
NatCAB 17
Bussom, Thomas Wainwright 1889-1951
WhAm 3
Bussotti, Sylvano 1931- *McGEWB*
Bustamante, Anastasio 1780-1853 *ApCAB*
Bustamante, Carlos Maria 1774-1848 *ApCAB*
Bustamante, Jose Maria 1777-1861 *ApCAB*
Bustamante Y Guerra, Jose 1759-1825 *ApCAB*
Bustamente, Anastasis 1782-1851 *Drake*
Bustamente, Don Carlos Maria De 1790?- *Drake*
Bustard, William Walter 1871-1935 *WhAm 1*
Busteed, Richard 1822-1898 *ApCAB, BiAUS,*
NatCAB 4, TwCBDA
Bustelo, Gregorio Menendez 1894-1965
NatCAB 51
Buster, Harry Crindlon *WhoColR*
Buswell, Arthur Moses 1888-1966 *WhAm 4*
Buswell, Henry Clark 1862-1940 *NatCAB 30,*
WhAm 4
Buswell, Henry Foster 1842-1919 *WhAm 1*
Butaud, Isaac *NewYHSD*
Butchart, James Baird 1905-1963 *NatCAB 50*
Butchart, William Arthur 1867-1945
NatCAB 35
Butcher, Edwin 1879- *WhAm 6*
Butcher, Howard, Jr. 1876- *WhAm 6*
Butcher, Ida Jane *WomWWA 14*
Butcher, John Anton 1910-1966 *NatCAB 53*
Butcher, Thomas Campbell 1910-1961 *WhAm 4*
Butcher, Thomas Walter 1867-1947 *BiDAmEd,*
NatCAB 39, WhAm 3
Butcher, William Lewis 1886-1931 *WhAm 1*
Bute, George Hering 1792-1876 *NatCAB 3*
Bute, James 1838-1915 *NatCAB 17*
Bute, John Stuart, Earl Of 1713-1792 *McGEWB*
Butenandt, Adolf Friedrich Johann 1903-
AsBiEn
Buteo, Johannes 1492?-1564? *DcScB*
Butet, John Francis *NewYHSD*
Butin, Mary Ryerson 1857- *AmWom*
Butin, Romain Francois 1871-1937 *WhAm 1*
Butlan, Abu'l-Hasan A A Ibn Sadun, Ibn *DcScB*
Butler *NewYHSD*
Butler, Albert Horace 1849- *NatCAB 10*
Butler, Alford Augustus 1845- *WhAm 1*
Butler, Amos William 1860-1937 *NatCAB 28,*
WhAm 1
Butler, Andrew Pickens 1796-1857 *ApCAB,*
BiAUS, BiDrAC, DcAmB, Drake,
NatCAB 3, TwCBDA, WhAm H,
WhAmP
Butler, Anne Balfour *WomWWA 14*
Butler, Anthony *BiAUS*
Butler, Arthur Pierce 1866-1953 *WhAm 3*
Butler, B D 1821?- *NewYHSD*
Butler, Benjamin F *NewYHSD*
Butler, Benjamin Franklin 1795-1858 *AmBi,*
ApCAB, BiAUS, BiDrUSE, DcAmB,
Drake, NatCAB 5, TwCBDA, WhAm H,
WhAmP
Butler, Benjamin Franklin 1818-1893 *AmBi,*
ApCAB, BiAUS, BiDrAC, DcAmB,
Drake, EncAB, NatCAB 1, TwCBDA,
WebAB, WebAMB, WhAm H, WhAmP
Butler, Bert Sylvanus 1877-1960 *NatCAB 49,*
WhAm 4
Butler, Burridge Davenal 1868-1948 *DcAmB S4,*
NatCAB 39, WhAm 2
Butler, Burridge Devenal 1868-1948 *EncAAH*
Butler, Caleb 1776-1854 *ApCAB, Drake*
Butler, Charles 1802-1897 *DcAmB, NatCAB 5,*

NatCAB 23, TwCBDA, WhAm H
Butler, Charles 1870-1953 *WhAm 3*
Butler, Charles Cicero 1865-1946 *NatCAB 33,*
WhAm 2
Butler, Charles Edwards 1818-1897 *NatCAB 3,*
NatCAB 18
Butler, Charles Henry 1859-1940 *NatCAB 33,*
WhAm 1
Butler, Charles St. John 1875-1944 *ApCAB X,*
NatCAB 33, WhAm 2
Butler, Charles Thompson 1884-1954 *WhAm 3*
Butler, Charles William 1873- *WhAm 5*
Butler, Chester Morris 1855-1918 *NatCAB 18*
Butler, Chester Pierce 1798-1850 *BiAUS,*
BiDrAC, WhAm H
Butler, Clement Moore 1810-1890 *ApCAB,*
NatCAB 10, TwCBDA, WhAm H
Butler, Clementina 1862- *AmWom*
Butler, Cora Waldo *WomWWA 14*
Butler, Cyrus 1767-1849 *ApCAB, TwCBDA*
Butler, Dan B 1879-1953 *WhAm 3*
Butler, David 1829-1891 *BiAUS, NatCAB 12*
Butler, Doris Lane 1904- *WhAm 6*
Butler, Edmond Borgia 1896-1956 *WhAm 3*
Butler, Edward 1763-1803 *ApCAB, NatCAB 1,*
NatCAB 8
Butler, Edward Burgess 1853-1928 *NatCAB 10,*
WhAm 1
Butler, Edward Crompton 1853- *NatCAB 8*
Butler, Edward Earl 1888-1953 *NatCAB 42*
Butler, Mrs. Edward H d1974 *WhAm 6*
Butler, Edward H 1841-1928 *WhAm 1*
Butler, Edward Hubert 1850-1914 *NatCAB 30,*
WhAm 1
Butler, Edward Hubert 1883-1956 *NatCAB 42,*
WhAm 3
Butler, Edward Mann 1784-1855 *BiDAmEd*
Butler, Ellis Parker 1869-1937 *AmBi,*
NatCAB 14, WhAm 1
Butler, Elmer Grimshaw 1900-1972 *WhAm 5*
Butler, Esteria *NewYHSD*
Butler, Ethan Flagg 1884-1964 *WhAm 4*
Butler, Ezra 1763-1838 *ApCAB, BiAUS,*
BiDrAC, DcAmB, Drake, NatCAB 8,
TwCBDA, WhAm H, WhAmP
Butler, F P *NewYHSD*
Butler, Fanny Kemble *ApCAB*
Butler, Frances Kemble *AmWom*
Butler, Francis 1810-1874 *ApCAB*
Butler, Francis Eugene 1825-1863 *ApCAB,*
TwCBDA
Butler, Frank Osgood 1861- *WhAm 5*
Butler, Frank Webster 1864-1934 *NatCAB 25*
Butler, Fred Lane 1868-1932 *NatCAB 34*
Butler, Fred Mason 1854-1932 *NatCAB 25,*
WhAm 1
Butler, Frederick 1766?-1843 *ApCAB*
Butler, G Montague 1881- *WhAm 6*
Butler, George Alfred 1911-1974 *WhAm 6*
Butler, George B 1809-1886 *ApCAB*
Butler, George Bernard, Jr. 1838-1907
NewYHSD, WhAm 1
Butler, George Frank 1857-1921 *WhAm 1*
Butler, George Harrison, Jr. 1877-1948
WhAm 2
Butler, George Morris 1869-1943 *NatCAB 34*
Butler, Glentworth Reeve 1855-1926 *WhAm 1*
Butler, Gordon Hubert 1889-1964 *NatCAB 51*
Butler, Harold Lancaster 1874-1957 *WhAm 3,*
WhAm 5
Butler, Henry Franklin 1896-1964 *NatCAB 50*
Butler, Henry Pierce 1872- *WhoColR*
Butler, Henry Rutherford 1862- *WhoColR*
Butler, Henry Varnum 1874-1957 *NatCAB 43,*
WhAm 3
Butler, Howard Crosby 1872-1922 *AmBi,*
BiDAmEd, DcAmB, NatCAB 20,
WhAm 1
Butler, Howard Russell 1856-1934 *IIBEAAW,*
NatCAB 13, NatCAB 28, WhAm 1
Butler, Hugh 1840-1913 *WhAm 1*
Butler, Hugh Alfred 1878-1954 *BiDrAC,*
WhAm 3, WhAmP
Butler, J B *NewYHSD*
Butler, J Glentworth 1821- *WhAm 4*
Butler, J Vernon 1868- *WhAm 4*
Butler, James d1781 *ApCAB*
Butler, James 1891-1940 *NatCAB 31*

Butler, James Davie 1815-1905 *ApCAB,*
NatCAB 9, TwCBDA, WhAm 1
Butler, James Gay 1840-1916 *NatCAB 12,*
NatCAB 24, WhAm 1
Butler, James Joseph 1862-1917 *BiDrAC,*
NatCAB 17, WhAm 2
Butler, James Orval 1928-1969 *WhAm 5*
Butler, Jerome Ambrose 1899-1949 *WhAm 3*
Butler, Jessie Storrs Ferris 1879-
WomWWA 14
Butler, Joe Beaty 1895-1955 *WhAm 3*
Butler, John d1794 *ApCAB, Drake*
Butler, John 1728-1796 *AmBi, DcAmB,*
McGEWB, WebAMB, WhAm H
Butler, John Ammi 1851-1922 *NatCAB 21*
Butler, John Ammi 1851-1923 *WhAm 1*
Butler, John B 1792-1870 *ApCAB*
Butler, John Cornelius 1887-1953 *BiDrAC,*
WhAm 3
Butler, John Gazzam 1842-1914 *WhAm 1*
Butler, John George 1826-1909 *NatCAB 1,*
WhAm 1
Butler, John Jay 1814-1891 *ApCAB,*
NatCAB 11, TwCBDA, WhAm H
Butler, John M *NewYHSD*
Butler, John Marshall 1897- *BiDrAC*
Butler, John Maynard 1834-1895 *NatCAB 2*
Butler, John Wesley 1851-1918 *DcAmB,*
WhAm 1
Butler, John Winchel Spencer 1876-1951
WhAm 3
Butler, Joline J *NewYHSD*
Butler, Joseph 1692-1752 *McGEWB*
Butler, Joseph Green, Jr. 1840-1927 *ApCAB X,*
WhAm 1
Butler, Josiah 1779-1854 *BiDrAC, TwCBDA,*
WhAm H
Butler, Josiah 1780-1854 *BiAUS*
Butler, Leroy Jefferson 1890-1960 *NatCAB 49*
Butler, Louis Fatio 1871-1929 *WhAm 1*
Butler, Mann d1835 *ApCAB, Drake*
Butler, Mother Marie Joseph 1860-1940
BiDAmEd, NotAW
Butler, Marion 1863-1938 *ApCAB Sup,*
BiDrAC, DcAmB S2, NatCAB 13,
TwCBDA, WhAm 1, WhAmP
Butler, Mary d1946 *WhAm 2*
Butler, Matthew Calbraith 1836-1909 *AmBi,*
ApCAB, BiDConf, BiDrAC, DcAmB,
NatCAB 1, TwCBDA, WhAm 1,
WhAmP
Butler, Millard Angle 1879-1943 *NatCAB 34*
Butler, Morgan Robert 1887-1965 *NatCAB 51*
Butler, Moses 1702-1756 *ApCAB, TwCBDA*
Butler, Mounce Gore 1849-1917 *BiDrAC*
Butler, Nathaniel 1853-1927 *NatCAB 8,*
TwCBDA, WhAm 1
Butler, Nicholas Murray 1862-1947 *ApCAB X,*
BiDAmEd, DcAmB S4, EncAB,
McGEWB, NatCAB 9, NatCAB 34,
TwCBDA, WebAB, WhAm 2
Butler, Noble 1810-1882 *BiDAmEd*
Butler, Noble 1819-1882 *ApCAB*
Butler, Noble Chase 1844-1933 *NatCAB 29*
Butler, Ovid 1801-1881 *NatCAB 33*
Butler, Ovid 1880-1960 *NatCAB 46, WhAm 6*
Butler, Paul M 1905-1961 *WhAm 4*
Butler, Percival 1760-1821 *ApCAB, Drake,*
NatCAB 1, NatCAB 8
Butler, Peter Walton 1856- *WhAm 4*
Butler, Pierce 1744-1822 *ApCAB, BiAUS,*
BiDrAC, DcAmB, Drake, NatCAB 2,
TwCBDA, WhAm H, WhAmP
Butler, Pierce 1807-1867 *ApCAB*
Butler, Pierce 1866-1939 *AmBi, DcAmB S2,*
NatCAB 44, WebAB, WhAm 1
Butler, Pierce 1873-1955 *NatCAB 44,*
WhAm 3
Butler, Pierce 1886-1953 *DcAmLiB, WhAm 3*
Butler, Pierce 1893-1957 *WhAm 3*
Butler, Pierce Mason 1798-1847 *ApCAB,*
BiAUS, DcAmB, Drake, NatCAB 12,
TwCBDA, WhAm H
Butler, Pinkney Ernest 1879- *WhoColR*
Butler, Ralph d1954 *WhAm 3*
Butler, Richard 1743-1791 *ApCAB, DcAmB,*
Drake, NatCAB 1, NatCAB 8, TwCBDA,
WhAm H

Butler, Richard 1831-1902 *NatCAB 1,*
WhAm 1
Butler, Robert 1897-1955 *NatCAB 49,*
WhAm 3
Butler, Robert Gordon 1860-1906 *NatCAB 38,*
WhAm 1
Butler, Robert Henry 1869- *WhoColR*
Butler, Robert Hiram 1881-1945 *NatCAB 36*
Butler, Robert Paul 1883-1971 *WhAm 5*
Butler, Robert Reyburn 1881-1933 *BiDrAC,*
WhAm 1
Butler, Roderick Randum 1827-1902 *BiAUS,*
BiDrAC
Butler, Rush Clark 1871-1953 *NatCAB 42,*
WhAm 3
Butler, Sampson Hale 1803-1848 *BiDrAC,*
WhAm H
Butler, Samson Hale 1803-1848 *BiAUS*
Butler, Samuel 1613-1680 *McGEWB*
Butler, Samuel 1835-1902 *McGEWB*
Butler, Samuel R 1868- *WhAm 4*
Butler, Sarah 1821-1876 *ApCAB*
Butler, Scot 1844-1931 *NatCAB 13, WhAm 1*
Butler, Simeon 1770-1847 *ApCAB, DcAmB,*
WhAm H
Butler, Smedley Darlington 1881-1940
DcAmB S2, NatCAB 38, WebAMB,
WhAm 1
Butler, Solomon 1895- *WhoColR*
Butler, Susan Dart 1888-1959 *DcAmLiB*
Butler, Tait 1862-1939 *NatCAB 34, WhAm 1*
Butler, Thomas 1754-1805 *ApCAB, Drake,*
NatCAB 1
Butler, Thomas 1785-1847 *BiAUS, BiDrAC,*
WhAm H
Butler, Thomas, Jr. 1748- *NatCAB 8*
Butler, Thomas Ambrose 1837- *ApCAB Sup*
Butler, Thomas B 1807-1873 *BiAUS*
Butler, Thomas Baldwin 1899-1968 *WhAm 5*
Butler, Thomas Belden 1806-1873 *ApCAB,*
BiDrAC, DcAmB, NatCAB 12, TwCBDA,
WhAm H
Butler, Thomas R *NewYHSD*
Butler, Thomas Stalker 1855-1928 *BiDrAC,*
TwCBDA, WhAm 1, WhAmP
Butler, Thomas W *NewYHSD*
Butler, Vincent Kingwell 1892-1935 *NatCAB 46*
Butler, Walter C 1892-1944 *WebAB*
Butler, Walter Halben 1852-1931 *BiDrAC*
Butler, Walter N 1752?-1781 *AmBi, ApCAB,*
DcAmB, WebAMB, WhAm H
Butler, Warren C 1826-1878 *NewYHSD*
Butler, Wentworth S 1826- *TwCBDA*
Butler, William *ApCAB*
Butler, William d1796 *Drake*
Butler, William 1745-1789 *NatCAB 8*
Butler, William 1759-1821 *ApCAB, BiAUS,*
BiDrAC, DcAmB, Drake, TwCBDA,
WhAm H
Butler, William 1790-1850 *BiAUS, BiDrAC,*
WhAm H
Butler, William 1818-1899 *DcAmB, WhAm H*
Butler, William 1819-1899 *ApCAB,*
NatCAB 12
Butler, William 1822-1909 *WhAm 1*
Butler, William Addison, Jr. 1847-1914
NatCAB 17
Butler, William Allen 1825-1902 *ApCAB,*
DcAmB, Drake, NatCAB 7, TwCBDA,
WhAm 1
Butler, William Allen 1853-1923 *NatCAB 29,*
WhAm 1
Butler, William Frederick d1926 *WhAm 1*
Butler, William John 1881-1948 *WhAm 2*
Butler, William Mill 1857-1946 *WhAm 2*
Butler, William Morgan 1861-1937 *BiDrAC,*
NatCAB 30, WhAm 1
Butler, William Morris 1850-1940 *NatCAB 6,*
WhAm 1
Butler, William Orlando 1791-1880 *AmBi,*
BiDrAC, DcAmB, NatCAB 6, TwCBDA,
WebAMB, WhAm H
Butler, William Orlando 1793-1880 *BiAUS,*
Drake
Butler, Willis Howard 1873-1930 *NatCAB 25,*
WhAm 1
Butler, Zebulon 1731-1795 *AmBi, ApCAB,*
DcAmB, Drake, NatCAB 1, WebAMB,

WhAm H
Butlerov, Aleksandr Mikhailovich 1828-1886
DcScB
Butlerov, Alexander Mikhailovich 1828-1886
AsBiEn
Butman, Arthur Benjamin 1865-1955 *WhAm 3*
Butman, Frederick A 1820-1871 *IIBEAAW,*
NewYHSD
Butman, Samuel 1788-1864 *BiAUS, BiDrAC,*
WhAm H
Butner, Henry W 1875-1937 *WhAm 1*
Butschli, Otto 1848-1920 *DcScB*
Butt, Archibald Willingham 1866-1912
WhAm 1
Butt, Emily 1867- *WomWWA 14*
Butt, Frederick *NewYHSD*
Butt, Israel LaFayette 1846- *WhoColR*
Butt, James Horton 1910-1966 *NatCAB 53*
Butt, John D d1967 *WhAm 4*
Butt, William 1880-1962 *WhAm 4*
Butte, George Charles 1877-1940 *NatCAB 33,*
WhAm 1
Butteese, Shearman 1870- *WhoColR*
Buttenheim, Edgar Joseph 1882-1964
NatCAB 53, WhAm 4
Buttenheim, Harold S 1876-1961 *WhAm 4*
Buttenwieser, Ellen Clune 1870- *WomWWA 14*
Buttenwieser, Moses 1862-1939 *WhAm 1*
Butterbaugh, Grant Illion 1893-1960
NatCAB 47
Butterfield, Consul Willshire 1824-1899 *ApCAB,*
TwCBDA, WhAm 1
Butterfield, Daniel 1831-1901 *ApCAB, DcAmB,*
Drake, NatCAB 4, TwCBDA, WhAm H,
WhAm 1
Butterfield, Emily Helen 1884- *WomWWA 14*
Butterfield, Ernest Warren 1874- *WhAm 5*
Butterfield, John 1801-1869 *AmBi, ApCAB,*
DcAmB, McGEWB, NatCAB 22,
REnAW, TwCBDA, WebAB, WhAm H
Butterfield, Kenyon Leech 1868-1935 *BiDAmEd,*
DcAmB S1, NatCAB 27, WhAm 1
Butterfield, Martin 1790-1866 *BiAUS, BiDrAC,*
WhAm H
Butterfield, Mellona Moulton 1853- *AmWom*
Butterfield, Ora Elmer 1870-1916 *NatCAB 16,*
WhAm 1
Butterfield, Roger Williams 1844-1920
NatCAB 8
Butterfield, Victor Lloyd 1904-1975 *WhAm 6*
Butterfield, Walter Hamblet 1875-1949
NatCAB 38
Butterick, Ebenezer 1826-1903 *AmBi, DcAmB,*
NatCAB 13, WhAm H
Butters, George 1849- *NatCAB 16*
Buttersworth, James E 1817-1894 *BnEnAmA,*
NewYHSD
Butterton, John *NewYHSD*
Butterworth, A H *NewYHSD*
Butterworth, Benjamin 1822- *ApCAB*
Butterworth, Benjamin 1837-1898 *BiDrAC,*
DcAmB, NatCAB 13, TwCBDA,
WhAm H
Butterworth, Charles Fred 1868-1959 *WhAm 3*
Butterworth, Edward Summers 1867-1950
NatCAB 38
Butterworth, Frank Willoughby 1870-1943
NatCAB 32
Butterworth, G Forrest 1892-1956 *NatCAB 46,*
WhAm 3
Butterworth, George Forrest 1853-1928
ApCAB X, NatCAB 28, WhAm 1
Butterworth, Hezekiah 1839-1905 *AmBi,*
ApCAB, DcAmB, NatCAB 2, TwCBDA,
WhAm 1
Butterworth, Julian Edward 1884-1961
WhAm 4
Butterworth, Mary Peck 1686-1775 *NotAW*
Butterworth, Samuel F d1875 *ApCAB*
Butterworth, William 1864-1936 *ApCAB X,*
NatCAB 28, WhAm 1
Butterworth, William Walton 1903-1975
WhAm 6
Buttfield, W J d1948 *WhAm 2*
Butti, Guido *NewYHSD*
Buttles, John S 1877-1949 *WhAm 2A*
Buttling, William J 1859- *NatCAB 7*
Button, Conyers 1836-1924 *NatCAB 22*

Button, Daniel Evan 1917- *BiDrAC*
Button, Frank Christopher 1863-1932 *WhAm 1*
Button, Frank Christopher 1864-1933
NatCAB 25
Button, Henry H 1818-1890 *NatCAB 3*
Button, John 1800-1882 *NatCAB 22*
Button, Joseph J 1822?- *NewYHSD*
Button, Joseph Priestley 1864-1931 *NatCAB 22*
Button, Richard Totten 1929- *WebAB*
Button, Stephen D 1803-1897 *WhAm H*
Button, Sir Thomas *ApCAB, Drake*
Button, William Henry 1871-1944 *NatCAB 33*
Buttram, Frank 1886-1966 *NatCAB 53,*
WhAm 4
Buttre, John Chester 1821-1893 *ApCAB,*
NewYHSD, TwCBDA, WhAm H
Buttrick, James Tyler 1875-1963 *WhAm 4*
Buttrick, John 1715-1791 *ApCAB, Drake,*
WebAMB
Buttrick, Stedman 1864-1925 *NatCAB 21*
Buttrick, Wallace 1853-1926 *BiDAmEd,*
DcAmB, NatCAB 22, WhAm 1
Butts, Alfred Benjamin 1890-1962 *WhAm 4*
Butts, Annice Esther Bradford 1844-1904
NatCAB 11, WhAm 1
Butts, Arthur Clarkson 1848- *WhAm 4*
Butts, Charles 1863-1946 *WhAm 3*
Butts, Charles Edwin 1884-1935 *NatCAB 29*
Butts, Charles Richards 1854-1938 *NatCAB 28*
Butts, Edmund Luther 1868-1950 *NatCAB 38,*
WhAm 4
Butts, Edward 1853- *WhAm 4*
Butts, Isaac 1816-1874 *ApCAB, DcAmB,*
NatCAB 21, TwCBDA, WhAm H
Butts, Ralph *NewYHSD*
Butts, Richard *NewYHSD*
Butts, Robert Freeman 1910- *BiDAmEd*
Butts, Willard Wilcox 1890-1956 *NatCAB 42*
Buttz, Charles Wilson 1837-1913 *BiDrAC,*
WhAmP
Buttz, Henry Anson 1835-1920 *DcAmB,*
NatCAB 13, TwCBDA, WhAm 1
Butz, Earl Lauer 1909- *EncAAH*
Butz, Jesse Samuel Cooper 1905-1963 *WhAm 4*
Butz, Reuben Jacob 1867-1957 *WhAm 3*
Butzel, Fred M 1877-1948 *WhAm 2*
Butzel, Henry Magnus 1871-1963 *WhAm 4*
Butzel, Leo Martin 1874-1961 *WhAm 4*
Butzer, Albert George 1893-1967 *WhAm 5*
Buwalda, John Peter 1886-1954 *WhAm 3*
Buxhowden, Friedrich Wilhelm, Graf Von
1750-1811 *WhoMilH*
Buxtehude, Dietrich 1637-1707 *McGEWB*
Buxton, Albert 1861-1930 *WhAm 1*
Buxton, Bertram Harrington 1883-1947
NatCAB 35
Buxton, Charles *NewYHSD*
Buxton, Charles Lee 1904-1969 *WhAm 5*
Buxton, Edward Timothy 1852-1935
NatCAB 27
Buxton, Edwin Orlando 1851- *WhAm 4*
Buxton, Eva Joanna 1863- *WomWWA 14*
Buxton, Frank W 1877-1974 *WhAm 6*
Buxton, G Edward 1849- *NatCAB 18*
Buxton, G Edward 1880-1949 *NatCAB 37,*
WhAm 2
Buxton, Herbert 1875-1928 *ApCAB X*
Buxton, Jarvis Barry 1792-1851 *ApCAB*
Buxton, John Anthony 1897-1966 *NatCAB 52,*
WhAm 4
Buxton, John Cameron 1852-1917 *NatCAB 48*
Buxton, Joseph Thomas 1875-1940 *NatCAB 35*
Buxton, L Haynes 1859-1924 *WhAm 1*
Buxton, Robert William 1909-1970 *WhAm 5*
Buxton, Warner Rockwell 1885-1941
NatCAB 30
Buys, John L 1897-1955 *WhAm 3*
Buys Ballot, Christoph Hendrik Diederik
1817-1890 *DcScB*
Buzbee, Thomas Stephen 1875-1948 *WhAm 2*
Buzby, George Carroll 1897-1970 *WhAm 5*
Buzby, Walter J 1865-1950 *NatCAB 41*
Buzzi, Alfred Antonio 1904-1964 *WhAm 4*
Buzznell, Reginald W d1959 *WhAm 3*
Byard, John Kenneth 1885-1959 *NatCAB 45*
Byars, Louis Thomas 1906-1969 *WhAm 5*
Byars, William Vincent 1857-1938 *WhAm 1*
Byas, Hugh d1945 *WhAm 2*

Bye, Carl Rollinson 1900-1960 *NatCAB 49,*
WhAm 4
Bye, Frank Paxson 1868-1931 *WhAm 1*
Byer *NewYHSD*
Byer, Herman Bailey 1893-1965 *WhAm 4*
Byerly, James Arthur 1880-1953 *NatCAB 41*
Byerly, Robert Wayne 1888-1957 *NatCAB 47*
Byerly, William Elwood 1849-1935 *ApCAB,*
BiDAmEd, DcAmB S1, NatCAB 27,
WhAm 1, WhAm 1C
Byerrum, Roswell Oertling 1889-1965
NatCAB 52
Byers, Alexander McBurney 1827-1900
NatCAB 11
Byers, Clovis Ethelbert 1899-1973 *NatCAB 57,*
WhAm 6
Byers, Gordon Leslie 1898-1973 *WhAm 6*
Byers, John Frederic 1881-1949 *WhAm 2*
Byers, John Winford 1875- *WhAm 5*
Byers, Joseph Perkins 1868- *WhAm 4*
Byers, Maxwell Cunningham 1878-1930
NatCAB 22, WhAm 1
Byers, Mortimer W d1962 *WhAm 4*
Byers, Morton Lewis 1868-1933 *NatCAB 25*
Byers, Noah Ebersole 1873-1962 *NatCAB 50*
Byers, Samuel Hawkins Marshall 1838-1933
ApCAB Sup, NatCAB 14, TwCBDA,
WhAm 1
Byers, Vincent Gerard 1892-1960 *WhAm 4*
Byers, Walter Louis 1910-1970 *WhAm 5*
Byers, William 1834?- *NewYHSD*
Byers, William Newton 1831-1903 *NatCAB 13,*
REnAW, WhAm 1
Byfield, Ernest Lessing 1889-1950 *WhAm 4*
Byfield, Joseph 1853-1926 *WhAm 1*
Byfield, N *NewYHSD*
Byfield, Nathaniel 1653-1733 *ApCAB, Drake,*
NatCAB 8, TwCBDA
Byford, Henry Turman 1853-1938 *NatCAB 2,*
WhAm 1
Byford, William Heath 1817-1890 *ApCAB,*
DcAmB, NatCAB 2, TwCBDA,
WhAm H
Byham, Steven 1906-1956 *NatCAB 49*
Byington, Cyrus 1793-1868 *ApCAB, DcAmB,*
NatCAB 8, WhAm H
Byington, Edwin Hallock 1861-1944 *WhAm 2*
Byington, Elia Goode 1858- *AmWom*
Byington, Ezra Hoyt 1828-1901 *TwCBDA,*
WhAm 1
Byington, Homer Morrison 1879-1966 *WhAm 4*
Byington, Jeannette Gregory 1880-
WomWWA 14
Byington, Lewis 1820-1886 *NatCAB 29*
Byington, Margaret Frances 1877-
WomWWA 14
Byington, Spring d1971 *WhAm 5*
Byington, Steven Tracy 1868- *WhAm 4*
Byington, Swift 1825-1895 *TwCBDA*
Byles, Axtell Julius 1880-1941 *NatCAB 30*
Byles, Axtell Julius 1881-1941 *WhAm 1*
Byles, Mather 1706-1788 *AmBi, DcAmB,*
Drake, NatCAB 7
Byles, Mather 1707-1788 *ApCAB, TwCBDA,*
WhAm H
Byles, Mather 1734-1814 *NatCAB 7*
Byles, Mather 1735-1814 *ApCAB*
Byllesby, Henry Marison 1859-1924
NatCAB 15, WhAm 1
Byllynge, Edward d1687 *ApCAB*
Bylot, Robert *ApCAB*
Bynam, Benjamin *NewYHSD*
Byne, Arthur 1883-1935 *WhAm 1*
Byng, John 1704-1757 *WhoMilH*
Byng, Julian Hedworth George 1862-1935
WhoMilH
Bynner, Edwin Lasseter 1842-1893 *ApCAB Sup*
Bynner, Edwin Lassetter 1842-1893 *NatCAB 7,*
WhAm H
Bynner, Witter 1881-1968 *WhAm 5*
Bynum, Curtis 1882-1964 *WhAm 4*
Bynum, Jesse Atherton 1797-1868 *BiAUS,*
BiDrAC, WhAm H
Bynum, John Gray 1846- *TwCBDA*
Bynum, Marshall Francis 1912-1969 *WhAm 5*
Bynum, William Dallas 1846-1927 *BiDrAC,*
TwCBDA, WhAm 1, WhAmP
Bynum, William Preston 1820-1909 *DcAmB,*

NatCAB 22
Bynum, William Preston 1861-1926 *WhAm 1*
Byoir, Carl 1888-1957 *WhAm 3*
Byram, George Logan 1862-1929 *WhAm 1*
Byram, Harry E 1865-1941 *WhAm 2*
Byram, Joseph H *NewYHSD*
Byrd, Adam Monroe 1859-1912 *BiDrAC,*
NatCAB 15, WhAm 1
Byrd, Anderson Floyd 1864- *WhAm 4*
Byrd, Charles W *BiAUS*
Byrd, Elon Eugene 1905-1974 *WhAm 6*
Byrd, Evelyn 1707-1737 *ApCAB*
Byrd, Frederick *NewYHSD*
Byrd, Harry Clifton 1889-1970 *WhAm 5*
Byrd, Harry Flood 1887-1966 *BiDrAC,*
WhAm 4, WhAmP
Byrd, Harry Flood, Jr. 1914- *BiDrAC*
Byrd, Harvey Leonidas 1820-1884 *ApCAB*
Byrd, Henry *NewYHSD*
Byrd, Mary Emma 1849- *WomWWA 14*
Byrd, Richard Evelyn 1860-1925 *WhAm 1*
Byrd, Richard Evelyn 1888-1957 *AsBiEn,*
EncAB, McGEWB, NatCAB 46, WebAB,
WebAMB, WhAm 3
Byrd, Robert Carlyle 1918- *BiDrAC*
Byrd, Samuel Craig 1868-1951 *NatCAB 38,*
WhAm 4
Byrd, William 1543?-1623 *McGEWB*
Byrd, William 1650-1704 *ApCAB, TwCBDA*
Byrd, William 1652-1704 *AmBi, DcAmB,*
McGEWB, WhAm H
Byrd, William 1674-1744 *AmBi, ApCAB,*
DcAmB, Drake, EncAAH, EncAB,
McGEWB, NatCAB 7, TwCBDA,
WebAB, WhAm H
Byrd, William 1728-1777 *ApCAB*
Byrd, William Clifton 1926-1974 *WhAm 6*
Byrd, William M 1817-1874 *BiAUS*
Byrd, William Paul Quinn *WhoColR*
Byrer, Charles Emory 1870- *WhAm 5*
Byrer, Harry Hopkins 1877- *WhAm 5*
Byrne *NewYHSD*
Byrne, Alice Hill 1876- *WhAm 5*
Byrne, Amanda Austin 1866- *WhAm 5*
Byrne, Andrew 1802-1862 *ApCAB, DcAmB,*
Drake, NatCAB 12, TwCBDA, WhAm H
Byrne, Austin Thomas 1859-1934 *WhAm 1*
Byrne, Barry 1892-1967 *WhAm 4A*
Byrne, Bernard Albert 1853-1910 *WhAm 1*
Byrne, Charles Alfred 1848-1909 *WhAm 1*
Byrne, Charles Christopher 1837-1921 *WhAm 1*
Byrne, Charles Thomas 1858-1943 *NatCAB 40*
Byrne, Christopher Edward 1867-1950
NatCAB 38, WhAm 3
Byrne, Cornelius James 1907- *WhAm 6*
Byrne, Donn 1889-1928 *AmBi, DcAmB,*
WhAm 1
Byrne, Edward 1802-1862 *WhAm H*
Byrne, Edwin Vincent 1891-1963 *WhAm 4*
Byrne, Emmet Francis 1896-1974 *BiDrAC,*
WhAm 6
Byrne, Eugene Hugh 1882-1952 *NatCAB 41*
Byrne, Frank Michael 1858-1927 *NatCAB 21,*
WhAm 1
Byrne, Harry Vincent 1904-1970 *WhAm 6*
Byrne, James 1857-1942 *NatCAB 31,*
WhAm 2
Byrne, James Aloysius 1906- *BiDrAC*
Byrne, John 1825-1902 *DcAmB, NatCAB 9,*
WhAm H
Byrne, John 1840?-1905 *WhAm 1*
Byrne, John Baird 1886-1963 *WhAm 4*
Byrne, John Bernardine 1877-1950 *NatCAB 38*
Byrne, Joseph 1870-1945 *WhAm 2*
Byrne, Joseph M, Jr. 1892-1963 *WhAm 4*
Byrne, Sister Marie Jose 1876-1951 *WhAm 3,*
WhAm 5
Byrne, Miriam 1884- *WomWWA 14*
Byrne, Richard 1832-1864 *WhAm H*
Byrne, Thomas 1853-1929 *NatCAB 22*
Byrne, Thomas Sebastian 1841-1924
ApCAB Sup, NatCAB 12, TwCBDA,
WhAm 1
Byrne, William 1780-1833 *ApCAB, TwCBDA,*
WhAm H
Byrne, William 1836-1912 *TwCBDA,*
WhAm 1
Byrne, William 1838-1912 *NatCAB 5*

Byrne, William Matthew 1896-1974 *WhAm 6*
Byrne, William Thomas 1876-1952 *BiDrAC,*
  WhAm 3, WhAmP
Byrnes, Allen William 1910-1971 *WhAm 5*
Byrnes, Charles Metcalfe 1881-1936
  NatCAB 30, WhAm 1
Byrnes, Clifford Hamilton 1893-1974 *WhAm 6*
Byrnes, Esther Russell 1866- *WomWWA 14*
Byrnes, Eugene Alexander 1862- *WhAm 4*
Byrnes, James Francis 1879-1972 *BiDrAC,*
  BiDrUSE, EncAB, McGEWB, WebAB,
  WhAm 5, WhAmP, WhWW-II
Byrnes, John William 1913- *BiDrAC*
Byrnes, Josephine Armstrong 1869-
  WomWWA 14
Byrnes, Ralph Leonidas 1878-1943 *ApCAB X,*
  WhAm 3
Byrnes, Robert Dennison 1900-1969 *WhAm 5*
Byrnes, Thomas 1842-1910 *DcAmB,*
  NatCAB 14
Byrnes, Timothy Edward 1853-1944 *WhAm 2*
Byrnes, William Joseph 1859- *NatCAB 16*
Byrnes, William M d1963 *WhAm 4*
Byrns, Clarence Franklin 1893-1964 *WhAm 4*
Byrns, Elinor *BiCAW*
Byrns, Joseph Wellington, Jr. 1903- *BiDrAC*
Byrns, Joseph Wellington, Sr. 1869-1936
  BiDrAC, DcAmB S2, WebAB, WhAm 1,
  WhAmP
Byrns, Samuel 1848-1914 *BiDrAC*
Byrom, James Leon 1893-1966 *NatCAB 53*
Byron, Arthur William 1872-1943 *WhAm 2A*
Byron, Charles Loomis 1884-1964 *WhAm 4*
Byron, Baron George Gordon Noel 1788-1824
  McGEWB
Byron, Henry *NewYHSD*
Byron, John 1723-1786 *ApCAB, Drake*
Byron, John W 1861-1895 *TwCBDA*
Byron, Joseph Wilson 1892-1951 *NatCAB 41,*
  WhAm 3
Byron, Katharine Edgar 1903- *BiDrAC*
Byron, Lewis Thomas 1870-1922 *NatCAB 36*
Byron, Robert Burns, Jr. 1916-1969 *WhAm 5*
Byron, William Devereux 1895-1941 *BiDrAC,*
  WhAm 1
Byron, William Fisher 1892-1968 *NatCAB 55*
Byrt, Arthur William 1864- *NatCAB 14*
Byrum, Enoch Edwin 1861- *WhAm 4*
Byrum, Paul Raymond 1892-1953 *NatCAB 40*
Bywaters, Jerry 1906- *IIBEAAW*

C

C, H *NewYHSD*
Caamano, Jose M Placido 1838- *ApCAB*
Caballero, Jose Agustin 1771-1835 *ApCAB*
Caballero Y Ocio, Juan 1644-1707 *ApCAB*
Cabana, Oliver, Jr. 1865-1938 *WhAm 1*
Cabanis, Pierre-Jean-Georges 1757-1808 *DcScB*
Cabaniss, Edward Harman 1857-1936 *WhAm 1*
Cabaniss, Edward McClernand 1885-1960
    NatCAB 50, WhAm 4
Cabaniss, Elbridge Gerry 1802-1872 *NatCAB 2*
Cabaniss, Henry Harrison 1848-1934
    NatCAB 7, WhAm 1
Cabaniss, Joseph Warren 1842-1916
    NatCAB 16
Cabaniss, Thomas Banks 1835-1915 *BiDrAC,*
    NatCAB 5, WhAm 4
Cabe, Charles Lee 1863-1950 *NatCAB 39*
Cabeen, Charles William 1859-1925 *WhAm 1*
Cabeen, David Clark 1886-1965 *WhAm 4*
Cabeen, Sarah Biddle 1867- *WomWWA 14*
Cabeen, Sarah Clark 1861- *WomWWA 14*
Cabell, Aaron Hall 1855- *WhoColR*
Cabell, Anne Branch 1860- *WomWWA 14*
Cabell, Benjamin Francis 1850-1909 *WhAm 1*
Cabell, Charles Arnold 1870-1946 *NatCAB 35*
Cabell, Charles Pearre 1903-1971 *WhAm 5*
Cabell, DeRosey Carroll 1861-1924 *WhAm 1*
Cabell, Earle 1906-1975 *BiDrAC, WhAm 6*
Cabell, Edward C 1817-1896 *BiAUS*
Cabell, Edward Carrington 1816-1896 *ApCAB,*
    BiDrAC, TwCBDA, WhAm H
Cabell, George C 1837-1906 *BiAUS*
Cabell, George Clarence 1860- *WhoColR*
Cabell, George Craghead 1837-1906 *WhAm 1*
Cabell, George Craighead 1836-1906 *BiDrAC,*
    TwCBDA, WhAmP
Cabell, George Craighead 1837-1906 *ApCAB*
Cabell, Isa Carrington 1860- *WhAm 4,*
    WomWWA 14
Cabell, James Alston 1852-1930 *NatCAB 16,*
    NatCAB 22, WhAm 1
Cabell, James Branch 1879-1958 *ApCAB X,*
    McGEWB, NatCAB 48, WebAB,
    WhAm 3
Cabell, James Laurence 1813-1889 *ApCAB,*
    NatCAB 12, TwCBDA
Cabell, James Lawrence 1813-1889 *DcAmB,*
    WhAm H
Cabell, Joseph 1732-1798 *ApCAB, TwCBDA*
Cabell, Joseph Carrington 1778-1856 *AmBi,*
    DcAmB, NatCAB 22, WhAm H
Cabell, Margaret 1862- *WomWWA 14*
Cabell, Mary Virginia Ellet 1839- *AmWom*
Cabell, Nathaniel Francis 1807-1891 *DcAmB,*
    WhAm H
Cabell, Robert Hervey 1865-1947 *NatCAB 38*
Cabell, Robert Hervey 1867-1947 *WhAm 2*
Cabell, Royal Eubank 1878-1950 *NatCAB 40,*
    WhAm 3
Cabell, Samuel Jordan 1756-1818 *ApCAB,*
    BiDrAC, DcAmB, Drake,
    NatCAB 2, TwCBDA, WhAm H
Cabell, William 1700-1774 *ApCAB, TwCBDA*
Cabell, William 1729?-1798 *DcAmB*
Cabell, William 1730-1798 *ApCAB, Drake,*
    TwCBDA, WhAm H
Cabell, William H 1772-1853 *ApCAB, BiAUS,*
    DcAmB, Drake, NatCAB 5, TwCBDA,
    WhAm H, WhAmP
Cabell, William Lewis 1827-1911 *BiDConf,*
    DcAmB, NatCAB 12, WhAm 1
Cabell, Wymond 1898-1956 *WhAm 3*
Cabeo, Niccolo 1586-1650 *DcScB*
Cabet, Etienne 1788-1856 *AmBi, DcAmB,*

EncAAH, McGEWB, WhAm H,
    WhAmP
Cabeza DeBaca, Ezequiel 1864-1917 *REnAW*
Cabeza DeVaca, Alvar Nunez *Drake*
Cabeza DeVaca, Alvar Nunez 1490?-1556?
    NatCAB 25
Cabeza DeVaca, Alvar Nunez 1490?-1557?
    McGEWB, REnAW
Cabeza DeVaca, Alvar Nunez 1507-1559
    ApCAB
Cabezas Altamirano, Juan DeLas d1615 *ApCAB*
Cabezon, Antonio 1510-1566 *McGEWB*
Cable, Arthur Goodrich 1887-1945 *NatCAB 35*
Cable, Benjamin Stickney 1872-1915 *WhAm 1*
Cable, Benjamin Taylor 1853-1923 *BiDrAC,*
    WhAm 1
Cable, Davis Arthur 1885-1946 *NatCAB 43*
Cable, Emmett James 1875- *WhAm 5*
Cable, Fayette S 1855-1920 *ApCAB X*
Cable, Frank Taylor 1863-1945 *DcAmB S3,*
    NatCAB 34, WhAm 2
Cable, George Washington 1844-1925 *AmBi,*
    ApCAB, ApCAB X, DcAmB, EncAAH,
    McGEWB, NatCAB 1, NatCAB 45,
    TwCBDA, WebAB, WhAm 1
Cable, Ida Tower 1860- *WomWWA 14*
Cable, John Levi 1884-1971 *BiDrAC, WhAm 5*
Cable, John Ray 1891-1951 *WhAm 3*
Cable, John W, III 1908-1967 *NatCAB 53*
Cable, Joseph 1801-1880 *BiAUS, BiDrAC,*
    WhAm H
Cable, Ransom R 1834-1909 *WhAm 1*
Cable, W Arthur 1890-1958 *NatCAB 47*
Cabot, Arthur Tracy 1852-1912 *DcAmB,*
    NatCAB 15, WhAm 1
Cabot, Caroline Sturgis 1846-1917
    WomWWA 14
Cabot, Carolyn Sturgis 1846-1917 *WhAm 1*
Cabot, Edward 1898-1965 *WhAm 4*
Cabot, Edward Clarke 1818-1901 *DcAmB,*
    NewYHSD, WhAm H
Cabot, Elinore Blake *WomWWA 14*
Cabot, Ella Lyman d1934 *BiCAW, WhAm 1,*
    WomWWA 14
Cabot, Elsie Pumpelly 1875- *WomWWA 14*
Cabot, Francis Higginson 1895-1956 *WhAm 3*
Cabot, Frederick Pickering 1868-1932 *WhAm 1*
Cabot, George 1751-1823 *ApCAB, BiDrAC,*
    NatCAB 2, TwCBDA, WhAm H,
    WhAmP
Cabot, George 1752-1823 *AmBi, BiAUS,*
    DcAmB, Drake
Cabot, George E 1861-1946 *WhAm 2*
Cabot, Godfrey Lowell 1861-1962 *ApCAB X,*
    NatCAB 14, NatCAB 57, WhAm 4
Cabot, Henry B 1894-1974 *WhAm 6*
Cabot, Henry Bromfield 1861-1932 *NatCAB 26,*
    WhAm 1
Cabot, Hugh 1872-1945 *DcAmB S3,*
    NatCAB 35, WhAm 2
Cabot, Hugh 1930- *IlBEAAW*
Cabot, John *ApCAB, Drake, McGEWB,*
    TwCBDA
Cabot, John 1450-1498 *AmBi, WhAm H*
Cabot, John 1450?-1499? *WebAB*
Cabot, Maria M 1866- *WomWWA 14*
Cabot, Philip 1872-1941 *NatCAB 30,*
    WhAm 1
Cabot, Richard Clarke 1868-1939 *ApCAB X,*
    DcAmB S2, McGEWB, WhAm 1
Cabot, Samuel 1815-1885 *NatCAB 25*
Cabot, Samuel 1850-1906 *NatCAB 23*
Cabot, Sebastian 1472?-1557? *Drake*
Cabot, Sebastian 1475?-1557? *ApCAB,*

NatCAB 7
Cabot, Sebastian 1476?-1557? *TwCBDA,*
    WhAm H
Cabot, Sebastian 1482?-1557 *McGEWB*
Cabot, Stephen Perkins 1869-1951 *WhAm 3*
Cabot, Ted 1917-1971 *WhAm 5*
Cabot, Thomas Handasyd 1864-1938
    NatCAB 41
Cabot, William Brooks 1858-1949 *NatCAB 38,*
    WhAm 2
Caboto, Giovanni 1450?-1499? *WebAB*
Cabral, Pedro Alvares 1467?-1520 *McGEWB*
Cabral, Pedro Alvarez De d1526? *ApCAB,*
    Drake
Cabrera, Blas 1878-1945 *DcScB*
Cabrera, Miguel d1730? *ApCAB*
Cabrera, Ramon 1806-1877 *WhoMilH*
Cabrera Quintero, Cayetano d1775? *ApCAB*
Cabrillo, Juan Rodriguez 1520-1543 *AmBi,*
    ApCAB, DcAmB, McGEWB, REnAW,
    WhAm H
Cabrini, Mother 1850-1917 *AmBi*
Cabrini, Frances Xavier 1850-1917 *McGEWB,*
    NotAW, WebAB, WhAm HA, WhAm 4
Cabrini, Frances Xavier 1850-1918 *DcAmReB*
Cabrini, Francis Xavier 1850-1917 *DcAmB S1*
Cabrini, Maria Francesca 1850-1917
    NatCAB 27
Cacade, George *NewYHSD*
Caccini, Giulio 1545?-1618 *McGEWB*
Caceres, Alonso De 1499-1554 *ApCAB*
Caceres, Andres Avelino 1831- *ApCAB*
Cadamosto, Alvise Da 1428?-1483 *McGEWB*
Cadbury, Anna Mary Moore *WomWWA 14*
Cadbury, Emma, Jr. 1875- *WomWWA 14*
Cadbury, Henry Joel 1883-1974 *DcAmReB,*
    WhAm 6
Cadbury, William Warder 1877-1959
    NatCAB 49
Caddell, Albert D 1888-1952 *WhAm 3*
Caddoo, William Henry 1908-1974 *WhAm 6*
Caddy, Edmund Harrington Homer 1902-1970
    WhAm 5
Cade, Cassius Marcellus 1856-1953 *WhAm 3*
Cade, Clayton Thomas 1868- *WomWWA 14*
Cade, George Newton 1876- *WhAm 5*
Cadek, Ottokar T 1897-1956 *WhAm 3*
Caden, William C *NewYHSD*
Cadena, Trinidad Garcia DeLa 1832-1886
    ApCAB
Cadenasso, Giuseppe 1858-1918 *IlBEAAW*
Cadet, Louis-Claude 1731-1799 *DcScB*
Cadet DeGassicourt, Charles-Louis 1769-1821
    DcScB
Cadet DeVaux, Antoine-Alexis-Francois
    1743-1828 *DcScB*
Cadillac, Sieur De *WhAm H*
Cadillac, Antoine DeLaMothe 1656?-1730 *AmBi,*
    DcAmB, WhAmP
Cadillac, Antoine DeLaMothe 1657?-1730
    TwCBDA
Cadillac, Antoine DeLaMothe 1660?-1717?
    ApCAB
Cadillac, Antoine DeLaMothe 1660?-1720?
    NatCAB 12
Cadillac, Antoine Laumet DeLaMothe
    1658-1730 *WebAB*
Cadisch, Gordon Francis 1894-1937 *WhAm 1*
Cadman, Charles Wakefield 1881-1946
    ApCAB X, DcAmB S4, WhAm 2
Cadman, Paul Fletcher 1889-1946 *NatCAB 36,*
    WhAm 2
Cadman, Samuel Parkes 1864-1936 *AmBi,*
    ApCAB X, DcAmB S2, NatCAB 14,

NatCAB 28, WhAm 1
Cadmus, A *NewYHSD*
Cadmus, Cornelius Andrew 1844-1902 *BiDrAC*
Cadmus, Paul 1904- *BnEnAmA*
Cadogan, William 1711-1797 *BiHiMed*
Cadorin, Ettore 1878- *WhAm 6*
Cadorna, Count Luigi 1850-1928 *WhoMilH*
Cadoux, Louis 1834?- *NewYHSD*
Cadwalader, Charles Evert 1839-1907 *WhAm 1*
Cadwalader, George d1879 *Drake*
Cadwalader, George 1804-1879 *ApCAB,*
TwCBDA
Cadwalader, George 1806-1879 *NatCAB 12*
Cadwalader, John 1742-1786 *ApCAB, DcAmB,*
NatCAB 1, TwCBDA, WhAm H
Cadwalader, John 1743-1786 *Drake*
Cadwalader, John 1805-1879 *ApCAB Sup,*
BiAUS, BiDrAC, DcAmB, NatCAB 15,
TwCBDA, WhAm H
Cadwalader, John 1843-1925 *NatCAB 15,*
WhAm 1
Cadwalader, John Lambert 1836-1914
ApCAB Sup, TwCBDA
Cadwalader, John Lambert 1837-1914
ApCAB X, BiAUS, NatCAB 33,
WhAm 1
Cadwalader, Lambert d1823 *BiAUS*
Cadwalader, Lambert 1741-1823 *Drake*
Cadwalader, Lambert 1742-1823 *BiDrAC,*
TwCBDA
Cadwalader, Lambert 1743-1823 *ApCAB,*
DcAmB, NatCAB 10, WhAm H
Cadwalader, Richard McCall 1839-1918
ApCAB Sup, TwCBDA, WhAm 1
Cadwalader, Thomas 1707?-1799 *DcAmB*
Cadwalader, Thomas 1708-1779 *ApCAB Sup,*
BiHiMed
Cadwalader, Thomas 1708-1799 *TwCBDA,*
WhAm H
Cadwalader, Thomas 1779-1841 *ApCAB Sup,*
TwCBDA
Cadwalader, Thomas 1795-1873 *ApCAB Sup,*
TwCBDA
Cadwalader, Thomas Francis 1880-1970
WhAm 5
Cadwallader, Alice A W 1832- *AmWom*
Cadwallader, Henry, Jr. 1881-1960 *NatCAB 49*
Cadwallader, Isaac Henry 1850-1919 *WhAm 1*
Cadwallader, Starr 1869-1926 *WhAm 1*
Cadwell, Charles Stewart 1901-1972 *WhAm 5*
Cadwell, Esbon Eugene 1846-1925 *NatCAB 21*
Cadwell, William Henry 1862-1941 *NatCAB 31*
Cady, Albemarle d1888 *Drake*
Cady, Albemarle 1807-1888 *TwCBDA*
Cady, Albemarle 1809?-1888 *ApCAB*
Cady, Burt Duward 1874- *NatCAB 17*
Cady, Calvin Brainerd 1851-1928 *BiDAmEd,*
NatCAB 21, WhAm 4
Cady, Claude Ernest 1878-1953 *BiDrAC,*
WhAm 6
Cady, Cornelia Ensign *WomWWA 14*
Cady, Daniel 1773-1859 *ApCAB, BiAUS,*
BiDrAC, DcAmB, TwCBDA, WhAm H
Cady, Daniel Leavens 1861-1934 *WhAm 1*
Cady, Edward Hammond 1866-1934
NatCAB 34, WhAm 1
Cady, Emma *NewYHSD*
Cady, Ernest 1842- *NatCAB 5*
Cady, Everett Ware 1902-1964 *WhAm 4*
Cady, George Luther 1868-1939 *WhAm 1*
Cady, Guy Brewster 1876-1954 *NatCAB 42*
Cady, Hamilton Perkins 1874-1943 *NatCAB 32,*
WhAm 2
Cady, Helena Maxwell 1849- *AmWom*
Cady, J Cleveland 1838-1919 *WhAm 1*
Cady, John Hutchins 1881-1967 *WhAm 5*
Cady, John Watts 1790-1854 *BiAUS, BiDrAC,*
WhAm H
Cady, Jonathan Rider 1851- *WhAm 4*
Cady, Josiah Cleveland 1838-1919 *TwCBDA*
Cady, Paget Kiersted 1895-1966 *NatCAB 52*
Cady, Philander Kinney 1826-1917 *WhAm 1*
Cady, Putnam 1863- *WhAm 4*
Cady, Ralph Howe 1893-1939 *NatCAB 30*
Cady, Samuel Howard 1870-1942 *WhAm 2*
Cady, Sarah Louise Ensign 1829-1912
BiDAmEd, DcAmB, NatCAB 9
Cady, Walter Guyton 1874- *WhAm 5*

Cady, William Byron 1860-1925 *NatCAB 20*
Cady, William Hamlin 1877-1969 *NatCAB 55*
Caesar, Doris 1893-1971 *WhAm 5*
Caesar, Gaius Julius 100BC-044BC *McGEWB*
Caesar, Kathleen d1960 *WhAm 4*
Caesar, Orville Swan 1892-1965 *NatCAB 51,*
WhAm 4
Caetani, Gelasio 1877-1934 *WhAm 1*
Caffee, Robert Henderson 1902-1957 *WhAm 3*
Cafferty, James H 1819-1869 *ApCAB,*
NewYHSD, WhAm H
Caffery, Donelson 1835-1906 *ApCAB Sup*
Caffery, Donelson 1835-1906 *BiDrAC, DcAmB,*
NatCAB 13, TwCBDA, WhAm 1,
WhAmP
Caffery, Eldon Lee 1924-1972 *WhAm 6*
Caffery, Jefferson 1886-1974 *WhAm 6*
Caffery, Patrick Thomson 1932- *BiDrAC*
Caffey, Eugene Mead 1895-1961 *WhAm 4*
Caffey, Francis Gordon 1868-1951 *NatCAB 5,*
WhAm 3
Caffin, Caroline 1864- *WomWWA 14*
Caffin, Charles Henry 1854-1918 *AmBi,*
DcAmB, NatCAB 22, WhAm 1
Caffrey, F *NewYHSD*
Caffrey, James Joseph 1897-1961 *WhAm 4*
Caffrey, T *NewYHSD*
Cage, Harry d1859 *BiAUS, BiDrAC,*
WhAm H
Cage, John Milton, Jr. 1912- *EncAB,*
McGEWB, WebAB
Cagger, Peter 1812-1868 *ApCAB*
Cagle, Alvah Penn 1896-1962 *NatCAB 51,*
WhAm 4
Cagle, Fred Ray 1915-1968 *WhAm 5*
Cagney, James 1904- *WebAB*
Cagniard DeLaTour, Charles 1777-1859 *DcScB*
Cagwin, Clara Joslyn 1884- *WomWWA 14*
Cagwin, Ward Jay 1873-1934 *NatCAB 26*
Cahalin, John Francis 1882-1950 *NatCAB 39*
Cahan, Abraham 1860-1951 *DcAmB S5,*
McGEWB, NatCAB 11, WebAB,
WhAm 3
Cahen, Alfred d1963 *WhAm 4*
Cahill, Arthur James 1878-1970 *IIBEAAW,*
WhAm 5
Cahill, Bernard J S 1866-1944 *WhAm 2*
Cahill, Daniel William 1802-1864 *Drake*
Cahill, Dennis John 1867-1942 *NatCAB 31*
Cahill, Edward 1843-1922 *WhAm 1*
Cahill, Edward A 1885-1961 *WhAm 4*
Cahill, Edward Cornelius 1900-1961 *WhAm 4*
Cahill, Edward Gustav 1882-1961 *NatCAB 53*
Cahill, Edward William 1880-1938 *NatCAB 28*
Cahill, George Francis 1890-1959 *NatCAB 44,*
WhAm 3
Cahill, Holger 1887-1960 *WhAm 4*
Cahill, Isaac Jasper 1868-1945 *WhAm 2*
Cahill, James Christopher 1885-1946 *WhAm 2*
Cahill, John Thomas 1903-1966 *WhAm 4*
Cahill, LeRoy 1841- *NatCAB 5*
Cahill, Marie 1870-1933 *NotAW, WhAm 1,*
WomWWA 14
Cahill, Michael Harrison 1874-1940
NatCAB 29, WhAm 1
Cahill, Michael Henry 1886-1939 *WhAm 1*
Cahill, Thaddeus 1867-1934 *WhAm 1*
Cahill, William Thomas 1912- *BiDrAC*
Cahn, Bertram Joseph 1875-1959 *WhAm 3*
Cahn, Edmond 1906-1964 *NatCAB 50,*
WhAm 4
Cahn, Gladys D Freeman 1901-1964 *WhAm 4*
Cahners, James Albert 1888-1963 *NatCAB 49*
Cahoon, Edward Augustus 1862-1934 *WhAm 1*
Cahoon, Grace Willson *WomWWA 14*
Cahoon, William 1774-1833 *BiAUS, BiDrAC,*
WhAm H
Cahoone, J Benjamin 1800-1873 *ApCAB,*
TwCBDA
Cahours, Auguste Andre Thomas 1813-1891
DcScB
Caicedo, Domingo 1783-1843 *ApCAB*
Caille, Augustus 1854- *WhAm 1*
Cailletet, Louis Paul 1832-1913 *AsBiEn, DcScB*
Caillie, Auguste Rene 1799-1838 *McGEWB*
Caillouet, Adrian Joseph 1883-1946 *WhAm 2*
Cain *NewYHSD*
Cain, Achilles Wade 1867-1929 *NatCAB 22*

Cain, Charles Cornelius, Jr. 1886-1971
NatCAB 55
Cain, George R 1910-1972 *WhAm 5*
Cain, Harry Pulliam 1906- *BiDrAC*
Cain, James Matthew 1885-1955 *NatCAB 43*
Cain, James William 1860-1938 *NatCAB 28,*
WhAm 1
Cain, Joseph Edward 1903-1963 *NatCAB 51,*
WhAm 4
Cain, Joseph Palmer, Jr. 1912-1971 *NatCAB 56*
Cain, Richard Harvey 1825-1887 *ApCAB,*
BiAUS, BiDrAC, DcAmB, NatCAB 11,
TwCBDA, WhAm H, WhAmP
Cain, Rolly Morton 1882-1947 *WhAm 2*
Cain, Walter 1862- *WhAm 1*
Cain, William 1847-1930 *BiDAmEd,*
DcAmB S1, WhAm 1
Caine, George Redfern 1845-1924 *NatCAB 20*
Caine, John Thomas 1829-1911 *BiDrAC,*
REnAW, TwCBDA, WhAmP
Caine, John Thomas, III 1882- *WhAm 3*
Caine, Milton A 1882-1955 *WhAm 3*
Caines, George 1771-1825 *ApCAB, DcAmB,*
Drake, WhAm H
Cairns, Alexander 1871-1957 *WhAm 3*
Cairns, Anna Sneed 1841-1930 *WhAm 1,*
WomWWA 14
Cairns, Charles Andrew d1933 *WhAm 1*
Cairns, Douglas Walker 1877-1947 *NatCAB 36*
Cairns, Frances V Shellabarger *WomWWA 14*
Cairns, Frederick Irvan 1865-1944 *WhAm 2*
Cairns, Leonard Stanley 1882-1918 *NatCAB 17*
Cairns, William B 1867-1932 *WhAm 1*
Cairns, William DeWeese 1871-1955
NatCAB 47, WhAm 3
Cairo, Frances Lillian Wilmer *WomWWA 14*
Caius, Johannes 1510-1573 *BiHiMed*
Caius, John 1510-1573 *DcScB*
Cajetan, Saint 1480-1547 *McGEWB*
Cajigal, Francisco Antonio 1695-1777 *ApCAB*
Cajigal Y Monserrate, Juan Manuel 1739-1811
ApCAB
Cajori, Florian 1859-1930 *BiDAmEd,*
DcAmB S1, NatCAB 27, WhAm 1,
WhAm 1C
Cake, Henry Lutz 1827-1899 *BiAUS, BiDrAC,*
NatCAB 5
Cake, Ralph Harlan 1891-1973 *WhAm 5*
Cake, Wallace Ellwood 1897-1973 *WhAm 6*
Caker, Thomas 1825?- *NewYHSD*
Calabrese, Giuseppe 1897-1966 *WhAm 4*
Calafquin 1540?-1602 *ApCAB*
Calahan, Harold Augustin 1889-1965
NatCAB 50
Calame, Justin L *NewYHSD*
Calamity Jane 1852-1903 *AmBi, McGEWB,*
NotAW, REnAW, WebAB
Calancha, Antonio DeLa *ApCAB*
Calandrelli, Giuseppe 1749-1827 *DcScB*
Calandrelli, Ignazio 1792-1866 *DcScB*
Calcidius *DcScB*
Caldani, Leopoldo Marcantonio 1725-1813
DcScB
Caldas, Francisco Jose De 1768-1816 *DcScB*
Caldas, Francisco Jose De 1770-1816 *Drake*
Caldas, Francisco Jose De 1771-1816 *ApCAB*
Caldas, Pereira DeSouza Antonia 1762-1814
Drake
Caldas Pereira DeSouza, Antonio 1762-1814
ApCAB
Caldemeyer, Daniel Henry 1885-1943
NatCAB 34
Calder, Alexander 1886-1962 *WhAm 4*
Calder, Alexander 1898- *BnEnAmA, EncAB,*
McGEWB, WebAB
Calder, Alexander Milne 1846-1923 *BnEnAmA,*
NatCAB 20, WhAm 1
Calder, Alexander Stirling 1870-1945
BnEnAmA, DcAmB S3, NatCAB 34,
WhAm 2
Calder, Curtis Ernest 1890-1955 *WhAm 3*
Calder, Helen Barnetson 1877- *WhAm 5*
Calder, Hugh Gordon 1902-1970 *WhAm 5*
Calder, James 1826-1893 *NatCAB 20*
Calder, John Knight 1882-1946 *NatCAB 35*
Calder, Louis 1879-1963 *WhAm 4*
Calder, Louis, Jr. 1919-1965 *WhAm 4*
Calder, May *NewYHSD*

Calder, Robert Scott 1870- *WhAm 5*
Calder, William Musgrave 1869-1945 *BiDrAC, NatCAB 44, WhAm 2, WhAmP*
Calderhead, William Alexander 1844-1928 *BiDrAC, TwCBDA, WhAm 4, WhAmP*
Calderon, Fernando 1809-1845 *ApCAB*
Calderon, Francisco Santiago d1736 *ApCAB*
Calderon, Ignacio 1848- *WhAm 4*
Calderon, Luis 1881- *WhAm 6*
Calderon, Manuel Alvarez 1852- *WhAm 4*
Calderon DeLaBarca, Frances Inglis 1818- *ApCAB, Drake*
Calderon DeLaBarca Y Henao, Pedro 1600-1681 *McGEWB*
Calderon Guardia, Rafael Angel 1900-1970 *WhAm 5*
Calderone, Mary Steichen 1904- *BiDAmEd*
Calderwood, Alva John 1873-1949 *WhAm 2*
Calderwood, James Park 1884-1934 *NatCAB 41*
Calderwood, William Robert 1866-1960 *NatCAB 49*
Caldicott, Thomas Ford 1803-1869 *ApCAB, Drake*
Caldwell, Doctor *NewYHSD*
Caldwell, Alexander d1839 *ApCAB, BiAUS*
Caldwell, Alexander 1830-1917 *ApCAB, BiDrAC, DcAmB, NatCAB 12, TwCBDA, WhAm 1, WhAmP*
Caldwell, Andrew Jackson 1837-1906 *BiDrAC*
Caldwell, Ben Franklin 1848-1924 *BiDrAC, TwCBDA, WhAm 4*
Caldwell, Benjamin Palmer 1875-1950 *WhAm 3*
Caldwell, Bert Wilmer 1875-1951 *WhAm 3*
Caldwell, Billy 1780-1841 *WhAm H*
Caldwell, Burns Durbin 1858-1922 *NatCAB 24, WhAm 1*
Caldwell, Charles 1772-1853 *ApCAB, DcAmB, Drake, NatCAB 7, TwCBDA, WhAm H*
Caldwell, Charles 1866-1956 *NatCAB 46*
Caldwell, Charles Albert 1863-1947 *NatCAB 37*
Caldwell, Charles Henry Bromedge 1823-1877 *ApCAB, DcAmB, Drake, NatCAB 11, TwCBDA, WhAm H*
Caldwell, Charles Pope 1875-1940 *BiDrAC, WhAm 1*
Caldwell, Charles Swan 1881-1950 *NatCAB 38*
Caldwell, Clarence B 1896-1968 *WhAm 4A*
Caldwell, Clifford Douglass 1872-1940 *WhAm 1*
Caldwell, Daniel Templeton 1892-1952 *WhAm 3*
Caldwell, David 1725-1824 *ApCAB, BiDAmEd, DcAmB, Drake, NatCAB 10, TwCBDA, WhAm H*
Caldwell, Edward 1861-1949 *NatCAB 38*
Caldwell, Edwin Valdivia 1907-1966 *WhAm 4*
Caldwell, Erskine Preston 1903- *EncAAH, McGEWB, WebAB*
Caldwell, Estella Riley 1873- *WomWWA 14*
Caldwell, Eugene Craighead 1876-1931 *WhAm 1*
Caldwell, Eugene Wilson 1870-1918 *DcAmB, NatCAB 18, WhAm 1*
Caldwell, Francis Cary 1868-1953 *WhAm 3*
Caldwell, Frank Congleton 1866- *WhAm 4*
Caldwell, Frank Merrill 1866-1937 *NatCAB 28, WhAm 1*
Caldwell, Fred T 1883-1951 *WhAm 3*
Caldwell, George Alexander 1864-1949 *NatCAB 37*
Caldwell, George Alfred 1814-1866 *BiAUS, BiDrAC, WhAm H*
Caldwell, George Brinton 1863-1933 *ApCAB X, NatCAB 15, WhAm 1*
Caldwell, George Chapman 1834-1907 *ApCAB, NatCAB 4, NatCAB 26, TwCBDA, WhAm 1*
Caldwell, George Overall 1883- *WhoColR*
Caldicott, George Walter 1866-1946 *NatCAB 33*
Caldwell, Greene W 1811- *BiAUS*
Caldwell, Greene Washington 1806-1864 *BiDrAC, WhAm H*
Caldwell, Henry Clay d1915 *BiAUS*
Caldwell, Henry Clay 1832-1915 *DcAmB, NatCAB 11, TwCBDA, WhAm 1*
Caldwell, Henry Clay 1835-1915 *ApCAB*
Caldwell, Howard H 1831- *Drake*
Caldwell, Howard Walter 1853-1927 *WhAm 1*
Caldwell, Hugh Milton 1881- *WhAm 3*

Caldwell, Ira Sylvester 1870-1944 *NatCAB 34*
Caldwell, J G 1913-1971 *WhAm 5*
Caldwell, James 1734-1781 *ApCAB, DcAmB, Drake, NatCAB 5, TwCBDA, WhAm H*
Caldwell, James 1770-1838 *BiAUS, BiDrAC, WhAm H*
Caldwell, James E 1854-1944 *WhAm 2*
Caldwell, James Emott 1882-1919 *NatCAB 33*
Caldwell, James Guthrie 1855-1926 *NatCAB 26*
Caldwell, James H 1793-1863 *WhAm H*
Caldwell, James Henry 1865-1931 *WhAm 1*
Caldwell, James Ralston 1900-1965 *NatCAB 51*
Caldwell, Jesse Cobb 1873-1941 *WhAm 1*
Caldwell, John d1804 *ApCAB, Drake, TwCBDA*
Caldwell, John A 1853-1927 *TwCBDA*
Caldwell, John Alexander 1852-1927 *BiDrAC, NatCAB 34, WhAmP*
Caldwell, John Curtis 1833-1912 *ApCAB, BiAUS, NatCAB 5, TwCBDA, WhAm 1*
Caldwell, John Handly d1954 *WhAm 3*
Caldwell, John Henry 1826-1902 *BiAUS, BiDrAC*
Caldwell, John Kenneth 1881- *WhAm 6*
Caldwell, John Lawrence 1875-1922 *WhAm 1*
Caldwell, John Livy *WhAm 5*
Caldwell, John W *BiAUS*
Caldwell, John William 1837-1903 *BiDrAC*
Caldwell, John Williamson 1842-1923 *WhAm 1*
Caldwell, Joseph 1773-1835 *ApCAB, BiDAmEd, DcAmB, Drake, NatCAB 13, TwCBDA, WhAm H*
Caldwell, Joseph Pearson 1808-1853 *BiAUS, BiDrAC, WhAm H*
Caldwell, Joseph Pearson 1853-1911 *WhAm 1*
Caldwell, Joshua William 1856-1909 *NatCAB 13, WhAm 1*
Caldwell, Josiah Samuel 1862- *WhAm 4, WhoColR*
Caldwell, Julian Carr 1870- *WhoColR*
Caldwell, Lisle Bones 1834- *ApCAB, TwCBDA, WhAm 4*
Caldwell, Louis Goldsborough 1891-1951 *WhAm 3*
Caldwell, Louise Orton 1877- *WomWWA 14*
Caldwell, Mary Gwendolin 1863-1909 *NotAW*
Caldwell, Mary Letitia 1890-1972 *WhAm 5*
Caldwell, Merritt 1806-1848 *ApCAB, TwCBDA*
Caldwell, Millard Fillmore 1897- *BiDrAC*
Caldwell, Morley Albert 1877-1938 *WhAm 1*
Caldwell, Oliver North 1869-1953 *NatCAB 41*
Caldwell, Orestes Hampton 1888-1967 *WhAm 4, WhAm 5*
Caldwell, Otis William 1869-1947 *BiDAmEd, DcAmB S4, NatCAB 35, WhAm 2*
Caldwell, Patrick Calhoun 1801-1855 *BiAUS, BiDrAC, WhAm H*
Caldwell, Perry DeFord 1879-1952 *NatCAB 45*
Caldwell, Robert Breckenridge 1882-1956 *WhAm 3*
Caldwell, Robert Dennis 1894-1953 *NatCAB 42*
Caldwell, Robert J 1875-1951 *WhAm 3*
Caldwell, Robert Porter 1821-1885 *BiAUS, BiDrAC, WhAm H*
Caldwell, Robert Tate 1882-1973 *WhAm 6*
Caldwell, Samuel *ApCAB, Drake*
Caldwell, Samuel Cushman 1836-1923 *WhAm 1*
Caldwell, Samuel Hawks 1904-1960 *WhAm 4*
Caldwell, Samuel Lunt 1820-1889 *ApCAB, NatCAB 5, TwCBDA, WhAm H*
Caldwell, Stephen Adolphus 1889-1956 *WhAm 3*
Caldwell, Thomas Jones 1882-1960 *WhAm 4*
Caldwell, Tod R 1818-1874 *BiAUS, NatCAB 4*
Caldwell, Victor Bush 1864-1915 *WhAm 1*
Caldwell, W D *NewYHSD*
Caldwell, Waller Cochran 1849- *WhAm 4*
Caldwell, Walter Lindsay 1871-1964 *WhAm 4*
Caldwell, William 1863- *WhAm 3*
Caldwell, William B 1808-1876 *NatCAB 7*
Caldwell, William E 1880-1943 *WhAm 2*
Caldwell, William Erwin 1858-1938 *NatCAB 42*
Caldwell, William Everette, Jr. 1916-1973 *NatCAB 57*
Caldwell, William H 1837-1899 *NewYHSD*
Caldwell, William Parker 1832-1903 *BiAUS, BiDrAC*

Caldwell, William Warner 1823- *ApCAB*
Caldwell, Willie Walker 1860- *WomWWA 14*
Caldwell, Winford Newman 1857-1927 *NatCAB 22*
Caldwell, Zenas 1800-1826 *ApCAB, TwCBDA*
Cale, George William, Jr. 1866-1935 *NatCAB 27*
Cale, Thomas 1848-1941 *BiDrAC, WhAm 4*
Calef, Robert d1720 *TwCBDA*
Calef, Robert d1723? *ApCAB, Drake*
Calef, Robert 1648-1719 *AmBi, DcAmB, NatCAB 8, WhAm H*
Caley, Katharine d1938 *WhAm 1*
Caley, Llewelyn N 1859-1932 *WhAm 1*
Calfe, Robert d1720 *TwCBDA*
Calfee, John Edward 1875-1940 *WhAm 1*
Calfee, Robert Martin 1876-1968 *NatCAB 57, WhAm 6*
Calhane, Daniel Francis 1869-1951 *WhAm 3*
Calhern, Louis 1895-1956 *NatCAB 45*
Calhern, Louis 1896-1956 *WhAm 3*
Calhoon, John 1797-1842 *BiDrAC, WhAm H*
Calhoon, Solomon Saladin 1838- *WhAm 4*
Calhoun, A R *IIBEAAW*
Calhoun, Abner Wellborn 1845-1910 *NatCAB 16, WhAm 1*
Calhoun, Albert Robert 1862- *WhoColR*
Calhoun, Alexander McConnell 1871-1935 *WhAm 1*
Calhoun, Byron E 1902-1957 *WhAm 3*
Calhoun, David Randolph 1858- *WhAm 1*
Calhoun, Edmund Rose 1821-1897 *NatCAB 4, TwCBDA*
Calhoun, Fred Harvey Hall 1873-1959 *WhAm 3*
Calhoun, Galloway 1894-1962 *WhAm 4*
Calhoun, George Miller 1886-1942 *NatCAB 41, WhAm 2*
Calhoun, Hall Laurie 1863-1935 *WhAm 1*
Calhoun, James S *BiAUS*
Calhoun, John *BiAUS*
Calhoun, John 1806-1859 *DcAmB, WhAm H*
Calhoun, John 1863-1937 *WhAm 1*
Calhoun, John Caldwell 1782-1850 *AmBi, ApCAB, BiAUS, BiDrAC, BiDrUSE, DcAmB, Drake, EncAAH, EncAB, McGEWB, NatCAB 6, REnAW, TwCBDA, WebAB, WhAm H, WhAmP*
Calhoun, John Caldwell 1843-1918 *NatCAB 13*
Calhoun, John Calwell 1843-1918 *WhAm 1*
Calhoun, John Darr 1920-1963 *WhAm 4*
Calhoun, John E 1749-1802 *BiAUS*
Calhoun, John Erwin 1749-1802 *ApCAB, TwCBDA*
Calhoun, John Ewing 1749-1802 *Drake*
Calhoun, John William 1871-1947 *WhAm 2*
Calhoun, Joseph 1750-1817 *BiAUS, BiDrAC, WhAm H*
Calhoun, Joseph Painter 1852- *WhAm 4*
Calhoun, Laura A 1847- *WomWWA 14*
Calhoun, Newell Meeker 1847- *WhAm 4*
Calhoun, Orange Van 1901-1953 *NatCAB 43*
Calhoun, Patrick 1856-1943 *DcAmB S3, NatCAB 1, NatCAB 34, WhAm 2*
Calhoun, Philo Clarke 1889-1964 *WhAm 4*
Calhoun, Ralph Emerson 1906-1968 *WhAm 5*
Calhoun, Randolph 1901-1961 *NatCAB 49*
Calhoun, Sallie Williams *WomWWA 14*
Calhoun, Simeon Howard 1804-1876 *ApCAB, TwCBDA*
Calhoun, Virginia Catherine *WomWWA 14*
Calhoun, William Barron 1795-1865 *DcAmB, Drake*
Calhoun, William Barron 1796-1865 *ApCAB, BiAUS, BiDrAC, NatCAB 11, TwCBDA, WhAm H, WhAmP*
Calhoun, William James 1848-1916 *DcAmB, NatCAB 14, WhAm 1*
Calhoun, William Lowndes 1885-1963 *WhAm 4*
Califano, Michael 1889- *ApCAB X*
Califf, Joseph Mark 1843-1914 *WhAm 1*
California Joe 1829-1876 *AmBi, DcAmB, WhAm H*
Caliga, Isaac Henry 1857- *NatCAB 12, WhAm 4*
Caligula 012-041 *McGEWB*
Calisch, Edward N 1865-1946 *WhAm 2*
Caliver, Ambrose 1894-1962 *BiDAmEd, WhAm 4*

Calkin, Henry C 1858- *BiAUS*
Calkin, Hervey Chittenden 1828-1913 *BiDrAC*
Calkin, John Burgess 1904-1959 *NatCAB 47*
Calkins, Adelaide Augusta Hosmer 1831-1909 *NatCAB 28*
Calkins, Alice Haile 1865-1934 *NatCAB 28*
Calkins, Allard A 1889-1973 *WhAm 6*
Calkins, Charles Walbridge 1842-1918 *NatCAB 17*
Calkins, Clinch 1895-1968 *NatCAB 54*
Calkins, Earnest Elmo 1868-1964 *WhAm 4*
Calkins, Emily Blackwell Lathrop *WomWWA 14*
Calkins, Emor L *WomWWA 14*
Calkins, Frank W *IlBEAAW*
Calkins, Franklin Welles 1857-1928 *WhAm 1*
Calkins, Frederick William 1831-1928 *NatCAB 21*
Calkins, Gary Nathan 1869-1943 *DcAmB S3, DcScB, NatCAB 33, WhAm 2*
Calkins, Harvey Reeves 1866-1941 *WhAm 1*
Calkins, Howard W 1902-1973 *WhAm 6*
Calkins, James E 1877- *WhAm 5*
Calkins, Leroy Adelbert 1894-1960 *NatCAB 50, WhAm 4*
Calkins, Lyman Darrow 1845-1917 *WhAm 1*
Calkins, Marshall 1828-1922 *NatCAB 28*
Calkins, Mary Whiton 1863-1930 *ApCAB X, BiDAmEd, DcAmB S1, NatCAB 13, NotAW, WhAm 1, WomWWA 14*
Calkins, Norman Allison 1822-1895 *ApCAB, BiDAmEd, DcAmB, NatCAB 10, TwCBDA, WhAm H*
Calkins, Phineas Wolcott 1831-1924 *DcAmB*
Calkins, Ransom M 1863-1932 *WhAm 1*
Calkins, Raymond 1869- *ApCAB X, WhAm 5*
Calkins, Truesdel Peck 1877-1942 *NatCAB 40, WhAm 2*
Calkins, William Henry 1842-1894 *BiDrAC, WhAm H*
Calkins, Wolcott 1831-1924 *DcAmB, WhAm 1*
Call, Annie Payson 1853- *WomWWA 14*
Call, Arthur Deerin 1869-1941 *NatCAB 31, WhAm 2*
Call, Charles Henry 1847-1925 *ApCAB X*
Call, Charles Warren, Jr. 1925-1975 *WhAm 6*
Call, Daniel D 1765?-1840 *ApCAB, Drake*
Call, Edward Payson 1855-1919 *ApCAB X, WhAm 1*
Call, Francis Marion 1843-1915 *NatCAB 17*
Call, Jacob d1826 *BiAUS, BiDrAC, WhAm H*
Call, Leland Everett 1881- *WhAm 6*
Call, Manfred 1876-1936 *NatCAB 39, WhAm 1*
Call, Margaret Fleming d1975 *WhAm 6*
Call, Norman 1880-1959 *NatCAB 44, WhAm 6*
Call, Rhydon Mays 1858-1928 *NatCAB 11, WhAm 1*
Call, Richard *Drake*
Call, Richard Ellsworth 1856- *WhAm 4*
Call, Richard Keith d1862 *BiAUS, Drake*
Call, Richard Keith 1757-1792 *ApCAB, TwCBDA*
Call, Richard Keith 1791-1862 *AmBi, ApCAB, DcAmB, NatCAB 11, TwCBDA, WhAm H*
Call, Richard Keith 1792-1862 *BiDrAC, REnAW, WhAmP*
Call, S Leigh 1872-1952 *WhAm 3*
Call, Wilkinson 1834-1910 *ApCAB, BiDrAC, NatCAB 2, TwCBDA, WhAm 1, WhAmP*
Callaghan, Alfred 1890-1959 *WhAm 3*
Callaghan, Bryan 1852-1913 *NatCAB 15*
Callaghan, Cornelius Henry 1872-1954 *NatCAB 40*
Callaghan, Daniel Judson 1890-1942 *WebAMB*
Callaghan, Daniel Judson 1892-1942 *WhWW-II*
Callaghan, Edward Morley 1903- *McGEWB*
Callaghan, Stephen 1876-1952 *WhAm 3*
Callaghan, Thomas Timothy 1900-1961 *NatCAB 48*
Callahan, Donald A 1876-1951 *WhAm 3*
Callahan, Ethelbert 1829-1918 *NatCAB 18, WhAm 1*

Callahan, Frank E 1898-1968 *NatCAB 54*
Callahan, Harry 1912- *BnEnAmA*
Callahan, Henry White 1856- *WhAm 4*
Callahan, James Morton 1864- *NatCAB 11*
Callahan, James Yancy 1852-1935 *BiDrAC, WhAm 4*
Callahan, Jeremiah Joseph 1878-1969 *WhAm 5*
Callahan, John 1865-1956 *WhAm 3*
Callahan, Patrick Henry 1865-1940 *DcAmB S2, DcAmReB*
Callahan, Patrick Henry 1866-1940 *WhAm 1*
Callahan, Samuel B 1834-1911 *BiDConf*
Callahan, William Paul, Jr. 1917-1971 *WhAm 5*
Callan, Albert Stevens 1884-1963 *WhAm 4*
Callan, Charles Jerome 1877-1962 *WhAm 4*
Callan, Clair Armstrong 1920- *BiDrAC*
Callan, Estella Folts *BiCAW*
Callan, Frank Hiram 1865-1927 *NatCAB 20*
Callan, John Gurney 1875-1940 *WhAm 1*
Callan, Nicholas 1799-1864 *DcScB*
Callan, Peter Augustus 1844-1932 *NatCAB 25*
Callan, Peter Augustus 1845-1932 *WhAm 1*
Callan, Robert Emmet 1874-1936 *NatCAB 26, WhAm 1*
Callanan, Carolyn Williams 1901-1959 *WhAm 4*
Callanan, Edward A 1889-1956 *WhAm 3*
Callander, Cyrus N 1865-1930 *WhAm 1, WhAm 2*
Callander, William Forrest 1880-1968 *WhAm 5*
Callandreau, Pierre Jean Octave 1852-1904 *DcScB*
Callas *NewYHSD*
Callas, Maria 1923- *WebAB*
Callaway, Andrew Wilson 1883-1958 *NatCAB 49*
Callaway, Cason Jewell 1894-1961 *NatCAB 53, WhAm 4*
Callaway, Ely Reeves, Sr. 1880-1956 *NatCAB 47, WhAm 3*
Callaway, Enoch 1892-1961 *NatCAB 47*
Callaway, Enoch Howard 1862- *WhAm 4*
Callaway, French Henry 1890-1960 *NatCAB 48*
Callaway, Fuller Earle 1870-1928 *NatCAB 21, WhAm 1, WhAm 1C*
Callaway, George *NewYHSD*
Callaway, George Samuel 1891-1962 *NatCAB 49*
Callaway, Howard Hollis 1927- *BiDrAC*
Callaway, Lea 1911-1964 *NatCAB 51*
Callaway, Llewellyn Link 1868-1951 *WhAm 3*
Callaway, Merrel Price 1872-1957 *WhAm 3*
Callaway, Morgan, Jr. 1862-1936 *DcAmB S2, WhAm 1*
Callaway, Oscar 1872-1947 *BiDrAC*
Callaway, Samuel Rodger 1850-1904 *DcAmB, NatCAB 21, WhAm 1*
Callaway, Samuel Roger 1850-1904 *ApCAB Sup*
Callaway, Trowbridge 1882-1963 *NatCAB 50, WhAm 4*
Callbreath, James Finch 1858-1940 *WhAm 1*
Callcott, Wilfrid Hardy 1895-1969 *WhAm 5*
Calleja, Emilio 1830?- *ApCAB*
Calleja, Felix DelRey 1750-1821? *ApCAB, Drake*
Callen, Alfred Copeland 1888-1951 *NatCAB 40, WhAm 3*
Callen, J Spencer 1854- *WhAm 4*
Callen, John Franklin 1854-1918 *NatCAB 19*
Callendar, Hugh Longbourne 1863-1930 *DcScB*
Callender, Benjamin 1773-1856 *NewYHSD*
Callender, Bessie Stough 1889-1951 *NatCAB 38*
Callender, Edward Belcher 1851-1917 *WhAm 1*
Callender, Estelle Victoria Hudgins 1873- *BiCAW*
Callender, Franklin D 1817?-1882 *ApCAB, TwCBDA*
Callender, George Russell 1884-1973 *WhAm 5*
Callender, Guy Stevens 1865-1915 *DcAmB, NatCAB 23, WhAm 1*
Callender, Harold 1892-1959 *WhAm 3*
Callender, James Thomas 1758-1813 *ApCAB*
Callender, James Thompson 1758-1803 *Drake*
Callender, James Thomson 1758-1803 *DcAmB, WhAm H, WhAmP*
Callender, John d1748 *Drake*
Callender, John 1700?-1748 *WhAm H*

Callender, John 1706-1748 *ApCAB, DcAmB, NatCAB 7, TwCBDA*
Callender, John Hill 1831-1896 *TwCBDA*
Callender, John Hill 1832-1896 *NatCAB 8*
Callender, Joseph 1751-1821 *NewYHSD*
Callender, Romaine 1857-1930 *WhAm 1*
Callender, Sherman D 1869-1952 *WhAm 3*
Callender, Walter 1834- *NatCAB 3*
Callender, Walter Reid 1872-1932 *WhAm 1*
Callender, William David 1871-1931 *NatCAB 24*
Caller, Mary Alice *WhAm 5*
Callery, Francis Anthony 1898-1971 *WhAm 5*
Callery, James Dawson 1857-1932 *NatCAB 13, WhAm 1*
Calles, Plutarco Elias 1877-1945 *McGEWB, WhAm 2*
Calley, Walter 1858-1928 *WhAm 1*
Callicot, J P *NewYHSD*
Callieres, Louis Hector De d1703 *Drake*
Callieres Bonnevue, Louis Hector De 1639-1703 *ApCAB, WhAm H*
Callimachus 310?BC-240BC *McGEWB*
Callinicos Of Heliopolis 620?- *DcScB*
Callinicus 620?- *AsBiEn*
Callippus 370?BC-300?BC *AsBiEn, DcScB*
Callis, James Augustus Braxston 1884- *WhoColR*
Callis, John Benton 1828-1898 *ApCAB Sup, BiAUS, BiDrAC, NatCAB 13*
Callison, Ferd Walter 1893-1969 *NatCAB 55*
Callison, Tolliver Cleveland 1884-1966 *WhAm 4*
Callister, Edward Henry 1862-1917 *WhAm 1*
Callos, George John 1909-1965 *NatCAB 53, WhAm 4*
Callow, John Michael 1867-1940 *WhAm 1*
Calloway, Alfred Woodward 1872-1926 *NatCAB 20, WhAm 1*
Calloway, Charles Henry 1878- *WhoColR*
Calloway, Thomas Clanton 1878- *WhAm 6*
Calloway, Thomas Junius 1866- *WhoColR*
Calloway, Walter Bowles 1873- *WhAm 5*
Callvert, Ronald Glenn 1873-1955 *WhAm 3*
Calm, Filen 1831?- *NewYHSD*
Calmes, Marquis 1755-1834 *ApCAB, Drake*
Calmette, Albert 1863-1933 *DcScB*
Calthrop, Samuel Robert 1829-1917 *ApCAB, TwCBDA, WhAm 1*
Calve, Emma 1866-1942 *WhAm 1, WhAm 2*
Calver, George Wehnes 1887-1972 *WhAm 5*
Calver, Homer Northup 1892-1970 *WhAm 5*
Calverley, Charles 1833-1914 *ApCAB, BnEnAmA, DcAmB, NewYHSD, TwCBDA, WhAm 1*
Calverley, Edwin Elliott 1882-1971 *NatCAB 56, NatCAB 57*
Calverley, Eleanor Jane Taylor 1887-1968 *NatCAB 57*
Calvert *ApCAB*
Calvert, Benedict d1732 *ApCAB, Drake*
Calvert, Benedict Leonard 1680?-1715 *NatCAB 7*
Calvert, Benedict Leonard 1700?-1731 *NatCAB 7*
Calvert, Cecil 1606-1675 *WhAm H*
Calvert, Cecil Kirk 1886-1948 *NatCAB 37*
Calvert, Cecilius 1606-1675 *DcAmReB*
Calvert, Cecilius, Lord Baltimore 1605?-1675 *AmBi*
Calvert, Cecilus 1606-1675 *NatCAB 7*
Calvert, Charles 1629-1715 *NatCAB 7, WhAm H*
Calvert, Charles 1699-1751 *NatCAB 7*
Calvert, Charles, Lord Baltimore 1637-1715 *AmBi, DcAmB, McGEWB, WebAB*
Calvert, Charles Baltimore 1843-1906 *NatCAB 16*
Calvert, Charles Benedict 1808-1864 *BiAUS, BiDrAC, DcAmB, EncAAH, WhAm H, WhAmP*
Calvert, Charles Cecil 1900-1954 *NatCAB 42*
Calvert, Edward Henry 1702-1730 *ApCAB, Drake*
Calvert, Eleanor Mackubin *WomWWA 14*
Calvert, Frances Adelia 1847- *WomWWA 14*
Calvert, Frederick 1731-1771 *Drake, NatCAB 7*
Calvert, George *TwCBDA*

Calvert, George 1579?-1632 *WebAB*
Calvert, George 1580?-1632 *AmBi, DcAmB, McGEWB, WhAm H*
Calvert, George 1581-1632 *NatCAB 7*
Calvert, Sir George 1582-1632 *Drake*
Calvert, George Henry 1803-1889 *ApCAB, DcAmB, Drake, NatCAB 5, TwCBDA, WhAm H*
Calvert, John Betts 1852-1928 *NatCAB 11, NatCAB 21, WhAm 1*
Calvert, John Fyfer 1898-1966 *NatCAB 53, WhAm 4*
Calvert, Leonard 1606-1647 *ApCAB, DcAmB, Drake, NatCAB 7, TwCBDA, WebAB, WhAm H*
Calvert, Mary Githens 1876- *WomWWA 14*
Calvert, Philip *NatCAB 7*
Calvert, Philip Powell 1871- *NatCAB 12, WhAm 5*
Calvert, Richard *NewYHSD*
Calvert, Richard Creagh Mackubin 1872- *WhAm 5*
Calvert, Robert 1889-1969 *WhAm 5*
Calvert, Thomas B *NewYHSD*
Calvert, Thomas Elwood 1849-1916 *WhAm 1*
Calvert, William Jephtha 1871- *WhAm 5*
Calverton, Victor Francis 1900-1940 *DcAmB S2, WhAm 1*
Calvery, Herbert Orion 1897-1945 *WhAm 2*
Calvin, Clementine *WomWWA 14*
Calvin, Delano Chipman 1824- *NatCAB 5, TwCBDA*
Calvin, Edgar Eugene 1858-1938 *WhAm 1*
Calvin, Henrietta Willard 1865-1947 *NatCAB 41, WhAm 5, WomWWA 14*
Calvin, John 1509-1564 *McGEWB*
Calvin, Melvin 1911- *AsBiEn, McGEWB, WebAB*
Calvin, Samuel 1811-1890 *BiAUS, BiDrAC, NatCAB 12, WhAm H*
Calvin, Samuel 1840-1911 *ApCAB, DcAmB, NatCAB 13, TwCBDA, WhAm 1*
Calvin, William Austin 1898-1962 *WhAm 4*
Calvo, Carlos 1824- *ApCAB*
Calvo, Joaquin Bernardo 1857-1915 *WhAm 1*
Calvo, Joaquin Bernardo 1858-1915 *ApCAB Sup*
Calvo DeLaPuerta, Sebastian De d1820 *ApCAB*
Calwell, Charles Sheridan 1871-1932 *WhAm 1*
Calyo, Hannibal W 1835?- *NewYHSD*
Calyo, John A 1818?-1893 *NewYHSD*
Calyo, Nicolino 1799-1884 *IlBEAAW, NewYHSD, WhAm H*
Cam, Helen Maud 1885-1968 *WhAm 4A*
Camac, Charles Nicoll Bancker 1868-1940 *NatCAB 32, WhAm 1*
Camacho, Manual Avila 1897-1955 *WhAm 3*
Camacho Roldan, Salvador 1827- *ApCAB*
Camak, David English 1880- *WhAm 6*
Camarco, Michael Leonardo 1874-1949 *NatCAB 38*
Camargo, Sergio 1833- *ApCAB*
Cambell *NewYHSD*
Cambell, Alexander 1779-1857 *BiAUS*
Cambell, Alexander see also Campbell, Alexander
Cambell, Brookins 1808-1853 *BiAUS*
Cambell, Brookins see also Campbell, Brookins
Cambell, George 1838?- *NewYHSD*
Cambon, Jules Martin 1845- *ApCAB Sup*
Cambreleng, Churchill C 1786-1862 *ApCAB, BiAUS*
Cambreleng, Churchill Caldain 1786-1862 *NatCAB 10*
Cambreleng, Churchill Caldom 1786-1862 *AmBi, BiDrAC, DcAmB, TwCBDA, WhAm H, WhAmP*
Cambreling, Churchill C 1786-1862 *Drake*
Cambridge, Charles Carroll 1868- *ApCAB X*
Cambridge, George William F C, Duke Of 1819-1904 *WhoMilH*
Cambronne, Pierre Jacques Etienne 1770-1842 *WhoMilH*
Camden, Harry Poole 1900-1943 *WhAm 2*
Camden, Johnson Newlon 1828-1908 *BiDrAC, DcAmB, NatCAB 6, NatCAB 20, REnAW, WhAm 1*
Camden, Johnson Newlon, Jr. 1865-1942 *BiDrAC, NatCAB 32, WhAm 2*

Camden, Johnson Newton 1828-1908 *TwCBDA*
Camden, Sprigg Despard 1874-1943 *NatCAB 33*
Camerarius, Rudolf Jakob 1665-1721 *DcScB*
Camerarius, Rudolph Jakob 1665-1721 *DcScB Sup*
Camerer, Eugene 1823-1898 *IlBEAAW, NewYHSD*
Camerer, Rudolph Jakob 1665-1721 *DcScB Sup*
Cameron, A Guyot 1864-1947 *WhAm 2*
Cameron, Adam Kirk 1874- *WhAm 5*
Cameron, Agnes Deans 1863- *WomWWA 14*
Cameron, Sir Alan d1828 *ApCAB, Drake*
Cameron, Albert Barnes 1925-1967 *WhAm 5*
Cameron, Alexander 1830-1890 *WhAm H*
Cameron, Alexander 1834- *NatCAB 7*
Cameron, Andrew Carr 1834-1890 *AmBi*
Cameron, Andrew Carr 1836-1892 *DcAmB, WhAm H*
Cameron, Angus 1824-1897 *NatCAB 12*
Cameron, Angus 1826-1897 *ApCAB, BiAUS, BiDrAC, TwCBDA, WhAm H*
Cameron, Archibald 1771?-1836 *ApCAB Sup, DcAmB, WhAm H*
Cameron, Augustus Garfield 1880- *WhAm 6*
Cameron, Beatrice *WomWWA 14*
Cameron, Benjamin Franklin 1890-1964 *WhAm 4*
Cameron, Bettie Garner *WomWWA 14*
Cameron, Charles Conrad 1869-1951 *WhAm 3*
Cameron, Charles Raymond 1875- *WhAm 5*
Cameron, Cora May Kent *WomWWA 14*
Cameron, D Ewen 1901-1967 *WhAm 5*
Cameron, Donald Forrester 1901-1974 *WhAm 6*
Cameron, Donald Palmer 1878-1951 *NatCAB 41*
Cameron, Duncan d1853 *BiAUS*
Cameron, Edgar Spier 1862-1944 *WhAm 2*
Cameron, Edith Virginia Buzzell *WomWWA 14*
Cameron, Edward Herbert 1875-1938 *WhAm 1*
Cameron, Edwin J 1895-1955 *WhAm 3*
Cameron, Elizabeth 1851- *AmWom, WomWWA 14*
Cameron, Emma *NewYHSD*
Cameron, Francis 1902-1975 *WhAm 6*
Cameron, Frank Kenneth 1869-1958 *WhAm 3*
Cameron, Frederick W 1859-1918 *NatCAB 19*
Cameron, George Hamilton 1861-1944 *WebAMB, WhAm 2*
Cameron, George Toland 1873-1955 *NatCAB 44, WhAm 3*
Cameron, Gordon Wyatt 1895-1955 *WhAm 3*
Cameron, Harold William 1902-1970 *WhAm 5*
Cameron, Hector 1833- *ApCAB*
Cameron, Henry Alvin 1872- *WhoColR*
Cameron, Henry Clay 1827-1906 *ApCAB Sup, TwCBDA, WhAm 1*
Cameron, J Walter 1895-1976 *WhAm 6*
Cameron, James 1801-1861 *ApCAB, Drake, NatCAB 4, TwCBDA*
Cameron, James 1816?- *NewYHSD*
Cameron, James Donald 1833-1918 *AmBi, ApCAB, BiDrAC, BiDrUSE, DcAmB, NatCAB 1, NatCAB 4, NatCAB 27, TwCBDA, WhAm 1, WhAmP*
Cameron, John 1827- *ApCAB*
Cameron, John 1828?- *NewYHSD, WhAm H*
Cameron, John A *BiAUS*
Cameron, John Andrew 1902-1961 *WhAm 4*
Cameron, John B 1830?- *NewYHSD*
Cameron, John Hillyard 1817-1876 *ApCAB*
Cameron, John M 1867-1939 *WhAm 1*
Cameron, Mabel Ward 1863-1923 *BiCAW*
Cameron, Malcolm 1808-1876 *ApCAB*
Cameron, Margaret *WomWWA 14*
Cameron, Matthew Crooks 1822- *ApCAB*
Cameron, Norman W 1876-1947 *WhAm 2*
Cameron, Ossian 1868- *WhAm 4*
Cameron, Ralph Henry 1863-1953 *ApCAB X, BiDrAC, WhAm 3, WhAmP*
Cameron, Ralph Henry 1864-1953 *NatCAB 42*
Cameron, Robert Alexander 1828-1894 *ApCAB, DcAmB, NatCAB 4, TwCBDA, WhAm H*
Cameron, Robert Buchanan 1871-1955 *NatCAB 49*

Cameron, Sir Roderick William 1825-1900 *ApCAB, ApCAB Sup, NatCAB 8, TwCBDA, WhAm 1*
Cameron, Ronald Brooks 1927- *BiDrAC*
Cameron, Shelton Thomas 1857-1944 *NatCAB 46, WhAm 2*
Cameron, Simon 1799-1889 *AmBi, ApCAB, BiAUS, BiDrAC, BiDrUSE, DcAmB, Drake, EncAB, McGEWB, NatCAB 2, TwCBDA, WebAB, WhAm H, WhAmP*
Cameron, Susan Elizabeth *WomWWA 14*
Cameron, Thomas Brown 1916-1973 *WhAm 6*
Cameron, Turner Christian, Jr. 1914-1971 *WhAm 5*
Cameron, Wilbert Frederick 1903-1971 *NatCAB 57*
Cameron, William 1795-1877 *NatCAB 8*
Cameron, William Donald 1846- *WhAm 4*
Cameron, William Evelyn 1842-1927 *DcAmB, WhAm 1*
Cameron, William Ewan 1842-1927 *NatCAB 5*
Cameron, William J 1889-1963 *WhAm 4*
Cameron, William John 1878-1955 *WhAm 3*
Cameron, William McCallum 1874-1950 *NatCAB 39, WhAm 3*
Cames, Vina 1908?- *IlBEAAW*
Camfferman, Margaret Gove 1895?- *IlBEAAW*
Camfferman, Peter Marienus 1890-1957 *IlBEAAW*
Camillo, Michael Francis 1928-1971 *WhAm 5*
Caminatzin d1521 *ApCAB*
Caminetti, Anthony 1854-1923 *BiDrAC, REnAW, WhAm 1*
Caminha DeMeneses, Antonio Telles Da 1790-1875 *ApCAB*
Camm, John 1718-1778 *DcAmB, NatCAB 3, WhAm H*
Cammack, Edmund Ernest 1881-1958 *WhAm 3*
Cammack, Ira Insco 1858-1939 *WhAm 1*
Cammack, James William 1869-1939 *WhAm 1*
Cammack, James William 1902-1958 *WhAm 3*
Cammack, John Walter 1875- *WhAm 5*
Cammann, Henry Julius 1835-1920 *NatCAB 19*
Cammann, Henry Lorillard 1864-1930 *NatCAB 23*
Cammerhof, Frederick d1751 *Drake*
Cammerhof, John Christoph Frederic 1721-1751 *NatCAB 5*
Cammerhoff, John Christopher Frederick 1721-1751 *DcAmB, WhAm H*
Cammerhoff, John Frederick 1721-1751 *ApCAB, TwCBDA*
Cammeyer, Augustus F *NewYHSD*
Cammeyer, DeWitt C 1828?- *NewYHSD*
Cammeyer, William, Jr. *NewYHSD*
Cammeyer, William, Sr. *NewYHSD*
Camoens, Luis Vaz De 1524-1580 *McGEWB*
Camore 1815?- *NewYHSD*
Camp, Albert Sidney 1892-1954 *BiDrAC, NatCAB 46, WhAm 3, WhAmP*
Camp, Charles Lewis 1893-1975 *WhAm 6*
Camp, Charles Wadsworth 1879-1936 *WhAm 1*
Camp, Constance Graham 1878- *WomWWA 14*
Camp, David Nelson 1820-1916 *BiDAmEd, DcAmB, NatCAB 2, TwCBDA, WhAm 1*
Camp, E C 1839- *NatCAB 1*
Camp, Edgar Whittlesey 1860- *WhAm 4*
Camp, Frederic Edgar 1904-1963 *NatCAB 50, WhAm 4*
Camp, Harold Manlove 1885-1959 *NatCAB 48*
Camp, Hiram 1811-1893 *DcAmB, NatCAB 8, TwCBDA, WhAm H*
Camp, Hugh Douglas 1903-1974 *WhAm 6*
Camp, Irving Luzerne 1879-1934 *WhAm 1*
Camp, James Leonidas 1857-1925 *NatCAB 37*
Camp, John Henry 1822-1881 *NewYHSD*
Camp, John Henry 1840-1892 *BiDrAC, WhAm H*
Camp, John Lafayette 1828-1891 *DcAmB, WhAm H*
Camp, John Lafayette 1855-1918 *DcAmB*
Camp, John Newbold Happy 1908- *BiDrAC*
Camp, John Newton 1824-1893 *NatCAB 26*
Camp, John Spencer 1858-1946 *NatCAB 12, WhAm 2*
Camp, Lawrence Sabyllia 1898-1947 *WhAm 2*

Camp, Mortimer Hart 1874-1966 *NatCAB 52,*
WhAm 4
Camp, Paul Douglas 1849-1924 *NatCAB 37*
Camp, Samuel Higby 1871-1944 *NatCAB 36*
Camp, Thomas James 1886-1974 *WhAm 6*
Camp, Thomas Ringgold 1895-1971 *WhAm 5*
Camp, Wallace Henry 1850-1924 *NatCAB 27*
Camp, Walter Chauncey 1859-1925 *AmBi,*
DcAmB, NatCAB 21, WebAB, WhAm 1
Camp, Walter John Richard 1897-1964
WhAm 4
Camp, Walter Mason 1867- *NatCAB 16*
Camp, Wendell H 1904-1963 *WhAm 4*
Camp, William Augustus 1822-1895 *NatCAB 9,*
TwCBDA
Camp, William Bacon 1913-1975 *WhAm 6*
Camp, William McCutcheon 1900-1966
WhAm 4
Campa, Arthur Leon 1905- *BiDAmEd*
Campa Y Caraveda, Miguel Angel 1882-1965
WhAm 4
Campagna, Anthony 1884-1969 *NatCAB 54*
Campanari, Giuseppe 1858-1927 *WhAm 1*
Campanella, Tommaso 1568-1639 *DcScB,*
DcScB Sup, McGEWB
Campani, Giuseppe 1635-1715 *DcScB*
Campanini, Cleofonte 1860-1919 *WhAm 1*
Campanius, Johan 1601-1683 *DcAmReB*
Campanius, John 1601-1683 *DcAmB, WebAB,*
WhAm H
Campanus Of Novara d1296 *DcScB,*
DcScB Sup
Camparet *IIBEAAW*
Campau, Daniel Joseph 1852-1927 *NatCAB 21,*
WhAm 1
Campau, Francis Denis 1880-1958 *WhAm 3*
Campau, Joseph 1769-1863 *DcAmB, WhAm H*
Campbell *NewYHSD*
Campbell, A G *NewYHSD*
Campbell, Albert H 1826-1899 *IIBEAAW,*
NewYHSD
Campbell, Albert H 1836-1899 *WhAm H*
Campbell, Albert James 1857-1907 *BiDrAC,*
NatCAB 11, WhAm 1
Campbell, Alexander *NewYHSD*
Campbell, Alexander 1707?-1790? *ApCAB*
Campbell, Alexander 1779-1857 *BiDrAC,*
NatCAB 4, TwCBDA, WhAm H,
WhAmP
Campbell, Alexander 1786-1866 *ApCAB,*
Drake, NatCAB 4, WhAm H
Campbell, Alexander 1788-1866 *AmBi, DcAmB,*
DcAmReB, McGEWB, REnAW,
TwCBDA, WebAB
Campbell, Alexander 1814-1898 *BiAUS,*
BiDrAC, WhAmP
Campbell, Sir Alexander 1822- *ApCAB*
Campbell, Alexander *see also* Cambell, Alexander
Campbell, Alexander Augustus 1789-1846
ApCAB, TwCBDA
Campbell, Alexander Bass 1888-1964
NatCAB 52
Campbell, Alexander Boyd 1889-1963 *WhAm 4*
Campbell, Alexander Morton 1907-1968
NatCAB 54, WhAm 5
Campbell, Alexander William 1828-1893
ApCAB Sup, BiDConf, TwCBDA
Campbell, Alfred Hills 1850- *WhAm 1*
Campbell, Allan 1815-1894 *DcAmB,*
NatCAB 9, WhAm H
Campbell, Allan B 1884-1962 *WhAm 4*
Campbell, Allen 1815-1894 *TwCBDA*
Campbell, Amasa B 1845-1912 *ApCAB X*
Campbell, Andrew 1821-1890 *ApCAB, DcAmB,*
NatCAB 9, TwCBDA, WhAm H
Campbell, Andrew Chambre 1856-1926
NatCAB 25
Campbell, Angus Kephart 1834-1926
NatCAB 44
Campbell, Annabel Thompson 1856-
WomWWA 14
Campbell, Sir Archibald 1739-1791 *ApCAB,*
Drake
Campbell, Archibald 1813-1887 *ApCAB Sup*
Campbell, Archibald Brush 1891-1965 *WhAm 4*
Campbell, Archibald Duncan 1919-1975
WhAm 6
Campbell, Archibald Murray 1843- *WhAm 4*

Campbell, Argyle 1874-1944 *NatCAB 37*
Campbell, Arthur 1742-1815 *Drake*
Campbell, Arthur Griffith 1884-1957 *WhAm 3*
Campbell, Bartley 1843-1888 *ApCAB, DcAmB,*
NatCAB 9, TwCBDA, WhAm H
Campbell, Ben Jonathan 1871-1934 *NatCAB 24*
Campbell, Benjamin 1858- *WhAm 4*
Campbell, Brookins 1808-1853 *BiDrAC,*
WhAm H
Campbell, Brookins *see also* Cambell, Brookins
Campbell, Bruce Alexander 1879-1955 *WhAm 3*
Campbell, Bruce Jones 1912-1968 *WhAm 5*
Campbell, Caroline Portman 1857-
WomWWA 14
Campbell, Catherine Mary 1887-
WomWWA 14
Campbell, Chandler 1880-1956 *WhAm 3*
Campbell, Charles 1807-1876 *ApCAB, DcAmB,*
Drake, NatCAB 19, TwCBDA, WhAm H
Campbell, Charles 1846-1913 *NatCAB 16*
Campbell, Charles Atwood 1872-1939 *WhAm 1*
Campbell, Charles Diven 1877-1919 *WhAm 1*
Campbell, Charles E 1885-1966 *WhAm 4*
Campbell, Charles King 1911-1972 *WhAm 5*
Campbell, Charles L 1877-1956 *WhAm 3*
Campbell, Charles Macfie 1876-1943
DcAmB S3, NatCAB 40, WhAm 2
Campbell, Charles Sherman 1863-1953
WhAm 3
Campbell, Charles Soutter 1887-1954
NatCAB 44, WhAm 3
Campbell, Charles Thomas 1823- *ApCAB,*
TwCBDA
Campbell, Chesser M 1897-1960 *WhAm 4*
Campbell, Chester I 1869- *WhAm 1*
Campbell, Clara Green *WomWWA 14*
Campbell, Clarence Gordon 1868-1956
NatCAB 45
Campbell, Cleveland J 1836-1865 *ApCAB,*
TwCBDA
Campbell, Clyde Henderson 1883-1946
NatCAB 42
Campbell, Colin 1792-1863 *WhoMilH*
Campbell, Courtney Warren 1895- *BiDrAC*
Campbell, D Scott d1965 *WhAm 4*
Campbell, Daisy Rhodes 1854- *WhAm 4*
Campbell, Dan Hampton 1907-1974 *WhAm 6*
Campbell, Daniel A 1863- *ApCAB X,*
NewYHSD, WhAm 4
Campbell, David *BiAUS*
Campbell, David 1779-1859 *BiAUS, Drake,*
NatCAB 5
Campbell, David A 1857- *TwCBDA*
Campbell, David Robert 1907-1963 *NatCAB 51*
Campbell, Delwin Morton 1880-1952
NatCAB 42, WhAm 3
Campbell, Doak Sheridan 1888-1973
NatCAB 57, WhAm 5
Campbell, Donald *NewYHSD*
Campbell, Donald 1735-1763 *ApCAB*
Campbell, Donald Francis 1867-1953
NatCAB 42, WhAm 5
Campbell, Donald J d1943 *WhAm 2*
Campbell, Donald Malcolm 1864-1942 *WhAm 2*
Campbell, Dorothy Iona *WomWWA 14*
Campbell, Douglas 1839-1893 *TwCBDA*
Campbell, Douglas 1873-1950 *NatCAB 41*
Campbell, Douglas Houghton 1859-1953
BiDAmEd, DcAmB S5, DcScB, WhAm 3
Campbell, Duncan Alexander 1876-1961
NatCAB 48
Campbell, Duncan R 1797?-1865 *Drake*
Campbell, Duncan R 1814-1865 *ApCAB,*
TwCBDA
Campbell, Dwight 1887-1964 *WhAm 4*
Campbell, E Ray 1895-1971 *WhAm 5*
Campbell, Ed Hoyt 1882-1969 *BiDrAC*
Campbell, Edmond Ernest 1859-1926 *WhAm 1*
Campbell, Edmund Schureman 1884-1950
WhAm 3
Campbell, Edward DeMille 1863-1925
NatCAB 28, WhAm 1
Campbell, Edward Everett 1883-1941
NatCAB 44
Campbell, Edward Hale 1872-1946 *NatCAB 36,*
WhAm 5
Campbell, Edward Hastings 1894-1963
NatCAB 50, WhAm 4

Campbell, Edward Kernan 1858-1938
NatCAB 29, WhAm 1
Campbell, Edward R 1820?- *NewYHSD*
Campbell, Edward Stelle 1854-1905 *NatCAB 18*
Campbell, Edward Williams 1900-1972
NatCAB 57
Campbell, Eldridge 1901-1956 *NatCAB 47,*
WhAm 3
Campbell, Eleanor Goodrich 1876-
WomWWA 14
Campbell, Eleanor Milbank Anderson 1878-1959
NatCAB 49
Campbell, Elizabeth 1862- *WhAm 4,*
WomWWA 14
Campbell, Elmer Bernard 1892-1960
NatCAB 50
Campbell, Elmer Grant 1876- *WhAm 5*
Campbell, Eugenia Steele 1843- *AmWom*
Campbell, Evelyn 1868- *AmWom*
Campbell, Felix 1829-1902 *BiDrAC, WhAm 1*
Campbell, Floyd D 1892-1962 *WhAm 4*
Campbell, Francis Joseph 1832-1914 *DcAmB,*
NatCAB 11
Campbell, Frank 1858-1924 *NatCAB 42,*
WhAm 4
Campbell, Frank L 1843- *WhAm 4*
Campbell, Gabriel 1838-1923 *WhAm 3*
Campbell, George 1848- *WhAm 4*
Campbell, George Alexander 1869-1943
WhAm 2
Campbell, George Ashley 1870-1954
NatCAB 45, WhAm 3
Campbell, George Hollister 1856-1930 *WhAm 1*
Campbell, George Washington 1768-1848
ApCAB, BiAUS, BiDrUSE, Drake,
NatCAB 5, TwCBDA
Campbell, George Washington 1769-1848 *AmBi,*
BiDrAC, DcAmB, WhAm H, WhAmP
Campbell, George Washington 1817-1898
DcAmB, WhAm H
Campbell, Georgine *AmWom*
Campbell, Sir Gerald 1879-1964 *WhAm 4*
Campbell, Gilbert Whitney 1883-1938 *WhAm 1,*
WhAm 1C
Campbell, Gordon Hensley 1880- *WhAm 6*
Campbell, Gordon Peter 1898-1964 *WhAm 4*
Campbell, Guy Edgar 1871-1940 *BiDrAC,*
WhAmP
Campbell, H Donald 1879-1969 *WhAm 5*
Campbell, Hamilton 1813?- *NewYHSD*
Campbell, Hardy Webster 1850- *NatCAB 16,*
WhAm 4
Campbell, Harold Denny 1895-1955
NatCAB 46, WhAm 3
Campbell, Harold George 1884-1942 *WhAm 2*
Campbell, Harriet Parker 1857- *WomWWA 14*
Campbell, Harry Huse 1859- *WhAm 1*
Campbell, Helen Stuart 1839-1918 *AmWom,*
ApCAB, NatCAB 9, NotAW, TwCBDA,
WhAm 4, WomWWA 14
Campbell, Henrietta Foster Crosman 1866-
WomWWA 14
Campbell, Henry Colin 1862-1923 *NatCAB 19,*
WhAm 1
Campbell, Henry Donald 1862-1923 *WhAm 1*
Campbell, Henry Fraser 1824-1891 *DcAmB,*
NatCAB 12, WhAm H
Campbell, Henry Munroe 1783-1842 *BiAUS*
Campbell, Henry Munroe 1854-1925
NatCAB 15
Campbell, Henry Munroe 1854-1926 *WhAm 1*
Campbell, Henry Wood 1866-1931 *WhAm 1*
Campbell, Herbert Grant 1868-1934 *WhAm 1*
Campbell, Herbert Johnston 1882-1941
NatCAB 31
Campbell, Howard Edmond 1890- *BiDrAC*
Campbell, Howell Hooper 1883-1961
NatCAB 50
Campbell, Hugh F 1760-1820 *Drake*
Campbell, Hugh George 1760-1820 *ApCAB,*
NatCAB 4
Campbell, Hugh Jones 1831-1898 *ApCAB Sup*
Campbell, Ira Alexander 1878-1963 *WhAm 4*
Campbell, J *NewYHSD*
Campbell, J Alan *NewYHSD*
Campbell, J K *NewYHSD*
Campbell, Jabez Pitt 1815-1891 *ApCAB,*
TwCBDA

Campbell, Jacob 1760-1788 *Drake*
Campbell, Jacob Miller 1821-1888 *BiDrAC, WhAm H*
Campbell, James *NatCAB 12*
Campbell, James 1812-1893 *BiDrUSE, DcAmB, NatCAB 4, TwCBDA, WhAm H*
Campbell, James 1813- *ApCAB, BiAUS, Drake*
Campbell, James 1826-1900 *NatCAB 40*
Campbell, James A 1854-1933 *WhAm 1*
Campbell, James Alexander 1847-1933 *NatCAB 7, WhAm 2*
Campbell, James Archibald 1811- *Drake*
Campbell, James Archibald 1862-1934 *WhAm 1*
Campbell, James Baxter 1808-1883 *ApCAB Sup*
Campbell, James C 1877-1961 *WhAm 4*
Campbell, James Cochran, Jr. 1894-1953 *NatCAB 43*
Campbell, James Daniels 1839-1925 *WhAm 1*
Campbell, James Edwin 1843-1924 *BiDrAC, NatCAB 1, WhAm 1*
Campbell, James Henry 1850-1923 *NatCAB 40*
Campbell, James Hepburn 1820-1895 *BiAUS, BiDrAC, DcAmB, NatCAB 4, TwCBDA, WhAm H*
Campbell, James Hobart 1910-1972 *WhAm 5*
Campbell, James Holmes 1914-1963 *NatCAB 51*
Campbell, James LeRoy 1870-1948 *WhAm 2*
Campbell, James Mann 1840-1926 *WhAm 2*
Campbell, James Phil 1878-1944 *WhAm 2*
Campbell, James Rickarby 1859-1934 *NatCAB 25*
Campbell, James Romulus 1853-1924 *BiDrAC, WhAm 1*
Campbell, James U 1866-1937 *WhAm 1*
Campbell, James Valentine 1823-1890 *ApCAB, BiAUS, DcAmB, NatCAB 9, TwCBDA, WhAm H*
Campbell, James Watson 1872- *WhAm 5*
Campbell, Jane *WomWWA 14*
Campbell, Jeremiah Rockwell 1827- *NatCAB 5*
Campbell, Jesse H 1807-1888 *ApCAB, TwCBDA*
Campbell, John *BiAUS, NewYHSD*
Campbell, John d1806 *ApCAB, Drake*
Campbell, John d1845 *BiAUS, BiDrAC, WhAm H*
Campbell, John 1653-1727? *DcAmB, WhAm H*
Campbell, John 1653-1728 *AmBi, ApCAB, Drake, NatCAB 7, TwCBDA*
Campbell, John 1705-1782 *DcAmB, WhAm H*
Campbell, John 1708-1775 *ApCAB, Drake*
Campbell, John 1765-1828 *BiAUS, BiDrAC, WhAm H*
Campbell, John 1821-1905 *TwCBDA, WhAm 1*
Campbell, John 1822?- *ApCAB*
Campbell, John 1839- *ApCAB*
Campbell, John 1848- *NatCAB 7*
Campbell, John 1853-1938 *NatCAB 12, WhAm 1*
Campbell, John A 1856-1938 *WhAm 1*
Campbell, John A, Jr. 1903-1974 *WhAm 6*
Campbell, John Allen 1835-1880 *ApCAB, BiAUS, TwCBDA, WhAm H*
Campbell, John Archibald 1811-1889 *AmBi, ApCAB, BiAUS, BiDConf, DcAmB, NatCAB 2, TwCBDA, WebAB, WhAm H*
Campbell, John B d1814 *ApCAB, Drake, TwCBDA*
Campbell, John Bayard Taylor 1880-1956 *NatCAB 45, WhAm 3*
Campbell, John Bradford 1856- *WhAm 4*
Campbell, John Bulow 1870-1940 *NatCAB 30, WhAm 1*
Campbell, John Charles 1867-1919 *WhAm 1*
Campbell, John Goulder 1827-1903 *BiDrAC*
Campbell, John Henry 1868-1928 *NatCAB 33, WhAm 1*
Campbell, John Hull 1800-1868 *BiAUS, BiDrAC, WhAm H*
Campbell, John Jock 1894-1942 *WhWW-II*
Campbell, John Logan 1863- *WhAm 4*
Campbell, John Lorne 1845- *NatCAB 11*
Campbell, John Lorne 1849- *WhAm 4*

Campbell, John Lyle 1818-1886 *ApCAB, TwCBDA*
Campbell, John Lyle 1827-1904 *WhAm 1*
Campbell, John Marie 1851- *NatCAB 16*
Campbell, John Neal 1893-1962 *WhAm 4*
Campbell, John Nicholson 1798-1864 *ApCAB, Drake, TwCBDA*
Campbell, John Otho 1899-1966 *NatCAB 54*
Campbell, John Pendleton 1863- *WhAm 4*
Campbell, John Pierce, Jr. 1820-1888 *BiAUS, BiDrAC, WhAm H*
Campbell, John Poage 1767-1814 *ApCAB, Drake, TwCBDA*
Campbell, John Preston 1849- *WhAm 4*
Campbell, John TenBrook 1833- *NatCAB 12, WhAm 1*
Campbell, John Thomas 1876- *WhAm 5*
Campbell, John W 1886- *WhAm 3*
Campbell, John Wilson 1782-1833 *ApCAB, BiAUS, BiDrAC, DcAmB, Drake, TwCBDA, WhAm H*
Campbell, Johnston B 1868-1953 *WhAm 3*
Campbell, Joseph Calvin 1852-1944 *NatCAB 35*
Campbell, Josiah Abigail Patterson 1830-1917 *BiDConf, DcAmB, NatCAB 7, WhAm 1*
Campbell, Kathleen Roseanne 1903-1975 *WhAm 6*
Campbell, Killis 1872-1937 *WhAm 1*
Campbell, L J 1906-1968 *WhAm 5*
Campbell, Leon 1881-1951 *WhAm 3*
Campbell, Leona Pelton 1879- *WomWWA 14*
Campbell, Leonard Lord 1881-1948 *NatCAB 35*
Campbell, LeRoy Brotzman 1873-1958 *WhAm 3*
Campbell, Leroy Walter d1967 *WhAm 5*
Campbell, Leslie Hartwell 1892-1970 *NatCAB 56*
Campbell, Lewis Davis 1811-1882 *ApCAB, BiAUS, BiDrAC, DcAmB, Drake, NatCAB 13, TwCBDA, WhAm H, WhAmP*
Campbell, Lily Bess 1883-1967 *WhAm 4*
Campbell, Louis Graham 1869-1952 *NatCAB 42*
Campbell, Lucien Quitman 1893-1945 *WhAm 2*
Campbell, Luther A 1872-1947 *WhAm 2*
Campbell, Macy 1879-1927 *WhAm 1*
Campbell, Marcus B d1944 *WhAm 2*
Campbell, Marguerite 1892-1965 *WhAm 4*
Campbell, Marius Robinson 1858-1940 *DcAmB S2, NatCAB 33*
Campbell, Marius Robison 1858-1940 *WhAm 1*
Campbell, Mary Edith 1875- *WhAm 6, WomWWA 14*
Campbell, Mary Isabella McPherson 1855- *WomWWA 14*
Campbell, Mattie Ormsby 1861- *WomWWA 14*
Campbell, Morton Carlisle 1876-1952 *NatCAB 39*
Campbell, Norman Robert 1880-1949 *DcScB*
Campbell, Orland 1890-1972 *NatCAB 57*
Campbell, Orson D 1876-1933 *IIBEAAW, NewYHSD*
Campbell, Oscar James, Jr. 1879-1970 *NatCAB 55, WhAm 5*
Campbell, Patrick *Drake, NewYHSD*
Campbell, Mrs. Patrick 1865-1940 *WhAm 1*
Campbell, Patrick Thomas 1871-1937 *WhAm 1*
Campbell, Persia 1898-1974 *WhAm 6*
Campbell, Peter 1855-1928 *ApCAB X, NatCAB 24*
Campbell, Peter Joseph 1859-1919 *NatCAB 25*
Campbell, Philip Pitt 1862-1941 *BiDrAC, WhAm 1, WhAmP*
Campbell, Price 1890-1964 *WhAm 4*
Campbell, Prince Lucian 1861-1925 *WhAm 1*
Campbell, Prince Lucien 1861-1925 *BiDAmEd, DcAmB, NatCAB 21*
Campbell, Pryse *NewYHSD*
Campbell, Ralph Emerson 1867-1921 *WhAm 1*
Campbell, Ralph Emerson 1897-1970 *NatCAB 55*
Campbell, Richard d1781 *ApCAB, Drake, TwCBDA*
Campbell, Richard 1872-1935 *WhAm 1*
Campbell, Richard Kenna 1853-1931 *WhAm 1*
Campbell, Richard Orme 1860-1912 *NatCAB 15*

Campbell, Robert *NewYHSD*
Campbell, Robert 1755-1831 *TwCBDA*
Campbell, Robert 1755-1832 *ApCAB, Drake*
Campbell, Robert 1804-1879 *DcAmB, REnAW, WhAm H*
Campbell, Robert Blair d1862 *BiAUS, BiDrAC, WhAm H*
Campbell, Robert Donald 1867- *WhAm 4*
Campbell, Robert Fishburne 1858-1947 *WhAm 2*
Campbell, Robert Granville 1879-1932 *WhAm 1*
Campbell, Robert L *NewYHSD*
Campbell, Robert Morrell 1899-1975 *WhAm 6*
Campbell, Robert Willis 1874-1947 *WhAm 2*
Campbell, Ronald Neil 1906-1965 *WhAm 4*
Campbell, Ross Turner 1863-1940 *WhAm 2*
Campbell, Rowland 1894-1943 *WhAm 2*
Campbell, Roy Davies 1872- *WhAm 5*
Campbell, Roy Hilton 1879- *WhAm 6*
Campbell, Sam 1895-1962 *WhAm 4*
Campbell, Samuel 1773-1853 *BiAUS, BiDrAC, WhAm H*
Campbell, Samuel L *NatCAB 3*
Campbell, Sidney S 1804-1887 *NatCAB 12*
Campbell, Stella Bogue *WomWWA 14*
Campbell, Sullivan Graham 1922-1972 *NatCAB 57*
Campbell, Theodorick Pryor 1861-1928 *WhAm 1*
Campbell, Thomas *NewYHSD*
Campbell, Thomas 1763-1854 *AmBi, ApCAB, DcAmB, DcAmReB, REnAW, WebAB, WhAm H*
Campbell, Thomas 1790-1858 *NewYHSD*
Campbell, Thomas A 1897-1972 *WhAm 5*
Campbell, Thomas Donald 1881-1966 *NatCAB 54*
Campbell, Thomas Donald 1882-1966 *WhAm 4*
Campbell, Thomas E 1833?- *NewYHSD*
Campbell, Thomas Edward 1878-1944 *WhAm 2*
Campbell, Thomas F *BiAUS*
Campbell, Thomas Huffman 1863-1944 *WhAm 2*
Campbell, Thomas Jefferson 1786-1850 *BiAUS, BiDrAC, WhAm H*
Campbell, Thomas Joseph 1848-1925 *DcAmB, NatCAB 2, TwCBDA, WhAm 1*
Campbell, Thomas Mitchell 1856-1923 *NatCAB 14, WhAm 1*
Campbell, Thomas W 1851-1918 *WhAm 1*
Campbell, Thompson 1811-1868 *ApCAB, BiAUS, BiDrAC, TwCBDA, WhAm H*
Campbell, Timothy John 1840-1904 *BiDrAC, TwCBDA, WhAmP*
Campbell, Viola Vaille Barnes *WomWWA 14*
Campbell, Wallace 1878-1950 *WhAm 3*
Campbell, Wallace Edwin 1896-1968 *WhAm 5*
Campbell, Walter Gilbert 1877- *WhAm 5*
Campbell, Walter Jenkins 1876-1939 *NatCAB 30*
Campbell, Walter Stanley 1887-1957 *REnAW, WhAm 3*
Campbell, Warren Malcolm 1911-1963 *NatCAB 51*
Campbell, Wayne 1872- *WhAm 5*
Campbell, Lord William d1778 *ApCAB, DcAmB, Drake, NatCAB 12, WhAm H*
Campbell, William 1745-1781 *AmBi, ApCAB, DcAmB, Drake, NatCAB 1, TwCBDA, WebAMB, WhAm H*
Campbell, Sir William 1758-1834 *ApCAB*
Campbell, William 1826?- *NewYHSD*
Campbell, William 1833?- *NewYHSD*
Campbell, William 1876-1936 *ApCAB X, DcAmB S2, WhAm 1*
Campbell, William Alexander 1881-1938 *WhAm 1*
Campbell, William B *NewYHSD*
Campbell, William Bedford 1881-1957 *NatCAB 46*
Campbell, William Bowen 1807-1867 *ApCAB, BiAUS, BiDrAC, DcAmB, Drake, NatCAB 7, TwCBDA, WhAm H, WhAmP*
Campbell, William Bucke 1888-1948 *NatCAB 36*
Campbell, William Carey 1854- *WhAm 4*

Campbell, William Edward March 1893-1954 DcAmB S5
Campbell, William Francis 1867-1926 WhAm 1
Campbell, William Harrison 1846-1906 NatCAB 15
Campbell, William Henry 1808-1890 ApCAB, DcAmB, NatCAB 3, TwCBDA, WhAm H
Campbell, William James 1877-1949 WhAm 2
Campbell, William Lyman 1892-1966 NatCAB 52, WhAm 4
Campbell, William Neal 1893-1947 NatCAB 37, WhAm 2
Campbell, William Purnell 1869- WhAm 5
Campbell, William Rogers 1855-1935 WhAm 1
Campbell, William Shaw 1818- NatCAB 9
Campbell, William Taggart 1836-1912 WhAm 1
Campbell, William W 1806-1881 AmBi, ApCAB, BiAUS, BiDrAC, DcAmB, Drake, NatCAB 11, TwCBDA, WhAm H, WhAmP
Campbell, William Wallace 1862-1938 DcAmB S2, DcScB, NatCAB 11, WebAB, WhAm 1
Campbell, William Wildman 1853-1927 BiDrAC, WhAm 4
Campbell, William Wilson 1889-1970 WhAm 5
Campbell, Willis Cohoon 1880-1941 NatCAB 31, WhAm 1
Campbell, Worthington 1890-1964 NatCAB 52, WhAm 4
Campeche, Jose 1752-1809 ApCAB
Campello, Count Solone Di 1871- WhAm 5
Camper, Peter 1722-1789 BiHiMed, DcScB
Camphausen, Edward 1823-1903 NatCAB 27
Camphor, Alexander Priestly 1865-1919 WhAm 1, WhoColR
Camphor, Mamie Anna Rebecca 1869- WhoColR
Campin, Robert 1375?-1444 McGEWB
Campion, James Walsh, Jr. 1905-1968 NatCAB 54
Campion, John Francis 1846-1916 NatCAB 21
Campion, Marguerite 1884- WomWWA 14
Campney, Ralph Osborne 1894-1967 WhAm 4A
Campos, Maria E 1891-1951 WhAm 3
Campos Salles, Manuel Ferras De 1841- ApCAB Sup
Camprubi, Jose Aymar 1879-1942 NatCAB 39
Campuzano, Baltasar d1666 ApCAB
Camrose, Viscount Of Hackwood Park 1879-1954 WhAm 3
Camsell, Charles 1876-1958 WhAm 3
Camus, Albert 1913-1960 McGEWB, WhAm 3
Camus, Charles-Etienne-Louis 1699-1768 DcScB
Canada, John Walter 1876-1944 NatCAB 35, WhAm 2
Canada, John William 1871-1958 WhAm 3, WhAm 5
Canada, Robert Owen, Jr. 1913-1972 WhAm 5
Canada, William Wesley 1871-1921 WhAm 1
Canaday, Paul O'Neal 1904-1962 WhAm 4
Canaga, Alfred Bruce 1850-1906 DcAmB, NatCAB 22
Canales, Servando 1830-1883 ApCAB
Canaletto 1697-1768 McGEWB
Canan, Denis Timothy 1884-1950 NatCAB 39
Canano, Giovan Battista 1515-1579 DcScB
Canaris, Wilhelm 1888-1945 WhWW-II, WhoMilH
Canarutto, Angelo 1909-1944 WhAm 2
Canary, Martha Jane 1852?-1903 REnAW, WebAB, WhAm H, WhAm 4
Canavan, Myrtelle May Moore 1879- WomWWA 14
Canby, Caleb Harlan 1856-1923 NatCAB 21
Canby, Edward Richard Sprigg 1817-1873 AmBi, DcAmB, NatCAB 5, TwCBDA, WebAMB, WhAm H
Canby, Edward Richard Sprigg 1819?-1873 ApCAB, Drake
Canby, Henry Seidel 1878-1961 ApCAB X, NatCAB 48, WhAm 4
Canby, Marion Gause 1885- WomWWA 14
Canby, Richard Sprigg 1808-1895 BiAUS, BiDrAC, WhAm H

Canby, Samuel 1837-1897 NatCAB 33
Canby, William Marriott 1831-1904 WhAm 1
Cancchaee ApCAB Sup
Cancer, Luis d1549 ApCAB
Cancrin, Franz Ludwig Von 1738-1812? DcScB
Canda, Ida Hammond Holmes 1867- WomWWA 14
Candage, Rufus George Frederick 1826- TwCBDA
Candee, Annie Chunn WomWWA 14
Candee, Charles Lucius 1874- WhAm 5
Candee, George Edward 1838- NewYHSD
Candee, Hamilton 1885-1930 NatCAB 29
Candee, Helen Churchill d1949 WhAm 2
Candee, Helen Churchill 1863- WomWWA 14
Candee, Helen Churchill 1868- BiCAW
Candee, Leverett 1795-1863 DcAmB, WhAm H
Candee, Lyman 1865-1943 WhAm 2
Candee, Marion Otis WomWWA 14
Candia, Pedro De d1542 ApCAB
Candidus, William 1840- ApCAB, TwCBDA
Candler, Allen Daniel 1834-1910 ApCAB Sup, BiDrAC, DcAmB, NatCAB 2, TwCBDA, WhAm 1, WhAmP
Candler, Asa Griggs 1851-1929 DcAmB, NatCAB 7, NatCAB 31, WebAB, WhAm 1
Candler, Asa Griggs, Jr. 1880-1953 NatCAB 47
Candler, Asa Warren 1885-1929 NatCAB 21
Candler, Charles Howard 1878-1957 NatCAB 46, WhAm 3
Candler, Charles Murphey 1858-1935 WhAm 1
Candler, Ezekiel Samuel, Jr. 1862-1944 BiDrAC, NatCAB 44, WhAm 1, WhAmP
Candler, Flamen Ball 1838-1914 NatCAB 16
Candler, Henry E 1870- WhAm 5
Candler, John Slaughter 1861-1941 NatCAB 49, WhAm 2
Candler, John Wilson 1828-1903 BiDrAC
Candler, Milton Anthony 1837-1909 BiAUS, BiDrAC
Candler, Samuel Charles 1895-1973 WhAm 5
Candler, Thomas Slaughter 1890-1971 WhAm 5
Candler, Warren Akin 1857-1941 ApCAB Sup, DcAmB S3, NatCAB 1, NatCAB 34, TwCBDA, WhAm 1
Candler, William 1890-1936 WhAm 1
Candolle, Alphonse De 1806-1893 DcScB
Candolle, Augustin Pyrame 1778-1841 AsBiEn
Candolle, Augustin-Pyramus De 1778-1841 DcScB
Candy, Albert Luther 1857- WhAm 2
Canedo, Juan DeDios 1786-1850 ApCAB
Canek ApCAB
Canek d1532? ApCAB
Canetta, Andres Hurtado DeMendoza d1560 ApCAB
Canevin, John Francis Regis 1852-1927 NatCAB 15, WhAm 1
Canfield, Abijah 1769-1830 NewYHSD
Canfield, Albert Homer 1875-1939 NatCAB 30
Canfield, Amos 1878-1942 NatCAB 31
Canfield, Arthur Graves 1859-1947 WhAm 2
Canfield, Austin Francis 1894-1953 NatCAB 41
Canfield, Byron Hilton 1879-1932 NatCAB 41
Canfield, Charles Adelbert 1848-1913 ApCAB X, NatCAB 16
Canfield, Corresta T 1833- AmWom
Canfield, Edward 1848- WhAm 4
Canfield, Elizabeth Norton 1874- WomWWA 14
Canfield, Francesca Anna 1803-1823 ApCAB, Drake
Canfield, Frederick Alexander 1849-1926 NatCAB 20
Canfield, George Folger 1854-1933 WhAm 1
Canfield, Gordon 1898- BiDrAC
Canfield, Harry Clifford 1875-1945 BiDrAC, WhAm 2
Canfield, Henry Judson 1789-1856 ApCAB, Drake
Canfield, Henry Monroe 1841-1920 NatCAB 6
Canfield, Henry Ogden 1847-1910 NatCAB 30
Canfield, James Hulme 1847-1909 DcAmB, NatCAB 7, TwCBDA, WhAm 1
Canfield, Nellie Heth WomWWA 14
Canfield, Richard Albert 1855-1914 AmBi,

DcAmB
Canfield, Robert Warren 1907-1943 NatCAB 37
Canfield, Roy Bishop 1874-1932 NatCAB 24, WhAm 1
Canfield, William Walker 1857-1937 WhAm 1
Canham, Charles Draper William 1901-1963 NatCAB 51, WhAm 4
Caniff, Milton Arthur 1907- WebAB, WebAMB
Caniff, William 1830- ApCAB
Canine, Ralph Julian 1895-1969 NatCAB 54
Canion, William George 1879- ApCAB X
Canjar, Lawrence Nicholas 1923-1972 NatCAB 57, WhAm 5
Cann, James Ferris 1868-1944 WhAm 2
Cann, John d1694? NatCAB 16
Cann, John William 1873- WhoColR
Cann, Norman D 1898-1956 WhAm 3
Cann, Richard Thompson 1856-1926 NatCAB 20
Cann, William Harvey 1877-1947 NatCAB 36
Cannada, Frank Booton 1870-1927 NatCAB 20
Cannady, Beatrice Hulon Morrow 1890- WhoColR
Cannady, Edward Daniel 1877- WhoColR
Cannan, Robert Keith 1894-1971 NatCAB 56, WhAm 5
Canniff, William Henry 1847-1925 ApCAB X, NatCAB 20, WhAm 4
Canning, George 1770-1827 McGEWB, WhAm H
Canning, John Bennet 1884-1962 NatCAB 50
Canning, John Edward 1865-1936 NatCAB 28
Cannizzaro, Stanislao 1826-1910 AsBiEn, DcScB
Cannon, A Benson 1888-1950 WhAm 3
Cannon, Annie Jump 1863-1941 BiCAW, DcAmB S3, DcScB, NotAW, WebAB, WhAm 1, WhAm 1C, WomWWA 14
Cannon, Arthur Monroe 1911-1963 NatCAB 51
Cannon, Arthur Patrick 1904-1966 BiDrAC
Cannon, Austin Victor 1869-1934 WhAm 1
Cannon, Cavendish Welles 1895-1962 WhAm 4
Cannon, Charles A d1971 WhAm 5
Cannon, Charles James 1800-1860 ApCAB, DcAmB, Drake, WhAm H
Cannon, Clarence Andrew 1879-1964 BiDrAC, EncAAH, NatCAB 52, WhAm 4, WhAmP
Cannon, Cornelia James 1876- WhAm 5
Cannon, Dana Hyde 1890-1943 NatCAB 34
Cannon, Edwin Bennion 1910-1963 NatCAB 51
Cannon, Frank Jenne 1859-1933 ApCAB Sup, BiDrAC, NatCAB 12, NatCAB 16, TwCBDA, WhAm 1
Cannon, George Epps 1869- WhoColR
Cannon, George Lyman, Jr. 1860- WhAm 4
Cannon, George Quayle 1827-1901 AmBi, BiAUS, BiDrAC, DcAmB, NatCAB 12, NatCAB 16, REnAW, TwCBDA, WhAm H, WhAmP
Cannon, George Randolph 1856-1917 NatCAB 27
Cannon, Grant Groesbeck 1911-1969 WhAm 5
Cannon, Harriet Starr 1823-1896 DcAmB, NotAW, WhAm H
Cannon, Harry Laws 1878-1944 NatCAB 35
Cannon, Henry White 1850-1934 NatCAB 1, NatCAB 33, TwCBDA, WhAm 1
Cannon, Howard Walter 1912- BiDrAC
Cannon, Hugh 1814?- NewYHSD
Cannon, James, III 1892-1960 NatCAB 49, WhAm 3
Cannon, James, Jr. 1864-1944 ApCAB X, DcAmB S3, DcAmReB, NatCAB 35, WhAm 2
Cannon, James Graham 1858-1916 DcAmB, WhAm 1
Cannon, James Hughes 1890-1950 NatCAB 38
Cannon, James Spencer 1776-1852 ApCAB, Drake, TwCBDA
Cannon, James William 1852-1921 NatCAB 33
Cannon, Jimmy 1909-1973 WhAm 6
Cannon, John 1872-1941 WhAm 1
Cannon, John Franklin 1851-1920 WhAm 1
Cannon, John Kenneth 1892-1955 NatCAB 46, WhAm 3

Cannon, Joseph Gurney 1836-1926 *AmBi,*
ApCAB X, BiAUS, BiDrAC, DcAmB,
EncAAH, EncAB, McGEWB,
NatCAB 13, NatCAB 22, TwCBDA,
WebAB, WhAmP
Cannon, Joseph Gurney 1836-1927 *WhAm 1*
Cannon, LeGrand Bouton d1906 *WhAm 1*
Cannon, Marion 1834-1920 *BiDrAC, TwCBDA,*
WhAmP
Cannon, Martin Luther 1885-1952 *NatCAB 40,*
WhAm 3
Cannon, Martin Luther, Jr. 1910-1957
NatCAB 46
Cannon, Newton 1781-1841 *BiDrAC, DcAmB,*
Drake, WhAm H, WhAmP
Cannon, Newton 1781-1842 *ApCAB, BiAUS,*
NatCAB 7, TwCBDA
Cannon, Raymond Joseph 1894-1951 *BiDrAC,*
WhAm 3, WhAmP
Cannon, Sylvester Quayle 1877-1943 *WhAm 2*
Cannon, Walter Bradford 1871-1945 *AsBiEn,*
BiHiMed, DcAmB S3, DcScB,
DcScB Sup, EncAB, NatCAB 15,
NatCAB 34, WebAB, WhAm 2
Cannon, William 1809-1865 *ApCAB, BiAUS,*
DcAmB, Drake, NatCAB 11, TwCBDA,
WhAm H
Cannon, William Cornelius 1873-1971 *WhAm 5*
Cannon, William Sherman 1869- *WhoColR*
Cannon, William Taylor 1856-1931 *NatCAB 30*
Canny, Joseph Francis 1888-1944 *NatCAB 49*
Cano, Juan Sebastian Del 1460?-1526 *AsBiEn*
Canonchet d1676 *DcAmB, NatCAB 10,*
WebAMB, WhAm H
Canonge, Louis Placide 1822-1893 *DcAmB,*
NatCAB 22, WhAm H
Canonicus 1565?-1647 *AmBi, ApCAB,*
DcAmB, Drake, NatCAB 11, WhAm H
Canot, Theodore 1804-1860 *McGEWB*
Canot, Theodore 1807?- *ApCAB*
Canova, Antonio 1757-1822 *McGEWB*
Canova, Dominico *NewYHSD*
Canova, Leon Joseph 1866- *WhAm 4*
Canright, Dudley Marvin 1840-1919 *WhAm 1*
Canrobert, Francois Certain 1809-1895
WhoMilH
Canse, John Martin 1869- *WhAm 5*
Cansler, Edwin Thomas 1866-1943 *NatCAB 39*
Cant, William Alexander 1863-1933 *WhAm 1*
Cantacuzene, Madame 1876- *WhAm 6*
Cantari *ApCAB Sup*
Cantelli, Guido 1920-1956 *WhAm 4*
Canter, Howard Vernon 1873- *WhAm 5*
Canter, John 1782?-1823 *NewYHSD*
Canter, Joshua d1826 *NewYHSD, WhAm H*
Canterac, Jose 1770?-1835 *ApCAB Sup*
Canterbury, Sam Shannon 1896-1954
NatCAB 41
Canterson, J *NewYHSD*
Cantey, James 1818-1874 *BiDConf,*
NatCAB 18
Cantey, Morgan Sabb 1911-1962 *WhAm 4*
Cantillon, William David 1861-1914 *WhAm 1*
Cantilo, Jose Maria 1877- *WhAm 5*
Cantine, Charles Freeman 1858-1912
NatCAB 25
Cantine, John *BiAUS*
Cantine, Martin 1866-1935 *NatCAB 25*
Cantir *NewYHSD*
Canton, Frank M 1849-1927 *REnAW*
Canton, John 1718-1772 *AsBiEn, DcScB*
Canton, Thomas 1815?- *NewYHSD*
Cantor, Eddie 1892-1964 *NatCAB 52, WebAB,*
WhAm 4
Cantor, Georg 1845-1918 *AsBiEn, DcScB,*
McGEWB
Cantor, Jacob Aaron 1854-1921 *BiDrAC,*
WhAm 1
Cantor, Moritz Benedikt 1829-1920 *DcScB*
Cantor, Nathaniel Freeman 1898-1957
NatCAB 45, WhAm 3
Cantrall, Arch Martin 1896-1967 *WhAm 5*
Cantrell, Charles E 1859- *WhAm 4*
Cantrell, Deaderick Harrell 1868-1934
NatCAB 38, WhAm 1
Cantril, Hadley 1906-1969 *NatCAB 55,*
WhAm 5

Cantril, Simeon Theodore 1908-1959
NatCAB 47
Cantrill, James Campbell 1870-1923 *BiDrAC,*
WhAm 1, WhAmP
Cantrill, James E d1908 *WhAm 1*
Cantwell, Alfred W 1902-1965 *WhAm 4*
Cantwell, Edwin 1834?- *NewYHSD*
Cantwell, James *NewYHSD*
Cantwell, James William 1868-1931 *WhAm 1*
Cantwell, John Joseph 1874-1947 *ApCAB X,*
NatCAB 35, WhAm 2
Cantwell, Robert Murray 1899-1954 *WhAm 3*
Canty, Thomas 1854- *WhAm 4*
Cany, Harriet *NewYHSD*
Caonabo d1494 *ApCAB*
Capa, Robert 1913-1954 *WhAm 4*
Caparo, Jose Angel 1888-1954 *WhAm 3*
Capdevielle, Armand 1851- *NatCAB 10*
Cape, Emily Palmer 1865- *WhAm 4*
Capehart, Edward Everett 1859-1917
NatCAB 26
Capehart, Homer Earl 1897- *BiDrAC*
Capehart, James 1847-1921 *BiDrAC, WhAmP*
Capehart, Wadleigh 1888-1952 *NatCAB 50*
Capek, Karel 1890-1938 *McGEWB*
Capek, Thomas 1861-1950 *WhAm 3*
Capell, Clarence Swift 1873-1956 *NatCAB 42*
Capellano, Antonio *NewYHSD*
Capen, Albert M 1857-1928 *ApCAB X*
Capen, Anne *WomWWA 14*
Capen, Azel *NewYHSD*
Capen, Chanie A 1843- *WomWWA 14*
Capen, Charles Laban 1845-1927 *WhAm 1*
Capen, Edward 1821-1901 *NatCAB 6,*
TwCBDA
Capen, Edward Warren 1870- *WhAm 5*
Capen, Elmer Hewitt 1838-1905 *ApCAB,*
BiDAmEd, DcAmB, NatCAB 6,
TwCBDA, WhAm 1
Capen, Francis L 1817-1889 *NatCAB 5*
Capen, George Dunn 1838-1893 *NatCAB 26*
Capen, John L 1822- *NatCAB 9*
Capen, Mary Warren 1874- *WomWWA 14*
Capen, Nahum 1804-1886 *ApCAB, DcAmB,*
NatCAB 24, TwCBDA, WhAm H
Capen, Oliver Bronson 1878-1953 *NatCAB 42,*
WhAm 3
Capen, Samuel Billings 1842-1914 *DcAmB,*
NatCAB 12, WhAm 1
Capen, Samuel Paul 1878-1956 *WhAm 3*
Capers, Ellison 1837-1908 *ApCAB Sup,*
BiDConf, DcAmB, NatCAB 12,
TwCBDA, WhAm 1
Capers, Gerald Mortimer 1909- *EncAAH*
Capers, John Gendron 1866-1919 *NatCAB 28,*
WhAm 1
Capers, Walter Branham 1870- *WhAm 5*
Capers, William 1790-1855 *ApCAB, DcAmB,*
Drake, NatCAB 13, TwCBDA, WhAm H
Capers, William Theodotus 1867-1943
NatCAB 41, WhAm 2
Caperton, Allen Taylor 1810-1876 *ApCAB,*
BiAUS, BiDConf, BiDrAC, NatCAB 7,
TwCBDA, WhAm H
Caperton, Helena Trench Lefroy 1878-
WomWWA 14
Caperton, Hugh 1780-1847 *BiAUS*
Caperton, Hugh 1781-1847 *BiDrAC,*
WhAm H
Caperton, Hugh John 1893-1944 *NatCAB 33*
Caperton, William Banks 1855-1941
NatCAB 36, WebAMB, WhAm 1
Capes, William Parr 1881-1946 *WhAm 2*
Capewell, George Joseph 1843- *NatCAB 16*
Capewell, Samuel *NewYHSD*
Capillana d1549 *ApCAB*
Caples, Grace Stelle *WomWWA 14*
Caples, Martin Joseph 1864-1931 *WhAm 1*
Caples, Ralph C 1872-1949 *NatCAB 39*
Caples, Robert Cole *IIBEAAW*
Caples, Russel B 1888-1968 *WhAm 5*
Caplin, Alfred Gerald 1909- *WebAB*
Capogrossi, Guiseppe 1900-1972 *WhAm 6*
Capon, William Albert 1863-1947 *NatCAB 35*
Capone, Al 1899-1947 *McGEWB*
Capone, Alphonse 1899-1947 *DcAmB S4,*
WebAB
Capote, Truman 1924- *WebAB*

Capozzoli, Louis Joseph 1901- *BiDrAC*
Capp, Al 1909- *WebAB*
Cappa, Carlo Alberto 1834-1893 *ApCAB,*
NatCAB 9, TwCBDA
Cappa, Victor Emanuel 1900-1965 *NatCAB 51*
Cappel, C Glenn 1892-1958 *NatCAB 48*
Cappelen, Frederick William 1857-1921
NatCAB 19
Cappelli *NewYHSD*
Cappellucci, Gabriel Orazio 1935-1975
WhAm 6
Cappelmann, F William 1888-1958 *NatCAB 48*
Capper, Arthur 1865-1951 *ApCAB X, BiDrAC,*
DcAmB S5, EncAAH, NatCAB 15,
NatCAB 41, REnAW, WhAm 3,
WhAmP
Capper, John Sheville 1867- *NatCAB 18*
Cappiani, Luisa *AmWom*
Cappleman, Josie Frazee 1861- *WomWWA 14*
Capps, Charles R 1871-1936 *WhAm 1*
Capps, Edward 1866-1950 *DcAmB S4,*
WhAm 3
Capps, Edwin Morris 1860-1938 *NatCAB 29*
Capps, Joseph Almarin 1872-1964 *WhAm 4*
Capps, Minnie Taliaferro Jossey 1878-
WomWWA 14
Capps, Samuel John 1844-1923 *NatCAB 6*
Capps, Stephen Reid 1881-1949 *NatCAB 36,*
WhAm 2
Capps, Washington Lee 1864-1935 *ApCAB X,*
DcAmB S1, NatCAB 26, WhAm 1
Capps, William 1858-1925 *NatCAB 21*
Capra, Baldassar 1580?-1626 *DcScB*
Capra, Frank 1897- *WebAB*
Capron, Adin Ballou 1841-1911 *BiDrAC,*
TwCBDA, WhAm 1, WhAmP
Capron, Allyn 1846-1898 *ApCAB Sup*
Capron, Allyn Kissam 1871-1898 *ApCAB Sup*
Capron, Charles Alexander 1886-1955 *WhAm 3*
Capron, Elisha S 1806- *Drake*
Capron, Erastus Allyn 1813-1847 *ApCAB Sup*
Capron, Fanny Littlefield 1858- *WomWWA 14*
Capron, Horace 1804-1885 *AmBi, BiAUS,*
DcAmB, EncAAH, WhAm H
Capstaff, Albert L 1912-1963 *WhAm 4*
Capstaff, John George 1879-1960 *NatCAB 49,*
WhAm 3
Capstick, John Henry 1856-1918 *BiDrAC,*
NatCAB 17, WhAm 1
Capt, James Clyde 1888-1949 *NatCAB 36,*
WhAm 2
Captain Jack 1837?-1873 *DcAmB, WebAMB,*
WhAm H
Captain Jack 1840?-1873 *REnAW*
Capwell, Irene Stoddard 1854- *WomWWA 14*
Caracalla 188-217 *McGEWB*
Caradeuc, James Achille De *NewYHSD*
Caradori, Anna 1822- *ApCAB*
Caradori-Allan, Maria 1800-1865 *ApCAB*
Caramuel Y Lobkowitz, Juan 1606-1682 *DcScB*
Carangeot, Arnould 1742-1806 *DcScB*
Caratheodory, Constantin 1873-1950 *DcScB*
Caravaggio 1573-1610 *McGEWB*
Caraway, Hattie Ophelia Wyatt 1878-1950
BiDrAC, DcAmB S4, NatCAB 44,
NotAW, WhAm 3, WhAmP
Caraway, Thaddeus Horatius 1871-1931
ApCAB X, BiDrAC, DcAmB S1,
NatCAB 44, WhAm 1, WhAmP
Carbajal, Fernando 1880- *WhAm 6*
Carbee, Scott Clifton 1860- *WhAm 4*
Carberry, Clifton Benjamin 1876-1940
NatCAB 30
Carberry, William Henry 1851- *NatCAB 12*
Carbery, J J 1823-1887 *ApCAB*
Carbo, Luis Felipe 1858- *WhAm 4*
Carbonara, E Vernon 1897-1968 *NatCAB 54,*
WhAm 5
Carbone, Agostino 1856-1915 *WhAm 1*
Carbone, Philip Lawrence 1867-1922 *ApCAB X*
Carbonnier, Claes Cecil 1912-1961 *WhAm 4*
Carbutt, John 1832-1905 *DcAmB, NatCAB 22*
Carcavi, Pierre De 1600?-1684 *DcScB*
Card, Benjamin Cozzens 1825-1916 *WhAm 1*
Card, Ernest Mason 1877- *WhAm 5*
Cardano, Geronimo 1501-1576 *McGEWB*
Cardano, Girolamo 1501-1576 *AsBiEn, DcScB*
Cardella, Liberato *NewYHSD*

Cardella, Liberto *NewYHSD*
Cardelli, Georgio 1791- *NewYHSD*
Cardelli, Pietro d1822 *NewYHSD, WhAm H*
Carden, Cap Robert 1866-1935 *BiDrAC, WhAm 1*
Carden, Edward Walter 1892-1957 *WhAm 3*
Carden, George Alexander 1865-1946 *NatCAB 17, WhAm 2*
Carden, William Thomas 1888-1924 *NatCAB 40, WhAm 1*
Cardenas, Bernardino De d1668 *ApCAB*
Cardenas, Francisco 1600?-1660? *ApCAB Sup*
Cardenas, Garcia Lopez De *AmBi, DcAmB, WhAm H*
Cardenas, Juan De *ApCAB*
Cardenas, Lazaro 1895-1970 *McGEWB, WhAm 5*
Cardenas, Louis, Penalver Y 1719-1810 *NatCAB 5*
Cardenas, Luis Ignacio Penalver Y 1749-1810 *ApCAB, TwCBDA*
Cardenas Y Rodriguez, Jose M De 1812-1882 *ApCAB*
Cardenas Y Rodriguez, Nicolas De 1814-1868 *ApCAB*
Carder, Clayton 1900-1959 *NatCAB 48*
Carder, Eugene Clayton 1881- *WhAm 6*
Carder, Frederick 1863-1963 *BnEnAmA*
Cardero, *NewYHSD*
Cardero, Jose *NewYHSD*
Cardew, Emily Craske 1907-1974 *WhAm 6*
Cardiff, Ira D 1873- *WhAm 5*
Cardigan, Thomas J Brudenell, Earl Of 1797-1868 *WhoMilH*
Cardinal, Joseph Narcisse 1808-1838 *ApCAB*
Cardoff, Thomas H 1904-1964 *WhAm 4*
Cardon, Philip Vincent 1889-1965 *WhAm 4*
Cardoso, Jose Joaquin 1802-1878 *ApCAB*
Cardozo, Benjamin Nathan 1870-1938 *AmBi, DcAmB S2, EncAB, McGEWB, NatCAB 27, WebAB, WhAm 1*
Cardozo, Ernest Abraham 1879- *NatCAB 19*
Cardozo, F Henry 1879- *WhoColR*
Cardozo, Francis Nunez 1882- *WhoColR*
Cardozo, Isaac Newton 1786-1850 *ApCAB, Drake, TwCBDA*
Cardozo, Jacob Newton 1786-1873 *DcAmB, WhAm H*
Cardozo, Michael Hart 1851-1906 *NatCAB 19*
Cardozo, Sidney B 1888-1952 *NatCAB 41*
Carducci, Giosue 1835-1907 *McGEWB*
Cardwell, Allen Donald 1896-1951 *NatCAB 39*
Cardwell, Byron 1833?- *NewYHSD*
Cardwell, Edward 1813-1886 *WhoMilH*
Cardwell, James R 1873-1957 *WhAm 3*
Cardwell, Richard Henry 1846-1931 *NatCAB 29*
Cardwill, Mary E *AmWom*
Cardy, Samuel d1764 *WhAm H*
Carelton, Mark Alfred 1866-1925 *EncAAH*
Carens, Thomas Henry 1893-1960 *WhAm 4*
Carew, Sir Benjamin Hallowell 1760-1834 *ApCAB, Drake*
Carew, Harold David 1890-1943 *WhAm 2*
Carew, James 1878-1938 *WhAm 1*
Carew, John 1820?- *NewYHSD*
Carew, John F 1876-1951 *WhAm 3*
Carew, John Francis 1873-1951 *BiDrAC, WhAmP*
Carew, Joseph d1870 *NewYHSD*
Carew, Thomas A *NewYHSD*
Carey, A Morris 1861-1930 *NatCAB 32*
Carey, Archibald 1884-1957 *WhAm 3*
Carey, Archibald James 1867-1931 *WhAm 1, WhoColR A*
Carey, Arthur Astor 1857-1923 *WhAm 1*
Carey, Asa Bacon 1835-1912 *ApCAB Sup, WhAm 1*
Carey, Charles Clinton 1905-1963 *NatCAB 50*
Carey, Charles Emerson 1893-1954 *WhAm 3*
Carey, Charles Henry 1857-1941 *ApCAB X, NatCAB 16, WhAm 1*
Carey, Charles Irving 1884-1970 *WhAm 5*
Carey, Eben James 1889-1947 *WhAm 2*
Carey, Emerson 1863-1933 *NatCAB 34*
Carey, Eustace W 1902-1964 *WhAm 4*
Carey, Francis King 1858-1944 *WhAm 2*
Carey, George d1844 *BiAUS*

Carey, Hampson 1896-1951 *WhAm 3*
Carey, Henry Ames 1890-1965 *NatCAB 52*
Carey, Henry Charles 1793-1879 *AmBi, ApCAB, DcAmB, Drake, EncAB, McGEWB, NatCAB 5, TwCBDA, WebAB, WhAm H*
Carey, Henry DeWitt 1844-1908 *NatCAB 8*
Carey, Henry Westonrae 1850-1911 *NatCAB 29, WhAm 1*
Carey, Homer Franklin 1894-1950 *NatCAB 42*
Carey, Hugh Leo 1919- *BiDrAC*
Carey, James Barron 1911-1973 *WhAm 6*
Carey, James F 1867- *WhAm 4*
Carey, James William 1892-1969 *WhAm 5*
Carey, Jeremiah E 1803- *BiAUS*
Carey, John 1792-1875 *BiAUS, BiDrAC*
Carey, John B *NewYHSD*
Carey, John Joseph 1894-1971 *WhAm 5*
Carey, John Newman 1855-1926 *NatCAB 23*
Carey, Joseph *NewYHSD*
Carey, Joseph 1839-1913 *TwCBDA, WhAm 1*
Carey, Joseph Maull 1845-1924 *AmBi, BiAUS, BiDrAC, DcAmB, EncAAH, NatCAB 1, NatCAB 4, NatCAB 29, REnAW, TwCBDA, WhAm 1, WhAmP*
Carey, Lawrence Bernard 1892-1973 *WhAm 6*
Carey, Liguori John 1893-1963 *WhAm 4*
Carey, Margaret Cheston Thomas *WomWWA 14*
Carey, Martin 1858-1922 *NatCAB 26*
Carey, Mathew 1760-1839 *AmBi, ApCAB, DcAmB, EncAB, WebAB, WhAm H*
Carey, Mathew 1760-1840 *NatCAB 6*
Carey, Matthew 1760-1839 *Drake, TwCBDA*
Carey, Miriam Eliza 1858-1937 *WhAm 1, WomWWA 14*
Carey, Peter Bernard 1886-1943 *WhAm 2*
Carey, Peyton *NewYHSD*
Carey, Robert 1862-1913 *NatCAB 16*
Carey, Robert 1872-1963 *WhAm 4*
Carey, Robert Davis 1878-1937 *AmBi, BiDrAC, NatCAB 28, WhAm 1, WhAmP*
Carey, Robert Lincoln 1898-1961 *WhAm 4*
Carey, William 1761-1834 *McGEWB*
Carey, William Francis 1878-1951 *NatCAB 41, WhAm 3*
Carey, William Gibson, Jr. 1896-1947 *NatCAB 36, WhAm 2*
Cargill, Frank Valentine 1885-1971 *WhAm 5*
Cargill, Oscar 1898-1972 *NatCAB 57, WhAm 5*
Cargill, Walter Hurt 1919-1959 *NatCAB 48*
Carhardt, Raymond T 1912-1975 *WhAm 6*
Carhart, Anna Georgine *WomWWA 14*
Carhart, Clara H Sully 1845- *AmWom*
Carhart, Daniel 1839-1926 *WhAm 1*
Carhart, Edith Noble 1879- *WomWWA 14*
Carhart, Frank Milton 1882-1965 *WhAm 4*
Carhart, Henry Smith 1844-1920 *ApCAB, NatCAB 4, TwCBDA, WhAm 1*
Carhart, Jeremiah 1813-1868 *ApCAB, TwCBDA*
Carhart, Margaret Sprague 1877- *WomWWA 14*
Carhart, Winfield Scott 1861- *WhAm 4*
Carhartt, Hamilton 1859- *ApCAB X, NatCAB 18, WhAm 1*
Carhartt, Hamilton, Jr. 1883-1961 *NatCAB 49*
Carhartt, John Ernest 1884-1943 *WhAm 2*
Carheil, Etienne De d1726 *ApCAB*
Cariani, Anthony 1918-1974 *WhAm 6*
Carias Andino, Tiburcio 1876- *WhAm 5*
Carillo, Braulio 1800-1845 *Drake*
Caris, Albert Garfield 1881- *WhAm 6*
Carissimi, Giacomo 1605-1674 *McGEWB*
Carkeek, Morgan James 1847-1931 *NatCAB 33*
Carkin, Seth Ballou 1885-1938 *WhAm 1*
Carkner, James W d1961 *WhAm 4*
Carl, Francis Augustus 1861-1930 *WhAm 1*
Carl, Katharine Augusta d1938 *WhAm 1, WomWWA 14*
Carl, Ludwig Leland 1876- *NatCAB 12*
Carl, Melvin Latshaw 1906-1959 *WhAm 3*
Carl, William Crane 1865-1936 *NatCAB 8, NatCAB 35, WhAm 1*
Carland, John Emmett 1853-1922 *WhAm 1*
Carlberg, Gotthold 1838-1881 *ApCAB*
Carle, E E 1880- *WhAm 6*

Carle, Frank Austin 1851-1930 *WhAm 1, WhAm 1C*
Carle, Nathaniel Allen 1875-1960 *NatCAB 51, WhAm 4*
Carle, Norman Levi 1867-1941 *NatCAB 51*
Carle, Richard 1871-1941 *WhAm 1*
Carles, Arthur B 1882-1952 *BnEnAmA, WhAm 3*
Carleton, Bukk G 1856-1914 *NatCAB 7, WhAm 1*
Carleton, Charles Ames 1836-1897 *ApCAB Sup*
Carleton, Clifford 1867- *WhAm 4*
Carleton, Edward Hercules 1904-1975 *WhAm 6*
Carleton, Emma Shields Nunemacher 1850- *WomWWA 14*
Carleton, Ezra Child 1838-1911 *BiDrAC*
Carleton, Francis Joseph 1899-1962 *NatCAB 50*
Carleton, Frank Henry 1849-1916 *NatCAB 6*
Carleton, Grace Haines *WomWWA 14*
Carleton, Guy 1857-1946 *WhAm 3*
Carleton, Guy, Lord Dorchester 1722-1808 *Drake*
Carleton, Guy, Lord Dorchester 1724-1808 *AmBi, ApCAB, McGEWB*
Carleton, Henry 1783-1863 *BiAUS*
Carleton, Henry 1785-1863 *ApCAB, DcAmB, Drake, TwCBDA, WhAm H*
Carleton, Henry Guy 1855-1910 *ApCAB Sup, NatCAB 13, TwCBDA*
Carleton, Henry Guy 1856-1910 *DcAmB, WhAm 1*
Carleton, James Henry 1814-1873 *ApCAB, Drake, REnAW, TwCBDA*
Carleton, Lillian Stewart 1873- *WomWWA 14*
Carleton, Mark Alfred 1866-1925 *NatCAB 23, WhAm 1*
Carleton, Monroe Guy 1833-1918 *NatCAB 16*
Carleton, Murray 1852-1926 *NatCAB 12, NatCAB 21, WhAm 1*
Carleton, Osgood 1742-1816 *ApCAB, Drake*
Carleton, Peter 1755-1828 *BiDrAC, WhAm H*
Carleton, Philip Greenleaf 1878-1965 *NatCAB 51, WhAm 6*
Carleton, Robert Andrew Wood 1881- *WhAm 6*
Carleton, Sprague 1881- *WhAm 6*
Carleton, Thomas 1736-1817 *ApCAB, Drake*
Carleton, Will 1845-1912 *AmBi, ApCAB, DcAmB, NatCAB 2, TwCBDA, WhAm 1*
Carley, Henry Thompson 1878-1953 *WhAm 4*
Carley, James Allen 1869-1952 *NatCAB 42*
Carley, Patrick J 1866-1936 *BiDrAC, WhAm 1*
Carley, W F d1954 *WhAm 3*
Carlile, John Snyder 1817-1878 *ApCAB, BiAUS, BiDrAC, DcAmB, NatCAB 4, TwCBDA, WhAm H*
Carlile, William Buford 1870- *WhAm 5*
Carlin, Andrew B 1816?- *NewYHSD, WhAm H*
Carlin, Anthony 1857-1938 *NatCAB 29*
Carlin, Charles Creighton 1866-1938 *BiDrAC, WhAm 1*
Carlin, Charles L 1847-1891 *WhAm H*
Carlin, Daniel 1826?- *NewYHSD*
Carlin, George Andrew 1890-1945 *WhAm 2*
Carlin, Henry A 1892-1965 *WhAm 4*
Carlin, James Joseph 1872-1930 *WhAm 1*
Carlin, John 1813-1891 *ApCAB, NewYHSD, TwCBDA, WhAm H*
Carlin, Thomas 1789-1852 *NatCAB 11, WhAm H*
Carlin, Thomas 1791-1852 *ApCAB, Drake*
Carlin, Walter Jeffreys d1958 *WhAm 3*
Carlin, William Passmore 1829-1903 *ApCAB, Drake, NatCAB 12, TwCBDA, WhAm 1*
Carlin, William Worth d1894 *WhAm H*
Carliner, Paul Elliott 1910-1956 *NatCAB 43*
Carling, Henry 1856-1932 *NatCAB 23*
Carling, John 1855- *NewYHSD*
Carling, John 1828- *ApCAB*
Carling, John 1877-1948 *NatCAB 37*
Carlisle, Anthony 1768-1840 *DcScB*
Carlisle, Burlington Majors 1886-1954 *NatCAB 45*
Carlisle, Charles Arthur 1864-1938 *WhAm 1*
Carlisle, Chester Lee 1876-1952 *WhAm 3*
Carlisle, Clifton Hugh 1869-1952 *WhAm 3*

Carlisle, Floyd Leslie 1881-1942 *DcAmB S3, NatCAB 31, WhAm 2*
Carlisle, Frederick Howard 1748-1825 *ApCAB, Drake*
Carlisle, G Lister, Jr. 1877-1954 *WhAm 3*
Carlisle, George Lister 1852-1930 *NatCAB 27*
Carlisle, Harold Walter 1910-1966 *WhAm 4*
Carlisle, Helen Grace 1898-1968 *WhAm 5*
Carlisle, Henry Coffin 1886-1964 *NatCAB 51*
Carlisle, Howard Bobo 1867- *WhAm 5*
Carlisle, J Mandeville 1879-1922 *NatCAB 49*
Carlisle, James Henry 1825-1909 *TwCBDA, WhAm 1*
Carlisle, James Mandeville 1814-1877 *DcAmB, WhAm H*
Carlisle, James McCoy 1851- *TwCBDA, WhAm 4*
Carlisle, John Griffin 1834-1910 *EncAB*
Carlisle, John Griffin 1835-1910 *AmBi, ApCAB, BiDrAC, BiDrUSE, DcAmB, NatCAB 1, TwCBDA, WebAB, WhAm 1, WhAmP*
Carlisle, John Nelson 1866-1931 *WhAm 1*
Carlisle, Marcus Lee 1863-1927 *WhAm 1*
Carlisle, Mary Jane 1835- *AmWom*
Carlisle, Richard Risley 1814-1874 *ApCAB*
Carlisle, Tyler Waterman 1885-1940 *NatCAB 30*
Carlisle, Woodson Studebaker 1897-1947 *NatCAB 37*
Carll, John Franklin 1828-1904 *ApCAB, DcAmB, NatCAB 12, TwCBDA, WhAm 1*
Carlo, William *NewYHSD*
Carlock, John Bruce 1882-1965 *WhAm 4A*
Carlough, David Jacobus 1869-1960 *WhAm 4*
Carlsen, Carl Laurence 1880- *WhAm 1*
Carlsen, Clarence J 1894-1959 *WhAm 4*
Carlsen, Dines 1901-1966 *WhAm 4*
Carlsen, Emil 1853-1931 *WhAm 1*
Carlsen, Emil 1853-1932 *AmBi, NatCAB 24*
Carlsen, Niels Christian 1884-1950 *WhAm 2A*
Carlson, Albert Sigfrid 1907- *WhAm 6*
Carlson, Anders Johan 1894- *WhAm 5*
Carlson, Anton Julius 1875-1956 *DcScB, NatCAB 18, NatCAB 45, WhAm 3*
Carlson, C Oscar 1874-1956 *NatCAB 46*
Carlson, Chester Floyd 1906-1968 *EncAB, WebAB, WhAm 5*
Carlson, Clarence Erick 1892-1958 *WhAm 3*
Carlson, E Leslie 1893-1967 *WhAm 5*
Carlson, Edward *NewYHSD*
Carlson, Evans Fordyce 1896-1947 *DcAmB S4, WebAMB, WhAm 2, WhWW-II*
Carlson, Frank 1893- *BiDrAC*
Carlson, George Alfred 1876-1926 *NatCAB 15, WhAm 1*
Carlson, Glen Everett 1896-1948 *NatCAB 37*
Carlson, Gunard Oscar 1895-1969 *WhAm 5*
Carlson, Gustav Waldemar 1884-1961 *NatCAB 52*
Carlson, Harry Johan 1869- *ApCAB X, WhAm 5*
Carlson, James Alfred 1907-1966 *WhAm 4*
Carlson, John Edwin 1897-1968 *NatCAB 55*
Carlson, John Fabian 1875-1945 *NatCAB 36, WhAm 2*
Carlson, Leonard Oliver 1892-1947 *NatCAB 41*
Carlson, Loren Daniel 1915-1972 *WhAm 5*
Carlson, Oscar William 1881-1950 *NatCAB 39*
Carlson, Samuel Augustus 1868-1961 *NatCAB 49*
Carlson, T C 1893-1970 *WhAm 5*
Carlson, Wally 1894-1967 *WhAm 4*
Carlston, Kenneth S 1904-1969 *WhAm 5*
Carlstrom, Oscar E 1878-1948 *WhAm 2*
Carlton, A C 1895-1958 *WhAm 3*
Carlton, Albert E 1866-1931 *WhAm 1*
Carlton, Caleb Henry 1836-1923 *WhAm 1*
Carlton, Caleb Sidney 1915-1966 *WhAm 5*
Carlton, Charles Elijah 1869- *ApCAB X*
Carlton, Clarence Clay 1882-1951 *NatCAB 40, WhAm 3*
Carlton, Doyle Elam 1885-1972 *NatCAB 57, WhAm 5*
Carlton, Ernest W 1897-1966 *WhAm 4*
Carlton, Frank Tracy 1873- *WhAm 5*
Carlton, Henry Fisk 1892-1973 *NatCAB 57*

Carlton, Henry Hull 1835-1905 *BiDrAC, NatCAB 2*
Carlton, Leslie Gilbert d1938 *WhAm 1*
Carlton, Lobel Alva 1860-1925 *NatCAB 6*
Carlton, Newcomb 1869-1953 *WhAm 3*
Carlton, Peter *BiAUS*
Carlton, Richard Paul 1893-1953 *NatCAB 43, WhAm 3*
Carlton, Romulus Lee 1881- *WhAm 6*
Carlton, Thomas 1808-1874 *ApCAB*
Carlton, Thomas 1810-1874 *NatCAB 11*
Carlton, William Newnham Chattin 1873-1943 *WhAm 2*
Carlton, William Tolman 1816-1888 *NewYHSD*
Carlyle, Frank Ertel 1897-1960 *BiDrAC*
Carlyle, Irving Edward 1891-1971 *WhAm 5*
Carlyle, Thomas 1795-1881 *McGEWB*
Carlyle, William Levi 1870- *WhAm 5*
Carmack, Edward Ward 1858-1908 *BiDrAC, DcAmB, NatCAB 13, TwCBDA, WhAm 1, WhAmP*
Carmack, George Washington 1860-1922 *NatCAB 19*
Carmack, Samuel W 1802-1849 *BiAUS*
Carmalt, James Walton 1872-1937 *WhAm 1*
Carmalt, William Henry 1836-1929 *NatCAB 14, NatCAB 29, TwCBDA, WhAm 1*
Carman, Captain d1645 *ApCAB, Drake*
Carman, Albert 1833- *ApCAB*
Carman, Albert Pruden 1861-1946 *WhAm 3*
Carman, Augustine Spencer 1859-1941 *WhAm 1*
Carman, Bliss 1861-1929 *NatCAB 18, NatCAB 21, TwCBDA, WhAm 1*
Carman, Eugene Moore 1886-1940 *NatCAB 34*
Carman, Ezra Ayers 1834-1909 *WhAm 1*
Carman, George Noble 1856-1941 *WhAm 2*
Carman, Harry James 1884-1964 *WhAm 4*
Carman, J *NewYHSD*
Carman, J Neale 1897-1972 *NatCAB 57*
Carman, Julius Frederick 1861-1928 *NatCAB 22*
Carman, Radcliff *NewYHSD*
Carman, Robert Baldwin 1843- *ApCAB*
Carman, Russell Daniel 1875-1926 *NatCAB 20*
Carman, Thadius Walter 1871-1929 *NatCAB 23*
Carman, William Bliss 1861-1929 *ApCAB Sup, ApCAB X*
Carmelia, Francis Albion 1889-1947 *WhAm 2*
Carmell, Daniel David 1898-1957 *NatCAB 49*
Carmichael, Annie Darling Cole *WomWWA 14*
Carmichael, Archibald Hill 1864-1947 *BiDrAC*
Carmichael, Archibald Hill 1864-1948 *WhAm 3*
Carmichael, Donald MacNevin 1902-1971 *NatCAB 57*
Carmichael, Francis Abbott, Jr. 1909-1973 *WhAm 6*
Carmichael, George Edgar 1875-1964 *WhAm 4*
Carmichael, George T 1889-1962 *WhAm 4*
Carmichael, Henry 1846-1924 *TwCBDA, WhAm 1*
Carmichael, Hoagland Howard 1899- *WebAB*
Carmichael, J W *NewYHSD*
Carmichael, James Henry 1859-1925 *NatCAB 24*
Carmichael, James S 1851-1922 *NatCAB 20*
Carmichael, James Vinson 1910-1972 *WhAm 6*
Carmichael, John Hugh 1868- *WhAm 5*
Carmichael, Leonard 1898-1973 *BiDAmEd, WhAm 6*
Carmichael, Oliver Cromwell 1891-1966 *BiDAmEd, WhAm 4*
Carmichael, Omer 1893-1960 *BiDAmEd, WhAm 3*
Carmichael, Richard Bennett 1807-1884 *BiAUS, BiDrAC, WhAm H*
Carmichael, Robert Daniel 1879-1967 *WhAm 4, WhAm 6*
Carmichael, T J *NewYHSD*
Carmichael, Thomas Harrison 1858-1942 *NatCAB 35, WhAm 2*
Carmichael, William d1795 *ApCAB, BiAUS, BiDrAC, DcAmB, Drake, NatCAB 11, TwCBDA, WhAm H, WhAmP*
Carmichael, William Donald, Jr. 1900-1961 *NatCAB 49, WhAm 4*
Carmichael, William Perrin 1858-1944 *WhAm 2*

Carmick, Daniel 1772-1816 *WebAMB*
Carmiencke, Johann Hermann 1810-1867 *NewYHSD*
Carmiencke, John Hermann 1810-1867 *ApCAB*
Carmody, Francis Terence 1908-1965 *NatCAB 53*
Carmody, John 1854-1920 *WhAm 3*
Carmody, John Michael 1881-1963 *NatCAB 56, WhAm 4*
Carmody, Martin Henry d1950 *WhAm 3*
Carmody, Terence Francis 1871-1943 *WhAm 2*
Carmody, Thomas 1859-1922 *WhAm 1*
Carmody, Thomas Edward 1875-1946 *WhAm 2*
Carmona, Alonso *ApCAB*
Carmona, Antonio Oscar DeFragoso d1951 *WhAm 3*
Carnaham, Herschel L 1879-1941 *WhAm 1*
Carnahan, Albert Sidney Johnson 1897-1968 *BiDrAC, WhAm 5*
Carnahan, Charles *NewYHSD*
Carnahan, David Hobart 1874- *WhAm 5*
Carnahan, George Holmes 1879-1941 *WhAm 1*
Carnahan, James 1775-1859 *ApCAB, DcAmB, Drake, NatCAB 5, TwCBDA, WhAm H*
Carnahan, James Richards 1840-1905 *WhAm 1*
Carnahan, Paul Harvey 1904-1965 *WhAm 4*
Carnahan, Robert Brown, Jr. 1871-1918 *NatCAB 17*
Carnahan, Wendell 1903-1961 *WhAm 4*
Carnahan, William Lane 1837-1897 *NatCAB 32*
Carnal, James Edward 1870-1926 *NatCAB 21*
Carnall, Rudolf Von 1804-1874 *DcScB*
Carnap, Rudolf 1891-1970 *McGEWB, WebAB, WhAm 5*
Carneades 213?BC-128?BC *McGEWB*
Carneal, William Leigh 1881-1958 *NatCAB 46*
Carnegie, Andrew 1835-1919 *AmBi, ApCAB, ApCAB X, DcAmB, DcAmLiB, EncAB, McGEWB, TwCBDA, WebAB, WhAm 1, WhAmP*
Carnegie, Andrew 1837-1919 *NatCAB 9*
Carnegie, Dale 1888-1955 *DcAmB S5, WebAB, WhAm 3*
Carnegie, Hattie 1889-1956 *WhAm 3*
Carnegie, Louise Whitfield 1857-1946 *NotAW, WhAm 2*
Carnegie, T Morris 1874-1944 *WhAm 5*
Carnegie, T Morrison 1874-1944 *NatCAB 41*
Carnegie, Thomas M 1843-1886 *ApCAB*
Carnell, Edward John 1919-1967 *WhAm 4*
Carnell, Laura Horner 1867-1929 *BiCAW, WhAm 1, WomWWA 14*
Carnes, Cecil 1909-1953 *WhAm 3*
Carnes, Edwin Hammond 1897-1959 *NatCAB 48*
Carnes, James *NewYHSD*
Carnes, Samuel Tate 1850- *NatCAB 8*
Carnes, Thomas Petters 1762-1822 *BiAUS, BiDrAC, Drake, WhAm H*
Carnett, John Berton 1876-1934 *NatCAB 26*
Carney, Claude Silas 1875-1940 *NatCAB 30*
Carney, Francis Joseph 1876-1939 *NatCAB 33, WhAm 1*
Carney, Frank 1868-1934 *WhAm 1*
Carney, Harry Howell 1910-1974 *WhAm 6*
Carney, James Lorring 1847- *WhAm 4*
Carney, Joseph Charles 1913- *BiDrAC*
Carney, Joseph Patrick 1876-1971 *NatCAB 56*
Carney, Leonard T d1964 *WhAm 4*
Carney, Robert Bostwick 1895- *WebAMB*
Carney, Thomas d1888 *BiAUS*
Carney, Thomas 1824-1888 *DcAmB*
Carney, Thomas 1827-1888 *NatCAB 8, WhAm H*
Carney, Thomas J 1886-1942 *WhAm 2*
Carney, William Roy 1889-1973 *WhAm 5*
Carnochan, Janet 1839- *WomWWA 14*
Carnochan, John Murray 1817-1887 *ApCAB, ApCAB X, DcAmB, Drake, NatCAB 9, TwCBDA*
Carnochran, John Murray 1817-1887 *WhAm H*
Carnot, Lazare Nicolas Marguerite 1753-1823 *DcScB, McGEWB, WhoMilH*
Carnot, Nicolas Leonard Sadi 1796-1832 *AsBiEn, DcScB, McGEWB*
Carnovsky, Leon 1903-1975 *DcAmLiB*
Carnwath, Robert, Jr. 1906-1973 *NatCAB 57*
Caro, Anthony 1924- *McGEWB*

Caro, Heinrich 1834-1910 *DcScB*
Caro, Joseph BenEphraim 1488-1575 *McGEWB*
Caro, Marcus Rayner 1903-1962 *WhAm 4*
Caro, Miguel Antonio 1843- *ApCAB*
Carochi, Horacio 1586-1666 *ApCAB Sup*
Carol II, King Of Rumania 1893-1957 *WhWW-II*
Carol, Kate *WhAm H*
Carollo, John Andrew 1906-1971 *NatCAB 56*
Caron, Adolphe 1843- *ApCAB*
Caron, Nettie Clark 1864- *WomWWA 14*
Caron, Rene Edward 1800-1876 *ApCAB*
Carondelet, Francisco L Hector, Baron De 1748?-1807 *DcAmB, WhAm H, WhAmP*
Carothers, Wallace Hume 1896-1937 *AsBiEn, DcAmB S2, DcScB, EncAB, McGEWB, NatCAB 38, WebAB, WhAm 1*
Carow, Isaac 1778-1850 *NatCAB 1*
Carp, Robert *NewYHSD*
Carpeaux, Charles *NewYHSD*
Carpeaux, Jean Baptiste 1827-1875 *McGEWB*
Carpender, Arthur S 1884-1960 *WhAm 3*
Carpender, Edward William 1797-1877 *ApCAB*
Carpenter, A *NewYHSD*
Carpenter, Aaron Everly 1883-1969 *WhAm 5*
Carpenter, Alfred George 1849-1918 *NatCAB 17*
Carpenter, Alfred Saint Vrain 1881- *WhAm 6*
Carpenter, Alice Caroline 1875- *BiCAW, WomWWA 14*
Carpenter, Alice Dimmick *AmWom*
Carpenter, Allen Fuller 1880-1949 *WhAm 2*
Carpenter, Allen Harmon 1876- *WhAm 5*
Carpenter, Alonzo Philetus 1829-1898 *NatCAB 12*
Carpenter, Alva Edwin 1855-1931 *WhAm 1*
Carpenter, Aretas Blood 1875-1965 *NatCAB 51*
Carpenter, Arthur 1920- *BnEnAmA*
Carpenter, Arthur DeVere 1866-1958 *WhAm 3*
Carpenter, Arthur Howe 1877-1956 *WhAm 3*
Carpenter, B *NewYHSD*
Carpenter, B Platt 1837-1921 *WhAm 1*
Carpenter, Benjamin *NewYHSD*
Carpenter, Benjamin 1725-1804 *TwCBDA*
Carpenter, Benjamin 1726-1823 *ApCAB, Drake*
Carpenter, Benjamin 1865-1927 *WhAm 1*
Carpenter, Benjamin F *NewYHSD*
Carpenter, Charles Carroll 1834-1899 *ApCAB Sup, TwCBDA*
Carpenter, Charles Carroll 1836-1918 *WhAm 1*
Carpenter, Charles Colcock Jones 1899-1969 *WhAm 5*
Carpenter, Charles E 1863-1929 *WhAm 1*
Carpenter, Charles Ernest 1878-1948 *WhAm 2*
Carpenter, Charles Ketchum 1826-1884 *ApCAB*
Carpenter, Charles Lincoln 1867-1929 *WhAm 1*
Carpenter, Clara Cornell 1860- *WomWWA 14*
Carpenter, Clarence 1906-1968 *WhAm 5*
Carpenter, Clarence Ray 1905-1975 *WhAm 6*
Carpenter, Clinton E 1892-1948 *WhAm 2*
Carpenter, Cora 1858- *WomWWA 14*
Carpenter, Coy Cornelius 1900-1971 *WhAm 5*
Carpenter, Cyrus Clay 1829-1898 *BiAUS, BiDrAC, DcAmB, NatCAB 11, NatCAB 11, WhAm H, WhAmP*
Carpenter, Daniel 1815?-1866 *ApCAB*
Carpenter, Davis 1799-1878 *BiAUS, BiDrAC, WhAm H*
Carpenter, Decatur Merritt Hammond *WhAm H*
Carpenter, Delph E 1877-1951 *WhAm 3*
Carpenter, Dudley Newcomb 1874-1955 *NatCAB 47*
Carpenter, Earl 1931- *IIBEAAW*
Carpenter, Edmund Janes 1845-1924 *DcAmB, NatCAB 19, WhAm 1*
Carpenter, Edmund Nelson 1865-1952 *BiDrAC*
Carpenter, Edward Childs 1872- *WhAm 5*
Carpenter, Edwin Fisher 1850-1927 *NatCAB 21*
Carpenter, Elbert Lawrence 1862-1945 *WhAm 2*
Carpenter, Elisha 1824-1897 *NatCAB 5*
Carpenter, Ellen M 1830- *ApCAB*
Carpenter, Ellen Maria 1836-1909? *AmWom, IIBEAAW, NewYHSD, TwCBDA, WhAm 4*
Carpenter, Emlen Newbold 1845-1891 *NatCAB 17*

Carpenter, Ernest Willoughby 1874-1942 *NatCAB 33*
Carpenter, Esther Bernon 1848- *NatCAB 2*
Carpenter, Eugene R 1873-1934 *WhAm 1*
Carpenter, Fanny Hallock *NatCAB 14, WhAm 5, WomWWA 14*
Carpenter, Florence Welles 1867- *WomWWA 14*
Carpenter, Ford Ashman 1868-1947 *ApCAB X, WhAm 2*
Carpenter, Francis Bicknell 1830-1900 *AmBi, ApCAB, DcAmB, Drake, NatCAB 11, NewYHSD, WhAm 1*
Carpenter, Francis Bicknell 1830-1901 *TwCBDA*
Carpenter, Francis Wood 1831-1922 *NatCAB 3, NatCAB 41*
Carpenter, Frank George 1855-1924 *DcAmB, TwCBDA, WhAm 1*
Carpenter, Frank Moody 1875-1947 *NatCAB 38*
Carpenter, Frank Oliver 1858- *WhAm 4*
Carpenter, Frank Pierce 1845-1938 *NatCAB 28, WhAm 1, WhAm 1C*
Carpenter, Frank Watson 1871- *WhAm 5*
Carpenter, Franklin Reuben 1848-1910 *DcAmB, WhAm 4*
Carpenter, Fred Green 1882-1965 *WhAm 4*
Carpenter, Fred Warner 1873- *WhAm 5*
Carpenter, Frederic Ives 1861-1925 *NatCAB 21, WhAm 1*
Carpenter, Frederic Walton 1876-1925 *NatCAB 20, WhAm 1*
Carpenter, Frederick Herbert 1876-1930 *NatCAB 51*
Carpenter, Frederick Wisner 1859-1939 *NatCAB 30*
Carpenter, George Albert 1867-1944 *NatCAB 43, WhAm 2*
Carpenter, George Ansel 1864-1927 *NatCAB 22*
Carpenter, George Moulton 1844-1896 *TwCBDA*
Carpenter, George O 1827-1896 *TwCBDA*
Carpenter, George Oliver 1852-1939 *WhAm 1*
Carpenter, George Rice 1863-1909 *BiDAmEd, DcAmB, NatCAB 23, WhAm 1*
Carpenter, George Thomas 1834-1893 *NatCAB 26, TwCBDA*
Carpenter, George Washington 1802-1860 *ApCAB, Drake, NatCAB 10, TwCBDA*
Carpenter, Gilbert Saltonstall 1836-1904 *TwCBDA, WhAm 1*
Carpenter, Grace Eleanor White *WomWWA 14*
Carpenter, H Beach 1892-1955 *WhAm 3*
Carpenter, Hannah Thayer *WomWWA 14*
Carpenter, Harlean 1911-1937 *WebAB*
Carpenter, Harry Melvin 1878-1929 *NatCAB 25*
Carpenter, Henry Alden 1867-1922 *NatCAB 19*
Carpenter, Henry Cort Harold 1875-1940 *DcScB*
Carpenter, Henry Otis 1852-1936 *NatCAB 42*
Carpenter, Homer Wilson 1880- *WhAm 6*
Carpenter, Horace Francis 1842-1937 *WhAm 1*
Carpenter, Hubert Vinton 1875-1941 *WhAm 2*
Carpenter, Imogene Hand 1867- *WomWWA 14*
Carpenter, J Henry 1893-1954 *NatCAB 46, WhAm 3*
Carpenter, J W *NewYHSD*
Carpenter, James D 1885-1972 *WhAm 5*
Carpenter, James Edward 1841- *ApCAB Sup*
Carpenter, James Edwin Ruthven 1867-1932 *NatCAB 24*
Carpenter, James W 1880-1961 *WhAm 4*
Carpenter, James W 1892-1965 *WhAm 4*
Carpenter, John Alden 1876-1951 *ApCAB X, DcAmB S5, NatCAB 40, WhAm 3*
Carpenter, John Slaughter 1860-1929 *WhAm 1*
Carpenter, John Thomas 1833- *ApCAB Sup*
Carpenter, John William 1881-1959 *NatCAB 48, WhAm 6*
Carpenter, Julia Wiltberger d1915 *WhAm 1, WomWWA 14*
Carpenter, Leslie E 1922-1974 *WhAm 6*
Carpenter, Levi D 1802-1856 *BiAUS, BiDrAC, WhAm H*
Carpenter, Lewis Cass 1836-1908 *BiAUS, BiDrAC*
Carpenter, Louis George 1861-1935 *ApCAB,*

Carpenter, *ApCAB X, NatCAB 14, TwCBDA, WhAm 1*
Carpenter, Louis Henry 1839-1916 *ApCAB Sup, WhAm 1*
Carpenter, Lucy A Boone 1852- *WomWWA 14*
Carpenter, Mary Frances *WomWWA 14*
Carpenter, Mary Noel 1874- *WomWWA 14*
Carpenter, Matthew Hale 1824-1881 *ApCAB, BiAUS, BiDrAC, DcAmB, NatCAB 4, TwCBDA, WhAm H, WhAmP*
Carpenter, Minnie Chamberlain 1869- *WomWWA 14*
Carpenter, Miriam Feronia 1881- *WhAm 6*
Carpenter, Myron Jay 1850- *WhAm 4*
Carpenter, Newel Underwood 1869-1957 *NatCAB 46*
Carpenter, Newton Henry 1853-1918 *WhAm 1*
Carpenter, Paul Chambers 1893-1952 *NatCAB 40*
Carpenter, Philip 1856- *NatCAB 12*
Carpenter, Philip Pearsall 1819-1877 *ApCAB*
Carpenter, R C 1852-1919 *NatCAB 4*
Carpenter, R R *NewYHSD*
Carpenter, Ralph Emerson 1882-1967 *WhAm 4*
Carpenter, Randolph 1894-1956 *NatCAB 47*
Carpenter, Ray Wilford 1894-1962 *WhAm 4*
Carpenter, Raymond VanArsdale 1875-1947 *NatCAB 37*
Carpenter, Reid 1853- *WhAm 1*
Carpenter, Reuben 1827?- *NewYHSD*
Carpenter, Robert Ruliph Morgan 1877-1949 *NatCAB 41, WhAm 2*
Carpenter, Robert Wilfred 1909-1970 *WhAm 5*
Carpenter, Rolla Clarton 1852-1919 *ApCAB*
Carpenter, Rolla Clinton 1852-1919 *TwCBDA, WhAm 1*
Carpenter, Samuel 1649-1714 *ApCAB Sup*
Carpenter, Samuel Barstow 1851-1912 *NatCAB 16*
Carpenter, Samuel H 1798?- *NewYHSD, WhAm H*
Carpenter, Samuel H, Jr. 1832?- *NewYHSD*
Carpenter, Stephen Cullen d1820 *DcAmB, Drake, WhAm H*
Carpenter, Stephen Cutter d1820? *ApCAB*
Carpenter, Stephen Haskins 1831-1878 *ApCAB, DcAmB, NatCAB 22, TwCBDA, WhAm H*
Carpenter, Terry McGovern 1900- *BiDrAC*
Carpenter, Thomas Preston 1804-1876 *ApCAB Sup*
Carpenter, W T Coleman 1872- *WhAm 6*
Carpenter, Walter Samuel, Jr. 1888-1976 *WhAm 6*
Carpenter, William Benjamin 1813-1885 *DcScB*
Carpenter, William E 1857-1937 *WhAm 1*
Carpenter, William H 1878-1965 *WhAm 4*
Carpenter, William Henry 1814- *NatCAB 11*
Carpenter, William Henry 1842-1923 *NatCAB 6*
Carpenter, William Henry 1853-1936 *NatCAB 8, WhAm 1*
Carpenter, William Howard 1871-1946 *NatCAB 34*
Carpenter, William Leland 1854-1936 *NatCAB 14, NatCAB 27, WhAm 1*
Carpenter, William Lewis 1844-1898 *ApCAB, TwCBDA*
Carpenter, William Randolph 1894-1956 *BiDrAC*
Carpenter, William Seal 1890-1957 *NatCAB 52, WhAm 3*
Carpenter, William Wallace Seymour 1868-1943 *NatCAB 32*
Carpenter, William Weston 1889-1968 *BiDAmEd, WhAm 5*
Carpentier, Charles Francis 1896-1964 *NatCAB 51, WhAm 4*
Carpi, Berengario Da *DcScB*
Carpio, Manuel 1791-1860 *ApCAB*
Carpmael, Charles 1846- *ApCAB*
Carr, Albert Zolotkoff 1902-1971 *WhAm 5*
Carr, Alexander 1880-1946 *WhAm 2*
Carr, Arthur Raymond 1893-1956 *NatCAB 44, WhAm 3*
Carr, Benjamin 1769-1831 *DcAmB, WhAm H*
Carr, Burt Wilbur 1875-1930 *NatCAB 22*
Carr, Caleb 1623-1695 *NatCAB 10, TwCBDA*

Carr, Camille Casatti Cadmus 1842-1914
  WhAm 1
Carr, Ceylon Spencer 1850- *WhAm 1*
Carr, Charles Carl 1884-1952 *NatCAB 42*
Carr, Charles Lancaster 1876-1951 *NatCAB 40*
Carr, Charlotte 1890-1957 *WhAm 3*
Carr, Clarence Alfred 1856-1930 *WhAm 1*
Carr, Clark Ezra 1836-1919 *NatCAB 12,*
  WhAm 1
Carr, Clifford Cheetham 1898-1960
  NatCAB 48
Carr, Clyde Mitchell 1869-1923 *WhAm 1*
Carr, Dabney d1773 *Drake*
Carr, Dabney 1743-1773 *TwCBDA*
Carr, Dabney 1744-1773 *ApCAB*
Carr, Dabney 1773-1837 *ApCAB, DcAmB,*
  TwCBDA, WhAm H
Carr, Dabney Smith d1854 *BiAUS, Drake*
Carr, Dabney Smith 1802-1854 *DcAmB,*
  NatCAB 11, TwCBDA, WhAm H
Carr, Dabney Smith 1803-1854 *ApCAB*
Carr, Earl Ingram 1886-1971 *NatCAB 57*
Carr, Edith Adele 1876-1965 *NatCAB 51*
Carr, Edson Worth 1892-1963 *NatCAB 50*
Carr, Elias 1839-1900 *DcAmB, NatCAB 4,*
  TwCBDA, WhAm 1, WhAmP
Carr, Emily 1871-1945 *McGEWB*
Carr, Emma Perry 1880-1972 *WhAm 5*
Carr, Ernest Leighton 1874-1914 *NatCAB 16*
Carr, Eugene Asa 1830-1910 *AmBi, ApCAB,*
  DcAmB, Drake, NatCAB 12, TwCBDA,
  WebAMB, WhAm 1
Carr, Ezra Slocum 1819- *ApCAB Sup*
Carr, Floyd LeVerne 1880-1948 *WhAm 2*
Carr, Francis 1751-1821 *BiAUS, BiDrAC,*
  WhAm H
Carr, Gene 1881-1959 *NatCAB 43, WhAm 3*
Carr, George H 1852-1918 *WhAm 1*
Carr, George Russell 1877-1965 *NatCAB 51*
Carr, George Wallace 1879-1958 *WhAm 3*
Carr, George Washington 1872-1942
  NatCAB 50
Carr, Harry 1877-1936 *WhAm 1*
Carr, Harry C 1886-1955 *WhAm 3*
Carr, Harvey 1873-1954 *WhAm 3*
Carr, Henrietta A 1868- *WomWWA 14*
Carr, Henry James 1849-1929 *DcAmLiB,*
  NatCAB 12, WhAm 1
Carr, Herbert Wildon 1857-1931 *DcScB,*
  WhAm 1
Carr, Imogen Mathewson *WomWWA 14*
Carr, Irving J 1875- *WhAm 5*
Carr, Jack Crouch 1893-1950 *NatCAB 38*
Carr, James 1777-1818 *BiAUS, BiDrAC,*
  WhAm H
Carr, James 1825-1891 *NatCAB 35*
Carr, James Angus 1867-1943 *NatCAB 35*
Carr, James O 1872-1949 *WhAm 3*
Carr, James Ozborn 1869-1949 *NatCAB 37,*
  WhAm 2
Carr, John d1837 *NewYHSD*
Carr, John 1793-1845 *BiAUS, BiDrAC,*
  WhAm H
Carr, John 1828-1913 *NatCAB 16*
Carr, John Foster 1869-1939 *WhAm 1*
Carr, John Gillian 1904-1967 *NatCAB 55*
Carr, John Wesley 1859-1960 *WhAm 3*
Carr, Joseph B 1824?-1895 *Drake*
Carr, Joseph Bradford 1828-1895 *ApCAB,*
  DcAmB, NatCAB 4, TwCBDA,
  WhAm H
Carr, Julian Shakespeare 1845-1924 *NatCAB 1,*
  NatCAB 17, WhAm 1
Carr, Julian Shakespeare 1878-1922
  NatCAB 40
Carr, Laura Whipple 1870- *WomWWA 14*
Carr, Lawrence 1917-1969 *WhAm 5*
Carr, Leland Walker 1883-1969 *NatCAB 54,*
  WhAm 5
Carr, Leo 1893-1970 *NatCAB 55*
Carr, Lewis E 1842-1929 *WhAm 1*
Carr, Lucien 1829-1915 *WhAm 1*
Carr, M Emily 1871-1945 *IIBEAAW*
Carr, Matthew 1750-1820 *DcAmB*
Carr, Matthew Lee 1892-1946 *NatCAB 36*
Carr, Nathan Tracy 1833-1885 *BiDrAC,*
  WhAm H
Carr, Ossian Elmer 1876- *WhAm 5*

Carr, Peter Petersen 1890-1966 *NatCAB 52*
Carr, Ralph L 1887-1950 *WhAm 3*
Carr, Reid Langdon 1880-1948 *WhAm 2*
Carr, Richard 1801?- *NewYHSD*
Carr, Sir Robert d1667 *ApCAB, Drake,*
  NatCAB 9
Carr, Robert Franklin 1871-1945 *NatCAB 18,*
  NatCAB 34, WhAm 2
Carr, Robert Manning 1907-1968 *NatCAB 54*
Carr, S Fay 1878-1937 *NatCAB 31*
Carr, Samuel 1771-1855 *ApCAB, ApCAB X,*
  TwCBDA
Carr, Samuel 1848-1922 *WhAm 1*
Carr, Sarah Pratt 1850- *WhAm 4,*
  WomWWA 14
Carr, Sterling Douglas 1876- *WhAm 5*
Carr, Sylvester Helicus 1850-1920 *ApCAB X*
Carr, Thomas Matthew 1750-1820 *DcAmB,*
  WhAm H
Carr, Trem 1891-1946 *NatCAB 36*
Carr, Walter Lester 1859- *WhAm 4*
Carr, Walter Scott d1960 *WhAm 4*
Carr, Wilbert Lester 1875- *WhAm 5*
Carr, Wilbur John 1870-1942 *DcAmB S3,*
  NatCAB 32, WhAm 2
Carr, William 1772?- *NewYHSD*
Carr, William 1823?- *NewYHSD*
Carr, William Finley 1848-1909 *NatCAB 24*
Carr, William George 1901- *BiDAmEd*
Carr, William Jarvis 1879- *WhAm 6*
Carr, William John 1862-1917 *WhAm 1*
Carr, William Kearny 1860-1915 *NatCAB 16,*
  WhAm 1
Carr, William Phillips 1858- *WhAm 4*
Carr, Wooda Nicholas 1871-1953 *BiDrAC,*
  WhAm 3
Carr-Saunders, Sir Alexander Morris 1886-1966
  McGEWB
Carracci, Agostino 1557-1602 *McGEWB*
Carracci, Annibale 1560-1609 *McGEWB*
Carracci, Ludovico 1555-1619 *McGEWB*
Carracross, Miss *NewYHSD*
Carrall, Robert William Weir 1839- *ApCAB*
Carranza, Diego 1569-1603 *ApCAB Sup*
Carranza, Jeronimo De 1535?-1600?
  ApCAB Sup
Carranza, Venustiano 1859-1920 *McGEWB*
Carratala, Jose d1845? *ApCAB*
Carre, Henry Beach 1871-1928 *WhAm 1*
Carre, Jean Marie 1887-1958 *WhAm 3*
Carre, Mathilde 1910- *WhWW-II*
Carreiro, Francis Joseph 1903-1967 *NatCAB 53*
Carrel, Alexis 1873-1944 *ApCAB X, AsBiEn,*
  DcAmB S3, DcScB, McGEWB,
  NatCAB 15, WhAm 2
Carrell, Columba 1810-1878 *ApCAB*
Carrell, George Aloysius 1803-1868 *ApCAB,*
  Drake, NatCAB 12, TwCBDA, WhAm H
Carrell, Horace Greeley 1873-1928 *NatCAB 21*
Carrell, Theodora M 1869- *WomWWA 14*
Carrell, William Beall 1883-1944 *WhAm 2*
Carreno, Teresa 1853-1917 *ApCAB X,*
  NotAW
Carrera, Jose Miguel 1782-1815 *ApCAB*
Carrera, Jose Miguel 1785-1821 *Drake,*
  McGEWB
Carrera, Jose Rafael 1814-1865 *McGEWB*
Carrera, Juan Jose d1817 *Drake*
Carrera, Louis d1817 *Drake*
Carrera, Martinez d1871 *Drake*
Carrera, Rafael 1814-1865 *ApCAB, Drake*
Carrere, John Merven 1858-1911 *AmBi,*
  ApCAB Sup, ApCAB X, BnEnAmA,
  DcAmB, NatCAB 11, WhAm 1
Carrere And Hastings *BnEnAmA*
Carrick, Alice VanLeer 1875- *WhAm 5*
Carrick, Carey Walton 1893-1966 *NatCAB 52*
Carrick, Lynn 1899-1965 *WhAm 4*
Carrick, Manton Marble 1879-1932 *WhAm 1*
Carrick, Samuel 1760-1809 *BiDAmEd,*
  DcAmB, WhAm H
Carrick, Samuel 1762-1809 *TwCBDA*
Carrico, Joseph Leonard 1881-1944 *WhAm 2*
Carriel, Mary Turner 1865- *WomWWA 14*
Carrier, Augustus Stiles 1857-1923 *WhAm 1*
Carrier, Chester Otto 1897- *BiDrAC*
Carrier, Lyman 1877-1963 *EncAAH*
Carrier, Thomas 1626-1735 *ApCAB, Drake*

Carrier, Wilbur Oscar 1860-1939 *WhAm 1*
Carrier, Willis Haviland 1876-1950 *DcAmB S4,*
  WhAm 3
Carriere, Leopold *NewYHSD*
Carrigain, Philip 1746-1806 *ApCAB*
Carrigain, Philip 1772-1842 *ApCAB, Drake*
Carrigan, Charles A 1872-1928 *ApCAB X*
Carrigan, Clarence 1880-1929 *WhAm 1*
Carrigan, Edward 1892-1944 *WhAm 2*
Carrigan, William L 1868-1939 *WhAm 1*
Carrigg, Joseph Leonard 1901- *BiDrAC*
Carrillo, Braulio 1800-1845 *ApCAB*
Carrillo, Edward John 1876-1964 *NatCAB 50*
Carrington, Abbie 1856- *AmWom*
Carrington, Alexander Berkeley 1862-1936
  NatCAB 38
Carrington, Alexander Berkeley, Jr. 1895-1974
  WhAm 6
Carrington, Anne Seddon 1842- *WomWWA 14*
Carrington, Edward 1748-1810 *BiDrAC,*
  TwCBDA, WhAm H, WhAmP
Carrington, Edward 1749-1810 *ApCAB,*
  BiAUS, NatCAB 5
Carrington, Edward Codrington 1872-1938
  WhAm 1
Carrington, Elaine d1958 *WhAm 3*
Carrington, Ellsworth Torrey 1875-1931
  NatCAB 24
Carrington, FitzRoy 1869-1954 *WhAm 3*
Carrington, Frances Courtney 1845-1911
  WhAm 1
Carrington, Francis Louis 1880- *WhAm 6*
Carrington, George Dart 1888-1945 *NatCAB 34*
Carrington, Gordon DeLaunay 1894-1944
  NatCAB 33, WhAm 2
Carrington, Henry Beebee 1824-1912 *AmBi,*
  ApCAB, DcAmB, NatCAB 22, REnAW,
  TwCBDA, WebAMB, WhAm 1
Carrington, Hereward 1880- *WhAm 6*
Carrington, James Beebee 1860-1929
  NatCAB 23, WhAm 1
Carrington, Paul 1733-1818 *ApCAB, BiAUS,*
  DcAmB, Drake, NatCAB 5, TwCBDA,
  WhAm H
Carrington, Paul 1764-1816 *ApCAB, TwCBDA*
Carrington, Richard Adams, Jr. 1889-1960
  WhAm 3A
Carrington, Richard Christopher 1826-1875
  AsBiEn, DcScB
Carrington, William J 1884-1947 *WhAm 2*
Carrington, William Thomas 1854-1937
  BiDAmEd, WhAm 1
Carris, Lewis Herbert 1869-1950 *NatCAB 38,*
  WhAm 3
Carrithers, Howard 1899-1963 *WhAm 4*
Carroll, Alfred Ludlow 1833- *NatCAB 3*
Carroll, Anna Ella 1815-1893 *NotAW*
Carroll, Anna Ella 1815-1894 *AmWom,*
  ApCAB Sup, NatCAB 5, TwCBDA,
  WhAm H
Carroll, Arthur Bertram 1893-1971 *NatCAB 57*
Carroll, Augustus John 1907-1968 *WhAm 5*
Carroll, B Harvey 1874-1922 *WhAm 1*
Carroll, Bartholomew Rivers 1800?-
  NatCAB 18
Carroll, Ben d1945 *WhAm 2*
Carroll, Benajah Harvey 1843-1914 *WhAm 1*
Carroll, Beryl Franklin 1860-1939 *NatCAB 34,*
  WhAm 1
Carroll, Caroline Moncure Benedict *BiCAW,*
  WhAm 5, WomWWA 14
Carroll, Charles *ApCAB*
Carroll, Charles 1660-1720 *NatCAB 2*
Carroll, Charles 1703-1783 *WhAm H*
Carroll, Charles 1723-1783 *BiDrAC,*
  NatCAB 11, WhAm H
Carroll, Charles 1737-1832 *AmBi, ApCAB,*
  BiAUS, BiDrAC, DcAmB, Drake,
  NatCAB 7, TwCBDA, WebAB,
  WhAm H, WhAmP
Carroll, Charles 1832-1889 *NatCAB 8*
Carroll, Charles Antoninus 1887-1954
  NatCAB 41
Carroll, Charles Chauncey 1876-1936 *WhAm 1*
Carroll, Charles Eden 1877-1946 *WhAm 2*
Carroll, Charles Hobart 1794-1865 *BiAUS,*
  BiDrAC, WhAm H
Carroll, Charles Joseph 1877-1941 *NatCAB 31*

Carroll, Daniel d1849 *Drake*
Carroll, Daniel 1730-1796 *BiDrAC, DcAmB, WhAm H, WhAmP*
Carroll, Daniel 1756-1829 *ApCAB, BiAUS, NatCAB 2, TwCBDA*
Carroll, Daniel Lynn 1797-1851 *Drake*
Carroll, David Lynn 1787-1851 *NatCAB 2*
Carroll, David Williamson 1816-1905 *BiDConf, NatCAB 5*
Carroll, Dudley DeWitt 1885-1971 *WhAm 5*
Carroll, Earl 1893-1948 *DcAmB S4, WhAm 2*
Carroll, Edward Ambrose 1888-1946 *WhAm 2*
Carroll, Elbert Henry 1867-1947 *NatCAB 36*
Carroll, Elizabeth Delia Dixon 1872- *WomWWA 14*
Carroll, Elizabeth M 1868- *WomWWA 14*
Carroll, Francis Patrick 1890-1967 *WhAm 4*
Carroll, Francis X d1971 *WhAm 5*
Carroll, Frank Victor 1887-1951 *NatCAB 42*
Carroll, Frederick Aloysius 1887-1945 *NatCAB 34, WhAm 2*
Carroll, George Martin 1881-1956 *NatCAB 43*
Carroll, George W 1855- *WhAm 4*
Carroll, Henry 1838-1908 *WhAm 1*
Carroll, Henry King 1848-1931 *WhAm 1*
Carroll, Horace Bailey 1903-1966 *WhAm 4, WhAm 5*
Carroll, Howard 1854-1916 *ApCAB X, DcAmB, NatCAB 3, WhAm 1*
Carroll, Howard Bertram 1898-1963 *NatCAB 49*
Carroll, Howard Joseph 1902-1960 *WhAm 3A*
Carroll, Isaac Squire 1879-1955 *NatCAB 45*
Carroll, J R *NewYHSD*
Carroll, James 1791-1873 *BiAUS, BiDrAC, WhAm H*
Carroll, James 1854-1907 *AmBi, DcAmB, DcScB, WhAm 1*
Carroll, James Bernard 1856-1932 *NatCAB 23, WhAm 1*
Carroll, James E 1878- *WhAm 6*
Carroll, James F 1890-1957 *WhAm 3*
Carroll, James John 1892-1949 *NatCAB 39*
Carroll, James Jordan d1913 *WhAm 1*
Carroll, James Milton 1852-1931 *WhAm 1*
Carroll, Jane Wall 1848-1927 *NatCAB 21*
Carroll, John *NewYHSD*
Carroll, John 1735-1815 *AmBi, DcAmB, DcAmReB, Drake, McGEWB, NatCAB 1, TwCBDA, WebAB, WhAm H*
Carroll, John 1735-1817 *ApCAB*
Carroll, John 1892-1959 *WhAm 3*
Carroll, John Albert 1901- *BiDrAC, WhAmP*
Carroll, John Alexander 1875-1944 *NatCAB 41*
Carroll, John Charles *NewYHSD*
Carroll, John D 1854-1927 *NatCAB 24, WhAm 1*
Carroll, John E 1912-1974 *WhAm 6*
Carroll, John F d1911 *WhAm 1*
Carroll, John Francis 1858-1917 *NatCAB 18, WhAm 1*
Carroll, John Haydock 1857-1931 *WhAm 1*
Carroll, John Joseph 1856- *NatCAB 7, WhAm 1*
Carroll, John Lee 1830-1911 *ApCAB, BiAUS, DcAmB, NatCAB 9, NatCAB 36, TwCBDA, WhAm 1*
Carroll, John M 1825- *BiAUS*
Carroll, John Michael 1823-1901 *BiDrAC*
Carroll, John Patrick 1864-1925 *NatCAB 15, WhAm 1*
Carroll, John Wesley 1832-1898 *NatCAB 10*
Carroll, Joseph Francis 1892-1955 *WhAm 3*
Carroll, Leo G 1892-1972 *WhAm 5*
Carroll, Lewis 1832-1898 *McGEWB*
Carroll, Louis Francis 1905-1971 *WhAm 5*
Carroll, Lydia Fritchie 1870- *WomWWA 14*
Carroll, Mary Dutcher 1882- *WomWWA 14*
Carroll, Mitchell 1870-1925 *NatCAB 24, WhAm 1*
Carroll, Monroe Spurgeon 1898-1968 *WhAm 5*
Carroll, Patrick John 1861-1916 *NatCAB 16*
Carroll, Paul E 1925-1972 *WhAm 6*
Carroll, Paul Thomas 1910-1954 *WhAm 3*
Carroll, Paul Vincent 1900-1968 *WhAm 5*
Carroll, Phil 1895-1971 *NatCAB 56, WhAm 5*
Carroll, Philip Acosta 1879-1957 *NatCAB 49, WhAm 3*

Carroll, R Emmett 1894-1947 *NatCAB 36*
Carroll, Raymond G d1943 *WhAm 2C*
Carroll, Raymond G d1945 *WhAm 2*
Carroll, Richard Augustine 1898-1959 *WhAm 3*
Carroll, Robert J 1913-1967 *NatCAB 53*
Carroll, Robert Paris 1886-1954 *WhAm 3*
Carroll, Robert Sproul 1869-1949 *WhAm 2C, WhAm 3*
Carroll, Samuel Sprigg 1832-1893 *ApCAB, DcAmB, Drake, NatCAB 5, TwCBDA, WhAm H*
Carroll, T K 1792-1873 *BiAUS*
Carroll, Thomas Benjamin 1873-1940 *NatCAB 35*
Carroll, Thomas Claude 1894-1960 *WhAm 4*
Carroll, Thomas Francis 1854- *NatCAB 11, WhAm 1*
Carroll, Thomas Henry, II 1914-1964 *WhAm 4*
Carroll, Thomas Joseph 1898-1971 *NatCAB 57*
Carroll, Thomas King 1792-1873 *NatCAB 9*
Carroll, Thomas Patrick 1922-1964 *WhAm 4*
Carroll, William 1788-1844 *ApCAB, BiAUS, DcAmB, Drake, NatCAB 7, TwCBDA, WhAm H*
Carroll, William H 1820?- *ApCAB*
Carroll, William Henry 1843-1916 *WhAm 1*
Carroll, William Simpson 1838-1911 *NatCAB 15*
Carroll, William Thomas d1863 *ApCAB*
Carroon, Frank 1869- *WhAm 5*
Carrothers, George Ezra 1880-1966 *WhAm 4*
Carrow, Fleming 1885- *WhAm 4*
Carrow, Howard 1860-1922 *NatCAB 30*
Carrow, Howard 1861- *NatCAB 4*
Carruth, Arthur Jay, Jr. 1887-1962 *WhAm 4*
Carruth, Charles Theodore 1851-1926 *WhAm 1*
Carruth, Fred Hayden 1862-1932 *DcAmB S1, WhAm 1*
Carruth, James Harrison 1807-1896 *ApCAB, TwCBDA*
Carruth, Louis 1850-1936 *WhAm 1*
Carruth, William Herbert 1859-1924 *NatCAB 14, WhAm 1*
Carruthers, John Alexander 1884-1951 *NatCAB 41*
Carruthers, John Franklin Bruce 1889-1960 *WhAm 3*
Carruthers, Thomas Neely 1900-1960 *WhAm 4*
Carruthers, William A 1800?-1850? *ApCAB, Drake, TwCBDA*
Carry, Charles Albert 1883-1949 *NatCAB 38*
Carry, Edward Francis 1867-1929 *NatCAB 35, WhAm 1*
Carryl, Charles Edward 1841-1920 *WhAm 2*
Carryl, Guy Wetmore 1873-1904 *AmBi, DcAmB, NatCAB 13, WhAm 1*
Carse, Elizabeth 1875- *WhAm 5*
Carse, Henry Ranney 1866-1942 *NatCAB 31*
Carse, John Bradley 1864- *ApCAB X*
Carse, Matilda Bradley 1835-1917 *AmWom, NotAW, TwCBDA, WhAm 1, WomWWA 14*
Carskaddon, Benjamin W 1858-1913 *NatCAB 16*
Carson, Adam Clarke 1869-1941 *WhAm 1*
Carson, Ann *NewYHSD*
Carson, Anna Lea 1854- *WomWWA 14*
Carson, Arthur Claypoole 1860-1939 *NatCAB 31*
Carson, Bernard 1820?- *NewYHSD*
Carson, C W *NewYHSD*
Carson, Cale Wellman 1891-1973 *WhAm 6*
Carson, Charles Averette 1891-1952 *WhAm 3*
Carson, Charles Clifton 1870-1944 *WhAm 2*
Carson, Charles L 1847-1891 *WhAm H*
Carson, Christopher 1809-1868 *AmBi, ApCAB, DcAmB, Drake, EncAAH, McGEWB, NatCAB 3, TwCBDA, WhAm H*
Carson, Christopher *see also* Carson, Kit
Carson, Clifford 1876- *WhAm 5*
Carson, Delia E 1833- *AmWom*
Carson, Frank L 1890-1952 *WhAm 3*
Carson, George Prentice 1864- *WhAm 4*
Carson, Gerald 1899- *EncAAH*
Carson, Hampton Lawrence 1852-1929 *DcAmB S1, NatCAB 3, WhAm 1*
Carson, Harry Roberts 1869-1948 *WhAm 2*

Carson, Henderson Haverfield 1893-1971 *BiDrAC*
Carson, Howard Adams 1842-1931 *NatCAB 14, WhAm 1*
Carson, James 1772-1843 *BiHiMed*
Carson, James Carlton 1847- *WhAm 4*
Carson, James Milton 1887-1950 *NatCAB 41*
Carson, James Oliver 1855-1943 *WhAm 2*
Carson, James S 1874- *WhAm 5*
Carson, Jessie M 1876- *WhAm 5*
Carson, John A 1860-1916 *NatCAB 18*
Carson, John Avery Gere 1856- *NatCAB 17*
Carson, John Fleming 1860-1927 *WhAm 1*
Carson, John Hargadine 1911-1972 *WhAm 5*
Carson, John Miller 1838-1912 *WhAm 1*
Carson, John Miller 1864-1956 *WhAm 3*
Carson, John Renshaw 1886-1940 *DcAmB S2*
Carson, John Renshaw 1887-1940 *WhAm 1*
Carson, Joseph 1808-1876 *ApCAB Sup, DcAmB, WhAm H*
Carson, Joseph 1809-1877 *NatCAB 5*
Carson, Joseph Kirtley, Jr. 1891-1956 *WhAm 3*
Carson, Kit 1809-1868 *REnAW, WebAB, WebAMB*
Carson, Kit *see also* Carson, Christopher
Carson, Luella Clay 1856- *WhAm 3, WomWWA 14*
Carson, Luther Festus 1873-1962 *NatCAB 50*
Carson, Matthew Vaughan, Jr. 1910-1971 *WhAm 5*
Carson, Norma Bright 1883- *WomWWA 14*
Carson, Norman Bruce 1844-1931 *WhAm 1*
Carson, R H *NewYHSD*
Carson, Rachel Louise 1907-1964 *EncAAH, EncAB, McGEWB, NatCAB 51, WebAB, WhAm 4*
Carson, Robert 1906-1960 *WhAm 3*
Carson, Samuel Price 1798-1838 *BiDrAC, WhAm H, WhAmP*
Carson, Samuel Price 1798-1840 *BiAUS, NatCAB 7*
Carson, Simeon Lewis 1882-1954 *DcAmB S5*
Carson, Stella Blanche Marbury *WomWWA 14*
Carson, Waid Edwin 1876-1946 *NatCAB 35*
Carson, Walter Lapsley 1894-1959 *WhAm 4*
Carson, Mrs. William A *NewYHSD*
Carson, William E d1942 *WhAm 2*
Carson, William Henry 1859- *WhAm 4*
Carson, William Pierce 1894-1971 *WhAm 5*
Carson, William Waller 1845-1930 *NatCAB 52, WhAm 1*
Carss, William Leighton 1865-1931 *BiDrAC, WhAm 1, WhAmP*
Carstairs, Carroll 1888-1948 *NatCAB 36*
Carstairs, James, Jr. 1834-1893 *NatCAB 16*
Carstarphen, Frederick Charles 1881-1942 *WhAm 3*
Carstarphen, William Turner 1875-1947 *WhAm 2*
Carstens, Albert Martin 1867-1956 *NatCAB 45*
Carstens, Christian Carl 1865-1939 *WhAm 1*
Carstens, Henry Rohnert 1888-1973 *WhAm 6*
Carstens, J Henry 1848-1920 *NatCAB 16, NatCAB 35, WhAm 1*
Carstensen, Gustav Arnold 1851-1941 *WhAm 1*
Carstensen, John 1854-1921 *WhAm 1*
Carstensen, Mary Rutherford Thomas *WomWWA 14*
Carstensen, Vernon 1907- *EncAAH*
Carswell, Henry Jones 1885-1948 *NatCAB 37*
Carswell, William Brown 1883-1953 *NatCAB 42*
Carswell, William Ross 1883-1956 *NatCAB 45*
Cartan, Elie 1869-1951 *DcScB*
Cartel, John *NewYHSD*
Carter *NewYHSD*
Carter, A Dewey 1899-1965 *NatCAB 51*
Carter, A F 1883-1966 *WhAm 4*
Carter, Alan 1904-1975 *WhAm 6*
Carter, Albert Edward 1881-1964 *BiDrAC, WhAm 6*
Carter, Albert Paine 1873- *WhAm 5*
Carter, Alfred Wellington 1867-1949 *NatCAB 40*
Carter, Alice Crosby 1887- *WomWWA 14*
Carter, Alice Draper 1883-1970 *NatCAB 55*
Carter, Alva John 1882-1943 *NatCAB 31*
Carter, Amon Giles 1879-1955 *NatCAB 43,*

WhAm 3

Carter, Anna Alice Chapin 1880-
   WomWWA 14
Carter, Arabella 1867- *WomWWA 14*
Carter, Arthur Bynum 1877-1939 *NatCAB 33*
Carter, Arthur Hazelton 1884-1965 *NatCAB 51,*
   WhAm 4
Carter, Asher 1805-1877 *WhAm H*
Carter, Augustus Henry 1862-1928 *NatCAB 21*
Carter, Benjamin Estes 1894-1943 *WhAm 2*
Carter, Bernard 1834-1912 *NatCAB 28,*
   WhAm 1
Carter, Bernard Shirley 1893-1961 *WhAm 4*
Carter, Berte Dean 1881-1963 *NatCAB 54*
Carter, Boake 1898-1944 *DcAmB S3,*
   WhAm 2
Carter, C C 1899-1963 *WhAm 4*
Carter, Caroline Louise Dudley 1862-1937
   DcAmB S2, NotAW
Carter, Charles 1830?- *NewYHSD*
Carter, Charles Bernard 1905-1969 *NatCAB 56*
Carter, Charles Blanchard 1880-1927
   NatCAB 21
Carter, Charles David 1868-1929 *BiDrAC,*
   WhAm 1, WhAmP
Carter, Charles Francis 1856-1928 *WhAm 1*
Carter, Charles Frederick 1863-1939 *WhAm 1*
Carter, Charles Henry 1874-1954 *NatCAB 44*
Carter, Charles Ignatius Hardman 1803-1879
   ApCAB
Carter, Charles Milton 1853-1929 *IlBEAAW*
Carter, Charles P *NewYHSD*
Carter, Charles Shirley 1840-1922 *NatCAB 21*
Carter, Clarence Edwin 1881-1961 *REnAW,*
   WhAm 4
Carter, Clifton Carroll 1876-1950 *WhAm 3*
Carter, Creed Fulton, Jr. 1909-1975 *WhAm 6*
Carter, D M 1827- *ApCAB*
Carter, Dale 1901-1971 *NatCAB 56*
Carter, Dennis Malone 1818?-1881 *NewYHSD*
Carter, DeWitt 1892-1957 *WhAm 3*
Carter, E Kemper 1884-1951 *NatCAB 39*
Carter, Edna 1872-1963 *NatCAB 52,*
   WomWWA 14
Carter, Edward Albert 1881- *WhoColR*
Carter, Edward Carlos 1854-1930 *NatCAB 22,*
   WhAm 1
Carter, Edward Clark 1878-1954 *NatCAB 46,*
   WhAm 3
Carter, Edwin A 1863-1943 *WhAm 2*
Carter, Edwin Farnham 1877-1956 *WhAm 3*
Carter, Elias 1781-1864 *DcAmB, WhAm H*
Carter, Elliott Cook, Jr. 1908- *McGEWB*
Carter, Emma Smuller d1928 *WhAm 1*
Carter, Emmet Thoroughman 1894-1961
   WhAm 4
Carter, Ernest Trow 1866-1953 *NatCAB 42,*
   WhAm 3
Carter, Frances Henderson *WomWWA 14*
Carter, Francis Beauregard 1861-1937
   NatCAB 41, WhAm 1
Carter, Francis Graves 1912-1960 *WhAm 4*
Carter, Franklin 1837-1919 *ApCAB,*
   ApCAB X, DcAmB, NatCAB 6,
   TwCBDA, WhAm 1
Carter, Franklin N 1827?- *NewYHSD*
Carter, Fred Afton 1870-1948 *NatCAB 36,*
   WhAm 2
Carter, Fred G 1888-1956 *WhAm 3*
Carter, Fred Mason 1868- *WhAm 3*
Carter, Frederick Gay 1888-1956 *NatCAB 45*
Carter, Gale H 1865- *WhAm 3*
Carter, Gardner Lloyd 1890-1953 *NatCAB 42*
Carter, Gardner Lloyd 1890-1957 *WhAm 4*
Carter, Garnet 1883-1954 *NatCAB 52*
Carter, George *NewYHSD*
Carter, George 1865-1942 *NatCAB 34*
Carter, George 1865-1948 *WhAm 3*
Carter, George Calvin 1876- *WhAm 5*
Carter, George Henry 1874-1948 *WhAm 2*
Carter, George Milton 1894-1958 *WhAm 3*
Carter, George Robert 1866-1933 *NatCAB 35,*
   WhAm 1
Carter, George Washington 1879-1955
   NatCAB 42
Carter, George William 1867-1930 *WhAm 1*
Carter, Grace Arvilla Banks *WomWWA 14*
Carter, Hannah Johnson *AmWom*

Carter, Harley H *BiAUS*
Carter, Harold Samuel 1896-1965 *WhAm 4*
Carter, Harriet Wilson 1873- *WomWWA 14*
Carter, Henry *NewYHSD*
Carter, Henry 1821-1880 *WebAB*
Carter, Henry 1889-1952 *NatCAB 41*
Carter, Henry Alpheus Peirce 1837-1891
   DcAmB
Carter, Henry Alpheus Pierce 1837-1891
   WhAm H
Carter, Henry Holland 1884-1952 *WhAm 3*
Carter, Henry Rose 1852-1925 *AmBi, DcAmB,*
   NatCAB 25, WhAm 1
Carter, Henry Rose, Jr. 1883-1956 *NatCAB 46*
Carter, Herbert DeWayne 1860-1914 *WhAm 1*
Carter, Herbert Keller 1881-1935 *NatCAB 26*
Carter, Herbert Swift 1869-1927 *WhAm 1*
Carter, Hodding 1907-1972 *WhAm 5*
Carter, Homer Munroe, Sr. 1901-1974 *WhAm 6*
Carter, Horace A 1869-1959 *WhAm 3*
Carter, Howell 1844-1918 *NatCAB 18*
Carter, Hubert Lazell 1877-1956 *WhAm 3*
Carter, James 1853-1944 *WhAm 2*
Carter, James Coolidge 1827-1905 *AmBi,*
   ApCAB, ApCAB X, DcAmB, NatCAB 7,
   NatCAB 22, TwCBDA, WhAm 1
Carter, James Francis 1896- *WhAm 5*
Carter, James G *WhoColR*
Carter, James Gordon 1795-1849 *ApCAB,*
   BiDAmEd, DcAmB, Drake, NatCAB 10,
   TwCBDA, WhAm H
Carter, James Madison Gore 1843-1919
   WhAm 1
Carter, James Richard 1849-1923 *NatCAB 33,*
   WhAm 1
Carter, Jay 1899-1958 *NatCAB 44*
Carter, Jesse Benedict 1872-1917 *DcAmB,*
   NatCAB 23, WhAm 1
Carter, Jesse Francis 1873-1943 *WhAm 2*
Carter, Jesse McIlvaine 1863-1930 *WhAm 1*
Carter, Jesse Washington 1888-1959 *WhAm 3*
Carter, Joel Walker 1845- *NatCAB 8*
Carter, John *ApCAB*
Carter, John 1713-1745 *ApCAB X*
Carter, John 1737-1781 *DcAmB, WhAm H*
Carter, John 1745-1814 *ApCAB X, DcAmB,*
   WhAm H
Carter, John 1792-1850 *BiAUS, BiDrAC,*
   WhAm H
Carter, John 1920-1973 *WhAm 6*
Carter, John C 1805-1870 *ApCAB, TwCBDA*
Carter, John Carpenter 1837-1864 *BiDConf*
Carter, John Franklin, Jr. 1897-1967 *WhAm 4A*
Carter, John H 1896-1959 *WhAm 4*
Carter, John Ridgely 1864-1944 *WhAm 2*
Carter, John Ridgely 1865- *NatCAB 14*
Carter, John S 1907- *WhAm 4*
Carter, John Wayn Flete 1905-1975 *WhAm 6*
Carter, John Wilkins 1843-1895 *NatCAB 40*
Carter, Joseph Newton 1843-1913 *NatCAB 5,*
   WhAm 1
Carter, Josiah Mason 1813-1868 *ApCAB*
Carter, Landon 1760-1800 *DcAmB, WhAm H*
Carter, Leon Marks 1855- *NatCAB 11*
Carter, Mrs. Leslie 1862-1937 *AmBi,*
   DcAmB S2, NotAW, WhAm 1
Carter, Levi 1829-1903 *ApCAB X*
Carter, Leyton E 1892-1953 *WhAm 3*
Carter, Lincoln Jared 1865-1926 *NatCAB 20*
Carter, Loren Frank 1893-1962 *NatCAB 50*
Carter, Lorenzo 1767-1814 *ApCAB,*
   NatCAB 23
Carter, Louise C *WomWWA 14*
Carter, Louise Wilson Lamica 1927-1975
   WhAm 6
Carter, Luther Cullen 1805-1875 *BiAUS,*
   BiDrAC, WhAm H
Carter, Lyndall Frederic 1902-1973 *WhAm 6*
Carter, Lyon 1892-1950 *NatCAB 39*
Carter, Marion Law 1880- *WomWWA 14*
Carter, Mary Adaline Edwarda *AmWom*
Carter, Mary Elizabeth 1836- *WhAm 4,*
   WomWWA 14
Carter, Mary Lupton 1854- *WomWWA 14*
Carter, Morris 1877- *WhAm 6*
Carter, Nathan A, Sr. 1885-1958 *WhAm 3*
Carter, Nathaniel Hazeltine 1787-1830 *Drake*
Carter, Nathaniel Hazeltine 1787-1830 *ApCAB,*

TwCBDA
Carter, Oberlin Montgomery 1856-1944
   WhAm 2
Carter, Oliver Clinton 1864- *WhAm 4*
Carter, Oma Belle Bixler 1913-1972 *WhAm 6*
Carter, Orra Lee 1855- *WomWWA 14*
Carter, Orrin Nelson 1854-1928 *NatCAB 17,*
   NatCAB 24, WhAm 1
Carter, Peter 1825-1900 *ApCAB, NatCAB 23,*
   TwCBDA
Carter, Philip Walker 1887-1951 *NatCAB 40*
Carter, Philips John 1888-1960 *NatCAB 48,*
   WhAm 4
Carter, Ponder Silas 1869-1933 *NatCAB 25*
Carter, Randall Albert 1867-1954 *WhAm 3,*
   WhoColR
Carter, Raymond Lanson 1886-1950 *WhAm 3*
Carter, Richard Burrage 1877-1949 *NatCAB 40*
   WhAm 2
Carter, Mrs. Robert *NewYHSD*
Carter, Robert 1663-1732 *DcAmB,*
   NatCAB 13, WhAm H
Carter, Robert 1807-1889 *NatCAB 8,*
   TwCBDA
Carter, Robert 1819-1879 *ApCAB, DcAmB,*
   TwCBDA, WhAm H
Carter, Robert Allen 1901-1961 *WhAm 4*
Carter, Robert Inglee 1868- *WhAm 4*
Carter, Roscoe Arnold 1880-1927 *NatCAB 21*
Carter, Russel Kelso 1849- *ApCAB, TwCBDA*
Carter, Russell Gordon 1892-1957 *WhAm 3*
Carter, Russell J 1892-1966 *NatCAB 52*
Carter, Samuel Fain 1857-1928 *WhAm 1*
Carter, Samuel Powhatan 1819-1891 *AmBi,*
   ApCAB, DcAmB, Drake, NatCAB 2,
   TwCBDA, WebAB, WebAMB, WhAm H
Carter, Sara Nelson 1880- *WomWWA 14*
Carter, Seth May 1854- *WhAm 4*
Carter, Shirley 1871-1940 *NatCAB 30*
Carter, Steven V 1915-1959 *BiDrAC, WhAm 3*
Carter, Thomas Coke 1851-1916 *WhAm 1*
Carter, Thomas Henry 1854-1911 *ApCAB Sup,*
   BiDrAC, DcAmB, NatCAB 13, TwCBDA
   WhAm 1, WhAmP
Carter, Tim Lee 1910- *BiDrAC*
Carter, Timothy Jarvis 1800-1838 *BiAUS,*
   BiDrAC, WhAm H
Carter, Vincent Michael 1891- *BiDrAC*
Carter, Vinson 1840-1932 *NatCAB 24*
Carter, Walter Frederick 1873-1936
   NatCAB 28
Carter, Walter Steuben 1833-1904 *NatCAB 12,*
   NatCAB 23, WhAm 1
Carter, Warren Ray 1922-1973 *WhAm 6*
Carter, Wilbert James 1902-1972 *WhAm 5*
Carter, Wilbur Lee 1879-1968 *NatCAB 54*
Carter, William 1830-1918 *ApCAB X,*
   NatCAB 15, NatCAB 31
Carter, William 1868-1949 *NatCAB 35,*
   WhAm 2
Carter, William B 1812-1848 *BiAUS*
Carter, William Blount 1792-1848 *BiDrAC,*
   WhAm H
Carter, William Curtis 1881-1970 *WhAm 5*
Carter, William Daniel 1911-1974 *WhAm 6*
Carter, William Francis 1867-1951 *WhAm 3*
Carter, William Harding 1851-1925 *ApCAB X,*
   NatCAB 21, WhAm 1
Carter, William Harrison 1905-1974 *WhAm 6*
Carter, William Henric 1829-1907 *WhAm 1*
Carter, William Henry 1864-1955 *BiDrAC,*
   NatCAB 46, WhAm 3
Carter, William Joseph, Jr. 1893-1971
   NatCAB 57
Carter, William Justin 1866- *WhoColR*
Carter, William Samuel 1859-1923 *DcAmB,*
   NatCAB 6, WhAm 1
Carter, William Spencer 1869-1944 *WhAm 2*
Carter, William Thornton 1829-1893
   NatCAB 27
Carter, William Thornton 1831-1893 *NatCAB 6*
Carter, William V 1883-1971 *WhAm 5*
Carter, Winthrop Lakey 1885-1944 *WhAm 2*
Carter, Worrall Reed 1885-1975 *WhAm 6*
Carter, Zoe Hamilton 1889- *WomWWA 14*
Cartereau, Peter *NewYHSD*
Carteret, Sir George 1610?-1680 *AmBi,*

WhAm H

Carteret, Philip 1639-1682 *AmBi, DcAmB, NatCAB 19, WhAm H, WhAmP*

Cartesius, Renatus *DcScB*

Cartier, Arthur Jean Baptiste 1886-1953 *NatCAB 42*

Cartier, Sir George Etienne 1814-1873 *ApCAB, Drake, McGEWB*

Cartier, Jacques 1491-1557 *McGEWB, WhAm H*

Cartier, Jacques 1494-1555? *ApCAB, Drake*

Cartland, Donald Lee 1911-1964 *WhAm 4*

Cartlidge, Harold Tyndale 1878- *WhAm 6*

Carton, Alfred Thomas 1884-1968 *WhAm 4A*

Carton, John Jay 1856-1934 *WhAm 1*

Carton DeWiart, Sir Adrian 1880-1963 *WhWW-II*

Cartotto, Ercole 1889-1946 *WhAm 2*

Cartter, David Kellogg 1812-1887 *ApCAB, BiAUS, BiDrAC, NatCAB 11, TwCBDA, WhAm H*

Cartwright, Alexander Joy 1820-1892 *WhAm H*

Cartwright, C Hawley 1904-1964 *WhAm 4*

Cartwright, Eakle Wesley 1899-1962 *NatCAB 49*

Cartwright, Emor Lopp 1887-1966 *NatCAB 52*

Cartwright, Florence Byrne 1863- *AmWom*

Cartwright, Frank Thomas 1884-1964 *WhAm 4*

Cartwright, George *Drake*

Cartwright, George 1739-1819 *ApCAB, Drake*

Cartwright, J *NewYHSD*

Cartwright, James Henry 1842-1924 *NatCAB 5, WhAm 1*

Cartwright, John 1740-1824 *ApCAB, Drake*

Cartwright, John Sheldon 1904-1970 *NatCAB 55*

Cartwright, Mabel *WomWWA 14*

Cartwright, Morse Adams 1890-1974 *BiDAmEd, WhAm 6*

Cartwright, Peter 1785-1872 *AmBi, ApCAB, DcAmB, DcAmReB, EncAAH, McGEWB, NatCAB 6, REnAW, TwCBDA, WebAB, WhAm H*

Cartwright, Sir Richard John 1835- *ApCAB*

Cartwright, Samuel Adolphus 1793-1863 *ApCAB, TwCBDA*

Cartwright, T *NewYHSD*

Cartwright, Wilburn 1892- *BiDrAC*

Carty, Donald Joseph 1908-1954 *WhAm 3*

Carty, John Joseph 1851-1932 *AmBi*

Carty, John Joseph 1861-1932 *DcAmB S1, NatCAB 15, NatCAB 23, WebAB, WhAm 1*

Carty, Martin *NewYHSD*

Carty, Roland Kenneth 1919-1972 *WhAm 5*

Caruana, George J 1882-1950 *WhAm 3*

Carus, Emma 1879-1927 *WhAm 1, WomWWA 14*

Carus, Julius Victor 1823-1903 *DcScB Sup*

Carus, Mary Hegeler 1861- *WomWWA 14*

Carus, Paul 1852-1919 *AmBi, ApCAB X, DcAmB, DcAmReB, DcScB, DcScB Sup, NatCAB 14, WhAm 1*

Carusi, Charles Francis 1873-1931 *NatCAB 22, WhAm 1*

Carusi, Eugene 1835-1931 *NatCAB 22*

Caruso, Enrico 1873-1921 *AmBi, ApCAB X, DcAmB, McGEWB, WhAm 1*

Caruth, Asher Graham 1844-1907 *BiDrAC*

Caruth, George William 1842-1921 *NatCAB 8*

Caruth, William Walter 1876-1949 *NatCAB 39*

Caruthers, Daisy Miller 1875- *WomWWA 14*

Caruthers, Eli Washington 1793-1865 *NatCAB 7*

Caruthers, Robert Looney 1800- *BiAUS*

Caruthers, Robert Looney 1800-1882 *ApCAB Sup, BiDConf, BiDrAC, NatCAB 8, WhAm H, WhAmP*

Caruthers, Robert Looney 1800-1892 *TwCBDA*

Caruthers, Sampel Sumner *WhoColR*

Caruthers, Samuel 1820-1860 *BiAUS, BiDrAC, WhAm H*

Caruthers, William Alexander 1800?-1846 *WhAm H*

Caruthers, William Alexander 1802-1846 *DcAmB*

Carvajal, Ciriaco Gonzalez *ApCAB*

Carvajal, Francis De 1464?-1548 *Drake*

Carvajal, Francisco De 1464?-1548 *ApCAB*

Carvajal, Gaspar De d1584 *ApCAB*

Carvajal, Manuel 1916-1971 *WhAm 6*

Carvalho, David Nunes 1848-1925 *WhAm 1*

Carvalho, Solomon Nunes 1815-1894 *IlBEAAW, NewYHSD, WhAm H*

Carvalho, Solomon Solis 1856-1942 *DcAmB S3, WhAm 2*

Carvallo, Manuel 1808- *Drake*

Carvallo Goveneche, Vicente 1742-1816 *ApCAB Sup*

Carvelle, Henry DeWolfe 1852-1923 *NatCAB 20*

Carver, Charles 1851-1932 *NatCAB 25*

Carver, Clara Belle Finney 1872- *WomWWA 14*

Carver, Clifford Nickels 1891-1965 *WhAm 4*

Carver, Eugene Pendleton 1860-1924 *NatCAB 20*

Carver, George 1888-1949 *WhAm 3*

Carver, George Washington 1861?-1943 *DcAmB S3*

Carver, George Washington 1864?-1943 *AsBiEn, EncAAH, EncAB, McGEWB, NatCAB 33, WebAB, WhAm HA, WhAm 2, WhAm 4A*

Carver, Jay Ward 1881-1942 *WhAm 2*

Carver, John 1576?-1621 *AmBi, DcAmB, Drake, WhAm H*

Carver, John 1590?-1621 *ApCAB, NatCAB 7, TwCBDA*

Carver, John E *NewYHSD*

Carver, John Stuart 1892-1957 *WhAm 3*

Carver, Jonathan 1710-1780 *AmBi, DcAmB, EncAAH, McGEWB, REnAW, WebAB, WebAMB, WhAm H*

Carver, Jonathan 1732-1780 *ApCAB, Drake, NatCAB 1, TwCBDA*

Carver, Leonard Dwight 1841- *TwCBDA*

Carver, Priscilla 1885- *WomWWA 14*

Carver, Thomas Nixon 1865-1961 *WhAm 4*

Carver, Walter Buckingham 1879-1961 *WhAm 4*

Carver, Walter Lexor 1889-1958 *WhAm 3*

Carver, William Owen 1868-1954 *NatCAB 44*

Carver, Williard 1866-1943 *WhAm 3*

Carveth, Hector Russell 1873-1942 *WhAm 2*

Carville, Edward Peter 1885-1956 *BiDrAC, WhAm 3, WhAmP*

Carwin, Joseph Lucian 1904-1964 *NatCAB 51*

Cary, Albigence Waldo 1801-1862 *ApCAB, TwCBDA*

Cary, Alice 1820-1871 *AmBi, AmWom, ApCAB, DcAmB, Drake, NatCAB 1, NotAW, TwCBDA, WebAB, WhAm H*

Cary, Anna May Gogley 1869- *WomWWA 14*

Cary, Annie Louise d1921 *AmWom*

Cary, Annie Louise 1841-1921 *NotAW, WhAm 1*

Cary, Annie Louise 1842-1921 *AmBi, ApCAB, DcAmB, NatCAB 1, TwCBDA, WomWWA 14*

Cary, Archibald 1721-1787 *DcAmB, WhAm H*

Cary, Archibald 1730?-1786 *ApCAB, Drake, NatCAB 5*

Cary, Austin 1865-1936 *WhAm 1*

Cary, Charles 1852-1931 *WhAm 1*

Cary, Charles Preston 1856- *WhAm 4*

Cary, Charles Reed 1881-1963 *NatCAB 48, WhAm 6*

Cary, Dale Emerson 1880-1958 *NatCAB 46*

Cary, Edward 1840-1917 *DcAmB, NatCAB 8, NatCAB 25, WhAm 1*

Cary, Edward Francis 1875-1952 *NatCAB 41*

Cary, Edward Henry 1872-1953 *NatCAB 49, WhAm 3*

Cary, Edward Richard 1865-1941 *NatCAB 30, WhAm 4*

Cary, Elisabeth Luther 1867-1936 *DcAmB S2, NotAW, WhAm 1, WomWWA 14*

Cary, Eugene 1886-1953 *NatCAB 44*

Cary, Frank 1857-1938 *NatCAB 32*

Cary, George d1945 *WhAm 2*

Cary, George 1789-1843 *BiDrAC, WhAm H*

Cary, George Archibald 1908-1959 *NatCAB 48*

Cary, George Booth 1811-1850 *BiAUS, BiDrAC, WhAm H*

Cary, George Foster 1867-1943 *WhAm 2*

Cary, George Hutchins 1900-1972 *NatCAB 56*

Cary, George Lovell 1830-1910 *TwCBDA, WhAm 1*

Cary, Glover H 1885-1936 *BiDrAC, WhAm 1*

Cary, Guy 1879-1950 *WhAm 3*

Cary, Harry Francis 1874- *WhAm 5*

Cary, Henry Nathaniel 1858-1922 *WhAm 1*

Cary, Isaac *NewYHSD*

Cary, Jeremiah Eaton 1803-1888 *BiDrAC, WhAm H*

Cary, John 1729-1843 *ApCAB, Drake*

Cary, Joseph Clinton 1828-1884 *ApCAB*

Cary, Joseph Clinton 1829-1884 *TwCBDA*

Cary, Joyce 1888-1957 *WhAm 3*

Cary, Lott 1780-1828 *ApCAB, DcAmB, Drake, WhAm H*

Cary, Lucian 1886-1971 *WhAm 5*

Cary, Martha Bryant *WomWWA 14*

Cary, Mary Ann Shadd 1823-1893 *NotAW*

Cary, Mary Harkness Flagler 1901-1967 *NatCAB 55*

Cary, Mary Stockly 1834- *AmWom*

Cary, Melbert Brinckerhoff 1852-1946 *WhAm 2*

Cary, Phoebe 1824-1871 *AmBi, AmWom, ApCAB, DcAmB, NatCAB 1, NotAW, TwCBDA, WebAB, WhAm H*

Cary, Phoebe 1825-1871 *Drake*

Cary, Richard 1747-1806 *Drake*

Cary, Robert John 1868-1929 *WhAm 1*

Cary, Robert Webster 1890-1967 *WhAm 4*

Cary, Russell Singer 1932-1972 *WhAm 6*

Cary, Samuel Fenton 1814-1900 *ApCAB, BiAUS, BiDrAC, NatCAB 11, TwCBDA*

Cary, Shepard 1805-1866 *BiAUS, BiDrAC, WhAm H*

Cary, Simeon 1719-1802 *Drake*

Cary, William DeLaMontagne 1840-1922 *IlBEAAW, NewYHSD, REnAW*

Cary, William Ernest 1888-1941 *NatCAB 31*

Cary, William Joseph 1865-1934 *BiDrAC, WhAm 1, WhAmP*

Cary, William Paxton 1882-1943 *NatCAB 33*

Casa Irujo, Carlos Maria, Marquis De 1765-1824 *Drake*

Casaday, Lauren Wilde 1905-1969 *NatCAB 54, WhAm 5*

Casadesus, Robert 1899-1972 *WhAm 5*

Casady, Thomas 1881-1958 *WhAm 3*

Casal, Manuel Ayres De 1750?-1850? *ApCAB, Drake*

Casal Julian, Gaspar Roque F Narciso 1680-1759 *DcScB*

Casale, John Baptist 1892-1948 *NatCAB 38*

Casals, Pablo 1876-1973 *WhAm 6*

Casamajor, George Holberton 1868- *WhAm 4*

Casamajor, Louis 1881-1962 *NatCAB 49, WhAm 6*

Casanova DeSeingalt, Giacomo J Girolamo 1725-1798 *McGEWB*

Casanowicz, Immanuel Moses 1853-1927 *DcAmB, WhAm 1*

Casante, Pedro Porter De *ApCAB*

Casas, Bartholomew DeLas 1474-1566 *Drake*

Casas, Bartolome DeLas 1474-1566 *ApCAB*

Casas Y Aragorri, Luis DeLas 1745-1800 *ApCAB*

Casault, Sir Louis Napoleon 1823- *ApCAB Sup*

Case, Adelaide Teague 1887-1948 *BiDAmEd, NotAW*

Case, Albert Hermon 1875- *WhAm 5*

Case, Albert Willard 1840-1925 *NatCAB 20*

Case, Anna Hubbell Lathrop *WomWWA 14*

Case, Arthur Ellicott 1894-1946 *WhAm 2*

Case, Augustus Ludlow 1812-1893 *Drake*

Case, Augustus Ludlow 1813-1893 *ApCAB, TwCBDA*

Case, Austin Edward 1857-1926 *NatCAB 20*

Case, Carl Delos 1868-1931 *WhAm 1*

Case, Charles 1817-1883 *BiAUS, BiDrAC, WhAm H*

Case, Charles 1859-1919 *NatCAB 19*

Case, Charles Clinton 1843- *WhAm 4*

Case, Charles Orlando 1860-1933 *BiDAmEd, NatCAB 24, WhAm 4*

Case, Clarence Edwards 1877-1961 *WhAm 4*

Case, Clarence Marsh 1874-1946 *WhAm 2*

Case, Clifford Philip 1873-1920 *WhAm 1*

Case, Clifford Philip 1904- *BiDrAC*

Case, Dwight Samuel 1843- *WhAm 4*
Case, Eckstein 1858- *WhAm 4*
Case, Edward Whitney 1888-1952 *NatCAB 42*
Case, Ermine Cowles 1871- *WhAm 5*
Case, Frances Powell *WomWWA 14*
Case, Francis Higbee 1896-1962 *BiDrAC, WhAm 4, WhAmP*
Case, Francis Owen 1894-1972 *WhAm 5*
Case, Frank Luther 1866-1930 *NatCAB 22*
Case, George Sessions 1882-1950 *NatCAB 39, WhAm 3*
Case, George Wilkinson 1880- *WhAm 6*
Case, Harold Claude 1902-1972 *WhAm 5*
Case, Harold Clayton M 1890-1966 *WhAm 4*
Case, Howard Gregory 1880-1943 *NatCAB 33, WhAm 2*
Case, J Herbert 1872-1972 *NatCAB 57, WhAm 5*
Case, James Herbert, Jr. 1906-1965 *WhAm 4*
Case, James Thomas 1882-1960 *WhAm 4*
Case, Jerome Increase 1818-1891 *DcAmB, EncAAH, WhAm H*
Case, Jerome Increase 1819-1891 *ApCAB X*
Case, John Francis 1876-1966 *WhAm 4*
Case, John Gail 1892-1959 *NatCAB 46*
Case, Josiah *NewYHSD*
Case, Katherine E LeMar 1844- *WomWWA 14*
Case, Lafayette Wallace 1845-1926 *NatCAB 20*
Case, Leonard 1786-1864 *DcAmB, NatCAB 11, WhAm H*
Case, Leonard 1820-1880 *DcAmB, NatCAB 11, WhAm H*
Case, Lorenzo Dow 1872- *WhAm 5*
Case, Lucius *NewYHSD*
Case, Marian Ward Ingersoll 1868- *WomWWA 14*
Case, Marietta Stanley 1845- *AmWom*
Case, Mary Emily 1857- *WhAm 4, WomWWA 14*
Case, Mary Sophia 1854- *TwCBDA*
Case, Maurice 1910-1968 *WhAm 5*
Case, Nelson 1845-1921 *ApCAB X, NatCAB 19, WhAm 1*
Case, Norman Stanley 1888-1967 *WhAm 4A*
Case, Ralph E 1887-1969 *WhAm 5*
Case, Rolland Webster 1882-1957 *WhAm 3*
Case, Shirley Jackson 1872-1947 *DcAmB S4, NatCAB 36, WhAm 2*
Case, Theodore Spencer 1832-1900 *ApCAB, TwCBDA, WhAm 1*
Case, Walter 1776-1859 *BiAUS, BiDrAC, WhAm H*
Case, Walter L 1863- *ApCAB X*
Case, Walter Summerhayes 1885-1937 *NatCAB 28, WhAm 1*
Case, Willard Erastus 1857-1918 *NatCAB 19*
Case, William 1780-1855 *ApCAB*
Case, William Scoville 1863-1921 *DcAmB, NatCAB 19, WhAm 1*
Caseau, Charles Felix 1807-1881 *ApCAB*
Casement, Dan Dillon 1868-1953 *WhAm 3*
Caser, Ettore 1880-1944 *WhAm 3*
Casesa, Philip Robert 1909-1973 *WhAm 5*
Casey, Charles Clinton 1881-1946 *WhAm 2*
Casey, Daniel Vincent 1874- *WhAm 5*
Casey, Douglas 1899-1963 *WhAm 4*
Casey, Edward O'Brien 1900-1960 *NatCAB 48*
Casey, Edward Pearce 1864-1940 *NatCAB 36, WhAm 1*
Casey, Ellenor Fairfax *WomWWA 14*
Casey, Francis DeSales 1882-1934 *WhAm 1, WhAm 1C*
Casey, George J 1903-1963 *WhAm 4*
Casey, John Francis 1872-1948 *WhAm 2*
Casey, John Joseph 1875-1929 *BiDrAC, WhAm 1, WhAmP*
Casey, John Schuyler 1880-1948 *WhAm 2*
Casey, Joseph 1814-1879 *BiAUS, BiDrAC, DcAmB, WhAm H*
Casey, Joseph Edward 1898- *BiDrAC*
Casey, Lee 1889-1951 *WhAm 3*
Casey, Levi d1807 *BiAUS*
Casey, Levi 1749-1807 *ApCAB, Drake*
Casey, Levi 1752?-1807 *BiDrAC, WhAm H*
Casey, Lyman Rufus 1837-1914 *ApCAB Sup, BiDrAC, NatCAB 1, TwCBDA, WhAm 1*
Casey, Mary Catherine Martin *WomWWA 14*

Casey, Richard 1890-1976 *WhWW-II*
Casey, Robert Joseph 1890-1962 *WhAm 4*
Casey, Robert Pierce 1897-1959 *WhAm 3*
Casey, Robert Randolph 1915- *BiDrAC*
Casey, Samuel *BiAUS*
Casey, Samuel Brown 1903-1963 *WhAm 4*
Casey, Samuel Lewis 1821-1902 *BiAUS, BiDrAC*
Casey, Silas 1807-1882 *ApCAB, DcAmB, Drake, NatCAB 4, TwCBDA, WebAMB, WhAm H*
Casey, Silas 1841-1913 *ApCAB, NatCAB 4, NatCAB 21, TwCBDA, WhAm 1*
Casey, Thomas Lincoln 1831-1896 *ApCAB Sup, DcAmB S1, NatCAB 4, TwCBDA, WebAMB*
Casey, Thomas Lincoln 1857-1925 *WhAm 1*
Casey, Thomas Wanton 1892-1954 *NatCAB 48*
Casey, William Joseph 1871-1959 *NatCAB 47, WhAm 3*
Casey, Zadoc 1796-1862 *BiAUS, BiDrAC, WhAm H*
Casgrain, Charles William 1859-1951 *NatCAB 40*
Casgrain, Henry Raymond 1831- *ApCAB*
Casgrain, Marie Emma *WomWWA 14*
Cash, Albert D 1897-1952 *WhAm 3*
Cash, James 1893-1975 *WhAm 6*
Cash, Johnny 1932- *WebAB*
Cash, Wilbur Joseph 1900-1941 *DcAmB S3*
Cash, Wilbur Joseph 1901-1941 *EncAB, WhAm 2*
Cash, William Levi *WhoColR*
Cash, William Thomas 1878-1951 *WhAm 3*
Cashen *NewYHSD*
Cashen, Thomas Cecil 1879-1959 *WhAm 3*
Cashen, Thomas Valentine 1835- *NatCAB 5*
Cashin, John Martin 1892-1970 *NatCAB 55, WhAm 5*
Cashman, Bender Zelotes 1886-1948 *NatCAB 36*
Cashman, Earl William 1891-1959 *WhAm 3*
Cashman, Edwin James 1904-1970 *WhAm 5*
Cashman, G H *NewYHSD*
Cashman, James Eugene 1876-1931 *NatCAB 25*
Cashman, Joseph Thomas 1876-1936 *WhAm 1*
Cashman, Louis Patrick 1886-1961 *NatCAB 56*
Cashman, William Timothy 1872-1928 *NatCAB 43*
Cashmore, Charles Henry 1883-1944 *NatCAB 33*
Cashmore, John d1961 *WhAm 4*
Cashwell, David Henry 1908-1972 *NatCAB 57*
Casilear, George W *NewYHSD*
Casilear, J W 1811-1893 *Drake*
Casilear, John William 1811-1893 *AmBi, ApCAB, BnEnAmA, DcAmB, IIBEAAW, NatCAB 12, NewYHSD, TwCBDA, WhAm H*
Casilear, Paul *NewYHSD*
Caskey, Fred Antrim 1886-1961 *NatCAB 47*
Caskey, John Fletcher 1902-1961 *WhAm 4*
Caskie, John Samuels 1821-1869 *BiAUS, BiDrAC, WhAm H*
Caskie, Marion Maxwell 1890-1966 *WhAm 4*
Casko, Stephen Frank 1908-1961 *NatCAB 49*
Caskoden, Edwin 1856-1913 *WhAm 1*
Casler, Anna Delia 1874- *WomWWA 14*
Casler, Herman 1867-1939 *NatCAB 36*
Casler, Lester Alonzo 1903-1974 *WhAm 6*
Casnelli, Victor *IIBEAAW*
Cason, Hulsey 1893-1950 *WhAm 3*
Cason, Thomas Jefferson 1828-1901 *BiAUS, BiDrAC*
Caspari, Charles, Jr. 1850-1917 *WhAm 1*
Caspari, Charles Edward 1871-1942 *WhAm 2*
Cass, Alonzo Beecher 1856-1924 *WhAm 1*
Cass, Charles Anderson 1880-1958 *WhAm 3*
Cass, George Nelson 1831?-1882 *ApCAB, NewYHSD*
Cass, George Washington 1810-1888 *ApCAB Sup, DcAmB, WhAm H*
Cass, Jonathan *ApCAB X*
Cass, Joseph Kerr 1848-1938 *WhAm 1*
Cass, Lewis 1782-1866 *AmBi, ApCAB, ApCAB X, BiAUS, BiDrAC, BiDrUSE, DcAmB, Drake, EncAAH, EncAB, McGEWB, NatCAB 5, REnAW,*

TwCBDA, WebAB, WhAm H, WhAmP
Cass, Lewis, Jr. 1810?- *BiAUS, NatCAB 7*
Cass, Louis S 1865- *WhAm 4*
Cassady, Harry James 1858- *NatCAB 17*
Cassady, John Howard 1896-1969 *WhAm 5*
Cassady, Morley Franklin 1900-1968 *WhAm 5*
Cassady, Thomas Gantz 1896-1972 *NatCAB 57, WhAm 5*
Cassandra *WhAm 4*
Cassard, Frances Wallace 1859- *WomWWA 14*
Cassatt, Alexander Johnson 1839-1906 *NatCAB 13*
Cassatt, Alexander Johnston 1839-1906 *ApCAB X, DcAmB, WhAm 1*
Cassatt, Mary d1926 *WhAm 1, WomWWA 14*
Cassatt, Mary 1844-1926 *NotAW, WebAB*
Cassatt, Mary Stevenson 1845-1926 *AmBi, BnEnAmA, DcAmB, EncAB, McGEWB, NatCAB 33*
Casse, Alfred *NewYHSD*
Casseday, Jennie 1840- *AmWom*
Cassedy, George 1783-1842 *BiAUS, BiDrAC, WhAm H*
Cassedy, John Irvin 1856-1916 *WhAm 1*
Cassegrain *DcScB*
Cassel, Abraham Harley 1820- *NatCAB 3*
Cassel, Henry Burd 1855-1926 *BiDrAC, WhAm 4*
Cassel, John H *WhAm 5*
Casselberry, Clarence Marmaduke 1875-1945 *NatCAB 34*
Casselberry, William Evans 1858-1916 *NatCAB 15, NatCAB 17, WhAm 1*
Cassell, Wallace Lewis 1899-1966 *WhAm 4*
Casselman, Arthur Vale 1874-1957 *WhAm 3*
Casselman, Elbridge Johnson 1893-1965 *NatCAB 52*
Cassels, Amy 1864- *WomWWA 14*
Cassels, Edwin Henry 1874-1947 *WhAm 2*
Cassels, Louis Welborn 1922-1974 *WhAm 6*
Casseri, Giulio 1552?-1616 *DcScB*
Casserly, Eugene 1820-1883 *BiDrAC, WhAm H*
Casserly, Eugene 1822-1883 *ApCAB, BiAUS, NatCAB 4*
Casserly, Eugene 1823-1883 *TwCBDA*
Cassett, Alexander Johnson 1839- *ApCAB Sup*
Cassidy, Butch 1866-1937? *REnAW*
Cassidy, Donald John 1903-1953 *NatCAB 43*
Cassidy, George Livingston 1902-1962 *WhAm 4*
Cassidy, George W *NewYHSD*
Cassidy, George Washington 1863-1941 *NatCAB 43, WhAm 1*
Cassidy, George Williams 1836-1892 *BiDrAC, WhAm H*
Cassidy, Gerald 1879-1934 *WhAm 1*
Cassidy, Gerald Ira Dymond 1869-1934 *NatCAB 26*
Cassidy, Ira Diamond Gerald 1879-1934 *IIBEAAW*
Cassidy, James E 1898-1951 *WhAm 3*
Cassidy, James Henry 1869-1926 *BiDrAC, NatCAB 30, WhAm 5*
Cassidy, Leslie Martin 1904-1967 *WhAm 4*
Cassidy, Lewis Cochran 1898-1949 *WhAm 2*
Cassidy, M Joseph 1893-1957 *WhAm 3*
Cassidy, Massilon Alexander 1856-1928 *WhAm 1*
Cassidy, Perlina Barnum Sizer 1869- *WomWWA 14*
Cassidy, Rosalind 1895- *BiDAmEd*
Cassidy, William 1815-1873 *ApCAB, DcAmB, NatCAB 22, TwCBDA, WhAm H*
Cassidy, William Joseph 1880- *WhAm 6*
Cassil, Hurd Alexander 1878- *WhAm 6*
Cassill, Harold E 1897-1957 *WhAm 3*
Cassilly, Francis 1860- *WhAm 4*
Cassilly, Philip Jacquemn 1904-1973 *WhAm 6*
Cassin, John *NewYHSD*
Cassin, John 1750?-1822 *Drake*
Cassin, John 1758?-1822 *ApCAB, TwCBDA*
Cassin, John 1813-1869 *AmBi, ApCAB, DcAmB, Drake, NatCAB 22, TwCBDA, WhAm H*
Cassin, Rene 1887-1976 *WhAm 6*
Cassin, Stephen 1783-1857 *ApCAB, Drake, NatCAB 13, TwCBDA, WebAMB*

Cassingham, John Wilson 1840-1930 *BiDrAC,*
WhAm 3
Cassingham, Roy B 1889-1967 *WhAm 4A*
Cassini, Gian Domenico 1625-1712 *DcScB*
Cassini, Giovanni Domenico 1625-1712 *AsBiEn*
Cassini, Jacques 1677-1756 *DcScB*
Cassini, Jean-Dominique 1748-1845 *DcScB*
Cassini DeThury, Cesar-Francois 1714-1784
DcScB
Cassino, Samuel Edson 1856-1937 *WhAm 1*
Cassiodorus, Flavus Magnus Aurelius 480?-575?
McGEWB
Cassiodorus Senator, Flavius M Aurelius
480?-575? *DcScB*
Cassirer, Ernst Alfred 1874-1945 *DcScB,*
McGEWB, WhAm 4
Cassoday, John Bolivar 1830-1907 *DcAmB S1,*
NatCAB 13, WhAm 1
Casson, Herbert Newton 1869- *WhAm 5*
Castaigne, J Andre 1860?-1930 *IlBEAAW*
Castaldi, Luigi 1890-1945 *DcScB*
Castaneda, Carlos Eduardo 1896-1958
BiDAmEd, WhAm 3
Castegnier, Georges 1851- *WhAm 4*
Castel, Louis-Bertrand 1688-1757 *DcScB*
Castellani, Aldo 1877-1971 *WhAm 5*
Castellanos, Juan De 1550?- *ApCAB Sup*
Castelle *NewYHSD*
Castelli, Benedetto 1578-1643 *DcScB*
Castelli, Frank Carlo 1893-1963 *NatCAB 49*
Castello, Eugene 1851-1926 *WhAm 1*
Castello Branco, Humberto DeAlencar
1900-1967 *WhAm 4*
Castellow, Bryant Thomas 1876-1962 *BiDrAC,*
WhAm 5
Castelnau, Francis *NewYHSD*
Castelnau, Noel Marie J E DeCurieres De
1851-1944 *WhoMilH*
Castelnuovo, Guido 1865-1952 *DcScB*
Castelnuovo-Tedesco, Mario 1895-1968
NatCAB 54, WhAm 5
Castelo Branco, Humberto 1900-1967
McGEWB
Casten, Daniel Francis 1906-1973 *WhAm 6*
Caster, George Brown 1894-1972 *WhAm 5*
Casterean, Alphonse *NewYHSD*
Castigliano, Alberto 1847-1884 *DcScB*
Castiglione, Baldassare 1478-1529 *McGEWB*
Castiglioni, Arturo 1874-1952 *WhAm 3*
Castilla, Ramon 1797-1867 *ApCAB, Drake,*
McGEWB
Castillo, Bernardo Diaz Del *ApCAB*
Castillo, Juan De 1615-1675 *ApCAB*
Castillo, Ramon S 1873-1944 *WhAm 2*
Castillo Najera, Francisco d1954 *WhAm 3*
Castillo Y Arteaga, Diego Del 1605-1670?
ApCAB
Castillo Y Lanzas, Joaquin M 1801-1878
ApCAB
Castillon, Johann 1704-1791 *DcScB*
Castin, Vincent, Baron De *Drake*
Castle, Alfred L 1884-1972 *WhAm 6*
Castle, Arthur S *NewYHSD*
Castle, Benjamin Frederick 1884-1966
NatCAB 52
Castle, Curtis Harvey 1848-1928 *BiDrAC*
Castle, Edward Sears 1903-1973 *WhAm 6*
Castle, Eugene Winston 1897-1960 *WhAm 3*
Castle, Frederick Albert 1842-1902 *ApCAB,*
WhAm 1
Castle, Frederick Augustus 1842- *TwCBDA*
Castle, Frederick Walker 1908-1944
NatCAB 34
Castle, Harold Kainalu Long 1886-1967
WhAm 4A
Castle, Henry Anson 1841-1916 *NatCAB 16,*
WhAm 1
Castle, Homer Levi 1859- *WhAm 4*
Castle, Howard Joel 1877-1942 *NatCAB 31*
Castle, Irene 1893-1969 *WebAB*
Castle, James Nathan 1836-1903 *BiDrAC*
Castle, John H, Jr. 1916-1968 *WhAm 5*
Castle, John Harvard 1830-1890 *ApCAB,*
NatCAB 19
Castle, Kendall Brooks 1868-1957 *NatCAB 49,*
WhAm 4
Castle, Lewis Gould 1889-1960 *WhAm 4*
Castle, Lydia 1840?- *NewYHSD*

Castle, Nicholas 1837-1922 *WhAm 1*
Castle, Samuel Northrup 1880- *WhAm 6*
Castle, Vernon Blythe 1887-1918 *DcAmB,*
WebAB, WebAMB, WhAm 4
Castle, Wendell 1932- *BnEnAmA*
Castle, William 1836-1909 *WhAm 1*
Castle, William Bathgate 1862-1953
NatCAB 40
Castle, William Ernest 1867-1962 *DcScB,*
NatCAB 16, WhAm 4
Castle, William Leon 1903-1959 *NatCAB 49*
Castle, William Richards 1849-1935
NatCAB 40, WhAm 1
Castle, William Richards 1878-1963 *WhAm 4*
Castle, Wilmot Vail 1889-1964 *NatCAB 51*
Castleberry, John Jackson 1877- *WhAm 1*
Castleberry, Winston 1912-1971 *WhAm 6*
Castleman, Alice Barbee 1843- *AmWom*
Castleman, Francis Lee, Jr. 1902-1954 *WhAm 3*
Castleman, John Breckinridge 1841-1918
WhAm 1
Castleman, John Warrant 1868-1920
NatCAB 18
Castleman, P F 1827?- *NewYHSD*
Castleman, Virginia Carter 1864- *WhAm 3,*
WomWWA 14
Castlemon, Harry *WhAm 1*
Castlereagh, Robert Stewart, Viscount 1769-1822
McGEWB
Castles, Alfred Guido Rudolph 1851-1933
ApCAB X, WhAm 2
Castles, John Wesley 1893-1965 *NatCAB 53*
Castner, Joseph Compton 1869-1946 *WhAm 2*
Casto, C Everett 1883-1958 *WhAm 3*
Casto, Frank Monroe 1875-1965 *NatCAB 52*
Caston, John Tolbert 1860- *WhoColR*
Caston, Saul 1901-1970 *NatCAB 56,*
WhAm 5
Castor, George Albert 1855-1906 *BiDrAC*
Castorena Y Ursua, Juan Ignacio 1668-1733
ApCAB
Castries, Armand Charles Augustin 1756-1842
ApCAB
Castries, Armand N Augustine, Duc De
1756-1842 *Drake*
Castries, Christian M F DeLaCroix De 1902-
WhoMilH
Castro, Agustin 1728-1790 *ApCAB*
Castro, Americo 1885-1972 *WhAm 5*
Castro, Andres 1500?-1577 *ApCAB*
Castro, Fidel 1926- *McGEWB*
Castro, Frank Monroe 1875- *WhAm 6*
Castro, Hector David 1894-1973 *WhAm 5*
Castro, Henri 1786-1861 *ApCAB*
Castro, Henry 1786-1861 *NatCAB 3*
Castro, Jose *WhAm H*
Castro, Juan 1799- *ApCAB*
Castro, Matilde 1879- *WhAm 6*
Castro, Ramon De *ApCAB*
Castro, Vaca De d1558 *ApCAB, Drake*
Castro Alves, Antonio De 1847-1871 *McGEWB*
Castro Lopes, Antonio De 1827- *ApCAB*
Caswall, Henry 1810-1870 *ApCAB*
Caswell, Albert Edward 1884-1954 *WhAm 3*
Caswell, Alexis 1799-1877 *ApCAB, DcAmB,*
Drake, NatCAB 1, NatCAB 8, TwCBDA,
WhAm H
Caswell, Caroline Matilda *BiCAW*
Caswell, Edward C 1880- *WhAm 6*
Caswell, Edward Thompson 1833-1887
NatCAB 12
Caswell, Edwin Whittier 1844- *NatCAB 7*
Caswell, Hollis Leland 1901- *BiDAmEd*
Caswell, Irving A 1870- *WhAm 5*
Caswell, John Wallace 1870-1943 *NatCAB 33*
Caswell, L B 1827-1919 *BiAUS*
Caswell, Lucien Bonaparte 1827-1919 *BiDrAC,*
NatCAB 3, NatCAB 16, TwCBDA,
WhAm 4, WhAmP
Caswell, Mary S d1924 *WhAm 1*
Caswell, Richard 1729-1789 *ApCAB, BiAUS,*
BiDrAC, DcAmB, Drake, NatCAB 4,
TwCBDA, WebAMB, WhAm H
Caswell, Thomas Hubbard 1825-1900 *WhAm 1*
Caswell, Thomas Thompson 1840-1913
WhAm 1
Caswell, William *ApCAB*

Caswell, Winafred Lyndia Sheldon 1875-
WomWWA 14
Catalan, Miguel Antonio 1894-1957 *DcScB*
Cataldi, Pietro Antonio 1552-1626 *DcScB*
Cataldo, Joseph Maria 1837-1928 *DcAmB S1,*
REnAW
Catchings, Thomas Clendinen 1847-1927
BiDrAC, TwCBDA, WhAm 4, WhAmP
Catchings, Waddill 1879-1967 *WhAm 4A*
Cate, Carrie Quincy *WomWWA 14*
Cate, George W 1824- *BiAUS*
Cate, George Washington 1825-1905 *BiDrAC*
Cate, George Washington 1834-1911
NatCAB 17
Cate, Horace Nelson 1863-1925 *WhAm 1*
Cate, L Maude 1863- *WomWWA 14*
Cate, Roscoe Simmons, Jr. 1906-1960 *WhAm 4*
Cate, William Henderson 1839-1899 *BiDrAC*
Catenacci, Alfred John 1912-1970 *NatCAB 55*
Catenhusen, Ernst 1841- *ApCAB*
Cater, James Tate 1889- *WhoColR*
Cates, Charles Theodore, Jr. 1863-1938
WhAm 1
Cates, Clifton Bledsoe 1893-1970 *WebAMB,*
WhAm 5
Cates, Dudley 1887-1954 *NatCAB 41*
Cates, Gordon Dell 1906-1970 *WhAm 5*
Cates, Junius Sidney 1877-1949 *WhAm 3*
Cates, Louis Shattuck 1881-1959 *NatCAB 47,*
WhAm 3
Cates, Walter Thruston 1913-1971 *WhAm 5*
Catesby, Mark 1679?-1749 *DcAmB, Drake,*
NewYHSD, WhAm H
Catesby, Mark 1680?-1749 *ApCAB*
Catesby, Mark 1683-1749 *DcScB*
Cathcart, Arthur Martin 1873-1949 *WhAm 2*
Cathcart, Charles Murray 1783-1859
ApCAB Sup
Cathcart, Charles Sanderson 1865-1945
WhAm 2
Cathcart, Charles William 1809-1888 *ApCAB,*
BiAUS, BiDrAC, NatCAB 4, TwCBDA,
WhAm H
Cathcart, James Leander 1767-1843 *DcAmB,*
WhAm H
Cathcart, Jane R 1874- *BiCAW*
Cathcart, Robert Spann 1871-1949 *NatCAB 47,*
WhAm 2
Cathcart, Stanley H 1889-1953 *WhAm 3*
Cathcart, Thomas Edward 1894-1968 *WhAm 5*
Cathcart, Wallace Hugh 1865- *WhAm 4*
Cathcart, William 1825-1908 *WhAm 1*
Cathcart, William 1826-1908 *ApCAB, DcAmB,*
TwCBDA
Cathcart, William Ledyard 1855-1925 *WhAm 1*
Cathcart, William Schaw 1755-1843 *ApCAB*
Cathcart, William Shaw 1755-1843 *Drake*
Cathell, Daniel Webster 1839- *WhAm 4*
Cathell, William T 1864- *WhAm 4*
Cather, David Clark 1879-1944 *WhAm 2*
Cather, T Russell 1888-1944 *NatCAB 34*
Cather, Willa Sibert 1873-1947 *DcAmB S4,*
EncAAH, EncAB, McGEWB,
NatCAB 44, NotAW, REnAW, WebAB
Cather, Willa Sibert 1875-1947 *WomWWA 14*
Cather, Willa Sibert 1876-1947 *ApCAB X,*
WhAm 2
Catherine De Medicis 1519-1589 *McGEWB*
Catherine Of Siena, Saint 1347-1380 *McGEWB*
Catherine II, The Great 1729-1796 *McGEWB*
Catheron, Alice Millett 1878- *WomWWA 14*
Catherwood, Frederick 1799-1854 *IlBEAAW,*
NewYHSD
Catherwood, Mary Hartwell 1847-1902 *AmBi,*
AmWom, ApCAB Sup, DcAmB,
NatCAB 9, NotAW, TwCBDA,
WhAm 1
Cathey, Cornelius Oliver 1908- *EncAAH*
Cathey, George Andrew 1882-1950 *NatCAB 39*
Cathles, Lawrence Maclagan 1877- *WhAm 5*
Cathrall, Isaac 1764-1819 *ApCAB, Drake*
Catiline 108?BC-062BC *McGEWB*
Catlett, Edward Tredick 1888-1949 *NatCAB 40*
Catlett, Fred Wayne 1882-1961 *NatCAB 48*
Catlett, Sidney 1910-1951 *DcAmB S5*
Catlin, Albertus Wright 1868-1933 *WhAm 1*
Catlin, Amos Parmalee 1823-1900 *NatCAB 8*
Catlin, Charles Albert 1849-1916 *WhAm 1*

Catlin, George 1796-1872 *AmBi, ApCAB, BnEnAmA, DcAmB, Drake, EncAAH, EncAB, IlBEAAW, McGEWB, NatCAB 3, NewYHSD, REnAW, TwCBDA, WebAB, WhAm H*

Catlin, George Byron 1857-1934 *NatCAB 30*

Catlin, George S 1809-1851 *BiAUS*

Catlin, George Smith 1808-1851 *BiDrAC, WhAm H*

Catlin, Henry Guy 1843- *WhAm 4*

Catlin, Isaac Swartwood 1835-1916 *NatCAB 3, WhAm 1*

Catlin, Laura Wood 1841- *AmWom*

Catlin, Louise Ensign 1861- *WhAm 4, WomWWA 14*

Catlin, Malcolm Bruce 1902-1960 *NatCAB 49*

Catlin, Randolph 1887-1961 *WhAm 4*

Catlin, Robert 1840-1903 *NatCAB 18*

Catlin, Robert Mayo 1853-1934 *ApCAB X, WhAm 1*

Catlin, Roy George 1883-1937 *WhAm 1*

Catlin, Sanford Robinson 1871-1951 *NatCAB 40*

Catlin, Theodore Burr *NewYHSD*

Catlin, Theron Ephron 1878-1960 *BiDrAC, WhAm 3*

Catlin, Warren Benjamin 1881-1968 *WhAm 5*

Cato, Marcus Porcius, The Elder 234BC-149BC *McGEWB*

Cato, Marcus Porcius, The Younger 095BC-046BC *McGEWB*

Cato, Sterling G *BiAUS*

Caton, Arthur J 1851-1904 *WhAm 1*

Caton, Harry Anderson 1881- *WhAm 6*

Caton, John Dean 1812-1895 *ApCAB, DcAmB, NatCAB 4, TwCBDA, WhAm H*

Caton, Martin Jennings 1863- *NatCAB 12*

Caton, Richard 1763-1845 *ApCAB*

Cator, George 1856-1932 *WhAm 1*

Cator, Thomas Vincent 1851- *TwCBDA*

Cator, William Whitfield 1864-1939 *NatCAB 42*

Catron, B Lacey 1912-1959 *NatCAB 48*

Catron, Bayard Lacey 1874-1944 *NatCAB 33*

Catron, Charles Christopher 1879-1951 *WhAm 4*

Catron, John 1778-1865 *ApCAB, BiAUS, Drake, TwCBDA, WhAm H*

Catron, John 1781-1865 *NatCAB 2*

Catron, John 1786?-1865 *AmBi, DcAmB, WebAB*

Catron, Thomas Benton 1840-1921 *BiDrAC, REnAW, WhAm 1*

Catroux, Georges 1877-1969 *WhWW-II*

Catt, Carrie Lane Chapman 1859-1947 *AmWom, ApCAB X, BiCAW, DcAmB S4, EncAB, McGEWB, NatCAB 15, NatCAB 38, NotAW, WebAB, WhAm 2, WhAmP, WomWWA 14*

Catt, George William 1860-1905 *NatCAB 10, WhAm 1*

Cattani, Gaetano 1696-1733 *ApCAB Sup*

Cattell, Alexander Gilmore 1816-1894 *ApCAB, BiAUS, BiDrAC, DcAmB, NatCAB 2, TwCBDA, WhAm H*

Cattell, Edward James 1856-1938 *WhAm 1*

Cattell, Henry Ware 1862-1936 *NatCAB 30, WhAm 1*

Cattell, J McKeen 1860-1944 *ApCAB X, NatCAB 34, WhAm 2*

Cattell, James McKeen 1860-1944 *BiDAmEd, DcAmB S3, DcScB, NatCAB 13, TwCBDA, WebAB*

Cattell, Jaques 1904-1960 *WhAm 4*

Cattell, Richard Bartley Channing 1900-1964 *NatCAB 52, WhAm 4*

Cattell, William Ashburner 1863-1920 *WhAm 1*

Cattell, William Cassaday 1827-1898 *DcAmB, WhAm H*

Cattell, William Cassady 1827-1898 *NatCAB 11, TwCBDA*

Cattell, William Cassidy 1827-1898 *ApCAB*

Cattelle, Wallis Richard 1848-1912 *WhAm 1*

Catterall, Helen Honor Tunnicliff 1870- *WomWWA 14*

Catterall, Ralph Charles Henry 1866-1914 *WhAm 1*

Cattie, Joseph 1881-1950 *NatCAB 39*

Cattle Kate 1862?-1888 *REnAW*

Catto, Lord Thomas Sivewright 1879- *WhAm 6*

Catton, Bruce 1899- *WebAB*

Catton, Charles, Jr. 1756-1819 *NewYHSD, WhAm H*

Catts, Sidney Johnston 1863-1936 *NatCAB 37, WhAm 1*

Catullus, Gaius Valerius 084?BC-054?BC *McGEWB*

Cauche, Francois 1615-1660? *ApCAB Sup*

Cauchon, Joseph Edward 1816-1885 *ApCAB*

Cauchy, Baron Augustin Louis 1789-1857 *AsBiEn, DcScB, McGEWB*

Cauffman, Frank Guernsey 1850- *WhAm 4*

Caughey, John *NewYHSD*

Caughey, John Walton 1902- *REnAW*

Caughey, Milton Hazeltine 1911-1958 *NatCAB 48*

Caughey, William *NewYHSD*

Caughey, William Thomas 1912-1963 *NatCAB 50*

Caughran, B Howard 1890-1973 *NatCAB 57*

Cauldwell, Frederic Wadsworth 1873- *WhAm 5*

Cauldwell, John Britton 1855- *WhAm 4*

Cauldwell, Leslie Giffen 1861-1941 *WhAm 1*

Cauldwell, Leslie Giffen 1864-1941 *NatCAB 3*

Cauldwell, Oscar Ray 1892-1959 *WhAm 3*

Cauldwell, S Milbank 1862-1916 *NatCAB 49*

Cauldwell, William 1824- *NatCAB 1*

Cauldwell, William Al Burtis 1827-1893 *NatCAB 15*

Caulfield, Bernard Gregory 1828-1887 *BiAUS, BiDrAC, WhAm H*

Caulfield, Henry Stewart 1873-1966 *BiDrAC, WhAm 4*

Caulfield, John Francis 1878- *WhAm 6*

Caulk, John Roberts 1881-1938 *WhAm 1*

Caulkins, Frances Mainwaring 1796-1869 *ApCAB*

Caulkins, Frances Manwaring 1795-1869 *Drake, NotAW, TwCBDA*

Caulkins, Horace James 1850-1923 *NatCAB 40*

Caullery, Maurice Jules Gaston Corneille 1868-1958 *DcScB, WhAm 3*

Caupolican d1558 *ApCAB*

Causey, Francis Frederick 1867-1933 *NatCAB 25*

Causey, James Campbell, Jr. 1902-1973 *WhAm 6*

Causey, James Henry 1873-1943 *NatCAB 32*

Causey, John Williams 1841-1908 *BiDrAC*

Causey, P F 1801-1871 *BiAUS*

Causey, Peter Foster 1801-1871 *NatCAB 11*

Causey, William Bowdoin 1865-1936 *WhAm 1*

Causici, Enrico *NewYHSD*

Causin, John M S 1811-1861 *BiAUS, BiDrAC, WhAm H*

Causler, Charles Warner 1871- *WhoColR*

Causse, Mrs. M S *NewYHSD*

Cauthorn, Joseph Lurton 1862-1969 *WhAm 5*

Cautley, Mabel MacLean *WomWWA 14*

Cavadas, Athenagoras 1885-1965 *WhAm 4*

Cavagnaro, James Francis 1883-1970 *NatCAB 56, WhAm 5*

Cavagnaro, Robert John 1905-1969 *WhAm 5*

Cavaignac, Jacques 1853-1905 *WhoMilH*

Cavaignac, Louis Eugene 1802-1857 *WhoMilH*

Cavalcante, Anthony 1897-1966 *BiDrAC*

Cavalcanti, Guido 1255?-1300 *McGEWB*

Cavaler, Paul *NewYHSD*

Cavalho *NewYHSD*

Cavalieri, Bonaventura 1598-1647 *DcScB*

Cavalieri, Lina 1874- *WhAm 5*

Cavallaro, Joseph B 1903-1957 *WhAm 3*

Cavallero, Ugo 1880-1943 *WhWW-II*

Cavalli, Pietro Francesco 1602-1676 *McGEWB*

Cavallito, Albino 1905-1966 *WhAm 4*

Cavallo, Tiberius 1749-1809 *DcScB*

Cavallon, Georgio 1904- *BnEnAmA*

Cavan, Marie 1889-1968 *WhAm 5*

Cavana, Martin 1849- *WhAm 4*

Cavanagh, C J 1908-1972 *WhAm 5*

Cavanagh, Helen 1907- *EncAAH*

Cavanagh, James 1853-1920 *NatCAB 18*

Cavanagh, John Alexis 1878- *WhAm 6*

Cavanagh, Richard Parkinson 1887-1953 *NatCAB 41*

Cavanaugh, George Walter 1870-1938 *NatCAB 30*

Cavanaugh, James Michael 1823-1879 *BiAUS, BiDrAC, WhAm H*

Cavanaugh, John *NewYHSD*

Cavanaugh, John William 1870-1935 *NatCAB 14, WhAm 1*

Cavanaugh, John William 1906-1969 *WhAm 5*

Cavanaugh, Michael 1834?- *NewYHSD*

Cavanaugh, Michael George 1896-1968 *NatCAB 54*

Cavanaugh, Robert Joseph 1905-1963 *WhAm 4*

Cavanaugh, William F *NewYHSD*

Cavanaugh, William John 1874-1949 *NatCAB 38*

Cavanilles, Antonio Jose 1745-1804 *DcScB*

Cave, C *NewYHSD*

Cave, Edward Powell 1880-1957 *NatCAB 47, WhAm 3*

Cave, H W 1890-1953 *WhAm 3*

Cave, Henry 1874-1963 *NatCAB 54, NatCAB 55*

Cave, Henry Wisdom 1887-1964 *WhAm 4*

Cave, Reuben Lindsay 1845- *NatCAB 4, TwCBDA, WhAm 4*

Cavelier, Rene Robert 1643-1687 *WebAB*

Cavelier, Robert *WhAm H*

Caven, William 1830- *ApCAB*

Cavender, John Hugus 1883-1940 *NatCAB 38*

Cavendish, Henry 1731-1810 *AsBiEn, DcScB, McGEWB*

Cavendish, Lord John d1796 *Drake*

Cavendish, Thomas 1564-1593 *ApCAB, Drake*

Caveness, Robert Lee 1866-1951 *NatCAB 38*

Caventou, Joseph-Bienaime 1795-1877 *DcScB*

Caverly, Charles Edward 1893-1946 *NatCAB 34*

Caverly, Robert Boodey 1806- *ApCAB Sup*

Caverno, Charles 1832-1916 *WhAm 1*

Caverno, Julia Harwood 1862- *WomWWA 14*

Cavett, Jesse William 1900-1963 *NatCAB 50*

Cavicchia, Peter Angelo 1879-1967 *BiDrAC, WhAm 4A*

Caviness, George Washington 1857- *TwCBDA*

Cavins, Lorimer Victor 1880-1945 *WhAm 2*

Cavins, William Livingston 1857-1929 *NatCAB 21*

Cavo, Andres 1739- *ApCAB Sup*

Cavour, Camillo Benso, Conte Di 1810-1861 *McGEWB*

Cawein, Madison Julius 1865-1914 *AmBi, DcAmB, NatCAB 8, TwCBDA, WhAm 1*

Cawl, Franklin Robert 1890-1961 *WhAm 4*

Cawley, Aloysius John 1884-1956 *NatCAB 47*

Cawley, Edgar Moore 1871- *WhAm 5*

Cawley, Robert Ralston 1893-1973 *WhAm 6*

Cawood, Richard Lawrence 1882-1968 *NatCAB 54*

Cawthon, Edly Wilkerson 1874-1951 *NatCAB 40*

Cawthorn, Joseph 1868-1949 *WhAm 2*

Caxias, L A DeLima E Silva, Duque De 1803-1880 *McGEWB*

Caxias, Luis Alves DeLima 1800?- *ApCAB*

Caxton, William 1422-1491 *McGEWB*

Cay, Florence Genovar *WomWWA 14*

Cayce, Edgar 1877-1945 *WhAm 4*

Caye, Woolsey Moorman 1885-1942 *NatCAB 33*

Cayeux, Lucien 1864-1944 *DcScB*

Cayia, Alfred Joseph 1892-1961 *NatCAB 49*

Cayley, Arthur 1821-1895 *DcScB*

Caylor, Charles Eli 1870-1944 *NatCAB 39*

Caylor, Harvey Wallace 1867-1932 *IlBEAAW*

Caylor, John 1894-1966 *WhAm 4*

Cayton, Herbert Cohen 1882-1947 *NatCAB 35*

Cayton, Horace Roscoe 1903-1970 *WhAm 5*

Cayvan, Georgia Eva 1857-1906 *NotAW*

Cayvan, Georgia Eva 1858-1906 *AmWom, DcAmB, NatCAB 2, WhAm 1*

Caywood, Roland Blanchard 1890-1952 *NatCAB 40, WhAm 3*

Cazedessus, Eugene Romain 1872-1938 *WhAm 1*

Cazenave, Alphee 1795-1877 *BiHiMed*

Cazenova, Edward *NewYHSD*

Cazenove, Theophile 1740-1811 *DcAmB,*

WhAm H

Caziarc, Louis Vasmer 1844-1935 *WhAm 1*
Cazier, Henry Hallowell 1885-1963 *REnAW*
Cazneau, Jane Maria E McManus Storms
  1807-1878 *NotAW*
Ce-Komo-Pyn *IlBEAAW*
Ceausescu, Nicolae 1918- *McGEWB*
Ceballos, Jose 1830- *ApCAB*
Cech, Eduard 1893-1960 *DcScB*
Cecil Of Chelwood, Viscount 1864-1958
  WhAm 3
Cecil, Charles Purcell 1893- *WhAm 3*
Cecil, Edgar A Robert Cecil, Viscount 1864-1958
  McGEWB
Cecil, Elizabeth Frances *NatCAB 3*
Cecil, George W 1891-1970 *WhAm 5*
Cecil, James McCosh 1891-1954 *WhAm 3*
Cecil, John Giles 1855-1913 *WhAm 1*
Cecil, Lamar 1902-1958 *NatCAB 52,*
  WhAm 3
Cecil, Russell 1853-1925 *WhAm 1*
Cecil, Russell LaFayette 1881-1965 *NatCAB 51,*
  WhAm 4
Cecoin, Michael *NewYHSD*
Cedarleaf, Edwin Swan 1879-1943 *NatCAB 32*
Cederberg, Elford Alfred 1918- *BiDrAC*
Cederberg, William Emanuel 1876- *WhAm 5*
Cedergren, Hugo 1891-1971 *WhAm 5*
Cederstrom, Albert Gustaf 1898-1965 *WhAm 4*
Cehrs, Charles Harold 1918-1970 *WhAm 5*
Cekada, Emil Bogomir 1903-1972 *WhAm 6*
Cela Y Trulock, Camilo Jose 1916- *McGEWB*
Celaya, Juan De 1490?-1558 *DcScB*
Celebrezze, Anthony Joseph 1910- *BiDrUSE*
Celentano, William C 1904-1972 *WhAm 5*
CeLeron DeBlainville, Pierre Joseph De
  WhAm H
Celeste 1814-1882 *ApCAB*
Celestin, Oscar Papa 1884-1954 *DcAmB S5*
Celine, Louis Ferdinand 1894-1961 *McGEWB,*
  WhAm 4
Cell, George C 1875-1937 *WhAm 1*
Cell, John Wesley 1907-1967 *NatCAB 54,*
  WhAm 5
Cella, John G 1909-1968 *WhAm 5*
Celler, Emanuel 1888- *BiDrAC*
Cellini, Benvenuto 1500-1571 *McGEWB*
Cellini, Renato 1912-1967 *WhAm 4*
Celoron DeBienville 1715?- *ApCAB*
Celoron DeBlainville, Pierre Joseph De 1693-1759
  DcAmB
Celoron DeBlainville, Pierre Joseph De see also
  DeCeleron
Cels, Jacques-Philippe-Martin 1740-1806 *DcScB*
Celsius, Anders 1701-1744 *AsBiEn, DcScB*
Celsus, Aulus Cornelius *DcScB*
Celsus, Aulus Cornelius 010?BC- *AsBiEn*
Celsus, Aulus Cornelius 025?BC-045?AD
  McGEWB
Celsus, Aulus Cornelius 030BC-050AD
  BiHiMed
Cenerazzo, Walter William 1913-1968
  NatCAB 55
Censorinus *DcScB*
Centeno, Diego 1505-1549 *ApCAB*
Centnerszwer, Mieczyslaw 1871-1944 *DcScB*
Cepeda, Fernando De *ApCAB*
Cephas, Benjamin A 1875- *WhoColR*
Ceracchi see also Cerrachi
Ceracchi, Giuseppe 1740- *NatCAB 8*
Ceracchi, Giuseppe 1751-1802 *NewYHSD*
Ceracchi, Giuseppe 1751-1802 *WhAm H*
Cerda, Alfonso DeLa d1592 *ApCAB*
Cerf, Barry 1881-1948 *NatCAB 37, WhAm 2*
Cerf, Bennett Alfred 1898-1971 *WebAB,*
  WhAm 5
Cerf, Edward Owen 1918-1959 *WhAm 3*
Cerf, Jay Henry 1923-1974 *WhAm 6*
Cerf, Katharine Agnew Martin 1886-
  WomWWA 14
Cermak, Anton Joseph 1873-1933 *DcAmB S1,*
  WhAm 1, WhAmP
Cerracchio, Enrico Filiberto 1880- *WhAm 6*
Cerrachi see also Cerachi
Cerrachi, Giuseppe 1760?- *Drake*
Cerrachi, Giuseppe 1760?-1801 *ApCAB*
Cerre, Jean Gabriel 1734-1805 *DcAmB,*
  WhAm H

Certain, Casper Carl 1885-1940 *DcAmLiB*
Certier, George 1831?- *NewYHSD*
Ceruti, Edward Burton 1875- *WhoColR*
Cervantes, Vicente 1755-1829 *DcScB*
Cervantes Saavedra, Miguel De 1547-1616
  McGEWB
Cervera, Pascual 1835?- *ApCAB Sup*
Cesalpino, Andrea 1519-1603 *DcScB,*
  DcScB
Cesare, Oscar Edward 1883-1948 *DcAmB S4*
Cesaro, Ernesto 1859-1906 *DcScB*
Cesi, Federico 1585-1630 *DcScB*
Cesnola, Louis Palma Di 1832-1904 *WhAm 1*
Cesnola, Luigi Palma Di 1832-1904 *AmBi,*
  ApCAB, DcAmB, NatCAB 1, TwCBDA
Cespedes, Carlos Manuel De 1819-1874 *ApCAB,*
  Drake Sup, McGEWB
Cespedes Y Ortiz, Carlos Miguel 1881-1955
  WhAm 3
Cessna, Clyde Vernon 1879-1954 *NatCAB 41*
Cessna, John 1821-1893 *BiAUS, BiDrAC,*
  WhAm H
Cessna, Orange Howard 1852-1932 *WhAm 1*
Cestaro, Michael Paul 1907-1974 *WhAm 6*
Cesti, Pietro 1623-1669 *McGEWB*
Cestoni, Giacinto 1637-1718 *DcScB*
Cetshwayo 1826?-1884 *McGEWB*
Cetti, Lewis *NewYHSD*
Ceulen, Ludolph Van 1540-1610 *DcScB*
Ceva, Giovanni 1647?-1734 *DcScB*
Ceva, Tomasso 1648-1737 *DcScB*
Cezanne, Paul 1839-1906 *McGEWB*
Chabanel, Natalis 1613- *ApCAB*
Chabert, Joseph Bernard, Marquis Of 1724-1805
  ApCAB, Drake
Chabot, Jean 1806-1860 *ApCAB Sup*
Chabrat, Guy Ignatius 1787-1868 *ApCAB,*
  TwCBDA, WhAm H
Chabry, Laurent 1855-1893 *DcScB*
Chace, Arnold Buffum 1845-1932 *NatCAB 17,*
  WhAm 1
Chace, Arthur Freeborn 1879- *WhAm 6*
Chace, Eliza Greene 1851- *WomWWA 14*
Chace, Elizabeth Buffum 1806-1899 *AmBi,*
  AmWom, DcAmB, NotAW, TwCBDA,
  WhAm H
Chace, George Hart 1883-1957 *WhAm 3*
Chace, George Ide 1808-1885 *ApCAB,*
  NatCAB 8, TwCBDA
Chace, Henry Thurston 1873-1955 *NatCAB 47*
Chace, Jonathan 1829-1917 *ApCAB, BiDrAC,*
  NatCAB 12, TwCBDA, WhAm 1
Chace, Kip Ingersoll 1888-1965 *NatCAB 51*
Chace, Malcolm Greene 1875-1955 *WhAm 3*
Chace, Robert Rhodes 1910-1954 *NatCAB 48*
Chace, Seth Howard 1871-1934 *NatCAB 25*
Chace, William N 1908-1976 *WhAm 6*
Chadbourn, Erlon R 1855- *WhAm 4*
Chadbourn, William Hobbs, Jr. 1865- *WhAm 4*
Chadbourne, Adeline M 1862- *WomWWA 14*
Chadbourne, George Storrs 1833-1923 *WhAm 1*
Chadbourne, Henrietta Topliff *WomWWA 14*
Chadbourne, Paul Ansel 1823-1883 *ApCAB,*
  BiDAmEd, DcAmB, NatCAB 6,
  TwCBDA, WhAm H
Chadbourne, Thomas Lincoln 1871-1938
  NatCAB 30, WhAm 1
Chadbourne, William Merriam 1879-1964
  WhAm 4
Chaddock, Charles Gilbert 1861-1936 *WhAm 1*
Chaddock, Robert Emmet 1879-1940 *WhAm 1*
Chadeayne, Henry Waring 1859-1945
  NatCAB 34
Chadman, Marion Lee 1863-1932 *NatCAB 25*
Chadsey, Charles Ernest 1870-1930 *WhAm 1*
Chadwick *NewYHSD*
Chadwick, Charles 1874-1953 *WhAm 3*
Chadwick, Charles Wesley 1861-1940 *WhAm 1*
Chadwick, Clarence Wells d1933 *WhAm 1*
Chadwick, Cornelia Jones 1856- *WomWWA 14*
Chadwick, E Wallace 1884-1969 *BiDrAC,*
  WhAm 5
Chadwick, Sir Edwin 1800-1890 *BiHiMed,*
  McGEWB
Chadwick, Ernest John 1913-1966 *NatCAB 54*
Chadwick, French Ensor 1844-1919 *AmBi,*
  ApCAB Sup, ApCAB X, DcAmB,
  NatCAB 9, WhAm 1

Chadwick, George Halcott 1876-1953 *WhAm 3*
Chadwick, George W 1854-1931 *ApCAB*
Chadwick, George Whitefield 1854-1931 *AmBi,*
  DcAmB S1, WhAm 1
Chadwick, George Whitfield 1854-1931
  BiDAmEd, NatCAB 7, TwCBDA
Chadwick, Henry 1824-1908 *DcAmB, WebAB*
Chadwick, Henry Dexter 1872-1969
  NatCAB 54, WhAm 5
Chadwick, Sir James 1891-1974 *AsBiEn,*
  McGEWB, WhAm 6
Chadwick, James Carroll 1915-1973 *WhAm 6*
Chadwick, James Read 1844-1905 *DcAmB,*
  NatCAB 12, WhAm 1
Chadwick, John Raymond 1896-1961 *WhAm 4*
Chadwick, John Rogers 1856- *NatCAB 14*
Chadwick, John White 1840-1904 *AmBi,*
  ApCAB, DcAmB, NatCAB 7, WhAm 1
Chadwick, Josh *NewYHSD*
Chadwick, Lee Sherman 1875-1958 *ApCAB X,*
  NatCAB 43, WhAm 5
Chadwick, Leigh E 1904-1975 *WhAm 6*
Chadwick, S Percy R 1870-1943 *NatCAB 32*
Chadwick, Stephen Fowler 1825-1895
  NatCAB 8
Chadwick, Stephen Fowler 1894-1975 *WhAm 6*
Chadwick, Stephen James 1863-1931 *WhAm 1*
Chadwick, Thomas Frederick 1871-1954
  NatCAB 44
Chadwick, William F 1828?- *NewYHSD*
Chafee, Henry Sharpe 1864-1964 *WhAm 4*
Chafee, Zechariah, Jr. 1885-1957 *WebAB,*
  WhAm 3
Chafer, Lewis Sperry 1871-1952 *WhAm 3*
Chaffe, Henry Hansell 1877- *WhAm 5*
Chaffee, Adna Lomanza 1842-1914 *TwCBDA*
Chaffee, Adna Romanza 1842-1914 *AmBi,*
  ApCAB Sup, DcAmB, NatCAB 10,
  NatCAB 30, WebAB, WebAMB,
  WhAm 1
Chaffee, Adna Romanza 1884-1941 *DcAmB S3,*
  NatCAB 30, WebAB, WebAMB,
  WhAm 1
Chaffee, Arthur Billings 1852- *WhAm 4*
Chaffee, Calvin Clifford 1811-1896 *BiAUS,*
  BiDrAC, WhAm H
Chaffee, Emma Hurd 1855- *WomWWA 14*
Chaffee, Emory Leon 1885-1975 *WhAm 6*
Chaffee, George Thrall 1857-1929 *ApCAB X,*
  NatCAB 21
Chaffee, H Almon 1876-1956 *NatCAB 45*
Chaffee, Hugh Goheen 1868-1937 *NatCAB 27*
Chaffee, James Franklin 1827-1911 *NatCAB 8*
Chaffee, Jerome B 1825-1886 *BiAUS, DcAmB*
Chaffee, Jerome Bonaparte 1825-1886 *REnAW*
Chaffee, Jerome Bunty 1825-1886 *ApCAB,*
  BiDrAC, NatCAB 6, WhAm H, WhAmP
Chaffee, Jerome Hunting 1825-1886 *TwCBDA*
Chaffee, Jerome Stuart 1873-1947 *NatCAB 36,*
  WhAm 2
Chaffee, Orel Nathan 1876-1965 *NatCAB 51*
Chaffee, Robert Emory 1918-1974 *WhAm 6*
Chaffee, Roger B 1935-1967 *WhAm 4*
Chaffereau, Peter *NewYHSD*
Chaffers, William Henry 1887-1947
  NatCAB 37
Chaffey, Andrew McCord 1874-1941
  NatCAB 40, WhAm 1
Chaffey, George 1848- *WhAm 4*
Chaffin, Clarence Eugene 1882-1943
  NatCAB 32
Chaffin, Lucien Gates 1846-1927 *WhAm 1*
Chafin, Eugene Wilder 1852-1920 *DcAmB,*
  WhAm 1
Chagall, Marc 1887- *McGEWB*
Chagas, Carlos Ribeiro Justiniano 1879-1934
  DcScB
Chaille, Stanford Emerson 1830-1911 *ApCAB,*
  NatCAB 9, TwCBDA, WhAm 1
Chaille-Long, Charles 1842-1917 *AmBi,*
  DcAmB, NatCAB 10, WebAMB,
  WhAm 1
Chain, Ernst Boris 1906- *AsBiEn*
Chain, Mrs. James Albert 1852-1892 *IlBEAAW*
Chainey, George 1851- *WhAm 4*
Chaisson, John Robert 1916-1972 *WhAm 5*
Chalcidius *DcScB*
Chalee *IlBEAAW*

Chalfant, Alexander Steele 1912-1963 *WhAm 4*
Chalfant, Floyd 1889-1954 *NatCAB 44*
Chalfant, George Alexander 1841-1904
  NatCAB 13
Chalfant, Harry Malcolm 1869-1932 *WhAm 1*
Chalfant, Henry 1867-1928 *NatCAB 22*
Chalfant, Jefferson David 1846-1931 *BnEnAmA*
Chalfant, John Weakley 1827-1898 *NatCAB 22*
Chalfant, John Weakley 1875-1933 *NatCAB 25*
Chalfant, Minnie List 1884- *WomWWA 14*
Chaliapin, Feodor 1873-1938 *WhAm 1*
Chalif, Louis Harvey 1876- *NatCAB 17*
Chalifour, Joseph Onesime 1889-1956 *WhAm 3*
Chalk, John Delber 1884-1956 *NatCAB 46*
Chalkley, Lyman 1861-1934 *NatCAB 33,*
  WhAm 1
Chalkley, Otway Hebron 1883-1956
  NatCAB 47, WhAm 3
Chalkley, Thomas 1675-1741 *AmBi, DcAmB,*
  Drake, NatCAB 11, WhAm H
Chalkly, Thomas 1675-1741 *ApCAB*
Chall, Alfred *NewYHSD*
Challener, William Albert 1866- *WhAm 4*
Challinor, Mercedes Crimmins 1885-1966
  NatCAB 52
Challis, James 1803-1882 *DcScB*
Challis, John 1907-1974 *WhAm 6*
Challoner, John 1856-1928 *NatCAB 28*
Chalmers, Allan Knight 1897-1972 *WhAm 5*
Chalmers, David Mark 1927- *EncAAH*
Chalmers, George 1742-1825 *ApCAB, Drake*
Chalmers, Gordon Keith 1904-1956 *NatCAB 46,*
  WhAm 3
Chalmers, Hamilton Henderson 1834-1885
  NatCAB 5
Chalmers, Harvey, II 1890-1971 *WhAm 5*
Chalmers, Hattie Elizabeth *WomWWA 14*
Chalmers, Henry 1892-1958 *NatCAB 43,*
  WhAm 3
Chalmers, Hugh 1873-1932 *ApCAB X,*
  NatCAB 24, WhAm 1
Chalmers, James 1859-1937 *WhAm 1*
Chalmers, James Ronald 1831-1898 *BiDConf,*
  BiDrAC, DcAmB, NatCAB 8, TwCBDA,
  WhAm H
Chalmers, James Valentine 1848-1927
  NatCAB 21
Chalmers, Joseph W d1853 *BiAUS*
Chalmers, Joseph W 1807-1853 *ApCAB,*
  NatCAB 4, TwCBDA
Chalmers, Joseph Williams 1806-1853 *BiDrAC,*
  WhAm H
Chalmers, Lionel 1715?-1777 *ApCAB, Drake,*
  TwCBDA
Chalmers, Louis Henry 1861-1934 *WhAm 1*
Chalmers, Neal 1891-1963 *NatCAB 53*
Chalmers, Robert Scott 1882-1935 *WhAm 1*
Chalmers, Stephen 1880-1935 *WhAm 1*
Chalmers, Thomas 1780-1847 *McGEWB*
Chalmers, Thomas 1869-1940 *WhAm 1*
Chalmers, Thomas Clark 1868- *WhAm 4*
Chalmers, Thomas Hardie d1966 *WhAm 4*
Chalmers, Thomas Mitchell 1858-1937
  WhAm 2
Chalmers, Thomas Stuart 1881-1923 *WhAm 1*
Chalmers, William Everett 1868-1928 *WhAm 1*
Chalmers, William James 1852-1938
  DcAmB S2, WhAm 1
Chalmers, William Wallace 1861-1944 *BiDrAC,*
  WhAm 4
Chambaud, T *NewYHSD*
Chambellan, Rene Paul d1955 *WhAm 3*
Chamberlain, Abiram 1837-1911 *NatCAB 13,*
  WhAm 1
Chamberlain, Alexander Francis 1865-1914
  DcAmB, TwCBDA, WhAm 1
Chamberlain, Allen 1867- *WhAm 3*
Chamberlain, Anna Mary Irwin *WomWWA 14*
Chamberlain, Anna V 1842- *WomWWA 14*
Chamberlain, Arthur Henry 1872-1942
  ApCAB X, WhAm 2
Chamberlain, Arthur Neville 1869-1940
  McGEWB
Chamberlain, Arthur VanDoorn 1891-1971
  WhAm 5
Chamberlain, Benjamin B 1833?- *NewYHSD*
Chamberlain, Charles Ernest 1917- *BiDrAC*

Chamberlain, Charles Joseph 1863-1943
  DcAmB S3, DcScB, WhAm 2
Chamberlain, Clark Wells 1870-1948
  NatCAB 37, WhAm 2
Chamberlain, Clarke Edmund 1895-1970
  NatCAB 56, WhAm 5
Chamberlain, D H 1835-1907 *BiAUS*
Chamberlain, Daniel Henry 1835-1907 *ApCAB,*
  DcAmB, NatCAB 12, TwCBDA,
  WhAm 1, WhAmP
Chamberlain, Dwight Lincoln 1877-1955
  WhAm 3
Chamberlain, Ebenezer Mattoon 1805-1861
  BiAUS, BiDrAC
Chamberlain, Ebenzer Mattoon 1805-1861
  WhAm H
Chamberlain, Eugene Tyler 1856-1929 *TwCBDA,*
  WhAm 1
Chamberlain, Francis Asbury 1855-1940
  WhAm 1
Chamberlain, Frank 1826-1910 *WhAm 1*
Chamberlain, Frederick Stanley 1872-1936
  WhAm 1
Chamberlain, George Agnew 1879-1966
  WhAm 4
Chamberlain, George Earle 1854-1928 *BiDrAC,*
  DcAmB, NatCAB 14, WhAm 1, WhAmP
Chamberlain, Glenn R 1877- *WhAm 3*
Chamberlain, Grace Wilmarth Caldwell 1870-
  WomWWA 14
Chamberlain, Henry 1824-1907 *WhAm 1*
Chamberlain, Henry Richardson 1859-1911
  DcAmB, WhAm 1
Chamberlain, Henry Thomas 1900-1961
  NatCAB 49, WhAm 4
Chamberlain, Herbert Marvin 1878-1951
  WhAm 3
Chamberlain, Hiram Sanborn 1835-1916
  WhAm 1
Chamberlain, Hope Summerell 1870- *WhAm 5*
Chamberlain, Houston Stewart 1855-1927
  McGEWB
Chamberlain, Isaac Dearborn 1840-1918
  WhAm 1
Chamberlain, Jacob 1835-1908 *ApCAB Sup,*
  DcAmB, NatCAB 35, TwCBDA,
  WhAm 1
Chamberlain, Jacob Chester 1860-1905
  NatCAB 24
Chamberlain, Jacob Payson 1802-1878 *BiAUS,*
  BiDrAC, WhAm H
Chamberlain, James Franklin 1869-1943
  WhAm 2
Chamberlain, James Mortimer Wills 1905-1974
  WhAm 6
Chamberlain, Jean Bosler *WomWWA 14*
Chamberlain, Jeremiah 1794-1850 *ApCAB,*
  TwCBDA
Chamberlain, John 1838-1921 *NatCAB 19*
Chamberlain, John 1927- *BnEnAmA*
Chamberlain, John Curtis 1772-1834 *BiAUS,*
  BiDrAC, WhAm H
Chamberlain, John Curtis 1847-1931
  NatCAB 23
Chamberlain, John Loomis 1858-1948
  ApCAB X, WhAm 2
Chamberlain, John M 1904-1959 *WhAm 3*
Chamberlain, Joseph 1836-1914 *McGEWB*
Chamberlain, Sir Joseph Austen 1863-1937
  McGEWB
Chamberlain, Joseph Perkins 1873-1951
  DcAmB S5, WhAm 3
Chamberlain, Joseph Redington 1861-1926
  NatCAB 39
Chamberlain, Joseph Scudder 1870- *WhAm 5*
Chamberlain, Joshua Lawrence 1824-1914 *AmBi*
Chamberlain, Joshua Lawrence 1828-1914
  ApCAB, BiDAmEd, DcAmB, Drake Sup,
  NatCAB 1, TwCBDA, WebAMB,
  WhAm 1, WhAmP
Chamberlain, Leander Trowbridge 1837-1913
  WhAm 1
Chamberlain, Lowell 1851-1922 *NatCAB 20*
Chamberlain, Lucy Jefferies 1893-1969
  WhAm 5
Chamberlain, Mary Crowinshield Endicott
  1864-1914 *WomWWA 14*

Chamberlain, Mary Crowninshield Endicott
  1864-1914 *WhAm 1*
Chamberlain, Mary E Bowman 1864-
  WomWWA 14
Chamberlain, Mellen 1821-1900 *DcAmB,*
  TwCBDA, WhAm 1
Chamberlain, Montague 1844-1924 *WhAm 1*
Chamberlain, Myron Levi 1844-1919
  NatCAB 19
Chamberlain, Nathan Henry 1828-1901 *DcAmB,*
  WhAm H
Chamberlain, Neville 1869-1940 *WhWW-II*
Chamberlain, Norman Stiles 1887-1961
  IlBEAAW
Chamberlain, Orville Tryon 1841- *WhAm 4*
Chamberlain, Oscar Pearl 1870-1932 *WhAm 1*
Chamberlain, Owen 1920- *AsBiEn, WebAB*
Chamberlain, Paul Mellen 1865-1940 *WhAm 1*
Chamberlain, Richard Hall 1915-1975 *WhAm 6*
Chamberlain, Robert F 1884-1967 *WhAm 4*
Chamberlain, Robert Linton 1871-1941
  NatCAB 31
Chamberlain, Rufus Nutting 1866-1931
  NatCAB 22
Chamberlain, Samuel 1895-1975 *WhAm 6*
Chamberlain, Samuel Selwyn 1851-1916
  WhAm 1
Chamberlain, Selah 1812-1890 *ApCAB,*
  TwCBDA
Chamberlain, Valentine Burt 1833-1893
  NatCAB 32
Chamberlain, W Lawrence 1878-1961 *WhAm 4*
Chamberlain, Webb Parks 1876-1948
  NatCAB 36
Chamberlain, Weston Percival 1871-1948
  NatCAB 38
Chamberlain, William d1828 *BiAUS*
Chamberlain, William 1753-1828 *NatCAB 8*
Chamberlain, William 1755-1828 *BiDrAC,*
  WhAm H
Chamberlain, William 1790- *NewYHSD*
Chamberlain, William 1878-1967 *WhAm 4*
Chamberlain, William Isaac 1837-1920 *AmBi,*
  DcAmB, NatCAB 28
Chamberlain, William Isaac 1862-1937
  WhAm 1
Chamberlain, William W 1876-1945 *WhAm 2*
Chamberlain, William Warren 1873-1951
  NatCAB 40
Chamberlain, Wilt 1936- *WebAB*
Chamberlain, Winthrop Burr 1864- *WhAm 4*
Chamberlaine, William 1871-1925 *NatCAB 20,*
  WhAm 1
Chamberlaine, William Wilson 1836-1923
  NatCAB 42
Chamberland, Charles Edouard 1851-1908
  DcScB
Chamberlayne, Catharine Jane d1920 *WhAm 1*
Chamberlayne, Churchill Gibson 1876-1939
  WhAm 1
Chamberlayne, Lewis Parke 1879-1917
  WhAm 1
Chamberlin, Brown 1827- *ApCAB*
Chamberlin, Charles Caswell 1848-1917
  NatCAB 34
Chamberlin, Chester Harvey 1859-1922
  WhAm 1
Chamberlin, Clayton Jenkins 1903-1958
  WhAm 4
Chamberlin, Edson Joseph 1852- *WhAm 4*
Chamberlin, Edward Hastings 1899-1967
  NatCAB 53
Chamberlin, F Tolles 1873-1961 *WhAm 4*
Chamberlin, Franklin 1821-1896 *NatCAB 2*
Chamberlin, Frederick 1870-1943 *WhAm 2*
Chamberlin, George Ellsworth 1872- *WhAm 5*
Chamberlin, Harry Dwight 1887-1944 *WhAm 2*
Chamberlin, Henry Barrett 1867-1941
  ApCAB X, NatCAB 30, WhAm 1
Chamberlin, Henry Harmon 1873-1951
  WhAm 3
Chamberlin, Humphrey Barker 1847-1897
  NatCAB 1, TwCBDA
Chamberlin, Jehiel Weston 1857-1921
  NatCAB 6
Chamberlin, Joseph Edgar 1851-1935
  NatCAB 25, TwCBDA, WhAm 1
Chamberlin, Joseph Hanson 1846-1932
  WhAm 3

Chamberlin, Joshua Lawrence 1828- *BiAUS*
Chamberlin, Lewis VanBuren 1890-1965
NatCAB 51
Chamberlin, McKendree Hypes 1838- *TwCBDA,
WhAm 4*
Chamberlin, Ralph Vary 1879- *WhAm 6*
Chamberlin, Rollin Thomas 1881-1948 *WhAm 2*
Chamberlin, Stephen Johnes 1907-1965
NatCAB 53
Chamberlin, Stephen Jones 1889-1971
NatCAB 57, WhAm 5
Chamberlin, Thomas Chrowder 1843-1928 *AmBi,
ApCAB X, AsBiEn, DcAmB, DcScB,
McGEWB, NatCAB 19, TwCBDA,
WhAm 1*
Chamberlin, Thomas Crowder 1843-1928
ApCAB, NatCAB 11
Chamberlin, Walter Howard 1866- *WhAm 4*
Chamberlin, Ward Bryan 1833-1903
NatCAB 25
Chamberlin, Ward Bryan 1843- *NatCAB 12*
Chamberlin, Ward Bryan 1881-1956
NatCAB 42
Chamberlin, William Bricker 1873-1939
NatCAB 31
Chamberlin, William H 1897-1969 *WhAm 5*
Chamberlin, Willis Arden 1868- *WhAm 4*
Chambers *NewYHSD*
Chambers, Alexander 1832-1888 *ApCAB,
TwCBDA*
Chambers, Benjamin 1800?- *NewYHSD*
Chambers, Charles Augustus 1873- *WhAm 5*
Chambers, Charles Carroll 1888-1958 *WhAm 3*
Chambers, Charles Edward 1883-1941
NatCAB 31, WhAm 2
Chambers, Charles Julius 1850-1920 *ApCAB,
DcAmB*
Chambers, Clarke 1921- *EncAAH*
Chambers, Cyrus, Jr. 1833-1911 *NatCAB 27*
Chambers, David 1780-1864 *BiAUS, BiDrAC,
WhAm H*
Chambers, David Laurance 1879-1963 *WhAm 4*
Chambers, Edward 1859-1927 *WhAm 1*
Chambers, Edward Francis Stapleton 1885-1962
NatCAB 50
Chambers, Ezekiel Forman 1788-1867 *ApCAB,
BiAUS, BiDrAC, DcAmB, Drake,
NatCAB 7, TwCBDA, WhAm H,
WhAmP*
Chambers, Francis T 1855-1939 *WhAm 1*
Chambers, Francis Taylor, Jr. 1897-1969
NatCAB 55, WhAm 5
Chambers, Frank Ross 1850-1940 *NatCAB 29*
Chambers, Frank Taylor 1870-1932 *NatCAB 46,
WhAm 1*
Chambers, Frank White 1908-1962 *WhAm 4*
Chambers, Franklin Smith 1876-1947
NatCAB 36
Chambers, George 1786-1866 *ApCAB, BiAUS,
BiDrAC, DcAmB, Drake, NatCAB 4,
TwCBDA, WhAm H*
Chambers, George Stuart 1841- *TwCBDA*
Chambers, Georgie Mar 1886- *WomWWA 14*
Chambers, Henry 1785?-1826 *ApCAB, BiAUS,
NatCAB 11, TwCBDA*
Chambers, Henry Cousins 1823-1871 *BiDConf*
Chambers, Henry Edward 1860-1929 *ApCAB X,
BiDAmEd, WhAm 1*
Chambers, Henry H 1790-1826 *BiDrAC,
WhAm H*
Chambers, I Mench 1865-1922 *WhAm 3*
Chambers, James 1851-1911 *WhAm 1*
Chambers, James Julius 1850-1920 *DcAmB*
Chambers, John d1765 *Drake*
Chambers, John 1700?-1764 *TwCBDA*
Chambers, John 1710?-1765 *ApCAB,
NatCAB 13*
Chambers, John 1779-1852 *ApCAB, BiAUS,
Drake, TwCBDA*
Chambers, John 1780-1852 *BiDrAC, DcAmB,
NatCAB 11, WhAm H, WhAmP*
Chambers, John 1797-1875 *NatCAB 15*
Chambers, John Storey 1823-1901 *NatCAB 13*
Chambers, Joseph Fleischmann 1862-1956
NatCAB 46
Chambers, Joseph T *NewYHSD*
Chambers, Julius 1850-1920 *DcAmB,
NatCAB 14, TwCBDA, WhAm 1*

Chambers, Lenoir 1891-1970 *WhAm 5*
Chambers, Mary 1870- *WomWWA 14*
Chambers, Mary Davoren 1865- *WhAm 1*
Chambers, Merritt Madison 1899- *BiDAmEd*
Chambers, Myron Gossette 1889-1960 *WhAm 4*
Chambers, Othniel Robert 1894-1951 *WhAm 3*
Chambers, Porter Flewellen 1853- *ApCAB X,
WhAm 4*
Chambers, R *NewYHSD*
Chambers, Robert 1802-1871 *DcScB*
Chambers, Robert 1849-1917 *NatCAB 17,
WhAm 1*
Chambers, Robert 1880-1957 *NatCAB 46*
Chambers, Robert 1881-1957 *WhAm 3*
Chambers, Robert Augustus 1894-1951
WhAm 3
Chambers, Robert Craig 1832-1901 *NatCAB 7,
WhAm 1*
Chambers, Robert Foster 1887-1947 *WhAm 2*
Chambers, Robert William 1865-1933 *AmBi,
ApCAB Sup, ApCAB X, DcAmB S1,
NatCAB 13, TwCBDA, WhAm 1*
Chambers, Sherman Daniel 1881- *WhAm 6*
Chambers, Smiley Newton, Jr. 1891-1955
NatCAB 42
Chambers, Stuart Munson 1887-1960
NatCAB 49, WhAm 4
Chambers, Susan *NewYHSD*
Chambers, Talbot Wilson 1819-1896 *ApCAB,
DcAmB, NatCAB 9, TwCBDA,
WhAm H*
Chambers, Thomas 1808?- *NewYHSD*
Chambers, Thomas 1815-1866? *BnEnAmA*
Chambers, Thomas Stryker 1852-1919
NatCAB 18
Chambers, Victor John 1869- *WhAm 5*
Chambers, Walter A 1878-1951 *NatCAB 39*
Chambers, Walter Boughton 1866-1945
WhAm 2
Chambers, Washington Irving 1856-1934
NatCAB 25, WhAm 4
Chambers, Will Grant 1867-1949 *ApCAB X,
WhAm 2*
Chambers, William 1800-1883 *ApCAB*
Chambers, William 1884-1951 *NatCAB 41,
WhAm 3*
Chambers, William B *NewYHSD*
Chambers, William Earl 1892-1952 *WhAm 3*
Chambers, William Harold 1894-1966
NatCAB 53
Chambers, William Kirtley 1875-1954
NatCAB 41
Chambers, William Lea 1852-1933 *ApCAB X,
NatCAB 25, WhAm 4*
Chambers, William Nesbitt 1853-1934 *WhAm 2*
Chambers, William Nesbitt 1914-1970
NatCAB 55
Chambers, William Royal 1882-1969
NatCAB 57
Chambless, John Robert 1911-1972 *WhAm 5*
Chamblin, Walter Williams, Jr. 1898-1955
WhAm 3
Chambliss, Alexander Wilds 1864-1947
NatCAB 40, WhAm 2
Chambliss, Charles Edward 1871- *WhAm 5*
Chambliss, Hardee 1872-1947 *NatCAB 35,
WhAm 2*
Chambliss, John Randolph 1833-1864 *ApCAB,
NatCAB 12, TwCBDA*
Chambliss, John Randolph, Sr. 1809-1875
BiDConf
Chambliss, William Parham 1827-1887 *ApCAB,
TwCBDA*
Chambodut, Louis Claude Marie 1821-1880
ApCAB
Chambre, A St. John d1912 *WhAm 1*
Chamisso, Adelbert Von 1781-1838 *DcScB,
DcScB Sup*
Chamlee, Aquila 1869- *WhAm 4*
Chamlee, Mario 1892-1966 *WhAm 4,
WhAm 5*
Chamorro, Fruto 1806-1855 *Drake*
Chamorro, Frutos 1806-1855 *ApCAB*
Chamot, Emile Monnin 1868- *WhAm 3*
Chamove, Arnold S 1902-1971 *WhAm 5*
Champagne, George *NewYHSD*
Champe, John 1752-1798? *ApCAB, Drake,
NatCAB 7, TwCBDA*

Champion, Aristarchus d1871 *NatCAB 13*
Champion, Charles Sumner 1871-1916 *WhAm 1*
Champion, Edwin VanMeter 1890- *BiDrAC*
Champion, Epaphroditus d1835 *BiAUS*
Champion, Epaphroditus 1756-1834 *BiDrAC,
WhAm H, WhAmP*
Champion, Fritz Roy 1878-1933 *WhAm 1*
Champion, John B 1868-1948 *WhAm 3*
Champion, Lee Rogers 1867-1940 *NatCAB 30*
Champlain, Samuel De 1567?-1635 *AmBi,
ApCAB, DcAmB, NewYHSD, WebAB,
WhAm H*
Champlain, Samuel De 1570?-1635 *Drake,
McGEWB*
Champlin, Charles Davenport 1885-1950
NatCAB 39
Champlin, Christopher Grant 1768-1840 *ApCAB,
BiAUS, BiDrAC, Drake, NatCAB 7,
TwCBDA, WhAm H*
Champlin, Edwin Ross 1854-1928 *WhAm 1*
Champlin, George B *ApCAB X*
Champlin, Herbert Hiram 1868-1944
NatCAB 40
Champlin, James Tift 1811-1882 *ApCAB,
NatCAB 8, TwCBDA*
Champlin, John 1863-1938 *NatCAB 31*
Champlin, John Denison 1834-1915 *ApCAB,
DcAmB, NatCAB 8, TwCBDA,
WhAm 1*
Champlin, John Wayne 1831-1901 *DcAmB,
NatCAB 4, WhAm 1*
Champlin, Stephen 1789-1870 *ApCAB,
DcAmB, Drake, NatCAB 4, TwCBDA,
WhAm H*
Champlin, Stephen G d1864 *Drake*
Champlin, Stephen Gardner 1797-1864
TwCBDA
Champlin, Stephen Gardner 1827-1864 *ApCAB*
Champney, Benjamin 1817-1907 *AmBi,
ApCAB, DcAmB, Drake, NatCAB 4,
NewYHSD, TwCBDA, WhAm 1*
Champney, Elizabeth Williams 1850-1922
*AmWom, NatCAB 11, TwCBDA,
WhAm 1, WomWWA 14*
Champney, James Wells 1843-1903 *AmBi,
ApCAB, DcAmB, Drake, IlBEAAW,
NatCAB 11, TwCBDA, WhAm 1*
Champney, Lizzie Williams 1850- *ApCAB*
Champney, W L *NewYHSD*
Champneys, Benjamin 1800-1871 *ApCAB,
TwCBDA*
Champollion, Jean Francois 1790-1832
McGEWB
Chanca, Diego Alvarez *WhAm H*
Chance, A Bishop 1873-1949 *NatCAB 38*
Chance, Britton 1913- *AsBiEn*
Chance, Edwin Mickley 1885-1954 *WhAm 3*
Chance, Henry Martyn 1856-1937 *NatCAB 30,
WhAm 1*
Chance, Jesse Clifton 1843-1914 *WhAm 1*
Chance, Julie Grinnell *NatCAB 14, WhAm 1,
WomWWA 14*
Chance, William Claudius 1880- *WhoColR*
Chancel, Gustav Charles Bonaventure 1822-1890
DcScB
Chancel, Ludovic 1901- *WhAm 5*
Chancellor, Charles Williams 1831-1915
NatCAB 28, WhAm 1
Chancellor, Charles Williams 1833- *ApCAB,
NatCAB 10, TwCBDA*
Chancellor, Eustathius A 1854- *NatCAB 5,
TwCBDA, WhAm 1*
Chancellor, Richard d1556 *McGEWB*
Chancellor, William Estabrook 1867-1963
WhAm 4
Chancey, Robert Edward Lee 1880-1948
WhAm 2
Chanche, John Mary Joseph 1795-1852 *DcAmB,
Drake, TwCBDA, WhAm H*
Chanche, John Mary Joseph 1795-1853 *ApCAB,
NatCAB 4*
Chancourtois, A E Beguyer De *DcScB*
Chandler, Abiel 1777-1851 *ApCAB, Drake,
TwCBDA*
Chandler, Ada May 1879- *WomWWA 14*
Chandler, Albert Benjamin 1898- *BiDrAC,*

WebAB

Chandler, Albert Brown 1840-1923 *NatCAB 3, WhAm 1*

Chandler, Albert Edward 1872-1954 *WhAm 3*

Chandler, Alexander John 1859-1950 *REnAW, WhAm 4*

Chandler, Alfred Dupont 1847-1923 *ApCAB X, NatCAB 43, WhAm 1*

Chandler, Alfred N 1858- *WhAm 5*

Chandler, Algernon Bertrand, Jr. 1870-1928 *WhAm 1*

Chandler, Alice Greene 1851- *WomWWA 14*

Chandler, Anna Curtis d1969 *WhAm 5*

Chandler, Anna Souther Pond 1848- *WomWWA 14*

Chandler, Asa Crawford 1891-1958 *WhAm 3*

Chandler, Bert D 1874-1947 *WhAm 2*

Chandler, Carl Beane 1876-1934 *NatCAB 26*

Chandler, Charles 1850-1938 *WhAm 1*

Chandler, Charles DeForest 1878-1939 *NatCAB 37, WhAm 1*

Chandler, Charles Frederick 1836-1925 *AmBi, ApCAB, DcAmB, NatCAB 13, NatCAB 23, TwCBDA, WebAB, WhAm 1*

Chandler, Charles Henry 1840-1885 *ApCAB, TwCBDA, WhAm 1*

Chandler, Charles Lyon 1883-1962 *NatCAB 50*

Chandler, Charles Quarles 1864-1943 *WhAm 2*

Chandler, Edward Barron 1800-1880 *ApCAB*

Chandler, Elbert Milam 1886-1968 *WhAm 5*

Chandler, Elizabeth Margaret 1807-1834 *ApCAB, DcAmB, Drake, NotAW, TwCBDA, WhAm H*

Chandler, Eva 1855- *WomWWA 14*

Chandler, Floyd C 1920- *IlBEAAW*

Chandler, Francis Ward 1844-1926 *WhAm 1*

Chandler, Frank Wadleigh 1873-1947 *WhAm 2*

Chandler, Frederick Charles 1874-1945 *NatCAB 36*

Chandler, Frederick Charles 1900-1942 *NatCAB 32*

Chandler, Fremont Augustus 1893-1954 *WhAm 3*

Chandler, G L *NewYHSD*

Chandler, George Brinton 1865-1943 *WhAm 2*

Chandler, George Fletcher 1872- *NatCAB 18*

Chandler, George Garvin, Jr. 1890-1973 *NatCAB 57, WhAm 5*

Chandler, George Henry 1869-1912 *NatCAB 31*

Chandler, George William 1882- *WhoColR*

Chandler, Grace Webster 1843- *WomWWA 14*

Chandler, Happy 1898- *WebAB*

Chandler, Harrison Tyler 1840-1912 *NatCAB 24*

Chandler, Harry 1864-1944 *DcAmB S3, NatCAB 40, WhAm 2*

Chandler, Henry Porter 1880-1975 *WhAm 6*

Chandler, Isaac N *NewYHSD*

Chandler, Izora d1906 *WhAm 1*

Chandler, James Gilbert 1856-1924 *NatCAB 23*

Chandler, Jefferson 1837-1912 *NatCAB 26*

Chandler, Jefferson Paul 1872-1948 *WhAm 2*

Chandler, Jessie Wallace 1886- *WomWWA 14*

Chandler, Joe Albert 1903-1974 *BiDAmEd*

Chandler, John d1841 *BiAUS*

Chandler, John 1693-1762 *NatCAB 13*

Chandler, John 1760-1841 *ApCAB, Drake*

Chandler, John 1762-1841 *BiDrAC, DcAmB, TwCBDA, WhAm H, WhAmP*

Chandler, John 1770?-1841 *NatCAB 4*

Chandler, John Gorham 1830-1915 *NatCAB 17, WhAm 1*

Chandler, Mrs. John Greene *NewYHSD*

Chandler, John Greene 1815-1879 *NewYHSD, WhAm H*

Chandler, John Scudder 1849-1934 *DcAmB S1*

Chandler, John Winthrop 1826-1877 *WhAm H*

Chandler, Joseph Goodhue 1813-1880? *NewYHSD*

Chandler, Mrs. Joseph Goodhue 1820-1868 *NewYHSD*

Chandler, Joseph Harvey 1842- *NatCAB 16*

Chandler, Joseph Hayes 1854- *WhAm 4*

Chandler, Joseph Ripley 1792-1880 *ApCAB, BiAUS, BiDrAC, DcAmB, Drake, NatCAB 11, TwCBDA, WhAm H, WhAmP*

Chandler, Julian Alvin Carroll 1872-1934 *DcAmB S1, NatCAB 24, WhAm 1*

Chandler, Katherine *WhAm 5, WomWWA 14*

Chandler, Kent 1892-1972 *WhAm 5*

Chandler, Lloyd Horwitz 1869-1947 *NatCAB 35, WhAm 2*

Chandler, Louise Prescott 1878- *WomWWA 14*

Chandler, Lucinda Banister 1828- *AmWom*

Chandler, Mary Alderson 1849- *AmWom*

Chandler, Mary Saxe 1863- *WomWWA 14*

Chandler, Norman 1899-1973 *WhAm 6*

Chandler, Peleg Whitman 1816-1889 *DcAmB, NatCAB 15, WhAm H*

Chandler, Percy Milton 1873-1944 *ApCAB X, WhAm 2*

Chandler, Philip 1907-1968 *WhAm 5*

Chandler, Ralph 1829-1889 *ApCAB, NatCAB 4, TwCBDA*

Chandler, Ralph Bradford 1891-1970 *WhAm 5*

Chandler, Raymond Thornton 1888-1959 *WebAB, WhAm 3*

Chandler, Samuel 1794-1867 *ApCAB*

Chandler, Samuel W 1803-1900 *NewYHSD*

Chandler, Seth Carlo 1846-1913 *DcAmB, DcScB, WhAm 1*

Chandler, Theodore Edson 1894-1945 *WhAm 2*

Chandler, Thomas 1772-1866 *BiAUS, BiDrAC, WhAm H*

Chandler, Thomas Alberter 1871-1953 *BiDrAC, WhAm 3*

Chandler, Thomas Bradbury 1726-1790 *ApCAB, DcAmB, Drake, TwCBDA, WhAm H*

Chandler, Victor L L 1836?- *NewYHSD*

Chandler, Walter 1887-1967 *BiDrAC, WhAm 4*

Chandler, Walter Marion 1867-1935 *BiDrAC, NatCAB 14, WhAm 1*

Chandler, William Eaton 1835-1917 *ApCAB, BiAUS, BiDrAC, BiDrUSE, DcAmB, NatCAB 4, TwCBDA, WhAm 1, WhAmP*

Chandler, William George 1882-1965 *WhAm 4*

Chandler, William Henry 1841-1906 *ApCAB, TwCBDA, WhAm 1*

Chandler, William Henry 1871-1939 *WhAm 1*

Chandler, William Jessup 1842- *WhAm 4*

Chandler, Winfield 1841?- *NewYHSD*

Chandler, Winthrop 1747-1790 *BnEnAmA, NewYHSD*

Chandler, Zachariah 1813-1879 *AmBi, ApCAB, BiAUS, BiDrAC, BiDrUSE, DcAmB, McGEWB, NatCAB 4, TwCBDA, WhAm H, WhAmP*

Chandor, Douglas 1897-1953 *WhAm 3*

Chandor, Valentine L *NewYHSD*

Chandragupta Maurya d298?BC *McGEWB*

Chandrasekhar, Subrahmanyan 1910- *AsBiEn*

Chanel, Adelbert Benjamin 1890-1967 *NatCAB 54*

Chanel, Gabrielle 1883-1971 *WhAm 5*

Chaney, Eugene 1868-1949 *NatCAB 39*

Chaney, Eugene 1885-1967 *NatCAB 53*

Chaney, George Leonard *ApCAB X*

Chaney, Gussie Scott 1865- *WomWWA 14*

Chaney, James Eugene 1885-1967 *WhAm 4*

Chaney, John 1790-1881 *BiAUS, BiDrAC, WhAm H*

Chaney, John Crawford 1853-1940 *BiDrAC*

Chaney, John Crawford 1854- *WhAm 3*

Chaney, Lon 1883-1930 *DcAmB S1, WebAB, WhAm HA, WhAm 4*

Chaney, Lucian West, Jr. 1857-1935 *ApCAB, NatCAB 27, TwCBDA, WhAm 1*

Chaney, Mary Ann Browne *NewYHSD*

Chaney, Morris J 1858-1941 *WhAm 3*

Chaney, Newcomb Kinney 1883-1966 *WhAm 4*

Chaney, Novetus Holland 1856-1925 *WhAm 1*

Chaney, Ralph Hill 1886-1961 *WhAm 4*

Chaney, Stewart 1910-1969 *WhAm 5*

Chaney, William Calvert 1889-1965 *NatCAB 51*

Chanfrau, Francis S 1824-1884 *DcAmB, WhAm H*

Chanfrau, Frank S 1824-1884 *ApCAB, NatCAB 7*

Chanfrau, Henrietta Baker 1837-1909 *ApCAB, DcAmB*

Chang And Eng 1811-1874 *ApCAB, DcAmB, WebAB, WhAm H*

Chang, Chien 1853-1926 *McGEWB*

Chang, Chih-Tung 1837-1909 *McGEWB*

Chang, Chu-Cheng 1525-1582 *McGEWB*

Chang, Hsin-Hai 1900-1973 *WhAm 5*

Chang, Hsueh-Ch'eng 1738-1801 *McGEWB*

Chang, John Myun 1899-1966 *WhAm 4*

Chang, Po-Go d846 *McGEWB*

Chang, Tso-Lin 1873-1928 *McGEWB*

Chanis, Daniel d1961 *WhAm 4*

Chanler, Amelie Rives 1863- *AmWom, NatCAB 1, TwCBDA, WomWWA 14*

Chanler, Beatrice Winthrop Ashley 1886-1946 *NatCAB 36*

Chanler, John Winthrop 1826-1877 *BiAUS, BiDrAC, NatCAB 12*

Chanler, Lewis Stuyvesant 1869-1942 *NatCAB 50, WhAm 3*

Chanler, Lewis Stuyvesant 1869-1963 *WhAm 4*

Chanler, Margaret 1862-1952 *WhAm 3*

Chanler, Robert Winthrop 1872-1930 *IlBEAAW*

Chanler, Theodore Ward 1902-1961 *NatCAB 49, WhAm 4*

Chanler, William Astor 1867-1934 *ApCAB Sup, BiDrAC, NatCAB 9, NatCAB 25, WhAm 1*

Chanler, Winthrop Astor 1863-1926 *NatCAB 50*

Channer, George Stanton 1882-1957 *NatCAB 47*

Channing, Edward 1856-1931 *AmBi, ApCAB, DcAmB S1, McGEWB, NatCAB 13, TwCBDA, WebAB, WhAm 1*

Channing, Edward Tyrrel 1790-1856 *ApCAB, Drake, NatCAB 13, TwCBDA*

Channing, Edward Tyrrell 1790-1856 *BiDAmEd, DcAmB, WhAm H*

Channing, George 1888-1957 *WhAm 3*

Channing, Grace Ellery 1862-1937 *WhAm 1*

Channing, J Parke 1863-1942 *WhAm 2*

Channing, Roscoe Henry 1832-1916 *NatCAB 26*

Channing, Walter 1786-1876 *ApCAB, DcAmB, Drake, TwCBDA, WhAm H*

Channing, Walter 1849-1921 *NatCAB 19, WhAm 1*

Channing, William 1751-1793 *NatCAB 8*

Channing, William Ellery 1780-1842 *AmBi, ApCAB, DcAmB, DcAmReB, Drake, EncAB, McGEWB, NatCAB 5, TwCBDA, WebAB, WhAm H*

Channing, William Ellery 1818-1901 *ApCAB, DcAmB, NatCAB 13, TwCBDA, WhAm 1*

Channing, William Francis 1820-1901 *ApCAB, DcAmB, Drake, NatCAB 23, TwCBDA, WhAm H*

Channing, William Henry 1810-1884 *ApCAB, DcAmB, Drake, NatCAB 13, TwCBDA, WhAm H*

Channon, Frank Ernest 1870-1920 *WhAm 1*

Channon, Vesta Miller Westover *BiCAW, WomWWA 14*

Chantry, Allan Joseph 1883-1959 *NatCAB 47*

Chanute, Octave d1832-1910 *AmBi, DcAmB, NatCAB 10, TwCBDA, WebAB, WhAm 1*

Chany, Jane Douglas Butler 1857- *WomWWA 14*

Chanzy, Antoine Eugene Alfred 1823-1883 *WhoMilH*

Chao, Meng-Fu 1254-1322 *McGEWB*

Chapais, Jean Charles 1825?- *ApCAB*

Chapeau, Ellen 1844- *WhAm 4*

Chapelle, Howard Irving 1900-1975 *WhAm 6*

Chapelle, Placide Louis 1842-1905 *ApCAB Sup, DcAmB, NatCAB 7, NatCAB 12, TwCBDA, WhAm 1*

Chapin, Aaron Lucius 1817-1892 *AmBi, ApCAB, BiDAmEd, DcAmB, NatCAB 3, TwCBDA, WhAm H*

Chapin, Alfred Clark 1848-1936 *BiDrAC, NatCAB 1, TwCBDA, WhAm 1*

Chapin, Alfred Hastings 1876-1962 *NatCAB 54, WhAm 4*

Chapin, Alice Delafield 1879-1964 *NatCAB 52, WomWWA 14*

Chapin, Alonzo Bowen 1808-1858 *ApCAB,
DcAmB, Drake, TwCBDA*
Chapin, Alpheus 1787?-1870 *NewYHSD*
Chapin, Angie Clara 1855- *WomWWA 14*
Chapin, Anna Alice 1880-1920 *WhAm 1,
WomWWA 14*
Chapin, Arthur Beebe 1868-1943 *WhAm 2*
Chapin, Augusta Jane 1836-1905 *AmWom,
NotAW, WhAm 1*
Chapin, Benjamin Chester 1874-1918 *ApCAB X,
WhAm 1*
Chapin, Benjamin M *NewYHSD*
Chapin, Calvin 1763-1851 *DcAmB, Drake,
WhAm H*
Chapin, Charles Augustus 1845-1913 *ApCAB X,
NatCAB 21*
Chapin, Charles Frederic 1852-1926 *WhAm 1*
Chapin, Charles Sumner 1859-1924 *WhAm 1*
Chapin, Charles Value 1856-1941 *DcAmB S3,
EncAB, NatCAB 39, WhAm 1*
Chapin, Chester W 1798-1883 *BiAUS*
Chapin, Chester William 1797-1883 *NatCAB 5,
WhAm H*
Chapin, Chester William 1798-1883 *DcAmB*
Chapin, Chester Williams 1798-1883 *BiDrAC*
Chapin, Clara Christiana 1852- *AmWom*
Chapin, Cornelia VanAuken d1972 *WhAm 5*
Chapin, Delia Lucretia 1854- *WomWWA 14*
Chapin, E Barton 1885-1967 *WhAm 5*
Chapin, Edward Whitman 1840-1924 *WhAm 3*
Chapin, Edward Young 1865-1954 *NatCAB 42,
WhAm 3*
Chapin, Edwin Hubbell 1814-1880 *ApCAB,
DcAmB, Drake, NatCAB 6, WhAm H*
Chapin, Edwin Hubbell 1814-1889 *TwCBDA*
Chapin, Emery David 1827-1883 *NatCAB 10,
NatCAB 11*
Chapin, Emily Coolidge 1849- *WomWWA 14*
Chapin, Flora Amorette Simmons
WomWWA 14
Chapin, Francis 1899-1965 *WhAm 4*
Chapin, Fred H d1958 *WhAm 3*
Chapin, Graham Hurd 1799-1843 *BiAUS,
BiDrAC, WhAm H*
Chapin, Henry 1811-1878 *ApCAB,
NatCAB 13, TwCBDA*
Chapin, Henry Austin 1813-1898 *NatCAB 10*
Chapin, Henry Barton 1827-1914 *WhAm 1*
Chapin, Henry Dwight 1857-1942 *DcAmB S3,
NatCAB 31, WhAm 2*
Chapin, Henry Edgerton 1859-1922 *WhAm 1*
Chapin, Howard Millar 1887-1940 *NatCAB 34,
WhAm 1*
Chapin, James 1887-1975 *WhAm 6*
Chapin, James Henry 1832-1892 *NatCAB 10*
Chapin, James Paul 1889-1964 *WhAm 4*
Chapin, Jane Catherine Louise Value 1814-1891
NewYHSD, WhAm H
Chapin, John Bassett 1829-1918 *ApCAB Sup,
WhAm 1*
Chapin, John Henry 1832-1892 *TwCBDA*
Chapin, John R 1823-1904 *IlBEAAW,
NewYHSD*
Chapin, Lindley Hoffman *ApCAB X*
Chapin, Lloyd Walter 1902-1963 *WhAm 4*
Chapin, Ralph Edwin 1863-1943 *NatCAB 34*
Chapin, Robert Coit 1863-1913 *WhAm 1*
Chapin, Rollin Coe 1888-1952 *NatCAB 42*
Chapin, Roy Dickeman 1880-1936 *ApCAB X*
Chapin, Roy Dikeman 1880-1936 *BiDrUSE,
DcAmB S2, NatCAB 34, WhAm 1*
Chapin, Sallie F *AmWom*
Chapin, Samuel M 1902-1975 *WhAm 6*
Chapin, Sarah Flournoy Moore 1830?-1896
NotAW
Chapin, Selden 1899-1963 *WhAm 4*
Chapin, Simeon Brooks 1865-1945 *NatCAB 34*
Chapin, Slocum 1913-1975 *WhAm 6*
Chapin, Stephen 1778-1845 *ApCAB, Drake,
NatCAB 3, TwCBDA*
Chapin, William 1802-1888 *ApCAB Sup,
NewYHSD*
Chapin, William Andrew Robertson 1890-1961
NatCAB 49
Chapin, William Reed 1900-1962 *NatCAB 51*
Chapin, William Wallace d1957 *WhAm 3*
Chapin, William Wisner 1851-1928 *NatCAB 23*
Chapin, Willis McDonald 1893-1960 *WhAm 4*

Chapin, Willis Ormel 1860-1917 *NatCAB 17*
Chapin, Winogene Grabill *WomWWA 14*
Chapleau, Joseph Adolphe 1840- *ApCAB*
Chaplin, Ada C 1842-1883 *ApCAB*
Chaplin, Carroll Sherman 1882-1953
NatCAB 43
Chaplin, Charles Spencer 1889- *EncAB,
McGEWB, WebAB*
Chaplin, Christine 1842- *ApCAB*
Chaplin, Claude Moore 1892-1966 *NatCAB 53*
Chaplin, F Stuart 1888-1974 *WhAm 6*
Chaplin, Henry Prescott 1885-1962 *NatCAB 48,
WhAm 4*
Chaplin, James Crossan 1863- *WhAm 5*
Chaplin, Jane Dunbar 1819-1884 *ApCAB,
TwCBDA*
Chaplin, Jeremiah 1776-1841 *ApCAB, DcAmB,
Drake, NatCAB 8, TwCBDA, WhAm H*
Chaplin, Jeremiah 1813-1886 *ApCAB,
TwCBDA*
Chaplin, John Howard 1893-1958 *WhAm 3*
Chaplin, William Edwards 1860-1948 *WhAm 3*
Chaplin, Winfield Scott 1847-1918 *NatCAB 11,
TwCBDA, WhAm 1*
Chapline, Jesse Grant 1870-1937 *WhAm 1*
Chapline, Vance Duncan 1887-1970 *WhAm 5*
Chaplygin, Sergei Alekseevich 1869-1942 *DcScB*
Chapman, Alfred Francis 1900-1974 *WhAm 6*
Chapman, Alice T Hall *WomWWA 14*
Chapman, Alva R *NewYHSD*
Chapman, Alvah H, Sr. d1961 *WhAm 4*
Chapman, Alvan Wentworth 1809-1899 *AmBi,
ApCAB, DcAmB, DcScB, NatCAB 13,
TwCBDA, WhAm H*
Chapman, Andrew Grant 1839-1892 *BiDrAC,
WhAm H*
Chapman, Arthur 1873-1935 *WhAm 1*
Chapman, Arthur 1873-1959 *WhAm 3*
Chapman, Arthur Levi 1856-1932 *NatCAB 26*
Chapman, Augustus Alexandria 1803-1876
BiAUS, BiDrAC, WhAm H
Chapman, Aurelie Reynaud *WomWWA 14*
Chapman, Berlin Basil 1900- *EncAAH*
Chapman, Bird Beers 1821-1871 *BiAUS,
BiDrAC, WhAm H*
Chapman, Carlton Theodore 1860-1925
NatCAB 22, WhAm 1
Chapman, Caroline 1818?-1876 *NotAW*
Chapman, Carrie Lane *AmWom*
Chapman, Charles 1799-1869 *BiAUS, BiDrAC,
Drake, WhAm H*
Chapman, Charles Brewster *ApCAB X*
Chapman, Charles C 1853-1944 *ApCAB X,
WhAm 2*
Chapman, Charles Edward 1880-1941
ApCAB X, WhAm 2
Chapman, Charles Hiram 1869- *WhAm 3*
Chapman, Charles Shepard 1879-1962
IlBEAAW, WhAm 4
Chapman, Clowry 1871-1950 *WhAm 3*
Chapman, Cloyd Mason 1874-1944 *NatCAB 33*
Chapman, Daniel Knowlton 1904-1969
NatCAB 55, WhAm 5
Chapman, David Carpenter 1876-1944 *WhAm 3*
Chapman, David Leonard 1869-1958 *DcScB*
Chapman, Dwight Ingersoll 1903-1934
NatCAB 26
Chapman, Dwight Westley, Jr. 1905-1973
NatCAB 57, WhAm 5
Chapman, E B 1884-1954 *WhAm 3*
Chapman, Edna Mae Coleman d1972 *WhAm 6*
Chapman, Edward Mortimer 1862-1952
NatCAB 42, WhAm 3
Chapman, Edwin 1841-1915 *NatCAB 17*
Chapman, Edwin Garner 1862- *WhAm 4*
Chapman, Edwin Nesbit 1819-1888
ApCAB Sup
Chapman, Elbridge Gerry 1895-1954 *WhAm 3*
Chapman, Eleanor Stickney *WomWWA 14*
Chapman, Elizabeth Kimball 1869-
WomWWA 14
Chapman, Elverton Romanta 1848-1928
NatCAB 38, WhAm 1
Chapman, Emmanuel 1905-1948 *WhAm 2*
Chapman, Ervin S 1838-1921 *NatCAB 19,
WhAm 1*
Chapman, Francis 1869-1939 *WhAm 1*
Chapman, Frank Elmo 1884-1931 *NatCAB 22,*

WhAm 1
Chapman, Frank Michler 1864-1945 *DcAmB S3,
NatCAB 9, NatCAB 36, WebAB,
WhAm 2*
Chapman, Frederic A 1818-1891 *IlBEAAW,
NewYHSD, WhAm H*
Chapman, Frederick Augustus 1818-1891
TwCBDA
Chapman, Frederick Braydon 1875-1957
NatCAB 47
Chapman, Frederick Lewis 1896-1965 *WhAm 4*
Chapman, Frederick Trench 1887- *IlBEAAW*
Chapman, George 1559?-1634 *McGEWB*
Chapman, George H *ApCAB*
Chapman, George Herbert 1898-1967 *WhAm 5*
Chapman, George Thomas 1786-1872 *ApCAB,
Drake, TwCBDA*
Chapman, Gerald Howard 1902-1965 *WhAm 4*
Chapman, Guy Wood 1894-1961 *NatCAB 49*
Chapman, Harold Ouida 1896-1963 *NatCAB 50*
Chapman, Harry Powell 1888-1952 *WhAm 3*
Chapman, Henry 1804-1891 *BiDrAC,
WhAm H*
Chapman, Henry 1805?- *BiAUS*
Chapman, Henry Cadwalader 1845-1909
*ApCAB, DcAmB, NatCAB 22, TwCBDA,
WhAm 1*
Chapman, Henry Leland 1845-1912 *WhAm 1*
Chapman, Henry Stanton *ApCAB X*
Chapman, Herman Haupt 1874-1963
NatCAB 49
Chapman, Horace Leet 1837-1917 *NatCAB 12*
Chapman, Horace Leete 1837-1917 *NatCAB 27,
WhAm 3*
Chapman, Howard Rufus 1868-1942 *WhAm 2*
Chapman, Ione Minervia 1900-1974 *WhAm 6*
Chapman, Ira T 1874-1957 *WhAm 3*
Chapman, J H d1895 *WhAm H*
Chapman, James Alfred 1893-1964 *WhAm 4*
Chapman, James Blaine 1884-1947 *WhAm 2*
Chapman, James Crosby 1889-1925 *NatCAB 20,
WhAm 1*
Chapman, James Russell 1851- *WhAm 4*
Chapman, James Wilkinson, Jr. 1871-1943
WhAm 2
Chapman, John 1740-1800 *BiAUS, BiDrAC,
WhAm H*
Chapman, John 1774-1845 *EncAAH, WebAB*
Chapman, John 1775?-1847 *AmBi, DcAmB,
WhAm H*
Chapman, John 1822-1894 *BiHiMed*
Chapman, John 1900-1972 *WhAm 5*
Chapman, John A 1873-1960 *WhAm 3*
Chapman, John Abney 1821-1906 *NatCAB 8*
Chapman, John Alfred Metcalf 1829-
NatCAB 4, TwCBDA
Chapman, John Gabsby 1808-1889 *BnEnAmA*
Chapman, John Gadsby 1808- *ApCAB, BiAUS,
Drake*
Chapman, John Gadsby 1808-1889 *AmBi,
BiDAmEd, DcAmB, IlBEAAW,
NewYHSD, TwCBDA, WhAm H*
Chapman, John Gadsby 1808-1890 *NatCAB 7*
Chapman, John Grant 1798-1856 *BiAUS,
BiDrAC, Drake, WhAm H, WhAmP*
Chapman, John Jay 1862-1933 *AmBi,
DcAmB S1, WebAB, WhAm 1*
Chapman, John Martin 1887-1970 *WhAm 5*
Chapman, John Stanton Higham 1891-1972
WhAm 6
Chapman, John Wayne 1889-1963 *WhAm 4*
Chapman, John Wilbur 1859-1918 *DcAmB,
DcAmReB, WhAm 1*
Chapman, Joseph 1871-1948 *NatCAB 43,
WhAm 2*
Chapman, Judson W 1900-1951 *WhAm 3*
Chapman, Katharine Hopkins 1872- *WhAm 5,
WomWWA 14*
Chapman, Kenneth Milton 1875-1968 *IlBEAAW,
WhAm 6*
Chapman, Kenneth William 1911-1959
WhAm 4
Chapman, Leonard Fielding, Jr. 1913-
WebAMB
Chapman, Levi S 1865- *WhAm 5*
Chapman, Lila May d1953 *WhAm 3*
Chapman, Maria Weston 1806-1885 *AmBi,
ApCAB, DcAmB, NatCAB 2, NotAW,*

TwCBDA, WhAm H

Chapman, Millie Jane 1845- *AmWom,*
WomWWA 14

Chapman, Moses 1783-1821 *NewYHSD*

Chapman, Nathaniel 1780-1853 *ApCAB,*
BiHiMed, DcAmB, Drake, NatCAB 3,
TwCBDA, WhAm H

Chapman, Nellie Stanley 1863- *WomWWA 14*

Chapman, Norton Everett 1858-1926
NatCAB 21

Chapman, Orlow W 1832-1890 *NatCAB 5,*
TwCBDA

Chapman, Oscar Littleton 1896- *BiDrUSE*

Chapman, Paul Wilber 1891-1953 *BiDAmEd,*
NatCAB 46, WhAm 3

Chapman, Pleasant Thomas 1854-1931 *BiDrAC,*
WhAm 1

Chapman, Reuben d1882 *BiAUS*

Chapman, Reuben 1799-1882 *ApCAB, BiDrAC,*
TwCBDA, WhAm H, WhAmP

Chapman, Reuben 1802-1882 *DcAmB,*
NatCAB 10

Chapman, Reuben Atwater 1801-1873 *ApCAB,*
NatCAB 7, TwCBDA

Chapman, Robert Hett 1771-1833 *ApCAB,*
Drake, NatCAB 13

Chapman, Robert Hett 1772-1833 *TwCBDA*

Chapman, Robert Hollister 1868-1920
NatCAB 18, WhAm 1

Chapman, Rosamond Low 1882-
WomWWA 14

Chapman, Ross McClure 1881-1948
NatCAB 38, WhAm 2

Chapman, Roy H 1885-1952 *WhAm 3*

Chapman, Roy Harrison 1883-1952 *NatCAB 44*

Chapman, Royal Norton 1889-1939 *NatCAB 29*

Chapman, Sydney 1888-1970 *McGEWB*

Chapman, Theodore S 1877-1943 *WhAm 2*

Chapman, Theron Taggert 1902-1964 *WhAm 4*

Chapman, Thomas Garfield 1886-1965 *WhAm 4*

Chapman, Valcour 1856- *WhoColR*

Chapman, Victor Emmanuel 1890-1916 *DcAmB,*
WebAMB

Chapman, Virgil Munday 1895-1951 *BiDrAC,*
NatCAB 38, WhAm 3, WhAmP

Chapman, W Louis 1874-1936 *NatCAB 32*

Chapman, W M 1910-1970 *WhAm 5*

Chapman, Walter Hopkins 1892-1943
NatCAB 32

Chapman, Warren Hosea 1821- *ApCAB*

Chapman, William *NewYHSD*

Chapman, William 1810-1887 *ApCAB,*
TwCBDA

Chapman, William Burr 1890-1946 *NatCAB 34*

Chapman, William Edgar 1877- *WhAm 5*

Chapman, William Gerard 1877-1945
NatCAB 34, WhAm 2

Chapman, William Harold 1890-1954
NatCAB 44

Chapman, William L 1866-1928 *ApCAB X*

Chapman, William Rogers 1855-1935
NatCAB 30

Chapman, William Williams 1808-1892 *BiAUS,*
BiDrAC, WhAm H, WhAmP

Chapman, Woodallen 1875-1923 *WhAm 1,*
WomWWA 14

Chappe D'auteroche, Jean-Baptiste 1728-1769
DcScB

Chappel, Alonzo 1828-1887 *IIBEAAW,*
NewYHSD, WhAm H

Chappel, James Edward 1885-1960 *WhAm 3*

Chappel, William *NewYHSD*

Chappell, Absalom Harris 1801-1878 *BiAUS,*
BiDrAC, DcAmB, NatCAB 6, WhAm H

Chappell, Bill 1919- *IIBEAAW*

Chappell, Charles Henry 1841-1904 *NatCAB 16*

Chappell, Chester Will 1845-1909 *NatCAB 8*

Chappell, Edward A 1886-1955 *WhAm 3*

Chappell, Edwin Barfield 1853-1936
NatCAB 46, WhAm 3

Chappell, George Shepard 1878-1946 *WhAm 3*

Chappell, Howard Field 1861-1924 *ApCAB X*

Chappell, John Joel 1782-1871 *BiAUS,*
BiDrAC, WhAm H

Chappell, Joseph John 1907-1962 *WhAm 4*

Chappell, Matthew Napoleon 1900-1968
NatCAB 54, WhAm 5

Chappell, Sara Lyon 1875- *WomWWA 14*

Chappell, Walter Franklin 1856-1918 *WhAm 1*

Chappell, Will Charles 1878- *WhAm 6*

Chappell, Will H 1866-1947 *WhAm 2*

Chappell, William Venroe, Jr. 1922- *BiDrAC*

Chappelle, Benjamin Franklin 1885-1948
WhAm 2

Chappelle, Charles Ward 1874- *WhoColR*

Chappelle, William David 1857-1925 *WhAm 1,*
WhoColR

Chappelsmith, John 1807?-1883? *NewYHSD*

Chapple, Joe Mitchell 1867-1950 *NatCAB 46,*
WhAm 3

Chapple, William Dismore 1868-1956
NatCAB 45

Chaptal, Jean Antoine Claude 1756-1832
AsBiEn, DcScB

Charbonneau, Jean Baptiste 1805-1866 *REnAW*

Charbonneau, Joseph d1959 *WhAm 3*

Charbonneau, Louis Henry 1897-1971 *WhAm 5*

Charbonneau, Toussaint 1759?-1840? *REnAW*

Charcot, Jean-Baptiste 1867-1936 *DcScB*

Charcot, Jean-Martin 1825-1893 *BiHiMed,*
DcScB, McGEWB

Chard, Marie Louise 1868- *WomWWA 14*

Chardenon, Jean Pierre 1714?-1769 *DcScB*

Chardin, Jean Baptiste Simeon 1699-1779
McGEWB

Chardon, Jean Baptiste 1672-1743 *WhAm H*

Chardonnet, Louis Marie H B, Comte De
1839-1924 *AsBiEn, DcScB*

Chargaff, Erwin 1905- *AsBiEn*

Charipper, Harry A 1900-1971 *WhAm 5*

Charlemagne 742?-814 *AsBiEn, McGEWB*

Charles *NewYHSD*

Charles I 1600-1649 *McGEWB, WhoMilH*

Charles II 1630-1685 *McGEWB*

Charles II 1661-1700 *McGEWB*

Charles III 1716-1788 *McGEWB*

Charles IV 1316-1378 *McGEWB*

Charles IV 1748-1819 *McGEWB*

Charles V 1337-1380 *McGEWB*

Charles V 1500-1558 *McGEWB, WhoMilH*

Charles VI 1368-1422 *McGEWB*

Charles VII 1403-1461 *McGEWB*

Charles VIII 1470-1498 *McGEWB*

Charles X 1757-1836 *McGEWB*

Charles XII 1682-1718 *McGEWB, WhoMilH*

Charles Albert 1798-1849 *McGEWB,*
WhoMilH

Charles, Archduke Of Austria 1771-1847
WhoMilH

Charles XIV John 1763-1884 *McGEWB*

Charles Martel 690?-741 *McGEWB*

Charles V, Prince Of Lorraine, A 1712-1780
WhoMilH

Charles The Bold 1433-1477 *McGEWB*

Charles, Alta Genevieve 1899-1963 *NatCAB 50*

Charles, Benjamin Hynes 1866-1937
NatCAB 28, WhAm 1

Charles, Carrie Lane Riggs *WomWWA 14*

Charles, Christina Howell 1864- *WomWWA 14*

Charles, Dorothy 1906-1956 *WhAm 3*

Charles, Emily Thornton 1845- *AmWom,*
TwCBDA

Charles, Frances 1872- *WhAm 5,*
WomWWA 14

Charles, H *NewYHSD*

Charles, Howard Warner 1867-1931
NatCAB 23

Charles, Jacques-Alexandre-Cesar 1746-1823
AsBiEn, DcScB

Charles, Joseph D 1907-1966 *WhAm 4*

Charles, Maurice *NewYHSD*

Charles, Ray 1932- *EncAB*

Charles, S M *NewYHSD*

Charles, William 1776-1820 *DcAmB,*
NatCAB 22, NewYHSD, WhAm H

Charles, William Barclay 1861-1950 *BiDrAC*

Charles, William Barclay 1862-1950 *WhAm 3*

Charless, Joseph 1772-1834 *DcAmB,*
NatCAB 21, REnAW, WhAm H

Charlesworth, James Clyde 1900-1974 *WhAm 6*

Charleton, Walter 1620-1707 *DcScB*

Charlevoix, Peter Francis Xavier 1682-1761
Drake

Charlevoix, Pierre Francois Xavier De 1682-1761
AmBi, ApCAB, DcAmB, WhAm H

Charlot, Jean 1898- *BnEnAmA*

Charls, George Herbert 1878-1944 *WhAm 2*

Charlton, Charles Magnus 1877- *WhAm 5*

Charlton, Clyde B 1899-1951 *WhAm 3*

Charlton, Earle Perry 1863-1930 *NatCAB 38,*
WhAm 1

Charlton, George James 1860-1929 *WhAm 1*

Charlton, James 1832-1913 *WhAm 1*

Charlton, John 1849-1910? *IIBEAAW*

Charlton, John William 1866-1922 *NatCAB 23*

Charlton, Joseph W 1892-1957 *WhAm 3*

Charlton, Loudon 1869-1931 *WhAm 1*

Charlton, Paul 1856-1917 *WhAm 1*

Charlton, Robert Milledge 1807-1854 *ApCAB,*
BiAUS, BiDrAC, Drake, NatCAB 4,
TwCBDA, WhAm H

Charlton, Thomas Usher Pulaski 1779-1835
DcAmB, NatCAB 13, WhAm H

Charlton, Walter Glasco 1851-1917 *WhAm 1*

Charlton, Wilhelmina Howell *WomWWA 14*

Charmaille, J B *NewYHSD*

Charnaux-Grillet, Raymond Paul 1922-
WhAm 5

Charnay, Desire 1828- *ApCAB Sup*

Charnisay, Charles DeMenou 1604?-1650
McGEWB

Charnise, Charles DeMenou, Aulnay De
1605-1650 *ApCAB*

Charnock, Donald Austin 1893-1968 *WhAm 5*

Charonton, Enguerrand 1410?- *McGEWB*

Charpentier, Johann De 1786-1855 *DcScB*

Charpentier, Marc Antoine 1634-1704
McGEWB

Charpiot, Mary Russell 1830-1908 *NatCAB 14*

Charpy, Augustin Georges Albert 1865-1945
DcScB

Charraud, John J *NewYHSD*

Charron, Pierre 1541-1603 *McGEWB*

Charshee, Thomas Amos 1853-1924
NatCAB 33

Charske, F W 1881-1953 *WhAm 3*

Chartener, William Huston 1924-1970
NatCAB 55

Charters, Werrett Wallace 1875-1952 *BiDAmEd,*
WhAm 3

Charters, William Arthur 1863-1925 *NatCAB 6*

Chartrand, Joseph 1870-1933 *WhAm 1*

Chartres, Robert Philippe L E Ferdinand
ApCAB

Chase, Adelaide Cole d1944 *WhAm 2,*
WomWWA 14

Chase, Agnes 1869-1963 *WhAm 4*

Chase, Alonzo 1839-1930 *NatCAB 24*

Chase, Ann 1809-1874 *ApCAB*

Chase, Arthur Horace 1864-1930 *WhAm 1*

Chase, Arthur Minturn 1873-1947 *WhAm 2*

Chase, Benjamin 1789-1870 *ApCAB*

Chase, Benjamin E 1843-1915 *WhAm 1*

Chase, Benjamin Franklin 1869-1925 *WhAm 1*

Chase, Beverley *NewYHSD*

Chase, Burr Linden 1891-1974 *WhAm 6*

Chase, Carlton 1794-1870 *ApCAB, Drake,*
NatCAB 11, TwCBDA

Chase, Charles Albert 1876-1955 *NatCAB 45*

Chase, Charles Amherst 1864-1937 *NatCAB 28*

Chase, Charles Edward 1857-1933 *NatCAB 16,*
WhAm 1

Chase, Charles Parker 1845-1923 *WhAm 1*

Chase, Charles Warren 1877-1942 *NatCAB 34*

Chase, Civilian Louis 1900-1965 *WhAm 4*

Chase, Clement Edwards 1888-1933
NatCAB 24

Chase, Cleveland King 1871-1951 *WhAm 3*

Chase, Daniel Cady 1859-1923 *NatCAB 20*

Chase, Darius 1808?- *NewYHSD*

Chase, Denison 1830- *NatCAB 4*

Chase, Dudley 1771-1846 *ApCAB, BiAUS,*
BiDrAC, Drake, NatCAB 8, TwCBDA,
WhAm H, WhAmP

Chase, E Frank 1878-1952 *NatCAB 42*

Chase, E Sherman 1884-1969 *NatCAB 55*

Chase, Edna Woolman 1877-1957 *WhAm 3*

Chase, Edward Averill 1869-1926 *NatCAB 20*

Chase, Edward Tilden 1884-1967 *NatCAB 54*

Chase, Elizabeth 1832-1911 *NotAW*

Chase, Elizabeth Hosmer Kellogg 1864- *BiCAW,*
WomWWA 14

Chase, Ellen 1863- *WhAm 4*

Chase, Elmer Ellsworth 1861-1939 *NatCAB 29*

WhAmP

Chavez, J Francisco 1833- *BiAUS*
Chavez Aparicio, Fray Trinidad 1508-1582
ApCAB
Chavin, Francois *NewYHSD*
Chavis, John 1762?-1838 *BiDAmEd*
Chavis, John 1763?-1838 *AmBi, DcAmB,*
NatCAB 7, WhAm H
Chayefsky, Paddy 1923- *WebAB*
Chayes, Nat 1876-1952 *NatCAB 42*
Chazy, Jean Francois 1882-1955 *DcScB*
Cheadle, John Begg 1874-1960 *NatCAB 49,*
WhAm 4
Cheadle, Joseph Bonaparte 1842-1904 *BiDrAC,*
NatCAB 2
Cheaney, Edgar Seymour 1858-1914
NatCAB 17
Cheatham, Benjamin Franklin 1820-1886
ApCAB, BiDConf, DcAmB, NatCAB 11,
TwCBDA, WebAMB, WhAm H
Cheatham, Benjamin Franklin 1867-1944
NatCAB 35, WhAm 2
Cheatham, Catharine S *ApCAB X*
Cheatham, Elliott Evans 1888-1972 *WhAm 5*
Cheatham, Goode Rutledge 1900-1955
NatCAB 43
Cheatham, Henry Plummer 1857-1935 *BiDrAC,*
WhAmP
Cheatham, John Henry 1882-1950 *WhAm 3*
Cheatham, Joseph Johnston 1872-1942
NatCAB 31, WhAm 2
Cheatham, Kitty Smiley 1869- *AmWom*
Cheatham, Mary Warren Denman 1879-
WomWWA 14
Cheatham, Owen Robertson 1903-1970
NatCAB 55, WhAm 5
Cheatham, Richard 1799-1845 *BiAUS,*
BiDrAC, NatCAB 2
Cheatum, Elmer Philip 1901-1973 *WhAm 6*
Cheavens, David Anderson 1907-1970 *WhAm 5*
Chebotaryov, Nikolai Grigorievich 1894-1947
DcScB
Chebyshev, Pafnuty Lvovich 1821-1894 *DcScB*
Checkley, John 1680-1753 *ApCAB, TwCBDA*
Checkley, John 1680-1754 *DcAmB, WhAm H*
Chedsey, Hubert Chauncey 1850-1929
NatCAB 23
Chee, Robert 1938- *IlBEAAW*
Cheek, F J, Jr. 1893-1959 *WhAm 3*
Cheek, Robert Stanley 1878- *WhAm 6*
Cheek, Tolbert Fanning 1833-1920 *NatCAB 27*
Cheeks, Robert Roy 1881- *WhoColR*
Cheer, Miss *WhAm H*
Cheer, Margaret *NotAW*
Cheeseborough, Mary Hugger 1824-1902
NewYHSD
Cheeshahteaumuck, Caleb 1646-1666 *ApCAB*
Cheesman, Forman 1763-1821 *DcAmB,*
NatCAB 24, WhAm H
Cheesman, Helen Kay 1863- *WomWWA 14*
Cheesman, John Cummings 1788-1862 *ApCAB*
Cheesman, Timothy Matlack 1853-1919
NatCAB 41
Cheesman, William James 1921-1974 *WhAm 6*
Cheetham, James 1772-1810 *ApCAB, DcAmB,*
Drake, TwCBDA, WhAm H, WhAmP
Cheever, Benjamin Harrison 1850-1930
NatCAB 22
Cheever, David 1876-1955 *NatCAB 52,*
WhAm 3
Cheever, David Williams 1831-1915 *NatCAB 13,*
TwCBDA, WhAm 1
Cheever, Ezekiel 1614-1708 *ApCAB,*
BiDAmEd, DcAmB, NatCAB 12,
TwCBDA
Cheever, Ezekiel 1615-1708 *WhAm H*
Cheever, Ezekiel 1616-1708 *Drake*
Cheever, George Barrell 1807-1890 *ApCAB,*
DcAmB, Drake, NatCAB 7, TwCBDA,
WhAm H
Cheever, Harriet A *WhAm 1*
Cheever, Henry Martyn 1832- *NatCAB 5*
Cheever, Henry Theodore 1814-1897 *ApCAB,*
DcAmB, Drake, NatCAB 13, TwCBDA,
WhAm H
Cheever, Louisa Sewall 1868- *WomWWA 14*
Cheever, Samuel 1639-1724 *ApCAB*
Cheever, Samuel 1787-1874 *NatCAB 2*

Chefdebien, Lewis *NewYHSD*
Cheffetz, Asa 1896-1965 *NatCAB 52,*
WhAm 4
Cheffey, John Howard 1916-1970 *WhAm 5*
Chegaray, Eloise Desabaye 1792-1889
ApCAB Sup
Chehab, Fuad 1902-1973 *WhAm 5*
Chekhov, Anton Pavlovich 1860-1904 *McGEWB*
Chekib Bey *WhAm 5*
Chel-Ab-Ku-Kil *ApCAB*
Cheldelin, Vernon H 1916-1966 *WhAm 4*
Cheley, Frank Howbert 1889-1941 *WhAm 2*
Cheley, Glen Evan 1892-1947 *NatCAB 39*
Chelf, Frank Leslie 1907- *BiDrAC, WhAmP*
Chelminski, Jan V De 1851-1925 *NatCAB 21*
Chelmsford, Baron Frederic A Thesiger
1827-1905 *WhoMilH*
Chelmsford, Frederic John Napier T 1868-1933
McGEWB
Ch'en, Tu-Hsiu 1879-1942 *McGEWB*
Chen, Yi 1902-1972 *WhAm 5*
Chenard, Anthony F *NewYHSD*
Chenault, Sarah Gibson Humphreys 1858-
WomWWA 14
Chenery, Christopher Tompkins 1886-1973
WhAm 5
Chenery, William Elisha 1864-1949 *NatCAB 37,*
WhAm 5
Chenery, William Ludlow 1884-1974 *WhAm 6*
Chenery, Winthrop Holt 1872-1953 *WhAm 3*
Chenevix, Richard 1774-1830 *DcScB*
Cheney, Abbey Perkins 1853- *AmWom*
Cheney, Albert Nelson 1849-1901 *WhAm 1*
Cheney, Archibald Myron 1880-1951
NatCAB 41, WhAm 3
Cheney, Armilla Amanda 1845- *AmWom*
Cheney, Arthur 1837-1878 *ApCAB*
Cheney, Azro E 1854- *WhAm 4*
Cheney, Benjamin Austin 1867- *WhAm 5*
Cheney, Benjamin Pierce 1815-1895
ApCAB Sup, ApCAB X, DcAmB,
NatCAB 10, TwCBDA, WhAm H
Cheney, Benjamin Pierce 1866-1942
NatCAB 32
Cheney, C L *NewYHSD*
Cheney, Charles 1803-1874 *NatCAB 19*
Cheney, Charles 1804-1874 *ApCAB, TwCBDA*
Cheney, Charles 1866-1942 *WhAm 2*
Cheney, Charles Baldwin 1872-1955 *WhAm 3*
Cheney, Charles Edward 1836-1916 *ApCAB,*
DcAmB, TwCBDA, WhAm 1
Cheney, Charles Henry 1884-1943 *WhAm 2*
Cheney, Clarence Orion 1887-1947 *NatCAB 34,*
WhAm 2
Cheney, Clifford D 1877-1948 *WhAm 2*
Cheney, Edna Dow 1824-1904 *AmWom*
Cheney, Ednah Dow Littlehale 1824-1904 *AmBi,*
ApCAB, DcAmB, NatCAB 9, NotAW,
TwCBDA, WhAm 1, WhAmP
Cheney, Elmer Erwood 1861-1934 *WhAm 1*
Cheney, Emma Smith Peters 1863-
WomWWA 14
Cheney, Everett Wethered 1888-1939
NatCAB 48
Cheney, Forest 1864-1925 *NatCAB 20*
Cheney, Frank 1817-1904 *NatCAB 19*
Cheney, Frank, Jr. 1860- *NatCAB 19,*
WhAm 5
Cheney, Frank Dexter 1878-1955 *NatCAB 51,*
WhAm 6
Cheney, Frank Woodbridge 1832-1909 *ApCAB,*
NatCAB 19, TwCBDA, WhAm 5
Cheney, George 1771-1829 *NatCAB 19*
Cheney, George Wells, Jr. 1825-1893
NatCAB 19
Cheney, Harold Clark 1877-1957 *WhAm 3*
Cheney, Harriet Elizabeth Cheney 1838-1913
NewYHSD
Cheney, Harriet V 1815?- *ApCAB, Drake*
Cheney, Horace Bushnell 1868-1936
NatCAB 31
Cheney, Howell 1870-1957 *WhAm 3*
Cheney, Irma Genette Port 1865-
WomWWA 14
Cheney, James William 1849-1917 *WhAm 1*
Cheney, James Woodbridge 1838-1919
NatCAB 19
Cheney, Jerome Lucius 1863-1932 *WhAm 1*

Cheney, John 1801-1885 *ApCAB, DcAmB,*
NatCAB 19, NewYHSD, WhAm H
Cheney, John Moses 1859-1922 *NatCAB 19,*
WhAm 1
Cheney, John Richard 1897-1966 *WhAm 4A*
Cheney, John Sherwood 1827-1910 *NatCAB 19*
Cheney, John Vance 1848-1922 *AmBi, DcAmB,*
NatCAB 6, TwCBDA, WhAm 1
Cheney, Knight Dexter 1837-1907 *NatCAB 19*
Cheney, Louis Richmond 1859-1944
NatCAB 18, NatCAB 34, WhAm 2
Cheney, Mary E 1845- *WomWWA 14*
Cheney, Monroe George 1893-1952 *NatCAB 42,*
WhAm 3
Cheney, Moses 1776-1856 *NatCAB 6*
Cheney, Oren Burbank 1816-1903 *DcAmB,*
NatCAB 8, TwCBDA
Cheney, Orion Howard 1869-1939 *WhAm 1*
Cheney, Person Colby 1828-1901 *ApCAB Sup,*
BiDrAC, DcAmB, NatCAB 11, TwCBDA,
WhAm 1
Cheney, Ralph 1806-1897 *NatCAB 19*
Cheney, Richard Otis 1841-1912 *NatCAB 19*
Cheney, Rush 1815-1882 *NatCAB 19*
Cheney, Russell 1881-1945 *IlBEAAW,*
WhAm 2
Cheney, Seth Wells 1810-1856 *AmBi, ApCAB,*
DcAmB, Drake, NatCAB 9, NewYHSD,
TwCBDA, WhAm H
Cheney, Sherwood Alfred 1873-1949
NatCAB 49, WhAm 2
Cheney, Simeon Pease 1818-1890 *NatCAB 6*
Cheney, Theseus Apoleon 1830-1878 *ApCAB*
Cheney, Thomas Perkins 1891-1942 *WhAm 2*
Cheney, Ward d1963 *WhAm 4*
Cheney, Ward 1813-1876 *ApCAB, DcAmB,*
NatCAB 19, TwCBDA, WhAm H
Cheney, Warren 1858-1921 *WhAm 1*
Cheney, William Atwell 1848-1925 *WhAm 1*
Cheney, William Fitch 1866-1941 *WhAm 1*
Cheney, William Henry 1872-1953 *NatCAB 45*
Cheng, Chen 1898-1965 *WhAm 4*
Cheng, Ho 1371-1433? *McGEWB*
Chenier, Andre Marie 1762-1794 *McGEWB*
Chenier, John-Oliver 1806-1837 *ApCAB*
Chennault, Claire Lee 1890-1958 *WebAMB,*
WhWW-II
Chennault, Claire Lee 1893-1958 *NatCAB 47,*
WhAm 3
Chennault, Claire Lee 1898-1953 *WhoMilH*
Chenoweth, Alexander Crawford 1849-1922
NatCAB 12, WhAm 1
Chenoweth, Caroline VanDeusen 1846-
AmWom, TwCBDA, WhAm 4,
WomWWA 14
Chenoweth, Catherine Richardson d1928
WhAm 1, WomWWA 14
Chenoweth, David Macpherson 1917-1969
WhAm 5
Chenoweth, Emma Leake 1861- *WomWWA 14*
Chenoweth, John Edgar 1897- *BiDrAC,*
WhAmP
Chenowith, F A *BiAUS*
Chentung, Sir Liang-Cheng *WhAm 5*
Cherenkov, Pavel Alekseevich 1904- *McGEWB*
Cherenkov, Pavel Alekseyevich 1904- *AsBiEn*
Cherington, Charles Richards 1913-1967
WhAm 4
Cherington, Paul Terry 1876-1943 *WhAm 2*
Cherington, Paul Whiton 1918-1974 *WhAm 6*
Chernick, Jack 1911-1971 *WhAm 6*
Chernoff, Hyman Mordecai 1918-1972
NatCAB 57
Chernov, Dmitri Konstantinovich 1839-1921
DcScB
Chernyaev, Ilya Ilyich 1893-1966 *DcScB*
Chernyakhovsky, Ivan 1906-1945 *WhWW-II*
Chernyshev, Feodosy Nikolaevich 1856-1914
DcScB
Chernyshevsky, Nikolai Gavrilovich 1828-1889
McGEWB
Cheronis, Nicholas Dimitrius 1896-1962
NatCAB 49, WhAm 4
Cherrie, George Kruck 1865-1948 *NatCAB 36,*
WhAm 2
Cherrill, Adolphus 1808- *NewYHSD*
Cherrington, Ernest Hurst 1877-1950
DcAmB S4, WhAm 2A

Cherrington, Murat Halstead 1876-1954
NatCAB 46
Cherrington, Virgil Arthur 1905-1973 *WhAm 6*
Cherry, C Waldo 1873-1944 *WhAm 2*
Cherry, Charles 1874- *WhAm 5*
Cherry, David King 1883- *WhoColR*
Cherry, Emma Richardson 1859- *IIBEAAW,*
WomWWA 14
Cherry, Francis Adams 1908-1965 *NatCAB 52,*
WhAm 4
Cherry, Henry Hardin 1864-1937 *BiDAmEd,*
NatCAB 39, WhAm 1
Cherry, Herbert Tilden 1877-1949 *NatCAB 55*
Cherry, Howard H 1880- *WhAm 6*
Cherry, James William 1872-1949 *NatCAB 39,*
WhAm 2
Cherry, Kathryn Evelyn d1931 *WhAm 1*
Cherry, Lloyd Benjamin 1915-1974 *WhAm 6*
Cherry, Robert Gregg 1891-1957 *NatCAB 44,*
WhAm 3
Cherry, S O 1882- *WhoColR*
Cherry, Talmadge Charles 1875-1941
NatCAB 30
Cherry, Thomas Crittenden 1862- *WhAm 4*
Cherry, Ulysses Simpson Grant 1863-1943
WhAm 2
Cherry, Walter Lorraine 1874-1946 *NatCAB 35,*
WhAm 2
Cherry, Wilbur Harkness 1887-1950 *WhAm 3*
Cherry, William Sinclair 1867-1941 *NatCAB 33*
Cherry, William Stamps 1868- *WhAm 4*
Cherryman, Myrtle Koon 1868- *WomWWA 14*
Cherubini, Luigi Carlo Zanobi Salvatore
1760-1842 *McGEWB*
Cherwell, Lord 1886-1957 *DcScB, WhWW-II,*
WhoMilH
Cherwell Of Oxford, Baron 1886-1957 *WhAm 3*
Chery, Louis 1829?- *NewYHSD*
Chesbrough, Ellis Sylvester 1813-1886 *ApCAB,*
NatCAB 9, TwCBDA
Cheseborough, Robert A 1837- *ApCAB X*
Chesebro, Caroline 1828?-1873 *ApCAB, Drake,*
TwCBDA
Chesebrough, Albert Stanton 1868-1916
NatCAB 17
Chesebrough, Caroline 1825-1873 *DcAmB,*
NatCAB 23, WhAm H
Chesebrough, Robert Augustus 1837-1933
NatCAB 3, NatCAB 25, TwCBDA,
WhAm 1
Cheselden, William 1688-1752 *BiHiMed*
Chesen, Doris Schimmel 1932-1975 *WhAm 6*
Cheshire, Fleming Duncan 1849-1922 *WhAm 1*
Cheshire, Joseph Blount 1814-1899 *NatCAB 6*
Cheshire, Joseph Blount, Jr. 1850-1932
DcAmB S1, NatCAB 13, TwCBDA,
WhAm 1
Cheshire, Leonard 1917- *WhWW-II*
Chesley, Albert Justus 1877-1955 *WhAm 3*
Chesley, Charles *BiAUS Sup*
Chesley, George William 1899-1966
NatCAB 52
Chesley, Mary Russell *WomWWA 14*
Chesner, William *NewYHSD*
Chesney, Alan Mason 1888-1964 *WhAm 4*
Chesney, Charles Cornwallis 1826-1876 *ApCAB*
Chesney, Chester Anton 1916- *BiDrAC*
Chesney, Cummings Coligny 1863-1947
NatCAB 38, NatCAB 47, WhAm 2
Chesnut, James, Jr. 1815-1885 *BiDConf,*
BiDrAC, DcAmB, TwCBDA, WhAm H
Chesnut, James Lyons 1897- *WhAm 2*
Chesnut, Mary Boykin Miller 1823-1886 *NotAW*
Chesnut, Victor King 1867-1938 *NatCAB 13,*
WhAm 1
Chesnut, William Calvin 1873-1962 *WhAm 4*
Chesnutt, Charles Waddell 1858-1932 *AmBi,*
NatCAB 12, WebAB, WhAm 1,
WhoColR
Chesnutt, Nelson Alexander 1872- *WhAm 5*
Chess, Mary 1878-1964 *NatCAB 52*
Chess, William 1828?- *NewYHSD*
Chessin, Alexander 1866- *WhAm 4*
Chessiti *NewYHSD*
Chessito *NewYHSD*
Chessman, Caryl Whittier 1921-1960 *WebAB*
Chessman, Frederick 1838?- *NewYHSD*

Chessman, William Allen 1830-1920
NatCAB 19
Chester, Albert Huntington 1843-1903 *ApCAB,*
NatCAB 11, WhAm 1
Chester, Alden 1848-1934 *NatCAB 24,*
WhAm 1
Chester, Colby M 1845-1932 *ApCAB*
Chester, Colby Mitchel 1844-1932 *TwCBDA,*
WhAm 4
Chester, Colby Mitchell 1844-1932 *ApCAB Sup,*
DcAmB S1, NatCAB 33, WhAm 1
Chester, Colby Mitchell 1877-1965 *NatCAB 52,*
WhAm 4
Chester, Edmund A, Sr. 1897-1973 *WhAm 6*
Chester, Eliza *WhAm 1*
Chester, Frank Dyer 1869-1938 *WhAm 1*
Chester, Frederick Walthill 1861-1943 *ApCAB*
Chester, Frederick Dixon Walthall 1861-1943
WhAm 2
Chester, Frederick Dixson Walthall 1861-1943
TwCBDA
Chester, George Randolph 1869-1924 *DcAmB,*
WhAm 1
Chester, Hawley Thomas 1889- *WhAm 3*
Chester, John 1749-1809 *ApCAB, Drake,*
TwCBDA
Chester, John 1785-1829 *NatCAB 20*
Chester, John Needels 1864- *ApCAB X,*
WhAm 5
Chester, Joseph Lemuel 1821-1882 *ApCAB,*
DcAmB, Drake, Drake Sup, NatCAB 10,
TwCBDA, WhAm H
Chester, K Starr 1906-1969 *WhAm 5*
Chester, Manley Earle 1876-1937 *NatCAB 28*
Chester, Samuel Hall 1851-1940 *WhAm 1*
Chester, Thomas Morris d1893 *TwCBDA*
Chester, Wayland Morgan 1870-1945 *WhAm 2*
Chester, William 1863- *NatCAB 13*
Chester, William Merrill 1891-1964 *WhAm 4*
Chesterman, Bennett 1873-1962 *NatCAB 56*
Chesterman, Bertram 1879-1949 *NatCAB 35*
Chesterman, Francis John 1884-1963 *WhAm 4*
Chesterman, William Dallas 1845-1904
TwCBDA, WhAm 1
Chesterton, Arthur Devereaux 1902-1969
NatCAB 54
Chesterton, Gilbert Keith 1874-1936 *McGEWB*
Chestnut, James, Jr. 1815- *ApCAB, BiAUS,*
NatCAB 5
Chestnut, Victor King d1938 *WhAm 1C*
Cheston, J Hamilton 1893-1966 *NatCAB 53,*
WhAm 4
Cheston, Radcliffe, Jr. 1889-1968 *WhAm 5*
Chetlain, Arthur Henry 1849- *TwCBDA,*
WhAm 4
Chetlain, Augustus Louis 1824-1914 *ApCAB,*
DcAmB, NatCAB 4, TwCBDA,
WhAm 1
Chetta, Nicholas John 1916-1968 *WhAm 5*
Chetwood, Charles Howard 1869- *ApCAB X,*
WhAm 5
Chetwood, John 1859- *WhAm 4*
Chetwood, John J 1800-1861 *ApCAB*
Chetwood, William 1769-1857 *ApCAB, BiAUS,*
NatCAB 11
Chetwood, William 1771-1857 *BiDrAC,*
WhAm H
Chevalier, Abraham *NewYHSD*
Chevalier, Alexander *NewYHSD*
Chevalier, Augustin *NewYHSD*
Chevalier, J B *NewYHSD*
Chevalier, John B 1887-1955 *WhAm 3*
Chevalier, Leonard 1820?- *NewYHSD*
Chevalier, Maurice 1888-1972 *WhAm 5*
Chevalier, Michel 1806-1879 *ApCAB, Drake*
Chevalier, Stuart 1879-1956 *NatCAB 49,*
WhAm 3
Chevalier, Willard Townshend 1886-1961
NatCAB 46, WhAm 4
Chevallier, Jean-Baptiste-Alphonse 1793-1879
DcScB
Chevallier, Temple 1794-1873 *DcScB*
Chevee, Charles Humbert 1859- *WhAm 4*
Chevenard, Pierre Antoine Jean Sylvestre
1888-1960 *DcScB*
Chever, James W 1791-1857 *DcAmB,*
WhAm H
Cheverton, Cecil Frank 1889-1953 *NatCAB 43,*

WhAm 3
Cheverus, Jean Louis Anne M Lefebre De
1768-1836 *NatCAB 6, WhAm H*
Cheverus, Jean Louis Anne M Lefebvre De
1768-1836 *AmBi, ApCAB*
Cheverus, Jean Louis Anne M Lefevre De
1768-1836 *Drake*
Cheverus, John Louis Ann M Lefebre De
1768-1836 *DcAmB, TwCBDA*
Cheves, Langdon 1776-1857 *AmBi, ApCAB,*
BiAUS, BiDrAC, DcAmB, Drake,
NatCAB 10, TwCBDA, WebAB,
WhAm H, WhAmP
Cheves, Langdon 1814-1863 *BiDConf*
Chevet, F *NewYHSD*
Chevigny, Hector 1904-1965 *WhAm 4*
Chevreul, Michel Eugene 1786-1889 *AsBiEn,*
DcScB
Chevrier, Edgar Rodolphe Eugene 1887-1958
WhAm 4
Chevrolet, Louis Joseph 1878-1941 *NatCAB 53*
Chew, Ada Knowlton 1876- *WomWWA 14*
Chew, Benjamin 1722-1810 *ApCAB, BiAUS,*
DcAmB, Drake, NatCAB 5, TwCBDA,
WhAm H
Chew, Beverly 1850-1924 *WhAm 1*
Chew, James Andrew 1882-1964 *NatCAB 50*
Chew, Mary Cady *WomWWA 14*
Chew, Ng Poon 1866-1931 *AmBi, WhAm 1*
Chew, Oswald 1880-1949 *WhAm 2*
Chew, Richard Smith 1843-1875 *ApCAB,*
TwCBDA
Chew, Robert Smith 1811-1873 *ApCAB,*
TwCBDA
Chew, Samuel 1690?-1744 *ApCAB*
Chew, Samuel Claggett 1837-1915 *WhAm 1*
Chew, Samuel Claggett 1888-1960 *NatCAB 47,*
WhAm 3
Chew, William Douglas 1874-1939 *NatCAB 36*
Chew, William White 1803-1851 *NatCAB 5*
Chewning, Edmund Taylor 1889-1970
NatCAB 55, WhAm 5
Cheydleur, Frederic D 1879-1949 *WhAm 2*
Cheyne, George 1671-1743 *BiHiMed, DcScB*
Cheyne, John 1777-1836 *BiHiMed*
Cheyney, Barton 1860- *WhAm 4*
Cheyney, Clyde Irwin 1885-1967 *NatCAB 56*
Cheyney, Edward Gheen 1878- *WhAm 2*
Cheyney, Edward Potts 1861-1947 *BiDAmEd,*
DcAmB S4, WhAm 2
Chez, Joseph 1869- *WhAm 5*
Ch'i, Pai-Shih 1863-1957 *McGEWB*
Chi-Ah-Kin, d1541? *ApCAB*
Ch'i-Ying, 1786?-1858 *McGEWB*
Chia, Ssu-Tao 1213-1275 *McGEWB*
Chialiquichiama d1533 *ApCAB*
Chiang, Kai-Shek 1887-1975 *McGEWB,*
WhAm 6, WhWW-II, WhoMilH
Chiang, Kai-Shek, Madame 1898- *WhWW-II*
Chiarugi, Giulio 1859-1944 *DcScB*
Chicheley, Henry 1615-1683 *NatCAB 13*
Chicherin, Georgi Vasilyevich 1872-1936
McGEWB
Chichester, Sir Francis 1901-1972 *WhAm 5*
Chichester, Richard Henry Lee 1876-1930
WhAm 1
Chichibabin, Alexei Yevgenievich 1871-1945
DcScB
Chichowski, Severin *NewYHSD*
Chickering, Allen Lawrence 1877-1958
NatCAB 47, WhAm 3
Chickering, Charles Addison 1843-1900 *BiDrAC,*
TwCBDA, WhAm 1
Chickering, Charles Francis 1827-1891
NatCAB 10
Chickering, Charles Frank 1827-1891 *TwCBDA*
Chickering, Henry Thorndike 1885-1954
NatCAB 43
Chickering, Jesse 1797-1855 *ApCAB, Drake,*
TwCBDA
Chickering, John White 1808-1888 *TwCBDA*
Chickering, John White 1831-1913 *TwCBDA,*
WhAm 1
Chickering, Jonas 1797-1853 *ApCAB,*
TwCBDA, WhAm H
Chickering, Jonas 1798-1853 *AmBi, DcAmB,*
Drake, NatCAB 6
Chickering, Thomas Edward 1824-1871 *ApCAB,*

TwCBDA
Chickering, William Elbridge 1895-1959
WhAm 3
Chickering, William Henry 1849-1915
NatCAB 24
Chidester, Drew 1880-1948 *NatCAB 38*
Chidester, John Young 1881-1948 *WhAm 3*
Chidley, Howard James 1878-1966 *NatCAB 51,*
WhAm 4
Chidsey, Andrew Dwight 1848-1926
NatCAB 21
Chidsey, D M *NewYHSD*
Chidsey, John Conley 1869-1931 *NatCAB 24*
Chidsey, John Tuttle 1866-1946 *NatCAB 39*
Chidsey, Thomas McKeen 1884-1958
NatCAB 48, WhAm 3
Chidwick, John Patrick Sylvester 1863-1935
ApCAB X, WhAm 1
Chief Joseph 1800?-1871 *REnAW*
Chief Joseph 1840?-1904 *EncAAH, REnAW,*
WhAm H
Ch'ien, Lung 1711-1799 *WhoMilH*
Ch'ien-Lung 1711-1799 *McGEWB*
Chiera, Edward 1885-1933 *DcAmB S1,*
NatCAB 24, WhAm 1
Chifley, Joseph Benedict 1885-1951 *McGEWB,*
WhAm 3, WhWW-II
Chignavitcelut, Oxiquieb *ApCAB*
Chiguaihue 1566?-1606 *ApCAB*
Chih-I 538-597 *McGEWB*
Chikamatsu Monzaemon 1653-1725 *McGEWB*
Chilam Balam d1430? *ApCAB*
Chilberg, John Edward 1867- *WhAm 4*
Chilcote, Sanford Marshall 1905-1974 *WhAm 6*
Chilcott, Ellery Channing 1859-1930
NatCAB 22, WhAm 1
Chilcott, George Miles 1828-1891 *ApCAB,*
BiAUS, BiDrAC, NatCAB 7, TwCBDA,
WhAm H
Child, Mrs. *NewYHSD*
Child, Calvin Goddard 1834-1880 *TwCBDA*
Child, Charles Manning 1869-1954 *DcAmB S5,*
DcScB, WhAm 3
Child, Clarence Griffin 1864-1948 *WhAm 2*
Child, Clement Dexter 1868-1933 *WhAm 1*
Child, Daniel Robert 1827-1914 *NatCAB 17*
Child, David Lee 1794-1874 *ApCAB, DcAmB,*
NatCAB 2, TwCBDA, WhAm H
Child, Edith *WomWWA 14*
Child, Edwin Burrage 1868-1937 *NatCAB 28,*
WhAm 1
Child, Eleanor Dodge 1902-1948 *WhAm 2*
Child, Elias Earle 1880- *WhAm 6*
Child, Florence Chapman 1883- *WomWWA 14*
Child, Francis James 1825-1896 *AmBi, ApCAB,*
DcAmB, NatCAB 8, TwCBDA, WebAB,
WhAm H
Child, Frank Samuel 1854-1922 *DcAmB,*
NatCAB 22, WhAm 1
Child, Frank Samuel 1882-1959 *NatCAB 47*
Child, Fred S 1893- *WhAm 4*
Child, George Newport 1869-1932 *WhAm 1*
Child, Georgie Boynton *WomWWA 14*
Child, Isaac 1792-1885 *NewYHSD*
Child, J M *NewYHSD*
Child, John *NewYHSD*
Child, Katherine Blake 1867- *WhAm 3,*
WomWWA 14
Child, Lewis 1781?-1829 *NewYHSD*
Child, Lydia Maria 1802-1880 *AmBi, AmWom,*
ApCAB, DcAmB, Drake, EncAB,
McGEWB, NatCAB 2, NotAW,
TwCBDA, WebAB, WhAm H
Child, Mary Lucy 1866- *WomWWA 14*
Child, Richard Washburn 1880-1935
NatCAB 26
Child, Richard Washburn 1881-1935
DcAmB S1, WhAm 1
Child, Robert 1613?-1654 *DcAmB S1*
Child, Shubael 1779-1876 *NatCAB 9*
Child, Thomas d1706 *NewYHSD*
Child, Thomas, Jr. 1818-1869 *BiDrAC,*
WhAm H
Child, Mrs. Willard *NewYHSD*
Childe, John 1802-1858 *DcAmB, NatCAB 16,*
WhAm H
Childe, Vere Gordon 1892-1957 *McGEWB*
Childers, Ben 1872-1917 *NatCAB 17*

Childers, David Marion 1867-1950 *NatCAB 39*
Childers, James Saxon 1899-1965 *NatCAB 53,*
WhAm 4
Childers, Marvin Alonzo 1885-1965 *WhAm 4*
Childers, Sylvester Earl 1886-1948 *WhAm 2*
Childress, Fielding Turner 1906-1968
NatCAB 54
Childress, John Whitsitt 1845- *WhAm 4*
Childress, L Wade 1876-1950 *WhAm 2*
Childrey, Joshua 1623-1670 *DcScB*
Childs, Albert H 1861-1927 *NatCAB 22*
Childs, Albert Henry d1921 *NatCAB 19*
Childs, Alvin 1909-1970 *NatCAB 57*
Childs, Arthur Edward 1869-1933 *WhAm 1*
Childs, Benjamin F 1814-1863 *NewYHSD*
Childs, C Frederick 1875-1955 *WhAm 3*
Childs, Caroline Goldsmith 1867-
WomWWA 14
Childs, Cephas Grier 1793-1871 *DcAmB,*
NatCAB 22, NewYHSD, WhAm H
Childs, Daniel Brewer 1843-1925 *NatCAB 20*
Childs, Donald Smythe 1888-1960 *NatCAB 50,*
WhAm 4
Childs, Edward Powell 1870- *WhAm 5*
Childs, Eleanor Stuart 1876-1920 *WhAm 1,*
WomWWA 14
Childs, Eversley 1867-1953 *NatCAB 42,*
WhAm 3
Childs, F *NewYHSD*
Childs, Francis Lane 1884-1973 *WhAm 6*
Childs, Frank Aiken 1875-1965 *WhAm 4*
Childs, Frank Hall 1859-1954 *NatCAB 17,*
WhAm 3
Childs, Geoffrey Stafford 1892-1957 *WhAm 3*
Childs, George Henshaw 1890-1963 *NatCAB 52*
Childs, George Theodore 1842- *WhAm 4*
Childs, George William 1829-1894 *AmBi,*
ApCAB, ApCAB X, DcAmB, NatCAB 2,
TwCBDA, WhAm H
Childs, Harwood Lawrence 1898-1972 *WhAm 5*
Childs, Henry A 1836-1906 *WhAm 1*
Childs, Henry Halsey 1783-1868 *ApCAB,*
Drake, NatCAB 20, TwCBDA
Childs, James Harold 1879-1963 *NatCAB 51*
Childs, John *NewYHSD*
Childs, John Lewis 1856-1921 *NatCAB 3,*
NatCAB 24, WhAm 4
Childs, Joseph William 1910-1960 *WhAm 4*
Childs, Mary Fairfax *WomWWA 14*
Childs, Orville Whitmore 1802-1870 *ApCAB*
Childs, Orville Whitmore 1803-1870 *NatCAB 3,*
TwCBDA
Childs, Prescott 1898-1969 *WhAm 5*
Childs, Randolph Willard 1886-1965
NatCAB 50
Childs, Robert Andrew 1845-1915 *BiDrAC*
Childs, Robert Gibbes 1897-1971 *NatCAB 57*
Childs, Ross Renfroe 1888-1942 *WhAm 2*
Childs, Samuel Beresford 1861- *WhAm 4*
Childs, Samuel Canning 1859-1932 *NatCAB 25*
Childs, Samuel Shannon 1863-1925 *NatCAB 5,*
NatCAB 20
Childs, Shubael D *NewYHSD*
Childs, Shubael D, Jr. *NewYHSD*
Childs, Thomas *BiAUS*
Childs, Thomas 1796-1853 *ApCAB, DcAmB,*
Drake, TwCBDA, WhAm H
Childs, Thomas Spencer 1825-1914 *TwCBDA,*
WhAm 1
Childs, Timothy 1748-1821 *ApCAB, Drake*
Childs, Timothy 1785-1847 *BiAUS, BiDrAC,*
WhAm H
Childs, William, Jr. 1865- *NatCAB 5*
Childs, William Hamlin 1857-1928 *WhAm 1*
Chiles, Harry Linden 1867-1945 *NatCAB 34,*
WhAm 2
Chiles, James Alburn 1877- *WhAm 5*
Chiles, John Overton 1901-1966 *NatCAB 51*
Chiles, Joseph B 1810- *WhAm H*
Chiles, Wilma Klein 1912-1974 *WhAm 6*
Chillas, David *NewYHSD*
Chiller, Godfrey *NewYHSD*
Chillman, James, Jr. 1891-1972 *WhAm 5*
Chilomacon, Charles *ApCAB*
Chilson, Gardner 1804-1877 *ApCAB,*
NatCAB 14
Chilton, Arthur Bounds 1890-1934 *WhAm 1,*
WhAm 1C

Chilton, Cecil Hamilton 1918-1972 *WhAm 5*
Chilton, Cleo Madison 1867-1962 *WhAm 4*
Chilton, Horace 1853-1932 *ApCAB Sup,*
BiDrAC, NatCAB 2, TwCBDA,
WhAm 1
Chilton, J Matt 1881- *WhAm 6*
Chilton, Robert Hall 1814-1879 *BiDConf*
Chilton, Robert Hall 1817-1879 *ApCAB Sup,*
TwCBDA
Chilton, Robert S 1861-1947 *WhAm 2*
Chilton, Samuel 1804-1867 *BiAUS, BiDrAC,*
WhAm H, WhAmP
Chilton, Thomas 1798-1854 *ApCAB, BiDrAC,*
TwCBDA, WhAm H
Chilton, Thomas Hamilton 1899-1972 *WhAm 5*
Chilton, William Edwin 1858-1939 *BiDrAC,*
NatCAB 15, WhAmP
Chilton, William Edwin, Jr. 1893-1950 *WhAm 3*
Chilton, William P 1810-1871 *ApCAB*
Chilton, William Paris 1810-1871 *DcAmB,*
WhAm H
Chilton, William Parish 1810-1871 *BiDConf,*
NatCAB 4, TwCBDA
Chilton, William Ransdell 1911-1973 *WhAm 6*
Chimalpain Quautlehuanitzin *ApCAB*
Chimalpopoca d1423 *ApCAB*
Ch'in, Chiu-Shao 1202?-1261? *DcScB*
Ch'in, Kuei 1090-1155 *McGEWB*
Ch'in, Shih Huang-Ti 259BC-210BC *McGEWB*
Chinard, Gilbert 1881-1972 *WhAm 5*
Chinchon, Countess Of *ApCAB*
Chindblom, Carl Richard 1870-1956 *BiDrAC,*
WhAm 3, WhAmP
Chinery, Isaac *NewYHSD*
Chinery, James *NewYHSD*
Ching, Cyrus Stuart 1876-1967 *WhAm 4A,*
WhAm 5
Chini, Eusebio Francisco 1645-1711 *DcAmB*
Chiniquy, Charles Paschal Telesphore 1809-1899
ApCAB Sup
Chinlund, Edwin F 1890-1960 *WhAm 3*
Chinn, Alexander Roderick 1857- *WhoColR*
Chinn, Armstrong 1894-1958 *WhAm 3*
Chinn, Clement Bell 1891-1953 *NatCAB 42,*
WhAm 3
Chinn, Joseph Graves 1797-1891 *TwCBDA*
Chinn, Joseph William 1798-1840 *BiAUS,*
BiDrAC, WhAm H
Chinn, Joseph William 1866- *WhAm 4*
Chinn, Thomas Withers 1791-1852 *BiAUS,*
BiDrAC, NatCAB 12, WhAm H
Chinoy, Ely 1921-1975 *WhAm 6*
Chiperfield, Burnett Mitchell 1870-1940
BiDrAC, WhAm 1
Chiperfield, Robert Bruce 1899-1971 *BiDrAC,*
WhAm 5, WhAmP
Chipley, William Dudley 1840-1897 *NatCAB 9,*
TwCBDA
Chipman *NewYHSD*
Chipman, Charles Albert 1891-1957
NatCAB 46
Chipman, Cline N 1882-1946 *NatCAB 39*
Chipman, Daniel 1763-1850 *TwCBDA,*
WhAm H
Chipman, Daniel 1765-1850 *ApCAB, BiAUS,*
BiDrAC, DcAmB, Drake, NatCAB 8
Chipman, Edna Earle Manners 1878-
WomWWA 14
Chipman, Henry 1785-1867 *ApCAB, BiAUS*
Chipman, John Logan 1830-1893 *BiDrAC,*
NatCAB 8, TwCBDA, WhAm H
Chipman, John Smith 1800-1869 *BiAUS,*
BiDrAC, WhAm H
Chipman, John Sniffen 1899-1940 *NatCAB 48,*
WhAm 1
Chipman, Nathaniel 1752-1843 *AmBi, ApCAB,*
BiAUS, BiDrAC, DcAmB, Drake,
NatCAB 2, TwCBDA, WhAm H
Chipman, Norris Bowie 1901-1957 *NatCAB 46,*
WhAm 3
Chipman, Norton Parker 1834-1924 *BiAUS*
Chipman, Norton Parker 1836-1924 *BiDrAC*
Chipman, Norton Parker 1838-1924 *WhAm 1*
Chipman, Ward 1754-1824 *ApCAB, DcAmB,*
WhAm H
Chipman, Ward 1787-1851 *ApCAB, Drake*
Chipman, William Evan 1871-1922 *NatCAB 24*

Christgau, Victor Laurence August 1894-
BiDrAC
Christian, Andrew Dunscomb 1892-1946
WhAm 2
Christian, Charles Henry 1884-1968
NatCAB 55
Christian, Edmund Adolph 1857-1935 *WhAm 1*
Christian, Elizabeth *WomWWA 14*
Christian, Eugene 1859-1930 *NatCAB 24*
Christian, Eugene 1860-1930 *WhAm 1*
Christian, Frank Lamar 1876-1955 *WhAm 4*
Christian, George Busby, Jr. 1873- *WhAm 5*
Christian, George Eastland 1888-1941 *WhAm 2*
Christian, George Llewellyn 1841-1924
NatCAB 20, WhAm 4
Christian, Henry Asbury 1876-1951 *DcAmB S5,*
NatCAB 18, NatCAB 39, WhAm 3
Christian, J H *NewYHSD*
Christian, John L 1910- *WhAm 5*
Christian, John Tyler 1854-1925 *NatCAB 20,*
WhAm 4
Christian, Joseph 1828- *ApCAB, TwCBDA*
Christian, Leo Gregory 1887-1962 *NatCAB 49*
Christian, Mary 1853- *WomWWA 14*
Christian, Palmer 1885-1947 *WhAm 2*
Christian, Robert J 1898-1964 *WhAm 4*
Christian, Sanders Lewis 1888- *WhAm 2*
Christian, William 1732-1782 *ApCAB, Drake,*
WhAm H
Christian, William 1743?-1786 *DcAmB,*
WebAMB
Christian, William Peter 1875-1945 *WhAm 2*
Christiancy, Isaac Peckham 1812-1890 *ApCAB,*
BiAUS, BiDrAC, DcAmB, NatCAB 12,
NatCAB 23, TwCBDA, WhAm H,
WhAmP
Christiania, Joseph *NewYHSD*
Christians, William F 1903-1956 *WhAm 3*
Christiansen, Arthur 1904-1963 *WhAm 4*
Christiansen, Christian 1843-1917 *DcScB Sup*
Christiansen, Edward S, IV 1909-1972 *WhAm 5*
Christiansen, F Melius 1871-1955 *WhAm 3*
Christiansen, Fredrik Melius 1871-1955
BiDAmEd
Christiansen, Harold Egbert 1898-1964
NatCAB 51
Christiansen, N Woodruff 1893-1955 *WhAm 4*
Christiansen, S Edward Smith, IV 1909-1972
NatCAB 57
Christianson, Adolph Marcus 1877-1954
NatCAB 49, WhAm 3
Christianson, John Oscar 1898-1961 *WhAm 4*
Christianson, Theodore 1883-1948 *BiDrAC,*
WhAm 2, WhAmP
Christianson, Theodore 1913-1955 *WhAm 3*
Christie, Agatha Mary Clarissa d1976 *WhAm 6*
Christie, Alexander *NewYHSD*
Christie, Alexander 1850-1925 *NatCAB 13,*
WhAm 1
Christie, Alexander Graham 1880-1964
WhAm 4
Christie, Arthur Carlisle 1879-1956 *WhAm 3*
Christie, Carmelite Brewer 1852-
WomWWA 14
Christie, Charles Johnson 1861- *WhAm 4*
Christie, Dan Edwin 1915-1975 *WhAm 6*
Christie, David 1818- *ApCAB*
Christie, Francis Albert 1858- *WhAm 4*
Christie, Gabriel d1798 *ApCAB, Drake*
Christie, Gabriel 1755-1808 *BiAUS, BiDrAC*
Christie, George Irving 1881- *WhAm 6*
Christie, Isabella Munro Lindsay 1841-
WomWWA 14
Christie, James 1840-1912 *WhAm 1*
Christie, Jane Johnstone 1860- *WhAm 4*
Christie, John 1786-1813 *ApCAB, Drake*
Christie, John Walter 1865-1944 *DcAmB S3*
Christie, John Watson 1883-1974 *WhAm 6*
Christie, Lansdell Kisner 1903-1965 *WhAm 4*
Christie, Luther Rice 1873-1939 *WhAm 1*
Christie, R E d1956 *WhAm 3*
Christie, Ralph Conklin 1882-1957 *NatCAB 49*
Christie, Robert 1788-1856 *ApCAB, Drake*
Christie, Robert 1837- *WhAm 4*
Christie, Robert Erskine, Jr. 1893-1934
NatCAB 26
Christie, Robert James 1864- *WhAm 4*
Christie, Samuel Hunter 1784-1865 *DcScB*

Christie, Thomas Davidson 1843-1921
NatCAB 19, WhAm 1
Christie, William Henry 1834- *NatCAB 13*
Christie, William Henry Mahoney 1845-1922
DcScB
Christie, William Wallace 1866-1925 *WhAm 1*
Christine De Pisan 1364?-1430? *McGEWB*
Christison, J Sanderson 1856-1908 *WhAm 1*
Christman, Charles E 1870- *WhAm 6*
Christman, Henry Jacob 1869-1945 *NatCAB 35,*
WhAm 2
Christman, Joseph Alonzo 1838-1888 *TwCBDA*
Christman, W W 1865-1937 *WhAm 1*
Christman, Warren Ursinus 1882-1944
WhAm 2
Christmann, Adam 1872-1950 *NatCAB 40*
Christmann, Jacob 1554-1613 *DcScB*
Christmas, Lee 1863-1924 *NatCAB 6*
Christoffel, Elwin Bruno 1829-1900 *DcScB*
Christofferson, Edward Albert 1885-1967
NatCAB 53
Christol, Carl 1872- *WhAm 5*
Christol, Jules De 1802-1861 *DcScB*
Christophe, Ferdinand *ApCAB*
Christophe, Frank Eugene 1877- *WhoColR*
Christophe, Henri 1767-1820 *ApCAB, Drake,*
McGEWB
Christophe, Herman 1874-1953 *NatCAB 42*
Christophe, Jacques Victor *ApCAB*
Christophe, William Rodolph 1879- *WhoColR*
Christopher, Frederick 1889-1967 *NatCAB 54,*
WhAm 4
Christopher, George H 1888-1957 *WhAm 3*
Christopher, George Henry 1888-1959 *BiDrAC,*
WhAmP
Christopher, George Thurman 1887-1954
NatCAB 44, WhAm 3
Christopher, John Case 1891-1926 *NatCAB 20*
Christopher, Max August 1878-1968
NatCAB 55
Christopher, William Rodolphus 1924-1973
WhAm 6
Christopherson, Charles Andrew 1871-1951
BiDrAC, WhAm 3, WhAmP
Christopherson, Conrad Hellick 1875-1922
NatCAB 6
Christus, Petrus 1410?-1473? *McGEWB*
Christy, Alexander *NewYHSD*
Christy, Bayard Henderson 1872-1943
NatCAB 32
Christy, David 1802-1868? *DcAmB, WhAm H*
Christy, Earl 1883-1961 *WhAm 4*
Christy, Edwin P 1815-1862 *AmBi, ApCAB,*
DcAmB, McGEWB, NatCAB 23,
WebAB, WhAm H
Christy, George Harvey 1837-1909 *NatCAB 32*
Christy, George N 1827-1868 *ApCAB,*
NatCAB 7
Christy, Grace 1883- *WomWWA 14*
Christy, Howard Chandler 1873-1952
DcAmB S5, IIBEAAW, NatCAB 11,
WhAm 3
Christy, John H *BiAUS*
Christy, Lloyd Bennett 1868-1945 *NatCAB 34*
Christy, Russ J 1862- *ApCAB X*
Christy, Samuel Benedict 1853-1914
NatCAB 20, WhAm 1
Christy, William 1791-1865 *ApCAB, Drake,*
NatCAB 11
Christy, William C 1885-1957 *WhAm 3*
Chritton, George Alvah 1870-1948 *WhAm 2*
Chronicle, William 1755-1780 *Drake*
Chronister, D J *NewYHSD*
Chrostwaite, Thomas Francis 1873-1958
NatCAB 53
Chrysippus 280?BC-206?BC *McGEWB*
Chrysler, Jack Forker 1912-1958 *WhAm 3*
Chrysler, Mintin Asbury 1871- *WhAm 5*
Chrysler, Morgan Henry 1826- *ApCAB*
Chrysler, Walter Percy 1875-1940 *DcAmB S2,*
McGEWB, WebAB, WhAm 1
Chryssa 1933- *BnEnAmA*
Chryst, Robert D 1890-1956 *WhAm 3*
Chrystal, George 1851-1911 *DcScB*
Chrystal, James 1832- *TwCBDA*
Chrystie, Thomas Ludlow 1872-1954 *WhAm 3*
Chrystie, Thomas Witter 1902-1956
NatCAB 42, WhAm 3

Chu, Hsi 1130-1200 *McGEWB*
Chu, Lan Jen 1913-1973 *WhAm 6*
Chu, Pak 1797-1866 *REnAW*
Chu, Shih-Chieh *DcScB*
Chu, Teh 1886-1976 *McGEWB, WhWW-II,*
WhoMilH
Chang, Tzu 369?BC-286?BC *McGEWB*
Chubb, Charles Frisbie 1877-1960 *NatCAB 49*
Chubb, Chester Niles 1878-1951 *WhAm 3*
Chubb, Edwin Watts 1865-1959 *NatCAB 48,*
WhAm 4
Chubb, Frederick Y 1838?- *NewYHSD*
Chubb, Hendon 1874-1960 *WhAm 4*
Chubb, Henry Stedman 1858- *NatCAB 5*
Chubb, Lewis Warrington 1882-1952
NatCAB 39, WhAm 3
Chubb, Percival 1860- *WhAm 4*
Chubb, Thomas 1809-1890 *TwCBDA*
Chubb, Thomas Caldecot 1899-1972 *WhAm 5*
Chubbuck, Emily *NotAW*
Chubbuck, Samuel W 1800-1875 *ApCAB*
Chubbuck, Thomas d1888 *NewYHSD,*
WhAm H
Chudoff, Earl 1907- *BiDrAC*
Chugaev, Lev Aleksandrovich 1873-1922 *DcScB*
Chuikov, Vasili 1900- *WhWW-II*
Chuikov, Vasilii Ivanovich 1900- *WhoMilH*
Chujoy, Anatole 1894-1969 *WhAm 5*
Chulalongkorn 1853-1910 *McGEWB*
Chundrigar, Ismail Ibrahim 1897-1960 *WhAm 4*
Chung, Margaret Jessie 1889-1959 *NatCAB 48*
Chupien, T *NewYHSD*
Chupp, Charles David 1886-1967 *WhAm 5*
Chuquet, Nicolas *DcScB*
Church, Albert Ensign 1807-1878 *ApCAB,*
Drake, TwCBDA
Church, Alonzo 1793-1862 *DcAmB,*
NatCAB 9, TwCBDA, WhAm H
Church, Alonzo 1870-1937 *WhAm 4*
Church, Alonzo Christy 1859-1916 *NatCAB 18*
Church, Alonzo Webster 1829- *TwCBDA*
Church, Aloysius Stanislaus 1909-1975
WhAm 6
Church, Angelica Schuyler 1877-1954 *WhAm 3*
Church, Archibald 1861- *WhAm 4*
Church, Arthur Latham 1858-1931 *WhAm 1*
Church, Augustus Byington 1858-1912 *WhAm 1*
Church, Benjamin 1639-1718 *AmBi, ApCAB,*
DcAmB, Drake, NatCAB 7, WebAMB,
WhAm H
Church, Benjamin 1734- *ApCAB, NatCAB 7*
Church, Benjamin 1734-1776 *Drake, WhAm H*
Church, Benjamin 1734-1778? *DcAmB,*
WebAB
Church, Benjamin Butler 1883- *WhAm 3*
Church, Benjamin Silliman 1836- *NatCAB 3,*
TwCBDA
Church, Charles Thomas 1874-1953
NatCAB 51
Church, Denver Samuel 1862-1952 *BiDrAC*
Church, Denver Samuel 1862-1952 *WhAm 3*
Church, Duane Herbert 1849- *NatCAB 12*
Church, Dwight *NewYHSD*
Church, Earl Douglas 1874-1930 *NatCAB 22,*
WhAm 1
Church, Edmund Tweedy 1864-1945
NatCAB 17, NatCAB 34
Church, Edward 1779-1845 *NatCAB 20*
Church, Edward Bentley 1844-1904 *NatCAB 1,*
WhAm 1
Church, Edwin Fayette, Jr. 1879- *WhAm 6*
Church, Elihu 1881- *WhAm 6*
Church, Elizabeth Hoyt 1881- *WomWWA 14*
Church, Elliott Bradford 1873-1955 *NatCAB 41*
Church, Francis Pharcellus 1839-1906 *ApCAB,*
TwCBDA, WhAm 1
Church, Frank Forrester 1924- *BiDrAC*
Church, Frank Henry 1858-1927 *WhAm 1*
Church, Frederic Edwin 1826-1900 *ApCAB,*
BnEnAmA, Drake, EncAAH, NatCAB 20,
NewYHSD
Church, Frederick Edwin 1826-1900 *AmBi,*
DcAmB, McGEWB, WebAB, WhAm 1
Church, Frederick Ewin 1826-1900 *TwCBDA*
Church, Frederick Fargo 1864-1925 *NatCAB 20*
Church, Frederick Stuart 1842- *ApCAB,*
ApCAB Sup, NatCAB 11, TwCBDA
Church, Frederick Stuart 1842-1923 *WhAm 1*

Church, Frederick Stuart 1842-1924 *DcAmB*
Church, George Dudley 1878- *WhAm 6*
Church, George Earl 1835-1910 *DcAmB, NatCAB 13*
Church, George Hervey 1855-1935 *WhAm 1*
Church, George Myers 1891-1946 *NatCAB 35*
Church, Gertrude Lee 1864- *WomWWA 14*
Church, Henry 1836-1908 *BnEnAmA, NewYHSD*
Church, Henry Ward 1887-1938 *WhAm 1*
Church, Irving Porter 1851-1931 *DcAmB S1, NatCAB 4, NatCAB 22, TwCBDA, WhAm 1*
Church, James Edward 1869-1959 *REnAW, WhAm 4*
Church, John Adams 1843-1917 *ApCAB, DcAmB, TwCBDA, WhAm 1*
Church, John Fertig 1917-1962 *WhAm 4*
Church, John Henry Coffin 1870-1946 *NatCAB 35*
Church, John Huston 1892-1953 *NatCAB 44, WhAm 3*
Church, Levi Ruggles 1836- *ApCAB*
Church, Louis Kossuth 1846-1897 *NatCAB 38, TwCBDA*
Church, Louise Akerly Husted *WomWWA 14*
Church, Marguerite Stitt 1892- *BiDrAC, WhAmP*
Church, Max 1888-1964 *NatCAB 53*
Church, Melville 1856-1935 *WhAm 1*
Church, Percy Clarke 1876-1951 *NatCAB 41*
Church, Pharcellus 1801-1886 *ApCAB, DcAmB, NatCAB 8, TwCBDA, WhAm H*
Church, Ralph Edwin 1883-1950 *BiDrAC, WhAm 2A, WhAmP*
Church, Randolph 1904-1969 *WhAm 5*
Church, Richard Cassius 1907-1976 *WhAm 6*
Church, Robert Reed, Jr. 1885- *WhoColR*
Church, Samuel 1785-1854 *BiAUS, Drake, NatCAB 7, TwCBDA*
Church, Samuel Harden 1858-1943 *NatCAB 9, NatCAB 33, WhAm 2*
Church, Sandford E 1815-1880 *BiAUS*
Church, Sanford Elias 1815-1880 *ApCAB, NatCAB 11, TwCBDA*
Church, Virginia Woodson Frame *WomWWA 14*
Church, William Conant 1836-1917 *ApCAB, DcAmB, NatCAB 8, TwCBDA, WhAm 1*
Church, William E 1841-1917 *WhAm 1*
Church, William Howell 1869- *WhAm 1*
Church, William Thorne 1866-1949 *NatCAB 39*
Churchill, Alfred Vance 1864-1949 *NatCAB 38, WhAm 2*
Churchill, Asaph 1866-1936 *NatCAB 29*
Churchill, Caroline M 1833- *AmWom*
Churchill, Carroll 1873-1969 *NatCAB 55*
Churchill, Charles Samuel 1856-1934 *WhAm 1*
Churchill, Edward Delos 1895-1972 *NatCAB 57*
Churchill, Edward Delos 1895-1973 *WhAm 5*
Churchill, Everett Avery 1892-1959 *WhAm 3*
Churchill, Florence 1873- *WomWWA 14*
Churchill, Frank Edwin 1901-1942 *WhAm 2*
Churchill, Frank Spooner 1864- *WhAm 4*
Churchill, George Bosworth 1866-1925 *BiDrAC, TwCBDA, WhAm 1*
Churchill, George Morton 1874- *WhAm 5*
Churchill, H W *NewYHSD*
Churchill, Henry Stern 1893-1962 *NatCAB 49, WhAm 4*
Churchill, J Edwin *NewYHSD*
Churchill, Jennie Jerome 1854-1921 *NotAW*
Churchill, John Charles 1821-1905 *BiAUS, BiDrAC, TwCBDA, WhAm 1*
Churchill, John Wesley 1839-1900 *NatCAB 10, WhAm 1*
Churchill, Joseph Richmond 1845-1933 *WhAm 1*
Churchill, Julia Patterson 1841- *WomWWA 14*
Churchill, Julius Alonzo 1862- *WhAm 4*
Churchill, Lida A 1859- *WhAm 5, WomWWA 14*
Churchill, Lide A 1859- *AmWom*
Churchill, Liska Stillman *WomWWA 14*
Churchill, Louise Nye *WomWWA 14*
Churchill, Mabel Harlakenden *WomWWA 14*

Churchill, Marlborough 1878-1942 *WhAm 2*
Churchill, Marlborough 1878-1947 *NatCAB 35*
Churchill, Owen Humphreys 1841-1916 *NatCAB 17*
Churchill, Peter Michel 1909-1972 *WhWW-II*
Churchill, Ralph Loren 1880- *WhAm 6*
Churchill, Lady Randolph Spencer 1853-1921 *AmWom, ApCAB Sup, WhAm 1*
Churchill, Sylvester 1783-1862 *ApCAB, Drake, TwCBDA*
Churchill, Thomas James 1824-1905 *BiDConf, DcAmB, NatCAB 10, NatCAB 34, WhAm 1, WhAmP*
Churchill, Thomas William 1862-1934 *WhAm 1*
Churchill, Warren Stanley 1894-1970 *NatCAB 57*
Churchill, William 1820?- *ApCAB*
Churchill, William 1859-1920 *DcAmB, WhAm 1*
Churchill, William Wilberforce 1867-1910 *NatCAB 18*
Churchill, William Worcester 1858- *NatCAB 18*
Churchill, Winston 1871-1947 *ApCAB Sup, ApCAB X, DcAmB S4, McGEWB, NatCAB 10, TwCBDA, WhAm 2*
Churchill, Sir Winston Leonard Spencer 1874-1965 *ApCAB Sup, McGEWB, WhAm 4, WhWW-II*
Churchman, James E 1874- *WhoColR*
Churchman, John 1705-1775 *ApCAB, Drake*
Churchman, John 1753-1805 *ApCAB, Drake, NatCAB 9*
Churchman, John Woolman 1877-1937 *WhAm 1*
Churchman, Philip Hudson 1874- *WhAm 5*
Churchman, William Henry 1818-1882 *ApCAB, DcAmB, NatCAB 22, WhAm H*
Churchwell, William Montgomery 1826-1862 *BiAUS, BiDrAC, WhAm H*
Churchyard, Ida Thompson 1856- *WomWWA 14*
Churriguera, Jose Benito De 1665-1725 *McGEWB*
Churruca Y Elorza, C Damian De 1761-1805 *Drake*
Churruca Y Elorza, Cosme Damian De 1761-1805 *ApCAB*
Chute, A Hamilton 1891-1968 *WhAm 5*
Chute, Arthur Hunt 1890-1929 *WhAm 1*
Chute, Arthur Lambert 1869-1934 *WhAm 1*
Chute, Charles Lionel 1882-1953 *WhAm 3*
Chute, Horatio Nelson 1847-1928 *ApCAB, NatCAB 11, WhAm 1*
Chute, Richard 1820-1893 *NatCAB 16*
Chutter, Reginald Frederick 1893-1963 *NatCAB 50*
Chwa, Daudi 1896- *WhoColR*
Chwistek, Leon 1884-1944 *DcScB*
Chworowsky, Martin Philip 1900-1975 *WhAm 6*
Chyle, John Joseph 1902-1969 *NatCAB 54*
Chynoweth, Henry William 1857-1932 *NatCAB 24*
Cialdini, Enrico 1811-1892 *WhoMilH*
Ciamician, Giacomo Luigi 1857-1922 *DcScB*
Cianca, Bernard Joseph 1916- *WhAm 6*
Ciano, Count Galeazzo 1903-1944 *WhWW-II*
Ciardi, John Anthony 1916- *WebAB*
Ciceri *NewYHSD*
Cicero, Marcus Tullius 106BC-043BC *McGEWB*
Cicerong *NewYHSD*
Cicognani, Amleto Giovanni 1883-1973 *WhAm 6*
Cid, The 1043-1099 *McGEWB*
Cieca DeLeon, Pedro 1520?- *ApCAB*
Cieza DeLeon, Pedro 1520?- *ApCAB, Drake*
Cifuentes, Fray Bernardino 1725-1780? *ApCAB*
Cil, Manuel *NewYHSD*
Cilley, Bradbury 1760-1831 *BiAUS, BiDrAC, TwCBDA, WhAm H*
Cilley, Bradbury Longfellow 1838-1899 *NatCAB 10, TwCBDA*
Cilley, C C d1969 *WhAm 5*
Cilley, Gordon Harper 1874-1938 *WhAm 1*
Cilley, Greenleaf 1829-1899 *ApCAB, NatCAB 10, TwCBDA, WhAm 4*
Cilley, Jonathan 1802-1838 *ApCAB, BiAUS,*

BiDrAC, NatCAB 10, TwCBDA, WhAmP
Cilley, Jonathan Longfellow 1838-1903 *TwCBDA, WhAm 1*
Cilley, Jonathan Prince 1835-1920 *ApCAB, NatCAB 10, TwCBDA, WhAm 1*
Cilley, Joseph 1734-1799 *DcAmB, Drake*
Cilley, Joseph 1735-1799 *ApCAB, NatCAB 10, TwCBDA, WhAm H*
Cilley, Joseph 1791-1887 *ApCAB, BiAUS, BiDrAC, NatCAB 10, TwCBDA, WhAm H*
Cilley, Leon H 1859-1917 *NatCAB 18*
Cimabue *McGEWB*
Cimarosa, Domenico 1749-1801 *McGEWB*
Cimiotti, Gustave 1875- *WhAm 5*
Cincannon *NewYHSD*
Cinelli, Albert Arthur 1900-1972 *NatCAB 56, WhAm 6*
Cinque 1800?- *ApCAB*
Cinque, Joseph 1813?-1879? *McGEWB*
Ciobanu, Ioan 1910-1974 *WhAm 6*
Ciocco, Antonio 1908-1972 *WhAm 5*
Cipollaro, Anthony Caesar 1900-1975 *WhAm 6*
Ciquard, Francois 1760?- *ApCAB*
Ciruelo, Pedro 1470-1554 *DcScB*
Cisneros, Eleonora De 1887- *ApCAB X, NotAW*
Cisneros, Jose 1910- *IIBEAAW*
Cist, Charles 1738-1805 *ApCAB, DcAmB, TwCBDA, WhAm H*
Cist, Charles 1792-1868 *DcAmB, Drake, NatCAB 22, WhAm H*
Cist, Charles 1793-1868 *ApCAB, TwCBDA*
Cist, Henry Martyn 1839-1902 *ApCAB, DcAmB, NatCAB 26, TwCBDA, WhAm 1*
Cist, Jacob 1782-1825 *DcAmB, NewYHSD, TwCBDA, WhAm H*
Cist, Lewis Jacob 1818-1885 *ApCAB, Drake, TwCBDA*
Citaroto, John *NewYHSD*
Citrino, Robert Joseph 1900-1963 *NatCAB 50*
Citron, William Michael 1896- *BiDrAC*
Citti, John *NewYHSD*
Citti, Louis 1827?- *NewYHSD*
Citti, Orelius *NewYHSD*
Ciudad Real, Antonio 1551-1617 *ApCAB*
Claar, Fae Wilson 1900-1946 *NatCAB 41*
Claassen, Harry Louis 1892-1947 *NatCAB 35*
Claassen, Peter Walter 1886-1937 *WhAm 1*
Clabaugh, Harry M 1856-1914 *WhAm 1*
Clabaugh, Hinton Graves d1946 *WhAm 2*
Claessens, Maria 1881- *WhAm 6*
Claffey, Harry William 1886-1961 *NatCAB 51*
Claflin, Adelaide Avery 1846- *AmWom*
Claflin, Albert Whitman 1885-1956 *NatCAB 45*
Claflin, Arthur Whitman 1852-1926 *NatCAB 20, WhAm 1*
Claflin, Edith Frances 1875- *WomWWA 14*
Claflin, Horace Brigham 1811-1885 *ApCAB, DcAmB, NatCAB 3, TwCBDA, WhAm H*
Claflin, John 1850-1938 *DcAmB S2, NatCAB 3, TwCBDA, WhAm 1*
Claflin, Lee 1791-1871 *ApCAB, NatCAB 11, TwCBDA*
Claflin, Mary Bucklin 1825-1896 *TwCBDA*
Claflin, Narcissa Adelaide Avery 1846- *WomWWA 14*
Claflin, Price Colby 1849-1914 *NatCAB 17*
Claflin, Tennessee 1845-1923 *DcAmB, NotAW*
Claflin, W Harold 1880-1950 *NatCAB 38, WhAm 6*
Claflin, William 1816- *TwCBDA*
Claflin, William 1818-1905 *ApCAB, BiDrAC, DcAmB, Drake, NatCAB 1, WhAm 1, WhAmP*
Claflin, William Bement 1872-1939 *NatCAB 31*
Clagett, Arthur Neville 1870-1953 *NatCAB 42*
Clagett, Brice 1889-1951 *NatCAB 44*
Clagett, Clifton 1762-1829 *BiDrAC, TwCBDA, WhAm H*
Clagett, John Rozier 1852-1902 *WhAm 1*
Clagett, Mary DuHamel *WomWWA 14*
Clagett, Thomas Holland 1875-1952 *NatCAB 41*
Clagett, William Horace 1838-1901 *BiAUS,*

BiDrAC, REnAW
Clagett, Wyseman 1721-1784 *DcAmB, WhAm H, WhAmP*
Claggett, Clifton d1829 *BiAUS*
Claggett, John Thomas 1742-1816 *Drake, NatCAB 6*
Claggett, Thomas John 1742-1816 *ApCAB, TwCBDA*
Claghorn, George 1748-1824 *DcAmB, NatCAB 25, WhAm H*
Claghorn, Kate Holladay 1863-1938 *TwCBDA, WhAm 1, WomWWA 14*
Clagstone, Cora Kirk 1878- *WomWWA 14*
Clague, Frank 1865-1952 *BiDrAC, WhAm 3, WhAmP*
Clague, Richard 1816-1878 *NewYHSD*
Claiborne, Ferdinand Leigh 1772-1815 *ApCAB, Drake, TwCBDA*
Claiborne, Hamilton Cabell 1888-1928 *NatCAB 38*
Claiborne, James Robert 1882-1944 *BiDrAC*
Claiborne, John 1777-1808 *BiAUS, BiDrAC, TwCBDA, WhAm H*
Claiborne, John Francis Hamtramck d1884 *BiAUS, Drake*
Claiborne, John Francis Hamtramck 1807-1884 *DcAmB, REnAW*
Claiborne, John Francis Hamtramck 1809-1884 *ApCAB, BiDrAC, NatCAB 11, TwCBDA, WhAm H, WhAmP*
Claiborne, John Herbert 1828-1905 *ApCAB, NatCAB 10, TwCBDA, WhAm 1*
Claiborne, John Herbert 1861- *NatCAB 3*
Claiborne, Nathaniel Herbert 1777-1858 *TwCBDA*
Claiborne, Nathaniel Herbert 1777-1859 *ApCAB, BiAUS, BiDrAC, DcAmB, Drake, NatCAB 12, WhAm H, WhAmP*
Claiborne, Thomas 1749-1812 *BiAUS, BiDrAC, TwCBDA, WhAm H*
Claiborne, Thomas 1780-1856 *BiAUS, BiDrAC, WhAm H*
Claiborne, Thomas Augustine 1779-1816 *TwCBDA*
Claiborne, William 1587?-1676 *NatCAB 11*
Claiborne, William 1587?-1677? *AmBi, DcAmB, WhAm H*
Claiborne, William 1589?-1676? *ApCAB*
Claiborne, William C C d1817 *BiAUS*
Claiborne, William Charles Cole d1817 *NatCAB 13*
Claiborne, William Charles Cole 1773-1817 *Drake*
Claiborne, William Charles Cole 1775-1817 *ApCAB, BiDrAC, NatCAB 10, TwCBDA, WhAmP*
Claiborne, William Charles Coles 1775-1817 *AmBi, DcAmB, REnAW, WhAm H*
Claiborne, William Stirling d1933 *WhAm 1*
Clair, Edward L 1894-1951 *WhAm 3*
Clair, Harry Cornelius 1865-1948 *NatCAB 37*
Clair, Matthew Wesley 1865-1943 *WhAm 2*
Clairaut, Alexis-Claude 1713-1765 *AsBiEn, DcScB*
Clairborne, John Herbert *ApCAB X*
Claire, Richard Shaw 1907-1969 *WhAm 5*
Clairville, William H *NewYHSD*
Claisen, Ludwig 1851-1930 *DcScB*
Clamer, Guilliam Henry 1875-1963 *WhAm 4*
Clampitt, Edward A *ApCAB X*
Clancy, Albert Worthington 1899- *WhAm 4*
Clancy, Donald Daniel 1921- *BiDrAC*
Clancy, Frank Bernard 1878-1945 *NatCAB 33*
Clancy, Frank J 1891-1958 *NatCAB 45, WhAm 3*
Clancy, Frank Willey 1852-1928 *WhAm 1*
Clancy, George Carpenter 1879-1961 *WhAm 4*
Clancy, John Matthew 1837-1903 *TwCBDA*
Clancy, John Michael 1837-1903 *BiDrAC*
Clancy, John Richard 1859-1932 *BiDrAC, WhAm 1*
Clancy, John W d1969 *WhAm 5*
Clancy, Paul Gormley 1897-1956 *NatCAB 42*
Clancy, Peter 1841?- *NewYHSD*
Clancy, Robert Henry 1882-1962 *BiDrAC, WhAm 4*
Clancy, William d1847 *NatCAB 6*
Clancy, William 1800?-1847 *ApCAB*

Clancy, William 1802-1847 *TwCBDA*
Clanton, James Holt 1827-1871 *BiDConf, TwCBDA*
Clanton, Orval Gene 1934- *EncAAH*
Clap, Miss *NewYHSD*
Clap, Nathaniel 1668-1745 *NatCAB 7, WhAm H*
Clap, Nathaniel 1669-1745 *ApCAB, Drake, TwCBDA*
Clap, Roger 1609-1691 *ApCAB, Drake, NatCAB 8*
Clap, Thomas 1703-1767 *ApCAB, BiDAmEd, DcAmB, Drake, NatCAB 1, TwCBDA*
Clap, Thoms 1703-1767 *WhAm H*
Clapeyron, Benoit-Pierre-Emile 1799-1864 *DcScB*
Clapham, Sir John Harold 1873-1946 *McGEWB*
Clapham, Lizzie Markley 1863- *WomWWA 14*
Clapham, Thomas 1838- *WhAm 4*
Clapp, Alexander Huntingdon 1818-1899 *NatCAB 6*
Clapp, Almon Mason 1811- *BiAUS, NatCAB 1*
Clapp, Asa 1762-1848 *ApCAB, DcAmB, Drake, NatCAB 5, TwCBDA, WhAm H*
Clapp, Asa William Henry 1805-1891 *BiAUS, BiDrAC, TwCBDA, WhAm H*
Clapp, Augustus Wilson 1877-1946 *NatCAB 38, WhAm 2*
Clapp, Charles Horace 1883-1935 *DcAmB S1, WhAm 1*
Clapp, Clift Rogers 1861-1945 *WhAm 2*
Clapp, Clyde Alvin 1880-1955 *WhAm 3*
Clapp, Cornelia Maria 1849- *WomWWA 14*
Clapp, Cornelia Maria 1849-1934 *NotAW*
Clapp, Cornelia Maria 1849-1935 *BiDAmEd, WhAm 1*
Clapp, Dexter Elisha 1830- *NatCAB 5*
Clapp, Dorlin Ferris 1820-1885 *NatCAB 23*
Clapp, Earle Hart 1877- *WhAm 5*
Clapp, Edward Allison 1883-1958 *NatCAB 47*
Clapp, Edward Bull 1856-1919 *WhAm 1*
Clapp, Edwin Jones 1881-1930 *WhAm 1*
Clapp, Eleanor Bassett *WomWWA 14*
Clapp, Elmer Frederick 1843-1917 *WhAm 1*
Clapp, Frank Leslie 1877-1937 *WhAm 1*
Clapp, Franklin Halsted 1871-1944 *WhAm 2*
Clapp, Frederick Gardner 1879-1944 *NatCAB 32, WhAm 2*
Clapp, George Alfred 1856-1924 *DcAmB*
Clapp, Gordon Rufus 1905-1963 *NatCAB 49, WhAm 4*
Clapp, H *NewYHSD*
Clapp, Harold L 1909-1961 *WhAm 4*
Clapp, Henry 1814-1875 *NatCAB 9*
Clapp, Henry Austin 1841-1904 *WhAm 1*
Clapp, Herbert Codman 1846-1929 *TwCBDA, WhAm 1*
Clapp, Jacob Crawford 1832- *TwCBDA, WhAm 4*
Clapp, James C *NewYHSD*
Clapp, James Ford 1876-1941 *NatCAB 30*
Clapp, James Gordon 1909-1970 *NatCAB 55*
Clapp, Jeremiah Watkins 1814-1898 *BiDConf*
Clapp, John Mantle 1870- *WhAm 5*
Clapp, Louise Amelia Knapp Smith 1819-1906 *NotAW*
Clapp, Margaret Antoinette 1910-1974 *BiDAmEd, WhAm 6*
Clapp, Moses Edwin 1851-1929 *BiDrAC, NatCAB 12, WhAm 1, WhAmP*
Clapp, Ozro Wright 1836- *NatCAB 5*
Clapp, Paul Spencer 1890-1953 *WhAm 3*
Clapp, Philip Greeley 1888-1954 *WhAm 3*
Clapp, Raymond Gustavus 1875-1967 *NatCAB 53*
Clapp, Theodore 1792-1866 *ApCAB, Drake, TwCBDA*
Clapp, Mrs. Thomas Calvin *WomWWA 14*
Clapp, Verner Warren 1901-1972 *DcAmLiB, NatCAB 57, WhAm 5*
Clapp, William Warland 1826-1891 *DcAmB, Drake, NatCAB 2, TwCBDA, WhAm H*
Clappe, Louise *REnAW*
Clapper, Raymond Lewis 1892-1944 *DcAmB S3, NatCAB 34, WhAm 2*
Clapper, Samuel Mott Duryea d1940 *WhAm 1*
Clapperton, Hugh 1788-1827 *McGEWB*

Clapperton, William R *NewYHSD*
Clarage, Harry Randall 1889-1959 *NatCAB 49*
Clarahan, Leo E 1891-1966 *WhAm 4*
Clardy, John Daniel 1828-1918 *BiDrAC, TwCBDA, WhAm 4*
Clardy, Kit Francis 1892-1961 *BiDrAC, WhAm 4*
Clardy, Martin Linn 1844-1914 *BiDrAC*
Clardy, Martin Luther 1844-1914 *TwCBDA*
Clare Joseph, Mother *NotAW*
Clare, Ada 1835?-1874 *NatCAB 6*
Clare, Ada 1836?-1874 *NotAW*
Clare, Arthur James 1864-1915 *WhAm 1*
Clare, Fulton Warren 1869-1916 *NatCAB 17*
Clare, Israel Smith 1847-1924 *WhAm 1*
Clarendon, Edward Hyde, Earl Of 1609-1674 *McGEWB*
Clarity, Frank Edmund 1877-1933 *WhAm 1*
Clark *NewYHSD*
Clark, A Schuyler 1874-1929 *NatCAB 24*
Clark, Abraham 1726-1794 *AmBi, ApCAB, BiAUS, BiDrAC, DcAmB, Drake, NatCAB 3, TwCBDA, WhAm H, WhAmP*
Clark, Addison 1842-1911 *NatCAB 6, TwCBDA, WhAm 4*
Clark, Albert Montgomery 1879-1950 *WhAm 3*
Clark, Albert Warren 1842-1921 *WhAm 1*
Clark, Alden Hyde 1878-1960 *WhAm 4*
Clark, Alexander 1826-1891 *NatCAB 5, TwCBDA*
Clark, Alexander 1834-1879 *ApCAB, TwCBDA*
Clark, Alfred Edward 1873-1951 *WhAm 3*
Clark, Allan 1896-1950 *NatCAB 39, WhAm 3*
Clark, Allan 1898?-1950 *IIBEAAW*
Clark, Allan Jay 1874-1950 *NatCAB 52, WhAm 3*
Clark, Allen Culling 1858-1943 *NatCAB 32, WhAm 2*
Clark, Alonzo 1807-1887 *ApCAB, NatCAB 1, TwCBDA*
Clark, Alonzo Howard 1850-1918 *ApCAB, TwCBDA, WhAm 1*
Clark, Alonzo Monroe 1868-1952 *NatCAB 42*
Clark, Alson Skinner 1876-1949 *IIBEAAW, NatCAB 36, WhAm 2*
Clark, Alva Benson 1890-1955 *WhAm 3*
Clark, Alvah Augustus 1840-1912 *BiDrAC*
Clark, Alvan 1804-1887 *AmBi, ApCAB, DcAmB, DcScB, Drake, NatCAB 6, NewYHSD, TwCBDA, WebAB, WhAm H*
Clark, Alvan Graham 1832-1897 *AmBi, ApCAB, AsBiEn, DcAmB, DcScB, NatCAB 5, TwCBDA, WebAB, WhAm H*
Clark, Ambrose Williams 1810-1887 *BiAUS, BiDrAC, TwCBDA, WhAm H*
Clark, Amelia Ray 1859- *WomWWA 14*
Clark, Amos, Jr. 1827-1912 *BiAUS*
Clark, Amos, Jr. 1828-1912 *BiDrAC*
Clark, Andrew Hill 1911-1975 *WhAm 6*
Clark, Anna Katherine Perkins *WomWWA 14*
Clark, Anna Newhall 1883- *WomWWA 14*
Clark, Anne Kinnier 1874- *WhAm 5*
Clark, Annie Maria Lawrence 1835- *WhAm 4, WomWWA 14*
Clark, Anson Luman 1836- *WhAm 3*
Clark, Arthur Bridgman 1866-1948 *WhAm 2*
Clark, Arthur Bryan 1880-1947 *NatCAB 38, WhAm 2*
Clark, Arthur Elwood 1871-1950 *WhAm 3*
Clark, Arthur Hamilton 1841-1922 *DcAmB*
Clark, Arthur Henry 1868-1951 *WhAm 3*
Clark, Asahel *NewYHSD*
Clark, Austin Hobart 1880-1954 *WhAm 3*
Clark, B Preston 1860-1939 *WhAm 1*
Clark, Badger, Jr. 1883-1957 *REnAW, WhAm 3*
Clark, Barrett H 1890-1953 *WhAm 3*
Clark, Barzilla Worth 1880-1943 *NatCAB 35*
Clark, Barzilla Worth 1881-1943 *WhAm 2*
Clark, Bennett Champ 1890-1954 *DcAmB S5, WhAm 3*
Clark, Benton Henderson 1895?-1964 *IIBEAAW*
Clark, Bert Boone 1872- *WhAm 5*
Clark, Bertha Winifred 1875- *WomWWA 14*

Clark, Billy James 1778-1867 *ApCAB*
Clark, Bobby 1888-1960 *WhAm 3*
Clark, Bonnell Wetmore 1883-1955 *WhAm 3*
Clark, Brackett Halford 1821-1900 *NatCAB 25*
Clark, Bruce Lawrence 1880-1945 *NatCAB 35*
Clark, Burton 1899-1950 *NatCAB 44*
Clark, Byron, III 1901-1967 *NatCAB 53*
Clark, C Carroll 1875-1973 *NatCAB 57*
Clark, Calvin Montague 1862-1947 *WhAm 2*
Clark, Cameron 1887-1957 *WhAm 3*
Clark, Caroline Richards *WhAm 5*
Clark, Cecil Pratt 1894-1962 *NatCAB 50,*
 WhAm 4
Clark, Cedric William 1895-1958 *NatCAB 43*
Clark, Champ 1850-1921 *AmBi, ApCAB X,*
 DcAmB, NatCAB 14, REnAW,
 TwCBDA, WebAB, WhAm 1, WhAmP
Clark, Charles 1810-1877 *DcAmB, WhAm H*
Clark, Charles 1811-1877 *BiDConf,*
 NatCAB 13
Clark, Charles Benjamin 1844-1891 *BiDrAC,*
 NatCAB 37, TwCBDA, WhAm H
Clark, Charles Benjamin 1882-1949
 NatCAB 37
Clark, Charles Cleveland 1875- *WhAm 5*
Clark, Charles Cotesworth Pinckney 1822-
 ApCAB
Clark, Charles Dickson 1847-1908 *NatCAB 13,*
 WhAm 1
Clark, Charles Edgar 1843-1922 *AmBi,*
 ApCAB Sup, DcAmB, NatCAB 9,
 NatCAB 25, TwCBDA, WebAMB,
 WhAm 1
Clark, Charles Edward 1889-1963 *WhAm 4*
Clark, Charles Erwin 1910-1965 *NatCAB 52*
Clark, Charles Finney 1836-1904 *WhAm 1*
Clark, Charles Francis 1868-1942 *NatCAB 31*
Clark, Charles Heber 1841-1915 *NatCAB 14,*
 NatCAB 35, WhAm 1
Clark, Charles Heber 1847-1915 *DcAmB*
Clark, Charles Hopkins 1848-1926 *DcAmB,*
 NatCAB 18, NatCAB 25, WhAm 1
Clark, Charles Martin 1873-1935 *WhAm 1*
Clark, Charles Nelson 1827-1902 *BiDrAC,*
 TwCBDA
Clark, Charles Peter 1836-1901 *NatCAB 33*
Clark, Charles Richard 1912-1960 *NatCAB 47*
Clark, Charles Upson 1875-1960 *WhAm 4*
Clark, Charles W *NewYHSD*
Clark, Charles Walker 1871-1933 *WhAm 1*
Clark, Charles William 1865-1925 *WhAm 1*
Clark, Chase Addison 1883-1966 *WhAm 4*
Clark, Chester 1828?- *NewYHSD*
Clark, Chester Floyd 1892-1956 *NatCAB 44*
Clark, Chester Frederic 1899-1957 *WhAm 3*
Clark, Christopher Henderson 1767-1828
 BiAUS, BiDrAC, WhAm H
Clark, Clara May *WomWWA 14*
Clark, Clarence Don 1851-1930 *ApCAB Sup,*
 BiDrAC, NatCAB 13, TwCBDA,
 WhAm 1, WhAmP
Clark, Clarence Munroe 1859-1937 *NatCAB 34,*
 WhAm 1
Clark, Clarence Sewall 1893-1960 *WhAm 4*
Clark, Claude Lester 1903-1966 *WhAm 4*
Clark, Clifford Pease 1872-1953 *WhAm 3*
Clark, Cyrus J 1900-1953 *WhAm 3*
Clark, Dan Elbert 1884-1956 *REnAW,*
 WhAm 3
Clark, Daniel 1766?-1813 *BiDrAC, DcAmB,*
 WhAm H
Clark, Daniel 1801-1891 *TwCBDA*
Clark, Daniel 1809-1891 *ApCAB, BiAUS,*
 BiDrAC, DcAmB, Drake, NatCAB 2,
 WhAm H, WhAmP
Clark, Daniel 1835- *ApCAB*
Clark, Daniel A 1779-1840 *ApCAB*
Clark, David 1877-1955 *NatCAB 49*
Clark, David L 1868-1936 *WhAm 1*
Clark, David Wasgate 1812-1871 *WhAm H*
Clark, David Worth 1902-1955 *BiDrAC,*
 NatCAB 40, WhAm 3, WhAmP
Clark, Davis Wasgate 1812-1871 *NatCAB 13*
Clark, Davis Wasgatt 1812-1871 *ApCAB,*
 Drake
Clark, Davis Wasgatt 1849-1935 *WhAm 1*
Clark, Davis Wesgatt 1812-1871 *TwCBDA*
Clark, Derral Leroy 1907-1967 *WhAm 5*

Clark, Donald Lemen 1888-1966 *WhAm 4*
Clark, Duncan Campbell 1920-1966 *WhAm 4*
Clark, Dwight Edwin 1910-1959 *WhAm 3A*
Clark, Edgar Charles 1903-1966 *NatCAB 53*
Clark, Edgar Erastus 1856-1930 *NatCAB 44,*
 WhAm 1
Clark, Edgar Milton 1868-1955 *NatCAB 42*
Clark, Edith Kirkwood Ormsby 1881- *WhAm 6*
Clark, Edmund Dougan 1869-1938 *NatCAB 28*
Clark, Edson Lyman 1827-1913 *ApCAB,*
 TwCBDA, WhAm 1
Clark, Edward *NatCAB 9, NewYHSD*
Clark, Edward 1822-1902 *BiAUS, WhAm 1*
Clark, Edward 1824- *NatCAB 11*
Clark, Edward Brayton *WhAm 5*
Clark, Edward Frank 1879-1960 *NatCAB 48*
Clark, Edward Gavion 1839-1915 *NatCAB 16*
Clark, Edward Gay 1872-1947 *WhAm 2*
Clark, Edward Hardy 1864-1945 *NatCAB 37,*
 WhAm 2
Clark, Edward Lee 1908-1962 *WhAm 4*
Clark, Edward Leonidas 1892-1952 *NatCAB 41,*
 WhAm 3
Clark, Edward Lord 1838-1910 *TwCBDA,*
 WhAm 1
Clark, Edward P 1847-1903 *WhAm 1*
Clark, Edward W d1946 *WhAm 2*
Clark, Edward W 1828- *NatCAB 6*
Clark, Edward Winter 1830- *TwCBDA*
Clark, Eleanor Phelps 1881- *WomWWA 14*
Clark, Eli P 1847- *ApCAB X*
Clark, Elijah 1733-1799 *WhAm H*
Clark, Eliot Candee 1883- *ApCAB X,*
 IIBEAAW
Clark, Eliot Round 1881-1963 *NatCAB 53,*
 WhAm 4
Clark, Elizabeth Conway Bent *WomWWA 14*
Clark, Elizabeth Morris *WomWWA 14*
Clark, Ella Cleveland 1860- *WomWWA 14*
Clark, Ellery Harding 1874-1949 *WhAm 2*
Clark, Elmer Talmage 1886-1966 *WhAm 4*
Clark, Elroy Newton 1860- *WhAm 4*
Clark, Embury Philip 1845-1928 *NatCAB 26*
Clark, Emily d1953 *WhAm 3*
Clark, Emily Anna 1878- *WomWWA 14*
Clark, Emma Kirkland *WomWWA 14*
Clark, Emmons 1827-1905 *ApCAB Sup,*
 NatCAB 26, TwCBDA, WhAm 1
Clark, Emory Wendell 1868-1958 *NatCAB 44,*
 WhAm 3
Clark, Enoch W 1802-1856 *NatCAB 6*
Clark, Ernest Collins 1911-1953 *NatCAB 42*
Clark, Eugene 1904-1972 *NatCAB 57*
Clark, Eugene Bradley 1873-1942 *NatCAB 31,*
 WhAm 2
Clark, Eugene Francis 1879-1930 *WhAm 1*
Clark, Evelyn 1885- *WomWWA 14*
Clark, Ezra, Jr. 1813-1896 *BiAUS, BiDrAC,*
 TwCBDA, WhAm H
Clark, Ezra W *WhAm 2*
Clark, Felicia Buttz 1862- *WhAm 4*
Clark, Felton Grandison 1903-1970 *NatCAB 57,*
 WhAm 5
Clark, Fontaine Riker 1893-1966 *WhAm 4*
Clark, Frances P 1836- *AmWom*
Clark, Francis Edward 1851-1927 *AmBi,*
 ApCAB X, DcAmB, DcAmReB,
 NatCAB 13, TwCBDA, WhAm 1
Clark, Francis Lewis 1861-1914 *WhAm 1*
Clark, Frank 1860-1936 *BiDrAC, WhAm 4,*
 WhAmP
Clark, Frank Hodges 1871- *WhAm 3*
Clark, Frank King 1870?- *NatCAB 14*
Clark, Frank Monroe 1915- *BiDrAC*
Clark, Frank Sylvester 1858-1958 *WhAm 3*
Clark, Frank William 1875- *WhAm 2*
Clark, Franklin 1801-1874 *BiAUS, BiDrAC,*
 WhAm H
Clark, Franklin Jones 1873-1962 *WhAm 4*
Clark, Fred 1914-1968 *WhAm 5*
Clark, Fred Emerson 1890-1948 *WhAm 2*
Clark, Fred George 1890-1973 *WhAm 5*
Clark, Fred Pope 1865-1929 *WhAm 1*
Clark, Frederic Simmons 1850-1929 *ApCAB X,*
 NatCAB 14, WhAm 1
Clark, Frederick Gorham 1819-1886 *TwCBDA*
Clark, Frederick Huntington 1877- *WhAm 5*
Clark, Frederick John 1857-1917 *WhAm 1*

Clark, Frederick M 1874- *WhAm 5*
Clark, Frederick Pareis 1908-1968 *WhAm 5*
Clark, Frederick Timothy 1874-1927 *ApCAB X,*
 WhAm 1
Clark, Friend Ebenezer 1876-1956 *NatCAB 44,*
 WhAm 5
Clark, G W *NewYHSD*
Clark, Gaylord Parsons 1856-1907 *WhAm 1*
Clark, George *NewYHSD*
Clark, George 1841- *TwCBDA, WhAm 4*
Clark, George Archibald 1864- *WhAm 1*
Clark, George Bassett 1827-1891 *DcScB,*
 TwCBDA
Clark, George Campbell 1862-1961 *NatCAB 49,*
 WhAm 4
Clark, George Crawford 1845-1919 *NatCAB 27,*
 WhAm 1
Clark, George Halford 1860-1953 *NatCAB 43*
Clark, George Halford 1860-1956 *WhAm 3*
Clark, George Hardy 1860- *WhAm 4*
Clark, George Harlow 1871- *WhAm 5*
Clark, George Henry 1819- *ApCAB, TwCBDA*
Clark, George Henry 1868-1924 *NatCAB 22*
Clark, George Hunt 1809-1881 *ApCAB, Drake*
Clark, George J d1949 *WhAm 3*
Clark, George Larkin 1849- *WhAm 4*
Clark, George Lindenberg 1892-1969 *WhAm 5*
Clark, George Luther 1877- *WhAm 5*
Clark, George Ramsey 1857-1945 *NatCAB 35,*
 WhAm 2
Clark, George Rogers 1752-1818 *AmBi,*
 ApCAB, DcAmB, EncAAH, EncAB,
 McGEWB, NatCAB 1, REnAW,
 TwCBDA, WebAB, WebAMB, WhAm H
Clark, George Thomas 1862-1940 *WhAm 1*
Clark, George Waldo 1837-1921 *NatCAB 41*
Clark, George Whitefield 1831-1911 *DcAmB,*
 WhAm 1
Clark, George Whitfield 1831-1911 *ApCAB,*
 NatCAB 11, TwCBDA
Clark, Gilbert Church 1897-1966 *NatCAB 51*
Clark, Gilbert John 1851- *NatCAB 7*
Clark, Glenn W 1905-1973 *WhAm 6*
Clark, Grace Miller 1860- *WomWWA 14*
Clark, Graves Glenwood 1894-1967 *NatCAB 54*
Clark, Greenleaf 1835-1904 *DcAmB,*
 NatCAB 22
Clark, Grenville 1882-1967 *WhAm 4,*
 WhAm 5
Clark, Grover 1891-1938 *WhAm 1,*
 WhAm 1C
Clark, Guy Ashley 1823-1902 *NatCAB 5*
Clark, Guy Gayler 1882-1945 *NatCAB 34*
Clark, H Chandler 1893-1958 *NatCAB 46*
Clark, Hamilton Burdick 1869- *WhAm 5*
Clark, Hannah Belle 1864- *WhAm 4*
Clark, Harold Benjamin 1878-1956 *WhAm 3*
Clark, Harold Johnson 1891-1958 *WhAm 3*
Clark, Harold Stevens 1896-1955 *NatCAB 49*
Clark, Harold Terry 1882-1965 *NatCAB 53,*
 WhAm 4
Clark, Harriet Merrell 1858- *WomWWA 14*
Clark, Harry A *NewYHSD*
Clark, Harry Camp 1883-1950 *NatCAB 40,*
 WhAm 3
Clark, Harry Elmore 1862-1944 *NatCAB 33*
Clark, Harry Granville 1875-1935 *WhAm 1*
Clark, Harry Henderson 1860-1952 *WhAm 3*
Clark, Harry Hivner 1889-1950 *NatCAB 39*
Clark, Harry Kenneth 1889-1961 *NatCAB 48*
Clark, Harry Willard 1863- *WhAm 4*
Clark, Harvey Cyrus 1869-1921 *WhAm 1*
Clark, Helen Taggart 1849- *AmWom*
Clark, Henry A 1865-1951 *WhAm 3*
Clark, Henry Alden 1850-1944 *BiDrAC*
Clark, Henry Benjamin 1874- *WhAm 5*
Clark, Henry Freeman 1834-1873 *NatCAB 21*
Clark, Henry Hunt 1875- *WhAm 5*
Clark, Henry James 1826-1873 *AmBi, ApCAB,*
 DcAmB, NatCAB 9, TwCBDA,
 WhAm H
Clark, Henry Lucius 1847-1926 *NatCAB 31*
Clark, Henry S d1874 *BiAUS*
Clark, Henry Selby 1809-1869 *BiDrAC,*
 WhAm H
Clark, Henry Toole 1808-1874 *BiDConf,*
 NatCAB 4, TwCBDA
Clark, Henry Wallace 1874-1942 *NatCAB 31,*

WhAm 2

Clark, Herbert Ralph 1868-1941 *NatCAB 48*
Clark, Herbert W 1882-1964 *WhAm 4*
Clark, Herbert Walter 1851-1935 *NatCAB 25*
Clark, Herma N d1959 *WhAm 3*
Clark, Homer Pierce 1868- *WhAm 6*
Clark, Horace Francis 1815-1873 *ApCAB, BiAUS, BiDrAC, DcAmB, TwCBDA, WhAm H*
Clark, Horace Mitchell 1883-1926 *NatCAB 21*
Clark, Horace Spencer 1840-1907 *WhAm 1*
Clark, Horatio David 1894-1957 *WhAm 3*
Clark, Howard J 1868-1940 *WhAm 1*
Clark, Howard V d1963 *WhAm 4*
Clark, Hubert Lyman 1870-1947 *WhAm 2*
Clark, Hugh Massey 1886-1956 *NatCAB 46*
Clark, Imogen d1936 *WhAm 1, WomWWA 14*
Clark, Isaac 1749-1822 *ApCAB, Drake*
Clark, Isaac 1833-1918 *WhAm 1*
Clark, Isaiah Raymond 1853-1933 *NatCAB 25, WhAm 1*
Clark, J Bayard 1869-1947 *NatCAB 38*
Clark, J Henry 1814-1869 *Drake*
Clark, J Henry *see also* Clark, James Henry
Clark, J R *NewYHSD*
Clark, J Reuben, Jr. 1871-1961 *WhAm 4*
Clark, J Scott 1854-1911 *TwCBDA, WhAm 1*
Clark, Jacob 1819?- *NewYHSD*
Clark, James 1730-1826 *ApCAB, Drake*
Clark, James 1770-1839 *BiDrAC, WhAmP*
Clark, James 1779-1839 *ApCAB, BiAUS, DcAmB, Drake, NatCAB 13, WhAm H*
Clark, James 1811-1850 *NatCAB 11*
Clark, James 1812-1892 *TwCBDA*
Clark, James 1816?- *NewYHSD*
Clark, James Beauchamp 1850-1921 *AmBi, BiDrAC, WebAB, WhAmP*
Clark, James Edward 1909-1970 *WhAm 5*
Clark, James Edwin 1871-1945 *WhAm 2*
Clark, James G *WhAm 5*
Clark, James Henry 1814-1869 *ApCAB, TwCBDA*
Clark, James Henry *see also* Clark, J Henry
Clark, James Jay 1889-1969 *NatCAB 56*
Clark, James Johnson 1828-1919 *NatCAB 19*
Clark, James Lippitt 1883-1969 *IlBEAAW, NatCAB 55*
Clark, James Noble 1885-1951 *NatCAB 39*
Clark, James Osgood Andrew 1827-1894 *TwCBDA*
Clark, James Ross 1850-1927 *NatCAB 21, WhAm 1*
Clark, James Truman 1852-1922 *WhAm 1*
Clark, James W d1844 *BiAUS*
Clark, James Waddey 1877-1939 *WhAm 1*
Clark, James West 1779-1843 *BiDrAC, TwCBDA, WhAm H*
Clark, Janet Howell 1889-1969 *WhAm 5*
Clark, Jerome Bayard 1882-1959 *BiDrAC, WhAmP*
Clark, Jesse Lewis 1869-1942 *NatCAB 30*
Clark, Jesse Redman 1854-1921 *WhAm 1*
Clark, Jesse Redman, Jr. 1885-1972 *NatCAB 57*
Clark, Joel Bennett 1890-1954 *BiDrAC, WhAmP*
Clark, John *NewYHSD*
Clark, John 1598-1664 *NatCAB 20*
Clark, John 1758-1833 *ApCAB, TwCBDA*
Clark, John 1761-1821 *NatCAB 11*
Clark, John 1766-1832 *DcAmB, WhAm H*
Clark, John Alden 1907-1974 *WhAm 6*
Clark, John Alonzo 1801-1843 *ApCAB, TwCBDA*
Clark, John Arvine 1889-1954 *WhAm 3*
Clark, John Bates 1847-1938 *AmBi, DcAmB S2, EncAB, McGEWB, NatCAB 13, TwCBDA, WebAB, WhAm 1*
Clark, John Brittan 1864-1944 *WhAm 2*
Clark, John Bullock 1802-1885 *ApCAB, BiAUS, BiDConf, BiDrAC, Drake, TwCBDA, WhAm H*
Clark, John Bullock, Jr. 1831-1903 *ApCAB, BiAUS, BiDrAC, TwCBDA, WhAm 1*
Clark, John Chamberlain 1793-1852 *BiDrAC, TwCBDA, WhAm H*

Clark, John Cheesman 1863-1946 *WhAm 2*
Clark, John Donavan 1874-1955 *NatCAB 45*
Clark, John Dustin 1882-1958 *NatCAB 52*
Clark, John Edward 1850-1934 *WhAm 1*
Clark, John Emory 1832-1921 *WhAm 1*
Clark, John Garretson 1932- *EncAAH*
Clark, John Goodrich 1867-1927 *NatCAB 21, WhAm 1*
Clark, John Howe 1837-1913 *WhAm 1*
Clark, John Jesse 1866- *WhAm 4*
Clark, John Lewis 1865- *NatCAB 14, WhAm 5*
Clark, John Marshall 1836-1918 *WhAm 1*
Clark, John Maurice 1884-1963 *McGEWB, NatCAB 48, WhAm 4*
Clark, John Robert 1888-1956 *WhAm 3*
Clark, John Spencer 1835- *WhAm 4*
Clark, John Thomas 1881- *WhoColR*
Clark, John W *NewYHSD*
Clark, Jonas 1730-1805 *ApCAB, DcAmB, Drake, TwCBDA*
Clark, Jonas 1731-1805 *WhAm H*
Clark, Jonas Gilman 1815-1900 *AmBi, DcAmB, NatCAB 9, TwCBDA, WhAm H*
Clark, Jonathan 1750-1811 *TwCBDA*
Clark, Joseph Bourne 1836-1923 *NatCAB 14, WhAm 1*
Clark, Joseph James 1893-1971 *WhAm 5, WhWW-II*
Clark, Joseph Leon 1896-1961 *WhAm 4*
Clark, Joseph Oscar 1871-1936 *NatCAB 27*
Clark, Joseph Sill 1901- *BiDrAC*
Clark, Joseph Sylvester 1800-1861 *DcAmB, WhAm H*
Clark, Josephine Adelaide 1856- *WhAm 4, WomWWA 14*
Clark, Josiah Latimer 1822-1898 *DcScB*
Clark, Julia Gilman 1873- *WomWWA 14*
Clark, Julian Jerome 1907-1971 *WhAm 5*
Clark, Kate Upson 1851-1935 *ApCAB X, WhAm 1, WomWWA 14*
Clark, Katharine Pickens Upson 1851-1935 *NatCAB 30*
Clark, Keith 1879- *WhAm 3*
Clark, Kenneth Bancroft 1914- *WebAB*
Clark, L Pierce 1870-1933 *WhAm 1*
Clark, Laban 1778-1868 *ApCAB, Drake, TwCBDA*
Clark, Lafayette 1801-1881 *NatCAB 19*
Clark, Lancaster Peter 1882-1950 *NatCAB 38*
Clark, Lee Hinchman 1895-1962 *NatCAB 49, WhAm 4*
Clark, LeGrand Lockwood 1868-1959 *NatCAB 47*
Clark, Lester Williams 1854-1922 *WhAm 1*
Clark, Lewis Gaylord 1808-1873 *AmBi, DcAmB, WhAm H*
Clark, Lewis Gaylord 1810-1873 *ApCAB, NatCAB 8, TwCBDA*
Clark, Lewis Sherman 1865- *WhoColR*
Clark, Lewis Whitehouse 1828-1900 *NatCAB 13, TwCBDA, WhAm 1*
Clark, Lincoln 1800-1886 *BiAUS, BiDrAC, TwCBDA, WhAm H*
Clark, Lincoln Romeiser 1882-1941 *NatCAB 30*
Clark, Lindley Daniel 1862- *WhAm 4*
Clark, Linwood Leon 1876-1965 *BiDrAC, WhAm 5*
Clark, Lloyd Montgomery 1895-1969 *WhAm 5*
Clark, Lot 1788-1862 *BiAUS, BiDrAC, WhAm H*
Clark, Louis Gaylord 1810- *Drake*
Clark, Louis Verdier 1862-1934 *NatCAB 31*
Clark, Louisa *NewYHSD*
Clark, Lucius Charles 1869-1949 *NatCAB 37, WhAm 2*
Clark, Luther Hale 1870-1933 *NatCAB 25*
Clark, Lyman Noble 1835-1914 *NatCAB 16*
Clark, M M *NewYHSD*
Clark, M S *BiAUS*
Clark, Mable Peters 1885- *WomWWA 14*
Clark, Mallie Adkin 1866- *WhAm 1*
Clark, Margaret Vaupel *WomWWA 14*
Clark, Marguerite d1940 *WhAm 1*
Clark, Marguerite 1883-1940 *NotAW*
Clark, Marguerite 1887-1940 *NatCAB 30*
Clark, Mark Wayne 1896- *McGEWB, WebAB, WebAMB, WhWW-II, WhoMilH*

Clark, Marvin R 1840- *TwCBDA*
Clark, Mary-Chase 1897-1945 *NatCAB 32*
Clark, Mary D *WomWWA 14*
Clark, Mary Frances 1873- *WhoColR*
Clark, Mary Kimber 1872- *WomWWA 14*
Clark, Mary Sheafer Whitcomb *WomWWA 14*
Clark, Mary Vida 1872- *WomWWA 14*
Clark, Matt 1903- *IlBEAAW*
Clark, Matthew 1810?- *NewYHSD*
Clark, Melville d1918 *WhAm 1*
Clark, Melville A 1883-1953 *ApCAB X, WhAm 3*
Clark, Melvin Green 1868-1931 *WhAm 1*
Clark, Meriweather Lewis *WhAm H*
Clark, Minna Minton Dyke *WomWWA 14*
Clark, Myra Almeda Smith *WomWWA 14*
Clark, Myron H 1881-1953 *WhAm 3*
Clark, Myron Holley 1806-1892 *ApCAB, DcAmB, NatCAB 3, WhAm H, WhAmP*
Clark, Myron Holly 1806-1892 *TwCBDA*
Clark, Natalie Lord Rice 1867- *WomWWA 14*
Clark, Nathaniel George 1825-1896 *ApCAB, NatCAB 6, TwCBDA*
Clark, Nathaniel Walling 1859-1918 *TwCBDA, WhAm 1*
Clark, Nora Graves 1877- *WomWWA 14*
Clark, Olynthus B 1864-1936 *WhAm 1*
Clark, Orange Marcus 1851-1929 *NatCAB 41*
Clark, Orrin Benner 1850-1894 *TwCBDA*
Clark, Orrin Melville 1870-1962 *NatCAB 49*
Clark, Patrick 1818-1887 *TwCBDA*
Clark, Paul Burroughs 1892-1962 *WhAm 4*
Clark, Paul Dennison 1901-1969 *WhAm 5*
Clark, Paul Foster 1892-1973 *NatCAB 57, WhAm 5*
Clark, Pearl Franklin 1886-1962 *NatCAB 47*
Clark, Percy Hamilton 1873-1965 *WhAm 4*
Clark, Peter 1796?- *NewYHSD*
Clark, Ralph Elden 1906-1954 *NatCAB 44*
Clark, Ralph Thurman 1896-1949 *NatCAB 37*
Clark, Randolph 1844- *WhAm 4*
Clark, Ray Henry 1896-1955 *WhAm 3*
Clark, Reed Paige 1878-1958 *WhAm 3*
Clark, Remington Alonzo 1900-1945 *NatCAB 40*
Clark, Rensselaer Weston 1885-1965 *NatCAB 51, WhAm 4*
Clark, Richard Francis Maplestone 1906-1974 *WhAm 6*
Clark, Richard H 1824-1896 *TwCBDA*
Clark, Richard T *NewYHSD*
Clark, Robert 1777-1836 *BiAUS*
Clark, Robert 1777-1837 *BiDrAC, WhAm H*
Clark, Robert Bruce *WhAm 5*
Clark, Robert Carlton 1877-1939 *WhAm 1*
Clark, Robert Fry 1880- *WhAm 6*
Clark, Robert Lanier 1903-1963 *WhAm 4*
Clark, Robert Thomas, Jr. 1906-1957 *WhAm 3*
Clark, Robert Watson 1884-1948 *NatCAB 36*
Clark, Roe Sidney 1887-1955 *NatCAB 44, WhAm 3*
Clark, Roland 1874-1957 *NatCAB 42*
Clark, Roland Eugene 1879-1958 *WhAm 3*
Clark, Rollin M 1899-1950 *WhAm 3*
Clark, Rose M *WomWWA 14*
Clark, Roy Wallace 1880-1948 *WhAm 2*
Clark, Rufus Wheelwright 1813- *Drake*
Clark, Rufus Wheelwright 1813-1866 *NatCAB 10, WhAm H*
Clark, Rufus Wheelwright 1813-1886 *ApCAB, TwCBDA*
Clark, Rufus Wheelwright 1844-1909 *WhAm 1*
Clark, Rush 1834-1879 *BiDrAC, TwCBDA, WhAm H*
Clark, Miss S D *NewYHSD*
Clark, Sam L 1898-1960 *WhAm 4*
Clark, Samuel 1777-1861 *NatCAB 19*
Clark, Samuel 1800-1870 *BiAUS, BiDrAC, WhAm H*
Clark, Samuel Adams 1822-1875 *ApCAB, Drake, TwCBDA*
Clark, Samuel C *NewYHSD*
Clark, Samuel Hicks 1879-1941 *NatCAB 31*
Clark, Samuel Mercer 1842-1900 *BiDrAC, TwCBDA*
Clark, Samuel Mercier 1842-1900 *WhAm 1*
Clark, Samuel Orman, Jr. 1900-1975 *WhAm 6*
Clark, Samuel Wesley 1872-1949 *WhAm 3*

Clark, Seth A *NewYHSD*
Clark, Seth H *NewYHSD*
Clark, Sheldon d1952 *WhAm 3*
Clark, Sheldon 1785-1840 *ApCAB, DcAmB, Drake, NatCAB 22, TwCBDA, WhAm H*
Clark, Silas C *NewYHSD*
Clark, Simeon Taylor 1836-1891 *TwCBDA*
Clark, Solomon Henry 1861-1927 *WhAm 1*
Clark, Stephen Carlton 1882-1960 *WhAm 4*
Clark, Stephen Cutter 1892-1950 *WhAm 3*
Clark, Susan Eliza 1844- *WomWWA 14*
Clark, Susie Champney *WomWWA 14*
Clark, Taliaferro 1867-1948 *WhAm 2*
Clark, Theodore 1895-1949 *WhAm 3*
Clark, Theodore Minot 1845-1909 *NatCAB 30, WhAm 1*
Clark, Thomas *ApCAB*
Clark, Thomas d1860 *Drake*
Clark, Thomas 1787-1860 *ApCAB, NatCAB 6*
Clark, Thomas 1789-1860 *TwCBDA*
Clark, Thomas 1801-1867 *DcScB*
Clark, Thomas Arkle 1862-1932 *WhAm 1*
Clark, Thomas Collier 1860-1915 *WhAm 1*
Clark, Thomas Curtis 1877-1954 *WhAm 3*
Clark, Thomas Dionysius 1903- *EncAAH, REnAW*
Clark, Thomas Edward 1869-1962 *NatCAB 53*
Clark, Thomas Frederic 1845- *NatCAB 14, WhAm 4*
Clark, Thomas Harvey 1857-1915 *WhAm 1*
Clark, Thomas March 1812-1903 *ApCAB, DcAmB, Drake, NatCAB 1, TwCBDA, WhAm 1*
Clark, Tom Campbell 1899- *BiDrUSE, WebAB*
Clark, Victor Selden 1868- *WhAm 3*
Clark, Virginia Keep 1878- *WomWWA 14*
Clark, Virginius E 1886-1948 *WhAm 2*
Clark, Wallace 1880-1948 *NatCAB 36, WhAm 2*
Clark, Walter 1846-1924 *AmBi, DcAmB, NatCAB 8, TwCBDA, WhAm 1*
Clark, Walter 1848-1917 *WhAm 1*
Clark, Walter 1885-1933 *NatCAB 25*
Clark, Walter Appleton 1876-1906 *WhAm 1*
Clark, Walter Eli 1869-1950 *NatCAB 14, NatCAB 38, WhAm 2A*
Clark, Walter Ernest 1873-1955 *NatCAB 51, WhAm 3*
Clark, Walter Eugene 1881-1960 *NatCAB 50, WhAm 4*
Clark, Walter Gordan 1876- *NatCAB 14*
Clark, Walter Haven 1872-1939 *NatCAB 29*
Clark, Walter Leighton 1859-1935 *DcAmB S1, NatCAB 27*
Clark, Walter Loane 1878-1941 *NatCAB 35, WhAm 1*
Clark, Walter VanTilburg 1909-1971 *NatCAB 57, REnAW, WhAm 5*
Clark, Walton 1856-1934 *NatCAB 28, WhAm 1*
Clark, Warren Dearborn 1850-1930 *NatCAB 27*
Clark, Washington A 1842-1931 *WhAm 2*
Clark, Wilbur 1908-1965 *WhAm 4*
Clark, Will L 1865- *WhAm 4*
Clark, William d1705? *NatCAB 16*
Clark, William d1841 *BiAUS*
Clark, William 1770-1838 *AmBi, ApCAB, DcAmB, EncAAH, McGEWB, NatCAB 12, REnAW, TwCBDA, WebAB, WebAMB, WhAm H, WhAmP*
Clark, William 1774-1851 *BiAUS, BiDrAC, TwCBDA, WhAm H*
Clark, William 1831-1884 *NatCAB 5*
Clark, William 1891-1957 *NatCAB 49, WhAm 3*
Clark, William A Graham 1879-1953 *WhAm 3*
Clark, William Albert, Jr. 1879-1960 *NatCAB 49*
Clark, William Alfred 1865-1934 *NatCAB 26*
Clark, William Andrews 1839-1925 *AmBi, ApCAB Sup, ApCAB X, BiDrAC, DcAmB, McGEWB, NatCAB 13, NatCAB 21, REnAW, WhAm 1, WhAmP*
Clark, William Andrews, Jr. 1877-1934 *NatCAB 25, WhAm 1*

Clark, William Anthony 1867- *WhAm 4*
Clark, William Arthur 1853-1918 *WhAm 1*
Clark, William Audley 1803-1887 *TwCBDA*
Clark, William Braddock 1841-1927 *NatCAB 18, WhAm 4*
Clark, William Bullock 1860-1917 *DcAmB, NatCAB 13, NatCAB 18, TwCBDA, WhAm 1*
Clark, William Clifford 1889-1952 *WhAm 3*
Clark, William E 1905-1966 *WhAm 4*
Clark, William Francis 1856- *WhAm 4*
Clark, William Heermans 1848-1928 *WhAm 1*
Clark, William Jr 1909-1969 *WhAm 5*
Clark, William Irving 1879-1958 *NatCAB 47, WhAm 3*
Clark, William John 1877-1956 *NatCAB 45*
Clark, William Mansfield 1884-1964 *DcScB, NatCAB 52, WhAm 4*
Clark, William Newton 1832-1920 *NatCAB 20*
Clark, William R *WhAm 5*
Clark, William Ramsey 1927- *BiDrUSE*
Clark, William Smith 1826-1886 *AmBi, ApCAB, DcAmB, NatCAB 5, TwCBDA, WhAm H*
Clark, William Smith, II 1900-1969 *WhAm 5*
Clark, William Squire 1807-1889 *NatCAB 24*
Clark, William T 1834- *BiAUS*
Clark, William Thomas 1831-1905 *BiDrAC, DcAmB, NatCAB 23, WhAm 4*
Clark, William Thomas 1867-1939 *NatCAB 30*
Clark, William Timothy 1831- *WhAm 4*
Clark, William Walker 1858-1949 *WhAm 3*
Clark, William Walton 1846-1932 *NatCAB 24*
Clark, William Washington 1853-1922 *NatCAB 20*
Clark, William White 1819-1883 *BiDConf*
Clark, Willis Gaylord d1841 *ApCAB*
Clark, Willis Gaylord 1808-1841 *DcAmB, WhAm H*
Clark, Willis Gaylord 1810-1841 *Drake, NatCAB 8, TwCBDA*
Clark, Willis Gaylord 1827-1898 *BiDConf*
Clark, Willis Winfield 1895-1964 *WhAm 4*
Clark, Wilson Warner 1878-1968 *NatCAB 57*
Clark, Winfred Newcomb 1876-1952 *WhAm 3*
Clark, Zachariah Harrison 1863-1916 *NatCAB 18*
Clarke, Albert 1840-1911 *NatCAB 11, TwCBDA, WhAm 1*
Clarke, Alfred 1848-1922 *NatCAB 20*
Clarke, Alfred 1849-1922 *WhAm 1*
Clarke, Sir Alured 1745-1832 *ApCAB, Drake*
Clarke, Alvah Augustus 1840- *TwCBDA*
Clarke, Andrew Stuart Currie 1859-1934 *WhAm 1*
Clarke, Archibald Smith 1788-1821 *BiAUS, BiDrAC, WhAm H*
Clarke, Arthur Edward 1872- *WhAm 2*
Clarke, Augustus Peck 1833-1912 *NatCAB 6, TwCBDA, WhAm 1*
Clarke, Bascom B 1851-1929 *WhAm 1*
Clarke, Bayard 1815-1884 *BiAUS, BiDrAC, TwCBDA, WhAm H*
Clarke, Benjamin Franklin 1831-1908 *NatCAB 10, TwCBDA, WhAm 1*
Clarke, Beverly Leonidas 1809-1860 *BiAUS, BiDrAC, NatCAB 12, TwCBDA, WhAm H*
Clarke, Sir Caspar Purdon 1846-1911 *DcAmB, WhAm 1*
Clarke, Caspar William 1892-1949 *NatCAB 38, WhAm 3*
Clarke, Charles 1826- *ApCAB*
Clarke, Charles Cameron 1861-1935 *WhAm 1*
Clarke, Charles Ezra 1790-1863 *BiAUS, BiDrAC, WhAm H*
Clarke, Charles Henry 1864-1946 *NatCAB 38*
Clarke, Charles Lorenzo 1853-1941 *NatCAB 30, WhAm 1*
Clarke, Charles S 1863-1920 *WhAm 3*
Clarke, Charles Walter 1887-1964 *WhAm 4*
Clarke, Charles Warrington Earle 1882-1965 *NatCAB 51, WhAm 4*
Clarke, Chester Raymond 1895-1956 *NatCAB 46*
Clarke, Clement George 1869-1940 *WhAm 1*
Clarke, Collins 1842?- *NewYHSD*
Clarke, Creston 1865-1910 *WhAm 1*

Clarke, Daniel *BiAUS*
Clarke, Daniel Boone 1825-1895 *NatCAB 2*
Clarke, David Andrew, Jr. 1919-1974 *WhAm 6*
Clarke, David Roland 1892- *WhAm 3*
Clarke, Donald Henderson 1887-1958 *WhAm 3*
Clarke, Dorus 1797-1884 *ApCAB, Drake, TwCBDA*
Clarke, Dumont 1840-1909 *NatCAB 15, WhAm 1*
Clarke, Dumont 1883-1960 *NatCAB 49*
Clarke, E L 1879- *WhAm 6*
Clarke, Edith Emily 1859-1932 *WhAm 1, WomWWA 14*
Clarke, Edmund Arthur Stanley 1862-1931 *WhAm 1*
Clarke, Edward Alexander 1861- *WhoColR*
Clarke, Edward Daniel 1769-1822 *DcScB*
Clarke, Edward Hammond 1820-1877 *ApCAB, NatCAB 8, TwCBDA*
Clarke, Edward Wight 1892-1946 *NatCAB 36*
Clarke, Edwin Leavitt 1888-1948 *WhAm 2*
Clarke, Elijah 1733-1799 *AmBi, ApCAB, DcAmB, Drake, WhAm H*
Clarke, Eliot Channing 1845-1921 *WhAm 1*
Clarke, Elizabeth Crocker Lawrence 1861- *WhAm 4, WomWWA 14*
Clarke, Ernest Perley 1859-1933 *WhAm 1*
Clarke, Ernest Swope 1872-1948 *NatCAB 37, WhAm 2*
Clarke, Francis Devereux 1849-1913 *DcAmB, NatCAB 22*
Clarke, Francis West 1885-1938 *WhAm 1*
Clarke, Frank Gay 1850-1901 *BiDrAC, TwCBDA, WhAm 1*
Clarke, Frank Wigglesworth 1847-1931 *AmBi, ApCAB, DcAmB S1, DcScB, NatCAB 3, NatCAB 26, TwCBDA, WhAm 1*
Clarke, Freeman 1809-1887 *BiAUS, BiDrAC, TwCBDA, WhAm H*
Clarke, George d1763 *ApCAB, Drake*
Clarke, George 1676-1760 *DcAmB, WhAm H*
Clarke, George Haven 1859-1929 *NatCAB 23*
Clarke, George Herbert 1873-1932 *WhAm 1*
Clarke, George Rogers 1752-1818 *Drake*
Clarke, George Washington 1852-1936 *ApCAB X, NatCAB 15, NatCAB 28, WhAm 1*
Clarke, Georgiana B *WomWWA 14*
Clarke, Grace Giddings Julian 1865-1938 *NotAW, WomWWA 14*
Clarke, Hans Thacher 1887-1972 *NatCAB 57, WhAm 5*
Clarke, Harley Lyman 1882-1955 *WhAm 3*
Clarke, Helen Archibald 1860-1926 *AmBi, DcAmB, WhAm 1, WomWWA 14*
Clarke, Henry Francis 1820-1887 *ApCAB, TwCBDA*
Clarke, Herbert Lincoln 1867-1945 *WhAm 2*
Clarke, Hermann Frederick 1882-1947 *WhAm 2*
Clarke, Hopewell 1854-1931 *WhAm 1*
Clarke, Horace Donald 1892-1957 *WhAm 3*
Clarke, Hugh Archibald 1839- *WhAm 4*
Clarke, Ida Clyde 1878-1956 *WhAm 3*
Clarke, J Alexander 1891-1943 *NatCAB 31*
Clarke, J Calvitt 1887-1970 *WhAm 5*
Clarke, James d1850 *BiAUS, Drake*
Clarke, James 1779-1839 *TwCBDA*
Clarke, James Alfred 1886-1969 *NatCAB 53*
Clarke, James Augustine 1871- *WhAm 5*
Clarke, James Everitt 1868- *WhAm 4*
Clarke, James Franklin 1832-1916 *WhAm 1*
Clarke, James Frederic 1864-1942 *WhAm 2*
Clarke, James Freeman 1810-1888 *AmBi, ApCAB, DcAmB, DcAmReB, Drake, NatCAB 2, TwCBDA, WebAB, WhAm H*
Clarke, James I 1885-1961 *WhAm 4*
Clarke, James Paul 1854-1916 *BiDrAC, DcAmB, NatCAB 10, WhAm 1, WhAmP*
Clarke, Jeremiah *NatCAB 10*
Clarke, Jeremy *ApCAB*
Clarke, Jessie Keziah *WomWWA 14*
Clarke, Joe Alexander 1897- *WhAm 5*
Clarke, John d1821 *BiAUS, Drake*
Clarke, John 1609-1676 *AmBi, ApCAB, DcAmB, DcAmReB, Drake, NatCAB 7, TwCBDA, WhAm H*

Clawson, Samuel George 1896-1942
NatCAB 31
Claxton, Alexander 1790?-1841 *ApCAB, Drake,
NewYHSD, TwCBDA*
Claxton, Allen Enes 1901-1966 *WhAm 4*
Claxton, Brooke 1898-1960 *WhAm 4*
Claxton, C Porter 1898-1963 *WhAm 4*
Claxton, F S *ApCAB*
Claxton, Hannah Johnson 1879- *BiCAW*
Claxton, Kate 1848-1924 *AmWom, ApCAB,
DcAmB, NatCAB 22, NotAW, WhAm 1,
WomWWA 14*
Claxton, Mary Hannah Johnson d1955
WhAm 3, WomWWA 14
Claxton, Philander Priestley 1862-1957
BiDAmEd, NatCAB 15, WhAm 3
Claxton, Thomas d1813 *ApCAB*
Clay, Albert Tobias 1866-1925 *DcAmB,
NatCAB 22, WhAm 1*
Clay, Alexander Stephens 1853-1910
*ApCAB Sup, BiDrAC, NatCAB 5,
TwCBDA, WhAm 1*
Clay, Boston 1879- *WhoColR*
Clay, Brutus Junius 1808-1878 *BiAUS,
BiDrAC, WhAm H*
Clay, Brutus Junius 1847-1932 *NatCAB 14,
WhAm 1*
Clay, Brutus Junius 1876-1926 *NatCAB 45*
Clay, Cassius Marcellus 1810-1903 *AmBi,
ApCAB, BiAUS, DcAmB, Drake,
NatCAB 2, TwCBDA, WebAB, WhAm 1,
WhAmP*
Clay, Cassius Marcellus 1942- *EncAB, WebAB*
Clay, Cassius Marcellus, Jr. 1846-1913
NatCAB 43
Clay, Cecil *NewYHSD*
Clay, Cecil 1842-1907 *TwCBDA, WhAm 1*
Clay, Christopher Field 1874-1939 *WhAm 1*
Clay, Mrs. Clement C *NotAW*
Clay, Clement Claiborne 1816-1882 *AmBi,
BiDConf, BiDrAC, DcAmB, WhAm H,
WhAmP*
Clay, Clement Claiborne 1817-1882 *TwCBDA*
Clay, Clement Claiborne 1819-1882 *ApCAB,
BiAUS, NatCAB 4*
Clay, Clement Comer 1789-1866 *ApCAB,
BiAUS, BiDrAC, DcAmB, Drake,
NatCAB 10, TwCBDA, WhAm H,
WhAmP*
Clay, Clement Comer 1819- *Drake*
Clay, Edward W 1792-1857 *ApCAB, Drake*
Clay, Edward Williams 1799-1857 *DcAmB,
NatCAB 22, NewYHSD, WhAm H*
Clay, Elizabeth Campbell 1871- *WomWWA 14*
Clay, George Strong 1860-1941 *NatCAB 30*
Clay, Green 1757-1826 *ApCAB, DcAmB,
Drake, NatCAB 4, TwCBDA, WhAm H*
Clay, Henry 1777-1851 *REnAW*
Clay, Henry 1777-1852 *AmBi, ApCAB,
BiAUS, BiDrAC, BiDrUSE, DcAmB,
Drake, EncAAH, EncAB, McGEWB,
NatCAB 5, TwCBDA, WebAB,
WhAm H, WhAmP*
Clay, Henry 1811-1847 *ApCAB, Drake,
TwCBDA*
Clay, Henry Brevard 1918-1967 *WhAm 5*
Clay, Jacob 1882-1955 *DcScB*
Clay, James Brown 1817-1864 *ApCAB, BiAUS,
BiDrAC, Drake, NatCAB 13, TwCBDA,
WhAm H*
Clay, James Franklin 1840-1921 *BiDrAC*
Clay, James Lloyd 1911-1974 *WhAm 6*
Clay, John 1851-1934 *REnAW, WhAm 1*
Clay, John Cecil 1875- *WhAm 5*
Clay, John Daniel 1879-1946 *NatCAB 37*
Clay, John Randolph 1808-1885 *BiAUS,
NatCAB 12, TwCBDA*
Clay, Joseph 1741-1804 *BiDrAC, DcAmB,
TwCBDA, WhAm H*
Clay, Joseph 1741-1805 *ApCAB, BiAUS,
Drake*
Clay, Joseph 1764-1811 *ApCAB, DcAmB,
Drake, TwCBDA, WhAm H*
Clay, Joseph 1769-1811 *BiDrAC, TwCBDA,
WhAm H*
Clay, Laura 1849-1941 *NotAW, WhAm 1,
WomWWA 14*
Clay, Lucius DuBignon 1897-1977 *WebAMB,*

WhWW-II
Clay, Mary Barr 1839- *AmWom*
Clay, Matthew 1754-1815 *BiAUS, BiDrAC,
DcAmB, NatCAB 22, WhAm H,
WhAmP*
Clay, Porter 1779-1850 *ApCAB*
Clay, Ryburn Glover 1891-1955 *WhAm 3*
Clay, Samuel 1840?- *NewYHSD*
Clay, Thomas Arthur 1880-1943 *NatCAB 34*
Clay, Thomas Hart 1803-1871 *BiAUS, Drake,
NatCAB 13, TwCBDA*
Clay, William Lacey 1931- *BiDrAC*
Clay, William Rogers 1864-1938 *NatCAB 30,
WhAm 1*
Clay-Clopton, Virginia Carolina 1825-1915
WhAm 4
Clay-Clopton, Virginia Caroline Tunstall
1825-1915 *NotAW*
Clayberg, John Bertrand 1853-1921 *NatCAB 11,
WhAm 1*
Clayberger, Raymond Pierce 1881-1965
NatCAB 51, WhAm 6
Clayborn, John Henry d1954 *WhAm 3*
Clayborne, William 1590?- *Drake, TwCBDA*
Claybourn, John Geronold 1886-1967
WhAm 4A, WhAm 5
Claycomb, Stephen Hugh 1847- *TwCBDA*
Clayland, John Martin 1860-1941 *NatCAB 30*
Claypole, Edith Jane 1870- *NatCAB 13,
WhAm 5, WomWWA 14*
Claypole, Edward Waller 1835-1901 *ApCAB,
DcAmB, NatCAB 13, TwCBDA,
WhAm 1*
Claypool, Harold Kile 1886-1958 *BiDrAC,
WhAm 3*
Claypool, Horatio Clifford 1859-1921 *BiDrAC,
WhAm 4*
Claypool, J Gordon 1916-1967 *NatCAB 56,
WhAm 5*
Claypool, James Vernon 1899-1965 *WhAm 4*
Claypoole, David Chambers 1757-1849
NatCAB 20
Claypoole, Elizabeth *NotAW*
Claypoole, James d1796? *NewYHSD*
Claypoole, James 1634-1686 *ApCAB*
Claypoole, James 1634-1687 *NatCAB 16*
Claypoole, James, Jr. 1743?-1800? *BnEnAmA*
Clayton, Alexander Mosby 1801-1889 *BiAUS,
BiDConf, TwCBDA*
Clayton, Augustin Smith 1783-1839 *BiAUS,
BiDrAC, DcAmB, Drake, TwCBDA,
WhAm H*
Clayton, Augustine Smith 1783-1839 *ApCAB*
Clayton, Bertram Tracy 1862-1918 *BiDrAC,
WhAm 1*
Clayton, Charles 1825-1885 *BiAUS, BiDrAC,
WhAm H*
Clayton, Charles O 1830?- *NewYHSD*
Clayton, Claude Feemster 1909-1969 *WhAm 6*
Clayton, Ernest 1889-1955 *NatCAB 45,
WhAm 3*
Clayton, Everett McCord, Jr. 1923-1974
WhAm 6
Clayton, Florence Andrews 1862- *AmWom*
Clayton, H G 1892-1961 *WhAm 4*
Clayton, Henry DeLamar 1827-1889 *BiDConf,
NatCAB 12, TwCBDA*
Clayton, Henry DeLamar 1857-1929 *AmBi,
BiDrAC, DcAmB S1, WhAm 1, WhAmP*
Clayton, Henry Helm 1861-1946 *ApCAB X,
WhAm 2*
Clayton, James Benjamin 1867- *WhAm 4*
Clayton, John 1685?-1773 *AmBi, DcAmB,
NatCAB 19, TwCBDA, WhAm H*
Clayton, John 1686-1773 *ApCAB, Drake*
Clayton, John Bell 1906-1955 *NatCAB 47*
Clayton, John Middleton 1796-1856 *AmBi,
ApCAB, BiAUS, BiDrAC, BiDrUSE,
DcAmB, Drake, McGEWB, NatCAB 4,
NatCAB 6, TwCBDA, WebAB,
WhAm H, WhAmP*
Clayton, John Middleton 1840-1889
ApCAB Sup
Clayton, Joseph Edward 1879- *WhoColR*
Clayton, Joshua 1744-1798 *ApCAB, BiAUS,
BiDrAC, DcAmB, Drake, NatCAB 11,
TwCBDA, WhAm H, WhAmP*
Clayton, Lawrence 1891-1949 *WhAm 2*

Clayton, Mabel Julia Andrews *WomWWA 14*
Clayton, Philip 1815-1877 *BiAUS, BiDConf,
TwCBDA*
Clayton, Philip Thomas Byard 1885-1972
WhAm 5
Clayton, Powell 1833-1914 *ApCAB, BiAUS,
BiDrAC, DcAmB, Drake, NatCAB 5,
NatCAB 10, NatCAB 16, REnAW,
TwCBDA, WhAm 1, WhAmP*
Clayton, Thomas d1854 *BiAUS*
Clayton, Thomas 1777-1854 *DcAmB*
Clayton, Thomas 1778-1854 *ApCAB, BiDrAC,
Drake, NatCAB 12, TwCBDA, WhAm H*
Clayton, Victoria Virginia 1832-1908 *WhAm 1*
Clayton, William Brasher 1888-1957 *WhAm 3*
Clayton, William Lockhart 1880-1966 *WhAm 4*
Clayton, Willis Sherman 1864-1940 *WhAm 1*
Claytor, Archer Adams 1893-1967 *NatCAB 53,
WhAm 4*
Claytor, Gertrude Boatwright 1889-1973
NatCAB 57
Claytor, Graham 1886-1971 *NatCAB 57*
Claytor, Thomas Ash 1869-1941 *WhAm 1*
Clearwater, Alphonso Trumphour 1848-1933
ApCAB X, NatCAB 18, WhAm 1
Clearwater, Anna Houghtaling Farrand 1858-
WomWWA 14
Cleary, Alfred John 1884-1941 *WhAm 1*
Cleary, Daniel Francis 1910-1953 *WhAm 3*
Cleary, George J 1896-1955 *WhAm 3*
Cleary, James Charles 1880-1949 *NatCAB 41*
Cleary, James M 1849- *WhAm 4*
Cleary, James Mansfield 1887-1972 *WhAm 5*
Cleary, James Vincent 1828- *ApCAB*
Cleary, John Joseph 1868-1917 *NatCAB 17*
Cleary, Kate McPhelim 1863- *AmWom*
Cleary, Michael Joseph 1876-1947 *WhAm 2*
Cleary, Owen J 1900-1960 *WhAm 4*
Cleary, Peter Joseph Augustine 1839-1914
WhAm 1
Cleary, Redmond 1829-1898 *NatCAB 9*
Cleary, William Edward 1849-1932 *BiDrAC,
WhAm 1*
Cleasby, Harold Loomis 1876- *WhAm 5*
Cleaveland, Agnes Morley 1874- *WhAm 5*
Cleaveland, Benjamin *Drake*
Cleaveland, Elisha Lord 1806-1866 *ApCAB,
Drake*
Cleaveland, Elizabeth Hannah Jocelyn d1911
WhAm 1
Cleaveland, Harry Hayes 1869-1946 *WhAm 2*
Cleaveland, Harry Hayes, Jr. 1898-1952
WhAm 3
Cleaveland, J F d1841 *BiAUS*
Cleaveland, John 1722-1799 *ApCAB, Drake,
TwCBDA*
Cleaveland, Livingston Warner 1860-1929
NatCAB 25, WhAm 1
Cleaveland, Moses 1754-1806 *AmBi, ApCAB,
DcAmB, TwCBDA, WhAm H*
Cleaveland, Nehemiah 1796-1877 *ApCAB,
TwCBDA*
Cleaveland, Newton 1874-1944 *NatCAB 44*
Cleaveland, Parker 1780-1858 *AmBi, ApCAB,
BiDAmEd, DcAmB, DcScB, Drake,
NatCAB 13, TwCBDA, WhAm H*
Cleaveland, Stephen 1740-1801 *Drake*
Cleaveland, William Waldo 1864- *NatCAB 5*
Cleaver, Leroy Eldridge 1935- *McGEWB*
Cleaves, Arthur Wordsworth 1876-1940
WhAm 1
Cleaves, Henry Bradstreet 1840-1912
NatCAB 6, TwCBDA, WhAm 1
Cleaves, Margaret Abagail 1848- *AmWom*
Cleaves, Margaret Abigail 1848-
WomWWA 14
Cleaves, Nelson Caldwell 1865- *WhAm 4,
WhoColR*
Cleaves, Willis Everett 1902-1966 *WhAm 4*
Cleavinger, John Simeon 1880-1954 *WhAm 3*
Cleborne, Christopher James 1838-1909
TwCBDA, WhAm 1
Clebsch, Rudolf Friedrich Alfred 1833-1872
DcScB
Cleburn, Patrick Ronayne 1828-1864 *WhAm H*
Cleburne, Patrick Ronayne 1828-1864 *AmBi,
ApCAB, BiDConf, DcAmB, Drake,
NatCAB 8, REnAW, TwCBDA,*

Cleveland, Jesse Franklin 1804-1841 *BiDrAC,*
WhAm H
Cleveland, John Bomar 1848- *WhAm 4*
Cleveland, John Fitch 1819-1876 *ApCAB,*
TwCBDA
Cleveland, Lemuel Roscoe 1892-1969 *WhAm 5*
Cleveland, Mary B 1873- *WomWWA 14*
Cleveland, Mason d1855 *ApCAB*
Cleveland, Moses 1754-1806 *NatCAB 6*
Cleveland, Newcomb 1865-1951 *NatCAB 38*
Cleveland, Orestes 1829- *BiAUS*
Cleveland, Orestes 1829-1895 *NatCAB 2*
Cleveland, Orestes 1829-1896 *BiDrAC,*
TwCBDA, WhAm H
Cleveland, Paul W d1952 *WhAm 3*
Cleveland, Reginald McIntosh 1886-1971
WhAm 5
Cleveland, Richard Jeffry 1773-1860 *ApCAB,*
DcAmB, WhAm H
Cleveland, Rose Elizabeth 1846-1918 *AmWom,*
ApCAB, ApCAB Sup, NatCAB 2,
TwCBDA, WhAm 1, WomWWA 14
Cleveland, Stephen 1740-1801 *ApCAB*
Cleveland, Stephen Grover 1837-1908 *DcAmB,*
EncAAH, EncAB, McGEWB, WhAmP
Cleveland, Treadwell, Jr. 1872- *WhAm 5*
Cleveland, William 1777-1845 *NewYHSD*
Cleveland, William Davis *WhAm 5*
Cleveley, John 1747-1786 *NewYHSD*
Cleven, Nels Andrew Nelson 1874- *WhAm 5*
Clevenger, Antoinette Brown Harlan
WomWWA 14
Clevenger, Cliff 1885-1960 *BiDrAC, WhAm 4,*
WhAmP
Clevenger, Galen Howell 1879- *WhAm 6*
Clevenger, Joseph R 1884-1974 *WhAm 6*
Clevenger, Raymond Francis 1926- *BiDrAC*
Clevenger, Shobal Vail 1812-1843 *AmBi,*
ApCAB, BnEnAmA, DcAmB, Drake,
NatCAB 8, NewYHSD, TwCBDA,
WhAm H
Clevenger, Shobal Vail 1843-1920 *ApCAB,*
DcAmB, NatCAB 5, TwCBDA,
WhAm 4
Clever, Charles P 1830-1874 *BiAUS, BiDrAC,*
WhAm H
Clever, Conrad 1848-1935 *WhAm 1*
Cleverley, Frank T 1903-1952 *WhAm 3*
Clewell, Edgar L 1896-1973 *WhAm 6*
Clewell, John Henry 1855-1922 *DcAmB,*
NatCAB 24, WhAm 1
Clewis, Alonzo Charles 1864-1944 *WhAm 2*
Clews, Henry 1830-1923 *ApCAB Sup*
Clews, Henry 1834-1923 *AmBi, DcAmB*
Clews, Henry 1840-1923 *ApCAB X,*
NatCAB 1, TwCBDA, WhAm 1
Clews, James Blanchard 1859-1934 *NatCAB 28*
Clews, James Blanchard 1869-1934 *WhAm 1*
Clews, Jessie Bradley *WomWWA 14*
Clexton, Edward William 1900-1966
NatCAB 52, WhAm 4
Cliffe, Adam C 1869-1928 *WhAm 1*
Clifford, Chandler R 1858-1935 *WhAm 1*
Clifford, Charles P d1971 *WhAm 5*
Clifford, Charles Warren 1844-1923 *TwCBDA,*
WhAm 1
Clifford, Clark McAdams 1906- *BiDrUSE,*
EncAB
Clifford, Donald Francis 1897-1960 *NatCAB 49*
Clifford, Edward 1873-1963 *WhAm 4*
Clifford, Edward P 1875-1928 *ApCAB X*
Clifford, Elmer Laurence 1874- *WhAm 5*
Clifford, George Henry 1881-1959 *NatCAB 48*
Clifford, George Sonntag 1858-1927
NatCAB 34
Clifford, Harriet Briggs Rogers 1867-
WomWWA 14
Clifford, Harry Ellsworth 1866-1952 *WhAm 3*
Clifford, John D d1820 *Drake*
Clifford, John David 1887-1956 *WhAm 3*
Clifford, John Henry 1809-1876 *ApCAB,*
BiAUS, DcAmB, Drake, NatCAB 1,
TwCBDA, WhAm H
Clifford, John Robert 1848- *WhoColR*
Clifford, Joseph Myers 1899-1955 *NatCAB 46*
Clifford, Josephine *NotAW*
Clifford, Leslie Forbes 1913-1966 *NatCAB 52,*
WhAm 5

Clifford, Nathan 1803-1881 *AmBi, ApCAB,*
BiAUS, BiDrAC, BiDrUSE, DcAmB,
Drake, NatCAB 2, TwCBDA, WebAB,
WhAm H, WhAmP
Clifford, R A *NewYHSD*
Clifford, Reese F 1891-1971 *WhAm 5*
Clifford, Sidney 1891-1966 *NatCAB 51*
Clifford, Walter 1849- *TwCBDA, WhAm 4*
Clifford, William Kingdon 1845-1879 *DcScB*
Clifford, William Schofield 1911-1972 *WhAm 6*
Cliffton, William 1772-1799 *DcAmB,*
NatCAB 10, WhAm H
Clift, Albert Earl 1869-1931 *WhAm 1*
Clift, David Horace 1907-1973 *DcAmLiB,*
WhAm 6
Clift, James Walter 1877-1944 *NatCAB 33*
Clift, Joseph W 1836-1908 *BiAUS*
Clift, Joseph Wales 1837-1908 *BiDrAC*
Clift, Montgomery 1920-1966 *WhAm 4*
Clift, William 1775-1849 *DcScB*
Clifton, Albert Turner 1879-1948 *NatCAB 48,*
WhAm 2
Clifton, Chalmers Dancy 1889-1966 *WhAm 4*
Clifton, Charles 1853-1928 *NatCAB 21,*
WhAm 1
Clifton, George 1880-1955 *NatCAB 45*
Clifton, Harriet Merrill 1874- *WomWWA 14*
Clifton, John Leroy 1881-1943 *NatCAB 34,*
WhAm 3
Clifton, John Lester, Jr. 1908-1957 *NatCAB 46*
Clifton, Joseph Clinton 1908-1967 *WhAm 4A*
Clifton, Josephine 1813-1847 *DcAmB,*
NatCAB 6, WhAm H
Clifton, Louis 1887-1957 *WhAm 3*
Clifton, William 1772-1799 *ApCAB, Drake*
Climo, Maurice Lorimore 1892-1960
NatCAB 49
Clinch, Charles Powell 1797-1880 *ApCAB,*
DcAmB, NatCAB 22, WhAm H
Clinch, Duncan Lamont 1787-1849 *ApCAB,*
BiAUS, BiDrAC, Drake, NatCAB 12,
TwCBDA, WhAm H
Clinch, Edward Sears 1846-1924 *WhAm 1*
Clinch, Richard Floyd 1865-1930 *NatCAB 29,*
WhAm 1
Cline, Allen Marshall 1881-1963 *NatCAB 54*
Cline, Cyrus 1856-1923 *BiDrAC, WhAm 4*
Cline, Genevieve R 1879- *WhAm 6*
Cline, Gloria Griffin 1929- *EncAAH*
Cline, Mrs. Henry A 1879- *WomWWA 14*
Cline, Henry Clayton 1888-1951 *NatCAB 44*
Cline, Howard Francis 1915-1971 *WhAm 5,*
WhAm 6
Cline, Isaac Monroe 1861-1955 *NatCAB 16,*
NatCAB 42, WhAm 3
Cline, John Wesley 1898-1974 *WhAm 6*
Cline, Lewis Manning 1909-1971 *NatCAB 57,*
WhAm 5
Cline, Louis Bernheim 1898-1963 *NatCAB 51*
Cline, Lyle Stanley 1908-1963 *WhAm 4*
Cline, Maggie 1857-1934 *NotAW*
Cline, Pierce 1890-1943 *WhAm 2*
Cline, Robert Alexander 1894-1958 *WhAm 3*
Cline, Russell Walter 1899-1966 *NatCAB 54,*
WhAm 4
Cline, Sheldon Scott 1874-1928 *WhAm 1*
Cline, Thomas Sparks 1877-1968 *WhAm 5*
Cline, Walter Branks 1862-1932 *WhAm 1*
Cline, Walter Branks 1863-1932 *NatCAB 37*
Cline, Yandell Cooperider 1897-1959
NatCAB 49
Clinedinst, Benjamin West 1859-1931
NatCAB 14, NatCAB 22
Clinedinst, Benjamin West 1860-1931 *AmBi,*
TwCBDA, WhAm 1
Clingan, Thomas Scott 1875-1947 *NatCAB 42*
Clingan, William d1790 *BiAUS, BiDrAC,*
NatCAB 7, WhAm H
Clingerman, Walter Hicks 1868-1927
NatCAB 21
Clingman, Thomas Lanier 1812-1897 *ApCAB,*
BiAUS, BiDConf, BiDrAC, DcAmB,
Drake, NatCAB 7, TwCBDA, WhAm H,
WhAmP
Clinkscales, John George 1855-1942
NatCAB 52, WhAm 1
Clinnin, John V 1876-1955 *WhAm 3*
Clinton, Alexander *ApCAB*

Clinton, Alexander 1793-1878 *ApCAB*
Clinton, Alexander James 1825- *NatCAB 11*
Clinton, Charles d1791 *ApCAB*
Clinton, Charles 1690-1773 *ApCAB, Drake,*
TwCBDA
Clinton, Delmar Smith 1874-1949 *NatCAB 39*
Clinton, DeWitt *NewYHSD*
Clinton, DeWitt 1769-1828 *AmBi, ApCAB,*
BiDAmEd, BiDrAC, DcAmB,
Drake, EncAB, McGEWB, NatCAB 3,
TwCBDA, WebAB, WhAm H, WhAmP
Clinton, Fred Severs 1874-1955 *NatCAB 41,*
WhAm 5
Clinton, George 1686?-1761 *ApCAB, DcAmB,*
Drake, NatCAB 5, WhAm H
Clinton, George 1739-1812 *AmBi, ApCAB,*
BiAUS, BiDrAC, BiDrUSE, DcAmB,
Drake, EncAB, McGEWB, NatCAB 3,
TwCBDA, WebAB, WebAMB, WhAm H,
WhAmP
Clinton, George 1771-1809 *BiAUS, BiDrAC,*
WhAm H
Clinton, George 1846-1934 *NatCAB 24,*
WhAm 1
Clinton, George Perkins 1867-1937 *WhAm 1*
Clinton, George Wiley 1859-1921 *TwCBDA*
Clinton, George William 1807-1885 *TwCBDA*
Clinton, George Wylie 1859-1921 *DcAmB,*
WhAm 1, WhoColR
Clinton, Harriet Pettibone 1896-1975 *WhAm 6*
Clinton, Sir Henry 1738?-1795 *AmBi, ApCAB,*
Drake, McGEWB, WhAm H, WhoMilH
Clinton, Henry Lauren 1820-1899 *ApCAB Sup*
Clinton, James 1733-1812 *AmBi, DcAmB,*
WebAMB, WhAm H
Clinton, James 1736-1812 *ApCAB, Drake,*
NatCAB 1, TwCBDA
Clinton, James Graham 1804-1849 *BiAUS,*
BiDrAC, WhAm H
Clinton, Jane Heard 1875- *WomWWA 14*
Clinton, John, Jr. 1867- *WhoColR*
Clinton, Joseph Jackson 1823-1881 *ApCAB*
Clinton, Joseph Jackson 1823-1887 *TwCBDA*
Clinton, Louis Adelbert 1868-1923 *WhAm 1*
Clinton, Marshall 1873-1943 *WhAm 2*
Clinton, Robert Hall 1817-1879 *NatCAB 12*
Clinton, Susan Merrill 1877- *WomWWA 14*
Clinton, Thomas *BiAUS*
Clippinger, Arthur Raymond 1878- *WhAm 6*
Clippinger, Donald Roop 1905-1967 *WhAm 5*
Clippinger, Erle Elsworth 1875-1939
NatCAB 29, WhAm 1
Clippinger, Roy 1886-1962 *BiDrAC,*
NatCAB 50
Clippinger, Walter Gillan 1873-1948
NatCAB 39, WhAm 2
Clirehugh, W S *NewYHSD*
Clise, James William 1900-1961 *WhAm 4*
Clitz, Henry Boynton 1824- *ApCAB, Drake,*
NatCAB 4, TwCBDA
Clitz, John M B 1820- *Drake*
Clitz, John Mellen Brady 1821-1897 *ApCAB,*
TwCBDA
Clive, Robert 1725-1774 *McGEWB, WhoMilH*
Cloak, Evelyn Kimmel Campbell 1907-1971
WhAm 6
Cloak, Frank Valentine Centennial 1876-1953
WhAm 3
Clock, Charles Henry 1878-1946 *NatCAB 39*
Clock, Ralph H 1878-1944 *WhAm 2*
Clodion 1738-1814 *McGEWB*
Clodius Pulcher, Publius d052BC *McGEWB*
Cloe, Charles Carroll 1878-1964 *NatCAB 50*
Cloke, Harvey Walton 1919-1975 *WhAm 6*
Cloke, Paul 1882-1963 *WhAm 4*
Cloman, Sydney Amos 1867-1923 *NatCAB 21*
Clonney, James Goodwyn 1812-1867 *BnEnAmA,*
NewYHSD, WhAm H
Cloonan, John Joseph 1881- *WhAm 6*
Cloos, Ernst 1898-1974 *WhAm 6*
Cloos, Hans 1885-1951 *DcScB*
Clopper, Edward Nicholas 1879-1953 *WhAm 3*
Clopton, David 1820-1892 *BiAUS, BiDConf,*
BiDrAC, DcAmB, NatCAB 22, TwCBDA,
WhAm H, WhAmP
Clopton, John d1816 *BiAUS*
Clopton, John 1755?-1816 *TwCBDA*
Clopton, John 1756-1816 *BiDrAC, DcAmB,*

WhAm H, WhAmP

Clopton, Malvern Bryan 1875-1947 *NatCAB 36, WhAm 2*

Clopton, Virginia Carolina Clay 1825- *WomWWA 14*

Clopton, Virginia Caroline Tunstall Clay *NotAW*

Cloran, Timothy 1869-1935 *NatCAB 40, WhAm 1*

Cloreviere, Father 1768-1826 *ApCAB*

Cloriviere, Joseph-P P DeLimoelan De 1768-1826 *NewYHSD, WhAm H*

Close, Charles Mollison 1903-1965 *WhAm 5*

Close, Charles William 1859- *WhAm 1*

Close, James William 1909-1972 *WhAm 5*

Close, Lewis Raymond 1881-1957 *WhAm 3*

Close, Lyman Withrow 1892-1968 *WhAm 5*

Close, Ralph William 1867-1945 *WhAm 2*

Close, Stuart 1860-1929 *NatCAB 15, NatCAB 30, WhAm 1*

Closse, Raphael Lambert 1620?-1662 *ApCAB*

Closson, Henry Whitney 1832-1917 *WhAm 1*

Closson, William Baxter 1848-1926 *AmBi, ApCAB X, DcAmB, NatCAB 8, NatCAB 28, WhAm 1*

Clossy, Samuel 1715-1776 *ApCAB*

Closterman, Donald Franks 1907-1974 *WhAm 6*

Clothier, Anita Porter 1886-1955 *NatCAB 50*

Clothier, Clarkson 1846- *NatCAB 9*

Clothier, Isaac Hallowell 1837-1921 *WhAm 1*

Clothier, Joseph Vaughan 1879-1951 *NatCAB 42*

Clothier, Mary Clapp Jackson *WomWWA 14*

Clothier, Morris Lewis 1868-1947 *NatCAB 37, WhAm 2*

Clothier, Robert Clarkson 1885-1970 *WhAm 5*

Clothier, William Jackson 1881-1962 *NatCAB 52, WhAm 6*

Clouchek, Emma Olds 1877- *WhAm 5*

Cloud, Ada A 1852- *WomWWA 14*

Cloud, Archibald Jeter 1878-1957 *NatCAB 46*

Cloud, Arthur David 1884-1966 *WhAm 4*

Cloud, Charles Henry 1879-1944 *NatCAB 33, WhAm 2*

Cloud, Henry Roe 1886-1950 *BiDAmEd, DcAmB S4, WhAm 2A*

Cloud, James Henry 1862-1926 *NatCAB 20, WhAm 1*

Cloud, John Hofer 1871- *WhAm 5*

Cloud, Marshall Morgan 1868-1937 *WhAm 1*

Cloud, Noah Bartlett 1809-1875 *DcAmB, EncAAH, WhAm H*

Cloud, Virginia Woodward *WomWWA 14*

Cloud, William Woodward d1957 *WhAm 3*

Cloudman, John J *NewYHSD*

Cloues, William Jacob 1860- *WhAm 4*

Clouet, Francois 1516?-1572? *McGEWB*

Clouet, Jean 1485?-1541? *McGEWB*

Clouet, Jean-Francois 1751-1801 *DcScB*

Clough, Arthur Hugh 1819-1861 *McGEWB*

Clough, Charles A 1903-1961 *WhAm 4*

Clough, Charles C d1954 *WhAm 3*

Clough, David Marston 1846-1924 *NatCAB 10, WhAm 1*

Clough, Dexter Jameson 1863-1949 *NatCAB 37*

Clough, Edna Coulter 1878- *WomWWA 14*

Clough, Francis Edgar 1878-1953 *WhAm 3*

Clough, Frank C 1900- *WhAm 3*

Clough, George Albert 1843-1910 *TwCBDA, WhAm 1*

Clough, George Hatch 1876-1948 *WhAm 3*

Clough, George L 1824-1901 *ApCAB, NewYHSD*

Clough, George Obadiah 1878- *WhAm 6*

Clough, Herbert Thorndike 1866-1945 *NatCAB 38*

Clough, John Everett 1836-1910 *ApCAB, DcAmB*

Clough, John H 1892-1975 *WhAm 6*

Clough, Mary Shepard 1872- *WomWWA 14*

Clough, Merrill H 1919-1972 *WhAm 5*

Clough, Moses T 1814- *NatCAB 3*

Clough, Paul Wiswall 1822- *WhAm 5*

Clough, Raphael Floyd 1886-1957 *WhAm 3*

Clough, S DeWitt 1879-1960 *WhAm 3*

Clough, William Pitt 1845-1916 *DcAmB, NatCAB 22, WhAm 1*

Clough, William Rockwell 1844-1920 *NatCAB 18*

Clough-Leighter, Henry 1874-1956 *WhAm 3*

Clous, John Walter 1837-1908 *WhAm 1*

Clouse, Alice Atkinson 1864- *WomWWA 14*

Clouse, Wynne F 1883-1944 *BiDrAC, WhAm 2*

Clover, Benjamin Hutchinson 1837-1899 *BiDrAC*

Clover, George Frederick 1866-1937 *NatCAB 39, WhAm 1*

Clover, Lewis Peter, Jr. 1819-1896 *ApCAB, NewYHSD, TwCBDA, WhAm H*

Clover, Philip 1832-1905 *NewYHSD*

Clover, Richardson 1846-1919 *TwCBDA, WhAm 1*

Clover, Samuel Travers 1859-1934 *WhAm 1*

Clover, William C *NewYHSD*

Clovis I 465-511 *McGEWB*

Clovis, Charles Homer 1885-1963 *NatCAB 50*

Clovis, Paul Curtis 1902-1975 *WhAm 6*

Clow, Allan Bowman 1906-1968 *WhAm 5*

Clow, Frederick Redman 1863-1930 *NatCAB 22*

Clow, Harry Beach 1870-1933 *WhAm 1*

Clow, James Beach 1903-1953 *WhAm 3*

Clow, Kent Sarver 1888-1952 *WhAm 3*

Clow, William Ellsworth, Jr. 1886-1953 *WhAm 3*

Cloward, Donald Bryan 1896-1956 *NatCAB 47*

Clowes, Edith Whitehill 1885-1967 *NatCAB 53*

Clowes, George Henry Alexander 1877-1958 *NatCAB 46, WhAm 3*

Clowes, George Hewlett 1842-1912 *NatCAB 8*

Clowes, Leo Clifford 1891-1953 *NatCAB 42*

Clowes, Timothy d1847 *Drake*

Clowney, William Kennedy 1797-1851 *BiAUS, BiDrAC, WhAm H*

Clowry, Robert Charles 1838-1925 *NatCAB 13, WhAm 1*

Clows, John *NewYHSD*

Cloyd, Genevieve *WomWWA 14*

Cloyes, Frederick 1828?- *NewYHSD*

Cloyes, Grace Gruber 1870- *WomWWA 14*

Clozel, Mister *NewYHSD*

Clozel, Mrs. *NewYHSD*

Clubb, Laura Abigail Rutherford 1873-1952 *NatCAB 38*

Clubb, Merrel Dare 1897-1970 *WhAm 5*

Clucas, Edward Welch 1880-1948 *NatCAB 36*

Cluesmann, Leo 1885-1966 *WhAm 4*

Cluett, Ernest Harold 1874-1954 *BiDrAC, WhAm 3*

Cluett, George B 1838- *NatCAB 13*

Cluett, Robert 1844-1927 *NatCAB 35, WhAm 1*

Cluett, Sanford Lockwood 1874-1968 *WhAm 5*

Cluett, W Scott 1912-1971 *WhAm 5*

Cluff, Alfred Thomas 1893-1954 *NatCAB 44*

Cluff, Ann 1843- *NatCAB 17*

Cluff, Harvey Harris 1872-1949 *NatCAB 38, WhAm 5*

Cluff, L Eggertsen 1886-1943 *NatCAB 33*

Cluff, William *NewYHSD*

Cluff, William 1856-1912 *NatCAB 16*

Cluff, William Wallace 1832-1915 *NatCAB 17*

Clugston, Herbert Andrews 1895-1964 *WhAm 4*

Clules, John *NewYHSD*

Clum, Blanche Stover 1867- *WomWWA 14*

Clum, Florence Brewster Corse 1880- *WomWWA 14*

Clum, Harold Dunstan 1879-1959 *NatCAB 44*

Clum, John P 1851-1932 *REnAW*

Clunie, Robert 1895?- *IIBEAAW*

Clunie, Thomas Jefferson 1852-1903 *BiDrAC, NatCAB 2, TwCBDA*

Cluseret, Gustave Paul 1823-1900 *ApCAB, Drake, NatCAB 4, TwCBDA*

Clusius, Carolus *DcScB*

Clusky, Michael Walsh 1832-1873 *BiDConf*

Cluss, Adolf 1825- *NatCAB 4*

Clute, Edward C *NewYHSD*

Clute, Howard Merrill 1890-1946 *NatCAB 35*

Clute, Robert Frary 1829-1892 *TwCBDA*

Clute, Walker Stillwell 1891-1964 *WhAm 4*

Clute, Walter Marshall 1870-1915 *WhAm 1*

Clute, Willard Nelson 1869-1950 *WhAm 3*

Clutts, Oliver Perry 1885-1959 *WhAm 4*

Clutz, Jacob Abraham 1848-1925 *NatCAB 20, TwCBDA, WhAm 1*

Cluverius, Wat Tyler 1874-1952 *NatCAB 39, WhAm 3*

Cluytens, Andre 1905-1967 *WhAm 4*

Clyatt, Claude Eugene 1883-1961 *NatCAB 49*

Clyce, Thomas Stone 1863-1946 *NatCAB 42, WhAm 2*

Clyde, Sir Colin Campbell 1792-1863 *ApCAB*

Clyde, George Dewey 1898-1972 *WhAm 5*

Clyde, Milton Adams 1815-1975 *NatCAB 32*

Clyde, Norman Asa 1885-1972 *WhAm 5*

Clyde, Samuel Dyer 1872-1955 *NatCAB 43*

Clyde, William Gray 1868-1931 *NatCAB 24, WhAm 1*

Clyde, William Pancoast 1839-1923 *NatCAB 20, WhAm 1*

Clyman, James 1792-1881 *DcAmB, EncAAH, REnAW, WhAm H*

Clymer, Ella Maria Dietz *AmWom*

Clymer, George 1739-1813 *AmBi, ApCAB, BiAUS, BiDrAC, DcAmB, Drake, NatCAB 3, TwCBDA, WhAm H, WhAmP*

Clymer, George E 1754-1834 *DcAmB, NatCAB 8, WhAm H*

Clymer, Hiester 1827-1884 *BiAUS, BiDrAC, TwCBDA, WhAm H*

Clymer, John 1907- *IIBEAAW*

Clymer, Meredith 1817-1902 *ApCAB, TwCBDA, WhAm 1*

Clymer, R Swinburne 1878-1966 *WhAm 5*

Clyne, Charles F 1877-1965 *WhAm 4, WhAm 5*

Clyne, James Francis, Jr. 1927-1971 *WhAm 5*

Cnut 995?-1035 *McGEWB*

Coad, J Allan 1884-1963 *NatCAB 50*

Coad, Merwin 1924- *BiDrAC*

Coad, William James 1879-1961 *NatCAB 48*

Coady, Charles Pearce 1868-1934 *BiDrAC, WhAm 1*

Coakley, Cornelius Godfrey 1862-1934 *DcAmB S1, NatCAB 26, WhAm 1*

Coakley, Daniel Henry 1906-1964 *WhAm 4*

Coakley, George Washington 1814-1893 *TwCBDA*

Coakley, John Aloysius 1881-1950 *NatCAB 40*

Coale, Esther Colston 1869- *WomWWA 14*

Coale, Griffith Baily 1890-1950 *WhAm 3*

Coale, Isaac, Jr. 1861- *WhAm 4*

Coale, James Johnson 1879-1947 *WhAm 2*

Coale, Robert Dorsey 1857- *ApCAB, WhAm 1*

Coalter, John 1775?-1813 *DcAmB*

Coan, Charles Florus 1886-1928 *WhAm 1*

Coan, Frederick Gaylord 1859- *WhAm 4*

Coan, George William 1867-1939 *NatCAB 30*

Coan, Ralph Alonzo 1881-1950 *NatCAB 40*

Coan, Sherwood 1830?-1874 *ApCAB*

Coan, Titus 1801-1882 *ApCAB, DcAmB, Drake Sup, NatCAB 2, TwCBDA, WhAm H*

Coan, Titus Munson 1836-1921 *ApCAB, NatCAB 11, TwCBDA, WhAm 1*

Coanacatzin *ApCAB*

Coapman, Eugene H 1865-1921 *WhAm 1*

Coar, John Firman 1863-1939 *WhAm 1*

Coard, Mary McKee Smith *WomWWA 14*

Coash, Louis Egbert 1904-1968 *NatCAB 54, WhAm 5*

Coast, Oscar Regan 1851-1931 *IIBEAAW*

Coat, Fannie Lorah 1865- *WomWWA 14*

Coate, Alvin Teague 1870- *WhAm 5*

Coate, Roland Eli 1890-1958 *WhAm 3*

Coate, S *NewYHSD*

Coates, Benjamin 1808-1887 *TwCBDA*

Coates, Benjamin Hornor 1797-1881 *NatCAB 17*

Coates, Charles Edward 1866-1939 *NatCAB 36, WhAm 1*

Coates, Charles F 1889-1957 *WhAm 3*

Coates, Charles Haskell 1872-1953 *NatCAB 42*

Coates, Charles Thomas 1847-1922 *NatCAB 19*

Coates, David C 1868- *WhAm 4*

Coates, E C *NewYHSD*

Coates, Edward Hornor 1846-1921 *NatCAB 19, WhAm 1*

Coates, Edwin Morton 1836-1913 *WhAm 1*

Coates, Eric 1886-1957 *WhAm 3*

Cocheu, Frank Sherwood 1871-1940 *WhAm 2*
Cocheu, Henry *NewYHSD*
Cochise d1874 *WhAm H*
Cochise 1812?-1874 *WebAB, WebAMB*
Cochise 1824?-1874 *REnAW*
Cochise 1825?-1874 *McGEWB*
Cochon DeLapparent *DcScB*
Cochran, Alexander G 1845-1928 *BiAUS*
Cochran, Alexander Gilmore 1846-1928 *BiDrAC, WhAm 1*
Cochran, Alexander Smith 1874-1929 *DcAmB, NatCAB 32*
Cochran, Almond D 1882-1955 *NatCAB 44*
Cochran, Andrew McConnell January 1854-1934 *WhAm 1*
Cochran, Archelaus M 1838- *WhAm 3*
Cochran, Archibald Prentice 1898-1970 *WhAm 5*
Cochran, Arthur Myron 1878- *WhoColR*
Cochran, Carlos Bingham 1854-1929 *WhAm 1*
Cochran, Charles Banister 1887-1963 *NatCAB 51*
Cochran, Charles Fremont 1846-1906 *BiDrAC, WhAmP*
Cochran, Charles Fremont 1848-1906 *TwCBDA, WhAm 1*
Cochran, Claude A 1884-1958 *WhAm 4*
Cochran, David Henry 1828-1909 *ApCAB, BiDAmEd, NatCAB 3, TwCBDA, WhAm 1*
Cochran, Eliza *NewYHSD*
Cochran, Ernest Ford 1865-1934 *WhAm 1*
Cochran, Fanny Travis *WomWWA 14*
Cochran, George G 1842-1905 *WhAm 1*
Cochran, George Ira 1863-1949 *ApCAB X, NatCAB 14, NatCAB 16, NatCAB 37, WhAm 2*
Cochran, H Merle 1892-1973 *WhAm 6*
Cochran, Harry King 1853-1913 *WhAm 1*
Cochran, Henry Jessup 1879-1952 *WhAm 3*
Cochran, Homer Pierce 1906-1969 *WhAm 5*
Cochran, J Lawrence 1908-1958 *NatCAB 48*
Cochran, Jacqueline 1910?- *WebAB, WebAMB*
Cochran, James 1763-1846 *ApCAB, Drake, NatCAB 7*
Cochran, James 1767?-1813 *BiDrAC, WhAm H*
Cochran, James 1769-1848 *BiAUS, BiDrAC, TwCBDA, WhAm H*
Cochran, James Chester 1886-1962 *WhAm 4*
Cochran, James Harvey 1913-1969 *WhAm 5*
Cochran, James Henry 1845-1911 *NatCAB 21*
Cochran, Jean Carter 1876- *WhAm 5*
Cochran, Jerome 1831- *NatCAB 5*
Cochran, John 1730-1807 *ApCAB, DcAmB, Drake, NatCAB 1, NatCAB 8, WhAm H*
Cochran, John 1813-1898 *ApCAB, NatCAB 8*
Cochran, John Joseph 1880-1947 *BiDrAC, WhAm 2, WhAmP*
Cochran, John Lewis 1857-1923 *NatCAB 20*
Cochran, John P 1809-1898 *NatCAB 11*
Cochran, John Webster 1814- *ApCAB, Drake Sup, NatCAB 11*
Cochran, Joseph William 1871-1926 *NatCAB 29*
Cochran, Katharine More 1869- *WomWWA 14*
Cochran, Robert 1739-1812 *TwCBDA*
Cochran, Robert LeRoy 1886-1963 *NatCAB 52, WhAm 4*
Cochran, Samuel Poyntz 1855-1936 *WhAm 1*
Cochran, Sarah Jane Bly 1878- *WhoColR*
Cochran, Sarah Marshall *WomWWA 14*
Cochran, Sophia Lee 1868- *WomWWA 14*
Cochran, Thomas 1871-1936 *NatCAB 27, WhAm 1*
Cochran, Thomas Baumgardner 1845-1910 *NatCAB 6, WhAm 4*
Cochran, Thomas Cunningham 1877-1957 *BiDrAC, WhAm 3*
Cochran, William Francis 1876-1950 *NatCAB 39*
Cochran, William J 1820?- *NewYHSD*
Cochran, William J Hamilton 1878-1925 *WhAm 1*
Cochran, William Wallace 1889-1973 *NatCAB 57*

Cochrane, Aaron VanSchaick 1858-1943 *BiDrAC, TwCBDA, WhAm 2*
Cochrane, Alexander 1840-1919 *ApCAB X, NatCAB 14, NatCAB 27*
Cochrane, Sir Alexander Forester Inglis 1758-1832 *ApCAB, Drake*
Cochrane, Archibald *DcScB*
Cochrane, Charles Henry 1856-1940 *WhAm 1*
Cochrane, Charles Stites 1879-1959 *NatCAB 48*
Cochrane, Clark B 1815-1867 *BiAUS*
Cochrane, Clark B 1817-1867 *ApCAB*
Cochrane, Clark Beaton 1815-1867 *TwCBDA*
Cochrane, Clark Betton 1815-1867 *BiDrAC, WhAm H*
Cochrane, Edward Gilbert 1853-1909 *NatCAB 14*
Cochrane, Edward Lull 1892-1959 *NatCAB 46, WhAm 3*
Cochrane, Edward W 1894-1954 *WhAm 3*
Cochrane, Elizabeth 1867-1922 *AmWom, DcAmB, NatCAB 1, NotAW*
Cochrane, F Douglas 1877- *WhAm 5*
Cochrane, Henry Clay 1842-1913 *DcAmB, NatCAB 17, WhAm 1*
Cochrane, John 1813-1898 *BiAUS, BiDrAC, DcAmB, Drake, TwCBDA, WhAm H, WhAmP*
Cochrane, John C 1835-1887 *WhAm H*
Cochrane, John Dundas 1780?-1825 *ApCAB*
Cochrane, John McDowell 1859-1904 *WhAm 1*
Cochrane, John Taylor 1873-1938 *WhAm 1*
Cochrane, Matthew Henry 1824- *ApCAB*
Cochrane, Robert Henry 1879- *WhAm 6*
Cochrane, Thomas, Earl Of Dundonald 1775-1860 *WhoMilH*
Cochrane, Thomas John 1790?-1872 *ApCAB*
Cochrane, Victor Hugo 1879-1948 *NatCAB 38*
Cochrane, William 1831- *ApCAB*
Cochrun, James Lee 1885-1964 *WhAm 4*
Cock, Thomas 1782-1869 *ApCAB, NatCAB 11, TwCBDA*
Cock, Thomas 1802-1869 *Drake*
Cockayne, Charles Alexander 1879-1949 *NatCAB 38, WhAm 2*
Cockburn, Alexander Peter 1837- *ApCAB*
Cockburn, Sir George 1771-1853 *Drake*
Cockburn, Sir George 1772-1853 *ApCAB*
Cockburn, George Ralph Richardson 1834- *ApCAB*
Cockburn, Jack Horton 1926-1959 *NatCAB 46*
Cockburn, James 1819-1883 *ApCAB*
Cockburn, James Pattison 1779?-1847 *NewYHSD*
Cockcroft, James 1842-1911 *NatCAB 15, WhAm 3*
Cockcroft, Sir John Douglas 1897-1967 *AsBiEn, McGEWB, WhAm 4, WhWW-II*
Cockcroft, Sir John Douglas *see also* Cockcroft, John Douglas
Cocke, C Francis 1886-1971 *NatCAB 56*
Cocke, Charles Hartwell 1881-1944 *WhAm 2*
Cocke, Charles Lewis 1820-1901 *NatCAB 29*
Cocke, John 1772-1854 *ApCAB, BiAUS, BiDrAC, Drake, NatCAB 11, TwCBDA, WhAm H, WhAmP*
Cocke, John Hartwell 1780-1866 *ApCAB, DcAmB, Drake, EncAAH, NatCAB 4, TwCBDA, WhAm H*
Cocke, Lucian Howard 1858-1927 *WhAm 1*
Cocke, M Estes 1876-1954 *NatCAB 45*
Cocke, Martha Louise 1855-1938 *NatCAB 29*
Cocke, Matty L 1855-1936 *WhAm 3*
Cocke, Norman Atwater 1884-1974 *WhAm 6*
Cocke, Philip Charles 1903-1963 *NatCAB 50*
Cocke, Philip St. George 1808-1861 *ApCAB, Drake*
Cocke, Philip St. George 1809-1861 *DcAmB, NatCAB 4, TwCBDA, WhAm H*
Cocke, Sarah Cobb Johnson *WomWWA 14*
Cocke, William d1828 *BiAUS*
Cocke, William 1740-1828 *ApCAB, NatCAB 11*
Cocke, William 1747-1828 *BiDrAC, TwCBDA, WhAmP*
Cocke, William 1748-1828 *DcAmB, WhAm H*
Cocke, William Horner 1874-1938 *NatCAB 27, WhAm 1*
Cocke, William Michael 1815-1896 *BiAUS,*

BiDrAC, *WhAm H*
Cocke, William Ruffin Coleman 1884-1967 *WhAm 5*
Cocke, Zitella *WomWWA 14*
Cocker, Benjamin Franklin 1821-1883 *TwCBDA*
Cocker, George *NewYHSD*
Cocker, George Baxendine 1870-1938 *NatCAB 29*
Cockerell, Theodore Dru Alison 1866-1948 *DcAmB S4, WhAm 2*
Cockerill, John Albert 1845-1896 *DcAmB, NatCAB 1, TwCBDA, WhAm H*
Cockerill, Joseph Randolph 1818-1875 *BiAUS, BiDrAC, WhAm H*
Cocking, Walter Dewey 1891-1964 *BiDAmEd, NatCAB 52, WhAm 4*
Cockran, Anne Ide 1878- *WomWWA 14*
Cockran, James *BiAUS*
Cockran, William Bourke 1854-1923 *ApCAB Sup, BiDrAC, DcAmB, NatCAB 5, NatCAB 28, TwCBDA, WhAm 1, WhAmP*
Cockrell, Egbert Railey 1872-1934 *NatCAB 39*
Cockrell, Egbert Railey 1872-1934 *WhAm 1*
Cockrell, Ewing 1874-1962 *WhAm 4*
Cockrell, Francis Marion 1834-1915 *AmBi, ApCAB, BiAUS, BiDConf, BiDrAC, DcAmB, NatCAB 3, NatCAB 35, TwCBDA, WhAm 1, WhAmP*
Cockrell, Francis Marion 1887-1940 *NatCAB 30*
Cockrell, Jeremiah Vardaman 1832-1915 *BiDrAC, TwCBDA*
Cockrell, Joseph Elmore 1859-1927 *NatCAB 21, WhAm 1*
Cockrell, Robert Spratt 1866-1957 *NatCAB 46, WhAm 5*
Cockrill, Ashley 1872-1932 *WhAm 1*
Cockrill, Sterling Robertson 1847-1901 *NatCAB 12*
Cockrill, Stirling Robertson 1847-1901 *TwCBDA*
Cockroft, John Douglas 1897-1967 *DcScB*
Cockroft, John Douglas *see also* Cockcroft, Sir John Douglas
Cockrum, John Barrett 1857-1937 *WhAm 1*
Cocks, Orrin Giddings 1877- *WhAm 5*
Cocks, William Willets 1861-1932 *BiDrAC, NatCAB 27, WhAm 1*
Cockshutt, C Gordon 1894-1967 *WhAm 4A*
Cockshutt, Henry 1868-1949 *WhAm 3*
Coco, Adolphe Valery 1857-1927 *WhAm 1*
Cocroft, Susanna *WomWWA 14*
Cocteau, Jean 1889-1963 *McGEWB, WhAm 4*
Codazzi, Agostine 1792-1859 *ApCAB*
Codazzi, Agostino 1792-1859 *Drake*
Codazzi, Delfino 1824-1873 *DcScB*
Codd, George Pierre 1869-1927 *BiDrAC, WhAm 1, WhAmP*
Codd, Leo A 1895-1971 *WhAm 5*
Coddaire, David Joseph 1893-1964 *NatCAB 52*
Codding, Ichabod 1811-1866 *ApCAB, Drake*
Codding, James Hodge 1849-1919 *BiDrAC, TwCBDA*
Coddington, Addison Epafro 1887-1952 *NatCAB 39*
Coddington, Charles Campbell 1878-1928 *NatCAB 28*
Coddington, David Smith 1823-1865 *ApCAB Sup*
Coddington, Edwin Broughton 1905-1967 *NatCAB 55, WhAm 4*
Coddington, Edwin DeWitt 1865-1943 *NatCAB 32*
Coddington, Edwin Foster 1870-1950 *NatCAB 40*
Coddington, Herbert Guibord 1865- *WhAm 5*
Coddington, Jonathan Inslee 1784-1856 *ApCAB Sup*
Coddington, Jonathan Insley 1783-1856 *NatCAB 12*
Coddington, Merrill Franklin 1901-1967 *WhAm 5*
Coddington, Paul 1892-1951 *NatCAB 40*
Coddington, Wellesley Perry 1840-1913 *NatCAB 2, NatCAB 15, TwCBDA, WhAm 1*
Coddington, William 1601-1678 *AmBi, ApCAB,*

DcAmB, Drake, NatCAB 7, NatCAB 10, TwCBDA, WhAm H

Coddington, William, Jr. 1651-1689 *NatCAB 10*
Code, Charles Joseph 1900-1966 *WhAm 4*
Code, James A, Jr. 1893-1971 *WhAm 5*
Code, William Henry 1865- *WhAm 4*
Codel, Martin 1902-1973 *WhAm 5*
Codere, Charles Francis 1886-1963 *NatCAB 52, WhAm 4*
Codington, William Reuben 1853- *NatCAB 4*
Codman, Charles 1800-1842 *BnEnAmA, NewYHSD, WhAm H*
Codman, Charles Russell 1829-1918 *NatCAB 28, WhAm 1*
Codman, Edmund Dwight 1864- *WhAm 5*
Codman, Ernest Amory 1869-1940 *NatCAB 30, WhAm 1*
Codman, John 1782-1847 *ApCAB, Drake, TwCBDA*
Codman, John 1814-1900 *ApCAB, DcAmB, NatCAB 13, TwCBDA, WhAm H*
Codman, John Amory 1824-1886 *NewYHSD*
Codman, John Sturgis 1868- *WhAm 4*
Codman, Julian 1870-1932 *NatCAB 26, WhAm 1*
Codman, Richard 1842-1928 *NatCAB 22*
Codman, Robert 1859-1915 *NatCAB 12, NatCAB 40, WhAm 1*
Codman, Russell Sturgis 1861-1941 *WhAm 1*
Codman, William P *NewYHSD*
Codner, William 1709-1769 *NewYHSD*
Codrington, Sir Edward 1770-1851 *WhoMilH*
Codrington, Frank T 1859- *WhAm 4*
Codrington, George W 1886-1961 *WhAm 4*
Cody, Buffalo Bill 1846-1917 *REnAW*
Cody, Buffalo Bill *see also* Cody, William Frederick
Cody, Claude Carr 1854- *NatCAB 1, WhAm 4*
Cody, Frank 1870-1946 *WhAm 2*
Cody, Grace Ethelwyn 1867- *WomWWA 14*
Cody, Henry John 1868-1951 *WhAm 3*
Cody, Hiram Alfred 1872-1948 *WhAm 2*
Cody, John Christopher 1899-1963 *WhAm 4*
Cody, Michael 1862-1932 *NatCAB 25*
Cody, Sherwin 1868-1959 *WhAm 3*
Cody, Thomas Edward 1855-1929 *NatCAB 33*
Cody, William Frederick 1845-1917 *ApCAB, ApCAB X, NatCAB 5, TwCBDA*
Cody, William Frederick 1846-1917 *AmBi, DcAmB, EncAAH, EncAB, WebAB, WebAMB, WhAm 1*
Cody, William Frederick *see also* Buffalo Bill
Cody, William Frederick *see also* Cody, Buffalo Bill
Cody, Zeachariah Thornton 1858- *WhAm 4*
Coe, Albert Buckner 1888-1970 *WhAm 5*
Coe, Benjamin Hutchins 1799-1883? *NewYHSD*
Coe, Charles Francis 1890-1956 *WhAm 3*
Coe, Charles Frederick 1910-1974 *WhAm 6*
Coe, David Benton 1814-1895 *TwCBDA*
Coe, Edward Benton 1842-1914 *NatCAB 12, TwCBDA, WhAm 1*
Coe, Edward Kirk 1868-1928 *NatCAB 21*
Coe, Emily M *AmWom*
Coe, Ethel Louise 1878-1938 *WomWWA 14*
Coe, Ethel Louise 1880?-1938 *IIBEAAW*
Coe, Frank Elmer 1872-1924 *NatCAB 6*
Coe, Frank Winston 1870-1947 *WhAm 2*
Coe, Frantz Hunt 1856-1904 *WhAm 1*
Coe, Fred Joiner 1870-1951 *NatCAB 47, WhAm 3*
Coe, Frederick Levi 1883-1970 *NatCAB 56*
Coe, George Albert 1862-1951 *BiDAmEd, DcAmB S5, WhAm 3*
Coe, George Simmons 1817-1896 *ApCAB Sup, DcAmB, NatCAB 7, WhAm H*
Coe, Henry Clarke 1856-1940 *NatCAB 34, WhAm 1*
Coe, Henry Waldo 1857-1927 *WhAm 1*
Coe, Howard Sheldon 1888-1918 *NatCAB 19*
Coe, Israel 1794-1891 *DcAmB, WhAm H*
Coe, John Allen 1868-1948 *WhAm 2*
Coe, John Parks 1889-1961 *WhAm 4*
Coe, Lord M 1828-1909 *ApCAB X*
Coe, Lyman Wetmore 1820-1893 *NatCAB 17*
Coe, Ralph Mortemer 1882-1959 *NatCAB 44*
Coe, Rensselaer Jay 1849-1923 *NatCAB 6*

Coe, Robert 1868- *WhAm 4*
Coe, Robert Lewis 1885-1965 *WhAm 4*
Coe, Schuyler Montgomery 1851-1922 *NatCAB 32*
Coe, Wesley Roswell 1869-1960 *NatCAB 47, WhAm 5*
Coe, William Robertson 1869-1955 *REnAW, WhAm 3*
Coe, William Rogers 1901-1971 *WhAm 5*
Coefield, John 1869-1940 *WhAm 1*
Coen, Jan Pieterszoon 1586?-1629 *McGEWB*
Coen, John Ralph 1885-1954 *NatCAB 42, WhAm 3*
Coen, Joseph Henry 1880-1957 *NatCAB 46*
Coenen, Frank 1867-1958 *NatCAB 47*
Coerne, Louis Adolphe 1870-1922 *ApCAB X, DcAmB, NatCAB 13, NatCAB 26, WhAm 1*
Coes, Harold Vinton 1883-1958 *NatCAB 46, WhAm 3*
Coes, John Henry 1840-1922 *NatCAB 29*
Coes, Loring 1812- *NatCAB 13*
Coes, Mary 1861-1913 *WhAm 1, WomWWA 14*
Coester, Alfred 1874- *WhAm 5*
Coetzee, Barzillai 1914- *WhAm 6*
Cofer, John Daly 1898-1971 *WhAm 5*
Cofer, Leland Eggleston 1869-1948 *ApCAB X, NatCAB 45, WhAm 2*
Cofer, Luisita Leland *BiCAW*
Cofer, Martin Hardin 1832-1881 *DcAmB, NatCAB 12, WhAm H*
Coffee, Harry Buffington 1890-1972 *BiDrAC, NatCAB 57, WhAm 5*
Coffee, John 1772-1833 *Drake*
Coffee, John 1772-1834 *ApCAB Sup*
Coffee, John 1782-1836 *BiAUS, BiDrAC*
Coffee, John Main 1897- *BiDrAC*
Coffee, Rudolph Isaac 1878-1955 *NatCAB 42, WhAm 3*
Coffee, Thomas 1800?- *NewYHSD*
Coffee, Thomas, Jr. 1839?- *NewYHSD*
Coffee, William J 1774?-1846? *NewYHSD, WhAm H*
Coffeen, Henry Asa 1841-1912 *BiDrAC, TwCBDA*
Coffen, T Homer 1877- *WhAm 5*
Coffey, Alexander Brainard *WhAm 1*
Coffey, Charles Shelby 1882-1961 *WhAm 4*
Coffey, Edward Hope 1896-1958 *WhAm 3*
Coffey, Finley H 1861-1943 *NatCAB 36*
Coffey, George Nelson 1875- *WhAm 5*
Coffey, Harry K 1895-1954 *WhAm 3*
Coffey, James V 1879-1937 *WhAm 1*
Coffey, James Vincent 1846-1919 *DcAmB, NatCAB 22, WhAm 1*
Coffey, John Will 1897- *WhAm 3*
Coffey, Martin Vincent 1896-1963 *WhAm 4*
Coffey, Robert Calvin 1869-1933 *NatCAB 25, WhAm 1*
Coffey, Robert Lewis, Jr. 1918-1949 *BiDrAC, WhAm 3*
Coffey, Titian James 1824-1867 *BiAUS, NatCAB 5*
Coffey, Walter Bernard 1868-1944 *WhAm 2*
Coffey, Walter Castella 1876-1956 *NatCAB 42*
Coffey, Walter Castella 1876-1957 *WhAm 3*
Coffin, Alfred Oscar 1861- *WhoColR*
Coffin, Charles 1775-1853 *Drake, TwCBDA*
Coffin, Charles Albert 1844-1926 *DcAmB, NatCAB 20, WhAm 1*
Coffin, Charles Carleton 1823-1896 *AmBi, ApCAB, DcAmB, NatCAB 1, TwCBDA*
Coffin, Charles Dustin 1805-1880 *BiDrAC, WhAm H*
Coffin, Charles E d1934 *WhAm 1*
Coffin, Charles Edward 1841-1912 *BiDrAC, TwCBDA*
Coffin, Charles Emmet 1849- *NatCAB 9*
Coffin, Charles Fisher 1823-1916 *DcAmB, NatCAB 22*
Coffin, Charles Franklin 1856-1835 *WhAm 1*
Coffin, Charles G *BiAUS*
Coffin, Charles Porter 1858-1940 *NatCAB 31*
Coffin, Charles Ransom 1847-1940 *NatCAB 30*
Coffin, Charlotte Rebecca 1855- *WomWWA 14*
Coffin, Elizabeth R 1850- *WomWWA 14*

Coffin, Fletcher Barker 1873-1944 *NatCAB 33*
Coffin, Frank Barbour 1871- *WhoColR*
Coffin, Frank G 1874-1941 *NatCAB 33, WhAm 1*
Coffin, Frank Morey 1919- *BiDrAC*
Coffin, Frederick M *NewYHSD*
Coffin, Freeman C 1856- *WhAm 4*
Coffin, George William 1845-1899 *NatCAB 29*
Coffin, Helen *WomWWA 14*
Coffin, Henry Sloane 1877-1954 *ApCAB X, DcAmB S5, DcAmReB, NatCAB 55, WhAm 3*
Coffin, Howard Aldridge 1877-1956 *BiDrAC, WhAm 3*
Coffin, Howard Earl 1873-1937 *NatCAB 16*
Coffin, Howard Earle 1873-1937 *DcAmB S2, NatCAB 30, WebAB, WhAm 1*
Coffin, Ida Willets 1856- *WomWWA 14*
Coffin, Sir Isaac 1759-1839 *AmBi, ApCAB, DcAmB, Drake, NatCAB 11, WhAm H*
Coffin, James Henry 1806-1873 *AmBi, ApCAB, DcAmB, NatCAB 8, TwCBDA, WhAm H*
Coffin, Joel Stephen 1861-1935 *NatCAB 29*
Coffin, John 1751-1838 *Drake*
Coffin, John 1756-1838 *ApCAB, DcAmB, NatCAB 11, WhAm H*
Coffin, John Huntington Crane 1815-1890 *ApCAB, BiAUS, NatCAB 5, TwCBDA, WhAm H*
Coffin, John Lambert 1852-1935 *WhAm 2*
Coffin, John Ruskin 1895-1962 *NatCAB 52*
Coffin, Joseph Herschel 1880- *WhAm 6*
Coffin, Joshua 1792-1864 *ApCAB, Drake, NatCAB 2*
Coffin, Levi 1789-1877 *AmBi, DcAmB, DcAmReB, McGEWB, WhAm H*
Coffin, Levi 1798-1877 *ApCAB, NatCAB 12, TwCBDA, WebAB*
Coffin, Lewis Augustus 1856-1933 *NatCAB 37*
Coffin, Lewis Augustus, Jr. 1892- *WhAm 4*
Coffin, Lonnie Alfonso 1890-1959 *NatCAB 48*
Coffin, Lorenzo S 1823-1915 *DcAmB, WebAB, WhAm 1*
Coffin, Marie T Brown d1959 *WhAm 3*
Coffin, Nathan Emery 1863-1931 *NatCAB 23*
Coffin, Nathaniel 1744-1826 *ApCAB, Drake*
Coffin, Oscar Jackson 1887-1956 *NatCAB 47, WhAm 3*
Coffin, Owen Tristram 1815- *TwCBDA*
Coffin, Owen Vincent 1836-1921 *NatCAB 10, TwCBDA, WhAm 1*
Coffin, Peleg, Jr. 1756-1805 *BiAUS, BiDrAC, WhAm H*
Coffin, Peter 1630-1715 *TwCBDA*
Coffin, Peter 1631-1715 *NatCAB 12*
Coffin, Phillip O 1881- *WhAm 6*
Coffin, Robert Allen 1801-1878 *ApCAB, TwCBDA*
Coffin, Robert Barry 1826-1886 *ApCAB, NatCAB 6, TwCBDA*
Coffin, Robert Peter Tristram 1892-1955 *DcAmB S5, NatCAB 45, WhAm 3*
Coffin, Robert Stevenson 1797-1827 *ApCAB, Drake*
Coffin, Roland Folger 1826-1888 *ApCAB, NatCAB 1, TwCBDA*
Coffin, S C *NewYHSD*
Coffin, Selden Jennings 1838-1915 *ApCAB, NatCAB 11, TwCBDA, WhAm 1*
Coffin, Sir Thomas Aston 1754-1810 *ApCAB, Drake*
Coffin, Thomas Chalkley 1887-1934 *BiDrAC, WhAm 1*
Coffin, Timothy Gardner 1788-1854 *ApCAB, Drake*
Coffin, Tristram 1605-1681 *ApCAB, NatCAB 6*
Coffin, Victor 1864- *WhAm 4*
Coffin, W H *NewYHSD*
Coffin, William 1877-1927 *WhAm 1*
Coffin, William A *NewYHSD*
Coffin, William Anderson 1855-1925 *AmBi, ApCAB, DcAmB, NatCAB 6, TwCBDA, WhAm 1*
Coffin, William Carey 1862-1944 *NatCAB 14, NatCAB 33, WhAm 2*

Coffin, William King 1850- *NatCAB 16*
Coffin, William Sloane 1879-1933 *NatCAB 26*,
WhAm 1
Coffin, William Tristram 1903-1961 *WhAm 4*
Coffinberry, Henry D 1841-1912 *NatCAB 15*
Coffinberry, James M 1818-1891 *NatCAB 3*
Coffman, DeWitt 1854-1932 *WhAm 1*
Coffman, George Raleigh 1880-1958 *WhAm 3*
Coffman, Guvarie Silas 1874-1964 *NatCAB 50*
Coffman, L Dale 1905-1949 *WhAm 2*
Coffman, Leroy Mallon 1867-1934 *WhAm 1*
Coffman, Lotus Delta 1875-1938 *BiDAmEd*,
DcAmB S2, *NatCAB 35*, *WhAm 1*
Coffman, Noah Beery 1857- *WhAm 4*
Coffman, Ray Harold 1918-1962 *WhAm 4*
Coffroth, Alexander Hamilton 1828-1906
BiAUS, *BiDrAC*, *TwCBDA*
Cogan, John Vincent 1890-1947 *NatCAB 36*
Cogan, William Neal 1856-1943 *NatCAB 32*
Cogdell, Gertrude 1881- *WomWWA 14*
Cogdell, John Stevens 1778-1847 *BnEnAmA*,
DcAmB, *NewYHSD*, *WhAm H*
Cogger, Edward P *NewYHSD*
Coggeshall, Allan 1881-1955 *NatCAB 43*
Coggeshall, Arthur Sterry 1873-1958
NatCAB 47, *WhAm 3*
Coggeshall, Chester 1909-1970 *WhAm 5*
Coggeshall, Edwin Walter 1842-1929 *WhAm 1*
Coggeshall, George 1784-1861 *ApCAB*,
DcAmB, *Drake*, *NatCAB 23*, *WhAm H*
Coggeshall, George Whiteley 1867-1944
NatCAB 33, *WhAm 2*
Coggeshall, Henry James 1845-1907 *NatCAB 3*,
WhAm 1
Coggeshall, John 1581?-1647 *TwCBDA*
Coggeshall, John 1599-1647 *NatCAB 10*
Coggeshall, John, Jr. 1618-1708 *NatCAB 10*,
TwCBDA
Coggeshall, Joshua 1631-1689 *TwCBDA*
Coggeshall, Mary Bancroft *WomWWA 14*
Coggeshall, Murray H 1873-1960 *WhAm 4*
Coggeshall, William Turner 1824-1867 *ApCAB*,
BiAUS, *DcAmB*, *NatCAB 12*, *TwCBDA*,
WhAm H
Coggeswell, William 1824?-1906 *NewYHSD*
Coggin, John Nelson Clark 1870- *WhoColR*
Coggins, Edward H *NewYHSD*
Coggins, Leslie Harriman 1904-1970
NatCAB 55
Coggins, Paschal Heston 1852-1917 *WhAm 1*
Coggs, Theodore Washington 1916-1968
NatCAB 55, *WhAm 5*
Coghill, George Ellett 1872-1941 *DcAmB S3*,
DcScB, *WhAm 1*
Coghill, Howard *ApCAB X*
Coghill, William Hawes 1876- *WhAm 5*
Coghlan, Charles F 1848-1899 *WhAm 1*
Coghlan, Charles Francis 1841-1899 *AmBi*
Coghlan, John Maxwell 1835-1879 *BiAUS*,
BiDrAC, *WhAm H*
Coghlan, Joseph Bullock 1844-1908
ApCAB Sup, *TwCBDA*, *WhAm 1*
Coghlan, Ralph 1896-1965 *WhAm 4*
Coghlan, Rose 1850-1932 *AmWom*,
NatCAB 13
Coghlan, Rose 1851-1932 *DcAmB S1*
Coghlan, Rose 1852-1932 *NotAW*
Coghlan, Rose 1853-1932 *WhAm 1*
Cogley, John Philip 1899-1968 *WhAm 6*
Cogolludo, Diego 1610?-1686? *ApCAB Sup*
Cogrossi, Carlo Francesco 1682-1769 *DcScB*
Cogshall, Frederick Charles 1875-1958
NatCAB 48
Cogshall, Wilbur Adelman 1874-1951 *WhAm 3*
Cogswell, Frederick Hull 1859-1907 *WhAm 1*
Cogswell, Hamlin Elisha 1852-1922 *WhAm 1*
Cogswell, Harry Jerome 1898-1971 *NatCAB 56*
Cogswell, Henry Daniel 1819-1900 *NatCAB 8*
Cogswell, James Kelsey 1847-1908 *WhAm 1*
Cogswell, John *NewYHSD*
Cogswell, Jonathan 1782-1864 *ApCAB*, *Drake*,
TwCBDA
Cogswell, Joseph Green 1786-1871 *AmBi*,
ApCAB, *DcAmB*, *DcAmLiB*, *Drake*,
NatCAB 11, *TwCBDA*, *WhAm H*
Cogswell, Laura Elizabeth *WomWWA 14*
Cogswell, Ledyard, Jr. 1878-1954 *WhAm 3*
Cogswell, Mariana 1858- *WomWWA 14*

Cogswell, Mason Fitch 1761-1830 *ApCAB*,
Drake, *NatCAB 8*, *TwCBDA*
Cogswell, Mason Fitch 1807-1865 *ApCAB*
Cogswell, Milton 1825-1882 *ApCAB*
Cogswell, Nathaniel 1773-1813 *ApCAB*, *Drake*
Cogswell, Parsons Brainard 1828-1895 *TwCBDA*
Cogswell, Thomas 1746-1810 *ApCAB*, *Drake*
Cogswell, Willard Goodrich 1881-1955
NatCAB 45
Cogswell, William 1760-1831 *ApCAB*
Cogswell, William 1787-1850 *ApCAB*, *Drake*,
TwCBDA
Cogswell, William 1838-1895 *ApCAB*, *BiDrAC*,
NatCAB 4, *TwCBDA*, *WhAm H*,
WhAmP
Cogswell, William Brown 1834-1921 *WhAm 1*
Cogswell, William Browne 1834-1921 *DcAmB*,
NatCAB 13
Cogswell, William F 1819-1903 *NewYHSD*,
WhAm H
Cogswell, William Sterling 1840-1935 *WhAm 1*
Cohan, George Michael 1878-1942 *DcAmB S3*,
EncAB, *McGEWB*, *NatCAB 15*, *WebAB*,
WhAm 1
Coheil, Charles *NewYHSD*
Coheil, John S *NewYHSD*
Cohelan, Jeffery 1914- *BiDrAC*
Cohen, A Broderick 1884-1956 *WhAm 3*
Cohen, Abraham 1870-1951 *NatCAB 40*,
WhAm 5
Cohen, Abraham Benjamin 1892-1960 *WhAm 4*
Cohen, Alfred *NewYHSD*
Cohen, Alfred Andrew 1829-1887 *NatCAB 35*
Cohen, Alfred Morton 1859-1949 *WhAm 3*
Cohen, Andrew Benjamin 1909-1968 *WhAm 5*
Cohen, Andrew Jacob 1860-1914 *NatCAB 16*
Cohen, Archie H 1889- *WhAm 3*
Cohen, Barnett 1891-1952 *NatCAB 42*,
WhAm 3
Cohen, Benjamin A 1896-1960 *WhAm 3*
Cohen, Charles Joseph 1847-1927 *WhAm 1*
Cohen, David Solis 1852- *WhAm 4*
Cohen, Dolly Lurie d1970 *WhAm 5*
Cohen, Ernst Julius 1869-1944? *DcScB*
Cohen, Felix Solomon 1907-1953 *DcAmB S5*,
WhAm 3
Cohen, Frances *WomWWA 14*
Cohen, Frank 1879-1960 *NatCAB 46*
Cohen, Frank 1893-1959 *NatCAB 43*
Cohen, Frederic 1904-1967 *NatCAB 53*
Cohen, Frederick E *NewYHSD*
Cohen, George 1860- *NewYHSD*
Cohen, George Harry 1892-1949 *WhAm 2*
Cohen, George Lion 1894-1945 *NatCAB 34*
Cohen, Harry 1884-1957 *NatCAB 43*
Cohen, Harry 1885-1969 *WhAm 5*
Cohen, Henry 1863-1952 *WhAm 3*
Cohen, Herbert Spencer 1901-1961 *WhAm 4*
Cohen, Hermann 1842-1918 *McGEWB*
Cohen, Irvin Joseph 1908-1970 *WhAm 5*
Cohen, Jacob DaSilva Solis 1838-1927 *ApCAB*,
DcAmB, *WhAm 1*
Cohen, John Sanford 1870-1935 *BiDrAC*,
DcAmB S1, *NatCAB 28*, *WhAm 1*,
WhAmP
Cohen, Joseph 1909-1966 *NatCAB 53*
Cohen, Julius Henry 1873-1950 *WhAm 3*
Cohen, Katherine Myrtilla 1859-1914
NatCAB 10, *WhAm 1*, *WomWWA 14*
Cohen, L Lewis 1891-1946 *NatCAB 35*
Cohen, Lawrence L *NewYHSD*
Cohen, Lee 1874-1943 *NatCAB 32*
Cohen, Lewis 1857-1915 *NatCAB 16*,
WhAm 1
Cohen, Lily Young d1930 *WhAm 1*
Cohen, Louis 1876-1948 *NatCAB 45*,
WhAm 2
Cohen, Louis 1891-1961 *NatCAB 50*
Cohen, Mary M 1854- *AmWom*
Cohen, Mendes 1831-1915 *DcAmB*,
NatCAB 13, *WhAm 1*
Cohen, Merrill Morris 1902-1963 *WhAm 4*
Cohen, Milton 1891-1942 *NatCAB 31*
Cohen, Morris Raphael 1880-1947 *DcAmB S4*,
DcScB, *McGEWB*, *NatCAB 40*, *WebAB*,
WhAm 2
Cohen, Mortimer J 1894-1972 *NatCAB 56*
Cohen, Murray 1905-1962 *WhAm 4*

Cohen, Nathaniel A 1912-1974 *WhAm 6*
Cohen, Octavus Roy 1891-1959 *NatCAB 46*,
WhAm 3
Cohen, Paul 1917-1968 *WhAm 5*
Cohen, Paul Pincus 1896-1971 *WhAm 5*
Cohen, Rebecca Ottolengui 1856-
WomWWA 14
Cohen, Samuel 1896-1965 *NatCAB 52*
Cohen, Sara Barr d1973 *WhAm 6*
Cohen, Sigmund 1899-1966 *NatCAB 54*
Cohen, Victor 1905-1970 *NatCAB 55*
Cohen, Wilbur Joseph 1913- *BiDrUSE*
Cohen, William Nathan 1857-1938 *WhAm 1*
Cohen, William W 1874-1940 *WhAm 1*
Cohen, William Wolf 1874-1940 *NatCAB 30*
Cohen, William Wolfe 1874-1940 *BiDrAC*
Cohill, Charles 1812?- *NewYHSD*
Cohill, Edmund Pendleton 1855-1943 *WhAm 2*
Cohn, Adolphe 1851-1930 *NatCAB 12*,
TwCBDA, *WhAm 1*
Cohn, Alfred A 1880-1951 *DcAmB S5*
Cohn, Alfred Einstein 1879-1957 *WhAm 3*
Cohn, Alfred I 1860- *WhAm 4*
Cohn, Charles Mittendorff 1873-1946 *WhAm 2*
Cohn, Edwin Joseph 1892-1953 *DcAmB S5*,
DcScB, *WebAB*, *WhAm 3*
Cohn, Essie White 1902-1963 *NatCAB 51*
Cohn, Ferdinand Julius 1828-1898 *AsBiEn*,
BiHiMed, *DcScB*
Cohn, Harry 1891-1958 *WhAm 3*
Cohn, Herman Michaels 1886-1966 *NatCAB 53*
Cohn, Jack 1889-1956 *WhAm 3*
Cohn, Joseph Hoffman 1886-1953 *WhAm 3*
Cohn, Lassar 1858-1922 *DcScB*
Cohn, Morris M 1852-1922 *WhAm 1*
Cohn, Ralph Morris 1914-1959 *WhAm 3*
Cohn, Saul 1885-1954 *NatCAB 45*, *WhAm 3*
Cohnheim, Julius 1839-1884 *BiHiMed*
Cohon, Morris 1904-1971 *WhAm 5*
Cohon, Samuel Solomon 1888-1959 *NatCAB 47*
WhAm 4
Cohu, LaMotte T 1895-1968 *WhAm 5*
Coil, Everett Johnston 1907-1950 *WhAm 3*
Coile, Samuel Andrew 1857-1923 *WhAm 1*
Coiner, Beverly Waugh 1857- *WhAm 4*
Coit, Alfred 1863-1947 *WhAm 2*
Coit, Alice Atwood 1870- *WomWWA 14*
Coit, Arthur Clinton 1869-1929 *WhAm 1*
Coit, Daniel Wadsworth *NewYHSD*
Coit, Elizabeth 1820- *AmWom*
Coit, George William 1836-1916 *NatCAB 17*
Coit, Harvey 1819- *NatCAB 11*
Coit, Henry Augustus 1830-1895 *DcAmB*,
TwCBDA, *WhAm H*
Coit, Henry Augustus 1831-1895 *ApCAB*
Coit, Henry Leber 1854-1917 *DcAmB*,
NatCAB 22
Coit, Irene Williams 1873- *AmWom*
Coit, J Eliot 1880- *WhAm 6*
Coit, James Milnor 1845-1925 *ApCAB*,
TwCBDA, *WhAm 1*
Coit, John Clarke 1872- *WhAm 5*
Coit, John Knox 1872- *WhAm 5*
Coit, John McLean 1869-1926 *WhAm 1*
Coit, Joseph Howland 1831-1906 *ApCAB*,
NatCAB 12, *TwCBDA*, *WhAm 1*
Coit, Joshua 1758-1798 *BiAUS*, *BiDrAC*,
NatCAB 2, *TwCBDA*, *WhAm H*
Coit, Joshua 1832-1907 *WhAm 1*
Coit, Judson Boardman 1849-1921 *TwCBDA*,
WhAm 1
Coit, Margaret 1922- *EncAAH*
Coit, Olin Burr 1855-1920 *NatCAB 6*,
TwCBDA, *WhAm 4*
Coit, Ruth 1868-1946 *WhAm 2*,
WomWWA 14
Coit, Stanton 1857-1944 *DcAmB S3*,
WhAm 4
Coit, Thomas Winthrop 1803-1885 *ApCAB*,
DcAmB, *Drake*, *NatCAB 4*, *TwCBDA*,
WhAm H
Coiter, Volcher 1534-1576 *DcScB*
Coke, Sir Edward 1552-1634 *McGEWB*
Coke, Edward Thomas 1807-1888 *NewYHSD*
Coke, Henry Cornick 1856-1933 *WhAm 1*
Coke, James L 1875- *WhAm 5*
Coke, John Archer 1842-1920 *NatCAB 33*
Coke, John Story 1867- *WhAm 5*

Coke, Richard 1829-1897 *AmBi, ApCAB, BiAUS, BiDrAC, DcAmB, NatCAB 9, TwCBDA, WhAm H, WhAmP*
Coke, Richard, Jr. 1790-1851 *BiAUS, BiDrAC, WhAm H*
Coke, Rogers 1867-1947 *NatCAB 41*
Coke, Thomas 1747-1814 *AmBi, ApCAB, DcAmB, DcAmReB, Drake, NatCAB 10, WhAm H*
Cokenower, James W 1851- *WhAm 3*
Cokenower, Katharine Eleanor Stalford 1866- *WomWWA 14*
Coker, Charles Westfield 1879-1931 *NatCAB 23*
Coker, David Robert 1870-1938 *DcAmB S2, NatCAB 29, WhAm 1*
Coker, Francis William 1878-1963 *WhAm 4*
Coker, James Lide 1837-1918 *DcAmB, NatCAB 17, WhAm 1*
Coker, James Lide 1904-1961 *NatCAB 49, WhAm 4*
Coker, James Lide, Jr. 1863-1931 *NatCAB 23*
Coker, Robert E 1876- *WhAm 5*
Coker, Robert Ervin, Jr. 1911-1966 *NatCAB 51*
Coker, Thomas *NewYHSD*
Coker, William Chambers 1872-1953 *NatCAB 42, WhAm 3*
Colac, Denis *NewYHSD*
Colacci, Mario 1910-1968 *WhAm 5*
Colahan, John Barron, Jr. 1848-1920 *WhAm 1*
Colaw, John Marvin 1860-1940 *WhAm 3*
Colbath, Jeremiah *EncAAH*
Colbern, William H 1895-1959 *WhAm 3*
Colbert, Carl Cato 1892-1968 *WhAm 5*
Colbert, Charles Caldwell 1878-1944 *NatCAB 37*
Colbert, Charles Francis, Jr. 1885-1971 *NatCAB 57, WhAm 5*
Colbert, Edouard, Comte DeMaulevrier 1758-1820 *NewYHSD*
Colbert, James William, Jr. 1920-1974 *WhAm 6*
Colbert, Jean Baptiste 1619-1683 *McGEWB*
Colbert, Leo Otis 1883-1968 *WhAm 5*
Colbert, Richard Gary 1915-1973 *WhAm 6*
Colbert, Richard Victor 1867- *WhAm 4*
Colborn, William 1828?- *NewYHSD*
Colborne, Sir John, Lord Seaton 1779-1863 *ApCAB, Drake*
Colbron, Grace Isabel d1948 *WhAm 2, WomWWA 14*
Colburn, Albert E *WhAm 3*
Colburn, Allan Philip 1904-1955 *WhAm 3*
Colburn, Anna Coder 1869- *WomWWA 14*
Colburn, Burnham Standish 1872-1959 *WhAm 3*
Colburn, Charles H 1822?- *NewYHSD*
Colburn, Dana Pond 1823-1859 *BiDAmEd, DcAmB, NatCAB 12, WhAm H*
Colburn, Hattie Leonard 1858- *WomWWA 14*
Colburn, Iola Burnham 1864- *WomWWA 14*
Colburn, Irving Wightman 1861-1917 *DcAmB, NatCAB 24*
Colburn, Jeremiah 1815-1891 *ApCAB, TwCBDA*
Colburn, Luke *NewYHSD*
Colburn, Warren 1793-1833 *ApCAB, BiDAmEd, DcAmB, Drake, NatCAB 10, TwCBDA, WhAm H*
Colburn, Warren 1824-1879 *NatCAB 11*
Colburn, Zerah 1804-1839 *DcAmB, Drake, WhAm H*
Colburn, Zerah 1804-1840 *ApCAB, NatCAB 7, TwCBDA*
Colburn, Zerah 1832-1870 *ApCAB, Drake, NatCAB 12, TwCBDA*
Colby, A 1793-1873 *BiAUS*
Colby, Albert Ladd 1860-1924 *WhAm 1*
Colby, Anthony 1792-1873 *ApCAB*
Colby, Anthony 1795-1873 *NatCAB 11*
Colby, Anthony 1795-1875 *TwCBDA*
Colby, Bainbridge 1869-1950 *BiDrUSE, DcAmB S4, NatCAB 48, WhAm 3*
Colby, Branch Harris 1854-1933 *WhAm 1*
Colby, Charles Carlyle 1884-1965 *NatCAB 51, WhAm 4*
Colby, Charles Galusha 1830-1866 *ApCAB, TwCBDA*
Colby, Charles Lewis 1839- *ApCAB*

Colby, Clara Dorothy Bewick 1846-1916 *NotAW, WhAm 1, WomWWA 14*
Colby, Edward Allen 1857-1935 *NatCAB 17, NatCAB 26*
Colby, Eleanor *WomWWA 14*
Colby, Eugene Chapman 1846-1930 *NatCAB 25*
Colby, Everett 1874-1943 *NatCAB 32, WhAm 2*
Colby, Francis Thompson 1882-1953 *NatCAB 40*
Colby, Frank C d1939 *WhAm 1*
Colby, Frank Harvey 1867- *WhAm 4*
Colby, Frank Moore 1865-1925 *AmBi, DcAmB, NatCAB 29, WebAB, WhAm 1*
Colby, Franklin Green 1858-1941 *WhAm 1*
Colby, Gardner 1810-1879 *ApCAB, DcAmB, NatCAB 8, TwCBDA, WhAm H*
Colby, Gardner 1864-1917 *WhAm 1*
Colby, H Maria George 1844- *AmWom*
Colby, Harrison Gray Otis 1846-1926 *NatCAB 23, TwCBDA, WhAm 1*
Colby, Henry Francis 1842-1915 *ApCAB, NatCAB 12, WhAm 1*
Colby, Irving Harold 1908-1968 *WhAm 5*
Colby, James 1822?- *NewYHSD*
Colby, James Adams 1885-1957 *NatCAB 45*
Colby, James Fairbanks 1850-1939 *WhAm 1*
Colby, Joseph Milton 1904-1974 *WhAm 6*
Colby, June Rose 1856-1940 *WhAm 1, WomWWA 14*
Colby, Kimball Gleason 1873-1928 *NatCAB 22*
Colby, Leonard Wright 1846-1925 *NatCAB 18, WhAm 1*
Colby, Leonard Wright 1848-1925 *ApCAB Sup*
Colby, Luther 1814-1894 *DcAmB, NatCAB 22, WhAm H*
Colby, Nathalie Sedgwick 1875-1942 *NatCAB 31, WhAm 2*
Colby, Sarah A 1824- *AmWom*
Colby, Stoddard B 1816-1867 *BiAUS*
Colby, Vincent V 1879- *IIBEAAW*
Colby, Walter Francis 1880-1970 *WhAm 5*
Colby, William Edward 1875- *WhAm 4, WhAm 5*
Colby, William Irving 1852- *WhAm 1*
Colby, Willoughby Amos 1896- *WhAm 4*
Colcleugh, Emma Shaw *WomWWA 14*
Colclough, Otho Thomas 1907-1974 *WhAm 6*
Colcock, F Horton 1855-1925 *WhAm 1*
Colcock, William Ferguson 1804-1889 *BiAUS, BiDrAC, TwCBDA, WhAm H*
Colcord, Bradford Claude 1897-1953 *NatCAB 45*
Colcord, Charles Francis 1859-1934 *NatCAB 26, REnAW, WhAm 1*
Colcord, Frank Forest 1877-1952 *WhAm 3*
Colcord, Joanna Carver 1882-1960 *WhAm 3A*
Colcord, Lincoln Ross 1883-1947 *DcAmB S4, NatCAB 39, WhAm 2*
Colcord, Roswell Keyes 1839-1939 *NatCAB 11, WhAm 1*
Colcord, Stella Gladys *WomWWA 14*
Colcord, William Claude 1897-1953 *WhAm 3*
Colcur 1555-1589 *Colcur*
Colden, Cadwalader 1688-1776 *NatCAB 2*
Colden, Cadwallader 1688-1776 *AmBi, ApCAB, BiHiMed, DcAmB, DcScB, Drake, EncAAH, McGEWB, REnAW, TwCBDA, WebAB, WhAm H, WhAmP*
Colden, Cadwallader David 1769-1834 *ApCAB, BiAUS, BiDrAC, DcAmB, Drake, NatCAB 7, TwCBDA, WhAm H*
Colden, Charles J 1870-1938 *BiDrAC, WhAm 1*
Colden, Charles S 1885-1960 *WhAm 4*
Colden, Jane 1724-1766 *DcAmB, NotAW, WhAm H*
Colding, Ludvig August 1815-1888 *DcScB Sup*
Coldren, Burt 1863-1952 *NatCAB 41*
Coldren, Philip 1882-1955 *WhAm 3*
Coldwell, Colbert 1883-1967 *NatCAB 53*
Coldwell, Thomas 1838-1905 *NatCAB 8*
Cole, A *NewYHSD*
Cole, Aaron Hodgman 1856-1913 *WhAm 1*
Cole, Ada Augusta 1876- *WomWWA 14*
Cole, Albert McDonald 1901- *BiDrAC*
Cole, Alfred Dodge 1861- *WhAm 1*

Cole, Alice Blanchard Merriam 1858-1936 *WhAm 1, WomWWA 14*
Cole, Ambrose N 1810?-1889 *NatCAB 2*
Cole, Angie Dresser 1876- *WomWWA 14*
Cole, Anna B Taylor 1852- *WomWWA 14*
Cole, Anna Virginia Russell 1846-1926 *BiCAW, NotAW*
Cole, Arlyn Edward 1908-1964 *NatCAB 53*
Cole, Arthur Vincent 1898-1955 *NatCAB 45*
Cole, Ashley Trimble 1876-1965 *WhAm 4*
Cole, Azel Dow 1818-1885 *ApCAB, TwCBDA*
Cole, Bart 1918-1968 *NatCAB 54*
Cole, Bertha Woolsey Dwight *WomWWA 14*
Cole, Betty Joy 1898-1970 *WhAm 5*
Cole, Birdie Haile 1866- *WomWWA 14*
Cole, Blase 1879-1937 *NatCAB 27*
Cole, Carlos Merton 1872- *WhAm 1*
Cole, Charles Briggs 1845-1928 *NatCAB 21*
Cole, Charles Cleaves 1841-1905 *WhAm 1*
Cole, Charles F 1871-1933 *WhAm 1*
Cole, Charles H 1871- *WhAm 5*
Cole, Charles Knox 1852-1920 *NatCAB 8, NatCAB 36, WhAm 1*
Cole, Charles Nelson 1871- *WhAm 5*
Cole, Charles Octavius 1814- *NewYHSD*
Cole, Charles Schneider 1886-1957 *NatCAB 43*
Cole, Chester Cicero 1824-1913 *DcAmB, NatCAB 13, WhAm 1*
Cole, Christopher Columbus 1878-1956 *NatCAB 46*
Cole, Clarence Alfred 1909-1963 *WhAm 4*
Cole, Clarence Lee 1863-1943 *NatCAB 33*
Cole, Cordelia Throop 1833- *AmWom*
Cole, Cornelius 1822-1924 *AmBi, ApCAB, BiAUS, BiDrAC, NatCAB 11, NatCAB 22, TwCBDA, WhAm 1, WhAmP*
Cole, Cyrenus 1863-1939 *BiDrAC, WhAm 1, WhAmP*
Cole, Cyrus W 1876- *WhAm 5*
Cole, David 1822- *WhAm 1*
Cole, Douglas Seaman 1893-1964 *WhAm 4*
Cole, Edward Ball 1879-1918 *NatCAB 20*
Cole, Edward F *ApCAB X*
Cole, Edward Hall 1831- *NatCAB 12*
Cole, Edward Smith 1871-1950 *WhAm 2A*
Cole, Eli Kelley 1867-1929 *NatCAB 24, WhAm 1*
Cole, Elizabeth 1856- *AmWom*
Cole, Ellis Calvin 1866- *WhoColR*
Cole, Elmer Ellsworth 1861-1941 *NatCAB 45, WhAm 4*
Cole, Ernest E 1871-1949 *WhAm 2*
Cole, Eugene Macon 1863-1944 *NatCAB 33*
Cole, Fay-Cooper 1881-1961 *WhAm 4*
Cole, Felix 1887-1969 *WhAm 5*
Cole, Francis Watkinson 1883-1966 *WhAm 4*
Cole, Frank Nelson 1861-1926 *DcAmB, DcScB, NatCAB 13, NatCAB 21, WhAm 1*
Cole, Franklin 1897-1968 *WhAm 5*
Cole, Fred 1901-1964 *NatCAB 50*
Cole, George Clarence 1872- *WhAm 5*
Cole, George Douglas Howard 1889-1959 *McGEWB, WhAm 3*
Cole, George E 1845-1930 *WhAm 1*
Cole, George Edward 1826-1906 *BiAUS, BiDrAC, TwCBDA, WhAm 1*
Cole, George Lamont 1849-1918 *WhAm 1*
Cole, George Lee 1910-1972 *WhAm 6*
Cole, George Stephen 1879-1955 *NatCAB 46*
Cole, George W 1858-1923 *WhAm 1*
Cole, George Watson 1850-1939 *DcAmB S2, DcAmLiB, NatCAB 16, TwCBDA, WhAm 1*
Cole, Glen Walker 1895-1955 *NatCAB 44, WhAm 3*
Cole, Harold Mercer 1905-1972 *WhAm 5*
Cole, Harry Outen 1874-1950 *WhAm 3*
Cole, Haydn Samuel 1861-1939 *NatCAB 33*
Cole, Henry Clay 1852-1924 *NatCAB 21*
Cole, Henry Tiffany 1870-1938 *WhAm 1*
Cole, Hermon Harrison 1893-1949 *NatCAB 38*
Cole, Howard Ellsworth 1873-1950 *NatCAB 39, WhAm 3*
Cole, Howard I 1892-1966 *WhAm 4*
Cole, Howard Norton 1873-1928 *NatCAB 21*
Cole, Howard Ware 1898- *WhAm 5*
Cole, Isaac P *NewYHSD*

Cole, Jack 1914-1974 *WhAm 6*
Cole, James Archibald Sterling 1876- *WhoColR*
Cole, James Reid 1839-1917 *NatCAB 41*
Cole, Jean Dean 1873-1939 *WhAm 1*
Cole, Jennie S 1852- *WomWWA 14*
Cole, John 1720?-1777 *NatCAB 4*
Cole, John Adams 1838-1932 *NatCAB 34, WhAm 4*
Cole, John Gully 1876-1924 *NatCAB 22*
Cole, John Melvin 1890-1956 *NatCAB 45*
Cole, John Nelson 1863-1922 *WhAm 1*
Cole, John Tupper 1895-1975 *WhAm 6*
Cole, Joseph Foxcroft 1837-1892 *ApCAB, DcAmB, Drake, IIBEAAW, NatCAB 22, NewYHSD, TwCBDA, WhAm H*
Cole, Joseph Greenleaf 1806-1858 *NewYHSD*
Cole, Lawrence Thomas 1869- *WhAm 5*
Cole, Lawrence Wooster 1870-1946 *WhAm 2*
Cole, Leland Howard 1863-1926 *NatCAB 20*
Cole, Leon J 1877-1948 *WhAm 2*
Cole, Lewis Gregory 1874-1954 *NatCAB 42, WhAm 3*
Cole, Louis Maurice 1870-1930 *NatCAB 22, WhAm 1*
Cole, Lyman Emerson 1812-1878? *NewYHSD*
Cole, Major *NewYHSD*
Cole, Mary Cross 1884- *WomWWA 14*
Cole, Mary Wallace 1878- *WomWWA 14*
Cole, Mary Watkinson Rockwell 1873- *WomWWA 14*
Cole, Moses Dupre 1783-1849 *NewYHSD*
Cole, Nat King 1919-1965 *WhAm 4*
Cole, Nathan 1825-1904 *BiDrAC*
Cole, Nathan, Jr. 1860-1921 *WhAm 1*
Cole, Nelson 1833-1899 *ApCAB Sup, WhAm 1*
Cole, Orsamus 1819- *ApCAB, BiAUS, TwCBDA*
Cole, Orsamus 1819-1892 *NatCAB 12*
Cole, Orsamus 1819-1903 *BiDrAC*
Cole, Phillip Gillett 1883-1940 *REnAW*
Cole, Ralph Dayton 1873-1932 *BiDrAC, WhAm 1*
Cole, Raymond Clinton 1870-1957 *BiDrAC*
Cole, Redmond Selecman 1881- *WhAm 6*
Cole, Richard Beverly 1829- *NatCAB 7, WhAm 1*
Cole, Robert Carl 1887-1966 *NatCAB 53*
Cole, Robert Edwin 1887-1959 *NatCAB 53*
Cole, Rossetter Gleason 1866-1952 *NatCAB 18, WhAm 3*
Cole, Roy 1915- *WhAm 6*
Cole, Roy Edward 1883-1950 *NatCAB 40*
Cole, Rufus 1872-1966 *WhAm 4, WhAm 5*
Cole, Russell David 1900-1962 *NatCAB 52, WhAm 4*
Cole, Samuel d1851 *Drake*
Cole, Samuel Valentine 1851-1925 *NatCAB 30, WhAm 1*
Cole, Samuel Winkley 1848- *WhAm 1*
Cole, Sarah *NewYHSD*
Cole, Theodore Lee 1852-1932 *WhAm 1*
Cole, Thomas 1801-1847 *Drake, NatCAB 7*
Cole, Thomas 1801-1848 *AmBi, ApCAB, BnEnAmA, DcAmB, EncAAH, EncAB, IIBEAAW, McGEWB, NewYHSD, TwCBDA, WebAB, WhAm H*
Cole, Thomas 1881- *WhAm 6*
Cole, Thomas Frederick 1862-1939 *NatCAB 31, WhAm 4*
Cole, Thomas Lafayette 1856-1923 *NatCAB 26*
Cole, Timothy 1852-1931 *AmBi, DcAmB S1, NatCAB 13, WhAm 1*
Cole, W O *NewYHSD*
Cole, Walton Adamson 1912-1963 *WhAm 4*
Cole, Whitefoord R 1874-1934 *WhAm 1*
Cole, Willard Glover 1906-1965 *NatCAB 51*
Cole, Willard W 1908-1973 *WhAm 6*
Cole, William Carey 1868-1935 *WhAm 1*
Cole, William Clay 1897-1965 *BiDrAC*
Cole, William Gregory 1902-1948 *NatCAB 35*
Cole, William H 1892-1967 *WhAm 4*
Cole, William Hinson 1837-1886 *BiDrAC, WhAm H*
Cole, William Isaac 1859-1935 *WhAm 1*
Cole, William Jacob 1883-1959 *NatCAB 47*
Cole, William Morse 1866-1960 *WhAm 4*

Cole, William Purington, Jr. 1889-1957 *BiDrAC, WhAmP*
Cole, William Purrington, Jr. 1889-1957 *WhAm 3*
Cole, William Sterling 1904- *BiDrAC*
Cole, Wilson Giffin 1884-1954 *WhAm 3*
Colean, James Russell 1891-1962 *NatCAB 49*
Colebaugh, Charles Henry 1892-1944 *WhAm 2*
Colegrove, Arthur Dana 1891-1955 *NatCAB 46*
Colegrove, Chauncey Peter 1855- *WhAm 4*
Colegrove, Emma Ridley 1866- *WomWWA 14*
Colegrove, Frederick Welton 1855- *WhAm 4*
Colegrove, Kenneth Wallace 1886-1975 *WhAm 6*
Colegrove, Mabel Eloise *WomWWA 14*
Colehandler, George A 1825?- *NewYHSD*
Coleman *NewYHSD*
Coleman, Algernon 1876-1939 *WhAm 1*
Coleman, Alice Blanchard Merriam 1858-1936 *NotAW*
Coleman, Ann Mary Butler 1813-1891 *NatCAB 4, TwCBDA*
Coleman, Anna William Edwards *WomWWA 14*
Coleman, Arch 1877-1966 *WhAm 4, WhAm 5*
Coleman, Arthur Philemon 1852-1939 *IIBEAAW*
Coleman, Arthur Prudden 1897-1974 *WhAm 6*
Coleman, B Dawson 1865-1933 *NatCAB 26*
Coleman, Benjamin Wilson 1869-1939 *NatCAB 28, WhAm 1*
Coleman, Chapman *WhAm 1*
Coleman, Charles d1874 *NewYHSD*
Coleman, Charles 1838?- *NewYHSD*
Coleman, Charles Caryl 1840-1928 *AmBi, DcAmB, NatCAB 21, NewYHSD, WhAm 1*
Coleman, Charles Caryll 1840-1928 *ApCAB, TwCBDA*
Coleman, Charles Elliott 1867- *WhAm 4*
Coleman, Charles Philip 1865-1929 *NatCAB 14, WhAm 1*
Coleman, Charles Washington 1862- *WhAm 4*
Coleman, Christopher Bush 1875-1944 *NatCAB 33, WhAm 2*
Coleman, Claude C 1879-1953 *WhAm 3*
Coleman, Corinne Hoyt *WomWWA 14*
Coleman, Cornelius Cunningham 1877- *WhAm 5*
Coleman, Cynthia Beverley Tucker 1832-1908 *WhAm 1*
Coleman, Cyril 1902-1958 *WhAm 3*
Coleman, D'Alton Corry 1879-1956 *WhAm 3*
Coleman, Daniel *BiAUS*
Coleman, David Augustus 1892-1938 *NatCAB 29*
Coleman, Edmund Thomas 1823-1892 *IIBEAAW*
Coleman, Edward A 1860- *NewYHSD*
Coleman, Edward Park 1867-1953 *NatCAB 44*
Coleman, Frank Joseph 1886-1934 *NatCAB 25, WhAm 1*
Coleman, Frederick William 1878-1945 *NatCAB 33, WhAm 2*
Coleman, Frederick William Backus 1874-1947 *NatCAB 33, WhAm 2*
Coleman, G Dawson 1825-1878 *NatCAB 25*
Coleman, George Preston 1870-1948 *WhAm 2*
Coleman, George Whitfield 1830-1907 *WhAm 1*
Coleman, George William 1867-1950 *ApCAB X, WhAm 3*
Coleman, Gilbert Payson 1866- *WhAm 4*
Coleman, Glenn Odem 1881-1932 *NatCAB 30*
Coleman, Hamilton Dudley 1845-1926 *BiDrAC, NatCAB 21, TwCBDA*
Coleman, Hannah Hemphill 1872- *WomWWA 14*
Coleman, Harry 1872-1918 *NatCAB 17*
Coleman, Helena *WomWWA 14*
Coleman, James Daniel Stetson 1904-1975 *WhAm 6*
Coleman, James Edmund 1863-1937 *NatCAB 31*
Coleman, James Harold 1871- *WhoColR*
Coleman, James Melville 1859- *WhAm 4*
Coleman, James William 1903-1962 *NatCAB 49*
Coleman, John 1803-1869 *ApCAB, Drake*

Coleman, John 1882-1961 *WhAm 4*
Coleman, John Crapser 1819-1896 *NatCAB 16*
Coleman, John Crisp 1823-1919 *NatCAB 18*
Coleman, John Dawson 1903-1963 *NatCAB 50, WhAm 4*
Coleman, John Francis 1866-1944 *WhAm 2*
Coleman, John Hamline 1847- *WhAm 4*
Coleman, John Shields 1894-1972 *WhAm 5*
Coleman, John Strider 1897-1958 *NatCAB 46, WhAm 3*
Coleman, John Wesley 1865- *WhoColR*
Coleman, Julia P H *WhoColR*
Coleman, Kathleen Blake 1864- *WhAm 4*
Coleman, Leighton 1837-1907 *ApCAB, DcAmB, NatCAB 11, TwCBDA, WhAm 1*
Coleman, Lewis Miner 1827-1863 *ApCAB*
Coleman, Lewis Minor 1861-1918 *WhAm 1*
Coleman, Lucy Newhall 1817- *NatCAB 4*
Coleman, Lyman 1796-1882 *ApCAB, DcAmB, Drake, NatCAB 11, TwCBDA, WhAm H*
Coleman, Mary Darter 1894- *IIBEAAW*
Coleman, Mary Willson 1885- *WomWWA 14*
Coleman, Nicholas Daniel 1800-1874 *BiAUS, BiDrAC, WhAm H*
Coleman, Norman Jay 1827-1911 *NatCAB 5, NatCAB 16, REnAW*
Coleman, Obed M 1817-1845 *ApCAB, NatCAB 7*
Coleman, Otho M 1817-1845 *Drake*
Coleman, Philip Frantz 1893-1956 *WhAm 3*
Coleman, Ralph Pallen 1892-1968 *WhAm 5*
Coleman, Richard B 1846- *WhAm 4*
Coleman, Robert 1900-1974 *WhAm 6*
Coleman, Robert Lewis, Jr. 1896-1950 *NatCAB 38*
Coleman, S Waldo 1881- *WhAm 6*
Coleman, Samuel 1832-1920 *NewYHSD*
Coleman, Satis Narrona Barton 1878-1961 *BiDAmEd, WhAm 4*
Coleman, Sidney Andrew 1879- *WhAm 6*
Coleman, Silas A *NewYHSD*
Coleman, Stewart P 1899-1969 *WhAm 5*
Coleman, Sydney Haines 1886-1955 *WhAm 3*
Coleman, Thomas 1808- *NatCAB 3*
Coleman, Thomas Davies 1865-1927 *WhAm 1*
Coleman, Thomas Emmet 1893-1964 *WhAm 4*
Coleman, Thomas Wilkes 1833-1920 *WhAm 1*
Coleman, Walter Moore 1863- *WhAm 1*
Coleman, Warren 1869-1948 *WhAm 2*
Coleman, William 1705?-1769 *NatCAB 17*
Coleman, William 1766-1829 *ApCAB, DcAmB, Drake, NatCAB 11, WhAm H, WhAmP*
Coleman, William 1870- *WhoColR*
Coleman, William Beecher 1887-1956 *NatCAB 43*
Coleman, William Caldwell 1884-1967 *WhAm 4A*
Coleman, William Coffin 1870-1957 *WhAm 3*
Coleman, William Emmette 1843- *NatCAB 5, WhAm 1*
Coleman, William Franklin 1838-1917 *NatCAB 16*
Coleman, William Harold 1885-1964 *WhAm 4*
Coleman, William Henry 1870-1923 *NatCAB 19*
Coleman, William Henry 1871-1943 *BiDrAC*
Coleman, William Henry 1888-1952 *WhAm 3*
Coleman, William John 1851- *WhAm 5*
Coleman, William Magruder 1874-1921 *WhAm 1*
Coleman, William Tell 1824-1893 *AmBi, ApCAB, DcAmB, NatCAB 8, REnAW, TwCBDA, WhAm H*
Coleman, William Tyler 1867- *WhoColR*
Coleman, William Wheeler 1873-1965 *NatCAB 53*
Coleman, William Wheeler 1873-1966 *WhAm 4*
Coleman-Norton, Paul Robinson 1898-1971 *NatCAB 56*
Colen, John H *NewYHSD*
Colepeper, Lord Thomas d1719 *NatCAB 12, NatCAB 13*
Coler, Bird Sim 1867- *WhAm 1*
Colerick, Walpole Gillespie 1845-1911 *BiDrAC*
Coleridge, Samuel Taylor 1772-1834 *McGEWB*
Coles, Abraham 1813-1891 *ApCAB, NatCAB 2, TwCBDA*

Coles, Alfred Porter 1861-1941 *WhAm 2*
Coles, David Smalley 1844- *WhAm 4*
Coles, Edward 1786-1868 *ApCAB, BiAUS, DcAmB, Drake, NatCAB 11, TwCBDA, WhAm H, WhAmP*
Coles, Edwin Sands 1828-1896 *NatCAB 30*
Coles, Isaac 1747-1813 *BiAUS, BiDrAC, WhAm H*
Coles, Isaac A 1780-1841 *Drake*
Coles, John, Jr. 1776?-1854 *NewYHSD*
Coles, John, Sr. 1749?-1809 *NewYHSD*
Coles, Jonathan Ackerman 1843-1925 *ApCAB Sup, NatCAB 2, TwCBDA, WhAm 1*
Coles, Malcolm Argyle 1869-1938 *NatCAB 27*
Coles, Stricker 1867-1937 *NatCAB 27*
Coles, Thomas 1752-1844 *Drake*
Coles, Walter d1857 *BiAUS*
Coles, Walter 1789-1857 *TwCBDA*
Coles, Walter 1790-1857 *BiDrAC, WhAm H*
Colesberry, Jean Walker 1867- *WomWWA 14*
Colestock, Henry Thomas 1868- *WhAm 4*
Colesworthy, Daniel Clement 1810- *ApCAB, Drake*
Colet, John 1446?-1519 *McGEWB*
Coletta, Paolo E U 1916- *EncAAH*
Colette, Sidonie Gabrielle 1873-1954 *McGEWB, WhAm 3*
Coletti, Joseph Arthur 1898-1973 *WhAm 6*
Coley, Bradley Lancaster 1892-1961 *WhAm 4*
Coley, Edward Huntington 1861-1949 *NatCAB 43, WhAm 2*
Coley, Francis Chase 1866-1934 *WhAm 1*
Coley, William Bradley 1862-1936 *ApCAB X, WhAm 1*
Colfax, Schuyler 1823-1885 *AmBi, ApCAB, BiAUS, BiDrAC, BiDrUSE, DcAmB, Drake, NatCAB 4, TwCBDA, WebAB, WhAm H, WhAmP*
Colfax, Schuyler 1870-1925 *NatCAB 20*
Colfelt, Lawrence Maclay 1849- *NatCAB 3, TwCBDA, WhAm 4*
Colflesh, Robert William 1900- *WhAm 4*
Colford, William Edward 1908-1971 *NatCAB 56, WhAm 5*
Colgate, Adele S 1883- *WomWWA 14*
Colgate, Austen 1863-1927 *ApCAB X*
Colgate, Gilbert 1858-1933 *NatCAB 26, WhAm 1*
Colgate, Henry A 1890-1957 *WhAm 3*
Colgate, James Boorman 1818-1904 *AmBi, ApCAB, DcAmB, NatCAB 24, TwCBDA, WhAm 1*
Colgate, James Colby 1853-1944 *NatCAB 34*
Colgate, James Colby 1863-1944 *WhAm 2*
Colgate, Russell d1941 *WhAm 1*
Colgate, S Bayard 1898-1963 *NatCAB 50, WhAm 4*
Colgate, Samuel 1822-1897 *ApCAB, NatCAB 13, TwCBDA*
Colgate, Sidney Morse 1862-1930 *ApCAB X, WhAm 1*
Colgate, William 1783-1857 *AmBi, ApCAB, DcAmB, NatCAB 13, TwCBDA, WebAB, WhAm H*
Colgate, William 1841- *NatCAB 18*
Colgrove, Philip Taylor 1858-1930 *WhAm 1*
Colhoun, Edmund K 1821- *Drake*
Colhoun, Edmund Ross 1821-1897 *ApCAB, NatCAB 10, TwCBDA*
Colhoun, John 1802-1872 *ApCAB*
Colhoun, John Ewing 1749-1802 *NatCAB 5, NatCAB 11*
Colhoun, John Ewing 1750-1802 *BiDrAC, WhAm H*
Colie, Edward Martin 1852-1931 *WhAm 1*
Colie, Rosalie Littell 1924-1972 *WhAm 5*
Coligny, Gaspard De 1519-1572 *McGEWB*
Colin, Therese F *WomWWA 14*
Colket, Edward Burton 1873- *WhAm 5*
Coll, Raymond S 1875-1962 *WhAm 4*
Colladay, Edward Francis d1961 *WhAm 4*
Colladay, Samuel Rakestraw 1868-1945 *WhAm 2*
Colladay, William Foulke 1873-1953 *NatCAB 39*
Collamer, Jacob 1791-1865 *AmBi, ApCAB, BiDrUSE, DcAmB, NatCAB 4,*

TwCBDA, *WhAm H*
Collamer, Jacob 1792-1865 *BiAUS, BiDrAC, Drake, WhAmP*
Collamore, Davis 1820-1887 *NatCAB 7*
Collamore, Harry Bacon d1975 *WhAm 6*
Collar, William Coe 1833-1916 *BiDAmEd, NatCAB 21, WhAm 1*
Collard, John *NewYHSD*
Collard, W *NewYHSD*
Collas, Louis Antoine 1775- *NewYHSD*
Collbran, Henry 1852-1925 *WhAm 1*
Colledge, William A 1859-1927 *WhAm 1*
Collens, Arthur Morris 1880- *WhAm 6*
Collens, Charles 1873-1956 *WhAm 3*
Collens, Clarence Lyman 1875-1972 *WhAm 5*
Collens, Thomas Wharton 1812-1879 *DcAmB, NatCAB 22, WhAm H*
Coller, Frederick Amasa 1887-1964 *NatCAB 51, WhAm 4*
Coller, Granville James 1853-1950 *NatCAB 45*
Coller, Julius A 1859- *WhAm 4*
Colleran, Harold Leo 1913-1960 *NatCAB 49*
Collers, Lewis *NewYHSD*
Colles, Abraham 1773-1843 *BiHiMed*
Colles, Christopher 1737?-1821 *TwCBDA*
Colles, Christopher 1738-1816 *AmBi, NatCAB 9*
Colles, Christopher 1738-1821 *ApCAB, Drake*
Colles, Christopher 1739-1816 *DcAmB, WhAm H*
Colles, John 1751-1807 *NewYHSD*
Collet, John Caskie 1898-1955 *NatCAB 46, WhAm 3*
Collet, Louis 1814?- *NewYHSD*
Collet-Descotils, Hippolyte-Victor 1773-1815 *DcScB*
Colleton, James *ApCAB, Drake, NatCAB 12*
Collett, Armand Rene 1895-1973 *NatCAB 57, WhAm 6*
Collett, George Richard 1872-1942 *NatCAB 52, WhAm 2*
Collett, John 1828-1899 *ApCAB, TwCBDA, WhAm 1*
Collett, Joshua 1781-1855 *NatCAB 12*
Collett, Robert Arthur 1922-1974 *WhAm 6*
Colley, Charles Clifford 1938- *EncAAH*
Collie, George Lucius 1857-1954 *WhAm 3*
Collie, John Norman 1859-1942 *DcScB*
Collie, Roy Munro 1884-1943 *NatCAB 39*
Collier *NewYHSD*
Collier, Ada Langworthy 1843- *AmWom*
Collier, Barron Gift 1873-1939 *DcAmB S2, NatCAB 39, WhAm 1*
Collier, Charles A 1848- *NatCAB 5*
Collier, Charles Fenton 1817-1899 *BiDConf*
Collier, Charles Myles 1836-1908 *NatCAB 35, NewYHSD*
Collier, Constance 1878-1955 *DcAmB S5*
Collier, Daniel Lewis 1796-1869 *WhAm H*
Collier, David Charles 1871-1934 *WhAm 1*
Collier, Edward Augustus 1835-1920 *WhAm 3*
Collier, Frank Wilbur 1870- *WhAm 2*
Collier, Sir George d1795 *ApCAB, Drake*
Collier, George Haskell 1827-1916 *WhAm 1*
Collier, Hannah C Shackleford *WomWWA 14*
Collier, Harold Reginald 1915- *BiDrAC*
Collier, Harry D 1876-1959 *WhAm 3*
Collier, Henry Lane 1886-1958 *NatCAB 47*
Collier, Henry Watkins 1801-1855 *ApCAB, BiAUS, DcAmB, Drake, NatCAB 10, TwCBDA, WhAm H*
Collier, Hiram Price 1860-1913 *DcAmB*
Collier, Howard Taylor 1869-1945 *NatCAB 37*
Collier, J Howard d1900 *NewYHSD*
Collier, James 1789-1873 *ApCAB*
Collier, James Currie 1869-1947 *NatCAB 37*
Collier, James William 1872-1933 *BiDrAC, WhAm 1, WhAmP*
Collier, John 1884-1968 *EncAB, NatCAB 54, REnAW, WebAB, WhAm 5*
Collier, John Allen 1787-1873 *ApCAB, BiAUS, BiDrAC, TwCBDA, WhAm H*
Collier, John Howard 1884-1955 *WhAm 3*
Collier, Joseph Avery 1828-1864 *ApCAB*
Collier, Laura Brownell 1851- *WomWWA 14*
Collier, Marie Elizabeth 1927-1971 *WhAm 5*
Collier, Mary Vail 1879- *WomWWA 14*
Collier, Nathaniel White 1871- *WhoColR*

Collier, Peter 1835-1896 *AmBi, ApCAB, DcAmB, NatCAB 8, TwCBDA, WhAm H*
Collier, Peter Fenelon 1849-1909 *DcAmB, NatCAB 10, WhAm 1*
Collier, Price 1860-1913 *DcAmB, NatCAB 15, WhAm 1*
Collier, Robert Joseph 1876-1918 *ApCAB X, NatCAB 21, WhAm 1*
Collier, Robert Laird 1835-1890 *TwCBDA*
Collier, Robert Laird 1837-1890 *ApCAB, NatCAB 7*
Collier, Theodore 1874-1963 *WhAm 4*
Collier, Thomas Stephens 1842-1893 *NatCAB 4, TwCBDA*
Collier, William 1771-1843 *ApCAB*
Collier, William 1866-1944 *WhAm 2*
Collier, William 1868- *NatCAB 17*
Collier, William Armistead 1847- *WhAm 4*
Collier, William Armistead Nelson 1874-1947 *NatCAB 49*
Collier, William Miller 1867-1956 *ApCAB X, NatCAB 13, WhAm 3*
Colliere, Lucien C *NewYHSD*
Colligan, Eugene Aloysius 1888-1959 *NatCAB 44*
Colligan, Francis James 1908-1974 *WhAm 6*
Collin *NewYHSD*
Collin, Alonzo 1837-1918 *WhAm 1*
Collin, Charles Avery 1846- *TwCBDA, WhAm 4*
Collin, Frederick 1850-1939 *NatCAB 33, WhAm 1*
Collin, Grace Lathrop *WomWWA 14*
Collin, Harry E 1885-1972 *WhAm 5*
Collin, John 1850- *NewYHSD*
Collin, John Francis 1802-1889 *BiAUS, BiDrAC, TwCBDA, WhAm H*
Collin, Nicholas 1744-1831 *NatCAB 13*
Collin, William Welch, Jr. 1887-1966 *NatCAB 53*
Collinge, Francis Vernon 1899-1966 *NatCAB 52*
Collinge, Patricia 1894-1974 *WhAm 6*
Collings, Charles John 1848-1931 *IIBEAAW*
Collings, Clyde Wilson 1892-1952 *WhAm 3*
Collings, Crittenden Taylor 1848-1924 *WhAm 1*
Collings, Gilbeart Hooper 1895-1964 *WhAm 4*
Collings, Harry Thomas 1880-1934 *NatCAB 25, WhAm 1*
Collings, Howard Paxton 1865- *WhAm 3*
Collings, John Ayres 1903-1971 *WhAm 5*
Collings, Kenneth Brown 1898-1941 *WhAm 1*
Collings, Samuel Posey 1845-1917 *NatCAB 8, WhAm 1*
Collingwood, Cuthbert 1758-1810 *WhoMilH*
Collingwood, Francis 1834-1911 *NatCAB 13, TwCBDA, WhAm 1*
Collingwood, G Harris 1890-1958 *WhAm 3*
Collingwood, Herbert Winslow 1857-1927 *WhAm 1*
Collingwood, James *ApCAB X*
Collingwood, Robin George 1889-1943 *McGEWB*
Collins, Mister *NewYHSD*
Collins, A Frederick 1869- *WhAm 5*
Collins, Abe, Sr. 1885-1956 *NatCAB 50*
Collins, Alan Copeland 1902-1968 *WhAm 4A*
Collins, Albert Hamilton 1894-1945 *WhAm 2*
Collins, Alfred Morris 1876-1951 *NatCAB 43, WhAm 2*
Collins, Alfred Quentin 1855-1903 *NatCAB 23*
Collins, Alfred Quinton d1903 *WhAm 1*
Collins, Alice Derfla Howes 1872- *WomWWA 14*
Collins, Alice Roger *WomWWA 14*
Collins, Andrew Dorr 1886-1960 *NatCAB 49*
Collins, Arnold *NewYHSD*
Collins, Atwood 1851-1926 *NatCAB 21, WhAm 1*
Collins, Bertrand Robson Torsey 1866- *WhAm 4*
Collins, Carter 1893-1973 *WhAm 6*
Collins, Charles *NewYHSD*
Collins, Charles 1813-1875 *ApCAB, Drake, NatCAB 6, TwCBDA*
Collins, Charles 1817-1891 *NatCAB 3*

Collins, Charles Alexander 1872-1958
  NatCAB 46
Collins, Charles Augustus 1878-1931
  NatCAB 24
Collins, Charles Bertine 1904-1975 *WhAm 6*
Collins, Charles E 1869- *WhAm 5*
Collins, Charles Edwin 1868- *WhAm 4*
Collins, Charles Sidney 1827-1889 *TwCBDA*
Collins, Charles Wallace 1879-1964 *NatCAB 51,*
  WhAm 6
Collins, Charles William 1880-1964 *WhAm 4*
Collins, Christopher Clark 1871-1930
  NatCAB 22
Collins, Clarence Lyman 1848- *NatCAB 5*
Collins, Clifford Ulysses 1867-1943 *WhAm 2*
Collins, Clinton DeWitt 1866-1932 *WhAm 1*
Collins, Conrad Green 1907-1971 *WhAm 5*
Collins, Cornelius Vallance 1856- *WhAm 4*
Collins, Cornelius VanSantvoord 1856-1926
  WhAm 1
Collins, Dean Albert 1904-1957 *NatCAB 50*
Collins, Delia 1830- *AmWom*
Collins, Donald Clark 1902-1964 *NatCAB 51*
Collins, Edgar Thomas 1873-1933 *WhAm 1*
Collins, Edward Day 1869-1940 *NatCAB 36,*
  WhAm 1
Collins, Edward Knight 1802-1878 *ApCAB,*
  DcAmB, McGEWB, NatCAB 23,
  TwCBDA, WhAm H
Collins, Edward Trowbridge 1887-1951
  DcAmB S5
Collins, Edwin R 1876-1933 *WhAm 1*
Collins, Ela 1786-1848 *BiAUS, BiDrAC,*
  TwCBDA, WhAm H
Collins, Elizabeth Ballinger 1755-1831 *ApCAB*
Collins, Ellen 1828-1912 *NotAW*
Collins, Emilie Moulton 1845- *WomWWA 14*
Collins, Emily Parmely 1814- *AmWom*
Collins, Emma Gowdy *WomWWA 14*
Collins, Everell Stanton 1866-1940 *NatCAB 38,*
  WhAm 1
Collins, Felix *NewYHSD*
Collins, Foster K 1871-1939 *WhAm 1*
Collins, Francis Arnold 1873-1957 *WhAm 3*
Collins, Francis D 1844-1891 *BiAUS*
Collins, Francis Dolan 1841-1891 *BiDrAC,*
  WhAm H
Collins, Francis Winfield 1878-1960
  NatCAB 48
Collins, Frank Shipley 1848-1920 *AmBi,*
  DcAmB, WhAm 3
Collins, Franklin Wallace 1860-1943
  NatCAB 32, WhAm 2
Collins, Frederick Lewis 1882-1950 *WhAm 3*
Collins, Frederick W 1846- *NatCAB 3*
Collins, Frederick William 1873-1948
  NatCAB 38
Collins, George C 1810-1875 *ApCAB*
Collins, George Franklin 1876- *WhoColR*
Collins, George J 1839- *NatCAB 1*
Collins, George Lewis 1852-1940 *WhAm 1*
Collins, George Stuart 1862- *WhAm 1*
Collins, George T *NewYHSD*
Collins, George Washington 1925-1972 *BiDrAC,*
  WhAm 5
Collins, George William 1902-1962 *WhAm 4*
Collins, Gilbert 1846-1920 *NatCAB 34,*
  WhAm 1
Collins, Guy N 1872-1938 *DcAmB S2,*
  WhAm 1
Collins, Harold Moorman 1894-1942 *WhAm 3*
Collins, Harry Otis 1873-1957 *NatCAB 47*
Collins, Henry Clovis 1909-1961 *NatCAB 50*
Collins, Henry John Alderton 1895-1952
  NatCAB 41
Collins, Henry W 1903-1971 *WhAm 5*
Collins, Herman LeRoy d1940 *WhAm 1*
Collins, Howard Dennis 1868- *WhAm 4*
Collins, Hubert Edwin 1872-1932 *WhAm 1*
Collins, Isaac 1746-1817 *ApCAB, Drake,*
  NatCAB 19
Collins, J Franklin 1863-1940 *WhAm 1,*
  WhAm 2
Collins, James Adams 1870-1946 *NatCAB 36*
Collins, James H 1873- *WhAm 5*
Collins, James Joshua 1891-1952 *NatCAB 39*
Collins, James Lawton 1882-1963 *WhAm 4*
Collins, James Mitchell 1916- *BiDrAC*

Collins, Jennie 1828-1887 *NotAW, TwCBDA*
Collins, Jennie Kendrick *WomWWA 14*
Collins, Jeremiah *NewYHSD*
Collins, Joe Lawton 1896-1963 *WhWW-II*
Collins, John *NewYHSD*
Collins, John 1625-1683 *DcScB*
Collins, John 1717-1795 *ApCAB, BiAUS,*
  BiDrAC, DcAmB, Drake, NatCAB 9,
  TwCBDA, WhAm H
Collins, John 1775-1822 *BiAUS, Drake,*
  NatCAB 11
Collins, John Anderson 1810?-1879? *DcAmB,*
  WhAm H
Collins, John Andrew 1877-1947 *NatCAB 36*
Collins, John Bartholomew 1850-1917 *WhAm 1*
Collins, John E 1895-1960 *NatCAB 49*
Collins, John H *NewYHSD*
Collins, John Joseph 1857-1934 *WhAm 1*
Collins, John M 1854- *WhoColR*
Collins, John Martin 1891-1952 *NatCAB 41*
Collins, John Martin 1892-1952 *WhAm 3*
Collins, John Mathewson 1880-1962 *WhAm 4*
Collins, John Stiles 1837-1928 *NatCAB 21*
Collins, John Timothy 1899-1965 *WhAm 4*
Collins, Joseph 1866-1950 *NatCAB 40,*
  WhAm 5
Collins, Joseph Edmund 1855- *ApCAB*
Collins, Joseph Henry 1851- *WhAm 4*
Collins, Joseph Howland 1898-1966 *WhAm 4*
Collins, Joseph Lawton 1896-1963 *WebAMB*
Collins, Joseph Martin 1907-1957 *WhAm 3*
Collins, Joseph Victor 1858-1943 *NatCAB 34,*
  WhAm 2
Collins, Joseph William 1839-1904 *TwCBDA,*
  WhAm 1
Collins, Joshua *WhAm H*
Collins, Julia Cope *WomWWA 14*
Collins, Justus 1857-1934 *NatCAB 42*
Collins, Kenneth Benedict 1885-1916
  NatCAB 18
Collins, Laura G 1826- *WhAm 4*
Collins, Laura Sedgwick *AmWom*
Collins, Lewis 1797-1870 *NatCAB 6*
Collins, Linton McGee 1902-1972 *NatCAB 57*
Collins, Loren Warren 1838-1912 *WhAm 1*
Collins, Lorin Cone 1848-1940 *WhAm 1*
Collins, Mark 1912-1970 *WhAm 5*
Collins, Mary Clementine 1846- *WomWWA 14*
Collins, Matthew Garrett 1874-1925 *WhAm 1*
Collins, Mauney Douglass 1885-1967 *BiDAmEd,*
  WhAm 4
Collins, Michael 1890-1922 *McGEWB,*
  WhoMilH
Collins, Michael 1930- *WebAMB*
Collins, Michael Francis 1854-1928 *WhAm 1*
Collins, Miriam O'Leary 1864- *AmWom*
Collins, Napoleon 1814-1875 *ApCAB, DcAmB,*
  Drake, NatCAB 4, TwCBDA, WebAMB,
  WhAm H
Collins, Nellie R 1855- *WomWWA 14*
Collins, Oliver Cromwell 1881-1949 *NatCAB 42*
Collins, Patrick Andrew 1844-1905 *ApCAB,*
  BiDrAC, DcAmB, NatCAB 11, TwCBDA,
  WhAm 1, WhAmP
Collins, Paul Fisk 1891-1971 *WhAm 5*
Collins, Paul Valorous 1860-1931 *WhAm 1*
Collins, Philip Sheridan 1864-1943 *WhAm 2*
Collins, Ralph L 1907-1963 *WhAm 4*
Collins, Robert Alexander 1891-1972 *WhAm 6*
Collins, Robert Moore 1867- *WhAm 4*
Collins, Ross Alexander 1880-1968 *BiDrAC,*
  WhAm 5, WhAm 6
Collins, Roy Charles 1903-1971 *WhAm 5*
Collins, Roy Taylor 1888-1954 *NatCAB 45*
Collins, Samuel Joseph 1881-1953 *NatCAB 42*
Collins, Samuel LaFort 1895-1965 *BiDrAC,*
  NatCAB 51
Collins, Stewart G 1880- *WhAm 2*
Collins, Thomas 1732-1789 *ApCAB, BiAUS,*
  Drake, NatCAB 5, TwCBDA
Collins, Thomas Wharton 1812-1879 *ApCAB*
Collins, Truman Wesley 1902-1964 *NatCAB 50,*
  WhAm 4
Collins, Varnum Lansing 1870-1936 *WhAm 1*
Collins, Victor Homer 1888- *WhoColR*
Collins, Virgil Dewey 1898-1954 *WhAm 4*
Collins, Vivian d1955 *WhAm 3*
Collins, W Herschel 1861-1953 *NatCAB 40*

Collins, W P *NewYHSD*
Collins, Walter P *NewYHSD*
Collins, Whitley Charles 1898-1959 *WhAm 3*
Collins, Wilbur M 1892-1973 *WhAm 6*
Collins, William *BiAUS, NewYHSD*
Collins, William 1721-1759 *McGEWB*
Collins, William 1818-1878 *BiAUS, BiDrAC,*
  WhAm H
Collins, William 1891-1952 *WhAm 3*
Collins, William 1893-1965 *WhAm 4*
Collins, William Dennis 1875- *WhAm 6*
Collins, William Henry 1859-1939 *WhAm 3*
Collins, William Steppes 1863-1952 *NatCAB 40*
Collins, William Wilkie 1824-1889 *McGEWB*
Collins, Winifred d1941 *WhAm 2*
Collins, Yvonne Deakins d1974 *WhAm 6*
Collins, Zaccheus 1764-1831 *ApCAB, Drake*
Collinson, Captain *NewYHSD*
Collinson, Peter 1693?-1768 *DcScB*
Collinson, Sir Richard 1811- *ApCAB*
Collinsworth, James 1806- *NatCAB 4*
Collip, James Bertram 1892-1965 *DcScB,*
  WhAm 4
Collipulle d1576 *ApCAB*
Collis, Charles H T 1838-1902 *WhAm 1*
Collis, George S *NewYHSD*
Collisi, Harrison Smith 1888-1972 *NatCAB 56*
Collison, Wilson 1893-1941 *WhAm 1*
Collisson, Norman Harvey 1900-1966
  NatCAB 54
Collisson, Norman Harvey 1902-1966 *WhAm 4*
Collitz, Hermann 1855-1935 *BiDAmEd,*
  WhAm 1
Collitz, Klara Hechtenberg 1863-1944
  BiDAmEd, WhAm 2, WomWWA 14
Collman, Frederick Albertus 1882-1968
  NatCAB 55
Colman, Gideon 1831?- *NewYHSD*
Collom, Eugenie Read 1874- *WomWWA 14*
Collom, Spencer Allen, Jr. 1904-1955
  NatCAB 45
Collopy, Paul Charles 1894-1957 *NatCAB 48*
Collot, A G 1796- *Drake*
Collot, George Henri Victor 1751?-1805
  NewYHSD
Collot, Victor 1751-1805 *ApCAB, Drake*
Collum, John *NewYHSD*
Collyer, Robert 1823-1912 *AmBi, ApCAB,*
  DcAmB, Drake, NatCAB 1, TwCBDA,
  WhAm 1
Colm, Gerhard 1897-1968 *WhAm 5*
Colman, Benjamin 1673-1747 *ApCAB, DcAmB,*
  Drake, NatCAB 7, TwCBDA, WhAm H
Colman, Charles 1818?- *NewYHSD*
Colman, Charles Lane 1826-1901 *ApCAB X*
Colman, Henry 1785-1849 *ApCAB, DcAmB,*
  Drake, NatCAB 22, WhAm H
Colman, James Douglas 1910-1972 *WhAm 5*
Colman, John 1670-1753? *DcAmB, WhAm H*
Colman, Julia 1828-1909 *AmWom, NotAW*
Colman, Lucy Newhall 1817-1906 *AmWom,*
  DcAmB, WhAmP
Colman, Norman Jay 1827-1911 *AmBi,*
  BiDrUSE, DcAmB, EncAAH, TwCBDA,
  WhAm 1
Colman, Ronald 1891-1958 *NatCAB 43,*
  WhAm 3
Colman, Samuel, Jr. 1832-1920 *AmBi, ApCAB,*
  ApCAB X, BnEnAmA, DcAmB, Drake,
  IlBEAAW, NatCAB 7, NewYHSD,
  TwCBDA, WhAm 1
Colman, William 1822?- *NewYHSD*
Colmer, William Meyers 1890- *BiDrAC*
Colmore, Charles Blayney 1879-1950 *WhAm 3*
Colnon, Aaron 1894-1950 *NatCAB 39,*
  WhAm 3
Colocolo 1515?-1561 *ApCAB*
Colomb, Christophe *NewYHSD*
Colombara, C *NewYHSD*
Colombo, Realdo 1510?-1559 *DcScB*
Colon, A *NewYHSD*
Colon, Cristobal 1451-1506 *WebAB*
Colonna, Benjamin Azariah 1843- *TwCBDA*
Colonna, Egidio *DcScB*
Colonna, Paul Crenshaw 1892-1966 *WhAm 4*
Colony, Horatio 1835-1917 *NatCAB 18*
Colpitts, Edwin Henry 1872-1949 *DcAmB S4,*
  WhAm 2

Colpitts, Walter William 1874-1951
NatCAB 41, WhAm 3
Colpitts, Walter William 1875-1951 *ApCAB X*
Colquhoun *NewYHSD*
Colquhoun, Walter Alexander 1898-1962
WhAm 4
Colquitt, Alfred Holt 1824-1894 *AmBi, ApCAB,
BiAUS, BiDConf, BiDrAC, DcAmB,
NatCAB 1, TwCBDA, WhAm H,
WhAmP*
Colquitt, Oscar Branch 1861-1940 *NatCAB 31,
WhAm 1*
Colquitt, Walter Terry 1799-1855 *ApCAB,
BiAUS, BiDrAC, DcAmB, Drake,
NatCAB 7, TwCBDA, WhAm H,
WhAmP*
Colquitt, Walter Terry 1874-1937 *NatCAB 28,
WhAm 1*
Colson, Clyde Lemuel 1902-1965 *WhAm 4*
Colson, David Grant 1861-1904 *BiDrAC,
TwCBDA, WhAm 1*
Colson, Jessie Lippincott 1866- *WomWWA 14*
Colson, Venila Spaulding Burrington
WomWWA 14
Colston, Edward 1786-1851 *TwCBDA*
Colston, Edward 1786-1852 *BiDrAC,
WhAm H*
Colston, Edward 1788-1851 *BiAUS*
Colston, Edward 1844-1928 *ApCAB X,
WhAm 1*
Colston, Lillian Elizabeth 1893- *WhoColR*
Colston, Raleigh Edward 1825-1896
*ApCAB Sup, BiDConf, DcAmB,
NatCAB 12, TwCBDA, WhAm H*
Colston, William Ainslie 1873-1934 *NatCAB 26,
WhAm 1*
Colt, Don Snell 1861-1937 *NatCAB 40*
Colt, Harris Dunscomb 1861-1959 *ApCAB X,
WhAm 3*
Colt, James Denison 1819-1881 *TwCBDA*
Colt, James Denison 1862-1936 *NatCAB 29*
Colt, James Dennison, Jr. 1894-1964
NatCAB 50
Colt, LeBaron Bradford 1846-1924 *ApCAB,
BiDrAC, DcAmB, NatCAB 15,
NatCAB 37, TwCBDA, WhAm 1*
Colt, Mary *NewYHSD*
Colt, Samuel 1814-1862 *AmBi, ApCAB,
DcAmB, Drake, EncAAH, McGEWB,
NatCAB 6, TwCBDA, WebAB,
WebAMB, WhAm H*
Colt, Samuel Pomeroy 1852-1921 *ApCAB X,
NatCAB 15, TwCBDA, WhAm 1*
Colt, Samuel Sloan 1892-1975 *WhAm 6*
Colt, William Edward 1873-1917 *NatCAB 17*
Colter, Fred Tuttle 1879- *WhAm 2*
Colter, John 1774?-1813 *REnAW*
Colter, John 1775?-1813 *DcAmB, WhAm H*
Coltman, Robert 1862- *WhAm 4*
Coltman, William George 1887-1956 *WhAm 4*
Colton, A M F 1823?-1896 *WhAm H*
Colton, A Marguerite *WomWWA 14*
Colton, Arthur Willis 1868-1943 *NatCAB 14,
WhAm 2*
Colton, Calvin 1789-1857 *ApCAB, DcAmB,
Drake, NatCAB 8, TwCBDA, WhAm H,
WhAmP*
Colton, Charles Adams 1852-1926 *NatCAB 24,
WhAm 4*
Colton, Charles Henry 1848-1915 *NatCAB 12,
WhAm 1*
Colton, Don Byron 1876-1952 *BiDrAC,
WhAm 5, WhAmP*
Colton, Elizabeth Avery 1872-1924 *BiDAmEd,
DcAmB, NotAW, WhAm 1,
WomWWA 14*
Colton, Elizabeth Sweetser d1927 *WhAm 3,
WomWWA 14*
Colton, Ethan Theodore 1872- *WhAm 5*
Colton, Ferry Barrows 1903-1954 *WhAm 3*
Colton, Gardner Quincy 1814-1898 *AmBi,
ApCAB, DcAmB, NatCAB 2, TwCBDA,
WhAm H*
Colton, George Henry 1848-1927 *WhAm 1*
Colton, George Hooker 1818-1847 *ApCAB,
Drake*
Colton, George Radcliffe 1865-1916 *DcAmB,
NatCAB 25*

Colton, George Radcliffe 1866-1916 *WhAm 1*
Colton, George Symonds 1845-1920 *NatCAB 19*
Colton, Harold Sellers 1881- *WhAm 6*
Colton, James Hooper 1875- *WhAm 6*
Colton, Julia M *WhAm 5, WomWWA 14*
Colton, Mary Russell Ferrell 1889- *IIBEAAW*
Colton, Sabin Woolworth, Jr. 1847-1925
NatCAB 40
Colton, Walter 1797-1851 *AmBi, ApCAB,
DcAmB, Drake, IIBEAAW, NatCAB 4,
NewYHSD, TwCBDA, WhAm H*
Colton, Winfred Rufus 1879- *WhAm 6*
Coltrane, David Stanton 1893-1968 *NatCAB 55*
Coltrane, Eugene J 1883-1960 *WhAm 4*
Coltrane, John William 1926-1967 *WebAB,
WhAm 4*
Colum, Mary M 1887-1957 *NatCAB 44,
WhAm 3*
Colum, Padraic 1881-1972 *McGEWB,
WhAm 5*
Columba, Saint 521?-597 *McGEWB*
Columban, Saint 543?-615 *McGEWB*
Columbus, Bartholomew 1436?-1514 *Drake*
Columbus, Christopher 1435?-1506 *Drake*
Columbus, Christopher 1436?-1506 *ApCAB,
NatCAB 3*
Columbus, Christopher 1446-1506 *TwCBDA*
Columbus, Christopher 1449?-1506 *WhAm H*
Columbus, Christopher 1451-1506 *AsBiEn,
DcScB, DcScB Sup, EncAB, McGEWB,
WebAB*
Columbus, Diego d1510? *WhAm H*
Columbus, Fernando Colon 1488-1539 *ApCAB,
WhAm H*
Colver, Benton Noble 1880- *WhAm 3*
Colver, Nathaniel 1794-1870 *ApCAB, DcAmB,
Drake, TwCBDA, WhAm H*
Colver, William Byron 1870-1926 *DcAmB,
NatCAB 28, WhAm 1*
Colvilie, Lord Alexander d1779 *Drake*
Colville, Alexander 1710?-1770 *ApCAB*
Colvin, Addison Beecher 1858- *WhAm 3*
Colvin, Allan DeWitt 1883-1950 *WhAm 3*
Colvin, D Leigh 1880-1959 *WhAm 3*
Colvin, Fred Herbert 1867-1965 *NatCAB 52,
WhAm 4*
Colvin, George 1875-1928 *NatCAB 21,
WhAm 1*
Colvin, H Milton 1886-1956 *WhAm 3*
Colvin, James G 1905-1968 *WhAm 5*
Colvin, Mamie White 1883-1955 *WhAm 3*
Colvin, Oliver Dyer 1867- *WhAm 4*
Colvin, Stephen Sheldon 1869-1923 *BiDAmEd,
DcAmB, NatCAB 27, WhAm 1*
Colvin, Verplanck 1847-1920 *ApCAB,
WhAm 1*
Colvin, William Henry 1870-1949 *NatCAB 37*
Colvin, William Henry, Jr. 1897-1972
NatCAB 57, WhAm 5
Colvine, A H *NewYHSD*
Colvocoresses, George Musalas 1816-1872
*ApCAB, DcAmB, Drake, NatCAB 23,
TwCBDA, WhAm H*
Colvocoresses, George Partridge 1847-1932
ApCAB, NatCAB 29, WhAm 1
Colwell, Ernest Cadman 1901-1974 *WhAm 6*
Colwell, Felton 1902-1974 *WhAm 6*
Colwell, James Irving 1881-1958 *NatCAB 46*
Colwell, John Bruner 1873-1959 *NatCAB 49*
Colwell, Nathan Porter 1870-1936 *WhAm 1*
Colwell, Robert Talcott 1903-1967 *WhAm 4*
Colwell, Stephen 1800-1871 *DcAmB, Drake,
TwCBDA, WhAm H*
Colwell, Stephen 1800-1872 *ApCAB,
NatCAB 4*
Colyar, Arthur St. Clair 1818-1907 *ApCAB,
BiDConf*
Colyar, Pauline Shackleford *AmWom*
Colyer, Douglas 1893-1956 *WhAm 3*
Colyer, Joel *NewYHSD*
Colyer, Vincent 1824-1888 *NatCAB 7,
WhAm H*
Colyer, Vincent 1825-1888 *ApCAB, IIBEAAW,
NewYHSD, TwCBDA*
Coman, Charlotte B 1845?- *ApCAB*
Coman, Charlotte Buell 1833-1924 *AmBi,
DcAmB, NatCAB 22, NewYHSD,
WhAm 1, WomWWA 14*

Coman, Edwin Truman 1869- *WhAm 5*
Coman, Henry Benjamin 1858-1912
NatCAB 25, WhAm 1
Coman, James Hilary 1895-1966 *NatCAB 52*
Coman, Katharine 1857-1915 *NotAW,
WhAm 1, WomWWA 14*
Coman, Mary Meriam 1861- *WhAm 4,
WomWWA 14*
Coman, Wilber Edmund d1939 *WhAm 1*
Comar, Jerome Morton 1911-1975 *NatCAB 57,
WhAm 6*
Comas Sola, Jose 1868-1937 *DcScB*
Comba, Richard 1837-1907 *WhAm 1*
Combacker, Leon Clinton 1883-1957
NatCAB 43
Combe, George 1788-1858 *ApCAB, Drake,
NatCAB 6*
Comber, Thomas Edward, Jr. 1892-1972
NatCAB 57
Combes, Abbott Carson, Jr. 1884-1959
NatCAB 44
Combes, Charles-Pierre-Mathieu 1801-1872
DcScB
Combes, Clinton DeRaismes 1886-1953
NatCAB 42
Combes, Raoul 1883-1964 *DcScB*
Combest, Earl Edgar 1899-1973 *WhAm 6*
Combs, Andy Lyndwood 1891-1969 *NatCAB 54*
Combs, Everett Randolph 1876- *WhAm 5*
Combs, Fielding 1896-1962 *NatCAB 50*
Combs, George Hamilton, Jr. 1899- *BiDrAC*
Combs, George W 1877-1958 *WhAm 3*
Combs, Gilbert Raynolds 1863-1934 *WhAm 1*
Combs, James Horton 1880- *WhAm 3*
Combs, James Milton 1889-1961 *NatCAB 50*
Combs, Jesse Martin 1889-1953 *BiDrAC,
WhAm 3*
Combs, Lee 1869-1931 *NatCAB 31*
Combs, Leslie 1793-1881 *DcAmB, WhAm H*
Combs, Leslie 1794-1881 *Drake*
Combs, Leslie 1852-1940 *NatCAB 13,
WhAm 1*
Combs, Morgan Lafayette d1955 *WhAm 3*
Combs, Moses Newell 1753-1834 *DcAmB,
NatCAB 23, WhAm H*
Combs, Pat 1908-1971 *WhAm 6*
Combs, Thomas Selby 1898-1964 *NatCAB 52,
WhAm 4*
Comeaux, C Stewart 1889-1954 *WhAm 3*
Comegys, Benjamin Bartis 1819-1900
NatCAB 15, TwCBDA
Comegys, Cornelius George 1816-1896 *ApCAB,
Drake, NatCAB 16, TwCBDA*
Comegys, Cornelius Parsons 1780-1851 *BiAUS,
NatCAB 11, TwCBDA*
Comegys, George H *NewYHSD*
Comegys, Joseph Parsons 1813-1893 *ApCAB,
BiAUS, BiDrAC, NatCAB 7, TwCBDA,
WhAm H, WhAmP*
Comenius, John Amos 1592-1670 *DcScB,
McGEWB*
Comer, Braxton Bragg 1848-1927 *BiDrAC,
DcAmB, NatCAB 14, WhAm 1, WhAmP*
Comer, Braxton Bragg, Jr. 1888-1954
NatCAB 43
Comer, Cornelia Atwood Pratt *WomWWA 14*
Comer, Donald 1877-1963 *NatCAB 51*
Comer, Edward Trippe 1856-1927 *NatCAB 35,
WhAm 1*
Comer, George Legare 1847- *WhAm 4*
Comer, Harry D 1897-1966 *WhAm 4*
Comer, Hugh Moss 1842-1900 *NatCAB 21*
Comer, Hugh Moss 1892-1962 *WhAm 4*
Comer, James McDonald 1877-1963 *WhAm 4*
Comer, John 1704-1734 *ApCAB*
Comer, Thomas 1790-1862 *ApCAB, Drake*
Comerford, Frank 1879-1929 *WhAm 1*
Comerford, Frank Dowd 1893-1941 *WhAm 2*
Comery, George Edward 1891-1950 *NatCAB 39*
Comey, Arthur Coleman 1886-1954 *WhAm 3*
Comey, Arthur Messinger 1861-1933 *WhAm 1*
Comfort, Anna Manning 1845-1931 *AmWom,
BiCAW, NatCAB 3, WhAm 1,
WomWWA 14*
Comfort, Bessie Marchant *WomWWA 14*
Comfort, Charlotte Walrath 1903-1973
WhAm 5
Comfort, Frank John 1890-1955 *NatCAB 45,*

WhAm 3

Comfort, George Fisk 1833-1910 *ApCAB,*
BiDAmEd, NatCAB 3, TwCBDA,
WhAm 1
Comfort, John Elijah 1837-1901 *NatCAB 18*
Comfort, Lucy Randall 1836-1914 *NatCAB 18*
Comfort, Mandred Whitset 1895-1957 *WhAm 3*
Comfort, Marian Coleman 1884-
WomWWA 14
Comfort, Randall 1871- *NatCAB 17,*
NatCAB 18
Comfort, Samuel 1837- *NatCAB 9*
Comfort, Walter Rockefeller 1858-1928
NatCAB 26, WhAm 4
Comfort, Will Levington 1878-1932 *DcAmB S1,*
NatCAB 16, WhAm 1
Comfort, William Wistar 1874-1955
NatCAB 45, WhAm 3
Comgmacker, August 1825?- *NewYHSD*
Comines, Philippe De 1445?-1511 *McGEWB*
Comingo, Abram 1820-1889 *BiAUS, BiDrAC,*
WhAm H, WhAmP
Comings, Lydia J Newcomb 1850-
WomWWA 14
Comins, Danforth William 1880-1971
NatCAB 57
Comins, Linus Bacon 1817-1892 *BiAUS,*
BiDrAC, WhAm H
Cominsky, Jacob R 1899-1968 *WhAm 5*
Comiskey, Charles Albert 1859-1931
NatCAB 24
Comley, James Madison 1832-1887 *TwCBDA*
Comley, William Henry 1875-1955 *NatCAB 48*
Comly, Ethan *NewYHSD*
Comly, Garrard *ApCAB X*
Comly, James M 1832- *NatCAB 12*
Comly, John 1774-1850 *ApCAB, Drake*
Comly, Rowland 1871-1926 *NatCAB 32*
Comly, Samuel Pancoast 1849-1918 *WhAm 1*
Comly, Thomas 1826?- *NewYHSD*
Commager, Henry S 1825?-1867 *ApCAB*
Commager, Henry Steele 1902- *BiDAmEd,*
WebAB
Commander, Lydia Kingsmill *WomWWA 14*
Commandino, Federico 1509-1575 *DcScB*
Commerson, Philibert 1727-1773 *DcScB*
Common, Andrew Ainslie 1841-1903 *DcScB*
Commons, Frank Watkin 1859-1930
NatCAB 22
Commons, John Rogers 1862- *NatCAB 13,*
TwCBDA
Commons, John Rogers 1862-1944 *WhAm 2*
Commons, John Rogers 1862-1945 *DcAmB S3,*
McGEWB, WebAB
Comonfort, Ygnacio 1812-1863 *ApCAB, Drake*
Comparette, Thomas Louis 1868-1922 *WhAm 1*
Compera, Alexis 1856-1906 *IIBEAAW*
Compere, Ebenezer Lattimore 1880- *WhAm 6*
Compher, Wilber G 1900- *WhAm 4*
Compostela, Diego Evelino De 1658-1704
ApCAB
Compton, Alfred Donaldson 1876-1949
WhAm 2
Compton, Alfred George 1835-1913 *WhAm 1*
Compton, Arthur Holly 1892-1962 *AsBiEn,*
BiDAmEd, DcScB, EncAB, McGEWB,
WebAB, WhAm HA, WhAm 4
Compton, Barnes 1830-1898 *BiDrAC,*
NatCAB 10, TwCBDA
Compton, C H Ranulf 1878- *BiDrAC*
Compton, Charles Elmer 1836-1909 *WhAm 1*
Compton, Charles Herrick 1880-1966 *DcAmLiB*
Compton, Charles Volantus 1873-1960
NatCAB 45
Compton, Elias 1856-1938 *NatCAB 41,*
WhAm 1
Compton, George Brokaw 1883-1938 *WhAm 1*
Compton, Irene Lathrop Smith *WomWWA 14*
Compton, James H *NewYHSD*
Compton, Karl Taylor 1887-1954 *BiDAmEd,*
DcAmB S5, DcScB, NatCAB 42,
WhAm 3
Compton, Lewis 1892-1942 *WhAm 2*
Compton, Loulie d1912 *WhAm 1*
Compton, Ranulf 1881-1974 *WhAm 6*
Compton, Richard J 1891-1951 *NewYHSD,*
WhAm 3
Compton, Walter 1912-1959 *WhAm 3*

Compton, William Alfred 1897-1970
NatCAB 55
Compton, William Randall 1899-1965
NatCAB 54
Compton, William Randall 1902-1974 *WhAm 6*
Compton, William Randolph 1866-1957
WhAm 3
Compton, Wilson Martindale 1890-1967
NatCAB 54, WhAm 4
Compton-Burnett, Ivy d1968 *WhAm 5*
Comri 1815?- *NewYHSD*
Comrie, Leslie John 1893-1950 *DcScB*
Comstock, A Barr 1886-1956 *WhAm 3*
Comstock, Ada Louise 1876-1973 *BiDAmEd,*
WhAm 6, WomWWA 14
Comstock, Adam d1819 *Drake*
Comstock, Addison J 1802-1867 *NatCAB 1*
Comstock, Albert H 1847-1926 *WhAm 1*
Comstock, Alzada 1888-1960 *WhAm 3*
Comstock, Andrew 1795- *ApCAB, Drake*
Comstock, Anna Botsford 1854-1930 *AmBi,*
BiDAmEd, NatCAB 11, NatCAB 22,
NotAW, TwCBDA, WhAm 1,
WomWWA 14
Comstock, Anthony 1844-1915 *AmBi, DcAmB,*
McGEWB, NatCAB 15, TwCBDA,
WebAB, WhAm 1
Comstock, Charles Carter 1818-1900 *BiDrAC,*
NatCAB 11
Comstock, Charles Whipple 1858-1917
NatCAB 17
Comstock, Clara Elizabeth 1866-
WomWWA 14
Comstock, Clarence Elmer 1866-1948 *WhAm 2*
Comstock, Cyrus Ballou 1831-1910 *ApCAB,*
NatCAB 22, TwCBDA, WhAm 1
Comstock, Daniel Frost 1883-1970 *ApCAB X,*
NatCAB 55, WhAm 5
Comstock, Daniel Webster 1840-1917 *BiDrAC*
Comstock, Elizabeth 1875- *WomWWA 14*
Comstock, Elizabeth Leslie Rous 1815-1891
DcAmB, NatCAB 22, NotAW, WhAm H,
WhAmP
Comstock, Elting Houghtaling 1876- *WhAm 5*
Comstock, Enos Benjamin 1879-1945 *IIBEAAW*
Comstock, F Ray 1880-1949 *WhAm 2*
Comstock, Frank Mason 1855-1929 *NatCAB 26,*
WhAm 1
Comstock, George Cary 1855-1934 *BiDAmEd,*
DcAmB S1, DcScB, NatCAB 12,
TwCBDA, WhAm 1
Comstock, George F 1811-1892 *BiAUS*
Comstock, George Francis 1811-1892 *TwCBDA*
Comstock, George Franklin 1811-1892 *DcAmB,*
NatCAB 13, WhAm H
Comstock, Gregory Jamieson 1893-1967
NatCAB 54
Comstock, Harriet Theresa *WhAm 5,*
WomWWA 14
Comstock, Henry Tompkins Paige 1820-1870
AmBi, DcAmB, McGEWB, WhAm H
Comstock, Hilliard 1891-1967 *NatCAB 54*
Comstock, John C *NewYHSD*
Comstock, John Henry 1849-1931 *AmBi,*
ApCAB, BiDAmEd, DcAmB S1,
NatCAB 4, NatCAB 22, TwCBDA,
WhAm 1
Comstock, John Lee 1787-1858 *BiDAmEd*
Comstock, John Lee 1789-1858 *AmBi, ApCAB,*
Drake, TwCBDA
Comstock, Louis Kossuth 1865-1964
NatCAB 14, WhAm 4
Comstock, Milton Lemmon 1824- *TwCBDA*
Comstock, Oliver Cromwell 1780-1860 *BiAUS,*
BiDrAC, TwCBDA, WhAm H
Comstock, Ralph J 1894-1962 *WhAm 4*
Comstock, Richard Borden 1854-1923
NatCAB 35
Comstock, Richard Williams 1834- *NatCAB 3*
Comstock, Samuel S *NewYHSD*
Comstock, Sarah d1960 *WhAm 3,*
WomWWA 14
Comstock, Solomon Gilman 1842-1933 *BiDrAC,*
TwCBDA, WhAm 1
Comstock, Theodore Bryant 1849-1915 *ApCAB,*
NatCAB 13, TwCBDA, WhAm 1
Comstock, Thomas Griswold 1829- *NatCAB 7*
Comstock, Willard Lee 1861-1927 *NatCAB 21*

Comstock, William Alfred 1877-1949
NatCAB 38, WhAm 2
Comte, Auguste 1798-1857 *McGEWB*
Comte, Isidore Auguste M Francois Xavier
1798-1857 *DcScB*
Comtois, Paul 1895-1966 *WhAm 4*
Conable, Barber Benjamin, Jr. 1922- *BiDrAC*
Conable, Florence Easton 1858- *WomWWA 14*
Conable, George Willard 1866- *NatCAB 16*
Conaghan, Brian Francis 1927-1973 *WhAm 6*
Conant, A *NewYHSD*
Conant, Alban Jasper 1821-1915 *AmBi,*
ApCAB, DcAmB, NewYHSD, WhAm 1
Conant, Carlos Everett 1870-1925 *WhAm 1*
Conant, Charles Arthur 1861-1915 *DcAmB,*
NatCAB 14, WhAm 1
Conant, Charles F 1835- *BiAUS*
Conant, Charles Perkins 1852-1930 *NatCAB 34*
Conant, Charlotte Howard 1862-1925 *WhAm 1,*
WomWWA 14
Conant, David Sloan 1866-1943 *NatCAB 39*
Conant, Edith M *WomWWA 14*
Conant, Edward 1829- *TwCBDA*
Conant, Edwin A *NewYHSD*
Conant, Eleanore Glasgow 1887-
WomWWA 14
Conant, Ernest Bancroft 1870- *WhAm 5*
Conant, Frances Augusta 1842- *AmWom*
Conant, Frederick Odell 1857-1928 *WhAm 1*
Conant, Gordon Daniel 1885-1953 *WhAm 4*
Conant, Grace Patten 1873- *WomWWA 14*
Conant, Grace Wilbur *WomWWA 14*
Conant, H Nelson 1894-1964 *NatCAB 49*
Conant, Hannah O'Brien Chaplin 1809-1865
ApCAB, DcAmB, NatCAB 22, NotAW,
TwCBDA, WhAm H
Conant, Hannah O'Brien Chaplin 1812-1865
Drake
Conant, Harold Wright 1888-1965 *WhAm 4*
Conant, Harriet Beecher 1852- *AmWom*
Conant, Harry Armitage 1844- *NatCAB 18*
Conant, Helen Charlotte Peters Stevens
1839-1899 *ApCAB, TwCBDA, WhAm 1*
Conant, Henry Dunning 1863- *WhAm 4*
Conant, Hezekiah 1827-1902 *DcAmB,*
NatCAB 22, WhAm H
Conant, Isabella Fiske *WomWWA 14*
Conant, James Bryant 1893- *BiDAmEd,*
EncAB, McGEWB, WebAB
Conant, John d1856 *ApCAB*
Conant, John Willis 1866- *WhAm 4*
Conant, Levi Leonard 1857-1916 *WhAm 1*
Conant, Maria *NewYHSD*
Conant, Mary Ellen Jones 1867- *WomWWA 14*
Conant, Roger 1591-1679 *NatCAB 11*
Conant, Roger 1592?-1679 *AmBi, DcAmB,*
WhAm H
Conant, Roger 1593-1679 *ApCAB, Drake*
Conant, Samuel Dozier 1897-1963 *NatCAB 52*
Conant, Samuel Stillman 1831- *ApCAB,*
TwCBDA
Conant, Thomas Jefferson 1802-1891 *AmBi,*
ApCAB, DcAmB, Drake, NatCAB 12,
TwCBDA, WhAm H
Conant, Thomas Oakes 1838-1913 *WhAm 1*
Conant, William Merritt 1856- *TwCBDA*
Conard, Frederick Underwood 1891-1954
WhAm 3
Conard, Henry Shoemaker 1874- *WhAm 5*
Conard, John 1773-1857 *BiDrAC, WhAm H,*
WhAmP
Conard, Laetitia Moon 1871- *WomWWA 14*
Conarro, Harry Wiborg 1890-1967 *WhAm 4A*
Conarroe, George W 1803-1882 *NewYHSD,*
WhAm H
Conaty, Thomas James 1847-1915 *ApCAB Sup,*
BiDAmEd, DcAmB, NatCAB 12,
TwCBDA, WhAm 1
Conaway, Asbury Bateman 1837-1897
NatCAB 17
Conaway, Charles Herman 1885-1958 *WhAm 3*
Conaway, Paul Brewer 1913-1971 *WhAm 6*
Conboy, Martin 1878-1944 *DcAmB S3,*
NatCAB 33, WhAm 2
Conboy, Philip 1868-1929 *NatCAB 22*
Conboy, Sara Agnes McLaughlin 1870-1928
DcAmB, WhAm 1, WhAmP
Concanen, Luke d1810 *ApCAB, Drake*

Concannen, Luke d1810 *NatCAB 1*
Concannen, Richard Luke 1740?-1810 *TwCBDA*
Concannon, Charles Cuthbert 1889-1957 *WhAm 3*
Concannon, Thomas 1841?- *NewYHSD*
Concha, Jose, Marquis DeLaHabana 1800- *Drake*
Concha, Jose Gutierrez DeLa 1809- *ApCAB*
Concha Toro, Melchor 1823- *ApCAB*
Concheso, Aurelio Fernandez d1955 *WhAm 3*
Concilio, Gennaro Luigi Vincenzo De 1835- *ApCAB*
Concklin, Jeremiah *NewYHSD*
Condamine, Charles Marie DeLa 1701-1774 *ApCAB, Drake*
Conde, Bertha *WhAm 5, WomWWA 14*
Conde, Daniel Toll 1807-1897 *TwCBDA*
Conde, Louis DeBourbon, II, Prince De 1621-1686 *McGEWB, WhoMilH*
Conde, Swits 1844- *NatCAB 5*
Condee, Robert Asa 1875-1930 *WhAm 1*
Condell, Aquila Hill 1849-1924 *NatCAB 22*
Condict *see also* Condit
Condict, George Herbert 1862-1934 *WhAm 1*
Condict, Ira 1764-1810 *NatCAB 3*
Condict, Ira 1764-1811 *ApCAB*
Condict, John 1755-1834 *ApCAB, BiAUS, Drake*
Condict, Lewis 1772-1862 *BiDrAC, WhAm H, WhAmP*
Condict, Lewis 1773-1862 *ApCAB, BiAUS, Drake*
Condict, Philip King 1880-1949 *NatCAB 44*
Condict, Silas 1738-1801 *BiAUS, BiDrAC, WhAm H*
Condict, Silas 1777-1861 *ApCAB, BiAUS, Drake*
Condie, David Francis 1796-1875 *ApCAB, Drake*
Condillac, Etienne Bonnot, Abbe De 1714-1780 *DcScB*
Condillac, Etienne Bonnot De 1715-1780 *McGEWB*
Condit *see also* Condict
Condit, Allen 1868-1935 *NatCAB 38*
Condit, Blackford 1829-1903 *NatCAB 38, WhAm 1*
Condit, Ira 1764-1811 *TwCBDA*
Condit, John 1755-1834 *BiDrAC, DcAmB, NatCAB 11, TwCBDA, WhAm H, WhAmP*
Condit, Jonathan Bailey 1808-1876 *TwCBDA*
Condit, Kenneth Hamilton 1888-1974 *WhAm 6*
Condit, L Irving 1885-1940 *NatCAB 30*
Condit, Lewis 1773-1862 *TwCBDA*
Condit, Silas 1778-1861 *BiDrAC, TwCBDA, WhAm H*
Condo, Gus S 1874-1957 *WhAm 3*
Condon, Eddie 1905-1973 *WhAm 6*
Condon, Edward J 1900-1965 *WhAm 4*
Condon, Edward Uhler 1902-1974 *WebAB, WhAm 6*
Condon, Francis Bernard 1891-1965 *BiDrAC, WhAm 4*
Condon, George Meflin Dallas 1859-1933 *NatCAB 29*
Condon, Herbert Thomas 1870-1952 *WhAm 3*
Condon, James *NewYHSD*
Condon, John Thomas 1865-1926 *WhAm 1*
Condon, Randall Judson 1862-1931 *NatCAB 23, WhAm 1*
Condon, Richard William 1867- *WhAm 4*
Condon, Robert Likens 1912- *BiDrAC*
Condon, Thomas 1822-1907 *DcAmB, NatCAB 13*
Condon, Thomas Gerald 1864- *WhAm 4*
Condon, William *NewYHSD*
Condorcanqui, Jose Gabriel *ApCAB*
Condorcanqui, Joseph Gabriel *Drake*
Condorcet, Marie J A Caritat, Marquis De 1743-1794 *DcScB, McGEWB*
Condra, George Evert 1869-1958 *NatCAB 47, WhAm 6*
Condron, Theodore Lincoln 1866- *WhAm 5*
Condy, Jonathan W *BiAUS*
Cone, Bernard Milton 1874-1956 *NatCAB 43*
Cone, Burtis Octavius 1892-1966 *WhAm 4*
Cone, Ceasar 1859-1917 *NatCAB 50*

Cone, Claribel 1864-1929 *DcAmB S4, NotAW*
Cone, Etta 1870-1949 *DcAmB S4*
Cone, Frank Lyman 1868-1936 *NatCAB 48*
Cone, Frederick Hayes 1873-1942 *NatCAB 32*
Cone, Frederick Preston 1871-1948 *NatCAB 38, WhAm 3*
Cone, George M *NewYHSD*
Cone, Helen Gray 1859-1934 *AmWom, WhAm 2, WomWWA 14*
Cone, Herman 1895-1955 *NatCAB 49, WhAm 3*
Cone, Hutchinson Ingham 1871-1941 *DcAmB S3, NatCAB 35, WhAm 1*
Cone, Joseph *NewYHSD*
Cone, Kate Morris 1857- *WomWWA 14*
Cone, Martin 1882-1963 *WhAm 4*
Cone, Marvin Dorwart 1891-1965 *NatCAB 52, WhAm 4*
Cone, Morris Huntington 1890-1949 *NatCAB 38*
Cone, Moses Herman 1857-1908 *DcAmB*
Cone, Orello 1835-1905 *DcAmB, NatCAB 10, TwCBDA, WhAm 1*
Cone, Russell Glenn 1896-1961 *NatCAB 51, WhAm 4*
Cone, Spencer Houghton 1785-1855 *ApCAB, DcAmB, Drake, NatCAB 12, NatCAB 22, TwCBDA, WhAm H*
Cone, Spencer Wallace 1819-1888 *ApCAB Sup*
Conely, William B 1830-1911 *NewYHSD*
Coney, Aims Chamberlain 1888-1965 *WhAm 4*
Coney, Donald 1901-1973 *DcAmLiB*
Coney, Harriot R 1870- *WomWWA 14*
Coney, Jabez 1804-1872 *DcAmB, NatCAB 23, WhAm H*
Coney, Jabez 1805-1872 *ApCAB*
Coney, John 1655-1722 *DcAmB, NewYHSD, WhAm H*
Coney, John 1656-1722 *BnEnAmA*
Coney, William DeVoe 1893-1921 *NatCAB 6*
Confrey, Edward Elzear 1895-1971 *WhAm 5*
Confucius 551BC-479BC *McGEWB*
Congar, Samuel Hayes 1796-1872 *ApCAB*
Congdon, Anne W *WomWWA 14*
Congdon, Charles Everett 1872-1944 *NatCAB 35*
Congdon, Charles Harris 1856-1928 *WhAm 1*
Congdon, Charles Howard 1870-1933 *NatCAB 26, WhAm 1*
Congdon, Charles Taber 1821-1891 *ApCAB, DcAmB, NatCAB 3, TwCBDA, WhAm H*
Congdon, Chester Adgate 1853-1916 *NatCAB 17, WhAm 1*
Congdon, Clement Hillman 1868- *WhAm 4*
Congdon, Edward Chester 1885-1940 *WhAm 1*
Congdon, Ernest Arnold 1866- *WhAm 4*
Congdon, Gilbert Maurice 1887-1961 *WhAm 4*
Congdon, Harriet Rice 1876- *WhAm 5*
Congdon, Joseph William 1844-1914 *WhAm 1*
Congdon, Laura D 1850- *WomWWA 14*
Congdon, Samuel B *NewYHSD*
Congdon, Thomas Richardson 1859- *NatCAB 11*
Conger, Abraham Benjamin 1887-1953 *WhAm 3*
Conger, Albert C 1920-1968 *WhAm 5*
Conger, Arthur L 1838-1899 *NatCAB 2*
Conger, Beach, III 1912-1969 *NatCAB 54, WhAm 5*
Conger, Charlotte Metcalf 1860- *WomWWA 14*
Conger, Edward A d1963 *WhAm 4*
Conger, Edwin Henry 1843- *ApCAB Sup*
Conger, Edwin Hurd 1843-1907 *BiDrAC, DcAmB, NatCAB 8, TwCBDA, WhAm 1, WhAmP*
Conger, Emily Bronson 1843- *WomWWA 14*
Conger, Everett Lorentus 1839-1914 *WhAm 1*
Conger, Frank 1849-1902 *NatCAB 11*
Conger, George Perrigo 1884-1960 *WhAm 4*
Conger, Harmon Sweatland 1816-1882 *BiAUS, BiDrAC, WhAm H*
Conger, James Lockwood 1805-1876 *BiAUS, BiDrAC, WhAm H*
Conger, John Leonard 1876- *WhAm 5*
Conger, John William 1857-1924 *TwCBDA, WhAm 1, WhAm 4*

Conger, Omar Dwight 1818-1898 *ApCAB, BiAUS, BiDrAC, NatCAB 12, TwCBDA, WhAmP*
Conger, Robert Alan 1911-1963 *WhAm 4*
Conger, Sarah Pike 1842- *WomWWA 14*
Conger, Seymour Beach 1876-1934 *WhAm 1*
Congleton, Jerome Taylor 1876-1936 *WhAm 1*
Congreve, William 1670-1729 *McGEWB*
Congreve, William 1772-1828 *DcScB*
Conick, Edward Gearing 1879- *WhoColR*
Conick, Harold C d1962 *WhAm 4*
Coningham, Sir Arthur 1895-1948 *WhWW-II, WhoMilH*
Conkey, Elizabeth A d1964 *WhAm 4*
Conkey, Henry Phillips 1885-1953 *WhAm 3*
Conkey, Samuel 1830-1904 *NewYHSD*
Conklin, Abram 1858- *WhAm 4*
Conklin, Arthur Stewart 1872-1960 *WhAm 4*
Conklin, Charles 1855-1930 *WhAm 1, WhAm 1C*
Conklin, Clifford Tremaine 1890-1956 *WhAm 3*
Conklin, Coursen Baxter 1884-1952 *NatCAB 40*
Conklin, Edmund Smith 1884-1942 *WhAm 2*
Conklin, Edwin Grant 1863-1952 *DcAmB S5, DcScB, NatCAB 12, TwCBDA, WhAm 3*
Conklin, Franklin 1869-1943 *NatCAB 31*
Conklin, Franklin, Jr. 1886-1966 *NatCAB 53, WhAm 4*
Conklin, G P 1830?- *NewYHSD*
Conklin, Horace Frederic 1904-1964 *NatCAB 51*
Conklin, Jane Elizabeth Dexter 1831- *AmWom*
Conklin, Jennie Maria Drinkwater 1841-1900 *DcAmB, WhAm 1*
Conklin, John F 1891-1973 *WhAm 5*
Conklin, John Woodruff 1851- *TwCBDA*
Conklin, Lena D Wells 1858- *WomWWA 14*
Conklin, Roland Ray 1858-1938 *NatCAB 15, WhAm 1*
Conklin, Viola A 1849- *WhAm 4*
Conklin, Viola Percy *WomWWA 14*
Conklin, William Augustus 1837-1913 *ApCAB, NatCAB 2, TwCBDA, WhAm 1*
Conklin, William Henry 1903-1951 *NatCAB 38*
Conklin, William Judkins 1844-1916 *ApCAB, WhAm 1*
Conkling, Alfred 1789-1874 *ApCAB, BiAUS, BiDrAC, DcAmB, Drake, NatCAB 11, TwCBDA, WhAm H, WhAmP*
Conkling, Alfred Ronald 1850- *ApCAB, TwCBDA, WhAm 4*
Conkling, Donald Herbert 1879- *WhAm 6*
Conkling, Frederick Augustus 1816-1891 *ApCAB, BiAUS, BiDrAC, TwCBDA, WhAm H, WhAmP*
Conkling, Grace Walcott Hazard 1878-1958 *WhAm 3, WomWWA 14, WomWWA 14a*
Conkling, Howard 1855- *TwCBDA*
Conkling, Mabel Viola Harris 1871-1966 *NatCAB 53, WomWWA 14*
Conkling, Margaret Cockburn 1814-1890 *ApCAB, TwCBDA*
Conkling, Mark LeRoy 1884-1960 *WhAm 4*
Conkling, Paul 1871-1926 *NatCAB 20*
Conkling, Roscoe 1828-1888 *BiAUS, Drake*
Conkling, Roscoe 1829-1888 *AmBi, ApCAB, BiDrAC, DcAmB, EncAB, McGEWB, NatCAB 3, TwCBDA, WebAB, WhAm H, WhAmP*
Conkling, Roscoe Powers 1889-1954 *WhAm 3*
Conland, Henry Holton 1882-1944 *NatCAB 34, WhAm 2*
Conlen, William J 1878-1956 *WhAm 3*
Conley, Alonzo Theodore 1847- *WhAm 4*
Conley, Benjamin 1815-1885 *NatCAB 1*
Conley, Benjamin 1815-1886 *TwCBDA*
Conley, Carey Herbert 1879- *WhAm 6*
Conley, Clyde d1969 *WhAm 5*
Conley, Clyde G 1879- *WhAm 6*
Conley, David VanBeuren 1875-1961 *NatCAB 53*
Conley, Dudley Steele 1878-1955 *NatCAB 47, WhAm 6*
Conley, Edgar Thomas 1874-1956 *WhAm 3*
Conley, Elmo Hansford 1896-1957 *WhAm 3*
Conley, George J 1872-1950 *WhAm 3*
Conley, John Dikeman 1843- *ApCAB*
Conley, John Dykeman 1843- *TwCBDA*

Conley, John Wesley 1852- *NatCAB 6,
WhAm 1*
Conley, John White 1836-1916 *NatCAB 17*
Conley, William Gustavus 1866-1940 *WhAm 1*
Conley, William H 1907-1974 *WhAm 6*
Conley, William Henry 1840-1897 *NatCAB 14*
Conley, William Maxwell 1866-1954 *WhAm 3*
Conlin, Bernard 1831-1891 *AmBi*
Conlin, Earl Edgar 1906-1974 *WhAm 6*
Conlin, John S *NewYHSD*
Conlon, John Francis 1861-1951 *NatCAB 41*
Conlon, John Francis 1908-1969 *NatCAB 55*
Conlon, Robert Joseph 1893-1948 *NatCAB 36*
Conlon, Mrs. William F 1901-1973 *WhAm 6*
Conn, Charles Fuller 1865-1945 *NatCAB 33*
Conn, Charles Gerard 1844-1931 *BiDrAC,
WhAmP*
Conn, Donald Deans 1894-1954 *WhAm 3*
Conn, George Chester 1867- *WhAm 4*
Conn, Granville Priest 1832-1916 *NatCAB 33,
WhAm 1*
Conn, Harry L 1869-1939 *WhAm 1*
Conn, Herbert William 1859-1917 *NatCAB 20,
TwCBDA, WhAm 1*
Conn, James *NewYHSD*
Conn, Ulysses Sylvester 1865-1936 *WhAm 1*
Connable, Alfred Barnes 1871-1951 *NatCAB 39*
Connah, Douglas John 1871-1941 *WhAm 1*
Connally, Ben C 1909-1975 *WhAm 6*
Connally, Elijah L 1837- *WhAm 4*
Connally, John Bowden 1917- *BiDrUSE*
Connally, Thomas Terry 1877-1963 *BiDrAC,
WhAmP*
Connally, Tom 1877-1963 *WhAm 4*
Connaroe *NewYHSD*
Connaway, Jay Hall 1893-1970 *NatCAB 55*
Conne, Philip A *ApCAB X*
Connell, Albert James 1882-1941 *WhAm 2*
Connell, Arthur J 1898-1962 *WhAm 4*
Connell, Carl W 1890-1946 *WhAm 2*
Connell, Charles Robert 1864-1922 *BiDrAC,
NatCAB 42, WhAm 1*
Connell, F Gregory 1875-1968 *NatCAB 54*
Connell, Francis J 1888-1967 *WhAm 4*
Connell, George Boyce 1905-1959 *WhAm 3*
Connell, Herbert John 1891-1945 *NatCAB 35*
Connell, Horatio 1876-1936 *WhAm 1*
Connell, James Mark 1863- *WhAm 4*
Connell, James Peter 1862-1916 *NatCAB 19*
Connell, Karl 1878-1941 *NatCAB 31,
WhAm 1*
Connell, Kenneth Hugh 1917-1973 *WhAm 6*
Connell, Richard 1893-1949 *NatCAB 36,
WhAm 2*
Connell, Richard Edward 1857-1912 *BiDrAC,
WhAm 1*
Connell, Wilfrid Thomas 1896-1963 *WhAm 4*
Connell, William 1827-1909 *BiDrAC,
NatCAB 8, TwCBDA, WhAm 1*
Connell, William Henry 1878-1943 *WhAm 2*
Connell, William James 1846-1924 *BiDrAC,
NatCAB 36, TwCBDA*
Connell, William John 1860-1934 *NatCAB 25*
Connell, William Lawrence 1862-1923
NatCAB 6, NatCAB 44, WhAm 1
Connell, William Phillips 1874-1932 *WhAm 1*
Connell, Wilson Edward 1858-1936 *WhAm 1*
Connelley, Clifford Brown 1866- *WhAm 1*
Connelley, Earl John 1892-1957 *WhAm 3*
Connelley, William Elsey 1855-1930 *WhAm 1*
Connelly, Augusta 1809-1879 *NatCAB 23*
Connelly, Celia Logan 1837-1904 *WhAm 4*
Connelly, Celia Logan 1840-1904 *AmWom*
Connelly, Celia Logan Kellogg d1904 *NotAW*
Connelly, Cornelia Augusta 1809-1879 *DcAmB,
NotAW, WebAB, WhAm H*
Connelly, Edward Michael 1892-1947 *WhAm 2*
Connelly, Emma Mary *AmWom, WhAm 5,
WomWWA 14*
Connelly, Henry 1800-1866 *AmBi, BiAUS,
DcAmB, NatCAB 23, WhAm H*
Connelly, James H 1840-1903 *WhAm 1*
Connelly, John 1750-1825 *ApCAB*
Connelly, John Patrick 1875-1948 *NatCAB 36*
Connelly, John Robert 1870-1940 *BiDrAC,
WhAm 5*
Connelly, Marc 1890- *WebAB*
Connelly, Pierce Francis 1840?- *ApCAB*

Connelly, Pierce Francis 1841- *DcAmB,
NatCAB 23*
Connelly, Pierce Francis 1841-1900 *WhAm H*
Connelly, Pierce Francis 1841-1902? *BnEnAmA*
Connelly, William 1839?- *NewYHSD*
Connelly, William Clement 1875-1964
NatCAB 53
Connelly, William Lawrence 1873-1964
NatCAB 51
Connely, Bertha Lillian 1863- *WomWWA 14*
Connely, Emmett Francis 1891-1960 *WhAm 3*
Connely, Pierce Francis *NewYHSD*
Connely, Willard 1888-1967 *WhAm 4*
Conner, Albert Holmes 1879- *WhAm 6*
Conner, Benjamin Coulbourn 1850-1921
WhAm 1
Conner, Benjamin Howe 1878- *WhAm 6*
Conner, Bruce 1933- *BnEnAmA, WhAm 5*
Conner, Charlotte Mary Sanford Barnes
1818-1863 *DcAmB*
Conner, David 1791-1856 *NatCAB 10*
Conner, David 1792-1856 *AmBi, ApCAB,
DcAmB, Drake, TwCBDA, WebAMB,
WhAm H*
Conner, Dennis M *NewYHSD*
Conner, Eli Taylor 1864-1938 *NatCAB 32,
WhAm 1*
Conner, Eliza Archard *AmWom*
Conner, Elizabeth Marney 1856- *AmWom*
Conner, Fox 1874- *WhAm 5*
Conner, Henry W 1793-1866 *ApCAB,
TwCBDA*
Conner, James 1798-1861 *ApCAB, NatCAB 5,
TwCBDA*
Conner, James 1829-1883 *ApCAB, BiDConf,
DcAmB, NatCAB 19, TwCBDA,
WhAm H*
Conner, James Keyes 1871-1925 *WhAm 1*
Conner, James L *NewYHSD*
Conner, James M 1865- *WhoColR*
Conner, James Moyer 1863- *WhAm 4*
Conner, James Perry 1851-1924 *BiDrAC,
WhAm 4*
Conner, John Coggswell 1842-1873 *BiAUS,
BiDrAC, WhAm H*
Conner, Lewis Atterbury 1867-1950 *ApCAB X,
WhAm 3*
Conner, Martin Sennett 1891-1950 *WhAm 3*
Conner, Patrick E 1820- *Drake Sup*
Conner, Phineas Sanborn 1839-1909
NatCAB 12, WhAm 1
Conner, Richard *NewYHSD*
Conner, Robert *NewYHSD*
Conner, Samuel Shepard 1783?-1820 *ApCAB,
BiAUS, BiDrAC, Drake, TwCBDA,
WhAm H*
Conner, Walter Thomas 1877- *WhAm 5*
Conners, William James 1857-1929 *ApCAB X,
NatCAB 21, WhAm 1*
Conners, William James, Jr. 1895-1951
NatCAB 45, WhAm 3
Connery, Alder Foster 1898-1971 *NatCAB 56*
Connery, Lawrence Joseph 1895-1941 *BiDrAC,
NatCAB 31, WhAm 1, WhAmP*
Connery, Thomas Bernard Joseph 1835-
NatCAB 3, WhAm 4
Connery, William Patrick, Jr. 1888-1937
BiDrAC, WhAm 1, WhAmP
Conness, John 1821-1909 *ApCAB, BiAUS,
BiDrAC, NatCAB 11, TwCBDA,
WhAm 1*
Conness, Leland Stanford 1880-1942 *WhAm 2*
Connet, Frederick Nevius 1867-1935
NatCAB 35
Connett, Albert Neumann 1859-1933
NatCAB 23
Connett, Eugene Virginius, III 1891-1969
NatCAB 54
Connett, Harold 1895-1972 *NatCAB 57*
Conney, John 1655-1722 *DcAmB*
Connick, Arthur Elwell 1882-1960 *WhAm 4*
Connick, Charles Jay 1875-1945 *DcAmB S3,
NatCAB 34, WhAm 4*
Connick, Harris DeHaven 1873-1965 *WhAm 4*
Conniff, Frank 1914-1971 *WhAm 5*
Conniff, Paul R 1871- *WhAm 5*
Conning, John Stuart 1862-1946 *WhAm 2*
Connole, Joseph Vincent 1889-1950 *NatCAB 40*

Connolley, Fred Davis 1877-1950 *NatCAB 39*
Connolly, Brendan 1913-1974 *WhAm 6*
Connolly, Christopher Powell 1863-1933
WhAm 1
Connolly, Daniel Ward 1847-1894 *BiDrAC,
TwCBDA, WhAm H*
Connolly, David Ward 1847- *NatCAB 5*
Connolly, Francis X 1909-1965 *WhAm 4*
Connolly, James Austin 1843-1914 *BiDrAC,
TwCBDA, WhAm 1*
Connolly, James Greenan 1886-1952
NatCAB 42
Connolly, James Joseph 1881-1952 *BiDrAC,
WhAm 3, WhAmP*
Connolly, John *Drake*
Connolly, John 1743-1813 *DcAmB S1,
WhAm H*
Connolly, John 1750-1825 *ApCAB, DcAmB,
Drake, NatCAB 1, TwCBDA, WhAm H*
Connolly, Joseph Peter 1890-1947 *WhAm 2*
Connolly, Joseph Vincent 1895-1945
NatCAB 36, WhAm 2
Connolly, Louise 1862- *WhAm 4,
WomWWA 14*
Connolly, Maureen Catherine 1934-1969
WebAB
Connolly, Maurice 1877-1921 *BiDrAC,
WhAm 1*
Connolly, Michael William 1853- *WhAm 1*
Connolly, Mike 1915-1966 *WhAm 4*
Connolly, Robert Emmet 1884-1950 *WhAm 3*
Connolly, Susan Cornelia 1885- *WomWWA 14*
Connolly, Terence Leo 1888-1961 *WhAm 4*
Connoly, Theodore 1846- *WhAm 4*
Connor, Aloysius J 1895-1967 *WhAm 4A*
Connor, Charles Ashley Richard 1905-1974
WhAm 6
Connor, Charles Francis 1881- *WhAm 6*
Connor, Charlotte Mary Sanford Barnes 1863-
ApCAB
Connor, Edmund Sheppard 1809- *ApCAB*
Connor, Edward 1908-1967 *WhAm 5*
Connor, Edward T 1869- *WhoColR*
Connor, Garland Daniel 1901-1963 *NatCAB 52*
Connor, George L 1846-1921 *WhAm 1*
Connor, George Whitfield 1872-1938 *WhAm 1*
Connor, Guy Leartus 1874-1943 *WhAm 2*
Connor, Hamilton Clark 1910-1964 *NatCAB 51*
Connor, Henry Groves 1852-1924 *DcAmB,
NatCAB 21, WhAm 1*
Connor, Henry William 1793-1866 *BiAUS,
BiDrAC, Drake, WhAm H, WhAmP*
Connor, Jacob Elon 1862- *WhAm 4*
Connor, John Thomas 1914- *BiDrUSE*
Connor, Laertus 1843-1911 *TwCBDA*
Connor, Leartus 1843-1911 *NatCAB 12,
WhAm 1*
Connor, Louis George 1883- *WhAm 3*
Connor, Margaret 1890- *WomWWA 14*
Connor, Miles Washington 1886- *WhoColR*
Connor, Patrick Edward 1820-1891 *AmBi,
ApCAB, DcAmB, NatCAB 23, REnAW,
TwCBDA, WhAm H*
Connor, Ray 1876-1933 *WhAm 1*
Connor, Robert Digges Wimberly 1878-1950
DcAmB S4, NatCAB 38, WhAm 2A
Connor, Selden 1839-1917 *ApCAB, BiAUS,
NatCAB 6, TwCBDA, WhAm 1*
Connor, Skeffington 1810-1863 *ApCAB*
Connor, Walter Thomas 1877-1952 *DcAmReB*
Connor, Washington Everett 1849-1935
ApCAB X, WhAm 1
Connor, William Durward 1874-1960
NatCAB 49, WhAm 4
Connor, William L 1889-1946 *NatCAB 42*
Connor, William Neil 1910-1967 *WhAm 4*
Connor, William Ott 1852-1934 *NatCAB 30,
WhAm 1*
Connors, Charles Garrett 1884-1949
NatCAB 38
Connors, Edwin Robert 1904-1967 *NatCAB 53*
Connors, James Joseph 1878- *WhAm 6*
Connors, James Joseph 1926-1974 *WhAm 6*
Connors, John Fox 1873-1935 *NatCAB 26*
Connors, John P 1857- *WhAm 4*
Connors, Joseph Matthew 1883-1967
WhAm 4A

Connors, Thomas 1836?- *NewYHSD*
Connover, Simon B 1840- *BiAUS*
Conny *NewYHSD*
Conolly, Richard L 1892-1962 *WhAm 4*
Conon Of Samos 300?BC- *AsBiEn, DcScB*
Conover *NewYHSD*
Conover, Adams Jewett 1850-1928 *NatCAB 32,*
WhAm 1
Conover, Charles H 1847-1915 *WhAm 1*
Conover, Charlotte Reeve *WomWWA 14*
Conover, Elbert Moore d1952 *WhAm 3*
Conover, Elisha 1860-1944 *NatCAB 34*
Conover, Frederic King 1857-1919 *NatCAB 19*
Conover, Grace Clark *WomWWA 14*
Conover, Harvey 1892-1958 *NatCAB 44,*
WhAm 3
Conover, Henry *NewYHSD*
Conover, Milton 1890-1972 *WhAm 5*
Conover, Obadiah Milton 1825-1884 *DcAmB*
Conover, Obediah Milton 1825-1884 *WhAm H*
Conover, Samuel Seymour 1869-1962
NatCAB 50, WhAm 4
Conover, Simon Barclay 1840-1908 *ApCAB,*
BiDrAC, NatCAB 12, TwCBDA
Conover, Thomas A 1794-1864 *ApCAB, Drake,*
NatCAB 4
Conover, Thomas H 1794-1864 *TwCBDA*
Conover, William 1900-1966 *NatCAB 53*
Conquest, Ida 1882-1937 *WhAm 1*
Conrad, Arcturus Z 1855-1937 *NatCAB 28,*
WhAm 1
Conrad, Augustus 1842?- *NewYHSD*
Conrad, Carl Nicholas 1858-1932 *ApCAB X,*
WhAm 1
Conrad, Casper Hauzer, Jr. 1872- *WhAm 3*
Conrad, Charles 1875-1954 *WhAm 3*
Conrad, Charles Edward 1879-1944 *NatCAB 37*
Conrad, Charles Magill 1804-1878 *ApCAB,*
BiAUS, BiDConf, DcAmB, Drake,
NatCAB 6, TwCBDA, WhAm H
Conrad, Charles Mynn 1804-1878 *BiDrAC,*
BiDrUSE, WhAmP
Conrad, Charles Wearne 1887-1957 *WhAm 3*
Conrad, Cuthbert Powell 1893-1956
NatCAB. 46, WhAm 3
Conrad, David 1928- *EncAAH*
Conrad, Elisabeth Whiting 1886-1964
NatCAB 52
Conrad, F 1833-1923 *ApCAB*
Conrad, Frank 1874-1941 *DcAmB S3,*
NatCAB 35, WhAm 1
Conrad, Frank Louis 1886-1949 *NatCAB 39,*
WhAm 2
Conrad, Frederick 1759-1827 *BiAUS, BiDrAC,*
WhAm H
Conrad, Frederick William 1816-1898
ApCAB Sup, TwCBDA
Conrad, Frowenus 1833-1923 *WhAm 1*
Conrad, G Miles 1911-1964 *NatCAB 52,*
WhAm 4
Conrad, George Washington Bryant 1867-
WhoColR
Conrad, Harry Lester 1889-1961 *NatCAB 49*
Conrad, Henry Clay 1852-1930 *NatCAB 4,*
WhAm 1
Conrad, Holmes 1840- *NatCAB 13*
Conrad, Holmes 1840-1915 *NatCAB 16*
Conrad, Holmes 1840-1916 *DcAmB, WhAmP*
Conrad, James Lawson 1900-1974 *WhAm 6*
Conrad, John *BiAUS*
Conrad, Joseph 1830-1897 *ApCAB, TwCBDA*
Conrad, Joseph 1857-1924 *McGEWB*
Conrad, Joseph Speed 1833-1891 *ApCAB,*
NatCAB 4, TwCBDA
Conrad, Laird Lewis 1884-1961 *NatCAB 49*
Conrad, Lowell Edwin 1879- *WhAm 6*
Conrad, Margaret May Dickson *WomWWA 14*
Conrad, Marus Edward 1896-1961 *NatCAB 49,*
WhAm 4
Conrad, Nicholas John 1883-1956 *WhAm 3*
Conrad, P *NewYHSD*
Conrad, Paul C 1906-1961 *WhAm 4*
Conrad, Robert Taylor 1810-1858 *ApCAB,*
DcAmB, Drake, NatCAB 11, TwCBDA,
WhAm H, WhAmP
Conrad, Roy Garman 1910-1965 *NatCAB 52*
Conrad, Stephen *WhAm 1*
Conrad, Timothy A *NewYHSD*

Conrad, Timothy Abbot 1803-1877 *NatCAB 8,*
WhAm H
Conrad, Timothy Abbott 1803-1877 *ApCAB,*
DcScB, Drake, TwCBDA
Conrad, Victor Allen 1900-1964 *WhAm 4*
Conrad, Victor Lafayette 1824-1900 *TwCBDA*
Conrad, William 1808-1865 *ApCAB*
Conrad VonHotzendorf, Franz 1852-1925
WhoMilH
Conrade, Mary Spencer 1863- *WomWWA 14*
Conradi, Edward 1869-1944 *NatCAB 33,*
WhAm 2
Conradt, Charles *NewYHSD*
Conried, Heinrich 1855-1909 *ApCAB X,*
DcAmB, NatCAB 11, WhAm H
Conrow, Aaron H 1824-1865 *BiDConf*
Conrow, Georgianna 1878- *WomWWA 14*
Conrow, J *NewYHSD*
Conrow, Leon Whitney 1899-1943 *NatCAB 33*
Conrow, Wilford Seymour 1880-1957 *WhAm 3*
Conroy, Frank Davies 1893-1953 *NatCAB 41*
Conroy, Frank Joseph 1859-1933 *NatCAB 27*
Conroy, J *NewYHSD*
Conroy, John Joseph 1819-1895 *ApCAB,*
NatCAB 12, TwCBDA, WhAm H
Conroy, Joseph H 1881-1939 *WhAm 1*
Conroy, Peter Joseph 1894-1955 *WhAm 3*
Conroy, Thomas Francis 1897-1953 *WhAm 3*
Conroy, Thomas Michael 1896-1970 *WhAm 5*
Conry, Joseph Aloysius 1868-1943 *BiDrAC,*
WhAmP
Conry, Michael Francis 1870-1917 *BiDrAC,*
WhAm 1, WhAmP
Conry, Thomas 1869-1947 *WhAm 2*
Cons, Louis 1879-1942 *NatCAB 31, WhAm 2*
Consaul, Charles Follett 1870-1945 *NatCAB 33*
Considerant, Victor Prosper 1808-1893 *AmBi,*
DcAmB, WhAm H
Considine, James Patrick 1863-1946
NatCAB 37
Considine, James W 1908-1971 *WhAm 5*
Considine, John William 1863-1943 *NatCAB 31*
Considine, Robert Bernard 1906-1975 *WhAm 6*
Consor, Herbert Austin 1883-1941 *NatCAB 30*
Constable, Albert 1805-1855 *BiAUS, BiDrAC,*
WhAm H
Constable, John 1776-1837 *McGEWB*
Constable, William George 1887-1976 *WhAm 6*
Constangy, Frank Alan 1911-1971 *WhAm 5*
Constant, Frank Henry 1869-1950 *WhAm 2A*
Constant, Samuel Victor 1857-1910 *WhAm 1*
Constantine 1919- *IIBEAAW*
Constantine I 274?-337 *McGEWB*
Constantine XI 1405-1453 *McGEWB*
Constantine The African *DcScB*
Constantine, Earl Gladstone 1885-1952
WhAm 3
Constantine, Kosciusko Walker 1877-1961
NatCAB 49
Constantinople, Panagiotes S 1901-1967
WhAm 4
Constas, John Nicholas 1877-1944 *NatCAB 34*
Conte, Richard 1916-1975 *WhAm 6*
Conte, Silvio Otto 1921- *BiDrAC*
Contecoeur 1730?- *ApCAB*
Contee, Benjamin 1755-1815 *ApCAB, BiAUS,*
BiDrAC, Drake, NatCAB 11, TwCBDA,
WhAm H
Conter, Augustus Eugene 1871-1948
NatCAB 43
Conti, Niccolo De 1396?-1469 *McGEWB*
Contzen, Fritz 1831-1909 *NatCAB 33*
Converse, Allan Dean 1880-1959 *NatCAB 47*
Converse, Amasa 1795-1872 *ApCAB,*
TwCBDA
Converse, Amasa R 1842-1885 *WhAm H*
Converse, Charles Crozat 1832-1918 *DcAmB,*
NatCAB 8, WhAm 1
Converse, Charles Crozat 1834-1918 *ApCAB,*
Drake
Converse, Clara Adra *WomWWA 14*
Converse, Costello C 1848-1931 *WhAm 1*
Converse, Dexter Edgar 1828-1899 *NatCAB 6*
Converse, Edmund Cogswell 1849-1921 *DcAmB,*
WhAm 1
Converse, Elisha Slade 1820- *NatCAB 10,*
TwCBDA
Converse, Emma Tudor 1872- *WomWWA 14*

Converse, Florence 1871- *NatCAB 13,*
WhAm 6, WomWWA 14
Converse, Francis Bartlett 1836-1907 *TwCBDA,*
WhAm 1
Converse, Frederick Shepherd 1871-1940
ApCAB X, DcAmB S2, NatCAB 14,
NatCAB 30, WhAm 1
Converse, George Albert 1844-1909 *NatCAB 36,*
WhAm 1
Converse, George Leroy 1827-1897 *BiDrAC,*
NatCAB 5, WhAm H
Converse, George Marquis 1872-1929
NatCAB 21
Converse, George Peabody 1902-1963 *WhAm 4*
Converse, Harriet Maxwell 1836-1903 *AmWom,*
NotAW, TwCBDA, WhAm 1
Converse, Harry E 1863-1920 *ApCAB X,*
WhAm 1
Converse, Harry Pollard 1876-1960 *WhAm 3*
Converse, James Booth 1844-1914 *DcAmB,*
TwCBDA, WhAm 1
Converse, Jesse *NewYHSD*
Converse, John Heman 1840-1910 *DcAmB,*
NatCAB 9, WhAm 1
Converse, Julius 1798-1885 *NatCAB 8,*
TwCBDA
Converse, Julius 1799-1885 *BiAUS*
Converse, Marquis Mills 1861-1931 *WhAm 1*
Converse, Mary Eleanor *WomWWA 14*
Converse, Miriam Sewall 1880- *WhAm 6*
Converse, Morton E 1837-1917 *NatCAB 20*
Converse, Myron Frederick 1876-1950
NatCAB 39, WhAm 3
Converse, Paul Dulaney 1889-1968 *NatCAB 54*
Converse, Thomas Edwards 1841- *TwCBDA*
Convery, Neil Joseph 1890-1966 *WhAm 4*
Conway, Albert 1889-1969 *WhAm 5*
Conway, Barret 1878-1949 *WhAm 2*
Conway, Carle Cotter 1877-1959 *ApCAB X,*
WhAm 3
Conway, Clara *AmWom*
Conway, Edwin Stapleton 1850-1919 *WhAm 1*
Conway, Elias Nelson 1812- *BiAUS*
Conway, Elias Nelson 1812-1892 *DcAmB,*
REnAW, TwCBDA
Conway, Elias Nelson 1812-1894 *NatCAB 10,*
WhAm H
Conway, Emeline Hoffman 1868-
WomWWA 14
Conway, Mrs. Frederick B 1834-1874
NatCAB 11
Conway, Mrs. Frederick B *see also* Crocker,
Sarah G
Conway, Frederick Bartlett 1819-1874 *ApCAB,*
DcAmB, NatCAB 7, WhAm H
Conway, Frederick Rector 1799-1874 *TwCBDA*
Conway, Henry Wharton 1793-1827 *BiAUS,*
BiDrAC, TwCBDA, WhAm H
Conway, Herbert 1904-1969 *WhAm 5*
Conway, James Ignatius 1908-1962 *WhAm 4*
Conway, James Sevier 1798-1855 *BiAUS,*
DcAmB, NatCAB 10, REnAW,
TwCBDA, WhAm H, WhAmP
Conway, John E 1892-1950 *WhAm 2A*
Conway, John Sebastian 1878- *WhAm 6*
Conway, John Severinus 1852-1925 *WhAm 1*
Conway, Joseph Michael 1890-1961 *NatCAB 47,*
WhAm 4
Conway, Joseph W 1898- *WhAm 2*
Conway, Katherine Eleanor 1853-1927 *AmWom,*
TwCBDA, WhAm 1
Conway, Louise Shoenberger 1886-
WomWWA 14
Conway, Martin F 1830?-1882 *BiAUS*
Conway, Martin Franklin 1827-1882 *BiDrAC,*
DcAmB, NatCAB 8, TwCBDA,
WhAm H, WhAmP
Conway, Moncure Daniel 1832-1907 *AmBi,*
ApCAB, DcAmB, NatCAB 1, TwCBDA,
WhAm 1
Conway, Patrick 1865-1929 *NatCAB 21*
Conway, Patrick 1867-1929 *WhAm 1*
Conway, Sarah Crocker 1834-1875 *ApCAB*
Conway, Thomas 1733-1800? *ApCAB, Drake,*
NatCAB 1, TwCBDA, WhAm H
Conway, Thomas 1735-1800? *AmBi, DcAmB,*
WebAB, WebAMB
Conway, Thomas, Jr. d1962 *WhAm 4*

Conway, Thomas Franklin 1859-1945 *NatCAB 34*
Conway, Thomas William 1840-1887 *TwCBDA*
Conway, Walter 1898-1956 *WhAm 3*
Conway, William 1802-1865 *ApCAB*
Conway, William Augustus 1789-1828 *ApCAB, Drake, NatCAB 7*
Conway, William B 1806?-1852 *TwCBDA*
Conwell, Henry 1745?-1842 *DcAmB, Drake, NatCAB 6, TwCBDA*
Conwell, Henry 1748-1842 *ApCAB*
Conwell, Hugh Earle 1893-1973 *WhAm 6*
Conwell, John William 1892-1958 *NatCAB 48*
Conwell, Leon Martin 1870-1953 *NatCAB 42*
Conwell, Russell H 1842-1925 *NatCAB 3*
Conwell, Russell Herman 1843-1925 *AmBi, DcAmB, DcAmReB, WebAMB, WhAm 1*
Conwell, Russell Herrman 1843-1925 *TwCBDA*
Conwell, Walter Lewis 1877-1948 *NatCAB 39, WhAm 2*
Cony *NewYHSD*
Cony, Daniel 1752-1842 *ApCAB Sup*
Cony, Samuel 1811-1870 *ApCAB, BiAUS, Drake, NatCAB 6, TwCBDA*
Conybeare, William Daniel 1787-1857 *DcScB*
Conyers, Christopher Bowen 1867-1945 *NatCAB 35*
Conyers, Edward 1590-1663 *NatCAB 8*
Conyers, James 1645-1706 *NatCAB 8*
Conyers, John, Jr. 1929- *BiDrAC*
Conyngham, Charles Miner 1840-1894 *NatCAB 26*
Conyngham, Gustavus 1744?-1819 *DcAmB, NatCAB 4, WebAMB, WhAm H*
Conyngham, John Butler 1827-1871 *ApCAB, TwCBDA*
Conyngham, John N 1798-1871 *BiAUS*
Conyngham, John Nesbit 1798-1871 *ApCAB Sup, NatCAB 9, NatCAB 28*
Conyngham, John Nesbitt 1798-1871 *TwCBDA*
Conyngham, John Nesbitt 1865-1935 *NatCAB 26*
Conyngham, Redmond 1781-1846 *ApCAB*
Conyngham, William Hillard 1868-1943 *WhAm 2*
Conyngham, William Lord 1829-1907 *NatCAB 26*
Cooch, Mary Evarts 1849- *WomWWA 14*
Coode, John d1709 *DcAmB*
Coogan, Edward Francis 1888-1960 *WhAm 4*
Coogan, Thomas James 1900-1974 *WhAm 6*
Cook *NewYHSD*
Cook, Aaron 1909-1959 *NatCAB 47*
Cook, Abraham 1774-1854 *NatCAB 11*
Cook, Albert John 1842-1916 *ApCAB, TwCBDA, WhAm 1*
Cook, Albert Samuel 1873-1952 *BiDAmEd, WhAm 3*
Cook, Albert St. Clair 1864-1941 *NatCAB 35*
Cook, Albert Stanburrough 1853-1927 *BiDAmEd, DcAmB, NatCAB 9, NatCAB 38, TwCBDA, WhAm 1*
Cook, Alfred A 1873-1950 *NatCAB 38, WhAm 2*
Cook, Alfred Newton 1866- *WhAm 1*
Cook, Alice Carter 1868- *WomWWA 14*
Cook, Alice Helena 1877- *WomWWA 14*
Cook, Alice Rice 1899- *WhAm 5*
Cook, Allan Behrands 1892-1967 *WhAm 4*
Cook, Alton 1905-1967 *WhAm 4*
Cook, Amelia Josephine *AmWom*
Cook, Andrew Bruce 1898-1969 *WhAm 5*
Cook, Ansel Granville 1862-1933 *NatCAB 24, WhAm 1*
Cook, Arthur Leroy 1878- *WhAm 6*
Cook, Burton Chauncey 1819-1894 *BiAUS, BiDrAC, NatCAB 13, TwCBDA, WhAm H, WhAmP*
Cook, C Kenneth 1901-1969 *NatCAB 55*
Cook, Carroll Blaine 1883-1922 *WhAm 1*
Cook, Cary Wilson 1862- *WhAm 4*
Cook, Charles 1810?- *NewYHSD*
Cook, Charles 1845-1928 *NatCAB 22*
Cook, Charles Alston 1848-1916 *WhAm 1*
Cook, Charles Augustus 1856-1940 *WhAm 1*
Cook, Charles Emerson *WhAm 5*
Cook, Charles Lee 1870-1928 *NatCAB 21*
Cook, Charles R 1884-1949 *WhAm 3*

Cook, Charles Sumner 1858-1939 *NatCAB 35, WhAm 1*
Cook, Charles T 1835-1907 *WhAm 1*
Cook, Charles William 1906-1968 *NatCAB 54*
Cook, Chauncey d1949 *WhAm 2*
Cook, Chester Aquila 1870-1953 *WhAm 3*
Cook, Clarence Chatham 1828-1900 *ApCAB, DcAmB, NatCAB 10, NewYHSD, TwCBDA, WhAm H*
Cook, Clarence Percy 1871-1950 *NatCAB 39*
Cook, Clinton Dana 1921-1969 *WhAm 5*
Cook, Coralie Franklin *WhoColR*
Cook, Daniel P d1827 *BiAUS*
Cook, Daniel Pope 1794-1827 *BiDrAC, WhAm H, WhAmP*
Cook, Daniel Pope 1795-1827 *ApCAB, TwCBDA*
Cook, David C 1850-1927 *WhAm 1*
Cook, David Charles 1881-1932 *NatCAB 23*
Cook, David Moie 1916-1967 *NatCAB 53*
Cook, Donald 1901-1961 *WhAm 4*
Cook, Douglas G 1847- *NatCAB 12*
Cook, Douglas P *ApCAB X*
Cook, Earl Kenneth 1901-1949 *NatCAB 42*
Cook, Ebenezer *WhAm H*
Cook, Edward Noble 1905-1972 *WhAm 5*
Cook, Elizabeth Christine 1876- *WomWWA 14*
Cook, Elizabeth Ellsworth 1884- *WomWWA 14*
Cook, Ellen Parmelee 1865- *WomWWA 14*
Cook, Elmer Jay 1901-1959 *NatCAB 48, WhAm 4*
Cook, Ermond Edson 1874-1931 *WhAm 1*
Cook, Ernest Fullerton 1879-1961 *NatCAB 49, WhAm 4*
Cook, Eugene 1904-1967 *WhAm 4*
Cook, Everett Richard 1894-1974 *WhAm 6*
Cook, Ezekiel Hanson 1845- *NatCAB 13*
Cook, Fannie 1893-1949 *WhAm 2*
Cook, Fayette Lamartine 1850-1922 *WhAm 1*
Cook, Flavius Josephus 1838-1901 *DcAmB*
Cook, Francis Ames 1843- *ApCAB Sup*
Cook, Francis Augustus 1843-1916 *NatCAB 9, TwCBDA, WhAm 1*
Cook, Frank Gaylord 1859-1948 *WhAm 2*
Cook, Frank Henry 1873- *WhoColR*
Cook, Frederic White 1873-1951 *WhAm 3*
Cook, Frederick 1833-1905 *NatCAB 17*
Cook, Frederick Albert 1865-1940 *DcAmB S2, NatCAB 13, WhAm 1*
Cook, G W E *NewYHSD*
Cook, George *NewYHSD*
Cook, George 1825?- *NewYHSD*
Cook, George Brinton 1868- *WhAm 1*
Cook, George Clarence 1895-1961 *NatCAB 46*
Cook, George Cram 1873-1924 *AmBi, DcAmB, NatCAB 22, WhAm 1*
Cook, George Crouse 1875-1960 *WhAm 4*
Cook, George Ezra 1875-1950 *NatCAB 39*
Cook, George Fox 1862- *WhAm 4*
Cook, George Francis 1896-1960 *NatCAB 48*
Cook, George Frederick 1846-1910 *WhAm 1*
Cook, George Hammell 1818-1889 *ApCAB, DcAmB, NatCAB 6, TwCBDA, WhAm H*
Cook, George Roy 1907-1973 *WhAm 5*
Cook, George Washington 1851-1916 *BiDrAC, NatCAB 18, WhAm 4*
Cook, George William 1855- *WhoColR*
Cook, George Wythe 1846- *WhAm 4*
Cook, Georgiana Hemingway *WomWWA 14*
Cook, Gilbert Richard 1889-1963 *WhAm 4*
Cook, Grant L 1894-1953 *WhAm 3*
Cook, H Earl 1886-1971 *WhAm 5*
Cook, H Weir 1892-1943 *NatCAB 32*
Cook, Harold *IlBEAAW*
Cook, Harold James 1887-1962 *WhAm 4*
Cook, Harold Jewett 1885-1933 *NatCAB 26*
Cook, Helen Noyes Currier 1876- *WomWWA 14*
Cook, Henry Clay 1837-1916 *WhAm 1*
Cook, Henry F d1863 *ApCAB, Drake*
Cook, Henry Mudd 1899- *WhAm 4*
Cook, Henry Webster 1872-1964 *WhAm 4*
Cook, Herman John 1880-1945 *NatCAB 35*
Cook, Mrs. Hosea *ApCAB*
Cook, Howard Garfield 1881-1952 *NatCAB 41*
Cook, Howard Norton 1901- *IlBEAAW*

Cook, Irving Sherburne 1858-1946 *NatCAB 35*
Cook, Irving Winthrop 1876- *WhAm 3*
Cook, Isaac 1810-1886 *DcAmB, NatCAB 12, WhAm H*
Cook, Isabel Vernon *WomWWA 14*
Cook, J Clinton, Jr. 1918-1965 *WhAm 4*
Cook, J M *NewYHSD*
Cook, James 1728-1779 *ApCAB, AsBiEn, BiHiMed, DcScB, Drake, McGEWB, WhAm H*
Cook, James Henry 1857-1942 *REnAW*
Cook, James Henry 1858-1942 *WhAm 2*
Cook, James Merrill 1807-1868 *ApCAB, DcAmB, WhAm H*
Cook, Jane A *NewYHSD*
Cook, Mrs. Jesse *ApCAB*
Cook, Joe 1862- *WhAm 4*
Cook, Joel 1842-1910 *BiDrAC, WhAm 1*
Cook, John *NewYHSD*
Cook, John 1810?- *ApCAB*
Cook, John 1825-1910 *ApCAB, Drake, TwCBDA, WhAm 1*
Cook, John 1889-1955 *WhAm 3*
Cook, John Belmont 1879- *WhAm 6*
Cook, John Calhoun 1846-1920 *BiDrAC*
Cook, John Henry 1874- *WhAm 5*
Cook, John Parsons 1817-1872 *BiAUS, BiDrAC, WhAm H*
Cook, John Williston 1844-1922 *ApCAB X, BiDAmEd, DcAmB, NatCAB 5, NatCAB 27, WhAm 1*
Cook, Joseph 1838-1901 *ApCAB, DcAmB, DcAmReB, NatCAB 2, TwCBDA, WhAm 1*
Cook, Joseph Platt 1730-1816 *BiDrAC, WhAm H*
Cook, Joshua Flood 1834- *TwCBDA*
Cook, Lemuel 1764-1866 *ApCAB*
Cook, Lora Mary Haines *BiCAW*
Cook, Marc 1854-1882 *ApCAB, NatCAB 13, WhAm H*
Cook, Marguerite 1853- *WomWWA 14*
Cook, Marguerite 1854- *BiCAW*
Cook, Marlow Webster 1926- *BiDrAC*
Cook, Marshall Lannis 1858-1955 *NatCAB 52*
Cook, Martha Elizabeth Duncan Walker 1806-1874 *ApCAB, DcAmB, WhAm H*
Cook, Martha M Giltner *WomWWA 14*
Cook, May A 1869- *AmWom*
Cook, May Elizabeth 1881- *WhAm 6*
Cook, May Estelle 1865- *WomWWA 14*
Cook, Mehitabel Jones 1809- *NewYHSD*
Cook, Melville Thurston 1869-1952 *NatCAB 40, WhAm 3*
Cook, Minnie Gathright *WomWWA 14*
Cook, Nelson 1817-1892 *NewYHSD*
Cook, Orator Fuller, Jr. 1867-1949 *NatCAB 38, WhAm 3*
Cook, Orchard 1763-1819 *BiAUS, BiDrAC, WhAm H*
Cook, Oscar Fremont 1878-1962 *NatCAB 50*
Cook, Otis Seabury 1873-1939 *WhAm 1*
Cook, Paul 1847-1926 *WhAm 1*
Cook, Paul Burns 1877-1930 *NatCAB 21*
Cook, Peter, Jr. 1898-1970 *WhAm 5*
Cook, Philip 1817-1894 *ApCAB, BiAUS, BiDrAC, DcAmB, NatCAB 4, TwCBDA, WhAm H*
Cook, Philip 1875-1938 *WhAm 1*
Cook, R Harvey 1870-1949 *WhAm 2*
Cook, Raymond Mack 1902-1965 *WhAm 4*
Cook, Raymond Rush 1898-1966 *NatCAB 51*
Cook, Richard Briscoe 1838-1916 *WhAm 1*
Cook, Richard Yerkes 1845-1917 *WhAm 1*
Cook, Robert *NewYHSD*
Cook, Robert Allen 1872-1949 *NatCAB 38*
Cook, Robert Carl 1887-1968 *NatCAB 54*
Cook, Robert Eugene 1920- *BiDrAC*
Cook, Robert George 1864-1940 *WhAm 1*
Cook, Robert Jay 1887-1951 *NatCAB 40*
Cook, Robert Johnson 1849-1922 *DcAmB*
Cook, Roderick Walker, Jr. 1925-1971 *NatCAB 57*
Cook, Roy Bird 1886-1961 *NatCAB 49, WhAm 4*
Cook, Roy H 1911-1964 *WhAm 4*
Cook, Russell Salmon 1811-1864 *ApCAB, DcAmB, Drake, NatCAB 7, TwCBDA,*

WhAm H

Cook, Samuel Andrew 1849-1918 *BiDrAC, WhAm 1*

Cook, Samuel C 1857-1924 *WhAm 1*

Cook, Samuel Ellis 1860-1946 *BiDrAC, WhAm 4*

Cook, Samuel Richard 1865- *WhAm 4*

Cook, Sarah A *NewYHSD*

Cook, Sidney Albert 1892-1944 *WhAm 2*

Cook, T B *NewYHSD*

Cook, Lady Tennessee Celeste Claflin 1845-1923 *DcAmB*

Cook, Theodore Augustus 1885-1959 *WhAm 4*

Cook, Theodore Pease 1844- *ApCAB*

Cook, Thomas d1870 *Drake*

Cook, Thomas B *BiAUS*

Cook, Valentine 1765-1820 *ApCAB*

Cook, Vernon 1870-1954 *NatCAB 45, WhAm 3*

Cook, Victor *NewYHSD*

Cook, Vincent 1841-1922 *NatCAB 21*

Cook, Virgil Young 1848-1922 *NatCAB 9, WhAm 1*

Cook, W H 1832- *Drake*

Cook, W H *see also* Cook, William Henry

Cook, Waldo Lincoln 1865-1951 *WhAm 3*

Cook, Walter 1846-1916 *DcAmB, NatCAB 14, WhAm 1*

Cook, Walter W 1899-1963 *WhAm 4*

Cook, Walter Wheeler 1873-1943 *DcAmB S3, NatCAB 32, WhAm 2*

Cook, Walter William Spencer 1888-1962 *WhAm 4*

Cook, Wesley *NewYHSD*

Cook, Will Marion 1869-1944 *DcAmB S3, WhoColR*

Cook, William 1807- *NewYHSD*

Cook, William Cassius 1882-1947 *WhAm 3*

Cook, William Decanter 1860- *WhoColR*

Cook, William Henry 1832-1899 *WhAm 1*

Cook, William Henry 1874-1937 *WhAm 1*

Cook, William Henry *see also* Cook, W H

Cook, William Joseph 1863-1932 *NatCAB 34*

Cook, William Loch 1869-1942 *NatCAB 41*

Cook, William Locke 1869-1942 *WhAm 2*

Cook, William Wallace 1867-1933 *WhAm 1*

Cook, William Wilson 1858-1930 *WhAm 1*

Cook, Willis Clifford 1874-1942 *WhAm 1, WhAm 2*

Cook, Zadock 1769-1863 *BiAUS, BiDrAC, WhAm H*

Cook, Zebedee 1786-1858 *ApCAB, DcAmB, WhAm H*

Cooke, A Wayland 1876-1940 *WhAm 1*

Cooke, Abigail Whipple *WomWWA 14*

Cooke, Amos Starr 1810-1871 *ApCAB*

Cooke, Anna Charlotte Rice 1853-1934 *NotAW*

Cooke, Arthur Bledsoe 1869- *WhAm 5*

Cooke, Augustus Paul 1836-1896 *NatCAB 6, TwCBDA*

Cooke, Bate d1841 *BiAUS*

Cooke, Bates 1787-1841 *BiDrAC, WhAm H*

Cooke, Bennett 1867-1946 *WhAm 2*

Cooke, C Montague, Jr. 1874-1948 *NatCAB 36, WhAm 2*

Cooke, Charles Henry 1878-1945 *NatCAB 35*

Cooke, Charles Maynard, Jr. 1886-1970 *WhAm 5*

Cooke, Charles Wallace 1890-1965 *NatCAB 51*

Cooke, Clara Dwight Sprague *WomWWA 14*

Cooke, Clarence Hyde 1876-1944 *WhAm 2*

Cooke, Clinton Tyng 1866-1963 *NatCAB 50*

Cooke, Dorothy Soden 1868- *WomWWA 14*

Cooke, Douglas Hageman 1886-1948 *NatCAB 37, WhAm 2*

Cooke, Ebenezer 1670-1732 *DcAmB S1, WhAm H*

Cooke, Edmund Francis 1885-1967 *BiDrAC*

Cooke, Edmund Vance 1866-1932 *NatCAB 23, WhAm 1*

Cooke, Edward 1812-1888 *ApCAB, TwCBDA*

Cooke, Edward Dean 1849-1897 *BiDrAC, WhAm H*

Cooke, Edwin Francis 1835-1867 *ApCAB*

Cooke, Elbridge Clinton 1854- *WhAm 4*

Cooke, Eleutheros 1787-1864 *ApCAB, BiDrAC, TwCBDA, WhAm H*

Cooke, Eleutheros 1787-1865 *BiAUS*

Cooke, Elisha 1637-1715 *ApCAB, DcAmB, Drake, WhAm H*

Cooke, Elisha 1678-1737 *ApCAB, DcAmB, WhAm H*

Cooke, Flora Juliette 1864-1953 *WhAm 3, WomWWA 14*

Cooke, George 1793-1849 *IIBEAAW, NewYHSD, WhAm H*

Cooke, George Anderson 1869-1938 *ApCAB X, NatCAB 17, WhAm 1*

Cooke, George Frederick 1756-1812 *ApCAB, Drake*

Cooke, George Henry 1836-1924 *WhAm 1*

Cooke, George Willis 1848-1923 *DcAmB, NatCAB 8, TwCBDA, WhAm 1*

Cooke, Grace MacGowan 1863- *WhAm 4, WomWWA 14*

Cooke, Harold Groves 1890-1958 *WhAm 3*

Cooke, Harrison Rice 1908-1973 *WhAm 5*

Cooke, Hedley Vicars 1862-1936 *NatCAB 29*

Cooke, Helen Temple 1865-1955 *WhAm 3, WomWWA 14*

Cooke, Henry D 1879-1958 *WhAm 3*

Cooke, Henry David 1825-1881 *ApCAB, BiAUS, DcAmB, NatCAB 10, TwCBDA, WhAm H*

Cooke, Hereward Lester 1879-1946 *WhAm 2*

Cooke, James Dee 1880- *WhoColR*

Cooke, James Francis 1875-1960 *WhAm 3*

Cooke, James Henry 1864-1930 *NatCAB 35*

Cooke, Jane Grosvenor *WomWWA 14*

Cooke, Jay 1821-1905 *AmBi, ApCAB, BiAUS, DcAmB, Drake, EncAB, McGEWB, NatCAB 1, TwCBDA, WebAB, WhAm 1*

Cooke, Jay 1897-1963 *NatCAB 51, WhAm 4*

Cooke, Jay, III 1872- *NatCAB 4*

Cooke, Jean Valjean 1883-1956 *NatCAB 45*

Cooke, John 1744-1812 *NatCAB 8*

Cooke, John Daniel 1892-1972 *WhAm 5*

Cooke, John Esten 1782-1853 *NatCAB 4*

Cooke, John Esten 1783-1853 *BiDAmEd, DcAmB, TwCBDA, WhAm H*

Cooke, John Esten 1830-1886 *AmBi, ApCAB, BiDConf, DcAmB, Drake, NatCAB 7, TwCBDA, WhAm H*

Cooke, John H d1866 *Drake*

Cooke, John P 1820-1865 *ApCAB, Drake*

Cooke, John Rogers 1788-1854 *ApCAB, DcAmB, TwCBDA, WhAm H*

Cooke, John Rogers 1833-1891 *ApCAB, BiDConf, TwCBDA*

Cooke, Joseph Brown 1868- *WhAm 4*

Cooke, Joseph Platt 1730-1816 *BiAUS, Drake, TwCBDA*

Cooke, Joseph Platt 1870-1918 *NatCAB 36*

Cooke, Joseph Platt 1896-1953 *WhAm 3*

Cooke, Josiah Parsons, Jr. 1827-1894 *AmBi, ApCAB, BiDAmEd, DcAmB, DcScB, NatCAB 6, TwCBDA, WhAm H*

Cooke, Josiah Platt 1730-1816 *ApCAB*

Cooke, Juan Isaac 1895-1957 *WhAm 3*

Cooke, Leslie Edward 1908-1967 *WhAm 4*

Cooke, Levi 1882-1932 *NatCAB 25*

Cooke, Lorenzo Wesley 1847-1915 *WhAm 1*

Cooke, Lorrin Alanson 1831-1902 *NatCAB 10, WhAm 1*

Cooke, Lucy Finkel 1918-1973 *WhAm 6*

Cooke, Marjorie Benton d1920 *WhAm 1, WomWWA 14*

Cooke, Martin Warren 1840- *NatCAB 5*

Cooke, Mary Jenckes 1859- *WomWWA 14*

Cooke, May Perry 1869- *WomWWA 14*

Cooke, Morris Llewellyn 1872-1960 *EncAAH, WhAm 3*

Cooke, Nicholas 1717-1782 *ApCAB, BiAUS, Drake, NatCAB 9, TwCBDA*

Cooke, Nicholas Francis 1829-1885 *ApCAB, TwCBDA*

Cooke, Parsons 1800-1864 *ApCAB, Drake, TwCBDA*

Cooke, Philip Pendleton 1816-1850 *ApCAB, DcAmB, NatCAB 7, TwCBDA, WhAm H*

Cooke, Philip St. George 1809-1895 *AmBi, ApCAB, DcAmB, Drake, NatCAB 4, REnAW, TwCBDA, WebAMB, WhAm H*

Cooke, Phillip Pendleton 1816-1850 *Drake*

Cooke, Richard Clarke *NewYHSD*

Cooke, Richard Dickson 1880-1958 *NatCAB 44, WhAm 3*

Cooke, Richard Joseph 1853-1931 *NatCAB 23, TwCBDA, WhAm 1*

Cooke, Robert Anderson 1880-1960 *WhAm 4*

Cooke, Robert Locke 1889-1955 *WhAm 3*

Cooke, Rose Terry 1827-1892 *AmBi, AmWom, ApCAB, DcAmB, NatCAB 6, NotAW, TwCBDA, WhAm H*

Cooke, Samuel 1815- *NatCAB 9*

Cooke, Samuel 1898-1965 *NatCAB 51, WhAm 4*

Cooke, Sidney Granger 1846-1926 *NatCAB 21*

Cooke, Stephen 1751-1816 *TwCBDA*

Cooke, Susan G *AmWom*

Cooke, Thomas Burrage 1778-1853 *BiDrAC, WhAm H*

Cooke, Thomas Burrage 1780-1853 *BiAUS Sup*

Cooke, Thomas Turner 1894-1965 *WhAm 4*

Cooke, Thomas Worthington 1872-1930 *NatCAB 50*

Cooke, Thornton 1873-1952 *WhAm 3*

Cooke, Walter Platt 1869-1931 *NatCAB 23, WhAm 1*

Cooke, Wells Woodbridge 1858-1916 *NatCAB 21*

Cooke, William Henry 1837-1889 *TwCBDA*

Cooke, William Mordecai 1823-1863 *BiDConf, NatCAB 16*

Cooke, William Parker 1859-1931 *WhAm 1*

Cooke, William Rule 1892-1948 *NatCAB 36*

Cookins, James *NewYHSD*

Cookins, James 1835?- *ApCAB*

Cookman, Alfred 1828-1871 *ApCAB, NatCAB 13, WhAm H*

Cookman, Emma Cornelius 1872- *WomWWA 14*

Cookman, George Grimston 1800-1841 *ApCAB, Drake*

Cookman, John Emory 1836-1891 *ApCAB, NatCAB 10*

Cooksey, George Robert d1941 *WhAm 2*

Cookson, Walter John 1876-1936 *WhAm 1, WhAm 1C*

Coolbaugh, Melville Fuller 1877-1950 *NatCAB 38, WhAm 3*

Coolbrith, Ina Donna d1928 *AmWom, TwCBDA, WhAm 1, WomWWA 14*

Coolbrith, Ina Donna 1841-1928 *DcAmB, DcAmLiB, NotAW*

Coolbrith, Ina Donna 1842-1928 *AmBi*

Coolbrith, Ina Donna 1845-1928 *ApCAB X, NatCAB 13*

Coole, Thomas Henry 1868-1930 *WhAm 1*

Cooley, Abiel A 1782-1858 *ApCAB, Drake*

Cooley, Alford Warriner 1873-1913 *WhAm 1*

Cooley, Anna Maria 1874- *WhAm 5, WomWWA 14*

Cooley, Arthur Henderson 1875- *WhAm 5*

Cooley, Benjamin Packard 1878-1941 *NatCAB 31*

Cooley, Charles Horton 1864-1929 *McGEWB, TwCBDA, WebAB, WhAm 1*

Cooley, Charles Parsons 1867- *WhAm 5*

Cooley, Charles Parsons, Jr. 1903-1975 *WhAm 6*

Cooley, Clara Aldrich 1830- *WomWWA 14*

Cooley, Dennis N *BiAUS*

Cooley, Edwin Gilbert 1857-1923 *BiDAmEd, DcAmB S1, NatCAB 14, WhAm 1*

Cooley, Elsie Jones 1864- *WomWWA 14*

Cooley, Emily M J 1831- *AmWom*

Cooley, Ethel Halcrow 1888-1970 *WhAm 5*

Cooley, Frederick Boyden 1875-1944 *WhAm 2*

Cooley, Harold Dunbar 1897-1974 *BiDrAC, EncAAH, WhAm 6, WhAmP*

Cooley, Hollis Eli 1859-1918 *WhAm 1*

Cooley, James d1828 *BiAUS*

Cooley, James Ewing 1802- *Drake*

Cooley, LeRoy Clark 1833-1916 *AmBi, ApCAB, BiDAmEd, NatCAB 11, TwCBDA, WhAm 1*

Cooley, Lyman Edgar 1850-1917 *DcAmB, NatCAB 9, WhAm 1*

Cooley, McWhorter Stephens 1907-1973 *WhAm 6*

Cooley, Mortimer Elwyn 1855-1944 *ApCAB X,*

DcAmB S3, NatCAB 51, WhAm 2
Cooley, Nellie Wooster *WomWWA 14*
Cooley, Robert Allen 1873-1968 *NatCAB 54, WhAm 5*
Cooley, Robert Lawrence 1869-1944 *WhAm 3*
Cooley, Roger William 1859-1931 *WhAm 1*
Cooley, Rossa B 1873- *WomWWA 14*
Cooley, Russell Henry 1889-1969 *NatCAB 55*
Cooley, Samuel Studdiford 1905-1958 *NatCAB 48*
Cooley, Stoughton 1861-1934 *WhAm 1*
Cooley, Theodore 1842- *NatCAB 9*
Cooley, Thomas Benton 1871-1945 *DcAmB S3, NatCAB 33, WhAm 2*
Cooley, Thomas M 1824-1898 *Drake*
Cooley, Thomas MacIntyre 1824-1898 *WhAm H*
Cooley, Thomas McIntyre 1824-1898 *AmBi, ApCAB, DcAmB, EncAB, NatCAB 9, TwCBDA, WebAB*
Cooley, Thomas Ross 1893-1959 *WhAm 3*
Cooley, William 1879-1964 *NatCAB 51*
Cooley, William Forbes 1857- *WhAm 4*
Cooley, Winnifred Harper *WomWWA 14*
Coolidge, Algernon 1860-1939 *NatCAB 29, WhAm 1*
Coolidge, Amory 1895-1952 *WhAm 3*
Coolidge, Archibald Cary 1866-1928 *AmBi, ApCAB X, DcAmB, WhAm 1*
Coolidge, Arthur William 1881-1952 *NatCAB 41, WhAm 3*
Coolidge, Asenath Carver 1830- *WomWWA 14*
Coolidge, C Earle 1892-1960 *NatCAB 49*
Coolidge, Calvin 1872-1933 *AmBi, ApCAB X, BiDrAC, BiDrUSE, DcAmB, EncAB, NatCAB 24, WebAB, WhAm 1, WhAmP*
Coolidge, Carlos 1792-1866 *ApCAB, BiAUS, Drake, NatCAB 8, TwCBDA*
Coolidge, Charles Allerton 1858-1936 *DcAmB S2, NatCAB 13, WhAm 1*
Coolidge, Charles Austin 1844-1926 *WhAm 1*
Coolidge, Cora Helen 1866-1933 *WhAm 1, WomWWA 14*
Coolidge, Cornelius 1778-1843? *WhAm H*
Coolidge, Dane 1873-1940 *NatCAB 35, WhAm 1*
Coolidge, David Hill 1833-1907 *NatCAB 19*
Coolidge, Edgar D 1881- *WhAm 6*
Coolidge, Elizabeth Penn Sprague 1864-1953 *DcAmB S5, WhAm 3*
Coolidge, Emelyn Lincoln 1873-1949 *WhAm 2, WomWWA 14*
Coolidge, Emma Downing d1968 *WhAm 4A*
Coolidge, F Gertrude *WomWWA 14*
Coolidge, Frank Wallace 1857-1926 *NatCAB 21*
Coolidge, Frederic Spaulding 1841-1906 *TwCBDA*
Coolidge, Frederick Spaulding 1841-1906 *BiDrAC*
Coolidge, George Greer 1885-1954 *NatCAB 48, WhAm 3*
Coolidge, Grace Goodhue 1879-1957 *WhAm 3*
Coolidge, Harold Jefferson 1870-1934 *NatCAB 45, WhAm 1*
Coolidge, Harriet Abbot Lincoln *AmWom*
Coolidge, Herbert 1875- *WhAm 5*
Coolidge, James Henry 1898-1961 *WhAm 4*
Coolidge, Jennie Adelaide Holmes 1866- *BiCAW, WomWWA 14*
Coolidge, John Calvin 1872-1933 *EncAAH, McGEWB*
Coolidge, John Gardner 1863-1936 *NatCAB 27, WhAm 1*
Coolidge, John Templeman 1856-1945 *NatCAB 35*
Coolidge, Joseph Bradford 1886-1965 *NatCAB 50, WhAm 4*
Coolidge, Joseph Randolph 1862-1928 *NatCAB 26, WhAm 1*
Coolidge, Joseph Randolph 1887-1936 *NatCAB 28*
Coolidge, Julian Lowell 1873-1954 *BiDAmEd, DcAmB S5, NatCAB 46, WhAm 3*
Coolidge, Julian Lowell 1873-1958 *DcScB*
Coolidge, Lawrence 1905-1950 *NatCAB 38, WhAm 3*
Coolidge, Louis Arthur 1861-1925 *ApCAB X,*

NatCAB 15, WhAm 1
Coolidge, Marcus Allen 1865-1947 *BiDrAC, NatCAB 35, WhAm 2*
Coolidge, Mary Elizabeth B Roberts 1860-1945 *WhAm 2, WomWWA 14*
Coolidge, Richard Bradford 1879-1957 *WhAm 4*
Coolidge, Richard H 1816-1866 *ApCAB*
Coolidge, Sherman 1863-1932 *WhAm 1*
Coolidge, Sidney 1830-1863 *ApCAB, TwCBDA*
Coolidge, Sidney 1864-1939 *NatCAB 29, WhAm 1*
Coolidge, Susan 1835-1905 *AmBi, AmWom, ApCAB, NotAW, TwCBDA*
Coolidge, T Jefferson 1893-1959 *NatCAB 47, WhAm 3*
Coolidge, T Jefferson, Jr. 1863-1912 *NatCAB 27, WhAm 1*
Coolidge, Thomas Jefferson 1831-1920 *ApCAB Sup, ApCAB X, DcAmB, NatCAB 12, TwCBDA, WhAm 1*
Coolidge, William David 1873-1975 *AsBiEn, WhAm 6*
Coolidge, William Henry 1859-1936 *WhAm 1*
Coom, Charles Sleeman 1853- *WhAm 4*
Cooman, Carl Conrad 1891-1953 *NatCAB 43*
Coomaraswamy, Ananda Kentish 1877-1947 *DcAmB S4, WhAm 2*
Coomb, William *NewYHSD*
Coombe, Harry E 1888-1969 *WhAm 5*
Coombe, Thomas 1747-1822 *DcAmB, Drake, WhAm H*
Coombe, Thomas 1748-1822 *NatCAB 7*
Coombe, Thomas 1758-1822 *ApCAB*
Coombe, Western Bascome 1859-1907 *NatCAB 22*
Coombes, Ethel Russell d1969 *WhAm 6*
Coombs, Charles Whitney 1859-1940 *TwCBDA, WhAm 1*
Coombs, Delbert Dana 1850-1938 *NatCAB 29*
Coombs, Frank Leslie 1853-1934 *BiDrAC, NatCAB 13, WhAm 1*
Coombs, George Holden 1863-1948 *WhAm 2*
Coombs, Harrison S 1921-1971 *WhAm 5*
Coombs, Leslie 1793-1881 *ApCAB, TwCBDA*
Coombs, Leslie Briggs 1888-1970 *NatCAB 56*
Coombs, Susan Bird 1880- *WomWWA 14*
Coombs, William Jerome 1832-1922 *NatCAB 26, WhAm 1*
Coombs, William Jerome 1833-1922 *BiDrAC, NatCAB 5, TwCBDA*
Coombs, Zelotes Wood 1865-1946 *NatCAB 35*
Coombs, Zelotes Wood 1865-1948 *WhAm 2*
Coon, Callie Prichard *WomWWA 14*
Coon, Charles Lee 1868-1927 *WhAm 1*
Coon, Daniel M *NewYHSD*
Coon, Eugene Henry 1890-1969 *NatCAB 56*
Coon, Frederick *NewYHSD*
Coon, Harold Macomber 1895-1962 *NatCAB 49*
Coon, Henry Clarke 1828-1898 *NatCAB 10*
Coon, J R d1961 *WhAm 4*
Coon, Jesse Drake 1885-1954 *WhAm 3*
Coon, John Henry 1831- *NatCAB 5*
Coon, John Sayler 1854- *WhAm 4*
Coon, Owen L 1894-1948 *WhAm 2*
Coon, Raymond Huntington 1883-1935 *NatCAB 38*
Coon, S *NewYHSD*
Coon, Samuel Harrison 1903- *BiDrAC*
Coon, Stephen Mortimer 1845-1913 *WhAm 1*
Coonan, Frederick Leo 1899-1961 *WhAm 4*
Coone, Henry Herbert 1869-1937 *WhAm 1*
Cooney, Charles Edwin 1873-1958 *WhAm 3*
Cooney, Dotia Trigg *WomWWA 14*
Cooney, Frank Henry 1872-1935 *NatCAB 26, WhAm 1*
Cooney, James 1848-1904 *BiDrAC, TwCBDA, WhAm 4*
Cooney, James D 1893-1971 *NatCAB 56, WhAm 5*
Cooney, Michael 1837-1928 *WhAm 1*
Cooney, Percival John 1871-1932 *WhAm 1*
Cooney, Russell Conwell 1892-1965 *WhAm 4*
Coonley, Avery 1870-1920 *NatCAB 24*
Coonley, Howard 1876-1966 *WhAm 4*
Coonley, John Clark 1838-1882 *NatCAB 25*
Coonley, Lydia Avery d1924 *WhAm 1*

Coonley, Prentiss Loomis 1880-1970 *WhAm 5*
Coonley, Queene Ferry 1874- *BiCAW*
Coonrad, Ralph Edward 1902-1958 *NatCAB 47*
Coonradt, Arthur Chapin 1887-1949 *NatCAB 37, WhAm 3*
Coons, Albert 1890-1959 *WhAm 3*
Coons, Arthur Gardiner 1900-1968 *NatCAB 55, WhAm 5*
Coons, H Westlake 1877-1957 *NatCAB 52*
Coons, Henry N 1853- *WhAm 4*
Coons, James Ephraim 1877- *WhAm 5*
Coons, Leroy Wilson 1872-1948 *WhAm 2*
Coons, Llewellyn 1847-1921 *NatCAB 6*
Coons, Samuel Warwick 1856- *WhAm 4*
Coontz, Robert Edward 1864-1935 *DcAmB S1, NatCAB 25, WebAMB, WhAm 1*
Coope, George Frederick 1893-1972 *WhAm 6*
Cooper, Alan Mills 1901-1960 *NatCAB 47*
Cooper, Albert Hudlburgh 1906-1974 *WhAm 6*
Cooper, Albert Warren 1879-1950 *NatCAB 39*
Cooper, Alfred Duff 1890-1954 *WhAm 3, WhWW-II*
Cooper, Allen Foster 1862-1917 *BiDrAC, WhAm 4*
Cooper, Anna Julia *WhoColR*
Cooper, Anna Wellington 1867- *WomWWA 14*
Cooper, Anne Thornhill 1873- *WomWWA 14*
Cooper, Armwell Lockwood 1870- *WhAm 5*
Cooper, Astley David Montague 1856-1924 *IIBEAAW, REnAW*
Cooper, Sir Astley Paston 1768-1841 *BiHiMed*
Cooper, B S *NewYHSD*
Cooper, Benjamin 1793-1850 *ApCAB, Drake*
Cooper, Bessie Dean 1874- *WomWWA 14*
Cooper, Beulah Keller *WomWWA 14*
Cooper, Brainard 1904-1967 *WhAm 4*
Cooper, Bryant Syms 1903-1952 *WhAm 3*
Cooper, Casper 1837?- *NewYHSD*
Cooper, Charles Champlin 1874-1930 *WhAm 1*
Cooper, Charles Hermance 1855- *WhAm 4*
Cooper, Charles Lawrence 1845- *WhAm 1*
Cooper, Charles Merian 1856-1923 *BiDrAC*
Cooper, Charles Philip 1827-1895 *BiDConf*
Cooper, Charles Phillips 1866-1950 *WhAm 3*
Cooper, Charles Proctor 1884-1966 *WhAm 4*
Cooper, Clayton Sedgwick 1869-1936 *NatCAB 27, WhAm 1*
Cooper, Colin Campbell 1856-1937 *IIBEAAW, WhAm 1*
Cooper, Cornelius V *NewYHSD*
Cooper, Cottie Albright 1885- *WomWWA 14*
Cooper, Courtney Ryley 1886-1940 *WhAm 1*
Cooper, Curtis Calvin 1882-1948 *NatCAB 39*
Cooper, Cyril Bernard 1898-1971 *WhAm 5*
Cooper, Dan 1901-1965 *NatCAB 51*
Cooper, Daniel C 1773-1818 *NatCAB 11*
Cooper, David *BiAUS*
Cooper, David Acron 1910-1974 *WhAm 6*
Cooper, David M *NewYHSD*
Cooper, David Young 1847-1920 *NatCAB 19*
Cooper, Dora Hauck 1870- *WomWWA 14*
Cooper, Douglas Hancock 1815-1879 *BiDConf*
Cooper, Douglas Harold 1915-1966 *WhAm 4*
Cooper, Drury Walls 1872-1957 *NatCAB 44, WhAm 3*
Cooper, Edgar Claudius 1887-1963 *NatCAB 48*
Cooper, Edmund 1821-1911 *BiAUS, BiDrAC*
Cooper, Edward 1824-1905 *ApCAB, DcAmB, NatCAB 3, WhAm 1*
Cooper, Edward 1873-1928 *BiDrAC, WhAm 3*
Cooper, Edward, Jr. 1897-1942 *NatCAB 41*
Cooper, Edward George 1883-1961 *NatCAB 47*
Cooper, Edward Nathan 1912-1971 *WhAm 5*
Cooper, Elias Samuel 1820-1862 *DcAmB, NatCAB 22, WhAm H*
Cooper, Elias Samuel 1821-1862 *ApCAB*
Cooper, Elisha Hilliard 1869-1947 *NatCAB 36, WhAm 2*
Cooper, Elizabeth 1877- *WhAm 5*
Cooper, Ellwood 1829-1918 *ApCAB, NatCAB 30, TwCBDA, WhAm 4*
Cooper, Emma Lampert 1865-1920 *IIBEAAW, WhAm 1, WomWWA 14*
Cooper, Ernest 1877-1939 *NatCAB 29*
Cooper, Ezekiel 1763-1847 *ApCAB, DcAmB, NatCAB 11, TwCBDA, WhAm H*
Cooper, Frank 1869-1946 *NatCAB 35, WhAm 2*

Cooper, Frank B 1855- *WhAm 4*

Cooper, Frank Edward 1910-1968 *NatCAB 54, WhAm 5*

Cooper, Frank Irving 1867-1933 *WhAm 1*

Cooper, Frank James 1901-1961 *WebAB*

Cooper, Frederic Taber 1864-1937 *TwCBDA, WhAm 1*

Cooper, Frederick William 1916-1961 *NatCAB 50*

Cooper, Gary 1901-1961 *NatCAB 48, WebAB, WhAm 4*

Cooper, George 1840- *NatCAB 8*

Cooper, George 1881-1959 *NatCAB 49, WhAm 3*

Cooper, George B 1808-1866 *BiAUS*

Cooper, George Bryan 1808-1866 *WhAm H*

Cooper, George Byran 1808-1866 *BiDrAC*

Cooper, George Franklin 1864-1953 *WhAm 3*

Cooper, George Henry 1821-1891 *ApCAB, Drake, NatCAB 4, TwCBDA*

Cooper, George Lotridge 1872-1937 *NatCAB 28*

Cooper, George Victor 1810-1878 *IIBEAAW, NewYHSD, WhAm H*

Cooper, George William 1851-1899 *BiDrAC*

Cooper, George William 1851-1901 *TwCBDA*

Cooper, Gladys d1971 *WhAm 5*

Cooper, H Wilbur 1871-1958 *NatCAB 47*

Cooper, Harold 1915-1969 *WhAm 5*

Cooper, Henry 1827-1884 *ApCAB, BiAUS, BiDrAC, NatCAB 12, TwCBDA, WhAm H*

Cooper, Henry Allen 1850-1931 *BiDrAC, WhAm 1, WhAmP*

Cooper, Henry Allen 1853?-1931 *TwCBDA*

Cooper, Henry Elliott 1873-1958 *WhAm 3*

Cooper, Henry Ernest 1857-1929 *AmBi, DcAmB, WhAm 1, WhAmP*

Cooper, Herman Charles 1875- *WhAm 5*

Cooper, Hermann 1895- *BiDAmEd*

Cooper, Homer Eber 1877-1953 *WhAm 3*

Cooper, Homer H 1868- *WhAm 5*

Cooper, Hugh Lincoln 1865-1937 *DcAmB S2, NatCAB 33, WhAm 1*

Cooper, Irving Steiger 1882-1935 *AmBi, WhAm 1*

Cooper, Isabelle Mitchell *WhAm 5*

Cooper, J *IIBEAAW*

Cooper, J 1695?- *NewYHSD*

Cooper, J Crossan 1863-1938 *NatCAB 31*

Cooper, Jacob 1830-1904 *DcAmB, NatCAB 22, TwCBDA, WhAm 1*

Cooper, James *NewYHSD*

Cooper, James 1810-1863 *ApCAB, BiAUS, BiDrAC, DcAmB, Drake, NatCAB 5, TwCBDA, WhAm H*

Cooper, James A 1874-1931 *NatCAB 36*

Cooper, James Allison 1894-1957 *NatCAB 46*

Cooper, James B 1753-1854 *ApCAB, Drake*

Cooper, James Campbell 1832- *ApCAB*

Cooper, James Earnest 1873-1943 *NatCAB 32*

Cooper, James Edward 1887-1940 *NatCAB 30*

Cooper, James Fenimore 1789-1851 *AmBi, ApCAB, DcAmB, Drake, EncAAH, EncAB, McGEWB, NatCAB 1, REnAW, TwCBDA, WebAB, WhAm H*

Cooper, James Graham 1830-1902 *DcAmB, IIBEAAW, NewYHSD, WhAm H*

Cooper, James Wesley 1842-1916 *WhAm 1*

Cooper, Jane Barnes 1843- *WomWWA 14*

Cooper, Jason Walker 1843-1925 *NatCAB 35*

Cooper, Jere 1893-1957 *BiDrAC, NatCAB 45, WhAm 3, WhAmP*

Cooper, Jesse Robert 1871-1956 *NatCAB 46*

Cooper, Job Adams 1843-1899 *NatCAB 6, NatCAB 33, TwCBDA, WhAm 1*

Cooper, John *NewYHSD*

Cooper, John 1729-1785 *BiAUS, BiDrAC, WhAm H, WhAmP*

Cooper, John Benjamin 1872- *WhoColR*

Cooper, John Cobb 1887-1967 *WhAm 4*

Cooper, John Downey 1849-1921 *NatCAB 42*

Cooper, John Fawcett 1822-1899 *NatCAB 12*

Cooper, John Gordon 1872-1955 *BiDrAC, WhAm 5, WhAmP*

Cooper, John Jesse 1867-1949 *NatCAB 40*

Cooper, John Montgomery 1881-1949 *DcAmB S4, WhAm 3*

Cooper, John Montgomery 1883-1950 *NatCAB 38*

Cooper, John Sherman 1901- *BiDrAC*

Cooper, Joseph Alexander 1823-1910 *ApCAB, DcAmB, TwCBDA*

Cooper, Joseph David 1917-1975 *WhAm 6*

Cooper, Julia Dean *NotAW*

Cooper, Kent 1880-1965 *WhAm 4*

Cooper, Lane 1875-1959 *NatCAB 47, WhAm 3*

Cooper, Leon N 1930- *WebAB*

Cooper, Linton Leander 1880- *WhAm 6*

Cooper, Lunsford Pitts 1830-1902 *NatCAB 8*

Cooper, Mark A 1800-1885 *BiAUS*

Cooper, Mark Anthony 1800-1885 *BiDrAC, DcAmB, WhAm H*

Cooper, Mark Antony 1800-1885 *ApCAB, TwCBDA*

Cooper, Merian C 1894-1973 *WhAm 5*

Cooper, Myers Young 1873-1958 *NatCAB 49, WhAm 3*

Cooper, Myles 1735-1785 *ApCAB, BiDAmEd, Drake, NatCAB 6, TwCBDA*

Cooper, Myles 1737-1785 *AmBi, DcAmB, WhAm H*

Cooper, Nathaniel M *NewYHSD*

Cooper, Ola Beth Capron *WomWWA 14*

Cooper, Oscar Henry 1852-1932 *BiDAmEd, NatCAB 30, WhAm 1*

Cooper, Oswald Bruce 1879-1940 *DcAmB S2*

Cooper, Peregrine F *NewYHSD*

Cooper, Peter *BnEnAmA, NewYHSD*

Cooper, Peter 1791-1883 *AmBi, ApCAB, DcAmB, Drake, EncAB, McGEWB, NatCAB 3, TwCBDA, WebAB, WhAm H*

Cooper, Philip 1908-1972 *WhAm 6*

Cooper, Philip Henry 1844-1912 *ApCAB, NatCAB 4, NatCAB 16, TwCBDA, WhAm 1*

Cooper, Prentice 1895-1969 *NatCAB 55, WhAm 5*

Cooper, Priscilla *NotAW*

Cooper, Richard Matlack 1768-1843 *BiDrAC, WhAm H*

Cooper, Richard Matlack 1768-1844 *BiAUS, TwCBDA*

Cooper, Richard Watson 1866-1954 *WhAm 3*

Cooper, Robert Archer 1874-1953 *NatCAB 40, WhAm 3*

Cooper, Robert Franklin 1881-1962 *WhAm 4*

Cooper, Robert Muldrow 1887-1966 *WhAm 4*

Cooper, Russell Morgan 1907-1975 *WhAm 6*

Cooper, Sam Bronson 1850-1918 *WhAm 1*

Cooper, Samuel 1725-1783 *ApCAB, DcAmB, Drake, TwCBDA, WhAm H*

Cooper, Samuel 1796?-1876 *Drake*

Cooper, Samuel 1798-1876 *AmBi, ApCAB, BiDConf, DcAmB, NatCAB 11, TwCBDA, WebAMB, WhAm H*

Cooper, Samuel Bronson 1850-1918 *BiDrAC, TwCBDA*

Cooper, Samuel Inman 1894-1974 *WhAm 6*

Cooper, Samuel Williams 1860-1939 *NatCAB 28, WhAm 1*

Cooper, Sanson Milligan 1858- *WhAm 4*

Cooper, Sarah Brown Ingersoll 1835-1896 *BiDAmEd, NotAW*

Cooper, Sarah Brown Ingersoll 1836-1896 *AmWom, DcAmB, NatCAB 3, WhAm H*

Cooper, Susan Fenimore 1813-1894 *ApCAB, DcAmB, NatCAB 6, NotAW, TwCBDA, WhAm H*

Cooper, Susan Fenimore 1815-1894 *Drake*

Cooper, Sydney Perry 1877-1944 *NatCAB 39*

Cooper, Theodore 1839-1919 *DcAmB, NatCAB 11, NatCAB 19, WhAm 1*

Cooper, Thomas 1759-1839 *AmBi, BiDAmEd, DcAmB, DcScB, Drake, EncAB, McGEWB, TwCBDA, WebAB, WhAm H, WhAmP*

Cooper, Thomas 1759-1840 *ApCAB, NatCAB 11*

Cooper, Thomas 1764-1829 *BiAUS, BiDrAC, WhAm H*

Cooper, Thomas Abthorpe 1776-1849 *DcAmB, NatCAB 10, TwCBDA, WhAm H*

Cooper, Thomas Apthorpe 1776-1849 *ApCAB, Drake*

Cooper, Thomas Buchecker 1823-1862 *BiAUS, BiDrAC, WhAm H*

Cooper, Tim E 1843- *NatCAB 5*

Cooper, W R 1793-1856 *BiAUS*

Cooper, W R *see also* Cooper, William Raworth

Cooper, Wade Hampton 1874-1960 *WhAm 4, WhAm 5*

Cooper, Washington Bogart 1802-1889 *NewYHSD*

Cooper, William 1632-1710 *NatCAB 4*

Cooper, William 1692-1743 *NatCAB 9, WhAm H*

Cooper, William 1694-1743 *ApCAB, Drake*

Cooper, William 1720-1809 *ApCAB*

Cooper, William 1754-1809 *BiAUS, BiDrAC, DcAmB, NatCAB 13, TwCBDA, WhAm H, WhAmP*

Cooper, William 1798- *WhAm H*

Cooper, William Albert 1843-1917 *NatCAB 17, WhAm 4*

Cooper, William Alpha 1868-1939 *NatCAB 29, WhAm 1*

Cooper, William B 1771-1849 *BiAUS, NatCAB 11*

Cooper, William Brown 1811-1900 *NewYHSD*

Cooper, William Craig 1832-1902 *BiDrAC, TwCBDA*

Cooper, William Frierson 1820- *NatCAB 9, TwCBDA*

Cooper, William Goodwin 1903-1971 *WhAm 5*

Cooper, William Irenaeus 1857-1931 *WhAm 1*

Cooper, William John 1882-1935 *DcAmB S1, NatCAB 28, WhAm 1*

Cooper, William Knowles 1867-1932 *NatCAB 24, WhAm 1*

Cooper, William Lee 1878- *WhAm 6*

Cooper, William Prentice 1870-1961 *NatCAB 49*

Cooper, William Raworth 1793-1856 *BiDrAC, WhAm H*

Cooper, William Raworth *see also* Cooper, W R

Cooper, Wyllis 1899-1955 *WhAm 3*

Cooper-Poucher, Matilda S 1839-1900 *DcAmB, WhAm H*

Cooperman, Morris Bernard 1884-1948 *NatCAB 36*

Cooperrider, George T 1852-1916 *WhAm 1*

Coors, D Stanley 1889-1960 *WhAm 4*

Coors, Henry George 1885-1961 *NatCAB 48*

Coote, Sir Eyre 1757-1823 *ApCAB, Drake*

Coote, Richard 1636-1701 *AmBi, DcAmB, NatCAB 7, WhAm H, WhAmP*

Cooter, James Thomas 1858- *NatCAB 7, TwCBDA, WhAm 4*

Coover, John Edgar 1872-1938 *NatCAB 27, WhAm 1*

Coover, Melanchthon 1861-1955 *WhAm 3*

Coowescoowe 1790-1866 *WebAB*

Copahue *ApCAB*

Copano 1511-1548 *ApCAB*

Copass, Alice Reynolds 1882- *WomWWA 14*

Copass, Benjamin Andrew 1865- *WhAm 5*

Copaux, Hippolyte Eugene 1872-1934 *DcScB*

Cope, Alexis 1841- *WhAm 4*

Cope, Arthur Clay 1909-1966 *NatCAB 53, WhAm 4*

Cope, Caleb Frederick 1797-1888 *DcAmB, NatCAB 22, WhAm H*

Cope, Edward Drinker 1840-1897 *AmBi, ApCAB, AsBiEn, DcAmB, DcScB, DcScB Sup, NatCAB 7, TwCBDA, WhAm H*

Cope, George 1855-1929 *BnEnAmA*

Cope, Gilbert 1840-1928 *ApCAB Sup, TwCBDA, WhAm 3*

Cope, Gordon Nicholson 1906- *IIBEAAW*

Cope, Harley Francis 1898-1963 *NatCAB 52*

Cope, Henry Frederick 1870-1923 *NatCAB 20, WhAm 1*

Cope, Kenneth Benedict 1901-1961 *NatCAB 49*

Cope, Millard 1905-1964 *WhAm 4*

Cope, Otis Merriam 1880-1950 *NatCAB 39*

Cope, Porter Farquharson 1869-1950 *NatCAB 46*

Cope, Quill Evan 1912-1968 *WhAm 5*

Cope, Robert S 1870-1952 *WhAm 3*

Cope, Thomas *NewYHSD*

Cope, Thomas Pym 1768-1854 *ApCAB,*
DcAmB, Drake, NatCAB 5, TwCBDA,
WhAm H
Cope, Walter 1860-1902 *DcAmB, NatCAB 27,*
WhAm H
Cope, Walter Burton 1861-1909 *NatCAB 15*
Cope, Warren W 1824-1903 *NatCAB 12*
Copelan, Robert W 1894-1967 *WhAm 4*
Copeland, Mister *NewYHSD*
Copeland, Alfred Bryant 1840-1909 *ApCAB,*
NewYHSD, WhAm 4
Copeland, Arthur H, Sr. 1898-1970 *WhAm 5*
Copeland, Charles 1858-1945 *NatCAB 36,*
WhAm 2
Copeland, Charles Daniel 1871-1937
NatCAB 28
Copeland, Charles Townsend 1860-1952
ApCAB X, DcAmB S5, WhAm 3
Copeland, Charles W 1815-1895 *DcAmB,*
TwCBDA, WhAm H
Copeland, D Graham 1885-1949 *NatCAB 38*
Copeland, Edward Rivers 1879-1952 *WhAm 3*
Copeland, Edwin Bingham 1873- *WhAm 5*
Copeland, Fayette 1895-1961 *WhAm 4*
Copeland, Foster 1858-1935 *WhAm 1*
Copeland, Frederick Kent 1855-1928 *WhAm 1*
Copeland, Guild Anderson 1862-1925 *WhAm 1*
Copeland, Henry Clay 1844- *ApCAB X*
Copeland, Isaac Seymour 1849-1919
NatCAB 18
Copeland, Joseph T 1830?- *ApCAB*
Copeland, Kenneth Wilford 1912-1973 *WhAm 6*
Copeland, Lennie Phoebe 1881-1951 *WhAm 3*
Copeland, Lucius Frederick 1841- *NatCAB 9*
Copeland, Manton 1881- *WhAm 6*
Copeland, Melvin Thomas 1884-1975 *WhAm 6*
Copeland, Oren Sturman 1887-1958 *BiDrAC,*
WhAm 3
Copeland, Paul L 1905-1964 *WhAm 4*
Copeland, Royal Samuel 1868-1938 *ApCAB X,*
BiDrAC, DcAmB S2, NatCAB 15,
WhAm 1, WhAmP
Copeland, Theodore 1867- *WhAm 1*
Copeland, Walter Scott 1856-1928 *WhAm 1*
Copeland, William Adams 1862- *WhAm 4*
Copeland, William Franklin 1872-1950
WhAm 3
Copeland, William Monroe 1859- *NatCAB 17*
Copernicus, Nicholas 1473-1543 *DcScB*
Copernicus, Nicolas 1473-1543 *AsBiEn*
Copernicus, Nicolaus 1473-1543 *McGEWB*
Copestick, Alfred *NewYHSD*
Copland, Aaron 1900- *EncAAH, EncAB,*
McGEWB, WebAB
Copland, Douglas Berry 1894-1971 *WhAm 5*
Copland, James 1791-1870 *BiHiMed*
Copland, Patrick *NatCAB 3*
Copley, Charles *NewYHSD*
Copley, Frederick S *NewYHSD*
Copley, Ira Clifton 1864-1947 *BiDrAC,*
DcAmB S4, NatCAB 36, WhAm 2,
WhAmP
Copley, James Strohn 1916-1973 *WhAm 6*
Copley, John Singleton 1737-1813 *Drake*
Copley, John Singleton 1737-1815 *ApCAB,*
NatCAB 6, TwCBDA
Copley, John Singleton 1738-1815 *AmBi,*
BnEnAmA, DcAmB, EncAB, McGEWB,
NewYHSD, WebAB, WhAm H
Copley, John Singleton, Jr. 1772-1863 *ApCAB*
Copley, Sir Lionel d1693? *DcAmB, NatCAB 7,*
WhAm H
Copley, Mary Singleton *NotAW*
Copley, Thomas 1595-1652? *DcAmB*
Coplin, John William 1865-1946 *NatCAB 34*
Coplin, William Michael Late 1864-1928
WhAm 1
Copmann, P *NewYHSD*
Copp, Andrew James 1846-1940 *NatCAB 45*
Copp, Andrew James, Jr. 1880-1971
NatCAB 57
Copp, Arthur Woodward 1868- *WhAm 1*
Copp, E F Foster 1899-1969 *NatCAB 56*
Copp, Evelyn Fletcher 1872- *WomWWA 14*
Copp, Helen Rankin 1853- *AmWom*
Copp, Maud Evelyn Fletcher 1872- *BiCAW*
Copp, Owen 1858-1933 *WhAm 1*

Coppage, Benjamin Denver 1872-1931
NatCAB 22
Coppee, Henry 1821-1895 *AmBi, ApCAB,*
BiDAmEd, DcAmB, Drake, NatCAB 7,
TwCBDA, WhAm H
Coppee, Henry St. Leger 1853-1901 *WhAm 1*
Coppell, Arthur 1872-1934 *NatCAB 26*
Coppens, Charles 1835-1920 *BiDAmEd,*
DcAmB, WhAm H
Copper, John C *NewYHSD*
Copper, Joseph Benjamin 1905-1968 *WhAm 5*
Coppernoll, William D 1864- *WhAm 4*
Coppers, George Henry 1902-1960 *WhAm 4*
Coppet, Edward J De 1855-1916 *DcAmB*
Coppin, Fanny Marion Jackson 1837?-1913
BiDAmEd, NotAW
Coppin, Levi J 1848-1924 *NatCAB 3,*
WhAm 3, WhoColR
Coppinger, John Joseph 1834-1909 *ApCAB Sup,*
TwCBDA, WhAm 1
Coppini, Pompeo 1870-1957 *NatCAB 48,*
WhAm 3
Coppock, Fred Douglass 1878- *WhAm 6*
Coppock, William Homer 1911-1975 *WhAm 6*
Coppridge, William Maurice 1893-1959
WhAm 3
Coppus, Frans Hubertus Cornelius 1880-1941
NatCAB 22
Copway, George d1863 *Drake*
Copway, George 1818-1863 *DcAmB,*
WhAm H
Copway, George 1820-1863 *ApCAB*
Coquard, Leon 1860- *WhAm 4*
Coquardon, A *NewYHSD*
Coquelin, Benoit Constant 1841-1909
WhAm HA, WhAm 4
Coquillard, Alexis 1795-1855 *NatCAB 11*
Coquillett, Daniel William 1856-1911 *DcAmB,*
WhAm 1
Coquillette, St. Elmo 1890-1971 *WhAm 5*
Coradi, L *NewYHSD*
Coram, Joseph A *WhAm 5*
Coram, Thomas 1667?-1751 *Drake*
Coram, Thomas 1668-1751 *AmBi, ApCAB,*
DcAmB, NatCAB 6, WhAm H
Coram, Thomas 1757-1811 *NewYHSD,*
WhAm H
Coras, Jose Zacarias 1752-1819 *ApCAB*
Corasaniti, Frank 1884-1955 *NatCAB 47*
Corbaley, Gordon Cook 1880-1964 *WhAm 4*
Corbaley, Kate Alaska Hinckley Hooper
1878-1938 *NatCAB 28*
Corbe, Zenan M 1876- *WhAm 5*
Corbet, Charles 1851-1927 *NatCAB 21*
Corbett, Frank Edward 1906-1952 *NatCAB 42*
Corbett, Gail Sherman *BiCAW, WhAm 5,*
WomWWA 14
Corbett, George *NewYHSD*
Corbett, Gerald Robert 1903-1973 *WhAm 6*
Corbett, Harvey Wiley 1873-1954 *DcAmB S5,*
WhAm 3
Corbett, Henry L 1881-1957 *WhAm 3*
Corbett, Henry Winslow 1827-1903 *ApCAB,*
BiAUS, BiDrAC, DcAmB, NatCAB 6,
TwCBDA, WhAm 1
Corbett, Hunter 1835-1920 *WhAm 1*
Corbett, James John 1866-1933 *AmBi,*
DcAmB S1, WebAB, WhAm HA,
WhAm 4
Corbett, Jim 1875-1955 *WhAm 3*
Corbett, John Thomas 1861-1940 *NatCAB 43*
Corbett, Lamert Seymour 1887-1945 *WhAm 2*
Corbett, Laurence Jay 1877-1951 *WhAm 3*
Corbett, Lee Cleveland 1867-1940 *WhAm 1*
Corbett, Mary Schofield White 1865-
WomWWA 14
Corbett, Paul McLain 1905-1972 *NatCAB 57*
Corbett, Robert James 1905-1971 *BiDrAC,*
WhAm 5
Corbett, Thomas H *NewYHSD*
Corbett, Timothy 1858-1939 *NatCAB 15,*
WhAm 1
Corbetta, Roger Henry 1896-1974 *WhAm 6*
Corbin *NewYHSD*
Corbin, Alberta Linton 1870- *WomWWA 14*
Corbin, Alvin LeRoy 1913-1969 *WhAm 5*
Corbin, Arthur Linton 1874-1967 *WhAm 4*
Corbin, Arthur Linton, Jr. 1902-1969 *WhAm 5*

Corbin, Austin 1827-1896 *ApCAB Sup,*
DcAmB, NatCAB 5, NatCAB 31,
TwCBDA, WhAm H
Corbin, Caroline Fairfield 1835- *WhAm 4,*
WomWWA 14
Corbin, Charles Russell 1893-1950 *WhAm 2A*
Corbin, Clement K 1879- *WhAm 6*
Corbin, Daniel C 1837-1918 *WhAm 1*
Corbin, Daniel Chase 1832-1918 *DcAmB,*
NatCAB 22
Corbin, Floyd Stewart 1869-1924 *NatCAB 16,*
NatCAB 19
Corbin, George Waldo 1859-1908 *NatCAB 21*
Corbin, Henry Clark 1842-1909 *AmBi,*
DcAmB S1, WhAm 1
Corbin, Henry Clarke 1842-1909 *ApCAB Sup,*
NatCAB 12
Corbin, Henry Clarke 1843-1909 *TwCBDA*
Corbin, Henry Pinkney 1867-1922 *WhAm 1*
Corbin, Hetty M 1883- *WomWWA 14*
Corbin, Horace Kellogg 1887-1960 *WhAm 3*
Corbin, John 1870-1959 *NatCAB 14,*
WhAm 3
Corbin, Joseph Carter 1833-1911 *BiDAmEd,*
WhAm 4
Corbin, Margaret 1750?- *ApCAB*
Corbin, Margaret 1751-1788? *NatCAB 6*
Corbin, Margaret Cochran 1751-1800? *AmBi,*
DcAmB, NotAW, WebAB, WebAMB,
WhAm H
Corbin, Philip 1824-1910 *WhAm 1*
Corbin, Thomas G 1820- *Drake*
Corbin, Thomas G 1820-1886 *ApCAB*
Corbin, Thomas G 1820-1901 *TwCBDA*
Corbin, William Herbert 1864-1945 *NatCAB 34,*
WhAm 2
Corbin, William Lee 1872-1952 *WhAm 3*
Corbino, Jon 1905-1964 *WhAm 4*
Corbit, John Darlington, Jr. 1910-1973
WhAm 6
Corbit, Ross 1899-1974 *WhAm 6*
Corbitt, Charles Linwood 1862-1934 *WhAm 1*
Corbitt, James Howard 1869-1945 *NatCAB 37,*
WhAm 2
Corbitt, Richard Johnson 1873-1961
NatCAB 50
Corbly, Lawrence Jugurtha 1863- *WhAm 4*
Corbus, Budd Clarke 1876-1954 *WhAm 3*
Corbus, Florence Josephine 1878-
WomWWA 14
Corby, William 1832-1897 *TwCBDA*
Corby, William 1833-1897 *AmBi, DcAmB,*
WhAm H
Corby, William Stephen 1867-1935 *NatCAB 25*
Corcilius, Inez 1879- *WomWWA 14*
Corcoran, Brewer 1877- *WhAm 5*
Corcoran, Francis Vincent 1879-1939 *WhAm 1*
Corcoran, George Francis 1900-1964 *WhAm 4*
Corcoran, James Andrew 1820-1889 *ApCAB,*
DcAmB, TwCBDA
Corcoran, James Augustine 1886-1953
NatCAB 44
Corcoran, John William 1853-1904 *WhAm 1*
Corcoran, Katherine *WhAm H*
Corcoran, Michael 1827-1863 *AmBi, ApCAB,*
Drake, NatCAB 4, TwCBDA, WhAm H
Corcoran, Sanford William 1876-1946 *WhAm 2*
Corcoran, Thomas J 1896-1956 *WhAm 3*
Corcoran, William Joseph 1895-1955
NatCAB 43
Corcoran, William Warwick 1884-1962
WhAm 4
Corcoran, William Wilson 1798-1888 *AmBi,*
ApCAB, BiAUS, DcAmB, NatCAB 3,
TwCBDA, WebAB, WhAm H
Corcos, Lucille 1908-1973 *WhAm 6*
Cord, Errett Lobban 1894-1974 *WhAm 6*
Cordano *NewYHSD*
Cordell, Eugene Fauntleroy 1843-1913
NatCAB 19
Cordell, L C 1808-1870 *NewYHSD*
Cordell, Wayne Wellington 1864- *WhAm 4*
Cordero, Jose *IIBEAAW, NewYHSD*
Cordero Y Molina, Rafael 1790-1868 *BiDAmEd*
Cordes, Frank 1870-1952 *WhAm 3*
Cordes, Frederick Carl 1892-1965 *NatCAB 52,*
WhAm 4
Cordes, H T A *NewYHSD*

Cordes, William 1873- *ApCAB X*
Cordice, John Walter Vincent 1881-1958 *NatCAB 47*
Cordier, Andrew Wellington 1901-1975 *WhAm 6*
Cordier, Auguste Julien 1854-1906 *NatCAB 14*
Cordier, Pierre-Louis-Antoine 1777-1861 *DcScB*
Cordiner, Ralph Jarron 1900-1973 *WhAm 6*
Cordingley, Ernest William 1899-1945 *NatCAB 37*
Cordley, Arthur Burton 1864-1936 *WhAm 1*
Cordner, John 1816-1894 *NatCAB 16*
Cordoba, Gonzalo Fernandez, Conde De 1453-1515 *WhoMilH*
Cordon, Guy 1890-1969 *BiDrAC, WhAm 5*
Cordon, Norman 1904-1964 *NatCAB 52*
Cordova, Francisco De d1514 *ApCAB*
Cordova, Francisco Fernandez De d1518 *ApCAB, Drake*
Cordova, Gabriel 1891-1953 *WhAm 3*
Cordova, Jorge Luis 1907- *BiDrAC*
Cordova, Jose M 1797-1829 *ApCAB, Drake*
Cordova, Jose Maria 1786-1846 *ApCAB*
Cordova, Pedro De 1460-1525 *ApCAB*
Cordova-Davila, Felix 1878-1938 *WhAm 1*
Cordts, John Nicholas 1865-1913 *NatCAB 17*
Corduba Y Salinas *ApCAB*
Cordus, Euricius 1486-1535 *DcScB*
Cordus, Valerius 1515-1544 *DcScB*
Core, Matilda McClure McKeehan 1874- *WomWWA 14*
Corea, George Claude Stanley 1894-1962 *WhAm 4*
Corea, Luis Felipe 1864-1932 *WhAm 1*
Coreal, Francisco 1648-1708 *ApCAB, Drake*
Corelli, Arcangelo 1653-1713 *McGEWB*
Corette, John Earl 1880- *WhAm 6*
Corey, Albert B 1898-1963 *WhAm 4*
Corey, Alfred Adams, Jr. 1878-1960 *NatCAB 47, WhAm 5*
Corey, Arthur Benjamin 1891-1950 *NatCAB 39*
Corey, Caroline Heberd 1868- *WomWWA 14*
Corey, Charles Henry 1834-1899 *ApCAB, TwCBDA, WhAm 1*
Corey, Delia Brigham 1858- *WomWWA 14*
Corey, Fred Daniel 1863-1936 *NatCAB 27, WhAm 1*
Corey, Giles 1649?-1692 *NatCAB 12*
Corey, Herbert 1872-1954 *WhAm 3*
Corey, Horace Harold 1893-1966 *WhAm 4*
Corey, James William 1891-1970 *WhAm 5*
Corey, Lester Spaulding 1880- *WhAm 6*
Corey, Lewis 1892-1953 *DcAmB S5*
Corey, Martha d1692 *NotAW*
Corey, Robert Brainard 1897-1971 *WhAm 5*
Corey, Stephen Jared 1873- *WhAm 5*
Corey, Wendell Reid 1914-1968 *WhAm 5*
Corey, William Butcher 1881-1967 *NatCAB 53*
Corey, William Ellis 1866-1934 *DcAmB S1, NatCAB 14, WhAm 1*
Corfman, Elmer Ellsworth 1863- *WhAm 5*
Corgan, Joseph Aloysius 1907-1975 *WhAm 6*
Cori, Carl Ferdinand 1896- *AsBiEn, WebAB*
Cori, Gerty Theresa Radnitz 1896-1957 *AsBiEn, DcScB, NatCAB 48, WebAB, WhAm 3*
Coriat, Isador Henry 1875-1943 *ApCAB X, DcAmB S3, NatCAB 32, WhAm 2*
Coriell, Louis Duncan 1878- *WhAm 6*
Coriolis, Gaspard Gustave De 1792-1843 *AsBiEn, DcScB*
Cork, James M 1894-1957 *WhAm 3*
Corker, Stephen Alfestus 1830-1879 *BiDrAC, WhAm H*
Corkery, Daniel *NewYHSD*
Corkery, Francis E 1903-1969 *WhAm 5*
Corkery, Thomas 1880-1947 *NatCAB 37*
Corkey, Alexander 1871-1914 *WhAm 1*
Corkill, James Frederick 1912-1964 *WhAm 4*
Corkill, William Andrew 1877-1967 *NatCAB 53*
Corkran, Anna M L 1858- *WomWWA 14*
Corle, Edwin 1906-1956 *NatCAB 46, WhAm 3*
Corlet, Elijah 1611-1687 *ApCAB, BiDAmEd, Drake*
Corlett, George Milton 1884-1955 *WhAm 3*
Corlett, Webster David 1891-1971 *NatCAB 57, WhAm 5*

Corlett, William Thomas 1854-1948 *NatCAB 14, NatCAB 38, WhAm 2*
Corlett, William Wellington 1842-1890 *BiDrAC, WhAm H*
Corley, Frederick Dexter 1882-1960 *WhAm 4*
Corley, James Henry 1904-1974 *WhAm 6*
Corley, Jesse Lee 1877-1943 *WhAm 2*
Corley, Manuel Simeon 1823-1902 *ApCAB, BiDrAC, TwCBDA*
Corley, Simeon *BiAUS*
Corlies, Benjamin F *NewYHSD*
Corliss, Augustus Whittemore 1837-1908 *WhAm 1*
Corliss, Charles Albert 1868-1936 *WhAm 1*
Corliss, Frederick William 1834- *WhAm 4*
Corliss, George Frost 1841-1927 *NatCAB 22*
Corliss, George Henry 1817-1888 *AmBi, ApCAB, ApCAB X, DcAmB, NatCAB 10, TwCBDA, WebAB, WhAm H*
Corliss, Guy Carleton Haynes 1858-1937 *NatCAB 13, NatCAB 32, WhAm 3*
Corliss, John Blaisdell 1851-1929 *BiDrAC, NatCAB 22, TwCBDA, WhAm 1*
Corliss, Leland Marchant 1905-1970 *NatCAB 55, WhAm 5*
Corliss, Maria Louisa 1839- *WomWWA 14*
Corliss, William 1835- *NatCAB 4*
Cormack, George 1870-1953 *NatCAB 44*
Corman, James Charles 1920- *BiDrAC*
Cormeny, Alvin E 1912-1973 *WhAm 5*
Cormier, Charles 1813- *ApCAB*
Corn, Hannah 1854- *WomWWA 14*
Corn, Herbert F 1897-1966 *WhAm 4*
Corn, N S 1884-1967 *WhAm 4A*
Corn, Samuel Thompson 1840-1925 *NatCAB 5, WhAm 1*
Corn, William Anderson 1892-1957 *NatCAB 50*
Cornbrooks, Ernest Ivon 1875-1939 *NatCAB 29*
Cornbrooks, Thomas Mullan 1876-1944 *WhAm 2*
Cornbury, Edward Hyde, Viscount 1661-1723 *ApCAB, DcAmB, Drake, WhAm H, WhAmP*
Corne, Michel Felice 1752?-1845 *NewYHSD, WhAm H*
Corneau, Barton 1878- *WhAm 6*
Corneille, Pierre 1606-1684 *McGEWB*
Cornelison, John M 1802-1875 *BiAUS*
Cornelison, Robert Wilson 1869-1946 *NatCAB 35*
Cornelius, Adam E 1882-1953 *WhAm 3*
Cornelius, Charles LeSueur 1888-1968 *WhAm 5*
Cornelius, Charles Over 1890-1937 *WhAm 1*
Cornelius, David William 1885-1942 *NatCAB 35*
Cornelius, Elias 1758-1823 *ApCAB*
Cornelius, Elias 1794-1832 *ApCAB, Drake, NatCAB 5, TwCBDA*
Cornelius, Harold Comfort 1873- *ApCAB X*
Cornelius, Martin Phelps 1883-1952 *WhAm 3*
Cornelius, Mary Ann 1827-1918 *WhAm 1*
Cornelius, Mary Ann 1829-1918 *AmWom, WomWWA 14*
Cornelius, Olivia Smith 1882- *WomWWA 14*
Cornelius, Ralph E 1869- *WhAm 5*
Cornelius, Samuel Anderson 1857-1932 *WhAm 1*
Cornelius, Willard M 1884-1957 *WhAm 3*
Cornelius, William Albert 1867-1947 *NatCAB 36*
Cornelius, William Harry, II 1919-1964 *NatCAB 52*
Cornelius, Yngve Ragnar 1905-1966 *NatCAB 53*
Cornell, Alonzo B 1832-1904 *AmBi, ApCAB, DcAmB, NatCAB 3, TwCBDA, WhAm 1, WhAmP*
Cornell, Beaumont Sandfield 1892-1958 *NatCAB 51*
Cornell, Charles James 1890-1972 *WebAB, WhAm 5*
Cornell, Clara Garfield 1880- *WomWWA 14*
Cornell, Edward Shelton, Jr. 1892-1972 *NatCAB 57*
Cornell, Ellen Frances 1835- *AmWom*
Cornell, Emma Butler 1868- *WomWWA 14*
Cornell, Ezekiel d1800 *ApCAB, BiAUS,*

Drake
Cornell, Ezekiel 1732-1800 *BiDrAC*
Cornell, Ezekiel 1733-1800 *DcAmB, WhAm H*
Cornell, Ezra 1807-1874 *AmBi, ApCAB, DcAmB, McGEWB, NatCAB 4, TwCBDA, WebAB, WhAm H*
Cornell, Franklin Cuthbert 1837-1908 *NatCAB 28*
Cornell, George Birdsall 1855-1929 *ApCAB X*
Cornell, Henry Watson 1866-1932 *NatCAB 24*
Cornell, Hughes *WhAm 5*
Cornell, Irwin H 1881-1963 *WhAm 4*
Cornell, James E *NewYHSD*
Cornell, John 1839- *ApCAB X*
Cornell, John Alfred 1886-1956 *NatCAB 45*
Cornell, John Black 1821-1887 *NatCAB 13, TwCBDA*
Cornell, John Black 1825?-1887 *ApCAB*
Cornell, John Black 1885-1963 *NatCAB 49*
Cornell, John Henry 1828-1894 *ApCAB, TwCBDA*
Cornell, John Joy 1884-1948 *NatCAB 38*
Cornell, John M 1846- *ApCAB X*
Cornell, John V *NewYHSD*
Cornell, Joseph 1903-1972 *WhAm 5*
Cornell, Joseph 1903-1973 *BnEnAmA*
Cornell, Katharine 1893-1974 *WhAm 6*
Cornell, Katharine 1898-1974 *WebAB*
Cornell, Lucinda Vail *WomWWA 14*
Cornell, Milton Longacre 1884-1958 *ApCAB X, NatCAB 44*
Cornell, Oliver Hazard Perry 1842-1911 *NatCAB 15*
Cornell, Ralph Dalton 1890-1972 *NatCAB 57*
Cornell, Thomas 1814-1890 *BiAUS, BiDrAC, TwCBDA, WhAm H*
Cornell, Walter Stewart 1877-1969 *WhAm 5*
Cornell, William Bouck 1883-1957 *WhAm 3*
Cornell, William Mason 1802-1895 *ApCAB, Drake, TwCBDA*
Cornell, William Wiggins 1823-1870 *ApCAB, TwCBDA*
Cornelson, George Henry 1869-1928 *WhAm 1*
Cornelson, George Henry 1870-1928 *NatCAB 21*
Cornelson, George Henry 1898-1954 *NatCAB 45*
Corner, George Washington 1862-1938 *WhAm 1*
Corner, Thomas Cromwell 1865-1938 *WhAm 1*
Cornet, Henry Louis 1856-1936 *NatCAB 28*
Cornetet, Noah E 1867-1931 *WhAm 1*
Cornets De Groot *DcScB*
Cornette, Claude-Melchior 1744-1794 *DcScB*
Cornick, Howard 1874- *WhAm 2*
Cornick, Philip H 1883-1971 *WhAm 5*
Cornil, Andre-Victor 1837-1908 *BiHiMed*
Corning, Charles Robert 1855-1924 *NatCAB 17, WhAm 1*
Corning, Edwin 1883-1934 *NatCAB 25*
Corning, Edwin 1919-1964 *WhAm 4*
Corning, Erastus 1794-1872 *ApCAB, BiAUS, BiDrAC, DcAmB, Drake, EncAB, McGEWB, TwCBDA, WhAm H, WhAmP*
Corning, Erastus 1795-1872 *AmBi*
Corning, Frederick Gleason 1857-1937 *WhAm 1*
Corning, Hanson Kelly 1860-1951 *NatCAB 39*
Corning, Hobart M 1889-1970 *WhAm 5*
Corning, James Leonard 1828- *TwCBDA*
Corning, James Leonard 1855-1923 *AmBi, ApCAB X, NatCAB 17, WhAm 1*
Corning, Parker 1874-1943 *BiDrAC, WhAmP*
Corning, Warren Holmes 1841- *NatCAB 7*
Cornish, Albert Judson 1855-1920 *NatCAB 37*
Cornish, Albert Judson 1856-1920 *WhAm 4*
Cornish, Charles L *NewYHSD*
Cornish, Ed 1871-1928 *WhAm 1*
Cornish, Edward Joel 1861-1938 *ApCAB X, NatCAB 16, NatCAB 30, WhAm 1*
Cornish, Gertrude Eleanor 1880- *WhAm 6*
Cornish, Ida Galpin Skilton *WomWWA 14*
Cornish, Joel Northrup 1828-1908 *ApCAB X, NatCAB 16*
Cornish, John *NewYHSD*
Cornish, Johnston 1858-1920 *BiDrAC*
Cornish, Leslie Colby 1854-1925 *NatCAB 22, WhAm 1*

Cornish, Lorenzo Dana 1877-1934 *WhAm 1*
Cornish, Louis Craig 1870-1950 *NatCAB 38,*
WhAm 2
Cornish, Nellie Centennial 1876-1956 *REnAW*
Cornish, Thomas Everett 1838-1924
NatCAB 21
Cornish, William D d1908 *WhAm 1*
Cornley, James Madison 1832-1887 *TwCBDA*
Cornman, Daniel 1852-1924 *WhAm 3*
Cornman, Noel 1927-1975 *WhAm 6*
Cornman, Oliver Perry 1866-1930 *WhAm 1*
Cornoyer, Paul 1864-1923 *DcAmB,*
NatCAB 24, WhAm 1
Cornplanter 1732-1836 *ApCAB, Drake,*
REnAW
Cornstalk 1720?-1777 *ApCAB Sup, DcAmB,*
REnAW, WebAMB, WhAm H
Cornu, Marie Alfred 1841-1902 *DcScB*
Cornwaleys, Thomas 1600?-1676 *ApCAB*
Cornwall, C Norman 1902-1967 *NatCAB 54*
Cornwall, Edward Everett 1866-1940 *WhAm 1*
Cornwall, George Mackie 1867-1950
NatCAB 38
Cornwall, Henry Bedinger 1844-1917 *ApCAB,*
TwCBDA, WhAm 1
Cornwall, William Tingley 1842-1918
NatCAB 25
Cornwallis, Charles 1737-1805 *ApCAB*
Cornwallis, Charles 1738-1805 *Drake,*
NatCAB 7, WhAm H, WhoMilH
Cornwallis, Charles Cornwallis, Marquess
1738-1805 *McGEWB*
Cornwallis, Charles Cornwallis, Marquis
1738-1805 *AmBi*
Cornwallis, Kinahan 1839-1917 *DcAmB,*
NatCAB 22, WhAm 1
Cornwell, Alfred L 1884-1968 *WhAm 5*
Cornwell, Dean 1892-1960 *IlBEAAW,*
NatCAB 46, WhAm 4
Cornwell, Forest Augustus 1921-1973 *WhAm 6*
Cornwell, John Jacob 1867-1953 *NatCAB 17,*
WhAm 3
Cornwell, Martha Jackson 1869-
WomWWA 14
Cornwell, Philip Morba 1909-1968 *NatCAB 54*
Cornwell, Willett Hastings 1875-1945
NatCAB 34
Cornwell, William Caryl 1851- *NatCAB 16,*
WhAm 4
Cornyn, John Hubert 1875-1941 *WhAm 1*
Coromilas, Lambros A 1857- *WhAm 4*
Corona, Ramon 1825?- *ApCAB*
Coronado, Francesco Vasquez De d1542 *Drake*
Coronado, Francisco Vasquez De 1500?-1554
AmBi
Coronado, Francisco Vasquez De 1510?-1542
ApCAB
Coronado, Francisco Vasquez De 1510-1554
McGEWB, REnAW, WebAB
Coronado, Francisco Vazquez De 1510-1554
DcAmB, WhAm H
Coronel, Luis Nunez d1531 *DcScB*
Coronel, Mariana W De 1851- *AmWom*
Coronelli, Vincenzo Maria 1650-1718 *DcScB*
Corot, Jean Baptiste Camille 1796-1875
McGEWB
Corp, Paul Metzger 1911- *WhAm 6*
Corpa, Peter De 1560?-1597 *ApCAB*
Corper, Harry John 1884-1973 *WhAm 6*
Corra, Francis *NewYHSD*
Corradi, Nestor *NewYHSD*
Corrado, Gaetano 1887-1938 *WhAm 1*
Corre, Joseph *WhAm H*
Correa, Antonio *ApCAB*
Correa, Juan *ApCAB*
Correa DaSerra, Joseph Francis 1750-1823
Drake
Correa DaSerra, Joseph Francisco 1750-1823
ApCAB
Correa DeSa Benavides, Salvador 1594-1668
ApCAB
Correale, Frank 1892-1952 *NatCAB 43*
Corregan, Charles Hunter 1860-1946 *WhAm 2*
Correggio 1494?-1534 *McGEWB*
Correia DeLacerda, Antonio 1777-1852 *ApCAB*
Correia DeSouza Costa, Antonio 1830?-
ApCAB
Correll, Charles James 1890-1972 *NatCAB 57*

Correns, Carl Franz Joseph Erich 1864-1933
DcScB
Correns, Karl Erich 1864-1933 *AsBiEn*
Corrick, Jeannette R Trowbridge 1861-
WomWWA 14
Corrie, Walter Samuel 1896-1966 *WhAm 4*
Corrigan, Charles Eugene 1863- *ApCAB X,*
NatCAB 17
Corrigan, Sir Dominic John 1802-1880 *BiHiMed*
Corrigan, Emmett 1891-1950 *WhAm 3*
Corrigan, Francis Patrick 1881-1968 *WhAm 4A*
Corrigan, Frank P 1881-1968 *NatCAB 54*
Corrigan, James 1848-1908 *NatCAB 22*
Corrigan, James Henry 1844-1890 *TwCBDA*
Corrigan, James William 1880-1928
NatCAB 22
Corrigan, John 1878-1959 *WhAm 3*
Corrigan, Jones Irwin Joseph 1878-1936
WhAm 2
Corrigan, Joseph Moran 1879-1942 *WhAm 2*
Corrigan, Leo Francis 1894-1975 *WhAm 6*
Corrigan, Archbishop Michael Augustine
1839-1902 *AmBi, ApCAB, DcAmB,*
DcAmReB, McGEWB, NatCAB 1,
TwCBDA, WhAm 1
Corrigan, Owen Bernard 1849-1929 *WhAm 1*
Corrigan, Severinus John 1852- *WhAm 4*
Corrigan, Walter Dickson, Sr. 1875-1951
WhAm 2
Corrigan, William John 1886-1961 *NatCAB 49*
Corrigan, William John 1886-1962 *WhAm 4*
Corrise, Jean 1834?- *NewYHSD*
Corroll, C H 1877- *WhoColR*
Corroon, Richard Aloysius 1882-1946 *WhAm 2*
Corrothers, James David 1869-1917 *DcAmB,*
NatCAB 23, WhAm 5, WhoColR
Corruccini, Roberto 1859-1926 *WhAm 1*
Corry, Earle Harrison 1890-1954 *NatCAB 41*
Corry, Edgar Clayton 1912-1968 *WhAm 5*
Corscaden, James Albert 1881-1964
NatCAB 52
Corse, John Murray 1835-1893 *ApCAB,*
DcAmB, Drake, NatCAB 4, TwCBDA,
WebAMB, WhAm H
Corse, Montgomery Dent 1816-1895 *ApCAB,*
BiDConf, Drake, TwCBDA
Corse, William Malcolm 1878-1944 *WhAm 2*
Corser, Charles Benjamin 1860-1954
NatCAB 41
Corser, Harry Prosper 1864-1936 *WhAm 1*
Corsi, Edward 1896-1965 *WhAm 4*
Corson, Allen 1881-1944 *NatCAB 35*
Corson, Caroline Rollins d1901 *WhAm 1*
Corson, David Birdsall 1864-1935 *WhAm 1*
Corson, Dighton d1915 *NatCAB 5*
Corson, Dighton 1827-1915 *NatCAB 16*
Corson, Dighton 1829-1915 *WhAm 1*
Corson, Edward T 1834-1864 *ApCAB*
Corson, Eugene Rollin 1855-1946 *NatCAB 35,*
WhAm 4
Corson, Harry Herbert 1898- *WhAm 5*
Corson, Hiram 1828-1911 *AmBi, ApCAB,*
DcAmB, NatCAB 1, TwCBDA,
WhAm 1
Corson, Juliet 1841-1897 *BiDAmEd, NotAW*
Corson, Juliet 1842-1897 *AmBi, ApCAB,*
DcAmB, NatCAB 8, TwCBDA,
WhAm H
Corson, Oscar Taylor 1857-1928 *NatCAB 12,*
WhAm 1
Corson, Robert Rodgers 1831-1904 *DcAmB,*
NatCAB 9
Corson, Rufus C 1826?- *NewYHSD*
Corson, William Russell Cone 1870-1945
WhAm 2
Corson-White, Ellen Pawling 1874-
WomWWA 14
Cort, Edwin Charles 1879-1950 *DcAmB S4*
Cort, Henry 1740-1800 *McGEWB*
Cort, Lottie Ambler 1860- *WomWWA 14*
Cort, Stewart Joseph 1881-1958 *NatCAB 47,*
WhAm 3
Cortambert, Louis Richard 1808-1881 *DcAmB,*
WhAm H
Corte Real, Gaspar d1501 *McGEWB*
Corte Real, Miguel d1502 *McGEWB*
Cortelyou, George Bruce 1862-1940 *ApCAB X,*
BiDrUSE, DcAmB S2, NatCAB 13,

NatCAB 14, TwCBDA, WebAB,
WhAm 1, WhAmP
Cortereal, Gaspar d1501 *ApCAB*
Cortereal, Gaspard d1501 *Drake*
Corterreal, Gaspar d1501 *ApCAB*
Cortes, Henry Cornelius 1892-1957 *NatCAB 48*
Cortes, Hernan 1485-1547 *ApCAB, McGEWB,*
WhoMilH
Cortes, Hernando 1485-1547 *Drake*
Cortes, Madariaga Jose 1784-1826 *ApCAB Sup*
Cortes DeAlbacar, Martin d1582 *DcScB*
Cortesi, Arnaldo 1897-1966 *WhAm 4*
Cortez, Gregorio 1875-1916 *REnAW*
Cortez, Hernando 1485-1547 *WhAm H*
Corthell, Arthur Bateman 1860-1924 *ApCAB X,*
WhAm 1
Corthell, Elmer Lawrence 1840-1916 *AmBi,*
ApCAB, DcAmB, NatCAB 9, TwCBDA,
WhAm 1
Corthell, Nellis Eugene 1861-1932 *WhAm 1*
Corti, Alfonso Giacomo Gaspare 1822-1876
DcScB
Corti, Bonaventura 1729-1813 *DcScB*
Cortilet, Michael P 1896- *WhAm 3*
Cortina, Jose M Justo Gomez DeLa 1799-1860
ApCAB
Cortina, Juan Nepomuceno 1824-1892 *REnAW*
Cortina, Juan Nepomuceno 1830-1892 *ApCAB*
Cortissoz, Ellen Mackay Hutchinson d1933
WhAm 1, WomWWA 14
Cortissoz, Royal 1869-1948 *DcAmB S4,*
NatCAB 36, WhAm 2
Cortney, Philip d1971 *WhAm 5*
Cortona, Pietro Da 1596-1669 *McGEWB*
Cortopassi, Andre John 1902-1966 *NatCAB 51*
Cortright, Ernest Everett 1873-1966
NatCAB 52, WhAm 5
Cortwright, J D *NewYHSD*
Coruja, Antonio Alvares Pereira 1806- *ApCAB*
Corum, Martene Windsor 1894-1958 *WhAm 3*
Corvisart, Jean-Nicholas 1755-1821 *BiHiMed*
Corvisart, Jean-Nicolas 1755-1821 *DcScB*
Corwin, Arthur Frank 1877-1957 *WhAm 3*
Corwin, Arthur Mills 1864-1933 *WhAm 1*
Corwin, Charles Abel 1857-1938 *IlBEAAW*
Corwin, Charles Edward 1868-1958 *WhAm 3*
Corwin, David Bruen 1839-1917 *ApCAB X,*
NatCAB 17
Corwin, Edward Samuel 1878-1963 *WebAB,*
WhAm 4
Corwin, Edward Tanjore 1834-1914 *DcAmB,*
NatCAB 23, TwCBDA, WhAm 1
Corwin, Franklin 1818-1879 *BiAUS, BiDrAC,*
TwCBDA, WhAm H
Corwin, George B d1972 *WhAm 5*
Corwin, John A *ApCAB*
Corwin, Mary Beatrice *WomWWA 14*
Corwin, Moses B 1790-1872 *ApCAB, BiAUS,*
TwCBDA
Corwin, Moses Biedso 1790-1872 *WhAm H*
Corwin, Moses Bledso 1790-1872 *BiDrAC,*
WhAmP
Corwin, Richard Warren 1852-1928 *WhAm 1*
Corwin, Robert Gilbert 1877-1940 *WhAm 1*
Corwin, Robert Nelson 1865-1944 *WhAm 2*
Corwin, Thomas 1794-1865 *AmBi, ApCAB,*
BiAUS, BiDrAC, BiDrUSE, DcAmB,
Drake, NatCAB 6, TwCBDA, WhAm H,
WhAmP
Corwine, Aaron H 1802-1830 *NewYHSD,*
WhAm H
Corwine, Amos Breckinridge 1815-1880 *ApCAB*
Corwith, Henry Nathan 1856-1944 *NatCAB 34*
Corwith, Howard Post 1892-1962 *NatCAB 49,*
WhAm 4
Corwith, James Carlton 1895-1966 *WhAm 4*
Cory, Abram Edward 1873- *WhAm 5*
Cory, Calvin M 1915-1968 *NatCAB 54*
Cory, Charles Barney 1857-1921 *AmBi,*
DcAmB, NatCAB 13, TwCBDA,
WhAm 1
Cory, Charles Edward 1878- *WhAm 5*
Cory, Clarence Linus 1872-1937 *WhAm 1*
Cory, David 1872-1966 *NatCAB 53, WhAm 4*
Cory, Florence Elizabeth 1851- *AmWom*
Cory, Harry Thomas 1870- *NatCAB 18,*
WhAm 5
Cory, John Michael 1871-1942 *NatCAB 31*

Cory, Kate T 1861- *IIBEAAW*

Cory, Lewis Lincoln 1861-1929 *NatCAB 23*

Cory, Russell Gherdes 1881-1946 *NatCAB 34*

Cory, Sarah Morris 1852- *WomWWA 14*

Cory, Thomas Judd 1914-1965 *NatCAB 51, WhAm 4*

Cory, Victor Edwin 1893-1968 *NatCAB 54*

Cory, Virgil 1893-1961 *WhAm 4*

Coryell, Charles DuBois 1912-1971 *NatCAB 56, WhAm 5*

Coryell, Horace Noble 1888-1965 *NatCAB 51*

Coryell, John Russell 1851-1924 *NatCAB 21*

Coryllos, Pol Nicholas 1880-1938 *NatCAB 30*

Cosa, Juan DeLa d1509 *ApCAB*

Cosby, Charles Mortimer 1847-1894 *NatCAB 28*

Cosby, Charlotte Malvina *WomWWA 14*

Cosby, Fortunatus, Jr. 1801-1871 *NatCAB 5*

Cosby, Frank Carvill 1840-1905 *WhAm 1*

Cosby, George Blake 1830-1909 *ApCAB Sup, TwCBDA, WhAm 1*

Cosby, Spencer 1867- *WhAm 4*

Cosby, Stanley Wallace 1890-1961 *NatCAB 49*

Cosby, William d1736 *Drake*

Cosby, William 1690?-1735? *DcAmB*

Cosby, William 1690-1736 *WhAm H*

Cosby, William 1695?-1736 *ApCAB, NatCAB 12*

Cosden, Jeremiah 1768-1824 *BiDrAC, WhAm H*

Cosden, Joshua S 1882-1940 *WhAm 1*

Cosenza, Mario Emilio 1880-1966 *WhAm 4*

Cosey, Auger Augustus 1876- *WhoColR*

Cosgrave, George 1870-1945 *WhAm 2*

Cosgrave, Jessica Garretson d1949 *WhAm 2*

Cosgrave, John O'Hara 1864-1947 *WhAm 2*

Cosgrave, John O'Hara, II 1908-1968 *WhAm 5*

Cosgrave, William Thomas 1880-1966 *WhAm 4*

Cosgriff, Edward Hall 1880-1947 *NatCAB 37*

Cosgriff, James Everett 1870-1938 *NatCAB 43, WhAm 1*

Cosgriff, Thomas Andrew 1854-1915 *NatCAB 19*

Cosgriff, Walter Everett 1914-1961 *NatCAB 46, WhAm 4*

Cosgrove, B G *NewYHSD*

Cosgrove, Edward Bradley 1888-1962 *WhAm 4*

Cosgrove, Emilie Dohrmann 1912-1969 *WhAm 5*

Cosgrove, Henrietta C 1849- *WomWWA 14*

Cosgrove, Henry 1834-1906 *ApCAB, NatCAB 12, TwCBDA, WhAm 1*

Cosgrove, James J 1887-1960 *WhAm 4*

Cosgrove, John 1839-1925 *BiDrAC*

Cosgrove, John Phillips 1897-1951 *WhAm 3*

Cosgrove, Michael Frank 1889-1961 *WhAm 4*

Cosgrove, Samuel Goodlove 1841-1909 *NatCAB 14*

Cosgrove, Terence Byrne 1881-1956 *NatCAB 45, WhAm 3*

Coshow, Oliver Perry 1863- *NatCAB 17, WhAm 1*

Cosler, William 1825?- *NewYHSD*

Coss, John J d1940 *WhAm 2*

Cosserat, Eugene Maurice Pierre 1866-1931 *DcScB*

Cossett, Franceway Ranna 1790-1863 *ApCAB*

Cossitt, Franceway Ranna 1790-1863 *TwCBDA*

Cosson, George 1876-1963 *NatCAB 49, WhAm 4*

Costa, Christovao Da *DcScB*

Costa, John Joseph 1893-1954 *NatCAB 44*

Costa, Joseph Louis 1897-1969 *NatCAB 55*

Costa Da, Claudio Manoel 1729-1789 *Drake*

Costa Ibn Luca *DcScB*

Costagni, Philippo 1839-1904 *NewYHSD*

Costain, Thomas Bertram 1885-1965 *WhAm 4*

Costanso, Miguel *DcAmB, WhAm H*

Costantin, Julien Noel 1857-1936 *DcScB*

Costar, George 1839?- *NewYHSD*

Coste, Paul F 1856- *WhAm 4*

Costello, Frederick Hankerson 1851-1921 *WhAm 1*

Costello, Harry Todd 1885-1960 *WhAm 4*

Costello, J F *WhAm 3*

Costello, John A 1891-1976 *WhAm 6*

Costello, John Cornelius 1894-1974 *WhAm 6*

Costello, John Martin 1903- *BiDrAC*

Costello, Joseph G 1836?- *NewYHSD*

Costello, Lou 1908-1959 *WhAm 3*

Costello, Louis B 1876-1959 *WhAm 3*

Costello, Michael *NewYHSD*

Costello, Peter Edward 1854-1935 *BiDrAC, WhAm 4*

Costello, William *NewYHSD*

Costello, William Aloysious 1904-1969 *WhAm 5*

Coster, Dirk 1889-1950 *AsBiEn, DcScB*

Coster, F Donald 1884-1938 *DcAmB S2*

Coster, Frank Donald 1884-1938 *WhAm 1*

Costigan, Daniel *NewYHSD*

Costigan, Edward 1885-1964 *NatCAB 50*

Costigan, Edward Prentiss 1874-1939 *BiDrAC, DcAmB S2, EncAAH, NatCAB 29, REnAW, WhAm 1, WhAmP*

Costigan, Francis 1810-1865 *WhAm H*

Costigan, George Purcell, Jr. 1870-1934 *DcAmB S1, NatCAB 26, WhAm 1*

Costigan, John 1835- *ApCAB*

Costigan, John Edward 1888-1972 *WhAm 5*

Costigan, Mabel Cory 1873- *WomWWA 14*

Costigan, Will Francis 1886-1956 *NatCAB 45*

Costikyan, S Kent 1867-1949 *WhAm 2*

Costin, William Gilmor 1875-1937 *NatCAB 28*

Costley, Elizabeth Christine 1920-1974 *WhAm 6*

Costolow, William Evert 1892- *WhAm 4*

Coston, Benjamin Franklin 1821-1848 *TwCBDA*

Coston, Henry Henry 1844-1896 *TwCBDA*

Coston, Martha Jay 1828- *TwCBDA*

Coston, Samuel Smith 1872-1951 *NatCAB 46*

Coston, William Franklin 1847-1901 *TwCBDA*

Cotabanama d1504 *ApCAB*

Cotchett, Louis Myers 1896-1958 *NatCAB 47*

Cote, Alcide 1903-1955 *WhAm 3*

Cotes, Roger 1682-1716 *DcScB*

Cotes, Sara Jeannette Duncan 1862- *AmWom*

Cotheal, Alexander Isaac 1804-1894 *NatCAB 1, TwCBDA*

Cothern, Leland 1900-1962 *WhAm 4*

Cothran, Frank Harrison 1878-1948 *NatCAB 37, WhAm 2*

Cothran, James Sproull 1830-1897 *BiDrAC, TwCBDA, WhAm H*

Cothran, Perrin Chiles 1886-1959 *WhAm 3*

Cothran, Thomas Perrin 1857-1934 *WhAm 1*

Cothren, Marion Benedict *WomWWA 14*

Cotillo, Salvatore A 1886-1939 *AmBi*

Cotnam, Perry 1855-1914 *NatCAB 18*

Cotnareanu, Leon 1891-1970 *WhAm 5*

Cotner, Samuel 1842-1912 *NatCAB 17*

Cott, George Ferdinant 1855-1921 *NatCAB 19*

Cott, Ted 1917-1973 *WhAm 6*

Cotta, Carl Bernhard Von 1808-1879 *DcScB*

Cottam, Charles Francis 1922-1971 *NatCAB 56*

Cottam, Clarence 1899-1974 *WhAm 6*

Cottam, Gilbert Geoffrey 1873-1949 *NatCAB 39, WhAm 2*

Cotte, Louis 1740-1815 *DcScB*

Cotten, Edythe Johns *WomWWA 14*

Cotten, Lyman Atkinson 1874-1926 *NatCAB 20*

Cotten, Robert Randolph 1839-1928 *NatCAB 31*

Cotten, Sallie Sims Southall 1846-1929 *NotAW, WhAm 1, WomWWA 14*

Cotten, Willis Frank 1895-1948 *NatCAB 39*

Cottenet, Rawlins Lowndes 1866-1951 *NatCAB 39*

Cotter, Carl Henry 1892-1965 *NatCAB 52, WhAm 4*

Cotter, Charles F *WhAm 3*

Cotter, James Edward 1847-1933 *NatCAB 14, WhAm 1*

Cotter, John F 1879-1957 *WhAm 3*

Cotter, John W 1861- *WhAm 4*

Cotter, Joseph Bernard 1844-1909 *ApCAB Sup, NatCAB 15, TwCBDA, WhAm 1*

Cotter, Richard Joseph 1879-1963 *NatCAB 51*

Cotter, William 1858- *WhAm 4*

Cotter, William Edward 1893-1957 *NatCAB 50, WhAm 3*

Cotteral, J L T *BiAUS*

Cotteral, John Hazleton 1864-1933 *WhAm 1*

Cotterell, William 1835?- *NewYHSD*

Cotterill, George Fletcher 1865- *ApCAB X, WhAm 5*

Cotterman, Charles Mason 1866- *WhAm 4*

Cottineau, Denis Nicholas 1746-1808 *ApCAB, Drake*

Cotting, John Ruggles 1783-1867 *ApCAB, NatCAB 5, WhAm H*

Cottingham, Arnold Douglas 1861-1915 *NatCAB 18*

Cottingham, Claybrook 1881-1949 *WhAm 2*

Cottingham, George W 1894-1948 *WhAm 2*

Cottingham, Harold Fred 1913- *BiDAmEd*

Cottingham, Irven A 1866-1934 *WhAm 1*

Cottingham, Thad Jerome 1883-1956 *NatCAB 43*

Cottingham, Walter Horace 1866-1930 *NatCAB 21*

Cottingham, Willard Sherwin 1899-1968 *NatCAB 54*

Cottis, George Wilbert 1880-1950 *NatCAB 39, WhAm 3*

Cottle, Brooks 1897-1967 *WhAm 4*

Cottle, George Franklin 1879-1945 *NatCAB 50*

Cottle, Marion Weston *BiCAW, WomWWA 14*

Cottman, Cary Chubb *WomWWA 14*

Cottman, James Hough 1847-1919 *WhAm 1*

Cottman, Joseph Stewart 1803-1863 *BiAUS, BiDrAC, WhAm H*

Cottman, Susan Powell *WomWWA 14*

Cottman, Vincendon Lazare 1852- *NatCAB 1*

Cottman, Vincendon Lazarus 1852-1917 *WhAm 1*

Cotton, Alfred Cleveland 1847-1916 *NatCAB 16, WhAm 1*

Cotton, Aylett Rains 1826-1912 *BiAUS, BiDrAC, TwCBDA, WhAmP*

Cotton, Aylett Rains 1874-1965 *NatCAB 53*

Cotton, Charles McGugin 1884-1951 *NatCAB 40*

Cotton, Charles Stanhope 1843-1909 *TwCBDA, WhAm 1*

Cotton, Clarence Arthur 1869- *NatCAB 17*

Cotton, Edward Howe 1880- *WhAm 6*

Cotton, Elizabeth Jane 1857- *WhAm 4, WomWWA 14*

Cotton, Fassett Allen 1862-1942 *BiDAmEd, WhAm 4*

Cotton, Francis Ridgely 1895-1960 *WhAm 4*

Cotton, Frederic Jay 1869-1938 *WhAm 1*

Cotton, Hattie Elizabeth 1854- *WomWWA 14*

Cotton, Henry Andrews 1869-1933 *WhAm 1*

Cotton, Henry Andrews 1876-1933 *ApCAB X, NatCAB 24*

Cotton, J S *NewYHSD*

Cotton, Jesse Lee 1862-1937 *WhAm 1*

Cotton, John 1584-1652 *AmBi, DcAmB, DcAmReB, EncAB, McGEWB, WhAm H*

Cotton, John 1585-1652 *ApCAB, Drake, NatCAB 7, TwCBDA, WebAB*

Cotton, John 1640-1699 *ApCAB, Drake, TwCBDA*

Cotton, John 1658-1710 *TwCBDA*

Cotton, John Wesley 1868-1931 *IIBEAAW*

Cotton, Joseph Bell 1865-1940 *NatCAB 17, WhAm 1*

Cotton, Joseph Potter 1875-1931 *DcAmB S1, NatCAB 23, WhAm 1*

Cotton, Josiah 1680-1756 *ApCAB, Drake, TwCBDA*

Cotton, Mary Hannah 1866- *WomWWA 14*

Cotton, Mary Slocomb 1863- *WomWWA 14*

Cotton, Norris 1900- *BiDrAC*

Cotton, Seaborn 1633-1686 *ApCAB, TwCBDA*

Cotton, Sir Stapleton 1773-1865 *WhoMilH*

Cotton, W Philip 1901-1958 *NatCAB 48*

Cotton, William Edwin 1866-1951 *WhAm 3*

Cotton, William H 1880-1958 *WhAm 3*

Cotton, William Joseph Henry 1878-1932 *WhAm 1*

Cotton, William Wick 1859-1918 *NatCAB 18, WhAm 1*

Cottrell, Calvert Byron 1821-1893 *DcAmB, NatCAB 3, WhAm H*

Cottrell, Calvert Byron, III 1888-1935 *NatCAB 44*

Cottrell, Charles Perkins 1858-1932 *NatCAB 37*

Cottrell, Charles Perkins, Jr. 1899-1955 *NatCAB 44*

Cottrell, Clarke Copeland 1885-1940 *NatCAB 30*

Cottrell, Donald Clark 1892-1956 *NatCAB 45, WhAm 3*

Cottrell, Edwin Angell 1881-1953 *NatCAB 42, WhAm 3*

Cottrell, Elias 1853-1937 *WhAm 1, WhoColR*

Cottrell, Frederick Gardner 1877-1948 *DcAmB S4, DcScB, NatCAB 38, WhAm 2*

Cottrell, George William 1876-1961 *NatCAB 49*

Cottrell, James LaFayette 1808-1885 *BiDrAC, WhAm H*

Cottrell, Jesse Samuel 1878-1944 *NatCAB 33, WhAm 2*

Cottrell, Leonard 1913-1974 *WhAm 6*

Cottrell, Mary James 1899-1952 *WhAm 3*

Cottrell, Samuel 1898-1974 *WhAm 6*

Cottrell, Will Rea, Jr. 1918-1970 *WhAm 5*

Cottrill, Charles A 1863- *WhoColR*

Cottu, Mister *NewYHSD*

Cotugno, Domenico Felice Antonio 1736-1822 *BiHiMed, DcScB*

Coty, Rene 1882-1962 *WhAm 4*

Couch, Albert Irving 1867-1936 *WhAm 1*

Couch, Benjamin Warren 1873-1945 *WhAm 2*

Couch, Charles Peter 1890-1955 *WhAm 4*

Couch, Darins Nash 1822-1897 *WhoMilH*

Couch, Darius Nash 1822-1897 *AmBi, ApCAB, DcAmB, Drake, NatCAB 4, TwCBDA, WhAm H*

Couch, George W, Jr. 1922-1973 *WhAm 6*

Couch, Harvey Crowley 1877-1941 *DcAmB S3, WhAm 1*

Couch, Harvey Crowley, Jr. 1908-1963 *NatCAB 51, WhAm 4*

Couch, Herbert Newell 1899-1959 *WhAm 3*

Couch, Joseph James 1828-1909 *NatCAB 15*

Couch, Nancy Henrietta 1845- *WomWWA 14*

Couchman, Charles Bennington 1879-1966 *WhAm 4*

Couden, Albert Reynolds 1846-1923 *WhAm 1*

Couden, Henry Noble 1842-1922 *WhAm 1*

Coudert, Amalia Kussner 1873- *WhAm 5, WomWWA 14*

Coudert, Frederic Rene 1832-1903 *AmBi, DcAmB, NatCAB 6, WhAm 1*

Coudert, Frederic Rene 1871-1955 *ApCAB X, DcAmB S5, WhAm 3*

Coudert, Frederic Rene, Jr. 1898-1972 *BiDrAC, NatCAB 55, WhAm 5*

Coudert, Frederick Rene 1832-1903 *TwCBDA*

Coudin, Robert 1805-1874 *ApCAB, TwCBDA*

Coudin, Robert Jackson 1839-1864 *ApCAB*

Coudrey, Harry Marcy 1867-1930 *BiDrAC, WhAm 4*

Coues, Elliott 1842-1899 *AmBi, ApCAB, DcAmB, DcScB, NatCAB 5, REnAW, TwCBDA, WhAm 1*

Coues, Mary Emily Bennett 1835- *AmWom*

Coues, Robert Wheaton 1872-1943 *NatCAB 32*

Coues, Samuel Elliott 1797-1867 *NatCAB 14*

Coues, Samuel Franklin 1825-1916 *WhAm 1*

Couey, Fred 1908-1964 *NatCAB 51*

Couey, James Henry, Jr. 1923-1971 *WhAm 5*

Coughlan, Jeremiah *NewYHSD*

Coughlan, Jeremiah A *NewYHSD*

Coughlan, Lawrence 1760?-1834 *ApCAB*

Coughlan, Robert Edward, Jr. 1899-1971 *WhAm 5*

Coughlin, Father Charles Edward 1891- *EncAAH, EncAB, McGEWB, WebAB*

Coughlin, Clarence Dennis 1883-1946 *BiDrAC, NatCAB 36, WhAm 3*

Coughlin, Edward Joseph, Jr. 1906-1974 *WhAm 6*

Coughlin, John Henry Famian 1883-1956 *NatCAB 46*

Coughlin, John William 1860-1920 *WhAm 1*

Coughlin, Robert Lawrence 1929- *BiDrAC*

Coughlin, Timothy J 1893-1951 *WhAm 3*

Coughlin, W G 1862- *WhAm 4*

Coughlin, Walter James 1901-1966 *WhAm 4*

Coughlin, William Thomas 1873-1940 *WhAm 1*

Cougle, Walter Driggs 1887-1964 *NatCAB 50*

Coulbourn, John Irvin 1876-1941 *NatCAB 33*

Couldock, Charles Walter 1815-1898 *ApCAB,*

DcAmB, NatCAB 2, TwCBDA, WhAm H

Coullon, John *NewYHSD*

Coulomb, Charles Augustin De 1736-1806 *AsBiEn, DcScB, McGEWB*

Coulon, George David 1823?-1904? *NewYHSD*

Coulson, Charles Alfred 1910-1974 *WhAm 6*

Coulson, E Jack 1904-1971 *NatCAB 56*

Coulson, Edwin Ray 1899-1969 *WhAm 5*

Coulson, Robert E 1884-1962 *WhAm 4*

Coulson, Sewell Briggs 1878-1958 *NatCAB 45*

Coulston, John Bishop 1869-1928 *WhAm 1*

Coulston, Melvin Herbert 1877-1952 *WhAm 3*

Coult, Joseph 1834- *NatCAB 12*

Coultas, Andrew Jackson 1853-1920 *WhAm 1*

Coulter, Benjamin Franklin 1832-1911 *NatCAB 36*

Coulter, Charles M 1897-1956 *WhAm 3*

Coulter, David Alexander 1846-1928 *NatCAB 21*

Coulter, Edith Margaret 1880-1963 *DcAmLiB, NatCAB 50*

Coulter, Ellis Merton 1890- *EncAAH*

Coulter, Elva Carter 1872- *WomWWA 14*

Coulter, Ernest Kent 1871-1952 *DcAmB S5, NatCAB 41*

Coulter, Herbert McKay 1877-1939 *NatCAB 44*

Coulter, John d1838 *BiAUS*

Coulter, John Lee 1881-1959 *ApCAB X, NatCAB 48, WhAm 3*

Coulter, John Merle 1851-1928 *AmBi, ApCAB, ApCAB X, BiDAmEd, DcAmB, NatCAB 11, TwCBDA, WhAm 1*

Coulter, John Stanley 1885-1949 *WhAm 2*

Coulter, John Wesley 1893-1967 *NatCAB 55*

Coulter, Mary Geigus 1859- *WhAm 4, WomWWA 14*

Coulter, Merle Crowe 1894-1958 *WhAm 3*

Coulter, Richard 1788-1852 *BiAUS, BiDrAC, NatCAB 16, WhAm H*

Coulter, Sidney Beech 1897-1968 *WhAm 5*

Coulter, Stanley 1853-1943 *NatCAB 33, WhAm 2*

Coulter, William S 1886-1975 *WhAm 6*

Coulthard, George William 1916-1972 *WhAm 5*

Coulton, George A d1933 *WhAm 5*

Coulton, George Gordon 1858-1947 *McGEWB*

Coulton, Thomas Evans 1891-1965 *WhAm 4*

Counce, Harvey 1821- *NewYHSD*

Council, Carl C 1895-1964 *WhAm 4*

Council, Commodore Thomas 1886-1960 *NatCAB 47*

Council, Walter Wooten *WhAm 2*

Councill, William Hooper 1848-1909 *BiDAmEd, WhAm 1*

Councilman, Halstead Powell 1883-1932 *NatCAB 26*

Councilman, Isabella Coolidge 1861- *WomWWA 14*

Councilman, William Thomas 1854-1933 *DcAmB S1, DcScB, NatCAB 5, WhAm 1*

Councilor, James Allan 1884-1945 *WhAm 2*

Counihan, Donald Morris 1917-1969 *NatCAB 54*

Counselman, Charles 1849-1904 *NatCAB 11, WhAm 1*

Countermine, John Donnan 1850- *WhAm 4*

Countess, Clem C 1884-1960 *NatCAB 49*

Countiss, Eugene Hendrix 1908-1972 *NatCAB 57*

Countryman, Edwin 1883-1914 *WhAm 1*

Countryman, Gratia Alta 1866-1953 *DcAmLiB, WhAm 3, WomWWA 14*

Countryman, John Everett 1903-1972 *NatCAB 57, WhAm 5*

Countryman, Marcellus L 1862- *WhAm 4*

Countryman, Willis Arthur 1884-1960 *NatCAB 48, WhAm 4*

Counts, George Sylvester 1889-1974 *BiDAmEd, WhAm 6*

Counts, Gerald Alford 1895-1964 *WhAm 4*

Counts, Noah Tilden 1876-1957 *NatCAB 47*

Countway, Francis A 1875-1955 *WhAm 3*

County, Albert John 1871-1944 *NatCAB 16, NatCAB 33, WhAm 2*

Coupal, James Francis 1884-1935 *WhAm 1*

Couper, Archibald Scott 1831-1892 *AsBiEn,*

DcScB, McGEWB

Couper, James Hamilton 1794-1866 *DcAmB, McGEWB, WhAm H*

Couper, Richard Hamilton 1886-1918 *NatCAB 38*

Couper, William 1853-1942 *ApCAB X, NatCAB 9, WhAm 2*

Couperin, Francois 1668-1733 *McGEWB*

Courant, Richard 1888-1972 *WhAm 5*

Courbet, Amedee Anatole Prosper 1827-1885 *WhoMilH*

Courbet, Jean Desire Gustave 1819-1877 *McGEWB*

Courcelles, Daniel DeRemi *ApCAB*

Courchesne, Georges 1880-1950 *WhAm 3*

Cournand, Andre Frederic 1895- *WebAB*

Cournand, Edward L 1897-1975 *WhAm 6*

Cournot, Antoine Augustin 1801-1877 *DcScB, McGEWB*

Coursault, Jesse Harliaman 1871-1937 *WhAm 1*

Coursen, A B *NewYHSD*

Coursey, Oscar William 1873- *WhAm 3*

Coursol, Michel Joseph Charles 1819- *ApCAB*

Court, Frank Willard 1875-1964 *WhAm 4*

Court DeGebelin, Antoine 1725-1784 *ApCAB, Drake*

Courtauld, Miss *NewYHSD*

Courtauld, Mrs. S L *NewYHSD*

Courtenay, Adrian Henry 1880-1939 *NatCAB 29*

Courtenay, Edward Henry 1803-1853 *ApCAB, Drake, TwCBDA*

Courtenay, Reginald 1813- *ApCAB*

Courtenay, T E *NewYHSD*

Courtenay, William Ashmead 1831-1908 *TwCBDA, WhAm 1*

Courtenay, William Howard 1858-1934 *WhAm 1*

Courteney, Edward Henry 1803-1853 *NatCAB 29*

Courter, Claude V 1888-1964 *WhAm 4*

Courter, Franklin C 1854- *NatCAB 5*

Courtis, Frank 1844-1908 *WhAm 1*

Courtis, Stuart Appleton 1874-1969 *BiDAmEd, WhAm 5*

Courtis, Thomas 1864-1929 *ApCAB X*

Courtis, William Munroe 1842-1922 *WhAm 1*

Courtivron, Gaspard LeC, Marquis De 1715-1785 *DcScB*

Courtleigh, William Louis 1869-1930 *WhAm 1*

Courtnay, Dominic Gerrold 1853-1906 *NatCAB 16*

Courtney, Charles Edward 1849-1920 *DcAmB*

Courtney, Frederick 1837-1918 *ApCAB Sup, WhAm 1*

Courtney, Joseph William 1868-1929 *WhAm 1*

Courtney, Luther Weeks 1880- *WhAm 6*

Courtney, Robert 1829?- *NewYHSD*

Courtney, Thomas J 1894-1971 *WhAm 5*

Courtney, Walter 1856-1924 *NatCAB 17, WhAm 1*

Courtney, William Wirt 1889-1961 *BiDrAC*

Courtois, Bernard 1777-1838 *AsBiEn, DcScB*

Courtright, Jim 1845?-1887 *REnAW*

Courts, Malon Clay 1908-1957 *WhAm 3*

Courville, Cyril Brian 1900-1968 *WhAm 5*

Courvoisier, Henry *NewYHSD*

Courvoisier, Ludwig 1843-1918 *BiHiMed*

Couse, Eanger Irving 1866-1936 *IIBEAAW, NatCAB 13, REnAW, WhAm 1*

Couse, Howard Ambrose 1871-1957 *NatCAB 46*

Couse, Walter Learned 1901-1967 *NatCAB 53*

Cousens, John Albert 1874-1937 *NatCAB 27, WhAm 1*

Cousin, Jean *ApCAB Sup*

Cousin, Victor 1792-1867 *McGEWB*

Cousin Alice *NotAW*

Cousino, Clayton 1902-1966 *NatCAB 51*

Cousins, Arthur George 1882-1949 *WhAm 3*

Cousins, Frank 1851- *WhAm 4*

Cousins, Glenn Thomas 1905-1965 *NatCAB 51*

Cousins, Norman 1912- *WebAB*

Cousins, Ralph P 1891-1964 *WhAm 4*

Cousins, Robert Bartow 1861-1932 *WhAm 1*

Cousins, Robert Gordon 1859-1933 *BiDrAC, TwCBDA, WhAm 1, WhAmP*

Cousins, Robert Winfield 1877-1936
  NatCAB 26
Cousland, William 1825?- NewYHSD
Cousley, Stanley W 1887-1958 WhAm 3
Coussin, Mister NewYHSD
Cousteau, Jacques-Yves 1910- AsBiEn
Cousy, Robert Joseph 1928- WebAB
Coutant, Frank Raymond 1885-1973 WhAm 6
Coutant, W H NewYHSD
Coutard, Henri 1876-1950 DcAmB S4
Couthouy, J P NewYHSD
Coutinho, Aureliano DeSousa E Oliveira
  1800-1855 ApCAB
Coutts, Alice IlBEAAW
Coutts, Gordon 1868?-1937 IlBEAAW
Couturat, Louis 1868-1914 DcScB
Couturier, Hendrick d1684? NewYHSD,
  WhAm H
Couzens, Frank 1902-1950 NatCAB 39,
  WhAm 3
Couzens, James 1872-1936 AmBi, ApCAB X,
  BiDrAC, DcAmB S2, EncAB,
  NatCAB 30, WebAB, WhAm 1, WhAmP
Couzins, Phoebe 1840?- AmWom
Couzins, Phoebe 1845?- WhAm 4
Couzins, Phoebe 1845-1915 NatCAB 15
Couzins, Phoebe Wilson 1839?-1913 NotAW
Covarrubias, Francisco Diaz 1833- ApCAB
Covarrubias, Miguel d1957 WhAm 3
Covel, Abbie Walker 1873- WomWWA 14
Covell, James 1796-1845 ApCAB
Covell, Louis Chapin 1875- WhAm 5
Covell, Maud Evelyn Clarke 1880-
  WomWWA 14
Covello, Leonard 1887- BiDAmEd
Coveney, Charles Carden 1874- WhAm 5
Cover, Loring Andrews 1867-1949 NatCAB 38
Cover, Ralph 1892-1969 WhAm 5
Cover, Rodney Addison 1905-1964 WhAm 4
Coverdale, Miles 1488-1569 McGEWB
Coverdale, William Hugh 1871-1949
  NatCAB 39, WhAm 2
Coverley, Robert 1863- TwCBDA
Coverley, Robert 1865- WhAm 4
Covernton, Charles William 1813- ApCAB
Covert, Charles Edward 1872- WhAm 5
Covert, E Blunn 1883-1940 NatCAB 38
Covert, James Way 1842-1910 BiDrAC,
  TwCBDA
Covert, John Cutler 1837-1919 NatCAB 18
Covert, John Cutler 1839-1919 TwCBDA,
  WhAm 1
Covert, John M 1832-1872 ApCAB
Covert, John Ralston 1878-1942 NatCAB 32
Covert, Lewis B NewYHSD
Covert, Lloyd Wesley 1906-1966 NatCAB 52,
  WhAm 4
Covert, William Chalmers 1864-1942 WhAm 1
Covey, Arthur Sinclair 1877-1960 WhAm 3
Covilhao, Pedro De 1455?-1530? McGEWB
Coville, Frederick Vernon 1867-1937
  ApCAB Sup, NatCAB 12, NatCAB 27,
  WhAm 1
Covington, Euclid M 1893-1975 WhAm 6
Covington, Eugene Clay 1872- WhoColR
Covington, Eugene Gray 1872- WhoColR A
Covington, George Washington 1838-1911
  BiDrAC
Covington, Harry Franklin 1870-1928 WhAm 1
Covington, Harry Stockdell 1892-1950 WhAm 3
Covington, James Harry 1870-1942 BiDrAC,
  NatCAB 40, WhAm 1
Covington, Leonard 1768-1813 ApCAB, BiAUS,
  BiDrAC, Drake, TwCBDA, WhAm H
Covode, James Henry 1858-1909 NatCAB 27
Covode, John 1808-1871 ApCAB, BiAUS,
  BiDrAC, DcAmB, Drake, NatCAB 23,
  TwCBDA, WhAm H, WhAmP
Cowan, Andrew 1841-1919 NatCAB 18,
  WhAm 1
Cowan, Clyde Lorrain 1919-1974 WhAm 6
Cowan, Edgar 1815-1885 ApCAB, BiAUS,
  BiDrAC, DcAmB, NatCAB 2, TwCBDA,
  WhAm H, WhAmP
Cowan, Edward Payson 1840- WhAm 4
Cowan, Frank 1844-1905 ApCAB, TwCBDA,
  WhAm 1
Cowan, Frank Augustus 1898-1957 NatCAB 43,

WhAm 3
Cowan, Frank Irving 1888-1948 WhAm 2
Cowan, George NewYHSD
Cowan, Isabel Eliot 1871- WomWWA 14
Cowan, Jacob Pitzer 1823-1895 BiAUS,
  BiDrAC, WhAm H
Cowan, James Raymo 1890-1955 WhAm 3
Cowan, John Francis 1858-1917 NatCAB 19
Cowan, John Francis 1879-1929 NatCAB 23
Cowan, John Franklin 1854- WhAm 4
Cowan, Robert d1846 NewYHSD
Cowan, Robert Ernest 1862-1942 WhAm 2
Cowan, Samuel Houston 1858-1928 NatCAB 21
Cowan, Samuel Kinkade 1869- WhAm 5
Cowan, William Thomas 1897-1964
  NatCAB 50
Coward, Edward Fales 1862-1933 NatCAB 25,
  WhAm 1
Coward, Jacob Meyer 1868-1943 NatCAB 33
Coward, James Smith 1847-1923 NatCAB 14,
  NatCAB 22
Coward, John Moore 1869-1925 NatCAB 22
Coward, John Mortimer 1900-1928 NatCAB 22
Coward, Joseph 1862-1944 NatCAB 33
Coward, Noel Peirce 1899-1973 McGEWB,
  WhAm 5
Coward, Thomas Ridgway 1896-1957 WhAm 3
Cowardin, James Andrew 1811-1882 NatCAB 2
Cowart, Harry Maciemore 1880- WhAm 6
Cowden, Howard Austin 1893-1972 WhAm 6
Cowden, John Brandon 1876- WhAm 5
Cowden, Robert E, Jr. 1910-1968 WhAm 5
Cowden, Roy William 1883-1961 NatCAB 48
Cowdery, Edward Gilmore 1856-1932 WhAm 1
Cowdery, Jonathan 1767-1852 ApCAB, Drake
Cowdery, Robert Holmes 1881- WhAm 6
Cowdery, Warren Hervey 1853-1937
  NatCAB 28
Cowdin, Elliot Christopher 1819-1880
  NatCAB 14
Cowdin, J Cheever 1889-1960 WhAm 4
Cowdin, John Elliot 1858-1941 NatCAB 39
Cowdin, Winthrop 1861-1922 ApCAB X,
  NatCAB 22
Cowdrey, Nathaniel Hartley 1876-1957
  NatCAB 44
Cowdry, Edmund Vincent 1888-1975 WhAm 6
Cowee, Willis Judson 1861-1931 NatCAB 42
Cowell, Alfred Lucius 1870- WhAm 5
Cowell, Benjamin 1781-1860 ApCAB
Cowell, Benjamin 1782-1860 Drake
Cowell, David 1704-1760 NatCAB 9
Cowell, Eugene Irving 1885-1954 NatCAB 47
Cowell, Henry Dixon 1897-1965 McGEWB,
  WebAB, WhAm 4
Cowell, Hervey Sumner 1855-1929 WhAm 1
Cowell, Hiram Augustus 1845-1926 NatCAB 23
Cowell, Joseph Leathley 1792-1863 ApCAB,
  Drake, NewYHSD, WhAm H
Cowell, Joseph S NewYHSD
Cowell, Maria I 1846- WomWWA 14
Cowell, Philip Herbert 1870-1949 DcScB
Cowell, Sidney Frances 1823-1881 DcAmB,
  NotAW
Cowell, Sylvester Eneix 1893-1970 NatCAB 55,
  WhAm 5
Cowell, Thomas J NewYHSD
Cowell, Thomas Richard 1873- ApCAB X
Cowen, Alma D 1872- WomWWA 14
Cowen, Benjamin Rush 1831-1908 BiAUS,
  TwCBDA, WhAm 1
Cowen, Benjamin Sprague 1792-1869
  NatCAB 12
Cowen, Benjamin Sprague 1793-1860 BiDrAC,
  WhAm H
Cowen, Benjamin Sprague 1793-1869 ApCAB,
  BiAUS, TwCBDA
Cowen, Benjamin Sprague 1861- WhAm 4
Cowen, Esek 1787-1844 ApCAB Sup,
  TwCBDA
Cowen, Esek 1788-1844 BiAUS
Cowen, John K 1844-1904 TwCBDA
Cowen, John King 1844-1904 ApCAB Sup,
  WhAm 1
Cowen, John Kissig 1844-1904 BiDrAC,
  DcAmB, NatCAB 18
Cowen, Joshua Lionel 1880-1965 WhAm 4
Cowen, Lawrence 1907-1970 WhAm 5

Cowen, Myron Melvin 1898-1965 WhAm 4
Cowen, William B 1861- WhAm 4
Cowger, William Owen 1922-1971 BiDrAC,
  WhAm 5
Cowgill, Calvin 1819-1903 BiDrAC
Cowgill, George Raymond 1893-1973 WhAm 6
Cowham, Robert Neil 1890-1957 NatCAB 51
Cowham, William Foster 1844-1913
  NatCAB 34
Cowherd, Fletcher 1859-1953 NatCAB 42
Cowherd, Russell 1894-1970 NatCAB 57
Cowherd, William Strother 1860-1915 BiDrAC,
  TwCBDA, WhAm 1, WhAmP
Cowie, Alexander Henderson 1872-1948
  NatCAB 48
Cowie, David Murray 1872-1940 NatCAB 37,
  WhAm 1
Cowie, Ernest Solon 1878-1951 NatCAB 38
Cowie, Jack Baron 1897-1966 WhAm 4
Cowie, Thomas Jefferson 1857-1936 WhAm 1
Cowin, John Clay 1846-1918 ApCAB X,
  WhAm 1
Cowin, William Benton 1874-1929 NatCAB 21
Cowing, Hugh Alvin 1860- WhAm 2
Cowing, Marie Antoinette 1875- WomWWA 14
Cowl, Jane 1883-1950 DcAmB S4, NotAW
Cowl, Jane 1884-1950 WhAm 3
Cowl, Jane 1889- NatCAB 17
Cowl, Jane 1890- ApCAB X
Cowles, Alfred 1865-1939 WhAm 1
Cowles, Alfred Abernethy 1845-1916
  NatCAB 18
Cowles, Alfred Hutchinson 1858-1929
  NatCAB 15, NatCAB 22, WhAm 1
Cowles, Augustus Woodruff 1819-1913
  ApCAB Sup, NatCAB 23, TwCBDA,
  WhAm 1
Cowles, Betsey Mix 1810-1876 NotAW
Cowles, Charles Holden 1875-1957 BiDrAC
Cowles, Cheney 1908-1943 WhAm 2
Cowles, Danforth Chauser 1875-1940
  NatCAB 31
Cowles, David Smith 1857-1911 NatCAB 24
Cowles, Dudley Redwood 1872- WhAm 6
Cowles, Edward 1837-1919 NatCAB 19,
  WhAm 1
Cowles, Edward Pitkin 1815-1874 ApCAB,
  BiAUS, TwCBDA
Cowles, Edward Spencer 1889-1954 WhAm 3
Cowles, Edwin 1825-1890 DcAmB, NatCAB 2,
  NatCAB 23, TwCBDA, WhAm H
Cowles, Emma Milton 1861- WhAm 4,
  WomWWA 14
Cowles, Eugene Chase 1860- WhAm 4
Cowles, Eugene Hutchinson 1855-1892
  NatCAB 23
Cowles, Frederic Albert 1881-1949 WhAm 3
Cowles, Gardner 1903- WebAB
Cowles, Gardner, Sr. 1861-1946 DcAmB S4,
  NatCAB 36, REnAW, WhAm 2
Cowles, Genevieve Almeda 1891-
  WomWWA 14
Cowles, George Washington 1823-1901 BiAUS,
  BiDrAC
Cowles, Giles Hooker 1766-1835 ApCAB
Cowles, Henry 1803-1881 ApCAB
Cowles, Henry Booth 1798-1873 BiAUS,
  BiDrAC, WhAm H
Cowles, Henry Chandler 1869-1939 DcAmB S2,
  NatCAB 39, WebAB, WhAm 1
Cowles, James Lewis 1843-1922 NatCAB 19,
  WhAm 1
Cowles, John Guiteau Welch 1836-1914
  NatCAB 9, WhAm 1
Cowles, John Henry 1863-1954 WhAm 3
Cowles, Mrs. Josiah Evans 1858- WhAm 4
Cowles, Julia Darrow 1862-1919 WhAm 1
Cowles, Julius Hatch 1859-1950 NatCAB 38
Cowles, LaMonte 1859- NatCAB 16
Cowles, LeRoy Eugene 1880-1957 BiDAmEd,
  NatCAB 42, WhAm 3
Cowles, Mabel Birdsall 1872- WomWWA 14
Cowles, Maude Alice 1871- WhAm 1
Cowles, Percival William 1880- WhAm 6
Cowles, Rheinart Parker 1872-1948 NatCAB 37
Cowles, Robert Lewis 1891-1962 NatCAB 50
Cowles, Russell 1887- IlBEAAW
Cowles, Torris Zalmon 1845-1919 WhAm 1

Cowles, Walter Cleveland 1853-1917
  NatCAB 23, WhAm 1
Cowles, William Henry Harrison 1840-1901
  BiDrAC, TwCBDA
Cowles, William Hutchinson 1866-1946
  NatCAB 35, WhAm 2
Cowles, William Hutchinson, Jr. 1902-1971
  NatCAB 57, WhAm 5
Cowles, William Lyman 1856-1926 *WhAm 1*
Cowles, William Sheffield 1846-1923
  NatCAB 23, WhAm 1
Cowley, Abraham 1618-1667 *McGEWB*
Cowley, Charles 1832-1908 *ApCAB Sup,*
  DcAmB, NatCAB 23, TwCBDA,
  WhAm 1
Cowley, Edward 1827-1891 *TwCBDA*
Cowley, Elizabeth Buchanan *WomWWA 14*
Cowley, Henry Thomas 1837-1917 *NatCAB 34*
Cowley, Howard Stephen 1913-1962
  NatCAB 50
Cowley, Malcolm 1898- *WebAB*
Cowley, Mary Junkin Buchanan 1853-
  WomWWA 14
Cowley, Matthew 1897-1953 *WhAm 3*
Cowley, Michael Mark 1841-1915 *NatCAB 17*
Cowling, Donald John 1880-1965 *BiDAmEd,*
  NatCAB 53, WhAm 4
Cowling, Lydia Hampton 1848- *WomWWA 14*
Cowman, Charles E 1868-1924 *NatCAB 19*
Cowper, George Vernon 1879-1948 *NatCAB 37*
Cowper, Harry Mattingly 1870-1934 *WhAm 1*
Cowper, Holmes 1870-1934 *NatCAB 31*
Cowper, William 1731-1800 *McGEWB*
Cowperthwait, John Howard 1848- *ApCAB X*
Cowperthwaite, Allen Corson 1848-
  NatCAB 11, WhAm 4
Cowpland, Caleb 1690?-1757 *NatCAB 16*
Cox, Abraham Beekman 1844-1906 *WhAm 1*
Cox, Abraham Siddon 1800-1864 *ApCAB,*
  NatCAB 12
Cox, Albert Lyman 1883-1965 *NatCAB 51,*
  WhAm 4
Cox, Albert Scott 1863- *WhAm 4*
Cox, Allen 1887-1974 *WhAm 6*
Cox, Alonzo Bettis 1884-1968 *NatCAB 55,*
  WhAm 5
Cox, Ann Caroline 1859- *WomWWA 14*
Cox, Archibald 1874-1931 *NatCAB 15,*
  WhAm 1
Cox, Argus 1856- *WhAm 4*
Cox, Attilla 1875- *WhAm 1*
Cox, Benjamin 1866-1944 *WhAm 2*
Cox, Catharine Elizabeth Bean 1865-
  WomWWA 14
Cox, Cedelia May 1875- *WomWWA 14*
Cox, Channing Harris 1879-1968 *WhAm 5*
Cox, Charles Brinton 1864-1905 *IlBEAAW*
Cox, Charles Elbridge 1860-1936 *NatCAB 26,*
  WhAm 1
Cox, Charles Finney 1846-1912 *WhAm 1*
Cox, Charles Hudson 1829-1901 *IlBEAAW,*
  NewYHSD
Cox, Charles Marshall 1859-1944 *NatCAB 33*
Cox, Charles Raymond 1891-1962 *NatCAB 51,*
  WhAm 4
Cox, Christopher Christian 1816-1881 *BiAUS,*
  NatCAB 10
Cox, Clara Ione 1879- *WomWWA 14*
Cox, Clark *IlBEAAW*
Cox, Clinton Vaylord 1888-1955 *NatCAB 43*
Cox, Creed Fulton 1877-1950 *WhAm 2A,*
  WhAm 5
Cox, Daniel Hargate 1872-1955 *WhAm 3*
Cox, Douglas Farley 1867-1940 *NatCAB 38,*
  WhAm 1
Cox, Edward Eugene 1880-1952 *BiDrAC,*
  DcAmB S5, NatCAB 42, WhAm 3,
  WhAmP
Cox, Edward Travers 1821- *ApCAB,*
  NatCAB 12
Cox, Edward Weston 1865- *WhAm 5*
Cox, Eleanor Rogers d1931 *WhAm 1*
Cox, Ephraim Jackson 1870- *WhoColR*
Cox, Eugene 1879-1930 *NatCAB 24*
Cox, Eugene R 1856-1921 *ApCAB X*
Cox, Forrest Dale 1902-1958 *WhAm 3*
Cox, Frank 1862-1940 *NatCAB 42*

Cox, Frank P 1866- *WhAm 4*
Cox, Frederick Irving 1870-1962 *WhAm 4*
Cox, G Howland 1854-1931 *WhAm 1*
Cox, Garfield V 1893-1970 *WhAm 5*
Cox, George Barnesdale 1853-1916 *NatCAB 17*
Cox, George Barnsdale 1853-1916 *DcAmB,*
  WhAmP
Cox, George Bryan 1896-1973 *WhAm 6*
Cox, George Clarke 1865-1943 *WhAm 2*
Cox, George Emerson 1870-1944 *NatCAB 42*
Cox, George Howland, Jr. 1883- *WhAm 2*
Cox, George James d1946 *WhAm 2*
Cox, Guy Henry 1882-1922 *WhAm 1*
Cox, Guy Wilbur 1871-1955 *ApCAB X,*
  WhAm 3
Cox, H F *NewYHSD*
Cox, Hannah 1776-1881 *ApCAB*
Cox, Hannah 1796-1876 *ApCAB*
Cox, Hannah Peirce 1797-1876 *DcAmB,*
  WhAmP
Cox, Hannah Pierce 1797-1876 *WhAm H*
Cox, Harvey Warren 1875-1944 *NatCAB 18,*
  WhAm 2
Cox, Henry G 1819-1866 *ApCAB*
Cox, Henry Hamilton 1750?-1822 *ApCAB*
Cox, Henry Hamilton 1769?-1821 *DcAmB,*
  WhAm H
Cox, Henry Joseph 1863-1930 *NatCAB 24,*
  TwCBDA, WhAm 1
Cox, Hudson Baynham 1909-1968 *WhAm 5*
Cox, Hugh 1905-1973 *WhAm 6*
Cox, Isaac Joslin 1873- *WhAm 5*
Cox, Isaac Newton 1846-1916 *BiDrAC*
Cox, J Elwood 1856-1932 *WhAm 1*
Cox, J Williard 1902-1960 *NatCAB 48*
Cox, Jacob 1810-1892 *NewYHSD, WhAm H*
Cox, Jacob 1812-1892 *IlBEAAW*
Cox, Jacob Dolson 1828-1900 *AmBi, ApCAB,*
  BiAUS, BiDrAC, BiDrUSE, DcAmB,
  Drake, NatCAB 3, NatCAB 4,
  NatCAB 22, TwCBDA, WebAB,
  WebAMB, WhAm 1, WhAmP
Cox, Jacob Dolson 1881-1953 *WhAm 3*
Cox, James 1751-1834 *ApCAB, NewYHSD*
Cox, James 1753-1810 *ApCAB, BiAUS,*
  BiDrAC, Drake, WhAm H
Cox, James 1838?- *NewYHSD*
Cox, James B 1861- *WhAm 4*
Cox, James Clifton 1873-1957 *NatCAB 43,*
  WhAm 3
Cox, James Estil 1872-1957 *NatCAB 47*
Cox, James Farley 1830-1898 *NatCAB 4*
Cox, James Franklin 1878- *WhAm 6*
Cox, James Middleton 1870-1957 *ApCAB X,*
  NatCAB 15, BiDrAC, NatCAB 51,
  WhAm 3, WhAmP
Cox, James Middleton, Jr. 1903- *WhAm 6*
Cox, James Monroe 1860-1948 *WhAm 2*
Cox, James Monroe 1896- *WhoColR*
Cox, James Sitgreaves 1822-1901 *NatCAB 49*
Cox, Jocelyn Meridith Nolting 1900- *WhAm 5*
Cox, John Harrington 1863- *WhAm 4*
Cox, John Isaac 1855-1946 *NatCAB 40*
Cox, John Lyman 1866-1955 *NatCAB 46*
Cox, Joseph Winston 1875-1939 *WhAm 1*
Cox, Katherine Hamilton Cabell d1925
  WhAm 1, WomWWA 14
Cox, Kenyon 1856-1919 *AmBi, ApCAB,*
  BnEnAmA, DcAmB, NatCAB 5,
  TwCBDA, WhAm 1
Cox, Leander Martin 1812-1865 *BiAUS,*
  BiDrAC, WhAm H
Cox, Leilyn Munns 1903-1972 *WhAm 5*
Cox, Lemuel 1736-1806 *ApCAB, DcAmB,*
  Drake, NatCAB 24, WhAm H
Cox, Lenore Hanna *WomWWA 14*
Cox, Leonard Martin 1870-1943 *WhAm 2*
Cox, Lester Edmund 1895-1968 *WhAm 5*
Cox, Linton A 1868- *WhAm 5*
Cox, Louis Lawrence 1907-1971 *NatCAB 55*
Cox, Louis Sherburne 1874-1961 *NatCAB 49,*
  WhAm 5
Cox, Louise Howland King 1865-1945
  NatCAB 11, TwCBDA, WhAm 2,
  WomWWA 14
Cox, Luella Alice Carr 1862- *WomWWA 14*
Cox, Manford E 1880-1958 *NatCAB 48*
Cox, Mary Brannon 1858- *WomWWA 14*

Cox, Mary Nichols 1869- *WomWWA 14*
Cox, Melville Beveridge 1799-1833 *ApCAB*
Cox, Millard, Jr. 1899-1972 *NatCAB 57*
Cox, Millard F 1856- *WhAm 4*
Cox, Nellie I McMaster d1968 *WhAm 5*
Cox, Nicholas Nichols 1837-1912 *BiDrAC,*
  TwCBDA, WhAm 4
Cox, Oliver Clemence 1887-1968 *NatCAB 54*
Cox, Oscar Larken 1877- *WhAm 5*
Cox, Oscar Sydney 1905-1966 *WhAm 4*
Cox, Palmer 1840-1924 *AmBi, ApCAB,*
  DcAmB, NatCAB 7, TwCBDA,
  WhAm 1
Cox, Philip Wescott Lawrence 1883-1975
  WhAm 6
Cox, Raymond Benjamin 1883-1948 *WhAm 3*
Cox, Robert *NewYHSD*
Cox, Robert Lynn 1865-1930 *NatCAB 22*
Cox, Rose Marion *WomWWA 14*
Cox, Ross 1793-1853 *REnAW*
Cox, Rowland 1842-1900 *DcAmB,*
  NatCAB 15, WhAm H
Cox, Samuel 1825-1903 *TwCBDA*
Cox, Samuel Hanson 1793- *Drake*
Cox, Samuel Hanson 1793-1880 *AmBi,*
  DcAmB, NatCAB 7, TwCBDA,
  WhAm H
Cox, Samuel Hanson 1793-1881 *ApCAB*
Cox, Samuel Sullivan 1824-1889 *AmBi,*
  ApCAB, BiAUS, BiDrAC, DcAmB,
  Drake, NatCAB 6, TwCBDA, WhAm H,
  WhAmP
Cox, T Newell 1898-1965 *NatCAB 52*
Cox, Taylor Harmon 1903-1962 *NatCAB 49,*
  WhAm 4
Cox, Theodore Sullivan 1894-1947 *NatCAB 36,*
  WhAm 2
Cox, Thomas, Jr. 1831?- *NewYHSD*
Cox, Thomas Lillard 1859- *NatCAB 7*
Cox, W H M *IlBEAAW*
Cox, W R 1829-1873 *NewYHSD*
Cox, W Rowland 1872- *WhAm 5*
Cox, Wally 1924-1973 *WhAm 5*
Cox, Walter Smith 1826-1902 *NatCAB 9,*
  TwCBDA, WhAm 1
Cox, Warren Edward 1907-1962 *NatCAB 49*
Cox, Wayne Wellington 1864- *WhoColR*
Cox, William d1851? *ApCAB, Drake*
Cox, William Alexander 1872- *WhoColR*
Cox, William Coburn 1905-1970 *NatCAB 57*
Cox, William Elijah 1861-1942 *BiDrAC,*
  WhAmP
Cox, William Elijah 1864- *WhAm 4*
Cox, William Ruffin 1831-1919 *BiDrAC*
Cox, William Ruffin 1832-1919 *ApCAB Sup,*
  BiDConf, DcAmB, NatCAB 7, TwCBDA,
  WhAm 1
Cox, William Stakely 1861-1938 *WhAm 3*
Cox, William VanZandt 1852-1923 *ApCAB X,*
  NatCAB 20, WhAm 1
Cox, William Wesley 1864- *WhAm 4*
Cox, Williston Madison 1877-1960 *NatCAB 49*
Cox, Wilson Naylor 1876-1938 *WhAm 1*
Cox-McCormack, Nancy 1885- *BiCAW*
Coxe, Alexander Brinton 1838-1906
  NatCAB 14
Coxe, Alfred Conkling *TwCBDA, WhAm 1*
Coxe, Alfred Conkling 1880-1957 *NatCAB 48,*
  WhAm 3
Coxe, Arthur Cleveland 1818-1896 *ApCAB,*
  DcAmB, Drake, NatCAB 3, TwCBDA,
  WhAm H
Coxe, Charles Sidney 1791-1879 *TwCBDA*
Coxe, Daniel 1673-1739 *DcAmB, WhAm H*
Coxe, Daniel 1674-1739 *ApCAB Sup*
Coxe, Eckley Brinton 1839-1895 *ApCAB,*
  DcAmB, NatCAB 11, WhAm H
Coxe, Frank Morrell 1844-1916 *WhAm 1*
Coxe, James Clarke Watson 1837-1914
  WhAm 1
Coxe, John Redman 1773-1864 *ApCAB,*
  BiHiMed, DcAmB, Drake, NatCAB 22,
  TwCBDA, WhAm H
Coxe, Lewis Crocker 1912-1974 *WhAm 6*
Coxe, Macgrane 1859-1923 *NatCAB 12,*
  WhAm 1
Coxe, Margaret 1800?- *ApCAB, Drake*
Coxe, Richard Smith 1792-1865 *DcAmB,*

NatCAB 19, WhAm H

Coxe, Samuel Hanson 1819-1895 TwCBDA
Coxe, Tench 1755-1824 AmBi, ApCAB,
  BiAUS, BiDrAC, DcAmB, Drake,
  EncAB, McGEWB, NatCAB 6,
  TwCBDA, WhAm H
Coxe, William, Jr. 1762-1831 AmBi, BiAUS,
  BiDrAC, DcAmB, WhAm H
Coxe, William Briscom 1869-1927 WhAm 1
Coxe, William Ellery C 1837-1904 WhAm 1
Coxetter, Louis Mitchell 1818-1873 AmBi,
  DcAmB, WhAm H
Coxey, Jacob Sechier 1854-1951 WebAB,
  WhAm 1
Coxey, Jacob Sechler 1854-1951 DcAmB S5,
  EncAB, McGEWB, NatCAB 46
Coxhead, Ralph Cramer 1892-1951 NatCAB 39
Coy, Edward Gustin 1844-1904 NatCAB 6,
  WhAm 1
Coy, Eliah Washburn 1832-1915 WhAm 1
Coy, Havelock George 1866-1926 NatCAB 20
Coy, Warren Deweese 1872-1953 NatCAB 47
Coy, Wayne 1903-1957 NatCAB 45, WhAm 3
Coy, William NewYHSD
Coye, William Henry 1863-1929 WhAm 1
Coykendall, Frederick 1872-1954 NatCAB 45,
  WhAm 3
Coyl, Horace Edward 1893-1964 WhAm 4
Coyle, David Cushman 1887-1969 WhAm 5
Coyle, Eugene 1847- WhAm 4
Coyle, Frank J 1900-1971 WhAm 5
Coyle, Henry 1865- WhAm 4
Coyle, James 1798-1828 NewYHSD
Coyle, James Edwin 1873-1921 WhAm 1
Coyle, James Frank 1846- NatCAB 12
Coyle, John Grant 1868- NatCAB 14
Coyle, John Patterson 1852-1895 TwCBDA
Coyle, Marvin E 1887-1961 WhAm 4
Coyle, Robert Francis 1850- NatCAB 12,
  WhAm 1
Coyle, Robert McCurdy 1860-1936 WhAm 1
Coyle, Susan Edmond 1871- WomWWA 14
Coyle, William Radford 1878-1962 BiDrAC,
  WhAm 4
Coyne, Frederick E 1860- WhAm 4
Coyne, George Albert 1883-1965 NatCAB 51
Coyne, Grace Margaret 1887- WomWWA 14
Coyne, John Anthony 1895-1954 NatCAB 43
Coyne, John Nicholas 1839-1907 WhAm 1
Coyner, Charles Luther 1853- WhAm 4
Coyriere, E Miriam AmWom
Coysevox, Antoine 1640-1720 McGEWB
Cozart, Reed 1904-1974 WhAm 6
Coze, Paul 1903-1975 IIBEAAW
Cozens, Frederick Warren 1890-1954 WhAm 3
Cozier, Robert V 1869- WhAm 5
Cozzens, Charles Owen 1890-1947 NatCAB 45
Cozzens, Frederick Schiller 1846- ApCAB
Cozzens, Frederick Swartwout 1818-1869
  ApCAB, DcAmB, Drake, NatCAB 6,
  TwCBDA, WhAm H
Cozzens, Issachar 1781- ApCAB, Drake
Cozzens, James Gould 1903- WebAB
Cozzens, Samuel Woodworth 1834-1878 ApCAB
Cozzens, William B 1787-1864 ApCAB
Cozzens, William Cole 1811-1876 ApCAB,
  BiAUS, NatCAB 9, TwCBDA
Crabb, Edward Joseph 1865- WhoColR
Crabb, George Melville 1882-1953 NatCAB 40
Crabb, George W BiAUS
Crabb, George W d1847 ApCAB
Crabb, George W 1802-1846 TwCBDA
Crabb, George Whitfield 1804-1846 BiDrAC,
  WhAm H
Crabb, Jeremiah 1760-1800 BiAUS, BiDrAC,
  WhAm H
Crabbe, George 1754-1832 McGEWB
Crabbe, George William 1875-1951 WhAm 3
Crabbe, John Grant 1865-1924 BiDAmEd,
  NatCAB 19, WhAm 1
Crabbe, Thomas 1788-1872 ApCAB,
  NatCAB 4, TwCBDA
Crabbe, Thomas 1809- Drake
Crabbe, Thomas Mackay 1905-1947
  NatCAB 40
Crabbs, Austin 1883-1960 NatCAB 48
Crabbs, George Dent 1875-1948 NatCAB 35,
  WhAm 2

Crabites, Pierre 1877-1943 WhAm 2
Crabtree, Charlotte 1847-1924 WhAm 1
Crabtree, Edgar Erman 1869-1946 NatCAB 35
Crabtree, Ernest Granville 1883-1947
  NatCAB 40, WhAm 2
Crabtree, Frederick 1867-1925 WhAm 1
Crabtree, Harold Roy 1918-1956 WhAm 3
Crabtree, James Anderson 1902-1966 WhAm 4
Crabtree, James William 1864-1945 BiDAmEd,
  WhAm 2
Crabtree, Lotta M 1849- WomWWA 14
Crabtree, Lotta Mignon 1847-1924 AmBi,
  AmWom, ApCAB, DcAmB, NotAW,
  TwCBDA, WebAB
Crabtree, Nate L 1906-1965 NatCAB 52,
  WhAm 4
Crabtree, Peter 1913-1955 NatCAB 46
Crabtree, William 1610-1644? DcScB
Cracchi, Guiseppe WhAm H
Crace, Sir John 1887-1968 WhWW-II
Craddock, Charles Egbert 1850-1922 AmBi,
  ApCAB Sup, DcAmB, NotAW,
  TwCBDA, WhAm 1
Craddock, John Derrett 1881-1942 WhAm 6
Craddock, John Durrett 1881-1942 BiDrAC
Cradlebaugh, John 1819-1872 BiAUS, BiDrAC,
  WhAm H
Cradock, Sir Christopher G F Maurice 1862-1914
  WhoMilH
Cradock, Matthew 1585?-1641 ApCAB, Drake,
  NatCAB 5
Cradock, Thomas d1760 ApCAB, Drake
Craft, Clarence Christian 1880-1935 WhAm 1
Craft, E A 1893-1954 WhAm 3
Craft, Edward Beech 1881-1929 NatCAB 22,
  WhAm 1
Craft, Ellen 1826?-1897? NotAW
Craft, Frost 1846-1919 NatCAB 13, WhAm 1
Craft, Marthanna 1868- WomWWA 14
Craft, R B NewYHSD
Craft, William Arthur 1894-1963 NatCAB 52
Crafton, Allen 1890-1966 WhAm 4
Crafts, Annetta Stratford 1865- WhAm 4
Crafts, Arthur Abram 1867-1940 NatCAB 30
Crafts, Clayton Edward 1848- NatCAB 2,
  WhAm 4
Crafts, Ebenezer 1740-1810 ApCAB
Crafts, Frederick, Jr. NewYHSD
Crafts, James Mason 1839-1917 AmBi,
  ApCAB, AsBiEn, DcAmB, NatCAB 13,
  TwCBDA, WhAm 1
Crafts, Leland Whitney 1892-1968 WhAm 5
Crafts, Leo Melville 1863-1938 NatCAB 15,
  WhAm 1
Crafts, Lettie May 1860- WomWWA 14
Crafts, Samuel Chandler 1768-1853 ApCAB,
  BiAUS, BiDrAC, Drake, NatCAB 8,
  TwCBDA, WhAm H, WhAmP
Crafts, Sara Jane WhAm 5, WomWWA 14
Crafts, Sarah J Timanus ApCAB
Crafts, Walter 1839- ApCAB
Crafts, Walter 1903-1963 WhAm 4
Crafts, Wilbur Fisk 1850-1922 ApCAB,
  NatCAB 14, TwCBDA, WhAm 1
Crafts, William 1787-1826 ApCAB, DcAmB,
  Drake, WhAm H
Cragen, Edward Leo 1882-1941 NatCAB 31
Craghan, George d1782 WhAm H
Cragin, Aaron Harrison 1821-1898 ApCAB,
  BiAUS, BiDrAC, Drake, NatCAB 12,
  TwCBDA, WhAmP
Cragin, Edward Bradford 1859-1918 ApCAB X
Cragin, Edwin Bradford 1859-1918 NatCAB 15,
  WhAm 1
Cragin, Francis Whittemore 1858- ApCAB,
  TwCBDA, WhAm 4
Cragin, Mary Randle Willard 1864-
  WomWWA 14
Crago, Alfred 1879- WhAm 6
Crago, Thomas Spencer 1866-1925 BiDrAC,
  NatCAB 49, WhAm 1
Cragun, John Wiley 1906-1969 WhAm 5
Craider, Frederick d1866 ApCAB
Craig, Agnes Houston WomWWA 14
Craig, Alexander Johnson 1823-1870 ApCAB
Craig, Alexander Kerr 1828-1892 BiDrAC,
  WhAm H

Craig, Alexander Righter 1868-1922
  NatCAB 19, WhAm 1
Craig, Alfred Edwin 1861- WhAm 1
Craig, Alfred M 1831-1911 ApCAB X,
  NatCAB 13
Craig, Alfred M 1833-1911 WhAm 1
Craig, Allan 1884-1970 NatCAB 57
Craig, Allen 1835- NatCAB 4
Craig, Anna WomWWA 14
Craig, Arthur Ulysses 1871- WhoColR
Craig, Asa Hollister 1847-1934 WhAm 1
Craig, Austin 1824-1881 DcAmB, NatCAB 13,
  WhAm H
Craig, Austin 1872-1949 WhAm 3
Craig, C Burns 1884-1936 NatCAB 30
Craig, Charity Rusk 1851?- AmWom
Craig, Charles 1846-1931 IIBEAAW,
  WhAm 4
Craig, Charles Curtis 1865-1944 ApCAB X,
  NatCAB 36, WhAm 4
Craig, Charles Franklin 1872-1950 WhAm 3
Craig, Charles Patton 1858-1935 WhAm 1
Craig, Clara Elizabeth 1873?-1943 BiDAmEd
Craig, Clarence Tucker 1895-1953 WhAm 3
Craig, Daniel Frank 1875-1929 WhAm 3
Craig, Daniel H 1814?-1895 DcAmB,
  WhAm H
Craig, David 1905-1964 NatCAB 52
Craig, Donald Alexander 1883-1936 WhAm 1
Craig, Dudley Irvine 1865-1954 NatCAB 47
Craig, Edward Chilton 1872- WhAm 3
Craig, Edward Marshall 1867-1928 NatCAB 21
Craig, Edwin Wilson 1893-1969 NatCAB 55,
  WhAm 5
Craig, Elijah 1743-1800 ApCAB
Craig, Elisabeth May d1975 WhAm 6
Craig, Frank 1870-1926 WhAm 1
Craig, Frank Ardary 1876-1959 NatCAB 47
Craig, Frank Myron 1877-1916 NatCAB 19
Craig, George Henry 1845-1923 BiDrAC
Craig, George M 1862-1950 WhAm 3
Craig, Hardin 1875-1968 WhAm 5
Craig, Hardin, Jr. 1907-1971 WhAm 6
Craig, Harry Raymond 1888-1954 NatCAB 47
Craig, Hector 1775-1842 BiAUS, BiDrAC,
  WhAm H
Craig, Henry Knox 1791-1869 ApCAB, Drake,
  TwCBDA
Craig, Hubert Maxton 1903-1968 NatCAB 54
Craig, Hugh 1816-1878 NatCAB 5
Craig, Hugh 1842-1920 NatCAB 19
Craig, Isaac Eugene 1830- ApCAB,
  NewYHSD, TwCBDA
Craig, James 1818-1888 BiDrAC, WhAm H
Craig, James 1820-1888 ApCAB, BiAUS,
  Drake, TwCBDA
Craig, James Alexander 1855- WhAm 4
Craig, James Alexander 1858- TwCBDA
Craig, James Douglas 1878-1940 NatCAB 29
Craig, James Edward 1881-1970 WhAm 5
Craig, Sir James Henry 1749-1812 ApCAB,
  Drake
Craig, James McIntosh 1848-1922 NatCAB 6
Craig, James William 1825-1891 NatCAB 19
Craig, John d1731 DcScB
Craig, John 1797-1872 ApCAB
Craig, John 1864-1912 WhAm 1
Craig, John D BiAUS
Craig, John Franklyn 1838-1934 NatCAB 25
Craig, John Joseph 1888-1948 NatCAB 36
Craig, John Newton 1831-1900 TwCBDA
Craig, Joseph Albert 1867-1958 NatCAB 47
Craig, Joseph Davis 1856-1923 WhAm 1
Craig, Joseph Edgar 1845-1925 WhAm 1
Craig, Jubal Early 1874- WhAm 6
Craig, Katherine L 1876-1934 WhAm 1,
  WomWWA 14
Craig, Katherine Taylor 1877- WomWWA 14
Craig, Lewis 1737-1828 ApCAB
Craig, Lewis S d1852 ApCAB
Craig, Locke 1860-1924 NatCAB 20
Craig, Locke 1860-1925 WhAm 1
Craig, Lyman Creighton 1906-1974 AsBiEn,
  WhAm 6
Craig, Malin 1875-1945 DcAmB S3,
  NatCAB 37, WebAMB, WhAm 2
Craig, Margaret 1880- WomWWA 14
Craig, Margaret Bell 1876- WomWWA 14

Craig, Mary Marsden Young 1879-
   WomWWA 14
Craig, Netta *WomWWA 14*
Craig, Ollison 1888-1956 *NatCAB 45*
Craig, Oscar John 1846-1911 *BiDAmEd,
   NatCAB 25, TwCBDA, WhAm 3*
Craig, Palmer Hunt 1901-1967 *WhAm 5*
Craig, Paul Frederick 1896-1974 *WhAm 6*
Craig, Robert *BiAUS*
Craig, Robert 1791?-1851 *TwCBDA*
Craig, Robert 1792-1852 *BiDrAC, WhAm H*
Craig, Robert 1882-1962 *NatCAB 49*
Craig, Robert B 1900-1973 *WhAm 6*
Craig, Robert 1842-1872 *ApCAB*
Craig, Robert Hall 1891-1944 *NatCAB 34*
Craig, Robert S 1905- *WhAm 5*
Craig, Samuel *NewYHSD*
Craig, Samuel Alfred 1839-1920 *BiDrAC*
Craig, Samuel G 1874-1960 *WhAm 4*
Craig, Talton Robert 1897-1952 *NatCAB 39*
Craig, Thomas d1832 *Drake*
Craig, Thomas 1853-1900 *TwCBDA*
Craig, Thomas 1855-1900 *DcAmB, WhAm H*
Craig, Thomas Bigalow 1849-1924 *WhAm 1*
Craig, Virginia Judith 1878- *WomWWA 14*
Craig, Wallace 1876- *WhAm 5*
Craig, Walter 1900-1972 *WhAm 5*
Craig, William 1829-1875 *ApCAB*
Craig, William Bayard 1846-1916 *NatCAB 21,
   TwCBDA, WhAm 1*
Craig, William Benjamin 1877-1925 *BiDrAC,
   WhAm 1*
Craig, William Edward 1874- *WhAm 1*
Craig, William Henry 1858-1928 *NatCAB 24*
Craig, Willis Green 1834-1911 *TwCBDA,
   WhAm 1*
Craig, Winchell McKendree 1892-1960
   NatCAB 46, WhAm 3
Craige, Burton 1875-1945 *NatCAB 33,
   WhAm 2*
Craige, Burton Francis 1811-1875 *BiAUS,
   NatCAB 28, TwCBDA*
Craige, Francis Burton 1811-1875 *BiDConf,
   BiDrAC, WhAm H*
Craige, Kerr 1843-1904 *NatCAB 28*
Craige, Kerr 1883-1943 *NatCAB 32*
Craighead, Edwin Boone 1861-1920 *AmBi,
   ApCAB X, DcAmB, NatCAB 14,
   TwCBDA, WhAm 3*
Craighead, Erwin 1852-1932 *NatCAB 24,
   WhAm 1*
Craighead, Ethel 1878- *WomWWA 14*
Craighead, James Geddes 1823-1895 *TwCBDA*
Craighead, Thomas 1750-1825 *NatCAB 8*
Craighill, George Bowdoin, Sr. 1882-1972
   NatCAB 56, WhAm 5
Craighill, William Edward 1863-1916
   NatCAB 18
Craighill, William Price 1833-1909 *ApCAB,
   Drake, NatCAB 12, TwCBDA, WhAm 1*
Craigie, Andrew 1743-1819 *DcAmB,
   WhAm H*
Craigie, David Johnston 1840-1913 *WhAm 1*
Craigie, Mary E Whitbeck *WomWWA 14*
Craigie, Pearl Mary Teresa 1867-1906 *AmBi,
   ApCAB Sup, NatCAB 10, WhAm 1*
Craigie, Pearl Richards 1867-1906 *TwCBDA*
Craigie, William 1799-1863 *ApCAB*
Craigie, Sir William Alexander 1867-1957
   WhAm 3
Craigmiles, John H 1825-1899 *BiDConf*
Craik, James 1730-1814 *AmBi, DcAmB,
   NatCAB 7, TwCBDA, WhAm H*
Craik, James 1731-1814 *ApCAB, Drake*
Craik, James 1806-1882 *TwCBDA*
Craik, William 1761-1814? *BiAUS, BiDrAC,
   TwCBDA, WhAm H*
Craik, William 1829?- *NewYHSD*
Crail, Joe 1877-1938 *BiDrAC, WhAm 1*
Crain, Carroll Francis 1895-1963 *NatCAB 50*
Crain, G D, Jr. 1885-1973 *WhAm 6*
Crain, Gustavus Dedman, Jr. 1885-1973
   NatCAB 57
Crain, James Kerr 1879- *WhAm 6*
Crain, John Hillier 1858- *WhAm 4*
Crain, L D 1868-1942 *NatCAB 43*
Crain, Robert 1865-1928 *NatCAB 21*
Crain, William Henry 1848-1896 *BiDrAC,*

TwCBDA, WhAm H, WhAmP
Craley, Nathaniel Neiman, Jr. 1927- *BiDrAC*
Cralle, Richard K d1864 *ApCAB, Drake*
Cram, Albert Monroe 1882-1957 *NatCAB 46*
Cram, Alice Estella 1861- *BiCAW*
Cram, Allan Gilbert 1886-1947 *IIBEAAW*
Cram, Elizabeth Carrington Read
   WomWWA 14
Cram, Franklin Webster 1846- *NatCAB 16,
   WhAm 4*
Cram, George F 1842-1928 *WhAm 1*
Cram, George Taylor 1834- *NatCAB 12*
Cram, Harold E 1890-1948 *WhAm 2*
Cram, Ralph Adams 1863- *NatCAB 15,
   WhAm HA, WhAm 4A*
Cram, Ralph Adams 1863-1938 *AmBi*
Cram, Ralph Adams 1863-1942 *BnEnAmA,
   DcAmB S3, WebAB, WhAm 2*
Cram, Ralph Warren 1869-1952 *NatCAB 41,
   WhAm 3*
Cram, Thomas Jefferson 1807?-1883 *ApCAB,
   TwCBDA*
Cram, Willard Gliden 1875- *WhAm 5*
Cram, William Everett 1871-1947 *WhAm 3*
Cram, Wingate Franklin 1887-1952 *WhAm 3*
Cramblet, Thomas E 1862-1919 *WhAm 1*
Cramblet, Wilbur Haverfield 1892-1975
   WhAm 6
Cramer, Ambrose 1857-1927 *NatCAB 22*
Cramer, Ambrose Coghill 1891-1970
   NatCAB 55
Cramer, Frank John 1863-1955 *NatCAB 43*
Cramer, Frederic 1874- *WhAm 5*
Cramer, Gabriel 1704-1752 *DcScB*
Cramer, Gustav 1838- *NatCAB 5*
Cramer, Harriet Laura 1848-1922 *WhAm 1*
Cramer, Ida Howell 1873- *WomWWA 14*
Cramer, Jacob Timothy 1881-1932 *NatCAB 24*
Cramer, Jesse Grant 1869- *TwCBDA*
Cramer, Johann Andreas 1710-1777 *DcScB Sup*
Cramer, John 1779-1870 *ApCAB, BiAUS,
   BiDrAC, NatCAB 1, TwCBDA,
   WhAm H*
Cramer, John Francis 1899-1967 *WhAm 5*
Cramer, John Luther 1864- *WhAm 4*
Cramer, John Wesley 1914-1966 *WhAm 4*
Cramer, Kenneth Frank 1894-1954 *NatCAB 45,
   WhAm 3*
Cramer, M J 1835-1898 *BiAUS*
Cramer, Michael John 1835-1898 *ApCAB,
   DcAmB, NatCAB 12, TwCBDA,
   WhAm H*
Cramer, Morley, Jr. 1894-1969 *NatCAB 55*
Cramer, Myron Cady 1881-1966 *WhAm 4*
Cramer, Sterling B 1881-1955 *WhAm 3*
Cramer, Stuart Warren 1868-1940 *NatCAB 33,
   WhAm 1*
Cramer, Stuart Warren, Jr. 1892-1957
   NatCAB 46, WhAm 3
Cramer, William 1878-1945 *WhAm 2*
Cramer, William Cato 1922- *BiDrAC*
Cramer, William E 1817- *NatCAB 1*
Cramer, William Stuart 1873-1930 *WhAm 1,
   WhAm 1C*
Cramer, Zadok 1773-1813 *REnAW*
Cramp, Arthur Joseph 1872- *WhAm 5*
Cramp, Charles Henry 1828- *ApCAB Sup,
   NatCAB 5, TwCBDA*
Cramp, Charles Henry 1828-1912 *WhAm 1*
Cramp, Charles Henry 1828-1913 *AmBi,
   DcAmB*
Cramp, Henry W *ApCAB Sup*
Cramp, John Mockett 1796-1881 *ApCAB*
Cramp, Thomas 1827-1885 *ApCAB Sup*
Cramp, Walter Concemore 1878-1941 *WhAm 1*
Cramp, William 1806-1879 *NatCAB 5*
Cramp, William 1807-1879 *DcAmB, TwCBDA,
   WhAm H*
Crampton, Albert M 1900-1953 *WhAm 3*
Crampton, C Ward 1877-1964 *WhAm 4*
Crampton, Charles Albert 1858-1915 *WhAm 1*
Crampton, George S 1874- *WhAm 5*
Crampton, Guy Chester 1881-1951 *WhAm 3*
Crampton, Henry Edward 1837-1899
   NatCAB 36
Crampton, Henry Edward 1875-1956
   NatCAB 42, WhAm 3

Crampton, Sir John Fiennes Twisleton 1807-1886
   ApCAB
Crampton, Louis William 1848-1912
   NatCAB 17
Cramton, Louis Convers 1875-1966 *BiDrAC,
   WhAm 5*
Cranach, Lucas, The Elder 1472-1553
   McGEWB
Cranch, A Girard 1880-1967 *NatCAB 54*
Cranch, Caroline A *ApCAB*
Cranch, Christopher Pearse 1813-1892 *AmBi,
   ApCAB, DcAmB, Drake, NatCAB 7,
   NewYHSD, TwCBDA, WhAm H*
Cranch, Jere 1821?- *NewYHSD*
Cranch, John d1883 *ApCAB*
Cranch, John 1807-1891 *NewYHSD,
   WhAm H*
Cranch, William 1769-1855 *AmBi, ApCAB,
   BiAUS, DcAmB, Drake, NatCAB 7,
   TwCBDA, WhAm H*
Crandall, A Julian 1864-1951 *NatCAB 40*
Crandall, Ada Allen 1879- *WomWWA 14*
Crandall, Albert Rogers 1840-1926 *WhAm 3*
Crandall, Andrew Wallace 1894-1963 *WhAm 4*
Crandall, Arthur FitzJames 1854-1951 *WhAm 3*
Crandall, Bruce Verne 1873-1945 *WhAm 2*
Crandall, Catharine Louise Patterson 1862-
   WomWWA 14
Crandall, Charles Henry 1858-1923 *DcAmB,
   TwCBDA, WhAm 1*
Crandall, Charles Lee 1850-1917 *NatCAB 4,
   TwCBDA, WhAm 1*
Crandall, Charles Spencer 1852-1929 *WhAm 1*
Crandall, Clifford Waldorf 1874- *WhAm 5*
Crandall, E *NewYHSD*
Crandall, Ella Phillips 1871-1938 *NotAW*
Crandall, Floyd Milford 1858-1921 *ApCAB X,
   NatCAB 15, WhAm 1*
Crandall, Francis Asbury 1837-1915 *WhAm 1*
Crandall, Fred Alonzo 1863-1957 *NatCAB 43*
Crandall, George Strachen 1880-1959
   NatCAB 48, WhAm 4
Crandall, H Burr 1834- *WhAm 4*
Crandall, Irving Bardshar 1890-1927
   NatCAB 22
Crandall, John J 1836-1922 *NatCAB 31*
Crandall, Lathan Augustus 1850-1923 *WhAm 1*
Crandall, Lee Saunders 1887-1969 *WhAm 5*
Crandall, Lucien Stephen 1844- *NatCAB 3*
Crandall, Prudence 1803- *ApCAB, TwCBDA*
Crandall, Prudence 1803-1889 *AmBi,
   BiDAmEd, NatCAB 2, WhAm H,
   WhAmP*
Crandall, Prudence 1803-1890 *DcAmB,
   McGEWB, NotAW, WebAB*
Crandall, Regina Katharine *WomWWA 14*
Crandall, Shannon 1871-1964 *NatCAB 51,
   WhAm 5*
Crandall, Shannon, Jr. 1902-1966 *NatCAB 51,
   WhAm 4*
Crandall, Willard Raymond 1894-1960
   NatCAB 47
Crandell, A William d1973 *WhAm 6*
Crandell, Walter Solomon 1879-1950
   NatCAB 38
Crandon, Franklin Philip 1834- *WhAm 4*
Crandon, LeRoi Goddard 1873-1939 *WhAm 1*
Crane, Aaron Martin 1839-1914 *WhAm 1*
Crane, Albert Sears 1868-1946 *WhAm 2*
Crane, Anne Moncure 1838-1872 *ApCAB,
   DcAmB, WhAm H*
Crane, Anne Moncure 1838-1873 *NatCAB 6*
Crane, Arthur Griswold 1877-1955 *WhAm 3*
Crane, Arthur Henry 1892-1964 *WhAm 4*
Crane, Augustus 1853- *WhAm 4*
Crane, Augustus W 1868-1937 *WhAm 1*
Crane, Benjamin E 1835-1885 *NatCAB 12*
Crane, Bruce 1857-1937 *ApCAB, BnEnAmA,
   WhAm 1*
Crane, Caroline Bartlett 1858-1935 *NatCAB 15,
   NotAW, WhAm 1, WomWWA 14*
Crane, Cephas Bennett 1833-1917 *NatCAB 16,
   WhAm 1*
Crane, Charles 1897-1960 *NatCAB 47*
Crane, Charles Alva 1853-1907 *WhAm 1*
Crane, Charles Henry 1825-1883 *ApCAB,
   NatCAB 4, TwCBDA*
Crane, Charles Howard 1885-1952 *WhAm 3*

Craven, Tunis Augustus Macdonough 1893-1972 *WhAm 5*
Craven, Tunis Augustus McDonough 1813-1864 *NatCAB 12*
Craven, Tunus Augustus Macdonough 1813-1864 *WhAm H*
Craven, William Reno 1862- *WhAm 4*
Cravens, Ben 1874-1939 *WhAm 1*
Cravens, DuVal Garland 1875- *WhAm 5*
Cravens, James Addison 1818-1893 *BiAUS, BiDrAC, TwCBDA, WhAm H*
Cravens, James H 1798- *BiAUS*
Cravens, James Harrison 1802-1876 *BiDrAC, TwCBDA, WhAm H*
Cravens, John Smith 1871-1946 *NatCAB 37*
Cravens, John William 1864-1937 *WhAm 1*
Cravens, Jordan Edgar 1830-1914 *BiDrAC, TwCBDA, WhAmP*
Cravens, Kenton Robinson 1904-1971 *WhAm 5*
Cravens, Oscar Henry 1869- *WhAm 5*
Cravens, William Ben 1872-1939 *BiDrAC, WhAmP*
Cravens, William Fadjo 1899- *BiDrAC, WhAmP*
Craver, Harrison Warwick 1875-1951 *DcAmLiB, NatCAB 40, WhAm 3*
Craver, Samuel Porch 1847-1919 *TwCBDA, WhAm 1*
Crawford, Adair 1748-1795 *DcScB Sup*
Crawford, Alexander d1809 *NewYHSD*
Crawford, Alice Arnold 1850- *AmWom*
Crawford, Andrew Murray 1853-1925 *WhAm 1*
Crawford, Andrew Wright 1873-1929 *WhAm 1*
Crawford, Angus 1850- *WhAm 4*
Crawford, Angus 1928-1970 *WhAm 5*
Crawford, Arch 1889-1965 *WhAm 4*
Crawford, Arthur 1867-1922 *WhAm 1*
Crawford, Benjamin Franklin 1843-1910 *NatCAB 36*
Crawford, Charles d1945 *WhAm 3*
Crawford, Charles Wallace 1888-1957 *NatCAB 47, WhAm 3*
Crawford, Clarence K 1864- *WhAm 4*
Crawford, Coe Isaac 1858-1944 *BiDrAC, REnAW, WhAm 4, WhAmP*
Crawford, Corie Isaac 1858-1944 *NatCAB 14*
Crawford, David A 1879-1957 *WhAm 3*
Crawford, David Bovaird 1872-1941 *NatCAB 34*
Crawford, David Eugene 1869- *WhoColR*
Crawford, David McLean 1889-1963 *WhAm 4*
Crawford, Dugald 1830- *NatCAB 7*
Crawford, E Stetson 1878-1966 *NatCAB 53*
Crawford, Earl Stetson 1877-1966 *WhAm 5*
Crawford, Eben G d1945 *WhAm 2*
Crawford, Edward Grant 1868-1923 *WhAm 1*
Crawford, Edwin Robert 1870-1936 *WhAm 1*
Crawford, Emma Walke 1881- *WomWWA 14*
Crawford, Eugene Lowther 1871-1934 *WhAm 1*
Crawford, Finia Goff 1894- *WhAm 5*
Crawford, Francis Marion 1854-1909 *AmBi, ApCAB, ApCAB X, DcAmB, NatCAB 2, TwCBDA, WebAB, WhAm 1*
Crawford, Fred Lewis 1888-1957 *BiDrAC, WhAm 3, WhAmP*
Crawford, Frederick Stuart 1876-1936 *WhAm 1*
Crawford, Genevieve Buckland 1861- *WomWWA 14*
Crawford, George Addison 1827-1891 *TwCBDA*
Crawford, George Gordon 1869-1936 *NatCAB 28, WhAm 1*
Crawford, George W 1798-1872 *BiAUS, Drake*
Crawford, George Walker 1798-1872 *AmBi, DcAmB*
Crawford, George Washington 1798-1872 *ApCAB, BiDrAC, BiDrUSE, NatCAB 4, TwCBDA, WhAm H, WhAmP*
Crawford, George Washington 1861-1935 *NatCAB 28*
Crawford, George Williamson 1877- *WhoColR*
Crawford, Georgina Lily Urquhart 1882- *WomWWA 14a*
Crawford, H Wadsworth 1884-1951 *NatCAB 40*
Crawford, Harold Duncan 1894-1946 *NatCAB 34*
Crawford, Harry Clement 1881- *WhAm 6*
Crawford, Harry James 1871-1954 *NatCAB 44,*

WhAm 3
Crawford, Harry Jennings 1867-1953 *NatCAB 40, WhAm 3*
Crawford, Harry Stuart 1873-1958 *NatCAB 49*
Crawford, Henry Benning 1874-1956 *NatCAB 43*
Crawford, Henry James 1902-1965 *NatCAB 51*
Crawford, Homer Caldwell 1852-1942 *NatCAB 32*
Crawford, Isabel 1865- *WhAm 4*
Crawford, Ivan Charles 1886-1960 *WhAm 4*
Crawford, J C 1880- *WhAm 6*
Crawford, Jack Randall 1878-1968 *WhAm 5*
Crawford, James Breckenridge 1885-1956 *NatCAB 44*
Crawford, James Laurence 1851-1905 *NatCAB 17*
Crawford, James Pollock 1855-1899 *NatCAB 34*
Crawford, James Pyle Wickersham 1882-1939 *BiDAmEd, DcAmB S2, NatCAB 29, WhAm 1*
Crawford, James Stoner 1872-1960 *WhAm 4*
Crawford, Jerry Tinder 1865-1938 *WhAm 1*
Crawford, Joel 1783-1858 *BiAUS, BiDrAC, TwCBDA, WhAm H*
Crawford, John 1746-1813 *DcAmB, WhAm H*
Crawford, John 1816-1877 *NatCAB 13*
Crawford, John 1838?- *NewYHSD*
Crawford, Mrs. John 1850- *AmWom*
Crawford, John Forsyth 1871- *WhAm 5*
Crawford, John Jones 1846- *WhAm 4*
Crawford, John Martin 1845-1916 *DcAmB, WhAm 1*
Crawford, John Martin 1846-1916 *NatCAB 23*
Crawford, John McLenahan 1867-1950 *NatCAB 38, WhAm 3*
Crawford, John Raymond 1886-1929 *NatCAB 37, WhAm 1*
Crawford, John Sydney 1839- *TwCBDA*
Crawford, John Wallace 1847-1917 *AmBi, DcAmB, NatCAB 8, WhAm 1*
Crawford, Joseph E 1876- *WhAm 5*
Crawford, Julia Townsend Hill 1860- *WomWWA 14*
Crawford, Kate Staples *WomWWA 14*
Crawford, Leonard Jacob 1860- *WhAm 1*
Crawford, Leonidas Wakefield 1877-1952 *WhAm 3*
Crawford, Martin Jenkins 1820-1883 *ApCAB, BiAUS, BiDConf, BiDrAC, DcAmB, NatCAB 2, TwCBDA, WhAm H, WhAmP*
Crawford, Mary Caroline 1874-1932 *BiCAW, WhAm 1, WomWWA 14*
Crawford, Mary J 1843- *AmWom*
Crawford, Mary Merritt 1884-1972 *NatCAB 57, WomWWA 14*
Crawford, Mary Rowan McCrackin 1860- *WomWWA 14*
Crawford, Mary Sinclair 1881-1964 *WhAm 4*
Crawford, Medorem 1844-1921 *WhAm 1*
Crawford, Meriwether Lewis 1841- *WhAm 4*
Crawford, Milo Hicks 1880-1961 *NatCAB 49, WhAm 6*
Crawford, Morris Barker 1852-1940 *WhAm 1, WhAm 2*
Crawford, Morris DeCamp 1882-1949 *NatCAB 37*
Crawford, Nathaniel Macon 1811-1871 *ApCAB, Drake, NatCAB 6, TwCBDA*
Crawford, Nelson Antrim 1853-1927 *NatCAB 22*
Crawford, Nelson Antrim 1888-1963 *NatCAB 53, WhAm 4*
Crawford, Porter James 1895-1946 *WhAm 2*
Crawford, Ralph Dixon 1873-1950 *WhAm 3*
Crawford, Ralston 1906- *BnEnAmA*
Crawford, Robert 1804-1896 *TwCBDA*
Crawford, Robert 1815-1892 *NatCAB 45*
Crawford, Robert A 1855-1937 *WhAm 1*
Crawford, Robert MacArthur 1899-1961 *NatCAB 49*
Crawford, Robert Murry 1917-1970 *NatCAB 55*
Crawford, Russell Tracy 1876-1958 *NatCAB 44, WhAm 3*
Crawford, S J *BiAUS*

Crawford, Samuel 1820-1861 *NatCAB 17*
Crawford, Samuel J 1835-1891 *TwCBDA*
Crawford, Samuel Johnson 1835-1913 *DcAmB, NatCAB 8, WhAm 1, WhAmP*
Crawford, Samuel Wylie 1827-1892 *TwCBDA*
Crawford, Samuel Wylie 1829-1892 *ApCAB, Drake, NatCAB 12*
Crawford, Stanton Chapman 1897-1966 *WhAm 4*
Crawford, Thomas 1813-1857 *AmBi, BnEnAmA, DcAmB, IlBEAAW, TwCBDA, WhAm H*
Crawford, Thomas 1814-1857 *ApCAB, BiAUS, Drake, NatCAB 8, NewYHSD*
Crawford, Thomas Dwight 1860-1936 *WhAm 1*
Crawford, Thomas Hartley 1786-1863 *ApCAB, ApCAB Sup, BiAUS, BiDrAC, Drake, TwCBDA, WhAm H*
Crawford, Thomas Henry 1840- *WhAm 4*
Crawford, Traverse Samuel 1871- *WhoColR*
Crawford, Walter Joshua 1873-1924 *WhAm 1*
Crawford, West James 1844-1923 *NatCAB 8*
Crawford, Will 1869-1944 *IlBEAAW*
Crawford, William d1849 *BiAUS*
Crawford, William 1732-1782 *AmBi, ApCAB, DcAmB, Drake, NatCAB 9, WhAm H*
Crawford, William 1760-1823 *BiAUS, BiDrAC, TwCBDA, WhAm H, WhAmP*
Crawford, William Alfred 1874-1926 *WhAm 1*
Crawford, William Campbell 1862-1938 *WhAm 1*
Crawford, William Gordon 1869- *NatCAB 17*
Crawford, William Harris 1772-1834 *AmBi, ApCAB, BiAUS, BiDrAC, BiDrUSE, DcAmB, Drake, EncAB, McGEWB, NatCAB 5, TwCBDA, WebAB, WhAm H, WhAmP*
Crawford, William Henry 1855-1944 *NatCAB 13, NatCAB 32, TwCBDA, WhAm 2*
Crawford, William Hopkins 1899-1964 *WhAm 4*
Crawford, William L 1839-1920 *WhAm 1*
Crawford, William T d1960 *WhAm 4*
Crawford, William Thomas 1856-1913 *BiDrAC, TwCBDA, WhAm 1*
Crawford, William Wait 1878-1944 *NatCAB 33*
Crawford, William Walt 1878- *WhAm 6*
Crawford, William Webb 1867-1934 *WhAm 1*
Crawford-Frost, William Albert 1863-1936 *WhAm 1*
Crawley, Clyde B 1907-1949 *WhAm 3*
Crawley, David Ephraim 1886-1946 *WhAm 2*
Crawley, Edwin Schofield 1862-1933 *NatCAB 24, WhAm 1*
Crawley, John 1784- *NewYHSD*
Crawley, John R, Jr. *NewYHSD*
Crawshaw, Fred Duane 1874- *WhAm 5*
Crawshaw, William Henry 1861-1940 *NatCAB 29, TwCBDA, WhAm 1*
Cray, James Robert 1860-1937 *NatCAB 28*
Craycroft, Robert Lee 1863- *ApCAB X*
Crayton, Jenkins Street 1928-1972 *WhAm 6*
Crazy Horse 1841?-1877 *REnAW*
Crazy Horse 1842?-1877 *ApCAB, McGEWB*
Crazy Horse 1849?-1877 *AmBi, DcAmB, EncAAH, WebAB, WebAMB, WhAm H, WhoMilH*
Creager, Charles Edward 1873-1964 *BiDrAC, WhAm 5*
Creager, John Oscar 1872-1943 *WhAm 2*
Creager, Marvin H 1882-1954 *WhAm 3*
Creager, Rentfro Banton 1877-1950 *NatCAB 39, WhAm 3*
Creager, William Pitcher 1878-1953 *NatCAB 45, WhAm 3*
Creal, Edward Wester 1883-1943 *BiDrAC, WhAm 2, WhAmP*
Creamer, David 1812-1887 *DcAmB, WhAm H*
Creamer, Thomas James 1843-1914 *BiAUS, BiDrAC, WhAm 4*
Creamer, William H 1882-1951 *NatCAB 39*
Crean, Robert d1974 *WhAm 6*
Creaser, Charles William 1897-1965 *NatCAB 51, WhAm 4*
Creasey, John 1908-1973 *WhAm 6*
Creasy, George 1895-1972 *WhWW-II*

Creasy, Raymond Claude 1885-1955
NatCAB 45
Creasy, William Neville 1908-1974 *WhAm 6*
Creath, Jacob 1777-1854 *DcAmB, NatCAB 22,*
WhAm H
Creath, Jacob 1799-1886 *DcAmB, WhAm H*
Crebassol, Prosper *NewYHSD*
Crebs, John Montgomery 1830-1890 *BiAUS,*
BiDrAC, TwCBDA, WhAm H
Crecraft, Earl Willis 1886-1950 *WhAm 3*
Crede, Carl S F 1819-1892 *BiHiMed*
Crede, Charles Edwin 1913-1964 *NatCAB 52*
Creditt, William Abraham 1864- *WhoColR*
Credner, Hermann Georg 1841-1913 *DcScB*
Cree, Archibald C 1872-1944 *WhAm 2*
Cree, William Harold 1894-1952 *NatCAB 42*
Creech, Harris 1874-1941 *WhAm 2*
Creech, John W 1849- *WhAm 3*
Creech, Oscar, Jr. 1916-1967 *WhAm 4A,*
WhAm 5
Creed, Georgie Ellis 1855- *WomWWA 14*
Creed, Thomas Percival 1897-1969 *WhAm 5*
Creed, Wigginton Ellis 1877-1927 *NatCAB 22,*
WhAm 1
Creed, William *NewYHSD*
Creede, Frank J 1892-1960 *WhAm 4*
Creeden, Daniel Woods 1891-1953 *NatCAB 41,*
WhAm 3
Creeden, John Berchmans 1871-1948
NatCAB 42
Creegan, Charles Cole 1850-1939 *WhAm 1*
Creek, Herbert Lesourd 1879- *WhAm 6*
Creel, Enrique C 1854-1931 *WhAm 2*
Creel, George 1875-1953 *NatCAB 41*
Creel, George Edward 1876-1953 *DcAmB S5,*
EncAB, McGEWB, WebAB, WhAm 3
Creel, Robert Calhoun 1913-1970 *WhAm 5*
Creelman, Harlan 1864-1950 *NatCAB 38,*
WhAm 3
Creelman, James 1859-1915 *DcAmB,*
NatCAB 14, TwCBDA, WhAm 1
Creely, John Vaudain 1839-1900 *BiAUS,*
BiDrAC, WhAmP
Creery, William Rufus 1824-1875 *ApCAB*
Creese, James 1896-1966 *WhAm 4*
Creese, Wadsworth 1883- *WhAm 5*
Creesy, Josiah Perkins 1814-1871 *DcAmB,*
WhAm H
Creevey, Caroline Alathea Stickney 1843-1920
NatCAB 30, WhAm 1
Creevey, George Mason 1872-1945 *NatCAB 35*
Creevey, John Kennedy 1841-1921 *NatCAB 30*
Cregier, DeWitt Clinton 1829-1897 *NatCAB 19*
Cregier, DeWitt Clinton 1829-1898 *TwCBDA*
Crego, Clarence Harrison 1895-1970
NatCAB 56
Crego, Floyd Stranahan 1856-1919 *NatCAB 17*
Cregor, Frank W 1873-1942 *NatCAB 33*
Crehan, Ada *TwCBDA, WebAB*
Crehen, Charles G 1829- *NewYHSD*
Crehen, E *NewYHSD*
Crehen, Lewis E *NewYHSD*
Crehore, Albert Cushing 1868- *WhAm 5*
Crehore, William Williams 1864-1918 *WhAm 1*
Creifield *NewYHSD*
Creighton, Albert Morton 1878-1966 *WhAm 4*
Creighton, Charles 1847-1927 *DcScB*
Creighton, Edward 1820-1874 *DcAmB,*
NatCAB 22, WhAm H
Creighton, Edward Bright 1866-1939
NatCAB 30
Creighton, Elmer Ellsworth Farmer 1873-1929
WhAm 1
Creighton, Frank Whittington 1879-1948
NatCAB 36, WhAm 2
Creighton, James Asbury 1846-1916
NatCAB 20
Creighton, James Edwin 1861-1924 *DcAmB,*
NatCAB 23, WhAm 1
Creighton, John Andrew 1831-1907 *DcAmB,*
NatCAB 11
Creighton, John Orde 1785?-1838 *ApCAB,*
Drake, TwCBDA
Creighton, John Thrale 1884-1941 *WhAm 1*
Creighton, Johnston B 1821- *Drake*
Creighton, Johnston Blakeley 1822-1883 *ApCAB,*
NatCAB 4, TwCBDA
Creighton, Martha Gladys 1894-1960 *WhAm 4*

Creighton, W *NewYHSD*
Creighton, William 1778-1851 *BiAUS, BiDrAC,*
DcAmB, NatCAB 23, TwCBDA,
WhAm H
Creighton, William 1793-1865 *ApCAB*
Creighton, William Henry 1859-1933 *WhAm 1*
Creighton, William J 1892-1955 *WhAm 3*
Creim, Ben Wilton 1898-1952 *WhAm 3*
Creitz, Charles Erwin 1865-1940 *WhAm 1*
Creker *NewYHSD*
Crele, Joseph 1725-1866 *ApCAB, Drake*
Crell, Lorenz Florenz Friedrich Von 1745-1816
DcScB
Crelle, August Leopold 1780-1855 *DcScB*
Crellin, Edward Webster 1863-1948
NatCAB 41, WhAm 2
Crellin, John 1828-1895 *NatCAB 7*
Cremazie, Octave 1827-1879 *McGEWB*
Cremer, Jacob Theodoor 1847-1923 *WhAm 1*
Cremona, Antonio Luigi G Giuseppe 1830-1903
DcScB
Cremony, John C 1815-1879 *REnAW*
Crenier, Henri 1873-1948 *WhAm 2*
Crenshaw, Anderson 1783-1847 *ApCAB,*
TwCBDA
Crenshaw, Ben Mills d1857 *NatCAB 12*
Crenshaw, Bolling Hall 1867-1935 *WhAm 1*
Crenshaw, Edward Hardage, Jr. 1883-1952
NatCAB 47
Crenshaw, H F 1875-1938 *WhAm 1*
Crenshaw, James Llewellyn 1887-1950 *WhAm 3*
Crenshaw, John Lewis 1882-1953 *NatCAB 42*
Crenshaw, Ollinger 1904-1970 *WhAm 5*
Crenshaw, Richard Parker 1856-1929
NatCAB 25
Crenshaw, Robert Walden 1885-1966
NatCAB 52
Crenshaw, Spottswood Dabney 1854-1940
NatCAB 36
Crenshaw, Thomas C 1849- *WhAm 4*
Crenshaw, Walter Henry 1817-1878 *ApCAB,*
TwCBDA
Crenshaw, William Graves *BiDConf*
Crepson, Leonard 1837?- *NewYHSD*
Crerar, Henry Duncan Graham 1888-1965
WhAm 4, WhWW-II
Crerar, John 1827-1889 *AmBi, ApCAB Sup,*
DcAmB, NatCAB 22, TwCBDA,
WhAm H
Crerar, John 1857-1932 *NatCAB 24*
Crerar, Marie Girvin 1871- *WomWWA 14*
Crerar, Thomas Alexander 1876- *McGEWB*
Cresap, Mark W, Jr. 1910-1963 *WhAm 4*
Cresap, Mark Winfield 1872-1942 *WhAm 2*
Cresap, Michael 1742-1775 *ApCAB, DcAmB,*
Drake, WebAMB, WhAm H
Cresap, Thomas 1702?-1790? *DcAmB,*
WhAm H
Crescas, Hasdai 1340?-1412 *DcScB*
Cresind *NewYHSD*
Creskoff, Adolph Jay 1908-1959 *NatCAB 44*
Cresmer, William Taylor 1876-1959
NatCAB 44
Creson, Larry Barkley 1906-1972 *WhAm 5*
Crespel, Emanuel 1700?- *ApCAB*
Crespel, Emmanuel *Drake*
Crespi, Juan 1721-1782 *DcAmB, WhAm H*
Crespi, Pio 1881-1969 *NatCAB 55*
Crespo Y Martinez, Gilberto 1853- *WhAm 4*
Cress, George Clifford 1873-1951 *WhAm 3*
Cress, George Oscar 1862-1954 *WhAm 3*
Cressey, George Babcock 1896-1963 *WhAm 4*
Cressey, George Croswell 1856-1938 *WhAm 1*
Cressler, Alfred Miller 1877-1939 *WhAm 1*
Cressler, Isabel Bonbrake 1872- *WhAm 3,*
WomWWA 14
Cresson, Charles Massey 1828-1893 *TwCBDA*
Cresson, Elliot 1796-1854 *Drake*
Cresson, Elliott 1796-1854 *ApCAB, DcAmB,*
TwCBDA, WhAm H
Cresson, Ezra Townsend 1838-1926 *DcAmB,*
NatCAB 23, WhAm 1
Cresson, John Chapman 1806-1876 *ApCAB,*
NatCAB 12, TwCBDA
Cresson, Margaret French 1889-1973 *WhAm 6*
Cresson, W Penn 1873-1932 *WhAm 1*
Cresswell, Robert 1897-1943 *WhAm 2*
Cressy, Josiah Perkins 1814- *NewYHSD*

Cressy, Warren Francis 1878-1952 *NatCAB 38,*
WhAm 3
Cressy, Wilfred Wesley 1867-1900 *WhAm 1*
Cressy, Will Martin 1863-1930 *WhAm 1*
Creswell, Andrew Sterrett 1891-1954
NatCAB 41
Creswell, Edward J 1905-1957 *WhAm 3*
Creswell, Harry I T 1891- *WhAm 5*
Creswell, Harry Lincoln 1864-1944 *NatCAB 36*
Creswell, John A J 1828-1891 *ApCAB, BiAUS,*
Drake, NatCAB 4
Creswell, John Andrew Jackson 1828-1891
BiDrAC
Creswell, John Angel James 1828-1891 *AmBi,*
BiDrUSE, DcAmB, TwCBDA, WhAm H
Creswell, Julia 1827-1886 *ApCAB*
Creswell, Mary E 1879- *WhAm 6*
Cret, Paul Philippe 1876-1945 *DcAmB S3,*
NatCAB 33, WhAm 2
Cretella, Albert William 1897- *BiDrAC*
Cretin, Joseph d1857 *Drake*
Cretin, Joseph 1799-1857 *DcAmB, TwCBDA,*
WhAm H
Cretin, Joseph 1800-1857 *ApCAB*
Cretin, Joseph 1810-1857 *NatCAB 9*
Cretin, Nestor Alexis 1895-1939 *NatCAB 28*
Creutzfeldt, Benjamin d1853 *IIBEAAW*
Crevaux, Jules Nicolas 1847-1882 *ApCAB*
Crevecoeur, Hector St. John De 1731-1813
Drake
Crevecoeur, Hector St. John De 1735-1813
McGEWB
Crevecoeur, J Hector St. John 1731-1813
EncAAH
Crevecoeur, J Hector St. John 1735-1813
DcAmB
Crevecoeur, Jean Hector St. John De 1731-1813
AmBi, ApCAB, NatCAB 8
Crevecoeur, Michel Guillaume Jean De
1731-1813 *DcAmB, WhAm H*
Crevecoeur, Michel Guillaume Jean De
1735-1813 *EncAAH, WebAB*
Creveling, Cyrus Robbins 1897-1952
NatCAB 42
Crew, Helen Coale 1866- *WomWWA 14*
Crew, Henry 1859-1953 *NatCAB 15,*
WhAm 3
Crew, Miriam Donalson 1886- *WomWWA 14*
Crew, William Binford 1852-1912 *NatCAB 21,*
WhAm 1
Crews, Floyd Houston 1899-1964 *WhAm 4*
Crews, Laura Hope 1879-1942 *NotAW*
Crews, Leslie F 1896-1968 *WhAm 5*
Crews, Nelson Caesar 1866- *WhoColR*
Crews, Ralph 1876-1926 *NatCAB 43,*
WhAm 1
Crews, Seth Floyd 1885?- *IIBEAAW*
Criado DeCastilla, Alonso *ApCAB*
Cribari, Wolfgang Edward 1903-1966
NatCAB 53
Crichton, Alexander Fraser 1878-1939 *WhAm 1*
Crichton, Andrew B 1882-1952 *NatCAB 42*
Crichton, Kyle Samuel 1896-1960 *WhAm 4*
Crichton, Kyle Samuel 1898-1960 *NatCAB 46*
Crick, Francis Harry Compton 1916- *AsBiEn,*
McGEWB
Crider, Blake 1902-1974 *WhAm 6*
Crider, Franklin Jacob 1883-1961 *NatCAB 49*
Crider, John Henshaw 1906-1966 *WhAm 4*
Crider, John Swan 1869-1952 *NatCAB 41*
Cridland, Charles 1915-1972 *WhAm 5*
Cridland, Charles E *NewYHSD*
Cridland, Leander, Jr. 1841?- *NewYHSD*
Cridler, Thomas Wilbur 1850- *NatCAB 12,*
WhAm 4
Crile, Austin Daniel 1870-1954 *WhAm 3*
Crile, Dennis Rider Wood 1891-1937
NatCAB 33, WhAm 1
Crile, George Washington 1864-1943 *ApCAB X,*
DcAmB S3, NatCAB 15, NatCAB 31,
WhAm 2
Crilley, A Cyril 1902-1951 *WhAm 3*
Crim, Frank Dwight 1855-1919 *NatCAB 18*
Crim, John William Henry 1879-1933 *WhAm 1*
Crimi, James Ernest 1916-1973 *WhAm 6*
Crimmins, Harry Benedict 1893-1960 *WhAm 4*
Crimmins, John Daniel 1844-1917 *DcAmB,*
NatCAB 3, NatCAB 23, WhAm 1

Crimont, Joseph Raphael 1858-1945 *WhAm 2*
Crinkley, Matthew S 1897-1967 *WhAm 4*
Crinnon, Peter Francis 1818-1882 *ApCAB*
Crippa, Edward David 1899-1960 *BiDrAC, WhAm 4*
Crippen, Caroline Winslow 1871- *WomWWA 14*
Crippen, Henry Durrell 1876-1935 *WhAm 1*
Crippen, Lloyd Kenneth 1895-1967 *WhAm 5*
Cripps, Sir Stafford 1889-1952 *WhAm 3, WhWW-II*
Crisand, Emil *NewYHSD*
Criscuolo, Luigi 1887- *WhAm 3*
Crisfield, John Woodland 1806-1897 *BiDrAC, WhAm H*
Crisfield, John Woodland 1808-1897 *BiAUS, NatCAB 13, TwCBDA*
Crisfield, Pearce 1864-1938 *NatCAB 28*
Crisler, Joseph Augustus 1868-1940 *NatCAB 33*
Crisman, Charles Henry 1854-1927 *NatCAB 20*
Crisp, Arthur 1881- *WhAm 6*
Crisp, Charles Frederick 1845-1896 *AmBi, ApCAB Sup, BiDrAC, DcAmB, NatCAB 1, TwCBDA, WebAB, WhAm H, WhAmP*
Crisp, Charles Robert 1870-1937 *BiDrAC, TwCBDA, WhAm 1, WhAmP*
Crisp, Donald d1974 *WhAm 6*
Crisp, John D 1858- *NatCAB 18*
Crisp, William Henry 1875-1951 *NatCAB 41*
Crispell, Cornelius Eltinge 1820- *TwCBDA*
Crispell, Reuben Bernard 1889-1967 *NatCAB 53*
Crispi, Francesco 1819-1901 *McGEWB*
Crispin, Carl N 1893-1961 *NatCAB 48*
Crispin, Clarence Gearhart 1879-1961 *NatCAB 50*
Crispin, Emma Fowler Weeks *WomWWA 14*
Crispin, M Jackson 1875-1953 *WhAm 3*
Crispin, Silas 1830?- *ApCAB*
Criss, Clair Carlton 1879-1952 *NatCAB 52, WhAm 3*
Criss, Neil Louis 1886-1966 *WhAm 5*
Criss, Nicholas Rittenhouse 1873-1958 *NatCAB 52*
Crissey, Forrest 1864-1943 *WhAm 2*
Crissinger, Daniel Richard 1860-1942 *DcAmB S3, NatCAB 45, WhAm 2*
Crist, Bainbridge 1883-1969 *WhAm 5*
Crist, Chester Garfield 1887-1970 *NatCAB 57*
Crist, Harris McCabe 1874-1946 *NatCAB 34, WhAm 2*
Crist, Henry 1764-1844 *BiAUS, BiDrAC, WhAm H*
Crist, John Letcher 1890-1961 *NatCAB 49*
Crist, Raymond Fowler 1871-1944 *WhAm 2*
Cristy, Albert Barnes 1853- *WhAm 4*
Cristy, Albert Moses 1889-1949 *NatCAB 40, WhAm 2*
Cristy, Joseph H *NewYHSD*
Criswell, George Stuart 1850-1928 *WhAm 1*
Critcher, Catharine Carter 1879?- *WomWWA 14*
Critcher, Catherine Carter 1879?- *IIBEAAW*
Critcher, John 1820-1901 *BiAUS, BiDrAC*
Critchett, James Hamilton 1886-1957 *NatCAB 43*
Critchfield, Howard Emmett 1886-1962 *WhAm 4*
Critchley, Bertha May *WomWWA 14*
Critchley, J Verner 1875-1948 *NatCAB 36*
Critchlow, Francis B 1888-1951 *WhAm 3*
Crites, Lowry Hyer 1906-1974 *WhAm 6*
Crittenberger, George Dale 1893-1965 *NatCAB 52, WhAm 4*
Crittenden, Albert Randolph 1843-1921 *NatCAB 20*
Crittenden, Charles Briggs 1889-1943 *NatCAB 33*
Crittenden, Christopher 1902-1969 *NatCAB 55, WhAm 5*
Crittenden, Eugene Casson 1880-1956 *NatCAB 53, WhAm 3*
Crittenden, George Bibb 1812-1880 *AmBi, ApCAB, BiDConf, DcAmB, Drake, NatCAB 4, TwCBDA, WebAMB, WhAm H*
Crittenden, John J 1786-1863 *BiAUS*

Crittenden, John Jordan 1787-1863 *AmBi, ApCAB, BiDrAC, BiDrUSE, DcAmB, EncAB, NatCAB 13, TwCBDA, WebAB, WhAm H, WhAmP*
Crittenden, John Jordon 1786-1863 *Drake*
Crittenden, Lisla Alice VanValkenburg 1879- *WomWWA 14*
Crittenden, Robert 1797-1834 *TwCBDA*
Crittenden, Thomas Leonidas 1815-1893 *ApCAB*
Crittenden, Thomas Leonidas 1819-1893 *AmBi, DcAmB, Drake, NatCAB 2, TwCBDA, WebAMB, WhAm H*
Crittenden, Thomas T 1828?- *ApCAB*
Crittenden, Thomas Theodore 1832-1909 *ApCAB Sup, BiDrAC, DcAmB, NatCAB 12, WhAm 1, WhAmP*
Crittenden, Thomas Theodore 1834-1909 *BiAUS, TwCBDA*
Crittenden, Walter Hayden 1859- *WhAm 2*
Crittenden, William Logan 1823-1851 *NatCAB 4*
Crittenton, Charles Nelson 1833-1909 *DcAmB*
Critz, Hugh 1876- *WhAm 5*
Critz, Richard 1877- *WhAm 5*
Croaff, Thomas Joseph 1889-1950 *NatCAB 41*
Croasdale, Jack Finch 1904-1959 *WhAm 4*
Croasdale, Samuel d1862 *ApCAB*
Croasdale, Stuart 1866-1934 *WhAm 1*
Croasdale, William Thomas 1844-1891 *TwCBDA*
Croce, Benedetto 1866-1952 *McGEWB, WhAm 3*
Crocheron, Henry 1772-1819 *BiAUS, BiDrAC, WhAm H*
Crocheron, Jacob 1774-1849 *BiAUS, BiDrAC, WhAm H*
Crockard, Frank Hearne 1873-1955 *WhAm 3*
Crockatt, Peter Campbell 1892-1926 *NatCAB 21*
Crocker, Mister *NewYHSD*
Crocker, Mrs. *NewYHSD*
Crocker, Alvah 1801-1874 *ApCAB, BiAUS, BiDrAC, DcAmB, TwCBDA, WhAm H*
Crocker, Alvah 1858-1931 *NatCAB 29*
Crocker, Arthur W 1902-1967 *WhAm 4*
Crocker, Augustus Luther 1850-1925 *NatCAB 21, WhAm 4*
Crocker, Bartow 1886-1939 *NatCAB 29*
Crocker, Bosworth 1871-1946 *NatCAB 37, WhAm 2*
Crocker, Charles 1822-1888 *AmBi, ApCAB, DcAmB, REnAW, TwCBDA, WebAB, WhAm H*
Crocker, Charles Frederick 1854-1897 *TwCBDA*
Crocker, Charles Henry 1865-1935 *WhAm 1*
Crocker, Charles Thomas 1833-1911 *NatCAB 29*
Crocker, Douglas 1888-1968 *NatCAB 55*
Crocker, Edward Savage 1895-1968 *WhAm 5*
Crocker, Ethel Willard *WomWWA 14*
Crocker, Francis Bacon 1861-1921 *DcAmB, NatCAB 12, TwCBDA, WhAm 1*
Crocker, Frank Longfellow 1876-1945 *WhAm 2*
Crocker, Frederick W 1846?-1896 *TwCBDA*
Crocker, George d1909 *WhAm 1*
Crocker, George Glover 1843-1913 *TwCBDA, WhAm 1*
Crocker, George Herbert 1853-1936 *NatCAB 41*
Crocker, Hannah Mather 1752-1829 *DcAmB, NotAW, WhAm H*
Crocker, Hannah Mather 1765-1847 *ApCAB, Drake*
Crocker, Henry E 1848-1918 *WhAm 1*
Crocker, Henry Graham 1868-1930 *NatCAB 23*
Crocker, J Denison 1823- *NewYHSD*
Crocker, John W *NewYHSD*
Crocker, Josiah Morse 1842-1920 *ApCAB X*
Crocker, Lawton Vincent 1890-1965 *NatCAB 52*
Crocker, Lucretia 1829-1886 *BiDAmEd, NotAW*
Crocker, Marcellus M 1830-1865 *ApCAB, Drake, NatCAB 4, TwCBDA*
Crocker, Nathan Bourne 1781-1865 *ApCAB, NatCAB 10*
Crocker, Samuel Leonard 1804-1883 *BiAUS, BiDrAC, TwCBDA, WhAm H*

Crocker, Samuel Sturgis 1890-1964 *NatCAB 50*
Crocker, Sarah G 1834-1874 *WhAm H*
Crocker, Sarah G *see also* Conway, Mrs. Frederick B
Crocker, Stuart Miller 1898-1956 *WhAm 3*
Crocker, Susan Elizabeth Wood 1836- *TwCBDA*
Crocker, Templeton 1884-1948 *WhAm 2*
Crocker, Theodore Doane 1878-1947 *NatCAB 34, WhAm 2*
Crocker, U Haskell 1901-1967 *NatCAB 53*
Crocker, Uriel 1796-1887 *ApCAB, DcAmB, NatCAB 11, TwCBDA, WhAm H*
Crocker, Uriel Haskell 1832-1902 *WhAm 1*
Crocker, Walter James 1885-1947 *NatCAB 47, WhAm 2*
Crocker, William 1859-1932 *NatCAB 24*
Crocker, William 1874-1950 *DcAmB S4*
Crocker, William 1876-1950 *WhAm 2A*
Crocker, William Henry 1861-1937 *NatCAB 36, WhAm 1*
Crocker, William Tufts 1862-1939 *NatCAB 29*
Crocker, William Willard 1893-1964 *NatCAB 52, WhAm 4*
Crockett, Albert Stevens 1873-1969 *WhAm 5*
Crockett, Arthur Jay 1865- *WhAm 4*
Crockett, Caroline Clark 1867- *WomWWA 14*
Crockett, Charles Winthrop 1862-1936 *NatCAB 39, WhAm 1*
Crockett, David 1786-1836 *AmBi, ApCAB, BiAUS, BiDrAC, DcAmB, Drake, EncAAH, EncAB, McGEWB, NatCAB 4, TwCBDA, WebAB, WebAMB, WhAm H, WhAmP*
Crockett, Davy 1786-1836 *REnAW*
Crockett, Emma Godwin Dickinson 1858- *WomWWA 14*
Crockett, Esther M 1883- *WomWWA 14*
Crockett, Eugene Anthony 1867-1932 *WhAm 1*
Crockett, Franklin Smith 1881- *WhAm 6*
Crockett, George Langtry 1870-1923 *NatCAB 6*
Crockett, Helen Ware 1859- *WomWWA 14*
Crockett, Horace Guy 1880-1966 *WhAm 4*
Crockett, Ingram 1856- *WhAm 4*
Crockett, James McGrath 1886-1949 *NatCAB 39*
Crockett, John W d1852 *ApCAB, BiAUS*
Crockett, John W 1811?-1852 *TwCBDA*
Crockett, John Watkins 1818-1874 *BiDConf*
Crockett, John Wesley 1807-1852 *BiDrAC, WhAm H, WhAmP*
Crockett, John Wesley 1860-1920 *NatCAB 18*
Crockett, Joseph Bryant 1850-1903 *NatCAB 8*
Crockett, Montgomery Adams 1860- *WhAm 4*
Crockett, Samuel Lane 1822-1855 *NewYHSD*
Crockett, Stuart 1854-1917 *NatCAB 18*
Crockett, Walter Hill 1870-1931 *WhAm 1*
Crockett, William Day 1869-1930 *NatCAB 23, WhAm 1*
Crockett, William Goggin 1888-1940 *WhAm 1*
Croes, John 1762-1832 *ApCAB, NatCAB 3, TwCBDA*
Croes, John 1763-1832 *Drake*
Croes, John James Robertson 1834-1906 *NatCAB 6, WhAm 1*
Croffut, William Augustus 1835-1915 *ApCAB, TwCBDA, WhAm 1*
Croft, Albert Jefferson 1877-1933 *WhAm 1*
Croft, Delmer Eugene 1864-1925 *WhAm 1*
Croft, Edward 1875-1938 *NatCAB 28, WhAm 1*
Croft, Effie McCall *WomWWA 14*
Croft, George William 1846-1904 *BiDrAC, WhAm 1*
Croft, Harry William 1865-1947 *NatCAB 36, WhAm 2*
Croft, Richard Graham 1901-1973 *WhAm 6*
Croft, Theodore Gaillard 1845-1915 *NatCAB 30*
Croft, Theodore Gaillard 1874-1920 *BiDrAC*
Croft, Theodore Gaillard 1887-1948 *NatCAB 38*
Croft, William Hilton 1877-1949 *NatCAB 42*
Croft, William Torbert 1897-1971 *NatCAB 55*
Croftan, Alfred Careno 1871-1938 *WhAm 1*
Crofton, Charles Borromeo 1898-1961 *NatCAB 46*
Crofts, Frederick Sharer 1883-1951 *WhAm 3*

Crofut, Sidney Winter 1847-1935 *NatCAB 26*
Crogan, Andrew *NewYHSD*
Croghan, George d1782 *ApCAB, DcAmB, Drake, EncAB, REnAW*
Croghan, George 1718?-1782 *AmBi*
Croghan, George 1720?-1782 *WebAB*
Croghan, George 1791-1849 *AmBi, ApCAB, DcAmB, Drake, NatCAB 4, TwCBDA, WebAMB, WhAm H*
Croghan, George St. John d1861 *ApCAB*
Croghan, Hubert McLeod 1906-1960 *WhAm 4*
Croghan, William 1752-1822 *TwCBDA*
Crogman, William Henry, Sr. 1841-1931 *NatCAB 14, WhAm 1, WhoColR*
Croissant, DeWitt Clinton 1876-1941 *WhAm 2*
Croissant, Sarah J Sands *WomWWA 14*
Croix, Jean Baptiste DeLa 1653-1727 *ApCAB*
Croix, John Baptist DeLa 1653-1727 *Drake*
Croix, Teodoro De 1730-1792 *DcAmB, WhAm H*
Croker, Bula Edmondson 1884- *ApCAB X*
Croker, Richard 1841-1922 *AmBi, ApCAB X, DcAmB, WhAm 1*
Croker, Richard 1843- *ApCAB Sup, NatCAB 13*
Croker, Richard 1844- *TwCBDA*
Croll, Frederick Warville 1893-1959 *NatCAB 49*
Croll, James 1821-1890 *DcScB*
Croll, Morris William 1872-1947 *WhAm 2*
Croll, Philip C 1852- *WhAm 4*
Croll, William Martin 1866-1929 *BiDrAC, WhAm 1*
Crollius, Oswald 1560?-1609 *DcScB*
Croly, David Goodman 1829-1889 *AmBi, ApCAB, DcAmB, NatCAB 11, TwCBDA, WhAm H*
Croly, Herbert David 1869-1930 *DcAmB S1, EncAB, McGEWB, WebAB, WhAm 1, WhAmP*
Croly, Jane Cunningham 1829-1901 *DcAmB, NotAW, WhAm 1*
Croly, Jane Cunningham 1831-1901 *ApCAB, NatCAB 6, TwCBDA*
Croly, Jennie Cunningham 1831- *AmWom*
Crombie, William Murray 1871- *ApCAB X*
Cromelin, Paul Bowen 1890-1956 *WhAm 3*
Cromer, Evelyn Baring, Earl Of 1841-1917 *McGEWB*
Cromer, George Benedict 1857-1935 *NatCAB 26, WhAm 1*
Cromer, George Washington 1856-1936 *BiDrAC, WhAm 4, WhAmP*
Cromer, Mary Elizabeth 1890- *WomWWA 14*
Cromer, S S 1887-1965 *WhAm 4*
Cromie, William James 1875- *WhAm 5*
Cromley, L Tate 1880-1957 *NatCAB 46*
Crommelin, Andrew Claude DeLaCherois 1865-1939 *DcScB*
Crommelin, Emiline Gifford *WomWWA 14*
Crommelin, Henry 1904-1971 *WhAm 5*
Crommett, Herbert Benton 1913-1968 *NatCAB 54*
Crompton, Alice Hastings 1874- *WomWWA 14*
Crompton, Charles 1865-1922 *NatCAB 21*
Crompton, George 1829-1886 *ApCAB, DcAmB, NatCAB 10, TwCBDA, WhAm H*
Crompton, George 1872-1953 *NatCAB 54, WhAm 3*
Crompton, William 1806-1891 *ApCAB, DcAmB, NatCAB 10, TwCBDA, WhAm H*
Cromwell *NewYHSD*
Cromwell, Arthur Dayton 1869- *WhAm 5*
Cromwell, Bartlett James 1841- *ApCAB Sup*
Cromwell, Bartlett Jefferson 1840-1917 *NatCAB 17, WhAm 1*
Cromwell, Charles 1849-1922 *NatCAB 23*
Cromwell, Emma Guy d1952 *WhAm 3*
Cromwell, Frank H 1878- *WhAm 6*
Cromwell, Frederic d1914 *WhAm 1*
Cromwell, Frederick 1909-1969 *WhAm 5*
Cromwell, George 1860-1934 *WhAm 1, WhAm 1C*
Cromwell, George R *NewYHSD*
Cromwell, Gladys Louise Husted 1885-1919 *DcAmB*
Cromwell, Henry Bowman 1828-1864 *ApCAB*

Cromwell, James Oliver 1905-1969 *NatCAB 55*
Cromwell, John L *NewYHSD*
Cromwell, John Wesley 1846- *WhoColR*
Cromwell, Lincoln 1865-1952 *NatCAB 38, WhAm 3*
Cromwell, Michael Jenkins 1901-1968 *WhAm 5*
Cromwell, Oliver 1599-1658 *McGEWB, WhoMilH*
Cromwell, Paul Crawford 1902-1974 *WhAm 6*
Cromwell, R Floyd 1898-1952 *NatCAB 41*
Cromwell, Thomas, Earl Of Essex 1485?-1540 *McGEWB*
Cromwell, William Nelson 1854-1948 *DcAmB S4, NatCAB 42, WhAm 2*
Cronau, Rudolf 1855-1939 *WhAm 1*
Cronbach, Abraham 1882-1965 *WhAm 4*
Crone, Frank Linden 1875- *WhAm 5*
Crone, R Bertram 1871- *WhAm 5*
Croneis, Carey 1901-1972 *WhAm 5*
Cronemeyer, William Christian 1847-1934 *NatCAB 31*
Cronemiller, Mary Maria 1861- *WomWWA 14*
Cronholm, Fredrik Norman 1883-1956 *NatCAB 43*
Cronin, Con P 1871-1932 *WhAm 1*
Cronin, David Edward 1839-1925 *ApCAB Sup, NewYHSD, WhAm 4*
Cronin, Edward Joseph 1912-1958 *WhAm 3*
Cronin, Eugene Augustus 1841-1879 *ApCAB Sup*
Cronin, James Farley 1906-1959 *NatCAB 47*
Cronin, John J 1895-1967 *WhAm 4*
Cronin, John William 1905-1953 *WhAm 3*
Cronin, Marcus Daniel 1865-1936 *WhAm 1*
Cronin, Ralph Marvin 1907-1973 *WhAm 6*
Cronin, Timothy T 1884-1955 *WhAm 3*
Cronin, William Francis 1905-1965 *WhAm 4*
Cronje, Piet 1835-1911 *WhoMilH*
Cronk, Clara L K 1863- *WomWWA 14*
Cronk, Katharine Scherer 1877- *WomWWA 14*
Cronk, Lucy Irene Morton 1864- *WomWWA 14*
Cronkhite, Adelbert 1861-1937 *WebAMB, WhAm 1*
Cronkhite, Leonard Wolsey 1882-1974 *WhAm 6*
Cronkite, Alfred Eugene 1912-1957 *NatCAB 47*
Cronkite, Walter Leland, Jr. 1916- *WebAB*
Cronstedt, Axel Fredrik 1722-1765 *AsBiEn, DcScB*
Cronstedt, Val 1897-1974 *WhAm 6*
Cronyn, Benjamin 1802-1871 *ApCAB, Drake*
Cronyn, George William 1888-1969 *WhAm 5*
Cronyn, William Jerome 1848-1918 *NatCAB 18*
Crook, Alja Robinson 1864-1930 *WhAm 1*
Crook, Frank Foster 1902-1950 *NatCAB 39*
Crook, George 1828-1890 *ApCAB, Drake, McGEWB, NatCAB 4, REnAW, TwCBDA*
Crook, George 1829-1890 *AmBi, DcAmB, WebAB, WebAMB, WhAm H, WhoMilH*
Crook, Harrison 1850-1924 *NatCAB 22*
Crook, Isaac 1833-1916 *WhAm 1*
Crook, Isaac 1840?- *NatCAB 13*
Crook, James King 1859-1908 *NatCAB 8, WhAm 1*
Crook, James Walter 1858-1933 *WhAm 1*
Crook, Jere Lawrence 1874-1953 *WhAm 4*
Crook, Thurman Charles 1891- *BiDrAC*
Crook, William McKissack 1875-1949 *WhAm 2*
Crook, Zeno Erskin 1874-1951 *NatCAB 39*
Crooke, Philip S 1810-1881 *BiAUS*
Crooke, Philip Schuyler 1810-1881 *BiDrAC, WhAm H*
Crooke, Philip St. John 1810-1881 *TwCBDA*
Crooker, Florence Kollock 1848-1925 *WhAm 1, WomWWA 14*
Crooker, George Hazard 1865-1939 *NatCAB 29*
Crooker, Joseph Henry 1850-1931 *WhAm 1*
Crookes, Sir William 1832-1919 *AsBiEn, DcScB, McGEWB*
Crooks, Adam 1827-1885 *ApCAB*
Crooks, Alexander Richard d1972 *WhAm 5*
Crooks, Annie Marcy 1876- *WomWWA 14*
Crooks, Arthur 1838?-1888 *WhAm H*
Crooks, Ezra Breckenridge 1874-1941 *WhAm 1, WhAm 2*
Crooks, George Richard 1822-1897 *ApCAB,*

DcAmB, Drake, NatCAB 22, TwCBDA, WhAm H
Crooks, George Wesley 1877-1936 *NatCAB 28*
Crooks, Harry Means 1878- *WhAm 6*
Crooks, James 1778-1860 *ApCAB*
Crooks, Ramsay 1787-1859 *DcAmB, WhAm H*
Crooks, Ramsey 1786-1859 *ApCAB Sup*
Crooks, Richard M 1905-1973 *WhAm 6*
Crooks, Samuel Stearns 1851- *NatCAB 6*
Crookshank, Angus James 1865- *WhAm 4*
Crookshanks, George 1773-1859 *ApCAB*
Croome, George L *NewYHSD*
Croome, William 1790-1860 *NewYHSD*
Croone, William 1633-1684 *DcScB*
Cropley, Charles Elmore 1894-1952 *WhAm 3*
Cropper, John 1756-1821 *ApCAB, Drake, NatCAB 2*
Cropper, Walter V 1886-1949 *WhAm 2*
Cropsey, Andrew George 1850- *NatCAB 5*
Cropsey, Emma F Rockwood *WomWWA 14*
Cropsey, James Church 1872-1937 *NatCAB 31, WhAm 1*
Cropsey, Jaspar Francis 1823-1900 *AmBi, DcAmB, EncAAH*
Cropsey, Jasper Francis 1823-1900 *ApCAB, BnEnAmA, Drake, NatCAB 1, NewYHSD, TwCBDA, WhAm 1*
Cropsey, Nebraska d1916 *WhAm 1*
Crosas, Andres Bernardino 1877- *WhAm 5*
Crosbie, Henry R *BiAUS*
Crosby, Albert Hastings 1900-1946 *NatCAB 40*
Crosby, Albert William 1870-1938 *NatCAB 28*
Crosby, Alpheus 1810-1874 *ApCAB, BiDAmEd, Drake, NatCAB 9, TwCBDA, WhAm H*
Crosby, Alpheus Benning 1832-1877 *ApCAB, NatCAB 9, TwCBDA*
Crosby, Arthur David 1875-1951 *NatCAB 41*
Crosby, Arthur Payne 1879-1953 *NatCAB 44*
Crosby, Bing 1904- *WebAB*
Crosby, Bob *REnAW*
Crosby, Charles H 1819-1896 *NewYHSD*
Crosby, Charles Noel 1876-1951 *BiDrAC, WhAm 3*
Crosby, Daisy *WomWWA 14*
Crosby, Dick J 1866-1926 *WhAm 1*
Crosby, Dixi 1800-1873 *ApCAB, NatCAB 9, TwCBDA*
Crosby, Eben d1872 *ApCAB*
Crosby, Ebenezer 1753-1788 *ApCAB, NatCAB 10, TwCBDA*
Crosby, Edward Harding 1901-1953 *NatCAB 41*
Crosby, Edward Harold 1859-1934 *WhAm 1*
Crosby, Edwin L 1908-1972 *WhAm 5*
Crosby, Edwin Stanislau 1887-1958 *WhAm 3*
Crosby, Elisha O *BiAUS*
Crosby, Elizabeth Coolidge 1889- *WomWWA 14*
Crosby, Emma Erskine *WomWWA 14*
Crosby, Enoch 1750-1835 *ApCAB, Drake*
Crosby, Enoch 1753-1835 *TwCBDA*
Crosby, Ernest Howard 1856- *NatCAB 10, TwCBDA*
Crosby, Ernest Howard 1856-1906 *WhAm 1*
Crosby, Ernest Howard 1856-1907 *AmBi, DcAmB*
Crosby, Evan 1898-1943 *WhAm 2*
Crosby, Everett Nathaniel 1900- *WhAm 5*
Crosby, Everett Uberto 1871-1960 *WhAm 4*
Crosby, Fanny 1820-1915 *AmBi, DcAmB, NotAW, WhAm 1, WomWWA 14*
Crosby, Fanny J 1823- *AmWom*
Crosby, Frances Jane 1820-1915 *ApCAB Sup, ApCAB X, TwCBDA*
Crosby, Franklin Muzzy 1875-1947 *WhAm 2*
Crosby, Frederic VanSchoonhoven 1860-1920 *WhAm 1*
Crosby, George Harrington d1927 *WhAm 1*
Crosby, George Heman 1849- *WhAm 4*
Crosby, George Howard 1865-1961 *NatCAB 49*
Crosby, Georgina 1876- *WomWWA 14*
Crosby, Harley Nutting 1873-1955 *NatCAB 47, WhAm 3*
Crosby, Harold E 1899-1958 *WhAm 3*
Crosby, Henry Grew 1898-1929 *NatCAB 31*
Crosby, Henry Lamar 1880- *WhAm 6*

Crosby, Henry Stetson 1904-1953 *NatCAB 44*
Crosby, Henry Wood 1896-1951 *NatCAB 45*
Crosby, Herbert Ball 1871-1936 *WhAm 1*
Crosby, Howard 1826-1891 *AmBi, ApCAB, DcAmB, Drake, NatCAB 4, TwCBDA, WhAm H*
Crosby, James L *NewYHSD*
Crosby, James Ott 1828-1921 *WhAm 1*
Crosby, John 1867-1962 *NatCAB 50, WhAm 4*
Crosby, John Crawford 1859-1943 *BiDrAC, NatCAB 33, TwCBDA, WhAm 4*
Crosby, John Schuyler 1839-1914 *ApCAB, DcAmB, NatCAB 11, NatCAB 24, TwCBDA, WhAm 1*
Crosby, Kenneth Howard 1906-1964 *NatCAB 51*
Crosby, Lucius Olen 1869-1948 *NatCAB 35*
Crosby, Maria *NewYHSD*
Crosby, Nathan 1798-1885 *ApCAB, NatCAB 8, WhAm H*
Crosby, Oscar Terry 1861-1947 *NatCAB 35, WhAm 2*
Crosby, Peirce 1823- *ApCAB*
Crosby, Peirce 1824-1899 *DcAmB, NatCAB 10, TwCBDA, WhAm 1*
Crosby, Pierce 1823- *Drake*
Crosby, Pierce 1824-1889 *WhAm H*
Crosby, Raymond Moreau 1874-1945 *WhAm 2*
Crosby, Robert Dewite 1880- *WhoColR*
Crosby, Sheldon Leavitt 1879-1936 *WhAm 1*
Crosby, Stephen Moody 1827-1909 *ApCAB, NatCAB 9, TwCBDA, WhAm 1*
Crosby, Sumner 1878-1954 *NatCAB 43*
Crosby, Thomas 1869-1947 *NatCAB 34*
Crosby, Thomas Russell 1816-1872 *ApCAB, NatCAB 9, TwCBDA*
Crosby, Victoria Robie 1856- *WomWWA 14*
Crosby, Walter Wilson 1872-1946 *NatCAB 33, WhAm 2*
Crosby, William Bedlow 1786-1865 *ApCAB, NatCAB 10*
Crosby, William Dorr 1857- *WhAm 4*
Crosby, William G *BiAUS*
Crosby, William George 1805-1881 *NatCAB 6, TwCBDA*
Crosby, William George 1806-1881 *ApCAB*
Crosby, William Hugh 1862- *WhAm 5*
Crosby, William Otis 1850-1925 *ApCAB, DcAmB, NatCAB 22, TwCBDA, WhAm 1*
Crose, William Michael 1867- *WhAm 4*
Crosier, Edwin Neil 1910-1956 *WhAm 3*
Croskey, John Welsh 1858-1951 *WhAm 3*
Crosland, Edward Throop 1893-1952 *NatCAB 40*
Crosland, John Everett 1902-1971 *WhAm 5*
Crosley, Ferdinand Swift 1872-1931 *NatCAB 29*
Crosley, Powel, Jr. 1886-1961 *WhAm 4*
Crosley, Walter Selwyn 1871-1939 *NatCAB 28, WhAm 1*
Crosman, Alexander Foster 1838-1872 *ApCAB*
Crosman, Charles Sumner 1858-1926 *WhAm 1*
Crosman, George Hampton 1798-1882 *ApCAB, TwCBDA*
Crosman, Henrietta 1866- *WomWWA 14*
Crosman, Henrietta 1870-1941 *WhAm 2*
Crosman, Henrietta Foster 1861-1944 *NotAW*
Croson, Carl Earl 1884-1954 *NatCAB 45*
Cross, A B *NewYHSD*
Cross, Alonzo Townsend 1846-1922 *NatCAB 20*
Cross, Anson Kent 1862-1944 *BiDAmEd, NatCAB 38, TwCBDA, WhAm 2*
Cross, Arthur Chester 1884-1951 *WhAm 3*
Cross, Arthur Lyon 1873-1940 *DcAmB S2, WhAm 1*
Cross, Asa Beebe 1826-1894 *WhAm H*
Cross, Cecil Frank 1895-1959 *NatCAB 45, WhAm 4*
Cross, Charles Clark 1879-1951 *NatCAB 39*
Cross, Charles E 1837-1863 *ApCAB*
Cross, Charles Frederick 1855-1935 *AsBiEn*
Cross, Charles Robert 1848-1921 *ApCAB, ApCAB X, NatCAB 11, TwCBDA, WhAm 1*
Cross, Charles Whitman 1854-1949 *DcAmB S4, DcScB*

Cross, Clarence Eland 1893-1962 *WhAm 4*
Cross, Claude B 1893-1974 *WhAm 6*
Cross, David W 1814- *ApCAB*
Cross, Dorothea Farquhar *WomWWA 14*
Cross, E A 1875- *WhAm 5*
Cross, Earle Bennett 1883-1946 *WhAm 2*
Cross, Edward 1798-1887 *BiAUS, BiDrAC, DcAmB, NatCAB 22, TwCBDA, WhAm H*
Cross, Edward Ephraim 1832-1863 *TwCBDA*
Cross, Edward Ephram 1832-1863 *ApCAB, NatCAB 4*
Cross, Edward Makin 1880-1965 *NatCAB 54, WhAm 4*
Cross, Edward Weeks 1885-1939 *WhAm 1*
Cross, Emily Redmond *WomWWA 14*
Cross, Frank 1870-1946 *NatCAB 35*
Cross, Frank Bradley 1871-1938 *NatCAB 28*
Cross, Frederic Stephen 1903-1968 *NatCAB 54*
Cross, Frederick Bowen 1877-1970 *NatCAB 55*
Cross, Frederick George 1881-1941 *IlBEAAW*
Cross, Frederick Holland 1852-1933 *NatCAB 25*
Cross, George 1838?- *NewYHSD*
Cross, George 1862-1929 *NatCAB 24, WhAm 1*
Cross, George Dilwyn 1799-1872 *ApCAB*
Cross, Grace Ella *BiCAW*
Cross, Hardy 1885-1959 *WhAm 3*
Cross, Harold Livingston 1890-1959 *NatCAB 49, WhAm 3*
Cross, Harry Gustav 1890-1959 *NatCAB 48*
Cross, Harry Parsons 1873-1955 *WhAm 3*
Cross, Henry H 1837-1918 *IlBEAAW, NewYHSD, REnAW, WhAm HA, WhAm 4*
Cross, Hiram *NewYHSD*
Cross, Jane Tandy Chinn 1817-1870 *ApCAB*
Cross, John W 1902-1971 *WhAm 5*
Cross, John Walter 1878-1951 *NatCAB 40, WhAm 3*
Cross, Joseph 1813- *ApCAB, TwCBDA*
Cross, Joseph 1843-1913 *WhAm 1*
Cross, Judson Lewis 1878-1947 *WhAm 2*
Cross, Judson Newell 1838-1901 *NatCAB 6, TwCBDA, WhAm 1*
Cross, Kate Smeed 1859- *AmWom*
Cross, Lewis Josephus 1874- *WhAm 5*
Cross, Louis John 1897- *WhAm 6*
Cross, Margaret Elsie *WomWWA 14*
Cross, Mary *NotAW*
Cross, Michael Hurley 1833-1897 *WhAm H*
Cross, Milton 1897-1975 *WhAm 6*
Cross, Minnie M 1871- *WomWWA 14*
Cross, Morton Robinson 1879- *WhAm 6*
Cross, Oliver Harlan 1868-1960 *BiDrAC*
Cross, Oliver Harlan 1870- *WhAm 5*
Cross, Osborne 1803-1876 *ApCAB, NewYHSD*
Cross, Peter F 1820?-1856 *NewYHSD, WhAm H*
Cross, Richard James 1845-1917 *WhAm 1*
Cross, Roselle Theodore 1844- *WhAm 4*
Cross, Roy 1884-1947 *NatCAB 37, WhAm 2*
Cross, Samuel Hazzard 1891-1946 *DcAmB S4, WhAm 2*
Cross, Thomas Joseph 1894-1963 *NatCAB 49, WhAm 4*
Cross, Tom Peete 1879-1951 *NatCAB 40, WhAm 6*
Cross, Trueman d1846 *ApCAB, Drake*
Cross, Walter Martin 1878-1931 *NatCAB 28*
Cross, Walter Martin, Jr. 1904-1954 *NatCAB 44*
Cross, Walter Snell d1971 *WhAm 5*
Cross, Whitman 1854-1949 *NatCAB 15, NatCAB 37, WhAm 2*
Cross, Wilbur Lucius 1862-1948 *BiDAmEd, DcAmB S4, WhAm 2*
Cross, William Campbell 1887-1959 *WhAm 3*
Cross, William Edward 1886-1955 *NatCAB 47*
Crosscup, Daniel L 1841?- *NewYHSD*
Crosscup, George W 1843?- *NewYHSD*
Crosse, Charles Washburn 1885-1949 *WhAm 2*
Crosse, Mentor 1866- *WhAm 4*
Crossen, George Edward 1905-1958 *WhAm 3*
Crossen, Harry Sturgeon 1869-1951 *WhAm 3*
Crossen, Henry Francis 1894-1954 *NatCAB 44*

Crossen, Robert James 1898-1959 *NatCAB 48*
Crosser, John Roach 1856- *WhAm 4*
Crosser, Robert 1874-1957 *BiDrAC, WhAm 3, WhAmP*
Crossett, Alexander *NewYHSD*
Crossett, Edward Clark 1882-1955 *NatCAB 43, WhAm 3*
Crossett, Edward Savage 1828-1910 *ApCAB X, NatCAB 43*
Crossett, Ella Hawley 1853- *WomWWA 14*
Crossett, Lewis Abbott 1859-1926 *NatCAB 29, WhAm 4*
Crossfield, Albert Scott 1921- *WebAMB*
Crossfield, Richard Henry 1868-1951 *NatCAB 14, WhAm 3*
Crosskey, William Winslow 1894-1968 *WhAm 4A*
Crossland, Edward 1827-1881 *BiAUS, BiDrAC, WhAm H*
Crossland, J R A 1864- *NatCAB 14*
Crossland, Paul Marion 1904-1968 *WhAm 5*
Crossland, Weldon Frank 1890-1961 *WhAm 4*
Crossley, Alfred 1893-1959 *NatCAB 47*
Crossley, Arthur Webster 1908-1971 *WhAm 5*
Crossley, Frederic Beers 1872- *WhAm 1*
Crossley, George Corliss 1881-1951 *NatCAB 39*
Crossley, James Judson 1869- *WhAm 5*
Crossley, Robert J 1902-1960 *WhAm 3*
Crossley, Robert Pierce 1914-1972 *WhAm 5*
Crossman, A Fred 1891-1950 *NatCAB 39*
Crossman, Charles *NewYHSD*
Crossman, Edgar Gibson 1895-1967 *WhAm 4*
Crossman, Edgar O 1864- *WhAm 4*
Crossman, Jerome Kenneth 1896-1972 *WhAm 5*
Crossman, John *NewYHSD*
Crossman, John C 1806?- *NewYHSD*
Crossman, Richard Howard Stafford 1907-1974 *WhAm 6*
Croswell, Edwin 1797-1871 *NatCAB 10*
Croswell, Harry 1778-1858 *NatCAB 10*
Croswell, William 1804-1851 *NatCAB 10, WhAm H*
Crosthwait, David Nelson, Sr. 1856- *WhoColR*
Crosthwait, Minnie Lou 1860- *WhoColR*
Crosthwait, Scott Washington 1856- *WhoColR*
Crosthwaite, Burwell Morgan 1881-1938 *NatCAB 39*
Croswell, Andrew 1709-1785 *ApCAB, Drake*
Croswell, Charles Miller 1825-1886 *ApCAB, NatCAB 5, TwCBDA*
Croswell, Edwin 1797-1871 *ApCAB, DcAmB, Drake, TwCBDA, WhAm H, WhAmP*
Croswell, Harry 1778-1858 *ApCAB, DcAmB, Drake, TwCBDA, WhAm H*
Croswell, James Greenleaf 1852-1915 *NatCAB 32, WhAm 1*
Croswell, Mary Sybel 1873- *WomWWA 14*
Croswell, William 1804-1851 *ApCAB, Drake, TwCBDA*
Crothers, Austin Lane 1860-1912 *NatCAB 14, WhAm 1*
Crothers, Bronson 1884-1959 *NatCAB 47, WhAm 3*
Crothers, George Edward 1870-1957 *WhAm 3*
Crothers, Harold Marion 1887-1964 *WhAm 4*
Crothers, John H *NewYHSD*
Crothers, Rachel *WomWWA 14*
Crothers, Rachel 1871-1958 *WhAm 3*
Crothers, Rachel 1878-1958 *WebAB*
Crothers, Samuel 1783-1856 *ApCAB*
Crothers, Samuel McChord 1857-1927 *AmBi, DcAmB, NatCAB 22, TwCBDA, WhAm 1*
Crothers, Thomas Davidson 1842-1918 *NatCAB 10, NatCAB 17*
Crothers, Thomas Davison 1842-1918 *WhAm 1*
Crott, Homer Daniel 1899-1972 *WhAm 5*
Crotti, Andre 1873-1958 *NatCAB 43, WhAm 3*
Crotty, Homer Daniel 1899-1972 *WhAm 6*
Crotty, Sister M Madeleine 1916-1973 *WhAm 6*
Crouch, Austin 1870-1957 *WhAm 3*
Crouch, Calvin Henry 1870-1937 *WhAm 1*
Crouch, Charles 1898-1957 *NatCAB 46*
Crouch, Charles T d1949 *WhAm 3*
Crouch, Courtney Chet 1912-1975 *WhAm 6*
Crouch, Edward 1764-1827 *BiAUS, BiDrAC, WhAm H*

Crouch, Edwin Gordon 1903-1962 *NatCAB 50*
Crouch, Frederick William Nicholls 1808-1896 *TwCBDA*
Crouch, Frederick William Nicolls d1896 *ApCAB Sup*
Crouch, John Baker 1880-1955 *NatCAB 47*
Crouch, Leonard Callender 1866-1953 *WhAm 3*
Crouch, Ralph B d1975 *WhAm 6*
Crouch, Richard Edwin 1894-1962 *WhAm 4*
Crouch, Sydney James Leonhardt 1889-1969 *WhAm 5*
Croughton, George Hanmer 1843-1920 *NatCAB 19*
Crounse, Lorenzo 1834-1909 *BiAUS, BiDrAC, DcAmB, NatCAB 12, TwCBDA, WhAm 1, WhAmP*
Crounse, Robert Mabie 1893-1974 *WhAm 6*
Crounse, William Livingston 1861- *TwCBDA*
Crousaz, Jean-Pierre De 1663-1750 *DcScB*
Crouse, Charles Mabie 1857-1920 *NatCAB 19*
Crouse, George N 1877-1945 *WhAm 2*
Crouse, George Washington 1832-1912 *BiDrAC, NatCAB 6*
Crouse, Huntington Beard 1872-1943 *NatCAB 34*
Crouse, John Bernard 1842-1921 *NatCAB 28*
Crouse, Lewis 1830?- *NewYHSD*
Crouse, Mary Elizabeth 1873- *WhAm 5, WomWWA 14*
Crouse, R Floyd 1892-1969 *NatCAB 56*
Crouse, Russel 1893-1966 *WhAm 4*
Crouta, John 1805?- *NewYHSD*
Crouter, Albert Louis Edgerton 1846-1925 *DcAmB, NatCAB 5, WhAm 1*
Crow, Carl 1883-1945 *NatCAB 36, WhAm 2*
Crow, Carl Chessley 1882-1953 *NatCAB 42*
Crow, Charles Augustus 1873-1938 *BiDrAC, WhAm 3*
Crow, Charles Langley 1866-1942 *WhAm 2*
Crow, DeWitt Smith 1891-1966 *NatCAB 54*
Crow, Herman Denton 1851- *WhAm 1*
Crow, James 1800?-1859 *ApCAB Sup*
Crow, Jim 1808-1860 *WebAB*
Crow, John McClusky 1846-1890 *TwCBDA*
Crow, Martha Emilie Foote 1854-1924 *TwCBDA*
Crow, Martha Emily Foote 1854-1924 *NatCAB 22, WhAm 1, WomWWA 14*
Crow, Moses Rockwell 1855- *NatCAB 4*
Crow, Orin Faison 1896-1955 *WhAm 3*
Crow, Randolph Fairfax 1877-1952 *WhAm 3*
Crow, William *NewYHSD*
Crow, William Evans 1870-1922 *BiDrAC, NatCAB 19, WhAm 1, WhAmP*
Crow, William Josiah 1902-1964 *BiDrAC*
Crowder, Enoch Herbert 1859-1932 *AmBi, ApCAB X, DcAmB S1, WebAMB, WhAm 1*
Crowder, Frank Warfield 1869-1932 *NatCAB 24, WhAm 1, WhAm 1C*
Crowder, John Batte 1904-1957 *WhAm 3*
Crowder, Mattee Saunders 1879- *WomWWA 14*
Crowder, Render Lewis, Jr. 1905-1968 *WhAm 5*
Crowder, Thomas Reid 1872- *WhAm 5*
Crowe, Eugene Burgess 1878-1970 *BiDrAC*
Crowe, Eyre 1824-1910 *NewYHSD*
Crowe, Francis Trenholm 1882-1946 *DcAmB S4, NatCAB 34, WhAm 2*
Crowe, Frederick d1858 *ApCAB, Drake*
Crowe, John A d1961 *WhAm 4*
Crowe, John Finley 1787-1860 *NatCAB 6, TwCBDA*
Crowe, R L 1887- *WhAm 3*
Crowe, Thomas Bennett 1876-1940 *NatCAB 30, WhAm 1*
Crowe, William 1871-1962 *WhAm 4*
Crowell, Bowman Corning 1879-1951 *WhAm 3*
Crowell, Chester Theodore 1888-1941 *WhAm 1*
Crowell, Edward Payson 1830-1911 *TwCBDA, WhAm 1*
Crowell, Evelyn Walker 1886- *WomWWA 14*
Crowell, Frank Grant 1869-1936 *NatCAB 26*
Crowell, Grace Noll 1877-1969 *WhAm 5*
Crowell, Grace Wenham 1872- *WomWWA 14*
Crowell, Henry Coleman 1897-1965 *WhAm 4*
Crowell, Henry Parsons 1855-1944 *NatCAB 33, WhAm 2*

Crowell, James Foster 1848-1915 *WhAm 1*
Crowell, James McMullin 1827-1908 *WhAm 1*
Crowell, John d1846 *BiAUS*
Crowell, John 1780-1846 *BiDrAC, WhAm H*
Crowell, John 1785?-1846 *TwCBDA*
Crowell, John 1801-1883 *BiAUS, BiDrAC, WhAm H*
Crowell, John 1814-1909 *WhAm 1*
Crowell, John Franklin 1857-1931 *ApCAB X, NatCAB 3, TwCBDA, WhAm 1*
Crowell, John Stephen 1850-1921 *NatCAB 19, WhAm 1*
Crowell, Katharine Roney d1926 *WhAm 1*
Crowell, Lena Annie 1863- *WomWWA 14*
Crowell, Lester Avant, Sr. 1867-1952 *WhAm 3*
Crowell, Luther Childs 1840-1903 *DcAmB, NatCAB 13, WhAm 1*
Crowell, Merle 1888-1956 *WhAm 3*
Crowell, Samuel Babcock 1868-1929 *NatCAB 22*
Crowell, Thomas Irving, Jr. 1894-1960 *WhAm 4*
Crowell, Wilbur Saunders 1872-1948 *NatCAB 37*
Crowell, William 1806-1871 *ApCAB, TwCBDA*
Crowell, William Hamblin 1877-1962 *NatCAB 51*
Crowl, Mabel Robinson 1876- *WomWWA 14*
Crowley, Charles Francis 1888-1954 *WhAm 3*
Crowley, Henry J 1865-1924 *WhAm 1*
Crowley, John 1869-1949 *NatCAB 38*
Crowley, John Dennis 1915-1969 *WhAm 5*
Crowley, John Gifford 1857-1921 *ApCAB X*
Crowley, Joseph Burns 1858-1931 *BiDrAC, WhAm 4*
Crowley, Karl Allen 1894-1948 *WhAm 2*
Crowley, Leo T d1972 *WhAm 5*
Crowley, Mary Catherine d1920 *WhAm 1, WomWWA 14*
Crowley, Miles 1859-1921 *BiDrAC*
Crowley, Patrick Edward 1864-1953 *WhAm 3*
Crowley, Patrick F 1911-1974 *WhAm 6*
Crowley, Richard 1836-1908 *BiDrAC, TwCBDA*
Crowley, Thomas Joseph 1894-1958 *NatCAB 44*
Crowley, William *NewYHSD*
Crowley, William M *NewYHSD*
Crowley, William Robert 1884-1968 *NatCAB 56*
Crowley, Xavier 1906-1958 *WhAm 3*
Crown, Edward A 1905-1975 *WhAm 6*
Crown, James Evans 1873-1945 *WhAm 2*
Crowne, John 1640-1712 *DcAmB, WhAm H*
Crowne, William 1617-1683 *DcAmB, WhAm H*
Crownfield, Gertrude d1945 *WhAm 2*
Crownhart, Charles Henry 1863-1930 *WhAm 1*
Crownhart, Charles Henry 1905-1974 *WhAm 6*
Crownhart, Jesse George 1896-1941 *WhAm 2*
Crowninshield, Arent Schuyler 1843-1908 *TwCBDA, WhAm 1*
Crowninshield, Arrant Schuyler 1843- *ApCAB*
Crowninshield, Benjamin W 1774-1851 *BiAUS*
Crowninshield, Benjamin William 1772-1851 *WhAmP*
Crowninshield, Benjamin Williams 1772-1851 *ApCAB, BiDrAC, BiDrUSE, DcAmB, Drake, NatCAB 5, WhAm H*
Crowninshield, Benjamin Williams 1773-1851 *TwCBDA*
Crowninshield, Bowdoin Bradlee 1867-1948 *WhAm 2*
Crowninshield, Caspar 1837-1897 *TwCBDA*
Crowninshield, Caspar Schuyler 1871-1910 *WhAm 1*
Crowninshield, Francis Welch 1872-1947 *DcAmB S4*
Crowninshield, Frank 1872-1947 *NatCAB 36, WhAm 2*
Crowninshield, Frederic 1845-1918 *AmBi, ApCAB, ApCAB X, DcAmB, NatCAB 14, TwCBDA, WhAm 1*
Crowninshield, George 1766-1817 *DcAmB, WhAm H*
Crowninshield, Hannah 1789-1834 *NewYHSD*
Crowninshield, Jacob 1770-1808 *ApCAB, BiAUS, BiDrAC, DcAmB, NatCAB 3, TwCBDA, WhAm H, WhAmP*

Crowninshield, Mary Bradford d1913 *WhAm 1, WomWWA 14, WomWWA 14a*
Crownover, Arthur, Jr. 1907-1965 *NatCAB 52, WhAm 4*
Crownover, Arthur, Sr. 1874-1942 *WhAm 2*
Crowson, Benjamin Franklin 1889-1938 *WhAm 1*
Crowther, Cyril Irwin 1895-1968 *WhAm 5*
Crowther, Frank 1870-1955 *BiDrAC, WhAm 3, WhAmP*
Crowther, George Calhoun 1849-1914 *BiDrAC*
Crowther, George H *NewYHSD*
Crowther, Henry *NewYHSD*
Crowther, J Chester 1897-1962 *NatCAB 52*
Crowther, James Edwin 1877-1947 *WhAm 2*
Crowther, Samuel d1947 *WhAm 2*
Crowther, Bishop Samuel Adjai 1806?-1891 *McGEWB*
Croxall, Agnes Brown *WomWWA 14*
Croxton, Fred Cleveland 1871-1960 *NatCAB 47, WhAm 4*
Croxton, John G 1839-1913 *ApCAB X*
Croxton, John Thomas 1837-1874 *ApCAB, BiAUS, NatCAB 7, TwCBDA*
Croxton, Thomas 1822-1903 *BiDrAC*
Croxton, William Nelson 1868- *ApCAB X*
Croy, Homer 1883-1965 *NatCAB 51, REnAW, WhAm 4, WhAm 5*
Croy, Ralph 1874-1947 *NatCAB 36*
Croyeau, Augustin *NewYHSD*
Crozat-Converse, Charles 1832- *ApCAB Sup*
Crozer, John Price 1793-1866 *ApCAB, DcAmB, NatCAB 10, TwCBDA, WhAm H*
Crozer, Samuel Aldrich 1825-1910 *WhAm 1*
Crozet, Claude d1863 *ApCAB*
Crozet, Claude 1790-1864 *BiDAmEd, DcAmB, WebAMB, WhAm H*
Crozet, Claudius 1790-1864 *NatCAB 18*
Crozier, Herbert William 1875-1939 *NatCAB 29, WhAm 1*
Crozier, John 1911-1971 *WhAm 6*
Crozier, John Hervey 1812-1889 *BiAUS, BiDrAC, WhAm H*
Crozier, Norman Robert 1877-1940 *WhAm 1*
Crozier, Robert 1827-1895 *BiDrAC, NatCAB 7, TwCBDA, WhAm H*
Crozier, W J 1892-1955 *WhAm 3*
Crozier, William 1855-1942 *ApCAB X, DcAmB S3, NatCAB 12, NatCAB 32, TwCBDA, WebAMB, WhAm 2*
Cru, Albert Louis 1881-1949 *NatCAB 37*
Cruce, Francisco DeLa 1600?-1660 *ApCAB*
Cruce, Lee 1863-1933 *NatCAB 16, WhAm 1*
Cruchaga-Tocornal, Miguel 1869- *WhAm 5*
Crudup, Josiah 1791-1872 *BiAUS, BiDrAC, WhAm H*
Cruft, Charles d1883 *ApCAB, NatCAB 4*
Cruger, Daniel 1780-1843 *BiAUS, BiDrAC, TwCBDA, WhAm H*
Cruger, Henry 1702-1780 *ApCAB*
Cruger, Henry 1739-1827 *ApCAB, DcAmB, Drake, NatCAB 7, WhAm H*
Cruger, John 1710-1791 *BiAUS, DcAmB, Drake, WhAm H*
Cruger, John 1710-1792 *ApCAB, NatCAB 1, TwCBDA*
Cruger, John Harris 1738-1807 *ApCAB, Drake*
Cruger, Julia Grinnell Storrow 1850?- *ApCAB Sup*
Cruger, Julie Grinnell *TwCBDA*
Cruger, Mary 1834-1908 *AmWom, WhAm 1*
Cruger, Mrs. S VanRensselaer *AmWom*
Cruger, Stephen VanRensselaer 1844- *NatCAB 7*
Cruickshank, H W 1893-1965 *WhAm 4*
Cruikshank, Alfred B 1847-1933 *WhAm 1*
Cruikshank, Edwin Allen 1843- *NatCAB 3*
Cruikshank, James 1831- *NatCAB 10*
Cruikshank, John McEliwaine 1865-1912 *NatCAB 15*
Cruikshank, Katharine Adams 1862- *WomWWA 14*
Cruikshank, Marcus Henderson 1826-1881 *BiDConf*
Cruikshank, Margaret d1955 *WhAm 3*
Cruikshank, R J 1898-1956 *WhAm 3*
Cruikshank, Russell V 1886-1965 *WhAm 4*

Cruikshank, William Cumberland 1745-1800
BiHiMed, DcScB
Cruikshank, William Mackey 1870-1943
ApCAB X, NatCAB 49, WhAm 2
Cruisin, C 1812?- *NewYHSD*
Crull, Harry Edward 1909-1972 *WhAm 5*
Crum, Bartley Cavanaugh 1900-1959 *WhAm 3*
Crum, Earl LeVerne 1891-1961 *NatCAB 50*
Crum, Roy W 1885-1951 *WhAm 3*
Crum, Walter 1796-1867 *DcScB*
Crum, William Demos 1859-1912 *WhAm 1*
Crum, William Leonard d1967 *WhAm 4*
Crum Brown, Alexander *DcScB*
Crumb, Frederick Waite 1909-1967 *WhAm 4*
Crumb, Geneva 1872- *WomWWA 14*
Crumbacker, William Pollock 1857-1920
WhAm 1
Crumbie, W D *NewYHSD*
Crumbine, Samuel Jay 1862-1954 *DcAmB S5,
WhAm 3*
Crumbly, Floyd Henry 1859- *WhoColR*
Crumbo, Woodrow Wilson 1912- *IIBEAAW,
REnAW*
Crumley, Thomas 1872-1954 *WhAm 3*
Crumley, Thomas Ralston 1878-1944 *WhAm 2*
Crummel, Alexander 1818-1898 *AmBi*
Crummell, Alexander 1819-1898 *ApCAB Sup,
DcAmReB, NatCAB 5, TwCBDA*
Crummer, LeRoy 1872-1934 *NatCAB 24,
WhAm 1*
Crummey, John D 1878- *WhAm 6*
Crump, Edward Hull 1874-1954 *BiDrAC,
DcAmB S5, WhAm 3, WhAmP*
Crump, George William d1850 *BiAUS*
Crump, George William 1786-1848 *BiDrAC,
WhAm H*
Crump, James Dobson 1848-1924 *NatCAB 28*
Crump, Jean 1892-1963 *NatCAB 52*
Crump, Malcolm Hart 1849- *NatCAB 2*
Crump, Richard 1805?- *NewYHSD*
Crump, Robert *NewYHSD*
Crump, Rousseau Owen 1843-1901 *BiDrAC,
TwCBDA, WhAm 1*
Crump, Samuel *NewYHSD*
Crump, Walter Gray 1869-1945 *WhAm 2*
Crump, William *BiAUS*
Crump, William Wood 1819-1897 *BiDConf,
DcAmB, WhAm H, WhAmP*
Crumpacker, Edgar Dean 1851-1920 *BiDrAC,
WhAm 1, WhAmP*
Crumpacker, Maurice Edgar 1886-1927 *BiDrAC,
WhAm 1*
Crumpacker, Shepard J, Jr. 1917- *BiDrAC*
Crumpton, Washington Bryan 1842- *WhAm 1*
Crumrine, Boyd 1838- *NatCAB 1*
Crunden, Elizabeth Chittenden 1865-
WomWWA 14
Crunden, Frederick Morgan 1847-1911 *DcAmB,
DcAmLiB, NatCAB 6, TwCBDA,
WhAm 1*
Crunelle, Leonard 1872-1944 *WhAm 2*
Cruse, Christian Frederic 1794-1864 *ApCAB*
Cruse, Edward *NewYHSD*
Cruse, Peter Hoffman 1793-1832 *Drake*
Cruse, Peter Hoffman 1795-1832 *ApCAB*
Cruse, Thomas 1857-1943 *WhAm 2*
Crusinberry, William Alfred 1850-1929
WhAm 3
Crusoe, Claude Allen 1891-1964 *NatCAB 51*
Crutchfield, James Stapleton 1874-1954
NatCAB 41, WhAm 3
Crutchfield, William 1824-1890 *BiDrAC,
WhAm H*
Crutchfield, William 1826- *BiAUS*
Crutchfield, William Gayle 1900-1972 *WhAm 5*
Crutchley, Victor 1893- *WhWW-II*
Cruthcer, Lewis Pinkerton 1874- *WhAm 5*
Cruttenden, Daniel Henry 1816-1874 *ApCAB*
Cruttenden, David H 1816- *Drake*
Cruttenden, Walter Barnes 1873-1949 *WhAm 2*
Cruveilhier, Jean 1791-1874 *BiHiMed, DcScB*
Cruz, Anibal 1865-1911 *WhAm 1*
Cruz, Juan Bautista Valerio DeLa 1517?-1572
ApCAB
Cruz, Juana Ines DeLa 1651-1695 *ApCAB*
Cruz, Oswaldo Goncalves 1872-1917
DcScB Sup, McGEWB
Cruz, Rodrigo DeLa 1637-1716 *ApCAB*

Cruze, James 1884-1942 *ApCAB X, WhAm 2*
Cryderman, Mackie Macintyre d1969 *WhAm 5*
Cryer, George Edward 1875-1961 *WhAm 4*
Cryer, Matthew Henry 1840-1921 *NatCAB 17,
WhAm 1*
Crystal, David 1883-1962 *NatCAB 49*
Crytzer, Harry Burnham 1904-1968
NatCAB 54
Csanadi, Gyorgy 1905-1974 *WhAm 6*
Csatorday, Karoly d1972 *WhAm 5*
Ctesibius *AsBiEn, DcScB*
Cuadra, Pedro Lucio 1842- *ApCAB*
Cuauhtemoc 1496?-1525 *McGEWB*
Cuauhtemotzin 1495-1524 *ApCAB*
Cuba, Dionisio Vives d1840 *ApCAB*
Cubberley, Ellwood Patterson 1868-1941
DcAmB S3, NatCAB 30, WhAm 1
Cubberly, Elwood Patterson 1868-1941
BiDAmEd
Cubberly, Fred 1869-1932 *WhAm 1*
Cubbins, William Robert 1874-1959 *WhAm 3*
Cubero, Pedro Rodriguez 1645-1704 *DcAmB*
Cuckson, John 1846-1907 *WhAm 1*
Cudahy, Edward A 1885-1966 *WhAm 4*
Cudahy, Edward Aloysius 1859-1941
NatCAB 11, NatCAB 35
Cudahy, Edward Aloysius, Sr. 1860-1941
WhAm 1
Cudahy, John 1843-1915 *NatCAB 11,
WhAm 1*
Cudahy, John 1887-1943 *NatCAB 33,
WhAm 2*
Cudahy, Joseph M 1878-1947 *WhAm 2*
Cudahy, Michael 1841-1910 *AmBi, DcAmB,
NatCAB 11, WhAm 1*
Cudahy, Michael Francis 1886-1970 *WhAm 5*
Cudahy, Patrick 1849-1919 *WhAm 1*
Cuddeback, Allan W 1868-1938 *WhAm 1*
Cuddeback, Cornelius Elting 1849-1918
NatCAB 18
Cuddeback, Samuel Mills 1877-1950
NatCAB 40
Cuddeback, William Herman 1852-1919
NatCAB 19, WhAm 1
Cuddihy, Herbert Lester 1896-1953 *NatCAB 42,
WhAm 3*
Cuddy, Loftus 1852-1917 *NatCAB 29*
Cuddy, Warren N 1886-1951 *WhAm 3*
Cudebach, Edith E 1874- *WomWWA 14*
Cudequala 1555?-1587 *ApCAB*
Cudlip, Merlin A d1968 *WhAm 5*
Cudworth, Frank Esekiel 1878-1972 *NatCAB 57*
Cudworth, James 1612?-1682 *ApCAB, Drake,
NatCAB 9*
Cudworth, Ralph 1617-1688 *DcScB, McGEWB*
Cue, Harold James 1887-1961 *IIBEAAW*
Cuellar, Jose T De 1835- *ApCAB*
Cuenecura 1578-1609 *ApCAB*
Cuenot, Lucien 1866-1951 *DcScB*
Cueny, Elizabeth d1931 *WhAm 1*
Cuesta, Karl Bernardo 1893-1971 *NatCAB 56*
Cuestas, Juan Lisboa 1837- *ApCAB Sup*
Cueva, Beatriz DeLa d1541 *ApCAB*
Cuevas Davalos, Alonso 1590-1665 *ApCAB*
Cuff, Harlan Austin 1888- *WhoColR*
Cuffe, Paul 1759-1817 *DcAmB, EncAB,
McGEWB, WhAm H, WhAmP*
Cuffe, Thomas E 1898-1959 *WhAm 4*
Cuffee, Paul 1757-1812 *ApCAB*
Cuffee, Paul 1759-1817 *AmBi*
Cuffee, Paul 1759-1818 *ApCAB, Drake,
NatCAB 12*
Cuffman, John Henry 1863-1917 *NatCAB 17*
Cugoano, Ottobah 1757?-1803? *McGEWB*
Cuicuitzcatzin *ApCAB*
Cuientur 1578-1627 *ApCAB*
Cuillamachu 1534-1603 *ApCAB*
Cuillavilu II 1580-1612 *ApCAB*
Cuiner, W *NewYHSD*
Cuinet, L Adele 1860- *WomWWA 14*
Cuinet, Louise Adele 1855- *AmWom*
Cuipers, Peter *NewYHSD*
Cuitlahuatzin 1490-1520 *ApCAB*
Culberson, Charles Allen 1855-1925 *BiDrAC,
DcAmB, NatCAB 9, WhAm 1, WhAmP*
Culberson, David Browning 1830-1900 *BiAUS,
BiDrAC, DcAmB, TwCBDA, WhAm H,
WhAmP*

Culberson, Olin 1886-1961 *NatCAB 50*
Culberson, Mrs. Sherwood Franklin 1846-
WomWWA 14
Culbert, Samuel L 1822?- *NewYHSD*
Culbertson, Albert L 1884-1956 *WhAm 3*
Culbertson, Alexander *WhAm H*
Culbertson, Anne Virginia 1864- *WhAm 4,
WomWWA 14*
Culbertson, Belle Caldwell 1857-
WomWWA 14
Culbertson, Eliza Mary 1866- *WomWWA 14*
Culbertson, Ely 1891-1955 *DcAmB S5,
NatCAB 46, WebAB, WhAm 3*
Culbertson, Emma Valeria Bicknell 1854-
WhAm 1, WomWWA 14
Culbertson, Henry Coe 1874-1933 *WhAm 1*
Culbertson, James Coe 1840-1908 *NatCAB 12,
WhAm 1*
Culbertson, James Gordon 1903-1969 *WhAm 5*
Culbertson, John James 1853-1932 *NatCAB 29,
WhAm 1*
Culbertson, Matthew Simpson 1818-1862
ApCAB
Culbertson, William 1905-1971 *NatCAB 56,
WhAm 5*
Culbertson, William Constantine 1825-1906
BiDrAC, TwCBDA
Culbertson, William H 1903-1973 *WhAm 6*
Culbertson, William Smith 1884-1966
ApCAB X, NatCAB 54, WhAm 4
Culbertson, William Wirt 1835-1911 *BiDrAC*
Culbreth, David Marvel Reynolds 1855-1943
NatCAB 32, WhAm 4
Culbreth, Thomas 1786-1843 *BiAUS, BiDrAC,
TwCBDA, WhAm H, WhAmP*
Culig, Ivan Conrad 1920-1964 *WhAm 4*
Culin, Alice Mumford 1875- *WhAm 5*
Culin, Frank Lewis 1892-1967 *NatCAB 54,
WhAm 4A*
Culin, Robert Stewart 1858-1929 *AmBi,
NatCAB 13*
Culin, Stewart 1858-1929 *NatCAB 29,
WhAm 1*
Culkin, Francis Dugan 1874-1943 *BiDrAC,
NatCAB 35, WhAm 2, WhAmP*
Culkins, William Clement 1868-1936 *WhAm 1*
Cull, Edwin Emory 1891-1956 *NatCAB 45*
Cull, Joseph Henry 1888-1941 *NatCAB 30*
Cullburg, Edwin *NewYHSD*
Cullen, Charles West 1865-1948 *NatCAB 38*
Cullen, Countee Porter 1903-1946 *DcAmB S4,
McGEWB, WhAm 2*
Cullen, Edgar Montgomery 1843-1922
NatCAB 13, WhAm 1
Cullen, Elisha Dickerson 1799-1862 *BiAUS,
BiDrAC, WhAm H*
Cullen, Frederick John d1968 *WhAm 5*
Cullen, Glenn Ernest 1890-1940 *NatCAB 41,
WhAm 1*
Cullen, Hugh Roy 1881-1957 *NatCAB 47,
WhAm 3*
Cullen, James Aloysius 1912-1974 *WhAm 6*
Cullen, John 1837- *NewYHSD*
Cullen, Matthew 1840-1918 *NatCAB 18*
Cullen, Maurice Galbraith 1866-1934 *McGEWB*
Cullen, Richard J d1948 *WhAm 2*
Cullen, Thomas Ernest 1874- *WhAm 5*
Cullen, Thomas Henry 1868-1944 *BiDrAC,
WhAm 2, WhAmP*
Cullen, Thomas Joseph Vincent 1892-1966
WhAm 4
Cullen, Thomas Stephen 1868-1953 *DcAmB S5,
WhAm 3*
Cullen, Victor Francis 1881-1949 *NatCAB 37*
Cullen, Vincent 1884-1962 *WhAm 4*
Cullen, William 1710-1790 *BiHiMed, DcScB*
Cullen, William 1826-1914 *BiDrAC*
Cullen, William George 1907-1973 *WhAm 6*
Culler, Arthur Jerome 1883-1946 *WhAm 2*
Culler, Arthur Merl 1899-1960 *WhAm 4*
Culler, Joseph Albertus 1858-1937 *WhAm 1*
Culler, Robert Martin 1877-1930 *NatCAB 23*
Culler, Roy Bunyan 1900-1959 *NatCAB 48*
Cullimore, Allan Reginald 1884-1956
NatCAB 42, WhAm 3
Cullimore, Clarence 1885-1963 *WhAm 4*
Cullin, Charles *NewYHSD*
Cullinan, Craig Francis 1894-1950 *WhAm 3*

Cullinan, Edith Phillips 1895-1949 *WhAm 3*
Cullinan, George Evans 1878-1941 *NatCAB 31*
Cullinan, Joseph Stephen 1860-1937 *DcAmB S2,* *WhAm 1*
Cullis, Charles 1833-1892 *DcAmB, WhAm H*
Cullison, James Buchanan 1857-1936 *NatCAB 29, WhAm 1*
Cullison, James Buchanan, Jr. 1883-1958 *NatCAB 46*
Cullman, Howard S 1891-1972 *ApCAB X,* *WhAm 5*
Cullman, Otto 1867-1963 *NatCAB 52*
Cullom, Alvan 1797-1877 *BiAUS, BiDrAC,* *WhAm H*
Cullom, Alvin 1797-1877 *TwCBDA*
Cullom, Marvin McTyeire 1868-1959 *NatCAB 47, WhAm 4*
Cullom, Shelby Moore 1829-1914 *AmBi,* *ApCAB, BiAUS, BiDrAC, DcAmB,* *EncAAH, NatCAB 1, NatCAB 11,* *TwCBDA, WhAm 1, WhAmP*
Cullom, William 1810-1896 *BiAUS, BiDrAC,* *TwCBDA, WhAm H*
Cullom, Willis Richard 1867- *WhAm 5*
Cullop, William Allen 1853-1927 *BiDrAC,* *WhAm 1*
Cullum, George Washington 1809-1892 *AmBi,* *ApCAB, DcAmB, NatCAB 4, TwCBDA,* *WhAm H*
Cullum, George Washington 1812- *Drake*
Cullum, John 1798?- *NewYHSD*
Culmann, Karl 1821-1881 *DcScB*
Culmer, Henry Lavender Adolphus 1854-1914 *IIBEAAW, WhAm 1*
Culp, Charles Cantrell 1891-1963 *WhAm 4*
Culp, John M 1849- *WhAm 1*
Culp, John Weaver 1888-1949 *NatCAB 39*
Culpeper, John *ApCAB, WhAm H*
Culpeper, John 1761-1837 *TwCBDA*
Culpeper, Nicholas 1616-1654 *BiHiMed*
Culpeper, Thomas d1719 *ApCAB*
Culpeper, Lord Thomas 1635-1689 *AmBi,* *DcAmB, WhAm H*
Culpepper, James Henry 1914-1974 *WhAm 6*
Culpepper, John *Drake, NatCAB 12*
Culpepper, John 1761- *BiAUS*
Culpepper, John 1761-1841 *BiDrAC,* *WhAm H, WhAmP*
Culpepper, Lord Thomas d1719 *Drake,* *NatCAB 12, NatCAB 13*
Culter, Mary McCrae 1858- *WhAm 4*
Culton, Jessie F 1860- *AmWom*
Cultzhayotl 1370-1421 *ApCAB*
Culver, Bernard Mott 1873-1951 *NatCAB 39,* *WhAm 3*
Culver, Bertram Beach 1875-1959 *WhAm 3*
Culver, Charles Aaron 1875- *WhAm 6*
Culver, Charles Beach 1908-1967 *WhAm 5*
Culver, Charles Mortimer 1856-1938 *NatCAB 12, NatCAB 28, WhAm 1*
Culver, Charles Vernon 1830-1909 *BiAUS,* *BiDrAC*
Culver, D Jay 1902-1968 *NatCAB 54*
Culver, E D *BiAUS*
Culver, Erastus D *BiAUS*
Culver, Erastus Dean 1803-1889 *BiDrAC,* *WhAm H*
Culver, Erastus Dean 1806-1889 *TwCBDA*
Culver, Essae Martha 1882-1973 *DcAmLiB*
Culver, Eugenia Margaret 1868- *WomWWA 14*
Culver, Frank Pugh 1863-1949 *WhAm 2*
Culver, Harry 1885-1959 *NatCAB 49*
Culver, Harry H d1946 *WhAm 2*
Culver, Helen 1832-1925 *NatCAB 17,* *TwCBDA, WhAm 1, WomWWA 14*
Culver, Henry S 1854- *WhAm 4*
Culver, John Chester 1932- *BiDrAC*
Culver, John Yapp 1839- *WhAm 4*
Culver, Montgomery Morton 1891-1950 *WhAm 3*
Culver, Raymond Benjamin 1887-1938 *NatCAB 27, WhAm 1, WhAm 1C*
Culver, Romulus Estep 1865-1957 *WhAm 4*
Culver, William Wallace 1835- *NatCAB 12*
Culverhouse, Johann Mongles *NewYHSD*
Culverhouse, John Burnett 1891-1950 *NatCAB 39*
Culvert, George 1744-1839 *Drake*

Culwer, Daniel 1793-1857 *ApCAB*
Culyer, John Yapp 1839- *ApCAB, TwCBDA*
Cumback, Will 1829-1905 *BiAUS*
Cumback, William 1829-1905 *BiDrAC,* *TwCBDA*
Cumberland, Frederic William 1820-1881 *ApCAB*
Cumberland, William Augustus, Duke Of 1721-1765 *WhoMilH*
Cumberland, William Wilson 1890-1955 *WhAm 3*
Cumbler, George William 1893-1958 *NatCAB 48*
Cume, Juan *NewYHSD*
Cuming, Sir Alexander 1690?-1775 *DcAmB,* *WhAm H*
Cuming, Sir Alexander 1700?- *ApCAB*
Cuming, Fortescue 1762-1828 *DcAmB,* *WhAm H*
Cumings, Edgar Roscoe 1874- *WhAm 5*
Cumings, Elizabeth *AmWom*
Cumings, Mrs. Henry Harrison 1846- *WomWWA 14*
Cummer, Arthur Gerrish 1873-1943 *NatCAB 31*
Cummer, Clyde Lottridge 1882-1958 *NatCAB 50, WhAm 3*
Cummer, Waldo Emerson 1875-1936 *NatCAB 31*
Cummin, Ellen Pearson 1849- *WomWWA 14*
Cumming *NewYHSD*
Cumming, Alexander 1726-1763 *ApCAB*
Cumming, Alfred 1802-1873 *ApCAB, DcAmB,* *TwCBDA, WhAm H, WhAmP*
Cumming, Alfred 1829- *ApCAB, TwCBDA*
Cumming, Alfred 1829-1864 *Drake*
Cumming, Alfred 1829-1910 *BiDConf*
Cumming, Charles Atherton 1858-1932 *IIBEAAW, WhAm 1*
Cumming, Ellen King *WomWWA 14*
Cumming, Gilbert W 1817- *ApCAB*
Cumming, Hugh S 1869-1948 *WhAm 2*
Cumming, James 1777-1861 *DcScB*
Cumming, John Noble d1821 *Drake*
Cumming, Kate 1828?-1909 *NotAW*
Cumming, Kate 1835?- *ApCAB*
Cumming, Mary Gairdner 1866- *WomWWA 14*
Cumming, Robert d1826 *Drake*
Cumming, Thomas William 1814?-1855 *BiAUS,* *BiDrAC, WhAm H*
Cumming, William *BiAUS, BiDrAC,* *WhAm H*
Cumming, William 1788-1863 *Drake,* *TwCBDA*
Cumming, William 1790?-1863 *ApCAB*
Cummings, Albert Baird 1850-1926 *WhAmP*
Cummings, Alexander *BiAUS, NatCAB 6*
Cummings, Alma Carrie 1857- *AmWom*
Cummings, Amos J 1838- *NatCAB 1*
Cummings, Amos Jay 1841-1902 *BiDrAC,* *DcAmB, TwCBDA, WhAm 1, WhAmP*
Cummings, Amos Jay 1842-1902 *ApCAB*
Cummings, Andrew Boyd 1830-1863 *ApCAB*
Cummings, Anna S 1860- *WomWWA 14*
Cummings, Anson Watson 1815-1894 *TwCBDA*
Cummings, Arthur Hibbard 1896-1956 *NatCAB 48*
Cummings, Asa 1790-1856 *Drake*
Cummings, Asa 1791-1856 *ApCAB*
Cummings, Bertrude Fields 1901-1963 *WhAm 4*
Cummings, Byron 1860-1954 *NatCAB 44*
Cummings, Charles *NewYHSD*
Cummings, Charles Amos 1833-1905 *DcAmB,* *NatCAB 20, WhAm 1*
Cummings, Charles Sumner 1856-1931 *NatCAB 24*
Cummings, Clara Eaton 1855-1906 *WhAm 1*
Cummings, Cornelius Theodore 1913-1967 *NatCAB 54*
Cummings, D Mark 1866-1932 *WhAm 1*
Cummings, Ebenezer Edson 1800-1886 *ApCAB*
Cummings, Edward 1861-1926 *ApCAB X,* *DcAmB, WhAm 1*
Cummings, Edward Estlin 1894-1962 *EncAB,* *McGEWB, WebAB, WhAm 4*
Cummings, Edward Josiah 1857-1928 *NatCAB 23*
Cummings, Emily *WomWWA 14*

Cummings, Fred Nelson 1864-1952 *BiDrAC*
Cummings, George Bain 1890-1974 *WhAm 6*
Cummings, George Donald 1904-1967 *WhAm 4*
Cummings, George W d1904 *WhAm 1*
Cummings, Gordon Parker *WhAm H*
Cummings, Harold Neff 1884-1962 *WhAm 4*
Cummings, Harry Sythe 1866- *TwCBDA,* *WhoColR*
Cummings, Henry 1739-1823 *Drake*
Cummings, Henry Johnson Brodhead 1831-1909 *BiDrAC, WhAm HA, WhAm 4*
Cummings, Herbert Wesley 1873-1956 *BiDrAC*
Cummings, Homer Stille 1870-1956 *BiDrUSE,* *WhAm 3*
Cummings, Horace Stuart 1840- *NatCAB 12*
Cummings, Jacob A 1772-1820 *Drake*
Cummings, James Howell 1867-1928 *NatCAB 14, NatCAB 24, WhAm 1*
Cummings, Jeremiah W 1823-1866 *ApCAB*
Cummings, Jeremiah Williams 1814-1866 *WhAm H*
Cummings, Joe Brown 1913- *WhAm 3*
Cummings, John 1785-1867 *ApCAB, DcAmB,* *WhAm H*
Cummings, John 1812-1898 *TwCBDA*
Cummings, John 1868-1936 *WhAm 1*
Cummings, Joseph 1817-1890 *AmBi, ApCAB,* *BiDAmEd, DcAmB, Drake, NatCAB 9,* *TwCBDA, WhAm H*
Cummings, Lucretia Stow Cummings *WomWWA 14*
Cummings, Mabel Homer 1872- *WomWWA 14*
Cummings, Marshall Baxter 1875- *WhAm 5*
Cummings, Marvin Earl 1876- *WhAm 5*
Cummings, Mary Augusta Marston 1855- *BiCAW, WomWWA 14*
Cummings, Michael Penn 1887-1958 *NatCAB 47*
Cummings, Moses 1816?-1867 *ApCAB*
Cummings, O Sam 1893-1964 *WhAm 4*
Cummings, Porter Emerson 1839-1918 *NatCAB 19*
Cummings, Ray 1887-1957 *NatCAB 43*
Cummings, Richard Osborn 1908- *EncAAH*
Cummings, Robert Augustus 1866-1962 *NatCAB 50*
Cummings, Thomas Augustus 1823-1859 *NewYHSD*
Cummings, Thomas James David 1867- *WhoColR*
Cummings, Thomas Seir 1804-1894 *AmBi,* *ApCAB, BnEnAmA, DcAmB, NatCAB 6,* *NewYHSD, TwCBDA, WhAm H*
Cummings, Walter J 1879-1967 *WhAm 4A*
Cummings, Wilbur Love 1881-1941 *NatCAB 36,* *WhAm 1*
Cummings, William Irving 1869-1946 *NatCAB 33*
Cummins, Albert Baird 1850-1926 *AmBi,* *ApCAB X, BiDrAC, DcAmB, EncAAH,* *NatCAB 13, NatCAB 31, WebAB,* *WhAm 1*
Cummins, Albert Wilson 1867-1935 *WhAm 1*
Cummins, Albert Wilson 1869-1935 *NatCAB 25*
Cummins, Alexander *WhAm H*
Cummins, Alexander Griswold 1869-1946 *NatCAB 35, WhAm 2*
Cummins, Alva Marvin 1869-1946 *NatCAB 36*
Cummins, Charles Albert 1882-1955 *NatCAB 56*
Cummins, Claude 1872-1960 *WhAm 4,* *WhAm 5*
Cummins, Clessie Lyle 1888-1968 *WhAm 5*
Cummins, Ebenezer Harlow 1790?-1835 *ApCAB,* *Drake*
Cummins, Francis 1732-1832 *ApCAB*
Cummins, Francis 1752-1832 *Drake*
Cummins, G Wyckoff 1865-1942 *NatCAB 32*
Cummins, George David 1822-1876 *ApCAB,* *DcAmB, NatCAB 7, TwCBDA,* *WhAm H*
Cummins, John 1838-1916 *BiAUS, WhAm 1*
Cummins, John Bigelow 1858-1958 *NatCAB 48*
Cummins, John D d1848 *BiAUS*
Cummins, John D 1791-1849 *BiDrAC,* *WhAm H*
Cummins, Joseph Michael 1881-1959 *WhAm 3*
Cummins, Maria S 1827-1866 *Drake*

Cummins, Maria Susan 1828-1866 *TwCBDA*
Cummins, Maria Susanna 1827-1866 *AmBi,
   ApCAB, DcAmB, NatCAB 6, NotAW,
   WhAm H*
Cummins, Mary Stuart 1854- *AmWom*
Cummins, Ralph 1887-1965 *WhAm 4*
Cummins, Robert James 1881-1960 *NatCAB 48*
Cummins, Robert Rankin 1884-1952 *WhAm 3*
Cummins, William Fletcher 1840- *WhAm 4*
Cummins, William J 1861-1936 *WhAm 1*
Cummins, William Taylor 1879-1953 *WhAm 3,
   WhAm 6*
Cumnock, Arthur James 1868-1930 *NatCAB 42*
Cumnock, Robert McLean 1840-1929 *WhAm 1*
Cumston, Charles McLaughlin 1824- *TwCBDA*
Cunard, Sir Edward 1816-1869 *ApCAB*
Cunard, Sir Samuel 1787-1865 *ApCAB*
Cundari, Dominic Anthony 1911-1962
   NatCAB 50
Cuneo, Cyrus Cincinnati 1878-1916 *IIBEAAW*
Cuneo, Rinaldo 1877-1939 *IIBEAAW*
Cunequeo d1612? *ApCAB*
Cuney, Joseph *WhoColR*
Cunha, Euclides Rodrigues Pimenta Da
   1866-1909 *McGEWB*
Cunha, Felix 1896-1960 *WhAm 4*
Cunha, Jose Anastacio Da 1744-1787
   DcScB Sup
Cunha Barbosa, Januario Da 1780-1846 *ApCAB,
   Drake*
Cunha DeAzevedo Coutinho, Jose J Da 1743-1821
   ApCAB
Cunha Mattos, Raimundo Jose Da 1776-1840
   ApCAB
Cunha Mattos, Raymunde Jose Da 1776-1840
   Drake
Cuninggim, Jesse Lee 1870-1950 *WhAm 3*
Cuningham, Alan 1864-1924 *NatCAB 6*
Cunliffe, John William 1865-1946 *WhAm 2*
Cunliffe-Owen, Frederick 1855-1926 *WhAm 1*
Cunliffe-Owen, Sir Hugo d1947 *WhAm 2*
Cunliffe-Owen, Philip Frederick 1855-1926
   DcAmB
Cunniff, Michael Glen 1875-1914 *WhAm 1*
Cunning, Edith May Klett *WomWWA 14*
Cunning, Kate Disher 1858- *WomWWA 14*
Cunningham, Mrs. *NewYHSD*
Cunningham, Sir Alan 1887- *WhWW-II,
   WhoMilH*
Cunningham, Albert Benjamin 1888-1962
   WhAm 4
Cunningham, Andrew Chase 1858-1917
   WhAm 1
Cunningham, Andrew Oswald 1866- *WhAm 1*
Cunningham, Ann Pamela 1816-1875 *DcAmB,
   NotAW, WhAm H*
Cunningham, Anna *WomWWA 14*
Cunningham, Annie Sinclair 1832- *AmWom*
Cunningham, Anthony W *NewYHSD*
Cunningham, Arthur 1865- *TwCBDA*
Cunningham, Augustine Joseph 1878-1957
   WhAm 3
Cunningham, Benjamin B 1874-1946 *WhAm 2*
Cunningham, Benjamin Frazier 1869- *WhAm 5*
Cunningham, Bert 1883-1943 *NatCAB 34,
   WhAm 2*
Cunningham, Briggs Swift 1839-1912
   NatCAB 27
Cunningham, Burris Bell 1912-1971 *NatCAB 57,
   WhAm 5*
Cunningham, C Frederick 1889- *WhAm 5*
Cunningham, Charles Barnard 1906-1972
   WhAm 6
Cunningham, Charles Henry 1885- *WhAm 2*
Cunningham, Cornelius Carman 1890-1958
   WhAm 3
Cunningham, David West 1829-1916 *WhAm 1*
Cunningham, Donnell LaFayette 1866-
   WhAm 2
Cunningham, Edward 1878-1960 *NatCAB 48*
Cunningham, Edward Henry 1869-1930
   WhAm 1
Cunningham, Edwin Shaddan 1868-1953
   WhAm 3
Cunningham, Edwin W 1901- *WhAm 4*
Cunningham, Edwin Wilbur 1842- *NatCAB 12*
Cunningham, Eileen Roach 1894-1965 *DcAmLiB*

Cunningham, Elijah William 1896-1960
   WhAm 4
Cunningham, Eric Alton 1898-1959 *NatCAB 50*
Cunningham, Eugene 1896-1957 *WhAm 3*
Cunningham, Firman *WhAm 6*
Cunningham, Francis Alanson 1804-1864 *BiAUS,
   BiDrAC, WhAm H*
Cunningham, Frank 1912-1965 *WhAm 4*
Cunningham, Frank Harrison 1911-1972
   WhAm 5
Cunningham, Frank Simpson 1866-1941
   NatCAB 30, WhAm 1
Cunningham, Gene Samuel 1887-1958
   NatCAB 46
Cunningham, George 1863-1924 *NatCAB 22*
Cunningham, George A 1855- *WhAm 4*
Cunningham, George Albert 1891-1943
   NatCAB 35
Cunningham, George William 1898-1958
   WhAm 3
Cunningham, Georgia Lee *WomWWA 14*
Cunningham, Glenn Clarence 1912- *BiDrAC*
Cunningham, Glenn Eugene 1888-1947
   NatCAB 52
Cunningham, Gustavus Watts 1881- *WhAm 6*
Cunningham, Harrison Edward 1877- *WhAm 6*
Cunningham, Harry A 1891-1964 *WhAm 4*
Cunningham, Helen M Benedict *WomWWA 14*
Cunningham, Henry Vincent 1865-1930
   WhAm 1
Cunningham, Holly Estil 1883-1952 *WhAm 3*
Cunningham, Horace Herndon 1913-1969
   WhAm 5
Cunningham, Howard 1900-1965 *NatCAB 54*
Cunningham, I A 1895- *WhAm 1*
Cunningham, Ida Cary 1853- *WomWWA 14*
Cunningham, Imogen 1883- *BnEnAmA*
Cunningham, Isaac Summerville 1877-
   WhoColR
Cunningham, J Harry 1865-1946 *NatCAB 35*
Cunningham, James 1815-1886 *NatCAB 12*
Cunningham, James A 1903-1961 *WhAm 4*
Cunningham, James Dalton 1887-1963 *WhAm 4*
Cunningham, John 1917- *WhWW-II*
Cunningham, John Charles 1910-1971
   NatCAB 57, WhAm 5
Cunningham, John Daniel 1840- *NatCAB 1*
Cunningham, John Ferguson 1877-1953
   WhAm 3
Cunningham, John Francis 1842- *NatCAB 13,
   NatCAB 15*
Cunningham, John Henry 1877- *WhAm 5*
Cunningham, John Lovell 1840- *WhAm 4*
Cunningham, Joseph Oscar 1830-1917 *WhAm 1*
Cunningham, Julian W 1893-1972 *WhAm 5*
Cunningham, Kate Richards O'Hare 1877-1948
   DcAmB S4, NotAW
Cunningham, Louis Wyborn 1863-1939
   WhAm 1
Cunningham, Mary Ann 1841- *WomWWA 14*
Cunningham, Merce 1919- *McGEWB*
Cunningham, Milton Joseph 1842-1916
   NatCAB 11, WhAm 1
Cunningham, Paul 1890-1960 *WhAm 4*
Cunningham, Paul Davis 1869-1901 *WhAm 1*
Cunningham, Paul Harvey 1890-1961 *BiDrAC,
   NatCAB 51, WhAmP*
Cunningham, Richard Hoope 1865-1937
   WhAm 1
Cunningham, Robert 1739?-1813 *ApCAB,
   Drake*
Cunningham, Robert Sydney 1891-1963
   WhAm 4
Cunningham, Ross MacDuffee 1907-1963
   WhAm 4
Cunningham, Russell McWhorter 1855-1922
   WhAm 1
Cunningham, Ruth Marion 1906-1956
   NatCAB 45
Cunningham, Samuel Robert 1872-1936
   NatCAB 30
Cunningham, Solomon M 1868- *WhAm 4*
Cunningham, Sumner Archibald 1843-1913
   WhAm 1
Cunningham, Susan Jane 1842-1921 *AmWom,
   NatCAB 6*
Cunningham, Thomas Francis 1864-1937
   NatCAB 30, WhAm 1

Cunningham, Thomas Mayhew 1869- *WhAm 5*
Cunningham, Thomas Oliver 1861-1939
   NatCAB 29
Cunningham, Wallace McCook 1881- *WhAm 6*
Cunningham, Walton 1883-1966 *NatCAB 52*
Cunningham, Warren W 1885-1953 *WhAm 3*
Cunningham, Wilfred Harris 1871- *WhAm 5*
Cunningham, William 1901-1967 *WhAm 4*
Cunningham, William Burgess 1883- *WhAm 2*
Cunningham, William Francis 1885-1961
   WhAm 4
Cunningham, William James 1875- *WhAm 5*
Cunningham, Zella May 1875- *WomWWA 14*
Cunninghan, Sir Andrew Browne 1883-1963
   WhWW-II, WhoMilH
Cunnyngham, Elizabeth Litchfield 1831-
   AmWom
Cunz, Dieter 1910-1969 *WhAm 5*
Cuppia, Jerome Chester 1890-1966 *WhAm 4*
Cupples, Samuel 1831-1912 *DcAmB,
   NatCAB 19, WhAm 1*
Cupples, Victor William 1863-1941 *NatCAB 31*
Cuppy, Hazlitt Alva 1863-1934 *WhAm 1,
   WhAm 1C*
Cuppy, William Jacob 1884-1949 *DcAmB S4,
   WhAm 2*
Cuprien, Frank W 1871-1948 *IIBEAAW*
Curam, George 1818?- *NewYHSD*
Curanteo 1726-1785 *ApCAB*
Cureton, Calvin Maples 1874-1940 *NatCAB 33,
   WhAm 2*
Cureton, Walter William 1875-1948
   NatCAB 36
Curie, Charles 1842- *NatCAB 5*
Curie, Marie Sklodowska 1867-1934 *AsBiEn,
   BiHiMed, DcScB, McGEWB*
Curie, Pierre 1859-1906 *AsBiEn, DcScB*
Curie, Robert James 1930-1974 *WhAm 6*
Curl, Gilbert Harold 1911-1968 *NatCAB 54*
Curl, Robert Floyd 1897-1971 *WhAm 5*
Curlee, Francis M 1877-1958 *WhAm 3*
Curless, Howard Marion 1903- *WhAm 6*
Curley, Daniel Joseph 1869-1932 *NatCAB 22,
   WhAm 1*
Curley, Edward Walter 1873-1940 *BiDrAC,
   WhAm 1*
Curley, Frank E 1877-1929 *WhAm 1*
Curley, James 1796-1889 *WhAm H*
Curley, James Michael 1874-1958 *BiDrAC,
   EncAB, McGEWB, WebAB, WhAm 3*
Curley, John Martin 1890-1969 *NatCAB 55*
Curley, Michael Joseph 1879-1947 *NatCAB 16,
   NatCAB 40, WhAm 2*
Curley, Walter J 1897-1970 *WhAm 5*
Curley, William A d1955 *WhAm 3*
Curling, Thomas Blizard 1811-1888 *BiHiMed*
Curme, George Oliver 1860-1948 *BiDAmEd,
   DcAmB S4, NatCAB 36, WhAm 2*
Curoe, Philip R V 1892-1969 *WhAm 5*
Curran, Charles Courtney 1861-1942 *ApCAB X,
   NatCAB 13, TwCBDA, WhAm 2*
Curran, Edward Lawrence 1879- *WhAm 6*
Curran, George Lally 1887-1938 *NatCAB 28*
Curran, Guernsey 1881-1950 *NatCAB 39*
Curran, Henry Hastings 1877-1966 *WhAm 4*
Curran, Ida M *AmWom*
Curran, James Augustus 1855-1930 *NatCAB 23*
Curran, John Emmett 1895-1956 *NatCAB 44*
Curran, John Harrison 1895-1962 *NatCAB 50*
Curran, John Joseph 1859-1936 *DcAmB S2*
Curran, John McCollum 1868-1935 *NatCAB 28*
Curran, Kenneth James 1903-1971 *NatCAB 56,
   WhAm 5*
Curran, Mary Katharine *NotAW*
Curran, Pearl Gildersleeve 1875-1941
   NatCAB 53
Curran, Peter Ferguson 1931-1974 *WhAm 6*
Curran, Robert Emmet 1889-1959 *NatCAB 49*
Curran, Thomas Jerome 1898-1958 *NatCAB 48,
   WhAm 3*
Curran, William Reid 1854- *WhAm 4*
Currell, William Spenser 1858-1943
   NatCAB 18, NatCAB 40, WhAm 2
Currey, Bradley Norton 1887-1967 *NatCAB 55*
Currey, Brownlee Own 1900-1952 *WhAm 3*
Currey, John 1814-1912 *NatCAB 12,
   WhAm 1*

Currey, Josiah Seymour 1844-1928 *WhAm 1*
Currick, Max Cohen 1877-1947 *WhAm 2*
Currie, Sir Arthur William 1875-1933
  McGEWB
Currie, Barton Wood 1877-1962 *WhAm 4*
Currie, Brainerd 1912-1965 *WhAm 4*
Currie, Carl Judson Barteaux 1898-1967
  NatCAB 53
Currie, Donald Herbert 1876-1918 *NatCAB 20,*
  WhAm 1
Currie, Edward James 1897-1967 *WhAm 4*
Currie, Emma Augusta 1829- *WomWWA 14*
Currie, George Graham 1867-1926 *WhAm 1*
Currie, Gilbert Archibald 1882-1960 *BiDrAC,*
  WhAm 4
Currie, James George 1827- *ApCAB*
Currie, John A *NewYHSD*
Currie, John S d1956 *WhAm 3*
Currie, Juan *NewYHSD*
Currie, Thomas White 1879-1943 *WhAm 2*
Currie, Wilbur Hoke 1896-1969 *NatCAB 55*
Currie, William *NewYHSD*
Currier, Albert Dean 1861-1931 *WhAm 1*
Currier, Albert Henry 1837- *TwCBDA,*
  WhAm 4
Currier, Amos Noyes 1832-1909 *NatCAB 20,*
  WhAm 1
Currier, Charles 1818-1887 *NewYHSD*
Currier, Charles Francis Adams 1862-1919
  WhAm 1
Currier, Charles Warren 1857-1918 *DcAmB,*
  WhAm 1
Currier, Edward Wilson 1857-1918 *IlBEAAW*
Currier, Enoch Henry 1849-1917 *BiDAmEd,*
  NatCAB 18
Currier, Frank Dunklee 1853-1921 *BiDrAC,*
  WhAm 1, WhAmP
Currier, George Harvey 1875- *WhAm 5*
Currier, J Frank 1843-1909 *WhAm 1*
Currier, John C 1842- *WhAm 4*
Currier, Moody 1806-1898 *DcAmB,*
  NatCAB 11, TwCBDA, WhAm H
Currier, Nathaniel 1813-1888 *AmBi,*
  BnEnAmA, DcAmB, EncAAH,
  McGEWB, NatCAB 21, NewYHSD,
  WebAB, WhAm H
Currier, Raymond Pillsbury 1891-1973
  WhAm 5
Currier, Richard Dudley 1877-1947 *NatCAB 38,*
  WhAm 2
Currier, Thomas Franklin 1873-1946 *WhAm 2*
Currier, Walter Barron 1879-1934 *IlBEAAW*
Currier And Ives *BnEnAmA, McGEWB*
Currin, David Maney 1817-1864 *BiDConf*
Curry, Adeline Jones Spencer *WomWWA 14*
Curry, Albert Bruce 1852-1939 *WhAm 1*
Curry, Allen 1871- *WhAm 5*
Curry, Arthur Mansfield 1866- *WhAm 4*
Curry, Charles Forrest 1858-1930 *BiDrAC,*
  WhAm 1, WhAmP
Curry, Charles Forrest, Jr. 1893- *BiDrAC*
Curry, Charles Madison 1869-1944 *WhAm 2*
Curry, Daniel 1809-1887 *ApCAB, Drake,*
  NatCAB 7, TwCBDA
Curry, David Alexander 1860-1917 *NatCAB 20*
Curry, Edward Rufus 1858- *WhAm 1*
Curry, Mrs. Edwin Rue *WomWWA 14*
Curry, George 1862-1948 *WhAm 2*
Curry, George 1863-1947 *BiDrAC, WhAmP*
Curry, George Law 1820-1878 *ApCAB, BiAUS,*
  DcAmB, NatCAB 8, TwCBDA,
  WhAm H, WhAmP
Curry, Grant 1884-1968 *NatCAB 54*
Curry, Henry Milo 1847-1900 *NatCAB 12,*
  NatCAB 24
Curry, Jabez L M 1825-1903 *BiAUS*
Curry, Jabez Lafayette Monroe 1825-1903
  Drake
Curry, Jabez Lamar Monroe 1815-1903
  McGEWB
Curry, Jabez Lamar Monroe 1825-1903 *AmBi,*
  ApCAB, BiDAmEd, BiDConf, BiDrAC,
  DcAmB, NatCAB 4, TwCBDA,
  WhAm 1, WhAmP
Curry, James Bernard 1856-1932 *WhAm 1*
Curry, James J d1962 *WhAm 4*
Curry, James Rowland 1903-1968 *WhAm 5*
Curry, John *NewYHSD*

Curry, John F 1873-1957 *WhAm 3*
Curry, John Francis 1886-1973 *WhAm 6*
Curry, John J *NewYHSD*
Curry, John Steuart 1897-1946 *BnEnAmA,*
  DcAmB S4, IlBEAAW, REnAW,
  WhAm 2
Curry, Louis Thomas 1888-1970 *NatCAB 56*
Curry, Michael John 1879-1954 *WhAm 3*
Curry, Nathaniel 1851- *NatCAB 17*
Curry, Neil James 1908-1965 *WhAm 4*
Curry, Otway 1804-1855 *ApCAB, NatCAB 8*
Curry, Peter H d1959 *WhAm 3*
Curry, R Granville 1890-1963 *WhAm 4*
Curry, Samuel Silas 1847-1921 *ApCAB X,*
  NatCAB 14, WhAm 1
Curry, Seaborn Jackson 1911-1970 *NatCAB 57*
Curry, Walker 1835-1902 *NatCAB 2*
Curry, William *NewYHSD*
Curry, William Melville 1867-1934 *WhAm 1,*
  WhAm 1C
Curtes, Henry 1831?- *NewYHSD*
Curti, Merle Eugene 1897- *BiDAmEd,*
  REnAW
Curtice, Harlow Herbert 1893-1962 *NatCAB 52,*
  WhAm 4
Curtin, Andrew Gregg 1815-1894 *AmBi,*
  ApCAB, DcAmB, McGEWB, TwCBDA,
  WhAm H
Curtin, Andrew Gregg 1817-1894 *BiAUS,*
  BiDrAC, Drake, NatCAB 2, NatCAB 24,
  WhAmP
Curtin, Austin 1896- *WhAm 4*
Curtin, Constans 1783-1842 *NatCAB 3*
Curtin, D Thomas 1886-1963 *WhAm 4*
Curtin, James Martin 1859-1924 *NatCAB 22*
Curtin, Jeremiah 1835?-1906 *ApCAB, DcAmB*
Curtin, Jeremiah 1838-1906 *TwCBDA*
Curtin, Jeremiah 1840-1906 *AmBi, WhAm 1*
Curtin, John Andrew 1870-1924 *NatCAB 23*
Curtin, John Joseph 1885-1945 *McGEWB,*
  WhWW-II
Curtin, Joseph Francis 1918-1973 *NatCAB 57*
Curtin, Roland Gideon 1839-1913 *NatCAB 3,*
  TwCBDA, WhAm 1
Curtin, Willard Sevier 1905- *BiDrAC, WhAmP*
Curtis, A J R 1887-1956 *WhAm 3*
Curtis, Alfred A 1833- *ApCAB*
Curtis, Alfred Allen 1831-1908 *DcAmB,*
  TwCBDA, WhAm 1
Curtis, Alfred Lee 1870-1953 *NatCAB 42*
Curtis, Alice Turner *WomWWA 14*
Curtis, Allen 1878-1936 *NatCAB 28*
Curtis, Alva 1797-1881 *ApCAB, Drake*
Curtis, Anna Louise 1882- *WomWWA 14*
Curtis, Anna Louise Anderson 1877-
  WomWWA 14
Curtis, Arthur Leo 1889- *WhoColR*
Curtis, Arthur Melvin 1886-1950 *WhAm 2A*
Curtis, Asahel 1874- *WhAm 5*
Curtis, Augustus Darwin 1865-1931
  NatCAB 23, WhAm 1
Curtis, Austin Maurice 1868- *WhoColR*
Curtis, Austin Maurice, Jr. 1890- *WhoColR*
Curtis, Austin Wingate 1872- *WhoColR*
Curtis, Benjamin B 1795?- *NewYHSD*
Curtis, Benjamin Robbins 1809-1874 *AmBi,*
  ApCAB, BiAUS, DcAmB, Drake,
  McGEWB, NatCAB 2, TwCBDA,
  WebAB, WhAm H
Curtis, Calvin 1822-1893 *ApCAB, NewYHSD*
Curtis, Carl Thomas 1905- *BiDrAC*
Curtis, Carlton Brandaga 1811-1883 *BiAUS,*
  BiDrAC, TwCBDA, WhAm H
Curtis, Carlton Clarence 1864-1945 *NatCAB 36,*
  WhAm 2
Curtis, Charles *NewYHSD*
Curtis, Charles 1860-1936 *AmBi, ApCAB X,*
  BiDrAC, BiDrUSE, DcAmB S2,
  NatCAB 14, NatCAB 47, TwCBDA,
  WebAB, WhAm 1, WhAmP
Curtis, Charles Albert 1835-1907 *NatCAB 18,*
  WhAm 1
Curtis, Charles Boyd 1827-1905 *WhAm 1*
Curtis, Charles Clarence 1893-1960 *WhAm 4*
Curtis, Charles Densmore 1875-1925
  NatCAB 19, WhAm 1
Curtis, Charles Gordon 1860-1953 *NatCAB 42,*
  WhAm 3

Curtis, Charles Henry 1812-1886 *NatCAB 16*
Curtis, Charles Minot 1859-1945 *WhAm 2*
Curtis, Charles Pelham 1860-1948 *WhAm 2*
Curtis, Charles Pelham 1891-1959 *WhAm 3*
Curtis, Charles Willis 1859-1953 *NatCAB 43*
Curtis, Clinton James 1870-1948 *NatCAB 37*
Curtis, Constance d1959 *WhAm 3,*
  WomWWA 14
Curtis, Cyrus Herman Kotzschmar 1850-1933
  EncAAH, NatCAB 13, WebAB
Curtis, Cyrus Hermann Kotzschmar 1850-1933
  AmBi, DcAmB S1, NatCAB 24, WhAm 1
Curtis, David A 1846-1923 *WhAm 1*
Curtis, DeWitt H 1839- *NatCAB 16*
Curtis, Earl A d1973 *WhAm 6*
Curtis, Edward 1801-1856 *BiAUS, BiDrAC,*
  WhAm H
Curtis, Edward 1838-1912 *ApCAB, NatCAB 9,*
  NatCAB 25, TwCBDA, WhAm 1
Curtis, Edward Clinton 1865-1920 *NatCAB 19*
Curtis, Edward Gilman 1886-1970 *WhAm 5*
Curtis, Edward Glion, Jr. 1909-1968 *WhAm 5*
Curtis, Edward Harvey 1843- *WhAm 4*
Curtis, Edward Lewis 1853-1911 *DcAmB,*
  TwCBDA
Curtis, Edward Sheriff 1868-1952 *DcAmB S5,*
  REnAW, WhAm 4
Curtis, Edward Upton 1861-1922 *WhAmP*
Curtis, Edwin Upton 1861-1922 *DcAmB,*
  WhAm 1
Curtis, Elizabeth *WomWWA 14*
Curtis, Elnora Whitman *WomWWA 14*
Curtis, Emma Ghent 1860- *WomWWA 14*
Curtis, Eugene Judson 1884-1951 *WhAm 3*
Curtis, Eugene Newton 1880-1944 *NatCAB 33,*
  WhAm 2
Curtis, F Kingsbury 1863-1936 *NatCAB 39,*
  WhAm 1
Curtis, Fayette Samuel 1843-1929 *NatCAB 23*
Curtis, Florence Rising 1873-1944 *DcAmLiB,*
  WhAm 2
Curtis, Frances Kellogg Small 1871- *BiCAW,*
  WomWWA 14
Curtis, Francis 1858- *WhAm 4*
Curtis, Francis Joseph 1894-1960 *WhAm 4*
Curtis, Frank George 1878-1922 *NatCAB 19*
Curtis, Frank Lionel 1856-1934 *NatCAB 25*
Curtis, Frederic Colton 1843- *NatCAB 2,*
  WhAm 4
Curtis, Frederick Smillie 1850-1930 *NatCAB 21,*
  WhAm 1
Curtis, George 1793?-1856 *NatCAB 2*
Curtis, George 1796-1856 *DcAmB, WhAm H*
Curtis, George 1826-1881 *NewYHSD*
Curtis, George Carroll 1872- *WhAm 1*
Curtis, George Lenox 1854- *WhAm 4*
Curtis, George Lewis 1878-1956 *WhAm 3*
Curtis, George Martin 1844-1921 *BiDrAC,*
  NatCAB 19, TwCBDA, WhAm 1
Curtis, George Martin, II 1905-1972 *WhAm 5*
Curtis, George Milton 1843-1915 *WhAm 1*
Curtis, George Morris 1890-1965 *WhAm 4*
Curtis, George Munson 1857-1915 *WhAm 1*
Curtis, George Ticknor 1812-1894 *AmBi,*
  ApCAB, DcAmB, Drake, NatCAB 1,
  TwCBDA, WebAB, WhAm H
Curtis, George William 1824-1892 *AmBi,*
  ApCAB, DcAmB, Drake, EncAB,
  McGEWB, NatCAB 3, TwCBDA,
  WebAB, WhAm H, WhAmP
Curtis, Georgina Pell 1859-1922 *WhAm 1,*
  WomWWA 14
Curtis, Gerald Beckwith 1882-1956 *WhAm 3*
Curtis, Greely Stevenson 1830-1897 *TwCBDA*
Curtis, Harry Alfred 1884-1963 *NatCAB 50,*
  WhAm 4
Curtis, Harry Lester 1896-1954 *NatCAB 44*
Curtis, Harvey 1806-1862 *ApCAB,*
  NatCAB 21, TwCBDA
Curtis, Harvey Lincoln 1875-1956 *WhAm 3*
Curtis, Heber Doust 1872-1942 *DcAmB S3,*
  DcScB, WhAm 1
Curtis, Heber Wooding 1880-1964 *NatCAB 50*
Curtis, Henry G 1839-1901 *WhAm 1*
Curtis, Henry Holbrook 1856-1920 *ApCAB X,*
  NatCAB 14, WhAm 1
Curtis, Henry Stoddard 1870-1954 *ApCAB X,*
  WhAm 3

Curtis, Horatio Greenough 1844-1922
NatCAB 29
Curtis, Howard James 1906-1972 *WhAm 5*
Curtis, Howard Junior 1857-1931 *WhAm 1*
Curtis, Ida Maynard *WomWWA 14*
Curtis, Isabel Gordon 1863-1915 *WhAm 1,*
WomWWA 14
Curtis, James Breckenridge 1859-1922
NatCAB 25
Curtis, James Breckenridge 1865- *NatCAB 16*
Curtis, James Freeman 1878-1952 *WhAm 3*
Curtis, James Langdon 1816- *ApCAB Sup*
Curtis, Jesse William 1865-1960 *NatCAB 50,*
WhAm 5
Curtis, John Birdseye 1871-1951 *NatCAB 47*
Curtis, John Green 1844-1913 *ApCAB,*
DcAmB, TwCBDA, WhAm 1
Curtis, John Jay 1857-1931 *WhAm 1*
Curtis, John Talbot 1900-1958 *NatCAB 43,*
WhAm 3
Curtis, John Thomas 1913-1961 *WhAm 4*
Curtis, John William 1879-1959 *NatCAB 44*
Curtis, Joseph Bridgham 1836-1862 *ApCAB,*
NatCAB 8, TwCBDA
Curtis, Josiah 1816-1883 *ApCAB, TwCBDA*
Curtis, Laura Elizabeth 1859- *WomWWA 14*
Curtis, Laurence 1893- *BiDrAC, WhAmP*
Curtis, Leland 1897- *IIBEAAW*
Curtis, Leonard Eager 1848-1923 *NatCAB 5,*
NatCAB 20
Curtis, Lester 1842-1930 *NatCAB 24*
Curtis, Loris Eugene 1904-1968 *NatCAB 54*
Curtis, Louis 1849-1931 *NatCAB 33*
Curtis, Mabel Gair 1866- *WomWWA 14*
Curtis, Martha E Sewall 1858- *AmWom*
Curtis, Mattoon Monroe 1858- *NatCAB 12,*
WhAm 4
Curtis, Melville Goss 1875-1950 *WhAm 3*
Curtis, Moses Ashley 1808-1872 *DcAmB,*
NatCAB 5, WhAm H
Curtis, Nannie Webb 1861- *WomWWA 14*
Curtis, Natalie 1875-1921 *NotAW,*
WomWWA 14
Curtis, Nathaniel Cortlandt 1881- *WhAm 6*
Curtis, Newton Martin 1835-1910 *ApCAB,*
BiDrAC, DcAmB, NatCAB 4, TwCBDA,
WhAm 1
Curtis, Oakley Chester 1865-1924 *NatCAB 22,*
WhAm 1
Curtis, Olin Alfred 1850-1918 *DcAmB,*
WhAm 1
Curtis, Otis Freeman 1888-1949 *WhAm 2*
Curtis, Philip Campbell 1907- *IIBEAAW*
Curtis, Raymond 1891-1971 *NatCAB 57*
Curtis, Richard Cary 1894-1951 *NatCAB 40,*
WhAm 3
Curtis, Robert J 1816?- *NewYHSD*
Curtis, Roy Emerson 1886-1960 *WhAm 4*
Curtis, Samuel Ryan 1805-1866 *BiDrAC,*
DcAmB, WebAMB, WhAm H
Curtis, Samuel Ryan 1807-1866 *ApCAB,*
BiAUS, Drake, NatCAB 4, TwCBDA
Curtis, Sumner 1868-1923 *WhAm 1*
Curtis, Thomas 1780?-1858 *ApCAB*
Curtis, Thomas Bradford 1911- *BiDrAC,*
WhAmP
Curtis, Thomas F 1815-1872 *ApCAB*
Curtis, Vivian Critz 1876- *WhAm 5*
Curtis, Wardon Allan 1867-1940 *WhAm 1*
Curtis, William Buckingham 1837-1900
WhAm 1
Curtis, William Edmond 1824-1880 *TwCBDA*
Curtis, William Edmond 1855-1923 *TwCBDA,*
WhAm 1
Curtis, William Edmund 1824-1880 *ApCAB*
Curtis, William Eleroy 1850-1911 *AmBi,*
ApCAB Sup, DcAmB, NatCAB 5,
TwCBDA, WhAm 1
Curtis, William Franklin 1873-1941 *WhAm 1*
Curtis, William Fuller 1873- *WhAm 5*
Curtis, William John 1854-1927 *WhAm 1*
Curtis, William Lewis 1848-1920 *NatCAB 23*
Curtis, William Rodolph 1908-1974 *WhAm 6*
Curtis, William Samuel 1850-1916 *WhAm 1*
Curtis, William Stanton 1815-1885 *NatCAB 21*
Curtis, William Stanton 1820-1885 *TwCBDA*
Curtis, Winterton Conway 1875- *WhAm 5*
Curtiss, Abby Allin 1820- *ApCAB, Drake*

Curtiss, Alice Bond *WomWWA 14*
Curtiss, Carl Henry 1872-1940 *NatCAB 34*
Curtiss, Charles Chauncey 1847-1928 *WhAm 1*
Curtiss, Charles Franklin 1863-1947 *WhAm 2*
Curtiss, Charles Romaine 1878-1957
NatCAB 46
Curtiss, David Raymond 1878-1953 *WhAm 3*
Curtiss, Elmer Lewis 1861-1943 *NatCAB 33*
Curtiss, Emma Frances Purington 1854-
WomWWA 14
Curtiss, George Boughton 1852-1920
NatCAB 18, WhAm 4
Curtiss, Glenn Hammond 1878-1930 *AmBi,*
ApCAB X, DcAmB S1, McGEWB,
NatCAB 15, NatCAB 22, WebAB,
WebAMB, WhAm 1
Curtiss, Julian Wheeler 1858-1944 *ApCAB X,*
NatCAB 33, WhAm 2
Curtiss, Lawrence Meredith 1903- *WhAm 5*
Curtiss, Lota Norton 1879- *WomWWA 14*
Curtiss, Philip 1885-1964 *WhAm 4*
Curtiss, Ralph Hamilton 1880-1929 *DcScB,*
NatCAB 21, WhAm 1
Curtiss, Richard Sydney 1864- *WhAm 4*
Curtiss, Samuel Ives 1844-1904 *AmBi, ApCAB,*
DcAmB, NatCAB 13, TwCBDA,
WhAm 1
Curtiss, William Hanford 1884-1960
NatCAB 49, WhAm 3
Curtiss, William John 1873-1947 *WhAm 3*
Curtius, Theodor 1857-1928 *DcScB*
Curtiz, Michael d1962 *WhAm 4*
Curtman, Louis Jacob 1878-1958 *NatCAB 43*
Curtright, Edward Eusebia 1873- *WhoColR*
Curtright, Felix Alonzo 1869- *WhoColR*
Curts, Jay Wilfred 1874-1930 *NatCAB 22*
Curts, Lewis 1847-1928 *WhAm 1*
Curts, Maurice Edwin 1898-1976 *WhAm 6*
Curts, Paul Holroyd 1884-1970 *NatCAB 55*
Curtze, E L W Maximilian 1837-1903 *DcScB*
Curtze, Frederick August 1894-1969
NatCAB 54
Curwen, John 1821-1901 *WhAm 1*
Curwen, Samuel 1715-1802 *ApCAB, DcAmB,*
Drake, NatCAB 8, WhAm H
Curwen, Samuel M d1932 *WhAm 1*
Curwood, James Oliver 1878-1927 *AmBi,*
ApCAB X, DcAmB, WhAm 1
Curwood, James Oliver 1879-1927 *NatCAB 21*
Curzon, George N Curzon, Marquess 1859-1925
McGEWB
Curzon, Mary Victoria Leiter 1870-1906
NotAW, WhAm 1
Cusa, Nicholas 1401?-1464 *DcScB*
Cusack, Mary Frances 1830- *ApCAB*
Cusack, Thomas 1858-1926 *BiDrAC*
Cusack, Thomas Francis 1862-1918 *NatCAB 15,*
WhAm 1
Cushard, William Green 1902-1965 *NatCAB 51*
Cushing, Abel 1785-1866 *NatCAB 18*
Cushing, Arthur Alden 1881-1955 *NatCAB 48*
Cushing, Caleb 1800-1879 *AmBi, ApCAB,*
BiAUS, BiDrAC, BiDrUSE, DcAmB,
Drake, NatCAB 4, TwCBDA, WebAB,
WhAm H, WhAmP
Cushing, Charles C S 1879-1941 *WhAm 1*
Cushing, Charles Phelps 1884-1973 *WhAm 6*
Cushing, Courtland *BiAUS, NatCAB 12*
Cushing, Daniel Francis 1879-1924 *NatCAB 6*
Cushing, Edmund Lambert 1807-1883
NatCAB 12, TwCBDA
Cushing, Edward Benjamin 1863-1924
NatCAB 21
Cushing, Edward Harvey 1898-1969 *WhAm 5*
Cushing, Eleanor Philbrook *WomWWA 14*
Cushing, Ernest Watson 1847-1916 *WhAm 1*
Cushing, Frank Hamilton 1857-1900 *AmBi,*
ApCAB, DcAmB, NatCAB 11, REnAW,
TwCBDA, WhAm 1
Cushing, George 1841-1920 *ApCAB X*
Cushing, George Holmes 1873- *WhAm 5*
Cushing, Grafton Dulany 1864-1939 *WhAm 1*
Cushing, Harry Alonzo 1870-1955 *WhAm 3*
Cushing, Harry Cooke 1895-1960 *WhAm 4*
Cushing, Harvey Williams 1869-1939 *AmBi,*
BiHiMed, DcAmB S2, DcScB, EncAB,
McGEWB, NatCAB 32, WebAB,
WhAm 1

Cushing, Henry Kirke 1827-1910 *NatCAB 25*
Cushing, Henry Platt 1860-1921 *NatCAB 19,*
WhAm 1
Cushing, Herbert Howard 1872-1926
NatCAB 20, WhAm 5
Cushing, Howard Gardiner 1869-1916
NatCAB 24, WhAm 1
Cushing, Howard Gardner 1869-1916 *IIBEAAW*
Cushing, John Eldridge 1887-1956 *NatCAB 46,*
WhAm 3
Cushing, John Pearsons 1861-1941 *WhAm 1*
Cushing, John Perkins 1787-1862 *DcAmB,*
WhAm H
Cushing, John Thayer 1887-1938 *NatCAB 28,*
WhAm 1
Cushing, Jonathan Peter 1793-1835 *ApCAB,*
Drake, NatCAB 2, TwCBDA
Cushing, Josiah Nelson 1840-1905 *DcAmB,*
NatCAB 12
Cushing, Juliet Clannon 1845-1934 *NatCAB 28*
Cushing, Luther Stearns 1803-1856 *AmBi,*
ApCAB, DcAmB, Drake, NatCAB 13,
TwCBDA, WhAm H
Cushing, Mary Gertrude 1870- *WomWWA 14*
Cushing, Nathan 1742-1812 *Drake*
Cushing, Nathaniel 1753-1814 *ApCAB, Drake*
Cushing, Nellie I Ferrell *WomWWA 14*
Cushing, Oscar K 1865-1948 *WhAm 2*
Cushing, Cardinal Richard James 1895-1970
DcAmReB, WhAm 5
Cushing, Samuel Dewey 1870-1933 *NatCAB 25*
Cushing, Samuel Tobey 1839-1901 *WhAm 1*
Cushing, Stephen S 1884-1957 *WhAm 3*
Cushing, Thomas 1725-1788 *ApCAB, BiAUS,*
BiDrAC, DcAmB, Drake, NatCAB 7,
TwCBDA, WhAm H, WhAmP
Cushing, Thomas Humphrey 1755-1822 *ApCAB,*
Drake, NatCAB 12
Cushing, Thomas Parkman 1787-1854 *ApCAB,*
Drake
Cushing, W T *NewYHSD*
Cushing, William 1732-1810 *AmBi, ApCAB,*
DcAmB, Drake, NatCAB 12, TwCBDA,
WebAB, WhAm H
Cushing, William 1733-1810 *BiAUS*
Cushing, William 1811-1895 *ApCAB Sup*
Cushing, William Barker 1842-1874 *AmBi,*
ApCAB, DcAmB, Drake, NatCAB 9,
TwCBDA, WebAB, WebAMB, WhAm H
Cushing, William Channing 1863-1940
NatCAB 29
Cushing, William Erastus 1853-1917 *WhAm 1*
Cushing, William Lee 1849-1921 *WhAm 1*
Cushman, Allerton Seward 1867-1930 *AmBi,*
NatCAB 26, WhAm 1
Cushman, Alonzo C *NewYHSD*
Cushman, Andrew Bernard 1856-1940
NatCAB 31
Cushman, Arlon Vannevar 1869-1950 *WhAm 3*
Cushman, Austin Sprague 1827-1907 *WhAm 1*
Cushman, Beulah 1890-1964 *WhAm 4*
Cushman, Burritt Alvin 1865-1945 *NatCAB 35*
Cushman, Charlotte Saunders 1816- *Drake*
Cushman, Charlotte Saunders 1816-1875 *AmBi*
Cushman, Charlotte Saunders 1816-1876
AmWom, ApCAB, DcAmB, McGEWB,
NatCAB 4, NotAW, TwCBDA, WebAB,
WhAm H
Cushman, Daniel Burr 1852-1927 *NatCAB 20*
Cushman, Edward Everett 1865-1944
NatCAB 35, WhAm 4
Cushman, Elisha 1788-1838 *ApCAB*
Cushman, Ella R Wylie *WomWWA 14*
Cushman, Elton Gray 1879-1946 *NatCAB 35*
Cushman, Everett Morton 1876-1948
NatCAB 37
Cushman, Francis Wellington 1867-1909
BiDrAC, WhAm 1, WhAmP
Cushman, Frank 1879-1953 *BiDAmEd,*
WhAm 3
Cushman, Frank Holmes 1891-1946 *NatCAB 41*
Cushman, George Hewitt 1814-1876 *DcAmB,*
NewYHSD, WhAm H
Cushman, Henry Otis 1865-1956 *NatCAB 45*
Cushman, Henry W 1868-1959 *WhAm 4*
Cushman, Henry Wyles 1805-1863 *Drake,*
NatCAB 10
Cushman, Herbert Ernest 1865- *WhAm 4*

Cushman, Horace O 1893-1972 *WhAm 5*
Cushman, Horatio Benzil 1831-1918 *ApCAB X*
Cushman, James Stewart 1871-1952 *ApCAB X,*
NatCAB 47
Cushman, Jessie Rathbun Manley 1870-
WomWWA 14
Cushman, John Franklin d1862 *BiAUS,*
NatCAB 5
Cushman, John Henry 1877-1963 *NatCAB 51*
Cushman, John Paine 1784-1848 *BiAUS,*
BiDrAC, TwCBDA, WhAm H
Cushman, Joseph Augustine 1881-1949
DcAmB S4, DcScB, NatCAB 37,
WhAm 2
Cushman, Joshua d1834 *BiAUS, WhAm H*
Cushman, Joshua 1758?-1834 *TwCBDA*
Cushman, Joshua 1761-1834 *BiDrAC, DcAmB*
Cushman, Lewis Arthur 1898-1963 *WhAm 4*
Cushman, Lucy D C 1861- *WomWWA 14*
Cushman, Pauline d1893 *TwCBDA*
Cushman, Pauline 1833-1893 *ApCAB, DcAmB,*
NatCAB 23, WhAm H
Cushman, Pauline 1835-1893 *AmBi*
Cushman, Ralph Spaulding 1879-1960
NatCAB 50, WhAm 4
Cushman, Robert 1579-1625 *DcAmB,*
WhAm H
Cushman, Robert 1580?-1625 *ApCAB, Drake,*
TwCBDA
Cushman, Robert Eugene 1889-1969
NatCAB 54, WhAm 5
Cushman, Robert Everton, Jr. 1914- *WebAMB*
Cushman, Rufus Packard 1857-1921
NatCAB 30
Cushman, Samuel 1783-1851 *BiAUS, BiDrAC,*
TwCBDA, WhAm H
Cushman, Susan Webb 1822-1859 *ApCAB,*
DcAmB, NatCAB 23, WhAm H
Cushman, Thomas 1608-1692 *ApCAB,*
TwCBDA
Cushman, Thomas Hastings 1815-1841
NewYHSD
Cushman, Vera Charlotte Scott 1876-1946
DcAmB S4, NotAW
Cushman, Victor Nilsson 1872-1933
NatCAB 27
Cushman, William Carroll Hall 1880-1950
NatCAB 41
Cushman, William Michael 1899-1964 *WhAm 4*
Cushny, Arthur Robertson 1866-1926 *DcAmB,*
DcScB, DcScB Sup
Cushwa, Charles B, Jr. 1909-1975 *WhAm 6*
Cushway, Charles Benton 1873-1951 *NatCAB 45*
Cushway, Bertram Charles 1873-1960
NatCAB 48
Cusick, David *ApCAB*
Cusick, James Francis 1898-1975 *WhAm 6*
Cusick, Nicholas 1756-1840 *ApCAB*
Custer, Edward L 1837-1881 *NewYHSD*
Custer, Elizabeth Bacon d1933 *AmWom,*
ApCAB
Custer, Elizabeth Bacon 1843-1933 *AmBi*
Custer, Elizabeth Bacon 1844?-1933 *WhAm 1*
Custer, George Armstrong 1839-1876 *AmBi,*
ApCAB, DcAmB, Drake, EncAAH,
EncAB, McGEWB, NatCAB 4, REnAW,
TwCBDA, WebAB, WebAMB, WhAm H,
WhoMilH
Custer, Omer N 1873-1942 *WhAm 2*
Custer, Thomas Ward 1845-1876 *ApCAB,*
TwCBDA
Custine, Adam Philip, Count De 1740-1793
Drake
Custine, Adam Philippe 1740-1793 *ApCAB*
Custine DeSarreck, Adam P, Comte De
1742-1793 *WhoMilH*
Custis, Edward Lewis 1853-1911 *WhAm 1*
Custis, Eleanor Parke 1779-1852 *NewYHSD*
Custis, George Washington Parke 1781-1857
AmBi, ApCAB, DcAmB, Drake,
NatCAB 7, TwCBDA, WhAm H
Custis, John Trevor 1875-1944 *WhAm 2*
Custis, Marvin A 1866-1956 *WhAm 3*
Custis, Vanderveer 1878-1961 *WhAm 4*
Cusumano, Stefano 1912-1975 *WhAm 6*
Cutbush, Edward *NewYHSD*
Cutbush, Edward 1772-1843 *NatCAB 18*
Cutbush, James 1788-1823 *ApCAB, DcAmB,*

Drake, *WhAm H*
Cutbush, Samuel *NewYHSD*
Cutcheon, Byron M 1836-1908 *BiDrAC,*
TwCBDA, WhAm 1, WhAmP
Cutcheon, Franklin Warner M 1864-1936
NatCAB 31, WhAm 1
Cuthbert, Alfred d1856 *BiAUS*
Cuthbert, Alfred 1780-1856 *TwCBDA*
Cuthbert, Alfred 1781?-1856 *ApCAB,*
NatCAB 11
Cuthbert, Alfred 1785-1856 *BiDrAC,*
WhAm H, WhAmP
Cuthbert, James Hazzard 1823- *ApCAB*
Cuthbert, John A 1778-1881 *BiAUS*
Cuthbert, John Alfred 1788-1881 *ApCAB,*
BiDrAC, TwCBDA, WhAm H
Cuthbert, Lucius Montrose 1856-1915 *WhAm 1*
Cuthell, Chester Welde 1884-1942 *NatCAB 31,*
WhAm 2
Cuthrell, Hugh Hamlin 1892-1953 *NatCAB 41,*
WhAm 3
Cutler, Anna Alice 1864-1957 *WhAm 3,*
WomWWA 14
Cutler, Arthur Hamilton 1849-1918 *WhAm 1*
Cutler, Augustus W 1829-1897 *BiAUS,*
NatCAB 7
Cutler, Augustus William 1827-1897 *BiDrAC,*
TwCBDA, WhAm H
Cutler, Benjamin Clarke 1798-1863 *ApCAB,*
Drake
Cutler, Bertram 1880-1952 *WhAm 3*
Cutler, Carroll 1829-1894 *DcAmB, NatCAB 7,*
TwCBDA, WhAm H
Cutler, Charles Frederic 1841-1907 *NatCAB 8,*
WhAm 1
Cutler, Condict Walker 1859-1930 *AmBi,*
NatCAB 22, TwCBDA, WhAm 1
Cutler, Condict Walker, Jr. 1888-1958 *WhAm 3*
Cutler, Elbridge Gerry 1846-1929 *WhAm 1*
Cutler, Elbridge Jefferson 1831-1870 *ApCAB,*
NatCAB 11, TwCBDA
Cutler, Elihu Herbert 1856-1936 *NatCAB 27*
Cutler, Elliott Carr 1888-1947 *BiDAmEd,*
DcAmB S4, NatCAB 36, WhAm 2
Cutler, Enos 1781-1860 *ApCAB, Drake*
Cutler, Ephraim 1767-1853 *ApCAB*
Cutler, Ephraim 1767-1853 *TwCBDA*
Cutler, Everett Alonzo 1873-1917 *WhAm 1*
Cutler, Frederic Farley 1866-1920 *ApCAB X*
Cutler, Frederick Morse 1874-1944 *WhAm 2*
Cutler, Garnet Homer 1882-1962 *WhAm 4*
Cutler, George Chalmers 1891-1956
NatCAB 45, WhAm 3
Cutler, George Younglove d1834 *NewYHSD*
Cutler, Hannah Maria Tracy 1815-1896 *ApCAB,*
NotAW, TwCBDA
Cutler, Harry Morton 1867-1930 *WhAm 1*
Cutler, Henry Edwin 1879-1959 *WhAm 3*
Cutler, Henry Franklin 1862-1945 *NatCAB 35,*
WhAm 4
Cutler, Henry Stephen 1824- *ApCAB*
Cutler, Ira Eugene 1863-1936 *WhAm 1*
Cutler, James Elbert 1876-1959 *NatCAB 45,*
WhAm 3
Cutler, James Goold 1848-1927 *DcAmB,*
WhAm 1
Cutler, James Gould 1848-1927 *WhAm HA,*
WhAm 4
Cutler, Jervis 1768-1844 *ApCAB, Drake,*
TwCBDA
Cutler, Jervis 1768-1846 *NewYHSD*
Cutler, John Christopher 1846-1928 *NatCAB 13,*
WhAm 1, WhAm 1C
Cutler, John W 1887-1950 *WhAm 3*
Cutler, Leland Whitman 1885-1959 *NatCAB 48*
Cutler, Lizzie Petit 1831-1902 *DcAmB,*
WhAm H
Cutler, Lizzie Petit 1836-1902 *ApCAB*
Cutler, Lysander 1806-1866 *ApCAB, Drake*
Cutler, Manasseh 1742-1823 *AmBi, ApCAB,*
BiAUS, BiDrAC, DcAmB, Drake,
McGEWB, NatCAB 3, TwCBDA,
WebAB, WhAm H
Cutler, Mary Goodnow 1874- *WomWWA 14*
Cutler, Mary Helen 1865- *WomWWA 14*
Cutler, Mary Salome *BiDAmEd, NotAW*
Cutler, Nathan 1775-1861 *NatCAB 6,*
TwCBDA

Cutler, Otis Henderson d1922 *WhAm 1*
Cutler, Ralph William 1853-1917 *WhAm 1*
Cutler, Robert 1895-1974 *WhAm 6*
Cutler, S Newton 1855- *NatCAB 15*
Cutler, Thomas Robinson 1844-1922
NatCAB 20
Cutler, Timothy 1683-1765 *ApCAB,*
NatCAB 1
Cutler, Timothy 1684-1765 *DcAmB,*
DcAmReB, Drake, TwCBDA, WhAm H
Cutler, Willard Walker 1856-1926 *NatCAB 28*
Cutler, William Frye 1888-1957 *WhAm 3*
Cutler, William P 1813-1889 *BiAUS*
Cutler, William Parker 1812-1889 *BiDrAC,*
TwCBDA, WhAm H
Cutright, Harold Glen 1900-1967 *WhAm 4*
Cutshall, H Walton, Jr. 1913-1963 *WhAm 4*
Cutt, Charles 1769-1846 *ApCAB*
Cutt, James Madison 1805-1863 *ApCAB*
Cutt, John 1625-1681 *ApCAB, Drake,*
TwCBDA
Cutt, Richard 1771-1845 *ApCAB*
Cutt, Richard Dominicus 1817-1883 *ApCAB*
Cutt, Thomas 1905-1965 *NatCAB 51*
Cutten, Arthur W d1936 *WhAm 1*
Cutten, George Barton 1874-1962 *WhAm 4*
Cutten, Ruloff Edward 1896-1961 *WhAm 4*
Cutter, Ammi Ruhamah 1705-1746 *TwCBDA*
Cutter, Ammi Ruhamah 1735-1819 *ApCAB,*
Drake
Cutter, Ammi Ruhamah 1735-1820 *TwCBDA*
Cutter, Anna Wheeler Alberger 1864-
WomWWA 14
Cutter, Benjamin 1857-1910 *WhAm 1*
Cutter, Calvin 1807-1872 *ApCAB, BiDAmEd,*
TwCBDA
Cutter, Charles Ammi 1837-1903 *AmBi,*
ApCAB, DcAmB, DcAmLiB, NatCAB 13,
TwCBDA, WhAm 1
Cutter, Donald C 1922- *REnAW*
Cutter, Ephraim 1832-1917 *DcAmB,*
NatCAB 3, NatCAB 27, WhAm 1
Cutter, Eunice Powers 1819-1893 *TwCBDA*
Cutter, Mrs. George Albert 1873- *WhAm 5*
Cutter, George F 1823?-1890 *NatCAB 8*
Cutter, George Francis 1819-1890 *TwCBDA*
Cutter, George Washington 1801-1865 *AmBi,*
ApCAB, DcAmB, Drake, NatCAB 22,
TwCBDA, WhAm H
Cutter, Irving Samuel 1875-1945 *NatCAB 34,*
WhAm 2
Cutter, John Ashburton 1863- *WhAm 4*
Cutter, John Hastings 1878-1958 *NatCAB 44*
Cutter, K K 1860-1939 *WhAm 1*
Cutter, Robert Kennedy 1898-1973 *WhAm 6*
Cutter, Victor Macomber 1881-1952
NatCAB 46, WhAm 3
Cutter, Victor Macomber, Jr. 1917-1962
WhAm 4
Cutter, William Dick 1878-1942 *WhAm 1*
Cutter, William Parker 1867- *WhAm 4*
Cutter, William Richard 1847- *TwCBDA*
Cutting, Alfred Leslie 1868-1926 *ApCAB X*
Cutting, Bronson Murray 1888-1935 *AmBi,*
BiDrAC, DcAmB S1, NatCAB 26,
WhAm 1, WhAmP
Cutting, Charles Sidney 1854-1936 *ApCAB X,*
NatCAB 26, WhAm 1
Cutting, Charles Suydam 1889-1972
NatCAB 57, WhAm 5
Cutting, Churchill Hunter 1842-1924 *WhAm 1*
Cutting, Elisabeth Brown 1871-1946 *WhAm 2*
Cutting, Elizabeth Brown 1871-1946
WomWWA 14
Cutting, Francis Brockholst 1804-1870 *BiDrAC,*
WhAm H
Cutting, Francis Brockholst 1805-1870 *ApCAB,*
BiAUS, Drake
Cutting, Fulton 1886-1967 *NatCAB 52*
Cutting, Helen McMahon 1894-1961
NatCAB 47
Cutting, Hiram Adolphus 1832-1892 *ApCAB,*
NatCAB 10, TwCBDA, WhAm H
Cutting, Hurlbut Barnes 1875-1950 *NatCAB 38*
Cutting, James Ambrose 1814-1867 *ApCAB,*
DcAmB, Drake, NatCAB 13, WhAm H
Cutting, John Tyler 1844-1911 *BiDrAC,*
TwCBDA

Cutting, Mary Stewart Doubleday 1851-1924
  WhAm 1, WomWWA 14
Cutting, May VanHorne 1867- *WomWWA 14*
Cutting, Olivia Murray 1855-1949 *NatCAB 38*
Cutting, Robert Fulton 1852-1934 *DcAmB S1,
  NatCAB 15, NatCAB 45, WhAm 1*
Cutting, Sewall Sylvester 1813-1882 *ApCAB,
  TwCBDA*
Cutting, Starr Willard 1858-1935 *TwCBDA,
  WhAm 1*
Cutting, W Bayard 1850-1912 *NatCAB 15,
  NatCAB 26, WhAm 1*
Cutting, William Bayard 1850-1912 *ApCAB X*
Cutting, Windsor Cooper 1907-1972 *WhAm 5*
Cuttle, Francis 1864- *WhAm 5*
Cutts, Charles 1769-1846 *BiAUS, BiDrAC,
  NatCAB 4, TwCBDA, WhAm H,
  WhAmP*
Cutts, Elmer Henry 1908-1960 *WhAm 4*
Cutts, Henry Eastman 1867-1946 *NatCAB 35*
Cutts, James Madison *BiAUS*
Cutts, John 1625-1681 *NatCAB 13*
Cutts, John 1794?- *NewYHSD*
Cutts, John, Jr. *NewYHSD*
Cutts, Love Pickman d1873 *NewYHSD*
Cutts, Maria 1811-1853 *ApCAB*
Cutts, Marsena Edgar 1833-1883 *BiDrAC,
  TwCBDA, WhAm H*
Cutts, Orillio *NewYHSD*
Cutts, Richard 1771-1845 *BiAUS, BiDrAC,
  Drake, TwCBDA, WhAm H, WhAmP*
Cutts, Richard Dominicus 1817-1883 *TwCBDA*
Cutts, Richard Malcolm 1903-1973 *WhAm 6*
Cutts, Wen Galaway *WhoColR*
Cuvier, Frederic 1773-1838 *DcScB*
Cuvier, Baron Georges Leopold 1769-1832
  AsBiEn, DcScB, McGEWB
Cuvillies, Francois 1695-1768 *McGEWB*
Cuyler, Sir Cornelius 1740?-1819 *ApCAB,
  Drake*
Cuyler, Cornelius 1783-1850 *ApCAB, Drake*
Cuyler, Cornelius Cuyler d1909 *WhAm 1*
Cuyler, Jeremiah d1839 *BiAUS*
Cuyler, John M 1810?-1884 *ApCAB*
Cuyler, Theodore 1819-1876 *DcAmB,
  NatCAB 17, WhAm H*
Cuyler, Theodore Ledyard 1822-1909 *ApCAB,
  DcAmB, NatCAB 5, TwCBDA,
  WhAm 1*
Cuyler, Thomas DeWitt 1854-1922 *ApCAB X,
  NatCAB 19, WhAm 1*
Cuyp, Aelbert 1620-1691 *McGEWB*
Cuypers, F H *NewYHSD*
Cuypers, Francis A *NewYHSD*
Cuzzort, Clyde Cecil 1899-1963 *NatCAB 53*
Cybis, Jan 1897-1972 *WhAm 6*
Cybulski, Waclaw Boleslaw 1901-1973 *WhAm 6*
Cyprian, Saint d258 *McGEWB*
Cyr, Louis Clement 1879-1947 *NatCAB 37*
Cyr, Paul Narcisse 1878-1946 *WhAm 2*
Cyriaque DeMangin, Clement *DcScB*
Cyril And Methodius, Saints *McGEWB*
Cyril Of Alexandria, Saint d444 *McGEWB*
Cyril, Saint 827-869 *McGEWB*
Cyrus The Great *McGEWB*
Cysat, Johann Baptist 1586?-1657 *DcScB*
Czapek, Emil 1891-1959 *NatCAB 51*
Czarnomska, Marie Elizabeth Josephine d1938
  WhAm 1, WomWWA 14
Czekanowski, Aleksander Piotr 1833-1876
  DcScB
Czermak, Johann Nepomuk 1828-1873 *DcScB*
Czernik, Stanislaw 1899-1969 *WhAm 6*
Czerski, Jan 1845-1892 *DcScB*
Czerwonky, Richard Rudolph 1886-1949
  WhAm 2

D

D'Abano, Pietro 1250?-1316? *AsBiEn*
Dabbs, Ellen Lawson 1853- *AmWom*
Dabich, George 1922- *IIBEAAW*
Dablon, Claude *Drake*
Dablon, Claude 1618?-1697 *WhAm H*
Dablon, Claude 1619?-1697 *DcAmB*
Dablon, Claude 1628-1700 *ApCAB*
Dabney, Archibald Douglas 1879-1955
 NatCAB 50
Dabney, Charles William 1794-1871 *ApCAB,*
 TwCBDA
Dabney, Charles William 1855-1945 *ApCAB,*
 ApCAB X, BiDAmEd, DcAmB S3,
 NatCAB 13, TwCBDA, WhAm 2
Dabney, Edith *WomWWA 14*
Dabney, Edwin 1876-1938 *WhAm 1*
Dabney, Francis Lewis 1907-1974 *WhAm 6*
Dabney, George Bigelow 1880-1939 *NatCAB 29*
Dabney, Julia Parker 1850- *TwCBDA,*
 WhAm 4, WomWWA 14
Dabney, Lewis Stackpole 1840-1908 *WhAm 1*
Dabney, Lillian Beatrice 1893- *WhoColR*
Dabney, Marye Yeamans 1884-1963
 NatCAB 50
Dabney, Richard 1787-1825 *ApCAB, DcAmB,*
 Drake, NatCAB 7, WhAm H
Dabney, Richard Heath 1860-1947 *NatCAB 13,*
 TwCBDA, WhAm 2
Dabney, Robert Lewis 1820-1898 *ApCAB,*
 BiDConf, DcAmB, DcAmReB,
 NatCAB 2, TwCBDA, WhAm H
Dabney, Samuel Gordon 1860-1935 *WhAm 2*
Dabney, Samuel Wyllys 1826-1893 *NatCAB 4,*
 TwCBDA
Dabney, Thomas Smith Gregory 1798-1885
 DcAmB, WhAm H
Dabney, Virginius 1835-1894 *ApCAB, DcAmB,*
 TwCBDA, WhAm H
Dabney, Wendell Phillips 1865- *WhoColR*
Dabney, William C d1963 *WhAm 4*
Dabney, William Henry 1817-1888 *TwCBDA*
Dabo, Leon 1868-1960 *WhAm 4*
Dabo, Theodore Scott 1877-1928 *WhAm 1*
Daboll, Celadon Leeds 1818-1866 *ApCAB*
Daboll, Charles Miner 1823- *ApCAB*
Daboll, David Austin 1813-1895 *ApCAB,*
 TwCBDA
Daboll, Nathan 1750-1818 *ApCAB, BiDAmEd,*
 DcAmB, Drake, NatCAB 23, TwCBDA,
 WhAm H
Daboll, Nathan 1780-1863 *TwCBDA*
Daboll, Nathan 1782-1863 *ApCAB*
Dabour, John 1837- *ApCAB*
Dabrowski, Joseph 1842-1903 *DcAmB,*
 WhAm H
Dacian, Jakob 1496-1562 *ApCAB*
DaCosta, Albert Lloyd 1928-1967 *WhAm 5*
DaCosta, Chalmers 1863-1933 *WhAm 1*
DaCosta, Jacob Mendez 1833-1900 *AmBi,*
 ApCAB, BiHiMed, DcAmB, NatCAB 9,
 TwCBDA, WhAm 1
DaCosta, John Chalmers 1863-1933 *DcAmB S1*
DaCosta, John Chalmers, Jr. 1871-1919
 WhAm 1
DaCosta, John Chalmers, Jr. 1871-1920
 NatCAB 18
Dacre, Henry 1820?- *NewYHSD*
Dacres, James Richard 1788-1853 *ApCAB,*
 Drake
Dacso, Michael Mihaly 1909-1975 *WhAm 6*
Dadant, Camille Pierre 1851-1938 *NatCAB 41,*
 WhAm 1
Dadd, George H 1813?- *ApCAB, Drake*
Daddario, Emilio Quincy 1918- *BiDrAC*

Daddow, Theodore R 1884-1952 *NatCAB 41*
Dade, Alexander Lucien 1863-1927 *WhAm 1*
Dade, Francis Langhorn d1835 *ApCAB*
Dade, Francis Langhorne 1793?-1835 *Drake,*
 NatCAB 12, WebAMB
Dadirrian, Markar Gevork 1839- *NatCAB 13*
Dadmun, Frances May 1875- *WhAm 5,*
 WomWWA 14
Dadourian, Haroutune Mugurdich 1878-1974
 WhAm 6
Daeger, Albert Thomas 1872-1932 *DcAmB S1,*
 WhAm 1
Daeger, Anthony Thomas 1872-1932
 NatCAB 25
Daffan, Katie *WomWWA 14*
Dafoe, Carmie R, Jr. 1920-1975 *WhAm 6*
Dafoe, John Wesley 1866-1944 *WhAm 2*
Daft, Leo 1843-1922 *DcAmB, WebAB,*
 WhAm HA, WhAm 4
DaGama, Vasco 1460?-1524 *WhAm H*
DaGama, Vasco *see also* Gama, Vasco Da
Dager, Forrest Eugene 1855-1936 *WhAm 1,*
 WhAm 1C
Dagg, John Leadley 1794-1881 *NatCAB 6*
Dagg, John Leadley 1794-1884 *ApCAB,*
 DcAmB, TwCBDA, WhAm H
Daggett, Aaron S 1839- *NatCAB 6*
Daggett, Aaron Simon 1837-1938 *NatCAB 28,*
 TwCBDA, WhAm 1
Daggett, Alfred 1799-1872 *NewYHSD*
Daggett, Athern Park 1904-1973 *WhAm 5*
Daggett, Charles Daniel 1851-1924 *NatCAB 33*
Daggett, David 1764-1851 *ApCAB, BiAUS,*
 BiDrAC, DcAmB, Drake, NatCAB 4,
 TwCBDA, WhAm H, WhAmP
Daggett, Ellsworth 1845-1923 *DcAmB,*
 WhAm 1
Daggett, Evelyn Eleanor Cutler *WomWWA 14*
Daggett, Frank Slater 1855-1920 *NatCAB 38*
Daggett, Griswold Templeton 1894-1941
 NatCAB 35
Daggett, Harriet Spiller 1891-1966 *WhAm 4*
Daggett, James Harry 1885-1965 *NatCAB 52*
Daggett, Jeannette 1852- *WomWWA 14*
Daggett, Leonard Mayhew 1863-1949 *WhAm 2*
Daggett, Mabel Potter d1927 *WhAm 1,*
 WomWWA 14
Daggett, Mary 1854-1922 *NatCAB 9*
Daggett, Mary Stewart 1856-1922 *WhAm 1,*
 WomWWA 14
Daggett, Naphtali 1727-1780 *ApCAB, DcAmB,*
 NatCAB 1, TwCBDA, WhAm H
Daggett, Napthali 1727-1780 *Drake*
Daggett, Oliver Ellsworth 1810-1880 *ApCAB,*
 NatCAB 4, TwCBDA
Daggett, Parker Hayward 1885-1964 *WhAm 4*
Daggett, Robert Frost 1875-1955 *WhAm 3*
Daggett, Rollin Mallory 1831-1901 *BiDrAC,*
 NatCAB 12, WhAmP
Daggett, Stuart 1881-1954 *NatCAB 44,*
 WhAm 3
Daggett, Volney Chapin 1859-1943 *ApCAB X,*
 NatCAB 35
Daggy, Maynard Lee 1874- *WhAm 5*
Dague, Paul Bartram 1898-1974 *BiDrAC,*
 WhAm 6, WhAmP
Daguerre, Louis Jacques Mande 1787-1851
 McGEWB
Daguerre, Louis Jacques Mande 1789-1851
 AsBiEn
Dagwell, Benjamin Dunlap 1890-1963 *WhAm 4*
Dahl, Francis W 1907-1973 *WhAm 5*
Dahl, George 1881-1962 *WhAm 4*
Dahl, Gerhard Melvin 1876-1953 *WhAm 3*

Dahl, J O 1893-1942 *NatCAB 32*
Dahl, Myrtle Hooper 1887-1952 *WhAm 3*
Dahl, Theodor Halvorson 1845-1923 *DcAmB*
Dahl, Theodore H 1845-1923 *WhAm 1*
Dahlberg, Arthur Chester 1896-1964
 NatCAB 51, WhAm 4
Dahlberg, Bror Gustave 1881-1954 *WhAm 3*
Dahle, Herman Bjorn 1855-1920 *BiDrAC,*
 NatCAB 18, WhAm HA, WhAm 3,
 WhAm 4
Dahlerup, Ioost Baron 1874-1944 *WhAm 2*
Dahlgreen, Charles W 1864-1955 *WhAm 3*
Dahlgren, B E d1961 *WhAm 4*
Dahlgren, Carl Christian 1841-1920 *IIBEAAW*
Dahlgren, Charles Bunker 1839- *NatCAB 9,*
 TwCBDA
Dahlgren, Charles Gustavus 1808-1888
 TwCBDA
Dahlgren, John A 1809-1870 *Drake*
Dahlgren, John Adolph 1809-1870 *ApCAB,*
 NatCAB 9, TwCBDA
Dahlgren, John Adolphus Bernard 1809-1870
 DcAmB, WebAB, WebAMB, WhAm H
Dahlgren, John Vinton 1868-1899 *NatCAB 9*
Dahlgren, Madeleine Vinton 1835?-1898
 AmWom, ApCAB, TwCBDA
Dahlgren, Marius 1844-1920 *IIBEAAW*
Dahlgren, Sarah Madeleine Vinton 1825-1898
 DcAmB, NatCAB 22, WhAm H
Dahlgren, Ulric 1842-1864 *ApCAB,*
 NatCAB 9, TwCBDA
Dahlgren, Ulric 1870-1946 *WhAm 2*
Dahlgren, Ulrich 1842-1864 *Drake*
Dahlman, James Charles 1856-1930 *WhAm 1*
Dahlquist, John E 1896-1975 *WhAm 6*
Dahlquist, Thomas Wilford 1893-1966 *WhAm 4*
Daicoviciu, Constantin 1898-1973 *WhAm 6*
Daigneau, Ralph H 1891-1955 *WhAm 3*
Daigo II 1288-1339 *McGEWB*
Dailey, Abram Hoagland 1831-1907 *NatCAB 9,*
 NatCAB 26
Dailey, Charlotte Field 1842- *AmWom*
Dailey, Francis Leo 1891-1964 *WhAm 4*
Dailey, Gibson Fuller 1910-1970 *NatCAB 55*
Dailey, Joseph Leonard 1896-1956 *NatCAB 45*
Dailey, Morris Elmer 1867-1919 *WhAm 1*
Dailey, William 1846-1919 *NatCAB 19*
Daille, Peter d1715 *Drake*
Daille, Pierre 1649-1715 *ApCAB*
Daily, Francis Leo 1891-1964 *NatCAB 51*
Daily, Joseph Earl 1888-1965 *WhAm 4*
Daily, Samuel G 1819-1865 *BiAUS, TwCBDA*
Daily, Samuel Gordon 1823-1866 *BiDrAC,*
 WhAm H
Daily, William H 1812-1877 *TwCBDA*
Daily, William Henry 1879-1937 *NatCAB 27*
Daily, William Mitchell 1812-1877 *NatCAB 13*
Daimler, Gottlieb Wilhelm 1834-1900 *AsBiEn,*
 McGEWB
Dain, Charles 1812-1873 *ApCAB*
Dain, Thomas Avery 1894-1957 *NatCAB 47*
Daine, Robert 1895-1957 *WhAm 3*
Dainelli, Giotto 1878-1968 *DcScB*
Daines, Lyman Luther 1883-1941 *WhAm 2*
Daines, Newel George 1895-1959 *NatCAB 48*
Daingerfield, Elliott 1859-1932 *AmBi,*
 ApCAB X, IIBEAAW, NatCAB 13,
 WhAm 1
Daingerfield, Foxhall Alexander 1887-1933
 WhAm 1
Dains, Frank Burnett 1869-1948 *WhAm 2*
Dainty, S *NewYHSD*
Daish, John Broughton 1867-1918 *WhAm 1*
Daisley, Robert Henry 1897-1961 *WhAm 4*

Dajety, F *NewYHSD*
Dake, Alvin Chamberlin 1849- *NatCAB 7*
Dake, Charles 1860-1937 *NatCAB 11,
   WhAm 2*
Dake, Charles Laurence 1883-1934 *WhAm 1*
Dake, Dumont Charles 1838- *NatCAB 2*
Dake, Frank Borland 1864- *NatCAB 11*
Dake, Jabez Philander 1827-1894 *NatCAB 11*
Dake, Walter Marshall 1855- *NatCAB 11*
Dake, William Church 1852- *NatCAB 11*
Dakin, Arthur Hazard 1862-1936 *NatCAB 27*
Dakin, Bertha Louise Kirkland *WomWWA 14*
Dakin, Emma Sahler *WomWWA 14*
Dakin, Henry Drysdale 1880-1952 *DcAmB S5,
   WhAm 3*
Dakin, James Harrison 1806-1852 *DcAmB S1,
   NewYHSD*
Dakin, Thomas Spencer 1831-1878 *ApCAB*
Dakins, John Gordon 1903-1965 *WhAm 4*
Daladier, Edouard 1884-1970 *McGEWB,
   WhWW-II*
Dalai Lama 1935- *McGEWB*
Daland, Judson 1860-1937 *ApCAB X,
   NatCAB 37, WhAm 1*
Daland, William Clifton 1860-1921 *WhAm 1*
Dalbey, A L *NewYHSD*
Dalbey, Josiah T 1898-1964 *WhAm 4*
Dalby, Zachary Lewis 1870- *WhAm 5*
Dalcho, Frederick 1770-1836 *ApCAB, DcAmB,
   Drake, NatCAB 23*
Dale, Alan 1861-1928 *WhAm 1*
Dale, Albert Ennis 1890-1954 *NatCAB 50,
   WhAm 3*
Dale, Anna 1851- *WomWWA 14*
Dale, Chalmers 1882- *NatCAB 17*
Dale, Chester 1832-1962 *WhAm 4*
Dale, Coudoashia Bernice Watts d1969
   WhAm 5
Dale, Edgar 1900- *BiDAmEd*
Dale, Edward Crathorne 1874-1947 *NatCAB 36*
Dale, Edward Everett 1879-1972 *EncAAH,
   REnAW, WhAm 5*
Dale, Essie Rock 1881- *WhAm 6*
Dale, Frank 1849-1930 *WhAm 1*
Dale, George Edward 1840-1873 *NewYHSD*
Dale, Harry Howard 1868-1935 *BiDrAC,
   WhAm 1*
Dale, Sir Henry Hallett 1875-1968 *AsBiEn,
   BiHiMed, DcScB, DcScB Sup, McGEWB,
   WhAm 5*
Dale, James Wilkinson 1812-1881 *ApCAB,
   NatCAB 10, TwCBDA, WhAm H*
Dale, John B d1848 *IlBEAAW, NewYHSD*
Dale, Mary Thompson 1881- *WomWWA 14*
Dale, Maud Murray Thompson 1875-1953
   DcAmB S5
Dale, Nelson Clark 1880- *WhAm 6*
Dale, Porter Hinman 1867-1933 *ApCAB X,
   BiDrAC, NatCAB 44, WhAm 1,
   WhAmP*
Dale, Richard 1756-1826 *AmBi, ApCAB,
   DcAmB, Drake, NatCAB 2, TwCBDA,
   WebAB, WebAMB, WhAm H*
Dale, Samuel 1772-1841 *ApCAB, DcAmB,
   Drake, NatCAB 4, WhAm H*
Dale, Sir Thomas d1619 *AmBi, DcAmB,
   NatCAB 13, WhAm H*
Dale, Sir Thomas d1620 *ApCAB, Drake,
   NatCAB 10*
Dale, Thomas Henry 1846-1912 *BiDrAC,
   WhAm 1*
Dale, Thomas Nelson 1845-1937 *NatCAB 15,
   WhAm 1*
Dale, Warren Jefferson 1896-1962 *WhAm 4*
Dale, William Johnson 1815- *ApCAB*
Dale, Wilton 1818?- *NewYHSD*
Dalechamps, Jacques 1513-1588 *DcScB*
Dalence, Joachim 1640?-1707? *DcScB*
Dales, John Blakely 1815-1893 *ApCAB Sup,
   TwCBDA*
D'Alesandro, Thomas, Jr. 1903- *BiDrAC*
Dalesio, Carmine 1887- *WhAm 4*
Daley, Arthur John 1904-1974 *WhAm 6*
Daley, George Henry 1844- *NatCAB 3*
Daley, John Francis 1895-1967 *NatCAB 55,
   WhAm 4A*
Daley, John Phillips 1910-1963 *NatCAB 51,
   WhAm 4*

Daley, Richard Joseph 1902- *EncAB, WebAB*
Daley, Robert Morris 1874-1950 *NatCAB 38,
   WhAm 3*
Daley, William Raymond 1892-1971 *WhAm 5*
Dalgleish, Oakley Hedley 1910-1963 *WhAm 4*
Dalhousie, George Ramsay 1770-1838 *ApCAB,
   Drake*
Dalhousie, James A Ramsay, Marquess Of
   1812-1860 *McGEWB*
Dali, Salvador 1904- *McGEWB*
Dalibard, Thomas Francois 1703-1779 *DcScB*
Dall, Caroline Wells Healey 1822-1912 *AmBi,
   AmWom, ApCAB, DcAmB, NatCAB 9,
   NotAW, TwCBDA, WhAm 4*
Dall, Charles Henry Appleton 1816-1886
   ApCAB, TwCBDA
Dall, William Healey 1845-1927 *AmBi,
   ApCAB, DcAmB, DcScB, NatCAB 10,
   NatCAB 27, TwCBDA, WhAm 1*
Dalla Valle, Joseph Maria 1906-1958 *WhAm 3*
Dalla Valle, Joseph Marius 1906-1958
   NatCAB 44
Dallam, Nannie Poultney Fisher 1874-
   WomWWA 14
Dallapiccola, Luigi 1904-1975 *McGEWB,
   WhAm 6*
Dallas, Alexander James 1759-1817 *AmBi,
   ApCAB, BiAUS, BiDrUSE, DcAmB,
   Drake, NatCAB 5, TwCBDA, WebAB,
   WhAm H, WhAmP*
Dallas, Alexander James 1791-1844 *ApCAB,
   Drake, NatCAB 8, TwCBDA*
Dallas, Alexander James 1830-1895 *TwCBDA*
Dallas, Alexander Robert Charles *ApCAB*
Dallas, Charles Donald 1881-1959 *NatCAB 7,
   WhAm 3*
Dallas, Sir George 1758-1833 *ApCAB*
Dallas, George Mifflin 1792-1864 *AmBi,
   ApCAB, BiAUS, BiDrAC, BiDrUSE,
   DcAmB, Drake, NatCAB 6, TwCBDA,
   WebAB, WhAm H, WhAmP*
Dallas, George Mifflin 1839- *WhAm 4*
Dallas, Hughes 1911-1958 *NatCAB 47*
Dallas, J Sanders 1905-1968 *NatCAB 54*
Dallas, Jacob A 1825-1857 *NewYHSD,
   WhAm H*
Dallas, John Thomson 1880-1961 *WhAm 4*
Dallas, Philip Nicklin 1825-1866 *ApCAB*
Dallas, Robert Charles 1754-1824 *ApCAB*
Dallas, Robert Frank 1855- *NatCAB 5*
Dallas, Trevanion Barlow 1843-1902 *NatCAB 8,
   NatCAB 42, TwCBDA, WhAm 4*
Dallenbach, Karl M 1887-1971 *WhAm 5*
Dallett, Morris 1864-1917 *NatCAB 17*
Dallin, Cyrus Edwin 1861- *ApCAB X,
   NatCAB 14*
Dallin, Cyrus Edwin 1861-1943 *IlBEAAW*
Dallin, Cyrus Edwin 1861-1944 *BnEnAmA,
   DcAmB S3, WhAm 2*
Dallin, David Julievich 1889-1962 *WhAm 4*
Dallin, Vittoria Colonna 1861- *WomWWA 14*
Dalling, Sir John d1798 *ApCAB, Drake*
Dallinger, Frederick William 1871-1955 *BiDrAC,
   WhAmP*
Dallman, Vincent Y 1873-1964 *WhAm 4*
Dallmann, William 1862-1952 *WhAm 3*
Dallstream, Andrew John 1893-1962
   NatCAB 46, WhAm 4
Dally, Abram 1795-1893 *ApCAB Sup*
Dalm, Jacob Arie 1892-1968 *NatCAB 54*
Dalmores, Charles 1871-1939 *WhAm 1*
D'Almaine, George d1893 *NewYHSD*
D'Aloes, Claude Jean 1622-1689 *DcAmB*
Dalrymple, Louis 1866-1905 *WhAm 1*
Dalrymple, William Haddock 1856-1925
   WhAm 1
Dalsheimer, Alice 1845-1880 *ApCAB*
Dalsimer, Allan Furth 1911-1963 *NatCAB 50*
Dalsimer, Philip T 1913-1975 *WhAm 6*
Dalsimer, Samuel 1908-1969 *WhAm 5*
Dalston, Alfred *NewYHSD*
Dalston, William B *NewYHSD*
Dalstrom, Oscar Frederick 1871- *WhAm 5*
Dalton, Albert Clayton 1867- *WhAm 5*
Dalton, David 1869-1959 *NatCAB 48*
Dalton, E *NewYHSD*
Dalton, Edward Barry 1832-1872 *AmBi*
Dalton, Edward Barry 1834-1872 *ApCAB,*

NatCAB 10, TwCBDA
Dalton, Edward Jerome 1879-1960 *NatCAB 49*
Dalton, Francis Warren 1891-1967 *NatCAB 54*
Dalton, Henry George 1862-1939 *WhAm 1*
Dalton, Ida May Hill 1868- *WomWWA 14*
Dalton, James *NewYHSD*
Dalton, James L 1910-1945 *WhAm 2*
Dalton, John d1869 *ApCAB, Drake*
Dalton, John 1766-1844 *AsBiEn, DcScB,
   McGEWB*
Dalton, John 1822-1884 *NatCAB 3*
Dalton, John Call 1795-1864 *TwCBDA*
Dalton, John Call 1825-1889 *AmBi, ApCAB,
   BiDAmEd, BiHiMed, DcAmB,
   DcScB Sup, Drake, NatCAB 10,
   TwCBDA, WhAm H*
Dalton, John Henry 1881- *WhAm 6*
Dalton, John Joseph 1856-1935 *IlBEAAW*
Dalton, John M 1900-1972 *WhAm 5*
Dalton, Joseph N 1892-1961 *WhAm 4*
Dalton, Mary Louise d1907 *WhAm 1*
Dalton, Robert 1867-1892 *DcAmB, WebAB,
   WhAm H*
Dalton, Samuel 1840- *TwCBDA*
Dalton, Sidna Poage 1892-1965 *WhAm 4*
Dalton, Test 1875-1945 *WhAm 2*
Dalton, Tristam 1738-1817 *Drake*
Dalton, Tristam 1743-1817 *BiAUS*
Dalton, Tristram 1738-1817 *ApCAB, BiDrAC,
   NatCAB 11, TwCBDA, WhAm H*
Dalton, W R Inge 1841-1931 *WhAm 1*
Dalton, William 1869- *WhAm 5*
Daltry, Joseph Samuel 1899-1967 *NatCAB 53*
Daly, Anthony Walter 1904-1960 *NatCAB 49*
Daly, Arnold 1875-1927 *AmBi, DcAmB,
   WhAm 1*
Daly, Augustin 1838-1899 *AmBi, ApCAB,
   DcAmB, NatCAB 1, TwCBDA, WebAB,
   WhAm 1*
Daly, Bernard John 1872-1942 *NatCAB 40*
Daly, Brenton L 1884-1956 *WhAm 3*
Daly, Carroll John 1889-1958 *WhAm 3*
Daly, Sister Cecilia 1905-1968 *WhAm 5*
Daly, Charles Frederick 1865-1928 *WhAm 1*
Daly, Charles Patrick 1816-1899 *AmBi,
   ApCAB, BiAUS, DcAmB, Drake,
   NatCAB 3, TwCBDA, WhAm 1*
Daly, David 1878- *WhAm 6*
Daly, Sir Dominick 1798-1868 *ApCAB*
Daly, Edward C 1894-1964 *WhAm 4*
Daly, Edward James 1892-1959 *NatCAB 46,
   WhAm 3*
Daly, Edwin King 1896-1960 *WhAm 3A*
Daly, Franklin Pierce 1858-1927 *NatCAB 21*
Daly, Howard J, Sr. 1897-1961 *WhAm 4*
Daly, Ivan DeBurgh 1893-1974 *WhAm 6*
Daly, J J d1948 *WhAm 2*
Daly, John Augustin 1838-1899 *DcAmB*
Daly, John Burrwood 1872-1939 *BiDrAC,
   WhAm 1*
Daly, John Fidlar 1905-1969 *WhAm 5*
Daly, John Francis 1879- *WhAm 6*
Daly, John J 1853- *NatCAB 7*
Daly, John J 1905-1964 *WhAm 4*
Daly, John Joseph 1852-1927 *NatCAB 23*
Daly, John Michael 1860-1916 *ApCAB X,
   NatCAB 19*
Daly, John Wallace 1868- *WhAm 4*
Daly, Joseph Francis 1840-1916 *NatCAB 1,
   TwCBDA, WhAm 1*
Daly, Kay Frances 1919-1975 *WhAm 6*
Daly, Marcus 1841-1900 *AmBi, DcAmB,
   McGEWB, REnAW, WebAB*
Daly, Marcus 1842-1900 *WhAm 1*
Daly, Paul Jay 1862-1915 *NatCAB 40*
Daly, Peter Christopher Arnold 1875-1927 *AmBi,
   DcAmB*
Daly, Reginald Aldworth 1871-1957 *DcScB,
   NatCAB 44, WhAm 3*
Daly, Thomas Augustine 1871-1948 *WhAm 2*
Daly, Thomas Franklin 1858-1921 *NatCAB 32*
Daly, William Augustine 1884-1947
   NatCAB 34
Daly, William Barry 1873- *WhAm 2*
Daly, William David 1851-1900 *BiDrAC,
   WhAm 1*
Daly, William Hudson 1842- *NatCAB 10*
Dalzel, Archibald 1740-1811 *McGEWB*

Dalzell, James d1763 *ApCAB*
Dalzell, John 1845-1927 *BiDrAC, DcAmB, NatCAB 34, TwCBDA, WhAm 1, WhAmP*
Dalzell, Lloyd Howland 1917-1968 *WhAm 4A*
Dalzell, Robert M 1793-1873 *ApCAB, DcAmB, WhAm H*
Dalzell, William Sage 1868-1934 *WhAm 1*
Dam, Carl Peter Henrik 1895- *AsBiEn, McGEWB*
Dam, Henry Jackson Wells d1906 *WhAm 1*
Damas, Joseph Francois L Charles Duc De 1758-1829 *Drake*
Damaskinos, Archbishop 1891-1949 *WhWW-II*
Dambach, Charles Arthur 1911-1969 *NatCAB 57, WhAm 5*
Dame, Elizabeth L 1904-1968 *WhAm 5*
Dame, Ella B 1859- *WomWWA 14*
Dame, Frank Libby 1867-1933 *NatCAB 27, WhAm 1*
Dame, Harriet Patience 1815-1900 *ApCAB Sup, WhAm 1*
Dame, J Frank 1905-1969 *WhAm 5*
Dame, Katharine 1874- *WomWWA 14*
Dame, Walter Reeves 1861-1924 *NatCAB 6*
Dame Shirley 1819-1906 *REnAW*
Damen, Arnold 1800?- *ApCAB*
Dameron, Frances Sublette 1870- *WomWWA 14*
Dameshek, William 1900-1969 *WhAm 5*
Damiano, Celestine Joseph 1911-1967 *WhAm 4A*
Damianov, Georgi d1958 *WhAm 3*
D'Amico, Carlos A 1844- *ApCAB*
Damien, Father 1840-1889 *AmBi, McGEWB*
Damino, Harry Orazio 1893-1968 *NatCAB 54*
Damiri, Muhammad Ibn Musa, Al- 1341-1405 *DcScB*
Damm, Carl Nelson 1891-1960 *NatCAB 50*
Damm, Henry Christian Augustus 1874-1929 *WhAm 1*
Damm, Max 1875-1969 *NatCAB 54*
Damm, Walter J 1893-1962 *WhAm 4*
Dammann, Isabel Adair Lynde 1882- *WomWWA 14*
Dammann, John Francis 1880-1963 *WhAm 4*
Dammann, Milton d1962 *WhAm 4*
Dammann, Theodore 1866-1946 *WhAm 3*
Dammert, Louis Arthur 1873-1956 *NatCAB 42*
Damon, Albert Forster, Jr. 1873-1954 *NatCAB 45*
Damon, Alexander M 1874-1947 *WhAm 2*
Damon, Alonzo Willard 1847-1924 *WhAm 1*
Damon, David 1788-1843 *ApCAB*
Damon, Edward Orne, Jr. 1876-1948 *NatCAB 43*
Damon, Frank Hardy 1870- *WhAm 5*
Damon, Frank Jesse 1869-1956 *NatCAB 45*
Damon, George Alfred 1871-1934 *NatCAB 33, WhAm 1*
Damon, George J 1858-1927 *NatCAB 36*
Damon, Howard Franklin 1833-1884 *ApCAB, NatCAB 3, WhAm H*
Damon, Joseph Almer 1882-1962 *NatCAB 51*
Damon, Lalia May *WomWWA 14*
Damon, Lindsay Todd 1871-1940 *WhAm 1*
Damon, Norman Clare 1897-1967 *WhAm 5*
Damon, Ralph Shepard 1897-1956 *WhAm 3*
Damon, Robert Hosken 1902-1960 *WhAm 3*
Damon, S Foster 1893-1971 *WhAm 5*
Damon, Samuel Mills 1845-1924 *NatCAB 37, WhAm 3*
Damon, Samuel Reed 1893-1967 *NatCAB 53*
Damon, Virgil Green 1895-1972 *NatCAB 57*
Damon, William Emerson 1838-1911 *NatCAB 15, WhAm 1*
Damoreau, Charles F *NewYHSD*
D'Amours, Ernest R 1904-1965 *WhAm 4*
Dampier, William 1652?- *ApCAB*
Dampier, William 1652-1712 *Drake*
Dampier, William 1652-1715 *McGEWB*
Damrell, Charles Lowe 1826-1896 *TwCBDA*
Damrell, William Shapleigh 1809-1860 *BiAUS, BiDrAC, TwCBDA, WhAm H*
Damrosch, Frank Heino 1859-1937 *AmBi, ApCAB X, BiDAmEd, DcAmB S2, NatCAB 2, NatCAB 31, WhAm 1*
Damrosch, Leopold 1832-1885 *AmBi, ApCAB,*

DcAmB, NatCAB 2, TwCBDA, WebAB, WhAm H
Damrosch, Walter Johannes 1862-1950 *ApCAB, ApCAB X, DcAmB S4, NatCAB 2, NatCAB 43, TwCBDA, WebAB, WhAm 3*
Damrow, Charles 1916- *IIBEAAW*
Dana, Alexander Hamilton 1807-1887 *ApCAB Sup*
Dana, Alexander Hope 1807-1887 *TwCBDA*
Dana, Amasa 1792-1867 *BiAUS, BiDrAC, TwCBDA, WhAm H*
Dana, Arnold Guyot 1862-1947 *NatCAB 36*
Dana, Charles Anderson 1819-1897 *AmBi, ApCAB, ApCAB X, BiAUS, DcAmB, Drake, McGEWB, NatCAB 1, TwCBDA, WebAB, WhAm H*
Dana, Charles Anderson 1881-1975 *WhAm 6*
Dana, Charles Edmund 1843-1914 *WhAm 1*
Dana, Charles Henry 1863-1946 *NatCAB 33*
Dana, Charles Loomis 1852-1935 *AmBi, ApCAB X, DcAmB S1, NatCAB 13, WhAm 1*
Dana, Daniel 1771-1859 *Drake, NatCAB 9*
Dana, David Michael 1926-1968 *NatCAB 54*
Dana, Denison Dean 1875-1938 *NatCAB 40*
Dana, Duncan 1891-1930 *NatCAB 24*
Dana, Edmund Lovell 1817-1889 *ApCAB Sup, TwCBDA*
Dana, Edmund Trowbridge 1779-1859 *NewYHSD*
Dana, Edmund Trowbridge 1818-1869 *ApCAB, Drake, TwCBDA*
Dana, Edward Salisbury 1849-1935 *AmBi, ApCAB, DcAmB S1, NatCAB 6, NatCAB 30, TwCBDA, WhAm 1*
Dana, Florence Hinkley *WomWWA 14*
Dana, Floyd G 1895-1967 *WhAm 4*
Dana, Frances Theodora *TwCBDA*
Dana, Francis 1743-1811 *AmBi, ApCAB, BiAUS, BiDrAC, DcAmB, Drake, NatCAB 3, TwCBDA, WhAm H, WhAmP*
Dana, Francis E 1836-1910 *WhAm 1*
Dana, Frank M 1906-1968 *WhAm 5*
Dana, Frank Whitmore 1863-1940 *NatCAB 30*
Dana, Harvey Eugene 1888-1945 *WhAm 2*
Dana, Henry Wadsworth Longfellow 1881-1950 *WhAm 3*
Dana, Henshaw 1846-1883 *TwCBDA*
Dana, Israel Thorndike 1827-1904 *ApCAB, TwCBDA, WhAm 1*
Dana, J F *NewYHSD*
Dana, James 1735-1812 *ApCAB, DcAmB, Drake, NatCAB 23, TwCBDA, WhAm H*
Dana, James Dwight 1813-1895 *AmBi, ApCAB, BiDAmEd, DcAmB, DcScB, Drake, NatCAB 6, NatCAB 30, NewYHSD, TwCBDA, WebAB, WhAm H*
Dana, James Dwight 1889-1954 *WhAm 3*
Dana, James Freeman 1793-1827 *ApCAB, DcAmB, Drake, NatCAB 10, TwCBDA, WhAm H*
Dana, John Cotton 1856-1929 *AmBi, DcAmB, DcAmLiB, NatCAB 22, TwCBDA, WebAB, WhAm 1*
Dana, John Fessenden 1877-1966 *WhAm 4*
Dana, John Winchester 1808-1867 *ApCAB, BiAUS, Drake, NatCAB 6, TwCBDA*
Dana, Joseph 1742-1827 *ApCAB*
Dana, Judah 1772-1845 *ApCAB, BiAUS, BiDrAC, Drake, NatCAB 11, TwCBDA, WhAm H*
Dana, Judith Bledsoe 1880- *WomWWA 14*
Dana, Luther 1763-1832 *NatCAB 10*
Dana, Lynn Boardman 1875-1941 *WhAm 1*
Dana, Malcolm 1869-1940 *NatCAB 29*
Dana, Malcolm McGregor 1838-1897 *ApCAB Sup*
Dana, Marshall Newport 1885-1966 *NatCAB 53*
Dana, Marvin 1867- *WhAm 4*
Dana, Myron T 1850- *WhAm 4*
Dana, Napoleon Jackson Tecumseh 1822-1905 *ApCAB, DcAmB, Drake, NatCAB 10, TwCBDA, WhAm H*
Dana, Olive Eliza 1859- *AmWom*
Dana, Paul 1852-1930 *AmBi, NatCAB 8,*

TwCBDA, WhAm 1
Dana, Richard 1699-1772 *ApCAB, Drake*
Dana, Richard 1700-1772 *DcAmB, NatCAB 10, TwCBDA, WhAm H*
Dana, Richard Henry 1787-1879 *AmBi, ApCAB, DcAmB, Drake, NatCAB 7, TwCBDA, WhAm H*
Dana, Richard Henry 1851-1931 *AmBi, ApCAB, NatCAB 7, NatCAB 24, TwCBDA, WhAm 1*
Dana, Richard Henry, Jr. 1815-1882 *AmBi, ApCAB, BiAUS Sup, DcAmB, Drake, EncAB, McGEWB, NatCAB 7, REnAW, TwCBDA, WebAB, WhAm H, WhAmP*
Dana, Richard Turner 1876-1928 *WhAm 1*
Dana, Samuel 1739-1798 *ApCAB, TwCBDA*
Dana, Samuel 1767-1825 *ApCAB, TwCBDA*
Dana, Samuel 1767-1835 *BiAUS, BiDrAC, Drake, WhAm H*
Dana, Samuel Luther 1795-1868 *AmBi, ApCAB, DcAmB, Drake, NatCAB 8, TwCBDA, WhAm H*
Dana, Samuel W 1747-1830 *BiAUS*
Dana, Samuel Whittelsey 1760-1830 *DcAmB, WhAm H*
Dana, Samuel Whittlesey 1757-1830 *Drake*
Dana, Samuel Whittlesey 1760-1830 *ApCAB, BiDrAC, NatCAB 2, TwCBDA, WhAmP*
Dana, Stephen Winchester 1840-1910 *ApCAB, NatCAB 10, WhAm 1*
Dana, William Franklin 1863-1920 *WhAm 1*
Dana, William H 1833-1872 *NatCAB 10*
Dana, William Henry 1846-1916 *NatCAB 18, TwCBDA, WhAm 1*
Dana, William Parsons Winchester 1833-1927 *AmBi, ApCAB, NewYHSD, TwCBDA, WhAm 1*
Dana, William Starr 1843-1890 *TwCBDA*
Dana, Woodbury Kidder 1840- *NatCAB 17*
Danaceau, Saul Samuel 1896-1965 *NatCAB 52*
Danaher, John Anthony 1899- *BiDrAC, WhAmP*
Dancel, Christian 1847-1898 *DcAmB, WhAm H*
Dancer, H M *WhAm 3*
Dancer, Herbert Allan 1874-1959 *NatCAB 49*
Dancer, Robert Clinton 1875-1926 *NatCAB 20*
Danckaerts, Jasper *NewYHSD, WhAm H*
Danco, Samuel 1912-1966 *NatCAB 53*
Dancy, Alexander Brown 1877-1933 *WhAm 1*
Dancy, Florence Nightingale *WomWWA 14*
Dancy, J C 1857- *WhoColR*
Dancy, John Campbell 1857- *TwCBDA*
Dancy, William Remshart 1877-1960 *NatCAB 52*
Dandelin, Germinal Pierre 1794-1847 *DcScB*
Dandolo, Enrico 1107?-1205 *McGEWB*
Dandreau, John Louis 1892-1968 *NatCAB 54*
Dandridge, Danske 1858- *WhAm 4, WomWWA 14*
Dandridge, Dorothy d1965 *WhAm 4*
Dandridge, Edmund Pendleton 1881-1961 *NatCAB 46*
Dandridge, Nathaniel Pendleton 1846-1910 *NatCAB 13, WhAm 1*
Dandurand, Josephine Marchand 1861- *WomWWA 14*
Dandy, George Brown 1830-1911 *NatCAB 2, TwCBDA, WhAm 1*
Dandy, John Percy 1902-1973 *WhAm 6*
Dandy, Walter Edward 1886-1946 *DcAmB S4, NatCAB 35, WhAm 2*
Dane, Carle Hamilton 1900-1968 *NatCAB 54*
Dane, Chester Linwood 1877-1953 *NatCAB 45*
Dane, Ernest Blaney 1868-1942 *NatCAB 31, WhAm 2*
Dane, John 1866-1939 *NatCAB 29*
Dane, Joseph 1778-1858 *BiAUS, BiDrAC, TwCBDA, WhAm H*
Dane, Nathan 1752-1834 *BiAUS*
Dane, Nathan 1752-1835 *ApCAB, BiDrAC, DcAmB, Drake, NatCAB 9, TwCBDA, WhAm H, WhAmP*
Dane, Walter Alden 1882-1971 *WhAm 5*
Danels, John Daniel 1786-1856 *ApCAB*
Danely, Alfred Marion 1841- *WhAm 4*
Danenhower, John Wilson 1849-1887 *ApCAB, DcAmB, NatCAB 3, WhAm H*

Daney, Eugene 1862-1946 *NatCAB 35,*
WhAm 2
Daney, T *NewYHSD*
Danford, Lorenzo 1829-1899 *BiAUS, BiDrAC,*
TwCBDA, WhAm 1, WhAmP
Danford, Robert Melville 1879-1974 *WhAm 6*
Danforth, Charles 1797-1876 *ApCAB, DcAmB,*
NatCAB 13, WhAm H
Danforth, Charles H 1876- *WhAm 5*
Danforth, Charles Haskell 1883-1969 *DcScB*
Danforth, Donald 1898-1973 *WhAm 6*
Danforth, Edward 1828-1898 *ApCAB Sup*
Danforth, Edward J *NewYHSD*
Danforth, Elliot 1850-1906 *ApCAB Sup,*
NatCAB 1
Danforth, Elliott 1850-1906 *WhAm 1*
Danforth, George Franklin 1819-1899 *ApCAB,*
TwCBDA
Danforth, George Jonathan 1875-1952
NatCAB 43, WhAm 3
Danforth, George Washington 1868- *WhAm 4*
Danforth, Henry Gold 1854-1918 *BiDrAC,*
WhAm 1
Danforth, Herman Wenger 1872-1949
NatCAB 41
Danforth, Isaac Newton 1835-1911 *WhAm 1*
Danforth, J B *NewYHSD*
Danforth, James Romeyn 1839-1915
NatCAB 17
Danforth, John 1660-1730 *ApCAB, TwCBDA*
Danforth, Joshua Noble 1798-1861 *ApCAB,*
NatCAB 2, TwCBDA, WhAm H
Danforth, Josiah Hays 1874-1935 *NatCAB 26*
Danforth, Loomis LeGrand 1849- *ApCAB X,*
WhAm 4
Danforth, Moseley Isaac 1800-1862 *AmBi,*
ApCAB, DcAmB, NatCAB 22,
NewYHSD, TwCBDA, WhAm H
Danforth, Richard Stevens 1885-1962
NatCAB 51
Danforth, Samuel 1626-1674 *ApCAB, Drake,*
TwCBDA
Danforth, Samuel 1666-1727 *ApCAB*
Danforth, Samuel 1696-1777 *ApCAB*
Danforth, Samuel 1740-1827 *ApCAB, Drake*
Danforth, Thomas 1622-1699 *ApCAB, Drake,*
TwCBDA
Danforth, Thomas 1623-1699 *DcAmB,*
WhAm H
Danforth, Thomas 1703-1786? *AmBi, DcAmB*
Danforth, Thomas 1742?-1825 *ApCAB*
Danforth, William H 1870-1955 *WhAm 3*
Dangaix, William Joseph 1864-1943 *WhAm 2*
Dangerfield, A D *NewYHSD*
Dangerfield, Royden 1902-1969 *WhAm 6*
Danhof, John James 1884-1973 *WhAm 6*
Danhof, Ralph John 1900-1971 *WhAm 5*
Daniel, Alice Maud Mary *WomWWA 14*
Daniel, Annie Sturges 1858-1944 *NotAW*
Daniel, Antony 1601-1648 *ApCAB*
Daniel, Charles Ezra 1895-1964 *BiDrAC,*
NatCAB 51, WhAm 4
Daniel, Charles William 1874- *WhAm 5*
Daniel, Charles Zollie 1877-1914 *NatCAB 16*
Daniel, Cullen Coleman 1879- *WhAm 6*
Daniel, David R 1902-1967 *WhAm 4*
Daniel, Delphine Lyon Minton 1887-
WomWWA 14
Daniel, Donald Snead 1897-1969 *NatCAB 54*
Daniel, Fannie V 1867- *WomWWA 14*
Daniel, Ferdinand Eugene 1839-1914
NatCAB 10, WhAm 1
Daniel, Harry 1868-1947 *NatCAB 36*
Daniel, Henry 1782?-1873 *TwCBDA*
Daniel, Henry 1786-1873 *BiDrAC, WhAm H*
Daniel, Henry 1793-1873 *BiAUS*
Daniel, Holy *NewYHSD*
Daniel, Isaac d1864 *Drake*
Daniel, J 1835?- *NewYHSD*
Daniel, J Frank 1873-1942 *WhAm 2*
Daniel, J McTyeire 1896-1970 *WhAm 5*
Daniel, James Jacquelin 1832-1888 *ApCAB Sup*
Daniel, James Jacquelin 1832-1888 *NatCAB 46*
Daniel, John 1862-1950 *WhAm 2A*
Daniel, John Hannah 1896-1972 *NatCAB 57*
Daniel, John Mobley 1883-1951 *NatCAB 43*
Daniel, John Moncure 1825-1865 *ApCAB,*
BiAUS, BiDConf, DcAmB, Drake,

NatCAB 10, TwCBDA, WhAm H
Daniel, John R J *BiAUS*
Daniel, John Reeve Jones 1802-1865 *TwCBDA*
Daniel, John Reeves Jones 1802?- *ApCAB*
Daniel, John Reeves Jones 1802-1868 *BiDrAC,*
WhAm H
Daniel, John Warwick 1842-1910 *ApCAB,*
BiDrAC, DcAmB, NatCAB 1, TwCBDA,
WhAm 1, WhAmP
Daniel, John William 1868-1954 *NatCAB 44*
Daniel, Joseph J 1783?-1848 *BiAUS, Drake*
Daniel, Joseph John 1784-1848 *NatCAB 9*
Daniel, Junius 1828-1864 *BiDConf, Drake,*
NatCAB 7, TwCBDA
Daniel, Lewis C 1901-1952 *WhAm 3*
Daniel, Pete 1938- *EncAAH*
Daniel, Peter Vivian 1784-1860 *ApCAB,*
DcAmB, NatCAB 2, TwCBDA, WebAB,
WhAm H
Daniel, Peter Vyvian 1785-1860 *BiAUS, Drake*
Daniel, Price Marion 1910- *BiDrAC*
Daniel, Raleigh Travers 1805-1877 *ApCAB,*
TwCBDA
Daniel, Richard Potts 1880-1968 *WhAm 5*
Daniel, Richard Tevia 1861-1949 *NatCAB 38*
Daniel, Robert *NatCAB 12*
Daniel, Robert Norman 1888-1956 *WhAm 3*
Daniel, Robert Prentiss 1902-1968 *WhAm 4A*
Daniel, Robert Towns 1859-1915 *NatCAB 18*
Daniel, Robert Williams 1884-1940 *NatCAB 39*
Daniel, T Cushing 1857-1923 *NatCAB 35*
Daniel, Walter Fletcher 1925-1974 *WhAm 6*
Daniel, Wilbur Clarence 1914- *BiDrAC*
Daniel, William 1770-1839 *ApCAB*
Daniel, William 1771-1839 *Drake*
Daniel, William 1806-1873 *ApCAB*
Daniel, William 1826- *ApCAB*
Daniel-Rops, Henry 1901-1965 *WhAm 4*
Danielian, Noobar Retheos 1906-1974 *WhAm 6*
Daniell, Francis Raymond 1901-1969 *WhAm 5*
Daniell, John Frederic 1790-1845 *AsBiEn,*
DcScB
Daniell, Mary Barnard 1862- *WomWWA 14*
Daniell, Moses Grant 1836-1909 *WhAm 1*
Daniell, Warren Fisher 1826-1913 *BiDrAC*
Daniells, Arthur Grosvenor 1858-1935 *WhAm 2*
Daniells, Helen West Kitchel *WomWWA 14*
Daniells, William Willard 1840-1912 *WhAm 1*
Daniels, A Millard 1887-1961 *NatCAB 50*
Daniels, Anson 1813-1884 *NewYHSD*
Daniels, Arthur Burdette 1861- *ApCAB X*
Daniels, Arthur Hill 1865-1940 *WhAm 1*
Daniels, Arthur Simpson 1905-1966
NatCAB 53, WhAm 4
Daniels, Benjamin 1898-1957 *WhAm 3*
Daniels, Charles 1825-1897 *BiDrAC,*
NatCAB 22, WhAm H
Daniels, Charles 1826-1897 *ApCAB Sup,*
TwCBDA
Daniels, Charles H *NewYHSD*
Daniels, Charles Herbert 1847-1914 *WhAm 1*
Daniels, Charles Neil 1878-1943 *NatCAB 33*
Daniels, Charles Nelson 1849-1916 *WhAm 1*
Daniels, Clarence White 1884-1966 *NatCAB 51*
Daniels, Cora Linn 1852- *AmWom, WhAm 4*
Daniels, Coralinn Morrison 1852-
WomWWA 14
Daniels, Dominick Vincent 1908- *BiDrAC*
Daniels, Edward 1854-1918 *NatCAB 36*
Daniels, Farrington 1889-1972 *WhAm 5*
Daniels, Francis Cummings 1896-1959 *WhAm 3*
Daniels, Francis Potter 1869- *WhAm 2*
Daniels, Frank 1860-1935 *WhAm 1*
Daniels, Frank Albert 1856-1935 *DcAmB S1*
Daniels, Fred Chapman 1898-1960 *NatCAB 47*
Daniels, Fred Harris 1853-1913 *AmBi, DcAmB,*
NatCAB 22, WhAm 1
Daniels, George Fisher 1821-1879? *NewYHSD*
Daniels, George Henry 1842-1908 *WhAm 1*
Daniels, Harold Kennan 1903-1965 *WhAm 4*
Daniels, Harriet McDougal *WomWWA 14*
Daniels, Henry H d1958 *WhAm 3*
Daniels, John 1881-1953 *WhAm 3*
Daniels, John H *NewYHSD*
Daniels, John Karl 1875- *WhAm 5*
Daniels, John William 1857-1931 *NatCAB 24*
Daniels, Joseph J 1890- *WhAm 5*
Daniels, Joseph Leonard 1833-1924 *TwCBDA,*

WhAm 1
Daniels, Josephus 1862-1948 *ApCAB X,*
BiDrUSE, DcAmB S4, EncAB,
McGEWB, NatCAB 39, TwCBDA,
WhAm 2, WhAmP
Daniels, Josephus, Jr. 1894-1964 *WhAm 4*
Daniels, Lewis Ernest 1886-1955 *NatCAB 44*
Daniels, Lilla Wood d1962 *WhAm 4*
Daniels, Mabel Wheeler 1879- *ApCAB X,*
WomWWA 14
Daniels, Mark 1881- *WhAm 6*
Daniels, Martin Edson 1871-1961 *NatCAB 50*
Daniels, Mary Louise 1857- *WomWWA 14*
Daniels, Milton John 1838-1914 *BiDrAC,*
WhAm 2
Daniels, Philip Brock 1904-1959 *NatCAB 47*
Daniels, Sarah E 1847- *WomWWA 14*
Daniels, Walter *NewYHSD*
Daniels, William Haven 1836- *ApCAB*
Daniels, William S 1861-1904 *WhAm 1*
Daniels, Winthrop More 1867-1944 *DcAmB S3,*
NatCAB 40, NatCAB 47, WhAm 2
Daniels, Wylie Johnston 1888-1951 *NatCAB 40*
Danielson, Clarence Hagbart 1889-1952
NatCAB 41, WhAm 3
Danielson, Frances Weld *WomWWA 14*
Danielson, Jacques 1875-1952 *WhAm 3*
Danielson, John Peter 1865-1940 *NatCAB 30*
Danielson, Ralph Raymond 1892-1965
NatCAB 52
Danielson, Ralph Wesley 1897-1970
NatCAB 57
Danielson, Reuben Gustaf 1884-1950 *WhAm 3*
Danielson, Richard Ely 1885-1957 *WhAm 3*
Danielson, Timothy 1733-1791 *ApCAB, Drake*
Danielson, Wilmot Alfred 1884-1966
NatCAB 51, WhAm 4
Danker, Daniel Joseph, Jr. 1903-1944
NatCAB 33
Danks, Hart Pease 1834-1903 *ApCAB,*
NatCAB 8
Dankworth, Frederick 1804?- *NewYHSD*
Danley, William L 1839- *WhAm 4*
Dann, Alexander William 1885-1965 *WhAm 4*
Dann, Clarence Burdette 1862-1931
NatCAB 33
Dann, Frode N 1892- *IIBEAAW*
Dann, Hollis Ellsworth 1861-1939 *BiDAmEd,*
WhAm 1
Dannat, William Turner 1853-1929 *AmBi,*
NatCAB 12, WhAm 1
Dannay, Frederic 1905- *WebAB*
Dannelly, Elizabeth Otis 1838- *AmWom*
Dannelly, John Milton 1855-1931 *WhAm 1*
Danneman, L *NewYHSD*
Dannenbaum, Walter 1892-1967 *WhAm 4*
Danner, Adam *NewYHSD*
Danner, Arthur Vincent 1911-1969 *WhAm 5*
Danner, Edward 1882-1952 *NatCAB 40*
Danner, George Herbert 1874-1941 *NatCAB 40*
Danner, Harris Leslie 1888-1941 *WhAm 1*
Danner, J A *NewYHSD*
Danner, Joel Buchanan 1804-1885 *BiAUS,*
BiDrAC, WhAm H
Danner, Peter C 1875-1939 *WhAm 1*
Dannreuther, Gustav 1853-1923 *DcAmB,*
WhAm HA, WhAm 4
Dannreuther, Nellie Morton 1858-
WomWWA 14
Dannreuther, Walter Taylor 1885-1960
NatCAB 43, WhAm 3
D'Annunzio, Gabriele 1863-1938 *McGEWB*
Danquah, Joseph B 1895-1965 *McGEWB*
Dansingberg, Paul d1945 *WhAm 2*
Dant, Michael Joseph 1882-1956 *NatCAB 46*
Dante Alighieri 1265-1321 *McGEWB*
Danti, Egnatio 1536-1586 *DcScB*
Danton, George Henry 1880- *WhAm 6*
Danton, Georges Jacques 1759-1794 *McGEWB*
Dantonet, A *NewYHSD*
D'Antoni, Salvador d1957 *WhAm 3*
Dantzig, Henry Poincare 1918-1973 *WhAm 6*
Dantzler, Lehre L 1878-1958 *NatCAB 49,*
WhAm 6
Dantzler, Lorenzo Nolley 1866-1943
NatCAB 32
Dantzler, Lorenzo Nolley 1899-1951
NatCAB 39

Danziger, Henry 1852-1935 *WhAm 1*
Daoust, Edward Chellis 1887-1947 *NatCAB 36*
Daoust, Jean Baptist 1817- *ApCAB*
Daponte *Drake*
DaPonte, Durant 1825?-1894 *TwCBDA*
DaPonte, Lorenzo 1749-1838 *ApCAB, DcAmB, TwCBDA, WhAm H*
DaPonte, Lorenzo Brooke 1878-1950 *WhAm 3*
Dapping, William Osborne 1880-1969 *WhAm 5*
Darboux, Jean-Gaston 1842-1917 *DcScB*
Darby, Ada Claire 1883-1953 *WhAm 3*
Darby, Ada Leonard *WomWWA 14*
Darby, Benjamin Edwin 1848- *NatCAB 16*
Darby, Edwin Tyler 1845-1929 *NatCAB 35, WhAm 1*
Darby, Ezra 1768-1808 *BiAUS, BiDrAC, WhAm H*
Darby, Harry 1895- *BiDrAC*
Darby, Henry F 1831?- *NewYHSD*
Darby, J G *NewYHSD*
Darby, John *WhAm H*
Darby, John 1804-1877 *ApCAB, DcAmB, TwCBDA, WhAm H*
Darby, John Eaton 1835-1918 *WhAm 1*
Darby, John Fletcher 1803-1882 *BiAUS, BiDrAC, WhAm H, WhAmP*
Darby, John Frederick 1872-1953 *NatCAB 42, WhAm 3*
Darby, John Joseph 1897-1950 *NatCAB 38*
Darby, Myron Guy 1889-1963 *NatCAB 51*
Darby, Nathaniel 1863- *WhoColR A*
Darby, William 1775-1854 *ApCAB, DcAmB, Drake, WhAm H*
Darby, William Daniel 1892-1950 *NatCAB 39*
Darby, William Johnson 1848-1921 *WhAm 1*
Darby, William Lambert 1875-1951 *WhAm 3*
Darbyshire, Leonard 1867- *WhAm 4*
D'Arcet, Jean 1725-1801 *DcScB*
Darcey, John S 1788-1863 *ApCAB*
D'Arcy, Julia Barclay 1886- *WomWWA 14*
D'Arcy, Patrick 1725-1779 *DcScB*
D'Arcy, Peter H 1854- *ApCAB X*
D'Arcy, William Cheever 1873-1948 *NatCAB 36, WhAm 2*
Darden, Colgate Whitehead, Jr. 1897- *BiDrAC*
Darden, Miles 1798-1857 *ApCAB, Drake*
Darden, Sam 1902-1956 *NatCAB 48*
Darden, Stephen Heard 1816-1902 *BiDConf*
Darden, Thomas Francis 1870-1943 *NatCAB 31, WhAm 2*
Dare, Ella 1842- *AmWom*
Dare, Virginia 1587-1587? *AmBi, ApCAB, DcAmB, Drake, NotAW, WebAB, WhAm H*
Dargan, Clara Victoria 1840?- *ApCAB*
Dargan, Edmond Strother 1805-1879 *WhAm H*
Dargan, Edmund Spawn 1805-1879 *ApCAB, NatCAB 4, TwCBDA*
Dargan, Edmund Strother 1805-1879 *BiDConf, BiDrAC, DcAmB*
Dargan, Edward S *BiAUS*
Dargan, Edwin Charles 1852-1930 *WhAm 1*
Dargan, Edwin Preston 1879-1940 *DcAmB S2, NatCAB 30, WhAm 1*
Dargan, George Washington 1841-1898 *TwCBDA*
Dargan, George William 1841-1898 *BiDrAC*
Dargan, Henry McCune 1879-1940 *WhAm 5*
Dargan, John Julius 1848-1925 *NatCAB 20*
Dargan, Kemp Strother 1883-1954 *NatCAB 43*
Dargan, Olive Tilford d1968 *WhAm 5, WomWWA 14*
Dargan, Theodore A 1823- *ApCAB*
Dargavel, John William 1894-1961 *WhAm 4*
Darge, Fred 1900- *IIBEAAW*
Dargeon, Harold William 1897-1970 *WhAm 5*
Dargon, George W 1801-1859 *BiAUS*
Dargue, Herbert Arthur 1886-1941 *NatCAB 40*
Dargue, Herbert Arthur 1886-1942 *WhAm 2*
Dargusch, Carlton Spencer, Jr. 1925-1975 *WhAm 6*
Darin, Bobby 1936-1973 *WhAm 6*
Darin, Frank Peter 1899-1958 *NatCAB 48*
Dario, Ruben 1867-1916 *McGEWB*
Darius I 522BC-486BC *McGEWB*
Darke, William 1736-1801 *ApCAB, DcAmB, Drake, WhAm H*

Darkenwald, Gordon Gerald 1906-1961 *WhAm 4*
Darlan, Jean Francois 1881-1942 *WhWW-II, WhoMilH*
Darley, E H *NewYHSD*
Darley, Ellen Westray d1849 *Drake*
Darley, Felix Octavius Carr 1822-1888 *AmBi, ApCAB, BnEnAmA, DcAmB, Drake, IIBEAAW, NatCAB 2, NewYHSD, REnAW, TwCBDA, WhAm H*
Darley, Jane Cooper 1807-1877 *NewYHSD, WhAm H*
Darley, John 1765-1853 *ApCAB*
Darley, John Clarendon 1808?- *NewYHSD*
Darley, Mrs. W H W *NewYHSD*
Darling, Alice O *AmWom*
Darling, Arthur Beebe 1873- *WhAm 5*
Darling, Arthur Burr 1892-1971 *WhAm 5*
Darling, Byron Clary 1875-1926 *NatCAB 26*
Darling, C Coburn 1887-1965 *WhAm 4*
Darling, Charles Ellett 1917-1974 *WhAm 6*
Darling, Charles Hial 1859-1944 *WhAm 2*
Darling, Charles Kimball 1864-1926 *WhAm 1*
Darling, Charles William 1830-1905 *NatCAB 6, TwCBDA, WhAm 1*
Darling, Charlotte Kelsey *WomWWA 14*
Darling, Chester Arthur 1880- *WhAm 6*
Darling, Edward 1907-1974 *WhAm 6*
Darling, Elmer Albert 1848-1931 *NatCAB 24*
Darling, Flora Adams 1840- *AmWom*
Darling, Flora Adams 1840-1909 *WhAm 1*
Darling, Flora Adams 1840-1910 *DcAmB, NatCAB 19, NotAW*
Darling, Frank Wilkinson 1865-1941 *NatCAB 31*
Darling, Grace 1867- *WomWWA 14*
Darling, Harriet L B 1872- *WomWWA 14*
Darling, Henry 1823-1891 *ApCAB, DcAmB, NatCAB 7, TwCBDA, WhAm H*
Darling, Herbert Franklin 1904-1968 *WhAm 5*
Darling, Ira Alphonso 1888-1941 *NatCAB 35*
Darling, J *NewYHSD*
Darling, James Sands 1899-1951 *NatCAB 42*
Darling, Jay Norwood 1876-1962 *WhAm 4*
Darling, John Adams 1802-1879 *NatCAB 9*
Darling, John Augustus 1835-1912 *NatCAB 8, WhAm 1*
Darling, John Henry 1847- *NatCAB 16*
Darling, Joseph Robinson 1872-1957 *NatCAB 43, WhAm 5*
Darling, Louis, Jr. 1916-1970 *WhAm 5*
Darling, Mae Sherman 1871- *WomWWA 14*
Darling, Mary Elizabeth *WomWWA 14*
Darling, Mary Greenleaf 1848- *WhAm 4*
Darling, Mason Cook 1801-1866 *BiAUS, BiDrAC, WhAm H*
Darling, Milton Alfred 1889-1963 *NatCAB 50*
Darling, Nelson Jarvie 1884-1942 *NatCAB 33*
Darling, Noyes 1782-1846 *ApCAB, Drake*
Darling, Philip Grenville 1878- *WhAm 6*
Darling, Robert Ensign 1904-1969 *WhAm 5*
Darling, Samuel Taylor 1872-1925 *ApCAB X, DcAmB, NatCAB 19, WhAm 1*
Darling, Sid L 1894-1971 *WhAm 5*
Darling, Thomas 1863- *ApCAB X*
Darling, Timothy Grenville 1842- *TwCBDA*
Darling, William 1815- *ApCAB*
Darling, William 1819-1885 *ApCAB*
Darling, William Augustus 1817-1895 *BiAUS, BiDrAC, WhAm H*
Darling, William Lafayette 1856-1938 *NatCAB 17, NatCAB 29, WhAm 1*
Darlington, Alice Benning 1906-1973 *NatCAB 57*
Darlington, Charles Francis 1860-1938 *WhAm 1*
Darlington, Charles Goodliffe 1892-1960 *WhAm 4*
Darlington, Charles Joseph 1894-1966 *WhAm 4*
Darlington, Edward 1795-1884 *BiAUS, BiDrAC, TwCBDA, WhAm H*
Darlington, Ella Louise Bearns 1859- *BiCAW, WomWWA 14*
Darlington, Frederick 1867-1943 *WhAm 3*
Darlington, Hannah Anne Goodliffe 1830-1900 *BiCAW*
Darlington, Henry 1889-1955 *NatCAB 45, WhAm 3*

Darlington, Henry Townsend 1875-1964 *NatCAB 51*
Darlington, Herbert Seymour 1876-1924 *NatCAB 36*
Darlington, Isaac 1781-1839 *BiAUS, BiDrAC, TwCBDA, WhAm H*
Darlington, Isabel 1865- *WomWWA 14*
Darlington, James Henry 1856-1930 *ApCAB X, NatCAB 1, NatCAB 15, TwCBDA, WhAm 1*
Darlington, Joseph James 1849-1920 *NatCAB 19, WhAm 1*
Darlington, O'Hara 1849-1916 *NatCAB 16*
Darlington, Smedley 1827-1899 *BiDrAC, NatCAB 32, TwCBDA*
Darlington, Thomas 1826-1903 *WhAm 1*
Darlington, Thomas 1858-1945 *NatCAB 2, NatCAB 34, TwCBDA, WhAm 2*
Darlington, Urban Valentine Williams 1870-1954 *NatCAB 41, WhAm 3*
Darlington, William 1782-1863 *AmBi, ApCAB, BiAUS, BiDrAC, DcAmB, DcScB, Drake, NatCAB 10, TwCBDA, WhAm H*
Darlington, William McCullough 1815-1889 *NatCAB 16*
Darlow, Albert Edward 1899-1966 *WhAm 4*
Darlow, Edward Ruff 1851-1933 *NatCAB 24*
Darms, John Martin George 1873- *WhAm 2*
Darnall, Carl Rogers 1867-1941 *WhAm 1*
Darnall, Marcy Bradshaw 1872-1960 *WhAm 4*
Darnall, William Edgar 1869-1937 *WhAm 1*
Darnand, Joseph 1897-1945 *WhWW-II*
Darnell, Henry Faulkner 1831-1917 *WhAm 1*
Darnell, Linda 1923-1965 *WhAm 4*
Darnell, Samuel Irwin 1884-1958 *NatCAB 45*
Darnton, Eleanor Choate 1907-1968 *WhAm 5*
Darr, Earl A 1883-1963 *WhAm 4*
Darr, Edward A 1890-1958 *WhAm 3*
Darr, John Whittier 1888-1972 *WhAm 5*
Darr, Loren Robert 1897-1968 *WhAm 5*
Darrach, Eugene Haslet 1866-1938 *NatCAB 28*
Darrach, James 1828- *TwCBDA*
Darrach, William 1876-1948 *WhAm 2*
Darragh, Archibald Bard 1840-1927 *BiDrAC, WhAm 4*
Darragh, Cornelius 1809-1854 *BiDrAC, WhAm H*
Darragh, Cornelius 1809-1855 *BiAUS, TwCBDA*
Darragh, John *NewYHSD*
Darragh, Lydia Barrington 1729-1789 *NotAW, WebAMB*
Darrah, Ann Sophia Towne 1819-1881 *NewYHSD, WhAm H*
Darrah, Charles Dana 1876-1924 *NatCAB 32*
Darrah, Leon Calvin 1889-1957 *NatCAB 46*
Darrah, Lydia *ApCAB*
Darrah, Thomas W 1873-1955 *WhAm 3*
Darrah, William Lee 1911-1973 *WhAm 6*
Darrall, Chester Bidwell 1842-1908 *BiAUS, BiDrAC, TwCBDA, WhAmP*
D'Arrigo, Andrew 1888-1965 *NatCAB 51*
Darrin, Erwin N 1895-1962 *WhAm 4*
Darrow, Anna Albertina Lindstedt 1876-1959 *NatCAB 48*
Darrow, Chester William 1893-1967 *WhAm 5*
Darrow, Clarence Seward 1857-1938 *AmBi, DcAmB S2, EncAB, McGEWB, NatCAB 27, WebAB, WhAm 1*
Darrow, Daniel Cady 1895-1965 *NatCAB 53, WhAm 4*
Darrow, George Frederick 1854-1924 *NatCAB 21*
Darrow, George Potter 1859-1943 *BiDrAC, WhAm 2, WhAmP*
Darrow, T H *NewYHSD*
Darrow, Walter Nicholas Paine 1863-1926 *NatCAB 24*
Darsey, Joseph Frederick 1926-1974 *WhAm 6*
Darsie, Darsie Lloyd 1896-1960 *WhAm 4*
Darsie, Marvin Lloyd 1887-1940 *WhAm 1*
Darst, Joseph Miltenberger 1889-1953 *WhAm 3*
Darst, Thomas Campbell 1875-1948 *NatCAB 35, WhAm 2*
Dart, Carlton Rollin 1862-1929 *WhAm 1*
Dart, Edward Dupaquier 1922-1975 *WhAm 6*
Dart, Frederick *NewYHSD*
Dart, Henry Plauche 1858-1934 *DcAmB S1,*

WhAm 1

Dart, John Lewis 1854- *WhoColR*
Dart, Maria Elizabeth Bond 1865-
 WomWWA 14
Dart, Raymond Arthur 1893- *AsBiEn*
Dart, Raymond Osborne 1890-1974 *WhAm 6*
Dart, William Crary 1869-1946 *NatCAB 35*
Darte, Franck George 1873-1936 *NatCAB 32*
Darton, Nelson Horatio 1865-1948 *DcAmB S4,*
 NatCAB 37, WhAm 2
D'Arusmont, Frances Wright *Drake, NotAW*
Darvas, Lili 1902-1974 *WhAm 6*
D'Arville, Camille 1863-1932 *WhAm 1*
Darvin, Erasmus *NewYHSD*
Darwin, C B *BiAUS*
Darwin, Charles Carlyle 1848- *WhAm 1*
Darwin, Charles Galton 1887-1962 *DcScB,*
 WhAm 4
Darwin, Charles Robert 1809-1882 *ApCAB Sup,*
 AsBiEn, DcScB, McGEWB
Darwin, Erasmus 1731-1802 *AsBiEn, DcScB*
Darwin, Francis 1848-1925 *DcScB*
Darwin, Sir George Howard 1845-1912 *AsBiEn,*
 DcScB
Darwin, Gertrude Bascom 1855-1911 *WhAm 1*
Darwin, Sir Robin 1910-1973 *WhAm 6*
Das, Chitta Ranjan 1870-1925 *McGEWB*
Das, Rajani Kanta 1881- *WhAm 6*
Das, Taraknath 1884-1958 *WhAm 3*
Dasabala *DcScB*
Dasburg, Andrew Michael 1887- *BnEnAmA,*
 IlBEAAW
D'Ascenzo, Nicola 1871-1954 *WhAm 3*
Dasch, George 1887-1955 *WhAm 3*
Daschbach, Estelle MacCloskey *WomWWA 14*
Dascomb, George Alfred 1861-1934
 NatCAB 27
Dashefsky, George Joseph 1899-1972
 NatCAB 56
Dasher, Benjamin Joseph 1912-1971 *WhAm 5*
Dasher, Charles Lanier, Jr. 1900-1968 *WhAm 5*
Dashiell, Alfred Sheppard 1901-1970
 NatCAB 55, WhAm 5
Dashiell, George 1780-1852 *ApCAB*
Dashiell, John Frederick 1888-1975 *WhAm 6*
Dashiell, Landon Randolph *WomWWA 14*
Dashiell, Paul Joseph 1867-1937 *WhAm 3*
Dashiell, Robert Laurenson 1825-1880
 NatCAB 6, TwCBDA
Dashiell, William Robert 1863-1939 *WhAm 1*
Dashiell, William Wailes 1856-1947
 NatCAB 14, NatCAB 34
Daskam, Walter Duryee 1865-1932 *WhAm 1*
Dassel, Herminia Borchard d1857 *NewYHSD*
Daston, Sarah 1613?- *ApCAB*
Dasypodius, Cunradus 1530?-1600 *DcScB*
Dater, Alfred Warner 1872-1938 *NatCAB 28,*
 WhAm 1
Dates, Henry Baldwin 1869- *WhAm 5*
Dattner, Bernhard 1887-1952 *WhAm 3*
Datus, Jay 1914-1974 *IlBEAAW*
Dau, William Herman Theodore 1864-1944
 WhAm 2
Daubenton, Louis Jean-Marie 1716-1800 *DcScB,*
 DcScB Sup
Daubeny, Charles Giles Bridle 1795-1867 *DcScB*
Daubigny, Charles Francois 1817-1878
 McGEWB
Daubin, Freeland Allen 1886-1959 *WhAm 3*
Daubrée, Gabriel Auguste 1814-1896 *AsBiEn,*
 DcScB
Daubresse, Isidore 1810-1895 *TwCBDA*
Dauch, Jacob Julius 1857-1918 *NatCAB 18*
Daucher, Louis 1837-1878 *ApCAB*
Dauchy, Walter Edward 1855-1941 *NatCAB 31*
Daudet, Alphonse 1840-1897 *McGEWB*
Daugette, Clarence William 1873-1942
 NatCAB 35, WhAm 2
Daughaday, Hamilton 1840-1904 *NatCAB 16*
Daugherty, Arthur Cornelius 1901-1970
 WhAm 5
Daugherty, Charles M 1854-1919 *WhAm 1*
Daugherty, Duncan W 1895-1969 *WhAm 5*
Daugherty, Edgar Fay 1874-1957 *WhAm 3*
Daugherty, Harry Kerr 1868-1945 *WhAm 3*
Daugherty, Harry Micajah 1860-1941
 ApCAB X, BiDrUSE, DcAmB S3, EncAB,
 NatCAB 33, WebAB, WhAm 1

Daugherty, James Alexander 1847-1920 *BiDrAC,*
 WhAm 4
Daugherty, James Henry 1889-1974 *IlBEAAW,*
 WhAm 6
Daugherty, Jerome 1849- *NatCAB 12,*
 WhAm 4
Daugherty, Lewis Sylvester 1857-1919 *WhAm 1*
Daughters, Freeman 1873-1951 *WhAm 3*
Daughton, Ralph Hunter 1885-1958 *BiDrAC*
Dauila, Alonso De d1536 *ApCAB*
Daulac, Adam 1635-1660 *ApCAB*
Daulton, Agnes McClelland 1867-1944
 WhAm 2, WomWWA 14
Daulton, George 1861-1913 *WhAm 1*
Daumier, Honore Victorin 1808-1879 *McGEWB*
Daumont, Simon Francois d1674 *WhAm H*
Daun, Leopold Joseph, Graf 1705-1766
 WhoMilH
D'Aunoy, Rigney 1890-1941 *WhAm 1*
Dauphin, W J *WhoColR*
Dauser, Sue Sophia 1888- *WebAMB*
Dausman, Ethan Allen 1861-1928 *NatCAB 22*
D'Autremont, Charles, Jr. 1851-1919
 NatCAB 17
D'Autremont, Hubert Hart 1889-1947
 NatCAB 36
Dauvray, Helen 1859- *AmWom, ApCAB*
Dauzvardis, Petras Paulius 1895-1971 *WhAm 5*
Davage, M S *WhoColR*
Davaine, Casimir Joseph 1812-1882 *DcScB*
Davalos, Gil De d1562 *ApCAB*
Davant, Thomas Stovell 1849-1921 *NatCAB 50,*
 WhAm 5
Davee, Henry A 1872-1955 *WhAm 3*
Davee, Thomas 1797-1841 *BiAUS, BiDrAC,*
 TwCBDA, WhAm H
Daveis, Charles Stewart 1788-1865 *DcAmB,*
 WhAm H
Daveiss, Joseph Hamilton 1774-1811 *DcAmB,*
 Drake, NatCAB 6, WhAm H
Daveiss, Maria 1814- *ApCAB, NatCAB 3*
Daveler, Erle Victor 1885-1957 *WhAm 3*
Davenport, Abraham 1715-1789 *ApCAB,*
 Drake
Davenport, Addington 1670-1736 *ApCAB,*
 Drake, TwCBDA
Davenport, Addington 1701-1746 *ApCAB,*
 Drake, TwCBDA
Davenport, Adolphus Hoyt 1828-1873 *ApCAB*
Davenport, Amzi Benedict 1817-1894
 NatCAB 2
Davenport, Basil 1905-1966 *WhAm 4*
Davenport, Bennett Franklin 1845-1927 *ApCAB,*
 ApCAB X, WhAm 1
Davenport, Blanche 1852- *ApCAB*
Davenport, Charles 1812-1903 *ApCAB Sup,*
 ApCAB X
Davenport, Charles Benedict 1866-1944
 ApCAB X, BiDAmEd, DcAmB S3, DcScB,
 NatCAB 15, WhAm 2
Davenport, Deodate Summerfield 1869-1949
 NatCAB 39
Davenport, Edgar Loomis 1816-1877 *NatCAB 9*
Davenport, Edgar Loomis 1862- *ApCAB*
Davenport, Edward John 1899-1953 *NatCAB 39*
Davenport, Edward L 1816-1877 *Drake*
Davenport, Edward Loomis 1814-1877 *ApCAB,*
 TwCBDA
Davenport, Edward Loomis 1815-1877 *AmBi,*
 DcAmB, WhAm H
Davenport, Erwin R 1875-1967 *WhAm 4*
Davenport, Esther C *WomWWA 14*
Davenport, Eugene 1856-1941 *BiDAmEd,*
 DcAmB S3, WhAm 1
Davenport, Fanny Elizabeth Vining 1829-
 ApCAB
Davenport, Fanny Lily Gipsy 1850-1898
 AmWom, ApCAB, NatCAB 4, TwCBDA
Davenport, Fanny Lily Gypsy 1850-1898 *AmBi,*
 DcAmB, NotAW, WhAm H
Davenport, Frances Gardiner 1870- *WhAm 1,*
 WomWWA 14
Davenport, Franklin d1829? *ApCAB, BiAUS,*
 Drake, NatCAB 2
Davenport, Franklin 1752?-1829? *TwCBDA*
Davenport, Franklin 1755-1832 *BiDrAC,*
 WhAm H

Davenport, Frederick Morgan 1866-1956
 BiDrAC, NatCAB 46, WhAm 3
Davenport, Frederick Parker 1853-1909
 WhAm 1
Davenport, George 1783-1845 *AmBi, DcAmB,*
 WhAm H
Davenport, George Edward 1833-1907 *WhAm 1*
Davenport, George Howe 1852-1932
 NatCAB 33
Davenport, George William 1870- *WhAm 5*
Davenport, Gertrude Crotty *WomWWA 14*
Davenport, Gideon I d1967 *WhAm 4*
Davenport, Harry James 1902- *BiDrAC*
Davenport, Henry George Bryant 1866- *ApCAB*
Davenport, Henry Joralemon 1880-1960
 WhAm 4
Davenport, Henry Kallock 1820-1872 *ApCAB,*
 Drake, TwCBDA
Davenport, Herbert Joseph 1861-1931 *AmBi,*
 DcAmB S1, NatCAB 26, WhAm 1
Davenport, Holton 1892-1966 *WhAm 4A*
Davenport, Homer Calvin 1867-1912 *AmBi,*
 DcAmB, NatCAB 11, WhAm 1
Davenport, Ira 1841-1904 *BiDrAC, TwCBDA,*
 WhAm 1
Davenport, Ira Erastus 1839-1911 *DcAmB,*
 WhAm HA, WhAm 4
Davenport, James 1716-1757 *ApCAB, DcAmB,*
 DcAmReB, TwCBDA, WhAm H
Davenport, James 1758-1797 *ApCAB, BiAUS,*
 BiDrAC, Drake, NatCAB 2, TwCBDA,
 WhAm H, WhAmP
Davenport, James Eggleston 1887-1956
 NatCAB 45
Davenport, James Henry 1862-1928 *WhAm 1*
Davenport, James J *BiAUS*
Davenport, James LeRoy 1845-1914
 NatCAB 20, WhAm 1
Davenport, James Sanford 1864-1940 *BiDrAC,*
 WhAm 1, WhAmP
Davenport, Jennie Woolston Rambo
 WomWWA 14
Davenport, John *NewYHSD*
Davenport, John 1597-1669? *DcAmB*
Davenport, John 1597-1670 *AmBi, ApCAB,*
 DcAmReB, Drake, McGEWB, NatCAB 1,
 TwCBDA, WhAm H
Davenport, John 1635-1677 *ApCAB*
Davenport, John 1668-1731 *ApCAB*
Davenport, John 1752-1830 *ApCAB, BiAUS,*
 BiDrAC, Drake, NatCAB 11, TwCBDA,
 WhAm H, WhAmP
Davenport, John 1788-1855 *BiAUS, BiDrAC,*
 WhAm H
Davenport, John 1888-1953 *NatCAB 40*
Davenport, John D *NewYHSD*
Davenport, John Gaylord 1840-1922 *WhAm 1*
Davenport, Joseph Jackson 1852-1921
 NatCAB 19
Davenport, Leroy Benjamin 1888-1966 *WhAm 4*
Davenport, Lily 1854-1879 *ApCAB*
Davenport, Louis Marks 1868-1951 *NatCAB 42,*
 WhAm 5
Davenport, May 1857- *ApCAB*
Davenport, Nicholas T 1831-1867 *ApCAB*
Davenport, Patrick Henry 1803-1890 *NewYHSD*
Davenport, R Briggs d1932 *WhAm 1*
Davenport, Richard 1606-1665 *ApCAB*
Davenport, Richard Graham 1849-1926
 ApCAB X, NatCAB 20, WhAm 1
Davenport, Roy Leonard 1898-1959 *NatCAB 47,*
 WhAm 4
Davenport, Russell Wheeler 1849-1904
 NatCAB 25
Davenport, Russell Wheeler 1899-1954
 DcAmB S5, NatCAB 40, WhAm 3
Davenport, Samuel Arza 1834-1911 *BiDrAC,*
 TwCBDA, WhAm 4
Davenport, Samuel Marshall 1892-1969
 NatCAB 55
Davenport, Stanley Woodward 1861-1921
 BiDrAC, WhAm 4
Davenport, Thomas d1838 *BiAUS, BiDrAC,*
 TwCBDA, WhAm H, WhAmP
Davenport, Thomas 1802-1851 *AmBi, ApCAB,*
 DcAmB, NatCAB 3, TwCBDA, WebAB,
 WhAm H
Davenport, Thomas 1805?- *NewYHSD*

Davenport, Walter 1889-1971 *WhAm 5*
Davenport, Walter Rice 1885-1942 *WhAm 2*
Davenport, William d1858 *ApCAB, Drake*
Davenport, William 1769-1859 *Drake*
Davenport, William 1770-1859 *ApCAB*
Davenport, William 1797-1869 *ApCAB*
Davenport, William Aiken 1869-1946
NatCAB 43
Davenport, William Bates 1847-1929 *ApCAB X,*
NatCAB 2
Davenport, William Francis 1854- *NatCAB 2*
Davenport, William Henry Harrison 1841-1877
DcAmB, WhAm H
Davenport, William Simeon 1861-1937
NatCAB 42
Daves, Edward Graham 1833-1894 *TwCBDA*
Daves, Jessica d1974 *WhAm 6*
Davey, George William *NewYHSD*
Davey, James Charles 1869-1935 *WhAm 1*
Davey, John 1846-1923 *AmBi, DcAmB,*
NatCAB 22, WhAm 1
Davey, Marie Augusta 1865-1932 *WebAB*
Davey, Martin Luther 1884-1946 *BiDrAC,*
NatCAB 34, WhAm 2, WhAmP
Davey, Randall 1887-1964 *IlBEAAW,*
WhAm 4
Davey, Robert Charles 1853-1908 *BiDrAC,*
TwCBDA, WhAm 1, WhAmP
Davey, Wheeler Pedlar 1886-1959 *NatCAB 47,*
WhAm 3
D'Avezac, Auguste Genevieve Valentin
1780-1851 *BiAUS, DcAmB, NatCAB 13,*
WhAm H
David *McGEWB*
David I 1084-1153 *McGEWB*
David, Edward *ApCAB*
David, Edward Wandell 1889-1960 *NatCAB 48,*
WhAm 4
David, Jacques Louis 1748-1825 *McGEWB*
David, Jean Baptist 1761-1841 *ApCAB*
David, John Baptist Maria 1761-1841 *Drake,*
NatCAB 12
David, John Baptist Mary 1761-1841 *AmBi,*
DcAmB, TwCBDA, WhAm H
David, L *NewYHSD*
David, Laurent Olivier 1842- *ApCAB Sup*
David, Louis P *NewYHSD*
David, S S *NewYHSD*
David, Tannatt William Edgeworth 1858-1934
DcScB
David, Vernon Cyrenius 1882-1961 *NatCAB 50,*
WhAm 4
David-Weill, Pierre S Desire Gerard 1900-1975
WhAm 6
Davidge, John Beale 1768-1829 *DcAmB,*
NatCAB 22, WhAm H
Davidge, Walter Dorsey 1823-1901 *NatCAB 13,*
Davidge, Walter Dorsey 1866-1945 *NatCAB 35*
Davidge, William 1847- *ApCAB*
Davidge, William Pleater 1814-1888 *ApCAB,*
DcAmB, NatCAB 11, WhAm H
Davidoff, Eugene 1901-1956 *NatCAB 46*
Davidoff, Leo Max 1898-1975 *WhAm 6*
Davidov, August Yulevich 1823-1885 *DcScB*
Davidow, H M 1900- *WhAm 3*
Davids, A J *NewYHSD*
Davids, James *WhAm H*
Davidson, Adaline White Allen *WomWWA 14*
Davidson, Alexander 1826-1893 *NatCAB 3,*
TwCBDA
Davidson, Alexander Caldwell 1826-1897
BiDrAC, TwCBDA, WhAm H
Davidson, Alfred James 1863- *WhAm 1*
Davidson, Allen Turner 1819-1905 *BiDConf*
Davidson, Anstruther 1860-1932 *NatCAB 14,*
WhAm 1
Davidson, Arnold 1840- *NatCAB 1, WhAm 4*
Davidson, Augustus Cleveland 1846-1938
TwCBDA, WhAm 1
Davidson, Benjamin 1859-1927 *WhAm 1*
Davidson, Bruce 1934- *BnEnAmA*
Davidson, Carter 1905-1965 *WhAm 4*
Davidson, Charles 1852-1919 *BiDAmEd,*
NatCAB 19, TwCBDA, WhAm 1
Davidson, Charles Jackson 1867-1935
NatCAB 39
Davidson, Clinton 1888-1967 *NatCAB 56*
Davidson, Clinton, Jr. 1911-1957 *NatCAB 56*

Davidson, Daniel Rogers 1820-1884 *NatCAB 12*
Davidson, David J 1899-1948 *WhAm 2*
Davidson, DeWitt A 1878- *WhAm 6*
Davidson, Donald 1893-1968 *WhAm 5*
Davidson, Donald Miner 1902-1960 *NatCAB 53,*
WhAm 4
Davidson, Edwin Lee 1863-1941 *WhAm 1*
Davidson, George d1800 *NewYHSD*
Davidson, George 1825-1911 *AmBi, ApCAB,*
DcAmB, NatCAB 7, TwCBDA,
WhAm 1
Davidson, George 1889-1965 *NatCAB 52,*
WhAm 4
Davidson, George A 1896-1963 *WhAm 4*
Davidson, Gratia E Andrews 1846-
WomWWA 14
Davidson, Hannah Amelia Noyes 1852-1932
BiDAmEd, NatCAB 19, WhAm 1,
WomWWA 14
Davidson, Harlan Page 1838-1913 *WhAm 1*
Davidson, Henry Alexander 1905-1973
WhAm 6
Davidson, Irville Fay 1875-1940 *WhAm 1*
Davidson, Irwin Delmore 1906- *BiDrAC*
Davidson, Israel 1870-1939 *DcAmB S2,*
WhAm 1
Davidson, J Brownlee 1880-1957 *NatCAB 43,*
WhAm 3
Davidson, James Edward 1865-1947 *WhAm 2*
Davidson, James Edward 1867-1947
NatCAB 34
Davidson, James Edward 1879-1949 *WhAm 3*
Davidson, James Hamilton 1839- *WhAm 3*
Davidson, James Henry 1858-1918 *BiDrAC,*
NatCAB 18, TwCBDA, WhAm 1,
WhAmP
Davidson, James Ole 1854-1922 *NatCAB 14,*
WhAm 1
Davidson, James Wheeler 1872-1933 *WhAm 1*
Davidson, James Wood 1829-1905 *ApCAB,*
DcAmB, NatCAB 9, TwCBDA,
WhAm 1
Davidson, Jo 1883-1952 *BnEnAmA,*
DcAmB S5, WebAB, WhAm 3
Davidson, John Keay, Sr. 1870-1961
NatCAB 49
Davidson, John S 1845?- *NatCAB 5*
Davidson, John Wynn 1823-1881 *DcAmB,*
WhAm H
Davidson, John Wynn 1824-1881 *ApCAB,*
Drake, TwCBDA
Davidson, Joseph G 1892-1969 *WhAm 5*
Davidson, Joseph Quentin 1905-1969
NatCAB 57, WhAm 5
Davidson, Kenneth Seymour Moorhead
1898-1958 *NatCAB 43*
Davidson, Laura Lee *WhAm 5*
Davidson, Levette Jay 1894-1957 *WhAm 3*
Davidson, Levi P 1817-1842 *ApCAB*
Davidson, Loucretia Isobel 1869- *WhAm 5*
Davidson, Louis Rogers 1866-1941 *NatCAB 31,*
WhAm 1
Davidson, Lucretia Maria 1808-1825 *ApCAB,*
DcAmB, Drake, NatCAB 7, NotAW,
TwCBDA, WhAm H
Davidson, Lyal Ament 1886-1950 *NatCAB 40,*
WhAm 3
Davidson, Margaret Miller 1823-1837 *Drake*
Davidson, Margaret Miller 1823-1838 *ApCAB,*
DcAmB, NatCAB 7, NotAW, WhAm H
Davidson, Mary Blossom d1968 *WhAm 5*
Davidson, Mary Brewin 1869- *WomWWA 14*
Davidson, Maurice Philip 1879-1956
NatCAB 46, WhAm 3
Davidson, Robert 1750-1812 *ApCAB, DcAmB,*
NatCAB 6, TwCBDA, WhAm H
Davidson, Robert 1808-1876 *ApCAB,*
NatCAB 4, TwCBDA, WhAm H
Davidson, Robert Hamilton McWhorta
1832-1908 *BiDrAC, TwCBDA, WhAmP*
Davidson, Robert Jackson 1850-1930 *ApCAB X*
Davidson, Robert James 1862-1915 *WhAm 1*
Davidson, Roy Elton 1901-1964 *WhAm 4*
Davidson, Royal Page d1943 *WhAm 2*
Davidson, Samuel Presley 1847- *WhAm 1*
Davidson, Shelby Jeames 1868- *WhoColR*
Davidson, Theodore Fulton 1845-1931 *WhAm 1*
Davidson, Thomas 1828-1874 *ApCAB,*

TwCBDA
Davidson, Thomas 1840-1900 *AmBi, ApCAB,*
BiDAmEd, DcAmB, NatCAB 23,
WhAm 1
Davidson, Thomas Green 1805-1883 *BiAUS,*
BiDrAC, TwCBDA, WhAm H
Davidson, Thomas Whitfield 1876-1974
WhAm 6
Davidson, Thomas William 1865- *WhAm 4*
Davidson, Victor H *WhAm 3*
Davidson, Ward Follett 1890-1960 *WhAm 4*
Davidson, Wilbur Leroy 1853-1913 *WhAm 1*
Davidson, William *DcScB*
Davidson, William 1746-1781 *ApCAB, Drake,*
NatCAB 1, TwCBDA
Davidson, William 1778-1857 *BiAUS, BiDrAC,*
TwCBDA, WhAm H
Davidson, William Andrew 1884-1957
NatCAB 47, WhAm 3
Davidson, William Clarence 1848- *TwCBDA*
Davidson, William Johnston 1885-1961
NatCAB 50
Davidson, William Joseph 1869-1968
NatCAB 54
Davidson, William L 1845-1921 *NatCAB 19*
Davidson, William Lee 1746-1781 *DcAmB,*
WhAm H
Davidson, William Mehard 1863-1930
NatCAB 22, WhAm 1
Davidson, William Murray 1869-1922
NatCAB 20
Davie, George Montgomery 1848-1900
NatCAB 10
Davie, John L 1850- *NatCAB 10*
Davie, Maurice R 1893-1964 *WhAm 4*
Davie, Preston 1881-1967 *NatCAB 53,*
WhAm 6
Davie, William R *BiAUS*
Davie, William Richardson 1756-1820 *AmBi,*
ApCAB, BiAUS, DcAmB, Drake,
TwCBDA, WebAMB, WhAm H,
WhAmP
Davie, William Richardson 1759-1820
NatCAB 1
Davies, Acton 1870-1916 *WhAm 1*
Davies, Arthur Bowen 1862-1928 *AmBi,*
BnEnAmA, DcAmB, IlBEAAW,
McGEWB, NatCAB 14, NatCAB 38,
WebAB, WhAm 1
Davies, Arthur Ernest 1867- *WhAm 4*
Davies, Arthur Powell 1902-1957 *WhAm 3*
Davies, Caroline Stodder 1864- *WhAm 4,*
WomWWA 14
Davies, Cecilia 1740-1836 *ApCAB*
Davies, Charles 1798-1876 *ApCAB, BiDAmEd,*
Drake, NatCAB 3, TwCBDA, WhAm H
Davies, Charles Frederick 1838-1865 *NatCAB 3,*
WhAm H
Davies, Charles Towson 1872-1950 *NatCAB 39*
Davies, Daniel Jenkin 1871-1959 *NatCAB 47*
Davies, David Charles 1866-1928 *WhAm 1*
Davies, David L *NewYHSD*
Davies, David Pryce 1870-1948 *NatCAB 36*
Davies, Edward 1779-1853 *BiAUS, BiDrAC,*
WhAm H
Davies, Elmer David 1899-1957 *NatCAB 45*
Davies, Ernest Coulter 1888-1962 *WhAm 4*
Davies, Frank Wesley 1896-1952 *NatCAB 42*
Davies, George Reginald 1876- *WhAm 5*
Davies, Harry William 1896-1956 *WhAm 3*
Davies, Henry Ebenezer 1805-1881 *NatCAB 3,*
TwCBDA
Davies, Henry Eugene 1805-1881 *ApCAB*
Davies, Henry Eugene 1836-1894 *ApCAB,*
DcAmB, NatCAB 3, TwCBDA,
WhAm H
Davies, Henry F 1822-1885? *NewYHSD*
Davies, Hyla Clara Armstrong *WomWWA 14*
Davies, Hywel 1859-1927 *WhAm 1*
Davies, J Clarence 1867- *ApCAB X*
Davies, James 1870-1940 *WhAm 1*
Davies, James William Frederick 1878-1967
WhAm 4
Davies, John Clay 1920- *BiDrAC*
Davies, John Eugene 1839-1900 *TwCBDA*
Davies, John Newton 1881- *WhAm 6*
Davies, John Pugh 1853-1908 *NatCAB 18*
Davies, John Richard 1879-1951 *NatCAB 40*

Davies, John Rumsey 1855-1919 *WhAm 1*
Davies, John Vipond 1862-1939 *ApCAB X, DcAmB S2, NatCAB 14, NatCAB 29, WhAm 1*
Davies, John William 1868-1959 *NatCAB 43*
Davies, Joseph Edward 1876-1958 *WhAm 3*
Davies, Julian Tappan 1845-1920 *WhAm 1*
Davies, Julien Tappan 1845-1920 *ApCAB X, NatCAB 2, TwCBDA*
Davies, Louis Henry 1845- *ApCAB*
Davies, Marianne 1736?-1792 *ApCAB*
Davies, Marion 1900-1961 *WhAm 4*
Davies, Martin 1908-1975 *WhAm 6*
Davies, Morgan Cryder 1895-1952 *NatCAB 41*
Davies, Paul Lewis 1899-1975 *WhAm 6*
Davies, Percy Albert 1896-1961 *WhAm 4*
Davies, Rodger Paul 1921-1974 *WhAm 6*
Davies, Samuel 1723-1761 *AmBi, DcAmB, DcAmReB, Drake, NatCAB 5, WebAB, WhAm H*
Davies, Samuel 1724-1761 *ApCAB, TwCBDA*
Davies, Thomas *NewYHSD*
Davies, Thomas 1736-1766 *ApCAB*
Davies, Thomas Alfred 1809-1899 *ApCAB, Drake, NatCAB 3, TwCBDA*
Davies, Thomas Frederick 1831-1905 *ApCAB Sup, NatCAB 5, TwCBDA, WhAm 1*
Davies, Thomas Frederick 1872-1936 *NatCAB 26, WhAm 1*
Davies, Thomas Stephen 1883-1967 *WhAm 5*
Davies, Thurston Jynkins 1893-1961 *NatCAB 49, WhAm 4*
Davies, Valentine 1905-1961 *NatCAB 50, WhAm 4*
Davies, William *ApCAB, BiAUS, Drake*
Davies, William Gilbert 1842-1910 *NatCAB 1, TwCBDA, WhAm 1*
Davies, William Preston 1862-1944 *WhAm 2*
Davies, William Rupert 1879-1967 *WhAm 4*
Davies, William Walter 1848-1922 *TwCBDA, WhAm 1*
Davies, William Watkins 1868-1945 *NatCAB 34*
Daviess, Joseph Hamilton 1774-1811 *ApCAB, DcAmB, TwCBDA*
Daviess, Maria Thompson 1872-1924 *BiCAW, DcAmB, WhAm 1*
Daviess, Marie Thompson 1872-1924 *WomWWA 14*
DaVigevano *DcScB*
D'Avignon, Francis 1814?- *NewYHSD*
Davila, Carlos 1887-1955 *WhAm 3*
Davila, Celeo 1880- *WhAm 6*
Davila, Charles Alexander 1886-1963 *WhAm 4*
Davila, Felix Cardova 1878-1938 *WhAmP*
Davila, Felix Cordova 1878-1938 *BiDrAC*
Davila, Gil Gonzalez 1570-1658 *ApCAB*
Davila, Nepomuceno 1574-1647 *ApCAB*
Davila, Pedro Franco 1713-1785 *ApCAB*
Davila Y Padilla, Agustin 1562-1604 *ApCAB*
Davila Y Padilla, Augustin 1562-1604 *Drake*
Davin, John Wysor 1892-1949 *NatCAB 37, WhAm 2*
Davin, Nicholas Flood 1843- *ApCAB Sup*
DaVinci, Leonardo 1452-1519 *BiHiMed*
DaVinci, Leonardo *see also* Leonardo DaVinci
Davion, Antony d1727 *ApCAB*
Davis *NewYHSD*
Davis, A M 1883-1971 *WhAm 5*
Davis, Abel 1874-1937 *NatCAB 27, WhAm 1*
Davis, Achilles Edward 1866-1941 *ApCAB X, NatCAB 29, WhAm 4*
Davis, Addison D 1883-1965 *WhAm 4*
Davis, Adelle 1904-1974 *WhAm 6*
Davis, Albert Gould 1871-1939 *WhAm 1*
Davis, Albert Milton 1880-1934 *NatCAB 26*
Davis, Alexander Jackson 1803-1892 *AmBi, ApCAB Sup, BnEnAmA, DcAmB, McGEWB, NatCAB 22, NewYHSD, TwCBDA, WhAm H*
Davis, Alexander Macdonald 1868- *WhAm 4*
Davis, Alexander Mathews 1833-1889 *BiDrAC, WhAm H*
Davis, Alfred Cookman 1875-1946 *WhAm 2*
Davis, Alice Brown 1852-1935 *NotAW*
Davis, Aloysia Mary Hoye *WomWWA 14*
Davis, Alton Frank 1889-1959 *NatCAB 48,*

WhAm 3
Davis, Alva Raymond 1887-1965 *WhAm 4*
Davis, Amos 1794-1835 *ApCAB, BiAUS, BiDrAC, WhAm H*
Davis, Andrew Jackson 1826-1910 *ApCAB, DcAmB, DcAmReB, Drake, NatCAB 8, TwCBDA*
Davis, Andrew Jay 1887-1956 *NatCAB 49, WhAm 3*
Davis, Andrew McFarland 1833-1920 *ApCAB, DcAmB, NatCAB 22, TwCBDA, WhAm 1*
Davis, Anna Beatrice Carter 1859- *WomWWA 14*
Davis, Annie Elizabeth Paret 1869- *WomWWA 14*
Davis, Arlene d1964 *WhAm 4, WhAm 5*
Davis, Arnold Lyman 1873-1940 *WhAm 1*
Davis, Arthur Cayley 1893-1965 *WhAm 4*
Davis, Arthur Kyle 1867-1953 *ApCAB X, WhAm 3*
Davis, Arthur Marshall 1907-1963 *WhAm 4*
Davis, Arthur Newton 1879- *WhAm 5*
Davis, Arthur Pattison 1895-1968 *NatCAB 54*
Davis, Arthur Powell 1861-1933 *AmBi, ApCAB X, DcAmB S1, NatCAB 24, TwCBDA, WhAm 1*
Davis, Arthur Vining 1867-1962 *WhAm 4, WhAm 5*
Davis, Arthur William 1873-1945 *NatCAB 35, WhAm 2*
Davis, Asa Barnes 1861-1930 *NatCAB 29, WhAm 1, WhAm 1C*
Davis, Asahel 1791- *ApCAB, Drake*
Davis, Augustine 1852-1933 *NatCAB 29*
Davis, Augustus Plummer 1835- *NatCAB 12*
Davis, Bancroft Chandler 1853-1934 *NatCAB 26*
Davis, Bancroft Gherardi 1864-1947 *NatCAB 41*
Davis, Beale 1886-1929 *WhAm 1*
Davis, Ben 1877-1950 *NatCAB 40*
Davis, Benjamin Franklin 1832-1863 *ApCAB, NatCAB 10*
Davis, Benjamin Franklin 1844-1934 *NatCAB 28*
Davis, Benjamin Marshall 1867- *WhAm 4*
Davis, Benjamin Oliver, Jr. 1912- *WebAMB*
Davis, Benjamin Oliver, Sr. 1877-1970 *EncAB, WebAB, WebAMB, WhoColR*
Davis, Benson Willis 1907-1959 *WhAm 3*
Davis, Bergen 1869-1958 *WhAm 3*
Davis, Bernard George 1906-1972 *WhAm 5*
Davis, Berry James 1892-1956 *NatCAB 43*
Davis, Bert Byron 1880-1944 *WhAm 2*
Davis, Bessie Blanch Scribner 1869- *WomWWA 14*
Davis, Bette 1908- *WebAB*
Davis, Boothe Colwell 1863-1942 *NatCAB 35, TwCBDA, WhAm 1*
Davis, Bradley Moore 1871-1957 *NatCAB 46, WhAm 3*
Davis, Brinton Beauregard 1872- *WhAm 5*
Davis, Bruce Gregory 1908-1975 *WhAm 6*
Davis, Byron Bennett 1859-1933 *ApCAB X, NatCAB 12, NatCAB 25, WhAm 1*
Davis, C K 1838-1900 *BiAUS*
Davis, C K *see also* Davis, Cushman Kellogg
Davis, C Roy 1882-1939 *NatCAB 30*
Davis, Caleb F *NewYHSD*
Davis, Calvin Olin 1871-1954 *BiDAmEd, WhAm 3*
Davis, Cameron Josiah 1873- *WhAm 3*
Davis, Carl Braden 1877-1950 *WhAm 3*
Davis, Carleton Emerson 1869-1957 *NatCAB 46*
Davis, Carlisle R 1903-1964 *WhAm 4*
Davis, Caroline E 1831- *ApCAB*
Davis, Carroll Campbell 1888-1957 *NatCAB 44*
Davis, Carroll Melvin 1857-1932 *WhAm 1*
Davis, Catherine *NewYHSD*
Davis, Cecil Clark 1877-1955 *WhAm 3*
Davis, Champion McDowell 1879-1975 *WhAm 6*
Davis, Charles 1789-1863 *ApCAB*
Davis, Charles A 1802-1867 *NatCAB 10*
Davis, Charles Albert 1861-1916 *WhAm 1*
Davis, Charles Augustus 1795-1867 *ApCAB,*

Drake
Davis, Charles B 1877-1943 *NatCAB 36, WhAm 2*
Davis, Charles Belmont 1868-1926 *WhAm 1*
Davis, Charles Bridge 1861-1943 *NatCAB 32*
Davis, Charles Edward Law Baldwin 1844-1925 *WhAm 1*
Davis, Charles Ernest, Jr. 1916-1968 *WhAm 5*
Davis, Charles Gilbert 1849-1928 *NatCAB 21, WhAm 1*
Davis, Charles Hague 1869-1957 *NatCAB 46*
Davis, Charles Harold 1856-1933 *AmBi, DcAmB S1, NatCAB 8, WhAm 1*
Davis, Charles Henry 1807-1877 *AmBi, ApCAB, BiAUS, DcAmB, Drake, NatCAB 4, TwCBDA, WebAMB, WhAm H*
Davis, Charles Henry 1845-1921 *AmBi, ApCAB, DcAmB, NatCAB 4, TwCBDA, WhAm 1*
Davis, Charles Henry Stanley 1840-1917 *ApCAB, DcAmB, NatCAB 25, TwCBDA, WhAm 1*
Davis, Charles Hubbard 1906-1976 *WhAm 6*
Davis, Charles K 1889-1968 *WhAm 4A*
Davis, Charles Lukens 1839-1919 *WhAm 1*
Davis, Charles Moler 1900-1972 *WhAm 5*
Davis, Charles Palmer 1859-1921 *WhAm 1*
Davis, Charles Russell 1849-1930 *BiDrAC, WhAm 1, WhAmP*
Davis, Charles Strout 1877-1954 *NatCAB 44, WhAm 3*
Davis, Charles Talcott 1865-1939 *NatCAB 29*
Davis, Charles Thornton 1863-1936 *NatCAB 27, WhAm 4*
Davis, Charles Wellington 1826-1897 *WhAm H*
Davis, Charles Wilder 1833-1898 *ApCAB Sup, TwCBDA*
Davis, Chester Charles 1887-1975 *EncAAH, WhAm 6*
Davis, Chester R 1896-1966 *WhAm 4*
Davis, Clara Marie 1878- *WomWWA 14*
Davis, Clarence Alba d1974 *WhAm 6*
Davis, Claude Jefferson 1923- *WhAm 5*
Davis, Cleland 1869-1948 *NatCAB 39*
Davis, Clifford 1897-1970 *BiDrAC, NatCAB 56, WhAm 5, WhAmP*
Davis, Clinton Wildes 1888-1958 *WhAm 3*
Davis, Clyde Brion 1894-1962 *WhAm 4*
Davis, Cornelia Cassady 1870-1920 *IlBEAAW*
Davis, Cushman Kellogg 1838-1900 *AmBi, ApCAB, BiDrAC, DcAmB, NatCAB 10, TwCBDA, WhAm 1, WhAmP*
Davis, Cushman Kellogg *see also* Davis, C K
Davis, Daniel d1814 *ApCAB, Drake*
Davis, Daniel 1762-1835 *ApCAB, Drake*
Davis, Daniel Franklin 1843-1897 *NatCAB 6, TwCBDA, WhAm H*
Davis, Daniel H 1839-1914 *NatCAB 18*
Davis, Daniel William 1866-1946 *NatCAB 33*
Davis, Darrell Haug 1879-1962 *WhAm 4*
Davis, David *NewYHSD*
Davis, David 1815-1886 *ApCAB, BiAUS, BiDrAC, DcAmB, Drake, EncAB, NatCAB 2, TwCBDA, WebAB, WhAm H, WhAmP*
Davis, David Jackson 1878-1938 *WhAm 1*
Davis, David John 1875-1954 *WhAm 3*
Davis, David William 1873-1959 *NatCAB 46, WhAm 5*
Davis, Dean William 1894-1953 *NatCAB 47*
Davis, Delbert Dwight 1908-1965 *WhAm 4*
Davis, Donald Derby 1888-1950 *WhAm 3*
Davis, Donald W 1882-1950 *WhAm 3*
Davis, Dwight Filley 1879-1945 *ApCAB X, BiDrUSE, DcAmB S3, NatCAB 40, WhAm 2*
Davis, E Asbury 1870-1955 *NatCAB 45, WhAm 3, WhAm 5*
Davis, Earl Fred 1905-1960 *WhAm 4*
Davis, Earl J 1885-1936 *WhAm 1*
Davis, Eben *NewYHSD*
Davis, Edgar Willingham 1896-1970 *NatCAB 55*
Davis, Edith Smith 1859-1917 *WhAm 1*
Davis, Edith Smith 1869-1917 *WomWWA 14*
Davis, Edmund 1824-1880 *NatCAB 12*
Davis, Edmund Jackson d1883 *BiAUS,*

NatCAB 9

Davis, Edmund Jackson 1827-1883 *DcAmB, WhAm H, WhAmP*

Davis, Edmund Jackson 1830-1883 *TwCBDA*

Davis, Edna Holmes 1870- *WomWWA 14*

Davis, Edward 1845-1918 *WhAm 1*

Davis, Edward C P 1898-1957 *WhAm 3*

Davis, Edward E d1969 *WhAm 5*

Davis, Edward Everett 1881-1950 *WhAm 3*

Davis, Edward Gorton 1880-1930 *NatCAB 26, WhAm 1*

Davis, Edward Jackson 1870- *WhoColR*

Davis, Edward Parker 1856-1937 *NatCAB 29, WhAm 4*

Davis, Edward Porter 1879- *WhoColR*

Davis, Edwin 1888-1964 *NatCAB 52, WhAm 4*

Davis, Edwin Adams 1904- *EncAAH*

Davis, Edwin G 1874- *WhAm 5*

Davis, Edwin Hamilton 1811-1888 *ApCAB, DcAmB, Drake, NatCAB 13, TwCBDA, WhAm H*

Davis, Edwin Weyerhaeuser 1895-1962 *WhAm 4*

Davis, Effa Vetina d1936 *WhAm 1*

Davis, Eliakim *NewYHSD*

Davis, Elisha Thomas 1856-1917 *NatCAB 18*

Davis, Elizabeth Brown *WomWWA 14*

Davis, Elizabeth R *WomWWA 14*

Davis, Ella Marion Briggs 1872- *WomWWA 14*

Davis, Ellery Williams 1857-1918 *NatCAB 8, WhAm 1*

Davis, Elmer Holmes 1890-1958 *EncAB, NatCAB 50, WebAB, WhAm 3*

Davis, Elmer Joseph 1869- *WhAm 5*

Davis, Elvert Mont 1875-1942 *NatCAB 31*

Davis, Emerson 1798-1866 *ApCAB, Drake, NatCAB 10, TwCBDA, WhAm H*

Davis, Ethel 1886- *WomWWA 14*

Davis, Eugene Keene 1895-1950 *NatCAB 37*

Davis, Ewin Lamar 1876-1949 *BiDrAC, NatCAB 36, WhAm 2, WhAmP*

Davis, Ezekiel Forman Chambers 1847-1895 *NatCAB 12*

Davis, Fannie Stearns 1884- *WomWWA 14*

Davis, Fay d1945 *WhAm 2*

Davis, Florence Harriet 1868- *WomWWA 14*

Davis, Floyd Macmillan 1896-1966 *IlBEAAW*

Davis, Frances Lewis *WomWWA 14*

Davis, Francis Breese, Jr. 1883-1962 *NatCAB 51, WhAm 4*

Davis, Frank, Jr. 1875-1929 *NatCAB 21, WhAm 1*

Davis, Frank Biddle 1857-1923 *ApCAB X*

Davis, Frank Coley 1868-1948 *NatCAB 40*

Davis, Frank DeMontibirt 1852- *WhAm 4*

Davis, Frank Garfield 1884-1957 *WhAm 3*

Davis, Frank Morgan 1850-1913 *NatCAB 17*

Davis, Frank Parker 1870-1958 *WhAm 3*

Davis, Fred Brownell 1872-1943 *NatCAB 32*

Davis, Fred Henry 1894-1937 *NatCAB 37, WhAm 1*

Davis, Frederick Barton 1909-1975 *WhAm 6*

Davis, Frederick Henry 1853-1935 *WhAm 1*

Davis, G Howlett 1865-1938 *NatCAB 31*

Davis, Garret 1801-1872 *BiAUS, DcAmB, Drake, WhAm H*

Davis, Garrett 1801-1872 *ApCAB, BiDrAC, NatCAB 2, TwCBDA, WhAmP*

Davis, Gaylord 1897-1972 *WhAm 5*

Davis, Gene 1920- *BnEnAmA*

Davis, George 1820-1896 *BiDConf, DcAmB, NatCAB 3, WhAm H*

Davis, George Allen 1858- *NatCAB 13*

Davis, George Arthur 1892-1969 *WhAm 6*

Davis, George Augustus 1858-1948 *NatCAB 36*

Davis, George Breckenridge 1847-1914 *AmBi, DcAmB, NatCAB 22, WhAm 1*

Davis, George Burwell 1852- *WhAm 4*

Davis, George Gilman 1881-1957 *NatCAB 47, WhAm 4*

Davis, George Gilman 1896-1968 *NatCAB 54*

Davis, George H 1863-1957 *WhAm 3*

Davis, George Harvey 1876-1955 *WhAm 3*

Davis, George Leonard 1833-1884 *NatCAB 11*

Davis, George Perrin 1842-1917 *NatCAB 18*

Davis, George Royal 1840-1899 *ApCAB Sup, BiDrAC, NatCAB 11, TwCBDA,*

WhAm 1

Davis, George Russell 1861- *WhAm 4*

Davis, George Samler 1858-1931 *NatCAB 32, WhAm 1*

Davis, George Solomon 1845- *NatCAB 18*

Davis, George Thomas 1810-1877 *ApCAB, BiAUS, BiDrAC, NatCAB 10, TwCBDA, WhAm H*

Davis, George Thompson Brown 1873- *WhAm 5*

Davis, George Trumbull Moore 1810-1888 *TwCBDA*

Davis, George Washington 1902-1960 *WhAm 4*

Davis, George Whitefield 1839-1918 *AmBi, ApCAB Sup, DcAmB, NatCAB 13, TwCBDA, WhAm 1*

Davis, George William 1858- *WhAm 4*

Davis, George William 1867-1948 *NatCAB 36*

Davis, Georgina A 1850?- *IlBEAAW*

Davis, Gertrude Kahn 1881- *WomWWA 14*

Davis, Gladys Rockmore 1901-1967 *WhAm 4*

Davis, Glenn Robert 1914- *BiDrAC*

Davis, Grace Spencer 1867- *WomWWA 14*

Davis, Graham Lee 1893-1958 *WhAm 3*

Davis, Gwilym George 1857-1918 *WhAm 1*

Davis, H L 1896-1960 *REnAW, WhAm 4*

Davis, Haim Iddell 1865-1938 *NatCAB 28*

Davis, Hal Strange 1900-1959 *WhAm 3*

Davis, Hallie Flanagan 1890-1969 *WhAm 5*

Davis, Hamilton Chace 1899-1953 *NatCAB 46*

Davis, Harlow Morrell 1885-1938 *NatCAB 27*

Davis, Harold Heath 1897-1969 *NatCAB 55*

Davis, Harold Thayer 1892-1974 *WhAm 6*

Davis, Harriet Winton *WomWWA 14*

Davis, Harriett Lobdell 1863- *WomWWA 14*

Davis, Harry 1861-1940 *NatCAB 30*

Davis, Harry Clayton 1868-1968 *NatCAB 56*

Davis, Harry Ellerbe 1905-1968 *WhAm 5*

Davis, Harry Lyman 1878-1950 *NatCAB 42, WhAm 3*

Davis, Harry Orville 1877-1964 *WhAm 4*

Davis, Harry Phillips 1868-1931 *NatCAB 25, WhAm 1*

Davis, Harvey Henry 1894-1969 *WhAm 5*

Davis, Harvey Louis 1861-1956 *NatCAB 47*

Davis, Harvey Nathaniel 1881-1952 *DcAmB S5, NatCAB 40, WhAm 3*

Davis, Hasbrouck 1827-1870 *ApCAB, TwCBDA*

Davis, Hassoldt 1907-1959 *NatCAB 47, WhAm 3*

Davis, Hayne 1868- *WhAm 5*

Davis, Helen Clarkson Miller 1879-1968 *WhAm 5*

Davis, Helen Lee 1876- *WomWWA 14*

Davis, Helen Lockwood 1865- *WomWWA 14*

Davis, Henrietta Vinton *WhoColR*

Davis, Henry 1771-1852 *ApCAB, BiDAmEd, DcAmB, Drake, NatCAB 7, TwCBDA, WhAm H*

Davis, Henry 1880-1960 *WhAm 4*

Davis, Henry Blaine 1884-1950 *NatCAB 40*

Davis, Henry Chandler 1849-1910 *NatCAB 16*

Davis, Henry Chase 1850-1932 *NatCAB 24*

Davis, Henry Edgar 1855- *WhAm 1*

Davis, Henry Gassaway 1823-1916 *AmBi, BiAUS, BiDrAC, DcAmB, NatCAB 10, NatCAB 40, WhAm 1, WhAmP*

Davis, Henry Gassett 1807-1896 *DcAmB, WhAm H*

Davis, Henry Gassoway 1823-1916 *ApCAB Sup, TwCBDA*

Davis, Henry Lyon 1775?-1836 *TwCBDA*

Davis, Henry Lyon 1775?-1837 *WhAm 1*

Davis, Henry Winter 1817-1865 *AmBi, ApCAB, BiAUS, BiDrAC, DcAmB, Drake, McGEWB, NatCAB 2, TwCBDA, WhAm H*

Davis, Herbert Burnham 1867-1928 *NatCAB 22, WhAm 1*

Davis, Herbert John 1893-1967 *WhAm 4*

Davis, Herbert Spencer 1875- *WhAm 5*

Davis, Herman S 1868-1933 *WhAm 1*

Davis, Hewitt Cuba 1902-1970 *NatCAB 55*

Davis, Highland Leonard 1889- *WhoColR*

Davis, Hoagland Cook 1878-1948 *NatCAB 39*

Davis, Horace 1831-1916 *ApCAB, ApCAB X, BiDrAC, DcAmB, NatCAB 7, TwCBDA,*

WhAm 1

Davis, Horace Andrew 1870-1957 *NatCAB 46*

Davis, Horace Meredith 1881-1935 *NatCAB 29*

Davis, Horace Webber 1883-1942 *NatCAB 33*

Davis, Howard 1876-1965 *WhAm 4*

Davis, Howard Benjamin Franklin 1893-1960 *NatCAB 48*

Davis, Howard Clarke 1881- *WhAm 6*

Davis, Howard Hubbell 1883-1945 *NatCAB 34*

Davis, Howland Shippen 1886-1969 *WhAm 5*

Davis, Hugh Orton 1899-1969 *WhAm 5*

Davis, Hymen DeBruin 1863-1916 *NatCAB 17*

Davis, Ida May 1857- *AmWom*

Davis, Ira Cleveland 1886-1961 *WhAm 4*

Davis, Irving Gilman 1885-1939 *WhAm 1*

Davis, Isaac 1745-1775 *ApCAB, TwCBDA*

Davis, Isaac 1799-1883 *ApCAB, NatCAB 11, TwCBDA*

Davis, Isabella Charles 1847- *WomWWA 14a*

Davis, J F d1972 *WhAm 5*

Davis, J Frank 1870-1942 *WhAm 1*

Davis, J Leslie 1872-1936 *NatCAB 27*

Davis, J Lionberger 1878-1973 *WhAm 5*

Davis, J M *NewYHSD*

Davis, J Wales 1890-1950 *NatCAB 40*

Davis, Jackson 1882-1947 *NatCAB 37, WhAm 2*

Davis, Jacob 1739-1814 *NatCAB 16*

Davis, Jacob 1887-1948 *NatCAB 36*

Davis, Jacob Cunningham 1820-1883 *BiDrAC, WhAm H*

Davis, Jacob Erastus 1905- *BiDrAC*

Davis, James 1721-1785 *NatCAB 7*

Davis, James 1852-1926 *NatCAB 16, WhAm 1*

Davis, James Cox 1857-1937 *NatCAB 28, WhAm 1*

Davis, James Curran 1895- *BiDrAC, WhAmP*

Davis, James Ellsworth 1875-1959 *NatCAB 49*

Davis, James Harvey 1853-1940 *BiDrAC, WhAm 4*

Davis, James John 1873-1947 *ApCAB X, BiDrAC, BiDrUSE, DcAmB S4, NatCAB 38, WhAm 2, WhAmP*

Davis, James Russell 1871-1924 *NatCAB 21*

Davis, James Sherman 1869-1969 *WhAm 5*

Davis, James Thomas 1880-1950 *WhAm 3*

Davis, Jeanne Frances West 1922-1975 *WhAm 6*

Davis, Jeff 1862-1913 *BiDrAC, DcAmB, REnAW, WhAm 1*

Davis, Jefferson 1808-1889 *AmBi, ApCAB, BiAUS, BiDConf, BiDrAC, BiDrUSE, DcAmB, Drake, EncAAH, EncAB, McGEWB, NatCAB 4, REnAW, TwCBDA, WebAB, WhAm H, WhAmP*

Davis, Jefferson 1862-1913 *NatCAB 13*

Davis, Jefferson C 1828-1879 *ApCAB, Drake, NatCAB 5*

Davis, Jefferson Clarke 1828-1879 *TwCBDA*

Davis, Jefferson Columbus 1828-1879 *DcAmB, WebAMB, WhAm H*

Davis, Jennie Eliza *WomWWA 14*

Davis, Jerome 1891- *ApCAB X*

Davis, Jerome Dean 1838-1910 *DcAmB*

Davis, Jess Harrison 1906-1972 *NatCAB 57, WhAm 5*

Davis, Jesse Buttrick 1871-1955 *BiDAmEd, WhAm 3*

Davis, Jesse Duke 1900-1960 *WhAm 4*

Davis, Jessie Bartlett 1860- *AmWom, TwCBDA*

Davis, Jessie Freemont Snow 1887- *IlBEAAW*

Davis, Jessie Fremont 1861-1905 *NatCAB 8*

Davis, Joan 1912-1961 *WhAm 4*

Davis, Joe L 1869-1941 *WhAm 2*

Davis, Joe Lee 1906-1974 *WhAm 6*

Davis, John 1550?-1605 *ApCAB, Drake, McGEWB*

Davis, John 1721-1809 *ApCAB*

Davis, John 1737-1772 *ApCAB*

Davis, John 1761-1847 *ApCAB, BiAUS, DcAmB, Drake, NatCAB 22, TwCBDA, WhAm H*

Davis, John 1780?-1838? *DcAmB, WhAm H*

Davis, John 1787-1854 *ApCAB, BiAUS, BiDrAC, DcAmB, Drake, NatCAB 1, TwCBDA, WhAm H, WhAmP*

Davis, John 1788-1878 *BiAUS, BiDrAC, WhAm H*
Davis, John 1826-1901 *BiDrAC, TwCBDA*
Davis, John 1851-1902 *ApCAB, NatCAB 5, TwCBDA, WhAm 1*
Davis, John A G 1801-1840 *ApCAB, Drake, NatCAB 5, WhAm H*
Davis, John Carlyle 1878-1948 *NatCAB 36*
Davis, John Chandler Bancroft 1822-1907 *ApCAB, BiAUS, DcAmB, NatCAB 11, TwCBDA, WhAm 1*
Davis, John Charles 1852-1909 *WhAm 1*
Davis, John D 1854-1926 *NatCAB 27, WhAm 1*
Davis, John David 1851- *NatCAB 12*
Davis, John DeWitt 1890-1965 *WhAm 4*
Davis, John Eayres 1891-1961 *NatCAB 46*
Davis, John Francis 1859-1930 *WhAm 1*
Davis, John Given 1810-1866 *BiAUS, BiDrAC, TwCBDA, WhAm H*
Davis, John Hart 1887-1964 *NatCAB 51*
Davis, John James 1835-1916 *BiAUS, BiDrAC*
Davis, John June 1885-1965 *NatCAB 52*
Davis, John Kennerly, Sr. 1906-1975 *WhAm 6*
Davis, John Ker 1882-1969 *WhAm 5*
Davis, John Lee 1825-1889 *ApCAB, DcAmB, NatCAB 23, TwCBDA, WhAm H*
Davis, John Marcus 1871-1944 *WhAm 2*
Davis, John McCan 1866-1916 *WhAm 1*
Davis, John Merrill 1846-1920 *TwCBDA, WhAm 1*
Davis, John Moore Kelso 1844-1920 *WhAm 1*
Davis, John Parker 1832-1910 *NewYHSD*
Davis, John Patterson 1862-1903 *WhAm 1*
Davis, John Rose Wilson 1868-1947 *NatCAB 38, WhAm 4*
Davis, John Staige 1872-1946 *DcAmB S4, NatCAB 36, WhAm 2*
Davis, John Warren 1867-1945 *NatCAB 33*
Davis, John Warren 1888- *BiDAmEd*
Davis, John Wesley 1799-1859 *AmBi, ApCAB, BiAUS, BiDrAC, DcAmB, Drake, NatCAB 8, TwCBDA, WhAm H, WhAmP*
Davis, John William 1826-1907 *NatCAB 9, TwCBDA, WhAm 1*
Davis, John William 1873-1955 *ApCAB X, BiDrAC, DcAmB S5, EncAB, NatCAB 45, WebAB, WhAm 3, WhAmP*
Davis, John William 1916- *BiDrAC*
Davis, John Williams 1887-1938 *NatCAB 33, WhAm 1*
Davis, John Woodbridge 1854-1902 *ApCAB, NatCAB 4, TwCBDA, WhAm 1*
Davis, Jonathan McMillan 1871-1943 *WhAm 2*
Davis, Joseph B *NewYHSD*
Davis, Joseph Baker 1845-1920 *NatCAB 18, WhAm 1*
Davis, Joseph D *NewYHSD*
Davis, Joseph Emory 1784-1870 *ApCAB, TwCBDA*
Davis, Joseph H *BnEnAmA, NewYHSD*
Davis, Joseph J 1840- *BiAUS*
Davis, Joseph John 1828-1892 *NatCAB 7, TwCBDA*
Davis, Joseph Jonathan 1828-1892 *BiDrAC, WhAm H*
Davis, Joseph Phineas 1837-1917 *ApCAB X, NatCAB 13, NatCAB 25, WhAm 1*
Davis, Joseph Robert 1825-1896 *BiDConf, DcAmB, WhAm H*
Davis, Joseph Slocum 1812-1884 *ApCAB*
Davis, Joseph Smith 1923-1969 *WhAm 5*
Davis, Joseph Stancliffe 1885-1975 *WhAm 6*
Davis, Joshua A 1903-1963 *WhAm 4*
Davis, Kary Cadmus 1867-1936 *WhAm 1*
Davis, Kate 1877- *WomWWA 14*
Davis, Kate Embry Dowdle 1871- *WomWWA 14*
Davis, Katharine Bement 1860-1935 *AmBi, BiCAW, DcAmB S1, NotAW, WhAm 1, WomWWA 14, WomWWA 14a*
Davis, Katherine Bement 1860-1935 *ApCAB X*
Davis, Keene West *NewYHSD*
Davis, L Clark 1835- *ApCAB*
Davis, LeCompte 1864- *ApCAB X, WhAm 3*
Davis, Lee Parsons 1882-1961 *NatCAB 50*
Davis, Lemuel Clarke 1835-1904 *WhAm 1*

Davis, Leonard Moore 1864-1938 *ApCAB X, IlBEAAW, WhAm 1*
Davis, Leonidas Cary 1901-1958 *NatCAB 48*
Davis, Lew E 1910- *IlBEAAW*
Davis, Lincoln 1872-1952 *NatCAB 41*
Davis, Llewellyn Farnum 1876-1953 *NatCAB 42*
Davis, Lowndes Henry 1836-1920 *BiDrAC, NatCAB 19, TwCBDA*
Davis, Lucia 1880- *WomWWA 14*
Davis, Lucy *WomWWA 14*
Davis, Lucy Belle Sizer *WomWWA 14*
Davis, Lucy Pryor McIlwaine 1867- *WomWWA 14*
Davis, Luther Cochran 1894-1932 *NatCAB 25*
Davis, Lydia Martin 1849- *WomWWA 14*
Davis, Lyman Edwyn 1854-1930 *WhAm 1*
Davis, M Louisa Robbins *WomWWA 14*
Davis, Malcolm McTear 1921-1973 *WhAm 5*
Davis, Malvin Edward 1901-1966 *WhAm 4*
Davis, Manton 1876-1957 *NatCAB 50, WhAm 3*
Davis, Manvel H 1891-1959 *WhAm 3*
Davis, Mary Evelyn Moore 1852-1909 *DcAmB, NatCAB 10, WhAm 1*
Davis, Mary Fenn 1824-1886 *NotAW*
Davis, Mary Gould 1882-1956 *WhAm 3*
Davis, Mary R Gale *WomWWA 14*
Davis, Matthew L 1766-1850 *ApCAB, Drake, NatCAB 3, NatCAB 5*
Davis, Matthew Livingston 1773-1850 *AmBi, DcAmB, WhAm H*
Davis, Maud Shepherd 1873- *WomWWA 14*
Davis, Merle Halsey 1893-1967 *NatCAB 56*
Davis, Mervyn 1881- *WhAm 6*
Davis, Michael Marks 1879-1971 *WhAm 5*
Davis, Miles Dewey, Jr. 1926- *WebAB*
Davis, Miles Lewis 1845-1923 *NatCAB 25*
Davis, Milton Daland 1902-1967 *NatCAB 53*
Davis, Milton Fennimore 1864-1938 *NatCAB 27, WhAm 1*
Davis, Minnie S 1835- *AmWom, WhAm 4, WomWWA 14*
Davis, Minor Meek 1858-1934 *NatCAB 25*
Davis, Minta S A 1864- *AmWom*
Davis, Miriam Maduro Peixotto 1842-1923 *BiCAW*
Davis, Mollie Evelyn Moore 1844-1909 *NotAW*
Davis, Mollie Evelyn Moore 1852-1909 *AmWom*
Davis, Monnett Bain 1893-1953 *NatCAB 47, WhAm 3*
Davis, Myron, Jr. 1872-1930 *ApCAB X*
Davis, N Evan 1875-1944 *NatCAB 34*
Davis, Nathan Smith 1817-1904 *AmBi, ApCAB, BiDAmEd, BiHiMed, DcAmB, NatCAB 10, NatCAB 35, TwCBDA, WhAm 1*
Davis, Nathan Smith 1858-1920 *NatCAB 13, NatCAB 16, NatCAB 35, TwCBDA, WhAm 1*
Davis, Nathan Smith 1889-1956 *WhAm 3*
Davis, Nathaniel French 1847-1921 *TwCBDA, WhAm 1*
Davis, Neal Balbach 1926-1969 *WhAm 5*
Davis, Nellie E 1862- *WomWWA 14*
Davis, Nellie Verrill *WomWWA 14*
Davis, Nelson Clifton 1882-1923 *ApCAB X*
Davis, Nelson Fithian 1872-1939 *WhAm 1*
Davis, Nelson Henry 1821-1890 *ApCAB, TwCBDA*
Davis, Newton Eads 1876-1959 *WhAm 3*
Davis, Nicholas, Jr. 1825-1874 *BiDConf*
Davis, Noah 1802-1830 *NatCAB 11*
Davis, Noah 1818-1902 *ApCAB, BiAUS, BiDrAC, DcAmB, NatCAB 11, TwCBDA, WhAm 1*
Davis, Noah Knowles 1830-1910 *ApCAB, BiDAmEd, DcAmB, NatCAB 4, TwCBDA, WhAm 1*
Davis, Norah 1873- *WomWWA 14*
Davis, Norah 1878- *WhAm 6*
Davis, Norman Hezekiah 1878-1944 *ApCAB X, DcAmB S3, WhAm 2*
Davis, Oakley *NewYHSD*
Davis, Oscar *NewYHSD*
Davis, Oscar Copeland 1870-1922 *NatCAB 19*
Davis, Oscar Franklyn 1861- *TwCBDA,*

WhAm 4
Davis, Oscar King 1866-1932 *DcAmB S1, WhAm 1*
Davis, Ossie 1917- *McGEWB*
Davis, Owen 1874-1956 *NatCAB 45, WhAm 3*
Davis, Ozora Stearns 1866-1931 *NatCAB 24, WhAm 1*
Davis, Paul 1896-1971 *WhAm 5*
Davis, Paul A, III 1872-1948 *WhAm 2*
Davis, Paul Arthur 1889-1967 *WhAm 4A*
Davis, Paul Hazlitt 1889-1969 *WhAm 5*
Davis, Paul Maclin 1882-1969 *NatCAB 55*
Davis, Paulina Kellogg Wright 1813-1876 *ApCAB, DcAmB, NatCAB 22, NotAW, WhAm H, WhAmP*
Davis, Pauline Kellogg Wright 1813-1876 *AmBi*
Davis, Pauline Morton Sabin 1887-1955 *DcAmB S5*
Davis, Perry 1791-1862 *NatCAB 12*
Davis, Philip 1876- *WhAm 5*
Davis, Philip Watkins, Jr. 1887-1964 *NatCAB 51*
Davis, Phineas 1800-1835 *DcAmB, WhAm H*
Davis, Pierpont 1884-1953 *WhAm 3*
Davis, Pierpont V 1884-1965 *WhAm 4*
Davis, R Hayes 1884-1963 *NatCAB 49*
Davis, Ralph Waldo 1895-1960 *NatCAB 48, WhAm 3*
Davis, Raymond Cazallis 1836-1919 *DcAmB, DcAmLiB, TwCBDA, WhAm 1*
Davis, Rebecca Blaine Harding 1831-1910 *AmBi, AmWom, ApCAB, DcAmB, NatCAB 8, NotAW, TwCBDA, WhAm 1*
Davis, Reuben 1813-1890 *ApCAB, BiAUS, BiDConf, BiDrAC, DcAmB, NatCAB 5, TwCBDA, WhAm H, WhAmP*
Davis, Reuben Nelson 1858-1934 *WhAm 1*
Davis, Richard 1904- *IlBEAAW*
Davis, Richard Beale 1845-1917 *WhAm 1*
Davis, Richard Bingham 1771-1799 *ApCAB, Drake, NatCAB 13, WhAm H*
Davis, Richard David 1799-1871 *BiAUS, BiDrAC, WhAm H*
Davis, Richard Hallock 1913-1972 *WhAm 5*
Davis, Richard Harding 1864-1916 *AmBi, ApCAB X, DcAmB, McGEWB, NatCAB 8, TwCBDA, WebAB, WhAm 1*
Davis, Richard Joseph 1883-1956 *NatCAB 44, WhAm 3*
Davis, Richmond Pearson 1866-1937 *WhAm 1*
Davis, Robert 1881- *WhAm 6*
Davis, Robert Asa 1885-1950 *NatCAB 39*
Davis, Robert Courtney 1876-1944 *NatCAB 42, WhAm 2*
Davis, Robert Fisher 1905-1974 *WhAm 6*
Davis, Robert Hobart Clarkson 1869-1942 *NatCAB 34, WhAm 2*
Davis, Robert Lee 1893- *BiDrAC*
Davis, Robert Luther 1903-1961 *NatCAB 50*
Davis, Robert McNair 1884-1959 *WhAm 3*
Davis, Robert Means 1849- *TwCBDA*
Davis, Robert Stewart 1839-1911 *WhAm 1*
Davis, Robert Stewart 1841-1911 *NatCAB 6*
Davis, Robert Thompson 1823-1906 *BiDrAC, TwCBDA*
Davis, Robert Wyche 1849-1929 *BiDrAC, TwCBDA, WhAm 4, WhAmP*
Davis, Roblin Henry 1885-1945 *NatCAB 34, WhAm 2*
Davis, Roger 1762-1815 *BiAUS, BiDrAC, WhAm H*
Davis, Roger Wolcott 1890-1959 *WhAm 3*
Davis, Roland C 1902-1961 *WhAm 4*
Davis, Roland Parker 1884-1974 *WhAm 6*
Davis, Rowland Lucius 1871-1954 *NatCAB 44, WhAm 3*
Davis, Roy 1876-1953 *WhAm 3*
Davis, Roy Tasco 1889-1975 *WhAm 6*
Davis, Royal Jenkins 1878-1934 *WhAm 1*
Davis, Royall Oscar Eugene 1880-1949 *WhAm 2*
Davis, Rufus Alonzo 1904-1967 *NatCAB 54*
Davis, S Hunter 1890-1949 *NatCAB 37*
Davis, Sam 1842-1863 *WhAm H*
Davis, Sammy, Jr. 1925- *WebAB*
Davis, Samuel 1774-1831 *BiAUS, BiDrAC, WhAm H*

Davis, Samuel 1842-1863 *ApCAB Sup*

Davis, Samuel 1844-1863 *NatCAB 8*

Davis, Samuel B *BiAUS*

Davis, Samuel Craft 1871-1940 *NatCAB 31*

Davis, Samuel Jacob 1874- *WhoColR*

Davis, Samuel Rosemond 1888- *WhoColR*

Davis, Samuel T 1838-1908 *NatCAB 3, WhAm 1*

Davis, Sarah Iliff 1820- *AmWom*

Davis, Sheldon Emmor 1876-1964 *WhAm 4*

Davis, Sherman Louis 1865-1940 *NatCAB 39*

Davis, Stephen Brooks 1874-1933 *WhAm 1*

Davis, Stilman George 1887-1955 *NatCAB 45*

Davis, Stuart 1894-1964 *BnEnAmA, EncAB, IlBEAAW, McGEWB, WebAB, WhAm 4*

Davis, Sturgiss Brown 1877- *WhAm 5*

Davis, Susan Topliff 1862- *WhAm 4, WomWWA 14*

Davis, Susie Burdick 1881- *WomWWA 14*

Davis, Sylvanus d1704 *ApCAB, Drake*

Davis, T Carroll 1881-1953 *NatCAB 41*

Davis, T Lawrence 1891-1953 *WhAm 3*

Davis, Tenney Lombard 1890-1949 *WhAm 2*

Davis, Theodore Russell 1840-1894 *IlBEAAW, NewYHSD, REnAW, WhAm H*

Davis, Thomas 1806-1895 *BiAUS, BiDrAC, TwCBDA, WhAm H*

Davis, Thomas Archibald 1858-1938 *NatCAB 29, WhAm 4*

Davis, Thomas Beall 1828-1911 *BiDrAC*

Davis, Thomas Bealle d1948 *WhAm 2*

Davis, Thomas Bodley 1856-1927 *NatCAB 21*

Davis, Thomas Crawley 1900-1964 *WhAm 4*

Davis, Thomas Davis 1846-1916 *NatCAB 14, WhAm 1*

Davis, Thomas Edward 1835-1917 *WhAm 1*

Davis, Thomas Francis 1853-1935 *WhAm 1*

Davis, Thomas Frederick 1804-1871 *ApCAB, Drake Sup, NatCAB 12, TwCBDA*

Davis, Thomas Harold 1880- *WhAm 6*

Davis, Thomas Jefferson 1869-1952 *NatCAB 45, WhAm 3*

Davis, Thomas Latham 1882-1955 *WhAm 3*

Davis, Thomas Terry 1789-1807 *BiAUS, BiDrAC, WhAm H*

Davis, Thomas Treadwell 1810-1872 *ApCAB, BiAUS, BiDrAC, TwCBDA, WhAm H*

Davis, Thomas Walker 1876-1951 *NatCAB 47, WhAm 3*

Davis, Timothy 1794-1872 *BiAUS, BiDrAC, WhAm H*

Davis, Timothy 1821-1888 *BiAUS, BiDrAC, TwCBDA, WhAm H*

Davis, Titus Elwood 1851- *WhAm 4*

Davis, Tobe Coller d1962 *WhAm 4*

Davis, Tom J 1888-1953 *WhAm 3*

Davis, Varina Anne Howell 1826-1906 *AmBi, AmWom, BiDConf, DcAmB, NotAW*

Davis, Varina Anne Jefferson 1864-1898 *AmBi, AmWom, ApCAB Sup, DcAmB, NatCAB 23, TwCBDA, WhAm H*

Davis, Varina Jefferson 1826-1906 *WhAm 1*

Davis, Vernon Mansfield 1855-1931 *NatCAB 33, WhAm 1*

Davis, Virginia Meriwether 1862- *AmWom*

Davis, Wallace McRae 1898-1966 *WhAm 5*

Davis, Walter Clay 1893-1952 *NatCAB 42*

Davis, Walter Gould 1851-1919 *NatCAB 2*

Davis, Walter Scott 1866-1943 *NatCAB 33*

Davis, Walton 1898-1962 *WhAm 4*

Davis, Warren Bartlett 1869-1944 *WhAm 2*

Davis, Warren Beagle 1881-1947 *NatCAB 36*

Davis, Warren Blair 1877-1939 *WhAm 1*

Davis, Warren Johnson 1861- *WhAm 4*

Davis, Warren Ransom 1793-1835 *BiAUS, BiDrAC, TwCBDA, WhAm H*

Davis, Watson 1896-1967 *WhAm 4*

Davis, Wayne Lambert 1904- *IlBEAAW*

Davis, Webster 1861- *TwCBDA*

Davis, Webster 1862-1923 *WhAm 1*

Davis, Werter Renick 1815-1893 *ApCAB, TwCBDA*

Davis, Westmoreland 1859-1942 *NatCAB 37, WhAm 2*

Davis, Whitman 1881- *WhAm 6*

Davis, Will Charles 1913-1951 *NatCAB 41*

Davis, William *NewYHSD*

Davis, William A 1873-1948 *NatCAB 37*

Davis, William Allison 1884-1947 *NatCAB 41*

Davis, William Augustine 1809-1875 *DcAmB, NatCAB 16, WhAm H*

Davis, William Bramwell 1832- *ApCAB*

Davis, William Church 1856-1958 *WhAm 3*

Davis, William Elias Brownlee 1863-1903 *NatCAB 13*

Davis, William Francis, Jr. 1909-1951 *WhAm 3*

Davis, William Garland 1904-1964 *WhAm 4*

Davis, William George Mackey 1812-1898 *BiDConf*

Davis, William H d1970 *WhAm 5*

Davis, William Hammatt 1879-1964 *WhAm 4*

Davis, William Harper 1877- *WhAm 5*

Davis, William Hawley 1880-1962 *NatCAB 50*

Davis, William Henry 1868- *WhAm 4*

Davis, William Herman 1867-1943 *NatCAB 32*

Davis, William Hersey 1887-1950 *WhAm 3*

Davis, William Holmes 1873- *WhAm 5*

Davis, William Horace 1871-1929 *WhAm 1*

Davis, William J *NewYHSD*

Davis, William J 1844-1919 *WhAm 1*

Davis, William Jennings 1853-1916 *NatCAB 17*

Davis, William Jonathan 1839-1900 *NatCAB 13*

Davis, William Joseph 1864-1948 *NatCAB 50*

Davis, William Leonard 1873- *WhoColR*

Davis, William Morris 1815-1891 *BiAUS, BiDrAC, WhAm H*

Davis, William Morris 1850-1934 *AmBi, ApCAB X, BiDAmEd, DcAmB S1, DcScB, McGEWB, NatCAB 24, TwCBDA, WebAB, WhAm 1*

Davis, William Nickels 1873-1949 *NatCAB 38*

Davis, William Philip 1897-1958 *WhAm 3*

Davis, William R 1850-1915 *WhAm 1*

Davis, William Rees 1877-1947 *WhAm 2*

Davis, William Riley 1886-1955 *NatCAB 44*

Davis, William Sidney 1832-1886 *NatCAB 8*

Davis, William Stearns 1877-1930 *ApCAB X, NatCAB 24, WhAm 1*

Davis, William Thomas 1822-1907 *DcAmB, WhAm 1*

Davis, William Thornwall 1877-1944 *NatCAB 34, WhAm 2*

Davis, William Warren 1862-1941 *WhAm 1*

Davis, William Watts Hart 1820-1910 *REnAW, WhAm 1*

Davis, William Whiting 1859- *WhAm 4*

Davis, William Z 1839-1926 *WhAm 1*

Davis, Winnie 1864-1898 *AmBi, DcAmB*

Davis, Wirt 1839-1914 *WhAm 1*

Davis, Wirt 1873-1945 *WhAm 2*

Davis, Woodbury 1818-1871 *ApCAB*

Davison, Albert Watson 1888-1960 *WhAm 4*

Davison, Alvah Eugene 1863-1928 *NatCAB 21*

Davison, Alvin 1868-1915 *NatCAB 18*

Davison, Archibald Thompson 1883-1961 *WhAm 4*

Davison, Charles 1858-1942 *WhAm 1*

Davison, Charles 1891-1965 *NatCAB 56*

Davison, Charles Stewart 1855-1942 *NatCAB 34, WhAm 2*

Davison, Chester Oliver 1888-1967 *NatCAB 53*

Davison, Clarence Maynard 1893-1964 *NatCAB 52*

Davison, Darius 1819- *NatCAB 2*

Davison, Donald Angus 1892-1944 *WhAm 2*

Davison, E Mora 1853-1927 *ApCAB X, NatCAB 34*

Davison, Edward 1898-1970 *WhAm 5*

Davison, F Trubee 1896-1974 *WhAm 6*

Davison, Francis Lyle 1911-1973 *WhAm 6*

Davison, Frank Elon 1887-1960 *WhAm 4*

Davison, George Mosby 1855-1912 *BiDrAC*

Davison, George Stewart 1856-1942 *NatCAB 33, WhAm 2*

Davison, George Willets 1872-1953 *DcAmB S5, NatCAB 42, WhAm 3*

Davison, Gregory Caldwell 1871-1935 *DcAmB S1, NatCAB 26, WebAMB*

Davison, Harry P 1898-1961 *WhAm 4*

Davison, Henry James 1835-1890 *NatCAB 28*

Davison, Henry Pomeroy 1867-1922 *AmBi, ApCAB X, DcAmB, NatCAB 20, WhAm 1*

Davison, Mrs. Henry Pomeroy 1871- *WhAm 5*

Davison, Homer R 1899-1972 *WhAm 5*

Davison, Hugh Loyd 1896-1944 *NatCAB 41*

Davison, John 1858-1924 *WhAm 1*

Davison, John A 1888-1947 *WhAm 2*

Davison, John Mason 1840-1915 *NatCAB 17*

Davison, Kate Trubee 1871- *BiCAW*

Davison, Marshall 1896-1946 *NatCAB 35*

Davison, Matthew 1839-1918 *NatCAB 38*

Davison, Peter Weimer 1869-1920 *WhAm 1*

Davison, R Winthrop 1880-1952 *NatCAB 40*

Davison, Sarah M *WomWWA 14*

Davison, Sarah Margaret 1880- *WhAm 6*

Davison, Thomas Callahan 1883-1953 *WhAm 3*

Davison, Wilburt Cornell 1892-1972 *WhAm 5*

Davison, William 1593-1669? *DcScB*

Davison, William Anthony 1866- *WhAm 4*

Davison, William Mercereau, Jr. 1876-1948 *NatCAB 40*

Davison, William Richardson 1876-1959 *NatCAB 47*

Davisson, Albert Eugene d1911 *WhAm 1*

Davisson, Clinton Joseph 1881-1958 *AsBiEn, DcScB, WebAB, WhAm 3*

Davisson, Oscar Fulton 1851-1932 *NatCAB 24*

Davock, Harlow Palmer 1848-1910 *NatCAB 18*

Davol, Joseph 1837-1909 *NatCAB 18*

Davol, Ralph 1874-1966 *WhAm 5*

Davol, William Canedy, Jr. 1841-1925 *NatCAB 20*

Davout, Louis Nicolas 1770-1823 *WhoMilH*

Davy, Sir Humphry 1778-1829 *AsBiEn, DcScB, McGEWB*

Davy, John 1790-1868 *DcScB*

Davy, John Madison 1835-1909 *BiAUS, BiDrAC, TwCBDA, WhAm 1*

Daw, George Weidman 1855-1914 *NatCAB 6*

Dawbarn, Charles 1833- *WhAm 4*

Dawbarn, Robert Hugh Mackay 1860-1915 *NatCAB 48*

Dawe, Grosvenor 1863-1948 *WhAm 2*

Dawe, Helen Cleveland 1909-1971 *WhAm 5*

Dawes, Anna Laurens 1851-1938 *AmWom, WhAm 1, WomWWA 14*

Dawes, Beman Gates 1870-1953 *ApCAB X, BiDrAC, WhAm 3, WhAmP*

Dawes, Charles Gates 1865-1951 *ApCAB Sup, ApCAB X, BiDrAC, BiDrUSE, DcAmB S5, EncAB, NatCAB 14, NatCAB 42, WebAB, WhAm 3, WhAmP*

Dawes, Chester Mitchell 1855-1917 *WhAm 1*

Dawes, H M *NewYHSD*

Dawes, Henry Laurens 1816-1903 *AmBi, ApCAB, BiAUS, BiDrAC, DcAmB, Drake, EncAAH, McGEWB, NatCAB 4, REnAW, TwCBDA, WebAB, WhAm 1, WhAmP*

Dawes, Henry May 1877-1952 *NatCAB 41, WhAm 3*

Dawes, Irving D 1892-1968 *WhAm 5*

Dawes, James William 1845- *ApCAB, NatCAB 12, TwCBDA, WhAm 3*

Dawes, Norman James 1874-1967 *WhAm 4*

Dawes, Rufus 1803-1859 *ApCAB, Drake, NatCAB 10, TwCBDA*

Dawes, Rufus Cutler 1867-1940 *DcAmB S2, NatCAB 14, NatCAB 30, WhAm 1*

Dawes, Rufus R 1838-1899 *ApCAB Sup, BiDrAC, TwCBDA, WhAmP*

Dawes, Thomas 1731-1809 *ApCAB, Drake*

Dawes, Thomas 1757-1825 *ApCAB, TwCBDA*

Dawes, Thomas 1758-1825 *Drake*

Dawes, Willard Crockett 1881-1960 *NatCAB 48*

Dawes, William 1745-1799 *AmBi, ApCAB, DcAmB, WebAMB, WhAm H*

Dawes, William Ruggles 1862-1951 *WhAm 3*

Dawes, William Rutter 1799-1868 *DcScB*

Dawkins, Benjamin Cornwell 1881- *WhAm 6*

Dawkins, Henry d1786? *BnEnAmA, DcAmB, NewYHSD, WhAm H*

Dawkins, James Baird 1820-1883 *BiDConf*

Dawkins, John Lee 1908-1951 *NatCAB 40*

Dawley, Frank E 1863-1936 *WhAm 1*

Dawley, Frank Fremont 1856- *ApCAB X, NatCAB 16*

Dawley, Robert Worthington 1897-1949 *NatCAB 40*

Dawley, Thomas Robinson, Jr. 1862-1930 *ApCAB X, WhAm 1*

Dawley, William Sanborn 1856-1927
NatCAB 26
Dawson, Aeneas MacDonell 1810- *ApCAB Sup*
Dawson, Agnes Wakefield Learned
WomWWA 14
Dawson, Albert Foster 1872-1949 *BiDrAC,*
WhAm 5
Dawson, Alden Benjamin 1892-1968
NatCAB 54
Dawson, Allan 1866-1923 *WhAm 1*
Dawson, Allan 1903-1949 *WhAm 2*
Dawson, Archie Owen 1898-1964 *WhAm 4*
Dawson, Arthur 1858-1922 *WhAm 1*
Dawson, Benjamin Elisha 1852-1922
NatCAB 21, WhAm 1
Dawson, Benjamin Frederick 1847-1888 *ApCAB*
Dawson, Cecil Forrest 1893-1960 *WhAm 4*
Dawson, Charles 1864-1916 *DcScB*
Dawson, Charles I 1881-1969 *WhAm 5*
Dawson, Claude Ivan 1877- *WhAm 5*
Dawson, Clyde C 1864-1927 *NatCAB 21,*
WhAm 1
Dawson, Daniel L 1855-1893 *NatCAB 6*
Dawson, Edgar 1872-1946 *WhAm 2*
Dawson, Edward 1871-1947 *WhAm 2*
Dawson, Francis Warrington 1840-1889 *DcAmB,*
NatCAB 12, NatCAB 23, TwCBDA,
WhAm H
Dawson, Fred 1891-1964 *WhAm 4*
Dawson, George 1813-1883 *ApCAB,*
NatCAB 2, TwCBDA, WhAm H
Dawson, George Ellsworth 1861-1936 *WhAm 1,*
WhAm 1C
Dawson, George Louis 1895-1963 *WhAm 4*
Dawson, George Mercer 1849- *ApCAB*
Dawson, George Walter 1870-1938 *WhAm 1*
Dawson, Henry Barton 1821-1889 *ApCAB,*
DcAmB, Drake, TwCBDA, WhAm H
Dawson, Homer Casner 1882-1966 *NatCAB 52*
Dawson, J Douglas 1906-1971 *WhAm 6*
Dawson, J W 1820-1899 *Drake*
Dawson, James Frederick 1874- *WhAm 5*
Dawson, John 1762-1814 *ApCAB, BiAUS,*
BiDrAC, DcAmB, Drake, NatCAB 2,
TwCBDA, WhAm H, WhAmP
Dawson, John B 1800-1845 *BiAUS, TwCBDA*
Dawson, John Bennett 1798-1845 *BiDrAC,*
WhAm H
Dawson, John Charles 1876- *WhAm 6*
Dawson, John Gilmer 1882-1966 *NatCAB 53*
Dawson, John Littleton 1813-1870 *ApCAB,*
BiAUS, BiDrAC, Drake, TwCBDA,
WhAm H
Dawson, John Shaw 1869-1960 *WhAm 4*
Dawson, Sir John William 1820-1899 *ApCAB,*
DcScB
Dawson, Joseph Martin 1879- *WhAm 6*
Dawson, Lemuel Orah 1865-1938 *WhAm 1*
Dawson, Louis Young, Jr. 1899-1969
NatCAB 57
Dawson, Marion Lindsay *WhAm 5*
Dawson, Martin Henry 1896-1945 *NatCAB 35*
Dawson, Mary d1922 *WhAm 1,*
WomWWA 14
Dawson, Miles Menander 1863-1942 *ApCAB X,*
WhAm 2
Dawson, Samuel Edward 1833- *ApCAB Sup*
Dawson, Samuel Kennedy 1818?-1889 *ApCAB,*
TwCBDA
Dawson, Sarah Morgan 1842-1909 *NatCAB 23*
Dawson, Simon James 1820?- *ApCAB*
Dawson, Susie Starke *WomWWA 14*
Dawson, Thomas d1761 *NatCAB 3, TwCBDA*
Dawson, Thomas 1800?- *NewYHSD*
Dawson, Thomas Cleland 1865-1912 *AmBi,*
DcAmB, NatCAB 13, WhAm 1
Dawson, Thomas S 1907-1963 *WhAm 4*
Dawson, Warrington 1878- *WhAm 6*
Dawson, William 1704-1752 *NatCAB 3,*
TwCBDA
Dawson, William 1848-1929 *BiDrAC*
Dawson, William 1885-1972 *WhAm 5*
Dawson, William Adams 1903- *BiDrAC*
Dawson, William C 1798-1856 *ApCAB, BiAUS,*
Drake, NatCAB 11
Dawson, William Causby 1798-1856 *TwCBDA*
Dawson, William Crosby 1798-1856 *BiDrAC,*
DcAmB, WhAm H

Dawson, William J d1798 *BiAUS*
Dawson, William James 1854- *WhAm 1*
Dawson, William Johnson d1798 *BiDrAC*
Dawson, William Johnston d1798 *WhAm H*
Dawson, William Leon 1873-1928 *WhAm 1*
Dawson, William Levi 1886-1970 *BiDrAC,*
WhAm 5
Dawson, William Levi 1899- *McGEWB*
Dawson, William Marcus 1875-1925
NatCAB 29
Dawson, William Mercer Owens 1853-1916
NatCAB 13, WhAm 1
Dawson, William W 1828-1893 *NatCAB 12*
Dawson, William Warren 1892-1947 *WhAm 2*
Dawson-Watson, Dawson 1864-1939 *IlBEAAW,*
NatCAB 34, WhAm 1
Day, Aaron *NewYHSD*
Day, Addison Blanchard 1874-1939 *WhAm 1*
Day, Albert Edward d1973 *WhAm 6*
Day, Anne Marjorie 1875- *WomWWA 14*
Day, Arthur Hiram 1890-1967 *NatCAB 53*
Day, Arthur Kehew 1862-1942 *NatCAB 34*
Day, Arthur Louis 1869-1960 *NatCAB 16,*
WhAm 4
Day, Arthur Morgan 1867-1942 *NatCAB 31*
Day, Augustus *NewYHSD*
Day, Benjamin *NewYHSD*
Day, Benjamin 1838-1916 *AmBi*
Day, Benjamin Franklin 1841-1933 *NatCAB 11,*
WhAm 1
Day, Benjamin Henry 1810-1889 *AmBi,*
DcAmB, NatCAB 13, TwCBDA, WebAB,
WhAm H
Day, Benjamin Henry, Jr. 1838-1916 *IlBEAAW,*
NewYHSD
Day, Bernard Pope 1902-1967 *NatCAB 53,*
WhAm 4
Day, Charles 1879-1931 *NatCAB 26,*
WhAm 1
Day, Charles Ivan 1882-1950 *WhAm 3*
Day, Charles Manley 1863-1945 *WhAm 2*
Day, Charles Orrin 1851-1910 *NatCAB 13,*
WhAm 1
Day, Charles Orrin 1880-1938 *NatCAB 31*
Day, Charles William *NewYHSD*
Day, Clarence 1874-1935 *NatCAB 28,*
WhAm 1
Day, Clarence Richmond 1872-1938
NatCAB 36
Day, Clarence Shepard 1874-1935 *DcAmB S1*
Day, Clarence Shephard, Jr. 1874-1935 *WebAB*
Day, Clifford Louis 1890-1964 *WhAm 4*
Day, Clive 1871-1951 *NatCAB 38, WhAm 5*
Day, Cornelia M 1859- *WomWWA 14*
Day, Cyrus Lawrence 1900-1968 *NatCAB 54,*
WhAm 5
Day, David Alexander 1851-1897 *DcAmB,*
WhAm H
Day, David Sheldon 1880-1962 *WhAm 4*
Day, David Talbot 1859-1925 *DcAmB, DcScB,*
WhAm 1
Day, Dorothy 1897- *WebAB*
Day, Edmund 1866-1923 *WhAm 1*
Day, Edmund Ezra 1883-1951 *DcAmB S5,*
NatCAB 44, WhAm 3
Day, Edward 1853- *WhAm 4*
Day, Edward Carroll 1884-1962 *NatCAB 52*
Day, Edward Cason 1862-1936 *WhAm 1*
Day, Edward Charles 1886- *WhAm 1*
Day, Edward Marvin 1872-1947 *WhAm 2*
Day, Elizabeth Dike Lewis 1873-
WomWWA 14
Day, Elizabeth Richards 1883- *BiCAW*
Day, Emily *NewYHSD*
Day, Erastus Sheldon 1836-1921 *WhAm 1*
Day, Ewing Wilber 1862-1942 *NatCAB 31,*
WhAm 2
Day, Fisk Holbrook 1826-1903 *WhAm 1*
Day, Florence Roberts 1898-1957 *WhAm 3*
Day, Floyd McArthur 1874-1946 *NatCAB 35*
Day, Francis 1863- *WhAm 2*
Day, Frank Leighton 1868- *WhAm 4*
Day, Frank Leslie 1856- *WhAm 4*
Day, Frank Miles 1861-1918 *DcAmB,*
NatCAB 14, WhAm 1
Day, Frank Parker 1881-1950 *WhAm 3*
Day, Fred Holland 1864- *TwCBDA*
Day, G Z *WhAm 2*

Day, George Armstrong 1859-1927 *WhAm 1*
Day, George Calvin 1871-1940 *WhAm 1*
Day, George Edward 1815-1905 *ApCAB,*
NatCAB 13, TwCBDA, WhAm 1
Day, George Edward 1864-1919 *WhAm 1*
Day, George Parmly 1876-1959 *NatCAB 48,*
WhAm 3
Day, George Tiffany 1822-1875 *ApCAB*
Day, Hannibal 1802-1891 *ApCAB*
Day, Hannibal 1804-1891 *TwCBDA*
Day, Harold Briggs 1907-1960 *WhAm 4*
Day, Harry Arnold 1859-1927 *NatCAB 32*
Day, Harry Kent 1851-1925 *NatCAB 24*
Day, Henry *NewYHSD*
Day, Henry 1820-1893 *ApCAB, NatCAB 2,*
WhAm H
Day, Henry E *NewYHSD*
Day, Henry Noble 1808-1890 *AmBi, ApCAB,*
BiDAmEd, DcAmB, Drake, NatCAB 22,
TwCBDA, WhAm H
Day, Henry Wright 1831- *ApCAB*
Day, Herbert James 1889-1954 *WhAm 3*
Day, Hilbert Francis 1879-1947 *NatCAB 36*
Day, Holman Francis 1865-1935 *DcAmB S1,*
WhAm 1
Day, Horace H 1813-1878 *ApCAB, DcAmB,*
WhAm H
Day, James E 1905-1967 *WhAm 4A*
Day, James Edward 1914- *BiDrUSE*
Day, James Gamble 1832-1898 *DcAmB,*
NatCAB 12, WhAm H
Day, James Roscoe 1845-1923 *ApCAB Sup,*
BiDAmEd, DcAmB, NatCAB 12,
TwCBDA, WhAm 1
Day, James W 1892-1962 *WhAm 4*
Day, Jeremiah 1738-1806 *ApCAB*
Day, Jeremiah 1773-1867 *AmBi, ApCAB,*
BiDAmEd, DcAmB, Drake, NatCAB 1,
TwCBDA, WhAm H
Day, Jerome James 1876-1941 *NatCAB 37,*
WhAm 1
Day, Jesse Erwin 1888-1935 *WhAm 1*
Day, John d1820 *Drake*
Day, John Boynton Wilson 1874-1957 *WhAm 1,*
WhAm 4A
Day, John C Mason 1859-1915 *NatCAB 16*
Day, John Dabney 1872-1929 *WhAm 1*
Day, John Francis 1853-1941 *WhAm 1*
Day, John William 1861- *WhAm 1*
Day, Joseph Paul 1873-1944 *NatCAB 38,*
WhAm 2
Day, Karl S 1896-1973 *WhAm 5*
Day, Katharine Beach 1853- *BiCAW*
Day, Kenneth 1901-1958 *NatCAB 46*
Day, Kenneth Bertram 1889-1955 *NatCAB 45*
Day, Kenneth Mosier 1896-1968 *NatCAB 55,*
WhAm 5
Day, L B 1889-1938 *WhAm 1*
Day, Lee Garnett 1890-1968 *NatCAB 55*
Day, Leigh Gross 1861- *WhAm 4,*
WomWWA 14
Day, Lillian Paschal *WomWWA 14*
Day, Luther 1813-1885 *DcAmB, NatCAB 4,*
TwCBDA, WhAm H
Day, Luther 1879-1965 *NatCAB 51, WhAm 4*
Day, Mahlon 1790-1854 *ApCAB, Drake*
Day, Malvina 1826- *NewYHSD*
Day, Marion M *NewYHSD*
Day, Martha 1813-1833 *ApCAB, Drake*
Day, Mary Anna 1852- *WhAm 4,*
WomWWA 14
Day, Mary Gage 1857- *WomWWA 14*
Day, Mary Robertson 1848-1927 *NatCAB 22*
Day, Moses Henry 1832-1882 *NatCAB 19*
Day, Osborne Atwater 1877-1950 *NatCAB 38*
Day, Oscar Fayette Gaines 1860- *WhAm 4*
Day, Philip Miller 1886-1966 *NatCAB 54*
Day, Ralph E 1885-1946 *WhAm 2*
Day, Richard Edwin 1852-1936 *NatCAB 8,*
WhAm 1
Day, Richard Ellsworth 1882-1965 *WhAm 4*
Day, Richard Hopper 1847-1924 *NatCAB 27*
Day, Robert Henry 1867-1933 *WhAm 1*
Day, Rowland 1779-1853 *BiAUS, BiDrAC,*
WhAm H
Day, Samuel Stearns 1808-1871 *ApCAB*
Day, Sarah J 1860-1940 *WhAm 1*
Day, Sarah Louise *WomWWA 14*

Day, Stephen 1594?-1668 *AmBi, DcAmB, WhAm H*
Day, Stephen Albion 1882-1950 *BiDrAC, NatCAB 17, WhAm 2*
Day, Thomas 1748-1789 *ApCAB, Drake*
Day, Thomas 1777-1855 *ApCAB, BiAUS, Drake, TwCBDA*
Day, Thomas Fleming 1861-1927 *WhAm 1*
Day, Thomas Franklin 1852- *WhAm 4*
Day, Timothy Crane 1819-1869 *BiAUS, BiDrAC, WhAm H*
Day, William A d1928 *WhAm 1*
Day, William A d1951 *WhAm 3*
Day, William Baker 1871-1938 *WhAm 1*
Day, William Cathcart 1857- *WhAm 1*
Day, William Cyrus 1849- *WhAm 4*
Day, William Edward 1865- *WhoColR*
Day, William Harrison 1842-1921 *ApCAB X*
Day, William Horace 1866-1942 *WhAm 2*
Day, William LaMotte 1863-1938 *NatCAB 29*
Day, William Lang 1907-1973 *NatCAB 57, WhAm 6*
Day, William Otis 1857-1939 *NatCAB 30*
Day, William Plummer 1848-1919 *WhAm 1*
Day, William Rufus 1849-1923 *AmBi, ApCAB Sup, ApCAB X, BiDrUSE, DcAmB, NatCAB 11, NatCAB 32, TwCBDA, WebAB, WhAm 1*
Day, Wilson Miles 1850- *NatCAB 7*
Day-Lewis, Cecil 1904-1972 *WhAm 5*
Day-Lewis, Cecil see also Lewis, Cecil Day
Daya, Ibn Al- *DcScB*
Dayan, Charles 1792-1877 *ApCAB, BiAUS, BiDrAC, TwCBDA, WhAm H*
Dayan, Moshe 1915- *McGEWB, WhoMilH*
Dayananda Saraswati, Swami 1824-1883 *McGEWB*
Daye, Stephen 1594?-1668 *AmBi*
Daye, Stephen 1611-1668 *ApCAB, Drake, TwCBDA*
Daye, Thomas J *NewYHSD*
Dayfoot, Herbert M 1846-1894 *NatCAB 25*
Dayton, Aaron O *BiAUS*
Dayton, Alston Gordon 1857-1920 *BiDrAC, NatCAB 17, TwCBDA, WhAm 1, WhAmP*
Dayton, Amos Cooper 1813-1865 *ApCAB, NatCAB 11*
Dayton, Arthur Spencer 1887-1948 *NatCAB 37, WhAm 2*
Dayton, Charles Willoughby 1846-1910 *NatCAB 11, NatCAB 36, WhAm 1*
Dayton, David Draper 1880-1923 *NatCAB 20*
Dayton, Edwin Winthrop 1865- *NatCAB 12*
Dayton, Elias d1807 *BiAUS*
Dayton, Elias 1735-1807 *Drake*
Dayton, Elias 1737-1807 *ApCAB, BiDrAC, DcAmB, NatCAB 11, TwCBDA, WhAm H, WhAmP*
Dayton, Elizabeth 1848- *AmWom*
Dayton, Frank 1851-1922 *NatCAB 23*
Dayton, George Draper 1857-1938 *WhAm 1*
Dayton, Henry 1834-1927 *NatCAB 21*
Dayton, Hughes 1873- *WhAm 5*
Dayton, James Henry 1846-1938 *WhAm 1*
Dayton, John 1762-1822 *ApCAB*
Dayton, John Havens 1869-1953 *WhAm 3*
Dayton, Jonathan 1760-1824 *AmBi, ApCAB, BiAUS, BiDrAC, DcAmB, Drake, NatCAB 1, TwCBDA, WebAB, WhAm H, WhAmP*
Dayton, Katharine 1890-1945 *NatCAB 34*
Dayton, Lewis Seeley 1894-1950 *WhAm 3*
Dayton, Nathan 1796-1859 *BiAUS*
Dayton, Roy 1883-1955 *WhAm 3*
Dayton, William A 1885-1958 *WhAm 3*
Dayton, William Lewis 1807-1864 *ApCAB, BiAUS, BiDrAC, DcAmB, Drake, NatCAB 4, TwCBDA, WhAm H*
Dayton, William Lewis 1839-1897 *ApCAB, NatCAB 4, TwCBDA*
Dayton, William Lewis 1864-1921 *WhAm 1*
Daza, Hilarion 1840- *ApCAB*
D'Azambuja, Lucien Henri 1884-1970 *WhAm 5*
Dazey, Charles Turner 1855-1938 *WhAm 4*
Dazey, Nathan Philip 1856-1945 *NatCAB 37*
Deach, Inez Rodgers 1853- *WomWWA 14*

Deacon, Charles Johnson 1849-1932 *NatCAB 51*
Deacon, Edward 1839- *NatCAB 5*
Deacon, William Henry 1861-1923 *ApCAB X*
Deaderick, James W 1812- *NatCAB 5*
Deaderick, William Heiskell 1876- *WhAm 2*
Deadrick, James W 1812-1890 *TwCBDA*
Deady, Matthew Paul 1824-1893 *AmBi, BiAUS, DcAmB, NatCAB 19, REnAW, TwCBDA, WhAm H*
Deagan, John Calhoun 1853-1934 *NatCAB 43*
Deahl, Floyd Anthony 1883-1933 *NatCAB 25*
Deahl, Orlo Rogers 1891-1961 *NatCAB 50*
Deak, Francis 1803-1876 *McGEWB*
Deak, Francis 1899-1972 *WhAm 5*
Deakin, Alfred 1856-1919 *McGEWB*
Deakin, Edwin 1838-1923 *IIBEAAW, NatCAB 22*
Deakin, Gerald 1883-1970 *WhAm 5*
Deakyne, Herbert 1867-1945 *NatCAB 34, WhAm 2*
Deal, Edson H 1903-1967 *WhAm 4*
Deal, Erastus Charles 1876-1952 *NatCAB 40, WhAm 5*
Deal, Herbert L 1906-1955 *WhAm 3*
Deal, Joseph Thomas 1860-1942 *BiDrAC, WhAm 2*
Deal, Roy Walter 1889-1966 *WhAm 4*
DeAlarcon, Hernando *WhAm H*
DeAlarcon, Hernando see also Alarcon, Hernando De
DeAlba, Pedro 1887-1960 *WhAm 4*
Dealey, Edward Musgrove 1892-1969 *NatCAB 57, WhAm 5*
Dealey, George Bannerman 1859-1946 *ApCAB X, DcAmB S4, WhAm 2*
Dealey, James Quayle 1861-1937 *NatCAB 27, WhAm 1*
Dealey, Walter Allen 1890-1934 *NatCAB 26*
Dealy, Jacob Henry 1872-1926 *NatCAB 20*
Dealy, Patrick Francis 1827-1891 *NatCAB 2, TwCBDA, WhAm H*
Dealy, Patrick Francis 1836- *ApCAB*
Dealy, William Joseph 1843-1918 *NatCAB 14, NatCAB 25*
Deam, Arthur Francis 1895- *WhAm 6*
DeAmorim Ferreira, Herculano 1895-1974 *WhAm 6*
Dean, Alexander 1893-1939 *WhAm 1*
Dean, Amos 1803-1868 *ApCAB, DcAmB, Drake, NatCAB 22, TwCBDA, WhAm H*
Dean, Arthur Davis 1872-1949 *WhAm 2*
Dean, Arthur Lyman 1878-1952 *WhAm 3*
Dean, Bashford 1867-1928 *AmBi, ApCAB X, DcAmB, DcScB, NatCAB 21, WhAm 1*
Dean, Basil 1915-1967 *WhAm 4A*
Dean, Ben d1956 *WhAm 3*
Dean, Benjamin 1794?-1866 *NewYHSD*
Dean, Benjamin 1824-1897 *BiDrAC, TwCBDA, WhAm H*
Dean, Carleton 1895-1961 *NatCAB 47*
Dean, Charles 1813-1889 *WhAm H*
Dean, Charles see also Deane, Charles
Dean, Charles Augustus 1844-1921 *NatCAB 29*
Dean, Charles James 1883-1948 *NatCAB 37*
Dean, Charles Leroy 1844-1909 *NatCAB 15*
Dean, Dizzy 1911- *WebAB*
Dean, Edward Clarence 1879-1950 *NatCAB 40*
Dean, Edward Francis 1874-1941 *NatCAB 30*
Dean, Edward N d1974 *WhAm 6*
Dean, Edwin Blanchard 1866-1948 *WhAm 2*
Dean, Elizabeth Whetten 1868- *WomWWA 14*
Dean, Emily Washburn 1870- *WomWWA 14*
Dean, Ernest Woodward 1888-1959 *NatCAB 50*
Dean, Ezra 1795-1872 *BiAUS, BiDrAC, WhAm H*
Dean, Francis Winthrop 1852-1940 *WhAm 1*
Dean, George Adam 1873- *WhAm 5*
Dean, George Cooper 1865-1940 *NatCAB 16, NatCAB 30*
Dean, George Reinald 1865- *WhAm 4*
Dean, George Washington 1825-1897 *TwCBDA*
Dean, George Washington 1828-1887 *NatCAB 5*
Dean, Gilbert 1819-1870 *ApCAB, BiAUS, BiDrAC, NatCAB 5, TwCBDA, WhAm H*
Dean, Gordon Evans 1905-1958 *NatCAB 47,*

WhAm 3
Dean, Graham M 1904-1974 *WhAm 6*
Dean, H Trendley 1893-1962 *WhAm 4*
Dean, Henry Ellsworth 1862-1923 *NatCAB 20*
Dean, Henry Stewart 1830-1915 *NatCAB 17*
Dean, Howard B 1897-1950 *WhAm 3*
Dean, Hugh 1888-1961 *NatCAB 50, WhAm 4*
Dean, James *NewYHSD*
Dean, James 1776-1849 *ApCAB, Drake, TwCBDA*
Dean, James Byron 1931-1955 *DcAmB S5, WhAm 4*
Dean, James Renwick 1862-1936 *WhAm 1*
Dean, James Theodore 1865-1939 *WhAm 1*
Dean, John *NewYHSD*
Dean, John 1835- *WhAm 1*
Dean, John Candee 1845-1928 *WhAm 1*
Dean, John Marvin 1875-1935 *WhAm 1*
Dean, John S W 1848- *TwCBDA*
Dean, John Ward 1815-1902 *Drake, TwCBDA, WhAm 1*
Dean, Josiah 1748-1818 *BiAUS, BiDrAC, TwCBDA, WhAm H*
Dean, Julia 1830-1868 *ApCAB, DcAmB, Drake, NotAW, WhAm H*
Dean, Julia 1830-1869 *NatCAB 3*
Dean, Lee Wallace 1873-1944 *NatCAB 32, WhAm 2*
Dean, Luther Lyon 1842-1912 *NatCAB 17*
Dean, Man Mountain 1889-1953 *DcAmB S5*
Dean, Man Mountain 1891-1953 *WebAB*
Dean, Marvin Ansel 1852- *NatCAB 17*
Dean, Myron E 1914- *WhAm 6*
Dean, Noble 1881-1942 *NatCAB 32*
Dean, Oliver 1783-1871 *TwCBDA*
Dean, Oliver Hayes 1845- *NatCAB 5*
Dean, Orville B *NewYHSD*
Dean, Paul d1860 *ApCAB, Drake*
Dean, Paul Dee *WebAB*
Dean, Philip Dale 1904-1952 *NatCAB 41*
Dean, Reginald Scott 1897-1961 *WhAm 4A*
Dean, Reuben *NewYHSD*
Dean, Richard Crain 1833-1910 *WhAm 1*
Dean, Richard Doggett 1884-1950 *WhAm 3*
Dean, Richmond 1862- *WhAm 4*
Dean, Robert Augustus 1881-1924 *WhAm 1*
Dean, Russell Hardy 1853-1918 *NatCAB 17*
Dean, Russell Jennings 1901-1958 *NatCAB 44*
Dean, S Ella Wood 1871- *WomWWA 14*
Dean, Sagar 1805?-1874 *NewYHSD*
Dean, Samuel E, Jr. d1975 *WhAm 6*
Dean, Sara 1870- *WhAm 5, WomWWA 14*
Dean, Sidney 1818-1901 *BiAUS, BiDrAC, DcAmB, TwCBDA, WhAm H*
Dean, Sidney Butler 1879- *WhAm 6*
Dean, Suzanne Ella Wood 1871- *BiCAW*
Dean, Vera Micheles 1903-1972 *WhAm 5*
Dean, Walter Carleton 1891-1971 *WhAm 5*
Dean, Walter Lofthouse 1854-1912 *NatCAB 10, WhAm 1*
Dean, William 1807-1895 *ApCAB, Drake, TwCBDA*
Dean, William Blake 1838-1922 *WhAm 1*
Dean, William Frishe 1899- *WebAMB*
Dean, William George 1868-1917 *NatCAB 17*
Dean, William Henry 1877- *WhoColR*
Dean, William Henry, Jr. 1910-1952 *DcAmB S5*
Dean, William John 1869-1941 *WhAm 1*
Dean, William Laird 1891-1963 *WhAm 4*
Dean, Willis Johnson d1944 *WhAm 2*
Dean, Willis Leonard 1857-1942 *WhAm 2*
Deandrade, Anthony J d1970 *WhAm 5*
DeAndreis, Andrew James Felix B 1778-1820 *WhAm H*
Deane, Bertha Louise *WomWWA 14*
Deane, Charles 1813-1889 *AmBi, ApCAB, DcAmB, Drake, NatCAB 3, TwCBDA*
Deane, Charles see also Dean, Charles
Deane, Charles Bennett 1898-1969 *BiDrAC, WhAm 5*
Deane, Charles J 1881-1966 *WhAm 4*
Deane, E *NewYHSD*
Deane, Edith Douglass 1875- *WomWWA 14*
Deane, Gardiner Andrus Armstrong 1840- *NatCAB 7, WhAm 4*
Deane, James 1748-1823 *ApCAB, Drake*
Deane, James 1801-1858 *ApCAB, Drake*
Deane, John d1761 *Drake*

Deane, John Hall d1923 *ApCAB, WhAm 1*
Deane, Mary Gray 1846- *WomWWA 14*
Deane, Rachel Shevelson *WomWWA 14*
Deane, Ruthven 1851-1934 *NatCAB 27, WhAm 1*
Deane, Samuel 1733-1814 *DcAmB, Drake, NatCAB 23, WhAm H*
Deane, Samuel 1784-1834 *ApCAB, Drake*
Deane, Sidney Norton 1878-1943 *NatCAB 33*
Deane, Silas 1737-1789 *ApCAB, BiAUS, BiDrAC, DcAmB, Drake, EncAB, McGEWB, NatCAB 12, TwCBDA, WebAB, WhAm H, WhAmP*
Deane, Silas 1739-1789 *AmBi*
Deane, Walter 1848-1930 *WhAm 1*
Deane, William Reed 1809-1871 *ApCAB, Drake, TwCBDA*
Deaner, John Jacob 1880-1949 *NatCAB 38*
DeAngelis, Jefferson 1859-1933 *ApCAB X, WhAm 1*
DeAngelis, Louis 1903-1970 *NatCAB 56*
DeAngelis, Pascal Charles Joseph 1850-1932 *WhAm 1*
DeAngelis, Thomas Jefferson 1859-1933 *DcAmB S1*
Deans, Clara Barr *WomWWA 14*
Deans, David Crocket 1853- *WhoColR*
Deans, John Sterling 1858-1918 *NatCAB 19*
DeAnza, Juan Bautista 1735-1781 *WhAm H*
Dear, Cleveland 1888-1950 *BiDrAC*
Dear, J Albert 1899-1959 *WhAm 3*
Dear, J Albert 1899-1967 *WhAm 4*
Dear, Joseph Albert 1871-1947 *WhAm 2*
Dear, Richard Brierly 1850-1909 *NatCAB 17*
Dear, Walter Moore 1876-1962 *NatCAB 48, WhAm 4*
DeAraujo Castro, Joao Augusto 1919-1975 *WhAm 6*
Dearborn, Benjamin 1754-1838 *NatCAB 4, WhAm H*
Dearborn, Benjamin 1755-1838 *ApCAB, Drake*
Dearborn, Brainerd Winslow 1842-1914 *NatCAB 16*
Dearborn, Donald Curtis 1910-1967 *WhAm 4A*
Dearborn, Earl Hamilton 1915-1973 *WhAm 5*
Dearborn, Ella Kyes 1858- *WomWWA 14*
Dearborn, Frederick Myers 1911-1958 *NatCAB 47*
Dearborn, George VanNess 1869-1938 *ApCAB X, WhAm 1*
Dearborn, Heman Allen 1831-1897 *TwCBDA*
Dearborn, Henry 1751-1829 *AmBi, ApCAB, BiAUS, BiDrAC, BiDrUSE, DcAmB, Drake, NatCAB 1, TwCBDA, WebAB, WebAMB, WhAm H, WhAmP, WhoMilH*
Dearborn, Henry Alexander Scammell 1783-1851 *ApCAB, BiAUS, BiDrAC, DcAmB, Drake, TwCBDA, WhAm H, WhAmP*
Dearborn, Henry Alexander Scamwell 1783-1851 *NatCAB 9*
Dearborn, Henry Martin 1846-1904 *NatCAB 9, WhAm 1*
Dearborn, John 1868-1930 *WhAm 1*
Dearborn, Nathaniel 1786-1852 *ApCAB, Drake, NewYHSD, WhAm H*
Dearborn, Nathaniel S *NewYHSD*
Dearborn, Ned 1865- *WhAm 4*
Dearborn, Ned Harland 1893-1962 *WhAm 4*
Dearborn, Richard Harold 1874-1946 *WhAm 2*
Dearborn, Samuel H *NewYHSD*
Dearborn, Walter Fenno 1878-1955 *WhAm 3*
Dearborn, William Lee 1812-1875 *NatCAB 9*
Deardorff, Neva Ruth 1887-1958 *WhAm 3*
Dearholt, Hoyt E 1879-1939 *WhAm 1*
Dearing, Anderson Chenault 1913-1963 *NatCAB 50*
Dearing, Charles Lee 1903-1972 *WhAm 5*
Dearing, Fred Morris 1879- *WhAm 6*
Dearing, James 1840-1865 *ApCAB, Drake, NatCAB 11, TwCBDA*
Dearing, John Lincoln 1858-1916 *DcAmB, WhAm 1*
Dearing, William *NewYHSD*
Dearing, William Prentice 1874-1958 *NatCAB 46, WhAm 3*
DeArment, Almon Whiting 1887-1950 *NatCAB 49*

DeArmond, David Albaugh 1844-1909 *BiDrAC, TwCBDA, WhAm 1, WhAmP*
Dearmont, Russell Lee 1891-1967 *WhAm 4*
Dearmont, Washington Strother 1859-1944 *BiDAmEd, WhAm 2*
Dearnley, Charles Edwin 1892-1961 *NatCAB 46*
Dearth, Henry Golden 1864-1918 *AmBi, DcAmB, NatCAB 20, WhAm 1*
Dearth, Walter Alfred 1881-1946 *NatCAB 34*
Deas, Charles 1818-1867 *ApCAB, BnEnAmA, Drake, IIBEAAW, NewYHSD, REnAW, WhAm H*
Deas, R H *NewYHSD*
Deas, Zachariah Cantey 1819-1882 *BiDConf, DcAmB, TwCBDA, WhAm H*
DeAshford, Maria Asuncion Lopez *WomWWA 14*
Deasy, Daniel Cornelius 1876-1936 *NatCAB 27*
Deasy, Frank Timothy 1889-1955 *NatCAB 43*
Deasy, John Francis 1882-1953 *NatCAB 44, WhAm 3*
Deasy, Luere Babson 1859-1940 *NatCAB 29, WhAm 1*
Death Valley Scotty 1872-1954 *WebAB*
Deaton, Sherman Samuel 1865-1942 *NatCAB 35*
Deaver, Bascom Sine 1882-1944 *NatCAB 36, WhAm 2*
Deaver, George Gilbert 1890-1973 *WhAm 6*
Deaver, John Blair 1855-1931 *DcAmB S1, NatCAB 22, WhAm 1*
Deaves, Edwin F *NewYHSD*
Deavitt, Edward Harrington 1871-1946 *NatCAB 44*
Deavours, Stone 1867-1933 *WhAm 1*
DeAyala, Juan Manuel *WhAm H*
DeAyllon, Lucas Vasquez 1475?-1526 *WhAm H*
DeAyolas, Juan *ApCAB*
Deb, Radhakant 1783-1867 *McGEWB*
DeBaca, Ezequiel Cabeza 1864-1917 *NatCAB 19*
DeBakey, Michael Ellis 1908- *McGEWB*
DeBar, B 1814?- *NewYHSD*
DeBar, Benedict 1812-1877 *ApCAB, NatCAB 3, TwCBDA*
DeBar, Florence 1828- *ApCAB*
DeBardeleben, Charles Fairchild 1876-1941 *WhAm 2*
DeBardeleben, Henry Fairchild 1840-1910 *DcAmB, NatCAB 37*
DeBardeleben, Henry Fairchild 1841-1910 *WhAm HA, WhAm 4*
DeBardeleben, Henry Ticknor 1874-1948 *NatCAB 37, WhAm 3*
DeBarenne, Joannes Gregorius Dusser 1885-1940 *DcAmB*
DeBarr, Edwin 1859- *WhAm 4*
DeBarrac, Henry d1800 *NewYHSD*
DeBarre, Joseph 1806?- *NewYHSD*
DeBary, Anton 1831-1888 *DcScB*
DeBastos, Emil 1931-1970 *WhAm 5*
DeBatz *NewYHSD*
DeBatz, Alexander 1685?- *IIBEAAW*
DeBault, Charles *NewYHSD*
DeBaun, John A 1833- *TwCBDA*
DeBazus, Baroness *WomWWA 14*
DeBeaumont, Charles Edouard 1821-1888 *IIBEAAW*
DeBeaumont, Guerin J Michel DuBosco 1896-1955 *WhAm 3*
Debeaune, Florimond 1601-1652 *DcScB*
DeBeck, William 1890-1942 *WhAm 2*
Debeerski, John *NewYHSD*
DeBegnis, Giuseppe 1795-1849 *ApCAB*
DeBelleville, Frederic 1857-1923 *WhAm 1*
DeBenedictis, Giosue 1874-1958 *NatCAB 44*
DeBenevides, Alonzo d1664 *WhAm H*
Debenham, Frank 1883-1965 *DcScB*
DeBerard, Wilford Willis 1874-1962 *NatCAB 51, WhAm 4*
DeBerdt, Dennis d1771 *ApCAB*
DeBerdt, Dennys 1694?-1770 *DcAmB, WhAm H*
Deberry, Edmund 1787-1859 *ApCAB, BiAUS, BiDrAC, WhAm H, WhAmP*
DeBerry, William Caleb 1873- *WhoColR*
DeBerry, William Nelson 1870- *WhAm 2,*

WhoColR
DeBessonies, John Francis August 1815- *ApCAB Sup*
Debevoise, Kendall Bush 1913-1973 *WhAm 6*
DeBevoise, P LeRoy 1892-1961 *WhAm 4*
Debevoise, Thomas 1874-1958 *WhAm 3*
DeBey, Cornelia Bernarda 1865- *WhAm 4*
DeBhaquiere, Peter Boyle 1784-1860 *ApCAB*
DeBibory *NewYHSD*
Debierne, Andre Louis 1874-1949 *AsBiEn*
DeBisschop, Frank J 1879-1955 *WhAm 3*
DeBlois, Austen Kennedy 1866-1945 *TwCBDA, WhAm 2*
DeBlois, George Lewis 1867-1939 *WhAm 1*
Deblois, Miss L *NewYHSD*
DeBlois, Rhoda Farquharson 1882- *WomWWA 14*
DeBoard, Elmer H 1892-1953 *WhAm 3*
DeBoe, Michael Price 1885-1955 *NatCAB 43*
Deboe, William Joseph 1849-1927 *ApCAB Sup, BiDrAC, NatCAB 13, TwCBDA, WhAm 1*
DeBoer, Augusta Featherly 1863- *WomWWA 14*
DeBoer, John James 1903-1969 *BiDAmEd, WhAm 5*
DeBoer, Joseph Arend 1861-1915 *NatCAB 17, WhAm 1*
DeBoer, Saco Rienk 1883-1974 *WhAm 6*
Deboest, Henry Frulan 1907-1973 *WhAm 6*
DeBogory, Eugene 1881-1956 *NatCAB 48*
Debolt, John T 1857- *WhAm 4*
DeBolt, Rezin A 1828-1891 *ApCAB, BiAUS, BiDrAC, TwCBDA, WhAm H*
DeBonne, P A 1750?- *ApCAB*
DeBonneville, Benjamin Louis Eulalie 1796-1878 *WhAm H*
DeBooy, Theodoor 1882-1919 *NatCAB 17, WhAm 1*
Deborre, Prudhomme *ApCAB*
DeBost, William Ludlam 1870-1951 *WhAm 3*
DeBow, Charles Louis 1881-1937 *WhAm 1*
DeBow, James Dunwoody Brownson 1820-1867 *AmBi, ApCAB, BiAUS, BiDConf, DcAmB, Drake, EncAB, McGEWB, NatCAB 8, TwCBDA, WebAB, WhAm H*
DeBow, Samuel P 1865- *WhoColR*
DeBower, Herbert Francis d1940 *WhAm 1*
DeBra, Harvey Rufus 1862- *WhAm 4*
DeBraekeleer, Ferdinand, Jr. 1828-1857 *NewYHSD*
DeBrahm, John Gerar William 1717-1799 *NatCAB 24*
DeBrahm, William Gerard 1717-1799 *AmBi, DcAmB*
DeBrahm, William Girard 1717-1799 *WhAm H*
Debray, Henri Jules 1827-1888 *DcScB*
DeBrehan, Marquise *WhAm H*
Debreul, Joseph Paul 1814-1878 *TwCBDA*
DeBroglie, Prince Louis Victor Pierre R 1892- *AsBiEn*
DeBruche, Winifred Sackville Stoner 1902- *BiCAW*
DeBruhl, Michael Samuel *NewYHSD*
DeBruls, Michael *NewYHSD*
Debry, Paul Constant 1880-1960 *NatCAB 48*
Debs, Eugene Victor 1855-1926 *AmBi, ApCAB X, DcAmB, EncAB, McGEWB, NatCAB 12, TwCBDA, WebAB, WhAm 1*
Debuchi, Katsuji 1878-1947 *WhAm 2*
DeBusk, Burchard Woodson 1877-1936 *WhAm 1*
Debussy, Achille Claude 1862-1918 *McGEWB*
DeButts, Henry *NatCAB 12*
DeBuys, Laurence Richard 1878-1957 *WhAm 3*
Debye, Peter Joseph Wilhelm 1884-1966 *AsBiEn*
Debye, Peter Joseph William 1884-1966 *DcScB, McGEWB, WhAm 4*
DeCaindry, William Augustin 1843-1915 *NatCAB 16*
DeCallieres Bonnevue, Louis Hector 1646-1703 *WhAm H*
DeCamp, George 1869- *WhAm 5*
DeCamp, John 1812-1875 *ApCAB, Drake, TwCBDA*
DeCamp, John A 1872-1953 *WhAm 3*

DeCamp, Joseph Rodefer 1858-1923 *DcAmB, NatCAB 13, WhAm 1*
DeCamp, Ralph Earll 1858-1936 *IIBEAAW*
DeCamp, William Scott 1846-1905 *WhAm 1*
DeCamp, William Val 1886-1944 *NatCAB 33*
Decanesora 1640?- *ApCAB*
DeCapriles, Jose Rafael 1912-1969 *WhAm 5*
DeCardenas, Garcia Lopez *WhAm H*
DeCardenas Y Rodriguez DeRivas, J F 1881- *WhAm 6*
DeCarondelet, Francisco Luis Hector 1748?-1807 *WhAm H*
DeCartier DeMarchienne, Baron Emile 1871-1946 *WhAm 2*
DeCarvalho, Estevao Leitao 1881- *WhAm 6*
DeCasseres, Benjamin d1945 *WhAm 2*
DeCastro, Hector 1849-1909 *WhAm 1*
Decastro, Josue 1908-1973 *WhAm 6*
DeCastro, Morris F 1902-1966 *WhAm 4*
Decatur, Emmett Daniel 1815-1904 *WhAm H*
Decatur, James d1804 *ApCAB*
Decatur, Stephen 1751-1808 *ApCAB*
Decatur, Stephen 1752-1808 *DcAmB, WhAm H*
Decatur, Stephen 1779-1820 *AmBi, ApCAB, DcAmB, Drake, McGEWB, NatCAB 4, TwCBDA, WebAB, WebAMB, WhAm H, WhoMilH*
Decatur, William Jefferson 1874- *WhoColR*
DeCazes, Paul 1841- *ApCAB Sup*
Decca, Marie *AmWom*
DeCeleron DeBlainville, Pierre Joseph 1694-1759 *WhAm H*
DeCeleron DeBlainville, Pierre Joseph see also Celeron
Decell, John Lloyd 1887-1945 *WhAm 2*
DeCelles, Alfred Duclos 1844- *ApCAB*
Decelles, Maxime 1849- *ApCAB Sup*
Dechales, Claude Francois Milliet 1621-1678 *DcScB*
DeChamplain, Samuel 1567?-1635 *WhAm H*
DeChant, Henry Gross 1876-1931 *NatCAB 34*
Dechant, John Aloysius 1917-1974 *WhAm 6*
DeCharlevoix, Pierre Francois Xavier 1682-1761 *WhAm H*
DeCharms, Richard 1796-1864 *ApCAB, Drake*
DeChatillon *NewYHSD*
DeChauliac, Guy 1300?-1368 *BiHiMed*
DeChavanne, Countess Loveau 1861- *WhAm 4*
Dechelette, Joseph 1862-1914 *DcScB*
Dechen, Heinrich Von 1800-1889 *DcScB*
Decherd, H Ben 1915-1972 *WhAm 5*
Dechert, Henry Martyn 1832-1918 *NatCAB 10, WhAm 1*
Dechert, Henry Taylor 1859-1915 *WhAm 1*
Dechert, Robert 1895-1975 *WhAm 6*
DeCheverus, Jean Louis Anne M Lefebre 1768-1836 *WhAm H*
DeCisneros, Eleonora 1878-1934 *NotAW, WhAm 1, WhAm 2*
Decker, A Clinton 1886-1950 *NatCAB 39*
Decker, Alfred 1871- *ApCAB X*
Decker, Alonzo Galloway 1884-1956 *NatCAB 46, WhAm 3*
Decker, Benton Clark 1867-1933 *NatCAB 24, WhAm 1*
Decker, Charles Elijah 1868-1958 *NatCAB 50, WhAm 3*
Decker, Charles Rutherford 1876-1956 *NatCAB 43*
Decker, Clarence Raymond 1904-1969 *WhAm 5*
Decker, Edward William 1869-1956 *WhAm 3, WhAm 5*
Decker, Ernest G *NewYHSD*
Decker, Estelle Remsen *WomWWA 14*
Decker, Floyd F 1881-1949 *WhAm 3*
Decker, Frank 1848-1919 *WebAB*
Decker, George Henry 1902- *WebAMB*
Decker, Joseph 1853-1924 *BnEnAmA*
Decker, Marion Emory 1902-1968 *WhAm 5*
Decker, Martin Snyder 1858-1928 *WhAm 1*
Decker, Orlady Paul 1903-1962 *WhAm 4*
Decker, Perl D 1875-1934 *BiDrAC, WhAm 5*
Decker, Philip Harold 1894-1960 *NatCAB 50*
Decker, Royal E 1889-1962 *NatCAB 49*
Decker, Sarah Sophia Chase Platt 1852-1912 *NotAW, WhAm 1*
Decker, Wilson Barney 1879-1962 *NatCAB 48*

DeClorivere *NewYHSD*
DeCloriviere, Joseph-Pierre P DeL 1768-1826 *WhAm H*
DeClouet, Alexander 1812-1890 *BiDConf*
Decombes *NewYHSD*
Decombes, J Mc *NewYHSD*
DeCoppet, Edward J 1855-1916 *DcAmB*
DeCora, Angel 1871-1919 *IIBEAAW*
DeCormis, Louis 1846-1916 *NatCAB 13, WhAm 1*
DeCosmos, Amor 1830?- *ApCAB*
DeCosta, Benjamin Franklin 1831-1904 *AmBi, ApCAB, DcAmB, NatCAB 22, TwCBDA, WhAm 4*
Decoto, Ezra William 1876-1948 *NatCAB 37*
DeCou, Anna May Pemberton 1867- *WomWWA 14*
DeCou, Branson 1892-1941 *WhAm 1*
DeCou, Edgar Ezekiel 1868-1947 *NatCAB 39, WhAm 2*
DeCoudres, Louis 1789-1872 *ApCAB*
DeCourcy, Charles A 1857-1924 *WhAm 1*
DeCoursey, Samuel Gerald 1839-1903 *NatCAB 16*
DeCreeft, Jose 1884- *BnEnAmA*
DeCrevecoeur, Michel-Guillaume Jean 1735-1813 *WhAm H*
Dedekind, Julius Wilhelm Richard 1831-1916 *AsBiEn*
Dedekind, Richard 1831-1916 *DcScB*
Dederer, Pauline Hamilton 1878- *WomWWA 14*
Dederick, Peter Kells 1838-1911 *NatCAB 19, WhAm 1*
Dee, John 1527-1608 *DcScB*
Dee, Thomas Joseph 1860-1952 *NatCAB 39*
Deeb, Paul Harold 1917-1974 *WhAm 6*
Deedmeyer, Frank 1863- *WhAm 4*
Deeds, Edward Andrew 1874-1960 *ApCAB X, NatCAB 49, WhAm 4*
Deegan, William Joseph 1885-1947 *WhAm 2*
Deeks, William Edgar 1866-1931 *WhAm 1*
Deeley, Caleb *NewYHSD*
Deemer, Elias 1838-1918 *BiDrAC, NatCAB 17, WhAm 3, WhAmP*
Deemer, Harold Davenport 1873-1946 *NatCAB 36*
Deemer, Horace Emerson 1858-1917 *DcAmB, NatCAB 13, NatCAB 18, WhAm 1*
Deems, Charles Force 1820-1893 *AmBi, ApCAB, DcAmB, Drake, NatCAB 9, TwCBDA, WhAm H*
Deems, Edward Mark 1852-1929 *WhAm 1*
Deems, James Harry 1848-1931 *TwCBDA, WhAm 1*
Deems, James Monroe 1818-1901 *TwCBDA*
Deen, Braswell Drue 1893- *BiDrAC*
Deen, Joshua Lee 1896-1951 *WhAm 3*
Deen, William Morris 1852- *NatCAB 5*
DeEnzling *NewYHSD*
Deeping, Werwick d1950 *WhAm 3*
Deer, George Harvison 1903-1966 *WhAm 4*
DeErdely, Francis 1904-1959 *WhAm 4*
Deere, Charles Henry 1837-1907 *NatCAB 3, NatCAB 28, WhAm 1*
Deere, John 1804-1886 *AmBi, ApCAB X, DcAmB, EncAAH, EncAB, McGEWB, NatCAB 20, WebAB, WhAm H*
Deerfoot 1828-1897 *AmBi, DcAmB, WhAm H*
Deering, Albert Benson 1874-1947 *NatCAB 41*
Deering, Charles 1852-1927 *NatCAB 33, WhAm 1*
Deering, Frank Prentiss 1855-1939 *NatCAB 36, WhAm 1*
Deering, James 1859-1925 *NatCAB 20, WhAm 1*
Deering, John Percy 1873-1947 *NatCAB 35*
Deering, John William 1833-1904 *NatCAB 6*
Deering, Mabel Craft *WomWWA 14*
Deering, Nathaniel 1791-1881 *ApCAB, DcAmB, Drake, NatCAB 10, WhAm H*
Deering, Nathaniel Cobb 1827-1887 *BiDrAC, TwCBDA, WhAm H*
Deering, Robert Waller 1865-1940 *NatCAB 30, WhAm 4*
Deering, William 1826-1913 *AmBi, ApCAB X, DcAmB, EncAAH, McGEWB,*

NatCAB 11, TwCBDA, WhAm 1
Dees, Randall Euesta 1893-1972 *WhAm 5*
Deesz, Louis A 1888-1950 *WhAm 3*
Deeter, Paxson 1880-1933 *WhAm 1*
Deeter, Paxson 1880-1935 *NatCAB 25*
Deetjen, Rudolph Henry 1897-1967 *WhAm 4*
Deetz, Charles Henry 1864-1946 *WhAm 3*
Deevy, William Joseph 1899-1961 *NatCAB 49*
DeFalco, Ralph Julius 1907-1971 *NatCAB 55*
Defan *NewYHSD*
Defandorf, Francis Marion 1897-1963 *NatCAB 50*
Defauw, Desire 1885-1960 *WhAm 4*
Defebaugh, James Elliott 1854-1909 *WhAm 1*
Defenbach, Byron 1870- *WhAm 5*
DeFere, Mrs. A Litsner *AmWom*
DeFere, Paul Eugene 1868-1952 *NatCAB 49*
Deferrari, Roy Joseph 1890-1969 *WhAm 5*
DeFerrit *NewYHSD*
Deffenbaugh, Walter Sylvanus 1872- *WhAm 5*
DeFlorat *NewYHSD*
DeFlorez, Luis 1889-1962 *WhAm 4*
Defoe, Daniel 1660-1731 *McGEWB*
Defoe, Harry Joseph 1875-1957 *WhAm 3*
DeFoe, Louis Vincent 1869-1922 *WhAm 1*
DeFontaine, Felix Gregory 1834-1896 *BiDConf, DcAmB*
DeFontaine, Felix Gregory 1834-1896 *WhAm H*
Deford, Miriam Allen 1888-1975 *WhAm 6*
DeForest, Albert Tracy 1863-1948 *NatCAB 37*
DeForest, Alfred Victor 1888-1945 *DcAmB S3, NatCAB 35, WhAm 2*
DeForest, Charles Mills 1878-1947 *NatCAB 37, WhAm 2*
DeForest, Charlotte Burgis *WomWWA 14*
DeForest, David Curtis 1774-1825 *DcAmB, WhAm H*
DeForest, Erastus Lyman 1834-1888 *DcAmB, WhAm H*
DeForest, Henry J 1860-1924 *IIBEAAW*
DeForest, Henry Lockwood 1875-1954 *WhAm 3*
DeForest, Henry Pelouze 1864-1948 *ApCAB X, NatCAB 36, WhAm 2*
DeForest, Henry Schermerhorn 1847-1917 *BiDrAC, WhAm 1*
DeForest, Henry Swift 1833-1896 *NatCAB 35, TwCBDA*
DeForest, Henry Wheeler 1855-1938 *NatCAB 27, WhAm 1*
DeForest, John Kinne Hyde 1844-1911 *DcAmB*
DeForest, John William 1826-1906 *AmBi, ApCAB, DcAmB, NatCAB 4, TwCBDA, WhAm HA, WhAm 4*
DeForest, Johnston 1873-1952 *WhAm 3*
DeForest, Katharine *WhAm 5*
DeForest, Lee 1873-1961 *ApCAB X, AsBiEn, DcScB, EncAB, McGEWB, NatCAB 13, NatCAB 17, WebAB, WhAm 4*
DeForest, Lockwood 1850-1932 *AmBi, IIBEAAW, WhAm 1*
DeForest, Marian d1935 *WhAm 1, WomWWA 14*
DeForest, Nora Blatch 1883- *WomWWA 14*
DeForest, Robert Elliott 1845-1924 *BiDrAC, TwCBDA*
DeForest, Robert Weeks 1848-1931 *ApCAB X, DcAmB S1, NatCAB 9, NatCAB 42, WhAm 1*
DeForest, William Henry 1857-1907 *ApCAB X*
DeFranca 1808-1865 *NewYHSD*
DeFranca, Manuel Joachim 1808-1865 *WhAm H*
DeFrancesco, Italo Luther 1901-1967 *WhAm 4*
DeFrancia *NewYHSD*
DeFrancisci, Anthony 1887-1964 *WhAm 4*
Defrasse, Auguste 1821?- *NewYHSD*
DeFrece, Abram Brougham 1850- *TwCBDA*
Defrees, Donald 1885-1968 *NatCAB 54, WhAm 5*
Defrees, John D 1810-1882 *BiAUS*
Defrees, John D 1811-1882 *ApCAB*
Defrees, Joseph Holton 1858-1929 *NatCAB 25, WhAm 1*
Defrees, Joseph Hutton 1812-1885 *BiAUS, BiDrAC, WhAm H*
Defrees, Joseph Rollie 1876-1958 *WhAm 3*
DeFreyre Y Santander, Manuel 1872-1944 *WhAm 2*

DeGalvez, Bernardo 1746-1786 *WhAm H*
DeGanahl, Charles Francis 1869-1939
 NatCAB 28
DeGarmo, Charles 1849-1934 *ApCAB X,*
 BiDAmEd, NatCAB 6, TwCBDA
DeGarmo, Ellwood 1872-1947 *NatCAB 36*
DeGarmo, Mrs. Frank *WomWWA 14*
DeGarmo, James M 1838- *WhAm 4*
DeGarmo, William 1849-1936 *WhAm 2*
Degas, Hilaire Germain Edgar 1834-1917
 McGEWB, WhAm HA, WhAm 4
DeGasperi, Alcide 1881-1954 *McGEWB,*
 WhAm 3
DeGaulle, Charles Andre Joseph Marie
 1890-1970 *McGEWB, WhAm 5, WhWW-II,*
 WhoMilH
DeGelleke, Gerrit Jacob 1872- *WhAm 5*
Degener, Edward 1809-1890 *BiAUS, BiDrAC,*
 TwCBDA, WhAm H
Degering, Edward Franklin 1894-1967
 NatCAB 53
Degering, Edward Franklind 1898-1967
 WhAm 4
DeGersdorff, Carl August 1865-1944 *WhAm 2*
DeGersdorff, Ernest Bruno Von *NewYHSD*
Degetau, Federico 1862-1914 *BiDrAC,*
 WhAm 4, WhAmP
DeGhelderode, Michel 1898-1962 *WhAm 4A*
Deglman, George Anthony 1877- *WhAm 5*
Degnon, Michael John 1856- *NatCAB 14*
DeGogorza, Emilio Eduardo 1874-1949
 WhAm 3, WhAm 5
DeGogorza, Emma Eames 1865- *BiCAW*
Degollado, Santos 1819-1861 *ApCAB*
DeGolyer, Everette Lee 1886-1956 *DcScB,*
 NatCAB 43, WhAm 3
DeGolyer, Robert Seeley 1876-1952 *WhAm 3*
Degout, Michel *NewYHSD*
DeGozzaldi, Mary Isabella *WomWWA 14*
DeGraeff, A C D 1872-1957 *WhAm 3*
DeGraff, Emma Christine 1870- *WomWWA 14*
DeGraff, John Isaac 1783-1848 *BiAUS,*
 BiDrAC, WhAm H
DeGraff, Lawrence 1871-1934 *WhAm 1*
DeGraff, Mark H 1890-1957 *WhAm 4*
DeGraffenreid, Claude Clarence 1875-1918
 NatCAB 18
DeGraffenreid, Edward 1899- *BiDrAC*
DeGraffenreid, Reese Calhoun 1859-1902
 BiDrAC
DeGraffenried, Christopher 1661-1743 *DcAmB*
DeGraffenried, Chrostopher 1661-1743
 WhAm H
DeGraffenried, Edward 1861-1922 *WhAm 1*
DeGraffenried, Mary Clare 1849-1921 *NotAW,*
 WhAm 4
DeGraffenried, Reese Calhoun 1859-1902
 TwCBDA, WhAm 1
DeGrailly, Victor *NewYHSD*
DeGrandmaison, Nicolas 1892?- *IIBEAAW*
DeGrasse, Francois Joseph Paul 1722-1788
 AmBi, WhAm H
DeGraw, Peter Voorhees 1853-1914 *WhAm 1*
DeGrazia, Ettore 1909- *IIBEAAW*
DeGroat, George Blewer 1898-1969 *WhAm 5*
DeGroat, Harry DeWitt 1873-1959 *NatCAB 49,*
 WhAm 5
DeGroff, Minnie Emily 1875- *WomWWA 14*
DeGroot, Albert 1813-1887 *ApCAB*
DeGroot, Jan Cornets 1554-1640 *DcScB*
DeGroot, John *NewYHSD*
DeGroot, William A 1869-1932 *WhAm 1*
DeGross, John 1828?- *NewYHSD*
DeGuingand, Francis 1900- *WhWW-II*
DeGuire, George Nicholas 1884-1941
 NatCAB 30
DeHaan, Chuck *IIBEAAW*
DeHaan, John, Jr. 1891-1945 *WhAm 2*
DeHaan, William 1907-1960 *NatCAB 48*
DeHaas, Alice Preble Tucker *WomWWA 14*
DeHaas, Jacob Judah Aaron 1872-1937
 WhAm HA, WhAm 4
DeHaas, John Philip 1735?-1786 *ApCAB,*
 DcAmB, WhAm H
DeHaas, John Philip 1735?-1794? *Drake*
DeHaas, Maurice F H 1830?-1895 *Drake*
DeHaas, Maurice Frederick Hendrick 1832-1895
 AmBi, ApCAB

DeHaas, Maurits Frederick Hendrick 1832-1895
 TwCBDA
DeHaas, Mauritz Frederick Hendrick 1832-1895
 NatCAB 9
DeHaas, Mauritz Frederik Hendrik 1832-1895
 NewYHSD
DeHaas, Wander J *DcScB*
DeHaas, William Frederick 1830-1880 *ApCAB,*
 NewYHSD, WhAm H
DeHart, John 1728-1795 *BiDrAC, WhAm H*
DeHart, John 1729-1795 *NatCAB 13*
DeHart, Sarah *NewYHSD*
DeHart, William 1746-1801 *ApCAB, Drake*
DeHart, William Chetwood 1800-1848 *ApCAB,*
 Drake
DeHart, William Henry 1837-1916 *WhAm 1*
DeHart, William Matthias 1838- *WhAm 4*
DeHass, Jacob Judah Aaron 1872-1937
 DcAmB S2
DeHass, Mauritz Frederick Hendrick 1832-1895
 WhAm H
DeHass, Wills 1817-1910 *WhAm 1*
DeHaven, David William 1872-1942 *WhAm 2*
DeHaven, Edwin Jesse 1816-1865 *AmBi,*
 DcAmB, WebAMB, WhAm H
DeHaven, Edwin Jesse 1819-1865 *ApCAB,*
 Drake
DeHaven, Frank 1856-1934 *WhAm 4*
DeHaven, Franklin 1856-1934 *IIBEAAW,*
 WhAm 1
DeHaven, John B *WhAm 2*
DeHaven, John Jefferson 1845-1913 *WhAm 1*
DeHaven, John Jefferson 1849-1913 *BiDrAC*
DeHavilland, Sir Geoffrey 1882-1965 *WhAm 4*
DeHevesy, George Charles 1885-1966 *WhAm 4*
Dehn, Adolf Arthur 1895-1968 *IIBEAAW,*
 NatCAB 54, WhAm 5
Dehn, Max 1878-1952 *DcScB*
DeHollosy, A *NewYHSD*
Dehon, Theodore 1776-1817 *ApCAB, Drake,*
 NatCAB 12, TwCBDA, WhAm H
Deibel, Cyril Paul 1894-1945 *NatCAB 33*
Deibler, Frederick Shipp 1876-1961 *WhAm 4*
Deichman, Carl F 1871- *WhAm 5*
Deierlein, Frederick *NewYHSD*
Deigert, Robert Campbell 1908-1974 *WhAm 6*
Deike, George James 1879-1963 *NatCAB 52*
Deiler, John Hanno 1849-1909 *NatCAB 9,*
 TwCBDA, WhAm 1
Deily, Curtis R *WhAm 6*
Deimel, Henry L 1858- *WhAm 4*
Deimler, Paul Ellas 1912-1969 *WhAm 5*
Deinard, Samuel Nathaniel 1872-1921
 NatCAB 19
Deindorfer, Johannes 1828-1907 *DcAmB*
Deines, Ernest Hubert 1894-1967 *WhAm 5*
Deines, John George 1861-1961 *NatCAB 51*
Deininger, William d1941 *WhAm 1*
Deinostratus *DcScB*
Deiss, Charles Frederick 1903-1959 *NatCAB 44,*
 WhAm 3
Deitrich, Theodore C 1876-1935 *WhAm 1*
Deitrick, Elizabeth Platt 1890- *WhAm 5*
Deitrick, Frederick Simpson 1875-1948 *BiDrAC,*
 WhAm 3
Deitrick, James 1864- *WhAm 4*
Deitrick, William Henley 1895- *WhAm 6*
Deitz *NewYHSD*
Deitz, Archibald Edwin 1869- *WhAm 5*
Deitz, John F *REnAW*
Deitz, William *BiAUS*
Deitzler, George Washington 1826-1884 *ApCAB,*
 DcAmB, NatCAB 5, TwCBDA,
 WhAm H
DeJarnette, Daniel Coleman 1822-1881 *BiAUS,*
 BiDConf, BiDrAC, TwCBDA, WhAm H
DeJarnette, Edmund Tompkins 1898-1966
 NatCAB 52
DeJarnette, Evelyn Magruder 1842- *AmWom*
DeJarnette, Joseph Spencer 1866- *WhAm 5*
Dejerine, Augusta Klumpke 1859-1927
 NatCAB 31
Dejerine, Joseph Jules 1849-1917 *BiHiMed*
DeJesus, Angel Roman 1891-1951 *WhAm 3*
DeJong, David Cornel 1901-1967 *NatCAB 53*
DeJong, David Cornel 1905-1967 *WhAm 4A*
DeJong, Yvonne Germaine d1973 *WhAm 6*
DeJurenev, Nicholas 1904-1954 *WhAm 3*

DeKalb, Baron 1721-1780 *WebAB*
DeKalb, Courtenay 1861-1931 *NatCAB 27,*
 WhAm 1
DeKalb, Frances Douglas 1870- *WhAm 5*
DeKalb, Johann *AmBi*
DeKay, Charles 1848-1935 *ApCAB,*
 ApCAB X, NatCAB 9, TwCBDA,
 WhAm 1
DeKay, Eckford Craven 1873-1951 *NatCAB 44*
DeKay, George C 1802-1849 *Drake*
DeKay, George Coleman 1802-1849 *ApCAB,*
 NatCAB 9, TwCBDA
DeKay, George Coleman 1842-1862 *ApCAB*
DeKay, George Colman 1802-1849 *DcAmB,*
 WhAm H
DeKay, James Ellsworth 1792-1851 *AmBi,*
 ApCAB, DcAmB, Drake, NatCAB 9,
 TwCBDA, WhAm H
DeKay, John Wesley 1872- *NatCAB 14,*
 WhAm 5
DeKay, Joseph Rodman Drake 1836-1886
 ApCAB, NatCAB 9
DeKay, Minna Craven 1844- *WomWWA 14*
DeKay, Sidney Brooks 1845-1890 *ApCAB,*
 NatCAB 9, TwCBDA
DeKay, Sidney Gilder 1880-1949 *NatCAB 38*
DeKermen, Valerie Louise 1857-
 WomWWA 14
DeKhotinsky, Achilles 1850-1933 *NatCAB 25*
Dekker, Albert 1905-1968 *WhAm 5*
Dekker, Thomas 1572?-1632? *McGEWB*
DeKleine, William 1877-1957 *WhAm 3*
Deknatel, Frederick Brockway 1905-1973
 WhAm 6
Deknatel, William Ferguson 1907-1973
 WhAm 6
DeKnight, Clarence Woods 1867-1936 *WhAm 1*
DeKooning, Willem 1904- *BnEnAmA, EncAB,*
 McGEWB, WebAB
DeKoven, Anna Farwell d1953 *WomWWA 14*
DeKoven, Anna Farwell 1860-1953 *ApCAB Sup,*
 BiCAW, NatCAB 16, NatCAB 48
DeKoven, Anna Farwell 1862-1953 *WhAm 3*
DeKoven, Henry 1819- *TwCBDA*
DeKoven, Henry Louis Reginald 1859-1920
 AmBi, ApCAB Sup, DcAmB
DeKoven, James 1831-1879 *ApCAB, DcAmB,*
 NatCAB 11, TwCBDA, WhAm H
DeKoven, Reginald 1859-1920 *NatCAB 5,*
 TwCBDA
DeKoven, Reginald 1861-1920 *ApCAB X,*
 NatCAB 26, WhAm 1
DeKrafft, Frances Blatchford 1855-
 WomWWA 14
DeKrafft, James Charles Philip 1826-1885
 ApCAB, TwCBDA
DeKrafft, William 1878-1963 *WhAm 4*
DeKraft, Charles *NewYHSD*
DeKroyft, Sarah Helen 1818-1915 *ApCAB*
DeKroyft, Susan Helen Aldrich 1818-1915
 NatCAB 11, WhAm 1, WomWWA 14
DeKruif, Paul 1890-1971 *WhAm 5*
DeLaBarra, Francisco Leon 1863- *WhAm 4*
DeLaBarre, Cecil Franzen 1900-1952 *WhAm 3*
Delabarre, Edmund Burke 1863-1945 *WhAm 2*
Delabarre, Frank Alexander 1868-1938
 WhAm 1
DeLaBeche, Henry Thomas 1796-1855 *DcScB*
DeLaboulaye, Andre Lefebvre 1876-1966
 WhAm 4, WhAm 5
DeLacour, Reginald Beardsley 1886-1948
 WhAm 2
Delacroix, C I *NewYHSD*
Delacroix, Ferdinand Victor Eugene 1798-1863
 McGEWB
Delacroix, Joseph C *NewYHSD*
DeLacy, Emerson Hugh 1910- *BiDrAC*
DeLacy, Walter Washington 1819-1892 *DcAmB,*
 NatCAB 3, WhAm H
Delafield, Albert 1846-1920 *NatCAB 29*
Delafield, E M d1943 *WhAm 2*
Delafield, Edward 1794-1875 *ApCAB, DcAmB,*
 NatCAB 10, TwCBDA, WhAm H
Delafield, Edward C 1877- *ApCAB X*
Delafield, Elizabeth Ray 1872- *WomWWA 14*
Delafield, Francis 1841-1915 *AmBi, ApCAB,*
 DcAmB, NatCAB 10, TwCBDA,
 WhAm 1

Delafield, Henry 1792-1875 *ApCAB,
NatCAB 11*
Delafield, John 1748-1824 *ApCAB, DcAmB,
TwCBDA*
Delafield, John 1749-1824 *WhAm H*
Delafield, John 1786-1853 *ApCAB, DcAmB,
Drake, NatCAB 11, TwCBDA, WhAm H*
Delafield, John Ross 1874-1964 *ApCAB X,
WhAm 4*
Delafield, Joseph 1790-1875 *ApCAB,
NatCAB 11, TwCBDA*
Delafield, Lewis Livingston 1834-1883
ApCAB X
Delafield, Lewis Livingston 1863-1944 *WhAm 2*
Delafield, Lewis Livingston 1886-1957 *WhAm 3*
Delafield, M Livingston 1901-1945 *WhAm 2*
Delafield, Maturin Livingston 1836-1917
ApCAB X
Delafield, Richard 1798-1873 *ApCAB, DcAmB,
NatCAB 11, TwCBDA, WhAm H*
Delafield, Richard 1853-1930 *ApCAB X,
Drake, NatCAB 14, WhAm 1*
Delafield, Rufus King 1802-1874 *ApCAB X*
Delafield, William 1792-1853 *ApCAB*
Delafosse, Gabriel 1796-1878 *DcScB Sup*
DeLaGarza, Eligio, II 1927- *BiDrAC*
Delage, Yves 1854-1920 *DcScB*
DeLaguna, Grace Andrus DeLeo 1878-
WomWWA 14
DeLaHaba, Gabriel 1896-1966 *WhAm 4*
Delahanty, William John 1895-1971 *WhAm 5*
Delahay, Mark W *BiAUS*
Delahay, Mark William 1817-1879 *WhAm H*
Delamain, Richard *DcScB*
Delamano, William *NewYHSD, WhAm H*
DeLamar, Alice Antoinette 1895- *BiCAW*
DeLamar, Joseph Rafael 1843-1918
NatCAB 28
DeLamar, Joseph Raphael 1843-1918 *DcAmB,
WhAm 1, WhAm 4*
DeLaMare, Walter 1873-1956 *WhAm 3*
Delamarter, Eric 1880-1953 *WhAm 3*
DeLamater, Cornelius Henry 1821-1889 *DcAmB,
TwCBDA, WebAB, WhAm H*
DeLamater, Jacqueline Montague Newton 1875-
WomWWA 14
Delamater, John 1787-1867 *ApCAB, Drake,
TwCBDA*
Delamater, Nicholas B 1847-1915 *WhAm 1*
DeLaMatyr, Gilbert 1825-1892 *BiDrAC,
WhAm H*
Delambre, Jean-Baptiste Joseph 1749-1822
DcScB
Delamere *NewYHSD*
DeLaMontanya, James 1798-1849 *BiDrAC*
DeLaMothe, Antoine 1660-1730 *WhAm H*
DeLaMotte, Anna Christesen 1862-
WomWWA 14
Delancey, Darragh 1870-1937 *WhAm 1*
DeLancey, Edward Floyd 1821-1905 *ApCAB,
TwCBDA, WhAm 1*
DeLancey, Etienne 1663-1741 *AmBi, ApCAB,
TwCBDA*
DeLancey, James 1703-1760 *AmBi, ApCAB,
DcAmB, Drake, NatCAB 4, TwCBDA,
WebAB, WhAm H, WhAmP*
DeLancey, James 1732-1800 *AmBi, ApCAB,
DcAmB, Drake, TwCBDA, WhAm H*
DeLancey, James 1746-1804 *DcAmB,
WhAm H*
DeLancey, James 1750?-1809 *ApCAB,
TwCBDA*
DeLancey, John 1741?-1829 *ApCAB*
DeLancey, John Peter 1753-1828 *ApCAB,
TwCBDA*
DeLancey, Oliver 1708-1785 *ApCAB,
TwCBDA*
DeLancey, Oliver 1717-1785 *Drake*
DeLancey, Oliver 1718-1785 *AmBi, DcAmB,
WhAm H*
DeLancey, Oliver 1752-1822 *ApCAB, Drake,
TwCBDA*
DeLancey, Peter 1705-1770 *ApCAB*
DeLancey, Stephen 1663-1741 *AmBi,
McGEWB*
DeLancey, Stephen 1740?-1798 *ApCAB, Drake,
TwCBDA*
DeLancey, Stephen 1740-1801 *ApCAB*

DeLancey, Warren d1855 *ApCAB*
DeLancey, William Heathcote 1797-1865
*ApCAB, DcAmB, Drake, NatCAB 1,
NatCAB 3, TwCBDA, WhAm H*
DeLancey, William Howe 1781?-1815 *ApCAB*
DeLand, Charles Edmund 1854- *WhAm 3*
DeLand, Charles Victor 1826-1903 *NatCAB 6*
DeLand, Charles Victor 1828-1903 *WhAm 1*
DeLand, Clyde Osmer 1872-1947 *WhAm 2*
Deland, Ellen Douglas 1860-1923 *TwCBDA,
WhAm 1, WomWWA 14*
DeLand, Helen Parce *WomWWA 14*
Deland, Margaret 1857-1945 *AmWom,
DcAmB S3, NotAW*
Deland, Margaretta Wade Campbell 1857-1945
*ApCAB Sup, NatCAB 3, NatCAB 33,
TwCBDA, WhAm 2, WomWWA 14*
Deland, Paul Stanley d1965 *WhAm 4*
Delander, N Paul 1890-1948 *WhAm 3*
Delaney, George A 1895-1974 *WhAm 6*
Delaney, George Philip 1909-1972 *WhAm 5*
Delaney, J E *NewYHSD*
Delaney, James *NewYHSD*
Delaney, James Joseph 1901- *BiDrAC*
Delaney, John Bernard 1864- *NatCAB 13*
Delaney, John Joseph 1878-1948 *BiDrAC,
WhAm 2, WhAmP*
DeLaney, Matthew A 1874-1936 *WhAm 1*
DeLaney, Paul 1865- *WhAm 4*
Delaney, Peter A 1864-1914 *WhAm 1*
Delaney, Sadie Peterson 1889-1958 *WhAm 3*
Delaney, Sadie Peterson 1889-1959 *DcAmLiB*
DeLanglade, Charles Michel 1729-1801 *AmBi,
DcAmB, WhAm H*
DeLannoy *NewYHSD*
Delano, Aline P 1845- *WhAm 4,
WomWWA 14*
Delano, Amasa 1763-1817 *ApCAB, Drake*
Delano, Amasa 1763-1823 *NatCAB 11*
Delano, Amassa 1763-1823 *AmBi, DcAmB,
WhAm H*
Delano, Charles 1820-1883 *BiAUS, BiDrAC,
WhAm H*
DeLano, Clayton Harris 1836-1920 *NatCAB 17*
Delano, Columbus 1809- *ApCAB, BiAUS,
Drake, NatCAB 4*
Delano, Columbus 1809-1893 *BiDrUSE*
Delano, Columbus 1809-1896 *BiDrAC,
DcAmB, TwCBDA, WhAm H, WhAmP*
Delano, Edith Barnard d1946 *WhAm 2*
Delano, Eugene d1920 *WhAm 1*
Delano, Frances Jackson 1857- *WhAm 4,
WomWWA 14*
Delano, Francis Henry 1848-1929 *WhAm 1*
Delano, Frederic Adrian 1863-1953 *ApCAB X,
NatCAB 40, WhAm 3*
Delano, Gerard Curtis 1890- *IIBEAAW*
Delano, Jane Arminda 1862-1919 *AmBi,
DcAmB, NatCAB 19, NotAW,
WhAm HA, WhAm 4*
Delano, Lyman 1883-1944 *NatCAB 36,
WhAm 2*
DeLano, Milton 1844-1922 *BiDrAC, TwCBDA*
Delano, Preston 1886-1961 *NatCAB 46*
Delano, Warren 1809-1898 *NatCAB 34*
Delano, William Adams 1874-1960 *BnEnAmA,
WhAm 3*
Delano And Aldrich *BnEnAmA*
Delanoy, Abraham, Jr. 1742-1795 *NewYHSD*
DeLany, Dorothy Celia 1901-1960 *NatCAB 47*
Delany, John Bernard 1864-1906 *WhAm 1*
Delany, John Joseph 1861-1915 *WhAm 1*
Delany, Joseph Francis 1866-1943 *WhAm 2*
Delany, Martin Robinson 1812-1885 *AmBi,
DcAmB, McGEWB, WebAB, WhAm H,
WhAmP*
Delany, Martin Robison 1812-1885 *EncAB*
Delany, Patrick Bernard 1845-1924 *ApCAB X,
DcAmB, NatCAB 13, WhAm 1*
Delany, Selden Peabody 1874-1935 *WhAm 1*
DeLaOssa, Ernesto 1891-1961 *WhAm 4*
Delaplaine, Isaac Clason 1817-1866 *ApCAB,
BiAUS, BiDrAC, WhAm H*
Delaplaine, John Ferris 1815-1885 *ApCAB*
Delaplaine, Joseph 1777-1824 *ApCAB, Drake*
DeLaporte, Helen Reed *WomWWA 14*
DeLaPuente, Don Juan Joseph Eligio 1724-1781
WhAm H

Delaquiert, Jules *NewYHSD*
DeLara *NewYHSD*
DeLaRey, Jacobus Hercules 1847-1914
WhoMilH
DeLarge, Robert Carlos 1842-1874 *BiAUS,
BiDrAC, TwCBDA, WhAm H, WhAmP*
DeLargentaye, Jean 1903-1970 *WhAm 5*
DeLaRichardie, Armand 1686-1758 *WhAm H*
DeLarme, Alonzo Alvin d1930 *WhAm 1*
DeLaRoche, Mazo Louise 1879-1961 *McGEWB,
WhAm 4*
DeLaRoche, Rene 1795-1872 *NatCAB 24*
DeLaRonde, Louis Denis 1675-1741 *WhAm H*
DeLaRosa, Oswaldo Arturo 1905-1963
NatCAB 48
DeLaRue, Warren 1815-1889 *AsBiEn, DcScB*
DeLashmutt, Basil Munson 1903-1956
NatCAB 42
DeLashmutt, VanBanks 1842-1921 *NatCAB 19*
DeLasRios *NewYHSD*
DeLatour *NewYHSD*
Delatour, Henry Beeckman 1866-1930
ApCAB X, WhAm 1, WhAm 1C
DeLaTour, LeBlond d1723 *NatCAB 25*
Delattre, Henri 1801?-1867 *NewYHSD*
DeLattre DeTassigny, Jean 1889-1952
WhWW-II
DeLaubenfels, Max W 1894-1958 *WhAm 3*
DeLaudonniere, Rene Goulaine *WhAm H*
Delaunay, Charles-Eugene 1816-1872 *DcScB*
Delaunay, Jules *NewYHSD*
Delaune, Jacques 1812-1849 *ApCAB*
DeLauny *NewYHSD*
Delaup, Sidney Philip 1863-1923 *WhAm 1*
Delavan, D Bryson 1850-1942 *NatCAB 48,
WhAm 2*
Delavan, Edward Cornelius 1793-1871 *ApCAB,
DcAmB, NatCAB 11, WhAm H*
Delavan, Nelson Breese 1897-1971 *NatCAB 56*
DeLaVega, Garcilaso *ApCAB*
DeLaVega, Manuel Mariano 1887-1951
NatCAB 39
DeLaVergne, Charles Edouard 1904-1958
NatCAB 47
DeLaVergne, John Chester 1840-1896
NatCAB 2
DeLaVergne, Paul Mason 1908-1972
NatCAB 56
Delavina, Frederick Valentine 1885-1945
NatCAB 35
Delaware, Lord Thomas West 1577-1618 *Drake,
TwCBDA, WebAB*
DeLaWarr, Baron 1577-1618 *WhAm H*
DeLaWarr, Lord 1577-1618 *NatCAB 13*
DeLaWarr, Baron Thomas West 1577-1618
*AmBi, ApCAB, DcAmB, NatCAB 10,
WebAB*
DeLawarre, Thomas West 1577-1618 *TwCBDA*
Delbos, Julius 1879-1970 *WhAm 5*
Delbruck, Max 1906- *WebAB*
Delcasse, Theophile 1852-1923 *McGEWB*
DeLee, Joseph Bolivar 1869-1942 *DcAmB S3,
NatCAB 31, WhAm 2*
DeLeeuw, Adolph Lodewyk 1861-1942
DcAmB S3
Delehanty, Edward 1868-1953 *NatCAB 42*
Delehanty, James Andrew 1878-1960
NatCAB 45
DeLeMontanya, James 1798-1849 *WhAm H*
DeLeon, Daniel 1852-1914 *AmBi, DcAmB,
EncAB, McGEWB, WebAB, WhAm 1,
WhAmP*
DeLeon, David Camden 1813-1872 *ApCAB,
BiDConf, TwCBDA*
DeLeon, Edwin 1818-1891 *BiDConf,
NatCAB 4, TwCBDA, WhAm H*
DeLeon, Edwin Warren 1868-1918 *WhAm 1*
DeLeon, Pablo Ocampo 1853- *WhAm 4*
DeLeon, Thomas Cooper 1839-1914 *DcAmB,
NatCAB 19, TwCBDA, WhAm 1*
Delepine, Stephane-Marcel 1871-1965 *DcScB*
DeLequerica Y Erquiza, Jose Felix 1891-1963
WhAm 4
Delery, Francois Charles 1815-1880 *ApCAB,
DcAmB, WhAm H*
DeLery, Joseph Gaspard Chaussegros 1721-1797
WhAm H
Delessard, Auguste Joseph 1827- *IIBEAAW,*

NewYHSD
DeLestry, Edmond Louis 1860-1933 *WhAm 1*
Deletombe, Alice S 1854- *AmWom*
DeLeuw, Charles Edmund 1891-1970 *WhAm 5*
Delevanne *NewYHSD*
Delfelder, Jacob Astor 1871-1921 *NatCAB 19*
Delgadillo, Diego d1533 *ApCAB*
Delgado, Francisco Afan 1886-1964 *BiDrAC*
Delgado, Pedro 1487-1552 *ApCAB*
DelGaudio, Matthew William 1889-1960
WhAm 4
DelGiudice, Guy Richard Mario 1905-1959
NatCAB 44
DeL'Halle, Constantin d1706 *WhAm H*
D'Elhuyar, Fausto 1755-1833 *AsBiEn*
Deli, Frank Carl 1886-1946 *NatCAB 35*
Delile, Alire 1778-1850 *DcScB*
DeLima, Edith Abinun 1889- *WomWWA 14*
DeLima E Silva, R d1935 *WhAm 1*
Deliniers, Jacques Antoine Marie 1756-1810
Drake
DeLiniers-Bremont, Jacques Antoine M
1756-1810 *ApCAB*
Delisle, Guillaume 1675-1726 *DcScB*
Delisle, Joseph-Nicolas 1688-1768 *DcScB*
DeLisle, Moreau *BiAUS*
DeLisser, Horace 1866-1923 *WhAm 1*
Delitisch, B *NewYHSD*
Delius, Frederick 1862-1934 *WhAm HA,*
WhAm 4
Delk, Edward Buehler 1885-1956 *WhAm 3*
Delk, Edwin Heyl 1859-1940 *WhAm 1*
Dell, Floyd 1887-1969 *WebAB, WhAm 5*
Dell, Francis William 1877-1945 *WhAm 2*
Dell, Harrison Leroy 1880-1957 *NatCAB 46*
Dell, Roger LeRoy 1897-1966 *WhAm 4,*
WhAm 5
Dell'agnese, F d1971 *WhAm 6*
DellaPietra, Alfonso 1917-1969 *WhAm 5*
DellaPorta, Giambattista *DcScB*
DellaTorre, Giovanni Maria 1713-1782 *DcScB*
DellaTorre, Marcantonio *DcScB*
DellaTorre Alta, Il Marchese 1873- *WhAm 5*
Dellay, Vincent John 1907- *BiDrAC*
Delleker, George *NewYHSD*
Dellenback, John Richard 1918- *BiDrAC*
Dellenbaugh, Frederick Samuel 1853-1935
DcAmB S1, IIBEAAW, NatCAB 32,
WhAm 1
Dellenbaugh, Harriet Rogers Otis d1930
WhAm 1, WomWWA 14
Dellet, James 1788-1848 *ApCAB, BiAUS,*
BiDrAC, TwCBDA, WhAm H
Dellinger, John Howard 1886-1962 *NatCAB 53,*
WhAm 4
Dellius, Godfreidus d1705? *ApCAB*
DelloJoio, Norman 1913- *WebAB*
Dellplain, Morse 1880-1968 *WhAm 5*
DelManzo, Milton Carl 1889-1963 *NatCAB 51*
DelMar, Alexander 1836-1926 *AmBi, ApCAB,*
BiAUS, DcAmB, Drake Sup, NatCAB 4,
NatCAB 11, TwCBDA, WhAm 1
DelMar, Algernon 1870- *WhAm 5*
DelMar, Eugene 1864-1941 *WhAm 2*
DelMar, Frances Paloma *WomWWA 14*
DelMar, John 1838- *NatCAB 8*
DelMar, William Arthur 1880- *WhAm 6*
Delmas, Delphin Michael 1844-1928 *DcAmB,*
WhAm 1
Delmas, Delphin Michel 1844-1928 *NatCAB 24*
Delmonico, Lorenzo 1813-1881 *DcAmB,*
WebAB, WhAm H
Delmonte, Felix Maria 1810?- *ApCAB*
Delmonte Y Tejada, Antonio 1783-1861 *ApCAB*
DelMue, Maurice August 1875-1955 *IIBEAAW*
Delnoce, Louis *NewYHSD*
Deloach, Robert John Henderson 1873-
WhAm 5
DeLom D'Arce, Louis-Armand 1666-1713?
WhAm H
DeLong, Charles E d1876 *BiAUS, TwCBDA*
DeLong, George Washington 1844-1881 *AmBi,*
ApCAB, DcAmB, NatCAB 3, TwCBDA,
WebAMB, WhAm H
DeLong, Ira Mitchell 1855-1942 *WhAm 2*
DeLong, Irwin Hoch 1873- *WhAm 5*
DeLongpre, Paul 1855-1911 *WhAm 1*
DeLongpre, Paul 1855-1912 *NatCAB 16*

DeLorenzi, Otto 1893-1963 *NatCAB 51*
Deloria, Vine, Jr. 1934- *REnAW*
DeLorimier, Alfred Alexandre 1901-1960
NatCAB 50
Delorme, Louis 1824- *ApCAB*
DeL'Orme, Philibert 1510?-1570 *McGEWB*
DeLosRios, Fernando 1879-1949 *WhAm 2*
Delougaz, Pinhas Pierre 1901-1975 *WhAm 6*
DeLoutherbourg *NewYHSD*
DeLoutherbourg, Annibale C Henry 1765-1813
WhAm H
DelPilar, Marcelo H 1850-1896 *McGEWB*
DelPino, Jose Moya 1891- *IIBEAAW*
Delpit, Louise *WomWWA 14*
Delporte, Eugene Joseph 1882-1955 *DcScB*
DelRio, Andres Manuel 1764-1849 *AsBiEn*
DelRio, Angel 1901-1962 *NatCAB 50*
Delsasso, Leo Peter 1895-1971 *WhAm 5*
DelSesto, Christopher 1907-1973 *WhAm 6*
DelSolar, June Eckart DeGonzalez 1918-1972
WhAm 6
DelTufo, Raymond, Jr. 1919-1970 *WhAm 5*
Deluc, Jean Andre 1727-1817 *DcScB*
DeLuca, Frank Wilfred 1892-1952 *NatCAB 47*
DeLuca, Giuseppe 1876-1950 *DcAmB S4,*
WhAm 3
Deluca, Patrick Augustus 1900-1972
NatCAB 57
DeLuna Y Arellano, Tristan *WhAm H*
Delurey, Laurence Augustine 1864-
NatCAB 11, WhAm 4
DeLussan, Zelie 1863-1949 *NotAW*
Delvalle, Aristobolo 1847- *ApCAB*
DelValle, Manuel Angel 1895-1964 *WhAm 5*
Delwiche, Edmond Joseph 1874-1950
NatCAB 41, WhAm 4
Delzell, James Ellis 1862- *WhAm 4*
Delzell, Thomas White 1901-1969 *NatCAB 54,*
WhAm 5
Demane, John *NewYHSD*
DeMar, John L 1865-1926 *WhAm 1*
Demarcay, Eugene Anatole 1852-1904 *AsBiEn*
DeMare, Jeanne 1884-1974 *WhAm 6*
DeMare, John *NewYHSD*
Demaree, Albert Lowther 1894-1964 *EncAAH,*
NatCAB 49, WhAm 4
Demarest, Abraham *NewYHSD*
Demarest, Alex *NewYHSD*
Demarest, Andrew J *NewYHSD*
Demarest, David D 1819-1898 *ApCAB,*
TwCBDA
Demarest, Frederick F Cornell 1856-1931
NatCAB 24
Demarest, George Stuart 1906-1972 *WhAm 5*
Demarest, Henry Samuel 1867-1937
NatCAB 31, WhAm 1
Demarest, John 1763-1837 *ApCAB*
Demarest, John Terhune 1813-1897 *TwCBDA*
Demarest, Mary Augusta Lee 1838-1888
ApCAB Sup, NatCAB 5
Demarest, Regina 1855- *WomWWA 14*
Demarest, S Emma 1856- *WomWWA 14*
Demarest, William Henry Steele 1863-1956
NatCAB 15, WhAm 3
Demarest, William Thomas 1866-1926 *WhAm 1*
Demartini, Luigi 1850-1948 *NatCAB 37*
DeMartino, Nobile Giacomo 1868-1957
WhAm 3, WhAm 4
DeMattia, Barthold 1882-1944 *NatCAB 33*
Dembitz, Lewis Naphtali 1833-1907 *WhAm 1*
Dembo, Leon H 1895-1973 *WhAm 6*
Dembowski, Ercole 1812-1881 *DcScB*
Demby, V E Thomas 1869-1957 *WhAm 3*
DeMeissner, Sophie Radford 1854- *WhAm 4*
DeMenasce, Jacques 1905-1960 *WhAm 3*
DeMenil, Alexander Nicholas 1849-1928
NatCAB 12
DeMenil, Alexander Nicolas 1849-1928
WhAm 1
DeMenil, John 1904-1973 *WhAm 6*
DeMenocal, Daniel Ammen 1867- *ApCAB X*
DeMent, Byron Hoover 1863-1933 *WhAm 1*
Demerec, Milislav 1895-1966 *WhAm 4*
DeMerell, Iantha Aldrich 1855- *WomWWA 14*
DeMeritte, Edwin 1846- *WhAm 4*
DeMerrall, Leo Cyril 1880- *WhAm 6*
DeMerry DelVal, Alfonse 1903-1975 *WhAm 6*
Demers, Albert Fox 1863-1943 *WhAm 2*

Demers, Jerome 1774-1853 *ApCAB*
Demers, M 1774-1871 *ApCAB, Drake*
Demers, Pierre Paul 1876- *WhAm 5*
Demeunier, Jean Nicolas 1751-1814 *ApCAB*
DeMezieres Y Clugny, Athanase 1715?-1779
AmBi, DcAmB, WhAm H
Demiashkevich, Michael John 1891-1938
BiDAmEd, WhAm 1
DeMilhau, Louis John DeGrenon 1884-1968
WhAm 5
DeMille, Agnes George 1905- *WebAB*
DeMille, Anna Angela George *WomWWA 14*
DeMille, Beatrice M *WomWWA 14*
DeMille, Cecil Blount 1881-1959 *ApCAB X,*
EncAB, NatCAB 47, WebAB, WhAm 3
DeMille, Henry Churchill 1850-1893 *TwCBDA*
DeMille, Henry Churchill 1853-1893 *DcAmB,*
NatCAB 41, WhAm H
DeMille, James 1837-1880 *ApCAB*
DeMille, William Churchill 1878-1955
NatCAB 45, WhAm 3
Demilliere, Ann *NewYHSD*
Demilliere, Auguste *NewYHSD*
Demilliere, Auguste, Jr. *NewYHSD*
DeMilt, Aida Rodman 1871- *WhAm 5*
Deming, Adelaide 1864- *WomWWA 14*
Deming, Benjamin F 1790-1834 *BiAUS,*
BiDrAC, WhAm H
Deming, Charlotte *NewYHSD*
Deming, Clarence 1848-1913 *NatCAB 12,*
WhAm 1
Deming, Clyde Leroy 1885-1969 *NatCAB 55*
Deming, Dudley Brainard 1874-1946
NatCAB 39
Deming, Edwin Willard 1860-1942 *IIBEAAW,*
WhAm 2
Deming, Eleanor *WomWWA 14*
Deming, Fred Curtiss 1868- *NatCAB 17*
Deming, Harold S 1883-1954 *WhAm 3*
Deming, Henry Champion 1815-1872 *ApCAB,*
BiAUS, BiDrAC, NatCAB 11,
TwCBDA, WhAm H, WhAmP
Deming, Henry Champion 1850-1931
NatCAB 29
Deming, Horace Edward 1850-1930 *ApCAB X,*
NatCAB 33, WhAm 1
Deming, Judson Keith 1858- *WhAm 4*
Deming, Katherine Burritt 1891-
WomWWA 14
Deming, Lucius Parmenias 1836- *WhAm 4*
Deming, Philander 1829-1915 *DcAmB,*
NatCAB 8, TwCBDA, WhAm 1
Deming, Richard Henry 1885-1943 *NatCAB 35*
Deming, Therese O d1945 *WhAm 2*
Deming, Thomas Harlan 1874-1949 *WhAm 3*
Deming, William 1736-1830 *ApCAB, DcAmB*
Deming, William Chapin 1869-1949 *WhAm 2*
Deming, Winifred Conwell Murray 1861-
WomWWA 14
Demint, James d1817 *NatCAB 12*
DeMiranda, Francisco 1750-1816 *WhAm H*
Demme, Charles Rudolph 1795-1863 *DcAmB,*
WhAm H
Demme, William *NewYHSD*
Demmler, Albert John 1855-1941 *NatCAB 31*
Demmon, Isaac Newton 1842-1920 *TwCBDA,*
WhAm 1
Democritus *DcScB*
Democritus 470?BC-380?BC *AsBiEn*
Democritus 494?BC-404?BC *McGEWB*
DeMoivre, Abraham 1667-1754 *DcScB,*
McGEWB
DeMokcsa, Agoston Haraszthy 1812?-1869
WhAm H
DeMonchy, W H *WhAm 5*
DeMondeville, Henri 1260?-1320 *BiHiMed*
DeMontpreville *NewYHSD*
DeMontule *NewYHSD*
Demorest, Alice Gilbert 1863- *WomWWA 14*
Demorest, Ellen Louise Curtis 1824-1898
NotAW
Demorest, Frederic Coe 1864-1915 *NatCAB 52,*
WhAm 4
Demorest, William Curtis 1859- *WhAm 4*
Demorest, William Jennings 1822-1895
NatCAB 10
Demorest, William Jennings 1890-1975
WhAm 6

DeMorgan, Augustus 1806-1871 *DcScB*
DeMorse, Charles 1816-1887 *NatCAB 5*
Demory, Adam Richard 1868-1935 *NatCAB 31*
Demos, Raphael 1892-1968 *WhAm 5*
DeMoscoso DeAlvarado, Luis *WhAm H*
DeMoss, Mary Hissem 1871- *NatCAB 14*
Demosthenes 384BC-322BC *McGEWB*
DeMott, John 1790-1870 *BiAUS, BiDrAC, WhAm H*
DeMott, Richard Hopper 1886-1968 *WhAm 5*
DeMotte, Harvey Clelland 1838-1904 *TwCBDA, WhAm 1*
DeMotte, Mark Lindsey 1832-1908 *BiDrAC, TwCBDA, WhAm 1*
DeMotte, William Holman 1830- *TwCBDA*
Dempsey, Clarence Haines 1871-1937 *WhAm 1*
Dempsey, Edward John 1858- *WhAm 4*
Dempsey, Edward Joseph 1878-1956 *WhAm 3*
Dempsey, Edward Wheeler 1911-1975 *WhAm 6*
Dempsey, Elam Franklin 1878- *WhAm 2*
Dempsey, F Kenneth 1906-1973 *WhAm 6*
Dempsey, George Christopher 1865-1928 *ApCAB X*
Dempsey, Jack 1895- *WebAB*
Dempsey, James Howard 1859-1920 *WhAm 1*
Dempsey, John *NewYHSD*
Dempsey, John Bourne 1888-1963 *NatCAB 51, WhAm 4*
Dempsey, John Corish 1859- *NatCAB 14*
Dempsey, John Joseph 1879-1958 *BiDrAC, NatCAB 47, WhAm 3, WhAmP*
Dempsey, John Stanley 1891-1950 *WhAm 3*
Dempsey, K Mary d1973 *WhAm 6*
Dempsey, Sister Mary Joseph 1856-1939 *NotAW*
Dempsey, Michael Ryan 1918-1974 *WhAm 6*
Dempsey, Miles 1896-1969 *WhWW-II*
Dempsey, Stephen Wallace 1862-1949 *BiDrAC, WhAmP*
Dempsey, William H *NewYHSD*
Dempsey, William Harrison Jack 1895- *McGEWB*
Dempsie, Ephraim 1854-1911 *WhAm 1*
Dempster, Arthur Jeffrey 1886-1950 *AsBiEn, NatCAB 38, WhAm 2A*
Dempster, Charles Brackett 1853-1933 *NatCAB 41*
Dempster, George Roby 1887-1964 *NatCAB 53*
Dempster, Harry Lee 1882-1946 *NatCAB 41*
Dempster, John 1794-1863 *ApCAB, DcAmB, NatCAB 11, TwCBDA, WhAm H*
Dempster, Wilfrid Taylor 1905-1965 *NatCAB 52*
Dempster, William John 1870-1932 *WhAm 1*
Dempster, William Richardson 1809-1871 *ApCAB*
Dempsy, Stephen Wallace 1862-1949 *WhAm 2*
Dempwolf, Reinhardt d1945 *WhAm 2*
Demuth, Charles 1883-1935 *BnEnAmA, DcAmB S1, EncAB, McGEWB, WebAB, WhAm HA, WhAm 4*
Demuth, John 1770?-1820 *NewYHSD*
DeMuth, Laurence Wheeler 1900-1961 *WhAm 4*
Demuth, Leopold 1872- *ApCAB X*
DeMuth, Peter Joseph 1892- *BiDrAC*
DeNancrede, Charles Beylard Guerard 1847- *NatCAB 14*
DeNancrede, Paul Joseph Guerard 1761-1841 *WhAm H*
Denari, Andrew F 1905-1958 *WhAm 3*
DeNarvaez, Panfilo 1478?-1528 *WhAm H*
Denaut, Peter 1743-1806 *ApCAB*
DeNavarro *WomWWA 14*
DeNavarro, Alfonso 1863-1926 *NatCAB 21*
DeNavarro, Jose Francisco 1823-1909 *NatCAB 15*
Denbigh, John Halliday 1868-1943 *WhAm 2*
Denby, Charles 1830-1904 *ApCAB Sup, DcAmB, NatCAB 8, TwCBDA, WhAm 1*
Denby, Charles, Jr. 1861-1938 *NatCAB 8, NatCAB 39, WhAm 1*
Denby, Edwin 1870-1929 *AmBi, BiDrAC, BiDrUSE, DcAmB, NatCAB 21, WhAm 1, WhAmP*
Denby, Edwin Hooper 1873-1957 *NatCAB 45*
Denby, William 1874-1948 *NatCAB 36*

Dench, Edward Bradford 1864-1936 *WhAm 1*
Dendramis, Vassili 1883-1956 *WhAm 3*
Dene, Shafto Henry Monckton 1898-1956 *WhAm 3*
Denechaud, Celesta *NewYHSD*
Denechaud, Charles Isidore 1879-1956 *WhAm 3*
DeNeckere, Leo Raymond 1800-1833 *WhAm H*
DeNeefe, Robert d1956 *WhAm 3*
Deneen, Charles Samuel 1863-1940 *BiDrAC, NatCAB 14, NatCAB 31, WhAm 1, WhAmP*
Denegan, Samuel *NewYHSD*
Denegre, George 1854-1930 *NatCAB 24*
Denegre, Walter Denis 1858-1934 *NatCAB 10, WhAm 1*
DeNeve, Felipe 1737-1784 *EncAAH*
Denfeld, Louis Emil 1891-1972 *WebAMB, WhAm 5*
Denfeld, Robert Edward 1853-1921 *WhAm 1*
Denfert-Rochereau, Pierre M P Aristide 1823-1878 *WhoMilH*
Dengler, Frank 1853- *ApCAB*
Denham, Edward 1849-1925 *ApCAB X, WhAm 1*
Denham, Harry Courtenay 1887-1957 *NatCAB 47*
Denham, Henry Henderson 1870- *WhAm 5*
Denham, Louis W *NewYHSD*
Denham, Robert Newton 1885-1954 *NatCAB 45, WhAm 3*
Denham, Thomas Mandell 1840- *ApCAB X*
Denham, Thomas Palmer 1862- *WhAm 4*
Denham, William Ernest 1881- *WhAm 6*
Denhard, Charles Edward 1840- *WhAm 1*
Denhard, Charles Edward 1849- *NatCAB 1*
Denhardt, Henry H 1876-1937 *WhAm 1*
Denig, Edwin T 1812-1858 *REnAW*
Denig, Robert Gracey 1851-1924 *WhAm 1*
Denig, Rudolf Charles Robert 1867- *ApCAB X, NatCAB 14*
Denig-Manoe, Rudolf Karl Robert 1867- *WhAm 4*
Denikin, Anton Ivanovich 1872-1947 *WhoMilH*
Denin, Kate 1837- *ApCAB*
Denin, Susan 1835-1875 *ApCAB*
Denio, Francis Brigham 1848-1936 *NatCAB 27, WhAm 1*
Denio, Hiram 1799-1871 *ApCAB, BiAUS, Drake Sup, NatCAB 4, TwCBDA*
Denious, Jess C 1879-1953 *WhAm 3*
Denious, Wilbur Franklin d1957 *WhAm 3*
Denis, George Jules 1859-1937 *NatCAB 27*
Denis, Jean *ApCAB Sup*
Denis, Jean-Baptiste 1640?-1704 *DcScB*
Denis, Jean Ferdinand 1798-1879 *ApCAB*
Denis, Julian N 1829?- *NewYHSD*
Denis, Nicolas 1600?- *ApCAB, Drake*
Denise, David Demarest 1840- *NatCAB 3*
Denise, Edith *WomWWA 14*
Denise, Ira Condit 1840- *NewYHSD*
Denise, Larimore Conover 1872- *WhAm 5*
Denison, A Rodger 1897-1962 *WhAm 4*
Denison, Andrew Woods 1831-1877 *ApCAB, NatCAB 4*
Denison, Arthur Carter 1861-1942 *WhAm 2*
Denison, Charles 1818-1867 *BiAUS, BiDrAC, TwCBDA, WhAm H*
Denison, Charles 1845-1909 *NatCAB 17, WhAm 1*
Denison, Charles Ellery 1858-1926 *NatCAB 20*
Denison, Charles Land 1866-1930 *NatCAB 22*
Denison, Charles Simeon 1849-1913 *WhAm 1*
Denison, Charles Wheeler 1809-1881 *AmBi, ApCAB, Drake, TwCBDA*
Denison, Daniel 1613-1682 *ApCAB, Drake*
Denison, Dudley Chase 1819-1905 *BiAUS, BiDrAC, TwCBDA*
Denison, Edward Everett 1873-1953 *BiDrAC, WhAm 5, WhAmP*
Denison, Elsa 1889- *WomWWA 14*
Denison, Enos Goble 1875-1948 *NatCAB 38*
Denison, Evelyn Mattocks 1872- *WomWWA 14*
Denison, Flora MacD 1867- *WomWWA 14*
Denison, Florence Howland 1875- *WomWWA 14*
Denison, Frederic 1819-1901 *ApCAB, WhAm 1*

Denison, Frederick Charles 1846- *ApCAB*
Denison, George 1790-1831 *BiDrAC, WhAm H*
Denison, George Taylor 1816-1873 *ApCAB*
Denison, George Taylor 1839- *ApCAB*
Denison, Henry Delmater 1822-1883 *NatCAB 3*
Denison, Henry Willard 1846-1914 *WhAm 1*
Denison, James Henry 1907-1975 *WhAm 6*
Denison, John Henry 1841-1924 *WhAm 1*
Denison, John Henry 1855-1935 *WhAm 1*
Denison, John Hopkins 1870-1936 *NatCAB 27, WhAm 1*
Denison, John Ledyard 1826-1906 *ApCAB, WhAm 1*
Denison, Lindsay 1873-1934 *WhAm 1*
Denison, Mrs. M A *NewYHSD*
Denison, Mary Andrews 1826-1911 *ApCAB, Drake, NatCAB 19, NotAW, TwCBDA, WhAm 1*
Denison, Robert Charles 1868-1936 *WhAm 1*
Denison, Robert Fuller 1876-1952 *NatCAB 54, WhAm 5*
Denison, Thomas Stewart 1848-1911 *WhAm 1*
Denison, William Cecil 1892-1963 *WhAm 4*
Denison, Winfred Thaxter 1873-1919 *WhAm 1*
DeNivernais, Edward James *BiDrAC*
DeNiza, Marcos d1558 *WhAm H*
Denkmann, Frederick Carl 1859-1929 *NatCAB 22*
Denkmann, Frederick Carl August 1822-1905 *NatCAB 22*
Denman, Burt J 1876-1938 *NatCAB 31, WhAm 1*
Denman, Ira O 1872-1933 *WhAm 1*
Denman, Leroy Gilbert 1855-1916 *WhAm 1*
Denman, William 1784-1870 *WhAm H*
Denman, William 1872-1959 *WhAm 3*
Denneman *NewYHSD*
Dennen, Ernest Joseph 1866-1937 *WhAm 1*
Dennen, Grace Atherton 1874- *WomWWA 14*
Dennen, Jeanne Whitney 1863-1929 *WhAm 1*
Denner, Norman Henry 1899-1967 *NatCAB 54*
Dennett, Miss A H *NewYHSD*
Dennett, Carl Pullen 1874-1955 *WhAm 3*
Dennett, Edward Power 1863-1947 *WhAm 3*
Dennett, Elisabeth Goodwin Redfern *WomWWA 14*
Dennett, Fred 1863-1928 *WhAm 2*
Dennett, John Richard 1837-1874 *ApCAB, WhAm H*
Dennett, John Richard 1838-1874 *NatCAB 8*
Dennett, Lewis Lincoln 1867-1942 *NatCAB 38*
Dennett, Mary Coffin Ware 1872-1947 *BiCAW, NotAW, WomWWA 14*
Dennett, Maybelle Raymond *WomWWA 14*
Dennett, Raymond 1913-1961 *WhAm 4*
Dennett, Roger Herbert 1876-1935 *WhAm 1*
Dennett, Tyler 1883-1949 *DcAmB S4, NatCAB 38, WhAm 2*
Denney, Charles Eugene 1879- *WhAm 6*
Denney, James Arlando 1857- *WhAm 4*
Denney, Jane Franklin 1878- *WomWWA 14*
Denney, Joseph Villiers 1862-1935 *NatCAB 44, WhAm 1*
Denney, Lawrence Vincent 1910-1973 *WhAm 5*
Denney, Oswald Evans 1889-1944 *WhAm 2*
Denney, Robert Vernon 1916- *BiDrAC*
Denney, Sam Harrison 1889-1956 *NatCAB 45*
Denney, William DuHamel 1873-1953 *NatCAB 42, WhAm 4*
Dennie, Charles Clayton 1883-1971 *NatCAB 57, WhAm 5*
Dennie, Joseph 1768-1812 *AmBi, ApCAB, DcAmB, Drake, NatCAB 7, TwCBDA, WebAB, WhAm H*
Denning *NewYHSD*
Denning, Forrest Wayne 1907-1967 *WhAm 4*
Denning, James Edwin 1912-1971 *WhAm 5*
Denning, Joseph M 1866-1927 *WhAm 1*
Denning, Reynolds McConnell 1916-1967 *NatCAB 54, WhAm 5*
Denning, William 1736-1830 *DcAmB, WhAm H*
Denning, William 1740-1819 *BiAUS, BiDrAC, WhAm H*
Dennis *NewYHSD*
Dennis, Adolphus 1857- *NatCAB 13*
Dennis, Agnes Miller *WomWWA 14*

Dennis, Alfred Lewis 1817-1890 *NatCAB 21*
Dennis, Alfred Lewis 1857-1939 *NatCAB 31*
Dennis, Alfred Lewis Pinneo 1874-1930 *AmBi, DcAmB S1, NatCAB 37, WhAm 1*
Dennis, Alfred Pearce 1869-1931 *WhAm 1*
Dennis, Andrew Jackson LaFayette 1861-1922 *NatCAB 20*
Dennis, Arthur Wellington 1846-1920 *NatCAB 35*
Dennis, Charles Henry 1860-1943 *NatCAB 32, WhAm 2*
Dennis, Clara Ellen 1844- *WomWWA 14*
Dennis, David Nichols 1858-1930 *NatCAB 22*
Dennis, David Worth 1849-1916 *NatCAB 38, WhAm 1*
Dennis, David Worth 1912- *BiDrAC*
Dennis, E Willard 1887-1965 *NatCAB 52, WhAm 4*
Dennis, Edgar *NewYHSD*
Dennis, Edward Wimberly 1923-1975 *WhAm 6*
Dennis, Fannie A Murdoch *WomWWA 14*
Dennis, Fred L 1890-1958 *WhAm 3*
Dennis, Frederic James 1888-1945 *NatCAB 44*
Dennis, Frederic Shepard 1850-1934 *DcAmB S1, NatCAB 13, WhAm 1*
Dennis, Gabriel Lafayette 1896-1954 *WhAm 3*
Dennis, George Robertson 1822-1882 *ApCAB, BiAUS, BiDrAC, NatCAB 7, TwCBDA, WhAm H*
Dennis, Graham Barclay 1855-1923 *DcAmB, NatCAB 7*
Dennis, Graham Barclay 1857-1923 *WhAm 1*
Dennis, Harold 1882-1947 *NatCAB 36*
Dennis, James M 1840- *NewYHSD*
Dennis, James Shepard 1842-1914 *AmBi, DcAmB, NatCAB 22, WhAm 1*
Dennis, James Teackle 1865-1918 *WhAm 1*
Dennis, John 1771-1806 *BiDrAC, WhAm H*
Dennis, John 1771-1807 *BiAUS, NatCAB 13, TwCBDA*
Dennis, John 1807-1859 *BiAUS, BiDrAC, TwCBDA, WhAm H*
Dennis, John Cobb 1892-1965 *WhAm 4*
Dennis, John Hancock 1835- *WhAm 4*
Dennis, John M 1866-1936 *WhAm 1*
Dennis, John Rhodes 1877-1945 *NatCAB 35*
Dennis, Joseph Charles 1877- *WhAm 5*
Dennis, Laban 1840-1925 *NatCAB 20*
Dennis, Lindley Hoag 1880-1955 *WhAm 3*
Dennis, Littleton Purnell 1786-1834 *BiAUS, BiDrAC, TwCBDA, WhAm H*
Dennis, Louis Munroe 1863-1936 *NatCAB 15, NatCAB 27, WhAm 1*
Dennis, Ralph 1876-1942 *WhAm 2*
Dennis, Rodney 1826- *NatCAB 5*
Dennis, Ruth 1877-1968 *WebAB*
Dennis, Samuel K 1874-1953 *WhAm 3*
Dennis, Samuel Shepard 1852-1924 *ApCAB X, NatCAB 35, WhAm 1*
Dennis, Thomas 1638?-1706 *BnEnAmA*
Dennis, Warren Egerton 1854-1932 *NatCAB 33*
Dennis, William B 1865-1937 *WhAm 1*
Dennis, William Cullen 1878-1962 *ApCAB X, WhAm 4*
Dennis, William Henry 1856-1919 *WhAm 1*
Dennis, William Henry, Jr. 1914-1965 *WhAm 4*
Dennison *NewYHSD*
Dennison, Aaron Lufkin 1812-1895 *DcAmB, WhAm H*
Dennison, Charles Melville 1873-1924 *NatCAB 22*
Dennison, Charles Sumner 1858-1912 *NatCAB 39*
Dennison, Clare 1891-1954 *WhAm 3*
Dennison, David Short 1918- *BiDrAC*
Dennison, E Haldeman 1872-1931 *WhAm 1*
Dennison, Ethan Allen 1881-1954 *NatCAB 43, WhAm 3*
Dennison, George d1831 *BiAUS*
Dennison, Henry Sturgis 1877-1952 *WhAm 3*
Dennison, Henry Sturgis 1877-1952 *DcAmB S5, NatCAB 40, WhAm 5*
Dennison, Jackson Belden 1891-1959 *WhAm 3*
Dennison, Walter 1869-1917 *DcAmB, WhAm 1*
Dennison, William 1815-1882 *AmBi, ApCAB, BiAUS, BiDrUSE, DcAmB, Drake, NatCAB 3, TwCBDA, WhAm H,*

WhAmP
Denniston, Henry Martyn 1840-1922 *WhAm 1*
Denno, Willard Joseph 1876-1951 *NatCAB 39*
Denny, Arthur Armstrong 1822-1899 *BiAUS, BiDrAC*
Denny, Charles Eugene 1879-1965 *WhAm 4*
Denny, Collins 1854-1943 *NatCAB 35, TwCBDA, WhAm 2*
Denny, Collins, Jr. 1899-1964 *WhAm 4*
Denny, Ebenezer 1761-1822 *NatCAB 12, WhAm H*
Denny, Elizabeth Bell Marshall *WomWWA 14*
Denny, Frank Lee 1858-1914 *WhAm 1*
Denny, George Hutcheson 1870-1955 *NatCAB 13, WhAm 3*
Denny, George Vernon, Jr. 1899-1959 *WhAm 3*
Denny, Harmar 1794-1852 *BiAUS, BiDrAC, TwCBDA, WhAm H*
Denny, Harmar Denny, Jr. 1886-1966 *BiDrAC, WhAm 4*
Denny, Harold Norman 1889-1945 *NatCAB 34, WhAm 2*
Denny, J G 1830-1886 *IIBEAAW*
Denny, James William 1838-1923 *BiDrAC, WhAm 1*
Denny, Ludwell 1894-1970 *WhAm 5*
Denny, Parkman Tyler 1851-1911 *NatCAB 17*
Denny, Reginald Leigh 1891-1967 *WhAm 4*
Denny, Robert H 1897-1956 *WhAm 3*
Denny, Roy 1878-1954 *NatCAB 43*
Denny, Thomas 1804-1874 *ApCAB*
Denny, Walter McKennon 1853-1926 *BiDrAC*
Denny, William *ApCAB*
DeNogales, Pedro Rafael 1879- *WhAm 6*
Denonville, Jacques R DeB, Marquis De *ApCAB, Drake*
DeNood, Neal Breaule 1904-1972 *NatCAB 57*
DeNoon, Charles *NewYHSD*
DeNormandie, James 1836-1924 *TwCBDA, WhAm 1*
DeNormandie, Robert L 1876-1953 *WhAm 3*
DeNoyan, Pierre-Jacques Payen 1695-1763? *WhAm H*
Denoyelles, Peter 1766-1829 *BiAUS, BiDrAC, WhAm H*
Denoyer, L Philip 1875-1964 *NatCAB 52, WhAm 4*
Denslow, Dorothea Henrietta 1900-1971 *WhAm 5*
Denslow, Herbert McKenzie 1852-1944 *WhAm 2*
Denslow, William Wallace 1856-1915 *WhAm 1*
Densmore, Amos 1825-1893 *NatCAB 3, TwCBDA*
Densmore, Emmet 1837-1911 *WhAm 1*
Densmore, Frances 1867-1957 *REnAW, WhAm 3*
Densmore, Harvey Bruce 1881- *WhAm 6*
Densmore, Hiram D 1862-1940 *WhAm 1*
Densmore, James 1820-1889 *NatCAB 3, TwCBDA*
Densmore, John B 1877-1937 *WhAm 3*
Densmore, John Hopkins 1880-1943 *WhAm 2*
Denson, Nimrod Davis 1856-1927 *WhAm 1*
Denson, Samuel Crawford 1839-1917 *WhAm 1*
Denson, William Henry 1846-1906 *BiDrAC*
Denstedt, Orville Frederick d1975 *WhAm 6*
Dent, Elmer Addison 1861- *NatCAB 11*
Dent, Frederick F 1786-1873 *ApCAB*
Dent, Frederick Rodgers, Jr. 1908-1969 *WhAm 5*
Dent, Frederick Tracy 1820-1892 *ApCAB, TwCBDA*
Dent, Frederick Tracy 1821-1892 *DcAmB, WhAm H*
Dent, George 1756-1813 *BiAUS, BiDrAC, WhAm H*
Dent, George 1760?-1813 *ApCAB, NatCAB 12*
Dent, Hawthorne K 1880-1958 *WhAm 3*
Dent, John Charles 1841-1888 *ApCAB*
Dent, John Herbert 1782-1823 *ApCAB, Drake*
Dent, John Herman 1908- *BiDrAC*
Dent, John Marshall, Jr. 1937-1974 *WhAm 6*
Dent, Louis 1822-1874 *ApCAB*
Dent, Louis Addison 1863- *NatCAB 11, WhAm 4*
Dent, Marmaduke Herbert 1849-1909 *WhAm 1*

Dent, Stanley Hubert, Jr. 1869-1938 *BiDrAC, WhAm 1, WhAmP*
Dent, Thomas 1831-1924 *NatCAB 17*
Dent, William Barton Wade 1806-1855 *BiAUS, BiDrAC, WhAm H*
Denton, Clara Janetta *WomWWA 14*
Denton, Daniel *ApCAB, Drake, NatCAB 8*
Denton, Franklin Evert 1859- *TwCBDA*
Denton, George Bion 1884-1963 *NatCAB 49*
Denton, George Kirkpatrick 1864-1926 *BiDrAC, WhAm 1*
Denton, J Furman 1914-1972 *WhAm 5*
Denton, James Clarence 1882-1942 *WhAm 2*
Denton, James Edgar 1855-1928 *WhAm 1*
Denton, James Way 1888-1950 *NatCAB 38*
Denton, Lyman Morse 1869- *WhAm 5*
Denton, Mary Florence 1857-1947 *NotAW*
Denton, Minna Caroline 1873-1958 *WhAm 3*
Denton, Richard 1586-1662 *ApCAB*
Denton, Sherman Foote 1856-1937 *NatCAB 27*
Denton, William 1823- *Drake*
Denton, Winfield Kirkpatrick 1896-1971 *BiDrAC, WhAm 5, WhAmP*
Dentz, Henri *WhWW-II*
Denver, James W 1818-1892 *ApCAB, BiAUS, Drake*
Denver, James William 1817-1892 *AmBi, BiDrAC, DcAmB, NatCAB 8, WhAm H, WhAmP*
Denver, James Wilson 1817-1892 *TwCBDA*
Denver, Matthew Rombach 1870-1954 *BiDrAC, WhAm 3*
Denver, William J 1841-1913 *NatCAB 16*
Denworth, Hugh Frederick 1891-1941 *NatCAB 32*
Denyer, Robert J *NewYHSD*
Denyes, John Russell 1869-1936 *WhAm 1*
Denys, F Ward 1854-1941 *NatCAB 38*
Deodoro DaFonseca, Manoel 1827-1892 *McGEWB*
DeOnate, Juan 1549?-1624? *WhAm H*
DeOnis, Federico 1885-1966 *WhAm 4*
DeOtermen, Antonio d1683 *WhAm H*
DePadilla, Juan 1500?-1544? *WhAm H*
DePalm, Joseph Henry Louis 1809-1876 *ApCAB*
DePaolis, Alessio 1893-1964 *WhAm 4*
Deparcieux, Antoine 1703-1768 *DcScB*
DeParis, Wilbur 1900-1973 *WhAm 5*
DePaugher, Adrien d1726 *WhAm H*
DePaula Gutierrez, Don Francisco *WhAm 6*
DePauw, Charles *ApCAB*
DePauw, John d1838 *ApCAB*
DePauw, Washington Charles 1822-1887 *AmBi, ApCAB, DcAmB, NatCAB 7, TwCBDA, WhAm H*
DePena, Carlos Maria 1852-1918 *WhAm 1*
DePenalosa Briceno, Diego Dioniso 1622?-1687 *WhAm H*
DePeralta, Pedro 1584?-1666 *WhAm H*
Deperet, Charles 1854-1929 *DcScB*
Depesseville *NewYHSD*
Depew, Charles Augustus 1804-1877 *NatCAB 23*
Depew, Chauncey Mitchell 1834-1928 *AmBi, ApCAB, BiDrAC, DcAmB, NatCAB 1, NatCAB 23, TwCBDA, WebAB, WhAm 1, WhAmP*
Depew, Claude Ira 1893-1956 *WhAm 3*
Depew, Harold 1883-1939 *NatCAB 33*
DePew, Joseph William 1889-1972 *WhAm 5*
DePeyster, Abraham 1657-1728 *DcAmB*
DePeyster, Abraham 1658-1728 *ApCAB, Drake, NatCAB 2, TwCBDA, WhAm H*
DePeyster, Abraham 1753-1799? *ApCAB*
DePeyster, Arent Schuyler 1736-1832 *ApCAB, NatCAB 2*
DePeyster, Frederic, Jr. 1796-1882 *ApCAB, NatCAB 2, NatCAB 3, TwCBDA*
DePeyster, Frederic James 1839-1905 *WhAm 1*
DePeyster, Frederick *ApCAB*
DePeyster, Frederick, Jr. 1843-1874 *NatCAB 2*
DePeyster, Frederick James 1839-1905 *NatCAB 2*
DePeyster, Gerard Beekman 1834-1870 *NewYHSD*
DePeyster, James d1793 *ApCAB*
DePeyster, Johannes 1600?-1685? *ApCAB, Drake, NatCAB 2*

DePeyster, John Watts 1821-1907 *ApCAB, DcAmB, Drake, NatCAB 2, TwCBDA, WhAm 1*
DePeyster, John Watts, Jr. 1841-1873 *ApCAB, NatCAB 2, TwCBDA*
DePeyster, Johnston Livingston 1846-1903 *NatCAB 2, TwCBDA*
Dephew, Chauncy Mitchell 1834-1928 *ApCAB X*
Depinet, Ned E 1890-1974 *WhAm 6*
DePinna, Leo Safati 1873-1939 *NatCAB 35*
DePodesta, Frank 1911-1963 *NatCAB 50*
DePolignac, Prince Camille Armand J M 1832-1913 *BiDConf*
Deponai, John Martin 1871-1917 *WhAm 1*
DePontelli *NewYHSD*
DePortola, Gaspar 1723?-1784 *WhAm H*
DePouilly, Jacques Nicholas Bussiere 1805-1875 *WhAm H*
DePourtales, Louis Francois 1823-1880 *WhAm H*
Deppermann, William Herman 1903-1971 *WhAm 5*
Depping, Charles William 1888-1964 *NatCAB 52*
Deprez, Marcel 1843-1918 *DcScB*
DePriest, Oscar Stanton 1871-1951 *BiDrAC, DcAmB S5, WhAm 3, WhAmP, WhoColR*
Depue, David A 1826-1902 *WhAm 1*
Depue, David Ayers 1826-1902 *TwCBDA*
Depue, David Ayres 1826-1902 *NatCAB 5*
Deputy, Manfred Wolfe 1868-1947 *WhAm 2*
DePuy, Henry Farr 1859-1924 *NatCAB 20*
DePuy, Henry Walter 1820-1876 *ApCAB*
DePuy, William Harrison 1821-1901 *WhAm 1*
Dequen, Jean d1659 *ApCAB*
DeQuille, Dan 1829-1898 *DcAmB S1, REnAW, WhAm H*
Derain, Andre 1880-1954 *McGEWB*
Deramus, William Neal 1888-1965 *NatCAB 51, WhAm 4*
Derbigny, Irving A 1900-1957 *WhAm 3*
Derbigny, Peter 1767-1829 *BiAUS, Drake, TwCBDA*
Derbigny, Pierre Auguste C Bourguignon 1767-1829 *DcAmB, NatCAB 10, WhAm H*
Derbigny, Pierre Auguste C Bourguinon 1767-1829 *WhAmP*
Derbigny, Pierre Auguste C Bourisgay 1767-1829 *ApCAB*
Derby, Ashton Philander 1878- *WhAm 6*
Derby, Charles Fretz 1886-1950 *NatCAB 40*
Derby, Donald 1908-1969 *WhAm 5*
Derby, Elias Hasket 1737-1799 *TwCBDA*
Derby, Elias Hasket 1739-1799 *AmBi, ApCAB, DcAmB, Drake, NatCAB 5, WhAm H*
Derby, Elias Hasket 1803-1880 *ApCAB, DcAmB, Drake, NatCAB 4, TwCBDA, WhAm H*
Derby, Elias Hasket, Jr. 1766-1826 *AmBi, ApCAB, DcAmB, Drake, NatCAB 4, TwCBDA, WhAm H*
Derby, George 1819-1874 *ApCAB, TwCBDA*
Derby, George H 1824-1861 *Drake*
Derby, George Horatio 1823-1861 *AmBi, ApCAB, DcAmB, EncAAH, NatCAB 5, REnAW, TwCBDA, WhAm H*
Derby, George Hunter 1823-1852 *NatCAB 11*
Derby, George McClellan 1856-1948 *WhAm 3*
Derby, George Strong 1875-1931 *WhAm 1*
Derby, Gertrude James 1867- *WomWWA 14*
Derby, Hasket 1835-1914 *NatCAB 17*
Derby, Ira Harris 1873-1950 *NatCAB 37*
Derby, James Cephas 1818-1892 *ApCAB, NatCAB 11, TwCBDA*
Derby, Jeanette Barr 1895-1965 *WhAm 4*
Derby, John Barton 1792-1867 *ApCAB, NatCAB 11*
Derby, Lillie Gill 1870- *WomWWA 14*
Derby, Margaret Leonard 1867- *WomWWA 14*
Derby, Mary 1814-1900 *NewYHSD*
Derby, Mary Jane 1807-1892 *NewYHSD*
Derby, Orville Adelbert 1851- *ApCAB Sup, NatCAB 10, TwCBDA, WhAm 4*
Derby, Perley 1823-1896 *NewYHSD*
Derby, Richard 1712-1783 *AmBi, ApCAB, DcAmB, TwCBDA, WhAm H*

Derby, Richard 1881-1963 *NatCAB 51, WhAm 4*
Derby, Samuel Carroll 1842-1921 *NatCAB 7, TwCBDA, WhAm 1*
Derby, Stephen Hasket 1877-1947 *WhAm 2*
Dercum, Francis Xavier 1856-1931 *DcAmB S1, NatCAB 22, WhAm 1*
DeReef, George Heriot 1869- *WhoColR*
DeRemer, John A 1835-1907 *WhAm 1*
DeRenne, Wymberley Jones 1853-1916 *NatCAB 18*
DeReszke, Edouard 1853-1917 *WhAm 1*
DeReszke, Eduard 1855-1917 *ApCAB Sup*
DeReszke, Jean 1850-1925 *WhAm 2*
DeReszke, Jean 1852-1925 *ApCAB Sup*
Derflinger, Lloyd Jackson 1891-1966 *NatCAB 51*
DeRham, Casimir 1896-1968 *NatCAB 54*
Derham, William 1657-1735 *DcScB*
Derick, Carrie Matilda 1862- *WomWWA 14*
Derickson, Donald 1878-1962 *WhAm 4*
Derickson, Samuel Hoffman 1879-1951 *WhAm 3*
Derieux, Samuel Arthur 1881-1922 *WhAm 1*
Deringer, J Paul 1903-1956 *NatCAB 43*
DeRivera, Belle *WomWWA 14*
DeRivera, Jose 1904- *BnEnAmA*
Derleth, August 1909-1971 *WhAm 5*
Derleth, Charles, Jr. 1874- *WhAm 5*
Dermitt, Granville 1830?- *NewYHSD*
Dern, Alfred L 1885-1947 *WhAm 2*
Dern, George Henry 1872-1936 *AmBi, BiDrUSE, DcAmB S2, NatCAB 26, REnAW, WhAm 1*
Dern, John 1850-1922 *NatCAB 33, WhAm 1*
Dern, John 1903-1958 *WhAm 3*
DeRoaldes, Abel 1804-1894 *NatCAB 7*
DeRoaldes, Arthur Washington 1849-1918 *NatCAB 7, WhAm 1*
DeRohan, William 1819-1891 *NatCAB 5*
DeRoover, Raymond 1904-1972 *NatCAB 56*
DeRos, John Frederick Fitzgerald 1804-1861 *Drake*
DeRose, Anthony Lewis 1803-1836 *NewYHSD*
DeRose, Peter d1953 *WhAm 3*
DeRose, Peter 1896-1953 *NatCAB 40*
DeRose, Peter 1900-1953 *DcAmB S5*
Derosne, Charles 1780-1846 *DcScB*
DeRosset, Armand John 1767-1859 *ApCAB, NatCAB 11*
DeRosset, Armand John 1807- *ApCAB*
DeRosset, Frederick Ancrum 1856-1915 *WhAm 1*
DeRosset, Mary Jane *ApCAB*
DeRosset, Moses John 1796-1826 *ApCAB*
DeRosset, Moses John 1838-1881 *ApCAB, DcAmB, NatCAB 11, TwCBDA, WhAm H*
DeRosset, William Lord 1832-1910 *NatCAB 11, WhAm 3*
DeRottenburg, Baron 1756?-1832 *ApCAB*
DeRouen, Rene Louis 1874-1942 *BiDrAC, WhAm 2, WhAmP*
Deroulet, Vincent W 1925-1975 *WhAm 6*
Derounian, Steven Boghos 1918- *BiDrAC, WhAmP*
DeRoussy DeSales, Raoul 1896-1942 *WhAm 2*
Derr, Cyrus George 1848-1933 *WhAm 1*
Derr, Homer Munro 1877- *WhAm 5*
Derr, Louis 1868-1923 *WhAm 1*
Derr, Thomas Sieger 1896-1948 *NatCAB 36*
Derr, Thompson 1834-1885 *NatCAB 9*
Derrick, Edward 1844-1914 *ApCAB X*
Derrick, Philip 1772-1819 *NewYHSD*
Derrick, Samuel Melanchthon 1896-1969 *WhAm 5*
Derrick, Sidney Jacob 1867-1948 *WhAm 2*
Derrick, W B 1840?- *NatCAB 12*
D'Errico, Emilio 1894-1954 *NatCAB 42*
Derry, George Hermann 1878-1949 *NatCAB 37, WhAm 2*
Derry, Joseph Tyrone 1841-1926 *NatCAB 21*
Derse, Alexander Anthony 1892-1962 *WhAm 4*
Dershem, Franklin Lewis 1865-1950 *BiDrAC, WhAm 4*
Derthick, Frank A 1844- *WhAm 4*
Derthick, Henry J 1872-1968 *NatCAB 54, WhAm 5*

Dertinger, Georg 1902-1968 *WhAm 4A*
DeRudio, Charles 1832-1910 *NatCAB 8*
Derujinsky, Gleb W 1888-1975 *WhAm 6*
DeRussy, Gustavus Adolphus 1818-1891 *ApCAB, TwCBDA*
DeRussy, Isaac Denniston 1840-1923 *WhAm 1*
DeRussy, Lewis G d1865 *Drake*
DeRussy, Louis G 1796-1864 *ApCAB, TwCBDA*
DeRussy, Rene Edward 1789-1865 *ApCAB*
DeRussy, Rene Edward 1790-1865 *NatCAB 4, TwCBDA*
DeRussy, Rene Edward 1791-1865 *Drake*
Derven, John Joseph 1882-1925 *NatCAB 6*
Derwent, Clarence 1884-1959 *WhAm 3*
Derwent, Emma Wilder 1859- *WomWWA 14*
Derwinski, Edward Joseph 1926- *BiDrAC*
Dery, D George *ApCAB X, WhAm 3*
DeRyke, Emma *IlBEAAW*
Deryugin, Konstantin Mikhailovich 1878-1938 *DcScB*
DeSabla, Eugene 1865-1956 *NatCAB 45*
Desaguliers, John Theophile 1683-1744 *AsBiEn*
Desaguliers, John Theophilus 1683-1744 *DcScB*
Desaignes *NewYHSD*
DeSaint Aubin, Percival Ovide 1887-1940 *WhAm 1*
DeSaint-Aulaire *NewYHSD*
DeSaint Denis, Louis Juchereau 1676-1744 *WhAm H*
DeSaint Exupery, Antoine 1900- *WhAm 2*
DeSaint-Memin, Charles B Julien Fevret 1770-1852 *NewYHSD, WhAm H*
DeSaint-Phalle, Francois 1884-1932 *NatCAB 32*
DeSaint Remy *NewYHSD*
DeSaint Vrain, Ceran DeHault Delassus 1802-1870 *WhAm H*
Desaix, Louis C A, Chevalier DeVeygoux 1768-1800 *WhoMilH*
DeSalazar *NewYHSD*
DeSalvio, Alfonso 1873- *WhAm 5*
DeSanctis, Adolph George 1893-1966 *WhAm 4*
DeSanctis, Francesco 1817-1883 *McGEWB*
Desandrouin, Viscount 1740- *ApCAB*
Desandrouins, Vicomte 1740- *Drake*
DeSantillana, Giorgio Diaz 1902-1974 *WhAm 6*
Desargues, Girard 1591-1661 *DcScB*
DeSaulles, Charles August Heckscher 1876- *WhAm 5*
Desaulniers, Louis Leon L 1823- *ApCAB*
Desaulniers, Lucien Lesieur 1875-1952 *NatCAB 40*
DeSaussure, Charles Alfred 1899-1959 *NatCAB 47*
Desaussure, Henry W d1839 *Drake*
Desaussure, Henry W 1764-1839 *BiAUS*
DeSaussure, Henry William 1763-1839 *ApCAB, DcAmB, NatCAB 13, TwCBDA, WhAm H*
DeSaussure, William Ford 1792-1870 *BiAUS, BiDrAC, NatCAB 5, TwCBDA*
DeSaussure, Wilmot Gibbes 1822-1886 *ApCAB, TwCBDA*
DeSautelle, William Thomas 1884-1959 *NatCAB 50*
DeSauze, Emile Blais 1878- *WhAm 6*
DeSavitsch, Eugene Constantine 1903-1959 *WhAm 4*
DesBarres, Joseph Frederic Wallet 1722-1824 *Drake*
DesBarres, Joseph Frederick Wallet 1722-1824 *ApCAB*
DesBarres, William Frederick 1800-1885 *ApCAB*
Desbrosses, Elias 1718-1778 *NatCAB 1*
Descartes, Rene DuPerron 1596-1650 *AsBiEn, BiHiMed, DcScB, McGEWB*
Deschamps, Isaac 1723-1801 *ApCAB, Drake*
Deschamps, Paul 1888-1975 *WhAm 6*
Deschaum, Ed *NewYHSD*
DeSchweinitz, Edmond Alexander 1825-1887 *WhAm H*
DeSchweinitz, Edmund Alexander 1825-1887 *DcAmB, NatCAB 27, TwCBDA*
DeSchweinitz, George Edmund 1858-1938 *DcAmB S2*
DeSchweinitz, Karl 1887-1975 *WhAm 6*

DeSchweinitz, Paul 1863-1940 *WhAm 1*
DesCloizeaux, Alfred-L-Olivier Legrand 1817-1897 *DcScB*
DesCombes *NewYHSD*
Descotils, Hippolyte Victor *DcScB*
Descourtilz, Michel Etienne 1775-1836 *DcScB*
DesEssarts, D D *NewYHSD*
DeSeversky, Alexander Procofieff 1894-1974 *WebAB, WebAMB*
DesGentils *NewYHSD*
Desha, John Rollin 1887-1958 *NatCAB 47*
Desha, Joseph 1768-1842 *ApCAB, BiAUS, BiDrAC, DcAmB, Drake, NatCAB 13, TwCBDA, WhAm H, WhAmP*
Desha, Mary d1910 *WhAm 1*
Desha, Robert 1791-1849 *ApCAB, BiAUS, BiDrAC, Drake, TwCBDA, WhAm H*
Deshayes, Gerard Paul 1797-1875 *DcScB*
DeShazo, Robert Mason 1886-1961 *NatCAB 49*
Deshler, Charles Franklin 1877-1947 *NatCAB 38*
Deshler, William Green 1827-1916 *NatCAB 17*
Deshon, George 1823-1903 *ApCAB, TwCBDA, WhAm 1*
Deshon, Harold Dudley 1887-1946 *NatCAB 37*
Deshon, Moses *NewYHSD*
DeSica, Vittorio 1902-1974 *WhAm 6*
Desiderio DaSettignano 1428?-1464 *McGEWB*
Desiderio, Anthony d1970 *WhAm 5*
DeSilver, Albert 1888-1924 *NatCAB 48*
DeSilver, Carll Harrison 1846-1913 *NatCAB 16*
Desiree, Sister 1815-1879 *ApCAB*
Desjardins, Arthur Ulderic 1884-1964 *WhAm 4*
DesJardins, Benjamin Myrrick 1858- *NatCAB 12*
Desjardins, T C Alphonse 1841- *ApCAB*
Deslandres, Henri 1853-1948 *DcScB*
Desloge, Jane Chambers Thatcher 1851- *WomWWA 14*
Desloge, Joseph 1889-1971 *WhAm 5*
DeSloovere, Frederick Joseph 1886-1945 *NatCAB 34*
Desmarest, Nicolas 1725-1815 *AsBiEn, DcScB*
DeSmet, Peter John 1801-1872 *NatCAB 11, TwCBDA*
DeSmet, Pierre Jean 1801-1873 *AmBi, DcAmB, DcAmReB, IlBEAAW, McGEWB, REnAW, WebAB, WhAm H*
Desmier DeSaint-Simon, Etienne J A *DcScB*
Desmond, Daniel Francis 1884-1945 *WhAm 2*
Desmond, Humphrey Joseph 1858-1932 *WhAm 1*
Desmond, Thomas Augustin 1884-1948 *NatCAB 37*
Desmond, Thomas Charles 1887-1972 *WhAm 5*
Desmond, Thomas Henry 1884-1950 *WhAm 3*
Desnoyers, Peter 1773-1880 *ApCAB*
Desobry, Prosper *NewYHSD*
DeSola, Abraham 1825-1882 *ApCAB*
DeSollar, Tenney Cook 1881-1966 *WhAm 4*
Desor, Pierre Jean Edouard 1811-1882 *DcScB*
Desormes, Charles-Bernard 1777-1862 *DcScB*
DeSoto, Ferdinand 1500?-1542 *AmBi*
DeSoto, Fernando 1496?-1542 *ApCAB, NatCAB 5*
DeSoto, Fernando 1500?-1542 *Drake*
DeSoto, Hernando 1496?-1542 *WebAB*
DeSoto, Hernando 1500?-1542 *AmBi, DcAmB, McGEWB, REnAW, WhAm H*
DeSoto, Hernando 1866-1928 *WhAm 1*
Despagnet, Jean *DcScB*
Despard, Clement L 1884-1957 *WhAm 3*
Despard, John 1745-1829 *ApCAB, Drake*
Despard, Victor Reginald 1888-1965 *NatCAB 52*
DeSpitzer, Ernestus 1709-1789 *NatCAB 11*
DeSpitzer, Garrett 1758-1801 *NatCAB 11*
DesPlanches, Baron Ed Mayor 1851- *WhAm 4*
DesPortes, Fay Allen 1890-1944 *NatCAB 34, WhAm 2*
Desportes, Henrietta *NewYHSD*
D'Esposito, Joshua 1878-1954 *WhAm 3*
Despradelle, Constant Desire 1862- *WhAm 1*
Despres, Emile 1909-1973 *WhAm 5*
Despres, Maurice Samuel 1901-1954 *WhAm 3*
Desprez-Crassier, Jean Etienne Philibert 1733-1803? *ApCAB, Drake*
DesRochers, John Mowbray 1859- *NatCAB 9*

Dessaignes, Victor 1800-1885 *DcScB*
Dessalines, Jean Jacques 1758-1806 *ApCAB, McGEWB*
Dessalines, Jean Jacques 1760?-1806 *Drake*
Dessar, Leo Charles *WhAm 5*
Dessar, Louis Paul 1867-1952 *WhAm 3*
Dessarts, C *NewYHSD*
Dessaur, Ferdinand *NewYHSD*
Desses, Jean 1904-1970 *WhAm 5*
Dessez, Elizabeth Richey 1879- *WhAm 6*
Dessez, Henriette Louise 1863- *WomWWA 14*
Dession, George Hathaway 1905-1955 *WhAm 3*
DesSmet, Peter John 1801-1872 *ApCAB*
D'Estaing, Count Charles Hector 1729-1794 *AmBi*
DeStefani, Rafael Esteva *NatCAB 5*
DeStefano, George Anthony 1912-1972 *NatCAB 57*
DeSteiguer, Louis Rodolph 1867-1947 *NatCAB 36, WhAm 2*
Destinn, Emmy 1878-1930 *WhAm 1*
Destrehan, Jean Noel 1780?-1824 *ApCAB, NatCAB 12*
Destrehan, John Noel 1780-1824 *BiDrAC, WhAm H*
Destrihan, John Noel 1780?-1824 *BiAUS*
Desty, Robert 1827-1895 *TwCBDA*
DeSuria, Tomas *NewYHSD*
Desvernine, Raoul Eugene 1891-1966 *WhAm 4*
DeSylva, George Gard Buddy 1896-1950 *DcAmB S4, WhAm 3*
Detchon, Adelaide *WhAm 5, WomWWA 14*
DeTejada *NewYHSD*
Detels, Martin Paul 1892-1971 *WhAm 5*
Dethmers, John R 1903-1971 *WhAm 5*
DeThulstrup, Thure 1848-1930 *IlBEAAW*
Detmer, Julian Francis 1851- *ApCAB X*
Detmer, Julian Francis 1865-1958 *WhAm 3*
Detmold, Christian Edward 1810-1887 *ApCAB, DcAmB, WhAm H*
Detmold, William Ludwig 1808- *ApCAB*
DeTocqueville, Alexis Henri Maurice C 1805-1859 *WhAm H*
DeTocqueville, Alexis Henri Maurice C see also Tocquevulle, A
DeTonty, Henry 1650-1704 *WhAm H*
DeTorrente, Henry 1893-1962 *WhAm 4*
DeToscano, Bettie Elizabeth 1867- *WhoColR*
DeTousard, Anne Louis 1749-1817 *WhAm H*
DeTransehe, Nicholas Alexander 1886-1960 *NatCAB 50*
Detre, Laszlo 1874-1939 *NatCAB 30*
Detre, Laszlo 1906-1974 *WhAm 6*
Detre, William 1664- *ApCAB*
DeTreville, Yvonne 1881-1954 *WhAm 3*
Detrick, Jacob Stoll 1839- *WhAm 4*
DeTrobriand, Philip Regis 1816-1897 *Drake, NatCAB 6*
DeTrobriand, Philippe Regis 1816-1897 *ApCAB*
DeTrobriand, Phillipe Regis 1816-1897 *TwCBDA*
DeTrobriand, Regis Denis DeKereden 1816-1897 *WhAm H*
DeTrobriand, Regis Denis DeKeredern 1816-1897 *DcAmB, IlBEAAW*
Dett, R Nathaniel 1882-1943 *WhoColR*
Dett, Robert Nathaniel 1882-1943 *BiDAmEd, DcAmB S3, McGEWB, WhAm 2*
Dettmann, Frank Carl Louis 1897-1967 *NatCAB 51*
Dettrith, William *NewYHSD*
Detweiler, Albert Henry 1906-1970 *NatCAB 55, WhAm 5*
Detweiler, Charles Samuel 1878-1962 *WhAm 4*
Detweiler, Frederick German 1881-1960 *WhAm 3A*
Detweiler, George H 1883-1953 *WhAm 3*
Detwiler, Augustus Kountze 1869-1922 *NatCAB 21*
Detwiler, Rollo William 1882-1959 *NatCAB 48*
Detwiler, Samuel Randall 1890-1957 *WhAm 3*
Detwiler, W Frank 1880-1950 *WhAm 4*
Detwiler, Ward Arnold 1880-1946 *NatCAB 37*
Detwiller, Frederick Knecht 1882-1953 *WhAm 3*
Detwiller, Henry 1795-1887 *NatCAB 5, TwCBDA*
Detwiller, John Jacob 1834-1916 *NatCAB 20*

Deuchen, Robert *NewYHSD*
Deuel, Alanson Chase 1874-1954 *WhAm 3*
Deuel, Diana Constable 1888- *WomWWA 14*
Deuel, Harry James, Jr. 1897-1956 *WhAm 3*
Deuel, Wallace Rankin 1905-1974 *WhAm 6*
DeUlloa, Antonio 1717-1795 *WhAm H*
Deupree, John Greer 1843- *WhAm 4*
Deupree, Richard Redwood 1885-1974 *WhAm 6*
Deupree, William James 1884-1953 *NatCAB 42*
DeUrso, James Joseph 1933- *WhAm 6*
Deuse, James Smith 1852-1937 *NatCAB 28*
Deussen, Alexander 1882-1959 *WhAm 4*
Deuster, Peter Victor 1831-1904 *BiDrAC, TwCBDA, WhAmP*
Deute, Arthur Herman 1889-1946 *NatCAB 35*
Deuterman, Joel LeRoy 1902-1955 *NatCAB 46*
Deutsch, Adolph 1881- *WhAm 6*
Deutsch, Albert 1905-1961 *WhAm 4*
Deutsch, Alcuin Henry 1877-1951 *WhAm 3*
Deutsch, Bernard Seymour 1884-1935 *WhAm 1*
Deutsch, Gotthard 1859-1921 *AmBi, DcAmB, WhAm 1*
Deutsch, Henry 1874-1928 *NatCAB 21, WhAm 5*
Deutsch, Herman Julius 1897- *EncAAH*
Deutsch, Joseph 1865- *NatCAB 17*
Deutsch, Monroe Emanuel 1879-1955 *WhAm 3*
Deutscher, Isaac 1907-1967 *WhAm 4*
Deuxponts, Christian, Count DeF Des 1752- *ApCAB, Drake*
Deuxponts, William, Count DeF Des 1754- *ApCAB, Drake*
DeVaca, Cabeza *ApCAB*
DeValera, Eamon 1882-1975 *McGEWB, WhAm 6, WhWW-II, WhoMilH*
Devan, Harriet Beecher Scoville *WhAm 5*
DeVane, William Clyde 1898-1965 *BiDAmEd, NatCAB 52, WhAm 4*
Devaney, John Patrick 1883-1941 *DcAmB S3, NatCAB 33, WhAm 1*
Devaney, Michael R 1876- *WhAm 5*
Devannie, Francis *NewYHSD*
DeVarennes, Pierre Gauthier d1749 *ApCAB Sup*
DeVargas, Diego 1650?-1704 *WhAmP*
DeVargas Zapata Y Lujan P DeL, Diego 1650?-1704 *DcAmB, WhAmP*
DeVarona, Ignatius M 1842- *NatCAB 10*
DeVaudricourt *NewYHSD*
DeVaudricourt, A *IlBEAAW*
DeVault, Samuel H 1889-1974 *WhAm 6*
Devaux, Henri 1862-1956 *DcScB*
Deveaux, David H *NewYHSD*
Deveaux, Jacques Martial 1825-1891 *NewYHSD*
Deveaux, James 1812-1844 *NewYHSD*
DeVeaux, James 1813-1844 *NatCAB 8*
DeVegh, Imrie 1906-1962 *WhAm 4*
Develin, Dora Harvey *WomWWA 14*
Develle, J *NewYHSD*
Devendorf, Earl 1888-1960 *NatCAB 45*
Devendorf, Irving R 1856-1932 *WhAm 1*
Devendorf, James Franklin 1856-1934 *NatCAB 29, WhAm 2*
Devens, Charles 1820-1891 *AmBi, ApCAB, BiDrUSE, DcAmB, Drake Sup, NatCAB 3, TwCBDA, WhAm H*
Dever, Paul Andrew 1903-1958 *WhAm 3*
Dever, William Emmett 1862-1929 *ApCAB X, WhAm 1*
DeVere, J *IlBEAAW, NewYHSD*
DeVere, Mary Aigne d1920 *NatCAB 8*
DeVere, Maximilian Schele 1820-1898 *DcAmB, Drake*
Devereaux, Anna White 1865- *WomWWA 14*
Devereaux, Helena Trafford 1885-1975 *WhAm 6*
Devereux, Annie Sinnott 1869- *WomWWA 14*
Devereux, F Ramsay 1891- *WhAm 4*
Devereux, George T 1810?- *NewYHSD*
Devereux, Henry Kelsey 1860-1932 *NatCAB 24*
Devereux, James Patrick Sinnott 1903- *BiDrAC, WhWW-II*
Devereux, John 1817?- *NewYHSD*
Devereux, John C 1774-1848 *WhAm H*
Devereux, John Henry 1832-1886 *ApCAB, DcAmB, NatCAB 12, WhAm H*
Devereux, Mary d1914 *WhAm 1,*

WomWWA 14
Devereux, Nicholas 1791-1855 *WhAm H*
Devereux, Nicholson B 1813?- *NewYHSD*
Devereux, Thomas Pollock 1793-1869 *ApCAB*
Devereux, Walter Bourchier 1853-1934
NatCAB 25
Devers, Jacob Loucks 1887- *WebAMB,*
WhWW-II
DeVeyra, Jaime Carlos 1873-1963 *BiDrAC*
Devilbiss, Howard P d1971 *WhAm 5*
Deville, Edward Gaston 1849- *ApCAB,*
ApCAB Sup
Deville, Felix 1820?- *NewYHSD*
Deville, Henri Etienne Sainte-Claire 1818-1881
DcScB
Deville, J *NewYHSD*
DeVilliers, Charles A 1826- *ApCAB*
Devin, Thomas Casimer 1822-1878 *ApCAB,*
DcAmB, TwCBDA, WhAm H
Devin, Thomas Casimir 1824-1878 *NatCAB 22*
Devin, Thomas Casimir *see also* Devine, Thomas
C
Devin, William Augustus 1871-1959
NatCAB 46, *WhAm 3*
Devine, Christopher Joseph 1905-1963
NatCAB 50
Devine, David Francis 1903-1973 *WhAm 6*
Devine, Edward Thomas 1867-1948 *DcAmB S4,*
NatCAB 18, *TwCBDA, WhAm 2*
Devine, James Gasper 1895-1972 *WhAm 5*
DeVine, James Herbert 1880-1943 *WhAm 2*
Devine, John James 1886-1954 *NatCAB 41*
Devine, John M 1895-1971 *WhAm 5*
Devine, John Patrick 1878-1955 *NatCAB 44*
Devine, Joseph McMurray 1861-1938
NatCAB 35, *TwCBDA, WhAm 4*
Devine, Samuel Leeper 1915- *BiDrAC*
Devine, Theodore Joseph 1904-1967 *NatCAB 55*
Devine, Thomas 1823- *ApCAB*
Devine, Thomas 1852- *NatCAB 1*
Devine, Thomas C *Drake*
Devine, Thomas C *see also* Devin, Thomas
Casimir
Devine, Thomas Hume 1860-1932 *WhAm 1*
Devine, Thomas Jefferson 1820-1890 *BiDConf*
Devine, William Henry 1860-1926 *NatCAB 6*
DeVinne, Daniel 1793-1883 *ApCAB, TwCBDA*
DeVinne, Theodore Low 1828-1914 *AmBi,*
ApCAB, DcAmB, NatCAB 7, TwCBDA,
WebAB, WhAm 1
Devins, John Bancroft 1856-1911 *WhAm 1*
Deviny, John Joseph 1882-1955 *NatCAB 45,*
WhAm 3
DeVisme, Henri Pierre Williamson 1874-1927
NatCAB 22
Devitt, Edward Ignatius 1841- *TwCBDA*
Devitt, Edward James 1911- *BiDrAC*
Devlan, Francis Daniel 1835-1870 *NewYHSD*
DeVlieg, Ray Albert 1886-1953 *NatCAB 41*
DeVlieg, Ray Albert 1888-1953 *WhAm 3*
Devlin, Arthur Coghlan 1898-1963 *NatCAB 51*
Devlin, Robert Thomas 1859-1938 *WhAm 1*
Devlin, Thomas Francis 1869-1952 *WhAm 3*
Devoe, Alan 1909-1955 *WhAm 3*
DeVoe, Emma Smith 1849- *AmWom*
DeVoe, Emma Smith 1858- *WhAm 4,*
WomWWA 14
Devoe, Frederick William 1828-1913 *NatCAB 8,*
NatCAB 29, *WhAm 1*
DeVoe, John M d1946 *WhAm 2*
DeVoe, Lucy Dillon *WomWWA 14*
DeVoe, Ralph Godwin 1883-1966 *WhAm 4*
Devoe, Robert W 1882-1957 *WhAm 3*
DeVoe, Thomas Farrington 1811-1892
ApCAB Sup
DeVoe, Walter 1874- *WhAm 5*
Devoe, William Beck 1884-1951 *WhAm 3*
DeVoin, Fillmore Stanley 1878-1950
NatCAB 38
Devol, Carroll Augustine 1859-1930
NatCAB 22, *WhAm 1*
Devol, Jonathan 1756-1824 *REnAW*
DeVoll, F Usher 1873-1941 *NatCAB 30,*
WhAm 1
Devonald, Ira Richard 1908-1967 *NatCAB 54*
Devoore, Ann 1872- *WhAm 5*
Devor, Donald Smith 1889- *WhAm 3*
Devore, Daniel Bradford 1860- *WhAm 4*

DeVore, Elsa Marion 1893- *WomWWA 14a*
DeVore, Harry S 1891-1947 *WhAm 2*
DeVore, Rebecca Jane *WhAm 5,*
WomWWA 14
DeVos, Julius Emilius 1848- *WhAm 4*
DeVoss, James Clarence 1884-1956 *WhAm 3*
DeVoto, Bernard Augustine 1897-1955
DcAmB S5, EncAAH, REnAW, WebAB,
WhAm 3
DeVou, James Laird 1821-1902 *NatCAB 32*
DeVou, Mary Ruth 1868- *WomWWA 14*
Devoy, John 1842-1928 *AmBi, DcAmB,*
WhAm HA, WhAm 4
Devree, Howard 1890-1966 *WhAm 4*
DeVries, David Pietersen 1592?- *DcAmB*
DeVries, David Pieterson 1592-1655 *WhAm H*
DeVries, David Pieterssen *ApCAB*
Devries, Herman 1858-1949 *WhAm 2*
DeVries, Hugo Marie 1848-1935 *AsBiEn*
Devries, Joseph C 1820?- *NewYHSD*
Devries, Louis 1885-1976 *WhAm 6*
DeVries, Marion 1865-1939 *BiDrAC,*
TwCBDA, WhAm 1
DeVries, Tiemen 1865- *WhAm 4*
DeVries, William Levering 1865-1937 *WhAm 1*
Devron, Alexander John Gustavus 1835-
NatCAB 10
DeVry, Herman Adolf 1876-1941 *NatCAB 31*
Dew, Louise E 1871-1962 *WhAm 4,*
WomWWA 14
Dew, Thomas R 1802-1846 *NatCAB 3*
Dew, Thomas Roderic 1802-1846 *Drake*
Dew, Thomas Roderick 1802-1846 *ApCAB,*
DcAmB, McGEWB, WhAm H
Dew, Thomas Roderick 1810-1846 *TwCBDA*
Dew, Thomas Roderick 1897-1961 *WhAm 4*
DeWaha, Baron Raymond 1877- *WhAm 5*
DeWald, John Adam 1849-1927 *NatCAB 22*
DeWalden, Thomas Blaides 1811-1873 *ApCAB*
DeWalt, Arthur Granville 1854-1931 *BiDrAC,*
NatCAB 24, *WhAm 1*
DeWan, Charles Henry 1892-1963 *NatCAB 54*
Dewar, Charles Edwin 1881-1944 *NatCAB 35*
Dewar, Henry Hamilton 1902-1975 *WhAm 6*
Dewar, Sir James 1842-1923 *AsBiEn, DcScB*
Dewart, Edward Hartley 1828- *ApCAB*
Dewart, Frederick Wesley 1867- *WhAm 5*
Dewart, Lewis 1780-1852 *BiAUS, BiDrAC,*
WhAm H
Dewart, Murray Wilder 1874-1927 *WhAm 1*
D'Ewart, Wesley Abner 1889-1973 *BiDrAC,*
WhAm 6
Dewart, William Herbert 1862-1941
NatCAB 30, *WhAm 1*
Dewart, William Lewis 1821-1888 *BiAUS,*
BiDrAC, WhAm H
Dewart, William Thompson 1875-1944
WhAm 2
Dewdney, Edgar 1835- *ApCAB*
DeWeerd, James A 1916-1972 *WhAm 5*
Dewees, William Potts 1768-1841 *AmBi,*
ApCAB, DcAmB, Drake, WhAm H
Deweese, John Thomas 1835-1906 *BiAUS,*
BiDrAC
DeWeese, Truman Armstrong 1860- *WhAm 4*
Dewein, Edward George 1903-1959 *NatCAB 45*
Dewesse, Arville Ottis 1888-1970 *WhAm 5*
DeWet, Christiaan 1854-1922 *WhoMilH*
Dewey, Alice Chipman 1858-1927 *NotAW*
Dewey, Alvin Hiram 1859-1928 *NatCAB 22*
Dewey, Annie *WomWWA 14*
Dewey, Bradley 1887-1974 *WhAm 6*
Dewey, Byrd Spilman *WhAm 5*
Dewey, Charles 1784-1862 *NatCAB 16*
Dewey, Charles 1826-1905 *WhAm 1*
Dewey, Charles Almon 1877-1958 *WhAm 3*
Dewey, Charles Andrew 1888-1946 *NatCAB 33*
Dewey, Charles Augustus 1793-1866 *ApCAB,*
Drake, TwCBDA
Dewey, Charles Melville 1849-1937 *AmBi,*
WhAm 1
Dewey, Charles Melville 1851-1936 *NatCAB 11,*
NatCAB 30
Dewey, Charles Schuveldt 1880- *BiDrAC,*
WhAm 6
Dewey, Charles Schuveldt 1885- *ApCAB X*
Dewey, Chester 1781-1867 *Drake*
Dewey, Chester 1784-1867 *AmBi, ApCAB,*

BiDAmEd, DcAmB, NatCAB 6,
TwCBDA, WhAm H
Dewey, Chester Pomeroy 1826-1899 *TwCBDA*
Dewey, Chester Robert 1888-1974 *WhAm 6*
Dewey, Christian Henry 1880-1949 *NatCAB 38*
Dewey, Daniel 1766-1815 *BiAUS, BiDrAC,*
Drake, TwCBDA, WhAm H
Dewey, Davis Rich 1858-1942 *NatCAB 13,*
TwCBDA, WhAm 2
Dewey, Francis Henshaw 1821-1887
NatCAB 35, *TwCBDA*
Dewey, Francis Henshaw 1856-1933
NatCAB 26, *WhAm 1*
Dewey, Frederic Perkins 1855- *ApCAB,*
TwCBDA, WhAm 1
Dewey, Frederick Lincoln 1860- *NatCAB 14*
Dewey, George 1837-1917 *AmBi, ApCAB Sup,*
ApCAB X, DcAmB, EncAB, McGEWB,
NatCAB 9, TwCBDA, WebAB,
WebAMB, WhAm 1, WhoMilH
Dewey, Harry Pinneo 1861-1937 *ApCAB X,*
NatCAB 27, WhAm 1, WhAm 1C
Dewey, Hattie Alice Chipman 1858-
WomWWA 14
Dewey, Henry Bingham 1864-1931 *BiDAmEd,*
WhAm 1
Dewey, Henry Sweetser 1856- *NatCAB 1,*
TwCBDA, WhAm 4
Dewey, Herbert Hopkins 1881-1933
NatCAB 25
Dewey, Hiram Todd 1816- *TwCBDA*
Dewey, Israel Otis 1824-1888 *NatCAB 4,*
TwCBDA
Dewey, James F 1887-1950 *WhAm 3*
Dewey, James French 1883-1956 *NatCAB 45,*
WhAm 3
Dewey, Jedediah 1714-1778 *ApCAB Sup,*
TwCBDA
Dewey, Joel Allen 1840-1873 *ApCAB Sup,*
TwCBDA
Dewey, John 1859-1952 *ApCAB X, BiDAmEd,*
DcAmB S5, EncAB, McGEWB,
NatCAB 11, NatCAB 40, TwCBDA,
WebAB, WhAm 3
Dewey, Julia *WomWWA 14*
Dewey, Julian Hiland 1867- *WhAm 4*
Dewey, Julius E 1831?- *NewYHSD*
Dewey, Lloyd Ellis 1897-1960 *NatCAB 45,*
WhAm 4
Dewey, Louis Marinus 1865- *TwCBDA*
Dewey, Lyster Hoxie 1865-1944 *NatCAB 13,*
WhAm 2
Dewey, Malcolm Howard 1881- *WhAm 6*
Dewey, Mary Elizabeth 1821-1910 *ApCAB,*
TwCBDA, WhAm 1
Dewey, Melvil 1851-1931 *AmBi, ApCAB,*
ApCAB X, BiDAmEd, DcAmB S1,
DcAmLiB, McGEWB, NatCAB 4,
NatCAB 23, TwCBDA, WebAB,
WhAm 1
Dewey, Nelson 1813-1889 *BiAUS, NatCAB 12,*
TwCBDA
Dewey, Orville 1794-1882 *ApCAB, DcAmB,*
Drake, NatCAB 5, TwCBDA, WhAm H
Dewey, Richard Smith 1845-1933 *DcAmB S1,*
NatCAB 39, *WhAm 1*
Dewey, Samuel Worthington 1807-1899
TwCBDA
Dewey, Sara Rousseau 1850- *WomWWA 14*
Dewey, Silas *NewYHSD*
Dewey, Stoddard 1853-1933 *WhAm 1*
Dewey, Thomas Edmund 1902-1971 *EncAB,*
McGEWB, WebAB, WhAm 5
Dewey, William Sabin 1869-1945 *NatCAB 46*
Dewey, Willis Alonzo 1858-1938 *NatCAB 27,*
WhAm 1, WhAm 1C
Dewhirst, Harry Thomas 1881-1947
NatCAB 36
Dewhurst, Frederic Eli 1855-1906 *WhAm 1*
Dewhurst, J Frederic 1895-1967 *WhAm 4*
Dewhurst, John Alfred 1885-1964 *NatCAB 51*
DeWild, Carel F L 1870-1922 *ApCAB X*
DeWilde, Brandon 1942-1972 *WhAm 5*
DeWindt, Delano 1892-1953 *WhAm 3*
DeWindt, Harold Clifford 1911-1971 *WhAm 5*
Dewing, Arthur Stone 1880-1971 *WhAm 5*
Dewing, Francis d1745? *AmBi, DcAmB,*
NewYHSD, WhAm H

DiCesnola, Emmanuele Pietro Luigi Palma 1832-
TwCBDA
Dick, Albert Blake 1856-1934 *NatCAB 34,*
WhAm 1
Dick, Albert Blake, Jr. 1894-1954 *NatCAB 45,*
WhAm 3
Dick, Allie Luse *WomWWA 14*
Dick, Archibald L 1805?-1855? *NewYHSD*
Dick, Archibald R *NewYHSD*
Dick, Carl Rankin 1884-1949 *NatCAB 41*
Dick, Charles Kissinger 1875-1947 *NatCAB 36*
Dick, Charles William Frederick 1858-1945
BiDrAC, NatCAB 13, WhAm 2, WhAmP
Dick, Elisha Cullen 1762-1825 *DcAmB,*
NatCAB 23, WhAm H
Dick, Everett 1898- *REnAW*
Dick, George *NewYHSD*
Dick, George 1916- *IIBEAAW*
Dick, George Alexander 1877-1948 *WhAm 2*
Dick, George Frederick 1829-1914 *NatCAB 15*
Dick, George Frederick 1881-1967 *NatCAB 54,*
WhAm 4A
Dick, George William 1864-1952 *NatCAB 46*
Dick, Gladys Rowena Henry 1881-1963
NatCAB 51, WhAm 4
Dick, Henry Kissinger 1886-1953 *WhAm 3*
Dick, Homer T 1870-1928 *WhAm 1*
Dick, Hugh Gilchrist 1909-1971 *WhAm 5*
Dick, James Chambers 1871-1935 *NatCAB 26*
Dick, James L 1834-1868 *NewYHSD*
Dick, James T 1834-1868 *ApCAB, Drake*
Dick, John 1794-1872 *BiAUS, BiDrAC,*
WhAm H
Dick, Mary Henrietta *WomWWA 14*
Dick, Paul Stephens 1877-1945 *NatCAB 35,*
WhAm 2
Dick, Robert 1814- *ApCAB*
Dick, Robert Paine 1823- *BiAUS, TwCBDA*
Dick, Robert Paine 1823-1898 *DcAmB,*
WhAm H
Dick, Robert Paine 1823-1900 *WhAm 1*
Dick, Samuel 1740-1812 *ApCAB, BiAUS,*
BiDrAC, Drake, WhAm H
Dick, Samuel Bernard 1836-1907 *BiDrAC,*
TwCBDA, WhAm H
Dick, Samuel Medary 1857- *WhAm 1*
Dick, Wallace Peter 1857- *NatCAB 7*
Dick, William Henry 1872-1951 *WhAm 3*
Dick, William Karl 1888-1953 *NatCAB 39,*
WhAm 3
Dick, Willis Virgil 1857-1919 *NatCAB 18*
Dick-Read, Grantly 1890-1959 *WhAm 3*
Dickason, John Howard 1867- *WhAm 4*
Dicke, Allen August 1891-1965 *NatCAB 51*
Dicken, Charles Ernest 1877- *WhAm 5*
Dicken, Clinton Orr 1885-1957 *NatCAB 46,*
WhAm 3
Dickens, Albert 1867-1930 *WhAm 1*
Dickens, Asbury 1773-1861 *BiAUS, Drake*
Dickens, Augustus N 1826-1866 *ApCAB*
Dickens, Charles John Huffam 1812-1870
McGEWB
Dickens, John Lunsford 1853- *WhAm 4*
Dickens, Samuel d1840 *BiAUS, BiDrAC,*
WhAm H
Dickenshied, Eugene Henry 1859-1944
NatCAB 33
Dickenson, Charles Monroe 1842-1924
ApCAB X
Dickenson, Daniel Stevens 1800-1866 *BiAUS*
Dickenson, Edward Fennick 1829-1891 *BiAUS*
Dickenson, Edwin Russel 1879-1956
NatCAB 42
Dickenson, Emily Elizabeth 1830-1886
McGEWB, NotAW
Dickenson, Helena Adell Snyder 1875-1957
WhAm 3
Dickenson, John Dean 1767-1841 *BiAUS*
Dickenson, Marquis Fayette, Jr. 1840-1915
TwCBDA, WhAm 1
Dickenson, Melville Pierce 1898-1968 *WhAm 5*
Dickenson, Robert Edward 1875- *WhAm 5*
Dickenson, Zenas Clark 1889-1966 *NatCAB 52*
Dicker, Samuel Byron 1889-1960 *WhAm 3*
Dickerman, Charles Heber 1843-1915
ApCAB X, BiDrAC, NatCAB 7,
WhAm 4
Dickerman, Elihu Elias 1887-1932 *NatCAB 24*

Dickerman, Elizabeth Street 1872-
WomWWA 14
Dickerman, Ezra *ApCAB X*
Dickerman, George Sherwood 1843-1937
WhAm 1
Dickerman, Mabel Stone 1878- *WomWWA 14*
Dickerman, Sherwood Owen 1874-1930
WhAm 1
Dickerman, Sumner *NewYHSD*
Dickerman, Watson B *ApCAB X*
Dickerman, William Carter 1874-1946
ApCAB X, NatCAB 37, WhAm 2
Dickerman, Wyatt *NewYHSD*
Dickerson, Charles Estell 1865-1939 *WhAm 1*
Dickerson, Daniel *NewYHSD*
Dickerson, Denver Sylvester 1872-1925
NatCAB 20, WhAm 1
Dickerson, Earl Burrus 1891- *WhoColR*
Dickerson, Edward Nicoll 1824-1889 *DcAmB,*
WhAm H
Dickerson, Emeline Fletcher *WomWWA 14*
Dickerson, James Spencer 1853-1933 *WhAm 1*
Dickerson, James Stokes 1825-1876 *ApCAB*
Dickerson, John Henry 1864- *WhoColR*
Dickerson, John J 1900-1966 *WhAm 4*
Dickerson, John Stiles 1828-1904 *NatCAB 42*
Dickerson, John Stiles 1879-1949 *NatCAB 40*
Dickerson, Luther L d1957 *WhAm 3*
Dickerson, Mahlon 1770-1853 *ApCAB, BiAUS,*
BiDrAC, BiDrUSE, DcAmB, Drake,
NatCAB 5, TwCBDA, WhAm H,
WhAmP
Dickerson, Mary Cynthia 1866-1923 *WhAm 1,*
WomWWA 14
Dickerson, Oliver Morton 1875-1966
NatCAB 53, WhAm 4
Dickerson, Philemon 1788-1862 *ApCAB,*
BiAUS, BiDrAC, DcAmB, Drake,
NatCAB 5, TwCBDA, WhAm H,
WhAmP
Dickerson, Robert Carl 1884-1953 *WhAm 3*
Dickerson, Rollin Peter 1869- *NatCAB 18*
Dickerson, Roy Ernest 1886-1965 *WhAm 4*
Dickerson, Samuel Newton 1866- *WhoColR*
Dickerson, W Mahlon 1908-1969 *NatCAB 54*
Dickerson, William Fisher 1844-1884 *ApCAB,*
TwCBDA
Dickerson, William Worth 1851-1923 *BiDrAC*
Dickert, David Augustus 1845- *WhAm 4*
Dickert, John George 1871-1947 *NatCAB 37*
Dickeson, Montroville Wilson 1810-1882
IIBEAAW, NewYHSD
Dickey, Adam Herbert 1864-1925 *WhAm 1*
Dickey, Alvin Oyer 1877-1946 *NatCAB 35*
Dickey, Arthur W 1897-1964 *WhAm 4*
Dickey, Charles Andrews 1838-1910 *TwCBDA,*
WhAm 1
Dickey, Charles Emmet 1871- *WhAm 5*
Dickey, Charles Hadley 1888-1937 *WhAm 1*
Dickey, Charles Henry 1842-1932 *NatCAB 37*
Dickey, Charles William 1871-1942 *NatCAB 39*
Dickey, Clement Cresson 1844-1893 *TwCBDA*
Dickey, Donald Ryder 1887-1932 *WhAm 1*
Dickey, Ebenezer 1772-1831 *ApCAB*
Dickey, Henry Luther 1832-1910 *BiDrAC*
Dickey, Herbert Spencer 1876-1948
NatCAB 36, WhAm 2
Dickey, James 1923- *WebAB*
Dickey, James Allen 1892-1943 *WhAm 2*
Dickey, James Edward 1864-1928 *NatCAB 13,*
WhAm 1
Dickey, James M 1870- *NatCAB 16*
Dickey, James Nathaniel 1840-1918
NatCAB 18
Dickey, Jane Murdock 1875- *WomWWA 14*
Dickey, Jesse Column 1808-1890 *BiAUS,*
BiDrAC, WhAm H
Dickey, John 1794-1853 *BiAUS, BiDrAC,*
WhAm H
Dickey, John Lindsay 1855-1929 *WhAm 1*
Dickey, John McElroy 1789-1849 *ApCAB*
Dickey, John Miller 1806-1878 *ApCAB,*
TwCBDA
Dickey, Lincoln Griffith 1884-1940 *WhAm 1*
Dickey, Lloyd Blackwell 1894-1974 *WhAm 6*
Dickey, Louise Atherton 1881- *WomWWA 14*
Dickey, Lyle Alexander 1868- *WhAm 4*
Dickey, Marcus 1859- *WhAm 4*

Dickey, Oliver James 1823-1876 *BiAUS,*
BiDrAC, TwCBDA, WhAm H
Dickey, Robert Barry 1811- *ApCAB*
Dickey, Robert Livingston 1861-1944
NatCAB 34
Dickey, Robert W 1891-1972 *WhAm 5*
Dickey, S 1840?- *NewYHSD*
Dickey, Samuel 1872-1944 *WhAm 2*
Dickey, Samuel Jackson 1882-1963 *WhAm 4*
Dickey, Sarah Ann 1838-1904 *BiDAmEd,*
NotAW
Dickey, Sarah Ida Phillips 1861-
WomWWA 14
Dickey, Solomon Cravens 1858-1920 *WhAm 1*
Dickey, T Lyle *BiAUS*
Dickey, Theophilus Lyle 1811-1885 *DcAmB,*
WhAm H
Dickey, Theophilus Lyle 1812-1885 *ApCAB,*
NatCAB 12
Dickey, Walter S d1931 *WhAm 1*
Dickey, William Donaldson 1845-1924
NatCAB 22, WhAm 1
Dickhout, George 1836?- *NewYHSD*
Dickie, Alexander Jack 1876-1948 *WhAm 2*
Dickie, Allan 1886-1959 *NatCAB 49*
Dickie, George William 1844-1918 *DcAmB,*
NatCAB 22, WhAm 1
Dickie, J Roy 1884-1962 *NatCAB 50,*
WhAm 4
Dickie, James Francis 1848-1933 *WhAm 1*
Dickie, John Jervis 1889-1947 *NatCAB 36*
Dickie, Samuel 1851-1925 *NatCAB 21,*
TwCBDA, WhAm 1
Dickie, Walter Murray 1875-1957 *NatCAB 46*
Dickins, Asbury 1780-1861 *ApCAB, TwCBDA*
Dickins, Francis William 1844-1911 *WhAm 1*
Dickins, John 1747-1798 *AmBi, ApCAB,*
DcAmB, NatCAB 3, TwCBDA,
WhAm H
Dickinson, Albert 1841-1925 *WhAm 1*
Dickinson, Albert Boyd 1895-1959 *NatCAB 48*
Dickinson, Alfred Elijah 1830-1906 *ApCAB,*
WhAm 1
Dickinson, Alfred James 1864- *WhAm 4*
Dickinson, Andrew B *BiAUS, NatCAB 12*
Dickinson, Andrew Glassel 1835- *NatCAB 7*
Dickinson, Anna Elizabeth 1842-1932 *AmBi,*
AmWom, ApCAB, DcAmB S1, Drake,
NatCAB 3, NotAW, TwCBDA,
WhAm 1
Dickinson, Anna M Juliand *WomWWA 14*
Dickinson, Anson 1779-1852 *DcAmB,*
NewYHSD, WhAm H
Dickinson, Asa Don 1876-1960 *DcAmLiB,*
WhAm 4
Dickinson, Augustus Edwin 1869- *WhAm 5*
Dickinson, Baxter 1795-1875 *ApCAB,*
TwCBDA
Dickinson, Calvin L 1914-1971 *WhAm 5*
Dickinson, Charles Henry 1857-1938 *WhAm 1*
Dickinson, Charles Monroe 1842-1924 *DcAmB,*
NatCAB 11, TwCBDA, WhAm 1
Dickinson, Clarence 1873-1969 *NatCAB 54,*
WhAm 5
Dickinson, Clement Cabell 1849-1938 *BiDrAC,*
WhAm 1, WhAmP
Dickinson, Daniel 1795- *NewYHSD*
Dickinson, Daniel Stevens 1800-1866 *AmBi,*
ApCAB, BiDrAC, DcAmB, Drake,
NatCAB 5, TwCBDA, WhAm H,
WhAmP
Dickinson, Darol 1942- *IIBEAAW*
Dickinson, David W 1808-1845 *BiAUS,*
BiDrAC, WhAm H
Dickinson, Don McDonald 1846-1917
NatCAB 2, WhAm 1
Dickinson, Donald McDonald 1846-1917
ApCAB X, BiDrUSE, DcAmB, TwCBDA,
WhAmP
Dickinson, Donald McDonald 1847-
ApCAB Sup
Dickinson, Dwight 1847- *WhAm 4*
Dickinson, Edward 1803-1874 *ApCAB, BiAUS,*
BiDrAC, NatCAB 11, TwCBDA,
WhAm H
Dickinson, Edward 1853-1946 *WhAm 3*
Dickinson, Edward Everett, Jr. 1891-1968
WhAm 5

Dickinson, Edward Fenwick 1829-1891 *BiDrAC, WhAm H*
Dickinson, Edward T, Jr. 1911-1969 *WhAm 5*
Dickinson, Edwin 1891- *BnEnAmA*
Dickinson, Edwin DeWitt 1887-1961 *WhAm 4*
Dickinson, Edwin Henry 1855- *WhAm 4*
Dickinson, Emily Elizabeth 1830-1886 *AmBi, DcAmB, EncAB, NatCAB 11, NatCAB 23, TwCBDA, WebAB, WhAm H*
Dickinson, Frances *NotAW*
Dickinson, Frances 1856- *WhAm 4*
Dickinson, Frank Greene 1899-1967 *NatCAB 53*
Dickinson, Frederick 1835-1916 *NatCAB 16*
Dickinson, Frederick 1879-1955 *NatCAB 42*
Dickinson, George Sherman 1888-1964 *BiDAmEd, DcAmLiB, NatCAB 51, WhAm 4*
Dickinson, Gordon Kimball 1855-1930 *NatCAB 22*
Dickinson, Helena Adell Snyder 1875-1957 *NatCAB 54, WomWWA 14*
Dickinson, Hester Benedict 1838- *WomWWA 14*
Dickinson, Hobart Cutler 1875-1949 *WhAm 2*
Dickinson, Horace Danforth 1866-1936 *WhAm 1*
Dickinson, Hunt Tilford 1899-1967 *WhAm 4*
Dickinson, Jacob McGavock 1851-1928 *AmBi, BiDrUSE, DcAmB, NatCAB 14, WhAm 1*
Dickinson, James Shelton 1818-1882 *BiDConf*
Dickinson, James Taylor 1861-1929 *WhAm 1*
Dickinson, John 1732-1808 *AmBi, ApCAB, BiAUS, BiDrAC, DcAmB, Drake, EncAAH, EncAB, McGEWB, NatCAB 2, TwCBDA, WebAB, WhAm H, WhAmP*
Dickinson, John 1894-1952 *DcAmB S5, WhAm 3*
Dickinson, John 1904-1960 *NatCAB 52*
Dickinson, John Dean 1767-1841 *BiDrAC, WhAm H*
Dickinson, John Lewis 1870-1954 *NatCAB 44*
Dickinson, John Quincy 1831-1925 *WhAm 1*
Dickinson, John Woodbridge 1825-1901 *BiDAmEd, DcAmB, WhAm H*
Dickinson, Jonathan d1722 *Drake, NatCAB 18*
Dickinson, Jonathan 1688-1747 *AmBi, ApCAB, DcAmB, DcAmReB, Drake, NatCAB 5, TwCBDA, WhAm H*
Dickinson, Julian George 1843- *NatCAB 4*
Dickinson, Katharine V *WomWWA 14*
Dickinson, Lester Jesse 1873-1968 *BiDrAC*
Dickinson, Lester Jesse 1873-1969 *WhAm 5*
Dickinson, Levi Call 1905-1974 *WhAm 6*
Dickinson, Loftus A 1830?- *NewYHSD*
Dickinson, Lucy Jennings d1971 *WhAm 5*
Dickinson, Luren Dudley 1859-1943 *NatCAB 33, WhAm 2*
Dickinson, Marquis Fayette, Jr. 1840-1915 *NatCAB 2*
Dickinson, Martha Gilbert *WomWWA 14*
Dickinson, Mary Clare 1755-1830 *ApCAB*
Dickinson, Mary Low 1839-1914 *WhAm 1, WomWWA 14*
Dickinson, May Bliss 1874- *WhAm 5*
Dickinson, Moss Kent 1822- *ApCAB*
Dickinson, Nellie Burnett 1877- *WomWWA 14*
Dickinson, Obadiah 1812-1850 *NewYHSD*
Dickinson, Oliver, Jr. 1757-1847 *NewYHSD*
Dickinson, Oliver Booth 1857-1939 *WhAm 1*
Dickinson, Philemon 1739-1809 *AmBi, ApCAB, BiAUS, BiDrAC, DcAmB, Drake, NatCAB 7, TwCBDA, WebAMB, WhAm H, WhAmP*
Dickinson, Preston 1889-1930 *DcAmB S1*
Dickinson, Preston 1891-1930 *BnEnAmA*
Dickinson, Richard William 1804-1874 *ApCAB*
Dickinson, Robert Edmunds 1868-1929 *NatCAB 24*
Dickinson, Robert Latou 1861-1950 *DcAmB S4, NatCAB 39, WhAm 3*
Dickinson, Robert Smith 1889-1971 *WhAm 5*
Dickinson, Rodolphus 1787-1863 *ApCAB*
Dickinson, Rodolphus 1797-1849 *BiDrAC, WhAm H*

Dickinson, Roscoe Gilkey 1894-1945 *DcScB, WhAm 2*
Dickinson, Roy 1888- *WhAm 2*
Dickinson, Rudolphus 1797-1849 *BiAUS*
Dickinson, Sackett Moore 1884-1955 *NatCAB 43*
Dickinson, Sarah Truslow 1863- *WomWWA 14*
Dickinson, Selden Stratton 1892-1964 *WhAm 4*
Dickinson, Susan E *AmWom*
Dickinson, Thomas H 1877-1961 *WhAm 4*
Dickinson, William *NewYHSD*
Dickinson, William Frederick 1876-1940 *WhAm 1*
Dickinson, William Hale, Jr. 1913-1972 *WhAm 5*
Dickinson, William Louis 1925- *BiDrAC*
Dickinson, Zenas Clark 1889-1966 *WhAm 4*
Dicklow, Adelaide Lynn 1859- *AmWom*
Dickman, Charles John 1863-1943 *IIBEAAW*
Dickman, Ernst d1885? *NatCAB 5*
Dickman, Franklin Jackson 1827?- *NatCAB 7*
Dickman, John William 1863-1931 *WhAm 1*
Dickman, Joseph Theodore 1857-1927 *AmBi, DcAmB, NatCAB 20, WebAMB, WhAm 1*
Dickman, W 1824?- *NewYHSD*
Dickmann, Bernard Francis 1888-1971 *NatCAB 56*
Dicks, J Oscar 1875-1938 *NatCAB 29*
Dicks, Robert Howe 1854-1938 *NatCAB 29*
Dicksee, Sir Francis Bernard 1853-1928 *WhAm 1*
Dickson, Agnes Lillian *WomWWA 14*
Dickson, Allan Hamilton 1851-1893 *NatCAB 9*
Dickson, Andrew Flinn 1825-1879 *ApCAB, TwCBDA*
Dickson, Archibald John 1879-1959 *NatCAB 49*
Dickson, Cyrus 1816-1881 *ApCAB*
Dickson, Dan Thorson Ringwalt 1895-1951 *NatCAB 38*
Dickson, David d1836 *BiAUS, BiDrAC, WhAm H*
Dickson, David 1809-1885 *DcAmB, WhAm H*
Dickson, Earle Ensign 1892-1961 *WhAm 4*
Dickson, Edith 1856- *WomWWA 14*
Dickson, Edward Augustus 1879-1956 *NatCAB 45, WhAm 3*
Dickson, Frank Dake 1882-1964 *WhAm 4*
Dickson, Frank Stoddard 1876-1953 *BiDrAC, WhAm 3*
Dickson, Fred Charles 1876-1936 *NatCAB 27*
Dickson, Frederick Stoever 1850-1925 *WhAm 1*
Dickson, Harris 1868- *ApCAB X, WhAm 5*
Dickson, James A 1774-1853 *ApCAB*
Dickson, James Anderson Ross 1839- *ApCAB*
Dickson, James Henderson 1806-1862 *NatCAB 9*
Dickson, James Pringle 1852-1907 *NatCAB 8*
Dickson, Jeanie A *ApCAB*
Dickson, John 1783-1852 *ApCAB, BiAUS, BiDrAC, NatCAB 11, TwCBDA, WhAm H*
Dickson, John Elmer 1882-1955 *NatCAB 43*
Dickson, John Fenwick 1832- *NatCAB 9*
Dickson, John Robinson 1819-1882 *ApCAB*
Dickson, Joseph 1745-1825 *BiDrAC, NatCAB 5, WhAm H*
Dickson, Joseph Benjamin 1861-1919 *NatCAB 25*
Dickson, Katharine Griswold Pratt 1882- *WomWWA 14*
Dickson, Leonard Eugene 1874-1954 *DcAmB S5, DcScB, NatCAB 18, WhAm 3*
Dickson, Raymond 1886-1956 *NatCAB 49*
Dickson, Reid Stuart 1885-1959 *WhAm 4*
Dickson, Robert 1765-1823 *DcAmB, WhAm H*
Dickson, Robert Barnes 1883-1950 *WhAm 3*
Dickson, Robert L 1911-1963 *WhAm 4*
Dickson, Rush Smith 1895-1966 *NatCAB 54, WhAm 4*
Dickson, Samuel 1807-1858 *BiAUS, BiDrAC, WhAm H*
Dickson, Samuel 1837-1915 *WhAm 1*
Dickson, Samuel Henry 1798-1872 *ApCAB, DcAmB, Drake, NatCAB 10, TwCBDA,*

Dickson, Samuel Henry 1849- *WhAm 4*
Dickson, Thomas 1822-1884 *ApCAB*
Dickson, Thomas 1824-1884 *DcAmB, NatCAB 8, WhAm H*
Dickson, Thomas Hunter 1884-1957 *NatCAB 47*
Dickson, Tracy Campbell 1868-1936 *WhAm 1*
Dickson, William 1770-1816 *BiAUS, BiDrAC, WhAm H*
Dickson, William Alexander 1861-1940 *BiDrAC, WhAm 4*
Dickson, William Brown 1865-1942 *NatCAB 31*
Dickstein, Samuel 1851-1939 *DcScB*
Dickstein, Samuel 1885-1954 *BiDrAC, NatCAB 42, WhAm 3, WhAmP*
Didama, Henry D d1905 *WhAm 1*
Didcoct, John Joseph 1882-1927 *WhAm 1*
Diddell, George *NewYHSD*
Diderot, Denis 1713-1784 *AsBiEn, DcScB, McGEWB*
Didier, E *NewYHSD*
Didier, Eugene Lemoine 1838-1913 *DcAmB, WhAm 4*
Didier, Eugene Lemoine 1848- *NatCAB 13, TwCBDA*
Didier, Franklin James 1794-1840 *ApCAB*
Didier, Franklin James 1794-1846 *NatCAB 13*
Didrikson, Babe 1914-1956 *WebAB*
Didusch, James Francis 1890-1955 *WhAm 3*
Didusch, Joseph Stephen 1879- *WhAm 6*
Diebenkorn, Richard 1922- *BnEnAmA*
Diebitsch, Hans Karl Friedrich Anton 1785-1831 *WhoMilH*
Diebitsch, Roberta Franc Watterson *WomWWA 14*
Diebold, Alfred John 1879-1966 *NatCAB 53*
Dieckmann, Johannes 1893-1969 *WhAm 5*
Dieckmann, William Joseph 1897-1957 *WhAm 3*
Diederich, Henry William 1845-1926 *WhAm 1*
Diederich, John Thomas 1888-1974 *WhAm 6*
Diederich, Wilhelm Hunt 1884-1953 *IIBEAAW*
Diederich, William Hunt 1884-1953 *WhAm 3*
Diederichs, Herman 1874-1937 *NatCAB 33, WhAm 1*
Diefenbach, Elmer G 1893-1949 *WhAm 2*
Diefenbach, Ruth Sinclair 1878- *WomWWA 14*
Diefenbaker, John George 1895- *McGEWB*
Diefenderfer, John Harold 1894-1954 *NatCAB 44*
Diefendorf, Allen Ross 1871- *WhAm 5*
Diefendorf, Dorr Frank 1874- *WhAm 5*
Diefendorf, Mary Riggs 1862- *WomWWA 14*
Dieffenbach, Albert Charles 1876- *WhAm 5*
Dieffenbach, Richard Hagen 1883-1959 *NatCAB 46*
Diego, Jose De 1868-1918 *WhAm 1*
Diego Y Moreno, Francisco Garcia 1785?-1845 *WhAm H*
Diego Y Moreno, Francisco Garcia 1800?-1846 *ApCAB*
Diehl, Charles Edward 1875- *WhAm 5*
Diehl, Charles Sanford 1854-1946 *REnAW, WhAm 2*
Diehl, Conrad 1843- *WhAm 4*
Diehl, Cora Victoria 1869- *AmWom*
Diehl, Edith 1876-1953 *WhAm 3*
Diehl, George Conrad 1873-1956 *NatCAB 44*
Diehl, Harold Sheely 1891-1973 *WhAm 6*
Diehl, Harvey John 1891-1963 *NatCAB 53*
Diehl, Jacob 1884-1946 *WhAm 2*
Diehl, John Casper *WhAm 5*
Diehl, Samuel Willauer Black 1851-1909 *WhAm 1*
Diehl, William Wells 1916-1974 *WhAm 6*
Diehm, Robert Adam 1903-1969 *NatCAB 57*
Dieke, Gerhard Heinrich 1901-1965 *WhAm 4*
Diekema, Gerrit John 1859-1930 *BiDrAC, NatCAB 23, WhAm 1*
Diekma, Gerrit John 1859-1930 *WhAmP*
Dielman, Frederick 1847-1935 *AmBi, ApCAB, DcAmB S1, NatCAB 7, TwCBDA, WhAm 1*
Dielman, Louis Henry 1864- *WhAm 5*
Diels, Otto Paul Hermann 1876-1954 *AsBiEn, DcScB, McGEWB, WhAm 3*
Diem, Ngo Dinh 1901-1963 *McGEWB*

Diem, William Roy 1890-1964 *WhAm 4*
Diemar, Richard *NewYHSD*
Diemer, George Willis 1885-1956 *WhAm 3*
Diemer, Hugo 1870-1939 *ApCAB X,*
WhAm 1
Diemer, Robert Bernard 1888-1966 *NatCAB 54*
Diemer, Robert Bernard 1888-1967 *NatCAB 53*
Diener, William Lewis 1903-1964 *WhAm 4*
Dienst, George Elias 1858-1932 *WhAm 1*
Diente, Juan 1497?-1542 *ApCAB*
Dierdorff, Ross Ainsworth 1896-1964
NatCAB 51
Diereville d1708 *Drake*
Diereville, Jean 1670?- *ApCAB*
Dierks, DeVere 1893-1957 *NatCAB 49,*
WhAm 3
Dierks, Frederick Henry 1890-1965 *WhAm 4*
Diers, Theodore Carl 1880- *NatCAB 6*
Dies, Martin, Jr. 1900-1972 *WhAm 5,*
WhAmP
Dies, Martin, Jr. 1901-1972 *BiDrAC, WebAB*
Dies, Martin, Sr. 1870-1922 *BiDrAC,*
WhAm 1, WhAmP
Diesel, Rudolf 1858-1913 *AsBiEn, McGEWB*
Diesel, William F 1877-1939 *WhAm 1*
Dieskau, Jean Erdman 1701-1767 *ApCAB*
Dieskau, Baron Ludwig August 1701-1767
Drake
Diestel, Hermann 1868- *WhAm 4*
Dieter, Berthold B 1909-1972 *WhAm 5*
Dieterich, Frederick Albrecht 1887-1960
NatCAB 45
Dieterich, William Henry 1876-1940 *BiDrAC,*
NatCAB 35, WhAmP
Dieterich, William Henry 1879-1940 *WhAm 1*
Dieterich, William Herbert 1897-1964
NatCAB 52, WhAm 4
Dieterle, George Frank 1858-1947 *NatCAB 50*
Dieterle, Robert Richard 1896-1969
NatCAB 56
Dieterle, William 1893-1972 *WhAm 5*
Dietl, Eduard 1890-1944 *WhWW-II*
Dietl, Ernest Lawrence 1909-1974 *WhAm 6*
Dietrich, Baron De *DcScB*
Dietrich Von Freiberg 1250?-1310? *DcScB*
Dietrich, Charles Elmer 1889-1942 *BiDrAC*
Dietrich, Charles Henry 1853-1924 *BiDrAC,*
NatCAB 12, NatCAB 37, TwCBDA,
WhAm 1, WhAmP
Dietrich, Frank Sigel 1863-1930 *NatCAB 33,*
WhAm 1
Dietrich, Herman Rudolph 1862-1938 *WhAm 3*
Dietrich, John Hassler 1878- *WhAm 6*
Dietrich, Margretta Straw 1881-
WomWWA 14
Dietrich, Sepp 1892-1976 *WhWW-II*
Dietrichson, Gustav Johan Fredrik 1855-1922
WhAm 3
Dietrichson, Johannes Wilhelm Christian
1815-1883 *DcAmB*
Dietrichson, Marthine Magdalena 1872-
WomWWA 14
Dietrick, Charles Robert 1920-1973 *WhAm 6*
Dietrickson, Johannes Wilhelm Christian
1815-1883 *WhAm H*
Dietsch, C Percival 1881- *WhAm 6*
Dietz, Arthur O d1967 *WhAm 4A*
Dietz, August *NewYHSD*
Dietz, August Andrew, Jr. 1902-1954
NatCAB 41
Dietz, Carl F 1880-1957 *WhAm 3*
Dietz, Gould Cooke 1868- *WhAm 5*
Dietz, John F 1861-1924 *REnAW*
Dietz, Joseph F 1909-1962 *WhAm 4*
Dietz, Joseph J 1790?- *NewYHSD*
Dietz, Peter Ernest 1878-1947 *DcAmB S4*
Dietz, Robert Edwin 1886-1970 *NatCAB 56*
Dietz, Sherl Melvin 1893-1962 *WhAm 4*
Dietz, William 1778-1848 *BiDrAC, WhAm H*
Dietzman, Richard Priest 1883-1943 *WhAm 2*
Dieudonne, Florence Carpenter 1850- *AmWom*
Difenderfer, Robert E 1849-1923 *WhAm 1*
Diffenderfer, George M 1869-1943 *WhAm 2*
Diffenderfer, Lloyd Herr 1902-1963 *WhAm 4*
Diffenderfer, Robert Edward 1849-1923 *BiDrAC*
Diffenderffer, Frank Ried 1833- *WhAm 4*
Diffendorfer, Ralph Eugene 1879-1951
NatCAB 39, WhAm 3

Digby, Kenelm 1603-1665 *DcScB*
Digby, Robert 1732-1814 *ApCAB Sup*
Digby, Seaborn Lee 1892-1958 *NatCAB 48*
DiGesare, Louis Anthony 1907-1968
NatCAB 54
Digges, Sir Dudley 1583-1639 *ApCAB*
Digges, Dudley 1612?-1643 *ApCAB*
Digges, Dudley 1880-1947 *DcAmB S4,*
WhAm 2
Digges, Edward 1620-1675 *ApCAB,*
NatCAB 13
Digges, Isaac Watlington 1897-1953 *WhAm 3*
Digges, Leonard 1520?-1559? *DcScB*
Digges, Thomas 1546?-1595 *DcScB*
Digges, Thomas Atwood 1741?-1821?
WhAm H
Digges, Walter Mitchell 1877-1934 *WhAm 1*
Diggle, Roland 1885-1954 *WhAm 3*
Diggle, Samuel Lewis 1887-1951 *NatCAB 39*
Diggs, Alberta Peck 1876- *WhoColR*
Diggs, Annie LaPorte 1853-1916 *REnAW*
Diggs, Annie LePorte *WomWWA 14*
Diggs, Annie LePorte 1848-1916 *NotAW*
Diggs, Annie LePorte 1853-1916 *AmWom,*
WhAm 1
Diggs, Charles Coles, Jr. 1922- *BiDrAC*
Diggs, Charles S 1873- *WhoColR*
Diggs, James Robert Lincoln 1866- *WhAm 4,*
WhoColR
Diggs, Marshall Ramsey 1888-1968 *WhAm 5*
Dight, Mary A G 1860- *AmWom*
DiGiorgio, Joseph 1874-1951 *WhAm 3*
Dignam, Mary Ella 1859- *WomWWA 14*
Dignan, Thomas G 1899-1960 *WhAm 4*
Dike, Alice Norton *WomWWA 14*
Dike, Chester Thomas 1870- *WhAm 5*
Dike, Cornelia Anthony *WomWWA 14*
Dike, George Phillips 1876- *WhAm 6*
Dike, Henry Albyn 1825-1887 *NatCAB 2*
Dike, Henry B 1847- *WhAm 4*
Dike, Jeannie Dean Scott 1837-1920
NatCAB 34
Dike, Jeannie Dean Scott 1838-1920 *BiCAW*
Dike, Norman Staunton 1862-1953 *NatCAB 44,*
WhAm 3
Dike, Samuel Warren 1839-1913 *DcAmB,*
NatCAB 22, WhAm 1
Diles, Dorothy Vernon 1906-1968 *WhAm 5*
Dilger, Raymond Joseph 1910-1965 *NatCAB 51*
Dilger, Walter Linnell 1906-1970 *WhAm 5*
Dilks, Walter Howard, Jr. 1902-1965 *WhAm 4*
Dill, Augustus Granville 1881- *WhoColR*
Dill, Bessie Williams 1880- *WomWWA 14*
Dill, Clarence Cleveland 1884- *ApCAB X,*
BiDrAC, WhAmP
Dill, Franklin Geselbracht 1876-1936
NatCAB 28, WhAm 1
Dill, Homer Ray 1878-1964 *WhAm 4*
Dill, James Brooks 1854-1910 *DcAmB,*
NatCAB 6, WhAm 1
Dill, James E *NewYHSD*
Dill, James Horton 1821-1863 *NatCAB 6*
Dill, Sir John Greer 1881-1944 *WhWW-II,*
WhoMilH
Dill, Leonard Carter, Jr. 1906-1974 *WhAm 6*
Dill, Lewis 1859-1929 *WhAm 1*
Dill, William 1866-1929 *NatCAB 23*
Dilla, Harriette May 1886- *WomWWA 14*
Dillard, Allyn 1905-1972 *WhAm 5*
Dillard, Frank Clifford d1938 *WhAm 1*
Dillard, George Henderson Lee 1915-1974
WhAm 6
Dillard, George T 1855- *WhoColR*
Dillard, James Edgar 1879-1953 *WhAm 3*
Dillard, James Hardy 1856-1940 *BiDAmEd,*
DcAmB S2, NatCAB 34, WhAm 1,
WhAmP
Dillard, John Henry 1819-1896 *NatCAB 8*
Dillard, Paul 1873-1938 *WhAm 1*
Dillaway, George W *NewYHSD*
Dillaway, William Edward Lovell 1852-
NatCAB 17
Dillaye, Blanche d1932 *AmWom, WhAm 1,*
WomWWA 14
Dille, J H 1820- *NewYHSD*
Dille, John Flint 1884-1957 *WhAm 3*
Dille, John Ichabod 1857- *NatCAB 16*

Dillehunt, Richard Benjamin 1886-1953
WhAm 3
Dillenius, Johann Jacob 1687-1747 *DcScB*
Diller, Burgoyne 1906-1965 *BnEnAmA*
Diller, Elizabeth Ann *WomWWA 14*
Diller, George E 1906-1969 *WhAm 5*
Diller, Joseph Silas 1850-1928 *ApCAB,*
DcAmB S1, NatCAB 3, TwCBDA,
WhAm 1
Diller, Neal V 1899-1959 *WhAm 3*
Diller, Theodore 1863-1943 *WhAm 2*
Dilley, Arthur Urbane 1873- *WhAm 5*
Dillin, Margaret Sidner *WomWWA 14*
Dillinger, John 1902-1934 *DcAmB S1, WebAB*
Dillinger, John 1903-1934 *McGEWB*
Dillingham, Albert Caldwell 1848-1925
ApCAB X, NatCAB 20, WhAm 1
Dillingham, Benjamin Franklin 1844-
NatCAB 11
Dillingham, Charles Bancroft 1866-1934
NatCAB 25
Dillingham, Charles Bancroft 1868-1934
DcAmB S1, WhAm 1
Dillingham, Frances Bent *WhAm 5,*
WomWWA 14
Dillingham, Frank 1849- *WhAm 4*
Dillingham, Frank Ayer 1869-1941 *NatCAB 18,*
WhAm 1
Dillingham, Frank S 1878- *ApCAB X*
Dillingham, Frederic William 1860-1918
NatCAB 18
Dillingham, James Darius 1865- *WhAm 4*
Dillingham, John E *NewYHSD*
Dillingham, John Hoag 1839- *WhAm 1*
Dillingham, Louise Olga Gaylord 1884-
WomWWA 14
Dillingham, Paul, Jr. 1799-1891 *BiDrAC,*
NatCAB 8, TwCBDA, WhAm H,
WhAmP
Dillingham, Paul, Jr. 1800-1891 *BiAUS, Drake*
Dillingham, Pitt 1852-1926 *NatCAB 45*
Dillingham, W O 1901-1975 *WhAm 6*
Dillingham, Walter Francis 1875-1963 *WhAm 4*
Dillingham, William Paul 1843-1923 *ApCAB X,*
BiDrAC, DcAmB, EncAAH, NatCAB 8,
TwCBDA, WebAB, WhAm 1, WhAmP
Dillistin, William Holms 1885-1964 *NatCAB 51*
Dillon, Arthur 1750-1794 *ApCAB*
Dillon, Arthur, Comte De 1750-1794 *Drake*
Dillon, Charles d1881 *ApCAB*
Dillon, Charles 1869-1942 *WhAm 2*
Dillon, Charles Hall 1853-1929 *BiDrAC,*
NatCAB 21, WhAm 1, WhAmP
Dillon, Charles Wesley 1865-1937 *NatCAB 29*
Dillon, Charlotte E *NewYHSD*
Dillon, Clarence Douglas 1909- *BiDrUSE*
Dillon, Edmond Bothwell 1869-1919 *WhAm 1,*
WhAm 2
Dillon, Fannie 1881-1947 *WhAm 2*
Dillon, George 1906-1968 *WhAm 5*
Dillon, Halle Tanner 1864- *NatCAB 3*
Dillon, J Clifford 1904-1960 *WhAm 3A*
Dillon, James 1918-1962 *WhAm 4*
Dillon, Jesse William 1904-1972 *WhAm 5*
Dillon, John B *NewYHSD*
Dillon, John B 1807?- *Drake*
Dillon, John Blake 1814-1866 *ApCAB*
Dillon, John Forrest 1831-1914 *AmBi, ApCAB,*
BiAUS, DcAmB, NatCAB 1, TwCBDA,
WhAm 1
Dillon, John Irving 1870-1938 *WhAm 1*
Dillon, John J 1856-1950 *WhAm 2A*
Dillon, John Jordan 1898-1944 *WhAm 2*
Dillon, John Richard 1890-1948 *WhAm 2*
Dillon, John Thomas 1884-1958 *NatCAB 48,*
WhAm 3
Dillon, Mary *WhAm 1, WomWWA 14*
Dillon, Michael Joseph 1891-1957 *NatCAB 44*
Dillon, Philip Robert 1868- *WhAm 5*
Dillon, Richard Charles 1877-1966 *WhAm 4*
Dillon, Robert E 1883-1952 *WhAm 3*
Dillon, Sidney 1812-1892 *DcAmB, REnAW,*
TwCBDA, WhAm H
Dillon, Theodore Harwood 1883-1961
NatCAB 52
Dillon, Thomas Joseph 1878-1949 *NatCAB 37,*
WhAm 2
Dillon, Thomas Joseph 1882-1961 *WhAm 4*

Dillon, Tony G 1891-1964 *NatCAB 51*
Dillon, William Thomas 1892-1964 *WhAm 4*
Dilloway, George W *NewYHSD*
Dillwyn, George 1738-1821 *ApCAB*
Dilnot, Frank 1875- *WhAm 5*
DiLoreto, Frank Joseph 1922-1964 *NatCAB 51*
Dilthey, Wilhelm Christian Ludwig 1833-1911 *McGEWB*
Dilweg, LaVern Ralph 1903-1968 *BiDrAC*
Dilworth, J Dale 1869-1949 *NatCAB 38*
Dilworth, Joseph Richardson 1860-1928 *NatCAB 31*
Dilworth, Richardson 1898-1974 *WhAm 6*
DiMaggio, Joseph Paul, Jr. 1914- *WebAB*
Diman, Byron 1795-1865 *ApCAB, BiAUS, NatCAB 9, TwCBDA*
Diman, Jeremiah Lewis 1831-1881 *ApCAB, DcAmB, NatCAB 8, TwCBDA, WhAm H*
Diman, John Hugh 1863-1949 *WhAm 2*
Diman, Louise 1869- *WomWWA 14*
Dimeck, Victor M *NewYHSD*
Diment, James Marshallsay 1850-1922 *NatCAB 19*
Dimick, Jeremiah Wood 1862-1914 *NatCAB 18*
Dimick, Justin 1800-1871 *ApCAB, TwCBDA*
Dimick, Justin E 1819-1863 *ApCAB, Drake*
DiMilla, Pasquale 1869- *NatCAB 16*
Dimitroff, George Zakharieff 1901-1968 *WhAm 4A*
Dimitrov, Georgi 1882-1949 *WhAm 3*
Dimitry, Alexander 1805-1883 *ApCAB, BiAUS, BiDAmEd, DcAmB, NatCAB 10, TwCBDA, WhAm H*
Dimitry, Charles Patton 1837-1910 *ApCAB, DcAmB, NatCAB 10, TwCBDA, WhAm 1*
Dimitry, John Bull Smith 1835-1901 *ApCAB, TwCBDA, WhAm 1*
Dimlich, H Karl 1898-1957 *NatCAB 46*
Dimmick, Eugene Dumont 1840-1935 *WhAm 1*
Dimmick, Forrest Lee 1893-1968 *NatCAB 54*
Dimmick, Francis Marion 1827- *NatCAB 1*
Dimmick, Joseph Benjamin 1858-1920 *ApCAB X, NatCAB 19*
Dimmick, Milo Melankthon 1811-1872 *BiAUS, BiDrAC, WhAm H*
Dimmick, William Harrison 1815-1861 *BiAUS, BiDrAC, TwCBDA, WhAm H*
Dimmitt, Charles Elliott 1862-1939 *NatCAB 28*
Dimmitt, Lillian English 1867- *WhAm 4*
Dimmock, Charles 1800-1863 *ApCAB, TwCBDA*
Dimmock, George 1852-1930 *ApCAB, NatCAB 26, TwCBDA, WhAm 1*
Dimmock, William Reynolds 1835-1878 *TwCBDA*
Dimnent, Edward D 1876- *WhAm 5*
Dimock, Anthony Weston 1842-1918 *WhAm 1*
Dimock, Davis, Jr. 1801-1842 *BiAUS, BiDrAC, WhAm H*
Dimock, Hedley S 1891-1958 *WhAm 3*
Dimock, Ira 1827-1917 *NatCAB 26*
Dimock, Susan 1847-1875 *ApCAB, NatCAB 19, NotAW*
Dimock, William Wallace 1880-1953 *WhAm 3*
Dimon, Abigail Camp 1874- *WomWWA 14*
Dimon, Raymond Clark 1895-1963 *WhAm 4*
Dimond, Anthony Joseph 1881-1953 *BiDrAC, WhAm 3, WhAmP*
Dimond, Douglas Marquand 1890-1962 *NatCAB 50*
Dimond, Francis M 1796-1858 *BiAUS, NatCAB 9, TwCBDA*
Dimond, Miss M *NewYHSD*
Dinakara 1550?- *DcScB*
Dinand, Joseph Nicholas 1869-1943 *WhAm 2*
DiNardo, Antonio 1889-1948 *NatCAB 37*
Dine, Jim 1935- *BnEnAmA*
Dinehart, Alan 1890-1944 *WhAm 2*
Diner, Jacob 1870-1937 *NatCAB 28*
Dinerman, Helen Schneider 1920-1974 *WhAm 6*
Dines, Homer Duncan 1877-1959 *WhAm 3*
Dines, Orville Lee 1871-1953 *NatCAB 42*
Dines, Thomas Anselm 1880-1961 *NatCAB 47, WhAm 6*
Dines, Tyson S 1858-1929 *WhAm 1*
Dinesen, Isak 1885-1962 *McGEWB*

Dinesen, Isak *see also* Blixen Finecke, Karen
Dingane 1795?-1840 *McGEWB*
Dingee, William Jackson 1853- *NatCAB 7*
Dingell, John David 1894-1955 *BiDrAC, NatCAB 42, WhAm 3, WhAmP*
Dingell, John David, Jr. 1926- *BiDrAC*
Dinger, Harold Eugene 1905-1975 *WhAm 6*
Dingle, John Holmes 1908-1973 *WhAm 6*
Dingler, Hugo Albert Emil Hermann 1881-1954 *DcScB*
Dingley, Anna Ladd 1868- *WomWWA 14*
Dingley, Edward Nelson 1862-1930 *NatCAB 8, NatCAB 21, WhAm 1*
Dingley, Frank Lambert 1840-1918 *WhAm 1*
Dingley, Henry McKenney 1858-1930 *NatCAB 38*
Dingley, Nelson 1832-1899 *AmBi, ApCAB, BiAUS, BiDrAC, DcAmB, EncAAH, NatCAB 6, TwCBDA, WhAm H, WhAmP*
Dings, Peter Conrad 1870-1938 *WhAm 1*
Dingwell, Laura Hale Stickney 1845- *WomWWA 14*
Dini, Ulisse 1845-1918 *DcScB*
Dinkelspiel, Lloyd William 1899-1959 *NatCAB 47, WhAm 3*
Dinkey, Alva Clymer 1866-1931 *NatCAB 22, WhAm 1*
Dinkins, James 1845-1939 *NatCAB 39, WhAm 1*
Dinkins, Philip M 1896-1969 *WhAm 5*
Dinkler, Carling d1961 *WhAm 4*
Dinkmeyer, Henry William 1892-1957 *WhAm 3*
Dinneen, Fitz-George 1866-1944 *WhAm 2*
Dinnies, Anna Peyre 1805-1886 *NatCAB 13*
Dinnies, Anna Peyre 1816- *ApCAB*
Dinostratus *DcScB*
Dinsmoor, Alice *WomWWA 14*
Dinsmoor, Robert 1757-1836 *ApCAB, DcAmB, Drake, NatCAB 7, WhAm H*
Dinsmoor, Samuel 1766-1835 *ApCAB, BiAUS, BiDrAC, Drake, NatCAB 11, TwCBDA, WhAm H, WhAmP*
Dinsmoor, Samuel 1799-1869 *ApCAB, BiAUS, Drake, NatCAB 11, TwCBDA*
Dinsmore, Carlos Millson 1875-1948 *WhAm 2*
Dinsmore, Charles Allen 1860-1941 *NatCAB 31, WhAm 1*
Dinsmore, Frank F 1869- *WhAm 6*
Dinsmore, Hugh Anderson 1850-1930 *BiDrAC, NatCAB 5, TwCBDA, WhAm 1, WhAmP*
Dinsmore, John Walker 1839-1922 *WhAm 1*
Dinsmore, John Wirt 1858- *WhAm 4*
Dinsmore, Joseph Campbell 1899-1973 *WhAm 5*
Dinsmore, Robert Scott 1892-1957 *WhAm 3*
Dinsmore, Samuel P 1822?-1882 *ApCAB*
D'Invilliers, Edward Vincent 1857-1928 *NatCAB 22, WhAm 1, WhAm 4*
Dinwiddie, Albert Bledsoe 1871-1935 *BiDAmEd, DcAmB S1, NatCAB 28, WhAm 1*
Dinwiddie, Courtenay 1882-1943 *DcAmB S3, WhAm 2*
Dinwiddie, Edwin Courtland 1867-1935 *AmBi, DcAmB S1, NatCAB 26, WhAm 1*
Dinwiddie, Emily Wayland 1879-1949 *NotAW, WomWWA 14*
Dinwiddie, George Summey 1909-1968 *NatCAB 57, WhAm 5*
Dinwiddie, John Ekin 1902-1959 *NatCAB 48, WhAm 4*
Dinwiddie, Robert 1690?-1770 *ApCAB, Drake*
Dinwiddie, Robert 1693-1770 *AmBi, DcAmB, McGEWB, NatCAB 13, WhAm H*
Dinwiddie, William 1867-1934 *WhAm 1*
Dinwiddie, William Stewart 1871-1932 *NatCAB 25*
Diocles *DcScB, DcScB Sup*
Diocles Of Carystus *DcScB*
Diocletian 245-313? *McGEWB*
Diogenes 400?BC-325?BC *McGEWB*
Dion, Cyrille 1843-1878 *ApCAB*
Dionis, Simon *NewYHSD*
Dionis DuSejour, Achille-Pierre 1734-1794 *DcScB*
Dionne, Narcisse Eutrope 1848- *ApCAB Sup*
Dionysodorus *DcScB*

Diop, Cheikh Anta 1923- *McGEWB*
Diophantus 210?-290? *AsBiEn*
Diophantus Of Alexandria *DcScB, DcScB Sup*
Dior, Christian 1905-1957 *WhAm 3*
Dioscorides *DcScB*
Dioscorides 020?- *AsBiEn*
Dioscorides 054?-068 *BiHiMed*
Dipalma, Joseph Alfred 1928- *WhAm 6*
Dippel, Andreas 1866-1932 *AmBi, NatCAB 14, WhAm 1*
Dippel, John Henry 1906-1964 *NatCAB 50*
Dippel, Michael William 1856-1933 *NatCAB 24*
Dippell, Victor William 1874-1966 *NatCAB 54*
Dirac, Paul Adrien Maurice 1902- *AsBiEn, McGEWB*
Dirbrell, George Gibbs 1822-1888 *BiAUS*
Dirck, Cornelius Lansing 1785-1857 *ApCAB*
Dirichlet, Gustav Peter Lejeune 1805-1859 *DcScB*
Dirks, Henry Bernhard 1884-1955 *NatCAB 44*
Dirks, Hermann John 1882-1968 *NatCAB 53*
Dirks, Louis Herman 1880-1967 *WhAm 4*
Dirksen, Everett McKinley 1896-1969 *BiDrAC, EncAAH, EncAB, NatCAB 55, WebAB, WhAm 5, WhAmP*
Dirr, Peter George 1915-1967 *WhAm 4A*
Dirstine, Pearl H 1886-1955 *NatCAB 47*
Disbrow, John B *NewYHSD*
Disbrow, Marie Angelina Williams *WomWWA 14*
Disbrow, William Stephen 1861-1922 *DcAmB*
Disbrowe, Samuel 1619-1690 *ApCAB*
Disdorf, Peter J *NewYHSD*
Diserens, Paul 1882-1958 *WhAm 3*
Dishman, John Wesley, Jr. 1864- *WhAm 4*
Diskin, Carlton Fine 1914-1967 *WhAm 4*
Dismukes, Douglas Eugene 1869-1949 *WhAm 2*
Disney, David Tiernan 1803-1857 *BiAUS, BiDrAC, TwCBDA, WhAm H*
Disney, Richard Randolph 1835- *ApCAB*
Disney, Roy Oliver 1893-1971 *NatCAB 57, WhAm 5*
Disney, Walt 1901-1966 *NatCAB 57, REnAW, WebAB*
Disney, Walter Elias 1901-1966 *EncAB, McGEWB, WhAm 4*
Disney, Wesley Ernest 1883-1961 *BiDrAC, WhAm 4, WhAmP*
Disosway, Gabriel Poillon 1799-1868 *ApCAB, TwCBDA*
Disque, Brice Pursell 1879-1960 *NatCAB 17, NatCAB 47, WhAm 3*
Disque, Robert Conrad 1883-1968 *WhAm 5*
Disraeli, Benjamin, Earl Of Beaconsfield 1804-1881 *McGEWB*
Dissette, Thomas Kemp 1838-1921 *NatCAB 27*
Disston, Henry 1819-1878 *AmBi, ApCAB, DcAmB, NatCAB 6, TwCBDA, WhAm H*
Disston, Jacob Steelman 1862-1938 *NatCAB 28*
Disston, William 1859-1915 *NatCAB 18*
DiStasio, Frank 1905-1951 *NatCAB 40*
Distler, Carl Martin 1886-1947 *WhAm 2*
Distler, John Cyrus 1884-1944 *NatCAB 35*
Disturnell, John 1801-1877 *ApCAB, DcAmB, NatCAB 23, WhAm H*
DiSuvero, Mark 1933- *BnEnAmA*
Ditchy, Clair William 1891-1967 *WhAm 4*
Dithmar, Edward Augustus 1854-1917 *WhAm 1*
Dithmer, Henry Louis 1869-1945 *NatCAB 35*
Ditisheim, Hanns 1901-1961 *NatCAB 49, WhAm 4*
Ditman, Norman Edward 1877-1944 *NatCAB 34*
Ditmars, Raymond Lee 1876-1942 *DcAmB S3, NatCAB 10, WhAm 2*
Ditmars, Walter Earl 1895-1962 *NatCAB 51, WhAm 4*
Ditrichstein, Leo 1865-1928 *DcAmB*
Ditrichstein, Leo 1867-1928 *NatCAB 22, WhAm 1*
Ditson, Charles Healy 1845-1929 *ApCAB X, WhAm 1*
Ditson, George Leighton 1812-1895 *ApCAB, DcAmB, NatCAB 13, WhAm H*
Ditson, Oliver 1811-1888 *ApCAB, DcAmB, NatCAB 7, TwCBDA, WhAm H*

Dittemore, John Valentine 1876-1937 *DcAmB S2, WhAm 1*
Dittenhaver, Sarah Louise 1901-1973 *WhAm 6*
Dittenhoefer, Abram Jesse 1836-1919 *NatCAB 7, NatCAB 14, NatCAB 36, WhAm 1*
Dittenhoefer, Irving Meade 1863- *NatCAB 14*
Ditter, John William 1888-1943 *BiDrAC, WhAm 2, WhAmP*
Dittmar, George Walter 1872-1949 *WhAm 2*
Dittmar, Paul Otto 1892-1972 *NatCAB 56*
Dittmar, William 1833-1892 *DcScB*
Ditto, Rollo C 1886-1947 *WhAm 2*
Ditto, Samuel Douglas 1861-1941 *NatCAB 30*
Dittrick, Howard 1877-1954 *WhAm 3*
Ditzion, Sidney Herbert 1908-1975 *DcAmLiB*
Ditzler, Charlotte Weber 1877- *WhAm 5*
Diven, Alexander Samuel 1809-1896 *ApCAB, BiAUS, BiDrAC, DcAmB, NatCAB 11, TwCBDA, WhAm H*
Diven, George Miles 1835-1909 *WhAm 1*
Diven, Robert Joseph 1869- *WhAm 5*
Divine, Father 1877?-1965 *DcAmReB, WebAB*
Divine, Frank Henry 1865-1941 *WhAm 1*
Divini, Eustachio 1610-1685 *DcScB*
Divis, Prokop 1698-1765 *DcScB*
Divol, Ira 1820-1871 *ApCAB*
Dix, Augustus J 1831- *NatCAB 5*
Dix, Beulah Marie *WomWWA 14*
Dix, Charles Temple 1838-1873 *ApCAB*
Dix, Charles Temple 1840-1873 *NewYHSD*
Dix, Cuno *NewYHSD*
Dix, Dorothea Lynde *Drake*
Dix, Dorothea Lynde 1794?-1887 *ApCAB*
Dix, Dorothea Lynde 1802-1887 *AmBi, AmWom, BiDAmEd, DcAmB, EncAB, McGEWB, NotAW, TwCBDA, WebAB, WhAm H*
Dix, Dorothy 1870-1951 *DcAmB S5*
Dix, Dorothy Lynde 1802-1887 *NatCAB 3*
Dix, Edgar Hutton, Jr. 1892-1963 *NatCAB 48*
Dix, Edwin Asa 1860-1911 *ApCAB X, NatCAB 8, WhAm 1*
Dix, Howard Whedon 1887-1956 *NatCAB 47*
Dix, John Adams 1798-1879 *AmBi, ApCAB, BiAUS, BiDrAC, BiDrUSE, DcAmB, Drake, NatCAB 5, TwCBDA, WebAB, WebAMB, WhAm H, WhAmP*
Dix, John Adams 1880-1945 *NatCAB 36*
Dix, John Alden 1860-1928 *NatCAB 15, NatCAB 23, WhAm 1*
Dix, John Homer 1810?-1884 *ApCAB, NatCAB 11*
Dix, John Homer 1811-1884 *DcAmB, WhAm H*
Dix, Morgan 1827-1908 *AmBi, ApCAB, DcAmB, NatCAB 3, NatCAB 23, TwCBDA, WhAm 1*
Dix, Otto 1891-1969 *WhAm 5*
Dix, Richard 1895-1949 *NatCAB 37*
Dix, William Frederick 1867-1945 *NatCAB 34, WhAm 2*
Dixey, George d1853? *NewYHSD*
Dixey, Henry Edward 1859-1943 *ApCAB, NatCAB 10, WhAm 2*
Dixey, John 1760?-1820 *NatCAB 9, NewYHSD, WhAm H*
Dixey, John V *NewYHSD*
Dixon *NewYHSD*
Dixon, Alexander 1820?- *ApCAB*
Dixon, Amzi Clarence 1854-1925 *DcAmReB, NatCAB 39, WhAm 1*
Dixon, Archibald 1802-1876 *ApCAB, BiAUS, BiDrAC, Drake, NatCAB 3, TwCBDA, WhAm H*
Dixon, Arminius Gray 1870- *WhAm 5*
Dixon, Arthur Mills 1882-1956 *NatCAB 46*
Dixon, Brandt VanBlarcom 1850-1941 *NatCAB 11, TwCBDA, WhAm 1*
Dixon, Charles Edward 1864- *TwCBDA*
Dixon, Charles F 1824- *WhoColR*
Dixon, Edgar H 1904-1962 *WhAm 4*
Dixon, Elijah *NewYHSD*
Dixon, Francis Stilwell 1879-1967 *NatCAB 52*
Dixon, Frank 1866-1925 *WhAm 1*
Dixon, Frank Haigh 1869-1944 *NatCAB 33, WhAm 2*
Dixon, Frank Joseph 1904-1966 *WhAm 4*

Dixon, Frank Murray 1892-1965 *WhAm 4*
Dixon, Franklin W *WebAB*
Dixon, Fred Willis 1888-1966 *NatCAB 52*
Dixon, Frederick d1923 *WhAm 1*
Dixon, G Gale 1885-1958 *NatCAB 43*
Dixon, George *NewYHSD*
Dixon, George d1800? *ApCAB, Drake*
Dixon, George Dallas 1857-1937 *WhAm 1*
Dixon, George Grady 1890-1958 *NatCAB 47*
Dixon, George Hall 1900-1965 *WhAm 4*
Dixon, George Peleg 1889-1956 *WhAm 3*
Dixon, George Sloan 1853-1944 *NatCAB 43*
Dixon, George W, Jr. 1908-1966 *WhAm 4*
Dixon, George Washington 1808?-1861 *ApCAB*
Dixon, George William 1866-1938 *WhAm 1*
Dixon, Harold Baily 1852-1930 *DcScB*
Dixon, Henry Aldous 1890-1967 *BiDrAC, WhAm 4*
Dixon, Henry Horatio 1869-1953 *DcScB*
Dixon, Henry Leander 1860-1930 *NatCAB 23*
Dixon, Hubert Allen 1904-1969 *NatCAB 55*
Dixon, Isaac Henry 1847-1910 *NatCAB 28*
Dixon, James 1814-1873 *ApCAB, BiAUS, BiDrAC, DcAmB, Drake, NatCAB 4, TwCBDA, WhAm H, WhAmP*
Dixon, James M 1873-1932 *WhAm 1*
Dixon, James Main 1856-1933 *WhAm 1*
Dixon, Jeremiah *ApCAB, WebAB*
Dixon, Jeremiah 1733-1779 *DcScB*
Dixon, John 1847- *WhAm 4*
Dixon, John Edward d1961 *WhAm 4*
Dixon, Jonathan 1839-1906 *NatCAB 28*
Dixon, Joseph 1799-1869 *AmBi, ApCAB, DcAmB, Drake, NatCAB 22, TwCBDA, WhAm H*
Dixon, Joseph 1828-1883 *BiAUS, BiDrAC, WhAm H*
Dixon, Joseph Andrew 1879-1942 *BiDrAC, WhAm 6*
Dixon, Joseph Henry *BiAUS*
Dixon, Joseph Moore 1867-1934 *BiDrAC, NatCAB 14, WhAm 1, WhAmP*
Dixon, Kay 1884-1957 *NatCAB 46*
Dixon, L A, Sr. 1898-1972 *WhAm 5*
Dixon, Lafayette Maynard 1875-1946 *IIBEAAW*
Dixon, Leon Snell 1886-1950 *NatCAB 40*
Dixon, Leon Suell 1886-1950 *NatCAB 47*
Dixon, Leonard Lee 1884-1944 *NatCAB 34*
Dixon, Lilian *WomWWA 14*
Dixon, Lincoln 1860-1932 *BiDrAC, WhAm 1, WhAmP*
Dixon, Luther C *BiAUS*
Dixon, Luther Swift 1825-1891 *DcAmB, NatCAB 12, WhAm H*
Dixon, Marion E Martin *WomWWA 14*
Dixon, Mary J Scarlett 1822- *AmWom*
Dixon, Mary Quincy Allen 1859- *WhAm 4*
Dixon, Maynard 1875-1946 *WhAm 2*
Dixon, N Walter 1858-1925 *NatCAB 6*
Dixon, Nathan Fellows 1774-1842 *ApCAB, BiAUS, BiDrAC, NatCAB 13, TwCBDA, WhAm H, WhAmP*
Dixon, Nathan Fellows 1812-1881 *ApCAB, BiAUS, BiDrAC, TwCBDA, WhAm H, WhAmP*
Dixon, Nathan Fellows 1847-1897 *BiDrAC, NatCAB 1, TwCBDA, WhAm H, WhAmP*
Dixon, Pierson 1904-1965 *WhAm 4*
Dixon, Robert Kenneth 1898-1960 *NatCAB 47*
Dixon, Robert M 1860-1918 *WhAm 1*
Dixon, Roland Burrage 1875-1934 *AmBi, DcAmB S1, NatCAB 14, NatCAB 39*
Dixon, Rolland Burrage 1875-1934 *WhAm 1*
Dixon, Royal 1885-1962 *WhAm 4*
Dixon, Russell Alexander 1898-1976 *WhAm 6*
Dixon, Sam Houston 1855- *WhAm 4*
Dixon, Samuel 1856-1934 *NatCAB 27*
Dixon, Samuel Gibson 1851-1918 *NatCAB 13, NatCAB 35, TwCBDA, WhAm 1*
Dixon, Sarah Ann *WomWWA 14*
Dixon, Sherwood 1896-1973 *WhAm 6*
Dixon, Susan Bullitt 1829-1907 *NatCAB 13, WhAm 1*
Dixon, Thomas, Jr. 1864-1946 *ApCAB X, DcAmB S4, NatCAB 13, WhAm 2*
Dixon, Wesley Moon 1896-1969 *NatCAB 55,*

WhAm 5
Dixon, William 1850-1913 *DcAmB, WebAMB, WhAm HA, WhAm 4*
Dixon, William Hepworth 1821-1879 *ApCAB*
Dixon, William Palmer 1847-1927 *WhAm 1*
Dixon, William Palmer 1902-1968 *WhAm 5*
Dixon, William Wirt 1838-1911 *BiDrAC, TwCBDA, WhAm 4*
Dixson, Zella Allen 1858-1924 *TwCBDA, WhAm 1, WomWWA 14*
Dixwell, John 1607?-1688? *DcAmB*
Dixwell, John 1607?-1689 *ApCAB, Drake, NatCAB 8, WhAm H*
Djerf, Frederick Joseph 1901-1946 *NatCAB 35*
Djilas, Milovan 1911- *McGEWB*
Djuanda Kartawidjaja, Raden Hadji 1911-1963 *WhAm 4*
Dmochowski *NewYHSD*
Do-Ne-Ho-Ga-Wa *WhAm H*
Doak, Archibald Alexander 1815-1866 *NatCAB 7, TwCBDA*
Doak, Henry Melvil 1841- *TwCBDA*
Doak, John Whitefield 1778-1820 *NatCAB 7*
Doak, Samuel *ApCAB*
Doak, Samuel 1749-1829 *BiDAmEd, NatCAB 7*
Doak, Samuel 1749-1830 *ApCAB, DcAmB, TwCBDA, WhAm H*
Doak, Samuel Witherspoon 1785-1864 *NatCAB 7, TwCBDA*
Doak, William Nuckles 1882-1933 *BiDrUSE, NatCAB 25, WhAm 1*
Doan, Fletcher Morris 1846-1924 *WhAm 1*
Doan, Frank Carleton 1877-1927 *WhAm 1*
Doan, Gilbert Everett 1897-1970 *WhAm 5*
Doan, James Burton 1870- *WhAm 5*
Doan, Jessie Ringen *WomWWA 14*
Doan, Leland Ira 1894-1974 *WhAm 6*
Doan, Murray Meredith 1866-1939 *NatCAB 44*
Doan, Robert Eachus 1831-1919 *BiDrAC*
Doan, William 1792-1847 *BiDrAC, WhAm H*
Doane, Augustus Sidney 1808-1852 *ApCAB, Drake*
Doane, Foster Baird 1893-1963 *NatCAB 52*
Doane, George Hobart 1830-1905 *ApCAB, NatCAB 8, TwCBDA, WhAm 4*
Doane, George Washington 1799-1859 *AmBi, ApCAB, DcAmB, Drake, NatCAB 3, TwCBDA, WhAm H*
Doane, George Washington 1853-1928 *NatCAB 45*
Doane, Ida Frances 1858-1942 *NatCAB 41*
Doane, Joseph *ApCAB*
Doane, Marguerite Treat 1868-1954 *NatCAB 41*
Doane, Ralph Harrington 1886-1941 *NatCAB 31, WhAm 2*
Doane, Richard Congdon 1898-1972 *WhAm 5*
Doane, Samuel Everett 1870-1952 *NatCAB 16, NatCAB 42, WhAm 5*
Doane, Thomas 1821-1897 *DcAmB, NatCAB 25, TwCBDA, WhAm H*
Doane, William *BiAUS*
Doane, William Croswell 1832-1913 *ApCAB, DcAmB, NatCAB 4, TwCBDA, WhAm 1*
Doane, William Howard 1831- *ApCAB*
Doane, William Howard 1832-1915 *NatCAB 7, NatCAB 41, TwCBDA, WhAm 4*
Dobbie, Elliott VanKirk 1907-1970 *WhAm 5*
Dobbie, George Alexander 1880-1951 *WhAm 3*
Dobbie, Robert Paul 1895-1956 *NatCAB 43*
Dobbie, Sir William 1879-1964 *WhWW-II*
Dobbin, Carroll Edward 1892-1967 *NatCAB 54, WhAm 5*
Dobbin, Elizabeth Calder 1878- *WomWWA 14*
Dobbin, George W 1870-1928 *WhAm 1*
Dobbin, George Washington 1809-1891 *TwCBDA*
Dobbin, James 1833- *WhAm 4*
Dobbin, James C 1814-1857 *BiAUS*
Dobbin, James Cochran 1814-1857 *BiDrUSE, DcAmB, WhAm H*
Dobbin, James Cochrane 1814-1857 *ApCAB, BiDrAC, Drake, NatCAB 4, TwCBDA, WhAmP*
Dobbins *NewYHSD*
Dobbins, Daniel 1776-1856 *ApCAB,*

NatCAB 13

Dobbins, Donald Claude 1878-1943 *BiDrAC, WhAm 2*

Dobbins, Harry Thompson 1865- *WhAm 5*

Dobbins, Horace Murrell 1868-1962 *NatCAB 50*

Dobbins, James Talmage 1888-1972 *NatCAB 57, WhAm 5*

Dobbins, John Leslie 1883-1938 *NatCAB 41*

Dobbins, John Young 1850-1917 *NatCAB 17*

Dobbins, Samuel Atkinson 1814-1886 *BiAUS, BiDrAC, WhAm H*

Dobbs, Amy Mary *WomWWA 14*

Dobbs, Arthur 1684-1765 *ApCAB, BiAUS, Drake, NatCAB 5*

Dobbs, Arthur 1689-1765 *AmBi, DcAmB, WhAm H*

Dobbs, Ella Victoria 1866-1952 *BiDAmEd*

Dobbs, Harrison Allen 1893-1963 *NatCAB 50*

Dobbs, Hoyt McWhorter 1878-1954 *WhAm 3*

Dobbs, John Francis 1870-1949 *WhAm 2*

Dobbs, Samuel Candler 1868- *WhAm 5*

Dobbs, Stuart Piper 1887-1955 *WhAm 4*

Dobell, Cecil Clifford 1886-1949 *DcScB*

Dobell, Richard Reid 1837- *ApCAB Sup*

Dobell, Sir William 1899-1970 *McGEWB*

Dobereiner, Johann Wolfgang 1780-1849 *AsBiEn, DcScB*

Doberstein, John Walter 1905-1965 *WhAm 4*

Dobi, Istvan 1898-1968 *WhAm 5*

Dobie, Armistead Mason 1881-1962 *WhAm 4*

Dobie, Charles Caldwell 1881-1943 *NatCAB 31, WhAm 2*

Dobie, Gilmour 1878-1948 *DcAmB S4*

Dobie, James Frank 1888-1964 *EncAAH, REnAW, WebAB, WhAm 4*

Doblado, Manuel 1818-1864 *ApCAB*

Doble, Kendall Dyer 1895-1960 *WhAm 4*

Doble, William Henry 1862-1950 *ApCAB X, NatCAB 40*

Dobnievski, David *WebAB*

Dobriner, Konrad 1902-1952 *WhAm 3*

Dobrizhoffer, Martin 1717-1791 *ApCAB*

Dobson *NewYHSD*

Dobson, Arthur Allan 1889-1956 *NatCAB 45*

Dobson, Fanita Duncan 1884- *WomWWA 14*

Dobson, George Frederick 1850-1928 *WhAm 1*

Dobson, John 1827-1911 *NatCAB 17*

Dobson, Mason Henry 1891-1952 *WhAm 3*

Dobson, Matthew 1735?-1784 *BiHiMed*

Dobson, Sir Roy Hardy 1891-1968 *WhAm 5*

Dobson, Thomas d1823 *Drake*

Dobson, Tom 1890-1918 *NatCAB 18*

Dobson, William Marshall 1883-1949 *NatCAB 41*

Dobyne, Margaret B 1870- *WomWWA 14*

Dobyns, A Webster 1879-1950 *WhAm 2A*

Dobyns, Fletcher 1872-1942 *WhAm 2*

Dobyns, John Robert 1850- *WhAm 1*

Dobyns, William Ray 1861-1932 *WhAm 1*

Dobzhansky, Theodosius Grigorievich 1900-1975 *WebAB, WhAm 6*

Docampo, Rodrigo d1545 *ApCAB*

Docharty, Gerardus Beekman 1804-1889 *TwCBDA*

Docherty, Edward 1891-1971 *NatCAB 55*

Dochez, Alphonse Raymond 1882-1964 *WhAm 4*

Dochterman, Frances May 1881- *WomWWA 14*

Dock, Christopher 1698-1771 *BiDAmEd, DcAmB, WhAm H*

Dock, George 1860-1951 *WhAm 3*

Dock, Howard 1889-1960 *NatCAB 55*

Dock, Lavinia L 1858- *WhAm 4, WomWWA 14*

Dock, Mira Lloyd 1853- *WomWWA 14*

Dockeray, Floyd Carlton 1880- *WhAm 6*

Dockery, Alexander Monroe 1845-1926 *BiDrAC, NatCAB 20, TwCBDA, WhAm 1, WhAmP*

Dockery, Alexander Monroe 1846-1926 *NatCAB 12*

Dockery, Alfred 1797- *BiAUS*

Dockery, Alfred 1797-1873 *TwCBDA*

Dockery, Alfred 1797-1875 *BiDrAC, WhAm H*

Dockery, Eva Hunt 1870- *WomWWA 14*

Dockery, Oliver Hart 1830-1906 *ApCAB, BiAUS, BiDrAC, TwCBDA*

Dockery, Will 1865-1936 *NatCAB 31*

Docking, George 1904-1964 *WhAm 4*

Docking, James Tippet 1861-1916 *WhAm 1*

Dockry, Patrick Francis 1906-1955 *NatCAB 45*

Dockstader, Ernest Ambrose 1890-1970 *NatCAB 55*

Dockstader, Lew 1856-1924 *DcAmB, NatCAB 23*

Dockweiler, Isidore Bernard 1867-1947 *WhAm 2*

Dockweiler, John Francis 1895-1943 *BiDrAC, WhAm 2*

Dockweiler, Thomas Aloysius Joseph 1892-1959 *NatCAB 48, WhAm 4*

Doctoroff, John 1893-1970 *WhAm 5*

Dod, Albert Baldwin 1805-1845 *ApCAB, DcAmB, Drake, TwCBDA, WhAm H*

Dod, Charles Squire 1814-1872 *TwCBDA*

Dod, Daniel 1778-1823 *DcAmB, NatCAB 24*

Dod, Daniel 1788-1823 *ApCAB, WhAm H*

Dod, Thaddeus 1740-1793 *ApCAB, BiDAmEd, DcAmB, NatCAB 7, TwCBDA*

Dod, Thaddeus 1741-1793 *WhAm H*

Dodart, Denis 1634-1707 *DcScB*

Dodd, Alvin Earl 1883-1951 *WhAm 3*

Dodd, Amzi 1823-1913 *NatCAB 2, TwCBDA, WhAm 1*

Dodd, Anna Bowman d1929 *AmWom, WhAm 2*

Dodd, Charles Harold 1884-1973 *WhAm 6*

Dodd, Charles Hastings 1859-1933 *WhAm 1*

Dodd, Cyrus Morris 1826-1897 *TwCBDA*

Dodd, David Rollin 1889-1967 *NatCAB 54*

Dodd, Edward 1805-1891 *BiAUS, BiDrAC, TwCBDA, WhAm H*

Dodd, Edward Howard 1869-1965 *WhAm 4*

Dodd, Edward Mills 1824-1865 *ApCAB*

Dodd, Edwin Merrick 1888-1951 *WhAm 3*

Dodd, Francis Joseph 1888-1962 *WhAm 4*

Dodd, Frank Courtenay 1875-1968 *WhAm 4A*

Dodd, Frank Howard 1844-1916 *DcAmB, WhAm 1*

Dodd, George Allan 1852-1925 *WhAm 1*

Dodd, Helen Chamberlin 1874- *WomWWA 14*

Dodd, Henry Martyn 1839-1920 *WhAm 1*

Dodd, Ira Seymour 1842- *WhAm 4*

Dodd, James B 1807-1872 *ApCAB, Drake, NatCAB 24*

Dodd, Jno Horace 1880- *WhoColR*

Dodd, John Edward 1887-1958 *NatCAB 47*

Dodd, John Morris 1866-1950 *WhAm 3*

Dodd, Katharine 1892-1965 *NatCAB 53*

Dodd, Lee Wilson 1879-1933 *DcAmB S1, NatCAB 40, WhAm 1*

Dodd, Mary Ann Hanmer 1813- *ApCAB, Drake*

Dodd, Monroe Elmon 1878-1952 *DcAmB S5, NatCAB 40, WhAm 3*

Dodd, Moses Woodruff 1813-1899 *TwCBDA*

Dodd, Norris Edward 1879-1968 *NatCAB 54, WhAm 5*

Dodd, Samuel 1797-1862 *NewYHSD*

Dodd, Samuel C T 1836-1907 *WhAm 1*

Dodd, Samuel Calvin Tait 1836-1907 *NatCAB 24*

Dodd, Samuel Calvin Tate 1836-1907 *DcAmB*

Dodd, Samuel Morris 1832-1912 *NatCAB 8, NatCAB 12*

Dodd, Stephen 1777-1856 *ApCAB*

Dodd, Thomas Joseph 1907-1971 *BiDrAC, WhAm 5, WhAmP*

Dodd, Verne Adams 1881-1957 *NatCAB 46, WhAm 6*

Dodd, Walter Fairleigh 1880-1960 *WhAm 4*

Dodd, Walter James 1869-1916 *NatCAB 17*

Dodd, William Clifton 1857-1919 *WhAm 1*

Dodd, William Edward 1869-1940 *DcAmB S2, NatCAB 38, WhAm 1*

Dodd, William George 1874-1963 *WhAm 4*

Dodd, William H C *NewYHSD*

Dodd, William Henry *NewYHSD*

Dodd, Wilson Farnsworth 1893-1958 *NatCAB 48*

Doddridge, Joseph 1769-1826 *ApCAB, DcAmB, WhAm H*

Doddridge, Philip 1772-1832 *ApCAB, BiAUS,*

NatCAB 2, TwCBDA, WhAm H

Doddridge, Philip 1773-1832 *BiDrAC, DcAmB, WhAmP*

Doddridge, William Brown 1848- *NatCAB 6, WhAm 4*

Doddrige, Joseph 1769-1826 *Drake*

Doddrige, Philip 1772-1832 *Drake*

Dodds, Alexander 1874-1920 *WhAm 1*

Dodds, B L 1903-1959 *WhAm 3*

Dodds, Chauncey Y 1892-1952 *WhAm 3*

Dodds, Eugene Maxwell 1892-1960 *WhAm 4*

Dodds, Francis Henry 1858-1940 *BiDrAC, WhAm 4*

Dodds, George William 1864-1947 *WhAm 2*

Dodds, Harold Willis 1889- *BiDAmEd*

Dodds, Ozro John 1840-1882 *BiAUS, BiDrAC, TwCBDA, WhAm H*

Dodds, Robert J 1877- *WhAm 5*

Dodds, Samuel 1858-1940 *WhAm 2*

Dodds, Susanna Way 1830- *AmWom*

Dodds, Warren 1898-1959 *WhAm 4*

DoDesterro, Antonio Reimas 1694-1773 *ApCAB*

Dodge, Arta Snyder 1852- *WomWWA 14*

Dodge, Arthur Farwell 1882-1960 *NatCAB 47*

Dodge, Arthur Murray 1852-1896 *NatCAB 15*

Dodge, Augustus C 1812-1883 *BiAUS*

Dodge, Augustus Caesar 1812-1883 *ApCAB, BiDrAC, DcAmB, TwCBDA, WhAmP*

Dodge, Augustus Ceasar 1812-1883 *WhAm H*

Dodge, Augustus Chester 1812-1883 *NatCAB 12*

Dodge, Aydee *IlBEAAW*

Dodge, Barnett Fred 1895-1972 *WhAm 5*

Dodge, Bayard 1888-1972 *NatCAB 57, WhAm 5*

Dodge, Bernard Ogilvie 1872-1960 *WhAm 4*

Dodge, C *NewYHSD*

Dodge, Caroline Louise 1866- *WomWWA 14*

Dodge, Charles Cleveland 1841- *ApCAB*

Dodge, Charles J 1806-1886 *NewYHSD*

Dodge, Charles Richards 1847- *WhAm 1*

Dodge, Charles Stuart 1864-1948 *NatCAB 38*

Dodge, Charles Wright 1863-1934 *WhAm 1*

Dodge, Clarence 1881-1964 *NatCAB 52*

Dodge, Clarence Phelps 1877-1939 *NatCAB 30, WhAm 1*

Dodge, Clayton Thomas Joseph 1890-1962 *NatCAB 51*

Dodge, Cleveland Hoadley 1860-1926 *NatCAB 26, WhAm 1*

Dodge, Daniel Kilham 1863-1933 *WhAm 1*

Dodge, David Child 1837-1918 *WhAm 1*

Dodge, David Low 1774-1852 *AmBi, ApCAB, DcAmB, NatCAB 20, WhAm H*

Dodge, David Stuart 1836-1921 *WhAm 1*

Dodge, Ebenezer 1819-1890 *ApCAB, BiDAmEd, DcAmB, NatCAB 5, TwCBDA, WhAm H*

Dodge, Edward Samuel 1816-1857 *NewYHSD*

Dodge, Edward Sherman 1852-1934 *NatCAB 26*

Dodge, Estelle Riddle 1880- *WomWWA 14*

Dodge, Etta Purinton *WomWWA 14*

Dodge, Francis Safford 1842-1908 *NatCAB 18, WhAm 1*

Dodge, Frederic 1847-1927 *NatCAB 22, WhAm 1*

Dodge, George Edward Payson 1839-1904 *NatCAB 14*

Dodge, Grace Hoadley 1856-1914 *AmBi, AmWom, ApCAB, ApCAB X, BiDAmEd, DcAmB, NatCAB 18, NotAW, WhAm 1, WomWWA 14*

Dodge, Grenville M 1831-1916 *BiAUS, Drake*

Dodge, Grenville Mellen 1831-1916 *ApCAB, BiDrAC, DcAmB, EncAAH, EncAB, NatCAB 11, NatCAB 16, REnAW, TwCBDA, WebAB, WebAMB, WhAm 1*

Dodge, Grenville Melton 1831-1916 *AmBi*

Dodge, Hannah P 1821- *AmWom*

Dodge, Harris T d1960 *WhAm 4*

Dodge, Henry 1782-1867 *AmBi, ApCAB, BiAUS, BiDrAC, DcAmB, Drake, NatCAB 3, NatCAB 12, REnAW, TwCBDA, WebAMB, WhAm H, WhAmP*

Dodge, Henry Chee 1860-1947 *DcAmB S4*

Dodge, Henry Irving 1861-1934 *WhAm 1*

Dodge, Henry Lee 1825- *ApCAB Sup*
Dodge, Henry Nehemiah 1843-1937 *NatCAB 28, WhAm 4*
Dodge, Henry Percival 1870-1936 *NatCAB 14, NatCAB 41, WhAm 1*
Dodge, Horace Elgin 1868-1920 *NatCAB 19*
Dodge, Jacob Richards 1823-1902 *DcAmB, WhAm 1*
Dodge, James Mapes 1852-1915 *ApCAB X, NatCAB 12, NatCAB 29, WhAm 1*
Dodge, Jeremiah 1781-1860 *NewYHSD, WhAm H*
Dodge, John Francis 1864-1920 *NatCAB 19*
Dodge, John Henry 1828-1863 *ApCAB*
Dodge, John Lanphere 1865-1940 *NatCAB 30*
Dodge, John Wood 1807-1893 *NewYHSD, WhAm H*
Dodge, Jonathan Sherman 1867-1935 *NatCAB 27*
Dodge, Joseph Morrell 1890-1964 *NatCAB 52, WhAm 4*
Dodge, Joseph Thompson 1833- *NatCAB 17*
Dodge, Josephine Marshall Jewell 1855-1928 *NotAW, WhAm 1, WomWWA 14*
Dodge, Joshua Eric 1854-1921 *TwCBDA, WhAm 1*
Dodge, Kern 1880-1958 *NatCAB 48, WhAm 6*
Dodge, Leon Alfred 1891-1958 *NatCAB 47*
Dodge, Lillian Sefton 1879-1960 *NatCAB 47*
Dodge, Louis 1870- *WhAm 5*
Dodge, M Hartley 1881-1963 *WhAm 4*
Dodge, Martha Miller 1859- *WomWWA 14*
Dodge, Martin 1851-1931 *NatCAB 22, WhAm 3*
Dodge, Martin 1892-1957 *WhAm 3*
Dodge, Mary Abby 1833-1896 *NatCAB 9, TwCBDA*
Dodge, Mary Abigail 1830-1896 *AmWom, ApCAB*
Dodge, Mary Abigail 1833-1896 *AmBi, DcAmB, NotAW, WhAm H*
Dodge, Mary Abigail 1838?-1896 *Drake*
Dodge, Mary Elizabeth Mapes 1831-1905 *AmBi, DcAmB, NotAW, WebAB*
Dodge, Mary Mapes d1905 *WhAm 1*
Dodge, Mary Mapes 1838-1905 *AmWom, ApCAB, NatCAB 1, TwCBDA*
Dodge, Melvin Gilbert 1868-1953 *TwCBDA, WhAm 3*
Dodge, Murray Witherbee 1878-1937 *NatCAB 30, WhAm 1*
Dodge, Nathan Phillips 1872-1950 *NatCAB 39, WhAm 3*
Dodge, Nathaniel Shatswell 1810-1874 *ApCAB*
Dodge, Nathaniel Shattswell 1810-1874 *NatCAB 11*
Dodge, Omenzo George 1856- *WhAm 4*
Dodge, Ossian Euclid 1820-1876 *ApCAB, NatCAB 4*
Dodge, Pauline Morgan 1893-1971 *NatCAB 56*
Dodge, Philip Tell 1851-1931 *NatCAB 24, WhAm 1*
Dodge, R E Neil 1867-1935 *WhAm 1*
Dodge, Raymond 1871-1942 *DcAmB S3, NatCAB 32, WhAm 2*
Dodge, Raynal 1844- *WhAm 4*
Dodge, Regina Lunt 1879- *WomWWA 14*
Dodge, Richard Elwood 1868-1952 *BiDAmEd, NatCAB 13, WhAm 3*
Dodge, Richard Irving 1827-1895 *ApCAB, NatCAB 11, TwCBDA*
Dodge, Robert 1820-1899 *TwCBDA*
Dodge, Robert Gray 1872-1964 *NatCAB 50, WhAm 4*
Dodge, Robert Perley 1817-1887 *ApCAB Sup*
Dodge, Ruby Porter Bridgman 1872- *WomWWA 14*
Dodge, Russell Alger 1893-1972 *NatCAB 57*
Dodge, Samuel *NewYHSD*
Dodge, Sherwood 1915-1968 *NatCAB 54, WhAm 5*
Dodge, Stanley Dalton 1897-1966 *NatCAB 54*
Dodge, Theodore Ayrault 1842-1909 *AmBi, ApCAB, DcAmB, TwCBDA, WhAm 1*
Dodge, Thomas Hutchins 1823-1910 *NatCAB 2*
Dodge, Walter Phelps 1869-1931 *NatCAB 11, NatCAB 29, WhAm 5*

Dodge, William DeLeftwich 1867-1935 *AmBi, DcAmB S1, IIBEAAW, NatCAB 38, WhAm 1*
Dodge, William Earl 1805-1883 *AmBi, ApCAB, BiAUS, DcAmB, NatCAB 1, NatCAB 3, TwCBDA, WhAm H*
Dodge, William Earl 1832-1903 *ApCAB, NatCAB 13, WhAm 1*
Dodge, William Earle 1805-1883 *BiDrAC*
Dodge, Willis Edward 1857- *WhAm 4*
Dodgson, Charles Lutwidge 1832-1898 *DcScB*
Dodoens, Rembert 1516-1585 *DcScB*
Dods, John Boree 1795-1872 *NatCAB 3*
Dods, John Bovee 1795-1872 *ApCAB, DcAmB, Drake, WhAm H*
Dodshon, Joseph Henry 1868-1948 *WhAm 2*
Dodson, Caroline Matilda 1845- *AmWom*
Dodson, Edwin Moseley 1882-1958 *NatCAB 47*
Dodson, George Rowland 1865-1939 *NatCAB 42, WhAm 1*
Dodson, Harry Lea *WhAm 3*
Dodson, John E d1931 *WhAm 1*
Dodson, John Milton 1859-1933 *WhAm 1*
Dodson, Loren Ralph 1897-1972 *WhAm 5*
Dodson, Louise M 1865- *WomWWA 14*
Dodson, Martha Ethel 1881- *WhAm 5, WomWWA 14*
Dodson, Nathaniel Barnett 1870- *WhoColR*
Dodson, Richard W 1812-1867 *NewYHSD*
Dodworth, Harvey B 1822-1891 *TwCBDA*
Dodworth, Thomas 1790-1876 *ApCAB*
Doe, Charles 1830-1896 *DcAmB, NatCAB 12, WhAm H*
Doe, Charles Henry 1838-1900 *ApCAB, TwCBDA*
Doe, Edward M 1850- *WhAm 1*
Doe, John *NewYHSD*
Doe, Joseph Bodwell 1855- *TwCBDA, WhAm 4*
Doe, Mary Lydia 1836- *AmWom, WomWWA 14*
Doe, Nicholas Bartlett 1786-1856 *BiAUS, BiDrAC, WhAm H*
Doe, Thomas Bartwell 1883-1966 *WhAm 4*
Doebler, Adeline Madeira 1858- *WomWWA 14*
Doehring, Carl Frederic 1903-1965 *NatCAB 51*
Doelter, Cornelio August Severinus 1850-1930 *DcScB*
D'Oench, Albert Frederick 1852-1918 *NatCAB 27*
Doenitz, Karl 1891- *WhWW-II*
Doepler, Carl Emil 1824-1905 *NewYHSD*
Doerfler, Christian 1862-1934 *WhAm 1*
Doerflinger, Charles Hermann 1843-1911 *WhAm 1*
Doerflinger, Jon Arno 1924-1973 *WhAm 6*
Doerhoefer, Basil 1850-1923 *NatCAB 30*
Doering, Edmund Janes 1854-1943 *NatCAB 16, WhAm 2*
Doering, Walter Charles 1886-1940 *NatCAB 31*
Doermann, Henry John 1890-1932 *NatCAB 25, WhAm 1*
Doern, William George 1878-1946 *NatCAB 39*
Doerner, Celia *WomWWA 14*
Doerr, George Valentine 1884-1967 *NatCAB 53*
Doerr, John Edward 1901-1964 *WhAm 4*
Doersam, Charles Henry 1878-1942 *WhAm 2*
Doerschuk, Anna Beatrice 1879-1974 *WhAm 6*
Doesburg, Theo Van 1883-1931 *McGEWB*
Doescher, Waldemar Oswald 1896-1967 *WhAm 4*
Doetsch, James F 1899-1967 *WhAm 4A*
Doflein, Philip *NewYHSD*
Dogan, Matthew Winfred 1863-1947 *WhAm 2, WhoColR*
Dogel, Valentin Alexandrovich 1882-1955 *DcScB*
Doggett, Andrew Capers 1852-1916 *NatCAB 34*
Doggett, Daniel Seth 1810-1880 *ApCAB, TwCBDA*
Doggett, John Locke 1868-1937 *ApCAB X, NatCAB 11, WhAm 1*
Doggett, Kate 1828-1884 *ApCAB*
Doggett, Laurence Locke 1864-1957 *WhAm 3*
Doggett, Simeon 1765-1852 *ApCAB*
Dogliotti, Achille Mario 1897-1966 *WhAm 4*
Dognaux, Rene Jean 1892-1965 *NatCAB 51*
Dohan, Edith Hayward Hall 1877-1943 *NotAW*

Dohan, Edward G 1870- *WhAm 5*
Doheny, Edward Laurence 1856-1935 *DcAmB S1, NatCAB 29, WhAm 1, WhAmP*
Doherty *NewYHSD*
Doherty, Edward J 1890-1975 *WhAm 6*
Doherty, Henry 1850-1915 *NatCAB 15*
Doherty, Henry Latham 1865-1921 *ApCAB X*
Doherty, Henry Latham 1870-1939 *AmBi, DcAmB S2, NatCAB 34, WebAB, WhAm 1*
Doherty, James L 1865-1921 *ApCAB X*
Doherty, Patrick 1838-1872 *ApCAB*
Doherty, Philip Joseph 1856-1928 *WhAm 1*
Doherty, Robert Ernest 1885-1950 *NatCAB 38, WhAm 3*
Doherty, Robert Remington 1848- *WhAm 4*
Dohme, Alfred Robert Louis 1867-1952 *NatCAB 41, WhAm 5*
Dohme, Charles Emil 1843-1911 *NatCAB 23*
Dohme, Louis 1837-1910 *NatCAB 28*
Dohnanyi, Erno 1877- *WhAm 5*
Dohr, James Lewis 1892-1961 *NatCAB 49*
Dohrn, Felix Anton 1840-1909 *DcScB Sup*
Dohse, John 1857-1902 *NatCAB 14*
Doidge, Frederick Widdowson 1884-1954 *WhAm 3*
Doig, Andrew Wheeler 1799-1875 *BiAUS, BiDrAC, WhAm H*
Doig, George *NewYHSD*
Doig, James Rufus 1903-1969 *WhAm 5*
Doig, Thomas W 1896-1955 *WhAm 3*
Doig, William Spencer 1849-1900 *ApCAB X*
Doing, Mahlon B 1894-1960 *WhAm 4*
Doissin, Louis 1721-1753 *ApCAB*
Doisy, Edward Adelbert 1893- *AsBiEn, WebAB*
Dokmo, Rolf Eugene 1904-1961 *NatCAB 49*
Dokuchaev, Vasily Vasilievich 1846-1903 *DcScB*
Dolak, Michael Charles 1891-1955 *WhAm 3*
Dolan, Arthur W 1876-1949 *NatCAB 2*
Dolan, Daniel Leo 1895-1966 *WhAm 4*
Dolan, Elizabeth Honor 1884-1948 *WhAm 3*
Dolan, Francis James 1893-1939 *WhAm 1*
Dolan, George W 1902-1948 *WhAm 2*
Dolan, James Edward 1864- *WhAm 4*
Dolan, Margaret Baggett 1914-1974 *WhAm 6*
Dolan, Robert Emmett 1908-1972 *WhAm 5*
Dolan, Rosalie Brown 1869- *WomWWA 14*
Dolan, Thomas *NewYHSD*
Dolan, Thomas 1834-1914 *DcAmB, NatCAB 2, WhAm 1*
Dolan, Tom 1912-1969 *WhAm 5*
Dolan, William Edward 1879-1952 *NatCAB 39*
Dolan, William Henry 1903-1968 *NatCAB 55*
Doland, James Joseph 1890-1960 *NatCAB 48, WhAm 4*
Dolanowski, Rudolph *NewYHSD*
Dolbear, Amos Emerson 1837-1910 *ApCAB, NatCAB 9, TwCBDA, WhAm 1*
Dolbeare, Harris Mason 1870-1938 *NatCAB 28*
Dolcho, Frederick 1770-1836 *WhAm H*
Dold, Jacob 1825-1909 *DcAmB*
Dold, Jacob Cyrus 1857-1924 *ApCAB X, NatCAB 21, WhAm 1*
Dole, Arthur, Jr. 1894-1972 *WhAm 5*
Dole, Caroline Fletcher 1817- *WomWWA 14*
Dole, Charles 1843- *NatCAB 18*
Dole, Charles Fletcher 1845-1927 *DcAmB, NatCAB 20, WhAm 1*
Dole, Charles Thurston 1869-1957 *NatCAB 49*
Dole, Edmund Pearson 1850-1928 *WhAm 1*
Dole, George Henry 1857-1942 *NatCAB 32*
Dole, Grace Weld Soper 1859- *WomWWA 14*
Dole, Helen James Bennett d1944 *WhAm 2, WomWWA 14*
Dole, James Drummond 1877-1958 *WhAm 3*
Dole, John Newton 1847-1931 *NatCAB 28*
Dole, Margaret Femald d1970 *WhAm 5*
Dole, Margaret Fernald 1896-1970 *NatCAB 56*
Dole, Nathan Haskell 1852-1935 *AmBi, ApCAB X, DcAmB S1, NatCAB 13, TwCBDA, WhAm 1*
Dole, Phebe Cobb Larry 1835- *AmWom*
Dole, Robert Joseph 1923- *BiDrAC*
Dole, Sanford Ballard 1844-1926 *AmBi, ApCAB Sup, ApCAB X, DcAmB, EncAB, McGEWB, NatCAB 12,*

TwCBDA, WebAB, WhAm 1, WhAmP
Dole, William P *BiAUS*
Doles, George E d1864 *Drake*
Doles, George Pierce 1830-1864 *ApCAB,
BiDConf, NatCAB 5*
Dolge, Alfred 1848-1922 *NatCAB 1, WhAm 1*
D'Olier, Franklin 1877-1953 *DcAmB S5,
NatCAB 50, WhAm 3*
Dolkart, Leo 1881-1966 *WhAm 4*
Doll, Alfred W 1903-1957 *WhAm 3*
Doll, Charles W *NewYHSD*
Doll, Frederick W *NewYHSD*
Doll, Jacob 1849-1911 *NatCAB 16*
Doll, William DeBerge 1897-1945 *WhAm 2*
Dollar, Dougal MacGregor 1892-1957
NatCAB 47
Dollar, R Stanley 1880-1958 *WhAm 3*
Dollar, Robert 1844-1932 *DcAmB S1,
NatCAB 37, WhAm 1*
Dollard, Paul M 1904-1965 *WhAm 4*
Dollard, Robert 1842-1915 *NatCAB 17*
Dollard, Stewart Edward 1905-1975 *WhAm 6*
Dollard, William d1851 *WhAm H*
Dollens, Burl Austin 1901-1952 *WhAm 3*
Dolley, Charles Sumner 1856- *WhAm 4*
Dolley, David Hough 1878-1927 *WhAm 1*
Dolley, Sarah Read Adamson 1829-1909
NotAW
Dollfuss, Engelbert 1892-1934 *McGEWB*
Dollier DeCasson, Francois 1630?- *ApCAB*
Dollinger, Ignaz 1770-1841 *DcScB*
Dollinger, Isidore 1903- *BiDrAC*
Dollinger, Johannes Josef Ignaz Von 1799-1890
McGEWB
Dolliver, George Benton 1880- *WhAm 6*
Dolliver, James Isaac 1894- *BiDrAC*
Dolliver, Jonathan Prentiss 1858-1910
*ApCAB X, BiDrAC, DcAmB, EncAAH,
NatCAB 12, TwCBDA, WhAm 1,
WhAmP*
Dolliver, Louise Pearsons *WomWWA 14*
Dolliver, Margaret Gay 1864- *WhAm 4,
WomWWA 14*
Dollo, Louis Antoine Marie Joseph 1857-1931
DcScB
Dolloff, David Ernest 1878-1948 *NatCAB 38*
Dollond, John 1706-1761 *AsBiEn, DcScB*
Dolman, John, Jr. 1888-1952 *WhAm 3*
Dolomieu, Dieudonne DeGratet De 1750-1801
DcScB
Dolowitz, Francis Marie Fleisher 1913-
WhAm 6
Dolph, Cyrus Abda 1840-1914 *NatCAB 16*
Dolph, John Henry 1835-1903 *ApCAB,
NatCAB 10, NewYHSD, TwCBDA,
WhAm 1*
Dolph, Joseph Norton 1835-1897 *ApCAB,
BiDrAC, DcAmB, NatCAB 1, TwCBDA,
WhAm H, WhAmP*
Dolphy, Eric Allan 1928-1964 *WhAm 4*
Dolsen, Torrey Lewis *WomWWA 14*
Domagk, Gerhard Johannes Paul 1895-1964
AsBiEn, DcScB, McGEWB, WhAm 4
Dombey, Joseph 1742-1793 *Drake*
Dombey, Joseph 1742-1794 *ApCAB, DcScB*
Dombroff, Joseph George 1896-1955
NatCAB 43
Dombrowski, Joseph 1842-1903 *DcAmB*
Dome, Lillian 1859- *NatCAB 9*
Domenec, Michael 1816-1878 *NatCAB 6,
TwCBDA, WhAm H*
Domenech, Emmanuel Henry Dieudonne
1825-1886 *ApCAB*
Domenech, Miguel 1816-1878 *ApCAB*
Domengeaux, James 1907- *BiDrAC*
Domenico Veneziano 1410?-1461 *McGEWB*
Domeratzky, Louis 1881- *WhAm 6*
Domers, Henry Russell 1905-1972 *WhAm 5*
Domeyko, Ignaz 1802-1889 *ApCAB Sup*
Domingo DeSoto *DcScB*
Dominian, Leon 1880-1935 *NatCAB 25,
WhAm 1*
Dominic Gundissalinus *DcScB*
Dominic, Saint 1170?-1221 *McGEWB*
Dominici, Santos Anibal 1869- *WhAm 5*
Dominick, Bayard 1873-1941 *NatCAB 41*
Dominick, Frank 1885-1937 *WhAm 1*
Dominick, Frederick Haskell 1877-1960 *BiDrAC,*

WhAm 5, WhAmP
Dominick, Gayer Gardner 1887-1961
NatCAB 50, WhAm 4
Dominick, James Robert 1863- *WhAm 5*
Dominick, Peter Hoyt 1915- *BiDrAC*
Dominick, Robert Lyon 1891-1965 *NatCAB 51*
Dominick, William Gayer 1845-1895
NatCAB 16
Dominicus DeClavasio *DcScB*
Dominis, Marko Antonije 1560-1626 *DcScB*
Domitian 051-096 *McGEWB*
Domninus Of Larissa *DcScB*
Domonoske, Arthur B 1884-1975 *WhAm 6*
Domville, James 1842- *ApCAB*
Don Carlos, Harlan Silcott 1890-1974
NatCAB 57
Don Carlos, Louisa Cooke *WomWWA 14*
Donaghey, Frederick d1937 *WhAm 1*
Donaghey, George W 1856-1937 *WhAm 1*
Donaghy, John 1838-1931 *NewYHSD*
Donaghy, William Andrew 1909-1975 *WhAm 6*
Donahey, Alvin Victor 1873-1946 *BiDrAC,
WhAmP*
Donahey, James Harrison 1875-1949 *WhAm 2*
Donahey, John William 1905-1967 *WhAm 4*
Donahey, Mary Dickerson 1876-1962
NatCAB 46, WhAm 4
Donahey, Vic 1873-1946 *NatCAB 44,
WhAm 2*
Donahoe, Daniel Joseph 1853-1930 *WhAm 1*
Donahoe, John Patrick 1875-1951 *NatCAB 42*
Donahoe, Patrick 1810-1901 *TwCBDA*
Donahoe, Patrick 1811-1901 *DcAmB,
NatCAB 13, WhAm H*
Donahue, Charles 1912-1972 *WhAm 5*
Donahue, Charles Henry 1877- *WhAm 5*
Donahue, John Bartholomew 1900-1970
WhAm 5
Donahue, Joseph Michael 1907-1963 *WhAm 4*
Donahue, Joseph P d1959 *WhAm 3*
Donahue, Maurice Herbert 1864-1928
NatCAB 28, WhAm 1
Donahue, Patrick James 1849-1922 *NatCAB 12,
WhAm 1*
Donahue, Patrick John 1861-1916 *NatCAB 17*
Donahue, Patrick Joseph 1849- *TwCBDA*
Donahue, Peter 1822-1885 *DcAmB, NatCAB 7,
WhAm H*
Donahue, Thomas Leo 1897-1959 *NatCAB 47*
Donahue, Vic 1917- *IIBEAAW*
Donald, David 1920- *EncAAH*
Donald, George H 1876- *WhAm 5*
Donald, James Mackie 1854-1918 *NatCAB 20*
Donald, Joseph Marion 1903-1961 *WhAm 4*
Donald, Malcolm 1877-1949 *NatCAB 37*
Donald, Norman Henderson 1881-1966
WhAm 4
Donald, William Goodricke 1889-1957 *WhAm 3*
Donald, William John Alexander 1890-1962
WhAm 4
Donaldson, Albert Eeeley 1876- *WhAm 6*
Donaldson, Alfred Lee 1866-1923 *NatCAB 20*
Donaldson, Allyn Capron 1898-1974 *WhAm 6*
Donaldson, Augustine 1843?- *NewYHSD*
Donaldson, Charles M 1879- *WhAm 6*
Donaldson, David L 1809?- *NewYHSD*
Donaldson, Eben Grantly 1887-1956
NatCAB 48
Donaldson, Edward 1816-1889 *ApCAB,
NatCAB 4, TwCBDA*
Donaldson, Edwards 1816-1889 *Drake*
Donaldson, Francis 1823-1891 *TwCBDA*
Donaldson, Frank 1823-1891 *ApCAB*
Donaldson, Fred Kermit 1901-1967 *WhAm 4A*
Donaldson, Henry Herbert 1857-1938
*DcAmB S2, DcScB, NatCAB 11,
NatCAB 28, WhAm 1*
Donaldson, Holland Hunter 1876-1961
NatCAB 49
Donaldson, J A 1894-1973 *WhAm 5*
Donaldson, James Lowry 1814-1885 *ApCAB,
NatCAB 11, TwCBDA*
Donaldson, James Oswell 1876-1929
NatCAB 22
Donaldson, James Rider 1920-1972 *WhAm 6*
Donaldson, Jesse Monroe 1885-1970 *BiDrUSE,
WhAm 5*
Donaldson, John 1892-1955 *NatCAB 42,*

WhAm 3
Donaldson, John Isaiah 1866- *WhoColR*
Donaldson, John McNaughton 1854-1941
NatCAB 39, WhAm 1
Donaldson, John Owen 1898-1930 *NatCAB 24*
Donaldson, Kenneth Hume 1888-1953 *WhAm 3*
Donaldson, McPherrin Hatfield 1889-1945
NatCAB 34
Donaldson, Norman Vaux 1891-1964 *WhAm 4*
Donaldson, Robert Golden 1876-1940 *WhAm 1*
Donaldson, Samuel Wright 1891-1961
NatCAB 48
Donaldson, Sidnor 1813?- *NewYHSD*
Donaldson, Thomas 1866-1950 *NatCAB 39*
Donaldson, Thomas Corwin 1843-1898
ApCAB Sup, REnAW, TwCBDA
Donaldson, Thomas Quint 1864-1934 *WhAm 1*
Donaldson, Thomas Quinton 1864-1934
NatCAB 24
Donaldson, Walter Foster 1873-1957
NatCAB 53, WhAm 6
Donaldson, Walter Joseph 1893-1947
NatCAB 38
Donaldson, Washington H 1840-1875 *ApCAB*
Donaldson, Welyn Hunter 1886-
WomWWA 14
Donaldson, William Jay 1880-1956 *NatCAB 48*
Donaldson, William Raymond 1893-1967
WhAm 4
Donalson, Erle Meldrim 1878- *WhAm 6*
Donalson, John Ernest 1846-1920 *WhAm 1*
Donat, Robert 1905-1958 *WhAm 3*
Donatello 1386-1466 *McGEWB*
Donati, Giovan Battista 1826-1873 *DcScB*
Donati, Giovanni Battista 1826-1873 *AsBiEn*
Donati, Pine 1907-1975 *WhAm 6*
Donato, Giuseppe d1965 *WhAm 4*
Donatto, Dewey Benjamin *WhoColR*
Donatus d355? *McGEWB*
Donchian, Paul Samuel 1895-1967 *NatCAB 53*
Donck, Adriaen VanDer 1620-1655 *DcAmB*
Dondanville, Laurence Aloysius 1892-1960
NatCAB 49
Donde Ibarra, Joaquin 1827-1875 *ApCAB*
Dondero, George Anthony 1883-1968 *BiDrAC,
WhAm 5*
Dondero, John Anthony 1900-1957 *NatCAB 46*
Donders, Franciscus Cornelis 1818-1889 *DcScB*
Dondi, Giovanni 1318-1389 *DcScB*
Dondlinger, Peter Tracy 1877-1954 *NatCAB 43,
WhAm 3*
Dondo, Mathurin 1884-1968 *WhAm 5*
Dondore, Dorothy Anne 1894-1946 *WhAm 2*
Donegan, C Henry 1876-1965 *NatCAB 51*
Donegan, Edmund Joseph 1888-1959 *WhAm 3*
Donegan, Harold Hand 1905-1967 *WhAm 4*
Donegan, Maurice Francis 1875-1950
NatCAB 38, WhAm 3
Donehoo, George Patterson 1862-1934 *WhAm 1*
Donehue, Francis McGarvey 1895-1973
WhAm 6
Donehue, Vincent Julian 1922-1966 *WhAm 4*
Donelson, Andrew Jackson 1799-1871 *AmBi,
BiAUS, DcAmB, Drake, WhAm H,
WhAmP*
Donelson, Andrew Jackson 1800-1871 *ApCAB,
NatCAB 7, TwCBDA*
Donelson, Daniel Smith 1801-1863 *BiDConf*
Dones, Sidney Preston 1889- *WhoColR*
Doney, Carl Gregg 1867-1955 *WhAm 3*
Doney, Thomas *NewYHSD*
Dongan, Thomas 1634-1715 *AmBi, ApCAB,
DcAmB, NatCAB 10, TwCBDA,
WhAm H, WhAmP*
Donges, Ralph Waldo Emerson 1875- *WhAm 5*
Donges, Theophilus Ebenaezer 1898-1968
WhAm 4A
Donham, C R 1898-1956 *WhAm 3*
Donham, Harold Gregory 1875-1946 *WhAm 2*
Donham, Wallace Brett 1877-1954 *WhAm 3*
Donhauser, J Lewi 1883-1964 *NatCAB 54,
WhAm 4*
Doniger, William 1908-1972 *WhAm 5*
Doniphan, Alexander William 1808-1887 *AmBi,
ApCAB, DcAmB, Drake Sup,
NatCAB 11, REnAW, TwCBDA,
WebAMB, WhAm H*

Donitz, Karl 1891- *WhoMilH*

Donizetti, Gaetano 1797-1848 *McGEWB*
Donkin, McKay 1904-1968 *WhAm 5*
Donkin, Robert 1727-1821 *ApCAB, Drake*
Donkin, Wilfred Thomas 1899-1962
 NatCAB 49
Donlevy, Alice Heighes 1846-1929 *AmWom,
 WhAm 1, WomWWA 14*
Donlevy, Harriet Farley 1817-1907 *DcAmB,
 NotAW, WhAm 1*
Donley, Angeline Scott *WomWWA 14*
Donley, Charles Sherman d1964 *WhAm 4*
Donley, Joseph Benton 1838-1917 *BiAUS,
 BiDrAC*
Donley, Nellie Wells *WomWWA 14*
Donley, William Henry 1863-1929 *WhAm 1*
Donlin, Thomas Alvin 1891-1966 *NatCAB 53*
Donlon, Alphonsus John 1867-1923 *WhAm 1*
Donn, Edward Wilton, Jr. 1868-1953
 NatCAB 40, WhAm 3
Donn-Byrne, Brian Oswald Patrick 1889-1928
 AmBi, DcAmB, NatCAB 22
Donnally, Harry Hampton 1877-1947
 NatCAB 36
Donnan, Elizabeth d1955 *WhAm 3*
Donnan, Frederick George 1870-1956 *DcScB*
Donnan, William G 1834-1908 *BiAUS,
 BiDrAC, TwCBDA*
Donnavan, C *NewYHSD*
Donne, John 1572-1631 *McGEWB*
Donnell, Annie Hamilton 1862-1943 *WhAm 3,
 WomWWA 14*
Donnell, Ben Dobyns 1881-1952 *WhAm 3*
Donnell, Clyde 1890-1971 *NatCAB 57*
Donnell, Forrest C 1884- *BiDrAC*
Donnell, Harold Eugene 1887-1966 *WhAm 4*
Donnell, James C 1854-1927 *DcAmB,
 NatCAB 24*
Donnell, James J 1840-1918 *WhAm 1*
Donnell, John R *BiAUS*
Donnell, Otto Dewey 1883-1961 *NatCAB 51,
 WhAm 4*
Donnell, Philip Stone 1889-1962 *WhAm 4*
Donnell, Richard Spaight 1820-1867 *BiAUS,
 BiDrAC, WhAm H*
Donnell, Robert 1784-1855 *DcAmB, WhAm H*
Donnell, S H *NewYHSD*
Donnelley, Elliott 1903-1975 *WhAm 6*
Donnelley, Reuben Hamilton 1864-1929
 NatCAB 22
Donnelley, Richard Robert 1837-1899
 NatCAB 22
Donnelley, Thomas Elliott 1867-1955
 NatCAB 41, WhAm 3
Donnelley, Thorne 1895-1963 *NatCAB 53*
Donnellon, James Augustine 1906-1971
 WhAm 5
Donnelly, Alice Moore *WomWWA 14*
Donnelly, Arthur Barrett 1875-1919 *WhAm 1*
Donnelly, Charles 1869-1939 *NatCAB 39,
 WhAm 1*
Donnelly, Charles Francis 1836-1909 *DcAmB,
 NatCAB 14*
Donnelly, Dorothy Agnes d1928 *WhAm 1*
Donnelly, Edward Calvin 1861-1927 *ApCAB X*
Donnelly, Edward Terence 1871-1929 *WhAm 1*
Donnelly, Eleanor Cecilia d1917 *TwCBDA,
 WhAm 1*
Donnelly, Eleanor Cecilia 1838-1917 *ApCAB,
 DcAmB*
Donnelly, Eleanor Cecilia 1848-1917 *AmWom,
 NatCAB 2*
Donnelly, Elizabeth McAllister 1878-
 WomWWA 14
Donnelly, Frederick William 1866-1935
 WhAm 1
Donnelly, George J d1950 *WhAm 3*
Donnelly, Harold Irvin 1892-1937 *WhAm 1*
Donnelly, Harry 1892-1955 *NatCAB 47*
Donnelly, Henry Edmund 1904- *WhAm 5*
Donnelly, Horace James 1879- *WhAm 6*
Donnelly, Ignatius 1831-1901 *AmBi, ApCAB,
 BiAUS, BiDrAC, DcAmB, EncAAH,
 EncAB, McGEWB, NatCAB 1, REnAW,
 TwCBDA, WebAB, WhAm 1, WhAmP*
Donnelly, James Corcoran 1881-1952
 NatCAB 41
Donnelly, James Ford, Jr. 1914-1966
 NatCAB 53

Donnelly, James Henry 1911-1968 *NatCAB 55*
Donnelly, James L d1972 *WhAm 5*
Donnelly, John C 1850-1924 *WhAm 1*
Donnelly, Joseph Gordon 1856-1915 *WhAm 1*
Donnelly, June Richardson 1872- *WhAm 5,
 WomWWA 14*
Donnelly, Lucy Martin 1870-1948 *NotAW,
 WhAm 2, WomWWA 14*
Donnelly, Phil Matthew 1891-1961 *NatCAB 49,
 WhAm 4*
Donnelly, Richard Carter *WhAm 5*
Donnelly, Samuel Bratton 1866-1946 *WhAm 2*
Donnelly, Simon Peter 1860- *WhAm 4*
Donnelly, T J *NewYHSD*
Donnelly, Thomas Frederick 1863-1924
 WhAm 1
Donnelly, Thomas James 1885-1963 *WhAm 4*
Donnelly, Thomas Ligouri 1905-1956
 NatCAB 46
Donnelly, Walter Joseph 1896-1970 *WhAm 5*
Donnelly, William Henry 1881-1940
 NatCAB 30
Donnelly, William Thomas 1863-1936
 NatCAB 26
Donnelson, J L *NewYHSD*
Donner, Georg Raphael 1693-1741 *McGEWB*
Donner, George 1784-1847 *WhAm H*
Donner, Philip Carl 1872-1945 *NatCAB 34*
Donner, Robert 1891-1964 *NatCAB 51*
Donner, Tamsen *WhAm H*
Donner, William Henry 1864-1953 *NatCAB 44,
 WhAm 3*
Donning, William d1830 *Drake*
Donoghue, John 1853-1903 *DcAmB*
Donoghue, Thomas J 1869- *WhAm 5*
Donoho, Ruger 1857-1916 *WhAm 1*
Donohoe, Denis 1861-1924 *WhAm 1*
Donohoe, James A 1877-1956 *WhAm 3*
Donohoe, Michael 1864-1958 *BiDrAC,
 WhAm 4*
Donohoe, Thomas Joseph 1870-1934 *WhAm 1*
Donohoe, William A d1965 *WhAm 4*
Donohoo, Harriet Grace Nichols 1878-
 WomWWA 14
Donohue, Anthony Joseph 1902-1965
 NatCAB 51
Donohue, Charles 1825-1910 *WhAm 1*
Donohue, Francis Michael 1859-1919 *WhAm 1*
Donohue, Francis Michael 1900-1958
 NatCAB 45
Donohue, Harold Daniel 1901- *BiDrAC*
Donohue, Jerry 1885-1943 *NatCAB 34*
Donohue, Patrick James 1851- *ApCAB Sup*
Donohue, Philip Francis 1895-1953 *NatCAB 40*
Donohue, William Edward 1882-1959
 NatCAB 48
Donohugh, Thomas Smith 1875- *WhAm 5*
Donop, Count d1777 *Drake*
Donop, Carl Emil Kurt Von 1740-1777 *ApCAB*
Donovan, Caroline 1803-1890 *TwCBDA*
Donovan, Cornelius 1850-1922 *NatCAB 15,
 NatCAB 20*
Donovan, Dennis D 1859-1941 *BiDrAC,
 TwCBDA*
Donovan, Edward Francis d1943 *WhAm 2*
Donovan, George Francis 1901-1972 *WhAm 5*
Donovan, Herman Lee 1887-1964 *WhAm 4*
Donovan, Hugh 1872-1949 *NatCAB 38*
Donovan, James Augustine 1889-1955
 NatCAB 43
Donovan, James Britt 1916-1970 *NatCAB 55,
 WhAm 5*
Donovan, James George 1898- *BiDrAC*
Donovan, James J 1909-1968 *WhAm 5*
Donovan, Jeremiah 1853-1935 *NatCAB 27*
Donovan, Jeremiah 1854-1935 *WhAm 1*
Donovan, Jeremiah 1857-1935 *BiDrAC*
Donovan, Jerome Francis 1872-1949 *BiDrAC,
 WhAm 2*
Donovan, John Ambrose 1871-1941 *NatCAB 30*
Donovan, John Joseph 1858-1937 *DcAmB S2,
 NatCAB 16, WhAm 1*
Donovan, John Joseph 1876-1949 *NatCAB 37*
Donovan, Michael R O *NewYHSD*
Donovan, Nellie Bakeman 1870- *WomWWA 14*
Donovan, Richard 1885-1949 *WhAm 2*
Donovan, Richard Joseph 1920?-1971 *WhAm 6*
Donovan, Thomas Leroy 1898-1975 *WhAm 6*

Donovan, Timothy Francis 1884-1936
 NatCAB 26
Donovan, William Francis 1861-1938
 NatCAB 49
Donovan, William Joseph 1883-1959
 *NatCAB 47, WebAB, WebAMB,
 WhAm 3, WhWW-II*
Donovan, Winfred Nichols 1869-1955 *WhAm 4*
Donshea, Clement *IIBEAAW*
Dontenville, Augustin 1857- *ApCAB Sup*
Donworth, George 1861-1947 *ApCAB X,
 NatCAB 5, WhAm 2*
Donworth, Grace d1945 *WhAm 2,
 WomWWA 14*
Doo, Waising 1868-1942 *NatCAB 47*
D'Ooge, Benjamin Leonard 1860-1940
 ApCAB X, WhAm 3
D'Ooge, Martin Luther 1839-1915 *DcAmB,
 NatCAB 12, TwCBDA, WhAm 1*
Doolan, John Calvin 1868-1947 *NatCAB 37,
 WhAm 2*
Doolan, Leonard Weakley 1872-1943 *WhAm 2*
Dooley, Augustine Xavier 1877-1947
 NatCAB 36
Dooley, Channing Rice 1878-1956 *WhAm 3*
Dooley, Edward James 1855-1927 *NatCAB 20*
Dooley, Edwin Benedict 1905- *BiDrAC,
 WhAmP*
Dooley, Harry Joseph 1888-1962 *NatCAB 49*
Dooley, Henry Williamson 1871-1932 *WhAm 1*
Dooley, Joseph Brannon 1889-1967 *WhAm 4*
Dooley, Lucy d1951 *WhAm 3*
Dooley, M S 1879-1958 *WhAm 3*
Dooley, Michael Francis 1852-1937 *NatCAB 27,
 WhAm 1, WhAm 1C*
Dooley, Mr. *WebAB*
Dooley, Patrick Callan 1842- *NatCAB 11*
Dooley, Thomas Anthony 1927-1961 *WebAB,
 WebAMB, WhAm 4A*
Dooley, Virginia Perrin Corttis *WhAm 6*
Dooley, William Francis 1872-1915 *WhAm 1*
Dooley, William Henry 1880-1944 *WhAm 2*
Doolin, John B 1879-1939 *WhAm 1*
Dooling, Maurice T 1860-1924 *WhAm 1*
Dooling, Peter Joseph 1857-1931 *BiDrAC,
 WhAm 1*
Doolittle, A B *NewYHSD*
Doolittle, Amos 1754-1832 *ApCAB, DcAmB,
 Drake, NewYHSD, WhAm H*
Doolittle, Benjamin 1695-1749 *ApCAB, Drake*
Doolittle, Charles Camp 1832-1902
 ApCAB Sup, TwCBDA, WhAm 1
Doolittle, Charles H 1816-1874 *BiAUS*
Doolittle, Charles Leander 1843-1919 *DcAmB,
 NatCAB 20, WhAm 1*
Doolittle, Clarence Everett 1863-1933
 NatCAB 29
Doolittle, Curtis M *NewYHSD*
Doolittle, Dudley 1881-1957 *BiDrAC,
 NatCAB 49, WhAm 3, WhAmP*
Doolittle, Edwin Stafford 1843-1880? *ApCAB*
Doolittle, Eric 1869-1920 *DcAmB,
 NatCAB 19, WhAm 1*
Doolittle, Frederick Benjamin 1825-1912
 NatCAB 15
Doolittle, Frederick William 1883-1950
 NatCAB 39, WhAm 3
Doolittle, Herbert Elliott 1864-1919
 NatCAB 18
Doolittle, Hilda 1886-1961 *McGEWB, WebAB,
 WhAm 4*
Doolittle, Hooker Austin 1889-1966 *WhAm 4*
Doolittle, Horace 1792- *NewYHSD*
Doolittle, Isaac *NewYHSD*
Doolittle, James Harold 1896- *WebAB,
 WebAMB, WhWW-II, WhoMilH*
Doolittle, James Rood 1815-1897 *ApCAB,
 BiAUS, BiDrAC, DcAmB, NatCAB 4,
 TwCBDA, WhAm H, WhAmP*
Doolittle, Lucy Salisbury 1832- *AmWom*
Doolittle, Mary Antoinette 1810-1886 *ApCAB*
Doolittle, Mortimer Leggett 1900-1950
 NatCAB 43
Doolittle, Roscoe Edward 1874- *WhAm 1*
Doolittle, Russell Comber 1886-1963
 NatCAB 50
Doolittle, S C *NewYHSD*
Doolittle, Samuel *NewYHSD*

Doolittle, Sears Polydore 1890-1961
NatCAB 49
Doolittle, Theodore Sandford 1834-1893
NatCAB 3, TwCBDA
Doolittle, Theodore Sandford 1836-1893 *ApCAB*
Doolittle, Thomas Benjamin 1839-1921
WhAm 1
Doolittle, William Hall 1848-1914 *BiDrAC,*
WhAmP
Doolittle, William Hall 1850-1914 *TwCBDA*
Dooly, John Mitchell 1772?-1827 *ApCAB*
Dooly, John Murray 1772?-1827 *TwCBDA*
Dooly, Oscar Earle 1900-1970 *WhAm 5*
Dooman, Eugene Hoffman 1890-1969
NatCAB 55
Doonan, Myra Knowlton 1875- *WomWWA 14*
Door, Julia Caroline Ripley 1825-1913 *AmWom*
Doorly, Henry 1879-1961 *NatCAB 48,*
WhAm 4
Doorman, Karel d1941 *WhWW-II*
Dopp, Katharine Elizabeth 1863-
WomWWA 14
Dopp, Katherine Elizabeth 1863- *WhAm 5*
Doppelmayr, Johann Gabriel 1671?-1750 *DcScB*
Doppler, Christian Johann 1803-1853 *AsBiEn*
Doppler, Johann Christian 1803-1853 *DcScB*
Doran, James *NewYHSD*
Doran, James Finton 1878-1931 *NatCAB 32*
Doran, James M 1885-1941 *WhAm 2*
Doran, James Maurice 1885-1942 *NatCAB 31*
Doran, John C 1826?- *NewYHSD*
Doran, John Charles 1874-1943 *NatCAB 32*
Doran, Joseph Ingersoll 1844-1919 *NatCAB 12,*
WhAm 1
Doran, Lant Hoxsey 1893-1959 *NatCAB 47*
Doran, Robert John 1895-1962 *NatCAB 50*
Doran, Thomas Francis 1856-1916 *NatCAB 15*
Doran, Thomas Francis 1862-1939 *WhAm 1*
Doran, William Thomas 1870-1949 *WhAm 3*
Dorantes, Pedro *ApCAB*
Doratt, Charles *NewYHSD*
Dorchester, Daniel 1827-1907 *DcAmB,*
TwCBDA, WhAm 1
Dorchester, Daniel, Jr. 1851-1944 *NatCAB 12,*
TwCBDA, WhAm 2
Dorchester, Liverus Hull 1864-1946 *WhAm 3*
Dorcus, Roy Melvin 1901-1968 *NatCAB 54*
Dore, John F 1881-1938 *WhAm 1*
Doremus, Abraham Fairbanks 1849-1933
NatCAB 26
Doremus, Charles Avery 1851-1925 *AmBi,*
ApCAB, NatCAB 10, TwCBDA,
WhAm 1
Doremus, Cornelius 1842-1918 *NatCAB 29*
Doremus, Cornelius 1862-1933 *NatCAB 25*
Doremus, Elias Osborn 1831- *NatCAB 5*
Doremus, Frank Ellsworth 1865-1947 *BiDrAC,*
WhAm 2, WhAmP
Doremus, Henry M 1851- *WhAm 4*
Doremus, John Edwards Caldwell 1816-1878
TwCBDA
Doremus, Robert Ogden 1824-1906 *AmBi,*
ApCAB, DcAmB, NatCAB 12,
NatCAB 28, TwCBDA, WhAm 1
Doremus, Sarah Platt Haines 1802-1877 *AmBi,*
ApCAB, DcAmB, NatCAB 6, NotAW,
TwCBDA, WhAm H
Doren, Dennis 1830- *NatCAB 3*
Doren, Electra Collins 1861-1927 *DcAmLiB,*
WhAm 1
Dorety, Frederic Gerber 1878- *WhAm 6*
Dorey, Halstead 1874-1946 *WhAm 2*
Dorf, Alfred Lawrence 1903-1956 *NatCAB 48*
Dorffel, Georg Samuel 1643-1688 *DcScB*
Dorfman, Julius 1908-1962 *NatCAB 52*
Dorgan, John Aylmer 1836-1867 *ApCAB,*
Drake, NatCAB 4
Dorgan, Thomas Aloysius 1877-1929 *DcAmB,*
WhAm HA, WhAm 4, WhAmP
Dorhman, Arnold Henry 1748-1813 *ApCAB,*
Drake
Doria, Andrea 1466-1560 *WhoMilH*
Doria, Clara *WhAm 1*
Dorigan, Harry William 1895-1966 *WhAm 4,*
WhAm 5
Dorion, Sir Antoine Aime 1818- *ApCAB*
Dorion, Eustache Charles Edouard 1872-1920
WhAm 1

Dorion, Jacques Edmond 1827- *ApCAB*
Dorion, Marie 1790?-1850 *NotAW*
Dorion, Marie 1791?-1850 *DcAmB, WhAm H*
Dorival, John *NewYHSD*
Dorizas, Michael Michael 1890-1957
NatCAB 49
Dorland, Ralph E, Sr. 1879-1948 *WhAm 2*
Dorland, William Alexander Newman 1864-
WhAm 4
D'Orleans, Antoine Philippe *NewYHSD*
D'Orleans, Louis Charles *NewYHSD*
Dorman, Alfred Allen 1891-1955 *NatCAB 43*
Dorman, Edmund Lawrence 1911-1962
WhAm 4
Dorman, Jessie Thomas *WomWWA 14*
Dorman, Joseph Harold 1889-1956 *NatCAB 46*
Dorman, Orlando P 1828- *NatCAB 5*
Dorman, Purman 1901-1964 *NatCAB 51*
Dorman, William Edwin 1875-1936 *WhAm 1*
Dorman-Smith, Sir Eric 1895-1969 *WhWW-II*
Dormer, Charles Joseph 1924-1973 *WhAm 6*
Dorn, Francis Edwin 1911- *BiDrAC*
Dorn, Friedrich Ernst 1848-1916 *AsBiEn*
Dorn, Gerard *DcScB*
Dorn, Harold F 1906-1963 *WhAm 4*
Dorn, John Emil 1909-1971 *WhAm 6*
Dorn, Norman Lester 1889-1952 *NatCAB 52*
Dorn, William Jennings Bryan 1916- *BiDrAC*
Dornbirer, James George 1867-1930
NatCAB 25
Dorne, Albert 1904-1965 *WhAm 4*
Dornette, George August 1886-1954
NatCAB 48
Dornin, Bernard 1761-1836 *WhAm H*
Dornin, Thomas Aloysius 1800-1874 *ApCAB,*
DcAmB, Drake, TwCBDA, WhAm H
Dorno, Carl W M 1865-1942 *DcScB*
Dorns, Francis 1815?- *NewYHSD*
Doroshaw, Jennis Milford 1901-1963 *WhAm 4*
Dorotheus Of Sidon *DcScB Sup*
Dorr, Benjamin 1796-1869 *ApCAB, Drake,*
NatCAB 11, TwCBDA
Dorr, Bradford Ripley 1881-1958 *NatCAB 48*
Dorr, Carl E 1879- *WhAm 6*
Dorr, Charles Philips 1852-1914 *BiDrAC,*
TwCBDA
Dorr, Dudley Huntington 1882-1961
NatCAB 50, WhAm 4
Dorr, Ebenezer Pearson 1817-1881 *ApCAB*
Dorr, Edward Monroe 1903-1964 *WhAm 4*
Dorr, George Bucknam 1853-1944 *WhAm 2*
Dorr, Harold M 1897-1973 *WhAm 5*
Dorr, John VanNostrand 1872-1962
NatCAB 48, WhAm 4
Dorr, Julia Caroline Ripley 1825-1913 *AmBi,*
ApCAB, DcAmB, NatCAB 6, TwCBDA,
WhAm 1, WomWWA 14
Dorr, Rheta Childe 1866-1948 *NotAW,*
WhAm 2, WomWWA 14
Dorr, Robert East Apthoep d1900 *WhAm 1*
Dorr, Robert John 1919-1960 *WhAm 4*
Dorr, Temple Emery 1840-1913 *NatCAB 17*
Dorr, Thomas Wilson 1805-1854 *AmBi,*
ApCAB, BiAUS, DcAmB, Drake,
EncAAH, NatCAB 8, TwCBDA, WebAB,
WhAm H, WhAmP
Dorrance, Arthur Calbraith 1893-1946
WhAm 2
Dorrance, George Morris 1877-1949 *WhAm 2*
Dorrance, Gordon 1765-1846 *ApCAB*
Dorrance, Gordon 1890-1957 *WhAm 3*
Dorrance, Henry Turner 1898-1961 *NatCAB 50*
Dorrance, John Thompson 1873-1930 *WhAm 1*
Dorrance, Sturges Dick 1881-1968 *WhAm 5*
Dorrance, W H *NewYHSD*
Dorrego, Manuel 1787-1829 *ApCAB*
Dorrel, William 1752-1846 *NatCAB 4*
Dorrell, Charles Earl 1890-1950 *NatCAB 39*
Dorrell, William 1752-1846 *DcAmB,*
WhAm H
Dorroh, John Hazard 1878- *WhAm 6*
D'Orsay, Lawrance d1931 *WhAm 1*
Dorsch, Eduard 1822-1887 *DcAmB, WhAm H*
Dorset, Marion 1872-1935 *DcAmB S1,*
EncAAH, NatCAB 26, WhAm 1
Dorsett, Ellen R Shepard *WomWWA 14*
Dorsett, P H 1862- *WhAm 4*

Dorsett, Walter Blackburn 1852-1915
NatCAB 13, WhAm 1
Dorsey, Anna Hanson 1816-1896 *AmWom*
Dorsey, Anna Hanson McKenney 1815-1896
ApCAB, DcAmB, NatCAB 11, TwCBDA
Dorsey, Charles Howard, Jr. 1904-1973
WhAm 6
Dorsey, Charles Marcellus 1876- *WhoColR*
Dorsey, Clarence Wilbur 1872- *WhAm 5*
Dorsey, Claude Eugene, Jr. 1914-1957
NatCAB 49
Dorsey, Clayton Chauncey 1871-1948 *WhAm 2*
Dorsey, Clement d1846 *BiAUS*
Dorsey, Clement 1778-1848 *BiDrAC,*
WhAm H, WhAmP
Dorsey, Edward 1849-1914 *NatCAB 40*
Dorsey, Ella Loraine 1850?- *AmWom*
Dorsey, Ella Loraine 1853- *WhAm 4,*
WomWWA 14
Dorsey, F Donald 1895-1959 *NatCAB 47*
Dorsey, Francis Oswald 1869-1915 *WhAm 1*
Dorsey, Frank Joseph Gerard 1891-1949
BiDrAC, WhAm 2
Dorsey, George Amos 1868-1931 *AmBi,*
ApCAB X, DcAmB S1, NatCAB 12,
NatCAB 22, WhAm 1
Dorsey, George Washington Emery 1842-1911
BiDrAC, TwCBDA
Dorsey, Godwin Volney 1812- *ApCAB*
Dorsey, Harry Woodward 1874- *WhAm 5*
Dorsey, Henry 1882-1959 *NatCAB 47*
Dorsey, Herbert Grove 1876- *WhAm 5*
Dorsey, Hugh Manson 1871-1948 *NatCAB 18,*
WhAm 2
Dorsey, Isabel Lovell 1866- *WomWWA 14*
Dorsey, Jack Sidney 1907-1974 *WhAm 6*
Dorsey, James Emmet 1889-1959 *WhAm 3*
Dorsey, James Owen 1848-1895 *ApCAB,*
DcAmB, REnAW, TwCBDA, WhAm H
Dorsey, Jesse Hook 1849- *NatCAB 6*
Dorsey, John *NewYHSD*
Dorsey, Father John Henry 1873- *WhoColR*
Dorsey, John Lloyd, Jr. 1891-1960 *BiDrAC*
Dorsey, John Richardson 1848-1917
NatCAB 26
Dorsey, John Syng 1783-1818 *ApCAB, DcAmB,*
Drake, NatCAB 10, NewYHSD,
WhAm H
Dorsey, Joseph 1863- *WhoColR*
Dorsey, Leo Patrick d1973 *WhAm 6*
Dorsey, LeRoy Howard 1887- *WhAm 3*
Dorsey, Maxwell J 1880-1966 *WhAm 4*
Dorsey, Rufus Thomas 1848- *NatCAB 12*
Dorsey, Sallie Webster *WomWWA 14*
Dorsey, Sarah Ann Ellis 1829-1879 *WhAm H*
Dorsey, Sarah Anne Ellis 1829-1879 *ApCAB,*
DcAmB, NatCAB 3, NotAW, TwCBDA
Dorsey, Stephen Palmer 1913-1968 *WhAm 4A*
Dorsey, Stephen Wallace 1842-1916 *ApCAB,*
BiAUS, BiDrAC, DcAmB, REnAW,
TwCBDA, WhAm 1, WhAmP
Dorsey, Stephen Wallace 1843-1916 *NatCAB 7*
Dorsey, Susan Almira Miller 1857-1946
ApCAB X, BiDAmEd, NotAW, WhAm 4,
WomWWA 14
Dorsey, Thomas *NewYHSD*
Dorsey, Thomas Beale 1780-1855 *Drake,*
NatCAB 12
Dorsey, Thomas Francis 1905-1956 *WhAm 3*
Dorsey, Thomas Manning 1887-1959
NatCAB 51
Dorsey, Vernon Martin 1869-1954 *NatCAB 41*
Dorsey, W Roderick 1868- *WhAm 4*
Dorsheimer, William Edward 1832-1888
ApCAB, BiDrAC, DcAmB, NatCAB 19,
TwCBDA, WhAm H
Dorsonnens, Eraste *ApCAB*
Dorst, Joseph Haddox 1852-1915 *WhAm 1*
Dorst, Joseph Haddox 1852-1916 *NatCAB 16*
Dort, Josiah Dallas 1861-1925 *ApCAB X,*
NatCAB 17, NatCAB 36, WhAm 1
Dortch, Ellen J 1868- *AmWom*
Dortch, William Theophilus 1824-1889 *BiDConf*
Dorward, William Thompson 1863- *WhAm 4*
Dorwin, Oscar John 1897-1974 *WhAm 6*
Doscher, Charles 1870-1922 *NatCAB 31*
Doscher, Claus 1830-1910 *NatCAB 27*
Doscher, Henry 1856-1937 *NatCAB 31*

Doscher, John 1865-1933 *NatCAB 30*
Dosdall, Chester Arthur 1882-1949 *WhAm 3*
Dositheus *DcScB*
Dosker, Henry Elias 1855-1926 *TwCBDA, WhAm 1*
DosPassos, John Randolph 1844-1917 *DcAmB, WhAm 1*
DosPassos, John Roderigo 1896-1970 *EncAB, McGEWB, WebAB, WhAm 5*
Dosquet, Peter Herman 1691-1777 *ApCAB*
Doss, Clay d1958 *WhAm 3*
Doss, James Houston 1875-1955 *NatCAB 43*
Doss, Roscoe James 1884-1949 *WhAm 2*
Dossert, Frank G 1861- *TwCBDA*
Dossin, Roy Lawrence 1893-1963 *NatCAB 50*
Dostal, Charles Antoine 1883-1962 *NatCAB 53*
Dostal, Charles Lewis 1916-1966 *NatCAB 51*
Dostal, Joseph Louis 1884-1949 *NatCAB 37*
Doster, Caroline Riddle 1847- *WomWWA 14*
Doster, Frank 1847-1933 *WhAm 1*
Doster, Frank 1849-1933 *NatCAB 12*
Doster, James Jarvis 1873-1942 *NatCAB 6, WhAm 2*
Doster, James Thomas 1867-1943 *NatCAB 32*
Dostert, Leon Emile 1904-1971 *WhAm 5*
Dostie, Anthony Paul d1866 *ApCAB, Drake*
Dostoevsky, Fyodor 1821-1881 *McGEWB*
Doten, Carroll Warren 1871-1942 *WhAm 2*
Doten, Lizzie 1829- *ApCAB*
Doten, Samuel Bradford 1875-1955 *WhAm 3*
D'Othon, A H *NewYHSD*
Doton, Hosea 1809-1886 *ApCAB*
Dotson, Mrs. E Milton 1861- *WomWWA 14*
Dotson, Floyd D 1909-1969 *WhAm 5*
Dotson, George Edgar 1904-1974 *WhAm 6*
Dotterweich, June 1918-1969 *WhAm 5*
Doty, Alvah Hunt 1854- *WhAm 4*
Doty, Carl Babcock 1901-1974 *WhAm 6*
Doty, Douglas Zabriskie 1874-1935 *WhAm 1*
Doty, Elihu 1809-1864 *ApCAB, DcAmB, WhAm H*
Doty, George H 1861-1923 *ApCAB X*
Doty, James D d1865 *BiAUS*
Doty, James Duane 1799-1865 *ApCAB, BiDrAC, DcAmB, NatCAB 12, REnAW, TwCBDA, WhAm H, WhAmP*
Doty, James Duane 1800-1865 *Drake*
Doty, John Williams 1879- *WhAm 6*
Doty, Lena Harris *WomWWA 14*
Doty, Lockwood Lyon 1827-1873 *ApCAB*
Doty, Madeleine Zabriskie 1879- *WhAm 6, WomWWA 14*
Doty, Paul 1869-1938 *NatCAB 16, WhAm 1*
Doty, Preston Beverly 1877-1947 *NatCAB 37*
Doty, Robert Clark 1915-1974 *WhAm 6*
Doty, Warren S *NewYHSD*
Doty, William Furman 1870- *WhAm 5*
Douai, Carl Daniel Adolf 1819-1888 *TwCBDA*
Doub, Peter 1796-1869 *NatCAB 7*
Doubleday, Abner 1819-1893 *AmBi, ApCAB, DcAmB, Drake, NatCAB 4, TwCBDA, WebAB, WebAMB, WhAm H*
Doubleday, Charles William 1829- *ApCAB*
Doubleday, Edward 1810-1849 *ApCAB, Drake*
Doubleday, Frank Nelson 1862-1934 *ApCAB X, DcAmB S1, NatCAB 13, WebAB, WhAm 1*
Doubleday, George 1866-1955 *WhAm 3*
Doubleday, Nelson 1889-1949 *DcAmB S4, NatCAB 37, WhAm 2*
Doubleday, Neltje Blanchan DeGraff 1865-1918 *AmBi, DcAmB, NatCAB 13, NotAW, WhAm 1, WomWWA 14*
Doubleday, Russell 1872-1949 *NatCAB 13, WhAm 2*
Doubleday, Thomas Donnelly 1816-1864 *ApCAB*
Doubleday, Ulysses 1824-1893 *ApCAB, TwCBDA*
Doubleday, Ulysses F 1794-1866 *BiAUS*
Doubleday, Ulysses Freeman 1792-1866 *ApCAB, BiDrAC, NatCAB 4, TwCBDA, WhAm H*
Doublet, Francois *ApCAB Sup*
Doucet, Edward Peter 1825-1890 *NatCAB 2, TwCBDA*
Doud, Ray Wilson 1899-1966 *NatCAB 51*
Doudna, Edgar George 1877-1948 *WhAm 2*

Doudoroff, Michael 1911-1975 *WhAm 6*
Dougal, William H 1822-1895 *IIBEAAW, NewYHSD, WhAm H*
Dougall, J Park 1874-1960 *NatCAB 47*
Dougall, John Bernard 1883-1964 *NatCAB 51*
Dougall, Lily *WomWWA 14*
Dougherty, Andrew Beach 1863-1928 *NatCAB 21*
Dougherty, Blanford Barnard 1870-1957 *BiDAmEd, WhAm 3*
Dougherty, Charles 1850-1915 *BiDrAC*
Dougherty, Curtis 1863-1919 *WhAm 1*
Dougherty, Daniel 1826-1892 *ApCAB, NatCAB 5, TwCBDA*
Dougherty, Denis Joseph 1865-1951 *NatCAB 16, WhAm 3*
Dougherty, Dennis Joseph 1865-1951 *DcAmB S5*
Dougherty, Edward Archer 1910-1969 *WhAm 5*
Dougherty, Edward E *WhAm 2*
Dougherty, George A 1861-1929 *WhAm 1*
Dougherty, George S 1865-1931 *WhAm 1*
Dougherty, Glenn 1892-1953 *NatCAB 42*
Dougherty, Hugh 1843?-1925 *NewYHSD*
Dougherty, Hugh 1844-1925 *NatCAB 14, NatCAB 27, WhAm 1*
Dougherty, James 1841?- *NewYHSD*
Dougherty, James Robert 1871-1950 *NatCAB 37*
Dougherty, John 1857-1905 *BiDrAC, WhAm 1, WhAmP*
Dougherty, John Hampden 1849-1918 *NatCAB 20, WhAm 1*
Dougherty, Joseph P 1905-1970 *WhAm 5*
Dougherty, Lee J 1881- *WhAm 6*
Dougherty, Lida 1873- *WomWWA 14*
Dougherty, Louis 1876-1948 *NatCAB 36*
Dougherty, Newton Charles 1847- *NatCAB 13*
Dougherty, Paul 1877-1947 *IIBEAAW, NatCAB 47, WhAm 2*
Dougherty, Proctor Lambert 1873- *WhAm 5*
Dougherty, Raymond Philip 1877-1933 *DcAmB S1, WhAm 1*
Dougherty, Richard Erwin 1880-1961 *NatCAB 49, WhAm 4*
Dougherty, Thomas *BiAUS*
Dougherty, Thomas Francis 1915-1974 *WhAm 6*
Dougherty, Walter Hampden *WebAB*
Dougherty, William 1832?- *NewYHSD*
Dougherty, William Edgeworth 1841-1915 *WhAm 1*
Dougherty, William H 1880- *WhAm 6*
Doughten, William Simpson 1876-1957 *NatCAB 47*
Doughtie, Charles Wilson 1877-1942 *NatCAB 39*
Doughton, Robert Lee 1863-1954 *BiDrAC, DcAmB S5, WhAm 3, WhAmP*
Doughty, Mrs. Alla *WhAm 1*
Doughty, Edmund *NewYHSD*
Doughty, Eva Craig Graves 1852- *AmWom*
Doughty, Grace Goble 1870- *WomWWA 14*
Doughty, Howard Waters 1871-1949 *WhAm 2*
Doughty, John 1754-1826 *ApCAB Sup, NatCAB 7, TwCBDA, WebAMB*
Doughty, Phebe VanVlack 1873- *WomWWA 14*
Doughty, Thomas 1793-1856 *AmBi, ApCAB, BnEnAmA, DcAmB, Drake, NatCAB 14, NewYHSD, WhAm H*
Doughty, Thomas, Jr. *NewYHSD*
Doughty, Walter Francis 1873-1931 *WhAm 1*
Doughty, William Ellison 1873- *WhAm 5*
Doughty, William Henry 1836-1905 *ApCAB, DcAmB, TwCBDA, WhAm 1*
Doughty, William Henry, Jr. 1856-1923 *WhAm 1*
Doughty, William Howard, Jr. d1961 *NatCAB 48*
Doughty, William McDowell 1881-1944 *NatCAB 34*
Douglas, Adele Cutts 1835-1899 *NotAW*
Douglas, Alanson 1779-1856 *TwCBDA*
Douglas, Albert 1852-1935 *BiDrAC, WhAm 4*
Douglas, Alexander 1848- *WhAm 4*
Douglas, Alice May 1865-1943 *AmWom, WhAm 2, WomWWA 14*

Douglas, Amanda Minnie 1831-1916 *DcAmB*
Douglas, Amanda Minnie 1837-1916 *NatCAB 2, WhAm 1, WomWWA 14*
Douglas, Amanda Minnie 1838-1916 *AmWom, ApCAB, TwCBDA*
Douglas, Archibald 1872-1943 *NatCAB 32, WhAm 2*
Douglas, Arthur F 1902-1956 *WhAm 3*
Douglas, Benjamin 1816-1894 *ApCAB, DcAmB, NatCAB 8, WhAm H*
Douglas, Beverly Browne 1822-1878 *BiAUS, BiDrAC, NatCAB 5, TwCBDA, WhAm H*
Douglas, Bruce Hutchinson 1892-1949 *NatCAB 38, NatCAB 47, WhAm 3*
Douglas, Byrd 1894-1965 *NatCAB 54*
Douglas, Sir Charles d1789 *ApCAB*
Douglas, Charles A 1862-1939 *WhAm 1*
Douglas, Charles Henry 1861-1954 *WhAm 3*
Douglas, Charles Winfred 1867-1944 *WhAm 2*
Douglas, Clarence Brown 1864- *WhAm 5*
Douglas, Corinne Williams 1860- *WomWWA 14*
Douglas, David 1798-1834 *ApCAB, Drake*
Douglas, David Dwight 1891-1951 *WhAm 3*
Douglas, Davison McDowell 1869-1931 *NatCAB 26, WhAm 1*
Douglas, Donald B 1892-1975 *WhAm 6*
Douglas, Donald Wills 1892- *McGEWB, WebAMB*
Douglas, Edward Osborn 1896-1949 *NatCAB 38*
Douglas, Emily Taft 1899- *BiDrAC*
Douglas, Ernest 1864- *WhAm 4*
Douglas, Fred James 1869-1949 *BiDrAC, WhAm 2, WhAmP*
Douglas, Frederic Huntington 1897-1956 *WhAm 3*
Douglas, Frederick A 1860- *WhAm 4*
Douglas, Frederick Alexander 1875-1954 *NatCAB 43*
Douglas, Gavin 1475?-1522 *McGEWB*
Douglas, George 1823- *NatCAB 6*
Douglas, George 1825- *ApCAB*
Douglas, George Bruce 1858-1923 *WhAm 1*
Douglas, George Perkins 1865-1951 *NatCAB 41*
Douglas, George William 1850-1926 *ApCAB X, NatCAB 12, WhAm 1*
Douglas, George William 1863-1945 *WhAm 2*
Douglas, Gertrude Douglas 1866- *WomWWA 14*
Douglas, Grace Parsons 1881- *WhAm 6*
Douglas, Hamilton 1887-1958 *WhAm 3*
Douglas, Helen Gahagan 1900- *BiDrAC, WhAmP*
Douglas, Henry Kyd 1838-1903 *DcAmB*
Douglas, Henry Kyd 1840-1903 *WhAm 1*
Douglas, Henry Trovert, Jr. 1863- *WhAm 4*
Douglas, Sir Howard 1776-1861 *ApCAB*
Douglas, Sir James 1286?-1330 *McGEWB*
Douglas, James 1675-1742 *DcScB*
Douglas, James 1800-1886 *ApCAB*
Douglas, Sir James 1803-1877 *ApCAB*
Douglas, James 1837-1918 *AmBi, ApCAB X, DcAmB, NatCAB 12, NatCAB 23, REnAW, WhAm 1*
Douglas, James Glass 1900-1960 *NatCAB 48*
Douglas, James H 1858-1930 *WhAm 1*
Douglas, James Marsh 1896-1974 *WhAm 6*
Douglas, James Stuart 1868-1948 *REnAW*
Douglas, James Stuart 1868-1949 *NatCAB 38, WhAm 2*
Douglas, Jesse 1897-1965 *DcScB*
Douglas, John *ApCAB*
Douglas, John 1826?- *NewYHSD*
Douglas, John 1875-1938 *WhAm 1*
Douglas, John Francis 1874-1952 *WhAm 3*
Douglas, John Frederic Howard 1884-1962 *WhAm 4*
Douglas, John Gray 1900-1974 *WhAm 6*
Douglas, John Hancock 1824-1892 *ApCAB, TwCBDA*
Douglas, Judith Hyams 1875- *WomWWA 14*
Douglas, Julia S 1852-1902 *WhAm 1*
Douglas, Katharine Ross Chrystie 1874- *WomWWA 14*
Douglas, Kenneth Wallace 1912-1974 *WhAm 6*
Douglas, Lavantia Densmore 1827- *AmWom*

Douglas, Lee 1885-1959 *WhAm 3*
Douglas, Lewis William 1894-1974 *REnAW*
Douglas, Lewis Williams 1894-1974 *BiDrAC,*
NatCAB 57, WhAm 6
Douglas, Lloyd Cassel 1877-1951 *DcAmB S5,*
WebAB, WhAm 3
Douglas, Lucy *NewYHSD*
Douglas, Marian *WomWWA 14a*
Douglas, Martin Francis 1886-1963 *NatCAB 50*
Douglas, Mary Teresa Peacock 1903-1970
DcAmLiB
Douglas, Orlando Benajah 1836-1920
NatCAB 6, TwCBDA, WhAm 1
Douglas, Oscar Berry 1892-1960 *WhAm 4*
Douglas, Paul Howard 1892- *BiDrAC*
Douglas, Percy Livingston 1903-1964 *WhAm 4*
Douglas, Richard 1860- *WhAm 4*
Douglas, Richard Leroy 1884-1961 *NatCAB 50*
Douglas, Robert *NewYHSD*
Douglas, Robert 1859-1929 *NatCAB 22*
Douglas, Robert 1865-1924 *ApCAB X*
Douglas, Robert Martin 1849-1917 *TwCBDA,*
WhAm 1
Douglas, Silas Hamilton 1816-1890 *ApCAB,*
NatCAB 11, TwCBDA, WhAm H
Douglas, Stephen Arnold 1813-1861 *AmBi,*
ApCAB, BiAUS, BiDrAC, DcAmB,
Drake, EncAAH, EncAB, McGEWB,
NatCAB 2, REnAW, TwCBDA, WebAB,
WhAm H, WhAmP
Douglas, Stephen Arnold 1850-1908 *WhAm 1*
Douglas, Thaddeus 1872-1949 *WhAm 2*
Douglas, Theodore Wayland 1897-1961
WhAm 4
Douglas, Thomas 1790-1855 *NatCAB 12*
Douglas, Wallace Barton 1852- *WhAm 4*
Douglas, Walter 1870-1946 *NatCAB 36,*
REnAW, WhAm 2
Douglas, Walter Donald 1861-1912 *NatCAB 16*
Douglas, Walter G d1966 *WhAm 5*
Douglas, Walter John 1922-1974 *WhAm 6*
Douglas, Walter Jules 1872-1941 *NatCAB 30*
Douglas, William 1742-1777 *ApCAB, DcAmB,*
NatCAB 7, TwCBDA
Douglas, William 1743-1777 *WhAm H*
Douglas, William Archer Sholte 1886-1951
WhAm 3
Douglas, William Bradley 1818- *TwCBDA*
Douglas, William Harris 1853-1944 *BiDrAC,*
NatCAB 12, WhAm 2
Douglas, William Kirtland 1827-1898 *TwCBDA*
Douglas, William Lewis 1845-1924 *DcAmB,*
NatCAB 13, NatCAB 25, WhAm 1
Douglas, William Orville 1898- *EncAAH,*
EncAB, McGEWB, WebAB
Douglas, Sir William Sholto 1893-1969
WhWW-II
Douglas, William Wilberforce 1841-1929
NatCAB 14, WhAm 1
Douglas, Winfred 1867-1944 *NatCAB 32*
Douglas Of Kirtleside, Lord 1893-1969 *WhAm 5*
Douglass *NewYHSD*
Douglass, Alonzo 1815?-1886 *NewYHSD*
Douglass, Andrew Ellicott 1867- *NatCAB 16*
Douglass, Andrew Ellicott 1867-1901 *WhAm 1*
Douglass, Andrew Ellicott 1867-1962 *AsBiEn,*
WhAm 4
Douglass, Aubrey Augustus 1887-1952
NatCAB 41, WhAm 3
Douglass, Benjamin 1816-1929 *NatCAB 24*
Douglass, Benjamin Wallace 1882-1939
WhAm 1
Douglass, Caroline *NewYHSD*
Douglass, Dana Carroll 1877- *WhAm 5*
Douglass, David 1720?- *ApCAB*
Douglass, David Bates 1790-1849 *ApCAB,*
DcAmB, Drake, NatCAB 7, NewYHSD,
TwCBDA, WhAm H
Douglass, Earl 1862-1931 *ApCAB X,*
NatCAB 26, WhAm 1
Douglass, Earl Leroy 1888-1972 *NatCAB 57,*
WhAm 5
Douglass, Edwin Herbert 1867- *WhAm 4*
Douglass, Frank Harvey 1899-1965 *NatCAB 51,*
WhAm 4
Douglass, Frederick 1817?-1895 *AmBi,*
ApCAB, DcAmB, Drake, EncAAH,
EncAB, McGEWB, NatCAB 2,

TwCBDA, WebAB, WhAm H, WhAmP
Douglass, Frederick Melvin 1890-1950 *WhAm 3*
Douglass, Frederick Melvin, Jr. 1919-1965
NatCAB 52
Douglass, Gaylord William 1876- *WhAm 5*
Douglass, George Angus 1876-1958 *NatCAB 48*
Douglass, George C 1876-1940 *WhAm 1*
Douglass, George Shearer 1895-1953 *WhAm 3*
Douglass, H Ellwood 1900-1969 *WhAm 5*
Douglass, H Paul 1871-1953 *WhAm 3*
Douglass, Mrs. Hallam *NotAW*
Douglass, Harl Roy 1892-1972 *BiDAmEd*
Douglass, I W 1827- *BiAUS*
Douglass, J Walter 1859- *NatCAB 12*
Douglass, James Clayton 1817-1874 *TwCBDA*
Douglass, John Joseph 1873-1939 *BiDrAC,*
WhAm 5, WhAmP
Douglass, John Watkinson 1827-1909 *WhAm 1*
Douglass, Joseph Henry 1871- *WhoColR*
Douglass, Joseph Henry 1917-1974 *WhAm 6*
Douglass, Leon Forrest 1869-1940 *NatCAB 44*
Douglass, Lucille Sinclair d1935 *WhAm 1*
Douglass, Mabel Smith 1877-1933 *BiDAmEd,*
NotAW, WhAm 5
Douglass, Malcolm 1825-1887 *NatCAB 18*
Douglass, Margaret Crittenden *ApCAB*
Douglass, Matthew Hale 1874-1945 *WhAm 2*
Douglass, Robert M J 1809-1887 *NewYHSD,*
WhAm H
Douglass, Rufus Collins 1837- *WhAm 4*
Douglass, Rush *NewYHSD*
Douglass, Samuel J *BiAUS*
Douglass, Sarah Mapps Douglass 1806-1882
NotAW
Douglass, Thomas Carter 1907-1954
NatCAB 43
Douglass, Thomas VanKirk 1912- *WhAm 4*
Douglass, Truman Bartlett 1901-1969
NatCAB 54, WhAm 5
Douglass, Truman Orville 1842-1925 *WhAm 1*
Douglass, W Tyler 1873-1955 *NatCAB 41*
Douglass, William 1691?-1752 *ApCAB,*
DcAmB, Drake, NatCAB 3, WhAm H
Douglass, William 1741-1777 *Drake*
Douglass, William Angus 1852-1935
NatCAB 44
Douhet, Giulio 1869-1930 *WhoMilH*
Doull, James Angus 1889-1963 *NatCAB 50,*
WhAm 4
Dounce, Harry Esty 1889-1957 *WhAm 3*
Douritch, Francis 1825?- *NewYHSD*
Dousman, Hercules Louis 1800-1868 *REnAW*
Douthirt, Walstein F 1867-1955 *WhAm 3*
Douthit, Claude 1879-1957 *NatCAB 48*
Douthit, Claude 1883-1957 *WhAm 3*
Douthit, Harold 1899-1962 *WhAm 4*
Douthit, Jasper Lewis 1834- *NatCAB 14,*
WhAm 4
Doutreleau, Gabriel 1700?- *ApCAB*
Doutrich, Isaac Hoffer 1871-1941 *BiDrAC,*
WhAm 1
Douty, Nicholas 1870- *WhAm 5*
Douville, Jean Baptiste 1794-1833? *ApCAB*
Douvillier *NewYHSD*
Douvillier, Suzanne Theodore Vaillande
1778-1826 *NotAW*
Douw, Volkert Peter 1720-1801 *TwCBDA*
Dove, Mrs. *NewYHSD*
Dove, Arthur Garfield 1880-1946 *BnEnAmA,*
DcAmB S4, McGEWB, WebAB
Dove, David James 1696?-1769 *BiDAmEd,*
DcAmB, WhAm H
Dove, Heinrich Wilhelm 1803-1879 *DcScB*
Dove, W Franklin 1897-1972 *WhAm 5*
Dovell, Ray C 1890-1968 *WhAm 5*
Dovener, Blackburn Barrett 1842-1914 *BiDrAC,*
TwCBDA, WhAm 4, WhAmP
Dover, Elmer 1873-1940 *WhAm 1*
Dover, John Randolph 1892-1963 *NatCAB 52*
Dover, Mary Violette *WomWWA 14*
Dover, Thomas 1662-1742 *BiHiMed*
Dow, Alex 1862-1942 *DcAmB S3, WhAm 2*
Dow, Allan Wade 1866-1955 *NatCAB 44,*
WhAm 3
Dow, Arthur Wesley 1857-1922 *BiDAmEd,*
IIBEAAW, WhAm 1
Dow, Blanche Hinman 1893-1973 *WhAm 6*
Dow, Caroline Bell 1858-1935 *WhAm 1,*

WomWWA 14
Dow, Charles Henry 1851-1902 *WebAB*
Dow, Charles Mason 1854-1920 *WhAm 1*
Dow, Cornelia M 1842- *AmWom*
Dow, Daniel 1772-1849 *ApCAB, NatCAB 11*
Dow, Dexter Douglass 1863-1941 *NatCAB 41*
Dow, Earle Wilbur 1868- *WhAm 4*
Dow, Edward Albert 1879-1945 *WhAm 2*
Dow, Edwin Barlow 1835- *NatCAB 13*
Dow, Eleanor Jones *WomWWA 14*
Dow, Fayette Brown 1881-1962 *WhAm 4*
Dow, Frank Fowler 1851-1928 *NatCAB 22*
Dow, Frederick Neal 1840-1934 *ApCAB X,*
NatCAB 26, WhAm 1
Dow, George Francis 1868-1936 *NatCAB 26,*
WhAm 1
Dow, Harriet Brown *WomWWA 14*
Dow, Harry Edward 1891-1944 *NatCAB 34*
Dow, Henry 1634-1707 *DcAmB, WhAm H*
Dow, Herbert Henry 1866-1930 *DcAmB S1,*
EncAB, NatCAB 24, WebAB, WhAm 1
Dow, Howard Malcolm 1837-1912 *WhAm 1*
Dow, James R 1820-1871 *ApCAB X*
Dow, Jennings Bryan 1897-1970 *NatCAB 55*
Dow, Jesse Erskine 1809- *ApCAB*
Dow, John Goodchild 1905- *BiDrAC*
Dow, John Reneau 1898-1973 *WhAm 6*
Dow, Lorenzo 1777-1834 *AmBi, ApCAB,*
DcAmB, Drake, NatCAB 10, TwCBDA
Dow, Lorenzo 1825-1899 *DcAmB, WhAm H*
Dow, Louis Henry 1872- *TwCBDA*
Dow, Martha Cora 1868- *WomWWA 14*
Dow, Mary E H G 1848- *AmWom*
Dow, Maud M 1865- *NatCAB 12*
Dow, Moses A 1810-1886 *ApCAB*
Dow, Neal 1803-1897 *Drake*
Dow, Neal 1804-1897 *AmBi, ApCAB,*
DcAmB, EncAB, McGEWB, NatCAB 5,
TwCBDA, WebAB, WhAm H
Dow, Peggy *ApCAB*
Dow, Roger 1906-1967 *WhAm 4*
Dow, Willard Henry 1897-1949 *NatCAB 37,*
WhAm 2
Dowd, Alice M 1855- *WomWWA 14*
Dowd, Charles Ferdinand 1825-1904
ApCAB Sup, NatCAB 18, TwCBDA,
WhAm 1
Dowd, Charles North 1858-1931 *WhAm 1*
Dowd, Clement 1832-1898 *BiDrAC*
Dowd, Daniel L 1854- *NatCAB 1*
Dowd, David L 1918-1968 *WhAm 5*
Dowd, Emma C *WomWWA 14*
Dowd, Fred A 1906-1974 *WhAm 6*
Dowd, H Laurence 1887-1968 *NatCAB 54*
Dowd, Heman 1854-1939 *NatCAB 29*
Dowd, James Edward 1899-1966 *WhAm 4*
Dowd, Jerome 1864- *WhAm 4*
Dowd, John Worthington 1847-1926 *WhAm 1*
Dowd, Mary Alice 1855- *AmWom*
Dowd, Olney Baldwin 1839-1918 *NatCAB 18*
Dowd, Patrick 1813- *ApCAB*
Dowd, Wallace Rutherford 1896-1962 *WhAm 4*
Dowd, William d1900 *WhAm 1*
Dowd, William Carey 1893-1949 *NatCAB 38,*
WhAm 3
Dowdall, Edward 1858- *WhAm 4*
Dowdall, Guy Grigsby 1875- *WhAm 5*
Dowdell, James Ferguson 1818-1871 *BiAUS,*
BiDrAC, NatCAB 11, TwCBDA,
WhAm H
Dowdell, James Render 1847-1921 *NatCAB 20,*
WhAm 3
Dowdell, William Shapard 1884-1937
NatCAB 31
Dowden, William Edgar 1865-1917 *NatCAB 17*
Dowding, Sir Hugh Caswell Tremenheere
1882-1970 *WhWW-II, WhoMilH*
Dowdney, Abraham 1841-1886 *BiDrAC,*
WhAm H
Dowdy, John Vernard 1912- *BiDrAC*
Dowe, Jennie Elizabeth Tupper 1845-1919
WhAm 1
Dowell, Alvis Yates 1896-1970 *WhAm 5*
Dowell, Benjamin B 1895-1958 *WhAm 3*
Dowell, Carr Thomas 1878- *WhAm 6*
Dowell, Cassius Clay 1864-1940 *BiDrAC,*
WhAm 1, WhAmP
Dowell, Floyd Dee 1910-1961 *WhAm 4*

Dowell, Greensville 1822-1881 *ApCAB, DcAmB, WhAm H*
Dowell, Spright 1878-1963 *WhAm 4*
Dower, John Lawrence 1867-1943 *NatCAB 32*
Dower, Walter H 1883-1934 *WhAm 1, WhAm 1C*
Dowie, John Alexander 1847-1907 *AmBi, DcAmB, NatCAB 13*
Dowland, John 1562-1626 *McGEWB*
Dowler, Bennet 1797-1879 *ApCAB, Drake*
Dowley, Francis Dwight 1863-1926 *NatCAB 6*
Dowling, Albert Lewis 1885-1948 *NatCAB 36*
Dowling, Alexander 1839-1917 *WhAm 1*
Dowling, Austin 1868-1930 *DcAmB S1, NatCAB 15, WhAm 1*
Dowling, Eddie 1894-1976 *WhAm 6*
Dowling, Edward C 1900-1974 *WhAm 6*
Dowling, Emmett Patrick 1917-1967 *WhAm 4*
Dowling, George Thomas 1849- *NatCAB 5, WhAm 4*
Dowling, J Ivimey 1872-1951 *NatCAB 42*
Dowling, John 1807-1878 *ApCAB, Drake, NatCAB 9, TwCBDA*
Dowling, John Charles Leonard 1880-1943 *NatCAB 32*
Dowling, John Joseph 1903-1949 *WhAm 2*
Dowling, John William 1864-1914 *WhAm 1*
Dowling, Joseph 1828-1877 *NatCAB 3*
Dowling, Judson Davie 1880-1946 *NatCAB 35, WhAm 6*
Dowling, Michael John 1866-1921 *NatCAB 20, WhAm 1*
Dowling, Noel Thomas 1885-1969 *NatCAB 53, WhAm 5*
Dowling, Oscar 1866-1931 *WhAm 1, WhAm 1C*
Dowling, Robert Whittle 1895-1973 *WhAm 6*
Dowling, Thomas Joseph 1840- *ApCAB Sup*
Dowling, Victor James 1866-1934 *WhAm 1*
Dowling, William Andrew 1859-1924 *NatCAB 45*
Dowling, William E d1963 *WhAm 4*
Dowman, Charles Edward 1849-1914 *NatCAB 16*
Dowman, Charles Edward 1882-1931 *NatCAB 23, WhAm 1*
Down, Frederick *NewYHSD*
Downard, C Paul 1894-1959 *NatCAB 47*
Downer, Alan Seymour 1912-1970 *WhAm 5*
Downer, Arthur Tiffany 1870- *ApCAB X*
Downer, Charles Alfred 1866-1930 *WhAm 1*
Downer, Eliphalet 1744-1806 *DcAmB, WhAm H*
Downer, Ezra Pierce 1816- *NatCAB 3*
Downer, James Walker 1864-1932 *WhAm 1*
Downer, Samuel 1807-1881 *ApCAB, DcAmB, NatCAB 11, WhAm H*
Downer, William Edwin 1871-1961 *NatCAB 49*
Downes, Anne Miller d1964 *WhAm 4*
Downes, Bruce 1899-1966 *WhAm 4*
Downes, Dennis Sawyer 1879- *WhAm 6*
Downes, Frances W *WomWWA 14*
Downes, J *NewYHSD*
Downes, James R 1883-1955 *WhAm 3*
Downes, John 1784-1854 *AmBi, DcAmB, Drake, WebAMB, WhAm H*
Downes, John 1784-1855 *TwCBDA*
Downes, John 1786-1855 *ApCAB, NatCAB 11*
Downes, John 1799-1882 *ApCAB*
Downes, John 1879-1954 *WhAm 3*
Downes, John A 1822-1865 *ApCAB, TwCBDA*
Downes, John Ireland Howe 1861-1933 *NatCAB 25*
Downes, Lewis Thomas 1824- *NatCAB 11*
Downes, Olin 1886-1955 *DcAmB S5, NatCAB 41, WhAm 3*
Downes, William Augustus 1872-1948 *NatCAB 36, WhAm 2*
Downes, William Elijah 1824-1904 *NatCAB 32*
Downes, William Howe 1854-1941 *NatCAB 32, WhAm 1*
Downey, David George 1858-1935 *WhAm 1*
Downey, Dennis Sebastian 1878-1959 *NatCAB 48*
Downey, Francis X 1902-1960 *WhAm 4*
Downey, Francis Xavier 1887-1942 *WhAm 2*
Downey, George Eddy 1860-1926 *WhAm 1*
Downey, George Faber 1866-1935 *WhAm 1*

Downey, Hal 1877-1959 *WhAm 3*
Downey, Hermon Horatio 1876- *WhAm 5*
Downey, James Henry 1864-1937 *NatCAB 33*
Downey, John 1765?-1826 *BiDAmEd, DcAmB, WhAm H*
Downey, John 1770-1827 *ApCAB*
Downey, John Florin 1846-1939 *WhAm 1*
Downey, John G 1826- *BiAUS, NatCAB 4, TwCBDA*
Downey, June Etta 1875-1932 *DcAmB S1, NotAW, WhAm 1, WomWWA 14*
Downey, Margaret Elsie 1873- *WomWWA 14*
Downey, Mary Elizabeth d1949 *WhAm 3, WomWWA 14*
Downey, Sabien B *NewYHSD*
Downey, Sheridan 1884-1961 *BiDrAC, WhAm 4, WhAmP*
Downey, Stanley Wilson Crowell d1927 *WhAm 1*
Downey, Stephen Wheeler 1839-1902 *BiDrAC, WhAmP*
Downey, Walter Francis 1884-1965 *WhAm 4*
Downey, William H 1896-1954 *WhAm 3*
Downie, George d1814 *ApCAB, Drake*
Downie, Robert C 1905-1965 *WhAm 4*
Downing, Colonel *ApCAB*
Downing, Andrew Jackson 1815-1852 *AmBi, ApCAB, BnEnAmA, DcAmB, Drake, EncAAH, McGEWB, NatCAB 11, TwCBDA, WebAB, WhAm H*
Downing, Arthur Matthew Weld 1850-1917 *DcScB*
Downing, Augustus S 1856-1936 *WhAm 1*
Downing, Benjamin Winans 1871-1948 *NatCAB 36*
Downing, Bertha Carol *WomWWA 14*
Downing, Charles d1841 *BiAUS*
Downing, Charles d1845 *BiDrAC, WhAm H*
Downing, Charles 1802-1885 *DcAmB, NatCAB 11, WhAm H*
Downing, Elliot Rowland 1868-1944 *BiDAmEd, NatCAB 37, WhAm 2*
Downing, Emma Hicks *WomWWA 14*
Downing, Fanny Murdaugh 1835?-1894? *ApCAB, NatCAB 7*
Downing, Finis Ewing 1846-1936 *BiDrAC*
Downing, Frances Murdaugh 1835?-1894? *WhAm H*
Downing, Sir George d1747 *ApCAB*
Downing, George 1623-1684 *DcAmB, WhAm H*
Downing, Sir George 1624-1684 *ApCAB, Drake*
Downing, Harold Kemp 1875- *WhAm 2*
Downing, Henry Hawkins 1853-1920 *NatCAB 18*
Downing, Jack *WhAm H*
Downing, Jerome Francis 1827-1913 *NatCAB 18*
Downing, John Franklin 1854-1935 *NatCAB 16, WhAm 1*
Downing, John Robert 1874-1939 *WhAm 1*
Downing, Lewis King 1896-1967 *WhAm 5*
Downing, Lilburn Liggins 1862- *WhoColR*
Downing, Lylburn Clinton 1889-1965 *NatCAB 53*
Downing, Major Jack *WebAB*
Downing, Paul M 1873-1944 *WhAm 2*
Downing, Robert Everard 1894- *WhAm 3*
Downing, Robert L 1857-1944 *WhAm 2*
Downing, Russell Vincent 1900-1968 *WhAm 5*
Downing, S Boardman *NewYHSD*
Downing, Samuel 1766-1867 *ApCAB*
Downing, Thomas Nelms 1919- *BiDrAC*
Downing, Warwick Miller 1875-1963 *WhAm 4*
Downs, Anthony John 1871-1939 *NatCAB 30*
Downs, Francis Shunk 1885-1960 *NatCAB 48, WhAm 4*
Downs, Mrs. George Sheldon 1843- *WhAm 4*
Downs, J Cloyd 1885-1957 *NatCAB 46*
Downs, Jere Arthur 1872-1935 *NatCAB 27*
Downs, John Ayman 1904-1966 *WhAm 4*
Downs, John Clayton 1865-1940 *NatCAB 34*
Downs, John William, Sr. 1888-1959 *WhAm 4*
Downs, Joseph 1895-1954 *NatCAB 46, WhAm 3*
Downs, Lawrence Aloysius 1872-1940 *NatCAB 33, WhAm 1*
Downs, LeRoy Donnelly 1900-1970 *BiDrAC,*

WhAm 5
Downs, Lynwood Gifford 1893-1961 *NatCAB 49*
Downs, Sallie Ward *AmWom*
Downs, Sarah Elizabeth 1843- *WomWWA 14*
Downs, Solomon Weathersbee 1801-1854 *BiAUS, BiDrAC, NatCAB 12, TwCBDA, WhAm H*
Downs, William Findlay 1887-1967 *WhAm 4*
Downs, William Fletcher, Jr. 1857-1925 *NatCAB 20*
Downs, William Smith 1883-1954 *WhAm 3*
Dowrie, George William 1880-1964 *WhAm 4*
Dows, Sutherland 1891-1969 *WhAm 5*
Dows, Tracy 1871-1937 *NatCAB 49*
Dowse, Edmund 1813-1905 *NatCAB 18*
Dowse, Edward 1756-1828 *BiAUS, BiDrAC, WhAm H*
Dowse, Thomas 1772-1856 *ApCAB, DcAmB, TwCBDA, WhAm H*
Dowse, William d1813 *BiAUS*
Dowse, William Bradford Homer 1852-1928 *ApCAB X, NatCAB 18, WhAm 1*
Dowsey, George Henry 1864- *ApCAB X*
Dowst, Frank Butland 1859-1929 *ApCAB X*
Dox, Charles Edward 1906-1968 *NatCAB 54, WhAm 5*
Dox, Peter Myndert 1813-1891 *ApCAB, BiAUS, BiDrAC, TwCBDA, WhAm H*
Doxey, Charles Taylor 1841-1898 *BiDrAC*
Doxey, Freeman B 1864- *WhoColR*
Doxey, Wall 1892-1962 *BiDrAC, NatCAB 56*
Doxiadis, Constantinos Apostolos 1913-1975 *WhAm 6*
Doxtater, Lee Walter 1885-1935 *WhAm 1*
Doyle, Albert Pryor Edward 1873- *WhAm 5*
Doyle, Alexander 1857-1922 *DcAmB, NatCAB 10, TwCBDA*
Doyle, Alexander 1858-1922 *WhAm 1*
Doyle, Alexander Patrick 1857-1912 *DcAmB, WhAm 1*
Doyle, Sir Arthur Conan 1859-1930 *BiHiMed, McGEWB*
Doyle, Bernard Wendell 1873-1949 *WhAm 3*
Doyle, C W 1852-1903 *WhAm 1*
Doyle, Sir Charles Hastings 1804?- *ApCAB*
Doyle, Clyde Gilman 1887-1963 *BiDrAC, WhAm 4, WhAmP*
Doyle, Cornelius James 1871-1938 *WhAm 1*
Doyle, Edward H 1849-1919 *WhAm 1*
Doyle, Edward John d1961 *WhAm 4*
Doyle, Gregory 1840-1913 *WhAm 1*
Doyle, Harold Kinyon 1899-1947 *NatCAB 44*
Doyle, Henry Grattan 1889-1964 *WhAm 4*
Doyle, Hobert Elliott 1889-1965 *NatCAB 52*
Doyle, Howard L 1894-1954 *WhAm 3*
Doyle, James Harold 1875- *WhAm 5*
Doyle, Sir John 1756-1834 *ApCAB, Drake*
Doyle, John Hardy 1844-1919 *ApCAB X, NatCAB 19, WhAm 1*
Doyle, John Thomas 1819-1906 *DcAmB, NatCAB 7, WhAm 1*
Doyle, Lawrence Oscar 1893-1964 *NatCAB 51*
Doyle, Manville 1831-1916 *NatCAB 16*
Doyle, Margaret Byron *NewYHSD*
Doyle, Martha Claire MacGowan 1869- *WhAm 4*
Doyle, Sister Mary Peter 1898-1971 *WhAm 5*
Doyle, Michael 1872-1943 *NatCAB 33*
Doyle, Michael Francis 1875-1960 *ApCAB X, NatCAB 46, WhAm 3A*
Doyle, Peter Cozzens 1842-1901 *NatCAB 34*
Doyle, Price 1896-1967 *WhAm 5*
Doyle, Rhederick Elwood, Jr. 1906- *WhAm 5*
Doyle, Richard Smith 1900-1966 *WhAm 5*
Doyle, Robert Morris 1853-1925 *WhAm 1*
Doyle, Roger Thomas 1901-1963 *NatCAB 49*
Doyle, Sarah Elizabeth 1830-1922 *DcAmB, NotAW, WhAm 1*
Doyle, Sherman Hoadley *WhAm 5*
Doyle, Thomas Aloysius 1886-1935 *BiDrAC, WhAm 1*
Doyle, Thomas Arthur 1827-1886 *TwCBDA*
Doyle, Thomas Henchion 1863- *WhAm 5*
Doyle, William *NewYHSD*
Doyle, William Edward 1844-1916 *NatCAB 16*
Doyle, William Jay 1881-1942 *NatCAB 31*
Doyle, William M S 1769-1828 *NewYHSD*

Doyne, John James 1858-1944 *BiDAmEd,*
WhAm 3
Dozier, Russell Shinnick 1908-1961 *WhAm 4*
Dozier, Curtis Merry 1883-1964 *WhAm 4*
Dozier, Edward P 1916-1971 *REnAW*
Dozier, Elizabeth Gist d1966 *WhAm 4*
Dozier, James Corde 1885-1974 *WhAm 6*
Dozier, Lewis David 1846- *NatCAB 12*
Dozier, Lewis David, Jr. 1887-1969 *NatCAB 55*
Dozier, Melville 1846- *WhAm 4*
Dozier, Orion Theophilus 1848-1925
NatCAB 22, WhAm 4
Dozier, Otis 1904- *IIBEAAW*
Dozier, Tennie Pinkerton 1861- *WomWWA 14*
Draa, Charles Clifton 1871- *ApCAB X,*
WhAm 6
Drabble, Martha Tenney Vance 1874-
WomWWA 14
Drabkin, Israel Edward 1905-1965 *WhAm 4*
Drabkin, Stella Molly Friedman d1971
WhAm 6
Dracass, Carrie E Tucker 1859- *WomWWA 14*
Drach, Edmund L 1887-1971 *WhAm 5*
Drach, George Edward 1906-1966 *NatCAB 52*
Drach, Jules Joseph 1871-1941 *DcScB*
Drach, S *NewYHSD*
Drache, Hiram Max 1924- *EncAAH*
Drachman, Bernard 1861-1945 *WhAm 2*
Drachsler, Julius 1889-1927 *WhAm 1*
Drackett, Harry Roger 1885-1948 *NatCAB 47*
Draddy, John G 1833-1904 *NewYHSD*
Draemel, Milo Frederick 1884-1971 *WhAm 5*
Draffan, George Livingston 1898-1963
NatCAB 50, WhAm 4
Drager, Walter Louis 1886-1953 *WhAm 3*
Dragging Canoe 1750-1792 *REnAW*
Drago, Harry Sinclair 1888- *REnAW*
Drago, Luis Maria 1859-1921 *McGEWB*
Dragomirov, Mikhail Ivanovich 1830-1905
WhoMilH
Dragstedt, Lester Reynold 1893-1975 *WhAm 6*
Dr'a'hms, August 1849- *WhAm 4*
Drain, James Andrew 1870-1943 *WhAm 2*
Drain, Jesse Cyrus 1883-1974 *WhAm 6*
Drake, A H Boyer 1900-1957 *NatCAB 47*
Drake, Alexander Wilson 1843-1916 *DcAmB,*
NatCAB 6, TwCBDA, WhAm 1
Drake, Archie Augustus, Jr. 1887-1961
WhAm 4
Drake, Benjamin 1794-1841 *ApCAB, Drake,*
NatCAB 7, TwCBDA
Drake, Benjamin 1795-1841 *DcAmB,*
WhAm H
Drake, Benjamin Michael 1800-1860 *ApCAB,*
TwCBDA
Drake, C St. Clair 1870-1935 *WhAm 1*
Drake, Charles Daniel 1811-1892 *ApCAB,*
BiAUS, BiDrAC, DcAmB, Drake,
NatCAB 3, TwCBDA, WhAm H,
WhAmP
Drake, Daniel 1785-1852 *AmBi, ApCAB,*
BiDAmEd, BiHiMed, DcAmB, Drake,
EncAAH, McGEWB, NatCAB 5, REnAW,
TwCBDA, WhAm H
Drake, Dula H Rae *BiCAW*
Drake, Durant 1878-1933 *WhAm 1*
Drake, Edwin Laurentine 1819-1880 *AmBi,*
DcAmB, NatCAB 26, WebAB, WhAm H
Drake, Elias Franklin 1813-1892 *NatCAB 6*
Drake, Emma Frances Angell 1849- *WhAm 4,*
WomWWA 14
Drake, Emmet Addis 1855- *WhAm 4*
Drake, Ernest Baylor 1853-1925 *NatCAB 24*
Drake, Frances Ann Denny 1797-1875 *ApCAB,*
DcAmB, NotAW, WhAm H
Drake, Sir Francis 1537?-1596 *Drake*
Drake, Sir Francis 1539?-1595 *ApCAB*
Drake, Sir Francis 1540?-1596 *WhAm H*
Drake, Sir Francis 1541?-1596 *McGEWB*
Drake, Sir Francis 1543?-1596 *WhoMilH*
Drake, Sir Francis 1545?-1595 *NatCAB 9*
Drake, Francis Marion 1830-1903 *AmBi,*
ApCAB Sup, DcAmB, NatCAB 5,
NatCAB 11, TwCBDA, WhAm 1,
WhAmP
Drake, Francis Samuel 1828-1885 *AmBi,*
ApCAB, DcAmB, NatCAB 4, TwCBDA,
WhAm H

Drake, Franklin Jeremiah 1846-1929 *WhAm 1*
Drake, Fred Raymond 1865-1932 *NatCAB 24,*
WhAm 1
Drake, Frederic Nelson 1887-1965 *NatCAB 51,*
WhAm 4
Drake, Harry LaBar 1897-1946 *NatCAB 38*
Drake, Harry Trevor 1889-1961 *WhAm 4*
Drake, Helen Virginia Frederick d1974
WhAm 6
Drake, Hervey John 1882-1963 *NatCAB 50*
Drake, J Frank 1880- *WhAm 6*
Drake, J Walter 1875-1941 *WhAm 2*
Drake, James Calhoun 1858-1921 *ApCAB X,*
WhAm 1
Drake, James Madison 1837-1913 *NatCAB 2,*
TwCBDA, WhAm 1
Drake, James Monroe 1883-1970 *NatCAB 57*
Drake, James Munroe 1823- *NatCAB 13*
Drake, Jeanie *WomWWA 14*
Drake, Jeannette May 1878- *WhAm 3*
Drake, John Burroughs 1826-1895 *DcAmB,*
WhAm H
Drake, John Louis 1892-1951 *NatCAB 40*
Drake, John Poad 1794?-1883 *NewYHSD,*
WhAm H
Drake, John Reuben 1782-1857 *BiAUS,*
BiDrAC, WhAm H
Drake, Joseph Horace, Sr. 1860-1947 *WhAm 2*
Drake, Joseph Rodman 1795-1820 *AmBi,*
ApCAB, DcAmB, Drake, NatCAB 5,
TwCBDA, WhAm H
Drake, Lauren J 1880-1953 *WhAm 3*
Drake, Louis Stoughton 1865-1933 *NatCAB 25*
Drake, Louis Stoughton 1865-1938 *ApCAB X*
Drake, Luther 1850-1921 *NatCAB 19*
Drake, Lyman Manley 1867-1943 *NatCAB 31*
Drake, Mary Eveline 1833- *AmWom*
Drake, Milton Jay 1906-1966 *NatCAB 51,*
WhAm 4
Drake, Nathan Lincoln 1898-1959 *WhAm 4*
Drake, Nelson Asaph 1842-1913 *NatCAB 16*
Drake, Noah Fields 1864-1945 *NatCAB 49,*
WhAm 2
Drake, Priscilla Holmes 1812-1892 *AmWom*
Drake, Russell Payson 1901-1971 *WhAm 5*
Drake, Samuel 1767-1854 *Drake*
Drake, Samuel 1768-1854 *ApCAB, DcAmB,*
WhAm H
Drake, Samuel Adams 1833-1905 *AmBi,*
ApCAB, DcAmB, NatCAB 25, TwCBDA,
WhAm 1
Drake, Samuel Gardner 1798-1875 *AmBi,*
ApCAB, DcAmB, Drake, NatCAB 7,
TwCBDA, WhAm H
Drake, Thomas J *BiAUS*
Drake, Tracy Corey 1864-1939 *NatCAB 30,*
WhAm 1
Drake, William *NewYHSD*
Drake, William A 1899-1965 *WhAm 4*
Drake, William Henry 1856-1925 *WhAm 1*
Drane, Herbert Jackson 1863-1947 *BiDrAC,*
WhAm 2, WhAmP
Drane, James Erasmus 1872-1947 *NatCAB 38*
Drane, Robert 1887-1970 *NatCAB 56*
Drane, Robert McVeigh 1885-1945 *NatCAB 34*
Dransfield, Jane 1875- *WhAm 5*
Dransfield, Thomas 1836-1923 *NatCAB 19*
Drant, Patricia Hart 1895-1955 *NatCAB 42,*
WhAm 3
Drapanas, Theodore 1930-1975 *WhAm 6*
Draparnaud, Jacques-Philippe-Raymond
1772-1804 *DcScB*
Drapeau, Raoul Laurent 1905-1966 *NatCAB 51*
Draper, Abijah Weld 1849-1925 *ApCAB X*
Draper, Alfred Pearman 1891-1955 *WhAm 3*
Draper, Alice Ames 1873- *WomWWA 14*
Draper, Alonzo Granville 1835-1865 *ApCAB*
Draper, Andrew Sloan 1848-1913 *AmBi,*
ApCAB, BiDAmEd, DcAmB,
NatCAB 12, TwCBDA, WhAm 1,
WhAmP
Draper, Arthur Joy 1875-1932 *NatCAB 29*
Draper, Bell Merrill 1857- *WomWWA 14*
Draper, Benjamin Helm Bristow 1885-1944
WhAm 2
Draper, Daniel 1841-1931 *AmBi, ApCAB,*
NatCAB 6, TwCBDA, WhAm 1
Draper, Dorothy 1889-1969 *WhAm 5*

Draper, Eben Sumner 1858- *NatCAB 14*
Draper, Eben Sumner 1858-1910 *NatCAB 23*
Draper, Eben Sumner 1858-1914 *DcAmB,*
WhAm 1, WhAmP
Draper, Eben Sumner 1893-1959 *NatCAB 51*
Draper, Ebenezer Daggett 1813-1887
NatCAB 23
Draper, Edward Bailey 1876-1947 *WhAm 2*
Draper, Ernest Gallaudet 1885-1954
NatCAB 40, WhAm 3
Draper, Frank Winthrop 1843-1909 *NatCAB 17,*
WhAm 1
Draper, George Otis 1867-1923 *NatCAB 12,*
WhAm 1
Draper, Helen Fidelia Hoffman 1871-1951
BiCAW, NatCAB 39
Draper, Henry 1837-1882 *AmBi, ApCAB,*
DcAmB, DcScB, NatCAB 6, TwCBDA,
WebAB, WhAm H
Draper, Ira 1764-1848 *DcAmB, WhAm H*
Draper, John *NewYHSD*
Draper, John 1702-1762 *DcAmB, NatCAB 19,*
WhAm H
Draper, John Christopher 1835-1885 *AmBi,*
ApCAB, NatCAB 6, TwCBDA
Draper, John William 1811-1882 *AmBi,*
ApCAB, AsBiEn, BiDAmEd, DcAmB,
DcScB, Drake, McGEWB, NatCAB 3,
TwCBDA, WebAB, WhAm H
Draper, Joseph 1794-1834 *BiAUS, BiDrAC,*
WhAm H
Draper, Joseph Rutter 1830-1886 *TwCBDA*
Draper, Lyman Copeland 1815-1891 *AmBi,*
ApCAB, DcAmB, DcAmLiB, Drake,
NatCAB 9, REnAW, TwCBDA,
WhAm H
Draper, Margaret d1800? *ApCAB*
Draper, Margaret Green 1730?-1807? *DcAmB,*
WhAm H, WhAmP
Draper, Mary Anna Palmer 1839-1914 *NotAW*
Draper, Norman 1893-1963 *WhAm 4*
Draper, Paul Arbuckle 1900-1972 *NatCAB 57*
Draper, Richard 1726?-1774 *DcAmB*
Draper, Richard 1727-1774 *ApCAB,*
WhAm H
Draper, Robert 1820?- *NewYHSD*
Draper, Ruth 1884-1956 *NatCAB 45,*
WhAm 3
Draper, Simeon 1804-1866 *ApCAB, Drake*
Draper, Warren Fales 1883-1970 *WhAm 5*
Draper, William *NewYHSD*
Draper, William Franklin 1842-1910 *BiDrAC,*
DcAmB, NatCAB 6, NatCAB 32,
TwCBDA, WhAm 1
Draper, William Henry 1801-1877 *ApCAB*
Draper, William Henry 1830- *ApCAB*
Draper, William Henry 1830-1901 *NatCAB 7,*
WhAm 1
Draper, William Henry 1830-1902 *TwCBDA*
Draper, William Henry 1841-1921 *BiDrAC,*
WhAm 1, WhAmP
Draper, William Henry, Jr. 1894-1974 *WhAm 6*
Draper, William Kinnicutt 1863-1926
ApCAB X, NatCAB 26, WhAm 1
Drath, Clara Louise F 1890- *WomWWA 14*
Dratt, Agnes Inez Lenore 1880- *WomWWA 14*
Draughon, Ralph Brown 1899-1968 *NatCAB 57,*
WhAm 5
Dravo, John Fleming 1819- *NatCAB 4*
Dravo, William McCray 1834-1904 *NatCAB 27*
Drawdy, Sherman 1903-1973 *NatCAB 57*
Drayer, Clarence Earl 1890- *WhAm 6*
Drayton, Charles O 1851-1928 *WhAm 1*
Drayton, Grace Gebbie 1877-1936 *WhAm 1,*
WomWWA 14
Drayton, Henry Shipman 1840-1923 *WhAm 1*
Drayton, Henry Sinclair 1839- *TwCBDA*
Drayton, J *NewYHSD*
Drayton, John *NewYHSD*
Drayton, John d1822 *BiAUS, Drake*
Drayton, John 1766-1822 *ApCAB, DcAmB,*
NewYHSD, TwCBDA
Drayton, John 1767-1822 *NatCAB 12,*
WhAm H
Drayton, Joseph *IIBEAAW, NewYHSD*
Drayton, Michael 1563-1631 *McGEWB*
Drayton, Percival 1812-1865 *ApCAB, DcAmB,*
Drake, NatCAB 4, TwCBDA, WhAm H

Drayton, Samuel d1949 *WhAm 2*
Drayton, Thomas Fenwick 1807?- *ApCAB*
Drayton, Thomas Fenwick 1807-1885 *NatCAB 12*
Drayton, Thomas Fenwick 1807?-1891 *TwCBDA, WhAm H*
Drayton, Thomas Fenwick 1808-1891 *DcAmB*
Drayton, William *BiAUS*
Drayton, William 1732-1790 *DcAmB, WhAm H*
Drayton, William 1733-1790 *ApCAB, Drake, NatCAB 11, TwCBDA*
Drayton, William 1776-1846 *ApCAB, BiAUS, BiDrAC, DcAmB, Drake, NatCAB 11, TwCBDA, WhAm H, WhAmP*
Drayton, William Henry 1742-1779 *AmBi, ApCAB, BiAUS, BiDrAC, DcAmB, Drake, NatCAB 7, TwCBDA, WhAm H*
Drebbel, Cornelius 1572-1633 *DcScB*
Dreer, Ferdinand Julius 1812-1902 *ApCAB X, NatCAB 10*
Drees, Charles William 1851-1926 *WhAm 1*
Drefs, Arthur George 1888-1950 *NatCAB 39, WhAm 3*
Dreher, E *NewYHSD*
Dreher, Julius Daniel 1846-1937 *NatCAB 10, TwCBDA, WhAm 1*
Dreher, LeRoy Herbert 1905-1965 *WhAm 4*
Dreher, Monroe Franklin 1899-1970 *WhAm 5*
Dreher, William Counts 1856-1929 *WhAm 1*
Dreibholz, Ernest William 1838-1926 *NatCAB 21*
Dreier, August 1841- *NatCAB 12*
Dreier, Christine Nielson 1866- *AmWom*
Dreier, Dorothea A 1870-1923 *BiCAW*
Dreier, H Edward 1872-1955 *NatCAB 42*
Dreier, Katherine Sophie 1877-1952 *BiCAW, DcAmB S5, NatCAB 42*
Dreier, Margaret *DcAmB S3*
Dreier, Mary Elisabeth 1875-1963 *WhAm 4*
Dreikurs, Rudolph d1972 *WhAm 5*
Dreis, Walter Herman 1888-1955 *NatCAB 42*
Dreiser, Herman Theodore 1871-1945 *McGEWB*
Dreiser, Theodore 1871-1945 *ApCAB X, DcAmB S3, EncAB, NatCAB 15, NatCAB 18, NatCAB 34, WebAB, WhAm 2*
Dreka, Louis 1839?- *NewYHSD*
Dreller, Louis 1897-1970 *WhAm 5*
Drennan, John Patton 1861-1919 *NatCAB 18*
Drennan, Michael Coyle 1838-1915 *NatCAB 16, WhAm 1*
Drennan, William 1872-1953 *NatCAB 41*
Drennen, D MacDonald 1857-1914 *NatCAB 30*
Drennen, W Melville 1859-1926 *NatCAB 20*
Dresbach, Glenn Ward 1889-1968 *WhAm 5*
Dresbach, Melvin 1874-1946 *WhAm 3*
Drescher, Henry Bernard 1884-1946 *NatCAB 37*
Drescher, Theodore Bausch 1894-1953 *WhAm 3*
Dresden, Arnold 1882-1954 *WhAm 3*
Dresel, Ellis Loring 1865-1925 *ApCAB X, WhAm 1*
Dresel, Emil *IlBEAAW, NewYHSD*
Dresel, Otto 1826?-1890 *DcAmB, WhAm H*
Dresen, Oswald Mathew 1899-1960 *WhAm 4*
Dreser, William 1820?- *NewYHSD*
Dresler, Earl Louis 1918-1972 *WhAm 5*
Dressel, Edwin Henry 1891-1959 *WhAm 4*
Dressel, Frederick Hermann 1861-1928 *ApCAB X*
Dressen, Charles Walter 1898-1966 *WhAm 4*
Dresser, Alice Reed 1870- *WomWWA 14*
Dresser, Charles 1800-1865 *TwCBDA*
Dresser, Daniel LeRoy 1866-1915 *WhAm 1*
Dresser, Horace d1877 *ApCAB*
Dresser, Horatio Willis 1866-1954 *ApCAB X, NatCAB 11, TwCBDA, WhAm 3*
Dresser, Louise 1882-1965 *WhAm 4*
Dresser, Paul 1857-1906 *WhAm HA, WhAm 4*
Dresser, Prudence Simpson *WomWWA 14*
Dresser, Raymond H 1901-1967 *WhAm 5*
Dresser, Solomon Robert 1842-1911 *BiDrAC, WhAm 4*
Dresslar, Fletcher Bascom 1858-1930 *WhAm 1*
Dresslar, Frank A, Sr. 1896- *WhAm 5*

Dressler, Louis Raphael 1861-1932 *WhAm 1, WhAm 1C*
Dressler, Marie 1869-1934 *NatCAB 27, NotAW, WebAB*
Dressler, Marie 1871-1934 *DcAmB S1*
Dressler, Marie 1873-1934 *AmBi, WhAm 1*
Dreuillettes, Gabriel 1593-1681 *ApCAB, Drake*
Drever, Thomas 1882-1965 *WhAm 4*
Dreves, Walter Julius 1897-1963 *WhAm 4*
Drew, Alfred Stanislaus 1921-1972 *WhAm 5*
Drew, Charles Aaron 1859-1952 *NatCAB 41*
Drew, Charles Myron 1868-1944 *NatCAB 33*
Drew, Charles Richard 1904-1950 *DcAmB S4, EncAB, McGEWB, WebAB, WhAm 3*
Drew, Charles Verner 1872-1937 *NatCAB 28*
Drew, Clement *NewYHSD*
Drew, Daniel 1788-1879 *ApCAB, Drake*
Drew, Daniel 1797-1879 *AmBi, DcAmB, McGEWB, NatCAB 11, TwCBDA, WebAB, WhAm H*
Drew, Edward *NewYHSD*
Drew, Edward B 1842-1924 *ApCAB X*
Drew, Francis A 1848-1910 *NatCAB 6*
Drew, Francis Webb 1851-1919 *NatCAB 18*
Drew, Frank Gifford 1872-1928 *WhAm 1*
Drew, Franklin Mellen 1837-1925 *WhAm 1*
Drew, Frederick Davenport 1913-1969 *NatCAB 55*
Drew, George Alexander 1827- *ApCAB*
Drew, George Alexander 1894-1973 *WhAm 5*
Drew, George Franklin 1827- *NatCAB 11*
Drew, George H 1833?- *NewYHSD*
Drew, Georgiana Emma 1856-1893 *DcAmB, NotAW, WebAB*
Drew, Gerald Augustin 1903-1970 *NatCAB 57, WhAm 5*
Drew, Gilman Arthur 1868-1934 *WhAm 1*
Drew, Horace Rainsford 1876-1951 *NatCAB 39*
Drew, Howard Porter 1890- *WhoColR*
Drew, Ira Walton 1878-1972 *BiDrAC, WhAm 5*
Drew, Irving Webster 1845-1922 *BiDrAC, NatCAB 21, WhAm 1*
Drew, James Byron 1877-1953 *NatCAB 40, WhAm 5*
Drew, Mrs. John 1820- *AmWom, NotAW*
Drew, John 1825-1862 *ApCAB, TwCBDA*
Drew, John 1827-1862 *AmBi, DcAmB, NatCAB 3, WhAm H*
Drew, John 1853-1927 *AmBi, ApCAB X, DcAmB, TwCBDA, WebAB, WhAm 1*
Drew, John 1854- *NatCAB 1, NatCAB 3*
Drew, John Graham 1864- *WhAm 4*
Drew, Lewis *NewYHSD*
Drew, Louisa Lane 1820-1897 *AmBi, ApCAB, DcAmB, NatCAB 8, NotAW, TwCBDA, WhAm H*
Drew, Maria Alice Kneen 1869- *WomWWA 14*
Drew, Morrill Newman 1862- *NatCAB 14*
Drew, Thomas Stevenson 1802-1879 *BiAUS, NatCAB 10*
Drew, Walter 1873-1961 *NatCAB 48*
Drewes, Alfred H 1913-1967 *WhAm 4, WhAm 5*
Drewry, Henry Harris 1901-1963 *NatCAB 50*
Drewry, Patrick Henry 1875-1947 *BiDrAC, NatCAB 41, WhAm 2, WhAmP*
Drewry, Raymond George 1894-1953 *NatCAB 40*
Drewry, William Francis 1860-1934 *WhAm 1*
Drexel, Alice Gordon Troth *WomWWA 14*
Drexel, Anthony *NewYHSD*
Drexel, Anthony Joseph 1826-1893 *AmBi, ApCAB, DcAmB, NatCAB 2, TwCBDA, WhAm H*
Drexel, Antony *NewYHSD*
Drexel, Francis Anthony 1824-1885 *WhAm H*
Drexel, Francis Martin 1792-1863 *ApCAB, DcAmB, NewYHSD, WhAm H*
Drexel, George W Childs 1868-1944 *WhAm 2*
Drexel, Joseph Wilhelm 1833-1888 *ApCAB, NatCAB 2, TwCBDA*
Drexel, Joseph William 1833-1888 *DcAmB, WhAm H*
Drexel, Katharine Mary 1858-1955 *DcAmB S5, DcAmReB, EncAB, REnAW*
Drexel, Mary Stretch Irick *BiCAW*
Drexler, Louis Phillippe 1836-1899 *NatCAB 41*

Dreyer, Elsa 1877- *WomWWA 14*
Dreyer, George Peter 1866-1931 *WhAm 1*
Dreyer, Henrietta Louise 1863- *WomWWA 14*
Dreyer, Johann Louis Emil 1852-1926 *DcScB*
Dreyer, Jorgan Christian 1878-1948 *WhAm 2*
Dreyer, Leslie Hayes 1902-1960 *WhAm 4*
Dreyer, Russell Paul 1916-1974 *WhAm 6*
Dreyer, Walter 1892-1966 *WhAm 4*
Dreyfous, Felix Jonathan 1857-1946 *NatCAB 54*
Dreyfous, Felix Julius 1896-1975 *WhAm 6*
Dreyfus, Alfred 1859-1935 *McGEWB, WhoMilH*
Dreyfus, Camille Edouard 1878-1956 *WhAm 3*
Dreyfus, Carl 1874-1951 *NatCAB 39*
Dreyfus, Carl 1876-1953 *WhAm 3*
Dreyfus, Louis 1877-1967 *NatCAB 53*
Dreyfus, Louis Goethe, Jr. 1889-1973 *WhAm 6*
Dreyfus, Max 1874-1964 *NatCAB 53*
Dreyfus, Theodore Frank 1878-1952 *NatCAB 41*
Dreyfus-Barney, Laura 1879- *WhAm 6*
Dreyfuss, Barney 1865-1932 *NatCAB 30*
Dreyfuss, Henry 1904-1972 *WhAm 5*
Dreyfuss, Leonard 1886-1969 *NatCAB 54, WhAm 5*
Dreyspring, Adolphe 1835-1906 *WhAm 1*
Dreystadt, Nicholas 1889-1948 *WhAm 2*
Driant, Emile August Cyprien 1855-1916 *WhoMilH*
Driemeyer, Henry 1888-1963 *WhAm 4*
Driesch, Hans Adolf Eduard 1867-1941 *DcScB, McGEWB*
Driggs, Edmund Hope 1865-1946 *BiDrAC, WhAm 2*
Driggs, Frank Howard 1895-1969 *WhAm 5*
Driggs, Frank Milton 1870- *WhAm 5*
Driggs, Howard Roscoe 1873-1963 *WhAm 4*
Driggs, John Fletcher 1813-1877 *BiAUS, BiDrAC, NatCAB 4, TwCBDA, WhAm H*
Driggs, Laurence LaTourette 1876-1945 *WhAm 2*
Driggs, Mary Ogden 1876- *WomWWA 14*
Driggs, Sarah Boardman Clark *WomWWA 14*
Drill, Lewis L 1877- *WhAm 5*
Drinard, J Elliott 1898-1967 *NatCAB 53*
Drinkard, Robert Uriel 1879-1935 *NatCAB 41*
Drinker, Anna 1827- *ApCAB, Drake*
Drinker, Anne 1827- *NatCAB 11*
Drinker, Catharine Ann 1841-1922 *DcAmB*
Drinker, Cecil Kent 1887-1956 *WhAm 3*
Drinker, Henry Sandwith 1880-1965 *NatCAB 52, WhAm 6*
Drinker, Henry Sturgis 1850-1937 *NatCAB 15, WhAm 1*
Drinker, John *NewYHSD*
Drinker, Katherine Rotan 1889- *WomWWA 14*
Drinker, Philip 1893-1972 *NatCAB 57*
Drinker, Philip 1894-1972 *WhAm 5*
Drinkwater, Jennie Maria 1841-1900 *DcAmB*
Dripps, Isaac L 1810-1892 *DcAmB, NatCAB 25, WhAm H*
Dripps, Joseph Frederick 1844- *TwCBDA, WhAm 4*
Dripps, Robert Dunning 1911-1973 *WhAm 6*
Drischel, Ora Manville 1879-1942 *NatCAB 31*
Driscol, Michael 1805-1880 *ApCAB, NatCAB 4, TwCBDA*
Driscoll, Alfred E 1902-1975 *WhAm 6*
Driscoll, Arthur Francis 1884-1967 *WhAm 4*
Driscoll, Charles Benedict 1885-1951 *WhAm 3*
Driscoll, Clara 1881-1945 *NotAW, WhAm 2*
Driscoll, Daniel Angelus 1875-1955 *BiDrAC, WhAm 5*
Driscoll, Denis Joseph 1871-1958 *BiDrAC, WhAm 3*
Driscoll, Donald Gotzian 1897-1974 *WhAm 6*
Driscoll, Frederick 1834-1907 *WhAm 1*
Driscoll, George Walter 1857- *WhAm 4*
Driscoll, H 1819?- *NewYHSD*
Driscoll, John Joseph 1911-1962 *NatCAB 49*
Driscoll, Joseph 1902-1954 *WhAm 3*
Driscoll, Louise 1875-1957 *WhAm 3*
Driscoll, Michael Edward 1851-1929 *BiDrAC, WhAm 1, WhAmP*
Driscoll, William H 1879-1950 *WhAm 3*
Drisius, Samuel 1602?-1673? *ApCAB,*

NatCAB 12

Drisler, Henry 1818-1897 *ApCAB, BiDAmEd, DcAmB, NatCAB 4, TwCBDA, WhAm H*
Driver, Godfrey Rolles 1892-1975 *WhAm 6*
Driver, James 1859-1925 *WhAm 1*
Driver, John Merritte 1858-1918 *NatCAB 17, WhAm 1*
Driver, Leeotis Lincoln 1867-1960 *WhAm 4*
Driver, Samuel Marion 1892-1958 *WhAm 3*
Driver, William Joshua 1873-1948 *BiDrAC, WhAm 5, WhAmP*
Driver, William Raymond 1839- *WhAm 4*
Droege, John Albert *WhAm 5*
Droke, George Wesley 1854-1936 *WhAm 3*
Droke, Maxwell 1896-1959 *WhAm 4*
Drolet, Gustave Adolphe 1844- *ApCAB*
Dromgoole, George Coke d1847 *BiAUS*
Dromgoole, George Coke 1795-1847 *NatCAB 19, TwCBDA*
Dromgoole, George Coke 1797-1847 *BiDrAC, WhAm H, WhAmP*
Dromgoole, Will Allen 1860-1934 *NatCAB 8, TwCBDA, WhAm 1, WomWWA 14*
Dromgoole, William Allen 1860-1934 *DcAmB S1*
Drone, Eaton Sylvester 1842-1917 *ApCAB, WhAm 1*
Drop Shot 1844-1925 *AmBi*
Droppers, Garrett 1860-1927 *NatCAB 20, WhAm 1*
Dropsie, Moses Aaron 1821-1905 *DcAmB*
Drossaerts, Arthur Jerome 1862-1940 *NatCAB 30, WhAm 1*
Drott, Edward Albert 1887-1956 *NatCAB 48*
Drouaillet, Gustav *NewYHSD*
Drouet, Robert 1870-1914 *WhAm 1*
Drought, Arthur Bernard 1914-1970 *WhAm 5*
Drought, Henry Patrick 1893-1957 *WhAm 3*
Drouin, Mark Robert 1903-1963 *WhAm 4*
Drown, Edward Staples 1861-1936 *WhAm 1*
Drown, Samuel Hilborn 1876- *NatCAB 16*
Drown, Solomon 1753-1834 *Drake*
Drown, Thomas Messinger 1842-1904 *ApCAB, DcAmB, NatCAB 7, TwCBDA, WhAm 1*
Drowne, Shem 1683-1774 *NewYHSD*
Drowne, Solomon 1753-1834 *ApCAB, NatCAB 8, TwCBDA*
Drowne, Thomas Stafford 1823-1897 *TwCBDA*
Droz, A *NewYHSD*
Droze, William Henry 1924- *EncAAH*
Drozniak, Edward 1902-1966 *WhAm 4*
Drucez, P J *NewYHSD*
Druckenmiller, Barton W 1891-1964 *WhAm 4*
Drucker, Arthur Eilert 1877-1949 *WhAm 2*
Drude, Paul Karl Ludwig 1863-1906 *DcScB*
Drueck, Charles 1906-1964 *WhAm 4*
Drueck, Charles John 1873-1945 *NatCAB 35*
Druffel, John Henry 1886-1967 *WhAm 4*
Druffel, John Henry, Jr. 1915-1965 *NatCAB 51*
Druillettes, Gabriel 1610-1681 *DcAmB, WhAm H*
Drukker, Dow Henry 1872-1963 *BiDrAC, NatCAB 49, WhAm 4, WhAm 5*
Drukker, Richard 1906-1973 *WhAm 5*
Druley, Garner Nicholas 1887-1946 *NatCAB 37*
Drum, A L 1875-1933 *WhAm 1*
Drum, Augustus 1815-1858 *BiAUS, BiDrAC, WhAm H*
Drum, Hugh Aloysius 1879-1951 *DcAmB S5, NatCAB 47, WhAm 3*
Drum, John Sylvester 1872- *WhAm 5*
Drum, Richard Coulter 1825-1909 *ApCAB, NatCAB 12, TwCBDA, WhAm 1*
Drum, Simon Henry 1807-1847 *ApCAB*
Drum, Walter 1870-1921 *WhAm 1*
Drumgoole, John C 1821-1888 *NatCAB 13*
Drumgoole, John C 1828-1888 *ApCAB, TwCBDA*
Drumgoole, John Christopher 1816-1888 *DcAmB, WhAm H*
Drumheller, Joseph 1900-1970 *WhAm 5*
Drumheller, Roscoe Maxson 1882-1943 *WhAm 2*
Drumm, Charles Palmer 1873-1960 *NatCAB 44*
Drumm, Thomas W 1871-1933 *WhAm 1*
Drummond, Lady *WomWWA 14*

Drummond, Alexander M 1884-1956 *WhAm 3*
Drummond, Amy McNally 1864- *WomWWA 14*
Drummond, Edmund John 1876-1938 *NatCAB 32*
Drummond, Sir Gordon 1771-1854 *ApCAB, Drake*
Drummond, Harrison Irwin 1868- *NatCAB 12*
Drummond, Harrison Irwin 1869- *WhAm 5*
Drummond, Huntly Redpath d1957 *WhAm 3*
Drummond, I Wyman 1855-1933 *WhAm 1*
Drummond, James Herbert 1865-1939 *WhAm 3*
Drummond, Joseph Blake 1884-1955 *NatCAB 43*
Drummond, Josiah Hayden 1827-1902 *WhAm 1*
Drummond, Richard Caldwell Steel 1879-1960 *NatCAB 50*
Drummond, Sara King Wiley 1871-1909 *WhAm 1*
Drummond, Sarah *ApCAB*
Drummond, Thomas 1809-1890 *ApCAB, BiAUS, NatCAB 20, TwCBDA*
Drummond, Thomas Russell 1873-1956 *NatCAB 46, WhAm 3*
Drummond, Wilbert Ivanhoe 1874- *WhAm 5*
Drummond, William d1677 *ApCAB, NatCAB 10*
Drummond, William d1814 *ApCAB*
Drummond, William W *BiAUS*
Drummond, Willis *BiAUS*
Drury, Alexander Greer 1844-1929 *WhAm 1*
Drury, Aubrey 1891-1959 *NatCAB 47, WhAm 3*
Drury, Augustus Waldo 1851-1935 *WhAm 1*
Drury, Dana Warren 1880-1963 *NatCAB 50*
Drury, Francis Edson 1850-1932 *NatCAB 24*
Drury, Francis Keese Wynkoop 1878-1954 *DcAmLiB, NatCAB 42, WhAm 3*
Drury, Frank Adams 1868-1936 *NatCAB 27*
Drury, J Henry 1862-1948 *NatCAB 36*
Drury, John 1898-1972 *WhAm 5*
Drury, John Benjamin 1838-1909 *DcAmB, NatCAB 15, TwCBDA, WhAm 1*
Drury, John H 1816- *NewYHSD*
Drury, Lacy 1758-1815 *WhAm H*
Drury, Marion Richardson 1849-1939 *NatCAB 7, WhAm 1*
Drury, Peter Arthur 1864-1942 *NatCAB 40*
Drury, Philo Walker 1876- *WhAm 6*
Drury, Robert Blee 1878-1933 *NatCAB 28*
Drury, Samuel Smith 1878-1938 *NatCAB 40, WhAm 1*
Drury, Theodore *WhoColR*
Drury, Victor Montague 1884-1962 *WhAm 4*
Drury, Walter Maynard 1880-1946 *WhAm 2*
Drury, Wells 1851-1932 *NatCAB 33, WhAm 1*
Drushel, J Andrew 1872-1940 *WhAm 1*
Drusus, Marcus Livius 124?BC-091BC *McGEWB*
Drybread, Ivory J 1875-1944 *NatCAB 39*
Dryden, Forrest Fairchild 1864-1932 *NatCAB 23, WhAm 1*
Dryden, George Bascomb 1869-1959 *WhAm 3*
Dryden, Helen *BiCAW*
Dryden, Hugh Latimer 1898-1965 *NatCAB 52*
Dryden, Hugh Latimer 1898-1966 *WhAm 4*
Dryden, James 1863-1935 *WhAm 1*
Dryden, John 1631-1700 *McGEWB*
Dryden, John Fairfield 1839-1911 *BiDrAC, DcAmB, NatCAB 9, TwCBDA, WhAm 1, WhAmP*
Dryden, John Lester *WhAm 3*
Dryden, John N 1856-1931 *WhAm 3*
Dryden, Mary Louise Clark 1876- *WomWWA 14*
Dryer, Charles Redaway 1850-1927 *NatCAB 23*
Dryer, Charles Redway 1850-1927 *WhAm 1*
Dryer, George William 1881-1959 *NatCAB 47, WhAm 3*
Dryer, Joseph Edward 1881- *WhAm 6*
Dryer, Rufus Keeler 1846-1937 *NatCAB 28*
Dryer, Thomas J *BiAUS*
Dryfoos, Orvil Eugene 1912-1963 *NatCAB 48, WhAm 4*
Drygalski, Erich Von 1865-1949 *DcScB*
Drysdale, Alexander Irvin 1841-1866 *ApCAB*

Drysdale, Alexander Irwin 1837-1886 *NatCAB 10*
Drysdale, George Arrowsmith 1873-1926 *NatCAB 20*
Drysdale, Sir George Russell 1912- *McGEWB*
Drysdale, Harry Hedgewick 1876-1945 *NatCAB 37*
Drysdale, Hugh d1726 *NatCAB 13*
Drysdale, Sir Matthew Watt 1892-1962 *WhAm 4*
Drysdale, Robert A d1964 *WhAm 4*
Drysdale, Thomas Murray 1831-1904 *ApCAB, WhAm 1*
Drysdale, William 1852-1901 *TwCBDA, WhAm 1*
Drysdale, William Tovey 1882-1948 *NatCAB 46*
Duaei, Alexander Julius 1890-1958 *NatCAB 50*
Duane, Alexander 1858-1926 *DcAmB, NatCAB 26, WhAm 1*
Duane, Charles Williams 1837-1915 *NatCAB 18*
Duane, James *NewYHSD*
Duane, James 1733-1797 *AmBi, ApCAB, BiAUS, BiDrAC, DcAmB, Drake, NatCAB 2, NatCAB 3, TwCBDA, WhAm H, WhAmP*
Duane, James Chatham 1824-1897 *AmBi, ApCAB, DcAmB, NatCAB 10, TwCBDA, WhAm H*
Duane, James Chatham 1876-1953 *NatCAB 40*
Duane, James May 1851-1912 *WhAm 1*
Duane, John William 1780-1865 *BiAUS*
Duane, Russell 1866-1938 *NatCAB 4, NatCAB 27, WhAm 1*
Duane, William 1760-1835 *AmBi, ApCAB, DcAmB, Drake, McGEWB, NatCAB 8, TwCBDA, WebAB, WhAm H, WhAmP*
Duane, William 1807-1882 *ApCAB*
Duane, William 1808-1882 *Drake, TwCBDA*
Duane, William 1872-1935 *AmBi, DcAmB S1, DcScB, WhAm 1*
Duane, William J 1868-1947 *NatCAB 40, WhAm 2*
Duane, William John 1780-1865 *AmBi, ApCAB, BiDrUSE, DcAmB, Drake, NatCAB 5, TwCBDA, WhAm H*
Duarte, Juan Pablo d1876 *ApCAB*
Duarte Coelho, Pereira d1554 *ApCAB*
Dub, Leonard Milton 1905-1962 *NatCAB 48*
DuBarry, Beekman 1824-1901 *TwCBDA, WhAm 1*
DuBarry, Joseph N 1830-1892 *NatCAB 7*
DuBarry, William H 1894-1958 *WhAm 4*
Dubbink, Gerrit Hendrik 1866-1910 *WhAm 1*
Dubbs, Henry Alfred 1868-1939 *NatCAB 47, WhAm 1*
Dubbs, Jesse Adams 1855-1918 *NatCAB 22*
Dubbs, Joseph Henry 1838-1910 *ApCAB, DcAmB, NatCAB 22, TwCBDA, WhAm 1*
Dubcek, Alexander 1921- *McGEWB*
Dube, John Langalibalele 1870-1949 *McGEWB*
Dube, Louis Theodore 1861- *IlBEAAW*
Dube, Paul Henderson 1908-1969 *NatCAB 55*
DuBellay, Joachim 1522?-1560 *McGEWB*
DuBignon, Fleming Grantland 1853- *NatCAB 1*
Dubilier, William 1888-1969 *WhAm 5*
Dubini, Angelo 1813-1902 *DcScB*
Dubinsky, David 1892- *EncAB, McGEWB, WebAB*
Duble, Lu 1896-1970 *WhAm 5*
Dubnov, Simon 1860-1941 *McGEWB*
Duboc, Frank Windsor 1894-1968 *WhAm 5*
DuBois, Albert 1831?- *NewYHSD*
Dubois, Augustus Jay 1849-1915 *AmBi, ApCAB, DcAmB, NatCAB 15, TwCBDA, WhAm 1*
Dubois, Charles Edward 1847-1885 *ApCAB*
DuBois, Charles Gilbert 1870-1940 *WhAm 1*
DuBois, Coert 1881-1960 *WhAm 3*
DuBois, Mrs. Cornelius *NewYHSD*
DuBois, Daniel N 1802?-1846 *NewYHSD*
DuBois, Durwood Carl 1902-1967 *WhAm 4A*
DuBois, Edward Church 1848-1914 *NatCAB 14, WhAm 1*
DuBois, Eugene Floyd 1882-1959 *BiHiMed, NatCAB 52, WhAm 3*

Dubois, Francois *DcScB*

Dubois, Fred Thomas 1851-1930 *BiDrAC, REnAW, TwCBDA, WhAm 1, WhAmP*

Dubois, Frederick T 1851-1930 *NatCAB 12*

DuBois, Gaston Frederic 1880-1953 *WhAm 3*

DuBois, George *NewYHSD*

DuBois, George Washington 1822- *TwCBDA*

DuBois, Gualterus 1666-1751 *ApCAB, NatCAB 12*

DuBois, Gussie Packard *WomWWA 14*

DuBois, Guy Pene 1884-1958 *BnEnAmA, NatCAB 43, WhAm 3*

DuBois, H W *NewYHSD*

Dubois, Henry Augustus 1808-1884 *ApCAB, TwCBDA*

Dubois, Jacques 1478-1555 *DcScB*

DuBois, James Taylor 1851-1920 *NatCAB 18, WhAm 1*

DuBois, Jean Joseph d1932 *WhAm 1*

DuBois, John 1764-1842 *ApCAB, DcAmB, Drake, NatCAB 1, TwCBDA, WhAm H*

DuBois, John Ezekiel 1861-1934 *WhAm 1*

DuBois, John Ezekiel 1865-1934 *NatCAB 27*

Dubois, Jules 1910-1966 *WhAm 4*

DuBois, Julian Arthur 1856-1937 *WhAm 3*

Dubois, Louis 1881-1949 *NatCAB 38*

Dubois, Marie Eugene Francois Thomas 1858-1940 *AsBiEn*

DuBois, Mary Ann Delafield 1813-1888 *NewYHSD*

DuBois, Mary Constance 1879-1959 *WhAm 3, WomWWA 14*

DuBois, Patterson 1847-1917 *WhAm 1*

DuBois, Phebe L 1883- *WomWWA 14*

DuBois, R P *NewYHSD*

DuBois, Samuel F 1805-1889 *NewYHSD, WhAm H*

DuBois, William Edward Burghardt 1868-1963 *BiDAmEd, EncAB, McGEWB, NatCAB 13, TwCBDA, WebAB, WhAm 4, WhAmP, WhoColR*

DuBois, William Ewing 1810-1881 *ApCAB, DcAmB, WhAm H*

DuBois-Reymond, Emil Heinrich 1818-1896 *AsBiEn, DcScB, McGEWB*

DuBois-Reymond, Paul David Gustav 1831-1889 *DcScB*

Duboise, Dudley M 1834- *BiAUS*

Dubord, Richard Joseph 1921-1970 *WhAm 5*

Duborg, Louis Guillaume Valentin 1766-1833 *DcAmB, WhAm H*

Dubos, Rene Jules 1901- *AsBiEn, McGEWB, WebAB*

Duboscq, Octave 1868-1943 *DcScB*

DuBose, Augusta Hines Wood *WomWWA 14*

Dubose, Catherine Anne 1826- *ApCAB, WhAm 4*

DuBose, Dudley McIver 1834-1883 *ApCAB, BiDrAC, WhAm H*

DuBose, Francis Goodwin 1873- *WhAm 5*

DuBose, Henry Wade 1884-1960 *WhAm 3*

DuBose, Horace Mellard 1858-1941 *NatCAB 18, NatCAB 30, WhAm 1*

DuBose, Joel Campbell 1855- *WhAm 4*

DuBose, John Witherspoon 1836- *WhAm 4*

Dubose, Marion 1878- *WhAm 6*

DuBose, Miriam Howard 1862- *AmWom*

DuBose, William Haskell 1870-1936 *WhAm 1*

DuBose, William Porcher 1836-1918 *AmBi, DcAmB, DcAmReB, NatCAB 18, TwCBDA, WhAm 1*

DuBose, William Richards 1854- *WhAm 4*

DuBosque, Francis LeBrun 1864-1940 *WhAm 1*

Dubost, Marie Louise 1793- *ApCAB*

Dubouchet, Florimand Langlois 1752-1826 *Drake*

Dubourg, Louis 1776-1883 *REnAW*

Dubourg, Louis Guillaume Valentin 1766-1833 *ApCAB, DcAmReB, NatCAB 4*

Dubourg, Louis William Valentine 1766-1833 *TwCBDA*

Dubourjal, Edme Savinien 1795-1865 *NewYHSD*

Dubourjal, Savinien Edme 1795-1865 *NewYHSD, WhAm H*

Dubousquet, Eugene *NewYHSD*

Dubray, Charles Albert 1875- *WhAm 5*

Dubreul, Joseph Paul 1814-1878 *ApCAB*

Dubs, Theodore Mathias 1877-1948 *NatCAB 39*

DuBuat, Pierre-Louis-Georges 1734-1809 *DcScB*

Dubuc, Joseph 1840- *ApCAB*

Dubufe, Claude Marie 1790-1864 *NewYHSD*

Dubuffet, Jean 1901- *McGEWB*

Dubuis, Claude Marie 1817-1895 *ApCAB, NatCAB 12*

Dubuis, Claude Mary 1817-1895 *TwCBDA, WhAm H*

Dubuisson, John Hugh 1904-1966 *NatCAB 53*

Dubuque, Julian 1762-1810 *AmBi*

Dubuque, Julien 1762-1810 *DcAmB, NatCAB 8, REnAW, WhAm H*

Ducachet, Henry William 1796-1865 *ApCAB*

Ducalvet, Pierre 1715?-1786 *ApCAB*

Ducasse, Curt John 1881-1969 *NatCAB 55, WhAm 5*

Ducasse, Jean Baptiste 1650-1715 *ApCAB*

DuCasse, Ralph Richelieu 1886-1954 *NatCAB 47*

Ducat, Arthur Charles 1830-1896 *TwCBDA*

Ducatel, Julius Timoleon 1796-1849 *ApCAB, NatCAB 8*

Duccio DiBuoninsegna 1255?-1319? *McGEWB*

Duce, Hugh Mario 1895-1965 *WhAm 4*

Duce, James Terry 1892-1965 *WhAm 4*

Ducey, Thomas James 1843-1909 *ApCAB, NatCAB 9, TwCBDA, WhAm 1*

DuChaillu, Paul Belloni 1835-1903 *AmBi, ApCAB, DcAmB, TwCBDA*

DuChaillu, Paul Belloni 1838-1903 *WhAm 1*

Duchamp, Marcel 1887-1967 *BnEnAmA*

Duchamp, Marcel 1887-1968 *McGEWB*

Duchamp-Villon, Raymond 1876-1918 *McGEWB*

Ducharme, Alphonse Napoleon 1881-1952 *NatCAB 41*

DuCharme, Charles Albert 1858- *NatCAB 17*

Duchassey, M J *NewYHSD*

Duche, Jacob 1737-1798 *ApCAB, DcAmB, NatCAB 4, TwCBDA, WhAm H, WhAmP*

Duche, Jacob 1739-1798 *Drake*

Duche, Thomas Spence, Jr. 1763-1790 *NewYHSD*

Duche DeVancy, Gaspard d1788 *NewYHSD*

Duchenne, Guillaume-Benjamin-Amand 1806-1875 *BiHiMed*

Duchesne, Mrs. *NewYHSD*

Duchesne, Joseph 1544?-1609 *DcScB*

Duchesne, Leon Chesnier 1840- *NatCAB 1*

Duchesne, Philippa Rose 1769-1852 *ApCAB, TwCBDA*

Duchesne, Rose Philippine 1769-1852 *AmBi, BiDAmEd, DcAmB, DcAmReB, NotAW, REnAW, WhAm H*

Duchin, Edward Frank 1909-1951 *DcAmB S5*

Duck, Allen Douglas 1884-1926 *NatCAB 22*

Ducker, Edward Augustus 1870-1946 *WhAm 2*

Ducker, Edward Augustus 1870-1948 *NatCAB 37*

Duckering, Florence West 1869-1951 *NatCAB 40, WomWWA 14*

Duckett, Allen B *BiAUS*

Duckinfield, Sir Nathaniel d1824 *ApCAB*

Duckwitz, Ferdinand Herman 1859-1915 *NatCAB 16*

Duckworth, George Eckel 1903-1972 *WhAm 5*

Duckworth, J Lon 1899-1964 *NatCAB 51*

Duckworth, Mary Walker Haines 1878- *WomWWA 14*

Duckworth, Roy Demarest 1899- *WhAm 6*

Duckworth, W Fred 1899-1972 *NatCAB 57*

Duckworth, William Henry 1894-1969 *WhAm 5*

Duckworth, William Lafayette 1834-1915 *NatCAB 17*

Duclary, Lepelletier 1824?- *NewYHSD*

Duclaux, Emile 1840-1904 *DcScB*

Duclerc, Jean-Baptiste 1662-1711 *ApCAB Sup*

Ducommun, Edmond Frederick 1880-1965 *WhAm 4*

Ducommun, Jesse Clarence 1904-1966 *WhAm 4*

DuCoudray, Philippe Charles J Tronson 1738-1777 *ApCAB, Drake, WebAMB, WhAm H*

Ducreux, Francois 1594-1666 *ApCAB Sup*

Ducreux, Francois 1596-1666 *Drake*

Ducro, John Peter 1865-1956 *NatCAB 45*

Ducrotay DeBlainville, Henri Marie *DcScB*

Ducrue, Bennon Francis 1721-1779 *ApCAB*

Ducrue, Francis Bennon 1721-1779 *WhAm H*

Duda, Herbert Wilhelm 1900-1975 *WhAm 6*

Duda, Michael 1909-1968 *NatCAB 54*

Duddy, Edward Augustin 1884-1966 *WhAm 4*

Dudensing, Richard d1899 *NewYHSD*

Dudgeon, Matthew Simpson 1871-1949 *DcAmLiB, WhAm 3*

Dudith, Andreas 1533-1589 *DcScB*

Dudley, A Dean 1878-1970 *WhAm 5*

Dudley, Albert Edward 1872-1925 *NatCAB 20*

Dudley, Albert Henry 1885-1945 *WhAm 3*

Dudley, Albertus True 1866-1955 *WhAm 3*

Dudley, Augustus Palmer 1853-1905 *NatCAB 2, WhAm 1*

Dudley, Benjamin Winslow 1785-1870 *AmBi, ApCAB, DcAmB, Drake, NatCAB 11, TwCBDA, WhAm H*

Dudley, Bide 1877-1944 *WhAm 2*

Dudley, Blandina 1783-1863 *ApCAB*

Dudley, Carl Ward 1910-1973 *WhAm 6*

Dudley, Charles Ashman 1839- *WhAm 4*

Dudley, Charles Benjamin 1842-1909 *ApCAB, DcAmB, NatCAB 12, TwCBDA, WhAm 1*

Dudley, Charles Edward 1780-1841 *ApCAB, BiAUS, BiDrAC, DcAmB, Drake, NatCAB 4, TwCBDA, WhAm H, WhAmP*

Dudley, Charles Rowland 1853- *TwCBDA, WhAm 1*

Dudley, Dean 1823- *ApCAB, Drake, TwCBDA*

Dudley, Edgar Swartwout 1845-1911 *WhAm 1, WhAm 4*

Dudley, Edward B d1855 *BiAUS, Drake*

Dudley, Edward Bishop 1769-1855 *BiDrAC, WhAm H, WhAmP*

Dudley, Edward Bishop 1787-1855 *ApCAB, NatCAB 4, TwCBDA*

Dudley, Edward Bishop 1789-1855 *DcAmB*

Dudley, Emelius Clark 1850-1928 *WhAm 1*

Dudley, Emilius Clark 1850-1928 *NatCAB 13, NatCAB 30*

Dudley, Frank Alonzo 1864-1945 *WhAm 2*

Dudley, Frank Church 1879-1949 *NatCAB 38*

Dudley, Frank Virgil 1868-1957 *WhAm 3*

Dudley, Frederick Merritt 1861- *WhAm 4*

Dudley, Mrs. Guilford 1876-1955 *WhAm 3*

Dudley, Guilford Swathel 1890-1961 *NatCAB 48*

Dudley, Guilford Swathel 1890-1962 *WhAm 4*

Dudley, Harold Merryman 1896-1970 *NatCAB 56*

Dudley, Helena Stuart 1858-1932 *NotAW, WhAm 3A, WomWWA 14*

Dudley, Henry C *WhAm H*

Dudley, Henry H 1891-1974 *WhAm 6*

Dudley, Henry Tyler *ApCAB X*

Dudley, Irving Bedell 1860-1911 *NatCAB 13*

Dudley, Irving Bedell 1861-1911 *TwCBDA, WhAm 1*

Dudley, Jack *IIBEAAW*

Dudley, James Benson 1859-1925 *BiDAmEd, TwCBDA, WhAm 1, WhoColR*

Dudley, James G 1848- *WhAm 4*

Dudley, Jessie Duncan *WomWWA 14*

Dudley, John Benton 1877-1960 *WhAm 4*

Dudley, John Gant 1909-1963 *WhAm 4*

Dudley, John Stuart 1893-1966 *NatCAB 52*

Dudley, Joseph 1647-1720 *AmBi, ApCAB, DcAmB, Drake, NatCAB 7, TwCBDA, WhAm H*

Dudley, Joseph Grassie 1869- *WhAm 5*

Dudley, Katharine *WomWWA 14*

Dudley, Lewis Joel 1815-1896 *TwCBDA*

Dudley, Lucy Bronson 1848-1920 *WhAm 1*

Dudley, Mary Henton 1846- *WomWWA 14*

Dudley, Mary Virginia Crawford 1868- *WomWWA 14*

Dudley, Nathan Augustus Monroe 1825-1910 *WhAm 1*

Dudley, Paul 1673-1751 *NatCAB 7*

Dudley, Paul 1675-1751 *AmBi, ApCAB, DcAmB, TwCBDA, WhAm H*

Dudley, Paul 1675-1752 *Drake*

Dudley, Pemberton 1837-1907 *NatCAB 3,*

TwCBDA, WhAm 1

Dudley, Pendleton 1876-1966 *WhAm 4*
Dudley, Plimmon Henry 1843-1924 *AmBi, NatCAB 13, NatCAB 19, WhAm 1*
Dudley, Richard Moberley 1838-1893 *NatCAB 5*
Dudley, Richard Moberly 1838-1893 *TwCBDA*
Dudley, Robert 1573-1649 *DcScB*
Dudley, Samuel Madison 1873-1947 *WhAm 2*
Dudley, Samuel William 1879-1963 *WhAm 4*
Dudley, Sarah Marie *AmWom*
Dudley, Thomas 1576-1652 *ApCAB*
Dudley, Thomas 1576-1653 *AmBi, DcAmB, Drake, McGEWB, NatCAB 7, TwCBDA, WebAB, WhAm H*
Dudley, Thomas Haines 1819-1893 *TwCBDA*
Dudley, Thomas Underwood 1837-1904 *ApCAB, NatCAB 3, TwCBDA, WhAm 1*
Dudley, Wesley Coleman 1867- *WhAm 4*
Dudley, William d1743 *NatCAB 7*
Dudley, William Henry 1811-1886 *ApCAB, TwCBDA*
Dudley, William Lofland 1859-1914 *ApCAB, NatCAB 8, TwCBDA, WhAm 1*
Dudley, William Russel 1849-1911 *AmBi, DcAmB, NatCAB 22, WhAm 1*
Dudley, William Russell 1849-1911 *ApCAB, TwCBDA*
Dudley, William Wade 1842-1897 *TwCBDA*
Dudley, William Wade 1842-1909 *NatCAB 2, WhAm 1*
Dudley, Winfield Ware 1879-1918 *WhAm 1*
Dudycha, George J 1903-1971 *WhAm 5*
Duehring, Frank Edward 1889-1945 *NatCAB 34*
Duel, Arthur Baldwin 1870-1936 *ApCAB X, NatCAB 37, WhAm 1*
Duell, Charles Halliwell 1905-1970 *WhAm 5*
Duell, Charles Holland 1850-1920 *ApCAB X, NatCAB 12, WhAm 1*
Duell, Prentice 1894-1960 *NatCAB 44, WhAm 4*
Duell, R Holland 1823-1891 *BiAUS*
Duell, Robert Holland 1824-1891 *ApCAB, TwCBDA, WhAm H*
Duell, Rodolphus Holland 1824-1891 *BiDrAC, NatCAB 12*
Duemler, George Ernest 1901-1966 *NatCAB 53*
Duemling, Hermann 1845- *WhAm 4*
Duenas, Francisco 1830?- *ApCAB*
Duer, Caroline King 1865-1956 *BiCAW, WhAm 3, WomWWA 14*
Duer, Catherine *ApCAB*
Duer, Douglas 1887-1964 *IIBEAAW*
Duer, Edward Louis 1836-1916 *ApCAB, NatCAB 10, NatCAB 25, WhAm 4*
Duer, John 1782-1858 *AmBi, ApCAB, DcAmB, Drake, NatCAB 11, TwCBDA, WhAm H*
Duer, William 1747-1799 *AmBi, ApCAB, BiAUS, BiDrAC, DcAmB, Drake, NatCAB 7, TwCBDA, WhAm H*
Duer, William 1805-1879 *ApCAB, BiAUS, BiDrAC, TwCBDA, WhAm H*
Duer, William Alexander 1780-1858 *AmBi, ApCAB, BiAUS, BiDAmEd, DcAmB, Drake, NatCAB 6, TwCBDA, WhAm H*
Duerink, John Baptist 1809-1857 *ApCAB*
Duerr, Alvan Emile 1872-1947 *WhAm 2*
Duerr, William Robert 1885-1958 *NatCAB 46*
Duesenberg, Fred Samuel 1877- *NatCAB 16*
DuFais, John 1855-1935 *NatCAB 40*
Dufal, Peter 1822- *TwCBDA*
Dufault, Joseph *IIBEAAW*
Dufay, Charles-Francois DeCisternai 1698-1739 *DcScB*
DuFay, Charles Francois DeCisternay 1698-1739 *AsBiEn*
Dufay, Guillaume 1400?-1474 *McGEWB*
Duff, Alexander 1806-1878 *McGEWB*
Duff, Alexander Wilmer 1864-1951 *NatCAB 38, WhAm 3*
Duff, Edward Aloysius 1885-1943 *WhAm 2*
Duff, G Lyman 1904-1956 *WhAm 3*
Duff, James Henderson 1883-1969 *BiDrAC, WhAm 5*
Duff, John 1787-1831 *ApCAB*
Duff, John T *NewYHSD*

Duff, Sir Lyman Poore 1865-1955 *WhAm 3*
Duff, Mary Ann d1832 *Drake*
Duff, Mary Ann 1795-1857 *ApCAB*
Duff, Mary Ann Dyke 1794-1857 *AmBi, DcAmB, NatCAB 6, NotAW, WhAm H*
Duff, Ned *NewYHSD*
Duff, Peter 1802-1869 *ApCAB*
Duff, Philip Grandy 1918-1964 *WhAm 4*
Duff, Philip Sheridan 1894-1962 *NatCAB 49, WhAm 4*
Duff, William Frederic 1855-1911 *NatCAB 16*
Duff, William McGill 1878-1948 *WhAm 3*
Duff, William McGill 1878-1949 *NatCAB 37*
Duffee, Mary Gordon 1840?- *ApCAB*
Duffee, Warren S 1917-1967 *WhAm 5*
Duffell, William R 1898-1973 *WhAm 6*
Duffens, Robert F 1897-1965 *NatCAB 51*
Dufferin, Frederick Temple H Blackwood 1826- *ApCAB*
Duffey, George Wallace 1912-1971 *WhAm 6*
Duffey, Warren Joseph 1886-1936 *BiDrAC, WhAm 1*
Duffie, Alfred Nattie 1835-1880 *ApCAB*
Duffield, Anna Vinacke 1865- *WomWWA 14*
Duffield, Divie Bethune 1821- *ApCAB*
Duffield, Edward *NewYHSD*
Duffield, Edward Dickinson 1871-1938 *ApCAB X, NatCAB 28, WhAm 1*
Duffield, Eugene Schulte 1908-1974 *WhAm 6*
Duffield, George *BiAUS*
Duffield, George 1732-1790 *ApCAB, DcAmB, Drake, TwCBDA, WhAm H*
Duffield, George 1767- *ApCAB*
Duffield, George 1794-1868 *ApCAB, DcAmB, Drake, TwCBDA, WhAm H*
Duffield, George 1816-1888 *ApCAB*
Duffield, George 1818-1888 *Drake, NatCAB 3, TwCBDA*
Duffield, Henry Martin 1842-1912 *ApCAB, TwCBDA*
Duffield, Henry Martyn 1842-1912 *WhAm 1*
Duffield, Howard 1854-1941 *WhAm 1*
Duffield, Isabella Graham Bethune *ApCAB*
Duffield, John Thomas 1823-1901 *ApCAB, TwCBDA, WhAm 1*
Duffield, Marcus McCampbell 1908-1973 *WhAm 6*
Duffield, Pitts 1869-1938 *WhAm 2*
Duffield, Samuel Augustus Willoughby 1843-1887 *DcAmB, NatCAB 9, WhAm H*
Duffield, Samuel Pearce 1833- *ApCAB, TwCBDA, WhAm 4*
Duffield, Samuel Willoughby 1843-1887 *ApCAB, TwCBDA*
Duffield, William Ward 1823-1907 *ApCAB, TwCBDA, WhAm 1*
Duffus, Robert Luther 1888-1972 *WhAm 5*
Duffy, Bernard Cornelius 1902-1972 *NatCAB 56, WhAm 5*
Duffy, Charles 1903-1972 *WhAm 5*
Duffy, Charles Gavan, Jr. 1909-1959 *NatCAB 46*
Duffy, Edmund 1899-1962 *WhAm 4*
Duffy, Edward Joseph 1906-1969 *NatCAB 55*
Duffy, Florence Armstrong 1876- *WomWWA 14a*
Duffy, Francis Patrick 1871-1932 *DcAmB S1, NatCAB 30, WebAMB, WhAm HA, WhAm 4*
Duffy, Francis Ryan 1888- *BiDrAC*
Duffy, Frank H d1950 *WhAm 3*
Duffy, Henry 1862-1948 *NatCAB 37*
Duffy, Herbert Smith 1900-1956 *NatCAB 48, WhAm 4*
Duffy, Hugh 1866-1954 *DcAmB S5*
Duffy, James Albert 1873-1968 *NatCAB 15, WhAm 4A, WhAm 5*
Duffy, James Joseph 1892-1941 *NatCAB 30*
Duffy, James O G 1864-1933 *WhAm 1*
Duffy, James Patrick Bernard 1878-1969 *BiDrAC, WhAm 6*
Duffy, John A d1944 *WhAm 2*
Duffy, Joseph Alexander 1903-1972 *WhAm 5*
Duffy, Joseph John 1896-1953 *NatCAB 44*
Duffy, Phillip B 1909-1973 *WhAm 6*
Duffy, Richard 1832?- *NewYHSD*
Duffy, Richard 1873-1949 *WhAm 2*
Duffy, Walter Bernard 1840-1911 *NatCAB 23*

Duffy, Ward Everett 1891-1961 *NatCAB 48, WhAm 4*
Duffy, William 1830?- *NewYHSD*
Duffy, William Core 1889-1956 *NatCAB 43*
Duffy, William Francis 1873-1934 *NatCAB 29*
Dufner, Edward 1871-1957 *WhAm 4*
Dufour, Amanda Louise Ruter 1822- *AmWom*
Dufour, Frank Oliver 1873-1952 *NatCAB 41, WhAm 3*
Dufour, Guillaume Henri 1787-1875 *DcScB, WhoMilH*
Dufour, John James 1763-1827 *DcAmB, WhAm H*
Dufour, William Cyprien 1871- *WhAm 5*
Dufourcq, Edward Leonce 1870-1919 *WhAm 1*
Dufrene, Edward *NewYHSD*
Dufrene, Thomas *NewYHSD*
Dufrenoy, Ours-Pierre-Armand 1792-1857 *DcScB*
Dufy, Raoul 1877-1953 *WhAm 3*
Dugan, Augustine A *NewYHSD*
Dugan, Caro Atherton *WhAm 5*
Dugan, Howard Francis 1894-1964 *WhAm 4*
Dugan, James 1912-1967 *WhAm 4*
Dugan, Larry Hull 1911-1968 *WhAm 5*
Dugan, Patrick Carroll 1866-1957 *NatCAB 47*
Dugan, Raymond Smith 1878-1940 *DcScB, NatCAB 36, WhAm 1*
Dugan, Thomas Buchanan 1858-1940 *WhAm 1*
Duganne, Augustine Joseph Hickey 1823-1884 *AmBi, ApCAB, DcAmB, Drake, NatCAB 4, TwCBDA, WhAm H*
Dugardin, Herve 1910- *WhAm 5*
Dugary *NewYHSD*
Dugas, Louis Alexander 1806- *ApCAB, TwCBDA*
Dugdale, Ralph E 1890-1964 *WhAm 4*
Dugdale, Richard L 1840-1883 *NatCAB 11*
Dugdale, Richard Louis 1841-1883 *AmBi, ApCAB, DcAmB, McGEWB, WhAm H*
Duggan, Arthur Pope 1876-1935 *NatCAB 27*
Duggan, B O d1949 *WhAm 3*
Duggan, Charles F 1895-1964 *WhAm 4*
Duggan, Edward Lloyd 1916-1968 *NatCAB 54*
Duggan, James 1825-1899 *ApCAB, NatCAB 9, TwCBDA*
Duggan, John J d1954 *WhAm 3*
Duggan, Laurence 1905-1948 *NatCAB 38, WhAm 2*
Duggan, Mell L 1857-1934 *WhAm 1*
Duggan, Paul Peter d1861 *NewYHSD*
Duggan, Peter Paul 1810?-1861 *ApCAB, Drake, NewYHSD*
Duggan, Sherman 1879- *WhAm 6*
Duggan, Stephen Pierce 1870-1950 *BiDAmEd, NatCAB 38, WhAm 3*
Duggan, Walter Teeling 1843-1915 *WhAm 1*
Duggan, William H 1899-1966 *WhAm 4*
Duggar, Benjamin Minge 1872-1956 *AsBiEn, DcScB, NatCAB 46, WhAm 3*
Duggar, John Frederick 1868-1945 *WhAm 2*
Duggar, Reuben Henry 1837-1921 *WhAm 3*
Dugmore, Arthur Radclyffe 1870- *WhAm 5*
Dugommier, Jean Francois Coquille 1736-1794 *ApCAB*
Dugro, Philip Henry 1855-1920 *BiDrAC*
Duguay-Trouin, Rene 1673-1736 *ApCAB Sup*
Dugue, Charles Oscar 1821-1872 *ApCAB, DcAmB, NatCAB 22, WhAm H*
DuHamel, Jean-Baptiste 1623-1706 *DcScB*
Duhamel, Jean-Marie-Constant 1797-1872 *DcScB*
Duhamel, Joseph 1836- *ApCAB*
Duhamel, Joseph Thomas 1841- *ApCAB*
DuHamel, William *WhAm 5*
Duhamel, William 1827-1883 *ApCAB*
Duhamel DuMonceau, Henri-Louis 1700-1782 *DcScB*
DuHautcilly *NewYHSD*
Duhem, Pierre Maurice Marie 1861-1916 *DcScB, McGEWB*
Duhring, Julia 1836-1892 *ApCAB, TwCBDA*
Duhring, Louis Adolphus 1845-1913 *AmBi, ApCAB, DcAmB, NatCAB 20, TwCBDA, WhAm 1*
Dujardin, Felix 1801-1860 *DcScB*
DuJardin, Rosamond Neal 1902-1963 *WhAm 4*
Duke, Alexandra Gamble 1881- *WomWWA 14*

Duke, Angier Buchanan 1884-1923 *NatCAB 29*
Duke, Basil C 1815- *BiDConf*
Duke, Basil Wilson 1838-1916 *BiDConf,*
DcAmB, WhAm 1
Duke, Benjamin Newton 1855-1929 *DcAmB,*
NatCAB 21, WhAm 1
Duke, Brodie Leonidas 1846-1919 *NatCAB 18*
Duke, Charles Wesley 1885-1956 *WhAm 3*
Duke, Claude Walter 1865-1936 *WhAm 1*
Duke, Edith Ridgeway 1863- *WomWWA 14*
Duke, James Buchanan 1856-1925 *AmBi,*
DcAmB, EncAAH, EncAB, McGEWB,
NatCAB 17, WebAB
Duke, James Buchanan 1857-1925 *WhAm 1*
Duke, James Thomas 1893-1970 *WhAm 5*
Duke, Nathaniel 1863- *WhAm 4*
Duke, Richard Thomas Walker 1822-1898
BiAUS, BiDrAC
Duke, Richard Thomas Walker, Jr. 1853-1926
WhAm 1
Duke, Samuel Page 1885-1955 *NatCAB 45,*
WhAm 3
Duke, T Seddon 1889-1966 *WhAm 4*
Duke, Vernon 1903-1969 *WhAm 5*
Duke, Victor LeRoy 1874-1933 *WhAm 1,*
WhAm 1C
Duke, Washington 1820-1905 *NatCAB 17*
Duke, William 1757-1840 *ApCAB*
Duke, William Mark 1879- *WhAm 6*
Duke, William Richard 1848-1929 *WhAm 1*
Duke, William Waddell 1882-1946 *NatCAB 37,*
WhAm 2
Dukelow, Charles Thomas 1865-1939 *WhAm 1*
Dukenfield, William Claude *WebAB*
Duker, J Edward 1862-1936 *NatCAB 36*
Dukes, Charles Alfred 1872-1942 *WhAm 2*
Dukes, J *NewYHSD*
Dukes, Joseph 1811- *ApCAB*
Dukes, Richard Gustavus 1871-1950 *WhAm 3*
Dukeshire, Wallace Benjamin 1892-1960
NatCAB 49
Dula, Robert Byron 1848- *NatCAB 12*
DuLac, Perrin *Drake*
Dulaney, Alice Hardeman 1877- *WomWWA 14*
Dulaney, Benjamin Lewis 1857-1930 *WhAm 1*
Dulaney, Daniel 1721-1797 *Drake*
Dulaney, Henry Stier 1849-1928 *WhAm 1*
Dulaney, William d1868 *Drake*
Dulaney, William LeRoy 1838- *TwCBDA,*
WhAm 4
Dulany, Daniel 1685-1753 *AmBi, DcAmB,*
WhAm H
Dulany, Daniel 1721-1797 *ApCAB, NatCAB 9*
Dulany, Daniel 1722-1797 *AmBi, DcAmB,*
WebAB, WhAm H
Dulany, George William, Jr. 1877-1959
WhAm 3
Dulany, Henry Rozier, Jr. 1889-1948 *WhAm 2*
Dulany, Lloyd d1782 *ApCAB*
Dulany, William d1868 *ApCAB*
Dulany, William Henry 1874-1948 *WhAm 2*
Dulcan, Charles Benjamin 1888-1957
NatCAB 44, WhAm 3
Dulce Y Garay, Domingo 1808-1869 *ApCAB*
DuLhut, Daniel Greysolon d1709 *ApCAB*
Dulin, Elijah Shelton 1821-1891 *TwCBDA*
Duling, G Harold 1909-1964 *WhAm 4*
Dull, Floyd Norman 1883-1957 *WhAm 6*
Dull Knife 1820?-1883 *REnAW*
Dullaert Of Ghent, Jean 1470?-1513 *DcScB*
Dulles, Allen Macy 1854-1930 *WhAm 1*
Dulles, Allen Welsh 1893-1969 *WhAm 5,*
WhWW-II
Dulles, Charles Winslow 1850-1921 *TwCBDA,*
WhAm 1
Dulles, John Foster 1888-1959 *BiDrAC,*
BiDrUSE, EncAB, McGEWB,
NatCAB 43, WebAB, WhAm 3, WhAmP
Dulles, John Welsh 1823-1887 *ApCAB,*
NatCAB 6
Dulles, Joseph Heatly 1853-1937 *TwCBDA,*
WhAm 2
Dullzell, Paul 1879-1961 *WhAm 4*
Dulon, Rudolf 1807-1869 *ApCAB*
Dulong, Pierre Louis 1785-1838 *AsBiEn,*
DcScB
Dulongpre, Louis 1754-1843 *NewYHSD*
Dulski, Thaddeus Joseph 1915- *BiDrAC*

Duluc, Andrew *NewYHSD*
DuLuth, Daniel DeGrecylon 1649-1709?
NatCAB 4
Duluth, Daniel Greysolon, Sieur 1636-1710
AmBi, DcAmB, WhAm H
Duluth, Daniel Greysolon, Sieur 1649-1709?
REnAW
Duluth, Daniel Greysolon, Sieur *see also* DuLhut,
Daniel G
Dumaine, Frederic Christopher 1866-1951
DcAmB S5, WhAm 3
Dumaresque, Philip *ApCAB*
Dumas, Alexandre 1803-1870 *McGEWB*
Dumas, Alexandre Davy 1762-1806 *ApCAB*
Dumas, Gustave 1858-1958 *WhAm 3*
Dumas, Henry J 1875- *WhoColR*
Dumas, Jack 1916- *IIBEAAW*
Dumas, Jean Baptiste Andre 1800-1884 *AsBiEn,*
DcScB, McGEWB
Dumas, Lawrence 1885-1953 *NatCAB 47*
Dumas, Count Mathieu 1753-1837 *ApCAB,*
Drake
Dumas, Valsin *NewYHSD*
Dumas, Walter A 1893-1952 *WhAm 3*
Dumas, William Thomas 1858- *WhAm 4*
Dumay, Alonzo Marion 1864-1933 *NatCAB 25*
Dumba, Constantin Theodor 1856-1915
WhAm 1
Dumbauld, Horatio Snyder 1869-1945 *WhAm 3*
Dumble, Edwin Theodore 1852-1927
NatCAB 21, WhAm 1
Dumbleton *DcScB*
Dumcke, John D *NewYHSD*
Dumeril, Andre-Marie-Constant 1774-1860
DcScB Sup
Dumetz, Francisco d1811 *WhAm H*
DuMez, Andrew Grover 1885-1948 *NatCAB 37,*
WhAm 2
Dumke *NewYHSD*
Dumler, Martin George 1868-1958 *NatCAB 49,*
WhAm 3
Dumm, Benjamin Alfred 1867- *WhAm 5*
Dummeier, Edwin F 1887-1946 *WhAm 2*
Dummer, Edwin Heyse 1902-1963 *WhAm 4*
Dummer, Jeremiah 1645-1718 *AmBi,*
BnEnAmA, DcAmB, NewYHSD,
WhAm H
Dummer, Jeremiah 1679?-1739 *AmBi, DcAmB,*
Drake, NatCAB 1, WhAm H
Dummer, Jeremiah 1680?-1739 *ApCAB*
Dummer, William 1677-1761 *ApCAB, Drake*
DuMoncel, Theodose Achille Louis 1821-1884
DcScB
Dumonchel, John Baptist 1784-1844 *ApCAB*
Dumond, Dwight Lowell 1895- *EncAAH*
DuMond, Frank Vincent 1865-1951 *IIBEAAW,*
NatCAB 41, WhAm 3
DuMond, Frederick Melville 1867-1927
IIBEAAW, NatCAB 27
DuMont, Allen Balcom 1901-1965 *WhAm 4*
Dumont, Conrad *NewYHSD*
Dumont, Ebenezer 1814-1871 *ApCAB, BiAUS,*
BiDrAC, Drake, TwCBDA, WhAm H
Dumont, Elizabeth 1876- *WomWWA 14*
Dumont, Frederick Theodore Frelinghuysen
1869-1939 *WhAm 1*
Dumont, John B *ApCAB X*
Dumont, Julia Louisa 1794-1857 *ApCAB*
Dumont, Paul Emile 1879- *WhAm 6*
DuMont, Randolph Eugene 1902-1961
NatCAB 48
Dumont, Wayne 1871-1929 *ApCAB X,*
WhAm 1
Dumont DeMontigny, Louis-F-Benjamin
NewYHSD
DuMotay, Cyprien Tessie 1819-1880 *ApCAB*
DuMouchel, Leandre Arthur 1844- *NatCAB 12,*
WhAm 5
DuMoulin, Bishop 1870-1947 *WhAm 2C*
DuMoulin, Frank 1870-1947 *NatCAB 35,*
WhAm 2
DuMoulin, John Philip 1834- *ApCAB Sup*
Dumouriez, Charles Francois 1739-1823
WhoMilH
Dun, Angus 1892-1971 *NatCAB 57, WhAm 5*
Dun, Edwin 1848-1931 *NatCAB 12, TwCBDA,*
WhAm 1
Dun, James 1844-1908 *WhAm 1*

Dun, Robert Graham 1826-1900 *DcAmB,*
NatCAB 2, WhAm 1
Dun, Walter Angus 1857-1887 *TwCBDA*
Dunagan, John Claiborne 1886-1965
NatCAB 57
Dunant, Jean Henri 1828-1910 *WhoMilH*
Dunaway, John Allder 1886-1969 *WhAm 5*
Dunaway, Thomas F 1851- *WhAm 4*
Dunbar, Alice Ruth Moore 1875- *WhoColR,*
WomWWA 14
Dunbar, Arthur White 1869- *WhAm 5*
Dunbar, Charles Edward, Jr. 1888-1959
NatCAB 47, WhAm 4
Dunbar, Charles Franklin 1830-1900 *AmBi,*
DcAmB, NatCAB 9, WhAm 1
Dunbar, Charles Robert 1873-1943 *NatCAB 32*
Dunbar, Duke Wellington 1894-1972 *WhAm 5*
Dunbar, Duncan 1791?-1864 *ApCAB*
Dunbar, Erroll *WhAm 1*
Dunbar, Miss F J *NewYHSD*
Dunbar, Flanders d1959 *WhAm 3*
Dunbar, George, Jr. *NewYHSD*
Dunbar, George, Sr. *NewYHSD*
Dunbar, James Robert 1847-1915 *WhAm 1*
Dunbar, James Whitson 1860-1943 *BiDrAC,*
WhAm 2
Dunbar, Janet 1888- *WomWWA 14*
Dunbar, Jesse Tuckwiller 1880-1928
NatCAB 21
Dunbar, John H 1890-1936 *WhAm 1*
Dunbar, Margaret Irene 1872- *WomWWA 14*
Dunbar, Mary Helena *WomWWA 14*
Dunbar, Moses 1746-1777 *ApCAB, DcAmB,*
WhAm H, WhAmP
Dunbar, Newell 1845-1925 *WhAm 1*
Dunbar, Olivia Howard 1873- *WomWWA 14*
Dunbar, Paul Brown 1882-1968 *NatCAB 54*
Dunbar, Paul Laurence 1872-1906 *AmBi,*
ApCAB Sup, DcAmB, McGEWB,
NatCAB 9, TwCBDA, WebAB, WhAm 1
Dunbar, Ralph McNeal 1890-1970 *DcAmLiB*
Dunbar, Ralph O 1845-1912 *NatCAB 5,*
WhAm 1
Dunbar, Reberta Johnson *WhoColR*
Dunbar, Robert 1812-1890 *DcAmB, WhAm H*
Dunbar, Saidie Orr 1880-1960 *NatCAB 51,*
WhAm 6, WomWWA 14
Dunbar, Thomas d1767 *ApCAB*
Dunbar, Ulric Stonewall Jackson 1862-1927
NatCAB 42, WhAm 1
Dunbar, William d1860 *BiAUS, NatCAB 3*
Dunbar, William 1460?-1520? *McGEWB*
Dunbar, Sir William 1740?-1810 *ApCAB*
Dunbar, William 1749-1810 *AmBi, DcAmB,*
McGEWB, WhAm H
Dunbar, William 1805-1861 *BiDrAC,*
WhAm H
Dunbar, William Harrison 1862- *WhAm 4*
Dunbar, William McLeish 1895-1951
NatCAB 41
Dunbar, Willis Frederick 1902-1970
NatCAB 55
Dunbaugh, Harry Joy 1877-1969 *NatCAB 54,*
WhAm 5
Dunca, Frederick S d1952 *WhAm 3*
Duncalf, Frederic 1882-1963 *WhAm 4*
Duncan, Albert Benjamin Ford 1903-1972
NatCAB 57
Duncan, Albert Greene 1868-1928 *NatCAB 21,*
WhAm 1
Duncan, Alexander d1852 *BiAUS, TwCBDA*
Duncan, Alexander 1788-1853 *BiDrAC,*
WhAm H
Duncan, Alexander Edward 1878-1972 *WhAm 5,*
WhAm 6
Duncan, Arch Adam 1884-1962 *NatCAB 50*
Duncan, Augustin 1873-1954 *NatCAB 42*
Duncan, Carson Samuel 1879-1958 *NatCAB 48,*
WhAm 3
Duncan, Catherine Gross 1908-1968
NatCAB 54
Duncan, Charles *BiAUS*
Duncan, Charles 1872-1936 *WhAm 1*
Duncan, Charles Miguel 1877-1960 *WhAm 4*
Duncan, Daniel 1806-1849 *BiAUS, BiDrAC,*
WhAm H
Duncan, David Shaw 1876-1941 *WhAm 1*
Duncan, Edward Carlton 1862-1920 *WhAm 1*

Duncan, Edwin 1905-1973 *WhAm 6*
Duncan, Ernest Allen 1885-1950 *NatCAB 39*
Duncan, Florence *WomWWA 14*
Duncan, Frances 1877- *WhAm 5,*
WomWWA 14
Duncan, Frederick Smyth 1868-1953
NatCAB 44
Duncan, Garnett 1800-1875 *BiAUS, BiDrAC,*
WhAm H
Duncan, George *NewYHSD*
Duncan, George Brand 1861-1950 *WhAm 2A*
Duncan, George Martin 1857-1928 *NatCAB 21,*
TwCBDA, WhAm 1
Duncan, George Stewart 1860-1946 *NatCAB 35*
Duncan, Gerald 1903-1970 *WhAm 5*
Duncan, Glenn A 1896-1956 *WhAm 3*
Duncan, Greer Assheton 1887-1962 *WhAm 4*
Duncan, Herman Cope 1846- *TwCBDA*
Duncan, Herschel Mills 1888-1957 *WhAm 3*
Duncan, Isaac Greenwood 1884-1955
NatCAB 42
Duncan, Isadora 1878-1927 *AmBi, DcAmB,*
EncAB, McGEWB, NatCAB 22, NotAW,
WebAB, WhAm HA, WhAm 4
Duncan, James 1756-1844 *BiDrAC, WhAm H*
Duncan, James 1810-1849 *ApCAB, Drake*
Duncan, James 1811-1849 *NatCAB 11*
Duncan, James 1857-1928 *DcAmB S1,*
WhAm 1, WhAmP
Duncan, James Armstrong 1830-1877 *ApCAB,*
TwCBDA
Duncan, James Cameron 1860-1937 *WhAm 1*
Duncan, James Floyd 1809- *WhAm 5*
Duncan, James Henry 1793-1869 *ApCAB,*
BiAUS, BiDrAC, TwCBDA, WhAm H
Duncan, James R 1901-1963 *WhAm 4*
Duncan, John Charles 1882-1967 *DcScB,*
NatCAB 54
Duncan, John Chester 1859-1942 *NatCAB 35*
Duncan, John Harris 1852-1919 *WhAm 1*
Duncan, John James 1919- *BiDrAC*
Duncan, John M 1796-1825 *ApCAB, Drake*
Duncan, John Mason 1853- *TwCBDA*
Duncan, John Saunders 1846-1914 *NatCAB 16*
Duncan, Johnson K 1826-1863 *Drake*
Duncan, Johnson Kelly 1827-1862 *ApCAB,*
NatCAB 12, TwCBDA
Duncan, Joseph *NewYHSD*
Duncan, Joseph 1789-1844 *ApCAB, TwCBDA*
Duncan, Joseph 1790?-1844 *BiAUS, Drake*
Duncan, Joseph 1794-1844 *BiDrAC, DcAmB,*
NatCAB 11, WhAm H, WhAmP
Duncan, Joseph Smith 1858-1950 *NatCAB 46*
Duncan, Joseph Wilson 1853-1912 *WhAm 1*
Duncan, Lena Elizabeth Hill 1871-
WomWWA 14
Duncan, Lewis Johnston 1875- *WhAm 5*
Duncan, Louis 1862-1916 *NatCAB 12,*
NatCAB 14, TwCBDA, WhAm 1
Duncan, Luther Noble 1875-1947 *WhAm 2*
Duncan, Norman 1871-1916 *WhAm 1*
Duncan, Oliver *NewYHSD*
Duncan, Oscar Dibble 1874-1947 *NatCAB 34,*
WhAm 2
Duncan, Richard Meloan 1889-1974 *BiDrAC,*
WhAm 6
Duncan, Robert Blackford 1920- *BiDrAC*
Duncan, Robert Kennedy 1868-1914 *AmBi,*
DcAmB, NatCAB 21, WhAm 1
Duncan, Ruth Henley 1908-1969 *WhAm 5*
Duncan, Sallie L 1877- *WhoColR*
Duncan, Samuel Edward 1904-1968 *WhAm 5*
Duncan, Samuel White 1838-1898 *ApCAB,*
TwCBDA
Duncan, Silas E d1834 *Drake*
Duncan, Simeon Winfield Scott 1848-1916
NatCAB 17
Duncan, Stuart *WhAm 3*
Duncan, Stuart English 1866-1963 *NatCAB 52*
Duncan, Thomas *NewYHSD*
Duncan, Thomas 1760-1827 *NatCAB 16*
Duncan, Thomas 1819-1887 *ApCAB,*
TwCBDA
Duncan, Thomas Shearer 1881-1957 *WhAm 4*
Duncan, Tracy Harry 1879-1942 *NatCAB 32*
Duncan, Walter Jack 1881-1941 *WhAm 1*
Duncan, Walter Wofford T d1945 *WhAm 2*
Duncan, Warren W 1857-1938 *WhAm 1*

Duncan, Watson Boone 1867-1930 *WhAm 1*
Duncan, Mrs. William *NewYHSD*
Duncan, William 1772-1864 *ApCAB*
Duncan, William Addison 1836-1884 *BiDrAC,*
WhAm H
Duncan, William Alexander 1837- *NatCAB 3*
Duncan, William Butler 1830-1912 *WhAm 1*
Duncan, William Cary 1874-1945 *WhAm 2*
Duncan, William Cecil 1824-1864 *ApCAB,*
Drake, TwCBDA
Duncan, William McKinley 1873-1945 *WhAm 2*
Duncan, William Stevens 1834- *ApCAB*
Duncan, William Wallace 1839-1908 *ApCAB,*
NatCAB 5, TwCBDA, WhAm 1
Duncan-Clark, Samuel John 1875-1938
WhAm 1
Duncanson, Robert S 1817?-1872 *BnEnAmA,*
IIBEAAW, NewYHSD, WhAm H
Duncanson, Thomas Sherriff 1896-1971
WhAm 5
Dunckerley *NewYHSD*
Duncklee, John Butler 1848- *WhAm 1*
Duncombe, Franklin 1897-1964 *NatCAB 50*
Duncombe, John Francis 1831-1902 *NatCAB 24*
Duncombe, Tyrrell Hubert Augustus 1867-1945
NatCAB 35
Dundas, Francis 1750?-1824 *ApCAB, Drake*
Dundas, James 1788-1865 *ApCAB*
Dundas, Thomas 1730-1794 *Drake*
Dundas, William H *BiAUS*
Dundee, John Graham Of C, Earl Of 1649-1689
WhoMilH
Dundey, Charles L 1872- *WhAm 5*
Dundonald, Archibald Cochrane, Earl Of
1749-1831 *DcScB*
Dundy, Elmer Scipio 1830-1896 *BiAUS,*
REnAW
Duner, Nils Christofer 1839-1914 *DcScB*
Dunfee, John 1851-1904 *NatCAB 14*
Dunford, Edward Bradstreet 1890-1966
WhAm 4
Dunford, Ernest 1884-1955 *NatCAB 43*
Dunford, Ralph Emerson 1896-1973 *WhAm 5*
Dungan, Albert Wallace 1894-1964 *WhAm 4*
Dungan, David Roberts 1837- *WhAm 4*
Dungan, Irvine 1844- *TwCBDA*
Dungan, James Irvine 1844-1931 *BiDrAC*
Dungan, Paul Baxter 1877-1941 *NatCAB 31,*
WhAm 2
Dungan, Susan Bray *WomWWA 14*
Dungan, Thomas Corwin 1840-1916
NatCAB 17
Dungay, Neil Stanley 1882-1958 *NatCAB 47,*
WhAm 3
Dungee, John Riley 1860- *WhoColR*
Dunglinson, George, Jr. 1882-1957 *NatCAB 45*
Dunglison, Richard James 1834-1901 *ApCAB,*
WhAm 1
Dunglison, Robley 1788-1869 *DcScB*
Dunglison, Robley 1798-1869 *AmBi, ApCAB,*
BiDAmEd, DcAmB, Drake, NatCAB 10,
WhAm H
Dunham, Adeline Frances 1879- *WomWWA 14*
Dunham, Amelia Hickenlooper 1874-
WomWWA 14
Dunham, Arthur 1875-1938 *WhAm 1*
Dunham, Carl Ernest 1898-1969 *NatCAB 55*
Dunham, Carroll 1828-1877 *ApCAB,*
NatCAB 3
Dunham, Carroll 1887-1948 *NatCAB 39*
Dunham, Charles Little 1906-1975 *WhAm 6*
Dunham, Clayton Aubra 1876-1946 *NatCAB 36*
Dunham, Cyrus Livingston 1817-1877 *BiAUS,*
BiDrAC, WhAm H
Dunham, Daniel H 1849-1924 *WhAm 1*
Dunham, David R *NewYHSD*
Dunham, Edward Kellogg 1860-1922
NatCAB 30, WhAm 1
Dunham, Edward Woodruff 1868-1944
NatCAB 34
Dunham, Emma Bedelia 1826- *AmWom*
Dunham, Franklin 1892-1962 *WhAm 4*
Dunham, Frederic Gibbons 1878-1943
NatCAB 35, WhAm 2
Dunham, George Clark 1887-1954 *NatCAB 44*
Dunham, George Earl 1859-1922 *NatCAB 19,*
WhAm 1
Dunham, George Lora 1859-1927 *NatCAB 21*

Dunham, Henry Goodrich 1862- *WhAm 4*
Dunham, Henry Kennon 1872-1944 *WhAm 2*
Dunham, Henry Morton 1853-1929 *DcAmB,*
NatCAB 21, WhAm 1
Dunham, Howard Potter 1878- *WhAm 6*
Dunham, J *NewYHSD*
Dunham, James Henry 1870-1953 *NatCAB 42,*
WhAm 3
Dunham, James Webb 1905-1963 *NatCAB 50,*
WhAm 4
Dunham, John Dudley 1873- *WhAm 1*
Dunham, Katherine 1910- *WebAB*
Dunham, Lawrence Boardman 1882-1959
NatCAB 44
Dunham, Lyndon Leon 1868-1950 *NatCAB 38*
Dunham, Marion Howard 1842- *AmWom*
Dunham, Otis E 1876- *ApCAB X*
Dunham, Ransom Williams 1838-1896 *BiDrAC,*
TwCBDA, WhAm H
Dunham, Ray E 1886-1956 *NatCAB 43*
Dunham, Robert James 1876-1948 *WhAm 3*
Dunham, Rowland Warren 1885-1967
NatCAB 54
Dunham, Russell H d1958 *WhAm 3*
Dunham, Samuel 1835-1936 *NatCAB 28*
Dunham, Samuel Clarke 1855- *WhAm 4*
Dunham, Sering Potter 1842-1913 *NatCAB 34*
Dunham, Sturges Sigler 1874-1944 *NatCAB 33,*
WhAm 2
Dunham, Sylvester Clark 1846-1915 *WhAm 1*
Dunham, Theodore 1862-1951 *NatCAB 41*
Dunham, Thomas *NewYHSD*
Dunham, William Russell 1833- *ApCAB,*
WhAm 4
Dunham, William S *NewYHSD*
Duniway, Abigail Jane Scott 1834-1915 *AmBi,*
AmWom, DcAmB, NotAW, REnAW,
WhAm 4, WhAmP, WomWWA 14
Duniway, Clyde Augustus 1866-1944
NatCAB 13, WhAm 2
Dunk, Alfred Owen 1873-1936 *NatCAB 26*
Dunk, Edith Watkins 1876- *NatCAB 17,*
WomWWA 14
Dunkel, J Ambrose 1871-1944 *WhAm 2*
Dunkerley, Joseph *NewYHSD*
Dunkin, Benjamin Franklin *NatCAB 5*
Dunkin, Christopher 1811-1880 *ApCAB*
Dunkin, Damon Duffield 1875-1933 *WhAm 1*
Dunkin, Paul Shaner 1905-1975 *DcAmLiB*
Dunklee, Edward Vaughan 1888-1963
NatCAB 50
Dunkley, Ferdinand Luis 1869-1956 *WhAm 3*
Dunklin, Daniel 1790-1844 *BiAUS, Drake,*
NatCAB 12
Dunklin, Hallie Milburn 1860- *WomWWA 14*
Dunlap, Alexander 1815- *ApCAB*
Dunlap, Andrew 1794-1835 *ApCAB, Drake,*
NatCAB 3
Dunlap, Andrew 1844-1914 *WhAm 1*
Dunlap, Anthony Bullock 1869-1960
NatCAB 48
Dunlap, Arthur Ray 1906-1974 *WhAm 6*
Dunlap, Boutwell 1877- *ApCAB X, WhAm 1*
Dunlap, Charles Bates 1863- *WhAm 1*
Dunlap, Charles Edward 1888-1966 *WhAm 4*
Dunlap, Charles Graham 1859- *WhAm 1*
Dunlap, Charles Kephart 1863-1940 *WhAm 2*
Dunlap, David Richardson 1879-1968 *WhAm 5*
Dunlap, Elbert 1872- *WhAm 5*
Dunlap, Flora 1874- *WomWWA 14*
Dunlap, Frederick 1881- *WhAm 6*
Dunlap, Frederick Levy 1870- *WhAm 5*
Dunlap, George McKenzie 1858-1924
NatCAB 49
Dunlap, George Washington 1813-1880 *ApCAB,*
BiAUS, BiDrAC, TwCBDA, WhAm H
Dunlap, Harry 1898-1960 *WhAm 4*
Dunlap, Hiram J 1841-1919 *WhAm 1*
Dunlap, James 1744-1818 *ApCAB, NatCAB 5,*
TwCBDA
Dunlap, James Boliver 1825-1864 *NewYHSD,*
WhAm H
Dunlap, John 1747-1812 *ApCAB, DcAmB,*
Drake, NatCAB 19, TwCBDA, WhAm H,
WhAmP
Dunlap, John 1852-1925 *NatCAB 21*
Dunlap, John A 1793?-1858? *ApCAB*
Dunlap, John Bettes 1903-1944 *WhAm 4*

DcAmB, McGEWB, NatCAB 19,
WhAm 1
Dunning, William Laughlin 1863-1931
NatCAB 24
Dunninger, Joseph 1896-1975 *WhAm 6*
Dunnington, Francis Perry 1851-1944 *ApCAB,*
NatCAB 34, TwCBDA, WhAm 4
Dunnington, Walter Grey 1891-1971 *WhAm 5*
Dunoyer DeSegonzac, Andre 1884-1974
WhAm 6
Dunoyer DeSegonzac, Louis D J Armand
1880-1963 *DcScB*
Dunphy, Charles 1878-1933 *NatCAB 26*
Dunphy, Charles 1879-1933 *WhAm 1*
Dunphy, Edward John 1856-1926 *BiDrAC,*
TwCBDA
Dunphy, Nicholas Reed 1891-1955 *NatCAB 43*
Dunphy, Richard L *NewYHSD*
Dunphy, Uriah *NewYHSD*
Dunphy, William Henry 1860-1915 *NatCAB 17,*
WhAm 1
Duns Scotus, John 1265?-1308 *McGEWB*
Duns Scotus, John 1266?-1308 *DcScB*
Dunscomb, Charles Ellsworth 1868-1938
WhAm 1
Dunscomb, Samuel Whitney, Jr. 1868-1936
NatCAB 18, WhAm 1
Dunshee, Jay Dee 1884-1956 *NatCAB 44,*
WhAm 3
Dunsmore, Andrew B 1866-1938 *WhAm 1*
Dunsmore, John MacArthur 1871-1949
NatCAB 37
Dunsmore, John Ward 1856-1945 *NatCAB 10,*
WhAm 2
Dunsmore, Philo Cordon 1895-1967 *WhAm 5*
Dunson, Walker Sanford 1881-1941 *NatCAB 36*
Dunstable, John 1390?-1453 *McGEWB*
Dunstan, Saint 909?-988 *McGEWB*
Dunstan, Arthur St. Charles 1871- *WhAm 5*
Dunstan, Edmund Fleetwood 1896-1969
WhAm 5
Dunstan, Richard Lee 1870-1949 *NatCAB 38*
Dunster, Edward Swift 1834-1888 *ApCAB,*
TwCBDA
Dunster, Henry d1659 *Drake*
Dunster, Henry 1609-1658? *DcAmB*
Dunster, Henry 1609-1659 *AmBi, BiDAmEd,*
DcAmReB, McGEWB, WebAB,
WhAm H
Dunster, Henry 1612?-1659 *ApCAB,*
NatCAB 6, TwCBDA
Dunston, Mary Alice Jackson *WhoColR*
Duntley, George Silas 1879-1957 *NatCAB 44*
Duntley, John Wheeler 1863-1921 *WhAm 1*
Dunton, Edith Kellogg 1873-1944
WomWWA 14
Dunton, Edith Kellogg 1875-1944 *WhAm 3A*
Dunton, Frank Holt 1827- *WhAm 4*
Dunton, Harold Francis 1888-1952 *NatCAB 41*
Dunton, John 1659-1733 *ApCAB, Drake*
Dunton, Larkin 1828-1899 *WhAm 1*
Dunton, Lewis Marion 1848- *TwCBDA,*
WhAm 4
Dunton, Walter Chipman 1830-1890 *TwCBDA*
Dunton, William Herbert 1878-1936 *IlBEAAW,*
WhAm 1
Dunton, William Rush, Jr. 1868-1966
NatCAB 53
Dunville, Robert Edwin 1906-1963 *NatCAB 51*
Dunwell, Charles Tappan 1852-1908 *BiDrAC,*
WhAm 1
Dunwell, James Winslow 1849-1907 *WhAm 1*
Dunwody, Thomas Edgar 1887-1959 *WhAm 4*
Dunwody, William Elliott 1870-1956 *WhAm 3*
Dunwood, Presley 1844- *WhoColR*
Dunwoody, Henry Harrison Chase 1842-1933
TwCBDA, WhAm 1
Dunwoody, William Hood 1841-1914 *DcAmB,*
NatCAB 22, WhAm 1
Dupalais, Virginia Poullard 1804-1864
NewYHSD, WhAm H
Duparquet, Jacques Diel 1600?-1658 *ApCAB*
Dupee, John *WhAm 5*
Duperly, Armand *NewYHSD*
Duperon, Thomas 1842-1898 *TwCBDA*
Duperrey, Louis Isidore 1786-1865 *ApCAB,*
DcScB

Dupin, Pierre-Charles-Francois 1784-1873
DcScB
Dupius, Charles W 1876- *WhAm 6*
Dupleix, Joseph Francois, Marquis De 1697-1763
McGEWB, WhoMilH
Duplessis, Maurice L 1890-1959 *WhAm 3*
DuPoisson 1695-1729 *ApCAB*
Duponceau, Peter Stephen 1760-1844 *AmBi,*
Drake, NatCAB 7
Duponceau, Pierre Etienne 1760-1844 *AmBi,*
ApCAB, DcAmB
DuPonceau, Pierre Etinne 1760-1844 *WhAm H*
Duponchel, Felix *NewYHSD*
DuPont *see also* DuPont DeNemours
DuPont, A Felix 1879-1948 *NatCAB 37,*
WhAm 2
Dupont, Aime *NatCAB 15*
DuPont, Alexis Irenee 1816-1856 *NatCAB 6*
DuPont, Alexis Irenee 1843-1904 *NatCAB 31*
DuPont, Alfred Irenee 1864-1935 *DcAmB S1,*
NatCAB 25, WhAm 1
DuPont, Alfred Rhett 1907-1972 *WhAm 5*
DuPont, Alfred Victor 1798-1856 *NatCAB 6*
DuPont, Alfred Victor 1900-1970 *NatCAB 57*
DuPont, Bessie Gardner 1864-1949 *NatCAB 38*
Dupont, Charles H 1805-1877 *NatCAB 12*
DuPont, Charles Irenee 1797-1869 *ApCAB Sup,*
NatCAB 6, TwCBDA
DuPont, Coleman 1863-1930 *NatCAB 22*
DuPont, Eleuthere Irenee 1771-1834 *AmBi,*
DcAmB, EncAB, McGEWB, WhAm H
DuPont, Emile Francis 1898-1974 *WhAm 6*
DuPont, Eugene 1873-1954 *NatCAB 44*
DuPont, Eugene Eleuthere 1882-1966
NatCAB 55
DuPont, Francis Gurney 1850-1905 *NatCAB 23*
DuPont, Francis Irenee 1873-1942 *DcAmB S3*
DuPont, Francis V 1894-1962 *WhAm 4*
DuPont, Gideon 1712-1790 *ApCAB X,*
NatCAB 6, TwCBDA
DuPont, Henry 1812-1889 *ApCAB Sup,*
ApCAB X, DcAmB, NatCAB 6,
TwCBDA, WhAm H
DuPont, Henry Algernon 1838-1926 *ApCAB X,*
BiDrAC, DcAmB, NatCAB 6, TwCBDA,
WebAMB, WhAm 1, WhAmP
DuPont, Henry Belin 1898-1970 *NatCAB 55,*
WhAm 5
DuPont, Henry Francis 1880-1969 *NatCAB 55,*
WhAm 5
DuPont, Irenee 1876-1963 *WhAm 4, WhAm 5*
DuPont, Jessie Ball d1970 *WhAm 5*
DuPont, Lammot 1880-1952 *NatCAB 56,*
WhAm 3
DuPont, Lammot 1880-1954 *DcAmB S5*
DuPont, Philip Francis 1878-1928 *NatCAB 37*
DuPont, Pierre Samuel 1870-1954 *DcAmB S5,*
EncAB, McGEWB, NatCAB 42,
WhAm 3
DuPont, Richard Chichester 1911-1943
NatCAB 32
DuPont, Samuel Francis 1803-1865 *AmBi,*
ApCAB X, DcAmB, Drake, NatCAB 5,
NewYHSD, TwCBDA, WebAB,
WhAm H
DuPont, Samuel Francis 1830-1865 *WebAMB*
DuPont, Thomas Coleman 1863-1930 *AmBi,*
ApCAB X, BiDrAC, DcAmB S1,
WhAm 1, WhAmP
DuPont, Victor 1828-1888 *ApCAB Sup,*
ApCAB X, NatCAB 21, TwCBDA
DuPont, Victor, Jr. 1852-1911 *NatCAB 21*
DuPont, Victor Marie 1767-1827 *DcAmB,*
WhAm H
DuPont, William 1855-1928 *NatCAB 29*
DuPont, William, Jr. d1965 *WhAm 4*
DuPont DeNemours *see also* DuPont
DuPont DeNemours, Eleuthere Irenee 1771-1834
ApCAB, ApCAB X, NatCAB 6,
TwCBDA, WebAB
DuPont DeNemours, Henry Algernon 1838-1926
ApCAB
DuPont DeNemours, Pierre Samuel 1739-1817
ApCAB, ApCAB X, McGEWB,
NatCAB 6, TwCBDA
DuPont DeNemours, Samuel Francis 1803-1865
ApCAB

DuPont DeNemours, Victor Marie 1767-1827
ApCAB, ApCAB X, NatCAB 6,
TwCBDA
Dupont-Grave, Francois *ApCAB Sup*
DuPortail *NewYHSD*
Duportail, Lebegue, Chevalier Louis d1802
Drake
Duportail, Louis Lebeque d1802 *NatCAB 9*
Duportail, Louis Lebeque 1736-1802 *ApCAB*
Duportail, Louis Lebeque 1743-1802 *WebAMB*
Dupouy, A L *NewYHSD*
Dupratz, Antoine Simon LePage 1689-1775
AmBi, ApCAB, DcAmB, NewYHSD
Dupratz, Antoine Simon LePage 1690?-1775?
WhAm H
Dupratz, LePage *Drake*
DuPre, Arthur Mason 1869-1949 *WhAm 2*
Dupre, Athanase Louis Victoire 1808-1869
DcScB
Dupre, Augustin *NewYHSD*
DuPre, Daniel Allston 1848-1930 *NatCAB 50,*
WhAm 4
Dupre, Eugene Charles *NewYHSD*
Dupre, Henry Garland 1873-1924 *BiDrAC,*
WhAm 1, WhAmP
Dupre, Jacques 1790?- *BiAUS, NatCAB 10*
Dupre, Julia Clarkson *NewYHSD*
Dupre, Lucius Jacques 1822-1869 *BiDConf*
Dupre, Marcel 1886-1971 *WhAm 5*
DuPriest, John Randolph 1882-1966
NatCAB 54
Dupuis, Mathias *ApCAB*
Dupuis, Nathan Fellowes 1836- *ApCAB*
Dupuis, Raymond 1907-1972 *WhAm 5*
Dupuis, Thomas R 1833- *ApCAB*
DuPuy, Charles Meredith 1884-1925
NatCAB 22
Dupuy, Eliza Ann 1814-1880 *Drake, NotAW*
Dupuy, Eliza Ann 1814-1881 *ApCAB, DcAmB,*
WhAm H
Dupuy, Eliza Ann 1815-1881 *NatCAB 6*
DuPuy, Harry Wilfred 1880-1920 *NatCAB 19*
DuPuy, Herbert 1856-1930 *NatCAB 22,*
WhAm 1
Dupuy, Pierre 1896-1969 *WhAm 5*
Dupuy, R Ernest 1887-1975 *WhAm 6*
DuPuy, Raymond 1860-1933 *WhAm 1*
Dupuy, Samuel Stuart 1912-1974 *WhAm 6*
DuPuy, William Atherton 1876-1941 *WhAm 1*
Dupuytren, Guillaume 1777-1835 *BiHiMed*
Duque, Henry O'Melveny 1904-1971 *WhAm 5*
Duquemy, John D *NewYHSD*
Duquesne, Abraham, Marquis De 1610-1688
WhoMilH
Duquesne, DeMenneville *Drake*
Duquesne, Joseph Marie Lazare 1804-1854
ApCAB
Duquesne DeMenneville, Marquis *ApCAB,*
WhAm H
Duquet, Joseph 1817-1838 *ApCAB*
Duran, F Mutis 1852- *WhAm 4*
Duran, John *NewYHSD*
Duran, Martin d1584 *ApCAB*
Duran, Narciso 1776-1846 *WhAm H*
Duran-Reynals, Francisco 1899-1958
NatCAB 46
Durand, Albert G *NewYHSD*
Durand, Alfred B 1826?- *NewYHSD*
Durand, Asher Brown 1796-1886 *AmBi,*
ApCAB, BnEnAmA, DcAmB, Drake,
McGEWB, NatCAB 4, NewYHSD,
TwCBDA, WebAB, WhAm H
Durand, Cyrus 1787-1868 *ApCAB, DcAmB,*
NewYHSD, TwCBDA, WhAm H
Durand, David *WhAm 5*
Durand, Edward Dana 1871- *NatCAB 14,*
WhAm 5
Durand, Elias 1794-1873 *ApCAB*
Durand, Elias Judah 1870-1922 *WhAm 1*
Durand, Elias W *NewYHSD*
Durand, Elie Magloire 1794-1873 *AmBi,*
DcAmB, WhAm H
Durand, Eugene *NewYHSD*
Durand, G Harrison 1868- *WhAm 5*
Durand, George Harman 1838-1903 *BiAUS,*
BiDrAC
Durand, Grace G *WomWWA 14*
Durand, Henry Calvin 1869-1929 *NatCAB 22*

Durand, Sir Henry Mortimer 1850-1924
WhAm 2
Durand, Henry Smith 1817-1900? *NatCAB 2*
Durand, James Harrison 1934-1974 *WhAm 6*
Durand, John *BnEnAmA, NewYHSD*
Durand, John 1822- *ApCAB*
Durand, Laura Bradshaw 1869- *WomWWA 14*
Durand, Loyal, Jr. 1902-1970 *WhAm 5*
Durand, Marie 1850?- *ApCAB*
Durand, Silas *NewYHSD*
Durand, Theodore *NewYHSD*
Durand, William *NewYHSD*
Durand, William Frederick 1859-1958 *WhAm 3*
Durang, Charles 1796-1870 *ApCAB*
Durang, E F *NewYHSD*
Duranquet, Hyacinthe 1809- *ApCAB*
Durant, Charles F *NewYHSD*
Durant, Charles Ferson 1805-1873 *DcAmB*
Durant, Charles Person 1805-1873 *WhAm H*
Durant, Charles S 1805?-1873 *ApCAB*
Durant, Frederick Clark, Jr. 1879-1961
WhAm 4
Durant, Henry 1802-1875 *BiDAmEd, DcAmB*
Durant, Henry 1803-1875 *NatCAB 7,
TwCBDA, WhAm H*
Durant, Henry Fowle 1822-1881 *AmBi,
DcAmB, NatCAB 7, TwCBDA,
WhAm H*
Durant, Henry Towle 1822-1881 *ApCAB*
Durant, John Waldo 1774?-1832 *NewYHSD*
Durant, Thomas Clark 1820-1885 *AmBi,
DcAmB, McGEWB, REnAW, WebAB,
WhAm H*
Durant, Thomas Jefferson 1817-1882 *ApCAB,
DcAmB, TwCBDA, WhAm H*
Durant, Will 1885- *WebAB*
Durant, William Crapo 1861-1947 *DcAmB S4,
EncAB, McGEWB, NatCAB 15,
NatCAB 36, WebAB, WhAm 2*
Durante, Jimmy 1893- *WebAB*
Durante, Oscar d1945 *WhAm 2*
Duranty, Walter 1884-1957 *WhAm 3*
Durao, Jose DaSanta-Rita 1737-1783 *ApCAB*
Duras, Victor Hugo 1880- *WhAm 6*
Durat *NewYHSD*
Durbin, Alexander Cook 1832- *TwCBDA*
Durbin, Elisha John 1800-1887 *ApCAB,
WhAm H*
Durbin, John Price 1800-1876 *ApCAB, DcAmB,
Drake, NatCAB 6, TwCBDA, WhAm H*
Durbin, Winfield Taylor 1847-1928 *NatCAB 13,
NatCAB 21, WhAm 1*
Durborow, Allan Cathcart, Jr. 1857-1908
BiDrAC, TwCBDA
Durbrow, Chandier Wolcott 1876- *WhAm 6*
Dureau DeLaMalle, Jean B Joseph Rene
1742-1807 *ApCAB*
Durell, Daniel Meserve 1769-1841 *BiAUS,
BiDrAC, TwCBDA, WhAm H*
Durell, Edward Henry 1810-1887 *ApCAB,
BiAUS, DcAmB, NatCAB 13, TwCBDA,
WhAm H, WhAmP*
Durell, Edward Hovey 1866- *WhAm 4*
Durell, George B 1861- *WhAm 4*
Durell, Laura Jackson *WomWWA 14*
DuRelle, George 1852- *WhAm 4*
Durer, Albrecht 1471-1528 *AsBiEn, DcScB,
McGEWB*
Duret, Miguel Lanz 1909-1959 *WhAm 3*
Durey, Cyrus 1864-1933 *BiDrAC, WhAm 4*
Durey, John Coleman 1880-1969 *NatCAB 55,
WhAm 5*
Durfee, Abby Slade Brayton 1870-
WomWWA 14
Durfee, Bradford Matthew Chaloner 1843-1872
ApCAB, TwCBDA
Durfee, Charles 1793-1849 *NewYHSD*
Durfee, Edgar Noble 1882-1958 *WhAm 3*
Durfee, Herbert Augustus 1856- *WhAm 4*
Durfee, Job 1790-1847 *ApCAB, BiAUS,
BiDrAC, DcAmB, Drake, NatCAB 7,
TwCBDA, WhAm H, WhAmP*
Durfee, Margaret Pyle 1883- *WomWWA 14*
Durfee, Nathan 1867-1948 *NatCAB 38*
Durfee, Nathaniel Briggs 1812-1872 *BiAUS,
BiDrAC, TwCBDA, WhAm H, WhAmP*
Durfee, Thomas 1826-1901 *DcAmB,
NatCAB 12, TwCBDA, WhAm 1*

Durfee, Walter Hetherington 1889-1974
WhAm 6
Durfee, William Franklin 1833-1899 *AmBi,
ApCAB, DcAmB, NatCAB 6, TwCBDA,
WhAm 1*
Durfee, William Pitt 1855-1941 *WhAm 1,
WhAm 2*
Durfee, Winthrop Carver 1858-1929 *WhAm 1*
Durfee, Zoheth Shearman 1831-1880 *ApCAB,
NatCAB 6, TwCBDA*
Durfee, Zoheth Sherman 1831-1880 *DcAmB,
WhAm H*
Durfey, John Cooper 1902-1960 *WhAm 4*
Durgan, George Richard 1872-1942 *BiDrAC*
Durgin, Calvin Thornton 1893-1965 *WhAm 4*
Durgin, Cyrus W 1907-1962 *WhAm 4*
Durgin, George Francis 1860- *WhAm 4*
Durgin, Harriet Thayer 1848- *AmWom*
Durgin, Lyle 1850- *AmWom*
Durgin, Samuel Holmes 1839- *NatCAB 13,
WhAm 4*
Durgo, Philip Henry 1855-1920 *WhAm 1*
Durham, Cady Burt 1872-1932 *NatCAB 25*
Durham, Caleb Wheeler 1848-1910 *DcAmB,
WhAm HA, WhAm 4*
Durham, Carl Thomas 1892-1974 *BiDrAC,
WhAm 6*
Durham, Charles Abercrombie 1921-1967
NatCAB 54
Durham, Charles Love 1872-1949 *WhAm 2*
Durham, Donald B 1883-1951 *WhAm 3*
Durham, Edward 1857-1933 *WhAm 1*
Durham, Edward Miall, Jr. 1875-1954 *WhAm 3*
Durham, Eleanor Hibbard Gregory 1882-
WomWWA 14
Durham, Ezra Daniel 1848-1919 *NatCAB 19*
Durham, Fred Stranahan 1884-1949 *WhAm 3*
Durham, Henry Welles 1874- *NatCAB 16,
WhAm 5*
Durham, Hobart Noble 1901-1969 *WhAm 5*
Durham, Israel W 1856- *WhAm 4*
Durham, James Ware 1875- *WhAm 5*
Durham, Jannie M *WomWWA 14*
Durham, John George Lambton, Earl Of
1792-1840 *ApCAB, McGEWB*
Durham, John Stephens 1861-1919 *NatCAB 4,
TwCBDA, WhAm 1*
Durham, Joseph Edward, Jr. 1882-1955
NatCAB 49
Durham, Knowlton 1880-1961 *NatCAB 50,
WhAm 4*
Durham, Milton J 1824-1911 *BiAUS*
Durham, Milton Jameson 1824-1911 *BiDrAC*
Durham, Milton Jamison 1824-1911 *ApCAB,
TwCBDA, WhAm 1*
Durham, Nelson Wayne 1859-1938 *WhAm 1*
Durham, Plato Tracy 1873-1930 *NatCAB 37,
WhAm 1*
Durham, Robert Lee 1870-1948 *WhAm 2*
Durham, Robert Lee 1870-1948 *NatCAB 37*
Durham, Silas Lucius 1884-1958 *NatCAB 48*
Durham, Thomas *NewYHSD*
Durham, Tyler *NewYHSD*
Durholz, Auguste *NewYHSD*
Durier, Anthony 1832-1904 *NatCAB 5*
Durier, Anthony 1833-1904 *TwCBDA*
Durier, Antoine 1833-1904 *ApCAB, WhAm 1*
Durivage, Francis Alexander 1814-1881 *ApCAB,
DcAmB, Drake, NatCAB 8, WhAm H*
Durivage, John E 1813-1869 *Drake*
Durkee, Charles 1805-1870 *BiDrAC,
WhAm H, WhAmP*
Durkee, Charles 1807-1870 *ApCAB, BiAUS,
Drake, NatCAB 11, TwCBDA*
Durkee, Eugene Winslow 1850-1926
NatCAB 20
Durkee, Frank Williams 1861-1939 *NatCAB 29,
WhAm 1*
Durkee, Henrietta Noble 1871- *WomWWA 14*
Durkee, J Stanley 1866- *WhAm 5*
Durkee, John 1728-1782 *AmBi, ApCAB,
DcAmB, Drake, NatCAB 12, TwCBDA,
WhAm H*
Durkee, Joseph Harvey 1837- *NatCAB 5*
Durkheim, Emile 1858-1917 *McGEWB*
Durkin, Edmund L *ApCAB X*
Durkin, John 1868-1903 *IIBEAAW*
Durkin, Martin Patrick 1894-1955 *BiDrUSE,*

DcAmB S5, NatCAB 45, WhAm 3
Durkin, Martin Thomas 1881-1931 *NatCAB 23*
Durland, Kellogg 1881-1911 *WhAm 1*
Durley, Ella Hamilton *AmWom,
WomWWA 14*
Durling, Edgar Vincent 1893-1957 *WhAm 3*
Durling, James Krotzer 1893-1951 *NatCAB 41*
Durman, Donald Charles 1898-1972
NatCAB 56
Durno, Edwin Russell 1899- *BiDrAC*
Durocher, Laurent 1786-1861 *ApCAB*
Durocher, Leo Ernest 1906- *WebAB*
Duroziez, Paul-Louis 1826-1897 *BiHiMed*
Durr, Clifford Judkins 1899-1975 *WhAm 6*
Durrant, Frances Miller 1857- *WomWWA 14*
Durrell, Irene Clark 1852- *AmWom*
Durrell, Joseph H 1879-1967 *WhAm 4*
Durrenmatt, Friedrich 1921- *McGEWB*
Durrett, Reuben Thomas 1824-1913 *AmBi,
ApCAB, DcAmB, NatCAB 2, TwCBDA,
WhAm 1*
Durrie, Daniel Steele 1819-1892 *AmBi, ApCAB,
DcAmB, NatCAB 11, TwCBDA,
WhAm H*
Durrie, George Henry 1820-1863 *BnEnAmA,
NewYHSD, WhAm H*
Durrie, John 1818- *NewYHSD*
Durst, William Arthur 1870-1940 *WhAm 1*
Durstine, Florence Sarles 1881- *WomWWA 14*
Durstine, Roy Sarles 1886-1962 *WhAm 4*
Durston, John Hurst 1848-1929 *WhAm 1*
Durthaler, Joseph 1819-1885 *ApCAB*
Durthaller, Joseph 1819-1885 *NatCAB 4,
TwCBDA*
Durward, Bernard Isaac 1817-1902 *NewYHSD*
Dury, Charles 1847-1931 *NatCAB 24,
WhAm 4*
Dury, George 1817-1894 *NewYHSD*
Duryea, Charles Edgar 1861-1938 *ApCAB X,
DcAmB S2, WebAB, WhAm HA,
WhAm 4*
Duryea, Dan 1907-1968 *WhAm 5*
Duryea, Edwin 1862- *WhAm 4*
Duryea, Harmanus Barkulo 1863-1916
ApCAB X, DcAmB
Duryea, Hiram 1834-1914 *WhAm 1*
Duryea, Jesse Townsend 1865- *NatCAB 14*
Duryea, Joseph Tuthill 1832-1898 *NatCAB 12,
TwCBDA*
Duryea, Nina Larrey 1874-1951 *BiCAW,
WhAm 3*
Duryea, Samuel Bowne 1845-1892 *TwCBDA*
Duryea, Wright 1896-1961 *WhAm 4*
Duryee, Abram 1815-1890 *ApCAB, DcAmB,
NatCAB 5, TwCBDA, WhAm H*
Duryee, Albert Plummer 1879-1949 *NatCAB 41*
Duryee, Joseph Rankin 1853-1935 *NatCAB 28*
Duryee, Peter Stanford 1874-1954 *NatCAB 44*
Duryee, William Rankin 1838-1897 *ApCAB,
TwCBDA*
DuSable, Jean Baptiste Point *WhAm H*
DuSable, Jean Baptiste Pointe 1745?-1818
WebAB
DuSacre Coeur, Mother Marie 1906-1964
WhAm 4
Duschak, Lionel Herman 1882-1948
NatCAB 37, WhAm 2
Duse, Eleonora 1859-1924 *WhAm HA,
WhAm 4*
Dusenberry, Charles Richard 1829-1924
NatCAB 22
Dusham, E H 1887-1974 *WhAm 6*
DuShane, Donald 1885-1947 *BiDAmEd,
WhAm 2*
DuShane, Graham 1910-1963 *NatCAB 50,
WhAm 4*
Dushman, Saul 1883-1954 *WhAm 3*
DuSimitiere, Pierre Eugene 1736?-1784 *DcAmB,
NewYHSD, WhAm H*
Duss, John Samuel 1860- *NatCAB 7*
Dussauce, Hippolyte d1869 *ApCAB*
Dusser DeBarenne, Joannes Gregorius 1885-1940
DcAmB S2, NatCAB 29, WhAm 1
Dussik, Karl Theo 1908-1968 *NatCAB 55*
Dussuchal, Eugenie 1860- *AmWom*
Dustan, Isaac K *NewYHSD*
Dustin, Guy King 1877-1944 *NatCAB 34*
Dustin, Hannah *NotAW*

Dustin, Hannah 1657- DcAmB, NatCAB 6
Dustin, Hannah 1657-1732? WhAm H
Dustin, Hannah 1657-1735? AmBi
Dustin, Hannah 1660?- ApCAB
Duston, Hannah Drake
Duston, Hannah 1657-1736? NotAW
Duston, Hannah 1660?- TwCBDA
Dusuau, Francis Emanuel Frederick 1801-1836
 ApCAB
DuSuaw NewYHSD
DuTant, Charles 1908- IlBEAAW
Dutcher, Addison Porter 1818-1884 ApCAB
Dutcher, Charles Mason 1862-1936 WhAm 1
Dutcher, Eva Olive 1880- WomWWA 14
Dutcher, Francis Edward 1909-1973 WhAm 6
Dutcher, Frank Jerome 1850-1930 NatCAB 28
Dutcher, George Matthew 1874-1959 WhAm 3
Dutcher, Jacob C 1820- ApCAB
Dutcher, John Gerow 1865-1928 ApCAB X,
 NatCAB 23
Dutcher, Silas Belden 1829-1909 NatCAB 2,
 TwCBDA, WhAm 1
Dutcher, William 1846-1920 WhAm 1
Dutchy ApCAB
Dutertre, Jean Baptiste 1610-1687 ApCAB
Duthie, James NewYHSD
DuToit, Alexander Logie 1878-1948 DcScB
DuToit, George Adolph 1847-1923 NatCAB 6
Dutra, Eurico Gaspar 1885-1974 WhAm 6
Dutra E Mello, Antonio Francisco 1823-1843
 ApCAB
DuTremblay, Pamphile-Real 1879-1955
 WhAm 3
Dutrochet, Rene-Joachim-Henri 1776-1847
 DcScB
Dutrow, Howard Victor 1880- WhAm 6
Dutton, Aaron 1780-1849 ApCAB
Dutton, Alice Dunbar 1874- WomWWA 14
Dutton, Arthur Henry 1838-1864 ApCAB,
 TwCBDA
Dutton, Benjamin Franklin 1831-1915
 NatCAB 2, WhAm 1
Dutton, Charles Judson 1888-1964 WhAm 4
Dutton, Clair C 1884-1973 WhAm 6
Dutton, Clarence Edward 1841-1912 AmBi,
 ApCAB, AsBiEn, DcAmB, DcScB,
 NatCAB 13, TwCBDA, WhAm 1
Dutton, David Cecil 1884-1953 NatCAB 42
Dutton, Edward A 1908-1954 WhAm 3
Dutton, Edward P 1831-1925 NatCAB 6
Dutton, Edward Payson 1831-1923 WhAm 1
Dutton, Emily Helen 1869-1947 WhAm 2
Dutton, Frank Kingsley 1892-1947 NatCAB 37
Dutton, George Burwell 1881-1930 NatCAB 24,
 WhAm 1
Dutton, George Elliott 1881-1944 WhAm 2
Dutton, George Washington 1826- ApCAB
Dutton, Henry 1796-1869 AmBi, ApCAB,
 BiAUS, DcAmB, Drake, NatCAB 10,
 TwCBDA, WhAm H
Dutton, Henry Worthington 1796-1875 ApCAB
Dutton, Ira Barnes 1843-1931 AmBi,
 NatCAB 22
Dutton, Joseph 1843-1931 WhAm 1
Dutton, Laura Ann Chapin 1860-
 WomWWA 14
Dutton, Lewis Richard 1873-1948 NatCAB 40
Dutton, Richard King 1919-1972 WhAm 5
Dutton, Samuel Train 1849-1919 AmBi,
 BiDAmEd, DcAmB, NatCAB 23,
 WhAm 1
Dutton, Samuel William Southmayd 1814-1866
 ApCAB, Drake
Dutton, Thomas NewYHSD
Dutton, Tom Whited 1893-1969 NatCAB 56
Dutton, Walter C 1889-1962 WhAm 4A
Dutton, William Jay 1847- NatCAB 16,
 WhAm 4
Dutzer, Frederick NewYHSD
Duval, Addie Hansbrough 1878- WomWWA 14
Duval, Ambrose NewYHSD
DuVal, Benjamin Livingston 1904-1966
 NatCAB 55
Duval, Charles Warren 1876- WhAm 5
Duval, E NewYHSD
DuVal, Frederic Beale 1847- WhAm 4
Duval, Gabriel 1752-1844 ApCAB, BiAUS,
 NatCAB 2, TwCBDA

Duval, H Reiman 1843-1924 ApCAB X
Duval, H Rieman 1843-1924 WhAm 1
Duval, Henry Rieman 1842- NatCAB 3
Duval, Horace Clark 1851- NatCAB 1
Duval, Isaac Hardin 1824-1902 ApCAB
Duval, Isaac Harding 1824-1902 BiDrAC,
 TwCBDA, WhAm 1
Duval, J NewYHSD
Duval, J H 1824- BiAUS
Duval, John NewYHSD
Duval, John Pope 1790-1854 TwCBDA
Duval, John Pope 1790-1855 ApCAB,
 NatCAB 3
Duval, Laurel 1887-1952 WhAm 3
Duval, Mathias Marie 1844-1907 DcScB
Duval, Peter S NewYHSD
Duval, Stephen NewYHSD
Duval, Stephen Orr 1832?- NewYHSD
Duval, Thomas H BiAUS
Duval, William Pope 1784-1854 AmBi, ApCAB,
 BiAUS, BiDrAC, DcAmB, NatCAB 11,
 REnAW, TwCBDA, WhAm H, WhAmP
Duvalier, Francois 1907-1971 McGEWB,
 WhAm 5
Duvall, Alvin 1813-1891 NatCAB 6
Duvall, Charles Raymond 1869-1940 WhAm 1
Duvall, Donald Chauncey 1915-1970 WhAm 5
Duvall, Gabriel 1752-1844 BiDrAC,
 DcAmB S1, Drake, WebAB, WhAm H,
 WhAmP
Duvall, James William 1844- WhAm 4
Duvall, Lulu Melick 1880- WomWWA 14
Duvall, Nannie W Goldborough 1868-
 WomWWA 14
Duvall, Trumbull Gillette 1861- TwCBDA,
 WhAm 4
Duvall, William P 1784-1854 Drake
Duvall, William Penn 1847-1920 WhAm 1
Duveen, Henry 1854- NatCAB 15
Duvel, Joseph William Tell 1873-1946 WhAm 2
Duveneck, Frank 1845?- ApCAB
Duveneck, Frank 1848-1919 AmBi, BiDAmEd,
 BnEnAmA, DcAmB, NatCAB 20,
 WebAB, WhAm 1
Duverger, Paul NewYHSD
Duvernay, Ludger 1799-1852 ApCAB,
 WhAm H
Duverney, Joseph-Guichard 1648-1730 DcScB
Duvernoy, Henry Grosclaude 1898-1958
 NatCAB 43
DuVigneaud, Vincent 1901- AsBiEn, WebAB
DuVillard, Henry Anthony 1859-1943
 NatCAB 32
Duvivier And Son NewYHSD
Duwe, George E 1897-1972 WhAm 5
Duxbury, George H 1893-1956 WhAm 3
Duyckinck, Evert 1621-1702 NewYHSD
Duyckinck, Evert, III 1677?-1727 NewYHSD
Duyckinck, Evert Augustus 1816-1878 AmBi,
 ApCAB, DcAmB, Drake, NatCAB 1,
 TwCBDA, WhAm H
Duyckinck, George Long 1823-1863 ApCAB,
 DcAmB, Drake, NatCAB 10, TwCBDA,
 WhAm H
Duyckinck, Gerardus 1695-1746? NewYHSD
Duyckinck, Gerardus, II 1723-1797 NewYHSD
Duyckinck, Gerrit 1660?-1710? WhAm H
Duyckinck, Gerrit 1663-1710? NewYHSD
Duzdein, John A NewYHSD
Dvorak, Antonin 1841-1904 McGEWB,
 WhAm H
Dvornik, Francis 1893-1975 WhAm 6
D'Vys, George Whitefield 1860-1941 WhAm 1
Dwan, Ralph Hubert 1901-1969 NatCAB 55,
 WhAm 5
Dwenger, Joseph 1837-1893 ApCAB, DcAmB,
 NatCAB 13, TwCBDA, WhAm H
Dwier, W Kirkland 1869-1950 NatCAB 39
Dwiggins, Clare Victor 1874-1958 WhAm 3
Dwiggins, William Addison 1880-1956 WhAm 3
Dwight, Miss NewYHSD
Dwight, Arthur Smith 1864-1946 DcAmB S4,
 NatCAB 33, WhAm 2
Dwight, Benjamin Franklin d1893 WhAm H
Dwight, Benjamin Woodbridge 1816-1889 AmBi,
 ApCAB, DcAmB, NatCAB 23, TwCBDA,
 WhAm H
Dwight, Benjamin Woolsey 1780-1850 ApCAB

Dwight, Charles 1842- ApCAB
Dwight, Charles Chauncey 1830- TwCBDA
Dwight, Edmund 1780-1849 ApCAB, DcAmB,
 NatCAB 12, TwCBDA, WhAm H
Dwight, Edmund 1824- ApCAB
Dwight, Edmund 1856-1938 NatCAB 29,
 WhAm 1
Dwight, Edward Strong 1853-1940 NatCAB 35
Dwight, Edwin Welles 1789-1841 ApCAB
Dwight, Edwin Welles 1863-1931 WhAm 1
Dwight, Elizabeth Amelia ApCAB
Dwight, Frances Ellen 1819- ApCAB
Dwight, Francis 1808-1845 ApCAB, BiDAmEd,
 DcAmB, NatCAB 12, WhAm H
Dwight, Harrison Gray Otis 1803-1862 AmBi,
 ApCAB, DcAmB, Drake, NatCAB 10,
 TwCBDA
Dwight, Harrison Griswold 1875-1959 WhAm 3
Dwight, Henry 1783-1857 NatCAB 13
Dwight, Henry Edwin 1797-1832 ApCAB,
 TwCBDA
Dwight, Henry Otis 1843-1917 AmBi, DcAmB,
 NatCAB 10, WhAm 1
Dwight, Henry Williams 1788-1845 ApCAB,
 BiAUS, BiDrAC, TwCBDA, WhAm H
Dwight, Howard 1837-1863 ApCAB
Dwight, James 1784-1863 ApCAB
Dwight, Jeremiah Wilbur 1819-1885 BiDrAC,
 WhAm H
Dwight, John 1819-1903 NatCAB 13,
 NatCAB 24
Dwight, John Sullivan 1813-1893 ApCAB,
 DcAmB, NatCAB 8, TwCBDA, WebAB,
 WhAm H
Dwight, John Wilbur 1859-1928 BiDrAC,
 WhAm 1, WhAmP
Dwight, Jonathan 1858-1929 NatCAB 22,
 WhAm 1
Dwight, Joseph 1703-1765 ApCAB, Drake,
 TwCBDA
Dwight, Julia Strong Lyman WomWWA 14
Dwight, Kirby 1879-1946 NatCAB 41
Dwight, Louis 1793-1854 ApCAB, TwCBDA
Dwight, Mabel 1876- WhAm 5
Dwight, Maitland 1889-1938 NatCAB 29
Dwight, Mary Ann 1806-1858 ApCAB, Drake
Dwight, Melatiah Everett 1841-1907
 NatCAB 23
Dwight, Minnie Ryan 1873-1957 WhAm 3,
 WomWWA 14
Dwight, N W NewYHSD
Dwight, Nathaniel 1770-1831 ApCAB, DcAmB,
 TwCBDA, WhAm H
Dwight, Ogden Graham 1915-1970 WhAm 5
Dwight, Richard Everett 1875-1951 NatCAB 41,
 WhAm 3
Dwight, Sereno Edwards 1786-1850 AmBi,
 ApCAB, DcAmB, Drake, NatCAB 7,
 TwCBDA, WhAm H
Dwight, Stephen NewYHSD
Dwight, Susan Edwards 1788-1839 ApCAB
Dwight, Theodore 1764-1846 AmBi, ApCAB,
 BiAUS, BiDrAC, DcAmB, Drake,
 NatCAB 11, TwCBDA, WhAm H,
 WhAmP
Dwight, Theodore 1796-1866 AmBi, ApCAB,
 DcAmB, Drake, NatCAB 11, TwCBDA,
 WhAm H
Dwight, Theodore William 1822-1892 AmBi,
 ApCAB, BiDAmEd, DcAmB, NatCAB 6,
 TwCBDA, WhAm H
Dwight, Thomas 1758-1819 BiAUS, BiDrAC,
 TwCBDA, WhAm H
Dwight, Thomas 1843-1911 ApCAB, DcAmB,
 NatCAB 12, TwCBDA, WhAm 1
Dwight, Timothy 1752-1817 AmBi, ApCAB,
 BiDAmEd, DcAmB, DcAmReB, Drake,
 EncAB, McGEWB, NatCAB 1,
 TwCBDA, WebAB, WhAm H
Dwight, Timothy 1778-1844 ApCAB
Dwight, Timothy 1828-1916 AmBi, ApCAB,
 BiDAmEd, DcAmB, NatCAB 1,
 TwCBDA, WhAm 1
Dwight, Walton 1838-1878 NatCAB 3
Dwight, Wilder 1833-1862 ApCAB
Dwight, William 1831-1888 ApCAB, DcAmB,
 TwCBDA, WhAm H
Dwight, William Buck 1833-1906 ApCAB,

NatCAB 10, TwCBDA, WhAm 1

Dwight, William George 1859-1930 NatCAB 23
Dwight, William Theodore 1795-1865 ApCAB, Drake, TwCBDA
Dwinell, Justin 1785-1850 BiAUS, BiDrAC, WhAm H
Dwinnell, Clifton Howard 1873-1928 WhAm 1
Dwire, Henry Rudolph 1882-1944 WhAm 2
D'Wolfe, James 1763-1837 ApCAB
Dworkis, Martin B 1919-1965 WhAm 4
Dworman, Irving 1879-1962 NatCAB 50
Dworshak, Henry Clarence 1894-1962 BiDrAC, WhAm 4, WhAmP
Dwyer, Ada WomWWA 14
Dwyer, Bessie Agnes AmWom
Dwyer, Charles d1916 WhAm 1
Dwyer, Edward Francis 1902-1967 NatCAB 52
Dwyer, Edward Martin 1906-1957 WhAm 3
Dwyer, Edward Raymond 1896-1956 NatCAB 45
Dwyer, Florence Price 1902- BiDrAC
Dwyer, James A 1896-1956 WhAm 3
Dwyer, James Francis 1874- WhAm 3
Dwyer, Jeremiah 1837- NatCAB 5
Dwyer, Jeremiah 1838- WhAm 4
Dwyer, John B 1910-1957 WhAm 3
Dwyer, John H 1843- ApCAB
Dwyer, John William 1865- WhAm 4
Dwyer, Margaret Adelaide 1857- WomWWA 14
Dwyer, P Florence 1902-1976 WhAm 6
Dwyer, Robert Arthur 1908-1960 WhAm 4
Dwyer, Robert E d1967 WhAm 4
Dwyer, Timothy John 1873-1928 NatCAB 22
Dwyer, William Joseph 1888-1948 NatCAB 35, WhAm 3
Dwyre, Dudley G 1880-1948 WhAm 2
Dyadkovsky, Iustin Evdokimovich 1784-1841 DcScB Sup
Dyal, Kenneth Warren 1910- BiDrAC
Dyar, Harrison Gray 1866-1929 AmBi, DcAmB, NatCAB 14, TwCBDA, WhAm 1
Dyar, John Beekman 1846-1898 NatCAB 24
Dyar, Mary A d1660 ApCAB
Dyas, Ada 1843-1908 WhAm HA, WhAm 4
Dyche, Howard Edward 1884-1954 NatCAB 45, WhAm 3
Dyche, James Edward 1866-1926 NatCAB 24
Dyche, Lewis Lindsay 1857-1915 NatCAB 21, TwCBDA
Dyche, Louis Lindsay 1857-1915 WhAm 1
Dyche, Russell 1884-1959 NatCAB 47
Dyche, William Andrew 1861-1936 WhAm 1
Dyck, Paul 1917- IIBEAAW
Dyck, Walther Franz Anton Von 1856-1934 DcScB
Dyckman, Fannie Blackwell 1832-1914 ApCAB X
Dyckman, Garrett W d1868 ApCAB
Dyckman, Henry MacPherson 1857-1923 NatCAB 20
Dyckman, Isaac Michael 1813-1899 NatCAB 34
Dyckman, Isaac Michael 1832-1914 ApCAB X
Dye, Alexander Vincent 1876-1956 WhAm 3
Dye, Charlie 1906-1972 IIBEAAW
Dye, Clair Albert 1869-1949 NatCAB 39, WhAm 2
Dye, Edward Randolph 1902-1961 NatCAB 53
Dye, Eugene Allen 1896-1960 WhAm 4
Dye, Eva Emery 1855-1947 NatCAB 13, REnAW, WhAm 3, WomWWA 14
Dye, Frank Ganes 1892-1947 NatCAB 41
Dye, Garnett Joel 1891-1962 NatCAB 50
Dye, John T 1835-1913 WhAm 1
Dye, John Walter 1878- WhAm 6
Dye, Mary Irene Clark 1837- AmWom
Dye, William Holton 1863- WhAm 4
Dye, William McEntyre 1831-1899 ApCAB, DcAmB, TwCBDA, WebAMB
Dyer, Albert Joseph 1910-1975 WhAm 6
Dyer, Albion Morris 1858-1912 NatCAB 18
Dyer, Alexander Brydie 1815-1874 ApCAB, DcAmB, NatCAB 4, TwCBDA, WebAMB, WhAm H
Dyer, Alexander Brydie 1852-1920 WhAm 1
Dyer, Arthur James 1868-1957 NatCAB 46
Dyer, Catherine Cornelia d1903 ApCAB,

WhAm 1

Dyer, Charles Brain 1806-1883 NatCAB 4
Dyer, Charles Gifford 1846- ApCAB
Dyer, Charles Volney 1808-1878 ApCAB
Dyer, Clara L Brown 1849- AmWom
Dyer, Clifton G 1885-1959 WhAm 3
Dyer, Clyde Percy 1884-1953 NatCAB 43
Dyer, David Patterson 1838-1924 ApCAB, BiAUS, BiDrAC, TwCBDA, WhAm 1
Dyer, Edward Franklin 1858- ApCAB X
Dyer, Eliphalet 1721-1807 AmBi, ApCAB, BiAUS, BiDrAC, DcAmB, Drake, NatCAB 11, TwCBDA, WhAm H
Dyer, Elisha 1811-1890 BiAUS, NatCAB 9, TwCBDA
Dyer, Elisha 1839-1906 NatCAB 9, TwCBDA, WhAm 1
Dyer, Elisha, Jr. 1862-1917 NatCAB 17
Dyer, Everett R 1907-1974 WhAm 6
Dyer, Francis John 1864-1924 WhAm 1
Dyer, Frank 1875- WhAm 5
Dyer, Frank Lewis 1870-1941 NatCAB 41, WhAm 1
Dyer, Franklin Benjamin 1858-1938 BiDAmEd, WhAm 4
Dyer, Frederick Rainey 1873-1934 WhAm 1
Dyer, George Leland 1849-1914 WhAm 1
Dyer, George Rathbone 1869-1934 NatCAB 14, NatCAB 30
Dyer, Gustavus Walker 1867- WhAm 4
Dyer, H Anthony 1872-1943 NatCAB 36, WhAm 2
Dyer, H Edward 1870-1948 NatCAB 37
Dyer, Heman 1810-1900 ApCAB, NatCAB 6, TwCBDA, WhAm 1
Dyer, Henry Knight 1846-1911 NatCAB 18, NatCAB 28
Dyer, Isaac Watson 1855-1937 WhAm 1
Dyer, Isadore 1865-1920 DcAmB, WhAm 1
Dyer, James Ballard 1905-1961 WhAm 4
Dyer, James Edward 1894-1970 NatCAB 55, WhAm 5
Dyer, Jesse Farley 1877- WhAm 5
Dyer, John H 1894-1952 WhAm 4
Dyer, John J BiAUS
Dyer, John LaFayette 1873- WhAm 1
Dyer, John Lewis 1914-1969 WhAm 5
Dyer, John Napier 1877-1954 WhAm 3
Dyer, Joseph Henry 1872-1947 WhAm 2
Dyer, Julia Knowlton 1829- AmWom
Dyer, Leonard Huntress 1873-1955 NatCAB 43, WhAm 3
Dyer, Leonidas Carstarphen 1871-1957 BiDrAC, WhAm 3, WhAmP
Dyer, Louis 1851-1908 DcAmB, NatCAB 22, WhAm 1
Dyer, Malvina Adeline WomWWA 14
Dyer, Mary 1610?-1660 DcAmB, DcAmReB, Drake, NatCAB 11, NotAW, WebAB, WhAm H
Dyer, Mattie 1842- ApCAB
Dyer, Nehemiah Mayo 1839-1910 ApCAB Sup, DcAmB, TwCBDA, WhAm 1
Dyer, Oliver 1824-1907 NatCAB 3, TwCBDA, WhAm 1
Dyer, Philip Sidney 1857-1919 NatCAB 17
Dyer, Richard NewYHSD
Dyer, Sallie 1891-1975 WhAm 6
Dyer, Samuel Eugene 1930-1973 WhAm 6
Dyer, Sidney 1814- ApCAB, TwCBDA
Dyer, Walter Alden 1878-1943 WhAm 2
Dyer, William Henry 1817-1899 TwCBDA
Dyett, Anthony Rainetaux 1824- TwCBDA
Dyett, Herbert Thomas 1875- WhAm 5
Dyhrenfurth, Gunter Oskar 1886-1975 WhAm 6
Dyke, Charles Bartlett 1870- WhAm 5
Dyke, Herbert H 1876-1965 WhAm 4
Dyke, Lodire Judson 1840-1927 NatCAB 21
Dyke, Samuel P NewYHSD
Dykema, Karl W 1906-1970 WhAm 5
Dykema, Peter William 1873-1951 BiDAmEd, NatCAB 40, WhAm 3
Dykema, Raymond K 1889-1972 WhAm 5
Dykeman, King 1874-1931 WhAm 1
Dykes, Jefferson C 1900- REnAW
Dykhuizen, Harold Daniel 1908-1967 NatCAB 54, WhAm 5

Dykstra, Clarence Addison 1883-1950 DcAmB S4, NatCAB 38, WhAm 3
Dykstra, Gerald Oscar 1906-1970 NatCAB 55, WhAm 5
Dykstra, John 1898-1972 WhAm 5
Dykstra, Ralph 1879- WhAm 6
Dykstra, Robert 1930- EncAAH
Dylan, Bob 1941- EncAB, WebAB
Dylan, Robert Zimmerman 1941- EncAAH
Dylander, John 1709?-1741 DcAmB, WhAm H
Dym, Aaron 1896-1951 WhAm 3
Dyment, Colin Victor 1879-1928 NatCAB 40, WhAm 1
Dymond, Alfred Hutchinson 1827- ApCAB
Dymond, Florence 1873- WhAm 5
Dymond, John 1836-1922 DcAmB, NatCAB 25
Dymond, John, Jr. 1867-1932 NatCAB 25
Dynes, Owen William 1869-1954 NatCAB 41, WhAm 5
Dyott, John 1812-1876 ApCAB
Dyott, Thomas W 1771-1861 DcAmB, WebAB, WhAm H
Dyre, William TwCBDA
Dyrenforth, Robert St. George 1844-1910 WhAm 1
Dysart, Robert 1872- NatCAB 16
Dysart, Thomas NewYHSD
Dysinger, Holmes 1853- WhAm 4
Dyson, Alfred Hartwell 1876-1941 NatCAB 31
Dyson, Charles Wilson 1861-1930 WhAm 1
Dyson, Frank Watson 1868-1939 DcScB
Dyson, James Lindsay 1912-1967 WhAm 4
Dyson, John Milnes 1903-1965 NatCAB 53
Dyson, John Rose 1874-1947 NatCAB 40
Dyson, Verne 1879- WhAm 6
Dyson, Walter 1882- WhoColR
Dzerzhinsky, Felix Edmundovich 1877-1926 McGEWB
Dzierozynskin, Francis 1779-1850 ApCAB
D'Zmura, Andrew Peter 1890-1961 NatCAB 50

E

Eastwick, Abram Trimble 1865-1948 *NatCAB 40*
Eastwick, Beatrice Hinkle *WomWWA 14*
Eastwick, Martha McIlvain 1855- *WomWWA 14*
Eastwood, Alice 1859-1953 *WhAm 3, WomWWA 14*
Eastwood, Andrew Jackson 1899-1966 *NatCAB 53, WhAm 4*
Eastwood, Everett Owen 1876- *WhAm 5*
Eastwood, George Anderson 1879-1961 *NatCAB 49, WhAm 4*
Eastwood, James 1867-1946 *NatCAB 33*
Eaton, Amasa Mason 1841-1914 *NatCAB 41, WhAm 1*
Eaton, Amos 1776-1842 *ApCAB, BiDAmEd, DcAmB, DcScB, Drake, NatCAB 5, TwCBDA, WhAm H*
Eaton, Amos Beebe 1806-1877 *ApCAB, Drake, TwCBDA*
Eaton, Anne Thaxter 1881-1971 *DcAmLiB*
Eaton, Arthur Wentworth Hamilton 1849-1937 *ApCAB X, WhAm 1*
Eaton, Asa 1778-1858 *ApCAB, TwCBDA*
Eaton, Barney Edward 1878-1944 *WhAm 2*
Eaton, Benjamin Harrison 1833-1904 *DcAmB, EncAAH, NatCAB 6, TwCBDA, WhAm 1*
Eaton, C Harry 1850-1901 *WhAm 1*
Eaton, Cecil LeRoy 1894-1947 *NatCAB 43*
Eaton, Charles Aubrey 1868-1953 *BiDrAC, DcAmB S5, NatCAB 12, WhAm 3, WhAmP*
Eaton, Charles Frederick 1842- *WhAm 4*
Eaton, Charles H 1813-1842 *NatCAB 6, WhAm H*
Eaton, Charles H 1852-1902 *WhAm 1*
Eaton, Charles Henry 1850-1901 *IIBEAAW*
Eaton, Charles Warren 1857-1937 *NewYHSD, WhAm 1*
Eaton, Clement 1898- *EncAAH*
Eaton, Cyrus 1784-1875 *ApCAB, Drake, NatCAB 11, WhAm H*
Eaton, Cyrus Stephen 1883- *WebAB*
Eaton, Daniel Cady 1834-1895 *AmBi, ApCAB, DcAmB, NatCAB 11, TwCBDA, WhAm H*
Eaton, Daniel Cady 1837-1912 *ApCAB, TwCBDA, WhAm 1*
Eaton, Dorman Bridgeman 1823-1899 *WhAm 1*
Eaton, Dorman Bridgman 1823-1899 *AmBi, ApCAB, DcAmB, McGEWB, NatCAB 7, NatCAB 21, TwCBDA*
Eaton, Edward Dwight 1851-1942 *ApCAB, NatCAB 3, TwCBDA, WhAm 2*
Eaton, Elon Howard 1866-1934 *NatCAB 28, WhAm 1*
Eaton, Emily Lovett 1874- *WomWWA 14*
Eaton, Emma Florance 1874-1933 *WomWWA 14*
Eaton, Emma Florence 1874-1933 *WhAm 3*
Eaton, Ephraim Llewellyn 1846- *NatCAB 12, WhAm 4*
Eaton, Ernest Theophilus 1877-1957 *NatCAB 48, WhAm 3*
Eaton, Frank Wales 1877-1940 *NatCAB 30*
Eaton, Fred Laurine 1859-1925 *WhAm 1*
Eaton, Frederick George 1893-1954 *NatCAB 43*
Eaton, Frederick Heber 1863-1916 *WhAm 1*
Eaton, George Daniel 1866-1930 *WhAm 1*
Eaton, George Francis 1872-1949 *WhAm 4*
Eaton, George Franklin 1892-1956 *WhAm 3*
Eaton, George Thomas 1856- *NatCAB 10*
Eaton, George Washington 1804-1872 *ApCAB, NatCAB 5, TwCBDA*
Eaton, H Douglas 1886-1952 *NatCAB 41*
Eaton, Harold Irving 1887-1951 *NatCAB 38*
Eaton, Harry Tupper 1901-1963 *NatCAB 50*
Eaton, Harvey Doane 1862-1953 *WhAm 3*
Eaton, Henry William d1926 *WhAm 1*
Eaton, Herbert Nelson 1892-1970 *NatCAB 55*
Eaton, Homer 1834-1913 *DcAmB, NatCAB 12, WhAm 1*
Eaton, Horace 1804-1855 *ApCAB, BiAUS, Drake, NatCAB 8, TwCBDA*
Eaton, Horace Ainsworth 1871- *WhAm 5*
Eaton, Hubert d1966 *WhAm 4*
Eaton, Hugh McDougal 1865-1924 *NatCAB 6*

Eaton, Isaac 1724-1772 *ApCAB*
Eaton, Isabella Graham 1845- *WomWWA 14*
Eaton, J N *NewYHSD*
Eaton, James Briggs 1856- *WhAm 4*
Eaton, James Demarest 1848-1928 *NatCAB 21*
Eaton, James Madison 1905-1961 *NatCAB 51*
Eaton, James Murchie 1888-1952 *WhAm 3*
Eaton, James Rodolphus 1834- *TwCBDA*
Eaton, James Shirley 1868-1933 *NatCAB 25, WhAm 3*
Eaton, James Tucker 1907-1968 *WhAm 5*
Eaton, James Webster 1856-1901 *WhAm 1*
Eaton, James Webster 1857-1901 *TwCBDA*
Eaton, John 1829-1906 *AmBi, ApCAB, BiAUS, BiDAmEd, DcAmB, DcAmLiB, NatCAB 8, TwCBDA, WhAm 1*
Eaton, John David d1973 *WhAm 6*
Eaton, John Henry d1856 *BiAUS, Drake*
Eaton, John Henry 1787-1856 *TwCBDA*
Eaton, John Henry 1790-1856 *AmBi, ApCAB, BiDrAC, BiDrUSE, DcAmB, NatCAB 5, WhAm H, WhAmP*
Eaton, John Wallace 1886-1948 *WhAm 2*
Eaton, Joseph Giles 1847-1913 *WhAm 1*
Eaton, Joseph Haywood 1812-1859 *ApCAB, TwCBDA*
Eaton, Joseph Horace 1815-1896 *NewYHSD, WhAm H*
Eaton, Joseph Oriel 1829-1875 *ApCAB, DcAmB, NewYHSD, TwCBDA, WhAm H*
Eaton, Joseph Oriel 1873-1949 *WhAm 1, WhAm 3*
Eaton, L McKendree 1905-1958 *WhAm 3*
Eaton, Leonard Hobart 1818-1895 *NatCAB 8*
Eaton, Lewis *BiAUS, BiDrAC, WhAm H*
Eaton, Lewis Tillson 1869-1934 *WhAm 1*
Eaton, Lucien 1831-1890 *TwCBDA*
Eaton, Lucien 1879-1952 *NatCAB 42, WhAm 3*
Eaton, Margaret L 1796-1879 *AmBi*
Eaton, Margaret L O'Neill 1796-1879 *ApCAB, DcAmB, NatCAB 6*
Eaton, Margaret O'Neale 1796-1879 *WebAB*
Eaton, Margaret O'Neale 1799-1879 *NotAW*
Eaton, Marion Durant Dow 1870- *WomWWA 14*
Eaton, Marquis 1876-1925 *ApCAB X, NatCAB 21, WhAm 1*
Eaton, Marquis G 1898- *WhAm 3*
Eaton, Melvin Carr 1891-1966 *NatCAB 52, WhAm 4*
Eaton, Nathaniel 1609?-1660 *ApCAB, NatCAB 6*
Eaton, Nathaniel 1609?-1674 *DcAmB, WhAm H*
Eaton, Nathaniel Johnson d1883 *ApCAB*
Eaton, Paul Blaine 1892-1960 *NatCAB 48, WhAm 4*
Eaton, Philip Bentley 1887-1958 *WhAm 3*
Eaton, Ralph Waldo 1880-1942 *NatCAB 32*
Eaton, Russell 1873- *WhAm 5*
Eaton, Samuel 1596?-1664? *DcAmB*
Eaton, Samuel 1596?-1665 *WhAm H*
Eaton, Samuel 1597?-1665 *ApCAB*
Eaton, Samuel John Mills 1820-1889 *ApCAB, TwCBDA*
Eaton, Serana D *NewYHSD*
Eaton, Seymour 1859-1916 *WhAm 1*
Eaton, Sherburne Blake 1840- *NatCAB 7*
Eaton, Theodore Hildreth 1877-1961 *WhAm 4*
Eaton, Theophilus d1657 *Drake*
Eaton, Theophilus 1590?-1658 *AmBi, DcAmB, WhAm H*
Eaton, Theophilus 1591?-1658 *ApCAB, NatCAB 6*
Eaton, Thomas Marion 1896-1939 *BiDrAC*
Eaton, Thomas Treadwell 1845-1907 *ApCAB, NatCAB 9, TwCBDA, WhAm 1*
Eaton, Walter Prichard 1878-1957 *NatCAB 51, WhAm 3*
Eaton, William 1764-1811 *AmBi, ApCAB, DcAmB, Drake, NatCAB 11, TwCBDA, WebAB, WebAMB, WhAm H*
Eaton, William Bradley 1836-1896 *NewYHSD*
Eaton, William Colgate 1851-1936 *WhAm 1*
Eaton, William H 1881-1963 *WhAm 4*
Eaton, William Hadley 1818-1896 *TwCBDA*

Eaton, William Hanmer 1879-1957 *WhAm 3*
Eaton, William Robb 1877-1942 *BiDrAC, WhAmP*
Eaton, William Robb 1877-1943 *WhAm 2*
Eaton, William Wallace 1816-1898 *ApCAB, BiAUS, BiDrAC, NatCAB 11, TwCBDA*
Eaton, Wyatt 1849-1896 *AmBi, ApCAB, BnEnAmA, DcAmB, NatCAB 8, TwCBDA, WhAm H*
Eavenson, Alban 1869-1958 *NatCAB 49*
Eavenson, Alben Taylor 1826-1910 *NatCAB 39*
Eavenson, Howard Nicholas 1873-1953 *NatCAB 39, WhAm 3*
Eavenson, Marvin Sample 1900-1947 *NatCAB 37*
Eavenson, Roscoe Llewellyn 1886-1961 *NatCAB 50*
Eaves, George 1858-1926 *WhAm 1*
Eaves, John *NewYHSD*
Eaves, Lucile 1869-1953 *NatCAB 41, WhAm 5, WomWWA 14*
Eaves, Lucille 1869-1953 *BiCAW*
Eaves, William *NewYHSD*
Ebaugh, Franklin Gessford 1895-1972 *NatCAB 56, WhAm 5*
Ebbert, Frank Baker 1879-1938 *NatCAB 31, WhAm 6*
Ebbinghaus, Hermann 1850-1909 *McGEWB*
Ebbott, Percy John 1887-1975 *WhAm 6*
Ebel, Johann Gottfried 1764-1830 *DcScB*
Ebel, William Kenneth 1899-1972 *NatCAB 57, WhAm 5*
Ebeling, Albert Henry 1883-1965 *NatCAB 53*
Ebeling, Christoph Daniel 1741-1817 *ApCAB*
Ebeling, Christopher Daniel 1741-1817 *Drake*
Ebeling, Herman Louis 1857-1945 *NatCAB 33*
Ebeling, Philip 1866-1937 *NatCAB 42*
Ebeling, Philip Calvin 1904-1963 *WhAm 4*
Ebeling, Willi Henry 1882-1961 *WhAm 4*
Eber, Elk 1892-1944 *IIBEAAW*
Eberbach, Carl Walter 1889-1962 *WhAm 4*
Eberhard, Ernst 1839- *NatCAB 5, TwCBDA, WhAm 4*
Eberhard, John *NewYHSD*
Eberhard, Theodore Philip 1904-1960 *NatCAB 47*
Eberhardt, Charles Christopher 1871-1965 *WhAm 4, WhAm 5*
Eberhardt, Frederick L'Hommedieu 1868-1946 *NatCAB 35, WhAm 2*
Eberhart, Adolph Olson 1870- *NatCAB 14*
Eberhart, Frederic George 1864-1933 *NatCAB 30*
Eberhart, John Frederick 1829- *NatCAB 9*
Eberhart, Nelle Richmond d1944 *WhAm 2*
Eberharter, Herman Peter 1892-1958 *BiDrAC, WhAm 3, WhAmP*
Eberle, Abastenia St. Leger 1878-1942 *BiCAW, WhAm 2*
Eberle, E G 1863- *WhAm 4*
Eberle, Edward Walter 1864-1929 *AmBi, DcAmB, NatCAB 21, WebAMB, WhAm 1*
Eberle, Frederick J 1902-1964 *WhAm 4*
Eberle, J Louis 1890-1964 *NatCAB 53, WhAm 4*
Eberle, John 1787-1838 *ApCAB, DcAmB, Drake, NatCAB 11, TwCBDA, WhAm H*
Eberle, Mary Abastenia St. Leger 1878-1942 *NotAW, WomWWA 14*
Eberlein, Harold Donaldson 1875-1964 *WhAm 4*
Eberly, George Agler 1871- *WhAm 5*
Eberly, Isaac C 1880-1958 *NatCAB 48*
Eberly, John Adam 1887-1949 *NatCAB 37*
Ebersole, Ezra Christian 1840-1919 *TwCBDA, WhAm 1*
Ebersole, J Scott 1869- *WhAm 5*
Ebersole, John Franklin 1884-1945 *WhAm 2*
Ebersole, William Stahl 1862-1952 *WhAm 3*
Eberson, John 1875-1954 *NatCAB 40*
Eberstadt, Ferdinand 1890-1969 *WhAm 5*
Eberstadt, Rudolph 1895-1961 *NatCAB 49*
Eberstadt, Rudolph 1896-1961 *WhAm 4*
Ebert, Caroline *NewYHSD*
Ebert, Edmund Francis 1911-1972 *WhAm 5*
Ebert, Friedrich 1871-1925 *McGEWB*
Ebert, Robert Edwin 1893-1968 *NatCAB 55,*

WhAm 5

Ebert, Rudolph Gustav 1854- *WhAm 4*
Eberth, Carl Joseph 1835-1926 *DcScB*
Eble, Frank Xavier A 1879- *WhAm 6*
Eboue, Adolphe Felix Sylvestre 1885-1944
   McGEWB
Ebright, George Elliott 1873-1954 *NatCAB 43*
Ebright, Homer Kingsley 1878- *WhAm 6*
Ebright, Leonidas Strickland 1844-1917
   NatCAB 17
Eby, Frederick 1874-1968 *BiDAmEd,*
   NatCAB 54, WhAm 4A, WhAm 5
Eby, Harvey Leatherman 1874-1966
   NatCAB 53
Eby, Ivan David 1887-1967 *WhAm 4A*
Eby, Kermit 1903-1962 *WhAm 4*
Eby, Kerr 1889-1946 *NatCAB 34, WhAm 2*
Eby, Robert Killian 1900-1962 *NatCAB 49,*
   WhAm 4
Eccles, David 1849-1912 *NatCAB 17*
Eccles, Henry 1817-1863 *ApCAB*
Eccles, James A 1887-1960 *WhAm 3*
Eccles, Sir John Carew 1903- *AsBiEn,*
   McGEWB
Eccles, Marriner Stoddard 1890- *EncAB*
Eccles, Robert Gibson 1848-1934 *NatCAB 10,*
   TwCBDA, WhAm 1
Eccleson, Samuel 1801-1851 *ApCAB*
Eccleston, James Houston 1837- *TwCBDA*
Eccleston, Samuel 1801-1851 *Drake,*
   NatCAB 1, TwCBDA, WhAm H
Echave, Baltasar De *ApCAB*
Echeandia, Manuel 1783-1850 *ApCAB*
Echenique, Jose Rufino 1808-1879 *ApCAB*
Echenique, Juan Martin 1841- *ApCAB*
Echeverria, Esteban 1809-1851 *ApCAB*
Echeverria, Jose Esteban 1805-1851 *McGEWB*
Echeverria, Manuel Mariano 1730?- *ApCAB*
Echohawk, Brummett 1920?- *IlBEAAW*
Echohawk, Brummett 1922- *REnAW*
Echols, Angus Blakey 1889-1967 *NatCAB 54,*
   WhAm 4
Echols, Charles Patton 1867-1940 *WhAm 1*
Echols, Edward 1849-1914 *NatCAB 17*
Echols, Ethel Umphress 1883- *WomWWA 14*
Echols, Francis Glenn 1854-1942 *NatCAB 32*
Echols, John 1823-1896 *BiDConf, DcAmB,*
   TwCBDA, WhAm H
Echols, John Warnock 1849-1932 *WhAm 1*
Echols, Joseph Hubbard 1816-1885 *BiDConf*
Echols, Leonard Sidney 1871-1946 *BiDrAC,*
   WhAm 1
Echols, Oliver P 1892-1954 *WhAm 3*
Echols, Robert 1874-1949 *WhAm 3*
Echols, William Holding, Jr. 1859-1934
   WhAm 1
Echols, William Joseph 1872-1933 *WhAm 1*
Ecija, Juan De 1510-1591 *WhAm H*
Eck, Johann Maier Von 1486-1543 *McGEWB*
Eck, William 1824?- *NewYHSD*
Eckard, Elisabeth Ellen Gilliland 1919-1968
   WhAm 5
Eckard, James Read 1805-1887 *ApCAB,*
   NatCAB 11, TwCBDA, WhAm H
Eckard, Leighton Wilson 1845-1925 *WhAm 1*
Eckard, Margaret Esther Bayard 1810-1872
   ApCAB
Eckardt, Lisgar Russell 1876-1946 *WhAm 2*
Eckart, Carl 1902-1973 *WhAm 6*
Eckart, Charles Franklin 1875-1934
   NatCAB 41
Eckart, E Albert 1902-1971 *WhAm 5*
Eckart, William Roberts 1841-1914 *DcAmB*
Eckburg, Charles Andrew 1897-1967
   NatCAB 54
Eckdall, Frank Albert 1872-1959 *NatCAB 49*
Eckel, Clarence Lewis 1892-1972 *WhAm 5*
Eckel, Edmond Jacques 1845-1934 *NatCAB 41*
Eckel, Edwin Clarence 1875-1941 *WhAm 2*
Eckel, J L *NewYHSD*
Eckel, John Leonard 1880-1935 *NatCAB 26*
Eckelberry, John Walter 1886-1957 *NatCAB 50*
Eckels, James Herron 1858-1907 *DcAmB,*
   NatCAB 21, WhAm 1
Eckels, James Herron 1859-1907 *TwCBDA*
Eckendorf, George *NewYHSD*
Eckenrode, Hamilton James 1881- *WhAm 6*
Ecker, Enrique E 1887-1966 *WhAm 4*

Ecker, Frederic W 1896-1964 *WhAm 4*
Ecker, Frederick H 1867-1964 *WhAm 4*
Eckerle, John 1870-1945 *NatCAB 32*
Eckersall, Edwin Robert 1908-1962 *NatCAB 47,*
   WhAm 4
Eckersall, Walter H 1887-1930 *WhAm 1*
Eckert, Charles Richard 1868-1959 *BiDrAC,*
   WhAm 4
Eckert, George Arthur 1889-1953 *NatCAB 42*
Eckert, George Nicholas 1802-1865 *BiAUS,*
   BiDrAC, WhAm H
Eckert, Howard Haines d1964 *WhAm 4*
Eckert, Robert Paul 1903-1966 *NatCAB 54*
Eckert, Thomas Thompson 1825-1910 *ApCAB,*
   DcAmB, NatCAB 12, TwCBDA,
   WhAm 1
Eckert, Wallace John 1902-1971 *DcScB Sup,*
   WhAm 5
Eckert, William D 1909-1971 *WhAm 5*
Eckfeldt, Howard 1873-1948 *WhAm 2*
Eckfeldt, Jacob Reese 1803-1872 *ApCAB*
Eckfeldt, John Wiegand 1851-1933 *NatCAB 25*
Eckfeldt, Thomas Hooper 1853-1923 *WhAm 1*
Eckford, Henry 1775-1832 *ApCAB, DcAmB,*
   Drake, NatCAB 1, TwCBDA, WhAm H
Eckford, Jessiejo 1895- *IlBEAAW*
Eckhard, George Frederick 1878-1945 *WhAm 2*
Eckhardt, Floyd Smith 1903-1969 *NatCAB 56*
Eckhardt, Robert Christian 1913- *BiDrAC*
Eckhardt, William George 1879-1959
   NatCAB 45
Eckhart, Bernard Albert 1852-1931 *NatCAB 18,*
   WhAm 1
Eckhart, Francis *NewYHSD*
Eckhart, Johann 1260?-1327? *McGEWB*
Eckhart, Otto *NewYHSD*
Eckhart, Percy Bernard 1877-1969 *NatCAB 17,*
   WhAm 5
Eckhart, William *NewYHSD*
Eckhouse, Joseph L 1907-1967 *WhAm 4*
Eckles, Clarence Henry 1875-1933 *WhAm 1*
Eckles, Delane R 1806-1888 *BiAUS, TwCBDA*
Eckles, Isabel Lancaster 1877- *WhAm 5*
Eckley, Ephraim Ralph 1811-1908 *BiDrAC*
Eckley, Ephraim Ralph 1812-1908 *BiAUS,*
   NatCAB 3
Eckley, Ephriam Ralph 1811-1908 *TwCBDA*
Eckley, Joseph 1750-1811 *ApCAB*
Eckley, Sophia May 1825?-1874 *NewYHSD*
Eckley, William Thomas 1855-1908 *WhAm 1*
Eckman, Donald Preston 1915-1962 *WhAm 4*
Eckman, George Peck 1860-1920 *NatCAB 19,*
   WhAm 1
Eckman, James Roy 1889-1929 *NatCAB 21*
Eckman, Julius 1805-1874 *ApCAB*
Eckmann, Janos 1905-1971 *WhAm 6*
Eckoff, William Julius 1853-1908 *WhAm 1*
Eckrich, Richard P 1914-1973 *WhAm 6*
Eckstein, Frederick 1775?-1852 *NewYHSD,*
   WhAm H
Eckstein, Henry Joseph 1885-1954 *NatCAB 42*
Eckstein, Johann 1736?-1817 *NewYHSD*
Eckstein, John 1750?-1817? *DcAmB,*
   WhAm H
Eckstein, Louis 1865-1935 *NatCAB 26,*
   WhAm 1
Eckstein, Louis Joseph 1883-1963 *NatCAB 50*
Eckstein, Nathan 1873-1945 *NatCAB 37,*
   WhAm 2
Eckstorm, Fannie Pearson Hardy 1865-1946
   DcAmB S4, NatCAB 36, NotAW,
   WhAm 2, WomWWA 14
Eckstrom, Lawrence Joel 1896-1966 *WhAm 4*
Ecob, James Henry 1844-1921 *NatCAB 19*
Ecton, Zales Nelson 1898-1961 *BiDrAC,*
   NatCAB 49, WhAm 4, WhAmP
Ector, Matthew Duncan 1822-1879 *BiDConf*
Ed, Carl Frank Ludwig 1890-1959 *WhAm 3*
Edbrooke, Willoughby J 1843-1896 *WhAm H*
Eddinger, Wallace 1881-1929 *WhAm 1*
Eddington, Sir Arthur Stanley 1882-1944
   AsBiEn, DcScB, McGEWB
Eddington, Jame 1866-1938 *WhAm 1*
Eddington, Royal Lacey 1878-1951 *NatCAB 47*
Eddins, Henry A 1908-1966 *WhAm 4*
Eddis, William 1745?- *ApCAB, DcAmB,*
   WhAm H

Eddleman, Thomas Stricker 1905-1974
   WhAm 6
Eddy, Alfred Delavan 1846-1918 *WhAm 1*
Eddy, Alfred Updike 1857-1937 *NatCAB 29*
Eddy, Allen 1870-1957 *WhAm 3*
Eddy, Ansel Doan 1798-1875 *ApCAB*
Eddy, Arthur Jerome 1859-1920 *WhAm 1*
Eddy, Benjamin F *NewYHSD*
Eddy, Brayton 1901-1950 *WhAm 3*
Eddy, C F *NewYHSD*
Eddy, Charles Brown 1872-1951 *NatCAB 49,*
   WhAm 3
Eddy, Clarence 1851-1937 *DcAmB S2,*
   NatCAB 7, TwCBDA, WhAm 1
Eddy, Clarence Leroy 1877-1958 *NatCAB 48*
Eddy, Condit Nelson 1890-1962 *WhAm 4*
Eddy, Daniel Clarke 1823-1896 *ApCAB,*
   DcAmB, NatCAB 9, TwCBDA,
   WhAm H
Eddy, David Brewer 1877-1946 *ApCAB X,*
   NatCAB 35, WhAm 2
Eddy, Edward 1821-1875 *ApCAB*
Eddy, Edward 1822-1875 *NatCAB 6*
Eddy, Ezra Butler 1827- *ApCAB*
Eddy, Forrest Greenwood 1853-1939
   NatCAB 30, WhAm 1
Eddy, Frank Marion 1856-1929 *BiDrAC,*
   TwCBDA, WhAmP
Eddy, Frank Woodman 1851-1914 *ApCAB X,*
   WhAm 1
Eddy, Harrison Prescott 1870-1937 *DcAmB S2,*
   NatCAB 28, WhAm 1
Eddy, Henry Brevoort 1872- *WhAm 5*
Eddy, Henry Clarence 1851- *ApCAB*
Eddy, Henry Stephens 1878-1944 *WhAm 2*
Eddy, Henry Turner 1844-1921 *ApCAB,*
   DcAmB, NatCAB 13, NatCAB 15,
   TwCBDA, WhAm 1
Eddy, Isaac 1777-1847 *NewYHSD, WhAm H*
Eddy, James 1806-1888 *NewYHSD, TwCBDA*
Eddy, John H 1782-1817 *ApCAB*
Eddy, Lee Moin 1881- *WhAm 6*
Eddy, Luther Devotion 1810-1892 *NatCAB 3*
Eddy, Lyman Kinsley 1848-1932 *NatCAB 24*
Eddy, Manton Sprague 1892-1962 *NatCAB 53,*
   WhAm 4
Eddy, Mary Baker 1821-1910 *AmBi,*
   ApCAB X, DcAmB, DcAmReB, EncAB,
   McGEWB, NatCAB 3, NotAW, WebAB,
   WhAm 1
Eddy, Mary Baker Glover 1827-1910 *TwCBDA*
Eddy, Mary Mathews d1865 *ApCAB*
Eddy, Mary Roberts Lawther *WomWWA 14*
Eddy, Milton Walker 1884-1964 *WhAm 4*
Eddy, Nathan Browne 1890-1973 *WhAm 5*
Eddy, Nelson 1901-1967 *NatCAB 53,*
   WhAm 4
Eddy, Norman 1810-1872 *ApCAB, BiAUS,*
   BiDrAC, TwCBDA, WhAm H
Eddy, Oliver Tarbell 1799-1868 *NewYHSD,*
   WhAm H
Eddy, Paul Dawson 1895-1975 *WhAm 6*
Eddy, Richard 1828-1906 *AmBi, ApCAB,*
   TwCBDA, WhAm 1
Eddy, Ruth Story Devereux 1875-
   WomWWA 14
Eddy, Samuel 1769-1839 *ApCAB, BiAUS,*
   BiDrAC, Drake, NatCAB 8, TwCBDA,
   WhAm H
Eddy, Sara Hershey *AmWom*
Eddy, Sarah Stoddard 1831- *AmWom*
Eddy, Sherwood 1871-1963 *WhAm 4*
Eddy, Spencer 1874-1939 *NatCAB 14,*
   NatCAB 31, WhAm 1
Eddy, Thomas 1758-1827 *AmBi, ApCAB,*
   DcAmB, Drake, NatCAB 3, TwCBDA,
   WhAm H
Eddy, Thomas Mears 1823-1874 *ApCAB,*
   NatCAB 11, WhAm H
Eddy, Walter Hollis 1877-1959 *WhAm 3*
Eddy, William Abner 1850-1909 *TwCBDA,*
   WhAm 1
Eddy, William Alfred 1896-1962 *NatCAB 49,*
   WhAm 4
Eddy, Zachary 1815-1891 *ApCAB,*
   NatCAB 10, WhAm H
Edebohls, George Michael 1853-1908 *DcAmB,*
   WhAm 1

Edeburn, Edith Lindsay 1877- *WomWWA 14*
Edeiken, Louis 1894-1955 *NatCAB 42*
Edelhertz, Bernard 1880-1931 *WhAm 1*
Edelman, Gerald Maurice 1929- *WebAB*
Edelman, John W 1893-1971 *WhAm 5*
Edelman, Maurice 1911-1975 *WhAm 6*
Edelman, Nathan 1911-1971 *WhAm 5*
Edelstein, Ludwig 1902-1965 *WhAm 4*
Edelstein, M Michael 1888-1941 *WhAm 2*
Edelstein, Morris Michael 1888-1941 *BiDrAC*
Eden, Anthony 1897-1977 *McGEWB, WhWW-II*
Eden, Charles 1673-1722 *ApCAB, BiAUS, DcAmB, Drake, WhAm H, WhAmP*
Eden, Sir Frederick 1814- *ApCAB*
Eden, John Carmen 1865-1929 *NatCAB 37*
Eden, John Rice 1826-1909 *BiAUS, BiDrAC, WhAmP*
Eden, Sir Robert 1741-1784 *AmBi, DcAmB, NatCAB 7, WhAm H, WhAmP*
Eden, Sir Robert 1741-1786 *ApCAB, Drake*
Eden, William, Lord Auckland 1744-1814 *ApCAB, Drake*
Edenborn, Harry Megargee 1890-1948 *NatCAB 36*
Edenborn, William 1848-1926 *NatCAB 18, WhAm 1*
Edens, Arthur Hollis 1901-1968 *WhAm 5*
Edens, J Drake 1899-1966 *NatCAB 52*
Edens, James Benjamin 1913-1972 *WhAm 5*
Edens, John Edward 1896-1963 *NatCAB 50*
Edens, William Grant 1863-1957 *WhAm 3*
Eder, Josef Maria 1855-1944 *DcScB*
Eder, Phanor James 1880- *WhAm 5*
Ederle, Gertrude Caroline 1906- *WebAB*
Edes, Benjamin 1732-1803 *ApCAB, DcAmB, Drake, NatCAB 11, WhAm H*
Edes, Edwin Lewis 1853-1929 *NatCAB 24*
Edes, Henry Herbert 1849-1922 *ApCAB, TwCBDA, WhAm 1*
Edes, Jonathan W *NewYHSD*
Edes, Peter 1756-1840 *ApCAB, Drake*
Edes, Richard Sullivan 1810-1877 *ApCAB, TwCBDA*
Edes, Robert Thaxter 1838-1923 *ApCAB, DcAmB, NatCAB 8, TwCBDA, WhAm 1*
Edes, William Cushing 1856-1922 *NatCAB 6, WhAm 1*
Edeson, Robert 1868-1931 *DcAmB S1, WhAm 1*
Edgar *NewYHSD*
Edgar, Alvin Randall 1903-1975 *WhAm 6*
Edgar, Mrs. C H *NewYHSD*
Edgar, Charles 1862-1922 *ApCAB X, DcAmB, NatCAB 19*
Edgar, Charles Bloomfield 1847-1923 *NatCAB 20, WhAm 1*
Edgar, Charles Leavitt 1860-1932 *NatCAB 27, WhAm 1*
Edgar, Cornelius Henry 1811-1884 *NatCAB 3*
Edgar, David Alexander 1865-1948 *NatCAB 37*
Edgar, David Stewart 1875-1944 *NatCAB 33*
Edgar, Elizabeth 1842- *AmWom*
Edgar, George Mathews 1837-1913 *NatCAB 26*
Edgar, Graham 1887-1955 *WhAm 3*
Edgar, Harold Thomas 1878-1957 *NatCAB 44*
Edgar, Henry Cornelius 1811-1884 *ApCAB*
Edgar, Herman LeRoy 1865-1938 *NatCAB 29*
Edgar, J Augustus 1872-1955 *NatCAB 43*
Edgar, James Clifton 1859-1939 *NatCAB 14, WhAm 1*
Edgar, James David 1841- *ApCAB*
Edgar, John Todd 1792-1860 *ApCAB*
Edgar, Margaret Belle 1861- *WomWWA 14*
Edgar, Randolph 1884-1931 *WhAm 1, WhAm 2*
Edgar, Robert Franklin 1894-1962 *WhAm 4*
Edgar, Thomas Delbert 1868-1932 *WhAm 1*
Edgar, Walter Samuel 1889-1951 *NatCAB 42*
Edgar, William Crowell 1856-1932 *TwCBDA, WhAm 1*
Edgar, William Francis 1823- *NatCAB 12*
Edgcomb, Ernest Isaac 1867- *WhAm 4*
Edgcomb, Harry Loring 1880-1952 *NatCAB 41*
Edge, Jacob 1885-1945 *NatCAB 34*
Edge, James Batcheller Dowsland 1874-1939 *NatCAB 29*

Edge, Rosalle 1881- *WhAm 6*
Edge, Walter Evans 1873-1956 *ApCAB X, BiDrAC, WhAm 3, WhAmP*
Edge, Walter Smith 1879-1956 *NatCAB 49*
Edgecomb, Willard W *BiAUS*
Edgecombe, Samuel Wheeler 1907-1959 *NatCAB 46, WhAm 3*
Edgell, George Harold 1887-1954 *NatCAB 45, WhAm 3*
Edgerly, Beatrice d1973 *WhAm 6*
Edgerly, Julian Campbell 1865-1913 *NatCAB 15*
Edgerly, Webster 1852-1926 *NatCAB 20*
Edgerly, Winfield Scot 1846-1927 *WhAm 1*
Edgerton, Alfred Peck d1897 *BiAUS*
Edgerton, Alfred Peck 1812-1897 *NatCAB 13*
Edgerton, Alfred Peck 1813-1897 *BiDrAC, DcAmB, WhAm H, WhAmP*
Edgerton, Alice Craig 1874-1946 *WhAm 2*
Edgerton, Alonzo Jay 1827-1896 *ApCAB Sup, BiDrAC, NatCAB 12, TwCBDA, WhAm H*
Edgerton, Charles Eugene 1861-1932 *WhAm 1*
Edgerton, Edward Keith 1925-1974 *WhAm 6*
Edgerton, Fannie Ida *WomWWA 14*
Edgerton, Franklin 1885-1963 *NatCAB 56, WhAm 4*
Edgerton, Halsey Charles 1884-1967 *WhAm 4*
Edgerton, Henry White 1888-1970 *WhAm 5*
Edgerton, Herbert Oliver 1862- *WhAm 5*
Edgerton, Hiram H 1847-1922 *WhAm 1*
Edgerton, James Arthur 1869-1938 *NatCAB 13, WhAm 1*
Edgerton, John Emmett 1879-1938 *ApCAB X, NatCAB 38, WhAm 1*
Edgerton, John Warren 1875-1920 *WhAm 1*
Edgerton, Joseph Ketchum 1818-1893 *BiAUS, BiDrAC, TwCBDA, WhAm H*
Edgerton, Justin Lincoln 1908-1970 *NatCAB 56, WhAm 5*
Edgerton, Ralph Harris 1887-1943 *NatCAB 32*
Edgerton, Sara Townsend *WomWWA 14*
Edgerton, Sidney 1818-1900 *AmBi, BiAUS, BiDrAC, DcAmB, NatCAB 11, WhAmP*
Edgerton, William Franklin 1893-1970 *WhAm 5*
Edgett, Edwin Francis 1867-1946 *WhAm 2*
Edgett, Grace Lawrence 1874- *WomWWA 14*
Edgeworth, Maria 1767-1849 *McGEWB*
Edgington, Thomas Benton 1837-1929 *WhAm 1*
Edgren, August Hjalmar 1840-1903 *AmBi, ApCAB, DcAmB, NatCAB 8, TwCBDA*
Edgren, John Alexis 1839-1908 *NatCAB 8*
Edholm, Mary Gow Charlton 1854- *AmWom, TwCBDA*
Edholm-Sibley, Mary G Charlton 1854- *WhAm 4*
Edie, Guy Lewis 1858-1930 *WhAm 1*
Edie, John Rufus 1814-1888 *BiAUS, BiDrAC, WhAm H*
Edie, Lionel Danforth 1893-1962 *WhAm 4*
Edings, William Seabrook 1859- *WhAm 4*
Edington, Arlo Channing 1890-1953 *WhAm 3*
Edison, Charles 1890-1969 *BiDrUSE, NatCAB 56, WhAm 5*
Edison, Charles B 1921-1971 *WhAm 5*
Edison, Harry 1891-1966 *WhAm 4*
Edison, Mark Aaron 1895-1951 *WhAm 3*
Edison, Mina Miller *WomWWA 14*
Edison, Oskar E 1892-1964 *WhAm 4*
Edison, Samuel Bernard 1888-1971 *WhAm 5*
Edison, Thomas Alva 1847-1931 *AmBi, ApCAB, ApCAB X, AsBiEn, DcAmB S1, DcScB, EncAB, McGEWB, NatCAB 3, NatCAB 25, TwCBDA, WebAB, WhAm 1*
Edison, Thomas Alva, Jr. 1876-1935 *NatCAB 39*
Edison, William Leslie 1878-1937 *NatCAB 28*
Edkin, Bert Clarence 1871-1951 *NatCAB 40*
Edlefsen, John Nicholas 1882-1942 *NatCAB 44*
Edlefsen, Niels Edlef 1893-1971 *NatCAB 57*
Edlund, Raymond Arthur 1899-1954 *NatCAB 42*
Edman, Irwin 1896-1954 *DcAmB S5, NatCAB 44, WhAm 3*
Edman, V Raymond 1900-1967 *WhAm 4*
Edmand, Paul Albert 1890-1956 *NatCAB 48*

Edmands, J Wiley 1809-1877 *BiAUS*
Edmands, John 1820-1915 *DcAmB, DcAmLiB, NatCAB 12, TwCBDA, WhAm 1*
Edmands, John Wiley 1809-1877 *BiDrAC, WhAm H*
Edmands, Samuel Sumner 1877-1938 *WhAm 1*
Edminster, Clothier Franklin 1865-1932 *NatCAB 24*
Edmister, Floyd 1881- *WhAm 6*
Edmiston, Althea Maria Brown *WhoColR*
Edmiston, Andrew 1892-1966 *BiDrAC, WhAm 4*
Edmiston, Robert Wentz 1894-1965 *NatCAB 51, WhAm 4*
Edmiston, William Sherman 1876- *WhAm 5*
Edmond, William 1755-1838 *BiAUS, BiDrAC, NatCAB 2, TwCBDA, WhAm H*
Edmonds, Charles *NewYHSD*
Edmonds, Claude Averill 1883-1967 *NatCAB 54*
Edmonds, Dean Stockett 1879-1972 *WhAm 5*
Edmonds, Douglas Lyman d1962 *WhAm 4*
Edmonds, Edward Ames 1868-1954 *NatCAB 44*
Edmonds, Francis William 1806-1860? *Drake*
Edmonds, Francis William 1806-1863 *ApCAB, BnEnAmA, DcAmB, NatCAB 11, NewYHSD, WhAm H*
Edmonds, Francis Williams 1806-1863 *TwCBDA*
Edmonds, Franklin Spencer 1874-1945 *NatCAB 35, WhAm 2*
Edmonds, George Washington 1864-1939 *BiDrAC, WhAm 1, WhAmP*
Edmonds, Harry Marcus Weston 1862-1945 *WhAm 2*
Edmonds, Henry Morris 1878-1960 *WhAm 4*
Edmonds, Herbert Augustus 1860-1924 *NatCAB 20*
Edmonds, Ira Clement 1880- *WhAm 6*
Edmonds, James E 1879- *WhAm 6*
Edmonds, John Worth 1799-1874 *ApCAB, BiAUS, DcAmB, Drake, NatCAB 10, TwCBDA, WhAm H*
Edmonds, Mary Derby 1862- *WomWWA 14*
Edmonds, Richard Hathaway 1857-1930 *NatCAB 2, WhAm 1*
Edmonds, Sarah Emma Evelyn 1841-1898 *NotAW, WebAMB*
Edmonds, Thomas Sechler 1899-1976 *WhAm 6*
Edmonds, William *NewYHSD*
Edmondson, Cathrine Elizabeth 1903-1968 *WhAm 5*
Edmondson, Clarence Edmund 1883-1946 *WhAm 2*
Edmondson, Edmond Augustus 1919- *BiDrAC*
Edmondson, Edward, Jr. *NewYHSD*
Edmondson, Frederick William 1876-1946 *NatCAB 36*
Edmondson, Harriette Codwise 1874- *WomWWA 14*
Edmondson, Henry A *BiAUS*
Edmondson, James Howard 1925-1971 *BiDrAC, WhAm 5*
Edmondson, Thomas William 1869-1938 *NatCAB 39, WhAm 1*
Edmondson, William 1882?-1951 *DcAmB S5*
Edmondson, William John 1868- *WhAm 5*
Edmonston, Edgar Davis 1876-1937 *NatCAB 27*
Edmonston, Laura 1860- *WomWWA 14*
Edmund, John H *NewYHSD*
Edmunds, Albert Joseph 1857-1941 *WhAm 1, WhAm 2*
Edmunds, Charles Carroll 1858- *WhAm 4*
Edmunds, Charles Dole 1859-1926 *NatCAB 20*
Edmunds, Charles Keyser 1876-1949 *NatCAB 37, WhAm 2*
Edmunds, Charles Wallis 1873-1941 *DcAmB S3, WhAm 1*
Edmunds, Franklin Davenport 1874-1948 *NatCAB 39*
Edmunds, G *BiAUS*
Edmunds, George Franklin 1828-1919 *AmBi, ApCAB, BiAUS, BiDrAC, DcAmB, NatCAB 2, TwCBDA, WebAB, WhAm 1, WhAmP*
Edmunds, H Spencer 1894-1950 *NatCAB 39*
Edmunds, Harry Nicholas 1876-1934 *WhAm 1*

Edmunds, Henry Littleton 1853-1902
  NatCAB 23
Edmunds, Henry Reeves 1840-1923 *NatCAB 20*
Edmunds, James Madison 1810-1879 *BiAUS,
  TwCBDA*
Edmunds, James Richard, Jr. 1890-1953
  NatCAB 42, WhAm 3
Edmunds, Newton 1819-1908 *BiAUS, REnAW*
Edmunds, Paul Carrington 1836-1899 *BiDrAC,
  TwCBDA*
Edmunds, Samuel Henry 1870-1935 *WhAm 1*
Edmunds, Sterling Edwin 1880-1944
  NatCAB 36, WhAm 2
Edmunds-Hemingway, Madame 1878-1958
  WhAm 3
Edmundson, Frank Busha 1887-1952
  NatCAB 41
Edmundson, Henry Alonzo 1814-1890 *BiDrAC,
  WhAm H, WhAmP*
Edmundson, James Depew 1838-1933 *WhAm 1*
Edouart, Alexander 1818-1892 *IIBEAAW,
  NewYHSD, WhAm H*
Edouart, Auguste 1789-1861 *NewYHSD,
  WhAm H*
Edrington, Nicholas Kuntz 1890-1955
  NatCAB 44
Edrington, William Reynolds 1872-1932
  WhAm 1
Edrop, Percy T 1883- *WhAm 5*
Edsall, Anne Comfort 1863- *WomWWA 14*
Edsall, David Linn 1869-1945 *DcAmB S3,
  WhAm 2*
Edsall, Joseph E 1789-1865 *BiAUS, BiDrAC,
  WhAm H*
Edsall, Preston William 1902-1972 *WhAm 5*
Edsall, Samuel Cook 1860-1917 *ApCAB Sup,
  NatCAB 12, TwCBDA, WhAm 1*
Edsen, Eduard Polonius 1856- *NatCAB 7,
  TwCBDA*
Edsforth, Charles Dugdale 1905-1961 *WhAm 4*
Edson, Allan Aaron 1842-1888 *ApCAB Sup*
Edson, Andrew Wheatley 1851-1924
  NatCAB 20, WhAm 1
Edson, Carroll Everett 1866-1930 *NatCAB 29,
  WhAm 1*
Edson, Cyrus 1857-1903 *NatCAB 3, TwCBDA,
  WhAm 1*
Edson, Franklin 1832-1904 *NatCAB 3,
  WhAm 1*
Edson, Gus 1901-1966 *WhAm 4*
Edson, Howard Austin 1875- *WhAm 5*
Edson, Job Adolphus 1854-1928 *NatCAB 21,
  WhAm 1*
Edson, John Joy 1846-1935 *WhAm 1*
Edson, Josiah 1710?-1778 *ApCAB*
Edson, Katherine Philips 1870-1933 *NotAW,
  WhAm 1, WomWWA 14*
Edson, Merritt Austin 1897-1955 *WhAm 3,
  WhWW-II*
Edson, Robert Clay 1906-1966 *WhAm 4*
Edson, Stephen Reuben 1895-1969 *WhAm 5*
Edson, Susan A 1823-1897 *TwCBDA*
Edson, Theodore 1838-1870 *ApCAB*
Edson, Tracy Robinson 1809-1881 *NatCAB 19,
  NewYHSD, WhAm H*
Edson, Winfield 1907-1956 *WhAm 3*
Edstrom, David 1873-1938 *WhAm 1*
Edstrom, Davis 1873-1938 *ApCAB X*
Edward I 1239-1307 *McGEWB*
Edward II 1284-1327 *McGEWB*
Edward III 1312-1377 *McGEWB*
Edward IV 1442-1483 *McGEWB*
Edward VI 1537-1553 *McGEWB*
Edward VII 1841-1910 *McGEWB*
Edward The Black Prince 1330-1376 *McGEWB*
Edward The Confessor d1066 *McGEWB*
Edward The Elder d924 *McGEWB*
Edward, Alexander *NewYHSD*
Edward, Harvey 1893- *WhAm 2*
Edward, John *BiAUS*
Edwardes, David 1502-1542? *DcScB*
Edwards, Abbie L M 1872- *WomWWA 14*
Edwards, Abner Beecher 1870- *WhoColR*
Edwards, Agustin 1816-1877 *ApCAB*
Edwards, Alanson W 1840-1908 *WhAm 1*
Edwards, Alba M 1872- *WhAm 5*
Edwards, Alfred Dunton 1867-1950 *NatCAB 38*
Edwards, Alfred Shenstone 1849- *WhAm 4*

Edwards, Anna Cheney 1835- *AmWom*
Edwards, Arthur 1834- *NatCAB 9*
Edwards, Arthur Robin 1867-1936 *NatCAB 39,
  WhAm 1*
Edwards, Bela Bates 1802-1852 *AmBi, ApCAB,
  DcAmB, Drake, NatCAB 10, TwCBDA,
  WhAm H*
Edwards, Benjamin 1752-1826 *BiAUS,
  TwCBDA*
Edwards, Benjamin 1753-1829 *BiDrAC,
  WhAm H*
Edwards, Benjamin D 1881-1930 *WhAm 1*
Edwards, Benjamin Franklin 1859- *WhAm 4*
Edwards, Benjamin Stevenson 1818-1886
  ApCAB
Edwards, Boyd 1876-1944 *NatCAB 34,
  WhAm 2*
Edwards, Bryan 1743-1800 *ApCAB, Drake*
Edwards, Burgess Allison 1892-1922 *ApCAB X*
Edwards, Caldwell 1841-1922 *BiDrAC*
Edwards, Caro Fries Buxton *WomWWA 14*
Edwards, Charles 1797-1868 *ApCAB, DcAmB,
  Drake, NewYHSD, WhAm H*
Edwards, Charles Gordon 1878-1931 *BiDrAC,
  WhAm 1, WhAmP*
Edwards, Charles Henry 1891-1947 *NatCAB 38*
Edwards, Charles Lincoln 1863-1937
  NatCAB 13, TwCBDA, WhAm 1
Edwards, Charles Vernon 1870- *WhAm 5*
Edwards, Charles William 1873-1955 *WhAm 3*
Edwards, Chauncey Theodore *WhAm 5*
Edwards, Clarence Ransom 1860-1931 *AmBi,
  ApCAB X, DcAmB S1, WhAm 1*
Edwards, Clement R *NewYHSD*
Edwards, Clement Stanislaus 1869- *WhAm 5*
Edwards, Cyrus 1793-1877 *ApCAB*
Edwards, Daniel Mann 1844-1919 *NatCAB 17*
Edwards, David 1877-1964 *NatCAB 55*
Edwards, David Frank 1881-1964 *NatCAB 51,
  WhAm 4*
Edwards, David George 1852- *WhAm 4*
Edwards, David Kitzmiller 1851-1932
  NatCAB 32
Edwards, David Morton 1871-1939 *WhAm 1*
Edwards, Dayton James 1882-1973 *NatCAB 57*
Edwards, Deltus Malin 1874- *WhAm 5*
Edwards, Don 1915- *BiDrAC*
Edwards, Don Calvin 1861-1938 *BiDrAC,
  WhAm 1*
Edwards, Duncan 1864-1931 *NatCAB 25*
Edwards, Edith 1873- *NatCAB 17,
  WomWWA 14*
Edwards, Edward Bartholomew 1873-1948
  NatCAB 36, WhAm 2
Edwards, Edward Irving 1863-1931 *ApCAB X,
  BiDrAC, NatCAB 24, WhAm 1,
  WhAmP*
Edwards, Edward Tudor 1877-1953 *NatCAB 46*
Edwards, Edward William 1874-1956
  ApCAB X, WhAm 3
Edwards, Edwin Washington 1927- *BiDrAC*
Edwards, Elijah Evan 1831- *TwCBDA*
Edwards, Elisha Jay 1847- *WhAm 4*
Edwards, Elizabeth Drake Morrill 1868-
  WomWWA 14
Edwards, Emma Atwood 1838- *AmWom*
Edwards, Everett Eugene 1900-1952 *DcAmB S5,
  EncAAH, WhAm 3*
Edwards, Francis Smith 1817-1899 *BiDrAC*
Edwards, Francis Smith 1818-1899 *BiAUS*
Edwards, Frank 1908-1967 *WhAm 4*
Edwards, Frank Wilson 1896-1957 *NatCAB 47*
Edwards, Frederick *WhAm 5*
Edwards, George Breed 1842-1887 *ApCAB X,
  NatCAB 32*
Edwards, George Clark 1846-1919 *NatCAB 6*
Edwards, George Herbert 1860-1941 *WhAm 2*
Edwards, George Lane 1868-1919 *NatCAB 33*
Edwards, George Lane 1869-1919 *NatCAB 12,
  WhAm 5*
Edwards, George Porter 1878-1941 *WhAm 1*
Edwards, George Sexton 1859-1930 *NatCAB 32*
Edwards, George Thornton 1868-1932 *WhAm 1*
Edwards, George Wharton 1859-1950
  NatCAB 11, TwCBDA, WhAm 2
Edwards, George William 1891-1954
  NatCAB 46, WhAm 3
Edwards, Gordon L 1884-1956 *WhAm 3*

Edwards, Granville Dennis 1868-1952 *WhAm 3*
Edwards, Gurney 1897-1955 *WhAm 3*
Edwards, Gus 1879-1945 *NatCAB 34*
Edwards, Harold 1893-1963 *NatCAB 51*
Edwards, Harrison Griffith 1907-1972
  NatCAB 57, WhAm 5
Edwards, Harry C 1868-1922 *IIBEAAW*
Edwards, Harry Ransom 1862-1919
  NatCAB 18
Edwards, Harry Stillwell 1855-1938 *NatCAB 8,
  NatCAB 39, TwCBDA, WhAm 1*
Edwards, Harry Taylor 1877-1949 *NatCAB 39*
Edwards, Heber L 1897-1962 *WhAm 4*
Edwards, Henriette Muir 1849- *WomWWA 14*
Edwards, Henry 1830-1891 *TwCBDA*
Edwards, Henry Lee 1856-1947 *NatCAB 36*
Edwards, Henry Pierrepont 1809-1855 *ApCAB*
Edwards, Henry Waggaman 1779-1847 *ApCAB,
  BiAUS, BiDrAC, DcAmB, Drake,
  NatCAB 10, TwCBDA, WhAm H,
  WhAmP*
Edwards, Howard 1854-1930 *WhAm 1*
Edwards, Howard Wesley 1879-1962 *WhAm 4*
Edwards, Ira 1893-1943 *WhAm 2*
Edwards, Isaac 1819-1879 *NatCAB 17*
Edwards, Jack 1928- *BiDrAC*
Edwards, Jack Coleman 1923-1968 *NatCAB 55*
Edwards, James Augustus 1854-1917
  NatCAB 17
Edwards, James Harvey 1864-1930 *NatCAB 27*
Edwards, James L *BiAUS*
Edwards, James Thomas 1838-1914
  *ApCAB Sup, NatCAB 9, TwCBDA,
  WhAm 1*
Edwards, Jesse 1819-1866 *ApCAB*
Edwards, John *BiAUS*
Edwards, John 1671?-1746 *BnEnAmA,
  DcAmB, WhAm H*
Edwards, John 1748-1837 *BiDrAC, DcAmB,
  WhAm H, WhAmP*
Edwards, John 1755-1837 *ApCAB, NatCAB 4,
  TwCBDA*
Edwards, John 1781-1850 *BiDrAC, WhAm H*
Edwards, John 1786-1843 *BiAUS, BiDrAC,
  WhAm H*
Edwards, John 1805-1894 *BiDrAC, WhAm H,
  WhAmP*
Edwards, John 1806-1887 *ApCAB*
Edwards, John 1815- *ApCAB, TwCBDA*
Edwards, John Cummins d1888 *BiAUS,
  TwCBDA*
Edwards, John Cummins 1804-1888 *BiDrAC,
  WhAm H, WhAmP*
Edwards, John Cummins 1806-1888
  NatCAB 12
Edwards, John Ellis 1814-1891 *ApCAB,
  TwCBDA*
Edwards, John Harrington 1834-1919
  NatCAB 14, NatCAB 33, WhAm 4
Edwards, John Homer 1869-1945 *WhAm 2*
Edwards, John Lewis 1879-1926 *NatCAB 23*
Edwards, John Palmer 1893-1962 *WhAm 4*
Edwards, John Richard 1853-1922 *NatCAB 6,
  WhAm 1*
Edwards, John Rogers 1871-1945 *WhAm 2*
Edwards, Jonathan 1703-1758 *AmBi, ApCAB,
  DcAmB, DcAmReB, Drake, EncAAH,
  EncAB, McGEWB, NatCAB 5,
  TwCBDA, WebAB, WhAm H*
Edwards, Jonathan 1745-1801 *AmBi, ApCAB,
  DcAmB, DcAmReB, Drake, NatCAB 7,
  TwCBDA, WhAm H*
Edwards, Jonathan 1798-1875 *ApCAB,
  TwCBDA*
Edwards, Jonathan 1817-1891 *NatCAB 2*
Edwards, Jonathan 1820-1894 *TwCBDA*
Edwards, Jonathan Patterson 1869-1948
  NatCAB 36
Edwards, Jonathan Walter 1772-1831 *ApCAB*
Edwards, Joseph, Jr. 1737-1783 *BnEnAmA*
Edwards, Joseph Lee 1870-1959 *NatCAB 50,
  WhAm 4, WhAmP*
Edwards, Julian 1855-1910 *DcAmB,
  NatCAB 7, TwCBDA, WhAm 1*
Edwards, Justin 1787-1853 *ApCAB, DcAmB,
  Drake, NatCAB 10, TwCBDA, WhAm H*
Edwards, Katharine May 1862- *WomWWA 14*
Edwards, Landon Brame 1845-1910 *ApCAB,*

WhAm 1

Edwards, Laura Ballou 1841- WomWWA 14
Edwards, Lawrence Kirkland 1878-1957
  NatCAB 50
Edwards, Leroy Delos 1897-1954 NatCAB 44,
  WhAm 4
Edwards, LeRoy Gardiner 1886-1964
  NatCAB 52
Edwards, LeRoy Mallory 1885-1962 WhAm 4
Edwards, LeRoy Sherman 1878-1953
  NatCAB 42
Edwards, Linden Forest 1899-1970 WhAm 5
Edwards, Llewellyn Nathaniel 1873-1952
  NatCAB 39
Edwards, Lonnie Joe IlBEAAW
Edwards, Loren McClain 1877-1945 WhAm 2
Edwards, Louise Betts d1928 WhAm 1
Edwards, Margaret Messenger 1890-1963
  WhAm 4
Edwards, Maurice Dwight 1847- NatCAB 16
Edwards, Merrick Knight 1880-1927
  NatCAB 23
Edwards, Michael 1893-1962 NatCAB 47
Edwards, Morgan 1722-1795 ApCAB, DcAmB,
  NatCAB 8, TwCBDA, WhAm H
Edwards, Murray French 1885-1963 WhAm 4
Edwards, Myrtle Sassman 1894-1969 WhAm 5
Edwards, Nathaniel Marsh 1837-1908 WhAm 1
Edwards, Newton 1889-1969 BiDAmEd
Edwards, Ninian 1775-1833 AmBi, ApCAB,
  BiAUS, BiDrAC, DcAmB, Drake,
  NatCAB 11, TwCBDA, WhAm H,
  WhAmP
Edwards, Ninian Wirt 1809-1889 ApCAB,
  DcAmB, NatCAB 10, TwCBDA,
  WhAm H
Edwards, Ogden 1781-1862 ApCAB, Drake,
  TwCBDA
Edwards, Ogden Matthias, Jr. 1869-1940
  NatCAB 31, WhAm 1
Edwards, Oliver 1835-1904 ApCAB, DcAmB
Edwards, Oliver Murray 1862-1938 NatCAB 27
Edwards, Orange 1870-1956 NatCAB 45
Edwards, Paul Kenneth 1898-1959 WhAm 3
Edwards, Percy Noyes 1889-1968 WhAm 5
Edwards, Philip R 1901-1966 WhAm 4
Edwards, Pierpont 1750-1826 AmBi, DcAmB,
  WhAm H
Edwards, Pierrepont 1750-1826 ApCAB,
  BiAUS, BiDrAC, Drake, TwCBDA,
  WhAmP
Edwards, R J 1868-1946 NatCAB 40
Edwards, Ray Gwyther 1872- WhAm 5
Edwards, Raymond Dorsey 1898-1968
  NatCAB 54
Edwards, Richard 1822-1908 WhAm 1
Edwards, Richard Henry 1877-1954 WhAm 3
Edwards, Richard Stanislaus 1885-1956
  NatCAB 45
Edwards, Richard Stanislaus 1885-1959
  WhAm 3
Edwards, Robert 1872-1935 NatCAB 34
Edwards, Robert Ernest 1923-1969 WhAm 5
Edwards, Robert Wilkinson 1914-1969 WhAm 5
Edwards, Robert William 1899-1955
  NatCAB 42
Edwards, Ronald Stanley 1910-1976 WhAm 6
Edwards, Samuel 1705-1762 BnEnAmA
Edwards, Samuel 1785-1850 BiAUS, BiDrAC,
  WhAm H
Edwards, Samuel 1839-1912 NatCAB 15,
  WhAm 1
Edwards, Samuel Lewis 1877- WhoColR
Edwards, Sarah Pierpont 1710-1758 NotAW
Edwards, Stephen Ostrom 1855-1916 WhAm 1
Edwards, Talmadge 1747-1821 DcAmB,
  WhAm H
Edwards, Thomas NewYHSD
Edwards, Thomas 1701?-1755 BnEnAmA
Edwards, Thomas Allison 1874-1955 WhAm 3
Edwards, Thomas Alvin 1856-1913 NatCAB 16
Edwards, Thomas Cynonfardd 1848-1927
  NatCAB 21, NatCAB 22, WhAm 1
Edwards, Thomas McKey 1795-1875 BiAUS,
  BiDrAC, WhAm H
Edwards, Thomas Owen 1810-1876 BiAUS Sup,
  BiDrAC, WhAm H, WhAmP
Edwards, Timothy 1669-1758 ApCAB,

TwCBDA

Edwards, Timothy 1738-1813 ApCAB
Edwards, Tom O 1738-1876 BiAUS
Edwards, Tryon 1809-1894 ApCAB, Drake,
  NatCAB 14, TwCBDA
Edwards, Velma Green 1914-1969 WhAm 5
Edwards, Vere Buckingham 1890-1946
  NatCAB 35, WhAm 2
Edwards, Victor Everett 1862-1931 NatCAB 24,
  WhAm 1
Edwards, W NewYHSD
Edwards, Wakeman Wakeman 1826-1921
  NatCAB 48
Edwards, Walter Alison 1862- TwCBDA,
  WhAm 4
Edwards, Weldon Nathaniel 1788-1873 ApCAB,
  BiAUS, BiDrAC, DcAmB, NatCAB 12,
  TwCBDA, WhAm H, WhAmP
Edwards, Willard Eldridge 1903-1975 WhAm 6
Edwards, William 1770-1851 AmBi, ApCAB,
  DcAmB, NatCAB 11, TwCBDA,
  WhAm H
Edwards, William 1830-1898 NatCAB 13
Edwards, William A 1902-1951 WhAm 3
Edwards, William Aloysius 1860-1933
  NatCAB 25
Edwards, William Augustus 1866-1939
  WhAm 1
Edwards, William Chalmers 1846-1910
  ApCAB X
Edwards, William Cunningham 1878- WhAm 6
Edwards, William David 1855- TwCBDA
Edwards, William Emory 1842- ApCAB
Edwards, William Franklin 1858-1933
  NatCAB 23
Edwards, William Frederic 1776-1842 DcScB
Edwards, William Hanford 1876- ApCAB X,
  WhAm 5
Edwards, William Henry 1822-1909 AmBi,
  DcAmB, TwCBDA, WhAm 1
Edwards, William P BiAUS
Edwards, William Pierrepont 1867-1950
  NatCAB 40
Edwards, William Posey 1835-1900 BiDrAC
Edwards, William Seymour 1856-1915 WhAm 1
Edwardsen, Charles, Jr. 1943- REnAW
Edwin, David 1776-1841 ApCAB, DcAmB,
  Drake, NewYHSD
Eeckhout, Jan NewYHSD
Eells, Cushing 1810-1893 BiDAmEd,
  DcAmReB, TwCBDA
Eells, Dan Parmelee 1825-1903 DcAmB,
  NatCAB 1
Eells, Dan Parmelee 1884-1959 NatCAB 48
Eells, Elsie Eusebia Spicer 1880-1963 WhAm 4
Eells, Hastings 1895-1970 WhAm 5
Eells, Howard Parmelee 1855-1919 NatCAB 19,
  WhAm 1
Eells, James 1822-1886 TwCBDA
Eells, Myron 1843-1907 TwCBDA, WhAm 1
Eells, Stillman Witt 1873-1937 WhAm 1
Eells, Walter Crosby 1886-1962 BiDAmEd
Eells, Walter Crosby 1886-1963 WhAm 4
Eerdmans, William Bernard 1882-1966
  WhAm 4
Effie, William NewYHSD
Effinger, John Robert 1869-1933 WhAm 1
Effingham, Lord 1630?-1694 NatCAB 13
Effler, Erwin R 1884-1956 WhAm 3
Effner, Valentine BiAUS
Efird, Cyprian Melanchton 1856-1941
  NatCAB 48
Efird, Edward Lilly 1880-1945 NatCAB 34
Efird, John Solomon 1857-1927 NatCAB 21
Efird, Paul Haywood 1886-1948 NatCAB 37
Efner, Valentine 1776-1865 BiDrAC,
  WhAm H
Efroymson, Abram B 1893-1964 WhAm 4
Efroymson, Gustave A 1870-1946 WhAm 2
Egan, Hannah M 1891-1949 WhAm 2
Egan, James Francis 1879-1945 NatCAB 34
Egan, John J IlBEAAW, NewYHSD
Egan, John M 1848- WhAm 6
Egan, Joseph B 1879- WhAm 6
Egan, Joseph L 1886-1948 WhAm 2
Egan, Lavinia Hartwell 1863- WomWWA 14
Egan, Louis Henry 1881- WhAm 3
Egan, Margaret Elizabeth 1905-1959 DcAmLiB

Egan, Martin 1872-1938 WhAm 1
Egan, Maurice Francis 1852-1924 AmBi,
  ApCAB, ApCAB X, DcAmB,
  NatCAB 11, TwCBDA, WhAm 1,
  WhAmP
Egan, Michael 1761-1814 ApCAB, DcAmB,
  NatCAB 5, TwCBDA, WhAm H
Egan, Patrick 1841-1919 AmBi, DcAmB,
  NatCAB 5, WhAmP
Egan, Raymond Blanning 1890-1952
  NatCAB 42
Egan, Thomas Aloysius 1884-1954 WhAm 3
Egan, Thomas Carby 1894-1961 NatCAB 53
Egan, Thomas H NewYHSD
Egan, Thomas P 1847- NatCAB 12
Egan, Thomas W 1836-1887 ApCAB
Egan, William Constantine 1841-1930
  NatCAB 22
Egan, William Joseph 1888-1960 NatCAB 48
Egana, Juan 1769-1836 ApCAB
Egana, Mariano 1793-1846 ApCAB
Egar, John Hodson 1832- WhAm 4
Egas, Camilo 1897-1962 WhAm 4
Egas Moniz, Antonio C DeAbreu Freire
  1874-1955 DcScB
Egbert, A G 1828-1896 BiAUS
Egbert, Albert Gallatin 1828-1896 BiDrAC,
  WhAm H
Egbert, Donald Drew 1902-1973 WhAm 5
Egbert, Henry 1826-1900 NewYHSD
Egbert, Henry Clay 1840?-1899 ApCAB Sup
Egbert, James Chidester 1859-1948 WhAm 2
Egbert, Joseph 1807-1888 BiAUS, BiDrAC,
  WhAm H
Egbert, Nelly Young 1843- WomWWA 14
Egbert, Percy T 1894-1970 WhAm 5
Egbert, Seneca 1863-1939 WhAm 1
Egbert, Sherwood Harry 1920-1969 WhAm 5
Egbert, W Grant 1869- WhAm 1
Ege, George 1748-1829 BiAUS, BiDrAC,
  WhAm H
Ege, Hattie B WhAm 5
Egeberg, Birger 1889-1969 NatCAB 55
Egede, Hans 1686-1758 ApCAB, Drake
Egede, Paul 1708-1789 ApCAB, Drake
Egekvist, Soren Andersen 1889-1955
  NatCAB 43
Egelson, Louis I 1885-1957 WhAm 3
Eger, Charles Michael 1843- NatCAB 14
Egerton, Graham 1861-1922 WhAm 1
Eggenhofer, Nick 1897- IlBEAAW
Eggerman, Donald Gilbert 1881-1953
  NatCAB 42
Eggers, Albert Herman 1892-1974 WhAm 6
Eggers, Carl 1879-1956 NatCAB 42
Eggers, George William 1883-1958 WhAm 3
Eggers, George William Nordholtz 1896-1963
  NatCAB 52
Eggers, Harold Everett 1882-1966 WhAm 4
Eggers, Henry Claus Thomas 1893-1964
  NatCAB 51
Eggers, John Hermann 1884-1959 NatCAB 47
Eggers, Otto Reinhold 1882-1964 NatCAB 50,
  WhAm 5
Eggerss, H A 1890- WhAm 5
Eggert, Carl Edgar 1868- WhAm 4
Eggert, Charles Augustus d1931 WhAm 1,
  WhAm 1C
Eggert, Harry T 1897-1969 WhAm 5
Eggert, Sylvania O 1845- WomWWA 14
Eggimann, Edward Daniel 1877-1948
  NatCAB 37, WhAm 2
Eggleston, Alice Adams 1866- WomWWA 14
Eggleston, Allan Arthur 1906-1965 WhAm 4
Eggleston, Allegra 1860- AmWom
Eggleston, Amy Whittington 1874-
  WomWWA 14
Eggleston, Aubrey Laurens 1888-1950
  NatCAB 40
Eggleston, Benjamin 1816-1888 BiAUS,
  BiDrAC, NatCAB 4, TwCBDA,
  WhAm H
Eggleston, Benjamin Osro 1867- NatCAB 8
Eggleston, Cary 1884-1966 NatCAB 52,
  WhAm 5
Eggleston, David Quinn 1857- WhAm 4
Eggleston, Edward 1837-1902 AmBi, ApCAB,
  DcAmB, EncAAH, McGEWB,

NatCAB 6, TwCBDA, WebAB, WhAm 1
Eggleston, Elmer Leslie 1874-1937 *NatCAB 28*
Eggleston, Sir Frederic William 1875-1954
WhAm 3
Eggleston, George Cary 1839-1911 *AmBi,
ApCAB, DcAmB, NatCAB 1, TwCBDA,
WhAm 1*
Eggleston, Joseph 1754-1811 *ApCAB, BiAUS,
BiDrAC, Drake, NatCAB 2, TwCBDA,
WhAm H*
Eggleston, Joseph Dupuy 1867-1953 *BiDAmEd,
NatCAB 42, WhAm 3*
Eggleston, Joseph Emmett 1847- *NatCAB 7*
Eggleton, Frank E 1893-1970 *WhAm 5*
Eglan, Max *NewYHSD*
Eglau, Max *NewYHSD*
Egle, William Henry 1830-1901 *ApCAB,
DcAmB, NatCAB 8, TwCBDA,
WhAm 1*
Egler, Ammiel *NewYHSD*
Egleston, Azariah 1757-1822 *NatCAB 3,
TwCBDA*
Egleston, Nathaniel Hillyer 1822- *NatCAB 13*
Egleston, Thomas 1832-1900 *AmBi, ApCAB,
DcAmB, NatCAB 3, TwCBDA,
WhAm 1*
Eglin, William Charles Lawson 1870-1928
WhAm 1
Eglof, Warren K 1899-1965 *WhAm 4*
Egloff, Gustav 1880-1955 *NatCAB 42,
WhAm 3*
Egloffstein, F W Von 1824?-1898 *NewYHSD*
Egloffstein, Frederick W Von 1824?-1898
WhAm H
Egly, Henry Harris 1893-1958 *WhAm 3*
Egmont, Lamoraal, Graaf Van 1522-1568
WhoMilH
Egner, Arthur Frederick 1882-1943 *WhAm 2*
Egner, Frank Lewis 1892-1957 *NatCAB 46,
WhAm 3*
Egolf, Arnold 1858-1924 *NatCAB 20*
Egolf, Willard Durre 1904-1964 *NatCAB 51*
Egorov, Dimitry Fedorovich 1869-1931 *DcScB*
Egtvedt, Clairmont Leroy 1892-1975 *WhAm 6*
Eguiara Y Eguren, Juan Jose d1763 *ApCAB*
Eguiguren, Victor 1860?- *ApCAB Sup*
Egusquiza, Juan Bautista 1845- *ApCAB Sup*
Ehegartner, Lawrence William 1895-1964
NatCAB 51
Ehlars, John D *NewYHSD*
Ehler, Annette Blackburn 1864- *WomWWA 14*
Ehler, Elmer Winfield 1882-1943 *NatCAB 33*
Ehlermann, Carl 1883-1950 *NatCAB 39*
Ehlers, Henry Edward 1879- *WhAm 6*
Ehlers, Victor Marcus 1884-1959 *NatCAB 48*
Ehnes, Morris Wellington 1873-1945 *WhAm 2*
Ehninger, John Whetten 1827-1889 *DcAmB,
NewYHSD*
Ehninger, John Whetton 1827-1889 *ApCAB,
Drake*
Ehninger, John Whitten 1827-1889 *TwCBDA*
Ehrenberg, Christian Gottfried 1795-1876
DcScB
Ehrenburg, Ilya Grigorievich 1891-1967
McGEWB
Ehrenfeld, Charles Hatch 1864-1937 *WhAm 1*
Ehrenfeld, Charles Lewis 1832-1914 *WhAm 1*
Ehrenfest, Paul 1880-1933 *DcScB*
Ehrenfried, Albert 1880-1951 *NatCAB 18,
WhAm 3*
Ehrenreich, Joseph 1907-1973 *WhAm 5*
Ehrenstein, Maximilian 1899-1968 *NatCAB 54*
Ehrensvard, Johan Jacob Albert 1867- *WhAm 4*
Ehrenzweig, Albert Armin 1906-1974 *WhAm 6*
Ehret, Adolph *NewYHSD*
Ehret, Georg Dionysius 1708-1770 *DcScB*
Ehret, George 1835-1927 *NatCAB 32*
Ehrgood, A Harry 1889-1964 *NatCAB 50*
Ehrgott, Peter *NewYHSD*
Ehrhardt, Julius George 1849-1922 *NatCAB 5,
WhAm 1*
Ehrhorn, Edward Macfarlane 1862-1941
WhAm 1
Ehrhorn, Oscar Weeks 1875-1957 *NatCAB 49*
Ehrich, Harold Louis 1880-1932 *WhAm 1*
Ehrich, Louis R 1849-1911 *WhAm 1*
Ehrich, Walter Louis 1878-1936 *NatCAB 27*
Ehrich, William E 1900-1967 *WhAm 5*

Ehringhaus, John Christoph Blucher 1882-1949
WhAm 2
Ehrlich, Arnold Bogumil 1848-1919 *DcAmB*
Ehrlich, Harry 1909-1952 *WhAm 3*
Ehrlich, Jacob W 1900-1971 *WhAm 5*
Ehrlich, Paul 1854-1915 *AsBiEn, BiHiMed,
DcScB, McGEWB*
Ehrlichman, Ben B 1895-1971 *WhAm 5*
Ehrman, Alfred 1872-1943 *NatCAB 32*
Ehrman, Frederick L 1906-1974 *WhAm 6*
Ehrman, Mary Bartholomew d1939 *WhAm 1*
Ehrman, Sidney M 1873- *WhAm 5*
Ehrmann, Herbert Brutus 1891-1970 *WhAm 6*
Ehrmann, Max 1872- *WhAm 5*
Eichbaum, George Calder 1837-1919
NewYHSD
Eichberg, Julius 1824- *ApCAB*
Eichberg, Julius 1824-1893 *DcAmB, TwCBDA,
WhAm H*
Eichberg, Julius 1824-1898 *NatCAB 13*
Eichberg, Julius 1825- *Drake Sup*
Eichberg, Solomon *NewYHSD*
Eichelberger, James W, Jr. 1886- *WhoColR*
Eichelberger, Robert Lawrence 1886-1961
*WebAMB, WhAm 4, WhWW-II,
WhoMilH*
Eichelberger, William Snyder 1865- *WhAm 5*
Eichelbrenner, Ernest A 1913-1974 *WhAm 6*
Eichenauer, Charles Frederick 1882-1945
WhAm 3
Eichenlaub, Frank Joseph 1894-1972 *WhAm 6*
Eichenwald, Aleksandr Aleksandrovich
1864-1944 *DcScB*
Eicher, Edward Clayton 1878-1944 *BiDrAC,
NatCAB 39, WhAm 2, WhAmP*
Eicher, Henry Martin 1858-1919 *WhAm 3*
Eicher, Henry Martin 1859-1919 *NatCAB 16*
Eichheim, Henry 1870-1942 *WhAm 2*
Eichholtz, Jacob 1776-1842 *BnEnAmA,
DcAmB, NewYHSD, WhAm H*
Eichhorn, William A 1897-1960 *WhAm 3*
Eichler, August Wilhelm 1839-1887 *DcScB*
Eichler, George Augustus 1892-1967
NatCAB 53
Eichmann, Adolf 1906-1962 *WhWW-II*
Eichwald, Karl Eduard Ivanovich 1795-1876
DcScB
Eickemeyer, Carl 1869- *NatCAB 11*
Eickemeyer, Rudolf 1831-1895 *DcAmB,
NatCAB 1, WhAm H*
Eickemeyer, Rudolf 1862-1932 *WhAm 1*
Eickhoff, Anthony 1827-1901 *BiDrAC*
Eickhoff, Henry 1856-1933 *NatCAB 25*
Eickhoff, Henry, Jr. 1898-1954 *NatCAB 43*
Eidem, Olaf 1875- *WhAm 5*
Eidlitz, Charles Leo 1866-1921 *WhAm 1*
Eidlitz, Cyrus Lazelle Warner 1853-1921
ApCAB, DcAmB
Eidlitz, Leopold 1823-1908 *ApCAB, DcAmB*
Eidlitz, Otto Marc 1860-1928 *ApCAB X,
NatCAB 16, WhAm 1*
Eidlitz, Robert James 1864-1935 *NatCAB 26*
Eidmann, Frank Lewis 1887-1941 *WhAm 1*
Eielsen, Elling 1804-1883 *AmBi, DcAmB,
WhAm H*
Eielson, Carl Ben 1897?-1929 *AmBi*
Eiesland, John 1867- *WhAm 5*
Eifert, Virginia Snider 1911-1966 *WhAm 4*
Eiffe, William *NewYHSD*
Eiffee, William *NewYHSD*
Eiffel, Alexandre Gustave 1832-1923 *McGEWB*
Eigen, Manfred 1927- *AsBiEn*
Eigenbrodt, Charles S 1825-1864 *ApCAB*
Eigenbrodt, David Lamberson 1810-1880
ApCAB
Eigenbrodt, Lewis Ernest Andrew 1773-1828
ApCAB
Eigenbrodt, William Ernest 1813-1894 *ApCAB,
TwCBDA*
Eigenmann, Carl H 1863-1927 *AmBi, DcAmB,
DcScB, NatCAB 13, NatCAB 21,
TwCBDA, WhAm 1*
Eigenmann, Rosa Smith 1858-1947 *NotAW,
WomWWA 14*
Eight, The *BnEnAmA*
Eights, James 1798-1882 *NewYHSD*
Eijkman, Christiaan 1858-1930 *AsBiEn, DcScB*
Eijkman, Christian 1858-1930 *McGEWB*

Eikenbary, Charles Franklin 1877-1933
WhAm 1
Eikenberry, Dan Harrison 1888-1963 *WhAm 4*
Eikenberry, William Lewis 1871-1957 *WhAm 3*
Eilberg, Joshua 1921- *BiDrAC*
Eilenberger, Clinton B 1876-1937 *WhAm 1*
Eilers, Anton Frederic 1839-1917 *NatCAB 14,
NatCAB 30, WhAm 1*
Eilers, Frederic Anton 1839-1917 *ApCAB,
DcAmB*
Eilers, Karl 1865-1941 *NatCAB 30, WhAm 1*
Eilert, Ernest Frederick 1866- *WhAm 4*
Eilshemius, Louis Michel 1864-1941 *BnEnAmA,
DcAmB S3, IIBEAAW, WhAm 1,
WhAm 2*
Eiman, John 1886-1954 *NatCAB 45*
Eimbeck, William 1841-1909 *DcAmB,
WhAm 4*
Eimer, August 1853- *NatCAB 14*
Eimermann, George Mickle *NewYHSD*
Eimermann, Ida F Buxton 1860- *WomWWA 14*
Einarsen, Arthur Skogman 1897-1965
NatCAB 53
Einaudi, Luigi 1874-1961 *WhAm 4*
Einert, Harry Edmond 1900-1952 *NatCAB 42*
Einhorn, David 1809-1879 *AmBi, ApCAB,
DcAmB, DcAmReB, NatCAB 12,
WhAm H*
Einhorn, Max 1862- *WhAm 4*
Einsidel, D 1852-1896 *WhAm H*
Einstein, Albert 1879-1955 *AsBiEn,
DcAmB S5, DcScB, EncAB, McGEWB,
WebAB, WhAm 3*
Einstein, Alfred 1880-1952 *WhAm 3*
Einstein, Edwin 1842-1905 *BiDrAC*
Einstein, Hannah Bachman 1862-1929 *BiCAW,
NotAW*
Einstein, Lewis 1877-1949 *WhAm 2*
Einstein, Morris 1826-1916 *NatCAB 17*
Einthoven, Willem 1860-1927 *AsBiEn,
BiHiMed, DcScB*
Einum, Lucille Grace Johnson 1907- *WhAm 6*
Eirick, William Frederick 1872-1955
NatCAB 45
Eis, Frederick 1843- *ApCAB Sup, WhAm 4*
Eisai 1141-1215 *McGEWB*
Eiselen, Frederick Carl 1872-1937 *WhAm 1*
Eiseley, Loren Corey 1907- *WebAB*
Eiseman, Benjamin 1833- *NatCAB 7*
Eiseman, Frederick Benjamin 1881- *WhAm 6*
Eiseman, Paul *NewYHSD*
Eisemann, Alexander 1886-1953 *NatCAB 41*
Eisen, Gustavus A 1847-1940 *WhAm 1*
Eisenberg, David Berton 1892-1975 *WhAm 6*
Eisenberg, Irwin Weinman 1906-1970 *WhAm 5*
Eisenberg, Maurice 1900-1972 *NatCAB 56*
Eisenberg, Maurice 1902-1972 *WhAm 5*
Eisenberg, Samuel Saul 1892-1964 *NatCAB 54*
Eisendrath, Daniel Nathan 1867-1939 *WhAm 1*
Eisendrath, David Benjamin 1890-1964
NatCAB 52
Eisendrath, Maurice Nathan 1902-1973
WhAm 6
Eisenhardt, Raymond 1901-1965 *WhAm 4*
Eisenhardt, Raymond F *WhAm 5*
Eisenhart, Charles Marion 1914-1967
WhAm 4A
Eisenhart, Luther Pfahler 1876-1965 *BiDAmEd,
DcScB, NatCAB 53, WhAm 4*
Eisenhart, Martin Herbert 1884-1975 *WhAm 6*
Eisenhauer, Charles Phillip 1891-1966
NatCAB 52
Eisenhour, B E 1878-1958 *NatCAB 48*
Eisenhower, Arthur B 1886-1958 *WhAm 3*
Eisenhower, David Dwight 1890-1969 *WhoMilH*
Eisenhower, Dwight David 1890-1969 *BiDrAC,
BiDrUSE, EncAAH, EncAB, McGEWB,
NatCAB 56, WebAB, WebAMB,
WhAm 5, WhAmP, WhWW-II*
Eisenhower, Edgar Nuton 1889-1971 *WhAm 5*
Eisenhower, Milton Stover 1899- *BiDAmEd*
Eisenlohr, Charles James 1864-1947
NatCAB 37
Eisenlohr, Edward G 1872-1961 *IIBEAAW*
Eisenman, William Hunt 1886-1958 *WhAm 3*
Eisenschiml, Otto 1880-1963 *WhAm 4*
Eisenstein, Ferdinand Gotthold Max 1823-1852
DcScB

Eisenstein, Sergei Mikhailovich 1898-1948 *McGEWB*
Eisentraut, John Philip 1870-1958 *NatCAB 47*
Eisfeld, Theodor 1816-1882 *WhAm H*
Eisfeld, Theodore 1816-1882 *ApCAB*
Eisfeldt, May Irwin 1862- *WomWWA 14*
Eisman, Sidney John 1879-1950 *NatCAB 38*
Eisner, H Raymond 1886-1948 *NatCAB 36*
Eisner, J Lester 1889-1955 *WhAm 3*
Eisner, Joseph 1900-1958 *NatCAB 43*
Eisner, Mark 1886-1953 *WhAm 3*
Eisner, Monroe 1893-1973 *WhAm 6*
Eisner, Sigmund 1859-1925 *ApCAB X*, *NatCAB 32*
Eitel, Emil 1865-1948 *NatCAB 41*
Eitel, George Gotthilf 1858-1928 *NatCAB 21*, *WhAm 1*
Eitel, Karl 1871-1954 *NatCAB 41*
Eitel, Max 1882-1954 *NatCAB 41*
Eitoku, Kano 1543-1590 *McGEWB*
Ekblaw, Walter Elmer 1882-1949 *NatCAB 41*, *WhAm 2*
Ekblom, John Olof 1894-1966 *WhAm 4*
Ekeberg, Anders Gustaf 1767-1813 *AsBiEn*, *DcScB*
Ekeberg, Lars Birger 1880- *WhAm 6*
Ekeley, John Bernard 1869-1951 *WhAm 3*
Ekengren, Wilhelm August Ferdinand 1861-1920 *WhAm 1*
Ekern, Herman Lewis 1872-1954 *WhAm 3*
Ekin, James Adams 1819-1891 *ApCAB*, *NatCAB 5*, *TwCBDA*
Ekin, John Jamison 1873- *WhAm 6*
Ekins, H R 1901-1963 *WhAm 4*
Eklund, Carl Robert 1909-1962 *NatCAB 48*
Eklund, Fred Nils 1904-1957 *WhAm 3*
Ekman, Vagn Walfrid 1874-1954 *DcScB*
Eksergian, Rupen 1889-1961 *WhAm 4*
Ekwall, William Alexander 1887-1956 *BiDrAC*, *NatCAB 48*, *WhAm 3*
Ekwensi, Cyprian 1921- *McGEWB*
El Azhari, Ismail 1900-1969 *WhAm 5*
El-Khoury, Bechara 1890-1964 *WhAm 4*
Ela, David Hough 1831- *WhAm 4*
Ela, Emerson 1875-1956 *NatCAB 46*
Ela, Jacob Hart 1820-1884 *BiAUS*, *BiDrAC*, *WhAm H*
Ela, John Whittier 1838-1902 *WhAm 1*
Elam, Emma Lee d1919 *WhAm 1*, *WomWWA 14*
Elam, John Babb 1845-1916 *NatCAB 18*, *WhAm 1*
Elam, Joseph Barton 1821-1885 *BiDrAC*, *WhAm H*
Elan, Meir 1918-1971 *WhAm 5*
Eland, John Shenton 1872-1933 *NatCAB 24*
Elander, Albin Eskel 1906-1966 *WhAm 4*
Elbee, Maurice Louis Joseph Gigost D' 1752-1794 *WhoMilH*
Elbert, Ella Lavinia 1865- *WomWWA 14*
Elbert, John Aloysius 1895-1966 *WhAm 4*
Elbert, Samuel 1740-1788 *DcAmB*, *Drake*
Elbert, Samuel 1743-1788 *ApCAB*, *BiDrAC*, *NatCAB 2*, *TwCBDA*, *WhAm H*, *WhAmP*
Elbert, Samuel Hitt 1833-1899 *NatCAB 6*, *TwCBDA*
Elcano, Juan Sebastian 1476-1526 *ApCAB*
Elcock, Thomas Edward 1887-1944 *NatCAB 34*
Elden, John Aten 1891-1935 *ApCAB X*, *WhAm 1*
Elder, Alfonso 1898-1974 *WhAm 6*
Elder, Bowman 1888-1954 *WhAm 3*
Elder, Cyrus 1833-1912 *ApCAB*, *WhAm 1*
Elder, Frank Ray 1885-1962 *WhAm 4*
Elder, George 1793-1838 *WhAm H*
Elder, George A M 1794-1838 *ApCAB*
Elder, James Walter 1882-1941 *BiDrAC*
Elder, John 1706-1792 *ApCAB*
Elder, John Adams 1833-1895 *IIBEAAW*, *NewYHSD*, *WhAm H*
Elder, Joseph *NewYHSD*
Elder, Joseph Freeman 1839-1910 *ApCAB*, *WhAm 1*
Elder, Orr Jay 1882-1957 *WhAm 3*
Elder, Paul 1872-1948 *WhAm 2*
Elder, Robert Henry 1877- *WhAm 5*
Elder, Samuel James 1850-1918 *DcAmB*,

NatCAB 21, *WhAm 1*
Elder, Susan Blanchard 1835-1923 *ApCAB*, *DcAmB*, *NatCAB 11*, *TwCBDA*, *WhAm 4*, *WomWWA 14*
Elder, William 1806-1885 *ApCAB*, *DcAmB*, *WhAm H*
Elder, William 1809- *Drake*
Elder, William 1822-1882 *ApCAB*
Elder, William 1840- *TwCBDA*
Elder, William Henry 1819-1904 *ApCAB*, *DcAmB*, *NatCAB 5*, *TwCBDA*, *WhAm 1*
Elder, William Line 1855-1940 *WhAm 1*
Elderkin, George Wicker 1879-1965 *WhAm 4*
Elderkin, John 1841- *WhAm 4*
Elderkin, Karl Osler 1895-1966 *NatCAB 53*, *WhAm 4*
Elderkin, Noble Strong 1878-1966 *WhAm 4*
Eldert, Cornelius 1849-1930 *ApCAB X*
Eldred, Byron E 1873-1956 *WhAm 3*
Eldred, Charles Dudley 1887-1938 *NatCAB 31*
Eldred, Lewis 1911-1966 *WhAm 4*
Eldred, Nathaniel B 1795-1867 *BiAUS*
Eldredge, Arch Bishop 1853-1919 *WhAm 1*
Eldredge, Barnabas 1843-1911 *NatCAB 6*
Eldredge, Charles Augustus 1820-1896 *BiDrAC*, *WhAm H*, *WhAmP*
Eldredge, Charles Henry 1839-1916 *WhAm 1*
Eldredge, Joseph Underwood, Jr. 1874-1933 *NatCAB 25*, *WhAm 1*
Eldredge, Nathaniel Buel 1813-1893 *BiDrAC*, *WhAm H*
Eldredge, Seneca Dutcher 1888-1931 *NatCAB 25*
Eldredge, Zoeth Skinner 1846- *WhAm 1*
Eldrerge, Elliott Minton 1878-1959 *WhAm 3*
Eldridge, Arthur Symons 1873-1954 *NatCAB 44*
Eldridge, Carl McKnight 1885-1965 *NatCAB 51*
Eldridge, Charles A 1821-1896 *ApCAB*, *BiAUS*, *NatCAB 8*, *TwCBDA*
Eldridge, Charles Judson 1893-1969 *NatCAB 55*
Eldridge, Charles William 1811-1883 *NewYHSD*
Eldridge, Edward Henry 1870- *WhAm 5*
Eldridge, Edwin 1811-1876 *ApCAB*
Eldridge, Francis Howard 1896-1944 *WhAm 2*
Eldridge, Francis Huyck 1905-1949 *NatCAB 37*
Eldridge, Frank Harold 1852-1921 *WhAm 1*
Eldridge, Frederick L 1860- *WhAm 4*
Eldridge, Frederick William 1877-1937 *WhAm 1*
Eldridge, George Homans 1854-1905 *WhAm 1*
Eldridge, Hamilton N 1831-1882 *ApCAB*
Eldridge, J *NewYHSD*
Eldridge, Maurice Owen 1873- *WhAm 5*
Eldridge, Muriel Tilden 1893-1972 *WhAm 6*
Eldridge, Seba 1885-1953 *WhAm 3*
Eldridge, Shalor Winchell 1816-1899 *DcAmB*, *NatCAB 21*, *WhAm H*
Eldridge, William Angevine 1900-1953 *WhAm 3*
Eleanor Of Aquitaine 1122?-1204 *McGEWB*
Elebash, Baisley Powell 1897-1953 *NatCAB 41*
Elena, Luigi *NewYHSD*
Elfe, Thomas, Sr. 1719?-1775 *BnEnAmA*
Elfe, Thomas, Sr. 1719?-1775 *BnEnAmA*
Elgar, Sir Edward 1857-1934 *McGEWB*
Elgar, Joseph *BiAUS*
Elghammer, H William 1894-1972 *WhAm 5*
Elgin, James Bruce, Earl Of 1811-1863 *ApCAB*, *Drake*, *McGEWB*
Elhuyar, Fausto D' 1755-1833 *DcScB*
Elhuyar, Juan Jose D' 1754-1796 *DcScB*
Elias, Albert Barnes 1875- *WhAm 5*
Elias, Domingo 1805-1867 *ApCAB*
Elias, Harold Lee 1891-1976 *WhAm 3*
Eliasberg, Wladimir Gottlieb 1887-1969 *NatCAB 54*, *WhAm 5*
Eliason, James Bayard 1885-1962 *NatCAB 49*, *WhAm 4*
Elie DeBeaumont, Jean-B-A-L-Leonce 1798-1874 *DcScB*
Eliel, Paul 1889-1953 *NatCAB 42*
Elijah BenSolomon 1720-1797 *McGEWB*
Elingham, Robert *NewYHSD*
Elion, Edward 1900-1961 *NatCAB 50*

Eliot, Amory 1856-1943 *WhAm 3*
Eliot, Andrew 1718-1778 *ApCAB*, *Drake*, *NatCAB 7*, *TwCBDA*
Eliot, Charles 1791-1813 *ApCAB*
Eliot, Charles 1857-1897 *AmBi*
Eliot, Charles 1859-1897 *DcAmB*, *NatCAB 13*, *WhAm H*
Eliot, Charles William 1834-1926 *AmBi*, *ApCAB*, *ApCAB X*, *BiDAmEd*, *DcAmB*, *EncAB*, *McGEWB*, *NatCAB 6*, *TwCBDA*, *WebAB*, *WhAm 1*
Eliot, Charlotte Champe Stearns 1843-1929 *NotAW*
Eliot, Christopher Rhodes 1856-1945 *WhAm 2*
Eliot, Douglas Fitch Guilford 1887-1971 *WhAm 5*
Eliot, Edward Cranch 1858-1928 *WhAm 1*
Eliot, Ellsworth, Jr. 1864-1945 *NatCAB 34*
Eliot, Ephraim *ApCAB*
Eliot, Ethel Cook 1890-1972 *NatCAB 56*
Eliot, Frederick May 1889-1958 *WhAm 3*
Eliot, George 1819-1880 *McGEWB*
Eliot, George Fielding 1894-1971 *NatCAB 56*, *WhAm 5*
Eliot, Gustavus 1857-1932 *NatCAB 28*
Eliot, Jared 1685-1763 *AmBi*, *ApCAB*, *DcAmB*, *Drake*, *TwCBDA*, *WhAm H*
Eliot, John d1690 *ApCAB*
Eliot, John 1603-1690 *Drake*
Eliot, John 1604-1690 *AmBi*, *BiDAmEd*, *DcAmB*, *DcAmReB*, *EncAAH*, *EncAB*, *McGEWB*, *NatCAB 2*, *REnAW*, *TwCBDA*, *WebAB*, *WhAm H*
Eliot, John 1754-1813 *ApCAB*, *Drake*, *TwCBDA*
Eliot, Samuel 1739-1820 *TwCBDA*
Eliot, Samuel 1821-1898 *AmBi*, *ApCAB*, *DcAmB*, *Drake*, *NatCAB 3*, *TwCBDA*, *WhAm H*
Eliot, Samuel Atkins 1798-1862 *ApCAB*, *BiAUS*, *BiDrAC*, *DcAmB*, *Drake*, *NatCAB 11*, *TwCBDA*, *WhAm H*
Eliot, Samuel Atkins 1862- *NatCAB 12*
Eliot, Thomas Dawes 1808-1870 *ApCAB*, *BiAUS*, *BiDrAC*, *Drake*, *NatCAB 12*, *TwCBDA*, *WhAm H*, *WhAmP*
Eliot, Thomas Hopkinson 1907- *BiDrAC*
Eliot, Thomas Lamb 1841- *WhAm 1*
Eliot, Thomas Stearns 1888-1965 *McGEWB*, *WebAB*, *WhAm 4*
Eliot, Walter Graeme 1857-1931 *TwCBDA*, *WhAm 1*, *WhAm 1C*
Eliot, William Greenleaf 1811-1887 *ApCAB*, *DcAmB*, *NatCAB 11*, *TwCBDA*, *WhAm H*
Eliot, William Greenleaf, Jr. 1866-1956 *WhAm 3*
Eliott, VanCourtlandt 1904-1970 *WhAm 5*
Elisofon, Eliot 1911-1973 *WhAm 5*
Elizabeth I 1533-1603 *McGEWB*
Elizabeth II 1926- *McGEWB*
Elizabeth Petrovna 1709-1761 *McGEWB*
Elizaga, Mariano 1781-1842 *ApCAB*
Elizalde, Joaquin Miguel 1896-1965 *BiDrAC*
Elizalde, Rafael Hector 1873- *WhAm 5*
Elkin, Daniel Collier 1893-1958 *WhAm 3*
Elkin, John Pratt 1860-1915 *WhAm 1*
Elkin, William Lewis 1855-1933 *ApCAB Sup*, *DcAmB S1*, *DcScB*, *NatCAB 12*, *NatCAB 24*, *TwCBDA*, *WhAm 1*
Elkin, William Simpson 1858- *WhAm 4*
Elkins, Davis 1876-1959 *ApCAB X*, *BiDrAC*, *NatCAB 46*, *WhAm 3*, *WhAmP*
Elkins, George W 1858-1919 *WhAm 1*
Elkins, Henry Arthur 1847-1884 *ApCAB*, *IIBEAAW*
Elkins, James Anderson 1879-1973 *WhAm 5*
Elkins, Stanley Maurice 1925- *EncAAH*
Elkins, Stephen Benton 1841-1911 *AmBi*, *ApCAB*, *BiAUS*, *BiDrAC*, *BiDrUSE*, *DcAmB*, *EncAAH*, *NatCAB 1*, *REnAW*, *TwCBDA*, *WhAm 1*, *WhAmP*
Elkins, William Joyce 1911-1966 *NatCAB 53*
Elkins, William Lukens 1832-1903 *DcAmB*, *NatCAB 9*, *WhAm 1*
Elkins, William McIntire 1882-1947 *WhAm 2*
Elkinton, Sarah West 1854- *WomWWA 14*
Elkus, Abram Isaac 1867-1947 *NatCAB 38*,

WhAm 2
Elkus, Albert Israel 1884-1962 *NatCAB 48*
Elkus, Charles DeYoung 1881-1963 *WhAm 4*
Elkus, Savilla Alice 1874- *WomWWA 14*
Ellabarger, Daniel Rudolph 1863-1949 *WhAm 3*
Ellard, Roscoe Cuffe Brabazon 1894-1962
    NatCAB 51, WhAm 4
Ellefson, Bennett Stanley 1911-1971
    NatCAB 55
Ellefson, Bennett Stanley 1911-1973 *WhAm 5*
Ellegood, Robert Griffith 1828- *WhAm 1*
Ellena, John Batista 1902-1971 *NatCAB 57*
Ellenberg, Samuel Lawrence 1903-1957
    NatCAB 46
Ellenbogen, Henry 1900- *BiDrAC*
Ellender, Allen Joseph 1890-1972 *BiDrAC,
    WhAm 5*
Ellender, Allen Joseph 1891-1972 *WhAmP*
Ellender, Raphael Theodore 1906-1972
    WhAm 5
Ellender, Willard Anthony 1905-1967
    NatCAB 53
Ellenstein, Meyer C 1886-1967 *WhAm 4*
Ellenwood, Charles 1825?- *NewYHSD*
Ellenwood, Frank Oakes 1878-1947 *NatCAB 36,
    WhAm 2*
Ellenwood, Fred Alden 1876-1946 *WhAm 2*
Eller, Adolphus Hill 1861-1941 *WhAm 2*
Eller VonBrockhausen, Johann Theodor
    1689-1760 *DcScB*
Ellerbe, Alma Martin 1871- *WhAm 5*
Ellerbe, James Edwin 1867-1917 *BiDrAC,
    WhAm 4*
Ellerbe, William Haselden 1862-1899
    NatCAB 12, TwCBDA, WhAm 1
Ellerhusen, Florence Cooney d1950 *WhAm 3*
Ellerhusen, Ulric Henry 1879-1957 *WhAm 3*
Ellerman, Ferdinand 1869-1940 *WhAm 1*
Ellerson, Henry Watkins 1875-1941
    NatCAB 30
Ellerton, Henry Howard 1861-1928 *NatCAB 42*
Ellery, Christopher 1768-1840 *ApCAB, BiAUS,
    BiDrAC, NatCAB 5, TwCBDA,
    WhAm H, WhAmP*
Ellery, Edward 1868- *WhAm 5*
Ellery, Eloise 1874- *WhAm 5, WomWWA 14*
Ellery, Frank 1794-1871 *ApCAB, DcAmB,
    NatCAB 5, TwCBDA, WhAm H*
Ellery, Frank 1812- *Drake*
Ellery, Nathaniel Bulkeley 1872-1956
    NatCAB 44
Ellery, William 1727-1820 *AmBi, ApCAB,
    BiAUS, BiDrAC, DcAmB, Drake,
    NatCAB 8, TwCBDA, WhAm H,
    WhAmP*
Ellery Queen *WebAB*
Ellet, Alfred W d1895 *ApCAB, NatCAB 4,
    TwCBDA*
Ellet, Charles 1810-1862 *AmBi, ApCAB,
    DcAmB, Drake, NatCAB 4, TwCBDA,
    WebAB, WebAMB, WhAm H*
Ellet, Charles R 1820-1877 *REnAW*
Ellet, Charles Rivers 1841-1863 *ApCAB, Drake*
Ellet, Charles Rivers 1843-1863 *NatCAB 4,
    TwCBDA, WebAMB*
Ellet, Elizabeth Fries Lummis 1812?-1877
    NotAW
Ellet, Elizabeth Fries Lummis 1818-1877
    *ApCAB, DcAmB, Drake, NatCAB 11,
    TwCBDA, WhAm H*
Ellet, Victor William 1880-1954 *NatCAB 42*
Ellet, William Henry 1804?-1859 *Drake*
Ellet, William Henry 1806-1859 *ApCAB,
    NatCAB 11, TwCBDA*
Ellett, Edward Coleman 1869-1947 *WhAm 2*
Ellett, Henry Thomas 1812-1887 *BiDrAC,
    WhAm H*
Ellett, Tazewell 1856-1914 *BiDrAC*
Ellett, Thomas Harlan 1880-1951 *WhAm 3*
Ellett, Walter Beal 1874-1943 *WhAm 2*
Ellick, Alfred George 1878-1942 *WhAm 2*
Ellickson, Raymond Thorwald 1910-1970
    WhAm 6
Ellicott, Andrew 1754-1820 *AmBi, ApCAB,
    BiAUS, DcAmB, Drake, NatCAB 13,
    TwCBDA, WhAm H*
Ellicott, Benjamin 1765-1827 *BiAUS, BiDrAC,
    WhAm H*

Ellicott, Edward Beach 1866-1926 *NatCAB 20*
Ellicott, Eugene 1846- *WhAm 4*
Ellicott, Henry Jackson 1847-1901 *NatCAB 12,
    TwCBDA*
Ellicott, John Morris 1859-1955 *WhAm 3*
Ellicott, Joseph 1760-1826 *AmBi, ApCAB,
    DcAmB, NatCAB 13, TwCBDA,
    WhAm H*
Ellicott, Joseph Remington 1858-1931
    NatCAB 23
Ellicott, Nancy Poultney 1872- *WomWWA 14*
Ellicott, William Miller 1863-1944 *NatCAB 33*
Elliff, Edgar Alonzo 1893-1966 *WhAm 5*
Elliff, Joseph Doliver 1863- *WhAm 5*
Elliman, Douglas Ludlow 1882-1972 *WhAm 5*
Elliman, Lawrence Bogert 1876-1954 *WhAm 3*
Elliman, Roland Franklin 1888-1966
    NatCAB 53
Elling, Christian 1901-1974 *WhAm 6*
Elling, Henry 1842-1900 *WhAm 1*
Ellinger, Moritz 1830- *WhAm 4*
Ellingham, Lewis Glendale 1868-1939 *WhAm 1*
Ellingham, William 1837-1922 *NatCAB 19*
Ellingson, Carl Herman 1883-1956 *WhAm 3*
Ellingson, Herman Edwin 1903-1970
    NatCAB 56
Ellingsworth, Carl W 1886-1948 *NatCAB 37*
Ellington, Buford 1907-1972 *WhAm 5*
Ellington, Duke 1899-1974 *WebAB*
Ellington, Edward Kennedy 1899-1974 *EncAB,
    McGEWB, WhAm 6*
Ellington, Jesse Thompson 1899-1968 *WhAm 5*
Ellingwood, Albert Russell 1887-1934 *WhAm 1*
Ellingwood, Finley 1852-1920 *WhAm 1*
Ellingwood, William Arthur 1883-1941
    NatCAB 32
Ellinson, Charles Norman 1836- *NatCAB 14*
Ellinwood, Eliza M *WomWWA 14*
Ellinwood, Everett E 1862-1943 *NatCAB 34,
    WhAm 2*
Ellinwood, Frank Field 1826-1908 *WhAm 1*
Ellinwood, Frank Fields 1826-1908 *TwCBDA*
Ellinwood, Henrietta Elizabeth 1876-
    NatCAB 16
Ellinwood, Lyman Watson 1874- *NatCAB 16*
Ellinwood, Ralph Everett 1893-1930 *WhAm 1*
Ellinwood, Truman Jeremiah 1830-1921
    WhAm 1
Elliot, Arthur Henry 1893-1962 *NatCAB 48*
Elliot, Benjamin 1786-1836 *ApCAB*
Elliot, Charles 1792-1869 *WhAm H*
Elliot, Charles 1801-1875 *ApCAB*
Elliot, Daniel Giraud 1835-1915 *AmBi,
    DcAmB, NatCAB 5, NatCAB 16,
    TwCBDA, WhAm 1*
Elliot, George 1776-1852 *NewYHSD*
Elliot, George Henry 1831-1900 *ApCAB,
    TwCBDA*
Elliot, George Thomson 1827-1871 *ApCAB*
Elliot, George Thomson 1855-1931 *WhAm 1*
Elliot, Henry Rutherford 1849-1906 *NatCAB 9,
    WhAm 1*
Elliot, James 1775-1839 *DcAmB, WhAm H*
Elliot, James *see also* Elliott, James
Elliot, John 1773?-1827 *ApCAB Sup, BiAUS*
Elliot, John *see also* Elliott, John
Elliot, John Wheelock 1852-1925 *ApCAB X,
    NatCAB 18, NatCAB 22, WhAm 1*
Elliot, Jonathan 1784-1846 *DcAmB, WhAm H*
Elliot, W P *NewYHSD*
Elliot, Washington L *Drake*
Elliot, William 1803- *Drake*
Elliot, William Henry 1850-1918 *ApCAB X,
    NatCAB 31*
Elliot, William Henry 1864-1926 *NatCAB 26*
Elliot, William Horace 1824-1852 *ApCAB*
Elliot Smith, Grafton 1871-1937 *DcScB*
Elliott, Aaron Marshall 1844-1910 *DcAmB,
    WhAm 1*
Elliott, Aaron Marshall 1846-1910 *BiDAmEd,
    NatCAB 14, TwCBDA*
Elliott, Ada Josephine 1852- *WomWWA 14*
Elliott, Alfred James 1895-1973 *BiDrAC,
    WhAm 5*
Elliott, Andrew *ApCAB*
Elliott, Anna *ApCAB*
Elliott, Arthur Richard 1869-1960 *WhAm 4*
Elliott, Bamford 1860-1944 *NatCAB 36*

Elliott, Benjamin 1787-1836 *DcAmB,
    WhAm H*
Elliott, Benjamin F 1829-1870 *NewYHSD*
Elliott, Byron Kosciusko 1835-1913 *NatCAB 22,
    WhAm 1*
Elliott, Carl Atwood 1913- *BiDrAC, WhAmP*
Elliott, Charles 1792-1869 *AmBi, ApCAB,
    DcAmB, Drake, NatCAB 11, TwCBDA*
Elliott, Charles 1815-1892 *ApCAB Sup,
    TwCBDA*
Elliott, Charles Addison 1873-1939 *WhAm 1*
Elliott, Charles Burke 1861-1935 *DcAmB S1,
    NatCAB 15, TwCBDA, WhAm 1*
Elliott, Charles Gleason 1850-1926 *NatCAB 21,
    WhAm 1*
Elliott, Charles Herbert 1878- *WhAm 6*
Elliott, Charles Loring 1812-1868 *AmBi,
    ApCAB, BnEnAmA, DcAmB, Drake,
    NatCAB 11, NewYHSD, TwCBDA,
    WhAm H*
Elliott, Charles Wyllys 1817-1883 *ApCAB,
    Drake, NatCAB 13, TwCBDA*
Elliott, Clarence Kilgore 1904-1962 *NatCAB 50*
Elliott, Claude 1896-1958 *WhAm 3*
Elliott, Clifford Withrow 1890-1948
    NatCAB 36
Elliott, Clinton Andrew 1892-1956 *NatCAB 46*
Elliott, Curtis Miller 1911-1968 *WhAm 5*
Elliott, Daniel Giraud *ApCAB X*
Elliott, Daniel Stanley 1893-1944 *WhAm 2*
Elliott, David 1787-1874 *ApCAB, TwCBDA*
Elliott, Donald Finley 1887-1947 *NatCAB 36*
Elliott, Douglas Hemphill 1921-1960 *BiDrAC*
Elliott, Edward 1874-1947 *WhAm 2*
Elliott, Edward Charles 1874-1960 *BiDAmEd,
    NatCAB 48, WhAm 4*
Elliott, Edward Loomis 1899-1959 *WhAm 3*
Elliott, Elizabeth Shippen Green
    WomWWA 14
Elliott, Ernest Eugene 1878- *ApCAB X,
    WhAm 1*
Elliott, Ernest Lamott 1869-1948 *NatCAB 36*
Elliott, Eugene Stanhope 1842-1902 *NatCAB 2*
Elliott, Ezekiel Brown 1823-1888 *ApCAB,
    NatCAB 2, TwCBDA*
Elliott, Ezra Taylor 1845-1923 *NatCAB 19*
Elliott, Francis Perry 1861-1924 *WhAm 1*
Elliott, Frank Rumsey 1878-1961 *WhAm 4*
Elliott, Franklin Reuben 1817-1878 *ApCAB*
Elliott, George 1851-1930 *WhAm 1*
Elliott, George Armstrong 1854-1943
    NatCAB 33
Elliott, George Blow 1873-1948 *NatCAB 38,
    WhAm 2*
Elliott, George Frank 1846-1931 *WebAMB,
    WhAm 1*
Elliott, George Frederick 1850- *NatCAB 10,
    WhAm 4*
Elliott, George Frederick 1892-1940
    NatCAB 37
Elliott, George Hood 1896-1960 *NatCAB 49*
Elliott, George Koch 1880-1926 *NatCAB 25*
Elliott, George Robert 1855-1935 *NatCAB 26*
Elliott, George Thomson 1855- *ApCAB X*
Elliott, Gertrude 1874-1950 *NotAW, WhAm 3,
    WomWWA 14*
Elliott, Gilbert Molleson 1840-1863 *ApCAB*
Elliott, Harold Hirsch 1886-1973 *WhAm 6*
Elliott, Harriet Wieseman 1884-1947 *WhAm 2*
Elliott, Harriet Wiseman 1884-1947 *NotAW*
Elliott, Harrison Sacket 1882-1951 *WhAm 3*
Elliott, Harry 1889-1948 *NatCAB 37*
Elliott, Hattie Hill 1862- *WomWWA 14*
Elliott, Henry 1884-1968 *NatCAB 54*
Elliott, Henry Wood 1841- *ApCAB, TwCBDA*
Elliott, Henry Wood 1846- *IlBEAAW,
    WhAm 4*
Elliott, Hiram 1857-1946 *NatCAB 36*
Elliott, Homer 1878-1952 *WhAm 3*
Elliott, Howard 1860-1928 *AmBi, NatCAB 12,
    NatCAB 20, WhAm 1*
Elliott, Huger 1877-1948 *NatCAB 37,
    WhAm 2*
Elliott, J M d1948 *WhAm 2*
Elliott, Jackson S 1876-1942 *WhAm 2*
Elliott, James *NewYHSD*
Elliott, James d1839 *BiAUS*
Elliott, James 1770-1839 *ApCAB*

Elliott, James 1775-1839 *BiDrAC, Drake, NatCAB 9, TwCBDA, WhAm H, WhAmP*
Elliott, James 1879-1929 *NatCAB 36*
Elliott, James *see also* Elliot, James
Elliott, James Douglas 1859-1933 *WhAm 1*
Elliott, James Habersham 1819-1876 *ApCAB*
Elliott, James Habersham 1819-1877 *TwCBDA*
Elliott, James Lewis 1863- *WhAm 5*
Elliott, James Robert 1924-1965 *WhAm 4*
Elliott, James Thomas 1823-1875 *BiAUS, BiDrAC, WhAm H*
Elliott, Jared Leigh 1807-1881 *TwCBDA*
Elliott, Jennie MacCracken 1866- *WomWWA 14*
Elliott, Jesse Duncan 1782-1845 *AmBi, ApCAB, DcAmB, Drake, NatCAB 7, WebAMB, WhAm H*
Elliott, Jesse Duncan 1785-1846 *TwCBDA*
Elliott, Jessie Gertrude *WomWWA 14*
Elliott, John 1768-1824 *ApCAB*
Elliott, John 1773-1827 *BiDrAC, NatCAB 4, WhAm H*
Elliott, John 1774?-1827 *TwCBDA*
Elliott, John 1858-1925 *AmBi, DcAmB, WhAm 1*
Elliott, John 1859-1925 *NatCAB 21*
Elliott, John *see also* Elliot, John
Elliott, John Arthur 1886-1956 *NatCAB 44*
Elliott, John Asbury 1887-1923 *WhAm 1*
Elliott, John B 1878-1967 *WhAm 4*
Elliott, John Barnwell 1870- *WhAm 5*
Elliott, John Brua 1884-1948 *NatCAB 39*
Elliott, John Henry 1853- *WhAm 4*
Elliott, John Henry 1866- *WhAm 4*
Elliott, John Lovejoy 1868-1942 *DcAmB S3, WhAm 2*
Elliott, John M 1877-1965 *WhAm 4*
Elliott, John Mackay 1844-1929 *WhAm 1*
Elliott, John Milton 1820-1879 *ApCAB Sup, BiAUS, BiDConf, BiDrAC, WhAm H, WhAmP*
Elliott, John Speed 1889-1951 *NatCAB 40*
Elliott, John Stuart 1859- *WhAm 4*
Elliott, John Wesley 1891-1967 *WhAm 4A, WhAm 5*
Elliott, Jonathan 1784-1846 *ApCAB, Drake, NatCAB 11*
Elliott, Joseph Alexander 1888-1961 *WhAm 4*
Elliott, Katharine Reed 1870- *WomWWA 14*
Elliott, Leo 1814?- *NewYHSD*
Elliott, Lewis Grimes 1872-1946 *WhAm 2*
Elliott, Martin Kelso 1908-1962 *WhAm 4*
Elliott, Maud Howe 1854-1948 *NatCAB 36, NotAW, WhAm 2, WomWWA 14*
Elliott, Maud Howe 1855-1948 *AmWom, TwCBDA*
Elliott, Maxine 1868-1940 *NotAW*
Elliott, Maxine 1871-1940 *AmBi, DcAmB S2*
Elliott, Maxine 1873-1940 *ApCAB X, NatCAB 14, WhAm 1, WomWWA 14*
Elliott, Middleton Stuart 1872-1952 *WhAm 3*
Elliott, Milton Courtright 1879-1928 *WhAm 1*
Elliott, Mortimer F 1841- *TwCBDA*
Elliott, Mortimer Fitzland 1839-1920 *BiDrAC*
Elliott, Oliver Morton 1867-1925 *WhAm 1*
Elliott, Orrin Leslie 1860-1940 *WhAm 1*
Elliott, Philip Lovin 1891-1961 *WhAm 4*
Elliott, Phillips Packer 1901-1961 *WhAm 4*
Elliott, Reuben James 1892-1965 *NatCAB 50*
Elliott, Richard Hammond 1893-1971 *WhAm 5*
Elliott, Richard Nash 1873-1948 *BiDrAC, WhAm 2, WhAmP*
Elliott, Robert Brown 1842-1884 *ApCAB, BiAUS, BiDrAC, NatCAB 10, TwCBDA, WhAm H, WhAmP*
Elliott, Robert Irving 1883-1944 *WhAm 2*
Elliott, Robert Michael 1863- *WhAm 4*
Elliott, Robert Woodward Barnwell 1840-1887 *ApCAB, NatCAB 13, TwCBDA*
Elliott, Roy Gordon 1899- *WhAm 3*
Elliott, Samuel Mackenzie 1811-1875 *ApCAB*
Elliott, Sarah Barnwell 1848-1928 *DcAmB, NatCAB 21, NotAW, WhAm 1, WhAmP, WomWWA 14*
Elliott, Shelden Douglass 1906-1972 *WhAm 5*
Elliott, Simon Bolivar 1830- *WhAm 4*
Elliott, Stephen 1771-1830 *ApCAB, DcAmB,*

Drake, *NatCAB 4, TwCBDA, WhAm H*
Elliott, Stephen 1804-1866 *TwCBDA*
Elliott, Stephen 1805-1866 *Drake*
Elliott, Stephen 1806-1866 *ApCAB, BiDConf, NatCAB 5, TwCBDA*
Elliott, Stephen 1830-1866 *TwCBDA*
Elliott, Stephen 1832-1866 *ApCAB, Drake*
Elliott, Stuart Rhett 1874- *WhAm 5*
Elliott, Susannah 1750?- *ApCAB*
Elliott, Theodore Bates 1836-1883 *NatCAB 2*
Elliott, Thomas 1851-1915 *NatCAB 16*
Elliott, Thompson Coit 1862-1943 *WhAm 2*
Elliott, Victor Alanson 1839- *NatCAB 12*
Elliott, W *NewYHSD*
Elliott, Walter Hackett Robert 1842-1928 *DcAmB, WhAm 1*
Elliott, Washington Lafayette 1821-1888 *ApCAB, NatCAB 13, TwCBDA*
Elliott, Washington Lafayette 1825-1888 *DcAmB, WhAm H*
Elliott, Wesley McKee 1888-1956 *NatCAB 46*
Elliott, William 1761-1808 *ApCAB, TwCBDA*
Elliott, William 1788-1863 *ApCAB, DcAmB, Drake, NatCAB 13, TwCBDA, WhAm H*
Elliott, William 1821-1890 *TwCBDA*
Elliott, William 1838-1907 *BiDrAC, TwCBDA, WhAm 1*
Elliott, William 1872-1943 *NatCAB 32, WhAm 2*
Elliott, William Arthur 1866-1935 *WhAm 1*
Elliott, William Frederick 1859-1927 *NatCAB 20*
Elliott, William Henry 1844-1914 *WhAm 1*
Elliott, William Herbert 1844-1901 *NatCAB 17*
Elliott, William Jennings 1901-1961 *NatCAB 51*
Elliott, William John 1856-1930 *NatCAB 25*
Elliott, William John 1878- *WhAm 6*
Elliott, William Sanders 1880-1957 *WhAm 3*
Elliott, William Swan 1863-1934 *WhAm 1*
Ellis, A Caswell 1871-1948 *WhAm 2*
Ellis, A Lee 1869-1947 *NatCAB 38*
Ellis, Abner *ApCAB*
Ellis, Abraham M 1880-1961 *NatCAB 49*
Ellis, Adrian Collier 1866-1941 *NatCAB 31*
Ellis, Albert Clarence 1881-1945 *NatCAB 35*
Ellis, Albert Joseph 1913-1969 *NatCAB 55*
Ellis, Alice Meribah James 1879- *WomWWA 14*
Ellis, Alston 1847-1920 *ApCAB X, BiDAmEd, NatCAB 13, NatCAB 26, WhAm 1*
Ellis, Anderson Nelson 1840-1927 *WhAm 2*
Ellis, Anna M B d1911 *WhAm 1*
Ellis, Arthur McDonald 1875-1932 *NatCAB 32, WhAm 1*
Ellis, Arthur Wakefield 1890-1955 *NatCAB 41*
Ellis, Bertram 1860-1920 *NatCAB 18*
Ellis, Caleb 1767-1816 *BiAUS, BiDrAC, WhAm H*
Ellis, Calvin 1826-1883 *ApCAB, DcAmB, NatCAB 17, WhAm H*
Ellis, Carleton 1876-1941 *DcAmB S3, NatCAB 32, WhAm 1*
Ellis, Carlos Bent 1900-1963 *NatCAB 50*
Ellis, Carlyle 1878- *WhAm 6*
Ellis, Challen Blackburn 1876-1948 *NatCAB 36, WhAm 2*
Ellis, Charles 1800-1874 *NatCAB 5*
Ellis, Charles Alton 1876-1949 *WhAm 2*
Ellis, Charles Calvert 1874-1950 *WhAm 3*
Ellis, Charles Mayo 1818-1878 *ApCAB*
Ellis, Charles S 1884-1962 *WhAm 4*
Ellis, Cheselden 1808-1854 *BiAUS*
Ellis, Chesselden 1808-1854 *BiDrAC, WhAm H*
Ellis, Cloyde Bryan 1896-1958 *NatCAB 45*
Ellis, Clyde Taylor 1908- *BiDrAC*
Ellis, Crawford Hatcher 1875-1966 *WhAm 4*
Ellis, David Abram 1873-1929 *WhAm 1*
Ellis, David Maldwyn 1914- *EncAAH*
Ellis, DeGoy Bowman 1876-1949 *NatCAB 38*
Ellis, Don Carlos 1883-1953 *WhAm 3*
Ellis, E John d1889 *BiAUS*
Ellis, E John 1841-1889 *ApCAB*
Ellis, E John *see also* Ellis, Ezekiel John
Ellis, Edgar Clarence 1854-1947 *BiDrAC, NatCAB 36, WhAm 2, WhAmP*
Ellis, Edith Anna Ellis *WomWWA 14*

Ellis, Edward Dimick 1801-1848 *ApCAB*
Ellis, Edward Sylvester 1840-1916 *DcAmB, NatCAB 19, TwCBDA, WhAm 1*
Ellis, Edwin Erastus 1883-1936 *WhAm 1*
Ellis, Edwin M *NewYHSD*
Ellis, Ellen Deborah 1878- *WomWWA 14*
Ellis, Ezekiel John 1840-1889 *BiDrAC, NatCAB 11, TwCBDA, WhAm H, WhAmP*
Ellis, Ezekiel John *see also* Ellis, E John
Ellis, Fay Ollie 1899-1969 *NatCAB 55*
Ellis, Francis Cutler 1890-1957 *NatCAB 48*
Ellis, Frank 1842-1919 *NatCAB 36*
Ellis, Frank Burton 1907-1969 *WhAm 5*
Ellis, Frank Wolcott 1865-1949 *NatCAB 41*
Ellis, Fremont F 1897- *IIBEAAW*
Ellis, G Corson 1899-1962 *WhAm 4*
Ellis, George Adams 1881-1955 *WhAm 3*
Ellis, George B *NewYHSD*
Ellis, George David 1897-1966 *WhAm 4*
Ellis, George Edward 1814-1894 *AmBi, ApCAB, DcAmB, Drake, NatCAB 8, TwCBDA, WhAm H*
Ellis, George Edwin 1864-1921 *NatCAB 19, WhAm 4*
Ellis, George Price, Sr. 1888-1959 *WhAm 3*
Ellis, George Washington 1875-1919 *AmBi, DcAmB, NatCAB 17, WhAm 1, WhoColR*
Ellis, George William 1870- *WhAm 5*
Ellis, Gordon 1915-1973 *WhAm 6*
Ellis, Grace Vinton 1867- *WomWWA 14*
Ellis, Griffith Ogden 1869-1948 *NatCAB 36, WhAm 2*
Ellis, H Bert 1863-1922 *WhAm 1*
Ellis, Harry Whittredge 1866-1949 *NatCAB 39*
Ellis, Harvey 1852-1904 *WhAm 1*
Ellis, Hayne 1877- *WhAm 5*
Ellis, Henry 1721-1806 *ApCAB, DcAmB, Drake, NatCAB 1, WhAm H*
Ellis, Henry Bertrand 1863-1922 *NatCAB 14*
Ellis, Horace 1861-1932 *WhAm 1*
Ellis, Howard 1892-1968 *NatCAB 56, WhAm 4A, WhAm 5*
Ellis, Hubert Summers 1887-1959 *BiDrAC, WhAmP*
Ellis, Ira Howell 1893-1966 *WhAm 4*
Ellis, Ivan George 1899-1950 *NatCAB 43*
Ellis, James 1898-1972 *WhAm 6*
Ellis, James Tandy 1868- *WhAm 4*
Ellis, James Willard 1869-1953 *NatCAB 49*
Ellis, Jennie Agnes Wilhite 1867- *WomWWA 14*
Ellis, Job Bicknell 1829-1905 *AmBi, DcAmB, TwCBDA, WhAm 1*
Ellis, John 1815- *NatCAB 3*
Ellis, John Breckenridge 1870-1956 *ApCAB X, WhAm 3*
Ellis, John D *NewYHSD*
Ellis, John Dayhuff 1886-1956 *WhAm 3*
Ellis, John Henry 1894-1975 *WhAm 6*
Ellis, John Millot 1793-1855 *ApCAB, TwCBDA*
Ellis, John Millott 1831-1894 *TwCBDA*
Ellis, John Tyler 1890-1958 *NatCAB 47*
Ellis, John Valentine 1835- *ApCAB Sup*
Ellis, John Washington 1817-1910 *DcAmB, WhAm HA, WhAm 4*
Ellis, John William 1839-1910 *TwCBDA, WhAm 1*
Ellis, John Willis 1820-1861 *ApCAB, BiAUS, BiDConf, DcAmB, Drake, NatCAB 4, TwCBDA, WhAm H, WhAmP*
Ellis, Julia Ada 1863- *WomWWA 14*
Ellis, Katharine Ruth 1879- *WhAm 6, WomWWA 14*
Ellis, Leighton Arthur 1862- *WhAm 4*
Ellis, Leland Wadsworth 1896-1958 *NatCAB 47*
Ellis, Leonard Augustine 1874-1943 *NatCAB 32*
Ellis, Leonora Beck 1872- *WomWWA 14*
Ellis, Louise Alverda Spencer 1860- *WomWWA 14*
Ellis, Lucy Morris 1878- *WomWWA 14*
Ellis, Lucy Terrill *WomWWA 14*
Ellis, Margaret Dye *WomWWA 14*
Ellis, Marion Durbin 1887- *WomWWA 14*

Ellis, Mary 1834-1917 *WhAm 1*
Ellis, Max Mapes 1887-1953 *NatCAB 42,*
WhAm 3
Ellis, Milton 1885-1947 *NatCAB 34,*
WhAm 2
Ellis, Milton Andrew 1910-1966 *WhAm 4*
Ellis, Olyette 1844- *WomWWA 14*
Ellis, Overton Gentry 1860-1940 *NatCAB 30,*
WhAm 1
Ellis, Perry Canby 1867- *WhAm 1*
Ellis, Powhatan *BiAUS, Drake*
Ellis, Powhatan 1790-1863 *BiDrAC, DcAmB,*
WhAm H
Ellis, Powhatan 1794?-1844? *ApCAB,*
NatCAB 11, TwCBDA
Ellis, Ralph 1879- *WhAm 3*
Ellis, Ralph Nicholson 1858-1930 *NatCAB 32*
Ellis, Reuben d1796 *ApCAB*
Ellis, Robert Fulton 1809-1854 *ApCAB*
Ellis, Robert Stephen 1899-1966 *NatCAB 57*
Ellis, Robert Walpole 1868-1937 *WhAm 1*
Ellis, Rudolph 1837-1915 *WhAm 1*
Ellis, Rufus 1819-1885 *ApCAB*
Ellis, Salathiel 1860- *NewYHSD*
Ellis, Samuel James 1870-1942 *NatCAB 32*
Ellis, Samuel Mervyl 1889-1944 *WhAm 2*
Ellis, Seth Hockett 1830-1904 *AmBi, DcAmB,*
WhAm 1, WhAmP
Ellis, Sherman Kingsbury 1892-1964
NatCAB 50
Ellis, Sumner 1828-1886 *ApCAB*
Ellis, Tharon J 1902-1965 *WhAm 4*
Ellis, Theodore Grenville 1829-1883 *TwCBDA*
Ellis, Theodore Gunville 1829-1883 *ApCAB*
Ellis, Theodore Thaddeus 1867-1934 *WhAm 1*
Ellis, Theodore Waterbury 1887-1965
NatCAB 51
Ellis, Thomas Cargill Warner 1836-
NatCAB 11, WhAm 4
Ellis, Thomas David 1868-1952 *WhAm 3*
Ellis, Vespasian *BiAUS*
Ellis, W R 1886-1955 *WhAm 3*
Ellis, Wade Hampton 1866-1948 *NatCAB 37,*
WhAm 2
Ellis, Warren Eugene 1866-1940 *NatCAB 29*
Ellis, Welbore d1802 *ApCAB*
Ellis, Willard Drake 1887-1947 *WhAm 2*
Ellis, William 1828-1916 *DcScB*
Ellis, William Cox 1787-1871 *BiAUS, BiDrAC,*
NewYHSD, WhAm H
Ellis, William D 1844- *WhAm 4*
Ellis, William H *NewYHSD*
Ellis, William Hull 1867-1948 *WhAm 2*
Ellis, William John 1892-1945 *NatCAB 34,*
WhAm 2
Ellis, William Russell 1850-1915 *BiDrAC,*
TwCBDA, WhAm 1
Ellis, William Thomas 1845-1925 *BiDrAC,*
TwCBDA
Ellis, William Thomas 1873-1950 *WhAm 3*
Ellis, Willis Stephens 1861-1944 *NatCAB 33*
Ellison, Andrew 1812-1860? *BiAUS, BiDrAC,*
WhAm H
Ellison, Daniel 1886-1960 *BiDrAC*
Ellison, Edward David 1869-1957 *NatCAB 47*
Ellison, Everett Monroe 1879-1939 *NatCAB 29,*
WhAm 1
Ellison, George Robb 1881-1957 *WhAm 3*
Ellison, Henry Clay 1842-1921 *NatCAB 28*
Ellison, Joseph Roy 1875- *WhAm 5*
Ellison, Laurence Ephraim 1879-1964
NatCAB 51
Ellison, Matthew 1804- *ApCAB*
Ellison, Ralph Waldo 1914- *EncAB, McGEWB,*
WebAB
Ellison, Robert Lewis 1831-1915 *NatCAB 17*
Ellison, Robert S 1875- *WhAm 5*
Ellison, Thomas Emmet 1852-1925 *WhAm 1*
Ellison, William Bruce 1857-1924 *WhAm 1*
Ellison, William H 1805-1884 *NatCAB 5,*
TwCBDA
Elliston, George *WhAm 2*
Elliston, Grace 1878-1950 *WhAm 3*
Elliston, Herbert Berridge 1895-1957
NatCAB 45, WhAm 3
Ellithorp, John Stafford, Jr. 1895-1962 *WhAm 4*
Ellithorp, Robert Lincoln 1871-1950
NatCAB 39

Ellmaker, Amos 1787-1851 *ApCAB, BiDrAC,*
NatCAB 7, TwCBDA, WhAm H
Ellmaker, Lee 1896-1951 *DcAmB S5,*
WhAm 3
Ellmore, Richard H *NewYHSD*
Ellms, Charles *NewYHSD*
Ellms, Joseph Wilton 1867-1950 *NatCAB 39*
Ells, Arthur Fairbanks 1879-1963 *WhAm 4*
Ellsasser, William John 1898-1970 *NatCAB 56*
Ellsberg, Edward 1891- *WebAMB*
Ellsberry, William Wallace 1833-1894 *BiDrAC,*
WhAm H
Ellskwatawa 1775- *ApCAB*
Ellsler, Effie *AmWom*
Ellsler, Effie 1854?-1942 *NotAW*
Ellsler, Effie 1858-1918 *WhAm 1*
Ellsler, Effie 1858-1942 *WhAm 2*
Ellsler, Fanny 1810-1884 *ApCAB*
Ellsworth, Albert LeRoy 1876- *WhAm 3*
Ellsworth, Charles Clinton 1824-1899 *BiDrAC,*
TwCBDA
Ellsworth, Clarence Arthur 1885-1961
IIBEAAW
Ellsworth, Clarence Eugene 1882-1960
NatCAB 48
Ellsworth, Elmer Ephraim 1837-1861 *AmBi,*
DcAmB, NatCAB 4, WebAMB,
WhAm H
Ellsworth, Ephraim Elmer 1837-1861 *ApCAB,*
Drake, TwCBDA
Ellsworth, Erastus Wolcott 1822- *ApCAB*
Ellsworth, Franklin Fowler 1879-1942 *BiDrAC,*
WhAm 3, WhAmP
Ellsworth, Fred Winthrop 1872- *WhAm 3*
Ellsworth, George Canning *NewYHSD*
Ellsworth, Henry Leavitt 1791-1858 *AmBi,*
ApCAB, BiAUS, DcAmB, Drake,
EncAAH, NatCAB 7, TwCBDA, WebAB,
WhAm H
Ellsworth, Henry William 1814-1864 *ApCAB,*
BiAUS, DcAmB, Drake
Ellsworth, Henry William 1837-1924
NatCAB 19
Ellsworth, James Drummond 1863-1940
WhAm 1
Ellsworth, James Sanford 1802-1874 *BnEnAmA,*
NewYHSD
Ellsworth, James William 1849-1925
NatCAB 26, WhAm 1
Ellsworth, John Jay 1894- *WhAm 5*
Ellsworth, John Lewis 1848-1921 *ApCAB X*
Ellsworth, John Orval 1891-1974 *WhAm 6*
Ellsworth, Lincoln 1880-1951 *DcAmB S5,*
McGEWB, NatCAB 39, WebAB,
WhAm 3
Ellsworth, Mary Wolcott 1830-1870 *ApCAB,*
Drake, NatCAB 11
Ellsworth, Mathew Harris 1899- *BiDrAC*
Ellsworth, Oliver 1745-1807 *AmBi, ApCAB,*
BiAUS, BiDrAC, DcAmB, Drake,
EncAB, NatCAB 1, TwCBDA, WebAB,
WhAm H, WhAmP
Ellsworth, Oliver B 1897-1969 *WhAm 5*
Ellsworth, Robert Fred 1926- *BiDrAC*
Ellsworth, Samuel Stewart 1790-1863 *BiAUS,*
BiDrAC, WhAm H
Ellsworth, Sidney Ernest 1862- *WhAm 4*
Ellsworth, William Webster 1855-1936
NatCAB 27, WhAm 1
Ellsworth, William Wolcott 1791-1868 *ApCAB,*
BiAUS, BiDrAC, DcAmB, Drake,
NatCAB 10, TwCBDA, WhAm H,
WhAmP
Ellwanger, George Herman 1848-1906
NatCAB 13, WhAm 1
Ellwanger, William DeLancey 1855-1913
NatCAB 13, WhAm 1
Ellwood, Charles Abram 1873-1946 *NatCAB 35,*
WhAm 2
Ellwood, Isaac Leonard 1833-1910 *WhAm 1*
Ellwood, John Kelley 1858- *WhAm 4*
Ellwood, Reuben 1821-1885 *BiDrAC,*
WhAm H
Ellwood, Walter Breckenridge 1902-1965
NatCAB 52
Ellwood, William Liddle 1851-1924 *NatCAB 19*
Ellyson, Charles Wright 1877-1959 *NatCAB 52*
Ellyson, Gideon Daniel 1861-1922 *NatCAB 19*

Ellyson, Henry Keeling 1823- *ApCAB*
Ellyson, James Taylor 1847-1918 *NatCAB 18*
Ellyson, James Taylor 1847-1919 *WhAm 1*
Ellyson, Lora Hotchkiss *WomWWA 14*
Ellyson, Selma Daum 1876- *WomWWA 14*
Ellzey, Lawrence Russell 1891- *BiDrAC*
Elman, Mischa 1891- *ApCAB X, WhAm 4*
Elman, Robert 1897-1956 *NatCAB 42,*
WhAm 3
Elmen, Gustaf Waldemar 1876-1957
NatCAB 43, WhAm 3
Elmendorf, A A *NewYHSD*
Elmendorf, Dwight Lathrop 1859-1929
WhAm 1
Elmendorf, Francis Littleton 1902-1972
WhAm 5
Elmendorf, Henry Livingston 1852-1906
NatCAB 21, WhAm 1
Elmendorf, Joachim 1827-1908 *ApCAB,*
TwCBDA, WhAm 1
Elmendorf, John E, Jr. 1893-1960 *WhAm 4*
Elmendorf, John James 1827-1896 *ApCAB*
Elmendorf, John Jay 1827-1896 *TwCBDA*
Elmendorf, Lucas Conrad 1758-1843 *BiAUS,*
BiDrAC, TwCBDA, WhAm H
Elmendorf, Theresa Hubbell West 1855-1932
DcAmLiB, NatCAB 23, WhAm 1,
WomWWA 14
Elmer, Ebenezer 1752-1843 *ApCAB, BiAUS,*
BiDrAC, DcAmB, Drake, NatCAB 5,
TwCBDA, WhAm H, WhAmP
Elmer, Edwin Romanzo 1850-1923 *BnEnAmA*
Elmer, Henry Whiteley 1847-1907 *WhAm 1*
Elmer, Herbert Charles 1860- *WhAm 4*
Elmer, Horace 1846-1898 *TwCBDA*
Elmer, Jonathan 1745-1807 *ApCAB, TwCBDA*
Elmer, Jonathan 1745-1817 *BiAUS, BiDrAC,*
DcAmB, Drake, NatCAB 11, WhAm H,
WhAmP
Elmer, Lucius Quintius Cincinnatus 1793-1883
ApCAB, BiAUS, BiDrAC, DcAmB, Drake,
NatCAB 5, TwCBDA, WhAm H,
WhAmP
Elmer, Rachel Robinson 1878- *WomWWA 14a*
Elmer, S Lewis 1877-1967 *WhAm 4, WhAm 5*
Elmer, Walter Gray 1872-1960 *NatCAB 48*
Elmer, William 1840-1908 *WhAm 1*
Elmer, William 1870-1947 *WhAm 3*
Elmer, William Price 1871-1956 *BiDrAC,*
WhAm 3, WhAmP
Elmes, Elias Morton 1857-1917 *ApCAB X*
Elmhirst, Leonard Knight 1893-1974 *WhAm 6*
Elmore, Cornelia Sylvester 1868- *WhoColR*
Elmore, Eltinge 1851-1937 *NatCAB 28*
Elmore, Franklin Harper 1799-1850 *ApCAB,*
BiAUS, BiDrAC, DcAmB, Drake,
NatCAB 11, TwCBDA, WhAm H,
WhAmP
Elmore, George Orton 1881-1932 *NatCAB 23*
Elmore, George Sutherland 1915-1955
NatCAB 45, WhAm 3
Elmore, Jefferson 1862- *WhAm 1*
Elmore, Lucie Ann Morrison 1829- *AmWom*
Elmore, Rush 1810?- *ApCAB, BiAUS*
Elmore, Samuel Edward 1833-1919 *NatCAB 8,*
NatCAB 33, WhAm 1
Elmore, Virginia Anita 1888- *WhoColR*
Elmore, Wilber Theodore 1871-1935 *WhAm 1*
Elmquist, Axel Louis 1884-1949 *WhAm 2*
Elmsley, John 1762-1805 *ApCAB*
Elmsley, John 1763-1805 *Drake*
Elmsley, John 1801-1863 *ApCAB*
Elmslie, George Grant 1871-1952 *DcAmB S5,*
WhAm 3
Eloesser, Herbert 1884-1956 *NatCAB 46*
Eloesser, Leo 1881- *WhAm 6*
Elofson, Carl L 1893-1954 *WhAm 3*
Elouis, Jean Pierre Henri 1755-1840 *NewYHSD*
Elphinstone, George Keith 1746-1823 *ApCAB*
Elphinstone, George Keith, Viscount 1747-1823
Drake
Elphinstone, Lewis Monteagle 1884-1949
NatCAB 40
Elrod, Henry Exall 1878-1944 *NatCAB 38*
Elrod, Morton John 1863- *ApCAB X,*
TwCBDA, WhAm 4
Elrod, Ralph 1913- *WhAm 3*
Elrod, Samuel Harrison 1856-1935 *NatCAB 13,*

WhAm 1

Elsaesser, Armin 1875-1952 NatCAB 41
Elsaesser, Edward Julius 1904- BiDrAC
Elsasser, Walter Maurice 1904- AsBiEn,
    McGEWB
Elsberg, Charles Albert 1871-1948 DcAmB S4,
    NatCAB 37, WhAm 2
Elsberg, Louis 1836-1885 AmBi, ApCAB,
    DcAmB, WhAm H
Elsenbast, Arthur S 1890-1973 WhAm 6
Elser, Albert Christian 1871-1942 NatCAB 45
Elser, Frank B 1885-1935 WhAm 1
Elser, Maximilian, Jr. 1889-1961 WhAm 4
Elser, William James 1872- WhAm 5
Elsey, Charles 1880- WhAm 6
Elsmore, Ray Thomas 1891-1957 NatCAB 46
Elsner, Henry Leopold 1855-1916 WhAm 1
Elsom, James Claude 1866- WhAm 4
Elson, Alfred Walter 1859-1944 WhAm 2
Elson, Arthur 1873-1940 WhAm 1
Elson, Henry William 1857-1954 WhAm 3
Elson, Louis Charles 1848-1920 AmBi, ApCAB,
    BiDAmEd, DcAmB, NatCAB 8,
    TwCBDA, WhAm 1
Elson, William Harris 1854-1935 BiDAmEd,
    NatCAB 26
Elson, William Harris 1856-1935 WhAm 1
Elssfeldt, Otto Hermann W Leonhard 1887-1973
    WhAm 6
Elstad, Rudolph T 1895-1959 WhAm 3
Elster, Johann Philipp Ludwig Julius 1854-1920
    DcScB
Elston, Charles Henry 1891- BiDrAC
Elston, Dorothy Andrews 1917-1971 WhAm 5
Elston, Isaac Compton 1836-1925 WhAm 1
Elston, Isaac Compton, Jr. 1873-1964
    NatCAB 51, WhAm 4
Elston, John Arthur 1874-1921 BiDrAC,
    WhAmP
Elston, John Arthur 1875-1921 WhAm 1
Elsworth, Edward 1840-1911 WhAm 1
Elthon, Leo 1898-1967 WhAm 4
Elting, Arthur Wells 1872-1948 WhAm 2
Elting, Howard 1869-1954 NatCAB 44,
    WhAm 3
Elting, Philip LeFevre 1866- NatCAB 18
Elting, Victor 1871-1956 WhAm 3
Elting, Winston 1907-1968 WhAm 5
Eltinge, Frank R 1883-1961 NatCAB 49
Eltinge, Julian 1883-1941 WhAm 1
Eltinge, LeRoy 1872-1931 WhAm 1
Eltinge, Louise WomWWA 14
Elton, Frederic Garfield 1881- WhAm 6
Elton, J O 1879-1956 WhAm 3
Elton, James Samuel 1838-1923 WhAm 1
Elton, John Prince 1809-1864 ApCAB
Elton, John Prince 1865-1948 WhAm 2
Elton, Prothesia S Goss 1800?-1867 ApCAB
Elton, Robert H NewYHSD
Elton, Romeo 1790-1870 ApCAB, Drake,
    NatCAB 9, TwCBDA
Eltse, Ralph Roscoe 1885- BiDrAC
Eltzholtz, Carl Frederick 1840-1929 WhAm 1
Eluyar Y Suvisa, Fausto De 1757-1833 ApCAB
Elvehjem, Conrad Arnold 1901-1962 AsBiEn,
    DcScB, NatCAB 52, WhAm 4
Elverson, James 1838-1911 NatCAB 2,
    WhAm 1
Elvert, Lewis NewYHSD
Elvey, Christian Thomas 1899-1970 WhAm 5
Elvins, Politte 1878-1943 BiDrAC, WhAm 2
Elwell, Abbie Miner 1858- WomWWA 14
Elwell, Charles Clement 1855-1931 WhAm 1
Elwell, Clarence Edward 1904-1973 WhAm 6
Elwell, Edward H 1825-1890 NatCAB 9
Elwell, Francis Edwin 1858-1922 NatCAB 10,
    WhAm 1
Elwell, Frank Edwin 1858-1922 AmBi,
    ApCAB X, DcAmB, TwCBDA
Elwell, George Herbert 1850-1926 NatCAB 20
Elwell, Herbert 1898-1974 WhAm 6
Elwell, John Johnson 1820-1900 DcAmB,
    WhAm H
Elwell, Levi Henry 1854-1916 WhAm 1
Elwell, Richard E 1895-1974 WhAm 6
Elwell, Robert Farrington 1874-1962 IlBEAAW
Elwell, William S 1810-1881 NewYHSD
Elwood, Everett Sprague 1881- WhAm 6

Elwood, John Worden 1895-1960 WhAm 4
Elwood, Philip Homer, Jr. 1884-1960 WhAm 4
Elwood, Robert Arthur 1873-1949 WhAm 3
Elwyn, Alfred William Langdon 1804-1884
    ApCAB, DcAmB, NatCAB 23, TwCBDA,
    WhAm H
Ely, A NewYHSD
Ely, Albert Heman 1860- WhAm 1
Ely, Albert Heman 1894-1964 NatCAB 52
Ely, Alfred 1778-1866 ApCAB
Ely, Alfred 1815-1892 ApCAB, BiAUS,
    BiDrAC, TwCBDA, WhAm H
Ely, Alfred 1884-1959 NatCAB 50
Ely, Charles C 1847- ApCAB X
Ely, Charles Russell 1870-1939 AmBi,
    NatCAB 29, WhAm 1
Ely, Charles Wright 1839-1912 BiDAmEd,
    NatCAB 15, WhAm 1
Ely, Dinsmore 1894-1918 NatCAB 17
Ely, Elizabeth L WhAm 5
Ely, Ezra Stiles 1786-1861 ApCAB, Drake,
    TwCBDA
Ely, Fordyce 1898-1968 NatCAB 56
Ely, Francis Argyle 1876-1952 NatCAB 42
Ely, Frederick David 1838-1921 BiDrAC,
    WhAm 1
Ely, George Henry 1844-1925 NatCAB 29
Ely, Griswold Lord 1842-1919 NatCAB 2
Ely, Grosvenor 1884-1959 WhAm 4
Ely, Hanson Edward 1867-1958 WhAm 3
Ely, Heman 1820-1894 NatCAB 25
Ely, Henry Guy 1842-1919 NatCAB 37
Ely, Horace S 1832-1904 ApCAB X
Ely, James Samuel Thomas Stranahan 1898-1963
    NatCAB 50
Ely, James Winchell Coleman 1820-
    NatCAB 10
Ely, John 1737-1800 TwCBDA
Ely, John 1774-1849 BiAUS, BiDrAC,
    WhAm H
Ely, John Hugh 1846-1906 WhAm 1
Ely, John Slade 1860- WhAm 1
Ely, Joseph Buell 1881-1956 WhAm 3
Ely, Lafayette G 1834- WhAm 4
Ely, Leonard Wheeler 1868-1944 NatCAB 34,
    WhAm 4
Ely, Lydia d1914 NewYHSD
Ely, Nathan C 1806-1886 NatCAB 14
Ely, Richard R 1892-1972 WhAm 5
Ely, Richard Sheldon 1818-1894 NatCAB 16
Ely, Richard Theodore 1854-1943 ApCAB,
    BiDAmEd, DcAmB S3, EncAB,
    NatCAB 9, TwCBDA, WebAB, WhAm 2
Ely, Robert Erskine 1861-1948 WhAm 2
Ely, Roy J W 1892-1959 WhAm 4
Ely, Rudolphine Scheffer 1872- WomWWA 14
Ely, Samuel Rose 1803-1873 ApCAB
Ely, Sims 1862-1954 WhAm 3
Ely, Smith, Jr. 1825-1911 BiAUS, BiDrAC,
    NatCAB 6, TwCBDA, WhAm 1,
    WhAmP
Ely, Sterling 1899-1961 WhAm 4
Ely, Sumner Boyer 1869- WhAm 5
Ely, Theodore Newel 1846-1916 NatCAB 32,
    WhAm 1
Ely, Thomas Southgate 1914-1974 WhAm 6
Ely, Wayne 1891-1959 WhAm 3
Ely, William 1765-1817 BiAUS, BiDrAC,
    WhAm H, WhAmP
Ely, William 1858-1949 NatCAB 37
Ely, William Caryl 1856-1921 NatCAB 21
Ely, William G 1835?- ApCAB
Ely, William Mather 1818-1872 ApCAB
Ely, William Newbold 1896-1947 NatCAB 37
Ely, Wilson C d1959 WhAm 3
Elzas, Barnett Abraham 1867-1936 WhAm 1
Elzey, Arnold 1816-1871 ApCAB, BiDConf,
    DcAmB, WebAMB, WhAm H
Elzner, Alfred Oscar 1862-1933 WhAm 1
Elzy, Arnold 1816-1871 NatCAB 6, TwCBDA
Emangard, Charles 1755-1837 ApCAB
Emanuel, David 1742-1808 NatCAB 1
Emanuel, Victor 1898-1960 WhAm 4
Emanuelli, Pio 1888-1946 DcScB
Embden, Gustav 1874-1933 DcScB
Ember, Aaron 1878-1926 WhAm 1
Embery, Frank 1867-1939 NatCAB 29
Embick, Stanley Dunbar 1877-1957 NatCAB 43

Embler, A H NewYHSD
Embleton, Harry 1888-1953 WhAm 3
Emblidge, William Robert 1902-1960
    NatCAB 47
Embody, George Charles 1876-1939 AmBi,
    WhAm 1
Embree, Charles Fleming 1874-1905 WhAm 1
Embree, Edwin Rogers 1883-1950 DcAmB S4,
    NatCAB 39, WhAm 2A
Embree, Elihu 1782-1820 DcAmB, NatCAB 8,
    WhAm H
Embree, Elisha 1801-1863 BiAUS, BiDrAC,
    WhAm H
Embree, William Dean 1880-1966 NatCAB 54
Embrey, Alvin Thomas 1874-1957 NatCAB 49
Embrie, Jonas Reece 1812-1869 WhAm H
Embry, Basil 1902-1977 WhWW-II
Embry, James Crawford 1834-1897 ApCAB,
    TwCBDA
Embry, John 1869-1960 WhAm 4
Embry, Julia A 1875- WhoColR
Embry, Talton, III 1860-1916 NatCAB 17
Embury, Aymar, II 1880-1966 WhAm 4
Embury, David A 1886-1960 WhAm 4
Embury, Emma Catharine 1806-1863 Drake
Embury, Emma Catherine 1806-1863 ApCAB,
    DcAmB, NatCAB 9
Embury, Gilbert William 1903-1967
    NatCAB 53
Embury, Philip 1728-1773 DcAmB, DcAmReB,
    WhAm H
Embury, Philip 1729-1775 ApCAB, NatCAB 3,
    TwCBDA
Emch, Arnold 1871- WhAm 5
Emch, Minna Elizabeth Libman 1904-1958
    NatCAB 47
Emch, Walter 1896-1961 NatCAB 50
Emden, Robert 1862-1940 DcScB
Emens, Homer Farnham 1862-1930 NatCAB 22
Emeree, Berla Ione 1899- IlBEAAW
Emeriau, Maurice Julien 1762-1845 ApCAB
Emerich, Ira 1894-1975 WhAm 6
Emerich, Martin 1846-1922 BiDrAC
Emerich, Martin 1847- WhAm 4
Emerick, Charles Franklin 1867-1920 WhAm 1
Emerick, Edson James 1863- WhAm 3
Emerman, David 1896-1974 WhAm 6
Emerson, Adaline Elizabeth Talcott
    WomWWA 14
Emerson, Alfred 1859- TwCBDA
Emerson, Benjamin Dudley 1781-1872 ApCAB,
    TwCBDA
Emerson, Benjamin Kendall 1843-1932 ApCAB,
    DcAmB S1, DcScB, NatCAB 12,
    NatCAB 29, TwCBDA, WhAm 1
Emerson, Brown 1778-1872 ApCAB
Emerson, Charles Franklin 1843-1922 ApCAB,
    NatCAB 9, NatCAB 51, TwCBDA,
    WhAm 1
Emerson, Charles Noble 1821-1869 ApCAB
Emerson, Charles Phillips 1872-1938 WhAm 1
Emerson, Charles Wesley 1837-1908 WhAm 1
Emerson, Cherry Logan d1959 WhAm 4
Emerson, Chester Burge 1882-1973 WhAm 6
Emerson, Clara Beardsley Count 1869-
    WomWWA 14
Emerson, Edgar Clark 1850-1923 NatCAB 19
Emerson, Edward Randolph 1856-1924
    NatCAB 14, WhAm 1
Emerson, Edward Waldo 1844-1930 AmBi,
    DcAmB, NatCAB 26, TwCBDA,
    WhAm 1
Emerson, Edwin 1869-1959 WhAm 4
Emerson, Edwin, Jr. WhAm 5
Emerson, Ellen Russell 1837-1907 AmWom,
    DcAmB, NatCAB 14, TwCBDA,
    WhAm 1
Emerson, Ellen Tucker WomWWA 14
Emerson, Evalyn WhAm 5
Emerson, Frank Collins 1882-1931 NatCAB 25,
    WhAm 1
Emerson, Frank Nelson 1876- WhAm 5
Emerson, Frederick 1788-1857 ApCAB
Emerson, George Barrell 1797-1881 ApCAB,
    BiDAmEd, DcAmB, Drake, NatCAB 11,
    TwCBDA, WhAm H
Emerson, George H WhAm 5

Emerson, George Harvey 1845-1914 *NatCAB 15*

Emerson, George Waldo 1861-1947 *NatCAB 37*

Emerson, Gouverneur 1795-1874 *DcAmB, WhAm H*

Emerson, Gouverneur 1796-1874 *ApCAB*

Emerson, Guy 1886-1969 *WhAm 5*

Emerson, Harold Logan 1893-1965 *WhAm 4*

Emerson, Harrington 1853-1931 *NatCAB 15, WhAm 1*

Emerson, Haven 1874-1957 *NatCAB 43, WhAm 3*

Emerson, Henry Ivory 1871-1953 *BiDrAC, WhAmP*

Emerson, Henry Pendexter 1846- *WhAm 1*

Emerson, Henry Pendexter 1847- *TwCBDA*

Emerson, Howard Foord 1875-1947 *NatCAB 38*

Emerson, Isaac Edward 1859-1931 *NatCAB 23*

Emerson, J *NewYHSD*

Emerson, Jabez Oscar 1875-1968 *WhAm 5*

Emerson, James Ezekiel 1823-1900 *ApCAB, DcAmB, NatCAB 12, WhAm 1*

Emerson, Jay N 1879-1947 *WhAm 2*

Emerson, John 1874-1956 *WhAm 3*

Emerson, John Smith 1800-1867 *ApCAB*

Emerson, Joseph 1777-1833 *ApCAB, BiDAmEd, DcAmB, WhAm H*

Emerson, Joseph 1821-1900 *NatCAB 11*

Emerson, Justin Edwards 1841- *NatCAB 12, WhAm 4*

Emerson, Kendall 1875-1962 *NatCAB 49, WhAm 5*

Emerson, Linn 1873- *WhAm 5*

Emerson, Louis Woodard 1857-1924 *BiDrAC*

Emerson, Lousis W 1857- *WhAm 4*

Emerson, Lowe 1837-1916 *NatCAB 18*

Emerson, Luther Orlando 1820-1915 *ApCAB, NatCAB 7, TwCBDA, WhAm 1*

Emerson, Maria Furman 1869- *WomWWA 14*

Emerson, Mary Alice 1865-1922 *NatCAB 20*

Emerson, Mary Moody 1774-1863 *DcAmB, NotAW*

Emerson, Merton Leslie 1882-1945 *NatCAB 34, WhAm 2*

Emerson, Nathaniel Bright 1839-1915 *WhAm 1*

Emerson, Nathaniel Waldo 1854-1930 *WhAm 1*

Emerson, Oliver Farrar 1860-1927 *DcAmB, NatCAB 13, NatCAB 24, WhAm 1*

Emerson, Orville Reddick 1894-1945 *NatCAB 45*

Emerson, Paul 1887-1937 *WhAm 1*

Emerson, Philip 1865- *WhAm 4*

Emerson, Philip H *BiAUS*

Emerson, Ralph 1787-1863 *ApCAB, ApCAB X, Drake, NatCAB 10, WhAm H*

Emerson, Ralph 1831-1914 *DcAmB, NatCAB 22, WhAm 1*

Emerson, Ralph Waldo 1803-1882 *AmBi, ApCAB, DcAmB, DcAmReB, Drake, EncAAH, EncAB, McGEWB, NatCAB 3, TwCBDA, WebAB, WhAm H*

Emerson, Robert 1903-1959 *DcScB, WhAm 3*

Emerson, Robert Alton 1911-1966 *WhAm 4*

Emerson, Robert E 1920?- *IIBEAAW*

Emerson, Robert Stephen 1876-1937 *NatCAB 30, WhAm 1*

Emerson, Rollins Adams 1873-1947 *DcAmB S4, NatCAB 39, WhAm 2*

Emerson, Sam W 1881- *WhAm 6*

Emerson, Samuel Franklin 1850-1939 *WhAm 1*

Emerson, Sarah H 1835- *WomWWA 14*

Emerson, Summer Brooks 1895-1969 *WhAm 5*

Emerson, Susan Mabel Hood 1876-1965 *WhAm 4, WomWWA 14*

Emerson, Teckla Hilbert 1879- *WomWWA 14*

Emerson, Ursula Sophia Newell 1806- *ApCAB*

Emerson, Victor Hugo 1866- *NatCAB 15*

Emerson, Wilimena Hannah Eliot 1853- *WomWWA 14*

Emerson, Willard I 1894-1966 *WhAm 4*

Emerson, William 1769-1811 *ApCAB, DcAmB, Drake, NatCAB 13, TwCBDA, WhAm H*

Emerson, William 1873-1957 *WhAm 3*

Emerson, Willis George 1856-1918 *WhAm 1*

Emert, Paul *NewYHSD*

Emerton, Ephraim 1851-1935 *AmBi, DcAmB S1, TwCBDA, WhAm 1*

Emerton, James H 1847-1930 *WhAm 1*

Emerton, James Heney 1847-1930 *ApCAB*

Emerton, James Henry 1847-1930 *DcAmB S1, NatCAB 22*

Emery, Albert Hamilton 1834-1926 *DcAmB, NatCAB 14, NatCAB 21, WhAm 1*

Emery, Albert Hamilton 1876-1945 *NatCAB 34*

Emery, Alden H 1901-1975 *WhAm 6*

Emery, Allan Comstock 1875-1952 *NatCAB 42*

Emery, Ambrose R 1883-1945 *WhAm 2*

Emery, Charles Edward 1838-1898 *ApCAB, DcAmB, NatCAB 9, TwCBDA, WhAm H*

Emery, Charles Henry 1862-1950 *NatCAB 40*

Emery, David F 1828?- *NewYHSD*

Emery, Dean 1874-1937 *NatCAB 28*

Emery, Delevan 1867-1911 *NatCAB 40*

Emery, DeWitt McKinley 1896-1955 *NatCAB 45, WhAm 3*

Emery, Edward Kellogg 1851-1919 *WhAm 1*

Emery, Edwin Wilbur 1858-1939 *NatCAB 31*

Emery, Eliza *NewYHSD*

Emery, Fred Azro 1875-1962 *WhAm 4*

Emery, Fred Parker 1865-1927 *WhAm 1*

Emery, George W *BiAUS*

Emery, Grenville C 1843-1927 *WhAm 1*

Emery, Henry Crosby 1872-1924 *DcAmB, NatCAB 21, WhAm 1*

Emery, Ina Capitola 1868-1941 *WhAm 1*

Emery, James Albert 1872-1943 *NatCAB 36*

Emery, James Augustan 1876-1955 *WhAm 3*

Emery, James Woodward 1808-1891 *NatCAB 14*

Emery, John Garfield 1881- *WhAm 6*

Emery, John Josiah 1835-1908 *NatCAB 26*

Emery, John Runkle 1842-1916 *WhAm 1*

Emery, John Walter 1866-1933 *NatCAB 24*

Emery, Joseph Welch 1850-1936 *NatCAB 31*

Emery, Lewis 1839-1924 *NatCAB 22, WhAm 1*

Emery, Lewis 1878-1941 *NatCAB 32*

Emery, Lucilius Alonzo 1840-1920 *DcAmB, NatCAB 14, TwCBDA, WhAm 1*

Emery, Mary Muhlenberg Hopkins 1844-1927 *NatCAB 24*

Emery, Matthew Gault 1818-1901 *NatCAB 5, WhAm 1*

Emery, Natt Morrill 1873-1935 *WhAm 1*

Emery, Richard Runkel 1910-1964 *WhAm 4*

Emery, Robert Lovett 1880-1948 *NatCAB 37*

Emery, Roe 1874-1953 *WhAm 3*

Emery, Rufus *NewYHSD*

Emery, Samuel Hopkins 1815-1901 *TwCBDA*

Emery, Sarah Anna 1821-1907 *WhAm 1*

Emery, Sarah Elizabeth VanDeVort 1838-1895 *NotAW*

Emery, Stephen Albert 1841-1891 *DcAmB, NatCAB 23, WhAm H*

Emery, Susan L 1846- *WhAm 1, WomWWA 14*

Emery, Thomas Josephus 1830-1906 *NatCAB 24*

Emery, Walter Byron 1907-1973 *NatCAB 57*

Emery, William B *NewYHSD*

Emery, William Marshall 1907-1966 *WhAm 4, WhAm 4A*

Emery, William Mills 1897-1970 *NatCAB 54*

Emery, William Morrell 1866- *WhAm 4*

Emery, William Orrin 1863-1946 *WhAm 3*

Emery, Woodward 1842- *NatCAB 14*

Emery, Zachary Taylor 1847-1924 *NatCAB 18, WhAm 1*

Emhardt, William Chauncey 1874-1950 *WhAm 3*

Emhardt, William Henry 1876-1951 *NatCAB 42*

Emidy, H Lorenzo 1897-1964 *NatCAB 51*

Emig, Arthur S 1887-1949 *WhAm 3*

Emig, Elmer Jacob 1898-1957 *WhAm 3*

Emil, Allan D 1898-1976 *WhAm 6*

Eminescu, Mihail 1850-1889 *McGEWB*

Emison, John C 1890-1966 *WhAm 4, WhAm 5*

Emken, Cecil Wheeler 1897-1970 *WhAm 5*

Emlaw, Harlan Stigand 1873-1953 *ApCAB X, WhAm 3*

Emlen, John Thompson 1878-1955 *NatCAB 42*

Emma 1836-1885 *NotAW*

Emmanuel, David *BiAUS*

Emmerich, Fred Joseph 1892-1970 *NatCAB 55, WhAm 5*

Emmerich, Herbert 1897-1970 *NatCAB 55, WhAm 5*

Emmerson, Henry Read 1883-1954 *WhAm 3*

Emmerson, Henry Robert 1853- *ApCAB Sup*

Emmerson, Louis Lincoln 1863-1941 *NatCAB 40, WhAm 1*

Emmert *NewYHSD*

Emmert, Howard Harbaugh 1869-1934 *NatCAB 27*

Emmert, John Harley 1858-1943 *NatCAB 32, WhAm 2*

Emmert, Max 1883-1940 *NatCAB 31*

Emmerton, James Arthur 1834-1888 *ApCAB, TwCBDA*

Emmerton, William Henry 1828- *NewYHSD*

Emmes, Henry *NewYHSD*

Emmes, Thomas *BnEnAmA, NewYHSD*

Emmet, Elizabeth *NewYHSD*

Emmet, Ellen Gertrude *NotAW*

Emmet, Grenville Temple 1877-1937 *NatCAB 30, WhAm 1*

Emmet, John M 1811?- *NewYHSD*

Emmet, John Patten 1797-1842 *NewYHSD, TwCBDA, WhAm H*

Emmet, John Patton 1797-1842 *ApCAB*

Emmet, John T 1854- *NatCAB 3*

Emmet, Joseph Kline 1841-1891 *NatCAB 5, TwCBDA*

Emmet, Lydia Field 1866-1952 *NatCAB 15, NatCAB 42, WhAm 3, WomWWA 14*

Emmet, Robert 1778-1803 *McGEWB*

Emmet, Robert 1792-1873 *ApCAB*

Emmet, Robert Temple 1854-1936 *ApCAB, NatCAB 27*

Emmet, Rosina 1854- *ApCAB, TwCBDA*

Emmet, Thomas Addis 1764-1827 *AmBi, ApCAB, DcAmB, NatCAB 5, TwCBDA, WhAm H*

Emmet, Thomas Addis 1765-1827 *Drake*

Emmet, Thomas Addis 1798-1863 *ApCAB*

Emmet, Thomas Addis 1818-1880 *ApCAB*

Emmet, Thomas Addis 1828-1919 *ApCAB, DcAmB, NatCAB 10, TwCBDA, WhAm 1*

Emmet, William LeRoy 1859-1941 *DcAmB S3, NatCAB 15, NatCAB 30, WhAm 1*

Emmet, William Temple 1869-1918 *WhAm 1*

Emmett, Burton 1871-1935 *DcAmB S1, NatCAB 29*

Emmett, Daniel Decatur 1815-1904 *AmBi, DcAmB, NatCAB 21, WebAB, WhAm H, WhAm 2*

Emmett, John 1804?-1853 *NewYHSD*

Emmett, John 1834- *NewYHSD*

Emmett, John Morehead 1893-1969 *NatCAB 54*

Emmett, Lafayette 1822- *NatCAB 13*

Emmons, Alexander Hamilton 1816- *NewYHSD*

Emmons, Arthur Brewster, III 1910-1962 *WhAm 4*

Emmons, Charles Demoss 1871-1933 *WhAm 1*

Emmons, Delos Carleton 1888-1965 *WebAMB, WhAm 4*

Emmons, Ebenezer 1799-1863 *AmBi, ApCAB, DcAmB, DcScB, Drake, NatCAB 8, TwCBDA, WhAm H*

Emmons, Ebenezer, Jr. *NewYHSD*

Emmons, Edward Ferguson 1889-1950 *NatCAB 39*

Emmons, Elizabeth Wales *WomWWA 14*

Emmons, Gardner Gage 1894-1963 *NatCAB 50*

Emmons, George *NewYHSD*

Emmons, George Edward 1857-1938 *NatCAB 29*

Emmons, George Foster 1811-1884 *ApCAB, DcAmB, Drake, NatCAB 4, TwCBDA, WhAm H*

Emmons, George Thorton 1874-1945 *WhAm 2*

Emmons, Grover Carlton 1886-1944 *WhAm 2*

Emmons, H H *BiAUS*

Emmons, Halmer Hull 1815-1877 *ApCAB, TwCBDA*

Emmons, Harold Hunter 1875-1962 *ApCAB X, WhAm 4*

Emmons, Lloyd C 1887-1957 *WhAm 3*

Emmons, Nathanael 1745-1840 *ApCAB,*
DcAmB, NatCAB 5, TwCBDA
Emmons, Nathanael 1746-1840 *WhAm H*
Emmons, Nathan 1704-1740 *BnEnAmA*
Emmons, Nathaniel 1704-1740 *NewYHSD*
Emmons, Nathaniel 1745-1840 *DcAmReB,*
Drake
Emmons, Nathaniel Henry 1870-1925
NatCAB 20
Emmons, Samuel Franklin 1841-1911 *ApCAB,*
DcAmB, DcScB, NatCAB 10, TwCBDA,
WhAm 1
Emmons, William *NewYHSD*
Emmons, William Harvey 1876-1948 *WhAm 2*
Emmons, William Henry Harrison 1841-1919
ApCAB X, NatCAB 19
Emory, Frederic 1853-1908 *WhAm 1*
Emory, Frederick Lincoln 1867-1921 *WhAm 1*
Emory, John 1789-1835 *ApCAB, DcAmB,*
Drake, NatCAB 10, TwCBDA, WhAm H
Emory, Reba Cornett *WomWWA 14*
Emory, Robert 1814-1848 *ApCAB, Drake,*
TwCBDA
Emory, Samuel T 1896-1957 *WhAm 3*
Emory, William Helmsley 1811-1887 *AmBi*
Emory, William Helmsley 1812?- *BiAUS,*
Drake
Emory, William Hemsley *ApCAB*
Emory, William Hemsley 1811-1887 *ApCAB,*
DcAmB, NatCAB 4, REnAW, TwCBDA,
WebAMB, WhAm H
Emory, William Hemsley 1846-1917
NatCAB 17, WhAm 1
Emott, James 1770-1850 *BiAUS*
Emott, James 1771-1850 *ApCAB, BiDrAC,*
DcAmB, Drake, NatCAB 11, TwCBDA,
WhAm H, WhAmP
Emott, James 1823-1884 *ApCAB, DcAmB,*
TwCBDA, WhAm H, WhAmP
Emparan, Diego De 1718-1807? *ApCAB*
Empedocles 490?BC-430?BC *AsBiEn*
Empedocles 493?BC-444?BC *McGEWB*
Empedocles Of Acragas 492?BC-432?BC *DcScB*
Empey, Arthur Guy 1883-1963 *WebAMB,*
WhAm 4
Empie, Adam 1785-1860 *NatCAB 3,*
TwCBDA
Empringham, James 1875- *WhAm 5*
Emrich, Frederick Ernest 1848-1933 *WhAm 1*
Emrich, Jeannette Wallace 1878-1946 *WhAm 2*
Emrie, J Reece 1812-1869 *BiAUS*
Emrie, Jonas Reece 1812-1869 *BiDrAC*
Emsweller, Samuel Leonar 1898-1966 *WhAm 5*
Enambuc, Pierre Vaudrosques Diel D' 1585-1636
ApCAB
Enander, John Alfred 1842-1910 *NatCAB 19,*
WhAm 1
Encalada, Manuel Blanco 1790-1876 *ApCAB*
Encina, Juan Del 1468-1529? *McGEWB*
Enciso, Martin Fernandez De d1525? *ApCAB*
Encke, Johann Franz 1791-1865 *AsBiEn,*
DcScB
Enckell, Carl J A 1876-1959 *WhAm 3*
Endalkachew, Makonnen 1927- *WhAm 6*
Endalkatchou, Bitwoded Makonnen *WhAm 4*
Ende, Louis *NewYHSD*
Endecott, John 1588-1655 *McGEWB*
Endecott, John 1588-1665 *Drake, WebAB,*
WhAmP
Endecott, John 1589?-1665 *AmBi, DcAmB,*
WhAm H
Endelman, Julio 1879-1948 *WhAm 2*
Enders, Frederick 1890-1960 *NatCAB 45*
Enders, George Christian 1869-1966 *WhAm 4*
Enders, Henry Cornelius 1871-1948 *NatCAB 39*
Enders, Howard Edwin 1877-1958 *NatCAB 47,*
WhAm 5
Enders, John Franklin 1897- *AsBiEn,*
McGEWB, WebAB
Enders, John Ostrom 1869-1958 *WhAm 3*
Enderton, S B *IlBEAAW*
Endicott, Charles Moses 1793-1863 *AmBi,*
ApCAB, DcAmB, WhAm H
Endicott, Francis 1832?- *NewYHSD*
Endicott, G *NewYHSD*
Endicott, George 1802-1848 *NewYHSD,*
WhAm H
Endicott, H Wendell 1880-1954 *WhAm 3*

Endicott, Henry 1824-1913 *NatCAB 11,*
WhAm 1
Endicott, Henry Bradford 1853-1920 *ApCAB X,*
NatCAB 19
Endicott, Israel *NewYHSD*
Endicott, John 1558-1665 *ApCAB, TwCBDA*
Endicott, John 1588?-1665 *WebAB*
Endicott, John 1589?-1665 *AmBi, DcAmB,*
NatCAB 5
Endicott, John 1867-1955 *NatCAB 44*
Endicott, Katharine Sears 1876- *WomWWA 14*
Endicott, Mordecai Thomas 1844-1926
ApCAB X, DcAmB, NatCAB 15,
WhAm 1
Endicott, Paul 1890-1958 *NatCAB 47*
Endicott, Sarah L *NewYHSD*
Endicott, W *NewYHSD*
Endicott, William 1816-1851 *NewYHSD,*
WhAm H
Endicott, William 1865-1941 *NatCAB 32,*
WhAm 1
Endicott, William Crowningshield 1826-1900
WhAmP
Endicott, William Crowninshield 1826-1900
BiDrUSE, DcAmB, NatCAB 2, TwCBDA,
WhAm 1
Endicott, William Crowninshield 1827- *ApCAB*
Endicott, William Crowninshield 1860-1936
WhAm 1
Endlich, Emma A *WomWWA 14*
Endlich, Gustav Adolf 1856-1929 *NatCAB 39,*
WhAm 1
Endore, Guy 1901-1970 *WhAm 5*
Endress, Christian Frederick Lewis 1775-1827
ApCAB, TwCBDA
Enelow, Heman Gerson 1877-1934 *WhAm 1*
Enelow, Hyman Gerson 1877-1934 *DcAmB S1*
Enesco, Georges 1881-1955 *WhAm 3*
Enfield, Gertrude Dixon d1969 *WhAm 5*
Enfield, William Lester 1879-1945 *NatCAB 33*
Engberg, Carl 1868-1943 *NatCAB 32*
Engberg, Carl Christian 1872-1929 *WhAm 1*
Engel, Adolph 1869-1928 *ApCAB X*
Engel, Albert Joseph 1888-1959 *BiDrAC,*
WhAm 3, WhAmP
Engel, Arthur Carsel 1891-1963 *NatCAB 53*
Engel, Carl 1883-1944 *DcAmB S3, WhAm 2*
Engel, Carl Henry 1924-1971 *WhAm 5*
Engel, Edward J 1874-1947 *WhAm 2*
Engel, Friedrich 1861-1941 *DcScB*
Engel, Fritz Franz 1877-1956 *NatCAB 45*
Engel, Jacob *NatCAB 7*
Engel, Johann *DcScB*
Engel, K August 1889-1968 *NatCAB 57,*
WhAm 4A
Engel, Katharine Asher 1898-1957 *WhAm 3*
Engel, Louis George 1859-1938 *NatCAB 30*
Engel, Max Robert 1868-1928 *ApCAB X*
Engel, Michael Martin 1896-1969 *WhAm 5*
Engel, Peter 1856-1921 *TwCBDA, WhAm 1*
Engel, Wilhelmina Lammert 1871-
WomWWA 14
Engel, William *NewYHSD*
Engelhard, Charles 1867-1950 *NatCAB 41*
Engelhard, Joseph Adolphus 1832-1879 *ApCAB*
Engelhardt, Francis Ernest 1835- *ApCAB,*
TwCBDA, WhAm 4
Engelhardt, Fred 1885-1944 *BiDAmEd,*
NatCAB 33, WhAm 2
Engelhardt, Nickolaus Louis 1882-1960
BiDAmEd, NatCAB 52, WhAm 3
Engelhardt, William R 1909- *WhAm 6*
Engelhardt, Zephyrin 1851-1934 *DcAmB S1,*
NatCAB 24, WhAm 1
Engelke, Ida Darling 1873- *WomWWA 14*
Engelkemeir, Donald William 1919-1969
WhAm 5
Engelmann, C F *NewYHSD*
Engelmann, George 1809-1884 *AmBi, ApCAB,*
DcAmB, DcScB Sup, NatCAB 6,
TwCBDA, WhAm H
Engelmann, George Julius 1847-1903 *ApCAB,*
DcAmB, NatCAB 11, TwCBDA,
WhAm 1
Engelmann, Theodor Wilhelm 1843-1909 *DcScB*
Engelmore, Irwin B 1910-1974 *WhAm 6*
Engels, Friedrich 1820-1895 *DcScB,*
DcScB Sup, McGEWB, WhoMilH

Engelsted, Knud 1889-1954 *NatCAB 45*
Engen, Hans Kristian 1912-1966 *WhAm 4*
Enger, Melvin Lorenius 1881-1956 *WhAm 3*
Engerrand, George C 1877-1961 *WhAm 4*
Engerud, Edward 1868- *WhAm 1*
England, Edward Theodore 1869-1934 *BiDrAC*
England, Edward Theodore 1870- *WhAm 5*
England, George Allan 1877-1936 *WhAm 1*
England, John 1786-1842 *AmBi, ApCAB,*
DcAmB, DcAmReB, Drake, McGEWB,
NatCAB 5, TwCBDA, WebAB,
WhAm H
England, Lynwood Earl 1905-1967 *NatCAB 54*
England, Octavia Grace Ritchie 1868-
WomWWA 14
England, Sir Richard 1750?-1812 *ApCAB,*
Drake
England, Sir Richard 1793-1883 *ApCAB*
England, William Henry 1876- *WhAm 5*
Englander, Ludwig 1853- *NatCAB 14*
Englar, D Roger 1883-1948 *WhAm 3*
Engle, Addie C Strong 1845- *AmWom*
Engle, Clair 1911-1964 *BiDrAC, WhAm 4,*
WhAmP
Engle, David Edwin 1909-1957 *NatCAB 47*
Engle, Earl Theron 1896-1957 *NatCAB 48,*
WhAm 3
Engle, Frederick 1799-1868 *ApCAB, Drake,*
TwCBDA
Engle, Jesse A 1901-1962 *WhAm 4*
Engle, John Summerfield 1869- *WhAm 5*
Engle, Wilbur Dwight 1870- *WhAm 5*
Englebright, Harry Lane 1884-1943 *BiDrAC,*
WhAm 2, WhAmP
Englebright, William Fellows 1855-1915
BiDrAC, WhAm 4, WhAmP
Englehard, Charles William 1917-1971
WhAm 5
Englehart, Robert William 1903-1965 *WhAm 4*
Engleken, Jacob *NewYHSD*
Engleman, James Ozro 1873-1943 *NatCAB 32,*
WhAm 2
Engler, Clarence William 1895-1957
NatCAB 46
Engler, Edmund Arthur 1856- *WhAm 1*
Engler, Heinrich Gustav Adolf 1844-1930
DcScB Sup
Engles, William Morrison 1797-1867 *ApCAB,*
Drake, TwCBDA
Englis, Charles Mortimer 1856-1926 *ApCAB X,*
NatCAB 16
Englis, Charles Mortimer 1857-1926 *NatCAB 9,*
WhAm 1
Englis, John 1808-1888 *DcAmB, NatCAB 9,*
WhAm H
Englis, John, Jr. 1833-1915 *NatCAB 9,*
NatCAB 16
English, Arthur 1863-1947 *NatCAB 36*
English, Calvin H 1857-1948 *NatCAB 38*
English, Charles Henry 1883-1944 *NatCAB 34,*
WhAm 2
English, Chester Ferrin 1888-1950 *NatCAB 40*
English, Conover 1877-1963 *WhAm 4*
English, David Combs 1842-1924 *WhAm 1*
English, Earl 1824-1893 *ApCAB, NatCAB 5,*
TwCBDA
English, Earle Walter 1904-1966 *WhAm 4*
English, Elbert Hartwell 1816-1884 *DcAmB,*
NatCAB 12, WhAm H
English, Frank A 1895-1959 *WhAm 3*
English, Frank Clare 1869-1949 *NatCAB 38,*
WhAm 5
English, George Bethune 1787-1828 *ApCAB,*
DcAmB, Drake, NatCAB 13, TwCBDA,
WhAm H
English, George Letchworth 1864-1944
WhAm 2
English, George Washington 1853- *NatCAB 7*
English, George Washington 1866- *WhAm 4*
English, Harold Thomas 1891-1956 *NatCAB 49*
English, Harry David Williams 1855-1926
WhAm 1
English, Henry Fowler 1851-1947 *NatCAB 38*
English, Horace Bidwell 1892-1961 *WhAm 4*
English, Isaac Buckingham 1836-1908
NatCAB 6
English, J *NewYHSD*
English, James 1853-1937 *NatCAB 28*

English, James Edward 1812-1890 *ApCAB,*
BiAUS, BiDrAC, DcAmB, Drake,
NatCAB 10, TwCBDA, WhAm H,
WhAmP
English, James Warren 1837-1925 *NatCAB 28*
English, Jennie Wright 1859- *WomWWA 14*
English, John Colin 1895- *BiDAmEd*
English, John Francis 1889-1969 *WhAm 5*
English, John Mahan 1845-1927 *WhAm 1*
English, Kate Vincent 1872- *WomWWA 14*
English, Lucy K 1855- *WomWWA 14*
English, Merle Neville 1878-1945 *WhAm 2*
English, Nereus Clarkson 1904-1965
NatCAB 51
English, Robert Byrns 1872-1952 *WhAm 3*
English, Robert Henry 1888-1943 *NatCAB 33,*
WhAm 2
English, Sara John 1872- *WhAm 5*
English, Stella Mae Williams 1875-
WomWWA 14
English, Thomas Dunn 1819-1902 *AmBi,*
ApCAB, BiDrAC, DcAmB, Drake,
NatCAB 4, TwCBDA, WhAm 1,
WhAmP
English, Virgil P 1858- *WhAm 4*
English, Warren Barkley 1840-1913 *BiDrAC,*
WhAmP
English, William Eastin 1850-1926 *BiDrAC,*
WhAmP
English, William Eastin 1854-1926 *WhAm 1*
English, William Elisha 1854- *NatCAB 10*
English, William Hayden 1822-1896 *AmBi,*
ApCAB, BiAUS, BiDrAC, DcAmB,
NatCAB 9, TwCBDA, WhAm H,
WhAmP
Engman, Martin Feeney 1868-1953 *NatCAB 42,*
WhAm 3
Engstad, Mathilda Charlotte 1868-
WomWWA 14
Engstrom, A B *NewYHSD*
Engstrom, Adolph 1880- *WhAm 6*
Engstrom, Howard Theodore 1902-1962
WhAm 4
Engstrom, Malcolm Carl 1901-1959
NatCAB 47
Engstrom, Sigfrid Emanuel 1907-1955 *WhAm 3*
Engstrom, William Weborg 1915-1974 *WhAm 6*
Enke, Ludwig *NewYHSD*
Enloe, Benjamin Augustine 1848-1922 *BiDrAC,*
NatCAB 11, TwCBDA, WhAm 1
Enloe, Eugene 1859-1945 *NatCAB 42*
Enloe, William Angel 1880-1952 *NatCAB 41*
Enlow, Robert Cooke 1905-1968 *NatCAB 54,*
WhAm 4A
Enlows, Harold Franklin 1884-1956 *NatCAB 47*
Enman, Florence Mabelle Holden 1875-
WomWWA 14
Enman, Horace Luttrell 1884-1960 *WhAm 4*
Enneking, John Joseph 1840-1916 *WhAm 1*
Enneking, John Joseph 1841-1916 *ApCAB,*
DcAmB, NatCAB 5, TwCBDA
Ennin 794-864 *McGEWB*
Ennis, Alfred 1837- *WhAm 4*
Ennis, Edith Mitchell *WomWWA 14*
Ennis, George *NewYHSD*
Ennis, George Pearse 1884-1936 *WhAm 1*
Ennis, H Robert 1870-1946 *WhAm 2*
Ennis, Joseph Burroughs 1879-1955 *NatCAB 45,*
WhAm 3
Ennis, Lambert High 1906-1954 *NatCAB 47*
Ennis, Luna May *WhAm 1*
Ennis, Thomas Leland 1891-1952 *WhAm 3*
Ennis, William Duane 1877-1947 *WhAm 2*
Ennius, Quintus 239BC-169BC *McGEWB*
Eno, Amos Richards 1810-1898 *ApCAB Sup,*
TwCBDA
Eno, Arthur Llewellyn 1870-1937 *NatCAB 28*
Eno, Clara Bertha 1854- *WomWWA 14*
Eno, Frank Harvey 1865-1943 *NatCAB 40*
Eno, Henry Lane 1871-1928 *NatCAB 22*
Eno, John Chester 1848-1914 *NatCAB 23*
Eno, William Phelps 1858-1945 *DcAmB S3,*
NatCAB 48, WhAm 2
Enochs, Herbert Alexander 1874- *WhAm 5*
Enochs, William Henry 1842-1893 *BiDrAC,*
WhAm H
Enos, Alanson Trask 1856- *NatCAB 14*
Enos, George M 1896-1952 *WhAm 3*
Enos, Pascal Paoli *ApCAB*

Enos, Roger 1729-1808 *ApCAB, Drake,*
NatCAB 5, TwCBDA
Enos, William Berkeley *WebAB*
Enrich, Walter Louis 1878- *WhAm 6*
Enrietto, John 1900-1975 *WhAm 6*
Enright, Earl F 1891-1961 *WhAm 4*
Enright, Elizabeth d1968 *WhAm 5*
Enright, Richard Edward 1871-1953 *WhAm 3*
Enright, Walter J 1879-1969 *WhAm 5*
Enrique *ApCAB*
Enriques, Federigo 1871-1946 *DcScB*
Enriquez DeAlmansa, Martin 1525?-1583
ApCAB
Enriquez DeRivera, Payo 1610?-1684 *ApCAB*
Ensey, Lot 1908-1970 *WhAm 5*
Ensign, Edward *NewYHSD*
Ensign, Forest Chester 1867-1961 *NatCAB 48,*
WhAm 5
Ensign, Joseph Ralph 1868-1941 *NatCAB 30*
Ensign, Josiah Davis 1833-1923 *NatCAB 17,*
WhAm 1
Ensign, Mary Jane 1916-1975 *WhAm 6*
Ensign, Moses 1794-1864 *NatCAB 16*
Ensign, Orville Hiram 1863-1935 *WhAm 1*
Ensign, Ralph Hart 1834-1917 *NatCAB 20*
Ensign, Timothy 1795?-1849 *NewYHSD*
Ensign, Willis Lee 1922-1973 *WhAm 6*
Enskog, David 1884-1947 *DcScB*
Ensle, James Frederick 1872-1935 *NatCAB 30*
Enslen, Eugene F 1858-1941 *WhAm 2*
Ensley, Enoch 1836-1891 *DcAmB, WhAm H*
Enslow, Linn Harrison 1891-1957 *NatCAB 47,*
WhAm 3
Ensor, Arthur John 1905- *IIBEAAW*
Ensor, James 1860-1949 *McGEWB, WhAm 4*
Ensor, Lawrence Edward 1898-1968
NatCAB 54
Ensor, Lowell Skinner 1907-1975 *WhAm 6*
Enstrom, William N 1888-1957 *WhAm 3*
Ent, George 1604-1689 *DcScB*
Ent, Uzal Girard 1900-1948 *WhAm 2*
Ent, Uzal Girard 1901-1948 *NatCAB 36*
Entizminger, Louis 1878- *WhAm 6*
Entratter, Jack 1914-1971 *WhAm 5*
Entrikin, John Bennett 1899-1966 *WhAm 4*
Entwistle, James 1837-1910 *DcAmB, WhAm 1*
Entz, John A 1880- *WhAm 6*
Enver Pasha 1881-1922 *McGEWB, WhoMilH*
Enwall, Hasse Octavius 1873-1947 *WhAm 2*
Enzing-Muller, Johann Michael 1804-1888
NewYHSD
Enzling, Monsieur De *NewYHSD*
Eoff, Alfred d1908 *NatCAB 16*
Eotvos, Baron Roland Von 1848-1919 *DcScB*
Epaminondas 425?BC-362BC *McGEWB*
Epes, James Fletcher 1842-1910 *BiDrAC,*
TwCBDA
Epes, Louis Spencer 1882-1935 *WhAm 1*
Epes, Sydney Parham 1865-1900 *BiDrAC,*
TwCBDA, WhAm 1
Epictetus 050?-135? *McGEWB*
Epicurus 341BC-270BC *AsBiEn, DcScB*
Epicurus 342?BC-270BC *McGEWB*
Epiphane, Louis Marie 1630-1692 *ApCAB*
Epler, Percy H 1872- *WhAm 5*
Epley, Lloyd L 1872- *WhAm 5*
Epling, Giles Thomas 1873-1933 *NatCAB 25*
Epp, George Edward 1885-1970 *WhAm 5*
Epperly, James Melvin 1900-1973 *WhAm 6*
Epperson, Uriah Spray 1861-1927 *NatCAB 21*
Eppes, John Wayles 1773-1823 *AmBi, ApCAB,*
BiAUS, BiDrAC, DcAmB, Drake,
NatCAB 11, TwCBDA, WhAm H,
WhAmP
Eppes, Richard 1864-1922 *NatCAB 6*
Eppley, Eugene C 1884-1958 *WhAm 3*
Eppley, Marion 1883-1960 *NatCAB 49*
Epps, Curtis Howard 1911-1959 *NatCAB 46*
Epstein, Abraham 1887-1958 *NatCAB 43*
Epstein, Abraham 1892-1942 *DcAmB S3,*
WhAm 2
Epstein, Albert Arthur 1880-1965 *NatCAB 51*
Epstein, Gustav 1885-1951 *NatCAB 40*
Epstein, Henry 1895-1961 *WhAm 4*
Epstein, Jacob 1864- *ApCAB X*
Epstein, Jacob 1880-1945 *WhAm 2*
Epstein, Jacob 1880-1959 *McGEWB,*
NatCAB 44, WhAm 3

Epstein, Joseph Hugo 1904-1961 *WhAm 4*
Epstein, Louis M 1887-1949 *WhAm 2*
Epstein, Max 1875-1954 *NatCAB 42,*
WhAm 3
Epstein, Paul Sophus 1883-1966 *WhAm 4*
Epstein, Philip G 1909-1952 *DcAmB S5*
Epstein, Ralph C 1899-1959 *WhAm 3*
Epstein, Stephan 1900-1973 *WhAm 6*
Epting, Monroe Jacob 1898-1958 *NatCAB 47*
Epton, Hicks 1906-1972 *NatCAB 57*
Equen, Murdock 1892-1964 *WhAm 4*
Equiano, Olaudah 1745-1801? *McGEWB*
Erard, Philip Valmore 1885-1951 *NatCAB 38*
Erasistratus 304?BC-250?BC *AsBiEn, DcScB*
Erasmus, Desiderius 1466-1536 *McGEWB*
Erasmus, Disiderius 1466-1536 *BiHiMed*
Erastus, Thomas 1523-1583 *DcScB*
Erath, George Bernard 1813-1891 *NatCAB 10*
Eratosthenes 276?BC-195?BC *DcScB*
Eratosthenes 276?BC-196?BC *AsBiEn*
Eratosthenes Of Cyrene 284?BC-205?BC
McGEWB
Erauzo, Catalina De 1585-1650 *ApCAB*
Erb, Carl Lee, Jr. 1913-1971 *NatCAB 55,*
WhAm 5
Erb, Donald Milton 1900-1943 *WhAm 2*
Erb, Frank Otis 1878-1950 *WhAm 3*
Erb, Frederick Baltus 1886-1937 *NatCAB 27*
Erb, Henry McKinley 1897-1961 *NatCAB 48*
Erb, John Lawrence 1877-1950 *WhAm 2A*
Erb, John Warren d1948 *ApCAB X, WhAm 2*
Erb, Lewis George 1883-1950 *NatCAB 39*
Erb, Nellie Kilsey 1870- *WomWWA 14*
Erb, Newman 1850-1925 *WhAm 1*
Erb, Wilhelm Heinrich 1840-1921 *BiHiMed*
Erba, Gaspar *NewYHSD*
Erben, Henry 1801-1883 *ApCAB*
Erben, Henry 1832- *TwCBDA*
Erben, Henry VanDerBogert 1898-1956
NatCAB 46, WhAm 3
Erben, Peter 1771-1863 *ApCAB*
Erbes, Philip Henry 1906-1971 *WhAm 5*
Erbsloh, Rudolf August 1858-1931 *NatCAB 25*
Ercilla Y Zuniga, Alonso De 1533-1594
McGEWB
Ercilla Y Zuniga, Alonso De 1533-1595? *ApCAB*
Ercilla Y Zuniga, Alonzo De *Drake*
Ercker, Lazarus 1530?-1594 *DcScB*
Erdland, Bernard August 1874- *WhAm 5*
Erdman, Charles Rosenbury 1866-1960
WhAm 4
Erdman, Constantine Jacob 1846-1911 *BiDrAC,*
TwCBDA
Erdman, Frederick Seward 1901-1968
NatCAB 54, WhAm 5
Erdman, Helga Mae 1929-1972 *WhAm 6*
Erdman, Jacob 1801-1867 *BiAUS, BiDrAC,*
WhAm H
Erdman, John Frederic 1864-1954 *WhAm 3*
Erdman, John Pinney 1874-1941 *NatCAB 47*
Erdmann, Charles Albert 1917-1967 *WhAm 4*
Erdmann, Charles Andrew 1866-1941
NatCAB 30
Erdmann, Otto Linne 1804-1869 *DcScB*
Erdmann, William Lawrence 1902-1961
WhAm 4
Erhard, Ludwig 1897- *McGEWB*
Erhardt, Joel Benedict *WhAm 5*
Erhardt, John George 1889-1951 *WhAm 3*
Eric *ApCAB*
Eric The Red *ApCAB, Drake, McGEWB,*
WhAm H
Erich, Augustus Frederick 1837-1886 *ApCAB,*
TwCBDA
Erichsen, Hugo 1860-1944 *WhAm 2*
Ericksen, O Charles 1896-1949 *NatCAB 42*
Erickson, Alfred William 1876-1936 *WhAm 1*
Erickson, Arthur Herman 1881-1965
NatCAB 50
Erickson, Arvel Benjamin 1905-1974 *WhAm 6*
Erickson, Benjamin William 1882-1945
NatCAB 38
Erickson, Carl Gustaf 1877-1936 *NatCAB 34*
Erickson, Charles John 1852- *ApCAB X*
Erickson, Charles Watt 1881- *WhAm 6*
Erickson, Clifford Eric 1907-1963 *NatCAB 53,*
WhAm 4
Erickson, Cyrus 1898-1959 *WhAm 3*

Erickson, E R 1900-1974 *WhAm 6*
Erickson, Emil Renhold 1888-1941 *NatCAB 33*
Erickson, Frank Morton 1870-1957 *WhAm 3*
Erickson, Hubbard Horace 1885-1960
 NatCAB 48
Erickson, J L E 1901-1968 *WhAm 5*
Erickson, John Albert 1891-1957 *NatCAB 50*
Erickson, John Edward 1863-1946 *BiDrAC,*
 WhAm 2, WhAmP
Erickson, Joseph Hyrum 1864-1948 *NatCAB 54*
Erickson, Knut Eric 1891-1965 *WhAm 4*
Erickson, Martina Cecelia *WomWWA 14*
Erickson, Peter W 1880- *WhAm 6*
Erickson, Reinhart 1700-1772 *WhAm H*
Erickson, Runar Carl 1914-1963 *NatCAB 49*
Ericson, Charles John Alfred 1840-1910
 WhAm 1
Ericson, John Ernst 1858-1927 *NatCAB 16,*
 WhAm 1
Ericson, Mauritz A 1836-1912 *NewYHSD*
Ericson, William Matthews 1880-1966
 NatCAB 17, NatCAB 53
Ericsson, Frans August 1883-1952 *NatCAB 40,*
 WhAm 3
Ericsson, John 1803-1889 *AmBi, ApCAB,*
 AsBiEn, DcAmB, Drake, McGEWB,
 NatCAB 4, TwCBDA, WebAB,
 WebAMB, WhAm H
Ericsson, Leif *AmBi, WebAB, WhAm H*
Erigena, John Scotus 810?-877? *McGEWB*
Erigena, John Scotus *see also* Eriugena, Johannes
 Scottus
Erik XIV d1577 *WhoMilH*
Erikson, Carl Anthony 1888-1958 *WhAm 3*
Erikson, David Junkin 1898-1961 *WhAm 4*
Erikson, Erik Homburger 1902- *EncAB,*
 McGEWB, WebAB
Erikson, Henry Anton 1869-1957 *NatCAB 46,*
 WhAm 3
Eriksson, Erik McKinley 1896-1941 *WhAm 1*
Eriksson, Herman d1949 *WhAm 2*
Eriugena, Johannes Scottus *DcScB*
Eriugena, Johannes Scottus *see also* Erigena, John
 Scotus
Erk, Edmund Frederick 1872-1953 *BiDrAC,*
 WhAm 3
Erlandsen, Clarita Knight 1872- *WomWWA 14*
Erlanger, Abraham Lincoln 1860-1930
 ApCAB X, DcAmB, WhAm 1
Erlanger, Charles 1857-1935 *NatCAB 26*
Erlanger, Joseph 1874-1965 *AsBiEn, DcScB,*
 McGEWB, NatCAB 51, WebAB,
 WhAm 4
Erlanger, Milton S 1888-1969 *WhAm 5*
Erlanger, Mitchell Louis d1940 *WhAm 1*
Erlanger, Sidney Charles 1884-1948
 NatCAB 36
Erlbacher, Robert William 1911-1968
 NatCAB 55
Erlenborn, John Neal 1927- *BiDrAC*
Erlenmeyer, Richard August Carl Emil
 1825-1909 *DcScB*
Erman, Georg Adolph 1806-1877 *DcScB*
Ermatinger, Francis 1798?-1838 *WhAm H*
Ermentrout, Daniel 1837-1899 *ApCAB Sup,*
 BiDrAC, TwCBDA, WhAm 1, WhAmP
Erminger, Howell B, Jr. 1882-1951 *WhAm 3*
Ern, Henri 1863- *WhAm 4*
Ernest, Albert 1904-1961 *WhAm 4*
Ernest, John Henry 1905-1974 *WhAm 6*
Ernest, Juan Watson 1852-1916 *NatCAB 17*
Ernest, Julius 1831?- *NewYHSD*
Ernesti, Richard 1856- *IIBEAAW*
Ernsberger, Millard Clayton 1862-1940
 WhAm 1
Ernst, Father *NewYHSD*
Ernst, Alwin Charles 1881-1948 *NatCAB 42,*
 WhAm 2
Ernst, August Frederic 1841-1924 *WhAm 3*
Ernst, Bernard Morris Lee 1879-1938
 NatCAB 57, WhAm 1
Ernst, Carl Clark 1897-1961 *NatCAB 53,*
 WhAm 4
Ernst, Carl Julius 1854- *NatCAB 17*
Ernst, Carl Wilhelm 1845-1919 *NatCAB 20,*
 WhAm 4
Ernst, Charles Augustus 1872-1939 *NatCAB 42*
Ernst, Clayton Holt 1886-1945 *WhAm 2*

Ernst, Edward Cranch 1886-1944 *WhAm 2*
Ernst, Edwin Charles 1885-1969 *WhAm 5*
Ernst, Fritz B 1877-1959 *WhAm 3*
Ernst, George Alexander Otis 1850-1912
 TwCBDA, WhAm 1
Ernst, George Goodman 1894-1944 *NatCAB 33*
Ernst, Harold Clarence 1855-1922 *NatCAB 20*
Ernst, Harold Clarence 1856-1922 *AmBi,*
 DcAmB, WhAm 1
Ernst, Henry 1842-1929 *WhAm 1*
Ernst, Julius 1831?- *NewYHSD*
Ernst, Max 1891- *McGEWB*
Ernst, Oliver Foerster 1876-1963 *NatCAB 51*
Ernst, Oswald Herbert 1842-1926 *AmBi,*
 DcAmB, NatCAB 4, TwCBDA,
 WhAm 1
Ernst, Oswald Hubert 1842-1926 *ApCAB*
Ernst, Richard Pretlow 1858-1934 *ApCAB X,*
 BiDrAC, NatCAB 33, WhAm 1,
 WhAmP
Ernst, Theodore Charles 1869-1946 *NatCAB 35*
Ernst, Thomas J 1829?- *NewYHSD*
Ernstene, Arthur Carlton 1901-1971 *WhAm 5*
Ernster, Nicholas 1885-1949 *NatCAB 40*
Erntson, Verland Volna 1908-1970 *NatCAB 57*
Erny, Charles G 1887-1963 *WhAm 4*
Erpf, Armand Grover 1897-1971 *WhAm 5*
Errani, Achille 1823- *ApCAB*
Errazuriz, Federico 1825-1877 *ApCAB*
Errera, Leo-Abram 1858-1905 *DcScB*
Errett, Edwin Reeder 1891-1944 *WhAm 2*
Errett, Isaac 1820-1888 *AmBi, ApCAB,*
 DcAmB, NatCAB 6, NatCAB 11,
 TwCBDA, WhAm H
Errett, Russell 1817-1891 *ApCAB, BiDrAC,*
 TwCBDA, WhAm H, WhAmP
Errol, Leon 1881-1951 *DcAmB S5*
Erskine, Albert Russel 1871-1933 *WhAm 1*
Erskine, Arthur Wright 1885-1952 *NatCAB 42*
Erskine, David Montagu 1776-1855 *ApCAB*
Erskine, David Montague 1776-1855 *Drake*
Erskine, Ebenezer 1821-1902 *ApCAB,*
 WhAm 1
Erskine, Emma Payne 1854-1924 *WhAm 1,*
 WomWWA 14
Erskine, Frances 1781-1843 *ApCAB*
Erskine, George Chester 1881- *WhAm 6*
Erskine, Graves Blanchard 1897-1973
 NatCAB 57, WhAm 6
Erskine, Harold Perry 1879-1951 *NatCAB 50*
Erskine, Howard Major 1893-1964 *WhAm 4*
Erskine, John 1813-1895 *BiAUS, DcAmB,*
 NatCAB 2, TwCBDA, WhAm H
Erskine, John 1879-1951 *BiDAmEd,*
 DcAmB S5, WebAB, WhAm 3
Erskine, Linwood Mandeville 1885-1956
 NatCAB 44
Erskine, Mary Louise 1880- *WomWWA 14*
Erskine, Morse 1895-1968 *NatCAB 54*
Erskine, Robert 1735-1780 *AmBi, ApCAB,*
 DcAmB, Drake, NatCAB 24, WebAMB,
 WhAm H
Erskine, Robert Scarborough 1889-1957
 NatCAB 46
Erskine, Sir William 1728-1795 *ApCAB, Drake*
Erskine, William Henry 1860-1927 *NatCAB 21*
Erstein, Moise Leopold 1878- *ApCAB X*
Ertegun, Mehmet Munir 1883-1944 *WhAm 2*
Ertz, Edward Frederick 1862- *IIBEAAW*
Ertz, R B A Edward 1862- *WhAm 4*
Erus, John *NewYHSD*
Ervin, Charles Edwin 1880-1946 *WhAm 2*
Ervin, James 1778-1841 *ApCAB, BiAUS,*
 BiDrAC, TwCBDA, WhAm H
Ervin, James S 1886-1961 *WhAm 4*
Ervin, Joe W 1901-1945 *WhAm 2*
Ervin, Joseph Wilson 1901-1945 *BiDrAC*
Ervin, Morris Donaldson 1894-1956 *WhAm 3*
Ervin, Paul Revere 1908-1970 *WhAm 6*
Ervin, Robert Tait 1863- *WhAm 4*
Ervin, Samuel James, Jr. 1896- *BiDrAC*
Ervin, Thomas Calloway 1890-1965 *NatCAB 51*
Ervin, William Carson 1859-1943 *NatCAB 35*
Ervine, St. John Greer 1883-1971 *WhAm 5*
Erving, Emma Lootz *WomWWA 14*
Erving, George William 1768-1850 *TwCBDA*
Erving, George William 1769-1850 *AmBi,*
 DcAmB, WhAm H

Erving, George William 1771-1850 *ApCAB,*
 BiAUS, Drake, NatCAB 12
Erving, Henry Wood 1851-1941 *NatCAB 30,*
 WhAm 4
Erving, John 1690?-1786 *ApCAB*
Erving, John 1727-1816 *ApCAB*
Erving, William Gage 1877-1923 *NatCAB 45,*
 WhAm 1
Erving, William VanRensselaer 1871-1940
 NatCAB 31
Erway, Richard Eugene 1907-1971 *WhAm 5*
Erwin, Alexander R 1820-1860 *ApCAB*
Erwin, Benoni *NewYHSD*
Erwin, Claude Mayo 1906-1972 *WhAm 5*
Erwin, Clyde Atkinson 1897-1952 *WhAm 3*
Erwin, Daniel Peart 1844- *NatCAB 9*
Erwin, David *BiAUS*
Erwin, George L, Jr. 1895-1956 *WhAm 3*
Erwin, George Z 1840- *NatCAB 3*
Erwin, Guy Burton 1872-1929 *WhAm 1*
Erwin, Henry Parsons 1881-1953 *NatCAB 42,*
 WhAm 3
Erwin, Herbert Jones 1912-1966 *NatCAB 51*
Erwin, Howell Cobb 1876-1957 *NatCAB 47,*
 WhAm 5
Erwin, James Brailsford 1856-1924 *ApCAB X,*
 NatCAB 19, WhAm 1
Erwin, John Caldwell 1898-1971 *NatCAB 57*
Erwin, Marion Corbett 1893-1954 *WhAm 3*
Erwin, Richard Kenney 1860-1917 *WhAm 1*
Erwin, Robert Gallaudet d1906 *WhAm 1*
Erwin, William Allen 1856-1932 *NatCAB 24*
Erzberger, Matthias 1875-1921 *McGEWB*
Esaki, Leo 1925- *AsBiEn*
Esarey, Logan 1873- *WhAm 5*
Esarey, Sol Hervey 1866-1954 *NatCAB 42*
Esberg, Alfred Isaac 1870-1955 *NatCAB 47*
Esberg, Milton Herman 1875-1939 *NatCAB 29,*
 WhAm 1
Esbjorn, Lars Paul 1808-1870 *DcAmB,*
 WhAm H
Escalante, Diogenes d1964 *WhAm 4*
Escalante, Juan d1519 *ApCAB*
Escalante, Juan D' d1519 *Drake*
Escalante, Silvestre Velez De *AmBi, DcAmB,*
 WhAm H
Escalante Y Colombres, Manuel d1708 *ApCAB*
Escalera, Antonio De 1506-1575 *ApCAB*
Escalona, Juan 1768-1834 *ApCAB*
Escalona Y Calatayud, Juan Jose 1675-1737
 ApCAB
Escandon, Antonio 1825-1882 *ApCAB*
Esch, John Jacob 1861-1941 *BiDrAC,*
 DcAmB S3, WhAm 1, WhAmP
Esch, Marvin Lionel 1927- *BiDrAC*
Escher, Franklin 1881-1952 *WhAm 3*
Escher VonDerLinth, Hans Conrad 1767-1823
 DcScB
Escherich, Theodor 1857-1911 *DcScB*
Escherick, A W *NewYHSD*
Escholier, Raymond 1882- *WhAm 6*
Escholt, Mikkel Pederson 1610?-1669 *DcScB*
Eschscholtz, Johann Friedrich 1793-1831 *DcScB*
Eschweiler, Alexander Chadbourne, Jr.
 1893-1951 *NatCAB 41*
Eschweiler, Franz Chadbourne 1863-1929
 WhAm 1
Esclangon, Ernest Benjamin 1876-1954 *DcScB*
Escobar, Adrian C 1881-1954 *WhAm 3*
Escobar, Bartolome De 1562-1624 *ApCAB*
Escobar, Maria De d1560? *ApCAB, Drake*
Escobar, Pedro Suarez De d1591 *ApCAB*
Escobedo, Mariano 1828- *ApCAB*
Escobedo Y Aguilar, Pedro Jose Alcantara
 1798-1844 *ApCAB*
Escobedo Y Alarcon, Jorge 1748-1806 *ApCAB*
Escobosa, Hector 1907-1963 *WhAm 4*
Escoffier, John *NewYHSD*
Escudero, Jose A 1801-1862 *ApCAB*
Esenin, Sergei Aleksandrovich 1895-1925
 McGEWB
Esenwein, Joseph Berg 1867-1946 *WhAm 2*
Esglis, Louis Philippe Mariaucheau D' 1710-1788
 ApCAB
Eshbach, Ovid Wallace 1893-1958 *NatCAB 46,*
 WhAm 3
Eshelman, Elmer T 1877- *WhAm 6*

Eshelman, Fayette Clinton 1890-1944
NatCAB 34
Eshelman, John William, Jr. 1869-1950
NatCAB 38
Eshelman, Paul Ward 1883-1962 *NatCAB 49*
Eshelman, Walter Witmer 1908-1971 *WhAm 5*
Esher, John Jacob 1823-1901 *DcAmB,*
TwCBDA
Esherick, Wharton 1887-1970 *BnEnAmA*
Eshkol, Levi 1895-1969 *WhAm 5*
Eshleman, Aaron 1827- *NewYHSD*
Eshleman, Charles L 1880- *WhAm 6*
Eshleman, Edwin Duing 1920- *BiDrAC*
Eshleman, Fred Koontz 1906-1964 *WhAm 4*
Eshleman, Isaac Stauffer 1820- *ApCAB*
Eshleman, John Morton 1876-1916 *WhAm 1*
Eshner, Augustus Adolph 1862-1949 *WhAm 2*
Eskew, Samuel Williams 1889-1968
NatCAB 55, WhAm 5
Eskildsen, Clarence Raymond 1913-1967
WhAm 4
Eskiminzin d1896 *REnAW*
Eskola, Pentti Eelis 1883-1964 *WhAm 4*
Eskola, Pentti Elias 1883-1964 *DcScB*
Eskridge, Belle Constant 1859- *WomWWA 14*
Eskridge, J T d1902 *WhAm 1*
Eskridge, James Burnette 1866-1952
NatCAB 50, WhAm 3
Eskridge, Marshall 1878-1958 *NatCAB 44*
Eskridge, Thomas P *BiAUS*
Eslaba, Sebastian 1698-1759 *ApCAB*
Esleeck, Augustine Washington 1848-1926
NatCAB 31
Eslick, Edward Everett 1872-1932 *BiDrAC,*
WhAm 1, WhAmP
Eslick, Willa McCord Blake 1878-1961 *BiDrAC,*
WhAmP
Esling, Catherine Harbeson 1812- *ApCAB*
Esling, Charles Henry Augustine 1845-1907
ApCAB, TwCBDA, WhAm 1
Esmay, Rhodolph Leslie 1898-1965 *WhAm 4*
Esmenard, Joseph Alphonse 1769-1811 *ApCAB*
Esmond, Bessie Archer *WomWWA 14*
Esmond, Rhoda Anna 1819- *AmWom*
Esmonde, Eugene 1909-1942 *WhWW-II*
Espada Y Landa, Juan J Diaz De 1756-1832
ApCAB
Espadero, Nicolas Ruiz 1833- *ApCAB*
Espartero, Baldomero 1793-1879 *ApCAB,*
WhoMilH
Espejo, Antonio De *AmBi, ApCAB, DcAmB,*
WhAm H
Espejo, Jeronimo 1801- *ApCAB*
Espelage, Bernard Theodore 1892-1971
WhAm 6
Espeleta, Antoine Froger 1676-1715 *ApCAB*
Espenhain, Frank Kempff 1879- *NatCAB 16*
Espenshade, Abraham Howry 1869- *WhAm 3*
Espil, Felipe A 1887-1972 *WhAm 5*
Espina, Concha 1869-1955 *WhAm 3*
Espinosa, Aurelio Macedonio 1880-1958
BiDAmEd, WhAm 3
Espinosa, Gaspar De 1484-1537 *ApCAB*
Espinosa, Juan 1804-1871 *ApCAB*
Espinosa, Pedro 1793-1866 *ApCAB*
Espinosa DeLosMonteros, Antonio 1903-1959
WhAm 3
Espinosa Y San Martin, Antonio 1908-1968
WhAm 5
Espivent, Louis Charles D' 1641-1677 *ApCAB*
Esposito, Vincent Joseph 1900-1965 *WhAm 4,*
WhAm 5
Espy, Arthur 1869-1944 *NatCAB 44*
Espy, James Pollard 1785-1860 *AmBi, ApCAB,*
BiAUS, DcAmB, DcScB, Drake, WebAB,
NatCAB 6, TwCBDA, WebAB,
WhAm H
Esquemeling, John *ApCAB, Drake*
Esquirol, John Henry 1900-1970 *WhAm 5*
Esquiu, Mamerto 1826-1883 *ApCAB*
Esquivel, Juan De 1480-1519? *ApCAB*
Ess, Henry N 1891-1963 *WhAm 4*
Essary, J Fred 1881-1942 *NatCAB 34*
Essary, Jesse Frederick 1881-1942 *WhAm 2*
Essary, John Thurman 1855-1919 *NatCAB 8*
Esselen, Gustavus John 1888-1952 *NatCAB 42,*
WhAm 5
Essen, Frederick 1863-1946 *BiDrAC*

Esser, Charles Hillegass 1892-1959 *NatCAB 47*
Esser, Sigurd Emanuel 1903-1972 *WhAm 5*
Esser, Theodore Clemens 1871-1955
NatCAB 45
Essery, Carl Vanstone 1886-1953 *WhAm 3*
Essex, Robert Devereux, Earl Of 1567-1601
McGEWB
Essex, William Leopold 1886-1959 *WhAm 3*
Essick, Samuel V 1841- *NatCAB 3*
Essick, William Wallace 1857-1941 *NatCAB 31*
Essig, Benjamin C 1892-1972 *WhAm 5*
Essig, Edward Oliver 1884-1964 *NatCAB 51,*
WhAm 4
Essig, George Emerick 1838- *NewYHSD*
Essig, Sanford F 1897-1961 *NatCAB 49*
Essington, Thurlow Gault 1886-1964
NatCAB 51, WhAm 4
Esson, William 1839?-1916 *DcScB*
Estabrook, Alma Martin *WomWWA 14*
Estabrook, Arthur F 1847-1919 *WhAm 1*
Estabrook, Charles Edward 1847-1918
NatCAB 11, NatCAB 31
Estabrook, Experience 1813-1894 *BiDrAC,*
NatCAB 14, WhAm H
Estabrook, Fred Watson 1852-1939 *WhAm 1*
Estabrook, Henry Dodge 1854-1917
NatCAB 14, WhAm 1
Estabrook, John Davis 1837-1918 *NatCAB 18,*
WhAm 5
Estabrook, Joseph 1793-1855 *DcAmB,*
WhAm H
Estabrook, Joseph Benedict 1889-1949
NatCAB 38
Estabrook, Leon Moyer 1869-1937 *NatCAB 28,*
WhAm 1
Estabrook, Merrick Gay, Jr. 1886-1947
WhAm 3
Estabrook, Robert Francis 1880- *WhAm 6*
Estabrooks, George Hoben 1895-1974 *WhAm 6*
Estabrooks, John F *NewYHSD*
Estaing, Charles Hector, Count D' 1729-1794
AmBi, ApCAB, WhAm H
Estaing, Charles Henry Theodat, Count D'
1729-1794 *Drake*
Estaing, Jean Baptiste C H H, Comte D'
1729-1794 *WhoMilH*
Estaugh, Elizabeth Haddon 1680?-1762 *AmBi,*
DcAmB, NotAW, WhAm H
Estaugh, Elizabeth Haddon 1682-1762 *ApCAB*
Estaugh, Elizabeth Haddon 1683-1762
NatCAB 17
Estberg, Edward Robert 1862-1944 *NatCAB 40,*
WhAm 2
Este, David Kirkpatrick 1785-1875 *ApCAB*
Este, George Peabody 1829-1881 *ApCAB Sup,*
TwCBDA
Estee, James Borden 1856-1933 *WhAm 1*
Estee, Morris M d1903 *WhAm 1*
Esten, James Christie Palmer 1805-1864 *ApCAB*
Estenson, Lyle Osbern 1915-1969 *WhAm 5*
Estep, Charles Lee 1884-1959 *NatCAB 49*
Estep, Ephraim James 1820- *NatCAB 7*
Estep, Harry Allison 1884-1968 *BiDrAC*
Estep, Helen DeCamp Lynch 1887-
WomWWA 14
Estep, Preston 1914-1970 *NatCAB 56,*
WhAm 5
Esterbrook, Edith Marsh 1877- *WomWWA 14*
Esterbrook, Richard 1813-1895 *DcAmB,*
WhAm H
Esterline, Blackburn 1877-1928 *WhAm 1*
Esterly, Calvin Olin 1879-1928 *WhAm 1*
Esterly, Charles Joseph 1888-1940 *BiDrAC*
Esterly, Elizabeth Norcross 1872-
WomWWA 14
Esterly, George 1809-1893 *ApCAB, DcAmB,*
WhAm H
Esterly, Henry Minor 1873- *WhAm 5*
Estermann, Immanuel 1900-1973 *NatCAB 57*
Esterquest, Ralph Theodore 1912-1968
DcAmLiB, WhAm 5
Esters, Bernard E 1899-1966 *WhAm 4*
Estes, Bedford Mitchell 1832- *NatCAB 10*
Estes, Charles Thompson 1891-1964 *WhAm 4*
Estes, Dana 1840-1909 *DcAmB, NatCAB 10,*
TwCBDA, WhAm 1
Estes, David Foster 1851-1926 *WhAm 1*
Estes, Frances York 1853- *WomWWA 14*

Estes, George Henson 1873- *WhAm 5*
Estes, Lewis Alden 1815-1891 *TwCBDA*
Estes, Ludovic 1849-1898 *TwCBDA*
Estes, Ludwell Hunter 1879-1965 *WhAm 4,*
WhAm 6
Estes, Maurice James 1910-1972 *WhAm 6*
Estes, Thomas *NewYHSD*
Estes, Webster Cummings 1855- *NatCAB 16,*
WhAm 1
Estes, William Lawrence 1855-1940 *WhAm 1*
Estes, William Lawrence, Jr. 1885-1971
NatCAB 57
Estes, William Lee 1870-1930 *NatCAB 23,*
WhAm 1
Estevez Y Ugarte, Pedro Agustin 1754-1827
ApCAB
Estey, Alexander R 1826-1881 *WhAm H*
Estey, Jacob 1814-1890 *DcAmB, NatCAB 1,*
WhAm H
Estey, James Arthur 1886-1961 *WhAm 4*
Estey, Stephen Sewall 1861-1932 *WhAm 1*
Estheham, Andrew *NewYHSD*
Estienne, Charles 1505?-1564 *DcScB*
Estigarribia, Jose Felix 1888-1940 *WhAm 2*
Estil, Benjamin 1780-1853 *BiAUS, BiDrAC,*
WhAm H
Estill, George Castleman 1881-1957 *WhAm 3*
Estill, Harry Fishburne 1861-1942 *WhAm 2*
Estill, John Holbrook 1840-1907 *NatCAB 2,*
TwCBDA, WhAm 1
Estill, Thomas 1859-1926 *NatCAB 17*
Estopinal, Albert 1845-1919 *BiDrAC,*
WhAm 1, WhAmP
Estorge, Joseph Leonard 1830-1880 *ApCAB*
Estrada, Bartolome Ruiz De *ApCAB*
Estrada, Jose Dolores 1787-1869 *ApCAB*
Estrada Cabrera, Manuel 1857-1924
ApCAB Sup, McGEWB
Estrada Palma, Tomas 1835-1908 *McGEWB*
Estrees, Jean, Count D' 1624-1707 *ApCAB Sup*
Estrem, Herbert William 1902-1973 *WhAm 6*
Estrem, Thomas Sabin 1894-1961 *WhAm 4*
Esty, Alice May 1866- *AmWom*
Esty, Charles Alexander 1883-1947 *NatCAB 36*
Esty, Constantine Canaris 1824-1912 *BiAUS,*
BiDrAC
Esty, Edward Tuckerman 1875-1942 *WhAm 2*
Esty, William 1868-1928 *WhAm 1*
Esty, William Cole 1838-1916 *WhAm 1*
Esty, William Cole, III 1895-1954 *WhAm 3*
Etcheverry, Bernard Alfred 1881-1954 *WhAm 3*
Etchison, Page McKendree 1892-1952 *WhAm 3*
Ethel, Agnes 1852-1903 *WhAm H*
Ethelred The Unready 968?-1016 *McGEWB*
Etheredge, M P 1897-1971 *WhAm 5*
Etheredge, Sumpter Price 1883-1953
NatCAB 42
Etheridge, Emerson 1819-1902 *ApCAB,*
BiAUS, BiDrAC, TwCBDA, WhAm 1
Ethridge, George H 1871- *WhAm 6*
Ethridge, W B *NewYHSD*
Ethridge, William Nathaniel, Jr. 1912-1971
WhAm 5
Etler, Alvin Derald 1913-1973 *WhAm 6*
Etling, Carl D 1911-1973 *WhAm 6*
Etnyre, Edward Daniel 1863-1933 *NatCAB 44*
Etranger And Graines *NewYHSD*
Etris, Joseph 1871-1951 *NatCAB 39*
Ets-Hokin, Louis 1893-1971 *WhAm 5*
Ettelberg, August Valentine 1901-1948
NatCAB 55
Ettelbrick, Nicholas 1876-1947 *NatCAB 38*
Ettelbrick, Nicholas Frank, Jr. 1909-1969
NatCAB 55
Ettelson, Samuel Aaron 1874- *NatCAB 17*
Ettenheim, George Patek 1892-1971
NatCAB 56
Etter, David Rent 1807-1881 *NewYHSD*
Etter, William Kirby 1874-1943 *NatCAB 54,*
WhAm 2
Ettinger, George Taylor 1860-1949 *NatCAB 37,*
WhAm 2
Ettinger, Richard Prentice 1893-1971 *WhAm 5*
Ettinger, William L 1862-1945 *ApCAB X,*
WhAm 2
Ettwein, John 1721-1802 *AmBi, ApCAB,*
DcAmB, NatCAB 5, TwCBDA,
WhAm H

Etz, Roger Frederick 1886-1950 *WhAm 3*

Etzell, George Ferdinand 1909-1975 *WhAm 6*

Eubank, Ambrose Eastin 1878-1953
NatCAB 40

Eubank, Earle Edward 1887-1945 *NatCAB 47,*
WhAm 2

Eubank, Jessie Burrall d1960 *WhAm 4*

Eubank, John Augustine *WhAm 3*

Eubank, Victor 1883-1955 *WhAm 3*

Eubanks, Elinor Mae 1911-1975 *WhAm 6*

Eubanks, Sam B 1904-1967 *WhAm 4*

Eucken, Arnold Thomas 1884-1950 *DcScB*

Euclid *AsBiEn, DcScB, McGEWB*

Euctemon *DcScB*

Eudemus Of Rhodes *DcScB*

Eudoxus Of Cnidus 400?BC-347?BC *DcScB*

Eudoxus Of Cnidus 408?BC-355?BC *AsBiEn,*
McGEWB

Eudy, Mary Cummings 1871-1952 *NatCAB 41*

Eugen, Prince Of Savoy-Carignon 1663-1736
WhoMilH

Eugene Of Savoy 1663-1736 *McGEWB*

Euler, Charles 1815- *NewYHSD*

Euler, Leonhard 1707-1783 *AsBiEn, DcScB,*
McGEWB

Euler, Ralph Stapleton 1888-1972 *WhAm 6*

Euler, William D 1875-1961 *WhAm 4*

Euler, William Gilman Badger 1883-1958
WhAm 3

Euler-Chelpin, Hans Karl A Simon Von
1873-1964 *AsBiEn, DcScB*

Eumenes *WhAm H*

Eunson, Robert Charles Romaine 1912-1975
WhAm 6

Eupalinus *AsBiEn*

Euphemia 1816-1887 *ApCAB*

Eurich, Alvin Christian 1902- *BiDAmEd*

Euripides 480BC-406BC *McGEWB*

Euritt, Edith Jones *WomWWA 14*

Europe, James Reese *WhoColR*

Eusden, Ray Anderson 1889-1971 *WhAm 5*

Eustace, Bartholomew Joseph 1887-1956
WhAm 3

Eustace, John Skey 1760-1805 *ApCAB, Drake,*
NatCAB 4

Eustachi, Bartolomeo 1500?-1574 *DcScB*

Eustachio, Bartolomeo 1524-1574 *AsBiEn*

Eustachio, Bartolomeo 1520?-1574 *BiHiMed*

Eustice, Alfred LeRoy 1884-1943 *NatCAB 32*

Eustis, Abraham 1786-1843 *ApCAB, Drake,*
TwCBDA

Eustis, Allan Chotard 1876-1966 *NatCAB 53*

Eustis, Allan Chotard, Jr. 1904-1974 *WhAm 6*

Eustis, Arthur Galen 1901-1959 *WhAm 3*

Eustis, Augustus Hemenway 1877-1969
WhAm 5

Eustis, Dorothy Leib Harrison Wood 1886-1946
DcAmB S4, NotAW

Eustis, Frederic Augustus 1877- *WhAm 5*

Eustis, George 1796-1858 *ApCAB, BiAUS,*
DcAmB, Drake, NatCAB 7, TwCBDA,
WhAm H

Eustis, George 1828-1872 *ApCAB, BiAUS,*
BiDrAC, DcAmB, TwCBDA, WhAm H,
WhAmP

Eustis, Henry Lawrence 1819-1885 *ApCAB,*
DcAmB, NatCAB 22, TwCBDA,
WhAm H

Eustis, James Biddle 1834-1899 *ApCAB,*
BiDrAC, DcAmB, NatCAB 1, TwCBDA,
WhAm H, WhAm 1, WhAmP

Eustis, John Edward 1847-1929 *WhAm 1*

Eustis, John Edwin 1847-1929 *NatCAB 25*

Eustis, John Peltz 1858-1923 *ApCAB X*

Eustis, Percy Sprague 1857- *WhAm 4*

Eustis, William 1753-1825 *AmBi, ApCAB,*
BiAUS, BiDrAC, BiDrUSE, DcAmB,
Drake, NatCAB 5, TwCBDA, WhAm H,
WhAmP

Eustis, William Corcoran 1862-1921
NatCAB 49

Eustis, William Henry 1845-1928 *NatCAB 6,*
NatCAB 25, WhAm 1

Eutocius Of Ascalon 480?- *DcScB*

Eutyches 380?-455 *McGEWB*

Euwer, Anthony Henderson 1877- *WhAm 5*

Evald, Emmy 1857-1946 *WhAm 2*

Evans, Adelaide Rebecca *WomWWA 14*

Evans, Alexander 1818-1888 *BiAUS, BiDrAC,*
WhAm H, WhAmP

Evans, Alexander Mason 1885-1938
NatCAB 29

Evans, Alexander William 1868-1959
DcScB Sup, NatCAB 50, WhAm 3

Evans, Alfred Randall 1849-1930 *NatCAB 23*

Evans, Alice Catherine 1881-1975 *WhAm 6*

Evans, Allan 1903-1970 *WhAm 5*

Evans, Alvin 1845-1906 *BiDrAC, WhAm 1*

Evans, Alvin Eleazer 1878-1953 *WhAm 3*

Evans, Andrew Browne 1888-1957 *NatCAB 46*

Evans, Andrew Wallace 1829- *WhAm 4*

Evans, Anne 1871-1941 *NotAW*

Evans, Anthony Harrison 1862-1942 *WhAm 2*

Evans, Anthony Walton White 1817-1886
ApCAB, NatCAB 10

Evans, Anthony Walton Whyte 1817-1886
DcAmB, WhAm H

Evans, Arthur Grant 1858-1928 *NatCAB 27,*
WhAm 1

Evans, Sir Arthur John 1851-1941 *McGEWB*

Evans, Arthur Maybury 1874-1967 *WhAm 4*

Evans, Arthur Seth 1887-1955 *NatCAB 44*

Evans, Arthur Thompson 1888-1943 *WhAm 2*

Evans, Augusta J 1836-1909 *Drake*

Evans, Augusta Jane d1909 *NotAW, TwCBDA*

Evans, Augusta Jane 1835-1909 *ApCAB,*
BiDConf, DcAmB

Evans, Aurelius Augustus 1862-1935 *WhAm 1,*
WhAm 1C

Evans, Austin Patterson 1883-1962 *NatCAB 52,*
WhAm 4

Evans, B R *NewYHSD*

Evans, Bernard *NewYHSD*

Evans, Beverly Daniel 1865-1922 *NatCAB 6,*
WhAm 1

Evans, Blanche Estelle Kahler *WomWWA 14*

Evans, Britton Duroc 1858-1920 *NatCAB 9,*
WhAm 1

Evans, Cadwallader, Jr. 1880-1966 *WhAm 4*

Evans, Caleb 1737-1791 *ApCAB, Drake*

Evans, Cecil Eugene 1871- *WhAm 6*

Evans, Charles 1850-1935 *DcAmB S1,*
DcAmLiB, NatCAB 38, WhAm 1

Evans, Charles 1870-1964 *WhAm 4*

Evans, Charles A *NewYHSD*

Evans, Charles Black 1866-1933 *NatCAB 25*

Evans, Charles Evan 1856- *NatCAB 11*

Evans, Charles Hawes 1897-1963 *NatCAB 51*

Evans, Charles Napoleon 1866- *WhAm 4*

Evans, Charles Robley 1866-1954 *BiDrAC,*
WhAm 4, WhAmP

Evans, Charles Rountree 1863-1920 *WhAm 1*

Evans, Clement Anselm 1833-1911 *BiDConf,*
DcAmB, NatCAB 22, TwCBDA,
WhAm 1

Evans, Clinton Buswell 1848-1923 *WhAm 1*

Evans, Cornelius Henry 1841-1902 *NatCAB 7*

Evans, Curtis Alban 1879-1947 *WhAm 2*

Evans, Dafydd Joshua 1846-1926 *WhAm 1*

Evans, Daniel 1866-1943 *WhAm 2*

Evans, Daniel Henry 1838- *WhAm 4*

Evans, David 1852-1923 *ApCAB X,*
NatCAB 6

Evans, David 1874-1958 *NatCAB 44*

Evans, David Ellicott 1788-1850 *BiAUS,*
BiDrAC, WhAm H

Evans, David Evan 1890-1960 *NatCAB 48*

Evans, David Lloyd 1854-1929 *NatCAB 22*

Evans, David Reid 1769-1843 *ApCAB, BiAUS,*
BiDrAC, WhAm H

Evans, DeScott 1847- *ApCAB, TwCBDA,*
WhAm 4

Evans, Donald 1882-1954 *NatCAB 44,*
WhAm 3

Evans, Donald 1884-1921 *WhAm 1*

Evans, Dudley 1838-1910 *NatCAB 6,*
WhAm 1

Evans, E S *NewYHSD*

Evans, Earle Wood 1873-1940 *NatCAB 31,*
WhAm 1

Evans, Edgar Hanks 1870-1954 *NatCAB 45,*
WhAm 3

Evans, Edith Brazwell 1912-1964 *WhAm 4*

Evans, Edith J Claggett *WomWWA 14*

Evans, Edward *BnEnAmA*

Evans, Edward 1860-1932 *NatCAB 49,*

WhAm 1

Evans, Edward Andrew 1892-1951 *WhAm 3*

Evans, Edward Baker 1861- *WhAm 4*

Evans, Edward Benjamin 1908-1971 *WhAm 5*

Evans, Edward Bering 1900-1966 *NatCAB 52*

Evans, Edward Payson 1831-1917 *AmBi,*
DcAmB, WhAm 4

Evans, Edward Payson 1833-1917 *ApCAB,*
NatCAB 9, TwCBDA

Evans, Edward Steptoe 1879-1945 *NatCAB 37,*
WhAm 2

Evans, Edwin 1860-1946 *IIBEAAW*

Evans, Elisha Nero 1857- *NatCAB 11*

Evans, Eliza 1887- *WomWWA 14*

Evans, Eliza T Sparc *WomWWA 14*

Evans, Elizabeth Edson Gibson 1832-1911
WhAm 1

Evans, Elizabeth Edson Gibson 1833-1911
ApCAB, TwCBDA

Evans, Elizabeth Gardiner 1856- *BiCAW,*
WhAm 4

Evans, Elizabeth Glendower 1856-1937 *NotAW*

Evans, Elizabeth Hewlings 1818-1855 *ApCAB*

Evans, Elmira Lee 1885- *WomWWA 14*

Evans, Elsa Elizabeth 1866- *WomWWA 14*

Evans, Elwyn 1895-1948 *WhAm 2*

Evans, Emory Gibbons 1928- *EncAAH*

Evans, Ernestine 1867-1967 *WhAm 4*

Evans, Evan *NatCAB 18*

Evans, Evan 1671-1721 *ApCAB, DcAmB*

Evans, Evan Alfred 1876-1948 *NatCAB 40,*
WhAm 2

Evans, Evan Wilhelm 1827-1874 *TwCBDA*

Evans, Evan William 1827-1874 *ApCAB*

Evans, Everett Idris 1909-1954 *NatCAB 42,*
WhAm 3

Evans, Everett James 1882-1951 *NatCAB 41*

Evans, Florence Wilkinson *WomWWA 14*

Evans, Frank 1873-1950 *WhAm 3*

Evans, Frank Alexander 1890-1956 *NatCAB 50*

Evans, Frank Edgar 1876-1941 *WhAm 2*

Evans, Frank Edward 1923- *BiDrAC*

Evans, Frank Williams 1877-1952 *NatCAB 40*

Evans, Fred M 1895- *WhAm 5*

Evans, Frederic Dahl 1866-1953 *WhAm 3*

Evans, Frederick 1865- *WhAm 4*

Evans, Frederick Huffman 1924-1971
NatCAB 57

Evans, Frederick John Owen 1815-1885 *DcScB*

Evans, Frederick Noble 1881-1946 *WhAm 2*

Evans, Frederick Walter 1880- *WhAm 6*

Evans, Frederick William 1808-1893 *ApCAB,*
DcAmB, NatCAB 11, TwCBDA,
WhAm H

Evans, Fremont 1878-1946 *NatCAB 36*

Evans, George 1797-1867 *ApCAB, BiAUS,*
BiDrAC, DcAmB, Drake, NatCAB 6,
TwCBDA, WhAm H, WhAmP

Evans, George 1844- *WhAm 4*

Evans, George Alfred 1850-1925 *DcAmB*

Evans, George Ballentine 1855- *WhAm 4*

Evans, Sir George DeLacy 1787-1870 *ApCAB,*
Drake

Evans, George E 1856-1931 *WhAm 1*

Evans, George Edward 1876-1945 *NatCAB 34,*
WhAm 2

Evans, George Henry 1805-1855 *ApCAB*

Evans, George Henry 1805-1856 *AmBi,*
DcAmB, McGEWB, WebAB, WhAm H

Evans, George L d1973 *WhAm 6*

Evans, George Watkin 1876-1951 *WhAm 3*

Evans, Griffith Conrad 1887-1973 *WhAm 6*

Evans, H David 1872- *WhAm 5*

Evans, H Sugden 1830- *ApCAB*

Evans, Hannah 1801-1860 *NewYHSD*

Evans, Harold Sulser 1895-1959 *WhAm 3*

Evans, Harry Carroll 1858-1932 *WhAm 1*

Evans, Harry Fifield 1884-1949 *NatCAB 38*

Evans, Harry G 1862-1930 *WhAm 1*

Evans, Harry Marshall Erskine 1876-1973
WhAm 6

Evans, Henry 1860-1924 *WhAm 1*

Evans, Henry Clay 1843-1921 *ApCAB Sup,*
BiDrAC, DcAmB, NatCAB 13,
NatCAB 28, TwCBDA, WhAm 1,
WhAmP

Evans, Henry Clay 1851- *WhAm 3*

Evans, Henry G 1812-1869 *ApCAB*

Evans, Henry Ridgely 1861-1949 *NatCAB 9,*
WhAm 2
Evans, Herbert Francis 1878-1958 *NatCAB 49,*
WhAm 4
Evans, Herbert McLean 1882-1971 *NatCAB 57*
Evans, Herbert P 1900-1959 *WhAm 3*
Evans, Herbert Silas 1875-1961 *NatCAB 49*
Evans, Hiram Kinsman 1863-1941 *BiDrAC,*
NatCAB 42, WhAm 1, WhAmP
Evans, Hiram Wesley 1881- *WhAm 6*
Evans, Holden Allen 1871- *ApCAB X*
Evans, Howard Rector 1897-1962 *WhAm 4*
Evans, Howell Gershom 1899-1963 *NatCAB 50,*
WhAm 4
Evans, Hugh Davey 1792-1868 *ApCAB,*
DcAmB, TwCBDA
Evans, Hugh Davy 1792-1868 *Drake,*
NatCAB 3
Evans, Hugh Ivan 1887-1958 *WhAm 3*
Evans, Ira Hobart 1844-1923 *WhAm 1*
Evans, Isaac Blair 1885-1941 *WhAm 1*
Evans, Isaac Newton 1827-1901 *BiDrAC*
Evans, J G *NewYHSD*
Evans, J M *NewYHSD*
Evans, James *NewYHSD*
Evans, James 1831-1909 *WhAm 1*
Evans, James B 1829?- *NewYHSD*
Evans, James LaFayette 1825-1903 *BiAUS,*
BiDrAC
Evans, Jervice Gaylord 1833-1910 *TwCBDA,*
WhAm 1
Evans, Jessie Benton 1866- *IIBEAAW,*
WhAm 5
Evans, Joe 1857-1898 *NatCAB 11, TwCBDA*
Evans, John *BiAUS, BiDrAC, DcAmB,*
NewYHSD, WhAm H
Evans, John 1678- *ApCAB, NatCAB 5*
Evans, John 1728-1783 *NatCAB 17*
Evans, John 1812-1861 *ApCAB, Drake,*
TwCBDA
Evans, John 1814-1897 *AmBi, DcAmB,*
NatCAB 6, REnAW, TwCBDA, WebAB,
WhAm H
Evans, John 1890-1965 *WhAm 4*
Evans, John Brooke 1872-1956 *WhAm 3*
Evans, John C d1957 *WhAm 3*
Evans, John Fairhurst 1891-1970 *WhAm 5*
Evans, John Gary 1863-1942 *NatCAB 12,*
WhAm 2
Evans, John Henry 1919-1973 *WhAm 6*
Evans, John Morgan 1863-1946 *BiDrAC,*
WhAm 4, WhAmP
Evans, John Morris 1877-1948 *WhAm 2*
Evans, John Norris d1953 *WhAm 3*
Evans, John Robert 1898-1967 *NatCAB 57*
Evans, John T *NewYHSD*
Evans, John W *NewYHSD*
Evans, John William 1855-1943 *WhAm 2*
Evans, Jonathan Henry 1830- *NatCAB 18*
Evans, Joseph E 1919-1971 *WhAm 5*
Evans, Joseph Spragg 1875-1948 *WhAm 2*
Evans, Joshua, Jr. 1777-1846 *BiAUS, BiDrAC,*
WhAm H
Evans, Joshua, Jr. 1877-1970 *WhAm 5*
Evans, Josiah James 1786-1858 *ApCAB,*
BiAUS, BiDrAC, Drake, NatCAB 7,
TwCBDA, WhAm H
Evans, Lawrence Boyd 1870-1928 *DcAmB,*
WhAm 1
Evans, Lawton Bryan 1862-1934 *BiDAmEd,*
NatCAB 13, WhAm 1
Evans, Lemuel Dale 1810-1877 *BiAUS,*
BiDrAC, NatCAB 4, WhAm H
Evans, Letitia Pate 1872-1953 *WhAm 3*
Evans, Lewis 1700?-1756 *AmBi, ApCAB,*
DcAmB, DcScB, NatCAB 11
Evans, Lewis Orvis d1931 *WhAm 1*
Evans, Lizzie P E 1846- *AmWom*
Evans, Louis 1700?-1756 *Drake*
Evans, Lynden 1858-1926 *BiDrAC*
Evans, Marcellus Hugh 1884-1953 *BiDrAC,*
WhAm 3
Evans, Margaret J 1842- *WomWWA 14*
Evans, Marguerite 1876- *WomWWA 14*
Evans, Marion Griffin 1877-1957 *NatCAB 43*
Evans, Marshall Blakemore 1874- *WhAm 5*
Evans, Mary 1841- *WhAm 4, WomWWA 14*
Evans, Mary Anna Buck 1857- *WomWWA 14*

Evans, Mary Elizabeth *BiCAW*
Evans, Milton G 1862-1939 *NatCAB 38,*
WhAm 1
Evans, Montgomery 1853- *WhAm 4*
Evans, Nathan 1804-1879 *BiAUS, BiDrAC,*
WhAm H
Evans, Nathan George 1824-1868 *ApCAB,*
DcAmB, NatCAB 12, WhAm H
Evans, Nathan George 1829?-1868 *Drake*
Evans, Nathaniel 1742-1767 *ApCAB, DcAmB,*
Drake
Evans, Nathaniel, Jr. *NewYHSD*
Evans, Nelson Frazer 1889-1922 *NatCAB 20*
Evans, Nelson Wiley 1842-1913 *WhAm 1*
Evans, Newton 1874-1945 *WhAm 2*
Evans, Nora Belle 1865- *WomWWA 14*
Evans, Norman West 1852-1915 *NatCAB 17*
Evans, Oliver 1755-1819 *AmBi, ApCAB,*
DcAmB, Drake, EncAAH, EncAB,
McGEWB, NatCAB 6, TwCBDA,
WebAB, WhAm H
Evans, Percy Henriques 1873- *WhAm 5*
Evans, Peyton Randolph 1892-1972 *WhAm 5*
Evans, Ralph Berrell 1883-1936 *NatCAB 28*
Evans, Ray O 1887-1954 *NatCAB 43,*
WhAm 3
Evans, Raymond Leslie 1895-1963 *NatCAB 51*
Evans, Richard 1923- *IIBEAAW*
Evans, Richard Bunton 1902-1967 *WhAm 4*
Evans, Richard Joseph 1837-1916 *TwCBDA,*
WhAm 1
Evans, Richard Laylord 1904-1969 *NatCAB 54*
Evans, Richard Louis 1906-1971 *WhAm 5*
Evans, Richard Taylor 1885-1940 *NatCAB 30*
Evans, Robert Dawson 1843-1909 *NatCAB 14*
Evans, Robert Emory 1856-1925 *BiDrAC,*
WhAm 1, WhAmP
Evans, Robert Kennon 1852-1926 *WhAm 1*
Evans, Robert T 1906-1967 *WhAm 4*
Evans, Robert Wilson 1888- *ApCAB X*
Evans, Robley Dunglison 1846-1912 *AmBi,*
ApCAB Sup, DcAmB, TwCBDA,
WebAMB, WhAm 1
Evans, Robley Dunglison 1847-1912 *NatCAB 9*
Evans, Ronald Krake 1889-1964 *NatCAB 52*
Evans, Rudolph Martin 1890-1956 *NatCAB 46,*
WhAm 3
Evans, Rudulph 1878-1960 *WhAm 3*
Evans, Sarah Anne *WomWWA 14*
Evans, Scott 1905-1968 *NatCAB 54*
Evans, Silas 1875-1959 *NatCAB 47*
Evans, Silas 1876-1959 *WhAm 3*
Evans, Silliman 1894-1955 *NatCAB 43,*
WhAm 3
Evans, Silliman, Jr. 1925-1961 *WhAm 4*
Evans, T Raymond 1878-1931 *NatCAB 40*
Evans, Thomas *BiAUS, BiDrAC, NewYHSD,*
WhAm H
Evans, Thomas 1798-1868 *ApCAB, DcAmB,*
Drake, NatCAB 3
Evans, Thomas 1842- *NatCAB 13, WhAm 4*
Evans, Thomas 1916-1973 *WhAm 6*
Evans, Thomas Crain 1860- *WhAm 4*
Evans, Thomas Lynn 1896-1970 *NatCAB 57*
Evans, Thomas William 1823-1897 *TwCBDA*
Evans, Thomas Wiltberger 1823-1897 *ApCAB,*
DcAmB, NatCAB 9
Evans, Thomas Wyche 1818- *NatCAB 3*
Evans, Titus Carr 1907-1975 *WhAm 6*
Evans, Victor Justice 1865- *NatCAB 16*
Evans, Walker 1903-1975 *BnEnAmA, EncAB,*
WebAB, WhAm 6
Evans, Walter *NewYHSD*
Evans, Walter 1842-1923 *BiDrAC, DcAmB,*
NatCAB 17, TwCBDA, WhAm 1,
WhAmP
Evans, Walter Chew 1898-1952 *WhAm 3*
Evans, Walter Harrison 1863- *WhAm 5*
Evans, Walter Howard 1870-1959 *WhAm 3*
Evans, Ward Vinton 1880-1957 *NatCAB 46,*
WhAm 3
Evans, Warren Felt 1817-1889 *DcAmB,*
DcAmReB, NatCAB 22
Evans, William *NewYHSD*
Evans, William 1786-1857 *ApCAB*
Evans, William 1870-1950 *NatCAB 40,*
NatCAB 47, WhAm 3
Evans, William Augustus 1865-1948 *WhAm 2*

Evans, William Carruthers 1871-1958
NatCAB 47
Evans, William Davis 1852-1936 *NatCAB 18,*
NatCAB 28, WhAm 1
Evans, William Dent, Jr. 1907-1969 *WhAm 5*
Evans, William Elmer 1877-1959 *BiDrAC,*
WhAm 3, WhAmP
Evans, William Frank 1859- *WhAm 1*
Evans, William Gray 1855-1924 *WhAm 1*
Evans, William Harry 1876-1956 *DcScB*
Evans, William John 1914-1963 *WhAm 4*
Evans, William Joseph 1880-1952 *NatCAB 39*
Evans, William Lloyd 1870-1954 *NatCAB 40,*
WhAm 3
Evans, William Ney 1898-1973 *WhAm 6*
Evans, William Pascoe 1886-1971 *NatCAB 55*
Evans, William Prentice 1861- *WhAm 4*
Evans, William Thomas 1843-1918 *ApCAB X,*
DcAmB, NatCAB 32
Evans, Wilmot Roby 1878- *WhAm 1*
Evans, Wilmoth Duane 1909-1974 *WhAm 6*
Evans-Pritchard, Sir Edward Evan 1902-
McGEWB
Evanturel, Francis Eugene Alfred 1849-
ApCAB Sup
Evarest, H G *NewYHSD*
Evarts, Allen Wardner 1848-1939 *WhAm 1*
Evarts, Edward Mark 1888-1933 *WhAm 1*
Evarts, Hal G 1887-1934 *WhAm 1*
Evarts, Jeremiah 1781-1831 *ApCAB, DcAmB,*
Drake, NatCAB 2
Evarts, Maxwell d1913 *WhAm 1*
Evarts, Prescott 1859-1931 *NatCAB 42*
Evarts, Richard Conover 1890-1972 *WhAm 5*
Evarts, William Maxwell 1818-1901 *AmBi,*
ApCAB, BiAUS, BiDrAC, BiDrUSE,
DcAmB, Drake, McGEWB, NatCAB 3,
NatCAB 27, TwCBDA, WebAB,
WhAm 1, WhAmP
Evatt, Clay Welborn 1898-1969 *NatCAB 53*
Evatt, Herbert Vere 1894-1965 *McGEWB,*
WhAm 4, WhWW-II
Evatt, William Steinwedell 1892-1970 *WhAm 5*
Eve, Duncan 1853- *WhAm 4*
Eve, Henry Prontaut 1917-1969 *WhAm 5*
Eve, Joseph *BiAUS*
Eve, Joseph 1760-1835 *DcAmB, WhAm H*
Eve, Joseph Adams 1805- *ApCAB*
Eve, Maria Lou 1848?- *ApCAB*
Eve, Maria Louise 1848- *AmWom*
Eve, Paul Fitzsimmons 1806-1877 *NatCAB 10,*
TwCBDA
Eve, Paul Fitzsimmons 1857- *NatCAB 10*
Eve, Paul Fitzsimons 1806-1877 *ApCAB,*
DcAmB, WhAm H
Eve, Robert Campbell 1843- *ApCAB*
Eveland, Samuel Schrack 1869-1932
NatCAB 42, WhAm 1
Eveland, William Perry 1864-1916 *WhAm 1*
Eveleigh, Nicholas 1748?-1791 *BiAUS,*
BiDrAC, WhAm H, WhAmP
Eveleth, Charles Edward 1876-1933 *NatCAB 24*
Eveleth, Louise Friend Parsons *WomWWA 14*
Eveleth, Malcolm Standish 1913-1956
NatCAB 47
Eveleth, True Ballentine 1904-1969 *WhAm 5*
Eveline, Robert *ApCAB*
Evelyn, John 1620-1706 *DcScB, McGEWB*
Evelyn, Judith d1967 *WhAm 4*
Evelyn, Sister Mary d1955 *WhAm 3*
Even, Louis *NewYHSD*
Even, Lucas *NewYHSD*
Evenden, Edward Samuel 1884-1957
NatCAB 46, WhAm 3
Evens, Alfred 1881- *WhAm 6*
Evens, Platt, Jr. *NewYHSD*
Evens, Theodore A *NewYHSD*
Everall, Amy Ford 1879- *WomWWA 14*
Everard, James 1829-1913 *NatCAB 16*
Everard, Lewis Charles 1884-1943 *WhAm 2*
Everard, Sir Richard d1733 *ApCAB, Drake,*
NatCAB 9
Everdell, Charles *NewYHSD*
Everdell, Frank *NewYHSD*
Everdell, George *NewYHSD*
Everdell, Henry *NewYHSD*
Everdell, James 1819?- *NewYHSD*
Everdell, Martin *NewYHSD*

Everdell, William *NewYHSD*
Everdell, William 1799?- *NewYHSD*
Everdell, William, Jr. *NewYHSD*
Everendon, Walter d1725 *DcAmB, WhAm H*
Everest, Charles Marvin 1852-1917 *NatCAB 22*
Everest, Charles William 1814-1877 *ApCAB, Drake*
Everest, David Clark 1883-1955 *NatCAB 45, WhAm 3*
Everest, Frank Fort 1869-1939 *WhAm 1*
Everest, Harold Philip 1893-1967 *WhAm 4A*
Everest, Harvey William 1831- *TwCBDA*
Everest, Herbert Austin 1885-1959 *NatCAB 47*
Everest, Hiram Bond 1830-1913 *NatCAB 17*
Everett, Alexander Hill 1790-1847 *AmBi, BiAUS, DcAmB, Drake, NatCAB 9, TwCBDA, WhAm H*
Everett, Alexander Hill 1792-1847 *ApCAB*
Everett, Arthur Greene 1855-1925 *WhAm 1*
Everett, Charles Carroll 1829-1900 *AmBi, ApCAB, DcAmB, NatCAB 9, TwCBDA, WhAm 1*
Everett, Charles Horatio 1855-1936 *WhAm 3*
Everett, Clara Winter *WomWWA 14*
Everett, David 1770-1813 *ApCAB, DcAmB, Drake, NatCAB 7*
Everett, Edward 1794-1865 *AmBi, ApCAB, BiAUS, BiDrAC, BiDrUSE, DcAmB, Drake, McGEWB, NatCAB 1, NatCAB 6, TwCBDA, WebAB, WhAm H, WhAmP*
Everett, Edward 1818-1900? *NewYHSD*
Everett, Edward Franklin 1840-1899 *ApCAB, TwCBDA*
Everett, Edward Warren 1872-1940 *ApCAB X, NatCAB 31*
Everett, Elizabeth Hawley 1857- *WomWWA 14*
Everett, Erastus 1813-1900 *ApCAB, TwCBDA*
Everett, Francis Dewey 1889-1974 *WhAm 6*
Everett, Frank Henry 1872-1957 *NatCAB 47*
Everett, George Abram 1875-1958 *WhAm 3*
Everett, Harry Harding 1875-1949 *NatCAB 37, WhAm 3*
Everett, Henry Azariah 1856-1917 *NatCAB 28, WhAm 1*
Everett, Henry Azarian 1856-1917 *NatCAB 13*
Everett, Henry Coffin 1859-1945 *NatCAB 34*
Everett, Henry Coffin, Jr. 1891-1963 *NatCAB 53*
Everett, Henry Sidney 1834-1898 *NatCAB 9*
Everett, Herbert Edward 1862-1932 *NatCAB 30*
Everett, Herbert Edward 1863-1932 *WhAm 1*
Everett, Hermon David 1891-1947 *NatCAB 37*
Everett, Homer 1884-1913 *NatCAB 28*
Everett, Horace 1779-1851 *BiDrAC, WhAm H, WhAmP*
Everett, Horace 1780-1851 *ApCAB, BiAUS, Drake, TwCBDA*
Everett, Howard 1870-1962 *WhAm 4*
Everett, Ida Josephine *WomWWA 14*
Everett, John 1801-1826 *ApCAB*
Everett, Joseph 1732-1809 *ApCAB*
Everett, Joseph Alma Freestone 1883?-1945 *IIBEAAW*
Everett, Leolyn Louise 1888- *WomWWA 14*
Everett, Louella Dorothea d1967 *WhAm 4A*
Everett, Marvin Niles 1828-1909 *NatCAB 17*
Everett, Raymond 1885- *IIBEAAW*
Everett, Robert 1791-1875 *DcAmB*
Everett, Robert Ashton 1915-1969 *BiDrAC, WhAm 5, WhAmP*
Everett, Robert William 1839-1915 *BiDrAC, NatCAB 2, TwCBDA*
Everett, Sidney Johnston 1862- *WhAm 2*
Everett, Walter Goodnow 1860- *WhAm 1*
Everett, William 1839-1910 *ApCAB, BiDrAC, NatCAB 9, TwCBDA, WhAm 1*
Everett, William Henry 1847-1912 *WhAm 1*
Everett, William Sprague 1839- *NatCAB 5*
Everett, William Wade 1871-1949 *WhAm 3*
Everett, Willis Mead 1863-1943 *WhAm 2*
Evergood, Philip 1901-1973 *BnEnAmA, McGEWB, WhAm 5*
Everhard, Caroline McCullough 1843- *AmWom*
Everhard, Eleanora S 1867- *WomWWA 14*
Everhart, Benjamin Matlack 1818-1904 *AmBi,*

ApCAB, NatCAB 10, TwCBDA, WhAm 1
Everhart, Isaiah Fawkes 1840- *NatCAB 5*
Everhart, James Bowen 1821-1888 *ApCAB, BiDrAC, NatCAB 3, TwCBDA, WhAm H*
Everhart, James Marion 1828- *NatCAB 5*
Everhart, John Roskell 1828- *NatCAB 3, TwCBDA*
Everhart, Mahlon Thatcher 1873-1955 *WhAm 3*
Everhart, William 1785-1867 *NatCAB 3, TwCBDA*
Everhart, William 1785-1868 *BiDrAC, WhAm H*
Everhartt, William *BiAUS*
Everill, Royal Burdette 1904-1969 *WhAm 5*
Everit, Edward Hotchkiss 1870- *WhAm 5*
Everite, G *NewYHSD*
Everitt, Charles Raymond 1901-1947 *WhAm 2*
Everitt, Chauncey Valentine 1878-1953 *NatCAB 40*
Everitt, Ella B *WomWWA 14*
Everitt, George Bain 1885-1941 *WhAm 1*
Everleigh, Ada 1876-1960 *DcAmB S4*
Everleigh, Minna 1878-1948 *DcAmB S4, NotAW*
Everly, Morton *NewYHSD*
Evermann, Barton Warren 1853-1932 *AmBi, DcAmB S1, NatCAB 13, TwCBDA, WhAm 1*
Evers, Charles 1923- *WebAB*
Evers, Helen Margaret *WomWWA 14*
Evers, John 1797-1884 *NatCAB 5, NewYHSD*
Evers, Medgar Wiley 1925- *WebAB*
Evers, Theodore *NewYHSD*
Evershed, John 1864-1956 *DcScB*
Eversman, Alice d1974 *WhAm 6*
Eversman, Walter A 1880-1960 *WhAm 4*
Everson, William Graham d1954 *WhAm 3*
Eversull, Frank Hubert 1903-1970 *NatCAB 56*
Eversull, Frank Lissenden 1892-1964 *WhAm 4*
Eversull, Harry Kelso 1893-1953 *WhAm 3*
Eversz, Moritz Ernst 1843- *WhAm 4*
Everts, Orpheus 1826-1903 *ApCAB, WhAm 1*
Everts, William Wallace 1814-1890 *ApCAB, NatCAB 11, TwCBDA*
Everts, William Wallace 1849- *TwCBDA*
Evertsen, Cornelis *ApCAB*
Evertson, Nicholas *NatCAB 3*
Everwijn, Jan Charles August 1873- *WhAm 5*
Evett, Robert 1922-1975 *WhAm 6*
Evins, John Hamilton 1830-1884 *BiDrAC, WhAm H, WhAmP*
Evins, Joseph Landon 1910- *BiDrAC*
Evins, Robert Benson 1875-1933 *WhAm 1*
Evison, Frances Millicent Marion 1880- *WhAm 6*
Evitt, James Edward, Jr. 1912-1973 *WhAm 6*
Evjen, John Oluf 1874-1942 *WhAm 1*
Evjue, William Theodore 1882-1970 *WhAm 5*
Evrett, Isaac 1820-1888 *TwCBDA*
Evvard, John Marcus 1884-1948 *ApCAB X, WhAm 2*
Ewald, Henry Theodore 1885-1953 *WhAm 3*
Ewald, Mark 1879-1941 *NatCAB 31*
Ewald, Martha Robinson *WomWWA 14*
Ewart, Frank Carman 1871-1942 *WhAm 2*
Ewart, Hamilton Glover 1849-1918 *BiDrAC, TwCBDA, WhAm 1*
Ewart, J Kaye 1907-1957 *WhAm 3*
Ewart, Mary Kirkpatrick 1865- *WomWWA 14*
Ewart, Thomas Alexander 1873-1958 *NatCAB 47*
Ewart, Thomas West 1816-1881 *ApCAB, TwCBDA*
Ewart, William Dana 1851-1908 *NatCAB 34*
Ewbank, Henry Lee 1893-1960 *WhAm 4*
Ewbank, James L *NewYHSD*
Ewbank, Louis B 1864- *WhAm 5*
Ewbank, Thomas 1792-1870 *AmBi, ApCAB, BiAUS, DcAmB, Drake, NatCAB 7, TwCBDA, WhAm H*
Ewell, Arthur Woolsey 1873- *WhAm 5*
Ewell, Benjamin Stoddert 1810-1894 *AmBi, ApCAB, BiDAmEd, DcAmB, Drake, NatCAB 3, TwCBDA*
Ewell, Elliott Gordon 1902-1965 *WhAm 4*
Ewell, Ervin Edgar 1867-1904 *WhAm 1*

Ewell, Glenn Blackmer 1880- *WhAm 6*
Ewell, James 1773-1832 *DcAmB, WhAm H*
Ewell, Joseph Emerson 1839- *NatCAB 12*
Ewell, Marshall Davis 1844-1928 *ApCAB, ApCAB X, NatCAB 12, TwCBDA, WhAm 1*
Ewell, Richard Stoddard 1820?-1872 *Drake, Drake Sup*
Ewell, Richard Stoddert 1817-1872 *AmBi, ApCAB, BiDConf, DcAmB, NatCAB 4, TwCBDA, WebAMB, WhAm H, WhoMilH*
Ewell, Thomas d1847 *ApCAB*
Ewell, Thomas 1785-1826 *DcAmB*
Ewen, Edward C 1897-1959 *WhAm 3*
Ewen, John 1810-1877 *NatCAB 16*
Ewen, John Meiggs 1859-1933 *WhAm 1*
Ewen, Mary Cecilia 1836-1866 *ApCAB*
Ewen, Melvin M 1904-1963 *WhAm 4*
Ewen, W C d1954 *WhAm 3*
Ewen, William 1720?- *ApCAB, Drake, NatCAB 1*
Ewen, William Richard Trotter 1880-1942 *NatCAB 32*
Ewer, Bernard Capen 1877- *WhAm 5*
Ewer, Ferdinand Cartwright 1826-1883 *ApCAB, DcAmB, NatCAB 9, TwCBDA, WhAm H*
Ewer, J Bertrand 1908-1958 *NatCAB 46*
Ewer, Warren Baxter 1814-1906 *WhAm 1*
Ewers, Ezra Philetus 1837-1912 *TwCBDA, WhAm 1*
Ewers, John Canfield 1909- *REnAW*
Ewers, John Ray 1877- *WhAm 5*
Ewing, Addie B 1869- *WomWWA 14*
Ewing, Alfred Cyril 1899-1973 *WhAm 6*
Ewing, Alonzo B 1894-1971 *WhAm 5*
Ewing, Amanda Woods 1850- *WomWWA 14*
Ewing, Andrew 1813-1864 *ApCAB, BiAUS, BiDrAC, NatCAB 8, WhAm H*
Ewing, Arthur Eugene 1855-1929 *NatCAB 22, WhAm 1*
Ewing, Arthur Henry 1864-1912 *WhAm 1*
Ewing, Catherine A Fay 1822- *AmWom*
Ewing, Charles 1780-1832 *ApCAB, BiAUS, DcAmB, Drake, NatCAB 7, TwCBDA, WhAm H*
Ewing, Charles 1835-1883 *ApCAB, TwCBDA, WhAm H*
Ewing, Charles Adlai 1878-1942 *NatCAB 31, WhAm 6*
Ewing, Charles H 1866-1935 *WhAm 1*
Ewing, Charles Oscar, Jr. 1897-1970 *NatCAB 55*
Ewing, Cortez Arthur Milton 1896-1962 *NatCAB 52, WhAm 4*
Ewing, David L 1877-1923 *WhAm 1*
Ewing, Dwight Tarbell 1888-1954 *NatCAB 44*
Ewing, Edwin Hickman 1809-1902 *BiAUS, BiDrAC*
Ewing, Emma Pike 1838- *AmWom, TwCBDA, WhAm 4*
Ewing, Ephraim M 1789-1860 *NatCAB 12*
Ewing, Fayette Clay 1862-1956 *WhAm 3*
Ewing, Finis 1773-1841 *ApCAB, DcAmB, NatCAB 11, TwCBDA, WhAm H*
Ewing, George Washington 1808-1888 *BiDConf*
Ewing, Henry Ellsworth 1883-1951 *NatCAB 41, WhAm 3*
Ewing, Hugh *BiAUS*
Ewing, Hugh Boyle 1826-1905 *AmBi, ApCAB, DcAmB, NatCAB 5, TwCBDA, WhAm 1*
Ewing, James 1736-1806 *ApCAB, DcAmB, Drake, TwCBDA, WhAm H*
Ewing, James 1866-1943 *BiHiMed, DcAmB S3, DcScB, NatCAB 18, NatCAB 32, WhAm 2*
Ewing, James Alfred 1855-1935 *DcScB*
Ewing, James Caruthers Rhea 1854-1925 *DcAmB, WhAm 1*
Ewing, James Dunlop 1899-1965 *WhAm 4*
Ewing, James Stevenson 1835-1918 *NatCAB 8, TwCBDA, WhAm 1*
Ewing, John d1857 *BiAUS*
Ewing, John 1732-1802 *AmBi, ApCAB, DcAmB, Drake, NatCAB 1, TwCBDA, WhAm H*

Ewing, John 1789-1858 *BiDrAC, WhAm H*
Ewing, John 1857-1923 *NatCAB 24, WhAm 1*
Ewing, John Alvin 1858-1935 *NatCAB 33*
Ewing, John Dunbrack 1892-1952 *WhAm 3*
Ewing, John Gillespie 1860- *WhAm 4*
Ewing, John Hoge 1796-1887 *BiAUS, BiDrAC, WhAm H*
Ewing, John Thomas 1856-1926 *WhAm 1*
Ewing, Lynn Moore 1903-1958 *WhAm 3*
Ewing, Majl 1903-1967 *WhAm 4*
Ewing, Margaret Wylie *WomWWA 14*
Ewing, Martin B *NewYHSD*
Ewing, Maurice 1906-1974 *WhAm 6*
Ewing, Nathaniel 1848-1914 *WhAm 1*
Ewing, Philemon 1820-1896 *WhAm H*
Ewing, Presley Kittredge 1860-1927 *NatCAB 17, WhAm 1*
Ewing, Presley Underwood 1822-1854 *BiAUS, BiDrAC, TwCBDA, WhAm H*
Ewing, Robert 1859-1931 *WhAm 1*
Ewing, Robert Legan 1878-1934 *WhAm 1*
Ewing, Russell Charles 1906-1972 *WhAm 5*
Ewing, Samuel Edgar 1865-1941 *WhAm 2*
Ewing, Sherman 1901-1975 *WhAm 6*
Ewing, Thomas 1789-1871 *AmBi, ApCAB, BiAUS, BiDrAC, BiDrUSE, DcAmB, Drake, NatCAB 3, NatCAB 25, TwCBDA, WhAm H, WhAmP*
Ewing, Thomas 1829-1896 *AmBi, ApCAB, BiAUS, BiDrAC, DcAmB, Drake, NatCAB 7, NatCAB 25, TwCBDA, WhAm H, WhAmP*
Ewing, Thomas 1862-1942 *ApCAB X, NatCAB 14, NatCAB 31, WhAm 2*
Ewing, Thomas, Jr. 1897-1933 *NatCAB 27*
Ewing, W Howard 1892-1955 *NatCAB 42*
Ewing, William 1853-1932 *WhAm 3*
Ewing, William 1880-1965 *WhAm 4*
Ewing, William Alexander 1842-1918 *ApCAB X, NatCAB 32*
Ewing, William Bellford 1776-1866 *ApCAB*
Ewing, William F C 1899-1965 *WhAm 4*
Ewing, William Green 1848-1914 *NatCAB 8*
Ewing, William Lee Davidson 1795-1846 *ApCAB, BiAUS, BiDrAC, NatCAB 11, TwCBDA, WhAm H*
Ewing, William Maurice 1906- *AsBiEn, McGEWB*
Ewing, William Wilson 1876-1952 *NatCAB 41*
Ewing, Wilson 1901-1952 *NatCAB 41*
Ewoldt, Harold Boaden 1908-1969 *NatCAB 57, WhAm 5*
Ewonwu, Benedict Chuka 1921- *McGEWB*
Ewry, Ray C 1873-1937 *WebAB*
Exall, Henry 1848-1913 *NatCAB 2, WhAm 1*
Exall, May Dickson 1859- *WomWWA 14*
Excell, Edwin Othello 1851-1921 *WhAm 1*
Exelmans, Remi Joseph Isidore 1775-1852 *WhoMilH*
Exilious, John G *NewYHSD*
Exline, Frank 1858- *WhAm 4*
Exman, Eugene 1900-1975 *WhAm 6*
Exmouth, Edward Pellew 1757-1833 *ApCAB, Drake*
Exner, Carl *NewYHSD*
Exner, Max Joseph 1871-1943 *WhAm 2*
Expilly, Jean Charles Marie 1814- *ApCAB*
Exton, James Anderson 1844- *WhAm 4*
Exton, William Gustav 1876-1943 *NatCAB 31, WhAm 2*
Eyanson, Charles Louis 1892-1959 *WhAm 4*
Eyck, Hubert Van d1426 *McGEWB*
Eyck, Jan Van 1390?-1441 *McGEWB*
Eycleshymer, Albert Chauncey 1867-1925 *WhAm 1*
Eyerly, Elmer Kendall 1865- *WhAm 4*
Eyerly, James Bryan 1895-1963 *NatCAB 53, WhAm 4*
Eyerman, John 1867- *NatCAB 9, TwCBDA, WhAm 4*
Eylar, Matthew Sample 1869-1948 *NatCAB 37*
Eyles, Don Edgar 1915-1963 *NatCAB 50*
Eyma, Louis Xavier 1816-1876 *ApCAB*
Eyman, Elmer Vail 1885-1955 *NatCAB 45*
Eyman, Frank P 1856- *WhAm 4*
Eyman, Henry Clinton 1856-1925 *NatCAB 21, WhAm 1*
Eyre, Edward John 1815-1901 *ApCAB,*

McGEWB
Eyre, Laurence d1959 *WhAm 3*
Eyre, Sir William 1805-1859 *ApCAB*
Eyre, Wilson 1858-1944 *BnEnAmA, NatCAB 11, TwCBDA, WhAm 2*
Eyring, Carl Ferdinand 1889-1951 *WhAm 3*
Eysmans, Julien L 1874- *WhAm 5*
Eyster, C S *BiAUS*
Eyster, George Senseny 1895-1951 *WhAm 3*
Eyster, John Augustine English 1881- *WhAm 6*
Eyster, Nellie Blessing *AmWom*
Eyster, Nellie Blessing 1831- *ApCAB, TwCBDA*
Eyster, Nellie Blessing 1836- *NatCAB 10, WhAm 4*
Eyster, Penelope Anna Blessing *WomWWA 14*
Eyster, William Henry 1889-1968 *WhAm 5*
Eytel, Carl 1862-1925 *IIBEAAW*
Eytelwein, Johann Albert C 1764-1848 *DcScB*
Eyth, Louis 1838-1889? *IIBEAAW*
Eytinge, Clarence *NewYHSD*
Eytinge, Ernest Oliver Joseph 1880-1935 *NatCAB 41*
Eytinge, Robert *NewYHSD*
Eytinge, Rose 1835-1911 *ApCAB, DcAmB, NotAW*
Eytinge, Rose 1838-1911 *TwCBDA, WhAm 1*
Eytinge, Solomon, Jr. 1833-1905 *IIBEAAW, NewYHSD*
Eyzaguirre, Agustin 1766-1837 *ApCAB*
Eyzaguirre, Domingo 1775-1854 *ApCAB*
Eyzaguirre, Jose Alejo 1783-1850 *ApCAB*
Eyzaguirre, Jose Ignacio 1787?-1850? *ApCAB*
Eyzaguirre, Jose Ignacio Victor 1824-1875 *ApCAB*
Eyzaguirre, Miguel 1770?-1821 *ApCAB*
Ezana *McGEWB*
Ezekiel *McGEWB*
Ezekiel, Mordecai Joseph Brill 1899-1974 *WhAm 6*
Ezekiel, Moses Jacob 1844-1917 *AmBi, ApCAB, DcAmB, NatCAB 18, TwCBDA, WhAm 1*
Ezekiel, Walter Naphtali 1901- *WhAm 4*
Ezell, B F 1886-1965 *WhAm 4*
Ezra *McGEWB*
Ezra, Abraham Ben Meir, Ibn 1090?-1164? *DcScB*

F

Fairbanks, Frank Perley 1875-1939 *WhAm 1*
Fairbanks, Franklin 1828-1895 *ApCAB,*
NatCAB 10, TwCBDA
Fairbanks, Frederick Cole 1881-1940
NatCAB 30, WhAm 1
Fairbanks, George Rainsford 1820- *NatCAB 10,*
TwCBDA, WhAm 4
Fairbanks, Harold Wellman 1860- *WhAm 4*
Fairbanks, Henry 1830-1918 *AmBi, ApCAB,*
DcAmB, NatCAB 10, TwCBDA,
WhAm 1
Fairbanks, Horace 1820-1888 *ApCAB,*
NatCAB 8, TwCBDA
Fairbanks, John Boylston 1855-1940 *IIBEAAW*
Fairbanks, John Leo 1878-1946 *IIBEAAW*
Fairbanks, John Leo 1880-1946 *NatCAB 38,*
WhAm 2
Fairbanks, Joseph Paddock 1806-1855 *ApCAB*
Fairbanks, Rebecca Pike 1841- *WomWWA 14*
Fairbanks, Richard 1883-1944 *NatCAB 33,*
WhAm 2
Fairbanks, Thaddeus 1796-1886 *AmBi,*
ApCAB, DcAmB, NatCAB 10, TwCBDA,
WhAm H
Fairbanks, Warren Charles 1878-1938
NatCAB 35, WhAm 1
Fairbrook, Iva Valeria Smith *WomWWA 14*
Fairbrother, Mary Lamkin Hatchett
WomWWA 14
Fairburn, William Armstrong 1876-1947
DcAmB S4, NatCAB 37, WhAm 2
Fairchild, Alice Bidwell *WomWWA 14*
Fairchild, Arthur Wilson 1876-1956 *WhAm 3*
Fairchild, Ashbel Green 1795-1864 *ApCAB*
Fairchild, Benjamin Lewis 1863-1946 *BiDrAC,*
WhAm 2
Fairchild, Blair 1877-1933 *DcAmB S1*
Fairchild, Cassius 1828-1868 *ApCAB,*
TwCBDA
Fairchild, Charles Grandison 1843-1933
NatCAB 28
Fairchild, Charles Stebbins 1842-1924 *ApCAB,*
ApCAB X, BiDrUSE, DcAmB,
NatCAB 2, TwCBDA, WhAm 1
Fairchild, Clarence A 1871- *WhAm 5*
Fairchild, David Grandison 1869-1954
ApCAB X, DcAmB S5, EncAAH,
WebAB, WhAm 3
Fairchild, David Sturges 1847-1930 *NatCAB 17,*
WhAm 1
Fairchild, David Sturges 1871-1940 *NatCAB 31*
Fairchild, Edward Henry 1815-1889
NatCAB 24, TwCBDA
Fairchild, Edward Thomson 1854-1917
BiDAmEd, NatCAB 19, WhAm 1
Fairchild, Fred Rogers 1877-1966 *NatCAB 54,*
WhAm 4
Fairchild, Fred Ross 1875-1959 *NatCAB 47*
Fairchild, George Thompson 1838-1901
BiDAmEd, DcAmB, NatCAB 25,
TwCBDA, WhAm 1
Fairchild, George Winthrop 1854-1924 *BiDrAC,*
NatCAB 14, WhAm 1, WhAmP
Fairchild, Henry Pratt 1880-1956 *NatCAB 47,*
WhAm 3
Fairchild, Herman LeRoy 1850-1943 *ApCAB,*
NatCAB 13, NatCAB 33, TwCBDA,
WhAm 4
Fairchild, Hoxie N 1894-1973 *WhAm 6*
Fairchild, Hurlstone 1893-1966 *IIBEAAW*
Fairchild, James Harris 1817-1902 *ApCAB,*
BiDAmEd, DcAmB, NatCAB 2,
TwCBDA, WhAm 1
Fairchild, John 1797-1847 *WhAmP*
Fairchild, John W *NewYHSD*
Fairchild, Joseph Schmitz 1903-1962
NatCAB 50, WhAm 4
Fairchild, Julian Douglas 1850-1926
NatCAB 29, WhAm 1
Fairchild, Lewis 1801?- *NewYHSD*
Fairchild, Lucius 1831-1896 *ApCAB, BiAUS,*
DcAmB, Drake, NatCAB 12, TwCBDA,
WhAm H
Fairchild, Maria Augusta 1834- *AmWom*
Fairchild, Mary Salome Cutler 1855-1921
BiDAmEd, DcAmB, DcAmLiB, NotAW
Fairchild, Milton 1865-1939 *WhAm 1*
Fairchild, Muir Stephen 1894-1950 *DcAmB S4,*

NatCAB 39, WhAm 2A
Fairchild, Nellie Rebecca 1875- *WomWWA 14*
Fairchild, Raymond Wilber 1889-1956
NatCAB 42, WhAm 3
Fairchild, Salome Cutler 1855-1921 *NatCAB 20,*
TwCBDA, WhAm 1, WomWWA 14
Fairchild, Samuel William 1853- *ApCAB X*
Fairchild, Sherman M 1896-1971 *WhAm 5*
Fairchild, Thomas Everett 1894-1934 *WhAm 1*
Fairchilds, John W *NewYHSD*
Faircloth, James M 1903-1964 *WhAm 4*
Faircloth, William Turner 1829-1900
NatCAB 12, TwCBDA
Faircloth, William Tyson d1900 *WhAm 1*
Fairclough, Ellen Louks 1905- *McGEWB*
Fairclough, George Herbert 1869- *WhAm 5*
Fairclough, Henry Rushton 1862-1938
BiDAmEd, NatCAB 28, WhAm 1
Faires, Virgil Moring 1897-1969 *WhAm 6*
Fairfax, Albert Kirby 1870-1939 *WhAm 5*
Fairfax, Beatrice *DcAmB S3, NotAW*
Fairfax, Bryan 1730?-1802 *ApCAB, Drake*
Fairfax, Charles Snowden 1829-1869 *ApCAB*
Fairfax, D R *NewYHSD*
Fairfax, Donald MacNeill 1821-1894
NatCAB 4
Fairfax, Donald MacNeill 1822-1894 *TwCBDA*
Fairfax, Donald McNeill 1821-1894 *DcAmB,*
WhAm H
Fairfax, Donald McNeill 1822-1894 *ApCAB,*
Drake
Fairfax, Ferdinand *NewYHSD*
Fairfax, George William d1787 *ApCAB*
Fairfax, John Contee 1830- *ApCAB*
Fairfax, Baron Thomas 1612-1671 *WhoMilH*
Fairfax, Thomas 1691-1781 *Drake*
Fairfax, Thomas 1691-1782 *ApCAB*
Fairfax, Thomas 1693-1781 *DcAmB,*
WhAm H
Fairfax, Thomas 1762-1846 *ApCAB*
Fairfax, W H *NewYHSD*
Fairfax Of Cameron, A K Fairfax, Baron
1870-1939 *AmBi*
Fairfax Of Cameron, T Fairfax, Baron 1693-1781
AmBi
Fairfield, Arthur Philip 1877-1946 *WhAm 2*
Fairfield, Edmund Burke 1821-1904 *DcAmB,*
NatCAB 8
Fairfield, Edward George 1890-1933 *WhAm 1*
Fairfield, Fanny Thompson Wagner
WomWWA 14
Fairfield, Francis Gerry 1844-1887 *ApCAB*
Fairfield, Genevieve Genevra 1832- *ApCAB,*
Drake
Fairfield, Hannah T *NewYHSD*
Fairfield, Jane Frazee *ApCAB*
Fairfield, John 1797-1847 *AmBi, ApCAB,*
BiAUS, BiDrAC, DcAmB, Drake,
NatCAB 6, TwCBDA, WhAm H
Fairfield, Louis William 1858-1930 *BiDrAC,*
WhAm 1, WhAmP
Fairfield, Sumner Lincoln 1803-1844 *ApCAB,*
DcAmB, Drake, NatCAB 12, TwCBDA,
WhAm H
Fairfield, Wynn Cowan 1886-1961 *WhAm 4*
Fairhall, Lawrence Turner 1888-1957
NatCAB 46
Fairhead, John Stirling 1841- *NatCAB 5*
Fairhurst, William 1891-1953 *WhAm 3*
Fairies, John *NewYHSD*
Fairlamb, James Remington 1838-1908 *DcAmB,*
NatCAB 10, WhAm 1
Fairlamb, James Remington 1839-1908 *ApCAB,*
TwCBDA
Fairleigh, David William 1853-1924 *WhAm 1*
Fairleigh, James Franklin 1879-1951
NatCAB 41
Fairless, Benjamin F 1890-1962 *WhAm 4*
Fairley, Edwin 1864-1941 *WhAm 1*
Fairley, William 1857-1918 *WhAm 1*
Fairlie, John Archibald 1872-1947 *DcAmB S4,*
NatCAB 34, WhAm 2
Fairman, David 1782-1815 *ApCAB, Drake,*
NewYHSD
Fairman, F E, Jr. 1899-1958 *WhAm 3*
Fairman, Gideon 1774-1827 *ApCAB, Drake,*
NewYHSD, WhAm H
Fairman, James 1826-1904 *NewYHSD,*

WhAm H
Fairman, James Ferdinand 1896-1967 *WhAm 4*
Fairman, Richard d1821 *Drake*
Fairman, Richard 1787-1821 *ApCAB*
Fairman, Richard 1788-1821 *NewYHSD*
Fairman, Seibert 1896-1961 *NatCAB 50*
Fairman, Selbert 1896-1961 *WhAm 4*
Fairthorne, William 1811?- *NewYHSD*
Fairweather, Clement Wilson 1882-1957
WhAm 3
Fairweather, Jack Hall Alliger Lee 1878-1948
WhAm 2
Faisal I 1883-1933 *McGEWB*
Faisal II, King Of Iraq *WhAm 3*
Faisal, Ibn Abdul Aziz Al Saud 1905-1975
WhAm 6
Faison, John Miller 1862-1915 *BiDrAC,*
WhAm 1
Faison, Samson Lane 1860-1940 *WhAm 1*
Faissler, Jane Byers 1871- *WomWWA 14*
Faith, Percy 1908-1976 *WhAm 6*
Faithorn, John Nicholson 1852-1914 *WhAm 1*
Fajans, Kasimir 1887-1975 *WhAm 6*
Fake, Guy Leverne 1879-1957 *WhAm 3*
Falardeau, Antony Sebastian 1822- *ApCAB*
Falayi, Samual Oladeie 1925- *WhAm 6*
Falck, Alexander Diven 1878-1950 *WhAm 3*
Falckner, Daniel 1666-1741? *DcAmB,*
WhAm H
Falckner, Justus 1662-1723 *WhAm H*
Falckner, Justus 1672-1723 *DcAmB*
Falcon, Juan Christomo d1870 *Drake*
Falconbridge, Elizabeth Porter 1879-
WomWWA 14
Falconbridge, Lady Mary Phoebe 1850-
WomWWA 14
Falconer, Bolivar Lang 1870-1953 *NatCAB 42*
Falconer, Douglas Platt 1889-1969 *WhAm 5*
Falconer, Hugh 1808-1865 *DcScB*
Falconer, Jacob Alexander 1869-1928 *BiDrAC,*
WhAm 5, WhAmP
Falconer, John Ironside 1888-1963 *WhAm 1,*
WhAm 4
Falconer, John Mackie 1820-1903 *ApCAB,*
NewYHSD, TwCBDA, WhAm 1
Falconer, Martha Platt 1862-1941 *NotAW*
Falconer, Robert Clemons 1874-1941 *WhAm 1*
Falconer, William Armistead 1869-1927
WhAm 1
Falconet, Etienne Maurice 1716-1791 *McGEWB*
Falconio, Diomede 1842-1917 *WhAm 1*
Fales, Almira L d1868 *ApCAB, Drake*
Fales, Almon Lawrence 1876-1949 *NatCAB 38*
Fales, Dean Abner 1890-1969 *NatCAB 56*
Fales, DeCoursey 1888-1966 *WhAm 4*
Fales, Elisha Noel 1887-1970 *NatCAB 57*
Fales, Frederick Sayward 1873-1955 *WhAm 3*
Fales, Haliburton, Jr. 1849-1929 *ApCAB X,*
NatCAB 24
Fales, Herbert Peck 1904-1971 *WhAm 5*
Fales, Jonathan Cilley 1836- *WhAm 4*
Fales, Lewis Fisher 1859-1930 *NatCAB 32*
Fales, Palmer Loren 1884-1933 *NatCAB 26*
Fales, Winnifred 1875- *WhAm 5*
Falinski, F *NewYHSD*
Falisi, J Vincent 1885-1957 *NatCAB 49*
Falize, Claudius *NewYHSD*
Falk, Arthur 1873-1946 *NatCAB 34*
Falk, Benjamin Joseph 1853- *NatCAB 5*
Falk, David Archer 1896-1960 *NatCAB 48*
Falk, Elisabeth Vogel 1878- *WomWWA 14*
Falk, Elmer M 1911-1968 *WhAm 6*
Falk, Frederick *NewYHSD*
Falk, Harold Sands 1883-1957 *WhAm 3*
Falk, K George 1880-1953 *NatCAB 42,*
WhAm 3
Falk, Leon 1870-1928 *NatCAB 23*
Falk, Louis 1848-1925 *WhAm 1*
Falk, Maurice 1866-1946 *DcAmB S4,*
WhAm 2
Falk, Myron Samuel 1878-1945 *WhAm 2*
Falk, Otto Herbert 1865-1940 *DcAmB S2,*
WhAm 1
Falk, Ralph 1884-1960 *WhAm 4*
Falk, Sawyer 1898-1961 *WhAm 4*
Falkenhainer, Victor Henry 1868-1931
NatCAB 23
Falkenhausen, Alexander Von 1878- *WhWW-II*

Falkenhayn, Erich Von 1861-1922 *WhoMilH*
Falkenhorst, Nikolaus Von 1885- *WhWW-II*
Falkenstein, Alfons Philip 1908-1960
 NatCAB 48
Falker, Fletiss *NewYHSD*
Falkner, Jefferson Manly 1843- *NatCAB 7,*
 WhAm 4
Falkner, Roland Post 1866-1940 *DcAmB S2,*
 TwCBDA, WhAm 1
Falkner, Thomas 1710-1784 *ApCAB*
Falkner, William Cuthbert *WebAB*
Fall, Albert Bacon 1861-1944 *BiDrAC,*
 BiDrUSE, DcAmB S3, EncAB,
 NatCAB 44, REnAW, WhAm 2,
 WhAmP
Fall, Anna Christy 1855- *AmWom*
Fall, Bernard B 1926-1967 *WhAm 4*
Fall, Charles Gershom 1845-1932 *NatCAB 23,*
 WhAm 1
Fall, Clifford Pervines 1863-1941 *WhAm 1*
Fall, Delos M S 1848-1921 *NatCAB 5,*
 TwCBDA, WhAm 1
Fall, Frank Andrews 1878-1959 *WhAm 3*
Fall, George *NewYHSD*
Fall, Gilbert Haven 1883-1956 *WhAm 3*
Fall, Henry Clinton 1862-1939 *WhAm 1*
Falla, Manuel De 1876-1946 *McGEWB*
Faller, Clement 1819-1901 *NewYHSD*
Fallers, Lloyd Ashton, Jr. 1925-1974 *WhAm 6*
Falley, George Frederick 1883-1962 *WhAm 4*
Falligant, Robert 1839-1902 *NatCAB 1,*
 WhAm 1
Fallis, Iva Campbell Doyle 1883- *WhAm 3*
Fallis, Laurence Sidney 1894-1974 *WhAm 6*
Fallis, William David 1909-1974 *WhAm 6*
Fallon, Bernard Joseph 1880-1956 *WhAm 3*
Fallon, Carlos Eugene 1901-1970 *NatCAB 55*
Fallon, George Hyde 1902- *BiDrAC*
Fallon, John 1901-1951 *NatCAB 40*
Fallon, Lester 1896- *WhAm 5*
Fallopius, Gabriel 1523-1562 *AsBiEn*
Falloppio, Gabriele 1523?-1562 *BiHiMed,*
 DcScB
Fallot, Arthur 1850-1911 *BiHiMed*
Fallows, Alice Katharine d1932 *WhAm 1,*
 WomWWA 14
Fallows, Edward Huntington 1865-1940
 NatCAB 11, WhAm 1
Fallows, Samuel 1835-1922 *AmBi, ApCAB,*
 ApCAB X, DcAmB, NatCAB 9,
 TwCBDA, WhAm 1
Falls, Charles Buckles 1874-1960 *WhAm 4,*
 WhAm 5
Falls, DeWitt Clinton 1864-1937 *ApCAB X,*
 WhAm 1
Falls, Frederick Howard 1885-1974 *WhAm 6*
Falls, Raymond Leonard 1899-1956 *WhAm 4*
Faloon, Dalton Boyles 1895-1952 *NatCAB 41*
False Geber *AsBiEn*
Falsey, William J 1894-1964 *WhAm 4*
Falstad, Clarence Henry 1896-1965 *NatCAB 51*
Falter, John Philip 1910- *IIBEAAW*
Falter, Philip Henry 1875-1958 *NatCAB 48*
Falvey, Daniel Patrick 1906-1962 *WhAm 4*
Falvey, Timothy J 1868-1947 *WhAm 2*
Falvey, Timothy James 1864-1947 *NatCAB 41*
Falvey, Wallace 1894-1958 *WhAm 3*
Fan, Chung-Yen 989-1052 *McGEWB*
Fancher, Albert Thomas 1859-1930 *NatCAB 25*
Fancher, Bertram Hull 1865-1932 *NatCAB 24,*
 WhAm 1
Fancher, Elvadore R 1864-1935 *WhAm 1*
Fancher, Enoch Lewis 1817-1900 *NatCAB 7,*
 TwCBDA
Fancher, Frederick Bartlett 1852- *NatCAB 13,*
 TwCBDA, WhAm 4
Fanciulli, Francesco 1853-1915 *NatCAB 16,*
 WhAm 1
Fane, Frances Gordon 1867- *WhAm 4,*
 WomWWA 14
Faner, Robert Dunn 1906-1967 *WhAm 5*
Faneuil, Peter 1700-1743 *AmBi, ApCAB,*
 DcAmB, Drake, McGEWB, NatCAB 1,
 TwCBDA, WhAm H
Fankuchen, Isidor 1905-1964 *DcScB*
Fannin, James W, Jr. d1836 *Drake*
Fannin, James W, Jr. 1800?-1836 *ApCAB,*
 NatCAB 4, TwCBDA

Fannin, James Walker 1804?-1836 *AmBi,*
 DcAmB, WebAMB, WhAm H
Fannin, Paul Jones 1907- *BiDrAC*
Fanning, Alexander Campbell Wilder 1788-1846
 ApCAB, DcAmB, Drake, WhAm H
Fanning, Cecil 1883-1931 *WhAm 1*
Fanning, Clara Elizabeth 1878- *WomWWA 14*
Fanning, David 1754?-1825 *ApCAB*
Fanning, David 1755?-1825 *AmBi, DcAmB,*
 NatCAB 7, WhAm H
Fanning, David 1756?-1825 *Drake*
Fanning, David Hale 1830-1926 *NatCAB 17*
Fanning, Edmund 1737-1818 *ApCAB, Drake,*
 NatCAB 5
Fanning, Edmund 1739-1818 *AmBi, DcAmB,*
 WhAm H
Fanning, Edmund 1769-1841 *AmBi, DcAmB,*
 WhAm H
Fanning, Golbert d1810 *Drake*
Fanning, John Thomas 1837-1911 *ApCAB,*
 DcAmB, NatCAB 9, TwCBDA,
 WhAm 1
Fanning, Lawrence Stanley 1914-1971 *WhAm 5*
Fanning, Nathaniel 1755-1805 *DcAmB,*
 WebAMB, WhAm H
Fanning, Ralph 1889-1971 *WhAm 5*
Fanning, Raymond Joseph 1893-1976 *WhAm 6*
Fanning, Solomon 1807- *NewYHSD*
Fanning, Thomas *ApCAB*
Fanning, Tolbert 1810-1874 *BiDAmEd,*
 DcAmB, WhAm H
Fanning, Wilmot Everett 1869-1962
 NatCAB 49
Fanny, Aunt *AmBi*
Fano, Gino 1871-1952 *DcScB*
Fanon, Frantz 1925-1961 *McGEWB*
Fanoni, Vincent 1884-1960 *NatCAB 48*
Fanshaw, Daniel 1789-1860 *ApCAB Sup*
Fanshaw, Hubert Valentine 1878-1940
 IIBEAAW
Fanshaw, Samuel Raymond 1814-1888
 NewYHSD
Fanshawe, Edmond Jones 1878- *ApCAB X*
Fansler, Michael Louis 1883-1963 *WhAm 4*
Fansler, Walter A 1889-1963 *NatCAB 50*
Fant, Clyde Edward 1905-1973 *WhAm 6*
Fant, John Clayton 1870-1929 *NatCAB 26,*
 WhAm 1
Fant, Lester Glenn 1875-1946 *WhAm 2*
Fantl, Alfred 1866- *ApCAB X*
Fanton, Mary Annable 1871- *WomWWA 14*
Farabee, Samuel Howard 1882-1939 *WhAm 1*
Farabee, William Curtis 1865-1925 *AmBi,*
 DcAmB, NatCAB 24, WhAm 1
Farabi, Al- *DcScB*
Farabi, Abu Nasr Muhammad Awzalagh, Al-
 870?-950 *DcScB*
Faraday, Michael 1791-1867 *AsBiEn, DcScB,*
 McGEWB
Faragher, Donald Qualtrough 1906-1971
 WhAm 5
Faragher, James Lawrence 1887-1959
 NatCAB 44
Faragher, Warren Fred 1884-1966 *WhAm 4*
Faran, James J d1892 *BiAUS*
Faran, James J 1799-1892 *TwCBDA*
Faran, James John 1808-1892 *BiDrAC,*
 DcAmB, WhAm H, WhAmP
Farber, Benjamin Franklin 1882- *ApCAB X*
Farber, John Clarke 1893-1969 *WhAm 5*
Farber, Sidney 1903-1973 *WhAm 5*
Farber, William Sims 1885-1963 *WhAm 4*
Farbstein, Leonard 1902- *BiDrAC*
Fardwell, Harry R 1902-1973 *WhAm 6*
Farenholt, Ammen 1871-1956 *NatCAB 45,*
 WhAm 5
Farenholt, Oscar Walter 1845-1920 *WhAm 1*
Farey, John 1766-1826 *DcScB*
Farghani, Abu'l-Abbas Ahmad Ibn M, Al- d861?
 DcScB
Fargo, Charles 1831-1900 *ApCAB, WhAm 1*
Fargo, James Congdel 1829-1915 *ApCAB,*
 WhAm 1
Fargo, Lucile Foster 1880-1962 *DcAmLiB,*
 WhAm 6
Fargo, William George 1818-1881 *AmBi,*
 ApCAB, DcAmB, EncAAH, McGEWB,
 NatCAB 12, REnAW, TwCBDA,

WebAB, WhAm H, WhAmP
Fargues, Thomas 1780-1847 *ApCAB, Drake*
Faribault, George Bartholomew 1789-1866
 ApCAB
Faribault, Jean Baptist 1775-1860 *WhAm H*
Faribault, Jean Baptiste 1775-1860 *DcAmB*
Faribault, John Baptist 1769?-1860 *ApCAB,*
 TwCBDA
Faries, David Reid 1891-1944 *NatCAB 37*
Farill, Juan Solares 1902-1973 *WhAm 6*
Farinacci, Nicholas Thomas 1903-1966
 NatCAB 51
Faris, Barry 1889-1966 *WhAm 4*
Faris, Charles Breckenridge 1864-1938
 NatCAB 42, WhAm 1
Faris, Ellsworth 1874-1953 *WhAm 3*
Faris, George Washington 1854-1914 *BiDrAC,*
 TwCBDA, WhAm 1, WhAmP
Faris, Herman Preston 1858-1936 *WhAm 1*
Faris, Hiram 1769-1800 *NewYHSD*
Faris, Hyram 1769-1800 *NewYHSD*
Faris, James Edge 1889-1952 *WhAm 3*
Faris, John Thomson 1871-1949 *NatCAB 42,*
 WhAm 2
Faris, Paul Patton 1877- *WhAm 5*
Faris, Robert Lee 1868-1932 *NatCAB 27,*
 WhAm 1
Faris, William *NewYHSD*
Faris, William Adam 1872-1944 *NatCAB 34*
Farish, Frederick Garesche 1866-1946 *WhAm 2*
Farish, Hunter Dickinson 1897- *WhAm 2*
Farish, William Stamps 1881-1942 *DcAmB S3,*
 NatCAB 32, WhAm 2
Farkas, Laszlo 1904-1948 *DcScB*
Farlee, Isaac Gray 1787-1855 *BiAUS, BiDrAC,*
 WhAm H
Farley, Arthur James 1885-1967 *NatCAB 53*
Farley, E Wilder 1818-1880 *BiAUS*
Farley, Edward Philip 1886-1956 *NatCAB 42,*
 WhAm 3
Farley, Edward Phillip 1886-1956 *NatCAB 17*
Farley, Eliot 1885-1952 *WhAm 3*
Farley, Ephraim Wilder 1817-1880 *BiDrAC,*
 WhAm H
Farley, Eugene Francis 1878-1928 *NatCAB 22*
Farley, Eugene Shedden 1899-1973 *NatCAB 57,*
 WhAm 6
Farley, Frank Edgar 1868-1943 *WhAm 2*
Farley, Franklin 1895-1960 *WhAm 4*
Farley, Frederic Henry Morton Stanley
 1895-1966 *WhAm 4*
Farley, Grace Colvin 1873- *WomWWA 14*
Farley, Harriet d1907 *Drake*
Farley, Harriet 1813?-1907 *NotAW*
Farley, Harriet 1815-1907 *ApCAB,*
 NatCAB 11
Farley, Harriet 1817-1907 *DcAmB*
Farley, Hugh D 1913-1966 *WhAm 4*
Farley, James Aloysius 1888- *BiDrUSE,*
 EncAB, WebAB
Farley, James Indus 1871-1948 *BiDrAC,*
 WhAm 2, WhAmP
Farley, James Thompson 1829-1886 *ApCAB,*
 BiDrAC, NatCAB 4, TwCBDA,
 WhAm H
Farley, John *NewYHSD*
Farley, John Murphy 1842-1918 *AmBi,*
 ApCAB Sup, ApCAB X, DcAmB,
 NatCAB 13, TwCBDA, WhAm 1
Farley, John Wells 1878-1959 *NatCAB 47,*
 WhAm 3
Farley, Joseph Francis 1889-1974 *WhAm 6*
Farley, Joseph Pearson 1839-1912 *WhAm 1*
Farley, Marcus Martin 1883-1941 *NatCAB 30*
Farley, Michael 1719-1789 *ApCAB, Drake*
Farley, Michael Francis 1863-1921 *BiDrAC,*
 WhAm 1
Farley, Richard Blossom 1875- *WhAm 5*
Farley, Robert E 1871-1933 *ApCAB X,*
 WhAm 1
Farley, Roland 1892-1932 *NatCAB 34*
Farley, Simon *NewYHSD*
Farlin, Dudley 1777-1837 *BiAUS, BiDrAC,*
 WhAm H
Farlinger, Alexander 1824- *ApCAB*
Farlow, Alfred d1919 *WhAm 1*
Farlow, Arthur Clark 1904-1967 *WhAm 4*
Farlow, John Woodford 1853-1937 *NatCAB 28*

Farrar, Eliza Ware 1792-1870 *Drake*
Farrar, Eliza Ware Rotch 1791-1870 *AmBi,
    ApCAB, NatCAB 13, NotAW*
Farrar, Frances 1855- *WomWWA 14*
Farrar, Fred 1877- *WhAm 5*
Farrar, Geraldine 1882-1967 *ApCAB X,
    NatCAB 16, WhAm 4, WomWWA 14*
Farrar, Gilbert Powderly 1886-1957 *WhAm 3*
Farrar, Henry 1843- *ApCAB*
Farrar, James McNall 1853-1921 *WhAm 1*
Farrar, John 1779-1853 *ApCAB, BiDAmEd,
    DcAmB, DcScB, Drake, TwCBDA,
    WhAm H*
Farrar, John Chipman 1896-1974 *WhAm 6*
Farrar, Lilian Katurah Pond 1871-1962
    NatCAB 48, WomWWA 14
Farrar, Roy Montgomery 1870-1943 *WhAm 2*
Farrar, Samuel 1773-1864 *ApCAB,
    NatCAB 10*
Farrar, Thomas Charles 1838- *ApCAB*
Farrar, Thomas James 1869- *NatCAB 6,
    WhAm 5*
Farrar, Timothy 1747-1849 *ApCAB, Drake,
    TwCBDA*
Farrar, Timothy 1788-1874 *ApCAB, DcAmB,
    Drake, NatCAB 23, TwCBDA, WhAm H*
Farrar, William Edmund 1866-1925 *WhAm 1*
Farras *NewYHSD*
Farrel, Alton 1851-1885 *NatCAB 24*
Farrel, Alton, Jr. 1879-1934 *NatCAB 24*
Farrel, Franklin 1828-1912 *NatCAB 24*
Farrel, Franklin, Jr. 1881-1967 *NatCAB 55,
    NatCAB 57, WhAm 6*
Farrell, Albert Martin 1876-1934 *NatCAB 25*
Farrell, Benjamin Peter d1947 *WhAm 2*
Farrell, Charles Henry 1873-1961 *NatCAB 49*
Farrell, Charles LeRoy 1874-1940 *WhAm 1*
Farrell, Eileen 1920- *WebAB*
Farrell, Francis David 1883-1976 *WhAm 6*
Farrell, Gabriel 1886-1968 *NatCAB 55,
    WhAm 5*
Farrell, George L 1824?- *NewYHSD*
Farrell, Glenda d1971 *WhAm 5*
Farrell, Henry Edward 1864- *WhAm 4*
Farrell, James Ambrose 1886-1960 *NatCAB 47*
Farrell, James Augustine 1862-1943 *DcAmB S3*
Farrell, James Augustine 1863-1943
    NatCAB 15, NatCAB 32, WhAm 2
Farrell, James Charles 1870-1918 *TwCBDA,
    WhAm 1*
Farrell, James Thomas 1904- *EncAB,
    McGEWB, WebAB*
Farrell, John D 1856- *WhAm 4*
Farrell, John Fletcher 1878-1938 *NatCAB 16,
    NatCAB 34, WhAm 1*
Farrell, John J 1890-1966 *WhAm 4*
Farrell, John P 1873- *ApCAB*
Farrell, Joseph D *WhAm 5*
Farrell, Patrick Joseph Hoshie 1863- *WhAm 5*
Farrell, Thomas d1880 *ApCAB*
Farrell, Thomas Francis 1891-1967 *NatCAB 53,
    WhAm 4*
Farrell, Walter Francis 1888-1965 *NatCAB 51*
Farrell, William Elliston 1870-1949 *WhAm 2*
Farrelly, John P 1856-1921 *NatCAB 15,
    WhAm 1*
Farrelly, John Wilson 1809-1860 *BiAUS,
    BiDrAC, WhAm H*
Farrelly, Patrick 1760-1826 *BiAUS*
Farrelly, Patrick 1770-1826 *BiDrAC,
    WhAm H*
Farren, George P *WhAm H*
Farren, Marie Ann Russell *WhAm H*
Farrens, Lida Pond 1863- *WomWWA 14*
Farrer, Edward 1850- *ApCAB*
Farrer, Henry 1843-1903 *AmBi, DcAmB*
Farrer, Henry 1844-1903 *WhAm 1*
Farrer, Thomas Charles 1840?-1891 *NewYHSD*
Farri, Louis Benjamin 1895-1969 *NatCAB 55*
Farrier, Henry Milton 1882-1926 *NatCAB 20*
Farrington, Carl Coleman 1905-1971 *WhAm 5*
Farrington, David *NewYHSD*
Farrington, Donald H 1914-1964 *WhAm 4*
Farrington, Dora Davis 1880- *WhAm 6*
Farrington, Edward Holyoke 1860-1934
    WhAm 1
Farrington, Edward Irving 1876- *WhAm 5*
Farrington, Edward Silsby 1856-1929 *WhAm 1*

Farrington, Ernest Albert 1880-1937 *WhAm 1*
Farrington, Ernest E 1847-1885 *NatCAB 3*
Farrington, Frank 1873-1955 *WhAm 4*
Farrington, Frank George 1872-1933
    NatCAB 25, WhAm 1
Farrington, Frederic Ernest 1872-1930 *WhAm 1*
Farrington, George Edward 1871-1930
    NatCAB 33
Farrington, Harold P 1885-1964 *WhAm 4*
Farrington, Harry Webb 1879-1930 *NatCAB 23*
Farrington, Harry Webb 1880-1931 *WhAm 1*
Farrington, Isabelle Scudder *WhAm 5*
Farrington, James 1791-1859 *BiAUS, BiDrAC,
    WhAm H*
Farrington, John D 1891-1961 *WhAm 4*
Farrington, Joseph Rider 1897-1954 *BiDrAC,
    DcAmB S5, WhAm 3, WhAmP*
Farrington, Leander Morton 1873-1921
    NatCAB 19
Farrington, Mary Elizabeth Pruett 1898-
    BiDrAC, WhAmP
Farrington, Mary Stone 1858- *WomWWA 14*
Farrington, Oliver Cummings 1864-1933
    TwCBDA, WhAm 1
Farrington, Robert Irving 1861-1948
    NatCAB 40, WhAm 3
Farrington, Wallace Rider 1871-1933
    DcAmB S1, WhAm 1, WhAmP
Farrington, William George 1832-1913 *ApCAB,
    TwCBDA, WhAm 1*
Farrington, William Giddings 1901-1967
    WhAm 4
Farris, Edmond John 1907-1961 *NatCAB 50,
    WhAm 4*
Farris, Frank Mitchell 1890-1950 *WhAm 3*
Farris, Harry Roswell 1874-1923 *NatCAB 20*
Farris, John Wallace DeBeque 1878-1970
    WhAm 5
Farris, Ralph W 1886-1968 *WhAm 5*
Farris, Robert Perry 1826-1903 *WhAm 1*
Farrisee, William James 1898-1958 *WhAm 4*
Farriss, Charles Sherwood 1856-1938 *WhAm 1*
Farrow, Edward Samuel 1855-1926 *ApCAB X,
    WhAm 1*
Farrow, Edward Samuel 1898-1962 *NatCAB 49,
    WhAm 4*
Farrow, James 1827-1892 *BiDConf*
Farrow, John Villiers 1906-1963 *WhAm 4*
Farrow, Miles 1871- *WhAm 5*
Farrow, Samuel 1759-1824 *ApCAB, BiDrAC,
    TwCBDA, WhAm H*
Farrow, Samuel 1760-1824 *BiAUS*
Farrukhan, Ibn Al- *DcScB*
Farson, Clara M J 1851- *WomWWA 14*
Farson, John 1855-1910 *WhAm 1*
Farwell, Arthur 1872- *ApCAB X,
    NatCAB 15*
Farwell, Arthur 1872-1951 *WhAm 3*
Farwell, Arthur 1872-1952 *DcAmB S5,
    NatCAB 40*
Farwell, Arthur Burrage 1852-1936 *NatCAB 40,
    WhAm 1*
Farwell, Arthur Lincoln 1863-1945 *NatCAB 39*
Farwell, Charles Alphonzo 1860-1917
    NatCAB 17
Farwell, Charles Benjamin 1823-1903 *ApCAB,
    BiAUS, BiDrAC, DcAmB, NatCAB 6,
    TwCBDA, WhAm 1, WhAmP*
Farwell, Frederick Marcus 1906-1965 *WhAm 4*
Farwell, James Benedict 1842-1919 *NatCAB 18*
Farwell, John Villiers 1825-1908 *ApCAB,
    DcAmB, WhAm 1*
Farwell, John Villiers 1858-1944 *NatCAB 34,
    WhAm 2*
Farwell, John W 1843-1929 *WhAm 1*
Farwell, Leonard J 1819-1889 *NatCAB 12*
Farwell, Nathan Allen 1812-1893 *ApCAB,
    BiAUS, BiDrAC, NatCAB 10, TwCBDA,
    WhAm H*
Farwell, Samuel 1800?-1875 *ApCAB*
Farwell, Sewall Spaulding 1834-1909 *BiDrAC*
Farwell, Thomas Abbot 1842-1904 *WhAm 1*
Farwell, William W *NewYHSD*
Faryon, Reginald Richard 1900-1962 *WhAm 4*
Fascell, Dante Bruno 1917- *BiDrAC*
Fasel, George Wilhelm *NewYHSD*
Fasnacht, Charles H 1842- *ApCAB*

Fasquelle, Jean Louis Francois Benoit 1808-1862
    ApCAB, Drake, TwCBDA
Fassel, Elgin George 1893-1968 *NatCAB 54*
Fassett, Bertha Chester 1871- *WomWWA 14*
Fassett, Charles Marvin 1858-1923 *WhAm 1*
Fassett, Cornelia Adele Strong 1831-1898 *AmBi,
    ApCAB, DcAmB, NewYHSD, TwCBDA,
    WhAm H*
Fassett, Fred Julius 1875-1926 *NatCAB 20*
Fassett, Helen Mary Revere 1875-1947
    WhAm 2
Fassett, Jacob Sloat 1853-1924 *BiDrAC,
    DcAmB, NatCAB 1, NatCAB 29,
    WhAm 1, WhAmP*
Fassett, James Hiram 1869-1930 *NatCAB 41,
    WhAm 1*
Fassett, Newton Pomeroy 1822-1894 *NatCAB 5*
Fassett, Norman C 1900-1954 *WhAm 3*
Fassett, William M 1876- *WhAm 5*
Fassig, Oliver Lanard 1860-1936 *WhAm 1*
Fassilat, Henry *NewYHSD*
Fasso, Guido 1915-1974 *WhAm 6*
Fast, Gustave 1884-1946 *NatCAB 34,
    WhAm 2*
Fast, Louisa Kimball *WomWWA 14*
Fasten, Nathan 1887-1953 *WhAm 3*
Fasting, George Frederick Kristoffer 1891-1958
    NatCAB 47
Fath, Edward Arthur 1880- *WhAm 6*
Fath, Jacques F 1912-1954 *WhAm 3*
Fatou, Pierre Joseph Louis 1878-1929 *DcScB*
Fatzer, Conrad *NewYHSD*
Faubel, Arthur Louis 1896- *WhAm 4*
Faucett, Max Albert 1899-1962 *NatCAB 50*
Faucette, William Dollison 1881-1947 *WhAm 2*
Faucher DeSaint Maurice, Narcisse H E 1844-
    ApCAB
Fauchet, Baron Jean Antoine Joseph 1763-
    ApCAB, Drake
Faugere, Monsieur *NewYHSD*
Faugeres, Margaretta VanWyck 1771-1801
    Drake, NatCAB 9, NotAW
Faught, Albert Smith 1883-1965 *NatCAB 51*
Faught, Walter Oliver 1897-1949 *NatCAB 38*
Faujas DeSaint-Fond, Barthelemy 1741-1819
    DcScB
Faulconer, Albert 1874- *WhAm 5*
Fauley, Wilber Finley 1872-1942 *WhAm 2*
Faulhaber, Johann 1580-1635 *DcScB*
Faulk, Andrew Jackson 1814-1898 *BiAUS,
    DcAmB, NatCAB 7, TwCBDA,
    WhAm H, WhAmP*
Faulk, C E 1878-1951 *WhAm 3*
Faulk, Odie 1933- *REnAW*
Faulkes, Fred Warren 1855-1905 *NatCAB 16*
Faulkes, James Nelson 1888-1956 *NatCAB 44,
    WhAm 3*
Faulkes, William Fred 1877-1961 *WhAm 4*
Faulkner, Barry 1881-1966 *IIBEAAW,
    WhAm 4*
Faulkner, Charles James 1806-1884 *AmBi,
    ApCAB, BiAUS, BiDrAC, DcAmB,
    NatCAB 2, TwCBDA, WhAm H,
    WhAmP*
Faulkner, Charles James 1840?- *ApCAB*
Faulkner, Charles James 1847-1929 *ApCAB X,
    BiDrAC, DcAmB, NatCAB 2,
    NatCAB 28, TwCBDA, WhAm 1,
    WhAmP*
Faulkner, Charles James 1877-1953 *WhAm 3*
Faulkner, Elisha Boyd 1841- *NatCAB 2*
Faulkner, Georgene 1873- *WhAm 5,
    WomWWA 14*
Faulkner, Harold Underwood 1890-1968
    WhAm 5
Faulkner, Harry Charles 1866- *WhAm 4*
Faulkner, Herbert Nelson 1902-1967 *WhAm 4*
Faulkner, Herbert Waldron 1860-1940
    NatCAB 31, WhAm 1
Faulkner, John Alfred 1857-1931 *NatCAB 22,
    WhAm 1*
Faulkner, Leon Charles 1884-1945 *WhAm 2*
Faulkner, Lester Bradner 1868- *WhAm 5*
Faulkner, Louis Edward 1883-1961 *NatCAB 49*
Faulkner, Roy H 1886-1956 *WhAm 3*
Faulkner, Sarah Elizabeth 1853-
    WomWWA 14

Faulkner, Whiting Carlyle 1895-1955 *NatCAB 43*

Faulkner, William 1897-1962 *EncAAH, McGEWB, NatCAB 57, WebAB, WhAm 4*

Faulkner, William Harrison 1874- *WhAm 5*

Faulkner, William Harrison 1897-1962 *EncAB*

Faulks, Theodosia 1874-1944 *WhAm 2*

Faull, Joseph Horace 1870-1961 *WhAm 4*

Faunce, Daniel Worcester 1829-1911 *AmBi, ApCAB, TwCBDA, WhAm 1*

Faunce, John 1807-1891 *TwCBDA*

Faunce, Sarah Edson *WomWWA 14*

Faunce, William Herbert Perry 1859-1930 *AmBi, DcAmB, NatCAB 10, NatCAB 32, TwCBDA, WhAm 1*

Fauntleroy, Archibald Magill 1837-1886 *ApCAB*

Fauntleroy, Mary Thurston *ApCAB*

Fauntleroy, Thomas T *ApCAB*

Fauntleroy, Thomas Turner 1796-1883 *ApCAB, TwCBDA*

Fauquier, Francis d1768 *Drake*

Fauquier, Francis 1703-1768 *NatCAB 13*

Fauquier, Francis 1704?-1768 *AmBi, DcAmB, WhAm H*

Fauquier, Francis 1720?-1768 *ApCAB, NatCAB 13*

Faure, Gabriel Urbain 1845-1924 *McGEWB*

Faure, John Peter 1846-1912 *NatCAB 15*

Fauset, Joseph Hartman 1896-1957 *NatCAB 49*

Fausett, Lynn 1894- *IIBEAAW*

Faust, Albert Bernhardt 1870-1951 *WhAm 3*

Faust, Allen Klein 1869-1953 *WhAm 3*

Faust, Charles Lee 1879-1928 *BiDrAC, WhAm 1, WhAmP*

Faust, Clarence Henry 1901-1975 *WhAm 6*

Faust, Elsie Ada 1865- *WomWWA 14*

Faust, Emma Beebe *WomWWA 14*

Faust, Frederick 1892-1944 *NatCAB 33*

Faust, Frederick Schiller 1892-1944 *REnAW, WebAB*

Faust, Frederick Shiller 1892-1944 *DcAmB S3*

Faust, John Bernard 1898-1957 *WhAm 3*

Faust, Paul E 1878-1952 *WhAm 3*

Faust, Samuel D 1852-1929 *WhAm 1*

Faust, Walter Livingston 1895-1956 *WhAm 3*

Faust, William *NewYHSD*

Faustina, Gilbert 1897- *WhoColR*

Faustmann, Edmund C d1946 *WhAm 2*

Fauvel, Sulpice Antoine 1813-1884 *BiHiMed*

Fauver, Edgar 1875-1946 *WhAm 2*

Fauver, Edwin 1875- *WhAm 5*

Fauvre, Frank Maus 1851-1938 *NatCAB 33*

Fauvre, Irving Maus 1895-1965 *NatCAB 53*

Faver, Harry Ernest 1898-1968 *NatCAB 54*

Faver, Henry Merrell 1880-1957 *NatCAB 46*

Faversham, Julie Opp *WomWWA 14*

Faversham, William Alfred 1868-1940 *AmBi, DcAmB S2, WhAm 1*

Favill, Henry Baird 1860-1916 *ApCAB X, DcAmB, NatCAB 10, WhAm 1*

Favill, John 1886-1946 *NatCAB 37*

Faville, Alpheus Davis 1880- *WhAm 6*

Faville, Cora Thornburg *WomWWA 14*

Faville, David Ernest 1899-1970 *NatCAB 57, WhAm 5*

Faville, Frederick F 1865- *WhAm 5*

Faville, Henry 1847- *WhAm 4*

Faville, John 1847-1927 *WhAm 1*

Faville, Oran 1817-1872 *ApCAB, TwCBDA*

Faville, William Baker 1866-1947 *NatCAB 38, NatCAB 47, WhAm 2*

Favorsky, Alexei Yevgrafovich 1860-1945 *DcScB*

Favour, Alpheus Hoyt 1880-1939 *NatCAB 37, WhAm 1*

Favre, Pierre Antoine 1813-1880 *DcScB*

Favreau, Guy 1917-1967 *WhAm 4*

Favrot, Charles Allen 1866-1939 *WhAm 1*

Favrot, George Kent 1868-1934 *BiDrAC, WhAm 1*

Favrot, Laurence Harrison 1900-1964 *WhAm 4*

Favrot, Leo Mortimer 1874- *WhAm 5*

Faw, Walter Wagner 1867-1956 *NatCAB 46, WhAm 3*

Fawcett, Angelo Vance 1846- *WhAm 1*

Fawcett, Edgar 1847-1904 *AmBi, ApCAB,*

DcAmB, NatCAB 7, TwCBDA, WhAm 1

Fawcett, Edna Hague *WomWWA 14*

Fawcett, George 1863- *ApCAB X*

Fawcett, George D 1861-1939 *WhAm 1*

Fawcett, George Deneal 1860-1939 *NatCAB 35*

Fawcett, Harold Pascoe 1894-1976 *WhAm 6*

Fawcett, Howard Samuel 1877-1948 *NatCAB 36, WhAm 2*

Fawcett, Jacob 1847- *WhAm 4*

Fawcett, M Edward 1865-1935 *NatCAB 13, WhAm 1*

Fawcett, Mary S 1829- *AmWom*

Fawcett, Owen 1838-1904 *WhAm 1*

Fawcett, Wilford Hamilton, Jr. 1908-1970 *WhAm 5*

Fawcett, William H 1883-1958 *WhAm 3*

Fawcett, William Vaughn Moody 1898-1965 *NatCAB 51*

Fawcett, William Vaughn Moody 1899-1965 *WhAm 4*

Faxon, Charles Edward 1846-1918 *TwCBDA, WhAm 1*

Faxon, Elihu J *NewYHSD*

Faxon, Eudora Meade *WomWWA 14*

Faxon, Frederick Winthrop 1866-1936 *DcAmLiB, WhAm 1*

Faxon, Henry Darlington 1873- *WhAm 5*

Faxon, Henry Hardwick 1823-1905 *NatCAB 18*

Faxon, Henry W 1830?-1864 *ApCAB*

Faxon, Nathaniel Wales 1880- *WhAm 6*

Faxon, Walter 1848-1920 *WhAm 1*

Faxon, William 1822- *BiAUS, NatCAB 5*

Faxon, William Bailey 1906-1941 *WhAm 1*

Faxon, William Otis, II 1910-1968 *WhAm 5*

Fay *NewYHSD*

Fay, Albert Hill 1871-1937 *NatCAB 28, WhAm 1*

Fay, Amy 1844-1928 *AmWom, NotAW, WhAm 3A, WomWWA 14*

Fay, Arthur Cecil 1896-1964 *NatCAB 51, WhAm 4*

Fay, Augustus 1824?- *NewYHSD*

Fay, Charles Ernest 1843-1931 *AmBi*

Fay, Charles Ernest 1846-1931 *NatCAB 22, WhAm 1*

Fay, Charles Norman 1848-1944 *WhAm 2*

Fay, Charles Robert 1900-1959 *NatCAB 48, WhAm 3*

Fay, Charles W 1903-1972 *WhAm 5*

Fay, Edward Allen 1843-1923 *BiDAmEd, DcAmB, NatCAB 20, WhAm 1*

Fay, Edwin Whitfield 1865-1920 *DcAmB, NatCAB 24, WhAm 1*

Fay, Eliphaz d1854 *NatCAB 8*

Fay, Emily Louise Bostwick 1850- *WomWWA 14*

Fay, Francis Ball 1793-1876 *ApCAB, BiAUS, BiDrAC, TwCBDA, WhAm H, WhAmP*

Fay, Frederic Harold 1872-1944 *NatCAB 34, WhAm 2*

Fay, George Morris 1909-1957 *WhAm 3*

Fay, Harold John Warren 1876-1947 *NatCAB 37*

Fay, Helen Carter 1876- *WomWWA 14*

Fay, Heman Allen 1778-1865 *ApCAB, Drake, TwCBDA*

Fay, Henry 1868-1939 *NatCAB 29, WhAm 4*

Fay, Henry Harrison 1835-1897 *TwCBDA*

Fay, Horace Byron 1888-1951 *NatCAB 45*

Fay, Irving Wetherbee 1861-1936 *WhAm 1*

Fay, James Herbert 1899-1948 *BiDrAC, WhAm 2*

Fay, John 1773-1855 *BiAUS, BiDrAC, WhAm H*

Fay, Jonas 1737-1818 *ApCAB, BiAUS, DcAmB, Drake, NatCAB 23, TwCBDA, WhAm H*

Fay, Katherine Carpender *WomWWA 14*

Fay, Lillian Watkins 1863- *WomWWA 14*

Fay, Lucy Ella 1875- *WhAm 5*

Fay, Mary Luella *WomWWA 14*

Fay, Oliver James 1874-1945 *NatCAB 35, WhAm 2*

Fay, Robert Joseph 1910-1970 *NatCAB 55*

Fay, Sidney Bradshaw 1876-1967 *WhAm 4, WhAm 5*

Fay, Temple 1895-1963 *NatCAB 48,*

WhAm 4

Fay, Theodore Sedgwick 1807-1898 *AmBi, ApCAB, BiAUS, DcAmB, Drake, NatCAB 7, TwCBDA, WhAm H*

Fay, Waldo Burnett 1858- *WhAm 4*

Fay, William Patrick 1909-1969 *WhAm 5*

Fayant, Frank H 1876-1965 *WhAm 4*

Faye, Herve 1814-1902 *DcScB*

Fayer, Margaret Wilson 1910-1964 *WhAm 4*

Fayerweather, Daniel B 1821-1890 *TwCBDA*

Fayerweather, Daniel Burton 1822-1890 *DcAmB, NatCAB 23, WhAm H*

Fayle, George Arthur 1881-1918 *NatCAB 19*

Fayolle, Marie Emile 1852-1928 *WhoMilH*

Fayssoux, Peter 1745-1795 *DcAmB, WhAm H*

Fazari, Muhammad Ibn Ibrahim, Al- *DcScB*

Fead, Louis H 1877-1943 *WhAm 2*

Feagin, Horace Cecil 1885-1951 *NatCAB 40*

Feagin, Noah Baxter 1843- *WhAm 1*

Feagin, William Francis 1869- *WhAm 5*

Fearey, Frederick Tysoe 1848- *NatCAB 5, NatCAB 14*

Fearing, Albert 1798-1875 *ApCAB*

Fearing, Benjamin Dana 1837-1881 *ApCAB, TwCBDA*

Fearing, Daniel Butler 1859-1918 *WhAm 1*

Fearing, Franklin 1892-1962 *NatCAB 48*

Fearing, Kenneth Flexner 1902-1961 *WebAB, WhAm 4*

Fearing, Lillian Blanche 1863- *AmWom*

Fearing, Paul 1762-1822 *BiAUS, BiDrAC, WhAm H*

Fearn, Anne Walter 1865-1939 *NatCAB 31, NotAW*

Fearn, Anne Walter 1867-1939 *AmBi*

Fearn, John Walker 1832-1899 *DcAmB, NatCAB 12, WhAm H*

Fearn, Richard Lee 1862- *WhAm 4*

Fearn, Thomas 1789-1868 *BiDConf*

Fearon, Henry Bradshaw 1770?- *ApCAB, Drake*

Fearon, Henry Dana 1864-1941 *WhAm 2*

Fearon, Mary Fuller 1865- *WomWWA 14*

Fearons, George Hadsall 1853- *ApCAB X, NatCAB 14*

Fearons, George Hadsall, Jr. 1900-1974 *NatCAB 57*

Fearrington, J C Pass 1898-1958 *NatCAB 47*

Fearrington, Mary Franklin Pass 1862- *WomWWA 14*

Feathers, William C 1870-1944 *WhAm 2*

Featherston, W S d1891 *BiAUS*

Featherston, Winfield Scott 1819-1891 *DcAmB, WhAm H*

Featherston, Winfield Scott 1820-1891 *ApCAB, BiDConf, BiDrAC*

Featherston, Winfield Scott 1821-1891 *TwCBDA*

Featherstone, Lewis Porter 1851-1922 *BiDrAC, WhAmP*

Featherstone, Robert Marion 1914-1974 *WhAm 6*

Featherstone, W S d1864 *Drake*

Featherstone, William B 1900-1951 *WhAm 3*

Featherstonhaugh, George William 1780-1866 *AmBi, ApCAB, DcScB Sup, Drake, NatCAB 8*

Feazel, William Crosson 1895-1965 *BiDrAC*

Febiger, Christian 1746-1796 *ApCAB, DcAmB, NatCAB 1, TwCBDA, WhAm H*

Febiger, Christian 1747-1796 *Drake*

Febiger, John Carson 1821-1898 *ApCAB, NatCAB 4, TwCBDA*

Fechet, James Edmond 1877-1948 *NatCAB 37, WhAm 2*

Fechheimer, S Marcus 1864-1932 *NatCAB 25*

Fechin, Nicolai Ivanovich 1881-1955 *IIBEAAW, NatCAB 45*

Fechner, Gustav Theodor 1801-1887 *AsBiEn, DcScB, McGEWB*

Fechner, Robert 1876-1939 *NatCAB 29, WhAm 1*

Fechteler, August Francis 1857-1921 *NatCAB 23*

Fechteler, Augustus Francis 1857-1921 *WhAm 1*

Fechteler, William Morrow 1896-1967 *WebAMB, WhAm 4*

Fechter, Charles 1823- *Drake*
Fechter, Charles Albert 1824-1879 *AmBi,*
 ApCAB, DcAmB, NatCAB 5, WhAm H
Fechter, Oscar Augustus 1864-1935 *WhAm 1*
Fedde, Sister Elizabeth 1850-1921 *NotAW*
Feddersen, Berend Wilhelm 1832-1918 *DcScB*
Feder, Daniel Dunn 1910- *BiDAmEd*
Federbush, Simon 1892-1969 *WhAm 5*
Federmann, Nicholas 1501-1550 *ApCAB*
Federspiel, Matthew Nicholas 1879-1951
 WhAm 3
Federspiel, Matthew Nicolas 1879-1951
 NatCAB 41
Fedigan, John J 1842-1908 *WhAm 1*
Fee, Antoine-Laurent-Apollinaire 1789-1874
 DcScB
Fee, Charles S 1853-1923 *WhAm 1*
Fee, Chester Anders 1893-1951 *WhAm 3*
Fee, James Alger 1888-1959 *WhAm 3*
Fee, Jerome John 1913-1971 *WhAm 5*
Fee, John Gregg 1816-1901 *AmBi, DcAmB,*
 McGEWB, NatCAB 24, TwCBDA,
 WhAm H, WhAmP
Fee, William Thomas 1854-1919 *WhAm 1*
Feehan, Daniel Francis 1855-1934 *NatCAB 15,*
 WhAm 1
Feehan, Patrick Augustine 1829-1902 *ApCAB,*
 DcAmB, DcAmReB, NatCAB 9,
 NatCAB 12, TwCBDA, WhAm 1
Feeley, James Patrick 1894-1962 *WhAm 4*
Feeley, Paul 1910-1966 *BnEnAmA*
Feeley, William P 1883-1968 *WhAm 5*
Feely, Edward Francis 1880-1964 *WhAm 4*
Feely, John *NewYHSD*
Feely, John Joseph 1875-1905 *BiDrAC,*
 WhAm 1
Feely, Raymond Thomas 1895-1965
 NatCAB 52
Feeman, Harlan Luther 1873- *WhAm 3*
Feemster, Robert M 1911- *WhAm 4*
Feeney, Daniel J 1894-1969 *WhAm 5*
Feeney, Joseph Gerald 1910-1968 *WhAm 5*
Fees, Walter Scott 1887-1964 *NatCAB 50*
Fegan, Hugh J 1881-1954 *WhAm 3*
Fegan, James 1827-1886 *ApCAB*
Fegan, Joseph Charles 1886-1949 *WhAm 2*
Fegtly, Samuel Marks 1867-1947 *WhAm 2*
Fehlandt, August Frederick 1869-1939 *WhAm 1*
Fehr, Arthur 1904-1969 *WhAm 5*
Fehr, Elizabeth Mandelkern 1887-
 WomWWA 14
Fehr, Frank 1844-1891 *NatCAB 7*
Fehr, Harrison Robert 1863-1930 *WhAm 1*
Fehr, Herman *WhAm 5*
Fehr, Julius 1825- *NatCAB 5*
Fehr, Rudolph Godfrey 1850-1916 *NatCAB 17*
Fehrenbach, John 1857- *TwCBDA, WhAm 4*
Feibelman, Herbert U 1889-1967 *WhAm 5*
Feibus, Arthur 1899-1972 *WhAm 6*
Feicht, Russell Stimson 1868-1949 *NatCAB 38*
Feickert, Edward Foster 1874-1942 *NatCAB 31*
Feidelson, Charles N 1886-1967 *WhAm 4*
Feidt, Josephine Thorpe *WomWWA 14*
Feierabend, Frank Leo 1897-1971 *NatCAB 56*
Feierabend, Raymond H d1972 *WhAm 5*
Feigenspan, Christian William 1876-1939
 NatCAB 29
Feighan, Michael Aloysius 1905- *BiDrAC*
Feigl, Georg 1890-1945 *DcScB*
Feigl, Hugo 1889-1961 *WhAm 4*
Feijo, Diogo Antonio 1784-1843 *ApCAB,*
 McGEWB
Feikema, Feike *REnAW*
Feiker, Frederick Morris 1881-1967 *WhAm 4*
Feilchenfeld, Ernst H 1898-1956 *WhAm 3*
Feinberg, Benjamin Franklin 1888-1959
 NatCAB 47
Feinberg, Louis 1909- *WhAm 6*
Feinberg, Samuel Maurice 1895-1973 *WhAm 6*
Feinbloom, William F 1895-1962 *NatCAB 52*
Feininger, Karl William Frederick 1844-
 ApCAB
Feininger, Lyonel Charles Adrian 1871-1956
 BnEnAmA, McGEWB, WhAm 3
Feis, Herbert 1893-1972 *NatCAB 57,*
 WhAm 5
Feisal II 1935-1958 *WhAm 3*
Feiss, Julius 1848-1931 *NatCAB 22*

Feiss, Paul Louis 1875-1952 *WhAm 3*
Feit, Louis James 1895-1964 *NatCAB 50*
Fejer, Lipot 1880-1959 *DcScB*
Fejos, Paul 1897-1963 *NatCAB 49, WhAm 4*
Feke, Robert *Drake*
Feke, Robert 1705?-1750? *AmBi, BnEnAmA,*
 DcAmB, NewYHSD, WhAm H
Feke, Robert 1725?-1770? *ApCAB,*
 NatCAB 8
Feland, Faris Robison, II 1887-1952 *WhAm 3*
Feland, Logan 1869-1936 *WhAm 1*
Felch, Alpheus 1804-1896 *BiDrAC, DcAmB,*
 WhAm H, WhAmP
Felch, Alpheus 1806-1896 *ApCAB, BiAUS,*
 Drake, NatCAB 3, TwCBDA
Felch, Carrie Innes 1873- *WomWWA 14*
Felch, J *NewYHSD*
Felch, John H *NewYHSD*
Feld, Jacob 1899-1975 *WhAm 6*
Feldberg, Morris d1969 *WhAm 5*
Feldbush, Harry A 1893-1960 *WhAm 4*
Felder, C S 1887- *WhAm 3*
Felder, John Myers 1782-1851 *ApCAB, BiAUS,*
 BiDrAC, TwCBDA, WhAm H
Felder, Thomas Brailsford 1864-1926 *ApCAB X,*
 NatCAB 20
Feldman, A Harry d1975 *WhAm 6*
Feldman, Charles K 1907-1968 *WhAm 5*
Feldman, Herman 1894-1947 *NatCAB 36,*
 WhAm 2
Feldman, Jacob Benjamin 1886-1954
 NatCAB 43
Feldman, William H 1892-1974 *WhAm 6*
Feldmann, Charles Russell 1898-1973 *WhAm 6*
Feldmann, Leonard George 1909-1972
 NatCAB 57, WhAm 5
Feldmann, Markus 1897-1958 *WhAm 3*
Feldmann, Robert Lincoln 1906-1973 *WhAm 6*
Feldmans, Jules 1889-1953 *WhAm 3*
Feldstein, David 1909-1972 *WhAm 6*
Feldstein, Theodore 1836- *NatCAB 3*
Felgar, James Huston 1874-1946 *WhAm 2*
Felipe 1508-1535 *ApCAB*
Felipillo 1508?-1535 *ApCAB*
Felitto, Raymond Nicholas 1921-1971 *WhAm 6*
Felix, Anthony G 1885-1958 *WhAm 3*
Felix, Douglas Duncan 1891-1957 *NatCAB 47*
Felix, Elizabeth Rachel 1820-1858 *WhAm H*
Felix, Louis 1765-1836 *ApCAB*
Felkel, Herbert 1889-1934 *WhAm 1*
Felkel, Edward Pearson 1891-1963 *NatCAB 48*
Felker, George Walton, Jr. 1886-1951
 NatCAB 40
Felker, Gertrude 1872- *WomWWA 14*
Felker, Samuel Demeritt 1859-1932 *WhAm 1*
Fell, Alpheus Gilbert 1846- *WhAm 1*
Fell, Charles Albert 1889-1969 *WhAm 5*
Fell, D Newlin 1840-1919 *NatCAB 17,*
 WhAm 1
Fell, Dora Cobb 1859- *WomWWA 14*
Fell, E Lawrence 1867-1943 *NatCAB 34*
Fell, Francis Jacob, Jr. 1878-1961 *NatCAB 49*
Fell, Frank J, Jr. 1878-1961 *WhAm 4*
Fell, George Edward 1850-1918 *NatCAB 12,*
 WhAm 1
Fell, Harold Bertels 1889-1959 *WhAm 3*
Fell, J Weldon *Drake*
Fell, John 1721-1798 *BiAUS, BiDrAC,*
 DcAmB, WhAm H, WhAmP
Fell, John R 1911-1961 *WhAm 4*
Fell, Olive 1900?- *IIBEAAW*
Fell, Thomas 1850-1942 *WhAm 2*
Fell, Thomas 1851-1942 *NatCAB 1, TwCBDA*
Felland, Ole Gunderson 1853-1938 *WhAm 1*
Feller, Abraham Howard 1904-1952
 NatCAB 39, WhAm 3
Feller, Alto Edmund 1910-1966 *WhAm 4*
Feller, Henrietta 1788?-1868 *ApCAB*
Feller, Robert William Andrew 1918- *WebAB*
Feller, William 1906-1970 *WhAm 5*
Fellers, Bonner Frank 1896-1973 *WhAm 6*
Fellers, Carl Raymond 1893-1960 *NatCAB 49,*
 WhAm 3
Fellheimer, Alfred 1895- *WhAm 3*
Fellingham, John Henry 1872- *WhAm 5*
Fellini, Federico 1920- *McGEWB*
Fellman, George Harry 1872-1957 *NatCAB 46*
Fellowes, Frank Wayland 1833-1900 *NewYHSD*

Fellows, Charles Gurnee 1863-1929 *WhAm 1*
Fellows, Dorkas 1873-1938 *WhAm 1*
Fellows, Edward B 1811- *NatCAB 2*
Fellows, Edwin Russell 1865-1945 *NatCAB 34*
Fellows, Eugene Hilpert 1879- *WhAm 6*
Fellows, Frank 1889-1951 *BiDrAC, WhAm 3,*
 WhAmP
Fellows, Fred 1935- *IIBEAAW*
Fellows, George Emery 1858-1942 *NatCAB 14*
Fellows, George Emory 1858-1942 *WhAm 1*
Fellows, Grant 1865-1929 *WhAm 1*
Fellows, Harold Everett 1899-1960 *NatCAB 47,*
 WhAm 3
Fellows, Jennie Dorcas 1873-1938 *DcAmLiB*
Fellows, John 1733-1808 *ApCAB, Drake,*
 TwCBDA
Fellows, John 1760-1844 *ApCAB, Drake,*
 NatCAB 4
Fellows, John Ernest 1899-1967 *WhAm 4*
Fellows, John R 1832-1896 *BiDrAC,*
 NatCAB 11, TwCBDA, WhAm H,
 WhAmP
Fellows, Olin Burt 1889-1962 *NatCAB 50*
Fellows, Oscar F 1857-1921 *WhAm 1*
Fellows, Ralph Manos 1894-1954 *NatCAB 44*
Fellows, Ray Stanley 1887-1958 *NatCAB 50*
Fellows, Samuel McGaffey 1818-1863
 NatCAB 7, TwCBDA
Fellows, William Bainbridge 1858-1921
 WhAm 1
Fellows, William Kinne 1870-1948 *WhAm 2*
Felmley, David 1857-1930 *WhAm 1*
Felmley, John Benjamin 1895-1958 *NatCAB 43*
Fels, Joseph 1853-1914 *NatCAB 20*
Fels, Joseph 1854-1914 *AmBi, DcAmB,*
 WhAm 1
Fels, Mary 1863- *BiCAW, WhAm 3*
Fels, Samuel Simeon 1860-1950 *DcAmB S4,*
 WhAm 3
Fels, William Carl 1916-1964 *WhAm 4*
Felsenthal, Bernhard 1822-1908 *DcAmB*
Felsing, William August 1891-1952 *WhAm 3*
Felt, Charles Frederick Wilson 1864-1928
 WhAm 1
Felt, Dorr Eugene 1862-1930 *AmBi,*
 NatCAB 40, WhAm 1
Felt, Dorr Eugene 1863-1930 *ApCAB X,*
 NatCAB 11
Felt, Edward Webster 1859-1926 *NatCAB 39,*
 WhAm 1
Felt, Ephraim Porter 1868-1943 *NatCAB 12,*
 WhAm 2
Felt, Henry William 1874-1959 *NatCAB 47*
Felt, Joseph Barlow 1789-1868 *NatCAB 23*
Felt, Joseph Barlow 1789-1869 *AmBi, ApCAB,*
 DcAmB, Drake, TwCBDA, WhAm H
Felt, Joseph Pollard 1850-1913 *NatCAB 15*
Felt, Truman Thomas 1899-1965 *WhAm 4*
Felter, Frederick Charles 1879-1948
 NatCAB 38
Felter, Harvey Wickes 1865-1927 *NatCAB 25,*
 WhAm 1
Felter, John D 1825?- *NewYHSD*
Felter, Lloyd King 1896-1965 *NatCAB 51*
Feltes, Nicholas Rudolph *WhAm 3*
Felthousen, Edward Greenough 1852-1930
 NatCAB 23
Feltin, Maurice 1883-1975 *WhAm 6*
Feltman, Bernhard *NewYHSD*
Felton, Charles B 1793?- *NewYHSD*
Felton, Charles N 1832-1914 *NatCAB 12,*
 TwCBDA, WhAm 1
Felton, Charles Norton 1828-1914 *BiDrAC*
Felton, Cornelius Conway 1807-1862 *AmBi,*
 ApCAB, DcAmB, Drake, NatCAB 6,
 TwCBDA, WhAm H
Felton, Edgar Conway 1858-1937 *WhAm 1*
Felton, George Hurlburt 1846- *TwCBDA,*
 WhAm 4
Felton, J Lang 1901-1948 *NatCAB 36*
Felton, John Brooks 1827-1877 *ApCAB*
Felton, Lloyd Derr 1885-1953 *NatCAB 40,*
 WhAm 3
Felton, Rebecca Latimer 1835-1930 *AmBi,*
 AmWom, BiDrAC, DcAmB, NatCAB 13,
 NatCAB 36, NotAW, WhAm 1, WhAmP
Felton, Robert *NewYHSD*
Felton, Samuel 1809-1877 *NatCAB 21*

Felton, Samuel Morse 1809-1889 *AmBi,*
ApCAB, DcAmB, WhAm H
Felton, Samuel Morse 1853-1930 *ApCAB X,*
NatCAB 5, NatCAB 12, NatCAB 33,
WhAm 1
Felton, Samuel Morse 1893-1971 *WhAm 5*
Felton, William C 1869- *WhoColR*
Felton, William Hamilton 1860- *WhAm 1*
Felton, William Harrell 1823-1909 *AmBi,*
BiDrAC, DcAmB, WhAmP
Fendall, Josias 1620?-1687? *ApCAB, DcAmB,*
Drake, NatCAB 7, WhAm H
Fendall, Philip Ricard 1794-1868 *ApCAB*
Fenderich, Charles *NewYHSD*
Fendler, Amelia Molly 1870- *WomWWA 14*
Fendler, August 1813-1883 *ApCAB*
Fendrich, Herrmann 1830-1889 *NatCAB 32*
Fenelon, Francois DeSalignac DeLaM 1651-1715
McGEWB
Fenerty, Clare Gerald 1895-1952 *BiDrAC*
Fenetry, Clare Gerald 1895-1952 *WhAm 3*
Feng, Kuei-Fen 1809-1874 *McGEWB*
Feng, Yu-Hsiang 1882-1948 *McGEWB*
Fenger, Christian 1840-1902 *BiHiMed,*
DcAmB, NatCAB 17, WhAm 1
Fenhagen, George Corner 1884-1956 *WhAm 3*
Fenhagen, James Corner 1875-1955 *WhAm 3*
Fenichel, Otto 1897-1946 *DcAmB S4*
Fenimore, James S *NewYHSD*
Fenkell, George Harrison 1873-1949
NatCAB 38, WhAm 3
Fenley, Oscar 1855-1931 *WhAm 1*
Fenlon, John F 1873-1943 *WhAm 2*
Fenn, Augustus Hall 1844-1897 *NatCAB 16*
Fenn, Edward Hart 1856-1939 *BiDrAC,*
WhAm 1, WhAmP
Fenn, Frederick C M *NewYHSD*
Fenn, George Karl 1890-1960 *WhAm 4*
Fenn, Harry 1837-1911 *NatCAB 6*
Fenn, Harry 1838-1911 *ApCAB, IIBEAAW,*
WhAm 1
Fenn, Harry 1840-1911 *TwCBDA*
Fenn, Mary *NotAW*
Fenn, Sarah Edna Howell 1874- *WomWWA 14*
Fenn, Sereno Peck 1844-1927 *NatCAB 21*
Fenn, Stephen Southmyd 1820-1892 *BiDrAC,*
WhAm H, WhAmP
Fenn, Wallace Osgood 1893-1971 *NatCAB 56,*
WhAm 5
Fenn, William Henry 1867-1946 *NatCAB 35*
Fenn, William Kemler 1859-1919 *NatCAB 18*
Fenn, William Wallace 1862-1932 *DcAmB S1,*
WhAm 1
Fenn, Wilson Lee 1858-1921 *NatCAB 40*
Fennamore *NewYHSD*
Fennebresque, John Drouet 1917-1971
NatCAB 56
Fennel, Eric Adolphus 1887-1957 *NatCAB 45*
Fennell, Earle James 1905-1972 *WhAm 6*
Fennell, Fannie Smith 1877- *WomWWA 14*
Fennell, James 1766-1816 *ApCAB, DcAmB,*
Drake, NatCAB 6, WhAm H
Fennell, Thomas Francis 1875-1936 *NatCAB 27*
Fennell, William George 1859-1917 *WhAm 1*
Fennelly, John Fauntleroy 1899-1974 *WhAm 6*
Fenneman, Nevin Melancthon 1865-1945
DcAmB S3, DcScB, WhAm 2
Fennemore *NewYHSD*
Fenner, Arthur 1745-1805 *ApCAB, BiAUS,*
DcAmB, Drake, NatCAB 9, TwCBDA,
WhAm H, WhAmP
Fenner, Burt Leslie 1869-1926 *DcAmB,*
NatCAB 33, WhAm 1
Fenner, Charles E 1876-1963 *WhAm 4*
Fenner, Charles Erasmus 1834-1911 *DcAmB,*
NatCAB 16, WhAm 1
Fenner, Charles Payne 1867-1927 *NatCAB 39,*
WhAm 1
Fenner, Clarence Norman 1870-1949 *DcScB,*
WhAm 3
Fenner, Cornelius George 1822-1847 *ApCAB,*
NatCAB 8
Fenner, Edward Blaine 1876-1943 *WhAm 2*
Fenner, Erasmus Darwin 1868-1944 *WhAm 2*
Fenner, George Potter 1855-1915 *NatCAB 16*
Fenner, Harlan K 1850- *WhAm 4*
Fenner, Herbert Nicholas 1843-1915
NatCAB 17

Fenner, Hiram Walter 1859-1929 *WhAm 1*
Fenner, James 1771-1846 *ApCAB, BiAUS,*
BiDrAC, DcAmB, Drake, NatCAB 9,
TwCBDA, WhAm H, WhAmP
Fenner, Jessie Gordon 1875- *WomWWA 14*
Fenner, Mary Galentine 1839- *AmWom*
Fenner, Robert Coyner 1880-1972 *WhAm 5*
Fenney, William H *NewYHSD*
Fenning, Frederick Alexander 1874-1944
WhAm 2
Fenning, Karl 1881-1963 *NatCAB 50*
Fenno, Charles Horace *NewYHSD*
Fenno, Edward Nicoll 1845-1931 *NatCAB 42*
Fenno, John 1751-1798 *DcAmB, NatCAB 19,*
WhAm H, WhAmP
Fenno, Lawrence Carteret 1858-1912
NatCAB 41
Fenno, William Augustus 1814-1873 *ApCAB*
Fenollosa, Ernest Francisco 1853-1908 *AmBi,*
DcAmB, WebAB, WhAm 1
Fenollosa, Mary McNeill d1954 *WhAm 3,*
WomWWA 14
Fenouillet, Emile De 1806-1859 *ApCAB, Drake*
Fensham, Florence 1861-1912 *WhAm 1*
Fenske, Merrell Robert 1904-1971 *WhAm 5*
Fenske, Theodore H 1904-1963 *WhAm 4*
Fenstermacher, R 1892-1961 *WhAm 4*
Fensterwald, Bernard 1890-1952 *WhAm 3*
Fenston, Earl J 1895-1958 *WhAm 3*
Fenton, Carroll Lane 1900-1969 *NatCAB 55*
Fenton, Charles L 1808?-1877 *NewYHSD*
Fenton, Daniel Higgins 1890-1956 *NatCAB 45*
Fenton, Hector Tyndale 1850- *WhAm 1*
Fenton, Henry Gilbert 1872-1951 *NatCAB 40*
Fenton, Howard Withrow 1877-1958
NatCAB 50, WhAm 3
Fenton, Ivor David 1889- *BiDrAC, WhAmP*
Fenton, Jerome D 1908-1967 *WhAm 4*
Fenton, Joseph Clifford 1906-1969 *WhAm 5*
Fenton, Lucien Jerome 1844-1922 *BiDrAC,*
TwCBDA, WhAm 1
Fenton, Ralph Albert 1880-1960 *WhAm 4*
Fenton, Reuben Eaton 1819-1885 *AmBi,*
ApCAB, BiAUS, BiDrAC, DcAmB,
Drake, NatCAB 3, TwCBDA, WhAm H,
WhAmP
Fenton, Robert *NewYHSD*
Fenton, Walter Samuel 1886-1940 *NatCAB 29*
Fenton, William David 1853-1925 *WhAm 1*
Fenton, William Matthew 1808-1871 *ApCAB,*
NatCAB 6
Fentress, Calvin 1879-1957 *WhAm 3*
Fentress, James 1871-1945 *NatCAB 34*
Fenwick, Benedict Joseph 1782-1846 *ApCAB,*
DcAmB, Drake, NatCAB 6, TwCBDA,
WhAm H
Fenwick, Charles Ghequiere 1880-1973
WhAm 5, WhAm 6
Fenwick, Charles H B *NewYHSD*
Fenwick, Charles Philip 1891-1954 *WhAm 3*
Fenwick, Cuthbert d1655 *ApCAB*
Fenwick, Edward Dominic 1768-1832 *AmBi,*
ApCAB, DcAmB, Drake, NatCAB 5,
TwCBDA, WhAm H
Fenwick, Edward Taylor 1869-1942 *NatCAB 32,*
WhAm 2
Fenwick, George 1603-1656? *DcAmB*
Fenwick, George 1603-1657 *ApCAB, Drake,*
WhAm H
Fenwick, George William 1848-1926
NatCAB 24
Fenwick, John 1618-1683 *AmBi, ApCAB,*
DcAmB, WhAm H
Fenwick, John R 1780-1842 *ApCAB, Drake,*
TwCBDA
Fenwick, Kenneth Neander 1852- *ApCAB*
Fenwick, Marin B *WomWWA 14*
Fenwicke, John 1618-1683 *DcAmB, Drake*
Feraud, Thomas, Jr. *NewYHSD*
Ferber, Edna 1887-1968 *ApCAB X, McGEWB,*
REnAW, WebAB, WhAm 5
Ferber, Herbert 1906- *BnEnAmA*
Ferbert, Adolph Henry 1883-1948 *WhAm 2*
Ferchault, Rene Antoine *DcScB*
Ferdinand 1865-1927 *McGEWB*
Ferdinand I 1503-1564 *McGEWB*
Ferdinand II 1578-1637 *McGEWB*
Ferdinand II 1810-1859 *McGEWB*

Ferdinand III 1608-1657 *McGEWB*
Ferdinand V 1452-1516 *McGEWB*
Ferdinand VII 1784-1833 *McGEWB*
Ferdinand Of Brunswick, Duke 1721-1792
WhoMilH
Ferdinand II Of Tuscany 1610-1670 *AsBiEn*
Ferdinand, Lorin W 1853-1925 *NatCAB 23*
Ferdon, John William 1826-1884 *BiDrAC,*
WhAm H
Ferebee, Enoch Emory 1903-1966 *WhAm 4*
Fereira, Alexandre Rodrigues 1756-1815 *Drake*
Ferenbaugh, Claude Birkett 1899-1975 *WhAm 6*
Ferento, August *NewYHSD*
Ferger, Roger H 1894-1974 *WhAm 6*
Fergus, Phyllis 1887-1964 *NatCAB 52*
Ferguson, Abbie Park 1837-1919 *NotAW*
Ferguson, Adam 1723-1816 *McGEWB*
Ferguson, Adam 1783-1862 *ApCAB*
Ferguson, Adam Johnston 1815-1867 *ApCAB*
Ferguson, Agnes Julia 1849- *WomWWA 14*
Ferguson, Alexander Hugh 1853-1911 *DcAmB,*
NatCAB 16, WhAm 1
Ferguson, Alfred Lynn 1884-1972 *NatCAB 57*
Ferguson, Catharine Lee *WomWWA 14*
Ferguson, Charles 1863- *WhAm 4*
Ferguson, Charles 1894-1973 *WhAm 6*
Ferguson, Charles Earl 1901-1951 *NatCAB 44*
Ferguson, Charles Eugene 1856- *WhAm 4*
Ferguson, Colin 1751-1806 *ApCAB, TwCBDA*
Ferguson, David Arthur 1875- *WhoColR*
Ferguson, DeLancey 1888-1966 *WhAm 4*
Ferguson, Donald 1839- *ApCAB*
Ferguson, Duncan *NewYHSD*
Ferguson, Edmund Sheppard 1871-1941
WhAm 1
Ferguson, Edward 1907-1968 *WhAm 5*
Ferguson, Edward Alexander 1826-1906
NatCAB 26
Ferguson, Edwin Hite 1852-1924 *NatCAB 21*
Ferguson, Elizabeth d1801 *Drake*
Ferguson, Elizabeth 1739-1801 *ApCAB,*
NatCAB 7
Ferguson, Elizabeth Graeme 1737-1801 *DcAmB,*
NotAW
Ferguson, Elsie 1885-1961 *WhAm 4*
Ferguson, Emma Henry 1840-1905 *WhAm 1*
Ferguson, Everard D 1843-1906 *WhAm 1*
Ferguson, Farquhar 1852- *WhAm 4*
Ferguson, Fenner 1814-1859 *BiAUS, BiDrAC,*
WhAm H
Ferguson, Finlay Forbes 1875-1936 *WhAm 1*
Ferguson, Francis Marion 1863-1910 *ApCAB X*
Ferguson, Frank Cardwell 1883-1964 *WhAm 4*
Ferguson, Frank William 1861-1926 *WhAm 1*
Ferguson, Franklin LaDu 1898- *WhAm 4*
Ferguson, Fred Swearengin 1887-1959 *WhAm 3*
Ferguson, Garland Sevier, Jr. 1878-1963
WhAm 4
Ferguson, George Albert 1868- *WhAm 1*
Ferguson, Georgia Ransom 1865- *WhAm 4,*
WomWWA 14
Ferguson, Harley B 1875- *WhAm 5*
Ferguson, Harriet R 1888-1966 *WhAm 4*
Ferguson, Harry George 1884-1960 *WhAm 4*
Ferguson, Harry Leroy 1881-1949 *NatCAB 37*
Ferguson, Henry 1848-1917 *TwCBDA,*
WhAm 1
Ferguson, Henry Augustus 1845-1911
NatCAB 25, WhAm 1
Ferguson, Henry Gardiner 1882-1966 *WhAm 4*
Ferguson, Hill 1877-1971 *WhAm 5*
Ferguson, Hiram *NewYHSD*
Ferguson, Homer 1889- *BiDrAC*
Ferguson, Homer Lenoir 1873- *NatCAB 17*
Ferguson, Homer Lenoir 1873-1952 *NatCAB 40*
Ferguson, Homer Lenoir 1873-1953 *WhAm 3*
Ferguson, Horace Stephen 1870- *WhoColR*
Ferguson, Ira Alfred 1896-1970 *WhAm 5*
Ferguson, James 1710-1776 *DcScB*
Ferguson, James 1797-1867 *ApCAB*
Ferguson, James 1834?- *NewYHSD*
Ferguson, James Edward 1871-1944 *DcAmB S3,*
EncAAH, NatCAB 15, REnAW,
WhAm 2
Ferguson, John *NewYHSD*
Ferguson, John Angus 1872-1955 *NatCAB 43*
Ferguson, John Calvin 1866-1945 *ApCAB X,*
DcAmB S3, NatCAB 3, NatCAB 34,

WhAm 2

Ferguson, John Donald 1890-1964 *NatCAB 52, WhAm 4*

Ferguson, John Haven 1915-1970 *NatCAB 55*

Ferguson, John Lambuth 1892-1950 *WhAm 3*

Ferguson, John Scott 1842- *NatCAB 5*

Ferguson, John Thacker 1908-1968 *NatCAB 57*

Ferguson, John William 1857-1942 *WhAm 1*

Ferguson, John Young *ApCAB*

Ferguson, Josiah Bunting 1836-1911 *NatCAB 16*

Ferguson, Kenneth Reinhard 1904-1954 *WhAm 3*

Ferguson, Louis Aloysius 1867-1940 *NatCAB 14, WhAm 1*

Ferguson, Lynn Adelbert 1891-1966 *NatCAB 52*

Ferguson, Margaret Clay 1862-1951 *WomWWA 14*

Ferguson, Margaret Clay 1863-1951 *WhAm 3A*

Ferguson, Meade 1869-1942 *NatCAB 31*

Ferguson, Melville Foster 1874-1968 *NatCAB 54, WhAm 5*

Ferguson, Milton James 1879-1954 *DcAmLiB, NatCAB 40, WhAm 3*

Ferguson, Miriam A 1875-1961 *WhAm 4, WhAmP*

Ferguson, Olin Jerome 1875-1965 *WhAm 4*

Ferguson, Patrick d1780 *ApCAB, Drake*

Ferguson, Phillip Colgan 1903- *BiDrAC*

Ferguson, R J 1898-1955 *WhAm 3*

Ferguson, Robert 1875-1939 *NatCAB 30*

Ferguson, Robert Gracey 1842-1926 *NatCAB 24, TwCBDA, WhAm 1*

Ferguson, Robert Gracey 1905-1972 *WhAm 5*

Ferguson, Roy King 1893-1974 *WhAm 6*

Ferguson, Samuel 1874-1950 *DcAmB S4, WhAm 2A*

Ferguson, Samuel David 1842-1916 *AmBi, ApCAB, NatCAB 13, TwCBDA, WhAm 1, WhoColR*

Ferguson, Samuel Wragg 1834-1917 *BiDConf*

Ferguson, Smith Farley 1872-1950 *WhAm 3*

Ferguson, Thomas Barker 1841-1922 *DcAmB, NatCAB 13*

Ferguson, Thomas Ewing 1885-1959 *WhAm 4*

Ferguson, Thompson B 1857-1921 *WhAm 1*

Ferguson, Walter Scott 1886-1936 *NatCAB 38, WhAm 1*

Ferguson, Wilbert 1857- *TwCBDA*

Ferguson, William *NewYHSD*

Ferguson, William Blair Morton 1881- *WhAm 6*

Ferguson, William Cashman 1861-1930 *NatCAB 23*

Ferguson, William H 1856- *WhAm 4*

Ferguson, William Jason 1844-1930 *DcAmB, WhAm 1*

Ferguson, William K *NewYHSD*

Ferguson, William Law 1865- *WhAm 4*

Ferguson, William P *NewYHSD*

Ferguson, William Porter Frisbee 1861-1929 *DcAmB, WhAm 1*

Ferguson, William Scott 1875-1954 *NatCAB 42, WhAm 3*

Ferguson, William Stanley 1880-1954 *NatCAB 43*

Ferguson, William Thomas 1847-1927 *NatCAB 27*

Fergusson, Arthur Walsh 1859-1908 *WhAm 1*

Fergusson, Bernard 1911- *WhWW-II*

Fergusson, E Morris 1864-1934 *WhAm 1*

Fergusson, Frank Kerby 1874-1937 *WhAm 1*

Fergusson, Harvey 1890-1971 *REnAW*

Fergusson, Harvey Butler 1848-1915 *BiDrAC, WhAm 1*

Fergusson, Robert Archibald 1920-1966 *NatCAB 52*

Fergusson, Sir William 1808-1877 *BiHiMed*

Feria, Pedro 1524-1588 *ApCAB*

Ferlaino, Frank Ralph 1900-1953 *NatCAB 39, WhAm 3*

Ferland, LAbbe 1805-1864 *Drake*

Ferland, John Antony Baptist 1805-1865 *ApCAB*

Ferm, Vergilius Ture Anselm 1896-1974 *WhAm 6*

Ferman, Joseph Wolfe 1906-1974 *WhAm 6*

Fermat, Pierre De 1601-1665 *AsBiEn, DcScB, McGEWB*

Fermi, Enrico 1901-1954 *AsBiEn, DcAmB S5, DcScB, EncAB, McGEWB, NatCAB 40, WebAB, WhAm 3*

Fermoy, Matthias Alexis Roche De 1737?-1778? *ApCAB Sup*

Fern, Fanny *AmBi, EncAB, NotAW, WebAB, WhAm H*

Fernald, Bert Manfred 1858-1926 *ApCAB X, BiDrAC, NatCAB 15, NatCAB 24, WhAm 1, WhAmP*

Fernald, Charles Henry 1838-1921 *ApCAB, BiDAmEd, DcAmB, NatCAB 9, TwCBDA, WhAm 1*

Fernald, Chester Bailey 1869-1938 *TwCBDA, WhAm 1*

Fernald, Frank Lysander 1835- *WhAm 1*

Fernald, Grace Maxwell *WomWWA 14*

Fernald, Gustavus Stockman 1857-1925 *WhAm 1*

Fernald, Guy Goodwin 1865-1939 *NatCAB 28*

Fernald, Henry Barker 1878-1967 *WhAm 4*

Fernald, Henry Torsey 1866-1952 *NatCAB 18, TwCBDA, WhAm 3*

Fernald, James Champlin 1838-1918 *DcAmB, TwCBDA, WhAm 1*

Fernald, Josiah Eastman 1856-1949 *NatCAB 37*

Fernald, Merritt Caldwell 1838-1916 *ApCAB, NatCAB 14, TwCBDA, WhAm 1*

Fernald, Merritt Lyndon 1873-1950 *DcAmB S4, DcScB, NatCAB 38, WhAm 3*

Fernald, Robert Foss 1890-1962 *WhAm 4*

Fernald, Robert Heywood 1871-1937 *WhAm 1*

Fernald, Roy Lynde 1901-1951 *NatCAB 39*

Fernald, Walter Elmore 1859-1924 *WhAm 1*

Fernan, T S *NewYHSD*

Fernandel 1903-1971 *WhAm 5*

Fernandes Calabar, Domingos d1635 *ApCAB*

Fernandes Pinheiro, Jose Feliciano 1774-1847 *ApCAB*

Fernandes-Sardinha, Pedro 1497-1556 *ApCAB*

Fernandez, Antonio Manuel 1902-1956 *BiDrAC, WhAm 3, WhAmP*

Fernandez, Diego 1530?-1581 *ApCAB, Drake*

Fernandez, Francisco Maria 1886-1937 *NatCAB 28*

Fernandez, Joachim Octave 1896- *BiDrAC*

Fernandez, John D 1848- *WhAm 4*

Fernandez, Juan 1490-1538 *ApCAB*

Fernandez, Juan 1526-1576 *ApCAB, Drake*

Fernandez, Manuel Lawrence 1876-1954 *NatCAB 43*

Fernandez, Prospero 1834-1885 *ApCAB*

Fernandez DeC Andrade Y Portugal, Pedro 1634-1672 *ApCAB*

Fernandez DeCordova, Diego d1650? *ApCAB*

Fernandez DeLizardi, Jose Joaquin 1776-1827 *McGEWB*

Fernandez DePiedrahita, Lucas 1624-1688 *ApCAB*

Fernandez Lizardi, Jose Joaquin 1771-1827 *ApCAB*

Fernandez Madrid, Jose 1789-1829 *ApCAB*

Fernandez Madrid, Pedro 1817-1875 *ApCAB*

Fernandez-Pena Y Angulo, Juan A Ignacio 1781-1849 *ApCAB*

Fernandis, Sarah Collins 1863- *WhoColR*

Fernau, Frederick *NewYHSD*

Fernbach, R Livingston 1876- *WhAm 5*

Fernberger, Samuel Weiller 1887-1956 *WhAm 3*

Fernel, Jean Francois 1497?-1558 *AsBiEn, BiHiMed, DcScB, McGEWB*

Fernholtz, Emil 1856- *NatCAB 18*

Fernley, George Anderson 1891-1972 *WhAm 5*

Fernoro, Thomas B *NewYHSD*

Fernos-Isern, Antonio 1895- *BiDrAC*

Fernow, Bernard Eduard 1851-1923 *ApCAB X, TwCBDA*

Fernow, Bernard Edward 1882-1964 *NatCAB 51*

Fernow, Bernhard Eduard 1851-1923 *AmBi, DcAmB, NatCAB 13, NatCAB 19, WebAB, WhAm 1*

Fernow, Bernice Pauahi Andrews 1881- *WomWWA 14*

Fernow, Berthold 1837-1908 *ApCAB, DcAmB,*

NatCAB 23, TwCBDA, WhAm 1

Fernstrom, Henning 1857-1932 *WhAm 1*

Feroe, Robert Augustus 1886-1950 *NatCAB 41*

Feron, Madame 1797- *WhAm H*

Ferran, Augusto 1813-1879 *IlBEAAW, NewYHSD*

Ferrana, Joseph 1800?- *NewYHSD*

Ferrana, Pilarene 1841?- *NewYHSD*

Ferrand, Marie Louis 1753-1808 *ApCAB*

Ferrara, Orestes 1876- *WhAm 5*

Ferrari, Louis 1879- *WhAm 3*

Ferrari, Ludovico 1522-1565 *DcScB*

Ferrari-Fontano, Edoardo 1878-1936 *WhAm 1*

Ferraris, Galileo 1847-1897 *DcScB*

Ferrata, Giuseppe 1865-1928 *WhAm 1*

Ferre, Nels Fredrik Solomon 1908-1971 *WhAm 5*

Ferree, Arris Idyl 1890-1965 *NatCAB 51*

Ferree, Barr d1924 *TwCBDA, WhAm 1*

Ferree, Clarence Errol 1877-1942 *DcAmB S3, NatCAB 33, WhAm 2*

Ferree, John Willard 1904-1975 *WhAm 6*

Ferree, Susan Frances Nelson 1844- *AmWom*

Ferrein, Antoine 1693-1769 *DcScB*

Ferreira, Alexandre Rodrigues 1756-1815 *ApCAB*

Ferreira DeAraujo Guimaraes, Manoel 1777-1838 *ApCAB*

Ferrel, William 1817-1891 *AmBi, ApCAB, DcAmB, DcScB, NatCAB 9, WhAm H*

Ferrell, Chiles Clifton 1865-1915 *WhAm 1*

Ferrell, John Appley 1865- *WhAm 1*

Ferrell, John Atkinson 1880-1965 *WhAm 4*

Ferrell, Thomas Merrill 1844-1916 *BiDrAC*

Ferrell, William 1817-1891 *TwCBDA*

Ferrelo, Bartolome 1499-1550 *ApCAB*

Ferren, John 1905-1970 *WhAm 5*

Ferren, Sallie Price 1854- *WomWWA 14*

Ferrer, Rafael 1570-1611 *ApCAB*

Ferrer, Ventura P 1772-1857 *ApCAB*

Ferrer-Maldonado, Lorenzo *ApCAB*

Ferrero, Edward 1831-1899 *ApCAB, DcAmB, NatCAB 4, TwCBDA, WhAm 1*

Ferrero, Edward 1832-1899 *Drake Sup*

Ferrero, Guglielmo 1871-1942 *McGEWB*

Ferreta, John *NewYHSD*

Ferreyros, Manuel B 1793-1872 *ApCAB*

Ferri, Antonio 1912-1975 *WhAm 6*

Ferrier, David 1843-1928 *DcScB*

Ferrier, Deborah Larimer 1878- *WomWWA 14*

Ferrier, Edsall 1831- *TwCBDA*

Ferrier, James 1800- *ApCAB*

Ferrier, Kathleen d1953 *WhAm HA, WhAm 4*

Ferrier, William Warren 1855-1945 *WhAm 2*

Ferril, William Columbus 1855- *NatCAB 18*

Ferrin, Albert Whitman 1851-1921 *NatCAB 28*

Ferrin, Augustin William 1875- *NatCAB 15, WhAm 5*

Ferrin, Dana Holman 1886-1960 *NatCAB 47, WhAm 4*

Ferrin, Mary Upton 1810-1881 *NotAW*

Ferrin, William Nelson 1854- *WhAm 4*

Ferris, Albert Warren 1856-1937 *WhAm 1*

Ferris, Amy 1879- *WomWWA 14*

Ferris, Benjamin d1867 *ApCAB*

Ferris, Charles Edward 1864-1951 *NatCAB 38, WhAm 5*

Ferris, Charles Goadsby 1796?-1848 *BiAUS, BiDrAC, WhAm H*

Ferris, Cornelius 1866- *WhAm 4*

Ferris, David 1821-1907 *WhAm 1*

Ferris, David Lincoln 1864-1947 *WhAm 2*

Ferris, Eleanor Amanda *WomWWA 14*

Ferris, Elmer Ellsworth 1861-1951 *WhAm 3*

Ferris, Eugene B, Jr. 1905-1957 *WhAm 3*

Ferris, Floyd Franklin 1898-1966 *NatCAB 52*

Ferris, George Floyd 1902-1967 *WhAm 4*

Ferris, George Hooper 1867-1917 *WhAm 1*

Ferris, George Washington Gale 1859-1896 *ApCAB Sup, DcAmB, NatCAB 13, WebAB, WhAm H*

Ferris, Gordon Floyd 1893-1958 *NatCAB 47*

Ferris, Harry Burr 1865-1940 *NatCAB 30, WhAm 1*

Ferris, Helen 1890-1969 *NatCAB 55, WhAm 5*

Ferris, Henry Lakin 1850-1932 *NatCAB 24*

Ferris, Ida May St. John 1849- *WomWWA 14*
Ferris, Isaac 1798-1873 *ApCAB, DcAmB, NatCAB 6, TwCBDA, WhAm H*
Ferris, Jean Leon Gerome 1863-1930 *AmBi, DcAmB, IlBEAAW, NatCAB 13, NatCAB 23, WhAm 1*
Ferris, Joel Edward 1874- *WhAm 6*
Ferris, John Mason 1825-1911 *ApCAB, TwCBDA, WhAm 1*
Ferris, John Wallace DeBeque 1878- *WhAm 6*
Ferris, Mary Lanman Douw 1855-1932 *WhAm 1, WomWWA 14*
Ferris, Morris Patterson 1855-1918 *NatCAB 6, NatCAB 32, TwCBDA, WhAm 1*
Ferris, Ralph Hall 1880- *WhAm 3*
Ferris, Robert Gaye 1905-1970 *NatCAB 55*
Ferris, Royal Andrew 1851- *NatCAB 18*
Ferris, Scott 1877-1945 *BiDrAC, WhAm 5, WhAmP*
Ferris, Stephen James 1835-1915 *NatCAB 33, NewYHSD*
Ferris, Theodore Ernest 1872-1953 *NatCAB 17, NatCAB 42*
Ferris, Theodore Parker 1908- *WhAm 5*
Ferris, Walter Rockwood 1869- *WhAm 5*
Ferris, Walton C 1900-1955 *WhAm 3*
Ferris, Warren Angus 1810-1873 *REnAW*
Ferris, William Henry 1874- *WhoColR*
Ferris, Woodbridge Nathan 1853-1928 *AmBi, ApCAB X, BiDrAC, DcAmB, NatCAB 15, WhAm 1, WhAmP*
Ferriss, Emory Nelson 1882-1946 *NatCAB 35*
Ferriss, Franklin 1849-1933 *WhAm 1*
Ferriss, Hugh 1889-1962 *BnEnAmA, WhAm 4*
Ferriss, James Henry 1849-1926 *WhAm 1*
Ferriss, Orange 1814-1894 *BiAUS, BiDrAC, TwCBDA, WhAm H*
Ferrit, Madame De *NewYHSD*
Ferro, Scipione 1465-1526 *DcScB*
Ferry, Abby Farwell 1851- *WomWWA 14*
Ferry, Charles Kinsley 1857-1940 *NatCAB 39*
Ferry, David William 1876-1955 *WhAm 3*
Ferry, Dexter Mason 1833-1907 *NatCAB 18, NatCAB 21, WhAm 1*
Ferry, Dexter Mason, Jr. 1872-1959 *NatCAB 49, WhAm 3*
Ferry, E Hayward 1864-1940 *WhAm 1*
Ferry, Elisha Peyre 1825-1895 *ApCAB X, DcAmB, NatCAB 1, TwCBDA, WhAm H, WhAmP*
Ferry, Ervin Sidney 1868-1956 *WhAm 3*
Ferry, Francis *NewYHSD*
Ferry, Frederick Carlos 1868- *WhAm 5*
Ferry, George Bowman 1851-1918 *WhAm 1*
Ferry, George Francis 1894-1954 *NatCAB 45, WhAm 3*
Ferry, Hugh J 1884-1970 *WhAm 5*
Ferry, Jules Francois Camille 1832-1893 *McGEWB*
Ferry, Mansfield 1882- *ApCAB X*
Ferry, Montague 1881-1949 *NatCAB 42*
Ferry, Orris S 1823-1875 *BiAUS*
Ferry, Orris Sandford 1823-1875 *TwCBDA*
Ferry, Orris Sanford 1823-1875 *ApCAB, BiDrAC, DcAmB, Drake, NatCAB 2, WhAm H, WhAmP*
Ferry, Thomas White 1826-1896 *NatCAB 9, TwCBDA*
Ferry, Thomas White 1827-1896 *ApCAB, BiAUS, BiDrAC, DcAmB, WhAm H, WhAmP*
Ferry, William Montague 1796-1867 *ApCAB*
Ferry, William Montague 1824-1905 *NatCAB 6*
Ferry, William Montague 1871-1938 *NatCAB 39, WhAm 1*
Fersen, Count Axel 1750-1810 *ApCAB, NatCAB 7*
Fersen, Count Axel 1755-1810 *Drake*
Fersen, Hans Axel, Count Von 1755-1810 *AmBi, DcAmB*
Fersman, Aleksandr Evgenievich 1883-1945 *DcScB*
Ferson, Merton Leroy 1876-1964 *WhAm 4*
Ferst, Monie Alan 1891-1965 *WhAm 4*
Fertig, David Irving 1910-1965 *NatCAB 53*
Fertig, John Henry 1882-1950 *NatCAB 39*
Fertitta, Charles Joseph 1899-1957 *NatCAB 50*
Fertman, Mildred Been 1916-1962 *NatCAB 49*

Ferullo, Francesco 1879- *NatCAB 15*
Fery, John 1865?-1934 *IlBEAAW*
Fesler, Bert 1866-1947 *NatCAB 51*
Fesler, John King 1899-1968 *NatCAB 54*
Fess, Lehr 1891-1965 *NatCAB 53*
Fess, Simeon Davidson 1861-1936 *ApCAB X, BiDAmEd, DcAmB S2, TwCBDA, WhAm 1*
Fess, Simeon Davison 1861-1936 *BiDrAC, NatCAB 27, WhAmP*
Fessenden, Benjamin 1809?- *NewYHSD*
Fessenden, Clementina *WomWWA 14*
Fessenden, Edwin Allan 1882-1967 *NatCAB 54, WhAm 5*
Fessenden, Francis 1839-1906 *ApCAB, DcAmB, Drake, NatCAB 22, TwCBDA, WhAm 1*
Fessenden, Franklin Goodridge 1849-1931 *WhAm 1*
Fessenden, Frederick J 1862- *WhAm 4*
Fessenden, James Deering 1833-1882 *ApCAB, DcAmB, NatCAB 10, TwCBDA, WhAm H*
Fessenden, Joshua Abbe *ApCAB*
Fessenden, Laura Dayton *WhAm 3, WomWWA 14*
Fessenden, Reginald Aubrey 1866-1932 *AsBiEn, DcAmB S1, DcScB, NatCAB 15, TwCBDA, WebAB, WhAm 1*
Fessenden, Reginald Aubrey 1868-1932 *AmBi*
Fessenden, Richard William 1902-1956 *NatCAB 45*
Fessenden, Russell Green 1869-1945 *WhAm 2*
Fessenden, Samuel 1784-1869 *ApCAB, DcAmB, Drake, NatCAB 10, TwCBDA, WhAm H*
Fessenden, Samuel 1841-1862 *ApCAB*
Fessenden, Samuel 1847-1908 *ApCAB, WhAm 1*
Fessenden, Samuel C 1815- *BiAUS*
Fessenden, Samuel Clement 1815-1881 *ApCAB*
Fessenden, Samuel Clement 1815-1882 *BiDrAC, TwCBDA, WhAm H, WhAmP*
Fessenden, Susan Snowden 1840- *WomWWA 14*
Fessenden, T A D 1826-1868 *BiAUS*
Fessenden, Thomas 1739-1813 *ApCAB*
Fessenden, Thomas Amory Deblois 1826-1868 *ApCAB, BiDrAC, TwCBDA, WhAm H, WhAmP*
Fessenden, Thomas Green 1771-1837 *AmBi, ApCAB, DcAmB, Drake, EncAAH, NatCAB 7, TwCBDA, WhAm H*
Fessenden, William Pitt 1806-1869 *AmBi, ApCAB, BiAUS, BiDrAC, BiDrUSE, DcAmB, Drake, EncAB, NatCAB 2, TwCBDA, WebAB, WhAm H, WhAmP*
Fest, Adam *NewYHSD*
Fest, Francis T B 1860- *WhAm 4*
Festner, Frederick C *NewYHSD*
Festorazzi, Angelo 1865-1919 *NatCAB 20*
Feters, W T *NewYHSD*
Fethers, Ogden Hoffman 1845-1911 *WhAm 1*
Fetherston, Edith Hedges 1885-1972 *WhAm 6*
Fetherston, Ernest Albert 1873-1954 *NatCAB 47*
Fetherston, John Patrick 1896-1966 *NatCAB 52*
Fetherston, John Turney 1874-1962 *NatCAB 50, WhAm 4*
Fetherston, William Thomas 1876-1959 *NatCAB 47*
Fetsch *NewYHSD*
Fette, Henry Gerhard *NewYHSD*
Fetter, Charles Harold 1895-1970 *NatCAB 55*
Fetter, Elizabeth Lean Fields Head 1904-1973 *WhAm 6*
Fetter, Frank Albert 1863-1949 *DcAmB S4, WhAm 2*
Fetter, George *NewYHSD*
Fetter, George W 1827- *NatCAB 5*
Fetter, John Henry 1892-1949 *NatCAB 38*
Fetter, John Sylvester 1911-1967 *NatCAB 53*
Fetter, Norman 1864- *WhAm 4*
Fetter, Theodore Roosevelt 1902-1967 *NatCAB 53*
Fetterman, John Davis 1920-1975 *WhAm 6*
Fetterman, William Judd 1833?-1866 *AmBi, DcAmB, WebAMB, WhAm H*
Fetterolf, Adam H 1842- *NatCAB 7*

Fetterolf, Adam Herman 1841-1912 *TwCBDA, WhAm 1*
Fetterolf, Laura Mangam *WomWWA 14*
Fetterolf, Paul Edward 1910-1960 *NatCAB 50*
Fetzer, Frank L 1886-1955 *WhAm 3*
Fetzer, Gottlob 1861- *WhAm 4*
Fetzer, Lewis William 1878- *WhAm 6*
Fetzer, Wade 1879-1956 *NatCAB 46, WhAm 3*
Fetzer, Wade, Jr. 1903-1968 *WhAm 5*
Feuchtwanger, Lewis 1805-1876 *ApCAB, TwCBDA*
Feuchtwanger, Lion 1884-1958 *WhAm 3*
Feuer, Mortimer 1909-1969 *WhAm 5*
Feuerbach, Karl Wilhelm 1800-1834 *DcScB*
Feuerbach, Ludwig Andreas 1804-1872 *McGEWB*
Feuille, Frank 1860-1954 *NatCAB 44*
Feuille, J F *NewYHSD*
Feuillee, Louis 1660-1732 *DcScB*
Feuillerat, Albert Gabriel 1874-1952 *WhAm 3*
Feuillet, Louis Econches 1660-1732 *ApCAB, Drake*
Feulgen, Robert Joachim 1884-1955 *DcScB*
Feuling, Alice Dynes 1869- *WomWWA 14*
Feurt, Seldon Dick 1923-1975 *WhAm 6*
Feustel, Robert Maximilian 1884-1932 *NatCAB 24, WhAm 1, WhAm 1C*
Few, Ignatius Alphonso 1789-1845 *DcAmB, NatCAB 1, TwCBDA, WhAm H*
Few, William 1748-1828 *AmBi, ApCAB, BiAUS, BiDrAC, DcAmB, Drake, NatCAB 2, TwCBDA, WhAm H, WhAmP*
Few, William Preston 1867-1940 *BiDAmEd, DcAmB S2, NatCAB 15, NatCAB 29, WhAm 1*
Fewell, Alexander Garrison 1884-1965 *NatCAB 51*
Fewkes, Jesse Walter 1850-1930 *AmBi, ApCAB Sup, DcAmB, NatCAB 15, REnAW, TwCBDA, WebAB, WhAm 1*
Fewsmith, Henry 1821-1846 *NewYHSD*
Fewsmith, Joseph 1889-1953 *WhAm 3*
Fey, Charles *NewYHSD*
Feyerherm, Harvey August 1919-1973 *WhAm 6*
Feynman, Richard Philips 1918- *AsBiEn*
Feynman, Richard Phillips 1918- *WebAB*
Fezandie, Clement 1865- *WhAm 4*
Ffirth, Stubbins H 1784-1820 *BiHiMed*
Ffoulke, Charles Mather 1841-1909 *DcAmB, NatCAB 16, WhAm 1*
Ffrench, Charles 1861-1916 *NatCAB 16*
Ffrench, Charles Dominic 1775-1851 *DcAmB, WhAm H*
Fiala, Anthony 1869-1950 *ApCAB X, NatCAB 38, WhAm 3*
Fiala, Joseph Charles 1906-1961 *NatCAB 49*
Fiala, Sigmund Nicholas 1900-1968 *WhAm 5*
Fibich, R *NewYHSD*
Fibonacci, Leonardo 1170?-1230? *AsBiEn*
Fibonacci, Leonardo 1170?-1240? *DcScB*
Fibonacci, Leonardo 1180?-1250? *McGEWB*
Fichot, Lazare-Eugene 1867-1939 *DcScB*
Ficht, Hartman *NewYHSD*
Ficht, John H *NewYHSD*
Ficht, Otto C *NewYHSD*
Fichte, Harold O 1914-1971 *WhAm 5*
Fichte, Johann Gottlieb 1762-1814 *McGEWB*
Fichter, Bessie Bleasdale 1879- *WomWWA 14*
Fichthorn, Luke Eberly 1871-1961 *NatCAB 46*
Ficino, Marsilio 1433-1499 *McGEWB*
Fick, Adolf Eugen 1829-1901 *DcScB*
Fick, Adolph 1829-1901 *BiHiMed*
Fick, George Henry 1889-1962 *WhAm 4*
Fick, Henry H 1849-1935 *WhAm 1*
Ficke, Arthur Davison 1883-1945 *NatCAB 35, WhAm 2*
Ficke, Charles August 1850-1931 *NatCAB 30*
Fickel, Jacob Earl 1883-1956 *WhAm 3*
Ficken, Clarence Elwood 1894-1975 *WhAm 6*
Ficken, George John 1900-1962 *WhAm 4*
Ficken, H Edwards d1929 *WhAm 1*
Ficken, Henry Horlbeck 1872-1940 *WhAm 3*
Fickert, Charles Marron 1873-1937 *NatCAB 33*
Fickes, Edwin Stanton 1872-1943 *NatCAB 35*
Fickes, Frank B *NewYHSD*
Fickes, Robert O 1908-1969 *WhAm 5*

Fickinger, James Albert 1853-1903 *NatCAB 21*
Ficklen, Bessie Alexander 1861- *AmWom*
Ficklen, John Rose 1858-1907 *TwCBDA, WhAm 1*
Ficklin, Benjamin F *REnAW*
Ficklin, Joseph 1833-1887 *ApCAB, TwCBDA*
Ficklin, Orlando B 1808- *BiAUS*
Ficklin, Orlando B 1808-1885 *TwCBDA*
Ficklin, Orlando Bell 1808-1886 *BiDrAC, WhAm H*
Fickling, Francis William 1811-1887 *NatCAB 6*
Ficsher, Mario McCaughin 1899-1968 *WhAm 5*
Fidler, Harry L 1870-1934 *WhAm 1*
Fidler, Roswell Schiedt 1898-1952 *NatCAB 44*
Fieandt, Rainer Von 1890-1972 *WhAm 5*
Fiebach, Albert H 1876-1955 *WhAm 3*
Fiebeger, Gustav Joseph 1858-1939 *WhAm 1*
Fiedler, Arthur 1894- *WebAB*
Fiedler, Edward Henry 1895-1973 *WhAm 6*
Fiedler, William Henry Frederick 1847-1919 *BiDrAC*
Fiekers, Bernard Albert 1906-1973 *WhAm 5*
Field, Ada Martitia *WomWWA 14*
Field, Albert Daniel 1853-1923 *NatCAB 20*
Field, Allan Bertram 1875- *WhAm 5*
Field, Allen Wescott 1853- *TwCBDA, WhAm 4*
Field, Archelaus G 1829- *ApCAB, WhAm 4*
Field, Benjamin 1816-1876 *ApCAB*
Field, Benjamin Hazard 1814-1893 *ApCAB, DcAmB, NatCAB 3, TwCBDA, WhAm H*
Field, Benjamin Rush 1861-1935 *NatCAB 12, WhAm 1*
Field, Betty 1918-1973 *WhAm 6*
Field, C Everett 1870- *NatCAB 16*
Field, Caroline Leslie 1853-1902 *TwCBDA, WhAm 1*
Field, Carter 1885-1957 *WhAm 3*
Field, Charles Neale 1849-1929 *WhAm 3*
Field, Charles William 1828-1892 *AmBi, BiDConf, DcAmB, WhAm H*
Field, Charlotte E 1838-1920 *NewYHSD*
Field, Cortlandt DePeyster 1839-1918 *TwCBDA, WhAm 1*
Field, Crosby 1889-1972 *WhAm 5*
Field, Cynthia 1926-1973 *WhAm 6*
Field, Cyrus West 1819-1892 *AmBi, ApCAB, AsBiEn, DcAmB, Drake, EncAB, McGEWB, NatCAB 4, TwCBDA, WebAB, WhAm H*
Field, Daniel F 1872-1937 *WhAm 1*
Field, David Dudley 1781-1867 *AmBi, ApCAB, DcAmB, Drake, NatCAB 4, TwCBDA*
Field, David Dudley 1805-1894 *AmBi, ApCAB, BiDrAC, DcAmB, Drake, McGEWB, NatCAB 4, TwCBDA, WebAB, WhAm H*
Field, David Mason 1849- *WhAm 4*
Field, Edmund Mills 1889-1972 *NatCAB 57*
Field, Edward 1858- *WhAm 4*
Field, Edward Bell 1850-1919 *NatCAB 18, WhAm 1*
Field, Edward Davenport 1879- *WhAm 6*
Field, Edward Pearsall, Jr. 1908-1965 *WhAm 4*
Field, Edward R *NewYHSD*
Field, Edward Salisbury 1840-1927 *NatCAB 32*
Field, Edwin Stanton 1869- *TwCBDA*
Field, Elias 1882-1949 *NatCAB 38*
Field, Elisha C 1842-1916 *WhAm 1*
Field, Mrs. Erastus Salisbury *NewYHSD*
Field, Erastus Salisbury 1805-1900 *BnEnAmA, NewYHSD, WebAB, WhAm H*
Field, Eugene 1850-1895 *AmBi, ApCAB Sup, DcAmB, NatCAB 1, TwCBDA, WebAB, WhAm H*
Field, F Bernice 1906-1974 *WhAm 6*
Field, Frank Harvey 1863- *WhAm 4*
Field, Fred Forest 1861-1934 *NatCAB 48*
Field, Fred Tarbell 1876-1950 *DcAmB S4, NatCAB 38, WhAm 3*
Field, George Wilton 1863- *WhAm 4*
Field, Gertrude Rugg *WomWWA 14*
Field, Hamilton Easter 1873-1922 *NatCAB 17, WhAm 1*
Field, Harold Crins 1872-1949 *NatCAB 48*
Field, Harry Ashby 1862-1936 *WhAm 1*
Field, Harry Hubert 1897-1946 *WhAm 2*

Field, Heman H 1857- *WhAm 4*
Field, Henry 1871-1949 *NatCAB 47, WhAm 2*
Field, Henry Alonzo 1870-1957 *WhAm 3*
Field, Mrs. Henry Martyn 1813?-1875 *NewYHSD*
Field, Henry Martyn 1822-1907 *AmBi, ApCAB, DcAmB, Drake, NatCAB 5, TwCBDA, WhAm 1*
Field, Henry Martyn 1837- *ApCAB, TwCBDA*
Field, Herbert H 1883-1955 *WhAm 3*
Field, Herbert Haviland 1868-1921 *DcAmB, WhAm 1*
Field, Hickson Woolman 1849-1925 *NatCAB 23*
Field, Hugh W 1906-1960 *WhAm 4*
Field, Isaac S 1860-1941 *WhAm 1*
Field, Isabel Louise *WomWWA 14*
Field, J A *NewYHSD*
Field, Jacob 1857- *WhAm 4*
Field, James Alfred 1880-1927 *NatCAB 29, WhAm 1*
Field, James Gaven 1826-1901 *ApCAB, NatCAB 12, WhAm 1*
Field, James Gavin 1826-1901 *TwCBDA*
Field, Jessie 1881- *WomWWA 14*
Field, Joseph M 1810-1856 *ApCAB, DcAmB, Drake, NatCAB 13, WhAm H*
Field, Julia A *NewYHSD*
Field, Kate 1838-1896 *DcAmB, NotAW, TwCBDA*
Field, Kate 1840-1896 *AmWom, ApCAB*
Field, Kate 1854-1896 *NatCAB 6*
Field, Laurence B 1905?- *IIBEAAW*
Field, Louise Maunsell *WomWWA 14*
Field, Lovasso 1849-1918 *NatCAB 28*
Field, Marriott *NewYHSD*
Field, Marshall 1834-1906 *AmBi, DcAmB, McGEWB, WebAB*
Field, Marshall 1835-1906 *ApCAB Sup, EncAB, NatCAB 6, TwCBDA, WhAm 1*
Field, Marshall 1893-1956 *WhAm 3*
Field, Marshall, IV 1916-1965 *WhAm 4*
Field, Martha R 1856- *AmWom*
Field, Martin 1773-1833 *ApCAB*
Field, Martin Thomas 1875-1958 *NatCAB 44*
Field, Mary Hickson Matthews *NatCAB 23*
Field, Mary Katherine Keemle 1838-1896 *DcAmB, WhAm H*
Field, Matthew C 1812-1844 *ApCAB*
Field, Maunsell B d1864 *BiAUS*
Field, Maunsell Bradhurst 1822-1875 *ApCAB, DcAmB, NatCAB 23, TwCBDA, WhAm H*
Field, Moses 1779-1833 *NatCAB 23*
Field, Moses W 1828-1889 *BiAUS*
Field, Moses Wheelock 1828-1889 *NatCAB 27*
Field, Moses Whelock 1828-1889 *BiDrAC, WhAm H, WhAmP*
Field, Nathaniel 1805-1888 *ApCAB*
Field, Neill Brooks 1854-1932 *WhAm 1*
Field, Oliver Peter 1897-1953 *NatCAB 46, WhAm 3*
Field, Mrs. P G d1859 *NewYHSD*
Field, Peter 1876-1949 *NatCAB 38*
Field, Rachel Lyman 1894-1942 *NatCAB 33, NotAW, WhAm 2*
Field, Richard Montgomery 1885-1961 *NatCAB 50*
Field, Richard Stockton 1803-1870 *ApCAB, BiAUS, BiDrAC, DcAmB, Drake, NatCAB 23, TwCBDA, WhAm H, WhAmP*
Field, Richard Stockton 1890- *WhAm 3*
Field, Robert 1769?-1819 *DcAmB, NewYHSD, WhAm H*
Field, Robert E Lee 1896-1962 *WhAm 4*
Field, Robert Michael d1949 *WhAm 2*
Field, Robert Patterson 1850- *WhAm 4*
Field, Roswell Martin 1851-1919 *DcAmB, NatCAB 22, WhAm 1*
Field, Salisbury 1878-1936 *NatCAB 32*
Field, Samuel 1823- *ApCAB*
Field, Sara Bard *BiCAW*
Field, Sara Buxton 1885- *WomWWA 14*
Field, Scott 1847-1931 *BiDrAC, WhAm 5*
Field, Stanley 1875-1964 *NatCAB 50, WhAm 4*
Field, Stephen Dudley 1846-1913 *DcAmB,*

WhAm 1
Field, Stephen Johnson 1816-1899 *AmBi, ApCAB, BiAUS, DcAmB, Drake, EncAB, McGEWB, NatCAB 1, REnAW, TwCBDA, WebAB, WhAm H*
Field, Theron Rockwell 1869-1940 *WhAm 1*
Field, Thomas Power 1814-1894 *TwCBDA*
Field, Thomas Warren 1820-1881 *ApCAB, NatCAB 24*
Field, Thomas Warren 1821-1881 *DcAmB, WhAm H*
Field, Walbridge Abner 1833-1899 *ApCAB Sup, BiAUS, BiDrAC, DcAmB, NatCAB 13, TwCBDA, WhAm 1*
Field, Walter Taylor 1861-1939 *WhAm 1*
Field, Wells Laflin 1846-1914 *WhAm 1*
Field, William *NewYHSD*
Field, William Henry 1877-1935 *WhAm 1*
Field, William Hildreth 1843-1900 *ApCAB Sup, WhAm 1*
Field, William Jefferson 1873-1964 *WhAm 4*
Field, William Lusk Webster 1876-1963 *WhAm 4*
Field, William Perez 1873- *WhAm 5*
Field, Winston Joseph 1904-1969 *WhAm 5*
Fielde, Adele Marion 1839-1916 *WhAm 1, WomWWA 14*
Fielder, Clarence Hunt 1884-1962 *WhAm 4*
Fielder, Frank Sidney 1866-1917 *NatCAB 25*
Fielder, George Bragg 1842-1906 *BiDrAC, NatCAB 3, TwCBDA*
Fielder, James Fairman 1867-1954 *NatCAB 15, WhAm 3*
Fielder, John W *NewYHSD*
Fielder, William 1852-1936 *WhAm 1*
Fielding, E M *NewYHSD*
Fielding, Henry 1707-1754 *McGEWB*
Fielding, Mantle 1865-1941 *WhAm 1*
Fielding, Michael Farlow 1896-1966 *WhAm 4*
Fielding, William John 1886-1973 *WhAm 6*
Fielding, William Stevens 1848- *ApCAB*
Fieldner, Arno Carl 1881-1966 *WhAm 4*
Fields, Annie Adams 1834-1915 *ApCAB, DcAmB, NotAW, TwCBDA, WhAm 2, WomWWA 14*
Fields, Dorothy 1905-1974 *WhAm 6*
Fields, Elijah H 1874- *WhoColR*
Fields, Ernest Seymour 1897-1963 *NatCAB 51, WhAm 4*
Fields, Harold 1890-1962 *WhAm 4*
Fields, Herbert 1897-1958 *WhAm 3*
Fields, James Thomas 1816-1881 *TwCBDA*
Fields, James Thomas 1817-1881 *AmBi, ApCAB, DcAmB, Drake, NatCAB 1, WhAm H*
Fields, John 1871-1934 *WhAm 1*
Fields, John Charles *WhoColR*
Fields, John Charles 1863-1932 *DcScB*
Fields, Joseph Edward 1878-1951 *NatCAB 40, WhAm 3*
Fields, Lew 1867-1941 *WhAm 1*
Fields, Lewis Maurice 1867-1941 *DcAmB S3, NatCAB 14*
Fields, Louis Glenn 1900-1956 *WhAm 3*
Fields, Mitchell 1901-1966 *WhAm 4*
Fields, W C 1879-1946 *McGEWB*
Fields, William Claude 1880-1946 *DcAmB S4, WebAB, WhAm 2*
Fields, William Craig 1804-1882 *BiAUS, BiDrAC, WhAm H*
Fields, William Henry 1869-1945 *WhAm 3*
Fields, William Jason 1874-1954 *BiDrAC, WhAm 3, WhAmP*
Fields, Willie 1877- *WomWWA 14*
Fiene, Ernest 1894-1965 *WhAm 4*
Fienzes, F *NewYHSD*
Fiero, James Newton 1847-1931 *TwCBDA, WhAm 1*
Fiero, Joshua, Jr. 1818-1886 *NatCAB 23*
Fiero, Joshua Milton 1849-1932 *NatCAB 23*
Fiero, William Pierson 1843-1912 *NatCAB 23*
Fieser, James Louis 1883-1965 *NatCAB 51, WhAm 4*
Fiesinger, William Louis 1877-1953 *BiDrAC*
Fiessinger, Noel 1881-1946 *DcScB*
Fife, Charles Andrew 1871-1935 *NatCAB 42*
Fife, Duncan *WebAB*
Fife, Elias 1882-1959 *NatCAB 46*

Fife, Eugene Morton 1916-1966 *NatCAB 52*

Fife, George Buchanan 1869-1939 *AmBi, WhAm 1*

Fife, Harvey Rowe 1899-1959 *NatCAB 47*

Fife, James 1897-1975 *WhAm 6*

Fife, Joseph Paull d1947 *WhAm 2*

Fife, Ray 1883-1950 *WhAm 3*

Fife, Robert Herndon 1871-1958 *WhAm 3*

Fifer, Joseph Wilson 1840-1938 *DcAmB S2, NatCAB 11, TwCBDA, WhAm 1*

Fifer, Orien Wesley 1868-1947 *WhAm 2*

Fifield, Albert Frank 1876-1958 *WhAm 3*

Fifield, Alice Ward Burnham 1864- *WomWWA 14*

Fifield, Benjamin Franklin 1832-1911 *TwCBDA, WhAm 1*

Fifield, Effie W Merriman 1857- *WomWWA 14*

Fifield, Henry Allen 1850- *WhAm 4*

Fifield, Lawrence Wendell 1891-1935 *WhAm 1*

Fifield, Lawrence Wendell 1891-1964 *WhAm 4*

Fifield, Samuel Stillman 1839-1915 *WhAm 1*

Fifield, Stella A Gaines 1845- *AmWom*

Figgatt, Tinney Cavenaugh 1882-1973 *WhAm 6*

Figge, Frank Henry John 1904-1973 *WhAm 6*

Figgins, Jesse Dade 1867- *WhAm 4*

Figgis, Dudley Weld 1883-1964 *WhAm 4*

Figl, Leopold 1902-1965 *WhAm 4*

Figueira, Luiz 1585-1643 *ApCAB*

Figueras-Chiques, Jose Maria 1851-1910 *WhAm 1*

Figueres Ferrer, Jose 1906- *McGEWB*

Figueroa, Francisco 1730?-1800? *ApCAB*

Figueroa, Francisco Acuna De 1791-1862 *ApCAB*

Figueroa, Geronimo 1604-1683 *ApCAB Sup*

Fihn, Joseph Adam 1918-1973 *WhAm 6*

Fike, Charles Laird 1902-1950 *WhAm 3*

Fike, Pierre Hicks 1873-1943 *WhAm 2*

Filbert, Ludwig Spang 1825-1903 *NatCAB 4, WhAm 1*

Filbert, William Jennings 1865-1944 *NatCAB 32, WhAm 2*

Filbey, Edward Joseph 1879-1959 *NatCAB 47, WhAm 3, WhAm 4*

Filbey, Emery Thomas 1878- *WhAm 6*

Filene, Edward Albert 1860-1937 *DcAmB S2, NatCAB 45, WebAB, WhAm 1, WhAmP*

Filene, Lincoln 1865-1957 *NatCAB 45, WhAm 3*

Filer, Harry Lambert 1891-1967 *WhAm 5*

Filer, Herbert Augustus 1870-1927 *WhAm 1*

Files, Duke Tarlton 1909-1971 *NatCAB 57*

Files, Howard Weston 1893-1957 *NatCAB 47, WhAm 3*

Filipowicz, Tytus 1873- *WhAm 5*

Fillebrown, Charles Bowdoin 1842-1917 *NatCAB 13, WhAm 1*

Fillebrown, Elizabeth P 1874- *WomWWA 14*

Fillebrown, Herbert Martin 1868- *ApCAB X*

Fillebrown, Thomas 1836-1908 *DcAmB, NatCAB 13*

Fillebrown, Thomas Scott 1834-1884 *ApCAB, TwCBDA*

Filler, Mervin Grant 1873-1931 *NatCAB 25, WhAm 1*

Filley, Chauncey Ives 1829-1923 *WhAm 1*

Filley, Everett Roswell 1894-1958 *NatCAB 47, WhAm 3*

Filley, Horace Clyde 1878-1973 *NatCAB 57, WhAm 6*

Filley, Mary A Powers 1821- *AmWom*

Fillion, Francis 1851- *WhAm 4*

Fillis, Ben Earle 1889-1969 *NatCAB 54, WhAm 5*

Fillmore, Abigail Powers 1798-1853 *AmWom, NatCAB 6, NotAW*

Fillmore, Charles Sherlock 1854-1948 *DcAmB S4, DcAmReB, WhAm 3*

Fillmore, Henry Daniel 1863-1935 *NatCAB 26*

Fillmore, John Comfort 1843-1898 *BiDAmEd, DcAmB, NatCAB 23, TwCBDA, WhAm H*

Fillmore, Millard 1800- *Drake*

Fillmore, Millard 1800-1871 *BiDrUSE*

Fillmore, Millard 1800-1872 *BiAUS*

Fillmore, Millard 1800-1874 *AmBi, ApCAB, BiDrAC, DcAmB, EncAAH, EncAB,*

McGEWB, *NatCAB 6, TwCBDA, WebAB, WhAm H, WhAmP*

Fillmore, Myrtle Page 1845-1931 *DcAmReB, NotAW*

Fillmore, Parker 1878-1944 *WhAm 2*

Fillmore, Waldo Rickert 1884-1965 *WhAm 4*

Fillmore, William *NewYHSD*

Fillot, Adolphe *NewYHSD*

Filmer, John *NewYHSD*

Filmer, Sir Robert d1653 *McGEWB*

Filon, Michael 1820-1893 *NatCAB 4*

Filsinger, Ernst B 1880-1937 *WhAm 2*

Filson, John 1747?-1788 *AmBi, DcAmB, NatCAB 10, TwCBDA, WebAB, WhAm H*

Fimple, John H 1903- *WhAm 4*

Finan, Joseph B 1869-1943 *WhAm 2*

Finch, Asahel 1809-1883 *NatCAB 3*

Finch, Doak 1898-1967 *NatCAB 54*

Finch, E E *NewYHSD*

Finch, Edward Ridley 1873-1965 *NatCAB 52, WhAm 4*

Finch, Francis Miles 1827-1907 *AmBi, ApCAB, DcAmB, NatCAB 11, TwCBDA, WhAm 1*

Finch, Frederick L 1905-1957 *WhAm 3*

Finch, George Augustus 1884-1957 *WhAm 3*

Finch, H Stanley 1853-1942 *NatCAB 31*

Finch, Henry LeRoy d1960 *WhAm 3*

Finch, Herbert Isaac 1875- *WhAm 5*

Finch, Irving A 1836-1904 *NatCAB 15*

Finch, Isaac 1783-1845 *BiAUS, BiDrAC, WhAm H*

Finch, James Kip 1883-1967 *WhAm 4*

Finch, Jessica Garretson 1873- *WomWWA 14*

Finch, John Aylard 1852-1915 *NatCAB 16*

Finch, John Aylard 1854-1915 *ApCAB X, WhAm 1*

Finch, John Wellington 1873-1951 *NatCAB 39, WhAm 5*

Finch, Morton Easley 1877-1949 *NatCAB 38, WhAm 3*

Finch, Nina Tree 1876- *WomWWA 14*

Finch, Opal Clair Lane 1907-1974 *WhAm 6*

Finch, Peyton Newell, Jr. 1921-1968 *WhAm 5*

Finch, Robert H 1925- *BiDrUSE*

Finch, Royal George 1884-1959 *WhAm 4*

Finch, Ruy Herbert 1890-1957 *WhAm 3*

Finch, Stanley Wellington 1872- *WhAm 5*

Finch, Thomas Austin 1890-1943 *WhAm 2*

Finch, Vernor Clifford 1883-1959 *WhAm 3*

Finch, Volney Cecil 1892-1953 *WhAm 3*

Finch, William Albert 1855-1912 *TwCBDA, WhAm 1*

Finch, William Rufus 1847-1913 *NatCAB 13, NatCAB 15, TwCBDA, WhAm 1*

Fincher, Edgar Franklin, Jr. 1900-1969 *NatCAB 56, WhAm 5*

Fincher, Joseph Wylie 1878-1948 *NatCAB 37*

Finck, Abbie Helen Cushman 1868- *WomWWA 14*

Finck, Edward Bertrand 1870- *WhAm 5*

Finck, Henry Theophilus 1854-1926 *AmBi, ApCAB, DcAmB, NatCAB 14, TwCBDA, WhAm 1*

Finck, William Edward 1822-1901 *BiDrAC*

Fincke, Clarence Mann 1874-1959 *WhAm 3*

Fincke, Mattie Brown 1875- *WomWWA 14*

Finckel, Martin Luther 1842-1926 *WhAm 1*

Findenegg, Ingomar 1896-1974 *WhAm 6*

Findlay, Hugh 1879-1950 *WhAm 3*

Findlay, James 1770-1835 *BiDrAC, DcAmB, WhAm H, WhAmP*

Findlay, James 1775?-1835 *ApCAB, BiAUS, Drake, NatCAB 5, TwCBDA*

Findlay, Jessica White *WomWWA 14*

Findlay, John 1766-1838 *ApCAB, BiAUS, BiDrAC, TwCBDA, WhAm H, WhAmP*

Findlay, John King 1803-1885 *ApCAB, TwCBDA*

Findlay, John VanLear 1839-1907 *ApCAB, BiDrAC, TwCBDA, WhAm 1*

Findlay, Louise Courtenaye O'Donnell 1885- *WomWWA 14*

Findlay, William d1821 *BiAUS*

Findlay, William 1768-1846 *ApCAB, BiAUS, BiDrAC, Drake, NatCAB 2, TwCBDA, WhAm H, WhAmP*

Findlay, William *see also* Findley, William

Findley, Alvin Irwin 1859-1940 *WhAm 1*

Findley, Earl Nelson d1956 *WhAm 3*

Findley, Guy Bernard 1885-1958 *NatCAB 43*

Findley, Howard Malcolm 1877-1958 *NatCAB 47*

Findley, John *REnAW*

Findley, Maud Kinsley *WomWWA 14*

Findley, Palmer 1868-1964 *WhAm 4*

Findley, Paul 1921- *BiDrAC*

Findley, Samuel 1818-1889 *ApCAB, TwCBDA*

Findley, Thomas Maskell 1847- *ApCAB, TwCBDA, WhAm 4*

Findley, Thomas Palmer, Jr. 1901-1974 *WhAm 6*

Findley, William 1741?-1821 *AmBi, BiDrAC, DcAmB, WhAm H, WhAmP*

Findley, William 1750?-1821 *ApCAB, Drake, NatCAB 2, TwCBDA*

Findley, William *see also* Findlay, William

Findley, William Thornton 1814-1893 *ApCAB, TwCBDA*

Findorff, Milton Bremer 1894-1967 *NatCAB 54*

Fine, Benjamin 1905-1975 *WhAm 6*

Fine, Henry Burchard 1858-1928 *AmBi, DcAmB, DcScB, NatCAB 14, WhAm 1*

Fine, Irving Gifford 1914-1962 *NatCAB 49, WhAm 4*

Fine, John 1784-1867 *BiAUS*

Fine, John 1794-1867 *ApCAB, BiDrAC, NatCAB 4, TwCBDA, WhAm H*

Fine, John 1889-1922 *NatCAB 21*

Fine, May Margaret 1869- *WomWWA 14*

Fine, Oronce 1494-1555 *DcScB Sup*

Fine, Sidney Asher 1903- *BiDrAC*

Finegan, James Emmet 1876-1940 *WhAm 1*

Finegan, Thomas Edward 1866-1932 *ApCAB X, BiDAmEd, NatCAB 23, WhAm 1*

Finer, Herman 1898-1969 *WhAm 5*

Finerty, John Frederick 1846-1908 *BiDrAC, NatCAB 13, REnAW, WhAm 1*

Fineshriber, William H 1878-1968 *NatCAB 54*

Finesilver, Benjamin 1898-1969 *WhAm 6*

Finesinger, Jacob Ellis 1902-1959 *WhAm 3*

Finfrock, Clarence Millard 1881-1948 *WhAm 2*

Finger, Aaron 1890-1969 *WhAm 5*

Finger, Charles Joseph 1869-1941 *NatCAB 46, WhAm 1*

Finger, Henry James 1853- *WhAm 4*

Fingerhood, Boris 1887-1946 *WhAm 2*

Fingold, George 1908-1958 *WhAm 3*

Fingold, Samuel 1911-1970 *WhAm 5*

Finigan, Thomas Henry 1896-1968 *NatCAB 55*

Fink, A J 1890-1963 *WhAm 4*

Fink, Albert 1827-1897 *AmBi, ApCAB, DcAmB, EncAB, NatCAB 9, TwCBDA, WebAB, WhAm H*

Fink, Bruce 1861-1927 *WhAm 1*

Fink, Colin Garfield 1881-1953 *WhAm 3*

Fink, Cornelius Winfield 1893-1955 *NatCAB 45*

Fink, David N 1868- *WhAm 4*

Fink, Denman 1880-1956 *WhAm 3*

Fink, Emil C d1942 *WhAm 2*

Fink, Francis A 1907-1971 *WhAm 5*

Fink, Frank Wolfe 1905-1974 *WhAm 6*

Fink, Frederick 1817-1849 *ApCAB, Drake, NewYHSD*

Fink, Frederick William 1846-1924 *NatCAB 27*

Fink, George Rupert 1886-1962 *NatCAB 54, WhAm 4*

Fink, Henry 1831-1912 *WhAm 1*

Fink, Homer Bernard 1881- *WhAm 6*

Fink, Joseph Lionel 1895-1964 *WhAm 4*

Fink, Louis Maria 1834-1904 *ApCAB Sup, WhAm 1*

Fink, Louis Mary 1834?- *TwCBDA*

Fink, Michael 1834- *ApCAB*

Fink, Mike 1770?-1823 *REnAW, WebAB*

Fink, Ollie Edgar 1898-1972 *WhAm 5*

Fink, Reuben 1889-1961 *WhAm 4*

Fink, Samuel Miles 1907-1959 *NatCAB 46*

Fink, Thomas 1561-1656 *DcScB*

Fink, William E 1822- *BiAUS*

Fink, William Green 1870-1949 *NatCAB 43, WhAm 3*

Finke, George 1869- *WhAm 5*

Finke, Walter William 1907-1972 *WhAm 5*

Finke, William F 1859- *WhAm 4*
Finkel, Benjamin Franklin 1865-1947 *TwCBDA, WhAm 2*
Finkeldey, John Frederick *NewYHSD*
Finkelnburg, G A 1837-1908 *BiAUS, WhAm 1*
Finkelnburg, Gustavus Adolphus 1837-1908 *BiDrAC*
Finkelstein, Jacob Joel 1922-1974 *WhAm 6*
Finkenauer, George *NewYHSD*
Finkernagel, Ernest *NewYHSD*
Finkle, Frederick Cecil 1865-1949 *NatCAB 37, WhAm 3*
Finkle, Kate Talbot *WomWWA 14*
Finkler, Rita V Sapiro 1888-1968 *WhAm 5*
Finks, Nettie Velier 1849- *WhAm 4*
Finlay, Carlos Juan 1833-1915 *BiHiMed, DcAmB, DcScB, McGEWB*
Finlay, Charles John 1833-1915 *WhAm 1*
Finlay, George Irving 1876-1961 *NatCAB 47, WhAm 5*
Finlay, Hugh 1731?-1801 *DcAmB, WhAm H*
Finlay, James Ralph 1869- *WhAm 5*
Finlay, John Borland 1826-1897 *NatCAB 2, TwCBDA*
Finlay, John Jerome 1893-1971 *WhAm 5*
Finlay, Kirkman George 1877-1938 *WhAm 1*
Finlay, Walter Stevenson, Jr. 1882-1953 *WhAm 3*
Finlayson, Alan Daniel 1881-1952 *NatCAB 41*
Finlayson, Frank Graham 1864-1947 *WhAm 2*
Finlayson, John Duncan 1886-1950 *NatCAB 39, WhAm 3*
Finley, Anthony *NewYHSD*
Finley, Charles 1865-1941 *BiDrAC, WhAm 1*
Finley, Charles R 1867-1927 *NatCAB 21*
Finley, Charles William 1880-1952 *WhAm 3*
Finley, Clement Alexander 1797-1879 *ApCAB, NatCAB 4, TwCBDA*
Finley, David Edward 1861-1917 *BiDrAC, WhAm 1, WhAmP*
Finley, Ebenezer Byron 1833-1916 *BiDrAC*
Finley, Emmet 1881-1950 *NatCAB 40, WhAm 3*
Finley, Ernest Latimer 1875-1942 *WhAm 2*
Finley, Harold Eugene 1905-1975 *WhAm 6*
Finley, Hugh Franklin 1833-1909 *BiDrAC, TwCBDA*
Finley, James *WhAm H*
Finley, James Bradley 1781-1856 *AmBi, ApCAB, DcAmB, DcAmReB, NatCAB 12, TwCBDA, WhAm H*
Finley, James Bradley 1781-1857 *Drake*
Finley, Jesse Johnson 1812-1904 *ApCAB, BiDConf, BiDrAC*
Finley, John 1722-1769? *ApCAB, REnAW*
Finley, John 1797-1866 *ApCAB*
Finley, John Barclay 1845-1919 *ApCAB X, NatCAB 18*
Finley, John Huston 1863-1940 *AmBi, ApCAB X, BiDAmEd, DcAmB S2, NatCAB 13, NatCAB 30, TwCBDA, WhAm 1, WhAm 2*
Finley, John Norville Gibson 1898-1971 *NatCAB 57*
Finley, John P 1783-1825 *ApCAB*
Finley, Joseph William 1896-1953 *WhAm 3*
Finley, Lorraine Noel 1899-1972 *WhAm 6*
Finley, Martha Farquharson 1828-1909 *AmWom, ApCAB, DcAmB, NatCAB 11, NotAW, TwCBDA, WhAm 1*
Finley, Robert 1772-1817 *AmBi, ApCAB, DcAmB, Drake, NatCAB 9, TwCBDA, WebAB, WhAm H*
Finley, Robert Smith 1804-1860 *ApCAB*
Finley, Robert W 1750-1840 *ApCAB*
Finley, Ruth Ebright 1884-1955 *WhAm 3*
Finley, Samuel 1715-1766 *AmBi, ApCAB, DcAmB, Drake, NatCAB 5, TwCBDA, WhAm H*
Finley, Samuel 1752-1829 *ApCAB, TwCBDA*
Finley, Solomon Henderson 1863-1944 *WhAm 2*
Finley, William Henry 1862-1926 *NatCAB 20, WhAm 1*
Finley, William Lovell 1876-1953 *WhAm 3*
Finley, William Wilson 1853-1913 *NatCAB 14, WhAm 1*
Finn, Francis James 1859-1928 *DcAmB, NatCAB 22, WhAm 1*

Finn, Henry J 1782-1840 *ApCAB, NatCAB 8*
Finn, Henry J 1785?-1840 *Drake*
Finn, Henry James William 1787-1840 *AmBi, DcAmB, NewYHSD, WhAm H*
Finn, Howard Joseph 1895- *WhAm 4*
Finn, John F X 1901-1956 *WhAm 3*
Finn, Matthew D *NewYHSD*
Finn, William Joseph 1881-1961 *WhAm 4*
Finnegan, Edward Rowan 1905-1971 *BiDrAC, WhAm 5*
Finnegan, James A 1906-1958 *WhAm 3*
Finnegan, James Edward 1892-1966 *WhAm 4*
Finnegan, James Francis 1893-1971 *WhAm 6*
Finnegan, John *NewYHSD*
Finnegan, Joseph Francis 1904-1964 *WhAm 4*
Finnegan, Philip J 1886-1959 *WhAm 3*
Finnegan, Richard James 1884-1955 *WhAm 3*
Finnegan, William A d1963 *WhAm 4*
Finnell, Thomas Constantine 1827-1890 *NatCAB 5*
Finnell, Woolsey 1866- *WhAm 4*
Finney, Benjamin Ficklin 1870-1943 *WhAm 2*
Finney, Charles Emery 1860- *NatCAB 12*
Finney, Charles Grandison 1792-1875 *AmBi, ApCAB, BiDAmEd, DcAmB, DcAmReB, Drake, EncAAH, EncAB, McGEWB, NatCAB 2, REnAW, TwCBDA, WebAB, WhAm H*
Finney, Darwin Abel 1814-1868 *BiAUS, BiDrAC, WhAm H*
Finney, David d1806 *ApCAB Sup*
Finney, Edward Clingan 1869- *WhAm 5*
Finney, Everett B 1867-1947 *NatCAB 39*
Finney, Frederick Norton 1832-1916 *WhAm 1*
Finney, James Imboden 1877-1931 *WhAm 1*
Finney, John d1774 *ApCAB Sup*
Finney, John Miller Train 1894-1969 *NatCAB 54*
Finney, John Miller Turpin 1863-1942 *DcAmB S3, WhAm 2*
Finney, Ross Lee 1875-1934 *WhAm 1*
Finney, Samuel d1734 *NatCAB 17*
Finney, Thomas Monroe 1827-1900 *NatCAB 7, NatCAB 26*
Finney, William Parker 1861-1944 *WhAm 2*
Finnigan, George Joseph 1885-1932 *WhAm 1*
Fino, Paul Albert 1913- *BiDrAC*
Finotti, Joseph Maria 1817-1879 *ApCAB, DcAmB, NatCAB 23, TwCBDA, WhAm H*
Finsen, Niels Ryberg 1860-1904 *AsBiEn, DcScB*
Finta, Alexander 1881-1958 *WhAm 3*
Finty, Tom, Jr. 1867-1929 *NatCAB 21, WhAm 1*
Fiocca, Nancy 1916- *WhWW-II*
Fioravanti, Albert 1907-1963 *NatCAB 49*
Fiorio, Franco Emilio 1912-1975 *WhAm 6*
Fiorito, Joseph Anthony 1910-1964 *NatCAB 49*
Fippin, Elmer Otterbein 1879-1949 *WhAm 3*
Firdausi 934-1020 *McGEWB*
Fireman, Peter 1863-1962 *NatCAB 52, WhAm 4*
Firestein, Alfred 1924-1973 *WhAm 5*
Firestone, Charles 1897-1952 *NatCAB 39*
Firestone, Charles E *WhAm 6*
Firestone, Clark Barnaby 1869-1957 *WhAm 3*
Firestone, Harvey Samuel 1868-1938 *AmBi, DcAmB S2, McGEWB, NatCAB 32, WebAB, WhAm 1*
Firestone, Harvey Samuel, Jr. 1898-1973 *WhAm 5*
Firestone, Ray Ernest 1906-1962 *NatCAB 48, WhAm 4*
Firestone, Roger Stanley 1912-1970 *WhAm 5*
Firfires, Nicholas S 1917- *IIBEAAW*
Firing, Thoralf Otmann 1890-1971 *WhAm 5*
Firkins, Oscar W d1932 *WhAm 1*
Firks, Henry *IIBEAAW, NewYHSD*
Firm, Joseph Lannison 1837- *ApCAB, NatCAB 7*
Firm, Joseph Lannison 1839- *WhAm 4*
Firmage, John Leonard 1884-1956 *NatCAB 50*
Firman, Robert John 1880-1955 *NatCAB 45*
Firmicus Maternus *DcScB*
Firmin, Albert Bancroft Wilcox 1868-1959 *WhAm 4*
Firmin, George Deazeley 1865- *TwCBDA*

Firmin, Giles 1615-1697 *ApCAB, Drake*
Firth, Louise Rodman *WomWWA 14*
Fisch, Joseph 1860-1927 *ApCAB X*
Fischel, Martha Ellis 1850- *WomWWA 14*
Fischel, Victor Arnold 1902-1969 *WhAm 5*
Fischel, Walter 1881-1950 *NatCAB 39*
Fischel, Walter Joseph 1902-1973 *WhAm 6*
Fischel, Washington Emil 1850-1914 *WhAm 1*
Fischer *NewYHSD*
Fischer, Alice 1869- *NatCAB 13*
Fischer, Ann Kindrick 1919-1971 *WhAm 6*
Fischer, Anton Otto 1882-1962 *IIBEAAW, WhAm 4*
Fischer, Arthur Frederick 1888-1962 *WhAm 4*
Fischer, Benedickt 1840- *NatCAB 11*
Fischer, Carl Daniel 1855-1921 *NatCAB 19*
Fischer, Carl Ditmar, Jr. 1881-1952 *NatCAB 4*
Fischer, Charles *NewYHSD*
Fischer, Charles Albert 1884-1922 *NatCAB 20*
Fischer, Charles Henry *NewYHSD*
Fischer, David Jule 1903-1964 *NatCAB 50*
Fischer, Earl Britzius 1892-1961 *NatCAB 49, WhAm 4*
Fischer, Earl W 1908-1970 *WhAm 5*
Fischer, Edgar 1873-1922 *NatCAB 19*
Fischer, Edward Louis 1870- *WhAm 5*
Fischer, Emil Friedrich August 1838-1914 *DcAmB*
Fischer, Emil Hermann 1852-1919 *AsBiEn, BiHiMed, DcScB, McGEWB*
Fischer, Ernst Georg 1815-1874 *NewYHSD*
Fischer, Ernst Georg 1852-1935 *WhAm 1*
Fischer, Frederic Philip 1908-1975 *WhAm 6*
Fischer, Frederick *NewYHSD*
Fischer, George Alexander d1922 *WhAm 1*
Fischer, George August 1870-1941 *WhAm 2*
Fischer, Gustave 1875-1971 *NatCAB 56*
Fischer, Hans 1881-1945 *AsBiEn, DcScB Sup, McGEWB*
Fischer, Helen Field 1876- *WomWWA 14a*
Fischer, Henry A Picking 1885-1959 *NatCAB 47*
Fischer, Henry W 1856- *WhAm 4*
Fischer, Herman Arthur 1882-1974 *WhAm 6*
Fischer, Herman George 1879-1950 *NatCAB 4?*
Fischer, Hermann Otto Laurenz 1888-1960 *DcScB, WhAm 4*
Fischer, Israel Frederick 1858-1940 *BiDrAC, TwCBDA, WhAm 4*
Fischer, J F *NewYHSD*
Fischer, Jacob 1871- *WhAm 5*
Fischer, John 1736-1808 *NewYHSD*
Fischer, John 1856-1938 *NatCAB 29*
Fischer, John G *NewYHSD*
Fischer, John Henry 1910- *BiDAmEd*
Fischer, Karl 1883-1950 *WhAm 3*
Fischer, Kermit 1905-1971 *WhAm 5*
Fischer, Laura E R *WomWWA 14*
Fischer, Leo H 1897-1970 *WhAm 5*
Fischer, Leo J d1948 *WhAm 2*
Fischer, Lewis *NewYHSD*
Fischer, Louis 1864-1945 *WhAm 2, WhAm 4*
Fischer, Louis Albert 1865-1921 *WhAm 1*
Fischer, Martin Henry 1879-1962 *WhAm 4*
Fischer, Mary Ellen Sigsbee 1876- *WhAm 5, WomWWA 14*
Fischer, Maurice Ritz 1903-1974 *WhAm 6*
Fischer, Murrel Justus 1906-1967 *NatCAB 55*
Fischer, Nicolaus Wolfgang 1782-1850 *DcScB*
Fischer, Oscar Anton 1889-1968 *NatCAB 55*
Fischer, Oscar Edward 1873-1946 *NatCAB 34*
Fischer, Philip *NewYHSD*
Fischer, Robert James 1943- *WebAB*
Fischer, Willy Hermann 1901-1955 *NatCAB 44*
Fischer-Hansen, Carl 1868- *NatCAB 12*
Fischer VonErlach, Johann Bernhard 1656-1723 *McGEWB*
Fischler, Peter Kalsch 1895-1950 *NatCAB 42, WhAm 3*
Fiset, Sir Eugene 1874- *WhAm 5*
Fiset, Louis Joseph Cyprien 1825- *ApCAB Sup*
Fish, Alfred Lawrence 1877-1955 *WhAm 3*
Fish, Asa Israel 1820-1879 *ApCAB, NatCAB 16*
Fish, Benjamin 1785-1880 *ApCAB*
Fish, Bert 1875-1943 *NatCAB 33, WhAm 2*
Fish, C B *IIBEAAW*
Fish, C W 1863- *WhAm 4*

Fish, Carl Russell 1876-1932 *AmBi,*
DcAmB S1, WhAm 1
Fish, Cary Brown 1867-1941 *NatCAB 31*
Fish, Charles *NewYHSD*
Fish, Charles Everett 1854- *NatCAB 10*
Fish, Daniel 1848-1924 *WhAm 1*
Fish, Edwards R 1870- *WhAm 5*
Fish, Elizabeth Meigs Porter *WomWWA 14*
Fish, Erland Frederick 1883-1942 *NatCAB 32*
Fish, Frank Leslie 1863-1927 *NatCAB 21,*
WhAm 1
Fish, Fred Alan 1875- *WhAm 5*
Fish, Frederick Perry 1855-1930 *ApCAB X,*
NatCAB 26, WhAm 1
Fish, Frederick Samuel 1852-1936 *WhAm 1*
Fish, George G *NewYHSD*
Fish, Hamilton 1808-1893 *AmBi, ApCAB,*
BiAUS, BiDrAC, BiDrUSE, DcAmB,
EncAB, McGEWB, NatCAB 4,
TwCBDA, WebAB, WhAm H, WhAmP
Fish, Hamilton 1809-1893 *Drake*
Fish, Hamilton 1849-1936 *BiDrAC, WhAmP*
Fish, Hamilton 1888- *BiDrAC, WhAmP*
Fish, Hamilton 1926- *BiDrAC*
Fish, Henry Clay 1820-1877 *ApCAB, Drake,*
NatCAB 3, TwCBDA
Fish, Herbert Henry 1870-1948 *NatCAB 36,*
WhAm 5
Fish, Horace 1885-1929 *WhAm 1*
Fish, Horace Walworth 1840-1927 *NatCAB 22*
Fish, Irving Andrews 1881-1948 *WhAm 2*
Fish, J *NewYHSD*
Fish, John Charles Lounsbury 1870- *WhAm 5*
Fish, Marian Graves Anthon 1853-1915 *NotAW*
Fish, May Ashworth 1878- *WomWWA 14*
Fish, May Hall 1885- *WomWWA 14*
Fish, Mayer Alvin 1905-1973 *WhAm 6*
Fish, Melanthon Williams 1828- *ApCAB*
Fish, Milton Ernest 1874- *WhAm 5*
Fish, Nicholas 1758-1833 *AmBi, ApCAB,*
DcAmB, Drake, NatCAB 2, TwCBDA,
WhAm H, WhAmP
Fish, Nicholas 1846-1902 *AmBi, ApCAB,*
NatCAB 11, TwCBDA
Fish, Nicholas 1848-1902 *WhAm 1*
Fish, Paul 1914-1971 *NatCAB 56*
Fish, Pierre Augustine 1865-1931 *NatCAB 23,*
WhAm 1
Fish, Preserved 1766-1846 *DcAmB, NatCAB 7,*
WhAm H
Fish, Stuyvesant 1851-1923 *AmBi, ApCAB X,*
DcAmB, NatCAB 19, TwCBDA,
WhAm 1
Fish, Walter Clark 1865- *WhAm 4*
Fish, William H 1812-1880 *NewYHSD*
Fish, William Hansell 1849- *NatCAB 18,*
WhAm 1
Fish, William Henry 1844- *WhAm 1*
Fish, Williston 1858-1939 *WhAm 1*
Fishback, Charles Fremont 1856- *NatCAB 16*
Fishback, George Welton 1860- *WhAm 4*
Fishback, William Meade 1831-1903
ApCAB Sup, DcAmB, NatCAB 10,
TwCBDA, WhAm 1
Fishbein, Morris 1889- *WebAB*
Fishberg, Maurice 1872-1934 *WhAm 1*
Fishbourne, R W *NewYHSD*
Fishburn, Blair Joshua 1876-1962 *NatCAB 48*
Fishburn, Ernest Boone 1874-1955 *NatCAB 46*
Fishburn, John Eugene 1859-1929 *WhAm 1*
Fishburn, Josephine Redmond *WomWWA 14*
Fishburn, Junius Blair 1865-1955 *NatCAB 41,*
WhAm 3
Fishburn, Junius Parker 1895-1954 *NatCAB 41,*
WhAm 3
Fishburn, Randolph Eugene 1862-1929
WhAm 1
Fishburn, William 1760-1819 *ApCAB, Drake*
Fishburne, Edward Bell 1874- *WhAm 5*
Fishburne, John Wood 1868-1937 *BiDrAC,*
WhAm 1
Fisher *NewYHSD*
Fisher, Adrian Posey 1901-1967 *NatCAB 53*
Fisher, Alanson 1807-1884 *NewYHSD*
Fisher, Albert Kenrick 1856-1948 *NatCAB 37,*
TwCBDA, WhAm 2
Fisher, Alexander H 1862-1929 *ApCAB X*
Fisher, Alexander Metcalf 1794-1822 *ApCAB,*

Drake, NatCAB 19
Fisher, Alphonse Louis 1886-1951 *WhAm 3*
Fisher, Alvan 1792-1863 *ApCAB, BnEnAmA,*
DcAmB, Drake, IlBEAAW, NatCAB 11,
NewYHSD, WhAm H
Fisher, Andrew 1862-1928 *McGEWB*
Fisher, Anna d1942 *WhAm 3*
Fisher, Anna A 1858- *AmWom*
Fisher, Anne B 1898-1967 *WhAm 4, WhAm 5*
Fisher, Arthur 1894-1960 *WhAm 4*
Fisher, Arthur Oscar 1884-1956 *NatCAB 46*
Fisher, Arthur William 1890-1967 *WhAm 5*
Fisher, Ben S 1890-1953 *WhAm 3*
Fisher, Bud 1884-1954 *DcAmB S5, WebAB,*
WhAm 3
Fisher, Bud 1885-1954 *NatCAB 43*
Fisher, Cassius Asa 1872-1930 *WhAm 1*
Fisher, Charles *NewYHSD*
Fisher, Charles 1789-1849 *BiAUS, BiDrAC,*
NatCAB 7, TwCBDA, WhAm H
Fisher, Charles 1808-1880 *ApCAB, Drake*
Fisher, Charles 1816-1891 *NatCAB 1,*
TwCBDA, WhAm H
Fisher, Charles A 1875-1940 *WhAm 1*
Fisher, Charles Asbury 1885-1948 *WhAm 2*
Fisher, Charles E 1853- *WhAm 4*
Fisher, Charles F *NewYHSD*
Fisher, Charles Harris 1822-1893 *ApCAB,*
TwCBDA
Fisher, Charles Lewis 1866- *WhoColR*
Fisher, Charles Thomas, Jr. 1907-1958 *WhAm 3*
Fisher, Charles Willis 1880- *WhAm 6*
Fisher, Clara 1811-1898 *ApCAB, DcAmB,*
NotAW, WhAm H
Fisher, Clarence Stanley 1876-1941 *DcAmB S3,*
NatCAB 40, WhAm 1
Fisher, Clark 1837-1903 *DcAmB*
Fisher, Clyde 1878-1949 *NatCAB 35,*
WhAm 2
Fisher, Daniel C 1887-1961 *WhAm 4*
Fisher, Daniel Robinson 1878-1967 *NatCAB 54*
Fisher, Daniel Webster 1838-1913 *DcAmB,*
NatCAB 2, TwCBDA, WhAm 1
Fisher, David 1794-1886 *ApCAB, BiAUS,*
BiDrAC, WhAm H, WhAmP
Fisher, Dorothy Canfield 1879-1958 *ApCAB X,*
NatCAB 18, NatCAB 44, WebAB,
WhAm 3, WomWWA 14
Fisher, Dorsey Gassaway 1907-1954 *WhAm 3*
Fisher, Ebenezer 1815-1879 *ApCAB,*
BiDAmEd, DcAmB, NatCAB 10,
TwCBDA, WhAm H
Fisher, Edgar Alexander 1866-1938 *NatCAB 28*
Fisher, Edgar Jacob 1885-1968 *NatCAB 55,*
WhAm 5
Fisher, Edmund Drew 1867- *WhAm 4*
Fisher, Edward Dix 1856- *ApCAB X,*
WhAm 4
Fisher, Edward Francis 1891-1972 *NatCAB 57,*
WhAm 5
Fisher, Edward Vincent 1892-1947 *NatCAB 37*
Fisher, Edwin 1883-1947 *WhAm 2*
Fisher, Edwin Lyle 1907-1962 *WhAm 4*
Fisher, Elam 1846-1923 *WhAm 1*
Fisher, Elijah John 1858- *WhoColR*
Fisher, Elizabeth Florette 1873- *WhAm 5,*
WomWWA 14
Fisher, Elwood 1808-1862 *Drake*
Fisher, Emory Devilla 1908-1969 *WhAm 5*
Fisher, Ernest Burdette 1847-1920 *NatCAB 20*
Fisher, Flavius J 1832-1905 *NewYHSD*
Fisher, Frances Christine *ApCAB, NotAW,*
TwCBDA
Fisher, Frank Cyril 1893-1967 *WhAm 5*
Fisher, Franklin L 1885-1953 *WhAm 3*
Fisher, Fred Douglas 1874- *WhAm 5*
Fisher, Frederic John 1878-1941 *DcAmB S3,*
WhAm 1
Fisher, Frederick Bohn 1882-1938 *DcAmB S2,*
NatCAB 28, WhAm 1
Fisher, Frederick Charles 1875- *WhAm 5*
Fisher, Frederick Vining 1866- *WhAm 4*
Fisher, G B *NewYHSD*
Fisher, Galen Merriam 1873-1955 *WhAm 3*
Fisher, Genevieve 1879- *WhAm 6*
Fisher, Geoffrey Francis 1887-1972 *WhAm 5*
Fisher, George 1788-1861 *BiAUS, BiDrAC,*
WhAm H

Fisher, George 1820-1898 *ApCAB X*
Fisher, George Egbert 1863-1920 *WhAm 1*
Fisher, George Harrison 1849-1925 *NatCAB 25*
Fisher, George J 1871-1960 *WhAm 4*
Fisher, George Jackson 1825-1893 *ApCAB,*
DcAmB, TwCBDA, WhAm H
Fisher, George Michael 1868-1940 *NatCAB 31*
Fisher, George Park 1827-1909 *AmBi, ApCAB,*
DcAmB, NatCAB 10, TwCBDA,
WhAm 1
Fisher, George Purnell 1817-1899 *BiAUS,*
BiDrAC, DcAmB, NatCAB 22,
WhAm H, WhAmP
Fisher, George Purnell 1856-1931 *NatCAB 22*
Fisher, Gordon 1873-1945 *NatCAB 34*
Fisher, Gordon 1874-1945 *WhAm 3*
Fisher, Haldane S d1953 *WhAm 3*
Fisher, Hammond Edward 1900-1955 *WhAm 3*
Fisher, Hammond Edward 1901?-1955
DcAmB S5
Fisher, Harold Henry 1890-1975 *WhAm 6*
Fisher, Harrison 1875-1934 *DcAmB S1*
Fisher, Harrison 1877-1934 *AmBi, WhAm 1*
Fisher, Harry Conway 1884-1954 *WebAB*
Fisher, Harry Linn 1885-1961 *WhAm 4*
Fisher, Harry Michael 1882-1958 *NatCAB 49*
Fisher, Harry William 1878-1948 *NatCAB 35*
Fisher, Hendrick 1703- *BiAUS, NatCAB 13*
Fisher, Henry 1843-1929 *NatCAB 52*
Fisher, Henry C 1867-1936 *WhAm 1*
Fisher, Henry Conroy 1884-1954 *DcAmB S5*
Fisher, Henry Johnson 1873-1965 *WhAm 4*
Fisher, Henry Wright 1861-1937 *WhAm 1*
Fisher, Herman Guy 1898-1975 *WhAm 6*
Fisher, Horace Newton 1836- *WhAm 4*
Fisher, Horatio Gates 1838-1890 *BiDrAC,*
TwCBDA, WhAm H
Fisher, Hubert Frederick 1877-1941 *BiDrAC,*
WhAm 1, WhAmP
Fisher, Hugo Antoine 1850?-1916 *IlBEAAW*
Fisher, Ira Rupert, Jr. 1919-1969 *NatCAB 55*
Fisher, Irving 1867-1947 *ApCAB X,*
BiDAmEd, DcAmB S4, McGEWB,
NatCAB 14, TwCBDA, WebAB,
WhAm 2
Fisher, Isaac 1877- *WhoColR*
Fisher, J Gurner 1832-1916 *NatCAB 17*
Fisher, J J *NewYHSD*
Fisher, Jacob Eli 1894-1964 *NatCAB 52*
Fisher, Jake 1871-1951 *NatCAB 47*
Fisher, James Blaine 1884-1953 *NatCAB 44,*
WhAm 3
Fisher, James Cogswell 1808-1880 *NatCAB 28*
Fisher, James Maxwell McConnell 1912-1970
WhAm 5
Fisher, Janon 1862-1943 *NatCAB 33*
Fisher, Jessie Weston 1872- *WomWWA 14*
Fisher, John *BiAUS*
Fisher, John 1806-1882 *BiAUS, BiDrAC,*
WhAm H
Fisher, John Arbuthnot 1841-1920 *WhoMilH*
Fisher, John Charlton d1849 *ApCAB, Drake*
Fisher, John Dix d1850 *Drake*
Fisher, John Dix 1797-1850 *AmBi, DcAmB,*
WhAm H
Fisher, John Dix 1799-1850 *ApCAB*
Fisher, John Frederick 1859- *WhAm 1*
Fisher, John Kenrick 1807- *NewYHSD*
Fisher, John King 1854-1884 *REnAW*
Fisher, John Roberts 1882-1942 *NatCAB 47*
Fisher, John Stuchell 1867-1940 *NatCAB 37,*
WhAm 1
Fisher, John Wesley 1907-1956 *WhAm 3*
Fisher, Jonathan 1768-1847 *ApCAB,*
BnEnAmA, Drake, NewYHSD,
WhAm H
Fisher, Joseph Anton 1895-1973 *WhAm 5*
Fisher, Joseph W *BiAUS, BiAUS Sup*
Fisher, Joshua 1748-1833 *ApCAB, TwCBDA*
Fisher, Joshua 1749-1833 *Drake*
Fisher, Joshua Francis 1807-1873 *AmBi,*
ApCAB, DcAmB, WhAm H
Fisher, Katharine Conner 1872- *WomWWA 14*
Fisher, Lawrence Frederick 1890-1969 *WhAm 6*
Fisher, Lawrence Peter 1888-1961 *WhAm 4*
Fisher, Leonard A 1885- *WhoColR*
Fisher, Lewis Beals 1857-1936 *WhAm 1*
Fisher, Lindale Carson 1899-1973 *WhAm 6*

Fisher, Louise Sanford 1882- *WomWWA 14*
Fisher, Lucius George 1808- *NatCAB 14*
Fisher, Lucius George, Jr. 1843-1916
  NatCAB 14, WhAm 1
Fisher, Lyle Harris 1912-1974 *WhAm 6*
Fisher, M Antoinette Schley *WomWWA 14*
Fisher, Mahlon Leonard 1874-1947 *WhAm 2*
Fisher, Mark 1841-1923 *NatCAB 19,
  WhAm 5*
Fisher, Martin Luther 1871-1942 *WhAm 2*
Fisher, Mary 1623?-1698 *NotAW*
Fisher, Mary 1858- *TwCBDA, WhAm 4*
Fisher, Metta DeBow 1877- *WomWWA 14*
Fisher, Michael Montgomery 1834-1891 *ApCAB,
  NatCAB 8, TwCBDA*
Fisher, Miles Bull 1870- *WhAm 5*
Fisher, Miles Mark 1899-1970 *EncAAH,
  NatCAB 56*
Fisher, Myles d1819 *Drake*
Fisher, Nathaniel 1742-1812 *ApCAB*
Fisher, Newton DeLorain 1843-1893
  NatCAB 16
Fisher, Oliver David 1875-1967 *NatCAB 53,
  WhAm 4*
Fisher, Oliver Mason 1855- *ApCAB X*
Fisher, Oliver William 1842-1922 *NatCAB 19*
Fisher, Olivia 1870- *WomWWA 14*
Fisher, Oscar Louis 1844-1907 *TwCBDA,
  WhAm 1*
Fisher, Otto Orren 1881-1961 *NatCAB 52*
Fisher, Ovie Clark Joseph 1903- *BiDrAC*
Fisher, Paul Julius 1899-1962 *NatCAB 50*
Fisher, Peter H *WhoColR*
Fisher, Philip 1595-1652? *ApCAB, DcAmB*
Fisher, Philip D *IIBEAAW*
Fisher, Ralph Lee 1897-1966 *NatCAB 52*
Fisher, Ralph Talcott 1877-1948 *WhAm 2*
Fisher, Raymond Antonio 1896-1959
  NatCAB 49
Fisher, Rebecca Jane Gilleland *AmWom*
Fisher, Redwood 1783-1856 *Drake*
Fisher, Redwood S 1782-1856 *ApCAB*
Fisher, Richard Thornton 1876-1934
  NatCAB 27, WhAm 1
Fisher, Robert 1894-1960 *WhAm 4*
Fisher, Robert Farley 1878-1953 *WhAm 4*
Fisher, Robert John 1915-1974 *WhAm 6*
Fisher, Robert Jones 1847-1932 *WhAm 1*
Fisher, Robert Joseph 1857-1932 *TwCBDA,
  WhAm 1*
Fisher, Robert Joseph, Jr. 1893-1963 *WhAm 4*
Fisher, Robert Welles 1863-1927 *WhAm 1*
Fisher, Robert Welles 1907-1960 *WhAm 4*
Fisher, Sir Ronald Aylmer 1890-1962 *DcScB,
  McGEWB*
Fisher, Russell Todd 1892-1951 *WhAm 3*
Fisher, S S 1832-1874 *BiAUS*
Fisher, Samuel Brownlee 1846-1926 *WhAm 1*
Fisher, Samuel Herbert 1867- *WhAm 5*
Fisher, Samuel Jackson 1847-1928 *WhAm 1*
Fisher, Samuel Reed 1810-1881 *ApCAB,
  TwCBDA*
Fisher, Samuel Sparks 1832-1874 *ApCAB,
  NatCAB 7, NatCAB 28*
Fisher, Samuel Ware 1814-1874 *ApCAB,
  NatCAB 7, TwCBDA, WhAm H*
Fisher, Sidney George 1809-1871 *ApCAB Sup,
  DcAmB, WhAm H*
Fisher, Sidney George 1856- *ApCAB Sup*
Fisher, Spencer Oliver 1843-1919 *BiDrAC*
Fisher, Stanley Parkins 1892-1958 *NatCAB 49*
Fisher, Stanley Ross 1880- *WhAm 6*
Fisher, Stokely S 1865-1924 *WhAm 1*
Fisher, Sydney Arthur 1850- *ApCAB Sup*
Fisher, Sydney George 1856-1927 *ApCAB,
  DcAmB, NatCAB 13, TwCBDA,
  WhAm 1*
Fisher, Theodore 1789-1819 *NewYHSD*
Fisher, Theodore Willis 1837-1914 *ApCAB,
  DcAmB, TwCBDA, WhAm 4*
Fisher, Thomas 1801-1856 *ApCAB, Drake*
Fisher, Thomas Edward 1869- *WhAm 4*
Fisher, Thomas Kaufman 1915-1964 *WhAm 4*
Fisher, Thomas Russell 1895-1967 *WhAm 4*
Fisher, Vardis 1895-1968 *REnAW, WhAm 5*
Fisher, Waldo Emanuel 1891-1964 *WhAm 4*
Fisher, Walter Kenrick 1878- *WhAm 6*
Fisher, Walter Lowrie 1862-1935 *AmBi,*

Fisher, *BiDrUSE, DcAmB S1, NatCAB 17,
  WhAm 1*
Fisher, Willard Clark 1865- *WhAm 1*
Fisher, William A d1969 *WhAm 5*
Fisher, William Alexander 1837-1901
  NatCAB 25
Fisher, William Alexander 1879- *WhAm 6*
Fisher, William Arms 1861-1948 *DcAmB S4,
  NatCAB 39, TwCBDA, WhAm 2*
Fisher, William Cummings 1876-1932 *WhAm 1,
  WhAm 1C*
Fisher, William Edwin 1878-1954 *NatCAB 41*
Fisher, William H 1854- *WhAm 4*
Fisher, William Mark 1841-1923 *AmBi,
  ApCAB, Drake*
Fisher, William Orris 1875- *WhAm 5*
Fisher, William Victor 1893- *WhAm 5*
Fisher, Willis Richardson 1875- *WhAm 1*
Fisher, Woolf 1912-1975 *WhAm 6*
Fishleigh, Walter Turner 1880-1947
  NatCAB 36
Fishler, Bennett Hill 1887-1969 *NatCAB 54*
Fishman, Leo 1914-1975 *WhAm 6*
Fishpaw, Kenneth B 1910-1975 *WhAm 6*
Fisk, Anna Louise Black 1868- *WomWWA 14*
Fisk, Archie Campbell 1836- *NatCAB 7,
  TwCBDA*
Fisk, Bradley 1904-1962 *WhAm 4*
Fisk, Charles Atwood 1879-1958 *NatCAB 49*
Fisk, Charles Henry 1843-1930 *WhAm 1*
Fisk, Charles Joseph 1862-1932 *WhAm 1*
Fisk, Clinton Bowen 1828-1890 *AmBi, ApCAB,
  DcAmB, NatCAB 6, TwCBDA,
  WhAm H, WhAmP*
Fisk, Daniel Moses 1846- *WhAm 4*
Fisk, Eugene Lyman 1867-1931 *AmBi,
  NatCAB 25, WhAm 1*
Fisk, Everett Olin 1850-1934 *NatCAB 15,
  WhAm 1*
Fisk, Ezra 1785-1833 *ApCAB*
Fisk, Fidelia 1816-1864 *ApCAB, Drake,
  WhAm H*
Fisk, Fidelia *see also* Fiske, Fidelia
Fisk, Franklin Woodbury 1820- *NatCAB 11*
Fisk, Frederick Mewborn 1897-1963
  NatCAB 50, WhAm 4
Fisk, George Clement 1831- *NatCAB 3*
Fisk, George Mygatt 1864- *WhAm 4*
Fisk, Gustaf Leonard 1887-1953 *NatCAB 40*
Fisk, Harlan Wilbur 1869-1932 *WhAm 1*
Fisk, Harold N 1908-1964 *WhAm 4*
Fisk, Harry T *IIBEAAW*
Fisk, Harvey 1831-1890 *NatCAB 11*
Fisk, Herbert Franklin 1840-1916 *WhAm 1*
Fisk, James 1762?-1844 *ApCAB, BiAUS,
  Drake*
Fisk, James 1763-1844 *BiDrAC, DcAmB,
  NatCAB 8, TwCBDA, WhAm H,
  WhAmP*
Fisk, James 1834-1872 *AmBi, DcAmB, Drake,
  EncAAH, McGEWB, NatCAB 22, WebAB,
  WhAm H*
Fisk, Janette 1832-1912 *BiCAW*
Fisk, Jessie 1895-1967 *WhAm 5*
Fisk, John *WebAB*
Fisk, Jonathan 1778-1832 *BiAUS, BiDrAC,
  WhAm H*
Fisk, Katharine 1861- *WhAm 4*
Fisk, Kerby H 1903-1962 *WhAm 4*
Fisk, Louisa Holman Richardson 1861-1955
  WhAm 3
Fisk, Mary Etta Doolittle 1851- *WomWWA 14*
Fisk, May Isabel *WomWWA 14*
Fisk, Nathan 1733-1799 *Drake*
Fisk, Nathan *see also* Fiske, Nathan
Fisk, Otis Harrison 1870-1944 *NatCAB 33*
Fisk, Photius Kavasales 1807?-1890 *TwCBDA*
Fisk, Pliny 1792-1825 *ApCAB, Drake*
Fisk, Pliny 1860- *NatCAB 14*
Fisk, Pliny *see also* Fiske, Pliny
Fisk, Richmond 1836- *NatCAB 10*
Fisk, Samuel 1828-1864 *ApCAB, Drake*
Fisk, Samuel Augustus 1856-1915 *NatCAB 6,
  WhAm 1*
Fisk, W *IIBEAAW*
Fisk, Wilbur 1792-1839 *AmBi, ApCAB,
  BiDAmEd, DcAmB, DcAmReB, Drake,
  NatCAB 3, TwCBDA, WhAm H*

Fiske, Adam Hastings 1894-1959 *WhAm 3*
Fiske, Amos Kidder 1842-1921 *DcAmB,
  NatCAB 20, TwCBDA, WhAm 1*
Fiske, Arthur Irving 1848- *WhAm 4*
Fiske, Asa Severance 1833- *WhAm 4*
Fiske, Augustus Henry 1880-1945 *NatCAB 33,
  WhAm 6*
Fiske, Beulah R 1886- *WomWWA 14*
Fiske, Bradley Allen 1854-1942 *DcAmB S3,
  NatCAB 13, NatCAB 31, TwCBDA,
  WebAMB, WhAm 2*
Fiske, Charles 1868-1941 *WhAm 1*
Fiske, Charles Albert 1837-1915 *NewYHSD*
Fiske, Charles Norman 1876-1964 *NatCAB 51*
Fiske, Charles Parker 1892-1968 *WhAm 5*
Fiske, Daniel Willard 1831-1904 *AmBi,
  ApCAB, DcAmB, NatCAB 25, TwCBDA,
  WhAm 4*
Fiske, David Luther 1840-1935 *NatCAB 26*
Fiske, Edmund Walter 1874-1940 *WhAm 1*
Fiske, Eugene Allen 1848- *WhAm 1*
Fiske, Eugene William 1892-1962 *NatCAB 50*
Fiske, Fidelia 1816-1864 *AmWom, DcAmB,
  NatCAB 3, NotAW*
Fiske, Fidelia *see also* Fisk, Fidelia
Fiske, G Walter 1872-1945 *NatCAB 35*
Fiske, George Converse 1872-1927 *DcAmB,
  WhAm 5*
Fiske, George McClellan 1850- *WhAm 4*
Fiske, George McClelland 1850- *ApCAB Sup*
Fiske, George Walter 1872-1945 *BiDAmEd,
  WhAm 2*
Fiske, Gertrude 1879-1961 *WhAm 4*
Fiske, Haley 1852-1929 *DcAmB, NatCAB 21,
  WebAB, WhAm 1*
Fiske, Harold Benjamin 1871-1960 *NatCAB 49,
  WhAm 5*
Fiske, Harrison Grey 1861-1942 *DcAmB S3,
  NatCAB 10, TwCBDA, WhAm 2*
Fiske, Horace Spencer 1859-1940 *NatCAB 15,
  WhAm 1*
Fiske, James Porter 1866-1941 *WhAm 1*
Fiske, John 1744-1797 *ApCAB, DcAmB,
  Drake, WebAMB, WhAm H*
Fiske, John 1842-1901 *AmBi, ApCAB,
  DcAmB, McGEWB, NatCAB 3,
  TwCBDA, WebAB, WhAm 1*
Fiske, John Sage 1870- *NatCAB 3*
Fiske, Lewis Ransom 1825-1901 *NatCAB 5,
  TwCBDA, WhAm 1*
Fiske, Louis Samuel 1844-1916 *NatCAB 34*
Fiske, Marie Antoinette *NewYHSD*
Fiske, Mary Augusta Davey 1865- *NatCAB 10,
  TwCBDA*
Fiske, Mary Duncan 1871- *WomWWA 14*
Fiske, Minnie Maddern 1865-1932 *AmBi,
  AmWom, DcAmB S1, NatCAB 35,
  NotAW, WebAB, WhAm 1,
  WomWWA 14*
Fiske, Nathan 1733-1799 *ApCAB, NatCAB 7*
Fiske, Nathan *see also* Fisk, Nathan
Fiske, Nathan W 1798-1847 *NatCAB 7*
Fiske, Nathan Welby 1798-1847 *ApCAB,
  NatCAB 5, TwCBDA*
Fiske, Nathan Wilby 1798-1847 *Drake*
Fiske, Oliver 1762-1836 *ApCAB*
Fiske, Pliny 1794-1825 *NatCAB 3*
Fiske, Pliny *see also* Fisk, Pliny
Fiske, Samuel 1828-1891 *NatCAB 11*
Fiske, Stephen Ryder 1840-1916 *DcAmB,
  TwCBDA, WhAm 1*
Fiske, Thomas Scott 1865-1944 *NatCAB 12,
  WhAm 2*
Fiske, W *NewYHSD*
Fiske, William F 1876- *WhAm 5*
Fiske, William H *NewYHSD*
Fiske, William Mead Lindsley 1841-1904
  NatCAB 3, WhAm 1
Fiske, William Mead Lindsley 1879-1940
  NatCAB 38
Fiske, Wyman P 1900-1972 *WhAm 5*
Fisken, John Barclay 1861-1946 *NatCAB 35,
  WhAm 2*
Fisker, Kay 1893-1965 *WhAm 4*
Fismer, Arnold Winkelried 1861-1930
  NatCAB 22
Fistell, Harry 1907-1971 *WhAm 5*
Fitch, Albert Parker 1877-1944 *WhAm 2*

Fitch, Alta Winchester 1840- *WomWWA 14*
Fitch, Amoretta Colby *WomWWA 14*
Fitch, Annie Loraine *WomWWA 14*
Fitch, Asa 1765-1843 *BiAUS, BiDrAC, WhAm H*
Fitch, Asa 1809-1878 *ApCAB*
Fitch, Asa 1809-1879 *DcAmB, DcScB, NatCAB 7, WebAB, WhAm H*
Fitch, Ashbel Parmelee 1848-1904 *ApCAB Sup, BiDrAC, TwCBDA, WhAm 1*
Fitch, Aubrey Wray 1883- *WebAMB, WhWW-II*
Fitch, Austin Elliot 1889-1966 *NatCAB 52*
Fitch, Benjamin 1802-1883 *ApCAB*
Fitch, Beriah *NewYHSD*
Fitch, Cecil 1885-1961 *WhAm 4*
Fitch, Charles Elliott 1825- *TwCBDA*
Fitch, Charles Elliott 1835-1918 *NatCAB 4, WhAm 1*
Fitch, Charles Hall 1854- *WhAm 4*
Fitch, Charles Luther 1873-1962 *NatCAB 55*
Fitch, Clifford Penny 1884-1940 *NatCAB 30, WhAm 1*
Fitch, Clyde 1865-1909 *AmBi, DcAmB, NatCAB 13, NatCAB 15, WhAm 1*
Fitch, Ebenezer 1756-1833 *AmBi, ApCAB, Drake, NatCAB 6, TwCBDA*
Fitch, Edward 1864-1946 *WhAm 2*
Fitch, Eleazar Thompson 1791-1871 *ApCAB*
Fitch, Eleazar Thompson 1791-1871 *TwCBDA*
Fitch, Elijah 1745-1788 *ApCAB, Drake, NatCAB 3*
Fitch, Ezra Charles 1847-1932 *NatCAB 13, WhAm 1*
Fitch, Florence Hopper 1876- *WomWWA 14*
Fitch, Florence Mary 1875-1959 *WhAm 3, WomWWA 14*
Fitch, Frank E 1841- *WhAm 4*
Fitch, George 1877-1915 *WhAm 1*
Fitch, George Hamlin 1852- *WhAm 4*
Fitch, Graham N 1810-1892 *BiAUS*
Fitch, Graham Newell 1809-1892 *ApCAB, BiDrAC, NatCAB 12, TwCBDA, WhAm H*
Fitch, Grant 1859-1940 *WhAm 1*
Fitch, Harriet Earling 1878- *WomWWA 14*
Fitch, James 1622-1702 *ApCAB, Drake*
Fitch, James Burgess 1888-1962 *NatCAB 49, WhAm 4*
Fitch, John 1743-1798 *AmBi, ApCAB, AsBiEn, DcAmB, Drake, EncAB, McGEWB, NatCAB 6, NewYHSD, TwCBDA, WebAB, WhAm H*
Fitch, John Andrews 1881-1959 *WhAm 3*
Fitch, John Hall 1909-1969 *WhAm 5*
Fitch, John Lee 1836-1895 *ApCAB, NatCAB 7, NewYHSD*
Fitch, Joseph Henry 1861- *WhAm 4*
Fitch, Lawrence 1874-1924 *NatCAB 20*
Fitch, Leroy 1835-1875 *AmBi, ApCAB, TwCBDA*
Fitch, Louise Norwood 1839- *WomWWA 14a*
Fitch, Mary Alida 1880- *WomWWA 14*
Fitch, Rachel Louise 1878- *WhAm 3, WomWWA 14*
Fitch, Ralph Roswell 1878- *WhAm 6*
Fitch, Reamy Curtis 1902-1957 *NatCAB 49*
Fitch, Samuel 1720-1786? *ApCAB*
Fitch, Samuel 1724-1799 *DcAmB, WhAm H*
Fitch, Simon 1758-1835 *BnEnAmA*
Fitch, Simon 1820- *ApCAB*
Fitch, Tecumseh Sherman 1908-1969 *NatCAB 55, WhAm 5*
Fitch, Thomas 1699-1774 *AmBi, ApCAB, Drake*
Fitch, Thomas 1700-1774 *DcAmB, NatCAB 10, WhAm H*
Fitch, Thomas 1838-1923 *BiAUS, BiDrAC, WhAmP*
Fitch, Thomas Davis 1829-1901 *ApCAB, WhAm 1*
Fitch, Thomas F 1885-1968 *WhAm 4A*
Fitch, Walter 1854-1937 *WhAm 1*
Fitch, Walter Quintin 1886-1937 *NatCAB 34*
Fitch, William Clyde 1865-1909 *AmBi, DcAmB, TwCBDA*
Fitch, William Edward 1867-1949 *NatCAB 39, WhAm 2*

Fitch, William Foresman 1839-1915 *WhAm 1*
Fitch, Mrs. William Grant 1836- *ApCAB X*
Fitch, William Henry 1843-1922 *NatCAB 6*
Fitch, William Henry 1876-1945 *NatCAB 33*
Fitch, William Kountz 1889-1969 *NatCAB 56, WhAm 5*
Fitch, Willis Bryan 1878-1952 *NatCAB 43*
Fitch, Winchester 1867-1963 *ApCAB X, NatCAB 50*
Fitchet, Seth Marshall 1887-1939 *NatCAB 29*
Fite, Alexander Green 1892-1962 *WhAm 4*
Fite, Emerson David 1874-1953 *WhAm 3*
Fite, Francis Bartow 1861-1938 *NatCAB 27*
Fite, Gilbert Courtland 1918- *EncAAH*
Fite, Samuel McClary 1816-1875 *BiDrAC*
Fite, Warner 1867-1955 *DcAmB S5, WhAm 3*
Fite, William Benjamin 1869-1952 *WhAm 3*
Fite, William Conyers 1893-1963 *WhAm 4*
Fithian, Edward 1820-1908 *WhAm 1*
Fithian, George Washington 1854-1921 *BiDrAC, TwCBDA*
Fithian, Philip Vickers 1747-1776 *NatCAB 18*
Fitkin, Abraham Edward 1878-1933 *WhAm 1*
Fitkin, Abram Edward 1878-1933 *NatCAB 27*
Fitler, Edwin Henry 1825-1896 *DcAmB, WhAm H*
Fitler, William Wonderly 1857-1931 *NatCAB 23*
Fitterer, J C 1871-1947 *WhAm 2*
Fittig, Rudolph 1835-1910 *DcScB*
Fitton, James 1803-1881 *ApCAB, WhAm H*
Fitton, James 1805-1881 *BiDAmEd, DcAmB*
Fitton, William Henry 1780-1861 *DcScB*
Fitts, Alice Evelina 1856- *WhAm 4*
Fitts, Charles Newton 1870- *WhAm 5*
Fitts, Clarke Cushing 1870-1916 *NatCAB 19*
Fitts, Dudley 1903-1968 *WhAm 5*
Fitts, Frederic Whitney 1872-1945 *NatCAB 35*
Fitts, George Henry 1851-1909 *WhAm 1*
Fitts, James Harris 1830-1912 *NatCAB 17*
Fitts, John Blair 1890-1943 *NatCAB 35*
Fitts, Maud Lenore Emerson 1870- *WomWWA 14*
Fitts, Oliver *BiAUS*
Fitts, Paul Morris, Jr. 1912-1965 *NatCAB 54*
Fitts, William Cochran 1866-1954 *WhAm 3*
Fitz, Austin Hervey 1875- *WhAm 5*
Fitz, Adeline Frances Slade 1861- *WomWWA 14*
Fitz, Benjamin Rutherford 1855-1891 *TwCBDA*
Fitz, Charles Newcomb 1871-1931 *NatCAB 26*
Fitz, Frederick William 1902-1955 *NatCAB 44*
Fitz, Henry 1808-1863 *ApCAB, DcAmB, Drake, WhAm H*
Fitz, Hugh Alexander 1876- *WhAm 5*
Fitz, Reginald 1885-1953 *NatCAB 39, WhAm 3*
Fitz, Reginald Heber 1843-1913 *AmBi, BiHiMed, DcAmB, NatCAB 10, WebAB, WhAm 1*
Fitz-Gerald, Aaron Ogden 1845-1932 *NatCAB 25, WhAm 1*
Fitz-Gerald, Daniel Michael 1910-1975 *WhAm 6*
Fitz-Gerald, John Driscoll, II 1873-1946 *BiDAmEd, NatCAB 37, WhAm 2*
Fitz-Patrick, Gilbert 1873-1936 *WhAm 1*
Fitz-Patrick, Hugh Louis 1861- *WhAm 4*
Fitz-Randolph, Corliss 1863-1954 *WhAm 3*
Fitz-Randolph, Louise 1851- *WomWWA 14*
Fitz-Randolph, Raymond Bernard 1872-1922 *NatCAB 6*
Fitzbutler, Henry 1837-1901 *NatCAB 14*
Fitzell, Lincoln 1903-1958 *NatCAB 47*
Fitzgerald, A Ann Strayer 1930-1974 *WhAm 6*
Fitzgerald, Adolphus Leigh 1840-1921 *ApCAB X, NatCAB 18, WhAm 4*
FitzGerald, Anne Campbell 1867- *WomWWA 14*
Fitzgerald, Anthony William 1911-1958 *NatCAB 43*
FitzGerald, Arthur Michael 1879-1957 *NatCAB 47*
Fitzgerald, Barry 1888-1961 *WhAm 4*
Fitzgerald, Benedict 1883-1967 *NatCAB 53*
Fitzgerald, D J *NewYHSD*
Fitzgerald, David Edward 1874-1942 *NatCAB 33, WhAm 2*

Fitzgerald, Desmond 1846-1926 *DcAmB, NatCAB 9, NatCAB 39*
Fitzgerald, Desmond 1846-1928 *WhAm 1*
Fitzgerald, E Roy 1893-1957 *WhAm 3*
Fitzgerald, Edward *WebAB*
Fitzgerald, Lord Edward 1763-1798 *ApCAB, Drake*
Fitzgerald, Edward 1833-1907 *ApCAB, DcAmB, NatCAB 12, TwCBDA, WhAm 1*
Fitzgerald, Edward Aloyslus 1893-1972 *WhAm 5*
Fitzgerald, Edward M 1881-1954 *NatCAB 49*
Fitzgerald, Edwin 1856-1928 *DcAmB*
Fitzgerald, Ella 1918- *EncAB, WebAB*
Fitzgerald, Francis Alexander James 1870-1929 *WhAm 1*
Fitzgerald, Francis Scott Key 1896-1940 *DcAmB S2, EncAB, McGEWB, WebAB, WhAm 1*
Fitzgerald, Frank Dwight 1885-1939 *NatCAB 35, WhAm 1*
Fitzgerald, Frank Thomas 1857-1907 *BiDrAC*
Fitzgerald, Fred Jesse Comfort 1874-1963 *NatCAB 51*
Fitzgerald, George Francis 1851-1901 *AsBiEn, DcScB*
Fitzgerald, Harrington 1847-1930 *WhAm 1*
Fitzgerald, Harrison Robertson 1873-1931 *NatCAB 35*
FitzGerald, James 1851-1922 *WhAm 1*
Fitzgerald, James J 1878-1942 *WhAm 2*
Fitzgerald, James Joseph 1869-1956 *NatCAB 55*
Fitzgerald, James Joseph 1909-1963 *NatCAB 51*
Fitzgerald, James Merlin 1870-1939 *WhAm 1*
FitzGerald, James Newbury 1837-1907 *NatCAB 12, TwCBDA, WhAm 1*
Fitzgerald, James Robert 1910-1973 *WhAm 6*
Fitzgerald, James Wilford 1862- *WhAm 4*
Fitzgerald, John Dillon 1897-1965 *NatCAB 52*
Fitzgerald, John Francis 1863-1950 *BiDrAC, DcAmB S4, WhAm 3, WhAmP*
Fitzgerald, John Francis 1865- *TwCBDA*
Fitzgerald, John Joseph 1872-1952 *BiDrAC, WhAm 3, WhAmP*
Fitzgerald, John Martin 1889-1955 *NatCAB 49*
Fitzgerald, John Morton 1877-1960 *WhAm 3*
Fitzgerald, Joseph 1837-1908 *WhAm 1*
Fitzgerald, Kent 1899-1957 *NatCAB 49*
Fitzgerald, Leo David 1896-1960 *WhAm 3*
FitzGerald, Leslie Maurice 1898-1972 *WhAm 5*
Fitzgerald, Lionel LeMoine 1890-1956 *IlBEAAW*
Fitzgerald, Louis 1838-1908 *ApCAB Sup, TwCBDA, WhAm 1*
Fitzgerald, Marie V 1884- *WomWWA 14*
Fitzgerald, Matthew Joseph 1901-1962 *WhAm 4*
Fitzgerald, Maurice A 1897-1951 *WhAm 3*
Fitzgerald, Michael Edward 1863-1945 *WhAm 2*
Fitzgerald, Oscar Penn 1829-1911 *ApCAB Sup, DcAmB, NatCAB 13, TwCBDA, WhAm 1*
Fitzgerald, Patrick Joseph 1879-1961 *NatCAB 46*
Fitzgerald, Pitt Loofbourrow 1893- *IlBEAAW*
Fitzgerald, Richard Y 1873-1942 *NatCAB 32*
Fitzgerald, Robert Mullins 1858-1934 *NatCAB 30, WhAm 1*
Fitzgerald, Roy Gerald 1875-1962 *BiDrAC, NatCAB 50, WhAm 4*
Fitzgerald, Rufus Henry 1890-1966 *NatCAB 52, WhAm 4*
Fitzgerald, Ruth 1885-1966 *WhAm 4*
Fitzgerald, Susan Grimes Walker 1871-1943 *NatCAB 32*
FitzGerald, Susan Walker 1871-1943 *WhAm 2, WomWWA 14*
Fitzgerald, Theodore Clinton 1903-1967 *WhAm 5*
Fitzgerald, Thomas 1796-1855 *ApCAB, BiAUS, BiDrAC, NatCAB 7, TwCBDA, WhAm H*
Fitzgerald, Thomas 1819-1891 *DcAmB, NatCAB 1, WhAm H*

Flanders, Alvin 1825-1884 *BiAUS*
Flanders, Benjamin Franklin 1816-1896 *ApCAB,*
BiAUS, BiDrAC, Drake, NatCAB 10,
TwCBDA, WhAm H, WhAmP
Flanders, Fred C 1883-1959 *WhAm 3*
Flanders, George Lovell 1856- *WhAm 4*
Flanders, Henry *Drake*
Flanders, Henry 1824-1911 *DcAmB,*
NatCAB 11
Flanders, Henry 1826-1911 *ApCAB, TwCBDA,*
WhAm 1
Flanders, James Greeley 1844-1920 *WhAm 1*
Flanders, Louis Warner 1864-1945 *NatCAB 36*
Flanders, Michael 1922-1975 *WhAm 6*
Flanders, Ralph Edward 1880-1970 *BiDrAC,*
WhAm 5
Flanders, Ralph Lindsay 1869- *WhAm 5*
Flanders, Ruth Stone d1975 *WhAm 6*
Flandin, Etienne 1889-1958 *WhWW-II*
Flandrau, Charles Eugene 1828-1903 *AmBi,*
ApCAB, DcAmB, NatCAB 22, TwCBDA,
WhAm 1
Flandrau, Charles Macomb 1871-1938
DcAmB S2, WhAm 5
Flandrau, Grace Hodgson d1971 *WhAm 5*
Flandrau, Thomas Macomb 1826- *ApCAB*
Flandraw, Charles E *BiAUS*
Flanigan, Edward Joseph 1874- *WhAm 1*
Flanigan, Georgia Hull 1875- *WomWWA 14*
Flanigan, Howard Adams 1889-1967 *WhAm 4*
Flannagan, Dallas 1866-1949 *NatCAB 40*
Flannagan, John Bernard 1895-1942 *BnEnAmA,*
DcAmB S3, McGEWB, WebAB
Flannagan, John William, Jr. 1885-1955 *BiDrAC,*
WhAm 3, WhAmP
Flannagan, William Walker 1843- *NatCAB 12*
Flannelly, Joseph F 1894-1973 *WhAm 6*
Flannery, Harry William 1900-1975 *WhAm 6*
Flannery, James Joseph 1854-1920 *ApCAB X,*
NatCAB 23
Flannery, John 1835-1910 *DcAmB, NatCAB 3,*
WhAm 4
Flannery, John Harold 1898-1961 *BiDrAC*
Flannery, John L 1847-1920 *NatCAB 31*
Flannery, John Rogers 1879-1947 *WhAm 2*
Flannery, John Spalding 1870-1954 *WhAm 3*
Flannery, Joseph Michael 1867-1920
NatCAB 23
Flannery, Lot 1836-1922 *NatCAB 19,*
NewYHSD
Flannery, May K 1881- *WomWWA 14*
Flannery, Vaughn 1898-1955 *WhAm 3*
Flannigan, Harris d1874 *BiAUS*
Flannigan, Richard Charles 1857-1927 *WhAm 1*
Flannigan, Richard Charles 1857-1928
NatCAB 21
Flansburg, Fonetta 1852- *WomWWA 14*
Flasch, Kilian 1831-1891 *ApCAB*
Flasch, Kilian Caspar 1831-1891 *NatCAB 12,*
TwCBDA
Flasch, Kilian Casper 1831-1891 *WhAm H*
Flash, Henry Lyden 1835- *ApCAB*
Flash, Henry Lynden 1835- *NatCAB 13*
Flath, Earl Hugo 1895- *WhAm 5*
Flather, Frederick Arthur 1867- *WhAm 5*
Flather, John Joseph 1862-1926 *DcAmB,*
NatCAB 22, WhAm 1
Flatt, Cornelius Judson 1829-1920 *NatCAB 19*
Flattery, Maurice Douglas 1870-1925
ApCAB X, NatCAB 16, WhAm 1
Flaubert, Gustave 1821-1880 *McGEWB*
Flaven, Allan Ervin 1910-1973 *WhAm 6*
Flavin, Dan 1933- *BnEnAmA*
Flavin, Martin 1883-1967 *WhAm 4*
Flavin, Thomas J 1906-1973 *WhAm 6*
Flebbe, Beulah Marie Dix 1876- *WhAm 5,*
WomWWA 14
Flechsig, Paul Emil 1847-1929 *DcScB*
Fleck, Alexander 1889-1968 *WhAm 5*
Fleck, Charles Everest 1879-1965 *NatCAB 51*
Fleck, Harry Willard 1873-1952 *NatCAB 41*
Fleck, Henry Thomas 1863-1937 *WhAm 1*
Fleck, Howard Leslie 1889-1958 *NatCAB 48*
Fleck, Joseph Amadeus 1893- *IIBEAAW*
Fleck, Wilbur H 1874- *WhAm 5*
Fleckles, Mary Elizabeth Fish 1864-
WomWWA 14
Fleeger, George Washington 1839-1894 *BiDrAC,*

WhAm H
Fleek, John Sherwood 1893-1957 *WhAm 3*
Fleeming, John *DcAmB*
Fleeson, Doris d1970 *WhAm 5*
Fleeson, Howard Tebbe 1895-1957 *WhAm 3*
Fleet, Alexander Frederick 1843-1911 *TwCBDA,*
WhAm 1
Fleet, Henry 1595?-1661? *NatCAB 19*
Fleet, Reuben Hollis 1887-1975 *WhAm 6*
Fleet, T Cecil 1890-1964 *NatCAB 50*
Fleet, Thomas *ApCAB*
Fleet, Thomas 1685-1758 *AmBi, ApCAB,*
DcAmB, Drake, NatCAB 20, TwCBDA,
WhAm H
Fleetwood, Anthony 1800?- *NewYHSD*
Fleetwood, Benjamin Franklin 1845-1923
WhAm 1
Fleetwood, Caleb V 1838?- *NewYHSD*
Fleetwood, Charles 1829?- *NewYHSD*
Fleetwood, Frederick Gleed 1868-1938 *BiDrAC,*
WhAm 1
Flegenheimer, Albert 1890-1972 *WhAm 5*
Flegenheimer, Arthur 1902-1935 *DcAmB S1,*
WebAB
Fleger, Anthony Alfred 1900-1963 *BiDrAC*
Fleischbein, Francois 1804?- *NewYHSD*
Fleischer, Carl 1883-1942 *WhWW-II*
Fleischer, Charles 1871-1942 *WhAm 2*
Fleischer, Isidor 1860-1928 *NatCAB 22*
Fleischer, Johannes 1539-1593 *DcScB*
Fleischman, E *NewYHSD*
Fleischmann, Charles Louis 1834-1896
WhAm H
Fleischmann, Charles Louis 1834-1897 *DcAmB,*
NatCAB 22
Fleischmann, Edwin Maurice 1892-1953
NatCAB 40
Fleischmann, Julian Ralph 1903-1967
NatCAB 51
Fleischmann, Julius 1872-1925 *NatCAB 26,*
WhAm 1
Fleischmann, Julius 1900-1968 *NatCAB 54*
Fleischmann, Max C 1887-1951 *WhAm 3*
Fleischmann, Raoul H 1885-1969 *WhAm 5*
Fleischmann, Simon 1859-1930 *NatCAB 33,*
WhAm 1
Fleischner, E Charles 1882-1926 *NatCAB 24*
Fleisher, Benjamin Wilfrid 1870-1946
DcAmB S4, WhAm 2
Fleisher, Samuel S 1872-1944 *WhAm 2*
Fleisher, Walter Louis 1880-1959 *WhAm 3*
Fleishhacker, Herbert 1872-1957 *WhAm 3*
Fleishhacker, Mortimer 1866- *WhAm 5*
Flemer, John Adolph 1859- *WhAm 5*
Fleming, Adrian Sebastian 1872-1940
NatCAB 31, WhAm 1
Fleming, Sir Alexander 1881-1955 *AsBiEn,*
DcScB, McGEWB, WhAm 3
Fleming, Andrew Magnus 1858- *NatCAB 2*
Fleming, Aretas Brooks 1839-1923 *DcAmB,*
NatCAB 1, NatCAB 12, TwCBDA,
WhAm 1
Fleming, Arthur Henry 1856-1940 *DcAmB S2,*
NatCAB 30, WhAm 1
Fleming, Bryant 1877-1946 *WhAm 2*
Fleming, Burton Percival 1881-1936 *WhAm 1*
Fleming, Caroline Pelgram 1872-
WomWWA 14
Fleming, Charles A 1868-1929 *WhAm 1*
Fleming, Daniel Johnson 1877-1969 *NatCAB 55,*
WhAm 5
Fleming, Dewey Lee 1898-1955 *WhAm 3*
Fleming, Dora Hartzell 1864- *WomWWA 14*
Fleming, Ernest Joseph 1871- *WhAm 5*
Fleming, Francis Philip 1841-1908 *NatCAB 1,*
NatCAB 11, TwCBDA, WhAm 1
Fleming, Francis Philip 1874-1948 *WhAm 2*
Fleming, Fred W 1866-1929 *WhAm 1*
Fleming, Frederic Sydney 1886-1956
NatCAB 45, WhAm 3
Fleming, Harvey Brown 1873-1947 *WhAm 2*
Fleming, Henry Craig 1881-1960 *NatCAB 48,*
WhAm 4
Fleming, Henry Stuart 1863-1938 *WhAm 1*
Fleming, Ian Lancaster 1908-1964 *WhAm 4*
Fleming, James R 1881-1973 *WhAm 6*
Fleming, James Wheeler 1867-1928 *WhAm 1*
Fleming, Jennie E 1862- *WomWWA 14*

Fleming, John *ApCAB, DcAmB, WhAm H*
Fleming, John 1785-1857 *DcScB*
Fleming, John 1806-1894 *NatCAB 19*
Fleming, John 1807-1894 *DcAmB, WhAm H*
Fleming, John 1836-1876 *IIBEAAW*
Fleming, John Adam 1877-1956 *NatCAB 42,*
WhAm 3
Fleming, Sir John Ambrose 1849-1945 *AsBiEn,*
DcScB
Fleming, John Donaldson 1851-1927 *WhAm 1*
Fleming, John Joseph 1851-1928 *NatCAB 30*
Fleming, Joseph Barclay 1881-1970 *WhAm 5*
Fleming, Lamar, Jr. 1892-1964 *WhAm 4*
Fleming, Luke Joseph 1868-1944 *NatCAB 33*
Fleming, Mark Lance 1880-1947 *NatCAB 38*
Fleming, Matthew Corry 1864-1946 *WhAm 2*
Fleming, Matthew John 1879- *WhAm 6*
Fleming, Maybury *ApCAB*
Fleming, Michael 1785?-1850 *ApCAB*
Fleming, Philip Bracken 1887-1955 *NatCAB 46,*
WhAm 3
Fleming, Robert Hull 1840-1928 *NatCAB 27*
Fleming, Robert Vedder 1890-1967 *WhAm 4*
Fleming, Rufus 1853-1920 *WhAm 1*
Fleming, Samuel Wilson, Jr. 1885-1966
WhAm 4
Fleming, Sir Sandford 1827-1915 *ApCAB,*
McGEWB
Fleming, Thomas 1727-1776 *ApCAB, Drake*
Fleming, Thomas Wallace 1874- *WhoColR*
Fleming, Victor d1949 *WhAm 2*
Fleming, Wallace Bruce 1872-1952 *NatCAB 43,*
WhAm 3
Fleming, Walter Lynwood 1874-1932 *AmBi,*
BiDAmEd, DcAmB S1, NatCAB 46,
WhAm 1
Fleming, Willard C 1899-1972 *WhAm 5*
Fleming, William 1729-1795 *DcAmB,*
NatCAB 22, WhAm H
Fleming, William 1734-1824 *ApCAB, Drake,*
TwCBDA
Fleming, William 1736-1824 *BiDrAC,*
NatCAB 12, WhAm H
Fleming, William 1881-1963 *NatCAB 51*
Fleming, William, Jr. 1880-1942 *NatCAB 33*
Fleming, William Bennett 1803-1886 *BiDrAC,*
WhAm H
Fleming, William Bowyer 1845- *WhAm 1*
Fleming, William Boyer 1843-1918 *NatCAB 17*
Fleming, William Hansell 1844-1915 *WhAm 1*
Fleming, William Henry 1855-1944 *NatCAB 33*
Fleming, William Henry 1856-1944 *BiDrAC,*
NatCAB 5, TwCBDA, WhAmP
Fleming, William Maybury 1817-1866 *ApCAB,*
DcAmB, WhAm H
Fleming, Williamina Paton Stevens 1857-1911
DcAmB, DcScB, NatCAB 7, NotAW,
TwCBDA, WhAm 1
Flemington, William Thomas Ross 1897-1971
WhAm 5
Flemming, Arthur Sherwood 1905- *BiDrUSE*
Flemming, Walther 1843-1905 *AsBiEn, DcScB*
Flemming, William *BiAUS*
Flenniken, Robert P *BiAUS*
Flenniker, Robert P *BiAUS*
Flerov, Georgii Nikolaevich 1913- *AsBiEn*
Flershem, Rudolph Byford 1876- *WhAm 6*
Fleshman, Mina Pepper 1879-1965 *NatCAB 50*
Fletcher, Aaron Dean 1817- *NewYHSD*
Fletcher, Alice Cunningham d1923
WomWWA 14
Fletcher, Alice Cunningham 1838-1923 *AmBi,*
DcAmB, McGEWB, NotAW
Fletcher, Alice Cunningham 1845?-1923
AmWom, ApCAB Sup, NatCAB 5,
TwCBDA, WhAm 1
Fletcher, Allen Miller 1853-1922 *NatCAB 19*
Fletcher, Andrew 1863- *ApCAB X*
Fletcher, Andrew 1864-1925 *WhAm 1*
Fletcher, Angus Somerville 1883-1960 *WhAm 4*
Fletcher, Asa E 1882-1955 *NatCAB 45*
Fletcher, Asaph 1746-1839 *ApCAB*
Fletcher, Austin Barclay 1852-1923 *NatCAB 1,*
WhAm 1
Fletcher, Austin Bradstreet 1871-1928
NatCAB 21
Fletcher, Austin Bradstreet 1872-1928 *WhAm 1*
Fletcher, Benjamin 1640-1703 *ApCAB,*

DcAmB S1, NatCAB 13, WhAm H
Fletcher, Benjamin E 1820?- NewYHSD
Fletcher, Calvin 1798-1866 DcAmB, WhAm H
Fletcher, Calvin 1882-1963 IlBEAAW
Fletcher, Calvin Ingram 1859-1913 NatCAB 16
Fletcher, Catharine Westinghouse 1883-
WomWWA 14
Fletcher, Charles Kimball 1902- BiDrAC
Fletcher, Charles William 1874-1942
NatCAB 31
Fletcher, Clara Irene Thompson 1900-
IlBEAAW
Fletcher, Cora Sechrist 1871- WomWWA 14
Fletcher, Daniel Howard 1872- WhAm 5
Fletcher, Daniel W NewYHSD
Fletcher, Dolphin Samuel 1847- NatCAB 5
Fletcher, Donald Gould 1898-1968 NatCAB 54
Fletcher, Duncan Upshaw 1859-1936 ApCAB X,
BiDrAC, DcAmB S2, EncAAH,
NatCAB 14, NatCAB 36, WhAm 1,
WhAmP
Fletcher, Edward Grove 1890-1948 NatCAB 37
Fletcher, Emerson Armor 1869-1946 WhAm 2
Fletcher, Frank Friday 1855-1928 NatCAB 15,
NatCAB 36, WebAMB, WhAm 1
Fletcher, Frank Jack 1885-1973 WebAMB,
WhAm 5, WhWW-II
Fletcher, Frank Morley 1866- WhAm 3
Fletcher, Frank Ward 1853- WhAm 4
Fletcher, Fred Leland 1911- WhAm 5
Fletcher, Frederick Charles 1874- WhAm 5
Fletcher, George 1796- NewYHSD
Fletcher, George Beard 1888-1960 NatCAB 52
Fletcher, George C NewYHSD
Fletcher, George Nichols 1813-1899
NatCAB 30
Fletcher, George Washington 1858-1916
NatCAB 16
Fletcher, Harold Augustus 1888-1951
NatCAB 41
Fletcher, Harvey Trunkey 1869-1946
NatCAB 35
Fletcher, Henry 1877-1953 ApCAB X,
WhAm 3
Fletcher, Henry Jesse 1860- WhAm 4
Fletcher, Henry Prather 1873-1959 NatCAB 15,
NatCAB 43, WhAm 3
Fletcher, Herbert Hervey 1855-1941
NatCAB 30
Fletcher, Horace 1796-1871 ApCAB
Fletcher, Horace 1849-1919 AmBi, ApCAB X,
DcAmB, NatCAB 14, WhAm 1
Fletcher, Inglis d1969 WhAm 5
Fletcher, Isaac 1784-1842 BiAUS, BiDrAC,
WhAm H
Fletcher, Jacob Guptil 1825- NewYHSD
Fletcher, James Cooley 1823-1901 ApCAB,
DcAmB, NatCAB 13, WhAm H
Fletcher, James Cooley 1825-1901 TwCBDA
Fletcher, James Donald 1895-1970 WhAm 5
Fletcher, Jefferson Butler 1865-1946 WhAm 2
Fletcher, John 1579-1625 McGEWB
Fletcher, John 1787-1844 ApCAB
Fletcher, John 1876- WhAm 5
Fletcher, John 1879- WhAm 6
Fletcher, John Gould 1886-1950 DcAmB S4,
NatCAB 42, WhAm 3
Fletcher, John Madison 1873-1944 WhAm 2
Fletcher, John Storrs 1879-1961 WhAm 4
Fletcher, Julia Constance 1850?- ApCAB
Fletcher, Julia Constance 1853- NatCAB 13,
TwCBDA
Fletcher, Julia Constance 1858- WhAm 4
Fletcher, Katharine Ogden 1877-
WomWWA 14
Fletcher, Lisa Anne 1844- AmWom
Fletcher, Loren 1833-1919 BiDrAC, TwCBDA,
WhAm 1, WhAmP
Fletcher, Louis DuBois 1899-1975 WhAm 6
Fletcher, Mabel Elizabeth Billings 1886-
WomWWA 14
Fletcher, Margaret Abert Beale 1879-
WomWWA 14
Fletcher, Mary Emily Moose 1854-
WomWWA 14
Fletcher, Mary Martha 1830-1885 TwCBDA
Fletcher, Mona d1965 WhAm 4
Fletcher, Montgomery 1830-1908 WhAm 1

Fletcher, Mordecai Hiatt 1849-1914 WhAm 1
Fletcher, Orlin Ottman 1847-1937 WhAm 1
Fletcher, Paul Franklin 1903-1962 NatCAB 48,
WhAm 4
Fletcher, Richard 1788-1861 WhAm H
Fletcher, Richard 1788-1869 ApCAB, BiAUS,
BiDrAC, DcAmB, Drake, NatCAB 12,
TwCBDA
Fletcher, Robert 1823-1912 DcAmB,
NatCAB 13, TwCBDA
Fletcher, Robert 1847-1936 DcAmB S2,
NatCAB 26, WhAm 1
Fletcher, Robert Howe 1850- WhAm 4
Fletcher, Robert S 1900-1959 WhAm 4
Fletcher, Robert Stillman 1874-1953 WhAm 3
Fletcher, Robert Virgil 1869-1960 NatCAB 18,
WhAm 4
Fletcher, Ryland 1799-1885 ApCAB, BiAUS,
NatCAB 8, TwCBDA
Fletcher, Samuel Johnson 1891-1958 WhAm 3
Fletcher, Stevenson Whitcomb 1875-1971
WhAm 5
Fletcher, Sydney E IlBEAAW
Fletcher, Thomas 1779- BiAUS, BiDrAC,
WhAm H
Fletcher, Thomas 1787-1866 BnEnAmA
Fletcher, Thomas 1819-1900 NatCAB 12
Fletcher, Thomas 1877-1947 NatCAB 44
Fletcher, Thomas Brooks 1879-1945 BiDrAC,
WhAm 6, WhAmP
Fletcher, Thomas Clement 1827-1899 AmBi,
ApCAB, BiAUS, DcAmB, NatCAB 12,
TwCBDA, WhAm H, WhAmP
Fletcher, Veron NewYHSD
Fletcher, Walter D 1896-1972 WhAm 5
Fletcher, Walter Morley 1873-1933 DcScB
Fletcher, William A d1855? ApCAB, Drake
Fletcher, William A 1788-1853 NatCAB 3
Fletcher, William Asa 1788-1852 DcAmB,
WhAm H
Fletcher, William Baldwin 1837-1907 ApCAB,
DcAmB, NewYHSD, WhAm 1
Fletcher, William Bartlett 1862-1957
NatCAB 46, WhAm 3
Fletcher, William Isaac 1844-1917 DcAmLiB,
NatCAB 12, TwCBDA, WhAm 1
Fletcher, William Meade 1870-1943 WhAm 2
Flett, John Smith 1869-1947 DcScB
Flett, Penelope McNaughton 1863-
WomWWA 14
Fleurieu, Charles Pierre Claret 1738-1810
ApCAB
Fleury, Albert Francois 1848- IlBEAAW
Fleury, Elsie NewYHSD
Fleury, Ernest De d1867 ApCAB
Fleury, Francois Louis Teisseidre De 1749-1794
NatCAB 13
Fleury, Louis De 1740?-1794 ApCAB, Drake
Flewelling, Ralph Carlin 1894-1960 WhAm 3A
Flewelling, Ralph Tyler 1871-1960 NatCAB 51,
WhAm 5
Flexner, Abraham 1866-1959 BiDAmEd,
EncAB, McGEWB, NatCAB 52, WebAB,
WhAm 3
Flexner, Anne Crawford d1955 WhAm 3,
WomWWA 14
Flexner, Bernard 1865-1945 DcAmB S3,
NatCAB 34, WhAm 2
Flexner, Gustav 1895-1960 NatCAB 49
Flexner, Helen Whitall Thomas WomWWA 14
Flexner, Jacob Aaron 1857-1934 NatCAB 52
Flexner, James 1906-1964 NatCAB 50
Flexner, Jennie Maas 1882-1944 DcAmB S3,
DcAmLiB, NotAW
Flexner, Magdalen Glaser Hupfel 1907-1972
WhAm 5
Flexner, Mary 1873- WomWWA 14
Flexner, Simon 1863-1946 ApCAB X,
DcAmB S4, DcScB, EncAB, NatCAB 52,
WhAm 2
Flexner, Washington 1869-1942 NatCAB 34
Flick, Alexander Clarence 1869-1942 WhAm 2
Flick, James Patton 1845-1929 BiDrAC,
TwCBDA, WhAmP
Flick, Lawrence Francis 1856-1938 DcAmB S2,
NatCAB 28, WhAm 1
Flick, Lawrence Francis 1917-1965 NatCAB 53
Flick, Lewis NewYHSD

Flick, Liddon 1858-1905 NatCAB 10,
NatCAB 29
Flick, Reuben Jay 1871-1940 ApCAB X,
NatCAB 29
Flick, Walter A 1895-1958 NatCAB 48,
WhAm 3
Flicker, Edward 1869-1939 NatCAB 29
Flickinger, Alice 1884- WomWWA 14
Flickinger, Daniel Kumler 1824-1911
ApCAB Sup, DcAmB, NatCAB 19,
WhAm 1
Flickinger, Martha Rodgers 1871-
WomWWA 14
Flickinger, Roy Caston 1876-1942 WhAm 2
Flickinger, Samuel Jacob 1848-1929 NatCAB 2,
WhAm 1
Flickinger, Samuel John 1892-1972 NatCAB 57
Flickinger, Smith M d1939 WhAm 1
Flickwir, David Williamson 1852-1935 WhAm 1
Flicon, Henry NewYHSD
Fliedner, William 1832-1914 NatCAB 17
Fliegel, Leslie 1912-1968 WhAm 5
Fliegler, Louis Aaron 1917- WhAm 6
Fliess, William Maynard 1833-1904 NatCAB 6
Flight, John William 1890-1964 NatCAB 50
Flikke, Julia O 1879- WhAm 4
Flinchbaugh, Edwin Flagler 1881-1959
NatCAB 45
Flinders, Matthew 1774-1814 McGEWB
Fling, Fred Morrow 1860-1934 NatCAB 13,
NatCAB 28, TwCBDA, WhAm 1
Flinn, Alfred Douglas 1869-1937 WhAm 1
Flinn, Andrew 1773-1820 ApCAB
Flinn, Irvine Moore, Jr. 1900-1970 NatCAB 56
Flinn, John Joseph 1851-1929 WhAm 1
Flinn, Mary Stephens 1888- WomWWA 14
Flinn, Ralph Emerson 1878-1949 NatCAB 38
Flinn, Richard Orme 1870-1948 NatCAB 36,
WhAm 2
Flinner, Ira Arthur 1884-1954 WhAm 3
Flint, Abel 1765-1825 ApCAB, Drake
Flint, Albert Stowell 1853-1923 DcAmB,
NatCAB 10, NatCAB 35, WhAm 1
Flint, Annie Austin 1866- BiCAW,
WomWWA 14
Flint, Austin 1812-1886 AmBi, ApCAB,
BiDAmEd, BiHiMed, DcAmB, Drake,
NatCAB 8, TwCBDA, WebAB,
WhAm H
Flint, Austin 1836-1915 ApCAB, DcAmB,
Drake, NatCAB 9, TwCBDA, WhAm 1
Flint, Austin 1868-1955 NatCAB 45,
WhAm 3
Flint, Billa 1805- ApCAB
Flint, Charles Lewis 1824-1889 Drake
Flint, Charles Louis 1824-1889 ApCAB,
DcAmB, NatCAB 25, TwCBDA,
WhAm H
Flint, Charles Ranlett 1850-1934 DcAmB S1,
NatCAB 37, TwCBDA, WhAm 1
Flint, Charles Roulette 1850- NatCAB 1
Flint, Charles Wesley 1878-1964 WhAm 4
Flint, Clarence Blake 1879-1952 NatCAB 38
Flint, David Bordman 1816- NatCAB 2
Flint, Edith Foster 1873- WhAm 5
Flint, Edward Austin 1832-1886 NatCAB 20
Flint, Frank Chapin 1872-1956 NatCAB 43
Flint, Frank Putnam 1862-1929 BiDrAC,
NatCAB 13, WhAm 1
Flint, Henry 1675-1760 ApCAB, Drake
Flint, Henry Martyn 1829-1868 ApCAB, Drake,
NatCAB 4
Flint, Jacob 1767-1835 ApCAB
Flint, Jacob 1768-1835 Drake
Flint, James Milton 1838-1919 WhAm 1
Flint, John Dexter 1826-1907 NatCAB 36
Flint, John James Bleecker 1838- ApCAB
Flint, Joseph Marshall 1872-1944 NatCAB 33,
WhAm 5
Flint, Joshua Barker 1801-1864 ApCAB, Drake
Flint, Kemp Russell Blanchard 1880- WhAm 6
Flint, Leon Nelson 1875-1955 NatCAB 45,
WhAm 3
Flint, Lillian C WomWWA 14
Flint, Marion Lenore WomWWA 14
Flint, Micah P 1807-1830 ApCAB, Drake
Flint, Motley H 1865- WhAm 4
Flint, Noel Leslie 1903-1964 WhAm 4

Flint, Timothy 1780-1840 *AmBi, ApCAB, DcAmB, Drake, EncAAH, NatCAB 6, REnAW, TwCBDA, WebAB, WhAm H*
Flint, Weston 1835-1906 *DcAmB, NatCAB 11, WhAm 1*
Flintoft, James 1919-1975 *WhAm 6*
Flippen, Edgar Lucas 1876- *WhAm 5*
Flipper, Joseph Simeon 1859-1944 *NatCAB 14, WhAm 2, WhoColR*
Flippin, Harrison Fitzgerald 1906-1968 *NatCAB 56*
Flippin, James Carroll 1878-1939 *WhAm 1*
Flippin, Percy Scott 1874- *WhAm 5*
Flitcraft, Allen J 1854- *NatCAB 10*
Flitcraft, Pembrook Reeves 1847-1908 *NatCAB 30*
Floan, John Peter 1872-1944 *NatCAB 34*
Flockhart, Thomas Alexander 1874-1955 *NatCAB 43*
Flocks, Rubin H 1907-1975 *WhAm 6*
Floersh, John A 1886-1968 *WhAm 5*
Floersheim, Otto 1853- *ApCAB Sup*
Floete, Franklin G 1889-1973 *WhAm 6*
Floherty, John Joseph 1882-1964 *WhAm 4*
Flohr, George Daniel 1759-1826 *ApCAB*
Flom, George Tobias 1871-1960 *WhAm 3*
Flood, Daniel John 1903- *BiDrAC*
Flood, Frances Otey *WomWWA 14*
Flood, Francis Arthur 1896-1956 *WhAm 3*
Flood, George Burnside 1880-1954 *NatCAB 43*
Flood, George H *BiAUS*
Flood, Gerald F 1898-1966 *WhAm 4*
Flood, Henry, Jr. 1887-1948 *WhAm 2*
Flood, Henry Delaware 1865-1921 *NatCAB 19, WhAm 1*
Flood, Henry DeLaWarr 1865-1921 *BiDrAC, WhAmP*
Flood, James Clair 1825-1888 *ApCAB Sup*
Flood, James Clair 1826-1889 *TwCBDA*
Flood, James Leary 1857-1926 *NatCAB 39*
Flood, Joel West 1894-1964 *BiDrAC*
Flood, Ned Arden 1870-1938 *WhAm 1*
Flood, Theodore L 1842- *WhAm 4*
Flood, Thomas Schmeck 1844-1908 *BiDrAC, TwCBDA*
Flood, Thomas William 1918-1963 *NatCAB 49*
Flood, Walter Vincent 1897- *WhAm 3*
Flood-Keyes, Regina *WomWWA 14*
Floody, Robert John 1859- *WhAm 4*
Flook, William M 1875-1962 *WhAm 4*
Flora, Abram Cline 1885-1971 *NatCAB 56*
Florance, Ernest Touro 1854-1918 *WhAm 1*
Florance, Howard 1885-1959 *WhAm 3*
Florance, William Edwin 1865-1943 *NatCAB 31*
Florat, J A De *NewYHSD*
Flore, Edward 1877-1945 *WhAm 2*
Florence, Elias 1797-1880 *BiAUS, BiDrAC, WhAm H*
Florence, Fred Farrel 1891-1960 *WhAm 4*
Florence, Malvina Pray 1830-1906 *NotAW*
Florence, Thomas Birch 1812-1875 *ApCAB, BiAUS, BiDrAC, DcAmB, NatCAB 23, TwCBDA, WhAm H, WhAmP*
Florence, Mrs. William J d1906 *WhAm 1*
Florence, William Jermyn 1831-1891 *AmBi, ApCAB, DcAmB, NatCAB 2, TwCBDA, WhAm H*
Florencia, Francisco 1620-1695 *ApCAB*
Florer, Jeannette Smith 1872- *WomWWA 14*
Florer, Warren Washburn 1869-1958 *WhAm 3*
Flores, Antonio 1833- *ApCAB*
Flores, Ignacio d1786 *ApCAB*
Flores, Jose 1730?-1795? *ApCAB*
Flores, Juan Jose 1800-1864 *ApCAB*
Flores, Juan Jose 1801-1864 *McGEWB*
Flores, Venancio 1809-1868 *ApCAB, Drake*
Flores-Alatorre, Juan Jose 1766-1854 *ApCAB*
Florey, Lord Howard Walter 1898-1968 *AsBiEn, DcScB, McGEWB, WhAm 4A, WhAm 5*
Florian *NewYHSD*
Floridablanca, Conde De 1728-1808 *WhAm H*
Floridia, Pietro 1860-1932 *WhAm 1, WhAm 1C*
Florimont, Austin *NewYHSD*
Florio, Caryl 1843- *WhAm 1*
Florio, Lloyd Joseph 1910-1975 *WhAm 6*
Florsheim, Irving S 1893-1959 *WhAm 3*

Florsheim, Leonard S 1879-1964 *WhAm 4*
Flory, Arthur Louis 1914-1972 *WhAm 5*
Flory, George Daniel 1867-1932 *WhAm 1*
Flory, Ira S 1883-1950 *WhAm 3*
Flory, John Samuel 1866-1961 *NatCAB 50, WhAm 4*
Flory, Joseph 1856-1925 *WhAm 1*
Flory, Robert Hewitt 1910-1962 *NatCAB 48*
Flory, Walter LeRoy 1880-1951 *NatCAB 40*
Flota, George W 1893-1955 *WhAm 3*
Floto, Otto Clement 1863-1929 *NatCAB 21*
Flourens, Marie-Jean-Pierre 1794-1867 *DcScB*
Flournoy, Anita Patterson *WomWWA 14*
Flournoy, Harry L 1878-1954 *WhAm 3*
Flournoy, Parke Poindexter 1839-1935 *WhAm 1*
Flournoy, Patrick Wood 1873-1947 *NatCAB 36*
Flournoy, Thomas S d1864 *BiAUS, Drake*
Flournoy, Thomas Stanhope 1811-1883 *ApCAB, BiDrAC, WhAm H*
Flournoy, William Walton 1874- *WhAm 5*
Flower, Anson Ranney 1843-1909 *WhAm 1*
Flower, Benjamin Orange 1858-1918 *DcAmB, NatCAB 9, TwCBDA, WhAm 1*
Flower, Benjamin Orange 1859-1918 *AmBi*
Flower, Edward Fordham 1805-1883 *ApCAB*
Flower, Elliott 1863-1920 *WhAm 1*
Flower, Frank Abial 1854-1911 *ApCAB, WhAm 1*
Flower, George 1780?-1862 *ApCAB, NatCAB 6*
Flower, George 1787-1862 *NewYHSD*
Flower, George 1788-1862 *AmBi, DcAmB, WhAm H*
Flower, Henry Corwin 1860-1938 *WhAm 2*
Flower, J Roswell 1888-1970 *WhAm 5*
Flower, Lucy Louisa Coues 1837-1921 *DcAmB, NatCAB 9, NotAW, WomWWA 14*
Flower, Richard 1761-1829 *DcAmB, WhAm H*
Flower, Rosewell Pettibone 1835-1899 *WhAm H*
Flower, Roswell Pettabone 1835-1899 *ApCAB*
Flower, Roswell Pettibone 1835-1899 *AmBi, ApCAB Sup, BiDrAC, DcAmB, NatCAB 2, TwCBDA, WhAmP*
Flower, Walter C 1850-1900 *WhAm 1*
Flower, William Henry 1831-1899 *DcScB*
Flowerman, Samuel Harold 1912-1958 *NatCAB 44*
Flowers, Alan Estis 1876-1945 *WhAm 2*
Flowers, Allen Gilbert 1869-1935 *WhAm 1*
Flowers, George W 1860- *ApCAB X*
Flowers, Herbert Baker 1881- *WhAm 1*
Flowers, James Nathaniel 1870-1952 *WhAm 3*
Flowers, John Garland 1895-1965 *WhAm 4*
Flowers, Montaville 1868-1934 *WhAm 1*
Flowers, Robert Lee 1870-1951 *WhAm 3*
Flowers, Samuel Bryce 1835- *ApCAB*
Flowers, Walter 1933- *BiDrAC*
Floy, Henry 1866-1916 *WhAm 1*
Floy, James 1806-1863 *ApCAB, DcAmB, Drake, NatCAB 23, TwCBDA, WhAm H*
Floyd, Arabella *ApCAB*
Floyd, Archibald Campbell 1857-1938 *NatCAB 28*
Floyd, Benjamin Levin Worth 1870-1926 *NatCAB 30*
Floyd, C Harold 1878-1944 *NatCAB 33*
Floyd, Charles Albert 1791-1873 *BiAUS, BiDrAC, WhAm H*
Floyd, Charles Miller 1861-1923 *NatCAB 20, WhAm 1*
Floyd, Charles Ranaldo 1796?-1845 *NewYHSD*
Floyd, Cleaveland 1880-1971 *NatCAB 56*
Floyd, David Bittle 1846-1922 *WhAm 1*
Floyd, David Richard 1764-1826 *ApCAB*
Floyd, Edward Elbridge 1834-1904 *NatCAB 15*
Floyd, Frank Monroe 1866- *WhAm 4*
Floyd, Ivy Knox 1885- *WhAm 3*
Floyd, John d1837 *BiAUS, Drake*
Floyd, John 1769-1829 *WhAm H*
Floyd, John 1769-1839 *ApCAB, BiAUS, BiDrAC, Drake, TwCBDA*
Floyd, John 1770-1837 *ApCAB*
Floyd, John 1783-1837 *AmBi, BiDrAC, DcAmB, NatCAB 5, TwCBDA, WhAm H, WhAmP*
Floyd, John Buchanan 1805-1863 *BiAUS, Drake*

Floyd, John Buchanan 1806-1863 *BiDrUSE, DcAmB, NatCAB 5, WebAMB, WhAm H*
Floyd, John Buchanan 1807-1863 *AmBi, ApCAB, TwCBDA*
Floyd, John C 1894-1964 *WhAm 4*
Floyd, John Charles 1858-1930 *BiDrAC, WhAm 1, WhAmP*
Floyd, John Gelston 1806-1881 *BiAUS, BiDrAC, WhAm H*
Floyd, Richard 1620-1690? *ApCAB*
Floyd, Richard 1661-1737 *ApCAB*
Floyd, Richard 1703-1771 *ApCAB*
Floyd, Richard 1736-1791 *ApCAB*
Floyd, Richard C 1886-1953 *WhAm 3*
Floyd, Robert Mitchell 1849- *WhAm 4*
Floyd, Sally Buchanan 1802-1879 *ApCAB*
Floyd, Silas Xavier 1869- *WhoColR*
Floyd, William 1734-1821 *ApCAB, BiAUS, BiDrAC, DcAmB, Drake, NatCAB 4, TwCBDA, WhAm H, WhAmP*
Floyd, William 1743-1821 *AmBi*
Floyd-Jones, David Richard 1813-1871 *ApCAB*
Floyd-Jones, DeLancey 1826-1902 *WhAm 1*
Floyd-Jones, Henry 1792-1862 *ApCAB*
Floyd-Jones, Thomas 1788-1851 *ApCAB*
Fludd, Robert 1574-1637 *DcScB*
Flug, Samuel S 1905-1952 *WhAm 4*
Flugel, Ewald 1863-1914 *DcAmB, WhAm 1*
Flugge-Lotz, Irmgard 1903-1974 *WhAm 6*
Flugler, Thomas T *BiAUS*
Fluhrer, John James 1919-1973 *WhAm 6*
Fluhrer, William Henry 1899-1948 *NatCAB 38*
Fluor, J Simon 1867-1944 *NatCAB 34*
Fluor, John Simon 1902-1974 *WhAm 6*
Fluor, Peter Earl 1895-1947 *NatCAB 34*
Flusser, Charles W 1833-1864 *ApCAB, Drake, NatCAB 5, TwCBDA*
Fly, James Lawrence 1898-1966 *NatCAB 53, WhAm 4*
Fly, Joel Orval 1883-1960 *NatCAB 49*
Fly, Murry Henderson 1886-1960 *NatCAB 48*
Flye, Edwin 1817-1886 *BiDrAC, WhAm H*
Flye, Louis Edwin 1881-1933 *NatCAB 24*
Flynn, Albert T 1894-1964 *WhAm 4*
Flynn, Benedict Devine 1880-1944 *WhAm 2*
Flynn, Dennis Joseph 1856-1911 *WhAm 1*
Flynn, Dennis T 1862-1939 *TwCBDA*
Flynn, Dennis Thomas 1861-1939 *BiDrAC, WhAm 1, WhAmP*
Flynn, Edmund Clarence 1893-1970 *NatCAB 56*
Flynn, Edmund James 1847- *ApCAB*
Flynn, Edmund W 1890-1957 *WhAm 3*
Flynn, Edward d1954 *WhAm 3*
Flynn, Edward Albert 1910-1971 *NatCAB 57*
Flynn, Edward Francis 1875-1964 *NatCAB 51, WhAm 4*
Flynn, Edward Joseph 1891-1953 *DcAmB S5, WhAm 3*
Flynn, Errol Leslie 1909-1959 *WhAm 3*
Flynn, Francis Joseph 1864- *NatCAB 12*
Flynn, Francis Marion 1903-1974 *WhAm 6*
Flynn, Frank Earl 1883-1965 *NatCAB 53, WhAm 4*
Flynn, Gerald Thomas 1910- *BiDrAC*
Flynn, J Cajetan 1871-1962 *NatCAB 49*
Flynn, James Augustin 1876-1964 *NatCAB 50*
Flynn, James Graham 1885-1957 *NatCAB 47*
Flynn, James Murray 1883-1946 *NatCAB 37*
Flynn, John Aloysius 1900-1965 *WhAm 4*
Flynn, John E 1897-1965 *WhAm 4*
Flynn, John Thomas 1882-1964 *WhAm 4*
Flynn, Joseph Anthony 1924-1974 *WhAm 6*
Flynn, Joseph Crane 1876-1948 *WhAm 2*
Flynn, Joseph Michael 1848- *WhAm 4*
Flynn, Joseph Vincent 1883-1940 *BiDrAC*
Flynn, P J 1856-1936 *WhAm 2*
Flynn, Patrick Henry 1861-1934 *NatCAB 29*
Flynn, Patrick John 1838- *NatCAB 4*
Flynn, Thomas *WhAm H*
Flynn, Thomas E 1906-1972 *WhAm 5*
Flynn, Thomas P 1868- *WhAm 4*
Flynn, Vincent Joseph 1901-1956 *NatCAB 44, WhAm 3*
Flynn, William James 1867-1928 *WhAm 1*
Flynn, William Smith 1885-1966 *WhAm 4*
Flynt, Charles Fremont 1857-1933 *WhAm 1*

Flynt, Fannie C 1863- *WomWWA 14*
Flynt, Henry Needham 1893-1970 *WhAm 5*
Flynt, John James, Jr. 1914- *BiDrAC*
Flynt, Josiah 1869-1907 *AmBi, DcAmB S1*
Flythe, William P 1893-1956 *WhAm 3*
Foard, Joseph Rasin 1853-1911 *NatCAB 29*
Fobes, Edwin Francis 1856-1926 *NatCAB 37*
Fobes, Francis Howard 1881-1957 *NatCAB 47*
Fobes, Harriet Keith *WomWWA 14*
Fobes, Joseph Henry 1878-1964 *WhAm 4*
Fobes, Peres 1752-1812 *Drake*
Fobes, Perez 1742-1812 *ApCAB*
Fobes, Philena 1811-1898 *NatCAB 6*
Foch, Ferdinand 1851-1929 *McGEWB,
WhoMilH*
Focher, Jean 1501-1572 *ApCAB*
Focht, Benjamin Kurtz 1863-1937 *BiDrAC,
WhAm 1, WhAmP*
Focht, John Brown 1851-1924 *WhAm 1*
Focke, Theodore Moses 1871-1949 *NatCAB 42,
WhAm 2*
Foelker, Otto Godfrey 1875-1943 *BiDrAC,
WhAm 5*
Foell, Charles Michael 1870-1937 *WhAm 1*
Foellinger, Oscar George 1885-1936
NatCAB 32, WhAm 1
Foelsch, Charles Berend 1891-1974 *WhAm 6*
Foerderer, Percival Edward 1884-1969 *WhAm 5*
Foerderer, Robert Herman 1860-1903
NatCAB 18
Foerderer, Robert Hermann 1860-1903 *BiDrAC*
Foerste, August Frederick 1862-1936 *DcScB,
NatCAB 29, WhAm 1*
Foerster, Adolph Martin 1854-1927 *ApCAB X,
NatCAB 11, TwCBDA, WhAm 1*
Foerster, Emil 1822-1906 *NewYHSD*
Foerster, Otto Hottinger 1876-1965 *NatCAB 51,
WhAm 4*
Foerster, Robert Franz 1883-1941 *NatCAB 30,
WhAm 1*
Foerster, Roland Constantine 1893-1961
WhAm 4
Fogarty, James Francis 1888-1960 *WhAm 4*
Fogarty, John Edward 1913-1967 *BiDrAC,
DcAmLiB, WhAm 4, WhAmP*
Fogarty, Thomas 1873-1938 *WhAm 1*
Fogdall, Sorenus P 1879-1947 *WhAm 2*
Fogel, Edwin Miller 1874-1949 *WhAm 2*
Fogel, Paul Martin 1881-1960 *NatCAB 49*
Fogg, Alden Knowlton 1892-1958 *NatCAB 43*
Fogg, Charles Sumner 1851- *ApCAB X*
Fogg, George Gilman 1813-1881 *AmBi,
BiDrAC, DcAmB, TwCBDA, WhAm H*
Fogg, George Gilman 1815-1881 *ApCAB,
BiAUS, Drake, NatCAB 4*
Fogg, Helen Moore *WomWWA 14*
Fogg, Heman Charles 1894-1952 *NatCAB 40*
Fogg, Isaac 1885-1962 *WhAm 4*
Fogg, Joseph *NewYHSD*
Fogg, Lawrence Daniel 1879-1914 *WhAm 1*
Fogg, Lloyd Clarke 1899-1960 *WhAm 4*
Fogg, Miller Moore, III 1868-1926 *NatCAB 21*
Fogg, William Perry 1826- *NatCAB 4,
TwCBDA*
Foght, Harold Waldstein 1869- *WhAm 3*
Fogle, Amanda Harter 1877- *WomWWA 14*
Foglesong, John E 1885-1956 *WhAm 3*
Fogliardi, J B *NewYHSD*
Fogo, James Gordon 1896-1952 *WhAm 3*
Fogwell, Harrison Harry 1885-1965 *NatCAB 53*
Fohs, Cora Baldauf 1882- *WomWWA 14*
Fohs, Ferdinand Julius 1884-1965 *WhAm 4*
Foik, Paul Joseph 1879-1941 *DcAmLiB*
Foik, Paul Joseph 1880-1941 *WhAm 1*
Foix, Gaston De, Duc DeNemours 1489-1512
WhoMilH
Fokine, Michel 1880-1942 *DcAmB S3,
WhAm 2*
Fokker, Anthony Herman Gerard 1890-1939
AmBi, WhAm 1
Fokma, Jan Jelle 1900-1972 *WhAm 5*
Fol, Hermann 1845-1892 *DcScB*
Folds, Charles Weston 1870-1928 *NatCAB 39,
WhAm 1*
Folds, George Robert 1870-1957 *NatCAB 46*
Foley, Arthur Lee 1867-1945 *NatCAB 43,
WhAm 2*
Foley, Edna Lois 1878- *WomWWA 14*

Foley, Edward Timothy 1887-1968 *NatCAB 57*
Foley, Ellen S McCarthy 1882-
WomWWA 14a
Foley, Francis B 1887-1973 *WhAm 5*
Foley, Frederick Clement 1904-1955 *WhAm 3*
Foley, George Cadwalader 1851-1935
NatCAB 39, WhAm 1
Foley, Harold Scanlon 1900-1974 *WhAm 6*
Foley, James *NewYHSD*
Foley, James A 1882-1946 *WhAm 2*
Foley, James Bradford 1807-1886 *BiAUS,
BiDrAC, WhAm H*
Foley, James Owen 1897-1961 *NatCAB 49,
WhAm 4*
Foley, James William, Jr. 1874-1939 *WhAm 1*
Foley, John Burton 1857-1925 *WhAm 1*
Foley, John Kennedy 1879-1950 *NatCAB 40*
Foley, John Robert 1917- *BiDrAC*
Foley, John Samuel 1833-1918 *NatCAB 13,
TwCBDA, WhAm 1*
Foley, Marcella M 1879- *WomWWA 14*
Foley, Margaret E d1877 *AmWom, ApCAB,
NatCAB 9*
Foley, Margaret F d1877 *NewYHSD,
WhAm H*
Foley, Margaret Mary 1918-1970 *WhAm 5*
Foley, Max Henry 1894-1968 *WhAm 5*
Foley, Nicholas *NewYHSD*
Foley, Raymond Michael 1890-1975 *WhAm 6*
Foley, Robert Emmett 1894-1960 *NatCAB 49*
Foley, Roger T 1886-1974 *WhAm 6*
Foley, Thomas 1823-1879 *ApCAB*
Foley, Thomas J 1866-1918 *WhAm 1*
Foley, Thomas Patrick Roger 1822-1879
NatCAB 9, TwCBDA, WhAm H
Foley, Thomas Stephen 1929- *BiDrAC,
EncAAH*
Foley, William Thomas 1908-1964 *NatCAB 50*
Folger, Abiah 1667- *ApCAB*
Folger, Alice Adele *WomWWA 14*
Folger, Alonzo Dillard 1888-1941 *BiDrAC,
NatCAB 42, WhAm 2*
Folger, Charles James 1818-1884 *AmBi,
ApCAB, BiDrUSE, DcAmB, NatCAB 4,
TwCBDA, WhAm H*
Folger, Edwin G *NewYHSD*
Folger, Emily Clara Jordan 1858-1936 *NotAW,
WomWWA 14*
Folger, Henry Clay 1857-1930 *AmBi, DcAmB,
NatCAB 23, WhAm 1*
Folger, James A 1900-1972 *WhAm 5*
Folger, John Hamlin 1880-1963 *BiDrAC,
WhAm 6*
Folger, L *NewYHSD*
Folger, Peleg 1733-1789 *ApCAB, Drake*
Folger, Peter 1617-1690 *AmBi, ApCAB,
DcAmB, Drake, NatCAB 7, WhAm H*
Folger, Walter 1765-1849 *ApCAB, BiAUS,
BiDrAC, DcAmB, TwCBDA, WhAm H*
Folger, William B *NewYHSD*
Folger, William Mayhew 1844-1928
*ApCAB Sup, NatCAB 31, TwCBDA,
WhAm 1*
Folie, A P *NewYHSD*
Folin, Laura Churchill Grant *WomWWA 14*
Folin, Otto Knut Olof 1867-1934 *BiHiMed,
DcAmB S1, DcScB, NatCAB 25,
WhAm 1*
Folingsby, Mrs. George Frederick *NewYHSD*
Folingsby, George Frederick 1830-1891
NewYHSD, WhAm H
Folinsbee, John Fulton 1892-1972 *WhAm 5*
Folk, Carey Albert 1867- *WhAm 4*
Folk, Edgar Estes 1856-1917 *WhAm 1*
Folk, George Billmyer 1887-1966 *NatCAB 53*
Folk, Joseph Wingate 1869-1923 *AmBi,
DcAmB, NatCAB 13, NatCAB 22,
WhAm 1*
Folk, Marion Hayne, Jr. 1899-1964 *WhAm 4*
Folkard, W *NewYHSD*
Folkers, Karl August 1906- *AsBiEn*
Folkes, Martin 1690-1754 *DcScB*
Folkmar, Daniel 1861-1932 *TwCBDA,
WhAm 1*
Folkmar, Elnora Cuddeback 1863- *BiCAW,
WhAm 4, WomWWA 14*
Folks, Homer 1867-1963 *EncAB, NatCAB 48,
WhAm 4*

Folland, William Henry 1877-1941 *NatCAB 30,
WhAm 2*
Follansbee, Benjamin Gilbert 1851-1939
ApCAB X, NatCAB 29
Follansbee, George Alanson 1843-1920
WhAm 1
Follansbee, George Edward 1871- *WhAm 5*
Follansbee, John 1868-1957 *WhAm 3*
Follansbee, Mitchell Davis 1870-1941 *WhAm 1*
Follansbee, Robert 1879-1952 *WhAm 4*
Follansbee, William Uhler 1859-1939
NatCAB 29
Follen, Charles 1796-1840 *AmBi, DcAmB*
Follen, Charles F C 1796-1840 *WhAm H*
Follen, Charles Theodore Christian 1796-1840
ApCAB, Drake, NatCAB 7, TwCBDA
Follen, Eliza Lee Cabot 1787-1860 *ApCAB,
DcAmB, Drake, NotAW, TwCBDA,
WhAm H*
Follen, Karl Theodor Christian 1796-1840
DcAmB
Follen, Karl Theodore Christian 1796-1840
AmBi, BiDAmEd
Follet, David Lyman 1836- *ApCAB*
Follett, Charles 1875-1952 *NatCAB 46*
Follett, Charles Walcott 1882-1952 *WhAm 3*
Follett, Darwin 1885-1959 *NatCAB 48*
Follett, John Dawson 1871-1918 *NatCAB 46*
Follett, John Fassett 1831-1902 *BiDrAC*
Follett, Martin Dewey 1826-1911 *WhAm 1*
Follett, Mary Parker 1868-1933 *DcAmB S1,
NotAW, WhAm 5*
Follett, William W 1856-1915 *WhAm 1*
Folley, Walter Clark 1897-1965 *NatCAB 52,
WhAm 4*
Follis, Richard Holden, Jr. 1909-1965
NatCAB 52
Follman, Matthew A d1964 *WhAm 4*
Follmer, Frederick Voris 1885-1971 *NatCAB 57*
Follmer, Harold Newton 1861-1933 *WhAm 1*
Folmer, William Frederic 1861-1936
NatCAB 33
Folsom, Abby 1792?-1867 *ApCAB, NatCAB 2*
Folsom, Abraham 1805-1886 *NewYHSD*
Folsom, Alfred Iverson 1883-1946 *NatCAB 35,
WhAm 2*
Folsom, Benjamin 1847-1922 *NatCAB 19,
WhAm 1*
Folsom, C A *NewYHSD*
Folsom, Charles 1794-1872 *ApCAB, DcAmB,
TwCBDA, WhAm H*
Folsom, Charles Follen 1842-1907 *ApCAB,
NatCAB 19, TwCBDA, WhAm 1*
Folsom, Charles William 1826- *ApCAB*
Folsom, Clara Abbott 1867- *WomWWA 14*
Folsom, David Morrill 1881- *WhAm 6*
Folsom, Elizabeth A 1812-1899 *NewYHSD*
Folsom, Elizabeth Irons 1878- *WhAm 6*
Folsom, Ellen Minot *WomWWA 14*
Folsom, Florens 1874- *WomWWA 14*
Folsom, Frank M 1894-1970 *NatCAB 55*
Folsom, G Winthrop 1846-1915 *NatCAB 31*
Folsom, George 1802-1869 *ApCAB, BiAUS,
DcAmB, Drake, NatCAB 12, TwCBDA,
WhAm H*
Folsom, H Lloyd 1888-1954 *NatCAB 45*
Folsom, Henry Titus 1859-1937 *NatCAB 33*
Folsom, Joseph L 1817-1855 *ApCAB*
Folsom, Justus Watson 1871- *WhAm 1*
Folsom, Marion Bayard 1893- *BiDrUSE*
Folsom, Nathaniel 1726-1790 *ApCAB, BiAUS,
BiDrAC, DcAmB, Drake, NatCAB 11,
TwCBDA, WhAm H, WhAmP*
Folsom, Nathaniel Smith 1806-1890 *ApCAB,
Drake, TwCBDA*
Folsom, Norton 1842- *ApCAB, TwCBDA*
Folsom, Sarah Blanton 1915-1969 *WhAm 5*
Folsom, Susannah Sarah *ApCAB*
Folsome, Clair Edwin 1903-1956 *NatCAB 52*
Folster, George Thomas 1906-1964 *WhAm 4*
Folts, Aubrey Fairfax 1901-1962 *WhAm 4*
Foltz, Clara Shortridge 1849-1934 *AmWom,
ApCAB, NotAW, TwCBDA, WhAm 5,
WomWWA 14*
Foltz, Frederick Steinman 1857-1952
NatCAB 41, WhAm 3
Foltz, Herbert Willard 1867-1946 *NatCAB 35*
Foltz, James A, Jr. 1903-1956 *WhAm 3*

Foltz, Jonathan Messersmith 1810-1877 *ApCAB,*
NatCAB 5, TwCBDA

Foltz, Moses Abraham 1837-1915 *NatCAB 16*

Folwell, Amory Prescott 1865-1960 *NatCAB 48,*
WhAm 5

Folwell, Arthur Hamilton 1877-1962 *WhAm 4*

Folwell, G *NewYHSD*

Folwell, P Donald 1881-1955 *NatCAB 43*

Folwell, Samuel 1765?-1813 *NewYHSD*

Folwell, Samuel 1768?-1813 *DcAmB,*
WhAm H

Folwell, Sarah Hubbard 1838- *WomWWA 14*

Folwell, William Hazelton 1876-1945 *WhAm 2*

Folwell, William Watts 1833-1929 *AmBi,*
ApCAB, BiDAmEd, DcAmB,
NatCAB 13, REnAW, TwCBDA,
WhAm 1

Folz, Stanley 1878-1954 *WhAm 3*

Fonck, Rene Paul 1894-1953 *WhoMilH*

Fonda, Henry 1905- *WebAB*

Fonda, John H 1797?-1868? *DcAmB,*
WhAm H

Fonda, Mary Alice 1837- *AmWom*

Fonde, C *NewYHSD*

Fonde, George 1873-1947 *WhAm 2*

Fondiller, Richard 1884-1962 *WhAm 4*

Fondren, Walter William 1877-1939
NatCAB 33

Fonerden, John 1804-1869 *ApCAB*

Fones, Daniel Gilbert 1837-1893 *NatCAB 7*

Fones, James A 1839- *NatCAB 7*

Fong, Hiram Leong 1907- *BiDrAC*

Fong, Jacob 1913-1967 *WhAm 4*

Fonseca, Juan Rodriguez 1451-1524 *ApCAB*

Fonseca, Mariano Jose Pereira Da 1773-1848
ApCAB

Fonseca Lima E Silva, Manoel Da 1793-1862
ApCAB

Font, Pedro d1781 *DcAmB, WhAm H*

Fontaine, Alexis 1704-1771 *DcScB*

Fontaine, Arthur Benjamin 1876- *WhAm 5*

Fontaine, Lamar 1829-1921 *ApCAB Sup,*
WhAm 3

Fontaine, Robert Anderson 1879-1955
NatCAB 46

Fontaine, William Morris 1835-1913
NatCAB 19, WhAm 1

Fontana, Felice 1730-1805 *DcScB*

Fontana, Lucio 1899-1968 *WhAm 5*

Fontana, Mark John 1849- *NatCAB 18*

Fontane, Theodor 1819-1898 *McGEWB*

Fontanne, Lynn 1887?- *WebAB*

Fontass, Jean *NewYHSD*

Fontelli, L De *NewYHSD*

Fontenelle, Bernard LeBouyer De 1657-1757
DcScB

Fontenelle, Lucien 1800-1840? *REnAW*

Fontius, Harry E 1887-1962 *NatCAB 50*

Fonville, Louis Eugene 1655-1711 *ApCAB*

Fonville, Richard Henry 1882-1954 *WhAm 3*

Fonville, William Drakeford 1849- *WhAm 4*

Fooks, D W 1874- *WhAm 5*

Fooks, Daniel James 1846-1915 *NatCAB 34*

Foord, Archibald Smith 1914-1969 *WhAm 5*

Foord, James Alfred 1872- *WhAm 5*

Foord, John 1842- *NatCAB 13*

Foos, Charles Schmeck 1863-1929 *NatCAB 21*

Foot, Andrew Hull *WebAB*

Foot, Edwin Hawley 1876-1957 *NatCAB 48,*
WhAm 3

Foot, Eliza Campbell *WomWWA 14*

Foot, Joseph Ives 1796-1840 *ApCAB*

Foot, Joseph Ives *see also* Foote, Joseph Ives

Foot, Nathan Chandler 1881-1958 *NatCAB 47,*
WhAm 3

Foot, Samuel Alfred 1790-1878 *ApCAB,*
NatCAB 7, TwCBDA

Foot, Samuel Augustus 1780-1846 *AmBi,*
BiAUS, DcAmB, WhAm H

Foot, Samuel Augustus *see also* Foote, Samuel
Augustus

Foot, Solomon 1802-1866 *AmBi, ApCAB,*
BiAUS, BiDrAC, DcAmB, Drake,
NatCAB 2, TwCBDA, WhAm H,
WhAmP

Foote, Allen Ripley 1842- *WhAm 4*

Foote, Andrew Hull 1806-1863 *AmBi, ApCAB,*
DcAmB, Drake, NatCAB 5, TwCBDA,

Foote, Anna Jenner 1881- *WomWWA 14*

Foote, Arthur Burling 1877-1964 *NatCAB 51*

Foote, Arthur William 1853-1937 *AmBi,*
ApCAB, ApCAB X, DcAmB S2,
NatCAB 7, NatCAB 27, TwCBDA,
WhAm 1

Foote, Charles Augustus 1785-1828 *BiAUS,*
BiDrAC, WhAm H

Foote, Charles Edwin 1858-1938 *NatCAB 35*

Foote, Charles Howard 1842-1921 *NatCAB 24*

Foote, Charles Jenkins 1861-1954 *NatCAB 43*

Foote, Dellizon Arthur 1860-1935 *WhAm 1*

Foote, Edward Augustus 1869-1937 *NatCAB 27*

Foote, Edward Bliss 1829-1906 *NatCAB 3,*
TwCBDA, WhAm 1

Foote, Edward Bond 1854- *NatCAB 3,*
TwCBDA, WhAm 4

Foote, Elial Todd 1796-1877 *ApCAB*

Foote, Elijah Hedding 1845-1920 *NatCAB 19*

Foote, Elisha 1809-1883 *ApCAB, NatCAB 7,*
NatCAB 21

Foote, Elizabeth Louisa 1866- *WhAm 4,*
WomWWA 14

Foote, Ellsworth Bishop 1898- *BiDrAC*

Foote, George Anderson 1835- *ApCAB*

Foote, Harry Ward 1875-1942 *WhAm 1,*
WhAm 2

Foote, Henry Stuart 1800-1880 *ApCAB,*
BiAUS, BiDConf, Drake, TwCBDA

Foote, Henry Stuart 1804-1880 *AmBi, BiDrAC,*
DcAmB, McGEWB, NatCAB 13,
REnAW, WhAm H, WhAmP

Foote, Henry Wilder 1838- *ApCAB*

Foote, Henry Wilder 1875-1964 *WhAm 4*

Foote, John Ambrose 1874-1931 *DcAmB S1,*
NatCAB 39, WhAm 1

Foote, John Howard 1833- *NatCAB 4*

Foote, John Johnson 1816- *NatCAB 5*

Foote, John Parsons 1783-1865 *NewYHSD*

Foote, John Taintor 1881-1950 *NatCAB 40,*
WhAm 2

Foote, Joseph Ives 1796-1840 *Drake*

Foote, Joseph Ives *see also* Foot, Joseph Ives

Foote, Lucius Harwood 1826-1913 *DcAmB,*
NatCAB 7, TwCBDA, WhAm 1

Foote, Mark 1882-1957 *WhAm 3*

Foote, Mary Hallock 1847-1938 *AmWom,*
IlBEAAW, NatCAB 6, NotAW, REnAW,
TwCBDA, WhAm 1, WomWWA 14

Foote, Morris Cooper 1843-1905 *WhAm 1*

Foote, Nathaniel 1849-1944 *WhAm 2*

Foote, Norman Landon 1915-1974 *WhAm 6*

Foote, Paul Darwin 1888-1971 *NatCAB 56,*
WhAm 5

Foote, Percy Wright 1879-1961 *WhAm 4*

Foote, Samuel Augustus 1780-1846 *AmBi,*
ApCAB, BiDrAC, DcAmB, Drake,
NatCAB 10, TwCBDA, WhAmP

Foote, Stephen Miller 1859- *WhAm 4*

Foote, Thomas Moses 1808-1858 *NatCAB 7*

Foote, Thomas Moses 1809-1858 *ApCAB,*
BiAUS

Foote, Wallace Turner, Jr. 1864-1910 *BiDrAC,*
NatCAB 34, TwCBDA

Foote, Wilder 1905-1975 *WhAm 6*

Foote, Will Howe 1874-1965 *WhAm 4*

Foote, William Augustine 1854-1915
NatCAB 17

Foote, William Henry 1794-1869 *ApCAB,*
DcAmB S1, Drake, WhAm H

Foote, William Wirt d1953 *WhAm 3*

Footner, Hulbert 1879-1944 *WhAm 2*

Foppl, August 1854-1924 *DcScB*

Fora, Louis *NewYHSD*

Foraker, Burch 1872-1935 *WhAm 1*

Foraker, Forest Almos 1881-1949 *WhAm 2*

Foraker, Joseph Benson 1846-1917 *AmBi,*
ApCAB, ApCAB X, BiDrAC, DcAmB,
NatCAB 3, TwCBDA, WhAm 1,
WhAmP

Foraker, Julia Bundy *WomWWA 14*

Foran, Joseph K 1857- *ApCAB*

Foran, Martin Ambrose 1844-1921 *BiDrAC,*
NatCAB 19

Forand, Aime Joseph 1895-1972 *BiDrAC,*
NatCAB 57, WhAm 5

Forbes, Alexander 1882-1965 *DcScB,*

Forbes, Alexander Stanton 1819-1848
NatCAB 9

Forbes, Allan 1874-1955 *WhAm 3*

Forbes, Allen Boyd 1866-1923 *NatCAB 20,*
WhAm 1

Forbes, Allyn Bailey 1897-1947 *WhAm 2*

Forbes, Arthur Henry Holland 1863-1927
NatCAB 22

Forbes, Arthur Whitton 1868-1946 *NatCAB 35*

Forbes, Bertie Charles 1880-1954 *NatCAB 47,*
WhAm 3

Forbes, Bruce Charles 1916-1964 *WhAm 4*

Forbes, Charles Edwin 1795-1881 *ApCAB*

Forbes, Charles Henry 1866-1933 *NatCAB 13,*
WhAm 1

Forbes, Edgar Allen 1872- *WhAm 5*

Forbes, Edward, Jr. 1815-1854 *AsBiEn, DcScB*

Forbes, Edward Abner 1867-1959 *NatCAB 46*

Forbes, Edward Waldo 1873-1969 *NatCAB 57,*
WhAm 5

Forbes, Edwin 1839-1895 *AmBi, ApCAB,*
DcAmB, IlBEAAW, NatCAB 5,
NewYHSD, TwCBDA, WhAm H

Forbes, Edwin Horace 1850-1935 *NatCAB 26*

Forbes, Eli 1726-1804 *ApCAB*

Forbes, Elisha *NewYHSD*

Forbes, Elizabeth Leslie 1867- *WomWWA 14*

Forbes, Elmer Severance 1860-1933 *WhAm 1*

Forbes, Ernest Browning 1876-1966 *WhAm 4*

Forbes, Esther 1891-1967 *NatCAB 53,*
WhAm 4

Forbes, Francis Murray 1874-1961 *NatCAB 49,*
WhAm 4

Forbes, Frederick Faber d1933 *WhAm 1*

Forbes, Frederick Levi 1854-1940 *WhAm 1*

Forbes, George Mather 1853-1934 *NatCAB 26,*
WhAm 1

Forbes, Georgie Hazel Scott 1873-
WomWWA 14

Forbes, Gerrit Angelo 1836-1906 *WhAm 1*

Forbes, Gordon 1738-1828 *ApCAB, Drake*

Forbes, Hannah Lucinda *NewYHSD*

Forbes, Harriette Merrifield 1856-1951
WhAm 1

Forbes, Harrye Rebecca Piper Smith *WhAm 5,*
WomWWA 14

Forbes, Helen Katherine 1891- *IlBEAAW*

Forbes, Henry Prentiss 1849-1913 *WhAm 1*

Forbes, James 1731?-1780 *BiAUS, BiDrAC,*
WhAm H

Forbes, James 1871-1938 *NatCAB 33,*
WhAm 1

Forbes, James David 1809-1868 *DcScB*

Forbes, James Fraser 1820- *ApCAB*

Forbes, Jesse Franklin 1847-1922 *WhAm 1*

Forbes, John 1710-1759 *AmBi, ApCAB,*
DcAmB, Drake, EncAAH, McGEWB,
NatCAB 12, WhAm H

Forbes, John 1740?-1783 *DcAmB, WhAm H*

Forbes, John 1769-1823 *DcAmB*

Forbes, John 1771-1824 *ApCAB*

Forbes, John Colin 1846- *ApCAB*

Forbes, John F 1876-1965 *WhAm 4*

Forbes, John Franklin 1853-1926 *BiDAmEd,*
NatCAB 5, NatCAB 22, TwCBDA,
WhAm 4

Forbes, John Murray 1771-1831 *BiAUS,*
DcAmB, NatCAB 13, WhAm H

Forbes, John Murray 1807-1885 *TwCBDA*

Forbes, John Murray 1813-1898 *ApCAB Sup,*
DcAmB, EncAB, NatCAB 35, REnAW,
TwCBDA, WhAm H

Forbes, John Samuel 1894-1948 *NatCAB 38*

Forbes, John Sims 1866- *WhAm 4*

Forbes, Myron E 1880- *WhAm 6*

Forbes, Philip Jones 1807-1877 *ApCAB*

Forbes, Richard Tasker 1868-1926 *WhAm 1*

Forbes, Robert 1844-1913 *WhAm 1*

Forbes, Robert Bennet 1804-1889 *AmBi,*
DcAmB, McGEWB, WhAm H

Forbes, Robert Humphrey 1867- *WhAm 5*

Forbes, Roger Sawyer 1878- *WhAm 6*

Forbes, Russell 1896-1957 *WhAm 3*

Forbes, Samuel Franklin 1829- *ApCAB*

Forbes, Stephen Alfred 1844-1930 *AmBi,*
ApCAB, DcAmB, DcScB, NatCAB 13,
NatCAB 22, TwCBDA, WhAm 1

Forbes, Theodore Frelinghuysen 1840-1917
WhAm 1
Forbes, W Cameron 1870-1959 *WhAm 3*
Forbes, W O 1852-1937 *WhAm 1*
Forbes, William Amariah 1853- *NatCAB 5*
Forbes, William C *WhAm H*
Forbes, William Hathaway 1840-1897 *TwCBDA*
Forbes, William Trowbridge 1850-1931
WhAm 1
Forbes, William Trowbridge Merrifield
1885-1968 *NatCAB 54*
Forbes-Robertson, Johnston 1853-1937
WhAm 1
Forbriger, Adolf *NewYHSD*
Forbriger, Adolphus *NewYHSD*
Forbush, Edward Howe 1858-1929 *AmBi,*
DcAmB, NatCAB 21, WhAm 1
Forbush, Gayle T 1870- *WhAm 5*
Forbush, William Byron 1868-1927 *NatCAB 23,*
WhAm 1
Forby, Theodore 1865-1942 *NatCAB 31*
Force, John Nivison 1877-1938 *NatCAB 30*
Force, Juliana Rieser 1876-1948 *DcAmB S4,*
NotAW, WhAm 2
Force, Manning Ferguson 1824-1899 *ApCAB,*
DcAmB, TwCBDA, WhAm 1
Force, Peter 1790-1868 *AmBi, ApCAB,*
BiAUS, DcAmB, Drake, TwCBDA,
WebAB, WhAm H
Force, Raymond Charles 1880-1951 *WhAm 3*
Force, William Quereau 1820-1880 *ApCAB,*
TwCBDA
Forchhammer, Johan Georg 1794-1865 *DcScB*
Forchheimer, Frederick 1853-1913 *NatCAB 16,*
WhAm 1
Ford, A *NewYHSD*
Ford, A Ward 1864-1948 *NatCAB 38*
Ford, Aaron Lane 1903- *BiDrAC*
Ford, Albert William 1879- *WhoColR*
Ford, Alexander Hume 1868-1945 *WhAm 2*
Ford, Amelia Clewley 1875- *WhAm 3*
Ford, Arthur Hillyer 1874-1930 *WhAm 1*
Ford, Arthur R 1880-1968 *WhAm 5*
Ford, Arthur Younger 1861-1926 *WhAm 1*
Ford, Bruce 1873-1931 *NatCAB 45*
Ford, Charles Algernon 1870-1927 *NatCAB 51*
Ford, Charles Edward 1898-1957 *NatCAB 48*
Ford, Charles F 1889-1971 *WhAm 5*
Ford, Charles Halsey Lindsley 1887-1939
WhAm 1
Ford, Clyde Ellsworth 1874-1927 *WhAm 1*
Ford, Corey 1902-1969 *WhAm 5*
Ford, Cornelius 1867- *WhAm 4*
Ford, Corydon La 1813- *ApCAB*
Ford, Daniel 1876- *WhAm 5*
Ford, Daniel Sharp 1822-1899 *AmBi, DcAmB,*
NatCAB 5, TwCBDA, WhAm 1
Ford, David McKechnie 1883-1953 *WhAm 3*
Ford, Donald 1889-1964 *NatCAB 50*
Ford, Edsel 1928-1970 *WhAm 5*
Ford, Edsel Bryant 1893-1943 *DcAmB S3,*
WhAm 2
Ford, Edward 1843-1920 *NatCAB 18*
Ford, Edward Emmons 1894-1963 *NatCAB 50*
Ford, Edward Lloyd 1845-1880 *ApCAB*
Ford, Edward Thomas 1879-1950 *NatCAB 40*
Ford, Elias Allen 1840- *WhAm 4*
Ford, Emily Ellsworth 1826- *ApCAB,*
NatCAB 13
Ford, Emory Low 1846-1900 *NatCAB 45*
Ford, Emory Moran 1906-1971 *NatCAB 56,*
WhAm 5
Ford, Eugene Amzi 1866-1948 *NatCAB 38*
Ford, Ford Madox 1873-1939 *McGEWB,*
WhAm HA, WhAm 2, WhAm 4A
Ford, Francis Chipman 1865-1922 *WhAm 1*
Ford, Francis J W 1882-1975 *WhAm 6*
Ford, Frank Richards 1871-1930 *WhAm 1*
Ford, Franklin *ApCAB X*
Ford, Frazer L 1883-1947 *WhAm 3*
Ford, Gabriel H 1764-1849 *BiAUS, Drake*
Ford, Gabriel Hogarth 1765-1849 *ApCAB*
Ford, George 1846-1917 *BiDrAC*
Ford, George Alfred 1851- *WhAm 4*
Ford, George Burdett 1879-1930 *AmBi,*
ApCAB X, DcAmB S1, NatCAB 25,
WhAm 1
Ford, George Michael 1871-1941 *WhAm 1*

Ford, George William 1847- *WhoColR*
Ford, Gerald Rudolph, Jr. 1913- *BiDrAC,*
EncAAH
Ford, Gertrude Seay *WomWWA 14*
Ford, Gordon Lester 1823-1891 *ApCAB,*
DcAmB, NatCAB 6, NatCAB 13,
TwCBDA, WhAm H
Ford, Guy Stanton 1873-1962 *NatCAB 50,*
WhAm 4
Ford, H Ward 1866-1930 *NatCAB 39*
Ford, Hannibal Choate 1877-1955 *DcAmB S5*
Ford, Harriet Chalmers Bliss 1876-
WomWWA 14
Ford, Harriet French 1868-1949 *WhAm 3,*
WomWWA 14
Ford, Heck 1886-1955 *NatCAB 49*
Ford, Henry 1845-1910 *NatCAB 18*
Ford, Henry 1863-1947 *AsBiEn, DcAmB S4,*
EncAAH, EncAB, McGEWB,
NatCAB 15, NatCAB 38, WebAB,
WhAm 2
Ford, Henry, II 1917- *EncAB, McGEWB*
Ford, Henry Chapman 1828-1894 *IIBEAAW,*
NewYHSD
Ford, Henry Clinton 1867-1936 *WhAm 1,*
WhAm 2
Ford, Henry Jones 1851-1925 *DcAmB,*
NatCAB 21, WhAm 1
Ford, Henry P 1837-1905 *WhAm 1*
Ford, Hiram Church 1884-1969 *WhAm 5*
Ford, Horace Sayford 1885-1969 *NatCAB 55*
Ford, Horatio 1881-1952 *NatCAB 41*
Ford, Horatio Clark 1853-1915 *ApCAB X,*
WhAm 1
Ford, Howard Egbert 1906-1975 *WhAm 6*
Ford, Hugh *WhAm 5*
Ford, Isaac Nelson 1848-1912 *WhAm 1*
Ford, Jacob 1738-1777 *DcAmB, WhAm H*
Ford, James d1781 *NewYHSD*
Ford, James 1783-1859 *BiAUS, BiDrAC,*
WhAm H
Ford, James 1884-1944 *NatCAB 42, WhAm 2*
Ford, James Albert 1869-1928 *NatCAB 24*
Ford, James Arthur 1892-1950 *NatCAB 39*
Ford, James Buchanan 1879-1947 *WhAm 2*
Ford, James Lauren 1854-1928 *WhAm 1*
Ford, James Rolla 1887-1956 *NatCAB 47*
Ford, James W d1866 *NewYHSD, WhAm H*
Ford, Jeremiah Denis Matthias 1873-1958
BiDAmEd, NatCAB 44, WhAm 3
Ford, Jessie Frances Smith *WomWWA 14*
Ford, John 1586-1639? *McGEWB*
Ford, John 1862-1941 *WhAm 1*
Ford, John Baptiste 1811-1903 *DcAmB,*
NatCAB 13, WhAm H
Ford, John Battice 1866-1941 *WhAm 2*
Ford, John Donaldson 1840-1918 *TwCBDA,*
WhAm 1
Ford, John Elijah 1862- *WhoColR*
Ford, John S 1815- *NatCAB 7*
Ford, John Sean O'Feeney *REnAW*
Ford, John Sean O'Feeney 1890?- *McGEWB*
Ford, John Sean O'Feeney 1895-1973 *EncAB,*
WebAB, WhAm 6
Ford, John Thompson 1829-1894 *TwCBDA,*
WhAm H
Ford, John Thomson 1829-1894 *AmBi, ApCAB,*
DcAmB, NatCAB 1
Ford, Joseph C 1889-1956 *WhAm 3*
Ford, Joshua Edwards 1825-1866 *ApCAB*
Ford, Julia Ellsworth 1859- *WhAm 5*
Ford, Leland Merritt 1893-1965 *BiDrAC,*
WhAm 4
Ford, Leonard Augustine 1904-1967 *WhAm 5*
Ford, Lewis DeSaussure 1801-1883 *ApCAB*
Ford, Mary Elizabeth Forker d1973 *WhAm 6*
Ford, Mary Hanford 1856- *WhAm 4*
Ford, Mason 1899-1951 *WhAm 3*
Ford, Melbourne Haddock 1849-1891 *BiDrAC,*
WhAm H
Ford, Minnie Smith 1853- *WomWWA 14*
Ford, Miriam Chase 1866- *AmWom*
Ford, Nancy Keffer 1906-1961 *WhAm 4*
Ford, Nicholas 1833-1897 *BiDrAC, WhAm H,*
WhAmP
Ford, Nixola Greeley-Smith 1880- *WhAm 6*
Ford, Patrick 1835-1913 *AmBi, DcAmB,*
NatCAB 22, WhAm 1

Ford, Paul Charles 1915-1972 *WhAm 5*
Ford, Paul Leicester 1865-1902 *AmBi, ApCAB,*
DcAmB, McGEWB, NatCAB 13,
TwCBDA, WebAB, WhAm 1
Ford, Peter J 1857- *WhAm 4*
Ford, Peyton 1911-1971 *WhAm 5*
Ford, Philip d1707? *ApCAB*
Ford, Richard 1915-1970 *WhAm 5*
Ford, Richard Clyde 1870-1951 *WhAm 3*
Ford, Robert Spivey 1902-1970 *NatCAB 55*
Ford, Sallie Rochester 1828- *NatCAB 12,*
TwCBDA, WhAm 4
Ford, Sally Rochester 1828- *ApCAB*
Ford, Samuel Clarence 1882-1961 *NatCAB 49,*
WhAm 4
Ford, Samuel Howard 1819-1905 *BiDConf,*
TwCBDA, WhAm 1
Ford, Samuel Howard 1823- *ApCAB*
Ford, Seabury 1801-1855 *ApCAB, BiAUS,*
Drake, NatCAB 3, TwCBDA
Ford, Seabury Cook 1834-1912 *NatCAB 16*
Ford, Sewell 1868-1946 *NatCAB 14,*
NatCAB 34, WhAm 4
Ford, Sheridan 1867-1922 *NatCAB 19*
Ford, Shirley Samuel 1887-1945 *NatCAB 34,*
WhAm 2
Ford, Simeon 1855-1933 *NatCAB 24,*
WhAm 1
Ford, Smith Thomas 1851-1929 *WhAm 1*
Ford, Stanley Myron 1906-1971 *WhAm 5*
Ford, Stella Dunbar *WomWWA 14*
Ford, Sumner 1887-1966 *WhAm 4*
Ford, T Francis 1878-1969 *NatCAB 55*
Ford, Thomas d1851 *ApCAB, BiAUS, Drake*
Ford, Thomas 1800-1850 *DcAmB, NatCAB 11,*
TwCBDA, WhAm H, WhAmP
Ford, Thomas Francis 1873-1958 *BiDrAC,*
WhAm 3, WhAmP
Ford, Thomas H *BiAUS*
Ford, Thomas J 1856-1930 *NatCAB 22*
Ford, Thomas Pownall 1856- *NatCAB 14*
Ford, Timothy 1762-1830 *ApCAB*
Ford, Tirey Lafayette 1857- *WhAm 1*
Ford, Walter Burton 1874-1971 *NatCAB 55,*
WhAm 5
Ford, Walter David 1877-1955 *NatCAB 44*
Ford, Webster *WebAB*
Ford, Willard Stanley 1890-1951 *WhAm 3*
Ford, William *NewYHSD*
Ford, William 1866-1935 *NatCAB 26*
Ford, William D 1779-1833 *BiAUS, BiDrAC,*
WhAm H
Ford, William David 1927- *BiDrAC*
Ford, William Ebenezer 1878-1939 *WhAm 1*
Ford, William Henry 1839- *ApCAB*
Ford, William Henry 1852- *WhAm 4*
Ford, William Jesse 1908-1972 *WhAm 6*
Ford, William John 1873-1961 *NatCAB 48*
Ford, William Mason 1874-1943 *NatCAB 40*
Ford, William Miller 1878-1938 *WhAm 1*
Ford, William Webber 1871-1941 *NatCAB 30,*
WhAm 1
Ford, Worthington Chauncey 1858-1941
ApCAB, DcAmB S3, NatCAB 13,
NatCAB 34, TwCBDA, WhAm 1
Forde, William *WhoColR*
Fordham, Elijah 1798-1879 *NewYHSD*
Fordham, George W *NewYHSD*
Fordham, Herbert 1869-1953 *WhAm 3*
Fordham, Hubbard L *NewYHSD*
Fordney, Joseph Warren 1853-1932 *AmBi,*
BiDrAC, DcAmB S1, EncAAH,
NatCAB 26, WhAm 1, WhAmP
Fordos, Mathurin-Joseph 1816-1878 *DcScB*
Fordyce, Charles 1857-1936 *WhAm 1*
Fordyce, Claude Powell 1883-1953 *WhAm 3*
Fordyce, James Paul 1892-1975 *WhAm 6*
Fordyce, John Addison 1858-1925 *DcAmB,*
NatCAB 20, WhAm 1
Fordyce, Robert H 1855-1928 *ApCAB X*
Fordyce, Samuel Wesley 1840-1919 *NatCAB 5,*
WhAm 1
Fordyce, Samuel Wesley 1877-1948 *WhAm 2*
Foregger, Richard V 1872-1960 *NatCAB 48*
Forehand, Brooks 1899-1957 *WhAm 3*
Forel, Auguste-Henri 1848-1931 *DcScB*
Forel, Francois Alphonse 1841-1912 *DcScB Sup*
Foreman, Albert Watson 1874-1950 *WhAm 3*

Foreman, Alvan Herbert 1878-1958 *WhAm 3*
Foreman, Edgar Franklin 1933- *BiDrAC*
Foreman, Edgar Seward 1870- *WhoColR*
Foreman, Edgar W *NewYHSD*
Foreman, Grant 1869-1953 *WhAm 3*
Foreman, Harold Edwin 1888-1958 *WhAm 3*
Foreman, Henry Gerhard 1857-1932
    NatCAB 24, WhAm 1
Foreman, Joseph *NewYHSD*
Foreman, Lester B d1969 *WhAm 5*
Foreman, Milton J 1863-1935 *WhAm 1*
Foreman, Oscar G 1863-1933 *WhAm 1*
Foreman, Miss S N *NewYHSD*
Foreman, Stephen 1807-1881 *ApCAB*
Forepaugh, Adam 1831-1890 *DcAmB,*
    WhAm H
Forepaugh, Joseph Lybrandt 1834-1892
    NatCAB 7
Foresman, Hugh Austin d1960 *WhAm 3*
Forest, John Anthony 1838-1911 *NatCAB 13,*
    TwCBDA, WhAm 1
Forester, Cecil Scott 1899-1966 *NatCAB 53,*
    WhAm 4
Forester, Edward Morgan 1879-1970 *WhAm 5*
Forester, Fanny 1817-1854 *AmBi, NotAW*
Forester, Frank 1807-1858 *AmBi, DcAmB,*
    WhAm H
Forester, J J *NewYHSD*
Forester, John B d1845 *BiAUS, BiDrAC,*
    WhAm H
Foresti, E Felice 1793-1858 *Drake*
Foresti, Eleutario Felice 1793-1858 *ApCAB,*
    DcAmB, WhAm H
Forestier, Auber *NotAW*
Forestier, Henri Joseph 1787-1874 *ApCAB*
Forey, Elie Frederic 1804-1872 *ApCAB*
Forgan, David Robertson 1862-1931
    NatCAB 18, WhAm 1
Forgan, James Berwick 1852-1924 *DcAmB,*
    NatCAB 18, WhAm 1
Forgan, James Russell 1900-1974 *WhAm 6*
Forgash, Morris 1898-1966 *WhAm 4*
Foringer, Alonzo Earl 1877-1948 *NatCAB 37*
Forio, Edgar Joseph 1901-1971 *WhAm 5*
Forker, John Norman 1885-1956 *WhAm 3*
Forker, Samuel Carr 1821-1900 *BiAUS,*
    BiDrAC
Forkner, Hamden Landon 1897-1975 *WhAm 6*
Forlong, John Alexander 1884-1956 *NatCAB 45*
Forman, Allan 1860-1914 *NatCAB 1,*
    WhAm 1
Forman, David d1812? *ApCAB, Drake*
Forman, David 1745-1797 *DcAmB, WebAMB,*
    WhAm H
Forman, Henry James 1879-1966 *WhAm 4*
Forman, Isador 1902-1960 *NatCAB 49*
Forman, John Newton 1905-1967 *NatCAB 53*
Forman, Joshua 1777-1848 *DcAmB,*
    NatCAB 6, WhAm H
Forman, Justus Miles 1875-1915 *DcAmB,*
    NatCAB 14, WhAm 1
Forman, Samuel Eagle 1858- *WhAm 4*
Forman, Thomas Marsh 1809-1875 *BiDConf*
Forman, William St. John 1847-1908 *BiDrAC,*
    NatCAB 28, TwCBDA, WhAm 1
Formento, Felix 1790-1888 *ApCAB Sup*
Formento, Felix 1837-1907 *ApCAB Sup,*
    NatCAB 12, TwCBDA, WhAm 1
Formes, Charles John 1810- *ApCAB*
Formes, Karl Johann 1816-1889 *WhAm H*
Fornance, Joseph 1804-1852 *BiAUS, BiDrAC,*
    WhAm H
Fornaris, Jose 1826- *ApCAB*
Fornell, Earl Wesley 1915-1969 *WhAm 5*
Fornes, Charles Vincent 1844-1929 *BiDrAC,*
    WhAmP
Fornes, Charles Vincent 1846-1929 *WhAm 1*
Forney *NewYHSD*
Forney, Daniel Munroe 1784-1847 *ApCAB,*
    BiAUS, BiDrAC, TwCBDA, WhAm H,
    WhAmP
Forney, Edward Hanna 1909-1965 *NatCAB 52*
Forney, James 1844-1921 *WhAm 1*
Forney, John Horace 1829-1902 *BiDConf,*
    WhAm 1
Forney, John W 1817-1881 *BiAUS*
Forney, John Wein 1817-1881 *NatCAB 3*
Forney, John Weiss 1817-1881 *ApCAB, Drake,*

TwCBDA
Forney, John Wien 1817-1881 *AmBi, DcAmB,*
    WhAm H
Forney, Mary Emma *WomWWA 14*
Forney, Matthias Nace 1835-1908 *DcAmB,*
    NatCAB 22
Forney, Peter 1756-1834 *ApCAB, BiAUS,*
    BiDrAC, NatCAB 7, TwCBDA,
    WhAm H, WhAmP
Forney, Tillie May 1861- *AmWom, NatCAB 3*
Forney, William Henry 1823-1894 *ApCAB,*
    BiAUS, BiDrAC, DcAmB, NatCAB 3,
    TwCBDA, WhAm H, WhAmP
Forney, William R 1878-1971 *WhAm 5*
Fornia, Rita 1876-1922 *WhAm 1*
Fornof, John W 1855-1921 *NatCAB 19*
Forres, Juan De d1560 *ApCAB*
Forrest, Aubrey Leland 1912-1957 *WhAm 3*
Forrest, Catherine Norton 1818-1891 *TwCBDA*
Forrest, Catherine Norton Sinclair 1817-1891
    NotAW
Forrest, Charles *NewYHSD*
Forrest, E Arnold 1896-1969 *NatCAB 55*
Forrest, Edwin 1806-1872 *AmBi, ApCAB,*
    DcAmB, Drake, EncAB, McGEWB,
    NatCAB 5, TwCBDA, WebAB,
    WhAm H
Forrest, Felicia H Brinton *WomWWA 14*
Forrest, French 1796-1866 *AmBi, ApCAB,*
    DcAmB, Drake, TwCBDA, WebAMB,
    WhAm H
Forrest, Jacob Dorsey 1866-1930 *WhAm 1*
Forrest, Baron John 1847-1918 *McGEWB*
Forrest, John B 1814?-1870 *NewYHSD*
Forrest, Joseph King Cummins 1820-1896
    NatCAB 7
Forrest, Nathan Bedford 1821-1877 *AmBi,*
    ApCAB, BiDConf, DcAmB, McGEWB,
    NatCAB 10, TwCBDA, WebAB,
    WebAMB, WhAm H, WhoMilH
Forrest, Nathan Bedford 1905-1944 *WhAm 2*
Forrest, Thomas 1747-1825 *BiAUS, BiDrAC,*
    WhAm H
Forrest, Thomas Francis 1906-1965 *NatCAB 53*
Forrest, Uriah 1756-1805 *ApCAB, BiAUS,*
    BiDrAC, Drake, TwCBDA, WhAm H,
    WhAmP
Forrest, William Mentzel 1868- *WhAm 4*
Forrest, William Sylvester 1852- *WhAm 4*
Forrestal, Frank Vincent d1959 *WhAm 3*
Forrestal, James Vincent 1892-1949 *BiDrUSE,*
    DcAmB S4, EncAB, McGEWB,
    NatCAB 42, WebAB, WebAMB,
    WhAm 2, WhAm 4A, WhWW-II
Forrester, D Bruce 1881- *WhAm 3*
Forrester, Elijah Lewis 1896-1970 *BiDrAC,*
    WhAm 5, WhAmP
Forrester, Fanny 1817-1854 *WebAB*
Forrester, Graham 1870-1948 *WhAm 2*
Forrester, Henry 1841- *WhAm 4*
Forrester, Izora L *WomWWA 14*
Forrester, James Joseph 1867-1939 *WhAm 1*
Forrester, Richard 1836-1914 *NatCAB 16*
Forrey, George C, Jr. 1882-1954 *WhAm 3*
Forrey, Harry Newcomer 1873-1964
    NatCAB 50
Forry, John Harold 1912-1965 *WhAm 4*
Forry, Samuel 1811-1844 *ApCAB, Drake*
Forsaith, Samuel Lincoln 1878-1960
    NatCAB 48
Forsander, Nils 1846-1926 *WhAm 1*
Forsbeck, Filip August 1873-1946 *NatCAB 47*
Forsberg, Harold Sigfrid 1886-1970 *NatCAB 55*
Forsch, Albert 1880- *WhAm 6*
Forse, Charles Thomas 1846-1925 *WhAm 1*
Forshey, Caleb Goldsmith 1812-1881 *ApCAB,*
    TwCBDA
Forshey, W *NewYHSD*
Forsskal, Peter 1732-1763 *DcScB*
Forstall, Armand William 1859-1948 *WhAm 2*
Forster, Alexius Mador 1880-1954 *WhAm 4*
Forster, Archibald McDonald 1843- *ApCAB*
Forster, Edward Morgan 1879-1870 *McGEWB*
Forster, Frank Joseph 1886-1948 *WhAm 2*
Forster, Georg Adam 1754-1794 *DcScB*
Forster, I G Gordon 1880-1953 *NatCAB 40*
Forster, James Franklin 1908-1972 *WhAm 5*
Forster, Johann Reinhold 1729-1798 *DcScB*

Forster, Rudolph 1872- *WhAm 5*
Forster, Thomas Edgar 1870-1946 *NatCAB 34*
Forster, Weidman Wallace 1895-1969
    NatCAB 55
Forster, Weidman Wallace 1899-1969 *WhAm 5*
Forster, William 1784-1854 *ApCAB*
Forster, William Andrew 1856- *NatCAB 5*
Forster, William Blair 1911-1975 *WhAm 6*
Forster, William Hays 1872-1943 *NatCAB 32*
Forstmann, Curt Erwin 1907-1950 *NatCAB 39,*
    WhAm 3
Forstmann, Julius 1871-1939 *NatCAB 29*
Forstmann, Julius George 1909-1962
    NatCAB 47, WhAm 4
Forsyth, Andrew Russell 1858-1942 *DcScB*
Forsyth, Benjamin d1814 *ApCAB, Drake*
Forsyth, David Dryden 1864-1926 *WhAm 1*
Forsyth, Donald William 1899-1956
    NatCAB 43
Forsyth, George Alexander 1837-1915 *AmBi,*
    REnAW, WebAMB, WhAm 1
Forsyth, Henry Hazlett 1877-1934 *WhAm 1*
Forsyth, Holmes 1867-1952 *NatCAB 38*
Forsyth, James 1817-1886 *ApCAB Sup*
Forsyth, James MacQueen 1842-1915 *TwCBDA*
Forsyth, James McQueen 1842-1915 *WhAm 1*
Forsyth, James N *ApCAB*
Forsyth, James W 1835-1906 *ApCAB*
Forsyth, James William 1834-1906 *NatCAB 4,*
    TwCBDA
Forsyth, James William 1836-1906 *WebAMB,*
    WhAm 1
Forsyth, Jessie 1849- *WhAm 4*
Forsyth, John *NewYHSD*
Forsyth, John 1780-1841 *AmBi, ApCAB,*
    BiAUS, BiDrAC, BiDrUSE, DcAmB,
    Drake, NatCAB 1, NatCAB 6, TwCBDA,
    WhAm H, WhAmP
Forsyth, John 1810-1886 *DcAmB, NatCAB 10,*
    WhAm H
Forsyth, John 1811-1886 *ApCAB, TwCBDA*
Forsyth, John 1812-1877 *NatCAB 8*
Forsyth, John 1812-1879 *BiDConf*
Forsyth, John 1813-1879 *ApCAB*
Forsyth, Raymond *NewYHSD*
Forsyth, Robert *NewYHSD*
Forsyth, Robert 1849-1927 *WhAm 1*
Forsyth, Thomas 1771-1833 *AmBi, DcAmB,*
    WhAm H
Forsyth, William d1935 *WhAm 1*
Forsyth, William 1852-1923 *NatCAB 20*
Forsythe, Albert Palaska 1830-1906 *BiDrAC*
Forsythe, Edwin Bell 1916- *BiDrAC*
Forsythe, George Elmer 1917-1972 *WhAm 5*
Forsythe, Grace C Strachan d1922 *BiCAW*
Forsythe, James 1934- *EncAAH*
Forsythe, Joseph Marion 1881-1941
    NatCAB 38
Forsythe, Matthew Leander 1840-1924
    NatCAB 19
Forsythe, Newton Melville 1902-1965 *WhAm 4*
Forsythe, Robert Stanley 1886-1941 *WhAm 1*
Forsythe, Victor Clyde 1885-1962 *IIBEAAW*
Forsythe, W B 1897-1959 *WhAm 3*
Fort, Carl Allen 1916-1973 *WhAm 6*
Fort, Frank Thomas 1871-1930 *NatCAB 23*
Fort, Franklin William 1880-1937 *BiDrAC,*
    WhAm 1
Fort, George Franklin 1809-1872 *ApCAB,*
    BiAUS, NatCAB 5, TwCBDA, WhAm H
Fort, George Hudson 1891-1975 *WhAm 6*
Fort, Gerrit 1865- *WhAm 3*
Fort, Greenberry Lafayette 1825-1883 *ApCAB,*
    BiAUS, TwCBDA
Fort, Greenbury Lafayette 1825-1883 *BiDrAC,*
    WhAm H
Fort, Jardine Carter 1889-1956 *WhAm 3*
Fort, Joel B, Jr. 1888-1951 *WhAm 3*
Fort, John Franklin 1852-1920 *NatCAB 14,*
    WhAm 1
Fort, John Henry 1851-1921 *NatCAB 19*
Fort, Marion Kirkland, Jr. 1921-1964
    NatCAB 51, WhAm 4
Fort, Rufus Elijah 1872-1940 *NatCAB 31,*
    WhAm 2
Fort, Tomlinson 1787-1859 *ApCAB, BiAUS,*
    BiDrAC, NatCAB 2, WhAm H
Fortas, Abe 1910- *WebAB*

Forten, Charlotte L NotAW

Forten, James 1766-1842 DcAmB, EncAB, McGEWB, WebAB, WhAm H, WhAmP

Fortenbaugh, Abraham 1838- WhAm 4

Fortenbaugh, Robert 1892-1959 NatCAB 47, WhAm 3

Fortenbaugh, Samuel Byrod 1869-1943 NatCAB 35

Fortescue, Charles LeGeyt 1876-1936 DcAmB S2

Fortescue, Granville 1875-1952 WhAm 3

Forth, Edward Walter 1919-1967 NatCAB 54, WhAm 4

Fortier, Alcee 1856-1914 AmBi, DcAmB, NatCAB 9, TwCBDA, WhAm 1

Fortier, George Ferdinand 1874-1928 NatCAB 22

Fortier, Louis J 1892-1974 WhAm 6

Fortier, Michel J 1903-1952 WhAm 3

Fortier, Samuel 1855-1933 WhAm 1

Fortin, Jean Nicolas 1750-1831 DcScB

Fortin, Philip Frederick 1906-1957 NatCAB 43

Fortin, Pierre 1823- ApCAB

Fortini, Charles NewYHSD

Fortique, Mariano Fernandez 1790-1866 ApCAB

Fortmiller, Hubert Clare 1901- WhAm 6

Fortoul, Pedro 1780-1837 ApCAB

Fortson, Bessie Washington Tompkins 1885- WomWWA 14

Fortson, Joseph Benjamin 1872-1950 NatCAB 48

Fortune, Alonzo Willard 1873-1950 WhAm 3

Fortune, J Robert 1871- WhAm 5

Fortune, Timothy Thomas 1856-1928 AmBi, EncAB, WhoColR

Fortune, William 1863-1942 WhAm 1

Forward, Chauncey 1793-1839 BiAUS, BiDrAC, TwCBDA, WhAm H, WhAmP

Forward, DeWitt Arthur 1894-1969 NatCAB 55

Forward, John F, Jr. 1876- WhAm 5

Forward, Walter 1783-1852 BiDrAC, TwCBDA, WhAm H, WhAmP

Forward, Walter 1786-1852 ApCAB, BiAUS, BiDrUSE, DcAmB, Drake, NatCAB 6

Forward, William A d1865 BiAUS

Forwood, William Henry 1838-1915 DcAmB, NatCAB 14, NatCAB 15, WhAm 1

Forwood, William Stump 1830-1892 ApCAB, TwCBDA

Fosbroke, Gerald Elton 1876-1964 WhAm 4

Fosbroke, Hughell Edgar Woodall 1875-1957 WhAm 3

Fosco, Peter 1892-1975 WhAm 6

Foscolo, Ugo 1778-1827 McGEWB

Foscue, Augustus William, Jr. 1895-1964 NatCAB 51

Foscue, Edwin Jay 1899-1972 WhAm 5

Fosdick, Charles Austin 1842-1915 DcAmB, NatCAB 33, WhAm 1

Fosdick, Charles B 1824- NatCAB 1

Fosdick, Frank Sheldon 1851- NatCAB 12

Fosdick, Harry Emerson 1878-1969 ApCAB X, DcAmReB, McGEWB, NatCAB 55, WebAB

Fosdick, James William 1858-1937 AmBi, NatCAB 28, WhAm 1

Fosdick, Leonard Samuel 1903-1969 NatCAB 54

Fosdick, Lucian John 1849- WhAm 4

Fosdick, Nicoll 1785-1868 BiAUS, BiDrAC, WhAm H

Fosdick, Raymond Blaine 1883-1972 NatCAB 57, WhAm 5

Fosdick, William Whiteman 1825-1862 ApCAB, DcAmB, Drake, NatCAB 13, WhAm H

Foshag, William Frederick 1894-1956 NatCAB 44, WhAm 3

Foshay, Arthur Wellesley 1912- BiDAmEd

Foshay, James A 1856-1914 NatCAB 8, WhAm 1

Foshay, Lee 1896-1960 NatCAB 48

Foskett, James Hicks 1898-1961 WhAm 4

Fosnot, Walter 1879-1950 NatCAB 41

Foss, Carrie M Conant 1854- WomWWA 14

Foss, Claude William 1855-1935 WhAm 1

Foss, Claus William 1855- TwCBDA

Foss, Cyrus David 1834-1910 ApCAB, DcAmB, NatCAB 9, TwCBDA, WhAm 1

Foss, Edgar Benjamin 1851-1915 NatCAB 17

Foss, Edgar Benjamin 1853-1915 ApCAB X

Foss, Emma Merrill 1855- WomWWA 14

Foss, Eugene Noble 1858-1939 BiDrAC, NatCAB 15, WhAm 1, WhAmP

Foss, Feodore Feodorovich 1874- WhAm 5

Foss, Frank Herbert 1865-1947 BiDrAC, WhAmP

Foss, Frederic Dearborn 1895-1954 NatCAB 47

Foss, George Edmund 1863-1936 BiDrAC, TwCBDA, WhAm 1, WhAmP

Foss, George Ernest 1873-1950 WhAm 3

Foss, Joseph Jacob 1915- WebAMB

Foss, Martin Howard 1877-1949 NatCAB 37

Foss, Martin Moore 1878- WhAm 6

Foss, Noble 1889-1969 WhAm 5

Foss, Sam Walter 1858-1911 AmBi, DcAmB, NatCAB 9, TwCBDA, WhAm 1

Foss, Walter Rolland 1897-1970 NatCAB 56

Foss, William Caleb 1897-1962 NatCAB 51

Foss, William Jay 1835-1859 ApCAB

Foss, Wilson, Jr. 1890-1957 WhAm 3

Fosseen, Carrie S 1875- WhAm 5, WomWWA 14

Fossette, H NewYHSD

Fossier, Albert Emile 1881-1966 NatCAB 53

Fossler, Laurence 1857-1933 WhAm 1

Fossum, Johan Kristian 1915-1964 NatCAB 50

Foster, A Lawrence BiAUS, BiDrAC, WhAm H

Foster, Abby Kelley 1810-1887 AmBi

Foster, Abby Kelley 1811-1887 ApCAB, TwCBDA

Foster, Abiel 1735-1806 ApCAB, BiAUS, BiDrAC, DcAmB, Drake, NatCAB 2, TwCBDA, WhAm H, WhAmP

Foster, Abigail Kelley 1810-1887 DcAmB, McGEWB, NotAW, WhAm H, WhAmP

Foster, Addison Gardner 1837-1917 ApCAB Sup, ApCAB X, BiDrAC, NatCAB 12, TwCBDA, WhAm 1, WhAmP

Foster, Adriance S 1901-1973 WhAm 6

Foster, Agnes Greene 1863-1933 WhAm 1, WomWWA 14

Foster, Albert Douglas 1875- WhAm 5

Foster, Alexis Caldwell 1867-1945 WhAm 2

Foster, Alfred Dwight 1852-1932 NatCAB 25, WhAm 1

Foster, Allyn King 1868-1934 WhAm 1

Foster, Antoine Lentilhon 1847-1928 NatCAB 22

Foster, Ardeen 1862- WhAm 4

Foster, Arthur Borders 1872-1956 NatCAB 48

Foster, Arthur Borders 1872-1958 WhAm 4

Foster, Asa Belknap 1817-1877 ApCAB

Foster, Austin Theophilus 1892-1967 WhAm 4

Foster, Ben 1852-1926 NatCAB 11, WhAm 1

Foster, Benjamin 1750-1798 ApCAB, Drake

Foster, Benjamin 1852-1926 AmBi, DcAmB, IlBEAAW

Foster, Bernard Augustus, Jr. 1909-1968 WhAm 5

Foster, Burnside 1861-1917 NatCAB 31

Foster, C G 1837-1899 BiAUS

Foster, Cassius G 1837-1899 WhAm 1

Foster, Cedric 1900-1975 WhAm 6

Foster, Charles NewYHSD

Foster, Charles 1828-1904 AmBi, ApCAB, BiAUS, BiDrAC, BiDrUSE, DcAmB, NatCAB 1, TwCBDA, WhAm 1, WhAmP

Foster, Charles Andrew 1817-1886 NewYHSD

Foster, Charles Dorrance 1836- NatCAB 9

Foster, Charles Elwood 1841- WhAm 1

Foster, Charles Fremont 1856-1927 NatCAB 21

Foster, Charles Henry Wheelright 1859-1955 NatCAB 51

Foster, Charles Henry Wheelwright 1859-1955 WhAm 3

Foster, Charles James 1820-1883 ApCAB, DcAmB, WhAm H

Foster, Charles Kendall 1867-1945 WhAm 2

Foster, Charles Richard 1879-1937 WhAm 1

Foster, Claiborne Jasper 1834-1898 NatCAB 11

Foster, Clair 1869-1935 NatCAB 28

Foster, Claud Hanscomb 1872-1965 NatCAB 55

Foster, Claudia Hills 1875- WomWWA 14

Foster, Clyde Tanner 1893-1975 WhAm 6

Foster, Curtis Smiley 1874-1929 NatCAB 23

Foster, Daniel Winthrop 1870-1927 NatCAB 22

Foster, David Johnson 1857-1912 BiDrAC, WhAm 1, WhAmP

Foster, David Nathaniel 1841-1934 NatCAB 41, WhAm 1

Foster, David Skaats 1852-1920 DcAmB, NatCAB 25

Foster, David Skaats 1862-1920 WhAm 1

Foster, Dwight 1757-1823 ApCAB, BiAUS, BiDrAC, Drake, NatCAB 2, TwCBDA, WhAm H, WhAmP

Foster, Edna A d1945 WhAm 2, WomWWA 14

Foster, Edward K 1907-1967 WhAm 4

Foster, Ellen Burroughs WomWWA 14

Foster, Ellen Horton 1840-1910 ApCAB

Foster, Ellen Horton see also Foster, J Ellen Horton

Foster, Ellsworth Decatur 1869-1936 NatCAB 27, WhAm 1

Foster, Elwin Carter 1852-1931 NatCAB 25

Foster, Emma Eastman 1850- WomWWA 14

Foster, Enoch 1839-1913 NatCAB 18, WhAm 1

Foster, Ephraim H d1854 BiAUS

Foster, Ephraim H 1794-1845 TwCBDA

Foster, Ephraim H 1795?-1854 ApCAB, NatCAB 7

Foster, Ephraim Hubbard 1794-1854 BiDrAC, DcAmB, WhAm H

Foster, Ernest Howard 1865-1949 NatCAB 39

Foster, Ernest LeNeve 1849- WhAm 4

Foster, Eugene 1850-1903 NatCAB 6

Foster, Eugene Clifford 1867-1927 WhAm 1

Foster, Fay BiCAW, WhAm 4

Foster, Finley M K 1892-1953 WhAm 3

Foster, Florence Josephine WomWWA 14

Foster, Florence Meritt 1875- WomWWA 14

Foster, Francis Appleton 1843-1921 NatCAB 19

Foster, Francis Apthorp 1872- WhAm 5

Foster, Frank Hugh 1851-1935 DcAmB S1, TwCBDA, WhAm 1

Foster, Frank Keyes 1854-1909 WhAm 1

Foster, Frank Pierce 1841-1911 DcAmB, NatCAB 22, WhAm 1

Foster, George Andrew 1879-1961 NatCAB 49

Foster, George Burgess, Jr. 1884-1949 WhAm 3

Foster, George Burman 1857-1918 NatCAB 18

Foster, George Burman 1858-1918 DcAmB, TwCBDA, WhAm 1

Foster, George Eulas 1847- ApCAB

Foster, George H 1862-1915 NatCAB 17

Foster, George Maynard 1899-1962 NatCAB 50

Foster, George Nimmons 1885-1952 WhAm 3

Foster, George P 1860- WhAm 4

Foster, George Peter 1858-1928 BiDrAC

Foster, George Sanford 1882-1945 NatCAB 39, WhAm 2

Foster, Gertrude Emslie Chapin 1858- WomWWA 14

Foster, Gideon, Jr. NewYHSD

Foster, Glen Edward 1897-1962 WhAm 4

Foster, Hannah d1840 Drake

Foster, Hannah Webster 1758-1840 NotAW

Foster, Hannah Webster 1759-1840 ApCAB, DcAmB, WhAm H

Foster, Harold Alfred 1880-1953 NatCAB 42

Foster, Harry Ellsworth 1898-1962 WhAm 4

Foster, Harry Howard 1857-1915 NatCAB 17

Foster, Harry LaTourette 1894-1932 WhAm 1

Foster, Henry 1797-1831 ApCAB, DcScB

Foster, Henry Allen 1800-1889 ApCAB, BiAUS, BiDrAC, NatCAB 4, TwCBDA, WhAm H

Foster, Henry Bacon 1863- WhAm 3

Foster, Henry Donnel 1808-1880 BiDrAC, WhAm H

Foster, Henry Donnel 1812-1880 BiAUS

Foster, Henry Hubbard 1876-1947 WhAm 2

Foster, Henry Vernon 1875-1939 NatCAB 37

Foster, Henry W NewYHSD

Foster, Herbert Darling 1863-1927 NatCAB 21,

TwCBDA, WhAm 1
Foster, Herbert Hamilton 1875-1942 *WhAm 2*
Foster, Horatio Alvah 1858- *WhAm 1*
Foster, Irving Lysander 1870-1929 *WhAm 1*
Foster, Isaac 1740?-1781 *ApCAB, TwCBDA*
Foster, Israel Moore 1873-1950 *BiDrAC, WhAm 3*
Foster, J *NewYHSD*
Foster, J Ellen Horton 1840-1910 *AmWom*
Foster, J Ellen Horton *see also* Foster, Judith Ellen
Foster, Jacob Post Giraud 1827-1886 *ApCAB*
Foster, James Anthony 1846-1919 *NatCAB 18*
Foster, James Martin 1831-1900 *NatCAB 11*
Foster, James P 1827-1869 *ApCAB, TwCBDA*
Foster, James Peers 1848- *WhAm 4*
Foster, James William 1890-1962 *WhAm 4*
Foster, Jeanne Robert 1884-1970 *WhAm 5*
Foster, Jedediah 1726-1779 *ApCAB, BiAUS, Drake*
Foster, John 1648-1681 *BnEnAmA, DcAmB, NatCAB 22, NewYHSD, WhAm H*
Foster, John 1763-1829 *TwCBDA*
Foster, John 1852-1914 *NatCAB 16*
Foster, John Barton 1822-1897 *TwCBDA*
Foster, John Calvin 1848- *NatCAB 12*
Foster, John Early 1864-1925 *WhAm 1*
Foster, John Gilman 1859-1931 *WhAm 1*
Foster, John Gray 1823-1874 *ApCAB, DcAmB, Drake, NatCAB 10, TwCBDA, WebAMB, WhAm H*
Foster, John Hopkins 1862-1917 *BiDrAC, WhAm 1*
Foster, John Hoskins 1876-1962 *NatCAB 50*
Foster, John McGaw 1860-1928 *NatCAB 27, WhAm 1*
Foster, John Morrell 1894-1958 *NatCAB 48, WhAm 4*
Foster, John Morton 1888-1971 *WhAm 5*
Foster, John Pierrepont Codrington 1847-1910 *DcAmB, WhAm 1*
Foster, John R *NewYHSD*
Foster, John Shaw 1870-1943 *WhAm 2*
Foster, John Shaw 1907-1957 *NatCAB 46*
Foster, John Watson 1836-1917 *AmBi, ApCAB, ApCAB X, BiAUS, BiDrUSE, DcAmB, NatCAB 3, TwCBDA, WhAm 1*
Foster, John Wells 1815-1873 *AmBi, ApCAB, NatCAB 10, TwCBDA, WhAm H*
Foster, John Winthrop 1880- *WhAm 6*
Foster, Johnson W *NewYHSD*
Foster, Joseph *NewYHSD*
Foster, Joseph 1841-1930 *WhAm 1*
Foster, Joseph Beverly 1895-1949 *NatCAB 43*
Foster, Joseph C 1906- *WhAm 6*
Foster, Joseph Franklin 1918-1975 *WhAm 6*
Foster, Joshua Hill 1819- *TwCBDA, WhAm 5*
Foster, Judith Ellen Horton 1840-1910 *AmBi, DcAmB, NatCAB 22, NotAW, TwCBDA, WhAm 1*
Foster, Judith Ellen Horton *see also* Foster, Ellen Horton
Foster, Julia Catharine Morris 1876- *WomWWA 14*
Foster, Julia E 1864- *WomWWA 14*
Foster, Julian Barringer 1897-1944 *WhAm 2*
Foster, LaFayette Sabine 1806-1880 *ApCAB, BiAUS, BiDrAC, DcAmB, Drake, NatCAB 2, TwCBDA, WhAm H, WhAmP*
Foster, Laurence 1903-1969 *WhAm 5*
Foster, Laurence Standley 1901-1973 *NatCAB 57*
Foster, Lloyd Elmore 1883-1956 *NatCAB 46*
Foster, Luther 1849- *WhAm 4*
Foster, Luther Ernest 1887-1943 *NatCAB 32*
Foster, Luther Hilton 1888-1949 *NatCAB 38*
Foster, Mabel Grace 1869- *WhAm 5, WomWWA 14*
Foster, Major Bronson 1892-1958 *WhAm 3*
Foster, Marcellus Elliott 1870-1942 *WhAm 2*
Foster, Margaret Bennett 1870- *WomWWA 14*
Foster, Marion Beattie 1871- *WomWWA 14*
Foster, Martin David 1861-1919 *BiDrAC, WhAm 1, WhAmP*
Foster, Mary Louise *WomWWA 14*
Foster, Matthias Lanckton 1859- *WhAm 4*
Foster, Maximilian 1872- *WhAm 5*

Foster, Sir Michael 1836-1907 *BiHiMed, DcScB*
Foster, Miller Clyde 1888-1965 *NatCAB 52*
Foster, Milton Hugh 1873- *WhAm 5*
Foster, Murphy James 1849-1921 *BiDrAC, DcAmB, NatCAB 10, TwCBDA, WhAm 1, WhAmP*
Foster, Nathaniel Dearborn Parker 1840-1926 *NatCAB 20*
Foster, Nathaniel Greene 1809-1869 *BiAUS, BiDrAC, WhAm H*
Foster, Nellis Barnes 1875-1933 *WhAm 1*
Foster, Norman 1888-1950 *NatCAB 39*
Foster, Paul F 1889-1971 *WhAm 5*
Foster, Paul Hadley 1868- *WhAm 4*
Foster, Paul Pinkerton 1875- *WhAm 5*
Foster, Percy Semple 1863- *WhAm 1*
Foster, Randolph Sinks 1820-1903 *ApCAB, DcAmB, Drake, NatCAB 13, TwCBDA, WhAm 1*
Foster, Reginald 1863-1944 *WhAm 2*
Foster, Reuben 1839-1915 *NatCAB 35*
Foster, Richard Clarke 1895-1941 *NatCAB 45, WhAm 2*
Foster, Robert Arnold 1877- *WhAm 5*
Foster, Robert Frederick 1853-1945 *WhAm 2*
Foster, Robert Sandford 1834-1903 *ApCAB, NatCAB 6, WhAm 1*
Foster, Robert Sanford 1834-1903 *DcAmB*
Foster, Robert Verrell 1845-1914 *NatCAB 17, TwCBDA, WhAm 1*
Foster, Roger Sherman Baldwin 1857-1924 *DcAmB, NatCAB 23, WhAm 1*
Foster, Rufus Edward 1871-1941 *NatCAB 18, WhAm 2*
Foster, Rufus James 1856- *WhAm 4*
Foster, Samuel B *NewYHSD*
Foster, Samuel Monell 1851-1935 *NatCAB 30, WhAm 1*
Foster, Sarah Elyot Betts *WomWWA 14*
Foster, Scott 1837- *NatCAB 3, WhAm 4*
Foster, Sheppard Walter 1861-1947 *NatCAB 36, WhAm 2*
Foster, Sophia Vernon Hammond 1867- *WomWWA 14*
Foster, Sophie Lee Jackson *WomWWA 14*
Foster, Stephen 1798-1835 *ApCAB, Drake*
Foster, Stephen Clark 1799-1872 *BiAUS, BiDrAC, WhAm H*
Foster, Stephen Collins 1826-1864 *AmBi, ApCAB, DcAmB, Drake, EncAAH, McGEWB, NatCAB 7, TwCBDA, WebAB, WhAm H*
Foster, Stephen Symonds 1809-1881 *AmBi, ApCAB, DcAmB, Drake, NatCAB 2, TwCBDA, WhAm H, WhAmP*
Foster, Susie E 1846- *AmWom*
Foster, T Jack 1902-1968 *NatCAB 54*
Foster, T Stewart 1903-1967 *WhAm 4*
Foster, Ted 1903-1976 *WhAm 6*
Foster, Theodore 1752-1828 *ApCAB, BiAUS, BiDrAC, DcAmB, NatCAB 2, TwCBDA, WhAm H, WhAmP*
Foster, Theodosia Toll 1838- *TwCBDA, WhAm 3, WhAm 4, WomWWA 14*
Foster, Thomas Arnold 1895-1973 *WhAm 5*
Foster, Thomas Flournoy 1790-1847 *ApCAB, BiAUS*
Foster, Thomas Flournoy 1790-1848 *BiDrAC, WhAm H, WhAmP*
Foster, Thomas Flournoy 1796-1847 *NatCAB 3, TwCBDA*
Foster, Thomas Henry 1875-1951 *WhAm 3*
Foster, Thomas Jefferson 1809-1887 *BiDConf*
Foster, Thomas Jefferson 1843-1936 *BiDAmEd, DcAmB S2, WhAm HA, WhAm 4*
Foster, Thomas Lewis 1875-1942 *NatCAB 32*
Foster, Thomas Sampson 1861-1913 *NatCAB 15*
Foster, Vernon Whit 1881- *WhAm 6*
Foster, Vernon Whitbeck 1881-1954 *NatCAB 43*
Foster, Virgll Elwood 1901-1970 *WhAm 5*
Foster, Volney William 1848-1904 *NatCAB 13, WhAm 1*
Foster, W Bert 1869- *WhAm 5*
Foster, Walter Herbert 1880- *WhAm 6*
Foster, Warren Dunham 1886-1961 *NatCAB 48*

Foster, Warren William 1859-1943 *WhAm 2*
Foster, Wilbur Fisk 1834- *NatCAB 8*
Foster, Wilder DeAyr 1819-1873 *BiAUS, BiDrAC, WhAm H*
Foster, William 1869-1937 *NatCAB 39, WhAm 1*
Foster, William Byron 1874-1937 *NatCAB 31*
Foster, William Davis 1841-1925 *WhAm 1*
Foster, William Eaton 1851-1930 *DcAmLiB, TwCBDA, WhAm 1*
Foster, William Edward 1839-1915 *WhAm 1*
Foster, William Edward 1864-1940 *WhAm 1*
Foster, William Frederick 1882-1953 *WhAm 3*
Foster, William Garnett 1884-1946 *WhAm 2*
Foster, William Heber Thompson 1873-1949 *NatCAB 49, WhAm 2*
Foster, William Henry 1866-1951 *NatCAB 40, WhAm 3*
Foster, William Howard 1858-1935 *NatCAB 27*
Foster, William James 1860-1943 *NatCAB 33, WhAm 3*
Foster, William James, Jr. 1899-1959 *NatCAB 49*
Foster, William Othello 1882- *WhoColR*
Foster, William Sewell d1839 *ApCAB, Drake*
Foster, William Trufant 1879-1950 *BiDAmEd, DcAmB S4, NatCAB 15, WhAm 3*
Foster, William Wallace 1873-1956 *WhAm 3*
Foster, William Wilson, Jr. 1849-1933 *WhAm 1*
Foster, William Zebulon 1881-1961 *McGEWB, WebAB, WhAm 4*
Fothergill, John 1712-1780 *BiHiMed*
Fothergill, John Vincent 1871-1953 *WhAm 3*
Fotitch, A Constantin 1891-1959 *WhAm 3*
Foucault, Jean Bernard Leon 1819-1868 *AsBiEn, DcScB, McGEWB*
Fouche, Glenn Robert 1901-1958 *NatCAB 47*
Fouche, Joseph 1759-1820 *McGEWB*
Foucher, Jean 1508-1567 *ApCAB*
Fouchy, Jean-Paul Grandjean De 1707-1788 *DcScB*
Fougner, Arne 1913-1965 *NatCAB 53*
Fougner, Ernest Hjalmar 1880-1967 *WhAm 5*
Fougner, G Selmer 1884-1941 *WhAm 1*
Fouilhoux, Jacques Andre 1879-1945 *WhAm 2*
Fouke, Philip Bond 1818-1876 *BiAUS, BiDrAC, WhAm H*
Fouke, William Hargrave 1851-1923 *WhAm 1*
Foulds, Henry W 1891-1959 *WhAm 3*
Foulk, Charles William 1869-1958 *WhAm 3*
Foulk, Claude Claude 1892-1969 *WhAm 5*
Foulk, Elma Perry 1878- *WomWWA 14*
Foulk, George Clayton 1856-1893 *DcAmB, WhAm H*
Foulk, William Henry 1897-1960 *WhAm 4*
Foulke, Amelia R *WomWWA 14*
Foulke, Elizabeth E *WhAm 5, WomWWA 14*
Foulke, William Dudley 1848-1935 *ApCAB X, DcAmB S1, NatCAB 8, NatCAB 26, TwCBDA, WhAm 1, WhAmP*
Foulkes, George Ernest 1878-1960 *BiDrAC*
Foulkrod, Harry Ellsworth 1903-1972 *WhAm 5*
Foulkrod, John Jacob 1876-1947 *NatCAB 36*
Foulkrod, William Walker 1846-1910 *BiDrAC, WhAm 1*
Foulois, Benjamin Delahauf 1879-1967 *WhAm 4*
Foulon, Clement 1557?-1632 *ApCAB Sup*
Foulon, Irenaeus Dielsechristo 1849- *TwCBDA*
Foulquier, V *NewYHSD*
Foulston, Robert Clare 1889-1947 *NatCAB 36*
Fountain, Claude Russell 1879-1947 *WhAm 2*
Fountain, Lawrence H 1913- *BiDrAC*
Fountain, Percy Coleman 1907-1956 *NatCAB 46, WhAm 3*
Fountain, Reginald Morton 1908-1969 *WhAm 5*
Fountain, Richard Tillman 1885-1945 *WhAm 2*
Fountain, Samuel Warren 1846-1920 *WhAm 1*
Fountain, William Alfred, Sr. 1870-1955 *WhAm 3, WhoColR*
Fouque, Ferdinand Andre 1828-1904 *DcScB*
Fouquet, Jean 1420?-1480? *McGEWB*
Fourcade, Anacharsis *NewYHSD*
Fourcade, Joseph *NewYHSD*
Fourcroy, Antoine Francois, Comte De 1755-1809 *AsBiEn, DcScB*
Fourier, Francois Charles Marie 1772-1837 *McGEWB*

Fourier, Baron Jean Baptiste Joseph 1768-1830
    AsBiEn, DcScB, McGEWB
Fourneau, Ernest 1872-1949 DcScB
Fourneyron, Benoit 1802-1867 DcScB
Fournier, Alexis Jean 1865-1948 WhAm 2
Fournier, Alphonse 1893-1961 WhAm 4
Fournier, Joseph NewYHSD
Fournier, Leslie Thomas 1901-1961 WhAm 4
Fournier, Telesphore 1823- ApCAB
Fouse, Levi Gardner 1850-1914 NatCAB 2
Fouse, Levi Garner 1850-1914 WhAm 1
Fouse, William Henry 1868- WhoColR
Fouse, Winfred Eugene 1877-1958 NatCAB 46,
    WhAm 3
Foust, Julius Isaac 1865-1946 BiDAmEd,
    NatCAB 35, WhAm 2
Fout, Henry H 1861-1947 WhAm 2
Foute, Mary DeKantzow WomWWA 14
Foute, Robert Chester 1841- NatCAB 7
Fouville, Jean Baptiste 1794-1837 ApCAB
Fowke, Gerard 1855-1933 DcAmB S1,
    NatCAB 23, WhAm 1
Fowke, Gerard 1855-1934 AmBi
Fowle, Daniel 1715-1787 ApCAB, DcAmB,
    Drake, NatCAB 23, WhAm H
Fowle, Daniel Gould 1831-1891 NatCAB 1,
    NatCAB 4, TwCBDA
Fowle, Edward A NewYHSD
Fowle, Elida Barker Rumsey 1842-1919 NotAW
Fowle, Frank Fuller 1877-1946 NatCAB 34,
    WhAm 2
Fowle, Isaac NewYHSD
Fowle, John D NewYHSD
Fowle, Luther Richardson 1886-1973 WhAm 5
Fowle, Robert ApCAB
Fowle, William Bentley 1795-1865 ApCAB,
    BiDAmEd, DcAmB, Drake, NatCAB 10,
    NewYHSD, WhAm H
Fowle, William H NewYHSD
Fowler, Mrs. NewYHSD
Fowler, Albert Perry 1866-1915 NatCAB 30
Fowler, Alfred 1868-1940 DcScB
Fowler, Alfred 1889- WhAm 3
Fowler, Andrew 1765?-1851 ApCAB
Fowler, Arthur Anderson 1878-1934
    NatCAB 32
Fowler, Arthur Thomas 1868- WhAm 5
Fowler, Asa 1811-1885 NatCAB 5
Fowler, Benjamin Austin 1843-1921 WhAm 1
Fowler, Benjamin Sherman 1875- ApCAB X
Fowler, Burton Philander 1887-1963 WhAm 4
Fowler, C Lewis 1877- WhAm 5
Fowler, Carl Hitchcock 1873-1942 WhAm 2
Fowler, Charles Anthony, Jr. 1884-1918
    NatCAB 17
Fowler, Charles Evan 1867-1944 WhAm 2
Fowler, Charles Henry 1837-1908 AmBi,
    ApCAB, DcAmB, NatCAB 7, TwCBDA,
    WhAm 1
Fowler, Charles Newell 1852-1932 BiDrAC,
    NatCAB 7, TwCBDA, WhAm 1,
    WhAmP
Fowler, Charles Rollin 1869-1950 WhAm 3
Fowler, Charles Wesley 1858- WhAm 4
Fowler, Chester Almeron 1862-1948 WhAm 2
Fowler, Clifton Lefevre 1882-1965 WhAm 4
Fowler, David 1836-1911 WhAm 1
Fowler, Edmund P, Jr. 1905-1964 WhAm 4
Fowler, Edmund Prince 1872-1966 WhAm 4
Fowler, Edson Brady 1865-1942 NatCAB 31
Fowler, Edson Fairbrother 1915-1964
    NatCAB 51
Fowler, Edward W NewYHSD
Fowler, Edwin 1847- NatCAB 7
Fowler, Elbert Hazelton 1883-1930 WhAm 1,
    WhAm 2
Fowler, Eldridge Merick 1833-1904 NatCAB 24
Fowler, Elting Alexander 1879-1916 WhAm 1
Fowler, Frank 1852-1910 AmBi, DcAmB,
    NatCAB 7, TwCBDA, WhAm 1
Fowler, Frank George 1872-1961 NatCAB 48
Fowler, Frederick Curtis, II 1901-1969 WhAm 5
Fowler, Frederick Hall 1879-1945 WhAm 2
Fowler, Gene 1890-1960 NatCAB 48,
    WhAm 4
Fowler, George Bingham 1847-1907 NatCAB 4
Fowler, George Little 1855-1926 WhAm 1
Fowler, George Ryerson 1848-1906 DcAmB,

NatCAB 4, WhAm 1
Fowler, George S 1884-1961 WhAm 4
Fowler, George W NewYHSD
Fowler, George W 1844- NatCAB 6
Fowler, H Robert d1925 WhAm 1
Fowler, Harold 1886-1957 NatCAB 47
Fowler, Harold North 1859-1955 NatCAB 44,
    TwCBDA, WhAm 3
Fowler, Harry Atwood 1872- WhAm 5
Fowler, Helen Frances Wose 1907-1968
    WhAm 5
Fowler, Henry 1824-1872 ApCAB
Fowler, Henry Hamill 1908- BiDrUSE
Fowler, Henry Thatcher 1867-1948 WhAm 2
Fowler, Hiram Robert 1851-1926 BiDrAC
Fowler, J NewYHSD
Fowler, James Alexander 1863-1955 WhAm 3
Fowler, James M 1845-1930 NatCAB 34
Fowler, Janet King WomWWA 14
Fowler, Jessie Allen 1856-1932 NatCAB 16,
    WhAm 1, WomWWA 14
Fowler, John 1755-1840 BiAUS, BiDrAC,
    WhAm H, WhAmP
Fowler, John 1858-1923 WhAm 1
Fowler, John Edgar 1866-1930 BiDrAC
Fowler, John Gordon 1905-1971 NatCAB 56
Fowler, Joseph Smith 1820-1902 BiDrAC,
    DcAmB, WhAm 1, WhAmP
Fowler, Joseph Smith 1822-1902 ApCAB,
    BiAUS, NatCAB 10, TwCBDA
Fowler, Laura 1878- WhAm 4
Fowler, Laurence Hall 1876-1971 WhAm 5
Fowler, Leonard Burke 1877-1942 WhAm 2
Fowler, Lewis Martin 1884-1951 NatCAB 38
Fowler, Lorenzo Niles 1811-1896 ApCAB,
    TwCBDA
Fowler, Ludlow Sebring 1896-1961 WhAm 4
Fowler, Lula A 1862- WomWWA 14
Fowler, Lydia Folger 1822-1879 NotAW
Fowler, Lydia Folger 1823-1879 ApCAB
Fowler, Lyttleton 1802-1846 ApCAB
Fowler, Marie Washburne WomWWA 14
Fowler, Nathaniel Clark, Jr. 1858-1918
    WhAm 1
Fowler, Orin 1791-1852 ApCAB, BiAUS,
    BiDrAC, DcAmB, Drake, NatCAB 4,
    TwCBDA, WhAm H
Fowler, Orson Squire 1809-1887 AmBi,
    ApCAB, DcAmB, Drake, NatCAB 3,
    TwCBDA, WhAm H
Fowler, Philemon Halstead 1814-1879 ApCAB
Fowler, Ralph Howard 1889-1944 DcScB
Fowler, Raymond Foster 1884-1949 WhAm 2
Fowler, Rex H 1893-1972 WhAm 5
Fowler, Richard Labbitt 1913- WhAm 5
Fowler, Robert Lambert 1876-1958 WhAm 3
Fowler, Robert Ludlow 1849-1936 NatCAB 29,
    WhAm 1
Fowler, Russell Story 1874-1959 ApCAB X,
    WhAm 3
Fowler, Samuel 1779-1844 ApCAB, BiAUS,
    BiDrAC, TwCBDA, WhAm H
Fowler, Samuel 1851-1919 BiDrAC
Fowler, Samuel Page 1800- ApCAB
Fowler, Susan 1875- WomWWA 14
Fowler, Thomas Powell 1851-1915 ApCAB,
    WhAm 1
Fowler, Trevor Thomas NewYHSD, WhAm H
Fowler, Walter Everett 1867-1946 NatCAB 35
Fowler, Walter William 1888- WhAm 3
Fowler, Warren Raymond 1815- NatCAB 2
Fowler, William Charles 1864-1937 WhAm 1
Fowler, William Chauncey 1793-1881 ApCAB,
    Drake, NatCAB 5, TwCBDA
Fowler, William Edward 1888-1967 WhAm 5
Fowler, William Eric 1874- ApCAB X,
    WhAm 6
Fowler, William Miles 1843- NatCAB 3
Fowler, William Worthington 1833-1881
    ApCAB, TwCBDA
Fowles, James H 1812-1854 ApCAB, Drake
Fownes, Edwin Stanton 1865-1937 NatCAB 36
Fownes, George 1815-1849 DcScB
Fownes, Henry Clay 1856-1935 NatCAB 35
Fownes, Jessie Gaither WomWWA 14
Fownes, William Clarke 1858-1928 NatCAB 29
Fox, A Manuel 1889-1942 WhAm 2
Fox, Adam NewYHSD

Fox, Albert Charles 1878-1934 WhAm 1
Fox, Alex Patrick 1893-1959 NatCAB 48,
    WhAm 4
Fox, Andrew Fuller 1849-1926 BiDrAC,
    TwCBDA, WhAm 3
Fox, Ann Leah 1818?-1890 NotAW
Fox, Augustus Henry 1902-1975 WhAm 6
Fox, Austen George 1849-1937 WhAm 1
Fox, B Blaine 1884-1933 NatCAB 37
Fox, B K NewYHSD
Fox, Carl 1876-1958 WhAm 3
Fox, Catherine 1839?-1892 NotAW
Fox, Charles Eben 1851-1916 NatCAB 16,
    WhAm 1
Fox, Charles Edwin 1882-1937 NatCAB 28
Fox, Charles Eli 1870-1926 NatCAB 21,
    WhAm 1
Fox, Charles James 1749-1806 McGEWB
Fox, Charles James 1811-1846 ApCAB, Drake,
    TwCBDA
Fox, Charles James 1877- WhAm 5
Fox, Charles Kemble 1833-1875 ApCAB,
    DcAmB, NatCAB 26, WhAm H
Fox, Charles Lewis 1854-1927 IlBEAAW
Fox, Charles Nelson 1829- NatCAB 7
Fox, Charles Shattuck 1868-1939 NatCAB 31,
    WhAm 1
Fox, Charles Welford 1894-1975 WhAm 6
Fox, Cyril Gattman 1893-1969 NatCAB 54
Fox, Daniel Frederick 1862-1939 WhAm 2
Fox, David Baird 1900-1949 NatCAB 38
Fox, Della 1872-1913 WhAm 1
Fox, Della May 1870-1913 NotAW
Fox, Dixon Ryan 1887-1945 DcAmB S3,
    NatCAB 53, WhAm 2
Fox, Donald L 1921-1972 WhAm 6
Fox, Donald Richard 1927-1973 WhAm 6
Fox, Early Lee 1890-1946 WhAm 2
Fox, Ebenezer 1763-1843 ApCAB
Fox, Edward BiAUS
Fox, Edward J 1858-1937 WhAm 1
Fox, Edward Jay, Jr. 1899-1962 NatCAB 48
Fox, Edwin Gordon 1887-1956 NatCAB 45
Fox, Elias Williams 1828- NatCAB 4
Fox, Emma Augusta Stowell 1847-1945 BiCAW,
    WhAm 2, WomWWA 14
Fox, Emmet 1886-1951 DcAmReB
Fox, Ernest Frederick 1880-1928 NatCAB 21
Fox, Errol Lionel 1892-1931 NatCAB 23
Fox, Fayburn L 1894-1961 WhAm 4
Fox, Felix 1876-1947 WhAm 2
Fox, Fontaine Talbot 1836-1926 NatCAB 21
Fox, Fontaine Talbot, Jr. 1884-1964
    NatCAB 51, WhAm 4
Fox, Frances Margaret 1870- WomWWA 14
Fox, Francis Morton 1866- WhAm 5
Fox, Fred C 1863- WhAm 4
Fox, Fred Lee 1876-1952 WhAm 3
Fox, Frederick E NewYHSD
Fox, Frederick S 1875-1968 WhAm 5
Fox, Genevieve d1959 WhAm 3
Fox, George 1624-1690 NatCAB 7
Fox, George 1624-1691 ApCAB, DcAmReB,
    McGEWB
Fox, George Henry 1846-1937 ApCAB,
    NatCAB 11, WhAm 1
Fox, George Levi 1852-1931 NatCAB 4,
    TwCBDA, WhAm 1
Fox, George Lingard 1825-1877 ApCAB,
    TwCBDA
Fox, George Walter NewYHSD
Fox, George Washington Lafayette 1825-1877
    DcAmB, WhAm H
Fox, Gilbert 1776-1806? NewYHSD
Fox, Gilbert 1776-1807? DcAmB, WhAm H
Fox, Gustav Theodore 1843-1917 NatCAB 18
Fox, Gustavus Vasa 1821-1883 AmBi, ApCAB,
    BiAUS, DcAmB, NatCAB 8, TwCBDA,
    WebAB, WebAMB, WhAm H
Fox, Harriet Gibbs 1848- WomWWA 14
Fox, Harry 1826-1883 DcAmB, WhAm H
Fox, Harry Joseph 1871-1941 NatCAB 44
Fox, Henry 1875- WhAm 5
Fox, Henry Stephen d1846 ApCAB, Drake
Fox, Herbert 1880-1942 WhAm 2
Fox, Herbert Henry Heywood 1871-1943
    WhAm 2
Fox, Herbert W 1873-1934 NatCAB 25

Fox, Howard 1873-1954 *WhAm 3*
Fox, I J 1888-1947 *NatCAB 34*
Fox, J Francke 1863-1959 *NatCAB 48*
Fox, Jabez 1850- *WhAm 1*
Fox, James Butler 1867- *WhAm 4*
Fox, James D 1847-1910 *WhAm 1*
Fox, James Harold 1900-1972 *WhAm 5*
Fox, Jane L 1875- *WomWWA 14*
Fox, Jared Copeland, III 1901-1969 *WhAm 5*
Fox, Jesse William 1867-1944 *WhAm 2*
Fox, John 1835-1914 *BiAUS, BiDrAC*
Fox, John 1853-1924 *WhAm 1*
Fox, John Herbert 1870-1957 *NatCAB 47*
Fox, John McDill 1891-1940 *WhAm 1*
Fox, John Pierce 1872- *WhAm 5*
Fox, John William, Jr. 1863-1919 *AmBi,*
    DcAmB, NatCAB 14, WhAm 1
Fox, Joseph Gale 1833-1889 *TwCBDA*
Fox, Joseph John 1855-1915 *NatCAB 15,*
    WhAm 1
Fox, Justus 1736- *NewYHSD*
Fox, Katherine 1839-1892 *WebAB*
Fox, Lawrence Webster 1835-1931 *NatCAB 4,*
    WhAm 1
Fox, Luke 1585?-1635? *ApCAB, Drake*
Fox, Luther Augustine 1882- *WhAm 4*
Fox, Margaret 1833-1893 *AmBi, DcAmB,*
    NotAW, WebAB, WhAm H
Fox, Margaret 1836-1893 *ApCAB*
Fox, Mary Hewins 1842- *ApCAB*
Fox, Matthew 1911-1964 *WhAm 4*
Fox, Morris 1909-1968 *NatCAB 54*
Fox, Netta Scott *WomWWA 14*
Fox, Norman 1836-1907 *WhAm 1*
Fox, Norman Arnold 1911-1960 *WhAm 3A*
Fox, Oscar Chapman 1830-1902 *NatCAB 1,*
    TwCBDA, WhAm 1
Fox, Philip 1878-1944 *NatCAB 14, WhAm 2*
Fox, R Atkinson 1860- *IIBEAAW*
Fox, Richard Kyle 1846-1922 *DcAmB, WebAB*
Fox, Robert Claybrook 1834- *NatCAB 3*
Fox, Robert Myron 1876- *WhAm 6*
Fox, Sherwood Dean 1917-1971 *WhAm 5*
Fox, Sidney W 1912- *AsBiEn*
Fox, Thomas Bailey 1808-1876 *ApCAB*
Fox, Thomas Bayley 1808-1876 *TwCBDA*
Fox, Victor Samuel 1893-1957 *WhAm 3*
Fox, Virginia Herrick 1863- *WomWWA 14*
Fox, Walter Dennis 1867-1912 *WhAm 1*
Fox, Walter Gordon 1863- *WhAm 4*
Fox, Walter Silvanus 1868-1940 *NatCAB 31*
Fox, William 1879-1952 *DcAmB S5,*
    WhAm 3
Fox, William Freeman 1840-1909 *WhAm 1*
Fox, William H 1906-1958 *WhAm 3*
Fox, William Henry 1858-1952 *ApCAB X,*
    WhAm 3
Fox, William Herrimon 1814-1883 *NatCAB 16*
Fox, William Joseph 1872-1947 *WhAm 2*
Fox, Williams Carlton 1855-1924 *DcAmB,*
    NatCAB 14, WhAm 1
Fox-Jencken, Katherine 1839-1892 *WebAB*
Foxall, Henry 1758-1823 *DcAmB, NatCAB 24,*
    WhAm H
Foxcroft, Frank 1850-1921 *NatCAB 19,*
    WhAm 1
Foxcroft, George Augustus 1815-1878 *ApCAB,*
    NatCAB 13
Foxcroft, Samuel d1807 *ApCAB*
Foxcroft, Thomas 1697-1769 *ApCAB, Drake*
Foxworthy, Alice S 1852- *AmWom*
Foxx, James Emory 1907-1967 *WebAB*
Foy, Byron Cecil 1893-1970 *WhAm 5*
Foy, Claudius E 1850-1930 *NatCAB 38*
Foy, Eddie 1856-1928 *DcAmB, WebAB*
Foy, Eddie 1857-1928 *WhAm 1*
Foy, Florville *NewYHSD*
Foy, George William 1902-1973 *NatCAB 57*
Foy, James Woodward 1901-1956 *NatCAB 50*
Foy, Mary Emily *WhAm 5, WomWWA 14*
Foy, Prosper *NewYHSD*
Foy, Robert Cherry 1876-1944 *WhAm 2*
Foye, Andrew Jay Coleman 1833-1905 *WhAm 1*
Foye, Andrew Jay Colman 1833-1905
    NatCAB 3
Foye, James Clark 1841-1896 *ApCAB*
Foye, James Clarke 1841-1896 *TwCBDA*
Foye, Wilbur Garland 1886-1935 *WhAm 1*

Foyt, Anthony Joseph, Jr. 1935- *WebAB*
FPA *WebAB*
Fracastorius, Hieronymus 1478?-1553 *BiHiMed*
Fracastoro, Girolamo 1478?-1553 *DcScB*
Frachon, Benoit 1893-1975 *WhAm 6*
Frachtenberg, Leo Joachim 1883-1930 *WhAm 1*
Frackelton, David Waddell 1871-1959
    NatCAB 45
Frackelton, Robert James 1868-1940
    NatCAB 30
Frackelton, Susan Stuart *WomWWA 14*
Frackelton, Susan Stuart 1848- *TwCBDA*
Fracker, Stanley Black 1889-1971 *WhAm 5*
Frackleton, Susan Stuart 1848- *WhAm 4*
Frackleton, Susan Stuart 1851- *AmWom*
Fradenburgh, Adelbert Grant 1868-1936
    WhAm 1
Fradenburgh, J N 1843- *WhAm 4*
Fraeb, Henry d1841 *REnAW*
Fraenkel, Adolf Abraham 1891-1965 *DcScB*
Fraenkel-Conrat, Heinz 1910- *AsBiEn*
Fragonard, Jean Honore 1732-1806 *McGEWB*
Frahm, Gustav Paul 1898-1962 *NatCAB 49*
Frailey, Carson Peter 1887-1954 *WhAm 3*
Frailey, James Madison 1809-1877 *ApCAB,*
    Drake, NatCAB 4, TwCBDA
Frailey, Leonard August 1843-1913 *WhAm 1*
Frain, Andrew Thomas 1904-1964 *NatCAB 52,*
    WhAm 4
Frain, H LaRue 1896-1965 *NatCAB 51*
Fraina, Louis C 1892-1953 *DcAmB S5*
Fraipont, Julien 1857-1910 *DcScB*
Fraker, George W 1874-1951 *WhAm 3*
Fraleigh, Arnold 1913-1973 *WhAm 5*
Fraley, Frederick 1804-1901 *ApCAB, DcAmB,*
    NatCAB 7, TwCBDA, WhAm H
Fralich, Charles Eugene 1902-1964 *NatCAB 51*
Frame, Alice Seymour Browne 1878-1941
    DcAmB S3, NotAW, WhAm 1
Frame, Andrew Jay 1844-1932 *NatCAB 10,*
    NatCAB 24, WhAm 1
Frame, Esther Gordon 1840- *AmWom*
Frame, James Everett 1868-1956 *NatCAB 45,*
    WhAm 3
Frame, Nat T 1877-1948 *WhAm 2*
Frame, Norman Renville 1895-1976 *WhAm 6*
Frame, Paul DeWitt 1899-1949 *NatCAB 37*
Frame, Stuart Maurer, Jr. 1925-1966
    NatCAB 53
Frame, Thomas Clark 1883-1955 *NatCAB 44*
Franca, Manuel Joachim De 1808-1865
    NewYHSD, WhAm H
Francais, Francois 1768-1810 *DcScB*
Francais, Jacques Frederic 1775-1833 *DcScB*
France, Anatole 1844-1924 *McGEWB*
France, Anna Edith Lapham *WomWWA 14*
France, Beulah Sanford 1891-1971 *WhAm 5*
France, Charles E 1900-1952 *WhAm 3*
France, Clemens James 1877-1959 *NatCAB 48*
France, Evalyn Smith d1927 *WhAm 1*
France, Harry Clinton 1890-1972 *WhAm 5*
France, Jacob 1882-1962 *NatCAB 48,*
    NatCAB 49, WhAm 4
France, Joseph 1797-1868 *ApCAB*
France, Joseph Irvin 1873-1939 *BiDrAC*
France, Joseph Irwin 1873-1939 *WhAm 1*
France, Lewis B 1833-1907 *WhAm 1*
France, Mary Adele 1880- *WhAm 6*
France, Melville Jefferson 1878-1955 *WhAm 3*
France, Mervin Blair 1901-1970 *NatCAB 55,*
    WhAm 5
France, Rachel Ann Noah 1842-1925
    NatCAB 20
France, Royal Wilbur 1883-1962 *WhAm 4*
Francesca, Piero Della 1410?-1492 *DcScB*
Franchere, Gabriel 1786- *Drake*
Franchere, Gabriel 1786-1856 *ApCAB*
Franchere, Gabriel 1786-1863 *AmBi, DcAmB,*
    REnAW, WhAm H
Franchet D'Esperey, Louis F M Francois
    1856-1942 *WhoMilH*
Franchot, Charles Pascal 1886-1953 *WhAm 3*
Franchot, Douglas Warner 1880-1928
    NatCAB 27
Franchot, Nicholas VanVranken 1855-1943
    NatCAB 31
Franchot, Richard 1816-1875 *BiAUS, BiDrAC,*
    WhAm H

Francia, Jose Gaspar Rodriguez 1757?-1840
    ApCAB, Drake
Francine, Albert Philip 1873- *WhAm 1*
Francis I 1494-1547 *McGEWB, WhoMilH*
Francis II 1768-1835 *McGEWB*
Francis Ferdinand 1863-1914 *McGEWB*
Francis Joseph 1830-1916 *McGEWB*
Francis Of Assisi, Saint 1182-1226 *McGEWB*
Francis Of Marchia *DcScB*
Francis Of Meyronnes 1285?-1330? *DcScB*
Francis Of Sales, Saint 1567-1622 *McGEWB*
Francis Xavier, Saint 1506-1552 *McGEWB*
Francis, Arthur J 1874- *WhAm 5*
Francis, Arthur W *NewYHSD*
Francis, Charles 1848-1936 *ApCAB X,*
    NatCAB 27
Francis, Charles Edward 1828-1905 *NatCAB 1,*
    NatCAB 9, WhAm 1
Francis, Charles Inge 1893-1969 *WhAm 5*
Francis, Charles Spencer 1853-1911 *DcAmB,*
    NatCAB 12, WhAm 1
Francis, Charles Stephen 1805-1887
    ApCAB Sup, DcAmB, WhAm H
Francis, Brother Clement 1906-1967 *WhAm 4*
Francis, Convers 1795-1863 *ApCAB, DcAmB,*
    Drake, NatCAB 9, TwCBDA, WhAm H
Francis, David G *ApCAB Sup*
Francis, David Rowland 1850-1927 *AmBi,*
    ApCAB Sup, BiDrUSE, DcAmB,
    NatCAB 1, NatCAB 12, NatCAB 24,
    TwCBDA, WhAm 1, WhAmP
Francis, Ebenezer d1777 *Drake*
Francis, Edward 1872- *WhAm 5*
Francis, Edward Stillman *NatCAB 3*
Francis, Emily A 1879-1966 *WhAm 4*
Francis, G Churchill *WhAm 5*
Francis, George 1790-1873 *NewYHSD*
Francis, George Blinn 1857-1913 *NatCAB 16,*
    TwCBDA
Francis, George Blinn 1883-1967 *BiDrAC*
Francis, George Judson 1862-1942 *NatCAB 31*
Francis, Harry C 1843-1916 *NatCAB 19*
Francis, Herbert Cadogan 1904-1961
    NatCAB 48, WhAm 4
Francis, James Allan 1864-1928 *NatCAB 5,*
    WhAm 1
Francis, James Bicheno 1815-1892 *AmBi,*
    ApCAB, DcAmB, NatCAB 9, TwCBDA,
    WhAm H
Francis, James Draper 1884-1958 *NatCAB 49,*
    WhAm 3
Francis, John 1763-1796 *ApCAB X*
Francis, John, Jr. 1875-1954 *WhAm 3*
Francis, John Brown 1791-1864 *ApCAB,*
    ApCAB X, BiDrAC, DcAmB, NatCAB 9,
    TwCBDA, WhAm H, WhAmP
Francis, John Brown 1794-1864 *BiAUS, Drake*
Francis, John F 1808-1886 *BnEnAmA,*
    NewYHSD, WhAm H
Francis, John Haywood 1867- *WhAm 1*
Francis, John Miller 1867-1924 *NatCAB 20,*
    WhAm 1
Francis, John Morgan 1823-1897 *ApCAB,*
    BiAUS, DcAmB, NatCAB 1, TwCBDA,
    WhAm H
Francis, John Morgan 1879-1925 *WhAm 1*
Francis, John R 1832-1910 *NatCAB 16*
Francis, John Wakefield 1789-1861 *AmBi,*
    ApCAB, DcAmB, Drake, NatCAB 1,
    TwCBDA, WhAm H
Francis, Joseph 1801-1893 *AmBi, ApCAB,*
    DcAmB, NatCAB 10, TwCBDA,
    WhAm H
Francis, Joseph G 1849- *WhAm 4*
Francis, Joseph Marshall 1862-1939
    NatCAB 12, TwCBDA, WhAm 1
Francis, Sir Josiah 1890-1964 *WhAm 4*
Francis, Kay d1968 *WhAm 5*
Francis, Lee Masten 1877- *WhAm 5*
Francis, Louise E 1869- *AmWom*
Francis, Mark 1863-1936 *WhAm 1*
Francis, Milly 1802?-1848 *NotAW*
Francis, Nellie Griswold 1874- *WhoColR*
Francis, Parker B 1886-1957 *WhAm 3*
Francis, Paul James 1863-1940 *DcAmB S2*
Francis, Richard Clarence 1904-1967 *WhAm 4*
Francis, Richard J 1910-1971 *WhAm 5*
Francis, Sam 1923- *BnEnAmA*

Francis, Samuel Ward 1835-1886 *ApCAB*, *DcAmB*, *NatCAB 4*, *WhAm H*
Francis, Sarah Dimon Chapman 1874-1962 *WhAm 4*
Francis, Tench d1758 *ApCAB*, *ApCAB X*, *DcAmB*, *NatCAB 5*, *WhAm H*
Francis, Tench 1730-1800 *ApCAB*, *ApCAB X*
Francis, Thomas, Jr. 1900-1969 *WhAm 5*
Francis, Turbutt 1740-1797 *ApCAB*
Francis, Valentine Mott 1834- *ApCAB*
Francis, Vida Hunt *WomWWA 14*
Francis, W A 1875-1957 *WhAm 3*
Francis, Warren Briggs 1908-1975 *WhAm 6*
Francis, William Allen 1861- *NatCAB 10*
Francis, William Bates 1860-1954 *BiDrAC*, *WhAm 5*
Francis, William Carson 1879-1945 *NatCAB 36*
Francis, William Howard 1885-1946 *NatCAB 42*, *WhAm 2*
Francis, William Howard, Jr. 1914-1958 *WhAm 3*
Francis, William Mursell 1870-1954 *WhAm 3*
Francis, William Trevanne 1870- *WhoColR*
Francisco, Clarence Benjamin 1880-1944 *NatCAB 34*
Francisco, Don 1891-1973 *WhAm 6*
Francisco, Henry d1820 *Drake*
Francisco, John Bond 1863-1931 *IIBEAAW*, *WhAm 1*
Francisco, Kate Bottomes 1869- *WomWWA 14*
Francisco, Lucy Hogarth 1872- *WomWWA 14*
Francisco, Peter d1831 *Drake*
Francisco, Peter 1761-1832 *ApCAB*
Franck, Cesar 1822-1890 *McGEWB*
Franck, Charles 1881-1972 *WhAm 5*
Franck, Harry Alverson 1881-1962 *NatCAB 52*, *WhAm 4*
Franck, Jacob W *NewYHSD*
Franck, James 1882-1964 *AsBiEn*, *DcScB*, *WhAm 4*
Franck, Sebastian 1499-1542 *DcScB*
Francke, Kuno 1855-1930 *AmBi*, *DcAmB*, *NatCAB 10*, *NatCAB 34*, *TwCBDA*, *WhAm 1*
Francksen, August Wilhelm Reinhard 1855-1929 *NatCAB 21*
Franco Of Cologne *McGEWB*
Franco, Bernardo DeSousa 1805-1875 *ApCAB*
Franco, Francisco 1892-1975 *McGEWB*, *WhoMilH*
Franco, Francisco-Bahamonde 1892-1975 *WhWW-II*
Franco, Francisco DeMello 1757-1823 *ApCAB*
Franco Bahamonda, Francisco 1892-1975 *WhAm 6*
Franco DeSa, Joaquim 1807-1851 *ApCAB*
Francois, Alexander 1824-1912 *NewYHSD*
Francois, Samson 1924-1970 *WhAm 5*
Francois, Victor Emmanuel 1866- *WhAm 4*
Francolini, Joseph Nocola 1856- *WhAm 4*
Frandsen, Julius Herman 1877-1962 *WhAm 4*
Frandsen, Peter 1876- *WhAm 5*
Franges, Ivan 1899-1972 *WhAm 5*
Frank, Aaron Meier 1891-1968 *NatCAB 56*
Frank, Abraham 1871-1932 *WhAm 1*
Frank, Alfred 1879- *WhAm 2*
Frank, Alfred Swift 1886-1962 *WhAm 4*
Frank, Anne 1929-1945 *WhWW-II*
Frank, Arthur Albert 1878-1962 *WhAm 4*
Frank, Augustus 1826-1895 *BiAUS*, *BiDrAC*, *WhAm H*
Frank, Bernard 1902-1964 *NatCAB 51*
Frank, Eli 1874-1958 *NatCAB 46*
Frank, Eli 1874-1959 *WhAm 3*
Frank, Everett 1893-1971 *WhAm 5*
Frank, Fritz John 1871-1939 *WhAm 1*
Frank, George P 1852- *NatCAB 7*
Frank, Glenn 1887-1940 *DcAmB S2*, *NatCAB 29*, *WebAB*, *WhAm 1*, *WhAmP*
Frank, Grace M 1886- *WomWWA 14*
Frank, Graham 1873- *WhAm 5*
Frank, Hans 1900-1946 *WhWW-II*
Frank, Helen Sophia d1973 *WhAm 6*
Frank, Henry 1854-1933 *ApCAB X*, *NatCAB 12*, *NatCAB 23*, *WhAm 1*
Frank, Ilya Mikhaylovich 1908- *AsBiEn*
Frank, Isaac William 1855-1930 *WhAm 1*
Frank, Israel Robert 1905-1968 *NatCAB 55*

Frank, James *NewYHSD*
Frank, Jerome N 1889-1957 *WhAm 3*
Frank, Johann Peter 1745-1821 *BiHiMed*
Frank, John Mayer 1886-1966 *WhAm 4*
Frank, Joseph Otto 1885-1949 *WhAm 3*
Frank, Karl Hermann 1898-1946 *WhWW-II*
Frank, Lawrence Kelso 1890-1968 *WhAm 5*
Frank, Lawrence Louis 1887-1970 *WhAm 5*
Frank, Lewis Crown, Jr. 1916-1970 *NatCAB 56*, *WhAm 5*
Frank, Maude Morrison *WhAm 5*
Frank, Melvin Porter 1841- *NatCAB 14*
Frank, Michael 1804-1894 *BiDAmEd*, *REnAW*
Frank, Nathan 1852-1931 *BiDrAC*, *NatCAB 12*, *WhAm 1*
Frank, Nelson 1906-1974 *WhAm 6*
Frank, Pat Harry Hart 1907-1964 *WhAm 4*
Frank, Philipp 1884-1966 *DcScB*
Frank, Rachel 1866- *AmWom*
Frank, Robert 1924- *BnEnAmA*
Frank, Royal Thaxter 1836-1908 *TwCBDA*, *WhAm 1*
Frank, Royall Thaxter 1836-1908 *ApCAB Sup*
Frank, Selby Harney 1891-1974 *WhAm 6*
Frank, Tenney 1876-1939 *DcAmB S2*, *NatCAB 19*, *WhAm 1*
Frank, Theodore 1894-1952 *WhAm 3*
Frank, Theodore McConnell 1901-1961 *WhAm 4*
Frank, Waldo 1889-1967 *WhAm 4*
Frank, Walter 1882-1969 *WhAm 5*
Frank, William George 1898-1970 *NatCAB 55*
Frank, William Klee 1890-1964 *NatCAB 51*
Frankau, Pamela 1908-1967 *WhAm 4*
Franke, Ann 1891-1973 *WhAm 6*
Franke, Gustav Henry 1888-1953 *NatCAB 42*, *WhAm 3*
Franke, Julius 1868-1936 *NatCAB 17*, *NatCAB 27*
Franke, Louis 1905-1965 *WhAm 4*
Frankel, Abigail Keasey *WomWWA 14*
Frankel, Bernard Louis 1895-1970 *WhAm 5*
Frankel, Emil 1886-1966 *WhAm 4*
Frankel, Joseph Jerome 1912-1975 *WhAm 6*
Frankel, Lee Kaufer 1867-1931 *NatCAB 23*, *WhAm 1*
Frankel, Louis 1880-1962 *NatCAB 49*
Frankel, Max 1900-1971 *WhAm 5*
Frankel, Rudolf 1901-1974 *WhAm 6*
Frankel, William Victor 1903-1972 *NatCAB 57*, *WhAm 5*
Frankenberg, Lloyd 1907-1975 *WhAm 6*
Frankenberg, Theodore Thomas 1877- *WhAm 5*
Frankenfeld, Frederick 1878- *WhAm 6*
Frankenfield, Harry Crawford 1862-1929 *WhAm 1*
Frankenheim, Moritz Ludwig 1801-1869 *DcScB*
Frankenstein, Eliza *NewYHSD*
Frankenstein, George L *NewYHSD*
Frankenstein, Godfrey N 1820-1873 *NewYHSD*, *WhAm H*
Frankenstein, Gustavus d1902? *NewYHSD*
Frankenstein, John Peter 1816?-1881 *NewYHSD*, *WhAm H*
Frankenstein, Marie M C *NewYHSD*
Frankenthal, Adolph Levy 1851- *WhAm 4*
Frankenthal, Lester Emanuel 1900-1967 *NatCAB 53*
Frankenthal, Tillie S *BiCAW*
Frankenthaler, Helen 1928- *BnEnAmA*, *McGEWB*
Frankfort, Henri 1897-1954 *WhAm 3*
Frankforter, George Bell 1859-1947 *NatCAB 42*, *WhAm 3*
Frankfurter, Felix 1882-1965 *EncAB*, *McGEWB*, *WebAB*, *WhAm 4*
Frankhauser, William Horace 1863-1921 *BiDrAC*, *NatCAB 6*, *NatCAB 20*, *NatCAB 21*
Frankl, Paul T 1887-1958 *BnEnAmA*
Frankl, Paul Theodore 1886-1958 *WhAm 3*
Frankland, Lady Agnes Surriage 1726-1783 *DcAmB*, *NotAW*, *WhAm H*
Frankland, Sir Charles Henry 1716-1768 *ApCAB*, *Drake*
Frankland, Sir Edward 1825-1899 *AsBiEn*, *DcScB*

Frankland, Frederick Herston 1882-1959 *WhAm 4*
Frankland, Frederick William 1854-1916 *WhAm 1*
Frankland, Percy Faraday 1858-1946 *DcScB*
Franklin, Alfred 1869- *WhAm 5*
Franklin, Alvin Bruce 1838-1921 *NatCAB 19*
Franklin, Ann Smith 1696-1763 *NotAW*
Franklin, B J 1839-1898 *BiAUS*
Franklin, Benjamin 1706-1790 *AmBi*, *ApCAB*, *AsBiEn*, *BiAUS*, *BiDAmEd*, *BiDrAC*, *BnEnAmA*, *DcAmB*, *DcAmLiB*, *DcScB*, *Drake*, *EncAB*, *McGEWB*, *NatCAB 1*, *NewYHSD*, *REnAW*, *TwCBDA*, *WebAB*, *WhAm H*, *WhAmP*
Franklin, Benjamin 1812-1878 *DcAmB*, *WhAm H*
Franklin, Benjamin 1819-1898 *TwCBDA*
Franklin, Benjamin A 1869-1940 *WhAm 1*
Franklin, Benjamin Joseph 1839-1898 *BiDrAC*, *WhAmP*
Franklin, Buck Colbert 1879- *WhoColR*
Franklin, Charles Amory 1881-1955 *NatCAB 41*
Franklin, Charles Greenlief 1883-1959 *NatCAB 47*
Franklin, Charles Thomas 1927-1971 *WhAm 6*
Franklin, Chester Arthur 1880-1955 *WhAm 3*
Franklin, Christine Ladd 1847-1930 *AmBi*, *NatCAB 5*, *NotAW*, *TwCBDA*
Franklin, Deborah Read 1707?-1774 *NotAW*
Franklin, Edward C 1822-1895 *NatCAB 7*
Franklin, Edward Curtis 1862-1937 *AmBi*, *DcAmB S2*, *NatCAB 30*, *WhAm 1*
Franklin, Effie Scott 1871- *WomWWA 14*
Franklin, Elizabeth Jennings 1887-1967 *NatCAB 53*
Franklin, Ezra Thomas 1881- *WhAm 6*
Franklin, Fabian 1853-1939 *DcAmB S2*, *TwCBDA*, *WhAm 1*
Franklin, Frank George 1861- *WhAm 4*
Franklin, Gertrude *AmWom*
Franklin, Harold B 1889- *ApCAB X*
Franklin, Henry James 1883-1958 *NatCAB 46*
Franklin, James 1696?-1735 *BnEnAmA*, *DcAmB*
Franklin, James 1697-1735 *NatCAB 8*, *WhAm H*
Franklin, James Alfred 1895-1964 *NatCAB 50*
Franklin, James Henry 1872- *WhAm 5*
Franklin, James M *NewYHSD*
Franklin, Jesse 1758-1823 *BiAUS*, *Drake*
Franklin, Jesse 1760-1823 *ApCAB*, *BiDrAC*, *DcAmB*, *NatCAB 4*, *TwCBDA*, *WhAm H*, *WhAmP*
Franklin, John 1749-1831 *ApCAB*
Franklin, Sir John 1786-1847 *ApCAB*, *Drake*, *McGEWB*
Franklin, John Eddy 1863- *WhAm 4*
Franklin, John Hope 1915- *EncAAH*, *WebAB*
Franklin, John Merryman 1895-1975 *WhAm 6*
Franklin, John Rankin 1820-1878 *BiAUS*, *BiDrAC*, *WhAm H*
Franklin, Joseph 1909-1957 *NatCAB 46*
Franklin, Laura C 1858- *WhoColR*
Franklin, Laura Merryman *BiCAW*
Franklin, Leo M 1870-1948 *WhAm 2*
Franklin, Lewis Battelle 1878-1959 *WhAm 3*
Franklin, Lindley Murray 1874-1960 *WhAm 4*
Franklin, Lucy Jenkins 1877- *WhAm 5*
Franklin, Lynn Winterdale 1888-1952 *WhAm 3*
Franklin, Marvin Augustus 1894-1972 *WhAm 5*
Franklin, Melvin M 1874-1938 *WhAm 1*
Franklin, Meshack 1772-1839 *BiAUS*, *BiDrAC*, *WhAm H*, *WhAmP*
Franklin, Miles 1879-1954 *McGEWB*
Franklin, Philip 1898-1965 *WhAm 4*
Franklin, Philip Albright Small 1871-1939 *AmBi*, *DcAmB S2*, *WhAm 1*
Franklin, Philip Lair 1911-1963 *NatCAB 50*
Franklin, Raymond Earl 1885-1960 *NatCAB 47*
Franklin, Richard 1831?- *NewYHSD*
Franklin, Richard West 1875-1943 *NatCAB 34*
Franklin, Rosalind Elsie 1920-1958 *DcScB*
Franklin, Ruth Barker 1865- *WomWWA 14*
Franklin, Samuel Petty 1895-1956 *WhAm 3*
Franklin, Samuel Rhoads 1825-1909 *ApCAB*, *WhAm 1*

Franklin, Samuel Rhodes 1825-1909 *NatCAB 4,*
TwCBDA
Franklin, Selim Maurice 1859-1927 *NatCAB 33*
Franklin, Sidney Arnold 1893-1972 *WhAm 5*
Franklin, Stella Maraia Sarah Miles 1879-1954
McGEWB
Franklin, Susan Braley *WomWWA 14*
Franklin, Thomas Levering 1822-1899 *ApCAB,*
WhAm 1
Franklin, Wallace Collin d1964 *WhAm 4*
Franklin, Walter Alexander 1891-1955
WhAm 3
Franklin, Walter S *BiAUS*
Franklin, Walter Scott 1878-1946 *NatCAB 35*
Franklin, Walter Simonds 1836-1911 *WhAm 1*
Franklin, Walter Simonds 1884-1972 *WhAm 5*
Franklin, William 1729-1813 *ApCAB,*
NatCAB 13
Franklin, William 1730?-1813 *AmBi, Drake*
Franklin, William 1731-1813 *DcAmB,*
McGEWB, WhAm H, WhAmP
Franklin, William Benjamin 1823- *Drake*
Franklin, William Buel 1823-1903 *AmBi,*
ApCAB, DcAmB, NatCAB 4, TwCBDA,
WebAMB, WhAm 1
Franklin, William Buel 1868-1942 *NatCAB 33*
Franklin, William Henderson 1852- *WhoColR*
Franklin, William Neil 1902- *EncAAH*
Franklin, William Suddards 1863-1930 *AmBi,*
NatCAB 22, WhAm 1
Franklin, William Temple 1760-1823 *AmBi,*
ApCAB
Franklin, Wirt 1883-1962 *WhAm 4*
Franko, Nahan 1861-1930 *NatCAB 22*
Franko, Sam 1857- *ApCAB X*
Franks, E T 1863- *WhAm 4*
Franks, F D 1836- *NewYHSD*
Franks, Fred Benjamin 1871-1968 *NatCAB 54*
Franks, Frederick *NewYHSD*
Franks, John B 1890-1946 *WhAm 2*
Franks, Rebecca 1760?-1823 *NotAW*
Franks, Robert A 1861-1935 *WhAm 1*
Franks, William *NewYHSD*
Franquinet, James *NewYHSD*
Franquinet, William Hendrik 1785-1854
NewYHSD
Fransioli, Joseph 1817-1890 *ApCAB,*
TwCBDA
Frant, Samuel 1898-1961 *NatCAB 50,*
WhAm 4
Frantz, Edward 1868- *WhAm 4*
Frantz, Frank 1872-1941 *NatCAB 35,*
WhAm 1
Frantz, Frank Flavius 1874-1957 *WhAm 3*
Frantz, Jacob Frick 1852-1914 *NatCAB 16*
Frantz, Joe Bertram 1917- *EncAAH, REnAW*
Frantz, Joseph Henry 1864-1938 *NatCAB 28,*
WhAm 1
Frantz, Oswin Stricker 1880- *WhAm 6*
Frantz, Robert Benjamin 1894-1971 *WhAm 5*
Frantz, Samuel Gibson 1897-1971 *NatCAB 56*
Frantz, Virginia Kneeland 1896-1967
NatCAB 53, WhAm 4, WhAm 6
Franz, Adolph 1862-1955 *NatCAB 42*
Franz, Elmer Franklin 1903-1968 *WhAm 5*
Franz, Frederick 1895-1971 *NatCAB 56*
Franz, Joseph 1882-1959 *NatCAB 50*
Franz, Shepherd Ivory 1874-1933 *DcAmB S1,*
WhAm 1
Franzen, August 1863-1938 *WhAm 1*
Franzen, Carl Gustave Frederick 1886-1966
NatCAB 54, WhAm 4
Franzen, Frank Clarence 1890-1959
NatCAB 50
Franzen, Ulrich 1921- *BnEnAmA*
Franzet, Louis *NewYHSD*
Franzheim, Kenneth 1890- *WhAm 3*
Franzoni, Carlo 1789-1819 *NewYHSD*
Franzoni, Charles William 1837- *WhAm 4*
Franzoni, Giuseppe d1815 *NewYHSD*
Fraprie, Frank Roy 1874-1951 *WhAm 3*
Fraps, George Stronach 1876- *WhAm 5*
Frary, Hobart Dickinson 1887-1920 *NatCAB 23*
Frary, Ihna Thayer 1873- *WhAm 5*
Frasca, William Robert 1911-1964 *WhAm 4*
Frasch, Herman 1851-1914 *AmBi, AsBiEn,*
DcAmB, NatCAB 19, WhAm HA,
WhAm 4

Frasch, Herman 1852-1914 *ApCAB X*
Frasch, William Frederick 1874-1953
NatCAB 43
Frasconi, Antonio 1919- *BnEnAmA*
Fraser, Abel McIver 1856-1933 *WhAm 1*
Fraser, Alexander David 1886-1955 *WhAm 3*
Fraser, Alexander Joseph 1869-1938
NatCAB 38
Fraser, Amorette E Harrington 1836-
WomWWA 14
Fraser, Archibald *NewYHSD*
Fraser, Arthur Cleveland 1859-1934
NatCAB 29
Fraser, Arthur McNutt 1915-1972 *NatCAB 57,*
WhAm 5
Fraser, Blair 1909-1968 *WhAm 5*
Fraser, Sir Bruce 1888- *WhWW-II*
Fraser, Carlyle 1894-1961 *WhAm 4*
Fraser, Cecil Eaton 1895-1947 *WhAm 2*
Fraser, Charles 1782-1860 *AmBi, ApCAB,*
BnEnAmA, DcAmB, Drake, NatCAB 4,
NewYHSD, WhAm H
Fraser, Chelsea Curtis 1876-1954 *WhAm 3*
Fraser, Christopher Finlay 1839- *ApCAB*
Fraser, Daniel 1855- *WhAm 1*
Fraser, Donald MacKay 1924- *BiDrAC*
Fraser, Duncan William 1875-1954 *WhAm 3*
Fraser, Elisha Alexander 1837-1916 *WhAm 1*
Fraser, Forrest L 1909-1956 *WhAm 3*
Fraser, Frank Edwin 1895-1972 *WhAm 5*
Fraser, Harold William 1872-1945 *NatCAB 36*
Fraser, Harry Wilson 1884-1950 *NatCAB 39,*
WhAm 3
Fraser, Horace John 1905-1969 *WhAm 5*
Fraser, Horatio Nelson 1851- *NatCAB 12,*
WhAm 4
Fraser, Hugh John 1897-1952 *WhAm 3*
Fraser, Hugh Wilson, Jr. 1904-1973 *WhAm 6*
Fraser, J *NewYHSD*
Fraser, James Earle 1876-1953 *DcAmB S5,*
IIBEAAW, NatCAB 16, NatCAB 40,
REnAW, WebAB, WhAm 3
Fraser, Jane Wells *WomWWA 14*
Fraser, John *NewYHSD*
Fraser, John 1750-1811 *NewYHSD*
Fraser, John 1823?-1878 *NatCAB 9*
Fraser, John 1827-1878 *BiDAmEd*
Fraser, John Arthur 1838?-1898 *IIBEAAW*
Fraser, John Falconer 1875- *WhAm 5*
Fraser, Laura Gardin 1889-1966 *WhAm 4*
Fraser, Leon 1889-1945 *DcAmB S3,*
NatCAB 56, WhAm 2
Fraser, Mabel Augusta Canada *WomWWA 14*
Fraser, Malcolm 1869-1949 *NatCAB 36,*
WhAm 3
Fraser, Margaret Ethel Victoria 1871-
WomWWA 14
Fraser, Melvin 1858-1936 *WhAm 1*
Fraser, Miss O H *NewYHSD*
Fraser, Peter 1884-1950 *McGEWB, WhAm 3*
Fraser, Philip *BiAUS*
Fraser, Samuel 1876-1959 *WhAm 3*
Fraser, Simon 1729-1777 *ApCAB*
Fraser, Simon 1776-1862 *McGEWB*
Fraser, Simon *see also* Frazer, Simon
Fraser, Thomas Boone 1860-1925 *NatCAB 20,*
WhAm 1
Fraser, Thomas Douglass 1883?-1955 *IIBEAAW*
Fraser, Wilber John 1869-1945 *WhAm 2*
Fraser, William 1790?-1857 *ApCAB*
Fraser, William Alexander 1886-1932 *WhAm 1*
Fraser, William Jocelyn Ian 1897-1974
WhAm 6
Fraser, William Lewis 1841-1905 *WhAm 1*
Frasier, George Willard 1890-1958 *NatCAB 47,*
WhAm 3
Frasier, Waldo 1902-1972 *WhAm 6*
Frassinelli, Attilio 1908-1976 *WhAm 6*
Frater, George Ellsworth 1900-1966 *WhAm 4*
Fratt, Frederick William 1859- *NatCAB 16*
Fraubel, M *NewYHSD*
Fraudendorfer, Alfred 1903-1971 *WhAm 6*
Frauenberger, G *NewYHSD*
Frauenheim, George Meyer 1912-1968 *WhAm 5*
Frauenthal, Henry William 1862-1927
NatCAB 23
Frauenthal, Ida Baridon *WomWWA 14*
Fraunces, Samuel 1722?-1795 *AmBi, DcAmB,*

WhAm H
Fraunhofer, Joseph Von 1787-1826 *AsBiEn,*
DcScB, McGEWB
Fravel, Roy Clyde 1882-1951 *NatCAB 40*
Frawley, John Edward 1894-1956 *NatCAB 46,*
WhAm 3
Frawley, John Milan 1891-1969 *WhAm 5*
Frawley, Michael P 1902-1971 *WhAm 5*
Frawley, William 1893-1966 *WhAm 4*
Frawley, William Henry 1865-1941 *NatCAB 33*
Fray, Ellen Sulley 1832- *AmWom*
Fray, William F 1844-1918 *NatCAB 18*
Frayne, Hugh 1869-1934 *DcAmB S1,*
WhAm 1
Frayser, Benjamin Hobson 1887-1937
NatCAB 29
Frazar, Everett Welles 1867-1951 *NatCAB 40,*
WhAm 3
Frazar, Lether Edward 1904-1960 *WhAm 4*
Frazee, Harry Herbert 1880-1929 *WhAm 1*
Frazee, John 1790-1852 *AmBi, ApCAB,*
ApCAB X, BnEnAmA, DcAmB, Drake,
NatCAB 8, NewYHSD, TwCBDA,
WhAm H
Frazee, P F *NewYHSD*
Frazer, Carl Byrd 1900-1964 *NatCAB 50*
Frazer, Charles Rivers 1879- *WhoColR*
Frazer, David Ruddach 1837-1916 *WhAm 1*
Frazer, Elizabeth d1967 *WhAm 4*
Frazer, Ephraim P *NewYHSD*
Frazer, George Enfield 1889-1972 *WhAm 5*
Frazer, Horace Southworth 1862-1931
NatCAB 27
Frazer, Sir James George 1854-1941 *DcScB,*
McGEWB
Frazer, James Somerville 1824-1893 *TwCBDA*
Frazer, John *NewYHSD*
Frazer, John 1882-1964 *WhAm 4*
Frazer, John Fries 1812-1872 *ApCAB, DcAmB,*
NatCAB 1, TwCBDA, WhAm H
Frazer, John G 1880-1942 *WhAm 4*
Frazer, John Stanley 1849-1927 *WhAm 1*
Frazer, Joseph Christie Whitney 1875-1944
NatCAB 34, WhAm 2
Frazer, Joseph Washington 1892-1971
NatCAB 57, WhAm 5
Frazer, Leslie 1889-1947 *WhAm 2*
Frazer, Mabel Pearl 1887- *IIBEAAW*
Frazer, Oliver 1808-1864 *DcAmB, NatCAB 24,*
NewYHSD, WhAm H
Frazer, Oscar Bryant 1886-1973 *WhAm 6*
Frazer, Persifor 1736-1792 *DcAmB, WhAm H*
Frazer, Persifor 1844-1909 *ApCAB, DcAmB,*
NatCAB 4, TwCBDA, WhAm 1
Frazer, Robert Sellers 1849-1936 *NatCAB 28,*
WhAm 1
Frazer, Simon 1729-1777 *Drake*
Frazer, Simon *see also* Fraser, Simon
Frazer, Spaulding 1881- *WhAm 6*
Frazer, Susan Carpenter *WomWWA 14*
Frazer, Thomas *NewYHSD*
Frazer, Tucker Henderson 1859- *NatCAB 12*
Frazer, William Henry 1873-1953 *WhAm 3*
Frazier *NewYHSD*
Frazier, Arthur Hugh 1868- *WhAm 4*
Frazier, Benjamin West 1841-1905 *WhAm 1*
Frazier, Charles Harrison 1870-1936
DcAmB S2, NatCAB 28, WhAm 1
Frazier, Chauncey Earl 1879-1961 *NatCAB 50*
Frazier, Chester North 1892-1973 *WhAm 5*
Frazier, Clarence Mackay 1903-1952 *WhAm 3*
Frazier, E Franklin 1894-1962 *WebAB*
Frazier, Edward Franklin 1894-1962 *BiDAmEd,*
EncAB, McGEWB, WhAm 4
Frazier, Esther Yates *IIBEAAW*
Frazier, Frank Pierce 1850-1923 *NatCAB 20*
Frazier, Fred Brennings 1880- *WhAm 6*
Frazier, Frederic Hiram 1873-1939 *NatCAB 34*
Frazier, George Harrison 1867-1934
NatCAB 25, WhAm 1
Frazier, James B 1858- *NatCAB 13*
Frazier, James Beriah, Jr. 1890- *BiDrAC,*
WhAmP
Frazier, James Beriah, Sr. 1856-1937 *BiDrAC,*
NatCAB 28, WhAm 1, WhAmP
Frazier, John Robinson 1889-1966 *WhAm 4*
Frazier, Kenneth 1867-1949 *WhAm 2*
Frazier, Lynn Joseph 1874-1947 *ApCAB X,*

BiDrAC, DcAmB S4, NatCAB 43,
WhAm 2, WhAmP
Frazier, Lynn Joseph 1875-1947 REnAW
Frazier, Martha M 1826- AmWom
Frazier, Raymond Robert 1873-1955 WhAm 3
Frazier, Reuben Eugene 1870- WhoColR
Frazier, Robert 1876-1940 NatCAB 34
Frazier, Robert Thomas 1863-1914 WhAm 1
Frazier, Samuel Jefferson 1886-1950
NatCAB 42
Frazier, Thomas Alexander 1894-1969
NatCAB 55
Frazier, William C 1776-1838 BiAUS
Frazier, William Fiske 1888-1962 WhAm 4
Frazin, Nathaniel Daniel 1889-1958
NatCAB 49
Frear, Charles Wright 1864-1944 NatCAB 35
Frear, Hugo Pinkney 1862-1955 NatCAB 46
Frear, James Archibald 1861-1939 BiDrAC,
WhAm 1, WhAmP
Frear, Joseph Allen, Jr. 1903- BiDrAC
Frear, Walter 1828- WhAm 4
Frear, Walter Francis 1863-1948 NatCAB 12,
NatCAB 40, WhAm 2
Frear, William 1860-1922 DcAmB, WhAm 1
Freas, Howard George 1900-1971 WhAm 5
Freas, Thomas Bruce 1868-1928 AmBi,
DcAmB, NatCAB 22, WhAm 1
Freas, William Streeper 1848-1911 WhAm 1
Frease, Donald William 1897-1968 WhAm 5
Frechette, Annie Thomas Howells WhAm 5,
WomWWA 14
Frechette, Louis-Honore 1839-1908 ApCAB,
McGEWB
Frechtel, Harry 1885-1958 NatCAB 47
Frechtling, Louis Henry 1880-1957 NatCAB 46
Fredenburg, George NewYHSD
Fredendall, Lloyd WhWW-II
Fredenhagen, Edward Adolph 1860-1916
NatCAB 17
Fredenthal, David 1914-1958 WhAm 3
Frederic, Harold 1856-1898 AmBi,
ApCAB Sup, DcAmB, NatCAB 5,
TwCBDA, WhAm H
Frederick I 1123-1190 McGEWB
Frederick II 1194-1250 AsBiEn, McGEWB
Frederick II 1712-1786 McGEWB
Frederick III 1415-1493 McGEWB
Frederick II Of Hohenstaufen 1194-1250 DcScB
Frederick II, The Great 1713-1786 WhoMilH
Frederick William, The Great Elector 1620-1688
McGEWB, WhoMilH
Frederick William I 1688-1740 McGEWB,
WhoMilH
Frederick William III 1770-1840 McGEWB
Frederick William IV 1795-1861 McGEWB
Frederick, Antoinette Elizabeth 1861-
WomWWA 14
Frederick, August Henry 1858- NatCAB 12
Frederick, Benjamin Todd 1834-1903 BiDrAC
Frederick, Charles NewYHSD
Frederick, Daniel Alfred 1855- WhAm 4
Frederick, Donald Edward 1860-1937
NatCAB 34
Frederick, Francis Harland 1907-1968
NatCAB 54
Frederick, George Aloysius 1842-1924
NatCAB 9, WhAm 1
Frederick, Harold 1856-1898 ApCAB X
Frederick, John L 1797?-1881? NewYHSD
Frederick, Karl Telford 1881-1962 WhAm 4
Frederick, Montgomery L NewYHSD
Frederick, Otto 1887-1954 NatCAB 41
Frederick, Pauline 1883-1938 NotAW
Frederick, Pauline 1885-1938 AmBi,
ApCAB X, WhAm 1
Frederick, Robert Tryon 1907-1971 WhAm 5
Frederick, Russell Adair 1901-1966 WhAm 4
Frederick, William Franklin 1861-1943
NatCAB 33
Fredericks, Alfred NewYHSD
Fredericks, John Donnan 1869-1945 BiDrAC,
WhAm 2
Fredericks, Mary Pate 1912-1972 WhAm 6
Fredericks, R N 1855- WhAm 4
Frederickson, Charles Richard 1875-1955
WhAm 3
Frederickson, George 1874-1961 WhAm 4

Frederickson, William 1865-1945 NatCAB 34
Fredericq, Leon 1851-1935 DcScB
Frederik IX 1899-1972 WhAm 5
Frederiksen, Ditlew Monrad 1866- WhAm 4
Frederiksen, Mary Monrad 1869- IlBEAAW
Frederycks, Kryn NewYHSD
Fredet, Peter 1801-1856 ApCAB
Fredholm, Ivar 1866-1927 DcScB
Fredo, Michael Angelo 1889-1965 NatCAB 51
Fredrick, John Eugene 1865-1943 NatCAB 31,
WhAm 2
Fredrick, Leopold 1876-1936 NatCAB 26,
WhAm 1
Fredricks, Charles D 1823-1894 NatCAB 2
Fredriks, Gerritt James 1882-1975 WhAm 6
Free, Arthur Monroe 1879-1953 BiDrAC,
WhAm 3, WhAmP
Free, Edward Elway 1883-1939 WhAm 1
Free, John D 1929- IlBEAAW
Free, John Edward 1894-1950 NatCAB 38
Free, Joseph L 1873- ApCAB X
Free, Joseph Paul 1911-1974 WhAm 6
Free, Lincoln Forrest 1903-1959 WhAm 3
Free, Montague 1885-1965 WhAm 4
Free, Spencer Michael 1856-1938 WhAm 1
Free, Walter Henry 1898-1965 WhAm 4
Freeborn, Stanley B 1891-1960 WhAm 4
Freebourn, Harrison J 1890- WhAm 3
Freeburg, Victor Oscar 1882-1953 WhAm 3
Freeburne, Cecil Max 1918-1974 WhAm 6
Freed, Allie Samuel 1891-1938 NatCAB 33
Freed, Arthur 1894-1973 WhAm 5
Freed, Cecil Forest 1893-1954 NatCAB 43
Freed, Charles Abram 1868-1938 WhAm 1
Freed, Emerich Burt 1897-1955 WhAm 3
Freed, Fred 1920-1974 WhAm 6
Freed, Harold 1890-1969 NatCAB 54
Freed, Isadore 1900-1960 WhAm 4
Freed, J Melvin 1888-1956 NatCAB 46
Freed, Nettie S 1881- WhAm 6
Freedlander, A L 1889-1971 WhAm 5
Freedlander, Joseph Henry d1943 WhAm 2
Freedlander, Samuel Oscar 1893-1971
NatCAB 56
Freedley, Angelo Tillinghast 1850-1907
WhAm 1
Freedley, Edwin Troxell 1827-1904 ApCAB,
NatCAB 10, WhAm 1
Freedley, George 1904-1967 WhAm 4
Freedley, John 1793-1851 BiAUS, BiDrAC,
WhAm H
Freedley, Vinton 1891-1969 WhAm 5
Freedman, Andrew 1860-1915 DcAmB,
WhAm 1
Freedman, Emanuel R 1910-1971 WhAm 5
Freedman, John Joseph 1835-1921 WhAm 1
Freedman, M Joel 1903-1973 NatCAB 57,
WhAm 6
Freedman, William Horatio 1867-1940
WhAm 1
Freehill, Joseph Hugh 1908-1959 NatCAB 49,
WhAm 4
Freeland, Anna C 1837-1911 NewYHSD
Freeland, O S NewYHSD
Freeland, Theodore NewYHSD
Freeling, Sargent Prentiss 1874- WhAm 5
Freely, John NewYHSD
Freeman, A F Patrick 1908-1965 WhAm 4
Freeman, Abraham Clark 1843-1911 TwCBDA,
WhAm 1
Freeman, Albert Clark 1883-1949 NatCAB 39
Freeman, Albert Howard 1866- WhAm 4
Freeman, Alden 1862- NatCAB 12, WhAm 4
Freeman, Alfred Bird 1881-1957 WhAm 3
Freeman, Alice Elvira 1855-1902 ApCAB,
TwCBDA, WebAB
Freeman, Allen Weir 1881-1954 DcAmB S5,
WhAm 3
Freeman, Anna Mary NewYHSD
Freeman, Arthur Merriman 1881- WhAm 6
Freeman, Barnardus 1660-1743 ApCAB
Freeman, Barnardus see also Freerman,
Barnardus
Freeman, Benjamin William 1890-1963
NatCAB 50
Freeman, Bernardus d1741 DcAmB
Freeman, Bernardus 1660-1742? WhAm H
Freeman, Bradford NewYHSD

Freeman, Chapman 1832-1904 BiAUS,
BiDrAC
Freeman, Charles Seymour 1878-1969 WhAm 5
Freeman, Charles West 1892-1960 WhAm 4
Freeman, Charles Yoe 1877-1964 WhAm 4
Freeman, Clara Augusta 1871- WomWWA 14
Freeman, Clarence Campbell 1862-1935
WhAm 1
Freeman, Clayton E 1872- WhAm 5
Freeman, Constant BiAUS
Freeman, Douglas Southall 1886-1953
DcAmB S5, McGEWB, WebAB,
WhAm 3
Freeman, E O NewYHSD
Freeman, Edmond Wroe 1866-1945 WhAm 2
Freeman, Edward Monroe 1875-1954
NatCAB 40, WhAm 4
Freeman, Elijah 1858- WhoColR
Freeman, Elizabeth Janette Child 1840-
WomWWA 14
Freeman, Ella Maria WomWWA 14
Freeman, Ellen Burrows BiCAW
Freeman, Elmer Burkitt 1875-1942 NatCAB 31
Freeman, Elmer Leslie 1876-1946 NatCAB 38
Freeman, Ernest Bigelow 1877- WhAm 5
Freeman, Ernest Harrison 1876- WhAm 3
Freeman, Florence 1836- ApCAB, NewYHSD
Freeman, Fortunatus d1874 ApCAB
Freeman, Francis Breakey 1867-1934 WhAm 2
Freeman, Francis O NewYHSD
Freeman, Frank 1862-1940 BnEnAmA
Freeman, Frank Nugent 1880-1961 BiDAmEd,
WhAm 4
Freeman, Frederick 1800-1883 ApCAB
Freeman, Frederick Kemper 1841-1928 DcAmB,
NatCAB 24
Freeman, Fulton 1915-1974 WhAm 6
Freeman, George 1789-1868 NewYHSD,
WhAm H
Freeman, George Fouche 1876-1930 WhAm 1
Freeman, George Washington 1789-1858
ApCAB, Drake, NatCAB 13, TwCBDA
Freeman, H Lawrence 1875- WhoColR
Freeman, Hadley Fairfield 1893-1951 WhAm 3
Freeman, Hal Elson 1907-1963 NatCAB 51
Freeman, Harrison Barber 1869-1942 WhAm 2
Freeman, Harrison Belknap 1838-1913
NatCAB 31
Freeman, Henry Blanchard 1837-1915 WhAm 1
Freeman, Henry Raymond 1860-1936 WhAm 1
Freeman, Henry Varnum 1842-1916 WhAm 1
Freeman, Hiram Guernsey 1844-1926
NatCAB 20
Freeman, Horatia Augusta Latilla 1826-
ApCAB
Freeman, Hovey Thomas 1894-1970
NatCAB 56
Freeman, James NewYHSD
Freeman, James 1759-1835 AmBi, ApCAB,
DcAmB, Drake, NatCAB 7, TwCBDA,
WhAm H
Freeman, James Crawford 1820-1885 BiAUS,
BiDrAC, WhAm H
Freeman, James Edward 1808-1884 ApCAB,
Drake, NatCAB 12, NewYHSD,
TwCBDA
Freeman, James Edward 1866-1943 ApCAB X,
NatCAB 12, NatCAB 32, WhAm 2
Freeman, James Edwards 1808-1884 DcAmB,
WhAm H
Freeman, James Henry 1909-1959 NatCAB 49
Freeman, James Midwinter 1827-1900 TwCBDA,
WhAm 1
Freeman, Joel Francis 1836- NatCAB 12
Freeman, John Charles 1842-1911 TwCBDA,
WhAm 1
Freeman, John D d1886 BiAUS, BiDrAC,
WhAm H
Freeman, John D, Jr. 1884-1974 WhAm 6
Freeman, John Dolliver 1864-1943 WhAm 2
Freeman, John Ripley 1855-1932 DcAmB S1,
NatCAB 36, WhAm 1
Freeman, John Ripley, Jr. 1895-1961
NatCAB 52
Freeman, John Shaw 1881-1964 NatCAB 51
Freeman, John William 1853-1926 WhAm 1
Freeman, John William 1900-1973 WhAm 6
Freeman, Jonathan 1745-1808 BiAUS, BiDrAC,

WhAm H, WhAmP

Freeman, Joseph 1897-1965 *WhAm 4*
Freeman, Joseph Hewett 1841- *WhAm 4*
Freeman, Joseph Wood 1863-1939 *NatCAB 31*
Freeman, Julia S Wheelock 1833-1900
NatCAB 7, WhAm 1
Freeman, Leonard 1860-1935 *WhAm 1,*
WhAm 4
Freeman, Lewis Ransome 1878- *WhAm 6*
Freeman, Lucy Jane 1872- *WomWWA 14*
Freeman, Luther 1866- *WhAm 4*
Freeman, Marilla Waite 1871-1961 *DcAmLiB*
Freeman, Mary Eleanor Wilkins 1852-1930
AmBi, DcAmB, NotAW, WebAB
Freeman, Mary Eleanor Wilkins 1862-1930
WhAm 1, WomWWA 14
Freeman, Mary L 1860- *WomWWA 14*
Freeman, Mattie A 1839- *AmWom*
Freeman, Miller 1875-1955 *WhAm 3*
Freeman, Monroe Edward 1906-1972 *WhAm 5*
Freeman, Nathaniel 1741-1820 *BiAUS*
Freeman, Nathaniel 1741-1827 *AmBi, ApCAB,*
DcAmB, Drake, NatCAB 2, TwCBDA,
WhAm H
Freeman, Nathaniel, Jr. 1766-1800 *BiDrAC,*
WhAm H, WhAmP
Freeman, Orville Lothrop 1918- *BiDrUSE,*
EncAAH
Freeman, Pliny 1798-1879 *NatCAB 11*
Freeman, R Austin 1862-1943 *WhAm 2*
Freeman, Ralph Evans 1894-1967 *NatCAB 53,*
WhAm 5
Freeman, Richard D 1910-1968 *WhAm 5*
Freeman, Richard Patrick 1869-1944 *BiDrAC,*
WhAm 2, WhAmP
Freeman, Robert 1878-1940 *WhAm 1*
Freeman, Rowland Godfrey 1859-1945 *WhAm 2*
Freeman, Rowland Godfrey 1894-1958
NatCAB 48
Freeman, Samuel 1743-1831 *ApCAB, BiAUS,*
Drake
Freeman, Sarah Jane 1867- *WomWWA 14*
Freeman, Sheldon Bower 1903-1964
NatCAB 50
Freeman, T W *NewYHSD*
Freeman, Talbot Otis 1890-1955 *WhAm 3*
Freeman, Thomas 1784-1821 *DcAmB,*
NatCAB 24, WhAm H
Freeman, Thomas J 1827-1891 *TwCBDA*
Freeman, Thomas J A 1841-1907 *WhAm 1*
Freeman, Thomas Jones 1859-1933 *WhAm 1*
Freeman, Thomas W 1824-1865 *BiDConf*
Freeman, W E 1927- *IIBEAAW*
Freeman, W Winans 1872- *WhAm 5*
Freeman, Walker Burford 1843-1935 *WhAm 1*
Freeman, Walter 1895-1972 *WhAm 5*
Freeman, Walter C *NewYHSD*
Freeman, Will 1897-1965 *WhAm 4*
Freeman, William Coleman 1881-1955
NatCAB 47
Freeman, William Grigsby 1815-1866 *ApCAB*
Freeman, William Perry 1858-1944 *WhAm 3*
Freeman, William R 1820?-1906? *NewYHSD*
Freeman, Winfield 1848-1926 *WhAm 1*
Freeman, Y Frank 1890-1969 *NatCAB 54,*
WhAm 5
Freeman, Zoheth Sparrow 1875- *NatCAB 16*
Freer, Arden 1888-1963 *NatCAB 51*
Freer, Charles Lang 1856-1919 *AmBi, DcAmB,*
NatCAB 15, WhAm 1
Freer, Eleanor Everest 1864-1942 *BiCAW,*
NatCAB 17, WhAm 2, WomWWA 14
Freer, Frederick Warren 1849-1908 *TwCBDA,*
WhAm 1
Freer, Hamline Hurlburt 1845-1920 *WhAm 1*
Freer, Howard Mortimer 1903-1960
NatCAB 48
Freer, Mrs. Otto *WomWWA 14*
Freer, Otto 1857-1932 *WhAm 1*
Freer, Paul Caspar 1862-1912 *NatCAB 19,*
TwCBDA, WhAm 1
Freer, Robert Elliott 1896-1963 *WhAm 4*
Freer, Romeo Hoyt 1845-1913 *WhAm 3*
Freer, Romeo Hoyt 1846-1913 *BiDrAC*
Freer, Romeo Hoyt 1847-1913 *TwCBDA*
Freer, William Davis 1880-1940 *WhAm 1*
Freericks, Frank Herman 1872-1941
NatCAB 31

Freerman, Barnardus 1660?-1734 *NatCAB 4*
Freerman, Barnardus *see also* Freeman,
Barnardus
Freese, John Henry 1876- *WhAm 5*
Freeston, William D 1910-1971 *WhAm 5*
Freestone, Fred James 1878-1961 *WhAm 4*
Frege, Friedrich Ludwig Gottlob 1848-1925
DcScB
Frege, Gottlob 1848-1925 *AsBiEn, McGEWB*
Frei Montalva, Eduardo 1911- *McGEWB*
Freiberg, Albert Henry 1868-1940 *NatCAB 30,*
WhAm 1
Freiberg, Joseph Albert 1898-1973 *WhAm 6*
Freiberg, Leonard Henry 1885-1954 *WhAm 3*
Freiberg, Maurice Julius 1861-1936 *NatCAB 27,*
WhAm 1
Freiberger, Isadore Fred 1879-1969 *WhAm 5*
Freidin, Jesse 1909-1968 *NatCAB 55,*
WhAm 5
Freiesleben, Johann Karl 1774-1846 *DcScB*
Freiler, Abraham J 1892-1962 *WhAm 4*
Freilich, Michael Leon 1912-1975 *NatCAB 57*
Freiman, Henry David 1913-1970 *WhAm 5*
Freimann, Frank Michael 1909-1968 *WhAm 5*
Frein, Pierre Joseph 1869-1954 *WhAm 3*
Freind, John 1675-1728 *DcScB*
Freire, Gomez 1685-1763 *ApCAB*
Freire, Luiz Jose Junqueira 1832-1855 *ApCAB*
Freire, Nicolas 1810-1880? *ApCAB*
Freire, Ramon 1787-1851 *ApCAB*
Freire DeAndrada, Gomez 1636-1702 *ApCAB*
Frejes, Francisco d1845 *ApCAB*
Freke, John 1688-1756 *BiHiMed*
Freley, Jasper Warren 1900- *WhAm 4*
Frelinghuysen, C Maria *NewYHSD*
Frelinghuysen, Frederick 1753-1804 *AmBi,*
ApCAB, BiAUS, BiDrAC, DcAmB,
Drake, NatCAB 7, TwCBDA, WhAm H,
WhAmP
Frelinghuysen, Frederick 1848-1924 *NatCAB 23*
Frelinghuysen, Frederick 1903-1966 *NatCAB 52,*
WhAm 4
Frelinghuysen, Frederick Theodore 1817-1885
AmBi, ApCAB, BiAUS, BiDrAC,
BiDrUSE, DcAmB, NatCAB 4,
NatCAB 43, TwCBDA, WhAm H,
WhAmP
Frelinghuysen, George Griswold 1851-1936
NatCAB 26
Frelinghuysen, John 1727-1754 *ApCAB*
Frelinghuysen, John 1776-1833 *ApCAB*
Frelinghuysen, Joseph Sherman 1869-1948
BiDrAC, NatCAB 42, WhAm 2, WhAmP
Frelinghuysen, Peter H Ballantine, Jr. 1916-
BiDrAC
Frelinghuysen, Peter Hood Ballantine 1882-1959
NatCAB 43
Frelinghuysen, Theodore 1787-1861 *ApCAB,*
BiDAmEd, NatCAB 3
Frelinghuysen, Theodore 1787-1862 *AmBi,*
BiAUS, BiDrAC, DcAmB, Drake,
TwCBDA, WhAm H, WhAmP
Frelinghuysen, Theodorus Jacobus 1691-1747
ApCAB
Frelinghuysen, Theodorus Jacobus 1691-1748?
DcAmB, McGEWB, NatCAB 12,
WhAm H
Frelinghuysen, Theodorus Jacobus 1691-1753
TwCBDA
Frelinghuysen, Theodorus Jacobus 1692-1748
DcAmReB
Fremd, Theodore 1863-1947 *NatCAB 35*
Fremin, Jacques d1691 *ApCAB*
Fremming, Morris A 1902-1953 *WhAm 3*
Fremont, Jessie Benton 1824-1902 *AmBi,*
AmWom, ApCAB, DcAmB, NatCAB 4,
NotAW, REnAW, WhAm 1
Fremont, Jessie Benton 1825-1902 *TwCBDA*
Fremont, John Charles 1813- *ApCAB, BiAUS,*
Drake
Fremont, John Charles 1813-1880 *WhoMilH*
Fremont, John Charles 1813-1890 *AmBi,*
BiDrAC, DcAmB, EncAAH, EncAB,
McGEWB, NatCAB 4, NewYHSD,
REnAW, TwCBDA, WebAB, WebAMB,

WhAm H, WhAmP

Fremont, John Charles 1849-1911 *WhAm 1*
Fremont, John Charles 1851- *TwCBDA*
Fremont-Smith, Frank 1895-1974 *WhAm 6*
Fremstad, Olive d1951 *WomWWA 14,*
WhAm 3
Fremstad, Olive 1868-1951 *NatCAB 40*
Fremstad, Olive 1870-1951 *ApCAB X*
Fremy, Edmond 1814-1894 *DcScB*
French, A C d1864 *BiAUS, Drake*
French, A C *see also* French, Augustus C
French, Aaron 1823-1902 *ApCAB X, DcAmB,*
NatCAB 24, WhAm H
French, Alice 1850-1934 *AmBi, AmWom,*
ApCAB Sup, ApCAB X, DcAmB S1,
NatCAB 10, NatCAB 25, NotAW,
TwCBDA, WhAm 1
French, Alice 1856- *WomWWA 14*
French, Alice Helm 1864- *WomWWA 14*
French, Allen 1870-1946 *NatCAB 34,*
WhAm 2
French, Amos Tuck 1863-1941 *WhAm 1,*
WhAm 2
French, Anne Warner 1869-1913 *WhAm 1*
French, Arthur Willard 1868- *WhAm 4*
French, Asa 1829-1903 *NatCAB 14*
French, Asa Palmer 1860-1935 *ApCAB X,*
WhAm 1
French, Augustus C 1808-1864 *WhAm H*
French, Augustus C 1808-1868 *NatCAB 11*
French, Augustus C *see also* French, A C
French, Benjamin B *BiAUS*
French, Benjamin Franklin 1799-1877 *ApCAB,*
Drake, NatCAB 3, TwCBDA
French, Blanche Cate 1864- *WomWWA 14*
French, Burton Lee 1875-1954 *BiDrAC,*
WhAm 3, WhAmP
French, C *NewYHSD*
French, C E G *BiAUS*
French, Calvin Hervey 1862-1934 *NatCAB 25,*
TwCBDA, WhAm 1
French, Carlos 1835-1903 *BiDrAC*
French, Charles Wallace 1858-1920 *NatCAB 18,*
WhAm 1
French, Clifton G A *WhoColR*
French, Daniel Chester 1850-1931 *AmBi,*
ApCAB, ApCAB X, BnEnAmA,
DcAmB S1, McGEWB, NatCAB 1,
NatCAB 8, NatCAB 31, TwCBDA,
WebAB, WhAm 1
French, Darwin Gallatin 1845-1933 *NatCAB 25*
French, David 1700-1742 *ApCAB*
French, David M 1827-1910 *NewYHSD*
French, Dudley Kimball 1881-1960 *NatCAB 49*
French, Edward L 1916- *WhAm 5*
French, Edward Sanborn 1883-1968
NatCAB 55, WhAm 5
French, Edward Vinton 1868-1957 *NatCAB 47,*
WhAm 3
French, Edwin Davis 1851-1906 *DcAmB,*
NatCAB 14, WhAm 1
French, Ezra Bartlett 1810-1880 *BiAUS,*
BiDrAC, WhAm H, WhAmP
French, Fanny Bartlett 1869- *WomWWA 14*
French, Ferdinand Courtney 1861-1927
TwCBDA, WhAm 1
French, Florence Kelsey 1868- *WomWWA 14*
French, Frances Graham d1919 *WhAm 1,*
WomWWA 14
French, Francis Henry 1857-1921 *WhAm 1*
French, Francis Ormond 1837-1893 *NatCAB 2*
French, Frank 1850-1933 *NatCAB 11,*
WhAm 1
French, Frank Chauncey 1876-1956 *WhAm 3*
French, George 1853-1935 *WhAm 1*
French, George Henry 1825-1888 *NatCAB 21*
French, George R *NewYHSD*
French, George Watson 1858- *ApCAB X*
French, Grace Preston 1876- *WomWWA 14*
French, Harlan Page 1843-1921 *WhAm 1*
French, Harley Ellsworth 1873- *WhAm 5*
French, Harry Banks 1857-1925 *NatCAB 20*
French, Helen Cornell 1875- *WomWWA 14*
French, Helen Goodwin *WomWWA 14*
French, Henry Flagg 1813-1885 *NatCAB 25,*
TwCBDA
French, Henry Willard 1854- *WhAm 4*
French, Herbert Greer 1872-1942 *NatCAB 31,*

WhAm 2
French, Hollis 1868-1940 *WhAm 1*
French, Horace S 1894-1966 *WhAm 4*
French, Howard Barclay 1848-1924 *NatCAB 5, WhAm 1*
French, J H *NewYHSD*
French, Jacob 1754- *WhAm H*
French, James Adolphus d1916 *WhAm 1*
French, James Benton 1863-1947 *NatCAB 36*
French, James J 1859- *WhAm 4*
French, John Charles 1854-1922 *NatCAB 27*
French, John Denton Pinkstone 1852-1925 *WhoMilH*
French, John Raymond 1825-1897 *NatCAB 2*
French, John Robert 1819-1890 *BiAUS, BiDrAC, WhAm H*
French, John Shaw 1873- *WhAm 5*
French, John Stewart 1872-1952 *NatCAB 51, WhAm 5*
French, John T *NewYHSD*
French, John William 1809-1871 *TwCBDA*
French, John William 1810?-1871 *ApCAB*
French, Jonathan 1740-1809 *NatCAB 10*
French, Joseph Lewis 1858-1936 *WhAm 4*
French, Joseph Milton 1895-1962 *WhAm 4*
French, L Virginia 1830-1881 *ApCAB, Drake, NatCAB 7*
French, Lafayette, Jr. 1887-1944 *NatCAB 33*
French, Leigh Hill 1863- *WhAm 4*
French, Lillie Hamilton 1854- *WhAm 4, WomWWA 14*
French, Lizzie H Norton 1856- *WomWWA 14*
French, Lucy Virginia Smith 1825-1881 *DcAmB, WhAm H*
French, Mansfield 1810-1876 *ApCAB, TwCBDA*
French, Mary Adams 1859- *WhAm 4*
French, Mary Montagu Billings 1869-1951 *WhAm 3, WomWWA 14*
French, Minnie Waller *WhoColR*
French, Nathaniel 1854-1920 *ApCAB X, NatCAB 21*
French, Nathaniel Stowers 1854-1905 *WhAm 1*
French, Owen Bert 1865- *WhAm 4*
French, Paul Comly 1903-1960 *WhAm 4*
French, Pearmeal Jane 1849- *WomWWA 14*
French, Peter 1849-1897 *REnAW*
French, Pinckney 1852- *NatCAB 11, WhAm 4*
French, Ralph Lines 1861-1945 *WhAm 2*
French, Ralph Winward 1883-1942 *NatCAB 41*
French, Richard 1792-1854 *BiAUS, BiDrAC, WhAm H, WhAmP*
French, Robert Dudley 1888-1954 *WhAm 3*
French, Roy Laverne 1888-1968 *WhAm 5*
French, Rufus Tyler 1881-1924 *NatCAB 20*
French, Samuel Gibbs 1818-1910 *ApCAB Sup, BiDConf, TwCBDA, WhAm 1*
French, Seward Haight, Jr. 1907-1954 *WhAm 3*
French, Shirley Smith 1881-1936 *NatCAB 27*
French, Stuart Whitney 1867-1946 *NatCAB 35*
French, Thomas 1639-1699 *WhAm H*
French, Thomas 1848- *TwCBDA*
French, Thomas Ewing 1871-1944 *WhAm 2*
French, W Shepard 1884-1957 *NatCAB 46*
French, Wilfred A 1855-1928 *ApCAB X*
French, Will J 1871-1947 *WhAm 2*
French, Willard 1854- *WhAm 4*
French, Willard S 1887-1959 *WhAm 3*
French, William 1917-1962 *WhAm 4*
French, William Cullen 1883-1950 *NatCAB 39*
French, William Henry 1815-1881 *ApCAB, DcAmB, NatCAB 4, TwCBDA, WhAm H*
French, William Henry 1818?-1881 *Drake*
French, William Henry 1850- *WhAm 4*
French, William John 1854-1928 *WhAm 1*
French, William Merchant Richardson 1843-1914 *DcAmB, NatCAB 14, NatCAB 15, WhAm 1*
French, William W, Jr. 1900-1970 *WhAm 5*
Freneau, Philip Morin 1752-1832 *AmBi, ApCAB, DcAmB, Drake, EncAB, McGEWB, NatCAB 6, WebAB, WhAm H*
Frenet, Jean-Frederic 1816-1900 *DcScB*
Frenger, Laura E 1873- *WomWWA 14*
Frenicle DeBessy, Bernard 1605?-1675 *DcScB*

Frenkel, Yakov Ilyich 1894-1954 *DcScB*
Frenzel, Friedrich August 1842-1902 *DcScB*
Frenzel, John Peter, Jr. 1881-1949 *WhAm 2*
Frenzeny, Paul 1840?-1902 *IlBEAAW, REnAW*
Frere, Sir Henry Bartle Edward 1815-1884 *McGEWB*
Frere, John 1740-1807 *DcScB*
Frere, Thomas *NewYHSD*
Freret, James 1839-1897 *WhAm H*
Freret, William Alfred 1833- *WhAm 4*
Freri, Joseph 1864- *WhAm 4*
Frerichs, Frederick William 1849-1939 *NatCAB 29*
Frerichs, William Charles Anthony 1829?-1905 *NewYHSD*
Frerichs, William Reinhard 1877- *WhAm 3*
Frerking, Herbert William 1915-1973 *WhAm 6*
Freschl, Robert 1881-1949 *NatCAB 37*
Frescobaldi, Girolamo 1583-1643 *McGEWB*
Freseman, William Langfitt 1901-1971 *WhAm 5*
Fresenius, Carl Remigius 1818-1897 *DcScB*
Freshwater, Robert Marquis 1899- *WhAm 4*
Fresnel, Augustin Jean 1788-1827 *AsBiEn, DcScB, McGEWB*
Fretter, Frank Bertram 1864-1935 *NatCAB 27, WhAm 1*
Fretwell, Elbert Kirtley 1878-1962 *BiDAmEd, NatCAB 49, WhAm 4*
Fretz, Franklin Kline 1876-1941 *WhAm 2*
Fretz, William Fox 1870-1951 *NatCAB 40*
Freuchen, Peter 1886-1957 *WhAm 3*
Freud, Sigmund 1856-1939 *AsBiEn, BiHiMed, DcScB, McGEWB, WhAm HA, WhAm 4*
Freudenberg, E G *NewYHSD*
Freudenberger, Clay Briscoe 1904-1946 *WhAm 2*
Freuler, John Rudolph 1872-1958 *WhAm 3*
Freund, Edmund Joseph 1889-1944 *NatCAB 34*
Freund, Ernst 1864-1932 *DcAmB S1, NatCAB 26, WhAm 1*
Freund, Erwin O 1888-1947 *WhAm 3*
Freund, Gustav, II 1913-1956 *NatCAB 45*
Freund, Henry *NewYHSD*
Freund, Hugo Abraham 1881-1952 *WhAm 3*
Freund, John Frederick 1874-1932 *NatCAB 24*
Freund, Jules 1890-1960 *WhAm 4*
Freund, Lillian A Myers 1874- *WomWWA 14*
Freund, Sanford H E 1880-1954 *WhAm 3*
Freundlich, Erwin Finlay 1885-1964 *DcScB*
Freundlich, Herbert Max Finlay 1880-1941 *DcScB Sup*
Freutel, Guy Scott 1921-1959 *WhAm 3*
Frevert, Harry Louis 1881-1947 *NatCAB 40, WhAm 6*
Frevet, William Alfred 1833- *ApCAB Sup*
Frew, Walter Edwin 1864-1941 *NatCAB 7, WhAm 1*
Frew, William 1881-1948 *WhAm 2*
Frew, William Nimick 1854-1915 *ApCAB X, NatCAB 36, WhAm 1*
Frey, Adolf 1865- *WhAm 4*
Frey, Adolph Julius 1875-1922 *NatCAB 22*
Frey, Albert R 1858- *WhAm 4*
Frey, Arthur Garfield 1883-1937 *NatCAB 28*
Frey, Calvin Alexander 1887-1947 *WhAm 2*
Frey, Charles Daniel 1886-1959 *WhAm 3*
Frey, Charles N 1885-1972 *NatCAB 56*
Frey, Erwin Mortimer 1906-1969 *WhAm 5*
Frey, Henry *NewYHSD*
Frey, Henry B 1845- *NatCAB 6*
Frey, John Philip 1871-1957 *NatCAB 47, WhAm 3*
Frey, John Walter 1892-1955 *WhAm 3*
Frey, John Weaver 1889-1971 *WhAm 5*
Frey, Joseph *BiAUS*
Frey, Joseph Samuel C F 1772-1850 *Drake*
Frey, Joseph Samuel Christian Frederick 1771-1850 *DcAmB, WhAm H*
Frey, Joseph Samuel Christian Frederick 1773-1850 *ApCAB*
Frey, Louis, Jr. 1934- *BiDrAC*
Frey, Maximilian Ruppert Franz Von 1852-1932 *DcScB*
Frey, Oliver W 1890-1939 *WhAm 1*
Frey, Oliver Walter 1887-1939 *BiDrAC*

Frey, Walter Guernsey, Jr. 1896-1965 *WhAm 4*
Freyberg, Sir Bernard 1889-1963 *WhAm 4, WhWW-II*
Freyburg, Bernard Cyril 1889-1963 *WhoMilH*
Freyer, William Norman 1903-1961 *WhAm 4*
Freyre, Gilberto 1900- *McGEWB*
Freytag, Gustav 1816-1895 *McGEWB*
Freyvogel, C Ernest Cecil 1888-1950 *WhAm 2*
Frezier, Amedee Francois 1682-1773 *ApCAB, Drake*
Frias, Felix 1820-1881 *ApCAB*
Frias, Francisco 1809-1877 *ApCAB*
Frias, Tomas 1805-1884 *ApCAB*
Friberg, Arnold 1913- *IlBEAAW*
Fribergius, Kalbius *DcScB*
Frick, Abraham Oppenlander 1852-1934 *NatCAB 24*
Frick, Bernard Armin 1910-1967 *NatCAB 53*
Frick, Bertha Margaret 1894-1975 *DcAmLiB*
Frick, Charles 1823-1860 *ApCAB, Drake*
Frick, Euclid Bernardo 1867-1954 *NatCAB 43*
Frick, Frank 1828- *NatCAB 1, WhAm 1*
Frick, Henry 1795-1844 *BiAUS, BiDrAC, WhAm H*
Frick, Henry Clay 1849-1919 *AmBi, ApCAB Sup, ApCAB X, DcAmB, EncAB, McGEWB, NatCAB 10, NatCAB 23, WebAB, WhAm 1*
Frick, John Henry 1845-1927 *WhAm 3*
Frick, Joseph E 1848-1927 *NatCAB 17, NatCAB 22, WhAm 1*
Frick, Mary Foster Gaylord *WomWWA 14*
Frick, Philip Louis 1874- *WhAm 5*
Frick, Wilhelm 1877-1946 *WhWW-II*
Frick, William Jacob d1942 *WhAm 2*
Frick, William Keller 1850-1918 *NatCAB 18, WhAm 1*
Fricke, William A 1857- *WhAm 4*
Fricks, Lunsford Dickson 1873-1947 *NatCAB 36, WhAm 2*
Friday 1822?-1881 *DcAmB, WhAm H*
Friday, Charles Bostwick 1921-1975 *WhAm 6*
Friday, David 1876-1945 *NatCAB 34, WhAm 2*
Friden, Carl Mauritz Fredrick 1891-1945 *NatCAB 54*
Friden, John H 1896-1962 *WhAm 4*
Fridenberg, Percy 1868-1960 *WhAm 4*
Fridge, Benjamin Franklin 1856- *WhAm 3*
Friebolin, Brookes 1910-1947 *NatCAB 35*
Friebolin, Carl D 1878- *WhAm 6*
Fried, George 1877- *WhAm 5*
Friedan, Betty Naomi Goldstein 1921- *EncAB, WebAB*
Friedberg, Robert 1912-1963 *NatCAB 50*
Friedeburg, Hans Von *WhWW-II*
Friedel, Charles 1832-1899 *AsBiEn*
Friedel, Francis Joseph 1897- *WhAm 3*
Friedel, Georges 1865-1933 *DcScB*
Friedel, Jacob Hyman 1892-1946 *NatCAB 36*
Friedel, Samuel Nathaniel 1898- *BiDrAC*
Frieden, Alexander 1895-1956 *WhAm 3*
Frieden, John Pierre 1844-1911 *WhAm 1*
Frieden, Pierre 1892-1959 *WhAm 3*
Friedenberg, Albert Marx 1881- *WhAm 6*
Friedenberg, Samuel 1886-1957 *NatCAB 43*
Friedenwald, Aaron 1836-1902 *DcAmB, NatCAB 23, WhAm H*
Friedenwald, Harry 1864-1950 *NatCAB 37, WhAm 3*
Friedenwald, Herbert 1870-1944 *WhAm 2*
Friedenwald, Jonas Stein 1897-1955 *NatCAB 42, WhAm 3*
Friedenwald, Julius 1866-1941 *NatCAB 30, WhAm 1*
Frieder, Marcus 1860-1940 *NatCAB 30*
Friedheim, Arthur 1859-1932 *NatCAB 24*
Friedlaender, Israel 1876-1920 *DcAmB, WhAm 1*
Friedlaender, Walter 1873-1966 *WhAm 4*
Friedland, Jacob Moses 1879-1964 *NatCAB 50*
Friedlander, Alfred 1871-1939 *NatCAB 32, WhAm 1*
Friedlander, Edwin M 1879-1928 *ApCAB X*
Friedlander, Israel 1888-1944 *WhAm 2*
Friedlander, Jackson H 1909-1972 *WhAm 6*
Friedlander, Lee 1934- *BnEnAmA*
Friedlander, Leo 1890-1966 *WhAm 4*

Friedlander, Rebecca *WomWWA 14*
Friedlander, Theodore 1886-1952 *WhAm 3*
Friedlein, Frederick 1851- *NatCAB 12*
Friedman, Bernard 1915-1966 *WhAm 4*
Friedman, Eli 1890-1972 *NatCAB 57*
Friedman, Elisha Michael 1889-1951
NatCAB 39, WhAm 3
Friedman, Emanuel David 1884- *WhAm 3*
Friedman, Esther Pauline 1918- *WebAB*
Friedman, Francis Lee 1918-1962 *WhAm 4*
Friedman, Harry G 1881-1965 *WhAm 4*
Friedman, Herbert 1916- *AsBiEn*
Friedman, Herbert Jacob 1876-1956 *WhAm 3*
Friedman, Herman 1855-1935 *NatCAB 27*
Friedman, Isaac Kahn 1869-1931 *NatCAB 23*
Friedman, Isaac Kahn 1870-1931 *WhAm 1*
Friedman, Jacob Henry 1903-1973 *WhAm 6*
Friedman, John Henry 1892-1962 *NatCAB 49*
Friedman, Lee Max 1871-1957 *WhAm 4*
Friedman, Louis 1889-1960 *NatCAB 46*
Friedman, Max 1888-1966 *NatCAB 52*
Friedman, Milton 1912- *EncAB, WebAB*
Friedman, Moses 1874- *WhAm 5*
Friedman, Pauline Esther 1918- *WebAB*
Friedman, Peter Henry 1882-1957 *NatCAB 46*
Friedman, Samuel 1906-1970 *WhAm 5*
Friedman, Sol H 1895-1957 *WhAm 3*
Friedman, Stanleigh Pohly 1884-1960 *WhAm 4*
Friedman, William 1880-1963 *NatCAB 50*
Friedman, William Frederic 1891-1969
WhWW-II
Friedman, William Frederick 1891-1969
WhAm 5
Friedman, William Henry 1886-1963 *WhAm 4*
Friedman, William Sterne 1868-1944
NatCAB 38, WhAm 2
Friedmann, Aleksandr Aleksandrovich 1888-1925
DcScB
Friedmann, Max E 1890-1954 *WhAm 3*
Friedmann, Wolfgang Gaston 1907-1972
WhAm 5
Friedrich Karl, Prinz 1828-1885 *WhoMilH*
Friedrich Wilhelm, Duke Of Brunswick
1771-1815 *WhoMilH*
Friedrich, Caspar David 1774-1840 *McGEWB*
Friedrich, Ferdinand August 1871- *WhAm 6*
Friedrich, Hans Rudolf 1911-1958 *NatCAB 46*
Friedsam, Michael d1931 *WhAm 1*
Friedson, Morris 1881-1947 *NatCAB 34*
Friees, Horace Leland 1900-1975 *WhAm 6*
Friel, Arthur Olney 1885-1959 *WhAm 3*
Friel, Francis DeSales 1894-1964 *NatCAB 50,
WhAm 4*
Friel, Henry Craig 1901-1971 *WhAm 5*
Frields, Eva Christine 1873- *WhAm 5*
Friend, Albert Mathias, Jr. 1894-1956 *WhAm 3*
Friend, Albert Wiley 1910-1972 *WhAm 5*
Friend, Clarence Lewis 1878-1958 *NatCAB 48*
Friend, Emanuel Michael 1853- *NatCAB 12*
Friend, Emil 1863-1921 *NatCAB 17, WhAm 1*
Friend, John Albert Newton 1881-1966 *DcScB*
Friend, Kate Harrison 1872- *WomWWA 14*
Friend, Leo Joseph 1872-1957 *NatCAB 43*
Friend, May Belle Willis 1872- *WomWWA 14*
Friend, Norman 1815?- *NewYHSD*
Friend, Oscar Jerome 1897-1963 *WhAm 4*
Friend, Robert Alonzo 1906-1964 *NatCAB 51*
Friend, Robert Elias 1886-1962 *NatCAB 53*
Friend, Robert Ellas 1886-1962 *WhAm 4*
Friend, Victor Alonzo 1870-1952 *NatCAB 42*
Friend, Washington F 1820?- *IlBEAAW*
Friendly, Edwin Samson 1884-1970 *WhAm 5*
Friendly, Oscar Nathan 1884-1975 *WhAm 6*
Frierson, Horace 1881-1956 *WhAm 3*
Frierson, James Nelson 1874-1960 *NatCAB 52,
WhAm 4*
Frierson, John Woods 1897-1959 *NatCAB 48,
WhAm 3*
Frierson, William Little 1868-1953 *NatCAB 47,
WhAm 3*
Fries, Adelaide Lisetta 1871-1949 *WhAm 2,
WomWWA 14*
Fries, Amos Alfred 1873- *WhAm 5*
Fries, Archibald 1864-1930 *WhAm 1*
Fries, Charles Carpenter 1887-1967 *NatCAB 54*
Fries, Elias Magnus 1794-1878 *DcScB*
Fries, Elmer Plumas 1884-1949 *WhAm 3*
Fries, Emma Riddell 1881- *WomWWA 14*

Fries, Francis 1812-1863 *DcAmB, WhAm H*
Fries, Francis Henry 1855-1931 *NatCAB 27,
WhAm 1*
Fries, Frank William 1893- *BiDrAC*
Fries, George 1799-1866 *BiAUS, BiDrAC,
WhAm H*
Fries, Gustave Wilhelm 1874-1941 *NatCAB 33*
Fries, Harold Harry 1866-1946 *NatCAB 33*
Fries, J Elias 1876-1932 *WhAm 1*
Fries, Jakob Friedrich 1773-1843 *DcScB,
McGEWB*
Fries, John 1750?-1818 *AmBi, DcAmB,
EncAAH, WhAm H*
Fries, John 1764?-1825? *ApCAB*
Fries, John William 1846-1927 *WhAm 1*
Fries, William Hayes 1878-1959 *NatCAB 47*
Fries, William Otterbein 1860-1925 *WhAm 1*
Frieseke, Frederick Carl 1874-1939 *DcAmB S2,
WhAm 1*
Friesell, H Edmund 1873-1946 *NatCAB 36,
WhAm 2*
Friesen, Abraham Penner 1887-1953 *WhAm 3*
Friesen, Henry J 1880-1951 *NatCAB 43*
Friesner, Isidore 1874-1945 *NatCAB 35*
Friesner, Ray Clarence 1894-1952 *WhAm 3*
Friessner, Johannes 1892- *WhWW-II*
Frietchie, Barbara 1776?-1862 *WhAm H*
Frietschie, Barbara Hauer 1766-1862 *NotAW*
Frieze, Henry Simmons 1817-1889 *ApCAB,
BiDAmEd, DcAmB, NatCAB 1,
TwCBDA, WhAm H*
Friley, Charles Edwin 1887-1958 *WhAm 3*
Frillmann, Paul William 1911-1972 *NatCAB 57*
Friml, Rudolf 1879-1972 *WebAB, WhAm 5*
Frinck, O E S *NewYHSD*
Frink, A *NewYHSD*
Frink, Carl Heman 1886-1958 *NatCAB 53*
Frink, Fred Goodrich 1862-1929 *NatCAB 25,
WhAm 1*
Frink, Henry Allyn 1844-1898 *TwCBDA*
Frink, Horace Westlake 1883-1936 *NatCAB 27*
Frink, John 1731-1807 *ApCAB*
Frink, John Melancthon 1845- *ApCAB X*
Frink, John Samuel Hatch 1832-1905 *WhAm 1*
Frink, Joy L 1866-1946 *NatCAB 36*
Fripp, Charles Edwin 1854-1906 *IlBEAAW*
Fripp, Thomas William 1864-1931 *IlBEAAW*
Fripp, William J 1863- *WhAm 4*
Frisbee, Samuel Hanna 1840- *NatCAB 4,
TwCBDA*
Frisbie, Alvan Lillie 1830-1917 *WhAm 1*
Frisbie, Edward Laurens, Jr. 1854-1929
NatCAB 23
Frisbie, Guy Stoddard 1903-1968 *NatCAB 54,
WhAm 5*
Frisbie, Henry Samuel 1863- *WhAm 4*
Frisbie, Levi 1748-1806 *ApCAB*
Frisbie, Levi 1783-1822 *ApCAB, DcAmB,
Drake, NatCAB 7, TwCBDA, WhAm H*
Frisbie, Martha C 1840- *WomWWA 14*
Frisbie, Robert Dean 1896- *WhAm 2*
Frisbie, William Albert 1867- *WhAm 4*
Frisby, Almah J 1857- *AmWom*
Frisby, Edgar 1837-1927 *ApCAB, TwCBDA,
WhAm 1*
Frisby, Leander F 1825-1889 *NatCAB 2*
Frisch, David 1902-1970 *NatCAB 56*
Frisch, Ephraim 1880-1957 *NatCAB 43*
Frisch, Hartvig 1893-1950 *WhAm 2A*
Frisch, Karl Von 1886- *AsBiEn, McGEWB*
Frisch, Martin 1899-1959 *WhAm 3*
Frisch, Max 1911- *McGEWB*
Frisch, Otto Robert 1904- *AsBiEn*
Frisch, Ragnar Anton Kittil 1895-1973
WhAm 4
Frisch, William 1854- *WhAm 1*
Frishmuth, Harriet Whitney 1880- *WhAm 6*
Frisi, Paolo 1728-1784 *DcScB*
Frisinger, Rolla Nathan 1890-1961 *NatCAB 48*
Frisius, Gemma *DcScB*
Frison, Theodore Henry 1895-1945 *WhAm 2*
Frissell, Algernon Sydney 1845-1932 *ApCAB X,
NatCAB 23, WhAm 1*
Frissell, Hollis Burke 1851-1917 *ApCAB X,
BiDAmEd, DcAmB, NatCAB 13,
NatCAB 18, TwCBDA, WhAm 1*
Frissell, Lewis Fox 1872-1943 *NatCAB 32*
Frissell, Lewis Varick 1903-1931 *NatCAB 23*

Frissell, Seraph 1840- *AmWom*
Fristoe, Edward T 1830-1892 *ApCAB,
TwCBDA*
Frisz, Frederick John 1887-1949 *NatCAB 38*
Fritch, Louis Charlton 1869- *WhAm 5*
Fritchie, Barbara 1766-1862 *NatCAB 10,
NotAW*
Fritsch, F J *NewYHSD*
Fritsch, Gustav Theodor 1838-1927 *DcScB*
Fritsch, Homer Charles 1894-1957 *WhAm 3*
Fritsch, Werner, Freiherr Von 1880-1939
WhoMilH
Fritsch, Werner Von 1880-1939 *WhWW-II*
Fritschel, Conrad Sigmund 1833-1900 *ApCAB,
DcAmB, WhAm H*
Fritschel, Constantine Sigmund 1833-1900
TwCBDA
Fritschel, George John 1867- *WhAm 4*
Fritschel, Gottfried Leonhard Wilhelm
1836-1889 *ApCAB, DcAmB, WhAm H*
Fritschel, Gottfried Wilhelm Leonhard
1836-1889 *TwCBDA*
Fritschel, Herman L 1869- *WhAm 5*
Fritts, Carl Emerson 1900-1970 *WhAm 5*
Fritts, Lewis Canfield 1903-1961 *NatCAB 50*
Fritz, Alfred Joseph 1871-1949 *NatCAB 38*
Fritz, Charles Bossert 1862-1944 *NatCAB 33*
Fritz, Herbert Daniel 1908-1969 *WhAm 5*
Fritz, Jacob *NewYHSD*
Fritz, John 1822-1913 *DcAmB, NatCAB 13,
WhAm 1*
Fritz, John Henry Charles 1874-1953 *WhAm 3*
Fritz, Lawrence G 1896-1970 *WhAm 5*
Fritz, Oscar Marion 1878-1957 *WhAm 3*
Fritz, Samuel 1653-1728 *ApCAB*
Fritz, William C 1866- *NatCAB 7*
Fritz, William Francis 1911-1972 *NatCAB 57*
Fritz, William Wallace 1872- *NatCAB 16*
Fritzsche, Carl Ferdinand 1903-1960 *WhAm 4*
Fritzsche, Carl Julius 1808-1871 *DcScB*
Frizell, Joseph Palmer 1832-1910 *DcAmB,
NatCAB 23, WhAm 1*
Frizol, Sylvester M 1906-1972 *WhAm 5*
Frizzell, Albert Burnett 1891-1934 *WhAm 1*
Frizzell, Bonner 1882-1968 *NatCAB 55*
Frizzell, Donald Leslie 1906-1972 *WhAm 5*
Frobenius, Georg Ferdinand 1849-1917 *DcScB*
Froberger, Johann Jakob 1616-1667 *McGEWB*
Frobisher, Sir Martin 1536?-1594 *ApCAB,
Drake, WhAm H*
Frobisher, Sir Martin 1538?-1594 *McGEWB*
Froebel, Friedrich Wilhelm August 1782-1852
McGEWB
Froebel, Julius 1806- *ApCAB*
Froedtert, Kurtis R 1887-1951 *WhAm 3*
Froehlich, Ava M 1863- *WomWWA 14*
Froehlich, Jack E 1921-1967 *WhAm 4*
Froehlinger, Richard Anthony 1887-1955
WhAm 3
Froelicher, Frances Mitchell 1854-
WomWWA 14
Froelicher, Francis Mitchell 1892-1960
WhAm 4
Froelicher, Hans 1865-1930 *NatCAB 37,
WhAm 1*
Froeligh, Solomon 1750-1827 *ApCAB*
Froggatt, Joseph 1868-1940 *NatCAB 29*
Froggett, Joseph Frederick 1870-1942
NatCAB 32
Frohlich, Alfred 1871-1953 *BiHiMed*
Frohlich, Ludwig William 1913-1971 *WhAm 5*
Frohman, Charles 1858-1915 *NatCAB 11*
Frohman, Charles 1860-1915 *AmBi, DcAmB,
WebAB, WhAm 1*
Frohman, Daniel 1851-1940 *DcAmB S2,
NatCAB 11, WhAm 1*
Frohman, Daniel 1853-1940 *TwCBDA*
Frohman, Philip Hubert 1887-1972 *WhAm 5*
Frohman, Sidney 1881-1964 *NatCAB 57,
WhAm 4*
Frohrieb, Louis Charles 1887-1966 *NatCAB 51*
Frohring, William Otto 1893-1959 *WhAm 3*
Froissart, Jean 1337?-1404? *McGEWB*
Frolich, Finn Haakon 1868-1947 *NatCAB 38,
WhAm 2*
Froman, Robert Hiram 1885-1949 *NatCAB 38*
Fromen, Anthony William 1880-1951
NatCAB 45

Froment, Jacques Victor Eugene 1820-1900
  IlBEAAW
Fromentin, Eligius d1822 ApCAB, BiAUS,
  BiDrAC, Drake, NatCAB 12, TwCBDA,
  WhAm H, WhAmP
Fromhagen, Frederick N NewYHSD
Fromkes, Maurice 1872-1931 WhAm 1
Fromm, Erich 1900- EncAB, WebAB
Fromm, Friedrich 1888-1945 WhWW-II
Fromme, Frederick W NewYHSD
Frommelt, Henry Julius 1911-1971 WhAm 5
Fromont, Charles H NewYHSD
Fromuth, Charles Henry 1861- WhAm 4
Fronczak, Francis Eustace 1874-1955
  NatCAB 43
Fronefield, W Roger 1864-1943 NatCAB 37
Froning, Henry Bernhardt 1884-1960
  NatCAB 48, WhAm 4
Frontenac, Louis DeBuade 1620-1698 WhAm H
Frontenac, Louis DeBuade, Comte De 1620-1698
  ApCAB
Frontenac, Louis DeBuade, Comte De 1622-1698
  McGEWB
Frontenac, Louis DeBuade, Count De 1620-1698
  Drake
Frontinus, Sextus Julius 030?-104 AsBiEn
Frontinus, Sextus Julius 035?-104? McGEWB
Frontz, William Archibald 1885-1934
  NatCAB 25
Frosh, Charles Franklin 1884-1947 NatCAB 35
Frost, Albert Dalbey 1889-1945 NatCAB 36,
  WhAm 2
Frost, Albert Ellis 1851-1917 WhAm 1
Frost, Albert Henry 1851-1912 NatCAB 15
Frost, Alfred Sidney 1858-1922 NatCAB 6,
  WhAm 1
Frost, Arthur Burdett 1851-1928 AmBi,
  DcAmB, IlBEAAW, NatCAB 11,
  WhAm 1
Frost, C K NewYHSD
Frost, C R NewYHSD
Frost, Charles 1632-1697 ApCAB, Drake
Frost, Charles Christopher 1806-1880 ApCAB
Frost, Charles Hamilton 1870-1926 ApCAB X
Frost, Charles Sumner 1856-1931 ApCAB X,
  NatCAB 17, NatCAB 26, WhAm 1
Frost, Cyrus 1820-1904 NatCAB 23
Frost, Daniel Marsh 1823- NatCAB 5
Frost, E Allen 1871-1963 NatCAB 50
Frost, Edward 1801-1868 BiAUS
Frost, Edward J 1873-1944 NatCAB 32,
  WhAm 2
Frost, Edward Justin 1869-1944 NatCAB 33
Frost, Edward Wheeler 1859- WhAm 4
Frost, Edwin Brant 1866-1935 AmBi,
  DcAmB S1, DcScB, NatCAB 9,
  NatCAB 25, TwCBDA, WhAm 1
Frost, Edwin Hunt 1874-1952 NatCAB 41
Frost, Edwin Parker 1846-1927 NatCAB 22
Frost, Eliott Park 1884-1926 NatCAB 21,
  WhAm 1
Frost, Frances 1905-1959 WhAm 3
Frost, Frederick George 1876-1966 NatCAB 51,
  WhAm 5
Frost, Fredric Worthen 1870-1938 WhAm 1
Frost, George 1720-1796 ApCAB, BiAUS,
  BiDrAC, Drake, TwCBDA, WhAm H
Frost, George Frederick 1872-1964 WhAm 4
Frost, George Henry 1838-1917 NatCAB 18,
  WhAm 1
Frost, Harold Locke 1875-1940 NatCAB 30
Frost, Harry Talfourd 1887-1943 WhAm 2
Frost, Henry Atherton 1883-1952 NatCAB 41,
  WhAm 3
Frost, Henry E 1877-1960 NatCAB 47
Frost, Henry Weston 1858-1945 WhAm 3
Frost, Hildreth 1880- WhAm 6
Frost, Holloway Halstead 1889-1935
  DcAmB S1
Frost, James Henry Paine 1825-1875 ApCAB
Frost, James Marion d1917 WhAm 1
Frost, James Nathan 1885-1949 NatCAB 41
Frost, Joel d1827 BiAUS, BiDrAC,
  WhAm H
Frost, John 1738-1810 ApCAB, NatCAB 1,
  TwCBDA
Frost, John 1800-1859 AmBi, ApCAB,
  BiDAmEd, Drake, NewYHSD, TwCBDA

Frost, John 1890-1937 IlBEAAW, WhAm 1
Frost, John Edward 1849-1921 WhAm 1
Frost, John Orne Johnson 1852-1928 BnEnAmA
Frost, Joseph Hardin 1881-1956 NatCAB 43,
  WhAm 3
Frost, Joshua NewYHSD
Frost, Kendal 1890-1945 NatCAB 34
Frost, Leonard Scott 1901-1964 NatCAB 50
Frost, Leslie Miscampbell 1895-1973 WhAm 5
Frost, Meigs Oliver 1882-1950 NatCAB 37
Frost, Norman 1887-1962 WhAm 4
Frost, Norman Burke 1897-1973 WhAm 6
Frost, Richard Graham 1851-1900 BiDrAC
Frost, Robert Lee 1874-1963 EncAAH, EncAB,
  McGEWB, WebAB, WhAm 4
Frost, Robert Lee 1875-1963 ApCAB X
Frost, Rufus S 1826-1893 NatCAB 13
Frost, Rufus Smith 1826- ApCAB, BiAUS
Frost, Rufus Smith 1826-1894 BiDrAC,
  TwCBDA, WhAm H
Frost, Ruth WomWWA 14
Frost, Stanley 1881-1942 WhAm 2
Frost, Thomas 1759-1804 ApCAB
Frost, Thomas C 1903- WhAm 5
Frost, Thomas Downs 1794-1819 ApCAB
Frost, Thomas Gold 1866-1948 NatCAB 14,
  WhAm 3
Frost, Timothy Prescott 1850-1937 WhAm 1
Frost, W Louis 1877-1954 NatCAB 42
Frost, Wade Hampton 1880-1938 DcAmB S2,
  WhAm 1
Frost, Wallace 1892-1962 NatCAB 49
Frost, Walter Archer 1875-1964 WhAm 4
Frost, Wesley 1884-1968 NatCAB 55,
  WhAm 4
Frost, William Dodge 1867-1957 NatCAB 46,
  WhAm 3
Frost, William Goodell 1854-1938 BiDAmEd,
  NatCAB 30, TwCBDA, WhAm 1
Frost, William Henry 1863-1902 WhAm 1
Frothingham, Arthur Lincoln 1859-1923 DcAmB,
  NatCAB 23, TwCBDA, WhAm 1
Frothingham, Benjamin, Jr. 1734-1809
  BnEnAmA
Frothingham, Benjamin Thompson 1843-1902
  NatCAB 27
Frothingham, Channing 1881-1959 WhAm 3
Frothingham, Ellen 1835-1902 ApCAB,
  WhAm 1
Frothingham, Eugenia Brooks 1874- BiCAW,
  WhAm 5, WomWWA 14
Frothingham, James 1781-1864 ApCAB
Frothingham, James 1786-1864 NewYHSD,
  WhAm H
Frothingham, James 1834-1920 WhAm 1
Frothingham, Jessie Peabody d1949 WhAm 2,
  WomWWA 14
Frothingham, John Whipple 1878-1935
  NatCAB 27
Frothingham, Langdon 1866-1935 NatCAB 46
Frothingham, Louis Adams 1871-1928
  ApCAB X, BiDrAC, NatCAB 21,
  WhAm 1
Frothingham, Nathaniel Langdon 1793-1870
  ApCAB, DcAmB, Drake, NatCAB 5,
  TwCBDA, WhAm H
Frothingham, Octavius Brooks 1822-1895 AmBi,
  ApCAB, DcAmB, Drake, NatCAB 2,
  TwCBDA, WebAB, WhAm H
Frothingham, Paul Revere 1864-1926 DcAmB,
  NatCAB 29, WhAm 1
Frothingham, Richard 1812-1880 AmBi,
  ApCAB, DcAmB, Drake, NatCAB 11,
  TwCBDA, WhAm H
Frothingham, Robert 1865-1937 WhAm 1
Frothingham, Sara C 1821-1861 NewYHSD
Frothingham, Theodore Longfellow 1863-1951
  WhAm 3
Frothingham, Thomas Goddard 1865-1945
  WhAm 3
Frothingham, Washington 1822- ApCAB
Froude, James Anthony 1818-1894 McGEWB
Froude, William 1810-1879 DcScB
Frudden, Conrad Erwin 1887-1971 NatCAB 56
Frueauff, Frank W 1874-1922 WhAm 1
Frueauff, Harry Day 1875-1959 WhAm 3
Frueh, Fred J 1882-1948 NatCAB 40
Fruehauf, Harry Richard 1896-1962 WhAm 4

Fruehauf, Harvey Charles 1893-1968 WhAm 5
Fruehauf, Roy A 1908-1965 WhAm 4
Fruend, Henry Louis 1885-1948 NatCAB 38
Fruit, John Phelps 1855- WhAm 4
Fruitnight, John Henry 1851-1900 NatCAB 3,
  WhAm 1
Fruits, George 1762-1876 ApCAB
Frumess, Gerald Myron 1906-1971 WhAm 6
Frune, George W NewYHSD
Frunze, Mikhail Vasilievich 1885-1925
  McGEWB, WhoMilH
Fry, Alfred Brooks 1860-1933 WhAm 1
Fry, Anson Clifton 1851- WhAm 5
Fry, Benjamin J NewYHSD
Fry, Benjamin St. James 1824-1892 ApCAB,
  NatCAB 5, TwCBDA
Fry, Birkett Davenport 1822-1891 BiDConf,
  DcAmB, WhAm H
Fry, C Luther 1894-1938 NatCAB 28,
  WhAm 1
Fry, Carl 1905-1966 WhAm 4
Fry, Cary Harrison 1813-1873 ApCAB,
  TwCBDA
Fry, Clements Collard 1892-1955 WhAm 3
Fry, Elizabeth Turner 1842- AmWom
Fry, Emma Viola Sheridan 1864- AmWom,
  BiCAW, WomWWA 14
Fry, Fielding Lewis 1892-1961 NatCAB 49
Fry, Francis Rhodes 1853-1937 NatCAB 30,
  WhAm 4
Fry, Franklin Clark 1900-1968 NatCAB 54,
  WebAB, WhAm 5
Fry, Franklin Foster 1864-1933 WhAm 1
Fry, George Washington 1881-1930 NatCAB 23
Fry, Georgia Timken 1864-1921 BiCAW
Fry, Georgiana Timken 1864-1921 WhAm 4,
  WomWWA 14
Fry, H Shipley 1876-1949 NatCAB 38
Fry, Harry Shipley 1878-1949 WhAm 3
Fry, Henry Clay 1840- NatCAB 12
Fry, Henry Davidson 1853-1919 WhAm 1
Fry, Henry Edmond 1870-1952 NatCAB 41
Fry, Howard Morton 1869-1943 NatCAB 33
Fry, Jacob 1834-1920 WhAm 1
Fry, Jacob, Jr. 1802-1866 BiAUS, BiDrAC,
  WhAm H
Fry, James Barnet 1827-1894 AmBi, ApCAB,
  DcAmB, NatCAB 4, TwCBDA,
  WebAMB, WhAm H
Fry, John A B 1870- WhAm 5
Fry, John Hemming 1860-1946 WhAm 2
Fry, Joseph 1828?-1873 AmBi, ApCAB,
  NatCAB 12
Fry, Joseph, Jr. 1781-1860 BiDrAC, WhAm H
Fry, Joseph Reese 1811-1865 ApCAB, Drake,
  TwCBDA
Fry, Joshua 1700?-1754 ApCAB, DcAmB,
  Drake, TwCBDA, WhAm H
Fry, Laura Ann 1857- AmWom
Fry, Lawford H 1873-1948 WhAm 2
Fry, Lynn Ward 1894-1967 NatCAB 53
Fry, Morton Harrison 1888-1971 WhAm 5
Fry, Richard d1745? DcAmB, WhAm H
Fry, Samuel Roeder 1901-1971 WhAm 5
Fry, Sherry Edmundson 1879- WhAm 6
Fry, Speed Smith 1817-1892 ApCAB,
  TwCBDA
Fry, W J NewYHSD
Fry, Wilfred Washington 1875-1936
  NatCAB 27, WhAm 1
Fry, William C 1822?- NewYHSD
Fry, William H 1905-1975 WhAm 6
Fry, William Henry 1813-1864 McGEWB
Fry, William Henry 1815-1864 AmBi, ApCAB,
  DcAmB, Drake, NatCAB 8, TwCBDA,
  WhAm H
Fry, William Justin 1918-1968 NatCAB 54
Fry, William Wallace, Jr. 1886-1953
  NatCAB 40, WhAm 3
Fryatt, Frances Elizabeth AmWom
Fryberger, Agnes Moore 1868- WhAm 1,
  WomWWA 14
Frydler, William Wladyslaw 1906-1973
  WhAm 6
Frye, Alexis Everett 1859-1936 BiDAmEd,
  NatCAB 40, WhAm 1
Frye, Annie Frances 1861- WomWWA 14
Frye, Benjamin Porter 1906-1969 WhAm 5

Frye, Charles Herman 1858-1940 *NatCAB 39*
Frye, Frank Augustus 1904-1970 *WhAm 5*
Frye, Jack d1959 *WhAm 3*
Frye, James 1709-1776 *ApCAB, Drake*
Frye, James Albert 1863-1933 *WhAm 1,
    WhAm 1C*
Frye, John H 1871-1943 *NatCAB 42,
    WhAm 2*
Frye, John William 1871-1925 *NatCAB 20*
Frye, Joseph 1711?-1794 *DcAmB, Drake*
Frye, Joseph 1712-1794 *ApCAB, WhAm H*
Frye, Louise Alexander 1884-1969 *WhAm 5*
Frye, Lucius Arnold 1885-1962 *NatCAB 49,
    WhAm 4*
Frye, Newton Phillips 1894-1957 *WhAm 3*
Frye, Prosser Hall 1866-1934 *WhAm 1*
Frye, Theodore Christian 1869- *WhAm 5*
Frye, William *NewYHSD*
Frye, William 1908-1961 *WhAm 4*
Frye, William Clinton 1877-1954 *NatCAB 41,
    WhAm 3*
Frye, William Pierce 1830-1911 *ApCAB,
    BiDrAC, TwCBDA, WhAmP*
Frye, William Pierce 1831-1911 *AmBi, BiAUS,
    DcAmB, NatCAB 1, WhAm 1*
Frye, William Wesley 1903-1975 *WhAm 6*
Fryer, Douglas 1891-1960 *WhAm 4*
Fryer, Eli Thompson 1878- *WhAm 5*
Fryer, Eugenie Mary 1879- *WhAm 6*
Fryer, Jane Eayre *WhAm 5*
Fryer, John 1839-1928 *NatCAB 21, TwCBDA,
    WhAm 4*
Fryer, Pauline Cushman 1833-1893 *TwCBDA*
Fryer, Robert Livingston 1847-1915
    NatCAB 26, WhAm 1
Fryett, Mrs. *NewYHSD*
Frymeier, G *NewYHSD*
Fryxell, Roald H 1934-1974 *WhAm 6*
Fteley, Alphonse 1837-1903 *NatCAB 13,
    WhAm 1*
Fthenakis, Emmanuel 1921-1972 *WhAm 6*
Fuad I 1868-1936 *McGEWB*
Fubini, Guido 1879-1943 *DcScB*
Fuca, Juan De d1632 *Drake*
Fuchida, Mitsuo 1902- *WhWW-II*
Fuchs, Emil 1866-1929 *WhAm 1*
Fuchs, F *NewYHSD*
Fuchs, Feodor *IIBEAAW*
Fuchs, Immanuel Lazarus 1833-1902 *DcScB*
Fuchs, Johann Nepomuk Von 1774-1856 *DcScB*
Fuchs, Leonhard 1501-1566 *AsBiEn*
Fuchs, Leonhart 1501-1566 *DcScB Sup*
Fuchs, Nathaniel 1898-1956 *NatCAB 44*
Fuchs, Otto 1839-1906 *NewYHSD*
Fuchs, Theo *NewYHSD*
Fuchsel, Georg Christian 1722-1773 *DcScB*
Fudge, Herbert William 1869-1948 *NatCAB 36*
Fuechsel, Hermann 1833-1915 *NewYHSD*
Fuellhart, William Clarke 1903-1967
    NatCAB 55
Fueloep-Miller, Rene 1891-1963 *NatCAB 56*
Fuenleal, Sebastian Ramirez d1547 *ApCAB*
Fuensalida, Luis 1490?-1545 *ApCAB*
Fuentes, Bartolome De *ApCAB*
Fuentes, Carlos 1928- *McGEWB*
Fuentes, Laureano 1825- *ApCAB*
Fuentes, Manuel Atanasio 1820- *ApCAB*
Fuerbringer, Ludwig Ernest 1864-1947 *WhAm 2*
Fuero, Francisco Fabian 1719-1801 *ApCAB*
Fuero, Joaquin 1814-1861 *ApCAB*
Fuerst, P Placidus 1868-1940 *WhAm 3*
Fuertes, Estevan Antonio 1838-1903 *BiDAmEd,
    DcAmB, NatCAB 4, WhAm 1*
Fuertes, James Hillhouse 1863-1932 *WhAm 1,
    WhAm 1C*
Fuertes, Louis Agassiz 1874-1927 *AmBi,
    DcAmB, NatCAB 21, WhAm 1*
Fuerth, Arthur Lawrence 1893-1959
    NatCAB 48
Fuess, Claude Moore 1885-1963 *WhAm 4*
Fuess, John Cushing 1912-1974 *WhAm 6*
Fuessle, Newton Augustus 1883-1924 *WhAm 1*
Fuessler, George Ludwig 1901-1970
    NatCAB 56
Fueter, Karl Rudolf 1880-1950 *DcScB*
Fugard, John Reed 1886-1968 *NatCAB 54,
    WhAm 5*
Fugate, Thomas Bacon 1899- *BiDrAC*

Fuhlrott, Johann Karl 1804-1877 *DcScB*
Fujiwara Kamatari 614-669 *McGEWB*
Fujiwara Michinaga 966-1027 *McGEWB*
Fulbright, J William 1905- *WebAB*
Fulbright, James Franklin 1877-1948 *BiDrAC,
    WhAm 2*
Fulbright, James William 1905- *BiDrAC,
    EncAB, McGEWB*
Fulbright, Jay 1866-1923 *NatCAB 20*
Fulbright, Roberta Waugh 1874-1953
    NatCAB 49
Fulcher, George Cordon 1909-1973 *WhAm 6*
Fulcher, Paul Milton 1895-1958 *WhAm 3*
Fuld, Carrie Bamberger Frank 1864-1944
    NotAW
Fuld, Felix 1868-1929 *NatCAB 21*
Fuld, Joseph Edward 1872-1937 *NatCAB 26*
Fuld, Leonhard Felix 1883-1965 *WhAm 4*
Fuld, William 1870-1927 *NatCAB 21*
Fulda, Carl Herman 1909-1975 *WhAm 6*
Fuleihan, Anis 1900-1970 *NatCAB 57,
    WhAm 5*
Fulford, Francis 1803-1868 *ApCAB, Drake*
Fulkerson, Abram 1834-1902 *BiDrAC*
Fulkerson, Clarke Bertern 1875-1962
    NatCAB 50
Fulkerson, Claude William 1862-1922
    NatCAB 19
Fulkerson, Frank Ballard 1866-1936 *BiDrAC,
    WhAm 4*
Fulkerson, Monroe 1867- *WhAm 4*
Fullam, Eben Joel 1871-1949 *NatCAB 37*
Fullam, Frank L 1870-1951 *DcAmB S5*
Fullam, James Edson 1890-1951 *NatCAB 39,
    WhAm 3*
Fullam, William Freeland 1855-1926
    NatCAB 20
Fullam, William Freeland 1855-1927 *WhAm 1*
Fullbrook, Earl S 1892-1964 *WhAm 4*
Fulle, Fred Albert 1892-1964 *NatCAB 50*
Fulle, Henry *ApCAB X*
Fuller, Abraham Lincoln 1863-1923
    NatCAB 20, WhAm 4
Fuller, Alfred 1817-1893 *NewYHSD*
Fuller, Alfred Carl 1885-1973 *WebAB,
    WhAm 6*
Fuller, Alfred Howard 1913-1959 *NatCAB 49,
    WhAm 3*
Fuller, Alvan Tufts 1878-1958 *BiDrAC,
    WhAmP*
Fuller, Alvin Tufts 1878-1958 *WhAm 3*
Fuller, Andrew S 1828-1896 *DcAmB,
    WhAm H*
Fuller, Anna 1853-1916 *TwCBDA, WhAm 1,
    WomWWA 14*
Fuller, Arthur Buckminster 1822-1862 *ApCAB,
    Drake, NatCAB 4, TwCBDA*
Fuller, Arthur Davenport 1889-1966 *WhAm 4*
Fuller, Augustus 1812-1873 *NewYHSD*
Fuller, Bartholomew *BiAUS*
Fuller, Ben Hebard 1870-1937 *NatCAB 44,
    WebAMB, WhAm 1*
Fuller, Benoni Stinson 1825-1903 *BiAUS,
    BiDrAC*
Fuller, Buckminster 1895- *WebAB*
Fuller, Caroline Macomber 1873- *WhAm 5,
    WomWWA 14*
Fuller, Charles A *NewYHSD*
Fuller, Charles E 1887-1968 *WhAm 5*
Fuller, Charles Eugene 1849-1926 *BiDrAC,
    WhAm 1, WhAmP*
Fuller, Charles Gordon 1856- *WhAm 1*
Fuller, Charles L 1877-1958 *NatCAB 46*
Fuller, Charlotte Anthony 1880- *WomWWA 14*
Fuller, Clara McLean Heath 1854-
    WomWWA 14
Fuller, Claude Albert 1876-1968 *BiDrAC,
    NatCAB 54, WhAm 4, WhAm 5,
    WhAmP*
Fuller, Clyde Dale 1915-1972 *WhAm 5*
Fuller, Crystal Eastman Benedict *NotAW*
Fuller, Edgar 1904-1973 *WhAm 6*
Fuller, Edward 1860-1938 *WhAm 1,
    WhAm 1C*
Fuller, Edward Hawley Laton 1851-1909
    NatCAB 18, WhAm 1
Fuller, Edward Reinow 1896-1964 *NatCAB 52*
Fuller, Edwin Wiley 1847-1875 *NatCAB 10*

Fuller, Ellis Adams 1891-1950 *NatCAB 39,
    WhAm 3*
Fuller, Emily Guillon 1860- *WhAm 4*
Fuller, Eugene 1858-1930 *NatCAB 23,
    WhAm 1*
Fuller, Eugene White 1888-1967 *NatCAB 54*
Fuller, Frank Lanneau 1868-1952 *WhAm 3*
Fuller, Frank Manly 1868-1946 *WhAm 3*
Fuller, Gardner 1833-1914 *NatCAB 15*
Fuller, Genevieve Morrill 1885- *WomWWA 14*
Fuller, George 1802-1888 *BiAUS, BiDrAC*
Fuller, George 1822-1884 *AmBi, ApCAB,
    BnEnAmA, DcAmB, NatCAB 6,
    NatCAB 39, NewYHSD, TwCBDA,
    WhAm H*
Fuller, George Freeman 1869- *WhAm 5*
Fuller, George Gregg 1886-1973 *WhAm 5*
Fuller, George Newman 1873- *WhAm 5*
Fuller, George Riley 1850-1927 *NatCAB 41,
    WhAm 1*
Fuller, George Warren 1868-1934 *DcAmB S1,
    WhAm 1*
Fuller, George Washington 1876-1940 *WhAm 1*
Fuller, H Harrison 1896-1961 *WhAm 4*
Fuller, Hadwen Carlton 1895- *BiDrAC*
Fuller, Harold DeWolf 1874-1957 *WhAm 3*
Fuller, Harry James 1907-1973 *WhAm 6*
Fuller, Harry Williams 1868-1936 *NatCAB 32*
Fuller, Hattie Smith 1869- *WomWWA 14*
Fuller, Hector 1856- *WhAm 4*
Fuller, Helen d1972 *WhAm 5*
Fuller, Henry Amzi 1855-1931 *WhAm 1*
Fuller, Henry Blake 1857-1929 *DcAmB,
    NatCAB 4, NatCAB 23, WhAm 1*
Fuller, Henry Brown 1867-1934 *WhAm 1*
Fuller, Henry Corbin 1879-1942 *NatCAB 42*
Fuller, Henry Frederick 1860- *NatCAB 16*
Fuller, Henry Jones 1873-1956 *NatCAB 43,
    WhAm 3*
Fuller, Henry Mills 1820-1860 *BiAUS, BiDrAC,
    WhAm H*
Fuller, Henry Starkey 1852- *WhAm 4*
Fuller, Henry Weld 1831-1829 *NatCAB 16*
Fuller, Hiram d1880 *Drake*
Fuller, Hiram 1814-1880 *DcAmB, WhAm H*
Fuller, Hiram 1815?-1880 *ApCAB*
Fuller, Homer Taylor 1838- *NatCAB 13,
    TwCBDA, WhAm 4*
Fuller, Horace Stevens 1844-1917 *NatCAB 17*
Fuller, Howard G 1851-1908 *NatCAB 5,
    WhAm 1*
Fuller, Hubert Bruce 1880-1957 *NatCAB 46*
Fuller, Hulbert 1865- *TwCBDA, WhAm 4*
Fuller, I C *NewYHSD*
Fuller, J *NewYHSD*
Fuller, J C *NewYHSD*
Fuller, J Douglas 1899-1967 *WhAm 5*
Fuller, James *NewYHSD*
Fuller, James Wheeler 1873-1929 *NatCAB 38*
Fuller, Jerome *BiAUS*
Fuller, John Frederick Charles 1878-1964
    WhoMilH
Fuller, John Wallace 1827-1891 *ApCAB,
    DcAmB, Drake, NatCAB 12, TwCBDA,
    WhAm H*
Fuller, Joseph Vincent 1890-1932 *DcAmB S1*
Fuller, Joseph Wiltsie 1821-1889 *NatCAB 29*
Fuller, Lawrence Campbell 1877-1952
    NatCAB 42
Fuller, Leo Charles 1889-1963 *WhAm 4*
Fuller, Leslie Elmer 1882-1936 *WhAm 1*
Fuller, Lester Edwin 1894-1956 *NatCAB 43*
Fuller, Levi Knight 1841-1896 *DcAmB,
    NatCAB 8, TwCBDA, WhAm H*
Fuller, Loie 1862-1928 *AmBi, DcAmB,
    NotAW, WhAm 1*
Fuller, Lucia Fairchild 1870-1924 *NotAW*
Fuller, Lucia Fairchild 1872-1924 *WhAm 1,
    WomWWA 14*
Fuller, Lucius Eckstein 1854- *WhAm 4*
Fuller, Lucy Derby 1851- *WomWWA 14*
Fuller, Marcellus Bunyan 1868-1935 *WhAm 1*
Fuller, Margaret d1954 *WhAm 1*
Fuller, Margaret 1810-1850 *AmBi, DcAmB,
    NotAW, WebAB*
Fuller, Mary Breese *WomWWA 14*
Fuller, Melville Weston 1833-1910 *AmBi,
    ApCAB Sup, DcAmB, NatCAB 1,*

NatCAB 33, *TwCBDA*, *WebAB*, *WhAm 1*
Fuller, Melvin Francis 1904-1953 *NatCAB 42*
Fuller, Meta Vaux Warrick 1877- *WhoColR*
Fuller, Metta Victoria *NotAW*
Fuller, Minnie U Oliver Scott Rutherford 1868-1946 *NotAW*
Fuller, Montie Sutton 1879- *WomWWA 14*
Fuller, Mortimer Bartine 1877-1931 *NatCAB 24*
Fuller, Myron Leslie 1873- *WhAm 5*
Fuller, Olive Beatrice Muir 1874- *WhAm 5*, *WomWWA 14*
Fuller, Oliver Clyde 1860-1942 *WhAm 2*
Fuller, Oliver Franklin 1829- *NatCAB 16*
Fuller, Paul 1847-1915 *NatCAB 16*
Fuller, Paul, Jr. d1947 *WhAm 2*
Fuller, Philo Case 1787-1855 *BiAUS*, *BiDrAC*, *WhAm H*
Fuller, R Buckminster 1895- *BnEnAmA*
Fuller, Ralph Lathrop 1865-1932 *NatCAB 23*
Fuller, Rathbun 1857-1937 *NatCAB 28*
Fuller, Raymond Garfield 1886-1960 *WhAm 4*
Fuller, Richard 1804- *Drake*
Fuller, Richard 1804-1876 *ApCAB*, *DcAmB*, *TwCBDA*, *WhAm H*
Fuller, Richard 1804-1896 *NatCAB 23*
Fuller, Richard Buckminster, Jr. 1895- *EncAB*, *McGEWB*, *WebAB*
Fuller, Richard Frederic 1821-1869 *Drake*
Fuller, Richard Frederick 1821-1869 *ApCAB*
Fuller, Richard Henry 1822-1871 *ApCAB*, *NewYHSD*
Fuller, Robert Higginson 1864-1927 *WhAm 1*
Fuller, Robert Mason 1845-1919 *DcAmB*, *NatCAB 12*
Fuller, Robert Nelson 1902-1970 *NatCAB 55*
Fuller, Robert Oliver 1829-1903 *NatCAB 13*
Fuller, Robert Stevens 1904-1969 *WhAm 5*
Fuller, Ruth Hamilton *WomWWA 14*
Fuller, Samuel 1802-1895 *TwCBDA*
Fuller, Samuel A *NewYHSD*
Fuller, Samuel Lester 1875-1963 *NatCAB 50*, *WhAm 4*
Fuller, Samuel Richard, Jr. 1879-1966 *NatCAB 54*
Fuller, Samuel W *NewYHSD*
Fuller, Sarah 1836-1927 *BiDAmEd*, *NotAW*, *WomWWA 14*
Fuller, Sarah E 1829?-1902 *NewYHSD*
Fuller, Sarah Margaret 1810-1850 *AmBi*, *ApCAB*, *DcAmB*, *Drake*, *EncAB*, *McGEWB*, *NatCAB 3*, *TwCBDA*, *WebAB*, *WhAm H*
Fuller, Solomon Carter 1872- *WhoColR*
Fuller, Stuart Jamieson 1880-1941 *WhAm 1*
Fuller, Sumner Francis 1892-1928 *NatCAB 22*
Fuller, Susan E W d1907 *NewYHSD*
Fuller, Teddy Ray 1924-1972 *WhAm 5*
Fuller, Thomas 1822- *WhAm 4*
Fuller, Thomas 1823- *ApCAB Sup*
Fuller, Thomas Brock 1810- *ApCAB*
Fuller, Thomas Charles 1832-1901 *BiDConf*, *DcAmB*, *WhAm H*
Fuller, Thomas James Duncan 1808-1876 *BiAUS*, *BiAUS Sup*, *BiDrAC*, *WhAm H*, *WhAmP*
Fuller, Thomas O 1867- *WhoColR*
Fuller, Thomas Staples 1881-1940 *WhAm 1*
Fuller, Timothy 1778-1835 *ApCAB*, *BiAUS*, *BiDrAC*, *Drake*, *TwCBDA*, *WhAm H*, *WhAmP*
Fuller, Walter Deane 1882-1964 *WhAm 4*
Fuller, Warner 1901-1957 *WhAm 3*
Fuller, Warren Graham 1920-1975 *WhAm 6*
Fuller, Wayne Edison 1919- *EncAAH*
Fuller, Weston Earle 1879-1935 *NatCAB 28*
Fuller, Wiley Madison 1890-1954 *WhAm 3*
Fuller, William 1864-1933 *NatCAB 30*
Fuller, William Alden 1836-1920 *NatCAB 35*
Fuller, William David 1873- *WhAm 5*
Fuller, William Eddy 1832- *WhAm 4*
Fuller, William Elijah 1846-1918 *BiDrAC*, *WhAm 1*
Fuller, William Hayes 1869- *WhAm 5*
Fuller, William Howe 1896-1962 *NatCAB 52*
Fuller, William Kendall 1792-1883 *BiAUS*, *BiDrAC*, *WhAm H*

Fuller, William Oliver 1856-1941 *NatCAB 35*, *WhAm 1*
Fuller, William Parmer 1827-1890 *NatCAB 39*
Fuller, William Parmer, Jr. 1888-1970 *WhAm 5*
Fuller, Williamson Whitehead 1858-1934 *WhAm 1*
Fullerton, Anna Martha 1853- *WhAm 5*, *WomWWA 14*
Fullerton, Baxter P 1851-1933 *WhAm 1*
Fullerton, Charles Alexander 1861-1945 *WhAm 3*
Fullerton, David 1771-1843 *BiAUS*
Fullerton, David 1772-1843 *BiDrAC*, *WhAm H*
Fullerton, E Dwight 1876-1940 *NatCAB 41*
Fullerton, Edith Loring 1876-1931 *WhAm 1*, *WomWWA 14*
Fullerton, George Stuart 1859-1925 *AmBi*, *DcAmB*, *NatCAB 12*, *TwCBDA*, *WhAm 1*
Fullerton, Hugh Stuart 1873- *WhAm 5*
Fullerton, Joseph Scott 1835-1897 *TwCBDA*
Fullerton, Kemper 1865-1940 *WhAm 1*
Fullerton, Mark A 1858-1931 *NatCAB 13*, *WhAm 1*
Fullerton, Nathaniel *NewYHSD*
Fullerton, Robert 1845-1945 *NatCAB 34*
Fullerton, Samuel Clyde 1877- *WhAm 5*
Fullerton, Samuel Holmes 1852-1939 *NatCAB 29*
Fullerton, William 1854-1888 *ApCAB Sup*
Fullerton, William Morton 1865- *WhAm 4*
Fullick, Elizabeth *WomWWA 14*
Fulmer, Clark Adelbert 1867-1940 *WhAm 1*
Fulmer, Ellis Ingham 1891-1953 *WhAm 3*
Fulmer, Elton 1864-1916 *WhAm 1*
Fulmer, Hampton Pitts 1875-1944 *BiDrAC*, *NatCAB 43*, *WhAm 2*, *WhAmP*
Fulmer, Joseph Henry 1876-1944 *NatCAB 32*
Fulmer, Willa Lybrand 1884-1968 *BiDrAC*
Fulmore, Zachary Taylor 1846-1923 *NatCAB 19*, *WhAm 4*
Fulp, James Douglas 1886- *WhAm 5*
Fulper, William Hill 1872-1928 *NatCAB 21*
Fulton, Albert Cooley 1872- *WhAm 5*
Fulton, Andrew Steele 1800-1884 *BiAUS*, *BiDrAC*, *WhAm H*
Fulton, Beatrice Joanna Shattuck 1860- *WomWWA 14*
Fulton, Charles Herman 1874- *WhAm 5*
Fulton, Charles William 1853-1918 *BiDrAC*, *NatCAB 13*, *WhAm 1*, *WhAmP*
Fulton, Chester Alan 1883-1951 *WhAm 3*
Fulton, David B 1865?- *WhoColR*
Fulton, Elisha M 1832-1913 *NatCAB 16*
Fulton, Elmer Lincoln 1863-1939 *WhAm 4*
Fulton, Elmer Lincoln 1865-1939 *BiDrAC*
Fulton, Frank Taylor 1867-1961 *WhAm 4*
Fulton, George 1900-1952 *NatCAB 41*
Fulton, George Hylton 1886-1955 *NatCAB 45*
Fulton, Hugh 1908-1962 *WhAm 4*
Fulton, James A 1889-1950 *WhAm 3*
Fulton, James Grove 1903-1971 *BiDrAC*, *WhAm 5*
Fulton, John 1834-1907 *ApCAB*, *TwCBDA*, *WhAm 1*
Fulton, John Allen 1878-1939 *WhAm 1*
Fulton, John Farquhar 1856-1932 *NatCAB 25*
Fulton, John Farquhar 1899-1960 *DcScB*, *NatCAB 53*, *WhAm 4*
Fulton, John Hall d1836 *BiAUS*, *BiDrAC*, *WhAm H*
Fulton, John Hamilton 1869-1927 *WhAm 1*
Fulton, John Samuel 1859-1931 *WhAm 1*
Fulton, Joseph Samuel 1866- *WhAm 4*
Fulton, Justin Dewey 1826-1901 *TwCBDA*
Fulton, Justin Dewey 1828-1901 *ApCAB*, *DcAmB*, *NatCAB 9*, *WhAm 1*
Fulton, Kerwin Holmes 1885-1955 *WhAm 3*
Fulton, Linda DeKowalewska 1858- *WomWWA 14*
Fulton, Mary Celia 1882- *WomWWA 14*
Fulton, Mary Hannah 1854-1927 *NotAW*
Fulton, Maurice Garland 1877- *WhAm 5*
Fulton, Richard Harmon 1927- *BiDrAC*
Fulton, Mrs. Robert *NewYHSD*
Fulton, Robert 1765-1815 *AmBi*, *ApCAB*, *AsBiEn*, *BnEnAmA*, *DcAmB*, *Drake*,

McGEWB, *NatCAB 3*, *NewYHSD*, *TwCBDA*, *WebAB*, *WebAMB*, *WhAm H*
Fulton, Robert Burwell 1849-1919 *ApCAB X*, *DcAmB*, *NatCAB 13*, *TwCBDA*, *WhAm 1*
Fulton, Robert Irving 1855-1916 *WhAm 1*
Fulton, Samuel Alexander 1877-1954 *WhAm 3*
Fulton, Sara Acer 1861- *WomWWA 14*
Fulton, Stanley Howes 1904-1971 *NatCAB 56*
Fulton, Wallace H 1896-1974 *WhAm 6*
Fulton, Walter Scott 1879-1950 *WhAm 3*
Fulton, Weston Miller, Sr. 1871-1946 *WhAm HA*, *WhAm 4*
Fulton, William 1802?-1868 *WhAm H*
Fulton, William Grosvenor 1860-1937 *NatCAB 29*
Fulton, William John 1875-1961 *WhAm 4*
Fulton, William Pomeroy 1856-1936 *WhAm 1*
Fulton, William Savin 1795-1844 *ApCAB*, *BiAUS*, *BiDrAC*, *Drake*, *NatCAB 10*, *TwCBDA*, *WhAm H*, *WhAmP*
Fulton, William Shirley 1880-1964 *WhAm 4*
Fulton, William Stewart d1938 *WhAm 1*, *WhAm 1C*
Fultz, Francis Marion 1857- *WhAm 4*
Fulwider, William Alexander 1844-1937 *NatCAB 38*
Fulwood, Charles Allen 1829- *WhAm 4*
Fumasoni-Biondi, Peter 1872-1960 *WhAm 4*
Funchess, Marion Jacob 1884-1953 *WhAm 3*
Funderburg, Hugh Kenneth 1890-1961 *NatCAB 51*
Funderburk, James Ernest 1887-1972 *WhAm 6*
Funes, Gregorio d1820? *ApCAB*
Fung, Ching 1863-1897 *REnAW*
Funk, Benjamin Franklin 1838-1909 *BiDrAC*, *TwCBDA*
Funk, Casimir 1884-1967 *AsBiEn*, *BiHiMed*, *DcScB*, *WebAB*, *WhAm 4*
Funk, Charles Earle 1881-1957 *NatCAB 45*, *WhAm 3*
Funk, Clarence Sidney 1866-1930 *WhAm 1*
Funk, Elmer Bramwell 1876-1962 *NatCAB 50*
Funk, Erwin Charles 1877- *WhAm 5*
Funk, Eugene Duncan 1867-1944 *EncAAH*, *WhAm 2*
Funk, Frank Hamilton 1869-1940 *BiDrAC*, *NatCAB 41*, *WhAm 1*
Funk, Henry Daniel 1875-1925 *WhAm 1*
Funk, Isaac 1797-1865 *EncAAH*, *TwCBDA*
Funk, Isaac Kauffman 1839-1912 *ApCAB X*, *DcAmB*, *NatCAB 11*, *WebAB*
Funk, Isaac Kaufman 1839-1912 *TwCBDA*, *WhAm 1*
Funk, John 1810?- *NewYHSD*
Funk, John Clarence 1884- *WhAm 3*
Funk, Miles Conrad 1887-1968 *WhAm 5*
Funk, Theron Hartzog 1902-1962 *NatCAB 48*
Funk, Vance Anderson 1882-1945 *NatCAB 35*
Funk, Wilfred 1883-1965 *NatCAB 52*, *WhAm 4*
Funk, Wilhelm Heinrich 1866- *NatCAB 12*, *WhAm 4*
Funk, William R 1861-1935 *WhAm 1*
Funke, Erich 1891-1974 *WhAm 6*
Funke, John 1873-1956 *NatCAB 46*
Funkhouser, Abram Paul 1853-1917 *NatCAB 34*, *WhAm 4*
Funkhouser, George A 1841-1927 *WhAm 1*
Funkhouser, John William 1926-1974 *WhAm 6*
Funkhouser, Raymond Joseph 1888-1968 *WhAm 4A*
Funkhouser, Robert Monroe 1850- *NatCAB 7*
Funkhouser, William Delbert 1881-1948 *NatCAB 40*, *WhAm 2*
Funsten, Benjamin Reed 1887-1969 *WhAm 5*
Funsten, David 1819-1866 *BiDConf*
Funsten, James Bowen 1856-1918 *NatCAB 12*, *NatCAB 26*, *TwCBDA*, *WhAm 1*
Funsten, James Bowen 1858-1918 *ApCAB Sup*
Funsten, Robert Vivian 1892-1949 *NatCAB 38*
Funston, Edward Hogue 1836-1911 *BiDrAC*, *NatCAB 11*, *TwCBDA*, *WhAm 1*, *WhAmP*
Funston, Frederick 1865-1917 *AmBi*, *ApCAB Sup*, *DcAmB*, *NatCAB 11*, *TwCBDA*, *WebAB*, *WebAMB*, *WhAm 1*
Fuqua, Don 1933- *BiDrAC*

Fuqua, Henry Luce 1865-1926 *NatCAB 22,*
WhAm 1
Fuqua, Isham W 1879- *WhAm 6*
Fuqua, James Henry 1837- *WhAm 4*
Fuqua, Stephen Ogden 1874-1943 *NatCAB 44,*
WhAm 2
Furay, James Henry 1879-1955 *WhAm 3*
Furay, John Baptist 1873- *WhAm 5*
Furber, Aurilla 1847- *AmWom*
Furber, Fred Nason 1882-1958 *WhAm 3*
Furber, Henry Jewett 1865-1956 *WhAm 3*
Furber, Pierce T d1893 *WhAm H*
Furbershaw, Virginia Lawton d1972 *WhAm 6*
Furbish, Kate 1834-1931 *NotAW*
Furbringer, Max Henry 1879-1957 *WhAm 3*
Furbush, Charles Lincoln 1863-1923
NatCAB 20, WhAm 1
Furches, David Moffat 1832-1908 *NatCAB 12*
Furches, David Moffatt 1832-1908 *TwCBDA,*
WhAm 1
Furcolo, Foster 1911- *BiDrAC*
Furer, Julius Augustus 1880-1965 *WhAm 4*
Furer, William Charles 1879-1963 *WhAm 4*
Furey, Francis Thomas 1852- *WhAm 4*
Furey, John Vincent 1839-1914 *WhAm 1*
Furguson, Elizabeth Graeme 1737-1801
WhAm H
Furlong, Atherton Bernard, Sr. 1849- *WhAm 4*
Furlong, Charles Wellington 1874-1967
IIBEAAW, NatCAB 54, WhAm 4
Furlong, Robert Grant 1886- *BiDrAC*
Furlong, Thomas J d1897 *WhAm H*
Furlong, William Rea 1881- *WhAm 6*
Furlow, Allen John 1890-1954 *BiDrAC*
Furlow, Floyd Charles 1877-1923 *ApCAB X,*
DcAmB, NatCAB 20, WhAm 1
Furman, Benjamin Applegate 1883-1967
NatCAB 53
Furman, Bess 1894-1969 *WhAm 5*
Furman, Charles M 1797-1872 *ApCAB*
Furman, Franklin DeRonde 1870-1943 *WhAm 2*
Furman, Gabriel 1800-1854 *ApCAB*
Furman, George Homan 1868-1941 *NatCAB 30*
Furman, Henry Marshall 1850-1916
NatCAB 29
Furman, James Cement 1809-1891 *WhAm H*
Furman, James Clement 1809-1891 *ApCAB,*
BiDConf, DcAmB, NatCAB 32,
TwCBDA
Furman, John Myers 1866-1933 *WhAm 1*
Furman, Lucy d1958 *WhAm 3*
Furman, Myrtie E 1860- *AmWom*
Furman, N Howell 1892-1965 *NatCAB 52,*
WhAm 4
Furman, Nellie E C 1871- *WomWWA 14*
Furman, Richard 1755-1825 *ApCAB, DcAmB,*
DcAmReB, NatCAB 12, WebAB,
WhAm H
Furnald, Henry Natsch d1945 *WhAm 2*
Furnas, Clifford Cook 1900-1969 *NatCAB 56,*
WhAm 5
Furnas, Elwood 1840-1902 *NatCAB 10,*
WhAm 1
Furnas, Robert Wilkinson 1824-1905 *DcAmB,*
NatCAB 12, REnAW, TwCBDA,
WhAm 1
Furnass, R W *BiAUS*
Furness, Caroline Ellen 1869-1936 *WhAm 1,*
WomWWA 14
Furness, Clifton Joseph 1898- *WhAm 3*
Furness, Frank 1839-1912 *BnEnAmA*
Furness, Helen Kate 1837-1883 *ApCAB*
Furness, Horace Howard 1833-1912 *AmBi,*
ApCAB, DcAmB, NatCAB 8, TwCBDA,
WebAB, WhAm 1
Furness, Horace Howard, Jr. 1865-1930 *DcAmB,*
NatCAB 23, WhAm 1
Furness, James Wilson 1874- *WhAm 5*
Furness, John Mason 1763-1804 *NewYHSD*
Furness, William Henry 1802-1896 *AmBi,*
ApCAB, DcAmB, Drake, NatCAB 2,
TwCBDA, WhAm H
Furness, William Henry 1827-1867 *Drake,*
NewYHSD
Furness, William Henry 1828-1867 *ApCAB,*
TwCBDA
Furness, William Henry, III 1866-1920
WhAm 1

Furniss, Edgar Stephenson 1890-1972 *WhAm 5*
Furniss, Edgar Stephenson, Jr. 1918-1966
WhAm 4
Furniss, Grace Livingston *WomWWA 14*
Furniss, Henry Dawson 1878-1942 *WhAm 1*
Furniss, Henry Watson 1868- *NatCAB 14,*
WhoColR
Furniss, Sumner Alexander 1874- *WhoColR*
Furphy, Joseph 1843-1912 *McGEWB*
Furr, Roy 1904-1975 *WhAm 6*
Furrer, Rudolph 1893-1965 *WhAm 4*
Furrow, Clarence Lee 1896-1955 *WhAm 3*
Furry, Elda *WebAB*
Furry, William Davis 1873- *WhAm 5*
Furscott, Mortimer Cuthbert 1879-1950
NatCAB 38
Furst, Clyde Bowman 1873-1931 *DcAmB S1,*
WhAm 1
Furst, Conrad 1829-1921 *NatCAB 26*
Furst, Frank Anthony 1845-1934 *NatCAB 31*
Furst, Joseph 1900-1967 *WhAm 4*
Furst, Michael *ApCAB X*
Furst, Moritz 1782- *NewYHSD, WhAm H*
Furst, Sidney Dale 1904-1969 *WhAm 5*
Furst, William Wallace 1852- *TwCBDA*
Furstenberg, Albert Carl 1890-1969 *NatCAB 55,*
WhAm 5
Furtado, Francisco Jose 1818-1870 *ApCAB*
Furtado DeMendonca, Hipolito J DaCosta
1773-1823 *ApCAB*
Furth, Albert Lavenson 1902-1962 *WhAm 4*
Furtseva, Yekaterina Alekseevna 1910-1975
WhAm 6
Furtwangler, Wilhelm 1886-1954 *WhAm 3*
Furuseth, Andrew 1854-1938 *DcAmB S2,*
WebAB, WhAm 1
Fuseli, Henry 1741-1825 *McGEWB*
Fushman, Arthur John 1898-1969 *NatCAB 54*
Fuson, Samuel Dillard 1890-1954 *WhAm 3*
Fusoris, Jean 1365?-1436 *DcScB Sup*
Fuss, Nicolaus 1755-1826 *DcScB*
Fussell, Bartholomew 1794-1871 *DcAmB,*
WhAm H
Fussell, Charles Lewis 1840-1909 *NewYHSD*
Fussell, Joseph Hall 1863-1942 *WhAm 2*
Fussell, Lewis 1882-1935 *WhAm 1*
Fussell, M Howard 1855-1921 *WhAm 1*
Fussell, Susan 1832-1889 *AmWom*
Fustel DeCoulanges, Numa Denis 1830-1889
McGEWB
Fusting, Frederick Erwin 1882-1953 *WhAm 3*
Futch, Charles Edward 1898-1948 *NatCAB 38*
Futcher, Marjorie Howard 1885-
WomWWA 14
Futcher, Thomas Barnes 1871-1938 *WhAm 1*
Futhey, Bruce 1913-1964 *WhAm 4*
Futhey, John Smith 1820-1888 *ApCAB,*
NatCAB 10, TwCBDA, WhAm H
Futrall, John Clinton 1873-1939 *NatCAB 18,*
WhAm 1
Futrell, Junius Marion 1872- *WhAm 3*
Futrelle, Jacques 1875-1912 *WhAm 1*
Futrelle, Louise May Peel 1876- *WomWWA 14*
Futrelle, May 1876- *WhAm 5*
Fux, Johann Joseph 1660-1741 *McGEWB*
Fuzy, Paul James 1893-1961 *NatCAB 48*
Fyan, Robert Washington 1835-1896 *BiDrAC,*
TwCBDA, WhAm H, WhAmP
Fyfe, Sir David Maxwell 1900-1967 *WhWW-II*
Fyfe, John William 1839- *WhAm 4*
Fyffe, Joseph 1832-1896 *ApCAB Sup,*
TwCBDA
Fyles, Franklin d1911 *WhAm 1*
Fyodorov, Evgraf Stephanovich 1853-1919
DcScB

G

Gaarde, Fred William 1887-1948 *WhAm 2*
Gaba, Meyer Grupp 1884-1962 *WhAm 4*
Gabaldon, Isauro 1875-1942 *BiDrAC,*
   WhAm 5, WhAmP
Gabaret, Jean De 1620-1697 *ApCAB*
Gabb, William More 1838-1878 *NatCAB 4*
Gabb, William More 1839-1878 *AmBi, ApCAB,*
   DcAmB, DcScB, TwCBDA, WhAm H
Gabbard, Elmer Everett 1880-1960 *WhAm 4*
Gabbert, Mont Robertson 1889-1955 *WhAm 3*
Gabbert, Monte Robertson 1889-1955
   NatCAB 47
Gabbert, William Henry 1849- *NatCAB 13,*
   WhAm 1
Gabel, Carl W 1906-1964 *WhAm 4*
Gabel, Siegfried Gerhard 1878-1957
   NatCAB 47
Gabel, Thomas Ring 1854- *NatCAB 17*
Gable, Amos 1840- *NewYHSD*
Gable, Clark 1901-1960 *McGEWB, WebAB,*
   WhAm 4
Gable, George Daniel 1863-1911 *WhAm 1*
Gable, Morgan Edwards 1862- *WhAm 1*
Gable, William Francis *ApCAB X*
Gable, William Russell 1924-1975 *WhAm 6*
Gableman, Edwin Wilson 1885-1954 *WhAm 3*
Gabo, Naum 1890- *BnEnAmA, McGEWB*
Gaboury, George Napoleon 1884-1935
   NatCAB 25
Gabriac, Paul Joseph DeCadoine 1792-1865
   ApCAB
Gabriel, Ange Jacques 1698-1782 *McGEWB*
Gabriel, Charles L 1891-1949 *WhAm 3*
Gabriel, George 1887- *WhoColR*
Gabriel, Gilbert Wolf 1890-1952 *NatCAB 41,*
   WhAm 3
Gabriel, John Huston 1862- *WhAm 4*
Gabriel, Mgrditch Simbad 1856- *WhAm 4*
Gabriel, Olive Scott *WomWWA 14*
Gabriel, Siegmund 1851-1924 *DcScB*
Gabrieli, Giovanni 1557?-1612 *McGEWB*
Gabriels, Henry 1838-1921 *ApCAB Sup,*
   NatCAB 4, TwCBDA, WhAm 1
Gabrielson, Carl 1869-1936 *NatCAB 28*
Gabrilowitsch, Ossip 1878-1936 *AmBi,*
   DcAmB S2, NatCAB 27, WhAm 1
Gabuzda, George Joseph, Jr. 1920-1975
   WhAm 6
Gachot, A M *NewYHSD*
Gaddesden, John Of 1280?-1361 *BiHiMed*
Gaddis, Cyrus Jacob 1868-1949 *NatCAB 38,*
   WhAm 4
Gade, Carl Johannes 1885-1955 *NatCAB 44*
Gade, John Allyne 1875-1955 *WhAm 3*
Gadlow, David Berman d1965 *WhAm 4*
Gadola, Paul Victor 1887-1968 *NatCAB 54*
Gadolin, Johan 1760-1852 *AsBiEn, DcScB*
Gadsby, Edward Northup 1900-1973
   NatCAB 57, WhAm 6
Gadsby, George M 1886-1960 *WhAm 3A*
Gadsby, Robert Charles 1916-1966 *WhAm 4*
Gadsden, Christopher 1723-1805 *BiDrAC,*
   WhAmP
Gadsden, Christopher 1724-1805 *AmBi,*
   ApCAB, BiAUS, DcAmB, Drake,
   NatCAB 1, TwCBDA, WhAm H
Gadsden, Christopher Edwards 1785-1852
   ApCAB, Drake, NatCAB 12, TwCBDA
Gadsden, James 1788-1858 *AmBi, ApCAB,*
   BiAUS, DcAmB, Drake, McGEWB,
   NatCAB 12, TwCBDA, WebAB,
   WhAm H, WhAmP
Gadsden, John 1787-1831 *ApCAB*
Gadsden, Philip Henry 1867-1945 *NatCAB 42,*

WhAm 2
Gadski, Johanna, Madame 1872-1932 *WhAm 1*
Gadski-Tauscher, Johanna 1872-1932
   NatCAB 14
Gaebelein, Arno Clemens 1861-1945 *WhAm 2*
Gaebelein, Paul Whitefield 1887-1947
   NatCAB 35
Gaede, William R 1891-1966 *WhAm 4*
Gaehr, Adolph Jonathan 1873-1936 *NatCAB 27*
Gaehr, Paul Frederick 1880-1955 *WhAm 3*
Gaenslen, Frederick Julius 1877-1937
   NatCAB 28, WhAm 1
Gaer, Joseph 1897-1969 *NatCAB 55*
Gaertner, Carl Frederick 1898-1952 *WhAm 3*
Gaertner, Fred, Jr. 1891-1963 *NatCAB 51,*
   WhAm 4
Gaertner, Frederick 1860-1929 *NatCAB 22*
Gaertner, Herman Julius 1866-1958 *WhAm 3*
Gaertner, Joseph 1732-1791 *DcScB*
Gaertner, Karl Friedrich Von 1772-1850 *DcScB*
Gaertner, Rudolf 1873-1932 *NatCAB 24*
Gaertner, William 1864-1948 *WhAm 2*
Gaerttner, Erwin Rudolf 1911-1974 *WhAm 6*
Gaff, Thomas Trueman 1854-1923 *NatCAB 23*
Gaffey, Hugh J 1895-1946 *WhAm 2*
Gaffey, John Tracy 1859-1935 *NatCAB 27*
Gaffky, Georg Theodor August 1850-1918
   AsBiEn, DcScB
Gaffney, Dale V 1894-1950 *WhAm 3*
Gaffney, Emmett Lawrence 1894-1965 *WhAm 4*
Gaffney, Hugh H 1894-1966 *WhAm 4*
Gaffney, John J 1891-1947 *WhAm 2*
Gaffney, John Marshall 1907-1967 *WhAm 5*
Gaffney, Leo Vincent 1903-1969 *WhAm 5*
Gaffney, Margaret *NotAW, TwCBDA*
Gaffney, Margaret 1814?-1882 *DcAmB*
Gaffney, Margaret 1825?-1882 *NatCAB 2*
Gaffney, Matthew Page 1891-1963 *WhAm 4*
Gaffney, T St. John 1864-1944 *WhAm 2*
Gafney, Milton V 1908-1963 *NatCAB 51*
Gag, Wanda Hazel 1893-1946 *DcAmB S4,*
   NotAW, WhAm 2
Gagarin, Yuri Alekseyevich 1934-1968 *AsBiEn,*
   WhAm 4
Gagarin, Yuri Alexeivich 1934-1968 *McGEWB*
Gage, Alfred Payson 1836-1903 *WhAm 1*
Gage, Benjamin F *NewYHSD*
Gage, Brownell 1874-1945 *WhAm 2*
Gage, Charles Amon 1872- *WhAm 5*
Gage, Elbert Mauney 1912-1972 *WhAm 5*
Gage, Elliot Howes 1891-1930 *NatCAB 22*
Gage, Frances Dana Barker 1808-1884 *AmBi,*
   AmWom, ApCAB, DcAmB, Drake,
   NatCAB 2, NotAW, TwCBDA,
   WhAm H
Gage, George Henry 1880-1956 *NatCAB 46*
Gage, George William 1887- *IlBEAAW*
Gage, George Williams 1856- *WhAm 4*
Gage, Harry Morehouse 1878-1961 *WhAm 4*
Gage, Henry Tifft 1852-1924 *WhAm 1*
Gage, Henry Tifft 1853-1924 *NatCAB 4*
Gage, Homer 1861-1938 *NatCAB 29,*
   WhAm 1
Gage, Idys Mims 1893-1957 *NatCAB 48*
Gage, John Bailey 1887-1970 *NatCAB 57,*
   WhAm 5
Gage, John Balley 1887-1970 *WhAm 6*
Gage, John H 1908-1966 *WhAm 4*
Gage, Joshua 1763-1831 *BiAUS, BiDrAC,*
   WhAm H
Gage, Lucy 1876-1945 *BiDAmEd*
Gage, Mrs. Lyman J *AmWom*
Gage, Lyman Judson 1836-1927 *AmBi,*
   ApCAB Sup, BiDrUSE, DcAmB,

NatCAB 11, NatCAB 26, TwCBDA,
   WhAm 1
Gage, Mary E Mott *WomWWA 14*
Gage, Matilda Joslyn 1826-1898 *AmBi,*
   AmWom, ApCAB, DcAmB, NatCAB 2,
   NotAW, TwCBDA, WhAm H, WhAmP
Gage, Nancy 1787-1845 *NewYHSD*
Gage, Sidney 1853-1923 *NatCAB 20*
Gage, Simon Henry 1851-1944 *NatCAB 4,*
   NatCAB 36, TwCBDA, WhAm 2
Gage, Stephen Thornton 1831-1916 *NatCAB 17*
Gage, Susanna Phelps 1857-1915 *TwCBDA,*
   WhAm 1, WomWWA 14
Gage, Thomas 1597-1655 *ApCAB, Drake*
Gage, Thomas 1719?-1787 *McGEWB*
Gage, Thomas 1720?-1787 *Drake*
Gage, Thomas 1721-1787 *AmBi, ApCAB,*
   DcAmB, NatCAB 7, WhAm H, WhAmP
Gage, Thomas Hovey 1826-1909 *NatCAB 33*
Gage, Thomas Hovey 1865-1938 *WhAm 1*
Gage, Victor Raymond 1882-1955 *NatCAB 43*
Gage, Walter Boutwell 1872- *WhAm 5*
Gage-Day, Mary Hannah 1857-1935
   NatCAB 26, WhAm 1
Gagel, Edward 1858-1931 *WhAm 1*
Gager, Charles Stuart 1872-1943 *NatCAB 38,*
   WhAm 2
Gager, Curtis H d1962 *WhAm 4*
Gager, Edwin Baker 1852-1922 *WhAm 1*
Gager, Nellie 1859- *WomWWA 14*
Gaggin, Edwin Hall 1866-1959 *WhAm 3*
Gagliardi, Domenico 1660-1725? *DcScB*
Gagliardi, Tommaso 1820-1895 *NewYHSD,*
   WhAm H
Gagnebin, Elie 1891-1949 *DcScB*
Gagnon, Ernest Amedee Frederic 1834-
   ApCAB Sup
Gagnon, J-Romeo 1903-1970 *WhAm 5*
Gagnon, Lucian d1842 *ApCAB*
Gagnon, Onesime 1888-1961 *WhAm 4*
Gagnon, Wilfrid 1898-1963 *WhAm 4*
Gahagan, Walter Hamer 1864-1930 *NatCAB 22*
Gahn, Harry Conrad 1880-1962 *BiDrAC,*
   WhAm 4
Gahn, Johan Gottlieb 1745-1818 *DcScB*
Gahn, Johann Gottlieb 1745-1818 *AsBiEn*
Gaiennie, Frank 1841- *NatCAB 12*
Gaige, Charlotte May *WomWWA 14*
Gaige, Crosby 1882-1949 *NatCAB 38,*
   WhAm 2
Gail, William Wallace 1880-1951 *WhAm 3*
Gailey, John Knox 1850-1926 *NatCAB 20*
Gailey, Watson 1882-1959 *NatCAB 47*
Gaillard, David DuBose 1859-1913 *AmBi,*
   DcAmB, NatCAB 15, WebAMB,
   WhAm 1
Gaillard, Edwin Samuel 1827-1885 *ApCAB,*
   DcAmB, NatCAB 24, TwCBDA,
   WhAm H
Gaillard, Edwin White 1872-1928 *WhAm 1*
Gaillard, Felix 1919-1970 *WhAm 5*
Gaillard, John 1765-1826 *ApCAB, BiAUS,*
   BiDrAC, DcAmB, Drake, NatCAB 4,
   TwCBDA, WhAm H, WhAmP
Gaillard, Peter Cordes 1815-1859 *ApCAB*
Gaillard, Samuel Gourdin 1853-1936
   NatCAB 29
Gaillard, Theodore *BiAUS*
Gaillard, William Dawson 1906-1975 *WhAm 6*
Gaillardet, Theodore Frederic 1808-1882
   ApCAB, DcAmB
Gaillardet, Theodore Frederick 1808-1882
   WhAm H

Gaillot, Aimable Jean-Baptiste 1834-1921 *DcScB*

Gailor, Frank Hoyt 1892-1954 *NatCAB 42, WhAm 3*

Gailor, Thomas Frank 1856-1935 *DcAmB S1, NatCAB 12, NatCAB 47, TwCBDA, WhAm 1*

Gaimard, Joseph Paul 1796-1858 *DcScB*

Gaine, Hugh 1726-1807 *ApCAB, DcAmB, Drake*

Gaine, Hugh 1727-1807 *NatCAB 23, WhAm H*

Gainer, Denzil Lee 1913-1972 *WhAm 6*

Gainer, Joseph Henry 1878-1945 *WhAm 2*

Gaines, Absalom Graves 1827- *NatCAB 10*

Gaines, Charles Kelsey 1854-1944 *WhAm 2*

Gaines, Clement Carrington 1857- *WhAm 4*

Gaines, Edmund Pendleton 1777-1849 *AmBi, ApCAB, DcAmB, Drake, NatCAB 9, TwCBDA, WebAMB, WhAm H*

Gaines, Edmund Pendleton 1824-1884 *NatCAB 18*

Gaines, Edward Franklin 1886-1944 *WhAm 2*

Gaines, Francis Pendleton 1892-1963 *WhAm 4*

Gaines, Frank Henry 1852-1923 *WhAm 1*

Gaines, George Strother 1784?-1872 *NatCAB 18*

Gaines, George Strother 1784?-1873 *AmBi, DcAmB, WhAm H*

Gaines, James Marshall 1911-1976 *WhAm 6*

Gaines, Janet Maxwell Harris *WomWWA 14*

Gaines, John P d1858 *ApCAB, BiAUS, Drake*

Gaines, John Paul 1795-1858 *NatCAB 8, TwCBDA*

Gaines, John Pollard 1795-1857 *AmBi, BiDrAC, DcAmB, WhAm H, WhAmP*

Gaines, John Wesley 1860-1926 *BiDrAC, WhAmP*

Gaines, John Wesley 1861-1926 *TwCBDA, WhAm 1*

Gaines, John William 1870- *WhAm 5*

Gaines, Joseph Holt 1864-1951 *BiDrAC, WhAm 4, WhAmP*

Gaines, L Ebersole 1893-1954 *WhAm 3*

Gaines, Lewis McFarland 1878-1937 *WhAm 1*

Gaines, Myra Clark Whitney 1805-1885 *AmWom, ApCAB, NatCAB 3, NotAW, TwCBDA*

Gaines, Paschal Clay 1898-1966 *WhAm 4*

Gaines, Reuben Ira 1858?- *WhoColR*

Gaines, Reuben Reid 1836-1914 *DcAmB, NatCAB 10, WhAm 1*

Gaines, Robert Edwin 1860- *WhAm 4*

Gaines, Ruth 1879- *WhAm 6*

Gaines, Walter Lee 1881-1950 *DcScB*

Gaines, Wesley John 1840-1912 *ApCAB Sup, DcAmB, NatCAB 2, TwCBDA, WhAm 1, WhoColR*

Gaines, William Embre 1844-1912 *BiDrAC*

Gainey, Percy Leigh 1887-1972 *WhAm 5*

Gains *NewYHSD*

Gainsborough, Thomas 1727-1788 *McGEWB*

Gainza, Gavino 1760?-1824? *ApCAB*

Gair, George West 1872-1940 *WhAm 1*

Gair, Robert 1839-1927 *ApCAB X, NatCAB 40*

Gairshofer, Maurice *NewYHSD*

Gaiseric d477 *McGEWB*

Gaisman, Henry Jacques 1869-1974 *WhAm 6*

Gaitan, Jorge Eliecer 1898-1948 *McGEWB*

Gaither, Burgess Sidney 1807-1892 *BiDConf, NatCAB 7, TwCBDA*

Gaither, Charles Thomas 1867-1955 *NatCAB 45*

Gaither, Frances 1889-1955 *WhAm 3*

Gaither, H Rowan, Jr. 1909-1961 *WhAm 4*

Gaither, Henry 1751-1811 *ApCAB, Drake*

Gaither, Henry Chew 1777-1845 *ApCAB*

Gaither, Nathan 1788-1862 *BiAUS, BiDrAC, WhAm H*

Gaither, P Stokes 1907-1967 *WhAm 5*

Gaither, William Cotter, Jr. 1914-1967 *WhAm 4*

Gaither, William Lingan 1813-1858 *ApCAB, Drake*

Gaitskell, Hugh Todd Naylor 1906-1963 *WhAm 4*

Gaitskill, Bennett S 1858- *WhAm 1*

Galarneault, John Toan 1899-1967 *WhAm 5*

Galatti, Stephen 1888-1964 *WhAm 4*

Galberry, Thomas 1833-1878 *ApCAB, DcAmB, NatCAB 10, TwCBDA, WhAm H*

Galbraith, Andrew 1692?-1747? *ApCAB*

Galbraith, Anna Mary *WhAm 1, WomWWA 14*

Galbraith, Archibald Victor 1877-1971 *NatCAB 56, WhAm 5*

Galbraith, C Blake 1897-1960 *NatCAB 50*

Galbraith, Clinton Alexander 1860-1923 *WhAm 1*

Galbraith, Frederick William 1874-1921 *NatCAB 19*

Galbraith, Jacob Garrettson 1856-1923 *NatCAB 6*

Galbraith, John 1794-1860 *ApCAB Sup, BiAUS, BiDrAC, WhAm H*

Galbraith, John Hughes 1886-1942 *NatCAB 41*

Galbraith, John Kenneth 1908- *EncAB, WebAB*

Galbraith, John Patrick 1865- *NatCAB 16*

Galbraith, Nettie May 1880-1943 *WhAm 2*

Galbraith, Victor 1823?- *NatCAB 8*

Galbraith, William Ayres 1823-1898 *ApCAB Sup*

Galbreath, Charles Burleigh 1858-1934 *AmBi, DcAmB S1, NatCAB 25, WhAm 1*

Galbreath, John Morrison 1848-1915 *WhAm 1*

Galbreath, Robert Ferguson 1884-1960 *NatCAB 48, WhAm 4*

Galbreath, William Robert 1884-1946 *NatCAB 40*

Galdos, Benito Perez 1843-1920 *McGEWB*

Gale, Ada Iddings *AmWom*

Gale, Agnes Spofford Cook 1873- *WomWWA 14*

Gale, Anthony 1782-1843? *WebAMB*

Gale, Arthur Sullivan 1877- *WhAm 5*

Gale, Benjamin 1715-1790 *ApCAB, DcAmB, Drake, NatCAB 23, WhAm H*

Gale, Charles William 1846-1919 *ApCAB X*

Gale, Christopher 1670?- *NatCAB 4*

Gale, Clement Rowland 1862- *WhAm 4*

Gale, Cyrus Ervin 1849-1929 *NatCAB 21*

Gale, Edward Chenery 1862-1943 *WhAm 2*

Gale, Edward Justus 1872- *WhAm 5*

Gale, Elbridge 1824-1907 *AmBi, DcAmB, NatCAB 23*

Gale, Esson McDowell 1884-1964 *NatCAB 51, WhAm 4*

Gale, Ezra Thompson 1819-1887 *NatCAB 3*

Gale, George 1756-1815 *BiAUS, BiDrAC, WhAm H, WhAmP*

Gale, George Washington 1789-1861 *AmBi, BiDAmEd, DcAmB, NatCAB 24, TwCBDA, WhAm H*

Gale, George Washington 1789-1862 *ApCAB*

Gale, Henry Gordon 1874-1942 *DcAmB S3, WhAm 2*

Gale, Hoyt Stoddard 1876-1952 *WhAm 3*

Gale, Sir Humphrey 1890-1971 *WhWW-II*

Gale, Jane Winsor 1868- *WomWWA 14*

Gale, John Elbridge 1841-1916 *ApCAB X*

Gale, Joseph Wasson 1900-1968 *WhAm 5*

Gale, Laurence Edward 1925-1967 *WhAm 4*

Gale, Levin 1784-1834 *BiAUS, BiDrAC, WhAm H, WhAmP*

Gale, Levin 1824-1875 *ApCAB*

Gale, Margaret Morris 1854- *WomWWA 14*

Gale, Minna K *WhAm 5*

Gale, Noel 1862- *WhAm 4*

Gale, Oliver Marble 1877- *WhAm 5*

Gale, Philip Bartlett 1873-1945 *NatCAB 34, WhAm 2*

Gale, Richard Pillsbury 1900-1973 *BiDrAC, WhAm 6*

Gale, Samuel 1783-1865 *ApCAB*

Gale, Samuel Chester 1895-1961 *WhAm 4*

Gale, Stephen Francis 1812- *ApCAB Sup*

Gale, Stephen Henry 1846-1920 *NatCAB 34, WhAm 1*

Gale, T C *NewYHSD*

Gale, Theophilus d1677 *ApCAB*

Gale, William Holt 1864-1932 *BiAUS, WhAm 1*

Gale, Willis Donald 1899-1966 *WhAm 4*

Gale, Zona 1874-1938 *AmBi, DcAmB S2,*

NatCAB 30, NotAW, WhAm 1, WomWWA 14

Galeazzi, Domenico Gusmano 1686-1775 *DcScB*

Galen 129?-200? *DcScB*

Galen 130?-200? *AsBiEn, McGEWB*

Galen, Albert John 1876-1936 *WhAm 1*

Galen, Claudius 130-200 *BiHiMed*

Galen, Archbishop Clemens Von 1878-1946 *WhWW-II*

Galeppi, Alexander *NewYHSD*

Galer, Roger Sherman 1863-1950 *WhAm 3*

Galerkin, Boris Grigorievich 1871-1945 *DcScB, DcScB Sup*

Gales, George M 1876-1954 *WhAm 3*

Gales, Joseph 1760-1841 *ApCAB*

Gales, Joseph 1761-1841 *AmBi, DcAmB, NatCAB 9, WhAm H, WhAmP*

Gales, Joseph 1786-1860 *AmBi, ApCAB, BiAUS, DcAmB, Drake, TwCBDA, WhAm H, WhAmP*

Gales, Seaton 1828-1878 *ApCAB*

Galey, John Henry 1840-1918 *NatCAB 18*

Gali, Francisco 1539-1591 *ApCAB*

Galifianakis, Nick 1928- *BiDrAC*

Galilei, Galileo 1564-1642 *DcScB*

Galilei, Vincenzio 1520?-1591 *DcScB*

Galileo 1564-1642 *AsBiEn, McGEWB*

Galinee *ApCAB*

Galitzen, Elizabeth 1797-1843 *WhAm H*

Galitzin, B B *DcScB*

Galitzin, Demetrius Augustine 1770-1840 *Drake*

Gall 1840?-1894 *AmBi, DcAmB, REnAW, WebAB, WebAMB, WhAm H*

Gall, Franz Joseph 1758-1828 *AsBiEn, DcScB*

Gall, Frederick P *NewYHSD*

Gall, John Christian 1901-1957 *NatCAB 48, WhAm 4*

Gallagher *NewYHSD*

Gallagher, Bernard John 1903-1963 *NatCAB 49*

Gallagher, Charles Eugene 1876-1951 *WhAm 3*

Gallagher, Charles Theodore 1851-1919 *NatCAB 11, WhAm 1*

Gallagher, Charles Wesley 1846-1916 *NatCAB 25, TwCBDA, WhAm 1*

Gallagher, Cornelius Edward 1921- *BiDrAC*

Gallagher, Daniel J 1873-1953 *WhAm 3*

Gallagher, Edward George 1922-1975 *WhAm 6*

Gallagher, Ferdinand H *NewYHSD*

Gallagher, Frances L 1881- *WomWWA 14*

Gallagher, Francis Edward 1884-1950 *WhAm 3*

Gallagher, Francis Xavier 1928-1972 *NatCAB 57*

Gallagher, H Clifford 1855-1931 *NatCAB 30*

Gallagher, Henry M 1885-1965 *WhAm 4*

Gallagher, Herbert Richard 1883-1949 *NatCAB 38*

Gallagher, Howard William 1903-1970 *WhAm 5*

Gallagher, Hugh 1888-1968 *WhAm 5*

Gallagher, Hugh Clifford 1855-1931 *WhAm 1*

Gallagher, Hugh Patrick 1815-1882 *AmBi, ApCAB, DcAmB, TwCBDA, WhAm H*

Gallagher, James A 1869-1957 *BiDrAC*

Gallagher, John d1842 *Drake*

Gallagher, John James 1891-1968 *WhAm 5*

Gallagher, Louis Joseph 1885-1972 *WhAm 5*

Gallagher, Michael 1870-1957 *WhAm 3*

Gallagher, Michael James 1866-1937 *WhAm 1*

Gallagher, Nettie *WomWWA 14*

Gallagher, Nicholas Aloysius 1846-1918 *ApCAB, NatCAB 12, TwCBDA, WhAm 1*

Gallagher, Ralph Aloysius 1896-1965 *WhAm 4*

Gallagher, Ralph W 1881-1952 *DcAmB S5, WhAm 3*

Gallagher, Sears 1869-1955 *WhAm 3*

Gallagher, Thomas 1850-1930 *BiDrAC, WhAm 1, WhAmP*

Gallagher, Thomas Francis 1855-1941 *NatCAB 30*

Gallagher, William 1849-1922 *WhAm 1*

Gallagher, William Davis 1808-1894 *AmBi, ApCAB, DcAmB, Drake, NatCAB 9, WhAm H*

Gallagher, William James 1875-1946 *BiDrAC, WhAm 2, WhAmP*

Gallaher, Edward Beach 1873-1953 *NatCAB 48*

Gallaher, Ernest Yale 1875- *WhAm 5*

Gallaher, Grace Margaret *WomWWA 14*

Gallaher, John Nicholas 1839- *ApCAB*
Gallaher, John S *BiAUS*
Gallaher, Sarah McCune 1864- *WomWWA 14*
Gallahue, Dudley Richard 1898-1972 *WhAm 5*
Gallahue, Edward Francis 1902-1971
NatCAB 56, WhAm 5
Gallalee, John Morin 1883-1961 *WhAm 4*
Galland, Adolf 1912- *WhWW-II*
Galland, John *NewYHSD*
Galland, Joseph Stanislaus 1883-1947 *WhAm 2*
Galland, Walter Isaac 1889-1962 *NatCAB 48*
Gallant, Albert Ernest 1861- *WhAm 1*
Gallant, W Erskine 1889-1901 *NatCAB 57*
Gallard, Gustave *NewYHSD*
Gallardo, Aurelio Luis 1831-1869 *ApCAB*
Gallatin, Abraham Alfonse Albert 1761-1849
DcAmB, EncAB
Gallatin, Albert 1761-1849 *AmBi, ApCAB,*
BiAUS, BiDrAC, BiDrUSE, Drake,
McGEWB, NatCAB 3, TwCBDA,
WebAB, WhAm H, WhAmP
Gallatin, Albert 1835-1905 *NatCAB 37*
Gallatin, Albert Eugene 1881-1952 *NatCAB 42,*
WhAm 3
Gallatin, Albert Horatio 1839- *TwCBDA*
Gallatin, Albert Rolaz 1800-1890 *TwCBDA*
Gallatin, Alberta 1860-1948 *NatCAB 39*
Gallatin, Francis Dawson 1870-1933 *ApCAB X,*
WhAm 1
Gallaudet, Bern Budd 1860-1934 *NatCAB 26,*
WhAm 1
Gallaudet, Edward 1809-1847 *NewYHSD*
Gallaudet, Edward Miner 1837-1917 *AmBi,*
ApCAB, BiDAmEd, DcAmB, NatCAB 9,
NatCAB 18, TwCBDA, WhAm 1
Gallaudet, Elisha 1730?-1805 *NewYHSD*
Gallaudet, Herbert Draper 1876-1944
NatCAB 33
Gallaudet, Sophia Fowler 1798-1877 *ApCAB*
Gallaudet, Thomas 1822-1902 *AmBi, ApCAB,*
DcAmB, NatCAB 9, TwCBDA,
WhAm 1
Gallaudet, Thomas Hopkins 1787-1851 *AmBi,*
ApCAB, BiDAmEd, DcAmB, Drake,
McGEWB, NatCAB 9, TwCBDA,
WebAB, WhAm H
Gallaway, George Ellis 1876-1950 *NatCAB 38*
Gallaway, Robert Macy 1837-1917 *WhAm 1*
Galle, Johann Gottfried 1812-1910 *AsBiEn,*
DcScB
Gallegos, Jose Manuel 1815-1875 *BiAUS,*
BiDrAC, REnAW, WhAm H, WhAmP
Gallegos Freire, Romulo 1884-1969 *McGEWB*
Galleher, John Nicholas 1839-1891 *NatCAB 11,*
TwCBDA
Gallen, John James 1905-1976 *WhAm 6*
Gallery, Daniel Vincent 1901-1977 *WebAMB*
Gallet, Louis 1904-1955 *NatCAB 45*
Galley, John Vessot 1897-1959 *NatCAB 44*
Galli, Stanley W 1912- *IlBEAAW*
Galli-Curci, Amelita 1889-1963 *WhAm 4*
Gallico, Poole 1868-1955 *WhAm 3*
Gallie, William Edward 1882-1959 *WhAm 3*
Gallieni, Joseph Simon 1849-1916 *WhoMilH*
Gallier, James 1798-1868 *BnEnAmA,*
DcAmB S1, WhAm H
Gallier, John *NewYHSD*
Galligan, Matthew James 1854- *WhAm 4*
Galliher, C Emery 1895-1952 *NatCAB 42*
Galliher, Charles Emery 1859-1935 *NatCAB 34*
Galliher, William Thompson 1856-1929
NatCAB 26, WhAm 1
Gallimore, Harry Charles 1887-1958
NatCAB 44
Gallinger, Jacob Harold 1837- *ApCAB Sup,*
TwCBDA
Gallinger, Jacob Harold 1837-1917 *NatCAB 2*
Gallinger, Jacob Harold 1837-1918 *BiDrAC,*
DcAmB, WhAm 1, WhAmP
Gallison, Henry Hammond 1850-1910 *WhAm 1*
Gallison, John 1788-1820 *ApCAB, Drake*
Gallissoniere, Rolland Michael Berrin 1693-1756
Drake
Gallitzin, Demetrius Augustine 1770-1840 *AmBi,*
DcAmB, NatCAB 23, TwCBDA,
WhAm H
Gallitzin, Demetrius Augustine 1770-1841
ApCAB

Gallitzin, Elizabeth 1795-1843 *ApCAB*
Gallivan, James Ambrose 1866-1928 *BiDrAC,*
WhAm 1, WhAmP
Galliver, George Alfred d1932 *WhAm 1*
Gallizier, Nathan 1866-1927 *WhAm 1*
Gallo, Fortune 1878-1970 *WhAm 5*
Gallo, Frank 1933- *BnEnAmA*
Gallois, Jean 1632-1707 *DcScB*
Gallop, John d1650 *ApCAB*
Galloway, Beverly Thomas 1863-1938
DcAmB S2, NatCAB 12, WhAm 1
Galloway, Charles Anderson 1876-1954
WhAm 3
Galloway, Charles Betts 1849-1909 *AmBi,*
ApCAB, DcAmB, NatCAB 5, TwCBDA,
WhAm 1
Galloway, Charles Henry 1871- *WhAm 5*
Galloway, Charles Mills 1875- *WhAm 5*
Galloway, Charles William 1868-1940 *WhAm 1*
Galloway, David Henry 1859- *WhAm 3*
Galloway, Emma Baker 1851- *WomWWA 14*
Galloway, Fannie Mead Delaplain 1857-
WomWWA 14
Galloway, Floyd Emerson 1890-1955 *WhAm 3*
Galloway, George Barnes 1898-1967
NatCAB 53
Galloway, Irene Oti'lia 1908-1963 *WhAm 4*
Galloway, J J 1882-1962 *WhAm 4*
Galloway, Jacob Scudder 1838-1919 *NatCAB 8*
Galloway, John D Brown 1907-1955
NatCAB 42
Galloway, John Debo 1869-1943 *NatCAB 40*
Galloway, John Stuart 1897-1965 *WhAm 4*
Galloway, Joseph 1729?-1803 *ApCAB,*
BiDrAC, NatCAB 1, TwCBDA, WhAmP
Galloway, Joseph 1730?-1803 *BiAUS, Drake*
Galloway, Joseph 1731?-1803 *AmBi, DcAmB,*
EncAB, McGEWB, WebAB, WhAm H
Galloway, Lee d1962 *WhAm 4*
Galloway, Robert E 1894-1965 *WhAm 4*
Galloway, Samuel 1811-1872 *ApCAB, BiAUS,*
BiDAmEd, BiDrAC, DcAmB,
NatCAB 23, WhAm H
Galloway, Samuel 1812-1872 *TwCBDA*
Galloway, Thomas Walton 1866-1929
NatCAB 22, WhAm 1
Gallowhur, Elizabeth Warner 1879-
WomWWA 14
Gallozzi, Tommaso 1873-1938 *WhAm 3*
Gallun, Albert Frederick 1865-1938 *NatCAB 50*
Gallup, Albert 1796-1851 *BiAUS, BiDrAC,*
WhAm H
Gallup, Anna Billings 1872-1956 *WhAm 3*
Gallup, Benjamin Ela 1826-1895 *NatCAB 18*
Gallup, Clarence Mason 1874-1947 *WhAm 2*
Gallup, Edward Hatton, Jr. 1898-1969 *WhAm 5*
Gallup, Frank Amner 1863-1951 *NatCAB 42,*
WhAm 3
Gallup, Fred D 1872-1949 *NatCAB 46*
Gallup, George Horace 1901- *EncAB, WebAB*
Gallup, Joseph Adam 1769-1849 *Drake*
Gallup, Joseph Adams 1769-1849 *ApCAB,*
DcAmB, NatCAB 5, TwCBDA,
WhAm H
Gallup, William Arthur 1851-1930 *ApCAB X,*
NatCAB 28, WhAm 1
Gallup, Willis Delancy 1899-1964 *NatCAB 51*
Gally, Merritt 1838-1916 *ApCAB, DcAmB,*
NatCAB 4, TwCBDA
Galois, Evariste 1811-1832 *DcScB*
Galpin, Charles Josiah 1864-1947 *DcAmB S4,*
WhAm 4
Galpin, Cromwell *IlBEAAW*
Galpin, Julia Bogart *WomWWA 14*
Galpin, Kate Tupper 1855-1906 *AmWom,*
WhAm 1
Galpin, Lloy 1876- *WomWWA 14*
Galpin, Perrin C 1889-1973 *WhAm 6*
Galpin, Stanley Leman 1878-1934 *WhAm 1*
Galpin, William Freeman 1890-1963 *WhAm 4*
Galston, Clarence G 1876-1964 *WhAm 4*
Galsworthy, John 1867-1933 *McGEWB*
Galt, Alexander 1827-1863 *NatCAB 19,*
NewYHSD, WhAm H
Galt, Sir Alexander Tilloch 1817-1893 *ApCAB,*
Drake, McGEWB
Galt, Arthur Thomas 1876- *WhAm 6*
Galt, Herbert Randolph 1881-1926 *WhAm 1*

Galt, Howard Spilman 1872- *WhAm 5*
Galt, Hugh Allan 1868-1947 *NatCAB 34*
Galt, John 1779-1839 *ApCAB*
Galt, John Minson 1744-1808 *NatCAB 20*
Galt, John Randolph 1867-1941 *WhAm 1*
Galt, Madeline Noyes 1878- *WomWWA 14*
Galt, Thomas 1815- *ApCAB*
Galton, Blanche *NotAW*
Galton, Sir Francis 1822-1911 *AsBiEn,*
BiHiMed, DcScB, McGEWB
Galusha, Elon d1859 *ApCAB*
Galusha, Hugh Duncan, Jr. 1919-1971
NatCAB 57, WhAm 5
Galusha, Jonas 1753-1834 *ApCAB, BiAUS,*
Drake, NatCAB 8, TwCBDA
Galvani, Aloysio Luigi 1737-1798 *BiHiMed*
Galvani, Charles 1805?- *NewYHSD*
Galvani, Luigi 1737-1798 *AsBiEn, DcScB,*
McGEWB
Galvez, Bernardo 1755-1786 *ApCAB*
Galvez, Bernardo De *WhAm H*
Galvez, Bernardo De 1746-1786 *AmBi, DcAmB,*
McGEWB, REnAW
Galvez, Bernardo De 1756-1786 *NatCAB 10*
Galvez, Bernardo De 1756-1794 *Drake*
Galvez, Jose De 1720-1787 *McGEWB*
Galvez, Jose De 1729-1786 *ApCAB*
Galvez, Mariano d1850? *ApCAB*
Galvez, Matias 1731-1784 *ApCAB*
Galvin, Charles Edward 1882-1941 *NatCAB 30*
Galvin, John 1862-1922 *WhAm 1*
Galvin, John E 1878- *WhAm 6*
Galvin, John Francis 1859- *WhAm 1*
Galvin, Joseph A 1883-1954 *WhAm 3*
Galvin, Leroy Spahr 1875-1952 *WhAm 3*
Galvin, Michael Joseph 1907-1963 *NatCAB 49,*
WhAm 4
Galvin, Paul Vincent 1895-1959 *WhAm 3*
Galway, Henri DeMassue, Earl Of 1648-1720
WhoMilH
Galwith, Sara Bailey 1862- *WomWWA 14*
Gama, Antonio Leon De 1735-1802 *ApCAB*
Gama, Domicio Da 1862-1925 *WhAm 1*
Gama, Jose Basilio Da 1740-1795 *ApCAB*
Gama, Jose Bernardo Fernandez 1802-1852
ApCAB
Gama, Vasco Da 1460?-1524 *McGEWB*
Gama, Vasco Da *see also* DaGama, Vasco
Gamache, George Paul 1929-1972 *WhAm 5*
Gamage, Frederick Luther 1860- *NatCAB 14,*
TwCBDA, WhAm 3
Gamaleya, Nikolay Fyodorovich 1859-1949
DcScB
Gamarra, Agustin 1785-1841 *ApCAB*
Gamarra Y Davalos, Juan Benito 1745-1793
ApCAB
Gambardella, Spiridione *NewYHSD*
Gambee, Martin 1905- *IlBEAAW*
Gambel, W *NewYHSD*
Gambel, William 1819?-1849 *WhAm H*
Gamber, Branson VanLeer 1893-1949 *WhAm 3*
Gamberini, Domenico *NewYHSD*
Gambetta, Leon 1838-1882 *McGEWB*
Gambey, Henri-Prudence 1787-1847 *DcScB*
Gambier, James 1756-1833 *ApCAB, Drake*
Gamble, Cecil Huggins 1884-1956 *NatCAB 46,*
WhAm 3
Gamble, Clarence James 1894-1966 *NatCAB 53*
Gamble, David *NewYHSD*
Gamble, David Samuel 1873-1945 *NatCAB 35*
Gamble, Donald Phelps 1899-1968 *WhAm 5*
Gamble, E Ross 1883-1964 *WhAm 4*
Gamble, Eleanor Acheson McCulloch 1868-1933
WhAm 1
Gamble, Eleanor Achison McCulloch 1868-1933
WomWWA 14
Gamble, Eliza Burt 1841-1920 *NatCAB 18*
Gamble, Francis G d1824 *ApCAB*
Gamble, Hamilton R d1874 *BiAUS*
Gamble, Hamilton Rowan 1798-1864 *AmBi,*
ApCAB, DcAmB, NatCAB 12, TwCBDA,
WhAm H
Gamble, Henry Floyd 1862- *WhoColR*
Gamble, Hugh Agnew 1876-1954 *NatCAB 44*
Gamble, James 1809- *BiAUS*
Gamble, James 1809-1882 *ApCAB, TwCBDA*
Gamble, James 1809-1883 *BiDrAC, WhAm H*
Gamble, James Lawder 1883-1959 *WhAm 3*

Gamble, James Norris 1836-1932 *NatCAB 40,*
WhAm 1
Gamble, John M 1791?-1836 *ApCAB*
Gamble, John Rankin 1848-1891 *BiDrAC,*
WhAm H, WhAmP
Gamble, Joseph Graham 1884-1946 *NatCAB 50*
Gamble, Maude Morey 1877- *WomWWA 14*
Gamble, Millard Gobert 1894-1974 *WhAm 6*
Gamble, Parker Blair 1886-1948 *NatCAB 37*
Gamble, Paul Gaston 1882-1957 *NatCAB 47*
Gamble, Peter d1814 *ApCAB*
Gamble, Ralph Abernethy 1885-1959 *BiDrAC,*
WhAm 3, WhAmP
Gamble, Robert 1861-1926 *NatCAB 21*
Gamble, Robert Bruce 1871-1940 *WhAm 1*
Gamble, Robert Howard 1888-1953 *WhAm 3*
Gamble, Robert Jackson 1851-1924 *BiDrAC,*
NatCAB 12, TwCBDA, WhAm 1,
WhAmP
Gamble, Roger Lawson 1787-1847 *BiAUS,*
BiDrAC, WhAm H
Gamble, Samuel Walter 1852-1932 *WhAm 1*
Gamble, Sidney David 1890-1968 *WhAm 5*
Gamble, Theodore Robert 1924-1969
NatCAB 57, WhAm 5
Gamble, Theodore Roosevelt 1906-1961
WhAm 4
Gamble, Thomas d1818 *ApCAB, Drake*
Gamble, Thomas Owen 1890-1961 *NatCAB 49*
Gamble, Willard Selden 1906-1948 *NatCAB 36*
Gamble, William 1818-1866 *ApCAB Sup*
Gamble, William Elliott 1860- *WhAm 4*
Gamboa, Francisco Javier 1717-1794 *ApCAB*
Gambrell, James Brueton 1841-1921 *NatCAB 6*
Gambrell, James Bruton 1841-1921 *DcAmB,*
TwCBDA, WhAm 1
Gambrell, Joel Halbert 1855-1923 *WhAm 1*
Gambrell, Mary Latimer 1898-1974 *WhAm 6*
Gambrill, Charles D 1832-1880 *WhAm H*
Gambrill, Howard 1867-1952 *NatCAB 41*
Gambrill, James Henry, Jr. 1866-1951
NatCAB 49, WhAm 3
Gambrill, John Montgomery 1880-1953
WhAm 3
Gambrill, Melville 1849-1925 *NatCAB 20*
Gambrill, Stephen Warfield 1873-1938 *BiDrAC,*
WhAm 1, WhAmP
Game, Josiah Bethea 1869-1935 *WhAm 1*
Gamel, W Warren 1906-1966 *WhAm 5*
Gamelin, Maurice Gustave 1872-1958
WhWW-II, WhoMilH
Gamer, Helena Margaret 1900-1966 *WhAm 4*
Gamertsfelder, Solomon Jacob 1851-1925
WhAm 1
Gamertsfelder, Walter Sylvester 1885-1967
WhAm 4
Gamewell, Francis Dunlap 1857-1950 *WhAm 3*
Gamewell, John N 1822-1896 *TwCBDA*
Gamlen, James Eli 1918-1973 *WhAm 6*
Gammack, Arthur James 1871-1927
NatCAB 21, WhAm 5
Gammack, James 1837-1923 *WhAm 1*
Gammage, Grady 1892-1959 *BiDAmEd,*
NatCAB 47, WhAm 3
Gammell, John 1872-1947 *NatCAB 36*
Gammell, Robert Ives 1852-1915 *WhAm 1*
Gammell, William 1812-1889 *ApCAB, Drake,*
NatCAB 8, TwCBDA
Gammell, William 1857-1943 *WhAm 2*
Gammeter, Harry Christian 1870-1937
NatCAB 27
Gammeter, John Rudolph 1876-1957
NatCAB 44
Gammill, Stewart 1865-1952 *NatCAB 42*
Gammino, Michael Anthony 1890-1949
NatCAB 39
Gammon, Burton Osmond 1881- *WhAm 6*
Gammon, Edgar Graham 1884-1962 *WhAm 4*
Gammon, Elijah Hedding 1819-1891 *DcAmB,*
NatCAB 23, WhAm H
Gammon, George Davis 1902-1974 *WhAm 6*
Gammon, Landon Haynes 1896-1975 *WhAm 6*
Gammon, Robert William 1867-1948 *WhAm 2,*
WhAm 2C
Gammons, Charles Clifford 1895-1964
NatCAB 51, WhAm 4
Gammons, Ferdinand Clinton 1845-1929
ApCAB X

Gamon, Wylena Clarissa d1968 *WhAm 5*
Gamoran, Emanuel 1895-1962 *WhAm 4*
Gamoran, Emmanuel 1895-1962 *BiDAmEd*
Gamow, George 1904-1968 *AsBiEn, DcScB,*
WebAB, WhAm 5
Gana, Domingo 1844- *ApCAB Sup*
Gana, Jose Francisco 1791-1862 *ApCAB*
Gancher, Jacob I 1882-1958 *NatCAB 47*
Gandara Y Navarro, Jose DeLa 1820- *ApCAB*
Gandek, Charles 1917-1973 *WhAm 6*
Gandhi, Indira Priyadarshini 1917- *McGEWB*
Gandhi, Mohandas Karamchand 1869-1948
McGEWB, WhWW-II
Gandhi, Mohandas Mahatma 1869-1948
WhAm 2
Gandolfi, Mauro 1764-1834 *NewYHSD*
Gandy, Charles Moore 1857-1937 *WhAm 1*
Gandy, Harry Luther 1881-1957 *BiDrAC,*
WhAm 6, WhAmP
Gandy, John Manuel 1870- *WhAm 5,*
WhoColR
Gandy, Joseph Edward 1904-1971 *WhAm 5*
Gane, Gertrude 1872- *WomWWA 14*
Gane, Marjory 1880- *WomWWA 14*
Ganesa 1507- *DcScB*
Ganev, Dimiter d1964 *WhAm 4*
Ganey, J Cullen 1899-1972 *WhAm 5*
Ganfield, William Arthur 1873-1940 *WhAm 1*
Gangel, Martha O'Donnell d1973 *WhAm 6*
Gangewere, Earnest Paul 1900-1973 *WhAm 6*
Gangwisch, John Paul 1868-1949 *NatCAB 38*
Ganiere, George Etienne d1935 *WhAm 1*
Ganiodaiio *WhAm H*
Ganley, J Howard 1892-1963 *NatCAB 52*
Ganly, James Vincent 1878-1923 *BiDrAC,*
WhAm 1
Gann, David Byron 1866-1945 *NatCAB 33*
Gann, Dewell, Jr. 1890-1960 *NatCAB 47*
Gann, Edward Everett 1880-1936 *ApCAB X,*
WhAm 1
Gannam, John 1905-1965 *WhAm 4*
Gannam, John 1907-1965 *IlBEAAW*
Gannaway, William Trigg 1825- *NatCAB 3*
Ganneaktena, Catharine d1673 *ApCAB*
Gannett, Abbie M 1845- *AmWom*
Gannett, Alice Peirson *WomWWA 14*
Gannett, Anne Macomber d1951 *WhAm 3*
Gannett, Barzilla 1764-1832 *BiAUS*
Gannett, Barzillai 1764-1832 *BiDrAC,*
WhAm H
Gannett, Deborah Sampson *NotAW*
Gannett, Ezra Stiles 1801-1871 *AmBi, ApCAB,*
DcAmB, Drake, NatCAB 10, TwCBDA,
WhAm H
Gannett, Farley 1880-1958 *NatCAB 47,*
WhAm 3
Gannett, Frank Ernest 1876-1957 *NatCAB 48,*
WhAm 3
Gannett, George 1819- *NatCAB 1*
Gannett, Guy Patterson 1881-1954 *NatCAB 44,*
WhAm 3
Gannett, Henry 1846-1914 *AmBi, DcAmB,*
NatCAB 19, TwCBDA, WebAB,
WhAm 1
Gannett, Lewis Stiles 1891-1966 *WhAm 4,*
WhAm 4A
Gannett, Thomas Brattle 1876-1931 *NatCAB 24,*
WhAm 1
Gannett, Thomas Brattle 1912-1968 *NatCAB 54*
Gannett, William Channing 1840-1923 *DcAmB,*
NatCAB 22, TwCBDA, WhAm 1
Gannett, William Henry 1854- *NatCAB 5*
Gannett, William Howard 1854-1948
NatCAB 38, WhAm 2
Gannon, Anna 1876- *WhAm 5*
Gannon, Frank Stanislaus 1851-1922 *WhAm 1*
Gannon, Fred Hall 1881- *WhAm 6*
Gannon, James Henry 1876-1935 *NatCAB 41*
Gannon, John Mark 1877-1968 *WhAm 5*
Gannon, Mary 1829-1868 *ApCAB,*
NatCAB 11
Gannon, Sinclair 1877-1948 *WhAm 2*
Gannon, Thomas Joseph 1853-1918 *NatCAB 2,*
TwCBDA, WhAm 1
Gannt, E W 1832-1874 *BiAUS*
Gano, D Curtis 1874-1948 *NatCAB 39*
Gano, John 1727-1804 *ApCAB, DcAmB,*
Drake, NatCAB 10, WhAm H

Gano, Roy A 1902-1971 *WhAm 5*
Gano, Seth Thomas 1879-1955 *WhAm 3*
Gano, Stephen 1762-1828 *ApCAB, DcAmB,*
NatCAB 10, WhAm H
Ganoe, William Addleman 1881-1966 *WhAm 5*
Ganong, Francis William 1864- *ApCAB Sup*
Ganong, William Francis 1864-1941
NatCAB 14, WhAm 1
Gans, Bird Stein 1868- *BiCAW*
Gans, Birdie Stein 1868- *WomWWA 14*
Gans, Edgar Hilary 1856-1914 *ApCAB X,*
WhAm 1
Gans, Emmett William 1861-1938 *NatCAB 38*
Gans, Julius 1879-1953 *NatCAB 42*
Gans, Marshall 1904-1970 *NatCAB 57*
Ganse, Hervey Doddridge 1822- *ApCAB*
Gansevoort, Guert C 1812-1868 *ApCAB, Drake,*
TwCBDA
Gansevoort, Henry Sanford 1834-1871
NatCAB 1
Gansevoort, Henry Sanford 1835-1871 *TwCBDA*
Gansevoort, Leonard 1751-1810 *ApCAB,*
BiAUS, BiDrAC, DcAmB, TwCBDA,
WhAm H, WhAmP
Gansevoort, Leonard 1754-1834 *ApCAB*
Gansevoort, Peter 1749-1812 *AmBi, ApCAB,*
DcAmB, Drake, NatCAB 1, TwCBDA,
WebAMB, WhAm H
Gansevoort, Peter 1788-1876 *NatCAB 1,*
TwCBDA
Ganso, Emil 1895-1941 *DcAmB S3*
Ganson, John 1818-1874 *BiAUS, BiDrAC,*
WhAm H
Ganson, John 1819-1874 *NatCAB 4*
Ganss, Henry George 1855-1912 *DcAmB*
Gant, Allen Erwin 1898-1972 *NatCAB 57*
Gant, Roger 1887-1960 *NatCAB 48*
Gant, Samuel Goodwin 1869- *WhAm 5*
Gante, Pedro De 1500?-1572 *ApCAB Sup*
Gantenbein, Calvin Ursinus 1865-1919 *WhAm 1*
Gantenbein, James Watson 1900-1960 *WhAm 4*
Ganter, Daniel *NewYHSD*
Gantt, Daniel 1814-1878 *NatCAB 13*
Gantt, Edward 1746-1837 *ApCAB*
Gantt, Ernest Sneed 1867-1947 *WhAm 2*
Gantt, Henry Laurence 1861-1919 *AmBi,*
DcAmB, WhAm 4
Gantt, Henry Lawrence 1861-1919 *NatCAB 18*
Gantt, James Britton 1845-1912 *NatCAB 12,*
WhAm 1
Gantt, L Rosa H 1875-1935 *WomWWA 14*
Gantt, Love Rosa Hirschmann 1875-1935
NotAW
Gantt, Matilda Weidemeyer 1857-
WomWWA 14
Gantt, Nicholas Jourdan, Jr. 1879- *WhAm 6*
Gantt, Robert Anderson 1881- *WhAm 6*
Gantvoort, Arnold Johann 1857-1937 *BiDAmEd,*
NatCAB 40, WhAm 1
Gantz, Hallie George 1910-1972 *WhAm 5*
Gantz, Helen Birney 1881- *WomWWA 14*
Gantz, Joseph 1888-1945 *NatCAB 33*
Gantz, Martin Kissinger 1862-1916 *BiDrAC*
Gantz, William Osger 1869-1957 *NatCAB 44*
Ganus, Clifton L 1903-1955 *WhAm 3*
Ganz, Albert Frederick 1872-1917 *WhAm 1*
Ganz, Rudolph 1877-1972 *WhAm 5*
Gara, Mrs. Isaac B *NewYHSD*
Garabedian, Garabed Arshag Zacar 1888-1938
NatCAB 34
Garakonthie, Daniel 1600?-1676 *AmBi,*
ApCAB, DcAmB, WhAm H
Garand, John Cantius 1888-1974 *WebAB,*
WebAMB, WhAm 6
Garanflo, William Henry 1865-1926
NatCAB 20
Garay, Francisco De d1523 *ApCAB*
Garay, John De 1541-1592? *Drake*
Garay, Jose De 1801-1858 *Drake*
Garay, Juan De 1541-1584 *ApCAB*
Garbeille, Philip *NewYHSD*
Garber, Daniel 1880-1958 *NatCAB 49,*
WhAm 3
Garber, Daniel Anderson 1860-1929
NatCAB 24
Garber, Earl Augustus 1893-1963 *WhAm 4*
Garber, Etelka Williar 1885- *WomWWA 14*
Garber, Frederick William d1950 *WhAm 3*

Garber, Harvey Cable 1865-1938 *NatCAB 31,*
  WhAm 4
Garber, Harvey Cable 1866-1938 *BiDrAC*
Garber, J Otis 1902-1969 *WhAm 5*
Garber, Jacob Aaron 1879-1953 *BiDrAC*
Garber, Jerry Mock 1872-1957 *NatCAB 45*
Garber, John 1833-1908 *NatCAB 25*
Garber, John Palmer 1858-1936 *WhAm 1*
Garber, Milton Cline 1867-1948 *BiDrAC,*
  NatCAB 38, WhAm 2, WhAmP
Garber, Ora Myers 1889-1941 *NatCAB 31*
Garber, Paul Neff 1899-1972 *WhAm 5*
Garber, Silas 1833- *BiAUS, NatCAB 12*
Garbisch, Norbert Samuel 1897-1967
  NatCAB 54
Garbo, Greta 1905- *McGEWB, WebAB*
Garbutt, Frank Alderman 1869-1947
  NatCAB 36
Garbutt, Frank Clarkson 1837-1920 *NatCAB 18*
Garbutt, Mary Alderman 1844- *WomWWA 14*
Garcelon, Alonzo 1813-1906 *DcAmB,*
  NatCAB 6, TwCBDA, WhAm 1,
  WhAmP
Garcelon, Harris 1879-1935 *NatCAB 40*
Garcelon, William Frye 1868-1949 *WhAm 2*
Garces, Francisco Tomas Hermenegildo
  1738-1781 *DcAmB, WhAm H*
Garces, Julian 1457-1547 *ApCAB*
Garcia, A M *NewYHSD*
Garcia, Alexo 1485-1526 *ApCAB*
Garcia, Carlos P 1896-1971 *McGEWB,*
  WhAm 5
Garcia, Diego 1471-1529 *ApCAB*
Garcia, Fabian 1871-1948 *WhAm 3*
Garcia, Hector Perez 1914- *REnAW*
Garcia, Manuel 1803-1872 *ApCAB*
Garcia, Manuel DePopulo Vicente 1775-1832
  ApCAB
Garcia, Miguel *NewYHSD*
Garcia-Calderon, Francisco 1829- *ApCAB*
Garcia-Conde, Pedro 1806-1851 *ApCAB*
Garcia-Cubas, Antonio 1832- *ApCAB*
Garcia DeQuevedo, Jose Heriberto 1819-1871
  ApCAB
Garcia DeSan Vicente, Nicolas 1793-1845
  ApCAB
Garcia-Granados, Miguel 1825-1878 *ApCAB*
Garcia Lorca, Federico 1898-1936 *McGEWB*
Garcia Lorca, Federico 1899-1936 *WhAm 4*
Garcia Marquez, Gabriel 1928- *McGEWB*
Garcia-Moreno, Gabriel 1821-1875 *ApCAB,*
  McGEWB
Garcia-Reyes, Antonio 1817-1855 *ApCAB*
Garcia-Rovira, Custodio 1780?-1816
  ApCAB Sup
Garcia-Velez, Carlos 1867- *WhAm 4*
Garcia Y Iniguez, Calixto 1839-1898
  ApCAB Sup
Garcias, Gregorio 1554-1627 *ApCAB*
Garcilaso DeLaVega 1540-1616 *Drake*
Garcilaso DeLaVega, Inca 1539-1616 *McGEWB*
Garcilaso DeLaVega, Sebastian 1495?-1559
  ApCAB
Garcin, Ramon David, Jr. 1899-1963
  NatCAB 50
Gard, George Edmond 1898-1959 *NatCAB 48*
Gard, Ida M *WomWWA 14*
Gard, Sanford Wayne 1899- *EncAAH*
Gard, Warren 1873-1929 *BiDrAC, WhAm 1,*
  WhAmP
Gard, Wayne 1899- *REnAW*
Gard, Willis Lloyd 1869-1936 *WhAm 1*
Garden, Alexander 1685?-1756 *ApCAB*
Garden, Alexander 1728-1791 *Drake*
Garden, Alexander 1730?-1791 *AmBi, ApCAB,*
  DcAmB, NatCAB 23, WebAB, WhAm H
Garden, Alexander 1757-1829 *AmBi, ApCAB,*
  DcAmB, Drake, NatCAB 8, TwCBDA,
  WhAm H
Garden, Francis *NewYHSD*
Garden, Henry Rhiel 1874-1941 *NatCAB 30*
Garden, Hugh Mackie Gordon 1873-1961
  WhAm 4
Garden, Hugh Richardson 1840-1910
  NatCAB 2, WhAm 4
Garden, Mary 1874-1967 *ApCAB X, WebAB,*
  WhAm 4
Garden, Mary 1877- *NatCAB 15*

Gardener, Cornelius 1849-1921 *NatCAB 19,*
  WhAm 1
Gardener, Helen Hamilton d1925 *WhAm 1,*
  WomWWA 14
Gardener, Helen Hamilton 1853-1925 *AmWom,*
  DcAmB, NatCAB 9, NotAW, WhAmP
Gardener, Helen Hamilton 1858-1925 *TwCBDA*
Gardenhire, Erasmus Lee 1815-1899 *BiDConf*
Gardenhire, Samuel Major 1855-1923 *WhAm 1*
Gardenier, Barent d1822 *BiAUS, BiDrAC,*
  WhAm H
Gardin, Francis *NewYHSD*
Gardin, John E *ApCAB X*
Gardiner, Addison 1797-1883 *ApCAB,*
  NatCAB 13
Gardiner, Arthur Z 1901-1975 *WhAm 6*
Gardiner, Asa Bird 1839-1919 *ApCAB Sup,*
  NatCAB 14, TwCBDA, WhAm 1
Gardiner, Charles Alexander 1855-1909
  WhAm 1
Gardiner, Charles Perkins 1836-1908
  NatCAB 14
Gardiner, Sir Christopher *AmBi, DcAmB,*
  WhAm H
Gardiner, Curtiss C 1874-1948 *WhAm 2*
Gardiner, David Lion 1816-1892 *ApCAB X*
Gardiner, Edmund Gibson 1844-1923
  NatCAB 21
Gardiner, Edward Gardiner 1854-1907
  NatCAB 14
Gardiner, Frederic 1822-1889 *NatCAB 9,*
  TwCBDA
Gardiner, Frederic 1858-1917 *WhAm 1*
Gardiner, George Hill 1869-1936 *ApCAB X,*
  NatCAB 27
Gardiner, George Schuyler 1854-1921
  NatCAB 19, WhAm 1
Gardiner, Glenn L 1896-1962 *WhAm 4*
Gardiner, Harry Norman 1855-1927 *DcAmB S1,*
  NatCAB 21, WhAm 1
Gardiner, James Garfield 1883-1962 *WhAm 4*
Gardiner, James L 1872- *WhAm 3*
Gardiner, James Terry 1842-1912 *ApCAB,*
  DcAmB, NatCAB 23, WhAm 1
Gardiner, John 1731-1793 *ApCAB, Drake*
Gardiner, John 1737-1793 *AmBi, DcAmB,*
  NatCAB 23, WhAm H
Gardiner, John 1747-1808 *BiDrAC, WhAm H*
Gardiner, John 1816-1915 *NatCAB 21*
Gardiner, John Hays 1863- *WhAm 4*
Gardiner, John Sylvester John 1765-1830
  ApCAB, DcAmB, Drake, NatCAB 8,
  TwCBDA, WhAm H
Gardiner, Lion 1599-1663 *AmBi, ApCAB,*
  DcAmB, NatCAB 23, WebAMB,
  WhAm H
Gardiner, Robert Hallowell 1782?-1864 *ApCAB,*
  DcAmB, WhAm H
Gardiner, Robert Hallowell 1855-1924 *WhAm 1*
Gardiner, Mrs. S W *NewYHSD*
Gardiner, Samuel Rawson 1829-1902 *McGEWB*
Gardiner, Sidney 1788?-1827 *BnEnAmA*
Gardiner, Silvester 1708-1786 *AmBi, DcAmB,*
  WhAm H
Gardiner, Sylvester 1707-1786 *ApCAB, Drake*
Gardiner, Sylvester 1717-1786 *NatCAB 8*
Gardiner, Sylvester 1730?-1803 *BiDrAC,*
  WhAm H
Gardiner, T Momolu 1870-1941 *WhAm 1*
Gardiner, Thomas Hazard 1893-1953
  NatCAB 44
Gardiner, Thomas William 1849-1924
  ApCAB X, NatCAB 20
Gardiner, William Howard 1875-1952 *WhAm 3*
Gardiner, William Munson 1871-1941
  NatCAB 37
Gardiner, William Saunders 1884-1953
  NatCAB 49
Gardiner, William Tudor 1892-1953
  NatCAB 42, WhAm 3
Gardinier, Barendt d1822 *NatCAB 13*
Gardner, Abraham 1912-1962 *NatCAB 50*
Gardner, Addison Leman 1866- *WhAm 5*
Gardner, Albert TenEyck 1909-1967 *WhAm 4*
Gardner, Alexander 1821-1882 *BnEnAmA*
Gardner, Alice Day 1873- *WomWWA 14*
Gardner, Anna 1816- *AmWom*
Gardner, Archibald K 1867-1962 *WhAm 4*

Gardner, Arthur 1889-1967 *WhAm 4*
Gardner, Augustus Kingsley 1812-1876 *ApCAB*
Gardner, Augustus Kinsley 1821-1876 *TwCBDA*
Gardner, Augustus Peabody 1865-1918 *BiDrAC,*
  WhAm 1, WhAmP
Gardner, B *NewYHSD*
Gardner, Bertie Charles 1884-1972 *WhAm 5*
Gardner, Caleb 1739-1806 *ApCAB, DcAmB,*
  NatCAB 23, WhAm H
Gardner, Celia Emmeline 1844- *WhAm 4*
Gardner, Charles Henry 1864- *WhAm 4*
Gardner, Charles K 1787-1869 *ApCAB, BiAUS,*
  Drake
Gardner, Charles Kitchel 1787-1869 *DcAmB,*
  WhAm H
Gardner, Charles Kitchell 1787-1869 *TwCBDA*
Gardner, Charles Kitchell 1789-1869 *NatCAB 5*
Gardner, Charles M 1872-1954 *WhAm 3*
Gardner, Charles Spurgeon 1859-1948 *WhAm 2*
Gardner, Constance 1872- *WomWWA 14*
Gardner, Dillard Scott 1906-1964 *WhAm 4*
Gardner, Donfred Huber 1900-1975 *WhAm 6*
Gardner, Dorsey 1842-1894 *ApCAB, TwCBDA*
Gardner, Earl Wentworth 1914-1970 *WhAm 5*
Gardner, Edmund Sherman 1892-1942
  NatCAB 31
Gardner, Edward Frederic 1904-1963 *WhAm 4*
Gardner, Edward Joseph 1898-1950 *BiDrAC,*
  NatCAB 51, WhAm 3
Gardner, Edward Tytus 1879-1960 *WhAm 3*
Gardner, Elizabeth Jane 1837-1922 *NewYHSD*
Gardner, Elizabeth Jane 1842- *ApCAB*
Gardner, Elliott 1892-1969 *NatCAB 53*
Gardner, Emily 1899-1956 *NatCAB 42*
Gardner, Erle Stanley 1889-1970 *WebAB,*
  WhAm 6
Gardner, Esther Bogue 1874- *WomWWA 14*
Gardner, Etta Brown Underwood
  WomWWA 14
Gardner, Eugene C 1836-1915 *WhAm 1*
Gardner, Eugene Elmore 1890-1955 *WhAm 3*
Gardner, Francis 1771-1835 *BiAUS, BiDrAC,*
  WhAm H
Gardner, Frank 1872-1937 *BiDrAC, WhAm 2,*
  WhAmP
Gardner, Frank Duane 1864-1963 *WhAm 4*
Gardner, Frank Saltus 1852-1927 *WhAm 1*
Gardner, Frank Williams 1874-1946
  NatCAB 36
Gardner, Franklin 1823-1873 *BiDConf*
Gardner, Fred 1867-1935 *NatCAB 26*
Gardner, Frederick Dozier 1869-1933
  NatCAB 45, WhAm 1
Gardner, George 1812-1849 *ApCAB*
Gardner, George Clinton 1834-1904 *NatCAB 13*
Gardner, George Peabody 1855-1939 *WhAm 1*
Gardner, George W 1834-1911 *WhAm 1*
Gardner, George Warren 1828-1895 *ApCAB,*
  TwCBDA
Gardner, Gideon 1759-1832 *BiAUS, BiDrAC,*
  WhAm H
Gardner, Gilson 1869-1935 *DcAmB S1,*
  WhAm 1
Gardner, Grandison 1892-1973 *WhAm 5*
Gardner, Halbert Paine 1867- *WhAm 4*
Gardner, Harold Ward 1877- *WhAm 5*
Gardner, Harriet Woodford *WomWWA 14*
Gardner, Harry Wentworth 1873- *WhAm 5*
Gardner, Helen 1878-1946 *BiDAmEd,*
  DcAmB S4, NotAW, WhAm 2
Gardner, Helen 1884-1968 *WhAm 6*
Gardner, Henry 1730?-1782 *ApCAB*
Gardner, Henry A 1883-1968 *WhAm 4*
Gardner, Henry Brayton 1863-1939 *WhAm 1*
Gardner, Henry Burchell 1891-1932
  NatCAB 33
Gardner, Henry Joseph d1892 *BiAUS*
Gardner, Henry Joseph 1818-1892 *DcAmB,*
  WhAm H, WhAmP
Gardner, Henry Joseph 1819-1892 *NatCAB 1,*
  TwCBDA
Gardner, Herbert Spencer 1872-1955 *WhAm 3*
Gardner, Herman d1947 *WhAm 2*
Gardner, Hilton Bowen 1902-1961 *WhAm 4*
Gardner, Horace Chase 1856-1936 *WhAm 1*
Gardner, Horace John d1950 *WhAm 3*
Gardner, Horace Tillman 1913-1970 *WhAm 5*
Gardner, Hugh Miller 1893-1947 *WhAm 2*
Gardner, Irvine C 1889-1972 *WhAm 5*

Gardner, Isabella Stewart 1840-1924 *AmBi,*
DcAmB, EncAB, NotAW, WebAB,
WhAm 1
Gardner, J Howland 1871-1944 *WhAm 2*
Gardner, Mrs. Jack *NotAW*
Gardner, James *NewYHSD*
Gardner, James Augustus 1870-1926
NatCAB 21, WhAm 1
Gardner, James Carson 1933- *BiDrAC*
Gardner, James Henry 1883-1964 *NatCAB 51,*
WhAm 4
Gardner, James Patterson 1858-1924
NatCAB 20
Gardner, Jessie Barker *WomWWA 14*
Gardner, John d1764 *NatCAB 8*
Gardner, John 1868- *WhAm 5*
Gardner, John Henry 1893-1944 *WhAm 2*
Gardner, John James 1845-1921 *BiDrAC,*
TwCBDA, WhAm 1, WhAmP
Gardner, John Lane 1793-1869 *ApCAB,*
DcAmB, Drake, TwCBDA, WhAm H
Gardner, John William 1912- *BiDrUSE,*
EncAB, WebAB
Gardner, Joseph *NewYHSD*
Gardner, Joseph 1752-1794 *ApCAB, BiAUS,*
BiDrAC, TwCBDA, WhAm H, WhAmP
Gardner, Julia Anna 1882- *WomWWA 14*
Gardner, Julia Streeter 1878- *WomWWA 14*
Gardner, Karl Dana 1892-1944 *WhAm 2*
Gardner, Kirtland C 1876-1955 *WhAm 3*
Gardner, Leroy Upson 1888-1946 *DcAmB S4,*
WhAm 2
Gardner, Lester Durand 1876-1956 *NatCAB 44,*
WhAm 3
Gardner, Lucie Marion *WomWWA 14*
Gardner, Lucien Dunbibbin 1876-1952
NatCAB 42
Gardner, Mary Carpenter 1865- *WomWWA 14*
Gardner, Mary Sewell 1871- *WhAm 5*
Gardner, Matthias Bennett 1897-1975 *WhAm 6*
Gardner, Mills 1830-1910 *BiDrAC*
Gardner, Murray MacGregor 1887-1957
NatCAB 47
Gardner, O Max 1882-1947 *NatCAB 36*
Gardner, Mrs. O Max 1885-1969 *WhAm 5*
Gardner, Obadiah 1850-1938 *BiDrAC*
Gardner, Obadiah 1852-1938 *NatCAB 15,*
WhAm 1
Gardner, Oliver Max 1882-1947 *WhAm 2,*
WhAm 2C
Gardner, Oliver Maxwell 1882-1947 *DcAmB S4*
Gardner, Patrick *NewYHSD*
Gardner, Percy Winchester 1881-1955
NatCAB 42, WhAm 3
Gardner, Rathbone 1856-1931 *WhAm 1*
Gardner, Richard Fisher 1874-1952 *NatCAB 43*
Gardner, Robert Abbe 1890-1956 *NatCAB 45,*
WhAm 3
Gardner, Robert Waterman 1866-1937
WhAm 1
Gardner, Russell Eugene 1866-1938 *NatCAB 48*
Gardner, Sally *NewYHSD*
Gardner, Samuel Hill 1876-1942 *NatCAB 31*
Gardner, Samuel Jackson 1788-1864 *ApCAB,*
Drake, NatCAB 13
Gardner, Thomas 1724-1775 *ApCAB, Drake*
Gardner, Trevor 1915-1963 *WhAm 4*
Gardner, Vernon O 1877- *WhAm 5*
Gardner, Wallace John 1883-1954 *NatCAB 40,*
WhAm 3
Gardner, Walter Edwin 1849-1927 *NatCAB 21,*
WhAm 1
Gardner, Walter Pennett 1869-1949 *NatCAB 39,*
WhAm 2
Gardner, Washington 1845-1928 *BiDrAC,*
NatCAB 5, TwCBDA, WhAm 1,
WhAmP
Gardner, Willard 1883-1964 *NatCAB 53*
Gardner, William Alexander 1859-1916
NatCAB 18, WhAm 1
Gardner, William Edward 1872-1965 *WhAm 4,*
WhAm 5
Gardner, William Emmett 1877-1947
NatCAB 34
Gardner, William Henry 1800-1870 *ApCAB,*
Drake, TwCBDA
Gardner, William Henry 1865-1932 *WhAm 1*
Gardner, William Henry 1882-1957 *NatCAB 46*

Gardner, William King 1898-1973 *NatCAB 57*
Gardner, William Marshall 1900-1946
NatCAB 34
Gardner, William Sisson 1861- *WhAm 4*
Gardner, Wright Austin 1878- *WhAm 6*
Garel, Leo 1917- *IlBEAAW*
Garesche, Claude Francis 1890-1962 *WhAm 4*
Garesche, Edward Francis 1876-1960 *WhAm 4*
Garesche, Julius Peter 1821-1862 *ApCAB,*
Drake, TwCBDA
Garey, Enoch Barton 1883- *WhAm 3*
Garey, Eugene Lester 1891-1953 *NatCAB 18,*
WhAm 3
Garey, John Charles 1911-1956 *NatCAB 43*
Garey, Thomas Andrew 1830-1909 *AmBi,*
DcAmB, NatCAB 23
Garfield, Abram 1872-1958 *WhAm 3*
Garfield, Charles Fowler 1872-1933 *WhAm 1*
Garfield, Charles William 1848-1934 *WhAm 1*
Garfield, Chester Arthur 1881-1962 *NatCAB 49*
Garfield, Harry Augustus 1863-1942 *ApCAB X,*
DcAmB S3, NatCAB 33, WhAm 2
Garfield, Irvin McDowell 1870-1951
NatCAB 40, WhAm 3
Garfield, James Abram 1831-1881 *AmBi,*
ApCAB, BiAUS, BiDrAC, BiDrUSE,
DcAmB, Drake, EncAAH, EncAB,
McGEWB, NatCAB 4, TwCBDA,
WebAB, WhAm H, WhAmP
Garfield, James Rudolph 1865-1950 *BiDrUSE,*
DcAmB S4, NatCAB 14, NatCAB 42,
WhAm 2A
Garfield, John 1913-1952 *DcAmB S5*
Garfield, Lucretia Rudolph 1832-1918 *AmWom,*
ApCAB, NatCAB 4, NotAW, TwCBDA,
WhAm 1
Garfield, Theodore Abbott 1913-1970
NatCAB 55
Garfield, Walter Thompson 1882-1947
NatCAB 35
Garfielde, Selucius 1822-1881 *BiAUS, BiDrAC,*
WhAm H
Garford, Arthur Lovett 1858-1933 *ApCAB X,*
WhAm 1
Gargan, Lucien Clair *WomWWA 14*
Garibaldi, Giuseppe 1807-1882 *ApCAB Sup,*
McGEWB, WhoMilH
Garibaldi, Guiseppe 1807-1882 *WhAm H*
Garibaldi, Joseph 1864-1939 *NatCAB 29*
Garibaldi, Lucinda *NewYHSD*
Garibaldi, Pietro A *NewYHSD*
Garibaldi, Mrs. Pietro A 1822?- *NewYHSD*
Garibi Y Rivera, Jose 1889-1972 *WhAm 6*
Garis, Charles Frederick Fleming 1881-1957
WhAm 3
Garis, Howard Roger 1873-1962 *WhAm 4*
Garis, Lilian C d1954 *WhAm 3*
Garl, Ernestine Julia Hicks 1859-
WomWWA 14
Garland, A H 1832-1899 *BiAUS*
Garland, Augustus Hill 1832-1899 *AmBi,*
ApCAB, BiDConf, BiDrAC, BiDrUSE,
DcAmB, NatCAB 2, NatCAB 10,
REnAW, TwCBDA, WhAm H, WhAmP
Garland, Cecil Raymond 1907-1972 *WhAm 5*
Garland, Charles Stedman 1898-1971
NatCAB 56, WhAm 5
Garland, Cornelius N *WhoColR*
Garland, Daniel Frank 1864-1928 *WhAm 1*
Garland, David Shepherd 1769-1841 *BiAUS,*
BiDrAC, WhAm H
Garland, Frank 1893-1962 *NatCAB 51*
Garland, Frank Milton 1855- *WhAm 4*
Garland, Hamlin 1860-1940 *AmBi,*
ApCAB Sup, ApCAB X, DcAmB S2,
EncAAH, NatCAB 8, REnAW,
TwCBDA, WebAB, WhAm 1
Garland, Hannibal Hamlin 1860-1940 *EncAB,*
McGEWB
Garland, Hugh A d1864 *ApCAB*
Garland, Hugh A 1805-1854 *ApCAB, BiAUS,*
Drake
Garland, James 1791-1885 *BiAUS, BiDrAC,*
WhAm H
Garland, James A 1870-1906 *WhAm 1*
Garland, James Powell 1835- *WhAm 4*
Garland, John 1792-1861 *ApCAB, Drake,*
TwCBDA

Garland, John Jewett 1902-1968 *NatCAB 54*
Garland, Joseph 1893-1973 *WhAm 6*
Garland, Judy 1922-1969 *WebAB, WhAm 5*
Garland, Landon Cabell 1810-1895 *ApCAB,*
BiDAmEd, BiDConf, DcAmB, NatCAB 8,
TwCBDA, WhAm H
Garland, Leo Henry 1903-1966 *NatCAB 53,*
WhAm 4
Garland, Mahlon Morris 1856-1920 *BiDrAC,*
WhAm 1, WhAmP
Garland, Mary J 1834-1901 *WhAm 1*
Garland, Peter Adams 1923- *BiDrAC*
Garland, Rice 1795?-1861 *BiAUS, BiDrAC,*
WhAm H, WhAmP
Garland, Robert 1862-1949 *NatCAB 50,*
WhAm 2
Garland, Robert 1895-1955 *WhAm 3*
Garland, Robert R d1862 *Drake*
Garland, Rufus King, Jr. 1830-1886 *BiDConf*
Garland, Samuel 1830-1862 *ApCAB,*
NatCAB 10, TwCBDA
Garland, Thomas James 1866-1931 *NatCAB 22,*
WhAm 1
Garland, William May 1866-1948 *NatCAB 40,*
WhAm 2
Garlick, Henry Manning 1848-1928
NatCAB 33, WhAm 1
Garlick, Samuel Middleton 1845-1924
NatCAB 35
Garlick, Theodatus 1805-1884 *DcAmB,*
NatCAB 24, NewYHSD, WhAm H
Garlington, Creswell 1887-1945 *WhAm 2*
Garlington, Ernest Albert 1853-1934
NatCAB 34, TwCBDA, WhAm 1
Garman, Charles Edward 1850-1907 *DcAmB,*
NatCAB 23, WhAm 1
Garman, Harrison 1856-1944 *NatCAB 33,*
WhAm 4
Garman, Harrison 1858-1944 *NatCAB 14*
Garman, Harry Otto 1880- *WhAm 6*
Garman, John Montgomery 1851-1926
NatCAB 20
Garman, Raymond Leroy 1907-1970 *WhAm 5*
Garman, Samuel 1843-1927 *AmBi, DcAmB,*
WhAm 1
Garman, Samuel 1846- *ApCAB, TwCBDA*
Garman, Samuel 1849- *NatCAB 10*
Garmatz, Edward Alexander 1903- *BiDrAC*
Garmhausen, Erwin John 1913-1972 *WhAm 5*
Garneau, Francois Xavier 1809-1866 *ApCAB,*
McGEWB
Garneau, Pierre 1823- *ApCAB*
Garneaux, Francis Xavier 1809-1866 *Drake*
Garner, Albert Rowland 1877-1950 *NatCAB 39*
Garner, Alfred Buckwalter 1873-1930 *BiDrAC,*
WhAm 5
Garner, Eliza A 1845- *AmWom*
Garner, Geston 1880-1958 *NatCAB 49*
Garner, Harry Hyman 1910-1973 *WhAm 6*
Garner, James Bert 1870- *WhAm 5*
Garner, James Wilford 1871-1938 *DcAmB S2,*
NatCAB 31, WhAm 1
Garner, John Nance 1868-1967 *BiDrAC,*
BiDrUSE, EncAB, WebAB, WhAm 4,
WhAmP
Garner, John Oakley 1889-1960 *NatCAB 50*
Garner, Peter M 1809-1868 *ApCAB*
Garner, Richard Lynch 1848- *NatCAB 13,*
WhAm 4
Garner, Robert Livingston 1894-1975 *WhAm 6*
Garner, Wightman Wells 1875- *WhAm 5*
Garneray, Ambrose Louis 1783-1857 *NewYHSD*
Garnerey *NewYHSD*
Garnet, Henry Highland 1815-1882 *AmBi,*
ApCAB, DcAmB, NatCAB 2, TwCBDA,
WhAm H, WhAmP
Garnet, Sarah J Smith Thompson 1831-1911
NotAW
Garnett, Alexander Yelverton Peyton 1819-1888
DcAmB, TwCBDA, WhAm H
Garnett, Alexander Yelverton Peyton 1820-1888
ApCAB, NatCAB 12
Garnett, Christopher Browne 1875-1955
NatCAB 43
Garnett, George Harrison 1866- *WhAm 4*
Garnett, James Mercer 1770-1843 *ApCAB,*
BiAUS, BiDrAC, DcAmB, Drake,
EncAAH, TwCBDA, WhAmP

Garnett, James Mercer 1840-1916 *DcAmB, NatCAB 1, TwCBDA, WhAm 1*
Garnett, James Mercur 1770-1843 *WhAm H*
Garnett, Joseph Blythe 1882-1954 *NatCAB 44*
Garnett, Judith Livingston Cox 1862- *WhAm 1*
Garnett, Louise Ayres d1937 *WhAm 1, WomWWA 14*
Garnett, Muscoe Russell Hunter 1821-1863? *ApCAB*
Garnett, Muscoe Russell Hunter 1821-1864 *BiAUS, BiDConf, BiDrAC, DcAmB, NatCAB 26, TwCBDA, WhAm H, WhAmP*
Garnett, Porter 1871-1951 *WhAm 3*
Garnett, Richard Brooke 1819-1863 *ApCAB, Drake, NatCAB 11, TwCBDA*
Garnett, Robert Selden 1789- *ApCAB, BiAUS*
Garnett, Robert Selden 1789-1840 *BiDrAC, WhAm H, WhAmP*
Garnett, Robert Selden 1789-1841 *TwCBDA*
Garnett, Robert Selden 1819-1861 *ApCAB, DcAmB, NatCAB 23, TwCBDA, WhAm H*
Garnett, Robert Selden 1820-1861 *Drake*
Garnett, Theodore Stanford 1844-1915 *WhAm 1*
Garnett, Thomas 1766-1802 *DcScB*
Garnier, Charles 1605-1649 *ApCAB*
Garnier, Jean Louis Charles 1825-1898 *McGEWB*
Garnier, Julien 1643?-1722? *ApCAB*
Garnier, Marie Joseph Francois 1839-1873 *McGEWB, WhoMilH*
Garnot, Prosper 1794-1838 *DcScB*
Garnsey, Daniel Greene 1779-1851 *BiAUS, BiDrAC, WhAm H*
Garnsey, Edward Grant 1869-1917 *NatCAB 18*
Garnsey, Edward Grant, Jr. 1897-1918 *NatCAB 18*
Garnsey, Elmer Ellsworth 1862-1946 *NatCAB 11, NatCAB 35, WhAm 2*
Garofalo, Emil 1898-1952 *NatCAB 41*
Garol, Hugh William 1910-1958 *NatCAB 47*
Garonhiague, Louis d1687 *ApCAB*
Garr, Charles Crain 1884-1957 *NatCAB 51*
Garrabrant, Arthur Anderson 1889-1951 *WhAm 3*
Garran, Frank W 1894-1945 *WhAm 2*
Garrard, Hector Lewis 1829-1887 *REnAW*
Garrard, James 1749-1822 *ApCAB, BiAUS, DcAmB, Drake, NatCAB 13, TwCBDA, WhAm H, WhAmP*
Garrard, Jeanne 1923- *WhAm 6*
Garrard, Jeptha d1915 *WhAm 1*
Garrard, Kenner 1827-1879 *NatCAB 23*
Garrard, Kenner 1828-1879 *AmBi, DcAmB, WhAm H*
Garrard, Kenner 1830-1879 *ApCAB, Drake, NatCAB 5, TwCBDA*
Garrard, Louis Ford 1847- *NatCAB 3*
Garrard, Theophilus Toulmin 1812- *ApCAB*
Garrard, William Mountjoy 1881-1958 *NatCAB 47*
Garratt, John Milton 1865-1919 *NatCAB 18*
Garreau, Armand 1817-1865 *DcAmB, WhAm H*
Garreau, Lazare 1812-1892 *DcScB*
Garrecht, Francis Arthur 1870-1948 *NatCAB 36, WhAm 2*
Garrels, Arthur 1873-1943 *WhAm 2*
Garretson, Abram Quick 1842-1907 *WhAm 1*
Garretson, Arthur Samuel 1851- *WhAm 4*
Garretson, Austin Bruce 1856-1931 *DcAmB S1, WhAm 1*
Garretson, Cornelius David 1882-1968 *WhAm 5*
Garretson, Freeborn 1752-1827 *ApCAB, TwCBDA*
Garretson, Garret James 1847-1922 *NatCAB 14, NatCAB 26, WhAm 1*
Garretson, George Armstrong 1844-1916 *NatCAB 21, WhAm 1*
Garretson, James Edmund 1828-1895 *AmBi, ApCAB, DcAmB, NatCAB 3, WhAm H*
Garretson, Joseph 1874-1931 *WhAm 1*
Garretson, Mary Rutherford 1783-1879 *ApCAB*
Garretson, Oliver Kelleam 1896-1975 *WhAm 6*
Garrett, Abraham Ellison 1830-1907 *BiAUS, BiDrAC*

Garrett, Alexander Charles 1832-1924 *ApCAB, NatCAB 13, TwCBDA, WhAm 1*
Garrett, Alfred Cope 1867-1946 *WhAm 2*
Garrett, Andrew 1823-1887 *ApCAB Sup, NatCAB 2*
Garrett, Arthur Sellers 1873-1955 *NatCAB 46*
Garrett, Campbell Deane 1900-1961 *WhAm 4*
Garrett, Clarence Coleman 1902-1954 *NatCAB 42*
Garrett, Clyde D 1887-1974 *WhAm 6*
Garrett, Clyde Leonard 1885-1959 *BiDrAC*
Garrett, Daniel Edward 1869-1932 *BiDrAC, NatCAB 24, WhAm 1, WhAmP*
Garrett, David Claiborne 1857-1930 *WhAm 1*
Garrett, Donald Wallace 1928-1973 *WhAm 5*
Garrett, Edmund Henry 1853-1929 *DcAmB, TwCBDA, WhAm 1*
Garrett, Edward Isaiah 1877- *WhAm 6*
Garrett, Eileen Jeanette 1893-1970 *NatCAB 55, WhAm 5*
Garrett, Emma 1846?-1893 *BiDAmEd, NotAW*
Garrett, Erastus R *NewYHSD*
Garrett, Erwin Clarkson 1879-1954 *WhAm 3*
Garrett, Eschen Boland 1896-1957 *NatCAB 48*
Garrett, Evan LaRue 1904-1967 *NatCAB 53*
Garrett, Finis James 1875-1956 *BiDrAC, WhAm 3, WhAmP*
Garrett, Garet 1878-1954 *NatCAB 43, WhAm 3*
Garrett, George *NewYHSD*
Garrett, George Angus 1888-1971 *NatCAB 56, WhAm 5*
Garrett, Harry Freeland 1887-1971 *WhAm 5*
Garrett, Henry E 1894-1973 *WhAm 6*
Garrett, Jack 1890-1954 *NatCAB 44*
Garrett, James Madison, Jr. 1892-1971 *WhAm 5*
Garrett, James William 1925-1970 *WhAm 5*
Garrett, John Biddle 1836-1924 *WhAm 1*
Garrett, John Clifford 1908-1963 *WhAm 4*
Garrett, John E 1817?- *NewYHSD*
Garrett, John W B *NewYHSD*
Garrett, John Work 1820-1884 *AmBi, ApCAB, DcAmB, McGEWB, NatCAB 18, TwCBDA, WhAm H*
Garrett, John Work 1872-1942 *WhAm 2*
Garrett, Joshua Tracy 1881-1941 *WhAm 1*
Garrett, Leroy Allin 1906-1963 *WhAm 4*
Garrett, Mary Elizabeth 1854-1915 *NotAW*
Garrett, Mary Smith 1839-1925 *NotAW, WomWWA 14*
Garrett, Mitchell Bennett 1881-1959 *NatCAB 50*
Garrett, Oliver Hart Palmer 1897-1952 *NatCAB 39*
Garrett, Pat 1850-1908 *REnAW*
Garrett, Paul Loos 1893-1955 *WhAm 3*
Garrett, Philip C 1834-1905 *WhAm 1*
Garrett, Ray 1889-1969 *NatCAB 55, WhAm 5*
Garrett, Robert 1783-1857 *DcAmB, WhAm H*
Garrett, Robert 1847-1896 *ApCAB, NatCAB 18, TwCBDA*
Garrett, Robert 1875-1961 *NatCAB 48, WhAm 4*
Garrett, Robert Edwin 1908-1973 *NatCAB 57, WhAm 6*
Garrett, Rufus Napoleon 1858-1942 *WhAm 2*
Garrett, Sylvester 1842-1910 *NatCAB 16*
Garrett, Thomas 1783-1871 *ApCAB, Drake*
Garrett, Thomas 1789-1871 *AmBi, DcAmB, McGEWB, WhAm H, WhAmP*
Garrett, Thomas Harrison 1849-1888 *NatCAB 9*
Garrett, Thomas Henry 1858-1934 *NatCAB 35*
Garrett, William Abner 1861-1924 *WhAm 1*
Garrett, William Adelor 1910-1972 *WhAm 5*
Garrett, William Robertson 1839-1904 *BiDAmEd, DcAmB, NatCAB 12, TwCBDA, WhAm 1*
Garrettson, Frederick Prime 1857-1930 *NatCAB 23*
Garrettson, Freeborn 1752-1827 *AmBi, DcAmB, DcAmReB, NatCAB 10, WhAm H*
Garrettson, John Archibald 1878-1945 *NatCAB 34*

Garrey, George Henry 1875-1957 *WhAm 3*
Garrey, Walter Eugene 1874-1951 *WhAm 3*
Garrick, James P 1875- *WhAm 2*
Garriga, Mariano Simon 1886-1965 *WhAm 5*
Garrigan, Philip Joseph 1840-1919 *DcAmB, NatCAB 12, WhAm 1*
Garrigue, Jean 1914-1972 *WhAm 5*
Garrigues, Henry Jacques 1831-1913 *ApCAB, WhAm 1*
Garrigues, James Edward 1852- *WhAm 4*
Garrigus, Harry Lucian 1876-1968 *NatCAB 54*
Garriott, Edward Bennett 1853-1910 *WhAm 1*
Garrison, Ada Hardemon *WomWWA 14*
Garrison, B *NewYHSD*
Garrison, Carl Louise *WhAm 5*
Garrison, Charles Grant 1849-1924 *WhAm 1*
Garrison, Cornelius Kingsland 1809-1885 *ApCAB, DcAmB, NatCAB 7, TwCBDA, WhAm H*
Garrison, Daniel 1782-1851 *BiAUS, BiDrAC, WhAm H*
Garrison, Daniel Mershon 1874-1927 *WhAm 1*
Garrison, Elisha Ely 1871-1935 *NatCAB 26*
Garrison, F Lynwood 1862- *WhAm 4*
Garrison, Fielding Hudson 1870-1935 *AmBi, DcAmB S1, NatCAB 26, WhAm 1*
Garrison, Francis Jackson 1848- *WhAm 1*
Garrison, George Pierce 1853-1910 *WhAm 1*
Garrison, George Tankard 1835-1889 *BiDrAC, TwCBDA, WhAm H*
Garrison, Harrell Edmond 1908-1972 *WhAm 5*
Garrison, Homer, Jr. 1901-1968 *WhAm 5*
Garrison, James Carr 1870-1929 *WhAm 1*
Garrison, James Harvey 1842-1931 *DcAmReB, NatCAB 18, WhAm 4*
Garrison, John Boggs 1849- *WhAm 3*
Garrison, John R 1838-1908 *WhAm 1*
Garrison, Joseph Fithian 1823-1892 *ApCAB, TwCBDA*
Garrison, Lemuel Addison 1871- *WhAm 5*
Garrison, Lindley Miller 1864-1932 *AmBi, ApCAB X, BiDrUSE, DcAmB S1, NatCAB 26, WhAm 1*
Garrison, Lloyd Amos 1903-1975 *WhAm 6*
Garrison, Lucy McKim 1842-1877 *NotAW*
Garrison, Mabel d1963 *WhAm 4*
Garrison, Mary Ridgely 1885- *WomWWA 14*
Garrison, Nicholas, Jr. *NewYHSD*
Garrison, Paul Adams 1927-1970 *NatCAB 56*
Garrison, Pleasant Austin 1868- *WhoColR*
Garrison, Sidney Clarence 1887-1945 *WhAm 2*
Garrison, Theodosia Pickering *WomWWA 14*
Garrison, Walter Raymond 1898-1946 *WhAm 4*
Garrison, Wendell Phillips 1840-1907 *NatCAB 1, TwCBDA, WhAm 1*
Garrison, William Dominick 1838-1892 *NatCAB 2*
Garrison, William Hart 1920-1970 *WhAm 5*
Garrison, William Lloyd 1804-1879 *Drake*
Garrison, William Lloyd 1805-1879 *AmBi, ApCAB, DcAmB, EncAAH, EncAB, McGEWB, NatCAB 2, TwCBDA, WebAB, WhAm H, WhAmP*
Garrison, William Lloyd 1838-1909 *WhAm 1*
Garrison, William Lloyd, Jr. 1874-1964 *NatCAB 50*
Garrison, William Retallack 1834-1882 *DcAmB, NatCAB 7, TwCBDA, WhAm H*
Garrison, Winfred Ernest 1874-1969 *WhAm 5*
Garritt, Joshua Bolles 1832- *NatCAB 3, TwCBDA*
Garritt, Walter Grant 1854-1917 *NatCAB 33*
Garrity, James *NewYHSD*
Garrod, Alfred Baring 1819-1909 *BiHiMed*
Garrott, Alva Curtis 1866- *WhoColR*
Garrow, James *NewYHSD*
Garrow, Nathaniel 1780-1841 *BiAUS, BiDrAC, WhAm H*
Garry, Harold Bernard 1923-1973 *WhAm 5*
Garry, Joseph R 1910- *REnAW*
Garry, Spokane 1811-1892 *AmBi, DcAmB, NatCAB 23, WhAm H*
Garshou, M *NewYHSD*
Garside, Alston Hill 1886-1946 *NatCAB 35*
Garside, Charles 1898-1964 *WhAm 4*
Garst, Perry 1848-1939 *WhAm 1*
Garst, Roswell 1898- *EncAAH*
Garst, Warren 1850-1924 *NatCAB 21,*

WhAm 1
Garstang, John 1876-1956 *WhAm 4*
Garth, George d1819 *ApCAB, Drake*
Garth, Sir Samuel 1661-1718 *BiHiMed*
Garth, Schuyler Edward 1898-1947 *WhAm 2*
Garth, Thomas Russell 1872-1939 *WhAm 1*
Garth, William Willis 1828-1912 *BiDrAC*
Garthe, Joseph Henry 1905-1961 *NatCAB 49*
Garthe, Louis 1861-1920 *WhAm 1*
Gartin, Carroll d1966 *WhAm 4*
Gartland, Francis Xavier 1805-1854 *ApCAB,
  Drake, NatCAB 12, TwCBDA*
Gartland, Joseph Francis 1880-1949 *WhAm 3*
Gartley, Alonzo 1869-1921 *NatCAB 41*
Gartley, Harold McKinley 1899-1972 *WhAm 5*
Gartlin, Alfred *BiAUS*
Gartner, Fred Christian 1896-1972 *BiDrAC,
  NatCAB 57*
Gartner, Karl Knox 1886-1937 *NatCAB 35*
Garton, Joseph *NewYHSD*
Garton, Will Melville 1875-1946 *WhAm 2*
Gartrell, Lucius Jeremiah 1821-1891 *BiAUS,
  BiDConf, BiDrAC, DcAmB, NatCAB 23,
  TwCBDA, WhAm H*
Garvan, Francis Patrick 1875-1937 *WhAm 1*
Garvan, Patrick 1836-1912 *NatCAB 17*
Garve, T Walter 1880-1961 *NatCAB 51*
Garver, Abraham Lincoln 1859-1920
  NatCAB 36
Garver, Austin Samuel 1847-1918 *WhAm 1*
Garver, Chauncey Brewster 1886-1973 *WhAm 5*
Garver, Earl Simeon 1911-1968 *NatCAB 54,
  WhAm 5*
Garver, Francis Marion 1875- *WhAm 5*
Garver, Frank Harmon 1875-1952 *WhAm 3*
Garver, Frederic Benjamin 1884-1950
  WhAm 2A
Garver, John Anson 1854-1936 *ApCAB X,
  NatCAB 39, WhAm 1*
Garver, John Newton, Jr. 1897-1957 *WhAm 3*
Garver, Milton 1879-1937 *NatCAB 32*
Garver, William Henry Harrison 1868-
  WhAm 4
Garver, William Lincoln 1867- *WhAm 4*
Garvey, Alberta Alexander 1864-
  WomWWA 14
Garvey, Eugene A 1845-1920 *WhAm 1*
Garvey, Helen Marie d1968 *WhAm 5*
Garvey, Henry *NewYHSD*
Garvey, James Allen 1912-1971 *WhAm 5*
Garvey, John L 1895-1964 *WhAm 4*
Garvey, Marcus Mosiah 1887-1940 *DcAmReB,
  McGEWB*
Garvey, Marcus Moziah 1887-1940 *DcAmB S2,
  EncAB, WebAB, WhAm HA, WhAm 4,
  WhAmP*
Garvey, Sister Mary Patricia 1888-1952
  WhAm 3
Garvey, Ray Hugh 1893-1959 *NatCAB 49*
Garvin, Amelia Warnock *WomWWA 14*
Garvin, Charles Herbert 1890-1968 *NatCAB 55*
Garvin, Edwin Louis 1877-1960 *NatCAB 47,
  WhAm 4*
Garvin, George Kinne 1897-1971 *WhAm 5*
Garvin, Jay Earle 1898-1957 *WhAm 3*
Garvin, Joseph F d1968 *WhAm 4*
Garvin, Lucius Fayette Clark 1841-1922 *DcAmB,
  NatCAB 13, NatCAB 26, WhAm 1*
Garvin, Margaret Root d1949 *WhAm 2*
Garvin, Victoria A 1874- *WomWWA 14*
Garvin, William Swan 1806-1883 *BiAUS,
  BiDrAC, WhAm H*
Garwood, Hiram Morgan 1864-1930 *WhAm 1*
Garwood, Irving 1883-1957 *WhAm 3*
Garwood, Sterling Marion 1893-1941 *WhAm 1*
Gary, Benjamin Roscoe 1869-1945 *NatCAB 45*
Gary, Clara Emerette *WomWWA 14*
Gary, Daniel Webster 1870- *WhoColR*
Gary, E Stanley 1862- *WhAm 4*
Gary, Elbert Henry 1846-1927 *AmBi,
  ApCAB X, DcAmB, EncAB, McGEWB,
  NatCAB 14, WebAB, WhAm 1*
Gary, Eugene Blackburn 1854-1926 *NatCAB 20,
  WhAm 1*
Gary, Frank Boyd 1860-1922 *BiDrAC,
  NatCAB 14, WhAm 1*
Gary, Frank Ephraim Herbert 1858-1927
  NatCAB 22

Gary, Franklin Newman 1828-1886 *NatCAB 4*
Gary, George 1793-1855 *ApCAB*
Gary, Hampson 1873-1952 *ApCAB X,
  NatCAB 41, WhAm 3*
Gary, Hunter Larrabee 1884-1946 *WhAm 2*
Gary, J Vaughan 1892-1973 *WhAm 6*
Gary, Mrs. James A *AmWom*
Gary, James Albert 1833-1920 *AmBi,
  ApCAB Sup, BiDrUSE, DcAmB,
  NatCAB 11, TwCBDA, WhAm 1*
Gary, John Everett 1916-1970 *NatCAB 56*
Gary, Joseph Easton 1821-1906 *WhAm 1*
Gary, Julian Vaughan 1892-1973 *BiDrAC,
  WhAmP*
Gary, Marco Bozzaris 1831-1909 *NatCAB 33*
Gary, Martin Witherspoon 1831-1881 *DcAmB,
  NatCAB 22, WhAm H*
Gary, Theodore d1952 *WhAm 3*
Garza, Lazaro DeLa 1785-1862 *ApCAB*
Gasaway, Howard Hamilton 1916-1966
  WhAm 4
Gasca, Pedro DeLa 1485-1567 *ApCAB*
Gasca, Pedro DeLa 1496?-1567 *McGEWB*
Gasch, Marie Manning *NotAW*
Gasche, Fred 1903-1966 *NatCAB 53*
Gascoigne, William 1612?-1644 *DcScB*
Gascoyne, John J 1872- *WhAm 5*
Gash, Abram Dale 1861- *NatCAB 17*
Gaskell, Elizabeth 1810-1865 *McGEWB*
Gaskell, Walter Holbrook 1847-1914 *DcScB*
Gaskill, Alfred 1861-1950 *WhAm 3*
Gaskill, Francis Almon 1846-1909 *WhAm 1*
Gaskill, Harold Vincent 1905-1975 *WhAm 6*
Gaskill, Harvey Freeman 1845-1889 *DcAmB,
  NatCAB 23, WhAm H*
Gaskill, Susanna Miller 1842- *WomWWA 14*
Gaskin, Dave 1902-1969 *NatCAB 57*
Gaskings, John A *NewYHSD*
Gaskins, Anna Robinson 1865- *WomWWA 14*
Gaskins, Lossie Leonard 1925-1975 *WhAm 6*
Gasner, George 1811-1861 *NewYHSD*
Gaspar Xiu, Antonio 1541?- *ApCAB*
Gaspard, Leon 1882-1964 *IIBEAAW*
Gasparian, Hagop Manoug 1904-1961
  NatCAB 50
Gaspe, Philip Aubert De 1786-1871 *ApCAB*
Gaspe, Philip Ignatius 1714-1787 *ApCAB*
Gasque, Allard Henry 1873-1938 *BiDrAC,
  WhAm 1, WhAmP*
Gasque, Elizabeth Hawley *BiDrAC*
Gass, Howard Allan 1852-1916 *WhAm 1*
Gass, John 1890-1951 *NatCAB 41*
Gass, Patrick 1771-1870 *AmBi, DcAmB,
  NewYHSD, WhAm H*
Gass, Sarah A *WomWWA 14*
Gass, Sherlock Bronson 1878-1945 *WhAm 2*
Gassaway, Percy Lee 1885-1937 *BiDrAC,
  WhAm 1*
Gassendi, Pierre 1592-1655 *AsBiEn, DcScB*
Gasser, Herbert Spencer 1888-1963 *AsBiEn,
  DcScB, WebAB, WhAm 4*
Gasser, Lorenzo Dow 1876-1955 *WhAm 3*
Gasser, Roy Cullen d1961 *WhAm 4*
Gassicourt *DcScB*
Gassiot, John Peter 1797-1877 *DcScB*
Gassner, John Waldhorn 1903-1967 *WhAm 4*
Gasson, Thomas Ignatius 1859-1930 *DcAmB,
  TwCBDA, WhAm 1*
Gast, August 1819- *NewYHSD*
Gast, Charles E 1848-1908 *WhAm 1*
Gast, Frederick Augustus 1835-1917
  ApCAB Sup, WhAm 1
Gast, Leopold *NewYHSD*
Gast, Paul Frederick 1916-1974 *WhAm 6*
Gast, Robert Shaeffer 1879-1948 *WhAm 2*
Gastine, Civique 1793-1822 *ApCAB*
Gaston, Arthur Lee 1876-1951 *WhAm 3*
Gaston, Athelston 1838-1907 *BiDrAC,
  TwCBDA, WhAm 4*
Gaston, Cecil Dulin 1887-1940 *NatCAB 31*
Gaston, Charles Robert 1874-1945 *WhAm 2*
Gaston, Edward Page 1868- *WhAm 4*
Gaston, Ernest B 1861-1937 *WhAm 1*
Gaston, Everett Thayer 1901-1970 *WhAm 5*
Gaston, George Albert 1875- *ApCAB X,
  WhAm 5*
Gaston, Herbert Earle 1881-1956 *NatCAB 45*
Gaston, James McFadden 1824-1903 *DcAmB,

NatCAB 12, WhAm 1
Gaston, James McFadden 1868-1946
  NatCAB 36
Gaston, John Brown 1834- *NatCAB 4*
Gaston, John Montgomery 1868- *WhAm 5*
Gaston, Joseph Alfred 1856-1937 *WhAm 1*
Gaston, Lloyd H 1906-1962 *WhAm 4*
Gaston, Lucy Page 1860-1924 *WhAm 1,
  WomWWA 14*
Gaston, Robert Kirkpatrick 1869-1951
  NatCAB 42
Gaston, William 1778-1844 *AmBi, ApCAB,
  BiAUS, BiDrAC, DcAmB, Drake,
  NatCAB 3, TwCBDA, WhAm H,
  WhAmP*
Gaston, William 1820-1894 *ApCAB,
  ApCAB X, DcAmB, NatCAB 1,
  TwCBDA, WhAm H*
Gaston, William Alexander 1859-1927
  *ApCAB X, NatCAB 15, NatCAB 26,
  WhAm 1*
Gasul, Benjamin Morris 1898-1962 *NatCAB 49*
Gatch, Lee 1902-1968 *BnEnAmA, WhAm 5*
Gatch, Thomas Leigh 1891-1954 *NatCAB 46,
  WhAm 3*
Gatch, Thomas Milton 1833-1913 *NatCAB 25,
  WhAm 1*
Gatch, Willis Dew 1878-1962 *WhAm 4*
Gatchell, Charles 1850- *TwCBDA*
Gatchell, Charles 1851- *WhAm 4*
Gatchell, George Washington 1865-1939
  WhAm 1
Gately, James Hayes 1882-1972 *WhAm 5*
Gatenby, John William, Jr. 1906-1975 *WhAm 6*
Gatens, William Nemier 1867-1927 *NatCAB 21*
Gates, Albert R 1869- *WhAm 5*
Gates, Arthur Irving 1890-1972 *BiDAmEd,
  WhAm 5*
Gates, Benjamin F 1821?- *NewYHSD*
Gates, C Ray 1885-1944 *WhAm 2*
Gates, Caleb Frank 1857-1946 *DcAmB S4,
  WhAm 2*
Gates, Caleb Frank 1903-1955 *WhAm 3*
Gates, Cassius Emerson 1886-1972 *NatCAB 56,
  WhAm 5*
Gates, Charles Cassius 1877-1961 *NatCAB 51,
  WhAm 4*
Gates, Charles Gilbert 1876-1913 *ApCAB X,
  WhAm 1*
Gates, Charles Winslow 1856-1927 *NatCAB 15,
  WhAm 1*
Gates, Clifford Elwood 1893-1968 *WhAm 5*
Gates, Collinson Reed 1816-1849 *ApCAB*
Gates, Earle Winslow 1909-1963 *WhAm 4*
Gates, Edmund O 1905-1966 *WhAm 5*
Gates, Eleanor 1875-1951 *NatCAB 15,
  WhAm 3, WomWWA 14*
Gates, Ellen M Huntington d1920 *WhAm 1,
  WomWWA 14*
Gates, Elmer 1858-1923 *NatCAB 10*
Gates, Elmer 1859-1923 *WhAm 1*
Gates, Erastus *NewYHSD*
Gates, Errett 1870- *WhAm 5*
Gates, Fanny Cook 1872-1931 *WhAm 1,
  WomWWA 14*
Gates, Frederick Taylor 1853-1929 *AmBi,
  DcAmB, NatCAB 23, WebAB, WhAm 1*
Gates, George Augustus 1851-1912 *AmBi,
  DcAmB, NatCAB 13, TwCBDA,
  WhAm 1*
Gates, Herbert Wright 1868-1948 *WhAm 2*
Gates, Horatio 1727-1793 *WhoMilH*
Gates, Horatio 1727?-1806 *WebAB, WebAMB*
Gates, Horatio 1728-1806 *ApCAB, DcAmB,
  Drake, NatCAB 1, TwCBDA, WhAm H*
Gates, Horatio 1729-1806 *AmBi*
Gates, Howard Baker 1867-1914 *NatCAB 16*
Gates, Isaac Edgar 1874-1933 *WhAm 1*
Gates, J George 1886-1961 *NatCAB 47*
Gates, James Henry 1851-1910 *NatCAB 16*
Gates, James Leslie 1850- *NatCAB 11*
Gates, Jasper Calvin 1850-1920 *NatCAB 18,
  WhAm 4*
Gates, Jemuel Clinton 1829-1915 *NatCAB 17*
Gates, John Gideon 1884-1969 *NatCAB 54*
Gates, John Howard 1865-1927 *NatCAB 18,
  WhAm 1*
Gates, John Warne 1855-1911 *AmBi,

*ApCAB X, DcAmB, NatCAB 18,
WebAB, WhAm 1*
Gates, Joseph Wilson 1862- *WhAm 4*
Gates, Josephine Scribner 1859-1930 *WhAm 1,
WomWWA 14*
Gates, Kermit Hoyt 1903-1965 *WhAm 4*
Gates, Lenna Florence Alexander 1862-
WomWWA 14
Gates, Lewis Edwards 1860- *WhAm 4*
Gates, Lulu Foster *WomWWA 14*
Gates, Mary Randall 1875- *WomWWA 14*
Gates, Merrill Edwards 1848-1922 *AmBi,
ApCAB, ApCAB X, NatCAB 5,
TwCBDA, WhAm 1*
Gates, Milo Hudson 1864-1939 *NatCAB 29*
Gates, Milo Hudson 1866-1939 *WhAm 1*
Gates, Moody Bliss 1879- *WhAm 6*
Gates, Noah Putnam 1832-1909 *BiDAmEd,
NatCAB 28*
Gates, Owen Hamilton 1862-1940 *WhAm 1*
Gates, Paul Hayden 1895-1956 *WhAm 3*
Gates, Paul Wallace 1901- *EncAAH, REnAW*
Gates, Philetus Warren 1857-1933 *WhAm 1*
Gates, Reginald Ruggles 1882-1962 *DcScB*
Gates, Robert 1841-1915 *NatCAB 8*
Gates, Robert McFarland 1883-1962
NatCAB 53, WhAm 4
Gates, Robert Moores 1871- *WhAm 5*
Gates, Robert S 1909-1968 *WhAm 5*
Gates, Seth Merrill 1800-1877 *ApCAB, BiAUS,
BiDrAC, TwCBDA, WhAm H*
Gates, Susa Young 1856-1933 *REnAW,
WhAm 1, WomWWA 14*
Gates, Sylvester Govett 1901-1972 *WhAm 6*
Gates, Sir Thomas 1560?-1621 *AmBi, ApCAB,
DcAmB, NatCAB 13, WhAm H*
Gates, Thomas G *NewYHSD*
Gates, Thomas Sovereign 1873-1948 *DcAmB S4,
NatCAB 42, WhAm 2*
Gates, Thomas Sovereign, Jr. 1906- *BiDrUSE*
Gates, W Francis 1865- *WhAm 4*
Gates, William 1788-1868 *ApCAB, Drake,
TwCBDA*
Gates, William Benjamin 1877-1959 *WhAm 3*
Gates, William Byram, Jr. 1917-1975 *WhAm 6*
Gates, William Clarence 1867-1919 *NatCAB 18*
Gates, William Frederick 1867-1938 *WhAm 3*
Gates, William Herbert 1867-1923 *NatCAB 20*
Gateson, Daniel Wilmot 1884-1954 *WhAm 4*
Gatewood, Arthur Randolph 1899-1970
WhAm 5
Gatewood, James Duncan 1857-1924 *WhAm 1*
Gatewood, James Edwin 1857- *WhAm 4*
Gatewood, William Beale 1876-1943
NatCAB 33
Gatewood, William Lawrence 1885-1964
NatCAB 51
Gathercoal, Edmund Norris 1874-1954
NatCAB 43, WhAm 3
Gathiel, Edward *NewYHSD*
Gathings, Ezekiel Candler 1903- *BiDrAC,
WhAmP*
Gathmann, Louis 1843- *WhAm 4*
Gathright, Josiah Baker 1838-1919 *NatCAB 19*
Gathright, Owen 1850-1931 *NatCAB 23*
Gatley, George Grant 1868-1931 *WhAm 1*
Gatley, H Prescott 1875-1940 *WhAm 1*
Gatlin, Alfred Moore 1790- *BiDrAC,
WhAm H*
Gatlin, Richard Caswell 1809-1896 *ApCAB Sup*
Gatling, Richard Jordan 1818-1903 *AmBi,
ApCAB, ApCAB X, AsBiEn, DcAmB,
McGEWB, NatCAB 4, TwCBDA,
WebAB, WebAMB, WhAm 1*
Gatschet, Albert Samuel 1832-1907 *AmBi,
ApCAB, DcAmB, NatCAB 21, TwCBDA,
WhAm 1*
Gattey, Henry *NewYHSD*
Gatti, Orville Clement 1909-1956 *NatCAB 48*
Gatti-Casazza, Giulio 1869-1940 *ApCAB X,
DcAmB S2*
Gatti-Casazza, Guilio 1869-1940 *WhAm 1*
Gattinger, Augustin 1825-1903 *NatCAB 15*
Gatto, Victor Joseph 1893-1965 *BnEnAmA*
Gatton, Roy Harper 1892-1965 *WhAm 4*
Gatts, Robert Roswell 1925-1974 *WhAm 6*
Gaty, John Pomeroy 1900-1963 *NatCAB 52*
Gaty, Lewis Rumsey 1902-1961 *WhAm 4*

Gauch, Donald Eugene 1937-1974 *WhAm 6*
Gauchat, Robert David 1922-1973 *WhAm 6*
Gauche, Edward Eugene 1877-1954 *NatCAB 44*
Gaudet, Frances Joseph 1861- *WhoColR*
Gaudi I Cornet, Antoni 1852-1926 *McGEWB*
Gaudin, Antoine Marc 1900-1974 *WhAm 6*
Gaudin, Marc Antoine Augustin 1804-1880
DcScB
Gaudrault, Gerard Louis 1901-1970 *NatCAB 56*
Gaudry, Albert Jean 1827-1908 *DcScB*
Gaugengigl, Ignaz Marcel 1855-1932 *WhAm 1*
Gauger, Alfred William 1892-1963 *NatCAB 50*
Gauger, John Anthony 1852-1914 *NatCAB 16*
Gaugler, Ray C 1892-1952 *WhAm 3*
Gauguin, Paul 1848-1903 *McGEWB*
Gauk, James *NewYHSD*
Gaul, Frederick *NewYHSD*
Gaul, Fritz George 1861-1928 *NatCAB 21*
Gaul, Gilbert William 1855-1919 *AmBi,
ApCAB, TwCBDA, WhAm 1*
Gaul, Harvey Bartlett 1881-1945 *NatCAB 36,
WhAm 2*
Gaul, William Gilbert 1855-1919 *DcAmB,
IIBEAAW, NatCAB 12*
Gaulden, Charles Lewis 1887-1941 *NatCAB 40*
Gauley, Robert David 1875-1943 *WhAm 3*
Gaulin, Alphonse, Jr. 1874- *WhAm 5*
Gaulli, Giovanni Battista 1639-1709 *McGEWB*
Gault, Arthur Eugene 1888-1973 *WhAm 6*
Gault, Edwin Sartain 1893-1958 *NatCAB 48*
Gault, Franklin Benjamin 1851-1918 *BiDAmEd,
NatCAB 18, TwCBDA, WhAm 1*
Gault, H Richard 1915-1961 *NatCAB 49*
Gault, James Sherman 1899-1951 *WhAm 3*
Gault, Jennie Perrett 1859- *WomWWA 14*
Gault, Lillien Mayhew Cox 1864-
WomWWA 14
Gault, Mark R d1969 *WhAm 5*
Gault, Matthew Hamilton 1822-1887 *ApCAB*
Gault, Norman Cox 1892-1968 *WhAm 5*
Gaultier DeClaubry, Henri-Francois 1792-1878
DcScB
Gaunt, Alfred Calvin 1882-1959 *WhAm 3*
Gaunt, Charles Lee 1883-1958 *NatCAB 43*
Gauntt, Jefferson *NewYHSD*
Gaupel, Henry John 1848-1921 *NatCAB 23*
Gaus, Charles H d1909 *WhAm 1*
Gaus, Daisy *WomWWA 14*
Gause, Frank Ales 1874- *WhAm 5*
Gause, Fred C 1879-1944 *WhAm 2*
Gause, Harry Lorenzo 1898-1964 *NatCAB 50*
Gause, Harry Taylor 1853-1925 *NatCAB 38*
Gause, Lucien Coatsworth 1836-1880 *BiDrAC,
WhAm H*
Gause, Lucien Cotesworth 1838-1880 *BiAUS*
Gause, Nora Trueblood 1851- *AmWom*
Gause, Owen B 1825- *NatCAB 3*
Gausewitz, Alfred LeRoy 1893-1960 *WhAm 4*
Gauss, Alice Sarah Hussey 1872-
WomWWA 14
Gauss, Carl Friedrich 1777-1855 *DcScB*
Gauss, Christian Frederick 1878-1951
DcAmB S5, WhAm 3
Gauss, Clarence Edward 1887-1960 *WhAm 3A*
Gauss, Johann Karl Friedrich 1777-1855 *AsBiEn,
McGEWB*
Gaut, Helen Lukens 1872- *WomWWA 14*
Gaut, John McReynolds 1841-1918 *DcAmB,
NatCAB 17, WhAm 1*
Gauthier, A F *NewYHSD*
Gauthier, Eva 1885-1958 *WhAm 3,
WomWWA 14*
Gauthier, Julie Celina 1857- *WomWWA 14*
Gautier, Armand E J 1837-1920 *DcScB*
Gautier, Paul Ferdinand 1842-1909 *DcScB*
Gautreau, J B *NewYHSD*
Gauvreau, Emile Henry 1891-1956 *WhAm 3*
Gaux, Jules A *NewYHSD*
Gavagan, Joseph Andrew 1892-1968 *BiDrAC,
WhAm 5*
Gavegan, Edward James 1863- *WhAm 4*
Gaver, Harry Hamilton 1886-1954 *WhAm 3*
Gaver, Jack 1906-1974 *WhAm 6*
Gavin, Ella Butler Lathrop 1853-
WomWWA 14
Gavin, Frank Stanton Burns 1890-1938
DcAmB S2, WhAm 1
Gavin, H *NewYHSD*

Gavin, James Maurice 1907- *WebAMB*
Gavin, Leon Harry 1893-1963 *BiDrAC,
WhAm 4, WhAmP*
Gavin, Michael Freebern 1844-1915 *NatCAB 15*
Gavisk, Francis Henry 1856-1932 *WhAm 1*
Gavit, Bernard Campbell 1893-1954
NatCAB 45, WhAm 3
Gavit, Daniel E 1819?- *NewYHSD*
Gavit, John E 1817-1874 *ApCAB, NatCAB 17,
NewYHSD, WhAm H*
Gavit, John Palmer 1868-1954 *WhAm 3*
Gavit, Joseph 1876- *WhAm 5*
Gavitt, Elmina M Roys 1828- *AmWom*
Gavitz, James *NewYHSD*
Gavrilovic, Stoyan 1894-1965 *WhAm 4*
Gaw, Allison 1877-1954 *WhAm 3*
Gaw, Chamber S *NewYHSD*
Gaw, Cooper 1877-1956 *WhAm 3*
Gaw, Esther Allen 1879- *WhAm 6*
Gaw, Robert M 1805?- *NewYHSD*
Gawtry, Harrison E d1919 *WhAm 1*
Gay, Byron 1886-1945 *NatCAB 34*
Gay, Carl Warren 1877- *WhAm 5*
Gay, Charles Merrick 1871-1951 *NatCAB 38*
Gay, Charles Richard 1875-1946 *NatCAB 36,
WhAm 2*
Gay, Claude 1800-1863 *ApCAB*
Gay, Claude 1800-1872 *ApCAB Sup*
Gay, Eben Howard 1858- *NatCAB 11*
Gay, Ebenezer 1696-1787 *ApCAB, DcAmB,
Drake, NatCAB 7, TwCBDA, WhAm H*
Gay, Edward 1837-1928 *AmBi, ApCAB,
NatCAB 10, NewYHSD, TwCBDA,
WhAm 1*
Gay, Edward James 1816-1889 *BiDrAC,
TwCBDA, WhAm H, WhAmP*
Gay, Edward James 1878-1952 *BiDrAC,
NatCAB 42, WhAmP*
Gay, Edward Randolph 1898-1966 *WhAm 4*
Gay, Edwin Francis 1867-1946 *DcAmB S4,
NatCAB 44, WhAm 2*
Gay, Francis 1852- *NatCAB 11*
Gay, Frank Butler 1856-1934 *NatCAB 25,
WhAm 1*
Gay, Fred Shinn 1878-1953 *NatCAB 43*
Gay, Frederick Lewis 1856-1916 *WhAm 1*
Gay, Frederick Parker 1874-1939 *DcAmB S2,
DcScB, WhAm 1, WhAm 3*
Gay, George Anderson 1852-1940 *NatCAB 34*
Gay, George Washington 1837-1899
NatCAB 10
Gay, George Washington 1842-1931 *ApCAB X,
WhAm 1*
Gay, H Nelson 1870-1932 *WhAm 1*
Gay, Henry B d1862 *NewYHSD*
Gay, John 1685-1732 *McGEWB*
Gay, John G *NewYHSD*
Gay, John Lewis 1865-1959 *NatCAB 48*
Gay, John Longdon 1866- *WhAm 4*
Gay, Jotham 1733-1802 *ApCAB*
Gay, Lucy Maria 1862- *WomWWA 14*
Gay, Maria d1943 *WhAm 3A*
Gay, Martin 1803-1850 *ApCAB, Drake*
Gay, Maude Clark 1876-1952 *WhAm 3,
WomWWA 14*
Gay, Norman Russell 1919-1966 *NatCAB 53,
WhAm 4*
Gay, Picard Du *ApCAB*
Gay, Robert Malcolm 1879-1961 *WhAm 4*
Gay, Samuel 1755-1847 *ApCAB*
Gay, Sidney Howard 1814-1888 *TwCBDA*
Gay, Sydney Howard 1814-1888 *AmBi,
ApCAB, DcAmB, NatCAB 2, WhAm H*
Gay, Taylor Scott 1907-1962 *WhAm 4*
Gay, Walter 1856-1937 *AmBi, ApCAB,
NatCAB 11, NatCAB 27, TwCBDA,
WhAm 1*
Gay, William Hovey 1863-1920 *NatCAB 18*
Gay, Wilson Riley 1859-1920 *NatCAB 19*
Gay, Winckworth Allan 1821-1910 *ApCAB,
DcAmB, Drake, NatCAB 11, NewYHSD,
TwCBDA, WhAm H*
Gay-Lussac, Joseph Louis 1778-1850 *AsBiEn,
BiHiMed, DcScB, McGEWB*
Gayant, Louis d1673 *DcScB*
Gayarre, Charles Etienne Arthur 1805-1895
*AmBi, ApCAB, BiAUS, DcAmB, Drake,
NatCAB 6, TwCBDA, WhAm H*

Gaydos, Joseph Matthew 1926- *BiDrAC*
Gayer, Arthur David 1903-1951 *WhAm 3*
Gayle, John 1792-1859 *ApCAB, BiAUS, BiDrAC, DcAmB, Drake, NatCAB 10, TwCBDA, WhAm H, WhAmP*
Gayle, June Ward 1865-1942 *BiDrAC*
Gayle, Mary Winn 1862- *WomWWA 14*
Gayle, R Finley, Jr. 1891-1957 *NatCAB 43, WhAm 3*
Gayler, Charles 1820-1892 *ApCAB, DcAmB, Drake, NatCAB 24, TwCBDA, WhAm H*
Gayles, George Washington 1844- *WhoColR*
Gayley, Charles Mills 1858-1932 *AmBi, BiDAmEd, NatCAB 23, TwCBDA, WhAm 1*
Gayley, Henry Clifford 1901-1974 *WhAm 6*
Gayley, James 1855-1920 *DcAmB, NatCAB 14, WhAm 1*
Gaylor, Charles Parson, II 1905-1971 *NatCAB 56*
Gaylord, Alice Brown *WomWWA 14*
Gaylord, Augustus S 1825- *BiAUS*
Gaylord, Charles Seely 1811-1862 *NewYHSD, WhAm H*
Gaylord, Clifford Willard 1883-1952 *WhAm 3*
Gaylord, Edward King 1873-1974 *WhAm 6*
Gaylord, Edward Lot 1827-1915 *NatCAB 22*
Gaylord, Franklin Augustus 1856-1943 *WhAm 2*
Gaylord, Harvey Russell 1872-1924 *NatCAB 20, WhAm 1*
Gaylord, Irving Champlin 1860-1933 *NatCAB 24*
Gaylord, James Madison 1811-1874 *BiAUS, BiDrAC, WhAm H*
Gaylord, Joseph Searle 1860- *WhAm 4*
Gaylord, Laurence Timmerman 1882-1968 *NatCAB 54*
Gaylord, Truman Penfield 1871-1931 *WhAm 1*
Gaylord, Willis 1792-1844 *DcAmB, NatCAB 23, WhAm H*
Gaynor, Francis Robert 1852-1920 *NatCAB 22*
Gaynor, Frank R 1852-1920 *WhAm 1*
Gaynor, Jessie Smith 1863-1921 *WhAm 1*
Gaynor, Paul, Sr. 1920-1975 *WhAm 6*
Gaynor, William Jay 1849-1913 *AmBi, DcAmB*
Gaynor, William Jay 1851-1913 *NatCAB 16, WhAm 1*
Gayoso DeLemos, Manuel 1752?-1799 *AmBi, DcAmB, WhAm H, WhAmP*
Gazlay, James William 1784-1874 *BiDrAC*
Gazlay, P M d1966 *WhAm 4*
Gazley, James William 1784-1874 *BiAUS, WhAm H*
Gazzam, Joseph Murphy 1842-1927 *NatCAB 3, NatCAB 15, TwCBDA, WhAm 1*
Gazzaniga, Signora 1825- *ApCAB*
Gear, Harry Barnes 1872-1959 *WhAm 3*
Gear, Hiram Lewis 1842- *TwCBDA, WhAm 4*
Gear, John Henry 1825-1900 *ApCAB, BiDrAC, DcAmB, NatCAB 11, TwCBDA, WhAm 1, WhAmP*
Gear, John William 1806-1866 *NewYHSD*
Gear, Joseph 1768-1853 *NewYHSD, WhAm H*
Gear, Luella Glasser 1874- *WomWWA 14*
Geare, Randolph Iltyd 1854-1917 *WhAm 1*
Gearhart, Bertrand Wesley 1890-1955 *BiDrAC, WhAm 3, WhAmP*
Gearhart, Ephraim Maclay 1880- *WhAm 6*
Gearin, John McDermeid 1851-1930 *BiDrAC, NatCAB 14, WhAm 1*
Geary, Donald 1891-1966 *NatCAB 53*
Geary, Edward Ratchford 1845-1863 *ApCAB*
Geary, George Reginald 1874- *WhAm 5*
Geary, Jessie May Ballard 1880- *WomWWA 14*
Geary, John White 1819-1873 *AmBi, ApCAB, DcAmB, NatCAB 2, TwCBDA, WebAB, WebAMB, WhAm H, WhAmP*
Geary, John White 1820?-1873 *BiAUS, Drake*
Geary, John White 1869-1940 *NatCAB 32*
Geary, Joseph James 1894-1958 *WhAm 4*
Geary, Thomas J 1854-1929 *BiDrAC, TwCBDA*
Gebelein, George Christian 1878-1945 *NatCAB 33, WhAm 2*
Geber 721?-815? *AsBiEn*

Gebert, Charles Adam 1892-1968 *NatCAB 54*
Gebert, Ernest 1901-1961 *NatCAB 46*
Gebert, Herbert George 1900-1962 *WhAm 4*
Gebhard, Charles August 1876-1919 *NatCAB 19*
Gebhard, Charles E 1810?- *NewYHSD*
Gebhard, Heinrich 1878- *WhAm 6*
Gebhard, John 1782-1854 *BiAUS, BiDrAC, WhAm H*
Gebhard, Louis 1826?- *NewYHSD*
Gebhard, Willrich 1853- *WhAm 4*
Gebhardt, Ernest A 1891-1961 *WhAm 4*
Gebhardt, F *NewYHSD*
Gebhardt, George Frederic 1874- *WhAm 5*
Gebhardt, Raymond L 1882-1953 *WhAm 3*
Geddes, Alice Spencer 1876- *WhAm 5, WomWWA 14*
Geddes, Sir Auckland Campbell d1954 *WhAm 3*
Geddes, Frederick Lyman 1850-1930 *NatCAB 30*
Geddes, Frederick Lyman 1850-1931 *WhAm 1*
Geddes, George 1809-1883 *ApCAB, NatCAB 10*
Geddes, George Washington 1824-1892 *BiDrAC, TwCBDA, WhAm H, WhAmP*
Geddes, James *NewYHSD*
Geddes, James 1763-1838 *AmBi, ApCAB, BiAUS, BiDrAC, DcAmB, NatCAB 10, TwCBDA, WhAm H*
Geddes, James, Jr. 1858-1948 *NatCAB 14, WhAm 2*
Geddes, James Loraine 1827-1887 *DcAmB, NatCAB 23, WhAm H*
Geddes, James Lorraine 1827-1887 *ApCAB, TwCBDA*
Geddes, John d1828 *BiAUS, Drake*
Geddes, John 1773?-1828 *ApCAB, TwCBDA*
Geddes, John 1777-1828 *NatCAB 12*
Geddes, John Joseph 1880-1950 *WhAm 2*
Geddes, Norman Bel 1893-1958 *NatCAB 44, WebAB, WhAm 3*
Geddes, Norman Bel *see also* Bel Geddes, Norman
Geddes, Sir Patrick 1854-1932 *McGEWB*
Geddes, Ross Campbell 1907-1975 *WhAm 6*
Geddes, William Findlay 1896-1961 *WhAm 4*
Geddes, William McGill 1856-1932 *NatCAB 23*
Geddes, Williamson Nevin 1836-1913 *WhAm 1*
Geddings, Eli 1799-1878 *ApCAB, TwCBDA*
Geddy, Vernon Meredith 1897-1952 *WhAm 3*
Gedney, Jonathan Haight 1798-1886 *ApCAB, NatCAB 5*
Gedye, George Eric Rowe 1890-1970 *WhAm 5*
Gee, A M 1889-1974 *WhAm 6*
Gee, Edward Artley 1893-1957 *NatCAB 49, WhAm 3*
Gee, Frederick Warren 1895-1945 *NatCAB 36*
Gee, Haldane 1901-1962 *NatCAB 50*
Gee, John Archer 1894-1944 *NatCAB 34*
Gee, Joshua 1698-1748 *ApCAB, Drake, TwCBDA*
Gee, Nathaniel Gist 1876-1937 *NatCAB 28, WhAm 1*
Gee, Walter Still 1883-1930 *NatCAB 23*
Gee, Wilson 1888-1961 *WhAm 4*
Gee, Winifred Neville Craig 1882- *WomWWA 14*
Geelan, James Patrick 1901- *BiDrAC*
Geer, Bennette Eugene 1873-1964 *WhAm 4*
Geer, Charles De 1720-1778 *DcScB*
Geer, Curtis Manning 1864-1938 *NatCAB 28, WhAm 1*
Geer, Danforth 1859- *WhAm 4*
Geer, Everett Kinne 1893-1950 *WhAm 3*
Geer, Ezra Harold 1886-1957 *WhAm 3*
Geer, George Jarvis 1821-1885 *ApCAB, NatCAB 11, WhAm H*
Geer, Gerhard Jakob De 1858-1943 *DcScB*
Geer, Grace Woodbridge 1854- *WomWWA 14*
Geer, Helen Hartley Jenkins 1894-1920 *BiCAW*
Geer, Helena 1881- *WomWWA 14*
Geer, Theodore Thurston 1851- *NatCAB 13, TwCBDA, WhAm 4*
Geer, Walter 1857-1937 *NatCAB 5, WhAm 1*
Geer, William Chauncey 1876-1964 *NatCAB 50, WhAm 4*
Geer, William Clarke 1859-1943 *WhAm 2*

Geer, William Henry 1885-1925 *WhAm 1*
Geer, William Montague 1848-1935 *WhAm 1*
Geerderts, John P *NewYHSD*
Geers, Edward Franklin 1851-1924 *DcAmB*
Geertgen Tot Sint Jans 1460?-1495? *McGEWB*
Geery, William Beckwith 1867- *WhAm 4*
Gees, J F S *NewYHSD*
Gefaell, John Eugene 1890-1960 *NatCAB 44*
Geffine, Victor Paul 1882-1967 *NatCAB 53*
Geffrard, Fabre 1806-1879 *ApCAB, Drake*
Gegenbaur, Carl 1826-1903 *DcScB Sup*
Gegenbaur, Karl 1826-1903 *AsBiEn, DcScB*
Gegenheimer, William 1877-1973 *NatCAB 57*
Gehan, John Francis 1893-1960 *WhAm 4*
Gehant, Grover William 1885-1967 *NatCAB 53*
Gehl, Edward John 1890-1956 *NatCAB 47, WhAm 3*
Gehlbach, Herman Hunter 1913-1965 *WhAm 4*
Gehle, Frederick W 1886-1960 *WhAm 4*
Gehlen, Adolf Ferdinand 1775-1815 *DcScB, DcScB Sup*
Gehlke, Charles Elmer 1884-1968 *WhAm 5*
Gehner, August 1846- *NatCAB 12*
Gehres, Leslie Edward 1898-1975 *WhAm 6*
Gehrig, Henry Louis 1903-1941 *DcAmB S3*
Gehrig, Lou 1903-1941 *WebAB, WhAm 4*
Gehring, Albert 1870-1926 *WhAm 1*
Gehring, Edwin Wagner 1876-1953 *NatCAB 43*
Gehring, John George 1857-1932 *WhAm 1*
Gehring, Norman John 1877-1961 *NatCAB 50*
Gehrkens, Karl Wilson 1882-1975 *BiDAmEd*
Gehrmann, Adolph 1868-1920 *WhAm 1*
Gehrmann, Bernard John 1880-1958 *BiDrAC, WhAm 3, WhAmP*
Gehrmann, George Howard 1890-1959 *NatCAB 48, WhAm 3*
Gehron, William 1887-1958 *WhAm 3*
Gehrs, John Henry 1882-1939 *WhAm 1*
Geib, G *NewYHSD*
Geibel, Adam 1855-1933 *AmBi, WhAm 1*
Geibel, Victor B 1896-1961 *WhAm 4*
Geier, Frederick August 1866-1934 *WhAm 1*
Geier, Oscar Arnold 1882-1942 *NatCAB 31*
Geier, Otto Philip 1874-1954 *NatCAB 49*
Geier, Philip Albert 1877-1942 *NatCAB 32*
Geier, Philip Otto 1876-1953 *WhAm 4*
Geier, Philip Otto 1876-1954 *WhAm 3*
Geiershofer, Maurice *NewYHSD*
Geiffert, Alfred, Jr. 1890-1957 *NatCAB 44, WhAm 3*
Geiger, Alfred Bernard 1891-1958 *NatCAB 48, WhAm 3*
Geiger, Arthur Henry 1878-1943 *NatCAB 33*
Geiger, C Harve 1893-1975 *WhAm 6*
Geiger, Emily 1760?- *ApCAB*
Geiger, Ernest 1896-1959 *NatCAB 47*
Geiger, Ferdinand August 1867-1939 *NatCAB 30, WhAm 1*
Geiger, Hans Wilhelm 1882-1945 *AsBiEn, DcScB*
Geiger, Jacob 1848-1934 *NatCAB 11, NatCAB 16, WhAm 1*
Geiger, Marlin George 1897-1960 *WhAm 4*
Geiger, Moritz 1880-1937 *NatCAB 28*
Geiger, Roy Stanley 1885-1947 *DcAmB S4, NatCAB 36, WebAMB, WhAm 2, WhWW-II*
Geiger, William Frederick 1870- *WhAm 5*
Geigle, Francis R 1906-1974 *WhAm 6*
Geijsbeek, John Bart 1872- *WhAm 5*
Geikie, Archibald 1835-1924 *DcScB*
Geikie, Cunningham 1826- *ApCAB*
Geikie, James 1839-1915 *DcScB*
Geil, Constance Emerson 1873- *WomWWA 14*
Geil, William Edgar 1865-1925 *ApCAB X, WhAm 1*
Geilfert, Charles 1787-1829 *NatCAB 9*
Geis, George 1875- *WhAm 5*
Geis, John Henry 1863-1930 *NatCAB 22*
Geisel, Carolyn d1932 *WhAm 1*
Geisel, Theodor Seuss 1904- *WebAB*
Geiseman, Otto Albert 1893-1962 *NatCAB 52*
Geiser, George Berger 1870-1938 *NatCAB 45*
Geiser, Karl Frederick 1869-1951 *WhAm 3*
Geiser, Karl Friedrich 1843-1934 *DcScB*
Geisinger, David 1790-1860 *ApCAB, Drake*
Geisler, John George 1886-1976 *WhAm 6*
Geisler, Joseph *NewYHSD*

Geisler, Mary C D 1848- *WomWWA 14*
Geismar, Herman 1872-1941 *NatCAB 30*
Geisness, John 1907-1956 *NatCAB 48*
Geissenhainer, Frederick Wilbono 1771-1838
 ApCAB, NatCAB 11
Geissenhainer, Jacob Augustus 1839-1917
 BiDrAC, WhAmP
Geissinger, James Allen 1873-1935 *WhAm 1*
Geissler, Arthur H 1877-1945 *WhAm 2*
Geissler, Heinrich 1814-1879 *AsBiEn*
Geissler, Johann Heinrich Wilhelm 1815-1879
 DcScB
Geissler, Louis Frederick 1861-1936
 NatCAB 40
Geissler, Ludwig Reinhold 1879-1932 *WhAm 1*
Geist, A Joseph 1886-1963 *NatCAB 48*
Geist, Clarence Henry 1874-1938 *WhAm 1*
Geist, Emil Sebastian 1878-1933 *WhAm 1*
Geist, Jacob Miller Willis 1824- *NatCAB 5*
Geist, Samuel Herbert 1885-1943 *NatCAB 32,*
 WhAm 2
Geist, Walter 1894-1951 *WhAm 3*
Geistlich, J C *NewYHSD*
Geitel, F K Hans 1855-1923 *DcScB*
Geitner, John George Harvey 1893-1957
 NatCAB 43
Gekler, Walter Albert 1884-1946 *NatCAB 50*
Gelatt, Philo Madison 1875-1944 *NatCAB 45*
Gelbach, Loring Lusk 1892-1966 *WhAm 4*
Gelderen, Adolphus Van 1835- *ApCAB*
Geldreich, Edward William 1908-1960
 NatCAB 48
Geleerd, Elisabeth Rozetta 1909-1969 *WhAm 5*
Gelelemend 1737-1811 *ApCAB*
Gelert, Johannes Sophus 1852-1923 *AmBi,*
 NatCAB 9, WhAm 1
Gelfond, Alexandr Osipovich 1906-1968 *DcScB*
Gell-Mann, Murray 1929- *AsBiEn, McGEWB,*
 WebAB
Gellatly, John 1853-1931 *DcAmB S1*
Gellatly, John Arthur 1869- *WhAm 5*
Geller, David 1888-1964 *WhAm 4*
Gellermann, William 1897-1961 *WhAm 4*
Gellert, N Henry 1889-1959 *WhAm 4*
Gelles, Paul P 1905-1966 *WhAm 4*
Gellhorn, Edith Fischel *WomWWA 14*
Gellhorn, Ernst 1893-1973 *WhAm 5*
Gellhorn, George 1870-1936 *WhAm 1*
Gellibrand, Henry 1597-1636 *AsBiEn, DcScB*
Gellis, Sidney Nathan 1911-1961 *NatCAB 48*
Gellman, Moses 1896-1960 *NatCAB 44*
Gelman, Samuel Joseph 1914-1971 *WhAm 5*
Gelmo, Paul Josef Jakob 1879-1961 *DcScB*
Gelshenen, William Henry 1848-1902
 NatCAB 12
Gelston, Clain Fanning 1890-1951 *NatCAB 41*
Gelston, David 1744-1828 *BiDrAC, WhAm H,*
 WhAmP
Gelz, John James 1883-1937 *NatCAB 38*
Gemeroy, Joseph Conrad 1901-1965
 NatCAB 51
Geminus *DcScB*
Geminus, Thomas 1510?-1562 *DcScB*
Gemma Frisius, Reiner 1508-1555 *DcScB*
Gemmell, John *NewYHSD*
Gemmell, Maude Hazlegrove *WomWWA 14*
Gemmell, Robert Campbell 1863-1922
 NatCAB 18, WhAm 1
Gemmell, William Henry 1866- *WhAm 4*
Gemmill, Benjamin McKee 1866-1940 *WhAm 1*
Gemmill, John Alexander 1847- *ApCAB*
Gemmill, Willard Beharrell 1875-1935 *WhAm 1*
Gemmill, William Billings 1898-1946
 NatCAB 36
Gemmill, William Headrick 1871-1945 *WhAm 3*
Gemmill, William Nelson 1860-1930
 NatCAB 41, WhAm 1
Gemmill, Worthy 1871-1955 *NatCAB 46*
Gemunder, August Martin 1862-1928
 NatCAB 21
Gemunder, August Martin Ludwig 1814-1895
 ApCAB, DcAmB, NatCAB 23, WhAm H
Gemunder, George 1816-1899 *ApCAB,*
 NatCAB 8
Genda, Minoru *WhWW-II*
Gendel, Samuel 1910-1965 *NatCAB 51*
Gendhart, Edward *NewYHSD*
Gendhart, Herman *NewYHSD*

Gendhart, John W *NewYHSD*
Genebach, George Jay 1874-1945 *NatCAB 37*
Generelly, Fleury *NewYHSD*
Genest, Edmond Charles 1763-1834 *Drake*
Genest, Edmond Charles 1765-1834 *ApCAB*
Genet, Arthur Samuel 1909-1968 *WhAm 5*
Genet, Edmond Charles 1763-1834 *AmBi,*
 DcAmB, EncAB, McGEWB, NatCAB 25,
 WhAm H
Genet, Jean 1910- *McGEWB*
Gengembre, Charles Antoine Colomb 1790-1863
 NewYHSD, WhAm H
Gengembre, Miss S *NewYHSD*
Gengenbach, Franklin Paul 1875-1955
 NatCAB 45
Genghis Khan 1167-1227 *McGEWB*
Gengler, Leonard d1973 *WhAm 6*
Genin, John Nicholas 1819-1878 *ApCAB,*
 DcAmB, NatCAB 11, WhAm H
Genin, Sylvester 1822-1850 *NewYHSD,*
 WhAm H
Gennes, Julien 1652-1704 *ApCAB*
Gennet, Charles Westcott, Jr. 1876-1943
 WhAm 2
Gennett, Nathaniel Chapman Weems, Jr.
 1915-1973 *WhAm 6*
Genot, Sebastian *NewYHSD*
Gensman, Lorrain Michael 1878-1954 *WhAm 6*
Gensman, Lorraine Michael 1878-1954 *BiDrAC*
Gensoul, Admiral *WhWW-II*
Gent, Sophia S Daniell 1818?- *NewYHSD,*
 WhAm H
Gentele, C Goran H A 1917-1972 *WhAm 5*
Genth, Frederick Augustus 1820-1893 *ApCAB,*
 DcAmB, DcScB, NatCAB 7, TwCBDA,
 WhAm H
Genth, Frederick Augustus, Jr. 1855- *WhAm 1*
Genth, Lillian Matilda d1953 *BiCAW,*
 WhAm 3, WomWWA 14
Genthe, Arnold 1869-1942 *DcAmB S3,*
 WhAm 2
Genthe, Karl Wilhelm 1871- *WhAm 5*
Gentile DaFabriano 1370?-1427 *McGEWB*
Gentile, Edward 1890-1968 *WhAm 5*
Gentile, Felix Michael 1910-1957 *WhAm 3*
Gentile, Giovanni 1875-1944 *McGEWB*
Gentilini, Joseph *NewYHSD*
Gentils *NewYHSD*
Gentilz, Jean Louis Theodore 1819-1906
 IlBEAAW
Gentilz, Theodore 1820?-1906 *NewYHSD*
Gentle, Alice True 1888-1958 *WhAm 3*
Gentry, Brady Preston 1896-1966 *BiDrAC*
Gentry, Charles Burt 1884-1955 *WhAm 3*
Gentry, Cyrus S 1892-1967 *WhAm 4*
Gentry, Elizabeth Butler 1874- *WomWWA 14*
Gentry, Emery Marcus 1880- *WhoColR*
Gentry, Franklin Marion 1898-1957 *NatCAB 46*
Gentry, Fred Bingham 1898-1970 *NatCAB 56*
Gentry, Martin Butler 1886-1956 *WhAm 3*
Gentry, Meredith P 1811-1866 *BiAUS*
Gentry, Meredith Poindexter 1809-1866 *ApCAB,*
 BiDConf, BiDrAC, TwCBDA, WhAm H,
 WhAmP
Gentry, North Todd 1866-1944 *NatCAB 34,*
 WhAm 2
Gentry, Richard d1837 *Drake*
Gentry, Susie *WomWWA 14*
Gentry, Thomas George 1843- *TwCBDA,*
 WhAm 4
Gentry, William Lee 1867- *WhAm 4*
Gentry, William Richard 1869-1959
 NatCAB 48, WhAm 4
Gentzen, Gerhard 1909-1945 *DcScB*
Genuario, Salvator Peter 1897-1959 *NatCAB 47*
Genung, George Frederick 1850-1935 *WhAm 1*
Genung, John Franklin 1850-1919 *AmBi,*
 DcAmB, TwCBDA, WhAm 1
Genung, Myrta Goodenough 1870-
 WomWWA 14
Genzmer, Sada Sevilla 1858- *WomWWA 14*
Geoffrey Of Monmouth 1100?-1155 *McGEWB*
Geoffrion, Felix P C 1832- *ApCAB*
Geoffroy, Claude Joseph 1685-1752 *DcScB*
Geoffroy, Etienne Francois 1672-1731 *DcScB*
Geoffroy, Etienne Louis 1725-1810 *DcScB*
Geoffroy, W J 1895-1952 *WhAm 3*

Geoffroy Saint-Hilaire, Etienne 1772-1844
 DcScB
Geoffroy Saint-Hilaire, Isidore 1805-1861
 DcScB
Geoghan, William F X d1959 *WhAm 3*
Geoghegan, A D 1877-1940 *NatCAB 33*
Geoghegan, Anthony Vincent Barrett 1897-1962
 WhAm 4
Geohegan, William Anthony 1859- *WhAm 4*
Georg, Walter Ferdinand 1874- *WhAm 5*
George I 1660-1727 *McGEWB, WhAm H*
George II 1683-1760 *McGEWB, WhAm H,*
 WhoMilH
George II 1889-1947 *WhWW-II*
George III 1738-1820 *McGEWB*
George IV 1762-1830 *McGEWB*
George V 1865-1936 *McGEWB*
George VI 1895-1952 *McGEWB, WhAm 3,*
 WhWW-II
George, Albert Bailey 1873- *WhoColR*
George, Albert Eugene 1857- *WhAm 4*
George, Albert Joseph 1913-1968 *WhAm 4*
George, Alice N 1866- *WomWWA 14*
George, Andrew Jackson 1855-1907 *TwCBDA,*
 WhAm 1, WhAm 4
George, Anne Everett 1880- *WomWWA 14*
George, Archibald *NewYHSD*
George, Arthur Alexander 1866-1955
 NatCAB 47
George, Charles Albert 1867-1950 *WhAm 3*
George, Charles Carlton 1863-1940 *WhAm 1*
George, Charles P 1886-1946 *WhAm 2*
George, Edgar Jesse 1863-1930 *WhAm 1*
George, Edwin Black 1896-1963 *WhAm 4*
George, Edwin Solomon 1873-1951 *NatCAB 43*
George, Ella Martin 1850- *WomWWA 14*
George, Enoch 1767-1828 *ApCAB, NatCAB 5,*
 TwCBDA
George, Enos 1768-1828 *Drake*
George, Eugene Sherman 1889-1959
 NatCAB 49
George, Eva G Neal 1855- *WomWWA 14*
George, Frank William 1878-1928 *NatCAB 22*
George, Gladys 1904-1954 *DcAmB S5*
George, Grace 1874-1961 *NatCAB 46*
George, Grace 1880-1961 *WomWWA 14*
George, Harold Coulter 1881-1937 *NatCAB 29,*
 WhAm 1
George, Harold Huston 1892-1942 *NatCAB 31*
George, Henry 1839-1897 *AmBi, ApCAB,*
 ApCAB X, DcAmB, EncAAH, EncAB,
 McGEWB, NatCAB 4, TwCBDA,
 WebAB, WhAm H, WhAmP
George, Henry 1862-1916 *BiDrAC, DcAmB,*
 TwCBDA, WhAm 1, WhAmP
George, Henry, III 1907-1968 *NatCAB 56*
George, Herbert 1853-1924 *WhAm 1*
George, James Zachariah 1826-1897 *AmBi,*
 ApCAB, BiDrAC, DcAmB, McGEWB,
 NatCAB 2, TwCBDA, WhAm H,
 WhAmP
George, Jennings Burton 1893-1971 *WhAm 5*
George, Jerome Rowley 1867-1942 *NatCAB 35*
George, John J 1897-1961 *WhAm 4*
George, John Jacob 1866-1932 *NatCAB 27*
George, John Malin 1802-1887 *ApCAB Sup*
George, Joseph Henry 1851-1923 *NatCAB 14*
George, Joseph Henry 1852-1923 *WhAm 1*
George, Joseph Johnson 1909-1975 *WhAm 6*
George, Joseph Warren 1869- *WhAm 5*
George, Lydia A 1839- *AmWom*
George, Manfred 1893-1965 *WhAm 4*
George, Marian M 1865- *WomWWA 14*
George, Melvin Clark 1849-1933 *BiDrAC,*
 WhAmP
George, Myron Virgil 1900- *BiDrAC*
George, Newell Adolphus 1904- *BiDrAC*
George, R Burns 1900-1963 *NatCAB 51*
George, Rebecca Rogers *WomWWA 14*
George, Robert James 1844-1911 *WhAm 1*
George, Robert Mabry 1908-1966 *WhAm 4*
George, Rufus Lambert 1868- *WhAm 4*
George, Russell D 1866- *WhAm 4*
George, Samuel Bolivar 1871-1964 *NatCAB 50*
George, Samuel Carr 1832- *ApCAB*
George, Stefan 1868-1933 *McGEWB*
George, Thomas *NewYHSD*
George, Thomas John 1873-1947 *NatCAB 35*

George, Vesper Lincoln 1865-1934 *WhAm 1, WhAm 1C*
George, W Kyle 1881- *WhAm 6*
George, Walter Franklin 1878-1957 *ApCAB X, BiDrAC, WhAm 3, WhAmP*
George, William 1861-1943 *WhAm 2*
George, William Perry 1895-1955 *WhAm 3*
George, William Reuben 1866-1936 *AmBi, DcAmB S2, WhAm 1, WhAmP*
Georges, Joseph 1875-1951 *WhWW-II, WhoMilH*
Georgeson, Charles Christian 1851-1931 *WhAm 1*
Georgey, Artur 1818-1912 *WhoMilH*
Gephart, S S *NewYHSD*
Geppert, Otto Emil 1889-1970 *WhAm 5*
Gepson, John Morgan 1913-1973 *WhAm 6*
Geraghty, James M d1940 *WhAm 1*
Geraghty, Martin John 1867-1914 *WhAm 1*
Gerald, Mother Mary d1961 *WhAm 4*
Geraldini, Alejandro 1455-1525 *ApCAB*
Geran, Elmer Hendrickson 1875-1954 *BiDrAC, WhAm 3*
Gerard, Madame *NewYHSD*
Gerard Of Brussels *DcScB*
Gerard Of Cremona 1114?-1187 *AsBiEn, DcScB, DcScB Sup*
Gerard Of Silteo *DcScB*
Gerard, Conrad Alexander d1790 *Drake*
Gerard, Felix Roy *WhAm 2*
Gerard, James Watson 1794-1874 *ApCAB, DcAmB, NatCAB 11, WhAm H*
Gerard, James Watson 1822-1900 *ApCAB, WhAm 1*
Gerard, James Watson 1823-1900 *NatCAB 11*
Gerard, James Watson 1867-1951 *ApCAB X, DcAmB S5, NatCAB 49, WhAm 3*
Gerard, Jessie Honor Bryant *WomWWA 14*
Gerard, John 1545-1612 *DcScB*
Gerard, Ralph Waldo 1900-1974 *WhAm 6*
Gerard DeRayneval, Conrad Alexandre d1790 *ApCAB*
Gerard-Thiers, Albert 1860- *NatCAB 4*
Gerardi, Joseph A 1896-1964 *WhAm 4*
Gerasimov, Mikhail Mikhaylovich 1907-1970 *WhAm 5*
Gerasimovich, Boris Petrovich 1889-1937 *DcScB*
Gerber, Daniel F 1898-1974 *DcAmB S5, WhAm 6*
Gerber, David 1861- *NatCAB 14*
Gerber, Frank 1873-1952 *DcAmB S5, NatCAB 41, WhAm 3*
Gerber, Joseph Roman 1891-1966 *NatCAB 53*
Gerber, Nathan B 1908-1961 *NatCAB 48*
Gerberding, George Henry 1847-1927 *WhAm 1*
Gerberding, Richard Henry 1889-1972 *WhAm 5*
Gerbereux, Denis F 1854-1928 *ApCAB X*
Gerbert 940?-1003 *AsBiEn*
Gerbert 945?-1003 *DcScB*
Gerbezius, Marcus 1658-1718 *DcScB*
Gerbrandy, P S 1885-1961 *WhAm 4*
Gercke, Daniel James 1874-1964 *WhAm 4*
Gerdemann, Herbert Edmund 1910-1972 *WhAm 5*
Gerdes, Henry Tienken 1877-1948 *NatCAB 37*
Gerdes, John 1886-1959 *WhAm 3*
Gerdine, L VanHorn 1873-1957 *NatCAB 43*
Gerdine, Thomas Golding 1872-1930 *WhAm 1, WhAm 1C*
Gere, Brewster Huntington 1910-1973 *WhAm 6*
Gere, Charles Henry 1838-1904 *TwCBDA, WhAm 1*
Gere, George Grant 1848-1918 *NatCAB 7, WhAm 3*
Gere, George Washington 1843- *WhAm 4*
Gere, Laura Ella *WomWWA 14*
Gere, Mary Elizabeth *WomWWA 14*
Geren, Paul Francis 1913-1969 *NatCAB 55, WhAm 5*
Gerfen, Richard Conrad 1911-1964 *NatCAB 51*
Gergen, John Jay 1903-1967 *WhAm 4*
Gergonne, Joseph Diaz 1771-1859 *DcScB*
Gerguson, Harry F *WebAB*
Gerhard, Benjamin 1812-1864 *ApCAB*
Gerhard, George 1830-1902 *NewYHSD*
Gerhard, Gerhard Russell 1906-1972 *WhAm 5*
Gerhard, William Paul 1854-1927 *AmBi, ApCAB, TwCBDA, WhAm 1*

Gerhard, William Wood 1809-1872 *AmBi, ApCAB, BiHiMed, DcAmB, Drake, NatCAB 23, WhAm H*
Gerhardt, August Edward 1882-1942 *WhAm 2*
Gerhardt, Charles 1863-1957 *NatCAB 43*
Gerhardt, Charles Frederic 1816-1856 *DcScB*
Gerhardt, Karl 1853- *ApCAB Sup, TwCBDA, WhAm 4*
Gerhardt, Paul, Jr. 1899-1966 *NatCAB 51, WhAm 4*
Gerhardt, Raymond 1905-1958 *NatCAB 47*
Gerhart, Emanuel Vogel 1817-1904 *AmBi, ApCAB, DcAmB, NatCAB 12, TwCBDA, WhAm 1*
Gerhauser, William Henry 1889-1952 *WhAm 3*
Gericault, Jean Louis Andre Theodore 1791-1824 *McGEWB*
Gericke, Wilhelm 1845-1925 *DcAmB, WhAm 1*
Gerig, John Lawrence 1878-1957 *NatCAB 46, WhAm 3*
Gerig, William 1866-1944 *NatCAB 46, WhAm 2*
Geriot, Achille *NewYHSD*
Gerity, James, Jr. 1904-1973 *WhAm 6*
Gerke, Johann Philip 1811- *NewYHSD*
Gerken, Frederick 1856-1918 *ApCAB X*
Gerken, Rudolph A 1887-1943 *WhAm 2*
Gerken, Walter Diedrick 1875- *WhAm 5*
Gerlach, Arch Clive 1911-1972 *NatCAB 57, WhAm 5*
Gerlach, Charles Lewis 1895-1947 *BiDrAC, WhAm 2, WhAmP*
Gerlach, George W 1879-1954 *WhAm 3*
Gerlach, Herman *NewYHSD*
Gerlach, John Joseph 1865-1931 *WhAm 1*
Gerlach, Richard Francis 1873-1957 *NatCAB 50*
Gerlaugh, Paul 1891-1951 *WhAm 3*
Gerling, Henry Joseph 1870-1948 *WhAm 3*
Gerlinger, Carl Frederick 1878-1951 *NatCAB 41*
Gerlinger, George Theodore 1876-1948 *NatCAB 51*
Gerlinger, Louis 1853-1941 *NatCAB 38*
Gerlinger, Louis, Jr. 1878-1953 *NatCAB 44*
Germain, George 1716-1785 *WhAm H*
Germain, Sophie 1776-1831 *DcScB*
Germaine, Lord George 1716-1785 *ApCAB, Drake*
German, Charles W *NewYHSD*
German, Henry LaVerne 1881-1955 *NatCAB 43*
German, John S 1879-1947 *WhAm 2*
German, Obadiah d1842 *BiAUS*
German, Obadiah 1766-1842 *BiDrAC, WhAm H*
German, Obadiah 1767-1842 *ApCAB, NatCAB 12, TwCBDA*
German, William J 1888-1963 *WhAm 4*
German, William Paxton Zacheus 1877-1953 *NatCAB 42*
Germane, Charles E 1885-1942 *WhAm 2*
Germann, Frank E E 1887-1974 *WhAm 6*
Germann, Melinda C Knapheide 1863- *WomWWA 14*
Germanos 1868-1951 *WhAm 3*
Germanus, Henricus Martellus *DcScB*
Germany, Eugene Benjamin 1892-1971 *WhAm 5*
Germer, Lester Halbert 1896-1971 *WhAm 5*
Germon, John D *NewYHSD*
Germon, Washington L *NewYHSD*
Germuth, Frederick George 1891-1964 *WhAm 4*
Gernerd, Fred Benjamin 1879-1948 *BiDrAC, WhAm 2*
Gernes, Alexander Bernard 1882-1947 *NatCAB 36*
Gernon, Frank E d1956 *WhAm 3*
Gernsback, Hugo 1884-1967 *WebAB, WhAm 4*
Geronimo 1829-1909 *AmBi, ApCAB, DcAmB, EncAB, McGEWB, NatCAB 23, REnAW, WebAB, WebAMB, WhAm HA, WhAm 4*
Gerosa, Giuseppe *NewYHSD*
Gerosa, John 1889-1969 *NatCAB 55*
Gerould, Gordon Hall 1877- *WhAm 3*

Gerould, James Thayer 1872-1951 *DcAmLiB, NatCAB 41, WhAm 3*
Gerould, John Hiram 1868-1961 *WhAm 4*
Gerould, Katharine Elizabeth Fullerton 1879-1944 *NotAW, WhAm 2, WomWWA 14*
Gerould, Winifred Gregory 1885-1955 *DcAmLiB, WhAm 3*
Gerow, John Young 1856-1944 *NatCAB 35*
Gerow, Leonard Townsend 1888-1972 *WebAMB, WhAm 5*
Gerrer, Gregory 1867-1946 *WhAm 3*
Gerrish, Frederic Henry 1845-1920 *DcAmB, NatCAB 12, WhAm 1*
Gerrish, Theodore 1846- *WhAm 4*
Gerrish, Thornton 1856-1955 *WhAm 3*
Gerrish, Willard Peabody 1866- *WhAm 5*
Gerrish, Woodbury *NewYHSD*
Gerrity, Thomas Patrick 1913-1968 *WhAm 4A*
Gerry, Elbridge 1744-1814 *AmBi, ApCAB, BiAUS, BiDrAC, BiDrUSE, DcAmB, Drake, EncAB, McGEWB, NatCAB 5, TwCBDA, WebAB, WhAm H, WhAmP*
Gerry, Elbridge 1813-1886 *BiDrAC, WhAm H*
Gerry, Elbridge 1815-1886 *BiAUS*
Gerry, Elbridge Thomas 1837-1927 *AmBi, ApCAB, ApCAB X, DcAmB, NatCAB 8, TwCBDA, WhAm 1*
Gerry, Eloise 1885- *WomWWA 14*
Gerry, James 1796-1873 *BiAUS, BiDrAC, WhAm H*
Gerry, Louis Cardell 1884-1966 *WhAm 4*
Gerry, Margarita Spalding 1870- *WhAm 5*
Gerry, Martin Hughes, Jr. 1868-1941 *WhAm 2*
Gerry, Peter Goelet 1879-1957 *BiDrAC, NatCAB 47, WhAm 3, WhAmP*
Gerry, Samuel Lancaster 1813-1891 *ApCAB, NewYHSD*
Gersbacher, Eva Nina Oxford d1973 *WhAm 5*
Gershom BenJudah 950?-1028 *McGEWB*
Gershon-Cohen, Jacob 1899-1971 *NatCAB 57, WhAm 5*
Gershovitz, Samuel D 1907-1960 *WhAm 4*
Gershoy, Leo 1897-1975 *WhAm 6*
Gershvin, Jacob *WebAB*
Gershwin, George 1898-1937 *DcAmB S2, EncAB, McGEWB, WebAB, WhAm 1*
Gershwin, George 1898-1938 *AmBi*
Gershwin, George 1900-1937 *NatCAB 29*
Gerson, Felix Napoleon 1862-1945 *WhAm 2*
Gerson, John 1363-1429 *McGEWB*
Gerson, Oscar 1874- *WhAm 5*
Gerson, Theodore Perceval 1872- *WhAm 5*
Gerst, Francis Joseph 1882-1968 *WhAm 5*
Gerst, Herbert Joseph 1888-1963 *NatCAB 51*
Gerstacker, Friedrich 1816-1872 *ApCAB*
Gerstell, Arnold Frederick 1861-1914 *ApCAB X*
Gerstell, Robert Sinclair 1893-1973 *WhAm 5*
Gersten, E Chester 1889-1971 *WhAm 5*
Gerstenberg, Alice *BiCAW, WomWWA 14*
Gerstenberg, Charles William 1882-1948 *WhAm 2*
Gerstenberg, Julia *BiCAW*
Gerstenberger, Henry John 1881-1954 *NatCAB 44, WhAm 3*
Gerstenfeld, Norman 1904-1968 *WhAm 5*
Gerster, Arpad Geyza Charles 1848-1923 *AmBi, DcAmB, NatCAB 11, NatCAB 26, WhAm 1*
Gerster, Jack Alan 1919-1971 *WhAm 5*
Gerstle, Lewis 1824-1902 *DcAmB, NatCAB 13, WhAm H*
Gerstle, Mark Lewis 1866- *WhAm 5*
Gertken, Severin 1881- *WhAm 6*
Gervais, John Lewis 1753-1798 *ApCAB, BiAUS, BiDrAC, WhAm H, WhAmP*
Gerwig, George William 1867-1950 *NatCAB 39, WhAm 3*
Gery, Louis 1830?- *NewYHSD*
Gescheidt, Louis Anthony 1808-1876 *ApCAB*
Gescheidt, Morris *NewYHSD*
Geschwindt *NewYHSD*
Gesell, Arnold Lucius 1880-1961 *AsBiEn, BiDAmEd, DcScB, NatCAB 49, WebAB, WhAm 4*
Gesell, Robert 1886-1954 *WhAm 3*
Geslain, The Younger *NewYHSD*
Gesleur, Clement *NewYHSD*

Gesner, Abraham 1797-1864 *ApCAB*, *Drake*
Gesner, Anthon Temple 1865-1939 *NatCAB 30*, *WhAm 1*
Gesner, Bertram Melvin 1931-1968 *WhAm 5*
Gesner, Konrad Von 1516-1565 *AsBiEn*, *DcScB*, *McGEWB*
Gesner, Virginia Brett *WomWWA 14*
Gessel, Udell Mathews 1911-1953 *NatCAB 42*
Gessler, A E 1885-1969 *WhAm 5*
Gessler, Theodore A K 1841-1925 *WhAm 1*
Gessner, Francis Emil 1890-1952 *NatCAB 39*
Gessner, Hermann Bertram 1872-1944 *WhAm 2*
Gessner, Johannes 1709-1790 *DcScB*
Gessner, Robert 1907-1968 *WhAm 5*
Gest, John Marshall 1859-1934 *WhAm 1*
Gest, Joseph Henry 1859-1935 *NatCAB 30*, *WhAm 1*
Gest, Morris 1881-1942 *DcAmB S3*, *NatCAB 38*, *WhAm 2*
Gest, William Harrison 1838-1912 *BiDrAC*
Gest, William Purves 1861-1939 *WhAm 1*
Gestefeld, Ursula Newell 1845-1921 *NotAW*, *WhAm 1*, *WomWWA 14*
Gestido, Oscar 1901-1967 *WhAm 4*
Gesualdo, Carlo, Prince Of Venosa 1560?-1613 *McGEWB*
Getchell, Charles Munro 1909-1963 *WhAm 4*
Getchell, Clara Augusta Furbish 1857- *WomWWA 14*
Getchell, Edward Leonard 1884-1954 *NatCAB 43*
Getchell, John Stirling 1899-1940 *NatCAB 30*, *WhAm 1*
Getchell, Margaret *NotAW*
Getchell, Noble Hamilton 1875- *WhAm 5*
Getchell, Warren Wick 1890-1960 *NatCAB 47*
Gethoefer, Louis Henry 1866-1946 *WhAm 2*
Gethro, Fred William 1873- *WhAm 5*
Getler, Charles d1967 *WhAm 4*
Getman, Frederick Hutton 1877-1941 *NatCAB 30*, *WhAm 2*
Getman, George Burrill 1879-1954 *NatCAB 41*
Getschow, Roy Martin 1894-1968 *WhAm 5*
Getsinger, Edward Christopher 1866- *WhAm 4*
Gettell, Raymond Garfield 1881-1949 *WhAm 3*
Gettemy, Charles Ferris 1868-1939 *WhAm 1*
Getty, George Franklin 1858- *ApCAB X*
Getty, George Franklin, II 1924-1973 *WhAm 6*
Getty, George Hale 1857-1920 *NatCAB 19*
Getty, George Washington 1819-1901 *AmBi*, *ApCAB*, *DcAmB*, *Drake*, *NatCAB 12*, *TwCBDA*, *WhAm H*
Getty, Jean Paul 1892-1976 *EncAB*, *WebAB*, *WhAm 6*
Getty, Robert 1916-1971 *WhAm 5*
Getty, Robert N 1855-1941 *WhAm 1*
Gettys, Thomas Smithwick 1912- *BiDrAC*
Getz, Charles S *NewYHSD*
Getz, Forry Rohrer 1877-1958 *WhAm 4*
Getz, George Fulmer 1863-1938 *NatCAB 27*
Getz, George Fulmer 1865-1938 *WhAm 1*
Getz, Hiram Landis 1850- *WhAm 4*
Getz, J Lawrence 1821-1891 *BiAUS*
Getz, J S *NewYHSD*
Getz, James Lawrence 1821-1891 *BiDrAC*, *WhAm H*, *WhAmP*
Getz, Mary Minnie 1862- *WomWWA 14*
Getz, Summers *NewYHSD*
Geuther, Anton 1833-1889 *DcScB*
Gevelot, Nicholas *NewYHSD*
Gevurtz, William Sanders 1910-1957 *NatCAB 44*
Gewehr, Wesley Marsh 1888-1961 *NatCAB 47*
Geyer, Andrew 1842-1919 *NatCAB 19*
Geyer, Bertram Birch 1891-1970 *WhAm 5*
Geyer, Ellen M 1879-1953 *WhAm 3*
Geyer, Frederick *NewYHSD*
Geyer, Henry Christian *NewYHSD*
Geyer, Henry Sheffie 1790-1859 *AmBi*, *ApCAB*, *BiDrAC*, *DcAmB*, *Drake*, *NatCAB 4*, *TwCBDA*, *WhAm H*, *WhAmP*
Geyer, Henry Sheffie 1798-1859 *BiAUS*
Geyer, Lee Edward 1888-1941 *BiDrAC*, *WhAm 1*, *WhAmP*
Geyl, Pieter 1887-1966 *WhAm 4*
Ghali, Paul 1905-1970 *WhAm 5*
Ghaster, Karl Leroy 1890-1959 *NatCAB 49*

Ghazali, Abu Hamid Muhammad, Al- 1058-1111 *McGEWB*
Gheen, Edward Hickman 1845-1920 *WhAm 1*
Ghent, William James 1866-1942 *DcAmB S3*, *WhAm 2*
Gheorghiu-Dej, Gheorghe 1901-1965 *WhAm 4*
Gherardi, Bancroft 1832-1903 *ApCAB*, *DcAmB*, *NatCAB 12*, *TwCBDA*, *WhAm 1*
Gherardi, Bancroft 1873-1941 *ApCAB X*, *DcAmB S3*, *NatCAB 34*, *WhAm 1*
Gherardi, Walter Rockwell 1875-1939 *WhAm 1*
Ghering, Leonard George 1909-1967 *NatCAB 54*
Gherky, William David 1868-1937 *NatCAB 28*
Ghetaldi, Marino 1566?-1626 *DcScB*
Ghiberti, Lorenzo 1381?-1455 *McGEWB*
Ghini, Luca 1490?-1556 *DcScB*
Ghio, James Christopher d1914 *NatCAB 16*
Ghirardelli, Alfred 1884-1956 *NatCAB 46*
Ghirardelli, Domingo 1849-1932 *NatCAB 37*
Ghirlandaio, Domenico 1449-1494 *McGEWB*
Ghiselin, George R 1824-1890 *NatCAB 2*
Ghisi, Martino 1715-1794 *DcScB*
Gholson, James Herbert 1798-1848 *BiAUS*, *BiDrAC*, *TwCBDA*, *WhAm H*
Gholson, S J 1808-1883 *BiAUS*
Gholson, Samuel James 1808-1883 *BiDConf*
Gholson, Samuel Jameson 1808-1883 *ApCAB*, *BiDrAC*, *DcAmB*, *NatCAB 23*, *TwCBDA*, *WhAm H*
Gholson, Thomas, Jr. d1816 *BiAUS*, *BiDrAC*, *TwCBDA*, *WhAm H*
Gholson, Thomas Saunders 1808-1868 *DcAmB*, *NatCAB 23*, *WhAm H*
Gholson, Thomas Saunders 1809-1868 *ApCAB*, *BiDConf*, *TwCBDA*
Gholson, William Yates 1807-1870 *ApCAB*, *DcAmB*, *Drake*, *NatCAB 11*, *TwCBDA*, *WhAm H*
Ghormley, Alfred M 1896-1965 *WhAm 4*
Ghormley, John Wallace 1899-1970 *WhAm 5*
Ghormley, Ralph K 1893-1959 *WhAm 3*
Ghormley, Robert Lee 1883-1958 *WebAMB*, *WhAm 3*, *WhWW-II*
Ghose, Aurobindo 1872-1950 *McGEWB*
Ghrist, Jennie G 1870- *WomWWA 14*
Ghulam Mohammed 1895-1956 *WhAm 3*
Giaccone, John S 1915-1973 *WhAm 6*
Giacometti, Alberto 1901-1966 *McGEWB*, *WhAm 4*
Giaimo, Robert Nicholas 1919- *BiDrAC*
Giampaoli, Dominicus *NewYHSD*
Gianella, John 1838-1914 *NatCAB 16*
Gianelli, Frostino *NewYHSD*
Gianelloni, Vivian Joseph 1892-1957 *WhAm 3*
Gianetti, Humbert Louis 1878-1951 *NatCAB 39*
Giannini, Amadeo Peter 1870-1949 *DcAmB S4*, *NatCAB 38*, *REnAW*, *WebAB*, *WhAm 2*
Giannini, Attilio Henry 1874-1943 *NatCAB 31*, *WhAm 2*
Giannini, Joseph *NewYHSD*
Giannini, Lawrence Mario 1894-1952 *NatCAB 41*, *WhAm 3*
Giannini, Vittorio 1903-1966 *WhAm 4*
Giap, Vo Nguyen 1910-1975 *WhWW-II*, *WhoMilH*
Giap, Vo Nguyen 1912-1975 *McGEWB*
Giard, Alfred 1846-1908 *DcScB*
Giauque, Florien 1843-1921 *WhAm 1*
Giauque, William Francis 1895- *AsBiEn*, *WebAB*
Giaver, Joachim Gotsche 1856-1925 *NatCAB 21*, *WhAm 1*
Gibault, Peter 1737-1804 *ApCAB*
Gibault, Pierre 1737-1804 *AmBi*, *DcAmB*, *WhAm H*
Gibb, Arthur Norman 1868-1949 *WhAm 3*
Gibb, Frederick William 1908-1968 *WhAm 5*
Gibb, Hamilton Alexander Rosskeen 1895-1971 *WhAm 5*
Gibb, John 1829- *NatCAB 4*
Gibberd, Eric Waters 1897-1972 *IlBEAAW*
Gibbes, Heneage d1912 *WhAm 1*
Gibbes, Robert 1644-1715 *NatCAB 12*
Gibbes, Robert Wilson 1809-1866 *ApCAB*, *DcAmB*, *Drake*, *NatCAB 11*, *TwCBDA*, *WhAm H*

Gibbes, Robert Wilson 1831-1875 *ApCAB*
Gibbes, William Hasell 1754-1831 *ApCAB*, *TwCBDA*
Gibbes, William Hasell 1754-1834 *DcAmB*, *NatCAB 23*
Gibbins, Henry 1877- *WhAm 2*
Gibbon, Edward 1737-1794 *McGEWB*
Gibbon, John 1826-1896 *Drake*
Gibbon, John 1827-1896 *AmBi*, *ApCAB*, *DcAmB*, *NatCAB 4*, *TwCBDA*, *WebAMB*, *WhAm H*
Gibbon, John Heysham 1871-1956 *NatCAB 47*, *WhAm 3*
Gibbon, John Heysham, Jr. 1903-1973 *WhAm 5*
Gibbon, Thomas Edward 1860-1921 *NatCAB 12*, *NatCAB 19*, *WhAm 1*
Gibboney, David Clarence 1868- *NatCAB 14*
Gibboney, Stuart Gatewood 1877-1944 *WhAm 2*
Gibbons, Abby Hopper 1801-1893 *AmWom*, *TwCBDA*
Gibbons, Abigail Hopper 1801-1893 *AmBi*, *ApCAB*, *DcAmB*, *NatCAB 7*, *NotAW*, *WhAm H*
Gibbons, Arthur Jarvis 1851-1933 *NatCAB 25*
Gibbons, Cedric *WhAm 3*
Gibbons, Charles 1814-1885 *ApCAB*
Gibbons, Charles Allen 1901-1962 *NatCAB 52*
Gibbons, Charles David 1895-1969 *WhAm 5*
Gibbons, Douglas 1883-1962 *WhAm 4*
Gibbons, Edmund F 1868-1964 *WhAm 4*, *WhAm 5*
Gibbons, Edward d1654 *ApCAB*, *Drake*
Gibbons, Emma F 1865- *WomWWA 14*
Gibbons, Floyd 1887-1939 *AmBi*, *DcAmB S2*, *WhAm 1*
Gibbons, George Rison 1879-1950 *WhAm 3*
Gibbons, Helen Davenport 1882- *WomWWA 14*
Gibbons, Henry 1808-1884 *ApCAB*, *NatCAB 7*, *TwCBDA*, *WhAm H*
Gibbons, Henry 1840-1911 *NatCAB 7*, *NatCAB 39*, *TwCBDA*, *WhAm 1*
Gibbons, Henry 1849-1926 *WhAm 1*
Gibbons, Henry Walter 1877-1958 *NatCAB 43*
Gibbons, Herbert Adams 1880-1934 *DcAmB S1*, *NatCAB 49*, *WhAm 1*
Gibbons, James 1736-1823 *ApCAB*, *TwCBDA*
Gibbons, James 1834-1921 *AmBi*, *ApCAB*, *ApCAB X*, *DcAmB*, *DcAmReB*, *EncAB*, *McGEWB*, *NatCAB 1*, *NatCAB 29*, *TwCBDA*, *WebAB*, *WhAm 1*
Gibbons, James Edmund 1890-1959 *WhAm 3*
Gibbons, James Sloan 1810-1892 *AmBi*, *ApCAB*, *DcAmB*, *NatCAB 9*, *TwCBDA*, *WhAm H*, *WhAmP*
Gibbons, John 1848-1917 *WhAm 1*
Gibbons, John Francis 1849-1909 *NatCAB 15*
Gibbons, John Henry 1904-1944 *NatCAB 33*
Gibbons, John Miles 1877-1945 *NatCAB 34*
Gibbons, Joseph 1818-1883 *ApCAB*, *TwCBDA*
Gibbons, Leo Patrick 1885-1968 *NatCAB 56*
Gibbons, Michael Joseph 1852-1925 *NatCAB 21*
Gibbons, Michael Joseph 1883-1967 *NatCAB 55*
Gibbons, Morton Raymond 1873-1949 *NatCAB 40*
Gibbons, Sam Melville 1920- *BiDrAC*
Gibbons, Stephen B d1958 *WhAm 3*
Gibbons, Thomas 1757-1826 *AmBi*, *BiAUS*, *DcAmB*, *NatCAB 24*, *WhAm H*, *WhAmP*
Gibbons, Vernette L 1874- *WomWWA 14*
Gibbons, Walter Bernard 1894-1972 *NatCAB 56*, *WhAm 5*
Gibbons, William 1726-1800 *ApCAB*, *BiAUS*, *BiDrAC*, *DcAmB*, *TwCBDA*, *WhAm H*, *WhAmP*
Gibbons, William 1781-1845 *ApCAB*, *DcAmB*, *NatCAB 13*, *TwCBDA*, *WhAm H*
Gibbons, William Cephus 1834- *WhAm 4*
Gibbons, William Futhey 1859- *WhAm 4*
Gibbs, A C 1825-1886 *BiAUS*
Gibbs, A Hamilton 1888-1964 *WhAm 4*
Gibbs, Addison Crandall 1825-1886 *NatCAB 8*
Gibbs, Alfred 1823-1868 *AmBi*, *ApCAB*, *Drake*, *NatCAB 12*, *TwCBDA*
Gibbs, Alfred Wolcott 1856-1922 *WhAm 1*

Gibbs, Carey A 1892- *WhAm 5*
Gibbs, Carl Cleveland 1882-1942 *NatCAB 31*
Gibbs, Charlotte Mitchell 1885- *WomWWA 14*
Gibbs, Edwin C 1859-1936 *WhAm 1*
Gibbs, Eleanor Churchill *AmWom*
Gibbs, Florence Reville 1890-1964 *BiDrAC*
Gibbs, Frederick Seymour 1845-1903
   NatCAB 12, WhAm 1
Gibbs, George 1776-1833 *ApCAB, DcAmB,*
   NatCAB 12, TwCBDA, WhAm H
Gibbs, George 1815-1873 *ApCAB, DcAmB,*
   IIBEAAW, NewYHSD, TwCBDA,
   WhAm H
Gibbs, George 1817-1873 *Drake*
Gibbs, George 1861-1940 *DcAmB S2,*
   WhAm 1
Gibbs, George Couper 1879-1946 *WhAm 2*
Gibbs, George Fort 1870-1942 *NatCAB 33,*
   WhAm 2
Gibbs, George Sabin 1875-1947 *WhAm 2*
Gibbs, Harry Drake 1872-1934 *WhAm 1*
Gibbs, Ione Elveda *WhoColR*
Gibbs, James 1682-1754 *McGEWB*
Gibbs, James Edward Allen 1829-1902
   NatCAB 19
Gibbs, James Ethan Allen 1829-1902 *DcAmB,*
   WhAm H
Gibbs, Jeannette Phillips 1892-1969 *WhAm 5*
Gibbs, John *NewYHSD*
Gibbs, John, Jr. *NewYHSD*
Gibbs, John Blair 1858-1898 *ApCAB Sup*
Gibbs, John Sears, Jr. 1876-1953 *WhAm 3*
Gibbs, Jonathan 1826?-1874 *REnAW*
Gibbs, Jonathan C 1827?-1874 *BiDAmEd*
Gibbs, Josiah Willard 1790-1861 *AmBi,*
   ApCAB, DcAmB, Drake, TwCBDA,
   WhAm H
Gibbs, Josiah Willard 1839-1903 *AmBi,*
   ApCAB, AsBiEn, DcAmB, DcScB,
   EncAB, McGEWB, NatCAB 4,
   TwCBDA, WebAB, WhAm 1
Gibbs, Lincoln Robinson 1868-1943 *WhAm 2*
Gibbs, Mifflin Wistar 1823- *NatCAB 10*
Gibbs, Mifflin Wister 1823- *WhoColR*
Gibbs, Norman 1828-1910 *NatCAB 17*
Gibbs, Oliver Wolcott 1822-1908 *AmBi,*
   ApCAB, DcAmB, NatCAB 10, TwCBDA,
   WebAB
Gibbs, Sir Philip 1877-1962 *WhAm 4*
Gibbs, Ralph Alvin 1894-1966 *NatCAB 53,*
   WhAm 4
Gibbs, Richard 1819-1894 *BiAUS, NatCAB 12*
Gibbs, Robert Adams 1871-1952 *WhAm 3*
Gibbs, Roswell Clifton 1878- *WhAm 6*
Gibbs, Sir Samuel d1815 *ApCAB, Drake*
Gibbs, Walter Abner 1869-1941 *NatCAB 30*
Gibbs, William Channing d1871 *BiAUS, Drake*
Gibbs, William Channing 1789-1871 *TwCBDA*
Gibbs, William Channing 1790-1871 *NatCAB 9*
Gibbs, William Francis 1886-1967 *NatCAB 53,*
   WebAMB, WhAm 4
Gibbs, William Hasell 1754-1824 *WhAm H*
Gibbs, Willis Benjamin 1889-1940 *BiDrAC,*
   WhAm 1
Gibbs, Winifred Stuart 1871-1928 *BiCAW,*
   WhAm 1, WomWWA 14
Gibbs, Wolcott 1822-1908 *DcAmB, DcScB,*
   WhAm 1
Gibbs, Wolcott 1902-1958 *NatCAB 44,*
   WhAm 3
Giberson, Earl Finch 1894-1957 *NatCAB 46*
Giberson, Philip Eugene 1899-1962 *NatCAB 49*
Gibert, A *NewYHSD*
Gibier, Paul d1900 *WhAm 1*
Giblin, Walter M 1901-1964 *WhAm 4*
Gibner, Herbert Charles 1879-1948 *NatCAB 39*
Gibney, Virgil Pendleton 1847-1927 *NatCAB 4,*
   NatCAB 21, TwCBDA, WhAm 1
Gibson, Addison Howard 1860-1936
   NatCAB 28
Gibson, Althea 1927- *WebAB*
Gibson, Anna Lemira 1875-1961 *WhAm 4*
Gibson, Arrell Morgan 1921- *EncAAH,*
   REnAW
Gibson, Augustus 1908-1972 *NatCAB 57*
Gibson, Axel Emil 1863- *WhAm 1*
Gibson, Bayard Kendall 1892-1964 *NatCAB 51*
Gibson, Ben J 1881-1949 *WhAm 2*

Gibson, C H *NewYHSD*
Gibson, Cable Morgan 1902-1967 *WhAm 5*
Gibson, Carleton Bartlett 1863-1927 *WhAm 1*
Gibson, Caroline 1836?- *NewYHSD*
Gibson, Charles 1825-1899 *NatCAB 5*
Gibson, Charles Bell 1815-1865 *TwCBDA*
Gibson, Charles Bell 1816-1865 *ApCAB*
Gibson, Charles Brockway 1854- *WhAm 4*
Gibson, Charles Dana 1867- *NatCAB 11,*
   TwCBDA
Gibson, Charles Dana 1867-1938 *AmBi*
Gibson, Charles Dana 1867-1944 *DcAmB S3,*
   WebAB, WhAm 2
Gibson, Charles Donnel 1863- *WhAm 4*
Gibson, Charles Hammond 1874-1954 *WhAm 3*
Gibson, Charles Henry 1884-1970 *NatCAB 55*
Gibson, Charles Hopper 1842-1900 *ApCAB Sup,*
   BiDrAC, NatCAB 5, TwCBDA,
   WhAm 1, WhAmP
Gibson, Charles Langdon 1864-1944 *WhAm 2*
Gibson, Cramer Watson 1908-1967 *NatCAB 53*
Gibson, Edgar J *WhAm 1*
Gibson, Edwin Thomas 1884-1959 *NatCAB 48,*
   WhAm 3
Gibson, Ernest Willard 1871-1940 *WhAm 1*
Gibson, Ernest Willard 1872-1940 *BiDrAC,*
   NatCAB 30, WhAmP
Gibson, Ernest William 1901-1969 *BiDrAC,*
   WhAm 5
Gibson, Eustace 1842-1900 *BiDrAC*
Gibson, Eva Katherine Clapp 1857- *AmWom,*
   WhAm 1
Gibson, Finley F 1876- *WhAm 5*
Gibson, Frank Markey 1857-1929 *WhAm 1*
Gibson, George 1747-1791 *ApCAB, DcAmB,*
   Drake, WhAm H
Gibson, George 1783-1861 *ApCAB, Drake,*
   TwCBDA
Gibson, George 1810?- *IIBEAAW, NewYHSD*
Gibson, George, Jr. *NewYHSD*
Gibson, George Harry 1865-1955 *NatCAB 42*
Gibson, George Jay 1873-1948 *NatCAB 37*
Gibson, George Miles 1860-1932 *WhAm 1*
Gibson, George Rutledge 1853- *NatCAB 3*
Gibson, Guy 1918-1944 *WhWW-II*
Gibson, Harvey Dow 1882-1950 *WhAm 3*
Gibson, Henry H 1855-1914 *NatCAB 17*
Gibson, Henry Richard 1837-1938 *BiDrAC,*
   NatCAB 28, TwCBDA, WhAm 1,
   WhAmP
Gibson, Horatio Gates 1827-1924 *WhAm 1*
Gibson, Hugh 1883-1954 *WhAm 3*
Gibson, J Bruce 1871-1927 *NatCAB 21*
Gibson, J J 1910-1971 *WhAm 5*
Gibson, James *NewYHSD*
Gibson, James d1814 *ApCAB, Drake*
Gibson, James 1690?-1752 *ApCAB*
Gibson, James 1700?-1752? *Drake*
Gibson, James Alexander 1852-1922 *NatCAB 8,*
   WhAm 1
Gibson, James Edgar 1875-1953 *NatCAB 44,*
   WhAm 3
Gibson, James King 1812-1879 *BiAUS,*
   BiDrAC, WhAm H
Gibson, James Lambert 1873-1945 *WhAm 2*
Gibson, John 1740-1822 *AmBi, ApCAB,*
   BiAUS, DcAmB, Drake, NatCAB 13,
   WebAMB, WhAm H
Gibson, John 1835?- *NewYHSD*
Gibson, John Aldridge 1876-1947 *NatCAB 38*
Gibson, John Bannister 1780-1853 *AmBi,*
   ApCAB, BiAUS, DcAmB, Drake,
   NatCAB 7, NatCAB 14, NewYHSD,
   TwCBDA, WhAm H
Gibson, John Graham 1854-1919 *NatCAB 19*
Gibson, John Jameson 1872-1939 *NatCAB 33*
Gibson, John Monro 1838- *ApCAB Sup*
Gibson, John Morison 1842- *ApCAB*
Gibson, John Strickland 1893-1960 *BiDrAC*
Gibson, Joseph Thompson 1844-1922 *WhAm 1*
Gibson, Joshua 1911-1947 *DcAmB S4*
Gibson, Lorenzo P 1855-1919 *WhAm 1*
Gibson, Louis Henry 1854- *WhAm 1*
Gibson, Mabel Leonard *WomWWA 14*
Gibson, Mary 1836?- *NewYHSD*
Gibson, Mary Adelaide 1853- *WomWWA 14*
Gibson, Nathan Adams 1867-1940 *NatCAB 31*
Gibson, Norman Rothwell 1880- *WhAm 6*

Gibson, Paris 1830-1920 *AmBi, ApCAB X,*
   BiDrAC, DcAmB, NatCAB 8, REnAW,
   WhAm 1, WhAmP
Gibson, Paul Emil 1908-1966 *WhAm 4*
Gibson, Philip Pendleton 1890-1963 *NatCAB 51*
Gibson, Preston 1879-1937 *WhAm 1*
Gibson, Randall Lee 1832-1892 *AmBi, ApCAB,*
   BiAUS, BiDConf, BiDrAC, DcAmB,
   NatCAB 1, TwCBDA, WhAm H,
   WhAmP
Gibson, Richard P *NewYHSD*
Gibson, Richard R 1795?- *NewYHSD*
Gibson, Robert 1834?- *NewYHSD*
Gibson, Robert Atkinson 1846-1919
   ApCAB Sup, NatCAB 12, TwCBDA,
   WhAm 1
Gibson, Robert Banks 1882-1959 *NatCAB 50*
Gibson, Robert Edward Lee 1864- *WhAm 4*
Gibson, Robert Murray 1869-1949 *WhAm 2*
Gibson, Robert Newcomb 1889-1963 *WhAm 4*
Gibson, Robert Williams 1854-1927
   ApCAB Sup, NatCAB 11, TwCBDA,
   WhAm 1
Gibson, Samuel Carrol 1857- *WhAm 4*
Gibson, Stanley 1883-1956 *NatCAB 45,*
   WhAm 3
Gibson, Stephen *NewYHSD*
Gibson, Susan Meta *WomWWA 14*
Gibson, Thomas d1811 *NewYHSD*
Gibson, Thomas L 1881- *WhAm 6*
Gibson, Tobias 1771-1804 *ApCAB*
Gibson, Truman Kella 1882-1972 *WhAm 5,*
   WhoColR
Gibson, Walter Murray 1823-1888 *ApCAB Sup,*
   DcAmB, NatCAB 23, WhAm H,
   WhAmP
Gibson, William 1788-1868 *ApCAB, BiDAmEd,*
   DcAmB, Drake, NatCAB 2, TwCBDA,
   WhAm H
Gibson, William Campbell 1838-1911 *WhAm 1*
Gibson, William Charles 1914-1961 *NatCAB 49*
Gibson, William Hamilton 1850-1896 *AmBi,*
   ApCAB, DcAmB, NatCAB 7, TwCBDA,
   WhAm H
Gibson, William Meredith 1856-1925 *WhAm 1*
Gibson, William Richie 1877-1940 *WhAm 1*
Gibson, William Wesley 1856- *WhAm 4*
Giddings, C M *NewYHSD*
Giddings, DeWitt Clinton 1827-1903 *BiAUS,*
   BiDrAC, WhAmP
Giddings, DeWitt Clinton, Jr. 1863-1927
   NatCAB 47
Giddings, Edward Leach 1835-1903 *NatCAB 16*
Giddings, Emanuel Martin 1886-1947
   NatCAB 36
Giddings, Franklin Henry 1855-1931 *AmBi,*
   BiDAmEd, DcAmB S1, McGEWB,
   NatCAB 15, NatCAB 39, TwCBDA,
   WhAm 1
Giddings, Harold Girard 1880-1949 *NatCAB 37*
Giddings, Howard Andrus 1868-1949 *WhAm 2*
Giddings, Joshua Reed 1775-1864 *TwCBDA*
Giddings, Joshua Reed 1795-1864 *AmBi,*
   ApCAB, BiAUS, BiDrAC, DcAmB,
   Drake, EncAAH, NatCAB 2, WebAB,
   WhAm H, WhAmP
Giddings, Marsh d1875 *BiAUS*
Giddings, Napoleon Bonaparte 1816-1897
   BiDrAC, WhAm H
Giddings, Rockwood 1812-1839 *TwCBDA*
Giddings, Salmon 1782-1828 *ApCAB*
Gide, Andre Paul Guillaume 1869-1951
   McGEWB, WhAm 3
Gideon, Abram 1867- *WhAm 4*
Gideon, Dave d1950 *WhAm 2*
Gideon, Peter Miller 1820-1899 *AmBi, DcAmB,*
   NatCAB 23, WhAm H
Gideon, Samuel Edward 1875- *IIBEAAW*
Gideon, Valentine 1859-1951 *NatCAB 48,*
   WhAm 3
Gideonse, Harry David 1901- *BiDAmEd*
Gidley, James Williams 1866-1931 *DcAmB S1,*
   NatCAB 24, WhAm 1
Gidney, Herbert Alfred 1881-1963 *WhAm 4*
Gie, Stefanus Francois Naude 1884-1945
   WhAm 2
Giebel, Frank Joseph 1861-1919 *NatCAB 18*
Giedion, Siegfried 1893-1968 *WhAm 5*

Giegengack, Augustus E 1890-1974 *WhAm 6*
Giegerich, Leonard Anthony 1855-1927
NatCAB 4, WhAm 1
Gielniak, Jozef 1932-1972 *WhAm 5*
Gielow, Martha Sawyer d1933 *WhAm 1,*
WomWWA 14
Giering, Eugene Thomas 1867-1934 *WhAm 1*
Gierke, Otto Von 1841-1921 *McGEWB*
Gierula, Jerzy Kazimierz 1917-1975 *WhAm 6*
Gies, William John 1872-1956 *WhAm 3*
Giese, Augustus Albert 1903-1966 *WhAm 4*
Giese, Charles Oscar 1875-1956 *NatCAB 48*
Giese, Gilbert Smith 1894-1963 *NatCAB 50*
Giese, Herman Robert 1904-1968 *WhAm 5*
Giese, Oscar W 1905-1956 *WhAm 3*
Giese, William Frederic 1864- *WhAm 4*
Giesecke, Frederick Ernest 1869-1953
NatCAB 41, WhAm 5
Giesecke, Friederich Ernst 1869-1953 *WhAm 5*
Gieseke, Ferdinand *NewYHSD*
Gieseking, Walter Wilhelm 1895-1956 *WhAm 3*
Giesel, Frederick W 1893-1963 *WhAm 4*
Giesel, Friedrich Oskar 1852-1927 *DcScB*
Giesler, Jean Verdi 1890-1965 *NatCAB 52*
Giesler, Jerry 1890-1963 *WhAm 4*
Giesler-Anneke, Mathilde Franzisha 1817-1884
WhAm H
Giesler-Anneke, Mathilde Franziska 1817-1884
DcAmB, NotAW
Giessing, Herbert William 1895-1954
NatCAB 45
Giesy, Andrew Jackson 1853-1933 *NatCAB 42*
Giesy, John Ulrich 1877-1947 *NatCAB 36,*
WhAm 2
Giesy, Samuel Hensel 1826-1888 *ApCAB Sup*
Giffard, Sir George 1886-1964 *WhWW-II*
Giffard, Walter LeMontais 1856-1929
NatCAB 46
Giffen, James Kelly 1885-1937 *WhAm 1*
Giffen, John Kelly 1853-1932 *WhAm 1*
Giffen, William Albert 1866-1929 *NatCAB 25*
Giffin, Etta Josselyn *WomWWA 14*
Giffin, Floye Josephine 1884- *ApCAB X*
Giffin, William M 1850- *WhAm 4*
Gifford, Albert Liscomb 1861-1959 *NatCAB 48*
Gifford, Archer 1797-1859 *ApCAB*
Gifford, Augusta Hale 1842-1915 *WhAm 1,*
WomWWA 14
Gifford, Charles B *NewYHSD*
Gifford, Charles B 1830- *IIBEAAW*
Gifford, Charles Laceille 1871-1947 *BiDrAC,*
NatCAB 37, WhAm 2, WhAmP
Gifford, Flora Sawyer 1880- *WomWWA 14*
Gifford, Frances Eliot 1844- *ApCAB,*
WhAm 4
Gifford, Franklin Kent 1861- *WhAm 4*
Gifford, George 1842-1924 *WhAm 1*
Gifford, George 1881-1951 *WhAm 3*
Gifford, Glen J 1877-1958 *WhAm 3*
Gifford, Harold 1858-1929 *NatCAB 22,*
WhAm 1
Gifford, Heman 1879-1954 *NatCAB 44*
Gifford, James Meacham 1856-1938 *WhAm 1*
Gifford, John Clayton 1870-1949 *WhAm 2*
Gifford, John Pearl 1871-1933 *NatCAB 27*
Gifford, Kenneth C 1897-1963 *WhAm 4*
Gifford, L C 1886-1969 *WhAm 5*
Gifford, Livingston 1855-1937 *ApCAB X,*
WhAm 1
Gifford, Miram Wentworth 1851- *WhAm 4*
Gifford, Myrnie Ada 1892-1966 *NatCAB 54*
Gifford, Nathaniel Howland 1878-1944
NatCAB 34
Gifford, Orrin Philip 1847-1932 *WhAm 1*
Gifford, Oscar Sherman 1842-1913 *BiDrAC,*
TwCBDA, WhAmP
Gifford, Porter William 1885-1941 *NatCAB 31*
Gifford, Ralph Clayton 1889-1959 *NatCAB 50,*
WhAm 3
Gifford, Ralph Waldo 1867-1925 *WhAm 1*
Gifford, Robert Ladd 1867-1963 *NatCAB 51,*
WhAm 4
Gifford, Robert Swain 1840-1905 *AmBi,*
ApCAB, DcAmB, IIBEAAW, NatCAB 2,
NewYHSD, TwCBDA, WhAm 1
Gifford, Roy Wellington 1883-1951 *WhAm 3*
Gifford, Sandford Robinson 1823-1880 *ApCAB,*
TwCBDA

Gifford, Sanford Robinson 1823-1880 *AmBi,*
BnEnAmA, DcAmB, Drake, NatCAB 2,
NewYHSD, WhAm H
Gifford, Sanford Robinson 1824-1880 *IIBEAAW*
Gifford, Sanford Robinson 1892-1944
DcAmB S3, NatCAB 32, WhAm 2
Gifford, Seth Kelley 1854-1933 *WhAm 1*
Gifford, Sidney Brooks 1836- *WhAm 4*
Gifford, Walter John 1884-1957 *WhAm 3*
Gifford, Walter Sherman 1885-1966 *WhAm 4*
Gifford, William Logan Rodman 1862-
WhAm 5
Gifft, Howard Merrill 1908-1956 *NatCAB 50*
Giger, George Musgrave 1822-1865 *ApCAB,*
TwCBDA
Gigli, Benjimino 1890-1957 *WhAm 3*
Gignilliat, Leigh R, Jr. 1899-1972 *WhAm 5*
Gignilliat, Leigh Robinson 1875- *WhAm 5*
Gignoux, Francois Regis 1816-1882 *ApCAB,*
Drake
Gignoux, Louise Fowler 1873- *WomWWA 14*
Gignoux, Regis Francois 1816-1882 *NewYHSD,*
WhAm H
Gigot, Francis Ernest 1859- *WhAm 1*
Gihon, Albert Dakin 1876- *WhAm 5*
Gihon, Albert Leary 1833-1901 *ApCAB,*
DcAmB, NatCAB 9, TwCBDA,
WhAm 1
Gihon, John L *NewYHSD*
Gihon, Thomas *NewYHSD*
Gihon, William B *NewYHSD*
Gil, Geronimo Antonio 1732-1798 *ApCAB*
Gil-Borges, Esteban 1879- *WhAm 6*
Gilber, James Henry 1874-1972 *WhAm 5*
Gilberg, Charles Alexander 1835- *ApCAB Sup,*
NatCAB 3
Gilbert *NewYHSD*
Gilbert, A *NewYHSD*
Gilbert, A N *NewYHSD*
Gilbert, Abijah 1806-1881 *ApCAB, BiAUS,*
BiDrAC, NatCAB 4, TwCBDA,
WhAm H
Gilbert, Addison 1808-1888 *ApCAB Sup*
Gilbert, Agnes Lowrie 1864- *WomWWA 14*
Gilbert, Albert Clark 1887-1952 *WhAm 3*
Gilbert, Alexander 1839- *NatCAB 4,*
WhAm 4
Gilbert, Alfred Carlton 1884-1961 *NatCAB 47,*
WebAB, WhAm 4
Gilbert, Alfred Carlton, Jr. 1919-1964 *WhAm 4*
Gilbert, Anne Jane Hartley 1821-1904 *AmBi,*
DcAmB, NotAW, TwCBDA
Gilbert, Annie Ward 1857- *WomWWA 14*
Gilbert, Arthur Hill 1894-1970 *WhAm 5*
Gilbert, Arthur Witter 1882-1936 *WhAm 1*
Gilbert, Benjamin 1711-1780 *ApCAB*
Gilbert, Benjamin Davis 1835- *WhAm 4*
Gilbert, Benjamin Thorne 1872-1961
NatCAB 50
Gilbert, Bradford Lee 1853- *NatCAB 14*
Gilbert, Carol Jeanne 1943-1975 *WhAm 6*
Gilbert, Cass 1859-1934 *AmBi, BnEnAmA,*
DcAmB S1, NatCAB 11, NatCAB 26,
TwCBDA, WebAB, WhAm 1
Gilbert, Charles Allan 1873-1929 *WhAm 1*
Gilbert, Charles Benajah 1855-1913 *WhAm 1*
Gilbert, Charles Calvin, Sr. 1877-1954 *WhAm 3*
Gilbert, Charles Champion 1822- *ApCAB,*
TwCBDA
Gilbert, Charles Henry 1859-1928 *DcAmB,*
NatCAB 28, TwCBDA, WhAm 1
Gilbert, Charles Kendall 1878-1958 *NatCAB 44,*
WhAm 3
Gilbert, Charles Pierrepont H 1863-1955
WhAm 3
Gilbert, Charles Smith 1861-1956 *NatCAB 45*
Gilbert, Charlotte *NewYHSD*
Gilbert, Clinton Wallace 1871-1933 *WhAm 1*
Gilbert, David McConaughy 1836- *ApCAB*
Gilbert, Donald Wood 1900-1957 *WhAm 3*
Gilbert, E J *NewYHSD*
Gilbert, Earl C 1895-1964 *WhAm 4*
Gilbert, Edward d1862 *ApCAB*
Gilbert, Edward 1819?-1852 *BiAUS, BiDrAC,*
NatCAB 5, WhAm H
Gilbert, Edward Martinius 1875-1956
NatCAB 42, WhAm 5
Gilbert, Edwin 1822-1906 *NatCAB 14*

Gilbert, Edwin M *NewYHSD*
Gilbert, Eliphalet Wheeler 1793-1853 *BiDAmEd,*
DcAmB, NatCAB 24, WhAm H
Gilbert, Elizabeth *NewYHSD*
Gilbert, Eugene Angelo 1889-1944 *NatCAB 41*
Gilbert, Ezekiel 1755-1842 *BiAUS*
Gilbert, Ezekiel 1756-1841 *BiDrAC, WhAm H*
Gilbert, Florence Anderson 1876-
WomWWA 14
Gilbert, Frances Baker *WomWWA 14*
Gilbert, Frank 1839-1899 *NatCAB 10*
Gilbert, Frank Bixby 1867-1927 *WhAm 1*
Gilbert, Frank Yuba 1878-1937 *NatCAB 18,*
NatCAB 27
Gilbert, Frederick Augustus 1912-1974
WhAm 6
Gilbert, Frederick Spofford 1912-1970 *WhAm 5*
Gilbert, G Burton 1881-1951 *NatCAB 39*
Gilbert, Mrs. G H *NotAW*
Gilbert, George *NewYHSD*
Gilbert, George Blodgett 1872-1948 *NatCAB 39,*
WhAm 2
Gilbert, George Burton 1881-1951 *NatCAB 18,*
WhAm 3
Gilbert, George Gilmore 1849-1909 *BiDrAC,*
WhAmP
Gilbert, George Gilmore 1850-1909 *TwCBDA,*
WhAm 1
Gilbert, Mrs. George Henry 1821-1904
NatCAB 1, WhAm 1
Gilbert, George Holley 1854-1930 *WhAm 1*
Gilbert, Grove Karl 1843-1918 *AmBi, ApCAB,*
DcAmB, DcScB, NatCAB 13, TwCBDA,
WebAB, WhAm 1
Gilbert, Grove Sheldon 1805-1885 *ApCAB,*
NewYHSD, TwCBDA
Gilbert, Harvey Wilbarger 1884-1955 *WhAm 3*
Gilbert, Henderson 1880-1962 *WhAm 4*
Gilbert, Henry Franklin Belknap 1868-1928
AmBi, ApCAB X, DcAmB, WebAB,
WhAm 1
Gilbert, Hiram Thornton 1850-1939 *WhAm 1*
Gilbert, Horace Mark 1862-1934 *WhAm 1*
Gilbert, Sir Humphrey 1537?-1583 *McGEWB*
Gilbert, Sir Humphrey 1539-1583 *Drake,*
WhAm H
Gilbert, Sir Humphrey 1539-1584 *ApCAB*
Gilbert, I *NewYHSD*
Gilbert, J *NewYHSD*
Gilbert, Jacob H 1920- *BiDrAC*
Gilbert, James A *NewYHSD*
Gilbert, James Eleazer 1839-1909 *WhAm 1*
Gilbert, James Henry 1878- *WhAm 6*
Gilbert, James Isham 1824-1887 *ApCAB Sup*
Gilbert, Jasper Willet 1812- *NatCAB 9*
Gilbert, John 1810-1959 *WhAm 4*
Gilbert, John 1897-1936 *AmBi, DcAmB S2,*
WhAm 1
Gilbert, Mrs. John Gibbs 1801-1866 *Drake*
Gilbert, John Gibbs 1809-1889 *Drake*
Gilbert, John Gibbs 1810-1889 *AmBi, ApCAB,*
DcAmB, NatCAB 1, TwCBDA,
WhAm H
Gilbert, John Ingersoll 1837-1904 *WhAm 1*
Gilbert, John S 1801-1891 *TwCBDA*
Gilbert, Joseph 1873-1951 *NatCAB 40*
Gilbert, Joseph Oscar 1888-1971 *WhAm 5*
Gilbert, Joseph Walter 1875-1944 *WhAm 2*
Gilbert, Joshua Judson 1861-1925 *NatCAB 25*
Gilbert, Katharine Everett 1886-1952
NatCAB 49, WhAm 3
Gilbert, L W *DcScB*
Gilbert, L Wolfe 1886-1970 *WhAm 5*
Gilbert, Levi 1852-1917 *WhAm 1*
Gilbert, Lewis Newton 1836- *NatCAB 17*
Gilbert, Linda 1847-1895 *AmBi, AmWom,*
ApCAB, DcAmB, NotAW, TwCBDA,
WhAm H
Gilbert, Louis *NewYHSD*
Gilbert, Lyman D 1845-1914 *WhAm 1*
Gilbert, Mahlon Norris 1848-1900 *ApCAB,*
NatCAB 2, TwCBDA, WhAm 1
Gilbert, Marie Dolores Eliza Rosanna *WebAB,*
WhAm H
Gilbert, Marion L 1882-1966 *WhAm 4*
Gilbert, Matthew William 1862-1917 *WhAm 1,*
WhoColR
Gilbert, Nathaniel *ApCAB*

Gilbert, Nelson Rust 1866- *WhAm 4*
Gilbert, Newell Clark 1880-1953 *NatCAB 48, WhAm 3*
Gilbert, Newton Whiting 1862-1939 *BiDrAC, WhAm 1, WhAmP*
Gilbert, Osceola Pinckney 1875-1947 *WhAm 2*
Gilbert, Paul Thomas 1876-1953 *NatCAB 43*
Gilbert, Prentiss Bailey 1883-1939 *NatCAB 30, WhAm 1*
Gilbert, Raleigh *ApCAB, Drake*
Gilbert, Ralph Waldo Emerson 1882-1939 *BiDrAC, WhAm 1, WhAmP*
Gilbert, Reuben S *NewYHSD*
Gilbert, Robert Randle 1888-1971 *WhAm 5*
Gilbert, Ruby I 1851- *AmWom*
Gilbert, Rufus Henry 1832-1885 *AmBi, ApCAB, DcAmB, NatCAB 11, TwCBDA, WhAm H*
Gilbert, Ruth Minnie 1886- *WhoColR*
Gilbert, S Price 1862-1951 *WhAm 3*
Gilbert, Samuel Augustus 1825-1868 *ApCAB Sup, TwCBDA*
Gilbert, Samuel Tilden 1881-1947 *NatCAB 36, WhAm 2*
Gilbert, Sarah Hughes 1858- *WomWWA 14*
Gilbert, Seymour Parker 1892-1938 *AmBi, DcAmB S2, NatCAB 28, WhAm 1*
Gilbert, Sue Racey *WomWWA 14*
Gilbert, Sylvester 1755-1846 *BiDrAC, WhAm H*
Gilbert, Sylvester 1756-1846 *BiAUS*
Gilbert, Theodore Markley 1900-1961 *NatCAB 50*
Gilbert, Thomas 1714?-1796 *ApCAB*
Gilbert, Thomas D 1815-1894 *NatCAB 10*
Gilbert, Vedder Morris 1914-1973 *WhAm 5*
Gilbert, Victor Byron 1889-1959 *NatCAB 49*
Gilbert, Virgil O 1861- *WhAm 4*
Gilbert, Virginia Banks 1852- *WomWWA 14*
Gilbert, Walter Bond 1829- *ApCAB, WhAm 4*
Gilbert, Walter Eugene 1902-1957 *NatCAB 48*
Gilbert, William 1544-1603 *AsBiEn, BiHiMed, DcScB, McGEWB*
Gilbert, William 1921-1964 *NatCAB 51*
Gilbert, William Augustus 1815-1875 *BiAUS, BiDrAC, WhAm H*
Gilbert, William Ball 1847-1931 *NatCAB 23, WhAm 1*
Gilbert, William Candee 1870-1940 *NatCAB 36*
Gilbert, William Edward 1870-1948 *WhAm 2*
Gilbert, William Kent 1830-1880 *ApCAB*
Gilbert, William Lewis 1806-1890 *ApCAB Sup, DcAmB, NatCAB 23, WhAm H*
Gilbert, William Markley 1852-1926 *NatCAB 30*
Gilbert, William Marshall 1879- *WhAm 6*
Gilbert, William Morris 1862-1924 *NatCAB 21*
Gilbert, Sir William Schwenck 1836-1911 *McGEWB*
Gilbertson, Gilbert S 1863-1917 *NatCAB 17*
Gilbertus Anglicus 1180?-1250 *BiHiMed*
Gilboy, Glennon 1902-1958 *WhAm 3*
Gilbreath, James Richard 1918-1965 *WhAm 4*
Gilbreath, Sidney Gordon 1869- *TwCBDA, WhAm 5*
Gilbreath, William Sydnor, Jr. 1895-1969 *NatCAB 55, WhAm 5*
Gilbreth, Frank Bunker 1868-1924 *WhAm 1*
Gilbreth, Frank Bunker 1868-1925 *NatCAB 26*
Gilbreth, Lillian Moller 1878-1972 *WhAm 5, WhAm 6*
Gilchrist, Albert Waller 1858-1926 *NatCAB 14, WhAm 1*
Gilchrist, Alexander 1856-1907 *WhAm 1*
Gilchrist, Beth Bradford 1879-1957 *NatCAB 47, WhAm 3, WomWWA 14*
Gilchrist, Charles 1893-1957 *NatCAB 47*
Gilchrist, Clarence Thomas 1893-1974 *WhAm 6*
Gilchrist, Donald Bean 1892-1939 *DcAmLiB, WhAm 1*
Gilchrist, Frank Rust 1871-1917 *NatCAB 24*
Gilchrist, Fred Cramer 1868-1950 *BiDrAC, WhAm 3, WhAmP*
Gilchrist, Fredericka 1846- *ApCAB Sup*
Gilchrist, Fredericka Raymond Beardsley 1845- *WomWWA 14*
Gilchrist, Harry Lorenzo 1870-1943 *NatCAB 45, WhAm 2*

Gilchrist, Huntington 1891-1975 *WhAm 6*
Gilchrist, Jack Cecil 1918-1968 *WhAm 5*
Gilchrist, John Foster 1868- *WhAm 4*
Gilchrist, John James 1809-1858 *ApCAB, BiAUS, Drake, NatCAB 7, TwCBDA*
Gilchrist, John Raymond 1906- *WhAm 5*
Gilchrist, Joseph Clough 1850-1919 *NatCAB 24*
Gilchrist, Maude 1861- *WomWWA 14*
Gilchrist, Robert 1825-1888 *ApCAB Sup, DcAmB, NatCAB 5, TwCBDA, WhAm H*
Gilchrist, Robert Budd 1796-1856 *ApCAB, BiAUS*
Gilchrist, Robert Cogdell *NewYHSD*
Gilchrist, Rosetta Grace 1851- *WomWWA 14*
Gilchrist, Rosetta Luce *AmWom*
Gilchrist, T Caspar 1862-1927 *WhAm 1*
Gilchrist, Thomas Byron 1885-1962 *NatCAB 52, WhAm 4*
Gilchrist, William Wallace 1846-1916 *ApCAB, DcAmB, NatCAB 10, TwCBDA, WhAm 1*
Gilcrease, Thomas 1890-1962 *REnAW, WhAm 4*
Gildea, James Hilary 1890- *BiDrAC*
Gildemeister, Charles 1820-1869 *NewYHSD*
Gildemeister, Karl 1820-1869 *NewYHSD*
Gilder, H *NewYHSD*
Gilder, Jeannette Leonard 1849-1916 *AmBi, AmWom, DcAmB, NatCAB 8, NotAW, TwCBDA, WhAm 1, WomWWA 14*
Gilder, John Francis 1837-1908 *NatCAB 7, TwCBDA, WhAm 1*
Gilder, Joseph B 1858-1936 *TwCBDA, WhAm 1*
Gilder, Richard Watson 1844-1909 *AmBi, ApCAB, ApCAB X, DcAmB, NatCAB 1, TwCBDA, WebAB, WhAm 1*
Gilder, Robert Fletcher 1856-1940 *IlBEAAW, WhAm 1*
Gilder, Rodman 1877-1953 *NatCAB 42, WhAm 3*
Gilder, William Henry 1812-1864 *ApCAB, TwCBDA*
Gilder, William Henry 1836-1900 *WhAm H*
Gilder, William Henry 1838-1900 *AmBi, ApCAB, DcAmB, NatCAB 3, TwCBDA*
Gildersleeve, Basil Lanneau 1831-1924 *AmBi, ApCAB, BiDAmEd, DcAmB, NatCAB 10, TwCBDA, WebAB, WhAm 1*
Gildersleeve, Benjamin 1791-1875 *ApCAB*
Gildersleeve, Ferdinand 1840-1919 *NatCAB 19, WhAm 1*
Gildersleeve, Henry Alger 1840-1923 *NatCAB 4, NatCAB 11, WhAm 1*
Gildersleeve, Oliver 1844-1912 *WhAm 1*
Gildersleeve, Virginia Crocheron 1877-1965 *ApCAB X, BiDAmEd, WhAm 4, WomWWA 14*
Gildner, Laura May 1877- *WomWWA 14*
Gile, Ernest Sidney 1871-1952 *NatCAB 41*
Gile, George Washington 1830-1896 *TwCBDA*
Gile, John Fowler 1893-1955 *NatCAB 44, WhAm 3*
Gile, John Martin 1864-1925 *WhAm 1*
Gile, M Clement 1858-1916 *WhAm 1*
Giles Of Lessines 1235?-1304? *DcScB*
Giles Of Rome 1247?-1316 *DcScB*
Giles, Anne H 1860- *AmWom*
Giles, Bessie Isabel *WomWWA 14*
Giles, Charles T 1827- *NewYHSD*
Giles, Chauncey 1813-1893 *ApCAB, DcAmB, NatCAB 9, TwCBDA, WhAm H*
Giles, David 1836- *NatCAB 13*
Giles, Dorothy 1892-1960 *WhAm 4*
Giles, Elizabeth Cynthia 1861- *WomWWA 14*
Giles, Ella A 1851- *AmWom*
Giles, Ellen Rose *WomWWA 14*
Giles, Ernest 1835-1897 *McGEWB*
Giles, Francis Fenard 1860- *WhoColR*
Giles, George 1863- *WhoColR*
Giles, H P *NewYHSD*
Giles, Henry 1809-1882 *ApCAB, Drake, NatCAB 2*
Giles, Howard Everett 1876-1955 *NatCAB 48, WhAm 3*
Giles, J B *NewYHSD*

Giles, J Edward 1853- *WhAm 4*
Giles, John 1788-1846 *BiAUS*
Giles, Malcolm R 1894-1953 *WhAm 3*
Giles, Mary Courtland Vanderbeek *WomWWA 14*
Giles, Robert 1855-1924 *NatCAB 24*
Giles, Rose Marie *WomWWA 14*
Giles, William Alexander 1836-1913 *WhAm 1*
Giles, William Branch 1762-1830 *AmBi, ApCAB, BiAUS, BiDrAC, DcAmB, Drake, NatCAB 5, TwCBDA, WhAm H, WhAmP*
Giles, William Fell 1807-1879 *BiAUS, BiDrAC, WhAm H, WhAmP*
Gilfallan, James 1829-1894 *NatCAB 4*
Gilfert, Agnes Holman 1793-1833 *ApCAB, NatCAB 2*
Gilfert, Charles 1787-1829 *ApCAB, NatCAB 9*
Gilfillan, C W 1832-1901 *BiAUS*
Gilfillan, Calvin Willard 1832-1901 *BiDrAC*
Gilfillan, George William 1899-1951 *NatCAB 49*
Gilfillan, James 1829-1894 *ApCAB, NatCAB 16*
Gilfillan, John Bachop 1835-1924 *BiDrAC, NatCAB 21*
Gilfillan, Margaret Neva *WomWWA 14*
Gilfillan, Silver Gloss 1853-1938 *NatCAB 30*
Gilford, Mary Penrose Hooton 1876- *WomWWA 14*
Gilford, Mary Penrose Hooton 1881- *BiCAW*
Gilfoyle, John *NewYHSD*
Gilhams, Clarence Chauncey 1860-1912 *BiDrAC, WhAm 3*
Gilkey, Charles Whitney 1882-1968 *WhAm 5*
Gilkey, Geraldine Gunsaulus Brown 1889-1955 *WhAm 3*
Gilkey, Mary C 1865- *WomWWA 14*
Gilkinson, Howard 1898-1958 *WhAm 4*
Gilkison, Frank E 1877-1955 *WhAm 3*
Gilkyson, Walter 1880-1969 *WhAm 5*
Gill, A Bruce 1876-1965 *NatCAB 53*
Gill, Adam Capen 1863-1932 *WhAm 1*
Gill, Augustus Herman 1864-1936 *NatCAB 27, WhAm 1*
Gill, Benjamin 1843-1912 *WhAm 1*
Gill, Bennett Lloyd 1862-1935 *WhAm 1*
Gill, Bessie Faunce *WomWWA 14*
Gill, Charles Clifford 1885-1948 *WhAm 2*
Gill, Charles R *BiAUS Sup*
Gill, Coleridge Mason 1909-1965 *NatCAB 52*
Gill, Corrington 1898-1946 *WhAm 2*
Gill, Sir David 1843-1914 *AsBiEn, DcScB*
Gill, Dorothea Ambos 1871- *WomWWA 14*
Gill, E W *NewYHSD*
Gill, Elbyrne Grady 1891-1966 *NatCAB 54, WhAm 4*
Gill, Ella Elizabeth Eaton *WomWWA 14*
Gill, Everett 1869-1958 *NatCAB 44, WhAm 3*
Gill, George 1866-1958 *NatCAB 45*
Gill, George Carleton 1858- *WhAm 4*
Gill, Georgine Belanger *WomWWA 14*
Gill, H Walter 1881-1944 *NatCAB 47*
Gill, Henry Z 1831-1907 *WhAm 1*
Gill, Irving J 1870-1936 *BnEnAmA*
Gill, James Presley 1896-1961 *WhAm 4*
Gill, James William 1906-1956 *NatCAB 46*
Gill, Joe Henry 1886-1944 *WhAm 2*
Gill, John 1732-1785 *DcAmB, WhAm H*
Gill, John 1831?- *NewYHSD*
Gill, John, Jr. 1850-1918 *BiDrAC, WhAm 1, WhAmP*
Gill, John Edward 1872-1934 *WhAm 1*
Gill, John Goodner 1905-1959 *NatCAB 48, WhAm 4*
Gill, John Loriman 1806-1895 *NatCAB 4*
Gill, Joseph Albert 1854-1933 *NatCAB 51*
Gill, Joseph John 1846-1920 *BiDrAC, WhAm 4*
Gill, Joseph Kaye 1841-1931 *ApCAB X, WhAm 1*
Gill, Jospeh Albert 1854-1933 *WhAm 1*
Gill, Kermode Frederic 1866- *WhAm 5*
Gill, Laura Drake 1860-1926 *DcAmB, NatCAB 24, WhAm 1, WomWWA 14*
Gill, Michael Joseph 1864-1918 *BiDrAC*
Gill, Moses *BiAUS*

Gill, Patrick Francis 1867-1923 *NatCAB 43*
Gill, Patrick Francis 1868-1923 *BiDrAC, WhAm 1*
Gill, Paul Ludwig 1894-1938 *WhAm 1*
Gill, Richard C 1901-1958 *WhAm 3*
Gill, Robert *NewYHSD*
Gill, Robert Lee 1870-1918 *NatCAB 24*
Gill, Rosalie Lorraine 1867- *NatCAB 7*
Gill, Theodore Nicholas 1837-1914 *AmBi, ApCAB, DcAmB, DcScB, NatCAB 12, TwCBDA, WebAB, WhAm 1*
Gill, Thomas Augustus 1840-1926 *NatCAB 27, WhAm 1*
Gill, Thomas Harvey 1891-1972 *WhAm 5*
Gill, Thomas Henry 1858- *NatCAB 16*
Gill, Thomas Ponce 1922- *BiDrAC*
Gill, Waltus Hughes 1860- *WhAm 1*
Gill, William Andrew 1859-1918 *WhAm 1*
Gill, William Dorman 1867-1915 *ApCAB X*
Gill, William Fearing 1844-1917 *TwCBDA, WhAm 1*
Gill, William Francis 1874-1917 *WhAm 1*
Gill, William Hanson 1886-1976 *WhAm 6*
Gill, William Hugh 1841-1904 *WhAm 1*
Gill, Wilson Lindsley 1851-1941 *NatCAB 4, WhAm 1*
Gillam, Bernhard 1856-1896 *DcAmB, NatCAB 8, TwCBDA, WhAm H*
Gillam, Bernhard 1858-1896 *ApCAB Sup*
Gillam, Manly Marcus 1846- *WhAm 4*
Gillan, Silas Lee 1883-1954 *WhAm 4*
Gilland, Nell Crawford Flinn 1885- *WomWWA 14*
Gillanders, John Gordon 1895-1946 *WhAm 2*
Gillard, Joseph Rogers Brown 1881-1947 *NatCAB 36*
Gilleaudeau, Raymond 1887-1958 *WhAm 3*
Gillem, Alvan Cullem 1830-1875 *AmBi, ApCAB, DcAmB, Drake, NatCAB 4, TwCBDA, WhAm H*
Gillem, Alvan Cullom, Jr. 1888-1973 *WhAm 5*
Gillen, Charles P 1876-1956 *WhAm 3*
Gillen, Courtland Craig 1880-1954 *BiDrAC, WhAm 3*
Gillen, Denver L 1914- *IIBEAAW*
Gillen, George Hamilton 1892-1969 *NatCAB 54*
Gillen, Ralph Keenor 1896-1950 *NatCAB 48*
Gillen, Wilfred Donnell 1900-1968 *WhAm 5*
Gillentine, William Howard 1908-1954 *NatCAB 50*
Gilles, Verner Arthur 1886-1954 *WhAm 3*
Gillespie, Alexander Garfield 1881-1956 *WhAm 3*
Gillespie, Mother Angela 1824-1887 *NotAW*
Gillespie, Barnes 1871-1932 *WhAm 1*
Gillespie, Charles Bowen 1872-1929 *WhAm 1*
Gillespie, Charles Pepper 1903-1954 *NatCAB 47*
Gillespie, Cora Haltom *WomWWA 14*
Gillespie, David Halliday Moffat 1875-1959 *NatCAB 49*
Gillespie, David Lindsay 1858-1926 *NatCAB 22*
Gillespie, Dean Milton 1884-1949 *BiDrAC, WhAm 2, WhAmP*
Gillespie, Eliza Maria 1824-1887 *AmBi, AmWom, ApCAB, BiDAmEd, DcAmB, TwCBDA*
Gillespie, Eugene Pierce 1852-1899 *BiDrAC, TwCBDA*
Gillespie, George 1683-1760 *ApCAB, NatCAB 4, WhAm H*
Gillespie, George Benjamin 1863-1944 *NatCAB 34, WhAm 3*
Gillespie, George DeNormandie 1819-1909 *ApCAB, NatCAB 13, TwCBDA, WhAm 1*
Gillespie, George Lewis 1841-1913 *NatCAB 12, WhAm 1*
Gillespie, I H *NewYHSD*
Gillespie, J H *NewYHSD*
Gillespie, James d1805 *BiAUS, BiDrAC, WhAm H*
Gillespie, James Edward 1887-1961 *WhAm 4*
Gillespie, James Frank 1869-1954 *BiDrAC, WhAm 3*
Gillespie, John Thomas 1874-1960 *NatCAB 47*
Gillespie, Julian Edgeworth 1893-1939 *WhAm 1*

Gillespie, Laura Anna Milam 1861- *WomWWA 14*
Gillespie, Lawrence Lewis 1876-1940 *NatCAB 30*
Gillespie, Leland Warwick 1903-1959 *NatCAB 48*
Gillespie, Leonard Glen 1899-1958 *NatCAB 48*
Gillespie, Lillian Stokes *WomWWA 14*
Gillespie, Louis 1906-1956 *NatCAB 43*
Gillespie, Louis Frank 1900- *WhAm 5*
Gillespie, Louis John 1886-1941 *NatCAB 30*
Gillespie, Mabel 1867-1923 *AmBi, DcAmB, NatCAB 23, WhAm HA, WhAm 4*
Gillespie, Mabel Edna 1877-1923 *NotAW*
Gillespie, Neal Henry 1831-1874 *WhAm H*
Gillespie, Neal Henry 1832-1874 *ApCAB, TwCBDA*
Gillespie, Oscar William 1858-1927 *BiDrAC, WhAm 4, WhAmP*
Gillespie, Richard Henry 1877-1941 *NatCAB 30*
Gillespie, Richard Thomas 1879-1930 *WhAm 1*
Gillespie, Robert Gracey 1857-1926 *NatCAB 30*
Gillespie, Robert L *NewYHSD*
Gillespie, Schuyler Wood 1884-1942 *NatCAB 30*
Gillespie, Sumter 1887-1958 *NatCAB 48*
Gillespie, T *NewYHSD*
Gillespie, Thad Reamy 1895-1955 *NatCAB 43*
Gillespie, Thomas Andrew 1852-1926 *ApCAB X, NatCAB 24, WhAm 1*
Gillespie, Thomas J 1847- *ApCAB X*
Gillespie, William 1817?- *NewYHSD*
Gillespie, William 1879-1947 *WhAm 2*
Gillespie, William Lane 1881-1949 *NatCAB 39, WhAm 3*
Gillespie, William Mitchell 1816-1868 *ApCAB, DcAmB, Drake, NatCAB 23, TwCBDA, WhAm H*
Gillessen, Karl 1842- *IIBEAAW*
Gillet, Charles 1879-1972 *WhAm 5*
Gillet, Charles William 1840-1908 *BiDrAC, TwCBDA, WhAm 1, WhAmP*
Gillet, Edgar P *NewYHSD*
Gillet, Guy Mark 1879-1973 *WhAm 5*
Gillet, Joseph Anthony 1837-1908 *NatCAB 23*
Gillet, Joseph Eugene 1888-1958 *NatCAB 44, WhAm 3*
Gillet, Paul 1874-1971 *WhAm 5*
Gillet, Ransom Hooker 1800-1876 *ApCAB, BiAUS, BiDrAC, DcAmB, TwCBDA, WhAm H*
Gillet, Ransome H 1800-1876 *NatCAB 3*
Gillett, Alfred S 1816-1914 *ApCAB X*
Gillett, Arthur Dudley Samuel 1881-1946 *WhAm 2*
Gillett, Arthur Lincoln 1859-1938 *NatCAB 28, WhAm 1*
Gillett, Charles Ripley 1855-1948 *DcAmLiB, TwCBDA, WhAm 4*
Gillett, Charles Warren 1876- *ApCAB X*
Gillett, Egbert W 1848- *ApCAB X*
Gillett, Emma Millinda 1852-1927 *NatCAB 17, NotAW*
Gillett, Ezra Hall 1823-1875 *AmBi, ApCAB, DcAmB, NatCAB 5, TwCBDA, WhAm H*
Gillett, Frederick Huntington 1851-1935 *AmBi, ApCAB X, BiDrAC, DcAmB S1, NatCAB 27, TwCBDA, WebAB, WhAm 1, WhAmP*
Gillett, Horace Wadsworth 1883-1950 *DcAmB S4, NatCAB 39*
Gillett, James Norris 1860-1937 *BiDrAC, NatCAB 14, NatCAB 28, WhAm 1, WhAmP*
Gillett, John Henry 1860-1920 *WhAm 1*
Gillett, Leonard Godfrey 1893-1956 *WhAm 3*
Gillett, Myron Eugene 1859-1922 *NatCAB 6*
Gillett, Omer Rand 1874-1948 *NatCAB 37*
Gillett, Paul W 1815-1882 *ApCAB X*
Gillett, Philip Goode 1833- *WhAm 1*
Gillett, William Kendall 1860-1914 *TwCBDA, WhAm 1*
Gillette, Abraham Dunn 1809- *Drake*
Gillette, Abram Dunn 1807-1882 *ApCAB*
Gillette, Albert Cooley 1876-1950 *WhAm 3*
Gillette, Arthur Jay 1864-1921 *NatCAB 19*

Gillette, Clarence Preston 1859-1941 *NatCAB 13, WhAm 1*
Gillette, Edward Hooker 1840-1918 *ApCAB, BiDrAC, TwCBDA, WhAm 1*
Gillette, Edwin Fraser 1863-1943 *NatCAB 40*
Gillette, Fanny Lemira 1828- *WhAm 4*
Gillette, Francis 1807-1879 *ApCAB, BiAUS, BiDrAC, DcAmB, NatCAB 4, TwCBDA, WhAm H*
Gillette, Frank Edward 1848- *WhAm 4*
Gillette, Gene 1907-1975 *WhAm 6*
Gillette, Gertrude Sanford 1869- *WomWWA 14*
Gillette, Grace Fidelia 1865- *WomWWA 14*
Gillette, Guy Mark 1879- *BiDrAC, WhAm 6*
Gillette, Halbert Powers 1869-1958 *WhAm 3*
Gillette, Howard Frank 1873-1943 *NatCAB 32*
Gillette, James Frank 1832-1894 *NatCAB 16*
Gillette, John Morris 1866-1949 *BiDAmEd, NatCAB 37, REnAW, WhAm 3*
Gillette, King Camp 1855-1932 *AmBi, DcAmB S1, NatCAB 10, WebAB, WhAm 1*
Gillette, L Fidelia Woolley 1827- *AmWom*
Gillette, Leon Narcisse 1877-1945 *NatCAB 49, WhAm 2*
Gillette, Lewis Singer 1854-1924 *NatCAB 20, WhAm 1*
Gillette, Walter Robarts 1840-1908 *WhAm 1*
Gillette, William 1851-1937 *NatCAB 2*
Gillette, William 1853-1937 *ApCAB, DcAmB S2, NatCAB 28, WebAB*
Gillette, William 1854-1937 *TwCBDA*
Gillette, William 1855-1937 *AmBi, WhAm 1*
Gillette, Wilson Darwin 1880-1951 *BiDrAC, NatCAB 42, WhAm 3, WhAmP*
Gillham, Charles Allen 1874-1936 *NatCAB 27*
Gillham, Robert 1854-1899 *NatCAB 3, WhAm 1*
Gilli, Filippo Salvatore d1764? *ApCAB*
Gilliam, David Tod 1844-1923 *AmBi, DcAmB, NatCAB 17, WhAm 4*
Gilliam, Donnell 1889-1960 *WhAm 4*
Gilliams, Jacob 1784-1868 *ApCAB*
Gilliams, John J *NewYHSD*
Gilliard, E Thomas 1912-1965 *WhAm 4*
Gillick, James T 1870-1956 *WhAm 3*
Gillick, Laurance Henry 1898-1971 *WhAm 5*
Gillie, George W 1880-1963 *BiDrAC, WhAm 6*
Gillie, John 1858- *ApCAB X*
Gillies, Andrew 1870-1942 *WhAm 2*
Gillies, Donald B 1872-1956 *WhAm 3*
Gillies, James Archibald 1877-1938 *NatCAB 31*
Gillies, James Lewis 1871-1946 *WhAm 2*
Gillies, John A 1889-1942 *WhAm 2*
Gillig, Edward M 1894-1938 *WhAm 1*
Gillig, George 1809-1862 *NatCAB 3*
Gilligan, Edmund 1899-1973 *WhAm 6*
Gilligan, John Joyce 1921- *BiDrAC*
Gillilan, Strickland 1869-1954 *NatCAB 52, WhAm 3*
Gilliland, Charles Edward, Jr. 1916-1975 *WhAm 6*
Gilliland, Charles Leslie 1874-1941 *NatCAB 31*
Gilliland, Clarence Vosburgh 1866-1939 *WhAm 1*
Gilliland, Edwin Richard 1909-1973 *NatCAB 57, WhAm 6*
Gilliland, John W 1881-1957 *WhAm 3*
Gilliland, William 1734-1796 *NatCAB 18*
Gillin, John Joseph, Jr. 1905-1950 *NatCAB 52*
Gillin, John Lewis 1871-1958 *NatCAB 49, WhAm 3*
Gillin, John P 1907-1973 *WhAm 6*
Gillingham, Anna 1878- *WhAm 6*
Gillingham, Clinton Hancock 1877- *WhAm 5*
Gillingham, Edwin D *NewYHSD*
Gillingham, Joseph Eddy 1830-1905 *NatCAB 25*
Gillingwater, Claude *ApCAB X*
Gillis, Alexander James 1888-1943 *NatCAB 33*
Gillis, James Henry Lawrence 1831-1910 *NatCAB 6, TwCBDA, WhAm 1*
Gillis, James Lisle 1792-1881 *BiAUS, BiDrAC, WhAm H*
Gillis, James Louis 1857-1917 *DcAmLiB, WhAm 1*
Gillis, James Martin 1876-1957 *WhAm 3*
Gillis, John Pritchet 1803-1873 *ApCAB, Drake,*

TwCBDA

Gillis, Mabel Ray 1882-1961 *DcAmLiB*
Gillispie, Robert Wallace 1882-1967 *WhAm 4*
Gilliss, James Melville 1811-1865 *AmBi,
ApCAB, DcAmB, NatCAB 9, TwCBDA,
WebAB, WebAMB, WhAm H*
Gilliss, James Melvin 1810-1865 *BiAUS, Drake*
Gilliss, Walter 1855-1925 *AmBi, DcAmB,
NatCAB 23*
Gillman, Henry 1833-1915 *DcAmB,
NatCAB 7, TwCBDA, WhAm 1*
Gillman, Robert Winthrop 1865- *TwCBDA,
WhAm 4*
Gillmer, Gipson Perry 1872-1936 *NatCAB 28,
WhAm 1*
Gillmor, C Stewart 1900-1964 *NatCAB 51*
Gillmor, Horatio Gonzalo 1870-1960 *WhAm 4,
WhAm 5*
Gillmor, Reginald E 1887-1960 *WhAm 3*
Gillmore, Frank 1867-1943 *WhAm 2*
Gillmore, Inez Haynes 1873- *WomWWA 14*
Gillmore, James Clarkson 1854-1927 *WhAm 1*
Gillmore, Quincy Adams 1825-1888 *AmBi,
ApCAB, DcAmB, Drake, NatCAB 4,
TwCBDA, WebAMB, WhAm H*
Gillmore, Quincy Adams 1881-1956 *WhAm 3*
Gillmore, Rufus 1879-1935 *WhAm 1*
Gillmore, William E 1876-1948 *WhAm 2*
Gillon, Alexander 1741-1794 *ApCAB, BiAUS,
BiDrAC, DcAmB, Drake, NatCAB 23,
TwCBDA, WhAm H, WhAmP*
Gillon, John William 1867-1931 *WhAm 1*
Gillpatrick, Wallace 1862- *WhAm 4*
Gills, Joe Pitzer 1913-1974 *WhAm 6*
Gillson, Joseph Lincoln 1895-1964 *WhAm 4*
Gillum, Robert Greene 1855-1924 *NatCAB 20*
Gilman, Albert Franklin 1871-1951 *WhAm 3*
Gilman, Alfred Alonzo 1878-1966 *WhAm 4*
Gilman, Andrew L 1886-1973 *WhAm 6*
Gilman, Arthur 1837-1909 *AmBi, ApCAB,
BiDAmEd, DcAmB, NatCAB 6,
TwCBDA, WhAm 1*
Gilman, Arthur Delevan 1821-1882 *ApCAB,
DcAmB, NatCAB 23, TwCBDA,
WhAm H*
Gilman, Benjamin Ives 1852-1933 *NatCAB 25,
TwCBDA, WhAm 1*
Gilman, Bradley 1857-1932 *WhAm 1*
Gilman, Caroline Howard 1794-1888 *ApCAB,
DcAmB, Drake, NatCAB 6, NotAW,
TwCBDA, WhAm H*
Gilman, Caroline Howard 1823-1877 *ApCAB*
Gilman, Chandler Robbins 1802-1865 *ApCAB,
Drake, TwCBDA*
Gilman, Charles Jervis 1824-1901 *BiAUS,
BiDrAC, WhAmP*
Gilman, Charlotte Anna Perkins Stetson
1860-1935 *AmBi, ApCAB X, DcAmB S1,
NatCAB 13, NotAW, WhAm 1, WhAmP,
WomWWA 14*
Gilman, Daniel Coit 1831-1908 *AmBi, ApCAB,
BiDAmEd, DcAmB, DcAmLiB, EncAB,
McGEWB, NatCAB 5, TwCBDA,
WebAB, WhAm 1*
Gilman, Edward Whiting 1823-1900 *TwCBDA*
Gilman, Elisabeth 1867-1950 *NotAW,
WomWWA 14*
Gilman, Florence 1878- *WomWWA 14*
Gilman, Francis Davidson 1888-1947
NatCAB 36
Gilman, George Everett 1909-1952 *NatCAB 41*
Gilman, George Thomas 1899-1948 *NatCAB 38*
Gilman, Harry A 1876- *WhAm 5*
Gilman, James Henry 1883-1972 *WhAm 5*
Gilman, Jeremiah Howard 1831-1909
NatCAB 24
Gilman, John E 1844-1921 *WhAm 1*
Gilman, John Ellis 1841-1916 *WhAm 1*
Gilman, John R 1895-1958 *WhAm 3*
Gilman, John Taylor 1753-1828 *AmBi, ApCAB,
BiAUS, BiDrAC, DcAmB, Drake,
NatCAB 11, TwCBDA, WhAm H,
WhAmP*
Gilman, Joseph *BiAUS*
Gilman, Julian Sturtevant 1882-1961
NatCAB 49
Gilman, Lawrence 1878-1939 *ApCAB X,
DcAmB S2, NatCAB 35, WhAm 1*

Gilman, Luthene Clairmont 1857-1942 *WhAm 2*
Gilman, Luthene Claremont 1857-1942
NatCAB 31
Gilman, Margaret 1866- *WomWWA 14*
Gilman, Margaret 1896-1958 *WhAm 3*
Gilman, Margaret May Rose 1873-
WomWWA 14
Gilman, Mary Rebecca Foster 1859-1943
WhAm 2, WomWWA 14
Gilman, Max M d1965 *WhAm 4*
Gilman, Nicholas 1755-1814 *ApCAB, BiAUS,
BiDrAC, DcAmB, Drake, NatCAB 2,
TwCBDA, WhAm H, WhAmP*
Gilman, Nicholas Paine 1849-1912 *NatCAB 8,
TwCBDA, WhAm 1*
Gilman, Roger 1874- *WhAm 5*
Gilman, Samuel 1791-1858 *ApCAB, DcAmB,
Drake, NatCAB 22, TwCBDA, WhAm H*
Gilman, Samuel P 1877-1941 *WhAm 1*
Gilman, Stella Scott 1844- *ApCAB,
NatCAB 10, WhAm 5, WomWWA 14*
Gilman, Stephen Warren 1857-1930
NatCAB 21, WhAm 1
Gilman, Theodore 1841-1930 *WhAm 1*
Gilman, William Stewart 1877-1945
NatCAB 37, WhAm 2
Gilman, Wilma Anderson 1883- *WomWWA 14*
Gilmartin, Eugene Richard 1902-1961 *WhAm 4*
Gilmer, Albert Hatton 1878-1950 *WhAm 3*
Gilmer, David J 1874- *WhoColR*
Gilmer, Elizabeth Meriwether d1951
WomWWA 14
Gilmer, Elizabeth Meriwether 1861-1951
WhAm 3
Gilmer, Elizabeth Meriwether 1870-1951
DcAmB S5, WhAm 5
Gilmer, Francis Meriwether 1810-1892 *BiDConf*
Gilmer, Francis Walker 1790-1826 *DcAmB,
NatCAB 19, WhAm H*
Gilmer, George Rockingham 1790-1859 *ApCAB,
BiAUS, BiDrAC, DcAmB, Drake,
NatCAB 1, TwCBDA, WhAm H,
WhAmP*
Gilmer, Jeremy Forbis 1818-1883 *TwCBDA*
Gilmer, Jeremy Francis 1818-1883 *ApCAB,
BiDConf*
Gilmer, John Adams 1805-1868 *BiAUS,
BiDConf, BiDrAC, DcAmB, TwCBDA,
WhAm H, WhAmP*
Gilmer, John Alexander 1805-1868 *ApCAB,
NatCAB 11*
Gilmer, John Coverdale 1875- *WhoColR*
Gilmer, John Lash 1872-1947 *NatCAB 37*
Gilmer, Thomas Lewis 1849-1931 *WhAm 1*
Gilmer, Thomas Walker 1802-1844 *AmBi,
ApCAB, BiAUS, BiDrAC, BiDrUSE,
DcAmB, Drake, NatCAB 5, NatCAB 6,
TwCBDA, WhAm H, WhAmP*
Gilmer, William Franklin 1901-1954 *BiDrAC,
WhAmP*
Gilmer, William Wirt 1863- *WhAm 4*
Gilmor, Harry 1837-1883 *TwCBDA*
Gilmor, Harry 1838-1883 *AmBi, ApCAB,
DcAmB, NatCAB 23, WhAm H*
Gilmor, Robert 1748-1822 *NatCAB 11*
Gilmor, Robert 1774-1848 *NatCAB 11*
Gilmor, Robert 1808-1874 *NatCAB 11*
Gilmor, Robert 1833- *NatCAB 11*
Gilmore, Albert Field 1868-1943 *NatCAB 42,
WhAm 2*
Gilmore, Alfred 1812-1890 *BiAUS, BiDrAC,
WhAm H*
Gilmore, Charles Whitney 1874-1945
NatCAB 34, WhAm 2
Gilmore, Eddy Lanier King 1907-1967 *WhAm 4*
Gilmore, Edward 1867-1924 *BiDrAC,
WhAm 4*
Gilmore, Eugene Allen 1871-1953 *NatCAB 44,
WhAm 3*
Gilmore, Eugene Allen, Jr. 1902-1971 *WhAm 5*
Gilmore, Evelyn Langdon *WomWWA 14*
Gilmore, George William 1857-1933 *TwCBDA*
Gilmore, George William 1858-1933 *WhAm 1*
Gilmore, James Lee 1884-1963 *NatCAB 49*
Gilmore, James Roberts 1822-1903 *AmBi,
DcAmB, NatCAB 10, TwCBDA,
WhAm 1*
Gilmore, James Roberts 1823-1903 *ApCAB*

Gilmore, John 1780-1845 *BiAUS, BiDrAC,
WhAm H*
Gilmore, John Curtis 1837-1922 *WhAm 1*
Gilmore, John Francis 1896-1962 *NatCAB 49*
Gilmore, John Washington 1872-1942
NatCAB 40, WhAm 2
Gilmore, Joseph Albree 1811-1867 *ApCAB,
DcAmB, NatCAB 11, TwCBDA,
WhAm H*
Gilmore, Joseph Atherton 1811-1867 *BiAUS,
Drake*
Gilmore, Joseph Henry 1834-1918 *AmBi,
ApCAB, DcAmB, NatCAB 22, TwCBDA,
WhAm HA, WhAm 1, WhAm 4*
Gilmore, Joseph Michael 1893-1962 *WhAm 4*
Gilmore, Marion Wilcox 1869- *WomWWA 14*
Gilmore, Maurice E 1878-1957 *WhAm 3*
Gilmore, Melvin Randolph 1868-1940 *WhAm 1*
Gilmore, Merrill Charles 1872-1960 *NatCAB 48*
Gilmore, Myron T 1847- *WhAm 4*
Gilmore, Pascal Pearl 1845- *WhAm 4*
Gilmore, Patrick Sarsfield 1829-1892 *AmBi,
ApCAB, DcAmB, Drake Sup, NatCAB 3,
TwCBDA, WebAB, WhAm H*
Gilmore, Robert 1856-1937 *NatCAB 18,
WhAm 2*
Gilmore, Robert Lee 1894-1955 *NatCAB 45*
Gilmore, Rodelphus Howard 1842- *NatCAB 18*
Gilmore, S A 1806-1873 *BiAUS*
Gilmore, Samuel Louis 1859-1910 *BiDrAC,
WhAm 1*
Gilmore, Thomas 1819-1890 *NatCAB 13*
Gilmore, Thomas Francis 1904-1959 *WhAm 3*
Gilmore, Thomas Mador 1858-1921 *WhAm 1*
Gilmore, William James 1821-1896 *NatCAB 12*
Gilmore, William Ross 1877-1950 *NatCAB 39*
Gilmour, Abram David Pollock 1876-1948
WhAm 3
Gilmour, George Peel 1900-1963 *WhAm 4*
Gilmour, James 1822-1885 *NatCAB 3*
Gilmour, Ray Bergantz 1888-1947 *WhAm 2*
Gilmour, Richard 1824-1891 *ApCAB, DcAmB,
NatCAB 5, TwCBDA, WhAm H*
Gilpatric, Guy 1896-1950 *NatCAB 38,
WhAm 3*
Gilpatrick, John Lord 1845- *WhAm 4*
Gilpin, C Monteith 1872- *WhAm 5*
Gilpin, Charles Sidney 1878-1930 *AmBi,
DcAmB, NatCAB 23, WebAB, WhAm 1*
Gilpin, Edward Woodward 1803-1876 *DcAmB,
NatCAB 7, WhAm H*
Gilpin, Edward Woodward 1805-1876 *ApCAB*
Gilpin, Friend Bennett 1877-1934 *NatCAB 26*
Gilpin, Garth Griffith 1882-1945 *NatCAB 42*
Gilpin, Henry D 1801-1859 *Drake*
Gilpin, Henry D 1801-1869 *BiAUS*
Gilpin, Henry Dilwood 1801-1860 *ApCAB,
NatCAB 6*
Gilpin, Henry Dilworth 1801-1860 *AmBi,
BiDrUSE, DcAmB, TwCBDA, WhAm H*
Gilpin, Joseph Elliott 1866-1924 *NatCAB 30,
WhAm 1*
Gilpin, Joshua 1765-1840 *ApCAB*
Gilpin, Kenneth Newcomer 1890-1947
NatCAB 38
Gilpin, Thomas 1728-1778 *ApCAB*
Gilpin, Thomas 1776-1853 *ApCAB*
Gilpin, William 1812-1894 *ApCAB Sup*
Gilpin, William 1813-1894 *DcAmB, WhAm H*
Gilpin, William 1814-1894 *NatCAB 6,
TwCBDA*
Gilpin, William 1815-1894 *REnAW*
Gilreath, Belton 1858-1920 *NatCAB 18*
Gilroy, Thomas F 1840-1911 *NatCAB 3,
WhAm 1*
Gilroy, William Edgar 1876- *WhAm 6*
Gilruth, Irwin Thoburn 1889-1957 *WhAm 3*
Gilsdorf, Walter Henry 1901-1957 *NatCAB 48*
Gilson, Etienne Henry 1884- *McGEWB*
Gilson, Helen Louise 1835-1868 *NotAW*
Gilson, Mary Barnett 1877- *WomWWA 14*
Gilson, Roy Rolfe 1875-1933 *WhAm 1*
Gilson, Sara Sumner Emery 1876-
WomWWA 14
Gilster, Adolph Louis 1885-1961 *NatCAB 48*
Gilster, Albert Henry 1872-1946 *NatCAB 41*
Gilster, August Emanuel 1877-1952 *NatCAB 40*
Gilstrap, W H 1840-1914 *NewYHSD*

Giltner, Clyde Haynes 1881-1967 *NatCAB 55*
Giltner, Frank Carlton 1876-1935 *WhAm 1*
Giltner, Leigh Gordon *WhAm 3,
WomWWA 14*
Giltner, Ward 1882-1950 *WhAm 3*
Gimbel, Adam Long 1893-1969 *WhAm 5*
Gimbel, Benedict, Jr. d1971 *WhAm 5*
Gimbel, Bernard Feustmann 1885-1966
NatCAB 53, WhAm 4
Gimbel, Charles d1932 *WhAm 1*
Gimbel, Ellis Adam 1865-1950 *NatCAB 43,
WhAm 2A*
Gimbel, Isaac 1856-1931 *NatCAB 23*
Gimbel, Jacob 1876-1943 *WhAm 2*
Gimber, Stephen Henry 1806?-1862 *NewYHSD*
Gimberman, Francois *NewYHSD*
Gimbrede, Joseph Napoleon 1820- *NewYHSD*
Gimbrede, Thomas 1781-1832 *Drake,
NewYHSD, WhAm H*
Gimmestad, Lars Monson 1868-1943 *WhAm 2*
Gimpey *NewYHSD*
Gimsley, George Perry 1868- *WhAm 4*
Ginastera, Alberto Evaristo 1916- *McGEWB*
Ginder, Floyd Edwin 1882-1953 *NatCAB 41*
Ginder, Philip Dewitt 1905-1968 *WhAm 5*
Gindhart, Francis Xavier *NewYHSD*
Gindhart, Isaac Dare, Jr. 1878-1964 *NatCAB 57*
Gindhart, Mary Wilhelmina 1878-1969
NatCAB 57
Ginenback, John V *NewYHSD*
Ginger, Ray d1975 *WhAm 6*
Gingery, Don 1884-1961 *BiDrAC*
Gingold, Joseph Randolph 1899-1952
NatCAB 41
Gingras, Adolphe Joseph 1896-1966 *NatCAB 54*
Gingrich, Curvin Henry 1880-1951 *WhAm 3*
Gingrich, John Edward 1897-1960 *NatCAB 43,
WhAm 4*
Ginn, Curtiss, Jr. 1908-1966 *WhAm 4*
Ginn, Edwin 1838-1914 *AmBi, DcAmB,
NatCAB 10, WhAm 1*
Ginn, Frank Hadley 1868-1938 *WhAm 1*
Ginn, James Theda 1909-1959 *WhAm 4*
Ginnel, Henry 1821- *NatCAB 4*
Ginott, Haim G 1922-1973 *WhAm 6*
Ginsberg, Allen 1926- *EncAB, McGEWB,
WebAB*
Ginsburg, William Irving 1898-1965
NatCAB 51, WhAm 4
Ginsburgh, A Robert 1895-1958 *WhAm 3*
Ginter, Lewis 1824-1897 *ApCAB Sup, DcAmB,
NatCAB 18, WhAm H*
Ginter, Ribert McNiel 1877- *WhAm 5*
Ginther, Mrs. Pemberton d1959 *WhAm 3*
Ginzberg, Louis 1873-1953 *McGEWB,
WhAm 3*
Ginzberg, Raphael 1895-1956 *NatCAB 45*
Giolitti, Giovanni 1842-1928 *McGEWB*
Giordano, Alfred Sabato 1893-1958 *NatCAB 47,
WhAm 3*
Giorgi, Giovanni 1871-1950 *DcScB*
Giorgione 1477-1510 *McGEWB*
Giotto 1267?-1337 *McGEWB*
Gioux, Olivier 1818- *ApCAB*
Giovanni DaBologna 1529-1608 *McGEWB*
Giovanni Pisano 1250?-1317? *McGEWB*
Gipprich, John L 1880-1950 *WhAm 3*
Gipson, Corwin Elroy 1890-1961 *NatCAB 48*
Gipson, Fred 1908-1973 *REnAW*
Gipson, James Herrick 1885-1965 *WhAm 4*
Gipson, Lawrence Henry 1880- *WhAm 6*
Girard, Albert 1595-1632 *DcScB*
Girard, Alexander H 1907- *BnEnAmA*
Girard, Alfred Conrad 1841-1914 *WhAm 1*
Girard, Andre 1901-1968 *NatCAB 55,
WhAm 5*
Girard, Charles Frederic 1822-1895 *AmBi,
ApCAB, DcAmB, Drake, NatCAB 16,
TwCBDA, WhAm H*
Girard, Felix Eloi 1869-1949 *NatCAB 38*
Girard, Joseph Basil 1846-1918 *WhAm 1*
Girard, Marc Amable 1822- *ApCAB*
Girard, Pierre-Simon 1765-1836 *DcScB*
Girard, Stephen 1750-1831 *AmBi, ApCAB,
DcAmB, Drake, EncAB, McGEWB,
NatCAB 7, TwCBDA, WebAB,
WhAm H*
Girardeau, John Lafayette 1825-1898 *DcAmB,*

NatCAB 23, WhAm H
Girardin, L H *Drake*
Girardin, Louis Hue *ApCAB*
Girardin, Ray d1971 *WhAm 5*
Girardon, Francois 1628-1715 *McGEWB*
Giraud, Henri 1879-1949 *WhWW-II,
WhoMilH*
Giraud, Louis Matthieux *NewYHSD*
Giraud-Soulavie, J L *DcScB*
Giraudoux, Jean 1882-1944 *McGEWB*
Girault, Louis Matthieux *NewYHSD*
Gird, Henry H 1801-1845 *Drake*
Gird, Richard 1836- *WhAm 4*
Girdler, Tom Mercer 1877-1965 *WhAm 4*
Girdler, Walter Higgins, Jr. 1913-1961 *WhAm 4*
Girdner, John Harvey 1856-1933 *WhAm 2*
Girl, Christian 1874-1946 *WhAm 2*
Girod, Jesse Calvin 1892-1968 *NatCAB 54*
Giron, Francisco Hernandez 1500?-1554
ApCAB
Giron, Marc *NewYHSD*
Girouard, Desire 1836- *ApCAB*
Girouard, John Joseph 1794-1855 *ApCAB*
Girouard, Joseph Arthur 1875-1953 *NatCAB 49*
Girsch, Frederick 1821-1895 *DcAmB,
NewYHSD*
Girsch, Frederick 1825-1895 *WhAm H*
Girtanner, Christoph 1760-1800 *DcScB*
Girty, George Herbert 1869-1939 *WhAm 1*
Girty, Simon 1741-1818 *AmBi, DcAmB,
McGEWB, NatCAB 2, REnAW,
WebAMB, WhAm H*
Girty, Simon 1750?-1815? *ApCAB*
Girvetz, Harry Kenneth 1910-1974 *WhAm 6*
Gisborne, Frederic Newton 1824- *ApCAB*
Gish, Dorothy 1898-1968 *WebAB*
Gish, Lillian Diana 1896- *WebAB*
Gish, Moses Napoleon 1851-1921 *NatCAB 19*
Gisser, Morris S 1901-1965 *NatCAB 51*
Gissing, Roland 1895- *IIBEAAW*
Gissler, F X *NewYHSD*
Gist, Annie Reavis 1865- *WomWWA 14*
Gist, Arthur Stanley 1883-1952 *NatCAB 42,
WhAm 3*
Gist, Christopher d1759 *ApCAB*
Gist, Christopher 1705?-1759 *REnAW*
Gist, Christopher 1706?-1759 *AmBi, DcAmB,
McGEWB, WebAB, WebAMB,
WhAm H*
Gist, Joseph 1775-1835 *BiAUS*
Gist, Joseph 1775-1836 *BiDrAC, WhAm H,
WhAmP*
Gist, Mordecai 1742?-1792 *DcAmB*
Gist, Mordecai 1743-1792 *AmBi, ApCAB,
Drake, NatCAB 6, TwCBDA, WhAm H*
Gist, Nathan Howard 1885-1962 *WhAm 4*
Gist, R Dennis 1882-1955 *NatCAB 43*
Gist, States Rights 1831-1864 *BiDConf*
Gist, William Henry d1874 *BiAUS*
Gist, William Henry 1807-1874 *AmBi, DcAmB,
WhAm H, WhAmP*
Gist, William Henry 1809-1874 *NatCAB 12*
Gistner, John C *NewYHSD*
Gitchell, Mazie 1894-1974 *WhAm 6*
Gitelson, Maxwell 1902-1965 *WhAm 4*
Gitelson, Moses Leo 1896-1964 *WhAm 4*
Githens, Alfred Morton 1876-1973 *DcAmLiB,
WhAm 5*
Githens, Perry 1901-1961 *WhAm 4*
Gitlin, Irving Joseph 1918-1967 *WhAm 4*
Gitlow, Benjamin 1891-1965 *WhAm 4*
Gitlow, Samuel 1889-1954 *NatCAB 42*
Gitsinger, The Misses *NewYHSD*
Gitt, Charles Moul 1915-1972 *WhAm 5*
Gitt, Josiah William 1884-1973 *WhAm 6*
Gittens, Mary Laurens *NewYHSD*
Gittens, Nathaniel *NewYHSD*
Gitterman, Alice Elsberg Sterne *WomWWA 14*
Gitti, Joseph *NewYHSD*
Gittinger, Roy 1878-1957 *WhAm 3*
Gittings, J Claxton 1874-1950 *WhAm 3*
Gittings, William George 1858-1918
NatCAB 17
Gittins, Robert Henry 1869-1957 *BiDrAC,
WhAm 4*
Givago-Grishina, Nadeshda *WhAm 1*
Givan, James Alexander 1899-1943 *NatCAB 37*
Givan, Thurman Boyd 1888-1975 *WhAm 6*

Given, Helen Dennis 1874- *WomWWA 14*
Given, John LaPorte 1871-1957 *WhAm 3*
Given, Josiah 1828- *NatCAB 12, WhAm 1*
Given, Leslie Emmett 1893-1962 *WhAm 4*
Given, William 1832-1863 *NatCAB 5*
Given, William Barns, Jr. 1886-1968 *WhAm 5*
Givens, James Martin 1876-1951 *NatCAB 40*
Givens, Raymond L 1884-1972 *WhAm 5*
Givens, Spencer Hollingsworth 1904-1968
WhAm 5
Givens, Willard Earl 1886-1971 *BiDAmEd,
WhAm 5*
Givler, J P 1882-1957 *WhAm 3*
Gjelsness, Rudolph H 1894-1968 *DcAmLiB,
WhAm 5*
Gjerset, Knut 1865-1936 *WhAm 1*
Glackens, William James 1870-1938 *AmBi,
BnEnAmA, DcAmB S2, McGEWB,
NatCAB 38, WebAB, WhAm 1*
Glad, Paul Wilbur 1926- *EncAAH*
Gladden, Adley H d1862 *ApCAB, Drake*
Gladden, Alice *WomWWA 14*
Gladden, George 1867-1924 *WhAm 1*
Gladden, Solomon Washington 1836-1918
DcAmReB, EncAB
Gladden, Washington 1836-1918 *AmBi,
ApCAB, ApCAB X, DcAmB, Drake Sup,
McGEWB, NatCAB 10, TwCBDA,
WebAB, WhAm 1*
Gladding, Albert Franklin 1843-1922 *NatCAB 6,
WhAm 1*
Gladding, Benjamin *NewYHSD*
Gladding, Ernest Knight 1888-1958 *WhAm 3*
Gladding, Freeman 1815-1881 *NewYHSD*
Gladding, Nelson Augustus 1863-1936
NatCAB 30
Gladding, Thomas Stantial 1853-1939
NatCAB 34
Gladding, Timothy 1775?-1846 *NewYHSD,
WhAm H*
Gladding, Timothy Allen 1818-1864 *NewYHSD*
Glade, Earl Joseph 1885-1966 *NatCAB 53*
Glading, John Reynolds 1885-1949 *NatCAB 37*
Gladson, Guy Allen 1891-1968 *NatCAB 54*
Gladson, Guy Allen 1892-1968 *WhAm 5*
Gladson, William Nathan 1866- *WhAm 4*
Gladstone, John Hall 1827-1902 *DcScB*
Gladstone, Robert William 1879-1951 *WhAm 4*
Gladstone, William Ewart 1809-1898 *McGEWB*
Gladwell, Thomas E *NewYHSD*
Gladwin, Henry 1729-1791 *ApCAB, DcAmB,
Drake, WebAMB, WhAm H*
Gladwin, Mary Elizabeth 1861-1939 *WhAm 1*
Gladwin, William Zachary *WhAm 1*
Glaenzer, Richard Butler 1876-1937 *WhAm 1*
Glaeser, Martin Gustave 1888-1967 *NatCAB 53,
WhAm 4*
Glaisher, James 1809-1903 *DcScB*
Glaisher, James Whitbread Lee 1848-1928
DcScB
Glaman, Eugenie Fish 1872-1956 *WhAm 3*
Glancy, Alfred Robinson 1881-1959 *NatCAB 44,
WhAm 3*
Glantz, Frederick William 1908-1970
NatCAB 55
Glanvill, Joseph 1636-1680 *DcScB*
Glanz, Louis Daniel 1872-1956 *NatCAB 47*
Glarner, Fritz 1899-1972 *BnEnAmA, WhAm 5*
Glascock, Hugh Grundy 1865-1934 *WhAm 1*
Glascock, John Raglan 1845-1913 *BiDrAC*
Glascock, Thomas 1790-1841 *BiAUS, BiDrAC,
WhAm H*
Glascock, Thomas 1888-1945 *NatCAB 34*
Glascock, Thomas Addison 1873-1958
NatCAB 47
Glascoff, Donald G 1898-1963 *WhAm 4*
Glaser, Christopher 1615?-1672? *DcScB*
Glaser, Donald Arthur 1926- *AsBiEn, WebAB*
Glaser, Edward 1918-1972 *NatCAB 57*
Glaser, Johann Heinrich 1629-1679 *DcScB*
Glaser, Lulu 1876-1958 *WhAm 3,
WomWWA 14*
Glaser, Otto 1880-1951 *WhAm 3*
Glasgow, Arthur Graham 1865-1955 *WhAm 3*
Glasgow, Benjamin Bascom 1880- *WhAm 6*
Glasgow, D 1834-1858 *NewYHSD*
Glasgow, Ellen Anderson Gholson d1945
WomWWA 14

Glasgow, Ellen Anderson Gholson 1873-1945 *DcAmB S3, McGEWB, NotAW, WebAB*
Glasgow, Ellen Anderson Gholson 1874-1945 *NatCAB 13, NatCAB 35, WhAm 2*
Glasgow, Fannie Englesing *WomWWA 14*
Glasgow, Frank Lawson 1906-1970 *WhAm 5*
Glasgow, Hugh 1769-1818 *BiAUS, BiDrAC, WhAm H*
Glasgow, Hugh 1884-1948 *WhAm 2*
Glasgow, J J *NewYHSD*
Glasgow, J T *NewYHSD*
Glasgow, McPheeters 1870-1949 *NatCAB 43*
Glasgow, Robert Pollock 1875-1922 *NatCAB 20*
Glasgow, S L 1838- *NatCAB 4*
Glasgow, William Anderson, Jr. 1865- *WhAm 1*
Glasgow, William Carr 1845- *NatCAB 5*
Glasgow, William Hargadine 1880-1947 *WhAm 2*
Glasgow, William Jefferson 1866-1967 *WhAm 4*
Glasier, Gilson Gardner 1873- *WhAm 5*
Glasmann, William 1858- *NatCAB 7*
Glasner, George *NewYHSD*
Glasner, Maude Wilcox 1876- *WomWWA 14*
Glasoe, Paul Maurice 1873- *WhAm 5*
Glaspell, Susan 1882-1948 *NatCAB 15, WhAm 2, WomWWA 14*
Glaspell, Susan Keating 1876?-1948 *DcAmB S4, NotAW*
Glass, Alexander 1859-1941 *NatCAB 31*
Glass, Carter 1858-1946 *ApCAB X, BiDrAC, BiDrUSE, DcAmB S4, EncAB, NatCAB 36, WebAB, WhAm 2, WhAmP*
Glass, Carter, Jr. 1893-1955 *WhAm 3*
Glass, Elwood Gray 1891-1956 *NatCAB 46*
Glass, Francis 1790-1825 *ApCAB*
Glass, Frank Potts 1858-1934 *NatCAB 43*
Glass, Franklin Potts 1858-1934 *DcAmB S1, WhAm 1*
Glass, Frederick Belo 1892-1963 *NatCAB 51*
Glass, Gilbert 1875-1934 *WhAm 1*
Glass, Henry 1844-1908 *TwCBDA, WhAm 1*
Glass, Hiram 1859-1919 *WhAm 1*
Glass, Hiram Bentley 1906- *BiDAmEd*
Glass, Hugh d1833 *DcAmB, REnAW, WebAB, WhAm H*
Glass, James Garfield 1884- *WhoColR*
Glass, James Henderson 1854-1931 *NatCAB 25, WhAm 1*
Glass, James W 1825-1857 *ApCAB, NatCAB 12*
Glass, James William, Jr. 1825?-1855 *NewYHSD, WhAm H*
Glass, Joseph 1894-1955 *NatCAB 41*
Glass, Joseph Sarsfield 1874-1926 *NatCAB 15, WhAm 1*
Glass, Julian Wood 1880-1952 *NatCAB 42*
Glass, Marvin d1974 *WhAm 6*
Glass, Meta 1880-1967 *NatCAB 53, WhAm 4*
Glass, Montague Marsden 1877-1934 *AmBi, DcAmB S1, WhAm 1*
Glass, Perly R 1873- *NatCAB 16*
Glass, Powell 1886-1945 *WhAm 2*
Glass, Presley Thornton 1824-1902 *BiDrAC*
Glass, Robert Camillus 1885-1958 *WhAm 3*
Glasscock, Carl Burgess 1884-1942 *WhAm 2*
Glasscock, Samuel Sampson 1862- *WhAm 4*
Glasscock, William Ellsworth 1862-1925 *NatCAB 23, WhAm 1*
Glasser, Otto 1895-1964 *WhAm 4*
Glassford, Pelham Davis 1883-1959 *NatCAB 49*
Glassford, William Alexander 1886-1958 *NatCAB 47, WhAm 3*
Glassie, Henry Haywood 1871-1938 *NatCAB 45, WhAm 1*
Glassman, Oscar 1901-1970 *WhAm 5*
Glasson, John J d1882 *ApCAB, Drake*
Glasson, William Henry 1874-1946 *WhAm 2*
Glatfelter, Philip Hollinger 1889-1971 *NatCAB 57*
Glatfelter, Samuel Feiser 1858-1927 *BiDrAC, WhAm 1*
Glatfelter, William Lincoln 1865-1930 *WhAm 1*
Glauber, Johann Rudolf 1604-1668 *AsBiEn*
Glauber, Johann Rudolph 1604-1670 *DcScB*
Glaubrecht, George J *NewYHSD*
Glavin, Charles Clarke 1911-1971 *NatCAB 55, WhAm 5*
Glavis, Louis Russell 1883-1971 *WhAm 5*

Glazebrook, Larkin White 1867-1943 *NatCAB 32*
Glazebrook, Otis Allan 1845-1931 *NatCAB 2, WhAm 1*
Glazebrook, Otis Allan, Jr. 1887-1954 *WhAm 3*
Glazebrook, Richard Tetley 1854-1935 *DcScB*
Glazebrook, Thomas Bradford 1849-1926 *NatCAB 20*
Glazer, Jack Solomon 1907-1956 *NatCAB 43*
Glazier, Robert Cromer 1870-1954 *WhAm 3*
Glazier, Willard 1841-1905 *AmBi, ApCAB, NatCAB 5, TwCBDA, WhAm 1*
Glazier, William S 1907-1962 *WhAm 4*
Gleason, Alfred Dwight 1846-1914 *NatCAB 16*
Gleason, Archie Leland 1891-1972 *WhAm 6*
Gleason, Arthur Huntington 1878-1923 *WhAm 1*
Gleason, Carlisle Joyslin 1874-1940 *WhAm 1*
Gleason, Charles Whitney 1841-1914 *NatCAB 18*
Gleason, Clara Belle 1859- *WomWWA 14*
Gleason, Clarence Willard 1866-1942 *WhAm 2*
Gleason, Daniel Angell 1836-1908 *WhAm 1*
Gleason, Edward Baldwin 1854-1934 *WhAm 1*
Gleason, Elliott Perry 1821-1901 *WhAm 1*
Gleason, Frederic Grant 1848-1903 *AmBi, ApCAB, DcAmB, TwCBDA*
Gleason, Frederic Grant 1849-1903 *WhAm 1*
Gleason, Frederick Grant 1848-1903 *NatCAB 7*
Gleason, Gay 1888-1955 *WhAm 3*
Gleason, Hattie May 1873- *WomWWA 14*
Gleason, Herbert John *WebAB*
Gleason, Herbert Wendell 1855- *WhAm 4*
Gleason, Jackie 1916- *WebAB*
Gleason, James 1886-1959 *WhAm 3*
Gleason, James E 1868-1964 *WhAm 4*
Gleason, John Hiram 1869-1925 *NatCAB 19*
Gleason, Joseph Michael 1869-1942 *NatCAB 31*
Gleason, Joseph Thomas 1844- *NatCAB 18*
Gleason, Kate 1865-1933 *DcAmB S1, NotAW, WhAm 1*
Gleason, Katherine Florence 1868- *WomWWA 14*
Gleason, Lafayette Blanchard 1863-1937 *NatCAB 28, WhAm 1*
Gleason, Lucius 1819- *NatCAB 3*
Gleason, Nellie Miles *WomWWA 14*
Gleason, Rachel Brooks 1820- *AmWom*
Gleason, Ralph Joseph 1917-1975 *WhAm 6*
Gleason, Rutherford Erwin 1889-1949 *NatCAB 37*
Gleason, Sarell Everett 1905-1974 *WhAm 6*
Gleason, Walter Burrell 1889-1942 *NatCAB 39*
Gleason, William B *NewYHSD*
Gleason, William E *BiAUS*
Gleason, William Palmer 1865-1936 *WhAm 1*
Gleason, William Thomas 1917-1975 *WhAm 6*
Gleason, William White 1882-1944 *NatCAB 33*
Gleave, John W *NewYHSD*
Gleaves, Albert 1858-1937 *ApCAB X, DcAmB S2, NatCAB 27, WebAMB, WhAm 1*
Gleaves, Evelina Heap 1863- *WomWWA 14*
Gleaves, John W *NewYHSD*
Gledhill, Franklin 1898-1975 *WhAm 6*
Gleed, Charles Sumner 1856-1920 *WhAm 1*
Gleed, James Willis 1859-1926 *WhAm 1*
Gleeson, Joseph Michael 1861-1917 *WhAm 1*
Gleeson, William 1828-1895 *TwCBDA*
Gleichen-Russworm, Wilhelm Friedrich Von 1717-1783 *DcScB*
Gleick, Esther 1869- *WomWWA 14*
Gleig, George Robert 1796-1888 *ApCAB, Drake*
Gleim, Christian 1780-1861 *ApCAB*
Gleim, George Christian 1736-1817 *ApCAB*
Gleim, John Godfried d1757 *ApCAB*
Gleis, Paul G 1887-1955 *WhAm 3*
Gleiss, Henry Crete 1870-1939 *WhAm 1*
Gleissner, John M 1893-1941 *WhAm 1*
Glen, Henry 1739-1814 *BiDrAC, WhAm H, WhAmP*
Glen, Irving Mackey 1871-1931 *WhAm 1*
Glen, James 1701- *NatCAB 12*
Glen, James 1749-1814 *ApCAB Sup*
Glen, James Allison 1877-1950 *WhAm 3*
Glen, John d1853 *BiAUS*
Glen, John King 1899-1969 *NatCAB 57*

Glendinning, John 1857-1916 *NatCAB 18*
Glendinning, Malcolm 1875-1953 *NatCAB 44, WhAm 5*
Glendinning, Robert 1867-1936 *NatCAB 35, WhAm 1*
Glendower, Owen 1359?-1415? *McGEWB*
Glendy, John 1755-1832 *ApCAB, NatCAB 20*
Glendy, William Marshall 1801-1873 *ApCAB*
Glenn, Charles Bowles 1871- *WhAm 5*
Glenn, Edgar Eugene 1896-1955 *WhAm 3*
Glenn, Edwin Forbes 1857-1926 *WhAm 1*
Glenn, Elias *BiAUS*
Glenn, Eugene Byron 1871-1924 *NatCAB 20, NatCAB 24*
Glenn, Garrard 1878-1949 *WhAm 2*
Glenn, Gustavus Richard 1848-1939 *BiDAmEd, NatCAB 13, WhAm 3*
Glenn, Helen Miller 1886- *WomWWA 14*
Glenn, Henry d1814 *BiAUS*
Glenn, Hugh 1788-1833 *DcAmB*
Glenn, Hugh James 1824-1883 *REnAW*
Glenn, J Lyles 1858-1927 *WhAm 1*
Glenn, James *ApCAB, Drake*
Glenn, James Dryden 1905-1958 *WhAm 3*
Glenn, James Walter 1882-1962 *NatCAB 47, WhAm 4*
Glenn, John Brodnax 1885-1962 *WhAm 4*
Glenn, John Herschel, Jr. 1921- *WebAB, WebAMB*
Glenn, John Mark 1858-1950 *DcAmB S4, WhAm 3*
Glenn, John McGaw 1859-1928 *WhAm 1*
Glenn, Joseph Burton 1896-1968 *NatCAB 53*
Glenn, Joseph Henry 1884-1921 *NatCAB 6*
Glenn, Joseph William 1879- *WhoColR*
Glenn, Leonidas Chalmers 1871-1951 *NatCAB 41, WhAm 3*
Glenn, Mary Willcox Brown 1869-1940 *NotAW, WhAm 1, WomWWA 14*
Glenn, Milton Willits 1903-1967 *BiDrAC, WhAm 4, WhAmP*
Glenn, Oliver Edmunds 1878- *WhAm 6*
Glenn, Otis Ferguson 1879-1959 *BiDrAC, WhAm 3*
Glenn, Robert Brodnax 1854-1920 *NatCAB 19, WhAm 1*
Glenn, Thomas Kearney 1868-1946 *WhAm 2*
Glenn, Thomas Louis 1847-1918 *BiDrAC, WhAm 4*
Glenn, William Schaeffer 1858-1931 *WhAm 1*
Glennan, Arthur Henry 1853- *WhAm 4*
Glennie, J S *NewYHSD*
Glennon, James Henry 1857-1927 *WhAm 1*
Glennon, James Henry 1857-1940 *NatCAB 42*
Glennon, John Joseph 1862-1946 *ApCAB Sup, DcAmB S4, NatCAB 13, TwCBDA, WhAm 2*
Glennon, Lawrence Edward 1880-1960 *NatCAB 49*
Glenny, Charlotte Miller 1864- *WomWWA 14*
Glenton *NewYHSD*
Glentworth, George 1735-1792 *ApCAB, Drake*
Glentworth, Harvey *NewYHSD*
Glentworth, Marguerite Linton 1882- *WomWWA 14*
Glessing, Thomas B 1817-1882 *NewYHSD, WhAm H*
Glessner, John Jacob 1843-1936 *WhAm 1*
Gleysteen, William Henry 1876-1948 *NatCAB 35*
Glick, Carl 1890-1971 *WhAm 5*
Glick, David 1895-1964 *NatCAB 50*
Glick, George Washington 1827-1911 *NatCAB 8, WhAm 1*
Glick, Harry Naylor 1893-1971 *NatCAB 56*
Glickman, Alfred Myron 1898-1954 *NatCAB 46*
Glickman, Irving 1914-1972 *NatCAB 57, WhAm 5*
Glickman, Mendel 1895-1967 *WhAm 4*
Glicksman, Harry 1882-1975 *WhAm 6*
Glidden, Charles Jaspar 1857-1927 *WebAB*
Glidden, Charles Jasper 1857-1927 *DcAmB, NatCAB 5, WhAm 1*
Glidden, George Dana Boardman 1844-1885 *ApCAB*
Glidden, Joseph Farwell 1813-1906 *AmBi, ApCAB X, DcAmB, EncAAH, NatCAB 23, WebAB, WhAm HA,*

WhAm 4
Glidden, Minnie Maud 1865- *WhAm 4*
Glidden, Stephen Clifton 1870-1917 *NatCAB 18*
Gliddon, Anna *NewYHSD*
Gliddon, George Robins 1809-1857 *ApCAB, Drake*
Glines, Earle Stanley 1889-1963 *WhAm 4*
Glinka, Mikhail Ivanovich 1804-1857 *McGEWB*
Glinsky, Vincent 1895-1975 *WhAm 6*
Glintenkamp, Hendrik 1887-1946 *NatCAB 42, WhAm 2*
Glisan, Rodney 1827- *ApCAB*
Glisson, Francis 1597?-1677 *BiHiMed, DcScB*
Glisson, Oliver S 1809-1890 *ApCAB, Drake, NatCAB 13, TwCBDA*
Glitchman, A *NewYHSD*
Glixon, S Arthur 1901-1964 *NatCAB 49*
Glock, Carl Edward 1892-1966 *NatCAB 53, WhAm 4*
Glockler, George 1890-1969 *NatCAB 55*
Glogauer, Fritz 1857-1926 *WhAm 1*
Glogger, John N *NewYHSD*
Gloninger, John 1758-1836 *BiAUS, BiDrAC, WhAm H*
Glore, Charles Foster 1887-1950 *WhAm 3*
Glorieux, Alphonse Joseph 1844-1917 *TwCBDA*
Glorieux, Alphonsus Joseph 1844-1917 *ApCAB Sup, NatCAB 5, WhAm 1*
Glorieux, Emilie Louise 1878- *WomWWA 14*
Glos, George Waldorf 1868-1957 *NatCAB 44*
Glose, Adolf 1854- *WhAm 4*
Glossbrenner, Adam John 1810-1889 *BiAUS, BiDrAC, WhAm H*
Glossbrenner, John Jacob 1813-1887 *ApCAB, TwCBDA*
Gloth, William Conrad 1886-1944 *NatCAB 38*
Glotzbach, William Edward *WhAm 1*
Gloucester, Humphrey, Duke Of 1391-1447 *McGEWB*
Glover, A T 1880- *WhoColR*
Glover, Arthur James 1873-1949 *WhAm 2*
Glover, Charles 1847-1922 *WhAm 1*
Glover, Charles Carroll 1846-1936 *ApCAB X, NatCAB 6, NatCAB 32, WhAm 1*
Glover, Clara Capitola *WomWWA 14*
Glover, David Delano 1868-1952 *BiDrAC, WhAm 3, WhAmP*
Glover, DeLay 1823?-1863? *NewYHSD*
Glover, DeLloyd Gage *NewYHSD*
Glover, DeWitt Clinton 1817-1836 *NewYHSD*
Glover, Edwin S 1845-1919 *IIBEAAW*
Glover, Fred Weston 1874-1941 *NatCAB 32*
Glover, Frederic Samuel 1879-1954 *WhAm 3*
Glover, George Henry 1864- *WhAm 5*
Glover, James Nettle 1837- *NatCAB 7*
Glover, James Waterman 1868-1941 *NatCAB 42, WhAm 1*
Glover, Jane Beale *WomWWA 14*
Glover, John 1732-1797 *AmBi, ApCAB, DcAmB, Drake, NatCAB 1, NatCAB 8, TwCBDA, WebAMB*
Glover, John George 1895-1970 *NatCAB 56, WhAm 5*
Glover, Sir John Hawley 1829-1885 *ApCAB*
Glover, John Milton 1852-1929 *BiDrAC*
Glover, John Montgomery 1822-1891 *BiDrAC, WhAm H*
Glover, John Montgomery 1824-1891 *BiAUS, TwCBDA*
Glover, Joseph 1780?-1840? *ApCAB*
Glover, Lloyd 1826- *NewYHSD*
Glover, Lyman Beecher 1846-1915 *WhAm 1*
Glover, Quinn 1897-1970 *NatCAB 56*
Glover, Robert Hall 1871-1947 *NatCAB 37, WhAm 2*
Glover, Roy Henry 1890-1958 *NatCAB 50, WhAm 4*
Glover, Samuel Taylor 1813-1884 *DcAmB, NatCAB 25*
Glover, Thomas Jefferson 1833-1899 *NatCAB 19*
Glover, Townend 1813-1883 *DcAmB, NatCAB 23, WhAm H*
Glover, Townsend 1813-1883 *EncAAH*
Glover, W Irving 1879- *WhAm 6*
Glover, William 1670?- *ApCAB*
Glover, William Howard 1819-1875 *WhAm H*
Glubb, Sir John Bagot 1897- *McGEWB*

Gluck, Alma 1884-1938 *AmBi, DcAmB S2, NatCAB 43, NotAW, WhAm 1*
Gluck, B *NewYHSD*
Gluck, Christoph Willibald 1714-1787 *McGEWB*
Gluck, Harold 1891-1953 *NatCAB 40*
Gluck, James Fraser 1852-1897 *ApCAB, TwCBDA*
Gluckin, William 1888-1963 *NatCAB 50*
Gluckmann, Grigory 1898-1973 *NatCAB 57*
Glucksmann, Olga Neyman 1860- *WomWWA 14*
Glueck, Bernard 1884-1972 *WhAm 5*
Glueck, Eleanor Touroff 1898-1972 *NatCAB 57, WhAm 5*
Glueck, Nelson 1900-1971 *NatCAB 56, WhAm 5*
Glueck, Sheldon 1896- *WebAB*
Gluhareff, Michael E 1892-1967 *WhAm 4*
Glyndon, Howard *WhAm 4*
Glynes, Ella Maria 1847- *NatCAB 13*
Glynn, James 1800?-1871 *ApCAB*
Glynn, James 1801-1871 *DcAmB, WebAMB, WhAm H*
Glynn, James Peter 1867-1930 *BiDrAC, WhAm 1, WhAmP*
Glynn, Martin Henry 1871-1924 *AmBi, ApCAB X, BiDrAC, DcAmB, NatCAB 15, NatCAB 24, WhAm 1, WhAmP*
Gmeiner, John 1847- *ApCAB, TwCBDA*
Gmeiner, John 1847-1913 *DcAmB*
Gmeiner, John 1847-1915 *WhAm 1*
Gmelin, Johann Georg 1709-1755 *DcScB*
Gmelin, Leopold 1788-1853 *AsBiEn, DcScB*
Gnade, Maude Fleming 1879- *WomWWA 14*
Gnagi, Will Bender 1898-1955 *NatCAB 43*
Gneisenau, Augustus Wilhelm 1760-1831 *WhoMilH*
Gnichtel, Frederick W 1860-1950 *NatCAB 37*
Goadby, William Henry 1849-1925 *ApCAB X*
Goan, Orrin S 1856- *WhAm 4*
Goater, John H *NewYHSD*
Gobble, Aaron Ezra 1856- *NatCAB 5, TwCBDA, WhAm 4*
Gobeil, Samuel 1875-1961 *WhAm 4*
Gobeille, Harrold LeFevre 1894-1958 *WhAm 3*
Gobel, Adolf 1864-1924 *NatCAB 22*
Gober, William Mathis 1875- *WhAm 5*
Gobetz, Wallace 1916-1973 *WhAm 6*
Gobin, Hillary Asbury 1842-1923 *NatCAB 7, TwCBDA, WhAm 1*
Gobin, John Peter Shindel 1837-1910 *ApCAB Sup, NatCAB 13, TwCBDA, WhAm 1*
Gobineau, Joseph Arthur, Comte De 1816-1882 *McGEWB*
Goble, Conrad *NewYHSD*
Goble, George Washington 1887-1963 *WhAm 4*
Gobley, Nicolas-Theodore 1811-1876 *DcScB*
Gobrecht, Christian 1784-1844 *NatCAB 12*
Gobrecht, Christian 1785-1844 *DcAmB, NewYHSD, WhAm H*
Gobright, Lawrence Augustus 1816-1879 *NatCAB 5*
Gochenour, Arthur Burchard 1879-1941 *NatCAB 40*
Gock, A J 1889-1962 *WhAm 4*
Gockeln, Frederick William 1820-1886 *NatCAB 2, TwCBDA*
Godard, George Seymour 1865-1936 *NatCAB 28, WhAm 1*
Godbe, William Samuel 1833-1902 *DcAmB, NatCAB 17, REnAW, WhAm H*
Godbeer, George H 1872-1961 *WhAm 4*
Godbey, Allen Howard 1864-1948 *NatCAB 42, WhAm 2*
Godbey, Earle d1941 *WhAm 2*
Godbey, John Campbell 1882-1970 *WhAm 5*
Godbey, John Emory 1839-1932 *WhAm 1*
Godbold, Edgar 1879-1952 *NatCAB 41, WhAm 3*
Godbold, Norman Dosier 1877-1936 *WhAm 1*
Godbout, Joseph Adelard 1892-1956 *WhAm 3*
Godcharles, Frederic Antes 1872-1944 *WhAm 2*
Godchaux, Charles 1869-1954 *NatCAB 41, WhAm 3*
Godchaux, Frank A 1879-1965 *WhAm 4*

Godchaux, Jules 1872-1951 *WhAm 3*
Goddard, Abby Rogers *WomWWA 14*
Goddard, Anson Morrill 1859-1932 *NatCAB 24*
Goddard, Calvin 1768-1842 *ApCAB, BiAUS, BiDrAC, Drake, NatCAB 5, TwCBDA, WhAm H*
Goddard, Calvin Hooker 1891-1955 *DcAmB S5, NatCAB 41, WhAm 3*
Goddard, Calvin Luther 1820-1895 *ApCAB*
Goddard, Calvin Luther 1822-1895 *DcAmB, WhAm H*
Goddard, Charles William 1825-1889 *NatCAB 27*
Goddard, Charles William 1879-1951 *NatCAB 39, WhAm 3*
Goddard, Christopher Marsh 1856- *WhAm 4*
Goddard, Clara Cecelia 1854- *WomWWA 14*
Goddard, Edwin Charles 1865-1942 *NatCAB 31*
Goddard, Emerson *NewYHSD*
Goddard, Emma *BiCAW*
Goddard, Emma Florence Robbins 1865- *WomWWA 14*
Goddard, Fannie Hermance 1855- *WomWWA 14*
Goddard, Fannie Walbridge *WomWWA 14*
Goddard, George Henry 1817-1906 *IIBEAAW, NewYHSD*
Goddard, Harold Clarke 1878-1950 *WhAm 2A*
Goddard, Harry Williams 1863-1927 *NatCAB 20, WhAm 1*
Goddard, Henry Herbert 1866-1957 *BiDAmEd, NatCAB 15, WhAm 4*
Goddard, Henry Newell 1867-1948 *NatCAB 39, WhAm 4*
Goddard, Henry Warren 1876-1955 *WhAm 3*
Goddard, John 1723?-1785 *AmBi, DcAmB, NatCAB 24*
Goddard, John 1724-1785 *WhAm H*
Goddard, John Calvin 1852-1945 *WhAm 2*
Goddard, Josiah 1813-1854 *ApCAB*
Goddard, Karl B 1886-1953 *WhAm 3*
Goddard, Leroy Albert 1854-1936 *WhAm 1*
Goddard, Loring Hapgood 1868- *WhAm 4*
Goddard, Louise Augustine 1880- *WomWWA 14*
Goddard, Luther Marcellus 1837-1917 *NatCAB 24*
Goddard, Luther Marcellus 1840-1917 *DcAmB*
Goddard, Mary Katherine 1738-1816 *NotAW*
Goddard, Morrill 1865-1937 *DcAmB S2, NatCAB 27*
Goddard, Morrill 1866-1937 *WhAm 1*
Goddard, O Fletcher 1853- *WhAm 4*
Goddard, Oscar Elmo 1867-1950 *WhAm 3*
Goddard, Paul Beck 1811-1866 *AmBi, ApCAB, DcAmB, NatCAB 23, WhAm H*
Goddard, Pliny Earle 1869-1928 *AmBi, DcAmB, NatCAB 17, WhAm 1*
Goddard, Ralph Bartlett 1861-1936 *NatCAB 27, WhAm 1*
Goddard, Ralph Willis 1887-1929 *WhAm 1*
Goddard, Robert Hale Ives 1837-1916 *WhAm 1*
Goddard, Robert Hale Ives 1880-1945 *WhAm 2*
Goddard, Robert Hutchings 1882-1945 *AsBiEn, DcAmB S3, DcScB, EncAB, McGEWB, NatCAB 35, WebAB, WhAm 2*
Goddard, Sarah Updike 1700?-1770 *NotAW*
Goddard, Stanhope Scott 1890-1946 *NatCAB 33*
Goddard, William 1740-1817 *ApCAB, DcAmB, Drake, WhAm H*
Goddard, William 1825-1907 *NatCAB 20, WhAm 1*
Goddard, William Giles 1794-1846 *ApCAB, Drake, NatCAB 8, TwCBDA*
Godden, A *NewYHSD*
Godding, Adelaide M Smith 1857- *WhAm 4*
Godding, John Granville 1853-1929 *NatCAB 22, WhAm 1*
Godding, William C *NewYHSD*
Godding, William Whitney 1831-1899 *NatCAB 23, WhAm 1*
Goddu, J H 1796-1882 *ApCAB*
Goddu, Louis 1837-1919 *DcAmB, NatCAB 13*
Godefroid, F *NewYHSD*
Godefroy, Charles Webb 1886-1964 *NatCAB 49*
Godefroy, Maximilian *DcAmB, NatCAB 23, WhAm H*

Godefroy, Maximilian 1765-1842? *BnEnAmA*
Godefroy, Maximilian 1770?-1837? *NewYHSD*
Godefroy, P M F *NewYHSD*
Godehn, Paul M 1891-1952 *WhAm 3*
Godel, Kurt 1906- *AsBiEn, McGEWB*
Godell, Albert *NewYHSD*
Godey, Louis Antoine 1804-1878 *AmBi, ApCAB, DcAmB, NatCAB 22, WebAB, WhAm H*
Godfrey Of Bouillon 1060?-1100 *McGEWB*
Godfrey, Alfred Laurance 1888-1970 *WhAm 5*
Godfrey, Arthur Michael 1903- *WebAB*
Godfrey, Benjamin 1794-1862 *DcAmB, NatCAB 6, TwCBDA, WhAm H*
Godfrey, E *NewYHSD*
Godfrey, Edward Settle 1843-1932 *NatCAB 25, WhAm 1*
Godfrey, Edward Settle, Jr. 1878-1960 *NatCAB 45*
Godfrey, Fletcher 1916-1962 *NatCAB 49, WhAm 4*
Godfrey, Freeman 1825-1898 *NatCAB 11*
Godfrey, Hollis 1874-1936 *WhAm 1*
Godfrey, Lincoln 1850-1916 *WhAm 1*
Godfrey, Stuart C 1886-1945 *WhAm 2*
Godfrey, Thomas 1704-1749 *AmBi, ApCAB, DcAmB, DcScB, Drake, NatCAB 23, WebAB, WhAm H*
Godfrey, Thomas 1736-1763 *ApCAB, DcAmB, Drake, NatCAB 8, WebAB, WhAm H*
Godfrey, William Truitt 1872-1943 *NatCAB 33*
Godfrey, Winona 1877- *WomWWA 14*
Godin, Isabel 1728- *ApCAB*
Godin, Jean Godin DesOdonais 1712-1792 *ApCAB*
Godin, Louis 1704-1760 *ApCAB, DcScB*
Goding, Frederic Webster 1858-1933 *NatCAB 12, WhAm 1*
Godkin, Edward L 1831-1902 *Drake Sup*
Godkin, Edwin Lawrence 1831-1902 *AmBi, ApCAB, DcAmB, EncAB, McGEWB, NatCAB 8, TwCBDA, WebAB, WhAm 1*
Godley, Frederick Augustus 1886-1961 *NatCAB 48, WhAm 4*
Godlove, Isaac Hahn 1892-1954 *NatCAB 43, WhAm 3*
Godman, John Davidson 1794-1830 *AmBi, ApCAB, DcAmB, Drake, NatCAB 7, TwCBDA, WhAm H*
Godman, Melvin M 1856-1914 *NatCAB 16*
Godman, William Davis 1829- *TwCBDA*
Godolphin, Francis Richard Borroum 1903-1974 *WhAm 6*
Godolphin, Sidney Godolphin, Earl Of 1645-1712 *McGEWB*
Godon, Sylvanus William 1809-1879 *ApCAB, Drake, NatCAB 9, TwCBDA*
Godowsky, Leopold 1870-1938 *AmBi, DcAmB S2, NatCAB 33, WhAm 1*
Godoy, Jose Francisco 1851- *WhAm 4*
Godoy Y Alvarez DeFaria, Manuel De 1767-1851 *McGEWB*
Godshalk, William 1817-1891 *BiDrAC, WhAm H*
Godshall, Lincoln Derstine 1865- *TwCBDA, WhAm 5*
Godshall, Wilson Leon 1895-1956 *NatCAB 45, WhAm 3*
Godunov, Boris 1551-1605 *McGEWB, WhoMilH*
Godwin, Abraham 1763-1835 *NewYHSD*
Godwin, Earl d1956 *WhAm 3*
Godwin, Edward Allison 1850-1923 *WhAm 1*
Godwin, Frank Whitney 1895-1958 *NatCAB 43*
Godwin, George William 1903-1968 *NatCAB 56*
Godwin, Hannibal Lafayette 1873-1929 *BiDrAC, WhAm 5, WhAmP*
Godwin, Harold 1857-1931 *WhAm 1*
Godwin, Harold 1858-1931 *NatCAB 24*
Godwin, Herbert 1869- *WhAm 5*
Godwin, Parke 1816-1904 *AmBi, ApCAB, DcAmB, Drake, NatCAB 11, NatCAB 35, TwCBDA, WhAm 1*
Godwin, William 1756-1836 *McGEWB*
Godwin-Austen, Robert Alfred Cloyne 1808-1884 *DcScB*
Goebbels, Joseph Paul 1897-1945 *McGEWB, WhWW-II*

Goebel, Frank J 1893-1962 *WhAm 4*
Goebel, Henry 1818-1893 *TwCBDA*
Goebel, Herman Philip 1853-1930 *BiDrAC, WhAm 1, WhAmP*
Goebel, Julius 1857-1931 *WhAm 1*
Goebel, Julius, Jr. 1892-1973 *WhAm 6*
Goebel, Karl 1855-1932 *DcScB*
Goebel, Louis William 1884-1973 *WhAm 6*
Goebel, Peter W 1859-1934 *WhAm 1*
Goebel, William 1854-1900 *TwCBDA*
Goebel, William 1856-1900 *AmBi, DcAmB, NatCAB 13, WhAm H, WhAmP*
Goedaert, Johannes 1617?-1668 *DcScB*
Goehring, Carl 1890-1962 *NatCAB 51*
Goehring, Raymond Russell 1892-1963 *NatCAB 49*
Goeke, John Henry 1869-1930 *BiDrAC, NatCAB 50, WhAm 1*
Goelet, Augustin Hardin 1854-1910 *WhAm 1*
Goelet, Raphael *NewYHSD*
Goelet, Robert 1880-1966 *WhAm 4*
Goelet, Robert Walton 1880-1941 *NatCAB 35, WhAm 1*
Goeller, John 1871-1927 *NatCAB 22*
Goens, Ernest 1892-1960 *NatCAB 49*
Goepp, Philip Henry 1798-1872 *NatCAB 2*
Goepp, Philip Henry 1864-1936 *WhAm 1*
Goeppert, Heinrich Robert 1800-1884 *DcScB*
Goeppert, Maria 1906-1972 *WebAB*
Goeppert-Mayer, Marie 1906-1972 *AsBiEn*
Goering, Hermann 1893-1946 *WhWW-II*
Goerke, Lenor Stephen 1912-1972 *WhAm 6*
Goertner, Francis Barnes 1893-1964 *NatCAB 51, WhAm 4*
Goertz, Raymond Corlis 1915-1970 *NatCAB 55, WhAm 5*
Goerz, David 1849-1914 *DcAmB*
Goes, Hugo VanDer *McGEWB*
Goes, Pedro De 1503-1554 *ApCAB*
Goesbriand, Louis De 1816-1899 *ApCAB, NatCAB 5, TwCBDA*
Goessmann, Charles Anthony 1827-1910 *ApCAB, DcAmB, NatCAB 11, TwCBDA, WhAm 1*
Goessmann, Helena Theresa d1926 *WhAm 3*
Goetchius, Henry Richard 1852-1925 *WhAm 1*
Goethals, George Washington 1858-1928 *AmBi, ApCAB X, DcAmB, EncAB, McGEWB, NatCAB 14, NatCAB 24, WebAB, WebAMB, WhAm 1*
Goethe, Charles Matthias 1875-1966 *WhAm 4*
Goethe, Johann Wolfgang Von 1749-1832 *AsBiEn, DcScB, McGEWB*
Goethe, Mary L Glide *WomWWA 14*
Goetsch, Frederick Albert 1882-1947 *NatCAB 38*
Goetschius, Johannes Henricus 1718-1800? *ApCAB*
Goetschius, John Henry 1718-1774 *DcAmB, WhAm H*
Goetschius, John Mauritius 1720-1800? *ApCAB*
Goetschius, Percy 1853-1943 *BiDAmEd, DcAmB S3, NatCAB 14, WhAm 4*
Goette, Alexander Wilhelm 1840-1922 *DcScB*
Goette, John 1896-1974 *WhAm 6*
Goetz, Albert Gillies 1892-1963 *WhAm 4*
Goetz, E Ray 1886-1954 *NatCAB 44*
Goetz, George 1900-1940 *DcAmB S2*
Goetz, George Washington 1855-1897 *NatCAB 24*
Goetz, George Washington 1856-1897 *DcAmB, WhAm H*
Goetz, Mina 1869- *WomWWA 14*
Goetz, Norman S 1887-1972 *WhAm 5*
Goetz, Philip Becker 1870-1950 *WhAm 3*
Goetz, William 1903-1969 *WhAm 5*
Goetze, Albrecht 1897-1971 *WhAm 5*
Goetze, Arthur Burton 1901-1959 *WhAm 3*
Goetze, Frederick Arthur 1870-1950 *WhAm 3*
Goetze, William August 1863-1934 *NatCAB 25*
Goetzman, William Harry 1930- *EncAAH*
Goetzmann, Jule Lawrence 1912-1956 *WhAm 3*
Goetzmann, William Harry 1930- *REnAW*
Goff, Abe McGregor 1899- *BiDrAC*
Goff, Bruce 1904- *BnEnAmA*
Goff, Charles Weer 1897-1975 *WhAm 6*
Goff, Emmet Stull 1852-1902 *AmBi, DcAmB, WhAm H*

Goff, Emmett Stull 1852-1902 *NatCAB 23*
Goff, Ernest Lucius 1907-1963 *WhAm 4*
Goff, Eugenia Wheeler 1844- *NatCAB 17*
Goff, Frederick Harris 1858-1923 *NatCAB 19, WhAm 1*
Goff, Guy Despard 1866-1933 *BiDrAC, NatCAB 24, WhAmP*
Goff, Guy Despard 1867-1933 *WhAm 1*
Goff, Harold 1884-1928 *WhAm 1*
Goff, Harriet Newell Kneeland 1828- *AmWom*
Goff, Henry Slade 1842-1917 *NatCAB 17*
Goff, Isaac Lewis 1852-1935 *NatCAB 26*
Goff, John William 1848-1924 *DcAmB, NatCAB 15, WhAm 1*
Goff, Lyman Bullock 1841-1927 *NatCAB 21*
Goff, Milton Browning 1831-1890 *BiDAmEd, NatCAB 21, TwCBDA*
Goff, Nathan 1843-1920 *AmBi, ApCAB, BiDrAC, BiDrUSE, NatCAB 13, NatCAB 29, TwCBDA, WhAm 1, WhAmP*
Goff, Thomas Theodore 1882-1945 *WhAm 2*
Goff, William Adams 1893-1947 *NatCAB 34*
Goffart, Edward *NewYHSD*
Goffe, James Riddle 1851-1931 *ApCAB X, NatCAB 25, WhAm 1*
Goffe, William 1605?-1679? *AmBi, ApCAB, DcAmB, Drake, NatCAB 11, WhAm H*
Goffigon, Page Nottingham 1903-1958 *NatCAB 47*
Goforth, John *BiAUS*
Goforth, William 1766-1817 *DcAmB, NatCAB 23, WhAm H*
Gogarty, Oliver St. John 1878-1957 *WhAm 3*
Goggin, Catharine *WhAm 5*
Goggin, William Leftwich 1807-1870 *BiAUS, BiDrAC, WhAm H*
Gogol, Nikolai 1809-1852 *McGEWB*
Gohdes, Conrad Bruno 1866- *WhAm 3*
Gohen, Charles Marsh 1875- *WhAm 5*
Gohory, Jacques 1520-1576 *DcScB*
Goicoechea, Jose Antonio DeLiendo Y 1735-1814 *ApCAB*
Goicouria, Domingo De 1799-1870 *Drake*
Goin, Edward Franklin 1873- *WhoColR*
Goin, Logwood Ulysses 1874- *WhoColR*
Goin, Sanford Williams 1908-1958 *WhAm 3*
Going, Charles Buxton 1863- *WhAm 5*
Going, Ellen Maud *WomWWA 14*
Going, Jonathan 1786-1844 *DcAmB, NatCAB 1, TwCBDA, WhAm H*
Going, Maud d1925 *WhAm 1*
Gokalp, Mehmet Ziya 1875?-1924 *McGEWB*
Gokhale, Gopal Krishna 1866-1915 *McGEWB*
Golatka, Walter Francis 1890-1960 *WhAm 4*
Golay, John Ford 1917-1969 *WhAm 5*
Golay, Juliette *WomWWA 14*
Gold, Edward E 1847- *NatCAB 14*
Gold, Egbert Habberton 1868-1928 *NatCAB 22*
Gold, Harry 1899-1972 *WhAm 5*
Gold, Howard R 1878-1959 *WhAm 3*
Gold, John Steiner 1898-1970 *NatCAB 56*
Gold, Nathan 1663-1723 *NatCAB 12*
Gold, Nathan Jules 1894-1970 *WhAm 5*
Gold, Pleasant Daniel, Jr. 1876- *WhAm 5*
Gold, Thomas 1920- *AsBiEn*
Gold, Thomas Ruggles 1764-1826 *BiAUS*
Gold, Thomas Ruggles 1764-1827 *BiDrAC, WhAm H*
Gold, William Henry 1865- *WhAm 4*
Gold, William Jason 1845-1903 *TwCBDA, WhAm 1*
Goldbach, Christian 1690-1764 *DcScB*
Goldbach, Leo John 1883-1966 *NatCAB 51*
Goldbacker, Barbara 1826?- *NewYHSD*
Goldbacker, Isaac 1834?- *NewYHSD*
Goldbeck, Albert Theodore 1885-1966 *WhAm 4*
Goldbeck, Edward 1886-1934 *WhAm 1*
Goldbeck, Robert 1839-1908 *BiDAmEd, DcAmB, NatCAB 23, WhAm 1*
Goldbecker, Herman Joseph 1905-1970 *NatCAB 55*
Goldberg, Abraham Isaac 1904-1973 *WhAm 6*
Goldberg, Arthur Joseph 1908- *BiDrUSE, EncAB, WebAB*
Goldberg, Dora *WebAB*
Goldberg, Isaac 1887-1938 *WhAm 1*
Goldberg, Isidor 1893-1961 *NatCAB 47*

Goldberg, Leo 1913-1971 *WhAm 5*
Goldberg, Louis Palatnik 1888-1957
NatCAB 44
Goldberg, Reuben Lucius 1883-1970 *WhAm 6*
Goldberg, Rube 1883-1970 *WebAB*
Goldberg, Samuel Auron 1898-1974 *WhAm 6*
Goldberg, Samuel James 1883-1958 *NatCAB 43*
Goldberg, Sol Harry 1880-1940 *NatCAB 32*
Goldberger, Isidore Harry 1888-1967 *WhAm 5*
Goldberger, Joseph 1874-1929 *AmBi, AsBiEn,*
DcAmB, DcScB, NatCAB 21, WebAB,
WhAm 1
Goldblatt, Maurice Henry 1883-1962 *WhAm 4*
Goldblatt, Nathan 1895-1944 *WhAm 2*
Golden, Ben Hale 1910-1970 *WhAm 5*
Golden, Benjamin Ira 1892-1973 *NatCAB 57*
Golden, Clinton Strong 1888-1961 *WhAm 4*
Golden, Elizabeth Lathrop 1874-
WomWWA 14
Golden, Emmett 1892-1950 *NatCAB 38*
Golden, Francis Leo 1900-1952 *NatCAB 40*
Golden, Grace *WhAm 5*
Golden, James Stephen 1891-1971 *BiDrAC,*
WhAm 5
Golden, John 1874-1955 *DcAmB S5,*
NatCAB 45, WhAm 3
Golden, Michael Joseph 1862- *WhAm 4*
Golden, Nora 1888- *BiCAW*
Golden, Richard 1854-1909 *WhAm 1*
Golden, Ross 1889-1975 *WhAm 6*
Golden, S Herbert 1875-1941 *WhAm 1*
Golden, S M d1950 *WhAm 3*
Goldenberg, Morris 1911-1969 *WhAm 5*
Goldenson, Samuel Harry 1873-1962
NatCAB 49
Goldenweiser, Alexander Alexandrovich
1880-1940 *DcAmB S2, WhAm 1*
Goldenweiser, Emanuel Alexander 1883-1953
DcAmB S5, NatCAB 42, WhAm 3
Golder, Benjamin Martin 1891-1946 *BiDrAC,*
WhAm 2
Golder, Frank Alfred 1877-1929 *AmBi,*
DcAmB, NatCAB 23, WhAm 1
Goldesberry, John Milford 1876- *WhAm 5*
Goldet, Antoine Gustave 1905-1963 *WhAm 4*
Goldfarb, Samuel Jesse 1882-1945 *NatCAB 35*
Goldfish, Samuel *WebAB*
Goldfogle, Henry Mayer 1856-1929 *BiDrAC,*
WhAm 1, WhAmP
Goldforb, Abraham Jules 1881- *WhAm 6*
Goldhaber, Maurice 1911- *AsBiEn*
Goldhorn, Ludwig Bernhard 1871-1944
NatCAB 34
Goldie, Sir George Dashwood Taubman
1846-1925 *McGEWB*
Goldin, Horace 1873-1939 *DcAmB S2*
Golding, Frank Henry 1875-1941 *WhAm 1*
Golding, Jerrold R d1967 *WhAm 4*
Golding, Louis 1895-1958 *WhAm 3*
Golding, Louis Thorn 1865-1961 *WhAm 4*
Golding, Samuel H d1970 *WhAm 5*
Goldman, Albert 1882-1960 *WhAm 4*
Goldman, Alfred d1973 *WhAm 6*
Goldman, Alvin D 1881- *WhAm 6*
Goldman, Ben 1893-1961 *NatCAB 46*
Goldman, Edward Alphonse 1873- *WhAm 2*
Goldman, Edwin Franko 1878-1956 *NatCAB 41,*
WebAB, WhAm 3
Goldman, Emma 1869-1940 *AmBi, DcAmB S2,*
EncAB, McGEWB, NotAW, WebAB,
WhAm HA, WhAm 4, WhAmP
Goldman, Frank 1890-1965 *WhAm 4*
Goldman, Hetty 1881-1972 *NatCAB 56,*
WhAm 5
Goldman, L Edwin 1883-1954 *NatCAB 48*
Goldman, Leon 1905-1975 *WhAm 6*
Goldman, Maurice Harry 1906-1962 *WhAm 4*
Goldman, May W 1876- *WomWWA 14*
Goldman, Mayer C 1874-1939 *DcAmB S2,*
WhAm 1
Goldman, Morris H 1906-1973 *WhAm 6*
Goldman, Samuel P 1877- *WhAm 5*
Goldman, Solomon 1893-1953 *WhAm 3*
Goldmann, Franz 1895-1970 *WhAm 5*
Goldmark, Carl 1875-1942 *NatCAB 33*
Goldmark, Henry 1857-1941 *DcAmB S3,*
NatCAB 38
Goldmark, Josephine Clara 1877-1950 *EncAB,*

NotAW, WomWWA 14
Goldmark, Pauline Dorothea d1962 *WhAm 4,*
WhAm 5, WomWWA 14
Goldmark, Rubin 1872-1936 *DcAmB S2,*
WhAm 1
Goldner, Jacob Henry 1871- *WhAm 5*
Goldoni, Carlo 1707-1793 *McGEWB*
Goldsberry, Louise Dunham *WhAm 5*
Goldsborough, Brice J 1803-1867 *BiAUS*
Goldsborough, Brice Worthington 1859-1929
NatCAB 49
Goldsborough, Charles 1760-1834 *ApCAB*
Goldsborough, Charles 1765-1834 *BiDrAC,*
DcAmB, NatCAB 9, TwCBDA,
WhAm H, WhAmP
Goldsborough, Charles Reubell 1892-1961
NatCAB 48
Goldsborough, Charles W d1834 *BiAUS,*
Drake
Goldsborough, Charles Washington 1779-1843
ApCAB, Drake
Goldsborough, Eleonora G *WomWWA 14*
Goldsborough, John R 1808-1877 *Drake*
Goldsborough, John Roberts 1809-1877
TwCBDA
Goldsborough, John Rodgers 1808-1877 *ApCAB*
Goldsborough, Laird Shields 1902-1950
NatCAB 38, WhAm 2A, WhAm 3
Goldsborough, Louis Malesherbes 1805-1877
AmBi, ApCAB, DcAmB, Drake,
NatCAB 2, TwCBDA, WebAMB,
WhAm H
Goldsborough, Phillips Lee 1865-1946 *BiDrAC,*
NatCAB 15, WhAm 2, WhAmP
Goldsborough, Richard Francis 1871-1931
WhAm 1
Goldsborough, Robert 1733-1788 *ApCAB,*
BiAUS, BiDrAC, DcAmB, Drake,
NatCAB 4, TwCBDA, WhAm H,
WhAmP
Goldsborough, Robert 1740-1798 *TwCBDA*
Goldsborough, Robert Henry 1779-1836 *BiDrAC,*
NatCAB 7, TwCBDA, WhAm H,
WhAmP
Goldsborough, Robert Henry 1780-1836 *ApCAB*
Goldsborough, Thomas Alan 1877-1951 *BiDrAC,*
DcAmB S5, WhAm 3, WhAmP
Goldsborough, Washington Laird 1869-
WhAm 5
Goldsborough, William Winder 1875-1943
NatCAB 32
Goldsborough, Winder Elwell 1871-1957
NatCAB 45, WhAm 3
Goldsborough, Worthington 1834-1918
WhAm 1
Goldschmidt, Hans 1861-1923 *AsBiEn*
Goldschmidt, Jakob 1882-1955 *DcAmB S5,*
WhAm 3
Goldschmidt, Richard Benedict 1878-1958
DcScB, WhAm 3
Goldschmidt, Samuel Anthony 1848-1933
WhAm 1, WhAm 1C
Goldschmidt, Victor 1853-1933 *DcScB*
Goldschmidt, Victor Moritz 1888-1947 *AsBiEn,*
DcScB
Goldsmith, Alan Gustavus 1892-1961 *WhAm 4*
Goldsmith, Allen LaVern 1910-1964
NatCAB 51
Goldsmith, Anna Rowena 1863- *WomWWA 14*
Goldsmith, Brooks P d1969 *WhAm 5*
Goldsmith, Clifford 1899-1971 *WhAm 5*
Goldsmith, Deborah 1808-1836 *NewYHSD,*
WhAm H
Goldsmith, Edward 1833-1925 *NatCAB 20*
Goldsmith, Elizabeth Edwards *BiCAW*
Goldsmith, Elmer LeGrand 1891-1950
NatCAB 38
Goldsmith, Evelyn M *WomWWA 14*
Goldsmith, Goldwin 1871- *WhAm 5*
Goldsmith, Grace Arabell 1904-1975 *WhAm 6*
Goldsmith, Jonothan 1783-1847 *WhAm H*
Goldsmith, Middleton 1818-1887 *DcAmB,*
NatCAB 23, WhAm H
Goldsmith, Milton 1861-1957 *WhAm 3*
Goldsmith, Oliver 1730-1774 *McGEWB*
Goldsmith, Oliver 1794-1861 *McGEWB*
Goldsmith, Philip Hess 1897-1958 *NatCAB 44,*
WhAm 3

Goldsmith, Robert 1882-1924 *WhAm 1*
Goldsmith, William *NewYHSD*
Goldsmith, William 1890-1961 *NatCAB 45*
Goldsmith, William E *NewYHSD*
Goldsmith, William Marion 1888-1955
NatCAB 46
Goldspohn, Albert 1851-1929 *ApCAB X,*
WhAm 1
Goldstein, Benjamin Franklin 1895-1974
WhAm 6
Goldstein, Betty Naomi *WebAB*
Goldstein, Eugen 1850-1930 *DcScB*
Goldstein, Eugen 1850-1931 *AsBiEn*
Goldstein, Irving 1897- *WhAm 5*
Goldstein, J Oscar 1888-1955 *NatCAB 44*
Goldstein, Jonah J 1886-1967 *NatCAB 53*
Goldstein, Kurt 1878-1965 *NatCAB 53*
Goldstein, Louis d1965 *WhAm 4*
Goldstein, Max Aaron 1870-1941 *BiDAmEd,*
DcAmB S3, NatCAB 37, WhAm 1
Goldstein, Molse Herbert 1882-1972 *WhAm 5*
Goldstein, Samuel Landman 1910-1965
NatCAB 51
Goldstein, Sidney Emanuel 1879-1955
NatCAB 43, WhAm 3
Goldstein, Sidney Schulim 1902-1963
NatCAB 49
Goldstine, Harry 1892-1959 *WhAm 3*
Goldstock, Samuel 1902-1972 *NatCAB 57*
Goldston, Eli 1920-1974 *WhAm 6*
Goldston, Walter Leon 1894-1957 *NatCAB 43*
Goldsworthy, William Arthur 1878- *WhAm 6*
Goldthwait, G H *NewYHSD*
Goldthwait, James Walter 1880-1947 *WhAm 2*
Goldthwait, Joel Ernest 1866-1961 *NatCAB 49,*
WhAm 5
Goldthwait, Nathan Edward 1872-1918
WhAm 3
Goldthwalt, Sheldon Forrest 1905-1965
WhAm 4
Goldthwaite, Anne Wilson 1869-1944
NatCAB 39, NotAW, WhAm 2
Goldthwaite, DuVal R 1893-1954 *WhAm 3*
Goldthwaite, George 1809-1879 *ApCAB,*
BiAUS, BiDrAC, DcAmB, TwCBDA,
WhAm H
Goldthwaite, George 1810-1879 *NatCAB 4*
Goldthwaite, George Edgar 1889-1960 *WhAm 4*
Goldthwaite, Henry 1798-1847 *ApCAB*
Goldthwaite, Henry Barnes 1802-1847 *DcAmB,*
WhAm H
Goldthwaite, Lucy Virginia *AmWom*
Goldthwaite, Nellie Esther d1946 *WhAm 2*
Goldthwaite, Vere 1870- *WhAm 5*
Goldwater, Barry Morris 1909- *BiDrAC,*
EncAAH, EncAB, REnAW, WebAB
Goldwater, Barry Morris, Jr. 1938- *BiDrAC*
Goldwater, Baron M 1867-1929 *REnAW*
Goldwater, Michael 1821-1903 *REnAW*
Goldwater, Morris 1852-1939 *REnAW*
Goldwater, Richard M 1904-1971 *WhAm 5*
Goldwater, Robert 1907-1973 *WhAm 5*
Goldwater, Sigismund Schultz 1873-1942
WhAm 2
Goldwater, Sigismund Schulz 1873-1942
DcAmB S3
Goldwater, Sigismund Shulz 1873-1942
NatCAB 31
Goldwyn, Samuel 1882-1974 *McGEWB,*
WebAB, WhAm 6
Goldzier, Julia 1863- *WomWWA 14*
Goldzier, Julius 1854-1925 *BiDrAC*
Goler, Frank Hall 1866-1944 *NatCAB 34*
Goler, George W 1864-1940 *WhAm 1*
Goler, William Harvey 1846- *WhAm 4,*
WhoColR
Golgi, Camillo 1843-1926 *AsBiEn, BiHiMed,*
DcScB
Golikov, Filipp 1900- *WhWW-II*
Golitsyn, Boris Borisovich 1862-1916 *DcScB*
Goll, Frederick P, Jr. *NewYHSD*
Golladay, Edward Isaac 1830-1897 *BiDrAC,*
WhAm H
Golladay, Edward Isaac 1831-1897 *BiAUS*
Golladay, Jacob Shall 1819-1887 *BiAUS,*
BiDrAC, WhAm H
Gollings, Elling William 1878-1932 *IIBEAAW*
Gollmann, Julius d1898 *NewYHSD*

Gollomb, Joseph 1881-1950 *WhAm 3*
Golovanov, Alexander 1903- *WhWW-II*
Golovin, Nicholas Erasmus 1912-1969 *WhAm 5*
Golschmann, Vladimir 1893-1972 *WhAm 5*
Goltman, Maximilian 1867-1933 *WhAm 1*
Goltra, Edward Field 1862-1939 *WhAm 1*
Goltz, Colmar Freiherr, VonDer 1843-1916 *WhoMilH*
Goltz, Friedrich Leopold 1834-1902 *DcScB*
Golub, Jacob Joshua 1891-1953 *WhAm 3*
Gomara, Francisco Lopez De 1510-1560? *ApCAB Sup, Drake*
Gomberg, Morris 1909-1974 *WhAm 6*
Gomberg, Moses 1866-1947 *AsBiEn, DcAmB S4, DcScB, NatCAB 16, WhAm 2*
Gombert, Nicolas 1500?-1557? *McGEWB*
Gombrowicz, Witold 1904-1969 *WhAm 5*
Gomer, John R *NewYHSD*
Gomez, Antonio 1805-1876 *ApCAB*
Gomez, Antonio Carlos 1839- *ApCAB*
Gomez, Esteban 1478?-1530? *ApCAB*
Gomez, Juan Vicente 1857-1935 *McGEWB*
Gomez, Laureano 1889-1965 *WhAm 4*
Gomez, Marco Antonio 1910-1972 *IlBEAAW*
Gomez, Maximo 1836-1905 *McGEWB*
Gomez, Valentin 1774-1833 *ApCAB*
Gomez Castro, Laureano Eleuterio 1889-1965 *McGEWB*
Gomez-Farias, Valentin 1781-1858 *ApCAB*
Gomez-Moreno Martinez, Manuel 1870-1970 *WhAm 5*
Gomez-Pedraza, Manuel 1789-1851 *ApCAB*
Gomez Y Baez, Maximo 1826- *ApCAB Sup*
Gomori, George 1904-1957 *NatCAB 42*
Gomorl, Pal 1905-1973 *WhAm 6*
Gompers, Samuel 1850-1924 *AmBi, ApCAB X, DcAmB, EncAB, McGEWB, NatCAB 11, WebAB, WhAm 1, WhAmP*
Gompert, William Henry 1875-1946 *WhAm 2*
Gompertz, Benjamin 1779-1865 *DcScB*
Gompertz, Louis Michael 1872-1931 *NatCAB 24*
Gomulka, Wladislaw 1905- *McGEWB*
Gonannhatenha, Frances d1692 *ApCAB*
Gonce, John Eugene, Jr. 1893-1956 *WhAm 3*
Goncharov, Ivan Aleksandrovich 1812-1891 *McGEWB*
Goncourt, Edmond De 1822-1896 *McGEWB*
Goncourt, Jules De 1830-1870 *McGEWB*
Gondelman, Sidney 1897-1970 *WhAm 5*
Gondolfi, Monro *NewYHSD*
Gongora Y Argote, Luis De 1561-1627 *McGEWB*
Gongwer, Lillian May 1871- *WhAm 5*
Gonneville, Binot Paulmier De *ApCAB Sup*
Gons, James Walker 1812-1870 *WhAm H*
Gonsalez, Domingo *DcScB*
Gonterman, Madison Gillham 1871-1941 *NatCAB 31*
Gonzaga, G F, II, Marchese DiMantua 1466-1519 *WhoMilH*
Gonzales, Ambrose Elliott 1857-1926 *AmBi, DcAmB, WhAm 1*
Gonzales, Boyer 1874-1934 *NatCAB 24*
Gonzales, Boyer 1878-1934 *IlBEAAW*
Gonzales, Corky 1928- *REnAW*
Gonzales, Richard Alonzo 1928- *WebAB*
Gonzales, William Elliott 1866-1937 *NatCAB 28, WhAm 1*
Gonzalez, Bienvenido M 1893-1953 *WhAm 3*
Gonzalez, Francisco Javier 1760-1832 *ApCAB*
Gonzalez, Henry Barbosa 1916- *BiDrAC*
Gonzalez, Jose Maria DeJesus 1803-1875 *ApCAB*
Gonzalez, Julio 1876-1942 *McGEWB*
Gonzalez, Manuel 1820- *ApCAB*
Gonzalez, Mario Flores 1925-1973 *WhAm 6*
Gonzalez, Rosa Mangual 1895-1966 *WhAm 4*
Gonzalez, Xavier 1898- *IlBEAAW*
Gonzalez Balcarce, Antonio 1774-1819 *ApCAB*
Gonzalez DelValle, Ambrosio 1822- *ApCAB*
Gonzalez DelValle, Jose Z 1820-1851 *ApCAB*
Gonzalez DelValle, Manuel 1802-1884 *ApCAB*
Gonzalez DeSanta Cruz, Roque 1576-1628 *ApCAB*
Gonzalez Prada, Manuel 1848-1918 *McGEWB*

Gonzalez-Vigil, Francisco DePaula 1792-1876 *ApCAB*
Gonzalo DeBerceo 1195?-1252? *McGEWB*
Gooch, Cecil Milton 1888-1969 *NatCAB 55*
Gooch, D Linn 1853-1913 *WhAm 4*
Gooch, Daniel Linn 1853-1913 *BiDrAC*
Gooch, Daniel Wheelwright 1820-1891 *BiAUS, BiDrAC, TwCBDA, WhAm H*
Gooch, Fanny Chambers *AmWom*
Gooch, Frank Austin 1852-1929 *ApCAB, NatCAB 12, TwCBDA, WhAm 1*
Gooch, George Peabody 1873-1968 *McGEWB*
Gooch, Robert 1784-1830 *BiHiMed*
Gooch, Stapleton Dabney 1888-1957 *NatCAB 46*
Gooch, Tom Carbry 1880-1952 *WhAm 3*
Gooch, Sir William 1681-1751 *AmBi, ApCAB, DcAmB, Drake, NatCAB 13, WhAm H*
Good, Adolphus Clemens 1856-1894 *AmBi, DcAmB, NatCAB 23, WhAm H*
Good, Alice Campbell 1878-1956 *NatCAB 42, WhAm 3*
Good, Carter Victor 1897- *BiDAmEd*
Good, Charles Winfred 1893-1956 *NatCAB 46, WhAm 3*
Good, Daniel 1862-1922 *NatCAB 35*
Good, David Martin 1850-1919 *NatCAB 18*
Good, Edward Ellsworth 1862-1937 *WhAm 1*
Good, Edwin Stanton 1871- *WhAm 5*
Good, Fredrick Hopkins 1911-1972 *WhAm 5*
Good, George Ross 1908-1950 *NatCAB 40*
Good, Harry Gehman 1880-1971 *BiDAmEd*
Good, Harry Hoyt 1872-1940 *NatCAB 32*
Good, Herman Bennett 1866-1937 *NatCAB 28*
Good, Howard Harrison 1888-1963 *WhAm 4*
Good, Irby J 1885-1945 *WhAm 2*
Good, J Dobson 1845- *NatCAB 11*
Good, James Isaac 1850-1924 *AmBi, DcAmB, NatCAB 5, TwCBDA, WhAm 1*
Good, James William 1866-1929 *BiDrAC, BiDrUSE, NatCAB 21, WhAm 1, WhAmP*
Good, Jeremiah Haak 1822-1888 *ApCAB Sup, DcAmB, WhAm H*
Good, John 1841-1908 *AmBi, DcAmB, NatCAB 2*
Good, John Walter 1879- *WhAm 6*
Good, Lloyd Andrew 1881-1951 *NatCAB 41*
Good, Paul Francis 1893-1971 *WhAm 5*
Good, Robert Hosea 1873-1947 *NatCAB 40*
Goodacre, William *NewYHSD*
Goodale, Charles William 1854-1929 *WhAm 1*
Goodale, Dora Read 1866- *AmWom, ApCAB, NatCAB 8, TwCBDA, WhAm 4, WomWWA 14*
Goodale, Elaine 1863- *ApCAB, TwCBDA*
Goodale, George Lincoln 1839-1923 *AmBi, ApCAB, BiDAmEd, DcAmB, NatCAB 6, TwCBDA, WhAm 1*
Goodale, George Pomeroy 1843-1919 *NatCAB 18, WhAm 1*
Goodale, Grace Harriet 1872- *WomWWA 14*
Goodale, Greenleaf Austin 1839-1915 *WhAm 1*
Goodale, Hubert Dana 1879- *WhAm 6*
Goodale, Joseph Lincoln 1868- *WhAm 4, WhAm 5*
Goodale, Nathan 1741-1806 *ApCAB*
Goodale, Stephen Lincoln 1815-1897 *DcAmB, NatCAB 24, TwCBDA, WhAm H*
Goodale, Stephen Lincoln 1875-1957 *WhAm 3*
Goodall, Albert Gallatin 1826-1887 *ApCAB, NatCAB 18, NewYHSD, WhAm H*
Goodall, Charles Edward 1876- *WhAm 5*
Goodall, Edwin Baker 1882-1947 *NatCAB 37*
Goodall, Harvey L 1836-1900 *DcAmB, NatCAB 23, WhAm H*
Goodall, Louis Bertrand 1851-1935 *ApCAB X, BiDrAC, NatCAB 26, WhAm 1*
Goodall, Thomas 1823-1910 *DcAmB, NatCAB 14*
Goodar, Francis Creighton 1903-1967 *NatCAB 52*
Goodard, Edwin Charles 1865-1942 *WhAm 2*
Goodard, Luther Marcellus 1840-1917 *WhAm 1*
Goodard, Paul Beck 1811-1866 *Drake*
Goodbar, Joseph Ernest 1890-1953 *WhAm 3*
Goodbar, Luan Joy *WomWWA 14*
Goodbody, Marcus 1876-1958 *NatCAB 46*

Goodbody, Robert 1850-1911 *NatCAB 32*
Goodcell, Marion Lamson 1872- *WomWWA 14*
Goodchild, Frank Marsden 1860-1928 *NatCAB 21, WhAm 1*
Goode, Charles Thomas 1835-1875 *TwCBDA*
Goode, Clement Tyson d1943 *WhAm 2*
Goode, Flavillus Sidney 1831-1886 *TwCBDA*
Goode, George Brown 1851-1896 *AmBi, ApCAB, DcAmB, NatCAB 3, TwCBDA, WhAm H*
Goode, George William 1870- *WhAm 5*
Goode, Henry Walton 1862-1907 *ApCAB X*
Goode, James Urquhart 1873-1944 *NatCAB 34*
Goode, John 1829-1909 *AmBi, ApCAB, BiAUS, BiDConf, BiDrAC, DcAmB, NatCAB 11, TwCBDA, WhAm 1, WhAmP*
Goode, John Paul 1862-1932 *BiDAmEd, DcAmB S1, NatCAB 23, WhAm 1*
Goode, Patrick Gaines 1798-1862 *BiAUS, BiDrAC, TwCBDA, WhAm H, WhAmP*
Goode, Patrick John 1880-1969 *NatCAB 55*
Goode, Richard Livingston 1855-1927 *NatCAB 20, WhAm 1*
Goode, Richard Urquhart 1858-1903 *WhAm 1*
Goode, Robert 1743-1809 *TwCBDA*
Goode, Samuel 1756-1822 *BiAUS, BiDrAC, TwCBDA, WhAm H*
Goode, Thomas 1789-1858 *TwCBDA*
Goode, William Athelstane Meredith 1875- *WhAm 5*
Goode, William Henry 1807-1879 *TwCBDA*
Goode, William Henry Collier 1843-1923 *NatCAB 20*
Goode, William Henry Collier 1888-1948 *NatCAB 45*
Goode, William Osborne 1798-1859 *ApCAB, BiAUS, BiDrAC, TwCBDA, WhAm H, WhAmP*
Goodell, Abigail P 1799-1871 *ApCAB*
Goodell, Abner Cheney 1805-1898 *TwCBDA*
Goodell, Arthur Augustus 1839-1882 *NatCAB 20*
Goodell, Charles Ellsworth 1926- *BiDrAC*
Goodell, Charles Elmer 1862-1931 *NatCAB 22, WhAm 1*
Goodell, Charles LeRoy 1854-1937 *WhAm 1*
Goodell, Constans Liberty 1830-1886 *ApCAB Sup*
Goodell, David Harvey 1834-1915 *NatCAB 11, WhAm 1*
Goodell, George Arthur 1871-1950 *NatCAB 40*
Goodell, Henry Hill 1839-1905 *ApCAB, BiDAmEd, DcAmB, NatCAB 8, TwCBDA, WhAm 1*
Goodell, Ira C 1810?- *NewYHSD*
Goodell, Nettie Delilah 1868- *WomWWA 14*
Goodell, Raymond Batchelder 1886-1958 *WhAm 3*
Goodell, Reginald Rusden d1945 *WhAm 2*
Goodell, Reginald Rusden 1869-1944 *NatCAB 33*
Goodell, Roswell Eaton 1825-1903 *WhAm 1*
Goodell, Thomas Dwight 1854-1920 *NatCAB 19, TwCBDA, WhAm 1*
Goodell, William 1792-1867 *AmBi, ApCAB, DcAmB, Drake, NatCAB 5, TwCBDA, WhAm H*
Goodell, William 1792-1878 *AmBi, DcAmB, WhAm H, WhAmP*
Goodell, William 1829-1894 *ApCAB, NatCAB 27, TwCBDA*
Gooden, Harriet Comegys 1863- *WomWWA 14*
Gooden, Robert Burton 1874- *WhAm 6*
Goodenough, Erwin Ramsdell 1893-1965 *NatCAB 52, WhAm 4*
Goodenough, George Alfred 1868-1929 *WhAm 1*
Goodenough, Luman W 1873-1947 *WhAm 3*
Goodenow, John Milton 1782-1835 *WhAm H*
Goodenow, John Milton 1782-1838 *ApCAB, BiAUS, BiDrAC, DcAmB, Drake, NatCAB 24*
Goodenow, Robert 1800-1874 *BiAUS, BiDrAC, WhAm H*
Goodenow, Rufus King 1790-1863 *BiAUS, BiDrAC, WhAm H*
Gooderham, Melvill Ross 1877-1951 *WhAm 3*

Goodes, Edward A *NewYHSD*
Goodfellow, Edward 1828- *ApCAB, TwCBDA*
Goodfellow, Edward 1828-1894 *NatCAB 3*
Goodfellow, Edward 1828-1899 *WhAm 1*
Goodfellow, Henry 1833-1885 *ApCAB, TwCBDA*
Goodfellow, Millard Preston 1892-1973
  WhAm 6
Goodfellow, Thomas John 1884-1957
  NatCAB 45
Goodfriend, Irving Frederick 1900-1951
  NatCAB 40
Goodhand, Charles Luther 1906-1965
  NatCAB 53
Goodhartz, Abraham Samuel 1910-1973
  WhAm 6
Goodheart, William Raymond, Jr. 1902-1960
  WhAm 4
Goodhue, Benjamin 1748-1814 *ApCAB, BiAUS,*
  BiDrAC, DcAmB, Drake, NatCAB 2,
  TwCBDA, WhAm H, WhAmP
Goodhue, Bertram Grosvenor 1869-1924 *AmBi,*
  BnEnAmA, DcAmB, NatCAB 19,
  WebAB, WhAm 1
Goodhue, Edward Solon 1863- *WhAm 4*
Goodhue, Everett Walton 1878- *WhAm 6*
Goodhue, Francis Abbot 1883-1963 *WhAm 4*
Goodhue, James Madison 1810-1852 *DcAmB,*
  NatCAB 24, WhAm H
Goodhue, Jonathan 1783-1848 *ApCAB,*
  NatCAB 5
Goodhue, William Joseph 1869- *WhAm 5*
Goodier, James Norman 1905-1969 *WhAm 5*
Goodin, John Randolph 1836-1885 *BiAUS,*
  BiDrAC, WhAm H
Gooding, Edith *WomWWA 14*
Gooding, Frank Robert 1859-1928 *BiDrAC,*
  NatCAB 14, NatCAB 21, REnAW,
  WhAm 1, WhAmP
Gooding, Fred William 1856-1927 *NatCAB 21*
Gooding, William C 1775-1861 *NewYHSD*
Goodkind, Gilbert E 1913-1951 *WhAm 3*
Goodkind, Maurice Louis 1867-1939 *WhAm 1*
Goodknight, James Lincoln 1846-1914 *TwCBDA,*
  WhAm 1
Goodland, Walter Samuel 1862-1947
  NatCAB 40, WhAm 2
Goodliff, John 1828?- *NewYHSD*
Goodling, George Atlee 1896- *BiDrAC*
Goodloe, Abbie Carter 1867- *WomWWA 14*
Goodloe, Daniel Reaves 1814-1902 *DcAmB,*
  NatCAB 10, WhAm H
Goodloe, Don Speed Smith 1878- *WhAm 6,*
  WhoColR
Goodloe, William Cassius 1841-1889 *DcAmB,*
  NatCAB 7, WhAm H, WhAmP
Goodman, Abe 1864-1943 *NatCAB 34*
Goodman, Benedict Kay 1891-1962 *WhAm 4*
Goodman, Benjamin David 1909- *EncAB*
Goodman, Benny 1909- *WebAB*
Goodman, Charles 1796-1835 *DcAmB,*
  NatCAB 23, NewYHSD, WhAm H
Goodman, Charles 1871-1945 *NatCAB 32,*
  WhAm 2
Goodman, Christian *NewYHSD*
Goodman, Daniel Carson 1883-1957 *WhAm 3*
Goodman, David 1894-1971 *WhAm 5*
Goodman, David Jerome 1913-1958 *NatCAB 43*
Goodhand, Edward 1830-1911 *ApCAB X,*
  NatCAB 19
Goodman, Edwin 1876-1953 *NatCAB 47*
Goodman, Ernest Long 1892-1963 *NatCAB 55*
Goodman, Frank Bartlett 1878-1954 *WhAm 3*
Goodman, Frank Croly 1878-1958 *WhAm 3*
Goodman, George Hill 1876- *WhAm 5*
Goodman, Grace Hastings Griswold 1854-
  WomWWA 14
Goodman, Herbert Edward 1862-1917
  ApCAB X, NatCAB 17
Goodman, Herman Sidney 1910-1965
  NatCAB 51
Goodman, Jack Arthur 1908-1957 *WhAm 3*
Goodman, James E 1904-1966 *WhAm 4*
Goodman, Jean R 1870-1934 *WhAm 1*
Goodman, Jess Dee 1917-1968 *WhAm 5*
Goodman, John *NewYHSD*
Goodman, John 1837- *ApCAB, WhAm 4*
Goodman, John Forest 1891-1947 *WhAm 2*

Goodman, Jules Eckert 1876-1962 *WhAm 4*
Goodman, Kenneth Sawyer 1883-1918 *DcAmB*
Goodman, Louis Earl 1892-1961 *WhAm 4*
Goodman, Marie Louise 1871- *WomWWA 14*
Goodman, Mary Ellen 1911-1969 *WhAm 5*
Goodman, Nathan Gerson 1899-1953
  NatCAB 40, WhAm 3
Goodman, Paul 1911-1972 *WhAm 5*
Goodman, Richard Johnston 1875- *NatCAB 17*
Goodman, Robert Walter 1914-1969
  NatCAB 55
Goodman, Sylvester Jacob 1876-1945
  NatCAB 35
Goodman, Theodore 1894-1952 *NatCAB 47*
Goodman, Theodosia *WebAB*
Goodman, Thomas 1789-1872 *ApCAB X*
Goodman, Walter 1838- *ApCAB*
Goodman, William Edward 1894-1966
  NatCAB 55, WhAm 4
Goodman, William Ernest 1838-1912
  NatCAB 15
Goodman, William M 1892-1958 *WhAm 3*
Goodman, William Owen 1848-1936
  NatCAB 33, WhAm 1
Goodnight, Charles 1836-1929 *AmBi, DcAmB,*
  EncAAH, McGEWB, REnAW, WebAB,
  WhAm HA, WhAm 4
Goodnight, Cloyd 1881-1932 *WhAm 1*
Goodnight, Ella Hoy *WomWWA 14*
Goodnight, Isaac Herschel 1849-1901 *BiDrAC,*
  TwCBDA, WhAm 1, WhAmP
Goodnight, Scott Holland 1875-1972 *WhAm 5*
Goodno, William Colby *NatCAB 3, WhAm 5*
Goodnough, Robert 1917- *BnEnAmA*
Goodnough, Xanthus Henry 1860-1935
  DcAmB S1
Goodnow, Charles Allen 1853-1918 *WhAm 1*
Goodnow, David Franklin 1888-1947
  NatCAB 37
Goodnow, Frank Johnson 1859-1939 *DcAmB S2,*
  NatCAB 15, NatCAB 29, WhAm 1
Goodnow, Isaac Tichenor 1814-1894 *BiDAmEd,*
  DcAmB, NatCAB 23, TwCBDA,
  WhAm H, WhAmP
Goodnow, John 1858-1907 *WhAm 1*
Goodnow, Minnie 1871- *WhAm 5*
Goodpaster, Andrew Jackson 1915- *WebAMB*
Goodpasture, Ernest William 1886-1960
  WhAm 4
Goodpasture, Wendell Williamson 1899-1970
  WhAm 5
Goodrell, Mancil Clay 1843-1925 *WhAm 1*
Goodrich *see also* Goodridge
Goodrich, Aaron 1807-1887 *ApCAB, BiAUS,*
  NatCAB 4
Goodrich, Albert Whaling 1868-1938
  NatCAB 27
Goodrich, Alfred Bailey 1828-1896 *NatCAB 6,*
  TwCBDA
Goodrich, Alfred John 1847-1920 *DcAmB,*
  NatCAB 23, WhAm 4
Goodrich, Alice Lyman 1877- *WomWWA 14*
Goodrich, Alva Curtis 1912-1973 *WhAm 6*
Goodrich, Annie Warburton 1866-1954
  BiDAmEd, DcAmB S5, NatCAB 42,
  WhAm 3
Goodrich, Arthur Frederick 1878-1941
  NatCAB 35, WhAm 1
Goodrich, Ben 1839- *WhAm 4*
Goodrich, Ben Elmer 1900-1953 *NatCAB 43*
Goodrich, Benjamin Franklin 1841-1888 *DcAmB,*
  NatCAB 28, WhAm H
Goodrich, Carter Lyman 1897-1971 *NatCAB 57,*
  WhAm 6
Goodrich, Caspar Frederick 1847-1925
  NatCAB 13, TwCBDA, WhAm 1
Goodrich, Casper Frederick 1847-1925
  ApCAB Sup
Goodrich, Charles Augustus 1790-1862 *ApCAB,*
  DcAmB, Drake, NatCAB 23, TwCBDA,
  WhAm H
Goodrich, Charles Rush 1829-1855 *ApCAB,*
  Drake
Goodrich, Charles Tice 1846-1911 *NatCAB 16*
Goodrich, Chauncey 1759-1815 *ApCAB,*
  BiAUS, BiDrAC, DcAmB, NatCAB 2,
  TwCBDA, WhAm H, WhAmP
Goodrich, Chauncey 1798-1858 *DcAmB,*

WhAm H
Goodrich, Chauncey 1817-1868 *ApCAB*
Goodrich, Chauncey 1836-1925 *DcAmB,*
  WhAm 1
Goodrich, Chauncey Allen 1790-1860 *AmBi,*
  ApCAB, BiDAmEd, DcAmB, Drake,
  NatCAB 4, TwCBDA, WhAm H
Goodrich, Chauncey William 1864-1956
  WhAm 3
Goodrich, Clarence Allen 1894-1946
  NatCAB 39
Goodrich, David Marvin 1876-1950 *NatCAB 39,*
  WhAm 3
Goodrich, Donald Reuben 1894-1945 *WhAm 2*
Goodrich, Edgar Jennings 1896-1969 *WhAm 5*
Goodrich, Edward Shields 1868-1953
  NatCAB 46
Goodrich, Edwin Stephen 1868-1946 *DcScB*
Goodrich, Elizur 1734-1797 *ApCAB, DcAmB,*
  Drake, TwCBDA, WhAm H
Goodrich, Elizur 1761-1849 *ApCAB, BiAUS,*
  BiDrAC, DcAmB, Drake, NatCAB 4,
  TwCBDA, WhAmP
Goodrich, Elizus 1761-1849 *WhAm H*
Goodrich, Ernest Payson 1874-1955 *WhAm 3*
Goodrich, Florence Ada 1850-1928 *NatCAB 23,*
  WomWWA 14
Goodrich, Foster Edward 1908-1972 *WhAm 5*
Goodrich, Francis Lee Dewey 1877-1962
  DcAmLiB, WhAm 5
Goodrich, Frank 1856-1929 *NatCAB 21,*
  WhAm 1
Goodrich, Frank Boot 1826-1894 *Drake,*
  NatCAB 13
Goodrich, Frank Boott 1826-1894 *ApCAB,*
  DcAmB, TwCBDA, WhAm H
Goodrich, Frederick William 1867- *WhAm 4*
Goodrich, George Clement 1858-1932
  NatCAB 24
Goodrich, Hale Caldwell 1904-1968 *WhAm 5*
Goodrich, Harry Clinton 1868-1938 *NatCAB 29*
Goodrich, Henry O 1814-1834 *NewYHSD*
Goodrich, Herbert F 1889-1962 *WhAm 4*
Goodrich, Hubert Baker 1887-1963 *NatCAB 50,*
  WhAm 4
Goodrich, James Clarence 1879-1931 *WhAm 3*
Goodrich, James Edward 1871-1952 *WhAm 3*
Goodrich, James Putnam 1864-1940
  NatCAB 30, WhAm 1
Goodrich, John Ellsworth 1831-1915
  NatCAB 17, TwCBDA, WhAm 1
Goodrich, John Wallace 1871- *NatCAB 13*
Goodrich, John Z 1801-1885 *BiAUS*
Goodrich, John Zacheus 1804-1885 *BiDrAC,*
  WhAm H
Goodrich, Joseph King 1850-1921 *WhAm 1*
Goodrich, Josephine Jolley *WomWWA 14*
Goodrich, Julia Irene 1874- *WomWWA 14*
Goodrich, L Keith 1906-1968 *WhAm 5*
Goodrich, Levi *NewYHSD*
Goodrich, Levi 1822-1887 *WhAm H*
Goodrich, Lowell Pierce 1891-1949 *WhAm 2*
Goodrich, Lucien Prichard 1881-1954
  NatCAB 45
Goodrich, Lucy Leonora Hutchinson 1831-
  WomWWA 14
Goodrich, Mary Ann *ApCAB*
Goodrich, Mary Hopkins 1814- *AmWom*
Goodrich, Milo 1814-1881 *BiDrAC, WhAm H*
Goodrich, Milo 1820-1881 *BiAUS*
Goodrich, Nathaniel Lewis 1880-1957
  NatCAB 43, WhAm 3
Goodrich, Percy Edgar 1861-1951 *NatCAB 50*
Goodrich, Pierre Frist 1894-1973 *WhAm 6*
Goodrich, Ralph Dickinson 1878-1961
  NatCAB 52, WhAm 6
Goodrich, Ralph Leland 1840- *NatCAB 7,*
  WhAm 4
Goodrich, Robert Eugene 1876- *WhAm 5*
Goodrich, Samuel Griswold 1793-1860 *AmBi,*
  ApCAB, BiDAmEd, DcAmB, Drake,
  NatCAB 5, TwCBDA, WebAB,
  WhAm H
Goodrich, Sarah 1788-1853 *DcAmB*
Goodrich, Sarah B Clapp *WomWWA 14*
Goodrich, Wallace 1871-1952 *WhAm 3*
Goodrich, William Henry 1825-1874 *ApCAB*
Goodrich, William Marcellus 1777-1833 *DcAmB,*

NatCAB 23, WhAm H
Goodrich, William W 1833-1906 WhAm 1
Goodricke, John 1764-1786 AsBiEn, DcScB
Goodridge see also Goodrich
Goodridge, Eliza 1798-1882 NewYHSD
Goodridge, John 1896-1960 WhAm 4
Goodridge, Malcolm 1873-1956 NatCAB 44,
WhAm 3
Goodridge, Sarah 1788-1853 BnEnAmA,
DcAmB, NatCAB 23, NewYHSD,
NotAW, WhAm H
Goodridge, Wallace Lloyd 1840- WhoColR
Goodridge, William Marcellus 1777-1833
DcAmB
Goodrum, James Jefferson, Jr. 1879-1928
NatCAB 22
Goodsell, Charles Townsend 1880-1955
NatCAB 42
Goodsell, Charles True 1886-1941 WhAm 1,
WhAm 2
Goodsell, Daniel Ayres 1840-1909 ApCAB Sup,
DcAmB, NatCAB 13, TwCBDA,
WhAm 1
Goodsell, Fred Field 1880- WhAm 6
Goodsell, Henry Guy 1880- WhAm 6
Goodsell, Josephine Bateham WomWWA 14
Goodsell, Willystine 1870- WhAm 5
Goodsir, John 1814-1867 DcScB
Goodson, Edward Fletcher 1865- WhAm 4
Goodson, John d1727 ApCAB
Goodson, William Alexander 1888-1966
NatCAB 52
Goodspeed, Arthur Willis 1860-1943
NatCAB 15, NatCAB 32, WhAm 4
Goodspeed, Charles Barnett 1885-1947
WhAm 2
Goodspeed, Charles TenBroeke 1869-1949
NatCAB 39, WhAm 2
Goodspeed, Edgar Johnson 1871-1962
NatCAB 52, WebAB, WhAm 4
Goodspeed, Frank Lincoln 1861-1941 WhAm 1
Goodspeed, George Stephen 1860-1905
WhAm 1
Goodspeed, Thomas Harper 1887-1966
WhAm 4
Goodspeed, Thomas Wakefield 1842-1927
DcAmB, NatCAB 22, WhAm 1
Goodspeed, Walter Stuart 1902-1971 WhAm 5
Goodwane, Mrs. NewYHSD
Goodwillie, David Herrick 1887-1952
NatCAB 55, WhAm 3
Goodwillie, David Lincoln 1863-1924 WhAm 1
Goodwillie, Frank 1866-1929 NatCAB 22
Goodwin NewYHSD
Goodwin, Angier Louis 1881- BiDrAC,
WhAm 6
Goodwin, Arthur C 1874- WhAm 1
Goodwin, Cardinal B 1880-1944 REnAW,
WhAm 2
Goodwin, Charles Archibald 1876-1954
WhAm 3
Goodwin, Charles Jaques 1866-1935 WhAm 1
Goodwin, Clarence LaRue 1859-1935
NatCAB 28
Goodwin, Clarence Norton d1956 WhAm 3
Goodwin, Daniel 1799-1887 ApCAB, BiAUS
Goodwin, Daniel 1832- ApCAB, TwCBDA
Goodwin, Daniel 1835-1922 WhAm 1
Goodwin, Daniel Raynes 1811-1890 ApCAB,
DcAmB, NatCAB 1, TwCBDA,
WhAm H
Goodwin, Edward C d1930 WhAm 1
Goodwin, Edward Jasper 1848-1931 WhAm 1
Goodwin, Edward Jewett 1864-1941 WhAm 1
Goodwin, Edward McKee 1859-1937 WhAm 1
Goodwin, Edwin Weyburn 1800-1845
NewYHSD
Goodwin, Elijah 1807-1879 DcAmB, WhAm H
Goodwin, Elliot H 1874-1931 WhAm 1
Goodwin, Ernest Vance 1896-1965 WhAm 4
Goodwin, F W NewYHSD
Goodwin, Forrest 1862-1913 BiDrAC
Goodwin, Francis Marion 1871-1962
NatCAB 49, WhAm 6
Goodwin, Frank Judson 1862-1953 WhAm 3
Goodwin, Frank Perry 1882-1959 NatCAB 48
Goodwin, Frederic Jordan 1812-1872 TwCBDA
Goodwin, Frederick C 1877-1942 WhAm 2

Goodwin, George Munro 1887-1947 NatCAB 43
Goodwin, Godfrey Gummer 1873-1933 BiDrAC,
WhAm 1, WhAmP
Goodwin, Grace Duffield 1869- WhAm 5,
WomWWA 14
Goodwin, Mrs. H B AmWom
Goodwin, Hannibal Williston 1822-1900 DcAmB,
NatCAB 23, WhAm H
Goodwin, Harold 1850-1935 WhAm 1
Goodwin, Harry Manley 1870-1949 NatCAB 38,
WhAm 3
Goodwin, Henry Charles 1824-1860 BiAUS,
BiDrAC, WhAm H
Goodwin, Hilliard Edward 1883- WhoColR
Goodwin, Ichabod d1882 BiAUS
Goodwin, Ichabod 1743-1829 BiAUS, Drake
Goodwin, Ichabod 1794-1882 DcAmB,
WhAm H
Goodwin, Ichabod 1796-1882 ApCAB,
NatCAB 11, TwCBDA
Goodwin, Isaac 1786-1832 ApCAB Sup, Drake
Goodwin, J B NewYHSD
Goodwin, James Junius 1835-1915 ApCAB X,
NatCAB 17, WhAm 1
Goodwin, John Abbott 1824-1884 ApCAB Sup
Goodwin, John Benjamin 1850-1921 WhAm 1
Goodwin, John Cheever 1850-1912 WhAm 1
Goodwin, John Edward 1876-1948 DcAmLiB,
WhAm 2
Goodwin, John Noble 1824-1887 ApCAB,
BiAUS, BiDrAC, DcAmB, Drake,
NatCAB 25, WhAm H, WhAmP
Goodwin, Kathryn Dickinson 1899- WhAm 5
Goodwin, Lavina Stella 1833-1911 AmWom
Goodwin, Lavinia Stella 1833-1911 WhAm 1
Goodwin, Leo, Sr. 1886-1971 WhAm 5
Goodwin, Mark London 1871- WhAm 5
Goodwin, Mary Elizabeth DePencier 1857-
WomWWA 14
Goodwin, Maud Wilder 1856-1935 TwCBDA,
WhAm 1, WomWWA 14
Goodwin, Minnie Newington WomWWA 14
Goodwin, Nat C 1857-1919 WhAm 1
Goodwin, Nathaniel 1782-1855 ApCAB, Drake
Goodwin, Nathaniel C 1857-1919 NatCAB 6
Goodwin, Nathaniel Carl 1857-1919 ApCAB X,
TwCBDA
Goodwin, Nathaniel Carll 1857-1919 AmBi,
DcAmB
Goodwin, Peterson d1818 BiAUS
Goodwin, Philip Arnold 1882-1937 BiDrAC,
WhAm 1
Goodwin, Philip Lippincott 1885-1958 WhAm 3
Goodwin, Philip Russell 1882-1935 IIBEAAW
Goodwin, Ralph Schuyler 1839-1904
NatCAB 16
Goodwin, Ralph Schuyler 1868- NatCAB 16
Goodwin, Richard Frederick 1888-1965
NatCAB 51
Goodwin, Richard LaBarre 1840-1910
IIBEAAW, NewYHSD
Goodwin, Richard Vanderburgh 1895-1952
WhAm 3
Goodwin, Robert Eliot 1878- WhAm 6
Goodwin, Robert Kingman 1905- BiDrAC
Goodwin, Russell Parker 1851-1916 WhAm 1
Goodwin, Ruth Sharpless 1875- WomWWA 14
Goodwin, Samuel NewYHSD
Goodwin, Sarah Storer 1870- WomWWA 14
Goodwin, T Martin 1905-1959 NatCAB 48
Goodwin, Thomas NewYHSD
Goodwin, Wilder 1887-1955 WhAm 3
Goodwin, Willard T 1893-1953 WhAm 3
Goodwin, William Archer Rutherfoord
1869-1939 NatCAB 31, WhAm 1
Goodwin, William Frederick 1823-1872 ApCAB
Goodwin, William Hall 1882-1937 WhAm 1,
WhAm 1C
Goodwin, William Jesse 1853-1928 NatCAB 21
Goodwin, William N 1909- WhAm 6
Goodwin, William Shields 1866-1937 BiDrAC,
WhAmP
Goodwin, William Watson 1831-1912 AmBi,
ApCAB, BiDAmEd, DcAmB, NatCAB 6,
TwCBDA, WhAm 1
Goodwyn, Albert Taylor 1842-1931 BiDrAC
Goodwyn, Peterson 1745-1818 BiDrAC,
WhAm H, WhAmP

Goodwyn, William Adolphus 1824-1898
NatCAB 18
Goodyear, Anson Conger 1877-1964
NatCAB 52, WhAm 4
Goodyear, Charles 1800-1860 AmBi, ApCAB,
AsBiEn, DcAmB, Drake, EncAB,
McGEWB, NatCAB 3, TwCBDA,
WebAB, WhAm H
Goodyear, Charles 1804-1876 BiDrAC,
WhAm H
Goodyear, Charles 1805-1876 BiAUS
Goodyear, Charles 1833-1896 AmBi, DcAmB,
WhAm H
Goodyear, Charles Waterhouse 1846-1911
NatCAB 4, NatCAB 27, WhAm 1
Goodyear, Frank Henry 1849-1907 NatCAB 25
Goodyear, Frank Henry 1891-1930 NatCAB 47
Goodyear, Jacob Morrett 1896-1956
NatCAB 46
Goodyear, John 1912-1964 WhAm 4
Goodyear, Robert Beardsley 1835-1923
NatCAB 6
Goodyear, William Harry 1872-1941
NatCAB 35
Goodyear, William Henry 1846-1923 DcAmB,
NatCAB 19, WhAm 1
Goodykoontz, Colin Brummitt 1885-1958
REnAW, WhAm 3
Goodykoontz, Wells 1872-1944 BiDrAC,
WhAm 2
Gookin, Charles ApCAB, NatCAB 5
Gookin, Daniel 1612-1686? DcAmB
Gookin, Daniel 1612?-1687 ApCAB, Drake,
NatCAB 7, WhAm H
Gookin, Edward Richard 1882-1945
NatCAB 34
Gookin, Nathaniel 1688-1734 ApCAB
Gookin, William Stoodley 1799- NewYHSD
Gookins, James Farrington 1840-1904
IIBEAAW, NewYHSD
Gookins, Samuel Barnes 1809-1880 NatCAB 18
Goold, James 1790-1879 NatCAB 18
Goold, Marshall Newton 1881-1935 WhAm 1
Goold, Paul Philip 1875-1925 NatCAB 20
Goold, William A 1830-1912 DcAmB
Goolrick, C O'Conor 1876-1960 WhAm 4
Goolsby, Robert Edwin Moorman 1908-1963
WhAm 4
Goossens, Sir Eugene 1893-1962 WhAm 4
Gopel, Adolph 1812-1847 DcScB
Goram, Thomas NewYHSD
Gorbach, Alfons 1898-1972 WhAm 5
Gorbett, W B NewYHSD
Gorby, Paul Ford 1904-1973 WhAm 5
Gorchakov, Mikhail 1793-1861 WhoMilH
Gordan, John Dozier, Jr. 1907-1968 NatCAB 54
Gordan, Paul Albert 1837-1912 DcScB
Gordeler, Karl 1884-1945 WhWW-II
Gordin, Harry Mann 1855-1923 WhAm 1
Gordin, Jacob M 1853-1909 AmBi, DcAmB,
NatCAB 23
Gordinier, Charles H 1867- WhAm 4
Gordinier, Hermon Camp 1864- WhAm 4
Gordon NewYHSD
Gordon, Aaron David 1856-1922 McGEWB
Gordon, Adoniram Judson 1836-1895 ApCAB,
DcAmReB, NatCAB 11, TwCBDA,
WhAm H
Gordon, Albert Isaac 1903-1968 NatCAB 55
Gordon, Alexander 1692?-1754 NewYHSD
Gordon, Alfred 1874- WhAm 5
Gordon, Ambrose 1750-1804 ApCAB Sup
Gordon, Andrew 1828-1887 DcAmB,
WhAm H
Gordon, Andrew Robertson 1851- ApCAB
Gordon, Anna Adams 1853-1931 AmWom,
NotAW, WhAm 1
Gordon, Anna Adams 1863-1931
WomWWA 14
Gordon, Archibald D 1835-1895 NatCAB 3,
WhAm H
Gordon, Armistead Churchill 1855-1931
NatCAB 8, TwCBDA, WhAm 1
Gordon, Armistead Churchill, Jr. 1897-1953
NatCAB 49, WhAm 3
Gordon, Arthur Horace 1863-1938 NatCAB 38,
NatCAB 47, WhAm 1
Gordon, Bennett Taylor 1902-1957 NatCAB 49

Gordon, Charles 1890-1945 *WhAm 2*
Gordon, Charles A 1879- *WhAm 6*
Gordon, Charles George 1833-1885 *McGEWB,*
WhoMilH
Gordon, Charles Henry 1857-1934 *WhAm 1*
Gordon, Clarence 1835-1920 *ApCAB,*
NatCAB 19, TwCBDA, WhAm 4
Gordon, Clarence McCheyne 1870- *WhAm 5*
Gordon, Colin Stuart 1904-1975 *WhAm 6*
Gordon, David Russell 1896-1966 *NatCAB 53*
Gordon, David Stuart 1832-1930 *WhAm 1*
Gordon, Donald 1879-1953 *NatCAB 44*
Gordon, Donald 1901-1969 *WhAm 5*
Gordon, Dorothy d1970 *WhAm 5*
Gordon, Douglas 1876-1944 *WhAm 2*
Gordon, Douglas Huntly 1866-1918 *ApCAB X,*
NatCAB 17
Gordon, Edward Clifford 1842-1922 *TwCBDA,*
WhAm 1
Gordon, Edwin Seamer 1867-1932 *WhAm 1*
Gordon, Eleanor Elizabeth 1852- *WhAm 4,*
WomWWA 14
Gordon, Eleanor Kinzie 1835-1917 *WhAm 1,*
WomWWA 14
Gordon, Elizabeth 1865-1922 *WhAm 1*
Gordon, Elizabeth P *AmWom*
Gordon, Emma Lelia Skinner 1860-
WomWWA 14
Gordon, Ernest 1867- *WhAm 5*
Gordon, Francis 1860-1931 *WhAm 1*
Gordon, Frank Malcolm 1876-1946 *WhAm 2*
Gordon, Fred George Russ 1870- *WhAm 4*
Gordon, Frederic Sutterle 1887-1951 *WhAm 3*
Gordon, Frederick Charles 1856-1924 *WhAm 1*
Gordon, Frederick Vernon 1875- *ApCAB X*
Gordon, G Arthur 1872-1941 *NatCAB 31*
Gordon, George Anderson 1885-1959 *WhAm 3*
Gordon, George Angier 1853-1929 *DcAmB,*
DcAmReB, NatCAB 11, NatCAB 22,
TwCBDA, WhAm 1
Gordon, George Breed 1860-1927 *WhAm 1*
Gordon, George Byron 1870-1927 *AmBi,*
DcAmB, WhAm 1
Gordon, George C 1872-1964 *WhAm 4*
Gordon, George Henry 1823-1886 *AmBi,*
DcAmB, WhAm H
Gordon, George Henry 1824-1886 *NatCAB 3,*
TwCBDA
Gordon, George Henry 1825-1886 *ApCAB,*
Drake
Gordon, George Phineas 1810-1878 *ApCAB,*
DcAmB, NatCAB 5, WhAm H
Gordon, George Washington 1836-1911 *BiDrAC,*
DcAmB, NatCAB 8, WhAm 1, WhAmP
Gordon, George William d1865 *ApCAB*
Gordon, Gordon 1874-1933 *NatCAB 32*
Gordon, Gurdon Wright 1871-1959 *WhAm 3*
Gordon, Harry Brace 1872-1954 *NatCAB 40*
Gordon, Hirsch Loeb 1896-1969 *NatCAB 54,*
WhAm 5
Gordon, Irwin Leslie 1888-1954 *WhAm 3*
Gordon, Isaac G 1819-1893 *NatCAB 13*
Gordon, J Riely 1863-1937 *NatCAB 28*
Gordon, J Wright 1807-1853 *NatCAB 5*
Gordon, Jacques d1948 *WhAm 2*
Gordon, James 1739-1810 *BiAUS, BiDrAC,*
WhAm H
Gordon, James 1833-1912 *BiDrAC, DcAmB,*
WhAm 1
Gordon, Sir James Alexander 1782?-1869
ApCAB, Drake
Gordon, James Bentley *Drake*
Gordon, James Byron 1822-1864 *BiDConf*
Gordon, James D d1872 *ApCAB*
Gordon, James Herndon 1868-1936 *WhAm 1*
Gordon, James Logan 1858-1930 *WhAm 1*
Gordon, James Marcus 1875-1951 *WhAm 3*
Gordon, James Waddell 1869-1952 *NatCAB 38*
Gordon, James Wright 1809-1853 *TwCBDA*
Gordon, Jean Margaret 1865-1931 *NotAW*
Gordon, John 1850-1923 *WhAm 1*
Gordon, John 1878-1956 *WhAm 3*
Gordon, John Brown 1832-1904 *AmBi, ApCAB,*
ApCAB X, BiAUS, BiDConf, BiDrAC,
DcAmB, McGEWB, NatCAB 1,
TwCBDA, WebAMB, WhAm 1, WhAmP
Gordon, John G *NewYHSD*
Gordon, John Weaver 1878-1944 *NatCAB 41*

Gordon, John Wotton 1847-1928 *NatCAB 30*
Gordon, Jonathan W 1820-1887 *NatCAB 18*
Gordon, Joseph Claybaugh 1842-1903 *TwCBDA,*
WhAm 1
Gordon, Julien d1920 *WhAm 1*
Gordon, Kate M 1861-1932 *NotAW*
Gordon, Laura DeForce 1838-1907 *AmBi,*
DcAmB, NatCAB 2, NotAW,
WhAm HA, WhAm 4, WhAmP
Gordon, Laura DeForce 1840-1907 *AmWom*
Gordon, Leon 1889-1943 *WhAm 2*
Gordon, Louis 1914-1966 *WhAm 4*
Gordon, Lyman Francis 1861-1914 *NatCAB 18*
Gordon, M Lafayette 1843-1900 *WhAm 1*
Gordon, Mack 1904-1959 *NatCAB 44*
Gordon, Mackenzie 1869-1943 *NatCAB 39*
Gordon, Margaret 1868- *WhAm 4*
Gordon, Margaret Blair 1861- *WomWWA 14*
Gordon, Marshall Peterson, Jr. 1904-1948
NatCAB 37
Gordon, Merritt James 1857-1925 *NatCAB 12,*
TwCBDA, WhAm 4
Gordon, Merritt James 1859-1925 *NatCAB 25*
Gordon, Nathan Harry 1872-1938 *NatCAB 29*
Gordon, Neil Elbridge 1886-1949 *WhAm 2*
Gordon, Ney Kingsley 1904-1962 *WhAm 4*
Gordon, Onslow Allen 1887-1948 *NatCAB 36*
Gordon, Patrick 1644-1736 *AmBi, ApCAB,*
Drake, NatCAB 2
Gordon, Peter *NewYHSD*
Gordon, Peter Benjamin 1907-1973 *WhAm 6*
Gordon, Peyton 1870-1946 *WhAm 2*
Gordon, Ray P 1904-1972 *WhAm 5*
Gordon, Richard Sammons 1931-1973 *WhAm 5*
Gordon, Robert 1875-1951 *WhAm 3*
Gordon, Robert Bryarly 1855-1923 *BiDrAC*
Gordon, Robert Greer 1879-1938 *NatCAB 28*
Gordon, Robert Loudon 1874-1946 *WhAm 2*
Gordon, S Anna 1832- *AmWom*
Gordon, S D 1859-1936 *WhAm 1*
Gordon, Samuel 1802-1873 *BiAUS, BiDrAC,*
WhAm H
Gordon, Seth Chase 1830-1921 *NatCAB 12,*
WhAm 1
Gordon, Seth Reed 1852-1929 *NatCAB 26*
Gordon, Sophia Park 1856- *WomWWA 14*
Gordon, Thomas d1722 *ApCAB, Drake,*
NatCAB 12
Gordon, Thomas Christian 1867-1929
NatCAB 21
Gordon, Thomas F 1787-1860 *ApCAB, Drake*
Gordon, Thomas F 1789-1860 *NatCAB 3*
Gordon, Thomas Robert 1854-1929 *NatCAB 25*
Gordon, Thomas Sylvy 1893-1959 *BiDrAC,*
WhAm 3, WhAmP
Gordon, Thurlow Marshall 1884-1975 *WhAm 6*
Gordon, Walter 1893-1940 *DcScB*
Gordon, Walter Henry 1863-1924 *NatCAB 21,*
WhAm 1
Gordon, Walter Scott 1848-1886 *NatCAB 2*
Gordon, Wilbur Clarance 1879- *WhoColR*
Gordon, William 1728-1807 *DcAmB,*
WhAm H
Gordon, William 1730-1807 *ApCAB, Drake,*
NatCAB 10
Gordon, William 1763-1802 *BiAUS, BiDrAC,*
TwCBDA, WhAm H
Gordon, William 1862-1942 *BiDrAC, WhAm 1,*
WhAm 2, WhAmP
Gordon, William Duncan 1892-1961
NatCAB 50, WhAm 4
Gordon, William Fitzhugh 1787-1858 *BiAUS,*
BiDrAC, DcAmB, NatCAB 8, TwCBDA,
WhAm H
Gordon, William Knox 1862-1949 *NatCAB 38,*
WhAm 2
Gordon, William Lawrence Sanford 1870-
WhAm 5
Gordon, William Robert 1811-1897 *ApCAB,*
NatCAB 5, TwCBDA, WhAm H
Gordon, William St. Clair 1858-1924 *WhAm 1*
Gordon, William Washington 1796-1842
ApCAB Sup, DcAmB, WhAm H
Gordon, William Washington 1834-1912
ApCAB Sup, NatCAB 15, TwCBDA,
WhAm 1
Gordon-Cummings, Constance Frederica
1837-1924 *IlBEAAW*

Gordon-Davis, Alfred Burwell 1872- *WhAm 5*
Gordy, Charles Burton 1893-1966 *NatCAB 48*
Gordy, John Pancoast 1851-1908 *BiDAmEd,*
DcAmB, WhAm 1
Gordy, Wilbur Fisk 1854-1929 *BiDAmEd,*
NatCAB 21, TwCBDA, WhAm 1
Gordy, William Sidney, Jr. 1873-1950
NatCAB 39
Gore, Albert Arnold 1907- *BiDrAC*
Gore, Christopher 1758-1827 *AmBi, ApCAB,*
BiAUS, BiDrAC, Drake, NatCAB 1,
TwCBDA, WhAm H
Gore, Claude 1878-1944 *WhAm 3*
Gore, Elbert Brutus 1867- *WhAm 4*
Gore, F Porter 1885-1960 *NatCAB 48*
Gore, George 1826-1908 *DcScB*
Gore, Herbert Charles 1877- *WhAm 5*
Gore, Howard Mason 1877-1947 *BiDrUSE,*
EncAAH, NatCAB 35
Gore, Howard Mason 1887-1947 *WhAm 2*
Gore, James Howard 1856- *NatCAB 12,*
TwCBDA, WhAm 4
Gore, John 1718-1796 *NewYHSD*
Gore, John Christopher *NewYHSD*
Gore, John Kinsey 1864-1943 *NatCAB 14,*
NatCAB 32, WhAm 2
Gore, Joshua *NewYHSD*
Gore, Joshua Walker 1852- *WhAm 1*
Gore, Quentin Pryor 1909-1967 *WhAm 4*
Gore, Ralph *NewYHSD*
Gore, Robert Hayes 1886-1972 *WhAm 6*
Gore, Samuel 1750?-1831 *NewYHSD*
Gore, Thomas Edwin 1888-1966 *NatCAB 53*
Gore, Thomas Pryor 1870-1949 *ApCAB X,*
BiDrAC, DcAmB S4, NatCAB 14,
NatCAB 36, REnAW, WhAm 2,
WhAmP
Gore, W A 1874-1928 *WhAm 1*
Goren, Charles Henry 1901- *WebAB*
Gorgas, Ferdinand James Samuel 1835-
TwCBDA, WhAm 4
Gorgas, Josiah 1818-1883 *ApCAB, BiDConf,*
DcAmB, McGEWB, NatCAB 12,
TwCBDA, WebAB, WebAMB, WhAm H
Gorgas, William Crawford 1854-1920 *AmBi,*
ApCAB X, AsBiEn, BiHiMed, DcAmB,
McGEWB, NatCAB 14, NatCAB 32,
WebAB, WebAMB, WhAm 1
Gorgeous George 1915?-1963 *WebAB*
Gorges, Sir Ferdinando d1647 *Drake*
Gorges, Sir Ferdinando 1565?-1647 *ApCAB,*
NatCAB 5, WhAm H
Gorges, Sir Ferdinando 1566?-1647 *AmBi*
Gorges, Sir Ferdinando 1568-1647 *McGEWB*
Gorges, Ferdinando 1629-1718 *ApCAB, Drake*
Gorgey, Arthur 1818-1916 *DcScB*
Gorgias 480?BC-376?BC *McGEWB*
Gorham, Benjamin 1775-1855 *ApCAB, BiAUS,*
BiDrAC, Drake, TwCBDA, WhAm H,
WhAmP
Gorham, Charles F *BiAUS Sup*
Gorham, Charles T 1812-1901 *NatCAB 7*
Gorham, Fred P *NewYHSD*
Gorham, Frederic Poole 1871-1933 *NatCAB 23,*
WhAm 1
Gorham, George Congdon 1832-1909 *BiAUS,*
WhAm 1
Gorham, George Elmer 1850- *NatCAB 12*
Gorham, Jabez 1792-1869 *DcAmB,*
NatCAB 23, WhAm H
Gorham, John 1709-1752? *ApCAB Sup*
Gorham, John 1783-1829 *ApCAB, DcAmB,*
Drake, NatCAB 12, TwCBDA, WhAm H
Gorham, Kate Foster 1860- *WomWWA 14*
Gorham, L Whittington 1885-1968 *NatCAB 56*
Gorham, Nathaniel d1826 *ApCAB*
Gorham, Nathaniel 1738-1796 *ApCAB, BiAUS,*
BiDrAC, BiDrUSE, DcAmB, Drake,
NatCAB 2, TwCBDA, WebAB,
WhAm H, WhAmP
Gorham, Nathaniel 1869-1931 *NatCAB 36*
Gorham, Shubael 1686-1746 *ApCAB Sup*
Gorham, Willett Noble 1909-1967 *NatCAB 53*
Gori, Ottaviano *NewYHSD*
Gorin, Orville B 1849-1935 *WhAm 1*
Goring, Hermann Wilhelm 1893-1946
McGEWB
Gorky, Arshile 1904-1948 *BnEnAmA,*

DcAmB S4, WebAB

Gorky, Arshile 1905-1948 *McGEWB, WhAm 4*

Gorky, Maxim 1868-1936 *McGEWB*

Gorman, Arthur Pue 1829-1906 *AmBi*

Gorman, Arthur Pue 1839-1906 *ApCAB, BiDrAC, DcAmB, EncAAH, NatCAB 1, TwCBDA, WhAm 1, WhAmP*

Gorman, Arthur Pue, Jr. 1873-1919 *WhAm 1*

Gorman, Charles Edmund 1844-1917 *WhAm 1*

Gorman, Cora Peticolas *WomWWA 14*

Gorman, Daniel M d1927 *WhAm 1*

Gorman, David *NewYHSD*

Gorman, Douglas 1882-1945 *NatCAB 34*

Gorman, Eugene John 1898-1971 *NatCAB 57*

Gorman, Eugene Judson Barney 1892-1965 *NatCAB 52*

Gorman, George Edmond 1873-1935 *WhAm 1*

Gorman, George Edmund 1873-1935 *BiDrAC*

Gorman, Grace Norris *WomWWA 14*

Gorman, Herbert Sherman 1893-1954 *NatCAB 42, WhAm 3*

Gorman, James Edward 1863-1943 *WhAm 2*

Gorman, James O *NewYHSD*

Gorman, James Sedgwick 1850-1923 *BiDrAC, TwCBDA*

Gorman, John Berry 1793-1864 *ApCAB*

Gorman, John Jerome 1883-1949 *BiDrAC*

Gorman, Joseph Vincent 1903-1969 *NatCAB 55*

Gorman, Lawrence Clifton 1898-1952 *WhAm 3*

Gorman, Michael Arthur 1892-1958 *WhAm 3*

Gorman, Robert Nestor 1896-1962 *WhAm 4*

Gorman, Thomas J d1972 *WhAm 5*

Gorman, William Henry 1843-1915 *NatCAB 32*

Gorman, Willis Arnold 1814-1876 *ApCAB, BiAUS, Drake, NatCAB 4, NatCAB 10, TwCBDA*

Gorman, Willis Arnold 1816-1876 *BiDrAC, DcAmB, WhAm H, WhAmP*

Gorostiza, Jose 1901-1973 *WhAm 5*

Gorostiza, Manuel Eduardo De 1789-1851 *ApCAB*

Gorrell, Edgar Staley 1891-1945 *DcAmB S3, NatCAB 34, WhAm 2*

Gorrell, Emilie C 1883- *WomWWA 14*

Gorrell, Faith Lanman 1881- *WhAm 6*

Gorrie, John 1803-1854 *NatCAB 15*

Gorrie, John 1803-1855 *ApCAB Sup, BiHiMed, DcAmB, EncAAH, WebAB, WhAm H*

Gorrie, Peter Douglas 1813-1884 *ApCAB, TwCBDA*

Gorrie, Peter Douglass 1813-1884 *NatCAB 3*

Gorrill, William Henry 1872-1961 *NatCAB 50*

Gorringe, Henry Honeychurch 1841-1885 *ApCAB, DcAmB, NatCAB 6, TwCBDA, WhAm H*

Gorriti, Jose Ygnacio 1770-1835 *ApCAB*

Gorshire, William R *BiAUS*

Gorski, Chester Charles 1906- *BiDrAC*

Gorski, Martin 1886-1949 *BiDrAC, WhAm 2, WhAmP*

Gorson, Herbert Hillel 1915-1958 *NatCAB 47*

Gorsuch, Ralph 1875-1957 *NatCAB 47*

Gort, John S S P Vereker, Viscount 1886-1946 *WhWW-II, WhoMilH*

Gortatowsky, Jacob Dewey 1885-1964 *WhAm 4*

Gorter, Nathan R 1860-1918 *ApCAB X*

Gorthy, Willis Charles 1908-1960 *WhAm 4*

Gortner, Ross Aiken 1885-1942 *DcAmB S3, NatCAB 33, WhAm 2*

Gorton, Cynthia M R 1826- *AmWom*

Gorton, David Allyn 1832- *WhAm 4*

Gorton, Eliot 1863-1917 *WhAm 1*

Gorton, George 1865- *ApCAB X*

Gorton, Othniel 1718-1797 *NatCAB 13*

Gorton, Samuel 1592?-1677 *AmBi, DcAmB*

Gorton, Samuel 1593-1677 *WhAm H*

Gorton, Samuel 1600?-1677 *ApCAB, Drake, NatCAB 7*

Gorton, Samuell 1592?-1677 *McGEWB*

Gorton, William Edward 1854-1933 *NatCAB 27*

Gorvett, Edmund Arthur 1906-1962 *NatCAB 49*

Gory, Emanuel G *NewYHSD*

Gory, Robert Earl 1891-1974 *WhAm 6*

Gosden, Freeman Fisher 1899- *WebAB*

Gose, J Gordon 1904-1963 *NatCAB 51*

Gose, Mack F 1859- *WhAm 3*

Gose, Thomas Phelps 1901-1970 *WhAm 5*

Gosford, Archibald Acheson 1775-1849 *ApCAB*

Goshen, Elmer Isaac 1872-1941 *WhAm 1*

Goshirakawa 1127-1192 *McGEWB*

Goshorn, Alfred Traber 1833-1902 *NatCAB 25, TwCBDA, WhAm 1*

Goshorn, Clarence Baker 1893-1949 *WhAm 3*

Goshorn, Edwin Clarence 1844-1924 *NatCAB 25*

Goshorn, Lenore Rhyno 1893-1959 *WhAm 3*

Goshorn, Robert Charles 1890-1953 *NatCAB 40, WhAm 3*

Goslee, Hart John 1871-1930 *WhAm 1*

Gosline, William A, Jr. 1873-1947 *WhAm 2*

Gosling, Glenn Donald 1909-1974 *WhAm 6*

Gosling, Joseph Woodley 1879-1938 *NatCAB 29*

Gosling, Thomas Warrington 1872-1940 *WhAm 1*

Gosnell, Cullen Bryant 1893-1963 *NatCAB 50*

Gosnell, John Ansley 1901-1969 *WhAm 5*

Gosney, Ezra Seymour 1855-1942 *NatCAB 31, WhAm 2*

Gosnold, Bartholomew d1607 *AmBi, ApCAB, DcAmB, Drake, NatCAB 12, WebAB, WhAm H*

Goss, Albert Simon 1882-1950 *DcAmB S4, WhAm 3*

Goss, Arthur 1866- *WhAm 4*

Goss, Audrey 1880- *WomWWA 14*

Goss, Bert Crawford 1907-1971 *NatCAB 56, WhAm 5*

Goss, Charles Albert 1863-1938 *NatCAB 30, WhAm 1*

Goss, Charles Carpenter 1871-1915 *NatCAB 17*

Goss, Charles Frederic 1852- *WhAm 1*

Goss, Chauncey P 1903-1964 *WhAm 4*

Goss, Chauncey Porter 1838-1918 *WhAm 1*

Goss, Edward Otis 1865-1938 *WhAm 1*

Goss, Edward Wheeler 1893- *BiDrAC*

Goss, Elbridge Henry 1830-1908 *WhAm 1*

Goss, Evan Benson 1872-1930 *WhAm 1*

Goss, Francis Webster 1842-1923 *WhAm 1*

Goss, Frederick Llewellyn 1847-1914 *NatCAB 18*

Goss, Harvey Theo 1900-1959 *WhAm 3*

Goss, Helen Louise *WomWWA 14*

Goss, James Hamilton 1820-1886 *BiAUS, BiDrAC*

Goss, James Walker 1812-1870 *DcAmB, NatCAB 25*

Goss, John Henry 1872-1944 *WhAm 2*

Goss, Nathaniel Stickney 1826-1891 *WhAm H*

Goss, Robert Whitmore 1891-1970 *WhAm 5*

Goss, Samuel G 1859- *WhAm 1*

Goss, Stanley Thomas 1884-1949 *NatCAB 38*

Goss, Warren Lee 1835-1925 *WhAm 1*

Goss, William Freeman Myrick 1859-1928 *NatCAB 20, WhAm 1*

Goss, William Middlebrook d1962 *WhAm 4*

Goss, Winifred Lane 1875- *WomWWA 14*

Gossard, Frank Phillip 1900-1950 *NatCAB 39*

Gossard, George Daniel 1868-1932 *NatCAB 26, WhAm 1*

Gossard, Harry Clinton 1884-1954 *WhAm 3*

Gosse, Philip Henry 1810- *ApCAB, Drake*

Gosselet, Jules-Auguste 1832-1916 *DcScB*

Gosser, Frank Israel 1865- *NatCAB 5*

Gossett, Alfred Newton 1861-1943 *WhAm 2*

Gossett, Benjamin Brown 1884-1951 *DcAmB S5, NatCAB 49, WhAm H*

Gossett, Charles Clinton 1888- *BiDrAC*

Gossett, Earl J 1887-1962 *WhAm 4*

Gossett, Ed Lee 1902- *BiDrAC*

Gossett, John Taylor 1896-1966 *WhAm 4*

Gossett, Ralph 1890-1963 *NatCAB 51*

Gossett, Robert Kenneth 1921-1967 *WhAm 5*

Gossett, William Sealy 1876-1937 *DcScB*

Gossler, Philip Green 1870-1945 *WhAm 2*

Gostelowe, Jonathan 1744-1795 *DcAmB, WhAm H*

Goszoler *NewYHSD*

Gotbut, Edward *NewYHSD*

Gotfredson, Benjamin 1863-1938 *NatCAB 34*

Goto, Joseph 1920- *BnEnAmA*

Gotsch, Arthur Edward 1900-1966 *WhAm 5*

Gotshal, Sylvan 1897- *WhAm 5*

Gotshalk, Dilman Water 1901- *WhAm 6*

Gotshall, William Charles 1870-1935 *DcAmB S1, NatCAB 26*

Gotshall, William Charles 1875-1935 *WhAm 1*

Gott, Charles 1887-1938 *WhAm 1*

Gott, Daniel 1794-1864 *BiAUS, BiDrAC, WhAm H*

Gott, Edgar Nathaniel 1887-1947 *NatCAB 36, WhAm 2*

Gott, John 1785-1860 *NewYHSD*

Gott, William Strafer 1897-1942 *WhWW-II*

Gott, William Thomas 1855-1933 *WhAm 1*

Gott, Winson Gilbert 1873-1928 *NatCAB 23*

Gottesman, D Samuel d1956 *WhAm 3*

Gottfried VonStrassburg 1165?-1215? *McGEWB*

Gottfried, Alexander *NewYHSD*

Gottfried, Anton 1862- *NatCAB 16*

Gottfried, Emil Henry 1898-1953 *NatCAB 44*

Gottfried, Louis Elio 1892-1970 *WhAm 5*

Gottheil, Gustav 1827-1903 *AmBi, DcAmB, TwCBDA*

Gottheil, Gustave 1827-1903 *ApCAB Sup, WhAm 1*

Gottheil, Richard James Horatio 1862-1936 *AmBi, DcAmB S2, NatCAB 14, WhAm 1*

Gottheil, William Samuel 1859- *WhAm 4*

Gotthold, Arthur Frederick 1879-1951 *NatCAB 40*

Gotthold, Florence Wolf 1858- *WomWWA 14*

Gottlieb, Abraham 1837-1894 *NatCAB 20*

Gottlieb, Adolph 1903-1974 *BnEnAmA, EncAB, WhAm 6*

Gottlieb, James E 1924-1975 *WhAm 6*

Gottlieb, Polly Rose d1971 *WhAm 6*

Gottschalk, Alfred 1894-1973 *WhAm 6*

Gottschalk, Alfred L Moreau 1873-1918 *WhAm 1*

Gottschalk, Louis 1899-1975 *WhAm 6*

Gottschalk, Louis Ferdinand 1868- *WhAm 4*

Gottschalk, Louis Moreau 1829-1869 *AmBi, ApCAB, DcAmB, Drake, McGEWB, TwCBDA, WebAB, WhAm H*

Gottschall, Morton 1894-1968 *WhAm 5*

Gottschall, Oscar M 1843- *WhAm 4*

Gottscho, Ira 1913-1971 *NatCAB 55*

Gottwald, Donald 1895-1953 *NatCAB 45*

Gottwald, Klement 1896-1953 *WhAm 3*

Gotwald, Luther Alexander 1833- *ApCAB, NatCAB 10*

Gotwald, Luther Alexander 1898-1966 *WhAm 4*

Gotwals, J Elmer 1882-1958 *NatCAB 46*

Gotwals, John C 1884-1946 *WhAm 3*

Gotzian, Conrad 1835-1887 *NatCAB 7*

Gotzsche, Kai G 1886- *IIBEAAW*

Goucher, John Franklin 1845-1922 *AmBi, BiDAmEd, DcAmB, NatCAB 3, NatCAB 24, WhAm 1*

Goudimel, Claude 1514?-1572 *McGEWB*

Goudkoff, Paul Pavel 1880-1955 *NatCAB 44*

Goudsmit, Samuel Abraham 1902- *AsBiEn*

Goudy, Alexander Kirkpatrick 1847-1906 *NatCAB 17*

Goudy, Frank Burris 1881-1944 *NatCAB 34, WhAm 2*

Goudy, Franklin Curtis 1852-1924 *NatCAB 33, WhAm 1*

Goudy, Frederic William 1865-1947 *DcAmB S4, NatCAB 33, WebAB, WhAm 2*

Goudy, William Charles 1824-1893 *DcAmB, NatCAB 16, WhAm H*

Gougar, Helen Mar Jackson 1843-1907 *AmWom, NotAW, WhAm 1*

Gouge, William M 1796-1863 *ApCAB, DcAmB, Drake, NatCAB 24, WhAm H*

Gougelmann, Pierre 1877-1963 *NatCAB 48*

Gough, Emile Jefferson 1889-1947 *WhAm 2*

Gough, Sir Hubert DeLaPoer 1870-1963 *WhoMilH*

Gough, Hugh 1779-1869 *WhoMilH*

Gough, John B 1817-1886 *Drake*

Gough, John Bartholemew 1817-1886 *TwCBDA*

Gough, John Bartholomew 1817-1886 *AmBi, ApCAB, DcAmB, NatCAB 3, WhAm H*

Gough, Lewis Ketcham 1908-1967 *WhAm 4*

Gough, Robert E d1973 *WhAm 5*

Gouinlock, William Chalk 1844-1914 *NatCAB 15*

Goujon, Jean 1510?-1568? *McGEWB*
Goulard, David *NewYHSD*
Goulart, Joao 1918- *McGEWB*
Gould, Albert Trowbridge 1885-1947 *NatCAB 38*
Gould, Alice Bache *WomWWA 14*
Gould, Anna Laura 1875- *WhAm 5*
Gould, Annie Westbrook 1844- *WomWWA 14*
Gould, Arthur Robinson 1857-1946 *BiDrAC, WhAm 2*
Gould, Ashley Mulgrave 1859-1921 *NatCAB 19, WhAm 1*
Gould, Augustus Addison 1805-1866 *AmBi, ApCAB, DcAmB, DcScB, Drake, NatCAB 3, TwCBDA*
Gould, Augustus Addison 1805-1886 *WhAm H*
Gould, Benjamin 1751-1841 *ApCAB, TwCBDA*
Gould, Benjamin Apthorp 1787-1859 *ApCAB, BiDAmEd, DcAmB, NatCAB 3, TwCBDA*
Gould, Benjamin Apthorp 1824-1896 *AmBi, ApCAB, DcAmB, DcScB, Drake, NatCAB 5, TwCBDA, WhAm H*
Gould, Carl Frelinghuysen 1873-1939 *WhAm 1*
Gould, Charles Albert 1849-1926 *ApCAB X, NatCAB 12, NatCAB 21*
Gould, Charles Duren 1807-1875 *ApCAB*
Gould, Charles Henry 1855-1919 *DcAmLiB*
Gould, Charles Newton 1868-1949 *WhAm 2*
Gould, Charles Winthrop 1849-1931 *WhAm 1*
Gould, Chester 1900- *WebAB*
Gould, Clarence Pembroke 1884-1971 *NatCAB 57, WhAm 5*
Gould, Cora Smith *BiCAW*
Gould, Edward Sherman 1805-1885 *DcAmB*
Gould, Edward Sherman 1808-1885 *ApCAB, Drake, NatCAB 4, TwCBDA*
Gould, Edward Sherman 1837-1905 *WhAm 1*
Gould, Edward Shuman 1805-1885 *WhAm H*
Gould, Edwin 1866-1933 *ApCAB Sup, NatCAB 24, WhAm 1*
Gould, Edwin Miner Lawrence 1886-1952 *WhAm 3*
Gould, Edwin Sprague 1844- *WhAm 1*
Gould, Elgin Ralston Lovell 1860-1915 *DcAmB, NatCAB 23, TwCBDA, WhAm 1*
Gould, Elizabeth Lincoln d1914 *WhAm 1, WomWWA 14*
Gould, Elizabeth Porter 1848- *AmWom*
Gould, Ellen M 1848- *AmWom*
Gould, Emily Bliss 1825-1875 *ApCAB*
Gould, Everett Willoughby 1873-1937 *NatCAB 30*
Gould, Ezra Palmer 1841-1900 *TwCBDA, WhAm 1*
Gould, Frank 1873-1960 *WhAm 4*
Gould, Frank Horace 1856-1918 *NatCAB 20, WhAm 1*
Gould, Frank Jay 1877-1956 *WhAm 3*
Gould, Frank Miller 1899-1945 *WhAm 2*
Gould, Franklin Pierce 1853-1916 *NatCAB 17*
Gould, Frederic Alvah 1852- *NatCAB 14*
Gould, George *NewYHSD*
Gould, George 1807-1868 *ApCAB Sup, NatCAB 2*
Gould, George 1811-1868 *BiAUS*
Gould, George Higginson Barker 1933-1971 *NatCAB 57*
Gould, George Jay 1864-1923 *AmBi, ApCAB Sup, DcAmB, NatCAB 13, WhAm 1*
Gould, George Milbry 1848-1922 *AmBi, DcAmB, NatCAB 10, WhAm 1*
Gould, Grace Margaret *WomWWA 14*
Gould, Hannah Flagg 1789-1865 *AmBi, ApCAB, DcAmB, Drake, NatCAB 8, WhAm H*
Gould, Harris Perley 1871-1946 *WhAm 2*
Gould, Harry 1869-1945 *NatCAB 34, WhAm 2*
Gould, Harry Edward 1898-1971 *NatCAB 57, WhAm 5*
Gould, Helen Miller 1868- *ApCAB Sup, NatCAB 13, TwCBDA, WomWWA 14*
Gould, Henry E 1908-1965 *NatCAB 52*
Gould, Henry William 1882-1951 *NatCAB 44*
Gould, Herman Day 1799-1852 *BiDrAC, WhAm H*

Gould, Howard 1867-1938 *WhAm 1*
Gould, James 1770-1838 *AmBi, ApCAB, BiAUS, BiDAmEd, DcAmB, Drake, NatCAB 19, WhAm H*
Gould, Jason *WebAB*
Gould, Jay 1836-1892 *AmBi, ApCAB, ApCAB X, DcAmB, EncAB, McGEWB, NatCAB 7, REnAW, TwCBDA, WebAB, WhAm H*
Gould, John 1804-1881 *DcScB*
Gould, John Stanton 1810-1874 *ApCAB*
Gould, John W 1814-1838 *ApCAB*
Gould, Joseph Edmund 1911- *EncAAH*
Gould, Kenneth Miller 1895-1969 *WhAm 5*
Gould, Kingdon 1887-1945 *NatCAB 49, WhAm 2*
Gould, Laura Stedman 1881- *WhAm 1*
Gould, Marion Josephine White 1845- *WomWWA 14*
Gould, Mary Hurst 1868- *WomWWA 14*
Gould, Moses Joseph 1887-1958 *WhAm 4*
Gould, Nathaniel Duren 1781-1864 *ApCAB, DcAmB, NatCAB 7, WhAm H*
Gould, Norman Judd 1877-1964 *BiDrAC, NatCAB 54, WhAm 4, WhAm 5*
Gould, Ralph Albert 1892-1958 *NatCAB 48*
Gould, Robert Simonton 1826-1904 *DcAmB, NatCAB 4*
Gould, Samuel Wadsworth 1852-1935 *BiDrAC, WhAm 1*
Gould, Theodore A *NewYHSD*
Gould, Theodore Pennock 1901-1962 *WhAm 4*
Gould, Thomas Ridgeway 1818-1881 *AmBi, BnEnAmA, DcAmB, NatCAB 1, NatCAB 8, NewYHSD, TwCBDA, WhAm H*
Gould, Walter 1829-1893 *ApCAB, NewYHSD, TwCBDA*
Gould, Will Daniel 1845- *ApCAB X*
Gould, William Edward 1867-1958 *WhAm 3*
Gould, William Henry Gulick 1869-1933 *NatCAB 25*
Gould, William Jonathan 1867-1925 *NatCAB 22*
Gould, William Stocking 1876-1955 *NatCAB 43*
Goulden, Edward Lewis 1857-1915 *NatCAB 17*
Goulden, Joseph Aloysius 1844-1915 *BiDrAC*
Goulden, Joseph Augustus 1844-1915 *WhAm 1*
Goulder, Harvey Danforth 1853-1928 *NatCAB 12, WhAm 1, WhAm 4*
Goulding, Edmund 1891-1959 *WhAm 3*
Goulding, Francis Robert 1810-1881 *AmBi, ApCAB, DcAmB, NatCAB 7, TwCBDA, WhAm H*
Goulding, Philip Sanford 1876-1937 *NatCAB 31*
Goulding, Thomas 1786-1848 *ApCAB*
Gouldy, Jennie Augusta *WomWWA 14*
Gouled, Peter 1876-1965 *NatCAB 50*
Goulett, Paul R 1896-1962 *WhAm 4*
Gouley, John William Severin 1832- *ApCAB, WhAm 4*
Goulston, Therese 1848- *WomWWA 14*
Gounod, Charles Francois 1818-1893 *McGEWB*
Goupil, Rene 1607?-1642 *AmBi, ApCAB, DcAmB, WhAm H*
Gouraud, Henri Joseph Eugene 1867-1946 *WhoMilH*
Gourden, Jean *NewYHSD*
Gourdin, Edward Orval 1897-1966 *NatCAB 53*
Gourdin, Theodore 1764-1826 *BiAUS, BiDrAC, WhAm H*
Gourgues, Dominique Chevalier De 1530?-1593 *ApCAB, Drake*
Gourko, Ossip Vladimirovich 1828-1901 *WhoMilH*
Gourlay, Robert Fleming 1778-1863 *ApCAB, Drake, McGEWB*
Gourley, Joseph Harvey 1883-1946 *NatCAB 35, WhAm 2*
Gourley, Louis Hill 1889-1950 *WhAm 3*
Gourley, Robert John 1878- *WhAm 6*
Gourley, William B 1856-1935 *WhAm 1*
Gourmont, Remy De 1858-1915 *McGEWB*
Goursat, Edouard Jean-Baptiste 1858-1936 *DcScB*
Gouverneur, Marian d1913 *WhAm 1, WomWWA 14*
Gouvion, Jean Baptiste 1747-1792 *ApCAB,*

Drake
Gouvion-Saint-Cyr, Laurent 1764-1830 *WhoMilH*
Gouy, Louis-Georges 1854-1926 *DcScB*
Gouyt, Theodore *NewYHSD*
Govan, A R 1794-1841 *BiAUS*
Govan, Andrew Robison 1794-1841 *BiDrAC, WhAm H*
Govan, Daniel Chevilette 1829-1911 *BiDConf, DcAmB*
Gove, Aaron Estellus 1839-1919 *BiDAmEd, DcAmB, NatCAB 12, WhAm 1*
Gove, Aaron M 1867- *NatCAB 12*
Gove, Anna M *WomWWA 14*
Gove, Charles Augustus 1854-1933 *WhAm 1*
Gove, Elma Mary *NewYHSD*
Gove, Frank Edward 1865- *WhAm 4*
Gove, George 1870-1956 *WhAm 3*
Gove, George 1881- *WhAm 6*
Gove, Philip Babcock 1902-1972 *WhAm 5*
Gove, Samuel Francis 1822-1900 *BiAUS, BiDrAC*
Gove, William Hazeltine 1817-1876 *ApCAB, ApCAB X*
Gover, William C *NewYHSD*
Govert, William Henry 1844-1921 *NatCAB 31*
Govin, Rafael R 1868-1926 *WhAm 1*
Govorov, Leonid 1897-1955 *WhWW-II*
Gow *NewYHSD*
Gow, Arthur Sidney 1892-1973 *WhAm 6*
Gow, Charles R 1872- *WhAm 5*
Gow, George Coleman 1860-1938 *NatCAB 28, WhAm 4*
Gow, James Steele 1895-1973 *WhAm 5*
Gow, John Russell 1855- *WhAm 1*
Gow, Paul Alexander 1883-1949 *NatCAB 39*
Gow, Robert Macgregor 1893-1964 *WhAm 4*
Gow-Smith, Francis William 1894-1939 *NatCAB 29*
Gowan, Alexander *NewYHSD*
Gowan, James Robert 1817- *ApCAB*
Gowan, Mary Olivia 1888-1977 *BiDAmEd*
Gowan, Ogle Robert 1796-1876 *ApCAB*
Gowans, Ephraim Gowan 1868- *WhAm 4*
Gowans, William 1803-1870 *ApCAB, DcAmB, TwCBDA, WhAm H*
Gowans, William 1805-1870 *NatCAB 26*
Gowdy, John Kennedy 1843-1918 *NatCAB 18, WhAm 1*
Gowdy, Robert Clyde 1886-1950 *WhAm 3*
Gowdy, Roy Cotsworth 1878-1939 *WhAm 1*
Gowen, Francis Innes 1855-1927 *WhAm 1*
Gowen, Franklin Benjamin 1836-1889 *ApCAB, DcAmB, NatCAB 13, TwCBDA, WhAm H*
Gowen, Herbert Henry 1864-1960 *NatCAB 51, WhAm 5*
Gowen, Isaac William 1858-1929 *TwCBDA, WhAm 1*
Gowen, James Bartholomew 1872-1958 *WhAm 3*
Gowen, James Emmet 1895-1971 *WhAm 5*
Gowen, John Knowles, Jr. 1894-1961 *WhAm 4*
Gowen, John Whittemore 1893-1967 *NatCAB 56, WhAm 4*
Gowen, Leo Francis 1911-1964 *NatCAB 50*
Gowen, Robert Fellows 1883-1966 *WhAm 4*
Gowen, Samuel Emmett 1902-1973 *WhAm 6*
Gowenlock, Thomas Russell 1887-1961 *WhAm 4*
Gower, Frederick Allan 1851-1884 *NatCAB 9*
Gower, John 1330?-1408 *McGEWB*
Gower, John Henry 1855-1922 *NatCAB 6, WhAm 4*
Gower, Lillian Norton *AmWom*
Gowers, Sir William 1845-1915 *BiHiMed*
Gowman, T Harry 1888-1960 *WhAm 4*
Goya Y Lucientes, Francisco DeP Jose De 1746-1828 *McGEWB*
Goyathlay *WebAB*
Goyen, Jan Van 1596-1656 *McGEWB*
Goyeneche Y Barreda, Jose Manuel 1775-1846 *ApCAB*
Goyeneche Y Barreda, Jose Sebastian 1784-1872 *ApCAB*
Goza, Anne 1872- *AmWom*
Gozzaldi, Mary Isabella De 1852- *WomWWA 14*

Graaf, Regnier De 1641-1673 *AsBiEn, DcScB*
Grabau, Amadeus William 1870-1946
  DcAmB S4, DcScB, NatCAB 34,
  WhAm 5
Grabau, Johannes Andreas August 1804-1879
  DcAmB, WhAm H
Grabau, Martin d1965 *WhAm 4*
Grabau, Mary Antin *NotAW*
Graber, Albert 1866-1959 *NatCAB 46*
Graber, Edward Darwin 1862-1926 *WhAm 1*
Graber, Fred August 1895-1950 *NatCAB 39*
Grabfelder, Samuel 1844- *WhAm 1*
Grabfield, G Philip 1892-1965 *NatCAB 52*
Grabill, Ethelbert Vincent 1874- *WhAm 5*
Grable, Betty 1916-1973 *WhAm 5*
Grable, E F 1866- *WhAm 4*
Grable, Errett Marion 1889-1959 *NatCAB 47,*
  WhAm 4
Grabner, August Lawrence 1849-1904 *DcAmB*
Grabo, Carl Henry 1881-1955 *NatCAB 52*
Grabowski, Bernard Francis 1923- *BiDrAC*
Gracchus, Gaius Sempronius 154?BC-121BC
  McGEWB
Gracchus, Tiberius Sempronius 163?BC-133BC
  McGEWB
Grace, Alonzo Gaskell 1896-1971 *BiDAmEd*
Grace, Atonzo G 1896-1971 *WhAm 5*
Grace, Carl Guy 1907-1970 *WhAm 5*
Grace, Charles Brown 1905-1969 *NatCAB 54*
Grace, Charles Emmanuel 1881-1960 *DcAmReB*
Grace, Edward Raymond 1892-1967 *WhAm 4*
Grace, Elizabeth Ross 1875- *WomWWA 14*
Grace, Eugene Gifford 1876-1960 *NatCAB 50,*
  WhAm 4
Grace, Francis Mitchell 1832-1904 *WhAm 1*
Grace, Frank W 1880- *WhAm 2*
Grace, Harry Holder 1856- *WhAm 4*
Grace, J D *NewYHSD*
Grace, James Thomas, Jr. 1923-1971 *WhAm 5*
Grace, John C *NewYHSD*
Grace, John Joseph 1902-1972 *WhAm 5*
Grace, Joseph Peter 1872-1950 *WhAm 3*
Grace, Louise Carol d1968 *WhAm 5*
Grace, Thomas 1841-1921 *ApCAB Sup,*
  TwCBDA, WhAm 1
Grace, Thomas Langdon 1814-1897 *ApCAB,*
  NatCAB 9, TwCBDA, WhAm H
Grace, Thomas Logan 1911-1971 *NatCAB 57,*
  WhAm 5
Grace, William 1847-1921 *WhAm 1*
Grace, William Joseph 1882-1959 *WhAm 3*
Grace, William Russell 1832-1904 *AmBi,*
  DcAmB, McGEWB, NatCAB 36,
  TwCBDA, WebAB, WhAm 1
Grace, William Russell 1833-1904 *NatCAB 1*
Grace, William Russell 1878-1943 *WhAm 2*
Gracey, Burton 1890-1960 *NatCAB 48*
Gracey, Samuel Levis 1835-1911 *WhAm 1*
Gracey, Wilbur Tirrell 1877- *WhAm 5*
Gracey, William Adolphe 1866-1944 *WhAm 2*
Gracian Y Morales, Baltasar Jeronimo 1601-1658
  McGEWB
Gracie, Archibald 1832-1864 *BiDConf, DcAmB,*
  WhAm H
Gracie, Archibald 1859-1912 *NatCAB 22*
Gradle, Harry Searls 1883-1950 *NatCAB 39,*
  WhAm 3
Gradle, Henry 1855-1911 *AmBi, DcAmB,*
  NatCAB 24, WhAm 1
Gradwohl, Rutherford Birchard Hayes 1877-1959
  NatCAB 46
Grady, Benjamin Franklin 1831-1914 *BiDrAC*
Grady, Daniel Henry 1872-1954 *WhAm 3*
Grady, Eleanor Hundson 1886-1970 *WhAm 5*
Grady, Henry Francis 1882-1957 *NatCAB 45,*
  WhAm 3
Grady, Henry W 1897-1967 *WhAm 4*
Grady, Henry Woodfern 1851-1889
  ApCAB Sup
Grady, Henry Woodfin 1850-1889 *AmBi,*
  DcAmB, EncAB, McGEWB, NatCAB 1,
  TwCBDA, WebAB, WhAm H
Grady, Henry Woodfin 1851-1889 *ApCAB X*
Grady, John C 1847- *NatCAB 5*
Grady, John Joseph 1913-1970 *NatCAB 56*
Grady, William Francis 1885-1950 *NatCAB 38*
Graebe, Karl James Peter 1841-1927 *AsBiEn,*
  DcScB

Graebner, August Lawrence 1849-1904 *DcAmB,*
  NatCAB 26, TwCBDA, WhAm 3
Graebner, Martin Adolph Henry 1879-1950
  WhAm 3
Graebner, Norman Arthur 1915- *EncAAH*
Graebner, Theodore 1876-1950 *WhAm 3*
Graefe, Charles 1859-1929 *NatCAB 47*
Graefe, Walter Louis 1893-1961 *NatCAB 51*
Graeff, Celestine *NewYHSD*
Graeff, Virginia E *WomWWA 14*
Graeffe, Edwin O 1900-1972 *WhAm 5*
Graeme, Elizabeth *NotAW*
Graeme, Thomas 1688-1772 *ApCAB,*
  TwCBDA
Graessel, Dominic Lawrence 1753-1793
  TwCBDA
Graesser, Roy French 1892-1972 *WhAm 5*
Graessl, Lawrence 1753-1793 *DcAmB,*
  WhAm H
Graetz, Heinrich Hirsch 1817-1891 *McGEWB*
Graf, Herbert 1903-1973 *WhAm 5*
Graf, Homer William 1894-1970 *WhAm 5*
Graf, Oskar Maria 1894-1967 *WhAm 5*
Graf, Robert Joseph 1882-1949 *NatCAB 41,*
  WhAm 2
Graf, Samuel Herman 1887-1966 *NatCAB 53*
Graff *NewYHSD*
Graff, Alexander M *NewYHSD*
Graff, Charles Everitt 1862-1946 *NatCAB 34*
Graff, Ellis U 1875- *WhAm 5*
Graff, Everett Dwight 1885-1964 *NatCAB 50,*
  REnAW, WhAm 4
Graff, Frederic 1774-1847 *NatCAB 25*
Graff, Frederic 1817-1890 *DcAmB, NatCAB 9,*
  WhAm H
Graff, Frederick 1774-1847 *DcAmB,*
  WhAm H
Graff, Frederick 1775-1847 *ApCAB, TwCBDA*
Graff, Fritz William 1887-1957 *NatCAB 42,*
  WhAm 3
Graff, George E 1865-1935 *WhAm 1*
Graff, John Francis 1857-1918 *NatCAB 17*
Graff, John Michael 1714-1782 *ApCAB,*
  NatCAB 5, TwCBDA
Graff, Joseph Verdi 1854-1921 *BiDrAC,*
  TwCBDA, WhAm 1, WhAmP
Graff, Kasimir Romuald 1878-1950 *DcScB*
Graffe, Karl Heinrich 1799-1873 *DcScB*
Graffenried, Christoph Von 1661-1743
  NewYHSD
Graffenried, Christopher, Baron De 1661-1735
  NatCAB 13
Graffenried, Christopher, Baron De 1661-1743
  DcAmB, WhAm H
Graffenried, Emanuel d1735 *ApCAB*
Graffenried, Mary Clare De *NotAW*
Grafflin, Douglas Gordon 1911-1959 *WhAm 3*
Grafly, Charles 1862-1929 *AmBi, ApCAB X,*
  DcAmB, NatCAB 12, NatCAB 22,
  WhAm 1
Grafton, Charles Chapman 1830-1912 *DcAmB,*
  NatCAB 12, TwCBDA, WhAm 1
Grafton, Edward C d1876 *ApCAB*
Grafton, John d1775 *NewYHSD*
Grafton, Joseph 1757-1836 *ApCAB*
Grafton, Robert Wadsworth 1876-1936
  WhAm 1
Graham *NewYHSD*
Graham, A W *NewYHSD*
Graham, Albert D d1957 *WhAm 3*
Graham, Alexander 1844-1934 *NatCAB 48*
Graham, Alexander William 1884-1949
  WhAm 2
Graham, Allen 1886-1961 *NatCAB 49*
Graham, Allen Jordan 1884-1931 *WhAm 1*
Graham, Andrew d1785 *ApCAB*
Graham, Arthur Butler 1878- *WhAm 6*
Graham, Augusta Strong 1866- *WomWWA 14*
Graham, B A d1970 *WhAm 5*
Graham, Balus Joseph Windsor 1862- *WhAm 5*
Graham, Ben George 1880-1942 *WhAm 2*
Graham, Bessie 1881-1966 *DcAmLiB*
Graham, Billy 1918- *McGEWB, WebAB*
Graham, Campbell 1800-1866 *TwCBDA*
Graham, Charles 1852-1911 *IIBEAAW,*
  REnAW
Graham, Charles Henry 1878-1948 *NatCAB 41*
Graham, Charles Jones 1878- *ApCAB X*

Graham, Charles Kinnaird 1824-1889 *ApCAB,*
  DcAmB, NatCAB 12, TwCBDA,
  WhAm H
Graham, Charles Vanderveer 1888-1967
  WhAm 4
Graham, Christopher 1856-1952 *WhAm 3*
Graham, Clarence Henry 1906-1971 *WhAm 5*
Graham, Curtis Burr 1814-1890 *NewYHSD*
Graham, Dale 1900-1958 *WhAm 3*
Graham, Daniel *BiAUS*
Graham, David 1808-1852 *ApCAB, DcAmB,*
  Drake, TwCBDA, WhAm H
Graham, David Brown 1846- *NatCAB 6*
Graham, David Wilson 1843-1925 *WhAm 1*
Graham, Donald Earl 1926-1974 *WhAm 6*
Graham, Donald Goodnow 1894- *WhAm 5*
Graham, Dorothy 1893-1959 *WhAm 3*
Graham, Edward Kidder 1876-1918 *BiDAmEd,*
  DcAmB, NatCAB 19, WhAm 1
Graham, Edward Montrose 1889-1961
  NatCAB 51
Graham, Edwin Charles 1871-1953 *WhAm 3*
Graham, Edwin Eldon 1864- *WhAm 3*
Graham, Edwin R 1854-1920 *WhAm 1*
Graham, Elijah James, Jr. 1884- *WhoColR*
Graham, Elizabeth T 1837- *WomWWA 14*
Graham, Ernest Robert 1866-1936 *ApCAB X,*
  DcAmB S2
Graham, Ernest Robert 1868-1936 *AmBi,*
  NatCAB 33, WhAm 1
Graham, Ethan Loughborough 1877-1955
  NatCAB 42
Graham, Evalyn Sarah Norton *WomWWA 14*
Graham, Evarts Ambrose 1883-1957
  NatCAB 42, WhAm 3
Graham, Florence *WebAB*
Graham, Frank 1894-1965 *WhAm 4*
Graham, Frank Dunstone 1890-1949 *WhAm 2*
Graham, Frank Porter 1886-1972 *BiDAmEd,*
  BiDrAC, WhAm 5
Graham, Frank Verne 1887-1944 *NatCAB 33*
Graham, Frederick J 1881- *WhAm 6*
Graham, George *NewYHSD*
Graham, George 1674?-1751 *DcScB*
Graham, George 1758-1826 *ApCAB*
Graham, George 1772-1830 *AmBi, ApCAB,*
  TwCBDA
Graham, George Edward 1866- *WhAm 4*
Graham, George Rex 1812-1894 *WhAm H*
Graham, George Rex 1813-1894 *AmBi,*
  ApCAB, DcAmB, NatCAB 6, TwCBDA,
  WebAB
Graham, George Scott 1850-1931 *BiDrAC,*
  NatCAB 3, TwCBDA, WhAm 1,
  WhAmP
Graham, Gwethalyn 1913-1965 *WhAm 4*
Graham, Hannah Isabel *WomWWA 14*
Graham, Hannah M 1874- *WomWWA 14*
Graham, Helen Tredway 1890-1971 *NatCAB 56*
Graham, Henry Hale 1731-1790 *ApCAB*
Graham, Henry Tucker 1865-1951 *NatCAB 14,*
  WhAm 3
Graham, Horace French 1862-1941 *NatCAB 33,*
  WhAm 1, WhAm 2
Graham, Horace Reynolds 1886-1954 *WhAm 3*
Graham, Hoyt Conlin 1899-1936 *WhAm 1*
Graham, Hugh 1878-1952 *WhAm 3*
Graham, Inez d1963 *WhAm 4*
Graham, Isabella Marshall 1742-1814 *ApCAB,*
  DcAmB, Drake, NatCAB 4, NotAW,
  TwCBDA, WhAm H
Graham, James d1700? *DcAmB*
Graham, James d1701 *NatCAB 23, WhAm H*
Graham, James 1793-1851 *ApCAB, BiAUS,*
  BiDrAC, TwCBDA, WhAm H, WhAmP
Graham, James 1866-1906 *NatCAB 19*
Graham, James B 1872- *WhAm 5*
Graham, James Duncan 1799-1865 *AmBi,*
  ApCAB, DcAmB, Drake, NatCAB 23,
  TwCBDA, WhAm H
Graham, James Francis 1915-1960 *WhAm 4*
Graham, James Harper 1812-1881 *BiAUS,*
  BiDrAC, TwCBDA, WhAm H
Graham, James Hiram d1960 *WhAm 4*
Graham, James Lorimer 1835-1876 *ApCAB,*
  TwCBDA
Graham, James McMahon 1852-1945 *BiDrAC,*
  WhAm 2

Graham, Jeanette Elizabeth 1872-
WomWWA 14
Graham, Joanna *ApCAB*
Graham, John 1694-1774 *ApCAB*
Graham, John 1718-1795 *DcAmB, WhAm H*
Graham, John 1774-1820 *ApCAB, BiAUS, DcAmB, NatCAB 11, TwCBDA, WhAm H*
Graham, John 1853-1924 *NatCAB 20*
Graham, John 1881-1961 *BnEnAmA*
Graham, John Andrew 1764-1841 *ApCAB, DcAmB, Drake, NatCAB 24, WhAm H*
Graham, John B *NewYHSD*
Graham, John H 1812- *Drake*
Graham, John Hodges 1794-1878 *ApCAB, TwCBDA*
Graham, John Howard 1880-1951 *WhAm 3*
Graham, John Hugh 1835-1895 *BiDrAC, WhAm H*
Graham, John Joseph 1915-1974 *NatCAB 57, WhAm 6*
Graham, John Lincoln 1866-1948 *NatCAB 38*
Graham, John Lorimer 1797-1876 *ApCAB, TwCBDA*
Graham, John Meredith 1873- *WhAm 5*
Graham, John Requa 1818-1909 *NewYHSD*
Graham, John William, Jr. 1915-1974 *WhAm 6*
Graham, Jonathan Thomas 1865-1938 *WhAm 1*
Graham, Joseph 1759-1836 *ApCAB, DcAmB, Drake, NatCAB 8, TwCBDA, WhAm H*
Graham, Joseph Alexander 1855- *WhAm 4*
Graham, Kelley 1889-1962 *WhAm 4*
Graham, Laurence Pike 1815-1905 *TwCBDA*
Graham, Lawrence Pike 1815-1905 *ApCAB, Drake, WhAm 1*
Graham, Lena Forney Reinhardt 1886-1970 *WhAm 5*
Graham, Louis Edward 1880-1965 *BiDrAC, WhAm 4*
Graham, Malbone Watson 1898-1965 *WhAm 4*
Graham, Malcolm Daniel 1827-1878 *BiDConf*
Graham, Malcolm Kintner 1872-1941 *NatCAB 33*
Graham, Margaret Collier 1850-1910 *WhAm 1*
Graham, Martha 1894?- *EncAB, McGEWB, WebAB*
Graham, Mary Owen *WhAm 5*
Graham, Minnie Almira 1875- *WomWWA 14*
Graham, Neil Ferguson 1840-1928 *NatCAB 1, NatCAB 24, WhAm 4*
Graham, Nellie Dean 1869- *WomWWA 14*
Graham, Patrick *NewYHSD*
Graham, Philip Joseph 1909-1966 *NatCAB 52*
Graham, Philip Leslie 1915-1963 *NatCAB 50, WhAm 4*
Graham, Ray Austin 1887-1932 *WhAm 1*
Graham, Robert A *NewYHSD*
Graham, Robert Cabel 1885-1967 *WhAm 4*
Graham, Robert Henry 1871- *WhAm 5*
Graham, Robert Lincoln 1899-1968 *NatCAB 54*
Graham, Robert Orlando 1853-1911 *TwCBDA, WhAm 1*
Graham, Robert Xavier 1902-1953 *NatCAB 44, WhAm 3*
Graham, S C 1862-1934 *NatCAB 28*
Graham, Samuel Jordan 1859-1951 *WhAm 3*
Graham, Shad Edmond 1896-1969 *NatCAB 54*
Graham, Stephen A 1873-1960 *WhAm 4*
Graham, Stephen Victor 1874- *WhAm 5*
Graham, Sterling Edward 1892-1971 *WhAm 5*
Graham, Sylvester 1794-1851 *AmBi, ApCAB, DcAmB, Drake, McGEWB, NatCAB 5, TwCBDA, WebAB, WhAm H*
Graham, Thomas 1805-1869 *AsBiEn, DcScB*
Graham, Thomas 1901-1969 *NatCAB 54*
Graham, Thomas Norris 1901-1970 *NatCAB 57*
Graham, Thomas Wesley 1882-1971 *WhAm 5*
Graham, Virgil Miller 1902-1970 *NatCAB 55*
Graham, Walter Emlen 1866-1927 *NatCAB 21*
Graham, Walter James 1885-1944 *NatCAB 34, WhAm 2*
Graham, Walter Waverly, Jr. 1906-1974 *WhAm 6*
Graham, Wesley Faul 1858- *WhoColR*
Graham, Willard J 1897-1966 *NatCAB 53, WhAm 4*
Graham, William *NewYHSD*
Graham, William 1745-1799 *NatCAB 3*

Graham, William 1746-1799 *TwCBDA*
Graham, William 1782-1858 *BiDrAC, WhAm H*
Graham, William 1783-1857 *BiAUS*
Graham, William Alexander 1804-1875 *AmBi, ApCAB, BiAUS, BiDConf, BiDrAC, BiDrUSE, DcAmB, Drake, NatCAB 4, NatCAB 6, TwCBDA, WhAm H, WhAmP*
Graham, William Alexander 1875-1954 *WhAm 3*
Graham, William Franklin 1918- *EncAAH, EncAB, WebAB*
Graham, William Harrison 1844-1923 *BiDrAC, TwCBDA, WhAm 4, WhAmP*
Graham, William Johnson 1872-1936 *ApCAB X, WhAm 1*
Graham, William Johnson 1872-1937 *BiDrAC, NatCAB 27*
Graham, William Joseph 1877-1963 *NatCAB 51, WhAm 4*
Graham, William Montrose 1798-1847 *ApCAB, Drake, TwCBDA*
Graham, William Montrose 1834-1916 *DcAmB, NatCAB 17, TwCBDA, WhAm 1*
Graham, William Pratt 1871-1962 *WhAm 4*
Graham, William Tate 1873-1953 *NatCAB 42, WhAm 5*
Graham, William Thompson 1850-1932 *NatCAB 27*
Grahame, David Caldwell 1912-1958 *NatCAB 47*
Grahame, James 1790-1842 *ApCAB, Drake*
Grahame, Laurance Hill 1867- *WhAm 4*
Graig, Frank Andrew 1914-1974 *WhAm 6*
Grain, Frederick *NewYHSD*
Grain, George *NewYHSD*
Grain, Peter, Jr. *NewYHSD*
Grain, Peter, Sr. 1786?- *NewYHSD*
Grain, Robert A *NewYHSD*
Grain, Urban A *NewYHSD*
Grainger, George Percy 1882- *ApCAB X*
Grainger, James 1723?-1767 *ApCAB*
Grainger, John Victor 1866-1942 *NatCAB 40*
Grainger, Minnie Starr 1869- *WomWWA 14*
Grainger, Percy 1882-1961 *WhAm 4*
Gram, Hans Christian Joachim 1853-1938 *AsBiEn, DcScB*
Gram, Lewis Merritt 1876-1953 *NatCAB 48*
Grambay, E A *NewYHSD*
Grambling, Allen Rowell 1891-1973 *WhAm 5*
Gramlich, Francis W 1911-1973 *WhAm 6*
Gramm, Edward M 1858- *NatCAB 3*
Gramme, Zenobe-Theophile 1826-1901 *DcScB*
Grammer, Allen Luther 1889-1969 *NatCAB 55, WhAm 5*
Grammer, Carl Eckhardt 1858-1944 *WhAm 2*
Grammer, Elijah Sherman 1868-1936 *BiDrAC, NatCAB 30, WhAm 1*
Grammer, Jacob 1871-1931 *WhAm 1*
Grammer, Julius Eckhardt 1831-1902 *NatCAB 14*
Gramont, Antoine Alfred A X Louis De 1861-1923 *DcScB*
Granahan, Kathryn Elizabeth *BiDrAC, WhAmP*
Granahan, William Thomas 1895-1956 *BiDrAC, WhAm 3, WhAmP*
Granata, Peter Charles 1898- *BiDrAC*
Granberg, Henry Olson 1860- *NatCAB 17*
Granberry, C Read 1899-1962 *WhAm 4*
Granbery, George 1794-1815 *NewYHSD*
Granbery, Henrietta Augusta 1829-1927 *NewYHSD*
Granbery, John Cowper 1829-1907 *ApCAB, NatCAB 13, TwCBDA, WhAm H*
Granbery, John Cowper 1874-1953 *WhAm 3*
Granbery, Virginia 1831-1921 *AmWom, NewYHSD*
Grand, Gordon 1883-1950 *NatCAB 42*
Grand, Gordon, Jr. 1917-1972 *WhAm 5*
Grand, Thomas *NewYHSD*
Grandee, Joe Ruiz 1929- *IIBEAAW*
Grandel, E *NewYHSD*
Grand'Eury, Cyrille 1839-1917 *DcScB*
Grandfield, Charles Paxton 1860-1925 *NatCAB 20*
Grandfield, Charles Paxton 1861-1925 *WhAm 4*

Grandgent, Charles Hall 1862-1939 *BiDAmEd, DcAmB S2, NatCAB 29, WhAm 4*
Grandi, Guido 1671-1742 *DcScB*
Grandin, Egbert Henry 1855- *WhAm 4*
Grandin, Elijah Bishop 1840-1917 *NatCAB 17*
Grandin, Vital Justin 1829- *ApCAB*
Grandjany, Marcel 1891-1975 *WhAm 6*
Grandma Moses *EncAAH*
Grandmont, Louis De 1645-1686? *ApCAB*
Grandy, Charles Rollin 1871-1932 *NatCAB 28*
Granfield, William Joseph 1889-1959 *BiDrAC, NatCAB 50, WhAm 3*
Grangaard, Oswald Ferdinand 1890-1960 *NatCAB 50*
Grange, Harold Edward 1903- *WebAB*
Granger, Alexis Louis 1867-1939 *NatCAB 30*
Granger, Alfred Hoyt 1867-1939 *ApCAB X, DcAmB S2, NatCAB 40, WhAm 1*
Granger, Amedee 1879- *WhAm 6*
Granger, Amos Phelps 1789-1866 *ApCAB, BiAUS, BiDrAC, TwCBDA, WhAm H*
Granger, Armour Townsend 1898-1966 *NatCAB 53, WhAm 5*
Granger, Arthur Otis 1846-1914 *WhAm 1*
Granger, Barlow 1816-1905 *WhAm 1*
Granger, Bradley Francis 1825-1882 *BiAUS, BiDrAC, WhAm H*
Granger, Caroline D Gregory 1850- *WomWWA 14*
Granger, Charles H *NewYHSD*
Granger, Charles Trumbull 1835-1915 *NatCAB 12, WhAm 1*
Granger, Daniel Larned Davis 1852-1909 *BiDrAC, WhAm 1, WhAmP*
Granger, Daniel Tristram 1807-1854 *ApCAB*
Granger, FitzHenry *NewYHSD*
Granger, Francis 1792-1868 *AmBi, ApCAB, BiAUS, BiDrAC, BiDrUSE, DcAmB, Drake, NatCAB 6, TwCBDA, WhAm H, WhAmP*
Granger, Francis H *NewYHSD*
Granger, Frank Butler 1875-1928 *WhAm 1*
Granger, Gideon 1767-1822 *AmBi, ApCAB, BiAUS, BiDrUSE, DcAmB, Drake, NatCAB 5, TwCBDA, WhAm H*
Granger, Gideon 1821-1868 *TwCBDA*
Granger, Gordon 1821-1876 *ApCAB, NatCAB 4*
Granger, Gordon 1822-1876 *AmBi, DcAmB, WebAMB, WhAm H*
Granger, Gordon 1823-1876 *TwCBDA*
Granger, Gordon 1825?-1876 *Drake*
Granger, Henry *NewYHSD*
Granger, James *NewYHSD*
Granger, Lester B 1896-1976 *WhAm 6*
Granger, Lottie E 1858- *AmWom*
Granger, Miles Tobey 1817-1895 *BiDrAC, NatCAB 5, TwCBDA, WhAm H*
Granger, Moses Moorhead 1831-1913 *NatCAB 27, TwCBDA, WhAm 1*
Granger, Robert Seaman 1816-1894 *AmBi, ApCAB, NatCAB 12, TwCBDA*
Granger, Robert Seaman 1817?-1894 *Drake*
Granger, Sherman Moorhead 1870- *WhAm 5*
Granger, Walter 1872-1941 *DcAmB S3, NatCAB 35, WhAm 1*
Granger, Walter Keil 1888- *BiDrAC*
Granger, Walter Willis 1872-1941 *DcScB*
Granger, William Alexander 1850-1922 *WhAm 1*
Granik, Theodore d1970 *WhAm 5*
Granit, Ragnar Arthur 1900- *AsBiEn*
Granja, Juan DeLa 1785?-1853 *ApCAB*
Granjon, Henry Regis 1863- *NatCAB 15, WhAm 4*
Grannan, Charles P *WhAm 5*
Grannis, Elizabeth Bartlett 1840-1926 *ApCAB X, WhAm 1*
Grannis, Florence Alvord 1866- *WomWWA 14*
Grannis, Robert Andrews 1840-1917 *WhAm 1*
Grannis, Robert Maitland 1903-1973 *WhAm 5*
Granniss, Anna Jane 1856- *WhAm 4, WomWWA 14*
Grant, Abraham 1848-1911 *TwCBDA, WhAm 1*
Grant, Abraham Phineas 1804-1871 *BiAUS, BiDrAC, WhAm H*
Grant, Albert Weston 1856-1930 *AmBi,*

DcAmB, WhAm 1

Grant, Alsie Raymond 1897-1967 *WhAm 4*
Grant, Amy 1880- *WhAm 6*
Grant, Anne 1755-1838 *AmBi, ApCAB, Drake*
Grant, Arthur Rogers 1871-1945 *WhAm 2*
Grant, Arthur Sheldon 1880-1947 *NatCAB 36*
Grant, Asahel 1807-1844 *AmBi, ApCAB, DcAmB, NatCAB 4, TwCBDA, WhAm H*
Grant, Bishop F 1897-1970 *WhAm 5*
Grant, Blanche Chloe 1874-1948 *IlBEAAW, WomWWA 14*
Grant, Carroll Walter 1900-1969 *WhAm 5*
Grant, Cary 1904- *WebAB*
Grant, Charles Henry 1866-1939 *WhAm 1*
Grant, Charles Leon 1915-1974 *WhAm 6*
Grant, Charles S 1845- *NatCAB 3*
Grant, Claudius Buchanan 1835-1921 *ApCAB X, DcAmB, NatCAB 12, NatCAB 18, TwCBDA, WhAm 1*
Grant, Clement Rollins 1849- *ApCAB*
Grant, Daniel *NewYHSD*
Grant, David Elias 1893-1968 *WhAm 5*
Grant, David Norvell Walker 1891-1964 *WhAm 4*
Grant, DeForest 1869-1960 *NatCAB 48, WhAm 5*
Grant, Duncan Campbell 1880- *WhAm 6*
Grant, Edward Maxwell 1839-1884 *ApCAB Sup*
Grant, Elihu 1873-1942 *WhAm 2*
Grant, Elizabeth Rhinehart *WomWWA 14*
Grant, Elliott Mansfield 1895-1969 *WhAm 5*
Grant, Ethel Watts M 1876- *WomWWA 14*
Grant, Fanny Etheridge *WomWWA 14*
Grant, Frederick Clifton 1891-1974 *DcAmReB, WhAm 6*
Grant, Frederick Dent 1850-1912 *AmBi, ApCAB, DcAmB, NatCAB 11, NatCAB 15, TwCBDA, WhAm 1*
Grant, George Barnard 1849-1917 *DcAmB, NatCAB 24, NatCAB 26, WhAm HA, WhAm 4*
Grant, George Camron 1893-1959 *WhAm 3*
Grant, George Ernest 1903-1955 *WhAm 3*
Grant, George McInvale 1897- *BiDrAC, WhAmP*
Grant, George Monroe 1835- *ApCAB*
Grant, Gordon 1875-1962 *WhAm 4*
Grant, Harry Johnston 1881-1963 *NatCAB 52, WhAm 4*
Grant, Heber Jeddy 1856-1945 *NatCAB 18, NatCAB 38, REnAW, WhAm 2*
Grant, Henry Fay 1882-1920 *NatCAB 19*
Grant, Henry Horace 1853-1921 *WhAm 1*
Grant, Henry William 1870- *WhAm 5*
Grant, Hiram Ulysses *WebAB*
Grant, Hugh John 1855- *WhAm 4*
Grant, J *NewYHSD*
Grant, J Jeffrey 1883-1960 *NatCAB 47*
Grant, James *NewYHSD*
Grant, James 1720-1806 *ApCAB, Drake*
Grant, Sir James Alexander 1829- *ApCAB*
Grant, James Benton 1848-1911 *DcAmB, NatCAB 6, TwCBDA, WhAm 1*
Grant, James Benton 1888-1947 *NatCAB 36, WhAm 2*
Grant, Sir James Hope 1805-1875 *WhoMilH*
Grant, James Richard 1880-1951 *WhAm 3*
Grant, Jeannie L Dailey *WomWWA 14*
Grant, Jedediah Morgan 1816-1856 *NatCAB 16*
Grant, Jesse R 1858- *WhAm 4*
Grant, John Black 1890-1962 *WhAm 4*
Grant, John Cowles 1848-1914 *WhAm 1*
Grant, John Gaston 1858-1923 *BiDrAC, WhAm 4*
Grant, John Henry 1857-1913 *WhAm 1*
Grant, John MacGregor 1874-1941 *WhAm 1*
Grant, John Prescott 1872-1946 *WhAm 2*
Grant, John Thomas 1813-1887 *DcAmB, NatCAB 1, WhAm H*
Grant, John William 1867- *NatCAB 17*
Grant, Joseph Donohoe 1858-1942 *WhAm 2*
Grant, Joseph Henry 1869-1933 *WhAm 1*
Grant, Julia Dent 1826-1902 *AmWom, ApCAB, NatCAB 4, NotAW, TwCBDA, WhAm H*
Grant, Lemuel Pratt 1817-1893 *NatCAB 4*
Grant, Lester Eames 1884-1965 *NatCAB 51*

Grant, Lester Strickland 1877- *WhAm 5*
Grant, Lewis A 1820- *ApCAB*
Grant, Lewis Addison 1829-1918 *DcAmB, NatCAB 10, TwCBDA, WebAMB, WhAm 1*
Grant, Lewis Alexander 1852-1904 *NatCAB 42*
Grant, Madison 1865-1937 *DcAmB S2, NatCAB 29, WhAm 1*
Grant, Malcolm Edward 1906-1962 *NatCAB 51*
Grant, Margaret d1967 *WhAm 4*
Grant, Owen *NewYHSD*
Grant, Percy Stickney 1860-1927 *ApCAB X, DcAmB, NatCAB 15, WhAm 1*
Grant, Peter Taylor 1884-1934 *NatCAB 25*
Grant, Richard Frank 1879-1957 *WhAm 3*
Grant, Richard Ralph Hallam 1878-1957 *WhAm 3*
Grant, Robert 1852-1940 *ApCAB, DcAmB S2, NatCAB 7, NatCAB 30, TwCBDA, WhAm 1*
Grant, Robert Allen 1905- *BiDrAC*
Grant, Robert Dyer 1862-1914 *NatCAB 16*
Grant, Robert John 1862-1949 *NatCAB 39, WhAm 2*
Grant, Robert Purves 1915-1966 *NatCAB 53*
Grant, Roderick McLellan 1901-1961 *WhAm 4*
Grant, Rollin P 1870-1936 *WhAm 1*
Grant, Samuel Arthur 1881- *WhoColR*
Grant, Thomas McMillan 1886-1952 *WhAm 3*
Grant, Ulysses S, III 1881-1968 *NatCAB 54, WhAm 5*
Grant, Ulysses S, Jr. 1852-1929 *WhAm 1*
Grant, Ulysses Sherman 1867-1932 *NatCAB 13, WhAm 1*
Grant, Ulysses Simpson 1822-1885 *AmBi, ApCAB, BiAUS, BiDrAC, BiDrUSE, DcAmB, Drake, EncAAH, EncAB, McGEWB, NatCAB 4, TwCBDA, WebAB, WebAMB, WhAm H, WhAmP, WhoMilH*
Grant, Vivian Verne 1882-1947 *NatCAB 36*
Grant, Walter Bruce 1859-1939 *AmBi, NatCAB 29, WhAm 1*
Grant, Walter Schuyler 1878- *WhAm 6*
Grant, Whit McDonough 1851-1927 *WhAm 1*
Grant, Wilbur Gill 1906-1964 *NatCAB 52*
Grant, William Daniel 1918-1973 *WhAm 6*
Grant, William Thomas 1876-1972 *WhAm 5*
Grant, William Thomas 1876-1954 *WhAm 3*
Grant, William West 1846-1934 *NatCAB 12, WhAm 1*
Grant, William West 1881-1957 *NatCAB 47, WhAm 3*
Grant, Zilpah Polly 1794-1874 *BiDAmEd, NotAW*
Grant-Smith, U 1870-1959 *WhAm 4*
Grantham, Edwin Lincoln 1866- *WhAm 1*
Grantham, Herbert Thomas 1868-1922 *NatCAB 6*
Grantham, Wilmer Lloyd 1883-1971 *NatCAB 57*
Grantland, Seaton 1782-1864 *BiAUS, BiDrAC, WhAm H*
Grantley, Charles *NewYHSD*
Grantz, Walter Anton Henry 1896-1957 *NatCAB 43*
Granville, Earl 1880-1953 *WhAm 3*
Granville, Charles Becard De *NewYHSD*
Granville, Joseph Desiderius 1874-1919 *NatCAB 18*
Granville, William Anthony 1863-1943 *WhAm 2*
Granville-Smith, W 1870-1938 *WhAm 1*
Granville-Smith, Walter, Jr. 1905-1974 *WhAm 6*
Graser, Hulda Regina 1869- *AmWom*
Grasett, Frederick LeMaitre 1851- *ApCAB Sup*
Grasett, Henry James 1808-1882 *ApCAB Sup*
Grashof, Franz 1826-1893 *DcScB*
Grask, Erwin Stephen 1897-1956 *NatCAB 42*
Grasmick, Jacob 1906-1967 *NatCAB 54*
Grason, C Gus 1881- *WhAm 3*
Grason, William 1786-1868 *NatCAB 9*
Grass, Gunter 1927- *McGEWB*
Grass, J D *NewYHSD*
Grass, John 1837-1918 *DcAmB, WhAm HA, WhAm 4*
Grass, John Aaron 1892-1949 *NatCAB 38*
Grasse, Augustus De *NewYHSD*

Grasse, Edwin 1884-1954 *WhAm 3*
Grasse, Francois Joseph Paul, Count De 1722-1788 *AmBi*
Grasse, Francois Joseph Paul, Count De 1723-1788 *NatCAB 2*
Grasse, Francois Joseph Paul De *WhAm H*
Grasse-Tilly, Francois J Paul, Comte De 1723-1788 *ApCAB, Drake*
Grasselli, Caesar Augustin 1850-1927 *ApCAB X, DcAmB, NatCAB 21, WhAm 1*
Grasselli, Eugene Ramiro 1810-1882 *NatCAB 21*
Grasselli, Eugene Ramiro 1872-1935 *NatCAB 27*
Grasselli, Thomas Fries 1903-1970 *WhAm 5*
Grasselli, Thomas Saxton 1874-1942 *ApCAB X, NatCAB 43, WhAm 2*
Grassham, Charles C 1871-1945 *WhAm 2*
Grasshoff, Frank O 1894-1952 *WhAm 3*
Grassi, Giovanni Battista 1854-1925 *DcScB*
Grassi, John 1778-1849 *ApCAB*
Grassie, Herbert J 1894-1973 *WhAm 6*
Grassie, Sarah Elizabeth 1829- *WomWWA 14*
Grassmann, Herman Gunther 1809-1877 *DcScB*
Grassmann, Hermann Gunther 1809-1877 *DcScB Sup*
Grasty, Charles Henry 1863-1924 *AmBi, DcAmB, NatCAB 22, WhAm 1*
Grasty, John Sharshall 1880-1930 *WhAm 1*
Gratacap, George G *NewYHSD*
Gratacap, Louis Pope 1850-1917 *ApCAB, TwCBDA*
Gratacap, Louis Pope 1851-1917 *WhAm 1*
Gratian d1155? *McGEWB*
Gratiolet, Louis Pierre 1815-1865 *DcScB*
Gratiot, Charles 1752-1817 *AmBi, DcAmB, WhAm H*
Gratiot, Charles 1786-1855 *AmBi, NatCAB 12*
Gratiot, Charles 1788-1855 *ApCAB, Drake, TwCBDA*
Gratke, Charles 1901-1949 *WhAm 2*
Graton, Caryl 1880-1970 *NatCAB 55*
Graton, Josephine Bowman 1877- *WomWWA 14*
Graton, L C 1880- *WhAm 6*
Grattan, Henry 1746-1820 *McGEWB*
Grattan, Thomas Colley 1796-1864 *ApCAB, Drake*
Gratwick, William Henry 1839-1899 *NatCAB 19*
Gratwick, William Henry 1870-1934 *NatCAB 24*
Gratz, Anderson 1852-1935 *NatCAB 26*
Gratz, Barnard 1738-1801 *AmBi, DcAmB*
Gratz, Bernard 1738-1801 *WhAm H*
Gratz, Hyman 1776-1857 *ApCAB Sup*
Gratz, John *NewYHSD*
Gratz, Michael 1740-1811 *AmBi, DcAmB, WhAm H*
Gratz, Rebecca 1781-1869 *AmBi, ApCAB Sup, BiDAmEd, DcAmB, NatCAB 10, NotAW, WhAm H*
Gratz, W Edward J 1873-1954 *WhAm 3*
Grau, Maurice 1849-1907 *ApCAB Sup, DcAmB, WhAm 1*
Grau, Miguel 1834-1879 *ApCAB*
Grau San Martin, Ramon 1882-1969 *WhAm 5*
Grau San Martin, Ramon 1887-1969 *McGEWB*
Graudan, Nikolai d1964 *WhAm 5*
Grauel, George Edward 1911-1967 *WhAm 4*
Grauer, A E 1906-1961 *WhAm 4*
Grauer, Natalie Eynon 1895-1955 *WhAm 3*
Grauer, Theophil Paul 1897-1963 *NatCAB 50, WhAm 4*
Grauman, Arthur Henry 1893-1967 *NatCAB 54*
Graunt, John 1620-1674 *DcScB*
Graupner, Adolphus Earhart 1875-1947 *WhAm 2*
Graupner, Gottlieb 1767-1836 *WebAB*
Graupner, Johann Christian Gottlieb 1767-1836 *DcAmB, WhAm H*
Graustein, Archibald R 1885-1969 *WhAm 5*
Graustein, William Caspar 1888-1941 *WhAm 1*
Gravatt, John James 1881- *WhAm 6*
Gravatt, William Loyall 1858-1942 *NatCAB 13, TwCBDA, WhAm 2*
Grave, Caswell 1870-1944 *WhAm 2*

Grave, Dmitry Aleksandrovich 1863-1939 *DcScB*
Grave, Frederick David 1849-1924 *NatCAB 33*
Grave, Frederick David 1889-1963 *WhAm 4*
Gravel, Elphige 1838- *ApCAB*
Gravel, Maurice Robert 1930- *BiDrAC*
Gravell, James Harvey 1880-1939 *NatCAB 38*
Gravell, William Henry 1883-1953 *NatCAB 43*
Gravely, Joseph Jackson 1828-1872 *BiAUS,*
BiDrAC, WhAm H
Gravely, Julian Stuart 1887-1947 *NatCAB 36*
Graven, Bruce 1881- *WhAm 6*
Graven, Henry Norman 1893-1970 *WhAm 5*
Gravener, Walter Ross 1872-1930 *NatCAB 25*
Gravenor, John *DcAmB*
Graver, James Philip 1869- *NatCAB 18*
Graver, Philip Sheridan 1878-1945 *NatCAB 47*
Graver, William 1842-1915 *NatCAB 18*
Graves, Abbott Fuller 1859-1936 *NatCAB 7,*
TwCBDA, WhAm 1
Graves, Adelia Cleopatra 1821-1895 *AmWom,*
ApCAB, TwCBDA
Graves, Albert Henry 1863-1919 *NatCAB 19*
Graves, Alexander 1844-1916 *BiDrAC*
Graves, Alice Amelia 1876- *WomWWA 14*
Graves, Alvin C 1909-1965 *WhAm 4*
Graves, Amos Maverick 1898-1956 *NatCAB 45*
Graves, Angeline Loesch 1875- *BiCAW,*
WomWWA 14
Graves, Anson Rogers 1842- *NatCAB 4,*
TwCBDA
Graves, Anson Rogers 1842-1931 *NatCAB 42*
Graves, Anson Rogers 1842-1932 *WhAm 1*
Graves, Benjamin Clifford 1886-1968
NatCAB 54
Graves, Benjamin Franklin 1817- *BiAUS,*
NatCAB 12
Graves, Benjamin Parker 1884-1954
NatCAB 46
Graves, Bibb 1873-1942 *NatCAB 31,*
WhAm 2
Graves, Carolyn Elliott *WomWWA 14*
Graves, Charles 1868-1948 *WhAm 2*
Graves, Charles Alfred 1850-1928 *NatCAB 22,*
WhAm 1
Graves, Charles Burleigh 1841-1912 *WhAm 1*
Graves, Charles Francis 1878- *WhoColR*
Graves, Charles Hinman 1839-1928 *NatCAB 14,*
NatCAB 22, WhAm 1
Graves, Charles Marshall d1952 *WhAm 3*
Graves, David Bibb 1873-1942 *DcAmB S3*
Graves, Dixie Bibb 1882-1965 *BiDrAC*
Graves, Eli Edwin 1847- *WhAm 4*
Graves, Eugene Silas 1876-1951 *WhAm 3*
Graves, Frank Pierrepont 1869-1956 *BiDAmEd,*
NatCAB 53, TwCBDA, WhAm 3
Graves, Frank Russell 1882-1962 *NatCAB 49*
Graves, Frederick Rogers 1858-1940 *DcAmB S2,*
NatCAB 13, TwCBDA, WhAm 1
Graves, Gaylord Willis 1884-1952 *NatCAB 39*
Graves, George Dana 1872-1970 *NatCAB 57*
Graves, George Keene 1865-1943 *WhAm 2*
Graves, George Olanda 1871-1950 *NatCAB 38*
Graves, Grant Ostrander 1905-1972 *NatCAB 56,*
WhAm 5
Graves, Harmon Sheldon 1870-1940
NatCAB 31
Graves, Harold Nathan 1887-1966 *WhAm 4*
Graves, Harriet S 1850- *WomWWA 14*
Graves, Henry Lee 1813-1881 *NatCAB 26*
Graves, Henry Solon 1871-1951 *NatCAB 39,*
WhAm 3
Graves, Herbert Cornelius 1869-1919 *WhAm 1*
Graves, Hiram Throop 1824-1902 *NatCAB 8*
Graves, Ireland 1885-1969 *NatCAB 57,*
WhAm 5
Graves, Jackson Alpheus 1852-1933 *WhAm 1*
Graves, James Clifford 1871-1947 *NatCAB 36*
Graves, James Quarles 1878-1958 *NatCAB 48*
Graves, James Robinson 1820- *ApCAB*
Graves, James Robinson 1820-1893 *DcAmB,*
DcAmReB, WhAm H
Graves, James Robinson 1820-1896 *TwCBDA*
Graves, James Wesley 1868-1950 *WhAm 3*
Graves, Jay P 1859-1948 *WhAm 2*
Graves, John 1901-1953 *WhAm 3*
Graves, John Temple 1856-1925 *DcAmB,*
NatCAB 2, WhAm 1
Graves, John Temple 1892-1961 *WhAm 4*

Graves, Lilyan Pratt *WomWWA 14*
Graves, Louis 1883-1965 *WhAm 4*
Graves, Lulu Grace d1949 *WhAm 2*
Graves, Marian Welch 1873- *WomWWA 14*
Graves, Mark 1877-1942 *WhAm 2*
Graves, Marvin Lee 1867- *WhAm 4*
Graves, Mary H 1839- *AmWom*
Graves, Mary Wheat 1911-1968 *WhAm 5*
Graves, Maude Miller 1878- *WomWWA 14*
Graves, Morris Cole 1910- *BnEnAmA 2,*
WebAB
Graves, Nathan Fitch 1813-1896 *NatCAB 2*
Graves, Nelson Zuingle 1849- *WhAm 4*
Graves, Ralph A 1882-1932 *WhAm 1*
Graves, Ralph H 1878-1939 *WhAm 1*
Graves, Robert James 1796-1853 *BiHiMed*
Graves, Robert John 1878-1950 *NatCAB 41,*
WhAm 3
Graves, Robert Ranke 1895- *McGEWB*
Graves, Robert Strickler 1882-1964 *NatCAB 51*
Graves, Rosewell Hobart 1833-1912 *DcAmB*
Graves, Schuyler Colfax 1858-1941 *WhAm 1*
Graves, Thomas 1605-1653 *ApCAB, Drake*
Graves, Lord Thomas 1725-1802 *Drake*
Graves, Baron Thomas Graves 1725?-1802 *AmBi*
Graves, Waller Washington 1860-1928
NatCAB 26, WhAm 1
Graves, Walter Haden 1851-1919 *NatCAB 18*
Graves, William Blair 1834-1915 *NatCAB 10,*
TwCBDA, WhAm 1
Graves, William Gurnell 1866-1945 *NatCAB 35*
Graves, William Jordan 1805-1848 *ApCAB,*
BiAUS, BiDrAC, NatCAB 12, TwCBDA,
WhAm H, WhAmP
Graves, William Leon 1876-1940 *NatCAB 29*
Graves, William Lucius 1872-1943 *WhAm 2*
Graves, William Phillips 1870-1933 *DcAmB S1,*
WhAm 1
Graves, William Sidney 1865-1940 *DcAmB S2,*
WebAMB, WhAm 1
Graves, William Washington 1865-1949
WhAm 3
Graves, Zuinglius Calvin 1815-1902 *NatCAB 24*
Graves, Zuinglius Calvin 1816-1902 *DcAmB,*
TwCBDA, WhAm H
Graves, Zwinglius Calvin 1816-1902 *ApCAB*
Gravesande, Willem Jacob, 's 1688-1742 *DcScB*
Gravett, Joshua 1863- *WhAm 5*
Gravett, Nettie K *WomWWA 14*
Gravier, Charles 1717-1787 *WhAm H*
Gravier, Jacques 1651-1708 *AmBi, ApCAB,*
DcAmB, WhAm H
Gravina, Carlos, Duque De 1756-1806 *WhoMilH*
Grawe, Oliver Rudolph 1901-1965 *NatCAB 56,*
WhAm 4
Grawn, Charles Theodore 1857-1942
NatCAB 31, WhAm 4
Grawoig, Isadore G 1891-1960 *NatCAB 51*
Gray *NewYHSD*
Gray, A H *NewYHSD*
Gray, Albert F 1886-1969 *WhAm 5*
Gray, Albert Zabriskie 1840-1889 *ApCAB,*
TwCBDA
Gray, Alexander 1882-1921 *WhAm 1*
Gray, Alfred G 1818-1876 *ApCAB*
Gray, Alfred Leftwich 1873-1932 *NatCAB 23,*
WhAm 1
Gray, Alfred Walter 1868-1941 *WhAm 1*
Gray, Alonzo 1808-1860 *ApCAB, Drake,*
TwCBDA
Gray, Amanda V *WhoColR*
Gray, Andrew Caldwell 1871-1929 *NatCAB 32,*
WhAm 1
Gray, Arthur Irving 1859- *WhAm 4*
Gray, Arthur Romeyn 1875-1923 *WhAm 1*
Gray, Arthur Smith 1869- *WhoColR*
Gray, Asa 1810-1888 *ApCAB, AsBiEn,*
BiDAmEd, BiHiMed, DcAmB, DcScB,
Drake, EncAAH, EncAB, McGEWB,
NatCAB 3, TwCBDA, WebAB,
WhAm H
Gray, Asa 1810-1898 *AmBi*
Gray, Augustus Clagett 1889-1964 *NatCAB 51*
Gray, Bahnson 1922-1970 *NatCAB 55*
Gray, Baron DeKalb 1855-1946 *WhAm 2*
Gray, Bernard Andrew 1889-1964 *NatCAB 50*
Gray, Bowman 1874-1935 *NatCAB 31,*
WhAm 1

Gray, Bowman 1907-1969 *NatCAB 54,*
WhAm 5
Gray, Campbell 1879-1944 *NatCAB 33,*
WhAm 2
Gray, Carl Raymond 1867-1939 *DcAmB S2,*
NatCAB 18, NatCAB 36, WhAm 1
Gray, Carl Raymond, Jr. 1889-1955 *WhAm 3*
Gray, Carroll Eugene 1891-1951 *NatCAB 41*
Gray, Charles Harold 1892-1959 *WhAm 3*
Gray, Charles J *NewYHSD*
Gray, Charles Oliver 1867- *WhAm 4*
Gray, Charlotte *NewYHSD*
Gray, Charlotte Elvira d1926 *WhAm 1*
Gray, Chester Earl 1881-1944 *WhAm 2*
Gray, Chester Harold 1879-1964 *NatCAB 50,*
WhAm 4
Gray, Chester Harvey 1898-1965 *NatCAB 51*
Gray, Clarence Truman 1877- *WhAm 5*
Gray, Clifton Daggett 1874-1948 *WhAm 2*
Gray, Clifton Merritt 1873-1933 *WhAm 1*
Gray, Clifton Sidney 1849- *NatCAB 12*
Gray, Cola Almon 1894-1967 *NatCAB 53*
Gray, Courtland Prentice 1882-1948
NatCAB 38
Gray, Cyrus S 1854-1918 *WhAm 1*
Gray, Daniel Thomas 1878- *WhAm 6*
Gray, David 1836-1888 *ApCAB, NatCAB 9,*
WhAm H
Gray, David 1870-1928 *NatCAB 31*
Gray, David 1870-1968 *WhAm 5*
Gray, David Lincoln 1870-1941 *NatCAB 31,*
WhAm 1
Gray, Dean Donald 1895-1955 *NatCAB 45*
Gray, Donald 1891-1939 *NatCAB 31*
Gray, Donald Joseph 1912-1967 *NatCAB 56,*
WhAm 4
Gray, Dudley Guy 1868-1930 *WhAm 1*
Gray, Duncan Montgomery 1898-1966 *WhAm 4*
Gray, E McQueen 1854- *WhAm 4*
Gray, Earle 1898-1967 *WhAm 5*
Gray, Eddie Camilla *WomWWA 14*
Gray, Edgar Harkness 1815-1894 *ApCAB,*
TwCBDA
Gray, Edward *BiAUS*
Gray, Edward Winthrop 1870-1942 *BiDrAC,*
WhAm 2
Gray, Edwin 1743- *BiDrAC, WhAm H*
Gray, Elisha 1835-1901 *AmBi, ApCAB,*
DcAmB, NatCAB 4, TwCBDA, WebAB,
WhAm 1
Gray, Elizabeth Chipman 1756-1823 *ApCAB*
Gray, Elizabeth Crittenden Cabell 1860-
WomWWA 14
Gray, Elizabeth Pearl Lewis 1889- *WhoColR*
Gray, Ernest Weston 1902-1974 *WhAm 6*
Gray, Finly H 1864-1947 *WhAm 3*
Gray, Finly Hutchinson 1863-1947 *BiDrAC,*
WhAmP
Gray, Francis Calley 1790-1856 *ApCAB,*
DcAmB, Drake, NatCAB 1, TwCBDA,
WhAm H
Gray, Frank Dorsey 1893-1962 *NatCAB 50*
Gray, George 1725-1800 *ApCAB*
Gray, George 1840-1925 *AmBi, ApCAB,*
BiDrAC, DcAmB, NatCAB 6,
NatCAB 26, TwCBDA, WhAm 1,
WhAmP
Gray, George Alexander 1851-1912 *DcAmB,*
NatCAB 37
Gray, George Edward 1818- *ApCAB,*
TwCBDA, WhAm 4
Gray, George Herbert 1868-1958 *NatCAB 48*
Gray, George Herbert 1874-1945 *NatCAB 34,*
WhAm 2
Gray, George William 1885-1960 *WhAm 4*
Gray, George Zabriskie 1838-1889 *ApCAB,*
NatCAB 12, TwCBDA, WhAm H
Gray, Giles Wilkeson 1889-1972 *WhAm 5*
Gray, Gordon 1877-1967 *WhAm 4*
Gray, Harold Edwin 1906-1972 *WhAm 5*
Gray, Harold Lincoln 1894-1968 *NatCAB 54,*
WebAB, WhAm 5
Gray, Harold Parker 1894-1967 *WhAm 4*
Gray, Helen *WomWWA 14*
Gray, Henry d1779 *NewYHSD*
Gray, Henry 1816-1892 *BiDConf*
Gray, Henry 1825?-1861 *DcScB*
Gray, Henry David 1873-1958 *NatCAB 46,*

WhAm 5

Gray, Henry G 1875-1954 *WhAm 3*

Gray, Henry Peeters 1819-1877 *WhAm H*

Gray, Henry Peters 1819-1877 *AmBi, ApCAB, BnEnAmA, DcAmB, Drake, NatCAB 5, NewYHSD, TwCBDA*

Gray, Hiram 1801-1890 *BiDrAC, WhAm H*

Gray, Hiram 1802-1890 *BiAUS*

Gray, Hob 1889-1973 *WhAm 5*

Gray, Horace 1828-1902 *AmBi, ApCAB, DcAmB, NatCAB 1, TwCBDA, WebAB, WhAm 1*

Gray, Horace Alfred 1875-1940 *NatCAB 35*

Gray, Horace Alfred, Jr. 1909-1958 *NatCAB 49*

Gray, Howard Adams 1878-1958 *WhAm 3*

Gray, Howard Kramer 1901-1955 *WhAm 3*

Gray, Hugh Matthias 1889- *WhoColR*

Gray, Isaac Pusey 1828-1895 *ApCAB, DcAmB, NatCAB 13, TwCBDA, WhAm H*

Gray, J F *NewYHSD*

Gray, J S 1890-1972 *WhAm 5*

Gray, Jacques Pierce 1900-1961 *NatCAB 49, WhAm 4*

Gray, James *NewYHSD*

Gray, James 1770-1824 *ApCAB*

Gray, James 1862-1916 *WhAm 1*

Gray, James Alexander 1846-1918 *NatCAB 31*

Gray, James Alexander 1889-1952 *WhAm 3*

Gray, James Burdis 1913-1967 *WhAm 4*

Gray, James Callam 1858-1925 *NatCAB 26*

Gray, James Martin 1851-1935 *DcAmReB, WhAm 1*

Gray, James Richard 1859-1917 *NatCAB 12, WhAm 1*

Gray, Jennie T 1857- *AmWom*

Gray, Jessie 1876-1948 *WhAm 2*

Gray, John 1764-1868 *ApCAB*

Gray, John Alexander 1848-1920 *NatCAB 19*

Gray, John Chipman 1793-1881 *ApCAB*

Gray, John Chipman 1839-1915 *AmBi, ApCAB X, DcAmB, NatCAB 16, WhAm 1*

Gray, John Clinton 1843-1915 *TwCBDA, WhAm 1*

Gray, John Cowper 1783-1823 *BiAUS, BiDrAC, WhAm H*

Gray, John Edward 1911-1955 *NatCAB 47*

Gray, John F 1804-1882 *NatCAB 6*

Gray, John Hamilton 1814- *ApCAB*

Gray, John Henry 1859-1946 *ApCAB X, NatCAB 15, WhAm 2*

Gray, John Lathrop 1875-1947 *NatCAB 36*

Gray, John Perdue 1825-1886 *ApCAB, NatCAB 7, TwCBDA*

Gray, John Pinkham 1880-1939 *WhAm 1*

Gray, John Purdue 1825-1886 *AmBi, DcAmB, WhAm H*

Gray, John Simson 1841-1906 *NatCAB 18, NatCAB 25*

Gray, John Stanley 1894-1968 *NatCAB 54*

Gray, Joseph Anthony 1884-1966 *BiDrAC*

Gray, Joseph M M 1877-1957 *WhAm 3*

Gray, Joseph Phelps 1851- *WhAm 4*

Gray, Joseph Preston 1855-1910 *WhAm 1*

Gray, Joseph W 1813-1862 *DcAmB, WhAm H*

Gray, Joseph W 1814-1862 *NatCAB 22*

Gray, Joslyn *WhAm 5*

Gray, Kennedy *NewYHSD*

Gray, Kenneth James 1924- *BiDrAC*

Gray, Landon Carter 1850-1900 *NatCAB 5*

Gray, Leon Fowler 1901-1969 *WhAm 5*

Gray, Lewis Cecil 1881-1952 *EncAAH, WhAm 6*

Gray, Lillie Putnam *WomWWA 14*

Gray, Louis Herbert 1875-1955 *NatCAB 15, WhAm 3*

Gray, Maria Freeman 1832- *WhAm 4, WomWWA 14*

Gray, Marion Clark 1876- *WomWWA 14*

Gray, Mary Tenney 1833- *AmWom*

Gray, Mat 1876- *WhAm 5*

Gray, Morris 1856-1931 *NatCAB 50, WhAm 1*

Gray, Myron Herbert 1881-1955 *NatCAB 45*

Gray, Myrtle M 1875- *WomWWA 14*

Gray, Oliver Crosby 1832-1905 *NatCAB 8*

Gray, Oscar Lee 1865-1936 *BiDrAC, WhAm 4*

Gray, Peter W 1819-1874 *BiDConf*

Gray, Philip Hayward 1865-1922 *NatCAB 23*

Gray, Prentiss Nathaniel 1884-1935 *WhAm 1*

Gray, Publius Rutilius Rufus 1795-1840 *BiAUS, Drake*

Gray, Ralph Weld 1880-1944 *NatCAB 42, WhAm 6*

Gray, Richard J 1887-1966 *WhAm 4*

Gray, Robert 1755-1806 *AmBi, ApCAB, DcAmB, Drake, McGEWB, NatCAB 5, REnAW, WebAB, WhAm H*

Gray, Roland 1874- *WhAm 5*

Gray, Samuel Merrill 1842-1921 *NatCAB 19*

Gray, Solomon S 1820- *ApCAB, NatCAB 13*

Gray, Stephen 1666-1736 *DcScB*

Gray, Stephen 1696?-1736 *AsBiEn*

Gray, Thomas 1716-1771 *McGEWB*

Gray, Thomas 1850-1908 *WhAm 1*

Gray, Thomas Kennedy 1883-1909 *NatCAB 17*

Gray, Thomas Tarvin 1881-1931 *NatCAB 24*

Gray, U *IlBEAAW*

Gray, W *NewYHSD*

Gray, Wade Hampton 1876-1923 *NatCAB 22*

Gray, Walter H 1898-1973 *WhAm 6*

Gray, Wilford Drury 1884-1939 *NatCAB 42*

Gray, Willard Franklin 1913-1973 *WhAm 6*

Gray, William *NewYHSD*

Gray, William 1750-1825 *ApCAB, DcAmB, Drake, NatCAB 5, WhAm H*

Gray, William Crane 1835- *NatCAB 13, TwCBDA*

Gray, William Cunningham 1830-1901 *TwCBDA, WhAm 1*

Gray, William Dodge 1878-1958 *NatCAB 47*

Gray, William H 1810-1889 *REnAW*

Gray, William Herbert, Jr. 1911-1972 *NatCAB 56*

Gray, William Houser 1847- *NatCAB 3*

Gray, William John 1857- *WhAm 1*

Gray, William Price, Jr. 1909-1962 *WhAm 4*

Gray, William Rensselaer 1879-1937 *WhAm 1*

Gray, William Scott 1885-1960 *BiDAmEd, NatCAB 48, WhAm 4*

Gray, William Steele 1897-1965 *WhAm 4*

Gray, William T *NewYHSD*

Gray, William Walden 1864-1942 *NatCAB 33*

Graybiel, Mary 1846- *ApCAB Sup*

Graybill, Harry Webster 1875-1938 *NatCAB 29*

Graybill, Kenneth Wayne 1898-1962 *NatCAB 52*

Graydon, Alexander 1752-1818 *ApCAB, DcAmB, Drake, NatCAB 7, NewYHSD, WhAm H*

Graydon, James Weir 1848- *WhAm 4*

Graydon, James Weir 1849- *NatCAB 13, TwCBDA*

Graydon, Joseph Spencer 1876- *WhAm 5*

Graydon, William 1759-1840 *ApCAB, NatCAB 11, WhAm H*

Grayson, Cary Travers 1878-1938 *NatCAB 28, WhAm 1*

Grayson, Charles Prevost 1859- *WhAm 4*

Grayson, Clifford Prevost 1857- *NatCAB 13, WhAm 4*

Grayson, David *EncAB, WebAB*

Grayson, J H Lee 1885?- *IlBEAAW*

Grayson, John Breckenridge 1807-1862 *ApCAB, Drake*

Grayson, Laurence Ayres 1895-1961 *NatCAB 49*

Grayson, Theodore Julius 1880-1937 *NatCAB 42, WhAm 1*

Grayson, Thomas Jackson 1896-1962 *WhAm 4*

Grayson, Thomas Wray 1871-1933 *WhAm 1*

Grayson, William 1736?-1790 *ApCAB, BiAUS, DcAmB, Drake, NatCAB 12, WhAm H*

Grayson, William 1740?-1790 *BiDrAC, TwCBDA, WhAmP*

Grayson, William 1786-1868 *ApCAB, BiAUS, Drake, TwCBDA*

Grayson, William Bandy 1897-1965 *WhAm 4*

Grayson, William John 1788-1863 *ApCAB, BiAUS, BiDrAC, Drake, NatCAB 7, TwCBDA, WhAm H, WhAmP*

Graziani, Rodolfo 1882-1955 *WhoMilH*

Greacen, Edmund 1876-1949 *NatCAB 37*

Greacen, Edmund 1877-1949 *WhAm 2*

Great Renegade *REnAW*

Greath *NewYHSD*

Greathouse, Charles A 1869-1931 *WhAm 1*

Greathouse, Clarence Ridgeby 1845?-1899 *DcAmB, WhAm H, WhAm 1*

Greathouse, Lucien 1843-1864 *ApCAB, Drake*

Greathouse, Mary Melissa Curtis 1857- *WomWWA 14*

Greaton, John 1741-1783 *ApCAB, DcAmB, NatCAB 1, WhAm H*

Greaton, John 1741-1784 *Drake*

Greaton, Joseph 1679-1753 *DcAmB, WhAm H*

Greatorex, Eliza Pratt 1819-1897 *AmWom, ApCAB, NatCAB 5, NewYHSD, NotAW, TwCBDA*

Greatorex, Eliza Pratt 1820-1897 *IlBEAAW, WhAm H*

Greatorex, Elizabeth Eleanor 1854- *ApCAB*

Greatorex, Henry Wellington 1811-1858 *NatCAB 6*

Greatorex, Henry Wellington 1816-1858 *ApCAB, TwCBDA*

Greatorex, Kathleen Honora 1851- *ApCAB, WhAm 3, WomWWA 14*

Greaves, Frederick Clarence 1896-1973 *WhAm 6*

Greaves, Jessie Royer 1874-1967 *NatCAB 53*

Greaves, Joseph Eames 1880-1954 *NatCAB 47, WhAm 3*

Grebe, Marguerite Luckett d1972 *WhAm 5*

Grebenstchikoff, George 1883-1964 *WhAm 4*

Greberman, David 1910-1970 *NatCAB 55*

Greble, Edwin St. John 1859-1931 *NatCAB 23, WhAm 1*

Greble, John Trout 1834-1861 *ApCAB, NatCAB 5, TwCBDA, WhAm H*

Grechko, Andrey 1903-1976 *WhWW-II*

Greco, El 1541-1614 *McGEWB*

Greear, Fred Bonham 1899-1960 *WhAm 4*

Greef, Robert Julius 1909-1966 *WhAm 4*

Greeley, Arthur Philip 1862- *NatCAB 12*

Greeley, Edwin Seneca 1832- *WhAm 4*

Greeley, Helen Katharine Hoy *WomWWA 14*

Greeley, Horace 1811-1872 *AmBi, ApCAB, BiAUS, BiDrAC, DcAmB, Drake, EncAAH, EncAB, McGEWB, NatCAB 3, REnAW, TwCBDA, WebAB, WhAm H, WhAmP*

Greeley, Jane Lincoln 1864- *WomWWA 14*

Greeley, Jonathan Clark 1833- *NatCAB 5*

Greeley, Louis May 1858-1939 *WhAm 1*

Greeley, Mary Elizabeth 1836-1924 *NewYHSD*

Greeley, Mellen Clark 1880- *WhAm 6*

Greeley, Philip Hartson 1870-1946 *NatCAB 35*

Greeley, Samuel Arnold 1882-1968 *WhAm 5*

Greeley, Samuel Sewall 1824-1916 *NatCAB 16*

Greeley, William B 1879-1955 *WhAm 3*

Greeley, William Bradford 1859- *NatCAB 16*

Greeley, William Roger 1881-1966 *WhAm 4*

Greeley-Smith, Nixola 1880-1919 *NotAW*

Greely, Adolphus Washington 1844-1935 *AmBi, ApCAB, ApCAB X, DcAmB S1, McGEWB, NatCAB 3, NatCAB 42, WebAB, WebAMB, WhAm 1*

Greely, Adolphus Washington 1847-1935 *TwCBDA*

Greely, Ann Frances 1831- *WomWWA 14*

Greely, Antoinette 1879- *WhAm 6*

Greely, Edward 1835-1888 *WhAm H*

Greely, John Nesmith 1885-1965 *WhAm 4*

Green, Abel 1900-1973 *WhAm 6*

Green, Addison Loomis 1862-1942 *WhAm 2*

Green, Adolphus Williamson 1843-1917 *NatCAB 15, WhAm 1*

Green, Adwin Wigfall 1900-1966 *WhAm 4, WhAm 5*

Green, Alexander 1807- *Drake*

Green, Alexander Little Page 1806-1874 *ApCAB, DcAmB, NatCAB 11, TwCBDA, WhAm H*

Green, Allen Percival 1875-1956 *NatCAB 44, WhAm 3*

Green, Andrew Haswell 1820-1903 *AmBi, ApCAB Sup, DcAmB, NatCAB 13, TwCBDA, WhAm 1*

Green, Andrew Heatley, Jr. 1867-1947 *NatCAB 36*

Green, Anna Katharine 1846-1935 *AmBi, AmWom, ApCAB, DcAmB S1, NotAW, TwCBDA, WomWWA 14*

WhAm 4

Green, Robert Stafford 1909-1964 *NatCAB 51*
Green, Robert Stockton 1831-1895 *BiDrAC, NatCAB 5, TwCBDA, WhAm H, WhAmP*
Green, Rolland Lester 1875- *WhAm 5*
Green, Roy Monroe 1889-1948 *WhAm 2*
Green, Rufus Lot 1862-1932 *WhAm 1*
Green, Rufus Smith 1848-1925 *NatCAB 9, NatCAB 39*
Green, Samuel 1614?-1702 *NatCAB 20*
Green, Samuel 1615-1701? *DcAmB*
Green, Samuel 1615-1702 *AmBi, ApCAB, Drake, WhAm H*
Green, Samuel 1648-1690 *NatCAB 20*
Green, Samuel Abbott 1830- *ApCAB, TwCBDA*
Green, Samuel Abbott 1830-1918 *DcAmB, NatCAB 2*
Green, Samuel Abbott 1830-1919 *WhAm 1*
Green, Samuel Bowdlear 1859-1910 *AmBi, BiDAmEd, DcAmB, WhAm 1*
Green, Samuel Swett 1837-1918 *AmBi, DcAmB, DcAmLiB, NatCAB 6, TwCBDA, WhAm 1*
Green, Sara Elizabeth 1868- *WomWWA 14*
Green, Sarah Letty *WomWWA 14*
Green, Seth 1817-1888 *AmBi, ApCAB, DcAmB, NatCAB 6, TwCBDA, WhAm H*
Green, Sidney Lewis 1914-1966 *NatCAB 51*
Green, Theodore Bliss 1877- *WhoColR*
Green, Theodore Francis 1867-1966 *BiDrAC, NatCAB 18, NatCAB 53, WhAm 4, WhAmP*
Green, Theodore Meyer 1897-1969 *WhAm 5*
Green, Thomas *ApCAB, NatCAB 7*
Green, Thomas 1735-1812 *DcAmB, NatCAB 17, WhAm H*
Green, Thomas 1814-1864 *BiDConf, NatCAB 4, TwCBDA*
Green, Thomas 1816-1864 *ApCAB, Drake*
Green, Thomas 1837-1916 *NatCAB 17*
Green, Thomas Dunbar 1870-1954 *WhAm 3*
Green, Thomas Edward 1857- *TwCBDA, WhAm 1*
Green, Thomas Hill 1836-1882 *McGEWB*
Green, Thomas Jefferson 1801-1863 *ApCAB, Drake, NatCAB 11*
Green, Thomas Jefferson 1802-1863 *TwCBDA*
Green, Thomas Jefferson 1870-1915 *NatCAB 16*
Green, Traill 1813-1897 *ApCAB, NatCAB 11, TwCBDA*
Green, W T *NewYHSD*
Green, Walter Lawrence 1894-1962 *WhAm 4*
Green, Walton Atwater 1881-1954 *WhAm 3*
Green, Warren Everett 1870-1945 *NatCAB 37, WhAm 2*
Green, Warren Kimball 1891-1964 *NatCAB 51*
Green, Wendell Elbert 1887-1959 *NatCAB 45*
Green, Wharton Jackson 1831-1910 *BiDrAC, TwCBDA, WhAm 1*
Green, Wharton Jackson 1840?- *ApCAB*
Green, William *NewYHSD*
Green, William 1806-1880 *DcAmB, NatCAB 22, WhAm H*
Green, William 1861-1925 *WhAm 1*
Green, William 1870-1952 *DcAmB S5, NatCAB 41, WhAm 3*
Green, William 1873-1952 *EncAB, WebAB*
Green, William Alexander 1834- *ApCAB*
Green, William Charles 1886-1952 *WhAm 3*
Green, William Cowan 1851- *NatCAB 6*
Green, William Elza 1845-1913 *WhAm 1*
Green, William H *NewYHSD*
Green, William Henry 1825-1900 *ApCAB, DcAmB, NatCAB 6, TwCBDA, WhAm 1*
Green, William Joseph 1938- *BiDrAC*
Green, William Joseph, Jr. 1910-1963 *BiDrAC, WhAm 4*
Green, William Louis 1874-1955 *NatCAB 43*
Green, William Marvin 1884-1946 *WhAm 2*
Green, William Mercer 1798-1887 *ApCAB, Drake, NatCAB 9, TwCBDA, WhAm H*
Green, William Mercer 1876-1942 *NatCAB 42, WhAm 2*

Green, William Ogden 1860-1943 *NatCAB 40*
Green, William R 1872-1952 *McGEWB*
Green, William Raymond 1856-1947 *BiDrAC, NatCAB 45, WhAm 2, WhAmP*
Green, William T 1857-1917 *NatCAB 17*
Green, Willis *BiAUS, BiDrAC, WhAm H*
Green, Wyman Reed 1881- *WhAm 6*
Greenacre, Isaiah Thomas 1863-1944 *NatCAB 43*
Greenawald, Paul Benjamin 1894-1952 *WhAm 3*
Greenawalt, E Paul 1895-1950 *NatCAB 39*
Greenawalt, Elmer Ellsworth 1862-1920 *WhAm 1*
Greenawalt, George Leiter 1851-1917 *NatCAB 17*
Greenawalt, Mary Eliza 1854- *WomWWA 14*
Greenbaum, David 1908-1974 *WhAm 6*
Greenbaum, Edward Samuel 1890-1970 *NatCAB 55, WhAm 5*
Greenbaum, Leo 1858- *WhAm 1*
Greenbaum, Max 1868-1937 *WhAm 1*
Greenbaum, Samuel 1854-1930 *WhAm 1*
Greenbaum, Sigmund Samuel 1890-1949 *WhAm 2*
Greenberg, Bernard Samuel 1913-1965 *WhAm 4*
Greenberg, David 1888-1959 *NatCAB 47*
Greenberg, Meyer 1872-1933 *NatCAB 27*
Greenberg, Noah 1919-1966 *WhAm 4*
Greenberg, Sarah K 1884-1971 *WhAm 6*
Greenberry, Nicholas 1627-1697 *NatCAB 10, WhAm H*
Greenbie, Marjorie Barstow 1891-1976 *WhAm 6*
Greenbie, Sydney 1889-1960 *WhAm 4*
Greenblatt, Jacob 1915-1972 *WhAm 6*
Greenblatt, Louis 1905-1972 *WhAm 5*
Greendlinger, Leo 1879-1935 *NatCAB 27, WhAm 1*
Greene *NewYHSD*
Greene, A Crawford 1885-1966 *NatCAB 54, WhAm 4*
Greene, Aella 1838-1903 *WhAm 1*
Greene, Albert Collins 1791-1863 *ApCAB, BiDrAC, Drake, TwCBDA, WhAm H*
Greene, Albert Collins 1792-1863 *BiAUS, NatCAB 8*
Greene, Albert Gorton 1802-1868 *AmBi, ApCAB, DcAmB, Drake, NatCAB 9, TwCBDA, WhAm H*
Greene, Anne Bosworth 1877- *WomWWA 14*
Greene, Anne Bosworth 1878- *WhAm 6*
Greene, Arthur Maurice, Jr. 1872- *WhAm 5*
Greene, Asa 1788-1837 *ApCAB, Drake*
Greene, Balcomb 1904- *BnEnAmA*
Greene, Belle C 1844- *AmWom*
Greene, Belle DaCosta 1883-1950 *DcAmB S4, DcAmLiB, NotAW*
Greene, Benjamin Allen 1845-1915 *WhAm 1*
Greene, Benjamin Daniel 1793-1862 *NatCAB 7*
Greene, Burch Ernest 1898-1954 *NatCAB 41*
Greene, Carolyn May Wygant 1874- *WomWWA 14*
Greene, Catherine Littlefield 1755-1814 *NotAW*
Greene, Charles Arthur 1875- *WhAm 5*
Greene, Charles Ezra 1842-1903 *ApCAB, DcAmB, NatCAB 26, TwCBDA, WhAm 1*
Greene, Charles Gordon 1804-1886 *ApCAB, Drake, NatCAB 4, TwCBDA*
Greene, Charles Jerome 1867-1944 *WhAm 2*
Greene, Charles Lyman 1862-1929 *ApCAB X, NatCAB 12, NatCAB 33, WhAm 1*
Greene, Charles Porter 1844-1915 *NatCAB 17*
Greene, Charles Samuel 1856-1930 *WhAm 1*
Greene, Charles Sumner 1868-1957 *BnEnAmA, DcAmB S5, NatCAB 48*
Greene, Charles Warren 1840- *ApCAB, TwCBDA, WhAm 4*
Greene, Charles Wilson 1866- *WhAm 4*
Greene, Chester W 1839- *WhAm 4*
Greene, Christopher 1737-1781 *AmBi, ApCAB, DcAmB, Drake, NatCAB 8, TwCBDA, WhAm H*
Greene, Clay Meredith 1850-1933 *WhAm 1*
Greene, Condon Lorntz 1895- *WhAm 6*
Greene, Daniel Crosby 1843-1913 *DcAmB, NatCAB 23, WhAm 1*

Greene, Daniel Crosby 1873-1941 *WhAm 1*
Greene, Dascom 1825-1900 *NatCAB 2, TwCBDA*
Greene, David 1791-1866 *ApCAB*
Greene, David Maxson 1832-1905 *WhAm 1*
Greene, Edward Allen 1873-1942 *NatCAB 33*
Greene, Edward Belden 1878-1957 *NatCAB 44, WhAm 3*
Greene, Edward D E 1823-1879 *NewYHSD*
Greene, Edward Lee 1843-1915 *DcAmB, NatCAB 19, TwCBDA, WhAm 1*
Greene, Edward Martin 1875-1952 *WhAm 3*
Greene, Edwin Farnham 1879-1953 *WhAm 3*
Greene, Ella Catherine *WomWWA 14*
Greene, Evarts Boutell 1870-1947 *WhAm 2*
Greene, Flora Hartley 1865- *WhAm 4, WomWWA 14*
Greene, Floyd L 1888-1954 *WhAm 3*
Greene, Frances Harriet Whipple *TwCBDA*
Greene, Frances Harriet Whipple 1805-1875 *ApCAB*
Greene, Frances Harriet Whipple 1805-1878 *DcAmB*
Greene, Frances Harriet Whipple *see also* Green, Frances H W
Greene, Frances Nimmo *AmWom, WomWWA 14*
Greene, Francis Vinton 1850-1921 *AmBi, ApCAB, ApCAB X, DcAmB, NatCAB 1, NatCAB 23, TwCBDA, WhAm 1*
Greene, Frank Lester 1870-1930 *ApCAB X, BiDrAC, NatCAB 25, WhAm 1, WhAmP*
Greene, Fred T 1903-1961 *WhAm 4*
Greene, Frederick Stuart 1870-1939 *NatCAB 37, WhAm 1*
Greene, Gardiner 1851-1925 *WhAm 1*
Greene, George C 1833-1909 *WhAm 1*
Greene, George Francis 1858-1926 *WhAm 1*
Greene, George Louis 1917- *WhAm 5*
Greene, George Sears 1801-1899 *AmBi, ApCAB, DcAmB, Drake, NatCAB 1, TwCBDA, WebAMB, WhAm H*
Greene, George Sears 1837-1922 *ApCAB, DcAmB, NatCAB 1, TwCBDA, WhAm 1*
Greene, George Shaw 1884-1933 *NatCAB 27*
Greene, George Washington 1811-1883 *AmBi, ApCAB, DcAmB, Drake, NatCAB 7, TwCBDA, WhAm H*
Greene, George Wellington 1866-1925 *WhAm 1*
Greene, George Woodward 1831-1895 *BiAUS, BiDrAC, WhAm H*
Greene, Gertrude Glass 1904-1956 *NatCAB 47*
Greene, Graham 1904- *McGEWB*
Greene, Hamilton 1904- *IIBEAAW*
Greene, Harry Irving 1868- *WhAm 4*
Greene, Harry Sylvestre Nutting 1904-1969 *WhAm 5*
Greene, Helen Culver Kerr 1896- *BiCAW*
Greene, Henry Alexander 1856-1921 *WhAm 1*
Greene, Henry Copley 1871-1951 *WhAm 3*
Greene, Henry F *NewYHSD*
Greene, Henry Fay 1859-1915 *WhAm 1*
Greene, Henry Mather 1870-1954 *BnEnAmA, DcAmB S5*
Greene, Henry Vincent 1888-1954 *WhAm 3*
Greene, Herbert Eveleth 1858-1942 *TwCBDA, WhAm 2*
Greene, Herbert Wilber 1851-1924 *WhAm 1*
Greene, Homer 1853-1940 *NatCAB 13, WhAm 1*
Greene, Howard 1864-1956 *WhAm 3*
Greene, Isabel Catherine 1842- *WhAm 4*
Greene, Jacob Lyman 1837-1905 *TwCBDA, WhAm 1*
Greene, James E 1900-1971 *WhAm 5*
Greene, James H 1895-1960 *WhAm 4*
Greene, James Leon 1861-1930 *WhAm 1, WhAm 1C*
Greene, James Nicholas 1906-1971 *WhAm 5*
Greene, James Sonnett 1880-1950 *WhAm 3*
Greene, Jerome Davis 1874-1959 *WhAm 3*
Greene, Jessie Rice 1862- *WomWWA 14*
Greene, John 1850- *WhAm 4*
Greene, John Ernest 1858-1921 *WhAm 1*
Greene, John Holden 1777-1850 *WhAm H*
Greene, John Morton 1830- *WhAm 4*

Greene, John Priest 1849-1933 *NatCAB 13,
TwCBDA, WhAm 1*
Greene, Joseph Chase 1829- *NatCAB 3*
Greene, Joseph Ingham 1897-1953 *WhAm 3*
Greene, Joseph Nathaniel 1893-1969 *WhAm 5*
Greene, Joseph Warren, Jr. 1897-1968
NatCAB 54
Greene, Josie Craig *WomWWA 14*
Greene, Katherine Glass 1865-1946 *WhAm 2*
Greene, Laurence Whitridge 1895-1971
WhAm 6
Greene, LeRoy E 1893- *IlBEAAW*
Greene, Lilyan Durrant 1876- *WomWWA 14*
Greene, Lionel Y 1892-1962 *WhAm 4*
Greene, Louisa Morton 1819- *AmWom*
Greene, Marc Tiffany 1881-1966 *WhAm 4*
Greene, Maria Louise *WhAm 5,
WomWWA 14*
Greene, Martha T 1859- *WomWWA 14*
Greene, Mary Anne 1857- *AmWom, WhAm 4,
WomWWA 14*
Greene, Mary E Lewis 1869- *WomWWA 14*
Greene, Mary Gertrude Munson *WomWWA 14*
Greene, Mary Jane *WhAm 4*
Greene, Milbury Miller 1831-1887 *NatCAB 12*
Greene, Minnie Waugh 1882- *WomWWA 14*
Greene, Mosely *NewYHSD*
Greene, Myron Wesley 1864-1935 *ApCAB X,
NatCAB 15, WhAm 1*
Greene, Mrs. N *NewYHSD*
Greene, Nancy Andrews 1858- *WomWWA 14*
Greene, Nathanael 1742-1786 *AmBi, ApCAB,
DcAmB, EncAB, McGEWB, NatCAB 1,
TwCBDA, WebAB, WebAMB, WhAm H,
WhoMilH*
Greene, Nathaniel 1742-1786 *Drake*
Greene, Nathaniel 1797-1877 *ApCAB, DcAmB,
Drake, NatCAB 11, TwCBDA, WhAm H*
Greene, Nellie Cady 1860- *WomWWA 14*
Greene, Nellie Weaver 1872- *WhoColR*
Greene, Nelson Lewis 1881-1947 *NatCAB 36*
Greene, Oliver D 1833- *WhAm 1*
Greene, Patterson 1898-1968 *WhAm 5*
Greene, Raleigh W 1893-1954 *WhAm 3*
Greene, Ray 1765-1829 *BiDrAC, WhAm H*
Greene, Ray 1765-1849 *ApCAB, BiAUS,
NatCAB 4, TwCBDA*
Greene, Richard Gleason 1829-1914 *WhAm 1*
Greene, Richard Henry 1839-1926 *NatCAB 24*
Greene, Richard Thurston 1867-1949 *WhAm 3*
Greene, Richard Ward 1792-1875 *NatCAB 4*
Greene, Robert Holmes 1861-1933 *WhAm 1*
Greene, Roger Sherman 1840-1930 *BiAUS,
NatCAB 24*
Greene, Roger Sherman 1881-1930 *WhAm 1*
Greene, Roger Sherman 1881-1947 *DcAmB S4,
WhAm 2*
Greene, S Harold 1880-1937 *NatCAB 30*
Greene, Sam 1895-1963 *WhAm 4*
Greene, Samuel Dana 1839-1884 *ApCAB,
TwCBDA*
Greene, Samuel Dana 1840-1884 *DcAmB,
NatCAB 2, WhAm H*
Greene, Samuel Harrison 1845- *NatCAB 2,
WhAm 4*
Greene, Samuel Stillman 1810-1883 *ApCAB,
BiDAmEd, DcAmB, Drake, NatCAB 8,
TwCBDA, WhAm H*
Greene, Samuel Webb 1876- *WhAm 5*
Greene, Sarah Pratt McLean 1856-1935 *AmBi,
NatCAB 13, NotAW, TwCBDA,
WhAm 1, WomWWA 14*
Greene, Stephen Harold 1880-1937 *WhAm 1*
Greene, Theodore Ainsworth 1890-1951
NatCAB 40, WhAm 3
Greene, Theodore Phinney 1809-1887 *ApCAB,
Drake, NatCAB 5, TwCBDA, WebAMB*
Greene, Thomas L d1904 *WhAm 1*
Greene, Thomas Marston 1758-1813 *BiAUS,
BiDrAC, WhAm H*
Greene, Wallace Martin, Jr. 1907- *WebAMB*
Greene, Walter E 1874- *NatCAB 18*
Greene, Ward 1892-1956 *WhAm 3*
Greene, Warwick 1879-1929 *NatCAB 24,
WhAm 1*
Greene, William d1758 *Drake*
Greene, William 1695-1758 *ApCAB, DcAmB,
NatCAB 10, TwCBDA*

Greene, William 1696-1758 *WhAm H*
Greene, William 1731-1809 *ApCAB, DcAmB,
NatCAB 9, TwCBDA, WhAm H*
Greene, William 1732-1809 *Drake*
Greene, William 1797-1881 *NatCAB 8*
Greene, William 1797-1883 *TwCBDA*
Greene, William Batchelder 1819-1878 *ApCAB,
NatCAB 7, TwCBDA*
Greene, William Brenton, Jr. 1854-1928
NatCAB 21, WhAm 4
Greene, William C *NewYHSD*
Greene, William Cornell 1851-1911 *DcAmB,
WhAm 1*
Greene, William Houston 1853-1918 *TwCBDA,
WhAm 1*
Greene, William Houston 1854-1918 *ApCAB*
Greene, William Laury 1849-1899 *BiDrAC,
TwCBDA, WhAm 1*
Greene, William Lyman 1828-1914 *NatCAB 17*
Greene, William Milbury 1858- *NatCAB 12,
WhAm 4*
Greene, William Stedman 1841-1924 *BiDrAC,
TwCBDA, WhAm 1, WhAmP*
Greene, Winfield Wardwell 1887-1965 *WhAm 4*
Greene, Zachariah 1760-1858 *Drake*
Greenebaum, Elias 1822-1919 *NatCAB 17*
Greenebaum, Henry Everett 1854-1931
WhAm 1
Greenebaum, Jacob Victor 1885-1972
NatCAB 57
Greenebaum, Leon Charles 1907-1968 *WhAm 5*
Greenebaum, Moses Ernest 1858-1934 *WhAm 1*
Greenebaum, Samuel Lewis 1902-1973 *WhAm 6*
Greenefield, Nathan R 1874-1938 *WhAm 1*
Greener, John Hunter 1906-1969 *WhAm 5*
Greener, Richard Theodore 1844-1922 *ApCAB,
DcAmB, NatCAB 13, TwCBDA,
WhAm 4, WhoColR*
Greenewalt, Mary Elizabeth Hallock 1871-1950
NatCAB 39, WomWWA 14
Greenfield, Albert Monroe 1887-1967 *WhAm 4*
Greenfield, Elizabeth Taylor 1808-1876 *ApCAB*
Greenfield, Elizabeth Taylor 1817?-1876
NotAW
Greenfield, Eric Viele 1881- *WhAm 6*
Greenfield, Joseph A 1879- *WhAm 6*
Greenfield, Kent Roberts 1893-1967 *WhAm 4*
Greenhalge, Frederic Brandlesome 1875-1954
NatCAB 42
Greenhalge, Frederic Thomas 1842-1896
BiDrAC, DcAmB, TwCBDA
Greenhalge, Frederick Thomas 1842-1896
ApCAB Sup, WhAm H
Greenhalgh, George Thomas 1864-1949
NatCAB 42
Greenhill, J P 1895-1975 *WhAm 6*
Greenhouse, Charles Abraham 1897-1966
NatCAB 52
Greenhow, Robert 1800-1854 *ApCAB, DcAmB,
Drake, WhAm H*
Greenhow, Rose O'Neal d1864 *WebAB*
Greenhow, Rose O'Neal 1815?-1864 *NotAW*
Greenhow, Rose O'Neal 1817-1864 *BiDConf*
Greenhow, William Henry 1845-1918
NatCAB 18
Greenhut, Benedict Joseph 1870-1932
NatCAB 23
Greening, Harry Cornell 1876- *WhAm 5*
Greening, Helen Eugene Haines *WomWWA 14*
Greening, J Neal 1896-1959 *NatCAB 48*
Greenlaw, Edwin Almiron 1874-1931 *BiDAmEd,
DcAmB S1, NatCAB 22, WhAm 1*
Greenlaw, Lowell M d1968 *WhAm 5*
Greenlaw, Ralph Milo 1875-1951 *NatCAB 39*
Greenleaf, Benjamin 1786-1864 *ApCAB,
BiDAmEd, DcAmB, Drake, NatCAB 8,
NewYHSD, TwCBDA, WhAm H*
Greenleaf, Carl Dimond 1876-1959 *WhAm 3*
Greenleaf, Charles Ravenscroft 1838-1911
TwCBDA, WhAm 1
Greenleaf, David 1763-1819 *TwCBDA*
Greenleaf, Edmund 1574?-1671 *NatCAB 8,
WhAm H*
Greenleaf, Ezekiel Price 1790-1886 *ApCAB,
TwCBDA*
Greenleaf, Franklin Lewis 1847-1908 *NatCAB 6*
Greenleaf, Georgie H Franck 1842-1913
WhAm 1

Greenleaf, Halbert Stevens 1827-1906 *BiDrAC,
DcAmB, NatCAB 8, TwCBDA*
Greenleaf, James 1765-1843 *TwCBDA*
Greenleaf, James Leal 1857-1933 *NatCAB 30,
WhAm 1*
Greenleaf, Jean Brooks 1832- *AmWom*
Greenleaf, Jonathan 1785-1865 *ApCAB, Drake,
NatCAB 8, TwCBDA, WhAm H*
Greenleaf, Joseph 1720-1809 *NatCAB 8*
Greenleaf, Moses 1755-1812 *NatCAB 8,
WhAm H*
Greenleaf, Moses 1777-1834 *DcAmB,
WhAm H*
Greenleaf, Moses 1778-1834 *ApCAB, Drake*
Greenleaf, Orick Herman 1823-1896 *NatCAB 8*
Greenleaf, Patrick Henry 1807-1869 *NatCAB 8*
Greenleaf, Simon 1783-1853 *AmBi, ApCAB,
BiDAmEd, DcAmB, Drake, NatCAB 7,
TwCBDA, WhAm H*
Greenleaf, Stephen 1704-1795 *NatCAB 8*
Greenleaf, Sue *WomWWA 14*
Greenleaf, Thomas 1755-1798 *DcAmB,
NatCAB 23, WhAm H*
Greenlee, John Reece 1916-1975 *WhAm 6*
Greenlee, Karl B 1902-1964 *WhAm 4*
Greenlee, William Brooks 1872-1953
NatCAB 41
Greenley, Howard 1874-1963 *WhAm 4*
Greenly, William L 1813-1883 *NatCAB 5,
TwCBDA*
Greenman, A V 1852- *WhAm 4*
Greenman, Edward Whitford 1840-1908
BiDrAC
Greenman, Frederick Francis 1892-1961
WhAm 4
Greenman, Jesse More 1867-1951 *WhAm 3*
Greenman, Milton Jay 1866-1937 *NatCAB 32,
WhAm 1*
Greenman, Walter Folger 1865-1945 *WhAm 2*
Greenough *NewYHSD*
Greenough, Allen Jackson 1905-1974 *WhAm 6*
Greenough, Benjamin F *NewYHSD*
Greenough, Charles Pelham 1844-1924
NatCAB 32
Greenough, Chester Noyes 1874-1938 *WhAm 1*
Greenough, Clara Mary 1870- *WomWWA 14*
Greenough, Francis Boott 1837- *ApCAB*
Greenough, George Bellas 1778-1855 *DcScB*
Greenough, George Gordon 1844-1912 *WhAm 1*
Greenough, Henry 1807-1883 *ApCAB, DcAmB,
NatCAB 20, TwCBDA, WhAm H*
Greenough, Horatio 1805-1852 *AmBi, ApCAB,
ApCAB X, BiAUS, BnEnAmA, DcAmB,
Drake, NatCAB 6, NewYHSD, TwCBDA,
WebAB, WhAm H*
Greenough, J James *NewYHSD*
Greenough, James Bradstreet 1833-1901 *DcAmB,
NatCAB 26, WhAm 1*
Greenough, James Carruthers 1829-1924
ApCAB X, NatCAB 27, WhAm 1
Greenough, Jane Ashley Bates 1835-
WomWWA 14
Greenough, Jeanie Ashley Bates 1835- *WhAm 4*
Greenough, John 1801-1852 *NewYHSD*
Greenough, John 1846-1934 *WhAm 1*
Greenough, Richard Saltonstall 1819-1904 *AmBi,
ApCAB, BnEnAmA, DcAmB, NatCAB 8,
NatCAB 23, NewYHSD, TwCBDA*
Greenough, Robert Battey 1871-1937
NatCAB 26, WhAm 1
Greenough, Sarah Dana 1827-1885 *ApCAB*
Greenough, William 1874-1949 *WhAm 2*
Greenough, William Bates 1866-1956
NatCAB 46
Greenough, William Israel 1821-1893
NatCAB 7
Greenquist, Kenneth Lloyd 1910-1968
NatCAB 54, WhAm 5
Greensfelder, Albert Preston 1879-1955
WhAm 3
Greensfelder, Louis Alexander 1867-1929
NatCAB 22
Greenshields, Donn D 1904-1961 *WhAm 4*
Greenslade, John Wills 1880-1950 *NatCAB 43,
WhAm 2*
Greenslet, Ferris 1875-1959 *WhAm 3*
Greenstein, Jesse Leonard 1909- *AsBiEn*
Greenstein, Jesse Philip 1902-1959 *NatCAB 45,*

WhAm 3

Greenstone, Julius Hillel 1873-1955 *WhAm 3*

Greenstreet, Sydney Hughes 1879-1954 *DcAmB S5*

Greenup, Christopher 1750?-1818 *ApCAB, BiAUS, BiDrAC, DcAmB, Drake, NatCAB 13, TwCBDA, WhAm H, WhAmP*

Greenville, Sir Richard 1540-1591 *Drake*

Greenwald *NewYHSD*

Greenwald, Emanuel 1811-1885 *ApCAB, DcAmB, TwCBDA, WhAm H*

Greenwald, Herbert S 1915-1959 *WhAm 3*

Greenwalt, John *NewYHSD*

Greenway, Charles Moore 1868-1934 *NatCAB 27, WhAm 1*

Greenway, Isabella Selmes 1886-1953 *BiDrAC, WhAm 3, WhAmP*

Greenway, James Cowan 1877- *WhAm 5*

Greenway, John Campbell 1872-1926 *DcAmB S1, NatCAB 18, REnAW, WhAm 1*

Greenway, Walter Burton 1876-1940 *WhAm 1*

Greenwell, Darrell J 1891-1961 *WhAm 4*

Greenwell, Hiliary Johnson 1840- *TwCBDA, WhAm 4*

Greenwood *NewYHSD*

Greenwood, A B 1811-1889 *BiAUS*

Greenwood, Alfred Burton 1811-1889 *BiDrAC, WhAm H, WhAmP*

Greenwood, Allen 1866-1942 *NatCAB 47, WhAm 2*

Greenwood, Arthur Herbert 1880-1963 *BiDrAC, NatCAB 52, WhAm 4*

Greenwood, Caleb 1763-1850 *REnAW*

Greenwood, Chester 1858-1937 *NatCAB 27*

Greenwood, Elizabeth Ward 1849- *AmWom*

Greenwood, Elizabeth Ward 1850- *WhAm 4, WomWWA 14*

Greenwood, Elmore Patrick 1875-1944 *NatCAB 34*

Greenwood, Ernest 1884-1955 *BiDrAC, WhAm 3*

Greenwood, Ethan Allen 1779-1856 *NewYHSD, WhAm H*

Greenwood, Francis William Pitt 1797-1843 *ApCAB, Drake, TwCBDA*

Greenwood, George Herbert 1884-1952 *NatCAB 41*

Greenwood, Grace *AmBi, AmWom, DcAmB, NotAW, WhAm 1*

Greenwood, Helen Evangeline 1872- *WomWWA 14*

Greenwood, Henry Burgess 1897-1961 *NatCAB 49*

Greenwood, Isaac 1702-1745 *ApCAB, BiDAmEd, DcAmB, DcScB, Drake, TwCBDA, WhAm H*

Greenwood, James 1878-1949 *NatCAB 42*

Greenwood, James M 1837- *WhAm 4*

Greenwood, James Mickleborough 1836-1914 *ApCAB, BiDAmEd, NatCAB 13*

Greenwood, John 1727-1792 *BnEnAmA, NewYHSD*

Greenwood, John 1760-1819 *DcAmB, WhAm H*

Greenwood, John 1798-1887 *NatCAB 6*

Greenwood, John Joseph 1917-1971 *WhAm 5*

Greenwood, Marion 1909-1970 *WhAm 5*

Greenwood, Miles 1807-1885 *ApCAB, DcAmB, Drake, TwCBDA, WhAm H*

Greenwood, Thomas Benton 1872-1946 *NatCAB 36, WhAm 2*

Greenwood, William Henry 1832-1880 *NatCAB 16*

Greer, Benjamin Brinton 1877-1932 *WhAm 1*

Greer, David Hummell 1844-1919 *AmBi, ApCAB Sup, ApCAB X, DcAmB, NatCAB 8, TwCBDA, WhAm 1*

Greer, Edith 1866- *WomWWA 14*

Greer, Frank U 1895-1949 *WhAm 2*

Greer, George 1844-1926 *NatCAB 20*

Greer, Herbert Chester 1877-1948 *NatCAB 37, WhAm 2*

Greer, Hilton Ross 1879-1949 *NatCAB 38, WhAm 3*

Greer, Isaac Garfield 1881- *WhAm 6*

Greer, James Agustin 1833-1904 *WhAm 1*

Greer, James Augustin 1833-1904 *ApCAB, DcAmB, NatCAB 4, TwCBDA*

Greer, James E *IIBEAAW*

Greer, Jefferson E 1905- *IIBEAAW*

Greer, Juliet *WomWWA 14*

Greer, Lawrence 1872-1925 *WhAm 1*

Greer, Margaret R 1891-1957 *WhAm 3*

Greer, Samuel Miller 1875-1948 *WhAm 2*

Greer, W Neal 1888-1964 *NatCAB 51*

Greer, William Kirk 1873-1945 *NatCAB 35*

Greet, William Cabell 1901-1972 *WhAm 5*

Greeter, Russell Franklin 1901-1958 *NatCAB 44*

Greever, Edgar Lee 1866-1943 *NatCAB 34*

Greever, Garland 1883-1967 *WhAm 4*

Greever, Paul Ranous 1891-1943 *BiDrAC, WhAmP*

Greever, Walton Harlowe 1870-1965 *NatCAB 53, WhAm 4*

Greever, William St. Clair 1916- *EncAAH*

Greey, Edward 1835-1888 *ApCAB, NatCAB 8*

Greger, Herbert Hans 1900-1972 *NatCAB 57*

Gregersen, Magnus Ingstrup 1903-1969 *WhAm 5*

Gregg, Alan 1890-1957 *WhAm 3*

Gregg, Alexander 1819-1893 *ApCAB, NatCAB 12, TwCBDA, WhAm H*

Gregg, Alexander White 1855-1919 *BiDrAC, WhAm 1, WhAmP*

Gregg, Alexander White, Jr. 1899-1958 *WhAm 3*

Gregg, Andrew 1755-1835 *ApCAB, BiAUS, BiDrAC, DcAmB, Drake, NatCAB 4, TwCBDA, WhAm H, WhAmP*

Gregg, Curtis Hussey 1865-1933 *BiDrAC, WhAm 4*

Gregg, David 1845-1919 *WhAm 1*

Gregg, David 1846-1919 *NatCAB 6*

Gregg, David Almus 1841-1928 *NatCAB 32*

Gregg, David L d1868 *BiAUS, NatCAB 13*

Gregg, David McM 1834- *Drake*

Gregg, David McMurtie 1833-1916 *NatCAB 4*

Gregg, David McMurtrie 1833-1916 *AmBi, ApCAB, DcAmB, TwCBDA, WhAm 1*

Gregg, Donald Cameron 1899-1954 *NatCAB 42*

Gregg, Earl Lamont 1878- *WhAm 6*

Gregg, Ellis Bailey 1856-1936 *NatCAB 27*

Gregg, Florence Clara d1974 *WhAm 6*

Gregg, Francis Whitlock 1873- *WhAm 5*

Gregg, Frank Moody 1864- *WhAm 4*

Gregg, Fred Marion 1867- *WhAm 4*

Gregg, Godfrey Robert 1923-1973 *WhAm 6*

Gregg, J A 1877-1953 *WhAm 3*

Gregg, James 1787-1852 *ApCAB*

Gregg, James Bartlett 1846-1922 *WhAm 1*

Gregg, James Edgar 1875-1946 *WhAm 2*

Gregg, James Madison 1806-1869 *BiAUS, BiDrAC, WhAm H*

Gregg, John 1828-1864 *BiDConf, DcAmB, Drake, WhAm H*

Gregg, John Andrew 1877-1953 *DcAmB S5, WhAm 3, WhoColR*

Gregg, John B 1888-1954 *WhAm 3*

Gregg, John Irvin 1826-1892 *ApCAB, Drake, NatCAB 10, TwCBDA*

Gregg, John Price 1891-1952 *NatCAB 41, WhAm 3*

Gregg, John Robert 1867-1948 *BiDAmEd, DcAmB S4, WhAm 2*

Gregg, John William 1880- *WhAm 6*

Gregg, Josiah 1806-1850 *AmBi, DcAmB, NatCAB 19, REnAW, WebAB, WhAm H*

Gregg, Maxcy 1814-1862 *BiDConf, DcAmB, Drake, NatCAB 10, TwCBDA, WhAm H*

Gregg, Maxey 1814-1862 *ApCAB*

Gregg, Norris Bradford 1856- *NatCAB 12*

Gregg, Paul L 1901-1955 *WhAm 3*

Gregg, Russell Taaffe 1903-1973 *WhAm 6*

Gregg, William 1800-1867 *AmBi, BiDConf, DcAmB, EncAB, McGEWB, TwCBDA, WebAB*

Gregg, William 1800-1877 *WhAm H*

Gregg, William 1817- *ApCAB*

Gregg, William C 1862-1946 *WhAm 2*

Gregg, William Henry 1831- *NatCAB 7, WhAm 4*

Gregg, Willis Ray 1880-1938 *DcAmB S2,*

NatCAB 32, WhAm 1

Greggs, Napoleon Payne 1880- *WhoColR*

Gregor, Elmer Russell 1878-1954 *WhAm 3*

Gregor, William 1761-1817 *AsBiEn*

Gregori, Luigi 1819- *ApCAB*

Gregory I 540?-604 *McGEWB*

Gregory VII 1020?-1085 *McGEWB*

Gregory XIII 1502-1585 *McGEWB*

Gregory Of Tours, Saint 538-594 *McGEWB*

Gregory, Lady Augusta 1852-1932 *McGEWB*

Gregory, Carl C 1888-1933 *WhAm 1*

Gregory, Caspar Rene 1846-1917 *DcAmB, TwCBDA, WhAm 1*

Gregory, Caspar Robue 1824-1882 *TwCBDA*

Gregory, Charles Alexander 1877-1956 *NatCAB 43*

Gregory, Charles Noble 1851-1932 *DcAmB S1, NatCAB 16, TwCBDA, WhAm 1*

Gregory, Chester Arthur 1880-1956 *WhAm 3*

Gregory, Clifford Verne 1883-1941 *DcAmB S3, EncAAH, NatCAB 31, WhAm 2*

Gregory, Daniel Seeley 1832-1915 *ApCAB*

Gregory, Daniel Seely 1832-1915 *TwCBDA*

Gregory, Daniel Seelye 1832-1915 *AmBi, DcAmB, NatCAB 19, WhAm 1*

Gregory, David 1659-1708 *DcScB*

Gregory, David 1661-1708 *AsBiEn*

Gregory, David Thomas 1889-1956 *WhAm 3*

Gregory, Donn 1918-1972 *NatCAB 57*

Gregory, Dudley S 1800-1874 *BiAUS*

Gregory, Dudley Sandford 1800-1874 *ApCAB*

Gregory, Dudley Sanford 1800-1874 *BiDrAC, WhAm H*

Gregory, Duncan Farquharson 1813-1844 *DcScB*

Gregory, Edith Holmes 1866- *WomWWA 14*

Gregory, Edmund Bristol 1882-1961 *WhAm 4*

Gregory, Eliot *NewYHSD*

Gregory, Eliot 1850-1915 *ApCAB X, NatCAB 8*

Gregory, Eliot 1854-1915 *AmBi, ApCAB, DcAmB, WhAm 1*

Gregory, Eliot 1856-1915 *TwCBDA*

Gregory, Elisha Hall 1824- *NatCAB 10, TwCBDA, WhAm 1*

Gregory, Elizabeth Goadby 1834- *AmWom*

Gregory, Emily Lovira 1841-1897 *TwCBDA*

Gregory, Emily Ray 1863- *WomWWA 14*

Gregory, Emma Helena *WomWWA 14*

Gregory, Francis Hoyt 1789-1866 *AmBi, ApCAB, Drake, NatCAB 4, TwCBDA*

Gregory, Frank M 1848- *ApCAB*

Gregory, Frederick Gugenheim 1893-1961 *DcScB*

Gregory, George Augustus 1865-1946 *NatCAB 35*

Gregory, George Craghead 1878-1956 *NatCAB 43*

Gregory, Helen Martha 1859- *WomWWA 14*

Gregory, Henry Duval 1819-1897 *TwCBDA*

Gregory, Herbert Bailey 1884-1951 *NatCAB 40, WhAm 3*

Gregory, Herbert E 1869-1952 *WhAm 3*

Gregory, Hiram Doyle 1858-1949 *NatCAB 41*

Gregory, Ida Leona Sturdavent 1860- *NatCAB 18*

Gregory, Jackson 1882-1943 *WhAm 2*

Gregory, James 1638-1675 *AsBiEn, DcScB*

Gregory, James Francis 1876- *WhoColR*

Gregory, John 1879-1958 *NatCAB 46, WhAm 3*

Gregory, John Goadby 1856-1947 *WhAm 3*

Gregory, John Harvey 1821-1900 *NatCAB 22*

Gregory, John Henry 1864-1934 *WhAm 1*

Gregory, John Herbert 1874-1937 *NatCAB 30, WhAm 1*

Gregory, John Lawrence 1913-1971 *NatCAB 56*

Gregory, John Milton 1822-1898 *ApCAB, BiDAmEd, DcAmB, NatCAB 12, TwCBDA, WhAm H*

Gregory, John Munford 1804-1887 *BiAUS, NatCAB 5, TwCBDA*

Gregory, L H d1975 *WhAm 6*

Gregory, Laurence Wilcoxson 1887-1946 *WhAm 2*

Gregory, Leslie Roscoe 1888-1954 *WhAm 3*

Gregory, Louis George *WhoColR*

Gregory, Louis Hoyt 1880-1954 *WhAm 3*

Gregory, Luther Elwood 1872-1960 *WhAm 4*

Gregory, Martin Leroy 1916-1967 *WhAm 5*
Gregory, Mary Rogers 1846- *AmWom*
Gregory, Maurice Clinton 1881- *WhAm 6*
Gregory, Menas Sarkas Boulgourjian 1872-1941 *DcAmB S3*
Gregory, Menas Sarkis 1872-1941 *WhAm 1*
Gregory, Montgomery 1887- *WhoColR*
Gregory, Noble Jones 1897-1971 *BiDrAC, WhAm 5, WhAmP*
Gregory, Olinthus Gilbert 1774-1841 *DcScB*
Gregory, Oliver Fuller 1844-1919 *WhAm 1*
Gregory, Raymond William 1893-1954 *WhAm 3*
Gregory, Samuel 1813-1872 *ApCAB, BiDAmEd, DcAmB, WhAm H*
Gregory, Stephen Strong 1849-1920 *DcAmB, NatCAB 18, WhAm 1*
Gregory, Tappan 1886-1961 *NatCAB 49, WhAm 4*
Gregory, Thomas Barger 1860-1951 *DcAmB S5, WhAm 3*
Gregory, Thomas Tingey Craven 1878-1933 *NatCAB 24, WhAm 1*
Gregory, Thomas Watt 1861-1933 *AmBi, ApCAB X, BiDrUSE, DcAmB S1, NatCAB 27, WhAm 1*
Gregory, Virginia Whitney 1912-1975 *WhAm 6*
Gregory, Warren 1864-1927 *NatCAB 30, WhAm 1*
Gregory, Warren Fenno 1863-1936 *WhAm 1*
Gregory, Waylande 1905-1971 *NatCAB 56*
Gregory, William 1803-1858 *DcScB*
Gregory, William 1849-1901 *NatCAB 13, TwCBDA, WhAm 1*
Gregory, William Benjamin 1871-1945 *WhAm 2*
Gregory, William C *NewYHSD*
Gregory, William Edward 1901-1956 *NatCAB 43, WhAm 3*
Gregory, William Hamilton, Jr. 1903-1962 *WhAm 4*
Gregory, William K d1970 *WhAm 5*
Gregory, William Logan 1898-1959 *NatCAB 49, WhAm 3*
Gregory, William Mumford 1876- *WhAm 5*
Gregory, William Voris 1877-1936 *BiDrAC, WhAm 1, WhAmP*
Gregory, Willis George 1857-1937 *WhAm 1*
Gregson, James *NewYHSD*
Gregson, John *NewYHSD*
Grehan, Bernard H 1893-1952 *WhAm 3*
Greig, Alexander Simpson 1860- *WhAm 4*
Greig, John 1779-1858 *ApCAB, BiAUS, BiDrAC, WhAm H*
Greigg, Stanley Lloyd 1931- *BiDrAC*
Greil, Gaston Jacob 1878-1932 *NatCAB 30*
Greiner, Christopher M d1864 *NewYHSD*
Greiner, John 1810-1871 *ApCAB, BiAUS*
Greiner, John Edwin 1859-1942 *ApCAB X, NatCAB 31, WhAm 2*
Greiner, Martha Nathalie 1869- *WomWWA 14*
Greiner, Tuisco 1846- *WhAm 4*
Greis, Henry Nauert 1880-1947 *WhAm 2*
Greiss, George Albert 1874-1950 *NatCAB 40*
Greist, John Milton 1850-1906 *ApCAB X, DcAmB, NatCAB 25*
Greive, George 1750-1793 *Drake*
Greiwe, John Ernest 1865-1937 *NatCAB 28*
Grell, Louis 1887-1960 *WhAm 4*
Grellet, Stephen 1773-1855 *AmBi, ApCAB, DcAmB, Drake, WhAm H*
Gremke, Henry Dietrich 1860-1933 *IlBEAAW*
Gren, Friedrich Albrecht Carl 1760-1798 *DcScB*
Grenell, William Horatio 1846-1915 *NatCAB 17*
Grenell, Zelotes 1841-1918 *WhAm 1*
Grenet, Edward Louis 1856?-1922 *IlBEAAW*
Grenfell, Anna E 1885- *WomWWA 14*
Grenfell, Helen Loring d1935 *AmBi, WhAm 1, WomWWA 14*
Grenfell, Nicholas Pirie, Jr. 1920-1970 *WhAm 6*
Grenfell, Sir Wilfred Thomason 1865-1940 *WhAm 1*
Grenier, Arthur Sylvester 1872-1935 *NatCAB 24, WhAm 1*
Grenier, John 1810-1871 *Drake*
Grennell, George 1786-1877 *ApCAB, BiAUS, BiDrAC, NatCAB 4, TwCBDA,*

WhAm H
Grenville, George 1712-1770 *ApCAB, Drake*
Grenville, Sir Richard 1540-1591 *ApCAB*
Grenville, Sir Richard 1541?-1591 *AmBi*
Grenville, Sir Richard 1542-1591 *WhoMilH*
Grenville, Thomas 1755-1846 *ApCAB*
Gresham, Alexis Tardy 1892-1943 *NatCAB 35*
Gresham, James Wilmer 1871-1958 *WhAm 3*
Gresham, LeRoy 1871-1955 *WhAm 3*
Gresham, Otto 1859-1946 *NatCAB 48*
Gresham, Thomas Dew 1879- *WhAm 6*
Gresham, Walter 1841-1920 *BiDrAC, NatCAB 17, TwCBDA*
Gresham, Walter Quintin d1895 *BiAUS*
Gresham, Walter Quintin 1832-1895 *AmBi, BiDrUSE, DcAmB, EncAB, NatCAB 24, WhAm H*
Gresham, Walter Quinton 1832-1895 *ApCAB, NatCAB 4*
Gresham, Walter Quinton 1833-1895 *TwCBDA*
Gress, Ernest Milton 1876- *WhAm 5*
Gress, George Valentine 1847- *NatCAB 7*
Gresser, Edward Bellamy 1898-1951 *NatCAB 38*
Gressley, Gene 1931- *EncAAH*
Gressly, Amanz 1814-1865 *DcScB*
Gresswell, Pearl Vere Burnham *WomWWA 14*
Greusel, John Hubert 1866-1946 *ApCAB X, NatCAB 17, WhAm 2*
Greuze, Jean Baptiste 1725-1805 *McGEWB*
Greve, Charles Theodore 1863-1930 *NatCAB 22, WhAm 1*
Greve, Harriet Fisher *WomWWA 14*
Greville, Mister *WhAm H*
Grevstad, Nicolay Andreas 1851-1940 *NatCAB 29*
Grevstad, Nicolay Andrew 1851-1940 *WhAm 1*
Grevyle, Lord Charles Montague 1741-1784 *ApCAB, Drake*
Grew, Henry S 1875-1953 *WhAm 3*
Grew, Henry Sturgis 1901-1966 *NatCAB 52*
Grew, Joseph Clark 1880-1965 *EncAB, NatCAB 55, WebAB, WhAm 4, WhWW-II*
Grew, Mary 1813-1896 *AmWom, NotAW*
Grew, Nehemiah 1641-1712 *AsBiEn, DcScB*
Grew, Randolph Clark 1873-1947 *NatCAB 36*
Grew, Theophilus d1759 *DcAmB, WhAm H*
Greweldt *NewYHSD*
Grey, Benjamin Edwards *BiAUS, BiDrAC, WhAm H*
Grey, Charles 1729-1807 *ApCAB, Drake*
Grey, Charles Grey, Earl 1764-1845 *McGEWB*
Grey, Elmer 1871-1962 *WhAm 4*
Grey, Elmer 1871-1963 *NatCAB 52*
Grey, Eula Ross *WhoColR*
Grey, Sir George 1812-1898 *McGEWB*
Grey, Idah 1889- *WhoColR*
Grey, James Parks 1860-1942 *NatCAB 31*
Grey, Odessa Warren 1883- *WhoColR*
Grey, Pearl *WebAB*
Grey, Samuel Howell 1836- *NatCAB 1, WhAm 4*
Grey, William Richard 1858-1944 *NatCAB 35*
Grey, Zane 1872-1939 *DcAmB S2, EncAAH*
Grey, Zane 1875-1939 *AmBi, REnAW, WebAB, WhAm 1*
Greyson, John *NewYHSD*
Gribbel, John 1858-1936 *NatCAB 17, NatCAB 27, WhAm 1*
Gribeauval, Jean Baptiste Vaquette De 1715-1789 *WhoMilH*
Grice, David Stephen 1914-1960 *WhAm 4*
Grice, John E 1911-1958 *NatCAB 44*
Grice, Mary VanMeter 1858- *WomWWA 14*
Grice, Warren 1875-1945 *WhAm 2*
Grider, George William 1912- *BiDrAC*
Grider, Henry 1796-1866 *BiAUS, BiDrAC, NatCAB 9, TwCBDA, WebAMB, WhAm H*
Grider, Rufus Alexander 1817-1900 *NewYHSD*
Gridley, Charles O 1897-1966 *WhAm 4*
Gridley, Charles Vernon 1844-1898 *DcAmB, NatCAB 9, TwCBDA, WebAMB, WhAm H*
Gridley, Charles Vernon 1845-1898 *ApCAB Sup*
Gridley, Enoch G *NewYHSD*
Gridley, Jeremiah 1701?-1767 *DcAmB*
Gridley, Jeremiah 1702-1767 *ApCAB,*

NatCAB 6, WhAm H
Gridley, Jeremy 1702-1767 *Drake*
Gridley, Josephine Bradley 1887- *WomWWA 14*
Gridley, Louise Dias 1862- *WomWWA 14*
Gridley, Marion Eleanor d1974 *WhAm 6*
Gridley, Philo 1796-1864 *ApCAB*
Gridley, Richard 1710?-1796 *DcAmB*
Gridley, Richard 1711-1796 *AmBi, ApCAB, Drake, NatCAB 1, NatCAB 6, TwCBDA, WebAMB, WhAm H*
Grieg, Edvard Hagerup 1843-1907 *McGEWB*
Griemsmann, John William Ernest 1916-1971 *NatCAB 56*
Griepenkerl, Florence Smith 1871- *WomWWA 14*
Grier, Albert Oliver Herman 1867-1953 *WhAm 3*
Grier, Alvan Ruckman 1860-1932 *WhAm 1*
Grier, Boyce McLaughlin 1894-1974 *WhAm 6*
Grier, David *NewYHSD*
Grier, David 1742-1790 *ApCAB*
Grier, Florencia A T Powella 1864- *WhoColR*
Grier, Francis Ebenezer 1899-1959 *NatCAB 50, WhAm 3*
Grier, Frank Layton 1870-1937 *NatCAB 28*
Grier, Harry Dobson Miller 1914-1972 *WhAm 6*
Grier, James Alexander 1846- *TwCBDA, WhAm 4*
Grier, James Harper 1882-1966 *WhAm 4*
Grier, Matthew Blackburn 1820-1899 *TwCBDA*
Grier, Norman MacDowell 1890-1951 *WhAm 3*
Grier, Robert Calvin 1817-1871 *TwCBDA*
Grier, Robert Cooper 1794-1870 *AmBi, ApCAB, BiAUS, DcAmB, Drake, NatCAB 2, TwCBDA, WebAB, WhAm H*
Grier, Robert David 1856-1920 *NatCAB 18*
Grier, Robert Maxwell 1898-1973 *WhAm 6*
Grier, Thomas Johnston 1849-1914 *NatCAB 16*
Grier, William 1816-1911 *WhAm 1*
Grier, William Moffatt 1843-1899 *TwCBDA, WhAm 1*
Grier, William Nicholson 1812-1885 *ApCAB, Drake, TwCBDA*
Grierson, Benjamin H 1837- *Drake*
Grierson, Benjamin Henry 1826-1911 *AmBi, ApCAB, DcAmB, NatCAB 13, REnAW, TwCBDA, WebAMB, WhAm 1, WhAm 4, WhoMilH*
Grierson, Francis 1848-1927 *AmBi, DcAmB*
Grierson, John 1898-1972 *WhAm 5*
Gries, George Gibson 1855-1955 *NatCAB 42*
Gries, John M *NewYHSD*
Gries, John Matthew 1877-1953 *NatCAB 41, WhAm 3*
Griesedieck, Alvin 1894-1961 *WhAm 4*
Grieshaber, Hugo Eugene 1880-1938 *NatCAB 28*
Griess, Ferdinand F 1883-1953 *NatCAB 40*
Griess, Johann Peter 1829-1888 *DcScB*
Griest, Theodore Reed 1898-1974 *WhAm 6*
Griest, William Walton 1858-1929 *BiDrAC, WhAmP*
Griest, William Walton 1859-1929 *WhAm 1*
Grieve, Lucia Catherine Graeme *WomWWA 14*
Grieve, Miller 1801-1878? *DcAmB, NatCAB 13, WhAm H*
Griffen, Henry E *NewYHSD*
Griffes, Charles Tomlinson 1884-1920 *DcAmB, NatCAB 33, WhAm HA, WhAm 4*
Griffeth, John M *NewYHSD*
Griffin, Angus Macivor 1910-1970 *WhAm 5*
Griffin, Anthony Jerome 1866-1935 *BiDrAC, WhAm 1, WhAmP*
Griffin, Appleton Prentiss Clark 1852-1926 *ApCAB Sup, DcAmB, DcAmLiB, WhAm 1*
Griffin, Arthur James 1877-1943 *NatCAB 32*
Griffin, Cardinal Bernard 1899-1956 *WhAm 3*
Griffin, Bulkley Southworth 1893-1967 *WhAm 5*
Griffin, Carroll Wardlaw 1900-1959 *WhAm 3*
Griffin, Charles 1825-1867 *AmBi, DcAmB, WhAm H*
Griffin, Charles 1826-1867 *ApCAB, Drake, NatCAB 4, TwCBDA*

Griffin, Charles Andrew 1884- *WhoColR*
Griffin, Charles Hudson 1926- *BiDrAC*
Griffin, Charles P 1842- *NatCAB 5*
Griffin, Clifford Henry 1870-1935 *NatCAB 28*
Griffin, Cyrus 1748-1810 *BiDrAC, BiDrUSE, DcAmB, TwCBDA, WhAm H*
Griffin, Cyrus 1749-1810 *ApCAB, BiAUS, Drake, NatCAB 5*
Griffin, Daniel Joseph 1880-1926 *BiDrAC, WhAm 1*
Griffin, Delia Isabel 1868- *WhAm 4*
Griffin, Ebenezer 1789- *ApCAB*
Griffin, Edmund Dorr 1804-1830 *ApCAB, Drake*
Griffin, Edward Dorr 1770-1837 *ApCAB, DcAmB, Drake, NatCAB 6, TwCBDA, WhAm H*
Griffin, Edward Herrick 1843-1929 *NatCAB 21, TwCBDA, WhAm 1*
Griffin, Emmet D 1880- *WhAm 6*
Griffin, Eugene 1855-1907 *AmBi, DcAmB, NatCAB 2, WhAm 1*
Griffin, Eugene Leonard 1912-1973 *WhAm 6*
Griffin, Francis Butler 1852- *NatCAB 12*
Griffin, Frank Abram 1854-1928 *NatCAB 38*
Griffin, Frank Loxley 1881-1969 *WhAm 5*
Griffin, Fred Benjamin 1873-1941 *NatCAB 41*
Griffin, Frederick Robertson 1876- *WhAm 5*
Griffin, George 1778-1860 *ApCAB, Drake*
Griffin, George Butler 1840-1893 *NatCAB 33*
Griffin, Gilderoy Wells 1840-1891 *ApCAB, TwCBDA*
Griffin, Heneage Mackenzie 1848- *NatCAB 8*
Griffin, Henry Lyman 1848-1917 *WhAm 1*
Griffin, Howard Cousens 1881-1954 *NatCAB 44*
Griffin, Howard Pardee 1890-1963 *NatCAB 52*
Griffin, Isaac 1756-1827 *BiAUS, BiDrAC, WhAm H, WhAmP*
Griffin, James Aloysius 1883-1948 *WhAm 2*
Griffin, James Arthur 1874-1958 *WhAm 3*
Griffin, James H 1889-1955 *WhAm 3*
Griffin, James Owen 1851- *WhAm 4*
Griffin, John *BiAUS*
Griffin, John 1858-1927 *WhAm 1*
Griffin, John B *NewYHSD*
Griffin, John Howard 1898-1954 *WhAm 3*
Griffin, John Joseph 1859- *WhAm 1*
Griffin, John King 1789-1841 *BiAUS, BiDrAC, WhAm H, WhAmP*
Griffin, John Philander 1821-1890 *NatCAB 2*
Griffin, John W 1893-1962 *WhAm 4*
Griffin, Lawrence Edmonds 1874-1949 *NatCAB 37, WhAm 5*
Griffin, Lee Henry 1891-1963 *WhAm 5*
Griffin, Levi Thomas 1837-1906 *BiDrAC, NatCAB 20, TwCBDA, WhAm 1*
Griffin, Malvern Ulysses 1889-1950 *NatCAB 42*
Griffin, Mark Alexander 1883-1968 *WhAm 5*
Griffin, Martin Eugene 1900-1964 *WhAm 4*
Griffin, Martin Ignatius Joseph 1842-1911 *DcAmB S1, TwCBDA, WhAm 1*
Griffin, Martin Luther 1859-1942 *WhAm 2*
Griffin, Mary Campbell Mossell *WhoColR*
Griffin, Michael 1842-1899 *BiDrAC, TwCBDA*
Griffin, Michael 1842-1901 *WhAm 1*
Griffin, Michael James 1852-1914 *ApCAB X*
Griffin, Nathaniel Edward 1873-1940 *WhAm 1*
Griffin, Nathaniel Herrick 1814-1876 *ApCAB, TwCBDA*
Griffin, Norval Burris 1887-1961 *NatCAB 50*
Griffin, Ralph Dustin 1878-1956 *NatCAB 47*
Griffin, Ramon 1903-1954 *NatCAB 45*
Griffin, Robert Melville 1890-1976 *WhAm 6*
Griffin, Robert Paul 1923- *BiDrAC*
Griffin, Robert Stanislaus 1857-1933 *DcAmB S1, WhAm 1*
Griffin, Samuel d1810 *BiAUS, BiDrAC, WhAm H*
Griffin, Samuel Paine 1826-1887 *ApCAB Sup*
Griffin, Simon Goddell 1824-1902 *WhAm 1*
Griffin, Simon Goodell 1824-1902 *ApCAB, DcAmB, NatCAB 11, TwCBDA*
Griffin, Solomon Bulkley 1852-1925 *ApCAB, DcAmB, NatCAB 9, NatCAB 21, WhAm 1*
Griffin, Thomas 1773-1837 *BiAUS, BiDrAC, WhAm H*

Griffin, Thomas A 1852-1914 *NatCAB 16*
Griffin, Thomas Musgrove 1823- *ApCAB Sup*
Griffin, Tracy Edward 1891-1957 *NatCAB 48*
Griffin, Walter 1861-1935 *WhAm 1*
Griffin, Walter Burley 1876-1937 *EncAB*
Griffin, William Aloysius d1950 *WhAm 2*
Griffin, William Hamilton 1853-1917 *NatCAB 18*
Griffin, William Morton 1870-1937 *NatCAB 31*
Griffin, William Ray 1881-1955 *NatCAB 47*
Griffin, William Richard 1883-1944 *WhAm 2*
Griffin, William Vincent 1886-1958 *WhAm 3*
Griffing, Josephine Sophia White 1814-1872 *NotAW*
Griffing, Josephine Sophie White 1814-1872 *AmBi, DcAmB, WhAm H*
Griffing, Josephine Sophie White 1816-1872 *NatCAB 6*
Griffing, Martin 1784-1859 *NewYHSD*
Griffis, Elliot 1893-1967 *WhAm 4*
Griffis, Frances King *WomWWA 14*
Griffis, Lawrence W 1895-1967 *WhAm 4*
Griffis, Margaret Clark 1838-1913 *WomWWA 14, WomWWA 14a*
Griffis, Stanton 1887-1974 *WhAm 6*
Griffis, William Elliot 1843-1928 *AmBi, ApCAB, ApCAB X, BiDAmEd, DcAmB, NatCAB 9, NatCAB 21, TwCBDA, WhAm 1*
Griffith, Alfred Patterson 1845-1914 *NatCAB 43*
Griffith, Armond Harold 1860- *NatCAB 15*
Griffith, Armond Harrold 1860- *WhAm 4*
Griffith, Ben Barret 1861-1923 *NatCAB 36*
Griffith, Benjamin 1668-1768 *WhAm H*
Griffith, Benjamin 1688-1768 *DcAmB*
Griffith, Benjamin Whitfield 1853-1931 *WhAm 1*
Griffith, C J 1865- *WhAm 4*
Griffith, Charles Marion 1882-1954 *NatCAB 43*
Griffith, Chauncey H 1879-1956 *WhAm 3*
Griffith, Clark Calvin 1869-1955 *DcAmB S5, WhAm 3*
Griffith, Coleman Roberts 1893-1966 *WhAm 4*
Griffith, D W 1875-1948 *WebAB*
Griffith, David 1742-1789 *ApCAB, TwCBDA*
Griffith, David F 1865-1949 *NatCAB 39*
Griffith, David Wark 1875-1948 *DcAmB S4, EncAB, McGEWB, WhAm HA, WhAm 4*
Griffith, David Wark 1880-1948 *ApCAB X, WhAm 2*
Griffith, Dickinson Ernest 1881-1950 *NatCAB 39*
Griffith, Earl L 1899-1966 *WhAm 4*
Griffith, Elmer Cummings 1869-1928 *WhAm 1*
Griffith, Emily 1880?-1947 *BiDAmEd, NotAW*
Griffith, Eva Kinney 1852- *AmWom*
Griffith, Francis Marion 1849-1927 *BiDrAC, TwCBDA, WhAm 4*
Griffith, Frank Carlos 1851-1939 *WhAm 1*
Griffith, Frank Leslie 1897-1969 *WhAm 5*
Griffith, Frank Libby 1873-1949 *NatCAB 38*
Griffith, Franklin Thomas 1870-1952 *NatCAB 44, WhAm 3*
Griffith, Frederic Richardson 1873- *WhAm 5*
Griffith, George 1853-1903 *WhAm 1*
Griffith, George Cupp 1898-1975 *WhAm 6*
Griffith, George John 1887-1950 *NatCAB 38*
Griffith, Goldsborough Sappington 1814-1904 *DcAmB, NatCAB 2*
Griffith, Griffith Jenkins 1850-1919 *NatCAB 32, WhAm 1*
Griffith, Griffith Pritchard 1840- *WhAm 4*
Griffith, Hall McAlister 1900-1957 *WhAm 3*
Griffith, Harriet Pomeroy 1842- *NatCAB 11*
Griffith, Harrison Patillo 1837-1928 *NatCAB 6*
Griffith, Harry Elmer 1908-1966 *WhAm 4*
Griffith, Harry Melvin 1873- *WhAm 5*
Griffith, Heber Emlyn 1887-1969 *WhAm 5*
Griffith, Helen Sherman 1873-1961 *WhAm 4*
Griffith, Herbert Eugene 1866- *WhAm 1*
Griffith, Hester T 1854- *WomWWA 14*
Griffith, Ivor 1891-1961 *NatCAB 49, WhAm 4*
Griffith, James *NewYHSD*
Griffith, Jefferson Davis 1850-1924 *NatCAB 11, WhAm 1*

Griffith, John *Drake, EncAB*
Griffith, John 1869- *WhAm 5*
Griffith, John Keller 1882-1942 *BiDrAC*
Griffith, John L d1944 *WhAm 2*
Griffith, John P Crozer 1856-1941 *WhAm 1*
Griffith, Josia *NewYHSD*
Griffith, Louis Oscar 1875-1956 *IlBEAAW*
Griffith, M Dison 1887-1975 *WhAm 6*
Griffith, Marcellus Alexander 1895-1949 *NatCAB 39*
Griffith, Martha E Hutchings 1842- *WomWWA 14*
Griffith, Mary Josephine 1865- *WomWWA 14*
Griffith, Mary Lillian 1854-1884 *AmWom*
Griffith, P Merrill 1872-1917 *WhAm 1*
Griffith, Paul Bartlett 1887-1957 *NatCAB 49*
Griffith, Paul Howard 1897-1974 *WhAm 6*
Griffith, Reginald Harvey 1873-1957 *WhAm 3*
Griffith, Richard 1912-1969 *WhAm 5*
Griffith, Richard John 1784-1878 *DcScB*
Griffith, Robert Eglesfeld 1798-1850 *TwCBDA*
Griffith, Robert Eglesfield 1798-1850 *ApCAB, NatCAB 12, WhAm H*
Griffith, Samuel 1816-1893 *BiAUS, BiDrAC, WhAm H*
Griffith, Samuel Henderson 1877- *WhAm 5*
Griffith, Sir Samuel Walker 1845-1920 *McGEWB*
Griffith, Thomas Morris 1895-1954 *NatCAB 41*
Griffith, Thomas Stuart 1862- *WhAm 4*
Griffith, Virgil A 1874- *WhAm 5*
Griffith, W M 1897-1954 *WhAm 3*
Griffith, Wendell Horace 1895-1968 *NatCAB 54, WhAm 5*
Griffith, William *BiAUS*
Griffith, William 1766-1826 *DcAmB, WhAm H*
Griffith, William 1810-1845 *DcScB*
Griffith, William 1876-1936 *WhAm 1*
Griffith, William Francis Roelofson 1876-1945 *NatCAB 35*
Griffith, William G d1964 *WhAm 4*
Griffith, William Hugh 1898-1967 *NatCAB 53*
Griffiths, Arthur Floyd 1878-1922 *WhAm 1*
Griffiths, Austin Edwards 1863-1952 *NatCAB 39*
Griffiths, David 1867-1935 *AmBi, WhAm 1*
Griffiths, Edwin Patterson 1880- *WhAm 6*
Griffiths, Edwin Stephen 1872-1930 *NatCAB 33, WhAm 1*
Griffiths, Farnham Pond 1884-1958 *NatCAB 47, WhAm 3*
Griffiths, Frederick J 1879-1949 *WhAm 2*
Griffiths, George Washington 1884-1947 *NatCAB 52*
Griffiths, Henry Holcombe 1868- *NatCAB 16*
Griffiths, James 1861-1943 *NatCAB 35*
Griffiths, James Henry 1903-1964 *NatCAB 49, WhAm 4*
Griffiths, John 1846-1937 *NatCAB 27*
Griffiths, John Lewis 1855-1914 *WhAm 1*
Griffiths, John Stephen 1860-1951 *NatCAB 42*
Griffiths, John Willis 1809-1882 *AmBi, ApCAB, DcAmB, Drake, NatCAB 8, TwCBDA, WebAB, WebAMB, WhAm H*
Griffiths, Martha Wright 1912- *BiDrAC*
Griffiths, Percy Wilfred 1893- *BiDrAC*
Griffiths, Thomas d1746 *NatCAB 17*
Griffiths, Wilfred Sharp 1857-1930 *NatCAB 23*
Griffiths, William John, Jr. 1915-1963 *WhAm 4*
Griffiths, Wilson Edwin 1851-1929 *NatCAB 22*
Griffitts, Samuel Powel 1759-1826 *TwCBDA*
Griffitts, Samuel Powell 1759-1826 *ApCAB, Drake*
Grigeby, Hugh Blair 1806-1881 *WhAm H*
Grigg, John 1792-1864 *ApCAB*
Grigg, John Warner 1819?-1869 *ApCAB*
Grigg, Walter 1892-1945 *NatCAB 38*
Griggs *NewYHSD*
Griggs, Allen Ralph 1852- *WhoColR*
Griggs, Arthur Irving 1835-1915 *ApCAB X*
Griggs, Chauncey Milton 1860-1931 *NatCAB 35*
Griggs, Chauncey Wright 1832-1910 *ApCAB X, WhAm 1*
Griggs, Clarence 1857-1939 *NatCAB 28*
Griggs, Clark Robinson 1824- *NatCAB 1*
Griggs, David Cullen 1871-1958 *WhAm 3*

Griggs, David Tressel 1911-1974 *WhAm 6*
Griggs, Edward Howard 1868-1951 *NatCAB 13, WhAm 3*
Griggs, Emily Clark d1912 *ApCAB X*
Griggs, Everett Gallup 1868-1938 *DcAmB S2, WhAm 1*
Griggs, Frederick 1867-1952 *WhAm 3*
Griggs, George Burnsides 1862-1919 *NatCAB 19*
Griggs, George King 1839-1914 *NatCAB 6*
Griggs, Herbert Lebau 1855-1944 *ApCAB X, NatCAB 33, WhAm 2*
Griggs, James Mathews 1861-1910 *BiDrAC, NatCAB 36, TwCBDA, WhAm 1, WhAmP*
Griggs, John 1792-1864 *Drake*
Griggs, John Leavitt 1876-1961 *NatCAB 48*
Griggs, John Stilwell 1870-1931 *NatCAB 30*
Griggs, John William 1849-1927 *AmBi, ApCAB Sup, BiDrUSE, DcAmB, NatCAB 11, TwCBDA, WhAm 1*
Griggs, Joseph Franklin 1822-1897 *TwCBDA*
Griggs, Lillian Baker 1876-1955 *DcAmLiB*
Griggs, Mary Amerman 1886-1962 *NatCAB 49*
Griggs, Nathan Kirk 1844-1910 *WhAm 1*
Griggs, Samuel Chapman 1819- *ApCAB*
Griggs, Samuel W d1898 *NewYHSD*
Griggs, Sutton E *WhoColR*
Griggs, Theodore Wright 1872-1934 *NatCAB 42*
Griggs, Thomas Newell 1903-1972 *WhAm 5*
Griggs, William Cornelius 1873-1955 *WhAm 4*
Grignard, Francois Auguste Victor 1871-1935 *AsBiEn, DcScB*
Grigsby, Bertram James 1884-1954 *WhAm 3*
Grigsby, George Barnes 1874-1962 *BiDrAC*
Grigsby, Hugh Blair 1806-1881 *ApCAB, DcAmB, Drake, NatCAB 19, TwCBDA*
Grigsby, Roll O 1891-1967 *NatCAB 54*
Grigsby, William Fred 1876-1940 *WhAm 3*
Grigware, Edward T 1889-1960 *IIBEAAW*
Grijalva, Juan De d1527 *ApCAB, Drake*
Grijns, Gerrit 1865-1944 *DcScB*
Grillet, Jean 1630?-1675? *ApCAB*
Grillparzer, Franz 1791-1872 *McGEWB*
Grim, Allan K 1904-1965 *WhAm 4*
Grim, Clifford Duval 1891-1950 *NatCAB 41*
Grim, David 1737-1826 *DcAmB, WhAm H*
Grim, Paul Ridgeway 1910-1956 *WhAm 3*
Grim, William Rhoads 1860-1924 *NatCAB 6*
Grima, Alfred Louis 1885-1945 *NatCAB 44*
Grimaldi, Francesco Maria 1618-1663 *AsBiEn, DcScB*
Grimball, Elizabeth Berkeley d1953 *WhAm 3*
Grime, Sarah Lois 1874-1953 *WhAm 4*
Grimes, Absalom Carlisle 1834-1911 *DcAmB*
Grimes, Bryan 1828-1880 *ApCAB, BiDConf, TwCBDA*
Grimes, Byran 1828-1880 *NatCAB 6*
Grimes, Charles Pennebaker 1904-1957 *WhAm 3*
Grimes, Charles Wilfred 1876-1953 *NatCAB 42*
Grimes, David 1896-1943 *NatCAB 32*
Grimes, Donald Robert 1906-1972 *WhAm 5*
Grimes, Fern Edith Munroe 1915-1975 *WhAm 6*
Grimes, Frances 1869-1963 *NatCAB 47, WhAm 4, WomWWA 14*
Grimes, Frank 1891-1961 *WhAm 4*
Grimes, George 1894-1964 *NatCAB 51, WhAm 4*
Grimes, George Simon 1846-1920 *WhAm 1*
Grimes, Hanson M 1852-1921 *NatCAB 19*
Grimes, J Frank 1881- *WhAm 6*
Grimes, James Stanley 1807-1903 *DcAmB, WhAm H*
Grimes, James Wilson 1816-1872 *ApCAB, BiAUS, BiDrAC, DcAmB, Drake, NatCAB 11, TwCBDA, WhAm H, WhAmP*
Grimes, John 1852-1922 *NatCAB 2, WhAm 1*
Grimes, John Bryan 1868-1923 *WhAm 1*
Grimes, John C 1804-1837 *NewYHSD*
Grimes, Thomas Wingfield 1844-1905 *BiDrAC, NatCAB 2*
Grimes, Waldo Ernest 1891-1947 *WhAm 2*
Grimes, William Hearne 1871-1952 *NatCAB 41*
Grimes, William Henry 1892-1972 *WhAm 5*

Grimes, William Middleton 1889-1951 *WhAm 3*
Grimke, Sisters *AmBi*
Grimke, Angelina Emily 1805-1879 *AmBi, DcAmB, DcAmReB, EncAB, McGEWB, NatCAB 2, NotAW, TwCBDA, WebAB, WhAm H, WhAmP*
Grimke, Angelina Weld 1880- *WhAm 6*
Grimke, Archibald Henry 1849-1930 *AmBi, DcAmB, McGEWB, NatCAB 26, WhAm 1, WhoColR*
Grimke, Charlotte L Forten 1837-1914 *BiDAmEd, NotAW*
Grimke, E Montague 1832-1896 *NatCAB 17*
Grimke, Francis James 1850- *WhAm 4, WhoColR*
Grimke, Frederic 1791-1863 *Drake*
Grimke, Frederick 1791-1863 *ApCAB, BiAUS, NatCAB 11, TwCBDA, WhAm H*
Grimke, John Faucheraud 1752-1819 *ApCAB, DcAmB, Drake, NatCAB 2, WhAm H*
Grimke, Sarah Moore 1792-1873 *AmBi, AmWom, ApCAB, DcAmB, DcAmReB, EncAB, McGEWB, NatCAB 2, NotAW, WebAB, WhAm H, WhAmP*
Grimke, Sarah Moore 1793-1873 *TwCBDA*
Grimke, Thomas Smith 1786-1834 *ApCAB, DcAmB, Drake, NatCAB 2, TwCBDA, WhAm H*
Grimm, Carl Robert 1849- *NatCAB 15*
Grimm, Carl William 1863- *WhAm 4*
Grimm, George 1859-1945 *NatCAB 37*
Grimm, J P P *NewYHSD*
Grimm, Jacob Luther 1842-1905 *WhAm 1*
Grimm, Jakob Karl 1785-1863 *McGEWB*
Grimm, John Crawford Milton 1891-1970 *WhAm 5*
Grimm, John Hugo 1864-1954 *WhAm 3*
Grimm, John Murchison 1866-1943 *NatCAB 37, WhAm 5*
Grimm, Paul *IIBEAAW*
Grimm, Wilhelm Karl 1786-1859 *McGEWB*
Grimmelshausen, H Jakob Christoffel Von 1621?-1676 *McGEWB*
Grimmelsman, Henry Joseph 1890-1972 *WhAm 5*
Grimmelsman, Joseph 1853-1918 *WhAm 1*
Grimmer, Ward Chipman Hazen 1858-1945 *WhAm 2*
Grimmons, Charles *NewYHSD*
Grimshaw, Austin 1905-1965 *WhAm 4*
Grimshaw, Robert 1850- *WhAm 4*
Grimshaw, William 1782-1852 *ApCAB, Drake, TwCBDA*
Grimsley, George Perry 1868- *TwCBDA*
Grimson, Samuel Bonarios 1879-1955 *NatCAB 42*
Grimston, John 1912-1973 *WhAm 6*
Grimwood, Henry Allen, Jr. 1873-1950 *NatCAB 38*
Grinager, Alexander 1865-1949 *NatCAB 38*
Grindal, Herbert W 1889-1959 *WhAm 3*
Grindall, Charles Sylvester 1849-1920 *WhAm 1*
Grindley, Harry Sands 1864- *WhAm 4*
Grindon, Joseph, Sr. 1858-1950 *WhAm 3*
Grindrod, Ida E 1852- *WomWWA 14*
Griner, John F 1907-1974 *WhAm 6*
Gringo, Harry 1819-1869 *AmBi*
Grinnell, Charles Edward 1841-1916 *WhAm 1*
Grinnell, Elizabeth 1851-1935 *WhAm 1*
Grinnell, Frank Washburn 1873-1964 *NatCAB 51, WhAm 4*
Grinnell, Frederick 1836-1905 *ApCAB Sup, DcAmB, WhAm 1*
Grinnell, George Bird 1849-1938 *AmBi, DcAmB S2, EncAAH, NatCAB 13, NatCAB 30, REnAW, TwCBDA, WebAB, WhAm 1*
Grinnell, George Blake 1823-1891 *NatCAB 3*
Grinnell, George Morton 1902-1953 *WhAm 3*
Grinnell, Harold C 1895-1970 *WhAm 5*
Grinnell, Henry 1799-1874 *AmBi, DcAmB, NatCAB 3, TwCBDA, WhAm H*
Grinnell, Henry 1800-1874 *ApCAB*
Grinnell, Henry Walton 1843-1920 *DcAmB, NatCAB 22*
Grinnell, Herbert Leroy 1881-1956 *NatCAB 44*
Grinnell, Ira Leonard 1848-1921 *NatCAB 41*
Grinnell, Joseph 1788-1885 *BiAUS, BiDrAC,*

DcAmB, TwCBDA, WhAm H
Grinnell, Joseph 1789-1885 *ApCAB*
Grinnell, Joseph 1877-1939 *DcScB, WhAm 1*
Grinnell, Josiah Bushnell 1821-1891 *AmBi, ApCAB, BiAUS, BiDrAC, DcAmB, NatCAB 8, TwCBDA, WhAm H, WhAmP*
Grinnell, Katherine VanAllen 1839- *AmWom*
Grinnell, Lloyd Garrison 1894-1966 *NatCAB 52*
Grinnell, Max *NewYHSD*
Grinnell, Morton 1855-1905 *WhAm 1*
Grinnell, Moses Hicks 1803-1877 *ApCAB, BiAUS, BiDrAC, DcAmB, Drake, NatCAB 1, TwCBDA, WhAm H*
Grinnell, Russell 1875-1948 *WhAm 2*
Grinnell, Susan B *WomWWA 14*
Grinnell, Sylvia *ApCAB*
Grinnell, William Henry 1841-1925 *NatCAB 20*
Grinnell, William Morton 1857-1906 *WhAm 1*
Grinnett, Max *NewYHSD*
Grinnis, Charles *NewYHSD*
Grinsfelder, H J 1902-1967 *WhAm 4*
Grinstead, James Fauntleroy 1845-1921 *NatCAB 19*
Grinstead, Minnie Johnson 1869- *WomWWA 14*
Grippen, A W *NewYHSD*
Grippo, Angelo 1894-1956 *NatCAB 43*
Gris, Juan 1887-1927 *McGEWB*
Grischy, William Brauch 1872-1949 *NatCAB 38*
Griscom, Clement Acton 1841-1912 *DcAmB, NatCAB 4, WhAm 1*
Griscom, Clement Acton 1868-1918 *WhAm 1*
Griscom, J Milton 1881-1943 *NatCAB 32*
Griscom, John 1774-1852 *ApCAB, BiDAmEd, DcAmB, Drake, NatCAB 10, TwCBDA, WhAm H*
Griscom, John Haskins 1809-1874 *ApCAB*
Griscom, John Hoskins 1809-1874 *Drake, TwCBDA*
Griscom, Lloyd Carpenter 1872- *ApCAB X, NatCAB 12, WhAm 5*
Griscom, Ludlow 1890-1959 *ApCAB X, WhAm 3*
Griscom, Rodman Ellison 1870-1944 *WhAm 3*
Griscom, S Milton 1894-1949 *NatCAB 39*
Grisebach, August Heinrich Rudolf 1814-1879 *DcScB*
Grisel, Louis *NewYHSD*
Griser, John Millen 1896-1957 *NatCAB 43, WhAm 3*
Griset, Ernest Henry 1844-1907 *IIBEAAW*
Grish, Joseph John 1893-1953 *NatCAB 42*
Grisha, Henry *NewYHSD*
Grisham, Orin Medicus 1866-1944 *NatCAB 33*
Grisham, Sadie Park 1859- *AmWom, WomWWA 14*
Grisham, Thomas Franklin 1884-1954 *NatCAB 44*
Grisley, Charles *NewYHSD*
Grismer, Joseph Rhode 1849-1922 *WhAm 1*
Grismore, Grover Cleveland 1888-1951 *WhAm 3*
Grisogono, Federico 1472-1538 *DcScB*
Grissinger, Elwood 1869-1934 *NatCAB 26*
Grissom, Eugene 1831-1902 *NatCAB 22*
Grissom, Irene Welch 1873- *WhAm 5*
Grissom, Pinkney 1897- *WhAm 6*
Grissom, Richard H 1881- *WhAm 6*
Grissom, Virgil Ivan 1926-1967 *WhAm 4*
Grist, Franklin R *NewYHSD*
Griswold, Alexander Veits 1766-1843 *TwCBDA*
Griswold, Alexander Viets 1766-1843 *ApCAB, DcAmB, DcAmReB, NatCAB 4, WhAm H*
Griswold, Alexander Vietts 1766-1843 *Drake*
Griswold, Alfred Whitney 1906-1963 *BiDAmEd, NatCAB 53, WhAm 4*
Griswold, Alphonso Miner 1834-1891 *ApCAB Sup, WhAm 4*
Griswold, Alphonso Miner 1836-1891 *NatCAB 6*
Griswold, Arthur Robbins 1884-1957 *NatCAB 45*
Griswold, Augustus H 1879-1940 *WhAm 1*
Griswold, Benjamin Howell, Jr. 1874-1946 *NatCAB 41, WhAm 2*

Griswold, C C 1834-1918 *Drake*
Griswold, Casimir Clayton 1834-1918 *ApCAB,*
IlBEAAW, NewYHSD, TwCBDA,
WhAm 1
Griswold, Chester 1844-1902 *NatCAB 15*
Griswold, Clayton Tracy 1901-1971 *WhAm 5*
Griswold, Dwight Palmer 1893-1954 *BiDrAC,*
WhAm 3
Griswold, Edith Anne 1878- *WomWWA 14*
Griswold, Edith Julia 1863- *BiCAW, WhAm 1,*
WomWWA 14
Griswold, F Gray 1854-1937 *WhAm 1*
Griswold, Frances Irene Burge 1826- *AmWom*
Griswold, Frederick, Jr. 1893-1952 *NatCAB 39*
Griswold, Gaylord 1767-1809 *BiAUS, BiDrAC,*
WhAm H
Griswold, George 1778?-1859 *NatCAB 3*
Griswold, George Monroe 1848-1932
NatCAB 33
Griswold, Glenn 1886-1950 *WhAm 3*
Griswold, Glenn Hasenfratz 1890-1940 *BiDrAC,*
WhAm 1
Griswold, Harry Wilbur 1886-1939 *BiDrAC*
Griswold, Hattie Tyng 1840-1909 *NatCAB 10,*
TwCBDA, WhAm 1
Griswold, Hattie Tyng 1842-1909 *AmWom,*
ApCAB
Griswold, Hervey DeWitt 1860-1945 *WhAm 3*
Griswold, Irving Harrington 1869-1947
NatCAB 36
Griswold, James Francis 1883-1957 *NatCAB 45,*
WhAm 3
Griswold, John Ashley 1822-1902 *BiDrAC*
Griswold, John Ashley 1827-1902 *BiAUS*
Griswold, John Augustus 1818-1872 *ApCAB,*
DcAmB, NatCAB 4, TwCBDA
Griswold, John Augustus 1822?-1872 *BiAUS,*
BiDrAC, Drake, WhAm H
Griswold, Joseph Lancaster 1843-1896
NatCAB 17
Griswold, Latta 1876-1931 *NatCAB 25,*
WhAm 1
Griswold, Leon Stacy 1865- *WhAm 4*
Griswold, Lyman William 1869-1944
NatCAB 33
Griswold, Matthew 1714-1799 *AmBi, ApCAB,*
DcAmB, NatCAB 10, TwCBDA,
WhAm H
Griswold, Matthew 1716-1799 *Drake*
Griswold, Matthew 1833-1919 *BiDrAC,*
WhAmP
Griswold, Merrill 1886-1962 *NatCAB 49,*
WhAm 4
Griswold, Merton Leon 1871-1951 *NatCAB 41*
Griswold, Morley 1890-1951 *NatCAB 48,*
WhAm 3
Griswold, Oscar Woolverton 1886- *WhAm 3*
Griswold, Oscar Woolverton 1886-1954
WhWW-II
Griswold, Oscar Woolverton 1886-1959
NatCAB 50
Griswold, Rettig Arnold 1898-1972 *NatCAB 57,*
WhAm 5
Griswold, Roger 1762-1812 *AmBi, ApCAB,*
BiAUS, BiDrAC, DcAmB, Drake,
NatCAB 10, TwCBDA, WhAm H,
WhAmP
Griswold, Rufus Wilmot 1815-1857 *AmBi,*
ApCAB, DcAmB, Drake, NatCAB 4,
TwCBDA, WebAB, WhAm H
Griswold, Sheldon Munson 1861-1930
NatCAB 13, WhAm 1
Griswold, Stanley 1763-1815 *ApCAB, BiDrAC,*
DcAmB, Drake, TwCBDA, WhAm H
Griswold, Stanley 1768-1814 *BiAUS,*
NatCAB 4
Griswold, Stephen Benham 1835-1912 *TwCBDA,*
WhAm 1
Griswold, Thomas, Jr. 1870-1967 *NatCAB 54,*
WhAm 5
Griswold, Victor Moreau 1819-1872 *NewYHSD,*
WhAm H
Griswold, Walter Stanley 1873-1957
NatCAB 47
Griswold, William Edward Schenck 1877-1964
NatCAB 50, WhAm 4
Griswold, William McCrillis 1853-1899 *DcAmB,*
NatCAB 23, WhAm H, WhAm 1

Griswold, William Tudor 1859-1931
NatCAB 29
Gritten, Henry *NewYHSD*
Groat, Benjamin Feland 1867-1949 *WhAm 2*
Groat, Carl D 1887-1953 *WhAm 3*
Groat, George Gorham 1871-1951 *WhAm 3*
Groat, William Avery 1876-1945 *WhAm 2*
Groath *NewYHSD*
Grob, Trautman *IlBEAAW, NewYHSD*
Grobe, M Alice Woolsey 1862- *WomWWA 14*
Grobschmidt, William 1868-1957 *NatCAB 48*
Grochowski, Leon M 1886-1969 *WhAm 5*
Groddeck, Albrecht Von 1837-1887 *DcScB*
Grodinsky, Julius 1896-1962 *NatCAB 51*
Grodzins, Morton 1917-1964 *WhAm 4*
Groedel, Franz Maximilian 1881-1951 *WhAm 3*
Groel, Frederick Henry 1899-1974 *WhAm 6*
Groener, Wilhelm 1867-1939 *WhoMilH*
Groenevelt, Sara *AmWom*
Groenland, Herrmann *NewYHSD*
Groesbeck, Alexander Joseph 1873-1953
NatCAB 41, WhAm 3
Groesbeck, Alice Wilson Thomas
WomWWA 14
Groesbeck, Clarence Edward 1876-1948
NatCAB 37, WhAm 2
Groesbeck, Harman VanSlyck 1849-
NatCAB 13
Groesbeck, Herman VanSlyck 1849- *WhAm 3*
Groesbeck, Stephen Walley 1840-1904 *WhAm 1*
Groesbeck, William S 1826?-1897 *BiAUS*
Groesbeck, William Slocomb 1815-1897 *ApCAB,*
TwCBDA
Groesbeck, William Slocum 1815-1897 *BiDrAC,*
DcAmB, WhAm H
Groesbeck, William Slocum 1816-1897
NatCAB 13
Groetz, Adolph August 1855-1926 *NatCAB 20*
Groezinger, Leland Becker 1907-1975 *WhAm 6*
Grofe, Ferde 1892-1972 *WebAB, WhAm 5*
Groff, George G 1851-1910 *NatCAB 12,*
WhAm 1
Groff, George Weidman 1884-1954 *WhAm 3*
Groff, Lewis Augustus 1841-1928 *NatCAB 21*
Grogan, Frank Willis 1857- *NatCAB 8*
Grogan, Henry Nathan 1886-1955 *NatCAB 45*
Grogan, James J 1884-1949 *WhAm 2*
Grogan, Nathaniel 1740?-1807 *NewYHSD*
Grogan, Starke McLaughlin 1880- *WhAm 6*
Groll, Albert Lorey 1866-1952 *IlBEAAW,*
WhAm 3
Gromaire, Marcel 1892-1971 *WhAm 5*
Gromer, Samuel David 1865-1928 *NatCAB 21,*
WhAm 1
Grondahl, Jens Kristian 1869-1941 *NatCAB 39,*
WhAm 1
Grondahl, Lars Olai 1880- *WhAm 6*
Groner, Duncan Lawrence 1873-1957
NatCAB 42, WhAm 5
Groner, Frank Shelby 1877-1943 *WhAm 2*
Groner, John Vaughan 1901-1972 *NatCAB 57,*
WhAm 5
Groninger, Taylor Ellis 1871-1958 *NatCAB 46*
Gronlund, Laurence 1846-1899 *AmBi, DcAmB,*
EncAB, NatCAB 11, WebAB, WhAm 1
Gronlund, Lawrence 1846-1899 *WhAm H*
Gronna, A J 1897-1965 *WhAm 4*
Gronna, Asle J 1853-1922 *WhAm 1*
Gronna, Asle Jorgen 1858-1922 *NatCAB 19*
Gronna, Asle Jorgenson 1858-1922 *BiDrAC,*
WhAmP
Gronouski, John A 1919- *BiDrUSE*
Gronwall, Thomas Hakon 1877-1933 *WhAm 1*
Groom, Thomas J 1899-1963 *WhAm 4*
Groombridge, Catherine 1760?-1837 *NewYHSD*
Groombridge, William 1748-1811 *NewYHSD,*
WhAm H
Groome, James Black 1838-1893 *ApCAB,*
BiAUS, BiDrAC, NatCAB 9, TwCBDA,
WhAm H, WhAmP
Grooms, Jessie Macy Roberts 1891-1955
NatCAB 45
Grooms, Red 1937- *BnEnAmA*
Groos, Franz Carl 1877-1947 *NatCAB 37*
Groote, Gerard 1340-1384 *McGEWB*
Groover, Paul 1898-1954 *NatCAB 45,*
WhAm 3

Gropius, Walter Adolf Georg 1883-1969
BiDAmEd, BnEnAmA, McGEWB, WebAB,
WhAm 5
Gropper, William 1897- *BnEnAmA,*
IlBEAAW, WebAB
Groppi, Pedro *NewYHSD*
Gros, Edmund Louis 1869-1942 *NatCAB 32*
Gros, John Daniel 1738-1812 *DcAmB,*
WhAm H
Grose, Charles Webster 1849-1930 *ApCAB X*
Grose, Clyde Leclare 1889-1942 *NatCAB 31,*
WhAm 2
Grose, D C *IlBEAAW*
Grose, George Richmond 1869-1953
NatCAB 15, NatCAB 42, WhAm 3,
WhAm 5
Grose, Howard Benjamin 1851-1939 *TwCBDA,*
WhAm 1
Grose, William 1812-1900 *AmBi, ApCAB,*
DcAmB, TwCBDA, WhAm H
Groseilliers, Medart Chouart, Sieur De *AmBi,*
DcAmB, WhAm H
Groset, John Pedersen 1876-1957 *NatCAB 47*
Grosh, Peter Lehn 1798-1859 *NewYHSD*
Grosjean, Florian 1824-1903 *NatCAB 14*
Gross, Albert Haller 1844-1918 *ApCAB,*
TwCBDA, WhAm 1
Gross, Alfred Otto 1883-1970 *WhAm 5*
Gross, Chaim 1904- *BnEnAmA*
Gross, Charles 1857-1909 *AmBi, DcAmB,*
NatCAB 22, TwCBDA, WhAm 1
Gross, Charles Edward 1847-1924 *NatCAB 20,*
WhAm 1
Gross, Charles Philip 1889-1975 *WhAm 6*
Gross, Charles Welles 1876-1957 *WhAm 3*
Gross, Chester Heilman 1888- *BiDrAC*
Gross, Christian 1895-1933 *WhAm 1*
Gross, Ezra Carter 1787-1829 *BiAUS, BiDrAC,*
WhAm H
Gross, Fred Louis 1878-1947 *WhAm 2*
Gross, Frederick William 1861- *WhoColR*
Gross, George *NewYHSD*
Gross, Harold Judson 1866-1927 *WhAm 1*
Gross, Harold Royce 1899- *BiDrAC*
Gross, Herman Frederick 1893-1967
NatCAB 53
Gross, Howard H 1853-1920 *NatCAB 19*
Gross, J *NewYHSD*
Gross, Jacob D *NewYHSD*
Gross, John Daniel 1737-1812 *ApCAB, Drake,*
NatCAB 12, TwCBDA
Gross, John E 1893-1967 *WhAm 4*
Gross, Joseph 1893-1972 *NatCAB 57*
Gross, Joseph Leonard 1862-1928 *WhAm 1*
Gross, Magnus 1817-1890 *NatCAB 8*
Gross, Mervin E 1900-1946 *WhAm 2*
Gross, Milt 1895-1953 *DcAmB S5, WhAm 3*
Gross, Myra Geraldine 1872- *WhAm 6,*
WomWWA 14
Gross, Nathan L 1907-1960 *WhAm 4*
Gross, Nels 1887-1970 *WhAm 6*
Gross, Onan Bowman 1851- *NatCAB 4*
Gross, Oskar 1871-1963 *WhAm 4*
Gross, Robert Ellsworth 1897-1961 *WhAm 4*
Gross, Robert John 1850-1930 *NatCAB 24*
Gross, Russell R 1897-1970 *NatCAB 55*
Gross, Samuel 1774-1844 *BiAUS, BiDrAC,*
WhAm H
Gross, Samuel David 1805-1884 *AmBi, ApCAB,*
BiDAmEd, BiHiMed, DcAmB, Drake,
EncAB, NatCAB 8, TwCBDA, WebAB,
WhAm H
Gross, Samuel E 1845- *NatCAB 1*
Gross, Samuel Elbely 1843- *WhAm 4*
Gross, Samuel Weissell 1837-1889 *ApCAB,*
DcAmB, TwCBDA, WhAm H
Gross, Sidney 1921-1969 *WhAm 5*
Gross, Walter W 1895-1956 *WhAm 3*
Gross, William Hickley 1837-1898 *ApCAB,*
NatCAB 13, TwCBDA
Gross, William Jennings 1897-1945 *NatCAB 36,*
WhAm 2
Grosscup, Benjamin Charles 1895-1965
NatCAB 50
Grosscup, Benjamin Sidney 1858-1935 *WhAm 1*
Grosscup, Peter Stenger 1852-1921 *ApCAB Sup,*
DcAmB, NatCAB 15, TwCBDA,
WhAm 1

Grosscup, Walter T 1883-1950 *WhAm 3*
Grosset, Alexander 1870-1934 *DcAmB S1, WhAm HA, WhAm 4*
Grosseteste, Robert 1168?-1253 *DcScB*
Grosseteste, Robert 1175?-1253 *AsBiEn, McGEWB*
Grossgebauer, Carl Hermann John 1871- *ApCAB X*
Grossi, Carmine James 1913- *WhAm 6*
Grossinger, Jennie 1892-1972 *WhAm 5*
Grosskopf, Homer Louis 1892-1953 *NatCAB 40*
Grossman, Althea Somerville 1880- *WomWWA 14*
Grossman, Georg Martin 1823-1897 *WhAm H*
Grossman, James Daniels 1884-1961 *NatCAB 49*
Grossman, Leo 1888-1967 *NatCAB 53*
Grossman, Marc Justin 1892- *WhAm 5*
Grossman, Mary Belle 1879- *WhAm 6*
Grossman, Maxwell Bernard 1897-1963 *NatCAB 51*
Grossman, Moses Henry 1873-1942 *WhAm 2*
Grossmann, Ernst A F W 1863-1933 *DcScB*
Grossmann, Georg Martin 1823-1897 *DcAmB*
Grossmann, Louis 1863-1926 *BiDAmEd, DcAmB, NatCAB 23, WhAm 1*
Grossmann, Marcel 1878-1936 *DcScB*
Grossmann, Marcus Aurelius 1890-1952 *NatCAB 42*
Grossmann, Rudolph 1867-1927 *WhAm 1*
Grosvenor, Abbie Johnston 1865- *WhAm 4*
Grosvenor, Charles Henry 1833-1917 *BiDrAC, DcAmB, NatCAB 13, TwCBDA, WhAm 1, WhAmP*
Grosvenor, Edwin Augustus 1845-1936 *NatCAB 10, TwCBDA, WhAm 1*
Grosvenor, Edwin Prescott 1875-1930 *DcAmB, NatCAB 21, WhAm 1*
Grosvenor, Frank Livingston 1875-1949 *NatCAB 40*
Grosvenor, Gilbert Hovey 1875-1966 *ApCAB X, WebAB, WhAm 4*
Grosvenor, Graham Bethune 1884-1943 *WhAm 2*
Grosvenor, Horace C *NewYHSD*
Grosvenor, John *DcAmB*
Grosvenor, Lemuel Conant 1833-1914 *NatCAB 7, WhAm 1*
Grosvenor, Mason 1800-1886 *NatCAB 20*
Grosvenor, Rose Dimond Phinney *WomWWA 14*
Grosvenor, Thomas P 1780-1817 *BiAUS*
Grosvenor, Thomas Peabody 1778-1817 *BiDrAC, WhAm H*
Grosvenor, William 1810-1888 *ApCAB X*
Grosvenor, William 1838-1906 *ApCAB X, NatCAB 31*
Grosvenor, William Mason 1835-1900 *DcAmB, NatCAB 20, WhAm H*
Grosvenor, William Mason 1873-1944 *NatCAB 33, WhAm 2*
Grosvenor, William Mercer 1863-1916 *WhAm 1*
Grosz, George 1893-1959 *BnEnAmA, McGEWB, NatCAB 48, WhAm 3*
Groszmann, Maximilian Paul Eugen 1855-1922 *WhAm 1*
Grote, August D 1888-1951 *WhAm 3*
Grote, Augustus Radcliffe 1841-1903 *DcAmB, DcScB, NatCAB 22, WhAm H*
Grote, Frances Fitzgibbon 1883- *WomWWA 14*
Grote, Henry Wallace 1869-1942 *NatCAB 32*
Grote, Irvine Walter 1899-1972 *NatCAB 57, WhAm 5*
Grotell, Maija 1899- *BnEnAmA*
Grotewohl, Otto 1894-1964 *WhAm 4*
Groth, Arnold William 1891-1972 *WhAm 5*
Groth, John August 1908- *IlBEAAW*
Groth, Paul Heinrich Von 1843-1927 *DcScB*
Grothjean, Francesca C R 1871- *WhAm 6*
Grotius, Hugo 1583-1645 *McGEWB*
Groton, William Mansfield 1850-1915 *WhAm 1*
Grotthuss, Theodor Von 1785-1822 *DcScB*
Grotz, William *IlBEAAW*
Grouard, Frank 1850-1905 *DcAmB, REnAW, WhAm H*
Grouard, John E *NewYHSD*

Grouchy, Emmanuel, Marquis De 1766-1847 *WhoMilH*
Grouitch, Slavko Y 1871- *WhAm 5*
Groustein, William 1824?- *NewYHSD*
Groustine, Z *NewYHSD*
Grout, Abel Joel 1867-1947 *WhAm 2*
Grout, Albert Philander 1848-1915 *NatCAB 18*
Grout, Daniel Alexander 1862- *WhAm 4*
Grout, Edward Marshall 1861-1931 *NatCAB 8, WhAm 1*
Grout, Frank F 1880-1958 *WhAm 3*
Grout, John H *NewYHSD*
Grout, John Henry 1857- *WhAm 4*
Grout, Jonathan 1737-1807 *BiAUS, BiDrAC, WhAm H*
Grout, Josiah 1841-1925 *NatCAB 8, WhAm 1*
Grout, Josiah 1842-1925 *TwCBDA*
Grout, Lewis 1815-1905 *TwCBDA, WhAm 1*
Grout, Paul 1866-1931 *NatCAB 23*
Grout, William Wallace 1836-1902 *BiDrAC, NatCAB 8, TwCBDA, WhAm 1, WhAmP*
Grove, Asa Porter 1819-1887 *WhAm H*
Grove, Benjamin Hershey 1854-1931 *NatCAB 27*
Grove, Charles Gordon 1890-1957 *WhAm 3*
Grove, Edwin Wiley 1850-1927 *NatCAB 21*
Grove, Frederick Philip 1871?-1948 *McGEWB*
Grove, James Harvey 1857- *TwCBDA, WhAm 4*
Grove, John Henry 1848- *TwCBDA*
Grove, Lon Woodfin 1890-1963 *WhAm 4*
Grove, Philip Harvey 1904-1975 *WhAm 6*
Grove, Robert Kellogg 1874-1951 *NatCAB 45*
Grove, William Barry 1764-1818 *BiAUS, BiDrAC, WhAm H, WhAmP*
Grove, Sir William Robert 1811-1896 *AsBiEn, DcScB*
Grove Vallejo, Marmaduke 1878- *WhAm 6*
Grover, Asa Porter 1819-1887 *BiAUS, BiDrAC*
Grover, Clayton D 1901-1965 *NatCAB 51*
Grover, Cuvier 1828-1885 *DcAmB, WhAm H*
Grover, Cuvier 1829-1885 *AmBi, ApCAB, Drake, NatCAB 5, TwCBDA*
Grover, Delo Corydon 1869-1955 *WhAm 3*
Grover, Eulalie Osgood 1873- *WhAm 5, WomWWA 14*
Grover, Frederick Orville 1868-1964 *WhAm 4*
Grover, Frederick Warren 1876- *WhAm 5*
Grover, James Hamilton 1873- *WhAm 5*
Grover, James Russell, Jr. 1919- *BiDrAC*
Grover, LaFayette 1823-1911 *ApCAB, BiAUS, BiDrAC, DcAmB, NatCAB 8, TwCBDA, WhAm 1, WhAmP*
Grover, Lewis C 1815- *NatCAB 3*
Grover, Lewis Clesson 1849-1909 *NatCAB 30*
Grover, Martin 1811-1875 *BiAUS, BiDrAC, NatCAB 11, WhAm H*
Grover, Nathan Clifford 1868-1957 *WhAm 3*
Grover, Oliver Dennett 1861-1927 *AmBi, IlBEAAW, NatCAB 11, NatCAB 48, WhAm 1*
Grover, Victor 1910-1967 *NatCAB 53*
Grover, Wayne Clayton 1906-1970 *NatCAB 55, WhAm 5*
Groves, Charles Stuart 1867-1948 *WhAm 2*
Groves, Ernest Rutherford 1877-1946 *WhAm 2*
Groves, Frank Malvon 1887- *WhAm 5*
Groves, Harold Martin 1897-1969 *NatCAB 55*
Groves, Hiram *NewYHSD*
Groves, James Henry 1837-1923 *BiDAmEd*
Groves, Junius George 1859- *WhoColR*
Groves, Leslie Richard 1896-1970 *NatCAB 56, WebAMB, WhAm 5*
Groves, Leslie Richard 1898-1970 *WhWW-II*
Groves, Owen Griffith 1893-1972 *WhAm 5*
Groves, Robert Walker 1883-1971 *WhAm 5*
Groves, Webber d1793 *Drake*
Grow, Caroline Windsor *WomWWA 14*
Grow, Galusha Aaron 1822-1907 *AmBi, DcAmB, WebAB, WhAm 1*
Grow, Galusha Aaron 1823-1907 *BiAUS, BiDrAC, Drake, NatCAB 2, TwCBDA, WhAmP*
Grow, Galusha Aaron 1824-1907 *ApCAB*
Grow, William Frederick 1881-1966 *NatCAB 53*
Growdon, Grace *ApCAB*

Growdon, Joseph d1730 *ApCAB, NatCAB 16*
Growdon, Joseph d1738 *ApCAB*
Growdon, Lawrence 1694-1770 *ApCAB, NatCAB 16*
Grower, Roy William 1890-1957 *WhAm 3*
Growoll, Adolf 1850-1909 *TwCBDA, WhAm 1*
Groza, Petre 1884-1958 *WhAm 3*
Grozelier, Leopold 1830-1865 *NewYHSD*
Grozelier, Sara 1821-1907 *NewYHSD*
Grozier, Edwin Atkins 1859-1924 *NatCAB 19, TwCBDA, WhAm 1*
Grozier, Richard 1887-1946 *WhAm 2*
Grubb, Edward Burd 1841- *ApCAB Sup, NatCAB 3, TwCBDA, WhAm 4*
Grubb, Eugene Housel 1850- *WhAm 4*
Grubb, George Albert 1880-1953 *WhAm 3*
Grubb, Howard 1844-1931 *DcScB*
Grubb, Ignatius Cooper 1841-1927 *NatCAB 20, TwCBDA, WhAm 1, WhAm 1C*
Grubb, Paul Nuzum 1889-1954 *NatCAB 47*
Grubb, Sophronia Farrington Naylor 1834- *AmWom*
Grubb, Thomas 1800-1878 *DcScB*
Grubb, Violet Burd *WomWWA 14*
Grubb, William Irwin 1862-1935 *AmBi, WhAm 1*
Grubbe, Emil Herman 1875-1960 *WhAm 3A*
Grubbs, Donald Hughes 1936- *EncAAH*
Grubbs, Harry Lindley, Jr. 1912-1966 *NatCAB 53*
Grubbs, Samuel Bates 1871-1942 *WhAm 2*
Grube, Bernhard Adam 1715-1808 *ApCAB, DcAmB, NatCAB 6, WhAm H*
Grube, Louis *NewYHSD*
Grube, Wallace McQuown 1917-1969 *NatCAB 54*
Grubenmann, Johann Ulrich 1850-1924 *DcScB*
Gruber, James M 1868- *NatCAB 17*
Gruber, John Lewis 1888-1944 *WhAm 3*
Gruber, L Franklin d1941 *WhAm 2*
Gruber, Leo Ray 1902-1966 *WhAm 4*
Gruber, Lewis 1895-1971 *WhAm 5*
Gruber, Max Von 1853-1927 *DcScB*
Gruber, Morris Manuel 1883-1961 *NatCAB 45*
Gruber, Thomas Keller 1887-1949 *NatCAB 39*
Gruby, David 1810-1898 *DcScB*
Gruehr, Anatole Rodolph 1897-1963 *WhAm 4*
Gruen, Christian *NewYHSD*
Gruen, Dietrich 1847-1911 *NatCAB 33*
Gruen, Frederick Gustavus 1872-1945 *NatCAB 33, WhAm 2*
Gruen, George John 1877-1952 *NatCAB 39, WhAm 3*
Gruenberg, Benjamin Charles 1875-1965 *BiDAmEd, WhAm 4*
Gruenberg, Louis 1884-1964 *NatCAB 50, WhAm 4*
Gruenberg, Sidonie Matsner 1881-1974 *BiDAmEd, WhAm 6*
Gruener, Charles *NewYHSD*
Gruener, Gustav 1863-1928 *WhAm 1*
Gruener, Hippolyte 1869- *WhAm 5*
Gruenewald, Edward Ralph Henry 1879-1938 *NatCAB 28*
Gruening, Emil 1842-1914 *DcAmB, NatCAB 19*
Gruening, Ernest 1887-1974 *BiDrAC, REnAW, WhAm 6*
Gruenstein, Siegfried Emanuel 1877-1957 *WhAm 3*
Gruenthaner, Michael J 1887-1962 *WhAm 4*
Gruenther, Alfred Maximilian 1899- *WebAMB*
Gruger, Frederic Rodrigo 1871- *WhAm 5*
Gruhl, Edwin 1886-1933 *WhAm 1*
Gruhn, William Theodore 1904- *BiDAmEd*
Gruitch, Jerry M 1904-1969 *WhAm 5*
Grulee, Clifford Grosselle G 1880-1962 *WhAm 4*
Grumbine, Annette Farwell 1855- *WomWWA 14*
Grumbine, Grant Bartholomew 1879- *WhAm 6*
Grumbine, Harvey Carson 1869-1941 *ApCAB X, WhAm 2*
Grumbine, Lee Light 1858-1904 *NatCAB 5*
Grumm, Arnold Henry 1893-1959 *WhAm 4*
Grumman, Leroy Randle 1895- *WebAMB*
Grund, Francis Joseph 1798-1863 *DcAmB S1, WhAm H*

Grund, Francis Joseph 1803?-1863 *Drake*
Grund, Francis Joseph 1805-1863 *ApCAB*, *NatCAB 23*, *TwCBDA*
Grundon, John Paul 1890-1950 *NatCAB 47*
Grundy, Blanche 1869- *WomWWA 14*
Grundy, Felix 1770-1840 *BiAUS*
Grundy, Felix 1777-1840 *AmBi*, *ApCAB*, *BiDrAC*, *BiDrUSE*, *DcAmB*, *Drake*, *EncAAH*, *NatCAB 6*, *TwCBDA*, *WhAm H*, *WhAmP*
Grundy, Joseph Ridgway 1863-1961 *BiDrAC*, *WhAm 4*
Gruner, C *NewYHSD*
Gruner, Ferdinand *NewYHSD*
Grunert, Francis Eugene 1859-1936 *WhAm 1*, *WhAm 1C*
Grunert, George 1881- *WhAm 6*
Grunert, Robert W 1903-1964 *WhAm 4*
Grunewald, Gustavus 1805-1878 *NewYHSD*, *WhAm H*
Grunewald, Matthias 1475?-1528 *McGEWB*
Grunewald, Max Eugene 1904-1971 *NatCAB 55*, *WhAm 5*
Grunitzky, Nicholas 1915-1969 *WhAm 5*
Grunn, Homer 1880-1944 *WhAm 2*
Grunsfeld, Ernest Alton, Jr. 1897-1970 *WhAm 6*
Grunsky, Carl Ewald 1855-1934 *NatCAB 13*, *NatCAB 32*, *WhAm 1*
Grunwald, Kurt 1881-1958 *WhAm 4*
Gruppe, Charles Paul 1860-1940 *NatCAB 30*, *WhAm 1*
Gruskin, Alan Daniel 1904-1970 *NatCAB 55*, *WhAm 5*
Gruver, Earl Shuman 1898-1963 *NatCAB 50*
Gruver, Harvey Snyder 1874- *WhAm 5*
Gruwell, Hugh Clifton 1891-1946 *WhAm 3*
Gruzen, Barnett Sumner 1903-1974 *WhAm 6*
Grylls, Humphry John Maxwell 1865-1942 *WhAm 2*
Grymes, John Randolph 1746?-1820 *ApCAB*, *NatCAB 12*
Grymes, John Randolph 1786-1854 *ApCAB*, *Drake*, *NatCAB 12*, *TwCBDA*
Gschwindt, Robert *NewYHSD*
Gua DeMalves, Jean Paul De 1712?-1786 *DcScB*
Guacanagari *ApCAB*
Gual, Pedro 1784-1862 *ApCAB*
Gualdi, Antonio *NewYHSD*
Guanoalca 1530-1591 *ApCAB*
Guard, Samuel R 1889-1966 *WhAm 4*, *WhAm 5*
Guardi, Francesco 1712-1793 *McGEWB*
Guardia, Tomas 1832-1882 *ApCAB*
Guardiola, Santos 1812-1862 *ApCAB*, *Drake*
Guareschi, Giovanni 1908-1968 *WhAm 5*
Guarini, Guarino 1624-1683 *McGEWB*
Guarionex d1502 *ApCAB*
Guasti, Secondo 1859-1927 *NatCAB 21*
Guasti, Secondo, III 1925-1973 *WhAm 6*
Guatala, Louis *NewYHSD*
Guatimozin d1522 *Drake*
Gubb, Larry E 1892-1966 *WhAm 4*
Guberlet, John Earl 1887-1940 *NatCAB 38*
Gubert, Louise d1882 *ApCAB*
Gubser, Charles Samuel 1916- *BiDrAC*
Guccia, Giovanni Battista 1855-1914 *DcScB*
Guck, Homer 1878-1949 *WhAm 2*
Gucker, Frank Thomson 1900-1973 *WhAm 5*
Guckes, P Exton 1901-1964 *NatCAB 51*
Gudakunst, Donald Welsh 1894-1946 *NatCAB 34*, *WhAm 2*
Gudde, Erwin Gustav 1889-1969 *WhAm 5*
Gudden, Johann Bernhard Aloys Von 1824-1886 *DcScB*
Gude, Gilbert 1923- *BiDrAC*
Gude, Ove 1853-1910 *WhAm 1*
Gudebrod, Charles Benjamin 1878-1945 *NatCAB 34*
Gudebrod, Edward David 1875-1958 *NatCAB 46*
Gudebrod, Louis Albert 1872- *WhAm 5*
Gudeman, Alfred 1862- *WhAm 4*
Gudeman, Edward 1865-1932 *WhAm 1*
Gudeman, Edward 1906-1974 *WhAm 6*
Guderian, Heinz 1888-1953 *WhWW-II*, *WhoMilH*
Gudermann, Christoph 1798-1852 *DcScB*
Gudernatsch, J Fredrick 1881-1962 *NatCAB 52*

Gudgell, Charles 1847-1916 *NatCAB 17*
Gudgen, Marjorie Gloria d1975 *WhAm 6*
Gudger, Eugene Willis 1866-1956 *WhAm 3*
Gudger, Hezekiah A 1850-1917 *WhAm 1*
Gudger, James Cassius Lowry 1837- *WhAm 4*
Gudger, James Madison, Jr. 1855-1920 *BiDrAC*, *WhAm 4*, *WhAmP*
Gue, Benjamin F 1828-1904 *DcAmB*, *REnAW*, *WhAm 1*
Gue, David John 1836-1917 *NewYHSD*
Guedalla, Philip 1889-1944 *WhAm 2*
Guedel, Arthur Ernest 1883-1956 *NatCAB 44*
Guell Y Rente, Juan 1815-1875 *ApCAB*
Guelpa, Jean B *NewYHSD*
Guemes, Martin 1785-1821 *McGEWB*
Guemes Y Horcasitas, Juan Francisco 1682-1768 *ApCAB*
Guemes Y Horcasitas, Juan Vicente 1734-1799 *ApCAB*
Guenard, H *NewYHSD*
Guendling, J H 1855- *WhAm 4*
Guenther, Adam Wilhelm Siegmund 1848-1923 *DcScB*
Guenther, August Ernest 1874- *WhAm 5*
Guenther, Francis Luther 1838-1918 *TwCBDA*, *WhAm 1*
Guenther, Henry Louis 1871-1945 *NatCAB 33*
Guenther, Louis 1874-1953 *WhAm 3*
Guenther, Richard William 1845-1913 *BiDrAC*, *TwCBDA*, *WhAm 1*
Guenther, Rudolph 1872-1966 *NatCAB 51*, *WhAm 4*
Guenucalquin 1599-1634 *ApCAB*
Guepin, Felix Alouis Caspar 1899-1966 *WhAm 4*
Guerard, Albert Leon 1880-1959 *WhAm 3*, *WhAm 3A*
Guerard, Benjamin d1789 *BiAUS*, *Drake*, *NatCAB 12*
Guerber, Helene Adeline d1929 *WhAm 1*, *WomWWA 14*
Guercino 1591-1666 *McGEWB*
Guericke, Otto Von 1602-1686 *AsBiEn*, *DcScB*, *McGEWB*
Guerin, Anne-Therese 1798-1856 *BiDAmEd*, *DcAmB*, *NatCAB 23*, *WhAm H*
Guerin, Edmond Hubert 1880-1935 *NatCAB 36*
Guerin, Jules 1866-1946 *ApCAB X*, *WhAm 2*
Guerin, Mother Theodore 1798-1856 *AmBi*
Guerin, William Estil 1847- *WhAm 4*
Guerin, William Eugene 1871-1960 *WhAm 4*
Guerisse, Albert 1911- *WhWW-II*
Guerlac, Othan Goepp 1870-1933 *WhAm 1*
Guermonprez, Trude *BnEnAmA*
Guernsey, Alfred Hudson 1818-1902 *NatCAB 12*
Guernsey, Alfred Hudson 1818-1903 *TwCBDA*
Guernsey, Alfred Hudson 1825- *ApCAB*
Guernsey, Alice Margaret 1850-1924 *WhAm 1*, *WomWWA 14*
Guernsey, Egbert 1823-1903 *AmBi*, *DcAmB*, *NatCAB 2*, *TwCBDA*, *WhAm 1*
Guernsey, Frank Edward 1866-1927 *BiDrAC*, *WhAm 1*, *WhAmP*
Guernsey, Henry Newell 1817-1885 *NatCAB 3*, *WhAm H*
Guernsey, James Seeley 1903-1959 *WhAm 4*
Guernsey, Joseph C 1849- *NatCAB 3*
Guernsey, Lucy Ellen 1826-1899 *NatCAB 6*, *WhAm 1*
Guernsey, Nathaniel Taylor 1857-1934 *WhAm 1*
Guernsey, Peter Buel 1899- *WhAm 4*
Guernsey, Rocellus Sheridan 1836-1918 *ApCAB Sup*, *NatCAB 12*, *TwCBDA*, *WhAm 1*
Guernsey, Samuel James 1868-1936 *NatCAB 30*, *WhAm 1*
Guernsey, Sarah Elizabeth 1860-1939 *WhAm 1*
Guerrant, Edward Owings 1838-1916 *NatCAB 18*, *WhAm 1*
Guerrero, Jose Custavo 1876-1958 *WhAm 3*
Guerrero, Teodoro 1825- *ApCAB*
Guerrero, Vicente 1783-1831 *ApCAB*, *Drake*, *McGEWB*
Guerrier, Edith 1870-1958 *WhAm 4*, *WomWWA 14*
Guerry, Alexander 1890-1948 *NatCAB 36*,

WhAm 2
Guerry, DuPont 1848-1920 *NatCAB 20*, *WhAm 4*
Guerry, John Benjamin 1882-1940 *NatCAB 30*
Guerry, LeGrand 1873-1947 *WhAm 2*
Guerry, William Alexander 1861-1928 *NatCAB 21*, *TwCBDA*, *WhAm 1*
Guertin, George Albert 1869-1931 *WhAm 1*
Guertler, William Minot 1880-1959 *DcScB*
Guess, George 1770?-1843 *AmBi*, *ApCAB*, *DcAmB*, *Drake*, *NatCAB 5*, *WebAB*, *WhAm H*
Guess, Harry Adelbert 1875-1946 *NatCAB 35*, *WhAm 2*
Guess, Henry Augustus 1869- *WhoColR*
Guess, Walter Eugene 1932-1975 *WhAm 6*
Guest, Edgar Albert 1881-1959 *NatCAB 44*, *WebAB*, *WhAm 3*
Guest, George Martin 1898-1966 *NatCAB 53*
Guest, Harold Walter 1895-1957 *WhAm 3*
Guest, John d1707 *ApCAB*, *NatCAB 16*
Guest, John 1821-1879 *ApCAB*, *Drake*, *TwCBDA*
Guest, Richard Clarence 1897-1962 *NatCAB 49*, *WhAm 4*
Guettard, Jean-Etienne 1715-1786 *AsBiEn*, *DcScB*
Guevara, Ernesto 1928-1967 *McGEWB*, *WhAm 4*, *WhoMilH*
Guevara, Pedro 1879-1937 *BiDrAC*, *WhAm 6*, *WhAmP*
Gueydan, Henri Louis 1867-1952 *NatCAB 39*
Gueye, Lamine 1891-1968 *McGEWB*
Guffey, James McClurg 1839-1930 *AmBi*, *DcAmB*, *NatCAB 10*, *NatCAB 14*, *WhAm 1*
Guffey, Joseph Finch 1870-1959 *BiDrAC*, *NatCAB 49*, *WhAm 3*, *WhAmP*
Guffey, Wesley S 1842- *NatCAB 14*
Guffy, Bayless Leander Durant 1832-1910 *NatCAB 12*, *TwCBDA*, *WhAm 1*
Gufler, Bernard 1903-1973 *WhAm 6*
Guggenheim, Benjamin 1865-1912 *NatCAB 12*, *NatCAB 21*
Guggenheim, Daniel 1856-1930 *AmBi*, *DcAmB*, *EncAB*, *NatCAB 12*, *NatCAB 22*, *WebAB*, *WhAm 1*
Guggenheim, Edmond Alfred 1888-1972 *WhAm 5*
Guggenheim, Florence Shloss 1863-1944 *NatCAB 33*
Guggenheim, Harry Frank 1890-1971 *NatCAB 57*
Guggenheim, Irene Rothschild 1868-1954 *NatCAB 44*
Guggenheim, Isaac 1854-1922 *NatCAB 12*, *NatCAB 21*, *WhAm 1*
Guggenheim, Louis Kaufman 1884-1952 *NatCAB 48*
Guggenheim, M Robert 1885-1959 *WhAm 3*
Guggenheim, Meyer 1828-1905 *AmBi*, *DcAmB*, *McGEWB*, *NatCAB 12*, *WebAB*
Guggenheim, Murry 1858-1939 *AmBi*, *NatCAB 12*, *WhAm 1*
Guggenheim, Olga H 1877-1970 *WhAm 5*
Guggenheim, Peggy 1898- *BnEnAmA*
Guggenheim, Simon 1867-1941 *BiDrAC*, *DcAmB S3*, *NatCAB 12*, *WebAB*, *WhAm 1*, *WhAmP*
Guggenheim, Solomon Robert 1861-1949 *DcAmB S4*, *NatCAB 12*, *NatCAB 39*, *WhAm 2*
Guggenheim, William 1868-1941 *WhAm 1*
Guggenheim, William 1869-1941 *NatCAB 12*
Guggenheimer, Charles S 1877-1953 *WhAm 3*
Guggenheimer, Max, Jr. 1842-1912 *NatCAB 16*
Guggenheimer, Minnie 1882-1966 *WhAm 4*
Guggenheimer, Randolph 1848-1907 *WhAm 1*
Gugler, Eric d1974 *WhAm 6*
Gugler, Henry 1816-1880 *NewYHSD*, *WhAm H*
Guglielmi, Louis O 1906-1956 *WhAm 3*
Guglielmi, O Louis 1906-1956 *BnEnAmA*
Guibert, John Clair 1888-1958 *NatCAB 44*
Guibert, Nicolas 1547?-1620? *DcScB*
Guicciardini, Francesco 1483-1540 *McGEWB*
Guider, John William 1900-1968 *NatCAB 57*
Guidi, Guido 1508-1569 *DcScB*

Guido D'Arezzo 995?-1050? *McGEWB*
Guido Y Spano, Carlos 1832- *ApCAB*
Guignard, Gabriel Alexander 1860-1926
 NatCAB 21
Guignard, Jean-Louis-Leon 1852-1928 *DcScB*
Guignas, Ignatius *ApCAB*
Guignas, Michel 1681-1752 *DcAmB, WhAm H*
Guigues, Joseph Eugene Bruno 1805-1874
 ApCAB
Guiher, James Morford 1897-1965 *WhAm 4*
Guilbert, Frank Warburton 1872-1940 *WhAm 1*
Guilbert, Yvette 1868-1944 *WhAm 4*
Guild, Benjamin Franklin 1833-1902
 NatCAB 20
Guild, Courtenay 1863-1946 *ApCAB X,
 WhAm 2*
Guild, Curtis 1827-1911 *ApCAB, DcAmB,
 NatCAB 9, TwCBDA, WhAm 1*
Guild, Curtis 1860-1915 *DcAmB, NatCAB 14,
 WhAm 1*
Guild, Curtis 1862-1915 *TwCBDA*
Guild, Edward Chipman 1832-1899 *NatCAB 19*
Guild, George A 1863-1944 *WhAm 2*
Guild, Harriet *NewYHSD*
Guild, Henry J 1891-1964 *WhAm 4*
Guild, Horace 1888-1966 *NatCAB 52*
Guild, James 1797-1841 *NewYHSD*
Guild, Josephus Conn 1802-1883 *NatCAB 8,
 TwCBDA*
Guild, Josephus Conn, Jr. 1887-1969
 NatCAB 55, WhAm 5
Guild, LaFayette 1825-1870 *DcAmB S1,
 WhAm H*
Guild, Lewis Thurber 1864-1944 *WhAm 2*
Guild, Reuben Aldridge 1822-1899 *ApCAB,
 DcAmB, DcAmLiB, Drake, NatCAB 3,
 TwCBDA, WhAm H, WhAm 1*
Guild, Roy Bergen 1871-1945 *WhAm 2*
Guild, Sarah Ann *NewYHSD*
Guild, Stacy Rufus 1890-1966 *NatCAB 53*
Guild, William Alva 1879- *WhAm 6*
Guild, William Huntoon 1883-1948 *WhAm 2*
Guild, Winifred Agnes 1869- *WomWWA 14*
Guilday, Peter Keenan 1884-1947 *DcAmB S4,
 WhAm 2*
Guilder, Joseph *NewYHSD*
Guiler, Henry Anderson 1877-1938 *WhAm 1*
Guilfoile, Francis Patrick 1875- *WhAm 5*
Guilford, Nathan 1786-1854 *BiDAmEd,
 DcAmB, NatCAB 12, WhAm H*
Guilford, Simeon Hayden 1841-1919 *WhAm 1*
Guill, Ben Hugh 1909- *BiDrAC*
Guill, John Hudson 1879-1959 *WhAm 3*
Guillandinus *DcScB*
Guillaumat, Marie Louis Adolphe 1863-1940
 WhoMilH
Guillaume De Lorris 1210?-1237? *McGEWB*
Guillaume, Charles Edouard 1861-1938 *AsBiEn,
 DcScB*
Guillaume, Clement Theodore 1857-1917
 NatCAB 17
Guillaume, Louis Mathieu Didier 1816-1892
 IlBEAAW, NewYHSD
Guille, Andrew J 1862- *WhAm 1*
Guille, Frances Vernor 1908-1975 *WhAm 6*
Guille, Peter 1911-1970 *NatCAB 54, WhAm 5*
Guillebeau, Joseph Edwin 1894-1956 *WhAm 3*
Guillen Y Alvarez, Jorge 1893- *McGEWB*
Guillet, Mrs. J *NewYHSD*
Guillet, Leon Alexandre 1873-1946 *DcScB*
Guilliermond, Marie Antoine Alexandre
 1876-1945 *DcScB*
Guilmette, Charles *NewYHSD*
Guiltinan, Daniel Aloysius 1873-1918
 NatCAB 17
Guinan, Mary Louise Cecilia 1884-1933 *NotAW*
Guinard, Emile *NewYHSD*
Guinee, William Fenton 1893-1956 *WhAm 3*
Guiney, Louise Imogen 1861-1920 *AmBi,
 AmWom, ApCAB Sup, DcAmB,
 NatCAB 9, NotAW, TwCBDA,
 WhAm 1, WomWWA 14*
Guiney, Patrick Robert 1835-1877 *WhAm H*
Guiney, Patrick William 1877-1936 *WhAm 1*
Guinizzelli, Guido 1230?-1276 *McGEWB*
Guinter, Joannes 1505?-1574 *DcScB*
Guinther, Robert 1890-1955 *NatCAB 44,
 WhAm 3*

Guinzberg, Aaron 1812-1873 *ApCAB*
Guinzburg, Harold K 1899-1961 *WhAm 4*
Guinzburg, Ralph Kleinert 1891-1957
 NatCAB 43, WhAm 3
Guinzburg, Roland Hay 1889-1965 *WhAm 4*
Guion, Clarence Child 1876-1958 *NatCAB 43*
Guion, Connie M 1882-1971 *WhAm 5*
Guion, David *NewYHSD*
Guion, John Isaac d1855 *NatCAB 13*
Guion, John J 1801-1855 *BiAUS*
Guion, Lewis 1838-1920 *WhAm 1*
Guion, Susan *NewYHSD*
Guion, Walter 1849-1927 *BiDrAC,
 NatCAB 24, WhAm 1, WhAm 1C*
Guiou, Arthur Pounsford 1870-1923
 NatCAB 19
Guiraldez, Ricardo 1886-1927 *McGEWB*
Guiraud, Ernest 1837-1892 *WhAm H*
Guiteau, Charles Julius 1840?-1882 *WhAm H*
Guiteras, Gregario Maria 1863-1934 *WhAm 1*
Guiteras, Juan 1852-1925 *AmBi, DcAmB,
 NatCAB 22, WhAm 1*
Guiteras, Ramon 1858-1917 *NatCAB 20*
Guiteras, Ramon 1860-1917 *WhAm 4*
Guiterman, Arthur 1871-1943 *ApCAB X,
 WhAm 2*
Guitry *NewYHSD*
Guittard, Horace Camille 1878-1950
 NatCAB 38
Guitteau, William Backus 1877-1963 *WhAm 4*
Guizade, Jose Ramon 1899-1964 *WhAm 4*
Guizot, Francois Pierre Guillaume 1787-1874
 McGEWB
Gulager, Charles *NewYHSD*
Guldager *NewYHSD*
Guldberg, Cato Maximilian 1836-1902 *AsBiEn,
 DcScB*
Guldin, John C 1799-1863 *ApCAB,
 NatCAB 11*
Guldin, Paul 1577-1643 *DcScB*
Gulick, Alice Winfield Gordon 1847-1903
 AmWom, NotAW
Gulick, Archibald A 1876-1959 *WhAm 4*
Gulick, Charles Burton 1868-1962 *NatCAB 49,
 WhAm 4*
Gulick, Charles Platt 1885-1955 *NatCAB 44,
 WhAm 3*
Gulick, David B 1829?- *NewYHSD*
Gulick, Edward Leeds 1862-1931 *WhAm 1*
Gulick, Eleanor Brooks 1876- *WomWWA 14*
Gulick, Elizabeth Milligan *NewYHSD*
Gulick, Harriet Farnsworth 1864-
 WomWWA 14
Gulick, John Duncan 1883-1954 *NatCAB 49*
Gulick, John Story 1817-1884 *NatCAB 5*
Gulick, John Thomas 1832-1923 *DcAmB,
 NatCAB 11, TwCBDA, WhAm 1*
Gulick, John Wiley 1874-1939 *NatCAB 31,
 WhAm 1*
Gulick, Lee Nelson 1893-1973 *WhAm 6*
Gulick, Luther Halsey 1828-1891 *DcAmB,
 NatCAB 26, WhAm H*
Gulick, Luther Halsey 1865-1918 *AmBi,
 ApCAB X, BiDAmEd, DcAmB,
 NatCAB 26, WebAB, WhAm 1*
Gulick, Peter Johnson 1797-1877 *ApCAB*
Gulick, S N *NewYHSD*
Gulick, Samuel W *NewYHSD*
Gulick, Sidney Lewis 1860-1945 *DcAmB S3,
 WhAm 2*
Gulick, Thomas Lafon 1839-1904 *WhAm 1*
Gull, Sir William 1816-1899 *BiHiMed*
Gullager, Christian 1759-1826 *NewYHSD,
 WhAm H*
Gullager, Christian 1762-1826 *BnEnAmA*
Gulland, John Masson 1898-1947 *DcScB*
Gullborg, John Sanfrid 1863-1940 *NatCAB 30*
Gullen, Augusta Stove *WomWWA 14*
Gullette, George Albert 1909-1969 *WhAm 5*
Gulley, Needham Yancey 1855-1945
 NatCAB 38, WhAm 4
Gullion, Allen Wyant 1880-1946 *NatCAB 37,
 WhAm 2*
Gulliver, Ashbel Green 1897-1974 *WhAm 6*
Gulliver, Charlotte Chester *WomWWA 14*
Gulliver, Frederic Putnam 1865- *WhAm 4*
Gulliver, John Putnam 1819-1894 *NatCAB 20,
 TwCBDA*

Gulliver, Julia Henrietta 1856-1940 *BiCAW,
 BiDAmEd, NotAW, WhAm 1,
 WomWWA 14*
Gulliver, Louisa Green 1857- *WomWWA 14*
Gulliver, Lucile 1882- *WomWWA 14*
Gulliver, Mary 1860- *WomWWA 14*
Gulliver, William Curtis 1847-1909 *NatCAB 16*
Gullstrand, Allvar 1862-1930 *DcScB*
Gum, Walter Clarke 1897-1969 *WhAm 5*
Gumbel, Irving 1895-1960 *WhAm 4*
Gumbleton, Henry A 1846- *NatCAB 3*
Gumilla, Jose 1690-1758 *ApCAB*
Gumm, Frances *WebAB*
Gummere, Amelia Mott 1859-1937 *NatCAB 46,
 WhAm 4, WomWWA 14*
Gummere, Francis Barton 1855-1919 *DcAmB,
 NatCAB 14, NatCAB 18, TwCBDA,
 WhAm 1*
Gummere, John 1784-1845 *ApCAB, BiDAmEd,
 DcAmB, Drake, NatCAB 23, TwCBDA,
 WhAm H*
Gummere, Samuel James 1811-1874 *DcAmB,
 NatCAB 25, TwCBDA, WhAm H*
Gummere, Samuel R 1789-1866 *ApCAB*
Gummere, Samuel Rene 1849-1920 *DcAmB,
 NatCAB 13*
Gummere, Samuel Rene 1853-1920 *WhAm 1*
Gummere, William 1876-1954 *NatCAB 45*
Gummere, William Stryker 1850-1933
 DcAmB S1
Gummere, William Stryker 1852-1933
 NatCAB 23, WhAm 1
Gummess, Karl Chester 1889-1957 *NatCAB 43*
Gummey, Henry Riley, Jr. 1870- *WhAm 5*
Gump, Louis Franklin 1913-1969 *WhAm 5*
Gumpert, Martin 1897-1955 *WhAm 3*
Gumplowicz, Ludwig 1838-1909 *McGEWB*
Gunby, Andrew Augustus 1849- *WhAm 4*
Gunckel, John Elstner 1846-1915 *WhAm 1*
Gunckel, Lewis B 1826-1903 *BiAUS, BiDrAC,
 NatCAB 2, WhAm 1*
Gund, George 1888-1966 *NatCAB 52,
 WhAm 4*
Gund, Henry 1840-1924 *NatCAB 20*
Gundell, Glenn 1904-1965 *WhAm 4*
Gunder, Dwight Francis 1905-1964 *NatCAB 53,
 WhAm 4*
Gunderman, John Francis, Jr. 1907-1960
 NatCAB 47
Gundersen, Adolf 1865-1938 *WhAm 1*
Gundersen, Henrick 1857-1925 *TwCBDA*
Gundersen, Henrik 1857-1925 *WhAm 1*
Gunderson, Adolf 1865-1938 *NatCAB 30*
Gunderson, B Harry 1906-1970 *WhAm 5*
Gunderson, Carl 1864-1933 *NatCAB 24,
 WhAm 1*
Gunderson, Charles John 1868-1927
 NatCAB 21
Gunderson, Clark Young 1908-1964 *WhAm 4*
Gunderson, Gertrude B 1871- *WomWWA 14*
Gunderson, Millard Fillmore 1902-1969
 NatCAB 55
Gundissalinus, Dominicus *DcScB*
Gundlach, Ernest Theodore 1876-1942
 NatCAB 31
Gundlach, Juan 1810- *ApCAB*
Gundrum, Lawrence Kramer 1893-1968
 NatCAB 54
Gundrum, Nellie Adams *WomWWA 14*
Gundry, Alfred Thomas 1870-1952 *NatCAB 42*
Gundry, Frances Ruth Gilchrist 1875-
 WomWWA 14
Gundry, John Murton 1859- *ApCAB X*
Gundry, Richard 1830-1891 *NatCAB 44*
Gundry, Richard FitzHarris 1866-1924
 WhAm 1
Gungel, B *NewYHSD*
Gunlock, Virgil Emmett 1905-1963 *NatCAB 49,
 WhAm 4*
Gunn, Alexander Hunter, III 1910-1966
 WhAm 4
Gunn, Archibald 1863- *WhAm 4*
Gunn, Donald 1797-1878 *ApCAB*
Gunn, E L, Jr. 1904-1964 *WhAm 4*
Gunn, Frederick William 1816-1881
 *ApCAB Sup, BiDAmEd, DcAmB,
 NatCAB 13, TwCBDA, WhAm H*
Gunn, George Purnell 1903-1973 *WhAm 6*

Gunn, Glenn Dillard 1879- *WhAm 6*
Gunn, Herbert Smith 1904-1962 *WhAm 4*
Gunn, James d1801 *BiAUS*
Gunn, James 1739-1801 *ApCAB, NatCAB 2, TwCBDA*
Gunn, James 1753-1801 *BiDrAC, WhAm H, WhAmP*
Gunn, James 1843-1911 *BiDrAC, WhAmP*
Gunn, James Albion 1883-1967 *NatCAB 54*
Gunn, James Newton 1867-1927 *DcAmB, NatCAB 24, WhAm HA, WhAm 4*
Gunn, John Edward 1863-1924 *NatCAB 15, WhAm 1*
Gunn, John W 1920-1970 *WhAm 5*
Gunn, John William 1903-1965 *WhAm 4*
Gunn, Katharine Miller 1872- *WomWWA 14*
Gunn, Levi Jewett 1830-1916 *ApCAB X*
Gunn, Milus Liddell 1895-1958 *NatCAB 44*
Gunn, Moses 1822-1887 *NatCAB 12*
Gunn, Ross 1897-1966 *NatCAB 52, WhAm 4*
Gunn, Selskar Michael 1883-1944 *DcAmB S3, NatCAB 34, WhAm 2*
Gunn, Thomas Butler *NewYHSD*
Gunn, Thomas McCheyne 1878-1943 *NatCAB 32*
Gunn, Walter Thomas 1879-1956 *WhAm 3*
Gunn, Will 1882-1957 *NatCAB 45*
Gunnell, Francis Mackall 1827-1922 *NatCAB 29, TwCBDA, WhAm 1*
Gunnell, George 1868-1921 *WhAm 1*
Gunner, Byron 1857- *WhoColR*
Gunning, Josiah Henry 1840-1910 *NatCAB 6*
Gunning, Thomas Brian 1814-1889 *TwCBDA*
Gunnington *NewYHSD*
Gunnison, Almon 1844-1917 *NatCAB 10, TwCBDA, WhAm 1*
Gunnison, Binney 1863- *WhAm 4*
Gunnison, Foster 1896-1961 *NatCAB 49, WhAm 4*
Gunnison, Frederic Everest 1869-1922 *NatCAB 19, WhAm 1*
Gunnison, Herbert Foster 1858-1932 *WhAm 1*
Gunnison, John W 1811-1853 *Drake*
Gunnison, John Williams 1812-1853 *ApCAB, DcAmB, NatCAB 23, WebAMB, WhAm H*
Gunnison, Raymond M 1887-1972 *WhAm 5*
Gunnison, Royal Arch 1873-1918 *WhAm 1*
Gunnison, Royal Arch 1909-1946 *WhAm 2*
Gunnison, Sarah Pierce *WomWWA 14*
Gunnison, Walter Balfour 1852-1916 *WhAm 1*
Gunnison, William Towne 1869-1928 *NatCAB 21*
Gunsaulus, Edwin Norton 1859-1930 *WhAm 1*
Gunsaulus, Frank Wakeley 1838- *TwCBDA*
Gunsaulus, Frank Wakeley 1856-1921 *AmBi, DcAmB, NatCAB 7, WhAm 1*
Gunsaulus, Frank Wakely 1856-1921 *ApCAB Sup*
Gunsett, Helen Tossey 1909-1971 *WhAm 5, WhAm 6*
Gunter, Archibald Clavering 1847-1907 *DcAmB, NatCAB 15, TwCBDA, WhAm 1*
Gunter, Clarence 1879-1955 *WhAm 3*
Gunter, Edmund 1581-1626 *DcScB*
Gunter, Felix Eugene 1876- *WhAm 5*
Gunter, Frederick *NewYHSD*
Gunter, John Havelock 1888-1949 *NatCAB 37*
Gunter, Julius Caldeen 1858-1940 *NatCAB 40, WhAm 1*
Gunter, Richmond Baker 1880- *WhAm 6*
Gunter, Thomas Montague 1826-1904 *BiAUS, BiDrAC*
Gunter, William Kensler 1875-1958 *NatCAB 48*
Gunther, Charles Frederick 1837-1920 *DcAmB, NatCAB 14, WhAm 1*
Gunther, Charles Godfrey 1822-1885 *NatCAB 3*
Gunther, Charles Otto 1879-1958 *WhAm 3*
Gunther, Ernest Ludolph 1887-1948 *WhAm 2*
Gunther, Franklin Mott 1885-1941 *NatCAB 32, WhAm 1*
Gunther, Ignaz 1725-1775 *McGEWB*
Gunther, Johann *DcScB*
Gunther, John 1901-1970 *WebAB, WhAm 6*
Gunther, Theodore John 1887-1956 *NatCAB 47*
Gunthrop, Horace 1881- *WhAm 6*
Gunton, George 1845-1919 *DcAmB, NatCAB 10*

Gunton, George 1847-1919 *AmBi, WhAm 1*
Gunton, Rebecca Douglas *WhAm 5*
Guptill, Arthur Leighton 1891-1956 *WhAm 3*
Gupton, William 1870- *WhAm 5*
Gurd, Fraser Baillie 1883-1948 *WhAm 2*
Gurewitsch, Arno David 1902-1974 *WhAm 6*
Gurian, Waldemar 1902-1954 *WhAm 3*
Gurkoff, Eugene 1921-1972 *WhAm 5*
Gurler, Henry Benjamin 1840-1928 *WhAm 1*
Gurley, Boyd 1880- *WhAm 6*
Gurley, Edwards Jeremiah 1824-1914 *NatCAB 16*
Gurley, Henry H 1787-1832 *BiAUS*
Gurley, Henry Hosford 1788-1833 *BiDrAC, WhAm H*
Gurley, John Addison 1813-1863 *BiAUS, BiDrAC, WhAm H*
Gurley, John Ward 1851-1903 *NatCAB 14*
Gurley, Phineas Densmore 1816-1868 *ApCAB, NatCAB 11, TwCBDA*
Gurley, Ralph Randolph 1797-1872 *AmBi, ApCAB, DcAmB, NatCAB 2, TwCBDA, WhAm H*
Gurley, Royal *NewYHSD*
Gurley, William Fitzhugh 1861-1927 *WhAm 1*
Gurley, William Wirt 1851-1923 *NatCAB 20, WhAm 1*
Gurney, Augustus M 1895-1967 *WhAm 4*
Gurney, Charles Edwin 1874-1945 *NatCAB 35*
Gurney, Charles Henry 1847- *WhAm 4*
Gurney, Claire Hubbard 1861- *WomWWA 14*
Gurney, Deloss Butler 1870- *WhAm 5*
Gurney, E Floyd d1969 *WhAm 6*
Gurney, Edward John 1914- *BiDrAC*
Gurney, Eliza Paul Kirkbride 1801-1881 *NotAW*
Gurney, Ephraim Whitman 1829-1886 *DcAmB, NatCAB 11, TwCBDA, WhAm H*
Gurney, Francis 1738-1815 *ApCAB, Drake, NatCAB 6, TwCBDA*
Gurney, Frederick William 1867-1944 *NatCAB 44*
Gurney, James Paul 1915-1972 *WhAm 5*
Gurney, John Chandler 1896- *BiDrAC*
Gurney, William 1821-1879 *ApCAB, TwCBDA*
Gurowski, Adam 1805-1866 *ApCAB, DcAmB S1, WhAm H*
Gurowski, Count Adam De 1805-1866 *Drake*
Gursel, Cemal d1966 *WhAm 4*
Gurteen, Stephen Humphreys 1842-1908 *NatCAB 17*
Gurvich, Aleksandr Gavrilovich 1874-1954 *DcScB*
Gurwitsch, Aron 1901-1973 *WhAm 6*
Gusel, Lewis *NewYHSD*
Gushee, Edward Manning 1836-1917 *WhAm 1*
Gushee, Edward Tisdale 1895-1954 *NatCAB 44, WhAm 3*
Guss, Uriah Cloyd 1860-1938 *WhAm 3*
Gussman, Charles 1889-1938 *NatCAB 28*
Gussow, Roy 1918- *BnEnAmA*
Gust, John Lewis 1878-1949 *WhAm 3*
Gustafson, Airik 1903-1970 *WhAm 5*
Gustafson, Axel Carl Johan 1847?- *ApCAB*
Gustafson, Axel Carl Johan 1849- *WhAm 4*
Gustafson, Carl Henry 1869- *WhAm 5*
Gustafson, Felix Gustav 1889-1969 *NatCAB 54*
Gustafson, Frank August 1871- *WhAm 5*
Gustafson, G Joseph 1910-1970 *WhAm 5*
Gustafson, Gerald Williams 1899-1954 *NatCAB 45*
Gustafson, Gilbert Eugene 1905-1958 *WhAm 3*
Gustafson, Wesley A 1909-1975 *WhAm 6*
Gustafson, William 1887-1931 *WhAm 1, WhAm 1C*
Gustafson, Zadel Barnes Buddington 1840?-1917 *ApCAB*
Gustafson, Zadel Barnes Buddington 1841-1917 *AmWom, WhAm 1, WomWWA 14*
Gustafsson, Greta Lovisa *WebAB*
Gustav Adolf VI 1882-1973 *WhAm 6*
Gustavson, Reuben Gilbert 1892-1974 *WhAm 6*
Gustavus I 1496-1560 *McGEWB*
Gustavus II 1594-1632 *McGEWB*
Gustavus III 1746-1792 *McGEWB*
Gustavus V 1858-1950 *WhAm 3*
Gustavus Adolphus 1594-1632 *WhoMilH*
Gustavus, A O *NewYHSD*
Guste, William Joseph 1893-1957 *NatCAB 44,*

WhAm 3
Gustin, Albert Lyman 1875-1943 *NatCAB 32*
Gustin, Albert Lyman, Jr. 1904-1966 *WhAm 4*
Gustin, Wilbert Hamilton 1860-1927 *NatCAB 20*
Gustine, Amos 1789-1844 *BiAUS, BiDrAC, WhAm H*
Gustine, Franklin Johns 1861-1939 *NatCAB 37*
Guston, Philip 1913- *BnEnAmA*
Gutbier, Felix Alexander 1876-1926 *DcScB*
Gutekunst, Frederick 1831-1917 *NatCAB 16, NewYHSD*
Gutelius, Frederick Passmore 1864-1935 *WhAm 1*
Gutelius, Jean Harrower 1846- *AmWom*
Gutenberg, Beno 1889-1960 *AsBiEn, DcScB, WhAm 3*
Gutenberg, Johann 1398?-1468? *AsBiEn, McGEWB*
Guterman, Carl Edward Frederick 1903-1957 *WhAm 3*
Gutermuth, Charles Sylvester 1890-1948 *NatCAB 42*
Guth, Henry Elias 1888-1969 *NatCAB 56*
Guth, William Westley 1871-1929 *NatCAB 23, WhAm 1*
Guthe, Carl Eugen 1893-1974 *WhAm 6*
Guthe, Karl Eugen 1866-1915 *BiDAmEd, DcAmB, NatCAB 22, WhAm 1*
Gutheil, Emilian Arthur 1899-1959 *WhAm 3*
Gutheim, James Koppel 1817-1886 *ApCAB*
Guthers, Karl 1844- *ApCAB*
Guthery, Erwin George 1878-1936 *NatCAB 27*
Gutherz, Carl 1844-1907 *DcAmB, NatCAB 19, TwCBDA, WhAm 1*
Guthiel, Andrew William 1900-1951 *NatCAB 42*
Guthmann, Walter S 1907-1976 *WhAm 6*
Guthner, William Ernest 1884-1951 *WhAm 3*
Guthrie, A B 1901- *REnAW*
Guthrie, Alfred 1805-1882 *ApCAB, DcAmB, NatCAB 11, TwCBDA, WhAm H*
Guthrie, Alfred Omega 1872- *WhoColR*
Guthrie, Anna Lorraine d1936 *WhAm 1, WomWWA 14*
Guthrie, Charles Claude 1880-1963 *WhAm 4*
Guthrie, Charles Ellsworth 1867-1940 *WhAm 1*
Guthrie, David Vance 1884-1962 *WhAm 4*
Guthrie, Donald 1880-1958 *WhAm 4*
Guthrie, Edward Sewall 1880-1964 *WhAm 4*
Guthrie, Edwin 1806-1847 *ApCAB*
Guthrie, Edwin Ray 1886-1959 *McGEWB*
Guthrie, Ernest Graham 1879-1944 *NatCAB 35, WhAm 2*
Guthrie, George James 1785-1856 *BiHiMed*
Guthrie, George Wilkins 1848-1917 *DcAmB, NatCAB 18, WhAm 1*
Guthrie, Hunter 1901-1974 *WhAm 6*
Guthrie, J Gordon 1874-1961 *NatCAB 49*
Guthrie, James 1782-1869 *DcAmB*
Guthrie, James 1792-1869 *AmBi, ApCAB, BiAUS, BiDrAC, BiDrUSE, Drake, NatCAB 4, TwCBDA, WhAm H, WhAmP*
Guthrie, James Alan 1888-1966 *WhAm 4, WhAm 5*
Guthrie, John Dennett 1878- *WhAm 6*
Guthrie, John Julius 1814-1877 *ApCAB, TwCBDA*
Guthrie, Joseph Edward 1871-1935 *WhAm 1*
Guthrie, Kenneth Sylvan 1871-1940 *WhAm 1*
Guthrie, Lewis VanGilder 1868-1930 *WhAm 1*
Guthrie, Lulu Galbraith 1872- *WomWWA 14*
Guthrie, Maria Elizabeth Seabury *WomWWA 14*
Guthrie, Marshall Crapon 1879- *WhAm 6*
Guthrie, Mary J 1895-1975 *WhAm 6*
Guthrie, Ramon 1896-1973 *WhAm 6*
Guthrie, Riley Henry 1895-1954 *NatCAB 40*
Guthrie, Robert R 1890-1968 *WhAm 5*
Guthrie, S Ashley 1889-1971 *WhAm 5*
Guthrie, Samuel 1782-1848 *AmBi, ApCAB, AsBiEn, DcAmB, Drake, NatCAB 11, TwCBDA, WhAm H*
Guthrie, Sarah Lewis 1854- *WomWWA 14*
Guthrie, Stanley Walter 1889-1952 *WhAm 3*
Guthrie, Thomas Joseph 1877-1958 *NatCAB 43, WhAm 5*

Guthrie, Walter James 1864-1940 *WhAm 1*
Guthrie, William 1852-1944 *NatCAB 33*
Guthrie, William Anderson 1851-1936 *WhAm 1*
Guthrie, William Buck 1869-1940 *WhAm 1*
Guthrie, William Dameron 1859-1935
 DcAmB S1, NatCAB 15, WhAm 1
Guthrie, William Norman 1868-1944 *WhAm 2*
Guthrie, William Tyrone 1900-1971 *WhAm 5*
Guthrie, Woodrow Wilson 1912-1967 *EncAB*
Guthrie, Woody 1912-1967 *REnAW, WebAB,*
 WhAm 4
Guthunz, Henry 1893-1957 *WhAm 3*
Gutierrez, Jose Nicolas 1800- *ApCAB*
Gutierrez, Rafael Antonio 1854- *ApCAB Sup*
Gutierrez, Santos 1820-1872 *ApCAB*
Gutierrez DeEstrada, Jose Maria 1800-1867
 ApCAB
Gutierrez DeLara, Bernardo 1778-1814 *ApCAB*
Gutierrez Ross, Francisco DePaula 1880-
 WhAm 6
Gutman, Monroe C 1885-1974 *WhAm 6*
Gutmann, Addis 1901-1971 *WhAm 5*
Gutmann, Bernhard 1869-1936 *NatCAB 26*
Gutmann, Frank 1832-1918 *NatCAB 20*
Gutsch, Milton Rietow 1885-1967 *WhAm 5*
Gutstadt, Richard E 1888-1954 *WhAm 3*
Gutt, Camille 1884-1971 *WhAm 5*
Gutten, Ernest *NewYHSD*
Gutteridge, John Ashton 1849- *NatCAB 10*
Gutterson, George Herbert 1847-1926
 NatCAB 21, WhAm 4
Gutterson, Henry Higby 1884-1954 *NatCAB 43,*
 WhAm 3
Gutterson, Herbert Lindsley 1881-1960
 NatCAB 49, WhAm 4
Guttmacher, Alan Frank 1898-1974 *WhAm 6*
Guttmacher, Manfred S 1898-1966 *WhAm 4*
Guttridge, G H 1898-1969 *WhAm 5*
Guy DeChauliac 1295?-1368 *DcScB,*
 McGEWB
Guy, Artemisia Stone *WomWWA 14*
Guy, Charles Lewis 1856-1930 *NatCAB 24,*
 WhAm 1
Guy, Francis 1760?-1820 *BnEnAmA,*
 NewYHSD, WhAm H
Guy, Harvey Hugo 1871-1936 *WhAm 1*
Guy, J Sam 1884-1953 *NatCAB 44, WhAm 3*
Guy, Louis 1768-1840 *ApCAB*
Guy, Peter 1738-1812 *ApCAB*
Guy, Seymour Joseph 1824-1910 *ApCAB,*
 DcAmB, NatCAB 11, NewYHSD,
 TwCBDA, WhAm 1
Guy, William 1689-1751 *ApCAB*
Guy, William Evans 1844-1928 *NatCAB 25,*
 WhAm 1
Guy, William George 1899-1969 *WhAm 5*
Guye, Charles-Eugene 1866-1942 *DcScB*
Guyer, Alfred Willard 1873-1938 *NatCAB 28*
Guyer, Caroline Clarkson *WomWWA 14*
Guyer, Michael Frederic 1874-1959 *DcScB,*
 WhAm 5
Guyer, Ulysses Samuel 1868-1943 *BiDrAC,*
 NatCAB 32, WhAm 2, WhAmP
Guyer, William Harris 1870-1926 *WhAm 1*
Guyles, William Bell 1815- *NatCAB 2*
Guyman, Clarence Lemuel 1889-1951
 NatCAB 42
Guynemer, Georges 1894-1917 *WhoMilH*
Guynn, Ray Frederick 1893-1962 *NatCAB 49*
Guyol DeGuiran, Francois M *NewYHSD*
Guyon, James, Jr. 1777-1846 *BiAUS*
Guyon, James, Jr. 1778-1846 *BiDrAC,*
 WhAm H
Guyonneau DePambour, F M *DcScB*
Guyot, Arnold 1807-1884 *ApCAB, NatCAB 4*
Guyot, Arnold Henri 1807-1884 *DcScB*
Guyot, Arnold Henry 1807-1884 *AmBi, AsBiEn,*
 BiDAmEd, DcAmB, Drake, TwCBDA,
 WhAm H
Guyton, David Edgar 1880-1964 *WhAm 4*
Guyton DeMorveau, Louis Bernard 1737-1816
 AsBiEn, DcScB
Guze, Henry 1919-1970 *WhAm 5*
Guzman, Agustin d1849 *ApCAB*
Guzman, Joaquin Eufrasio 1801-1875 *ApCAB*
Guzman, Marie Ester *AmWom*
Guzman, Nuno Beltran De d1544 *ApCAB*
Guzman, Rui Diaz De 1544- *ApCAB*

Guzman Blanco, Antonio 1829-1899 *McGEWB*
Guzman-Blanco, Antonio 1830-1899 *ApCAB*
Guzy, Isaac 1878-1945 *NatCAB 35*
Gwaltney, Eugene Cleveland 1881-1951
 NatCAB 41
Gwaltney, Leslie Lee 1876-1955 *WhAm 3*
Gwaltney, Pembroke Decatur 1836-1914
 NatCAB 17
Gwathmey, Basil Manly 1861-1949 *NatCAB 38*
Gwathmey, Edward Moseley 1891-1956
 WhAm 3
Gwathmey, Edward Smith 1909-1973 *WhAm 6*
Gwathmey, James Tayloe 1863-1944 *WhAm 2*
Gwathmey, Robert 1903- *BnEnAmA*
Gwin, Earl Stimpson 1875-1928 *NatCAB 40*
Gwin, Earl Stimson 1875-1928 *WhAm 1*
Gwin, William 1831-1863 *Drake*
Gwin, William 1832-1863 *ApCAB,*
 NatCAB 13, TwCBDA
Gwin, William M 1805-1885 *BiAUS*
Gwin, William McKendree 1805-1885 *AmBi,*
 ApCAB, BiDrAC, DcAmB, REnAW,
 TwCBDA, WhAm H, WhAmP
Gwin, William McKendry 1805-1885 *Drake,*
 NatCAB 5
Gwinn, Joseph Marr 1870- *WhAm 5*
Gwinn, Ralph Waldo 1884-1962 *BiDrAC,*
 NatCAB 46, WhAm 4
Gwinnett, Button 1732?-1777 *ApCAB, BiAUS,*
 BiDrAC, Drake, NatCAB 1, TwCBDA,
 WhAmP
Gwinnett, Button 1735?-1777 *AmBi, DcAmB,*
 WebAB, WhAm H
Gwyn, Charles Redding 1874-1968 *NatCAB 54*
Gwyn, Francis Edward d1822 *Drake*
Gwyn, Herbert Britton 1873-1934 *WhAm 1*
Gwyn, John d1849 *Drake*
Gwyn, Thomas Lenoir 1881- *WhAm 6*
Gwynn, J Minor 1897-1971 *WhAm 5*
Gwynn, Joseph Kean 1854- *NatCAB 6*
Gwynne, Charles Thomas 1874-1945 *WhAm 2*
Gwynne, Edmund L *NewYHSD*
Gwynne, John Wellington 1814- *ApCAB*
Gwynne, John Williams 1889- *BiDrAC*
Gwynne, Samuel Carlton 1889-1962
 NatCAB 49
Gwynne, Walker 1845-1931 *WhAm 1*
Gwynne-Vaughan, David Thomas 1871-1915
 DcScB
Gye, Marie Emma 1851- *NatCAB 9*
Gyger, Edward Grant d1941 *WhAm 1*
Gyllenhaal, Leonhard 1752-1840 *DcScB*
Gzowski, Sir Casimir Stanislaus 1813-1898
 ApCAB Sup
Gzowskie, Casimir Stanislaus 1813-1898
 ApCAB

H

Haddock, John A 1823- *ApCAB*
Haddock, John Courtney 1893-1959 *WhAm 4*
Haddock, John Courtney 1894-1959 *NatCAB 47*
Haddon, Elizabeth 1680?-1762 *AmBi, DcAmB, NotAW*
Haddon, Michael d1750 *NewYHSD*
Haddow, Alexander 1907-1976 *WhAm 6*
Hadduck, A T *NewYHSD*
Haden, Annie Bates 1873- *WhAm 5, WomWWA 14*
Haden, Charles Jones 1863- *WhAm 5*
Haden, Llewellyn Pugh 1914-1956 *NatCAB 45*
Haden, Russell Landram 1888-1952 *NatCAB 45, WhAm 3*
Hader, Berta Hoerner d1976 *WhAm 6*
Hadfield, Barnabas Burrows 1906-1961 *WhAm 4*
Hadfield, George d1826 *BiAUS*
Hadfield, George 1763-1826 *BnEnAmA*
Hadfield, George 1764?-1826 *DcAmB, NatCAB 23, WhAm H*
Hadfield, John 1874-1947 *NatCAB 36*
Hadfield, Sir Robert Abbott 1858-1940 *AsBiEn, DcScB*
Hading, Jane 1861- *WhAm 4*
Hadjimarkos, Demetrios Markos 1912-1973 *WhAm 6*
Hadkins, Annie Louise 1864- *WomWWA 14*
Hadley, Arthur Twining 1856-1930 *AmBi, ApCAB, ApCAB X, BiDAmEd, DcAmB, NatCAB 9, NatCAB 32, TwCBDA, WebAB, WhAm 1*
Hadley, Carleton Sturtevant 1902-1945 *WhAm 2*
Hadley, Cassius Clay 1863-1913 *WhAm 1*
Hadley, Chalmers 1872-1958 *DcAmLiB, NatCAB 53, WhAm 3*
Hadley, Charles William 1875-1951 *WhAm 3*
Hadley, Cynthia Alice 1867- *WomWWA 14*
Hadley, Edwin Marshall 1872-1953 *NatCAB 17, WhAm 3*
Hadley, Edwin Marshall 1907-1967 *NatCAB 54*
Hadley, Ernest Elvin 1894-1954 *WhAm 3*
Hadley, Everett Addison 1879-1932 *NatCAB 24, WhAm 1*
Hadley, Hamilton 1896-1975 *WhAm 6*
Hadley, Helen Harrison Morris 1863- *WomWWA 14*
Hadley, Henry Hamilton 1826-1864 *ApCAB, NatCAB 13, TwCBDA*
Hadley, Henry Harrison d1903 *WhAm 1*
Hadley, Henry Harrison 1875-1934 *WhAm 1, WhAm 1C*
Hadley, Henry Kimball 1871-1937 *AmBi, DcAmB S2, WhAm 1*
Hadley, Henry Kimball 1874-1937 *ApCAB X, NatCAB 14*
Hadley, Herbert Spencer 1872-1927 *AmBi, ApCAB X, DcAmB, NatCAB 14, WhAm 1*
Hadley, Hiram 1833-1922 *BiDAmEd, NatCAB 21, WhAm 1*
Hadley, Hiram Elwood 1854-1929 *NatCAB 24, WhAm 1*
Hadley, Homer More 1884-1967 *NatCAB 54*
Hadley, Horace Webster 1835-1921 *NatCAB 19*
Hadley, James 1821-1872 *AmBi, ApCAB, BiDAmEd, DcAmB, Drake, NatCAB 1, TwCBDA, WhAm H*
Hadley, John 1682-1744 *DcScB*
Hadley, John Vestal 1841-1915 *NatCAB 14*
Hadley, John Vestal 1842-1915 *WhAm 1*
Hadley, Lindley Hoag 1861-1948 *BiDrAC, WhAm 2, WhAmP*
Hadley, O A 1826- *BiAUS*
Hadley, Ozro A 1826- *NatCAB 10*
Hadley, Philip Bardwell 1881- *WhAm 6*
Hadley, Sara *NewYHSD*
Hadley, Sarah Louise 1871- *WomWWA 14*
Hadley, William Flavius Leicester 1847-1901 *TwCBDA*
Hadley, William Flavius Lester 1847-1901 *BiDrAC*
Hadley, William Spencer 1866-1933 *NatCAB 34*
Hadlin, W Ad *NewYHSD*
Haddock, Harvey Denning 1843- *NatCAB 1*

Hadra, Ida Weisselberg 1861-1885 *IIBEAAW*
Hadrian 076-138 *McGEWB*
Hadsall, Harry Hugh 1875- *WhAm 5*
Hadsell, Irving W 1893-1967 *WhAm 4*
Hadzsits, George Depue 1873-1954 *NatCAB 41, WhAm 3*
Haeberle, Arminius T 1874- *WhAm 5*
Haeberle, Frederick Edward 1893-1975 *WhAm 6*
Haeckel, Ernest 1834-1919 *BiHiMed*
Haeckel, Ernst Heinrich 1834-1919 *AsBiEn, DcScB*
Haecker, Theophilus Levi 1846-1938 *WhAm 2*
Haedden, Bingham *NewYHSD*
Haeger, Edmund Henry 1886-1954 *NatCAB 44*
Haehnlen, Jacob 1824- *NewYHSD*
Haenke, Thaddeus 1761-1817 *ApCAB*
Haensel, Fitzhugh William 1879-1944 *WhAm 2*
Haensel, Paul 1878-1949 *WhAm 2*
Haensler, Arminta Victoria Scott 1842- *AmWom*
Haenszel, Allen Lee 1885-1959 *NatCAB 50*
Haentjens, Otto 1879-1957 *NatCAB 45*
Haering, David *NewYHSD*
Haering, George *NewYHSD*
Haering, George John 1895-1963 *WhAm 4*
Haering, Robert *NewYHSD*
Haertlein, Albert 1895-1960 *WhAm 4*
Haesche, William Edwin 1867-1929 *WhAm 1*
Haeseler, A Elisabeth Lipman *WomWWA 14*
Haessler, Carl 1888-1972 *WhAm 6*
Haeussler, Armin 1891-1967 *WhAm 4*
Haeussler, Herman A 1838- *NatCAB 16*
Hafen, Ann Woodbury 1893-1970 *WhAm 5*
Hafen, John 1856-1910 *IIBEAAW*
Hafen, LeRoy R 1893- *EncAAH, REnAW*
Hafey, William Joseph 1888-1954 *WhAm 3*
Haff, Charles Alfred 1875-1946 *NatCAB 36*
Haff, Delbert James 1859-1943 *NatCAB 16, NatCAB 32, WhAm 2*
Haffen, John Mathias 1872-1932 *NatCAB 34*
Haffenreffer, Rudolf Frederick 1874-1954 *WhAm 3*
Haffkine, Waldemar Mordecai Wolfe 1860-1930 *DcScB*
Hafiz, Shams Al-Din 1320?-1390 *McGEWB*
Hafner, John A 1892-1955 *WhAm 3*
Haga, Godfrey 1745-1825 *ApCAB*
Haga, Oliver Owen 1872-1943 *NatCAB 32, WhAm 2*
Hagan, Edward James 1879-1956 *WhAm 3*
Hagan, George Elliott 1916- *BiDrAC*
Hagan, Horace Henry 1891-1936 *WhAm 1*
Hagan, Janie Moore Gray 1874- *WomWWA 14*
Hagan, John Campbell, Jr. 1899-1959 *WhAm 3*
Hagan, Oliver Crumwell 1853-1923 *NatCAB 19*
Hagan, Ralph 1872-1944 *NatCAB 34*
Hagan, William Arthur 1893-1963 *WhAm 4*
Hagans, John Marshall 1838-1900 *BiDrAC*
Hagar, Daniel Barnard 1820-1896 *BiDAmEd, NatCAB 13*
Hagar, Edward McKim d1918 *WhAm 1*
Hagar, George Jotham 1847-1921 *TwCBDA, WhAm 1*
Hagar, Gerald Hanna 1892-1965 *NatCAB 52, WhAm 4*
Hagar, Stansbury 1869- *WhAm 5*
Hagarty, Clara Sophia *WomWWA 14*
Hagarty, John Hawkins 1816- *ApCAB*
Hageboeck, Alfons Ludwig 1867-1938 *WhAm 1*
Hagedorn, H C *NewYHSD*
Hagedorn, Hermann 1882-1964 *WhAm 4*
Hageman, Harry Andrew 1877- *WhAm 5*
Hageman, Louis *NewYHSD*
Hageman, Richard 1882-1966 *WhAm 4*
Hagemann, Harry H 1900-1970 *WhAm 5*
Hagemeyer, Frank Ernest 1867-1955 *NatCAB 44*
Hagemeyer, Jesse Kalper 1908-1973 *WhAm 6*
Hagen, Ernest *BnEnAmA*
Hagen, Harlan Francis 1914- *BiDrAC, WhAmP*
Hagen, Harold Christian 1901-1957 *BiDrAC, NatCAB 46, WhAm 3*
Hagen, Hermann August 1817-1893 *AmBi, ApCAB, DcAmB, NatCAB 5, TwCBDA, WhAm H*
Hagen, J Stewart 1877-1941 *NatCAB 30*

Hagen, Jere 1908-1969 *WhAm 5*
Hagen, Johann Georg 1847-1930 *AmBi*
Hagen, John C *NewYHSD*
Hagen, John George 1847-1930 *TwCBDA, WhAm 4*
Hagen, Oskar Frank Leonard 1888-1957 *NatCAB 47, WhAm 3*
Hagen, Sam 1891-1952 *WhAm 3*
Hagen, Theodore 1823-1871 *ApCAB, NatCAB 6*
Hagen, Walter Charles 1892-1969 *WebAB*
Hagen, Winston Henry 1859-1918 *NatCAB 25*
Hagenah, William John 1881- *WhAm 6*
Hagenbarth, Francis Joseph 1868-1934 *NatCAB 26, WhAm 4*
Hager *NewYHSD*
Hager, Albert David 1817-1888 *ApCAB, TwCBDA*
Hager, Albert Davis 1817-1888 *NatCAB 3, WhAm H*
Hager, Albert Ralph 1874- *WhAm 5*
Hager, Alice Rogers d1969 *WhAm 5*
Hager, Alva Licander 1850-1923 *TwCBDA*
Hager, Alva Lysander 1850-1923 *BiDrAC*
Hager, Chauncey Alexander 1909-1966 *NatCAB 53*
Hager, Clint Wood 1890-1945 *WhAm 2*
Hager, Eric Hill 1918-1973 *WhAm 6*
Hager, George Caldwell 1893-1958 *NatCAB 46, WhAm 3*
Hager, John Sharpenstein 1818- *BiAUS*
Hager, John Sharpenstein 1818-1890 *BiDrAC, DcAmB, WhAm H*
Hager, John Sharpenstein 1818-1897 *TwCBDA*
Hager, John Sharpenstein 1818-1901 *NatCAB 13*
Hager, John Sharpenstien 1818- *ApCAB*
Hager, Lee 1874-1944 *NatCAB 36*
Hager, Lucie Caroline 1853- *AmWom*
Hager, Luther George 1885-1945 *WhAm 2*
Hager, Titus Wagner 1896-1972 *NatCAB 56*
Hager, William Morris 1868-1942 *NatCAB 31*
Hagerman, Barton Campbell 1853-1922 *NatCAB 19*
Hagerman, Edward Thomson 1857- *WhAm 4*
Hagerman, Frank 1857- *WhAm 1*
Hagerman, Herbert James 1871-1935 *NatCAB 25, WhAm 1*
Hagerman, James 1848-1913 *NatCAB 16, WhAm 1*
Hagerman, Rosa Bullock 1865- *WomWWA 14*
Hagert, Henry Schell 1826-1885 *ApCAB*
Hagerty, Christian Dane 1876- *WhAm 1*
Hagerty, Edward Daniel 1909-1970 *NatCAB 55, WhAm 5*
Hagerty, George James 1861- *TwCBDA, WhAm 4*
Hagerty, James Edward 1869-1946 *NatCAB 37, WhAm 2*
Hagerty, John Francis 1869-1937 *NatCAB 31*
Hagerty, Thomas Harvey 1828-1917 *NatCAB 17*
Haggard, Alfred Martin 1851-1933 *WhAm 1*
Haggard, Fred Porter 1862- *WhAm 4*
Haggard, Sir Godfrey Digsby Napier d1969 *WhAm 5*
Haggard, Howard Wilcox 1891-1959 *WhAm 3*
Haggard, Sewell 1879-1928 *NatCAB 20, WhAm 1*
Haggard, William David 1872-1940 *NatCAB 33, WhAm 1*
Haggart, G Edmund 1894-1970 *NatCAB 55*
Haggart, John Graham 1836- *ApCAB Sup*
Haggart, William Waugh 1897-1955 *NatCAB 44*
Hagge, Hans Jergen 1886-1959 *WhAm 3*
Haggenjos, Frank 1873-1952 *NatCAB 42*
Haggerson, Fred H 1884-1952 *WhAm 3*
Haggerty, Cornelius J 1894-1971 *WhAm 5*
Haggerty, James E 1898- *WhAm 5*
Haggerty, John James 1905-1973 *WhAm 6*
Haggerty, Melvin Everett 1875-1937 *DcAmB S2, WhAm 1*
Haggerty, William J 1908-1975 *WhAm 6*
Haggett, Arthur Sewall 1870-1917 *WhAm 1*
Haggin, Ben Ali 1882-1951 *WhAm 3*
Haggin, James Ben Ali 1821-1914 *NatCAB 19*
Haggin, James Ben Ali 1827-1914 *DcAmB,*

WebAB, WhAm 1
Haggin, Louis Terah 1847-1929 *WhAm 1*
Hagglund, Joel Emmanuel *WebAB*
Haggott, Warren Armstrong 1864-1958 *BiDrAC, WhAm 4*
Hagin, Fred Eugene 1869-1938 *WhAm 1*
Hagler, Kent Rolla Dunlap 1866- *WomWWA 14*
Hagler, Thomas Waterman 1906-1971 *NatCAB 58*
Haglin, Charles Frederick 1890-1957 *NatCAB 48*
Hagner, Alexander Burton 1826-1915 *TwCBDA, WhAm 1*
Hagner, Francis Randall 1873-1940 *WhAm 1*
Hagner, Isabella Louisa 1876- *WomWWA 14*
Hagner, Leonard Gawthrop 1894-1965 *NatCAB 51*
Hagner, Peter 1772-1850 *ApCAB, BiAUS, DcAmB, NatCAB 22, WhAm H*
Hagner, Peter Valentine 1815-1893 *ApCAB, Drake, NatCAB 4, TwCBDA*
Hagny, J *NewYHSD*
Hagood, Johnson 1771-1816 *ApCAB*
Hagood, Johnson 1829-1898 *ApCAB Sup, DcAmB, NatCAB 12, TwCBDA, WhAm H*
Hagood, Johnson 1873-1948 *WhAm 2*
Hagsner, John *NewYHSD*
Hagspiel, Bruno Martin 1885-1961 *WhAm 4*
Hagstrom, G Arvid 1867-1953 *WhAm 3*
Hague, Arnold 1840-1917 *AmBi, ApCAB, DcAmB, DcScB, NatCAB 3, TwCBDA, WhAm 1*
Hague, Eliott Baldwin 1902-1974 *WhAm 6*
Hague, Frank 1876-1956 *McGEWB, WhAm 3*
Hague, James Duncan 1836-1908 *ApCAB, DcAmB, NatCAB 2, NatCAB 23, TwCBDA, WhAm 1*
Hague, Louis Marchand 1899-1967 *WhAm 4*
Hague, Maurice Stewart 1862-1943 *WhAm 2*
Hague, Parthenia Antoinette Vardaman 1838- *WhAm 4*
Hague, Raoul 1905- *BnEnAmA*
Hague, Robert Lincoln 1880-1939 *DcAmB S2*
Hague, William 1805?-1887 *Drake*
Hague, William 1808-1887 *ApCAB, NatCAB 3, TwCBDA, WhAm H*
Hague, William Bailey 1848-1923 *NatCAB 20*
Hagy, Henry B 1864-1955 *WhAm 3*
Hagyard, Edward Weddall 1863-1951 *NatCAB 40*
Hahn, Adolf d1934 *WhAm 1C*
Hahn, Adolf 1872-1934 *NatCAB 27*
Hahn, Adolf 1875-1934 *WhAm 1*
Hahn, Albert George 1893-1969 *NatCAB 55, WhAm 5*
Hahn, Benjamin Daviese 1856-1938 *WhAm 1*
Hahn, Calvin 1925-1974 *WhAm 6*
Hahn, Conrad Velder 1890-1933 *WhAm 1*
Hahn, Dorothy Anna 1876-1950 *NotAW*
Hahn, E Adelaide 1893-1967 *WhAm 4*
Hahn, E Vernon 1891-1959 *NatCAB 47*
Hahn, Emma Erskine *WomWWA 14*
Hahn, Frederic Halsted 1896-1972 *WhAm 5*
Hahn, Frederick E 1869-1942 *WhAm 2*
Hahn, Georg Michael Decker 1830-1886 *DcAmB*
Hahn, George Philip 1879-1937 *WhAm 1*
Hahn, Herman F 1902-1954 *WhAm 3*
Hahn, J Elmer 1894-1964 *NatCAB 50*
Hahn, J Jerome 1868-1938 *WhAm 1*
Hahn, John 1776-1823 *BiAUS, BiDrAC, WhAm H*
Hahn, Lew 1882-1956 *WhAm 3*
Hahn, Michael 1830-1886 *ApCAB, BiAUS, BiDrAC, Drake, NatCAB 10, TwCBDA, WhAm H*
Hahn, Nancy Coonsman d1976 *WhAm 6*
Hahn, Otto 1879-1968 *AsBiEn, DcScB, McGEWB, WhAm 5*
Hahn, Paul M 1895-1963 *WhAm 4*
Hahn, Willard E 1901-1967 *WhAm 4*
Hahn, Willard Steele 1909-1968 *NatCAB 57*
Hahn, William 1829-1887 *IIBEAAW*
Hahne, Ernest Herman 1890-1952 *NatCAB 40, WhAm 3*

Hahnemann, Christian Friedrich Samuel 1755-1843 *DcScB*
Hahr, Emma *AmWom*
Haid, Leo 1849-1924 *ApCAB Sup, DcAmB, NatCAB 12, NatCAB 26, TwCBDA, WhAm 1*
Haid, Paul L 1887-1942 *WhAm 2*
Haidar Ali 1721?-1782 *McGEWB*
Haidinger, Wilhelm Karl 1795-1871 *DcScB*
Haidt, John Valentin 1700-1780 *BnEnAmA*
Haidt, John Valentine 1700-1780 *ApCAB, NewYHSD, WhAm H*
Haig 1877- *WhAm 5*
Haig, Alexander Meigs, Jr. 1924- *WebAMB*
Haig, Douglas 1861-1928 *McGEWB, WhoMilH*
Haig, John T 1877-1962 *WhAm 4*
Haig, Robert Murray 1887-1953 *NatCAB 45, WhAm 3*
Haigh, George Carmelich 1877-1957 *NatCAB 51*
Haigh, Henry Allyn 1854-1942 *NatCAB 31*
Haight, Aaron R *NewYHSD*
Haight, Albert 1842-1926 *TwCBDA, WhAm 1*
Haight, Andrew Levi 1884-1950 *NatCAB 41*
Haight, Benjamin Isaacs 1809-1879 *ApCAB, TwCBDA*
Haight, Cameron 1901-1970 *WhAm 5*
Haight, Charles 1838-1891 *BiAUS, BiDrAC, WhAm 1*
Haight, Charles Coolidge 1841-1917 *AmBi, ApCAB, DcAmB, WhAm 1*
Haight, Charles S 1903-1968 *WhAm 5*
Haight, Edward 1817-1885 *BiAUS, BiDrAC, WhAm H*
Haight, Elizabeth Hazelton 1872-1964 *WhAm 4, WomWWA 14*
Haight, Fletcher M *BiAUS*
Haight, George Ives 1878-1955 *ApCAB X, WhAm 3*
Haight, George W 1842-1913 *NatCAB 15*
Haight, Harold Warren 1902-1970 *NatCAB 55, WhAm 5*
Haight, Helen Ives *WomWWA 14*
Haight, Henry Huntley 1825-1878 *ApCAB, NatCAB 4, TwCBDA*
Haight, Henry Huntly 1825-1878 *BiAUS, DcAmB, Drake, WhAm H, WhAmP*
Haight, Louis 1867-1952 *NatCAB 41*
Haight, Raymond LeRoy 1897-1947 *WhAm 2*
Haight, Thomas Griffith 1879-1942 *WhAm 1*
Haight, Vincent Wymand 1894-1958 *NatCAB 45*
Haigis, John William 1881-1960 *WhAm 4*
Hailandiere, Celestine Rene L G DeLa 1798-1882 *NatCAB 12, TwCBDA*
Haile Selassie 1892- *McGEWB*
Haile Selassie, Emperor Of Abyssinia 1891-1976 *WhWW-II*
Haile Sellassie 1892-1975 *WhAm 6*
Haile, Columbus 1860-1931 *WhAm 1*
Haile, Henry Chapin 1868-1940 *NatCAB 30*
Haile, William 1797-1837 *BiAUS, BiDrAC, WhAm H*
Haile, William 1807-1876 *NatCAB 11*
Hailes, Patrick Buchan-Hepburn 1901-1974 *WhAm 6*
Hailey, Howard 1898-1967 *NatCAB 53*
Hailey, J K *NewYHSD*
Hailey, John 1835-1921 *BiAUS, BiDrAC, REnAW*
Hailey, Orren Luico 1852-1934 *WhAm 1*
Hailey, Thomas Griffith 1865- *WhAm 4*
Hailman, Johanna Knowles *WomWWA 14*
Hailmann, William Nicholas 1836-1920 *AmBi, BiDAmEd, DcAmB, WhAm 4*
Hailperin, Herman 1899-1973 *WhAm 5*
Hails, Raymond Richard 1889-1959 *WhAm 4*
Hain, Edward Wiles 1910-1973 *WhAm 6*
Hain, Jacob L 1902-1972 *WhAm 5*
Hainds, John Robert 1896-1974 *WhAm 6*
Hainer, Bayard Taylor 1860-1933 *NatCAB 11*
Hainer, Bayard Taylor 1866-1933 *WhAm 1*
Hainer, Eugene Jeremiah 1851-1929 *TwCBDA*
Hainer, Eugene Jerome 1851-1929 *BiDrAC, NatCAB 17, WhAmP*
Haines, Alanson Austin 1830- *ApCAB*
Haines, Anna Jones *WomWWA 14*

Haines, Carroll Fogg 1895-1972 *NatCAB 57*
Haines, Charles Delemere 1856-1929 *BiDrAC, NatCAB 9*
Haines, Charles Glidden 1792-1825 *DcAmB, NatCAB 22, WhAm H*
Haines, Charles Glidden 1793-1852 *Drake*
Haines, Charles Grove 1879-1948 *NatCAB 42, WhAm 2*
Haines, Charles Henry 1851- *WhAm 4*
Haines, D *NewYHSD*
Haines, Daniel 1801-1877 *ApCAB, BiAUS, DcAmB, NatCAB 5, TwCBDA, WhAm H*
Haines, Edith Key 1882- *WomWWA 14*
Haines, Edmund Thomas 1914-1974 *WhAm 6*
Haines, Elwood Lindsay 1893-1949 *NatCAB 40, WhAm 2*
Haines, Francis Stoddard 1857-1941 *NatCAB 31*
Haines, Frank David 1866-1959 *WhAm 3*
Haines, George W *NewYHSD*
Haines, Harry Burdette 1882-1972 *NatCAB 56, WhAm 5*
Haines, Harry Luther 1880-1947 *BiDrAC, WhAm 2*
Haines, Helen Elizabeth 1872-1961 *DcAmLiB, WhAm 5*
Haines, Helen Stuart Colby *WhAm 5, WomWWA 14*
Haines, Henry Cargill 1859-1926 *WhAm 1*
Haines, Isabel Burton 1848- *WomWWA 14*
Haines, Jane Bowne 1869- *WomWWA 14*
Haines, Jennie Day 1853- *WhAm 4*
Haines, John Allen 1877-1936 *WhAm 1, WhAm 1C*
Haines, John Michener 1863-1917 *NatCAB 15, WhAm 1*
Haines, John Peter 1851-1921 *NatCAB 13, WhAm 1*
Haines, Lilian Smith 1868- *WomWWA 14*
Haines, Lynn 1876-1929 *DcAmB*
Haines, Mahlon Nathaniel 1875-1962 *NatCAB 52*
Haines, Marie Bruner 1885- *IIBEAAW*
Haines, Matthias Loring 1850-1941 *NatCAB 31, WhAm 4*
Haines, Oliver Sloan 1860- *NatCAB 3*
Haines, Ray Edward 1891-1962 *NatCAB 49*
Haines, Richard Townley 1795-1870 *ApCAB*
Haines, Robert Terrel 1870- *WhAm 5*
Haines, Stella B 1876- *WomWWA 14*
Haines, Thomas Harvey 1871-1951 *WhAm 3*
Haines, Thomas Jefferson 1827-1883 *ApCAB, TwCBDA*
Haines, Thomas Ryerson 1838-1862 *ApCAB*
Haines, Townsend *BiAUS*
Haines, Walter Stanley 1850-1923 *WhAm 1*
Haines, William 1778-1848 *NewYHSD*
Haines, William Thomas 1854-1919 *NatCAB 19, WhAm 1*
Hains, Peter Conover 1840-1921 *TwCBDA, WhAm 1*
Hains, Thornton Jenkins 1866- *WhAm 4*
Haionhwat'ha *WebAB*
Haire, Andrew J 1881-1956 *WhAm 3*
Haire, Norman Washington 1855-1921 *NatCAB 19*
Hairgrove, John Whitlock 1856-1938 *NatCAB 32*
Hairston, Laura Peters *WomWWA 14*
Haish, Jacob 1826-1926 *DcAmB, WhAm HA, WhAm 4*
Haish, Jacob 1827-1926 *NatCAB 5*
Haislip, Wade Hampton 1889-1971 *NatCAB 57, WhAm 5*
Haiss, Catherine Nugent d1973 *WhAm 6*
Haji Ali d1815 *WhAm H*
Hakansson, Erik Gosta 1886-1950 *NatCAB 46, WhAm 3*
Hake, Harry 1871-1955 *NatCAB 45, WhAm 3*
Hakes, George W *NewYHSD*
Hakluyt, Richard 1552?-1616 *DcScB, McGEWB, WhAm H*
Hakluyt, Richard 1553?-1616 *ApCAB*
Hakluyt, Richard 1555-1616 *Drake*
Halas, George Stanley 1895- *EncAB, WebAB*
Halberstadt, Baird 1860-1934 *WhAm 1*

Halbert, Augustus *NewYHSD*
Halbert, Henry Sale 1837-1916 *WhAm 1*
Halbert, Homer Valmore 1858-1927 *WhAm 1*
Halbleib, Edward Andrew 1882-1957
 NatCAB 47
Hald, Henry Martin 1893-1967 *WhAm 4*
Haldane, John Burdon Sanderson 1892-1964
 AsBiEn, DcScB, McGEWB
Haldane, John Scott 1860-1936 *BiHiMed,*
 DcScB
Haldane, Richard Burdon, Viscount 1856-1928
 DcScB, WhoMilH
Haldane, William George 1877-1961
 NatCAB 48
Haldane, William George 1879-1961 *WhAm 6*
Haldeman, Bruce 1862-1948 *NatCAB 38,*
 WhAm 2
Haldeman, Frederick Dwight 1859- *WhAm 4*
Haldeman, Harry Marston 1871-1930
 NatCAB 37, WhAm 1
Haldeman, Isaac Massey 1845-1933
 NatCAB 25, WhAm 1
Haldeman, Jacob Samils 1827-1889 *BiAUS,*
 NatCAB 13
Haldeman, Richard Jacobs 1831-1886 *BiAUS,*
 BiDrAC, WhAm H
Haldeman, S S 1812-1880 *Drake*
Haldeman, Samuel Stehman 1812-1880 *ApCAB,*
 BiDAmEd, NatCAB 9, TwCBDA
Haldeman, Samuel Steman 1812-1880 *AmBi,*
 DcAmB, WhAm H
Haldeman, Sarah Alice 1853-1915 *ApCAB X,*
 WomWWA 14
Haldeman, Walter Newman 1821-1902
 NatCAB 18, WhAm 1
Haldeman, William Birch 1846-1924
 NatCAB 18, WhAm 1
Haldeman-Julius, Emanuel 1889-1951
 DcAmB S5, WebAB, WhAm 3
Halden, Alfred A 1895-1956 *WhAm 3*
Halden, Leon Gilbert 1893-1954 *WhAm 3*
Halder, Franz 1884-1971 *WhWW-II,*
 WhoMilH
Halder, Rudolph *NewYHSD*
Halderman, John A 1833-1908 *DcAmB*
Halderman, John A 1838- *NatCAB 7,*
 WhAm 1
Halderman, John Acoming 1833- *ApCAB*
Halderman, John Adams 1833- *TwCBDA*
Haldimand, Sir Frederick 1718-1791 *ApCAB,*
 Drake
Hale, Albert 1860-1929 *WhAm 1*
Hale, Albert Cable 1845-1921 *NatCAB 10,*
 TwCBDA, WhAm 1
Hale, Anne Gardner d1914 *WhAm 1*
Hale, Annie Riley 1859-1944 *WhAm 2*
Hale, Artemas 1783-1882 *BiAUS, BiDrAC,*
 WhAm H
Hale, B F *NewYHSD*
Hale, Benjamin 1797-1863 *AmBi, ApCAB,*
 BiDAmEd, DcAmB, Drake, NatCAB 13,
 TwCBDA, WhAm H
Hale, Chandler 1873-1951 *WhAm 3*
Hale, Charles 1831-1882 *ApCAB, BiAUS,*
 DcAmB, Drake, TwCBDA, WhAm H
Hale, Charles Reuben 1837-1900 *DcAmB,*
 NatCAB 7, TwCBDA, WhAm 1
Hale, Clarence 1848-1934 *NatCAB 35,*
 WhAm 1
Hale, David 1791-1849 *ApCAB, DcAmB,*
 Drake, NatCAB 11, WhAm H
Hale, David C d1896 *WhAm H*
Hale, Earl Melvin 1884-1961 *NatCAB 54,*
 WhAm 4
Hale, Edward Everett 1822-1909 *AmBi,*
 ApCAB, DcAmB, Drake, McGEWB,
 NatCAB 1, TwCBDA, WebAB, WhAm 1
Hale, Edward Everett 1863-1932 *WhAm 1*
Hale, Edward Joseph 1839-1922 *DcAmB,*
 NatCAB 19, WhAm 1
Hale, Edward Russell 1884-1963 *WhAm 4*
Hale, Edwin Butler 1819-1891 *NatCAB 25*
Hale, Edwin Moses 1829-1899 *ApCAB,*
 DcAmB, NatCAB 11, TwCBDA,
 WhAm H, WhAm 1
Hale, Ellen Day 1855-1940 *ApCAB, TwCBDA,*
 WhAm 2, WomWWA 14
Hale, Enoch 1790-1848 *ApCAB, DcAmB,*

Drake, *NatCAB 3, WhAm H*
Hale, Eugene 1836-1918 *ApCAB, BiAUS,*
 BiDrAC, DcAmB, NatCAB 1,
 NatCAB 20, TwCBDA, WhAm 1,
 WhAmP
Hale, Fletcher 1883-1931 *BiDrAC, WhAm 1,*
 WhAmP
Hale, Florence Maria 1880-1959 *BiDAmEd,*
 WhAm 3
Hale, Floyd Orlin 1882-1938 *WhAm 1*
Hale, Frances Ward 1873- *WomWWA 14*
Hale, Frank J 1899- *WhAm 6*
Hale, Frank Judson 1862-1954 *NatCAB 43,*
 WhAm 5
Hale, Franklin Darius 1854-1940 *NatCAB 46,*
 WhAm 1
Hale, Fred Douglas 1855- *WhAm 4*
Hale, Frederick 1874-1963 *ApCAB X,*
 BiDrAC, NatCAB 52, WhAm 4,
 WhAmP
Hale, Gardner 1894-1931 *NatCAB 23,*
 WhAm 1
Hale, George 1844-1927 *NatCAB 22*
Hale, George Clyde 1891-1948 *NatCAB 42*
Hale, George Ellery 1868-1938 *AmBi, AsBiEn,*
 DcAmB S2, DcScB, EncAB, NatCAB 11,
 NatCAB 38, TwCBDA, WebAB,
 WhAm 1
Hale, George Hamilton 1883-1954 *NatCAB 45*
Hale, George Silsbee 1825-1897 *ApCAB,*
 NatCAB 13, TwCBDA
Hale, H *NewYHSD*
Hale, Harriet Swinburne *WomWWA 14*
Hale, Harris Grafton 1865- *WhAm 4*
Hale, Harrison 1879- *WhAm 6*
Hale, Harry Clay 1861-1946 *NatCAB 43,*
 WhAm 2
Hale, Henry 1814-1890 *NatCAB 18*
Hale, Horace Morrison 1833-1901 *BiDAmEd,*
 NatCAB 6, TwCBDA
Hale, Horatio Emmons 1817-1896 *AmBi,*
 ApCAB, DcAmB, NatCAB 3, TwCBDA,
 WhAm H
Hale, Hugh Ellmaker *WhAm 3*
Hale, Irving 1861- *ApCAB Sup, ApCAB X,*
 NatCAB 6, TwCBDA, WhAm 4
Hale, James Tracy 1810-1865 *BiAUS, BiDrAC,*
 WhAm H
Hale, John 1636-1700 *ApCAB, Drake,*
 NatCAB 11
Hale, John Blackwell 1831-1905 *BiDrAC*
Hale, John D 1847-1929 *REnAW*
Hale, John Henry 1879- *WhoColR*
Hale, John Howard 1853-1917 *WhAm 1*
Hale, John Parker 1806-1873 *AmBi, ApCAB,*
 BiAUS, BiDrAC, DcAmB, Drake,
 EncAAH, NatCAB 3, TwCBDA, WebAB,
 WhAm H, WhAmP
Hale, John Philetus 1850- *WhAm 4*
Hale, Ledyard Park 1854-1926 *WhAm 1*
Hale, Lilian Westcott 1881-1963 *WomWWA 14*
Hale, Lillian Westcott 1881-1963 *WhAm 4*
Hale, Lincoln Bell 1899-1958 *WhAm 3*
Hale, Louise Closser 1872-1933 *AmBi,*
 DcAmB S1, WhAm 1
Hale, Lucretia Peabody 1820-1900 *AmBi,*
 ApCAB, DcAmB, NatCAB 5, NotAW,
 TwCBDA, WebAB, WhAm 1
Hale, Marshal 1866-1945 *NatCAB 37,*
 WhAm 2
Hale, Matthew 1829-1897 *TwCBDA*
Hale, Matthew 1882-1925 *WhAm 1*
Hale, Maud Frances 1879- *WomWWA 14*
Hale, Morris Smith 1895-1948 *WhAm 2*
Hale, Nathan 1755-1776 *AmBi, ApCAB,*
 DcAmB, Drake, NatCAB 1, TwCBDA,
 WebAB, WebAMB, WhAm H
Hale, Nathan 1784-1863 *AmBi, ApCAB,*
 DcAmB, Drake, NatCAB 11, TwCBDA,
 WhAm H
Hale, Nathan 1818-1871 *ApCAB, Drake,*
 TwCBDA
Hale, Nathan 1818-1873 *NatCAB 11*
Hale, Nathan Wesley 1860-1941 *BiDrAC,*
 WhAm 4
Hale, Oliver Ambrose 1852-1907 *NatCAB 6*
Hale, Oscar 1867-1950 *WhAm 3*
Hale, Philip 1854-1934 *AmBi, ApCAB X,*

DcAmB S1, NatCAB 14, TwCBDA,
 WhAm 1
Hale, Philip Leslie 1865-1931 *AmBi, DcAmB,*
 NatCAB 31, WhAm 1
Hale, Philip Thomas 1857-1926 *WhAm 1*
Hale, Philo 1785-1847 *NatCAB 25*
Hale, Prentis Cobb 1858-1936 *WhAm 1*
Hale, Ralph Tracy 1880-1951 *WhAm 3*
Hale, Reuben Brooks 1869-1950 *WhAm 3*
Hale, Richard Walden 1871-1943 *WhAm 2*
Hale, Robert 1703-1767 *ApCAB, Drake*
Hale, Robert 1889- *BiDrAC*
Hale, Robert Lee 1884-1969 *WhAm 5*
Hale, Robert Safford 1822-1881 *ApCAB,*
 BiAUS, BiDrAC, DcAmB, NatCAB 4,
 TwCBDA, WhAm H
Hale, Rose Perkins *WomWWA 14*
Hale, Salma 1787-1866 *ApCAB, BiAUS,*
 BiDrAC, Drake, NatCAB 11, TwCBDA,
 WhAm H
Hale, Samuel Whitney 1823-1891 *NatCAB 11*
Hale, Sarah Josepha Buell 1788-1879 *AmBi,*
 ApCAB, DcAmB, EncAB, McGEWB,
 NatCAB 3, NatCAB 22, NotAW,
 TwCBDA, WebAB, WhAm H
Hale, Sarah Josepha Buell 1790-1879 *Drake*
Hale, Stephen Fowler 1816-1862 *BiDConf*
Hale, Susan 1833-1910 *NotAW, WhAm 1*
Hale, Susan 1834-1910 *NewYHSD*
Hale, Susan 1838-1910 *ApCAB, TwCBDA*
Hale, Walter 1869-1917 *WhAm 1*
Hale, Will T 1880-1967 *WhAm 4*
Hale, William 1765-1848 *BiAUS, BiDrAC,*
 WhAm H
Hale, William 1797-1870 *DcScB*
Hale, William 1837-1885 *WhAm H*
Hale, William Barton 1860-1938 *NatCAB 29,*
 WhAm 1
Hale, William Bayard 1869-1924 *AmBi,*
 DcAmB, NatCAB 15, WhAm 1
Hale, William Benjamin 1871-1924 *WhAm 1*
Hale, William Browne 1875-1944 *WhAm 2*
Hale, William Ellery 1836-1898 *NatCAB 26*
Hale, William Gardner 1849-1928 *AmBi,*
 BiDAmEd, DcAmB, NatCAB 11,
 NatCAB 23, TwCBDA, WhAm 1
Hale, William Green 1881-1952 *NatCAB 41,*
 WhAm 3
Hale, William Harlan 1910-1974 *WhAm 6*
Hale, William Henry 1840-1919 *WhAm 1*
Hale, William Jay 1876-1955 *NatCAB 44,*
 WhAm 3
Hale, William Thomas 1857-1926 *ApCAB Sup,*
 WhAm 1
Hale, Willis H 1893-1961 *WhAm 4*
Hale, Wyatt Walker 1901-1943 *WhAm 2*
Hale-White, Sir William 1857-1949 *BiHiMed*
Halecki, Oscar 1891-1973 *WhAm 6*
Hales, Jesse Collins 1897-1956 *NatCAB 45*
Hales, Stephen 1677-1761 *AsBiEn, BiHiMed,*
 DcScB, McGEWB
Halevy, Elie 1870-1937 *McGEWB*
Haley, Andrew Gallagher 1904-1966 *WhAm 4*
Haley, Charles Little, Jr. 1889-1958
 NatCAB 49
Haley, Dennis C 1893-1966 *WhAm 4*
Haley, Elisha 1776-1860 *BiAUS, BiDrAC,*
 WhAm H
Haley, George Franklin 1856- *WhAm 1*
Haley, George Phineas 1853-1920 *NatCAB 19*
Haley, James Andrew 1899- *BiDrAC*
Haley, James Evetts 1901- *REnAW*
Haley, James Frederick 1926-1969 *WhAm 5*
Haley, Jesse James 1851-1924 *WhAm 1*
Haley, Lella Byrd 1869- *WomWWA 14*
Haley, Mrs. Lovick Pierce 1880- *WhAm 6*
Haley, Margaret Angela 1861-1939 *BiDAmEd,*
 NotAW
Haley, Olive L 1873- *WomWWA 14*
Haley, Ora 1845-1919 *NatCAB 20, WhAm 1*
Haley, Thomas Preston 1832-1913 *NatCAB 6*
Haley, Victoria Clay 1877- *WhoColR*
Haley, William J 1891-1957 *WhAm 3*
Halffter, Christobal 1930- *McGEWB*
Halfhill, Albert Powers 1847-1924 *NatCAB 33*
Halfhill, James Wood 1861-1923 *WhAm 1*
Halford, Albert James 1851-1910 *WhAm 1*
Halford, Elijah Walker 1843-1938 *NatCAB 1,*

WhAm 1

Halford, Sir Henry 1766-1844 *BiHiMed*
Halford, John Henry 1885-1968 *WhAm 5*
Haliburton, Sir Arthur Laurence 1832-
  ApCAB Sup
Haliburton, Brenton 1773-1860 *ApCAB*
Haliburton, John 1739-1808 *ApCAB*
Haliburton, Robert Grant 1831- *ApCAB Sup*
Haliburton, Thomas Chandler 1796-1865
  McGEWB, *NatCAB 5*
Haliburton, Thomas Chandler 1797-1865
  ApCAB, *Drake*
Halifax, Earl Of 1881-1959 *McGEWB*,
  WhAm 3, *WhWW-II*
Halkett, A *NewYHSD*
Halkett, John 1768-1852 *ApCAB*, *Drake*
Halkett, Sir Peter d1755 *ApCAB*, *Drake*
Hall, A Neely 1883-1959 *WhAm 3*
Hall, Abraham Oakey 1826-1898 *ApCAB Sup*,
  DcAmB, *NatCAB 3*, *TwCBDA*, *WebAB*,
  WhAm H
Hall, Adaline M 1866- *WomWWA 14*
Hall, Adelaide S 1857- *WomWWA 14*
Hall, Alastair Cameron 1903-1971 *WhAm 5*
Hall, Albert Acton 1860-1923 *ApCAB X*,
  NatCAB 20
Hall, Albert Heath 1858-1920 *NatCAB 20*
Hall, Albert Richardson 1884-1969 *BiDrAC*
Hall, Alexander Wilford 1819-1902 *NatCAB 3*,
  TwCBDA, *WhAm 1*
Hall, Alice Linscott 1857- *WomWWA 14*
Hall, Allen A d1867 *BiAUS*, *Drake*,
  NatCAB 7
Hall, Allen Garland 1862-1915 *WhAm 1*
Hall, Alton Parker 1900-1951 *WhAm 3*
Hall, Alvin Percy McDonald 1910-1973
  WhAm 6
Hall, Alvin William 1888-1969 *NatCAB 55*,
  WhAm 5
Hall, Andrew Douglass 1833- *ApCAB*
Hall, Ann 1792-1863 *NewYHSD*
Hall, Anne 1792-1863 *ApCAB Sup*,
  NatCAB 10, *NotAW*
Hall, Ansel Franklin 1894-1962 *WhAm 4*
Hall, Arethusa 1802-1891 *ApCAB*, *DcAmB*,
  NatCAB 22, *TwCBDA*, *WhAm H*
Hall, Arnold Bennett 1881-1936 *NatCAB 30*,
  WhAm 1
Hall, Arthur Benedict 1881- *WhAm 6*
Hall, Arthur Cleveland 1865-1910 *WhAm 1*
Hall, Arthur Crawshay Alliston 1847-1930
  ApCAB Sup, *DcAmB*, *NatCAB 11*,
  TwCBDA, *WhAm 1*
Hall, Arthur Fletcher 1872-1942 *WhAm 2*
Hall, Arthur Graham 1865-1925 *WhAm 1*
Hall, Arthur Jackson 1874- *WhAm 2*
Hall, Arthur Pinckney 1858- *WhAm 4*
Hall, Arthur Raymond 1869-1955 *NatCAB 47*
Hall, Asaph 1829-1907 *AmBi*, *ApCAB*,
  AsBiEn, *DcAmB*, *DcScB*, *McGEWB*,
  NatCAB 11, *NatCAB 22*, *TwCBDA*,
  WebAB, *WhAm 1*
Hall, Asaph 1830-1907 *BiAUS*
Hall, Asaph, Jr. 1859-1930 *NatCAB 27*,
  WhAm 1
Hall, Augustus 1814-1861 *BiAUS*, *BiDrAC*,
  WhAm H
Hall, Augustus R 1824- *NatCAB 4*
Hall, Basil 1788-1844 *ApCAB*, *Drake*,
  NewYHSD
Hall, Baynard Rush 1798-1863 *DcAmB*,
  TwCBDA, *WhAm H*
Hall, Baynard Rust 1798-1863 *ApCAB*, *Drake*,
  NatCAB 3
Hall, Benjamin Franklin 1814-1891 *BiAUS*,
  NatCAB 13
Hall, Benjamin Homer 1830-1893 *ApCAB*,
  NatCAB 3, *TwCBDA*
Hall, Benjamin Mortimer 1853-1929 *WhAm 1*
Hall, Benton Jay 1835-1894 *BiDrAC*,
  NatCAB 12, *WhAm H*
Hall, Bolling 1767-1836 *BiAUS*, *BiDrAC*,
  WhAm H, *WhAmP*
Hall, Bolton 1854-1938 *DcAmB S2*, *TwCBDA*,
  WhAm 1
Hall, C Lester 1845-1922 *WhAm 1*
Hall, Carlotta Case 1880- *WomWWA 14*
Hall, Cecil Langton 1904-1969 *NatCAB 55*

Hall, Chaffee E 1888-1969 *WhAm 5*
Hall, Channing Moore 1890-1953 *NatCAB 42*
Hall, Chapin 1816-1879 *BiAUS*, *BiDrAC*,
  WhAm H
Hall, Charles Badger 1844-1914 *WhAm 1*
Hall, Charles Bingley 1815-1883 *NatCAB 13*
Hall, Charles Bryan 1840-1906? *NewYHSD*
Hall, Charles Cuthbert 1852-1908 *DcAmB*,
  NatCAB 6, *TwCBDA*, *WhAm 1*
Hall, Charles Edward 1852- *WhAm 4*
Hall, Charles F *NewYHSD*
Hall, Charles Francis 1821-1871 *AmBi*,
  ApCAB, *DcAmB*, *NatCAB 3*, *TwCBDA*,
  WhAm H
Hall, Charles Henry 1820-1895 *ApCAB*,
  DcAmB, *NatCAB 10*, *TwCBDA*,
  WhAm H
Hall, Charles Hershall 1833- *WhAm 1*
Hall, Charles Hershall 1835- *ApCAB*
Hall, Charles Martin 1863-1914 *AmBi*, *AsBiEn*,
  DcAmB, *DcScB*, *NatCAB 13*, *WebAB*,
  WhAm 1
Hall, Charles Mercer 1864-1929 *WhAm 1*
Hall, Charles Philip 1886-1953 *NatCAB 42*,
  WhAm 3
Hall, Charles Winslow 1843- *WhAm 4*
Hall, Chester Wallace 1883-1963 *WhAm 4*
Hall, Christopher Webber 1845-1911 *ApCAB*,
  NatCAB 9, *TwCBDA*, *WhAm 1*
Hall, Clara Wendel 1868- *WomWWA 14*
Hall, Claude Caleb 1871- *WhAm 5*
Hall, Colby Dixon 1975- *WhAm 6*
Hall, Cornelius *NewYHSD*
Hall, Custis Lee 1888-1951 *NatCAB 40*
Hall, Cyrenius 1830- *IIBEAAW*
Hall, Damon Everett 1875-1953 *NatCAB 42*,
  WhAm 3
Hall, Daniel 1832-1920 *ApCAB X*, *WhAm 1*
Hall, Darwin Scott 1844-1919 *BiDrAC*,
  NatCAB 9
Hall, David 1714-1772 *ApCAB*, *DcAmB*,
  NatCAB 23, *TwCBDA*, *WhAm H*
Hall, David 1752-1817 *BiAUS*, *NatCAB 11*,
  TwCBDA
Hall, David McKee 1918-1960 *BiDrAC*,
  NatCAB 45, *WhAm 3*
Hall, Dominick Augustin 1765?-1820 *DcAmB*,
  WhAm H
Hall, Dominick Augustine 1765-1820 *ApCAB*,
  BiAUS, *Drake*, *NatCAB 13*, *TwCBDA*
Hall, Durward Gorham 1910- *BiDrAC*
Hall, E W *NewYHSD*
Hall, Edith Babbitt 1885- *WomWWA 14*
Hall, Edith Hayward *NotAW*, *WomWWA 14*
Hall, Edmond 1902-1967 *WhAm 4*
Hall, Edward *ApCAB*
Hall, Edward Bigelow 1886-1969 *WhAm 5*
Hall, Edward Brooks 1800-1866 *Drake*,
  NatCAB 8
Hall, Edward Hagaman 1858-1936 *WhAm 1*,
  WhAm 1C
Hall, Edward Henry 1831-1912 *WhAm 1*
Hall, Edward Kimball 1870-1932 *NatCAB 26*,
  WhAm 1
Hall, Edward S *NewYHSD*
Hall, Edwin 1802-1877 *ApCAB*, *TwCBDA*
Hall, Edwin Arthur 1909- *BiDrAC*
Hall, Edwin Cesar Malan 1858-1939
  NatCAB 29
Hall, Edwin Herbert 1855-1938 *DcAmB S2*,
  DcScB, *NatCAB 39*, *WhAm 1*
Hall, Edwin S d1953 *WhAm 3*
Hall, Elbert John 1882-1955 *ApCAB X*,
  NatCAB 43
Hall, Elbert Rufus 1881- *WhoColR*
Hall, Elliott Holmes, Jr. 1903-1971 *NatCAB 57*
Hall, Elmer Edwards 1890-1958 *WhAm 3*
Hall, Emery Stanford 1869-1939 *NatCAB 17*,
  WhAm 1
Hall, Emma Amelia 1837-1884 *NotAW*
Hall, Ernest 1844-1920 *NatCAB 10*, *WhAm 1*
Hall, Ernest Mosiah 1885-1961 *NatCAB 50*
Hall, Everett Wesley 1901-1960 *WhAm 4*
Hall, Fanny Southard Hay 1872-
  WomWWA 14
Hall, Fitzedward 1825-190? *AmBi*, *ApCAB*,
  DcAmB, *NatCAB 11*, *TwCBDA*,
  WhAm H

Hall, Fitzgerald 1889-1946 *WhAm 2*
Hall, Florence Marion Howe 1845-1922 *DcAmB*,
  NatCAB 19, *WhAm 1*, *WomWWA 14*
Hall, Ford Poulton 1898-1951 *WhAm 3*
Hall, Francis 1785-1866 *ApCAB*
Hall, Francis Joseph 1857-1932 *WhAm 1*
Hall, Frank 1836-1917 *REnAW*
Hall, Frank A 1894-1972 *WhAm 5*
Hall, Frank Haven 1841-1911 *ApCAB X*
Hall, Frank Herbert 1890-1964 *WhAm 4*
Hall, Frank Hillman 1870-1957 *WhAm 3*
Hall, Frank Lorenzo 1850- *NatCAB 9*
Hall, Frank Lucas 1856-1929 *NatCAB 22*,
  WhAm 1
Hall, Frank M 1852-1928 *WhAm 1*
Hall, Frank Oliver 1860-1941 *WhAm 1*
Hall, Franklin 1872- *WhAm 5*
Hall, Fred L 1916-1970 *WhAm 5*
Hall, Fred Smith 1870- *WhAm 5*
Hall, Frederic Aldin 1854-1925 *NatCAB 20*,
  WhAm 1
Hall, Frederic Byron 1843-1913 *NatCAB 22*,
  WhAm 1
Hall, Frederick 1779-1843 *TwCBDA*
Hall, Frederick 1780-1843 *ApCAB*, *Drake*
Hall, Frederick Garrison 1878-1946 *NatCAB 35*
Hall, Frederick Perry 1859-1939 *NatCAB 31*
Hall, Frieda P C 1879- *WomWWA 14*
Hall, Gaylord Crawford 1879-1946 *NatCAB 35*
Hall, Gene W 1898-1951 *WhAm 3*
Hall, George 1770-1840 *BiAUS*, *BiDrAC*,
  WhAm H
Hall, George 1795-1868 *ApCAB*, *NatCAB 8*
Hall, George B 1826-1864 *ApCAB*
Hall, George Chalmers 1864-1939 *NatCAB 30*
Hall, George Cleveland 1864- *WhoColR*
Hall, George Edward 1868- *WhAm 4*
Hall, George Edward 1907-1972 *WhAm 5*
Hall, George Eli 1863- *WhAm 1*
Hall, George Elisha 1870-1944 *WhAm 2*
Hall, George Gilman 1866- *WhAm 4*
Hall, George Henry 1825-1913 *ApCAB*,
  BnEnAmA, *DcAmB*, *NatCAB 15*,
  NewYHSD, *TwCBDA*, *WhAm 1*
Hall, George Houston 1854-1930 *NatCAB 24*
Hall, George Martin 1891-1941 *WhAm 1*
Hall, George R 1818- *NewYHSD*
Hall, George Washington 1869-1941
  NatCAB 31, *WhAm 1*
Hall, Gertrude 1863- *WhAm 4*,
  WomWWA 14
Hall, Gertrude Ella 1877- *WomWWA 14*
Hall, Gordon 1784-1826 *Drake*, *NatCAB 10*
Hall, Granville Stanley 1844-1924 *AmBi*,
  BiDAmEd, *DcAmB*, *McGEWB*,
  NatCAB 39, *WebAB*
Hall, Granville Stanley 1845-1924 *ApCAB Sup*,
  NatCAB 9
Hall, Granville Stanley 1846-1924 *ApCAB X*,
  AsBiEn, *DcScB*, *EncAB*, *TwCBDA*,
  WhAm 1
Hall, Grover Cleveland 1888-1941 *WhAm 1*
Hall, Grover Cleveland, Jr. 1915-1971 *WhAm 5*
Hall, Halliett Deraxa Ellis 1861-
  WomWWA 14
Hall, Harold d1958 *WhAm 4*
Hall, Harriet Baker 1877- *WomWWA 14*
Hall, Harrison 1785-1866 *ApCAB*
Hall, Harrison 1787-1866 *Drake*
Hall, Harry Alvan 1861-1917 *NatCAB 18*,
  WhAm 1
Hall, Harry Hinckley 1846-1911 *NatCAB 16*,
  WhAm 1
Hall, Harry Melville 1877-1931 *WhAm 1*
Hall, Harvey Monroe 1874-1932 *WhAm 1*
Hall, Hazel 1886-1924 *DcAmB*, *NatCAB 22*
Hall, Henri Mason 1884-1972 *NatCAB 57*
Hall, Henry 1845-1920 *TwCBDA*, *WhAm 1*
Hall, Henry B 1851-1934 *WhAm 1*
Hall, Henry B 1916-1964 *WhAm 4*
Hall, Henry Bryan 1808-1884 *ApCAB*, *DcAmB*,
  NewYHSD, *WhAm H*
Hall, Henry Bryan, Jr. *NewYHSD*
Hall, Henry Clay 1860-1936 *WhAm 1*
Hall, Henry Cook *NatCAB 5*
Hall, Henry Harrington 1846-1906 *WhAm 1*
Hall, Henry Noble 1872-1949 *WhAm 2*
Hall, Herbert Edwin 1893-1963 *WhAm 4*

Hall, Herbert James 1870-1923 *ApCAB X, NatCAB 20, WhAm 1*
Hall, Herman 1864-1928 *NatCAB 21, WhAm 4*
Hall, Hiland 1795-1885 *AmBi, ApCAB, BiAUS, BiDrAC, DcAmB, Drake, NatCAB 8, TwCBDA, WhAmP*
Hall, Hilland 1795-1885 *WhAm H*
Hall, Holworthy *WhAm 1*
Hall, Homer William 1870-1954 *BiDrAC, WhAm 5*
Hall, Howard 1895-1971 *WhAm 5*
Hall, Howard Judson 1869-1942 *WhAm 2*
Hall, Ida Dickinson *WomWWA 14*
Hall, Irving Frank 1892-1959 *NatCAB 47*
Hall, Isaac Harry 1845- *WhAm 4*
Hall, Isaac Hollister 1837-1896 *AmBi, ApCAB, DcAmB, NatCAB 12, TwCBDA, WhAm H*
Hall, Isaac Staples 1882-1963 *NatCAB 50*
Hall, J F *NewYHSD*
Hall, James d1823 *NewYHSD*
Hall, James 1744-1826 *ApCAB, DcAmB, NatCAB 22, TwCBDA, WhAm H*
Hall, Sir James 1761-1832 *AsBiEn, DcScB*
Hall, James 1793-1868 *AmBi, ApCAB, DcAmB, Drake, NatCAB 7, REnAW, TwCBDA, WebAB, WhAm H*
Hall, James 1811-1898 *AmBi, ApCAB, DcAmB, DcScB, Drake, NatCAB 3, TwCBDA, WebAB, WhAm H*
Hall, James 1869-1917 *WhAm 1*
Hall, James A 1835-1893 *ApCAB Sup, NatCAB 4*
Hall, James Alexander 1888-1936 *WhAm 1*
Hall, James D *NewYHSD*
Hall, James Frederick 1822-1884 *ApCAB*
Hall, James Frederick 1824-1884 *NatCAB 3, TwCBDA*
Hall, James Glenn 1902-1953 *WhAm 3*
Hall, James Jabez 1849-1921 *WhAm 1*
Hall, James King 1875-1948 *NatCAB 37, WhAm 2*
Hall, James Knox Polk 1844-1915 *BiDrAC, NatCAB 41, WhAm 4*
Hall, James Lowell 1892-1965 *NatCAB 53*
Hall, James Morris Whiton 1842- *WhAm 4*
Hall, James Norman 1887-1951 *DcAmB S5, WhAm 3*
Hall, James Parker 1871-1928 *NatCAB 38, WhAm 1*
Hall, James Pierre 1849- *WhAm 4*
Hall, James Whitney 1869-1936 *WhAm 1*
Hall, Jeanie Stewart Boyd 1857- *WomWWA 14*
Hall, Jennie 1875-1921 *WhAm 1, WomWWA 14*
Hall, Jeremiah 1805-1881 *NatCAB 1, TwCBDA*
Hall, John *BiAUS, NewYHSD*
Hall, John 1729-1797 *BiDrAC, WhAm H, WhAmP*
Hall, John 1767-1833 *ApCAB, NatCAB 7*
Hall, John 1769-1833 *Drake*
Hall, John 1806- *ApCAB*
Hall, John 1829-1898 *ApCAB, ApCAB Sup, DcAmB, Drake Sup, NatCAB 6, TwCBDA, WhAm H*
Hall, John Dean 1842- *WhAm 4*
Hall, John Elihu 1783-1827 *NatCAB 3*
Hall, John Elihu 1783-1829 *ApCAB, DcAmB, Drake, WhAm H*
Hall, John Ellsworth 1876-1945 *WhAm 2*
Hall, John Ewing 1873-1829 *TwCBDA*
Hall, John H *NewYHSD, WhAm H*
Hall, John Howe 1881-1953 *NatCAB 42*
Hall, John Hudson 1828-1891 *NatCAB 2*
Hall, John Hudson 1897-1952 *NatCAB 41*
Hall, John L *NewYHSD*
Hall, John Leslie 1856-1928 *WhAm 1*
Hall, John Lesslie 1856-1928 *TwCBDA*
Hall, John Lincoln 1860-1943 *NatCAB 33*
Hall, John Loomer 1872-1960 *NatCAB 49, WhAm 4*
Hall, John Manning 1841-1905 *NatCAB 15*
Hall, John P *NewYHSD*
Hall, John Raymond 1879-1936 *WhAm 1*
Hall, John Smith 1863-1924 *NatCAB 24*

Hall, John W 1802-1886 *TwCBDA*
Hall, John W 1817-1893 *TwCBDA*
Hall, John Walter 1859- *NatCAB 14*
Hall, John William *WhAm 5*
Hall, John Wood 1817-1892 *NatCAB 11*
Hall, Jonathan Prescott 1796-1862 *ApCAB*
Hall, Joseph 1793-1859 *BiAUS, BiDrAC, WhAm H*
Hall, Joseph Kevin 1906-1965 *WhAm 4*
Hall, Josephine d1920 *WhAm 1*
Hall, Joshua Gilman 1828-1898 *BiDrAC, TwCBDA*
Hall, Josiah Newhall 1859-1939 *WhAm 1*
Hall, Joyce Clyde 1891- *WebAB*
Hall, Juanita d1968 *WhAm 4A*
Hall, Kate Cowling 1878- *WomWWA 14*
Hall, Lawrence Washington 1819-1863 *BiAUS, BiDrAC, WhAm H*
Hall, Lee Davis 1893-1963 *NatCAB 51, WhAm 4*
Hall, Leland 1883-1957 *WhAm 3*
Hall, Lemuel C 1874-1946 *WhAm 2*
Hall, Leonard Wood 1900- *BiDrAC*
Hall, Lester W 1876- *WhAm 5*
Hall, Lillian Popenoe 1865- *WomWWA 14*
Hall, Lloyd Augustus 1894-1971 *WhAm 5*
Hall, Lolabel House 1877- *WomWWA 14*
Hall, Lot 1757-1809 *TwCBDA*
Hall, Louis Dixon 1878- *WhAm 6*
Hall, Louis Harrison 1875-1949 *NatCAB 43, WhAm 3*
Hall, Louis Phillips 1860-1941 *WhAm 1*
Hall, Louis Phillips 1860-1944 *WhAm 2*
Hall, Louisa Jane Park 1802-1892 *ApCAB, Drake, NatCAB 11, WhAm H*
Hall, Lucia Wheeler 1876- *WomWWA 14*
Hall, Lucile Carol Reynolds 1876- *WomWWA 14*
Hall, Lucy Howe 1874- *WomWWA 14*
Hall, Lucy M *AmWom*
Hall, Luella Jemima 1890-1973 *WhAm 6*
Hall, Luther Egbert 1869-1921 *DcAmB, NatCAB 15, WhAm 1*
Hall, Lyman 1724-1790 *AmBi, BiDrAC, DcAmB, NatCAB 2, TwCBDA, WhAm H, WhAmP*
Hall, Lyman 1725-1790 *ApCAB, Drake*
Hall, Lyman 1725-1791 *BiAUS*
Hall, Lyman 1859-1905 *NatCAB 29, TwCBDA, WhAm 1*
Hall, Lyman Beecher 1852-1935 *WhAm 1*
Hall, Margaret Thompson 1854- *AmWom*
Hall, Margaret Woodburn 1879- *WomWWA 14*
Hall, Marshall 1790-1857 *AsBiEn, BiHiMed, DcScB*
Hall, Mary 1848- *NatCAB 12*
Hall, Mary 1850?- *AmWom*
Hall, Mary Bowers 1871- *WomWWA 14*
Hall, Mary Evelyn 1874-1956 *DcAmLiB*
Hall, Mary Hunter *WomWWA 14*
Hall, Mary Keney *WomWWA 14*
Hall, Mary Louise *WomWWA 14*
Hall, Matthew Alexander 1862-1942 *WhAm 2*
Hall, Matthew Walton 1853- *WhAm 4*
Hall, Maurice Crowther 1881-1938 *NatCAB 29, WhAm 1, WhAm 1C*
Hall, Mollie Margaret Baker 1866- *WomWWA 14*
Hall, Nathan Kelsey 1810-1874 *AmBi, ApCAB, BiAUS, BiDrAC, BiDrUSE, DcAmB, Drake, NatCAB 6, TwCBDA, WhAm H*
Hall, Nathaniel 1805-1875 *ApCAB*
Hall, Nellie N 1870- *WomWWA 14*
Hall, Newman 1816- *ApCAB*
Hall, Newton Marshall 1865-1926 *WhAm 1*
Hall, Nichols 1903-1965 *WhAm 5*
Hall, Norman 1829-1917 *BiDrAC*
Hall, Norman Brierley 1886-1962 *WhAm 4*
Hall, Oakel Fowler 1878- *WhAm 6*
Hall, Obed 1757-1828 *BiAUS, BiDrAC, WhAm H*
Hall, Oliver Gray 1834-1914 *NatCAB 30*
Hall, Oliver Leigh 1870-1946 *WhAm 2*
Hall, Ollie Goodloe Gregory *WomWWA 14*
Hall, Orson Loftin 1877- *WhAm 5*
Hall, Osee Matson 1847-1914 *BiDrAC*
Hall, Pauline 1860-1919 *WhAm 1*

Hall, Pauline 1862-1919 *AmWom*
Hall, Percival 1872-1953 *WhAm 3*
Hall, Peter 1828-1895 *NewYHSD*
Hall, Philip Louis 1850-1923 *WhAm 1*
Hall, Philo 1865-1938 *BiDrAC, WhAm 3, WhAmP*
Hall, Prescott Farnsworth 1868-1921 *WhAm 1*
Hall, Randall Cooke 1842-1921 *WhAm 1*
Hall, Ray Ovid 1891-1952 *WhAm 3*
Hall, Reynold Thomas 1858-1934 *NatCAB 44, WhAm 1*
Hall, Richard Cartwright 1856-1931 *WhAm 1*
Hall, Richard Smith 1855-1910 *NatCAB 33*
Hall, Robert Anderson 1880-1944 *NatCAB 33*
Hall, Robert Bernard 1812-1868 *ApCAB, BiAUS, BiDrAC, NatCAB 2, TwCBDA, WhAm H*
Hall, Robert Burnett 1896-1975 *WhAm 6*
Hall, Robert Henry 1837-1914 *NatCAB 16, WhAm 1*
Hall, Robert Newton 1836- *ApCAB*
Hall, Robert Pleasants 1825-1854 *ApCAB, Drake*
Hall, Robert Samuel 1876-1941 *NatCAB 42*
Hall, Robert Samuel 1879-1941 *BiDrAC, WhAm 1*
Hall, Robert William 1853- *TwCBDA*
Hall, Robert William 1872-1963 *NatCAB 51, WhAm 5*
Hall, Roland William 1875-1942 *NatCAB 38*
Hall, Rufus Bartlett 1849- *NatCAB 13, WhAm 4*
Hall, Ruth 1858- *WhAm 4, WomWWA 14*
Hall, Ruth Marion 1880- *WomWWA 14*
Hall, Samuel 1740-1807 *ApCAB, DcAmB, Drake, TwCBDA, WhAm H*
Hall, Samuel 1797-1855? *ApCAB*
Hall, Samuel 1800-1870 *DcAmB, WhAm H*
Hall, Samuel Read 1795-1877 *AmBi, ApCAB, BiDAmEd, DcAmB, Drake, TwCBDA, WhAm H*
Hall, Samuel Reed 1793-1877 *NatCAB 3*
Hall, Sarah 1761-1830 *ApCAB, NatCAB 11*
Hall, Sarah C 1832- *AmWom*
Hall, Sarah Deborah Trowbridge 1841- *WomWWA 14*
Hall, Sarah Elizabeth *AmWom*
Hall, Sarah Ewing 1761-1830 *DcAmB, WhAm H*
Hall, Sharlot Mabridth 1870-1943 *WhAm 3*
Hall, Sharlot Mabridth 1875-1943 *WomWWA 14*
Hall, Sherman 1800-1879 *DcAmB, WhAm H*
Hall, Sherman Rogers 1874-1928 *NatCAB 33*
Hall, Sidney *NewYHSD*
Hall, Sidney Bartlett 1895-1946 *WhAm 3*
Hall, Stephen Crosby 1834-1888 *NatCAB 26*
Hall, Sydney Prior 1842-1922 *IIBEAAW*
Hall, Sylvester 1778- *NewYHSD*
Hall, Thomas 1791-1874 *ApCAB*
Hall, Thomas 1834-1911 *DcAmB, NatCAB 3, WhAm 1*
Hall, Thomas 1869-1911 *WhAm 1*
Hall, Thomas 1869-1958 *BiDrAC, WhAm 3, WhAmP*
Hall, Thomas Bartlett 1824- *WhAm 1*
Hall, Thomas Cuming 1858-1936 *WhAm 1*
Hall, Thomas H 1773-1853 *BiAUS, BiDrAC, WhAm H, WhAmP*
Hall, Thomas Lee 1895- *NatCAB 19*
Hall, Thomas Mifflin 1798-1828 *ApCAB*
Hall, Thomas Seavey 1827-1880 *DcAmB, WhAm H*
Hall, Thomas Winthrop 1862-1900 *WhAm 1*
Hall, Tomas Proctor 1858-1931 *WhAm 1*
Hall, Uriel Sebree 1852-1932 *BiDrAC, TwCBDA, WhAmP*
Hall, Violette *WomWWA 14*
Hall, Walter Henry 1862-1935 *AmBi, WhAm 1*
Hall, Walter Perley 1867-1942 *NatCAB 33, WhAm 3*
Hall, Warren Esterly 1881-1956 *NatCAB 49*
Hall, Wilbur Curtis 1892-1972 *WhAm 5*
Hall, Wilburn Briggs 1838-1912 *NatCAB 8, TwCBDA*
Hall, Willard 1780-1875 *ApCAB, BiAUS, BiDAmEd, BiDrAC, DcAmB, Drake,*

NatCAB 11, TwCBDA, WhAm H
Hall, Willard Merrill 1896-1953 *WhAm 3*
Hall, Willard Preble 1820-1882 *BiAUS,
BiDrAC, DcAmB, NatCAB 22, TwCBDA,
WhAm H, WhAmP*
Hall, William *NewYHSD*
Hall, William 1774-1856 *ApCAB, BiAUS,
Drake, NatCAB 7, TwCBDA*
Hall, William 1775-1856 *BiDrAC, WhAm H,
WhAmP*
Hall, William 1796-1874 *ApCAB, NatCAB 13*
Hall, William 1914- *IlBEAAW*
Hall, William Augustus d1888 *BiAUS*
Hall, William Augustus 1815-1888 *BiDrAC,
WhAm H, WhAmP*
Hall, William Augustus 1816-1889 *TwCBDA*
Hall, William Baldwin Fletcher 1905-1969
WhAm 5
Hall, William Bonnell 1866- *WhAm 4*
Hall, William Dickson 1876- *WhAm 5*
Hall, William Edward 1796-1874 *NatCAB 3*
Hall, William Edwin 1878-1961 *WhAm 4*
Hall, William Henry 1881-1933 *NatCAB 29*
Hall, William Leroy 1847- *WhAm 4*
Hall, William O 1880- *WhAm 6*
Hall, William P 1820?-1865 *ApCAB*
Hall, William Phillips 1864-1937 *WhAm 1*
Hall, William Preble 1848-1927 *WhAm 1*
Hall, William Shafer 1861-1948 *NatCAB 37,
TwCBDA, WhAm 2*
Hall, William Thomas 1874- *WhAm 5*
Hall, William Whitty 1810-1876 *ApCAB,
DcAmB, Drake, NatCAB 11, TwCBDA,
WhAm H*
Hall, Willis 1801-1868 *ApCAB*
Hall, Wilmer Lee 1885-1957 *WhAm 3*
Hall, Wilton Earle 1901- *BiDrAC*
Hall, Winfield Scott 1861-1942 *NatCAB 13,
NatCAB 31, WhAm 4*
Hall, Young Lafayette, Jr. 1910-1971 *WhAm 6*
Halladay, Daniel Sawyer 1866-1954
NatCAB 50
Hallaert, Charles 1894-1948 *WhAm 2*
Hallagan, Frank Berry 1889-1957 *NatCAB 47*
Hallaj, Al-Husayn Ibn Mansur, Al- 857-922
McGEWB
Hallam, Clement Benner 1876- *WhAm 5*
Hallam, John *NewYHSD*
Hallam, Julia Clark 1860-1927 *WhAm 1,
WomWWA 14*
Hallam, Mrs. Lewis d1774 *NotAW*
Hallam, Lewis 1705?-1755 *McGEWB*
Hallam, Lewis 1714?-1756 *ApCAB*
Hallam, Lewis 1736-1808 *NatCAB 10*
Hallam, Lewis 1755-1808 *ApCAB, TwCBDA*
Hallam, Lewis 1740?-1808 *AmBi, DcAmB,
McGEWB, WebAB, WhAm H*
Hallam, Oscar 1865-1945 *WhAm 2*
Hallam, Peter *NewYHSD*
Hallam, Robert Alexander 1807-1877 *ApCAB,
NatCAB 11, TwCBDA, WhAm H*
Hallam, William 1712?-1758? *ApCAB*
Hallam, Wirt Willard 1866- *NatCAB 17*
Hallam Family *Drake*
Hallanan, Walter Simms 1890-1962 *WhAm 4*
Hallaren, Mary Agnes 1907- *WebAMB*
Hallauer, Carl S 1894-1971 *WhAm 5*
Hallbeck, Elroy Charles 1902-1969 *WhAm 5*
Hallberg *NewYHSD*
Hallberg, Carl Savante Nicanor 1856-1910
WhAm 1
Hallden, Karl William 1884-1970 *NatCAB 57,
WhAm 5*
Halle, Edward Gustav 1844-1917 *WhAm 1*
Halle, Louis 1885-1949 *NatCAB 36*
Halle, Salmon Portland 1866-1949 *NatCAB 42*
Halle, Samuel H 1868-1954 *WhAm 3*
Halle, Stanley Jacques 1891-1972 *WhAm 5*
Halle, Walter Murphy d1972 *WhAm 5*
Halleck, Charles Abraham 1900- *BiDrAC,
WhAmP*
Halleck, Fitz-Greene 1790-1867 *AmBi,
ApCAB, DcAmB, NatCAB 3, TwCBDA,
WhAm H*
Halleck, Fitzgreene 1790-1867 *Drake*
Halleck, Henry Wager 1814-1872 *Drake,
Drake Sup*
Halleck, Henry Wager 1815-1872 *AmBi,*

*ApCAB, DcAmB, EncAB, NatCAB 4,
TwCBDA, WebAB, WebAMB, WhAm H,
WhoMilH*
Halleck, Maria 1788-1870 *ApCAB*
Halleck, Reuben Post 1859-1936 *BiDAmEd,
NatCAB 27, WhAm 1*
Hallenbach, J F *NewYHSD*
Hallenbeck, Earl 1876-1934 *NatCAB 25*
Hallenbeck, Edwin Forrest 1864- *WhAm 4*
Hallenborg, Charles Edward 1898- *WhAm 6*
Haller, Albrecht Von 1708-1777 *AsBiEn,
DcScB, McGEWB*
Haller, Frank Louis 1861-1922 *WhAm 1*
Haller, Granville O 1819-1897 *NatCAB 11*
Haller, H L 1894-1972 *WhAm 5*
Haller, William 1885-1974 *WhAm 6*
Halleran, Laurence Basil 1887-1963
NatCAB 48
Hallet, Etienne Sulpice 1755-1825 *AmBi,
DcAmB, WhAm H*
Hallet, Richard Matthews 1887-1967 *WhAm 4*
Hallet, Stephen 1755-1825 *BiAUS, DcAmB*
Hallett, Benjamin 1760-1849 *ApCAB, DcAmB,
WhAm H*
Hallett, Benjamin Franklin 1797-1862 *ApCAB,
DcAmB, Drake, NatCAB 3, TwCBDA,
WhAm H*
Hallett, George Hervey 1870-1947 *NatCAB 38,
WhAm 4*
Hallett, Herbert Kimball 1867-1950
NatCAB 38, WhAm 3
Hallett, Moses 1834-1913 *BiAUS, DcAmB,
NatCAB 12, REnAW, WhAm 1*
Hallett, Robert Leroy 1881-1952 *WhAm 3*
Halley, Edmond 1656-1742 *BiHiMed*
Halley, Edmond 1656?-1743 *DcScB*
Halley, Edmund 1656-1742 *AsBiEn, McGEWB*
Halley, George 1839- *NatCAB 4, WhAm 4*
Halley, James 1854-1920 *WhAm 1*
Halley, Rudolph 1913-1956 *WhAm 3*
Halley, Sara Dalsheimer 1867- *WomWWA 14*
Halley, William J 1897-1966 *WhAm 4*
Hallgarten, George Wolfgang Felix 1901-1975
WhAm 6
Hallgren, Mauritz Alfred 1899-1956 *WhAm 3*
Halliburton, Erle Palmer 1892-1957 *WhAm 3*
Halliburton, Richard 1900-1939 *AmBi,
NatCAB 35, WhAm 1, WhAm 1C*
Halliday, Ernest Milton 1878-1961 *NatCAB 48,
WhAm 6*
Halliday, Richard 1905-1973 *WhAm 5*
Halliday, Samuel Dumont 1847-1907 *WhAm 1*
Hallidie, Andrew Smith 1836-1900 *DcAmB,
NatCAB 7, WhAm H*
Hallier, Ernst Hans 1831-1904 *DcScB*
Halligan, Harold Joseph 1902-1946 *NatCAB 33*
Halligan, Howard Ansel 1874-1950 *WhAm 3*
Halligan, James Edward 1879- *WhAm 6*
Halligan, John 1876-1934 *WhAm 1*
Hallinan, Joseph Daniel 1886-1952 *NatCAB 41*
Hallinan, Paul John 1911-1968 *WhAm 5*
Hallinan, William Wayne 1896-1959
NatCAB 43
Halliwell, Ashleigh C 1861- *WhAm 4*
Hallman, Franklin B *NewYHSD*
Hallman, Henderson 1870-1940 *NatCAB 32*
Hallman, John *NewYHSD*
Hallman, William A *NewYHSD*
Hallmark, Harrydele 1867- *WomWWA 14*
Hallock, Charles 1834-1917 *AmBi,
ApCAB Sup, DcAmB, NatCAB 9,
TwCBDA, WhAm 1*
Hallock, Frank Hudson 1877-1944 *WhAm 2*
Hallock, Frank Kirkwood 1860-1937
NatCAB 27, WhAm 1
Hallock, Gerard 1800-1866 *AmBi, ApCAB,
DcAmB, Drake, TwCBDA, WhAm H*
Hallock, Gerard 1800-1886 *NatCAB 11*
Hallock, Gerard 1867- *WhAm 1*
Hallock, Gerard Benjamin Fleet 1856-
WhAm 5
Hallock, Henry Galloway Comingo 1870-1951
WhAm 3
Hallock, Homan 1803-1894 *NatCAB 11*
Hallock, Jeremiah 1758-1826 *ApCAB, Drake,
NatCAB 11*
Hallock, John, Jr. 1783-1840 *BiAUS, BiDrAC,
WhAm H*

Hallock, Joseph Newton 1834-1913 *NatCAB 8,
NatCAB 11, TwCBDA, WhAm 1*
Hallock, Julia Isabel 1846- *WhAm 4*
Hallock, Lewis 1803-1897 *NatCAB 9*
Hallock, Mary Angeline 1810- *ApCAB*
Hallock, Mary Elizabeth d1950 *WhAm 3*
Hallock, Moses 1760-1837 *ApCAB, Drake,
NatCAB 11*
Hallock, Robert Crawford 1857-1932 *WhAm 1*
Hallock, William 1857-1913 *TwCBDA,
WhAm 1*
Hallock, William Allen 1794-1880 *AmBi,
ApCAB, DcAmB, NatCAB 10, TwCBDA,
WhAm H*
Hallopeau, Henri 1842-1919 *BiHiMed*
Halloran, Edward Roosevelt 1895-1972
WhAm 5
Halloran, Edward Roosevelt 1895-1975
WhAm 6
Halloran, Paul James 1896-1971 *WhAm 5*
Halloway, Ransom 1793?-1851 *BiAUS,
BiDrAC, WhAm H*
Halloway, Thomas *NewYHSD*
Hallowell, Alfred Irving 1892-1974 *WhAm 6*
Hallowell, Anna 1831-1905 *BiDAmEd, NotAW*
Hallowell, Anna Davis 1838- *WhAm 4,
WomWWA 14*
Hallowell, Benjamin d1799 *Drake*
Hallowell, Benjamin 1799-1877 *DcAmB,
NatCAB 22, WhAm H*
Hallowell, Edward Needles 1837-1871 *ApCAB,
TwCBDA*
Hallowell, Edwin 1844-1916 *BiDrAC*
Hallowell, George Hawley 1872- *WhAm 5*
Hallowell, Howard Thomas 1877-1955
NatCAB 46
Hallowell, John White 1878-1927 *WhAm 1*
Hallowell, Norwood Penrose 1839-1914
NatCAB 17
Hallowell, Norwood Penrose 1875-1961
NatCAB 49, WhAm 4
Hallowell, Richard Price 1835-1904 *ApCAB,
DcAmB, NatCAB 22, WhAm 1*
Hallowell, Robert 1886-1939 *WhAm 1*
Hallowell, Sara Catherine Fraley 1833-
WhAm 4
Hallowell, William 1801-1890 *NewYHSD*
Hallstead, William F 1836- *NatCAB 4,
WhAm 4*
Hallum, John 1833- *TwCBDA*
Hallwachs, Wilhelm Ludwig Franz 1859-1922
DcScB
Hallwig, Oscar *NewYHSD*
Hallworth, Joseph Bryant 1872- *WhAm 5*
Hallyburton, James D *BiAUS*
Halm, Jacob Karl Ernst 1866-1944 *DcScB*
Halper, Benzion 1884-1924 *WhAm 1*
Halpern, Alexander 1908-1970 *NatCAB 56*
Halpern, Jacob 1915-1970 *NatCAB 55,
WhAm 5*
Halpern, Julius 1912-1972 *WhAm 5*
Halpern, Michael 1892-1960 *WhAm 4*
Halpern, Philip 1902-1970 *WhAm 4*
Halpern, Seymour 1913- *BiDrAC*
Halpert, Edith Gregor 1900-1970 *WhAm 5*
Halphen, Georges-Henri 1844-1889 *DcScB*
Halpin, Frederick W 1805-1880 *NewYHSD*
Halpin, George H 1889-1959 *WhAm 3*
Halpin, James Anthony 1890-1934 *NatCAB 25*
Halpin, James Garfield 1882-1961 *NatCAB 49*
Halpin, James Garfield 1883-1961 *WhAm 4*
Halpin, John *NewYHSD*
Halpine, Charles Graham 1829-1868 *AmBi,
ApCAB, DcAmB, Drake, NatCAB 6,
TwCBDA, WhAm H*
Hals, Frans 1581?-1666 *McGEWB*
Halsall, Mary E 1865- *WomWWA 14*
Halsall, William Formby 1841- *WhAm 4*
Halsall, William Formby 1844- *ApCAB,
TwCBDA*
Halsell, John Edward 1826-1899 *BiDrAC*
Halsey, Abram Woodruff 1853-1921 *WhAm 1*
Halsey, Benjamin Schuyler 1873-1956 *WhAm 3*
Halsey, Charles Day 1865- *NatCAB 15*
Halsey, Charles Duffield Wrenn 1876-1961
NatCAB 46
Halsey, Charles Storrs 1834- *NatCAB 1*
Halsey, Don Peters 1870-1938 *NatCAB 42*

Halsey, Edmund Drake 1840-1896 *NatCAB 16*
Halsey, Edwin Alexander 1881-1945
  NatCAB 34
Halsey, Forrest 1878- *WhAm 6*
Halsey, Francis Whiting 1851-1919 *NatCAB 9,*
  TwCBDA, WhAm 1
Halsey, Frederick Arthur 1856-1935 *DcAmB S1,*
  NatCAB 26, WhAm 1
Halsey, Frederick Douglass 1877- *WhoColR*
Halsey, George Armstrong 1827-1894 *ApCAB,*
  BiAUS, BiDrAC, TwCBDA, WhAm H
Halsey, Harlan Page 1837-1898 *NatCAB 9*
Halsey, Henrietta A 1839- *WomWWA 14*
Halsey, Jehiel Howell 1788-1867 *BiAUS,*
  BiDrAC, WhAm H
Halsey, Jesse 1882-1954 *NatCAB 47,*
  WhAm 3
Halsey, Job Foster 1800-1881 *ApCAB*
Halsey, John *NewYHSD*
Halsey, John 1670-1716 *DcAmB, WhAm H*
Halsey, John Julius 1848-1919 *TwCBDA,*
  WhAm 1
Halsey, John Taylor 1870- *WhAm 5*
Halsey, Leroy Jones 1812-1896 *ApCAB,*
  NatCAB 3, TwCBDA, WhAm H
Halsey, Levi Wright 1860-1955 *NatCAB 42*
Halsey, Luther 1794-1880 *ApCAB, TwCBDA*
Halsey, Nicoll 1782-1865 *BiAUS, BiDrAC,*
  WhAm H
Halsey, Noah Wetmore 1856-1911 *NatCAB 16,*
  WhAm 1
Halsey, Rena Isabelle d1932 *WhAm 1*
Halsey, Richard T Haines 1865-1942 *WhAm 1*
Halsey, Silas 1743-1832 *BiAUS, BiDrAC,*
  WhAm H
Halsey, Thomas J 1864- *WhAm 4*
Halsey, Thomas Jefferson 1863-1951 *BiDrAC*
Halsey, Thomas Lloyd 1776?-1855 *DcAmB,*
  WhAm H
Halsey, William 1770-1843 *BiAUS*
Halsey, William Armstrong 1849-1928
  NatCAB 24
Halsey, William Bull 1882-1959 *WhWW-II*
Halsey, William C 1820?- *NewYHSD*
Halsey, William Frederick 1882-1959 *McGEWB,*
  WebAB, WebAMB, WhAm 3, WhoMilH
Halstead, Albert 1867-1949 *NatCAB 42,*
  WhAm 2
Halstead, Albert Edward 1868-1926 *WhAm 1*
Halstead, Alexander Seaman 1861-1923
  WhAm 1
Halstead, Alexander Seaman 1861-1949
  WhAm 2
Halstead, Benton 1834-1919 *NatCAB 19*
Halstead, Kenneth Burt 1880-1967 *WhAm 4*
Halstead, Laurence 1875-1954 *WhAm 3*
Halstead, Murat 1829-1908 *ApCAB, DcAmB,*
  Drake Sup, NatCAB 1, TwCBDA,
  WhAm 1
Halstead, Schureman 1805-1868 *ApCAB*
Halstead, Ward Campbell 1908-1969
  NatCAB 55, WhAm 5
Halstead, Willard George 1841-1910
  NatCAB 23
Halstead, William 1794-1878 *BiDrAC,*
  WhAm H
Halstead, William Riley 1848-1931 *WhAm 1*
Halsted, Abel Stevens 1870-1932 *WhAm 1*
Halsted, Byron David 1852-1919 *ApCAB,*
  NatCAB 10, TwCBDA, WhAm 1
Halsted, David Crane 1863-1938 *NatCAB 30*
Halsted, George Bruce 1853-1922 *AmBi,*
  ApCAB, BiDAmEd, DcAmB, DcScB,
  NatCAB 3, TwCBDA, WhAm 1
Halsted, Leonora B *WomWWA 14*
Halsted, Nathaniel Norris 1816-1884 *ApCAB,*
  TwCBDA
Halsted, Oliver Spencer 1792-1877 *ApCAB,*
  NatCAB 13, TwCBDA
Halsted, Oliver Spencer 1827-1871 *ApCAB*
Halsted, Thomas Henry 1865-1956 *NatCAB 53,*
  WhAm 3
Halsted, William *BiAUS*
Halsted, William Stewart 1852-1922 *AmBi,*
  AsBiEn, BiDAmEd, BiHiMed, DcAmB,
  DcScB, EncAB, NatCAB 20, WebAB,
  WhAm 1
Halterman, Frederick 1831-1907 *BiDrAC*

Haltom, William Lorenz 1904-1970 *WhAm 5*
Halton, Mary 1878- *WomWWA 14*
Halton, Samuel 1738-1816 *NatCAB 11*
Halverson, Wilton Lee 1896-1961 *NatCAB 49,*
  WhAm 4
Halvorsen, Raymond George 1906-1974
  WhAm 6
Halvorson, Halvor Orin 1897-1975 *WhAm 6*
Halvorson, Kittel 1846-1936 *BiDrAC*
Ham, Adeline Putnam 1876- *WomWWA 14*
Ham, Arthur Harold 1882-1951 *WhAm 3*
Ham, Bertram Lamar 1910-1974 *WhAm 6*
Ham, Clifford Dudley 1861- *WhAm 2A*
Ham, Edward Billings 1902-1965 *NatCAB 53,*
  WhAm 4
Ham, Guy Andrews 1878-1926 *WhAm 1*
Ham, Helen Willard 1875- *WomWWA 14*
Ham, John *BiAUS*
Ham, Marion Franklin 1867-1956 *WhAm 3*
Ham, Roscoe James 1875-1953 *WhAm 3*
Ham, William Felton 1870-1949 *NatCAB 38,*
  WhAm 2
Ham, William Ross 1879- *WhAm 6*
Hamachek, Frank 1853- *NatCAB 18*
Hamachek, Frank Wencel 1888-1952
  NatCAB 41
Hamady, Kamol Cassam 1893-1969
  NatCAB 57
Hamady, Michael Hassau 1884-1968
  NatCAB 53
Hamady, Robert Michael 1908-1967
  NatCAB 53
Hamaker, John Irvin 1869-1956 *WhAm 3*
Hamaker, Lawrence Sandford 1896-1964
  NatCAB 50
Hamaker, Winters D 1859- *WhAm 4*
Haman, B Howard 1857-1932 *NatCAB 25,*
  WhAm 1
Haman, Ralph Wright 1901-1961 *NatCAB 48*
Hamann, Anna 1894-1969 *WhAm 5*
Hamann, Carl Ampt 1908-1962 *NatCAB 50*
Hamann, Carl August 1868-1930 *NatCAB 21,*
  WhAm 1
Hamann, Carl Ferdinand 1857- *WhAm 1*
Hamann, Johann Georg 1730-1788 *McGEWB*
Hamar, Irene 1919-1973 *NatCAB 57*
Hamber, Eric Werge 1879- *WhAm 6*
Hamberg, Axel 1863-1933 *DcScB*
Hambidge, Edward John 1867-1924 *IlBEAAW*
Hambidge, Gove 1890-1970 *WhAm 5*
Hambidge, Jay 1867-1924 *AmBi, DcAmB,*
  WhAm 4
Hamblen, Archelaus L 1894-1971 *WhAm 5*
Hamblen, Edwin Crowell 1900-1963 *WhAm 4*
Hamblen, Eli 1804?-1839 *NewYHSD*
Hamblen, Herbert Eliott 1849- *WhAm 4*
Hamblen, Herbert Elliott 1849- *TwCBDA*
Hamblen, Joseph G 1817?- *NewYHSD*
Hamblen, Joseph H 1817?- *NewYHSD*
Hamblen, Nathaniel *NewYHSD*
Hamblen, Sturtevant J *NewYHSD*
Hambleton, Frank Sherwood 1855- *NatCAB 9*
Hambleton, Howard Francis 1906-1972
  NatCAB 57
Hambleton, John Adams 1827- *NatCAB 1,*
  NatCAB 9
Hambleton, Samuel 1812-1886 *BiAUS,*
  BiDrAC, WhAm H
Hambleton, Thomas Edward 1829-1906 *DcAmB,*
  NatCAB 1, NatCAB 9, WhAm 1
Hamblin, Charles Henry 1859- *WhAm 4*
Hamblin, Joseph Eldridge 1828-1870 *AmBi,*
  ApCAB, DcAmB, NatCAB 10, TwCBDA,
  WhAm H
Hamblin, L J *NewYHSD*
Hamblin, Thomas Sowerby 1800-1853 *ApCAB,*
  DcAmB, Drake, NatCAB 3, TwCBDA,
  WhAm H
Hambrecht, Fred 1904-1955 *NatCAB 45*
Hambrecht, George Philip 1871-1943 *WhAm 2*
Hambro, C J 1885-1964 *WhAm 4*
Hambro, Sir Charles Jocelyn 1897-1963
  WhAm 4
Hambrook, Richard Edward 1899-1968
  WhAm 5
Hamburger, Louis Philip 1873- *WhAm 5*
Hamburger, Walter Wile 1881-1941 *WhAm 1*
Hamby, William Henry 1875-1928 *WhAm 1*

Hamdani, Abu Muhammad Al-Hasan Ibn, Al-
  893?-951? *DcScB*
Hamel *NewYHSD*
Hamel, Charles Dennis 1881-1970 *WhAm 5*
Hamele, Ottamar 1878-1964 *WhAm 4*
Hamer, Edward Everett 1877- *WhAm 5*
Hamer, Francis Gregg 1843-1918 *WhAm 1*
Hamer, Homer G 1880- *WhAm 6*
Hamer, James Henry 1847- *NatCAB 3,*
  WhAm 4
Hamer, Jesse Dewey 1898-1966 *WhAm 4*
Hamer, Philip May 1891-1971 *NatCAB 55,*
  WhAm 5
Hamer, Rawthmall *NewYHSD*
Hamer, Thomas Lyon 1800-1846 *ApCAB,*
  BiAUS, BiDrAC, Drake, NatCAB 6,
  TwCBDA, WhAm H, WhAmP
Hamer, Thomas Lyon 1800-1847 *BiDrAC*
Hamer, Thomas Ray 1864-1950 *BiDrAC,*
  WhAm 4, WhAmP
Hamerschlag, Arthur Acton 1869-1927
  BiDAmEd
Hamerschlag, Arthur Arton 1867-1927
  WhAm 1
Hamerschlag, Arthur Arton 1872-1927
  ApCAB X, NatCAB 23
Hamerschlag, Robert Joseph 1894-1973
  WhAm 5
Hamerslag, Victor 1904-1953 *WhAm 3*
Hamersley, Andrew 1725-1819 *ApCAB X,*
  NatCAB 7
Hamersley, Andrew Gordon 1806-1880
  ApCAB X
Hamersley, Andrew Gordon 1806?-1883
  NatCAB 7
Hamersley, James Hooker 1844-1901 *ApCAB X,*
  NatCAB 7, NatCAB 31, WhAm 1
Hamersley, John William 1808-1889 *ApCAB X,*
  NatCAB 7
Hamersley, Lewis Carre 1767-1853 *ApCAB X,*
  NatCAB 7
Hamersley, Lewis Carre 1840-1883 *ApCAB X*
Hamersley, Louis Gordon 1892-1942 *ApCAB X,*
  NatCAB 31
Hamersley, William 1687-1752 *ApCAB X,*
  NatCAB 7
Hamersley, William 1838-1920 *NatCAB 19,*
  WhAm 1
Hamet Karamanli *WhAm H*
Hamff, Christian F 1882-1961 *WhAm 4*
Hamid, George Abou 1896-1971 *WhAm 5*
Hamid Ibn Khidr Al-Khujandi *DcScB*
Hamilburg, Ira M 1897-1962 *WhAm 4*
Hamilburg, Joseph M 1902-1968 *WhAm 5*
Hamilcar Barca 285?BC-228?BC *McGEWB*
Hamill, Alfred Ernest 1883-1953 *WhAm 3*
Hamill, Chalmers Martin 1884-1954
  NatCAB 46
Hamill, Charles Aden 1896-1963 *NatCAB 51*
Hamill, Charles Davisson 1839-1905
  NatCAB 28
Hamill, Charles Humphrey 1868-1941 *WhAm 1*
Hamill, Charles Pace 1882-1965 *NatCAB 51*
Hamill, Ernest Alfred 1851-1927 *NatCAB 24,*
  WhAm 1
Hamill, Howard M 1847-1915 *NatCAB 16*
Hamill, Howard M 1849-1915 *WhAm 1*
Hamill, Hugh Henderson 1851-1909
  NatCAB 28
Hamill, James Alphonsus 1877-1941 *BiDrAC,*
  WhAm 1, WhAmP
Hamill, Patrick 1817-1895 *BiAUS, BiDrAC,*
  NatCAB 3, WhAm H
Hamill, Ralph C 1877-1961 *NatCAB 49*
Hamill, Robert Lyon 1899-1974 *WhAm 6*
Hamill, Samuel McClintock 1864-1948
  NatCAB 46, WhAm 2
Hamill, William *NewYHSD*
Hamilton, A H 1834-1895 *BiAUS*
Hamilton, A H see also Hamilton, Andrew
  Holman
Hamilton, A J *WhAm 5*
Hamilton, Albert Hine 1859-1938 *NatCAB 28,*
  WhAm 1
Hamilton, Alexander 1712-1756 *DcAmB,*
  NewYHSD, WhAm H
Hamilton, Alexander 1755-1804 *DcAmB,*
  EncAB, McGEWB, WebAB, WhAmP

Hamilton, Alexander 1757-1804 *AmBi,*
ApCAB, BiAUS, BiDrAC, BiDrUSE,
Drake, NatCAB 1, TwCBDA, WhAm H
Hamilton, Alexander 1786-1875 *ApCAB*
Hamilton, Alexander 1815-1907 *WhAm 1*
Hamilton, Alexander 1847-1928 *NatCAB 21*
Hamilton, Alexander 1851-1916 *NatCAB 11,*
WhAm 1
Hamilton, Alexander 1903-1970 *WhAm 5*
Hamilton, Alice 1869-1970 *EncAB, McGEWB,*
WhAm 5
Hamilton, Allan McLane 1848-1919 *AmBi,*
ApCAB, DcAmB, NatCAB 9, TwCBDA,
WhAm 1
Hamilton, Alston 1871-1937 *AmBi, WhAm 1*
Hamilton, Amos *NewYHSD*
Hamilton, Andrew d1703 *AmBi, ApCAB,*
DcAmB, NatCAB 5, WhAm H
Hamilton, Andrew d1709 *Drake*
Hamilton, Andrew 1676?-1741 *AmBi, ApCAB,*
DcAmB, Drake, NatCAB 13, TwCBDA,
WhAm H
Hamilton, Andrew Holman 1834-1895 *BiDrAC,*
WhAm H
Hamilton, Andrew Holman *see also* Hamilton, A
H
Hamilton, Andrew Jackson 1815-1875 *AmBi,*
ApCAB, BiAUS, BiDrAC, DcAmB,
Drake, NatCAB 9, TwCBDA, WhAm H
Hamilton, Anna D 1863- *WomWWA 14*
Hamilton, Anna J 1860- *AmWom*
Hamilton, Anna Sanborn *WomWWA 14*
Hamilton, Archibald 1793-1815 *ApCAB Sup*
Hamilton, Arthur Louis 1881-1947 *NatCAB 37*
Hamilton, Arthur Stephen 1872-1940 *WhAm 2*
Hamilton, Aymer Jay 1876-1965 *WhAm 4*
Hamilton, B Wallace 1877-1951 *NatCAB 40*
Hamilton, Bertha Nelson 1868- *WomWWA 14*
Hamilton, Bertis Frank 1884- *WhAm 3*
Hamilton, Carl Lewis 1888-1946 *NatCAB 34*
Hamilton, Caroline Frances *WomWWA 14*
Hamilton, Charles *NewYHSD*
Hamilton, Charles 1834- *ApCAB*
Hamilton, Charles Anglin 1876-1942
NatCAB 35
Hamilton, Charles Dingee Pennock 1851-1940
NatCAB 29
Hamilton, Charles Edgar 1886-1969
NatCAB 56
Hamilton, Charles Elbert 1865-1933 *WhAm 1*
Hamilton, Charles Lyman 1865-1932
NatCAB 24
Hamilton, Charles Mann 1874-1942 *BiDrAC*
Hamilton, Charles Memorial 1840-1875 *BiAUS,*
BiDrAC, WhAm H
Hamilton, Charles Robert 1872-1954 *WhAm 3*
Hamilton, Charles S 1824?- *Drake*
Hamilton, Charles Smith 1822-1891 *ApCAB,*
DcAmB, NatCAB 8, TwCBDA,
WhAm H
Hamilton, Charles Sumner 1863-1936 *WhAm 1*
Hamilton, Charles Whiteley 1907-1971
WhAm 5
Hamilton, Clarence Grant 1865-1935
NatCAB 38, WhAm 1
Hamilton, Clayton 1881-1946 *DcAmB S4,*
NatCAB 18, WhAm 2
Hamilton, Cora Perry 1861- *WomWWA 14*
Hamilton, Cornelius Springer 1821-1867 *BiAUS,*
BiDrAC, WhAm H
Hamilton, Daniel Webster 1861-1936 *BiDrAC,*
WhAm 4
Hamilton, David Gilbert 1842-1915 *WhAm 1*
Hamilton, David Wiley 1878- *WhAm 6*
Hamilton, Dexter 1879- *WhAm 6*
Hamilton, Donald Ross 1914-1972 *WhAm 5*
Hamilton, E Wilbur Dean 1863-1943 *WhAm 2*
Hamilton, Edith 1867-1963 *EncAB,*
NatCAB 52, WebAB, WhAm 4
Hamilton, Edward John 1834-1918 *ApCAB Sup,*
DcAmB, TwCBDA, WhAm 1
Hamilton, Edward LaRue 1857-1923 *BiDrAC,*
WhAm 1, WhAmP
Hamilton, Elizabeth Schuyler 1757-1854
ApCAB, NotAW
Hamilton, Elwood 1883- *WhAm 2*
Hamilton, Estelle Brown 1883- *WhoColR A*
Hamilton, Eugene Harrison 1880- *WhoColR*

Hamilton, F F 1853-1899 *WhAm H*
Hamilton, Finley 1886-1940 *BiDrAC,*
WhAm 1
Hamilton, Francis Frazee 1891-1960 *WhAm 4*
Hamilton, Frank 1883-1952 *NatCAB 41*
Hamilton, Frank D 1858-1928 *NatCAB 22*
Hamilton, Frank Hastings 1813-1886 *ApCAB,*
DcAmB, NatCAB 9, TwCBDA,
WhAm H
Hamilton, Frank Hastings 1865-1931 *WhAm 1*
Hamilton, Frank Judson 1853-1946 *NatCAB 38*
Hamilton, Franklin Elmer Ellsworth 1866-1918
NatCAB 14, WhAm 1
Hamilton, Frederic Rutherford 1881-1952
WhAm 3
Hamilton, Frederick William 1860-1940
NatCAB 14, WhAm 1
Hamilton, Gail 1833-1896 *AmBi, DcAmB,*
NotAW, WhAm H
Hamilton, Garrison W 1859- *WhAm 4*
Hamilton, George Anson 1843-1935 *WhAm 1*
Hamilton, George E 1855-1946 *WhAm 2*
Hamilton, George Hall 1884-1935 *WhAm 1*
Hamilton, George Henry 1875-1948 *WhAm 2*
Hamilton, George Livingstone 1874-1940
WhAm 1
Hamilton, George W *NewYHSD*
Hamilton, Gilbert VanTassel 1877-1943
NatCAB 32, WhAm 2
Hamilton, Grant E 1862- *WhAm 4*
Hamilton, Grover Cleveland 1888-1958
NatCAB 48
Hamilton, Hamilton 1847-1928 *ApCAB,*
TwCBDA, WhAm 1
Hamilton, Harold Lee 1890-1969 *NatCAB 55,*
WhAm 5
Hamilton, Harry Heber 1878- *WhAm 6*
Hamilton, Henry d1796 *AmBi, ApCAB,*
Drake, WhAm H
Hamilton, Hollister Adelbert 1870-1939
WhAm 1
Hamilton, Hugh Gerard 1905-1960 *NatCAB 48*
Hamilton, Hugh Ralston 1904-1964 *WhAm 4*
Hamilton, Sir Ian Standish Monteith 1853-1947
WhoMilH
Hamilton, Isaac Miller 1864-1952 *WhAm 3*
Hamilton, J G DeRoulhac 1878- *WhAm 6*
Hamilton, James *NewYHSD*
Hamilton, James 1710?-1783 *ApCAB, DcAmB,*
Drake, TwCBDA, WhAm H
Hamilton, James 1710?-1793 *NatCAB 5*
Hamilton, James 1786-1857 *AmBi, ApCAB,*
BiDrAC, DcAmB, Drake, NatCAB 12,
TwCBDA, WhAm H, WhAmP
Hamilton, James 1789-1857 *BiAUS*
Hamilton, James 1793-1873 *ApCAB*
Hamilton, James 1819-1878 *ApCAB,*
BnEnAmA, IIBEAAW, NewYHSD,
WhAm H
Hamilton, James 1820?-1878 *Drake*
Hamilton, James 1866-1943 *NatCAB 32*
Hamilton, James Alexander 1788-1878 *ApCAB,*
DcAmB, WhAm H
Hamilton, James Alexander 1906-1973
WhAm 5
Hamilton, James E d1959 *WhAm 3*
Hamilton, James Edward 1852-1940 *WhAm 1*
Hamilton, James Henry 1861- *WhAm 4*
Hamilton, James Inglis d1803 *Drake*
Hamilton, James Kent 1839-1918 *NatCAB 18*
Hamilton, James Kent 1839-1919 *WhAm 1*
Hamilton, James Lemmon, Jr. 1907-1964
WhAm 4
Hamilton, James McLellan 1861-1940
ApCAB X, WhAm 1
Hamilton, James Wallace 1900-1968 *WhAm 5*
Hamilton, Jamin Hannibal 1836- *WhAm 4*
Hamilton, Jay Benson 1847-1920 *WhAm 1*
Hamilton, John d1746 *ApCAB, Drake,*
NatCAB 5, WhAm H
Hamilton, John 1692?-1747 *TwCBDA*
Hamilton, John 1754-1837 *BiAUS, BiDrAC,*
WhAm H
Hamilton, John 1802-1882 *ÅpCAB*
Hamilton, John 1827-1887 *ApCAB*
Hamilton, John 1843-1921 *WhAm 1*
Hamilton, John Alan 1871-1930 *WhAm 1*
Hamilton, John Brown 1847-1898 *NatCAB 23,*

TwCBDA
Hamilton, John C 1903-1968 *WhAm 5*
Hamilton, John Carroll 1891-1957 *WhAm 3*
Hamilton, John Church 1792-1882 *ApCAB,*
Drake
Hamilton, John Daniel Miller 1892-1973
WhAm 6
Hamilton, John Lawrence 1862-1927
NatCAB 20, WhAm 1
Hamilton, John Leonard 1878- *WhAm 3*
Hamilton, John M 1855-1916 *BiDrAC*
Hamilton, John Marshall 1847-1905
NatCAB 11, WhAm 1
Hamilton, John McLure 1853-1936 *AmBi,*
ApCAB, TwCBDA, WhAm 1
Hamilton, John Sherman 1870- *WhAm 5*
Hamilton, John Taylor 1843-1925 *BiDrAC,*
WhAm 1
Hamilton, John Taylor 1859-1951 *NatCAB 38,*
WhAm 3
Hamilton, John William 1845-1934 *ApCAB,*
DcAmB S1, NatCAB 13, TwCBDA,
WhAm 1, WhAm 1C
Hamilton, Joseph 1763- *TwCBDA*
Hamilton, Joseph Gilbert 1907-1957
NatCAB 46
Hamilton, Kate Waterman *ApCAB, WhAm 5,*
WomWWA 14
Hamilton, Kate Waterman 1835?- *NatCAB 4*
Hamilton, Kate Waterman 1841- *TwCBDA*
Hamilton, Kenneth Gardiner 1893-1975
WhAm 6
Hamilton, Lee Herbert 1931- *BiDrAC*
Hamilton, Louis Franklin 1907-1975 *WhAm 6*
Hamilton, Lydia *NewYHSD*
Hamilton, Margaret *WomWWA 14*
Hamilton, Margaret Porch 1867-
WomWWA 14
Hamilton, Mary E *WomWWA 14*
Hamilton, Maud *WomWWA 14*
Hamilton, Maxwell McGaughey 1896-1957
NatCAB 46, WhAm 3
Hamilton, Morgan Calvin 1809-1893 *ApCAB,*
BiAUS, BiDrAC, NatCAB 12, TwCBDA,
WhAm H
Hamilton, Morris Robeson 1820- *NatCAB 1,*
TwCBDA
Hamilton, Norman Rond 1877-1964 *BiDrAC,*
WhAm 4
Hamilton, Otho 1700?-1770 *ApCAB Sup*
Hamilton, Paul 1762-1816 *AmBi, ApCAB,*
BiAUS, BiDrUSE, DcAmB, Drake,
NatCAB 5, TwCBDA, WhAm H
Hamilton, Paul Myron 1894-1951 *NatCAB 39*
Hamilton, Peter 1817-1888 *DcAmB,*
NatCAB 12, WhAm H
Hamilton, Peter Joseph 1859-1927 *NatCAB 13,*
WhAm 1
Hamilton, Peter Myers 1812-1878 *WhAm H*
Hamilton, Philip 1782-1801 *ApCAB,*
NatCAB 12
Hamilton, Philip 1802-1884 *ApCAB*
Hamilton, Ralph Scott 1879-1960 *WhAm 4*
Hamilton, Ray Leroy 1900-1958 *NatCAB 47*
Hamilton, Robert 1809-1878 *BiDrAC,*
NatCAB 3, TwCBDA, WhAm H
Hamilton, Robert 1816- *BiAUS*
Hamilton, Robert Patrick 1896-1970
NatCAB 55, WhAm 5
Hamilton, Rolland Jerome 1879-1962 *WhAm 4*
Hamilton, Roy William 1883-1952 *NatCAB 40,*
NatCAB 47, WhAm 3
Hamilton, Sadie Black 1859- *WhoColR*
Hamilton, Samuel 1856-1922 *NatCAB 19*
Hamilton, Samuel King 1837-1922 *NatCAB 14,*
WhAm 1
Hamilton, Samuel Lowrie 1885-1953
NatCAB 39, WhAm 3
Hamilton, Samuel Warren 1878-1951
NatCAB 40
Hamilton, Schuyler 1822-1903 *AmBi, ApCAB,*
DcAmB, Drake, NatCAB 4, TwCBDA,
WhAm 1
Hamilton, Sophie *NewYHSD*
Hamilton, Stanislaus Murray 1855-1909
WhAm 1
Hamilton, Susanna Boyle 1869- *WomWWA 14*
Hamilton, Theo 1905-1961 *NatCAB 52*

TwCBDA, WhAm H
Hammond, Jabez Delno 1778-1855 *BiDrAC*
Hammond, Jack 1916-1973 *WhAm 5*
Hammond, James, Jr. 1892-1951 *WhAm 3*
Hammond, James Bartlett 1829-1913
WhAm HA
Hammond, James Bartlett 1839-1913 *DcAmB,*
NatCAB 3, WhAm 4
Hammond, James H 1807-1864 *BiAUS*
Hammond, James Hamilton 1807-1864 *Drake*
Hammond, James Henry 1807-1864 *AmBi,*
ApCAB, BiDrAC, DcAmB, EncAAH,
EncAB, McGEWB, NatCAB 12,
TwCBDA, WhAm H, WhAmP,
WhoColR
Hammond, Jason E 1862- *WhAm 4*
Hammond, John d1707 *NatCAB 10*
Hammond, John 1827-1889 *BiDrAC, TwCBDA,*
WhAm H
Hammond, John 1843-1939 *IIBEAAW*
Hammond, John A *NewYHSD*
Hammond, John Dennis 1850- *WhAm 4*
Hammond, John Fox 1821-1886 *ApCAB*
Hammond, John Hays 1855-1936 *AmBi,*
ApCAB X, DcAmB S2, NatCAB 10,
NatCAB 26, WhAm 1
Hammond, John Hays, Jr. 1888-1965
NatCAB 15, WhAm 4
Hammond, John Henry 1871-1949 *NatCAB 37,*
WhAm 2
Hammond, John Lawrence LeBreton 1872-1952
McGEWB
Hammond, John LeRoy 1843-1891 *NatCAB 36*
Hammond, John T 1820?- *NewYHSD*
Hammond, John Wilkes 1837-1921 *WhAm 1*
Hammond, John Winthrop 1887-1934 *WhAm 1*
Hammond, Johnson Francis 1882-1961
NatCAB 49
Hammond, Josiah Shaw 1844- *NatCAB 11*
Hammond, Juliet *WomWWA 14*
Hammond, Laurens 1895-1973 *WhAm 6*
Hammond, Lawrence 1872-1952 *McGEWB*
Hammond, LeRoy 1740?-1800? *ApCAB, Drake*
Hammond, Lily Hardy 1859-1925 *DcAmReB,*
WhAm 1
Hammond, Loretta Mann 1842- *AmWom*
Hammond, Lucy Barbara 1873-1961 *McGEWB*
Hammond, Lyman Pierce 1880-1952 *WhAm 3*
Hammond, Marcus Claudius Marcellus
1814-1876 *ApCAB*
Hammond, Mary Virginia Spitler 1847-
AmWom
Hammond, Matthew Brown 1868-1933
WhAm 1
Hammond, Monroe Percy 1888-1935 *WhAm 1*
Hammond, Natalie Harris 1861-1931 *ApCAB X,*
NatCAB 24, WomWWA 14
Hammond, Nathaniel Job 1833-1899 *BiDrAC,*
DcAmB, TwCBDA, WhAm H
Hammond, Norma Mae 1907-1960 *WhAm 4*
Hammond, Ogden Haggerty 1869-1956
WhAm 3
Hammond, Percy Hunter 1873-1936 *DcAmB S2,*
NatCAB 27, WhAm 1
Hammond, Peter Francis 1887- *BiDrAC*
Hammond, Philip 1871-1937 *NatCAB 31*
Hammond, Richard Pindell 1820-1891
NatCAB 12
Hammond, Robert Hanna 1791-1847 *BiAUS,*
BiDrAC, WhAm H
Hammond, Roland 1875-1956 *WhAm 4*
Hammond, Roland 1875-1957 *NatCAB 46*
Hammond, Samuel 1757-1842 *AmBi, ApCAB,*
BiAUS, BiDrAC, DcAmB, Drake,
NatCAB 10, TwCBDA, WhAm H
Hammond, Schuyler Weston 1866-1936
NatCAB 27
Hammond, Stevens Hill 1910-1958 *WhAm 3*
Hammond, Theodore Augustus 1861-1932
NatCAB 25, WhAm 1
Hammond, Thomas 1843-1909 *BiDrAC*
Hammond, Thomas Stevens 1883-1950
NatCAB 47, WhAm 3
Hammond, William 1900-1973 *WhAm 6*
Hammond, William Alexander 1828-1900 *AmBi,*
ApCAB, ApCAB X, BiHiMed, DcAmB,
Drake, NatCAB 9, NatCAB 26,
TwCBDA, WhAm 1, WhAm 4A

Hammond, William Churchill 1860-1949
NatCAB 37, WhAm 2
Hammond, William Gardiner 1829-1894
BiDAmEd, DcAmB, NatCAB 9, TwCBDA,
WhAm H
Hammond, William Robinson 1848-1923
NatCAB 8
Hammond, William Thomas 1886-1959
NatCAB 49
Hammond, Winfield Scott 1863-1915 *BiDrAC,*
NatCAB 16, WhAm 1, WhAmP
Hammonds, Oliver Overstreet 1880-1949
NatCAB 37
Hammons, David 1807-1888 *BiAUS*
Hammons, David 1808-1888 *BiDrAC,*
WhAm H
Hammons, Earle Wooldridge 1892-1962
WhAm 4
Hammons, Earle Woolridge 1882- *WhAm 1*
Hammons, Joseph 1787-1836 *BiAUS, BiDrAC,*
WhAm H
Hammons, Paul Edward 1925-1974 *WhAm 6*
Hammurabi 2250BC- *BiHiMed, McGEWB*
Hamner, Salley B *WomWWA 14*
Hamond, Sir Andrew Snape 1738-1828 *ApCAB,*
Drake
Hamp, Mrs. Francis *IIBEAAW*
Hamp, Sidford Frederick 1855-1919 *WhAm 1*
Hampden, John 1594-1643 *McGEWB*
Hampden, Walter 1879-1955 *DcAmB S5,*
NatCAB 44, WebAB, WhAm 3
Hampel, Everett Keeler 1898-1964 *NatCAB 51*
Hampson, Alfred Aubert 1882-1946
NatCAB 35, WhAm 2
Hampson, Philip F 1894-1974 *WhAm 6*
Hampson, William 1854?-1926 *DcScB*
Hampton, Aubrey Otis 1900-1955 *WhAm 3*
Hampton, Benjamin Bowles 1875-1932
WhAm 1
Hampton, Bill 1925- *IIBEAAW*
Hampton, Edgar Lloyd 1872- *WhAm 3*
Hampton, Florence Estelle 1853-
WomWWA 14
Hampton, Fred Jordan 1889-1937 *NatCAB 42*
Hampton, George 1902-1962 *WhAm 4*
Hampton, Ireland 1871-1943 *WhAm 2*
Hampton, Isabel Adams *NotAW*
Hampton, James Giles 1814-1861 *BiAUS,*
BiDrAC, WhAm H
Hampton, John W 1918- *IIBEAAW*
Hampton, Moses 1803-1878 *BiAUS, BiDrAC,*
WhAm H
Hampton, Thomas Earle 1890-1963 *NatCAB 50*
Hampton, Wade 1751?-1835 *DcAmB,*
McGEWB, WebAMB
Hampton, Wade 1752-1835 *AmBi, BiDrAC,*
WhAm H, WhAmP
Hampton, Wade 1754-1835 *ApCAB, Drake,*
TwCBDA
Hampton, Wade 1775-1834 *BiAUS*
Hampton, Wade 1791-1858 *ApCAB*
Hampton, Wade 1818-1902 *AmBi, ApCAB,*
BiDConf, BiDrAC, DcAmB, Drake,
EncAB, McGEWB, NatCAB 12,
TwCBDA, WebAB, WebAMB, WhAm 1,
WhAmP, WhoMilH
Hampton, William Wade 1856-1928
NatCAB 47
Hamre, Haken 1914-1972 *NatCAB 57*
Hamrick, Hayward Russell 1907-1957
NatCAB 48
Hamrin, Shirley Austin 1900-1958 *BiDAmEd,*
NatCAB 47, WhAm 3
Hamsun, Knut 1859-1952 *McGEWB,*
WhAm 3, WhAm 4
Hamtramck, John Francis 1757-1803 *ApCAB,*
Drake
Hamtramck, John Francis 1798-1858 *ApCAB,*
DcAmB, NatCAB 22, WhAm H
Hamuda Pasha d1814 *WhAm H*
Hamy, Maurice Theodore Adolphe 1861-1936
DcScB
Han, Fei Tzu 280?BC-233BC *McGEWB*
Han, Kao-Tsu 247?BC-195BC *McGEWB*
Han, Wu-Ti 157BC-087BC *McGEWB*
Han, Yu 768-824 *McGEWB*
Hanaford, Mary E Neal *WomWWA 14*
Hanaford, Phebe Ann 1829-1921 *NotAW,*

TwCBDA
Hanaford, Phebe Anne 1829-1921 *AmWom,*
ApCAB, NatCAB 13
Hanaford, Phoebe Ann 1829-1921 *AmBi,*
DcAmB
Hanaford, Phoebe Anne 1829-1921
WomWWA 14
Hanahan, Kate Louisa 1870- *WomWWA 14*
Hanan, Addison Garthwaite 1876-1923
NatCAB 34
Hanan, Herbert Wilmer 1872-1933 *NatCAB 24*
Hanan, John Henry 1849-1920 *NatCAB 19,*
WhAm 1
Hanan, Robert Wilmer 1903-1933 *NatCAB 24*
Hanatschek, Herman Carl 1873-1963
NatCAB 50
Hanau, Emma French 1867- *WomWWA 14*
Hanau, Kenneth John 1895-1957 *WhAm 3*
Hanauer, Jerome Jonas 1875-1938 *ApCAB X,*
NatCAB 46, WhAm 1
Hanavan, William Lawrence 1882-1966
NatCAB 52
Hanaw, Henry 1856-1916 *WhAm 1*
Hanback, Lewis 1839-1897 *BiDrAC,*
WhAm H
Hanbeck, William *NewYHSD*
Hanbury, Harry Alfred 1863-1940 *BiDrAC*
Hanby, Albert Thatcher 1881- *WhAm 6*
Hanby, Benjamin Russel 1833-1867 *DcAmB,*
WhAm H
Hanby, Benjamin Russell 1833-1867
NatCAB 23
Hance, Irwin Howell 1861-1929 *ApCAB X,*
NatCAB 24
Hance, James Harold 1880-1955 *NatCAB 44*
Hancey, Carlos 1905-1966 *WhAm 4*
Hanch, Charles Connard 1867-1946
NatCAB 35, WhAm 2
Hancher, John William 1856- *WhAm 4*
Hancher, Virgil Melvin 1896-1965 *NatCAB 52,*
WhAm 4
Hanchett, Benjamin Sawtell 1868-1933
NatCAB 27
Hanchett, Benton 1835-1931 *WhAm 1*
Hanchett, Edwin Lani 1919-1975 *WhAm 6*
Hanchett, George Tilden 1871- *WhAm 5*
Hanchett, Harry Bigelow 1879-1960
NatCAB 46
Hanchett, Henry Granger 1853-1918 *BiDAmEd,*
DcAmB, WhAm 1
Hanchett, Lafayette 1868- *WhAm 3*
Hanchett, Lewis Edward 1872-1956 *NatCAB 46*
Hanchett, Luther 1825-1862 *BiAUS, BiDrAC,*
WhAm H
Hancock, Albert Elmer 1870- *WhAm 1*
Hancock, Arthur Boyd 1875- *WhAm 5*
Hancock, Arthur Murray 1874-1939
NatCAB 29
Hancock, Belle Clay 1872- *WomWWA 14*
Hancock, Clarence Eugene 1885-1948 *BiDrAC,*
NatCAB 36, WhAm 2, WhAmP
Hancock, Cornelia 1840-1927 *NotAW*
Hancock, Elizabeth Hazlewood 1871-1915
WhAm 1
Hancock, Emma Louise 1881- *WomWWA 14*
Hancock, Franklin Wills, Jr. 1894-1969 *BiDrAC*
Hancock, G Allan 1875-1965 *WhAm 4*
Hancock, George d1820 *BiAUS*
Hancock, George 1754-1820 *BiDrAC,*
WhAm H
Hancock, George 1755-1820 *ApCAB*
Hancock, George Leverett 1877-1955
NatCAB 45
Hancock, Glover Dunn 1878-1955 *WhAm 3*
Hancock, H Irving 1868-1922 *WhAm 1*
Hancock, Harris 1867- *NatCAB 16, WhAm 4*
Hancock, Ida Stebbins *WomWWA 14*
Hancock, James Cole 1865-1933 *WhAm 1*
Hancock, James Denton 1837-1929 *NatCAB 23*
Hancock, John 1671-1752 *ApCAB*
Hancock, John 1702-1744 *Drake*
Hancock, John 1703-1744 *ApCAB*
Hancock, John 1736?-1793 *DcAmB, WhAm H*
Hancock, John 1737-1793 *AmBi, ApCAB,*
BiAUS, BiDrAC, BiDrUSE, Drake,
EncAB, McGEWB, NatCAB 1,
TwCBDA, WebAB, WebAMB, WhAmP
Hancock, John 1824-1893 *ApCAB, BiAUS,*

BiDrAC, DcAmB, NatCAB 4, TwCBDA, WhAm H, WhAmP

Hancock, John 1825-1891 *BiDAmEd, NatCAB 5*

Hancock, John Milton 1883-1956 *NatCAB 46, WhAm 3*

Hancock, Joy Bright 1898- *WebAMB*

Hancock, LaToucha 1860- *WhAm 4*

Hancock, Lawrence Peres 1866-1953 *NatCAB 42*

Hancock, Mary B Hollingshead 1874- *WomWWA 14*

Hancock, Nathaniel *NewYHSD*

Hancock, Parker Cross 1843-1908 *NatCAB 45*

Hancock, Sarah *NewYHSD*

Hancock, T *NewYHSD*

Hancock, Theodore E 1847-1916 *NatCAB 49, WhAm 1*

Hancock, Thomas 1702-1764 *ApCAB*

Hancock, Thomas 1703-1764 *DcAmB, NatCAB 22, WhAm H*

Hancock, Thomas Hightower 1869- *WhAm 2*

Hancock, W Scott 1869- *WhAm 5*

Hancock, William Wayne 1886-1965 *WhAm 4*

Hancock, Winfield Scott 1824-1886 *AmBi, ApCAB, DcAmB, Drake, NatCAB 4, TwCBDA, WebAB, WebAMB, WhAm H*

Hancox, Joseph Wright *ApCAB X*

Hand, Alfred 1835-1917 *NatCAB 4, WhAm 1*

Hand, Augustus C 1806- *BiAUS*

Hand, Augustus Cincinnatus 1803-1878 *ApCAB, BiDrAC, TwCBDA, WhAm H*

Hand, Augustus Noble 1869-1954 *ApCAB X, DcAmB S5, WhAm 3*

Hand, Billings Learned 1872-1961 *McGEWB*

Hand, Carlton Harper 1859-1924 *NatCAB 20*

Hand, Chauncey Harris 1893-1961 *WhAm 4*

Hand, Daniel 1801-1891 *ApCAB Sup, DcAmB, NatCAB 3, TwCBDA, WhAm H*

Hand, Daniel Whilldin 1834- *ApCAB*

Hand, David Bishop 1848-1923 *NatCAB 39*

Hand, Edward 1744-1802 *ApCAB, BiAUS, BiDrAC, DcAmB, Drake, NatCAB 1, TwCBDA, WebAMB, WhAm H*

Hand, Edward Patrick 1889-1949 *NatCAB 39*

Hand, Frances Amelia Fincke *WomWWA 14*

Hand, George Trowbridge 1872-1945 *NatCAB 35, WhAm 5*

Hand, Harold Curtis 1901-1967 *BiDAmEd, WhAm 5*

Hand, John Pryor 1850-1923 *NatCAB 13, WhAm 1*

Hand, Joseph *NewYHSD*

Hand, Judson Larrabee 1850-1916 *NatCAB 18*

Hand, Learned Billings 1872-1961 *EncAB, WebAB, WhAm 4*

Hand, Richard Lockhart 1839-1914 *ApCAB X, WhAm 1*

Hand, Samuel 1834-1886 *ApCAB, TwCBDA*

Hand, Thomas Millet 1902-1956 *BiDrAC, WhAm 3, WhAmP*

Hand, William Flowers 1873-1948 *WhAm 2*

Hand, William Morgan 1864-1949 *NatCAB 38*

Handal, Nicholas Solomon 1899-1956 *NatCAB 42*

Handbury, John D *WhAm 5*

Handel, George Frederick 1685-1759 *McGEWB*

Handerson, Henry Ebenezer 1837-1918 *DcAmB, WhAm 4*

Handforth, Thomas 1897-1948 *WhAm 2*

Handlery, Harry 1888-1965 *NatCAB 52*

Handley, Carroll Alfred 1911-1961 *WhAm 4*

Handley, George 1752-1793 *ApCAB, Drake, NatCAB 2, TwCBDA*

Handley, Harold Willis 1909-1972 *WhAm 5*

Handley, William Anderson 1834-1909 *BiAUS, BiDrAC*

Handley, William White 1872-1919 *WhAm 1*

Handlin, Frank Augustine 1860-1925 *WhAm 3*

Handlin, Oscar 1915- *EncAAH, McGEWB, WebAB*

Handly, Albert 1900-1957 *NatCAB 46*

Handman, Max Sylvius 1885-1939 *NatCAB 38, WhAm 1*

Handschin, Charles H 1873-1964 *WhAm 4*

Handsome Lake 1735-1815 *AmBi, DcAmReB*

Handwork, Bentley S 1885-1956 *WhAm 3*

Handwork, Bently Smith 1885-1956 *NatCAB 49*

Handy, Albert Montgomery 1870-1956 *NatCAB 52*

Handy, Alexander Hamilton 1809-1883 *ApCAB, DcAmB, NatCAB 13, TwCBDA, WhAm H*

Handy, Anson Burgess 1883-1946 *WhAm 2*

Handy, Burton 1884-1955 *WhAm 3*

Handy, Cortlandt Waite 1888-1973 *NatCAB 57*

Handy, George Charles 1886-1958 *NatCAB 43*

Handy, Henry Hunter Smith 1856-1935 *WhAm 1*

Handy, James Anderson 1826-1911 *NatCAB 6, TwCBDA, WhAm 1*

Handy, Levin Irving 1861-1922 *BiDrAC, TwCBDA*

Handy, Moses Purnell 1847-1898 *ApCAB Sup, NatCAB 10, NatCAB 16, TwCBDA*

Handy, Parker Douglas 1858-1929 *NatCAB 28, WhAm 1*

Handy, Ray D 1877- *WhAm 5*

Handy, Thomas Troy 1892- *WebAMB*

Handy, Truman Parker 1890-1959 *NatCAB 49*

Handy, William Christopher 1873-1958 *EncAB, McGEWB, WebAB, WhAm 3*

Hanecy, Elbridge 1852-1925 *WhAm 1*

Hanelton, Peter *NewYHSD*

Haneman, Frederick Theodore 1862- *WhAm 4*

Haner, Frank Henry 1872-1960 *NatCAB 50*

Hanes, Alexander Stephen 1881-1944 *NatCAB 33*

Hanes, Edward L 1871-1947 *NatCAB 36*

Hanes, Frederic Meir 1883-1946 *WhAm 2*

Hanes, Frederic Moir 1883-1946 *NatCAB 37*

Hanes, James Gordon 1886-1972 *WhAm 5*

Hanes, Leigh 1893-1967 *WhAm 5*

Hanes, P H 1880- *WhAm 6*

Hanes, Pleasant Henderson 1845-1925 *NatCAB 22*

Hanes, Ralph Philip 1898-1973 *WhAm 6*

Hanes, Robert March 1890-1959 *NatCAB 47, WhAm 3*

Hanes, S B, Jr. d1966 *WhAm 4*

Hanes, Thomas Andrews 1896-1972 *WhAm 6*

Hanes, William Marvin 1882-1931 *NatCAB 30*

Haney, Bert Emory 1879-1943 *NatCAB 35, WhAm 2*

Haney, Carol 1924-1964 *WhAm 4*

Haney, Dick 1852-1948 *NatCAB 13, WhAm 2*

Haney, George Jacob 1914-1973 *WhAm 6*

Haney, James Parton 1869-1923 *WhAm 1*

Haney, Jennie Pomerene 1866- *WomWWA 14*

Haney, John Louis 1877- *WhAm 5*

Haney, Lewis Henry 1882-1969 *WhAm 5*

Haney, Oramel Elisha 1876-1945 *NatCAB 37*

Hanford, A Chester 1891-1975 *WhAm 6*

Hanford, Ben 1861-1910 *WhAm 1*

Hanford, Charles Barnum 1859-1926 *WhAm 1*

Hanford, Cornelius Holgate 1849- *WhAm 1*

Hanford, Franklin 1844-1928 *NatCAB 26, WhAm 1*

Hanford, George Arthur 1875-1949 *NatCAB 47*

Hanford, Henry Samuel 1847-1927 *NatCAB 22*

Hanford, James Holly 1882-1969 *WhAm 5*

Hanford, Russell Bratton 1905-1965 *NatCAB 51*

Hanford, Samuel *ApCAB X*

Hangarter, Andrew Henry 1883-1950 *NatCAB 39*

Hanger, Franklin M 1894-1971 *WhAm 5*

Hanger, G Wallace William 1866-1935 *WhAm 1*

Hanger, George, Lord Coleraine 1750-1824 *ApCAB, Drake*

Hanger, Harry Baylor 1864-1925 *NatCAB 37, WhAm 1*

Hanger, Robert Kittrell 1894-1969 *WhAm 5*

Hanger, William A d1944 *WhAm 2*

Hanifan, Lyda Judson 1879-1932 *WhAm 1*

Hanington, Henry *NewYHSD*

Hanington, Robert *NewYHSD*

Hanington, William J *NewYHSD*

Hanisch, Arthur Oscar 1895-1966 *NatCAB 53, WhAm 4*

Hank, Frederick Borter 1893-1962 *WhAm 4*

Hank, Oscar Charles 1877-1946 *WhAm 2*

Hankel, Hermann 1839-1873 *DcScB*

Hankel, Wilhelm Gottlieb 1814-1899 *DcScB*

Hankins, Edward Robert 1882-1954 *NatCAB 42*

Hankins, Frank Hamilton 1877-1970 *WhAm 5*

Hankison, Otto Leroy 1886-1955 *NatCAB 47*

Hanks, Abbot Atherton 1886- *WhAm 1*

Hanks, Mrs. Bernard 1884-1967 *WhAm 4*

Hanks, Bryan Cayce 1896-1972 *WhAm 5*

Hanks, Charles Stedman 1856-1908 *NatCAB 14, WhAm 1*

Hanks, Henry Garber 1826-1907 *NatCAB 13, WhAm 1*

Hanks, Horace Tracy 1837-1900 *NatCAB 2*

Hanks, James Millander 1833-1909 *BiAUS, BiDrAC*

Hanks, Jarvis F 1799- *NewYHSD*

Hanks, Julia Dana Godfrey 1845- *WomWWA 14*

Hanks, Lucien Mason 1868-1950 *NatCAB 39, WhAm 3*

Hanks, Lucien Stanley 1838-1925 *NatCAB 39*

Hanks, Marshall Bernard 1884-1948 *NatCAB 37, WhAm 2*

Hanks, Marshall Wilfred 1875-1952 *NatCAB 39*

Hanks, Mary Elizabeth 1862- *WomWWA 14*

Hanks, Mary Esther Vilas 1873-1959 *NatCAB 49*

Hanks, Owen G 1815?-1865? *NewYHSD*

Hanks, Rodney 1782-1846 *NatCAB 23*

Hanks, Stanley Charles 1872-1945 *NatCAB 34*

Hankwitz, Arthur Walter 1907-1970 *WhAm 5*

Hanley, Charles Clark 1851-1934 *NatCAB 26*

Hanley, Deloss Reed 1903-1972 *WhAm 6*

Hanley, Diana Pomeroy 1876- *WomWWA 14*

Hanley, Elijah Andrews 1871- *WhAm 5*

Hanley, Frances Gordon Fane 1867- *WomWWA 14*

Hanley, Gerald Thomas 1884-1950 *NatCAB 38*

Hanley, Herbert Russell 1874- *WhAm 5*

Hanley, James Hugh 1881- *WhAm 6*

Hanley, James Michael 1920- *BiDrAC*

Hanley, John Chaney d1949 *WhAm 3*

Hanley, Joseph Rhodes 1876-1961 *WhAm 4*

Hanley, L E 1880-1952 *WhAm 3*

Hanley, Miles Lawrence 1893-1954 *NatCAB 46, WhAm 3*

Hanley, Sarah Bond 1865-1959 *WhAm 3*

Hanley, Stewart 1881-1931 *WhAm 1*

Hanley, Thomas Edward 1893-1969 *NatCAB 55*

Hanley, Thomas James, Jr. 1893-1969 *WhAm 5*

Hanley, Walter *NewYHSD*

Hanley, William Andrew 1886-1967 *WhAm 4*

Hanley, William H *NewYHSD*

Hanley, William Scott 1879- *WhAm 6*

Hanlin, Merton L 1876-1955 *WhAm 3*

Hanlon, Edward Ignatius 1880-1963 *NatCAB 51, WhAm 4*

Hanlon, Edward K 1891-1956 *WhAm 3*

Hanlon, Francis Woodward 1904-1958 *NatCAB 47*

Hanlon, Lawrence Wilson 1914-1970 *WhAm 5*

Hanlon, Michael J 1886-1967 *NatCAB 54*

Hanlon, Thomas 1832- *NatCAB 5*

Hanlon, Thomas J, Jr. 1884-1960 *WhAm 4*

Hanly, George *NewYHSD*

Hanly, J Frank 1863-1920 *WhAm 1*

Hanly, James Franklin 1863-1920 *BiDrAC, NatCAB 14, WhAmP*

Hanly, Thomas Burton 1812-1880 *BiDConf*

Hanmer, Lee Franklin 1871- *WhAm 5*

Hann, Charles 1888-1957 *WhAm 3*

Hann, Julius Ferdinand Von 1839-1921 *DcScB*

Hann, Rosa Dean 1868- *WomWWA 14*

Hanna, Bayless W 1830-1891 *TwCBDA*

Hanna, Bayliss W 1830-1891 *NatCAB 12*

Hanna, Charles Augustus 1863-1950 *WhAm 3*

Hanna, Dan R d1921 *WhAm 1*

Hanna, Daniel Rhodes 1866-1921 *ApCAB X*

Hanna, Daniel Rhodes, Jr. 1894-1962 *WhAm 4*

Hanna, Delphine 1854-1941 *BiDAmEd, WomWWA 14*

Hanna, Dora Myers *WomWWA 14*

Hanna, Edward Joseph 1860-1944 *ApCAB X, DcAmB S3, NatCAB 15, NatCAB 32, WhAm 2*

Hanna, Frank Willard 1867-1944 *WhAm 2*

Hanna, Guy Carleton 1879-1961 *WhAm 4*
Hanna, H Melville 1840-1921 *NatCAB 32*
Hanna, Howard Melville 1877-1945 *WhAm 2*
Hanna, Howard Melville 1887-1945
NatCAB 34
Hanna, Hugh Henry 1848-1920 *WhAm 1*
Hanna, Hugh Sisson 1879-1948 *WhAm 2*
Hanna, J Lindsay 1889-1955 *NatCAB 44*
Hanna, James B 1854-1931 *NatCAB 23*
Hanna, James Francis 1886-1952 *NatCAB 41*
Hanna, James Robert 1866-1931 *WhAm 1*
Hanna, John 1827-1882 *BiDrAC, WhAm H*
Hanna, John 1891-1964 *WhAm 4*
Hanna, John Andre 1762-1805 *BiAUS,*
BiDrAC, WhAm H, WhAmP
Hanna, John Hunter 1871-1947 *WhAm 2*
Hanna, Mrs. John M 1869-1957 *WhAm 3*
Hanna, Kathryn Abbey 1895-1967 *WhAm 5*
Hanna, Leonard Colton 1850-1919 *NatCAB 34*
Hanna, Leonard Colton, Jr. 1889-1957
NatCAB 44, WhAm 3
Hanna, Louis Benjamin 1861-1948 *ApCAB X,*
BiDrAC, NatCAB 15, NatCAB 48,
WhAm 2, WhAmP
Hanna, Marcus Alonzo 1837-1904 *AmBi,*
ApCAB Sup, ApCAB X, BiDrAC,
DcAmB, EncAB, McGEWB, NatCAB 11,
NatCAB 22, REnAW, TwCBDA,
WhAm 1, WhAmP
Hanna, Marcus Alonzo, II 1888-1936
NatCAB 26
Hanna, Margaret M d1950 *WhAm 3*
Hanna, Mark 1837-1904 *WebAB*
Hanna, Matthew Elting 1873-1936 *NatCAB 27,*
WhAm 1
Hanna, Max Ross 1881-1949 *NatCAB 38*
Hanna, Paul Glenn 1890-1968 *NatCAB 54*
Hanna, Paul Robert 1902- *BiDAmEd*
Hanna, Phil Townsend 1896-1957 *NatCAB 46*
Hanna, Philip C 1857-1929 *WhAm 1*
Hanna, Philip Sidney 1887-1958 *WhAm 3*
Hanna, R *NewYHSD*
Hanna, Richard Henry 1878-1946 *NatCAB 36,*
WhAm 2
Hanna, Richard Thomas 1914- *BiDrAC*
Hanna, Robert 1786-1858 *ApCAB, BiAUS,*
BiDrAC, NatCAB 4, TwCBDA,
WhAm 1
Hanna, Sarah Jackson 1847- *AmWom*
Hanna, Septimus James 1844-1921 *NatCAB 19,*
WhAm 1
Hanna, Thomas King, Jr. 1872-1951 *IIBEAAW*
Hanna, William Brantley 1835-1906 *TwCBDA*
Hanna, William Brantly 1835-1906 *ApCAB,*
WhAm 1
Hanna, William Stiffler 1860-1932 *NatCAB 24*
Hannaford, Charles Edward 1860- *WhAm 1*
Hannaford, Jule Murat 1850-1934 *ApCAB X,*
NatCAB 25, WhAm 1
Hannagan, Stephen Jerome 1899-1953
DcAmB S5, WhAm 3
Hannah, Edwin *NewYHSD*
Hannah, Harvey Horatio 1868-1936 *WhAm 2*
Hannah, Jane Osborn 1876- *NatCAB 15*
Hannahs, Elizabeth Helen 1862-
WomWWA 14
Hannan, Emma J 1860- *WomWWA 14*
Hannan, Frederick Watson 1866-1929 *WhAm 1*
Hannan, Jerome Daniel 1896-1965 *WhAm 4*
Hannan, John J *NewYHSD*
Hannan, John Lawrence 1886-1949 *NatCAB 39*
Hannan, Robert Winslow 1874-1948
NatCAB 36
Hannan, William W 1854- *NatCAB 5*
Hannauer, George 1872-1929 *NatCAB 21*
Hannay, James 1842- *ApCAB*
Hannay, Neilson Campbell 1880-1962
NatCAB 50, WhAm 4
Hannegan, Edward Allen 1807-1859 *ApCAB,*
BiAUS, BiDrAC, DcAmB, Drake,
NatCAB 11, TwCBDA, WhAm H,
WhAmP
Hannegan, Robert Emmet 1903-1949 *BiDrUSE,*
DcAmB S4, WhAm 2
Hanners, A Ross 1877-1956 *NatCAB 50*
Hannett, James Wallace 1882-1956 *NatCAB 46*
Hannibal Barca 247BC-183BC *McGEWB*
Hannigan, Francis James 1880-1940 *WhAm 1*

Hannigan, Judson 1892-1959 *NatCAB 50*
Hannikainen, Tauno 1896-1969 *WhAm 5*
Hanning, Maurice Francis 1894-1968
NatCAB 54
Hanno 530?BC- *AsBiEn*
Hannoch, Julius 1921-1969 *NatCAB 55*
Hannon, W H 1864- *WhAm 4*
Hannon, William Garrett 1919-1973 *WhAm 6*
Hannum, Warren Thomas 1880- *WhAm 6*
Hano, Edward 1891-1954 *NatCAB 41*
Hanover, Clinton DeWitt, Jr. 1901-1965
WhAm 4
Hanoway, John *NewYHSD*
Hanrahan, Edward Mitchell 1892-1952
WhAm 3
Hanrahan, John David 1844-1923 *NatCAB 6*
Hans, Edmund 1886-1959 *NatCAB 49*
Hansberry, Lorraine 1930-1965 *WhAm 4*
Hansbrough, Henry Clay 1848-1933
ApCAB Sup, BiDrAC, NatCAB 4,
TwCBDA, WhAm 1, WhAmP
Hanscom, Charles Ridgely 1850-1918 *WhAm 1*
Hanscom, Elizabeth Deering 1865-1960
WhAm 3, WomWWA 14
Hanscom, Frank Edward 1863-1940 *WhAm 1*
Hanscom, John Forsyth 1842-1912 *WhAm 1*
Hansel, Charles 1859-1936 *WhAm 1*
Hansel, Charles Francis 1893-1954 *NatCAB 41*
Hansel, Miss H M *NewYHSD*
Hansel, John Washington 1853-1932 *WhAm 1*
Hansel, John Washington 1889-1957 *WhAm 3*
Hansell, Clarence Weston 1898-1967
NatCAB 54
Hansell, George H *NewYHSD*
Hansell, Granger 1901-1968 *NatCAB 56,*
WhAm 5
Hansell, Howard Forde 1855-1932 *WhAm 1*
Hansell, William Henry 1873-1933 *NatCAB 27*
Hanselman, George 1862-1923 *NatCAB 19*
Hanselman, Joseph Francis 1856-1923 *WhAm 1*
Hansen, A B 1896-1948 *WhAm 2*
Hansen, Alice G 1913-1953 *WhAm 3*
Hansen, Alvin Harvey 1887-1975 *EncAB,*
McGEWB, WebAB, WhAm 6
Hansen, Arild Edsten 1899-1962 *WhAm 4*
Hansen, Armin Carl 1886-1957 *IIBEAAW,*
WhAm 3
Hansen, Arthur Edmond 1891-1959 *NatCAB 48*
Hansen, Augie Louis 1879-1965 *WhAm 4*
Hansen, Bertie *WomWWA 14*
Hansen, Carl Ludwig, Jr. 1920-1973 *WhAm 6*
Hansen, Carl W 1901-1961 *WhAm 4*
Hansen, Clifford Peter 1912- *BiDrAC*
Hansen, Einar A 1895-1958 *WhAm 4*
Hansen, Ejnar 1870-1938 *NatCAB 28*
Hansen, Elmer Frank 1906-1967 *NatCAB 53*
Hansen, Emil Christian 1842-1909 *DcScB*
Hansen, Eric H 1903-1965 *WhAm 4,*
WhAm 5
Hansen, Florence Froney 1887-1971 *WhAm 5*
Hansen, George 1863-1908 *DcAmB,*
NatCAB 22, WhAm 4
Hansen, George 1899-1972 *WhAm 5*
Hansen, George Troup 1881-1963 *WhAm 4*
Hansen, George Vernon 1930- *BiDrAC*
Hansen, Gerhard Henrik Armauer 1841-1912
BiHiMed, DcScB
Hansen, Hans Christian Svane 1906-1960
WhAm 3, WhAm 4
Hansen, Hans Immanuel 1904-1970
NatCAB 56
Hansen, Hans Winnes 1886-1955 *NatCAB 44*
Hansen, Hazel Dorothy 1899-1962 *NatCAB 49*
Hansen, Herman Wendelborg 1854-1924
IIBEAAW
Hansen, Homer Alfred 1872-1960 *NatCAB 44*
Hansen, John *NewYHSD*
Hansen, John Morrison 1873-1929 *NatCAB 37*
Hansen, John Robert 1901-1974 *BiDrAC,*
WhAm 6
Hansen, Julia Butler 1907- *BiDrAC*
Hansen, Marcus Lee 1892-1938 *DcAmB S2,*
REnAW, WebAB
Hansen, Niels Ebbesen 1866-1950 *DcAmB S4,*
WhAm 3
Hansen, Orval Howard 1926- *BiDrAC*
Hansen, Oscar J W 1892-1971 *IIBEAAW*
Hansen, Oskar J W 1892-1971 *WhAm 5*

Hansen, Paul 1879-1944 *WhAm 2*
Hansen, Peter Andreas 1795-1874 *DcScB*
Hansen, Robert Rochester 1883-1970
NatCAB 55
Hansen, Sara Jenner 1878- *WomWWA 14*
Hansen, Walter William 1901-1967 *WhAm 4*
Hansen, William Webster 1909-1949
DcAmB S4, DcScB, WhAm 3
Hansen-Pruss, Oscar Carl Edvard 1900-1970
NatCAB 55
Hanshue, Harris Mathewson 1881-1937
NatCAB 27
Hansky, Aleksey Pavlovich 1870-1908 *DcScB*
Hansmann, Elwood 1899-1954 *NatCAB 44*
Hansmann, William H 1888-1952 *WhAm 3*
Hanson, Abel Aaron 1903-1973 *NatCAB 57*
Hanson, Albert Hoit 1846- *WhAm 4*
Hanson, Albert Murray 1904-1971 *NatCAB 57*
Hanson, Alexander Contee 1749-1806 *ApCAB,*
DcAmB, NatCAB 12, WhAm H
Hanson, Alexander Contee 1786-1819 *AmBi,*
ApCAB, BiAUS, BiDrAC, DcAmB,
Drake, NatCAB 12, TwCBDA, WhAm H,
WhAmP
Hanson, Andrew P 1858-1926 *NatCAB 20*
Hanson, Arthur Edwin 1894-1966 *WhAm 4*
Hanson, Bert 1867-1938 *WhAm 1*
Hanson, Burton 1851-1922 *WhAm 1*
Hanson, Carl Oscar 1902-1954 *NatCAB 45*
Hanson, Charles Lane 1870- *WhAm 5*
Hanson, Elisha 1888-1962 *WhAm 4*
Hanson, Eliza Rice 1825-1865 *ApCAB*
Hanson, Ephraim 1872- *WhAm 5*
Hanson, Felix Valentine 1877-1956 *WhAm 3*
Hanson, Frank Blair 1886-1945 *WhAm 2*
Hanson, Frank Herbert 1861- *NatCAB 5*
Hanson, George Charles 1883-1935 *WhAm 1*
Hanson, George McKay 1856-1924 *NatCAB 20,*
WhAm 1
Hanson, Grace Payne 1880- *WomWWA 14*
Hanson, Henry W A 1882-1962 *WhAm 4*
Hanson, Herman Herbert 1876-1972
NatCAB 57
Hanson, Howard Harold 1896- *BiDAmEd,*
McGEWB, WebAB
Hanson, James Christian Meinich 1864-1943
DcAmB S3, DcAmLiB, NatCAB 34,
WhAm 2
Hanson, James H 1816- *NatCAB 5*
Hanson, John d1783 *BiAUS, Drake*
Hanson, John 1715-1783 *ApCAB, BiDrAC,*
BiDrUSE, NatCAB 10, TwCBDA,
WhAmP
Hanson, John 1721-1783 *AmBi, DcAmB,*
WebAB, WhAm H
Hanson, John F 1842- *NatCAB 13*
Hanson, John Fletcher 1840-1910 *WhAm 1*
Hanson, John Wesley 1823- *ApCAB*
Hanson, Joseph Miles 1868-1921 *NatCAB 19,*
WhAm 1
Hanson, Julia 1843- *WomWWA 14*
Hanson, Justus Greeley 1870-1955 *NatCAB 44*
Hanson, Karl P 1905-1967 *WhAm 5*
Hanson, Leonard G 1891-1964 *WhAm 4*
Hanson, Loring Outbier 1906-1975 *WhAm 6*
Hanson, Louis 1890-1963 *NatCAB 50*
Hanson, Martin Gustav 1859- *WhAm 4*
Hanson, Martin H 1864-1931 *WhAm 1*
Hanson, Michael Francis 1867-1950 *WhAm 2A*
Hanson, Miles 1866- *WhAm 4*
Hanson, Murray 1904-1971 *WhAm 5*
Hanson, Norwood Russell 1924- *WhAm 4*
Hanson, O B 1894-1961 *WhAm 4*
Hanson, Ole 1874-1940 *DcAmB S2, WhAm 1*
Hanson, Paul M 1878- *WhAm 4*
Hanson, Peter 1821-1887 *NewYHSD*
Hanson, Peter 1875-1954 *NatCAB 42*
Hanson, Richard Burpee 1879-1948 *WhAm 2*
Hanson, Richard Locke 1899-1958 *WhAm 3*
Hanson, Roger d1862 *Drake*
Hanson, Roger Weightman 1827-1863
ApCAB Sup, DcAmB, NatCAB 22,
WhAm H
Hanson, Thomas Grafton 1865-1945 *WhAm 2*
Hanson, Victor Emerson 1879-1926 *NatCAB 20*
Hanson, Victor Henry 1876-1945 *NatCAB 34,*
WhAm 2
Hansteen, Christopher 1784-1873 *DcScB*

Hanton, Andrew *NewYHSD*
Hantz, Jacob F 1831-1887 *NewYHSD*
Hantzsch, Arthur Rudolf 1857-1935 *DcScB*
Hanus, Paul Henry 1855-1941 *BiDAmEd,
DcAmB S3, NatCAB 35, TwCBDA,
WhAm 1, WhAm 2*
Hanway, J E 1866-1946 *WhAm 2*
Hanzlik, Paul John 1885-1951 *NatCAB 39,
WhAm 3*
Hanzsche, William Thomson 1891-1954
WhAm 3
Hapai, Henry Chase 1873- *NatCAB 17*
Hapgood, Hutchins 1869-1944 *DcAmB S3,
NatCAB 35, WhAm 2*
Hapgood, Isabel Florence 1850-1928 *AmWom,
DcAmB, NatCAB 21, NotAW, WhAm 1,
WomWWA 14*
Hapgood, Isabel Florence 1851-1928 *TwCBDA*
Hapgood, Marshall Jay 1850-1926 *WhAm 1*
Hapgood, Neith Boyce 1872-1951 *WhAm 3,
WomWWA 14*
Hapgood, Norman 1868-1937 *AmBi,
ApCAB X, DcAmB S2, McGEWB,
NatCAB 27, TwCBDA, WhAm 1*
Hapgood, William Powers 1872-1960
NatCAB 49
Haplacher, George I *NewYHSD*
Happel, Carl 1819- *IlBEAAW*
Happel, Thomas Knight, Jr. 1914-1970
NatCAB 56
Happer, Andrew Patton 1818-1894 *DcAmB,
NatCAB 22, WhAm H*
Happy, Cyrus Prickett 1888-1965 *NatCAB 53*
Hara, Kei 1856-1921 *McGEWB*
Harada, Tasuku 1863- *WhAm 4*
Haraden, Jonathan 1744-1803 *DcAmB,
NatCAB 22, WhAm H*
Haraden, Jonathan 1745-1803 *ApCAB, Drake*
Harahan, James Theodore 1841-1912 *DcAmB,
NatCAB 15, WhAm 1*
Harahan, James Theodore 1843-1912
NatCAB 14
Harahan, William Johnson 1867-1937
DcAmB S2, NatCAB 27, WhAm 1
Haralson, Charles Herndon 1892-1952
NatCAB 42
Haralson, Hugh Anderson 1805-1854 *BiAUS,
BiDrAC, TwCBDA, WhAm H, WhAmP*
Haralson, Jeremiah 1846-1916 *BiDrAC,
WhAmP*
Haralson, Joe John 1895-1955 *NatCAB 42*
Haralson, Jonathan 1830-1912 *WhAm 1*
Haralsson, Jeremiah 1846-1916 *BiAUS*
Haram, Benjamin Lewis 1901-1953 *NatCAB 43*
Harap, Henry 1893- *BiDAmEd*
Haraszthy, Agostin 1812-1869 *ApCAB*
Haraszthy DeMokcsa, Agoston 1812?-1869
AmBi, DcAmB
Haraux, Alfred *NewYHSD*
Harb, Alfred Abdou 1888-1965 *NatCAB 51*
Harbach, Abram Alexander 1841-1933
WhAm 1
Harbach, Horatio M *NewYHSD*
Harbach, Otto Abels 1873-1963 *NatCAB 52,
WhAm 4*
Harbaugh, Charles Hamilton 1870-1943
NatCAB 32
Harbaugh, Charles William 1914-1972
WhAm 5
Harbaugh, Henry 1817-1867 *ApCAB, DcAmB,
Drake, NatCAB 12, TwCBDA, WhAm H*
Harbaugh, James Fleming Linn 1860- *WhAm 4*
Harbaugh, Marion Dwight 1892-1952
NatCAB 43
Harbaugh, Thomas Chalmers 1849-1924
NatCAB 10, WhAm 1
Harben, Mabelle Chandler 1879-
WomWWA 14
Harben, Will N 1858-1919 *WhAm 1*
Harben, William Nathaniel 1858-1919 *DcAmB,
NatCAB 10*
Harber, Clinton Edward 1888-1966 *NatCAB 53*
Harber, Giles Bates 1849-1925 *NatCAB 20,
WhAm 1*
Harber, Winford Elmer 1892-1974 *WhAm 6*
Harbert, Elizabeth Boynton 1843- *AmWom,
WomWWA 14*

Harbert, Elizabeth Morrisson Boynton 1845-1925
WhAm 1
Harbert, William Soesbe 1842-1919
NatCAB 18
Harbeson, James P *NewYHSD*
Harbeson, William Page 1882-1972 *WhAm 5*
Harbison, Alexander 1840-1910 *NatCAB 16*
Harbison, E Harris 1907-1964 *WhAm 4*
Harbison, Hugh 1833-1903 *NatCAB 16*
Harbison, John Pooler 1837-1914 *NatCAB 16*
Harbison, Ralph Warner 1876-1959 *ApCAB X,
WhAm 3*
Harbison, Robert Cleland 1866-1937 *WhAm 1*
Harbison, Samuel Pollock 1840-1905 *ApCAB X,
NatCAB 14*
Harbison, William Albert 1874-1950 *ApCAB X,
WhAm 3*
Harbo, Elias Peter 1856-1927 *WhAm 1*
Harbold, Peter Monroe 1873-1956 *NatCAB 45,
WhAm 5*
Harbord, James Guthrie 1866-1947 *DcAmB S4,
NatCAB 36, WebAMB, WhAm 2*
Harborough-Sherard, Mrs. Robert d1922
WhAm 1
Harbottle, John 1880- *WhAm 6*
Harbour, Jefferson Lee 1857-1931 *WhAm 1*
Harbridge, Delamere Forest 1872-1959
NatCAB 50
Harby, Isaac 1788-1828 *ApCAB, DcAmB,
Drake, NatCAB 3, WhAm H*
Harby, Lee Cohen 1849- *ApCAB Sup,
WhAm 4*
Harcourt, A G Vernon 1834-1919 *DcScB*
Harcourt, Alfred 1881-1954 *DcAmB S5,
WhAm 3*
Harcourt, Guy Nichols 1889-1957 *NatCAB 44*
Harcourt, Ralph Eldridge 1887-1952
NatCAB 41
Harcourt, William 1743-1830 *Drake*
Harcum, Edith Hatcher d1958 *WhAm 3*
Hard, Anne 1877-1961 *NatCAB 57*
Hard, Elvene Curtis 1853- *WomWWA 14*
Hard, Gideon 1797- *BiAUS*
Hard, Gideon 1797-1885 *BiDrAC*
Hard, Gideon 1797-1887 *WhAm H*
Hard, William 1878-1962 *NatCAB 56,
WhAm 4*
Hardaway, R Travis 1904-1961 *NatCAB 47*
Hardaway, Robert Hamilton 1883-1955
NatCAB 43
Hardaway, William Augustus 1850-1923
WhAm 1
Hardee, Cary Augustus 1876-1957 *WhAm 3*
Hardee, Henry Marion 1867-1949 *NatCAB 41*
Hardee, Theodore 1868- *WhAm 4*
Hardee, William 1845-1922 *NatCAB 35*
Hardee, William Joseph 1815-1873 *BiDConf,
DcAmB, NatCAB 4, WebAMB,
WhAm H*
Hardee, William Joseph 1817?-1873 *AmBi,
ApCAB*
Hardee, William Joseph 1818?-1873 *Drake*
Hardee, William Joseph 1819-1873 *TwCBDA*
Hardeman, Nicholas Brodie 1874- *WhAm 5*
Hardeman, Robert Ulla 1838- *NatCAB 3*
Hardeman, Thomas, Jr. 1825-1891 *BiAUS,
BiDrAC, NatCAB 5, WhAm H*
Harden, Sir Arthur 1865-1940 *AsBiEn, DcScB*
Harden, Cecil Murray 1894- *BiDrAC*
Harden, Edward Walker 1868- *WhAm 5*
Harden, Graham 1892-1963 *NatCAB 50*
Harden, John Henry 1836- *WhAm 4*
Harden, Komuria Albert 1905-1974 *WhAm 6*
Harden, Orville 1894-1957 *WhAm 3*
Harden, William 1844-1936 *WhAm 1*
Harden, William Dearing 1907-1962
NatCAB 48
Hardenberg, Prince Karl August Von 1750-1822
McGEWB
Hardenbergh, Augustus Albert 1830-1889
BiAUS, BiDrAC, NatCAB 14, TwCBDA
Hardenbergh, Cornelius Low 1790-1860
TwCBDA
Hardenbergh, Henry Janeway 1847-1918 *AmBi,
BnEnAmA, DcAmB, NatCAB 11,
TwCBDA, WhAm 1*
Hardenbergh, Jacob Rutsen 1736-1790 *DcAmB,
TwCBDA, WhAm H*

Hardenbergh, Jacob Rutsen 1738-1790 *ApCAB,
NatCAB 3*
Hardenbergh, Jacob Rutsen 1767-1841
TwCBDA
Hardenbergh, Jacobus Rutsen d1790 *Drake*
Hardenbergh, James Bruyn 1800-1870 *TwCBDA*
Hardenbergh, John Andrew 1878-1950
NatCAB 39
Hardenbergh, John Gerard 1892-1963 *WhAm 4*
Hardenbergh, Lewis Randolph 1878-1931
NatCAB 25
Hardenbrook, Edward Richard 1870-1929
NatCAB 22
Hardenbrook, Margaret *NotAW*
Hardenburgh, Augustus Albert 1830-1889
WhAm H
Harder, Howard Charles 1916-1974 *WhAm 6*
Hardesty, Cecilia Fairbrother *WomWWA 14*
Hardesty, Frederick A 1893-1956 *WhAm 3*
Hardesty, Irving 1866-1944 *WhAm 2*
Hardesty, Marshall Glade 1910-1972 *WhAm 6*
Hardesty, Shortridge 1884-1956 *WhAm 3*
Hardesty, William Couzens 1891-1962
NatCAB 50
Hardey, Mother Mary Aloysia 1809-1886
*ApCAB, BiDAmEd, DcAmB, NotAW,
TwCBDA, WhAm H*
Hardgrove, George P 1878-1963 *WhAm 4*
Hardgrove, John Gilbert 1877- *WhAm 5*
Hardie, Fernando *NewYHSD*
Hardie, George Robert 1869-1935 *WhAm 1*
Hardie, James 1750?-1832 *ApCAB, Drake*
Hardie, James A 1843- *Drake*
Hardie, James Allen 1823-1876 *ApCAB,
DcAmB, TwCBDA, WhAm H*
Hardie, James Finley 1880- *WhAm 6*
Hardie, James Keir 1856-1915 *McGEWB*
Hardie, John T 1829- *NatCAB 7*
Hardie, Lorenzo, Jr. *NewYHSD*
Hardie, Lorenzo, Sr. *NewYHSD*
Hardie, Robert Gordon 1854-1904 *TwCBDA,
WhAm 1*
Hardie, William Vincent 1881- *WhAm 6*
Hardigg, Carl Adolphus 1890-1967 *NatCAB 53*
Hardiman, Frank Murray 1889-1948
NatCAB 38
Hardin, Ben 1784-1852 *DcAmB, NatCAB 12*
Hardin, Benjamin 1784-1852 *ApCAB, BiAUS,
BiDrAC, TwCBDA, WhAm H, WhAmP*
Hardin, Charles Henry 1820-1892 *ApCAB,
BiAUS, DcAmB, NatCAB 12, TwCBDA,
WhAm H*
Hardin, Charles Roe 1894-1951 *WhAm 3*
Hardin, Clifford Morris 1915- *BiDrUSE,
EncAAH*
Hardin, E R *BiAUS*
Hardin, Everitt C 1869-1941 *WhAm 1*
Hardin, George Anson 1832-1901 *TwCBDA,
WhAm 1*
Hardin, Hugh H 1883-1964 *NatCAB 53*
Hardin, John 1753-1792 *AmBi, ApCAB,
DcAmB, Drake, TwCBDA, WebAMB,
WhAm H*
Hardin, John J 1810-1847 *ApCAB, BiAUS,
BiDrAC, DcAmB, Drake, NatCAB 12,
TwCBDA, WhAm H*
Hardin, John Ralph 1860-1945 *WhAm 2*
Hardin, John Ralph 1897-1970 *WhAm 5*
Hardin, John Wesley 1853-1895 *EncAAH,
REnAW, WhAm H*
Hardin, L Sage 1873-1937 *NatCAB 28*
Hardin, Martin D 1780-1823 *ApCAB, BiAUS,
DcAmB, Drake, NatCAB 12, TwCBDA,
WhAm H*
Hardin, Martin D 1837-1923 *NatCAB 12,
WhAm 1*
Hardin, Martin D 1873-1935 *WhAm 1*
Hardin, Martin Davis 1780-1823 *BiDrAC*
Hardin, Mordecai Robert d1875? *NatCAB 12*
Hardin, Oliver R 1903-1960 *NatCAB 51*
Hardin, Robert Allen 1899-1972 *WhAm 5*
Hardin, Willett Lepley 1868- *WhAm 4*
Harding, Aaron 1805-1875 *BiAUS, BiDrAC,
WhAm H*
Harding, Abner Clark 1807-1874 *ApCAB,
BiAUS, BiDrAC, DcAmB, NatCAB 4,
TwCBDA, WhAm H*
Harding, Albert Austin 1880-1958 *WhAm 3*

Harding, Alfred *NewYHSD*
Harding, Alfred 1852-1923 *NatCAB 15,*
WhAm 1
Harding, Alfred 1892-1969 *WhAm 5*
Harding, Amos Joseph 1839- *NatCAB 9*
Harding, Arthur McCracken 1884-1947
WhAm 2
Harding, Benjamin Fosdick 1875-1923
ApCAB X
Harding, Benjamin Franklin 1823-1899 *ApCAB,*
BiAUS, BiDrAC, NatCAB 12, TwCBDA
Harding, C Francis 1881-1942 *WhAm 2*
Harding, Carl Ludwig 1765-1834 *DcScB*
Harding, Carroll Rede 1888-1963 *WhAm 4*
Harding, Charles Henry 1862-1935 *NatCAB 28*
Harding, Charles L 1906-1953 *WhAm 3*
Harding, Charles Lewis 1879-1944 *NatCAB 32*
Harding, Chester 1792-1866 *AmBi, ApCAB,*
BnEnAmA, DcAmB, Drake, IIBEAAW,
NatCAB 4, NewYHSD, TwCBDA,
WebAB, WhAm H
Harding, Chester 1866-1936 *WhAm 1*
Harding, Christopher *NewYHSD*
Harding, Clara B Whipple *WomWWA 14*
Harding, Dexter 1796-1862 *NewYHSD*
Harding, Edwin Forrest 1886-1970 *WhAm 5*
Harding, Edwin Tyler 1911-1973 *WhAm 6*
Harding, Esther Gordon 1875- *WomWWA 14*
Harding, Evilela 1855-1920 *NatCAB 21*
Harding, Ferdinand Rockwell 1902-1968
NatCAB 55
Harding, Florence Kling 1860-1924 *NatCAB 20,*
NotAW
Harding, Frank 1858-1923 *NatCAB 39*
Harding, Frank Waller 1870-1951 *NatCAB 39*
Harding, Garrick Mallery 1827- *NatCAB 10,*
WhAm 4
Harding, George 1827-1902 *ApCAB, DcAmB,*
WhAm 1
Harding, George Franklin 1830-1915
NatCAB 19
Harding, George Franklin 1862-1940
NatCAB 29
Harding, George Franklin 1868-1939 *WhAm 1*
Harding, George Hosken 1902-1962
NatCAB 51
Harding, George Matthews 1882-1959
NatCAB 48, WhAm 3
Harding, Harry Alexis 1871- *WhAm 5*
Harding, Harry Patrick 1874- *WhAm 5*
Harding, Harvey A *NewYHSD*
Harding, Henry 1837-1910 *WhAm 1*
Harding, Henry H *NewYHSD*
Harding, Henry Morgan 1872- *WhoColR*
Harding, Horace 1794-1857? *NewYHSD*
Harding, J C *NewYHSD*
Harding, J Horace 1863-1929 *NatCAB 26,*
WhAm 1
Harding, J M 1887-1964 *WhAm 4*
Harding, Jeremiah d1830 *NewYHSD*
Harding, Jesper 1799-1865 *ApCAB, DcAmB,*
NatCAB 22, WhAm H
Harding, John Cowden 1873-1960 *WhAm 4*
Harding, John Eugene 1877-1959 *BiDrAC,*
WhAm 5
Harding, John Francis 1908-1975 *WhAm 6*
Harding, John L *NewYHSD*
Harding, John Philip 1866-1943 *NatCAB 32*
Harding, John Thomas 1866-1946 *WhAm 2*
Harding, John Ward 1863-1926 *NatCAB 21*
Harding, John William 1864- *WhAm 4*
Harding, Louis A 1876- *WhAm 3*
Harding, Mary Boak 1875- *WomWWA 14*
Harding, Minnie Lahm *WomWWA 14*
Harding, Nelson 1879-1944 *WhAm 2*
Harding, Norman G 1888-1949 *NatCAB 40*
Harding, Ralph R 1929- *BiDrAC*
Harding, Rebecca Blaine *NotAW*
Harding, Robert 1701-1772 *DcAmB,*
WhAm H
Harding, Robert Ellison 1883-1952 *WhAm 3*
Harding, Russell 1856-1908 *WhAm 1*
Harding, Samuel Bannister 1866-1927 *TwCBDA,*
WhAm 1
Harding, Seth 1734-1814 *DcAmB, NatCAB 21,*
WebAMB, WhAm H
Harding, Spencer S *NewYHSD*
Harding, Stephen Selwyn 1808-1893 *BiAUS,*

NatCAB 5
Harding, Warren Gamaliel 1865-1923 *AmBi,*
ApCAB X, BiDrAC, BiDrUSE, DcAmB,
EncAAH, EncAB, McGEWB,
NatCAB 19, WebAB, WhAm 1, WhAmP
Harding, William Barclay 1906-1967 *WhAm 4*
Harding, William Lloyd 1877-1934 *NatCAB 28,*
WhAm 1
Harding, William Procter Gould 1864-1930
DcAmB
Harding, William Proctor Gould 1864-1930
NatCAB 28, WhAm 1
Harding, William White 1830-1889 *ApCAB,*
DcAmB, NatCAB 1, NatCAB 22,
TwCBDA, WhAm H
Hardinge, Belle Boyd 1844-1900 *BiDConf*
Hardinge, Hal Williams 1855-1943 *WhAm 2*
Hardinge, Harry Williams 1855-1943
NatCAB 33
Hardison, Allen Crosby 1869- *WhAm 6*
Hardison, James Archibald 1896-1958
NatCAB 49
Hardison, Osborne Bennett 1892-1959 *WhAm 3*
Hardman, Catherine Virginia Stone 1863-
WomWWA 14
Hardman, Dwight Harrison 1897-1955
NatCAB 49
Hardman, Lamartine Griffin 1856-1937
WhAm 1
Hardon, Henry Winthrop 1861-1934
NatCAB 25
Hardrick, John Wesley 1891- *WhoColR*
Hardt, Frank McCulley 1879-1949 *WhAm 2*
Hardt, John William 1884-1960 *WhAm 3*
Hardt, Walter Keller 1881- *WhAm 6*
Hardwick, Charles Cheever, Jr. 1904-1970
WhAm 5
Hardwick, Charles Z 1900-1967 *WhAm 4*
Hardwick, Clifford Emerson 1904-1971
WhAm 5
Hardwick, Francis Tiley 1868-1948 *NatCAB 37*
Hardwick, Katharine Davis 1886-1974 *WhAm 6*
Hardwick, Thomas William 1872-1944 *BiDrAC,*
DcAmB S3, WhAm 2, WhAmP
Hardwicke, Sir Cedric Webster 1893-1964
WhAm 4
Hardy, Alexander George 1920-1973 *WhAm 6*
Hardy, Alexander Merrill 1847-1927 *BiDrAC*
Hardy, Alfred *NewYHSD*
Hardy, Alpheus Holmes 1840-1917 *NatCAB 32*
Hardy, Alpheus Sumner 1864-1943 *NatCAB 45*
Hardy, Anna Eliza 1839-1934 *NewYHSD,*
NotAW
Hardy, Arthur Schuyler 1868-1943 *NatCAB 32*
Hardy, Arthur Sherburne 1847-1930 *AmBi,*
ApCAB, DcAmB, NatCAB 2, TwCBDA,
WhAm 1
Hardy, Arthur Sturgis 1837- *ApCAB*
Hardy, Ashley Kingsley 1871-1940 *NatCAB 30,*
WhAm 1
Hardy, Benjamin Franklin 1808-1886 *ApCAB*
Hardy, Caldwell 1852-1923 *NatCAB 13,*
WhAm 1
Hardy, Carroll Foster 1907-1964 *NatCAB 50*
Hardy, Sir Charles 1705-1780 *ApCAB, Drake*
Hardy, Charles J d1956 *WhAm 3*
Hardy, Charles J, Jr. 1895-1973 *WhAm 6*
Hardy, Charles Oscar 1884-1948 *NatCAB 49,*
WhAm 2
Hardy, Claude 1598?-1678 *DcScB*
Hardy, David Keith 1924-1970 *WhAm 6*
Hardy, David Phillip 1890-1957 *NatCAB 47,*
WhAm 3
Hardy, Don 1912-1966 *NatCAB 53*
Hardy, Edward Lawyer 1868- *WhAm 5*
Hardy, Edwin Noah 1861-1950 *NatCAB 39,*
WhAm 3
Hardy, Elias 1746-1799 *ApCAB*
Hardy, Ewing Lloyd 1892-1968 *WhAm 5*
Hardy, George Erastus 1868- *WhAm 4*
Hardy, George Fiske 1865-1947 *WhAm 2*
Hardy, Godfrey Harold 1877-1947 *DcScB*
Hardy, Guy Urban 1872-1947 *BiDrAC,*
NatCAB 37, WhAm 2, WhAmP
Hardy, H Claude 1887-1973 *WhAm 6*
Hardy, Helen Avery 1873- *WomWWA 14*
Hardy, Howard Cecil 1911-1962 *NatCAB 52*
Hardy, Ira May 1874-1948 *NatCAB 43*

Hardy, Irene 1841- *WhAm 4, WomWWA 14*
Hardy, J Alex 1861-1934 *NatCAB 33*
Hardy, James Edward 1895-1951 *NatCAB 38*
Hardy, James Graham 1874-1953 *WhAm 3*
Hardy, James Ward 1815-1853 *ApCAB*
Hardy, Jennie Amelia Whitcomb 1860-
WomWWA 14
Hardy, Jenny C Law 1869- *WomWWA 14*
Hardy, Jeremiah Pearson 1800-1887 *BnEnAmA,*
NewYHSD
Hardy, Jessie Mack 1875- *WomWWA 14*
Hardy, John 1835-1913 *BiDrAC*
Hardy, John Crumpton 1864-1938 *WhAm 1*
Hardy, John Henry 1847-1917 *WhAm 1*
Hardy, Joseph Johnston 1844-1915 *WhAm 1*
Hardy, Josiah *ApCAB, NatCAB 13,*
WhAm H
Hardy, Karl John 1906-1950 *NatCAB 39*
Hardy, Kenneth Burnham 1908- *WhAm 5*
Hardy, Lamar 1879-1950 *WhAm 3*
Hardy, LeGrand Haven 1894-1954 *WhAm 3*
Hardy, Marjorie 1888-1948 *WhAm 2*
Hardy, Martha Eugenia Sidebottom 1911-1969
WhAm 5
Hardy, Mary Ann 1809-1887 *NewYHSD*
Hardy, Mary Chapman *WomWWA 14*
Hardy, Mary Earle 1846-1928 *WhAm 1,*
WomWWA 14
Hardy, Oliver 1892-1957 *WebAB*
Hardy, Oscar Jacob 1874-1950 *NatCAB 38,*
WhAm 3
Hardy, Osgood 1889-1955 *NatCAB 46*
Hardy, Porter, Jr. 1903- *BiDrAC, WhAmP*
Hardy, Ralph W 1916-1957 *WhAm 3*
Hardy, Robert Marion 1883-1960 *WhAm 4*
Hardy, Robert Monroe 1911-1967 *NatCAB 54*
Hardy, Rosswell Eric 1893-1961 *NatCAB 48*
Hardy, Rufus 1855-1943 *BiDrAC, WhAm 4,*
WhAmP
Hardy, Samuel 1758?-1785 *ApCAB, BiAUS,*
BiDrAC, DcAmB, NatCAB 5, TwCBDA,
WhAm H
Hardy, Sarah Drown Belcher 1864-
WomWWA 14
Hardy, Summers 1875-1950 *NatCAB 38,*
WhAm 3
Hardy, Thomas 1840-1928 *McGEWB*
Hardy, Thomas Walter 1881-1960 *WhAm 4*
Hardy, Walter Manly 1877-1933 *NatCAB 25*
Hardy, Warren Follansbee 1879-1933 *WhAm 1*
Hardy, William Bate 1864-1934 *DcScB Sup*
Hardy, William Edwin 1863-1934 *WhAm 1*
Hardy, William Harris 1837-1917 *DcAmB,*
NatCAB 22
Hare, Arley Munson 1871- *WhAm 5*
Hare, Butler Black 1875-1967 *BiDrAC*
Hare, Clifford LeRoy 1869-1948 *WhAm 2*
Hare, D O 1811?- *NewYHSD*
Hare, Darius Dodge 1843-1897 *BiDrAC,*
TwCBDA, WhAm H
Hare, David 1917- *BnEnAmA*
Hare, Emlen Spencer 1882-1962 *WhAm 4*
Hare, Evanetta 1862- *WomWWA 14*
Hare, George Andrew 1857-1936 *NatCAB 29,*
WhAm 1
Hare, George Emlen 1808-1892 *ApCAB,*
DcAmB, NatCAB 6, TwCBDA,
WhAm H
Hare, Hobart Amory 1862-1931 *AmBi,*
NatCAB 13, NatCAB 32, WhAm 1
Hare, Horace Binney 1876-1956 *NatCAB 47*
Hare, Hugh F 1902-1967 *WhAm 4*
Hare, James Butler 1918-1966 *BiDrAC*
Hare, James H 1856-1946 *DcAmB S4,*
WhAm 2
Hare, James Madison 1859- *WhAm 4*
Hare, John Innes Clark 1816-1905 *ApCAB,*
BiAUS, DcAmB, Drake, TwCBDA
Hare, John Innes Clark 1817-1905 *WhAm 4*
Hare, Marmaduke 1856-1942 *WhAm 3*
Hare, Maud Cuney 1879- *WhoColR*
Hare, Montgomery 1870-1932 *NatCAB 42*
Hare, Robert 1781-1858 *AmBi, ApCAB,*
AsBiEn, DcAmB, DcScB, Drake,
McGEWB, NatCAB 5, TwCBDA,
WhAm H
Hare, S Herbert 1888-1960 *WhAm 4*
Hare, Silas 1827-1907 *BiDrAC*

Hare, T Truxtun 1878- *WhAm 6*
Hare, Thomas Joseph 1877-1942 *NatCAB 31*
Hare, William *NewYHSD*
Hare, William Hobart 1838-1909 *AmBi,*
ApCAB, DcAmB, NatCAB 3, TwCBDA,
WhAm 1
Harer, William Benson 1896-1968 *NatCAB 56,*
WhAm 5
Hares, Charles Joseph 1881-1970 *NatCAB 56*
Harford, Sir Henry 1762- *NatCAB 7*
Hargadon, I Leo 1880-1952 *WhAm 3*
Harger, Charles Moreau 1863-1955 *WhAm 3*
Harger, Maria McDonald 1861- *WomWWA 14*
Harger, Oscar 1843-1887 *ApCAB Sup,*
TwCBDA
Hargest, William M 1868-1948 *WhAm 2*
Hargett, Ira Mason 1881- *WhAm 6*
Hargis, Denver David 1921- *BiDrAC*
Hargis, Thomas Frazier 1842-1903 *ApCAB,*
NatCAB 12
Hargis, Thomas Frazier 1843-1903 *WhAm 1*
Hargitt, Charles Wesley 1852-1927 *NatCAB 5,*
TwCBDA, WhAm 1
Hargitt, George Thomas 1881-1971 *NatCAB 57,*
WhAm 6
Hargrave, Frank Flavius 1878- *WhAm 6*
Hargrave, Homer Pearson 1895-1964
NatCAB 50, WhAm 4
Hargrave, Thomas *NewYHSD*
Hargrave, Thomas Jean 1891-1962 *NatCAB 49,*
WhAm 4
Hargrave, William Loftin 1903-1975 *WhAm 6*
Hargraves, Edward Hammond 1816-1891
McGEWB
Hargreaves, John Morris 1901-1959 *WhAm 3*
Hargreaves, Mary Wilma Massey 1914-
EncAAH
Hargreaves, Richard T 1875- *WhAm 5*
Hargrove, Reginald Henry 1897-1954
NatCAB 42, WhAm 3
Hargrove, Robert Kennon 1829-1905 *ApCAB,*
DcAmB, NatCAB 8, TwCBDA,
WhAm 1
Haridatta I *DcScB*
Haridatta II *DcScB*
Haring, Alexander 1871-1960 *WhAm 3A*
Haring, Clarence Henry 1885-1960 *WhAm 4*
Haring, Clarence Melvin 1878-1951 *WhAm 3*
Haring, Douglas Gilbert 1894-1970 *WhAm 5*
Haring, Jacob Conrad 1846-1926 *NatCAB 6*
Haring, John 1739-1809 *ApCAB, BiAUS,*
BiDrAC, TwCBDA, WhAm H
Haring, Philip Erwin 1916-1967 *WhAm 5*
Hariot, Thomas 1560-1621 *DcScB, NatCAB 7*
Harison, Beverly Drake 1855-1924 *WhAm 1*
Harjes, H Herman 1875-1926 *NatCAB 20*
Harjes, John Henry 1830-1914 *NatCAB 19*
Hark, J Max 1849-1930 *WhAm 1*
Hark, Joseph Maximilian 1849-1930 *TwCBDA*
Harker, Alfred 1859-1939 *DcScB*
Harker, Catharine d1938 *WomWWA 14*
Harker, Catherine d1938 *WhAm 1*
Harker, Charles G 1837-1864 *ApCAB, Drake,*
NatCAB 5, TwCBDA
Harker, John Coates 1833-1913 *EncAAH*
Harker, Joseph Ralph 1853-1938 *WhAm 1*
Harker, Oliver Albert 1844-1936 *WhAm 1*
Harker, Ray Clarkson 1866- *WhAm 5*
Harker, Samuel *ApCAB, Drake*
Harkey, Simeon Walcher 1811-1889 *ApCAB,*
NatCAB 5, WhAm H
Harkins, Albert Glendye 1884-1967 *NatCAB 53*
Harkins, Edward Francis 1872- *WhAm 5*
Harkins, Henry Nelson 1905-1967 *NatCAB 54,*
WhAm 4
Harkins, Mathew 1845-1921 *ApCAB,*
TwCBDA
Harkins, Matthew 1845-1921 *NatCAB 13,*
WhAm 1
Harkins, Robert *NewYHSD*
Harkins, Thomas J 1879- *WhAm 6*
Harkins, William Dickey 1894-1973
NatCAB 57
Harkins, William Draper 1873-1951 *AsBiEn,*
DcAmB S5, DcScB, NatCAB 42,
Harkisheimer, William John 1838- *NatCAB 5*
Harkness, Albert 1822-1907 *AmBi, ApCAB,*

BiDAmEd, DcAmB, NatCAB 6,
TwCBDA, WhAm 1
Harkness, Albert Granger 1856-1923 *ApCAB X,*
NatCAB 19, WhAm 1
Harkness, Albert Granger 1857-1923 *ApCAB,*
TwCBDA
Harkness, Anna M Richardson 1837-1926
NotAW
Harkness, Charles William 1860-1916 *WhAm 1*
Harkness, David Weild 1844-1919 *NatCAB 8*
Harkness, Edward Stephen 1874-1940 *AmBi,*
DcAmB S2, WhAm 1
Harkness, Georgia Elma 1891-1974 *DcAmReB,*
WhAm 6
Harkness, Gordon Follette 1880-1962 *WhAm 4*
Harkness, Harvey W d1901 *WhAm 1*
Harkness, James 1803-1878 *ApCAB*
Harkness, James Stewart 1867- *WhAm 4*
Harkness, Lamon Vanderburg 1850-1915
NatCAB 24
Harkness, Mary Emma Stillman 1874-1950
NotAW
Harkness, Robert Baskin 1872-1956
NatCAB 48
Harkness, Una McMahan 1871-
WomWWA 14
Harkness, William 1837-1903 *AmBi, ApCAB,*
BiAUS, DcAmB, DcScB, NatCAB 8,
TwCBDA, WhAm 1
Harkness, William Hale 1900-1954 *NatCAB 46,*
WhAm 3
Harkness, William Lamon 1858-1919
NatCAB 25
Harl, Maple Talbot 1893-1957 *WhAm 3*
Harl, Virgil Anderson 1889-1958 *NatCAB 49*
Harlan, Aaron 1802-1868 *BiAUS, BiDrAC,*
WhAm H
Harlan, Andrew Jackson 1815-1907 *BiAUS,*
BiDrAC, TwCBDA, WhAmP
Harlan, Byron Berry 1886-1949 *BiDrAC,*
WhAm 2
Harlan, Campbell Allen 1907-1972 *WhAm 5*
Harlan, Edgar Rubey 1869-1941 *WhAm 1*
Harlan, George Cuvier 1835-1909 *ApCAB,*
NatCAB 24, TwCBDA, WhAm 1
Harlan, Henry David 1858-1943 *NatCAB 9,*
NatCAB 39, WhAm 2
Harlan, Herbert 1856-1923 *NatCAB 30*
Harlan, Ida Carter *WomWWA 14*
Harlan, James 1800-1863 *ApCAB, BiAUS,*
BiDrAC, DcAmB, NatCAB 11, TwCBDA,
WhAm H
Harlan, James 1820- *ApCAB, BiAUS, Drake*
Harlan, James 1820-1889 *WhAm H*
Harlan, James 1820-1899 *AmBi, BiDrAC,*
BiDrUSE, DcAmB, NatCAB 2,
TwCBDA, WhAm H, WhAmP
Harlan, James Elliott 1845-1933 *WhAm 1*
Harlan, James S 1861-1927 *WhAm 1*
Harlan, John Marshall 1833-1911 *AmBi,*
ApCAB, DcAmB, EncAB, McGEWB,
NatCAB 1, TwCBDA, WebAB, WhAm 1
Harlan, John Marshall 1899-1971 *NatCAB 57,*
WebAB, WhAm 5
Harlan, John Maynard 1864-1934 *NatCAB 45,*
WhAm 1
Harlan, Joseph Gibbons 1825-1857 *NatCAB 33*
Harlan, Josiah 1799-1871 *DcAmB, WhAm H*
Harlan, Marie Hall 1859- *WomWWA 14*
Harlan, N Robert 1880-1942 *NatCAB 32*
Harlan, Otis d1940 *WhAm 1*
Harlan, Richard 1796-1843 *ApCAB, DcAmB,*
DcScB, Drake, TwCBDA, WhAm H
Harlan, Richard Davenport 1859-1931 *ApCAB,*
NatCAB 33, WhAm 1
Harlan, Rolvix 1876- *WhAm 5*
Harland, Edward 1832-1915 *WhAm 1*
Harland, Henry 1861-1905 *AmBi, ApCAB,*
DcAmB, NatCAB 13, TwCBDA,
WhAm 1
Harland, James Penrose 1891-1973 *WhAm 5*
Harland, Lewis E 1905-1974 *WhAm 6*
Harland, Marion 1830-1922 *AmBi, DcAmB,*
NotAW, TwCBDA, WhAm 1
Harland, Thomas 1735-1807 *DcAmB,*
WhAm H
Harless, Richard Fielding 1905-1970 *BiDrAC*
Harless, William Frank 1881-1962 *NatCAB 50*

Harley, Charles Richard 1864-1930 *WhAm 1*
Harley, George 1829-1896 *BiHiMed*
Harley, Halvor Larson 1882-1957 *NatCAB 48*
Harley, James Kimball 1828-1889 *NewYHSD*
Harley, John B *NatCAB 2*
Harley, Joseph Emile 1880-1942 *NatCAB 37*
Harley, Joseph S *NewYHSD*
Harley, Lewis Reifsneider 1866- *WhAm 4*
Harley, Robert, Earl Of Oxford 1661-1724
McGEWB
Harline *NewYHSD*
Harling, W Franke 1887-1958 *WhAm 3*
Harllee, William Curry 1877- *WhAm 5*
Harlow, Alvin Fay 1875-1963 *WhAm 4*
Harlow, Arthur Harold, Jr. 1907-1966
NatCAB 53
Harlow, Ellwood 1873-1943 *NatCAB 32*
Harlow, George Arthur 1867-1950 *NatCAB 38*
Harlow, Jean 1911-1937 *DcAmB S2,*
NatCAB 27, NotAW, WebAB,
WhAm HA, WhAm 4
Harlow, John Brayton 1844- *WhAm 4*
Harlow, Justin Edwards, Jr. 1908-1961
NatCAB 51
Harlow, Louis Kinney 1850- *WhAm 4*
Harlow, Ralph Volney 1884-1956 *NatCAB 47,*
WhAm 3
Harlow, Richard Austin 1859-1932 *NatCAB 34*
Harlow, Richard Cresson 1889-1962 *WhAm 4*
Harlow, S Ralph 1885-1972 *WhAm 5*
Harlow, Sarah Havens 1867- *WomWWA 14*
Harlow, Victor Emmanuel 1876-1958 *WhAm 3*
Harlow, William Burt 1856-1928 *NatCAB 2,*
NatCAB 24, WhAm 4
Harlow, William Elam 1860-1922 *WhAm 3*
Harlow, William Page 1867-1924 *WhAm 1*
Harman, Arthur Fort 1875-1948 *WhAm 2*
Harman, Byron Mentzer 1893-1964 *NatCAB 50*
Harman, Fred, Jr. 1902- *IIBEAAW*
Harman, George Amos 1842-1919 *NatCAB 18*
Harman, Gerald Jerome 1897-1961 *NatCAB 49*
Harman, Harvey John 1900-1969 *WhAm 5*
Harman, Henry A 1845-1922 *NatCAB 20*
Harman, Henry Elliott 1866- *WhAm 1*
Harman, Henry Martyn 1822- *TwCBDA*
Harman, Jacob Anthony 1866- *WhAm 5*
Harman, James Lewie 1874- *WhAm 5*
Harman, Pinckney Jones 1879-1938 *NatCAB 28,*
WhAm 1
Harman, Pinckney Jones 1913-1966 *WhAm 4*
Harman, Ralph Augustus 1857-1929
NatCAB 32
Harman, Sayers French 1892-1948 *NatCAB 36*
Harmand, Louis Gustave 1503-1549 *ApCAB*
Harmanson, John Henry 1803-1850 *BiAUS,*
BiDrAC, WhAm H, WhAmP
Harmar, Josiah 1753-1813 *AmBi, ApCAB,*
BiAUS, DcAmB, Drake, NatCAB 5,
REnAW, TwCBDA, WebAMB,
WhAm H
Harmati, Sandor 1892-1936 *NatCAB 26,*
WhAm 1
Harmeling, Henry 1864- *WhAm 4*
Harmeling, Stephen John 1851-1940 *WhAm 3*
Harmer, Alexander Francis 1856-1925
IIBEAAW, NatCAB 42
Harmer, Alfred Crout 1825-1900 *BiAUS,*
BiDrAC, TwCBDA, WhAm 1, WhAmP
Harmer, James Torr 1856-1937 *NatCAB 27*
Harmer, Torr Wagner 1881-1940 *NatCAB 30*
Harmon, Andrew Davidson 1870- *WhAm 3*
Harmon, Arthur Loomis 1878-1958 *WhAm 3*
Harmon, Austin Morris 1878-1950 *WhAm 3*
Harmon, Benjamin Smith 1859-1916 *WhAm 1*
Harmon, Cameron 1876- *WhAm 5*
Harmon, Charles H *IIBEAAW*
Harmon, Claude Moore 1868-1951 *WhAm 3*
Harmon, Daniel Williams 1778-1845 *DcAmB,*
WhAm H
Harmon, Darrell Victor 1922-1971 *WhAm 6*
Harmon, Eleazar 1853- *NatCAB 16*
Harmon, Ernest Nason 1894- *WebAMB*
Harmon, Frank Wilson 1851-1931 *WhAm 1*
Harmon, Harold Elliott 1905-1967 *NatCAB 53,*
WhAm 4
Harmon, Henry Gadd 1901-1964 *WhAm 4*
Harmon, Hubert Reilly 1892-1957 *WhAm 3*
Harmon, John Francis 1858-1943 *WhAm 3*

Harmon, John Hanchett 1819-1888
ApCAB Sup
Harmon, John Millard 1895-1974 *WhAm 6*
Harmon, Judson 1846-1927 *AmBi,*
ApCAB Sup, ApCAB X, BiDrUSE,
DcAmB, NatCAB 13, TwCBDA,
WhAm 1
Harmon, Julia R Riker *WomWWA 14*
Harmon, Kenneth Allen 1903-1955 *NatCAB 41*
Harmon, Leo Clinton 1871- *WhAm 5*
Harmon, Millard Fillmore 1888-1945 *WebAMB,*
WhAm 2, WhWW-II
Harmon, Paul M 1892-1964 *WhAm 4*
Harmon, Randall S 1903- *BiDrAC*
Harmon, Rollin E 1845-1923 *ApCAB X*
Harmon, William Elmer 1862-1928 *AmBi,*
WhAm 1
Harmony, David Buttz 1832-1917 *ApCAB,*
TwCBDA, WhAm 1
Harms, Ernst 1872-1928 *NatCAB 22*
Harms, Eugene Henry 1883-1937 *NatCAB 35*
Harms, Herman 1873-1934 *NatCAB 25*
Harms, John Henry 1876-1946 *WhAm 2*
Harn, Orlando Clinton 1871-1955 *WhAm 3*
Harnack, Adolf Von 1851-1930 *McGEWB*
Harnagel, George, Jr. 1903-1962 *NatCAB 51*
Harnden, Arthur DeWitt 1879-1929
NatCAB 22
Harnden, William Frederick 1812-1845 *DcAmB,*
NatCAB 13, TwCBDA, WhAm H
Harnden, William Frederick 1813-1845 *ApCAB*
Harned, Perry L 1866- *WhAm 4*
Harned, Robert Ellsworth 1877- *WhAm 5*
Harned, Thomas Biggs 1851- *NatCAB 5,*
WhAm 4
Harned, Virginia 1896-1946 *WhAm 2*
Harned, William Biechele 1907-1956
NatCAB 48
Harner, Nevin Cowger 1901-1951 *WhAm 3*
Harness, Forest Arthur 1895- *BiDrAC*
Harnett, Cornelius 1723-1781 *AmBi, ApCAB,*
BiAUS, BiDrAC, DcAmB, Drake,
NatCAB 7, TwCBDA, WhAm H,
WhAmP
Harnett, William Michael 1848-1892 *BnEnAmA,*
McGEWB, WebAB
Harney, Benjamin Robertson 1871-1938
DcAmB S2
Harney, George Edward 1840-1924 *NatCAB 1,*
WhAm 1
Harney, John Hopkins 1806-1867 *ApCAB*
Harney, John Hopkins 1806-1868 *Drake,*
TwCBDA
Harney, John Milton 1789-1825 *ApCAB,*
Drake, NatCAB 10, WhAm H
Harney, Thomas Porter 1893-1960 *NatCAB 49*
Harney, William Selby 1798-1889 *Drake*
Harney, William Selby 1800-1889 *AmBi,*
ApCAB, DcAmB, NatCAB 5, REnAW,
TwCBDA, WebAMB, WhAm H
Harney, William Wallace 1831- *ApCAB*
Harnisch, Albert E 1843- *NewYHSD*
Harnisch, Albert Ernest 1842- *ApCAB,*
TwCBDA
Harnisch, Carl 1800-1883 *NewYHSD*
Harnly, Andrew Hoerner 1864- *WhAm 4*
Harno, Albert James 1889-1966 *WhAm 4*
Haro, Alonso Nunez De 1729-1800 *ApCAB*
Haro, Gonzalo Lopez De 1734-1796 *ApCAB*
Haro Y Tamariz, Antonio De 1810-1872?
ApCAB
Harold I 840?-933 *McGEWB*
Harold II d1066 *McGEWB*
Harold III 1015-1066 *McGEWB*
Harold, Frank Walker 1862-1927 *NatCAB 22*
Harold, Raymond Paget 1898-1972 *WhAm 5*
Haroutunian, Joseph 1904-1968 *WhAm 5*
Harper, Albert Bering 1896-1950 *NatCAB 37*
Harper, Albert Metcalf 1843-1871 *NatCAB 3*
Harper, Alexander 1786-1860 *BiAUS, BiDrAC,*
WhAm H, WhAmP
Harper, Alexander James 1877-1940
NatCAB 30
Harper, Blanche B 1879- *WomWWA 14*
Harper, Carrie Anna d1918 *WhAm 1,*
WomWWA 14
Harper, Clara Moore 1854- *WomWWA 14*
Harper, Clarence Lee 1864-1940 *NatCAB 33*

Harper, Cora Stickney 1859- *WomWWA 14*
Harper, Cornelius Allen 1864- *WhAm 3*
Harper, Donald 1868-1954 *WhAm 3*
Harper, Earl Enyeart 1895-1967 *WhAm 4*
Harper, Edward Bascom 1842-1895 *NatCAB 7*
Harper, Edward Thomson 1857-1921 *WhAm 1*
Harper, Evangeline Coates 1853-
WomWWA 14
Harper, Fletcher 1804-1877 *Drake*
Harper, Fletcher 1806-1877 *DcAmB,*
NatCAB 1, TwCBDA, WebAB,
WhAm H
Harper, Floyd Arthur 1905-1973 *WhAm 5*
Harper, Fowler Vincent 1897-1965 *NatCAB 52,*
WhAm 4
Harper, Frances Ellen Watkins 1825-1911
DcAmReB, NotAW
Harper, Francis Alexander 1874- *ApCAB X*
Harper, Francis Jacob 1800-1837 *BiAUS,*
BiDrAC, WhAm H
Harper, Frederick Butler 1857-1928
NatCAB 23
Harper, George Andrew 1879-1939 *WhAm 1*
Harper, George McLean 1863-1947 *TwCBDA,*
WhAm 2
Harper, George Washington Finley 1834-1921
WhAm 3
Harper, H Mitchell 1901-1964 *WhAm 4*
Harper, Harold 1885-1971 *WhAm 5*
Harper, Harry Clayton 1895-1963 *NatCAB 48*
Harper, Harry F d1949 *WhAm 2*
Harper, Harvey W 1878-1958 *WhAm 3*
Harper, Henry Winston 1859-1943 *WhAm 2*
Harper, Herbert E 1901-1974 *WhAm 6*
Harper, Ida Husted 1851-1931 *AmBi, AmWom,*
BiCAW, DcAmB, NatCAB 25, NotAW,
WhAm 1, WomWWA 14
Harper, Jacob Chandler 1858-1939 *NatCAB 30,*
WhAm 1
Harper, James 1779-1872 *BiAUS*
Harper, James 1795-1869 *AmBi, ApCAB,*
DcAmB, Drake, EncAB, NatCAB 1,
TwCBDA, WebAB, WhAm H
Harper, James Byall 1848-1918 *NatCAB 17*
Harper, James Clarence 1819-1890 *BiAUS,*
BiDrAC, WhAm H
Harper, James Patterson, Jr. 1863-1934
WhAm 1
Harper, James R 1869- *WhAm 5*
Harper, John 1797-1875 *DcAmB, Drake,*
NatCAB 1, TwCBDA, WebAB
Harper, John 1811-1891 *NatCAB 3*
Harper, John Adams 1779-1816 *BiAUS,*
BiDrAC, WhAm H
Harper, John Erasmus 1851-1921 *WhAm 1*
Harper, John Geddes 1848- *NatCAB 5*
Harper, John Lyell 1873-1924 *DcAmB,*
NatCAB 20, WhAm 1
Harper, John M 1845- *ApCAB*
Harper, Joseph Hotchkiss 1845-1921
NatCAB 19
Harper, Joseph Morrill 1787-1865 *ApCAB,*
BiAUS, BiDrAC, TwCBDA, WhAm H
Harper, Joseph Morrill 1789-1865 *NatCAB 11*
Harper, Joseph Wesley 1801-1870 *DcAmB,*
Drake, NatCAB 1, TwCBDA, WebAB
Harper, Joseph Wesley 1830-1896 *TwCBDA*
Harper, Katherine Medill Patrick 1863-
WomWWA 14
Harper, Mabel Herbert Urner *WomWWA 14*
Harper, Marion Sampson 1862-1940
NatCAB 30
Harper, Martha Matilda 1857-1950 *NatCAB 39*
Harper, Mary McKibbin *WhAm 5*
Harper, Merritt Wesley 1877-1938 *WhAm 1*
Harper, Olive *NatCAB 5*
Harper, Orlando Metcalf 1846- *NatCAB 3*
Harper, Paul Tompkins 1881-1931 *WhAm 1*
Harper, Paul Vincent 1889-1949 *WhAm 2*
Harper, Robert Almer 1862-1946 *DcScB,*
WhAm 2
Harper, Robert Francis 1864-1914 *DcAmB,*
NatCAB 22, WhAm 1
Harper, Robert Goodloe 1765-1825 *AmBi,*
ApCAB, BiAUS, BiDrAC, DcAmB,
Drake, NatCAB 5, TwCBDA, WebAB,
WhAm H, WhAmP

Harper, Robert N 1861-1940 *WhAm 1*
Harper, Robert Story 1899-1962 *NatCAB 50,*
WhAm 4
Harper, Roland McMillan 1878-1966
ApCAB X, DcScB, WhAm 4
Harper, Samuel H *BiAUS*
Harper, Samuel Northrup 1882-1943 *WhAm 2*
Harper, Samuel Williams 1874-1950
NatCAB 40, WhAm 3
Harper, Theodore Acland 1871-1942 *WhAm 2*
Harper, Thomas Henry 1868- *WhAm 4*
Harper, Wesley 1801-1870 *WebAB*
Harper, Wilhelmina d1973 *WhAm 6*
Harper, William 1790-1847 *AmBi, ApCAB,*
BiAUS, BiDrAC, DcAmB, Drake,
NatCAB 11, TwCBDA, WhAm H
Harper, William Allen 1880-1942 *WhAm 2*
Harper, William Durbin 1862-1939 *NatCAB 36*
Harper, William Edward 1865-1938
NatCAB 28
Harper, William Rainey 1856-1906 *AmBi,*
ApCAB, BiDAmEd, DcAmB, EncAB,
McGEWB, NatCAB 11, TwCBDA,
WebAB, WhAm 1
Harper, William St. John 1851-1910
NatCAB 13, TwCBDA, WhAm 1
Harper, William Wade 1868-1941 *WhAm 1*
Harper Brothers *WebAB*
Harpestraeng, Henrik d1244 *DcScB*
Harpham, Gertrude Tressel Rider *WhAm 5*
Harpster, Charles Melvin 1873-1926 *WhAm 1*
Harpster, John Henry 1843-1911 *WhAm 1*
Harpster, John Henry 1844-1911 *DcAmB,*
NatCAB 15
Harpster, M Julia Jacobs 1846- *WomWWA 14*
Harpur, Robert 1731?-1825 *DcAmB,*
WhAm H
Harr, Luther 1896-1950 *WhAm 3*
Harr, William R 1872-1950 *WhAm 3*
Harrah, Charles Clayton 1900-1969
NatCAB 54
Harrah, Charles Jefferson 1817-1890 *ApCAB,*
DcAmB, NatCAB 24, WhAm H
Harrah, Charles Jefferson 1855- *WhAm 4*
Harrah, William Ferguson 1871-1959
NatCAB 18, WhAm 3
Harral, Jared Alphonso 1842- *WhAm 4*
Harral, Stewart 1906-1964 *NatCAB 53,*
WhAm 4
Harrar, Ellwood Scott 1905-1975 *WhAm 6*
Harre, T Everett 1884- *WhAm 2*
Harreld, John William 1872-1950 *ApCAB X,*
BiDrAC, WhAm 5, WhAmP
Harrell, Alfred 1863-1946 *WhAm 2*
Harrell, David 1852- *WhoColR*
Harrell, H Voss 1895-1966 *NatCAB 52*
Harrell, Joel Ellis 1891-1968 *WhAm 5*
Harrell, John 1806-1876 *DcAmB, WhAm H*
Harrell, Linwood Parker 1908-1970 *WhAm 5*
Harrell, Mack 1909-1960 *WhAm 4*
Harrell, Sarah Carmichael 1844- *AmWom*
Harrelson, John William 1885-1955 *WhAm 3*
Harrer, Gustave Adolphus 1886-1943 *WhAm 2*
Harries, George Herbert 1860-1934 *AmBi,*
WhAm 1
Harries, John 1815-1904 *NatCAB 23*
Harries, William Henry 1843-1921 *BiDrAC*
Harriet 1823-1896 *ApCAB Sup*
Harrigan, Edward 1845-1911 *DcAmB,*
NatCAB 11, WhAm 1
Harrigan, Nolan 1894-1966 *NatCAB 52,*
WhAm 4
Harriman, Alice 1861-1925 *WhAm 1,*
WomWWA 14
Harriman, Alonzo Jesse 1898-1966 *WhAm 5*
Harriman, Averell 1891- *WebAB*
Harriman, Averell *see also* Harriman, William
Averell
Harriman, Benjamin *NewYHSD*
Harriman, Bertha Ray 1866- *WomWWA 14*
Harriman, Charles Conant 1876-1946 *WhAm 2*
Harriman, Cora Elizabeth 1876-
WomWWA 14
Harriman, Edward Avery 1869- *WhAm 5*
Harriman, Edward Henry 1848-1909 *AmBi,*
ApCAB X, DcAmB, EncAB, McGEWB,
NatCAB 14, REnAW, WebAB, WhAm 1

Harriman, Florence Jaffray 1870-1967
NatCAB 53, WhAm 4, WomWWA 14
Harriman, Frank Black 1861- *WhAm 4*
Harriman, Frederick William 1852-1931
WhAm 1
Harriman, Henry Ingraham 1871-1950
NatCAB 39, WhAm 3
Harriman, Henry Ingrahm 1872-1950
ApCAB X
Harriman, Hiram Putnam 1846-1907
NatCAB 14
Harriman, Job 1861-1925 *WhAm 1*
Harriman, John Walter 1898-1972 *WhAm 5*
Harriman, Joseph Wright 1867-1949 *WhAm 2*
Harriman, Karl Edwin 1875-1935 *NatCAB 13,
WhAm 1*
Harriman, Lewis Gildersleeve 1889-1973
WhAm 5
Harriman, Louis Howard 1868-1940
NatCAB 31
Harriman, Mary Williamson Averell 1851-1932
*NatCAB 23, NotAW, WhAm 1,
WomWWA 14*
Harriman, Oliver 1862-1940 *ApCAB X,
WhAm 1*
Harriman, Raymond Davis 1888- *WhAm 5*
Harriman, W Averell 1891- *McGEWB*
Harriman, Walter 1817-1884 *ApCAB, BiAUS,
DcAmB, Drake, NatCAB 11, TwCBDA,
WhAm H*
Harriman, William Averell 1891- *BiDrUSE,
EncAB, WebAB, WhWW-II*
Harrington, Arlan Foster 1910-1961
NatCAB 50
Harrington, Arthur William 1888-1964
WhAm 4
Harrington, Calvin Sears 1826-1886 *TwCBDA*
Harrington, Charles 1856-1908 *DcAmB,
WhAm 1*
Harrington, Charles, Earl Of 1753-1829 *ApCAB*
Harrington, Charles A 1874- *WhAm 5*
Harrington, Charles Kendall 1858-1920
WhAm 1
Harrington, Charles Medbury 1855-1928
WhAm 1, WhAm 1C
Harrington, Charles Stanhope 1753-1829 *Drake*
Harrington, Daniel 1878- *WhAm 6*
Harrington, David L 1894-1961 *WhAm 4*
Harrington, Denis Joseph 1883-1946
NatCAB 38
Harrington, Ebenezer Burke 1813-1844 *ApCAB*
Harrington, Edward Michael 1928- *EncAB*
Harrington, Edwin Ira 1894-1958 *NatCAB 47*
Harrington, Emerson Columbus 1864-
NatCAB 15, WhAm 4
Harrington, Francis Bishop 1854-1914 *WhAm 1*
Harrington, Francis Clark 1887-1940 *WhAm 1*
Harrington, Francis Edward 1879-1947
NatCAB 36
Harrington, Frank Annibal 1895-1959 *WhAm 3*
Harrington, G *NewYHSD*
Harrington, George 1815-1892 *BiAUS,
NatCAB 12*
Harrington, George 1833-1911 *NewYHSD*
Harrington, George Bates 1881-1960 *WhAm 4*
Harrington, Mrs. George F *WomWWA 14*
Harrington, Harry Franklin 1882-1935
BiDAmEd, WhAm 1
Harrington, Henry Hill 1859-1939 *NatCAB 33,
TwCBDA, WhAm 4*
Harrington, Henry William 1825-1882 *BiAUS,
BiDrAC, WhAm H*
Harrington, Howard Dewitt 1907-1974
WhAm 6
Harrington, James 1611-1677 *McGEWB*
Harrington, James Taylor 1877-1948
NatCAB 37
Harrington, John *NewYHSD*
Harrington, John Lyle 1868-1942 *DcAmB S3,
WhAm 2*
Harrington, John Thomas 1858-1947 *WhAm 2*
Harrington, John Truesdale 1873-1932
NatCAB 24, WhAm 1
Harrington, John Walker 1868-1952 *WhAm 3*
Harrington, Jonathan 1757-1854 *NatCAB 1*
Harrington, Joseph 1841-1900 *IlBEAAW*
Harrington, Joseph 1873-1959 *NatCAB 56,
WhAm 5*

Harrington, Joseph J 1813-1852 *ApCAB,
NatCAB 11*
Harrington, Karl Pomeroy 1861-1953
NatCAB 42, TwCBDA, WhAm 4
Harrington, Laura Frick 1851- *WomWWA 14*
Harrington, Leon W 1882-1965 *WhAm 4*
Harrington, Louis Clare 1879-1951 *NatCAB 42*
Harrington, Louis Clare 1880-1951 *WhAm 3*
Harrington, Lucy Irwin 1858- *WomWWA 14*
Harrington, Mark Raymond 1882-1971
WhAm 5
Harrington, Mark Walrod 1848-1926 *AmBi,
ApCAB, DcAmB, NatCAB 10, TwCBDA,
WhAm HA, WhAm 4*
Harrington, Michael Joseph 1936- *BiDrAC*
Harrington, Milton Alexander 1884-1942
NatCAB 31
Harrington, Philip 1886-1949 *WhAm 2*
Harrington, Purnell Frederick 1844-1937
NatCAB 27, TwCBDA, WhAm 1
Harrington, Russell Chase 1890-1971
NatCAB 56, WhAm 5
Harrington, Samuel M 1802-1865 *BiAUS*
Harrington, Samuel Maxwell 1803-1865 *ApCAB,
DcAmB, Drake, NatCAB 13, WhAm H*
Harrington, Samuel Milby 1882-1948 *WhAm 2*
Harrington, Sara Maria 1863- *WomWWA 14*
Harrington, Stuart William 1889-1973 *WhAm 5*
Harrington, Thomas Francis 1866-1919
*ApCAB X, DcAmB, NatCAB 22,
WhAm 1*
Harrington, Thomas Francis 1902-1955
NatCAB 44, WhAm 3
Harrington, Timothy 1715-1795 *ApCAB*
Harrington, Vernon Charles 1871-1942
NatCAB 32
Harrington, Vincent Francis 1903-1943 *BiDrAC,
NatCAB 33, WhAm 2, WhAmP*
Harrington, William H *NewYHSD*
Harrington, William Watson 1874-1959
NatCAB 49, WhAm 5
Harrington, Willis F 1882-1960 *WhAm 4*
Harriot, Josephine Ladenburg 1881-
WomWWA 14
Harriot, Samuel Carman 1863- *NatCAB 9*
Harriot, Thomas 1560-1621 *ApCAB, DcScB,
Drake*
Harriott, Frank 1842- *WhAm 4*
Harris, Mrs. *NewYHSD*
Harris, Abram Lincoln 1899-1963 *WhAm 4*
Harris, Abram Winegardner 1858-1935 *AmBi,
NatCAB 14, TwCBDA, WhAm 1*
Harris, Addison Clay 1840-1916 *ApCAB X,
NatCAB 12, NatCAB 17, TwCBDA,
WhAm 1*
Harris, Agnes Ellen 1883-1952 *WhAm 3,
WomWWA 14*
Harris, Albert Hall 1861-1931 *WhAm 1*
Harris, Albert Lewis 1869-1933 *NatCAB 24*
Harris, Albert Mason 1868-1945 *WhAm 2*
Harris, Albert Wadsworth 1867-1958
NatCAB 50, WhAm 5
Harris, Alexander 1885-1969 *WhAm 5*
Harris, Alfred F 1860-1943 *NatCAB 33,
WhAm 2*
Harris, Alfred Stull 1891-1947 *NatCAB 36,
WhAm 2*
Harris, Alfred William 1912-1966 *NatCAB 51*
Harris, Amanda Bartlett 1824-1917 *TwCBDA,
WhAm 1*
Harris, Andrew Lintner 1835-1915 *NatCAB 14,
WhAm 1*
Harris, Sir Arthur 1892- *WhWW-II,
WhoMilH*
Harris, Arthur Emerson 1870-1954 *NatCAB 40,
WhAm 3*
Harris, Arthur I 1882-1963 *WhAm 4*
Harris, Arthur Merriman 1865-1941
NatCAB 30, WhAm 1
Harris, Arvil Ernest 1898-1964 *WhAm 4*
Harris, B Felix 1894-1960 *NatCAB 48*
Harris, Basil 1889-1948 *NatCAB 38,
WhAm 2*
Harris, Belinda *NewYHSD*
Harris, Belle C 1856- *WomWWA 14*
Harris, Benjamin *DcAmB, NatCAB 25,
NewYHSD, WebAB, WhAm H*
Harris, Benjamin Bee 1886-1967 *WhAm 4*

Harris, Benjamin Franklin 1868-1920 *WhAm 1*
Harris, Benjamin Gwinn 1805-1895 *BiDrAC,
WhAm H, WhAmP*
Harris, Benjamin Gwinn 1806-1895 *BiAUS*
Harris, Benjamin Winslow 1823-1907 *BiAUS,
BiDrAC, WhAmP*
Harris, Bertha Wright Carr 1863-
WomWWA 14
Harris, Beverly Dabney 1872-1948 *NatCAB 38,
WhAm 2*
Harris, Bravid Washington 1896-1965
NatCAB 53, WhAm 4
Harris, Broughton Davis 1822- *NatCAB 4*
Harris, Burton Kenneth 1891-1948 *NatCAB 37*
Harris, Caleb Fiske 1818-1881 *ApCAB,
DcAmB, NatCAB 22, WhAm H*
Harris, Carl Alfred 1902-1967 *NatCAB 54*
Harris, Carl Wainwright 1881-1937
NatCAB 28
Harris, Carlton Danner 1864-1928 *WhAm 1*
Harris, Cary A *BiAUS*
Harris, Chapin Aaron 1806-1860 *AmBi,
ApCAB, BiDAmEd, DcAmB, Drake,
NatCAB 22, WebAB, WhAm H*
Harris, Chapman 1802-1890 *NatCAB 5*
Harris, Charles 1762-1825 *NatCAB 7*
Harris, Charles 1772-1827 *ApCAB*
Harris, Charles 1859-1943 *WhAm 2*
Harris, Charles Butler 1843- *WhAm 4*
Harris, Charles Cuthbert 1886-1959 *WhAm 4*
Harris, Charles Joseph 1853-1944 *NatCAB 34,
WhAm 2*
Harris, Charles Kassell 1865-1930 *AmBi,
DcAmB, NatCAB 23, WhAm 1*
Harris, Charles Miller 1868-1923 *NatCAB 17*
Harris, Charles Murray 1821-1896 *BiAUS,
BiDrAC, WhAm H*
Harris, Charles Nathan 1851-1929 *NatCAB 22*
Harris, Charles Tillman, Jr. 1884-1961
WhAm 4
Harris, Charles Willis 1873-1954 *WhAm 4*
Harris, Christina Phelps 1902-1972 *NatCAB 57*
Harris, Christopher Columbus 1842-1935
BiDrAC, WhAm 4
Harris, Cicero Richardson 1844-1917
ApCAB Sup, WhAm 1, WhoColR
Harris, Clinton Lee 1886-1944 *NatCAB 35*
Harris, Cora May White 1869-1935
WomWWA 14
Harris, Cornelia Burton 1882- *WomWWA 14*
Harris, Corra May White 1869-1935
NatCAB 26, NotAW, WhAm 1
Harris, Credo Fitch d1956 *WhAm 3*
Harris, D D 1887-1974 *WhAm 6*
Harris, Dallas Dale 1917-1959 *NatCAB 47*
Harris, Daniel Lester 1818-1879 *DcAmB,
WhAm H*
Harris, Daniel Lester 1894-1958 *NatCAB 47*
Harris, Daniel Smith 1808-1891 *REnAW*
Harris, David Bullock 1814-1864 *ApCAB,
TwCBDA*
Harris, David Urquhart 1888-1926 *NatCAB 20*
Harris, Dawson Bailey 1891-1953 *WhAm 3*
Harris, DeLancey Pike 1868-1949 *NatCAB 40*
Harris, Duncan G 1878-1970 *WhAm 5*
Harris, Edward *BiAUS*
Harris, Edward 1801-1872 *NatCAB 12*
Harris, Edward D *Drake*
Harris, Edwin Ewell 1867-1938 *WhAm 2*
Harris, Elbridge 1817?- *NewYHSD*
Harris, Elijah Paddock 1832-1920 *WhAm 1*
Harris, Elisha *BiAUS*
Harris, Elisha 1791-1861 *NatCAB 9*
Harris, Elisha 1824-1884 *AmBi, ApCAB,
DcAmB, NatCAB 9, TwCBDA,
WhAm H*
Harris, Eliza Burton *WomWWA 14*
Harris, Ella Isabel *WhAm 5*
Harris, Elliott 1914-1970 *NatCAB 55*
Harris, Elmer Blaney 1878-1966 *NatCAB 52*
Harris, Emerson Pitt 1853-1937 *WhAm 1*
Harris, Emma Gale 1848- *WomWWA 14*
Harris, Ethel Hillyer *AmWom*
Harris, Eugene Dennis 1911-1971 *WhAm 5*
Harris, Everett Earl 1887- *WhAm 3*
Harris, Florence Nightingale Knight 1872-
WomWWA 14
Harris, Francis Waller 1886-1959 *NatCAB 47*

Harris, Frank 1854-1931 *WhAm 1*
Harris, Frank 1856-1931 *AmBi, McGEWB*
Harris, Franklin Stewart 1884-1960 *BiDAmEd, NatCAB 53, WhAm 4*
Harris, Fred Roy 1930- *BiDrAC*
Harris, Frederic Robert 1875-1949 *NatCAB 38, WhAm 2*
Harris, Frederick Brown 1883-1970 *NatCAB 55, WhAm 5*
Harris, Garrard 1875-1927 *WhAm 1*
Harris, George *NewYHSD*
Harris, Lord George 1746-1829 *ApCAB, Drake*
Harris, George 1844-1922 *DcAmB, NatCAB 10, TwCBDA, WhAm 1*
Harris, George B 1848-1918 *WhAm 1*
Harris, George Barnes 1881-1970 *WhAm 5*
Harris, George D *NewYHSD*
Harris, George DeLancey 1894-1958 *NatCAB 47*
Harris, George Ellsworth 1892-1964 *WhAm 4*
Harris, George Emrick 1827-1911 *BiAUS, BiDrAC*
Harris, George Francis 1818-1888 *ApCAB Sup*
Harris, George Simmons 1881-1950 *NatCAB 38, WhAm 2*
Harris, George Stiles 1887-1957 *WhAm 3*
Harris, George Upham 1898-1971 *WhAm 5*
Harris, George W 1805-1869 *Drake*
Harris, George Waldo 1876-1950 *WhAm 3*
Harris, George Washington 1814-1869 *AmBi, ApCAB, DcAmB, NatCAB 4, WhAm H*
Harris, George Wesley 1884- *WhoColR*
Harris, George William 1849-1917 *TwCBDA, WhAm 1*
Harris, George William 1872-1964 *NatCAB 51, WhAm 4*
Harris, George Winans 1868-1957 *NatCAB 52*
Harris, Gilbert Dennison 1864-1952 *NatCAB 41, TwCBDA, WhAm 3*
Harris, Grady DeWitt, Jr. 1926-1974 *WhAm 6*
Harris, Guy W 1878- *WhAm 5*
Harris, Hamilton 1820-1900 *ApCAB, NatCAB 1, TwCBDA, WhAm 1*
Harris, Hannah Margaret 1865- *WomWWA 14*
Harris, Harriette D 1864- *WomWWA 14*
Harris, Harry Ezekiel, Sr. 1878- *WhAm 6*
Harris, Hayden Bartlett 1885-1951 *NatCAB 40*
Harris, Heaton W 1858- *WhAm 4*
Harris, Henrietta Clark *WomWWA 14*
Harris, Henry Archibald 1885- *NatCAB 17*
Harris, Henry Burkhardt 1866-1912 *NatCAB 19, WhAm 1*
Harris, Henry Fauntleroy 1867- *WhAm 4*
Harris, Henry Herbert 1837-1897 *TwCBDA*
Harris, Henry Hickman 1899-1965 *NatCAB 53*
Harris, Henry Hiter 1893-1952 *WhAm 3*
Harris, Henry Richard 1828-1909 *BiAUS, BiDrAC*
Harris, Henry Schenck 1850-1902 *BiDrAC*
Harris, Henry Tudor Brownell 1845-1920 *WhAm 1*
Harris, Herbert Eugene 1875- *WhAm 5*
Harris, Hugh Henry 1875- *WhAm 5*
Harris, Ira 1802-1875 *ApCAB, BiAUS, BiDrAC, DcAmB, Drake, NatCAB 2, TwCBDA, WhAm H*
Harris, Isaac Burt 1873-1953 *NatCAB 41*
Harris, Isaac Faust 1879-1953 *NatCAB 42*
Harris, Isham Green 1818-1897 *AmBi, ApCAB, BiAUS, BiDConf, BiDrAC, DcAmB, Drake, NatCAB 2, NatCAB 7, TwCBDA, WhAm H, WhAmP*
Harris, Iverson Louis 1860-1921 *NatCAB 19*
Harris, J Morrison 1821-1898 *BiAUS, NatCAB 3*
Harris, James *NewYHSD*
Harris, James 1808?-1846 *NewYHSD*
Harris, James A 1870-1947 *WhAm 2*
Harris, James Alexander 1863-1914 *NatCAB 8*
Harris, James Armstrong 1847-1921 *NatCAB 19*
Harris, James Arthur 1880-1930 *DcAmB, NatCAB 22, WhAm 1*
Harris, James Coffee 1858-1940 *WhAm 1*
Harris, James F *NewYHSD*
Harris, James Morrison 1817-1898 *BiDrAC*
Harris, James William 1854-1943 *NatCAB 32*

Harris, Jane Howell *WomWWA 14*
Harris, Janet Simons 1869- *WomWWA 14*
Harris, Joel Chandler 1848-1908 *AmBi, ApCAB, ApCAB X, DcAmB, EncAAH, EncAB, McGEWB, NatCAB 1, TwCBDA, WebAB, WhAm 1*
Harris, John 1666?-1719 *DcScB*
Harris, John 1716-1791 *ApCAB*
Harris, John 1726-1791 *DcAmB, NatCAB 12, WhAm H*
Harris, John 1760-1824 *BiAUS, BiDrAC, WhAm H*
Harris, John 1795?-1864 *WebAMB*
Harris, John A 1826- *BiAUS*
Harris, John Andrews 1834- *WhAm 4*
Harris, John Andrews, Jr. d1940 *WhAm 1*
Harris, John Augustus 1890-1951 *WhAm 3*
Harris, John Barnes 1877-1952 *NatCAB 41*
Harris, John Burke 1887-1957 *WhAm 3*
Harris, John Campbell 1840-1916 *ApCAB X*
Harris, John David 1889-1962 *NatCAB 49*
Harris, John Dennis *ApCAB Sup*
Harris, John Harper 1910-1970 *WhAm 5*
Harris, John Howard 1847-1925 *NatCAB 12, NatCAB 22, TwCBDA, WhAm 1*
Harris, John Huggins 1898-1959 *NatCAB 47*
Harris, John Peter 1901-1969 *WhAm 5*
Harris, John Royall 1869-1926 *WhAm 1*
Harris, John Spafford 1825-1906 *ApCAB, BiDrAC, NatCAB 4*
Harris, John Thomas 1823-1899 *BiAUS, BiDrAC, NatCAB 10, TwCBDA, WhAmP*
Harris, John Thomas 1825-1899 *ApCAB*
Harris, John Warton 1891-1955 *WhAm 3*
Harris, John Woods 1810-1887 *ApCAB, DcAmB, WhAm H*
Harris, Jonathan Newton 1815-1896 *ApCAB Sup, NatCAB 3, TwCBDA*
Harris, Joseph 1828-1892 *DcAmB, WhAm H*
Harris, Joseph 1854-1936 *WhAm 1*
Harris, Joseph B 1859- *WhAm 4*
Harris, Joseph Hastings 1870-1941 *WhAm 1*
Harris, Joseph Smith 1836-1910 *WhAm 1*
Harris, Joseph T *NewYHSD*
Harris, Julia Collier 1875- *WhAm 5*
Harris, Julia Fillmore 1878- *WhAm 6*
Harris, Julian Hartwell 1876-1933 *NatCAB 25*
Harris, Julian LaRose 1874-1963 *WhAm 4*
Harris, LaDonna 1931- *REnAW*
Harris, Lancelot Minor 1868- *WhAm 4*
Harris, Lawren Stewart 1885-1970 *IIBEAAW*
Harris, Leavitt *BiAUS*
Harris, Lee A 1880-1944 *WhAm 2*
Harris, Leon Abraham 1886-1935 *NatCAB 26*
Harris, Leon R 1886- *WhoColR*
Harris, Leslie Huntington 1883-1920 *WhAm 1*
Harris, Lillie Coyle Hench *WomWWA 14*
Harris, Lina Small 1882- *WomWWA 14*
Harris, Linnie Sarah 1868- *WomWWA 14*
Harris, Lloyd Webb 1922-1974 *WhAm 6*
Harris, Lorin Benjamin 1870-1950 *NatCAB 40*
Harris, Louis 1921- *WebAB*
Harris, Louis Israel 1882-1939 *NatCAB 28, WhAm 1*
Harris, Louis Marshall 1900-1955 *WhAm 3*
Harris, Lucy A Bailey 1858- *WomWWA 14*
Harris, M Anstice 1857-1956 *NatCAB 45, WhAm 3*
Harris, Malcolm LaSalle 1862-1936 *NatCAB 26, WhAm 1*
Harris, Mark 1779-1843 *BiAUS, BiDrAC, WhAm H*
Harris, Mary Belle d1957 *WhAm 3, WomWWA 14*
Harris, Mattie Powell *WhAm 5*
Harris, Maurice Henry 1859-1930 *DcAmB, WhAm 1*
Harris, May 1873- *WhAm 5*
Harris, Maynard Lawrence 1902-1974 *WhAm 6*
Harris, Merriman Colbert 1846-1921 *DcAmB, NatCAB 14, WhAm 1*
Harris, Minnie Greenwood *WomWWA 14*
Harris, Miriam Coles 1834-1925 *ApCAB, DcAmB, NatCAB 11, TwCBDA, WhAm 4, WomWWA 14*
Harris, Montefiore M 1884-1956 *WhAm 3*
Harris, Morris Bedford 1866-1941 *WhAm 2*

Harris, Moses Henry 1845-1911 *WhAm 1*
Harris, Nathaniel Edwin 1846-1929 *NatCAB 23, WhAm 1*
Harris, Nathaniel Harrison 1834-1900 *BiDConf, DcAmB*
Harris, Newton Megrue 1872- *WhAm 5*
Harris, Norman Dwight 1870- *ApCAB X, WhAm 5*
Harris, Norman W 1894-1965 *WhAm 4*
Harris, Norman Wait 1846-1916 *ApCAB X, NatCAB 17, WhAm 1*
Harris, Oren 1903- *BiDrAC, WhAmP*
Harris, Orion Wendell 1908-1962 *NatCAB 52*
Harris, Overton 1856-1931 *WhAm 1*
Harris, Paul Percy 1868-1947 *ApCAB X, DcAmB S4, NatCAB 33, WhAm 2*
Harris, Peter 1750?-1830 *ApCAB*
Harris, Peter Charles 1865-1951 *WhAm 3*
Harris, Philander Abbey 1852-1924 *NatCAB 40*
Harris, Philip Howard 1881-1956 *NatCAB 42, WhAm 3*
Harris, Philip Spooner 1824-1884 *NewYHSD*
Harris, Pierce 1895-1971 *WhAm 5*
Harris, Prince Edward 1871-1952 *NatCAB 39*
Harris, Mrs. Ralph A d1952 *WhAm 3*
Harris, Ralph Scott 1889-1961 *WhAm 4*
Harris, Reese Harvey 1883- *WhAm 3*
Harris, Richard Lamar 1896-1955 *NatCAB 44*
Harris, Robert 1768-1851 *BiAUS, BiDrAC, WhAm H*
Harris, Robert 1849- *ApCAB*
Harris, Robert Alfred 1905-1969 *WhAm 5*
Harris, Robert George 1911- *IIBEAAW*
Harris, Robert Lee, Jr. 1909-1965 *NatCAB 51*
Harris, Robert LeRoy 1874-1948 *NatCAB 37, WhAm 2*
Harris, Robert Orr 1854-1926 *BiDrAC, WhAm 1, WhAmP*
Harris, Rollin Arthur 1863-1918 *DcAmB, NatCAB 22, WhAm 1*
Harris, Roscoe Everett 1896-1949 *NatCAB 42*
Harris, Rowland Hill 1878-1961 *NatCAB 49*
Harris, Roy Ellsworth 1898- *McGEWB, WebAB*
Harris, Ruth Miriam 1898-1972 *WhAm 5*
Harris, Sam Henry 1872-1941 *DcAmB S3, WhAm 1*
Harris, Sampson Willis 1809-1857 *BiAUS, BiDrAC, WhAm H, WhAmP*
Harris, Samuel 1724-1794 *ApCAB, Drake*
Harris, Samuel 1783-1810 *NewYHSD*
Harris, Samuel 1814-1899 *ApCAB, BiDAmEd, DcAmB, Drake, NatCAB 1, TwCBDA, WhAm H, WhAm 1*
Harris, Samuel Arthur 1847-1908 *NatCAB 6*
Harris, Samuel Henry 1858-1939 *WhAm 1*
Harris, Samuel Smith 1841-1888 *ApCAB, NatCAB 13, TwCBDA, WhAm H*
Harris, Seale 1870-1957 *WhAm 3*
Harris, Seward 1882-1962 *NatCAB 51*
Harris, Seymour Edwin 1897-1974 *WhAm 6*
Harris, Sherwin Bentley 1909-1970 *WhAm 5*
Harris, Silas Adelbert 1888-1942 *NatCAB 35*
Harris, Squire Rush 1854-1930 *NatCAB 21*
Harris, Stanley G 1890-1971 *WhAm 5*
Harris, Stephen Ross 1824-1905 *BiDrAC, TwCBDA*
Harris, Thaddeus Mason 1768-1842 *ApCAB, DcAmB, Drake, NatCAB 8, TwCBDA, WhAm H*
Harris, Thaddeus William 1795-1856 *AmBi, ApCAB, DcAmB, Drake, TwCBDA, WhAm H*
Harris, Theona Clare Peck *WomWWA 14*
Harris, Thomas Alexander 1826-1895 *BiDConf*
Harris, Thomas Cadwalader 1825-1875 *ApCAB, TwCBDA*
Harris, Thomas Green 1854- *WhAm 4*
Harris, Thomas Jefferson 1865-1943 *NatCAB 33, WhAm 2*
Harris, Thomas K d1816 *BiAUS, BiDrAC, WhAm H*
Harris, Thomas L 1824-1906 *Drake*
Harris, Thomas Lake 1823-1906 *AmBi, ApCAB, DcAmB, NatCAB 53*
Harris, Thomas Langrell 1816-1858 *BiAUS, BiDrAC, Drake, WhAm H*

Harris, Thomas LeGrand 1863-1941
NatCAB 41, WhAm 1
Harris, Thomas Luther 1876-1955 *NatCAB 43,*
WhAm 4
Harris, Thomas Mealey 1817- *ApCAB*
Harris, Titus Holliday 1892-1969 *NatCAB 55,*
WhAm 5
Harris, Townsend d1878 *BiAUS*
Harris, Townsend 1803-1878 *ApCAB,*
NatCAB 5
Harris, Townsend 1804-1878 *AmBi, DcAmB,*
EncAB, McGEWB, TwCBDA, WebAB,
WhAm H
Harris, Uriah Rose 1849-1930 *WhAm 1*
Harris, Victor 1869- *WhAm 5*
Harris, W John 1852-1946 *NatCAB 7*
Harris, W John *see also* Harris, William John
Harris, W L *BiAUS*
Harris, Wade Hampton 1858-1935 *WhAm 1*
Harris, Wade Negley 1906-1967 *NatCAB 54,*
WhAm 5
Harris, Walter 1647-1732 *BiHiMed*
Harris, Walter Alexander 1875-1958 *WhAm 3*
Harris, Walter Butler 1865-1935 *WhAm 1*
Harris, Walter Edward 1868-1939 *WhAm 1*
Harris, Walter William 1894-1952 *WhAm 3*
Harris, Wiley Pope 1818-1891 *BiAUS,*
BiDConf, BiDrAC, DcAmB, NatCAB 4,
WhAm H
Harris, William 1765-1829 *ApCAB, DcAmB,*
Drake, NatCAB 6, TwCBDA, WhAm H
Harris, William, Jr. 1884-1946 *NatCAB 35,*
WhAm 2
Harris, William Alexander 1805-1864 *BiAUS,*
BiDrAC, NatCAB 12, WhAm H,
WhAmP
Harris, William Alexander 1841-1909
ApCAB Sup, BiDrAC, DcAmB,
NatCAB 13, TwCBDA, WhAm 1,
WhAmP
Harris, William Anderson 1827-1895 *ApCAB,*
TwCBDA
Harris, William Charles 1830-1905 *WhAm 1*
Harris, William Delaware 1890-1953
NatCAB 42
Harris, William Detwiler 1883-1949
NatCAB 39
Harris, William Fenwick 1868-1923 *WhAm 1*
Harris, William Hall 1852-1938 *WhAm 1*
Harris, William Henry 1876-1959 *NatCAB 48*
Harris, William John 1852-1946 *WhAm 3*
Harris, William John *see also* Harris, W John
Harris, William Julius 1868-1932 *ApCAB X,*
BiDrAC, NatCAB 24, WhAm 1,
WhAmP
Harris, William Laurel 1870-1924 *NatCAB 15,*
WhAm 1
Harris, William Lee 1880-1954 *NatCAB 44*
Harris, William Littleton 1807-1868 *DcAmB,*
NatCAB 22, WhAm H
Harris, William Logan 1817-1887 *ApCAB,*
DcAmB, NatCAB 10, TwCBDA,
WhAm H
Harris, William R d1868 *BiAUS*
Harris, William Thaddeus 1826-1854 *ApCAB,*
Drake
Harris, William Torrey 1835-1909 *AmBi,*
ApCAB, BiDAmEd, DcAmB, DcAmLiB,
EncAB, McGEWB, NatCAB 4,
NatCAB 15, TwCBDA, WebAB,
WhAm 1
Harris, William Welton 1866-1932 *WhAm 1*
Harris, Willis Overton 1847-1911 *WhAm 1*
Harris, Winder Russell 1888-1973 *BiDrAC,*
WhAm 5
Harrison, Adelia Leftwich 1868-
WomWWA 14
Harrison, Albert Galliton 1800-1839 *BiAUS,*
BiDrAC, WhAm H
Harrison, Albert Micajah 1849-1916
NatCAB 17
Harrison, Alexander 1853-1930 *AmBi, DcAmB,*
NatCAB 11, WhAm 1
Harrison, Alfred Craven 1846-1927 *NatCAB 32*
Harrison, Alfred Craven, Jr. 1875- *WhAm 5*
Harrison, Alice Sinclair 1882-1967 *DcAmLiB*
Harrison, Anna Symmes 1775-1864 *AmWom,*
ApCAB, NatCAB 3, NotAW, TwCBDA

Harrison, Archibald Cunningham 1864-1926
NatCAB 20
Harrison, B George 1889- *WhAm 3*
Harrison, Belle Richardson 1856- *WhAm 4*
Harrison, Benjamin d1791 *BiAUS*
Harrison, Benjamin 1726?-1791 *AmBi,*
BiDrAC, DcAmB, NatCAB 10, TwCBDA,
WhAm H, WhAmP
Harrison, Benjamin 1740?-1791 *ApCAB,*
Drake
Harrison, Benjamin 1833-1901 *AmBi, ApCAB,*
ApCAB Sup, BiDrAC, BiDrUSE,
DcAmB, EncAAH, EncAB, McGEWB,
NatCAB 1, TwCBDA, WebAB, WhAm 1,
WhAmP
Harrison, Benjamin 1888-1960 *WhAm 4*
Harrison, Benjamin Franklin 1875- *WhAm 5*
Harrison, Benjamin Inabnit 1902-1965
WhAm 4
Harrison, Benjamin J *NewYHSD*
Harrison, Bernard Johnston 1875-1941
NatCAB 39
Harrison, Beverley Randolph 1900-1968
NatCAB 54
Harrison, Birge 1854-1929 *AmBi, DcAmB,*
NatCAB 11, NatCAB 26, TwCBDA,
WhAm 1
Harrison, Bruce Magill 1881- *WhAm 6*
Harrison, Burr Powell 1875-1942 *NatCAB 32*
Harrison, Burr Powell 1904-1973 *BiDrAC,*
WhAm 6, WhAmP
Harrison, Mrs. Burton *NotAW*
Harrison, Burton Norvell 1838-1909 *ApCAB X*
Harrison, Byron Patton 1881-1941 *ApCAB X,*
BiDrAC, DcAmB S3, WhAmP
Harrison, Caroline Lavinia Scott 1832-1892
AmWom, ApCAB Sup, NatCAB 1,
NotAW, TwCBDA
Harrison, Carrie *WomWWA 14*
Harrison, Carter B *BiAUS*
Harrison, Carter Bassett d1804 *TwCBDA*
Harrison, Carter Bassett d1808 *BiDrAC,*
WhAm H
Harrison, Carter Henry 1825-1893 *AmBi,*
ApCAB, BiAUS, BiDrAC, DcAmB,
NatCAB 10, TwCBDA, WhAm H,
WhAmP
Harrison, Carter Henry 1860-1953 *DcAmB S5,*
TwCBDA, WhAm 3
Harrison, Charles *Drake, NewYHSD*
Harrison, Charles A 1893-1955 *WhAm 3*
Harrison, Charles Curtis 1844-1929 *NatCAB 13*
Harrison, Charles Custis 1844-1929 *DcAmB,*
NatCAB 29, TwCBDA, WhAm 1
Harrison, Charles Custis, III 1907-1972
NatCAB 57
Harrison, Charles Custis, Jr. 1877-1948
NatCAB 48
Harrison, Charles Luce 1883-1944 *NatCAB 39*
Harrison, Charles P 1783-1854 *NewYHSD*
Harrison, Charles Yale 1898-1954 *WhAm 3*
Harrison, Christopher 1775-1863 *NewYHSD,*
WhAm H
Harrison, Constance Cary d1920 *ApCAB X*
Harrison, Constance Cary 1835?-1920 *AmWom,*
ApCAB
Harrison, Constance Cary 1843-1920 *AmBi,*
DcAmB, NotAW, WhAm 1
Harrison, Constance Cary 1845?-1920
NatCAB 4
Harrison, Constance Cary 1846-1920
WomWWA 14
Harrison, Constance Cary 1848-1920 *TwCBDA*
Harrison, David R *NewYHSD*
Harrison, DeSales 1899-1973 *WhAm 5*
Harrison, Earl Grant 1899-1955 *NatCAB 41,*
WhAm 3
Harrison, Edith Ogden d1955 *WhAm 3,*
WomWWA 14
Harrison, Edward Tyler 1878-1959 *WhAm 4*
Harrison, Edwin 1836-1905 *NatCAB 15,*
WhAm 1
Harrison, Elizabeth 1849-1927 *BiDAmEd,*
DcAmB, NatCAB 21, NotAW, WhAm 1
Harrison, Fairfax 1869-1938 *ApCAB X,*
DcAmB S2, WhAm 1
Harrison, Florence *WomWWA 14*
Harrison, Floyd Reed 1889-1961 *NatCAB 46,*

WhAm 4
Harrison, Francis Burton 1873-1957 *ApCAB X,*
BiDrAC, NatCAB 46, WhAm 3,
WhAmP
Harrison, Fred 1874-1929 *WhAm 1*
Harrison, Gabriel 1818-1902 *DcAmB,*
NatCAB 5, NewYHSD, TwCBDA
Harrison, Gabriel 1825-1902 *ApCAB,*
WhAm 1
Harrison, George d1830 *NewYHSD*
Harrison, George 1599?-1624 *ApCAB Sup*
Harrison, George Billingsley 1870- *WhAm 5*
Harrison, George Leib 1811-1885 *ApCAB*
Harrison, George Leslie 1887-1958 *NatCAB 51,*
WhAm 3
Harrison, George McGregor 1895-1968
WhAm 5
Harrison, George Moffett 1847-1923
NatCAB 20, WhAm 1
Harrison, George Paul 1841-1922 *BiDrAC,*
DcAmB, NatCAB 8, TwCBDA,
WhAm 4
Harrison, George Torrence 1847-1902
NatCAB 26
Harrison, George Tucker 1835-1925
NatCAB 12, NatCAB 22
Harrison, Gertrude Freutagh VanVleek
WomWWA 14
Harrison, Gertrude Gordon Grayson 1892-1961
NatCAB 51
Harrison, Gessner 1807-1862 *ApCAB, DcAmB,*
TwCBDA, WhAm H
Harrison, Gilbert Newton 1866-1927
NatCAB 21
Harrison, Hall 1837-1900 *ApCAB, TwCBDA,*
WhAm 1
Harrison, Hamlett 1910-1970 *WhAm 5*
Harrison, Harold Charles 1907-1970
NatCAB 56
Harrison, Harold Everus 1904-1972 *WhAm 6*
Harrison, Harry 1877-1957 *NatCAB 47*
Harrison, Harry Lincoln 1867-1952 *NatCAB 42*
Harrison, Harry P 1878-1968 *WhAm 5*
Harrison, Harvey Thomas 1884-1942 *WhAm 2*
Harrison, Henry *NewYHSD*
Harrison, Henry Baldwin 1821-1901 *DcAmB,*
NatCAB 10, TwCBDA
Harrison, Henry Sydnor 1880-1930 *AmBi,*
ApCAB X, DcAmB, NatCAB 21,
WhAm 1
Harrison, Herbert Champion 1876-1927
NatCAB 24
Harrison, Horace Harrison 1829-1885 *BiAUS,*
BiDrAC, WhAm H
Harrison, Ida Withers 1851-1927 *WhAm 1,*
WomWWA 14
Harrison, Ike H 1909-1971 *WhAm 5*
Harrison, J Max 1914-1966 *NatCAB 55*
Harrison, J P *NewYHSD*
Harrison, James 1803-1870 *DcAmB,*
NatCAB 22, WhAm H
Harrison, James Albert 1848-1911 *AmBi,*
ApCAB, DcAmB, TwCBDA, WhAm 1
Harrison, James D d1972 *WhAm 5*
Harrison, James Jabez 1891-1943 *WhAm 2*
Harrison, James Leftwich 1895-1973 *WhAm 6*
Harrison, James Orlando 1804-1888
NatCAB 21
Harrison, James Pinckney 1896-1968
NatCAB 54
Harrison, James Thomas 1811-1879 *ApCAB,*
BiDConf, NatCAB 12, TwCBDA
Harrison, Jamison Richard 1903-1966 *WhAm 4*
Harrison, Jay Smolens 1927-1974 *WhAm 6*
Harrison, Jerome Gabriel 1883-1961
NatCAB 51
Harrison, Jesse Burton 1805-1841 *ApCAB X*
Harrison, John 1693-1776 *AsBiEn, DcScB*
Harrison, John 1773-1833 *ApCAB, DcAmB,*
NatCAB 13, WhAm H
Harrison, John B 1861-1947 *NatCAB 40,*
WhAm 2
Harrison, John Cleves Short 1829-1904
NatCAB 8
Harrison, John DeHart 1889-1943 *NatCAB 35*
Harrison, John Ellis 1854- *WhAm 4*
Harrison, John Green 1869-1934 *WhAm 1*
Harrison, John Higgins 1867-1930 *WhAm 1*

Harrison, John Hoffman 1808-1849 *ApCAB*

Harrison, John Scott 1804-1878 *ApCAB, BiAUS, BiDrAC, TwCBDA, WhAm H, WhAmP*

Harrison, John Smith 1877- *WhAm 5*

Harrison, John Thomas 1877- *WhoColR*

Harrison, Jonathan Baxter 1835-1907 *WhAm 1*

Harrison, Joseph 1810-1874 *AmBi, ApCAB, DcAmB, NatCAB 12, WhAm H*

Harrison, Joseph LeRoy 1862-1950 *NatCAB 9, TwCBDA, WhAm 3*

Harrison, Leland 1883-1951 *NatCAB 38*

Harrison, Leland 1893-1951 *WhAm 3*

Harrison, Leon 1866-1928 *WhAm 1*

Harrison, Leonard Vance 1891-1969 *NatCAB 55*

Harrison, Lester Stanley 1889-1966 *WhAm 4*

Harrison, Lillian Byrn *WomWWA 14*

Harrison, Louise 1875- *WomWWA 14*

Harrison, Louise Thatcher 1883- *WomWWA 14*

Harrison, Lovell Birge 1854-1929 *AmBi, DcAmB, IIBEAAW*

Harrison, Lucy d1826 *ApCAB*

Harrison, Lucy Gray *WomWWA 14*

Harrison, Luther 1877-1959 *WhAm 3*

Harrison, Lynde 1837-1906 *NatCAB 8, TwCBDA, WhAm 1*

Harrison, M F *NewYHSD*

Harrison, Marion Myrl 1890-1946 *NatCAB 35*

Harrison, Mark Robert 1819-1894 *NewYHSD, WhAm H*

Harrison, Mary Middleton 1860- *WomWWA 14*

Harrison, Mary Scott Lord Dimmick 1858-1948 *BiCAW, NotAW, WhAm 2, WomWWA 14*

Harrison, Maurice Edward 1888-1951 *NatCAB 39, WhAm 3*

Harrison, Max Clark 1905-1966 *NatCAB 53*

Harrison, Miller Thurman 1897-1948 *NatCAB 39*

Harrison, Milton 1889-1949 *WhAm 2*

Harrison, Milton F 1817?- *NewYHSD*

Harrison, Napoleon Bonaparte 1823-1870 *ApCAB, Drake, TwCBDA*

Harrison, Orla Ellsworth 1873-1925 *WhAm 1*

Harrison, Pat 1881-1941 *DcAmB S3, WhAm 1*

Harrison, Pearl Adele Landers 1874- *WomWWA 14*

Harrison, Peleg Dennis 1843- *WhAm 4*

Harrison, Perry Galbraith 1885-1959 *NatCAB 45, WhAm 3*

Harrison, Persis Jones 1875- *WomWWA 14*

Harrison, Peter 1716-1775 *BnEnAmA, DcAmB, McGEWB, NatCAB 23, WebAB, WhAm H*

Harrison, Preston 1869-1940 *NatCAB 29*

Harrison, R A 1833-1878 *Drake*

Harrison, Ralph Chandler 1831-1918 *NatCAB 21, WhAm 1*

Harrison, Ray 1895-1957 *WhAm 3*

Harrison, Raymond Leyden 1896-1960 *WhAm 4*

Harrison, Richard 1750-1841 *ApCAB, BiAUS, Drake*

Harrison, Richard A 1827-1904 *BiAUS*

Harrison, Richard Almgill 1824-1904 *BiDrAC, NatCAB 12, WhAm 1*

Harrison, Richard Berry 1864-1935 *AmBi, DcAmB S1, NatCAB 26, WhAm 1*

Harrison, Richard G 1790?- *NewYHSD*

Harrison, Richard G, Jr. *NewYHSD*

Harrison, Robert A *NewYHSD*

Harrison, Robert Alexander 1833-1878 *ApCAB*

Harrison, Robert Dinsmore 1897- *BiDrAC*

Harrison, Robert Hanson 1745-1790 *AmBi, ApCAB, BiAUS, Drake, NatCAB 1*

Harrison, Robert Waite 1872-1969 *NatCAB 55*

Harrison, Roger Wayles 1876-1961 *NatCAB 50*

Harrison, Roland Rathbun 1878-1940 *WhAm 1*

Harrison, Roland Rathbun 1878-1941 *NatCAB 30*

Harrison, Roland Wendell 1897-1964 *WhAm 4*

Harrison, Ross Granville 1870-1959 *DcScB, NatCAB 15, WebAB, WhAm 3*

Harrison, Roy Bertrand 1891-1954 *NatCAB 43*

Harrison, Roy Joseph 1893-1968 *NatCAB 55*

Harrison, Russell Benjamin 1854-1936 *NatCAB 27, WhAm 1*

Harrison, S D *NewYHSD*

Harrison, S S 1780-1853 *BiAUS*

Harrison, Samuel *NewYHSD*

Harrison, Samuel 1789?-1818 *NewYHSD*

Harrison, Samuel Bealy 1802-1867 *ApCAB*

Harrison, Samuel Smith 1780-1853 *BiDrAC, WhAm H*

Harrison, Sarah 1748?-1812 *ApCAB*

Harrison, Shelby Millard 1881-1970 *WhAm 5*

Harrison, Stephen Noble 1910-1962 *WhAm 4*

Harrison, Susie Frances 1860?- *ApCAB Sup, WomWWA 14*

Harrison, Thomas *NewYHSD*

Harrison, Thomas 1823-1891 *BiDConf*

Harrison, Thomas 1839- *ApCAB, ApCAB Sup*

Harrison, Thomas Alexander 1853-1930 *AmBi, DcAmB, TwCBDA*

Harrison, Thomas Asbury 1811-1887 *NatCAB 6*

Harrison, Thomas Perrin 1864-1949 *TwCBDA, WhAm 2*

Harrison, Thomas Samuel 1881-1964 *NatCAB 52*

Harrison, Thomas Skelton 1837-1919 *NatCAB 27, WhAm 1*

Harrison, Thomas Walter 1856-1935 *BiDrAC, WhAm 1, WhAmP*

Harrison, V F *NewYHSD*

Harrison, Virgil F 1817?- *NewYHSD*

Harrison, W Vernon 1879-1929 *WhAm 1*

Harrison, Walter Hamilton 1863-1955 *NatCAB 42*

Harrison, Walter Munford 1888-1961 *WhAm 4*

Harrison, Ward 1888-1970 *WhAm 5*

Harrison, Wayles Randolph 1895-1949 *NatCAB 38*

Harrison, William *BiAUS, NewYHSD*

Harrison, William 1873-1945 *NatCAB 35*

Harrison, William, Jr. *BiDrAC, NewYHSD, WhAm H*

Harrison, William, Sr. d1803 *NewYHSD*

Harrison, William Benjamin 1889-1948 *WhAm 2*

Harrison, William F 1812?- *NewYHSD*

Harrison, William Gilpin 1802-1883 *NatCAB 18*

Harrison, William Groce 1871- *WhAm 5*

Harrison, William Henry 1773-1841 *AmBi, ApCAB, BiAUS, BiDrAC, BiDrUSE, DcAmB, Drake, EncAAH, EncAB, McGEWB, NatCAB 3, REnAW, TwCBDA, WebAB, WebAMB, WhAm H, WhAmP*

Harrison, William Henry 1813-1891 *NatCAB 28*

Harrison, William Henry 1880-1955 *WhAm 3*

Harrison, William Henry 1892-1956 *WhAm 3*

Harrison, William Henry 1896- *BiDrAC, WhAmP*

Harrison, William Moore 1912-1974 *WhAm 6*

Harrison, William Mortimer 1892-1965 *WhAm 4*

Harrison, William P 1887-1955 *NatCAB 45*

Harrison, William Pope 1830-1895 *DcAmB, NatCAB 22, TwCBDA, WhAm H*

Harrison, William Preston 1869-1940 *WhAm 1*

Harrison, William Robert 1869-1937 *WhAm 1*

Harrison, William Thomas 1890-1959 *NatCAB 48*

Harrison, Zadok Daniel 1842- *WhAm 4*

Harriss, Richard Tompkins 1879- *ApCAB X*

Harriss, Robert Raines 1907-1960 *NatCAB 46*

Harrisse, Henri 1829-1910 *NatCAB 18*

Harrisse, Henry 1829-1910 *DcAmB S1, DcAmLiB*

Harrisse, Henry 1830-1910 *AmBi, ApCAB Sup*

Harrity, William Francis 1850-1912 *NatCAB 3, NatCAB 25, WhAm 1*

Harrod, Benjamin Morgan 1837-1912 *DcAmB, NatCAB 12, WhAm 1*

Harrod, James 1742?-1793 *AmBi, DcAmB, Drake, NatCAB 12, REnAW, WhAm H*

Harrod, James 1746-1825? *ApCAB*

Harroff, Fred F 1896-1955 *WhAm 3*

Harrold, Charles Cotton 1878-1948 *NatCAB 36, WhAm 2*

Harrold, Charles Walter 1881-1956 *NatCAB 45*

Harrold, Helen Shaw 1878- *WomWWA 14*

Harrold, Orville 1877-1933 *NatCAB 25, WhAm 1*

Harron, Julia Augusta Scofield *WomWWA 14*

Harron, Marion Janet 1903-1972 *WhAm 5*

Harrop, George Argale, Jr. 1890-1945 *WhAm 2*

Harrop, Leslie DeVottie 1901-1964 *WhAm 4*

Harroun, Gilbert King 1835-1901 *NatCAB 11*

Harrow, Benjamin 1888- *WhAm 5*

Harrow, William 1820?- *ApCAB*

Harrower, David 1857-1937 *NatCAB 33*

Harry, Joseph Edward 1863-1949 *TwCBDA, WhAm 2*

Harry, Lee Cohen 1849- *AmWom*

Harry, Philip *NewYHSD*

Harsch, Leila Katherine Close 1875- *WomWWA 14*

Harsh, David Newby 1897-1972 *WhAm 5*

Harsh, James Birney 1845-1923 *WhAm 1*

Harsh, Philip Whaley 1905-1960 *NatCAB 48, WhAm 4*

Harsha 590?-647 *McGEWB*

Harsha, David Addison 1827- *ApCAB, Drake*

Harsha, William Howard 1921- *BiDrAC*

Harsha, William McIntire 1855-1943 *NatCAB 16, WhAm 2*

Harsha, William Thomas 1884-1950 *WhAm 3*

Harshaw, William Andrew 1861-1940 *NatCAB 34*

Harshaw, William Jacob 1891-1965 *WhAm 4*

Harshbarger, Charles Lester 1896-1950 *NatCAB 39*

Harshbarger, William Asbury 1862- *WhAm 4*

Harshberger, John William 1869-1929 *DcAmB, NatCAB 13, NatCAB 21, TwCBDA, WhAm 1*

Harshe, Robert Bartholow 1879-1938 *DcAmB S2, WhAm 1*

Harshman, Walter Scott Dean 1859-1924 *NatCAB 27, WhAm 1*

Harson, M Joseph 1856-1930 *WhAm 1*

Harston, Charles Grenville 1844- *ApCAB*

Harstrom, Carl Axel 1863-1926 *WhAm 1*

Hart, A G *NewYHSD*

Hart, Abraham 1810-1885 *ApCAB, DcAmB, WhAm H*

Hart, Alan L 1890-1962 *NatCAB 51*

Hart, Albert Bushnell 1854-1943 *ApCAB X, BiDAmEd, DcAmB S3, NatCAB 11, NatCAB 47, TwCBDA, WebAB, WhAm 2*

Hart, Alden Leonard 1888-1967 *WhAm 4*

Hart, Alfred 1816- *IIBEAAW, NewYHSD*

Hart, Alonzo Jay 1849-1919 *NatCAB 18*

Hart, Alphonso 1830-1910 *BiDrAC*

Hart, Archibald Chapman 1873-1935 *BiDrAC, NatCAB 18, WhAm 1*

Hart, Artemas Elijah 1842-1920 *NatCAB 18*

Hart, Augustus Brewster 1846- *NatCAB 12*

Hart, Bertha Platt 1851- *WomWWA 14*

Hart, Boies Chittenden 1885-1946 *WhAm 2*

Hart, Burdette 1821-1906 *NatCAB 25, WhAm 1*

Hart, C O *NewYHSD*

Hart, Charles 1869-1950 *NatCAB 44*

Hart, Charles A 1893- *WhAm 3*

Hart, Charles Allan 1880- *WhAm 6*

Hart, Charles Arthur 1859-1918 *WhAm 3*

Hart, Charles Burdett 1850- *NatCAB 13*

Hart, Charles Byerly 1846-1918 *NatCAB 17*

Hart, Charles Delucena 1871-1951 *NatCAB 45*

Hart, Charles Edward 1838-1916 *WhAm 1*

Hart, Charles Henry 1847-1918 *AmBi, ApCAB, DcAmB, NatCAB 18, TwCBDA, WhAm 1*

Hart, Crawford Avery 1891-1962 *NatCAB 50*

Hart, David Steele 1911-1969 *NatCAB 57*

Hart, Dwight Howard 1874-1942 *NatCAB 32*

Hart, Edmund Hall 1839-1898 *DcAmB, NatCAB 24, WhAm H*

Hart, Edward 1854-1931 *DcAmB S1, NatCAB 11, TwCBDA, WhAm 1*

Hart, Edward Joseph 1893-1961 *BiDrAC, WhAm 4, WhAmP*

Hart, Edward Payson 1835- *WhAm 4*
Hart, Edwin Bret 1874-1953 *DcAmB S5, DcScB, NatCAB 43, WhAm 3*
Hart, Elias Burton 1834- *NatCAB 12*
Hart, Eliza *NewYHSD*
Hart, Elizur Kirke 1841-1893 *BiDrAC, WhAm H*
Hart, Emanuel B 1811-1897 *BiAUS*
Hart, Emanuel Bernard 1809-1897 *ApCAB, BiDrAC, NatCAB 3, TwCBDA, WhAm H*
Hart, Ernest Eldred 1859-1913 *NatCAB 16, WhAm 1*
Hart, Estelle May 1865- *WomWWA 14*
Hart, Frances Noyes 1890-1943 *WhAm 2*
Hart, Francis Russell 1868-1938 *WhAm 1*
Hart, Franklin Augustus 1894-1967 *WhAm 4*
Hart, Freeman H 1889-1965 *WhAm 4*
Hart, George H 1883-1959 *WhAm 3*
Hart, George Overbury 1868-1933 *BnEnAmA, DcAmB S1, WhAm 1*
Hart, George Spencer 1837- *NatCAB 12*
Hart, Harris *WhAm 5*
Hart, Harry William 1885-1937 *NatCAB 27*
Hart, Hastings Hornell 1851-1932 *AmBi, DcAmB S1, NatCAB 23, WhAm 1*
Hart, Henry *NewYHSD*
Hart, Henry Clay 1878-1965 *NatCAB 52, WhAm 4*
Hart, Henry D *NewYHSD*
Hart, Henry Hersch 1886-1968 *WhAm 5*
Hart, Henry Joseph 1880- *WhAm 6*
Hart, Henry Martyn 1838-1920 *WhAm 1*
Hart, Henry Melvin, Jr. 1904-1969 *WhAm 5*
Hart, Hornell 1888-1967 *WhAm 4*
Hart, Howard Stanley 1867-1944 *NatCAB 37, WhAm 2*
Hart, Irving Harlow 1877-1958 *WhAm 3*
Hart, J Sol 1874-1957 *NatCAB 44*
Hart, James 1896-1959 *NatCAB 49*
Hart, James, Jr. *NewYHSD*
Hart, James A 1900-1960 *WhAm 3*
Hart, James Hill 1878- *WhAm 6*
Hart, James M 1828-1901 *Drake*
Hart, Mrs. James M 1829-1921 *NewYHSD*
Hart, James MacDougal 1828-1901 *AmBi, BnEnAmA, DcAmB*
Hart, James MacDougall 1828-1901 *WhAm 1*
Hart, James McDougal 1828-1901 *ApCAB, NatCAB 7, NewYHSD*
Hart, James McDougall 1828-1901 *TwCBDA*
Hart, James Morgan 1839-1916 *DcAmB, NatCAB 9, TwCBDA, WhAm 1*
Hart, James Norris 1861- *WhAm 4*
Hart, Jay Hiscox 1847-1918 *NatCAB 27*
Hart, Jerome Alfred 1854-1937 *NatCAB 28, WhAm 1*
Hart, Jesse Cleveland 1864-1933 *NatCAB 30, WhAm 1*
Hart, Joel Tanner 1801-1877 *WhAm H*
Hart, Joel Tanner 1810-1877 *AmBi, ApCAB, BnEnAmA, DcAmB, Drake, NatCAB 6, NewYHSD, TwCBDA*
Hart, John *NatCAB 7, NewYHSD*
Hart, John 1707?-1779? *BiDrAC, TwCBDA, WhAmP*
Hart, John 1708-1779 *NatCAB 5*
Hart, John 1708-1780 *ApCAB, BiAUS, Drake*
Hart, John 1711?-1779 *AmBi, DcAmB, WhAm H*
Hart, John Francis 1867- *WhAm 4*
Hart, John Marion 1895- *WhAm 5*
Hart, John Nathaniel 1909-1971 *WhAm 5*
Hart, John Seely 1810-1877 *ApCAB, BiDAmEd, DcAmB, Drake, NatCAB 9, TwCBDA, WhAm H*
Hart, John William 1866-1936 *WhAm 2*
Hart, Jonathan 1744-1791 *TwCBDA*
Hart, Jonathan 1748-1791 *ApCAB, Drake*
Hart, Joseph C d1855 *Drake*
Hart, Joseph Johnson 1859-1926 *BiDrAC*
Hart, Joseph Kinmont 1876-1949 *BiDAmEd, WhAm 2*
Hart, Joseph W *NewYHSD*
Hart, Julie *NewYHSD*
Hart, Lasher 1879- *WhAm 1*
Hart, Laura B Norris 1855- *WomWWA 14*
Hart, Leo 1883-1935 *NatCAB 26*

Hart, Levi d1808 *Drake*
Hart, Lorenz Milton 1895-1943 *DcAmB S3, WhAm 4*
Hart, Louis Bret 1869-1939 *WhAm 1*
Hart, Louis Edward 1871-1957 *NatCAB 46*
Hart, Louis Folwell 1862-1929 *NatCAB 23, WhAm 1*
Hart, Louisa Helena 1870- *WomWWA 14*
Hart, Luke Edward 1880-1964 *WhAm 4*
Hart, Luther 1783-1834 *ApCAB*
Hart, Marie Theresa *NewYHSD*
Hart, Marion Weddell 1890-1938 *WhAm 1*
Hart, Marx M *NewYHSD*
Hart, Mary Ward 1865- *NatCAB 18*
Hart, Maurice J 1849-1912 *NatCAB 16*
Hart, Merwin Kimball 1881-1962 *WhAm 4*
Hart, Michael James 1877-1951 *BiDrAC, WhAm 3*
Hart, Moss 1904-1961 *NatCAB 46, WebAB, WhAm 4*
Hart, Nancy 1735?-1830 *NotAW*
Hart, Nancy 1750?- *NatCAB 13*
Hart, Nancy 1755-1840? *ApCAB*
Hart, O B 1821-1874 *BiAUS*
Hart, Oliver 1723-1795 *ApCAB, Drake*
Hart, Oliver Philip 1898-1951 *WhAm 3*
Hart, Ossian Bingley 1821-1874 *NatCAB 11*
Hart, Percie 1870- *WhAm 5*
Hart, Philip Aloysius 1912- *BiDrAC*
Hart, Phoebe Alder *WomWWA 14*
Hart, Ray 1872-1948 *NatCAB 37*
Hart, Rebecca Mitchell 1865- *WomWWA 14*
Hart, Ringgold 1886-1965 *WhAm 4*
Hart, Roswell 1824-1883 *BiAUS, BiDrAC, WhAm H*
Hart, Roy Meldrum 1876-1947 *NatCAB 35*
Hart, Russell Eason 1872-1955 *NatCAB 43*
Hart, Samuel 1845-1917 *DcAmB, NatCAB 13, TwCBDA, WhAm 1*
Hart, Simeon Thompson 1878-1970 *WhAm 5, WhAm 6*
Hart, Sophie Chantal 1868-1948 *WhAm 2, WomWWA 14*
Hart, Theodore Stuart 1869-1951 *WhAm 3*
Hart, Thomas 1894-1975 *WhAm 6*
Hart, Thomas Charles 1877-1971 *BiDrAC, NatCAB 56, WebAMB, WhAm 5, WhWW-II*
Hart, Thomas Norton 1829-1927 *WhAm 1*
Hart, Thomas Patrick *WhAm 5*
Hart, Verling Kersey 1894-1971 *NatCAB 57*
Hart, Virgil Chittenden 1840-1904 *DcAmB, NatCAB 22*
Hart, Walter Morris 1872- *WhAm 5*
Hart, Willard 1898-1957 *NatCAB 44*
Hart, William *NewYHSD*
Hart, William 1823-1894 *AmBi, ApCAB, BnEnAmA, DcAmB, Drake, NatCAB 7, NewYHSD, TwCBDA, WhAm H*
Hart, William H 1864-1926 *WhAm 1*
Hart, William Henry 1834- *ApCAB X*
Hart, William Henry Harrison 1848-1919 *NatCAB 9, NatCAB 18*
Hart, William Henry Harrison 1857- *WhAm 4*
Hart, William Lee 1881-1957 *WhAm 3*
Hart, William Lincoln 1867- *WhAm 5*
Hart, William Michael 1889-1962 *WhAm 4*
Hart, William Octave 1857-1929 *WhAm 1*
Hart, William Richard 1853-1929 *BiDAmEd*
Hart, William Richard 1893-1965 *WhAm 4*
Hart, William S 1872-1946 *WhAm 2*
Hart, William Surrey 1862?-1946 *DcAmB S4*
Hart, William Surrey 1870-1946 *WebAB*
Hartdegen, Adolf 1849- *TwCBDA*
Hartdegen, Carl 1851-1925 *NatCAB 20*
Harte, Bret 1836-1902 *DcAmB, EncAAH, REnAW, WebAB*
Harte, Bret 1839-1902 *TwCBDA, WhAm 1*
Harte, Emmet Forrest 1876- *WhAm 5*
Harte, Francis Bret 1837-1902 *ApCAB, Drake, NatCAB 1*
Harte, Francis Brett 1836-1902 *AmBi, DcAmB*
Harte, Francis Brett 1837-1902 *McGEWB*
Harte, Houston 1893-1972 *WhAm 5*
Harte, Richard 1894-1970 *NatCAB 55, WhAm 5*
Harte, Richard Hickman 1855-1925 *NatCAB 22, WhAm 1*

Harte, Thomas John 1888-1962 *WhAm 4*
Hartenbower, George Earl 1892-1966 *NatCAB 52*
Hartenbower, Jeremiah J 1843-1914 *NatCAB 16*
Hartenstein, Robert Franklin 1900-1965 *WhAm 4*
Harter, Clarence Jacob 1881-1935 *NatCAB 26*
Harter, Dow Watters 1885-1971 *BiDrAC, WhAm 5*
Harter, George Abram 1853-1943 *TwCBDA, WhAm 2*
Harter, Isaac 1880-1957 *NatCAB 47, WhAm 3*
Harter, John Francis 1897-1947 *BiDrAC, WhAm 2*
Harter, Michael Daniel 1846-1896 *BiDrAC, TwCBDA, WhAm H*
Hartfield, August Julius 1875-1939 *NatCAB 30*
Hartfield, John McCallum 1868- *WhAm 4*
Hartfield, Joseph Manuel 1882-1964 *WhAm 4*
Hartford, Edward Vassallo 1870-1922 *ApCAB X, NatCAB 40*
Hartford, Fernando Wood 1872-1938 *WhAm 1*
Hartford, George Huntington 1833-1917 *DcAmB S5, WhAm HA, WhAm 4*
Hartford, George Ludlum 1864-1957 *DcAmB S5, WhAm 3*
Hartford, John Augustine 1872-1951 *DcAmB S5, WhAm 3*
Hartford, William Hatton 1860-1927 *NatCAB 21*
Harth, H Addison 1861-1940 *NatCAB 39*
Harthorn, Drew Thompson 1871- *WhAm 5*
Hartig, Theodor 1805-1880 *DcScB*
Hartigan, Charles Conway 1882-1944 *NatCAB 45, WhAm 2*
Hartigan, Grace 1922- *BnEnAmA*
Hartigan, James William 1863-1950 *NatCAB 40*
Hartigan, John Patrick 1887-1968 *NatCAB 55*
Hartigan, Raymond Harvey 1915-1971 *WhAm 5*
Harting, Marinus *NewYHSD*
Harting, Pieter 1812-1885 *DcScB*
Harting, Rial *NewYHSD*
Hartinger, William Calvert 1875- *WhAm 5*
Hartke, Rupert Vance 1919- *BiDrAC*
Hartle, Russell Peter 1889-1961 *NatCAB 49*
Hartley, Charles Pinckney 1870- *WhAm 5*
Hartley, David 1705?-1757 *DcScB, McGEWB*
Hartley, David 1729-1813 *ApCAB, Drake*
Hartley, Ellis Taylor 1848-1914 *WhAm 1*
Hartley, Eugene Fuller 1879-1961 *WhAm 4*
Hartley, Frank 1856-1913 *DcAmB, NatCAB 15, WhAm 1*
Hartley, Fred Allan, Jr. 1902-1969 *BiDrAC*
Hartley, Fred Allan, Jr. 1903-1969 *WhAm 5*
Hartley, G Inness 1887-1949 *NatCAB 38*
Hartley, German Smith 1881-1964 *NatCAB 51*
Hartley, Harold H 1902-1964 *WhAm 4*
Hartley, Henry Alexander Saturnin 1861- *WhAm 4*
Hartley, Isaac Smithson 1830-1899 *WhAm 1*
Hartley, James Joseph 1858-1944 *WhAm 2*
Hartley, John F *BiAUS*
Hartley, Jonathan Scott 1845-1912 *AmBi, ApCAB, ApCAB Sup, DcAmB, NatCAB 7, NatCAB 38, TwCBDA, WhAm 1*
Hartley, Leslie Poles 1895-1972 *WhAm 5*
Hartley, Lowrie C 1871- *WhAm 5*
Hartley, Marsden 1877-1943 *BnEnAmA, DcAmB S3, IIBEAAW, McGEWB*
Hartley, Rachel 1884- *BiCAW*
Hartley, Raphael Benedict 1900-1962 *NatCAB 49*
Hartley, Robert Willard 1911-1971 *WhAm 5*
Hartley, Roland H 1864-1952 *WhAm 3*
Hartley, Thomas 1748-1800 *ApCAB, ApCAB Sup, BiAUS, BiDrAC, DcAmB, Drake, NatCAB 2, TwCBDA, WhAm H, WhAmP*
Hartley, William *NewYHSD*
Hartlib, Samuel d1662 *DcScB*
Hartline, Haldan Keffer 1903- *AsBiEn, WebAB*
Hartman, A O *NewYHSD*

Hartman, Adam *NewYHSD*
Hartman, Adolph *NewYHSD*
Hartman, Albert Carl 1863-1937 *NatCAB 28*
Hartman, Carl G 1879-1968 *WhAm 4A*
Hartman, Charles F *NewYHSD*
Hartman, Charles Sampson 1861-1929 *BiDrAC, NatCAB 21, TwCBDA, WhAm 1, WhAmP*
Hartman, Charles William 1924-1970 *WhAm 5*
Hartman, Conrad Fried *NewYHSD*
Hartman, Douglas William 1902-1965 *WhAm 4*
Hartman, Edwin Mitman 1869-1947 *WhAm 2*
Hartman, Ernest Herman 1893-1967 *WhAm 5*
Hartman, Frank Alexander 1883-1971 *WhAm 5*
Hartman, Frank Edward 1890-1952 *NatCAB 39*
Hartman, George Willis 1872-1965 *NatCAB 52*
Hartman, Gertrude d1955 *WhAm 3*
Hartman, Harold Hoover 1890-1965 *WhAm 4*
Hartman, Harvey Clarence 1900-1961 *WhAm 4*
Hartman, Helen Stahr 1873- *WomWWA 14*
Hartman, Henry 1889-1966 *WhAm 4*
Hartman, Howard Russell 1887-1959 *WhAm 3*
Hartman, Irvin Henry 1869-1962 *NatCAB 50*
Hartman, J W *NewYHSD*
Hartman, James Henry 1880-1946 *NatCAB 39*
Hartman, Jesse Lee 1853-1930 *BiDrAC, NatCAB 22, WhAm 4*
Hartman, John A 1907-1967 *WhAm 5*
Hartman, John Clark 1861-1941 *WhAm 1*
Hartman, John Daniel 1878- *WhAm 6*
Hartman, John Peter 1857-1945 *WhAm 2*
Hartman, John VanHorn 1877-1953 *NatCAB 42*
Hartman, Lee Foster 1879-1941 *NatCAB 43, WhAm 1*
Hartman, Leon Wilson 1876-1943 *NatCAB 35, WhAm 2*
Hartman, Lewis Oliver 1876-1955 *NatCAB 46, WhAm 3*
Hartman, Louis Francis 1901-1970 *WhAm 5*
Hartman, Louis H 1884-1964 *WhAm 4*
Hartman, Martin *NewYHSD*
Hartman, Paul William 1904-1973 *WhAm 6*
Hartman, Robert S 1910-1973 *WhAm 6*
Hartman, Samuel Brubaker 1830-1918 *ApCAB X, NatCAB 13*
Hartman, Sara 1872- *WhAm 5*
Hartman, Siegfried Frisch 1888-1953 *WhAm 3*
Hartman, Theodore 1822?- *NewYHSD*
Hartman, W Emory 1900-1958 *NatCAB 44*
Hartman, Wiley Virgil 1875-1925 *NatCAB 6*
Hartman, William Dell 1817-1899 *ApCAB, TwCBDA*
Hartman, William Louis 1864- *NatCAB 14*
Hartmann, Alexis Frank 1898-1964 *WhAm 4*
Hartmann, Carl Friedrich Alexander 1796-1863 *DcScB*
Hartmann, Carl Sadakichi 1867?-1944 *DcAmB S3*
Hartmann, F M 1870-1932 *WhAm 1, WhAm 1C*
Hartmann, F Norman 1906-1974 *WhAm 6*
Hartmann, Georg 1489-1564 *DcScB*
Hartmann, George W 1904-1955 *WhAm 3*
Hartmann, Heinz 1894-1970 *NatCAB 55*
Hartmann, Herman *NewYHSD*
Hartmann, Herman 1886-1966 *NatCAB 52*
Hartmann, Hermann Henry 1870-1956 *NatCAB 43*
Hartmann, Jacob Wittmer 1881-1934 *WhAm 2*
Hartmann, Johannes 1568-1631 *DcScB*
Hartmann, Johannes Franz 1865-1936 *DcScB*
Hartmann, Louis Frederick 1894-1949 *NatCAB 39*
Hartmann, Reina Kate Goldstein 1880- *WhAm 6*
Hartmann, Sadakichi 1869- *WhAm 5*
Hartmann, William V 1871- *WhAm 5*
Hartness, James 1861-1934 *DcAmB S1, NatCAB 15, NatCAB 30, WhAm 1*
Hartnett, J Henry 1876-1949 *NatCAB 38*
Hartnett, Timothy V 1890-1974 *WhAm 6*
Hartney, Harold Evans 1888-1945 *NatCAB 34, WhAm 2*
Hartney, James Bradley 1921-1972 *NatCAB 56*
Hartranft, Chester David 1839-1914 *BiDAmEd, DcAmB, NatCAB 6, TwCBDA, WhAm 1*

Hartranft, John Frederick 1830-1889 *ApCAB, BiAUS, DcAmB, NatCAB 2, TwCBDA, WhAm H*
Hartrath, Joseph *NewYHSD*
Hartrath, Lucie d1962 *WhAm 4*
Hartrauft, John Frederick 1830- *Drake*
Hartree, Douglas Rayner 1897-1958 *DcScB, WhAm 3*
Hartridge, Clifford Wayne 1866-1937 *NatCAB 27, WhAm 4*
Hartridge, Emelyn Battersby 1871-1942 *WhAm 2*
Hartridge, Emelyn Bettersby 1871-1942 *WomWWA 14*
Hartridge, John Earle 1849-1929 *WhAm 1*
Hartridge, John Earle 1850-1929 *NatCAB 10*
Hartridge, Julian 1829-1879 *BiAUS, BiDConf, BiDrAC, WhAm H*
Hartridge, Julian 1869-1942 *NatCAB 30*
Hartridge, Walter Charlton 1870-1932 *NatCAB 33*
Harts, David Hazleton 1878-1962 *NatCAB 52*
Harts, Martha Hale 1873- *WomWWA 14*
Harts, William Wright 1866-1961 *NatCAB 55, WhAm 4*
Hartsell, Luther Thompson, Jr. 1902-1961 *NatCAB 50*
Hartsfield, William Berry 1890-1971 *WhAm 5*
Hartshorn, Charles Henry 1859-1946 *NatCAB 35*
Hartshorn, Edwin Simpson 1874- *WhAm 6*
Hartshorn, Stanley Denton 1899-1961 *NatCAB 47*
Hartshorn, Stewart 1840-1937 *NatCAB 36*
Hartshorn, Stewart Henry 1876-1929 *NatCAB 28*
Hartshorn, William Henry 1863-1926 *NatCAB 20, WhAm 1*
Hartshorn, William Newton 1843-1920 *ApCAB X, WhAm 1*
Hartshorne, Charles 1829-1908 *ApCAB, TwCBDA, WhAm 1*
Hartshorne, Charles Hopkins 1851-1918 *WhAm 1*
Hartshorne, Douglas 1883-1950 *NatCAB 43*
Hartshorne, Edward 1818-1885 *ApCAB, Drake, TwCBDA*
Hartshorne, Edward Yarnall 1861-1933 *NatCAB 50*
Hartshorne, Francis Cope 1868-1950 *NatCAB 38*
Hartshorne, Henry 1823-1897 *ApCAB, DcAmB, Drake, NatCAB 8, TwCBDA, WhAm H*
Hartshorne, Hugh 1885-1967 *WhAm 4*
Hartshorne, Joseph 1779-1850 *ApCAB, Drake*
Hartshorne, Robert 1866-1927 *NatCAB 39*
Hartsock, Harvey Barton 1887-1966 *NatCAB 53*
Hartsoeker, Nicolaas 1656-1725 *DcScB*
Hartson, Dorr Parmelee 1889-1953 *NatCAB 44*
Hartstene, Henry J d1868 *ApCAB, Drake, TwCBDA*
Hartsuff, Albert 1827-1908 *WhAm 1*
Hartsuff, George Lucas 1830-1874 *ApCAB, DcAmB, Drake, NatCAB 5, TwCBDA, WebAMB, WhAm H*
Hartt, Charles Frederick 1840-1878 *ApCAB, NatCAB 11, TwCBDA, WhAm H*
Hartt, George Montgomery 1877-1954 *WhAm 3*
Hartt, Henry Allen 1813-1892 *NatCAB 8*
Hartt, Jessie Knight 1874- *WomWWA 14*
Hartt, Mary Bronson 1873- *WhAm 5, WomWWA 14*
Hartt, Rollin Lynde 1869-1946 *WhAm 2*
Hartung, Albert Michael d1958 *WhAm 3*
Hartung, F *IIBEAAW*
Hartwell, Alfred Stedman 1836-1912 *NatCAB 40, TwCBDA, WhAm 1*
Hartwell, Alonzo 1805-1873 *ApCAB, Drake, NewYHSD*
Hartwell, Arthur Mowry 1890-1969 *NatCAB 54*
Hartwell, Burt Laws 1865-1939 *NatCAB 29, WhAm 4*
Hartwell, Edward Mussey 1850-1922 *BiDAmEd, NatCAB 20, WhAm 1*

Hartwell, Ernest Clark 1883-1964 *WhAm 4*
Hartwell, Everett Smith 1882-1954 *NatCAB 43*
Hartwell, Frederick Willard 1850-1911 *NatCAB 41*
Hartwell, G G *NewYHSD*
Hartwell, Harold Elbert 1885-1964 *NatCAB 51*
Hartwell, Henry Walker 1833-1919 *WhAm 3*
Hartwell, John Augustus 1869-1940 *NatCAB 29, WhAm 1*
Hartwell, Joseph Charles 1874-1952 *NatCAB 41*
Hartwell, Mary Ann 1871- *WomWWA 14*
Hartwell, Maud Louise Ray *WomWWA 14*
Hartwell, Maude Appleton *WomWWA 14*
Hartwell, Robert McClay 1874-1948 *NatCAB 39*
Hartwell, Shattuck Osgood 1865-1946 *WhAm 3*
Hartwich, Herman 1853-1926 *WhAm 2*
Hartwick, Edward Edgar 1871-1918 *NatCAB 19*
Hartwick, Gunther *NewYHSD*
Hartwick, John Christopher 1714-1796 *ApCAB, TwCBDA*
Hartwick, T B *NewYHSD*
Hartwig, Ernst 1851-1923 *DcScB*
Hartwig, Johann Christoph 1714-1796 *DcAmB, WhAm H*
Harty, Jeremiah J 1853-1927 *NatCAB 15, WhAm 1*
Harty, Russell Alzue 1877-1918 *NatCAB 18*
Harty, William Albert 1880-1949 *NatCAB 38*
Hartz, Irving Thomas 1861-1929 *NatCAB 22*
Hartz, John Frederick 1864-1944 *NatCAB 33*
Hartz, William Homer 1887-1970 *WhAm 5*
Hartzel, Benjamin Franklin 1856-1923 *NatCAB 22*
Hartzell, Charles 1862-1932 *WhAm 1*
Hartzell, Joseph Crane 1842- *ApCAB X, NatCAB 13*
Hartzell, Joseph Crane 1842-1928 *DcAmB*
Hartzell, Joseph Crane 1842-1929 *WhAm 1*
Hartzell, Joseph Culver 1870- *WhAm 1*
Hartzell, Milton Bixler 1854- *WhAm 4*
Hartzell, Robert Norris 1896-1968 *NatCAB 56*
Hartzell, Solomon Mayer 1879-1956 *NatCAB 45*
Hartzell, Thomas B 1866- *WhAm 5*
Hartzell, William 1837-1903 *BiAUS, BiDrAC*
Hartzler, Henry Burns 1840-1920 *WhAm 1*
Hartzler, John Ellsworth 1879-1963 *WhAm 4*
Hartzog, Henry Simms 1866- *TwCBDA, WhAm 4*
Hartzog, Justin R 1892-1963 *WhAm 4*
Harun Al-Rashid 766-809 *McGEWB*
Harunobu, Suzuki 1725?-1770 *McGEWB*
Harvard, John 1607-1638 *AmBi, ApCAB, DcAmB, NatCAB 6, TwCBDA, WebAB, WhAm H*
Harvard, John 1608?-1638 *Drake*
Harvey, Alexander 1868-1949 *WhAm 2*
Harvey, Alfred 1848-1915 *NatCAB 38*
Harvey, Andrew Magee 1868-1949 *WhAm 2*
Harvey, Anne Catherine Roberta 1849- *WomWWA 14*
Harvey, Arlington Coryell 1873-1943 *NatCAB 33*
Harvey, Arthur 1834- *ApCAB*
Harvey, Basil Coleman Hyatt 1875-1958 *WhAm 3*
Harvey, Byron, Jr. 1903-1965 *NatCAB 51, WhAm 4*
Harvey, Byron Schermerhorn 1876-1954 *WhAm 3*
Harvey, Charles Edward 1880-1949 *NatCAB 37*
Harvey, Charles Henry 1861-1935 *WhAm 1*
Harvey, Charles Milton 1869-1952 *NatCAB 42, WhAm 3*
Harvey, Charles Mitchell 1848- *WhAm 1*
Harvey, Coin 1851-1936 *DcAmB S2, WebAB*
Harvey, Daniel Robert 1891-1959 *WhAm 4*
Harvey, David Archibald 1845-1916 *BiDrAC*
Harvey, Don Stuart 1867-1943 *NatCAB 32*
Harvey, Dwight B 1834- *NatCAB 1*
Harvey, Edmund Newton 1887-1959 *NatCAB 45, WhAm 3*
Harvey, Edward Lee 1898-1970 *NatCAB 56*
Harvey, Edward Maris 1888-1959 *NatCAB 48*
Harvey, Edward S 1870- *WhoColR*

Harvey, Edwin Bayard 1834-1913 *NatCAB 15*
Harvey, Eli 1860-1957 *ApCAB X, IlBEAAW, NatCAB 12, WhAm 3*
Harvey, Erwin Maurice 1872-1945 *NatCAB 35*
Harvey, Ethel Browne 1885-1965 *WhAm 4*
Harvey, Ford Ferguson 1866-1928 *NatCAB 38, REnAW, WhAm 1*
Harvey, Fred Addison 1882-1945 *NatCAB 50*
Harvey, Frederick Henry 1835-1901 *WebAB*
Harvey, Frederick Loviad 1856-1923 *WhAm 1*
Harvey, George 1800?-1878 *IlBEAAW, NewYHSD, WhAm H*
Harvey, George 1801-1878 *BnEnAmA*
Harvey, George 1835?-1920? *NewYHSD*
Harvey, George Booth 1875-1951 *NatCAB 43*
Harvey, George Brinton McClellan 1864-1928 *AmBi, DcAmB, NatCAB 18, WhAm 1*
Harvey, George Cockburn 1858-1935 *WhAm 1*
Harvey, George Lockwood 1870-1947 *NatCAB 37*
Harvey, George U d1946 *WhAm 2*
Harvey, Gerald 1933- *IlBEAAW*
Harvey, Harold Brown 1884-1949 *WhAm 2*
Harvey, Harold Charles 1891-1949 *NatCAB 37*
Harvey, Hayward Augustus 1824-1893 *ApCAB Sup, DcAmB, NatCAB 13*
Harvey, Haywood Augustus 1824-1893 *WhAm H*
Harvey, Hezekiah 1821-1893 *ApCAB Sup, TwCBDA*
Harvey, Holman 1894-1973 *WhAm 5*
Harvey, Horace 1863-1949 *WhAm 3*
Harvey, I J, Jr. 1896-1964 *NatCAB 52, WhAm 4*
Harvey, James 1922- *BiDrAC*
Harvey, James E 1820- *BiAUS*
Harvey, James Madison 1833-1894 *ApCAB, BiAUS, BiDrAC, NatCAB 8, TwCBDA, WhAm H, WhAmP*
Harvey, Jean Charles 1891-1967 *WhAm 5*
Harvey, Sir John d1646 *AmBi, ApCAB, DcAmB S1, Drake, NatCAB 13, WhAm H*
Harvey, Sir John 1778-1852 *ApCAB, Drake*
Harvey, John 1840-1905 *NatCAB 18*
Harvey, John 1899-1971 *WhAm 5*
Harvey, Jonathan 1780-1859 *ApCAB, BiAUS, BiDrAC, TwCBDA, WhAm H, WhAmP*
Harvey, Kate Benedict Hanna 1871-1936 *NatCAB 34*
Harvey, Kenneth G 1900-1967 *WhAm 5*
Harvey, Laurence 1928-1973 *WhAm 6*
Harvey, Lawson Moreau 1856-1920 *NatCAB 35, WhAm 1*
Harvey, Leo Heartt 1899-1959 *NatCAB 44*
Harvey, Leo M 1886-1974 *WhAm 6*
Harvey, LeRoy 1873-1928 *NatCAB 31, WhAm 1, WhAm 1C*
Harvey, Lillian A d1968 *WhAm 5*
Harvey, Lorenzo Dow 1848-1922 *ApCAB X, BiDAmEd, NatCAB 14, WhAm 1*
Harvey, Louis Powell 1820-1862 *ApCAB, BiAUS, DcAmB, Drake, NatCAB 12, TwCBDA, WhAm H*
Harvey, Matthew 1781-1866 *ApCAB, BiAUS, BiDrAC, Drake, NatCAB 11, TwCBDA, WhAm H, WhAmP*
Harvey, Moses 1820- *ApCAB*
Harvey, P Casper 1889-1975 *WhAm 6*
Harvey, Paul 1878-1948 *WhAm 2*
Harvey, Perry Williams 1869-1932 *NatCAB 25*
Harvey, Peter 1810-1877 *ApCAB*
Harvey, Philip Francis 1844-1922 *WhAm 1*
Harvey, Ralph 1901- *BiDrAC, WhAmP*
Harvey, Ralph Hicks 1893-1950 *WhAm 3*
Harvey, Ray Forrest 1905-1968 *WhAm 5*
Harvey, Rodney Beecher 1890-1945 *NatCAB 44, WhAm 2*
Harvey, Roger Allen 1910-1973 *WhAm 6*
Harvey, Roland Bridenall 1870-1917 *WhAm 1*
Harvey, Rowland Hill 1889-1943 *WhAm 2*
Harvey, Samuel Clark 1886-1953 *NatCAB 42, WhAm 3*
Harvey, Thomas Burgess 1827-1889 *NatCAB 35*
Harvey, Thomas Wadleigh 1821-1892 *BiDAmEd*
Harvey, Thomas William 1795-1854 *NatCAB 12*

Harvey, Turlington Walker 1835-1909 *NatCAB 21*
Harvey, W W 1869- *WhAm 5*
Harvey, William 1578-1657 *AsBiEn, BiHiMed, DcScB, McGEWB*
Harvey, William Edwin 1871-1922 *WhAm 1*
Harvey, William Henry 1811-1866 *DcScB*
Harvey, William Hope 1851-1936 *DcAmB S2, EncAAH, NatCAB 18, WebAB, WhAm 1*
Harvey, William Lemuel 1871-1938 *WhAm 1*
Harvey, William Patrick 1843- *WhAm 4*
Harvey, William Riggs 1877-1953 *WhAm 3*
Harvey, Wilson Godfrey 1866-1932 *NatCAB 44*
Harvie, Eliza J 1840- *WomWWA 14*
Harvie, Eric Lafferty 1892-1975 *WhAm 6*
Harvie, John 1742-1807 *ApCAB, BiDrAC, DcAmB, NatCAB 7, TwCBDA, WhAm H*
Harvie, John Bruce 1857-1941 *WhAm 2*
Harvie, Peter Lyons 1885-1944 *WhAm 2*
Harward, Thomas 1789-1891 *NatCAB 5*
Harwell, Earl Palmer 1882-1950 *NatCAB 39*
Harwood, Andrew Allen 1802-1884 *ApCAB, Drake, NatCAB 4, TwCBDA, WebAMB, WhAm H*
Harwood, Burt S 1897-1924? *IlBEAAW*
Harwood, Charles 1880-1950 *NatCAB 38, WhAm 3*
Harwood, Charles Edward 1830-1933 *ApCAB X, NatCAB 33*
Harwood, Charles McHenry 1864- *WhAm 4*
Harwood, Cole Leslie 1866- *WhAm 4*
Harwood, Edward Charles 1872-1944 *NatCAB 33*
Harwood, Edwin 1822-1902 *WhAm 1*
Harwood, Francis Laird 1883-1957 *NatCAB 45*
Harwood, Frank Haswell 1875-1948 *NatCAB 39*
Harwood, Frank James 1855-1940 *WhAm 1*
Harwood, Frederick Hollister 1863-1925 *NatCAB 21*
Harwood, George Alexander 1875-1926 *WhAm 1*
Harwood, Herbert Joseph 1854- *NatCAB 14*
Harwood, James Taylor 1860-1940 *IlBEAAW*
Harwood, John *WhAm H*
Harwood, John Edmund 1771-1809 *ApCAB, Drake, WhAm H*
Harwood, Joseph Alfred 1827-1896 *NatCAB 14*
Harwood, R Henry 1868-1951 *NatCAB 40*
Harwood, Sydney 1860-1929 *ApCAB X, NatCAB 47*
Harwood, Thomas Armine 1894-1964 *NatCAB 53, WhAm 4*
Harwood, William Sumner 1857-1908 *WhAm 1*
Harza, Leroy Francis 1882-1953 *NatCAB 42, WhAm 3*
Hasan Ibn Al-Haytham, Al- 966?-1039 *McGEWB*
Hasan Ibn Muhammad Al-Wazzen, Al- *DcScB*
Hasan Ibn Musa Ibn Shakir, Al- *DcScB*
Hasbrouck, Abraham Bruyn 1791-1879 *ApCAB, BiAUS, BiDrAC, DcAmB, NatCAB 3, TwCBDA, WhAm H*
Hasbrouck, Abraham Joseph 1773-1845 *BiAUS, BiDrAC, WhAm H*
Hasbrouck, Alfred 1858-1920 *WhAm 1*
Hasbrouck, Charles Alfred 1864- *WhAm 4*
Hasbrouck, Cornelius Jansen 1852-1925 *NatCAB 31*
Hasbrouck, David Schoonmaker 1850-1922 *NatCAB 19*
Hasbrouck, Gertrude M 1876- *WomWWA 14*
Hasbrouck, Gertrude Shaw 1869- *WomWWA 14*
Hasbrouck, Gilbert David Blauvelt 1860-1942 *NatCAB 40, WhAm 2*
Hasbrouck, Henry Cornelius 1839-1910 *NatCAB 15, TwCBDA, WhAm 1*
Hasbrouck, James Foster 1870-1945 *NatCAB 36*
Hasbrouck, Josiah 1755-1821 *BiAUS, BiDrAC, WhAm H*
Hasbrouck, Lydia Sayer 1827-1910 *DcAmB, NotAW, WhAm HA, WhAm 4*
Hasbrouck, Oscar 1882-1961 *NatCAB 49*
Hascall, Augustus Porter 1800-1872 *BiAUS,*

BiDrAC, WhAm H
Hascall, Daniel 1782-1852 *ApCAB, TwCBDA*
Hascall, Milo S 1833?- *Drake*
Hascall, Milo Smith 1829-1904 *ApCAB, DcAmB, TwCBDA, WhAm 1*
Hascall, Wilbur Fisk 1854-1925 *NatCAB 6, WhAm 1*
Hascall, William Hosmer Shailer 1850-1927 *NatCAB 21*
Hasche, Rudolph Leonard 1896-1959 *NatCAB 52, WhAm 3*
Hase, William Frederick 1874-1935 *WhAm 1*
Haselden, Kyle Emerson 1913-1968 *WhAm 5*
Haseltine, Burton 1874-1941 *WhAm 2*
Haseltine, Charles Field 1840-1915 *NewYHSD*
Haseltine, Elizabeth Stanley 1811-1882 *NewYHSD*
Haseltine, George 1829-1915 *WhAm 1*
Haseltine, Herbert 1877-1962 *WhAm 4*
Haseltine, James Henry 1833-1907 *ApCAB, DcAmB, NewYHSD, WhAm 1*
Haseltine, Nathan Stone 1911-1970 *WhAm 5*
Haseltine, William Stanley 1835-1900 *ApCAB, NatCAB 12, NewYHSD, TwCBDA*
Haselton, Barton 1877-1939 *NatCAB 30*
Haselton, Jonathan Sawyer 1847-1908 *NatCAB 35*
Haselton, Page Smith 1896-1967 *WhAm 5*
Haselton, Seneca 1848-1921 *DcAmB, NatCAB 13, WhAm 1*
Haseman, Charles 1880-1931 *WhAm 1*
Hasenclever, Peter 1716-1793 *DcAmB, NatCAB 25, WhAm H*
Hasenohrl, Friedrich 1874-1915 *DcScB*
Haserot, Francis Henry 1860-1954 *NatCAB 43*
Hasford, Carl Boyce 1894-1955 *NatCAB 48*
Haskel, Daniel 1784-1848 *NatCAB 2, TwCBDA*
Haskell, Abraham 1746-1834 *ApCAB*
Haskell, Charles Nathaniel 1860-1933 *DcAmB S1, NatCAB 14, WhAm 1, WhAmP*
Haskell, Clement Caldwell 1847- *NatCAB 5*
Haskell, Clinton Howard 1888-1952 *WhAm 3*
Haskell, Daniel 1784-1848 *ApCAB, Drake*
Haskell, Daniel Noyes 1818-1874 *ApCAB, TwCBDA*
Haskell, Duane Hedrick 1905-1974 *WhAm 6*
Haskell, Dudley Chase 1842-1883 *BiDrAC, DcAmB, NatCAB 10, WhAm H*
Haskell, E Kirk 1877-1941 *NatCAB 38*
Haskell, Earl Stanley 1886-1965 *WhAm 4*
Haskell, Edward Howard 1845- *NatCAB 16, TwCBDA*
Haskell, Edward Howard 1845-1924 *ApCAB X*
Haskell, Edward Howard 1845-1925 *WhAm 1*
Haskell, Edwin Bradbury 1837-1907 *TwCBDA, WhAm 1*
Haskell, Ella Louise 1862- *NatCAB 11*
Haskell, Ella Louise Knowles 1860-1911 *DcAmB, WhAm HA, WhAm 4*
Haskell, Ernest 1876-1925 *DcAmB, IlBEAAW, NatCAB 23*
Haskell, Eugene Elwin 1855-1933 *WhAm 1*
Haskell, Freda Rew 1900-1967 *WhAm 5*
Haskell, Frederick Tudor 1854-1935 *NatCAB 40, WhAm 1*
Haskell, Glenn Leach 1883-1972 *WhAm 5*
Haskell, Harold Clifford 1885-1957 *NatCAB 49, WhAm 3*
Haskell, Harriet Newell 1835-1907 *AmWom, NatCAB 6, WhAm 1*
Haskell, Harry Garner 1870-1951 *NatCAB 47, WhAm 3*
Haskell, Harry Garner, Jr. 1921- *BiDrAC*
Haskell, Harry Leland 1840-1908 *WhAm 1*
Haskell, Helen Eggleston 1871- *WhAm 5*
Haskell, Henry Joseph 1874-1952 *DcAmB S5, WhAm 3*
Haskell, Hiram Betts 1823-1873 *NewYHSD*
Haskell, Horace Bray 1869- *WhAm 5*
Haskell, Horace Stewart 1860-1940 *NatCAB 30*
Haskell, James Richards 1825-1897 *ApCAB Sup, NatCAB 13, TwCBDA*
Haskell, Jessica Josephine 1880- *WomWWA 14*
Haskell, Jonathan Amory 1861-1923 *NatCAB 15, WhAm 1*

Haskell, Joseph Allen 1808-1894 *NewYHSD*
Haskell, Joseph Theodore 1838-1898
ApCAB Sup
Haskell, Lewis Wardlaw 1868- *WhAm 4*
Haskell, Llewellyn Frost 1842- *ApCAB,
TwCBDA, WhAm 4*
Haskell, Llewellyn Solomon 1815-1872 *ApCAB*
Haskell, Lyman *NewYHSD*
Haskell, Margaret Bell 1841- *WomWWA 14*
Haskell, Mellen Woodman 1863-1948
NatCAB 37, WhAm 2
Haskell, Oreola Williams 1875- *WomWWA 14*
Haskell, Raymond 1878-1945 *NatCAB 35*
Haskell, Reuben Locke 1878- *BiDrAC,
WhAm 6*
Haskell, Thomas Hawes 1842-1900 *WhAm 1*
Haskell, Thomas J *NewYHSD*
Haskell, Thomas Nelson 1826- *TwCBDA*
Haskell, William Cook 1869-1933 *NatCAB 27*
Haskell, William Edwin 1862-1933 *NatCAB 27,
WhAm 1*
Haskell, William Edwin, Jr. 1889-1953
WhAm 3
Haskell, William Nafew 1878-1952 *NatCAB 40,
WhAm 3*
Haskell, William T 1818-1859 *BiAUS, BiDrAC,
Drake, WhAm H*
Hasket, Elias 1670-1739? *DcAmB, WhAm H*
Haskill, Julia Ellen Smart 1861- *WomWWA 14*
Haskin, Frederic Jennings 1872-1944
NatCAB 33, WhAm 2
Haskin, Helen C *ApCAB X*
Haskin, John Bussing 1821-1895 *BiAUS,
BiDrAC, WhAm H*
Haskin, Joseph A 1817-1874 *ApCAB,
TwCBDA*
Haskin, William Lawrence 1841-1931 *WhAm 1*
Haskins, Caryl Davis 1867-1911 *NatCAB 28,
WhAm 1*
Haskins, Charles Homer 1870-1937 *AmBi,
DcAmB S2, McGEWB, NatCAB 28,
TwCBDA, WhAm 1*
Haskins, Charles Nelson 1874-1942 *WhAm 2*
Haskins, Charles Waldo 1852-1903 *NatCAB 9,
WhAm 1*
Haskins, Clara Allen *WomWWA 14*
Haskins, David Greene 1818-1896 *TwCBDA*
Haskins, Kittredge 1836-1916 *BiDrAC,
WhAm 1, WhAmP*
Haskins, Samuel Moody 1813-1900 *NatCAB 10*
Haskins, Samuel Moody 1872-1948 *WhAm 3*
Haslam, Charles Raymond 1880-1962 *WhAm 4*
Haslam, Edward Thomas 1915-1971
NatCAB 57
Haslam, George James 1858-1923 *NatCAB 20*
Haslam, Robert Thomas 1888-1961 *NatCAB 55,
WhAm 4*
Hasler, Frederick Edward 1882-1973 *WhAm 5*
Hasler, Henry 1846- *WhAm 4*
Hasler, Maurice Fred 1907-1968 *NatCAB 54*
Hasler, Robert Tabor 1891-1955 *NatCAB 42*
Haslet, George Warren 1859-1928 *ApCAB X*
Haslet, Joseph d1823 *NatCAB 11, TwCBDA*
Haslett, John d1777 *ApCAB, Drake*
Haslett, John 1799-1878 *ApCAB*
Haslett, Joseph d1823 *ApCAB, BiAUS*
Haslett, Samuel Montgomerie 1863-1947
NatCAB 43
Hasley, Henry 1904-1962 *NatCAB 50*
Haslup, Alice Elma *WomWWA 14*
Haslup, Lemuel A 1896-1953 *WhAm 3*
Haspel, Joseph 1884-1959 *NatCAB 48,
WhAm 4*
Hass, Bernard *NewYHSD*
Hassam, Childe 1859-1935 *AmBi, ApCAB X,
BnEnAmA, NatCAB 10, WebAB,
WhAm 1*
Hassam, Frederick Childe 1859-1935
*DcAmB S1, IIBEAAW, McGEWB,
TwCBDA*
Hassam, John Tyler 1841-1902 *WhAm 1*
Hassan, Muhammad Abdille 1864-1920
McGEWB
Hassard, John Rose Greene 1836-1888 *ApCAB,
DcAmB, NatCAB 3, TwCBDA,
WhAm H*
Hassard, Samuel 1806-1847 *ApCAB*
Hassaurek, Frederick *BiAUS*

Hassaurek, Friedrich 1831-1885 *DcAmB,
WhAm H*
Hassaurek, Friedrich 1832-1885 *ApCAB,
NatCAB 11*
Hasse, Adelaide Rosalie 1868-1953 *DcAmLiB,
WhAm 3, WomWWA 14*
Hasse, Hermann Edward 1836-1915
NatCAB 16
Hassel, Karl Elmer 1896-1975 *WhAm 6*
Hasselbring, Heinrich 1875- *WhAm 5*
Hassell, Cushing Biggs 1809-1880 *NatCAB 7*
Hassell, Baron Ulrich Von 1881-1944
WhWW-II
Hasselmans, Louis 1878-1957 *WhAm 3*
Hasselquist, Toovay Nelsson 1816- *ApCAB*
Hasselquist, Toovay Nelsson 1816-1898
TwCBDA
Hasselquist, Tufve Nilsson 1816-1891
NatCAB 24
Hasselquist, Tuve Nilsson 1816-1891 *DcAmB,
WhAm H*
Hasseltine, Ann *WebAB*
Hasseltine, Hermon Erwin 1881-1968 *WhAm 5*
Hassen, William *NewYHSD*
Hassenfratz, Jean-Henri 1755-1827 *DcScB*
Hassett, Charles Estel 1906-1960 *NatCAB 48*
Hassett, William D 1880- *WhAm 6*
Hassig, John Franklin 1875-1950 *NatCAB 39*
Hasskarl, Joseph F 1863-1926 *WhAm 1*
Hasslacher, George *NewYHSD*
Hasslacher, Jacob Pius Maria 1852-
NatCAB 15
Hassler, Elizabeth Emily 1865- *WhAm 4*
Hassler, Ferdinand Augustus 1844-1919
TwCBDA, WhAm 1
Hassler, Ferdinand Rudolph 1770-1843 *AmBi,
ApCAB, BiAUS, DcAmB, DcScB, Drake,
NatCAB 3, TwCBDA, WebAB,
WhAm H*
Hassler, Russell Herman 1906-1969 *WhAm 5*
Hassler, Simon 1832-1901 *ApCAB, WhAm 1*
Hassler, William Charles 1868-1931
NatCAB 23
Hastie, William Henry 1904- *EncAB, WebAB*
Hastings *NewYHSD*
Hastings, Caroline Eliza *BiCAW*
Hastings, Charles Douglas 1858-1940
NatCAB 40, WhAm 1
Hastings, Charles Harris 1867- *WhAm 5*
Hastings, Charles Sheldon 1848-1932
DcAmB S1, WhAm 1
Hastings, Daniel *NewYHSD*
Hastings, Daniel Hartman 1849-1903
NatCAB 5, TwCBDA, WhAm 1
Hastings, Daniel Oren 1874-1966 *BiDrAC,
WhAm 4*
Hastings, Earl Freeman 1908-1961 *WhAm 4*
Hastings, Edgar Morton 1882- *WhAm 3*
Hastings, Edgar Morton 1883-1954 *NatCAB 41*
Hastings, Edward Richard 1881-1954
NatCAB 43
Hastings, Edwin George 1872- *WhAm 5*
Hastings, Ella 1856- *WomWWA 14*
Hastings, F Rawdon-Hastings, Marquess Of
1754-1826 *AmBi*
Hastings, Francis William 1848- *WhAm 4*
Hastings, Frank Seymour 1853-1924 *ApCAB X,
NatCAB 14, WhAm 1*
Hastings, Frank Warren 1856-1925 *WhAm 1*
Hastings, George 1807-1866 *BiAUS, BiDrAC,
WhAm H*
Hastings, George Aubrey 1885-1956
NatCAB 46, WhAm 3
Hastings, George Buckland 1892-1967 *WhAm 4*
Hastings, George Everett 1878-1942 *WhAm 2*
Hastings, George Henry 1848-1926 *WhAm 1*
Hastings, Harold William 1887-1949
NatCAB 37
Hastings, Harry George 1869-1962 *WhAm 4*
Hastings, Henry 1818-1887 *ApCAB Sup*
Hastings, Henry Panet 1891-1942 *NatCAB 32*
Hastings, Hester Jane Mercer 1877-
WomWWA 14
Hastings, Holman Kelley 1853- *NatCAB 7*
Hastings, Hugh 1856- *TwCBDA, WhAm 4*
Hastings, Hugh J 1820-1883 *ApCAB,
TwCBDA*
Hastings, James *NewYHSD*

Hastings, James Fred 1926- *BiDrAC*
Hastings, John 1778-1854 *BiAUS, BiDrAC,
WhAm H*
Hastings, John Russel 1873-1942 *NatCAB 36*
Hastings, John Russel 1878-1942 *WhAm 2*
Hastings, Lansford Warren 1818?-1868?
REnAW
Hastings, Matthew 1834-1919 *NewYHSD*
Hastings, Paul Pardee 1872-1947 *WhAm 2*
Hastings, Reuben C M 1867- *WhAm 4*
Hastings, Robert Frank 1914-1973 *NatCAB 57*
Hastings, Russell 1835- *ApCAB*
Hastings, Samuel Clinton *BiAUS*
Hastings, Samuel Dexter 1816-1903 *DcAmB,
NatCAB 10, WhAm 1*
Hastings, Samuel Miles 1860-1943 *WhAm 2*
Hastings, Serramus Clinton 1813-1893
WhAm H
Hastings, Serranus Clinton 1813-1893 *BiDrAC*
Hastings, Serranus Clinton 1814-1893 *AmBi,
ApCAB, DcAmB, NatCAB 31, TwCBDA*
Hastings, Seth 1762-1831 *BiAUS, BiDrAC,
WhAm H*
Hastings, Syranus Clinton 1814- *NatCAB 3*
Hastings, T Mitchell 1876-1950 *NatCAB 41*
Hastings, Thomas 1784-1872 *ApCAB, DcAmB,
Drake, NatCAB 7, TwCBDA, WhAm H*
Hastings, Thomas 1787-1872 *AmBi*
Hastings, Thomas 1860-1929 *AmBi,
ApCAB X, DcAmB, NatCAB 11,
NatCAB 33, WhAm 1*
Hastings, Thomas Samuel 1827-1911 *ApCAB,
NatCAB 7, TwCBDA, WhAm 1*
Hastings, Thomas Wood 1873- *WhAm 5*
Hastings, Warren 1732-1818 *McGEWB*
Hastings, Wells Southworth 1878-1923
WhAm 1
Hastings, William Granger 1853-1937
ApCAB X, WhAm 1
Hastings, William Henry 1874-1929
NatCAB 22
Hastings, William Henry Howe 1840-1900
NatCAB 21
Hastings, William Soden 1798-1842 *BiAUS,
BiDrAC, WhAm H*
Hastings, William Thomson 1881-1969
NatCAB 56
Hastings, William Walter 1865- *WhAm 4*
Hastings, William Wirt 1866-1938 *BiDrAC,
DcAmB S2, WhAm 1, WhAmP*
Hastings, Wilmot Reed 1860-1922 *NatCAB 19*
Haswell, Alanson Mason 1847- *WhAm 4*
Haswell, Anthony 1756-1816 *DcAmB,
NatCAB 8, WhAm H*
Haswell, Charles Haynes 1809-1907 *AmBi,
ApCAB, DcAmB, NatCAB 9, TwCBDA,
WhAm 1*
Haswell, John Chace 1867-1936 *NatCAB 27*
Haswell, Kanah Elizabeth Marcum d1969
WhAm 5
Haswell, Robert *NewYHSD*
Haswin, Frances R 1852- *AmWom*
Hatathli, Ned 1923-1972 *WhAm 6*
Hatch, Abbie A *WomWWA 14*
Hatch, Abram 1830-1911 *NatCAB 8,
TwCBDA, WhAm 4*
Hatch, Albert Sydney 1866- *WhAm 4*
Hatch, Alden 1898-1975 *WhAm 6*
Hatch, Alta May 1863- *WomWWA 14*
Hatch, Arthur Joel 1874-1947 *NatCAB 35*
Hatch, Carl Atwood 1889-1963 *BiDrAC,
WhAm 4*
Hatch, Charles Everett 1902-1962 *NatCAB 50*
Hatch, D Arthur 1877-1957 *NatCAB 48*
Hatch, Edward *Drake*
Hatch, Edward 1832-1889 *AmBi, DcAmB,
NatCAB 12, TwCBDA, WhAm H*
Hatch, Edward 1832-1890 *ApCAB*
Hatch, Edward, Jr. 1859- *WhAm 4*
Hatch, Edward Sparhawk 1875-1937
NatCAB 29
Hatch, Edward Wingate 1851-1924 *NatCAB 20*
Hatch, Edward Wingate 1852-1924 *WhAm 1*
Hatch, Edwin Glentworth 1886-1933 *WhAm 1*
Hatch, Elisha *NewYHSD*
Hatch, Emily Nichols d1959 *WhAm 3*
Hatch, Eric 1901-1973 *NatCAB 57*
Hatch, Everard E 1859- *WhAm 1*

Hatch, Everett Norman 1906-1956 *NatCAB 44*
Hatch, Floyd Frost 1892-1963 *NatCAB 51*
Hatch, Francis March 1852-1923 *WhAm 1*
Hatch, Frederick Thomas 1855-1920 *WhAm 1*
Hatch, Frederick Winslow 1822-1885 *ApCAB*
Hatch, George W 1805-1867 *NewYHSD*
Hatch, George W, Jr. *NewYHSD*
Hatch, Harry C 1884-1946 *WhAm 2*
Hatch, Henry James 1869-1931 *WhAm 1*
Hatch, Herschel Harrison 1837-1920 *BiDrAC*
Hatch, Israel Thompson 1808-1875 *ApCAB,*
BiAUS, BiDrAC, TwCBDA, WhAm H
Hatch, James Noble 1868- *WhAm 4*
Hatch, Jethro Ayers 1837-1912 *BiDrAC*
Hatch, John Fletcher 1879- *WhAm 6*
Hatch, John Porter 1822-1901 *AmBi, ApCAB,*
DcAmB, Drake, NatCAB 12, TwCBDA,
WebAMB, WhAm 1
Hatch, John Wood 1864- *WhAm 4*
Hatch, Katy Gower 1863- *WomWWA 14*
Hatch, Kirk Lester 1871-1956 *NatCAB 46*
Hatch, L Boyd 1897-1957 *WhAm 3*
Hatch, Leonard Williams 1869-1958 *WhAm 3*
Hatch, Lloyd A 1901- *WhAm 4*
Hatch, Louis Clinton 1872-1931 *NatCAB 22,*
WhAm 5
Hatch, Martin Fellows 1907-1968 *NatCAB 54*
Hatch, Mary R P 1848- *AmWom*
Hatch, P H *NewYHSD*
Hatch, Pascal Enos 1867-1952 *WhAm 3*
Hatch, Philander Ellsworth 1861- *WhAm 4*
Hatch, Robert Seymour 1907-1968 *WhAm 5*
Hatch, Roger Conant 1878-1943 *NatCAB 38*
Hatch, Roy Winthrop 1878-1955 *WhAm 4*
Hatch, Rufus 1832-1893 *DcAmB, WhAm H*
Hatch, Samuel Grantham 1865-1918 *WhAm 1*
Hatch, Stephen D 1839-1894 *WhAm H*
Hatch, Uriel Chittenden 1854-1939 *NatCAB 29*
Hatch, Vermont 1893-1959 *WhAm 3*
Hatch, Warner D *NewYHSD*
Hatch, William Edwin 1852-1923 *ApCAB X*
Hatch, William Henry 1833-1896 *AmBi,*
BiDrAC, DcAmB, EncAAH, McGEWB,
NatCAB 8, TwCBDA, WebAB,
WhAm H, WhAmP
Hatch, William Henry Paine 1875-1972
NatCAB 57
Hatcher, Anna Denson 1879- *WomWWA 14*
Hatcher, Cornelia Templeton 1867-
WomWWA 14
Hatcher, Eldridge Burwell 1865-1943 *WhAm 2*
Hatcher, James Fulton 1890-1955 *WhAm 3*
Hatcher, John Bell 1861-1904 *NatCAB 21,*
WhAm 1
Hatcher, John Henry 1875- *WhAm 5*
Hatcher, Julian Sommerville 1888-1963
NatCAB 50, WhAm 4
Hatcher, Latham 1868-1946 *WhAm 2*
Hatcher, Orie Latham 1868-1946 *BiDAmEd,*
DcAmB S4, NotAW, WomWWA 14
Hatcher, Robert Anthony 1819-1886
ApCAB Sup, BiAUS, BiDConf, BiDrAC,
TwCBDA, WhAm H, WhAmP
Hatcher, Robert Anthony 1868-1944
DcAmB S3, NatCAB 33, WhAm 2
Hatcher, Samuel Claiborne 1869-1952 *WhAm 3*
Hatcher, William Bass 1888-1947 *NatCAB 34,*
WhAm 2
Hatcher, William Eldridge 1834-1912 *DcAmB,*
NatCAB 19, WhAm 1
Hatcher, Wirt Hargrove 1894-1973 *WhAm 6*
Hatchett, Charles 1765-1847 *AsBiEn, DcScB*
Hatchett, James Brier 1853- *WhoColR*
Hatfield, Charles Albert Phelps 1850- *WhAm 4*
Hatfield, Charles Folsom 1862-1939 *WhAm 1,*
WhAm 1C
Hatfield, Charles James 1867-1951 *WhAm 3*
Hatfield, Charles Sherrod 1882-1950 *WhAm 2*
Hatfield, Edwin Francis 1807-1883 *ApCAB,*
DcAmB, NatCAB 10, TwCBDA,
WhAm H
Hatfield, George 1875-1957 *WhAm 3*
Hatfield, George Juan 1887-1953 *WhAm 3*
Hatfield, Henry Drury 1875-1962 *BiDrAC,*
NatCAB 53, WhAm 4
Hatfield, Henry Rand 1866-1945 *WhAm 2*
Hatfield, James Taft 1862-1945 *TwCBDA,*
WhAm 2

Hatfield, James Tobias 1865-1938 *WhAm 1*
Hatfield, Joseph Clayton 1877-1952 *WhAm 3*
Hatfield, Joshua Alexander 1863-1931
NatCAB 28, WhAm 1
Hatfield, Lansing d1954 *WhAm 3*
Hatfield, Malcolm 1900-1962 *NatCAB 52*
Hatfield, Marcus Patten 1849-1909 *TwCBDA,*
WhAm 1
Hatfield, Mark Odom 1922- *BiDrAC*
Hatfield, Oliver Perry 1819-1894 *WhAm H*
Hatfield, R G 1815-1879 *WhAm H*
Hatfield, Theophilus David 1855-1929
ApCAB X
Hathaway *NewYHSD*
Hathaway, Arthur Stafford 1855-1934 *WhAm 1*
Hathaway, Benjamin 1822- *ApCAB*
Hathaway, Charles Montgomery, Jr. 1874-1954
WhAm 3
Hathaway, Charles Wesley 1821-1899
NatCAB 17
Hathaway, Evangeline 1869- *WhAm 5,*
WomWWA 14
Hathaway, Fons A 1875- *WhAm 5*
Hathaway, Forrest Henry 1844-1912 *WhAm 1*
Hathaway, George Edgar 1871-1928
NatCAB 22
Hathaway, George Henry 1843-1931 *WhAm 1*
Hathaway, Harle Wallace 1866-1945 *WhAm 2*
Hathaway, Isaac Scott 1874- *WhoColR*
Hathaway, James S *NewYHSD*
Hathaway, Joseph *NewYHSD*
Hathaway, Joseph Henry 1875- *WhAm 5*
Hathaway, King 1878-1944 *NatCAB 33,*
WhAm 2
Hathaway, Lester Gordon 1878- *WhAm 6*
Hathaway, Norman Edward 1920-1969
NatCAB 54
Hathaway, Robert Joseph 1874-1955 *WhAm 3*
Hathaway, Rufus 1770-1822 *BnEnAmA,*
NewYHSD
Hathaway, Samuel Gilbert 1780-1867 *BiAUS,*
BiDrAC, WhAm H
Hathaway, Stewart Southworth 1885-1963
WhAm 4
Hathaway, Warren 1828-1909 *WhAm 3*
Hathaway, William Dodd 1924- *BiDrAC*
Hathaway, William Lee 1867- *WhAm 4*
Hatherty, Henry *NewYHSD*
Hatheway, Samuel Gilbert 1780-1867 *ApCAB,*
NatCAB 11, TwCBDA
Hatheway, Samuel Gilbert 1810-1864 *ApCAB,*
NatCAB 11, TwCBDA
Hathorn, Henry Harrison 1813-1887 *BiAUS,*
BiDrAC, WhAm H
Hathorn, John 1749-1825 *BiAUS, BiDrAC,*
WhAm H
Hathorne, George d1889 *WhAm H*
Hathorne, John 1641-1717 *ApCAB, Drake*
Hathorne, Nathaniel *WebAB*
Hathorne, William d1681 *Drake*
Hathorne, William 1607?-1681 *DcAmB,*
NatCAB 22, WhAm H
Hathorne, William 1608-1681 *ApCAB*
Hathorne, William *see also* Hawthorne, William
Hathway, Calvin Sutliff 1907-1974 *WhAm 6*
Hathway, George Wilson 1906-1968
NatCAB 53, WhAm 5
Hathway, Marion 1895-1955 *WhAm 3*
Hatlo, Jimmy 1898-1963 *WhAm 4*
Hatoyama, Ichiro 1883-1959 *WhAm 3*
Hatschek, Berthold 1854-1941 *DcScB*
Hatshepsut *McGEWB*
Hatt, Paul Kitchener 1914-1953 *WhAm 3*
Hatt, Rafe Nelson 1889-1949 *NatCAB 39*
Hatt, William Kendrick 1868- *WhAm 5*
Hattan, Michael *NewYHSD*
Hatton, Augustus Rutan 1873-1946 *WhAm 2*
Hatton, Charles Harold 1880-1936 *WhAm 1*
Hatton, E Roy 1887-1961 *WhAm 4*
Hatton, Fanny Cottinet Locke 1869-1939
NatCAB 42
Hatton, Frank 1846-1894 *ApCAB, BiDrUSE,*
DcAmB, NatCAB 4, TwCBDA,
WhAm H
Hatton, Moses Wesley 1866- *WhAm 4*
Hatton, Robert 1827-1862 *ApCAB, BiAUS,*
Drake
Hatton, Robert Hopkins 1826-1862 *BiDrAC,*

TwCBDA, WhAm H
Hatton, T Chalkley 1860- *WhAm 1*
Hatton, Thomas d1655 *ApCAB*
Hattstaedt, John James 1851-1931 *WhAm 1*
Hatuey d1512 *ApCAB*
Hauberg, John Henry 1869- *WhAm 3*
Hauberg, Susanne Christine Denkmann
1872-1942 *NatCAB 42*
Haubisen, Christopher 1830-1913 *NewYHSD*
Haubold, Herman A 1867-1931 *WhAm 1*
Hauck, Cornelius John 1893-1967 *NatCAB 53*
Hauck, Eugene Frederick 1856-1939
NatCAB 51
Hauck, Fred 1905-1960 *WhAm 4*
Hauck, Louis John 1867-1942 *NatCAB 30*
Hauck, Louise Platt 1883-1943 *WhAm 2*
Hauck, Minnie d1929 *Drake*
Hauck, Minnie 1852-1929 *ApCAB*
Hauck, Minnie 1853-1929 *WhAm 2*
Hauck, Minnie *see also* Hauk, Minnie
Hauenstein, Minnie Ferris *WomWWA 14*
Haug, Gustave Emile 1861-1927 *DcScB*
Haugaard, William Edward 1889-1948
NatCAB 40
Haugan, Henry Alexander 1878-1928 *WhAm 1*
Hauge, Hjalmar Christian 1862- *WhAm 4*
Haugen, Gilbert Nelson 1859-1933 *BiDrAC,*
DcAmB S1, EncAAH, WhAm 1,
WhAmP
Haugen, Nils Pederson 1849-1931 *BiDrAC,*
DcAmB S1, TwCBDA, WhAm 1,
WhAmP
Haugg, Louis *NewYHSD*
Haugh, Jesse Lee 1887-1965 *WhAm 4*
Haughery, Margaret d1882 *ApCAB*
Haughery, Margaret Gaffney 1813-1882
NotAW
Haughery, Margaret Gaffney 1814?-1882
DcAmB
Haughery, Margaret Gaffney 1825?-1882
TwCBDA
Haughey, James M 1915?- *IlBEAAW*
Haughey, Thomas 1826-1869 *BiAUS, BiDrAC,*
WhAm H
Haught, Benjamin Franklin 1881-1961 *WhAm 4*
Haught, Thomas William 1871-1957 *WhAm 3*
Haughton, Louisa Courlauld Osburne 1866-
WomWWA 14
Haughton, Percy Duncan 1876-1924 *DcAmB*
Haughwout, Frank Goddard 1877-1960
NatCAB 46
Haugsten, Harry George 1890-1955 *NatCAB 44*
Hauhart, William Frederic 1873- *WhAm 5*
Hauk, Minnie 1851?-1929 *NotAW*
Hauk, Minnie 1852?-1929 *AmBi, AmWom,*
DcAmB, WhAm HA, WhAm 4
Hauk, Minnie 1853-1929 *NatCAB 8*
Hauk, Minnie *see also* Hauck, Minnie
Hauke, Robert Charles 1924-1975 *WhAm 6*
Hauksbee, Francis 1666?-1713 *DcScB*
Hauksbee, Francis 1670?-1713? *AsBiEn*
Hauksbee, Francis 1688-1763 *DcScB*
Haulenbeek, P Raymond 1899-1966 *NatCAB 51,*
WhAm 4
Haulick, Christian J *NewYHSD*
Haun, Burton Oliver 1877- *WhAm 5*
Haun, H P 1815-1860 *BiAUS*
Haun, Henry Peter 1815-1860 *ApCAB,*
BiDrAC, NatCAB 11, TwCBDA,
WhAm H
Haun, Paul 1906-1969 *NatCAB 55*
Haupert, Raymond Samuel 1902-1972 *WhAm 5*
Haupt, Alexander James Derbyshire 1859-1934
WhAm 1
Haupt, Caspar Wistar 1895-1965 *NatCAB 51*
Haupt, Charles Elvin 1852- *WhAm 1*
Haupt, Herman 1817-1905 *AmBi, ApCAB,*
DcAmB, NatCAB 10, TwCBDA,
WhAm 1
Haupt, Hermann 1817-1905 *Drake*
Haupt, Ira 1889-1963 *WhAm 4*
Haupt, Lewis Muhlenberg 1844-1937 *AmBi,*
ApCAB, NatCAB 13, TwCBDA,
WhAm 1
Haupt, Louis 1851- *NatCAB 15*
Haupt, Paul 1858-1926 *AmBi, ApCAB,*
ApCAB X, DcAmB, NatCAB 22,
TwCBDA, WhAm 1

Haupt, Sarah Minerva 1874- *WhAm 5*
Hauptmann, Alfred 1881-1948 *NatCAB 36*
Hauptmann, Bruno Richard 1900-1936 *AmBi*
Hauptmann, Gerhart Johann Robert 1862-1946
  McGEWB, WhAm 2
Hauschel, Alphonse Robert 1877-1956
  NatCAB 48
Hausdorfer, Walter 1898-1970 *WhAm 5*
Hausdorff, Felix 1868-1942 *DcScB*
Hauser, Charles R 1900-1970 *WhAm 5*
Hauser, Conrad Augustine 1872-1943 *WhAm 2*
Hauser, Elizabeth J 1873- *WomWWA 14*
Hauser, Ernst Alfred 1896-1956 *NatCAB 44,
  WhAm 3*
Hauser, Harry 1904-1971 *WhAm 5*
Hauser, John 1858?-1913 *IIBEAAW*
Hauser, John 1859-1913 *NatCAB 16*
Hauser, Samuel Thomas 1833-1914 *DcAmB,
  NatCAB 3, NatCAB 11, REnAW,
  WhAm 1*
Hauser, Walter 1893-1959 *WhAm 4*
Hauserman, Fredric Martin 1909-1972
  WhAm 5
Haushofer, Karl 1869-1946 *McGEWB*
Hauskens, Peter Bert 1919-1972 *WhAm 5*
Hauslein, Clara Dawson 1868- *WomWWA 14*
Hausman, E C *NewYHSD*
Hausman, Leon Augustus 1888-1966 *WhAm 4*
Hausman, Louis 1891-1972 *NatCAB 57,
  WhAm 5*
Hausman, William A, Jr. 1878-1949 *WhAm 2A*
Hausmann, Erich 1886-1962 *WhAm 4*
Haussermann, John William 1867-1965
  NatCAB 52, WhAm 4
Haussermann, Oscar William 1888-1975
  WhAm 6
Haussler, Arthur Glenn 1899-1974 *WhAm 6*
Haussling, Jacob 1855-1921 *WhAm 1*
Haussmann, Alfred Carl 1897-1963 *WhAm 4*
Haussmann, Baron Georges Eugene 1809-1891
  McGEWB
Haut, Irvin Charles 1906-1972 *WhAm 5*
Hautecoeur, Louis 1884-1973 *WhAm 6*
Hautefeuille, Paul Gabriel 1836-1902 *DcScB*
Hauver, Robert Beebe 1896-1961 *NatCAB 53*
Hauxhurst, Henry Austin 1881- *WhAm 6*
Hauxhurst, Stanley Cottrill 1880-1930
  NatCAB 23
Hauy, Rene Just 1743-1822 *AsBiEn, DcScB*
Havard, Valery 1846-1927 *WhAm 1*
Havas, George 1903-1962 *NatCAB 47,
  WhAm 4*
Haveland, Joseph H *NewYHSD*
Haveland, Laura Smith 1808- *ApCAB*
Havell, Henry Augustus *NewYHSD*
Havell, Robert 1793-1878 *DcAmB,
  NatCAB 22, NewYHSD, WhAm H*
Havelock, Sir Henry 1795-1857 *WhoMilH*
Havemeyer, Arthur 1882-1955 *NatCAB 44*
Havemeyer, Clara Martha Herrick 1884-
  WomWWA 14
Havemeyer, Frederick Christian 1807-1891
  NatCAB 13
Havemeyer, Henry 1838-1886 *ApCAB*
Havemeyer, Henry Osborne 1847-1907 *AmBi,
  DcAmB, EncAB, WhAm 1*
Havemeyer, Henry Osborne 1876-1965
  ApCAB X, WhAm 4
Havemeyer, Horace 1886-1956 *NatCAB 45,
  WhAm 3*
Havemeyer, John Craig 1833-1922 *NatCAB 3,
  NatCAB 17, WhAm 1*
Havemeyer, Loomis 1886-1971 *WhAm 5*
Havemeyer, Louisine Waldron Elder 1855-1929
  NotAW
Havemeyer, Theodore Augustus d1936
  WhAm 1
Havemeyer, William Frederick 1804-1874
  *ApCAB, DcAmB, NatCAB 13,
  NatCAB 17, TwCBDA, WhAm H*
Havemeyer, William Frederick 1850-1913
  WhAm 1
Haven, Alfred Coles 1858-1918 *NatCAB 19*
Haven, Alice B *NotAW*
Haven, Alice B 1827-1863 *DcAmB*
Haven, Alice Bradley 1828-1863 *ApCAB,
  Drake, NatCAB 5, TwCBDA*
Haven, Emily Bradley Neal 1827-1863 *DcAmB,*

NotAW, WhAm H
Haven, Erastus Otis 1820-1881 *ApCAB,
  DcAmB, Drake, NatCAB 1, TwCBDA,
  WhAm H*
Haven, Franklin d1908 *WhAm 1*
Haven, George Bartholomew 1871-1953
  NatCAB 45
Haven, George Griswold d1908 *WhAm 1*
Haven, Gilbert 1821-1880 *ApCAB, DcAmB,
  DcAmReB, NatCAB 13, TwCBDA,
  WhAm H*
Haven, Hale 1902-1964 *NatCAB 51*
Haven, Henry Philemon 1815-1876 *DcAmB,
  WhAm H*
Haven, Joseph 1816-1874 *ApCAB, DcAmB,
  NatCAB 2, TwCBDA, WhAm H*
Haven, Joseph Emerson 1885-1937 *WhAm 1*
Haven, Joshua P *NewYHSD*
Haven, Mary Emerson 1819- *AmWom*
Haven, Nathaniel Appleton 1762-1831 *BiAUS,
  BiDrAC, WhAm H*
Haven, Nathaniel Appleton 1790-1826 *ApCAB,
  Drake*
Haven, Samuel 1727-1806 *ApCAB*
Haven, Samuel Forster 1806-1881 *ApCAB*
Haven, Samuel Foster 1806-1881 *DcAmLiB,
  Drake*
Haven, Solomon George 1810-1861 *ApCAB,
  BiAUS, BiDrAC, NatCAB 11, TwCBDA,
  WhAm H, WhAmP*
Haven, William Ingraham 1856-1928 *WhAm 1*
Havenhill, L D 1870-1950 *WhAm 3*
Havenner, Franck Roberts 1882-1967 *BiDrAC,
  WhAm 4*
Havenner, George Clement 1866- *WhAm 5*
Havens, Donald 1892-1959 *WhAm 3*
Havens, Frank Colton 1848-1918 *WhAm 1*
Havens, Harrison Eugene 1837-1916 *BiAUS,
  BiDrAC*
Havens, James 1763-1864 *ApCAB*
Havens, James Dexter 1900-1960 *WhAm 4*
Havens, James Smith 1859-1927 *BiDrAC,
  DcAmB, WhAm 1*
Havens, Jonathan Nicoll 1757-1799 *BiAUS,
  BiDrAC, WhAm H*
Havens, Lizzie M 1862- *WomWWA 14*
Havens, Paul Egbert 1839-1913 *WhAm 1*
Havens, Raymond Dexter 1880-1958 *WhAm 3*
Havens, Ruth Ginivia Dowd 1845-
  WomWWA 14
Havens, Valentine Britton 1889-1948
  NatCAB 36, WhAm 2
Havens, Verne Leroy 1881-1944 *NatCAB 34*
Havens, William Louis 1893-1958 *NatCAB 46*
Haverly, Christopher 1837-1901 *DcAmB,
  WhAm H*
Haverly, Jack H 1837-1901 *DcAmB*
Havers, Clopton 1655?-1702 *DcScB*
Haverstick, Edward Everett 1873-1955
  WhAm 3
Haverty, Clarence 1881-1960 *WhAm 4*
Havestad, Bernhard 1715-1778 *ApCAB*
Havighurst, Freeman Alfred 1869- *WhAm 5*
Havighurst, Robert James 1900- *BiDAmEd*
Haviland, Charles Edward 1839- *NatCAB 13*
Haviland, Clarence Floyd 1875-1930 *DcAmB,
  NatCAB 24, WhAm 1*
Haviland, James Thomas 1889-1957
  NatCAB 44, WhAm 3
Haviland, John 1792-1852 *ApCAB, BnEnAmA,
  DcAmB, Drake, NatCAB 11, WhAm H*
Haviland, John 1792-1853 *NewYHSD*
Haviland, Laura Smith 1808-1898 *NotAW*
Haviland, Thomas Heath 1822- *ApCAB*
Haviland, William 1718-1784 *ApCAB, Drake*
Havner, Horace Moore 1871-1949 *NatCAB 37,
  WhAm 3*
Haw, George Edwin 1881-1971 *WhAm 5*
Haw, Stanley Alfred 1902-1955 *NatCAB 48*
Hawes, Albert Gallatin 1804-1849 *BiAUS,
  BiDrAC, WhAm H*
Hawes, Austin Foster 1879- *WhAm 6*
Hawes, Aylett 1768-1833 *BiAUS, BiDrAC,
  WhAm H*
Hawes, Charles Boardman 1889-1923 *DcAmB*
Hawes, Charles Henry 1867-1943 *WhAm 2*
Hawes, Charlotte W *AmWom*
Hawes, Elizabeth 1903-1971 *WhAm 5*

Hawes, Flora Harrod 1863- *AmWom*
Hawes, Franc P *AmWom*
Hawes, George Edward 1864- *WhAm 4*
Hawes, Granville P 1839- *NatCAB 3*
Hawes, Harriet Ann Boyd 1871-1945
  *DcAmB S3, NotAW, WhAm 3A,
  WomWWA 14*
Hawes, Harry Bartow 1869-1947 *BiDrAC,
  NatCAB 41, WhAm 2, WhAmP*
Hawes, James Morrison 1824-1889 *BiDConf*
Hawes, James William 1844-1918 *WhAm 1*
Hawes, Jesse 1843-1901 *NatCAB 57*
Hawes, Joel 1789-1867 *ApCAB, Drake,
  NatCAB 11, TwCBDA, WhAm H*
Hawes, John Bromham, II 1877-1938 *WhAm 1*
Hawes, Josiah Johnson 1808-1901 *BnEnAmA,
  NatCAB 28, NewYHSD*
Hawes, Peter 1768-1829 *NatCAB 8*
Hawes, Richard 1797-1877 *ApCAB, BiAUS,
  BiDConf, BiDrAC, TwCBDA, WhAm H,
  WhAmP*
Hawes, Richard Simrall 1873-1949 *NatCAB 46,
  WhAm 2*
Hawes, S P *NewYHSD*
Hawes, Sarah E *NewYHSD*
Hawes, Stewart S 1898-1967 *WhAm 4,
  WhAm 5*
Hawes, William Post 1803-1842 *ApCAB,
  Drake, NatCAB 11, WhAm H*
Hawgood, Harry 1853-1931 *WhAm 1*
Hawk, Eugene Blake 1881- *WhAm 6*
Hawk, Philip Bovier 1874-1966 *WhAm 4*
Hawk, Robert Moffett Allison 1839-1882
  BiDrAC, WhAm H
Hawk, Sydney *NewYHSD*
Hawk, Wilbur C 1881-1936 *WhAm 1*
Hawke, Anne Shoemaker 1882- *WomWWA 14*
Hawke, James Albert 1841-1910 *WhAm 1*
Hawkes, Albert Wahl 1878-1971 *BiDrAC,
  WhAm 6*
Hawkes, Benjamin Carleton 1875-1931
  WhAm 1
Hawkes, Clarence 1869-1954 *WhAm 3*
Hawkes, Edith Granger *WomWWA 14*
Hawkes, Elden Earl 1908-1972 *WhAm 5*
Hawkes, Forbes 1865-1940 *NatCAB 30,
  WhAm 1*
Hawkes, Herbert Edwin 1872-1943 *NatCAB 32,
  WhAm 2*
Hawkes, James 1776-1865 *BiAUS, BiDrAC,
  WhAm H*
Hawkes, McDougall 1862-1929 *NatCAB 24,
  WhAm 1*
Hawkes, William *NewYHSD*
Hawkes, William F 1898-1950 *WhAm 3*
Hawkesworth, Alan Spencer 1867-1942
  WhAm 2
Hawkins, Alfred Lamb 1873-1948 *NatCAB 36*
Hawkins, Alvin 1821-1905 *NatCAB 7,
  TwCBDA, WhAm 1*
Hawkins, Arthur Elliott 1888-1966 *NatCAB 51*
Hawkins, Arthur Hanson 1868-1952
  NatCAB 39, WhAm 3
Hawkins, Augustus Freeman 1907- *BiDrAC*
Hawkins, Avis A 1857- *WomWWA 14*
Hawkins, Benjamin 1754-1816 *ApCAB,
  BiAUS, BiDrAC, DcAmB, Drake,
  NatCAB 4, TwCBDA, WebAB,
  WhAm H, WhAmP*
Hawkins, Benjamin Waterhouse 1807-1889
  ApCAB, NatCAB 11, WhAm H
Hawkins, Charles Martyr 1858- *WhAm 4*
Hawkins, Chauncey Jeddie 1876-1930 *WhAm 1*
Hawkins, Coleman 1904-1969 *WhAm 5*
Hawkins, Dexter Arnold 1825-1886 *ApCAB,
  DcAmB, NatCAB 7, WhAm H*
Hawkins, Dexter Arnoll 1825-1886 *TwCBDA*
Hawkins, Dexter Clarkson 1898-1965
  NatCAB 52, WhAm 4
Hawkins, Earle T 1903-1972 *WhAm 5*
Hawkins, Edward Russell 1908-1963
  NatCAB 51, WhAm 4
Hawkins, Emmet Lefevre 1887-1949
  NatCAB 41
Hawkins, Ernest 1802?- *ApCAB, Drake*
Hawkins, Eugene Dexter 1860-1919 *ApCAB X*
Hawkins, Evangel Lee Bristow 1875-
  WomWWA 14

Hawkins, Ezekiel C *NewYHSD*
Hawkins, George Knight 1862-1940 *NatCAB 32, WhAm 1*
Hawkins, George Lawrence 1859-1941 *NatCAB 31*
Hawkins, George Sydney 1808-1878 *BiAUS, BiDrAC, WhAm H*
Hawkins, Hamilton Smith 1834-1910 *ApCAB Sup, TwCBDA, WhAm 1*
Hawkins, Hamilton Smith 1872-1950 *WhAm 3*
Hawkins, Harry Benjamin 1871-1941 *NatCAB 31*
Hawkins, Henry 1873-1947 *NatCAB 34*
Hawkins, Henry Gabriel 1866- *WhAm 4*
Hawkins, Horace Norman 1867-1947 *WhAm 2*
Hawkins, Ira 1894-1967 *WhAm 4*
Hawkins, Isaac *NewYHSD*
Hawkins, Isaac Roberts 1818-1880 *BiAUS, BiDrAC, NatCAB 13, WhAm H*
Hawkins, J Dawson 1868- *WhAm 4*
Hawkins, J E 1899-1961 *WhAm 4*
Hawkins, Jack 1910-1973 *WhAm 5*
Hawkins, Sir John 1520-1595 *ApCAB, Drake*
Hawkins, Sir John 1532-1595 *McGEWB*
Hawkins, John Henry Willis 1797-1858 *Drake, NatCAB 11, TwCBDA*
Hawkins, John Henry Willis 1799-1858 *ApCAB*
Hawkins, John J 1855-1935 *WhAm 1*
Hawkins, John Parker 1830-1914 *ApCAB, TwCBDA, WhAm 1*
Hawkins, John Russell 1862- *WhoColR*
Hawkins, Joseph 1781-1832 *BiAUS, BiDrAC, WhAm H*
Hawkins, Joseph H d1823 *BiAUS, BiDrAC, WhAm H*
Hawkins, Laurence Ashley 1877-1958 *NatCAB 47, WhAm 3*
Hawkins, Layton S 1877-1960 *WhAm 4*
Hawkins, M T 1790-1858 *BiAUS*
Hawkins, Mason Albert 1874- *WhoColR*
Hawkins, Micajah Thomas 1790-1858 *ApCAB, BiDrAC, TwCBDA, WhAm H*
Hawkins, Morris Seymour 1882-1946 *WhAm 2*
Hawkins, Philemon 1717-1801 *ApCAB*
Hawkins, Philemon 1752-1833 *BiAUS, Drake*
Hawkins, Prince Albert 1871-1939 *NatCAB 36, WhAm 1*
Hawkins, Richard Fenner 1837- *NatCAB 3*
Hawkins, Richard Hays 1879-1933 *NatCAB 26*
Hawkins, Rush Christopher 1831-1920 *ApCAB, DcAmB, NatCAB 5, TwCBDA, WhAm 1*
Hawkins, Thomas *NewYHSD*
Hawkins, Thomas Hayden *WhAm 5*
Hawkins, Walter Everette 1883- *WhoColR*
Hawkins, Wilford Judson 1877-1959 *NatCAB 47*
Hawkins, William *NewYHSD*
Hawkins, William d1814? *BiAUS*
Hawkins, William 1770-1819 *ApCAB, Drake, NatCAB 4, TwCBDA*
Hawkins, William Ashbie 1862- *WhoColR*
Hawkins, William Bruce 1900-1971 *WhAm 6*
Hawkins, William Edward 1863-1937 *WhAm 1*
Hawkins, William George 1823- *ApCAB, TwCBDA, WhAm 4*
Hawkins, William John 1851- *WhAm 4*
Hawkins, William Waller 1883-1953 *NatCAB 46, WhAm 3*
Hawkridge, Leslie Dean 1891-1952 *NatCAB 40*
Hawks, Annie Sherwood 1835-1918 *AmWom, NatCAB 17*
Hawks, Charles, Jr. 1899-1960 *BiDrAC, WhAm 3*
Hawks, Cicero Stephen 1812-1868 *Drake, NatCAB 8*
Hawks, Cicero Stephens 1812-1868 *ApCAB, TwCBDA*
Hawks, Emma Beatrice 1871- *WomWWA 14*
Hawks, Emma Lucinda *WomWWA 14*
Hawks, Francis Lister 1798-1866 *ApCAB, DcAmB, Drake, NatCAB 7, TwCBDA, WhAm H*
Hawks, Frank Monroe 1897-1938 *AmBi, NatCAB 29, WhAm 1*
Hawks, Howard Winchester 1896- *WebAB*
Hawks, James Dudley 1847- *WhAm 4*
Hawks, John 1707-1784 *NatCAB 9*

Hawks, John 1731-1790 *DcAmB, WhAm H*
Hawks, John 1832-1922 *NatCAB 19*
Hawks, Rachel Marshall *WomWWA 14*
Hawksett, S, Jr. *NewYHSD*
Hawksmoor, Nicholas 1661-1736 *McGEWB*
Hawley, Alan Ramsay 1864-1938 *NatCAB 32*
Hawley, Alan Ramsay 1869-1938 *WhAm 1*
Hawley, Albert Henry 1866-1931 *WhAm 1*
Hawley, Bostwick 1814-1910 *ApCAB, TwCBDA, WhAm 1*
Hawley, Cameron 1905-1969 *NatCAB 54, WhAm 5*
Hawley, Charles 1819-1885 *ApCAB*
Hawley, Charles Anthony 1832- *WhAm 4*
Hawley, Charles Augustus 1861-1929 *NatCAB 22*
Hawley, Charles B 1858- *WhAm 4*
Hawley, Chester Warner 1834- *NatCAB 7*
Hawley, Cyrus M *BiAUS*
Hawley, Donly Curtis 1855-1926 *NatCAB 14, NatCAB 27, WhAm 4*
Hawley, Edwin 1850-1912 *WhAm 1*
Hawley, Frances Mallette 1843- *AmWom*
Hawley, Fred Horace 1873-1961 *NatCAB 49*
Hawley, Fred Vermillia 1862-1927 *WhAm 1*
Hawley, Frederick William 1866-1953 *WhAm 3*
Hawley, George 1869-1934 *NatCAB 26*
Hawley, George Maxwell Blackstock 1870-1941 *NatCAB 31*
Hawley, Gideon 1727-1807 *AmBi, ApCAB, DcAmB, Drake, WhAm H*
Hawley, Gideon 1785-1870 *ApCAB, BiDAmEd, DcAmB, Drake, TwCBDA, WhAm H*
Hawley, Gideon 1785-1890 *NatCAB 13*
Hawley, Harry Franklin 1870-1970 *WhAm 5*
Hawley, Henry Stephen 1851-1915 *NatCAB 19*
Hawley, James Henry 1847-1929 *DcAmB, NatCAB 15, REnAW, WhAm 1*
Hawley, John Baldwin 1831-1895 *BiAUS, BiDrAC, WhAm H, WhAmP*
Hawley, John Blackstock 1866-1941 *NatCAB 30, WhAm 1*
Hawley, John Mitchell 1846-1925 *WhAm 1*
Hawley, John Savage 1836-1913 *NatCAB 17*
Hawley, Joseph 1723-1788 *AmBi, ApCAB, DcAmB, NatCAB 4, WhAm H*
Hawley, Joseph 1724-1788 *BiAUS, Drake*
Hawley, Joseph Boswell 1826-1905 *WhAm 1*
Hawley, Joseph Roswell 1826-1905 *ApCAB, BiAUS, BiDrAC, DcAmB, Drake, NatCAB 1, TwCBDA, WhAmP*
Hawley, Julius Sargent 1844-1935 *WhAm 1*
Hawley, Lewis Tanner 1807-1891 *NatCAB 3*
Hawley, Marcus Clinton 1834-1899 *ApCAB X*
Hawley, Margaret Foote 1880- *WhAm 6*
Hawley, Newton Fremont 1859-1918 *NatCAB 17, WhAm 1*
Hawley, Paul Ramsey 1891-1965 *WhAm 4*
Hawley, Ralph Chipman 1880-1971 *WhAm 5*
Hawley, Ralph Waldo 1888-1949 *NatCAB 50*
Hawley, Ransom Smith 1881- *WhAm 6*
Hawley, Robert Bradley 1849-1921 *BiDrAC*
Hawley, Thomas Porter 1830-1907 *NatCAB 12, WhAm 1*
Hawley, William Merrill 1802-1869 *ApCAB*
Hawley, Willis Chatman 1864-1941 *BiDrAC, DcAmB S3, NatCAB 32, TwCBDA, WhAm 1, WhAmP*
Hawn, Henry Gaines d1930 *WhAm 1C*
Hawn, Henry Gaines 1862-1930 *NatCAB 14*
Hawn, Henry Gaines 1864-1930 *WhAm 1*
Hawn, Russell John 1878-1938 *NatCAB 27*
Haworth, Adrian Hardy 1768-1833 *DcScB*
Haworth, Eleanor Frothingham 1860- *WomWWA 14*
Haworth, Erasmus 1855-1932 *WhAm 1*
Haworth, George *NewYHSD*
Haworth, Joseph 1855-1903 *DcAmB, TwCBDA*
Haworth, Joseph 1858-1903 *WhAm 1*
Haworth, Sir Norman 1883-1950 *WhAm 2*
Haworth, Paul Leland 1876-1938 *ApCAB X, NatCAB 28, WhAm 1*
Haworth, Sir Walter Norman 1883-1950 *AsBiEn, DcScB*
Hawqal, Abu'l-Qasim Muhammad, Ibn *DcScB*
Haws, J H Hobart 1809-1858 *BiAUS*
Haws, John Henry Hobart 1809-1858 *BiDrAC,*

WhAm H
Hawthorn, Charles *NewYHSD*
Hawthorne, Alice 1827-1902 *AmBi*
Hawthorne, Charles Webster 1872-1930 *AmBi, BnEnAmA, DcAmB, NatCAB 22, WhAm 1*
Hawthorne, Edith G 1874- *IIBEAAW*
Hawthorne, Frank Warren 1852-1911 *NatCAB 6*
Hawthorne, Hildegarde d1952 *WhAm 3, WomWWA 14*
Hawthorne, Hugh Robert 1885-1962 *WhAm 4*
Hawthorne, James Boardman 1837- *NatCAB 2*
Hawthorne, James Cossett 1819-1881 *NatCAB 7*
Hawthorne, Julian 1846-1934 *AmBi, ApCAB, DcAmB S1, NatCAB 2, NatCAB 25, TwCBDA, WhAm 1*
Hawthorne, Mrs. Nathaniel *NewYHSD*
Hawthorne, Nathaniel 1804-1864 *AmBi, ApCAB, BiAUS, DcAmB, Drake, EncAAH, EncAB, McGEWB, NatCAB 3, TwCBDA, WebAB, WhAm H*
Hawthorne, Rose 1851-1926 *AmBi, DcAmB, NotAW, WhAm HA, WhAm 4*
Hawthorne, Sophia Amelia Peabody 1809-1871 *NotAW*
Hawthorne, Sophia Peabody 1810-1871 *ApCAB*
Hawthorne, William 1607-1681 *NatCAB 8*
Hawthorne, William see also Hathorne, William
Hawtrey, Charles Henry 1858-1923 *WhAm 1*
Hawtrey, Sir Ralph George 1879- *WhAm 6*
Hawxhurst, Robert, Jr. 1875- *WhAm 5*
Haxall, Robert William 1802-1872 *ApCAB*
Haxo, Henry Emile 1881-1958 *NatCAB 48, WhAm 6*
Haxton, Milton 1826-1898 *TwCBDA*
Hay, Andrew Kessler 1809-1881 *BiAUS, BiDrAC, WhAm H*
Hay, Arthur Douglas 1884-1952 *WhAm 3*
Hay, Charles Augustus 1821-1893 *ApCAB, DcAmB, TwCBDA, WhAm H*
Hay, Charles Edward 1841-1916 *NatCAB 16*
Hay, Charles Martin 1879-1945 *WhAm 2*
Hay, Clarence Leonard 1884-1969 *NatCAB 54, WhAm 5*
Hay, David G 1798?- *NewYHSD*
Hay, DeWitt Clinton 1819?- *NewYHSD*
Hay, Donald Leith 1893-1938 *NatCAB 28*
Hay, Earl Downing 1886-1953 *WhAm 3*
Hay, Edward Northup 1891-1958 *NatCAB 47*
Hay, Eleanor Humbird 1877- *WomWWA 14*
Hay, Elzey *NotAW*
Hay, Eugene Gano 1853-1933 *WhAm 1*
Hay, George 1765-1830 *ApCAB, BiAUS, DcAmB, Drake, NatCAB 11, WhAm H*
Hay, Henry Clinton 1853-1935 *WhAm 1*
Hay, James 1856-1931 *BiDrAC, NatCAB 23, TwCBDA, WhAm 1, WhAmP*
Hay, James, Jr. 1881-1936 *NatCAB 28, WhAm 1*
Hay, John 1839- *Drake*
Hay, John Breese 1834-1916 *BiAUS, BiDrAC*
Hay, John Milton 1838-1905 *AmBi, ApCAB, ApCAB X, BiDrUSE, DcAmB, EncAB, McGEWB, NatCAB 3, NatCAB 11, NatCAB 14, NatCAB 36, TwCBDA, WebAB, WhAm 1, WhAmP*
Hay, John W 1864-1951 *WhAm 3*
Hay, Lawrence Gano 1823-1897 *TwCBDA*
Hay, Logan 1871-1942 *WhAm 2*
Hay, Malcolm 1907-1972 *WhAm 5*
Hay, Marion E 1865-1933 *NatCAB 14, WhAm 1*
Hay, Mary Garrett 1857-1928 *ApCAB X, BiCAW, DcAmB, NotAW, WhAm 1, WhAmP, WomWWA 14*
Hay, Mary Ridgely 1844- *WomWWA 14a*
Hay, Oliver Perry 1846-1930 *AmBi, DcAmB, NatCAB 22, WhAm 1*
Hay, Samuel Ross 1865-1944 *WhAm 2*
Hay, Stephen John 1864-1916 *WhAm 1*
Hay, Thomas Abraham Horn 1855-1925 *NatCAB 39, WhAm 1*
Hay, Valentine 1834-1916 *NatCAB 18*
Hay, Walter 1830- *ApCAB*
Hay, Walter Fulton Whittimore 1897-1944 *NatCAB 34*

Hay, William *NewYHSD*
Hay, William H *NewYHSD*
Hay, William Henry 1860-1946 *WhAm 2*
Hay, William Perry 1872-1947 *WhAm 2*
Haya DeLaTorre, Victor Raul 1895- *McGEWB*
Hayakawa, Samuel Ichiye 1906- *BiDAmEd, WebAB*
Hayakawa, Sessue 1890-1973 *WhAm 6*
Haycox, Ernest 1899-1950 *NatCAB 39, REnAW, WhAm 3*
Haycraft, Julius Everette 1871- *WhAm 5*
Hayden, Miss *NewYHSD*
Hayden, Amos Sutton 1813-1880 *DcAmB, NatCAB 22, WhAm H*
Hayden, Anexamander Montgomery 1852-1937 *NatCAB 30*
Hayden, Arthur Gunderson 1874-1964 *NatCAB 51, WhAm 4*
Hayden, Austin Albert 1881-1940 *WhAm 1*
Hayden, Carl Trumbull 1877-1972 *BiDrAC, REnAW, WhAm 5, WhAm 6, WhAmP*
Hayden, Charles 1870-1937 *AmBi, ApCAB X, DcAmB S2, NatCAB 14, WhAm 1*
Hayden, Charles Henry 1856-1901 *DcAmB, WhAm 1*
Hayden, Charles Sidney 1880-1937 *WhAm 1*
Hayden, Charles Trumbull 1825-1900 *REnAW*
Hayden, Clara May 1880- *WomWWA 14*
Hayden, Dorothea Hoaglin *WomWWA 14*
Hayden, Edward Daniel 1833-1908 *BiDrAC*
Hayden, Edward Everett 1858-1932 *DcAmB S1, NatCAB 8, NatCAB 27, TwCBDA, WhAm 1*
Hayden, Edward Simeon 1851-1899 *NatCAB 25*
Hayden, Ferdinand V 1829-1887 *BiAUS Sup*
Hayden, Ferdinand Vandeveer 1829-1887 *ApCAB, REnAW, TwCBDA, WebAB*
Hayden, Ferdinand Vandiveer 1829-1887 *AmBi, DcAmB, DcScB, EncAAH, NatCAB 11, WhAm H*
Hayden, Frank 1874-1936 *WhAm 1*
Hayden, Frederick Smith 1846- *WhAm 4*
Hayden, George Dickerson 1878-1962 *NatCAB 51*
Hayden, Gillette 1880-1929 *NatCAB 24*
Hayden, Harriet Clark Winslow 1840-1906 *NewYHSD*
Hayden, Hezekiah Sidney 1816-1896 *NatCAB 6*
Hayden, Hiram Washington 1820-1904 *DcAmB, NatCAB 25*
Hayden, Horace Edwin 1837-1917 *ApCAB Sup, NatCAB 10, TwCBDA, WhAm 1*
Hayden, Horace Henry 1769-1844 *ApCAB, BiDAmEd, DcAmB, NatCAB 13, TwCBDA, WhAm H*
Hayden, J H *NewYHSD*
Hayden, Jay G 1884-1971 *WhAm 5*
Hayden, Jerome William 1901-1962 *NatCAB 49*
Hayden, Jesse Franklin 1875-1952 *NatCAB 41*
Hayden, Joel Babcock 1888-1950 *NatCAB 38, WhAm 2*
Hayden, John Louis 1866-1936 *WhAm 1*
Haycox, Joseph Ralston 1887-1945 *WhAm 2*
Hayden, Joseph Shepard 1802-1877 *DcAmB, WhAm H*
Hayden, Josiah Willard 1874-1955 *WhAm 3*
Hayden, Mother Mary Bridget 1814-1890 *NotAW*
Hayden, Merrill A 1913-1974 *WhAm 6*
Hayden, Moses 1786-1830 *BiAUS, BiDrAC, WhAm H*
Hayden, Perry Mead 1901-1954 *NatCAB 47*
Hayden, Philip Cady 1854- *WhAm 4*
Hayden, Ruth Eleanor *WomWWA 14*
Hayden, Velma Denison 1912-1966 *WhAm 4*
Hayden, Warren Sherman 1870-1933 *WhAm 1*
Hayden, William 1799-1863 *DcAmB, WhAm H*
Hayden, William Frederick 1870-1937 *NatCAB 31*
Haydn, Franz Joseph 1732-1809 *McGEWB*
Haydn, Hiram 1907-1973 *WhAm 6*
Haydn, Hiram Collins 1831-1913 *ApCAB Sup, NatCAB 7, TwCBDA, WhAm 1*
Haydock, George Sewell 1876- *WhAm 5*
Haydon, Albert Eustace 1880-1975 *WhAm 6*

Haydon, Glen 1896-1966 *BiDAmEd, WhAm 4*
Haydon, William *NewYHSD*
Hayes, Agnes Hayes Stone 1876- *WomWWA 14*
Hayes, Alexander L 1793-1875 *BiAUS*
Hayes, Alfred 1873-1936 *WhAm 1*
Hayes, Allison John 1885-1928 *NatCAB 23*
Hayes, Anson 1882-1960 *WhAm 4*
Hayes, Arthur Badley 1859-1942 *WhAm 2*
Hayes, Augustus Allen 1806-1882 *ApCAB, DcAmB, Drake, NatCAB 11, TwCBDA, WhAm H*
Hayes, Basil Augustus 1890-1970 *NatCAB 55*
Hayes, Carlton Joseph Huntley 1882-1964 *BiDAmEd, WhAm 4*
Hayes, Carroll 1889-1965 *NatCAB 50*
Hayes, Catharine 1825-1861 *ApCAB*
Hayes, Catherine 1825-1861 *NatCAB 4*
Hayes, Charles Harris 1868-1910 *WhAm 1*
Hayes, Charles Miller 1877-1957 *NatCAB 48*
Hayes, Charles Willard 1858-1916 *DcAmB*
Hayes, Charles Willard 1859-1916 *WhAm 1*
Hayes, Clara Lyon 1857- *WomWWA 14, WhAm 4*
Hayes, Clifford Barron 1895-1961 *NatCAB 50, WhAm 4*
Hayes, Daniel Webster 1874-1938 *WhAm 1*
Hayes, David J A 1900-1959 *WhAm 3*
Hayes, Doremus Almy 1863-1936 *WhAm 1*
Hayes, Edward Arthur 1893-1955 *WhAm 3*
Hayes, Edward Cary 1868-1928 *DcAmB S1, NatCAB 41, WhAm 1*
Hayes, Edward Dixon 1872-1941 *WhAm 1*
Hayes, Edward Francis 1881- *WhAm 6*
Hayes, Edward Mortimer 1842-1912 *WhAm 1*
Hayes, Edwin Patrick 1886-1958 *NatCAB 43*
Hayes, Ellen 1851- *TwCBDA, WhAm 1, WomWWA 14*
Hayes, Ethel Munroe 1873- *WomWWA 14*
Hayes, Eugene Jeffers 1909-1964 *NatCAB 50*
Hayes, Everis Anson 1855-1942 *BiDrAC, NatCAB 39, WhAm 4, WhAmP*
Hayes, Francis Little 1858-1926 *NatCAB 20, WhAm 1*
Hayes, Frank Herbert 1859-1927 *NatCAB 23*
Hayes, Frederick Albert 1889-1966 *WhAm 4*
Hayes, George H *NewYHSD*
Hayes, George Miller 1897-1957 *WhAm 3*
Hayes, H Jay 1869-1957 *NatCAB 43*
Hayes, Hammond Vinton 1860-1947 *WhAm 2*
Hayes, Harold M 1894-1963 *WhAm 4*
Hayes, Harvey Cornelius 1878-1968 *WhAm 5*
Hayes, Helen 1900- *WebAB*
Hayes, Helen Hayden 1881- *WhAm 6*
Hayes, Henry *WhAm 4*
Hayes, Henry Reed 1879-1955 *ApCAB X, WhAm 3*
Hayes, Ira 1923-1955 *REnAW*
Hayes, Ira Hamilton 1922-1955 *WebAMB*
Hayes, Isaac Israel 1832-1881 *AmBi, ApCAB, DcAmB, Drake, NatCAB 3, TwCBDA, WhAm H*
Hayes, J Harry 1904-1963 *NatCAB 52*
Hayes, James *NewYHSD*
Hayes, James E 1827?- *NewYHSD*
Hayes, James Edward 1872-1948 *WhAm 2*
Hayes, James Henry *NewYHSD*
Hayes, James Henry 1883-1949 *NatCAB 38*
Hayes, James Leo 1895-1971 *WhAm 5*
Hayes, Jay Orley 1857-1948 *NatCAB 39, WhAm 2*
Hayes, John Herman 1890-1965 *WhAm 4*
Hayes, John Lord 1812-1887 *ApCAB, DcAmB, NatCAB 14, TwCBDA, WhAm H*
Hayes, John Russell 1866-1945 *WhAm 3*
Hayes, John William 1854-1942 *DcAmB S3, WhAm 2*
Hayes, Johnson Jay 1886-1970 *NatCAB 55, WhAm 5*
Hayes, Joseph 1835- *ApCAB, TwCBDA, WhAm 4*
Hayes, Joseph Magnor 1846-1920 *NatCAB 6*
Hayes, Joseph P 1895- *WhAm 5*
Hayes, Kenneth Aurand 1894-1966 *NatCAB 53*
Hayes, Lucy Ware Webb 1831-1879 *AmWom*
Hayes, Lucy Ware Webb 1831-1889 *ApCAB, NatCAB 3, NotAW, TwCBDA, WhAm H*

Hayes, Mary Coulbourn Conner 1878- *WomWWA 14*
Hayes, Mary Sanders 1876- *WhAm 5*
Hayes, Max Sebastian 1866-1945 *DcAmB S3, NatCAB 37, WhAm 2*
Hayes, Montrose W 1874-1936 *WhAm 1*
Hayes, Myron Joseph 1891-1956 *NatCAB 48, WhAm 3*
Hayes, Patrick Joseph 1867-1938 *AmBi, ApCAB X, DcAmB S2, McGEWB, NatCAB 16, WhAm 1*
Hayes, Philip 1887-1949 *NatCAB 38, WhAm 2*
Hayes, Philip Cornelius 1833-1916 *ApCAB, BiDrAC, TwCBDA, WhAm 1*
Hayes, Pliny Harold 1824-1894 *NatCAB 12*
Hayes, R S d1972 *WhAm 5*
Hayes, Robert Benjamin 1876- *WhoColR*
Hayes, Robert Hunter 1880-1955 *NatCAB 46*
Hayes, Roland 1887- *WebAB*
Hayes, Rutherford Birchard 1822-1893 *AmBi, ApCAB, BiAUS, BiDrAC, BiDrUSE, DcAmB, Drake, EncAAH, EncAB, McGEWB, NatCAB 3, TwCBDA, WebAB, WhAm H, WhAmP*
Hayes, Rutherford Platt 1858-1927 *NatCAB 21*
Hayes, Samuel *BiAUS*
Hayes, Samuel H 1825?- *NewYHSD*
Hayes, Samuel Perkins 1874-1958 *WhAm 3*
Hayes, Samuel Walter 1875-1941 *NatCAB 32, WhAm 1*
Hayes, Simeon Mills 1862- *WhAm 4*
Hayes, Stanley Wolcott 1865-1963 *NatCAB 51*
Hayes, Stephen Quentin 1873-1936 *WhAm 1*
Hayes, Thomas Gordon 1844-1915 *NatCAB 11, WhAm 1*
Hayes, Thomas Sumner 1902-1959 *WhAm 3*
Hayes, Timothy Michael 1892-1965 *NatCAB 52*
Hayes, Wade Hampton 1879-1956 *WhAm 3*
Hayes, Walter Ingalls 1841-1901 *BiDrAC, NatCAB 2, TwCBDA*
Hayes, Warren Howard 1847-1899 *NatCAB 6, NatCAB 7, WhAm 1*
Hayes, Watson McMillan 1857-1944 *WhAm 2*
Hayes, Wayland J 1893-1972 *WhAm 5*
Hayes, Webb Cook 1856-1934 *NatCAB 25, WhAm 1*
Hayes, Webb Cook, II 1890-1957 *NatCAB 42, WhAm 3*
Hayes, William Augustus 1877-1946 *NatCAB 35*
Hayes, William Christopher 1903-1963 *NatCAB 51*
Hayes, William Ebenezer 1846- *NatCAB 16*
Hayes, William H 1800-1828 *NewYHSD*
Hayes, William Henry 1829-1877 *DcAmB*
Hayes, William Preston 1881-1963 *NatCAB 49, WhoColR*
Hayford, J E Casely 1866-1903 *McGEWB*
Hayford, John Fillmore 1868-1925 *DcAmB, DcScB, NatCAB 14, WhAm 1*
Haygarth, John 1740-1827 *BiHiMed*
Haygood, Atticus Green 1839-1896 *ApCAB, BiDAmEd, DcAmB, WhAm H*
Haygood, Atticus Greene 1839-1896 *DcAmReB, NatCAB 1, TwCBDA*
Haygood, Laura Askew 1845-1900 *DcAmB, NotAW, WhAm H*
Hayhow, Edgar Charles 1894-1957 *WhAm 3*
Hayhurst, Emery Roe 1880-1961 *NatCAB 48, WhAm 4*
Haykin, David Judson 1896-1958 *DcAmLiB, WhAm 3*
Hayler, Guy Wilfrid 1877- *WhAm 5*
Hayley, John William 1834-1927 *WhAm 1*
Haymaker, H Henley 1892-1964 *NatCAB 51*
Haymaker, Jesse N 1858-1930 *WhAm 1*
Hayman, Al d1917 *WhAm 1*
Hayman, George Washington 1866- *WhoColR*
Hayman, J Lester 1896-1963 *NatCAB 50*
Hayman, Samuel Brinkle 1820-1895 *ApCAB, TwCBDA*
Haymond, Creed 1836- *ApCAB Sup*
Haymond, Frank Cruise 1887-1972 *WhAm 5*
Haymond, Thomas S 1869- *WhAm 5*
Haymond, Thomas Sherwood 1794-1869 *BiAUS, BiDrAC, WhAm H*

Haymond, W S 1823-1885 *BiAUS*
Haymond, William Stanley 1852-1928
   NatCAB 32
Haymond, William Summerville 1823-1885
   BiDrAC, *WhAm H*
Haynau, Julius Jacob Von 1786-1853 *WhoMilH*
Hayne, Arthur P 1790-1867 *BiAUS,* *Drake*
Hayne, Arthur Peronneau 1790-1867 *ApCAB,*
   BiDrAC, *TwCBDA,* *WhAm H*
Hayne, Arthur Perroneau 1790-1867
   NatCAB 11
Hayne, Coe 1875- *WhAm 5*
Hayne, Daniel Harvey 1863- *NatCAB 16*
Hayne, Franklin Brevard 1858-1935
   NatCAB 26
Hayne, Isaac 1745-1781 *AmBi,* *ApCAB,*
   DcAmB, *Drake,* *NatCAB 1,* *TwCBDA,*
   WhAm H
Hayne, Isaac William 1809- *NatCAB 13*
Hayne, James Adams 1872- *WhAm 5*
Hayne, Julia Dean *NotAW*
Hayne, Paul H 1831- *Drake*
Hayne, Paul Hamilton 1830-1886 *AmBi,*
   ApCAB, *DcAmB,* *NatCAB 4,* *TwCBDA,*
   WhAm H
Hayne, Robert Young 1791-1839 *AmBi,*
   ApCAB, *BiAUS,* *BiDrAC,* *DcAmB,*
   Drake, *EncAAH,* *EncAB,* *McGEWB,*
   NatCAB 3, *NatCAB 12,* *TwCBDA,*
   WebAB, *WhAm H,* *WhAmP*
Hayne, William Hamilton 1856-1929 *WhAm 1*
Hayner, Rutherford 1877-1939 *WhAm 1*
Haynes, Arthur Edwin 1849-1915 *WhAm 1*
Haynes, Benjamin Rudolph 1897-1962
   BiDAmEd, *WhAm 4*
Haynes, C Younglove *NewYHSD*
Haynes, Carlyle Boynton 1882-1958 *WhAm 3*
Haynes, Caroline Coventry *WomWWA 14*
Haynes, Charles Eaton 1784-1841 *BiAUS,*
   BiDrAC, *WhAm H*
Haynes, Charles H 1878- *WhAm 6*
Haynes, Daniel H 1882-1959 *WhAm 3*
Haynes, David Oliphant 1858-1932 *NatCAB 25,*
   WhAm 1
Haynes, Edgar John 1866-1919 *NatCAB 18*
Haynes, Eli Stuart 1880-1956 *WhAm 3*
Haynes, Elizabeth A Ross d1953 *WhAm 3*
Haynes, Elwood 1857-1925 *AmBi,* *ApCAB X,*
   NatCAB 13, *NatCAB 25,* *WhAm 1*
Haynes, Emory James 1847-1914 *TwCBDA,*
   WhAm 1
Haynes, Evan 1895-1955 *NatCAB 53,*
   WhAm 3
Haynes, Francis G *NewYHSD*
Haynes, Frank Jay 1853-1921 *NatCAB 19*
Haynes, Fred Emory 1868- *WhAm 4*
Haynes, George Edmund 1880-1960
   NatCAB 44, *WhAm 3,* *WhoColR*
Haynes, George Henry 1866-1947 *NatCAB 38,*
   TwCBDA, *WhAm 2*
Haynes, Harley Armand 1875-1965 *NatCAB 56,*
   WhAm 5
Haynes, Henry Williamson 1831-1912 *ApCAB,*
   NatCAB 8, *TwCBDA,* *WhAm 1*
Haynes, Herbert Hodge 1878-1949 *NatCAB 38*
Haynes, Ira Allen 1859-1955 *WhAm 3*
Haynes, Irving Samuel 1861-1946 *WhAm 2*
Haynes, James Clark 1848-1913 *ApCAB X,*
   NatCAB 18
Haynes, John 1594?-1653? *DcAmB,* *WhAm H*
Haynes, John 1594?-1654 *AmBi,* *ApCAB,*
   Drake, *NatCAB 7,* *TwCBDA*
Haynes, John Cummings 1829-1907 *ApCAB X,*
   NatCAB 5, *TwCBDA*
Haynes, John Henry 1849-1910 *DcAmB*
Haynes, John Randolph 1853-1937 *WhAm 1*
Haynes, Joseph 1638-1679 *ApCAB*
Haynes, Joseph Walton 1917- *WhAm 5*
Haynes, Justin O'Brien 1902-1972 *WhAm 5*
Haynes, Landon Carter 1816-1875 *BiDConf,*
   TwCBDA
Haynes, Lemuel 1753-1833 *ApCAB,* *Drake,*
   TwCBDA
Haynes, Lemuel 1753-1834 *NatCAB 12*
Haynes, Lorenza 1820- *AmWom*
Haynes, Martin Alonzo 1842-1919 *BiDrAC*
Haynes, Myron Wilbur 1855- *WhAm 1*
Haynes, Myrte Rice 1866- *WomWWA 14*

Haynes, Nathaniel Smith 1844-1925 *WhAm 1*
Haynes, Robert Blair 1898- *WhAm 3*
Haynes, Rowland 1878-1963 *NatCAB 50,*
   WhAm 4
Haynes, Roy Asa 1881-1940 *WhAm 1*
Haynes, Thornwell 1870-1953 *WhAm 3*
Haynes, Tilly 1828-1901 *NatCAB 2*
Haynes, William Elisha 1829-1914 *BiDrAC,*
   TwCBDA
Haynie, Henry 1841-1912 *WhAm 1*
Haynie, Isham Nicolas 1824-1868 *ApCAB*
Haynsworth, Clement Furman 1886-1953
   NatCAB 42
Hays, Albert Theodore 1907-1972 *WhAm 6*
Hays, Alexander 1819-1864 *ApCAB,*
   ApCAB X, *DcAmB,* *NatCAB 4,*
   TwCBDA, *WhAm H*
Hays, Alexander 1820-1864 *Drake*
Hays, Arthur Alexander 1875-1959 *WhAm 3*
Hays, Arthur Garfield 1881-1954 *DcAmB S5,*
   NatCAB 44, *WebAB,* *WhAm 3*
Hays, Barton S 1826-1914 *NewYHSD*
Hays, Calvin Cornwell 1861-1935 *WhAm 1*
Hays, Charles 1834-1879 *BiAUS,* *BiDrAC,*
   WhAm H, *WhAmP*
Hays, Charles Melville 1856-1912 *NatCAB 4,*
   WhAm 1
Hays, Charles Thomas 1869-1949 *NatCAB 41,*
   WhAm 2
Hays, Daniel Peixotto 1854-1923 *NatCAB 24,*
   WhAm 1
Hays, Edde K 1906-1965 *WhAm 4*
Hays, Edward Dixon 1872-1941 *BiDrAC*
Hays, Edward Retilla 1847-1896 *BiDrAC,*
   WhAm H
Hays, Elmer D 1891-1937 *WhAm 1*
Hays, Frank Lazmer 1889-1951 *WhAm 3*
Hays, Frank W 1861- *WhAm 4*
Hays, George Arthur 1854-1945 *NatCAB 35*
Hays, George Price 1838-1897 *NatCAB 2,*
   TwCBDA
Hays, George Washington 1863-1927
   NatCAB 20, *WhAm 1,* *WhAm 1C*
Hays, Harold M 1880-1940 *NatCAB 30*
Hays, Harry Thompson 1820-1876 *ApCAB Sup,*
   BiDConf, *DcAmB,* *WhAm H*
Hays, Henry, Jr. *NewYHSD*
Hays, Henry, Sr. *NewYHSD*
Hays, Henry Blake 1829-1881 *NatCAB 16*
Hays, Howard H 1883-1969 *WhAm 5*
Hays, I Minis 1847-1925 *WhAm 1*
Hays, Isaac 1796-1879 *ApCAB,* *DcAmB,*
   Drake, *NatCAB 11,* *TwCBDA,* *WhAm H*
Hays, Jack Newton 1917-1970 *WhAm 5*
Hays, Jacob 1772-1850 *ApCAB,* *Drake,*
   NatCAB 12
Hays, James Buchanan 1838-1888 *ApCAB Sup*
Hays, John 1837-1921 *WhAm 1*
Hays, John C d1861? *NatCAB 2*
Hays, John Coffee 1817-1883 *DcAmB,*
   EncAAH, *WebAB,* *WebAMB*
Hays, John Coffee 1817-1885 *WhAm H*
Hays, John W 1884- *WhoColR*
Hays, Josephine 1860- *WomWWA 14*
Hays, L Samuel *BiAUS*
Hays, Lawrence Brooks 1898- *BiDrAC*
Hays, Margaret Gebbie d1925 *WhAm 1,*
   WomWWA 14
Hays, Molly 1754-1832 *AmBi*
Hays, Mortimer 1897-1962 *WhAm 4*
Hays, Samuel 1783-1868 *BiDrAC,* *WhAm H*
Hays, Samuel Lewis 1794-1871 *BiDrAC,*
   WhAm H
Hays, Silas B 1902-1964 *WhAm 4*
Hays, Steele 1872-1959 *NatCAB 49*
Hays, Walter B 1882-1960 *NatCAB 50*
Hays, Walter Lee 1895-1964 *WhAm 4*
Hays, Wayne Levere 1911- *BiDrAC*
Hays, Will H 1879-1954 *ApCAB X,*
   DcAmB S5, *WhAm 3*
Hays, Will Shakespeare 1837-1907 *ApCAB,*
   TwCBDA
Hays, Willet Martin 1859- *WhAm 4*
Hays, William 1819-1875 *ApCAB,* *TwCBDA*
Hays, William Charles 1873-1963 *WhAm 4*
Hays, William H *NewYHSD*
Hays, William Harrison 1879-1954 *BiDrUSE*
Hays, William Jacob 1830-1875 *AmBi,* *ApCAB,*

   DcAmB, *Drake,* *IIBEAAW,* *NatCAB 4,*
   NewYHSD, *REnAW,* *TwCBDA,*
   WhAm H
Hays, William Jacob 1872-1934 *WhAm 1*
Hays, William Shakespeare 1837-1907 *AmBi,*
   DcAmB, *WhAm 1*
Hays, William Shakspeare 1837-1907
   NatCAB 3
Hayse, Martha S *NewYHSD*
Hayt, Charles Denison 1850- *NatCAB 12,*
   WhAm 1
Hayter, Earl Wiley 1901- *EncAAH*
Haytham, Abu Ali Al-Hasan, Ibn Al- 965-1040?
   DcScB
Haythorne, Robert Poore 1815- *ApCAB*
Hayton, Charles Henry 1869-1944 *NatCAB 36*
Hayward, Benjamin Dover 1860-1916 *WhAm 1*
Hayward, Celia Adelia *WomWWA 14*
Hayward, David *NewYHSD*
Hayward, E Bartlett 1862-1946 *NatCAB 38*
Hayward, Edward Farwell 1851-1923 *WhAm 1*
Hayward, Elijah *BiAUS*
Hayward, Florence 1865- *WhAm 1,*
   WomWWA 14
Hayward, Fred Preston 1871- *WhAm 5*
Hayward, George *NewYHSD*
Hayward, George 1791-1863 *ApCAB,* *DcAmB,*
   Drake, *NatCAB 11,* *TwCBDA,* *WhAm H*
Hayward, H Josephine 1869- *WomWWA 14*
Hayward, Harry 1869-1932 *WhAm 1*
Hayward, Harry Taft 1868-1930 *NatCAB 26,*
   WhAm 1
Hayward, Henry George Augustus 1906-1966
   NatCAB 53
Hayward, Ione 1879- *WomWWA 14*
Hayward, James 1786-1866 *ApCAB,* *TwCBDA*
Hayward, John 1781-1862 *ApCAB*
Hayward, John 1781-1869 *Drake*
Hayward, John 1784-1869 *NatCAB 10*
Hayward, John B *NewYHSD*
Hayward, John Balcom 1874-1966 *NatCAB 53*
Hayward, Joseph Warren 1841-1905 *TwCBDA,*
   WhAm 1
Hayward, Joshua Henshaw 1797-1856
   NewYHSD
Hayward, Lemuel 1749-1821 *ApCAB,* *Drake,*
   NatCAB 11
Hayward, Lillian Woolson *WomWWA 14*
Hayward, Mary E Smith 1849- *AmWom*
Hayward, Mary E Smith 1853- *WomWWA 14*
Hayward, Mildred Marshall 1889-1967
   NatCAB 53
Hayward, Monroe Leland 1840-1899
   ApCAB Sup, *BiDrAC,* *NatCAB 12,*
   TwCBDA, *WhAm 1*
Hayward, Nathan 1872-1944 *WhAm 2*
Hayward, Nathaniel Manley 1808-1865 *ApCAB,*
   DcAmB, *Drake,* *NatCAB 12,* *WhAm H*
Hayward, Ralph Allington 1895-1951
   NatCAB 38, *WhAm 3*
Hayward, Susan 1919-1975 *WhAm 6*
Hayward, Thomas, Jr. 1746-1809 *Drake*
Hayward, Thomas Jonas 1847-1909 *NatCAB 37*
Hayward, Walter Brownell 1877- *WhAm 5*
Hayward, William 1877-1944 *NatCAB 33,*
   WhAm 2
Hayward, William, Jr. 1787-1836 *BiDrAC,*
   WhAm H
Hayward, William Edwin 1839-1925
   NatCAB 32
Hayward, William Eugene 1842-1914
   NatCAB 17
Hayward, William Leete 1870- *WhAm 3*
Haywood, Alfred Williams 1853-1916
   NatCAB 19
Haywood, Allan Shaw 1888-1953 *DcAmB S5*
Haywood, Allen S d1953 *WhAm 3*
Haywood, Benjamin 1792-1878 *ApCAB*
Haywood, Edmund Burke 1825-1894 *ApCAB,*
   NatCAB 9, *NatCAB 29,* *TwCBDA*
Haywood, Ernest 1860- *NatCAB 18*
Haywood, Harry LeRoy 1886-1955 *WhAm 3*
Haywood, John d1826 *Drake*
Haywood, John 1684-1758 *NatCAB 4*
Haywood, John 1753-1826 *ApCAB,*
   NatCAB 4
Haywood, John 1762-1826 *DcAmB,* *TwCBDA,*
   WhAm H

Haywood, John Kerfoot 1873-1928 *WhAm 1*
Haywood, John Wilfred 1881-1972 *WhAm 5*
Haywood, Marshall, Jr. 1912-1970 *NatCAB 57, WhAm 5*
Haywood, Marshall DeLancey 1871-1933 *WhAm 1*
Haywood, Martha Helen 1872- *WomWWA 14*
Haywood, William 1730?-1779 *NatCAB 4*
Haywood, William Dudley 1869-1928 *AmBi, DcAmB, EncAB, McGEWB, REnAW, WebAB, WhAm HA, WhAm 4*
Haywood, William Henry 1801-1852 *ApCAB, BiAUS, BiDrAC, NatCAB 4, TwCBDA, WhAm H*
Hayworth, Donald 1898- *BiDrAC*
Hazard, Alida Blake 1861- *WomWWA 14*
Hazard, Arthur Potter 1841-1921 *ApCAB X*
Hazard, Augustus George 1802-1868 *DcAmB, WhAm H*
Hazard, Benjamin 1770-1841 *NatCAB 8*
Hazard, Bertha *WomWWA 14*
Hazard, Caroline 1856-1945 *BiDAmEd, NatCAB 12, NatCAB 34, NotAW, TwCBDA, WhAm 2, WomWWA 14*
Hazard, Clifton T 1885-1963 *WhAm 4*
Hazard, Daniel Lyman 1865-1951 *WhAm 3*
Hazard, Ebenezer 1744-1817 *AmBi, ApCAB, DcAmB, TwCBDA, WhAm H*
Hazard, Ebenezer 1745-1817 *BiAUS, Drake*
Hazard, Elmer Clarke 1879- *WhAm 6*
Hazard, Frederick Rowland 1858-1917 *WhAm 1*
Hazard, Frederick Rowland 1858-1918 *ApCAB X*
Hazard, Henry Bernard 1880-1954 *WhAm 3*
Hazard, Henry Thomas 1844-1921 *NatCAB 6*
Hazard, J T *NewYHSD*
Hazard, Jeffrey *ApCAB X*
Hazard, John Gibson 1877-1918 *NatCAB 23*
Hazard, Jonathan J 1728-1812 *ApCAB, TwCBDA*
Hazard, Jonathan J 1744-1824 *BiAUS, BiDrAC, DcAmB, WhAm H*
Hazard, Lauriston Hartwell 1866-1937 *WhAm 1*
Hazard, Marshall Curtiss 1839-1929 *WhAm 1*
Hazard, Nathaniel 1776-1820 *BiAUS, BiDrAC*
Hazard, Rebecca N 1826- *AmWom*
Hazard, Roland Gibson 1801-1888 *NatCAB 9*
Hazard, Rowland 1829-1898 *ApCAB X, NatCAB 12, TwCBDA*
Hazard, Rowland Gibson 1801-1888 *ApCAB, ApCAB X, DcAmB, Drake, TwCBDA, WhAm H*
Hazard, Rowland Gibson 1855-1918 *ApCAB X, NatCAB 43, WhAm 1*
Hazard, Samuel 1713?-1758 *TwCBDA*
Hazard, Samuel 1714-1758 *ApCAB*
Hazard, Samuel 1784-1870 *AmBi, ApCAB, DcAmB, Drake, NatCAB 13, TwCBDA, WhAm H*
Hazard, Samuel 1834-1876 *TwCBDA*
Hazard, Samuel F 1811-1867 *Drake*
Hazard, Spencer Peabody 1872-1957 *WhAm 3*
Hazard, Thomas 1720-1798 *DcAmB, WhAm H*
Hazard, Thomas Pierrepont 1892-1968 *WhAm 5*
Hazard, Thomas Robinson 1784-1876 *ApCAB, Drake*
Hazard, Thomas Robinson 1797-1886 *DcAmB, TwCBDA, WhAm H*
Hazard, William Douglas 1883-1948 *NatCAB 38*
Hazard, Willis Hatfield 1866-1950 *WhAm 3*
Hazard, Willis Pope 1825- *TwCBDA*
Hazel, Fred C 1884- *WhoColR*
Hazel, John Raymond 1860- *WhAm 4*
Hazel, Melvin Ronald 1904-1959 *NatCAB 48*
Hazelbaker, Norval Denver 1915-1970 *WhAm 5*
Hazelett, C William 1892-1956 *NatCAB 43*
Hazelett, Earl Tuttle 1882-1943 *NatCAB 34*
Hazelius, Ernest Lewis 1777-1853 *ApCAB, DcAmB, Drake, TwCBDA, WhAm H*
Hazell, Joseph William 1895-1930 *NatCAB 49*
Hazelrigg, Clara H 1861- *AmWom*
Hazelrigg, James Hervey 1848- *NatCAB 12, WhAm 4*

Hazeltine, Abner 1793-1879 *BiAUS, BiDrAC, WhAm H*
Hazeltine, Abner 1836-1915 *NatCAB 17*
Hazeltine, Alan 1886-1964 *WhAm 4*
Hazeltine, Elizabeth Hallock *WomWWA 14*
Hazeltine, George Cochran 1833- *NatCAB 5*
Hazeltine, Harold Dexter 1871- *WhAm 5*
Hazeltine, Horace *WhAm 4*
Hazeltine, Hugh Vincent 1877-1952 *NatCAB 39*
Hazeltine, Ira Sherwin 1821-1899 *BiDrAC*
Hazeltine, Mary Emogene 1868-1949 *DcAmLiB, NotAW, WhAm 2, WomWWA 14*
Hazeltine, Mayo Williamson 1841-1909 *DcAmB, WhAm 1*
Hazeltine, Moses B 1865-1949 *NatCAB 52*
Hazelton, George Cochrane 1832-1922 *BiDrAC*
Hazelton, George Cochrane, Jr. 1868-1921 *DcAmB, WhAm 1*
Hazelton, Gerry Whiting 1829-1920 *BiAUS, BiDrAC*
Hazelton, John Hampden 1871-1957 *NatCAB 44, WhAm 3*
Hazelton, John Morton 1866-1940 *NatCAB 30*
Hazelton, John W 1819- *BiAUS*
Hazelton, John Wright 1814-1878 *BiDrAC, WhAm H*
Hazelton, William French 1860-1925 *NatCAB 22*
Hazelwood, John 1726?-1800 *AmBi, ApCAB, DcAmB, TwCBDA, WebAMB, WhAm H*
Hazen, Allen 1869-1930 *AmBi, DcAmB S1, NatCAB 28, WhAm 1*
Hazen, Annah Putnam *WomWWA 14*
Hazen, Azel Washburn 1841-1928 *WhAm 1*
Hazen, Charles Downer 1868-1941 *NatCAB 13, NatCAB 30, TwCBDA, WhAm 2*
Hazen, Edward Warriner 1860-1929 *NatCAB 42*
Hazen, Ella Jay 1856- *WomWWA 14*
Hazen, Emily Hall *WomWWA 14*
Hazen, Frances Mary 1844-1925 *NatCAB 6*
Hazen, Gaines Homer 1847-1921 *NatCAB 19*
Hazen, Henry Allen 1832-1900 *TwCBDA, WhAm 1*
Hazen, Henry Allen 1849-1900 *DcAmB, NatCAB 8*
Hazen, Henry Honeyman 1879-1951 *WhAm 3*
Hazen, I *NewYHSD*
Hazen, J *NewYHSD*
Hazen, John Norman 1893-1966 *NatCAB 52*
Hazen, John Vose 1850-1919 *NatCAB 31, WhAm 1*
Hazen, Joseph Chalmers 1874-1967 *WhAm 4*
Hazen, Louise Coleman 1877- *WomWWA 14*
Hazen, Marshman Williams 1845-1911 *WhAm 1*
Hazen, Maynard Thompson 1887-1960 *NatCAB 49, WhAm 4*
Hazen, Moses 1733-1802 *ApCAB, NatCAB 1*
Hazen, Moses 1733-1803 *DcAmB, Drake, TwCBDA, WhAm H*
Hazen, Pauline Browne 1881- *WomWWA 14*
Hazen, Rush Strong 1854-1932 *NatCAB 42*
Hazen, William Babcock 1830-1887 *AmBi, ApCAB, DcAmB, Drake, NatCAB 3, TwCBDA, WebAMB, WhAm H*
Hazen, William Elton 1873-1940 *NatCAB 32*
Hazen, William Livingston 1861-1944 *WhAm 2*
Hazen, William Patterson Clark 1853-1944 *NatCAB 33*
Hazewell, Charles Creighton 1814-1883 *ApCAB, TwCBDA*
Hazlehurst, Thomas Huger 1906-1949 *NatCAB 39*
Hazlet, Stewart E 1910-1974 *WhAm 6*
Hazlett, Almon Cyrus 1891-1950 *NatCAB 39*
Hazlett, Edgar Marion 1869-1946 *NatCAB 39*
Hazlett, Harry Fouts 1884-1960 *WhAm 4*
Hazlett, James Miller 1864-1940 *BiDrAC*
Hazlett, Robert 1863-1944 *WhAm 2*
Hazlett, Samuel M 1879-1956 *WhAm 3*
Hazlewood, Charlotte Williams *WomWWA 14*
Hazlewood, Craig Beebe 1883-1953 *WhAm 3*
Hazlewood, John 1726?-1800 *NatCAB 13*
Hazlitt, John 1767-1837 *NewYHSD*
Hazlitt, William 1778-1830 *McGEWB*
Hazzard, Charles 1871-1938 *NatCAB 29,*

WhAm 1
Hazzard, Daniel 1781-1864 *TwCBDA*
Hazzard, David 1781-1864 *BiAUS, NatCAB 11*
Hazzard, Jesse Charles 1871- *WhAm 5*
Hazzard, John Edward 1881-1935 *WhAm 1*
HD *WebAB*
H'Doubler, Francis Todd 1887-1962 *NatCAB 48, WhAm 4*
Heacock, Edward Morton 1876-1939 *NatCAB 29*
Heacock, Frank Ahern 1893-1966 *WhAm 4*
Heacock, Roger Lee 1906-1961 *WhAm 4*
Heacox, Arthur Edward 1867- *WhAm 5*
Head, Annie Lyndesay Wilkinson *WomWWA 14*
Head, Sir Edmund Walker 1805-1868 *ApCAB, Drake*
Head, Sir Francis Bond 1793-1875 *ApCAB, Drake*
Head, Franklin Harvey 1832-1914 *ApCAB X, NatCAB 41*
Head, Franklin Harvey 1835-1914 *WhAm 1*
Head, Sir George 1782-1875 *ApCAB*
Head, Hayden Wilson 1882-1922 *NatCAB 6*
Head, Sir Henry 1861-1940 *BiHiMed*
Head, Henry Oswald 1851-1929 *WhAm 1*
Head, James Butler 1846-1902 *WhAm 1*
Head, James Marshall 1855-1930 *NatCAB 9, WhAm 1*
Head, James Milne 1925-1969 *WhAm 5*
Head, Jerome Reed 1893-1974 *WhAm 6*
Head, John Benedict 1855- *WhAm 1*
Head, John Frazier 1821-1908 *WhAm 1*
Head, Leon Oswald 1879-1961 *WhAm 4*
Head, Mabel 1873- *WhAm 5*
Head, Natt 1828-1883 *ApCAB, NatCAB 11, TwCBDA*
Head, Ozella Shields 1869- *AmWom*
Head, Sallie Cary Wilson 1856- *WomWWA 14*
Head, Samuel *NewYHSD*
Head, T Grady 1897-1965 *NatCAB 51, WhAm 4*
Head, Walter Dutton 1881-1967 *WhAm 4*
Head, Walter William 1877-1954 *NatCAB 45, WhAm 3*
Head, Walton O 1909-1972 *WhAm 5*
Headden, William Parker 1850-1932 *WhAm 1*
Heade, Martin Johnson 1819-1904 *ApCAB, BnEnAmA, McGEWB, NewYHSD, WhAm H*
Heade, William P *NewYHSD*
Headings, Donald Moore 1899-1955 *NatCAB 43*
Headland, Isaac Taylor 1859-1942 *WhAm 2*
Headlee, Thomas Jefferson 1877-1946 *NatCAB 40, WhAm 2*
Headley, Cleon 1887-1954 *NatCAB 41, WhAm 3*
Headley, Hal Price 1888-1962 *NatCAB 50*
Headley, Joel Tyler 1813-1897 *AmBi, ApCAB, DcAmB, TwCBDA, WhAm H*
Headley, Joel Tyler 1814- *Drake, NatCAB 3*
Headley, John William 1901-1957 *WhAm 3*
Headley, Joseph H *NewYHSD*
Headley, Leal Aubrey 1884-1965 *WhAm 4*
Headley, Phineas Camp 1819- *ApCAB, Drake*
Headley, Phineas Camp 1819-1902 *WhAm 1*
Headley, Phineas Camp 1819-1903 *DcAmB, NatCAB 11, TwCBDA*
Headley, Roy 1878-1951 *WhAm 3*
Headman, Sam Sasha 1887-1954 *NatCAB 42*
Heady, Morrison 1829- *NatCAB 11*
Heafford, George Henry 1845- *WhAm 4*
Heaford, Vincent *NewYHSD*
Heagy, Alice M R 1860- *WomWWA 14*
Heal, Gilbert B 1887-1951 *WhAm 3*
Heald, Charles Mercer 1849- *NatCAB 18*
Heald, Charles Wesley 1876-1957 *NatCAB 47*
Heald, Daniel Addison 1818-1900 *NatCAB 1, WhAm 1*
Heald, Edward Payson 1843-1925 *NatCAB 6*
Heald, Frederick DeForest 1872-1954 *NatCAB 44, WhAm 3*
Heald, Henry Townley 1904-1975 *BiDAmEd, WhAm 6*
Heald, James *NewYHSD*
Heald, Kenneth Conrad 1888-1971 *WhAm 5*

Hecht, Julius Lawrence 1881-1955 *WhAm 3*
Hecht, Moses S d1954 *WhAm 3*
Hecht, Rudolf S 1885-1956 *WhAm 3*
Hecht, Selig 1892-1947 *DcAmB S4,*
NatCAB 38, WhAm 2
Hecht, Wilbur Hudson 1905-1974 *WhAm 6*
Heck, Barbara d1804 *ApCAB*
Heck, Barbara 1744-1804 *NatCAB 13*
Heck, Barbara Ruckle 1734-1804 *DcAmB,*
NotAW, WhAm H
Heck, Nicholas Hunter 1882-1953 *NatCAB 45,*
WhAm 3
Heck, Robert Culbertson Hays 1870-1951
WhAm 3
Heck, Walter Emil 1915-1964 *NatCAB 50*
Heck, William Harry 1879-1919 *WhAm 1*
Hecke, Erich 1887-1947 *DcScB*
Hecke, G H 1870-1953 *WhAm 4*
Heckel, Albert Kerr 1880- *WhAm 6*
Heckel, Edward Balthasar 1865-1935 *WhAm 1*
Heckel, George Baugh 1858-1941 *WhAm 1*
Heckel, George Philip 1909-1963 *NatCAB 50*
Heckel, Norris Julius 1896-1966 *WhAm 4*
Hecker, Frank Joseph 1846-1927 *WhAm 1*
Hecker, Friedrich Karl Franz 1811-1881
ApCAB, DcAmB, Drake, WhAm H
Hecker, Isaac Thomas 1819-1888 *AmBi,*
ApCAB, DcAmB, DcAmReB, Drake,
McGEWB, NatCAB 9, TwCBDA,
WebAB, WhAm H
Hecker, John Valentine 1848- *WhAm 4*
Heckert, Charles Girven 1863-1920 *WhAm 1*
Heckert, John Walter 1872-1952 *WhAm 3*
Heckett, Eric Harlow 1892-1961 *WhAm 4*
Heckewelder, John Gottlieb Ernestus 1743-1823
AmBi, ApCAB, DcAmB, NatCAB 9,
TwCBDA, WhAm H
Heckler, Edwin Little 1902-1964 *WhAm 4*
Heckler, Margaret M 1931- *BiDrAC*
Heckman, Charles Adam 1822- *ApCAB*
Heckman, Dayton Eyster 1909-1956
NatCAB 45
Heckman, George C 1825-1902 *NatCAB 2,*
TwCBDA
Heckman, James Robert 1866-1939 *WhAm 2*
Heckman, Samuel B 1870-1957 *WhAm 3*
Heckman, Samuel Harry 1872-1958
NatCAB 43
Heckman, Wallace 1851-1927 *WhAm 1*
Heckscher, August 1848-1941 *DcAmB S3,*
NatCAB 14, WhAm 1, WhAm 2
Heckscher, Austin Stevens 1858-1910
NatCAB 29
Heckscher, Celeste DeLongpre 1860-1928
ApCAB X, NatCAB 21, WhAm 1
Heckwelder, John 1743-1823 *Drake*
Hector, Francisco Luis 1748?-1807 *DcAmB*
Hedback, Axel Emanuel 1874-1951 *WhAm 3*
Hedblom, Carl Arthur 1879-1934 *WhAm 1*
Hedbrooke, Andrew *WhAm H*
Hedden, Charles Rohrbach 1852-1930
NatCAB 23
Hedden, Ralph Clyde 1878-1947 *NatCAB 36*
Hedden, Rose C DelPino 1866- *WomWWA 14*
Hedding, Elijah 1780-1852 *ApCAB, DcAmB,*
Drake, NatCAB 10, TwCBDA
Hedenstrom, Paul Henry 1926-1969 *WhAm 5*
Hederman, T M 1878-1948 *WhAm 2*
Hederman, Thomas Martin 1878-1948
NatCAB 36
Hedgcock, George Grant 1863-1946
NatCAB 37, WhAm 4
Hedge, Charles Gorham 1852-1921 *NatCAB 35,*
WhAm 1
Hedge, Franklin 1830?- *NewYHSD*
Hedge, Frederic Henry 1805-1890 *AmBi,*
ApCAB, DcAmB, DcAmReB, Drake,
NatCAB 8, TwCBDA, WhAm H
Hedge, Frederic Henry 1831- *TwCBDA,*
WhAm 4
Hedge, Henry Rogers 1876- *WhAm 5*
Hedge, Levi 1766-1844 *ApCAB, DcAmB,*
Drake, TwCBDA, WhAm H
Hedge, Thomas 1844-1920 *BiDrAC, WhAm 4,*
WhAmP
Hedge, William Russell 1876-1943 *NatCAB 41,*
WhAm 2
Hedgeman, Anna Arnold *WhAmP*

Hedgepeth, Levi Larndon 1899-1958
NatCAB 51
Hedger, Caroline 1868- *WomWWA 14*
Hedges, Agnes Jane 1873- *WomWWA 14*
Hedges, Benjamin VanDoren 1907-1969
WhAm 5
Hedges, Cornelius 1831-1907 *BiDAmEd,*
NatCAB 4, NatCAB 12
Hedges, Frank Hinckley 1895-1940 *WhAm 1*
Hedges, Isaac Angel 1811-1882 *NatCAB 30*
Hedges, James Blaine 1894-1965 *WhAm 4*
Hedges, Job Elmer 1862-1925 *WhAm 1*
Hedges, Joseph Edward 1904-1966 *WhAm 4*
Hedges, Joseph Harold 1862-1956 *WhAm 3*
Hedges, Marion Hawthorne 1888-1959
WhAm 3
Hedges, Samuel Hamilton 1866- *WhAm 2*
Hedges, William W 1835?- *NewYHSD*
Hedin, Sven Anders 1865-1952 *DcScB,*
McGEWB
Hedinger, Hugh 1897-1959 *NatCAB 49*
Hedinger, John H *NewYHSD*
Hedleston, Winn David 1862- *WhAm 1*
Hedley, Evalena Fryer *WomWWA 14*
Hedley, Frank 1864-1955 *WhAm 3*
Hedley, Joseph H *NewYHSD*
Hedly, Arthur Howard 1881-1960 *NatCAB 51,*
WhAm 4
Hedrich, Kenneth d1972 *WhAm 5*
Hedrich, Walter Alfred 1895-1962 *NatCAB 49*
Hedrick, Bayard Murphy 1880-1967 *WhAm 4*
Hedrick, Benjamin Sherwood 1827-1886
NatCAB 9, TwCBDA
Hedrick, Burl Vance 1876-1944 *NatCAB 33*
Hedrick, Charles Baker 1877-1943 *WhAm 2*
Hedrick, Charles Embury 1881- *WhAm 3*
Hedrick, E H 1894-1954 *WhAm 3*
Hedrick, Earle Raymond 1876-1943 *BiDAmEd,*
NatCAB 32, WhAm 2
Hedrick, Ellen A *WomWWA 14*
Hedrick, Erland Harold 1894-1954 *BiDrAC,*
WhAmP
Hedrick, Hannah Fancher Mace 1870-
WomWWA 14
Hedrick, Henry Benjamin 1865-1936
NatCAB 27
Hedrick, Ira Grant 1868-1937 *NatCAB 36,*
WhAm 1
Hedrick, Lawrence E 1916- *WhAm 6*
Hedrick, T Wade 1890-1958 *NatCAB 49*
Hedrick, Tubman Keene 1873- *WhAm 5*
Hedrick, Ulysses Prentiss 1870-1951
NatCAB 42, WhAm 3
Hedrick, Wyatt Cephas 1888-1964 *NatCAB 51,*
WhAm 4
Hedstrom, Carl Oscar 1871- *WhAm 5*
Hedstrom, Oscar Carl 1871- *NatCAB 15*
Hedtoft, Hans 1903-1955 *WhAm 3*
Hedwig, Johann 1730-1799 *DcScB*
Heebner, Charles 1859-1933 *WhAm 1*
Heed, J *NewYHSD*
Heed, J M *NewYHSD*
Heed, M J *NewYHSD*
Heed, Thomas Daugherty 1875-1957
NatCAB 46, WhAm 3
Heekin, Albert Edward, Jr. 1914-1971 *WhAm 5*
Heekin, Daniel M 1886-1968 *NatCAB 54*
Heelan, Edmond 1868-1948 *WhAm 2*
Heely, Allan Vanderhoef 1897-1959 *WhAm 3*
Heely, Emma A *NewYHSD*
Heenan, John Carmel 1835-1873 *DcAmB,*
WhAm H
Heenehan, James T 1891-1958 *WhAm 3*
Heeney, Arnold Danford Patrick 1902-1970
WhAm 5
Heer, Oswald 1809-1883 *DcScB*
Heerman, Ritz Edwin 1892-1959 *NatCAB 47,*
WhAm 4
Heermance, Edgar Laing 1876- *WhAm 5*
Heermance, Radcliffe 1882-1958 *NatCAB 48*
Heermann, Adolphus L 1827?-1865 *WhAm H*
Heermans, Augustin 1605?-1686 *NatCAB 4*
Heermans, Augustyn 1605?-1686 *NewYHSD,*
WhAm H
Heermans, Charles Abram 1843- *NatCAB 3,*
WhAm 4
Heermans, Forbes 1856-1928 *WhAm 1*

Heermans, Josephine Woodbury 1859-
WhAm 4
Heery, Bernice Branch 1895-1970 *NatCAB 57*
Hees, James Ledlie 1862- *NatCAB 17*
Hees, William Rathbun 1867-1947 *WhAm 2*
Hees, William Rathbun, Jr. 1894-1954
NatCAB 43
Heeter, Silvanus Laurabee 1870- *WhAm 5*
Heezen, Bruce C 1924- *AsBiEn*
Hefelbower, Samuel Gring 1871-1950
NatCAB 40, WhAm 3
Heffelfinger, Frank Totton 1869-1959 *WhAm 3*
Heffelfinger, George W P 1901-1970 *WhAm 5*
Heffelfinger, William Walter Pudge 1867-1954
DcAmB S5, WebAB
Hefferan, Helen Maley 1870- *WomWWA 14*
Hefferan, Mary *WomWWA 14*
Hefferan, Thomas 1831-1915 *NatCAB 16*
Hefferan, Thomas Hume 1908-1969 *WhAm 5*
Hefferan, W S, Jr. 1893-1961 *WhAm 4*
Hefferline, Ralph Franklin 1910-1974 *WhAm 6*
Heffern, Andrew Duff 1856-1920 *WhAm 1*
Heffernan, James Joseph 1885-1967 *WhAm 4*
Heffernan, James Joseph 1888-1967 *BiDrAC*
Hefflon, George Henry 1865-1925 *NatCAB 22*
Heffron, John Lorenzo 1851-1924 *WhAm 1*
Heffron, Patrick Richard 1860-1927
NatCAB 15, WhAm 1
Heflin, Aubrey Newbill 1912-1973 *WhAm 6*
Heflin, James Thomas 1869-1951 *ApCAB X,*
BiDrAC, DcAmB S5, NatCAB 43,
WhAm 3, WhAmP
Heflin, Robert Stell 1815-1901 *ApCAB,*
BiAUS, BiDrAC
Heflin, Van 1910-1971 *WhAm 5*
Hefling, Arthur William 1899-1974 *WhAm 6*
Hefner, Hugh Marston 1926- *WebAB*
Hefner, Ralph A 1902-1967 *WhAm 5*
Hefner-Alteneck, Friedrich Franz Von 1845-1904
DcScB
Hefty, Thomas Rudolph 1885-1967 *NatCAB 53,*
WhAm 4
Heg, Elmer Ellsworth 1861-1922 *NatCAB 20,*
WhAm 4
Heg, Hans C 1829-1863 *ApCAB*
Hegan, Alice Caldwell *NotAW*
Hegardt, William Gustaf 1860-1926
NatCAB 23
Hegel, Georg Wilhelm Friedrich 1770-1831
McGEWB
Hegeler, Edward Carl 1835-1910 *ApCAB X,*
NatCAB 23
Hegeler, Herman 1872-1913 *NatCAB 25*
Hegeler, Julius Weisbach 1867-1943
NatCAB 32
Hegeman, Benjamin Arrowsmith, Jr. 1860-1929
ApCAB X
Hegeman, George *NewYHSD*
Hegeman, John Rogers 1844-1919 *ApCAB X,*
DcAmB, NatCAB 24, WhAm 1
Heger, Anthony 1828-1908 *WhAm 1*
Heger, Joseph 1835- *IIBEAAW, NewYHSD*
Hegge, Olav Hans 1872-1963 *NatCAB 52*
Heggen, Thomas Orlo 1919-1949 *NatCAB 38,*
WhAm 2
Hegland, Martin 1880-1967 *WhAm 5*
Hegler, John Jacob 1812-1856 *NewYHSD*
Hegner, Bertha Hofer 1862- *WhAm 4*
Hegner, Casper Frank 1879-1960 *NatCAB 52*
Hegner, Robert William 1880-1942 *NatCAB 36,*
WhAm 2
Heher, Harry 1889-1972 *WhAm 5*
Hehir, Martin Aloysius 1855-1935 *NatCAB 29,*
WhAm 1, WhAm 1C
Hehl, Matthew 1705-1787 *ApCAB, NatCAB 5*
Heide, Henry 1846- *ApCAB X, NatCAB 15*
Heidegger, Martin 1889-1976 *McGEWB,*
WhAm 6
Heidel, Frank William 1859-1927 *NatCAB 21*
Heidel, William Arthur 1868-1941 *NatCAB 30,*
WhAm 1
Heidemans, Henri P *NewYHSD*
Heiden, Konrad 1901-1975 *WhAm 6*
Heidenhain, Martin 1864-1949 *DcScB*
Heidenhain, Rudolf Peter Heinrich 1834-1897
BiHiMed, DcScB
Heidenreich, Carl Schmelzle 1890-1954
NatCAB 40

Heidenreich, Frederick John 1859-1952
  NatCAB 40
Heidenstam, Carl Gustaf Verner Von 1859-1940
  McGEWB
Heider, Raphael 1903-1971 *WhAm 5*
Heidinger, James Vandaveer 1882-1945 *BiDrAC,*
  WhAm 2, WhAmP
Heidinger, William Ernest 1885-1955
  NatCAB 44
Heidingsfield, Myron Samuel 1914-1969
  NatCAB 54, WhAm 5
Heidler, Joseph Bunn 1896-1956 *NatCAB 46*
Heifetz, Benar 1899-1974 *WhAm 6*
Heifetz, Jascha 1901- *WebAB*
Heikes, Victor Conrad 1867-1948 *WhAm 2*
Heikka, Earle Erik 1910-1941 *IIBEAAW*
Heil, Charles Emile 1870-1950 *NatCAB 49,*
  WhAm 3
Heil, Julius Peter 1876-1949 *NatCAB 40,*
  WhAm 2
Heil, William Franklin 1857-1930 *WhAm 1*
Heiland, Carl August 1899-1956 *WhAm 3*
Heilbron, George H 1860-1895 *NatCAB 8*
Heilbronner, Louis 1866- *WhAm 5*
Heilbrunn, Lewis Victor 1892-1959 *WhAm 3*
Heileman, Frank A 1891-1961 *WhAm 4*
Heilge, George *IIBEAAW, NewYHSD*
Heilig, Sterling 1864- *WhAm 4*
Heill, Carl *NewYHSD*
Heill, George *NewYHSD*
Heill, Jacob *NewYHSD*
Heill, Philip *NewYHSD*
Heilman, Fordyce Russell 1905-1960
  NatCAB 51, WhAm 4
Heilman, Jacob Daniel 1875-1960 *NatCAB 48*
Heilman, Marlin Webster 1883-1964
  NatCAB 51
Heilman, Mary Erskine *WomWWA 14*
Heilman, Ralph Emerson 1886-1937 *WhAm 1*
Heilman, Russell Howard 1893-1966 *WhAm 4*
Heilman, William 1824-1890 *BiDrAC,*
  WhAm H
Heilman, William Clifford 1877-1946 *WhAm 2*
Heilmann, Harry 1894-1951 *DcAmB S5*
Heilner, Samuel 1855-1938 *WhAm 1*
Heilner, VanCampen 1899- *WhAm 4*
Heilprin, Angelo 1853-1907 *AmBi, ApCAB,*
  DcAmB, NatCAB 12, TwCBDA,
  WhAm 1
Heilprin, Louis 1851-1912 *ApCAB, WhAm 1*
Heilprin, Michael 1823-1888 *ApCAB, DcAmB,*
  NatCAB 8, WhAm H
Heilprin, Phineas Mendel 1801-1863 *ApCAB*
Heim, Albert 1849-1937 *DcScB*
Heim, Albert Arnold 1882-1965 *DcScB*
Heim, C Henry 1844-1918 *NatCAB 41*
Heim, Herbert E 1906-1970 *WhAm 5*
Heim, Jacques 1899-1967 *WhAm 4*
Heim, William Louis 1879-1950 *NatCAB 41*
Heiman, Joseph David 1896-1962 *NatCAB 50*
Heimann, Henry Herman 1891-1958
  NatCAB 47, WhAm 3
Heimbach, Arthur E 1902-1958 *WhAm 3*
Heimbach, Howard Anders 1909-1970 *WhAm 5*
Heimberger, William Wengerd 1894-1971
  NatCAB 57
Heimerich, John James 1906-1972 *WhAm 5*
Heimhold, George *NewYHSD*
Heimke, William 1853-1931 *NatCAB 28,*
  WhAm 1
Heimrod, George 1845- *WhAm 4*
Hein, Carl 1864-1945 *NatCAB 34, WhAm 2*
Hein, Carl Christian 1868-1937 *WhAm 1*
Hein, Illo 1893-1948 *NatCAB 34*
Hein, Otto Louis 1847- *WhAm 4*
Hein, Peter Leo 1884-1957 *NatCAB 43*
Hein, Piet 1570-1629 *ApCAB*
Hein, Walter Jacob 1891-1962 *WhAm 4*
Heinberg, John Gilbert 1901-1953 *WhAm 3*
Heinbokel, John Frederick William 1889-1944
  NatCAB 33
Heindel, Augusta Foss 1865-1949 *WhAm 2*
Heindle, William Albert 1869-1956 *NatCAB 45*
Heine, Heinrich 1797-1856 *McGEWB*
Heine, Heinrich Eduard 1821-1881 *DcScB*
Heine, Peter Bernard William 1827-1885
  NewYHSD, WhAm H
Heine, Sebastian *NewYHSD*

Heine, Webster Raymond 1895-1953
  NatCAB 41
Heine, William *NewYHSD*
Heineman, Walter Ben 1879-1930 *WhAm 1*
Heinemann, Barbara 1795-1883 *NotAW*
Heinemann, Benjamin 1850-1919 *NatCAB 29*
Heinemann, E 1848-1912 *WhAm 1*
Heinemann, Ernst 1848-1912 *DcAmB,*
  NatCAB 33
Heiner, Daniel Brodhead 1854-1944 *BiDrAC*
Heiner, Gordon Graham 1869-1943 *WhAm 2*
Heiner, Mary Pershing *WomWWA 14*
Heiner, Moroni 1877-1948 *NatCAB 37,*
  WhAm 5
Heingartner, Robert Wayne 1881-1945
  WhAm 2
Heinicke, Arthur John 1892- *WhAm 5*
Heinigke, Jessie Weir 1851- *WomWWA 14*
Heinisch, Don 1923-1974 *WhAm 6*
Heinisch, Frank Cletus 1905-1964 *NatCAB 52*
Heinke, George Henry 1882-1940 *BiDrAC*
Heinl, Robert D 1880-1950 *WhAm 3*
Heinle, Robert Walter 1909-1972 *NatCAB 57*
Heinlein, Mary Virginia 1903-1961 *WhAm 4*
Heinlein, Robert Anson 1907- *WebAB*
Heinmiller, Louis Edward 1890-1939 *WhAm 1*
Heinmueller, William *NewYHSD*
Heinmuller, John P V 1892-1960 *WhAm 4*
Heinmuller, William *NewYHSD*
Heino, Albert Frederic 1905-1955 *WhAm 3*
Heinrich, Anthony Philip 1778?-1858
  NatCAB 8
Heinrich, Anthony Philip 1781-1861 *McGEWB*
Heinrich, Antony Philip 1781-1861 *AmBi,*
  DcAmB, WhAm H
Heinrich, Edward Oscar 1881-1953 *WhAm 3*
Heinrich, Francis H *NewYHSD*
Heinrich, Max 1853-1916 *DcAmB,*
  NatCAB 22
Heinrich, Roy Frederic 1881-1943 *IIBEAAW*
Heinrich, Wilhelm 1865- *WhAm 1*
Heinrichs, Charles E 1898-1963 *WhAm 4*
Heinrichs, Jacob 1860-1947 *WhAm 2*
Heinrici, Gotthard *WhWW-II*
Heinritz, Stuart Franklin 1894-1972
  NatCAB 57
Heinroth, Charles 1874- *WhAm 5*
Heins, George Lewis 1860-1907 *TwCBDA,*
  WhAm 1
Heinsheimer, Edward Lewis 1861-1917
  WhAm 1
Heinsohn, Alvin Frederick 1900-1967 *WhAm 5*
Heinsohn, Dora Henninges 1861- *AmWom*
Heintish, George W, Jr. 1903-1974 *WhAm 6*
Heintz, Philip Benjamin 1861-1943 *NatCAB 32,*
  WhAm 2
Heintz, Victor 1876-1968 *BiDrAC*
Heintzelman, Arthur William 1890-1965
  WhAm 4
Heintzelman, Samuel Peter 1805-1880 *AmBi,*
  ApCAB, DcAmB, Drake, NatCAB 12,
  TwCBDA, WebAMB, WhAm H
Heintzelman, Stuart 1876-1935 *DcAmB S1,*
  WhAm 1
Heintzleman, Percival Stewart 1880-1942
  WhAm 2
Heinz, Fred C 1899-1961 *WhAm 4*
Heinz, Henry John 1844-1919 *DcAmB,*
  NatCAB 5, NatCAB 26, WebAB,
  WhAm 1
Heinz, Howard 1877-1941 *ApCAB X,*
  WhAm 1
Heinz, John Bernard 1890-1965 *WhAm 4*
Heinze, Adolph 1887- *IIBEAAW*
Heinze, Frederick Augustus 1869-1914 *DcAmB,*
  REnAW, WhAm 1
Heinze, Otto Charles 1866- *WhAm 5*
Heinzelman, Karl John, Jr. 1922-1957
  NatCAB 46
Heinzen, Karl Peter 1809-1880 *DcAmB,*
  NatCAB 12, WhAm H
Heischbein, F *NewYHSD*
Heischmann, John J 1858-1929 *WhAm 1*
Heise, Fred H 1883-1946 *WhAm 2*
Heisel, Thomas Bayard 1868-1921 *WhAm 1*
Heisen, Aaron Jonah 1917-1970 *WhAm 5*
Heisenberg, Werner Karl 1901-1976 *AsBiEn,*
  McGEWB, WhAm 6

Heiser, Victor George 1873- *WhAm 5*
Heiserman, Arthur Ray 1929-1975 *WhAm 6*
Heiserman, Clarence Benjamin 1862-1950
  WhAm 3
Heisey, Augustus Henry 1842-1922 *NatCAB 28*
Heising, Raymond Alphonsus 1888-1965
  WhAm 4
Heiskell, Frederick Hugh 1851-1933 *WhAm 1*
Heiskell, Henry Lee 1850-1914 *WhAm 1*
Heiskell, John Netherland 1872-1972 *BiDrAC,*
  WhAm 5
Heiskell, Joseph Brown 1823-1913 *BiDConf*
Heiskell, Samuel G 1858-1923 *WhAm 1*
Heisler, Charles Louis 1863-1931 *NatCAB 25*
Heisler, Charles Washington 1857- *NatCAB 12*
Heisler, John Clement 1862-1938 *WhAm 1*
Heiss, Austin Elmer 1868- *WhAm 4*
Heiss, George G 1823?- *NewYHSD*
Heiss, Gerson Kirkland 1896-1971 *WhAm 5*
Heiss, Marion Welch 1898-1959 *NatCAB 48,*
  WhAm 4
Heiss, Michael 1818-1890 *ApCAB, DcAmB,*
  NatCAB 12, TwCBDA, WhAm H
Heissenbuttel, John Diedrich 1834- *WhAm 4*
Heissig, Mabel Stevens Haynes *WomWWA 14*
Heistand, Henry Olcot Sheldon 1856-1924
  WhAm 1
Heister, Daniel *BiAUS*
Heister, Daniel 1747-1804 *BiAUS, Drake*
Heister, Edward *NewYHSD*
Heister, George 1822?- *NewYHSD*
Heister, John 1746-1821 *BiAUS*
Heister, Joseph 1752-1832 *BiAUS, Drake*
Heister, Leopold Philip De 1707-1777 *ApCAB,*
  Drake
Heister, Lorenz 1683-1758 *BiHiMed, DcScB*
Heister, William d1853 *BiAUS*
Heit, Benjamin *NewYHSD*
Heitfeld, Henry 1859-1938 *BiDrAC,*
  NatCAB 13, WhAm 1, WhAmP
Heitfield, Henry 1859-1938 *ApCAB Sup,*
  TwCBDA
Heitman, Charles Easton 1874-1948 *WhAm 3*
Heitman, Francis Bernard 1838- *WhAm 4*
Heitman, Harvie Earnhardt 1872-1922
  NatCAB 19
Heitman, John Franklin 1840- *NatCAB 3,*
  TwCBDA
Heitmann, John 1871-1955 *NatCAB 41*
Heitschmidt, Earl T 1894-1972 *WhAm 5*
Heitz, Frederick F *NewYHSD*
Heitzman, Charles 1836- *ApCAB*
Heizer, Oscar Stuart 1868- *WhAm 4*
Heizmann, Charles Lawrence 1846- *WhAm 4*
Hekking, J Antonio *NewYHSD*
Hekking, William Mathews 1885-1970
  WhAm 5
Hekking, William Mathews 1885-1971
  NatCAB 57
Hekma, Jacob 1879-1949 *WhAm 2*
Hekman, John 1886-1951 *WhAm 3*
Hektoen, Ludvig 1863-1951 *DcScB,*
  NatCAB 14, NatCAB 18, WhAm 3
Helbig, Bud 1915?- *IIBEAAW*
Helbron, Peter 1739-1816 *DcAmB, WhAm H*
Helburn, Theresa d1959 *WhAm 3*
Held, Al 1928- *BnEnAmA*
Held, Anna 1865?-1918 *NotAW*
Held, Anna 1877-1918 *WhAm 1,*
  WomWWA 14
Held, George August 1862-1948 *NatCAB 35*
Held, John, Jr. 1889-1958 *WebAB, WhAm 3*
Helder, H A 1886-1961 *WhAm 4*
Hele, Edward *NewYHSD*
Helfant, Reuben 1902-1968 *NatCAB 54*
Helfen, Mathias 1889-1955 *WhAm 3*
Helfenstein, Charles Philip 1820- *NatCAB 8*
Helfenstein, Edward Trail 1865-1947
  NatCAB 41, WhAm 2
Helfenstein, Ernest *WhAm H*
Helfenstein, John Conrad Albert 1748-1790
  ApCAB
Helff, Joseph *NewYHSD*
Helffenstein, John Albert Conrad 1748-1790
  DcAmB, WhAm H
Helfrich, Howard 1891-1939 *NatCAB 29*
Helgesen, Henry Thomas 1857-1917 *BiDrAC,*
  WhAm 1, WhAmP

Helgeson, Dean Arlan C 1921- *EncAAH*
Helias D'Humonde, Ferdinand Mary 1796-1874 *ApCAB*
Hell, Maximilian 1720-1792 *DcScB*
Helland, Andreas 1870- *WhAm 5*
Hellbaum, Arthur Alfred 1904-1964 *WhAm 4*
Hellem, Charles B *NewYHSD*
Hellems, Fred Burton Renney 1872-1929 *WhAm 1*
Hellems, Fred Burton Rennie 1872-1929 *NatCAB 37*
Hellenthal, John Albertus 1874-1945 *WhAm 2*
Heller, A Arthur 1867- *WhAm 4*
Heller, Edmund 1875-1939 *NatCAB 35,* *WhAm 1*
Heller, Edward Hellman 1900-1961 *WhAm 4*
Heller, Edward Peter 1892-1948 *NatCAB 37*
Heller, Florence Grunsfeld 1897-1966 *NatCAB 51,* *WhAm 5*
Heller, Frank Henry 1907-1971 *WhAm 5*
Heller, Frank Morley 1870- *WhAm 5*
Heller, George 1905-1955 *WhAm 3*
Heller, George Phillip Fred 1893-1954 *NatCAB 43*
Heller, George Washington 1860-1928 *ApCAB X*
Heller, Helen West d1955 *WhAm 3*
Heller, Irma Irene 1870- *WomWWA 14*
Heller, James Gutheim 1892-1971 *WhAm 5*
Heller, Joseph Milton 1872-1943 *WhAm 2*
Heller, Louis Benjamin 1905- *BiDrAC*
Heller, Maximilian 1860-1929 *DcAmB,* *WhAm 1*
Heller, Otto 1863-1941 *WhAm 1*
Heller, Robert 1899-1973 *WhAm 6*
Heller, Siegfried 1868-1924 *NatCAB 20*
Heller, Mrs. T *NewYHSD*
Heller, Victor H 1886-1967 *WhAm 4*
Heller, Walter E 1890- *WhAm 5*
Heller, William 1885-1962 *NatCAB 48,* *WhAm 4*
Heller, William Jacob 1857-1920 *NatCAB 6*
Hellerman, Robert *NewYHSD*
Hellge, George *NewYHSD*
Hellier, Charles Edward 1864-1940 *NatCAB 15,* *WhAm 1*
Hellier, Mary Harmon 1864- *WomWWA 14*
Hellinger, Ernst D 1883-1950 *DcScB,* *WhAm 2A*
Hellinger, Mark 1903-1947 *WhAm 2*
Hellman, Alfred Myer 1880-1955 *NatCAB 41*
Hellman, C Doris 1910-1973 *WhAm 6*
Hellman, F J 1901-1965 *WhAm 4*
Hellman, Frances 1853- *BiCAW*
Hellman, George Sidney 1878-1958 *WhAm 3*
Hellman, Herman W 1843-1906 *NatCAB 16*
Hellman, Hugo Edward 1908-1975 *WhAm 6*
Hellman, Isaias William 1842-1920 *WhAm 1*
Hellman, Isaias William, Jr. 1871-1920 *WhAm 1*
Hellman, Lillian 1905- *EncAB, McGEWB,* *WebAB*
Hellman, Marco H 1878- *WhAm 6*
Hellman, Maurice S 1864- *WhAm 4*
Hellman, Milo 1872-1947 *WhAm 2*
Hellman, Sam 1885-1950 *NatCAB 39*
Hellmann, Carl August 1885-1955 *NatCAB 42*
Hellmund, Rudolph Emil 1879-1942 *WhAm 2*
Hellmuth, Harriet Fowler *WomWWA 14*
Hellmuth, Isaac 1819- *ApCAB*
Hellot, Jean 1685-1766 *DcScB*
Hellriegel, Hermann 1831-1895 *DcScB*
Hellstrom, Carl Reinhold 1895-1963 *WhAm 4*
Hellweg, J F 1879- *WhAm 6*
Hellwig, C Alexander 1889-1963 *NatCAB 51*
Helm, Augustus L *NewYHSD*
Helm, Ben Hardin 1830-1863 *ApCAB, Drake,* *NatCAB 5*
Helm, Benjamin 1767-1858 *TwCBDA*
Helm, Benjamin Hardin 1830-1863 *TwCBDA*
Helm, Benjamin Hardin 1831-1863 *BiDConf*
Helm, Charles John 1817-1868 *DcAmB*
Helm, Grover Cleveland 1884-1955 *NatCAB 43*
Helm, Gustave Adolph 1861-1926 *ApCAB X*
Helm, Harry Sherman 1867-1947 *NatCAB 35,* *WhAm 2A*
Helm, Harvey 1865-1919 *BiDrAC, WhAm 1,* *WhAmP*

Helm, Israel d1693? *ApCAB*
Helm, Jacob Anton 1761-1831 *BiHiMed*
Helm, James Meredith 1855-1927 *WhAm 1*
Helm, Jenny M Hanson *WomWWA 14*
Helm, John Charles 1817-1868 *WhAm H*
Helm, John Larue 1802-1867 *ApCAB, BiAUS,* *DcAmB, NatCAB 13, TwCBDA,* *WhAm H*
Helm, Joseph Church 1848-1915 *NatCAB 13,* *TwCBDA, WhAm 1*
Helm, Julius Felix 1887-1956 *NatCAB 45*
Helm, Lucinda Barbour 1839-1897 *AmWom,* *TwCBDA*
Helm, Nathan Wilbur 1879- *WhAm 6*
Helm, Nelson 1903-1965 *NatCAB 51,* *WhAm 4*
Helm, Roy 1888-1951 *WhAm 3*
Helm, Thaddeus Geary 1866- *WhAm 4*
Helm, Thomas Kennedy 1874-1939 *WhAm 1*
Helm, Wilbur 1879-1970 *WhAm 5*
Helm, William P 1883-1958 *WhAm 3*
Helmer, Bessie Bradwell 1858-1927 *DcAmB,* *WhAm 1, WomWWA 14*
Helmer, Elizabeth Bradwell 1858-1927 *BiCAW*
Helmer, Frank Ambrose 1854-1925 *NatCAB 18,* *WhAm 1*
Helmer, George Jacob 1866- *NatCAB 10*
Helmer, Nellie Fitzhugh *BiCAW*
Helmersen, Grigory Petrovich 1803-1885 *DcScB*
Helmert, Friedrich Robert 1843-1917 *DcScB*
Helmholtz, Hermann Ludwig Ferdinand Von 1821-1894 *AsBiEn, DcScB, McGEWB*
Helmholtz-Phelan, Anna Augusta *WomWWA 14*
Helmholz, Henry Frederic 1882-1958 *WhAm 3*
Helmick, Eli Alva 1863-1945 *WhAm 2*
Helmick, John Pierpont 1904-1961 *NatCAB 50*
Helmick, Milton John 1885-1954 *WhAm 3*
Helmick, William 1817-1888 *BiAUS, BiDrAC,* *WhAm H*
Helming, Oscar Clemens 1867-1935 *WhAm 1*
Helmle, Frank J 1869-1939 *WhAm 1*
Helmle, Henry Richardson 1888-1949 *NatCAB 37*
Helmont, Jan Baptista Van 1577-1644? *AsBiEn*
Helmont, Jan Baptista Van 1579-1644 *McGEWB*
Helmont, Johannes Baptista Van 1579-1644 *DcScB*
Helmpraecht, Joseph 1820-1884 *DcAmB,* *WhAm 1*
Helms, Edgar James 1863- *WhAm 4*
Helms, Elmer Ellsworth 1863- *WhAm 3*
Helms, Paul Hoy 1889-1957 *WhAm 3*
Helms, William d1813 *BiAUS, BiDrAC,* *WhAm H*
Helmsley, William 1737-1812 *WhAm H*
Helmuth, Fannie Ida 1838- *NatCAB 12*
Helmuth, Justus Christian Henry 1745-1825 *ApCAB, TwCBDA*
Helmuth, Justus Henry Christian 1745-1825 *DcAmB, NatCAB 22, WhAm H*
Helmuth, William Tod 1833-1901 *WhAm 1*
Helmuth, William Tod 1833-1902 *DcAmB,* *NatCAB 12, NewYHSD*
Helmuth, William Tod 1862-1932 *NatCAB 12,* *WhAm 1*
Helper, Hinton Rowan 1829-1909 *AmBi,* *ApCAB, DcAmB, Drake Sup, EncAAH,* *EncAB, McGEWB, TwCBDA, WebAB,* *WhAm 1*
Helpman, Dell A 1867-1924 *WhAm 1*
Helps, Sir Arthur 1817-1875 *ApCAB*
Helser, Albert D 1897-1969 *WhAm 5*
Helser, Maurice David 1890-1956 *WhAm 3*
Helstoski, Henry 1925- *BiDrAC*
Heltman, Harry Joseph 1885-1962 *WhAm 4*
Heltzen, Oscar Leonard 1882-1968 *NatCAB 55*
Helvering, Guy Tresillian 1878-1946 *BiDrAC,* *WhAm 2, WhAmP*
Helvetius, Claude Adrien 1715-1771 *McGEWB*
Helwig, Clarence Franklin 1872- *NatCAB 18*
Helwig, Frank Jay 1874-1954 *NatCAB 45*
Helyar, Frank G 1883-1963 *WhAm 4*
Hem, Halvor Olsen 1863-1952 *NatCAB 42*
Hemans, Lawton Thomas 1864-1916 *WhAm 1*
Hembdt, Phil Harold 1875-1927 *WhAm 1*
Hembel, William 1764-1851 *ApCAB, Drake,*

NatCAB 11
Hemborg, Carl August 1847- *NatCAB 13,* *WhAm 4*
Hemelright, Frank H 1870-1930 *NatCAB 23*
Hemelt, Francis Joseph 1879-1948 *NatCAB 37*
Hemen, Frank Joseph 1870-1939 *NatCAB 29*
Hemenway, Abby Maria 1828-1890 *NotAW,* *TwCBDA*
Hemenway, Alfred 1839-1927 *WhAm 1*
Hemenway, Asa *NewYHSD*
Hemenway, Augustus 1853- *WhAm 1*
Hemenway, Charles d1887 *NewYHSD*
Hemenway, Charles Carroll 1850- *TwCBDA*
Hemenway, Charles Clifton 1883-1968 *WhAm 5*
Hemenway, Charles Reed 1875-1947 *NatCAB 37, WhAm 2*
Hemenway, Henry Bixby 1856-1931 *WhAm 1*
Hemenway, Herbert Daniel 1873-1943 *WhAm 2*
Hemenway, James Alexander 1860-1923 *BiDrAC, NatCAB 14, TwCBDA,* *WhAm 1, WhAmP*
Hemenway, John Francis *ApCAB X*
Hemenway, Kenneth Harlow 1904-1957 *NatCAB 49*
Hemenway, Mary Porter Tileston 1820-1894 *DcAmB, NotAW, WhAm H*
Hemenway, Mary Porter Tileston 1822-1894 *TwCBDA*
Hemenway, Ralph Wilbur 1881-1952 *NatCAB 41*
Heming, Arthur Henry Howard 1870-1940 *IIBEAAW, WhAm 1*
Hemington, Francis 1866-1942 *WhAm 2*
Hemingway, Alfred Tyler 1877-1922 *NatCAB 19*
Hemingway, Allan 1902-1972 *WhAm 5*
Hemingway, Ernest Miller 1898-1961 *McGEWB*
Hemingway, Ernest Miller 1899-1961 *EncAB,* *NatCAB 57, WebAB, WhAm 4*
Hemingway, Gertrude Clapp 1884- *WomWWA 14*
Hemingway, Grace Hall 1872- *WomWWA 14*
Hemingway, Harold Edgar 1887- *WhAm 2*
Hemingway, Harry J 1905-1965 *WhAm 4*
Hemingway, James S 1899-1961 *WhAm 4*
Hemingway, Reginald Stanley 1884-1955 *NatCAB 45*
Hemingway, Roy Willet 1881-1942 *NatCAB 34*
Hemingway, Samuel 1858-1930 *NatCAB 25*
Hemingway, Samuel Burdett 1883-1958 *WhAm 3*
Hemingway, Walter Clarke 1887-1951 *WhAm 3*
Hemingway, Willet Alvord 1858-1930 *NatCAB 33*
Hemingway, Wilson Edwin 1854-1922 *NatCAB 18, WhAm 1*
Hemingway, Wilson Linn 1880-1954 *WhAm 3*
Heminway, Bartow Lewis 1899-1970 *NatCAB 56*
Heminway, Buell 1838- *NatCAB 12*
Hemley, Cecil 1914-1966 *WhAm 4, WhAm 5*
Hemley, Samuel 1898-1970 *WhAm 5*
Hemmens, Elsie Berlin *WomWWA 14*
Hemmenway, Moses 1735-1811 *ApCAB*
Hemmenway, Moses 1736-1811 *Drake*
Hemmerich, Hugo 1887-1951 *NatCAB 39*
Hemmeter, Henry Bernard 1869-1948 *WhAm 2*
Hemmeter, John Cohn 1863-1931 *NatCAB 11*
Hemmeter, John Conrad 1863-1931 *DcAmB,* *NatCAB 30*
Hemmeter, John Conrad 1864-1931 *AmBi,* *WhAm 1*
Hemmick, Laura Alice Pike Barney 1860- *WomWWA 14*
Hemming, H *NewYHSD*
Hemming, Richard *NewYHSD*
Hemminger, Charles John 1873-1951 *NatCAB 40*
Hemminger, J Ross 1875-1953 *NatCAB 42*
Hemminghaus, Roy George 1908-1960 *NatCAB 46*
Hemon, Louis 1880-1913 *McGEWB*
Hempel, Charles Julius 1811-1879 *ApCAB,* *DcAmB, Drake, WhAm H*
Hempel, Edward Henry 1895-1951 *NatCAB 39*
Hempel, Frieda 1885-1955 *ApCAB X,* *WhAm 3*

Hemphill, Alexander Julian 1856-1920
ApCAB X, WhAm 1
Hemphill, Anna Emily 1874- *WomWWA 14*
Hemphill, Ashton Erastus 1849- *NatCAB 11*
Hemphill, Charles Robert 1852-1932 *TwCBDA,*
WhAm 1
Hemphill, Clifford d1966 *WhAm 4*
Hemphill, Elsie Beale 1872- *WomWWA 14*
Hemphill, James 1827-1900 *ApCAB X*
Hemphill, James Calvin 1850-1927 *NatCAB 2,*
TwCBDA, WhAm 1
Hemphill, John 1803-1862 *AmBi, ApCAB,*
BiAUS, BiDConf, BiDrAC, DcAmB,
NatCAB 4, TwCBDA, WhAm H,
WhAmP
Hemphill, John James 1849-1912 *BiDrAC,*
WhAm 1, WhAmP
Hemphill, Joseph 1770-1842 *ApCAB, BiAUS,*
BiDrAC, Drake, NatCAB 1,
TwCBDA, WhAm H, WhAmP
Hemphill, Joseph Newton 1847-1931 *WhAm 1*
Hemphill, Robert Witherspoon 1915- *BiDrAC*
Hemphill, Victor Herman 1882-1957
NatCAB 47, WhAm 3
Hemphill, William Arnold 1842-1902
NatCAB 1, WhAm 1
Hemphill, William P d1961 *WhAm 4*
Hemphill, William Ramsey 1806-1876 *TwCBDA*
Hempl, Anna Belle 1865- *WomWWA 14*
Hempl, George 1859-1921 *DcAmB,*
NatCAB 13, TwCBDA, WhAm 1
Hempstead, Clark 1873-1952 *WhAm 3*
Hempstead, Edward 1780-1817 *BiAUS,*
BiDrAC, TwCBDA, WhAm H
Hempstead, Fay 1847-1934 *WhAm 1*
Hempstead, Harry Newton 1868-1938
NatCAB 28
Hempstead, Helen *WomWWA 14*
Hempstead, Louise *WomWWA 14*
Hempstead, Stephen 1812-1883 *BiAUS,*
NatCAB 11, TwCBDA
Hemry, Alice Squire 1851- *WomWWA 14*
Hemry, Charles W 1841- *WhAm 4*
Hemsath, Frederick Augustus 1894-1971
NatCAB 57
Hemsley, William 1737-1812 *BiAUS, BiDrAC*
Hemstreet, Charles 1866- *WhAm 4*
Henard, Charles *NewYHSD*
Hench, Atcheson Laughlin 1891-1974 *WhAm 6*
Hench, George Allison 1866-1899 *TwCBDA*
Hench, Jay Lyman 1885-1961 *WhAm 4*
Hench, Philip Showalter 1896-1965 *AsBiEn,*
WebAB, WhAm 4
Henchman, Daniel 1689-1761 *DcAmB S1,*
WhAm H
Henck, John Benjamin 1815-1903 *DcAmB,*
Drake, TwCBDA
Henck, John Benjamin 1816-1903 *ApCAB*
Henck, John Benjamin 1854- *TwCBDA,*
WhAm 4
Henckel, Carl 1862- *IlBEAAW*
Henckel, Johann Friedrich 1678-1744 *DcScB*
Hendee, Mrs. 1754- *ApCAB, TwCBDA*
Hendee, George Ellsworth 1841-1916 *WhAm 1*
Hendee, George Mallory 1866-1943 *NatCAB 32*
Hendee, George Whitman 1832-1906 *BiAUS,*
BiDrAC, NatCAB 8, TwCBDA
Hendel, John William 1740-1798 *DcAmB,*
WhAm H
Hendel, William 1730?-1798 *ApCAB*
Hendelson, William H 1904-1975 *WhAm 6*
Henderlite, James Henry 1872- *WhAm 3*
Hendershott, Howard Ernst 1896-1954
NatCAB 42
Henderson, Abigail *NewYHSD*
Henderson, Alexander Iselin 1892-1961
WhAm 4
Henderson, Alfred Edwin 1877- *WhAm 5*
Henderson, Algo Donmyer 1897- *BiDAmEd*
Henderson, Annie Heloise Abel *NotAW*
Henderson, Archibald 1768-1822 *ApCAB,*
BiAUS, BiDrAC, DcAmB, NatCAB 7,
TwCBDA, WhAm H
Henderson, Archibald 1783-1859 *WebAMB*
Henderson, Archibald 1785-1859 *ApCAB,*
Drake, NatCAB 4
Henderson, Archibald 1877-1963 *WhAm 4*
Henderson, Arthur 1863-1935 *McGEWB*

Henderson, Augusta A Fox 1843- *AmWom*
Henderson, Bennett H 1784- *BiAUS, BiDrAC,*
WhAm H
Henderson, Burton Waters 1866-1927
NatCAB 21
Henderson, Byrd Everett 1889-1967 *WhAm 4*
Henderson, Charles 1860-1937 *NatCAB 35,*
WhAm 1
Henderson, Charles Belknap 1873-1954 *BiDrAC,*
NatCAB 44, WhAm 3, WhAmP
Henderson, Charles E 1871-1939 *NatCAB 39*
Henderson, Charles English 1844-1919
NatCAB 16, WhAm 1
Henderson, Charles Hanford 1861-1941
WhAm 1
Henderson, Charles J 1903-1960 *WhAm 4*
Henderson, Charles Mather 1834- *NatCAB 1*
Henderson, Charles Richmond 1848-1915
DcAmB, NatCAB 11, TwCBDA,
WhAm 1
Henderson, Charles Stephen 1874-1946
NatCAB 41
Henderson, Charles William 1866-1949
NatCAB 39
Henderson, Charles William 1885-1945
WhAm 2
Henderson, Daniel 1880-1955 *WhAm 3*
Henderson, Daniel McIntyre 1851-1906 *DcAmB*
Henderson, David 1853-1908 *WhAm 1*
Henderson, David Bremner 1840-1906 *AmBi,*
ApCAB Sup, BiDrAC, DcAmB,
NatCAB 11, TwCBDA, WebAB,
WhAm 1, WhAmP
Henderson, David E 1879- *WhAm 6*
Henderson, David English 1832-1887
NewYHSD, WhAm H
Henderson, David Newton 1921- *BiDrAC*
Henderson, David Williams 1881-1947
NatCAB 36
Henderson, Earl C 1892-1955 *WhAm 3*
Henderson, Edward 1896-1973 *WhAm 5*
Henderson, Edward Henry 1886-1959
NatCAB 48
Henderson, Eldon Hazelton 1908- *WhAm 5*
Henderson, Elias Franklin 1848- *WhoColR*
Henderson, Elmer Lee 1885-1953 *WhAm 3*
Henderson, Ernest 1897-1967 *WhAm 4*
Henderson, Ernest Flagg 1861-1928 *WhAm 1*
Henderson, Ernest Norton 1869-1938 *WhAm 1*
Henderson, Everette Lee 1896-1966 *NatCAB 53*
Henderson, Fletcher Hamilton 1897-1952
DcAmB S5
Henderson, Frances Cox 1820- *AmWom*
Henderson, Francis Freeman 1885-1947
NatCAB 37
Henderson, Fred Charles 1877- *WhoColR*
Henderson, George Bunsen 1894-1972 *WhAm 5*
Henderson, George Livingston 1878-1954
NatCAB 48
Henderson, George Logan 1891-1965 *WhAm 4*
Henderson, Gerard Carl 1891-1927 *NatCAB 39,*
WhAm 1
Henderson, Grace Mildred 1901-1971 *WhAm 5*
Henderson, Harold Gould 1889-1974 *WhAm 6*
Henderson, Harry Peters 1879- *WhAm 6*
Henderson, Helen Weston 1874- *WhAm 5,*
WomWWA 14
Henderson, Henry Parry 1843-1909 *NatCAB 17*
Henderson, Howard Andrew Millet 1836-1912
BiDAmEd, WhAm 1
Henderson, Isaac 1850-1909 *NatCAB 5,*
WhAm 1
Henderson, J Pinckney 1808-1858 *BiAUS*
Henderson, J W *NatCAB 9*
Henderson, Jacob 1681?-1751 *ApCAB*
Henderson, James 1871-1951 *IlBEAAW*
Henderson, James Alexander 1821- *ApCAB*
Henderson, James Alexander 1907-1956
NatCAB 42
Henderson, James Fletcher 1898-1952 *WhAm 4*
Henderson, James Henry Dickey 1810-1885
BiDrAC, WhAm H
Henderson, James Monroe 1859- *WhAm 4*
Henderson, James Pinckney 1808-1858 *AmBi,*
ApCAB, BiDrAC, DcAmB, Drake,
TwCBDA, WhAm H, WhAmP
Henderson, James Pinkney 1809-1858
NatCAB 1

Henderson, Jane Grace VanWoert
WomWWA 14
Henderson, John 1795-1857 *ApCAB, DcAmB,*
NatCAB 11, TwCBDA, WhAm H
Henderson, John 1795-1866 *BiDrAC*
Henderson, John 1864-1934 *NatCAB 25*
Henderson, John Armstrong 1853-1939
WhAm 1
Henderson, John Blythe Halton 1905-1955
NatCAB 44
Henderson, John Brooks 1826-1913 *ApCAB,*
BiAUS, BiDrAC, DcAmB, NatCAB 13,
TwCBDA, WhAm 1, WhAmP
Henderson, John Brooks 1870-1923 *WhAm 1*
Henderson, John Earl 1917- *BiDrAC*
Henderson, John H 1848- *WhAm 4*
Henderson, John H D 1810- *BiAUS*
Henderson, John Joseph 1843-1928 *WhAm 1*
Henderson, John Moreland 1840-1934
NatCAB 25, WhAm 1
Henderson, John O 1909-1974 *WhAm 6*
Henderson, John R *IlBEAAW*
Henderson, John Steele 1846-1916 *BiDrAC,*
NatCAB 9, TwCBDA, WhAm 1,
WhAmP
Henderson, John Thomas 1876- *NatCAB 16*
Henderson, John Thompson 1858- *WhAm 3*
Henderson, Joseph 1791-1863 *BiAUS, BiDrAC,*
TwCBDA, WhAm H
Henderson, Joseph Lindsey 1869-1965 *WhAm 4*
Henderson, Joseph Welles 1890-1957
NatCAB 47, WhAm 3
Henderson, Junius 1865-1937 *WhAm 1*
Henderson, Kenneth Manning 1893-1968
WhAm 5
Henderson, Laura Parker Montgomery
WomWWA 14
Henderson, Lawrence Joseph 1878-1942
BiDAmEd, BiHiMed, DcAmB S3, DcScB,
WhAm 1
Henderson, Leland John 1874- *WhAm 5*
Henderson, Leon N 1906-1960 *WhAm 4*
Henderson, Leonard 1772-1833 *ApCAB,*
BiAUS, DcAmB, Drake, NatCAB 4,
TwCBDA, WhAm H
Henderson, Lester Dale 1886-1945 *BiDAmEd*
Henderson, Lightner 1866-1916 *NatCAB 17*
Henderson, Lizzie George 1863- *WhAm 4,*
WomWWA 14
Henderson, Lucia Tiffany 1869- *WomWWA 14*
Henderson, Mary Foote 1835- *ApCAB*
Henderson, Mary Foote 1846- *TwCBDA*
Henderson, Mary N Foote 1844- *WhAm 4,*
WomWWA 14
Henderson, Matthew 1736-1795 *ApCAB*
Henderson, Melvin Starkey 1883-1954 *WhAm 3*
Henderson, Sir Nevile 1882-1942 *WhWW-II*
Henderson, Paul 1884-1951 *DcAmB S5*
Henderson, Peronneau Finley 1877-1968
NatCAB 55, WhAm 5
Henderson, Peter 1822-1890 *AmBi, DcAmB,*
NatCAB 6, WhAm H
Henderson, Peter 1823-1890 *ApCAB,*
TwCBDA
Henderson, Philip Eldon 1901-1955 *WhAm 3*
Henderson, Pleasant 1756-1842 *ApCAB, Drake*
Henderson, Reuben Andrew 1876- *WhoColR*
Henderson, Richard 1734-1785 *ApCAB*
Henderson, Richard 1735-1785 *AmBi, DcAmB,*
McGEWB, NatCAB 8, REnAW,
TwCBDA, WebAB, WhAm H
Henderson, Robert 1871-1942 *WhAm 2*
Henderson, Robert 1878-1956 *WhAm 3*
Henderson, Robert Burns 1877-1940
NatCAB 32, WhAm 1
Henderson, Robert Miller 1827-1906 *ApCAB,*
WhAm 1
Henderson, Samuel 1764-1841 *BiAUS,*
BiDrAC, WhAm H
Henderson, Samuel Jones 1880-1942
NatCAB 41
Henderson, Theodore Sommers 1868-1929
NatCAB 25, WhAm 1
Henderson, Thomas 1743-1824 *ApCAB,*
BiAUS, BiDrAC, DcAmB, Drake,
TwCBDA, WhAm H, WhAmP
Henderson, Thomas 1798-1844 *AsBiEn, DcScB*

Henderson, Thomas Howard 1910-1970
WhAm 5
Henderson, Thomas Jefferson 1824-1911
ApCAB, BiAUS, BiDrAC, TwCBDA,
WhAm 1, WhAmP
Henderson, Thomas Stalworth 1859-1937
NatCAB 36, WhAm 1
Henderson, Vivian Wilson 1923-1976 *WhAm 6*
Henderson, W B Drayton 1887-1939 *WhAm 2*
Henderson, Walter C 1876- *WhAm 3*
Henderson, William 1748-1787? *TwCBDA*
Henderson, William Albert 1836-1921
NatCAB 37
Henderson, William D 1866-1944 *WhAm 2*
Henderson, William James 1855-1937 *AmBi,*
DcAmB S2, NatCAB 14, TwCBDA,
WhAm 1
Henderson, William Olin 1850-1934 *WhAm 1*
Henderson, William Penhallow 1877-1943
IIBEAAW, WhAm 2
Henderson, William Price 1867-1943 *WhAm 2*
Henderson, William Thomas 1874- *WhAm 5*
Henderson, William Titus 1885-1961
NatCAB 49
Henderson, William Williams 1879-1944
WhAm 2
Henderson, Yandell 1873-1944 *DcAmB S3,*
DcScB, NatCAB 36, WhAm 2
Hendler, L Manuel 1885-1962 *WhAm 4*
Hendley, Charles *NewYHSD*
Hendley, John Walter 1826-1899 *NewYHSD*
Hendren, Gilbert Hiram 1857-1923 *NatCAB 6*
Hendren, John Newton 1822-1898 *TwCBDA*
Hendren, Linville Laurentine 1880-1958
NatCAB 47, WhAm 6
Hendren, Paul 1889-1958 *WhAm 3*
Hendren, William Foster 1889-1941
NatCAB 41
Hendren, William Mayhew 1871-1939 *WhAm 1*
Hendrick 1680?-1755 *AmBi, ApCAB,*
DcAmB, Drake, NatCAB 10, WhAm H
Hendrick, Archer Wilmot 1871-1937
NatCAB 29, WhAm 1
Hendrick, Burton Jesse 1870-1949 *DcAmB S4,*
WhAm 2
Hendrick, Burton Jesse 1871-1949 *NatCAB 38,*
NatCAB 47
Hendrick, Calvin Wheeler 1865- *NatCAB 12,*
WhAm 1
Hendrick, Ellwood 1861-1930 *AmBi, DcAmB,*
NatCAB 22, WhAm 1
Hendrick, Frank 1874- *WhAm 5*
Hendrick, Ives 1898-1972 *WhAm 5*
Hendrick, James Paul 1828-1898 *NatCAB 10*
Hendrick, John Kerr 1849-1921 *BiDrAC*
Hendrick, John Thilman 1876-1944 *NatCAB 32,*
WhAm 2
Hendrick, Michael J 1847-1922 *WhAm 1*
Hendrick, Peter Aloysius 1858-1923
NatCAB 20, WhAm 1
Hendrick, Rhoda Grace 1874- *WomWWA 14*
Hendrick, Thomas Augustine 1849-1909
WhAm 1
Hendrick, William Jackson 1855- *NatCAB 10,*
WhAm 4
Hendricken, Thomas Francis 1827-1886 *ApCAB,*
NatCAB 8, TwCBDA
Hendricks, Allan Barringer, Jr. 1874- *WhAm 5*
Hendricks, Eldo Lewis 1866-1938 *WhAm 1*
Hendricks, Eliza C Morgan 1823- *AmWom*
Hendricks, Emma Stockman 1869- *IIBEAAW*
Hendricks, Francis 1834-1920 *NatCAB 3,*
NatCAB 21, WhAm 4
Hendricks, Ira King 1900-1970 *WhAm 5*
Hendricks, Joseph Edward 1903- *BiDrAC*
Hendricks, T Arthur 1889-1935 *NatCAB 26*
Hendricks, Thomas A 1819-1885 *BiAUS*
Hendricks, Thomas Andrew 1819-1885 *AmBi*
Hendricks, Thomas Andrews *NatCAB 13*
Hendricks, Thomas Andrews 1819-1885 *ApCAB,*
BiDrAC, BiDrUSE, DcAmB, NatCAB 2,
TwCBDA, WebAB, WhAm H, WhAmP
Hendricks, Thomas Armstrong 1871- *WhAm 2*
Hendricks, William 1782-1850 *BiDrAC,*
DcAmB, NatCAB 13, WhAm H,
WhAmP
Hendricks, William 1783-1850 *ApCAB,*
BiAUS, Drake, TwCBDA

Hendrickson, Charles Elvin 1843-1919 *WhAm 1*
Hendrickson, George Lincoln 1865-1963
NatCAB 47, TwCBDA, WhAm 4
Hendrickson, Homer O 1890-1958 *WhAm 3*
Hendrickson, Robert Clymer 1898-1964 *BiDrAC,*
WhAm 4
Hendrickson, Samuel Armstrong 1838-1913
NatCAB 24
Hendrickson, William Woodbury 1844-1920
WhAm 1
Hendrie, George 1834-1914 *NatCAB 16*
Hendrie, Lilian Margaret 1869- *WomWWA 14*
Hendrix, Eugene Russell 1847-1927
ApCAB Sup, DcAmB, NatCAB 13,
TwCBDA, WhAm 1
Hendrix, Herman Elert 1880-1948 *BiDAmEd*
Hendrix, Jimi 1942-1970 *WhAm 5*
Hendrix, Joseph Clifford 1853-1904 *BiDrAC,*
DcAmB, NatCAB 12, TwCBDA,
WhAm 1
Hendrix, William Samuel 1887-1948 *WhAm 2*
Hendrixson, Walter Scott 1859- *WhAm 1*
Hendron, Carroll 1871-1956 *NatCAB 44*
Hendryx, Andrew Benedict 1834-1907
NatCAB 38
Hendryx, James Beardsley 1880-1963 *WhAm 4*
Hendryx, Nathan Wilbur 1880-1929
NatCAB 35
Hendy, John 1757-1840 *NatCAB 12*
Henes, John Edwin 1881-1948 *NatCAB 37*
Heney, Francis Joseph 1859-1937 *AmBi,*
DcAmB S2, NatCAB 33, WhAm 1,
WhAmP
Henfrey, Arthur 1819-1859 *DcScB*
Hengst, James McCleery 1884-1964
NatCAB 51, WhAm 4
Henican, Joseph Padrick, Jr. 1903-1963
WhAm 4
Henie, Sonja 1912-1969 *WhAm 5*
Henigan, George Francis d1973 *WhAm 6*
Hening, Benjamin Cabell 1863-1949 *WhAm 2*
Hening, William Waller 1767?-1828 *ApCAB,*
DcAmB, Drake, WhAm H
Henius, Arthur 1870-1949 *NatCAB 37*
Henius, Henry Robert 1884-1962 *NatCAB 50*
Henius, Lillian Grace 1879-1926 *NatCAB 21*
Henius, Max 1859-1935 *NatCAB 27,*
WhAm 1
Henke, Frederick Goodrich 1876-1963 *WhAm 4*
Henkel, Alice *WomWWA 14*
Henkel, Carl Henry 1880-1962 *NatCAB 51*
Henkel, Moses Montgomery 1798-1864 *ApCAB*
Henkel, Paul 1754-1825 *ApCAB, DcAmB,*
DcAmReB, WhAm H
Henkin, Leo Justin 1906-1952 *NatCAB 41*
Henking, Hermann 1858-1942 *DcScB*
Henkle, Charles Zane 1892-1949 *WhAm 3*
Henkle, Eli James 1828-1893 *NatCAB 11*
Henkle, Eli Jones 1828-1893 *ApCAB, BiAUS,*
BiDrAC, TwCBDA, WhAm H
Henkle, Moses Montgomery 1798- *Drake*
Henkle, Rae DeLancey 1883-1935 *WhAm 1*
Henle, Friedrich Gustav Jacob 1809-1885 *DcScB*
Henle, Friedrich Gustav Jakob 1809-1885
AsBiEn
Henle, Friedrich Gustave Jacob 1809-1885
BiHiMed
Henle, James 1891-1973 *WhAm 5*
Henley, Anna F Adams 1865- *WhoColR*
Henley, Barclay 1843-1914 *BiDrAC*
Henley, David 1748-1823 *ApCAB, Drake*
Henley, John Dandridge 1781-1835 *ApCAB,*
Drake, TwCBDA
Henley, Robert 1783-1828 *ApCAB, DcAmB,*
Drake, NatCAB 13, TwCBDA, WhAm H
Henley, Robert Edward 1886-1965 *NatCAB 52,*
WhAm 4
Henley, Samuel 1740-1815 *NatCAB 18*
Henley, Thomas d1776 *ApCAB*
Henley, Thomas J 1810- *BiAUS*
Henley, Thomas Jefferson 1807-1875 *TwCBDA*
Henley, Thomas Jefferson 1810-1865 *BiDrAC,*
WhAm H
Henley, Walter Ervin 1877- *WhAm 6*
Henmon, Vivian Allen Charles¶1877-1950
WhAm 3
Henn, Albert William 1865-1947 *WhAm 3*
Henn, Bernhart 1817-1865 *BiAUS, BiDrAC,*

TwCBDA, WhAm H
Hennan, Clarence William 1894-1956
NatCAB 46
Henneberger, Herman 1852-1924 *ApCAB X*
Hennegan, B K *BiAUS*
Henneman, Alexander 1868- *NatCAB 13*
Henneman, John Bell 1864-1908 *WhAm 1*
Hennemuth, Robert George 1921-1975 *WhAm 6*
Hennen, Alfred 1786-1870 *ApCAB*
Hennenberger, Martin *NewYHSD*
Hennepin, Louis 1640?-1699 *Drake*
Hennepin, Louis 1640?-1701? *AmBi, ApCAB,*
DcAmB, WebAB, WhAm H
Hennequin, Alfred 1846- *WhAm 4*
Hennessey, Thomas Michael 1901-1974
WhAm 6
Hennessy, Frank J 1880- *WhAm 6*
Hennessy, James William 1897-1965
NatCAB 53
Hennessy, John 1823-1900 *WhAm 1*
Hennessy, John 1825-1900 *ApCAB, DcAmB,*
NatCAB 10, TwCBDA
Hennessy, John Francis 1902-1973 *WhAm 5*
Hennessy, John Joseph 1847-1920 *ApCAB Sup,*
NatCAB 12, TwCBDA, WhAm 1
Hennessy, John Lawrence 1886-1955 *WhAm 3*
Hennessy, Michael Edmund 1866-1955
WhAm 3
Hennessy, Roland Burke 1870- *WhAm 5*
Hennessy, William John 1837-1917 *WhAm 1*
Hennessy, William John 1839-1917 *ApCAB,*
DcAmB, NewYHSD, TwCBDA
Hennessy, William Thomas 1887-1962 *WhAm 4*
Henneuse, Clarence Alvin 1879-1939
NatCAB 29
Henney, Charles William Francis 1884-1969
BiDrAC
Henney, William Franklin 1852-1928 *WhAm 1*
Henni, John Martin 1805-1881 *ApCAB,*
DcAmB, NatCAB 7, TwCBDA,
WhAm H
Hennig, Julian Henry 1894-1971 *NatCAB 57*
Henning, A *NewYHSD*
Henning, Albin 1886-1943 *IIBEAAW*
Henning, Arthur Sears 1876-1966 *WhAm 4*
Henning, Carl 1880-1956 *NatCAB 49*
Henning, Edward J 1868-1935 *WhAm 1*
Henning, George Neely 1871-1950 *NatCAB 38,*
WhAm 3
Henning, William Cleveland 1869-1949
NatCAB 37
Hennings, Ernest Martin 1886-1956 *IIBEAAW,*
WhAm 3
Hennings, Joseph Everett 1865-1929
NatCAB 22
Hennings, Thomas Carey, Jr. 1903-1960
BiDrAC, WhAm 4, WhAmP
Hennings, Thomas Carey, Sr. 1874- *WhAm 6*
Henningsen, Charles Frederic 1815-1877 *Drake*
Henningsen, Charles Frederick 1815-1877
ApCAB, DcAmB, NatCAB 9, TwCBDA,
WhAm H
Hennisee, Argalus Garey 1839-1913 *WhAm 1*
Hennock, Frieda B 1904-1960 *WhAm 4*
Hennrich, Kilian Joseph 1880-1946 *WhAm 2*
Henny, David Christiaan 1860-1935 *DcAmB S1,*
NatCAB 26
Henny, David Christian 1860-1935 *WhAm 1*
Henoch, Eduard Heinrich 1820-1910 *BiHiMed*
Henretta, James Edward 1874-1971 *WhAm 5*
Henri *DcScB*
Henri, Pierre *NewYHSD*
Henri, Robert 1865-1929 *AmBi, BiDAmEd,*
BnEnAmA, DcAmB, EncAB, IIBEAAW,
NatCAB 15, WebAB, WhAm 1
Henrich, V C 1899-1966 *WhAm 4*
Henrichs, Henry Frederick 1876-1970 *WhAm 6*
Henrichsen, Sophus 1845-1928 *DcScB*
Henrici, Arthur Trautwein 1889-1943
DcAmB S3, WhAm 2
Henricks, Coleman Bresee 1907-1969 *WhAm 5*
Henricks, Harold H 1889-1955 *WhAm 3*
Henrikson, Seved Henry 1904-1965 *NatCAB 51*
Henrion, Denis 1580?-1632? *DcScB*
Henrion, Nicolas 1733-1793 *ApCAB*
Henriques, Robert David Quixano 1905-1967
WhAm 4
Henriquez, Camilo 1769-1825 *ApCAB*

Henriquez-Urena, Max 1885-1968 *WhAm 5*
Henriquez-Urena, Pedro 1884-1947 *WhAm 2*
Henrotin, Charles 1843-1914 *DcAmB,*
WhAm 1
Henrotin, Ellen M Martin 1847-1922 *NotAW,*
WhAm 1, WomWWA 14
Henrotin, Fernand 1847-1906 *DcAmB,*
WhAm 1
Henry I 876-936 *McGEWB*
Henry I 1068-1135 *McGEWB*
Henry II 1133-1189 *McGEWB*
Henry III 1017-1056 *McGEWB*
Henry III 1207-1272 *McGEWB*
Henry IV 1050-1106 *McGEWB*
Henry IV 1367-1413 *McGEWB*
Henry IV 1553-1610 *McGEWB, WhoMilH*
Henry V 1081-1125 *McGEWB*
Henry V 1387-1422 *McGEWB*
Henry VI 1421-1471 *McGEWB*
Henry VII 1274?-1313 *McGEWB*
Henry VII 1457-1509 *McGEWB*
Henry VIII 1491-1547 *McGEWB*
Henry Bate Of Malines 1246-1310? *DcScB*
Henry Of Denmark *DcScB*
Henry Of Hesse 1325-1397 *DcScB*
Henry Of Mondeville 1260?-1320? *DcScB*
Henry The Navigator 1394-1460 *AsBiEn,*
McGEWB
Henry, Abigail Thomas Moss 1867-
WomWWA 14
Henry, Albert P 1836-1872 *NewYHSD,*
WhAm H
Henry, Alexander 1739-1814 *TwCBDA*
Henry, Alexander 1739-1824 *AmBi, ApCAB,*
DcAmB S1, Drake, WhAm H
Henry, Alexander 1766-1847 *ApCAB, Drake,*
NatCAB 13
Henry, Alexander 1823-1883 *ApCAB,*
NatCAB 4
Henry, Alexander 1850-1925 *WhAm 1*
Henry, Alfred Hylas 1865- *WhAm 4*
Henry, Alfred Judson 1858-1931 *NatCAB 22,*
WhAm 1
Henry, Alice 1857-1943 *BiCAW, DcAmB S3,*
NotAW, WomWWA 14
Henry, Ambrose Dyer 1863-1939 *NatCAB 39*
Henry, Andrew 1775?-1833 *DcAmB, REnAW,*
WebAB, WhAm H
Henry, Arnold Kahle 1898-1971 *WhAm 5*
Henry, Arthur 1867- *WhAm 4*
Henry, Aurelia *WomWWA 14*
Henry, Barklie McKee 1902-1966 *NatCAB 53,*
WhAm 4
Henry, Bayard 1857-1926 *WhAm 1*
Henry, Benjamin West 1777-1806 *NewYHSD*
Henry, Caleb Sprague 1804-1884 *ApCAB,*
DcAmB, Drake, NatCAB 11, TwCBDA,
WhAm H
Henry, Carl French 1867-1929 *WhAm 1*
Henry, Charles Lewis 1849-1927 *BiDrAC,*
NatCAB 22, TwCBDA, WhAm 1
Henry, Charles William 1878-1935 *NatCAB 42,*
WhAm 1
Henry, Charles Wolcott 1852-1903 *NatCAB 35*
Henry, Claude Morrison 1873- *WhAm 1*
Henry, Daniel Maynadier 1823-1899 *BiDrAC*
Henry, David Dodds 1905- *BiDAmEd*
Henry, David W 1885-1955 *WhAm 3*
Henry, Douglas Selph 1890-1971 *WhAm 5*
Henry, Edgar Schall 1890-1965 *NatCAB 51*
Henry, Edward *NewYHSD*
Henry, Edward Atwood 1881- *WhAm 6*
Henry, Edward Lamson 1841-1919 *AmBi,*
ApCAB, ApCAB X, BnEnAmA, DcAmB,
NatCAB 5, NewYHSD, TwCBDA,
WhAm 1
Henry, Edward Stevens 1836-1921 *BiDrAC,*
TwCBDA, WhAm 1, WhAmP
Henry, Erastus *NewYHSD*
Henry, Eugene John 1866- *WhAm 4*
Henry, Francis Augustus 1847-1936
NatCAB 27
Henry, Frank Forrest 1870-1961 *NatCAB 54*
Henry, Franklin Sylvester 1846-1914
NatCAB 18
Henry, Frederick Augustus 1867-1949
NatCAB 46, WhAm 2
Henry, Frederick Porteous 1844- *WhAm 4*

Henry, George *NewYHSD*
Henry, George Francis 1894-1965 *WhAm 4*
Henry, George Frederick 1870-1945 *WhAm 2*
Henry, George McClellan 1877- *WhAm 5*
Henry, George William 1889-1964 *WhAm 4*
Henry, Georgia Johnson *WomWWA 14*
Henry, Gustavus Adolphus 1804-1880 *ApCAB,*
BiDConf, NatCAB 13, TwCBDA
Henry, Guy Vernor 1839-1899 *ApCAB,*
NatCAB 9, TwCBDA, WhAm 1
Henry, Guy Vernor 1875-1967 *NatCAB 54,*
WhAm 4
Henry, Harold Augustus 1895-1966 *NatCAB 53*
Henry, Helen Natalie 1879- *WomWWA 14*
Henry, Henry A 1801-1879 *ApCAB*
Henry, Heth 1825-1899 *WhAm H*
Henry, Horace Chapin 1844-1928 *ApCAB X,*
NatCAB 11, NatCAB 33, WhAm 1
Henry, Howard James 1911-1969 *WhAm 5*
Henry, Howell Meadors 1879-1956 *WhAm 3*
Henry, Hugh 1838-1920 *NatCAB 39*
Henry, Hugh Carter 1875-1945 *WhAm 2*
Henry, Hugh Thomas 1862- *WhAm 4*
Henry, J Porter 1884-1969 *WhAm 5*
Henry, James d1805 *BiAUS, Drake*
Henry, James 1731-1804 *BiDrAC, TwCBDA,*
WhAm H
Henry, James 1809- *ApCAB*
Henry, James Addison 1835-1906 *WhAm 1*
Henry, James Buchanan 1833-1915 *NatCAB 22*
Henry, James Harrison 1845- *NatCAB 7*
Henry, James McClure 1880-1958 *WhAm 3*
Henry, Jerry Maurice 1880- *WhAm 6*
Henry, John *NewYHSD*
Henry, John d1794 *Drake*
Henry, John 1731-1829 *ApCAB, Drake*
Henry, John 1738?-1795 *ApCAB*
Henry, John 1746?-1794 *DcAmB, WhAm H*
Henry, John 1750-1798 *BiAUS,*
BiDrAC, DcAmB, Drake, NatCAB 2,
NatCAB 9, TwCBDA, WhAm H,
WhAmP
Henry, John 1776?- *ApCAB, DcAmB, Drake,*
WhAm H
Henry, John 1800-1882 *BiDrAC, WhAm H*
Henry, John B *NewYHSD*
Henry, John Flournoy 1793-1873 *ApCAB,*
BiAUS, BiDrAC, TwCBDA, WhAm H
Henry, John Joseph 1758-1810? *Drake*
Henry, John Joseph 1758-1811 *ApCAB*
Henry, John Norman 1873-1938 *NatCAB 28,*
WhAm 1
Henry, John Pennington 1898-1947 *NatCAB 36*
Henry, John Robert, Jr. 1913-1974 *WhAm 6*
Henry, John Robertson 1868- *WhAm 4*
Henry, John Williams 1825-1902 *NatCAB 12*
Henry, Joseph 1797-1878 *AmBi, ApCAB,*
AsBiEn, BiAUS, DcAmB, DcScB, Drake,
EncAB, McGEWB, NatCAB 3, WebAB,
WhAm H
Henry, Joseph 1799-1873 *TwCBDA*
Henry, Josephine Kirby Williamson 1846-
AmWom
Henry, Jules 1904-1969 *WhAm 5*
Henry, Kate Kearney 1840- *WhAm 1,*
WomWWA 14
Henry, Langdon Chapin 1878-1967 *NatCAB 54,*
WhAm 4
Henry, Lemuel H 1871-1929 *WhAm 1*
Henry, Lewis 1885-1941 *BiDrAC*
Henry, Loris LaVerne 1894-1958 *NatCAB 48*
Henry, Mary Gibson 1884- *WomWWA 14*
Henry, Matthew George 1910-1975 *WhAm 6*
Henry, Morris *NewYHSD*
Henry, Morris Henry 1835-1895 *ApCAB,*
DcAmB, WhAm H
Henry, Morris Henry 1836-1895 *NatCAB 2*
Henry, Myron Ormell 1893-1953 *WhAm 3*
Henry, Nelson Herrick 1855-1933 *WhAm 1*
Henry, O 1862-1910 *AmBi, DcAmB,*
McGEWB, WebAB, WhAm 1
Henry, Patrick 1736-1799 *AmBi, ApCAB,*
BiAUS, BiDrAC, DcAmB, Drake,
EncAAH, EncAB, McGEWB, NatCAB 1,
REnAW, TwCBDA, WebAB, WhAm H,
WhAmP
Henry, Patrick 1843-1930 *BiDrAC, TwCBDA,*
WhAm 3

Henry, Patrick 1861-1933 *BiDrAC*
Henry, Paul Pierre 1848-1905 *DcScB*
Henry, Peter *NewYHSD*
Henry, Philip Solomon 1863-1933 *WhAm 1*
Henry, Philip Walter 1864-1947 *NatCAB 10,*
NatCAB 15, NatCAB 36, WhAm 2
Henry, Pierre Francois 1759-1833 *ApCAB*
Henry, Prosper Mathieu 1849-1903 *DcScB*
Henry, Ralph Coolidge 1875- *WhAm 5*
Henry, Robert 1792-1856 *ApCAB, DcAmB,*
Drake, NatCAB 11, TwCBDA, WhAm H
Henry, Robert Evelyn 1880-1955 *NatCAB 45*
Henry, Robert Kirkland 1890-1946 *BiDrAC,*
WhAm 2
Henry, Robert Lee 1864-1931 *BiDrAC,*
TwCBDA, WhAm 1, WhAmP
Henry, Robert Llewellyn, Jr. 1882-1969
WhAm 5
Henry, Robert Patterson 1911-1973 *WhAm 6*
Henry, Robert Pryor 1788-1826 *ApCAB,*
BiAUS, BiDrAC, TwCBDA, WhAm H
Henry, Robert Selph 1889-1970 *NatCAB 55,*
WhAm 5
Henry, Samuel Clements 1872- *WhAm 5*
Henry, Sarepta Myrenda 1839-1900 *AmWom,*
NatCAB 9, TwCBDA
Henry, Sidney Morgan 1878-1959 *WhAm 3*
Henry, Stuart Oliver 1860-1953 *NatCAB 9,*
TwCBDA, WhAm 3
Henry, Thomas *NewYHSD*
Henry, Thomas 1734-1816 *DcScB*
Henry, Thomas 1779-1849 *BiDrAC, WhAm H*
Henry, Thomas 1781-1849 *TwCBDA*
Henry, Thomas 1785-1849 *BiAUS*
Henry, Thomas Charlton 1790-1827 *ApCAB,*
Drake
Henry, Thomas Patrick 1877-1945 *NatCAB 34,*
WhAm 2
Henry, Vincent *NewYHSD*
Henry, Waights Gibbs 1879-1960 *WhAm 4*
Henry, William *NewYHSD*
Henry, William 1729-1786 *ApCAB, BiAUS,*
BiDrAC, DcAmB, NatCAB 11, TwCBDA,
WhAm H
Henry, William 1757-1827 *ApCAB*
Henry, William 1761-1824 *ApCAB, Drake,*
TwCBDA
Henry, William 1774-1836 *DcScB*
Henry, William 1788-1861 *BiAUS, BiDrAC,*
TwCBDA, WhAm H
Henry, William Alexander 1816- *ApCAB,*
Drake
Henry, William Arnon 1850-1932 *DcAmB S1,*
TwCBDA, WhAm 1
Henry, William Elmer 1857-1936 *NatCAB 26,*
WhAm 1
Henry, William M 1890-1970 *WhAm 5*
Henry, William Seaton 1816-1851 *ApCAB,*
Drake
Henry, William Thomas 1849- *WhAm 4*
Henry, William Wirt 1831-1900 *ApCAB,*
DcAmB, NatCAB 9, TwCBDA,
WhAm 1
Henry, Winder Laird 1864-1940 *BiDrAC*
Henry-Ruffin, Margaret Ellen *WomWWA 14*
Henschel, George 1850-1934 *WhAm 2*
Henschel, Lillian June Bailey 1860-1901
AmWom, WhAm H
Hensel, Arthur 1870-1927 *NatCAB 22*
Hensel, Daniel 1831?- *NewYHSD*
Hensel, Kurt 1861-1941 *DcScB*
Hensel, William Uhler 1851-1915 *WhAm 1*
Hensell, G H *NewYHSD*
Hensen, Victor 1835-1924 *DcScB*
Henshall, James Alexander 1836-1925 *DcAmB,*
WhAm 1
Henshaw, Albert Melville 1879-1950 *WhAm 3*
Henshaw, Daniel 1782-1863 *ApCAB, Drake*
Henshaw, Daniel 1822- *TwCBDA*
Henshaw, David 1791-1852 *ApCAB, BiAUS,*
BiDrUSE, DcAmB, Drake, TwCBDA,
WhAm H
Henshaw, David 1791-1862 *NatCAB 6*
Henshaw, Flora Alice Newlin 1867-
WomWWA 14
Henshaw, Frederic Rich 1872-1938 *WhAm 1*
Henshaw, Frederick Valdemar 1868-1941
NatCAB 30

Herlihy, John Albert 1904-1962 *WhAm 4*
Herlin, August *NewYHSD*
Herline, Edward *NewYHSD*
Herlong, Albert Sydney, Jr. 1909- *BiDrAC,*
  WhAmP
Herly, Louis 1881-1952 *WhAm 3*
Herman, Mister *IIBEAAW*
Herman, Abraham 1878-1947 *WhAm 2*
Herman, Alexander C 1897-1974 *WhAm 6*
Herman, Augustin 1605?-1686 *NatCAB 4*
Herman, Harry L *ApCAB X*
Herman, Henry Edson Todd 1891-1950
  WhAm 3
Herman, James R 1898-1951 *WhAm 3*
Herman, John Gottlieb 1789-1854 *ApCAB,*
  NatCAB 1, TwCBDA
Herman, Lebrecht Frederick 1761-1848 *DcAmB,*
  WhAm H
Herman, Leon Emerson 1887-1956 *WhAm 3*
Herman, Ralph Edward 1891-1960 *NatCAB 47*
Herman, Raphael 1865-1946 *WhAm 2*
Herman, Stewart Winfield 1878- *WhAm 6*
Herman, Theodore Frederick 1872-1948
  NatCAB 37, WhAm 2
Hermance, Harry Putnam 1867-1937
  NatCAB 28
Hermance, W Oakley 1872-1953 *NatCAB 43*
Hermance, William Ellsworth 1862-1927
  WhAm 1
Hermandt, Ph *NewYHSD*
Hermann The Lame 1013-1054 *DcScB*
Hermann, Binger 1843-1926 *BiDrAC,*
  TwCBDA, WhAm 1, WhAmP
Hermann, Carl Heinrich 1898-1961 *DcScB*
Hermann, Edward Adolph 1856- *WhAm 4*
Hermann, Harold Nathaniel 1896-1963
  NatCAB 50
Hermann, Jakob 1678-1733 *DcScB*
Hermann, Otto John 1884-1973 *NatCAB 57*
Hermannsson, Halldor 1878-1958 *WhAm 3*
Hermannus Contractus *DcScB*
Hermany, Charles 1830- *NatCAB 13*
Hermbstadt, Sigismund Friedrich 1760-1833
  DcScB
Hermbstaedt, Sigismund Friedrich 1760-1833
  DcScB Sup
Hermes Trismegistus *DcScB*
Hermite, Charles 1822-1901 *AsBiEn, DcScB*
Herms, William Brodbeck 1876-1949 *ApCAB X,*
  NatCAB 36, WhAm 3
Hermsen, Edward Herman 1911- *WhAm 5*
Hermstaedt, Nicholas Piet 1521-1589 *ApCAB*
Hernandez, Benigno Cardenas 1862-1954
  BiDrAC, NatCAB 43, WhAm 4, WhAmP
Hernandez, Francisco d1587 *Drake*
Hernandez, Francisco 1517-1587 *DcScB*
Hernandez, Francisco 1530-1587 *ApCAB*
Hernandez, Jose 1834-1886 *McGEWB*
Hernandez, Jose Conrado 1849-1932 *WhAm 1*
Hernandez, Joseph Marion 1793-1857 *ApCAB,*
  BiAUS, BiDrAC, Drake, TwCBDA,
  WhAm H, WhAmP
Hernandez, Roberto 1884-1960 *WhAm 4*
Hernandez, Vicente 1480?-1543 *ApCAB*
Herndon, Alonzo Franklin 1858- *WhoColR*
Herndon, Charles Traverse 1857-1936 *WhAm 3*
Herndon, James B, Jr. 1898-1953 *WhAm 3*
Herndon, John Goodwin 1896-1957 *NatCAB 44,*
  WhAm 3
Herndon, Mary Eliza 1820- *ApCAB*
Herndon, Thomas Hord 1828-1883 *BiDrAC,*
  WhAm H
Herndon, William Henry 1818-1891 *AmBi,*
  ApCAB Sup, DcAmB, NatCAB 23,
  WhAm H
Herndon, William Lewis 1813-1857 *ApCAB,*
  BiAUS, DcAmB, Drake, NatCAB 4,
  TwCBDA, WhAm H
Herndon, William S 1837- *BiAUS*
Herndon, William Smith 1835-1903 *BiDrAC*
Herne, Chrystal Katharine 1882-1950
  DcAmB S4, NotAW
Herne, James A 1839-1901 *AmBi, DcAmB,*
  NatCAB 5, TwCBDA, WebAB, WhAm 1
Herne, Katherine Corcoran *WhAm H*
Hernon, Joseph Martin 1901-1963 *NatCAB 50*
Hernon, William Seton 1891-1952 *WhAm 3*
Hero Of Alexandria 020?- *AsBiEn, DcScB*

Hero, Alfred Olivier 1887-1941 *NatCAB 41*
Hero, Andrew, Jr. 1868-1942 *NatCAB 43,*
  WhAm 1
Hero, Ann 1875- *WomWWA 14*
Hero, George Alfred 1854- *NatCAB 15*
Hero, William Sommer 1870-1949 *NatCAB 38*
Herod The Great 073?BC-004BC *McGEWB*
Herod, William 1801-1871 *BiAUS, BiDrAC,*
  WhAm H
Herod, William Pirtle 1864-1931 *WhAm 1,*
  WhAm 2
Herod, William Rogers 1898-1974 *NatCAB 57,*
  WhAm 6
Herodotus 484?BC-425?BC *McGEWB*
Herodotus Of Halicarnassus d420?BC *DcScB*
Herold, David E *DcAmB*
Herold, Don 1889-1966 *WhAm 4*
Herold, Herman Christian Henry 1854-
  NatCAB 5
Herold, Jean Christopher 1919-1964 *WhAm 4*
Herold, Stanley Carrollton 1883-1959
  NatCAB 47
Heron Of Alexandria *DcScB, McGEWB*
Heron, Ernest Alvah 1851-1917 *ApCAB X*
Heron, James 1853-1915 *NatCAB 16*
Heron, James Henry 1877- *WhAm 5*
Heron, Matilda Agnes 1830-1877 *ApCAB,*
  DcAmB, Drake, NatCAB 8, NotAW,
  TwCBDA, WhAm H
Heron, S D 1891-1963 *WhAm 4*
Heron, William 1742-1819 *DcAmB, WhAm H*
Herophilus 320?BC- *AsBiEn, DcScB*
Heroult, Paul Louis Toussaint 1863-1914
  AsBiEn, DcScB
Heroy, James Harold 1881-1950 *NatCAB 38,*
  WhAm 3
Heroy, William Bayard 1883-1971 *WhAm 5*
Heroy, William Ward 1853-1923 *NatCAB 42*
Herpolsheimer, Henry B 1868-1920 *NatCAB 18*
Herpolsheimer, William G 1842-1920
  NatCAB 18
Herr, Albert Hiram *ApCAB X*
Herr, Edwin Musser 1860-1932 *NatCAB 23,*
  WhAm 1
Herr, George *NewYHSD*
Herr, Herbert Thacker 1876-1933 *DcAmB S1,*
  WhAm 1
Herr, Hiero Benjamin 1842-1920 *NatCAB 20,*
  WhAm 1
Herr, John 1781-1850 *DcAmB, NatCAB 7,*
  WhAm H
Herr, John Knowles 1878-1955 *NatCAB 43,*
  WhAm 6
Herr, John Kohr 1882-1970 *NatCAB 55*
Herr, Martin L 1838- *NatCAB 5*
Herr, Theodore Witmer 1833-1917 *NatCAB 23*
Herr, Vincent V 1901-1970 *WhAm 5*
Herr, Willis Benjamin 1863-1929 *NatCAB 23*
Herran, Jeronimo *ApCAB*
Herran, Pedro Alcantara 1800-1872 *ApCAB*
Herre, Albert William Christian Theodore
  1868-1962 *NatCAB 52, WhAm 4*
Herreid, Charles N 1857-1928 *NatCAB 13,*
  WhAm 1
Herreid, Myron Tillman 1895-1964 *WhAm 4*
Herrell, John Eli 1830-1909 *NatCAB 2*
Herrera, Alfonso Luis 1868-1942 *DcScB*
Herrera, Bartolome 1808-1864 *ApCAB*
Herrera, Joe Hilario 1923- *IIBEAAW*
Herrera, Jose Joaquin De d1851 *Drake*
Herrera, Jose Joaquin De 1792-1854 *ApCAB*
Herrera, Juan De 1530?-1597 *McGEWB*
Herrera, Miguel DaFonseca E Silva 1763-1822
  ApCAB
Herrera, Nicolas 1780-1832 *ApCAB*
Herrera, Tordesillas Antony 1549-1625 *Drake*
Herrera, Velino Shije 1902-1973 *IIBEAAW*
Herrera Lane, Felipe 1922- *McGEWB*
Herrera Y Cabrera, Desiderio 1792-1856
  ApCAB
Herrera Y Olalla, Alonso De 1500?-1580
  ApCAB
Herrera Y Tordesillas, Antonio De 1559-1625
  ApCAB
Herreshoff, Charles Frederick 1809-1888
  NatCAB 12, TwCBDA
Herreshoff, Charles Frederick 1876-1954
  WhAm 3

Herreshoff, Charles Frederick 1880- *ApCAB X*
Herreshoff, J B Francis 1850-1932 *ApCAB X,*
  NatCAB 24
Herreshoff, James Brown 1834-1930 *DcAmB,*
  NatCAB 12, NatCAB 42, TwCBDA,
  WhAm 1
Herreshoff, John Brown 1841-1915 *AmBi,*
  ApCAB Sup, DcAmB, NatCAB 12,
  TwCBDA, WhAm 1
Herreshoff, John Brown Francis 1850-1932
  NatCAB 12, TwCBDA, WhAm 1
Herreshoff, Julian Lewis 1854- *NatCAB 12,*
  TwCBDA
Herreshoff, Nathanael Greene 1848-1938 *AmBi,*
  DcAmB S2, NatCAB 30, TwCBDA,
  WhAm 1
Herreshoff, Nathaniel Greene 1848-1938
  NatCAB 12
Herrick, Ada Elizabeth 1873- *WomWWA 14*
Herrick, Albert Bledsoe 1862-1938 *NatCAB 38,*
  WhAm 4
Herrick, Anson 1812-1868 *ApCAB, BiAUS,*
  BiDrAC, TwCBDA, WhAm H
Herrick, Charles Judson 1868-1960 *DcScB,*
  NatCAB 47, WhAm 3
Herrick, Cheesman Abiah 1866-1956
  NatCAB 47, WhAm 3
Herrick, Christine Terhune 1859-1944 *AmWom,*
  NatCAB 8, NotAW, TwCBDA,
  WhAm 2, WomWWA 14
Herrick, Clarence Luther 1858- *TwCBDA*
Herrick, Clarence Luther 1858-1903 *WhAm 1*
Herrick, Clarence Luther 1858-1904 *DcScB,*
  NatCAB 26
Herrick, Clinton B 1859- *WhAm 4*
Herrick, Curtis James 1909-1971 *WhAm 5*
Herrick, D Cady 1846-1926 *TwCBDA,*
  WhAm 1
Herrick, Ebenezer 1785-1839 *BiAUS, BiDrAC,*
  TwCBDA, WhAm H
Herrick, Edward Claudius 1811-1862 *ApCAB,*
  DcAmB, Drake, NatCAB 11, TwCBDA,
  WhAm H
Herrick, Elias Hicks 1866- *NatCAB 14*
Herrick, Elinore Morehouse 1895-1964
  WhAm 4
Herrick, Elizabeth 1874- *WhAm 5*
Herrick, Everett Carleton 1876-1957 *WhAm 3*
Herrick, Francis Hobart 1858-1940 *NatCAB 3,*
  NatCAB 31, TwCBDA, WhAm 1
Herrick, Frank Rufus 1865-1926 *NatCAB 21*
Herrick, Frederick Cowles 1872-1943
  NatCAB 32, WhAm 2
Herrick, Gamaliel Ephraim 1827-1900
  NatCAB 31
Herrick, Genevieve Forbes 1894- *WhAm 5*
Herrick, George Frederic 1834-1926
  ApCAB Sup
Herrick, George Frederick 1834-1926 *WhAm 1*
Herrick, George Marsh 1856- *TwCBDA,*
  WhAm 4
Herrick, Glenn Washington 1870- *NatCAB 18,*
  WhAm 5
Herrick, Harold 1853-1933 *WhAm 1*
Herrick, Henry W 1824-1906 *IIBEAAW,*
  NewYHSD, WhAm 1
Herrick, Huldah *WhAm 4*
Herrick, James Bryan 1861-1954 *BiHiMed,*
  NatCAB 42, WhAm 3
Herrick, John Origen 1898- *WhAm 5*
Herrick, John Pierce 1868-1961 *NatCAB 50*
Herrick, John Russell 1822- *ApCAB,*
  TwCBDA
Herrick, Joshua 1793-1874 *ApCAB, BiDrAC,*
  TwCBDA, WhAm H
Herrick, Joshua 1794-1874 *BiAUS*
Herrick, Lott Russell 1871-1937 *NatCAB 30,*
  WhAm 1
Herrick, Lucius Carroll 1840-1903 *ApCAB,*
  WhAm 1
Herrick, Mabel Hurd Walker 1866-
  WomWWA 14
Herrick, Manuel 1876-1952 *BiDrAC,*
  WhAm 5, WhAmP
Herrick, Margaret Perkins 1875-1968
  NatCAB 54
Herrick, Marvin Theodore 1899-1966
  NatCAB 52, WhAm 4

Herrick, Myron Timothy 1854-1929 *AmBi,*
ApCAB X, DcAmB, NatCAB 13,
NatCAB 32, WebAB, WhAm 1
Herrick, Parmely Webb 1881-1937 *WhAm 1*
Herrick, Paul Murray 1898-1972 *WhAm 5*
Herrick, Ray W 1890-1973 *WhAm 5*
Herrick, Richard Platt 1791-1846 *BiAUS,*
BiDrAC, WhAm H
Herrick, Robert 1591-1674 *McGEWB*
Herrick, Robert Frederick 1866-1942
NatCAB 33, WhAm 2
Herrick, Robert Frederick 1893-1941
NatCAB 36
Herrick, Robert Welch 1868-1938 *ApCAB X,*
DcAmB S2, NatCAB 13, NatCAB 42,
TwCBDA, WhAm 1
Herrick, Samuel 1779-1851 *BiAUS*
Herrick, Samuel 1779-1852 *BiDrAC,*
TwCBDA, WhAm H
Herrick, Samuel, Jr. 1911-1974 *WhAm 6*
Herrick, Samuel Edward 1841-1904 *ApCAB,*
WhAm 1
Herrick, Sophia McIlvaine Bledsoe 1837-1919
DcAmB, TwCBDA
Herrick, Sophia M'Ilvaine Bledsoe 1837-1919
WhAm 1, WomWWA 14
Herrick, Sophie McIlvaine Bledsoe 1837-1919
ApCAB
Herrick, Stephen Solon 1833-1906 *ApCAB,*
WhAm 1
Herrick, Walter R 1877- *WhAm 5*
Herrick, William Francis 1826-1906
NatCAB 33, NewYHSD
Herrick, William Worthington 1879-1945
NatCAB 37
Herrick, Wirt 1889-1966 *WhAm 4*
Herridge, William Duncan 1888-1961 *WhAm 4*
Herrig, Peter 1848-1915 *NatCAB 16*
Herriman, Abbie Frances *WomWWA 14*
Herriman, George 1878-1944 *WebAB*
Herriman, George Joseph 1880-1944 *DcAmB S3*
Herriman, Helen Strange *WomWWA 14*
Herrin, William Franklin 1854-1927 *WhAm 1*
Herring, Mrs. *NewYHSD*
Herring, Augustus Moore 1867-1926 *DcAmB*
Herring, Clyde LaVerne 1879-1945 *BiDrAC,*
NatCAB 34, WhAm 2, WhAmP
Herring, Donald Grant, Jr. 1918-1962
NatCAB 50
Herring, Elbert 1777-1876 *ApCAB, BiAUS,*
BiAUS Sup, TwCBDA
Herring, Frances Elizabeth 1851-
WomWWA 14
Herring, Frederick William 1821-1899 *ApCAB,*
NewYHSD
Herring, Herbert James 1899-1966 *WhAm 5*
Herring, Hubert Clinton 1859-1920 *WhAm 1*
Herring, Hubert Clinton 1889-1967 *WhAm 5*
Herring, James 1794-1867 *ApCAB, DcAmB,*
Drake, NewYHSD, WhAm H
Herring, Katherine M 1876- *WomWWA 14*
Herring, Lewis *NewYHSD*
Herring, Louis *NewYHSD*
Herring, Silas Clark 1803-1881 *DcAmB,*
WhAm H
Herring, Silas Clarke 1803-1881 *NatCAB 9*
Herring, William 1833-1912 *NatCAB 33,*
WhAm 1
Herrington, Arthur William Sidney 1891-1970
WhAm 5
Herrington, Bertram Almar 1869-1923
NatCAB 19
Herrington, Cass E 1856-1934 *WhAm 1*
Herrington, Lewis Butler 1880- *WhAm 6*
Herrington, Timothy A *NewYHSD*
Herriot, Edouard Marie 1872-1957 *McGEWB,*
WhAm 3
Herriott, Frank Irving 1868-1941 *WhAm 2*
Herriott, Irving 1886-1953 *WhAm 3*
Herriott, J *NewYHSD*
Herriott, James Homer 1895-1973 *WhAm 5*
Herriott, Maxwell Haines 1899-1973 *WhAm 6*
Herrle, Colin 1892-1952 *WhAm 3*
Herrlein, Edward *NewYHSD*
Herrlein, Gustav *NewYHSD*
Herrlein, Julius *NewYHSD*
Herrlinger, Roth Frederick 1904-1961
NatCAB 50

Herrman, Augustine 1605?-1686 *AmBi,*
ApCAB, DcAmB, NewYHSD, WhAm H
Herrman, Casparus 1656-1704 *ApCAB*
Herrman, Ephraim Augustine d1735 *ApCAB*
Herrman, Ephraim George 1652-1689 *ApCAB*
Herrman, Esther d1911 *WhAm 1*
Herrmann, Alexander 1844-1896 *DcAmB,*
NatCAB 9, WhAm H
Herrmann, Amos Wallick 1885-1948
NatCAB 37
Herrmann, August 1859- *NatCAB 12*
Herrmann, Bernard 1911-1975 *WhAm 6*
Herrmann, Elizabeth Adelaide 1880-
WomWWA 14
Herrmann, Ernest Edward 1896-1952 *WhAm 3*
Herrmann, Hajo *WhWW-II*
Herrmann, Henry Bradley 1902-1966
NatCAB 53
Herrmann, Henry Francis 1890-1964 *WhAm 4*
Herrmann, Louis George 1900-1965
NatCAB 51
Herrmann, Richard 1849-1941 *WhAm 2*
Herrold, Gordon William 1902-1968 *WhAm 5*
Herron, Anna Fish 1845- *WomWWA 14*
Herron, Carrie Rand *NotAW*
Herron, Charles 1863-1942 *WhAm 2*
Herron, Charles Douglas 1877- *WhAm 5*
Herron, Clark Lincoln 1861-1936 *WhAm 1*
Herron, D *NewYHSD*
Herron, Francis 1774-1860 *ApCAB, TwCBDA*
Herron, Francis Jay d1902 *Drake*
Herron, Francis Jay 1837-1902 *AmBi, ApCAB,*
DcAmB, NatCAB 12, WebAMB
Herron, Francis Jay 1838-1902 *TwCBDA*
Herron, George Davis 1862-1925 *AmBi,*
DcAmB, DcAmReB, NatCAB 9,
TwCBDA, WhAm 1
Herron, James Hervey 1875-1948 *NatCAB 36,*
WhAm 2
Herron, John S 1887-1954 *WhAm 3*
Herron, John Williamson 1827-1912
NatCAB 24
Herron, Rufus Hills 1849- *WhAm 4*
Herron, William Christie 1843-1909
NatCAB 15
Hersam, John Edward 1872-1949 *NatCAB 39*
Herschdorfer, Manuel 1896-1958 *WhAm 3*
Herschel *DcScB*
Herschel, Caroline Lucretia 1750-1848 *AsBiEn,*
DcScB
Herschel, Clemens 1842-1930 *DcAmB,*
NatCAB 11, NatCAB 22, WhAm 1
Herschel, Sir John Frederick William 1792-1871
AsBiEn, DcScB, McGEWB
Herschel, Sir William 1738-1822 *AsBiEn,*
DcScB, McGEWB
Herschell, William 1873-1939 *WhAm 1*
Herschman, Walter R 1883-1932 *NatCAB 23*
Hersey, Abner 1722-1787 *ApCAB*
Hersey, Ada Harvey 1858- *WomWWA 14*
Hersey, Alfred Cushing 1804-1888 *ApCAB Sup*
Hersey, Annie Louise 1864- *WomWWA 14*
Hersey, Charles Henry 1831-1916 *NatCAB 17*
Hersey, Ezekiel 1709-1770 *ApCAB, Drake*
Hersey, George Dallas 1847-1919 *NatCAB 1,*
WhAm 1
Hersey, Harold Brainerd 1893-1956
NatCAB 45
Hersey, Heloise Edwina 1855-1933 *WhAm 1,*
WomWWA 14
Hersey, Henry Blanchard 1861-1948 *WhAm 2*
Hersey, Henry Johnson 1863- *WhAm 1*
Hersey, Ira Greenlief 1858-1943 *BiDrAC,*
WhAm 2, WhAmP
Hersey, Jacob Daniel Temple 1821-1902
NatCAB 3, WhAm 1
Hersey, John Richard 1914- *WebAB*
Hersey, Mark Leslie 1863-1934 *WhAm 1*
Hersey, Mayo Dyer 1886- *ApCAB X*
Hersey, Rexford 1895-1965 *NatCAB 52*
Hersey, Samuel Freeman 1812-1875 *ApCAB,*
BiAUS, BiDrAC, NatCAB 11, TwCBDA,
WhAm H
Hersh, A H 1891-1955 *WhAm 3*
Hersh, John Lewis 1888-1949 *NatCAB 44*
Hershberger, Lloyd Ralph 1906-1953
NatCAB 42
Hershey, Alfred Day 1908- *WebAB*

Hershey, Amos Shartle 1867-1933 *WhAm 1*
Hershey, Burnet 1896-1971 *WhAm 5*
Hershey, Charlie Brown 1878-1955 *NatCAB 45,*
WhAm 3
Hershey, David Unger 1874-1949 *NatCAB 38*
Hershey, Harry Bryant 1885-1967 *WhAm 4*
Hershey, Harry Ellis 1889-1955 *NatCAB 50*
Hershey, J Willard 1876-1943 *WhAm 2*
Hershey, Lewis Blaine 1893-1977 *WebAMB*
Hershey, Milton Snavely 1857-1945 *DcAmB S3,*
NatCAB 33, WebAB, WhAm 2
Hershey, Omer F 1867- *WhAm 4*
Hershey, Oscar H 1874-1939 *NatCAB 29,*
WhAm 1
Hershey, Paris Nissley 1883-1956 *NatCAB 43,*
WhAm 3
Hershey, Robert Landis 1901-1973 *WhAm 6*
Hershey, Scott F 1852-1931 *WhAm 1*
Hershey, Sylvia Schaffer 1870- *WomWWA 14*
Hershfield, Abraham 1848-1932 *NatCAB 24*
Hershman, Abraham Moses 1880-1959
NatCAB 44
Hershman, Oliver Sylvester 1859-1930
NatCAB 12, NatCAB 21, WhAm 1
Hersholt, Jean 1886-1956 *NatCAB 42,*
WhAm 3
Herskovits, Melville Jean 1895-1963 *EncAB,*
McGEWB, WebAB, WhAm 4
Hersman, Charles Campbell 1838- *WhAm 4*
Hersman, Christopher C 1853- *WhAm 4*
Hersman, Hugh Steel 1872-1954 *BiDrAC,*
WhAm 3
Hersom, Jane Lord 1840- *AmWom,*
WomWWA 14
Hert, Mrs. Alvin T d1948 *WhAm 2*
Hert, Alvin Tobias 1865-1921 *WhAm 1*
Hertel, Robert Russell 1919-1965 *WhAm 4*
Hertel DeRouville, Francis 1643-1722 *ApCAB*
Herter, Adele 1869- *WomWWA 14*
Herter, Albert 1871-1950 *NatCAB 43,*
WhAm 3
Herter, Christian 1839-1883 *NatCAB 5*
Herter, Christian 1840-1883 *BnEnAmA,*
DcAmB, WhAm H
Herter, Christian Archibald 1865-1910 *DcAmB,*
WhAm 1
Herter, Christian Archibald 1895-1966 *BiDrAC*
Herter, Christian Archibald 1895-1967
BiDrUSE, WhAm 4, WhAmP
Herter, Gustave 1830-1898 *NatCAB 6*
Herterick, Vincent Richard 1922-1971 *WhAm 5*
Hertner, John Henry 1877-1963 *NatCAB 46*
Herts, Alice Minnie *WomWWA 14*
Herts, B Russell 1888-1954 *WhAm 3*
Hertwig, Karl Wilhelm Theodor R Von
1850-1937 *DcScB*
Hertwig, Wilhelm August Oscar 1849-1922
DcScB
Herty, Charles Holmes 1867-1938 *DcAmB S2,*
NatCAB 18, NatCAB 41, WhAm 1
Herty, Charles Holmes, Jr. 1896-1953 *WhAm 3*
Hertz, Alfred 1872-1942 *ApCAB X,*
DcAmB S3, NatCAB 31, WhAm 2
Hertz, Emanuel 1870-1940 *WhAm 1*
Hertz, Gustav 1887- *AsBiEn*
Hertz, Gustav Crane 1918-1967 *WhAm 4*
Hertz, Heinrich Rudolf 1857-1894 *AsBiEn,*
DcScB, McGEWB
Hertz, John, Jr. 1908-1968 *WhAm 5*
Hertz, John Daniel 1879-1961 *WhAm 4*
Hertz, Richard Otto 1898-1961 *WhAm 4*
Hertz, Stanton S 1894-1943 *NatCAB 33*
Hertzberg, Anna Goodman 1864-
WomWWA 14
Hertzberg, Hans Rudolph Reinhart 1871-1920
WhAm 1
Hertzka, Wayne Solomon 1907-1973 *WhAm 6*
Hertzler, Arthur Emanuel 1870-1946
NatCAB 16, WhAm 2
Hertzler, Charles William 1867- *TwCBDA,*
WhAm 4
Hertzler, William 1858-1940 *NatCAB 31*
Hertzog, Charles D 1897-1970 *WhAm 5*
Hertzog, James Barry Munnik 1866-1942
McGEWB
Hertzog, Walter Scott 1874- *WhAm 5*
Hertzog, Walter Sylvester 1881- *ApCAB X,*
WhAm 6

Hertzsprung, Ejnar 1873-1967 *AsBiEn, DcScB*
Heruy Walda-Sellase 1878-1938 *McGEWB*
Hervas Y Panduro, Lorenzo 1735-1809 *ApCAB, WhAm H*
Herve *NewYHSD*
Herve, H *NewYHSD*
Herve, Walter R *NewYHSD*
Hervey, Alpheus Baker 1839-1931 *NatCAB 10, WhAm 1*
Hervey, Antoinette Bryant *WomWWA 14*
Hervey, Daniel Edward 1845-1914 *NatCAB 31, WhAm 4*
Hervey, Donald Franklin 1917-1974 *WhAm 6*
Hervey, Eliphalet Williams, Jr. 1834-
ApCAB X
Hervey, Harcourt 1892-1970 *WhAm 5*
Hervey, Harcourt, Jr. 1920-1968 *WhAm 5*
Hervey, Harry Clay 1900-1951 *WhAm 3*
Hervey, James Madison 1874- *WhAm 5*
Hervey, Walter Lowrie 1862-1952 *WhAm 3*
Hervey, William Addison 1870-1918 *WhAm 1*
Hervey, William Rhodes 1870-1953 *WhAm 3*
Hervieu, Auguste *NewYHSD*
Herwitz, Harry Kruskal 1889-1947 *NatCAB 39*
Herzberg, Max J 1886-1958 *WhAm 3*
Herzberg, Sarah Pearson 1868- *WomWWA 14*
Herzen, Aleksandr Ivanovich 1812-1870 *McGEWB*
Herzig, Arthur J 1881-1954 *NatCAB 40*
Herzig, Charles Simon 1874- *WhAm 5*
Herzl, Theodor 1860-1904 *McGEWB*
Herzog, Anna Edes d1955 *WhAm 3*
Herzog, Felix Benedict 1859-1912 *WhAm 1*
Herzog, George 1851-1920 *WhAm 1*
Herzog, Hermann 1832-1932 *IIBEAAW*
Herzog, Maximilian Joseph 1858-1918 *WhAm 1*
Herzstein, Joseph 1893-1971 *WhAm 5*
Heschel, Abraham Joshua 1907-1972 *DcAmReB, McGEWB, WhAm 5*
Heselton, John Walter 1900-1962 *BiDrAC, NatCAB 49*
Hesing, Washington 1849-1897 *NatCAB 18*
Hesiod *McGEWB*
Heskett, Rolland McCartney 1871-1966
NatCAB 52
Heslin, Thomas 1847-1911 *ApCAB Sup, NatCAB 13, TwCBDA, WhAm 1*
Hess, Alfred Fabian 1875-1933 *DcAmB S1, NatCAB 32, WhAm 1*
Hess, B *NewYHSD*
Hess, Bertha Greyson *WomWWA 14*
Hess, Dean Elmer 1917- *WebAMB*
Hess, Elmer 1889-1961 *NatCAB 51, WhAm 4*
Hess, Finley Baird 1905-1968 *NatCAB 54, WhAm 5*
Hess, Frank L 1871- *WhAm 3*
Hess, Franklin 1870-1931 *WhAm 1*
Hess, George 1832- *ApCAB, NewYHSD*
Hess, George Alexander 1888-1958 *NatCAB 47*
Hess, Germain Henri 1802-1850 *AsBiEn, DcScB*
Hess, Harry Hammond 1906-1969 *AsBiEn, NatCAB 55, WhAm 5*
Hess, Henry 1863-1922 *WhAm 1*
Hess, Herbert William 1880-1949 *WhAm 2*
Hess, Jerome Sayles 1882-1970 *NatCAB 55, WhAm 5*
Hess, Julia *WomWWA 14*
Hess, Julius Hays 1876-1955 *WhAm 3*
Hess, Leslie Elsworth 1869-1952 *WhAm 3*
Hess, Max 1911-1968 *NatCAB 55, WhAm 5*
Hess, Myra d1965 *WhAm 4*
Hess, Rudolf 1896- *WhWW-II*
Hess, Sara M 1880- *IIBEAAW*
Hess, Victor Francis 1883-1964 *AsBiEn, McGEWB, WhAm 4*
Hess, Victor Franz 1883-1964 *DcScB*
Hess, Walter J 1901- *WhAm 6*
Hess, Walter Rudolf 1881-1973 *McGEWB, WhAm 6*
Hess, Wendell Frederick 1903-1954 *WhAm 3*
Hess, William Emil 1898- *BiDrAC*
Hessberg, Albert 1856-1920 *WhAm 1*
Hessberg, Irving Kapp 1894-1948 *WhAm 2*
Hesse, Bernard Conrad 1869-1934 *WhAm 1*
Hesse, Frank McNeil 1894-1952 *WhAm 3*
Hesse, Herman Carl 1900-1972 *WhAm 6*
Hesse, Hermann 1877-1962 *McGEWB,*

WhAm 4
Hesse, Ludwig Otto 1811-1874 *DcScB*
Hesse, Richard 1895-1975 *WhAm 6*
Hesse, Seymour David 1901-1967 *WhAm 4*
Hessel, Johann Friedrich Christian 1796-1872
DcScB
Hesselberg, Edouard Gregory 1870- *WhAm 1*
Hesselius, Gustavus 1682-1755 *AmBi, BnEnAmA, DcAmB, IIBEAAW, NewYHSD, WhAm H*
Hesselius, John 1728-1778 *BnEnAmA, DcAmB, NatCAB 23, NewYHSD, WhAm H*
Hessellund-Jensen, Aage 1911-1974 *WhAm 6*
Hessels, Louis *NewYHSD*
Hesseltine, Francis S 1833-1916 *NewYHSD*
Hesseltine, William Best 1902-1963 *NatCAB 50, WhAm 4*
Hesser, Frederic William 1904-1954 *WhAm 3*
Hessler, John Charles 1869-1944 *NatCAB 34, WhAm 2*
Hessler, Maud C 1870- *WomWWA 14*
Hessler, Potter Strobridge 1858- *NatCAB 18*
Hessler, William Henry 1904-1965 *NatCAB 51, WhAm 4*
Hesson, Ivan Raymond 1898-1968 *NatCAB 54*
Hesson, Samuel Moodie 1906-1975 *WhAm 6*
Hessoun, Joseph 1830-1906 *DcAmB*
Hester, Clinton Monroe 1895-1971 *WhAm 5*
Hester, Ewart Atkins 1896-1957 *NatCAB 44*
Hester, Jackson Boling 1904-1962 *NatCAB 49*
Hester, John Hutchison 1886-1976 *WhAm 6*
Hester, John Kenton 1916-1965 *WhAm 4*
Hester, St. Clair 1868-1933 *NatCAB 12, WhAm 1*
Hester, William 1835-1921 *ApCAB X, NatCAB 19, WhAm 1*
Hester, William John 1902- *WhAm 3*
Hester, William VanArden 1858-1924 *WhAm 1*
Heston, J Edgar 1910-1972 *WhAm 5*
Heston, Jacob *NewYHSD*
Heston, John William 1854-1920 *WhAm 1*
Heterick, Robert Hynton d1957 *WhAm 3*
Heterick, Vincent Richard 1922-1971 *WhAm 5*
Hetfield, Mrs. E H *NewYHSD*
Heth, Henry 1825-1899 *ApCAB, BiDConf, DcAmB, Drake, NatCAB 4, TwCBDA, WhAm H*
Heth, Nannie Randolph *WomWWA 14*
Heth, William d1807 *Drake*
Heth, William 1735-1808 *ApCAB*
Hetherington, Clark Wilson 1870-1942
BiDAmEd
Hetherington, John Aikman 1907-1974
WhAm 6
Hetherington, John Edwin 1840-1903 *WhAm 1*
Hetherington, Leon Hughes 1900-1969
NatCAB 54
Hetler, Donald McK 1896-1956 *WhAm 3*
Hettinger, Edwin Levi 1879-1951 *NatCAB 41*
Hettinger, Frederick C 1891-1959 *WhAm 4*
Hettinger, Herman Strecker 1902-1972
NatCAB 57, WhAm 6
Hettrick, Elwood Harrison 1909-1972 *WhAm 5*
Hetzel, Carl Christian 1872-1939 *NatCAB 40*
Hetzel, Edgar Bauer 1869-1948 *NatCAB 37*
Hetzel, George 1826-1899 *NewYHSD*
Hetzel, George Christian 1858- *NatCAB 4*
Hetzel, Joseph Linn 1862-1912 *NatCAB 26*
Hetzel, Ralph Dorn 1882-1947 *BiDAmEd, WhAm 2*
Hetzler, Howard George 1863-1926 *WhAm 1*
Hetzler, Theodore 1875-1945 *WhAm 2*
Heublein, Arthur Carl 1879-1932 *NatCAB 31*
Heuchling, Fred G 1886-1970 *WhAm 5*
Heuck, Robert 1892-1964 *NatCAB 51*
Heuer, George Julius 1882-1950 *NatCAB 48, WhAm 3*
Heuer, John Harland 1917-1972 *WhAm 5*
Heuer, William Henry 1843- *WhAm 4*
Heulan, J J *NewYHSD*
Heuraet, Hendrik Van 1633-1660? *DcScB*
Heurne, Jan Van 1543-1601 *DcScB*
Heuser, Emil 1892-1953 *WhAm 3*
Heuser, Frederick William Justus 1878-1961
NatCAB 48, WhAm 4
Heuser, Gustave A 1879-1972 *WhAm 5*
Heusner, A Price 1910-1963 *NatCAB 52*
Heusner, William Samuel 1872- *WhAm 5*

Heuss, John 1908-1966 *WhAm 4*
Heuss, Theodor 1884-1963 *WhAm 4*
Heustis, Charles Herbert 1855- *WhAm 4*
Heustis, Jabez Wiggins 1784-1841 *ApCAB*
Heustis, James Fountain 1829- *ApCAB*
Heustis, Louise Lyons *WomWWA 14*
Hevelius, Johannes 1611-1687 *AsBiEn, DcScB*
Heverin, James Henry 1844- *NatCAB 3*
Hevesy, Georg Von 1885-1966 *AsBiEn*
Hevesy, George Charles De 1885-1966
McGEWB, WhAm 4
Hevesy, Gyorgy 1885-1966 *DcScB*
Hewat, Alexander 1745?-1829 *ApCAB, DcAmB, WhAm H*
Hewe, Laurence Ilsey 1876-1950 *WhAm 3*
Hewes, Amy 1877-1970 *WhAm 5*
Hewes, Clarence Bussey 1890-1962 *WhAm 4*
Hewes, David 1822- *NatCAB 18*
Hewes, Fletcher Willis 1838-1910 *WhAm 1*
Hewes, George Robert Twelve 1742-1840 *Drake*
Hewes, George Robert Twelves 1731-1840
ApCAB
Hewes, George Robert Twelves 1742-1840
NatCAB 5
Hewes, Harry Bartram 1866-1953 *NatCAB 40*
Hewes, Henry Fox 1867-1926 *ApCAB X*
Hewes, Joseph 1730-1779 *AmBi, ApCAB, BiDrAC, BiDrAC, DcAmB, Drake, NatCAB 10, TwCBDA, WhAm H, WhAmP*
Hewes, M Lewin 1861-1940 *WhAm 1*
Hewes, Robert 1751-1830 *DcAmB, NatCAB 23, WhAm H*
Hewes, Thomas d1957 *WhAm 3*
Hewet, H W *NewYHSD*
Hewetson, H H 1896-1971 *WhAm 5*
Hewett, Donnel Foster 1881-1971 *WhAm 5*
Hewett, Edgar Lee 1865-1946 *WhAm 2*
Hewett, Edward Osborne 1835- *ApCAB*
Hewett, Edwin Crawford 1828-1905 *TwCBDA, WhAm 1*
Hewett, Hobart 1900-1967 *WhAm 4*
Hewett, I *NewYHSD*
Hewett, Katherine Mary 1869- *WomWWA 14*
Hewett, Waterman Thomas 1846-1921 *ApCAB, BiDAmEd, DcAmB, NatCAB 8, TwCBDA, WhAm 1*
Hewett, William Wallace 1897-1962 *WhAm 4*
Hewett-Thayer, Harvey Waterman 1873-1960
WhAm 4
Hewins, Amasa 1795-1855 *NewYHSD*
Hewins, Caroline Maria 1846-1926 *DcAmLiB, NatCAB 1, NatCAB 21, NotAW, TwCBDA, WhAm 1, WomWWA 14*
Hewins, Nellie Priscilla *WomWWA 14*
Hewins, Philip 1806-1850 *NewYHSD*
Hewins, Sara *NewYHSD*
Hewit, Augustine Francis 1820-1897 *DcAmB, NatCAB 11, TwCBDA, WhAm H*
Hewit, Henry Stewart 1825-1873 *ApCAB, NatCAB 11*
Hewit, Henry Stuart 1825-1873 *TwCBDA*
Hewit, Nathaniel 1788-1867 *ApCAB, Drake, NatCAB 11, TwCBDA*
Hewit, Nathaniel Augustus 1820- *ApCAB*
Hewitt *NewYHSD*
Hewitt, A d1947 *WhAm 2*
Hewitt, Abram Stevens 1822-1903 *AmBi, ApCAB, BiAUS, BiDrAC, DcAmB, EncAB, McGEWB, NatCAB 3, TwCBDA, WebAB, WhAm 1, WhAmP*
Hewitt, Alexander *Drake*
Hewitt, C C *BiAUS*
Hewitt, Charles Edmund 1836-1911
NatCAB 17
Hewitt, Charles Morgan 1857-1916 *NatCAB 16*
Hewitt, Charles Nathaniel 1835-1910 *WhAm 1*
Hewitt, Charles Nathaniel 1836-1910 *ApCAB, NatCAB 13*
Hewitt, Clarence Horace 1890-1952 *WhAm 3*
Hewitt, Edward Crawford 1828- *ApCAB*
Hewitt, Edward Ringwood 1866-1957 *WhAm 3*
Hewitt, Edward Shepard 1877-1962 *WhAm 4*
Hewitt, Edwin Hawley 1874-1939 *WhAm 1*
Hewitt, Emma Churchman 1850- *AmWom, WhAm 4, WomWWA 14*
Hewitt, Erastus Henry 1888-1969 *WhAm 5*
Hewitt, Erskine 1871-1938 *WhAm 1*

Hewitt, Fayette 1831-1909 *NatCAB 11,*
WhAm 1
Hewitt, Frederick F *NewYHSD*
Hewitt, George Ayres 1899-1963 *WhAm 4*
Hewitt, George Walter 1886-1954 *NatCAB 43*
Hewitt, Goldsmith Whitehouse 1834-1895
BiAUS, BiDrAC, WhAm H
Hewitt, Harrison 1877-1938 *NatCAB 32*
Hewitt, Harvey 1885-1954 *WhAm 3*
Hewitt, Henry, Jr. 1840-1918 *ApCAB X,*
NatCAB 35, WhAm 1
Hewitt, Henry Kent 1887-1972 *NatCAB 57,*
WebAMB, WhAm 5
Hewitt, Herbert Edmund 1871-1944 *WhAm 2*
Hewitt, James 1770-1827 *DcAmB, WhAm H*
Hewitt, John Edmond 1886-1967 *NatCAB 53*
Hewitt, John Haskell 1835-1920 *TwCBDA,*
WhAm 1
Hewitt, John Henry 1801-1890 *NatCAB 11*
Hewitt, John Hill 1801-1890 *ApCAB Sup,*
DcAmB, WhAm H
Hewitt, John Napoleon Brinton 1859- *WhAm 4*
Hewitt, John Vance 1884-1964 *NatCAB 50*
Hewitt, Joseph William 1875-1938 *WhAm 1*
Hewitt, Kent 1887-1972 *WhWW-II*
Hewitt, Leland Hazelton 1894-1964 *WhAm 4*
Hewitt, Louis Percy 1883-1945 *NatCAB 35*
Hewitt, Margaret L 1873- *WomWWA 14*
Hewitt, Martha Elizabeth 1841- *WomWWA 14*
Hewitt, Mary Elizabeth 1818- *ApCAB, Drake*
Hewitt, Ogden Blackfan 1893-1963 *WhAm 4*
Hewitt, Peter Cooper 1861-1921 *AmBi,*
ApCAB X, DcAmB, NatCAB 14,
WhAm 1
Hewitt, Richard Miner 1892-1970 *WhAm 5*
Hewitt, Theodore Brown 1881- *WhAm 3*
Hewitt, William 1853-1922 *NatCAB 19,*
WhAm 1
Hewitt, William Keesey 1817-1893 *NewYHSD,*
WhAm H
Hewitt, William Stirling 1880-1955 *NatCAB 43*
Hewlett, A Walter 1874-1925 *WhAm 1*
Hewlett, Cleora M 1855- *WomWWA 14*
Hewlett, James Howell 1888-1948 *WhAm 3*
Hewlett, James Monroe 1868-1941 *NatCAB 11,*
WhAm 1
Hewlett, Mortimer Clifton 1864-1928
ApCAB X
Hewlett, Richard 1712?-1789 *ApCAB*
Hewlett, Thomas d1780 *ApCAB*
Hewson, Addinell 1828-1889 *ApCAB,*
TwCBDA
Hewson, Addinell 1855-1938 *NatCAB 42,*
TwCBDA, WhAm 1
Hewson, Robert John 1900-1960 *NatCAB 48*
Hewson, Thomas Tickell 1773-1848 *ApCAB,*
Drake, TwCBDA
Hewson, William 1739-1774 *BiHiMed, DcScB*
Hexamer, Charles John 1862-1921 *WhAm 1*
Hexner, Ervin Paul 1893-1968 *WhAm 5*
Hexter, Irving Bernard 1897-1960 *NatCAB 47,*
WhAm 4
Hexter, Joseph 1887-1954 *WhAm 3*
Hey, William d1797 *ApCAB*
Hey, William 1736-1819 *BiHiMed*
Heyburn, Gheretein Yeatman *WomWWA 14*
Heyburn, John Gilpin 1895-1952 *NatCAB 47*
Heyburn, Weldon Brinton 1852-1912 *BiDrAC,*
NatCAB 13, REnAW, WhAm 1,
WhAmP
Heyd, Conrad 1837-1912 *NewYHSD*
Heyde, Charles L *NewYHSD*
Heydecker, Edward LeMoyne 1863- *WhAm 4*
Heydler, Charles 1861- *WhAm 5*
Heydon, Henry Darling 1851-1925 *WhAm 1*
Heydrich, Reinhard 1904-1942 *WhWW-II*
Heydrick, Benjamin Alexander 1871- *WhAm 5*
Heydt, Hans Jost d1760 *DcAmB*
Heydt, Herman A 1868-1941 *WhAm 1*
Heye, Carl T 1871-1946 *WhAm 2*
Heye, George Gustav 1874-1957 *NatCAB 42,*
WhAm 3
Heyer, Christian Frederick 1793-1873 *ApCAB*
Heyer, Frederick William 1887-1948
NatCAB 36
Heyer, Georgette 1902-1974 *WhAm 6*
Heyer, John Christian Frederick 1793-1873
DcAmB, WhAm H

Heyke, John Ericson, Jr. 1910-1974 *WhAm 6*
Heyl, Bernard Chapman 1905-1966 *WhAm 4*
Heyl, Henry Livingston 1906-1975 *WhAm 6*
Heyl, Paul Renno 1872- *WhAm 5*
Heyliger, Joseph *NewYHSD*
Heylman, Henry Budelman 1872-1944
NatCAB 33
Heyman, Charles *NewYHSD*
Heyman, Clarence Henry 1891-1964
NatCAB 51, WhAm 4
Heyman, Herman 1898-1968 *NatCAB 54*
Heyman, Lazarus Samuel 1906-1968
NatCAB 55
Heyman, Marcus Babcock 1866-1925
ApCAB X
Heyman, Seymour Caesar 1861-1912
NatCAB 16
Heymann, Edgar d1969 *WhAm 5*
Heymann, Hans 1885-1949 *WhAm 2*
Heymans, Corneille J F 1892-1968 *BiHiMed,*
WhAm 5
Heymsfeld, Ralph Taft 1908-1962 *WhAm 4*
Heyn, Emil 1867-1922 *DcScB*
Heyn, John Miller 1862-1931 *NatCAB 23*
Heyne, Maurice 1891-1972 *WhAm 5*
Heyne, Roland 1912-1962 *WhAm 4*
Heynitz, Friedrich Anton Von 1725-1802 *DcScB*
Heyns, Garrett 1891-1969 *NatCAB 57,*
WhAm 5
Heyrovsky, Jaroslav 1890-1967 *AsBiEn, DcScB,*
WhAm 4
Heyse, Paul Johann Ludwig 1830-1914
McGEWB
Heysham, Theodore 1864-1935 *WhAm 1*
Heysinger, Isaac Winter 1842- *WhAm 4*
Heytesbury, William *DcScB*
Heyward, Dorothy 1890-1961 *WhAm 4*
Heyward, DuBose 1885-1940 *DcAmB S2,*
WebAB, WhAm 1
Heyward, Duncan Clinch 1864-1943
NatCAB 15, NatCAB 31, WhAm 2
Heyward, Thomas, Jr. 1746-1809 *AmBi,*
ApCAB, BiAUS, BiDrAC, DcAmB,
NatCAB 1, TwCBDA, WhAm H,
WhAmP
Heyward, William, Jr. *BiAUS*
Heywood, Abbot Rodney 1855-1923
NatCAB 19, WhAm 1
Heywood, Alba 1859-1921 *WhAm 1*
Heywood, Albert Samuel 1867-1938 *WhAm 1*
Heywood, Benjamin 1792-1878 *NatCAB 3*
Heywood, Charles 1839-1915 *ApCAB,*
ApCAB Sup, NatCAB 27, WebAMB,
WhAm 1
Heywood, Curtis Milton 1892-1957 *NatCAB 44*
Heywood, Ezra Hervey 1829-1893 *DcAmB,*
NatCAB 23, WhAm H
Heywood, Frank 1857- *NatCAB 8*
Heywood, Gene Bryant 1897-1971 *WhAm 5*
Heywood, George *NewYHSD*
Heywood, George Henry 1862-1898 *NatCAB 18*
Heywood, Henry 1836-1904 *NatCAB 18*
Heywood, John Healy 1818-1880 *ApCAB*
Heywood, Levi 1800-1882 *ApCAB, DcAmB,*
NatCAB 10, WhAm H
Heywood, Thomas 1573?-1641 *McGEWB*
Heywood, Walter 1804- *ApCAB*
Heyworth, James Ormerod 1866-1928
ApCAB X, WhAm 1
HH *WebAB*
Hiacoomes 1610?-1690? *ApCAB, DcAmB,*
Drake, NatCAB 11, WhAm H
Hiarne, Urban 1641-1724 *DcScB*
Hiatt, Walter Sanders 1878-1956 *WhAm 3*
Hiawatha *WebAB*
Hibbard, Addison 1887-1945 *WhAm 2*
Hibbard, Aldro Thompson 1886-1972
NatCAB 57, WhAm 5
Hibbard, Alfred Tyler 1890-1968 *NatCAB 54*
Hibbard, Angus Smith 1860-1945 *WhAm 2*
Hibbard, Benjamin Horace 1870-1955
NatCAB 43, WhAm 3
Hibbard, Carlisle V 1876-1954 *WhAm 3*
Hibbard, Charles Jared 1855-1924 *NatCAB 6*
Hibbard, Claude William 1905-1973
NatCAB 57, WhAm 6
Hibbard, David Sutherland 1868-1967 *WhAm 4*
Hibbard, Ellery Albee 1826-1903 *ApCAB,*

BiAUS, BiDrAC, TwCBDA, WhAm 1,
WhAmP
Hibbard, Frank 1873-1957 *WhAm 3*
Hibbard, Frederick Cleveland 1881-1950
WhAm 3
Hibbard, Freeborn Garretson 1811-1895 *ApCAB,*
Drake, TwCBDA
Hibbard, Freeborn Garrettson 1811-1895
DcAmB, WhAm H
Hibbard, George 1858-1928 *NatCAB 3,*
NatCAB 11, WhAm 1
Hibbard, George Albee 1864- *WhAm 1*
Hibbard, Grace *AmWom*
Hibbard, H Wade 1863-1929 *WhAm 1*
Hibbard, Harry 1816-1872 *BiAUS, BiDrAC,*
TwCBDA, WhAmP
Hibbard, Isaac Lester 1857-1924 *ApCAB X*
Hibbard, Laura Alandis 1883- *WomWWA 14*
Hibbard, Mary Eastman Gale 1860-
WomWWA 14
Hibbard, Rufus Percival 1875- *WhAm 5*
Hibbard, Susan Davis Follansbee
WomWWA 14
Hibben, Harold Barcroft 1855-1916 *NatCAB 16*
Hibben, John Grier 1861-1933 *AmBi,*
ApCAB X, BiDAmEd, DcAmB S1,
NatCAB 15, NatCAB 33, TwCBDA,
WhAm 1
Hibben, John Severy 1888-1956 *NatCAB 46*
Hibben, Paxton Pattison 1880-1928 *AmBi,*
DcAmB, NatCAB 22, WhAm 1
Hibben, Samuel Galloway 1888-1972 *WhAm 5*
Hibberd, Isaac Norris 1861-1933 *NatCAB 31*
Hibberd, James Farquhar 1816-1903
NatCAB 12, WhAm 1
Hibbert, Harold 1877-1945 *NatCAB 33*
Hibbins, Ann d1656 *DcAmB, WhAm H*
Hibbitt, George Whiting 1895-1965 *NatCAB 51*
Hibbs, Ben 1901-1975 *WhAm 6*
Hibbs, Harold Dickson 1901-1968 *WhAm 5*
Hibbs, Henry C 1882-1949 *WhAm 2*
Hibbs, Louis E 1893-1970 *WhAm 5*
Hibinta, Ibn *DcScB*
Hibler, Nellie 1858- *AmWom*
Hibshman, Jacob 1772-1852 *BiAUS, BiDrAC,*
WhAm H
Hicetas Of Syracuse *DcScB*
Hichborn, Franklin 1869- *WhAm 5*
Hichborn, Herman Granville 1861-1920
ApCAB X
Hichborn, Philip 1839-1910 *AmBi,*
ApCAB Sup, DcAmB, TwCBDA,
WhAm 1
Hickam, John Bamber 1914-1970 *WhAm 5*
Hickam, Willis 1852-1927 *NatCAB 37*
Hickcox, John Howard 1832-1897 *ApCAB,*
TwCBDA
Hickcox, Thomas N *NewYHSD*
Hickel, Walter J 1919- *BiDrUSE*
Hickenlooper, Andrew 1837-1904 *ApCAB,*
DcAmB, WhAm 1
Hickenlooper, Bourke Blakemore 1896-1971
BiDrAC, WhAm 5, WhAmP
Hickenlooper, Lucy Mary Olga Agnes
BiDAmEd
Hickenlooper, Smith 1880-1933 *NatCAB 33,*
WhAm 1
Hickernell, Latimer Farrington 1899-1963
NatCAB 52, WhAm 4
Hickerson, J Roy 1893-1962 *NatCAB 50*
Hickey, Mister *NewYHSD*
Hickey, Andrew James 1872-1942 *BiDrAC,*
WhAm 2, WhAmP
Hickey, Daniel Francis Bray 1887-1966
NatCAB 53
Hickey, Doyle Overton 1892-1961 *NatCAB 50*
Hickey, James Burke 1848-1928 *WhAm 1*
Hickey, Jeremiah Griffin 1866-1960 *WhAm 3A*
Hickey, John F 1893-1966 *WhAm 4*
Hickey, John Joseph 1911-1970 *BiDrAC,*
WhAm 5
Hickey, Joseph Aloysious 1883-1955 *WhAm 3*
Hickey, Lee Cole 1911-1970 *WhAm 5*
Hickey, Leo Joseph 1888-1937 *NatCAB 28,*
WhAm 1
Hickey, Matthew, Jr. 1896-1969 *WhAm 5*
Hickey, Patrick Valentine 1846-1889
NatCAB 29

Hickey, Philip J 1896-1965 *WhAm 4*
Hickey, Preston Manasseh 1865-1930
  NatCAB 26, WhAm 1
Hickey, Thomas d1776 *ApCAB*
Hickey, Thomas Francis 1861- *NatCAB 15*
Hickey, Thomas M d1842 *BiAUS*
Hickey, Turner Paul 1873- *WhAm 5*
Hickey, William *NewYHSD*
Hickey, William Augustine 1869-1933 *WhAm 1*
Hickey, William Augustus 1883-1959
  NatCAB 48
Hickley, Arthur Samuel 1852- *NatCAB 7*
Hickling, D Percy 1863- *WhAm 1*
Hickman, Adam Clark 1837- *WhAm 1*
Hickman, Amy Williams Hall 1854-
  WomWWA 14
Hickman, Cuthbert Wright 1888-1956 *WhAm 3*
Hickman, Emily 1880-1947 *WhAm 2,
  WomWWA 14*
Hickman, Eugene Christian 1881-1937
  WhAm 1
Hickman, Francis Gould 1896-1969 *NatCAB 55*
Hickman, Hamilton Hilliard 1818-1904
  NatCAB 2
Hickman, Herman Michael 1911-1958 *WhAm 3*
Hickman, John 1810-1875 *ApCAB, BiAUS,
  BiDrAC, TwCBDA, WhAm H*
Hickman, John Edward 1883-1962 *WhAm 4*
Hickman, John Henry 1857- *WhoColR*
Hickman, John Samuel 1887-1946 *NatCAB 35*
Hickman, Josiah Edwin 1862-1937 *NatCAB 27*
Hickman, Mary Catharine 1838- *AmWom*
Hickman, Norman 1890-1953 *WhAm 3*
Hickman, Paschal d1813 *ApCAB*
Hickman, Robert S 1813-1873 *ApCAB*
Hickman, William 1747-1830 *ApCAB*
Hickman, William Howard 1844- *NatCAB 3,
  TwCBDA*
Hickman, William Howard 1845- *WhAm 4*
Hickok, Charles Thomas 1869-1958 *WhAm 3*
Hickok, Francis *NewYHSD*
Hickok, James Butler 1837-1876 *AmBi,
  DcAmB, McGEWB, WebAB, WhAm H*
Hickok, Laurens Perseus 1798-1888 *ApCAB,
  DcAmB, Drake, NatCAB 7, WhAm H*
Hickok, Laurens Perseus 1799-1888 *TwCBDA*
Hickok, Milo Judson 1809-1873 *TwCBDA*
Hickok, Paul Robinson 1877-1945 *WhAm 2*
Hickok, Ralph Kiddoo 1880-1947 *NatCAB 42,
  WhAm 2*
Hickok, S Rae 1883-1945 *NatCAB 46*
Hickok, Wild Bill 1837-1876 *DcAmB, REnAW,
  WebAB*
Hickox, John Howard 1832- *Drake*
Hickox, Ralph W 1850- *WhAm 1*
Hicks, Amanda Malvina 1841- *WomWWA 14*
Hicks, Ami Mali *WhAm 5*
Hicks, Amy Mali *WomWWA 14*
Hicks, Archie Ray, Jr. 1915-1974 *WhAm 6*
Hicks, Benjamin Doughty 1836-1906
  NatCAB 14
Hicks, Bobby 1934- *IlBEAAW*
Hicks, C *NewYHSD*
Hicks, Charles C *NewYHSD*
Hicks, Clarence John 1863-1944 *WhAm 2*
Hicks, Clifford E 1887-1969 *WhAm 5*
Hicks, Douglas Mallory 1902-1964 *WhAm 4*
Hicks, Edith Stearns *WomWWA 14*
Hicks, Edward 1780-1849 *BnEnAmA,
  IlBEAAW, McGEWB, NewYHSD,
  WebAB, WhAm H*
Hicks, Elias 1748-1830 *AmBi, ApCAB,
  DcAmB, DcAmReB, Drake, NatCAB 11,
  TwCBDA, WebAB, WhAm H*
Hicks, Floyd Verne 1915- *BiDrAC*
Hicks, Francis Marion 1826- *NatCAB 9*
Hicks, Francis Marion 1856- *WhAm 4*
Hicks, Frank M 1893-1959 *WhAm 3*
Hicks, Frederick Charles 1863- *TwCBDA*
Hicks, Frederick Charles 1875-1956 *WhAm 3*
Hicks, Frederick Cocks 1872-1925 *BiDrAC,
  NatCAB 20, WhAm 1*
Hicks, George 1905-1965 *WhAm 4*
Hicks, Gilbert *NewYHSD*
Hicks, Hanne John 1910-1966 *WhAm 5*
Hicks, Helen Gertrude 1900-1964 *NatCAB 51*
Hicks, Henry *NewYHSD*
Hicks, Irl R 1844-1916 *NatCAB 17*

Hicks, John *NewYHSD*
Hicks, John 1750?- *ApCAB*
Hicks, John 1847-1917 *DcAmB, NatCAB 12,
  WhAm 1*
Hicks, John Braxton 1823-1897 *BiHiMed*
Hicks, John Clayton 1869-1935 *NatCAB 25*
Hicks, John Donald 1890-1972 *EncAAH,
  REnAW, WhAm 5*
Hicks, John Edgar 1850-1894 *ApCAB X*
Hicks, Joseph Emerson 1874- *WhAm 5*
Hicks, Joseph Winstead 1899-1959 *WhAm 4*
Hicks, Josiah Duane 1844-1923 *BiDrAC,
  NatCAB 12, TwCBDA, WhAm 4*
Hicks, Katharine Adams 1871- *WomWWA 14*
Hicks, Lawrence Emerson 1905-1957 *WhAm 3*
Hicks, Leonard 1886-1966 *WhAm 4*
Hicks, Lewis Ezra 1839- *WhAm 4*
Hicks, Lewis Wenman 1871- *WhAm 6*
Hicks, Lucius Sumner 1881- *WhoColR*
Hicks, Marshall 1865-1930 *WhAm 1*
Hicks, Mary Amelia Dana 1862- *AmWom,
  NotAW*
Hicks, R Randolph 1870-1951 *NatCAB 41*
Hicks, Richard Burton 1883-1959 *NatCAB 48*
Hicks, Robert Emmet 1858- *WhAm 4*
Hicks, Sheila 1934- *BnEnAmA*
Hicks, Thomas 1823- *ApCAB, Drake*
Hicks, Thomas 1823-1890 *AmBi, BnEnAmA,
  DcAmB, NewYHSD, TwCBDA,
  WhAm H*
Hicks, Thomas 1823-1891 *NatCAB 5*
Hicks, Thomas E 1900-1965 *WhAm 4*
Hicks, Thomas Holliday 1798-1865 *AmBi,
  ApCAB, BiDrAC, DcAmB, NatCAB 9,
  TwCBDA, WhAm H, WhAmP*
Hicks, Thomas Holliday 1869- *WhAm 3*
Hicks, Thomas Hollyday 1798-1865 *BiAUS,
  Drake*
Hicks, Verser 1892-1965 *NatCAB 51*
Hicks, Vonnie Monroe 1895-1971 *NatCAB 57*
Hicks, W B 1932-1969 *WhAm 5*
Hicks, Walter Scott 1827-1914 *NatCAB 17*
Hicks, Whitehead 1728-1780 *ApCAB, Drake*
Hicks, William Arthur 1880-1952 *WhAm 3*
Hicks, William Minor 1903-1969 *WhAm 5*
Hicks, William Norwood 1901-1973 *WhAm 6*
Hicks, William Winston 1877-1954 *NatCAB 42*
Hicks, Wilson 1897-1970 *WhAm 5*
Hicks, Xenophon 1872-1952 *WhAm 3*
Hickson, Lady Catherine *WomWWA 14*
Hickson, Sir Joseph 1830-1877 *ApCAB Sup*
Hickson, William James 1874-1935 *WhAm 1*
Hidalgo, Ignacio Xavier 1698-1759 *ApCAB*
Hidalgo Y Costilla, Miguel 1753-1811 *ApCAB,
  Drake, McGEWB*
Hidayat, Sadiq 1903-1951 *McGEWB*
Hidden, Harry B 1839-1862 *NatCAB 4*
Hidden, Henry A *NewYHSD*
Hidden, Isabel Dinwiddee McKee 1861-
  WomWWA 14
Hidden, James E *NewYHSD*
Hidden, Lowell Mason 1839-1923 *NatCAB 20*
Hidden, William Earl 1853-1918 *WhAm 1*
Hider, William 1844-1916 *WhAm 1*
Hideyoshi, Toyotomi 1536-1598 *WhoMilH*
Hidlay, William Clair 1896-1969 *NatCAB 55*
Hidley, Joseph H 1830-1872 *BnEnAmA,
  NewYHSD*
Hiebert, Joelle C 1892-1944 *WhAm 2*
Hiebert, Peter Cornelius 1878-1963 *WhAm 4*
Hiemenz, John W 1850-1919 *NatCAB 19*
Hier, Frank 1899-1960 *NatCAB 48*
Hieronimus, Leonard *NewYHSD*
Hieronymus, Robert Enoch 1862-1941 *WhAm 2*
Hieronymus, William Peter 1893-1957 *WhAm 3*
Hiestand, Edgar Willard 1888-1970 *BiDrAC,
  WhAm 5, WhAmP*
Hiestand, Jean Carter 1893-1959 *WhAm 3*
Hiestand, John Andrew 1824-1890 *BiDrAC,
  WhAm H*
Hiester, Anselm Vinet 1866-1927 *NatCAB 21,
  WhAm 1*
Hiester, Daniel 1747-1804 *ApCAB, BiDrAC,
  DcAmB, TwCBDA, WhAm H, WhAmP*
Hiester, Daniel 1774-1834 *ApCAB, BiDrAC,
  TwCBDA, WhAm H*
Hiester, Gabriel 1749-1824 *TwCBDA*
Hiester, Gabriel 1779-1834 *TwCBDA*

Hiester, Isaac Ellmaker d1871 *BiAUS*
Hiester, Isaac Ellmaker 1820?-1871 *ApCAB*
Hiester, Isaac Ellmaker 1824-1871 *BiDrAC,
  TwCBDA, WhAm H*
Hiester, John 1745-1821 *BiDrAC, TwCBDA,
  WhAm H*
Hiester, John 1746-1821 *ApCAB*
Hiester, Joseph 1752-1832 *ApCAB, BiDrAC,
  DcAmB, NatCAB 2, TwCBDA,
  WhAm H, WhAmP*
Hiester, William 1790-1853 *ApCAB, BiDrAC,
  TwCBDA, WhAm H, WhAmP*
Higbee, Albert Enos 1842-1924 *WhAm 1*
Higbee, Anna Marie 1847- *WomWWA 14*
Higbee, Chester Goss 1835-1908 *NatCAB 17*
Higbee, Elnathan Elisha 1830-1889 *ApCAB,
  TwCBDA*
Higbee, Frederic Goodson 1881-1968
  NatCAB 55, WhAm 6
Higbee, Harry 1854-1929 *WhAm 1*
Higbee, Irving Jackson 1881-1955 *WhAm 3*
Higbee, Jesse Edward 1882-1943 *NatCAB 37*
Higbee, Lenah Agnew Wiseman Sutcliffe 1874-
  WomWWA 14
Higbee, Netta Wetherbee *WomWWA 14*
Higbee, Roscoe Bacon 1878- *NatCAB 16*
Higbee, William Tryon 1867-1956 *NatCAB 46*
Higbie, Carlton M 1890-1955 *WhAm 3*
Higbie, Edgar Creighton 1875-1944 *WhAm 2*
Higbie, Robert Winfield 1863-1936 *WhAm 1*
Higby, Chester Penn 1885-1966 *WhAm 4*
Higby, Gilbert C d1952 *WhAm 3*
Higby, William 1813-1887 *BiAUS, BiDrAC,
  NatCAB 5, TwCBDA, WhAm H*
Higby, William Riley 1825-1902 *NatCAB 6*
Higginbotham, Alfred Leslie 1895-1967
  WhAm 4
Higginbotham, Ethel Lattimore 1876-
  WomWWA 14
Higginbotham, Jay Cee 1906-1973 *WhAm 6*
Higginbottom, Sam 1874-1958 *NatCAB 44,
  WhAm 3*
Higginbottom, William *NewYHSD*
Higgins, Aldus Chapin 1872-1948 *NatCAB 36,
  WhAm 2*
Higgins, Alice Louise 1870-1920 *NotAW,
  WhAm 1, WomWWA 14*
Higgins, Allan Herbert Webster 1904-1959
  WhAm 4
Higgins, Alma Margaret *WomWWA 14*
Higgins, Alvin McCaslin 1866-1938
  NatCAB 29, WhAm 1
Higgins, Andrew Foster 1831-1916 *WhAm 1*
Higgins, Andrew Jackson 1885-1952
  NatCAB 41
Higgins, Andrew Jackson 1886-1952 *DcAmB S5,
  WhAm 3*
Higgins, Anthony 1840-1912 *ApCAB Sup,
  BiDrAC, NatCAB 1, TwCBDA,
  WhAm 1*
Higgins, Archibald Thomas *WhAm 2*
Higgins, Arthur M 1867- *NatCAB 16*
Higgins, Bryan 1737?-1818 *DcScB*
Higgins, Carter Chapin 1914-1964 *NatCAB 54*
Higgins, Charles Houchin 1879-1961
  NatCAB 16, WhAm 4
Higgins, Charles Melbourne 1857- *WhAm 4*
Higgins, Charles Michael 1854-1929 *ApCAB X,
  NatCAB 35*
Higgins, Christopher P 1830-1889 *ApCAB X*
Higgins, Clara Carter 1882- *WomWWA 14*
Higgins, Daniel Paul 1886-1953 *DcAmB S5,
  WhAm 3*
Higgins, Edward 1856-1919 *WhAm 1*
Higgins, Edward Charles 1866-1944
  NatCAB 33
Higgins, Edwin Werter 1874-1954 *BiDrAC,
  WhAm 3*
Higgins, Elmore Fitzpatrick 1882-1941
  WhAm 1
Higgins, Eugene 1874-1958 *IlBEAAW,
  NatCAB 43, WhAm 3*
Higgins, Floyd Halleck 1886- *EncAAH*
Higgins, Francis G 1863- *WhAm 4*
Higgins, Frank *NewYHSD*
Higgins, Frank James 1869-1937 *WhAm 1*
Higgins, Frank Wayland 1856-1907 *DcAmB,
  NatCAB 13, WhAm 1*

Higgins, George F *NewYHSD*
Higgins, George Frederick 1862- *WhAm 4*
Higgins, George Thomas 1924-1971 *WhAm 5*
Higgins, Harry B 1882-1963 *WhAm 4*
Higgins, Herbert Newton 1913-1964 *WhAm 4*
Higgins, James Bennett 1872- *WhAm 5*
Higgins, James Henry 1876-1927 *NatCAB 14,*
WhAm 1
Higgins, James Henry, Jr. 1910-1975 *WhAm 6*
Higgins, John Allen 1913-1965 *NatCAB 52*
Higgins, John Clark 1838-1924 *WhAm 3*
Higgins, John Martin 1899-1973 *WhAm 6*
Higgins, John Patrick 1893-1955 *BiDrAC,*
WhAm 3
Higgins, John Wilfred 1864-1936 *WhAm 1*
Higgins, John Woodman 1874-1961 *NatCAB 49,*
WhAm 4
Higgins, Joseph 1872-1946 *WhAm 2*
Higgins, Joseph Ignatius 1884-1947 *NatCAB 36*
Higgins, Katharine Elizabeth Chapin 1847-1925
ApCAB X, BiCAW, WhAm 1
Higgins, Leon Forrest 1870-1923 *NatCAB 20*
Higgins, Lewis Eleon 1852-1924 *ApCAB X*
Higgins, Marguerite d1966 *WhAm 4*
Higgins, Milton Prince 1842-1912 *ApCAB X,*
NatCAB 31, WhAm 1
Higgins, Montgomery Earle 1879- *WhAm 6*
Higgins, Nathan Bert 1885-1957 *NatCAB 48*
Higgins, Pattillo 1862-1955 *NatCAB 44*
Higgins, Raymond Walker 1881-1946
NatCAB 35
Higgins, Richard Thomas 1865-1934 *WhAm 1*
Higgins, Robert Barnard 1868-1928 *WhAm 1*
Higgins, Robert William 1868- *WhAm 4*
Higgins, Rodney Gonzales 1911-1964 *WhAm 4*
Higgins, Samuel 1860- *WhAm 4*
Higgins, Samuel George 1880-1954 *NatCAB 43*
Higgins, Stanley Carmen, Jr. 1913-1972
WhAm 5
Higgins, Victor 1884-1949 *NatCAB 45,*
REnAW, WhAm 2
Higgins, Wilbur Warren 1883-1930 *ApCAB X*
Higgins, William 1762?-1825? *DcScB*
Higgins, William Edward 1865-1920 *WhAm 1*
Higgins, William Harvey 1872- *WhoColR*
Higgins, William Lincoln 1867-1951 *BiDrAC,*
NatCAB 41, WhAm 3
Higgins, William Victor 1884-1949 *IIBEAAW*
Higginson, Ella Rhoads 1862-1940 *AmWom,*
TwCBDA, WhAm 1, WomWWA 14
Higginson, Francis 1586-1630 *AmBi, DcAmB,*
DcAmReB, WhAm H
Higginson, Francis 1587-1630 *NatCAB 1*
Higginson, Francis 1588-1630 *ApCAB, Drake,*
TwCBDA
Higginson, Francis John 1843-1931 *ApCAB,*
ApCAB X, TwCBDA, WhAm 1
Higginson, Francis Lee 1841-1925 *WhAm 1*
Higginson, Francis Lee 1877-1969 *WhAm 5*
Higginson, George 1864-1936 *NatCAB 27*
Higginson, Henry Lee 1834-1919 *AmBi,*
ApCAB, DcAmB, NatCAB 14, WhAm 1
Higginson, John 1616-1708 *ApCAB, DcAmB,*
Drake, NatCAB 8, TwCBDA, WhAm H
Higginson, Mary P Thacher 1844-1941
WhAm 1, WomWWA 14
Higginson, Nathaniel 1652-1708 *DcAmB,*
WhAm H
Higginson, Stephen 1743-1828 *ApCAB, BiAUS,*
BiDrAC, DcAmB, Drake, NatCAB 5,
TwCBDA, WhAm H
Higginson, Stephen 1770-1834 *ApCAB*
Higginson, Thomas Wentworth Storrow
1823-1911 *AmBi, ApCAB, DcAmB, Drake,*
McGEWB, NatCAB 1, TwCBDA,
WebAB, WhAm 1
High, B F *NewYHSD*
High, E Nelson 1871-1943 *NatCAB 32*
High, George *NewYHSD*
High, Robert King 1924-1967 *WhAm 4*
High, Stanley 1895-1961 *WhAm 4*
High, Suzanne Frances *WomWWA 14*
Higham, Sydney *IIBEAAW*
Highet, Frank Brewster 1858-1934 *NatCAB 24*
Highet, Mary Elizabeth 1869- *WomWWA 14*
Highet, William W *NewYHSD*
Highfill, Robert David 1889-1963 *WhAm 4*
Highland, Cecil Blaine 1876-1957 *WhAm 3*

Highland, Virgil Lee 1870-1930 *WhAm 1*
Highley, Aida Evans 1876- *WomWWA 14*
Highmore, Nathaniel 1613-1685 *DcScB*
Highsmith, J Henry 1877-1953 *WhAm 3*
Highsmith, Jacob Franklin 1868-1939 *WhAm 1*
Hight, Clarence Albert 1868-1945 *WhAm 2*
Hightower, Emmett 1866-1929 *WhAm 1*
Hightower, Louis Victor 1909-1972 *WhAm 5*
Hightower, Robert E 1890-1952 *WhAm 4*
Hightower, William Harrison 1887-1947
WhAm 2
Highwood, Charles *NewYHSD*
Higier, Daniel Herman 1893-1949 *NatCAB 42*
Higinbotham, Erwin Hayward 1869-
WomWWA 14
Higinbotham, Harlow Niles 1838-1919
ApCAB Sup, DcAmB, NatCAB 18,
WhAm 1
Higinbotham, John U 1867- *WhAm 4*
Higley, Adelbert Pankey 1872-1944 *WhAm 2*
Higley, Albert Maltby 1895-1969 *WhAm 5*
Higley, Brodie Gilman 1872-1946 *WhAm 2*
Higley, Cyrus Martin 1894-1971 *WhAm 5*
Higley, Henry Grant 1903-1969 *WhAm 5*
Higley, L Allen 1871-1955 *NatCAB 43*
Higley, Miles M 1867- *WhAm 3*
Higley, Walter Maydole 1899-1969 *WhAm 5*
Higley, Warren 1833-1911 *NatCAB 3,*
WhAm 1
Higman, Nellie *WomWWA 14*
Higuaihue 1576?-1616 *ApCAB*
Hiketas *DcScB*
Hiland, James H 1848-1929 *WhAm 1*
Hilb, Emanuel 1834-1919 *NatCAB 18*
Hilbernaz, Francisco DeFaria 1669-1731
ApCAB
Hilberry, Clarence Beverly 1902-1966
NatCAB 51
Hilberseimer, Ludwig Karl 1885-1967 *WhAm 4*
Hilbert, Carl Emil 1872-1927 *NatCAB 23*
Hilbert, David 1862-1943 *AsBiEn, DcScB*
Hilbert, Frederic Leon 1882-1956 *NatCAB 44*
Hilbert, George H 1881- *WhAm 6*
Hilbert, Pierre Alphonse 1865-1921 *NatCAB 19*
Hilborn, Samuel Greeley 1834-1899 *BiDrAC,*
TwCBDA
Hilbrant, Robert Edward 1900-1970 *WhAm 5*
Hilbun, Ben Frank 1890-1963 *WhAm 4*
Hilbun, William Bryan 1931-1971 *WhAm 6*
Hild, Frederick Henry *WhAm 5*
Hild, Oscar F 1901-1950 *WhAm 3*
Hildasmith, Josephine *WomWWA 14*
Hildebrand, Arthur Sturges 1887-1924
NatCAB 37
Hildebrand, Daniel Munroe 1880-1942 *WhAm 2*
Hildebrand, H Edward 1895-1965 *WhAm 4*
Hildebrand, Ira Polk 1876-1944 *WhAm 2*
Hildebrand, Jesse Richardson 1888-1951
WhAm 3
Hildebrandt, Cornelia Trumbull Ellis 1876-
WomWWA 14
Hildebrandt, Fred H 1882-1956 *WhAm 3*
Hildebrandt, Fred Herman 1874-1956 *BiDrAC,*
WhAmP
Hildebrandt, Georg Friedrich 1764-1816 *DcScB*
Hildebrandt, Harvey Thornton 1898-1965
WhAm 4
Hildebrandt, Howard Logan 1872-1958
NatCAB 43
Hildebrandt, Johann Lucas Von 1663-1745
McGEWB
Hildebrant, Charles Quinn 1864-1953 *BiDrAC,*
WhAm 4
Hildebrant, Howard Logan 1872-1958 *WhAm 3*
Hildeburn, Charles Swift Riche 1855-1901
ApCAB, TwCBDA, WhAm 1
Hildeburn, Mary Jane 1821-1882 *ApCAB*
Hildegard Of Bingen 1098-1179 *DcScB*
Hilder, Gottfried Julius 1859-1921 *NatCAB 51*
Hilder, Howard 1866-1935 *WhAm 1*
Hilder, John Chapman 1892-1936 *WhAm 1*
Hilderburn, Mary Jane 1821-1882 *NatCAB 13*
Hildinger, Wade Wheeler 1912-1963 *WhAm 4*
Hilditch, Thomas Percy 1886-1965 *DcScB*
Hildreth, Alfred Hitchcock 1874-1955
NatCAB 42
Hildreth, Arthur Grant 1863-1941 *NatCAB 40*
Hildreth, Charles Lotin 1856-1896 *ApCAB Sup*

Hildreth, David Merrill 1862-1923 *WhAm 1*
Hildreth, Eugenius Augustus 1821-1885 *ApCAB*
Hildreth, Ezekiel 1784-1856 *Drake*
Hildreth, Harold Mowbray 1906-1965 *WhAm 4*
Hildreth, Helen Rebecca 1864- *WomWWA 14*
Hildreth, Hosea 1782-1835 *ApCAB,*
NatCAB 10, TwCBDA
Hildreth, John 1851-1942 *NatCAB 31*
Hildreth, John Lewis 1838-1925 *WhAm 1*
Hildreth, Joseph S d1960 *WhAm 4*
Hildreth, Melvin Andrew 1859-1944 *WhAm 2*
Hildreth, Melvin Davis 1890-1959 *WhAm 3*
Hildreth, Mrs. Richard *NewYHSD*
Hildreth, Richard 1807-1865 *AmBi, ApCAB,*
DcAmB, Drake, McGEWB, NatCAB 1,
NatCAB 10, TwCBDA, WhAm H
Hildreth, Samuel Clay 1866-1929 *DcAmB*
Hildreth, Samuel Prescott 1783-1863 *ApCAB,*
DcAmB, Drake, TwCBDA, WhAm H
Hildreth, William Sobieski 1893-1966 *WhAm 4*
Hildrup, William Thomas 1822- *NatCAB 3*
Hildrup, William Thomas, Jr. 1862-1920
NatCAB 18
Hildt, John Coffey 1882-1938 *WhAm 1*
Hildum, Clayton Edward 1871-1952 *WhAm 3*
Hilen, Andrew Reuben 1887-1949 *NatCAB 40*
Hiles, George Howard 1877-1930 *NatCAB 23*
Hiles, Osia Joslyn 1832- *AmWom*
Hilgard, Ernest Ropriequet 1904- *BiDAmEd*
Hilgard, Eugene Woldemar 1833-1916 *AmBi,*
ApCAB, DcAmB, NatCAB 10, TwCBDA,
WhAm 1
Hilgard, Ferdinand Heinrich Gustav *WebAB,*
WhAm H
Hilgard, Julius Erasmus 1825-1891 *ApCAB,*
BiAUS, DcAmB, NatCAB 10, TwCBDA,
WhAm H
Hilgard, Theodor Erasmus 1790-1873 *DcAmB*
Hilgard, Theodore Charles 1828-1875 *ApCAB,*
NatCAB 22
Hilgard, Theodore Erasmus 1790-1873 *ApCAB*
Hilgartner, Henry Louis 1868-1937 *WhAm 1*
Hilgemeier, George August 1876-1948
NatCAB 39
Hilken, Henry Gerhard 1847-1937 *NatCAB 31*
Hilkey, Charles Joseph 1880-1964 *NatCAB 53,*
WhAm 4
Hill, A *NewYHSD*
Hill, Abby Williams 1861- *IIBEAAW*
Hill, Adams Sherman 1833-1910 *TwCBDA,*
WhAm 1
Hill, Agnes Leonard 1842-1917 *AmWom,*
NatCAB 17, WhAm 1
Hill, Albert Hudgins 1866-1933 *WhAm 1*
Hill, Albert Ross 1869-1943 *NatCAB 14,*
NatCAB 32, WhAm 2
Hill, Alferd J 1881-1953 *WhAm 3*
Hill, Alfred Gibson 1893-1971 *WhAm 5*
Hill, Alice Polk 1854- *WomWWA 14*
Hill, Alice Stewart 1850?-1921? *IIBEAAW*
Hill, Ambrose Powell 1824-1865 *Drake*
Hill, Ambrose Powell 1825-1865 *AmBi,*
ApCAB, BiDConf, DcAmB, NatCAB 4,
TwCBDA, WebAB, WebAMB, WhAm H
Hill, Amelia Robertson *NewYHSD*
Hill, Andrew Henry 1870- *WhoColR*
Hill, Anne *NewYHSD*
Hill, Archibald Vivian 1886- *AsBiEn,*
McGEWB
Hill, Arthur Asa 1853-1917 *NatCAB 17*
Hill, Arthur B 1879- *WhAm 6*
Hill, Arthur Dehon 1869-1947 *NatCAB 36,*
WhAm 2
Hill, Arthur Edward 1880-1939 *WhAm 1*
Hill, Arthur Joseph 1888-1964 *WhAm 4*
Hill, Arthur Middleton 1892-1972 *WhAm 5*
Hill, Arthur Turnbull 1868-1929 *NatCAB 25,*
WhAm 1
Hill, Aymer Seth Columbus 1876-1958
NatCAB 47
Hill, Bancroft 1887-1957 *NatCAB 46,*
WhAm 3
Hill, Benjamin Dionysius 1842- *ApCAB*
Hill, Benjamin Harvey 1823-1882 *AmBi,*
ApCAB, BiAUS, BiDConf, BiDrAC,
DcAmB, McGEWB, NatCAB 10,
TwCBDA, WhAm H, WhAmP
Hill, Benjamin Jefferson 1825-1880 *BiDConf*

Hill, Bert Hodge 1874-1958 *WhAm 3*
Hill, Britton Armstrong 1816-1888 *ApCAB Sup*
Hill, Miss C *NewYHSD*
Hill, Calvin Heywood 1857-1929 *NatCAB 22*
Hill, Carlton 1894-1971 *WhAm 5*
Hill, Caroline Miles 1866-1951 *WhAm 3, WomWWA 14*
Hill, Carolyn Bailey d1961 *WhAm 4*
Hill, Charles 1862- *WhAm 4*
Hill, Charles Augustus 1833-1902 *BiDrAC*
Hill, Charles Ebenezer 1848-1917 *NatCAB 22*
Hill, Charles Edward 1881-1936 *NatCAB 27, WhAm 1*
Hill, Charles Geraldus 1849-1925 *NatCAB 20*
Hill, Charles Hubbard 1869-1944 *NatCAB 35*
Hill, Charles Leander 1906-1956 *NatCAB 43, WhAm 3*
Hill, Charles Lewis 1869-1957 *WhAm 3*
Hill, Charles Otis 1869-1939 *NatCAB 29*
Hill, Charles Phillips 1871-1933 *NatCAB 25*
Hill, Charles Shattuck 1868- *WhAm 4*
Hill, Chester James, Jr. 1914-1969 *WhAm 5*
Hill, Claiborne Milton 1857-1950 *NatCAB 38, WhAm 3*
Hill, Clara Mossman 1871- *WomWWA 14*
Hill, Claude Eugene 1874-1957 *WhAm 3*
Hill, Clement Sidney 1813-1892 *BiAUS, BiDrAC*
Hill, Clyde Milton 1885-1965 *BiDAmEd, WhAm 4*
Hill, Crawford 1862-1922 *WhAm 1*
Hill, Daniel Harvey 1821-1889 *AmBi, ApCAB, BiDAmEd, BiDConf, DcAmB, NatCAB 4, TwCBDA, WebAMB, WhAm H*
Hill, Daniel Harvey 1824-1889 *Drake*
Hill, Daniel Harvey 1859-1924 *NatCAB 19, WhAm 1*
Hill, Daniel Webster 1865- *WhoColR*
Hill, David Bennett 1843-1910 *AmBi, ApCAB, BiDrAC, DcAmB, NatCAB 1, TwCBDA, WhAm 1, WhAmP*
Hill, David Garrett 1902-1973 *WhAm 5*
Hill, David Jayne 1850-1932 *AmBi, ApCAB, ApCAB X, DcAmB S1, NatCAB 12, TwCBDA, WhAm 1*
Hill, David Spence 1873-1951 *BiDAmEd, NatCAB 40, WhAm 3*
Hill, Donald MacKay 1877- *WhAm 6*
Hill, Eben Clayton 1882-1940 *NatCAB 29, WhAm 1*
Hill, Ebenezer J 1845-1917 *BiDrAC, NatCAB 18, TwCBDA, WhAm 1, WhAmP*
Hill, Ed Sperry 1870-1952 *NatCAB 44*
Hill, Edgar Goodspeed 1883-1955 *NatCAB 49*
Hill, Edgar Preston 1861-1938 *WhAm 1*
Hill, Edith Thatcher 1879- *WomWWA 14*
Hill, Edmund Walton 1896-1973 *WhAm 6*
Hill, Edward Augustus 1845-1910 *NatCAB 16*
Hill, Edward Burlingame 1872-1960 *NatCAB 14, WhAm 4*
Hill, Edward Curtis 1863- *WhAm 4*
Hill, Edward Everett 1906-1967 *NatCAB 54*
Hill, Edward Gurney 1847-1933 *WhAm 1*
Hill, Edward Lee 1904-1974 *WhAm 6*
Hill, Edward Llewellyn 1900-1958 *WhAm 3*
Hill, Edward Rufus 1852-1908 *IIBEAAW*
Hill, Edward Yates 1868-1941 *NatCAB 30, WhAm 1*
Hill, Edwin Allston 1850-1929 *NatCAB 22*
Hill, Edwin Conger 1884-1957 *WhAm 3*
Hill, Eliza Trask 1840- *AmWom*
Hill, Elizabeth Fitz 1846- *WomWWA 14*
Hill, Elsie Mary 1883- *WomWWA 14*
Hill, Emma Linton 1860- *WomWWA 14*
Hill, Emory 1883-1940 *WhAm 1*
Hill, Ernest Rowland 1872-1948 *ApCAB X, DcAmB S4, NatCAB 37, WhAm 2*
Hill, Ernest W 1876-1964 *WhAm 4*
Hill, Ernie 1908-1958 *WhAm 3*
Hill, Eugene Lott 1878- *WhAm 6*
Hill, Evelyn Corthell 1886- *IIBEAAW*
Hill, Felix Robertson, Jr. 1869- *WhAm 5*
Hill, Frances Maria Mulligan 1799-1884 *NotAW*
Hill, Frances Mulligan 1807?-1884 *ApCAB*
Hill, Francis 1842?- *NewYHSD*
Hill, Francis 1875- *WhAm 5*

Hill, Francis C *NewYHSD*
Hill, Frank Alpine 1841-1903 *BiDAmEd, DcAmB, NatCAB 23, WhAm 1*
Hill, Frank Davis 1862-1912 *WhAm 1*
Hill, Frank Ernest 1888-1969 *WhAm 5*
Hill, Frank Pierce 1855-1941 *DcAmLiB, NatCAB 2, TwCBDA, WhAm 4*
Hill, Fred Burnett 1876-1919 *WhAm 1*
Hill, Frederic Stanhope 1805-1851 *DcAmB, WhAm H*
Hill, Frederic Stanhope 1829-1913 *NatCAB 15, TwCBDA, WhAm 4*
Hill, Frederick Sinclair 1888-1951 *WhAm 3*
Hill, Frederick Thayer 1889-1969 *WhAm 5*
Hill, Frederick Trevor 1866-1930 *DcAmB, WhAm 1*
Hill, G Albert 1892-1965 *WhAm 4*
Hill, George 1796-1871 *ApCAB, Drake, TwCBDA*
Hill, George 1815-1895 *TwCBDA*
Hill, George 1861- *NatCAB 10*
Hill, George Alfred, Jr. 1892-1949 *NatCAB 39, WhAm 2*
Hill, George Andrews 1858-1927 *WhAm 1*
Hill, George Anthony 1842-1916 *WhAm 1*
Hill, George Edwin 1864-1916 *NatCAB 33*
Hill, George Griswold 1868-1935 *WhAm 1*
Hill, George Handel 1799-1849 *Drake*
Hill, George Handel 1809-1848 *NatCAB 1*
Hill, George Handel 1809-1849 *ApCAB, DcAmB, TwCBDA, WhAm H*
Hill, George Robert 1913-1975 *WhAm 6*
Hill, George Snow 1898-1969 *NatCAB 53*
Hill, George W 1815-1893 *NewYHSD*
Hill, George W 1824- *ApCAB*
Hill, George Washington 1884-1946 *DcAmB S4, WebAB, WhAm 2*
Hill, George William 1838-1914 *ApCAB, DcAmB, DcScB, NatCAB 13, TwCBDA, WhAm 1*
Hill, George William 1845-1914 *WhAm 1*
Hill, Gershom Hyde 1846-1925 *NatCAB 20, WhAm 1*
Hill, Grace Livingston 1865-1947 *DcAmB S4, NatCAB 40, NotAW, WhAm 2*
Hill, Grover Bennett 1889-1961 *WhAm 4*
Hill, Hamilton Andrews 1827- *TwCBDA*
Hill, Harold O 1887-1963 *WhAm 4*
Hill, Harry Granison 1874-1951 *WhAm 3*
Hill, Harry Harrison 1888-1965 *WhAm 4*
Hill, Harry R W 1797-1853 *NatCAB 2*
Hill, Harry W 1890-1971 *WhAm 5*
Hill, Hattie 1874- *ApCAB X*
Hill, Henry Albert 1896-1959 *WhAm 3*
Hill, Henry Alexander 1844- *NatCAB 7*
Hill, Henry Alexander 1849- *WhAm 4*
Hill, Henry Arthur 1850-1928 *NatCAB 23*
Hill, Henry Barker 1849-1903 *ApCAB, DcAmB, TwCBDA, WhAm 1*
Hill, Henry Clarke 1877- *WhAm 3*
Hill, Henry Garland 1885-1951 *NatCAB 42*
Hill, Henry Root 1876-1918 *NatCAB 20*
Hill, Henry Wayland 1853- *NatCAB 8, WhAm 4*
Hill, Herbert E 1845-1895 *NatCAB 12*
Hill, Herbert Malcolm 1856-1927 *NatCAB 20*
Hill, Herbert Wynford 1875-1943 *WhAm 2*
Hill, Hiram Warner 1858-1934 *WhAm 1*
Hill, Horace Greeley 1873-1942 *NatCAB 51, WhAm 2*
Hill, Howard Copeland 1878-1940 *BiDAmEd, NatCAB 30, WhAm 1*
Hill, Hugh Clement *BiAUS*
Hill, Hugh Lawson White 1810-1892 *BiAUS, BiDrAC, WhAm H*
Hill, I *NewYHSD*
Hill, I W *NewYHSD*
Hill, Ida Alma 1889- *WhoColR*
Hill, Irving 1876- *WhAm 5*
Hill, Isaac 1788-1851 *ApCAB, BiAUS, BiDrAC, Drake, NatCAB 11, TwCBDA, WhAmP*
Hill, Isaac 1789-1851 *DcAmB, WhAm H*
Hill, Isaac William 1861- *WhAm 4*
Hill, J *NewYHSD*
Hill, J H *NewYHSD*
Hill, J Leubrie *WhoColR*
Hill, J Murray 1891-1961 *WhAm 4*

Hill, James *NewYHSD, WhAm 4*
Hill, James 1734-1811 *DcAmB, WhAm H*
Hill, James 1889-1962 *NatCAB 50*
Hill, James, Jr. 1898-1960 *WhAm 3*
Hill, James Brents 1878-1952 *WhAm 3*
Hill, James Ewing 1837-1916 *WhAm 1*
Hill, James Gilbert 1872-1933 *WhAm 1*
Hill, James Hamilton 1858-1926 *NatCAB 20*
Hill, James Jerome 1838-1916 *AmBi, ApCAB X, DcAmB, EncAB, McGEWB, NatCAB 13, NatCAB 33, REnAW, WebAB, WhAm 1*
Hill, James Langdon 1848-1931 *WhAm 1*
Hill, James Michael 1899-1962 *WhAm 4*
Hill, James Norman 1870-1932 *WhAm 1*
Hill, James Perminter 1878-1950 *WhAm 3*
Hill, James S *NewYHSD*
Hill, James W 1895-1951 *WhAm 3*
Hill, Janet McKenzie 1852-1933 *WhAm 1, WomWWA 14*
Hill, Jared Winburn 1856-1932 *NatCAB 41*
Hill, Jennie Justina Robinson *WomWWA 14*
Hill, Jesse Hooper 1875-1958 *NatCAB 43*
Hill, Joe 1872?-1915 *WebAB*
Hill, Joe 1879-1915 *REnAW, WhAm HA, WhAm 4*
Hill, John 1707?-1775 *DcScB*
Hill, John 1770-1850 *DcAmB, NatCAB 23, NewYHSD, WhAm H*
Hill, John 1797-1861 *BiAUS, BiDrAC, WhAm H*
Hill, John 1800-1880 *BiAUS, BiDrAC, WhAm H*
Hill, John 1821-1884 *ApCAB, BiAUS, BiDrAC, TwCBDA, WhAm H*
Hill, John 1874-1931 *NatCAB 24*
Hill, John Alexander 1858-1916 *WhAm 1*
Hill, John Arthur 1880-1951 *NatCAB 40, WhAm 3*
Hill, John Boynton Philip Clayton 1879-1941 *BiDrAC, WhAm 1, WhAmP*
Hill, John Calvin 1921-1973 *WhAm 6*
Hill, John Edward 1864-1934 *WhAm 1*
Hill, John Ethan 1865- *WhAm 4*
Hill, John Fremont 1855-1912 *NatCAB 13, WhAm 1*
Hill, John Godfrey 1870- *WhAm 5*
Hill, John Henry 1791-1882 *ApCAB Sup, DcAmB, NatCAB 24, TwCBDA, WhAm H*
Hill, John Henry 1839-1922 *IIBEAAW, NewYHSD*
Hill, John Leonard 1878- *WhAm 6*
Hill, John Lindsay 1840- *NatCAB 3, WhAm 4*
Hill, John McClary 1821- *ApCAB*
Hill, John R 1840?- *NewYHSD*
Hill, John Roy 1910-1969 *NatCAB 55*
Hill, John Sprunt 1869-1961 *WhAm 4*
Hill, John Wesley 1863-1936 *ApCAB X, NatCAB 7, WhAm 1*
Hill, John William 1812-1879 *BnEnAmA, NewYHSD, WhAm H*
Hill, John Wilson 1857- *NatCAB 16*
Hill, Johnson Washington 1865- *WhoColR*
Hill, Joseph Adna 1860-1938 *DcAmB S2, NatCAB 29, WhAm 1*
Hill, Joseph Henry 1858-1927 *WhAm 1*
Hill, Joseph Herbert 1858-1958 *NatCAB 49*
Hill, Joseph Knoerle 1918-1971 *WhAm 5*
Hill, Joseph Lister 1894- *BiDrAC*
Hill, Joseph Morrison 1863-1951 *NatCAB 43*
Hill, Joseph Morrison 1864-1951 *NatCAB 13, WhAm 5*
Hill, Joseph St. Clair 1860- *WhAm 4*
Hill, Joseph Stacy 1862-1939 *WhAm 1*
Hill, Joshua 1812-1891 *ApCAB, BiAUS, BiDrAC, DcAmB, NatCAB 4, TwCBDA, WhAm H, WhAmP*
Hill, Judson Sudborough 1854-1931 *WhAm 1*
Hill, Julien Harrison 1877-1943 *NatCAB 38, WhAm 2*
Hill, Kate Donahue 1870- *WomWWA 14*
Hill, Kittie C Ellis *WomWWA 14*
Hill, Knute 1876-1963 *BiDrAC, WhAm 5*
Hill, Lamar 1885-1937 *WhAm 1*
Hill, Laurance Landreth 1887-1932 *WhAm 1*
Hill, Lawrence 1879- *WhAm 6*

Hill, Lee H 1899-1974 *WhAm 6*
Hill, Leslie Pinckney 1880-1960 *WhAm 3,
WhoColR*
Hill, Lester Sanders 1890-1961 *DcScB*
Hill, Lew Cass 1852-1923 *NatCAB 19*
Hill, Lewis Dana 1870-1945 *NatCAB 34*
Hill, Louis A 1865- *WhAm 4*
Hill, Louis Clarence 1865-1938 *DcAmB S2,
NatCAB 33, WhAm 1*
Hill, Louis Warren 1872-1948 *NatCAB 36,
WhAm 2*
Hill, Louise Bethell Sneed *WomWWA 14*
Hill, Luther Leonidas 1862-1946 *NatCAB 8,
NatCAB 36*
Hill, Lysander 1834-1914 *NatCAB 16,
WhAm 1*
Hill, Mabel Jones 1864-1957 *WomWWA 14*
Hill, Mabel Jones 1884-1957 *WhAm 3*
Hill, Marianna Nicholson Buffum 1881-
WomWWA 14
Hill, Marion 1870-1918 *WhAm 1,
WomWWA 14*
Hill, Mark Langdon 1772-1842 *ApCAB,
BiAUS, BiDrAC, TwCBDA, WhAm H*
Hill, Mary Dorsey Anderson *WomWWA 14*
Hill, Max 1904-1949 *WhAm 2*
Hill, Millard Daniel 1901-1969 *NatCAB 54*
Hill, Minnie Speer *WomWWA 14*
Hill, Mozell Clarence 1911-1969 *WhAm 5*
Hill, Myrle Kauffman 1880- *WomWWA 14*
Hill, Napoleon 1830- *NatCAB 12*
Hill, Napoleon 1883-1970 *NatCAB 57*
Hill, Nathaniel Parker 1832- *ApCAB*
Hill, Nathaniel Peter 1781-1842 *TwCBDA*
Hill, Nathaniel Peter 1832-1900 *BiDrAC,
DcAmB, NatCAB 6, REnAW, TwCBDA,
WhAm H, WhAm 1, WhAmP*
Hill, Nicholas 1766-1857 *NatCAB 3*
Hill, Nicholas 1806-1859 *ApCAB*
Hill, Nicholas Snowden, Jr. 1869- *NatCAB 16*
Hill, Noadiah Moore 1815-1889 *NatCAB 1*
Hill, Noble 1859- *WhAm 4*
Hill, Norman Newton 1863-1950 *NatCAB 39*
Hill, Norman Stewart 1889-1972 *WhAm 5*
Hill, Owen Aloysius 1863-1930 *WhAm 1,
WhAm 1C*
Hill, Owen Duffy 1865- *WhAm 4*
Hill, Pamelia E 1803-1860 *NewYHSD*
Hill, Patty Smith 1868-1946 *BiDAmEd,
DcAmB S4, NotAW, WhAm 2*
Hill, Percival Smith 1862-1925 *NatCAB 15,
NatCAB 32, WhAm 1*
Hill, Philip Samuel 1879-1954 *NatCAB 41*
Hill, Pierre Bernard 1877-1958 *WhAm 3*
Hill, Ralph 1827-1899 *BiAUS, BiDrAC*
Hill, Ralph Lee 1876-1958 *NatCAB 48*
Hill, Ralph Waldo Snowden 1882-1954
WhAm 3
Hill, Randolph William 1854-1926 *WhAm 3*
Hill, Reese Franklin 1908-1969 *WhAm 5*
Hill, Reuben L 1888-1953 *WhAm 3*
Hill, Richard 1673-1729 *ApCAB, DcAmB,
NatCAB 16, WhAm H*
Hill, Richard 1864- *WhoColR*
Hill, Richard, Jr. 1887- *WhoColR*
Hill, Robert Andrews 1811-1900 *BiAUS,
DcAmB, NatCAB 2, TwCBDA,
WhAm H*
Hill, Robert Carmer 1869-1947 *WhAm 2*
Hill, Robert E Lee 1890-1957 *WhAm 3*
Hill, Robert H 1856- *NatCAB 3*
Hill, Robert Jerome 1878- *IlBEAAW*
Hill, Robert Leon 1872- *WhoColR*
Hill, Robert Potter 1874-1937 *BiDrAC,
NatCAB 40, NatCAB 47, WhAm 1*
Hill, Robert Stockwell Reynolds 1876-1938
WhAm 1
Hill, Robert Thomas 1858-1941 *NatCAB 14,
NatCAB 40, WhAm 1*
Hill, Robert Tudor 1881-1945 *NatCAB 33*
Hill, Robert William 1882-1966 *WhAm 4*
Hill, Rolla Bennett 1891-1963 *WhAm 4*
Hill, Roscoe R 1880-1960 *WhAm 4*
Hill, Samuel *NewYHSD*
Hill, Samuel 1678-1752 *NatCAB 19*
Hill, Samuel 1857-1931 *WhAm 1*
Hill, Samuel Billingsley 1875-1958 *BiDrAC,
WhAmP*

Hill, Sherwin Alonzo 1885-1961 *NatCAB 47,
WhAm 4*
Hill, Stephen G *NewYHSD*
Hill, Theophilus Hunter 1836-1901 *ApCAB,
TwCBDA, WhAm 1*
Hill, Thomas *BiAUS*
Hill, Thomas 1818-1891 *AmBi, ApCAB,
BiDAmEd, DcAmB, Drake, NatCAB 6,
TwCBDA, WhAm H*
Hill, Thomas 1829-1908 *ApCAB, DcAmB,
Drake, IlBEAAW, NatCAB 3,
NewYHSD, REnAW, WhAm 1*
Hill, Thomas Edie 1832-1915 *WhAm 1*
Hill, Thomas Guthrie Franklin 1865-1900
WhAm 1
Hill, Thomas Jefferson 1805-1894 *NatCAB 9*
Hill, Thomas Russell 1894-1975 *WhAm 6*
Hill, Thomas William 1847-1921 *ApCAB X*
Hill, Tom Burbridge 1898-1957 *WhAm 3*
Hill, Tyler Edward 1883- *WhoColR*
Hill, Ureli Corelli 1802?-1875 *DcAmB,
NatCAB 22, WhAm H*
Hill, Uriah C 1802?-1875 *ApCAB, TwCBDA*
Hill, Vassie James 1875-1954 *WhAm 3*
Hill, W *NewYHSD*
Hill, Walker 1855-1922 *NatCAB 12,
WhAm 1*
Hill, Walter Barnard 1851-1905 *DcAmB,
NatCAB 19, WhAm 1*
Hill, Walter Bradley 1875-1949 *NatCAB 38*
Hill, Walter Briggs 1866-1950 *NatCAB 40*
Hill, Walter Clay 1880-1962 *WhAm 4*
Hill, Walter Henry 1822-1907 *ApCAB,
TwCBDA, WhAm 1*
Hill, Walter Newell 1881-1955 *WhAm 3*
Hill, Walter Nickerson 1846-1884 *NatCAB 12*
Hill, Warren Eames 1902-1962 *NatCAB 47,
WhAm 4*
Hill, Whitmel 1743-1797 *BiDrAC, TwCBDA,
WhAm H*
Hill, Whitmell 1743-1797 *BiAUS, Drake,
NatCAB 12*
Hill, Whitmill 1743-1797 *ApCAB*
Hill, William 1741-1816 *DcAmB, NatCAB 24,
WhAm H*
Hill, William 1769-1852 *ApCAB*
Hill, William A 1864-1932 *NatCAB 26,
WhAm 1*
Hill, William Alexander 1875- *ApCAB X*
Hill, William Austin 1873-1951 *NatCAB 40,
WhAm 3*
Hill, William Bancroft 1857-1945 *NatCAB 34,
WhAm 2*
Hill, William David 1833-1906 *BiDrAC*
Hill, William Edwin 1880-1940 *WhAm 1*
Hill, William Free 1867-1935 *WhAm 1*
Hill, William Henry 1767-1809 *BiAUS,
BiDrAC, TwCBDA, WhAm H*
Hill, William Henry 1838-1913 *NatCAB 11,
WhAm 1*
Hill, William Henry 1877-1972 *BiDrAC,
WhAm 5*
Hill, William Lee 1899-1964 *NatCAB 50*
Hill, William Luther 1873-1951 *BiDrAC*
Hill, William Oakley 1892-1968 *NatCAB 54*
Hill, William S 1863-1940 *WhAm 1*
Hill, William Silas 1886-1972 *BiDrAC,
WhAm 5*
Hill, Wilson Shedric 1863-1921 *BiDrAC,
WhAm 1*
Hill, Winfield Scott 1839-1911 *NatCAB 16*
Hill, Wyman Newton 1891-1958 *NatCAB 47*
Hillard, Charles W d1921 *WhAm 1*
Hillard, George Stillman 1808-1879 *ApCAB,
BiDAmEd, DcAmB, Drake, NatCAB 3,
TwCBDA, WhAm H*
Hillard, Mary Robbins d1932 *WhAm 1*
Hillary, Sir Edmund Percival 1919- *AsBiEn*
Hillary, William 1700-1763 *BiHiMed*
Hillas, Robert M 1884-1956 *WhAm 3*
Hillbrand, Earl K 1894-1962 *WhAm 4*
Hille, Gustav 1852- *WhAm 4*
Hille, Hermann 1871-1962 *WhAm 4*
Hilleary, Edgar D 1877- *WhAm 5*
Hilleary, Louis Raymond 1886-1961
NatCAB 49
Hilleary, Mary Esta 1861- *WomWWA 14*

Hilleboe, Herman Ertresvaag 1906-1974
WhAm 6
Hillebrand, Harold Newcomb 1887-1953
WhAm 3
Hillebrand, William Francis 1853-1925 *AmBi,
ApCAB Sup, DcAmB, NatCAB 14,
WhAm 1*
Hillegas, Howard Clemens 1872-1918 *WhAm 1*
Hillegas, Michael d1804 *BiAUS, Drake*
Hillegas, Michael 1728-1804 *ApCAB,
NatCAB 11*
Hillegas, Michael 1729-1804 *DcAmB,
TwCBDA, WhAm H, WhAmP*
Hillel I 060?BC-010?AD *McGEWB*
Hillelson, Jeffrey Paul 1919- *BiDrAC*
Hillen, Edward 1818?- *NewYHSD*
Hillen, J T E 1818?- *NewYHSD*
Hillen, Solomon, Jr. 1810-1873 *BiDrAC,
WhAm H*
Hillen, Solomon, Jr. 1813-1873 *BiAUS*
Hillenbrand, John 1843-1910 *NatCAB 33*
Hillenkoetter, Roscoe Henry 1897- *WebAMB*
Hillenmeyer, Louis Edward 1885-1965 *WhAm 4*
Hiller, Mrs. *NewYHSD*
Hiller, Alfred 1831-1920 *ApCAB, TwCBDA,
WhAm 3*
Hiller, Clara Louise 1862- *WomWWA 14*
Hiller, Ernest Theodore 1883-1966 *NatCAB 52*
Hiller, Hiram Milliken 1867-1921 *WhAm 1*
Hiller, Joseph, Jr. 1777-1795 *NewYHSD*
Hiller, Joseph, Sr. 1748-1814 *NewYHSD*
Hillerich, John Frederick 1833-1924
NatCAB 19
Hillern, Bertha Von 1857- *ApCAB Sup*
Hilles, Charles Dewey 1867-1949 *WhAm 2*
Hilles, Florence Bayard 1865-1954 *NatCAB 45*
Hilles, Frederick VanTyne Holbrook 1908-1969
WhAm 5
Hilles, Frederick Whiley 1900- *WhAm 6*
Hilles, William Samuel 1865-1928 *NatCAB 45,
WhAm 1*
Hillhouse, Augustus Lucas 1791-1859 *ApCAB,
NatCAB 4*
Hillhouse, James 1687?-1740 *ApCAB*
Hillhouse, James 1754-1832 *ApCAB, BiAUS,
BiDrAC, DcAmB, Drake, NatCAB 2,
TwCBDA, WhAm H, WhAmP*
Hillhouse, James 1854-1938 *NatCAB 28*
Hillhouse, James Abraham 1730-1775 *ApCAB*
Hillhouse, James Abraham 1789-1841 *ApCAB,
DcAmB, Drake, NatCAB 7, TwCBDA,
WhAm H*
Hillhouse, John TenBroeck 1848-1932
NatCAB 23
Hillhouse, Thomas 1816-1897 *NatCAB 8*
Hillhouse, William 1728-1816 *ApCAB, BiAUS,
BiDrAC, NatCAB 11, TwCBDA,
WhAm H, WhAmP*
Hilliard, Benjamin Clark 1868-1951 *BiDrAC,
NatCAB 41, WhAm 3*
Hilliard, Benjamin Clark, Jr. 1898-1969
WhAm 5
Hilliard, Curtis Morrison 1887-1969 *WhAm 5*
Hilliard, D'Auberteuil 1740?-1789? *Drake*
Hilliard, Edmund Bayfield 1878- *WhAm 6*
Hilliard, Francis 1806?-1878 *DcAmB,
NatCAB 3, WhAm H*
Hilliard, Francis 1808?-1878 *ApCAB, Drake*
Hilliard, Henry *NewYHSD*
Hilliard, Henry Washington 1808-1892 *AmBi,
ApCAB, BiAUS, BiDrAC, DcAmB,
Drake, NatCAB 2, TwCBDA, WhAm H*
Hilliard, Isaac 1879-1970 *WhAm 5*
Hilliard, John Gerald 1858-1926 *NatCAB 20*
Hilliard, John Northern 1872-1935 *WhAm 1*
Hilliard, Nicholas 1547?-1619 *McGEWB*
Hilliard, Raymond Marcellus 1907-1966
WhAm 4
Hilliard, Robert Cochran 1857-1927
NatCAB 22, WhAm 1
Hilliard, Thomas C 1908-1965 *WhAm 4*
Hilliard, Thomas Montgomery 1865- *ApCAB X*
Hilliard, William Henry 1836-1905 *ApCAB,
NewYHSD*
Hilliard D'Auberteuil, Michel Rene 1751-1785
ApCAB
Hillier, James 1915- *AsBiEn*
Hillinger, Raymond Peter 1904-1971 *WhAm 5*

Hillings, Patrick Jerome 1923- *BiDrAC*
Hillis, Annie Patrick 1862-1930 *WomWWA 14*
Hillis, David 1788-1845 *DcAmB, WhAm H*
Hillis, David 1789-1845 *ApCAB*
Hillis, David B *ApCAB*
Hillis, Glen Raymond 1891-1965 *NatCAB 52*
Hillis, Newell Dwight 1858-1929 *AmBi,
DcAmB, NatCAB 9, NatCAB 21,
TwCBDA, WhAm 1*
Hillis, Mrs. Newell Dwight 1862-1930 *WhAm 1*
Hillix, Clara Z *WomWWA 14*
Hillkowitz, Morris *WebAB*
Hillkowitz, Philip 1873-1948 *NatCAB 39*
Hillman, Alex L 1900-1968 *WhAm 5*
Hillman, Bessie Abramowitz 1889-1970
NatCAB 56
Hillman, Christine Huff 1908-1975 *WhAm 6*
Hillman, James 1762-1848 *NatCAB 11*
Hillman, James Frazer 1888-1972 *NatCAB 57,
WhAm 5*
Hillman, James Noah 1883-1959 *NatCAB 48*
Hillman, John Hartwell, Jr. 1880-1959
NatCAB 48, WhAm 3
Hillman, John William 1921-1970 *NatCAB 55,
WhAm 5*
Hillman, Lucy Rosaltha 1881-1964 *WhAm 4*
Hillman, Richard S *NewYHSD*
Hillman, Sidney 1887-1946 *DcAmB S4,
EncAB, McGEWB, WebAB, WhAm 2*
Hillman, Swan 1887-1965 *NatCAB 52*
Hillman, Thomas Tennessee 1844-1905 *DcAmB,
NatCAB 23*
Hillman, William 1895-1962 *WhAm 4*
Hillquit, Morris 1869-1933 *AmBi, DcAmB S1,
McGEWB, NatCAB 44, WebAB,
WhAm 1, WhAmP*
Hills, Ada Isadore Ayer 1857- *WhAm 4,
WomWWA 14*
Hills, Charles Turner 1821-1902 *NatCAB 33*
Hills, Cordelia M 1866- *WomWWA 14*
Hills, Edgar Samuel 1870-1958 *NatCAB 46*
Hills, Elijah Clarence 1867-1932 *BiDAmEd,
DcAmB S1, NatCAB 23, WhAm 1*
Hills, Franklin Grant 1868-1941 *NatCAB 30,
WhAm 4*
Hills, George 1816- *ApCAB*
Hills, George Morgan 1825-1890 *ApCAB,
TwCBDA*
Hills, James H 1814?- *NewYHSD*
Hills, James Mandly 1875-1951 *NatCAB 39*
Hills, Jonas Coolidge 1851-1913 *NatCAB 16*
Hills, Joseph Lawrence 1861-1954 *NatCAB 41,
WhAm 3*
Hills, Laura Coombs 1859-1952 *WhAm 3,
WomWWA 14*
Hills, Laurence 1879-1941 *WhAm 1*
Hills, Lewis Samuel 1836-1915 *WhAm 1*
Hills, Oscar Armstrong 1837-1919 *WhAm 3*
Hills, Richard Charles 1848-1923 *WhAm 1*
Hills, Thomas McDougall 1881- *WhAm 6*
Hills, Victor Gardiner 1855-1930 *WhAm 1*
Hills, William Henry 1859-1930 *NatCAB 4,
WhAm 1*
Hillsborough, Wills Hill, Earl Of 1718-1793
ApCAB, Drake
Hillstrom, Joseph *WebAB*
Hillyar, Sir James 1769-1843 *ApCAB Sup*
Hillyard, Henry 1806?- *NewYHSD*
Hillyard, J *NewYHSD*
Hillyer, Asa 1763-1840 *ApCAB, Drake*
Hillyer, Dotha Bushnell 1843- *WomWWA 14*
Hillyer, Edgar Winters 1830- *BiAUS*
Hillyer, Ernest Cain 1901-1960 *NatCAB 49*
Hillyer, George 1835- *NatCAB 10*
Hillyer, H Stanley 1887-1955 *WhAm 3*
Hillyer, Henry L *NewYHSD*
Hillyer, Homer Winthrop 1859-1949 *WhAm 2*
Hillyer, John Freeman 1805-1893 *TwCBDA*
Hillyer, Junius 1807-1886 *ApCAB, BiAUS,
BiDrAC, DcAmB, NatCAB 10, TwCBDA,
WhAm H*
Hillyer, Robert Silliman 1895-1961 *WhAm 4*
Hillyer, Shaler Granby 1809-1900 *TwCBDA*
Hillyer, Thomas Arthur 1868- *WhAm 4*
Hillyer, Virgil Mores 1875-1931 *WhAm 1*
Hillyer, William, Jr. *NewYHSD*
Hillyer, William Hurd 1880-1959 *WhAm 4*
Hillyer, William Silliman 1831-1874 *ApCAB,*

NatCAB 8
Hilmer, William Charles 1871- *WhAm 5*
Hilpert, Elmer Ernest 1905-1975 *WhAm 6*
Hilpert, Frank Moth 1914-1969 *NatCAB 57*
Hilprecht, Herman Volrath 1859-1925 *DcAmB,
WhAm 1*
Hilprecht, Hermann Vollrat 1859-1925 *ApCAB,
NatCAB 10*
Hilprecht, Hermann Volrath 1859-1925 *AmBi*
Hilsberg, Alexander 1900-1961 *NatCAB 46,
WhAm 4*
Hilson, Edwin I 1895-1952 *WhAm 3*
Hilson, Ellen Augusta 1801-1837 *ApCAB*
Hilson, Thomas 1784-1834 *ApCAB, Drake*
Hilson, Mrs. Thomas 1801-1837 *Drake*
Hiltman, John Wolfe 1862-1941 *NatCAB 41,
WhAm 1*
Hiltner, Walter Garfield 1881-1951 *NatCAB 42*
Hilton, Alexander 1865-1922 *WhAm 1*
Hilton, Charles Henry 1871-1942 *NatCAB 31*
Hilton, Clifford L 1866- *WhAm 2*
Hilton, Conrad Nicholson 1887- *WebAB*
Hilton, David Clark 1877-1945 *WhAm 2*
Hilton, George Porter 1859-1909 *NatCAB 16*
Hilton, Harriet M Kent 1873- *WomWWA 14*
Hilton, Henry 1824-1899 *TwCBDA*
Hilton, Henry Hoyt 1868-1948 *NatCAB 37,
WhAm 2*
Hilton, Hugh Gerald 1889-1966 *WhAm 5*
Hilton, James 1900-1954 *WhAm 3*
Hilton, John William 1904- *IlBEAAW*
Hilton, Robert B 1821-1894 *BiDConf*
Hilton, Robert William 1873-1923 *NatCAB 28*
Hilton, Thomas Harrison 1881- *WhoColR*
Hilton, Warren 1874-1958 *WhAm 3*
Hilton, William Atwood 1878- *WhAm 6*
Hilyard, George Dilwyn 1830-1898 *NatCAB 6*
Hilyer, Andrew F 1859- *WhoColR*
Himebaugh, Keith 1901-1974 *WhAm 6*
Himel, Sanford Zygmunt 1914-1963
NatCAB 55
Himely, Henry Alexander 1850-1927 *ApCAB X*
Himes, Charles Francis 1838-1918 *ApCAB,
BiDAmEd, DcAmB, NatCAB 4,
TwCBDA, WhAm H, WhAm 3*
Himes, George Henry 1844- *NatCAB 16*
Himes, John Andrew 1848-1923 *WhAm 1*
Himes, Joseph Hendrix 1885-1960 *BiDrAC,
NatCAB 47, WhAm 4*
Himes, Joshua Vaughan 1805-1895 *DcAmB,
WhAm H*
Himes, Norman Edwin 1899-1949 *WhAm 2*
Himes, William Daniel 1887-1957 *NatCAB 46*
Himler, Leonard E 1904-1967 *WhAm 5*
Himmel, Joseph 1855- *WhAm 1*
Himmelberger, John Henry 1861-1930
NatCAB 51
Himmelblau, David 1889-1965 *WhAm 4*
Himmelwright, Abraham Lincoln Artman 1865-
WhAm 4
Himmler, Heinrich 1900-1945 *McGEWB,
WhWW-II*
Himpler, Francis George 1833-1916 *NatCAB 18*
Himstead, Ralph E 1893-1955 *WhAm 3*
Himsworth, Winston E 1912-1970 *WhAm 5*
Hinchee, Fred Lee 1919-1973 *WhAm 6*
Hinchey, William J 1829-1893 *NewYHSD*
Hinchman, Walter Swain 1879- *WhAm 6*
Hinckes, John *NatCAB 12*
Hinckle, Charles *NewYHSD*
Hinckle, William 1906-1961 *WhAm 4*
Hinckley *NewYHSD*
Hinckley, Allen Carter 1877-1954 *NatCAB 41,
WhAm 3*
Hinckley, Cornelius T 1820?- *NewYHSD*
Hinckley, Edwin Smith 1868- *WhAm 2*
Hinckley, F H *NewYHSD*
Hinckley, Frank Erastus 1871-1950 *WhAm 3*
Hinckley, Frank L 1869-1959 *WhAm 3*
Hinckley, Frederic Allen 1845-1917 *WhAm 1*
Hinckley, Frederick Wheeler 1878-1933
WhAm 1
Hinckley, George Lyman 1879-1936 *WhAm 1*
Hinckley, George W 1853-1950 *WhAm 4*
Hinckley, Harriet Elma 1855- *WomWWA 14*
Hinckley, Isabella 1840-1862 *ApCAB, Drake,
NatCAB 1*
Hinckley, Livingston Spraker 1855- *NatCAB 5*

Hinckley, Robert 1853-1941 *NewYHSD,
WhAm 1*
Hinckley, Thomas 1618?-1706 *ApCAB, Drake,
NatCAB 7, TwCBDA*
Hinckley, Thomas 1888-1918 *WhAm 1*
Hinckley, Thomas Hewes 1813-1896 *ApCAB,
IlBEAAW, NewYHSD*
Hinckley, Watson Dexter 1854-1920
NatCAB 19
Hinckman *NewYHSD*
Hincks, Carroll Clark 1889-1964 *WhAm 4*
Hincks, Clarence Meredith 1885-1964 *WhAm 4*
Hincks, Edward Winslow 1830-1894 *ApCAB,
TwCBDA*
Hincks, Edward Young 1844-1927 *NatCAB 10,
WhAm 1*
Hincks, Sir Francis 1795- *Drake*
Hincks, Francis 1807-1885 *ApCAB*
Hincks, Maud Morris 1873- *WomWWA 14*
Hincks, Robert Beresford 1880-1957
NatCAB 46
Hincks, William 1801-1871 *ApCAB*
Hincks, William Thurston 1870-1931
NatCAB 24
Hind, Ella Cora 1861- *WomWWA 14*
Hind, Henry Youle 1823- *ApCAB, Drake,
IlBEAAW*
Hind, John 1858-1933 *NatCAB 37*
Hind, John Russell 1823-1895 *DcScB*
Hind, William George Richardson 1833-1888?
IlBEAAW
Hindemith, Paul 1895-1963 *McGEWB,
WhAm 4*
Hindenburg, Carl Friedrich 1741-1808 *DcScB*
Hindenburg, Paul Ludwig Hans Von 1847-1934
McGEWB, WhoMilH
Hinderlider, Michael Creed 1876- *WhAm 5*
Hindes, Earle Pease 1888-1962 *NatCAB 50*
Hindle, Charles Frederic 1875-1946 *NatCAB 41*
Hindle, Norman Frederick 1902-1960 *WhAm 4*
Hindley, George 1852- *WhAm 4*
Hindley, Howard Lister 1870-1943 *WhAm 2*
Hindley, John Henry 1847-1917 *NatCAB 17*
Hindman, Albert Clare 1884-1923 *WhAm 1*
Hindman, Albert Delmer 1870-1921
NatCAB 19
Hindman, Baker Michael 1902-1969 *WhAm 5*
Hindman, Biscoe 1861-1932 *NatCAB 24*
Hindman, Jacob d1766 *TwCBDA*
Hindman, James Edward 1875-1962
NatCAB 50, WhAm 4
Hindman, Thomas Carmichael 1818-1868
ApCAB, BiAUS, Drake
Hindman, Thomas Carmichael 1826?-1868
TwCBDA
Hindman, Thomas Carmichael 1828-1868 *AmBi,
BiDConf, BiDrAC, DcAmB, NatCAB 22,
REnAW, WhAm H*
Hindman, William d1822 *BiAUS, Drake*
Hindman, William 1742-1823 *NatCAB 2*
Hindman, William 1743-1822 *ApCAB,
BiDrAC, DcAmB, TwCBDA, WhAm H*
Hindmarsh, Harry Comfort 1887-1956 *WhAm 3*
Hindry, Hayes Ralph 1909-1962 *NatCAB 57*
Hinds, Anna Bolender *WomWWA 14*
Hinds, Anthony Keith 1910-1964 *WhAm 4*
Hinds, Asher Crosby 1863-1919 *BiDrAC,
DcAmB, NatCAB 22, WhAm 1, WhAmP*
Hinds, Ellen Maria *WomWWA 14*
Hinds, Ernest 1864-1941 *NatCAB 37,
WhAm 1*
Hinds, Frederick Wesley 1888-1943 *WhAm 2*
Hinds, Henry 1883-1964 *WhAm 4*
Hinds, James 1833-1868 *ApCAB, BiAUS,
BiDrAC, WhAm H*
Hinds, John Iredel Dillard 1847-1921
NatCAB 7, TwCBDA
Hinds, John Iredelle Dillard 1847-1921
NatCAB 26, WhAm 1
Hinds, Julian 1881- *WhAm 6*
Hinds, Mary E 1839- *WomWWA 14*
Hinds, Paul *NewYHSD*
Hinds, Thomas d1840 *Drake*
Hinds, Thomas 1775-1840 *BiAUS, TwCBDA*
Hinds, Thomas 1780-1840 *BiDrAC, WhAm H*
Hinds, Warren Elmer 1876-1936 *NatCAB 29,
WhAm 1*
Hinds, William Alfred 1833-1910 *WhAm 1*

Hinds, William Lawyer 1874- *WhAm 5*
Hindus, Maurice Gerschon 1891-1969 *WhAm 5*
Hine, Charles 1827-1871 *NewYHSD*
Hine, Charles Daniel 1845-1923 *BiDAmEd,*
NatCAB 19, WhAm 1
Hine, Charles DeLano 1867-1927 *DcAmB,*
NatCAB 38, WhAm 1
Hine, Clint C 1884-1935 *WhAm 1*
Hine, Francis Lyman d1927 *WhAm 1*
Hine, Henry George 1811-1895 *IlBEAAW*
Hine, James Wallace 1850-1937 *NatCAB 28*
Hine, Lewis Wickes 1874-1940 *BnEnAmA,*
DcAmB S2, WebAB
Hine, Robert V 1921- *EncAAH, REnAW*
Hine, Samuel Kirtland 1867-1942 *NatCAB 34*
Hine, Samuel P *NewYHSD*
Hinebaugh, William Henry 1867-1943 *BiDrAC,*
WhAm 1
Hiner, Edwin Morrison 1871-1948 *NatCAB 36*
Hinerfeld, Benjamin 1896-1957 *WhAm 3*
Hines, Charles 1888-1966 *WhAm 4*
Hines, Cloyd Albert 1886-1947 *NatCAB 36*
Hines, Duncan 1880-1959 *NatCAB 43,*
WebAB, WhAm 3
Hines, Earl Kenneth 1905- *EncAB*
Hines, Earle Garfield 1880-1962 *WhAm 4*
Hines, Edgar Alphonso 1867-1940 *WhAm 1*
Hines, Edward 1863-1931 *NatCAB 42,*
WhAm 1
Hines, Edward Norris 1870-1938 *NatCAB 28,*
WhAm 1
Hines, Edward Warren 1858- *WhAm 1*
Hines, Frank Thomas 1879-1960 *WhAm 3A*
Hines, Franklin Bannon 1890-1964 *NatCAB 52*
Hines, Harry Hayes 1876-1929 *NatCAB 23*
Hines, Harry Matlock 1893-1963 *WhAm 4*
Hines, James Kollock 1852-1932 *WhAm 1*
Hines, John Fore 1870- *WhAm 5*
Hines, John Leonard 1868-1968 *ApCAB X,*
WebAMB, WhAm 5
Hines, Laurence Edward 1896-1955 *WhAm 3*
Hines, Linnaeus Neal 1871-1936 *WhAm 1*
Hines, Murray Arnold 1876- *WhAm 5*
Hines, Ralph J 1900-1950 *WhAm 3*
Hines, Richard d1851 *BiAUS, BiDrAC,*
WhAm H
Hines, Russell Jack 1906-1965 *NatCAB 51*
Hines, Thomas Henry 1838-1898 *NatCAB 12*
Hines, Walker Downer 1870-1934 *AmBi,*
ApCAB X, DcAmB S1, NatCAB 24,
WhAm 1
Hines, William Henry 1856-1914 *BiDrAC*
Hingeley, Joseph Beaumont 1856-1929
WhAm 1
Hingham *NewYHSD*
Hingston, Lady Margaret Josephine
WomWWA 14
Hingston, Sir William Hales 1829- *ApCAB Sup*
Hiniker, Jerome Joseph 1912-1969 *NatCAB 54*
Hinitt, Frederick William 1866-1928
NatCAB 14, NatCAB 22, WhAm 1
Hinke, Frederick William 1900-1960 *WhAm 4*
Hinke, William John 1871-1947 *WhAm 2*
Hinkel, Charles Luther 1910-1956 *NatCAB 45*
Hinkel, David *NewYHSD*
Hinkle, Abbie A *WomWWA 14*
Hinkle, Anthony Howard 1842-1911
NatCAB 17
Hinkle, Beatrice Moses 1874-1953 *DcAmB S5,*
WhAm 3, WomWWA 14
Hinkle, Clarence Keiser 1880-1960 *IlBEAAW,*
NatCAB 49
Hinkle, Elmer Forry 1907-1957 *NatCAB 47,*
WhAm 4
Hinkle, Frederick Wallis 1870-1950 *WhAm 3*
Hinkle, James Fielding 1862-1951 *NatCAB 41*
Hinkle, James Fielding 1862-1951 *WhAm 4*
Hinkle, Ross Oel 1883- *WhAm 3*
Hinkle, Thomas Clark 1876-1949 *WhAm 2*
Hinkle, Thornton Mills 1840-1920 *WhAm 1*
Hinkley *NewYHSD*
Hinkley, Alonzo Gibbs 1876-1965 *WhAm 4*
Hinkley, H Lawrence 1896-1962 *NatCAB 50,*
WhAm 4
Hinkley, Holmes 1793-1866 *ApCAB,*
NatCAB 5
Hinkley, J William, III 1905-1967 *WhAm 4*
Hinkley, James *NewYHSD*

Hinkley, John 1864-1940 *NatCAB 30,*
WhAm 1
Hinkley, Susan Heywood 1861- *WomWWA 14*
Hinks, Edward W 1830- *Drake*
Hinkson, J H Ward 1895-1973 *NatCAB 57*
Hinkson, Joseph Humphrey 1865-1926
NatCAB 22
Hinman, Alice Hamlin d1934 *WomWWA 14*
Hinman, Alice Hamlin 1867-1934 *NatCAB 26*
Hinman, Alice Hamlin 1868-1934 *WhAm 1*
Hinman, Beach Isaac 1829-1905 *NatCAB 17*
Hinman, Benjamin 1720-1810 *ApCAB, Drake,*
NatCAB 11, TwCBDA
Hinman, Charles 1932- *BnEnAmA*
Hinman, Clark Titus 1817-1854 *NatCAB 5*
Hinman, Clarke Titus 1817-1854 *ApCAB,*
TwCBDA
Hinman, Dale Durkee 1891-1949 *WhAm 3*
Hinman, David C *NewYHSD*
Hinman, E Harold 1904-1971 *NatCAB 57,*
WhAm 5
Hinman, Edward Chauncey 1852-1921
NatCAB 19
Hinman, Elisha 1734-1805 *DcAmB, TwCBDA,*
WhAm H
Hinman, Elisha 1734-1807 *ApCAB, Drake,*
NatCAB 11
Hinman, George Elijah 1870- *WhAm 5*
Hinman, George Warren 1869-1940 *WhAm 1*
Hinman, George Wheeler 1863-1927
NatCAB 11
Hinman, George Wheeler 1864-1927 *DcAmB,*
WhAm 1
Hinman, Harold J 1877-1955 *WhAm 3*
Hinman, Harvey DeForest 1864-1954 *WhAm 3*
Hinman, Hazen Beecher 1892-1964 *NatCAB 51*
Hinman, Ida *AmWom*
Hinman, Joel 1802-1870 *ApCAB, DcAmB,*
NatCAB 11, WhAm H
Hinman, John 1802-1870 *BiAUS, Drake*
Hinman, Royal Ralph 1785-1868 *ApCAB,*
Drake, NatCAB 11, TwCBDA
Hinman, Russell 1853-1912 *WhAm 1*
Hinman, Thomas Philip 1870-1931 *NatCAB 25,*
WhAm 1
Hinmatonyalakit *WebAB*
Hinojosa, Pedro De d1553 *ApCAB*
Hinoyossa, Alexander D' *ApCAB*
Hinrichs, Carl Gustav 1878- *WhAm 6*
Hinrichs, Charles F A 1814- *NatCAB 1*
Hinrichs, Gustav 1850-1942 *NatCAB 38*
Hinrichs, Gustavus Detlef 1836-1923 *ApCAB,*
NatCAB 21, WhAm 1, WhAm 4
Hinrichs, Henry Frederick 1866-1940
NatCAB 31
Hinrichsen, Annie 1879- *WomWWA 14*
Hinrichsen, Walter 1907- *WhAm 5*
Hinrichsen, William Henry 1850-1907 *BiDrAC,*
WhAm 4
Hinsch, Charles Arthur 1865-1928 *NatCAB 22,*
NatCAB 24, WhAm 1
Hinsdale, Burke Aaron 1837-1900 *AmBi,*
ApCAB, BiDAmEd, DcAmB,
NatCAB 10, TwCBDA, WhAm 1
Hinsdale, Ellen Clarinda 1864- *WhAm 4,*
WomWWA 14
Hinsdale, Grace Webster 1832- *NatCAB 9,*
WhAm 4
Hinsdale, Guy 1858-1948 *WhAm 2*
Hinsdale, John Wetmore 1843-1921 *TwCBDA,*
WhAm 1
Hinsdale, Lester Jesse 1870-1929 *NatCAB 23*
Hinsdale, Richard Law 1826-1856 *NewYHSD*
Hinsdale, Robert Graham 1833-1889
NatCAB 30, TwCBDA
Hinsdale, Wilbert B 1851-1944 *WhAm 2*
Hinshaw, Carl 1894-1956 *WhAm 3*
Hinshaw, David Schull 1882-1953 *DcAmB S5,*
WhAm 3
Hinshaw, Edmund Howard 1860-1932 *BiDrAC,*
WhAm 4, WhAmP
Hinshaw, John Carl Williams 1894-1956
BiDrAC, WhAmP
Hinshaw, Joseph Howard 1890-1973 *WhAm 5*
Hinshaw, Melvin Taliaferro 1878- *WhAm 6*
Hinshaw, Virgil Goodman 1876-1952
NatCAB 42, WhAm 3
Hinshaw, William Wade 1867-1947 *NatCAB 38,*

WhAm 2
Hinshelwood, Sir Cyril Norman 1897-1967
AsBiEn, DcScB, McGEWB, WhAm 4,
WhAm 5
Hinshelwood, Robert 1812-1875? *NewYHSD*
Hinsman, Carl B 1873- *WhAm 5*
Hinson, Charles Wesley 1884-1914 *NatCAB 16*
Hinson, M R 1891-1952 *WhAm 4*
Hinson, Noel Bertram 1885-1958 *WhAm 3*
Hinson, Walter Benwell 1862-1926 *WhAm 1*
Hintenach, Andrew 1844- *ApCAB Sup*
Hintenach, Tobias 1844- *TwCBDA*
Hinton, Charles Louis 1869-1950 *WhAm 3*
Hinton, Sir Christopher 1901- *AsBiEn*
Hinton, Edward Wilcox 1868-1936 *NatCAB 26,*
WhAm 1
Hinton, H D 1895-1965 *WhAm 4*
Hinton, Harold Boaz 1898-1954 *NatCAB 42,*
WhAm 3
Hinton, Mrs. Howard 1834-1921 *NewYHSD*
Hinton, Isaac Taylor 1799-1847 *ApCAB*
Hinton, James William 1894-1973 *WhAm 5*
Hinton, John Henry 1827-1905 *NatCAB 2*
Hinton, John Howard 1791-1873 *ApCAB,*
Drake
Hinton, L W 1907-1972 *WhAm 6*
Hinton, Mary Hilliard *WomWWA 14*
Hinton, Oscar Myers 1883-1947 *NatCAB 38*
Hinton, Raymond J d1958 *WhAm 3*
Hintz, Alfred Edward 1906-1962 *WhAm 4*
Hintz, Howard William 1903-1964 *WhAm 4*
Hipp, Harold Richard 1913-1968 *NatCAB 56*
Hippach, Louis Albert 1864-1935 *NatCAB 26*
Hipparchus *McGEWB*
Hipparchus d127?BC *DcScB Sup*
Hipparchus 190?BC-120?BC *AsBiEn*
Hipparchus Of Rhodes *DcScB*
Hippenheimer *NewYHSD*
Hipper, Franz 1863-1932 *WhoMilH*
Hippias Of Elis *DcScB*
Hipple, Alpheus Hugh 1865- *WhAm 1*
Hipple, Frank K 1839-1906 *WhAm 1*
Hippocrates 460BC-370?BC *AsBiEn*
Hippocrates 460BC-375BC *BiHiMed*
Hippocrates 460?BC-377?BC *McGEWB*
Hippocrates Of Chios *DcScB*
Hippocrates Of Cos 460BC-370?BC *DcScB*
Hippolyte, Louis Mondestin Florvil 1827-1896
ApCAB Sup
Hipsher, Edward Ellsworth 1871-1948 *WhAm 2*
Hipsley, Elmer R 1913- *WhAm 5*
Hirayama, Kiyotsugu 1874-1943 *DcScB*
Hird, Lewis Arthur 1889-1954 *NatCAB 41*
Hire, Charles 1887-1952 *WhAm 3*
Hires, Charles Elmer 1851-1937 *DcAmB S2,*
WebAB, WhAm HA, WhAm 4
Hires, George 1835-1911 *BiDrAC*
Hires, Harrison Streeter 1887-1962 *WhAm 4*
Hirn, Gustave Adolfe 1815-1890 *DcScB*
Hirnoe, Mabel Stevens 1874- *WomWWA 14*
Hirohito 1901- *McGEWB, WhWW-II*
Hirons, Frederic C 1882-1942 *WhAm 1,*
WhAm 2
Hiroshige, Ando 1797-1858 *McGEWB*
Hirsch, Alcan 1885-1938 *WhAm 1*
Hirsch, Charles Sidney 1863-1938 *NatCAB 29*
Hirsch, Daniel 1861-1940 *NatCAB 34*
Hirsch, Edwin Frederick 1886-1972 *WhAm 5*
Hirsch, Emil Gustav 1851-1923 *AmBi, DcAmB,*
WhAm 1
Hirsch, Emil Gustav 1852-1923 *NatCAB 2,*
TwCBDA
Hirsch, Frank E 1864- *WhAm 4*
Hirsch, Gustav 1876-1959 *NatCAB 47,*
WhAm 3
Hirsch, Harold 1881-1939 *NatCAB 37,*
WhAm 1
Hirsch, Irene Dorothea 1903-1970 *WhAm 5*
Hirsch, Isaac Einstein 1859-1942 *NatCAB 49,*
WhAm 2
Hirsch, Isaac Seth 1880-1942 *DcAmB S3,*
WhAm 6
Hirsch, Jerome Byron 1885-1950 *NatCAB 47*
Hirsch, John Frederick 1851- *WhAm 4*
Hirsch, Julius 1882-1961 *NatCAB 50,*
WhAm 4
Hirsch, Max 1877-1968 *WhAm 5*
Hirsch, Morris 1906-1967 *NatCAB 54*

Hirsch, Samuel 1815-1889 *ApCAB*
Hirsch, Solomon 1839-1902 *NatCAB 13*
Hirschbein, Peretz 1880-1948 *DcAmB S4*
Hirschberg, Alice 1856- *AmWom*
Hirschberg, Francis D 1854- *NatCAB 12*
Hirschberg, Henry 1879-1963 *NatCAB 52*
Hirschberg, Michael Henry 1847-1929
  NatCAB 41, WhAm 1
Hirschberg, Sanford Leon 1906-1965 *WhAm 4*
Hirschensohn, Chaim 1857-1935 *DcAmB S1*
Hirschey, Urban Carl 1881-1944 *NatCAB 40*
Hirschfeld, Hans M 1899-1961 *WhAm 4*
Hirschfelder, Arthur Douglass 1879-1942
  WhAm 2
Hirschfelder, Joseph Oakland 1854-1920
  WhAm 1
Hirschhorn, Fred 1870-1946 *WhAm 2*
Hirschler, Daniel Arthur 1883-1955
  NatCAB 44
Hirschler, Frederic Salz 1902-1968 *WhAm 5*
Hirschman, Frank Henry 1875-1948
  NatCAB 47
Hirschman, Louis Jacob 1878- *WhAm 6*
Hirschy, Noah Calvin 1867-1925 *NatCAB 20*
Hirsh, Allan Mortimer 1878-1951 *NatCAB 41*
Hirsh, David 1859-1917 *NatCAB 17*
Hirsh, Harry Bernheim 1864-1944 *NatCAB 40*
Hirsh, Herbert William 1902-1971 *WhAm 5*
Hirsh, Hugo 1848-1933 *WhAm 1*
Hirsh, Leonard Frederick 1901-1962
  NatCAB 50
Hirsh, Samuel 1852-1916 *NatCAB 24*
Hirsh, Siegfried *NewYHSD*
Hirshberg, Albert Simon 1909-1973 *WhAm 6*
Hirshberg, Herbert Simon 1879-1955 *DcAmLiB,
  WhAm 3*
Hirshberg, Leonard Keene 1877- *WhAm 5*
Hirshfeld, Clarence Floyd 1881-1939
  NatCAB 29, WhAm 1
Hirshfeld, Elizabeth 1878- *WomWWA 14*
Hirshfield, Benjamin Lewis 1873-1937
  NatCAB 27
Hirshfield, Morris 1872-1946 *BnEnAmA*
Hirshheimer, Albert 1840-1924 *NatCAB 42*
Hirson, Herbert Lester 1912-1960 *NatCAB 48*
Hirst, Barton Cooke 1861-1935 *DcAmB S1,
  NatCAB 45, WhAm 1*
Hirst, Mrs. Charles D 1865- *WomWWA 14*
Hirst, Edgar Clarkson 1882-1972 *NatCAB 57*
Hirst, Henry Beck 1813-1874 *ApCAB, Drake*
Hirst, Henry Beck 1817-1874 *DcAmB,
  NatCAB 13, WhAm H*
Hirst, Jesse Watson 1864-1952 *NatCAB 42*
Hirst, Otto Christian 1890-1961 *NatCAB 48*
Hirst, Robert Lincoln 1864- *WhAm 4*
Hirszfeld, Ludwig 1884-1954 *DcScB*
Hirt, Arthur 1903-1950 *NatCAB 39*
Hirt, L *NewYHSD*
Hirt, William Elmer 1881-1963 *NatCAB 50*
Hirt, Zoe Isabella 1877- *WomWWA 14*
Hirth, Emma P d1951 *WhAm 3*
Hirth, Friedrich 1845-1927 *WhAm 1*
Hirth, William Andrew 1875-1940 *DcAmB S2*
His, Wilhelm, Jr. 1863-1934 *BiHiMed*
His, Wilhelm, Sr. 1831-1904 *BiHiMed, DcScB*
Hisaw, Frederick Lee 1891-1972 *WhAm 5*
Hiscock, Charles Eber 1854-1920 *NatCAB 19*
Hiscock, Frank 1834-1914 *ApCAB, BiDrAC,
  NatCAB 12, TwCBDA, WhAm 1,
  WhAmP*
Hiscock, Frank Harris 1856-1946 *DcAmB S4,
  WhAm 2*
Hiscox, David 1837- *NatCAB 1*
Hiscox, Gardner Dexter *NewYHSD*
Hise, Elijah 1801-1867 *DcAmB, NatCAB 12,
  TwCBDA*
Hise, Elijah 1802-1867 *BiAUS, BiDrAC,
  WhAm H*
Hisgen, Thomas Louis 1858-1925 *NatCAB 42,
  WhAm 1*
Hisinger, Wilhelm 1766-1852 *AsBiEn, DcScB*
Hislop, Thomas *NewYHSD*
Hiss, Alger 1904- *EncAB, WebAB*
Hiss, Philip Hanson, Jr. 1868-1913 *NatCAB 16*
Hitch, Arthur Martin 1875-1956 *WhAm 3*
Hitch, Calvin Milton 1869- *WhAm 5*
Hitch, Emmet Francis 1882-1956 *NatCAB 42*
Hitch, Henry Charles 1884-1967 *NatCAB 55*

Hitch, Mayhew Robinson 1867-1956
  NatCAB 47
Hitch, Robert Mark 1872-1940 *ApCAB X,
  NatCAB 17, NatCAB 36, WhAm 1*
Hitchcock, Abner Edward 1853- *WhAm 4*
Hitchcock, Albert Harvey 1856-1926
  NatCAB 20
Hitchcock, Albert Spear 1865-1935 *AmBi,
  DcScB Sup, NatCAB 26, WhAm 1*
Hitchcock, Alfred 1813-1874 *ApCAB,
  NatCAB 4, WhAm H*
Hitchcock, Alfred 1814-1874 *TwCBDA*
Hitchcock, Alfred Joseph 1899- *McGEWB,
  WebAB*
Hitchcock, Alfred Marshall 1868-1941
  WhAm 3
Hitchcock, Alvirus Nelson 1854- *WhAm 4*
Hitchcock, Caroline Hanks 1863- *WhAm 4,
  WomWWA 14*
Hitchcock, Caroline Judson 1857-
  WomWWA 14
Hitchcock, Charles *NewYHSD*
Hitchcock, Charles A 1859-1932 *WhAm 1,
  WhAm 1C*
Hitchcock, Charles Baker 1906-1969 *WhAm 5*
Hitchcock, Charles Henry 1836-1919 *AmBi,
  ApCAB, DcAmB, NatCAB 12, TwCBDA,
  WhAm 1*
Hitchcock, Charles Wilcox 1871-1955
  NatCAB 49
Hitchcock, Curtice 1892-1946 *WhAm 2*
Hitchcock, D Howard 1861-1943 *NatCAB 41*
Hitchcock, Daniel 1741-1777 *ApCAB, Drake*
Hitchcock, David 1773-1832? *ApCAB*
Hitchcock, DeWitt C *NewYHSD*
Hitchcock, Edward *NewYHSD*
Hitchcock, Edward 1793-1864 *AmBi, ApCAB,
  BiDAmEd, DcAmB, DcAmReB, DcScB,
  Drake, NatCAB 5, TwCBDA, WhAm H*
Hitchcock, Edward 1828-1911 *AmBi, ApCAB,
  BiDAmEd, DcAmB, NatCAB 13,
  TwCBDA, WhAm 1*
Hitchcock, Edward 1854- *NatCAB 4,
  TwCBDA*
Hitchcock, Embury Asbury 1866-1948 *WhAm 2*
Hitchcock, Enos 1744-1803 *ApCAB, DcAmB,
  Drake, NatCAB 9, TwCBDA, WhAm H*
Hitchcock, Ernest Dexter 1884-1967
  NatCAB 53
Hitchcock, Ethan Allen 1798-1870 *AmBi,
  ApCAB, DcAmB, Drake, NatCAB 11,
  TwCBDA, WebAMB, WhAm H*
Hitchcock, Ethan Allen 1835-1909 *AmBi,
  ApCAB Sup, BiDrUSE, DcAmB,
  NatCAB 11, NatCAB 32, TwCBDA,
  WhAm 1, WhAmP*
Hitchcock, Frank d1872 *DcAmB*
Hitchcock, Frank Harris 1867-1935 *BiDrUSE,
  DcAmB S1, NatCAB 14, NatCAB 27,
  WhAmP*
Hitchcock, Frank Harris 1869-1935 *AmBi,
  WhAm 1*
Hitchcock, Frank Lauren 1875-1957 *WhAm 3*
Hitchcock, Frederick Collamore 1864-1937
  WhAm 1
Hitchcock, Frederick Hills 1867-1928 *WhAm 1*
Hitchcock, Frederick Lyman 1837-1924
  NatCAB 19
Hitchcock, Gad d1803 *Drake*
Hitchcock, George 1850-1913 *NatCAB 15,
  WhAm 1*
Hitchcock, George Collier 1867- *WhAm 5*
Hitchcock, Gilbert Monell 1859-1934 *AmBi,
  BiDrAC, DcAmB S1, McGEWB,
  NatCAB 15, NatCAB 25, REnAW,
  WhAm 1, WhAmP*
Hitchcock, Halbert Kellogg 1865-1930
  NatCAB 24
Hitchcock, Harold Homer 1893-1955
  NatCAB 51
Hitchcock, Helen Sanborn Sargent 1870-
  BiCAW, NatCAB 18
Hitchcock, Henry 1791-1839 *NatCAB 11*
Hitchcock, Henry 1829-1902 *DcAmB,
  NatCAB 11, WhAm 1*
Hitchcock, Henry Booth 1887-1933 *WhAm 1*
Hitchcock, Henry Ethan 1822-1907 *NatCAB 8,
  TwCBDA*

Hitchcock, Henry Lawrence 1813-1873
  NatCAB 7, TwCBDA
Hitchcock, Herbert Emery 1867-1958 *BiDrAC,
  NatCAB 48, WhAm 4, WhAmP*
Hitchcock, James Ripley Wellman 1857-1918
  ApCAB, DcAmB
Hitchcock, Jane Elizabeth 1863-
  WomWWA 14
Hitchcock, Jessica M 1874- *WomWWA 14*
Hitchcock, Lauren Blakely 1900-1972 *WhAm 5*
Hitchcock, Lucius Wolcott 1868-1942 *WhAm 2*
Hitchcock, Mary Antoinette 1834- *AmWom*
Hitchcock, Mary E *WomWWA 14*
Hitchcock, Orra White 1796- *NewYHSD*
Hitchcock, Peter 1780-1853 *BiAUS*
Hitchcock, Peter 1781-1853 *AmBi, ApCAB,
  DcAmB, Drake, NatCAB 1*
Hitchcock, Peter 1781-1854 *BiDrAC,
  TwCBDA, WhAm H*
Hitchcock, Philip 1916-1960 *NatCAB 49*
Hitchcock, Phineas W 1831-1881 *BiAUS*
Hitchcock, Phineas Warren 1831-1881 *BiDrAC,
  REnAW, WhAmP*
Hitchcock, Phineas Warrener 1831-1881
  *ApCAB, DcAmB, NatCAB 7, TwCBDA,
  WhAm H*
Hitchcock, Raymond 1865-1929 *DcAmB*
Hitchcock, Reuben *NewYHSD*
Hitchcock, Ripley 1857-1918 *AmBi, DcAmB,
  NatCAB 18, TwCBDA, WhAm 1*
Hitchcock, Robert Bradley 1803-1888 *ApCAB,
  Drake*
Hitchcock, Robert Bradley 1804-1888 *TwCBDA*
Hitchcock, Romyn 1851-1923 *NatCAB 19,
  WhAm 4*
Hitchcock, Roswell Dwight 1817-1887 *ApCAB,
  DcAmB, NatCAB 2, NatCAB 7,
  TwCBDA, WhAm H*
Hitchcock, Samuel 1755-1813 *BiAUS,
  NatCAB 11*
Hitchcock, Samuel Austin 1784-1873 *ApCAB*
Hitchcock, Samuel Austin 1794-1873
  NatCAB 5, TwCBDA
Hitchcock, Samuel J *NewYHSD*
Hitchcock, Thomas 1831-1910 *NatCAB 17*
Hitchcock, Thomas 1860-1941 *NatCAB 36*
Hitchcock, Thomas, Jr. 1900-1944 *DcAmB S3,
  NatCAB 38, WebAB, WebAMB*
Hitchcock, William E 1823?- *NewYHSD*
Hitchcock, William Edwin 1869-1953
  NatCAB 41
Hitchens, Arthur Parker 1877-1949 *NatCAB 36,
  WhAm 2*
Hitchens, Ethel Bennett *WomWWA 14*
Hitchens, Joseph 1838-1893 *IIBEAAW*
Hitching, William R *NewYHSD*
Hitchings, Edson Fobes 1853-1937 *NatCAB 30*
Hitchings, Hector Morrison 1855- *NatCAB 17*
Hitchings, Henry d1902 *NewYHSD*
Hitchler, Theresa *WhAm 3*
Hitchler, Walter Harrison 1883-1959 *WhAm 3*
Hite, Bert Holmes 1866-1921 *WhAm 1*
Hite, George E, Jr. 1886-1950 *WhAm 3*
Hite, George Harrison d1880? *NewYHSD*
Hite, Jost d1760 *DcAmB, WhAm H*
Hite, Lewis Field 1852-1945 *WhAm 2*
Hiter, Frank Ambrose 1892-1955 *WhAm 3*
Hiteshew, Harry Otis 1882-1960 *NatCAB 47*
Hitler, Adolf 1889-1945 *McGEWB, WhAm 4,
  WhWW-II, WhoMilH*
Hitrec, Joseph George 1912-1972 *WhAm 5*
Hitschmann, Edward E 1871-1957 *NatCAB 46*
Hitt, Edward Greenway 1886-1962 *NatCAB 52*
Hitt, Ida A *WomWWA 14*
Hitt, Robert Melvin, Jr. 1914-1968 *WhAm 5*
Hitt, Robert Roberts 1834-1906 *BiDrAC,
  DcAmB, NatCAB 5, TwCBDA,
  WhAm 1, WhAmP*
Hitt, Robert Stockwell Reynolds 1876-1938
  NatCAB 14, NatCAB 28
Hittel, Charles J 1861-1938 *WhAm 4*
Hittell, Charles J 1861-1938 *IIBEAAW*
Hittell, John Shertzer 1825-1901 *DcAmB,
  REnAW, TwCBDA*
Hittell, John Sherzer 1825-1901 *NatCAB 22,
  WhAm 1*
Hittell, Theodore Henry 1830-1917 *DcAmB,
  NatCAB 22, TwCBDA*

Hittle, Harry Faron 1886-1957 *NatCAB 49*
Hittorf, Johann Wilhelm 1824-1914 *AsBiEn, DcScB*
Hitz, Henry Barnard 1867-1944 *NatCAB 33*
Hitz, John 1820?-1864 *ApCAB*
Hitz, John 1828-1908 *NatCAB 12, WhAm 1*
Hitz, Ralph 1891-1940 *WhAm 1*
Hitz, William 1872-1935 *WhAm 1*
Hitzig, Eduard 1838-1907 *DcScB*
Hively, John Lewis 1866- *NatCAB 17*
Hix, Asa Witt 1893-1960 *WhAm 4*
Hix, Charles H 1862-1933 *WhAm 1*
Hixon, Ernest Howard 1922-1972 *WhAm 5*
Hixon, Frank Pennell 1862-1931 *ApCAB X, NatCAB 34*
Hixson, Arthur Warren 1880- *WhAm 6*
Hixson, Fred Whitlo 1874-1924 *NatCAB 20, WhAm 1*
Hixson, William Aase 1922-1975 *WhAm 6*
Hjelm, Peter Jacob 1746-1813 *AsBiEn*
Hjorn, Oscar 1741-1792 *ApCAB*
Hjort, Alf 1877-1944 *NatCAB 33*
Hjort, Johan 1869-1948 *DcScB*
Hlavaty, Vaclav 1894-1969 *WhAm 5*
Ho, Chi Minh 1890-1969 *McGEWB, WhAm 5, WhWW-II*
Ho-Shen 1750-1799 *McGEWB*
Hoad, William Christian 1874-1962 *WhAm 4*
Hoadley, Charles Wesson 1878-1942 *NatCAB 31*
Hoadley, David 1774-1839 *DcAmB, NatCAB 25, WhAm H*
Hoadley, David 1806- *NatCAB 5*
Hoadley, George 1826- *ApCAB*
Hoadley, George Arthur 1848-1936 *WhAm 1*
Hoadley, John Chipman 1818-1886 *ApCAB, DcAmB, NatCAB 23, TwCBDA, WhAm H*
Hoadley, Leigh 1895-1975 *WhAm 6*
Hoadley, Loammi Ives 1790-1883 *ApCAB, Drake*
Hoadly, Benjamin 1706-1757 *BiHiMed*
Hoadly, Charles Jeremy 1828-1900 *ApCAB, TwCBDA*
Hoadly, Genevieve Groesbeck 1865- *WomWWA 14*
Hoadly, George 1826-1902 *DcAmB, NatCAB 3, TwCBDA, WhAm 1*
Hoadly, George 1858-1935 *NatCAB 27*
Hoag, Arthur Edmund 1885-1963 *NatCAB 50*
Hoag, Clarence Gilbert 1873- *WhAm 6*
Hoag, David Doughty 1848-1933 *WhAm 1*
Hoag, David Edward 1868-1932 *NatCAB 22*
Hoag, Ernest Bryant 1868-1924 *NatCAB 19, WhAm 1*
Hoag, Frank Stephen 1871-1963 *WhAm 4*
Hoag, George Grant 1872-1948 *NatCAB 36, WhAm 5*
Hoag, Gilbert Thomas 1899-1952 *WhAm 3*
Hoag, Helen Elisabeth *WomWWA 14*
Hoag, Joseph 1762-1846 *DcAmB, WhAm H*
Hoag, Junius Clarkson 1858-1930 *WhAm 1*
Hoag, Lynne Arthur 1892-1936 *NatCAB 30*
Hoag, Truman Harrison 1816-1870 *BiAUS, BiDrAC, WhAm H*
Hoag, William 1870-1953 *NatCAB 41*
Hoag, William Burnham 1876-1955 *NatCAB 42*
Hoag, William Ricketson 1859- *WhAm 4*
Hoage, Robert J 1877- *WhAm 5*
Hoagland, Charles Lee 1907-1946 *DcAmB S4*
Hoagland, Cornelius Nevius 1828- *NatCAB 2*
Hoagland, Denis Robert 1884-1949 *WhAm 3*
Hoagland, Dennis Robert 1884-1949 *DcAmB S4, DcScB, NatCAB 47*
Hoagland, Henry E 1886-1975 *WhAm 6*
Hoagland, John Hurle 1900-1962 *WhAm 4*
Hoagland, Mahlon Bush 1921- *AsBiEn*
Hoagland, Moses 1812-1865 *BiAUS, BiDrAC, WhAm H*
Hoagland, W *NewYHSD*
Hoagland, Warren Eugene 1904-1967 *NatCAB 53, WhAm 5*
Hoaglund, Joel Emmanuel *WebAB*
Hoan, Daniel Webster 1881-1961 *WhAm 4*
Hoar, Ebenezer Rockwood 1816-1895 *AmBi, ApCAB, BiAUS, BiDrAC, BiDrUSE, DcAmB, Drake, NatCAB 4, TwCBDA,*

WebAB, WhAm H, WhAmP
Hoar, George F 1826-1904 *Drake*
Hoar, George Frisbee 1826-1904 *NatCAB 1*
Hoar, George Frisbie 1826-1904 *AmBi, ApCAB, BiAUS, BiDrAC, DcAmB, EncAB, TwCBDA, WebAB, WhAm 1, WhAmP*
Hoar, Jonathan 1708-1771 *Drake*
Hoar, Jonathan 1720?-1771 *ApCAB*
Hoar, Leonard *Drake*
Hoar, Leonard 1629?-1675 *ApCAB*
Hoar, Leonard 1630-1675 *DcAmB, NatCAB 6, TwCBDA, WhAm H*
Hoar, Rockwood 1855-1906 *BiDrAC, WhAm 1, WhAmP*
Hoar, Roger Sherman 1887-1963 *ApCAB X, NatCAB 50*
Hoar, Samuel 1778-1856 *AmBi, BiDrAC, DcAmB, Drake, NatCAB 22, WebAB, WhAm H, WhAmP*
Hoar, Samuel 1788-1856 *ApCAB, BiAUS, TwCBDA*
Hoar, Samuel 1845-1904 *NatCAB 20*
Hoar, Sherman 1860-1898 *BiDrAC, TwCBDA, WhAmP*
Hoard, Charles Brooks 1805-1886 *BiAUS, BiDrAC, TwCBDA, WhAm H*
Hoard, Charles DeVillers 1857-1915 *NatCAB 17*
Hoard, William Dempster 1836-1918 *AmBi, DcAmB, NatCAB 12, NatCAB 16, TwCBDA, WebAB, WhAm 1*
Hoard, William Demptster 1836-1918 *EncAAH*
Hoare, Elmer Joseph 1902-1971 *WhAm 5*
Hoban, Edward Francis 1878-1966 *WhAm 4*
Hoban, James d1831 *BiAUS*
Hoban, James 1758-1831 *NatCAB 24*
Hoban, James 1762-1831 *AmBi, BnEnAmA, DcAmB, WebAB, WhAm H*
Hoban, Michael John 1853-1926 *ApCAB Sup, NatCAB 12, TwCBDA, WhAm 1*
Hobart, Aaron 1787-1858 *ApCAB, BiAUS, BiDrAC, Drake, TwCBDA, WhAm H*
Hobart, Alice Tisdale 1882-1967 *WhAm 4*
Hobart, Alvah Sabin 1847-1930 *WhAm 1*
Hobart, Augustus Charles 1822-1886 *ApCAB*
Hobart, Elijah *NewYHSD*
Hobart, Fannie Tuttle *AmWom*
Hobart, Franklin Gatfield 1864-1960 *NatCAB 48, WhAm 4*
Hobart, Garret Augustus 1844-1899 *AmBi, ApCAB Sup, BiDrAC, BiDrUSE, DcAmB, NatCAB 11, TwCBDA, WebAB, WhAm 1, WhAmP*
Hobart, George Vere 1867-1926 *WhAm 1*
Hobart, Henry Metcalf 1868-1946 *WhAm 2*
Hobart, Horace Reynolds 1839-1928 *WhAm 1*
Hobart, Ida Sprague 1856- *WomWWA 14*
Hobart, John Henry 1775-1830 *ApCAB, DcAmB, DcAmReB, Drake, McGEWB, NatCAB 1, TwCBDA, WhAm H*
Hobart, John Henry 1817-1889 *ApCAB, TwCBDA*
Hobart, John Sloss 1738-1805 *ApCAB, BiAUS, BiDrAC, DcAmB, Drake, NatCAB 2, TwCBDA, WhAm H*
Hobart, Lewis Parsons 1873-1954 *WhAm 3*
Hobart, Mrs. Lowell Fletcher 1869- *WhAm 5*
Hobart, Marie Elizabeth Jefferys 1860-1928 *WhAm 1*
Hobart, Marie Elizabeth Jeffreys 1860-1928 *WomWWA 14*
Hobart, Noah 1705-1773 *ApCAB, Drake*
Hobart, Peter 1604-1678 *ApCAB*
Hobart, Sarah Dyer 1845- *AmWom*
Hobbes, John Oliver 1867-1906 *AmBi, ApCAB Sup*
Hobbes, Thomas 1588-1679 *DcScB, McGEWB*
Hobbie, Henry Martin 1880-1944 *WhAm 3*
Hobbie, Selah Reeve 1797-1854 *ApCAB, BiAUS, BiDrAC, Drake, WhAm H*
Hobbins, James R 1883-1949 *WhAm 3*
Hobbins, Mary Newton 1858- *WomWWA 14*
Hobble, Deborah Sharp 1918-1969 *WhAm 5*
Hobbs, Alfred Charles 1812-1891 *DcAmB, NatCAB 23, WhAm H*
Hobbs, Allan Wilson 1885-1960 *WhAm 4*

Hobbs, Anna Nightingale Warren 1882- *WomWWA 14*
Hobbs, Charles Seright 1909-1971 *WhAm 5*
Hobbs, Charles Wood 1842-1929 *WhAm 1*
Hobbs, Clarence Whitman 1878-1944 *NatCAB 33*
Hobbs, Edward H 1835-1907 *WhAm 1*
Hobbs, Elizabeth Kittredge 1876- *WomWWA 14*
Hobbs, Elon St. Clair 1863-1948 *NatCAB 37*
Hobbs, Franklin Warren 1868-1955 *WhAm 3*
Hobbs, G W *NewYHSD*
Hobbs, George Sayward 1859-1945 *NatCAB 34, WhAm 4*
Hobbs, Gustavus Warfield, Jr. 1876-1957 *WhAm 3*
Hobbs, Ichabod Goodwin 1843-1918 *WhAm 1*
Hobbs, James Randolph d1942 *WhAm 2*
Hobbs, John Edward 1829-1919 *WhAm 1*
Hobbs, John Weston 1889-1968 *NatCAB 53, WhAm 4A*
Hobbs, John William 1882-1951 *NatCAB 38*
Hobbs, Leland Stanford 1892-1966 *WhAm 4*
Hobbs, Lewis Lyndon 1849- *TwCBDA, WhAm 4*
Hobbs, Lucy B *NotAW*
Hobbs, Marabeth 1888- *WomWWA 14*
Hobbs, Mary Everett Marshall 1863- *BiCAW, WomWWA 14*
Hobbs, Morris Henry 1892-1967 *WhAm 4*
Hobbs, Nathan *NewYHSD*
Hobbs, Perry Lynes 1861-1912 *NatCAB 16, WhAm 4*
Hobbs, Ralph Waller 1872-1936 *WhAm 1*
Hobbs, Roe Raymond 1871-1933 *WhAm 1*
Hobbs, Roscoe Conklin 1880- *WhAm 6*
Hobbs, Samuel 1854-1929 *ApCAB X, NatCAB 23*
Hobbs, Samuel Francis 1887-1952 *BiDrAC, WhAm 3, WhAmP*
Hobbs, William Henry 1846-1915 *NatCAB 17*
Hobbs, William Herbert 1864-1953 *NatCAB 42, TwCBDA, WhAm 3*
Hobbs, William J 1854- *WhAm 4*
Hobbs, Willis Farrar 1854-1939 *NatCAB 30*
Hobby, Sir Charles 1650?-1714 *ApCAB, Drake*
Hobby, Oveta Culp 1905- *BiDrUSE, WebAMB*
Hobby, Oveta Culp 1931- *WhAmP*
Hobby, William 1707-1765 *ApCAB, Drake*
Hobby, William Pettus 1878-1964 *WhAm 4*
Hobdy, John Buford 1875- *WhAm 5*
Hobdy, William Cotton 1870-1938 *NatCAB 29*
Hobein, Charles Augustus 1881-1946 *NatCAB 35*
Hoben, Allan 1874-1935 *WhAm 1*
Hoben, Lindsay 1902-1967 *WhAm 4*
Hoberg, Ingemar Eric 1903-1971 *NatCAB 57*
Hoberg, Oscar William 1889-1963 *NatCAB 50*
Hoberman, Lewis Karl 1905-1969 *NatCAB 55*
Hobgood, Charles Goyne 1911-1972 *WhAm 6*
Hobgood, Frank P 1872- *WhAm 5*
Hobgood, Franklin P 1847-1924 *NatCAB 19*
Hobhouse, Leonard Trelawny 1864-1929 *McGEWB*
Hobler, Atherton W 1890-1974 *WhAm 6*
Hobler, Harriet Wells 1862- *WomWWA 14*
Hoblit, Harris Keys 1882-1960 *NatCAB 46*
Hoblitzell, Fetter Schrier 1838-1900 *BiDrAC*
Hoblitzell, John Dempsey, Jr. 1912-1962 *BiDrAC, WhAm 4*
Hoblitzelle, Harrison 1896-1949 *WhAm 2*
Hoblitzelle, Karl 1879-1967 *WhAm 4*
Hobson, A Augustus 1877- *WhAm 5*
Hobson, Alfred Norman 1848-1918 *WhAm 1*
Hobson, Benjamin Lewis 1859-1918 *WhAm 1*
Hobson, Carvie Gustavus 1838-1900 *WhoColR*
Hobson, Charles Walter 1867-1935 *NatCAB 28*
Hobson, Edward Henry 1825-1901 *ApCAB, DcAmB, NatCAB 5, TwCBDA, WhAm 1*
Hobson, Elizabeth Christophers Kimball 1831-1912 *NotAW*
Hobson, Elizabeth Macgill Bridges *WomWWA 14*
Hobson, Ernest William 1856-1933 *DcScB*
Hobson, Jesse Edward 1911-1970 *WhAm 5*
Hobson, John Peyton 1850-1934 *NatCAB 13,*

WhAm 1

Hobson, Joseph Reid Anderson 1867- *WhAm 4*
Hobson, Milburn 1883-1964 *NatCAB 51*
Hobson, Richmond Pearson 1870-1937 *AmBi, ApCAB Sup, BiDrAC, DcAmB S2, NatCAB 9, TwCBDA, WebAMB, WhAm 1*
Hobson, Robert Louis 1918-1973 *WhAm 5*
Hobson, Robert P 1893-1966 *WhAm 4*
Hobson, Sarah Matilda 1861- *BiCAW, WhAm 4*
Hobson, Stanley H 1892-1961 *WhAm 4*
Hobson, T Francis 1900-1966 *WhAm 4*
Hobson, Thayer 1897-1967 *WhAm 4*
Hobson, Wilder 1906-1964 *WhAm 4*
Hobson, William 1793-1842 *McGEWB*
Hobson, William Andrew 1862- *ApCAB X, WhAm 5*
Hobson, William Horace 1888-1960 *WhAm 4*
Hoca, Myron Myroslaw 1912-1969 *WhAm 5*
Hoch, August 1868-1919 *DcAmB, NatCAB 23, WhAm 1*
Hoch, Daniel Knabb 1866-1960 *BiDrAC, WhAm 5*
Hoch, Edward Wallis 1849-1925 *NatCAB 14, WhAm 1*
Hoch, Homer 1879-1949 *BiDrAC, WhAm 2, WhAmP*
Hoch, Paul H 1902-1964 *WhAm 4*
Hochbaum, Hans Weller 1881-1952 *WhAm 3*
Hochdoerfer, Richard 1854- *WhAm 4*
Hoche, Herman Emanuel 1913-1963 *WhAm 4*
Hoche, Louis Lazare 1768-1797 *WhoMilH*
Hochmuth, Bruno Arthur 1911-1967 *WhAm 4*
Hochschild, Berthold 1860-1928 *NatCAB 42*
Hochstein, Anthony *NewYHSD*
Hochstetter, Robert William 1873- *WhAm 5*
Hochwald, Fritz G 1897-1968 *WhAm 5*
Hochwalt, Albert Frederick 1869-1938 *WhAm 1*
Hochwalt, Frederick 1909-1966 *WhAm 4*
Hockaday, Ela 1876-1956 *NatCAB 42, WhAm 5*
Hockaday, Hugh 1892-1968 *IIBEAAW*
Hockema, Frank C 1892-1956 *NatCAB 43, WhAm 3*
Hockenbeamer, August Frederick 1871-1935 *NatCAB 27, WhAm 1*
Hockensmith, Wilbur Darwin 1878-1951 *WhAm 3*
Hocker, Elizabeth Key Hansbrough 1875- *WomWWA 14*
Hocker, Lon O 1873-1948 *NatCAB 37, WhAm 2*
Hocker, Ulysses Washington 1869-1955 *NatCAB 49*
Hocker, William Adam 1844-1918 *NatCAB 27, WhAm 4*
Hockett, Homer Carey 1875- *WhAm 5*
Hocking, Brian 1914-1974 *WhAm 6*
Hocking, William Ernest 1873-1966 *BiDAmEd, NatCAB 54, WebAB, WhAm 4*
Hockley, Chester Fox 1882-1963 *WhAm 4*
Hockstader, Leonard Albert 1879-1962 *WhAm 4*
Hodder, Alfred 1866-1907 *NatCAB 18, WhAm 1*
Hodder, Frank Heywood 1860-1935 *NatCAB 41, WhAm 1*
Hodder, Jessie Donaldson 1867-1931 *NotAW*
Hodder, Mary Gwinn 1861- *WomWWA 14*
Hoddinott, Mary Loretta 1934-1968 *WhAm 5*
Hoddock *NewYHSD*
Hodell, Charles Wesley 1872- *WhAm 1*
Hodes, Henry Irvng 1899-1962 *WhAm 4*
Hodes, Robert 1915-1966 *NatCAB 52*
Hodgdon, Anderson Dana 1890-1948 *WhAm 2*
Hodgdon, Charles 1866-1953 *NatCAB 42, WhAm 3*
Hodgdon, Frank Wellington 1856-1923 *WhAm 1*
Hodgdon, Frank Wilbert 1868- *WhAm 4*
Hodgdon, Frederick Crosby 1873-1946 *NatCAB 35*
Hodgdon, Sylvester Phelps 1830-1906 *NewYHSD*
Hodge, Archibald Alexander 1823-1886 *ApCAB, DcAmB, NatCAB 10, TwCBDA, WhAm H*

Hodge, Bachman Gladstone 1893-1961 *WhAm 4*
Hodge, Benjamin Louis 1824-1864 *BiDConf*
Hodge, Caspar Wistar 1830-1891 *NatCAB 10, TwCBDA*
Hodge, Caspar Wistar 1870-1937 *NatCAB 28, WhAm 1*
Hodge, Charles 1797-1878 *AmBi, ApCAB, DcAmB, DcAmReB, Drake, TwCBDA, WhAm H*
Hodge, Charles 1798-1878 *NatCAB 10*
Hodge, Charles Watson 1856-1936 *NatCAB 27*
Hodge, Clifton Fremont 1859- *WhAm 4*
Hodge, Clifton Tremont 1859- *TwCBDA*
Hodge, Edward B 1841-1906 *WhAm 1*
Hodge, Edward Blanchard 1875-1945 *WhAm 2*
Hodge, Edwin Rose, Jr. 1916-1965 *WhAm 4*
Hodge, Emma Carol 1857- *WomWWA 14*
Hodge, Frederick Webb 1864-1956 *ApCAB Sup, NatCAB 10, NatCAB 43, REnAW, TwCBDA, WhAm 3*
Hodge, George Baird 1828-1892 *ApCAB, BiDConf*
Hodge, George Washington 1845- *NatCAB 7*
Hodge, George Woolsey 1845-1929 *NatCAB 22*
Hodge, Helen Henry 1877- *WomWWA 14*
Hodge, Henry Wilson 1865-1919 *WhAm 1*
Hodge, Hugh Lenox 1796-1873 *ApCAB, DcAmB, TwCBDA, WhAm H*
Hodge, Hugh Lenox 1836-1881 *ApCAB, NatCAB 10, TwCBDA*
Hodge, Hugh Lenox 1864-1934 *WhAm 1*
Hodge, James Thatcher 1816-1871 *ApCAB, NatCAB 4*
Hodge, John Aspinwall 1831-1901 *TwCBDA, WhAm 1*
Hodge, John Reed 1893-1963 *NatCAB 51, WebAMB, WhAm 4*
Hodge, Kenneth LaVern 1912-1964 *WhAm 4*
Hodge, Mary DeVeaux 1848- *WomWWA 14*
Hodge, Oliver 1901-1968 *BiDAmEd, WhAm 4*
Hodge, Richard Morse 1864- *TwCBDA, WhAm 4*
Hodge, Samuel 1829-1892 *ApCAB, NatCAB 7*
Hodge, Tobe *WhAm 1*
Hodge, Virginia S Shedd 1854- *WomWWA 14*
Hodge, Walter Hartman 1896-1975 *WhAm 6*
Hodge, Walter Roberts 1884-1940 *WhAm 1*
Hodge, Willard Wellington 1884-1961 *WhAm 4*
Hodge, William Beach 1872-1947 *NatCAB 36*
Hodge, William Irvine 1905-1970 *WhAm 5*
Hodge, William Thomas 1874-1932 *DcAmB S1, NatCAB 14, WhAm 1*
Hodge, William Vallance Douglas 1903-1975 *WhAm 6*
Hodgen, John Thompson 1826-1882 *DcAmB, NatCAB 8, WhAm H*
Hodges, Abel Bixby Ward 1862-1942 *NatCAB 31*
Hodges, Addiear Lena 1889- *WhoColR*
Hodges, Adele Louise Goepper 1858- *WomWWA 14*
Hodges, Amory Glazier 1852-1917 *NatCAB 23*
Hodges, Anne Lamson DuBois 1877- *WomWWA 14*
Hodges, Arthur 1868- *WhAm 4*
Hodges, Asa 1822-1900 *BiDrAC*
Hodges, Asa 1823-1900 *BiAUS*
Hodges, Benjamin K 1814?- *NewYHSD*
Hodges, Brandon Patton 1903-1957 *WhAm 3*
Hodges, Campbell Blackshear 1881-1944 *WhAm 2*
Hodges, Charles 1894-1964 *NatCAB 52, WhAm 4*
Hodges, Charles Drury 1810-1884 *BiAUS, BiDrAC, WhAm H*
Hodges, Charles H 1859-1937 *WhAm 1*
Hodges, Charles Libbens 1847-1911 *WhAm 1*
Hodges, Courtney Hicks 1887-1966 *WebAMB, WhAm 4, WhWW-II, WhoMilH*
Hodges, Edward 1796-1876 *ApCAB*
Hodges, Edward Francis 1851-1916 *NatCAB 17*
Hodges, Frank 1863-1962 *NatCAB 50, WhAm 5*
Hodges, Frederick Walter 1864-1943 *NatCAB 32*
Hodges, George 1856-1919 *AmBi, DcAmB, NatCAB 22, TwCBDA, WhAm 1*

Hodges, George Hartshorn 1866-1947 *NatCAB 15, WhAm 2*
Hodges, George Tisdale 1789-1860 *BiAUS, BiDrAC, TwCBDA, WhAm H*
Hodges, Gilbert d1972 *WhAm 5*
Hodges, Gilbert Tennent 1872-1959 *WhAm 3*
Hodges, Harry Foote 1860-1929 *DcAmB, WebAMB, WhAm 1*
Hodges, Harry Marsh 1855-1923 *NatCAB 6, WhAm 4*
Hodges, Helen B *WomWWA 14*
Hodges, Henry Clay 1831-1917 *WhAm 1*
Hodges, Herbert Marion 1906-1966 *NatCAB 54*
Hodges, James Leonard 1790-1846 *BiAUS, BiDrAC, TwCBDA, WhAm H*
Hodges, John Cunyus 1892-1967 *NatCAB 53, WhAm 4, WhAm 5*
Hodges, John Sebastian Bach 1830-1915 *WhAm 1*
Hodges, Johnny 1907-1970 *WhAm 5*
Hodges, Joseph Gilluly 1909-1972 *WhAm 5*
Hodges, Leigh Mitchell 1876-1954 *NatCAB 40, WhAm 3*
Hodges, LeRoy 1888-1944 *WhAm 2*
Hodges, Lizzie Wetmore *WomWWA 14*
Hodges, Louise Threete *WhAm 5*
Hodges, Luther Hartwell 1898-1974 *BiDrUSE, WhAm 6*
Hodges, Margaret Roberts *WomWWA 14*
Hodges, Nathaniel 1629-1688 *BiHiMed*
Hodges, Nathaniel Dana Carlile 1852-1927 *DcAmLiB, NatCAB 12, WhAm 1*
Hodges, Richard Edward 1903-1962 *WhAm 4*
Hodges, Richard Gilbert 1909-1966 *WhAm 6*
Hodges, S H 1804-1875 *BiAUS*
Hodges, Silas Henry 1804-1875 *ApCAB, NatCAB 5*
Hodges, Thomas Edward 1858- *WhAm 4*
Hodges, Walter Edward 1860-1942 *WhAm 2*
Hodges, William Franklin 1877-1954 *WhAm 3*
Hodges, William Hamilton 1879-1943 *NatCAB 39*
Hodges, William Thomas 1881-1947 *NatCAB 34, WhAm 2*
Hodges, William V 1877-1965 *WhAm 4*
Hodghead, Beverly Lacy 1865-1928 *WhAm 1*
Hodgin, Charles Elkanah 1858-1934 *BiDAmEd, WhAm 4*
Hodgin, Cyrus Wilburn 1842-1908 *TwCBDA, WhAm 1*
Hodgin, Emily Caroline Chandler 1838- *AmWom*
Hodgins, Eric 1899-1971 *WhAm 5*
Hodgins, John George 1821- *ApCAB*
Hodgins, Thomas 1835- *ApCAB*
Hodgkin, Alan Lloyd 1914- *AsBiEn, McGEWB*
Hodgkin, Dorothy Crowfoot 1910- *AsBiEn*
Hodgkin, Henry Theodore 1877-1933 *WhAm 1*
Hodgkin, Thomas 1798-1866 *BiHiMed*
Hodgkin, Wilfred Reginald Haughton 1879- *WhAm 6*
Hodgkin, William Newton 1890-1961 *WhAm 4*
Hodgkins, Alton Ross 1890-1952 *WhAm 3*
Hodgkins, Howard Lincoln 1862-1931 *NatCAB 23, TwCBDA, WhAm 1*
Hodgkins, Louise Manning 1846-1935 *AmWom, TwCBDA, WhAm 1, WomWWA 14*
Hodgkins, William Candler 1854- *WhAm 1*
Hodgkinson, Arabella 1765?-1804 *ApCAB*
Hodgkinson, Eaton 1789-1861 *DcScB*
Hodgkinson, Francis 1867-1949 *DcAmB S4, WhAm 2*
Hodgkinson, John 1766-1805 *ApCAB*
Hodgkinson, John 1767-1805 *DcAmB, Drake, NatCAB 3, WhAm H*
Hodgkiss, James 1883-1961 *NatCAB 49*
Hodgman, Abbott 1834- *NatCAB 1*
Hodgman, Adelaide Knight 1858- *WomWWA 14*
Hodgman, Arthur Winfred 1869-1948 *NatCAB 37*
Hodgman, Burns Plummer 1875-1938 *NatCAB 29, WhAm 1*
Hodgman, George Barker 1866- *NatCAB 14*
Hodgman, Jennie Stanley 1857- *WomWWA 14*
Hodgman, T Morey 1859- *WhAm 4*

Hodgman, William Lansing 1854-1936
WhAm 1
Hodgsdon, Daniel Bascome 1836-1916 *TwCBDA,*
WhAm 1
Hodgson, Albert James 1858-1943 *WhAm 2*
Hodgson, Carey Vandervort 1880-1929
WhAm 1
Hodgson, Caspar Wistar 1868-1938 *WhAm 1*
Hodgson, Christman William 1830-1914
NewYHSD
Hodgson, Edward Reginald 1846-1920
NatCAB 36
Hodgson, Frances Eliza *NotAW*
Hodgson, Francis 1805-1877 *ApCAB*
Hodgson, Frank Corrin 1884-1968 *WhAm 5*
Hodgson, Fred Grady 1878-1965 *WhAm 4*
Hodgson, Harry 1874- *WhAm 5*
Hodgson, Hyland Lorraine 1892-1961
NatCAB 51
Hodgson, James D 1915- *BiDrUSE*
Hodgson, Joseph 1788-1869 *BiHiMed*
Hodgson, Joseph Frederick 1929-1970 *WhAm 5*
Hodgson, Joseph Park 1869- *WhAm 5*
Hodgson, Laurence Curran 1874-1937 *WhAm 1*
Hodgson, Marshall Goodwin Simms 1922-1968
WhAm 5
Hodgson, Mary Arthur McCullough 1881-
WomWWA 14
Hodgson, Morton Strahan 1889-1954
NatCAB 54, WhAm 3
Hodgson, Richard 1855-1905 *WhAm 1*
Hodgson, Sir Robert 1798-1880 *ApCAB*
Hodgson, Robert Willard 1893-1966 *WhAm 4*
Hodgson, Telfair 1840-1893 *NatCAB 2,*
TwCBDA
Hodgson, Thekla Roese 1901-1971 *WhAm 5*
Hodgson, William Brown 1801-1871 *DcAmB S1,*
WhAm H
Hodgson, William Roy 1892-1958 *WhAm 3*
Hodierna, Giovanni *DcScB*
Hoding, Thomas *NewYHSD*
Hodler, Ferdinand 1853-1918 *McGEWB*
Hodnette, John K 1902-1966 *WhAm 4*
Hodous, Lewis 1872-1949 *WhAm 2*
Hodson, Clarence 1868-1928 *ApCAB X,*
NatCAB 21, WhAm 1
Hodson, George Emerson 1853-1942
NatCAB 31
Hodson, William 1891-1943 *DcAmB S3,*
WhAm 2
Hodur, Francis 1866-1953 *DcAmB S5,*
DcAmReB, WhAm 5
Hoe, Evelyn Perry 1886- *WomWWA 14*
Hoe, Richard March 1812-1886 *AmBi, ApCAB,*
DcAmB, McGEWB, NatCAB 7,
TwCBDA, WebAB, WhAm H
Hoe, Robert 1784-1833 *AmBi, ApCAB,*
DcAmB, Drake, NatCAB 7, WhAm H
Hoe, Robert 1815-1884 *ApCAB*
Hoe, Robert 1839-1909 *AmBi, ApCAB,*
DcAmB, NatCAB 3, NatCAB 45,
TwCBDA, WhAm 1
Hoe, Robert 1876-1960 *WhAm 3*
Hoeber, Arthur 1854-1915 *WhAm 1*
Hoechst, Edward John 1915-1968 *WhAm 5*
Hoeck, Theodor Albert 1868- *WhAm 4*
Hoecken, Adrian 1815-1897 *REnAW*
Hoecken, Christian 1808-1851 *ApCAB,*
DcAmB, WhAm H
Hoecker, Wade Lee 1887-1958 *NatCAB 47*
Hoefeld, Norman 1897-1956 *WhAm 3*
Hoefer, Charles Wenzel 1891- *WhAm 3*
Hoefer, Elmer George 1882-1962 *NatCAB 49*
Hoefer, U W C *NewYHSD*
Hoeffler, Adolf 1825-1898 *NewYHSD*
Hoeffler, Adolf Johann 1826-1898 *IIBEAAW*
Hoeh, George *NewYHSD*
Hoehler, Fred Kenneth 1892-1969 *WhAm 5*
Hoehling, Adolph August 1839-1920 *WhAm 1*
Hoehling, Adolph August 1868-1941 *WhAm 2*
Hoehn, Kenneth William 1918-1972 *WhAm 5*
Hoeing, Charles 1871-1938 *WhAm 1*
Hoeing, Frederick Waldbridge 1907-1962
WhAm 4
Hoek, Martinus 1834-1873 *DcScB*
Hoekendijk, Johannes Christiaan 1912-1975
WhAm 6
Hoel, Libbie Beach 1858- *AmWom*

Hoelscher, Randolph Philip 1890-1972 *WhAm 5*
Hoelzel, John Philip 1883-1950 *NatCAB 43,*
WhAm 3
Hoen, Albert Berthold 1864-1956 *NatCAB 45*
Hoen, August 1817-1886 *DcAmB, NatCAB 24,*
WhAm H
Hoen, August 1825?- *NewYHSD*
Hoen, Ernest *NewYHSD*
Hoen, Henry *NewYHSD*
Hoene-Wronski, Jozef Maria 1776-1853
DcScB Sup
Hoenecke, Gustav Adolf Felix Theodor
1835-1908 *DcAmB*
Hoenig, Arthur Vincent 1877-1954 *NatCAB 44*
Hoenshel, Eli J 1846-1924 *WhAm 1,*
WhAm 1C
Hoeper, Matilda 1860- *WomWWA 14*
Hoepner, Erich 1886-1944 *WhoMilH*
Hoeppel, John Henry 1881- *BiDrAC,*
WhAm 6
Hoerman, Carl 1885-1955 *NatCAB 43*
Hoerman, Louise 1879- *WomWWA 14*
Hoermann, Rudolph Bernard 1872-1958
NatCAB 46
Hoerr, Charles Ferdinand 1869-1919
NatCAB 18
Hoerr, Normand Louis 1902-1958 *WhAm 4*
Hoerter, Charles Richard 1904-1974 *WhAm 6*
Hoes, Rose Gouverneur *BiCAW,*
WomWWA 14
Hoeven, Charles Bernard 1895- *BiDrAC,*
WhAmP
Hoeven, Jan VanDer 1801-1868 *DcScB*
Hoey, Clyde Roark 1877-1954 *BiDrAC,*
DcAmB S5, NatCAB 50, WhAm 3,
WhAmP
Hoey, James J 1877-1941 *WhAm 2*
Hoey, Mrs. John 1824- *Drake*
Hoey, Josephine 1824- *ApCAB*
Hoey, Matthew Joseph 1882-1920 *NatCAB 19*
Hof, Samuel 1870-1937 *WhAm 1*
Hofeller, Eli David 1867-1918 *NatCAB 19*
Hofer, Mari Ruef *WomWWA 14*
Hoff, Charles Worthington 1898-1965 *WhAm 4*
Hoff, Emanuel Buechley 1860-1928 *WhAm 1*
Hoff, Henry *NewYHSD*
Hoff, Henry Kuhn 1809-1878 *ApCAB, Drake,*
NatCAB 4, TwCBDA
Hoff, Jacobus H Van't 1852-1911 *BiHiMed*
Hoff, John Edward 1906-1966 *WhAm 4*
Hoff, John Francis 1814-1881 *TwCBDA*
Hoff, John VanRensselaer 1848-1920 *DcAmB,*
NatCAB 18, NatCAB 21, WhAm 1
Hoff, Karl Ernst Adolf Von 1771-1837 *DcScB*
Hoff, Nelville Soule 1854-1926 *WhAm 1*
Hoff, Olaf 1859-1924 *NatCAB 14, WhAm 1*
Hoff, William Bainbridge 1846-1903 *TwCBDA,*
WhAm 1
Hoffa, James Riddle 1913- *WebAB*
Hoffay, A A *NewYHSD*
Hoffecker, John Henry 1827-1900 *BiDrAC,*
WhAm 1
Hoffecker, Walter Oakley 1854-1934 *BiDrAC*
Hoffenstein, Samuel 1890-1947 *WhAm 2*
Hoffer, Eric 1902- *WebAB*
Hoffherr, Frederic G 1887-1956 *WhAm 3*
Hofflund, John Leslie 1892-1963 *WhAm 4*
Hoffman, Abram 1875-1958 *WhAm 3*
Hoffman, Abram J *NewYHSD*
Hoffman, Adolphus *NewYHSD*
Hoffman, Albert Adolph 1880-1954 *NatCAB 41*
Hoffman, Arnold 1903-1962 *WhAm 4*
Hoffman, Arthur G d1947 *WhAm 2*
Hoffman, Arthur Sullivant 1876- *WhAm 6*
Hoffman, Beekman Verplanck 1789-1834
ApCAB, Drake, TwCBDA
Hoffman, Burton C 1911-1953 *WhAm 3*
Hoffman, C W *NewYHSD*
Hoffman, Carl 1882-1946 *NatCAB 41,*
WhAm 2
Hoffman, Carl Henry 1896- *BiDrAC*
Hoffman, Catherine A Hopkins 1855-
WomWWA 14
Hoffman, Charles *NewYHSD*
Hoffman, Charles Fenno 1806-1884 *AmBi,*
ApCAB, DcAmB, Drake, NatCAB 8,
TwCBDA, WhAm H
Hoffman, Charles Frederick *NewYHSD*

Hoffman, Charles Frederick 1830-1897
NatCAB 7, TwCBDA
Hoffman, Charles Frederick 1834-1897
ApCAB Sup
Hoffman, Charles Frederick 1856-1919
WhAm 1
Hoffman, Charles Wesley 1870-1962
NatCAB 49, WhAm 5
Hoffman, Christian Balzac 1851-1915 *WhAm 1*
Hoffman, Clara Cleghorn 1831- *AmWom*
Hoffman, Clare Eugene 1875-1967 *BiDrAC,*
WhAm 4, WhAmP
Hoffman, Clifford Pierson 1903-1954
NatCAB 43
Hoffman, David *NewYHSD*
Hoffman, David 1784-1854 *ApCAB, DcAmB,*
Drake, NatCAB 7, TwCBDA, WhAm H
Hoffman, David Bancroft 1827- *ApCAB*
Hoffman, David Murray 1791-1878 *DcAmB,*
WhAm H
Hoffman, Dean Meck 1880-1968 *WhAm 5*
Hoffman, Doretta Schlaphoff 1912-1975
WhAm 6
Hoffman, Edward George 1878-1931
NatCAB 40, WhAm 1
Hoffman, Edward Richard 1879-1953 *WhAm 3*
Hoffman, Elmer Joseph 1899- *BiDrAC,*
WhAmP
Hoffman, Eugene Augustus 1829-1902
ApCAB Sup, DcAmB, NatCAB 6,
TwCBDA, WhAm 1
Hoffman, Frances Othenia 1890- *WhoColR*
Hoffman, Frank B 1888-1958 *IIBEAAW*
Hoffman, Frank Sargent 1852-1928 *NatCAB 21,*
TwCBDA, WhAm 1
Hoffman, Fred William 1887-1961 *NatCAB 53,*
WhAm 4
Hoffman, Frederick *NewYHSD*
Hoffman, Frederick John 1909-1967 *WhAm 5*
Hoffman, Frederick Ludwig 1865-1946
DcAmB S4, NatCAB 34, WhAm 2
Hoffman, George Edward 1863-1929
NatCAB 21
Hoffman, George Matthias 1870-1936 *WhAm 1*
Hoffman, George W 1823?- *NewYHSD*
Hoffman, Gustavus Adolphus 1832?-
NewYHSD
Hoffman, Harold Giles 1896-1954 *BiDrAC,*
WhAm 3, WhAmP
Hoffman, Harry Clyde 1877-1942 *NatCAB 35*
Hoffman, Harry Leslie 1871-1964 *WhAm 4*
Hoffman, Heman Leslie 1905-1971 *WhAm 5*
Hoffman, Henry William 1825-1895 *BiAUS,*
BiDrAC, TwCBDA, WhAm H
Hoffman, Herman S 1841-1912 *WhAm 1*
Hoffman, Horace Addison 1855- *TwCBDA,*
WhAm 2
Hoffman, Hugh French T 1896-1951 *WhAm 3*
Hoffman, Hugo William G 1863-1917
NatCAB 17
Hoffman, J Ogden 1858-1909 *NatCAB 30*
Hoffman, Jacob *NewYHSD*
Hoffman, James David 1868-1938 *WhAm 1*
Hoffman, James Franklin 1876- *WhAm 5*
Hoffman, James I 1893-1964 *WhAm 4*
Hoffman, John C 1883-1961 *WhAm 4*
Hoffman, John N 1804-1857 *ApCAB*
Hoffman, John Thompson 1828-1888 *ApCAB,*
BiAUS, DcAmB, Drake, NatCAB 3,
TwCBDA, WhAm H
Hoffman, John W 1871- *WhoColR*
Hoffman, John Washington 1867-1953
WhAm 3
Hoffman, John Wesley 1869- *TwCBDA*
Hoffman, John Wesley 1870- *WhAm 5*
Hoffman, John Wessley 1870- *WhoColR*
Hoffman, Josef Casimir 1876-1957 *WhAm 3*
Hoffman, Joseph Gilbert 1909-1974 *WhAm 6*
Hoffman, Josiah Ogden 1766-1837 *DcAmB,*
NatCAB 3, WhAm H
Hoffman, Josiah Ogden 1793-1856 *BiDrAC*
Hoffman, Josiah Ogden *see also* Hoffman, Ogden
Hoffman, Leon Walter 1915-1970 *NatCAB 55*
Hoffman, Leroy E 1893-1971 *WhAm 5*
Hoffman, Malvina Cornell d1966 *BiCAW,*
WomWWA 14
Hoffman, Malvina Cornell 1885-1966
NatCAB 55

Hoffman, Malvina Cornell 1887-1966
BnEnAmA, IlBEAAW, WhAm 4
Hoffman, Mark 1904-1975 *WhAm 6*
Hoffman, Mary Grohs 1857- *WomWWA 14*
Hoffman, Michael 1787-1848 *BiDrAC,*
NatCAB 11, TwCBDA, WhAm H
Hoffman, Michael 1788-1848 *ApCAB, BiAUS,*
Drake
Hoffman, Michael Joseph 1861-1925
NatCAB 35
Hoffman, Milton J 1886-1973 *WhAm 6*
Hoffman, Murray 1791-1878 *ApCAB,*
NatCAB 11, TwCBDA
Hoffman, Ogden d1856 *BiAUS*
Hoffman, Ogden 1793-1856 *ApCAB, DcAmB,*
NatCAB 11, WhAm H
Hoffman, Ogden 1794-1856 *BiAUS, TwCBDA*
Hoffman, Ogden 1799-1856 *Drake*
Hoffman, Ogden *see also* Hoffman, Josiah Ogden
Hoffman, Paul 1882-1943 *NatCAB 32*
Hoffman, Paul Gray 1891-1974 *WhAm 6*
Hoffman, Philip 1892-1968 *NatCAB 54*
Hoffman, Ralph 1870-1932 *WhAm 4*
Hoffman, Ralph *see also* Hoffmann, Ralph
Hoffman, Richard Curzon 1839-1926 *WhAm 1*
Hoffman, Richard H 1831-1909 *AmBi, ApCAB,*
DcAmB, NatCAB 26, WhAm 1
Hoffman, Richard William 1893-1975 *BiDrAC,*
WhAm 6
Hoffman, Roy 1869- *WhAm 5*
Hoffman, Samuel David 1900-1957 *WhAm 3*
Hoffman, Samuel Verplanck 1866-1942
NatCAB 12, NatCAB 31
Hoffman, Sarah 1742- *ApCAB*
Hoffman, Sophia Curtiss 1836- *AmWom*
Hoffman, Victor *NewYHSD*
Hoffman, W D 1884-1952 *WhAm 3*
Hoffman, Walter James 1846-1899 *TwCBDA*
Hoffman, Wickham 1821-1900 *ApCAB,*
DcAmB, NatCAB 12, TwCBDA,
WhAm H
Hoffman, William 1807-1884 *ApCAB,*
TwCBDA
Hoffman, William George 1882-1954 *WhAm 3*
Hoffman, William Henry 1881-1956
NatCAB 45
Hoffman, Zelia Krumbhaar 1867-1929
NatCAB 32
Hoffmann, E *NewYHSD*
Hoffmann, Ernst 1899-1956 *WhAm 3*
Hoffmann, Ernst Theodor Amadeus 1776-1822
McGEWB
Hoffmann, Francis Arnold 1822-1903 *DcAmB,*
WhAm 1
Hoffmann, Friedrich 1660-1742 *DcScB*
Hoffmann, John Adam 1882-1946 *NatCAB 35*
Hoffmann, Martha Muerman *WomWWA 14*
Hoffmann, Martin Hugh 1898-1963
NatCAB 50
Hoffmann, Max 1869-1927 *WhoMilH*
Hoffmann, Ralph 1870-1932 *WhAm 1*
Hoffmann, Ralph *see also* Hoffman, Ralph
Hoffmann, Robert 1865-1946 *NatCAB 35*
Hoffmann, William Frederick 1869-1939
NatCAB 29
Hoffmayer, W *NewYHSD*
Hofford, Martin Lowrie 1825- *ApCAB*
Hoffs, Marimus Adrian 1902-1971 *NatCAB 56*
Hoffses, Granville Ernest 1872-1956
NatCAB 45
Hoffstot, Frank Norton 1861-1938 *NatCAB 32,*
WhAm 1
Hoffstot, Henry Phipps 1886-1967 *NatCAB 54*
Hofft, Fred Bernhardt 1878-1955 *NatCAB 49*
Hoffy, Alfred M 1790?- *NewYHSD,*
WhAm H
Hoffzimmer, Ernest K 1877- *WhAm 5*
Hofhaimer, Paul 1459-1537 *McGEWB*
Hofman, Heinrich Oscar 1852-1924 *DcAmB,*
NatCAB 20, WhAm 1
Hofmann, August Wilhelm Von 1818-1892
AsBiEn, DcScB, McGEWB
Hofmann, Charles C *BnEnAmA*
Hofmann, Hans 1880-1966 *BnEnAmA,*
McGEWB, WebAB, WhAm 4
Hofmann, Herbert Andrew 1917-1971 *WhAm 5*
Hofmann, Hugo 1898-1972 *WhAm 5*
Hofmann, Josef Casimir 1876-1957 *NatCAB 53*

Hofmann, Julius 1865-1928 *WhAm 1*
Hofmann, Julius Valentine 1882-1965
NatCAB 53
Hofmannsthal, Hugo Von 1874-1929 *McGEWB*
Hofmeister, Henry 1890-1962 *NatCAB 48*
Hofmeister, Wilhelm Friedrich Benedikt
1824-1877 *DcScB*
Hofstadter, Richard 1916-1970 *EncAB,*
WebAB, WhAm 5
Hofstadter, Richard 1916-1972 *EncAAH*
Hofstadter, Robert 1915- *AsBiEn, WebAB*
Hofstatter, Theodore 1848- *NatCAB 5*
Hogaboom, George Byron 1874-1953
NatCAB 40
Hogan, Aloysius Gonzaga Joseph 1891-1943
NatCAB 37, WhAm 2
Hogan, Bernard Francis 1885-1955 *WhAm 3*
Hogan, Cornelia Sara Heslep 1862-
WomWWA 14
Hogan, Dana 1891-1945 *WhAm 2*
Hogan, Daniel Wise 1867- *WhAm 6*
Hogan, Denis Patrick 1869- *WhAm 5*
Hogan, Earl Lee 1920- *BiDrAC*
Hogan, Edgar Poe 1872- *WhAm 5*
Hogan, Edward A, Jr. 1908-1957 *WhAm 3*
Hogan, Edward Leslie 1891-1970 *NatCAB 55*
Hogan, Frank J 1877-1923 *WhAm 1*
Hogan, Frank Joseph 1877-1944 *NatCAB 33,*
WhAm 2
Hogan, Frank Smithwick 1902-1974 *WhAm 6*
Hogan, George Archibald 1871- *WhAm 5*
Hogan, George Maynard 1874-1953
NatCAB 41
Hogan, Gertrude May 1865- *WomWWA 14*
Hogan, Henry Michael 1896-1968 *WhAm 5*
Hogan, James Joseph 1837-1914 *ApCAB X*
Hogan, John 1805-1892 *ApCAB, BiAUS,*
BiDrAC, DcAmB, Drake, NatCAB 22,
TwCBDA, WhAm H
Hogan, John Henry 1882-1940 *WhAm 1*
Hogan, John Joseph 1829-1913 *ApCAB,*
NatCAB 12, TwCBDA, WhAm 1
Hogan, John Philip 1881-1961 *NatCAB 52*
Hogan, John Philip 1881-1966 *WhAm 4*
Hogan, John Sheridan 1815?-1859 *ApCAB*
Hogan, John Vincent Lawless 1890-1960
WhAm 4
Hogan, Lawrence Joseph 1928- *BiDrAC*
Hogan, Louise E Shimer 1855-1929 *WhAm 1*
Hogan, Martin Edward 1910-1965 *NatCAB 51*
Hogan, Michael Joseph 1871-1940 *BiDrAC,*
WhAm 1
Hogan, O T d1971 *WhAm 5*
Hogan, Thomas 1839?- *IlBEAAW,*
NewYHSD
Hogan, William 1788-1848 *DcAmReB*
Hogan, William 1792- *BiAUS*
Hogan, William 1792-1874 *BiDrAC,*
WhAm H
Hogan, William 1792-1875? *ApCAB*
Hogan, William Benjamin 1912- *WebAB*
Hogan, William Ransom 1908-1971 *WhAm 5*
Hogart, George *NewYHSD*
Hogarth, William 1697-1764 *BiHiMed,*
McGEWB
Hogate, Enoch George 1849-1924 *WhAm 1*
Hogate, Kenneth Craven 1897-1947 *WhAm 2*
Hogben, Lancelot 1895-1975 *WhAm 6*
Hoge, Albert Hammond 1885-1943 *NatCAB 36*
Hoge, Arthur Franklin 1887-1954 *NatCAB 44*
Hoge, Arthur Kenworthy 1889-1932 *WhAm 1*
Hoge, James 1784-1863 *ApCAB, NatCAB 10,*
TwCBDA
Hoge, James Doster 1871-1929 *NatCAB 13,*
NatCAB 27, WhAm 1
Hoge, James Fulton 1901-1972 *NatCAB 57,*
WhAm 5
Hoge, Jane Currie Blaikie 1811-1890 *NotAW*
Hoge, John 1760-1824 *ApCAB, BiAUS,*
BiDrAC, TwCBDA, WhAm H
Hoge, John 1840-1917 *WhAm 1*
Hoge, John Blair 1790-1826 *NatCAB 10,*
TwCBDA
Hoge, John Blair 1825-1896 *BiDrAC,*
TwCBDA, WhAm H
Hoge, Joseph Pendleton 1810-1891 *BiAUS,*
BiDrAC, WhAm H
Hoge, Mary Lochary 1853- *WomWWA 14*

Hoge, Moses 1752-1820 *ApCAB, DcAmB,*
Drake, NatCAB 2, TwCBDA, WhAm H
Hoge, Moses Drury 1818-1899 *NatCAB 10,*
TwCBDA
Hoge, Moses Drury 1819-1899 *ApCAB,*
DcAmB, WhAm H
Hoge, Peyton Harrison 1858- *TwCBDA,*
WhAm 4
Hoge, Samuel Davies 1791-1826 *ApCAB*
Hoge, Samuel Davies 1792?-1826 *NatCAB 10,*
TwCBDA
Hoge, Solomon LaFayette d1909 *BiAUS*
Hoge, Solomon LaFayette 1836-1909 *BiDrAC,*
TwCBDA
Hoge, Solomon LaFayette 1837?-1909 *ApCAB*
Hoge, Vane Morgan 1902-1970 *WhAm 5*
Hoge, William 1762-1814 *ApCAB, BiAUS,*
BiDrAC, TwCBDA, WhAm H
Hoge, William James 1821-1864 *ApCAB*
Hoge, William James 1824-1864 *NatCAB 10,*
WhAm H
Hoge, William James 1825-1864 *TwCBDA*
Hogeboom, Henry 1808-1872 *ApCAB*
Hogeboom, James Lawrence 1766-1839 *BiAUS,*
BiDrAC, WhAm H
Hogeland, Albert Harrison 1858-1930
NatCAB 41, WhAm 1
Hogeland, Horace Binney 1862-1958
NatCAB 47
Hogg, Astor 1901-1972 *WhAm 5*
Hogg, Charles Edgar 1852-1935 *BiDrAC,*
NatCAB 7
Hogg, David 1886- *BiDrAC*
Hogg, George 1784-1849 *DcAmB, WhAm H*
Hogg, Herschel Millard 1853-1934 *BiDrAC,*
WhAm 4
Hogg, James Stephen 1851-1906 *DcAmB,*
EncAAH, NatCAB 9, NatCAB 29,
REnAW, TwCBDA, WhAm 1
Hogg, John Webb 1893-1964 *NatCAB 50*
Hogg, Robert Letcher 1873-1956 *NatCAB 45*
Hogg, Robert Lynn 1893- *BiDrAC*
Hogg, Samuel 1783-1842 *BiAUS, BiAUS Sup,*
BiDrAC, WhAm H
Hogg, Walter 1872-1949 *NatCAB 38*
Hogg, William Clifford 1875-1930 *WhAm 1*
Hogg, William James 1851- *NatCAB 6*
Hogg, William Stetson 1856-1921 *WhAm 1*
Hogg, Wilson Thomas 1852- *TwCBDA*
Hoggard, John Thomas 1876-1965 *NatCAB 53*
Hoggatt, Wilford Bacon 1865-1938 *NatCAB 28,*
WhAm 1
Hoggson, Noble Foster 1865- *NatCAB 18*
Hoggson, Samuel James 1830-1911 *NatCAB 33*
Hoggson, William John 1861-1933 *WhAm 1*
Hogle, Berton Mason 1899-1966 *NatCAB 53*
Hogle, James Albert 1876-1955 *NatCAB 45,*
WhAm 3
Hogle, Kate Asma Mason 1859- *WomWWA 14*
Hoglund, Arthur William 1926- *EncAAH*
Hogner, Nils 1893- *IlBEAAW*
Hogness, Thorfin Rusten 1894-1976 *WhAm 6*
Hogsett, William Sloan 1883-1960 *WhAm 4*
Hogshire, Russell Blake 1903-1966 *NatCAB 53*
Hogue, Addison 1849- *TwCBDA, WhAm 4*
Hogue, Alexandre 1898- *IlBEAAW*
Hogue, J David 1898-1958 *NatCAB 46*
Hogue, Lydia Evans 1856- *AmWom*
Hogue, Martha Bradley *WomWWA 14*
Hogue, Mary J 1883- *WomWWA 14*
Hogue, Richard Wallace 1905-1961 *NatCAB 49*
Hogue, S Fred 1872-1941 *WhAm 1*
Hogue, Walter Jenkins 1878-1936 *WhAm 1*
Hogue, Wilson Thomas 1852-1920 *DcAmB,*
WhAm 1
Hoguet, Henry Louis 1816- *ApCAB*
Hoguet, J Peter 1882-1946 *NatCAB 34*
Hoguet, Ramsay 1880-1937 *NatCAB 28*
Hoguet, Robert Louis 1878-1961 *NatCAB 45,*
WhAm 4
Hogun, James d1780 *NatCAB 9*
Hogun, James d1781 *DcAmB, WhAm H*
Hoh, Paul Jacob 1893-1952 *WhAm 3*
Hohein, George Franklin 1907-1955
NatCAB 43
Hohenberg, A Elkan 1899-1961 *WhAm 4*
Hohenheim, Bombastus Von *DcScB*

Hohenlohe-Ingelfingen, Karl Augustus Von 1827-1892 *WhoMilH*
Hohenlohe-Ingelfingen, Prinz F L Von 1746-1818 *WhoMilH*
Hohenstein, Anton 1823?- *NewYHSD*
Hohenthal, Emil Louis George 1864-1928 *WhAm 1*
Hohf, Silas Matthew 1872- *WhAm 5*
Hohfeld, Edward 1875-1966 *NatCAB 51, WhAm 4*
Hohfeld, Wesley Newcomb 1879-1918 *DcAmB, NatCAB 27, WhAm HA, WhAm 4*
Hohl, August *NewYHSD*
Hohlfeld, Alexander Rudolf 1865-1956 *WhAm 2, WhAm 3*
Hohlfeld, Alexander Rudolph 1865-1956 *NatCAB 46*
Hohlfeld, J Maurice 1909-1973 *NatCAB 57*
Hohman, Leslie B 1891-1972 *WhAm 5*
Hoidale, Einar 1870-1952 *BiDrAC, NatCAB 45, WhAm 3*
Hoiles, Raymond Cyrus 1878-1970 *WhAm 5*
Hoisington, Henry Richard 1801-1858 *DcAmB, NatCAB 24, WhAm H*
Hoisington, Jacob 1736-1777 *NatCAB 19*
Hoisington, Roy Donald 1909-1962 *NatCAB 50*
Hoit, Albert Gallatin 1809-1856 *ApCAB, Drake, NewYHSD*
Hoit, Henry Ford 1872- *NatCAB 16, WhAm 5*
Hoit, Sewel 1807-1875 *NatCAB 23*
Hoit, William B *NewYHSD*
Hoitash, Frederick John 1883-1952 *NatCAB 45*
Hoitt, Charles William 1847- *WhAm 4*
Hoke, Elmer Rhodes 1892-1931 *WhAm 1*
Hoke, J Fred 1870-1966 *NatCAB 51*
Hoke, Kremer J 1878-1944 *WhAm 2*
Hoke, Mac 1891-1945 *NatCAB 37*
Hoke, Martha Harriet 1861- *NatCAB 5*
Hoke, Michael 1874-1944 *WhAm 2*
Hoke, Robert Frederick 1837-1912 *ApCAB Sup, BiDConf, DcAmB, NatCAB 12, NatCAB 38, TwCBDA, WhAm 2*
Hoke, Travis Henderson 1892-1947 *WhAm 3*
Hoke, William Alexander 1851-1925 *NatCAB 24, WhAm 1*
Hokeah, Jack 1902- *IlBEAAW*
Hokinson, Helen 1899?-1949 *WebAB*
Hokinson, Helen Elna 1893-1949 *DcAmB S4, NatCAB 41, NotAW*
Hokusai, Katsushika 1760-1849 *McGEWB*
Holabird, John Augur 1886-1945 *WhAm 2*
Holabird, Samuel Beckley 1826-1907 *AmBi, ApCAB, NatCAB 10, TwCBDA, WhAm 1*
Holabird, William 1854-1923 *DcAmB, NatCAB 24, WebAB, WhAm 1*
Holaday, Ross Edgar 1869-1929 *WhAm 1*
Holaday, William Perry 1882-1946 *BiDrAC, WhAm 2, WhAmP*
Holahan, Maurice Fenelon 1873-1957 *WhAm 3*
Holand, Hjalmar Rued 1872-1963 *WhAm 4, WhAm 5*
Holbach, Paul Henri Thiry, Baron D' 1723-1789 *DcScB, McGEWB*
Holbein, Hans, The Younger 1497?-1543 *McGEWB*
Holben, Ralph Penrose 1891-1965 *WhAm 4*
Holberg, Edmond Arthur 1883-1949 *NatCAB 38*
Holberg, Richard Almberg 1886-1942 *NatCAB 31*
Holbert, James Ransom 1890-1957 *NatCAB 49*
Holberton, Wakeman 1839-1898 *NewYHSD*
Holborn, Hajo 1902-1969 *WhAm 5*
Holborn, Ludwig Christian Friedrich 1860-1926 *DcScB*
Holbourne, Francis d1771 *Drake*
Holbrock, Greg John 1906- *BiDrAC*
Holbrook, Alfred 1816-1909 *ApCAB, BiDAmEd, DcAmB, TwCBDA, WhAm 1*
Holbrook, Alice Marion 1874- *WomWWA 14*
Holbrook, Amos 1754-1842 *ApCAB, NatCAB 13*
Holbrook, Arthur Tenney 1870- *WhAm 6*
Holbrook, Charles Henry 1871-1943 *NatCAB 33*
Holbrook, Donald 1897-1970 *WhAm 5*

Holbrook, Dwight 1853- *WhAm 4*
Holbrook, E D 1836-1870 *BiAUS*
Holbrook, E Everett 1835-1919 *NatCAB 6*
Holbrook, Edward Dexter 1836-1870 *BiDrAC, WhAm H, WhAmP*
Holbrook, Eliza Jane Poitevent *NotAW*
Holbrook, Elmer Allen 1881-1957 *WhAm 3*
Holbrook, Evans 1875-1932 *WhAm 1*
Holbrook, Florence d1932 *WhAm 1, WomWWA 14*
Holbrook, Frederick 1813-1909 *BiAUS, DcAmB, NatCAB 8, TwCBDA, WhAm 1, WhAmP*
Holbrook, Frederick 1861-1920 *NatCAB 18, WhAm 1*
Holbrook, Henry Crosby 1857- *WhAm 4*
Holbrook, James 1812-1864 *ApCAB, Drake*
Holbrook, John 1909-1970 *NatCAB 56, WhAm 5*
Holbrook, John Edwards 1794-1871 *ApCAB, DcAmB, DcScB Sup, Drake, NatCAB 13, TwCBDA, WhAm H*
Holbrook, John Swift 1875- *WhAm 1*
Holbrook, Josiah 1788-1854 *BiDAmEd, DcAmB, McGEWB, WebAB, WhAm H*
Holbrook, Lucius Roy 1875- *WhAm 5*
Holbrook, Martin Luther 1831-1902 *ApCAB Sup, NatCAB 12, WhAm 1*
Holbrook, Ralph Waldo 1880-1934 *NatCAB 27*
Holbrook, Richard Thayer 1870-1934 *WhAm 1*
Holbrook, Roland C 1898-1956 *WhAm 3*
Holbrook, Silas Pinckney 1796-1835 *ApCAB, Drake, NatCAB 7, TwCBDA, WhAm H*
Holbrook, Stewart Hall 1893-1964 *REnAW, WhAm 4*
Holbrook, Theodore Lewis 1839-1912 *NatCAB 15*
Holbrook, W Paul 1898-1963 *NatCAB 50*
Holbrook, Willard Ames 1860-1932 *WhAm 1*
Holch, Arthur Everett 1891-1958 *WhAm 3*
Holcomb, Amasa 1787-1875 *DcAmB, WhAm H*
Holcomb, Carlos Sanford 1889-1966 *NatCAB 52*
Holcomb, Elizabeth Miller *WomWWA 14*
Holcomb, Elton Dewitt 1878-1941 *NatCAB 31*
Holcomb, George 1786-1828 *BiAUS*
Holcomb, Horace Hale 1865-1955 *WhAm 3*
Holcomb, J Ross 1882-1951 *NatCAB 52*
Holcomb, Lynn Howe 1903-1948 *WhAm 2*
Holcomb, Marcus Hensey 1844-1932 *ApCAB X, NatCAB 15, NatCAB 23, WhAm 1*
Holcomb, Oscar Raymond 1867- *WhAm 5*
Holcomb, Richard Roy d1960 *WhAm 4*
Holcomb, Richmond Cranston 1874-1945 *NatCAB 34*
Holcomb, Silas Alexander 1858-1920 *DcAmB, NatCAB 12, TwCBDA, WhAm 1, WhAmP*
Holcomb, Thomas 1879-1965 *WebAMB, WhAm 4*
Holcombe, Amasa 1787- *Drake*
Holcombe, Amasa 1787-1873 *NatCAB 3, TwCBDA*
Holcombe, Amasa 1787-1875 *ApCAB*
Holcombe, Amasa Maynard 1882-1971 *WhAm 5*
Holcombe, Armstead Richardson 1876-1936 *WhAm 1*
Holcombe, Carolyn Crossett *WomWWA 14*
Holcombe, Chester 1843-1912 *NatCAB 3, TwCBDA*
Holcombe, Chester 1844-1912 *DcAmB, WhAm 1*
Holcombe, Curtis Wilson 1840- *NatCAB 3*
Holcombe, Elizabeth J 1827- *AmWom*
Holcombe, Emily Seymour Goodwin 1852- *NatCAB 16, NatCAB 18*
Holcombe, Frederick 1786-1872 *NatCAB 3, TwCBDA*
Holcombe, George 1786-1828 *BiDrAC, TwCBDA, WhAm H, WhAmP*
Holcombe, George Obed 1851- *NatCAB 3*
Holcombe, Harold Goodwin 1873-1960 *NatCAB 49*
Holcombe, Henry 1680-1750 *NatCAB 3*
Holcombe, Henry 1762-1824 *DcAmB, Drake, TwCBDA, WhAm H*

Holcombe, Henry 1762-1826 *ApCAB, NatCAB 3*
Holcombe, Hosea 1780-1841 *ApCAB, NatCAB 3, TwCBDA*
Holcombe, Hugh Hamilton 1825-1857 *NatCAB 3*
Holcombe, James Foote 1837- *NatCAB 3*
Holcombe, James Philemon 1820-1873 *ApCAB, DcAmB, Drake Sup, NatCAB 3, NatCAB 24, TwCBDA, WhAm H, WhAmP*
Holcombe, James Philemon 1820-1883 *BiDConf*
Holcombe, John Hite Lee 1856- *NatCAB 3*
Holcombe, John Lavallee 1911-1964 *WhAm 4*
Holcombe, John Marshall 1848-1926 *NatCAB 3, NatCAB 18, WhAm 1*
Holcombe, John Walker 1853- *NatCAB 3*
Holcombe, John Winslow 1836- *NatCAB 3*
Holcombe, Jonathan 1762-1847 *NatCAB 3*
Holcombe, Joseph Gales 1862- *NatCAB 3*
Holcombe, Judson 1819- *NatCAB 3*
Holcombe, Origen Pinney 1794-1869 *NatCAB 3*
Holcombe, Oscar Fitzallen 1888-1968 *WhAm 5*
Holcombe, Reuben 1752-1824 *NatCAB 3, TwCBDA*
Holcombe, Silas Wright 1842- *NatCAB 3*
Holcombe, Solomon 1789-1871 *NatCAB 3*
Holcombe, Theodore Isaac *NatCAB 3*
Holcombe, Thomas d1657 *NatCAB 3*
Holcombe, Thomas 1843- *NatCAB 3*
Holcombe, Virgil Eugene 1894-1959 *NatCAB 45*
Holcombe, Walter Pearce 1874-1951 *NatCAB 40*
Holcombe, William Frederic 1827-1904 *ApCAB, Drake, NatCAB 3, TwCBDA, WhAm 1*
Holcombe, William Henry 1825-1893 *ApCAB, DcAmB, Drake Sup, NatCAB 3, TwCBDA, WhAm H*
Holdaway, Charles William 1880- *WhAm 6*
Holden, Albert Fairchild 1867-1913 *NatCAB 22*
Holden, Albert James 1841-1916 *WhAm 1*
Holden, Alice M 1882-1951 *WhAm 3*
Holden, Amos F 1848-1921 *NatCAB 20*
Holden, Ann *NewYHSD*
Holden, Benedict Michael 1874- *NatCAB 18*
Holden, Carl Frederick 1895-1953 *WhAm 3*
Holden, Charles Arthur 1872-1960 *WhAm 4*
Holden, Charles Revell 1871- *WhAm 2*
Holden, Clifford C *NewYHSD*
Holden, Edgar 1838-1909 *NatCAB 15, WhAm 1*
Holden, Edward Henry 1858- *WhAm 1*
Holden, Edward Singleton 1846-1914 *AmBi, ApCAB, BiAUS, DcAmB, DcScB, NatCAB 7, TwCBDA, WhAm 1*
Holden, Edwin Chapin 1872- *WhAm 2*
Holden, Erastus Franklin 1826-1899 *NatCAB 13*
Holden, Florence Heywood *WomWWA 14*
Holden, Fox 1849- *TwCBDA*
Holden, Frederick Clark 1868-1944 *WhAm 2*
Holden, George Parker 1869-1935 *WhAm 1*
Holden, George Walter 1866-1934 *WhAm 1*
Holden, Gerry Rounds 1874-1945 *WhAm 2*
Holden, Gertrude Lynde 1874- *WomWWA 14*
Holden, Hale 1869-1940 *DcAmB S2, NatCAB 30, WhAm 1*
Holden, Hale 1900-1954 *WhAm 3*
Holden, Horace Moore 1866-1936 *WhAm 1*
Holden, James 1856-1925 *WhAm 1*
Holden, James Austin 1861-1918 *WhAm 2*
Holden, James Franklin 1861- *WhAm 4*
Holden, James Stansbury 1875- *WhAm 5*
Holden, John Burt 1873-1928 *WhAm 1*
Holden, John J 1810?-1855 *NewYHSD*
Holden, Katherine Cramer 1871- *WomWWA 14*
Holden, Liberty Emery 1833-1913 *DcAmB, NatCAB 11, NatCAB 22, WhAm 1*
Holden, Louis Edward 1863- *TwCBDA*
Holden, Louis Edward 1863-1942 *NatCAB 31, WhAm 1*
Holden, Louis Edward 1863-1943 *WhAm 2*
Holden, Louis Halsey 1873- *WhAm 5*
Holden, Mary Barnes 1875- *WomWWA 14*
Holden, Oliver 1765-1831 *ApCAB, Drake*
Holden, Oliver 1765-1844 *AmBi, DcAmB,*

NatCAB 13, TwCBDA, WhAm H
Holden, Perry Greeley 1865-1959 *WhAm 4*
Holden, Roy Jay 1870-1945 *NatCAB 34,*
WhAm 2
Holden, Thomas Steele 1886-1958 *NatCAB 46,*
WhAm 3
Holden, Ward Andrews 1866-1937 *WhAm 1,*
WhAm 1C
Holden, William Burroughs 1873-1955
NatCAB 46
Holden, William Henry 1859-1925 *NatCAB 22*
Holden, William Woods 1818-1892 *ApCAB,*
BiAUS, BiDConf, DcAmB, NatCAB 4,
TwCBDA, WhAm H
Holden, Willis Sprague 1909-1973 *WhAm 6*
Holder, Arthur Ernest 1860-1937 *WhAm 1*
Holder, Charles Adams 1872-1955 *WhAm 3*
Holder, Charles Frederick 1851-1915 *AmBi,*
ApCAB, DcAmB, NatCAB 7, TwCBDA,
WhAm 1
Holder, Charles Wesley 1904-1948 *NatCAB 37*
Holder, Edward Perry 1892-1951 *NatCAB 50,*
WhAm 3
Holder, Francis Jerome 1876-1931 *WhAm 1*
Holder, Ivan Wendell 1906-1973 *WhAm 6*
Holder, Joseph Basset 1824-1888 *WhAm H*
Holder, Joseph Bassett 1824-1888 *ApCAB,*
DcAmB, TwCBDA
Holder, Joseph Bassett 1829-1888 *NatCAB 7*
Holder, Oscar Curtis 1911-1962 *WhAm 4*
Holder, Otto Ludwig 1859-1937 *DcScB*
Holder, William Dunbar 1824-1900 *BiDConf*
Holderby, Andrew Roberdeau 1838- *WhAm 4*
Holderby, William Matthew 1880-1933
WhAm 1
Holderlin, Johann Christian Friedrich 1770-1843
McGEWB
Holderman, Elizabeth Sinclair *WomWWA 14*
Holdich, Joseph 1804-1893 *ApCAB, TwCBDA*
Holding, Archibald M 1862-1935 *WhAm 1,*
WhAm 1C
Holding, Elisabeth Sanxay d1955 *WhAm 3*
Holding, Herbert Holmes 1867-1949
NatCAB 37
Holding, Robert Powell 1896-1957 *WhAm 3*
Holdom, Jesse 1851-1930 *NatCAB 11,*
WhAm 1
Holdredge, Ransom Gillet 1836-1899 *IIBEAAW*
Holdrege, George Ward 1847-1926 *DcAmB S1,*
WhAm 1
Hole, Agnes Christine Atwood 1870-
WomWWA 14
Hole, Willitts J 1858-1936 *NatCAB 27*
Hole, Winston LeRoy 1910-1970 *NatCAB 55*
Hole-In-The-Day 1827?-1868 *ApCAB*
Holenstein, Thomas 1896-1962 *WhAm 4*
Holes, Wilbur Warren 1898-1970 *NatCAB 57*
Holgate, Edwin Headley 1892- *IIBEAAW*
Holgate, J F H *NewYHSD*
Holgate, Thomas Franklin 1859-1945 *WhAm 2*
Holguin, Carlos 1832- *ApCAB*
Holguin, Diego Gonzalez 1560?-1620? *ApCAB*
Holiday, Billie 1915-1959 *WebAB*
Holiday, Eleanor 1915-1959 *WhAm 4*
Holiday, Herman Joe 1915-1966 *WhAm 4*
Holifield, Chester Earl 1903- *BiDrAC*
Holk, Heinrich 1599-1633 *WhoMilH*
Holl, Carl Waldo 1892-1961 *WhAm 4*
Holl, Dio Lewis 1895-1954 *WhAm 3*
Hollabaugh, Andrew Newton 1876-1928
NatCAB 23
Holladay, Albert Lewis 1805-1856 *NatCAB 2*
Holladay, Alexander Quarles 1839-1949
TwCBDA, WhAm 3
Holladay, Alexander Richmond 1811-1877
BiAUS, BiDrAC, TwCBDA, WhAm H
Holladay, Ben 1819-1887 *DcAmB, REnAW,*
WebAB, WhAm H
Holladay, Ben *see also* Holliday, Ben
Holladay, Edmund Burke 1862-1945
NatCAB 33
Holladay, James 1893-1963 *NatCAB 50,*
WhAm 4
Holladay, Lewis L 1832-1891 *NatCAB 2*
Holladay, Waller 1840- *TwCBDA, WhAm 4*
Hollaman, Mary L 1857- *WomWWA 14*
Hollaman, Rich William 1885-1947 *WhAm 2*
Holland, Arrie Ellsworth 1876- *WhoColR*

Holland, Cecilia Gaines *WomWWA 14*
Holland, Charles Hubert 1878-1951 *NatCAB 40,*
WhAm 6
Holland, Clifford Milburn 1883-1924 *AmBi,*
ApCAB X, DcAmB, NatCAB 19,
WhAm 1
Holland, Cornelius 1782-1870 *BiAUS*
Holland, Cornelius 1783-1870 *BiDrAC,*
WhAm H
Holland, Dorothy Stebbins 1877-
WomWWA 14
Holland, Edmund Milton 1848-1913 *AmBi,*
DcAmB, NatCAB 11, WhAm 1
Holland, Edward Clifford 1794-1824 *ApCAB,*
TwCBDA
Holland, Edward Everett 1861-1941 *BiDrAC,*
WhAm 1, WhAmP
Holland, Edwin Clifford 1793-1824 *Drake*
Holland, Edwin Clifford 1794?-1824 *DcAmB,*
WhAm H
Holland, Eldridge Vanleer 1880-1965
NatCAB 51
Holland, Elihu G 1817- *Drake*
Holland, Elmer Joseph 1894-1968 *BiDrAC,*
WhAm 5, WhAmP
Holland, Elmer Leonard, Jr. 1918-1966
WhAm 4
Holland, Elsie Nichols 1876- *WomWWA 14*
Holland, Ernest Otto 1874-1950 *BiDAmEd,*
NatCAB 39, WhAm 3
Holland, Francis P *NewYHSD*
Holland, Frank Pierce 1852-1928 *NatCAB 33,*
WhAm 1
Holland, Frederic May 1836-1908 *ApCAB,*
TwCBDA, WhAm 1
Holland, Frederic West 1811-1895 *Drake*
Holland, Frederick West 1811-1895 *ApCAB,*
TwCBDA
Holland, George *NewYHSD*
Holland, George 1791-1870 *AmBi, DcAmB,*
Drake, NatCAB 3, WhAm H
Holland, George 1791-1871 *ApCAB*
Holland, George Frank 1871-1936 *NatCAB 47*
Holland, Henry Finch 1912-1962 *WhAm 4*
Holland, James 1754-1823 *BiAUS, BiDrAC,*
TwCBDA, WhAm H, WhAmP
Holland, James Buchanan 1857-1914 *WhAm 1*
Holland, James M 1859- *WhAm 4*
Holland, James William 1849-1922 *NatCAB 19,*
WhAm 1
Holland, John Francis 1858-1912 *NatCAB 23*
Holland, John Joseph 1776?-1820 *NewYHSD,*
WhAm H
Holland, John Philip 1840-1914 *AmBi, DcAmB,*
McGEWB, WebAB, WebAMB,
WhAm HA, WhAm 4
Holland, John Philip 1841-1914 *ApCAB X*
Holland, John Philip 1842-1914 *NatCAB 15*
Holland, Joseph Jefferson 1860-1926 *DcAmB,*
WhAm 1
Holland, Josiah Gilbert 1819-1881 *AmBi,*
ApCAB, DcAmB, Drake, NatCAB 1,
TwCBDA, WebAB, WhAm H
Holland, Josiah Gilbert 1900-1975 *WhAm 6*
Holland, Lancelot 1887-1941 *WhWW-II*
Holland, Laurier Fox-Strangways d1957
WhAm 3
Holland, Leicester Bodine 1882-1952
NatCAB 41, WhAm 3
Holland, Louis Edward 1878-1960 *WhAm 4*
Holland, Madeline Oxford 1916-1968 *WhAm 5*
Holland, Martin Luther 1886-1954 *NatCAB 41*
Holland, Nelson Clarke 1875-1949 *NatCAB 42*
Holland, Peter Olai 1878-1939 *WhAm 1*
Holland, Philip 1877- *WhAm 5*
Holland, Robert Afton 1844-1909 *TwCBDA,*
WhAm 1
Holland, Robert Allen 1868-1959 *WhAm 3*
Holland, Roy Anthony 1912-1965 *NatCAB 53*
Holland, Rupert Sargent 1878-1952 *WhAm 3*
Holland, Rush LaMotte 1867-1944 *WhAm 2*
Holland, Samuel d1801 *ApCAB*
Holland, Samuel Eugene 1889-1958 *NatCAB 49*
Holland, Samuel Hyman 1892-1973 *WhAm 6*
Holland, Sidney George 1893-1961 *WhAm 4*
Holland, Spessard Lindsey 1892-1971 *BiDrAC,*
WhAm 5, WhAmP
Holland, St. Clair Cecil 1894-1974 *WhAm 6*

Holland, Thomas *NewYHSD*
Holland, Thomas Leroy 1879-1944 *WhAm 2*
Holland, Thomas R 1816?- *NewYHSD*
Holland, Travis 1874- *WhAm 5*
Holland, Ubert Cecil 1889-1957 *WhAm 3*
Holland, W Bob 1868-1932 *WhAm 1*
Holland, William Jacob 1848-1932 *AmBi,*
DcAmB S1, NatCAB 13, TwCBDA,
WhAm 1
Holland, William Merideth 1875- *WhAm 5*
Holland-Moritz, Charles John 1876-1948
NatCAB 38
Hollander, Franklin 1899-1966 *NatCAB 51,*
WhAm 4
Hollander, Jacob Harry 1871-1940 *DcAmB S2,*
NatCAB 13, TwCBDA, WhAm 1
Hollander, Peter 1600?- *ApCAB*
Hollander, Sidney 1881-1972 *NatCAB 57,*
WhAm 5
Hollands, Edmund Howard 1879- *WhAm 6*
Holleman, Howard Ivanhoe 1885-1955
NatCAB 45
Holleman, Joel 1799-1844 *BiAUS, BiDrAC,*
WhAm H
Holleman, Willard Roy 1909- *WhAm 5*
Hollen, John E *NewYHSD*
Hollenback, George Matson 1791-1866
WhAm H
Hollenback, John Welles 1827-1923 *NatCAB 19,*
TwCBDA, WhAm 4
Hollenback, Matthias 1752-1829 *WhAm H*
Hollenbeck, Conrad 1847-1915 *NatCAB 20*
Hollenbeck, Don 1905-1954 *WhAm 3*
Hollenbeck, Willard Fletcher 1898-1966
NatCAB 53
Holleran, Leslie Gilbert 1881-1959 *NatCAB 47*
Holleran, Walter Martin 1889-1957 *NatCAB 47*
Hollerith, Charles 1893-1972 *NatCAB 57*
Hollerith, Herman 1860-1929 *DcAmB S1,*
WebAB, WhAm HA, WhAm 4
Hollerith, Herman 1890- *WhAm 2*
Hollett, Roderick Peregrine 1856-1934
NatCAB 39
Holley, Alexander Hamilton 1804-1887
NatCAB 10, TwCBDA
Holley, Alexander Lyman 1832-1882 *AmBi,*
ApCAB, DcAmB, NatCAB 11, TwCBDA,
WebAB, WhAm H
Holley, Earl 1881-1958 *NatCAB 57*
Holley, Francis 1863-1923 *WhAm 1*
Holley, George Malvin 1878-1963 *NatCAB 53,*
WhAm 4
Holley, Horace 1781-1827 *ApCAB, BiDAmEd,*
DcAmB, Drake, NatCAB 4, TwCBDA,
WhAm H
Holley, Horace 1887-1960 *WhAm 4*
Holley, John Milton 1802-1848 *BiAUS,*
BiDrAC, WhAm H
Holley, John Milton 1845-1914 *WhAm 1*
Holley, Marietta d1926 *AmWom, WhAm 1,*
WomWWA 14
Holley, Marietta 1836-1926 *AmBi, DcAmB,*
NotAW
Holley, Marietta 1844-1926 *NatCAB 9,*
TwCBDA
Holley, Mary Phelps Austin 1784-1846 *ApCAB,*
NotAW
Holley, Myron 1779-1841 *ApCAB, DcAmB,*
NatCAB 2, TwCBDA, WhAm H
Holley, Orville Luther 1791-1861 *ApCAB,*
Drake, TwCBDA
Holley, Robert William 1922- *AsBiEn, WebAB*
Holley, Sallie 1818-1893 *NotAW*
Holley, William Welles 1841-1916 *WhAm 1*
Hollick, Arthur 1857-1933 *WhAm 1*
Hollick, Charles Arthur 1857-1933 *DcAmB S1,*
NatCAB 24, TwCBDA
Holliday, Ben 1819-1887 *ApCAB*
Holliday, Ben *see also* Holaday, Ben
Holliday, Carl 1879-1936 *WhAm 1*
Holliday, Cyrus Kurtz 1826-1900 *DcAmB,*
NatCAB 23, WhAm H
Holliday, Doc 1851-1887 *REnAW*
Holliday, Edith Wray *WomWWA 14*
Holliday, Elias Selah 1842-1936 *BiDrAC,*
WhAm 4, WhAmP
Holliday, Frederick Taylor 1897-1951
NatCAB 40

Holliday, Frederick William Mackey 1828-1899
  BiDConf, NatCAB 5, TwCBDA
Holliday, Houghton 1889-1972 *WhAm 5*
Holliday, Jaquelin Smith 1867-1944
  NatCAB 33
Holliday, John Hampden 1846-1921
  NatCAB 19, WhAm 1
Holliday, Judy 1923-1965 *WhAm 4*
Holliday, Robert Cortes 1880-1947 *WhAm 2*
Holliday, Robert Paul 1894-1959 *NatCAB 52,
  WhAm 3*
Holliday, Wallace Trevor 1884-1950 *WhAm 3*
Holliday, William Harrison 1863- *WhAm 4*
Holliday, William Helmus 1843-1916
  WhAm HA, WhAm 4
Holliday, William Helmus 1843-1925 *WhAm 1*
Holliday, William Jaquelin 1829-1918
  NatCAB 33
Holling, Holling C *IIBEAAW*
Holling, Thomas Leslie 1889-1966 *WhAm 4*
Hollings, Ernest Frederick 1922- *BiDrAC*
Hollingshead, Gordon 1890-1952 *NatCAB 42*
Hollingshead, Richard Milton 1869-1945
  NatCAB 34
Hollingshead, Stewart 1904-1968 *WhAm 4A*
Hollingsworth, Amor 1880-1955 *WhAm 3*
Hollingsworth, David Adams 1844-1929 *BiDrAC,
  WhAm 4*
Hollingsworth, Frank 1892-1964 *WhAm 4*
Hollingsworth, George 1813-1882 *NewYHSD*
Hollingsworth, James M 1830- *NatCAB 10*
Hollingsworth, Levi 1739-1824 *ApCAB*
Hollingsworth, Orlando Newton 1836-
  BiDAmEd
Hollingsworth, Robert Emmett 1874-1952
  NatCAB 45
Hollingsworth, William Franklin 1867-
  WhAm 4
Hollington, Richard Deming 1870-1944
  WhAm 2
Hollingworth, Harry Levi 1880-1956
  NatCAB 45, WhAm 3
Hollingworth, Leta Anna Stetter 1886-1939
  BiDAmEd, DcAmB S2, NotAW, WhAm 1
Hollins, George N 1799-1878 *Drake*
Hollins, George Nicholas 1799-1878 *TwCBDA*
Hollins, George Nichols 1799-1878 *AmBi,
  ApCAB, BiDConf, DcAmB, NatCAB 11,
  WebAMB, WhAm H*
Hollis, Allen 1871-1955 *WhAm 3*
Hollis, Bertha Poole 1877- *WomWWA 14*
Hollis, Charles J 1815?- *NewYHSD*
Hollis, Ernest Victor 1895-1965 *WhAm 4*
Hollis, Grace Weston 1869- *WomWWA 14*
Hollis, Henry French 1869-1949 *BiDrAC,
  NatCAB 15, WhAm 2*
Hollis, Henry Leonard 1866-1958 *WhAm 3*
Hollis, Ira Nelson 1856-1930 *DcAmB,
  NatCAB 22, WhAm 1*
Hollis, John *ApCAB*
Hollis, Nathaniel *ApCAB*
Hollis, Thomas d1735 *ApCAB*
Hollis, Thomas 1659-1731 *ApCAB, Drake*
Hollis, Thomas 1720-1774 *ApCAB*
Hollis, W Stanley 1866-1930 *WhAm 1*
Hollis, William Allen 1878-1925 *NatCAB 20*
Hollis, William Dennard 1850-1925 *NatCAB 26*
Hollister, Buell 1883-1966 *WhAm 4*
Hollister, Clay Harvey 1863-1940 *NatCAB 36,
  WhAm 1*
Hollister, Clay Harvey 1902-1967 *NatCAB 53*
Hollister, Frank Canfield 1866- *NatCAB 13*
Hollister, Fred H 1865-1955 *WhAm 3*
Hollister, Frederick Kellogg 1869-1934
  NatCAB 30
Hollister, George C 1871-1935 *NatCAB 26*
Hollister, Gertrude Bullen 1868-
  WomWWA 14
Hollister, Gideon Hiram d1881 *BiAUS, Drake*
Hollister, Gideon Hiram 1817-1881 *ApCAB,
  DcAmB, WhAm H*
Hollister, Gideon Hiram 1818-1881 *NatCAB 12*
Hollister, Granger A 1854-1924 *WhAm 1*
Hollister, Horace Adelbert 1857- *WhAm 4*
Hollister, Howard Clark 1856-1919 *NatCAB 39,
  WhAm 1*
Hollister, John Baker 1890- *BiDrAC*
Hollister, John Hamilcar 1824-1911 *WhAm 1*

Hollister, Joseph 1877-1946 *NatCAB 35,
  WhAm 3*
Hollister, Lillian 1853- *AmWom*
Hollister, Madison E 1808- *BiAUS*
Hollister, Ned 1876-1924 *NatCAB 20,
  WhAm 1*
Hollister, Orlando Knapp 1865- *WhAm 1*
Hollister, Ovando James 1834-1892 *TwCBDA*
Hollister, Richard Dennis Teall 1878- *WhAm 6*
Hollister, Seymour Walter 1845-1916
  NatCAB 17
Hollister, William Henry, Jr. 1847-1925
  WhAm 1
Hollister, William Welles 1818-1886 *REnAW*
Hollmann, Harry Triebner 1878-1942 *WhAm 2*
Hollmann, Henry Abraham 1881-1951
  NatCAB 40
Holloman, Delmar Winston 1913-1975 *WhAm 6*
Holloman, Reed 1871-1953 *NatCAB 44*
Hollomon, James Arthur 1873-1929 *WhAm 1,
  WhAm 1C*
Hollon, William Eugene 1913- *EncAAH,
  REnAW*
Hollopeter, William Clarence 1858-1927
  WhAm 1
Holloway, Asher Earl 1887-1966 *NatCAB 53*
Holloway, David Pierson 1809-1883 *ApCAB,
  BiAUS, BiDrAC, NatCAB 7, WhAm H*
Holloway, Edward Stratton d1939 *WhAm 1*
Holloway, H E *NewYHSD*
Holloway, Harry Vance 1875-1966 *WhAm 4*
Holloway, Henry Wesley 1868- *WhoColR*
Holloway, Isaac H 1875- *WhoColR*
Holloway, Jacob James 1857-1927 *WhAm 1*
Holloway, James Lemuel, III 1922- *WebAMB*
Holloway, James Montgomery 1834- *ApCAB*
Holloway, John 1666-1734 *DcAmB, WhAm H*
Holloway, John Lindesay 1898-1960 *WhAm 4*
Holloway, John Wesley 1865- *WhoColR*
Holloway, John Woodford 1896-1949
  NatCAB 37
Holloway, Joseph Flavius 1825-1896 *DcAmB,
  WhAm H*
Holloway, Josephus Flavius 1825-1896
  NatCAB 12
Holloway, Laura Carter 1848- *ApCAB*
Holloway, Richard Jones *WhoColR A*
Holloway, Ross L 1866-1936 *NatCAB 27*
Holloway, Thomas Beaver 1872-1936 *WhAm 1*
Holloway, Ward Beecher 1864-1909
  NatCAB 15
Holloway, William A 1897-1966 *WhAm 4*
Holloway, William Grace 1886-1959 *WhAm 3*
Holloway, William Harvard 1875- *WhoColR*
Holloway, William James 1873- *WhAm 5*
Holloway, William Judson 1888-1970 *WhAm 5*
Holloway, William Lawson 1867-1926 *WhAm 1*
Holloway, William M 1862- *WhAm 4*
Holloway, William Robeson 1836- *WhAm 4*
Hollowell, Amos Kendall 1844-1921
  NatCAB 19
Holls, Frederick William 1857-1903 *DcAmB,
  NatCAB 11*
Holls, George Charles 1824-1886 *ApCAB,
  NatCAB 3*
Holls, George Frederick William 1857-1903
  AmBi, DcAmB, TwCBDA, WhAm 1
Hollums, Ellis Clyde 1893-1949 *WhAm 2A*
Holly, Alexander Hamilton 1804-1887 *BiAUS*
Holly, Alonzo Potter Burgess 1865- *WhoColR*
Holly, Birdsall 1822-1894 *NatCAB 26*
Holly, Charles F *BiAUS*
Holly, Charles Harden 1936-1959 *WhAm 4*
Holly, Flora Mai *WomWWA 14*
Holly, Henry Hudson d1892 *WhAm H*
Holly, James Theodore Augustus 1829-1911
  *ApCAB, DcAmB, NatCAB 5, TwCBDA,
  WhAm 1*
Holly, John I 1843- *NatCAB 2*
Holly, William H 1869-1958 *WhAm 3*
Hollyday, Richard Carmichael 1859- *WhAm 4*
Hollyer, Samuel 1826-1919 *DcAmB,
  NewYHSD, WhAm 4*
Hollzer, Harry Aaron 1880-1946 *WhAm 2*
Holm, Charles Ferdinand 1862- *NatCAB 14*
Holm, Frits Vilhelm 1881-1930 *WhAm 1*
Holm, George Elmer 1891-1955 *WhAm 3*
Holm, Henry Jesse 1876- *WhAm 5*

Holm, John Campanius 1601-1683 *ApCAB*
Holm, Saxe *WebAB*
Holm, Theodor 1854-1932 *WhAm 1*
Holm, Thomas Campanius *ApCAB*
Holm, Victor S 1876-1935 *WhAm 1*
Holman, Albert William 1896-1952 *NatCAB 42*
Holman, Alfred 1857-1930 *NatCAB 24,
  WhAm 1*
Holman, Austin Webster 1868-1952
  NatCAB 42
Holman, Charles Thomas 1882-1968 *WhAm 4A*
Holman, Charles William 1886-1971
  NatCAB 55
Holman, David 1904-1969 *NatCAB 55*
Holman, Eugene 1895-1962 *WhAm 4*
Holman, Frank 1865- *WhAm 4*
Holman, Frank E 1886-1967 *WhAm 4*
Holman, Frederick VanVoorhies 1852-1927
  WhAm 1
Holman, Howard Francis 1878-1954 *WhAm 3*
Holman, James Duval 1814-1882 *NatCAB 7*
Holman, Jesse Lynch d1842 *BiAUS*
Holman, Jesse Lynch 1783-1842 *TwCBDA*
Holman, Jesse Lynch 1784-1842 *ApCAB,
  DcAmB, NatCAB 22, WhAm H*
Holman, Jonas W *NewYHSD*
Holman, Joseph George 1764-1817 *ApCAB,
  Drake*
Holman, Joseph Palmer 1850-1933 *NatCAB 27*
Holman, Josephine McArthur 1867-
  WomWWA 14
Holman, Jud McCarty 1886-1950 *WhAm 3*
Holman, Louis Arthur 1866-1939 *WhAm 1*
Holman, Madge Timmerman 1876-
  WomWWA 14
Holman, Minard Lafever 1852-1925 *WhAm 1*
Holman, Minard Lafevre 1852-1925
  NatCAB 14
Holman, Rufus Cecil 1877-1959 *BiDrAC,
  WhAm 3, WhAmP*
Holman, Russell Lowell 1907-1960 *WhAm 4*
Holman, Silena Moore 1850-1915 *NatCAB 17,
  WomWWA 14*
Holman, William Duran 1896-1966 *NatCAB 51*
Holman, William Henry 1889-1962 *WhAm 4*
Holman, William Kunkel 1877- *WhAm 5*
Holman, William Steele 1822-1897 *ApCAB,
  BiAUS, BiDrAC, DcAmB, NatCAB 5,
  TwCBDA, WhAm H, WhAmP*
Holmberg, Adrian Otis 1900- *WhAm 5*
Holmberg, Allan Richard 1909-1966 *WhAm 4*
Holmberg, George Clarence 1882-1953
  NatCAB 45, WhAm 4
Holmberg, Gustaf Fredrik 1872-1936 *WhAm 1*
Holmboe, Bernt Michael 1795-1850 *DcScB*
Holmboe, Jens Anthon 1866-1948 *NatCAB 37*
Holme, John d1701 *ApCAB*
Holme, John Francis 1868-1904 *IIBEAAW,
  WhAm 1*
Holme, Thomas d1695 *NatCAB 24*
Holme, Thomas 1624-1695 *DcAmB, WhAm H*
Holme, Thomas 1625-1695 *ApCAB*
Holmes, Abiel 1763-1837 *ApCAB, DcAmB,
  Drake, NatCAB 7, TwCBDA, WhAm H*
Holmes, Adeline Morehouse *WomWWA 14*
Holmes, Adoniram Judson 1842-1902 *BiDrAC,
  WhAmP*
Holmes, Andrew Fernando 1797-1860 *ApCAB,
  Drake*
Holmes, Andrew Owens 1906-1965 *NatCAB 53*
Holmes, Arthur 1890-1965 *DcScB, McGEWB,
  WhAm 4*
Holmes, Bayard Paul 1869-1931 *NatCAB 23*
Holmes, Bayard Taylor 1852-1924 *DcAmB,
  NatCAB 10, WhAm 1, WhAmP*
Holmes, Burton 1870-1958 *NatCAB 44,
  WhAm 3*
Holmes, Champneys Holt 1894-1950 *WhAm 3*
Holmes, Charles Elmer 1863-1927 *NatCAB 21,
  WhAm 4*
Holmes, Charles Horace 1827-1874 *BiDrAC,
  WhAm H*
Holmes, Charles Mason 1864-1945 *ApCAB X,
  NatCAB 37*
Holmes, Charles Nevers 1872-1930 *NatCAB 22*
Holmes, Charles Shiveley 1916-1976 *WhAm 6*
Holmes, Charlotte Rebecca 1877-
  WomWWA 14

Holmes, Christian Rasmus 1857-1920
NatCAB 18, WhAm 1
Holmes, Clarence Leroy 1879-1938 *NatCAB 30,
WhAm 1*
Holmes, Daniel Henry 1851-1908 *DcAmB,
NatCAB 23*
Holmes, David d1832 *ApCAB, BiAUS, Drake*
Holmes, David 1769-1832 *BiDrAC,
NatCAB 13, REnAW, TwCBDA,
WhAm H, WhAmP*
Holmes, David 1770-1832 *DcAmB*
Holmes, David 1810-1873 *ApCAB*
Holmes, David Eugene 1859- *WhAm 4*
Holmes, Donald Safford 1888-1949 *WhAm 2*
Holmes, Dorothy Lees Dole 1868-
WomWWA 14
Holmes, Dwight Oliver Wendell 1877- *WhAm 5,
WhoColR*
Holmes, E W *NewYHSD*
Holmes, Edward 1797-1859 *WhAm H*
Holmes, Edward Britain 1872-1934 *NatCAB 26*
Holmes, Edward Jackson 1873-1950 *WhAm 3*
Holmes, Edward Marion, Jr. 1907-1971
WhAm 5
Holmes, Edward Thomas 1870- *WhAm 5*
Holmes, Edwin Francis 1843- *WhAm 4*
Holmes, Edwin Sanford, Jr. 1862- *WhAm 5*
Holmes, Elias Bellows 1807-1866 *BiAUS,
BiDrAC, WhAm H*
Holmes, Elias Bellows 1810-1866 *TwCBDA*
Holmes, Elias Burton 1870- *TwCBDA*
Holmes, Ernest Shurtleff 1887-1960 *DcAmReB*
Holmes, Ernest Shurtliff 1887-1960 *WhAm 4*
Holmes, Ernest Walter 1883-1945 *NatCAB 37*
Holmes, Ezekiel 1801-1865 *DcAmB,
NatCAB 24, WhAm H*
Holmes, Francis Clinton 1869-1950 *NatCAB 39*
Holmes, Francis Howland *ApCAB X*
Holmes, Frank Graham 1878-1954 *NatCAB 40,
WhAm 3*
Holmes, Fred Gooding 1889-1955 *NatCAB 48*
Holmes, Frederick 1889-1958 *WhAm 3*
Holmes, Frederick Lionel 1883-1946 *WhAm 2*
Holmes, Frederick Morgan 1877-1948
NatCAB 36
Holmes, Frederick S 1865- *WhAm 4*
Holmes, Gabriel 1769-1829 *ApCAB, BiAUS,
BiDrAC, Drake, NatCAB 4, TwCBDA,
WhAm H, WhAmP*
Holmes, George Bass 1794-1879 *NatCAB 12*
Holmes, George Ellsworth 1862-1898
NatCAB 10
Holmes, George Frederick 1820-1897 *ApCAB,
BiDAmEd, DcAmB, NatCAB 13,
TwCBDA, WhAm H*
Holmes, George Isabell 1903-1966 *NatCAB 55*
Holmes, George Kirby 1856-1927 *WhAm 1*
Holmes, George Robert 1895-1939 *AmBi,
WhAm 1*
Holmes, George Sanford 1883-1955 *WhAm 3*
Holmes, George W 1812?- *NewYHSD*
Holmes, George William 1880-1964 *WhAm 4*
Holmes, George William 1880-1965
NatCAB 56
Holmes, Georgiana Klingle *AmWom*
Holmes, Gerald Anderson 1887-1948 *WhAm 2*
Holmes, Gideon Francis 1843- *NatCAB 14*
Holmes, Sir Gordon 1876-1965 *BiHiMed*
Holmes, Gustavus S 1860- *WhAm 4*
Holmes, Guy Earl 1873-1945 *WhAm 2*
Holmes, Harry Nicholls 1879-1958 *WhAm 4*
Holmes, Hector Adams 1829- *NatCAB 10*
Holmes, Henry 1832?- *NewYHSD*
Holmes, Henry Alfred 1883-1963 *WhAm 4*
Holmes, Henry Wyman 1880-1960 *WhAm 4*
Holmes, Howard Carleton 1854-1921
NatCAB 14, WhAm 1
Holmes, Isaac E 1786-1867 *BiAUS*
Holmes, Isaac Edward 1796-1867 *ApCAB,
BiDrAC, DcAmB, Drake, NatCAB 23,
TwCBDA, WhAm H, WhAmP*
Holmes, Israel 1800-1874 *DcAmB, WhAm H*
Holmes, J D *NewYHSD*
Holmes, Jack Alroy 1911-1967 *WhAm 5*
Holmes, Jack David Lazarus 1930- *EncAAH*
Holmes, James Thomas 1890-1970 *WhAm 5*
Holmes, Jay Vanderbilt 1887-1954 *NatCAB 41*
Holmes, Jennie Florella 1842-1892 *AmWom*

Holmes, Jesse Herman 1864-1942 *WhAm 2*
Holmes, John 1773-1843 *ApCAB, BiAUS,
BiDrAC, DcAmB, Drake, NatCAB 10,
TwCBDA, WhAm H, WhAmP*
Holmes, John 1789-1870 *ApCAB*
Holmes, John 1799-1852 *ApCAB*
Holmes, John 1891-1961 *WhAm 4*
Holmes, John 1904-1962 *WhAm 4*
Holmes, John A *NatCAB 12*
Holmes, John Grier 1849-1904 *NatCAB 27*
Holmes, John Haynes 1879-1964 *DcAmReB,
McGEWB, NatCAB 15, WhAm 4*
Holmes, John Laird 1868-1958 *NatCAB 48*
Holmes, John McClellan 1834-1911 *ApCAB,
WhAm 1*
Holmes, John P 1905-1960 *WhAm 4*
Holmes, John Simcox 1868- *WhAm 5*
Holmes, Joseph Addison 1900-1964 *WhAm 4*
Holmes, Joseph Austin 1859-1915 *DcAmB,
NatCAB 23, WhAm 1*
Holmes, Joses B S *WhAm 5*
Holmes, Julius Cecil 1899-1968 *NatCAB 54,
WhAm 5*
Holmes, Kate Osgood 1858- *WomWWA 14*
Holmes, Keturah Beers 1878- *WomWWA 14*
Holmes, Lawrence 1865-1950 *NatCAB 38*
Holmes, Ludvig 1858-1910 *WhAm 1*
Holmes, Major Edward 1882-1946 *WhAm 2*
Holmes, Malcolm Haughton 1906-1953
WhAm 3
Holmes, Marshall Fuller 1857-1912 *NatCAB 17*
Holmes, Mary Caroline d1927 *WhAm 1*
Holmes, Mary Elisabeth 1870-1927 *WhAm 1*
Holmes, Mary Elizabeth 1870-1927
WomWWA 14
Holmes, Mary Emilie 1850-1906 *AmWom,
WhAm 1*
Holmes, Mary Emma 1839- *AmWom*
Holmes, Mary Jane Hawes d1907 *AmWom,
ApCAB, TwCBDA, WhAm 1*
Holmes, Mary Jane Hawes 1825-1907 *DcAmB,
NotAW*
Holmes, Mary Jane Hawes 1838-1907
NatCAB 8
Holmes, Merrill Jacob 1886-1962 *NatCAB 47,
WhAm 4*
Holmes, Morris Grant 1862-1945 *WhAm 2*
Holmes, Myrta Whitney 1871- *WomWWA 14*
Holmes, Nathaniel 1814-1901 *ApCAB,
NatCAB 3*
Holmes, Nathaniel 1815-1901 *DcAmB,
TwCBDA, WhAm 1*
Holmes, Nathaniel, Jr. *NewYHSD*
Holmes, Nathaniel, Sr. *NewYHSD*
Holmes, Oliver Wendell 1809-1894 *AmBi,
ApCAB, AsBiEn, BiHiMed, DcAmB,
Drake, EncAB, McGEWB, NatCAB 2,
TwCBDA, WebAB, WhAm H*
Holmes, Oliver Wendell 1841-1935 *AmBi,
ApCAB, ApCAB X, DcAmB S1, EncAB,
McGEWB, NatCAB 12, NatCAB 27,
TwCBDA, WebAB, WhAm 1, WhAmP*
Holmes, Otis Halbert 1902- *BiDrAC*
Holmes, Pehr Gustaf 1881-1952 *BiDrAC,
WhAm 3, WhAmP*
Holmes, Philip Henry 1870-1939 *NatCAB 38*
Holmes, Phillips 1909-1942 *WhAm 2*
Holmes, Ralph Clinton 1874-1950 *WhAm 3*
Holmes, Ralph Maynard 1887-1967
NatCAB 55
Holmes, Ralph Williams 1876-1966 *NatCAB 51*
Holmes, Ralston Smith 1882-1966 *WhAm 4*
Holmes, Richard Edwin 1908-1954 *NatCAB 46*
Holmes, Richard Sill 1842-1912 *WhAm 1*
Holmes, Robert 1903-1965 *WhAm 4*
Holmes, Robert Shailor 1870-1939 *WhAm 1*
Holmes, Robert Thomas 1857-1918 *NatCAB 19*
Holmes, Rudolph Wieser d1953 *WhAm 3*
Holmes, Ruth Vickery 1888- *WomWWA 14*
Holmes, Samuel Foss 1881- *WhAm 6*
Holmes, Samuel Jackson 1868- *WhAm 5*
Holmes, Samuel VanVranken 1862-1935
NatCAB 26, WhAm 1
Holmes, Sidney Tracy 1815-1890 *BiAUS,
BiDrAC, WhAm H*
Holmes, Simon H 1843- *ApCAB*
Holmes, Theophilus Hunter 1804-1880 *AmBi,
ApCAB, BiDConf, DcAmB, NatCAB 10,*

TwCBDA, WebAMB, WhAm H
Holmes, Theophilus Hunter 1805-1864 *Drake*
Holmes, Thomas James 1874-1959 *WhAm 3*
Holmes, Urban Tigner 1900-1972 *WhAm 5*
Holmes, Uriel 1764-1827 *BiAUS, BiDrAC,
TwCBDA, WhAm H*
Holmes, W Raymond 1902-1973 *NatCAB 57*
Holmes, Walton Hezekiah 1861-1934
NatCAB 26, WhAm 4
Holmes, Wilbur Fisk 1849- *WhAm 4*
Holmes, William 1844- *NatCAB 14*
Holmes, William Henry 1846-1933 *AmBi,
ApCAB, DcAmB S1, IIBEAAW,
NatCAB 16, TwCBDA, WhAm 1*
Holmes, William Henry 1874-1948 *WhAm 2*
Holmes, Zacheus, Jr. 1839?- *NewYHSD*
Holmgren, Frithiof 1831-1897 *DcScB*
Holmgren, John Rueben 1897-1963 *NatCAB 51,
WhAm 4*
Holmquist, Claire Walfred 1906-1972 *WhAm 5*
Holmquist, Fred Nels 1884-1955 *NatCAB 44*
Holmstrom, Andrew Birger 1895-1970
NatCAB 56, WhAm 4
Holmstrom, Gus Edgar 1897-1967 *WhAm 5*
Holsapple, Cortell King 1900-1962 *WhAm 4*
Holsapple, Lloyd Burdwin 1884-1959
NatCAB 47
Holschuh, Louis William 1881-1971 *WhAm 5*
Holsclaw, Charles H 1904-1973 *WhAm 6*
Holsey, Hopkins 1779-1859 *BiDrAC,
WhAm H*
Holsey, Hopkins 1799-1859 *BiAUS*
Holsey, Lucius Henry 1842?-1920 *DcAmB*
Holsey, Lucius Henry 1845-1920 *WhAm 4,
WhoColR*
Holsman, Henry K 1866- *WhAm 5*
Holst, Amy M 1858- *WomWWA 14*
Holst, Edvard 1843-1899 *WhAm H*
Holst, Engelhardt Wilboren 1872-1932
NatCAB 29
Holst, Gustav 1874-1934 *McGEWB*
Holst, Hermann Edouard Von 1841-1904
NatCAB 11
Holst, Hermann Eduard Von 1841-1904 *AmBi,
ApCAB, DcAmB*
Holst, Johan-Bernt 1842-1919 *NatCAB 18*
Holste, Peter Caspar 1775?- *NewYHSD*
Holstead, Lula 1860- *WomWWA 14*
Holstein, Henry Lincoln 1865- *WhAm 4*
Holstein, Joseph Samuel 1877-1948 *NatCAB 38*
Holstein, LaFayette Villaume 1763-1839
ApCAB
Holstein, Otto 1883-1934 *WhAm 1*
Holstein-Ducoudray, H L V d1839 *Drake*
Holswade, James Frederick 1878-1942
NatCAB 34
Holt, Adoniram Judson 1847-1933 *WhAm 1*
Holt, Alexina Crawford 1869- *WomWWA 14*
Holt, Andrew 1855-1948 *NatCAB 37,
WhAm 2*
Holt, Andrew Hall 1890-1956 *WhAm 3*
Holt, Arthur Erastus 1876-1942 *DcAmB S3,
NatCAB 31, WhAm 1*
Holt, Byron Webber 1857-1933 *WhAm 1*
Holt, Calvert 1892-1938 *NatCAB 42*
Holt, Camilla McPherson 1860- *WomWWA 14*
Holt, Charles *NewYHSD*
Holt, Charles Scott 1879-1952 *NatCAB 46*
Holt, Charles Sumner 1855-1918 *WhAm 1*
Holt, Dan 1802-1853 *NatCAB 9*
Holt, Edwin Bissell 1873-1946 *DcAmB S4,
WhAm 3*
Holt, Edwin Cameron 1861-1944 *NatCAB 35*
Holt, Edwin Michael 1807-1884 *DcAmB,
WhAm H*
Holt, Ellen 1869- *WomWWA 14*
Holt, Erastus Eugene, Sr. 1849-1931 *TwCBDA,
WhAm 1*
Holt, Erwin Allen 1873- *WhAm 5*
Holt, Eugene 1875-1948 *NatCAB 37*
Holt, Frank O 1883-1948 *WhAm 2*
Holt, Fred Park 1860- *WhAm 4*
Holt, George Chandler 1843-1931 *NatCAB 24,
WhAm 1*
Holt, George Hubbard 1852-1924 *WhAm 1*
Holt, Guy 1892-1934 *WhAm 1*
Holt, Hamilton 1872-1951 *DcAmB S5,
NatCAB 15, NatCAB 40, WhAm 3*

Holt, Hamilton Tatum 1897-1963 *WhAm 4*
Holt, Harold Edward 1908-1967 *WhAm 4*
Holt, Harry Howard, Jr. 1904-1964 *WhAm 4*
Holt, Henry 1840-1926 *AmBi, DcAmB,*
NatCAB 9, NatCAB 31, TwCBDA,
WhAm 1
Holt, Henry Chandler 1881-1955 *NatCAB 45,*
WhAm 3
Holt, Henry Winston 1864-1947 *NatCAB 40,*
WhAm 2
Holt, Hines 1805-1865 *BiDrAC, WhAm H*
Holt, Hines 1805-1868 *BiDConf*
Holt, Homer Adams 1898-1975 *WhAm 6*
Holt, Isabella 1892-1962 *NatCAB 46*
Holt, Ivan Lee 1886-1967 *WhAm 4*
Holt, J J d1868 *BiAUS*
Holt, J Seaborn 1884-1963 *NatCAB 51*
Holt, John 1721-1784 *ApCAB, DcAmB,*
Drake, NatCAB 23, WhAm H
Holt, John Herrimon 1860- *WhAm 4*
Holt, John Saunders 1826-1886 *ApCAB, Drake,*
NatCAB 6
Holt, Joseph 1807-1894 *AmBi, ApCAB,*
BiAUS, BiDrUSE, DcAmB, Drake,
NatCAB 1, TwCBDA, WhAm H
Holt, Joseph Franklin, III 1924- *BiDrAC*
Holt, L Banks 1842-1920 *NatCAB 30*
Holt, L Emmett, Jr. 1895-1974 *WhAm 6*
Holt, Lawrence Shackleford 1851-1937
WhAm 1
Holt, Lee Cone 1880-1957 *WhAm 3*
Holt, Lucius Hudson 1881-1953 *WhAm 3*
Holt, Luther Emmett 1855-1924 *ApCAB X,*
DcAmB, NatCAB 13, NatCAB 20,
WebAB, WhAm 1
Holt, Marshall Keyser 1874- *BiCAW,*
WhAm 5
Holt, Mary Roxy Wilkins 1869- *WomWWA 14*
Holt, Orren Thaddeus 1849- *WhAm 4*
Holt, Orrin 1792-1855 *BiAUS, BiDrAC,*
WhAm H
Holt, Percy William 1895?- *IIBEAAW*
Holt, Rackham 1899-1963 *WhAm 4*
Holt, Robert Harold 1889-1973 *WhAm 6*
Holt, Roland 1867-1931 *NatCAB 23,*
WhAm 1
Holt, Rosa Belle *WhAm 5, WomWWA 14*
Holt, Rush Dew 1905-1955 *BiDrAC,*
NatCAB 50, WhAm 3
Holt, Samuel 1801- *NewYHSD*
Holt, Thomas Michael 1831-1896 *NatCAB 4,*
TwCBDA
Holt, Thomas Worsley 1887-1944 *NatCAB 37*
Holt, Walter Vincent 1857- *WhAm 4*
Holt, Ward Parsons 1899-1960 *NatCAB 48*
Holt, William Franklin 1864-1951 *DcAmB S5,*
NatCAB 48, WhAm 3
Holt, William Henry 1842-1919 *NatCAB 13,*
WhAm 1
Holt, William Joseph 1891-1955 *WhAm 3*
Holt, William Leland 1878-1946 *NatCAB 39*
Holt, William Sylvester 1848-1931 *WhAm H*
Holt, Winifred 1870-1945 *BiCAW, DcAmB S3,*
NotAW, WhAm 2, WomWWA 14
Holten, Samuel 1738-1816 *BiAUS, BiDrAC,*
DcAmB, NatCAB 13, WhAm H,
WhAmP
Holter, Edwin Olaf 1871-1964 *NatCAB 53*
Holter, Norman B 1868-1957 *WhAm 3*
Holthusen, Henry Frank 1894-1971 *WhAm 5*
Holtman, Dudley Frank 1889-1963 *WhAm 4*
Holtman, Louis 1851-1901 *WhAm 4*
Holton, Edward Dwight 1815-1892 *NatCAB 2*
Holton, Edwin Lee 1876-1950 *WhAm 3*
Holton, Elizabeth Curran d1970 *WhAm 5*
Holton, George VanSyckel 1890-1972 *WhAm 5*
Holton, Hart Benton 1835-1907 *BiDrAC*
Holton, Henry *NewYHSD*
Holton, Henry Dwight 1838-1917 *WhAm 1*
Holton, Holland 1888-1947 *WhAm 2*
Holton, Jessie Moon 1866-1951 *BiCAW,*
WhAm 3
Holton, Jessie Moore 1866-1951 *WomWWA 14*
Holton, Luther Hamilton 1817-1880 *ApCAB*
Holton, M Adelaide 1860- *WhAm 4*
Holton, Samuel 1738-1816 *ApCAB, Drake,*
NatCAB 13, TwCBDA

Holton, Winfred Byron, Jr. 1888-1957
NatCAB 54, WhAm 3
Holtzapple, George Emanuel 1862-1946
NatCAB 34
Holtzclaw, Jack Gilbert 1886-1955 *NatCAB 46,*
WhAm 4
Holtzclaw, James Thadeus 1832-1893 *BiDConf,*
NatCAB 18
Holtze *NewYHSD*
Holtzman, John W 1858- *WhAm 4*
Holtzman, Lester 1913- *BiDrAC, WhAmP*
Holtzmann, F *NewYHSD*
Holtzmann, Jacob L 1888-1963 *WhAm 4*
Holtzoff, Alexander 1886-1969 *WhAm 5*
Holtzworth, Bertram Arthur 1904-1971
WhAm 5
Holubar, Allen 1889-1923 *ApCAB X*
Holwerda, John Jacob 1910-1971 *NatCAB 56*
Holy, Thomas Celestine 1887-1973 *WhAm 6*
Holyland, C J *NewYHSD*
Holyoke, Edward 1689-1769 *ApCAB, Drake,*
NatCAB 6, TwCBDA
Holyoke, Edward 1858-1940 *NatCAB 31,*
WhAm 1
Holyoke, Edward Augustus 1728-1829 *ApCAB,*
DcAmB, Drake, NatCAB 7, TwCBDA,
WhAm H
Holyoke, Edward Augustus, Jr. 1827-
NewYHSD
Holyoke, Samuel 1762-1820 *AmBi, ApCAB,*
DcAmB, Drake, NatCAB 13, WhAm H
Holzapple, Joseph Randall 1914-1973 *WhAm 6*
Holzberg, Jules Donald 1915-1973 *WhAm 5*
Holzer, Charles Elmer 1887-1956 *WhAm 3*
Holzheimer, William Andrew 1870- *WhAm 2*
Holzinger, Karl John 1892-1954 *BiDAmEd,*
WhAm 3
Holzknecht, Karl J 1899-1956 *WhAm 3*
Holzman, Benjamin Grad 1910-1975 *WhAm 6*
Holzman, Jerome Leopold 1895-1964
NatCAB 50
Holzman, Mark Benjamin 1882-1957
NatCAB 48
Holzwart, F A *NewYHSD*
Holzworth, Ernest Harvey 1891-1969
NatCAB 55
Homan, Earl Wilson 1898-1960 *NatCAB 48*
Homan, Fletcher 1868- *WhAm 5*
Homan, Paul Thomas 1893-1969 *WhAm 5*
Homan, Samuel V *NewYHSD*
Homan, Walter Joseph 1895-1963 *NatCAB 48*
Homans, Amy Morris 1848-1933 *BiDAmEd,*
WhAm 4, WomWWA 14
Homans, Charles Dudley 1826-1886 *ApCAB*
Homans, Isaac Smith 1832-1879 *NatCAB 30*
Homans, John 1793-1868 *ApCAB, Drake*
Homans, Nancy 1861- *WomWWA 14*
Homans, Sheppard 1831-1898 *NatCAB 6*
Homans, Sheppard 1870-1952 *NatCAB 39*
Homans, Thomas Simmons 1871-1927
NatCAB 21
Homberg, Wilhelm 1652-1715 *DcScB*
Homberger, Alfred William 1887-1952
WhAm 3
Homberger, Ludwig Maximillian 1882-1954
WhAm 3
Home, Daniel Douglas 1833-1886 *ApCAB,*
Drake
Home, Daniel Dunglas 1833-1886 *AmBi*
Home, Everard 1756-1832 *DcScB*
Home, Francis 1719-1813 *BiHiMed*
Home, Mrs. M A *NewYHSD*
Homer *McGEWB*
Homer, Arthur Bartlett 1896-1972 *NatCAB 57,*
WhAm 5
Homer, Charles Christopher 1847-1914
NatCAB 16
Homer, Charles Savage 1834-1917 *ApCAB X*
Homer, Francis Theodore 1872- *WhAm 5*
Homer, Henrietta Maria 1809-1884 *NewYHSD*
Homer, Horatio Julius 1848- *WhoColR*
Homer, James *NewYHSD*
Homer, John L 1888-1961 *WhAm 4*
Homer, Jonathan 1759-1843 *ApCAB*
Homer, Louise Dilworth Beatty d1947 *WhAm 2,*
WomWWA 14
Homer, Louise Dilworth Beatty 1871-1947
DcAmB S4, NotAW

Homer, Louise Dilworth Beatty 1872?-1947
ApCAB X
Homer, Louise Dilworth Beatty 1874?-1947
NatCAB 14
Homer, Mary Frances Wellington 1842-
WomWWA 14
Homer, Philena Fletcher 1877- *WomWWA 14*
Homer, Sidney 1864-1953 *WhAm 3*
Homer, Soloman Jones 1870- *WhAm 5*
Homer, William Bradford 1817-1841 *ApCAB,*
Drake
Homer, William John 1869-1919 *NatCAB 18,*
WhAm 1
Homer, William Oscar 1881- *WhAm 6*
Homer, Winslow 1836-1910 *AmBi, ApCAB,*
BnEnAmA, DcAmB, EncAB, McGEWB,
NatCAB 11, NewYHSD, TwCBDA,
WebAB, WhAm 1
Homes, Henry Augustus 1812-1887 *ApCAB,*
DcAmB, DcAmLiB, NatCAB 13,
TwCBDA, WhAm H
Homes, Mary Sophie Shaw 1830?- *ApCAB*
Homes, William 1663-1746 *ApCAB, Drake*
Homma, Masaharu 1888-1946 *WhWW-II*
Hommel, Ida May *WomWWA 14*
Hommel, Oscar 1868-1941 *NatCAB 50*
Hommell, Philemon Emile 1863-1935
NatCAB 25
Honan, James Henry 1859-1917 *WhAm 1*
Honan, William Francis d1935 *WhAm 1*
Honda, Kotaro 1870-1954 *AsBiEn, DcScB*
Honda, Masaki *WhWW-II*
Honda, Masujiro 1866- *WhAm 4*
Hondius, Gerrit 1891-1970 *NatCAB 55*
Hondorp, Peter 1903-1970 *WhAm 5*
Hone, Philip 1780-1851 *AmBi, DcAmB,*
WebAB, WhAm H
Hone, Philip 1781-1851 *ApCAB, Drake*
Honegger, Arthur 1892-1955 *McGEWB,*
WhAm 4
Honen 1133-1212 *McGEWB*
Hones, Charles Julius 1894-1954 *NatCAB 42*
Honest Abe *EncAAH*
Honey, Robertson 1870-1941 *WhAm 1*
Honey, Samuel Robertson 1842-1927 *WhAm 1*
Honeycutt, Charles Fletcher 1909-1960
NatCAB 51
Honeycutt, Francis Webster 1883-1940
WhAm 1
Honeycutt, Jesse Vernon 1893-1969 *WhAm 5*
Honeycutt, John Thomas 1882-1964
NatCAB 52
Honeyman, Nan Wood 1881-1970 *BiDrAC,*
WhAm 6
Honeyman, Paul Depue 1870-1933 *NatCAB 29*
Honeywell, Alba 1821-1916 *NatCAB 17*
Honeywell, Clara E 1873- *WomWWA 14*
Honeywell, Miss M A 1787?- *NewYHSD,*
WhAm H
Honeywell, Mark Charles 1874-1964
NatCAB 52, WhAm 4
Honeywood, St. John 1763-1798 *ApCAB,*
Drake, NatCAB 9
Honfleur, Mr. *NewYHSD*
Honfleur, Mrs. *NewYHSD*
Honig, George Honig 1881- *WhAm 6*
Honigschmid, Otto 1878-1945 *DcScB*
Honline, Moses Alfred 1873-1932 *WhAm 1*
Honnen, George 1897-1974 *WhAm 6*
Honnold, William Lincoln 1866-1950 *ApCAB X,*
WhAm 3
Honnoll, Hodges Hafford 1883-1956
NatCAB 47
Honold, J Frank 1903-1964 *NatCAB 51*
Honor, Leo Lazarus 1894-1956 *NatCAB 43*
Honor, William Hilliard 1877-1955 *NatCAB 43*
Honore, Henry Hamilton 1824-1916 *ApCAB X,*
NatCAB 12
Honore, Paul 1885-1956 *WhAm 3*
Hontan, Louis DeL D'Arce, Baron DeLa
1666-1713? *AmBi, DcAmB*
Honzik, Charles H 1897-1968 *NatCAB 55*
Hoo, Victor Chi-Tsai 1894-1972 *WhAm 5*
Hoober, John Aaron 1867-1950 *NatCAB 40*
Hoobler, B Raymond 1872-1943 *NatCAB 32,*
WhAm 2
Hooch, Pieter, De 1629-1684? *McGEWB*
Hood, Alice Watkins 1877- *WomWWA 14*

Hood, Arthur A 1891-1965 *WhAm 4*
Hood, Arthur Needham 1868-1950 *NatCAB 39*
Hood, Charles Crook 1841-1927 *NatCAB 21,*
  WhAm 1
Hood, Charles Emerson 1878-1965 *WhAm 4*
Hood, Charles Harvey 1860-1937 *NatCAB 28*
Hood, E Lyman 1858-1931 *WhAm 1*
Hood, Edwin Milton 1858-1923 *WhAm 1*
Hood, Francis George 1878-1938 *NatCAB 35*
Hood, Frazer 1875-1944 *NatCAB 51,*
  WhAm 2
Hood, Frederic Clark 1865-1942 *WhAm 2*
Hood, George 1815?-1869 *ApCAB, Drake*
Hood, George Ezekial 1875-1960 *BiDrAC,*
  WhAm 3
Hood, Harry 1876- *IIBEAAW*
Hood, Helen *NatCAB 8*
Hood, Horace 1853-1924 *NatCAB 20*
Hood, Horace 1853-1925 *WhAm 1*
Hood, J Douglas 1889-1966 *WhAm 4*
Hood, James Walker 1831-1918 *AmBi, ApCAB,*
  DcAmB, TwCBDA, WhAm 1, WhoColR
Hood, John 1859-1919 *WhAm 1*
Hood, John Bell 1830?-1879 *Drake*
Hood, John Bell 1831-1879 *AmBi, ApCAB,*
  BiDConf, DcAmB, NatCAB 4, TwCBDA,
  WebAB, WebAMB, WhAm H, WhoMilH
Hood, John Mifflin 1843-1906 *NatCAB 30*
Hood, John Mifflin 1880-1941 *NatCAB 30*
Hood, Kenneth Ogilvie 1906- *WhAm 6*
Hood, Matilda *NewYHSD*
Hood, Oliver Roland 1867- *WhAm 5*
Hood, Ozni Porter 1865-1937 *WhAm 1*
Hood, Raymond Mathewson 1881-1934 *AmBi,*
  BnEnAmA, DcAmB S1, NatCAB 28,
  WhAm 1
Hood, Robert Thurlow 1887-1930 *NatCAB 26*
Hood, Samuel 1724-1816 *ApCAB*
Hood, Samuel 1800?-1875 *ApCAB*
Hood, Solomon Porter 1853-1943 *NatCAB 36,*
  WhAm 4, WhoColR
Hood, Washington 1808-1840 *DcAmB,*
  NatCAB 24, NewYHSD, WebAMB,
  WhAm H
Hood, William 1846-1926 *NatCAB 20,*
  WhAm 1
Hoogewerff, John Adrian 1860-1933
  NatCAB 25, WhAm 1
Hoogland, William 1795?-1832 *NewYHSD*
Hook, Charles Ruffin 1880-1963 *NatCAB 52*
Hook, Charles Ruffin, Jr. 1914-1961
  NatCAB 50, WhAm 4
Hook, Enos 1804-1841 *BiAUS, BiDrAC,*
  WhAm H
Hook, Frances *NatCAB 6*
Hook, Frank Eugene 1893- *BiDrAC*
Hook, Ida MacDonald *WomWWA 14*
Hook, James Schley 1834- *NatCAB 2*
Hook, James William 1884-1957 *NatCAB 51,*
  WhAm 3
Hook, Mary Elizabeth Burton 1850-
  WomWWA 14
Hook, Sidney 1902- *BiDAmEd*
Hook, Walter Williams 1902-1963 *WhAm 4*
Hook, William Cather 1857-1921 *NatCAB 34,*
  WhAm 1
Hooke, Ethel M Wagoner *WomWWA 14*
Hooke, Robert 1635-1702 *DcScB*
Hooke, Robert 1635-1703 *AsBiEn, BiHiMed,*
  McGEWB
Hooke, William 1600-1677 *NatCAB 5*
Hooke, William 1601-1678 *ApCAB, Drake*
Hooker, Albert Huntington 1865-1936
  NatCAB 28
Hooker, Arthur Myreenus 1904-1962
  NatCAB 50
Hooker, Blanche Ferry 1871- *BiCAW*
Hooker, Brian 1880-1946 *WhAm 2*
Hooker, Charles *NewYHSD*
Hooker, Charles 1779-1863 *ApCAB*
Hooker, Charles 1799-1863 *TwCBDA*
Hooker, Charles Edward 1825-1914 *ApCAB,*
  BiAUS, BiDrAC, NatCAB 4, TwCBDA,
  WhAm 4, WhAmP
Hooker, Donald Russell 1876-1946 *DcAmB S4,*
  WhAm 2
Hooker, Edith Houghton *WomWWA 14*
Hooker, Edward 1822-1903 *ApCAB, TwCBDA,*

  WhAm 1
Hooker, Edward Beecher 1855-1927 *WhAm 1*
Hooker, Edward William 1794-1875 *ApCAB,*
  Drake, TwCBDA
Hooker, Edward Williams 1865-1915
  NatCAB 16
Hooker, Ellen Kelley 1833-1918 *NatCAB 4,*
  TwCBDA, WhAm 1, WomWWA 14
Hooker, Elon Huntington 1869-1938 *ApCAB X,*
  DcAmB S2, WhAm 1
Hooker, Forrestine Cooper 1867-1932 *WhAm 1*
Hooker, Frank Arthur 1844-1911 *NatCAB 12,*
  TwCBDA, WhAm 1
Hooker, George Ellsworth 1861-1939 *WhAm 1*
Hooker, George Washington 1863-1946
  NatCAB 41
Hooker, Harold Louis 1869-1950 *NatCAB 39*
Hooker, Harry Mix 1872-1949 *WhAm 2*
Hooker, Henry Clay 1828-1907 *REnAW*
Hooker, Henry Stewart 1879-1964 *WhAm 4*
Hooker, Herman 1804-1865 *ApCAB,*
  NatCAB 7
Hooker, Herman 1806?-1865 *Drake, TwCBDA*
Hooker, Horace 1793-1864 *ApCAB*
Hooker, Isabella Beecher 1822-1907 *AmWom,*
  ApCAB, DcAmB, NotAW, TwCBDA,
  WhAm 1, WhAmP
Hooker, James Murray 1873-1940 *BiDrAC,*
  WhAm 1
Hooker, John Daggett 1838-1911 *NatCAB 22,*
  WhAm 1
Hooker, John Jay 1903-1971 *WhAm 5*
Hooker, John Williams 1914-1959 *NatCAB 46*
Hooker, Joseph 1814-1879 *AmBi, ApCAB,*
  DcAmB, NatCAB 4, TwCBDA, WebAB,
  WebAMB, WhAm H, WhoMilH
Hooker, Joseph 1815-1879 *Drake*
Hooker, Joseph Dalton 1817-1911 *DcScB*
Hooker, Margaret Huntington 1869- *WhAm 5,*
  WomWWA 14
Hooker, Mary Agnes 1867- *WomWWA 14*
Hooker, Mildred Phelps Stokes 1881-
  WomWWA 14
Hooker, Philip 1766-1836 *DcAmB,*
  NatCAB 24, NewYHSD, WhAm H
Hooker, Philip 1766-1837 *BnEnAmA*
Hooker, Ransom Spafard 1873-1957
  NatCAB 46
Hooker, Richard 1554-1600 *McGEWB*
Hooker, Richard 1878-1967 *WhAm 4*
Hooker, Samuel 1632-1697 *ApCAB*
Hooker, Samuel Cox 1864-1935 *DcAmB S1*
Hooker, Thomas 1585?-1647 *TwCBDA*
Hooker, Thomas 1586-1647 *AmBi, ApCAB,*
  DcAmB, DcAmReB, Drake, EncAB,
  McGEWB, NatCAB 6, WebAB,
  WhAm H
Hooker, Thomas 1849-1924 *NatCAB 20,*
  WhAm 1
Hooker, Thomas 1882-1936 *NatCAB 29*
Hooker, Warren Brewster 1856-1920 *BiDrAC,*
  NatCAB 18, TwCBDA, WhAm 1,
  WhAmP
Hooker, William *DcAmB, NewYHSD,*
  WhAm H
Hooker, William Jackson 1785-1865 *DcScB*
Hooker, William P 1905-1965 *WhAm 4*
Hooker, Worthington 1806-1867 *ApCAB,*
  BiDAmEd, DcAmB, Drake, NatCAB 13,
  WhAm H
Hooks, Charles d1851 *BiAUS, TwCBDA*
Hooks, Charles 1768-1843 *BiDrAC, WhAm H,*
  WhAmP
Hoole, Celia Dame 1846- *WomWWA 14*
Hoole, Edmund *NewYHSD*
Hoole, John R *NewYHSD*
Hooley, Abraham George 1862-1918
  NatCAB 17
Hooley, Arthur 1874- *WhAm 5*
Hooley, Edwin Strange 1863- *WhAm 4*
Hooley, Francis George 1882-1962 *NatCAB 50*
Hooley, Helen Therese *WomWWA 14*
Hoon, Clarence Earl 1880-1934 *WhAm 1*
Hooper, Alcaeus 1859-1938 *NatCAB 29*
Hooper, Archibald Maclaine 1775-1853
  TwCBDA
Hooper, Ben Walter 1870-1957 *NatCAB 48,*
  WhAm 3

Hooper, Benjamin Stephen 1835-1898 *BiDrAC*
Hooper, Bert Leslie 1892-1975 *WhAm 6*
Hooper, Blanche Heard 1881- *WomWWA 14*
Hooper, C E 1898-1954 *WhAm 3*
Hooper, Charles Edward 1867-1920 *WhAm 1*
Hooper, Claude Ernest 1898-1954 *DcAmB S5*
Hooper, Edward 1829-1870 *ApCAB,*
  NewYHSD
Hooper, Edward James 1803- *ApCAB, Drake*
Hooper, Elizabeth Mae Merritt 1860-
  WomWWA 14
Hooper, Ellen Sturgis 1812-1848 *NotAW*
Hooper, Everett 1868- *WhAm 4*
Hooper, Francis Xavier 1854-1916 *NatCAB 17*
Hooper, Frank Finley 1877- *WhAm 3*
Hooper, Franklin Henry 1862-1940 *WhAm 1*
Hooper, Franklin William 1851-1914
  NatCAB 13, TwCBDA, WhAm 1
Hooper, Sir Frederic Collins 1892-1963
  WhAm 4
Hooper, George DeBerniere 1809-1892
  TwCBDA
Hooper, Horace Everett 1859-1922 *AmBi*
Hooper, James Ripley 1854-1934 *NatCAB 27*
Hooper, Jessie Annette Jack 1865-1935
  DcAmB S1, NotAW, WhAm 1, WhAmP
Hooper, John *NewYHSD*
Hooper, John 1802-1869 *ApCAB*
Hooper, John Albert 1838- *ApCAB X*
Hooper, John DeBerniere 1811-1886 *TwCBDA*
Hooper, John E d1848 *NewYHSD*
Hooper, John W d1868 *BiAUS*
Hooper, John William 1896-1959 *WhAm 3*
Hooper, Johnson Jones 1815-1862 *DcAmB,*
  NatCAB 11, TwCBDA, WhAm H
Hooper, Johnson Jones 1815-1863 *ApCAB*
Hooper, Joseph Albert 1840-1916 *NatCAB 17*
Hooper, Joseph Lawrence 1877-1934 *BiDrAC,*
  WhAm 1, WhAmP
Hooper, Louis Leverett 1867- *WhAm 4*
Hooper, Lucy 1816-1841 *ApCAB, Drake*
Hooper, Lucy Hamilton 1835-1893 *AmWom,*
  ApCAB, DcAmB, NatCAB 8, TwCBDA,
  WhAm H
Hooper, Osman Castle 1858-1941 *WhAm 1*
Hooper, Philo O 1833-1902 *NatCAB 7,*
  WhAm 1
Hooper, Robert 1709-1790 *NatCAB 19*
Hooper, Robert Lettice *ApCAB*
Hooper, Robert Lettice d1739 *Drake*
Hooper, Robert Lettice 1709-1785 *ApCAB*
Hooper, Robert Lettis 1709-1785 *NatCAB 12*
Hooper, Robert P 1872-1958 *WhAm 3*
Hooper, Samuel 1808-1875 *ApCAB, BiAUS,*
  BiDrAC, DcAmB, Drake, NatCAB 4,
  TwCBDA, WhAm H, WhAmP
Hooper, Shadrach K 1841- *WhAm 1*
Hooper, Stanford Caldwell 1884-1955
  NatCAB 47, WhAm 3
Hooper, Timothy Joseph 1871-1940 *NatCAB 30*
Hooper, W H 1813-1882 *BiAUS*
Hooper, W W *NewYHSD*
Hooper, Will Phillip 1855?-1938 *IIBEAAW*
Hooper, William 1702-1767 *ApCAB*
Hooper, William 1704-1767 *TwCBDA*
Hooper, William 1742-1790 *AmBi, ApCAB,*
  BiAUS, BiDrAC, DcAmB, Drake,
  NatCAB 5, TwCBDA, WhAm H,
  WhAmP
Hooper, William 1792-1876 *NatCAB 20,*
  TwCBDA
Hooper, William Davis 1843-1893 *NatCAB 16*
Hooper, William Henry 1813-1882 *ApCAB,*
  BiDrAC, REnAW, TwCBDA, WhAm H,
  WhAmP
Hooper, William Leslie 1855-1918 *WhAm 1*
Hooper, William Thomas 1886-1938
  NatCAB 28, WhAm 1
Hoopes, Benjamin 1820-1898 *NatCAB 6*
Hoopes, John Wilfred 1875-1948 *NatCAB 37*
Hoopes, Josiah 1832-1904 *ApCAB, TwCBDA,*
  WhAm 1
Hoopes, Maurice 1870-1949 *NatCAB 37*
Hoopes, William 1867-1924 *NatCAB 19*
Hoopes, Wilmer Worthington 1870-1955
  NatCAB 43
Hoopingarner, Dwight Lowell 1893-1955
  WhAm 3

Hoopingarner, Newman Leander 1891-1958
WhAm 3
Hoople, Gordon Douglass 1895-1973 *WhAm 6*
Hoose, James Harmon 1835-1915 *WhAm 1*
Hooton, Caradine Ray 1895-1966 *WhAm 4*
Hooton, Earnest Albert 1887-1954 *DcAmB S5,
NatCAB 40, WebAB, WhAm 3*
Hooton, Mott 1838-1920 *WhAm 1*
Hoover, Arthur McCall 1901-1972 *WhAm 5*
Hoover, Benjamin Andrew 1873-1962
NatCAB 50
Hoover, Bessie Ray 1874- *WhAm 5*
Hoover, Blaine 1893-1950 *WhAm 3*
Hoover, Calvin Bryce 1897-1974 *WhAm 6*
Hoover, Charles Franklin 1865-1927 *DcAmB,
NatCAB 42, WhAm 1*
Hoover, Charles Lewis 1872-1949 *WhAm 2*
Hoover, Charles Ruglas 1885-1942 *NatCAB 31,
WhAm 2*
Hoover, Donald Douglas 1904-1969 *NatCAB 54,
WhAm 5*
Hoover, Frank Garfield 1883-1954 *NatCAB 43,
WhAm 3*
Hoover, Frank Kryder 1854-1931 *NatCAB 41*
Hoover, George Pendleton d1943 *WhAm 3*
Hoover, Harvey Daniel 1880-1958 *WhAm 3*
Hoover, Herbert, Jr. 1903-1969 *WhAm 5*
Hoover, Herbert Clark 1874-1964 *ApCAB X,
BiDrAC, BiDrUSE, EncAAH, EncAB,
McGEWB, NatCAB 56, WebAB,
WhAm 4, WhAmP*
Hoover, Herbert William 1877-1954 *DcAmB S5,
WhAm 3*
Hoover, Hubbard 1888-1951 *NatCAB 39*
Hoover, Hubert Don 1887-1971 *WhAm 5*
Hoover, James Matthews 1872-1935 *DcAmB S1*
Hoover, Jeremiah Franklin 1879-1964
NatCAB 50
Hoover, John Crittenden 1861-1942 *NatCAB 36*
Hoover, John Edgar 1895-1972 *EncAB,
McGEWB, WebAB, WhAm 5*
Hoover, John Howard 1887-1970 *WhAm 5*
Hoover, Lou Henry 1874-1944 *NotAW,
WhAm 2*
Hoover, Ray 1894-1965 *WhAm 4*
Hoover, Samuel Earle 1879-1945 *WhAm 2*
Hoover, Simon Robert 1867-1936 *WhAm 1*
Hoover, Stuart 1920-1965 *WhAm 4*
Hoover, Theodore Jesse 1871-1955 *WhAm 3*
Hoover, Vincent Keyes 1864-1934 *NatCAB 26*
Hoover, William David 1864-1943 *NatCAB 46,
WhAm 2*
Hoover, William H 1889-1952 *WhAm 3*
Hoover, William Henry 1849-1932 *NatCAB 27*
Hope, Bob 1903- *WebAB*
Hope, Chester Raines 1881-1963 *WhAm 4*
Hope, Clifford Ragsdale 1893-1970 *BiDrAC,
WhAm 5*
Hope, Clifford Ragsdale 1893-1972 *EncAAH*
Hope, Eliza Milford Tatum 1908-1975 *WhAm 6*
Hope, Elizabeth Willard 1880- *WomWWA 14*
Hope, Francis Moffat 1877-1968 *WhAm 5*
Hope, Henry 1736-1811 *Drake*
Hope, J W 1812-1892 *NewYHSD*
Hope, James 1801-1841 *BiHiMed*
Hope, James 1818-1892 *ApCAB, NewYHSD,
TwCBDA, WhAm H*
Hope, James Barron 1827-1887 *ApCAB,
NatCAB 7*
Hope, James Barron 1829-1887 *DcAmB,
TwCBDA, WhAm H*
Hope, James Haskell 1874- *WhAm 5*
Hope, James William 1895-1964 *WhAm 4*
Hope, John 1868-1936 *AmBi, BiDAmEd,
DcAmB S2, McGEWB, NatCAB 28,
WebAB, WhAm 1*
Hope, Laura Lee *WebAB*
Hope, Leslie Townes *WebAB*
Hope, Matthew Boyd 1812-1859 *ApCAB,
TwCBDA*
Hope, Minnie Gazelle Welborn 1872- *WhAm 5,
WomWWA 14*
Hope, R DeVere 1884-1951 *NatCAB 40*
Hope, Richard 1895-1955 *WhAm 3*
Hope, Robert Hervey 1906-1970 *WhAm 6*
Hope, Robert Meek 1903-1964 *NatCAB 52*
Hope, Thomas *NewYHSD*
Hope, Thomas Charles 1766-1844 *DcScB*

Hope, Thomas W *NewYHSD*
Hope, Walter Ewing 1879-1948 *WhAm 2*
Hopekirk, Helen 1856-1945 *NotAW,
WhAm 3A, WomWWA 14*
Hopewell, Frank 1857-1918 *NatCAB 20*
Hopewell, Frank Blake 1873-1934 *NatCAB 33*
Hopewell, John 1845-1916 *NatCAB 14,
WhAm 1*
Hopewell-Smith, Arthur 1865- *WhAm 1*
Hopf, Harry Arthur 1882-1949 *WhAm 2*
Hopf, Heinz 1894-1971 *DcScB*
Hopfenbeck, George M 1900-1963 *WhAm 4*
Hopke, Theodore Mathias 1858-1940
NatCAB 30
Hopkin, Robert 1832-1909 *NatCAB 17,
NewYHSD*
Hopkins, Abel Grosvenor 1844-1899 *TwCBDA*
Hopkins, Abner Crump 1835-1911 *WhAm 1*
Hopkins, Albert 1807-1872 *ApCAB,
NatCAB 6, TwCBDA*
Hopkins, Albert Cole 1837-1911 *BiDrAC,
TwCBDA*
Hopkins, Albert Jarvis 1846-1922 *ApCAB X,
BiDrAC, NatCAB 11, TwCBDA,
WhAm 1, WhAmP*
Hopkins, Albert Lloyd 1871-1915 *NatCAB 37*
Hopkins, Alden 1905-1960 *NatCAB 46*
Hopkins, Alphonso Alva 1843-1918 *TwCBDA,
WhAm 1*
Hopkins, Altis Skiles 1872- *WhAm 5*
Hopkins, Amos Lawrence 1844- *WhAm 4*
Hopkins, Anderson Hoyt 1861- *WhAm 4*
Hopkins, Andrew Delmar 1857-1948
NatCAB 13, NatCAB 41, WhAm 4
Hopkins, Andrew Winkle 1880- *WhAm 6*
Hopkins, Archibald 1842-1926 *NatCAB 14,
WhAm 1*
Hopkins, Archibald Wilson 1845-1926
NatCAB 20
Hopkins, Arthur 1848-1930 *IlBEAAW*
Hopkins, Arthur F 1796-1866 *ApCAB*
Hopkins, Arthur Francis 1794-1865 *DcAmB,
WhAm H*
Hopkins, Arthur Francis 1794-1866 *NatCAB 4*
Hopkins, Arthur John 1864-1939 *WhAm 1*
Hopkins, Arthur Melancthon 1878-1950
NatCAB 39, WhAm 2A
Hopkins, B Smith 1873-1952 *WhAm 3*
Hopkins, Benjamin Franklin 1829-1870 *BiAUS,
BiDrAC, WhAm H*
Hopkins, Benjamin Franklin 1876-1955
WhAm 3
Hopkins, Berne Hudson 1880-1956 *NatCAB 46*
Hopkins, Caspar Thomas 1826-1893 *ApCAB,
TwCBDA*
Hopkins, Cecil Blaine 1883-1953 *NatCAB 47*
Hopkins, Charles Jerome 1836-1898 *ApCAB,
NatCAB 4, TwCBDA*
Hopkins, Charlotte Everett 1851-1935 *WhAm 1,
WomWWA 14*
Hopkins, Clarence Victor 1880- *WhAm 6*
Hopkins, Cyril George 1866-1919 *DcAmB,
WhAm 1*
Hopkins, Daniel 1734-1814 *ApCAB, Drake*
Hopkins, David William 1897-1968 *BiDrAC*
Hopkins, Edna Boies 1878- *WhAm 1*
Hopkins, Edward 1600-1657 *AmBi, ApCAB,
DcAmB, Drake, NatCAB 10, WhAm H*
Hopkins, Edward Augustus 1822-1891 *ApCAB,
DcAmB, WhAm H*
Hopkins, Edward Jerome 1836-1898 *WhAm H*
Hopkins, Edward Washburn 1857-1932 *AmBi,
DcAmB S1, NatCAB 14, TwCBDA,
WhAm 1*
Hopkins, Edward Whiting 1848-1926
NatCAB 42
Hopkins, Edwin Butcher 1882-1940 *NatCAB 30,
WhAm 1*
Hopkins, Edwin Mortimer 1862-1946 *WhAm 2*
Hopkins, Eleanor Scribner *WomWWA 14*
Hopkins, Ellen Dunlap 1858-1939 *AmBi,
WomWWA 14*
Hopkins, Emily Linnard *WomWWA 14*
Hopkins, Emma Curtis 1853-1925 *DcAmReB,
NotAW*
Hopkins, Erasmus Guy 1877- *WhAm 1*
Hopkins, Erastus 1810-1872 *ApCAB*
Hopkins, Erastus 1867-1937 *NatCAB 29,*

WhAm 4
Hopkins, Ernest Martin 1877-1964 *BiDAmEd,
WhAm 4*
Hopkins, Esek 1718-1802 *AmBi, ApCAB,
DcAmB, Drake, McGEWB, NatCAB 2,
TwCBDA, WebAB, WebAMB, WhAm H*
Hopkins, Evan Henry 1864-1938 *NatCAB 39,
WhAm 1*
Hopkins, Ferdinand T 1834- *NatCAB 2*
Hopkins, Ferdinand Travis 1879-1971
NatCAB 55
Hopkins, Florence May 1865- *NatCAB 18,
WomWWA 14*
Hopkins, Frances Ann Beechey 1856-1918
IlBEAAW
Hopkins, Francis Alexander 1853-1918 *BiDrAC*
Hopkins, Frank A 1853- *WhAm 4*
Hopkins, Frank Tucker 1857-1945 *NatCAB 34*
Hopkins, Franklin 1879- *WhAm 6*
Hopkins, Franklin Whetstone 1857- *WhAm 4*
Hopkins, Fred Mead 1875-1954 *WhAm 3*
Hopkins, Frederick Eli 1857- *WhAm 4*
Hopkins, Sir Frederick Gowland 1861-1947
AsBiEn, BiHiMed, DcScB, McGEWB
Hopkins, Frederick Vincent 1839- *ApCAB*
Hopkins, George Cyril 1866-1919 *AmBi*
Hopkins, George Hiram 1842- *NatCAB 5*
Hopkins, George Washington 1804-1861 *BiAUS,
BiDrAC, NatCAB 4, TwCBDA,
WhAm H*
Hopkins, Gerard Manley 1844-1889 *McGEWB*
Hopkins, Grace Porter *WomWWA 14*
Hopkins, Grant Sherman 1865- *WhAm 4*
Hopkins, Harry Lloyd 1890-1946 *BiDrUSE,
DcAmB S4, EncAAH, EncAB, McGEWB,
NatCAB 42, WebAB, WhAm 2, WhAmP,
WhWW-II*
Hopkins, Henry 1837-1908 *NatCAB 13,
NatCAB 38, WhAm 1*
Hopkins, Henry, Jr. 1882-1949 *NatCAB 38*
Hopkins, Herbert Cornwell 1880-1946
NatCAB 34
Hopkins, Herbert Muller 1870-1910 *TwCBDA,
WhAm 1*
Hopkins, I *NewYHSD*
Hopkins, Isaac Stiles 1841-1914 *DcAmB,
NatCAB 1, TwCBDA, WhAm 1*
Hopkins, James Campbell 1819-1877 *BiAUS,
DcAmB, WhAm H*
Hopkins, James E *NewYHSD*
Hopkins, James Frederick 1868-1931 *WhAm 1*
Hopkins, James Herron 1831-1904 *BiAUS*
Hopkins, James Herron 1832-1904 *BiDrAC*
Hopkins, James Love 1868-1931 *WhAm 1*
Hopkins, James R 1877-1969 *WhAm 5*
Hopkins, Jay Paul 1875- *WhAm 5*
Hopkins, Jennie Chandler White 1860-
WomWWA 14
Hopkins, Jesse Lamb 1860-1946 *NatCAB 36*
Hopkins, John Appleton Haven 1872-1960
NatCAB 53, WhAm 5
Hopkins, John Burroughs 1742-1796 *ApCAB,
DcAmB, WebAMB, WhAm H*
Hopkins, John Henry 1792-1868 *ApCAB,
DcAmB, Drake, NatCAB 11, NewYHSD,
TwCBDA, WhAm H*
Hopkins, John Henry 1861-1945 *WhAm 2*
Hopkins, John Henry, Jr. 1820-1891 *ApCAB,
NewYHSD, TwCBDA, WhAm H*
Hopkins, John Jay 1893-1957 *NatCAB 47,
WhAm 3*
Hopkins, John Morgan 1861-1929 *NatCAB 21*
Hopkins, Johns 1794-1873 *NatCAB 5*
Hopkins, Johns 1795-1873 *AmBi, ApCAB,
DcAmB, TwCBDA, WhAm H*
Hopkins, Joseph Gardner 1882-1951 *WhAm 3*
Hopkins, Josiah 1786-1862 *ApCAB*
Hopkins, Julia Anna 1870- *WomWWA 14*
Hopkins, Juliet Ann Opie 1818-1890 *DcAmB,
NotAW, WebAMB, WhAm H*
Hopkins, Lemuel 1750-1801 *AmBi, ApCAB,
BiHiMed, DcAmB, Drake, NatCAB 7,
TwCBDA, WhAm H*
Hopkins, Lewis Neill 1834- *NatCAB 3*
Hopkins, Lindsey 1879-1937 *WhAm 1*
Hopkins, Lodica Seely 1883- *WomWWA 14*
Hopkins, Louis Bertram 1881-1940 *WhAm 1*
Hopkins, Louisa Payson 1812-1862 *ApCAB,*

NatCAB 5
Hopkins, Louise Virginia Martin 1860-
WomWWA 14
Hopkins, Louise Virginia Martin 1861-
WhAm 4
Hopkins, M W *NewYHSD*
Hopkins, Margaret Hall Daly *WomWWA 14*
Hopkins, Margaret Sutton Briscoe 1864-
WhAm 4, WomWWA 14
Hopkins, Mark 1802-1887 *AmBi, ApCAB,*
BiDAmEd, DcAmB, DcAmReB, Drake,
McGEWB, NatCAB 6, TwCBDA,
WebAB, WhAm H
Hopkins, Mark 1813-1878 *NatCAB 20,*
REnAW
Hopkins, Mark 1832-1914 *NatCAB 18*
Hopkins, Mary Murray 1878- *WomWWA 14*
Hopkins, Miriam 1902-1972 *WhAm 5*
Hopkins, Moses Aaron 1846-1886 *ApCAB,*
NatCAB 12, TwCBDA
Hopkins, Nanette 1860-1938 *WhAm 1*
Hopkins, Nathan Thomas 1852-1927 *BiDrAC*
Hopkins, Nevil Monroe 1873-1945 *NatCAB 35,*
WhAm 2
Hopkins, Pauline Bradford Mackie 1873-
WomWWA 14
Hopkins, Percy Earl 1892-1967 *WhAm 4*
Hopkins, Porter William 1880-1957 *NatCAB 49*
Hopkins, Richard Joseph 1873-1943
NatCAB 33, WhAm 2
Hopkins, Robert Emmet 1833-1901 *NatCAB 30,*
WhAm 1
Hopkins, Robert Holbrook 1902-1968 *WhAm 5*
Hopkins, Robert Milton 1878-1955 *WhAm 3*
Hopkins, Roy Samuel 1881-1947 *NatCAB 35*
Hopkins, Samuel d1819 *BiAUS, Drake*
Hopkins, Samuel 1693-1755 *Drake*
Hopkins, Samuel 1721-1803 *AmBi, ApCAB,*
DcAmB, DcAmReB, Drake, McGEWB,
NatCAB 7, TwCBDA, WebAB,
WhAm H
Hopkins, Samuel 1750?-1819 *ApCAB,*
TwCBDA
Hopkins, Samuel 1753-1819 *BiDrAC, DcAmB,*
WhAm H
Hopkins, Samuel 1807-1887 *ApCAB,*
NatCAB 7, WhAm H
Hopkins, Samuel 1887-1927 *NatCAB 22*
Hopkins, Samuel Augustus 1858-1921 *WhAm 1*
Hopkins, Samuel Isaac 1843-1914 *BiDrAC*
Hopkins, Samuel Miles 1772-1837 *ApCAB,*
BiAUS, BiDrAC, TwCBDA, WhAm H
Hopkins, Samuel Miles 1813-1901 *ApCAB,*
TwCBDA, WhAm 1
Hopkins, Scott 1860-1917 *WhAm 1*
Hopkins, Selden G 1862- *WhAm 4*
Hopkins, Sherburne Gillette 1868-1932
WhAm 1
Hopkins, Stanley Marshall 1896-1973 *WhAm 6*
Hopkins, Stephen 1707-1785 *AmBi, ApCAB,*
ApCAB X, BiAUS, BiDrAC, DcAmB,
Drake, NatCAB 10, TwCBDA, WhAm H,
WhAmP
Hopkins, Stephen Tyng 1849-1892 *BiDrAC,*
WhAm H
Hopkins, Theodore Eli 1874-1958 *NatCAB 49*
Hopkins, Theodore Weld 1841- *ApCAB,*
WhAm 4
Hopkins, Thomas Cramer 1861-1935 *WhAm 3*
Hopkins, Thomas Snell 1845-1925 *WhAm 1*
Hopkins, Timothy 1859-1936 *NatCAB 26*
Hopkins, Una Nixson *WomWWA 14*
Hopkins, W Lathrop 1895-1944 *NatCAB 37*
Hopkins, W Wylie 1881-1938 *NatCAB 29*
Hopkins, Walter Lee 1889-1949 *WhAm 3*
Hopkins, William 1793-1866 *DcScB*
Hopkins, William Evelyn 1858-1940
NatCAB 31
Hopkins, William Fenn 1802-1859 *ApCAB,*
Drake, TwCBDA
Hopkins, William Henry 1841-1919 *NatCAB 1*
Hopkins, William Hersey 1841-1919 *WhAm 1*
Hopkins, William John 1863-1926 *WhAm 1*
Hopkins, William Karl 1879- *WhAm 6*
Hopkins, William Rowland 1869-1961 *WhAm 4*
Hopkinson, Charles 1869-1962 *NatCAB 53,*
WhAm 4

Hopkinson, Edward, Jr. 1885-1966 *NatCAB 54,*
WhAm 4
Hopkinson, Ernest 1872-1933 *WhAm 1*
Hopkinson, Francis 1737-1791 *AmBi, ApCAB,*
BiDrAC, DcAmB, McGEWB, NatCAB 5,
NewYHSD, TwCBDA, WebAB,
WhAm H, WhAmP
Hopkinson, Francis 1738-1791 *BiAUS, Drake*
Hopkinson, Harold 1918- *IIBEAAW*
Hopkinson, John 1849-1898 *DcScB*
Hopkinson, Joseph 1770-1842 *AmBi, ApCAB,*
BiAUS, BiDrAC, DcAmB, Drake,
NatCAB 7, TwCBDA, WhAm H,
WhAmP
Hopkinson, Thomas 1709-1751 *ApCAB,*
NatCAB 7
Hopkirk, Howard William 1894-1963 *WhAm 4*
Hopler, William C *NewYHSD*
Hopley, Elizabeth Sheppard 1870-1922
WhAm 1, WomWWA 14
Hopley, John Edward 1850-1927 *WhAm 1*
Hopley, Russell James 1895-1949 *WhAm 2*
Hopner, Erich 1886-1944 *WhWW-II*
Hoppe, Herman Henry 1867-1929 *NatCAB 22,*
WhAm 1
Hoppe, William Frederick 1887-1959 *WebAB*
Hoppe-Seyler, Ernst Felix Immanuel 1825-1895
AsBiEn
Hoppe-Seyler, Felix 1825-1895 *BiHiMed,*
DcScB
Hoppenstedt, Alfred Wienhold 1879-1934
NatCAB 26
Hopper, Bruce Campbell 1892-1973 *WhAm 6*
Hopper, David Claude 1888-1968 *WhAm 5*
Hopper, DeWolf 1858-1935 *AmBi, DcAmB S1,*
NatCAB 10, WebAB, WhAm 1
Hopper, Edna Wallace d1959 *WhAm 3*
Hopper, Edward 1818-1888 *ApCAB Sup*
Hopper, Edward 1882-1967 *BnEnAmA, EncAB,*
IIBEAAW, McGEWB, WebAB, WhAm 4
Hopper, Frances Peters 1889-1970 *WhAm 5*
Hopper, Franklin Ferguson 1878-1950
DcAmLiB, WhAm 3
Hopper, H Boardman 1884-1962 *NatCAB 49*
Hopper, Hedda 1890-1966 *WebAB, WhAm 4*
Hopper, Henry Shelmire 1858- *NatCAB 10*
Hopper, Isaac Tatem 1771-1852 *AmBi,*
ApCAB, DcAmB, Drake, NatCAB 2,
TwCBDA, WhAm H
Hopper, James Marie 1876-1956 *NatCAB 46,*
WhAm 4
Hopper, James Woodson 1888-1965 *NatCAB 52*
Hopper, Martha Wentworth *WomWWA 14*
Hopper, Rex Devern 1898-1966 *WhAm 4*
Hopper, Vincent Foster 1906-1976 *WhAm 6*
Hopper, William DeWolf 1858-1935 *ApCAB X*
Hopper, William D'Wolf *WebAB*
Hopper, William Lewers 1856-1938 *NatCAB 37*
Hoppes, John J 1857- *WhAm 4*
Hoppin, Augustus 1828-1896 *AmBi, ApCAB,*
DcAmB, Drake, IIBEAAW, NatCAB 9,
NewYHSD, TwCBDA, WhAm H
Hoppin, Emily Anna 1854- *WomWWA 14*
Hoppin, Francis Laurens Vinton 1866-1941
NatCAB 31
Hoppin, Frederick Street 1875-1946
NatCAB 34
Hoppin, Gerard Beekman 1869-1950
NatCAB 38
Hoppin, James Mason 1820-1906 *ApCAB,*
DcAmB, NatCAB 1, TwCBDA,
WhAm 1
Hoppin, Joseph Clark 1870-1925 *DcAmB,*
WhAm 1
Hoppin, Thomas Frederick 1816-1872 *ApCAB,*
NewYHSD, TwCBDA
Hoppin, William Jones 1813-1895 *ApCAB,*
NatCAB 5, TwCBDA
Hoppin, William Warner d1913 *WhAm 1*
Hoppin, William Warner 1807-1890 *ApCAB,*
BiAUS, DcAmB, NatCAB 9, TwCBDA,
WhAm H
Hoppin, William Warner 1878-1948 *WhAm 2*
Hopping, Andrew Daniel 1894-1951
NatCAB 40, WhAm 3
Hopping, Clyde Everett 1886-1955 *NatCAB 43*
Hopping, Enos D 1805?-1847 *ApCAB*
Hopps, Charles *NewYHSD*

Hopson, George Bailey 1838-1916 *NatCAB 17,*
TwCBDA, WhAm 1
Hopson, Howard Colwell 1882-1949 *DcAmB S4,*
NatCAB 38
Hopson, Mary Adams 1850- *WomWWA 14*
Hopson, William Charles 1856-1948
NatCAB 36
Hopson, William Fowler 1849-1935 *WhAm 1*
Hopson, Winthrop Hartly 1823- *ApCAB*
Hopton, Edwin Franklin 1861-1931 *NatCAB 44*
Hopton, Lord Ralph 1598-1652 *WhoMilH*
Hopwood, Avery 1882-1928 *DcAmB*
Hopwood, Avery 1884-1928 *WhAm 1*
Hopwood, Erie Clark 1877-1928 *NatCAB 20,*
WhAm 1
Hopwood, Herbert Gladstone 1898-1966
WhAm 4
Hopwood, Josephus 1843- *TwCBDA,*
WhAm 4
Hopwood, Robert Freeman 1856-1940 *BiDrAC,*
WhAm 4
Hopwood, Mrs. William *NewYHSD*
Horace 065BC-008BC *McGEWB*
Horack, Frank Edward 1873-1956 *WhAm 3*
Horack, Frank Edward, Jr. 1907-1957 *WhAm 3*
Horack, H Claude 1877-1958 *NatCAB 46*
Horan, Eduard John 1817-1875 *ApCAB*
Horan, Hubert Joseph, Jr. 1889-1971 *WhAm 5*
Horan, Mary Austin 1820-1874 *ApCAB*
Horan, Philip Edward 1885-1972 *WhAm 5*
Horan, Walter Franklin 1898-1966 *BiDrAC,*
NatCAB 53, WhAm 4, WhAmP
Horan, William Francis 1904-1958 *NatCAB 47*
Horbaczewski, Jan 1854-1942 *DcScB*
Horberg, Leland 1910-1955 *WhAm 3*
Horch, Charles Martin 1856-1944 *NatCAB 32*
Hord, Donal 1902-1966 *IIBEAAW, WhAm 4*
Horden, John 1828- *ApCAB*
Hordyk, Gerard 1899-1958 *WhAm 3*
Hore-Belisha, Sir Leslie 1894-1957 *WhWW-II*
Horelick, Samuel 1886-1962 *NatCAB 47*
Horenstein, Jascha 1899- *WhAm 5*
Horenstein, Perry Samuel 1905-1959
NatCAB 47
Horgan, Daniel Stephen 1909-1973 *WhAm 6*
Horgan, Paul 1903- *REnAW*
Horgan, Stephen Henry 1854-1941 *NatCAB 30*
Horine, John Winebrenner 1869- *WhAm 5*
Horine, Merrill Castleberry 1893-1958
NatCAB 44
Horkan, George Anthony 1894-1974 *WhAm 6*
Horkheimer, Arthur Philip 1904-1974 *WhAm 6*
Horlick, Alexander James 1873-1950
NatCAB 39, WhAm 3
Horlick, William 1846-1936 *DcAmB S2,*
NatCAB 27, WhAm 1
Horlick, William, Jr. 1875-1940 *WhAm 1*
Horlor, Edward C *NewYHSD*
Horlor, Henry P *NewYHSD*
Hormel, George Albert 1860-1946 *DcAmB S4,*
WhAm 2
Hormel, Jay Catherwood 1892-1954 *DcAmB S5,*
WhAm 3
Hormell, Duane Couzens 1890-1969
NatCAB 55
Hormell, Orren Chalmer 1879-1975 *WhAm 6*
Hormell, William Garfield 1861-1933 *WhAm 1*
Horn, A *NewYHSD*
Horn, Aaron Charles 1876-1952 *WhAm 3*
Horn, Aaron Charles 1878-1952 *NatCAB 41*
Horn, Albert Frederick 1867-1950 *NatCAB 40*
Horn, Carlton William 1905-1969 *WhAm 5*
Horn, Charles Edward 1776-1848 *ApCAB*
Horn, Charles Edward 1786-1849 *NatCAB 6,*
WhAm H
Horn, Charles J 1912-1970 *WhAm 5*
Horn, Clinton Morris 1885-1970 *WhAm 5*
Horn, David Wilbur 1877-1962 *NatCAB 49*
Horn, Edward Charles 1916-1969 *WhAm 5*
Horn, Edward Traill 1850-1915 *ApCAB,*
DcAmB, WhAm 1
Horn, Ellen Marvin Ropes *WomWWA 14*
Horn, Frank Churchill 1861-1919 *WhAm 1*
Horn, George Henry 1840-1897 *DcAmB,*
DcScB, NatCAB 7, WhAm H
Horn, Henry 1786-1862 *BiAUS, BiDrAC,*
WhAm H
Horn, Henry J *NewYHSD*

Horn, Henry John 1864-1940 *WhAm 1,*
WhAm 2
Horn, John 1843- *NatCAB 13*
Horn, John Louis 1881- *WhAm 6*
Horn, John McPherson 1893-1963 *NatCAB 50*
Horn, Lois Farnham 1877- *WomWWA 14*
Horn, Maude A 1875- *WomWWA 14*
Horn, Nelson Paxson 1890-1958 *WhAm 3*
Horn, Paul Whitfield 1870-1932 *WhAm 1*
Horn, Raymond Edwin 1886-1960 *WhAm 4*
Horn, Robert Chisolm 1881-1959 *WhAm 4*
Horn, Roy DeSaussure 1894-1973 *WhAm 6*
Horn, Sallie M *WomWWA 14*
Horn, Tiemann Newell 1868-1923 *WhAm 1*
Horn, Tom 1860-1903 *DcAmB, REnAW*
Horn, Trader *IIBEAAW*
Horn, Van De 1635?-1683 *ApCAB*
Horn, William C 1888-1965 *WhAm 4*
Horn, William Melchior 1882-1932 *WhAm 1*
Horn D'Arturo, Guido 1879-1967 *DcScB*
Hornaday, Clifford Lee 1879- *WhAm 6*
Hornaday, James Parks 1863-1935 *WhAm 1*
Hornaday, William Temple 1854-1937 *AmBi,*
ApCAB, DcAmB S2, NatCAB 4,
TwCBDA, WhAm 1
Hornady, John Randolph 1872-1948 *WhAm 2*
Hornbeak, Samuel Lee 1865-1949 *WhAm 2*
Hornbeck, Donald Warner 1903-1966 *WhAm 4*
Hornbeck, James Sylvanus 1908-1971
NatCAB 57
Hornbeck, John Wesley 1881-1951 *WhAm 3*
Hornbeck, John Westbrook 1804-1848 *BiAUS,*
BiDrAC, WhAm H
Hornbeck, Marquis D 1849- *WhAm 4*
Hornbeck, Stanley K 1883-1966 *WhAm 4*
Hornbeck, Vivienne B 1896-1970 *WhAm 5*
Hornberger, Theodore 1906-1975 *WhAm 6*
Hornblow, Arthur d1941 *WhAm 2*
Hornblower, Henry 1863-1941 *WhAm 1*
Hornblower, Joseph C 1777-1864 *BiAUS*
Hornblower, Joseph Coerten 1777-1864 *ApCAB,*
DcAmB, TwCBDA, WhAm H
Hornblower, Joseph Coerten 1848-1908
WhAm 1
Hornblower, Joseph Coerton 1777-1864
NatCAB 13
Hornblower, Joseph Courten 1777-1864 *Drake*
Hornblower, Josiah 1729-1809 *ApCAB, BiAUS,*
BiDrAC, DcAmB, Drake, NatCAB 6,
TwCBDA, WhAm H
Hornblower, Ralph 1891-1960 *WhAm 4*
Hornblower, William Butler 1851-1914
ApCAB X, DcAmB, NatCAB 7,
NatCAB 31, TwCBDA, WhAm 1
Hornblower, William Henry 1820-1883 *ApCAB,*
TwCBDA
Hornbostel, Henry Frederick 1867-1961
NatCAB 48, WhAm 4
Hornbrook, Henry Hallam 1870-1935
NatCAB 28, WhAm 1
Hornby, Henry Crook 1866-1952 *NatCAB 41*
Hornby, Squire T *NewYHSD*
Horndy, J R 1832?- *NewYHSD*
Horne, Alice Merrill 1868- *WomWWA 14*
Horne, Antoine 1608-1697 *ApCAB*
Horne, Ashley 1841-1913 *NatCAB 15*
Horne, Burchard Everett 1887-1951
NatCAB 40
Horne, Charles Francis 1870-1942 *WhAm 2*
Horne, Edmund Campion 1898-1948 *WhAm 2*
Horne, Florence Wentworth 1867-
WomWWA 14
Horne, Frank Alexander 1869-1939 *NatCAB 41,*
WhAm 1
Horne, Frank S 1899-1974 *WhAm 6*
Horne, Frederick Joseph 1880-1959 *WhAm 3*
Horne, Henry Abbott 1878- *WhAm 6*
Horne, Herman Harrell 1874-1946 *BiDAmEd,*
NatCAB 44, WhAm 2
Horne, Johannes Van 1621-1670 *DcScB*
Horne, Joseph A 1869-1950 *WhAm 3*
Horne, Josh L 1887-1974 *WhAm 6*
Horne, Mary Tracy Earle 1864- *WhAm 4,*
WomWWA 14
Horne, Nellie Mathes 1870- *WhAm 5*
Horne, Perley Leonard 1866-1932 *WhAm 1*
Horne, Sarah C 1839- *WomWWA 14*
Horne, William Titus 1876-1944 *NatCAB 33*

Horner, Miss *NewYHSD*
Horner, Albert 1863-1930 *NatCAB 40*
Horner, Bernard Justine 1895-1968 *WhAm 5*
Horner, Charles Francis 1878-1967 *WhAm 4*
Horner, Harlan Hoyt 1878- *WhAm 6*
Horner, Henry 1878-1940 *DcAmB S2,*
NatCAB 30, WhAm 1, WhAmP
Horner, J Richey 1861-1947 *WhAm 2*
Horner, James B *NewYHSD*
Horner, Johann Friedrich 1831-1886 *BiHiMed*
Horner, John B 1856-1933 *WhAm 1*
Horner, John Scott 1802-1883 *NatCAB 5,*
TwCBDA
Horner, Junius Moore 1859-1933 *NatCAB 11,*
TwCBDA, WhAm 1
Horner, Leonard 1785-1864 *DcScB*
Horner, Leonard Sherman 1875-1943 *WhAm 2*
Horner, Leonard Sherman 1876-1943
NatCAB 41
Horner, Walter Augustus 1876-1950
NatCAB 39
Horner, Wesley Winans 1883-1958 *WhAm 3*
Horner, William Edmonds 1793-1853 *ApCAB,*
BiHiMed, DcAmB, TwCBDA, WhAm H
Horner, William Edmunds 1793-1853 *Drake,*
NatCAB 6
Horner, William George 1786-1837 *DcScB*
Horner, William Stewart 1868-1944
NatCAB 34
Horney, Karen 1885-1952 *WhAm 3*
Horney, Karen Danielsen 1885-1952 *McGEWB*
Horney, Karen Danielssen 1885-1952
DcAmB S5
Horney, Odus Creamer 1866-1957 *WhAm 3*
Hornibrook, William Harrison 1884-1946
WhAm 2
Hornibrooke, Isabel *WhAm 5*
Hornick, Charles W 1863-1916 *WhAm 1*
Horning, Harry LeVan 1880-1936 *NatCAB 44*
Horning, William Allen 1904-1959 *WhAm 4*
Hornor, Harry Archer 1874-1939 *NatCAB 29*
Hornor, Lynn Sedwick 1874-1933 *BiDrAC*
Hornor, Lynn Sedwick 1877-1933 *WhAm 1*
Hornor, Thomas *NewYHSD*
Hornsby, John Allen 1859-1939 *WhAm 1*
Hornsby, Rogers 1896-1963 *WebAB,*
WhAm HA, WhAm 4
Hornsby, Thomas 1733-1810 *DcScB*
Hornten, Robert *NewYHSD*
Hornung, Christian 1845- *WhAm 4*
Hornung, John Albert 1872-1930 *NatCAB 23*
Horowitz, Louis Jay 1875-1956 *WhAm 3*
Horowitz, Saul, Jr. 1925-1975 *WhAm 6*
Horr, Alfred Reuel 1875-1958 *NatCAB 50,*
WhAm 3
Horr, Asa 1817-1896 *ApCAB, NatCAB 13*
Horr, George Edwin 1856-1927 *DcAmB,*
NatCAB 24, WhAm 1
Horr, Ralph Ashley 1884-1960 *BiDrAC,*
WhAm 3
Horr, Roswell Gilbert 1830-1896 *BiDrAC,*
TwCBDA, WhAm H
Horrax, Gilbert 1887-1957 *WhAm 3*
Horrebow, Christian 1718-1776 *DcScB*
Horrebow, Peder Nielsen 1679-1764 *DcScB*
Horrell, George Robert 1905-1970 *WhAm 5*
Horrocks, Sir Brian 1895- *WhWW-II*
Horrocks, Harry Sykes 1883-1959 *NatCAB 49*
Horrocks, James 1734?-1772 *DcAmB,*
NatCAB 3, TwCBDA, WhAm H
Horrocks, Jeremiah 1618-1641 *DcScB*
Horrocks, Jeremiah 1619-1641 *AsBiEn*
Horrworth, Charles A 1900-1967 *WhAm 4*
Horry, Elias 1743-1834 *ApCAB, Drake*
Horry, Peter *ApCAB, NatCAB 6*
Horsburgh, Robert Homer 1883-1949
NatCAB 37, WhAm 2
Horsey, Outerbridge 1777-1842 *ApCAB,*
BiAUS, BiDrAC, Drake, NatCAB 4,
TwCBDA, WhAm H, WhAmP
Horsfall, Frank Lappin, Jr. 1906-1971 *WhAm 5*
Horsfall, I Owen 1885-1972 *WhAm 5*
Horsfall, R Bruce 1868-1948 *WhAm 2*
Horsfall, Robert Bruce 1869-1948 *IIBEAAW*
Horsfield, Thomas 1773-1859 *ApCAB, DcAmB,*
WhAm H
Horsford, Cornelia 1861- *BiCAW, TwCBDA,*
WhAm 3, WomWWA 14

Horsford, Eben Norton 1818-1893 *ApCAB,*
DcAmB, DcScB, Drake, NatCAB 6,
TwCBDA, WhAm H
Horsford, Jedediah 1791-1874 *ApCAB*
Horsford, Jerediah 1791-1875 *BiDrAC,*
TwCBDA, WhAm H
Horsford, Mary L'Hommedieu Gardiner
1824-1855 *ApCAB*
Horsky, Antone Joseph 1882-1967 *NatCAB 54*
Horsky, Edward 1873-1948 *NatCAB 11,*
NatCAB 53, WhAm 2
Horsley, Charles Edward 1821-1876 *ApCAB*
Horsley, John Shelton 1870-1946 *NatCAB 35,*
WhAm 2
Horsley, Sir Victor Alexander Haden 1857-1916
BiHiMed, DcScB
Horsman, Edward Imerson 1843- *NatCAB 3*
Horsman, Ellett Wallace 1890-1967
NatCAB 55
Horsman, Reginald 1931- *EncAAH*
Horsmanden, Daniel 1691-1778 *ApCAB, Drake,*
NatCAB 7
Horsmanden, Daniel 1694-1778 *DcAmB,*
WhAm H
Horst, Emil Clemens 1867-1940 *WhAm 1*
Horst, Enos Henry 1911-1967 *NatCAB 53*
Horst, George Philip 1884-1936 *WhAm 1*
Horst, Henry William 1864-1949 *NatCAB 44*
Horst, John Joseph 1880-1945 *WhAm 2*
Horst, Louis 1884-1964 *WhAm 4*
Horst, Miles 1891-1968 *WhAm 5*
Horstman, Albert Adam 1888-1960 *WhAm 4*
Horstman, Herman *NewYHSD*
Horstmann, August Friedrich 1842-1929 *DcScB*
Horstmann, Ignatius Frederick 1840-1908
ApCAB Sup, NatCAB 5, TwCBDA,
WhAm 1
Horstmann, William H 1815-1852 *NatCAB 13,*
WhAm H
Horswell, Charles 1857- *WhAm 4*
Hortensius, Martinus 1605-1639 *DcScB*
Hortenstine, Raleigh 1887-1969 *WhAm 5*
Horter, Charles D *NewYHSD*
Horthy, Miklos 1868-1946 *WhWW-II*
Horthy DeNagybanya, Nicholas 1868-1957
McGEWB
Hortigosa, Peter De 1546-1626 *ApCAB*
Horton, Albert Howell 1837-1902 *NatCAB 6,*
TwCBDA, WhAm 1
Horton, Alonzo Erastus 1813- *NatCAB 12*
Horton, Arthur d1973 *WhAm 6*
Horton, Azariah 1715-1777 *ApCAB*
Horton, Benjamin Jason 1873-1963 *NatCAB 49,*
WhAm 5
Horton, Bryson Dexter 1871-1945 *NatCAB 34*
Horton, Charles *NewYHSD*
Horton, Charles Bertram 1899-1959
NatCAB 48
Horton, Charles C *NewYHSD*
Horton, Clarence Herbert 1879-1949
NatCAB 38
Horton, Clark Willis 1899-1966 *NatCAB 53*
Horton, Clinton Thompson 1876-1953
NatCAB 42
Horton, Dexter 1825-1904 *ApCAB X*
Horton, Douglas 1891-1968 *WhAm 5*
Horton, Edmund Prior 1863-1949 *NatCAB 38*
Horton, Edward Augustus 1843-1931
NatCAB 14, TwCBDA, WhAm 1
Horton, Edward Everett 1886-1970 *WhAm 5*
Horton, Elmer Grant 1868-1949 *WhAm 2*
Horton, Frank Jefferson 1919- *BiDrAC*
Horton, Frank Ogilvie 1882-1948 *BiDrAC,*
WhAm 2, WhAmP
Horton, George 1859-1942 *WhAm 2*
Horton, George Firman 1806-1886 *ApCAB*
Horton, George Monroe 1865-1927 *NatCAB 21*
Horton, George Moses 1798?-1880? *NatCAB 7*
Horton, George Terry 1873-1945 *WhAm 2*
Horton, Harris Leonidas 1879-1939 *NatCAB 36*
Horton, Harry Lawrence 1832- *NatCAB 1,*
NatCAB 14
Horton, Henry Hollis 1866-1934 *NatCAB 25,*
WhAm 1
Horton, Herbert L 1893-1957 *WhAm 3*
Horton, Herman DeWitt 1889-1959
NatCAB 47, WhAm 3
Horton, Horace Babcock 1885-1959 *WhAm 3*

Horton, Horace Ebenezer 1843- *NatCAB 14*
Horton, J Warren 1889-1967 *WhAm 5*
Horton, James *NewYHSD*
Horton, James Madison 1835- *NatCAB 7*
Horton, Jesse M 1889-1959 *WhAm 4*
Horton, Jesse Maxwell 1875-1969 *NatCAB 54*
Horton, John S *NewYHSD*
Horton, Judith Carter 1866- *WhoColR*
Horton, Katharine Loren Pratt d1931 *WhAm 1*
Horton, Katharine Lorenz Pratt d1931 *BiCAW, WomWWA 14*
Horton, Kathrine L P d1931 *WhAm 1C*
Horton, Lillias Sterling *NotAW*
Horton, Loton 1854-1926 *NatCAB 35*
Horton, Lydia M 1846- *WomWWA 14*
Horton, Lydiard Heneage 1879-1945 *WhAm 2*
Horton, Mrs. M N *NewYHSD*
Horton, Marcus 1879- *WhAm 6*
Horton, Sir Max 1883-1951 *WhWW-II*
Horton, McDavid 1884-1941 *WhAm 1*
Horton, Mildred Helen McAfee 1900- *WebAMB*
Horton, O Lee 1899-1964 *NatCAB 52*
Horton, Oliver Harvey 1835-1915 *NatCAB 16, WhAm 1*
Horton, Richard *NewYHSD*
Horton, Robert Elmer 1875-1945 *WhAm 2*
Horton, Samuel Dana 1844-1895 *AmBi, ApCAB Sup, DcAmB, NatCAB 5, TwCBDA, WhAm H*
Horton, Thomas Attwood 1876-1959 *NatCAB 47*
Horton, Thomas Corwin 1848-1932 *WhAm 1*
Horton, Thomas Raymond 1822-1894 *BiAUS, BiDrAC, WhAm H*
Horton, Tudor *NewYHSD*
Horton, Valentine Baxter 1802-1888 *ApCAB, BiAUS, BiDrAC, DcAmB, NatCAB 13, TwCBDA, WhAm H*
Horton, Walter Marshall 1895-1966 *WhAm 4*
Horton, Walter Shurts 1857- *WhAm 4*
Horton, Wilkins P 1889-1950 *WhAm 2*
Horton, William Edward 1868-1935 *WhAm 1*
Horton, William S 1865- *WhAm 4*
Horvath, Imre 1901-1958 *WhAm 3*
Horvitz, Aaron 1888-1968 *WhAm 5*
Horvitz, Samuel Aaron 1889-1956 *NatCAB 43*
Horwich, Bernard 1861- *NatCAB 18*
Horwitz, Carolyn Norris *WomWWA 14*
Horwitz, Phineas Jonathan 1822-1904 *ApCAB, NatCAB 11, TwCBDA, WhAm 1*
Horwitz, Solis 1910-1972 *WhAm 5*
Horwood, Murray Philip 1892-1957 *NatCAB 43, WhAm 3*
Hosack, Alexander Eddy 1805-1871 *ApCAB, DcAmB, NatCAB 9, TwCBDA, WhAm H*
Hosack, David 1769-1835 *AmBi, ApCAB, BiHiMed, DcAmB, DcScB, Drake, NatCAB 3, NatCAB 9, TwCBDA, WhAm H*
Hosafros, Wayne Orville 1926-1972 *WhAm 6*
Hosea *McGEWB*
Hosea, H N *NewYHSD*
Hosea, Lewis Montgomery 1842-1924 *NatCAB 19*
Hosemann *DcScB*
Hosford, Bradley *NewYHSD*
Hosford, Charles Franklin, Jr. 1887-1953 *WhAm 3*
Hosford, Charles Henry 1853-1927 *NatCAB 22*
Hosford, Harry Lindley 1877-1945 *WhAm 2*
Hosford, Harry William 1886-1955 *NatCAB 44*
Hosford, Henry Hallock 1859- *TwCBDA*
Hosford, Hester E 1883- *WomWWA 14*
Hosford, Jedediah *BiAUS*
Hosford, Jennie Chamberlain 1865- *WomWWA 14*
Hosford, Oramel 1820- *ApCAB*
Hosford, Willard Deere 1882-1951 *WhAm 3*
Hosford, William Fuller 1882-1958 *WhAm 3*
Hoshour, Harvey Sheely 1890-1951 *WhAm 3*
Hoshour, Samuel Kleinfelder 1803-1883 *NatCAB 19*
Hoshour, Samuel Klinefelter 1803-1883 *DcAmB, WhAm H*
Hosic, James Fleming 1870-1959 *BiDAmEd, NatCAB 47, WhAm 3*

Hosier, Abraham *NewYHSD*
Hosket, Charles Frederick 1860-1923 *NatCAB 19*
Hoskier, Herman C 1864-1938 *WhAm 1*
Hoskin, Arthur Joseph 1869-1935 *WhAm 1*
Hoskin, Robert *NewYHSD*
Hoskin, Robert 1842- *ApCAB, WhAm 4*
Hosking, P W *NewYHSD*
Hoskins, Fermin Lincoln 1865-1935 *WhAm 1*
Hoskins, Franklin Evans 1858-1920 *WhAm 1*
Hoskins, Fred 1906-1966 *WhAm 4*
Hoskins, Gayle Porter 1887-1962 *IIBEAAW, NatCAB 48*
Hoskins, George Gilbert 1824-1893 *ApCAB, BiAUS, BiDrAC, TwCBDA, WhAm H*
Hoskins, Halford Lancaster 1891-1967 *WhAm 4*
Hoskins, James Dickason 1870-1960 *NatCAB 47*
Hoskins, James Dickcason 1870-1960 *WhAm 3A*
Hoskins, James Preston 1864-1948 *WhAm 2*
Hoskins, John Deane Charles 1846-1937 *WhAm 1*
Hoskins, John Hobart 1896-1957 *WhAm 3*
Hoskins, John K 1884-1958 *WhAm 3*
Hoskins, John Madison 1898-1964 *NatCAB 50, WhAm 4*
Hoskins, John Preston 1867-1935 *WhAm 1*
Hoskins, Leander Miller 1860-1937 *NatCAB 28, WhAm 1*
Hoskins, Nathan 1795-1869 *ApCAB, Drake*
Hoskins, Roy Graham 1880- *WhAm 6*
Hoskins, Sydney *NewYHSD*
Hoskins, William 1862-1934 *WhAm 1*
Hoskins, William Horace 1860-1921 *WhAm 1*
Hosman, Everett Mills 1888-1965 *NatCAB 52*
Hosmer, Alfred 1832-1891 *NatCAB 19*
Hosmer, Charles Bridgham 1889-1942 *WhAm 2*
Hosmer, Craig 1915- *BiDrAC*
Hosmer, Frank Alvin 1874-1958 *WhAm 3*
Hosmer, Frederick Lucian 1840-1929 *DcAmB, NatCAB 21, TwCBDA, WhAm 1*
Hosmer, George 1781-1861 *ApCAB*
Hosmer, George Leonard 1874-1935 *NatCAB 25*
Hosmer, George Stedman 1855-1921 *NatCAB 19, WhAm 1*
Hosmer, George Washington 1803-1881 *NatCAB 7, TwCBDA*
Hosmer, George Washington 1804-1881 *ApCAB*
Hosmer, Gladys Eleanor Holden 1886- *WomWWA 14*
Hosmer, H L 1814-1893 *BiAUS*
Hosmer, Harriet Goodhue 1830-1908 *AmBi, AmWom, ApCAB, BnEnAmA, DcAmB, Drake, NatCAB 1, NatCAB 8, NewYHSD, NotAW, TwCBDA, WhAm 1*
Hosmer, Hezekiah Lord 1765-1814 *BiAUS, BiDrAC, WhAm H*
Hosmer, Hezekiah Lord 1814-1893 *DcAmB, NatCAB 13, WhAm H*
Hosmer, James Jackson 1881-1930 *NatCAB 23*
Hosmer, James Kendall 1834-1927 *ApCAB, DcAmB, DcAmLiB, NatCAB 6, TwCBDA, WhAm 1*
Hosmer, Jean 1842- *ApCAB, Drake, NatCAB 4*
Hosmer, Katherine Tipton 1867- *WomWWA 14*
Hosmer, Lucius Everett 1870-1935 *NatCAB 26*
Hosmer, Lydia *NewYHSD*
Hosmer, Margaret 1830- *ApCAB*
Hosmer, Ralph Sheldon 1874-1963 *WhAm 4*
Hosmer, Samuel Monroe 1846-1916 *TwCBDA, WhAm 1*
Hosmer, Stephen Titus 1763-1834 *ApCAB, BiAUS, Drake, NatCAB 7*
Hosmer, Timothy 1740-1820 *ApCAB*
Hosmer, Titus 1736-1780 *ApCAB, BiAUS, BiDrAC, Drake, TwCBDA*
Hosmer, Titus 1737-1780 *DcAmB, NatCAB 4, WhAm H*
Hosmer, William Henry Cuyler 1814-1877 *ApCAB, Drake, TwCBDA*
Hosmer, William Howe Cuyler 1814-1877 *DcAmB, NatCAB 8, WhAm H*

Hoss, Elijah Embree 1849-1919 *NatCAB 13, NatCAB 25, WhAm 1*
Hoss, George Washington 1824-1906 *TwCBDA, WhAm 1*
Hosset, Gillis d1631 *ApCAB*
Hossinger, Joseph Humphrey 1870-1920 *NatCAB 18*
Hoster, Herman Albert 1912-1951 *NatCAB 41, WhAm 3*
Hostetler, Abraham Jonathan 1818-1899 *BiDrAC*
Hostetler, Erwin Case 1904-1968 *WhAm 5*
Hostetler, Joseph Cleveland 1885-1958 *NatCAB 46, WhAm 3*
Hostetler, Lowell Coy 1928-1968 *WhAm 5*
Hostetler, Theodore Allen 1864-1948 *WhAm 2*
Hostetter, Anita Miller 1889-1963 *DcAmLiB*
Hostetter, Harry Benjamin 1893-1946 *NatCAB 35*
Hostetter, Jacob 1754-1831 *BiAUS, BiDrAC, WhAm H*
Hostetter, John Clyde 1886-1962 *NatCAB 53*
Hostetter, Thomas *NewYHSD*
Hostlot, Louis 1848-1884 *ApCAB*
Hostmann, Jeannot 1876-1926 *NatCAB 20*
Hostos, Eugenio Maria De 1839-1903 *BiDAmEd, McGEWB*
Hosty, Thomas Edward 1891-1971 *WhAm 5*
Hotchener, Henry 1881- *WhAm 6*
Hotchener, Marie Russak 1867- *WhAm 4*
Hotchkin, Samuel Fitch 1833-1912 *ApCAB Sup, NatCAB 15, TwCBDA, WhAm 1*
Hotchkiss, Andrew 1822-1858 *NatCAB 8*
Hotchkiss, Benjamin Berkeley 1826-1885 *AmBi, DcAmB, NatCAB 6, TwCBDA, WhAm H*
Hotchkiss, Benjamin Berkely 1826-1885 *ApCAB*
Hotchkiss, Berkeley William 1905-1960 *NatCAB 48*
Hotchkiss, Chauncey Crafts 1852-1920 *WhAm 1*
Hotchkiss, Clarence Francis 1859-1928 *NatCAB 22*
Hotchkiss, Clarence Roland 1880-1952 *ApCAB X, NatCAB 39, WhAm 3*
Hotchkiss, George Burton 1884-1953 *WhAm 3*
Hotchkiss, George W 1831-1926 *WhAm 1*
Hotchkiss, Giles Waldo 1815-1878 *BiAUS, BiDrAC, TwCBDA, WhAm H*
Hotchkiss, H Stuart 1878-1947 *WhAm 2*
Hotchkiss, Henry DeWitt 1856-1922 *WhAm 1*
Hotchkiss, Henry Greene 1863-1963 *WhAm 4*
Hotchkiss, Horace Leslie 1842-1929 *DcAmB, NatCAB 23, WhAm 1*
Hotchkiss, J Elizabeth *WhAm 5*
Hotchkiss, James Harvey 1781-1851 *ApCAB, Drake*
Hotchkiss, Jean Jewel 1837- *WomWWA 14*
Hotchkiss, Jed 1827?-1899 *TwCBDA*
Hotchkiss, Jedediah 1828-1899 *BiDConf*
Hotchkiss, Julius 1810-1878 *BiAUS, BiDrAC, WhAm H*
Hotchkiss, Loyal Durand 1893-1964 *WhAm 4*
Hotchkiss, Lucius Wales 1859-1926 *WhAm 1*
Hotchkiss, Mary Ashley 1887- *WomWWA 14*
Hotchkiss, Milo 1802-1874 *NewYHSD*
Hotchkiss, Norton Royce 1870-1912 *NatCAB 34*
Hotchkiss, Robert James 1872-1942 *NatCAB 32*
Hotchkiss, T H d1869 *NewYHSD*
Hotchkiss, Velona Roundy 1815-1882 *ApCAB*
Hotchkiss, Wales 1826- *NewYHSD*
Hotchkiss, Willard Eugene 1874-1956 *NatCAB 43, WhAm 3*
Hotchkiss, William Horace 1864-1950 *NatCAB 39, WhAm 3*
Hotchkiss, William Otis 1878-1954 *NatCAB 53, WhAm 3*
Hotchkiss, Willis R 1873- *WhAm 5*
Hotelling, Harold 1895-1973 *WhAm 6*
Hoth, Hermann *WhWW-II*
Hott, Maxwell Rhoades 1897-1969 *NatCAB 54*
Hottenroth, Adolph Christian 1869- *WhAm 5*
Hottes, Charles Frederick 1870- *WhAm 5*
Hotton, Harriet Jane 1870- *WomWWA 14*
Hotz, Ferdinand Carl 1843-1909 *DcAmB, WhAm 1*

Hotz, H G 1880-1972 *WhAm 5*
Hotz, John William 1900-1951 *NatCAB 41*
Hotz, Robert Schuttler 1870-1918 *WhAm 1*
Hotze, Henry 1833-1887 *BiDConf*
Houchin, Clarence Elmer 1884-1953
    NatCAB 42
Houck, Emma Myra Bence 1864-
    WomWWA 14
Houck, George Elza 1865-1958 *NatCAB 43*
Houck, Irvin Elmer 1901-1970 *WhAm 5*
Houck, Jacob, Jr. 1801-1857 *BiAUS, BiDrAC,*
    WhAm H
Houck, Louis 1840-1925 *REnAW, WhAm 1*
Houdan, Luc Du 1811-1846 *ApCAB*
Houde, Camillien 1889-1958 *WhAm 3*
Houde, Frederick 1847- *ApCAB*
Houdetot, Francois Lauriot De 1617-1659
    ApCAB
Houdini, Harry 1874-1926 *AmBi, DcAmB,*
    NatCAB 22, WebAB, WhAm 1
Houdon, Jean Antoine 1740-1828 *ApCAB,*
    NatCAB 8
Houdon, Jean Antoine 1741-1828 *Drake,*
    McGEWB, NewYHSD
Houel, Guillaume-Jules 1823-1886 *DcScB*
Hough, Alfred Lacey 1826-1908 *WhAm 1*
Hough, Charles Egerton 1864-1945 *NatCAB 34*
Hough, Charles Merrill 1858-1927 *DcAmB,*
    NatCAB 20, WhAm 1
Hough, Charles Pinckney 1845-1926
    NatCAB 20
Hough, David 1753-1831 *BiAUS, BiDrAC,*
    TwCBDA, WhAm H
Hough, E K *NewYHSD*
Hough, Emerson 1857-1923 *AmBi, ApCAB X,*
    DcAmB, NatCAB 13, NatCAB 19,
    REnAW, WebAB, WhAm 1
Hough, Franklin Benjamin 1820-1885 *ApCAB*
Hough, Franklin Benjamin 1822-1885 *AmBi,*
    DcAmB, Drake, NatCAB 13, TwCBDA,
    WhAm H
Hough, George Anthony 1868- *WhAm 5*
Hough, George W 1808-1878 *TwCBDA*
Hough, George Washington 1836-1909 *AmBi,*
    ApCAB, DcAmB, DcScB, NatCAB 8,
    TwCBDA, WhAm 1
Hough, Henry Hughes 1871-1943 *WhAm 2*
Hough, Jacob B 1829- *ApCAB*
Hough, John Stockton 1845- *ApCAB*
Hough, Lynn Harold 1877-1971 *NatCAB 57,*
    WhAm 6
Hough, M Leslie 1886-1937 *NatCAB 27*
Hough, Marshall Lewis 1899-1955 *NatCAB 46*
Hough, Mary Elizabeth 1868- *WomWWA 14*
Hough, Mary P H 1858- *WomWWA 14*
Hough, Robert Lee, Jr. 1924-1975 *WhAm 6*
Hough, Romeyn Beck 1857-1924 *NatCAB 20,*
    WhAm 1
Hough, Samuel Strickler 1864-1944 *WhAm 2*
Hough, Theodore 1865-1924 *DcAmB,*
    NatCAB 23, WhAm 1
Hough, Walter 1859-1935 *DcAmB S1,*
    NatCAB 25, TwCBDA, WhAm 1
Hough, Warwick 1836-1915 *DcAmB,*
    NatCAB 7, TwCBDA, WhAm 1
Hough, Will Millan 1882-1962 *NatCAB 54*
Hough, William Jervis 1795-1869 *BiAUS,*
    BiDrAC, WhAm H
Hough, Williston Samuel 1860-1912 *WhAm 1*
Houghston, Walter *WebAB*
Houghteling, James Lawrence 1855-1910
    NatCAB 15, WhAm 1
Houghteling, James Lawrence 1883-1962
    WhAm 4
Houghten, Ferry Charles 1888-1945
    NatCAB 32
Houghton, Alanson Bigelow 1863-1941
    ApCAB X, BiDrAC, DcAmB S3,
    NatCAB 31, WhAm 1, WhAmP
Houghton, Albert Balch 1882-1969 *WhAm 5*
Houghton, Albert Charles 1844-1914
    NatCAB 50
Houghton, Albert Fyler 1850-1937 *NatCAB 32*
Houghton, Alice 1849- *AmWom*
Houghton, Alice Bucknam 1858-
    WomWWA 14
Houghton, Arthur Boyd 1836-1875 *IlBEAAW*

Houghton, Augustus Seymour 1866-1948
    NatCAB 38
Houghton, David *NewYHSD*
Houghton, Dorothy Deemer 1890-1972
    WhAm 5
Houghton, Douglas 1809-1845 *ApCAB,*
    NatCAB 5
Houghton, Douglass 1809-1845 *DcAmB,*
    DcScB, Drake, TwCBDA, WhAm H
Houghton, E Mark 1867-1937 *NatCAB 31*
Houghton, Edna M 1873- *WomWWA 14*
Houghton, Edward Franklin 1849-1929
    NatCAB 22
Houghton, Edward Lovell 1858- *WhAm 4*
Houghton, Edward Rittenhouse 1871-1955
    WhAm 3
Houghton, Elizabeth Harris 1858-
    WomWWA 14
Houghton, Frank Wilbur 1849-1932
    NatCAB 24
Houghton, Frederick Boies 1866- *WhAm 4*
Houghton, Frederick Lowell 1859-1927
    WhAm 1
Houghton, Frederick Percival *WhAm 5*
Houghton, George Clarke 1852-1923 *WhAm 1*
Houghton, George Frederick 1820-1870 *ApCAB,*
    Drake
Houghton, George H 1820-1897 *NatCAB 6*
Houghton, George Heindric 1820-1897
    WhAm H
Houghton, George Hendric 1820-1897 *DcAmB*
Houghton, George Hendricks 1820-1897
    ApCAB Sup
Houghton, George Washington Wright
    1850-1891 *ApCAB, NatCAB 4*
Houghton, H Seymour 1862- *WhAm 4*
Houghton, Henry Clark 1837-1901 *ApCAB*
Houghton, Henry Clarke 1837-1901 *TwCBDA,*
    WhAm 1
Houghton, Henry Oscar 1823-1895 *AmBi,*
    ApCAB, DcAmB, NatCAB 1, TwCBDA,
    WhAm H
Houghton, Henry Spencer 1880-1975 *WhAm 6*
Houghton, Herbert Pierrepont 1880-1964
    NatCAB 51, WhAm 4
Houghton, James Franklin 1827- *NatCAB 7*
Houghton, James Warren 1856-1913 *WhAm 1*
Houghton, John Henry 1848-1917 *WhAm 1*
Houghton, Louise Phillips 1870- *WhAm 5,*
    WomWWA 14a
Houghton, Louise Seymour 1838-1920 *WhAm 1,*
    WomWWA 14
Houghton, Lucile C 1879- *WhAm 6*
Houghton, Mary Hayes 1837- *AmWom*
Houghton, Merritt Dana 1846-1918 *IlBEAAW*
Houghton, Sherman Otis 1828-1914 *ApCAB,*
    BiAUS, BiDrAC, NatCAB 7, TwCBDA,
    WhAm 4
Houghton, Stanley Washington 1872-1951
    NatCAB 38
Houghton, Will Henry 1887-1947 *NatCAB 34,*
    WhAm 2
Houghton, William Addison 1852-1917
    TwCBDA, WhAm 1
Houghton, William Morris 1882-1960 *WhAm 4*
Houk, Eliza Phillips Thruston 1833- *WhAm 1,*
    WomWWA 14
Houk, George Washington 1825-1894 *BiDrAC,*
    TwCBDA, WhAm H
Houk, John Chiles 1860-1923 *BiDrAC,*
    NatCAB 20, TwCBDA, WhAmP
Houk, Leonidas Campbell 1836-1891 *BiDrAC,*
    DcAmB, NatCAB 24, TwCBDA,
    WhAmP
Houk, Leonidas Campbell 1836-1896 *WhAm H*
Houkom, John Asbjorn 1890-1950 *WhAm 3*
Houlahan, James Michael 1898-1965
    NatCAB 50
Houlahan, Patrick Henry 1855-1939
    NatCAB 28
Houlden, Robert Taylor 1875-1949 *NatCAB 38*
Houlihan, D F 1902-1964 *WhAm 4*
Houlihan, Raymond Florence 1902-1955
    NatCAB 43
Houlton, Ruth 1881- *WhAm 6*
Houphouet-Boigny, Felix 1905- *McGEWB*
Hourigan, John Aloysius 1872-1951 *NatCAB 41,*
    WhAm 3

Hourwich, Isaac Aaronovich 1860-1924 *DcAmB,*
    WhAm 1
House, A G 1901-1962 *WhAm 4*
House, Albert Virgil, Jr. 1906- *EncAAH*
House, Arthur Everett 1896-1967 *NatCAB 54*
House, Augustus Farlin 1847-1932 *NatCAB 24*
House, Boyce 1896-1961 *WhAm 4*
House, Byron Orvil 1901-1969 *WhAm 5*
House, Edward Howard 1836-1901 *ApCAB,*
    DcAmB, NatCAB 13, TwCBDA,
    WhAm 1
House, Edward John 1879- *WhAm 6*
House, Edward Mandell 1858-1938 *AmBi,*
    ApCAB X, DcAmB S2, EncAB,
    McGEWB, WebAB, WhAm 1, WhAmP
House, Elwin Lincoln 1861-1932 *WhAm 1*
House, Francis Edwin 1855-1926 *NatCAB 36,*
    WhAm 1
House, Garry Campbell 1871- *WhAm 5*
House, Henry Alonzo 1840-1930 *DcAmB,*
    NatCAB 23, WhAm 4
House, Herbert Crossby 1883-1957 *NatCAB 49*
House, Homer Clyde 1871-1939 *WhAm 1*
House, Homer Doliver 1878-1949 *WhAm 2*
House, James *NewYHSD*
House, James 1775?-1834 *ApCAB, NewYHSD*
House, James Alford 1838-1906 *ApCAB,*
    WhAm 1
House, James Arthur 1871- *WhAm 5*
House, Jay Elmer 1870-1936 *WhAm 1*
House, John F 1827-1904 *BiAUS*
House, John Ford 1827-1904 *BiDConf,*
    BiDrAC, WhAmP
House, John Forde 1827-1904 *WhAm 1*
House, John Henry 1845-1936 *NatCAB 26,*
    WhAm 1
House, Joseph Warren 1886-1954 *WhAm 3*
House, Ralph Emerson 1873-1940 *WhAm 1*
House, Robert Ernest 1875-1930 *WhAm 1*
House, Roy Temple 1878-1963 *WhAm 4*
House, Royal Earl 1814-1895 *ApCAB, DcAmB,*
    NatCAB 12, WebAB, WhAm H
House, Samuel Reynolds 1817-1899 *DcAmB,*
    WhAm H
House, Timothy 1814-1864 *NewYHSD,*
    TwCBDA
House, Willie Durham 1856- *WomWWA 14*
Housekeeper, Cheney H *NewYHSD*
Houseman, Julius 1832-1891 *BiDrAC,*
    WhAm H
Houser, Allan C 1915- *IlBEAAW*
Houser, Daniel M 1834-1915 *NatCAB 12,*
    WhAm 1
Houser, Frederick Wilhelm 1871-1942 *WhAm 2*
Houser, Frederick William 1871-1942
    NatCAB 34
Houser, Gerald Fred Tillman 1902-1971
    WhAm 5
Houser, Gilbert Logan 1866-1951 *NatCAB 40,*
    WhAm 3
Houser, Karl Musser 1893-1967 *WhAm 4*
Houser, Shaler Charles 1879-1948 *WhAm 2*
Houser, Theodore Virgil 1892-1963 *NatCAB 51,*
    WhAm 4
Houser, Walter L 1855- *WhAm 4*
Houseworth, Mortimer *NewYHSD*
Housh, Esther T *AmWom*
Housh, S Henrietta *WomWWA 14*
Housman, Alfred Edward 1859-1936 *McGEWB*
Housman, Laurence 1865-1959 *WhAm 3*
Houssay, Bernardo Alberto 1887-1971 *AsBiEn,*
    DcScB Sup, McGEWB, WhAm 5
Houston, A *NewYHSD*
Houston, Andrew Jackson 1854-1941 *BiDrAC*
Houston, Bernard John 1912-1962 *NatCAB 50*
Houston, Bryan 1899-1974 *WhAm 6*
Houston, Charles Albert 1881-1951 *WhAm 3*
Houston, Charles Hamilton 1895-1950
    DcAmB S4, NatCAB 38, WhAm 3
Houston, Charles Robb 1850-1932 *NatCAB 36*
Houston, Charlotte Harding Shepherd
    WomWWA 14
Houston, Clarence Preston 1891-1965
    NatCAB 51, WhAm 4
Houston, David Crawford 1835-1893 *ApCAB,*
    TwCBDA
Houston, David Franklin 1866-1940 *BiDrUSE,*
    DcAmB S2, EncAAH, WhAm 1

Houston, Delmar Elmor 1917-1972 *NatCAB 57*
Houston, Edwin James 1844-1914 *NatCAB 13, TwCBDA*
Houston, Edwin James 1847-1914 *BiDAmEd, DcAmB, WhAm 1*
Houston, Edwin Samuel 1845- *WhAm 1*
Houston, Frances C 1851-1906 *WhAm 1*
Houston, Francis A 1858-1919 *WhAm 1*
Houston, George Harrison 1883-1949 *NatCAB 38, WhAm 2*
Houston, George Smith 1808-1879 *BiDrAC, WhAm 1, WhAmP*
Houston, George Smith 1811-1879 *ApCAB, BiAUS, DcAmB, Drake, NatCAB 10, TwCBDA*
Houston, Gordon David 1880- *WhoColR*
Houston, Grant 1864-1953 *WhAm 3*
Houston, H H *NewYHSD*
Houston, Harry Rutherford 1878- *WhAm 6*
Houston, Henry Aydelotte 1847-1925 *BiDrAC, WhAm 3*
Houston, Henry Howard 1820-1895 *DcAmB, NatCAB 3, NatCAB 35, TwCBDA, WhAm H*
Houston, Herbert Sherman 1866-1955 *WhAm 3*
Houston, Herbert Sherman 1866-1956 *NatCAB 41*
Houston, James *BiAUS*
Houston, James Garfield 1881- *WhAm 6*
Houston, John 1744-1796 *ApCAB, BiAUS, Drake, NatCAB 1*
Houston, John *see also* Houstoun, John
Houston, John Alexander 1859-1937 *NatCAB 28*
Houston, John Mills 1890-1975 *BiDrAC, WhAm 6*
Houston, John Wallace 1814-1896 *BiAUS, BiDrAC, TwCBDA, WhAm H, WhAmP*
Houston, Margaret Bell d1966 *WhAm 4*
Houston, Mary Asenath Sabin *WomWWA 14*
Houston, Minnie Gertrude Adams *WomWWA 14*
Houston, Nathan Foster 1829-1916 *NatCAB 18*
Houston, Nelly Macdonald 1886- *WomWWA 14*
Houston, Oscar Rempel 1883-1969 *NatCAB 54, WhAm 5*
Houston, Paul Leon 1890-1944 *NatCAB 33*
Houston, Persis Daniel 1874-1956 *NatCAB 45*
Houston, Persis Daniel 1874-1957 *WhAm 3*
Houston, Philip Douglas 1893-1966 *NatCAB 52*
Houston, Robert Griffith 1867-1946 *BiDrAC, NatCAB 35, WhAm 2, WhAmP*
Houston, Sam 1793-1863 *BiAUS, EncAB, REnAW, TwCBDA*
Houston, Samuel 1793-1863 *AmBi, ApCAB, BiDrAC, DcAmB, Drake, EncAAH, McGEWB, NatCAB 9, WebAB, WebAMB, WhAm H, WhAmP*
Houston, Samuel Frederic 1866-1952 *NatCAB 39, WhAm 3*
Houston, Victor Steuart Kaleoaloha 1876-1959 *WhAm 5*
Houston, Victor Stewart Kaleoaloha 1876-1959 *BiDrAC, WhAmP*
Houston, William 1755-1813 *BiAUS, NatCAB 3*
Houston, William C *NewYHSD*
Houston, William Cannon 1852-1931 *BiDrAC, WhAm 3, WhAmP*
Houston, William Churchill d1788 *BiAUS, Drake*
Houston, William Churchill 1740-1788 *ApCAB, NatCAB 3*
Houston, William Churchill 1745?-1788 *BiDrAC*
Houston, William Churchill 1746?-1788 *DcAmB, TwCBDA, WhAm H*
Houstoun, John 1744-1796 *BiDrAC, DcAmB, TwCBDA, WhAm H, WhAmP*
Houstoun, John *see also* Houston, John
Houstoun, William 1755-1813 *ApCAB, BiDrAC, TwCBDA, WhAm H*
Housum, Bird White 1860-1927 *NatCAB 21*
Houts, Charles Alfred 1868-1932 *WhAm 1*
Houx, Frank L 1860- *WhAm 3*
Houze, Armand Leon 1887-1957 *NatCAB 48*
Houze, Roger Joseph 1890-1945 *NatCAB 52*

Hovannes, John 1900-1973 *WhAm 5*
Hovde, Bryn Jacob 1896-1954 *NatCAB 52, WhAm 3*
Hove, Elling 1863-1927 *DcAmB*
Hovel, Cleo Wayne 1921-1970 *NatCAB 55*
Hovell, Albert Armand 1877- *WhAm 3*
Hovenden, Alfred 1824-1885 *NatCAB 18*
Hovenden, Thomas 1840-1895 *AmBi, ApCAB, BnEnAmA, DcAmB, NatCAB 6, TwCBDA, WhAm H*
Hover, C Watson 1908-1968 *NatCAB 54*
Hover, Herbert Austin 1868-1951 *NatCAB 40*
Hover, John Calvin 1866-1949 *NatCAB 37*
Hover, John Milton 1885-1940 *NatCAB 37*
Hover, William Adgate 1856-1952 *WhAm 3*
Hoverman, Russell Maas 1918-1974 *WhAm 6*
Hovey, Alvah 1820-1903 *ApCAB, DcAmB, Drake, NatCAB 8, TwCBDA, WhAm 1*
Hovey, Alvin Peterson 1821-1891 *ApCAB, BiAUS, BiDrAC, DcAmB, Drake, NatCAB 1, NatCAB 13, TwCBDA, WhAm H*
Hovey, C Earl 1897-1959 *NatCAB 49*
Hovey, Chandler 1880-1971 *NatCAB 56, WhAm 5*
Hovey, Charles Edward 1827-1897 *ApCAB, BiDAmEd, DcAmB, TwCBDA, WhAm H*
Hovey, Charles Mason 1810-1887 *AmBi, ApCAB, DcAmB, EncAAH, NatCAB 26, TwCBDA, WhAm H*
Hovey, Chester Ralph 1872- *ApCAB X, WhAm 5*
Hovey, Edmund Otis 1801-1877 *TwCBDA*
Hovey, Edmund Otis 1862-1924 *NatCAB 22, WhAm 1*
Hovey, Esther Lancraft 1863- *WomWWA 14*
Hovey, George Rice 1860-1943 *WhAm 2*
Hovey, Harriette Spofford d1916 *NatCAB 6*
Hovey, Henriette 1849- *WhAm 5, WomWWA 14*
Hovey, Horace Carter 1833-1914 *NatCAB 12, TwCBDA, WhAm 1*
Hovey, John *NewYHSD*
Hovey, Otis 1788- *NewYHSD*
Hovey, Otis Ellis 1864-1941 *DcAmB S3, NatCAB 32, WhAm 2*
Hovey, Rexford William 1892-1957 *WhAm 3*
Hovey, Richard 1864-1900 *AmBi, ApCAB Sup, DcAmB, NatCAB 6, TwCBDA, WhAm 1*
Hovey, William Simmons 1875-1954 *WhAm 3*
Hovgaard, William 1857-1950 *DcAmB S4, NatCAB 41, WebAMB, WhAm 2*
Hovick, Rose Louise *WebAB*
Hoving, Johannes Walter Wilhelm 1868- *ApCAB X, NatCAB 15, WhAm 5*
Hovis, William Forney 1872-1960 *WhAm 4*
Hovland, Carl Iver 1912-1961 *McGEWB, NatCAB 52, WhAm 4*
How, James Flintham 1842- *NatCAB 5*
How, Louis d1947 *WhAm 2*
How, Samuel Blanchard 1790-1868 *ApCAB, NatCAB 6, TwCBDA*
Howard, A Philo 1878- *WhAm 6*
Howard, A T 1893-1951 *WhAm 3*
Howard, Abram Claude 1880-1942 *NatCAB 35*
Howard, Ada Lydia 1829-1907 *BiDAmEd, DcAmB, NatCAB 7, TwCBDA, WhAm 1*
Howard, Adams Bailey Lothrop 1860- *NatCAB 16*
Howard, Albert Andrew 1858-1925 *WhAm 1*
Howard, Alfred Franklin 1842-1919 *NatCAB 19*
Howard, Alfred Taylor 1868-1948 *WhAm 2*
Howard, Alice Sturtevant 1878-1945 *NatCAB 33*
Howard, Alice Sturtevant *see also* Howard, Mrs. Henry
Howard, Alvin Hayward 1915-1969 *NatCAB 56, WhAm 5*
Howard, Arthur Ethelbert, Jr. 1891-1972 *WhAm 5*
Howard, Arthur Platt 1869- *WhAm 5*
Howard, B *NewYHSD*
Howard, Bailey Kneiriem 1914-1974 *WhAm 6*
Howard, Belle 1857- *AmWom*
Howard, Ben Odell 1904-1970 *WhAm 5*

Howard, Benjamin 1760-1814 *ApCAB, BiAUS, BiDrAC, DcAmB, Drake, NatCAB 12, TwCBDA, WhAm H, WhAmP*
Howard, Benjamin Chew 1791-1872 *ApCAB, BiAUS, BiDrAC, DcAmB, Drake, NatCAB 6, TwCBDA, WhAm H, WhAmP*
Howard, Blanche Willis 1847-1898 *AmWom, ApCAB, DcAmB, NatCAB 1, NotAW, TwCBDA, WhAm H*
Howard, Bronson Crocker 1842-1908 *AmBi, ApCAB, DcAmB, NatCAB 3, TwCBDA, WhAm 1*
Howard, Burt Estes 1862-1913 *WhAm 1*
Howard, Burton James 1872-1950 *WhAm 2A*
Howard, C McHenry 1870-1942 *NatCAB 31*
Howard, Campbell 1889-1965 *NatCAB 51*
Howard, Campbell Palmer 1877- *WhAm 5*
Howard, Caroline Emily Fox *NotAW*
Howard, Cecil DeBlaquiere 1888-1956 *WhAm 3*
Howard, Charles Abner 1881- *WhAm 6*
Howard, Charles Benjamin 1885-1964 *WhAm 4*
Howard, Charles Danforth 1873-1944 *NatCAB 34, WhAm 2*
Howard, Charles Eliot 1885-1962 *NatCAB 50*
Howard, Charles J 1875-1919 *NatCAB 18*
Howard, Charles Lowell 1881- *WhAm 6*
Howard, Charles Pagelsen 1887-1966 *NatCAB 52, WhAm 4*
Howard, Charles Perry 1879-1938 *DcAmB S2*
Howard, Charles S 1865-1951 *WhAm 3*
Howard, Charles Stewart 1877-1950 *NatCAB 38*
Howard, Charles Turner 1832-1885 *NatCAB 9*
Howard, Clara Eliza 1879-1935 *WhAm 1*
Howard, Clarence Henry 1863-1931 *WhAm 1*
Howard, Claud 1888- *WhAm 3*
Howard, Clifford 1868-1942 *WhAm 2*
Howard, Clinton Norman 1868-1955 *WhAm 3*
Howard, Clinton Wilbur 1890-1949 *WhAm 2*
Howard, Cordelia 1848-1941 *NotAW*
Howard, Daniel Edward 1861- *WhoColR*
Howard, Dowell J 1897-1957 *WhAm 3*
Howard, E D *NewYHSD*
Howard, Earl Dean 1876-1956 *WhAm 3*
Howard, Ed 1866-1948 *NatCAB 40*
Howard, Eddy 1914-1963 *WhAm 4*
Howard, Edgar 1858-1951 *BiDrAC, DcAmB S5, WhAm 3, WhAmP*
Howard, Edgar Billings 1887-1943 *NatCAB 32, WhAm 2*
Howard, Edward Daniel 1877- *ApCAB X, WhAm 6*
Howard, Edward Lloyd 1837-1881 *NatCAB 15*
Howard, Edward Orson d1946 *WhAm 2*
Howard, Eleanor Frasier 1866- *WomWWA 14*
Howard, Ella M 1864- *WomWWA 14*
Howard, Elmira Y 1841- *AmWom*
Howard, Emil Washington 1878-1958 *NatCAB 52*
Howard, Emma *NewYHSD*
Howard, Emma Lovell Shafter 1842- *WomWWA 14*
Howard, Emma Pease 1860- *WhAm 4*
Howard, Eric 1895-1943 *WhAm 2*
Howard, Ernest Emmanuel 1880-1953 *NatCAB 42, WhAm 3*
Howard, Erving Melville 1848- *NatCAB 3*
Howard, Sir Esme William 1863- *WhAm 4*
Howard, Everett *NewYHSD*
Howard, Everette Burgess 1873-1950 *BiDrAC, WhAm 3, WhAmP*
Howard, Ezra Lee 1869- *WhAm 5*
Howard, Francis, Lord Effingham 1630?-1694 *ApCAB, Drake, NatCAB 13*
Howard, Francis W d1944 *WhAm 2*
Howard, Frank Atherton 1890-1964 *WhAm 4*
Howard, Frank Eugene 1878-1963 *NatCAB 50, WhAm 4*
Howard, Frank Turner 1855- *NatCAB 9*
Howard, Fred Leslie 1849- *WhAm 1*
Howard, Frederic Hollis 1876- *WhAm 5*
Howard, G Turner 1877-1946 *NatCAB 34*
Howard, George 1789-1846 *BiAUS, NatCAB 9, TwCBDA*
Howard, George Bronson 1884-1922 *WhAm 1*
Howard, George C *WhAm H*
Howard, George Elliott 1849-1928 *AmBi,*

DcAmB, NatCAB 23, TwCBDA,
WhAm 1
Howard, George H 1844-1925 WhAm 1
Howard, George H 1884-1960 WhAm 4
Howard, George Rumsey 1861-1933
NatCAB 25
Howard, Georgena Myrtle 1868-
WomWWA 14
Howard, Graeme Keith 1896-1962 WhAm 4
Howard, Guy C 1878-1943 WhAm 2
Howard, Guy Victor 1879-1954 BiDrAC
Howard, H Maxwell 1867-1944 NatCAB 36
Howard, Hamilton Gay 1845-1926 NatCAB 21
Howard, Harry Clay 1866-1930 WhAm 1
Howard, Harry Herbert 1887-1971 NatCAB 56
Howard, Harvey James 1880-1956 WhAm 3
Howard, Hazel Antoinette 1885-
WomWWA 14
Howard, Hector Holdbrook 1873-1960 WhAm 4
Howard, Helen Margaret Willard 1872-
NatCAB 29
Howard, Henry 1815-1884 ApCAB
Howard, Henry 1818-1884 WhAm H
Howard, Henry 1826-1905 BiAUS, NatCAB 9,
TwCBDA, WhAm 1
Howard, Henry 1859-1933 WhAm 1
Howard, Henry 1868-1951 DcAmB S5,
NatCAB 47, WhAm 3
Howard, Mrs. Henry 1878-1945 WhAm 2
Howard, Mrs. Henry see also Howard, Alice
Sturtevant
Howard, Henry Clay 1860-1928 WhAm 1
Howard, Herbert Burr 1855-1923 WhAm 1
Howard, Howell Hoffman 1898-1937
NatCAB 42
Howard, J Edward 1870-1926 NatCAB 20
Howard, Jacob Merritt 1805-1871 ApCAB,
BiAUS, BiDrAC, DcAmB, Drake,
NatCAB 4, TwCBDA, WhAm H,
WhAmP
Howard, James 1814-1876 REnAW
Howard, James E 1851-1930 WhAm 1,
WhAm 1C
Howard, James H W 1859- WhoColR
Howard, James John 1927- BiDrAC
Howard, James Leland 1818-1906 NatCAB 6
Howard, James Lindt 1878- WhAm 6
Howard, James Quay d1912 WhAm 4
Howard, James Raley 1873-1954 NatCAB 18,
NatCAB 48, WhAm 3
Howard, John 1726?-1790 BiHiMed
Howard, John Dalphin 1869- WhoColR
Howard, John Don 1903-1974 WhAm 6
Howard, John Eager 1752-1827 AmBi, ApCAB,
BiAUS, BiDrAC, DcAmB, Drake,
NatCAB 3, NatCAB 9, TwCBDA,
WebAMB, WhAm H, WhAmP
Howard, John Galen 1864-1931 NatCAB 14,
WhAm 1
Howard, John George 1803- ApCAB
Howard, John Purple 1814-1885 ApCAB
Howard, John Raymond 1837-1926 WhAm 1
Howard, John Tasker 1890-1964 WhAm 4
Howard, Jonas George 1825-1911 BiDrAC
Howard, Joseph NewYHSD
Howard, Joseph, Jr. 1833-1908 NatCAB 4,
TwCBDA, WhAm 1
Howard, Joseph Henry 1860-1949 WhAm 3
Howard, Joseph Kinsey 1906-1951 DcAmB S5,
REnAW
Howard, Joseph Whitney 1889-1968 WhAm 5
Howard, Josiah W NewYHSD
Howard, Judson NewYHSD
Howard, Julia Palmer 1917-1971 WhAm 5
Howard, Justin H NewYHSD
Howard, Karl Sharpe 1887-1962 NatCAB 47
Howard, Kathleen d1956 WhAm 3
Howard, Lawrence Augustus 1881- WhAm 6
Howard, Lawrence Clayton 1894-1959
NatCAB 49
Howard, Leland Ossian 1857-1950 ApCAB Sup,
DcAmB S4, DcScB, NatCAB 12,
TwCBDA, WhAm 3
Howard, Leslie 1893-1943 DcAmB S3,
WhAm 2
Howard, Louis Orrin 1884-1944 WhAm 2
Howard, Lowry Samuel 1891-1949 WhAm 2
Howard, Margaret Douglas 1944-1972 WhAm 6

Howard, Maria A Chase 1872- WomWWA 14
Howard, Marion Edith 1899-1959 WhAm 3
Howard, Mary Katharine Foster 1845-
WomWWA 14
Howard, Mary M AmWom
Howard, McHenry 1838-1923 NatCAB 31
Howard, Mildred Langford 1916-1975 WhAm 6
Howard, Milford Wriarson 1862-1937 BiDrAC,
TwCBDA, WhAm 4
Howard, Nathaniel Lamson 1884-1949
NatCAB 38, WhAm 2
Howard, Nelson Willard 1872-1937 NatCAB 29
Howard, Oliver Otis 1830-1909 AmBi, ApCAB,
DcAmB, Drake, EncAB, McGEWB,
NatCAB 4, REnAW, TwCBDA, WebAB,
WebAMB, WhAm 1
Howard, Orson 1853-1923 NatCAB 20
Howard, Oscar Robert 1875-1950 NatCAB 38
Howard, Perry Wilbon 1877-1961 WhAm 4,
WhAm 5
Howard, Perry Wilbur 1878-1961 WhoColR
Howard, Philip Eugene 1870-1946 WhAm 2
Howard, Ralph Hills 1870-1928 WhAm 1
Howard, Rebecca F 1839?- NewYHSD
Howard, Robert Boardman 1896- IIBEAAW
Howard, Robert Mayburn 1878-1963
NatCAB 52, WhAm 4
Howard, Roger Strong 1807-1880 NatCAB 18
Howard, Rossiter 1878-1950 NatCAB 41,
WhAm 2
Howard, Roy Wilson 1883-1964 WebAB,
WhAm 4
Howard, Seth NewYHSD
Howard, Seth Edwin 1884-1935 WhAm 1
Howard, Sidney Coe 1891-1939 AmBi,
ApCAB X, DcAmB S2, NatCAB 28,
WebAB, WhAm 1
Howard, Simeon 1733-1804 ApCAB, Drake
Howard, Solomon 1811-1873 NatCAB 4,
TwCBDA
Howard, Thomas Benton 1854-1920
NatCAB 15, WhAm 1
Howard, Tilghman Ashurst 1797-1844 BiAUS,
BiDrAC, NatCAB 18, WhAm H
Howard, Timothy Edward 1837-1916 DcAmB,
NatCAB 16, TwCBDA, WhAm 1
Howard, Velma Swanston 1868-1937 WhAm 1,
WomWWA 14
Howard, Volney Erskine d1889 BiAUS
Howard, Volney Erskine 1805-1889 NatCAB 4
Howard, Volney Erskine 1808?-1889 ApCAB,
TwCBDA
Howard, Volney Erskine 1809-1889 BiDrAC,
DcAmB, WhAm H
Howard, Walter 1870-1902 WhAm 1
Howard, Walter Eugene 1849-1912 WhAm 1
Howard, Walter Lafayette 1872-1949
NatCAB 42, WhAm 2
Howard, Wayne Cox 1882- WhoColR
Howard, Wendell Stanton 1867- WhAm 4
Howard, Wesley O 1863-1933 WhAm 1
Howard, Wilbert Harvard 1890-1966 WhAm 4
Howard, William 1817-1891 BiAUS, BiDrAC,
WhAm H
Howard, William A 1807-1871 ApCAB,
BiAUS
Howard, William Alanson 1813-1880 ApCAB,
BiDrAC, DcAmB, NatCAB 4, TwCBDA,
WhAm H, WhAmP
Howard, William Clyde d1953 WhAm 3
Howard, William Eager, Jr. 1906-1972
WhAm 5
Howard, William Gibbs 1887-1948 WhAm 2
Howard, William James 1875-1935 NatCAB 27
Howard, William Lauriston 1860-1930
WhAm 1
Howard, William Lee 1860-1918 NatCAB 17,
WhAm 1
Howard, William Marcellus 1857-1932 BiDrAC,
TwCBDA, WhAm 1, WhAmP
Howard, William Schley 1875-1953 BiDrAC,
WhAm 5
Howard, William Travis 1821-1907 DcAmB S1,
NatCAB 12
Howard, William Travis 1867- WhAm 5
Howard, William Washington 1817-1871
ApCAB, TwCBDA
Howard, Willie 1886-1949 DcAmB S4,

WhAm 3
Howarth, Ellen Clementine 1827-1899
ApCAB Sup, NatCAB 7, WhAm 1
Howarth, Francis Andrew 1849-1927
NatCAB 22
Howat, Philip Yvonne Kirkpatrick 1891-1970
NatCAB 55, NatCAB 56
Howat, William Frederick 1860-1929 WhAm 1
Howbert, Irving 1846-1934 WhAm 1
Howdell, Thomas NewYHSD
Howden, Frederick Bingham 1869-1940
WhAm 2
Howe, Achibald Murray 1848- NatCAB 14
Howe, Albert Richards 1840-1884 BiAUS,
BiDrAC, WhAm H
Howe, Albion Paris 1818-1897 ApCAB, Drake,
NatCAB 6, TwCBDA
Howe, Albion Parris 1818-1897 AmBi, DcAmB,
WhAm H
Howe, Amelia Ely 1874- WomWWA 14
Howe, Andrew Jackson 1825-1892 DcAmB,
NatCAB 8, WhAm H
Howe, Anna Belknap 1849-1927 WhAm 1,
WomWWA 14
Howe, Anne Sturm Rotan 1881- WomWWA 14
Howe, Archibald Murray 1848-1916 WhAm 1
Howe, Arthur 1890-1955 WhAm 3
Howe, Arthur Millidge 1867-1947 WhAm 2
Howe, B D NewYHSD
Howe, Burton Alonzo 1886-1957 WhAm 3
Howe, Carl 1870-1946 WhAm 2
Howe, Carl Ellis 1898-1966 WhAm 4
Howe, Charles Sumner 1858-1939 NatCAB 15,
TwCBDA, WhAm 1
Howe, Church 1839-1915 WhAm 1
Howe, Clarence Decatur 1886-1960 WhAm 4
Howe, Daniel Wait 1839-1921 NatCAB 13,
WhAm 1
Howe, Delia Akeley 1875-1970 NatCAB 57
Howe, Edgar F 1862- WhAm 5
Howe, Edgar Watson 1853-1937 AmBi,
DcAmB S2, EncAAH, McGEWB,
WebAB, WhAm 1
Howe, Edgar Watson 1854-1937 ApCAB,
NatCAB 10
Howe, Edmund Grant 1883-1950 NatCAB 39,
WhAm 3
Howe, Edward Cole 1866-1959 NatCAB 49
Howe, Edward Gardiner 1849-1931 NatCAB 24
Howe, Edward Gardner 1849-1931 WhAm 4
Howe, Edward Leavitt 1870-1952 WhAm 3
Howe, Elias 1819-1867 AmBi, ApCAB,
AsBiEn, DcAmB, Drake, EncAB,
McGEWB, NatCAB 4, TwCBDA,
WebAB, WhAm H
Howe, Elmer Parker 1851-1918 ApCAB X,
NatCAB 19
Howe, Emeline Harriet 1844- AmWom
Howe, Ernest 1875-1932 NatCAB 25,
WhAm 1
Howe, Fannie Gay 1851- WomWWA 14
Howe, Fisher 1798-1871 ApCAB
Howe, Frank William 1865- WhAm 4
Howe, Frederic Clemson 1867-1940 DcAmB S2,
WhAm 1
Howe, Frederic William 1872-1957 WhAm 3
Howe, Frederick William, Jr. 1905-1972
WhAm 5
Howe, Frederick Stanley 1885-1957 WhAm 3
Howe, Frederick Webster 1822-1891 DcAmB,
WhAm H
Howe, G Allen 1876-1934 NatCAB 30
Howe, Gene Alexander 1886-1952 NatCAB 41,
WhAm 3
Howe, George 1802-1883 DcAmB, WhAm H
Howe, George 1876-1936 WhAm 1
Howe, George 1881-1967 NatCAB 53,
WhAm 5
Howe, George 1886-1955 WhAm 3
Howe, George Augustus 1724?-1758 ApCAB,
DcAmB, Drake, WhAm H
Howe, George Maxwell 1873- WhAm 5
Howe, George Rowland 1847-1917 NatCAB 29
Howe, Harland Bradley 1873-1946 WhAm 2
Howe, Harley Earl 1882-1965 WhAm 4
Howe, Harold 1913-1968 WhAm 5
Howe, Harriet Emma 1881-1965 DcAmLiB
Howe, Harrison Estell 1881-1942 WhAm 2

Howe, Helen 1905-1975 *WhAm 6*
Howe, Henry 1816-1893 *AmBi, ApCAB, DcAmB, Drake, NatCAB 3, NewYHSD, TwCBDA, WhAm H*
Howe, Henry Marion 1848-1922 *ApCAB, DcAmB, NatCAB 13, TwCBDA, WhAm 1*
Howe, Henry Saltonstall 1848-1931 *WhAm 1*
Howe, Henry V 1896-1974 *WhAm 6*
Howe, Herbert Alonzo 1858-1926 *DcAmB, NatCAB 20, TwCBDA, WhAm 1*
Howe, Herbert Crombie 1872-1940 *NatCAB 29, WhAm 1*
Howe, Herbert DeForest 1876-1922 *ApCAB X*
Howe, Herbert Marshall 1844-1916 *ApCAB X, WhAm 1*
Howe, James Blake 1860-1930 *WhAm 1*
Howe, James H *BiAUS*
Howe, James Lewis 1859-1955 *DcScB, NatCAB 9, NatCAB 47, TwCBDA, WhAm 3*
Howe, James Robinson 1839-1914 *BiDrAC, TwCBDA*
Howe, John d1843 *ApCAB*
Howe, John 1753-1835 *ApCAB*
Howe, John Badlam 1813-1882 *ApCAB*
Howe, John Badlam 1813-1883 *TwCBDA*
Howe, John Benedict 1859-1943 *WhAm 2*
Howe, John H d1873 *WhAm H*
Howe, John Ireland 1793-1876 *ApCAB, DcAmB, NatCAB 4, TwCBDA, WhAm H*
Howe, John Kasson 1850-1917 *NatCAB 17*
Howe, John Lynn 1880- *WhAm 6*
Howe, John W 1801-1873 *BiAUS, BiDrAC, WhAm H*
Howe, Jonas Holland 1821-1898 *NewYHSD, WhAm H*
Howe, Joseph 1804-1873 *ApCAB, Drake, McGEWB*
Howe, Joseph C *NewYHSD*
Howe, Joseph Olin 1875-1930 *WhAm 1*
Howe, Joseph P *NewYHSD*
Howe, Julia Romana 1844-1886 *ApCAB*
Howe, Julia Ward 1819-1910 *AmBi, AmWom, ApCAB, ApCAB X, BiCAW, DcAmB, Drake, EncAB, McGEWB, NatCAB 1, NotAW, TwCBDA, WebAB, WhAm 1, WhAmP*
Howe, Leon Bruce 1875-1949 *NatCAB 39*
Howe, Lois Lilley 1864-1964 *WhAm 4*
Howe, Louis McHenry 1871-1936 *DcAmB S2, NatCAB 27, WhAm 1, WhAmP*
Howe, Lucien 1848-1928 *DcAmB, NatCAB 23, WhAm 1*
Howe, Malverd Abijah 1863- *NatCAB 17, WhAm 4*
Howe, Malvina A *WomWWA 14*
Howe, Marie Jenney *WomWWA 14*
Howe, Mark Anthony DeWolfe 1808-1895 *DcAmB, NatCAB 13, WhAm H*
Howe, Mark Antony DeWolfe 1808-1895 *TwCBDA*
Howe, Mark Antony DeWolfe 1809-1895 *ApCAB*
Howe, Mark Antony DeWolfe 1864-1960 *WhAm 4*
Howe, Mark DeWolfe 1906-1967 *WhAm 4*
Howe, Marshall Avery 1867-1936 *WhAm 1*
Howe, Mary 1882-1964 *WhAm 4*
Howe, Mary Ann 1835-1870 *NatCAB 8*
Howe, Maud 1854-1948 *NotAW*
Howe, Maud 1855-1948 *ApCAB*
Howe, May Louise *WomWWA 14*
Howe, Nathanael 1764-1837 *ApCAB*
Howe, Nathaniel 1764-1837 *Drake*
Howe, Oliver Hunt 1860- *NatCAB 18*
Howe, Orville *NewYHSD*
Howe, Oscar 1915- *IIBEAAW*
Howe, Percival S, Jr. 1895-1965 *WhAm 4*
Howe, Percival Spurr 1863- *WhAm 4*
Howe, Percy Rogers 1864-1950 *DcAmB S4, WhAm 2A*
Howe, Ralph Sawyer 1891-1959 *NatCAB 47, WhAm 4*
Howe, Ralph Wilson 1885-1935 *NatCAB 31*
Howe, Reginald Heber 1846-1924 *TwCBDA, WhAm 1*

Howe, Reginald Heber 1875-1932 *TwCBDA, WhAm 1*
Howe, Richard 1725-1799 *ApCAB, Drake*
Howe, Richard Flint 1863-1943 *WhAm 2*
Howe, Richard Howe, Earl 1726-1799 *AmBi, McGEWB, WhoMilH*
Howe, Robert d1787 *Drake*
Howe, Robert 1732-1785 *ApCAB, NatCAB 6, TwCBDA*
Howe, Robert 1732-1786 *AmBi, DcAmB, WebAMB, WhAm H*
Howe, Samuel 1785-1828 *DcAmB, WhAm H*
Howe, Samuel Burnett 1879-1941 *WhAm 1*
Howe, Samuel Gridley 1801-1876 *AmBi, ApCAB, BiDAmEd, Drake, EncAB, McGEWB, NatCAB 8, TwCBDA, WebAB, WhAm H*
Howe, Stanley H 1890-1955 *WhAm 3*
Howe, Stewart Samuel 1905-1973 *WhAm 5*
Howe, Thomas Carr 1867-1934 *WhAm 1*
Howe, Thomas Marshall 1808-1877 *BiAUS, BiDrAC, NatCAB 18, WhAm H*
Howe, Thomas Y, Jr. 1801-1860 *BiAUS, BiDrAC, WhAm H*
Howe, Timothy Otis 1816-1883 *AmBi, ApCAB, BiAUS, BiDrAC, BiDrUSE, DcAmB, NatCAB 4, TwCBDA, WhAm H, WhAmP*
Howe, Wallis Eastburn 1868-1960 *WhAm 4*
Howe, Walter 1846-1915 *NatCAB 17, WhAm 1*
Howe, Walter 1907-1966 *NatCAB 52, WhAm 4*
Howe, Walter Bruce 1879-1954 *NatCAB 47, WhAm 3*
Howe, Walter Clarke 1872- *NatCAB 18*
Howe, Will David 1873-1946 *WhAm 2*
Howe, Willard B 1864-1929 *WhAm 1*
Howe, William 1729-1814 *NatCAB 7, WhAm H, WhoMilH*
Howe, William 1786-1843 *ApCAB*
Howe, William 1803-1852 *DcAmB, NatCAB 7, WhAm H*
Howe, William Augustus 1862-1940 *NatCAB 38, WhAm 1*
Howe, William Bell White 1823-1894 *ApCAB, NatCAB 12, TwCBDA*
Howe, William Francis 1888-1952 *WhAm 3*
Howe, William Frederick 1821-1902 *NatCAB 22*
Howe, William Frederick 1828-1902 *DcAmB*
Howe, William Henry 1844-1929 *TwCBDA*
Howe, William Henry 1846-1929 *DcAmB, NatCAB 13, WhAm 1*
Howe, William Howe, Viscount 1729-1814 *AmBi, ApCAB, Drake, McGEWB*
Howe, William Wirt 1833-1909 *DcAmB, NatCAB 13, WhAm 1*
Howe, Wirt 1875- *WhAm 1*
Howe, Zadoc *NewYHSD*
Howel, Clayton James 1878- *WhAm 6*
Howelcke, Johann *DcScB*
Howell, A Brazier 1886-1961 *WhAm 4*
Howell, Albert Summers 1879-1951 *DcAmB S5*
Howell, Alfred Corey 1884-1961 *NatCAB 50, WhAm 4*
Howell, Arthur 1748-1816 *ApCAB*
Howell, Arthur Holmes 1872-1940 *WhAm 1*
Howell, Benjamin Franklin 1844-1933 *BiDrAC, TwCBDA, WhAm 1, WhAmP*
Howell, Charles Cook 1890-1965 *WhAm 4*
Howell, Charles Fish 1868-1943 *NatCAB 32, WhAm 2*
Howell, Charles Robert 1904-1973 *BiDrAC, WhAm 6*
Howell, Clark 1863-1936 *AmBi, DcAmB S2, NatCAB 1, WhAm 1, WhAmP*
Howell, Clark 1894-1966 *WhAm 4*
Howell, Corwin 1881-1961 *NatCAB 50, WhAm 6*
Howell, Daniel Lane 1853- *WhAm 4*
Howell, Daniel William 1861-1949 *WhAm 2*
Howell, David 1747-1824 *BiAUS, BiDrAC, DcAmB, Drake, NatCAB 8, TwCBDA, WhAm H, WhAmP*
Howell, David 1747-1826 *ApCAB*
Howell, Edward 1792-1871 *BiAUS, BiDrAC, WhAm H*

Howell, Edward Vernon 1872- *WhAm 2*
Howell, Edwin Eugene 1845-1911 *WhAm 1*
Howell, Edwin Hite 1901-1965 *NatCAB 52, WhAm 4*
Howell, Elias 1792-1844 *BiAUS, BiDrAC, WhAm H*
Howell, Elizabeth *Drake*
Howell, Elizabeth Myra Brown *WomWWA 14*
Howell, Evan Park 1839-1905 *DcAmB, NatCAB 1, TwCBDA, WhAm 1*
Howell, Francis Singleton 1863-1937 *WhAm 1*
Howell, Frederica Burckle Gilchrist 1871- *WomWWA 14*
Howell, Frederick Hunting 1848-1929 *ApCAB X*
Howell, George 1859-1913 *BiDrAC, WhAm 4*
Howell, George Blaine 1893-1961 *WhAm 4*
Howell, George Evan 1905- *BiDrAC*
Howell, George Rogers 1833-1899 *ApCAB, NatCAB 3, TwCBDA*
Howell, Henry Clay 1845-1900 *NatCAB 2*
Howell, Henry Wilson, Jr. 1903-1958 *NatCAB 46*
Howell, Herbert P 1874-1944 *WhAm 2*
Howell, Hilton Emory 1897-1968 *WhAm 5*
Howell, J B *NewYHSD*
Howell, James Albert, Jr. 1931-1969 *WhAm 6*
Howell, James Bruen 1816-1880 *ApCAB, BiAUS, BiDrAC, DcAmB, NatCAB 9, TwCBDA, WhAm H*
Howell, James Edward 1848-1916 *WhAm 1*
Howell, Jeremiah Brown d1822 *BiAUS*
Howell, Jeremiah Brown 1771-1822 *BiDrAC, NatCAB 9, TwCBDA, WhAm H, WhAmP*
Howell, Jeremiah Brown 1772-1822 *ApCAB*
Howell, John Adams 1840-1918 *AmBi, ApCAB, DcAmB, NatCAB 6, TwCBDA, WebAMB, WhAm 1, WhAm 4*
Howell, John Carnett 1901-1961 *WhAm 4*
Howell, John Cumming 1819-1892 *ApCAB, Drake, NatCAB 2, TwCBDA*
Howell, John White 1857-1937 *NatCAB 27, WhAm 1*
Howell, Joseph d1798 *Drake*
Howell, Joseph 1857-1918 *BiDrAC, WhAm 1, WhAmP*
Howell, Joseph A 1901-1960 *WhAm 3*
Howell, Joseph B *NewYHSD*
Howell, Joseph Morton 1863-1937 *NatCAB 27, WhAm 1*
Howell, Joshua B 1799-1864 *Drake*
Howell, Julius Franklin 1846-1948 *TwCBDA, WhAm 2*
Howell, Mabel Katharine *WomWWA 14*
Howell, Mary Seymour 1844-1913 *AmWom*
Howell, Mary Seymour 1850-1913 *WhAm 1*
Howell, Max Don 1887-1967 *WhAm 4*
Howell, Meta Pauline 1899-1968 *WhAm 5*
Howell, Nathaniel Woodhull 1770-1851 *BiAUS, BiDrAC, TwCBDA, WhAm H*
Howell, P *NewYHSD*
Howell, Rednap *ApCAB*
Howell, Reese M 1889-1967 *WhAm 4*
Howell, Richard 1753-1802 *ApCAB*
Howell, Richard 1754-1802 *BiAUS, DcAmB, WhAm H*
Howell, Richard 1754-1803 *NatCAB 5, TwCBDA*
Howell, Richard 1755-1802 *Drake*
Howell, Richard Lewis *ApCAB*
Howell, Robert Beecher 1864-1933 *ApCAB X, BiDrAC, NatCAB 43, WhAm 1*
Howell, Robert Boyte Crawford 1801-1868 *ApCAB, DcAmB, Drake, TwCBDA, WhAm H*
Howell, Roger William 1911-1970 *WhAm 5*
Howell, Smith Allen 1860- *WhoColR*
Howell, Stanley Evans 1906-1967 *NatCAB 53*
Howell, Theodore Pike 1819-1878 *NatCAB 2*
Howell, Thomas 1868-1948 *NatCAB 36*
Howell, Thomas Jefferson 1842-1912 *DcAmB*
Howell, Walter Rufus 1888-1949 *WhAm 2*
Howell, William Barberie 1865-1927 *WhAm 1*
Howell, William F *BiAUS*
Howell, William Henry 1860-1945 *DcAmB S3, DcScB, WhAm 2*
Howell, Williamson S, Jr. d1947 *WhAm 2*

Howells, David P *ApCAB X*
Howells, John Mead 1868-1959 *NatCAB 45,
WhAm 3*
Howells, Mildred 1872- *WhAm 5,
WomWWA 14*
Howells, Sophia Brookes 1884- *WomWWA 14*
Howells, William Dean 1837- *ApCAB, Drake,
NatCAB 1, TwCBDA*
Howells, William Dean 1837-1919 *WhAm 1*
Howells, William Dean 1837-1920 *AmBi,
ApCAB X, DcAmB, EncAB, McGEWB,
WebAB*
Hower, Frank Benjamin 1858-1932 *NatCAB 25*
Hower, Harry 1877-1941 *WhAm 2*
Hower, Milton Otis 1859-1916 *WhAm 1*
Hower, Paul Allen 1917-1967 *WhAm 4A*
Hower, Ralph M 1903-1973 *WhAm 6*
Howerth, Cora Olive 1864- *WomWWA 14*
Howerth, Ira Woods 1860-1938 *NatCAB 28,
WhAm 1*
Howerton, James Robert 1861- *WhAm 1*
Howes, Benjamin Alfred 1875-1952 *WhAm 3*
Howes, Bertha Sage Bell *WomWWA 14*
Howes, Edith Mary 1855- *BiCAW*
Howes, Edwin Alliston 1871-1962 *NatCAB 47*
Howes, Ernest Grant 1871-1951 *NatCAB 39*
Howes, Ernest Grant 1871-1956 *WhAm 3*
Howes, Ethel Dench Puffer 1872-1950
WhAm 3A, WomWWA 14
Howes, Frank Stewart 1891-1974 *WhAm 6*
Howes, Frank Warner 1858-1933 *NatCAB 45*
Howes, George Edwin 1865- *WhAm 4*
Howes, Hannah Nichols Cushman 1886-
WomWWA 14
Howes, Herbert Harold 1881-1940 *WhAm 1*
Howes, Josephine Holt 1887- *WomWWA 14*
Howes, Maria Adelaide 1846- *WomWWA 14*
Howes, Royce B 1901-1973 *WhAm 5*
Howes, Samuel P *NewYHSD*
Howes, Warren Lincoln 1904-1963 *NatCAB 52*
Howes, William Edward 1894-1952 *NatCAB 41*
Howes, William Washington 1887-1962
WhAm 4
Howey, Benjamin Franklin 1828-1895 *BiDrAC,
WhAm H*
Howey, Walter Crawford 1882-1954 *DcAmB S5,
WhAm 3*
Howey, William John 1876-1938 *WhAm 2*
Howie, Robert George 1890-1954 *WhAm 3*
Howison, George Holmes 1834- *TwCBDA,
WhAm 1*
Howison, George Holmes 1834-1916 *BiDAmEd,
DcAmB*
Howison, George Holmes 1834-1917
NatCAB 23
Howison, Henry Lycurgus 1837-1914
ApCAB Sup, TwCBDA, WhAm 1
Howison, Robert Reid 1820-1906 *Drake,
NatCAB 19, WhAm 1*
Howkins, Elizabeth Penrose 1906-1972
WhAm 5
Howlan, George William 1835- *ApCAB*
Howland, Alfred Cornelius 1838-1909 *ApCAB,
DcAmB, NatCAB 7, NewYHSD,
TwCBDA, WhAm 1*
Howland, Alfred R *NewYHSD*
Howland, Alice Gulielma 1883- *WomWWA 14*
Howland, Arthur Charles 1869-1952 *WhAm 3*
Howland, B F *NewYHSD*
Howland, Benjamin d1821 *BiAUS*
Howland, Benjamin 1755-1821 *BiDrAC,
WhAm H*
Howland, Benjamin 1756-1821 *ApCAB,
NatCAB 4, TwCBDA*
Howland, Charity *NewYHSD*
Howland, Charles Follen 1841-1921 *NatCAB 35*
Howland, Charles P 1869-1932 *WhAm 1*
Howland, Charles Roscoe 1871-1946
NatCAB 46, WhAm 2
Howland, Clara Ward 1841- *WomWWA 14*
Howland, Edward 1832-1890 *WhAm 4*
Howland, Edward DeMonte 1858-1952
NatCAB 41
Howland, Emily 1827-1929 *AmWom,
BiDAmEd, DcAmB, NatCAB 25,
NotAW, WhAm 1*
Howland, Frances Louise *WhAm 4*

Howland, Francis Nathaniel 1844-1913
NatCAB 18
Howland, Frank *NewYHSD*
Howland, Fred Arthur 1864-1953 *NatCAB 41,
WhAm 3*
Howland, Frederick Hoppin 1871-1916
WhAm 1
Howland, French *NewYHSD*
Howland, Gardiner Greene 1767-1851
WhAm H
Howland, Gardiner Greene 1787-1851 *DcAmB,
NatCAB 25*
Howland, Gardiner Greene 1834-1903 *WhAm 1*
Howland, Garth A 1887-1950 *WhAm 3*
Howland, George 1824-1892 *ApCAB,
NatCAB 20, TwCBDA*
Howland, Harold 1877-1966 *WhAm 4*
Howland, Henry Elias 1835-1913 *NatCAB 9,
WhAm 1*
Howland, Henry Raymond 1844-1930
NatCAB 22, WhAm 1
Howland, Hewitt Hanson 1863-1944 *WhAm 2*
Howland, James *NewYHSD*
Howland, John 1757-1854 *ApCAB, BiDAmEd,
Drake, NatCAB 8, TwCBDA*
Howland, John 1873-1926 *DcAmB,
NatCAB 21, WhAm 1*
Howland, John Dare 1843-1914 *IIBEAAW*
Howland, Joseph Briggs 1873-1963 *NatCAB 50,
WhAm 5*
Howland, Joseph T *NewYHSD*
Howland, Leonard Paul 1865-1942 *BiDrAC*
Howland, Leroy Albert 1879- *WhAm 6*
Howland, Louis 1857-1934 *WhAm 1*
Howland, Louise *WomWWA 14*
Howland, Marguerite Elizabeth Smith 1915-1972
WhAm 6
Howland, Mary Woolsey *ApCAB*
Howland, Murray Shipley 1874-1953 *WhAm 3*
Howland, Oliver Aiken 1847- *ApCAB Sup*
Howland, Paul 1865-1942 *WhAm 2*
Howland, Peleg C 1830-1885 *ApCAB X*
Howland, Richard Smith 1847- *WhAm 4*
Howland, Robert Southworth 1820-1887
ApCAB, TwCBDA
Howland, Sarah Maud *WomWWA 14*
Howland, Silas Wilder 1879-1938 *WhAm 1*
Howland, Thomas Smith 1844-1921 *WhAm 1*
Howland, William *NewYHSD*
Howland, William 1871-1945 *WhAm 2*
Howland, William Bailey 1849-1917 *WhAm 1*
Howland, William Legrand 1872-1915
NatCAB 21
Howland, Sir William Pearce 1811- *ApCAB,
Drake*
Howle, Paul Williamson 1874-1954 *NatCAB 43*
Howlett, Freeman Smith 1900-1970
NatCAB 57, WhAm 5
Howlett, James David 1874- *WhAm 5*
Howlett, Walter Main 1883-1972 *WhAm 5*
Howley, Richard 1740?-1784 *BiAUS, BiDrAC,
DcAmB, NatCAB 2, TwCBDA,
WhAm H*
Howley, Richard 1740?-1790? *ApCAB*
Howorth, George 1791?- *NewYHSD*
Howorth, John 1836?- *NewYHSD*
Howry, Charles Bowen 1844-1928 *DcAmB,
NatCAB 22, TwCBDA, WhAm 1*
Howry, Charles Bowen 1845-1928 *NatCAB 2*
Howry, James Moorman 1804-1884 *TwCBDA*
Hows, John Augustine 1831-1874 *TwCBDA*
Hows, John Augustus 1831-1874 *ApCAB*
Hows, John Augustus 1832-1874 *NewYHSD*
Hows, John William Stanhope 1797-1871
ApCAB, Drake
Howse, Hilary Ewing 1866-1938 *WhAm 1,
WhAm 1C*
Howse, John Wordsworth 1873- *WhoColR*
Howse, William Massy Godwin 1879- *WhAm 6*
Howson, Elmer Thomas 1884-1944 *WhAm 2*
Howson, Hubert 1856-1943 *NatCAB 31*
Howson, Roger 1882-1962 *WhAm 4*
Howze, Augustin Clayton 1846- *NatCAB 6*
Howze, Henry Russell 1870- *WhAm 5*
Howze, Robert Lee 1864-1926 *DcAmB,
NatCAB 23, WebAMB, WhAm 1*
Hoxha, Enver 1908- *WhWW-II*
Hoxie, Charles A 1867-1941 *NatCAB 39*

Hoxie, George Howard 1872-1959 *NatCAB 49*
Hoxie, George Luke 1872- *WhAm 5*
Hoxie, Harold Jennings 1908-1967 *WhAm 5*
Hoxie, Joseph 1795-1870 *ApCAB*
Hoxie, Richard Leveridge 1844-1930
NatCAB 23, WhAm 1
Hoxie, Robert Franklin 1868-1916 *AmBi,
DcAmB, NatCAB 23, WhAm 1*
Hoxie, Solomon 1829-1917 *WhAm 1*
Hoxie, Stansbury *NewYHSD*
Hoxie, Vinnie Ream d1914 *NotAW,
WomWWA 14*
Hoxie, Vinnie Ream 1846-1914 *ApCAB,
TwCBDA*
Hoxie, Vinnie Ream 1847-1914 *AmBi,
AmWom, DcAmB, IlBEAAW, WhAm 1*
Hoxie, William Dixie 1866-1925 *DcAmB,
NatCAB 24*
Hoxton, Archibald Robinson 1875- *WhAm 5*
Hoxton, Llewellyn Griffith 1878-1966 *WhAm 4*
Hoxton, William Winslow 1871-1935 *WhAm 1*
Hoxworth, Stephen Arnold 1860-1930 *BiDrAC,
WhAm 4*
Hoy, Albert Harris *WhAm 5*
Hoy, Anne Harris 1866- *WomWWA 14*
Hoy, Carson 1902-1966 *NatCAB 52,
WhAm 4*
Hoy, Claribel Wright 1879- *WomWWA 14*
Hoy, Frank Clement 1891-1954 *NatCAB 41*
Hoy, Patrick Henry 1914-1973 *WhAm 6*
Hoy, Philo Romayn 1816-1892 *ApCAB Sup*
Hoy, Philo Romayne 1816-1892 *NatCAB 15*
Hoyer, Theodore 1883-1963 *WhAm 4*
Hoyle, Eli DuBose 1851-1921 *WhAm 1*
Hoyle, Fred 1915- *AsBiEn*
Hoyle, Raphael 1804-1838 *NewYHSD*
Hoyme, Gjermund 1847-1902 *DcAmB,
WhAm H*
Hoyne, Archibald Lawrence 1878-1963
WhAm 4
Hoyne, Maclay 1872- *NatCAB 18*
Hoyne, Thomas 1817-1883 *ApCAB, TwCBDA*
Hoyne, Thomas Maclay 1843-1941 *WhAm 1*
Hoyne, Thomas Temple 1875-1946 *WhAm 2*
Hoynes, William 1846-1933 *WhAm 1*
Hoyns, Henry d1945 *WhAm 2*
Hoyo, John Charles 1891-1958 *WhAm 3*
Hoyt, A G *NewYHSD*
Hoyt, Albert Ellis 1865- *WhAm 4*
Hoyt, Albert Harrison 1826-1915 *ApCAB,
DcAmB, TwCBDA, WhAm 4*
Hoyt, Alex Crawford 1881- *WhAm 6*
Hoyt, Allen Grey 1876-1941 *WhAm 1*
Hoyt, Arthur Stephen 1851-1923 *WhAm 1*
Hoyt, Benjamin Thomas 1820-1867 *ApCAB,
Drake*
Hoyt, Benjamin Thomas 1821-1867 *TwCBDA*
Hoyt, Burnham 1887-1960 *WhAm 3A*
Hoyt, Charles Albert 1839-1903 *NatCAB 3,
WhAm 1*
Hoyt, Charles Edgar 1869-1955 *NatCAB 43*
Hoyt, Charles Hale 1860-1900 *DcAmB,
NatCAB 30, TwCBDA, WhAm 1*
Hoyt, Charles Kimball 1846- *WhAm 4*
Hoyt, Charles Oliver 1856-1927 *WhAm 1*
Hoyt, Charles Wilson 1872-1928 *ApCAB X,
NatCAB 21*
Hoyt, Colgate 1849-1922 *ApCAB X,
WhAm 1*
Hoyt, Colgate 1883-1963 *WhAm 4*
Hoyt, Creig Simmons 1894-1957 *WhAm 3*
Hoyt, David Webster 1833-1921 *WhAm 1*
Hoyt, Deristhe Lavinta *WhAm 5*
Hoyt, Doristhe Lavinta *WomWWA 14*
Hoyt, Mrs. E C *NewYHSD*
Hoyt, Edward C 1853-1925 *WhAm 1*
Hoyt, Edwin 1896-1964 *NatCAB 50*
Hoyt, Elizabeth Orpha 1834- *ApCAB*
Hoyt, Elizabeth Stone 1905-1972 *WhAm 6*
Hoyt, Elton, II 1888-1955 *NatCAB 41,
WhAm 3*
Hoyt, Epaphras 1765-1850 *ApCAB, Drake*
Hoyt, Florence Smith 1863- *WomWWA 14*
Hoyt, Francis Southack 1822- *ApCAB,
TwCBDA, WhAm 4*
Hoyt, Franklin Chase 1876-1937 *NatCAB 27,
WhAm 1*
Hoyt, H Spencer 1895-1965 *NatCAB 54*

Hoyt, Harold Wardwell 1885-1953 *WhAm 3*
Hoyt, Harry Barzillai 1874-1952 *NatCAB 42*
Hoyt, Helen Brown 1858- *WhAm 4*
Hoyt, Henry Augustus 1914-1967 *WhAm 4*
Hoyt, Henry E 1833?-1906 *NewYHSD*
Hoyt, Henry Martyn 1830-1892 *ApCAB, DcAmB, NatCAB 2, TwCBDA, WhAm H*
Hoyt, Henry Martyn 1856-1910 *WhAm 1*
Hoyt, James Alfred 1877-1959 *WhAm 3*
Hoyt, James Humphrey 1850-1917 *NatCAB 17, NatCAB 27*
Hoyt, James Humphrey 1852-1917 *WhAm 1*
Hoyt, James Phillips 1844- *WhAm 4*
Hoyt, John Clayton 1874-1946 *WhAm 2*
Hoyt, John Philo 1841- *NatCAB 11, WhAm 4*
Hoyt, John Sherman 1869-1954 *DcAmB S5, NatCAB 43, WhAm 3*
Hoyt, John Wesley 1831-1912 *AmBi, ApCAB, BiDAmEd, DcAmB, NatCAB 13, TwCBDA, WhAm 1*
Hoyt, Joseph Gibson 1815-1862 *ApCAB, Drake, NatCAB 11, TwCBDA*
Hoyt, Laurence Brackett 1891-1936 *NatCAB 29*
Hoyt, Loy Eugene 1884-1955 *NatCAB 43*
Hoyt, Lucius Warner 1860-1910 *WhAm 1*
Hoyt, Maud Buckingham *WomWWA 14*
Hoyt, Merrill Hubert 1881-1933 *NatCAB 24*
Hoyt, Minerva Lockhart Hamilton 1866-1945 *NatCAB 35, WhAm 2*
Hoyt, Myra Corliss *WomWWA 14*
Hoyt, Oliver 1823-1887 *ApCAB, TwCBDA*
Hoyt, Phillis Lucille 1923-1970 *WhAm 5*
Hoyt, Purdy B 1829?- *NewYHSD*
Hoyt, Ralph 1806-1878 *ApCAB, NatCAB 7, WhAm H*
Hoyt, Ralph Edwin 1894-1961 *NatCAB 49*
Hoyt, Ralph Wilson 1849-1920 *NatCAB 20, WhAm 1*
Hoyt, Richard Farnsworth 1888-1935 *NatCAB 29, WhAm 1*
Hoyt, Robert Stephens 1916-1971 *NatCAB 56*
Hoyt, Robert Stuart 1918-1971 *WhAm 5*
Hoyt, Stewart Ellison 1863- *WhoColR*
Hoyt, Thomas *NewYHSD*
Hoyt, Thomas R, Jr. *NewYHSD*
Hoyt, W Henry 1884-1957 *WhAm 3*
Hoyt, Walter Stiles 1873-1920 *NatCAB 33*
Hoyt, Walter Stiles 1879-1928 *NatCAB 43*
Hoyt, Warren Albert 1868-1933 *NatCAB 25*
Hoyt, Wayland 1838-1910 *TwCBDA, WhAm 1*
Hoyt, Wilbur Franklin 1864-1930 *WhAm 1*
Hoyt, William Ballard 1858-1915 *NatCAB 22*
Hoyt, William Dana 1880-1945 *WhAm 2*
Hoyt, William Greeley 1859-1935 *WhAm 1*
Hoyt, William H *NewYHSD*
Hoyt, William Henry 1855-1929 *NatCAB 23*
Hoyt, William S *NewYHSD*
Hrdlicka, Ales 1869-1943 *ApCAB X, DcAmB S3, DcScB, NatCAB 35, WebAB, WhAm 2*
Hromadka, Josef Luki 1889-1969 *WhAm 5*
Hruby, Allan Joseph 1890-1939 *NatCAB 30*
Hruska, Roman Lee 1904- *BiDrAC*
Hsia, David Yi-Yung 1925-1972 *WhAm 5*
Hsia, Kuei *McGEWB*
Hsieh, Ling-Yun 385-433 *McGEWB*
Hsu, Mo 1893- *WhAm 3*
Hsuan, Tsang 602?-664 *McGEWB*
Hsuan-Tsung, T'ang 685-762 *McGEWB*
Hsun-Tzu 312?BC-235?BC *McGEWB*
Hu, Shih 1891-1962 *McGEWB*
Hu-Shih 1891-1962 *WhAm 4*
Huang, Ch'ao d884 *McGEWB*
Huang, Tsung-Hsi 1610-1695 *McGEWB*
Huard, Leo A 1916-1969 *WhAm 5*
Huascar 1490?-1533 *ApCAB*
Huayna Capac d1523 *ApCAB*
Hubard, Edmund Wilcox 1806- *BiAUS*
Hubard, Edmund Wilcox 1806-1872 *NatCAB 20*
Hubard, Edmund Wilcox 1806-1878 *BiDrAC, WhAm H*
Hubard, Robert Thruston 1839-1921 *WhAm 1*
Hubard, William 1740-1802 *ApCAB*
Hubard, William James 1807-1862 *BnEnAmA,*

NewYHSD, WhAm H
Hubban, Miss E A *NewYHSD*
Hubbard, Adolphus Skinner 1840-1913 *WhAm 1*
Hubbard, Alice 1861-1915 *WhAm 1, WomWWA 14*
Hubbard, Alice Clarke *WomWWA 14*
Hubbard, Allen 1860-1930 *NatCAB 24*
Hubbard, Anita Day 1889-1965 *WhAm 4*
Hubbard, Arthur Lucius 1872-1931 *NatCAB 24*
Hubbard, Asahel Wheeler 1819-1879 *BiAUS, BiDrAC, TwCBDA, WhAm H, WhAmP*
Hubbard, Bela 1739-1812 *ApCAB*
Hubbard, Bela 1814-1896 *ApCAB, NatCAB 5, TwCBDA*
Hubbard, Bernard Rosecrans 1888-1962 *WhAm 4*
Hubbard, Burritt Seymour 1891-1956 *NatCAB 47*
Hubbard, Carlisle LeCompte 1881- *WhAm 6*
Hubbard, Charles 1801-1876 *NewYHSD*
Hubbard, Charles Francis Wayland 1857-1927 *NatCAB 21*
Hubbard, Charles Gillette 1883-1967 *NatCAB 54*
Hubbard, Charles Joseph 1902-1950 *NatCAB 39, WhAm 3*
Hubbard, Charles Wells 1856-1933 *NatCAB 29, WhAm 3*
Hubbard, Chester Dorman 1814-1891 *BiAUS, BiDrAC, NatCAB 5, TwCBDA, WhAm H*
Hubbard, David *NewYHSD*
Hubbard, David d1874 *BiAUS*
Hubbard, David 1790-1874 *TwCBDA*
Hubbard, David 1792-1874 *BiDConf, BiDrAC, DcAmB, WhAm H*
Hubbard, David 1806- *ApCAB*
Hubbard, Demas, Jr. 1806-1873 *BiAUS, BiDrAC, WhAm H*
Hubbard, Edna Post 1854- *WomWWA 14*
Hubbard, Elbert 1856-1915 *AmBi, ApCAB X, DcAmB, NatCAB 13, NatCAB 16, WebAB*
Hubbard, Elbert 1859-1915 *TwCBDA, WhAm 1*
Hubbard, Elbert Hamilton 1849-1912 *BiDrAC, WhAm 1, WhAmP*
Hubbard, Elijah Kent 1835-1915 *NatCAB 18*
Hubbard, Elijah Kent 1869-1941 *NatCAB 32, WhAm 1*
Hubbard, Emma Lucretia *WomWWA 14*
Hubbard, Etta Belle Ross *ApCAB X*
Hubbard, Eugene 1876-1946 *NatCAB 35*
Hubbard, F Elmore 1877-1943 *NatCAB 33*
Hubbard, Fordyce Mitchell 1809-1888 *NatCAB 7*
Hubbard, Frances Johnson 1885- *WomWWA 14*
Hubbard, Frances Virginia *WhAm 5*
Hubbard, Frank Gaylord 1859- *TwCBDA, WhAm 4*
Hubbard, Frank McKinney 1868-1930 *AmBi, DcAmB, WebAB, WhAm 1*
Hubbard, Frank Watson 1863-1943 *NatCAB 33, WhAm 2*
Hubbard, Frederick A d1956 *WhAm 3*
Hubbard, Gardiner Greene 1822-1897 *AmBi, ApCAB Sup, DcAmB, NatCAB 5, TwCBDA, WebAB, WhAm H*
Hubbard, George David 1871-1958 *WhAm 3*
Hubbard, George Henry 1857- *WhAm 4*
Hubbard, George Warner 1818-1888 *TwCBDA*
Hubbard, George Whipple 1841- *WhAm 4*
Hubbard, Giles Munro 1887-1953 *WhAm 3*
Hubbard, Grace Amanda *WomWWA 14*
Hubbard, Gurdon Saltonstall 1802-1886 *AmBi, ApCAB, DcAmB, NatCAB 25, TwCBDA, WhAm H*
Hubbard, Harry 1816-1872 *WhAm H*
Hubbard, Harry Appleton 1859-1935 *NatCAB 27*
Hubbard, Havrah William Lines 1867- *WhAm 5*
Hubbard, Helen Fahnestock 1872-1955 *NatCAB 45*
Hubbard, Henry 1784-1857 *ApCAB, BiAUS, BiDrAC, Drake, NatCAB 11, TwCBDA,*

WhAm H
Hubbard, Henry Griswold 1814-1891 *DcAmB, NatCAB 10, WhAm H*
Hubbard, Henry Guernsey 1850-1899 *DcAmB, WhAm H*
Hubbard, Henry Vincent 1875-1947 *NatCAB 46, WhAm 2*
Hubbard, Henry Wright 1844-1913 *WhAm 1*
Hubbard, Howard S 1912-1967 *WhAm 4*
Hubbard, Ida Blanche Harroun 1862- *WomWWA 14*
Hubbard, Ira Stoddard 1871-1966 *NatCAB 53*
Hubbard, Joel Douglas 1860-1919 *BiDrAC*
Hubbard, John 1759-1810 *ApCAB, Drake, WhAm H*
Hubbard, John 1794-1869 *ApCAB, BiAUS, DcAmB, Drake, NatCAB 6, NatCAB 30, TwCBDA, WhAm H*
Hubbard, John 1849-1932 *WhAm 1*
Hubbard, John 1870-1933 *NatCAB 30*
Hubbard, John Barrett 1837-1863 *NatCAB 6*
Hubbard, John Charles 1879-1954 *NatCAB 44, WhAm 3*
Hubbard, John Clarence 1884-1959 *NatCAB 48*
Hubbard, John Henry 1804-1872 *BiDrAC, TwCBDA, WhAm H*
Hubbard, John Henry 1805-1872 *BiAUS*
Hubbard, John W d1947 *WhAm 2*
Hubbard, Jonathan Hatch 1768-1849 *ApCAB, BiAUS, BiDrAC, Drake, WhAm H*
Hubbard, Joseph Stiles 1823-1863 *NatCAB 9*
Hubbard, Joseph Stillman 1823-1863 *ApCAB, BiAUS, DcAmB, Drake, TwCBDA, WhAm H*
Hubbard, Joshua Clapp 1869-1934 *NatCAB 25*
Hubbard, Josiah Clark 1853-1928 *NatCAB 23*
Hubbard, Kin *AmBi, DcAmB, WebAB, WhAm 1*
Hubbard, L Marsden 1882-1973 *WhAm 6*
Hubbard, Leslie Elmer 1879-1962 *WhAm 4*
Hubbard, Lester Thomas 1877-1958 *NatCAB 46*
Hubbard, Levi 1762-1836 *BiAUS, BiDrAC, WhAm H*
Hubbard, Louis Vaughan 1865-1929 *NatCAB 22*
Hubbard, Lucius Frederick 1836-1913 *ApCAB, DcAmB, NatCAB 10, TwCBDA, WhAm 1*
Hubbard, Lucius Lee 1849-1933 *TwCBDA, WhAm 1*
Hubbard, Marian Elizabeth 1868- *WomWWA 14*
Hubbard, Mary Bradley 1859- *WomWWA 14*
Hubbard, Mary Tenney 1855- *WomWWA 14*
Hubbard, Moses Gilbert 1893-1967 *WhAm 4*
Hubbard, Nathaniel Mead, Jr. 1860- *WhAm 3*
Hubbard, Nehemiah 1752-1837 *ApCAB Sup*
Hubbard, Newton K 1839-1909 *ApCAB X*
Hubbard, Oliver Payson 1809-1900 *ApCAB, TwCBDA, WhAm 1*
Hubbard, Prevost 1881-1971 *NatCAB 56*
Hubbard, R W 1816-1888 *Drake*
Hubbard, Richard Bennet 1835-1901 *TwCBDA*
Hubbard, Richard Bennet 1836-1901 *WhAm 1*
Hubbard, Richard Bennett 1832-1901 *DcAmB, WhAm H*
Hubbard, Richard Bennett 1834-1901 *NatCAB 9*
Hubbard, Richard Dudley 1818-1884 *ApCAB, BiAUS, BiDrAC, NatCAB 10, TwCBDA, WhAm H*
Hubbard, Richard William 1810-1888 *ApCAB, TwCBDA*
Hubbard, Richard William 1816-1888 *DcAmB, NewYHSD*
Hubbard, Robert 1826-1897 *NatCAB 25*
Hubbard, Russell Sturgis 1863-1918 *NatCAB 26*
Hubbard, Russell Sturgis 1902-1972 *WhAm 5*
Hubbard, S Dana 1869-1937 *WhAm 1*
Hubbard, Samuel 1785-1847 *ApCAB, Drake, TwCBDA*
Hubbard, Samuel Birdsey 1833- *NatCAB 5*
Hubbard, Samuel Dickinson 1799-1855 *AmBi, ApCAB, BiAUS, BiDrAC, BiDrUSE, Drake, NatCAB 6, TwCBDA, WhAm H*
Hubbard, Samuel Fairfield 1846-1928 *WhAm 1*

Hubbard, Sara Anderson 1832-1918 *WhAm 1*
Hubbard, Susan Platt 1865- *WomWWA 14*
Hubbard, Theodora Kimball 1887-1935 *AmBi,*
NatCAB 28, WhAm 1
Hubbard, Thomas 1776-1838 *ApCAB*
Hubbard, Thomas 1859- *WhAm 4*
Hubbard, Thomas Hamlin 1838-1915 *DcAmB,*
NatCAB 2, NatCAB 30, WhAm 1
Hubbard, Thomas Hill d1857 *BiAUS*
Hubbard, Thomas Hill 1780-1857 *ApCAB*
Hubbard, Thomas Hill 1781-1857 *BiDrAC,*
TwCBDA, WhAm H
Hubbard, Walter Comstock 1851-1927 *WhAm 1*
Hubbard, Walter John 1862-1951 *NatCAB 52*
Hubbard, Walton d1954 *WhAm 3*
Hubbard, Wilbur Watson 1860- *ApCAB X*
Hubbard, William 1621-1704 *AmBi, ApCAB,*
DcAmB, Drake, NatCAB 11, TwCBDA,
WhAm H
Hubbard, William Barrington 1898-1968
NatCAB 55
Hubbard, William H 1860- *WhAm 1*
Hubbard, William Henry 1851-1913
NatCAB 15, WhAm 1
Hubbard, William J *NewYHSD*
Hubbard, William Norris 1861-1948
NatCAB 49
Hubbard, William Pallister 1843-1921 *BiDrAC,*
WhAm 1
Hubbard, William Stimpson 1866-1944
NatCAB 34
Hubbard, Wynant Davis 1900-1961 *WhAm 4*
Hubbart, Henry Clyde 1882-1960 *WhAm 4*
Hubbart, Ralph 1881-1956 *WhAm 3*
Hubbell, Alvin Allace 1846-1911 *WhAm 1*
Hubbell, Benjamin S 1868- *WhAm 4*
Hubbell, Burt G 1867-1925 *WhAm 1*
Hubbell, Charles Bulkley 1853-1939 *WhAm 1*
Hubbell, Clarence W 1870-1950 *WhAm 3*
Hubbell, DeWitt 1876-1952 *NatCAB 42*
Hubbell, Edwin Nelson 1815- *BiAUS, BiDrAC,*
WhAm H
Hubbell, Frederick Cooper 1864-1947
NatCAB 41
Hubbell, Frederick Marion 1839-1930
ApCAB X, NatCAB 28, WhAm 1
Hubbell, Frederick Windsor 1891-1959
WhAm 3
Hubbell, George Allen 1862- *ApCAB X*
Hubbell, Grover Cooper 1883-1956 *WhAm 3*
Hubbell, Harry Mortimer 1881-1971 *WhAm 5*
Hubbell, Harvey 1857-1927 *NatCAB 22*
Hubbell, Harvey 1901-1968 *NatCAB 54,*
WhAm 5
Hubbell, Henry Salem 1870-1949 *WhAm 2,*
WhAm 5
Hubbell, Henry Wilson 1842-1917 *WhAm 1*
Hubbell, James Floyd 1876-1948 *NatCAB 37*
Hubbell, James Randolph 1824- *BiAUS*
Hubbell, James Randolph 1824-1890 *BiDrAC*
Hubbell, James Randolph 1824-1896 *WhAm H*
Hubbell, James Wakeman 1881- *WhAm 2*
Hubbell, Jay Abel 1829-1900 *ApCAB, BiAUS,*
BiDrAC, NatCAB 4, TwCBDA,
WhAm 1, WhAmP
Hubbell, John Lorenzo 1853-1930 *DcAmB S1*
Hubbell, Levi 1808-1876 *ApCAB, TwCBDA*
Hubbell, Martha Stone 1814-1856 *ApCAB*
Hubbell, Raymond 1879-1954 *NatCAB 44,*
WhAm 3
Hubbell, Sidney A *BiAUS*
Hubbell, William 1750?-1835? *ApCAB*
Hubbell, William N 1862-1934 *NatCAB 25*
Hubbell, William Spring 1801-1873 *BiAUS,*
BiDrAC, WhAm H
Hubbell, William Wheeler 1821-1902
NatCAB 16
Hubbert, James Monroe 1850-1934 *WhAm 1*
Hubble, Edwin Powell 1889-1953 *AsBiEn,*
DcAmB S5, DcScB, McGEWB,
NatCAB 42, WebAB, WhAm 3
Hubbs, John Brewster 1856-1938 *WhAm 1*
Hubbs, Orlando 1840-1930 *BiDrAC*
Hubbs, Rebecca 1772-1852 *DcAmB, WhAm H*
Hubbuch, Otto Joseph 1888-1970 *NatCAB 55*
Hubeny, Maximilian John 1880-1942
NatCAB 31, WhAm 2
Huber *NewYHSD*

Huber, Carl Parker 1903-1974 *WhAm 6*
Huber, Caroline Stephens *WomWWA 14*
Huber, Charles Frederick 1871-1966 *WhAm 4*
Huber, Charles Henry 1871- *WhAm 5*
Huber, Charles Joseph 1886-1953 *NatCAB 42*
Huber, Conrad *NewYHSD*
Huber, Edward Godfrey 1882-1946 *WhAm 2*
Huber, Erwin 1886-1951 *NatCAB 40*
Huber, Gotthelf Carl 1865-1934 *DcAmB S1,*
NatCAB 42, WhAm 1
Huber, Harold 1907-1962 *NatCAB 52,*
WhAm 4
Huber, Harvey Evert 1884-1953 *WhAm 3*
Huber, Henry Allen 1869-1933 *WhAm 1*
Huber, Jacques 1851- *NatCAB 14*
Huber, Johann Jacob 1707-1778 *DcScB*
Huber, John Bessner 1864-1924 *WhAm 1*
Huber, John Greenleaf 1865- *WhAm 4*
Huber, Lucretia Marshall 1869- *WomWWA 14*
Huber, Maksymilian Tytus 1872-1950 *DcScB*
Huber, Max d1960 *WhAm 3*
Huber, Michael Joseph 1905-1957 *NatCAB 47*
Huber, Miriam Blanton d1969 *WhAm 5*
Huber, Phil d1952 *WhAm 3*
Huber, Ray Allen 1883-1958 *WhAm 3*
Huber, Seba Cormany 1871-1944 *WhAm 2*
Huber, Walter B 1903- *BiDrAC*
Huber, Walter Leroy 1883-1960 *WhAm 4*
Huberich, Charles Henry 1877-1945 *WhAm 2*
Huberman, Leo 1903-1968 *WhAm 5*
Hubert *NewYHSD*
Hubert, Benjamin Franklin 1884-1958 *WhAm 3,*
WhoColR
Hubert, Charles *NewYHSD*
Hubert, Conrad 1855-1928 *DcAmB,*
WhAm HA, WhAm 4
Hubert, Conrad 1856-1928 *NatCAB 24*
Hubert, Joseph *NewYHSD*
Hubert, Philip Aklis 1860- *WhAm 1*
Hubert, Philip Gengembre 1830-1911
NatCAB 15
Hubert, Philip Gengembre 1852-1925 *WhAm 1*
Huberth, Martin Francis 1875-1960 *WhAm 4*
Huberty, Martin R 1894-1960 *WhAm 4*
Hubler, Edward Lorenzo 1902-1965 *WhAm 4*
Hubley, Adam 1740-1798 *ApCAB*
Hubley, Edward Burd 1792-1856 *BiAUS,*
BiDrAC, WhAm H
Hubley, George Wilbur 1870-1944 *WhAm 2*
Hubner, Charles William 1835-1929 *DcAmB,*
NatCAB 2, WhAm 1
Hubner, Cleo Laverne 1902-1968 *NatCAB 54*
Hubrecht, Ambrosius Arnold Willem 1853-1915
DcScB
Hubschman, Albert 1899-1956 *WhAm 3*
Hubschman, Herbert 1912-1964 *NatCAB 52*
Huch, Ricarda 1864-1947 *McGEWB*
Huchingson, James Edwin 1881- *WhAm 6*
Huck, Ferdinand *NewYHSD*
Huck, Winnifred Sprague Mason 1882-1936
BiDrAC, NotAW, WhAmP
Huckabee, Edgar Clarke 1855-1925 *NatCAB 20*
Huckabee, Hattie J 1875- *WhoColR*
Huckel, Oliver 1864-1940 *WhAm 1*
Huckins, Jennie Thomas *WomWWA 14*
Hucles, Henry B 1856- *WhoColR*
Hudd, Thomas Richard 1835-1896 *BiDrAC,*
WhAm H
Hudde, Andreas 1600?-1663 *ApCAB*
Hudde, Andries 1608-1663 *AmBi, DcAmB,*
WhAm H
Hudde, Jan 1628-1704 *DcScB*
Huddle, J Klahr 1891-1959 *NatCAB 43,*
WhAm 3
Huddle, William Henry 1847-1892 *IIBEAAW*
Huddleson, I Forest 1893-1965 *WhAm 4*
Huddleston, George 1869-1960 *BiDrAC,*
NatCAB 50, WhAm 3, WhAmP
Huddleston, George, Jr. 1920-1971 *BiDrAC,*
WhAm 5
Huddleston, John Henry 1864-1915 *WhAm 1*
Huddy, George Henry, Jr. 1872- *WhAm 5*
Huddy, R T 1904-1974 *WhAm 6*
Huddy, William M *NewYHSD*
Hude, James 1695-1762 *TwCBDA*
Huden, Lucas Van 1509-1553 *ApCAB*
Hudgens, John Allison 1872-1946 *NatCAB 35*
Hudgens, Robert Smith 1900-1966 *WhAm 4*

Hudgins, Edward Wren 1882- *WhAm 3*
Hudgins, Houlder 1900-1963 *NatCAB 49,*
WhAm 4
Hudgins, Lavinia A Bess 1874- *WhoColR*
Hudgins, Morgan Hughes 1878- *WhAm 6*
Hudnut, Joseph 1886-1968 *WhAm 4*
Hudnut, Richard Alexander 1855- *NatCAB 14*
Hudnut, William Herbert 1864-1963 *WhAm 4*
Hudnutt, Dean 1891-1943 *NatCAB 33*
Hudon, Henry 1823- *NatCAB 4*
Hudson, Albert Blellock 1875-1947 *WhAm 2*
Hudson, Birney Stillmon 1868-1946 *NatCAB 35*
Hudson, Buell W 1902-1966 *WhAm 4*
Hudson, C Alan 1847-1970 *NatCAB 57*
Hudson, Ceylon E 1901-1973 *WhAm 6*
Hudson, Charles 1795-1881 *ApCAB, BiAUS,*
BiDrAC, DcAmB, Drake, NatCAB 24,
TwCBDA, WhAm H
Hudson, Charles Bannus 1898-1968 *NatCAB 54*
Hudson, Charles Bradford 1865-1939
NatCAB 29
Hudson, Charles Henry 1833- *NatCAB 10*
Hudson, Clara Elizabeth 1880- *WomWWA 14*
Hudson, Claude Silbert 1881-1952 *DcAmB S5,*
DcScB, NatCAB 40, WhAm 3
Hudson, Daniel Eldred 1849-1934 *DcAmB S1,*
WhAm 1
Hudson, Edward 1772-1833 *DcAmB,*
WhAm H
Hudson, Erasmus Darwin 1805-1880 *ApCAB,*
NatCAB 2, TwCBDA, WhAm H
Hudson, Erasmus Darwin 1843-1887 *ApCAB,*
TwCBDA
Hudson, Eric d1932 *WhAm 1, WhAm 1C*
Hudson, Frederic 1819-1875 *ApCAB,*
DcAmB S1, WhAm H
Hudson, Frederick 1819-1875 *NatCAB 11*
Hudson, Frederick Auld 1884-1959 *NatCAB 49*
Hudson, Frederick Mitchell 1871- *WhAm 6*
Hudson, G H *NewYHSD*
Hudson, Gardner Kirk 1875-1926 *NatCAB 20*
Hudson, George Elford 1907-1974 *WhAm 6*
Hudson, Grace Carpenter 1865-1937 *IIBEAAW*
Hudson, Grant Martin 1868-1955 *BiDrAC,*
WhAm 3
Hudson, Harry 1878-1951 *NatCAB 38*
Hudson, Hendrik 1575?-1611 *TwCBDA*
Hudson, Henry 1575?-1611 *AmBi, ApCAB,*
DcAmB, Drake, EncAB, McGEWB,
NatCAB 9, TwCBDA, WebAB,
WhAm H
Hudson, Henry Norman 1814-1886 *AmBi,*
ApCAB, DcAmB, Drake, NatCAB 9,
TwCBDA, WhAm H
Hudson, Hoyt Hopewell 1893-1944 *NatCAB 36,*
WhAm 2
Hudson, J Cramer 1896-1943 *NatCAB 32*
Hudson, James Alexander 1853-1922
NatCAB 6
Hudson, James Fairchild 1846-1915 *WhAm 1*
Hudson, James Henry 1878-1947 *WhAm 2*
Hudson, Jay William 1874-1958 *WhAm 3*
Hudson, John Bradley 1832-1903 *NewYHSD*
Hudson, John Elbridge 1839-1900 *NatCAB 5,*
TwCBDA, WhAm 1
Hudson, John Rogers 1859- *WhAm 4*
Hudson, John Walter 1905-1972 *NatCAB 57*
Hudson, Joseph Kennedy 1840-1907 *NatCAB 1,*
TwCBDA, WhAm 1
Hudson, Joseph Lowthian 1846-1912
NatCAB 47, WhAm 1
Hudson, Jules *NewYHSD*
Hudson, Julien *NewYHSD*
Hudson, Laura Agnes Shaw 1846-
WomWWA 14
Hudson, Manley Ottmer 1886-1960 *WebAB,*
WhAm 4
Hudson, Mary Clemmer Ames d1884 *NotAW,*
TwCBDA
Hudson, Mary Clemmer Ames 1839-1884
DcAmB
Hudson, Mary Clemmer Ames 1840-1884
AmWom
Hudson, Maurice 1892-1954 *NatCAB 43*
Hudson, Millard Fillmore 1889-1951 *WhAm 3*
Hudson, Oscar 1876- *WhoColR, WhoColR A*
Hudson, Paul Bateman 1907-1970 *WhAm 5*
Hudson, Ralph 1908-1968 *WhAm 5*

Hughes, Howard Wingett 1891-1945
NatCAB 34

Hughes, I Lamont 1878- *WhAm 6*

Hughes, J W 1881- *WhAm 6*

Hughes, James 1823-1873 *BiAUS, BiDrAC, DcAmB, NatCAB 23, WhAm H*

Hughes, James 1830-1895 *TwCBDA*

Hughes, James Anthony 1861-1930 *BiDrAC, WhAm 1, WhAmP*

Hughes, James Frederic 1883-1940 *BiDrAC*

Hughes, James Fredric 1883-1940 *WhAm 1*

Hughes, James Hurd 1867-1953 *BiDrAC, WhAm 3, WhAmP*

Hughes, James Hurd 1889-1938 *NatCAB 29*

Hughes, James Langston 1902-1967 *EncAB*

Hughes, James Langston *see also* Hughes, Langston

Hughes, James Laughlin 1846- *ApCAB*

Hughes, James Madison 1809-1861 *BiAUS, BiDrAC, WhAm H*

Hughes, James Mercer Langston *WebAB*

Hughes, James Monroe 1890-1971 *NatCAB 56, WhAm 5*

Hughes, James P 1874-1961 *WhAm 4*

Hughes, Jesse Knight 1864-1942 *NatCAB 32*

Hughes, John 1797-1864 *ApCAB, Drake, NatCAB 1, TwCBDA, WebAB*

Hughes, John 1830-1889 *TwCBDA*

Hughes, John Chambers 1891-1971 *WhAm 5*

Hughes, John H 1876-1952 *WhAm 3*

Hughes, John Henry 1904-1972 *WhAm 5*

Hughes, John Joseph 1797-1864 *AmBi, BiDAmEd, DcAmB, DcAmReB, McGEWB, WhAm H*

Hughes, John Newton 1867-1947 *NatCAB 37, WhAm 2*

Hughes, John T 1874- *WhAm 5*

Hughes, Joseph E 1894-1963 *WhAm 4*

Hughes, Josiah Simpson 1884-1965 *NatCAB 53*

Hughes, Julian 1888-1958 *NatCAB 48*

Hughes, Kate Duval 1837- *AmWom*

Hughes, Katherine *WomWWA 14*

Hughes, Lafayette Menefee, Jr. 1916-1965 *NatCAB 53*

Hughes, Langston 1902-1967 *McGEWB, WebAB, WhAm 4*

Hughes, Langston *see also* Hughes, James Langston

Hughes, Levi Allen 1858-1934 *NatCAB 28, WhAm 1*

Hughes, Louis C 1844- *WhAm 1*

Hughes, Louis Cameron 1843- *TwCBDA*

Hughes, Mack F 1923-1973 *WhAm 6*

Hughes, Marc Ray 1878- *NatCAB 12*

Hughes, Marietta E *AmWom*

Hughes, Matt Simpson 1863-1920 *WhAm 1*

Hughes, Matthew Simpson 1863-1920 *NatCAB 21*

Hughes, Maude Howard 1868- *WomWWA 14*

Hughes, Merritt Yerkes 1893-1971 *WhAm 5*

Hughes, Mildred B d1972 *WhAm 5*

Hughes, Nicholas Collin 1822-1893 *TwCBDA*

Hughes, Nina Vera B *AmWom*

Hughes, Oliver John Davis *WhAm 1*

Hughes, Owen Rogers 1888-1958 *NatCAB 44*

Hughes, Owen Wroten 1888-1957 *NatCAB 48*

Hughes, Patrick *NewYHSD*

Hughes, Percy 1872-1952 *WhAm 3*

Hughes, Percy Meredith 1864-1928 *WhAm 1*

Hughes, Peter Davis 1855-1911 *WhAm 1*

Hughes, Phillip Samuel 1917-1967 *WhAm 4*

Hughes, Price d1715 *DcAmB, WhAm H*

Hughes, Ray Osgood 1879-1959 *BiDAmEd, WhAm 3*

Hughes, Raymond Mollyneaux 1873-1958 *NatCAB 43, WhAm 3*

Hughes, Rees Hopkins 1892-1973 *WhAm 6*

Hughes, Reynold King 1890-1966 *WhAm 4*

Hughes, Richard Cecil 1861-1920 *TwCBDA, WhAm 1*

Hughes, Robert Ball 1806-1868 *DcAmB, Drake, NatCAB 24, NewYHSD, WhAm H*

Hughes, Robert Ball *see also* Hughes, Ball

Hughes, Robert Elkin 1869-1925 *NatCAB 20*

Hughes, Robert Hugh 1880- *WhAm 6*

Hughes, Robert M, Jr. 1880-1951 *WhAm 3*

Hughes, Robert Morton 1855-1940 *NatCAB 29, WhAm 1*

Hughes, Robert Patterson 1839-1909 *WhAm 1*

Hughes, Robert William 1821-1901 *ApCAB, BiAUS, DcAmB, NatCAB 7, TwCBDA, WhAm 1*

Hughes, Rowland Roberts 1896-1957 *WhAm 3*

Hughes, Royal Delaney 1884-1938 *WhAm 1*

Hughes, Rupert 1872-1956 *ApCAB X, WhAm 3*

Hughes, Russell Houston 1891-1970 *WhAm 5*

Hughes, Shelly Gleason 1893-1967 *NatCAB 54*

Hughes, Simon P 1830-1906 *NatCAB 10, TwCBDA, WhAm 1*

Hughes, Stanley Carnaghan 1869-1944 *NatCAB 32*

Hughes, Talmage Coates 1887-1963 *WhAm 4*

Hughes, Thomas 1823- *ApCAB*

Hughes, Thomas Aloysius 1849- *TwCBDA, WhAm 4*

Hughes, Thomas Hurst 1769-1839 *BiAUS, BiDrAC, TwCBDA, WhAm H*

Hughes, Thomas Patrick 1838-1911 *WhAm 1*

Hughes, Thomas Welburn 1858-1943 *WhAm 2*

Hughes, Wilburn Patrick 1892-1940 *WhAm 1*

Hughes, William 1872-1918 *BiDrAC, NatCAB 21, WhAm 1, WhAmP*

Hughes, William Arthur 1892-1960 *NatCAB 50*

Hughes, William Edgar 1840-1918 *NatCAB 18, WhAm 4*

Hughes, William F 1874-1929 *WhAm 1*

Hughes, William Joseph 1863-1938 *WhAm 1*

Hughes, William Joseph, Jr. 1897-1974 *NatCAB 57*

Hughes, William Lee 1866-1922 *NatCAB 19*

Hughes, William Leonard 1895-1957 *BiDAmEd, NatCAB 47, WhAm 3*

Hughes, William Morris 1864-1952 *McGEWB*

Hughes, Winfred Otis 1906-1971 *NatCAB 56*

Hughett, Joseph Lynn 1883-1954 *NatCAB 46*

Hughey, Allen Harrison 1881- *WhAm 6*

Hughitt, Marvin 1837-1928 *NatCAB 20, WhAm 1*

Hughitt, Marvin, Jr. 1861-1949 *NatCAB 40, WhAm 2*

Hughs, Fannie May Barbee *WomWWA 14*

Hughson, Frank Campbell 1861-1945 *NatCAB 36*

Hughston, Jonas Abbott 1808-1862 *BiAUS, BiDrAC, WhAm H*

Hughston, Wallace 1874-1959 *NatCAB 49*

Hugo, Albert Carl 1896-1957 *WhAm 3*

Hugo, Nicholas Frederic 1860-1921 *NatCAB 19*

Hugo, Trevanion William 1848- *WhAm 4*

Hugo, Victor Marie 1802-1885 *McGEWB*

Hugoniot, Pierre Henri 1851-1887 *DcScB*

Huguelet, Guy Alexander 1891-1955 *WhAm 3*

Huguerin, Edward *NewYHSD*

Hugues, Victor 1761-1826 *ApCAB*

Huguet-Latour, Louis A 1830?- *ApCAB*

Hugunin, Daniel, Jr. 1790-1850 *BiAUS, BiDrAC, WhAm H*

Hugus, Wright 1890-1958 *WhAm 4*

Huhlein, Charles Frederick 1858-1938 *NatCAB 53, WhAm 1*

Huhn, F *NewYHSD*

Huhn, John Ernest 1880- *WhAm 6*

Huhne, Bernhard 1547-1611 *ApCAB*

Huhner, Leon 1871-1957 *WhAm 3*

Huhner, Max 1873-1947 *WhAm 2*

Hui, Ka Kwong 1922- *BnEnAmA*

Hui-Tsung 1082-1135 *McGEWB*

Hui-Yuan 334-416 *McGEWB*

Huidekoper, Arthur Clarke 1845-1928 *WhAm 1*

Huidekoper, Frederic 1817-1892 *ApCAB, DcAmB, TwCBDA, WhAm H*

Huidekoper, Frederic Louis 1874-1940 *NatCAB 30, WhAm 1*

Huidekoper, Frederic Wolters 1840-1908 *NatCAB 15, WhAm 1*

Huidekoper, Harm Jan 1776-1854 *ApCAB, DcAmB, WhAm H*

Huidekoper, Henry Shippen 1839-1918 *ApCAB, TwCBDA, WhAm 1*

Huidekoper, Reginald Shippen 1876-1943 *NatCAB 32, WhAm 2*

Huidekoper, Rush Shippen 1854-1901 *WhAm 1*

Huiginn, Eugene Joseph Vincent 1860-1927 *NatCAB 21*

Huitzilihuitl *ApCAB*

Huitzilihuitzin d1448 *ApCAB*

Huitziton *ApCAB*

Huizenga, Lee Sjoerds 1881-1945 *WhAm 2*

Huizinga, Arnold VanC P 1876-1953 *WhAm 3*

Huizinga, Faith Trumbull 1873- *WomWWA 14*

Huizinga, Henry 1873-1945 *WhAm 2*

Huizinga, Johan 1872-1945 *McGEWB*

Hukill, Edwin Martin 1840- *WhAm 4*

Hukill, Ralph Leroy 1901-1968 *WhAm 5*

Hukriede, Theodore Waldemar 1878-1945 *BiDrAC, WhAm 6*

Hulagu Khan 1216?-1265 *McGEWB*

Hulanski *NewYHSD*

Hulbert, Archer Butler 1873-1933 *DcAmB S1, WhAm 1*

Hulbert, Calvin Butler 1827-1917 *NatCAB 12, TwCBDA, WhAm 1*

Hulbert, Edith Josephine *WomWWA 14*

Hulbert, Edmund Daniel 1858-1923 *NatCAB 19, WhAm 1*

Hulbert, Edwin James 1829-1910 *DcAmB*

Hulbert, Eri Baker 1841-1907 *NatCAB 11, TwCBDA, WhAm 1*

Hulbert, George Murray 1881-1950 *BiDrAC, WhAm 3*

Hulbert, Harold Stacey 1887-1949 *NatCAB 41*

Hulbert, Henry Carlton 1831-1912 *NatCAB 3, NatCAB 30, WhAm 1*

Hulbert, Henry Woodward 1858-1937 *NatCAB 29, TwCBDA, WhAm 1*

Hulbert, Homer B 1863-1949 *WhAm 2*

Hulbert, John Whitefield 1770-1831 *BiAUS, BiDrAC, WhAm H*

Hulbert, Milan Hulbert 1867-1931 *NatCAB 23, WhAm 1*

Hulbert, Roscoe Conkling 1891-1955 *NatCAB 44*

Hulbert, William Davenport 1868-1913 *WhAm 1*

Hulburd, Alice L *WomWWA 14*

Hulburd, Anna Kilian 1862- *WomWWA 14*

Hulburd, Calvin Tilden 1809-1897 *BiAUS, BiDrAC, NatCAB 4, TwCBDA, WhAm H*

Hulburd, Charles Henry 1850-1923 *WhAm 1*

Hulburd, Charles Henry 1850-1924 *NatCAB 20*

Hulburd, Hiland R *BiAUS*

Hulburt, David Willey 1853-1936 *WhAm 1*

Hulburt, Lorrain Sherman 1858-1942 *WhAm 2*

Hulburt, Ray Garland 1885-1947 *WhAm 2*

Hulen, John Augustus 1871-1957 *WhAm 3*

Hulen, Rubey Mosley 1894-1956 *WhAm 3*

Hulett, Alta M 1854-1877 *ApCAB*

Hulett, Edwin Lee 1870-1942 *WhAm 2*

Hulett, George Augustus 1867-1955 *NatCAB 44, WhAm 3*

Hulick, George Washington 1833-1907 *BiDrAC, TwCBDA, WhAm 3*

Hulick, Peter Vaughn 1909-1971 *WhAm 5*

Huling, Caroline Augusta 1856- *AmWom*

Huling, Ellen Paine 1880- *WomWWA 14*

Huling, James Hall 1844-1918 *BiDrAC*

Huling, Ray Greene 1847-1915 *WhAm 1*

Huling, Sara Hawks 1872-1940 *BiCAW, WhAm 1*

Hulings, Clark *IIBEAAW*

Hulings, Garnet 1889-1932 *NatCAB 24, WhAm 1, WhAm 1C*

Hulings, Willis James 1850-1924 *BiDrAC, WhAm 1, WhAm 4*

Hull, Albert Wallace 1880-1966 *DcScB, NatCAB 53, WhAm 4*

Hull, Alexander 1887-1953 *WhAm 3*

Hull, Alexander C 1858- *NatCAB 9*

Hull, Amos Girard 1815- *ApCAB*

Hull, Asa *NewYHSD*

Hull, Asbury 1797-1866 *ApCAB*

Hull, Blake D 1882-1952 *NatCAB 40*

Hull, Charles Henry 1864-1936 *NatCAB 27, TwCBDA, WhAm 1*

Hull, Clark Leonard 1884-1952 *BiDAmEd, DcAmB S5, McGEWB, NatCAB 41, WhAm 3*

Hull, Cordell 1871-1955 *BiDrAC, BiDrUSE, EncAAH, EncAB, McGEWB, WebAB, WhAm 3, WhAmP, WhWW-II*

Hull, Cordell 1872-1955 *DcAmB S5*

Hull, David Carlisle 1869-1928 *NatCAB 47,*

WhAm 1

Hull, David Denton 1872-1945 *WhAm 2*
Hull, Fannie Fitzalan Johnston *WomWWA 14*
Hull, George Huntington 1840-1921
 NatCAB 19, *WhAm 1*
Hull, George Malcolm 1865-1923 *NatCAB 20*
Hull, George Ross 1888-1952 *WhAm 3*
Hull, Gordon Ferrie 1870-1956 *WhAm 3*
Hull, Hannah Clothier 1872- *WomWWA 14*
Hull, Harry Charles 1894-1963 *NatCAB 50*
Hull, Harry Edward 1864-1938 *BiDrAC*,
 WhAm 1, *WhAmP*
Hull, Helen Lamb 1875- *WomWWA 14*
Hull, Henry 1798-1881 *ApCAB*
Hull, Holmer 1815-1877 *NatCAB 4*
Hull, Hope 1763-1818 *ApCAB*
Hull, Isaac 1773-1843 *AmBi*, *ApCAB*,
 DcAmB, *NatCAB 13*, *TwCBDA*, *WebAB*,
 WebAMB, *WhAm H*
Hull, Isaac 1775-1843 *Drake*, *NatCAB 3*
Hull, James Meriwether 1885-1975 *WhAm 6*
Hull, John 1624-1682 *Drake*
Hull, John 1624-1683 *AmBi*, *ApCAB*,
 BnEnAmA, *DcAmB*, *TwCBDA*,
 WhAm H
Hull, John 1839-1921 *NatCAB 19*
Hull, John Adley 1874-1944 *WhAm 2*
Hull, John Albert Tiffin 1841-1928 *ApCAB Sup*,
 BiDrAC, *NatCAB 23*, *TwCBDA*,
 WhAm 1, *WhAmP*
Hull, John Clarence 1878-1945 *NatCAB 34*
Hull, John Edwin 1895-1975 *WhAm 6*
Hull, John MacIntyre 1861-1944 *NatCAB 35*
Hull, Joseph Bartine 1802-1890 *ApCAB*, *Drake*,
 TwCBDA
Hull, Josephine Sherwood 1886-1957 *WhAm 3*,
 WomWWA 14
Hull, Lawrence Cameron 1857- *WhAm 4*
Hull, Mary Josephine *WomWWA 14*
Hull, Merlin 1870-1953 *BiDrAC*, *WhAm 3*,
 WhAmP
Hull, Morton Denison 1867-1937 *BiDrAC*,
 WhAm 1
Hull, Nathan P 1867-1954 *WhAm 3*
Hull, Noble Andrew 1827-1907 *BiDrAC*
Hull, Richard Ostrander 1905-1957 *NatCAB 46*
Hull, Robert Johnson 1901-1965 *WhAm 4*
Hull, Robert William 1924-1970 *WhAm 5*
Hull, Roger 1907-1972 *WhAm 5*
Hull, Roger Benton 1885-1942 *WhAm 1*
Hull, Theodore Young 1860-1938 *WhAm 1*
Hull, Thomas Everett 1893-1964 *WhAm 4*
Hull, William 1753-1825 *AmBi*, *ApCAB*,
 BiAUS, *DcAmB*, *Drake*, *McGEWB*,
 NatCAB 1, *TwCBDA*, *WebAB*,
 WebAMB, *WhAm H*
Hull, William Chase 1880- *WhAm 6*
Hull, William Edgar 1866-1942 *BiDrAC*,
 NatCAB 31, *WhAm 2*
Hull, William Hope 1820-1877 *ApCAB*
Hull, William Isaac 1868-1939 *NatCAB 38*,
 TwCBDA, *WhAm 1*
Hull, William Raleigh, Jr. 1906- *BiDrAC*
Hulley, Lincoln 1865-1934 *NatCAB 24*,
 WhAm 1
Hullfish, Henry Gordon 1894-1962 *BiDAmEd*,
 WhAm 4
Hullihen, Simon P 1810-1857 *DcAmB*,
 WhAm H
Hullihen, Walter 1875-1944 *WhAm 2*
Hullinger, Edwin Ware 1893-1968 *WhAm 5*
Hullings, Edward Peak 1885-1942 *NatCAB 33*
Hulman, Anton 1864-1942 *NatCAB 31*
Hulman, Herman 1831-1913 *NatCAB 38*
Hulme, Edward Maslin 1868-1951 *WhAm 5*
Hulme, Edward Maslin 1869-1951 *NatCAB 40*
Hulme, Harold 1898-1969 *NatCAB 55*
Hulme, John J *NewYHSD*
Hulme, Thomas Wilkins 1868-1939 *WhAm 1*
Hulme, William Henry 1862-1934 *TwCBDA*,
 WhAm 1
Hulse, C J *NewYHSD*
Hulse, Frederick 1868-1933 *NatCAB 24*
Hulse, George Egbert 1877-1965 *WhAm 4*
Hulse, Hiram Richard 1868-1938 *WhAm 1*
Hulse, Jesse *NewYHSD*
Hulse, Wilfred Cohn 1900-1962 *NatCAB 50*
Hulseman, Edward *NewYHSD*

Hulshizer, Stanford 1903-1967 *WhAm 5*
Hulst, Cornelia Steketee 1865- *WomWWA 14*
Hulst, Henry 1859-1949 *NatCAB 37*
Hulst, Nelson Powell 1842-1923 *WhAm 1*
Hulswit, Charles Louis 1901-1974 *WhAm 6*
Hulswit, Frank Theodore 1875-1933 *WhAm 1*
Hult, Adolf 1869-1943 *WhAm 2*
Hult, Gottfried Emanuel 1869-1950 *WhAm 3*
Hulten, Charles Morris 1909-1967 *NatCAB 53*,
 WhAm 4
Hulten, Herman H 1874- *WhAm 5*
Hultgrenn, Elmer Frederick 1876-1951
 NatCAB 41
Hultman, Ivar Ninus 1893-1965 *WhAm 4*
Hultquist, Earle Oscar 1891-1963 *NatCAB 50*
Hultz, Fred Samuel 1893-1961 *WhAm 4*
Hulvey, Otey Crawford 1873- *WhAm 5*
Humason, H Monroe 1887-1955 *NatCAB 45*
Humason, Harry Byrd 1875- *WhAm 5*
Humason, M L 1891-1972 *WhAm 5*
Humason, Milton LaSalle 1891-1972 *AsBiEn*
Humber, Robert Lee 1898-1970 *NatCAB 57*,
 WhAm 5
Humberger, Frank Owen 1884-1953
 NatCAB 42
Humbert, Adele *NewYHSD*
Humbert, Jean Joseph Amable 1755-1823
 ApCAB, *DcAmB*
Humbert, Jean Joseph Amable 1775-1823
 WhAm H
Humbert, Joseph Amable 1755-1823 *Drake*
Humbert, Marie-Georges 1859-1921 *DcScB*
Humbert, Pierre 1891-1953 *DcScB*
Humbert, Russell J 1905-1962 *WhAm 4*
Humbird, John Alexander 1888-1963 *WhAm 4*
Humboldt, Baron Friedrich W H A Von
 1769-1859 *ApCAB Sup*, *AsBiEn*, *DcScB*,
 Drake, *McGEWB*
Humboldt, Baron Wilhelm Von 1767-1835
 McGEWB
Hume, Alfred 1866-1950 *NatCAB 38*,
 TwCBDA, *WhAm 3*
Hume, Annette Ross 1858- *WomWWA 14*
Hume, Cyril 1900-1966 *WhAm 4*
Hume, David 1711-1776 *DcScB*, *McGEWB*
Hume, David 1915-1972 *WhAm 5*
Hume, David Milford 1917-1973 *WhAm 6*
Hume, Edgar Erskine 1889-1952 *DcAmB S5*,
 WebAMB, *WhAm 3*
Hume, Edward Hicks 1876-1957 *NatCAB 42*,
 WhAm 3
Hume, Frank 1843-1906 *NatCAB 1*,
 NatCAB 38
Hume, H Harold 1875- *WhAm 5*
Hume, Henry C *NewYHSD*
Hume, James Cleland 1862- *WhAm 3*
Hume, Jessie Fremont *WomWWA 14*
Hume, John *NewYHSD*
Hume, Julia Cracraft *WomWWA 14*
Hume, Leland 1864-1939 *NatCAB 34*,
 WhAm 4
Hume, Lida Munson 1858- *WomWWA 14*
Hume, Nelson 1881-1948 *NatCAB 37*,
 WhAm 2
Hume, Omer Forest d1959 *WhAm 3*
Hume, Robert Allen 1847-1929 *ApCAB X*,
 DcAmB, *NatCAB 26*, *WhAm 1*
Hume, Robert Ernest 1877-1948 *NatCAB 36*,
 WhAm 2
Hume, Samuel James 1885-1962 *NatCAB 50*
Hume, Sophia Wigington 1702-1774 *NotAW*
Hume, Thomas 1836-1912 *BiDConf*,
 NatCAB 37, *WhAm 1*
Hume, William 1830-1902 *DcAmB*, *WhAm H*
Hume, William 1888-1950 *WhAm 2A*
Hume-Rothery, William 1899-1968 *DcScB*
Humes, Augustine Leftwich 1874-1952
 WhAm 3
Humes, Augustine Leftwich 1874-1952
 NatCAB 41
Humes, Edward Crouch 1810-1895 *NatCAB 16*
Humes, Harold Louis 1900- *WhAm 4*
Humes, Samuel Hamilton 1901-1943
 NatCAB 34
Humes, Thomas William 1815-1892 *DcAmB*,
 NatCAB 24, *TwCBDA*, *WhAm H*
Humes, William Young Conn 1830-1883
 BiDConf, *TwCBDA*

Humfrey, John 1600?-1661 *ApCAB*, *Drake*
Humiston, Charles Edward 1868-1940
 NatCAB 30
Humiston, William Henry 1855-1943
 NatCAB 32
Humiston, William Henry 1869-1923 *DcAmB*
Hummel, Abraham Henry 1850-1926 *DcAmB*,
 NatCAB 25
Hummel, Arthur William 1884-1975 *WhAm 6*
Hummel, George F 1882-1952 *WhAm 3*
Hummel, George Henry d1946 *WhAm 2*
Hummel, R A d1959 *WhAm 3*
Hummel, William Grandville 1882- *WhAm 3*
Hummer, Harry Reid 1878-1957 *NatCAB 48*
Humming-Bird 1742-1827 *ApCAB*, *Drake*
Hummons, Henry Lytle 1873- *WhoColR*
Humpage, Frederic Richard 1875-1954
 NatCAB 46
Humphrey, Adele Alice *WomWWA 14*
Humphrey, Alexander Pope 1848-1928
 NatCAB 21, *WhAm 1*
Humphrey, Arthur Luther 1860-1939 *WhAm 1*
Humphrey, Augustin Reed 1859-1937 *BiDrAC*
Humphrey, Caroline Louise 1875- *WhAm 5*
Humphrey, Charles 1712?-1786 *BiAUS*, *Drake*
Humphrey, Charles 1792-1850 *BiDrAC*,
 WhAm H
Humphrey, Charles Frederic 1844-1926
 WhAm 1
Humphrey, Charles Frederick, Jr. 1876-1968
 WhAm 5
Humphrey, Doris 1895-1958 *WhAm 3*
Humphrey, Dudley Sherman 1852-1933
 NatCAB 24
Humphrey, Edward Frank 1878-1960 *WhAm 3*
Humphrey, Edward Porter 1809-1887 *ApCAB*,
 TwCBDA
Humphrey, Edward W 1877-1961 *NatCAB 50*
Humphrey, Elizabeth B 1850?- *ApCAB*,
 IIBEAAW
Humphrey, Evan H 1875- *WhAm 5*
Humphrey, George Colvin 1875-1947 *WhAm 2*
Humphrey, George Duke 1897-1973 *BiDAmEd*,
 WhAm 6
Humphrey, George Magoffin 1890-1970
 BiDrUSE, *NatCAB 55*, *WhAm 5*
Humphrey, George Thomas 1917-1973 *WhAm 5*
Humphrey, Harriette Zephine 1874-
 WomWWA 14
Humphrey, Harry Baker 1873-1955 *WhAm 3*
Humphrey, Harry Jasper 1879- *WhAm 6*
Humphrey, Helen F 1909-1963 *WhAm 4*
Humphrey, Heman 1779-1861 *ApCAB*,
 DcAmB, *Drake*, *NatCAB 5*, *TwCBDA*,
 WhAm H
Humphrey, Henry H 1862-1947 *WhAm 2*
Humphrey, Henry Martyn 1846-1928
 NatCAB 38
Humphrey, Herbert Sidney 1864-1942
 NatCAB 32
Humphrey, Herman Leon 1830-1902 *BiDrAC*,
 WhAm H
Humphrey, Herman Loin 1830-1902 *ApCAB*,
 NatCAB 11, *TwCBDA*, *WhAm 1*
Humphrey, Hubert Horatio, Jr. 1911- *BiDrAC*,
 BiDrUSE, *EncAAH*, *EncAB*, *WebAB*
Humphrey, J M 1819-1899 *BiAUS*
Humphrey, J Otis 1850-1918 *WhAm 1*
Humphrey, James 1747-1810 *ApCAB*
Humphrey, James 1811-1866 *ApCAB*, *BiAUS*,
 BiDrAC, *TwCBDA*, *WhAm H*
Humphrey, James Morgan 1819-1899 *BiDrAC*
Humphrey, Josiah *NewYHSD*
Humphrey, Lewis Craig 1875-1927 *WhAm 1*,
 WhAm 1C
Humphrey, Lyman Underwood 1844-1915
 NatCAB 1, *NatCAB 8*, *TwCBDA*,
 WhAm 1
Humphrey, Maria Hyde *NewYHSD*
Humphrey, Marie E Ives d1941 *WhAm 1*,
 WomWWA 14
Humphrey, Mary Vance 1846- *WomWWA 14*
Humphrey, Maud 1868- *AmWom*
Humphrey, Nina S 1880- *WhAm 6*
Humphrey, Reuben *BiAUS*
Humphrey, Reuben 1757-1831 *BiDrAC*
Humphrey, Reuben 1757-1832 *WhAm H*
Humphrey, Richard Lewis 1869-1928 *WhAm 1*

Humphrey, Seth King 1864-1932 *NatCAB 23, WhAm 1*
Humphrey, W Berlin 1881- *WhoColR*
Humphrey, Walter R 1904-1971 *WhAm 5*
Humphrey, Watts Sherman 1844-1916 *NatCAB 36*
Humphrey, William Armine 1860- *WhAm 4*
Humphrey, William Brewster 1867- *WhAm 4*
Humphrey, William Ewart 1862-1934 *BiDrAC, NatCAB 27, WhAm 1, WhAmP*
Humphrey, William Francis d1960 *WhAm 3*
Humphrey, William Otho 1874-1956 *NatCAB 45*
Humphrey, Wirt E 1868-1940 *NatCAB 30*
Humphrey, Wolcott Julius 1877-1959 *NatCAB 51*
Humphrey, Zephaniah Moore 1824-1881 *TwCBDA*
Humphreys, Abram Stephanus 1868- *WhAm 4*
Humphreys, Albert Edmund 1860-1927 *NatCAB 22, WhAm 1*
Humphreys, Albert Edmund 1893-1968 *WhAm 5*
Humphreys, Alexander Crombie 1851-1927 *DcAmB, NatCAB 13, WhAm 1*
Humphreys, Andrew 1821-1904 *BiDrAC*
Humphreys, Andrew Atkinson 1810-1883 *AmBi, ApCAB, DcAmB, NatCAB 7, TwCBDA, WebAMB, WhAm H*
Humphreys, Andrew Atkinson 1812?-1883 *Drake*
Humphreys, Benjamin Grubb 1808-1882 *BiDConf, DcAmB, NatCAB 13, TwCBDA, WhAm H, WhAmP*
Humphreys, Benjamin Grubb 1865-1923 *BiDrAC, WhAm 1, WhAmP*
Humphreys, Benjamin Grubb *see also* Humphries, Benjamin G
Humphreys, Charles *NewYHSD*
Humphreys, Charles d1786 *BiAUS*
Humphreys, Charles 1712-1786 *ApCAB, NatCAB 3, TwCBDA*
Humphreys, Charles 1714-1786 *BiDrAC, WhAm H, WhAmP*
Humphreys, Clement 1777-1803 *ApCAB*
Humphreys, David 1752-1818 *AmBi, ApCAB, DcAmB, Drake, TwCBDA, WhAm H*
Humphreys, David 1753-1818 *BiAUS, NatCAB 1*
Humphreys, David C *BiAUS*
Humphreys, David Carlisle 1855-1921 *TwCBDA, WhAm 1*
Humphreys, Edward Rupert 1820- *ApCAB*
Humphreys, Francis 1815?- *NewYHSD*
Humphreys, Frank Landon 1858-1937 *NatCAB 27, TwCBDA, WhAm 1*
Humphreys, Frederick 1816- *NatCAB 7*
Humphreys, Frederick Brown 1878-1951 *NatCAB 45*
Humphreys, H E, Jr. 1900-1967 *WhAm 4*
Humphreys, Harrie Moreland 1868-1943 *WhAm 2*
Humphreys, Hector 1797-1857 *ApCAB, Drake, NatCAB 1, TwCBDA*
Humphreys, Jacob *BiAUS*
Humphreys, James 1748-1810 *DcAmB, TwCBDA, WhAm H*
Humphreys, John J 1860-1896 *WhAm H*
Humphreys, Joshua 1751-1838 *AmBi, ApCAB, DcAmB, NatCAB 5, TwCBDA, WebAB, WebAMB, WhAm H*
Humphreys, Lester Warren 1883-1929 *NatCAB 40, WhAm 1*
Humphreys, Marie Champney 1876-1906 *WhAm 1*
Humphreys, Mary Gay d1915 *WhAm 1, WomWWA 14*
Humphreys, Milton Wylie 1844-1928 *AmBi, ApCAB, DcAmB, NatCAB 13, TwCBDA, WhAm 1, WhAm 1C*
Humphreys, Parry Wayne 1778-1839 *BiDrAC, WhAm H*
Humphreys, Perry W 1778-1839 *BiAUS*
Humphreys, Richard 1749-1832 *BnEnAmA*
Humphreys, Richard F 1911-1968 *WhAm 5*
Humphreys, Robert 1893- *BiDrAC*
Humphreys, Robert 1905-1965 *WhAm 4*

Humphreys, Robert Wade 1875-1950 *NatCAB 40*
Humphreys, Samuel 1778-1846 *ApCAB, TwCBDA*
Humphreys, Sarah Gibson 1830- *AmWom*
Humphreys, Solon 1821-1900 *WhAm 1*
Humphreys, T Hadden 1865- *WhAm 5*
Humphreys, Thomas Basil 1840- *ApCAB*
Humphreys, Walter 1874- *WhAm 5*
Humphreys, West Hughes 1806-1882 *DcAmB, WhAm H*
Humphreys, West Hughes 1806-1883 *ApCAB Sup, NatCAB 7, TwCBDA*
Humphreys, Willard Cunningham 1867-1902 *TwCBDA, WhAm 1*
Humphreys, William Jackson 1862-1949 *DcAmB S4, NatCAB 38, WhAm 2*
Humphreys, William Yerger 1890-1933 *BiDrAC, WhAm 1, WhAmP*
Humphries, G C *NewYHSD*
Humphries, John David 1873-1942 *NatCAB 34*
Humphries, John Edmund 1852-1915 *WhAm 1*
Humphries, Joseph H 1857-1925 *NatCAB 20*
Humphries, Rolfe 1894-1969 *WhAm 5*
Humphriss, Charles Harry 1867-1934? *IIBEAAW, WhAm 4*
Humphry, Sir George Murray 1820-1896 *BiHiMed*
Humphrys, William 1794-1865 *NewYHSD*
Humpries, Benjamin G 1808-1882 *BiAUS*
Humpries, Benjamin G *see also* Humphreys, Benjamin Grubb
Humpstone, Henry Judson 1870-1952 *WhAm 3*
Humpstone, John 1850-1929 *NatCAB 21*
Humpton, Richard 1733?-1804 *ApCAB, Drake*
Humstone, Walter Coutant 1849-1925 *NatCAB 21, WhAm 1*
Hun, Edward Reynolds 1842-1880 *ApCAB*
Hun, Henry 1854-1924 *NatCAB 19, WhAm 1*
Hun, Henry Hand 1893-1972 *NatCAB 57*
Hun, John Gale 1877-1945 *WhAm 2*
Hun, Marcus Tullius 1845-1920 *NatCAB 28*
Hun, Thomas 1883-1936 *NatCAB 28*
Hunayn Ibn Ishaq 809?-877 *DcScB*
Hunayn Ibn Ishaq Al-Ibadi, Abu Zayd 808-873 *DcScB Sup*
Hunckel, George *NewYHSD*
Hunckel, Otto *NewYHSD*
Hund, August 1887-1952 *NatCAB 41*
Hund, H E 1888-1954 *WhAm 3*
Hundley, Frank Martin 1882-1958 *NatCAB 48*
Hundley, Henry Rhodes 1867-1934 *WhAm 1*
Hundley, John Robinson, Jr. 1917-1972 *WhAm 5*
Hundley, John Trible Thomas 1868-1945 *NatCAB 41, WhAm 4*
Hundley, Oscar R 1855-1921 *NatCAB 17, WhAm 1*
Hundt, Magnus 1449-1519 *DcScB*
Hune, J H C *NewYHSD*
Huneke, William August 1864-1946 *WhAm 2*
Huneker, James Gibbons 1859-1921 *TwCBDA*
Huneker, James Gibbons 1860-1921 *AmBi, ApCAB X, DcAmB, NatCAB 14, WebAB, WhAm 1*
Huner, John Theodore 1856- *NatCAB 14*
Hung, Hsiu-Ch'uan 1814-1864 *McGEWB*
Hung-Wu 1328-1398 *McGEWB*
Hungate, William Leonard 1922- *BiDrAC*
Hungerford, Charles Stuart 1874-1957 *NatCAB 43*
Hungerford, Charles William 1885-1971 *WhAm 5*
Hungerford, Clark 1899-1962 *NatCAB 50, WhAm 4*
Hungerford, Edward 1875-1948 *WhAm 2*
Hungerford, Frank Louis 1843-1909 *NatCAB 16, WhAm 1*
Hungerford, Herbert Barker 1885-1963 *NatCAB 50*
Hungerford, John Newton 1825-1883 *BiDrAC, WhAm H*
Hungerford, John P d1833 *Drake*
Hungerford, John P 1769-1833 *BiAUS*
Hungerford, John Pratt 1760-1833 *ApCAB, TwCBDA*
Hungerford, John Pratt 1761-1833 *BiDrAC, WhAm H*

Hungerford, Orville 1790-1851 *BiDrAC, TwCBDA, WhAm H*
Hungerford, Orville 1790-1855 *BiAUS*
Hungerford, Samuel James 1872- *WhAm 3*
Hungerford, Walter 1873-1950 *NatCAB 37*
Hungerford, William 1786-1873 *ApCAB*
Hungerford, William Churchill 1871-1932 *NatCAB 25*
Hunicke, William George 1856- *NatCAB 5*
Hunkeler, Edward J 1894-1970 *WhAm 5*
Hunker, Jacob John 1849-1933 *NatCAB 27*
Hunker, John Jacob 1844-1916 *WhAm 1*
Hunley, Horace Lawson 1823-1863 *WebAMB*
Hunn, David Lathrop 1789-1888 *TwCBDA*
Hunn, John 1847- *NatCAB 11*
Hunn, John 1849- *WhAm 4*
Hunn, Myrta Eleanor 1878- *WomWWA 14*
Hunneman, William Cooper 1892-1958 *NatCAB 45, WhAm 3*
Hunner, Guy LeRoy 1868-1957 *NatCAB 43, WhAm 3*
Hunneus, George 1831- *ApCAB*
Hunnewell, Henry Sargent 1854-1931 *NatCAB 38*
Hunnewell, Horatio Hollis 1810-1902 *DcAmB, NatCAB 25, WhAm H*
Hunnewell, James 1794-1869 *DcAmB, WhAm H*
Hunnewell, James Frothingham 1832-1910 *NatCAB 6, NatCAB 32, TwCBDA, WhAm 1*
Hunnewell, James Melville 1879-1954 *NatCAB 40*
Hunnewell, Walter 1844-1921 *WhAm 1*
Hunnicutt, Warren Towers 1862- *WhAm 5*
Hunsaker, Jerome Clarke 1886- *WebAB, WebAMB*
Hunsaker, Walter Jerome 1857-1939 *WhAm 1*
Hunsaker, William Jefferson 1855-1933 *NatCAB 44*
Hunsicker, Alvin 1864- *NatCAB 14*
Hunsicker, William Cosgrove 1873-1939 *NatCAB 29*
Hunsicker, William Cosgrove, Jr. 1902-1974 *WhAm 6*
Hunt, Albert Clarence 1888-1956 *WhAm 3*
Hunt, Albert Henry 1892-1959 *WhAm 4*
Hunt, Albert Sanford 1827-1898 *NatCAB 4, TwCBDA*
Hunt, Alexander Cameron 1825-1894 *NatCAB 6*
Hunt, Alfred Ephraim 1855-1899 *ApCAB X, DcAmB, NatCAB 25, WhAm H*
Hunt, Alice Elizabeth Palmer 1867- *WomWWA 14*
Hunt, Alice Winsor 1872- *WomWWA 14*
Hunt, Andrew Murray 1859-1930 *NatCAB 18, WhAm 1*
Hunt, Andrew William 1866-1934 *NatCAB 25*
Hunt, Arthur Prince 1874-1925 *WhAm 1*
Hunt, Augusta Merrill 1842- *AmWom*
Hunt, Azor Ruggles 1848-1925 *NatCAB 20*
Hunt, Benjamin Faneuil 1792-1857 *ApCAB*
Hunt, Benjamin Powel 1849-1921 *NatCAB 19*
Hunt, Benjamin Weeks 1847-1934 *DcAmB S1, WhAm 1, WhAm 1C*
Hunt, Carleton 1836-1921 *BiDrAC, DcAmB, WhAm 1*
Hunt, Caroline Louisa 1865-1927 *WhAm 1, WomWWA 14*
Hunt, Charles D 1840-1914 *NewYHSD*
Hunt, Charles Jack 1876-1951 *NatCAB 40*
Hunt, Charles Sedgwick 1842-1876 *ApCAB*
Hunt, Charles Taylor 1873-1957 *NatCAB 44*
Hunt, Charles Wallace 1841-1911 *DcAmB, NatCAB 13, TwCBDA, WhAm 1*
Hunt, Charles Warren 1858-1932 *NatCAB 13, WhAm 1*
Hunt, Charles Wesley 1880-1973 *WhAm 6*
Hunt, Clara Whitehill 1871-1958 *DcAmLiB, WhAm 3*
Hunt, Clyde DuVernet 1861- *WhAm 4*
Hunt, D F 1899-1959 *WhAm 3*
Hunt, Duane Garrison 1884-1960 *WhAm 3A*
Hunt, Ebenezer Kingsbury 1810-1889 *ApCAB X*
Hunt, Edward Bissell 1822-1863 *ApCAB, Drake, NatCAB 11, TwCBDA*

Hunt, Edward Eyre 1885-1953 *WhAm 3*
Hunt, Edward Livingston 1871- *ApCAB X*
Hunt, Emory William 1862-1938 *NatCAB 13,
WhAm 1*
Hunt, Ernest Leroi 1877-1948 *WhAm 2*
Hunt, Evert Merle 1907-1972 *WhAm 5*
Hunt, Ezra Mundy 1830-1894 *ApCAB,
NatCAB 12, TwCBDA*
Hunt, Frank Williams 1861-1906 *NatCAB 12,
WhAm 1*
Hunt, Frazier 1885-1967 *WhAm 4*
Hunt, Fred Lawrence 1879-1944 *NatCAB 33*
Hunt, Frederick Salisbury 1868-1944 *WhAm 2*
Hunt, Frederick Vinton 1905-1972 *WhAm 5*
Hunt, Freeman 1804-1858 *ApCAB, DcAmB,
Drake, NatCAB 24, TwCBDA, WhAm H*
Hunt, Gaillard 1862-1924 *AmBi, DcAmB,
NatCAB 19, WhAm 1*
Hunt, George Edwin 1864-1914 *NatCAB 15,
WhAm 1*
Hunt, George Llewellyn 1878-1954 *NatCAB 44*
Hunt, George Radford 1872-1946 *NatCAB 38*
Hunt, George Smith 1829- *NatCAB 5*
Hunt, George Warren 1875-1942 *NatCAB 52*
Hunt, George Washington 1842-1910
NatCAB 17
Hunt, George Wiley Paul 1859-1934 *REnAW*
Hunt, George Wylie Paul 1859-1934 *DcAmB S1,
NatCAB 29, WhAm 1, WhAmP*
Hunt, Grace Usborne 1875- *WomWWA 14*
Hunt, Graham Putnam 1873-1953 *WhAm 3*
Hunt, H Lyons 1882-1954 *NatCAB 44*
Hunt, Hannah 1903-1973 *DcAmLiB*
Hunt, Harold Otis 1882-1950 *NatCAB 38*
Hunt, Haroldson Lafayette 1889-1974 *EncAB,
REnAW, WebAB, WhAm 6*
Hunt, Harriet E 1889-1974 *WomWWA 14*
Hunt, Harriet Larned 1893-1960 *WhAm 4*
Hunt, Harriot Kezia 1805-1875 *ApCAB,
DcAmB, NatCAB 9, NotAW, WhAm H*
Hunt, Harriot Keziah 1805-1875 *TwCBDA*
Hunt, Harry Burleigh 1875-1929 *NatCAB 24*
Hunt, Harry Edison 1889-1951 *NatCAB 40*
Hunt, Harry Hampton 1868-1937 *WhAm 1*
Hunt, Helen Fiske *NotAW*
Hunt, Henry Alexander 1866-1938 *BiDAmEd,
NatCAB 27*
Hunt, Henry Jackson 1819-1889 *AmBi,
ApCAB, DcAmB, Drake, NatCAB 9,
TwCBDA, WhAm H*
Hunt, Henry P *NewYHSD*
Hunt, Henry Thomas 1878- *WhAm 6*
Hunt, Henry Warren 1844-1915 *WhAm 1*
Hunt, Hiram 1860-1919 *NatCAB 20*
Hunt, Hiram Paine 1796-1865 *BiAUS, BiDrAC,
WhAm H*
Hunt, Isaac 1742?-1809 *AmBi, ApCAB,
DcAmB, WhAm H*
Hunt, Isaac Hamilton 1868-1935 *WhAm 1*
Hunt, James 1833-1869 *DcScB*
Hunt, James B d1857 *BiAUS*
Hunt, James Bennett 1798-1857 *TwCBDA*
Hunt, James Bennett 1799-1857 *BiDrAC,
WhAm H*
Hunt, James Gallaway 1870-1949 *WhAm 3*
Hunt, James Gillespie 1845- *NatCAB 7*
Hunt, James Ramsay 1874-1937 *NatCAB 29,
WhAm 1*
Hunt, James Stone 1897-1972 *WhAm 5*
Hunt, James Winford 1875-1934 *WhAm 1*
Hunt, Jedediah 1815- *ApCAB, Drake*
Hunt, Joe Byron 1907-1975 *WhAm 6*
Hunt, John Edmund 1908- *BiDrAC*
Hunt, John Oliver 1886-1957 *NatCAB 47*
Hunt, John Thomas 1860-1916 *BiDrAC,
WhAm 4*
Hunt, John W *NewYHSD*
Hunt, John Wesley 1834- *ApCAB*
Hunt, John Wilson 1879-1924 *NatCAB 20*
Hunt, Jonathan d1832 *BiAUS*
Hunt, Jonathan 1780-1832 *TwCBDA*
Hunt, Jonathan 1787-1832 *BiDrAC, WhAm H,
WhAmP*
Hunt, Leigh 1881-1959 *WhAm 3*
Hunt, Leigh S J 1855-1933 *NatCAB 24,
WhAm 1*
Hunt, LeRoy Philip 1892-1968 *WhAm 4*
Hunt, Lester Callaway 1892-1954 *BiDrAC,*

Hunt, *DcAmB S5, NatCAB 43, WhAm 3,
WhAmP*
Hunt, Levi Clarence 1873-1948 *NatCAB 38,
WhAm 5*
Hunt, Lewis Cass 1824-1886 *ApCAB,
NatCAB 4, TwCBDA*
Hunt, Livingston 1859-1943 *NatCAB 32,
WhAm 2*
Hunt, Mabel Leigh 1892-1971 *WhAm 5*
Hunt, Marion Palmer 1860- *WhAm 5*
Hunt, Marita Trotter 1852- *WomWWA 14*
Hunt, Mary H d1906 *AmWom*
Hunt, Mary Hannah Hanchett 1830-1906
BiDAmEd, DcAmB, NotAW, WhAm 1
Hunt, Mary Hannah Hanchett 1831-1906
NatCAB 9, TwCBDA
Hunt, Mary Leland *WomWWA 14*
Hunt, Memucan 1807-1856 *NatCAB 10*
Hunt, Myron 1868-1952 *ApCAB X, WhAm 3*
Hunt, Nathan 1758-1853 *DcAmB, NatCAB 9,
WhAm H*
Hunt, O E 1872- *WhAm 5*
Hunt, Ormond Edson 1883-1967 *WhAm 4*
Hunt, Rachel McMasters Miller 1882-
WomWWA 14
Hunt, Ralph Hudson 1869-1928 *WhAm 1*
Hunt, Ralph Leslie 1880- *WhAm 6*
Hunt, Ralph Waldo Emerson 1884- *WhAm 5*
Hunt, Randall 1825-1892 *ApCAB*
Hunt, Randell 1825-1892 *TwCBDA*
Hunt, Reid 1870-1948 *DcAmB S4, WhAm 2*
Hunt, Reuben Harrison 1862-1937 *NatCAB 28*
Hunt, Richard Carley 1886-1954 *NatCAB 45,
WhAm 3*
Hunt, Richard Howland 1862-1931 *AmBi,
ApCAB Sup, WhAm 1*
Hunt, Richard Morris 1827-1895 *AmBi,
DcAmB, McGEWB, WebAB, WhAm H*
Hunt, Richard Morris 1828-1895 *ApCAB,
BnEnAmA, NatCAB 6, TwCBDA*
Hunt, Richard Morris 1829-1895 *Drake*
Hunt, Ridgely 1854-1916 *NatCAB 16*
Hunt, Robert 1568?-1608 *DcAmB, WhAm H*
Hunt, Robert D 1874- *WhoColR*
Hunt, Robert Irving 1864-1937 *NatCAB 28*
Hunt, Robert Woolston 1838-1923 *ApCAB,
DcAmB, NatCAB 1, NatCAB 19,
WhAm 1*
Hunt, Rockwell Dennis 1868-1966 *NatCAB 53,
TwCBDA*
Hunt, Roy Arthur 1881-1966 *NatCAB 53,
WhAm 4*
Hunt, Samuel 1765-1807 *BiAUS, BiDrAC,
WhAm H*
Hunt, Samuel 1810-1878 *ApCAB, NatCAB 13,
TwCBDA*
Hunt, Samuel Furman 1844-1907 *TwCBDA,
WhAm 1*
Hunt, Samuel Valentine 1803-1893 *NewYHSD*
Hunt, Sandford 1825-1896 *NatCAB 12*
Hunt, Sanford Bebee 1825-1884 *TwCBDA*
Hunt, Seth Bliss 1871-1948 *WhAm 2*
Hunt, Sumner P 1865-1938 *WhAm 1*
Hunt, Theodore Gaillard 1805-1893 *BiAUS,
BiDrAC, WhAm H*
Hunt, Theodore Whitefield 1844-1930 *ApCAB,
DcAmB, TwCBDA, WhAm 1*
Hunt, Theodore Whitfield 1844-1930
NatCAB 8
Hunt, Thomas d1808 *Drake*
Hunt, Thomas 1808-1867 *ApCAB, Drake,
NatCAB 30, TwCBDA*
Hunt, Thomas Forsyth 1862-1927 *BiDAmEd,
WhAm 1*
Hunt, Thomas Poage 1794-1876 *ApCAB*
Hunt, Thomas Russell 1896-1952 *NatCAB 41*
Hunt, Thomas Sterry 1826-1892 *AmBi,
ApCAB, DcAmB, DcScB, Drake,
NatCAB 3, TwCBDA, WhAm H*
Hunt, Thomasa Haydock 1885- *WomWWA 14*
Hunt, Timothy Atwater 1805-1884 *ApCAB,
NatCAB 3, TwCBDA*
Hunt, Verne Carlton 1888-1943 *NatCAB 32*
Hunt, W *NewYHSD*
Hunt, Walter 1796-1859 *NatCAB 19, WebAB*
Hunt, Walter Reid 1867- *WhAm 5*
Hunt, Ward 1810-1886 *AmBi, ApCAB,
BiAUS, DcAmB, NatCAB 2, TwCBDA,*

WebAB, WhAm H
Hunt, Ward Evans 1868-1921 *NatCAB 19*
Hunt, Washington 1811-1867 *ApCAB, BiAUS,
BiDrAC, DcAmB, Drake, NatCAB 3,
TwCBDA, WhAm H, WhAmP*
Hunt, Wayne 1904- *IlBEAAW*
Hunt, Westley Marshall 1888-1950 *WhAm 3*
Hunt, William *NewYHSD*
Hunt, William 1825- *ApCAB*
Hunt, William Chamberlin 1856- *WhAm 4*
Hunt, William Floyd 1851-1951 *NatCAB 40*
Hunt, William Gibbes 1791-1833 *DcAmB,
Drake, WhAm H*
Hunt, William H *WhoColR*
Hunt, William Henry 1823-1884 *AmBi,
BiDrUSE, DcAmB, WhAm H*
Hunt, William Henry 1824-1884 *ApCAB,
NatCAB 4, TwCBDA*
Hunt, William Henry 1857-1949 *NatCAB 37,
WhAm 2*
Hunt, William Hill 1864- *NatCAB 18*
Hunt, William Holman 1827-1910 *McGEWB*
Hunt, William Morris 1804-1879 *NatCAB 3*
Hunt, William Morris 1824-1879 *AmBi,
ApCAB, BiDAmEd, BnEnAmA, DcAmB,
Drake, NewYHSD, TwCBDA, WebAB,
WhAm H*
Hunt, William Peter d1966 *WhAm 4*
Hunt, William Prescott 1827- *NatCAB 10,
WhAm 4*
Hunt, William Southworth 1879-1940 *WhAm 1*
Hunt, Wilson Price 1782?-1842 *AmBi, DcAmB,
WhAm H*
Hunt, Wilson Price 1783-1842 *REnAW*
Hunter, A *NewYHSD*
Hunter, A Stuart 1897-1958 *NatCAB 46*
Hunter, Aaron Burtis 1854-1933 *WhAm 3*
Hunter, Adison I 1860- *WhAm 1*
Hunter, Alexander Stuart d1926 *WhAm 1*
Hunter, Alfred M 1864-1929 *WhAm 1*
Hunter, Alice Cushman 1874- *WomWWA 14*
Hunter, Allan Oakley 1916- *BiDrAC*
Hunter, Andrew 1751-1823 *DcAmB, WhAm H*
Hunter, Andrew 1752-1823 *ApCAB, TwCBDA*
Hunter, Andrew Jackson 1831-1913 *BiDrAC,
TwCBDA, WhAm 4*
Hunter, Anna Rogers *WomWWA 14*
Hunter, Arthur 1869-1964 *WhAm 4*
Hunter, Ashley Pechin 1851-1914 *NatCAB 18*
Hunter, Charles 1813-1873 *ApCAB,
NatCAB 9, TwCBDA*
Hunter, Charles Francis 1913-1975 *WhAm 6*
Hunter, Charles O 1853- *WhAm 4*
Hunter, Clingham *WebAB*
Hunter, Corinne Smith *WomWWA 14*
Hunter, Croil 1893-1970 *NatCAB 56,
WhAm 5*
Hunter, Dard 1883-1966 *WhAm 4*
Hunter, David 1802-1886 *AmBi, ApCAB,
DcAmB, Drake, NatCAB 4, TwCBDA,
WebAMB, WhAm H*
Hunter, Edward 1839- *WhAm 4*
Hunter, Eugene Griggs 1905-1967 *NatCAB 53*
Hunter, Fannie Dundas *WomWWA 14*
Hunter, Francis Tennery 1896-1954 *NatCAB 44*
Hunter, Fred Heaton 1869- *WhAm 5*
Hunter, Frederick Maurice 1879-1964
BiDAmEd, WhAm 6
Hunter, George Bowditch 1879-1965 *WhAm 4*
Hunter, George King 1855-1940 *WhAm 1*
Hunter, George Leland 1867-1927 *WhAm 1*
Hunter, George McPherson 1864- *WhAm 4*
Hunter, George William 1873-1948 *WhAm 2*
Hunter, Guy Breckenridge 1891-1967 *WhAm 4*
Hunter, Guy Oliver 1887-1955 *NatCAB 41*
Hunter, H Blount 1873-1955 *NatCAB 45*
Hunter, Harry 1866-1921 *NatCAB 21*
Hunter, Henry Claude 1867-1936 *NatCAB 28*
Hunter, Herbert Davis 1906-1969 *NatCAB 54*
Hunter, Hiram Tyram 1883-1947 *WhAm 2*
Hunter, Horace Talmage 1881-1961 *WhAm 4*
Hunter, Howard Louis 1904-1975 *WhAm 6*
Hunter, Howard Owen 1895-1964 *WhAm 4*
Hunter, Hubert Samuel 1886- *WhAm 1*
Hunter, James Boyd 1863-1933 *WhAm 1*
Hunter, James Francis 1876-1961 *NatCAB 48*
Hunter, James Franklin 1856- *NatCAB 11*
Hunter, James Joseph 1881- *WhAm 6*

Hunter, Jay Tyler 1873-1953 *NatCAB 41,*
WhAm 3
Hunter, Jesse Coleman 1890-1945 *WhAm 2*
Hunter, Joel *WhAm 5*
Hunter, John 1728-1793 *BiHiMed, DcScB*
Hunter, John 1732-1802 *BiAUS, BiDrAC,*
WhAm H
Hunter, John 1760?- *ApCAB, NatCAB 12*
Hunter, John 1866- *WhAm 4*
Hunter, John 1881-1945 *NatCAB 35*
Hunter, John Dunn 1798?-1827 *ApCAB, Drake*
Hunter, John Edwared 1864- *WhoColR*
Hunter, John Farrar 1860-1918 *NatCAB 18*
Hunter, John Feeney 1896-1957 *BiDrAC,*
WhAm 3
Hunter, John Howard 1839- *ApCAB*
Hunter, John Lathrop 1834-1903 *WhAm 1*
Hunter, John Ward 1807-1900 *ApCAB, BiAUS,*
BiDrAC, NatCAB 3, TwCBDA
Hunter, Joseph 1783-1861 *ApCAB, Drake*
Hunter, Joseph Henry 1867-1952 *NatCAB 40*
Hunter, Joseph Rufus 1865-1951 *TwCBDA,*
WhAm 3
Hunter, Joshua Rollin 1904-1967 *NatCAB 53*
Hunter, Kent A 1892-1958 *WhAm 3*
Hunter, Lewis Boudinot 1804-1887 *ApCAB,*
TwCBDA
Hunter, Lillian Acomb *WomWWA 14*
Hunter, Livingston Legrand 1861-1902
NatCAB 18
Hunter, Louis James d1972 *WhAm 5*
Hunter, Lucy Robins *WomWWA 14*
Hunter, Sir Martin 1757-1846 *ApCAB, Drake*
Hunter, Matthew Albert 1878-1961 *WhAm 4*
Hunter, Merlin Harold 1887-1948 *NatCAB 41,*
WhAm 2
Hunter, Morton Craig 1825-1896 *ApCAB,*
BiAUS, BiDrAC, NatCAB 5, TwCBDA,
WhAm H
Hunter, Naisworthy d1802 *BiAUS*
Hunter, Narsworthy d1802 *BiDrAC,*
WhAm H
Hunter, Oscar Benwood 1888-1951 *NatCAB 49,*
WhAm 3
Hunter, Paull Stuart 1877-1923 *WhAm 1*
Hunter, Peter 1746-1805 *ApCAB*
Hunter, R M 1895-1952 *WhAm 3*
Hunter, Reuben B 1869-1934 *NatCAB 25*
Hunter, Richard *WhAm H*
Hunter, Richard Charles 1884-1941 *BiDrAC*
Hunter, Richard Stockton 1845- *WhAm 4*
Hunter, Robbins 1880-1954 *NatCAB 49*
Hunter, Robert d1734 *AmBi, ApCAB,*
DcAmB, Drake, NatCAB 7, WhAm H
Hunter, Robert 1826- *NatCAB 7*
Hunter, Robert 1851-1925 *NatCAB 6*
Hunter, Robert 1874-1942 *DcAmB S3,*
NatCAB 14, NatCAB 31, WhAm 2
Hunter, Robert Earl 1895-1945 *NatCAB 34*
Hunter, Robert Henry 1869-1931 *NatCAB 24*
Hunter, Robert M T 1809-1887 *BiAUS*
Hunter, Robert Mercer Taliafaro 1809-1887
BiDConf
Hunter, Robert Mercer Taliaferro 1809-1887
AmBi, ApCAB, BiDrAC, DcAmB, Drake,
NatCAB 9, TwCBDA, WebAB,
WhAm H, WhAmP
Hunter, Roy Deneale 1875-1944 *NatCAB 34*
Hunter, Rudolph Melville 1856-1935
NatCAB 10, NatCAB 25, WhAm 1
Hunter, Russell Vernon 1900-1955 *IIBEAAW*
Hunter, Samuel John 1866-1946 *WhAm 2*
Hunter, Stephen Alexander 1851-1923 *WhAm 1*
Hunter, Taliaferro *BiAUS*
Hunter, Thomas *WhAm 5*
Hunter, Thomas 1831-1915 *BiDAmEd,*
DcAmB, NatCAB 22, WhAm HA,
WhAm 4
Hunter, Thomas Lomax 1875-1948 *NatCAB 38*
Hunter, W Godfrey 1841-1917 *WhAm 4*
Hunter, Walter David 1875-1925 *ApCAB X,*
DcAmB, NatCAB 21, WhAm 1
Hunter, Walter L 1868-1962 *REnAW*
Hunter, Walter Samuel 1889-1954 *NatCAB 42,*
WhAm 3
Hunter, Warren *IIBEAAW*
Hunter, Warren Clair 1895-1970 *WhAm 5*
Hunter, Whiteside Godfrey 1841-1917 *BiDrAC,*

DcAmB, NatCAB 5, WhAmP
Hunter, William 1718-1783 *BiHiMed, DcScB,*
McGEWB
Hunter, William 1754-1827 *BiAUS, BiDrAC,*
WhAm H
Hunter, William 1774-1849 *ApCAB, BiDrAC,*
DcAmB, Drake, NatCAB 9, TwCBDA,
WhAm H, WhAmP
Hunter, William 1775-1849 *BiAUS*
Hunter, William 1805-1886 *ApCAB, BiAUS,*
NatCAB 3, NatCAB 5, TwCBDA
Hunter, William Adams 1896-1964 *NatCAB 50*
Hunter, William Armstrong 1855-1920
WhAm 1
Hunter, William Boyd 1876- *WhAm 5*
Hunter, William C 1812-1891 *DcAmB*
Hunter, William Forrest 1808-1874 *BiAUS,*
BiDrAC, WhAm H
Hunter, William Forrest 1839-1904 *WhAm 1*
Hunter, William H d1842 *BiAUS, BiDrAC,*
WhAm H
Hunter, William M d1849 *Drake*
Hunting, Ethel Parker 1877- *WomWWA 14*
Hunting, Fred Stanley 1867-1951 *WhAm 3*
Hunting, Gardner 1872-1958 *WhAm 4*
Hunting, George Coolidge 1871-1924
NatCAB 21, WhAm 1
Hunting, Nathaniel Stevens 1863-1937
NatCAB 28
Hunting, Walter Judson 1874- *WhAm 5*
Huntington, Abel 1777-1858 *BiAUS, BiDrAC,*
TwCBDA, WhAm H
Huntington, Adoniram Judson 1818-1903
TwCBDA, WhAm 1
Huntington, Agnes 1863- *AmWom,*
NatCAB 2
Huntington, Albert Tracy 1878- *WhAm 6*
Huntington, Andrew 1745-1824 *ApCAB*
Huntington, Anna Hyatt 1876-1973 *WhAm 6*
Huntington, Archer Milton 1870-1955
ApCAB X, NatCAB 15, NatCAB 44,
WhAm 3
Huntington, Arria Sargent 1848- *WhAm 4,*
WomWWA 14
Huntington, Arthur Elon 1868-1939 *NatCAB 39*
Huntington, Arthur Franklin 1877- *WhAm 5*
Huntington, Baldwin Gwynne 1879-1958
WhAm 3
Huntington, Benjamin 1736-1800 *ApCAB,*
BiAUS, BiDrAC, Drake, TwCBDA,
WhAm H, WhAmP
Huntington, Benjamin 1736-1801 *NatCAB 13*
Huntington, Benjamin 1777-1850 *ApCAB*
Huntington, Charles Clifford 1873-1956
WhAm 4
Huntington, Charles Pratt 1871-1919 *WhAm 1*
Huntington, Clarence William 1857-1927
WhAm 1
Huntington, Collis Porter 1821-1900 *AmBi*
Huntington, Collis Potter 1821-1900 *ApCAB,*
DcAmB, EncAB, McGEWB, NatCAB 15,
REnAW, TwCBDA, WebAB, WhAm 1
Huntington, Constant 1876-1962 *NatCAB 50*
Huntington, Daniel 1788-1858 *ApCAB, Drake*
Huntington, Daniel 1816-1906 *AmBi, ApCAB,*
BnEnAmA, DcAmB, Drake, NatCAB 5,
NewYHSD, TwCBDA, WhAm 1
Huntington, Daniel Trumbull 1868-1950
NatCAB 40, WhAm 3
Huntington, David Lynde 1870-1929 *WhAm 1*
Huntington, DeWitt Clinton 1830-1912
TwCBDA, WhAm 1
Huntington, Dorothy Phillips 1893-1972
WhAm 5
Huntington, Dwight Williams 1851-1938
NatCAB 53
Huntington, E M 1808-1862 *BiAUS*
Huntington, Ebenezer 1754-1834 *ApCAB,*
BiAUS, BiDrAC, Drake, TwCBDA,
WhAm H
Huntington, Edward Vermilye 1874-1952
DcAmB S5, DcScB, WhAm 3
Huntington, Eleazer *NewYHSD*
Huntington, Elisha 1796-1865 *ApCAB,*
DcAmB, Drake, WhAm H
Huntington, Elisha Mills 1806-1862 *ApCAB,*
BiAUS, TwCBDA

Huntington, Eliza Prentiss 1858-
WomWWA 14
Huntington, Ellsworth 1876-1947 *BiDAmEd,*
DcAmB S4, NatCAB 37, WebAB,
WhAm 2
Huntington, Emily 1841-1909 *NotAW,*
WhAm 1
Huntington, Ezra Abel 1813-1901 *TwCBDA*
Huntington, Faye *WhAm 4*
Huntington, Ford 1867-1949 *WhAm 2*
Huntington, Frances Carpenter 1890-1972
WhAm 5
Huntington, Frank 1848-1928 *WhAm 1*
Huntington, Frederic Dan 1819-1904 *DcAmB,*
DcAmReB, Drake, NatCAB 3, TwCBDA,
WhAm 1
Huntington, Frederick Dan 1819-1904 *AmBi,*
ApCAB
Huntington, George 1835-1916 *WhAm 1*
Huntington, George 1850-1916 *BiHiMed*
Huntington, George Herbert 1878-1953
NatCAB 42, WhAm 3
Huntington, George Sumner 1861-1927
BiHiMed, NatCAB 12, WhAm 1
Huntington, Harwood 1861-1923 *ApCAB X,*
NatCAB 29, WhAm 1
Huntington, Helen *WomWWA 14*
Huntington, Henry Alonzo 1840-1907 *WhAm 1*
Huntington, Henry Barrett 1875-1965
NatCAB 50, WhAm 4
Huntington, Henry Edwards 1850-1927 *AmBi,*
DcAmB, NatCAB 15, WebAB, WhAm 1
Huntington, J A *NewYHSD*
Huntington, J D *NewYHSD*
Huntington, Jabez 1719-1786 *ApCAB, DcAmB,*
Drake, WhAm H
Huntington, Jabez Williams 1788-1847 *ApCAB,*
BiAUS, BiDrAC, Drake, NatCAB 4,
TwCBDA, WhAm H, WhAmP
Huntington, James Otis Sargent 1854-1935
WhAm 1
Huntington, Jedediah 1743-1818 *AmBi,*
DcAmB, Drake, WhAm H
Huntington, Jedediah Vincent 1815-1862
ApCAB, DcAmB, Drake, NatCAB 13,
TwCBDA
Huntington, Jedidiah 1743-1818 *ApCAB,*
NatCAB 1, TwCBDA
Huntington, John 1832-1893 *NatCAB 9*
Huntington, Joseph 1735-1794 *ApCAB, Drake*
Huntington, Joshua 1751- *ApCAB*
Huntington, Joshua 1786-1819 *ApCAB, Drake,*
TwCBDA
Huntington, Julia Bradlee Weld 1878-
WomWWA 14
Huntington, Lloyd Lee 1924-1963 *WhAm 4*
Huntington, Lucius Seth 1827-1886 *ApCAB*
Huntington, Margaret Jane Evans 1842-1926
DcAmB, WhAm 1
Huntington, Oliver Whipple 1858-1924
WhAm 1
Huntington, Philip Weatherly 1876-1948
NatCAB 37
Huntington, Richard Lee 1896-1972 *WhAm 5*
Huntington, Robert Watkinson 1866-1949
NatCAB 38, WhAm 2
Huntington, Ruth *WomWWA 14*
Huntington, Samuel d1796 *BiAUS*
Huntington, Samuel 1731-1796 *AmBi, ApCAB,*
BiDrAC, BiDrUSE, DcAmB, Drake,
NatCAB 10, TwCBDA, WhAm H,
WhAmP
Huntington, Samuel 1732-1796 *BiAUS*
Huntington, Samuel 1765-1817 *AmBi, ApCAB,*
BiAUS, DcAmB, Drake, NatCAB 3,
TwCBDA, WhAm H
Huntington, Susan Mansfield 1791-1823 *ApCAB*
Huntington, Theodore Sollace 1873-1937
WhAm 1
Huntington, Thomas Waterman 1849-1929
NatCAB 22, WhAm 1
Huntington, Thomas Waterman 1893-1973
WhAm 6
Huntington, Tuley Francis 1870-1938 *WhAm 1*
Huntington, Warner Dare 1874-1938 *WhAm 1*
Huntington, Whitney Clark 1887-1967 *WhAm 4*
Huntington, Willard Vincent 1856-1915
NatCAB 33

Huntington, William Chapin 1884-1958
WhAm 3
Huntington, William Edwards 1844-1930
DcAmB, NatCAB 11, WhAm 1
Huntington, William Henry 1820-1885 *ApCAB,*
TwCBDA
Huntington, William Reed 1838-1909 *ApCAB,*
DcAmB, DcAmReB, NatCAB 8,
NatCAB 38, TwCBDA, WhAm 1
Huntley, Benjamin Franklin 1863-1925
NatCAB 29
Huntley, Charles R 1853-1926 *WhAm 1*
Huntley, Chester Robert 1911-1974 *WhAm 6*
Huntley, Elias DeWitt 1840-1909 *ApCAB,*
TwCBDA, WhAm 1
Huntley, Florence d1912 *AmWom, WhAm 1*
Huntley, Mary Sutton 1852- *AmWom*
Huntley, Samantha Littlefield d1949 *WhAm 2*
Huntley, Victoria Hutson 1900-1971 *WhAm 5*
Huntley, William Russell 1879- *WhAm 6*
Huntly, George Gordon, Earl Of 1514-1562
WhoMilH
Hunton, Addie D Waites 1870-1943 *WhoColR*
Hunton, Addie D Waites 1875-1943 *NotAW*
Hunton, Eppa 1822-1908 *BiDConf, BiDrAC,*
DcAmB, WhAm 1, WhAmP
Hunton, Eppa 1823-1908 *ApCAB, BiAUS,*
NatCAB 13, TwCBDA
Hunton, Eppa, Jr. 1855-1932 *NatCAB 35,*
WhAm 1
Hunton, Grace 1878- *WomWWA 14*
Hunton, Jonathan Glidden 1781-1851 *BiAUS,*
Drake, NatCAB 6, TwCBDA
Hunton, Logan 1806-1880 *ApCAB*
Hunton, Virginia Semmes Payne
WomWWA 14
Hunton, William Alphaeus 1865- *WhoColR*
Hunton, William Lee 1864-1930 *DcAmB,*
WhAm 1
Huntoon, Benjamin Bussey 1836-1919 *WhAm 1*
Huntoon, Gardner A 1874- *WhAm 5*
Huntoon, Lew Addison 1862-1913 *NatCAB 18*
Huntoon, Louis Doremus 1869-1947 *WhAm 2*
Huntress, Carroll Benton 1885-1952 *WhAm 3*
Huntress, Frank G 1870-1955 *WhAm 3*
Huntress, Leonard 1848-1927 *NatCAB 21*
Huntsman, Adam *BiAUS, BiDrAC,*
WhAm H
Huntsman, Elizabeth VanBuskirk 1876-
WomWWA 14
Huntsman, Owen Benjamin 1871-1935
ApCAB X, WhAm 1
Huntsman, Robert F R 1868-1945 *WhAm 2*
Huntzinger, George Frederick 1878-1949
NatCAB 37
Hunyadi, John 1385?-1456 *McGEWB*
Hunziker, Otto Frederick 1873-1959
NatCAB 47, WhAm 3
Hunziker, Richard Overton 1916-1971 *WhAm 6*
Huon DePenanster, Charles Henry 1727-1771
ApCAB
Huot, Joseph Oliva 1917- *BiDrAC*
Hupp, Frank LeMoyne 1865-1929 *NatCAB 22*
Hupp, John Cox 1819- *ApCAB, NatCAB 10,*
WhAm 4
Hupper, Roscoe Henderson 1883-1967 *WhAm 4*
Huppertz, John William 1927- *WhAm 6*
Huppuch, Winfield A 1861- *WhAm 4*
Hurban, Vladimir S 1883-1949 *WhAm 2*
Hurd, Albert Arthur 1849-1915 *WhAm 1*
Hurd, Annah 1871- *WomWWA 14*
Hurd, Archer Willis 1883-1953 *WhAm 3*
Hurd, Arthur William 1858-1924 *WhAm 1*
Hurd, Benjamin 1739-1781 *BnEnAmA,*
NewYHSD
Hurd, Charles Edwin 1833-1910 *WhAm 1*
Hurd, Charles W B 1903-1968 *WhAm 5*
Hurd, E *NewYHSD*
Hurd, Edward Melville 1873-1933 *WhAm 1*
Hurd, Edward Payson d1899 *WhAm 1*
Hurd, Edward Payson 1841-1927 *ApCAB X,*
NatCAB 20, WhAm 1
Hurd, Ethel Edgerton 1845- *WomWWA 14*
Hurd, Eugene 1881-1941 *WhAm 1*
Hurd, Francis William 1831- *NatCAB 14*
Hurd, Frank Hunt 1840-1896 *BiDrAC,*
WhAm H
Hurd, Frank Hunt 1841-1896 *ApCAB, BiAUS,*

NatCAB 4, TwCBDA
Hurd, George Arthur 1869-1929 *WhAm 1,*
WhAm 1C
Hurd, George Edward 1872- *WhAm 5*
Hurd, Gildersleeve *NewYHSD*
Hurd, Guilford Lansing 1877- *WhAm 5*
Hurd, Harriette Collin Seward 1849-
WomWWA 14
Hurd, Harry Boyd 1875-1943 *NatCAB 17,*
NatCAB 32, WhAm 2
Hurd, Harvey Bostwick 1828-1906 *ApCAB Sup,*
NatCAB 10, WhAm 1
Hurd, Helen Mar 1839- *AmWom*
Hurd, Henry Mills 1843-1927 *NatCAB 12,*
WhAm 1
Hurd, Jacob 1702?-1758 *BnEnAmA*
Hurd, John Codman 1816-1892 *ApCAB,*
DcAmB, NatCAB 13, TwCBDA,
WhAm H
Hurd, Katherine Hatfield *WomWWA 14*
Hurd, L P *IIBEAAW*
Hurd, Lee Maidment 1873-1945 *WhAm 2*
Hurd, Louis Guthrie 1847- *WhAm 1*
Hurd, Nathaniel 1729?-1777 *BnEnAmA,*
NewYHSD
Hurd, Nathaniel 1730-1777 *ApCAB, DcAmB,*
Drake, WhAm H
Hurd, Peter 1904- *IIBEAAW*
Hurd, Richad Melancthon 1865-1941 *WhAm 1*
Hurd, William Daniel 1875-1924 *NatCAB 27,*
WhAm 1
Hurd-Mead, Kate Campbell 1867-1941 *NotAW*
Hurdle, James Ernest 1913-1970 *WhAm 5*
Hurdon, Elizabeth 1868-1941 *NotAW,*
WhAm 4, WomWWA 14
Hurff, Lindley Scarlett 1895-1968 *WhAm 5*
Hurford, Etta B 1853- *WomWWA 14*
Hurich, Oscar John 1892-1927 *NatCAB 23*
Hurie, Wiley Lin 1885-1954 *WhAm 3*
Hurlbatt, Ethel *WomWWA 14*
Hurlbert, Henry Francis 1854-1924 *ApCAB X*
Hurlbert, William Henry 1827-1895 *DcAmB,*
NatCAB 5, WhAm H
Hurlburt, Elizabeth *NewYHSD*
Hurlburt, Frederick Butler 1866-1925
NatCAB 28
Hurlburt, Henry Francis 1854-1924 *NatCAB 20*
Hurlburt, Katherine Maria *WomWWA 14*
Hurlburt, Stephen Augustus 1815-1882 *BiAUS*
Hurlbut, Byron Satterlee 1865-1929 *NatCAB 23,*
WhAm 1
Hurlbut, Mrs. Clarke Stanley 1868-
WomWWA 14
Hurlbut, Edwin Wilcox 1854-1925 *WhAm 1*
Hurlbut, Harriette Persis 1862- *AmWom*
Hurlbut, Henry Augustus 1808- *NatCAB 4*
Hurlbut, Hinman Barrett 1819-1884 *NatCAB 2*
Hurlbut, Jed Walter 1858-1950 *NatCAB 38*
Hurlbut, Jesse Lyman 1843-1930 *DcAmB,*
NatCAB 11, TwCBDA, WhAm 1
Hurlbut, Louise McCollom 1875-
WomWWA 14
Hurlbut, Stephen Augustus 1815-1882 *AmBi,*
ApCAB, BiDrAC, DcAmB, Drake,
NatCAB 4, TwCBDA, WebAMB,
WhAm H, WhAmP
Hurlbut, William Henry 1827-1895 *ApCAB,*
Drake, TwCBDA
Hurlbut, William N 1889-1956 *WhAm 3*
Hurley, Charles Francis 1893-1946 *NatCAB 35,*
WhAm 2
Hurley, Denis Michael 1843-1899 *BiDrAC*
Hurley, Dennis M 1843-1899 *TwCBDA*
Hurley, Edward Nash 1864-1933 *DcAmB S1,*
NatCAB 40, WhAm 1
Hurley, Edward Nash, Jr. 1892-1948
NatCAB 37
Hurley, Edward Timothy 1869-1950 *WhAm 3*
Hurley, Francis Eugene 1877-1928 *NatCAB 23*
Hurley, Frank James 1883-1953 *NatCAB 43*
Hurley, George 1884-1954 *NatCAB 40,*
WhAm 3
Hurley, George Ira 1877-1958 *NatCAB 48*
Hurley, James E 1860-1910 *WhAm 1*
Hurley, James Franklin 1870-1936 *WhAm 1*
Hurley, Jeremiah Joseph 1869-1950 *NatCAB 39*
Hurley, John Joseph 1868-1948 *NatCAB 37*
Hurley, John Patrick 1878-1944 *WhAm 2*

Hurley, John Richard 1908-1953 *NatCAB 42,*
WhAm 3
Hurley, Joseph Patrick 1894-1967 *WhAm 4*
Hurley, Lawrence Francis 1897-1953 *WhAm 3*
Hurley, Leonard B 1893-1960 *WhAm 4*
Hurley, Margaret Helene 1908-1967 *WhAm 4*
Hurley, Neil C d1948 *WhAm 2*
Hurley, Neil Charles, Jr. 1911-1965 *NatCAB 51,*
WhAm 4
Hurley, Patrick Jay 1883-1963 *BiDrUSE,*
NatCAB 53, WhAm 4, WhWW-II
Hurley, Pearley B 1878- *WhAm 6*
Hurley, Raymond Joseph 1895-1956
NatCAB 43
Hurley, Robert Augustine 1895-1968 *WhAm 5*
Hurley, Roy T 1896-1971 *WhAm 5*
Hurley, Stephen Edward 1892-1955 *WhAm 3*
Hurley, William E 1875-1957 *WhAm 3*
Hurley, William Leonard 1862-1928
NatCAB 22
Hurley, William Rowe 1889-1952 *NatCAB 42*
Hurley, Wilson 1924- *IIBEAAW*
Hurll, Estelle May 1863-1924 *WhAm 1,*
WomWWA 14
Hurok, Sol 1888-1974 *WhAm 6*
Hurok, Solomon 1888-1974 *WebAB*
Hurrell, Alfred 1874-1938 *WhAm 1*
Hurrey, Clarence Barzillai 1876- *WhAm 5*
Hurry, Edmund 1807-1875 *ApCAB Sup*
Hurry, Randolph 1854- *ApCAB X*
Hurry, William 1805-1893 *ApCAB Sup*
Hursh, Catherine S McGuigan 1856-
WomWWA 14
Hursh, Ralph Kent 1885-1956 *NatCAB 44,*
WhAm 4
Hurst, Albert S 1866-1944 *WhAm 2*
Hurst, Carlton Bailey 1867-1943 *WhAm 2*
Hurst, Charles Warner 1875-1947 *WhAm 2*
Hurst, Clarence Thomas 1895-1949 *WhAm 2*
Hurst, David Wiley 1819-1882 *BiDConf*
Hurst, Fannie d1968 *WhAm 4*
Hurst, Harold Emerson 1912-1972 *WhAm 5*
Hurst, John 1863-1930 *WhAm 1, WhoColR*
Hurst, John Edward 1832-1904 *NatCAB 2*
Hurst, John Fletcher 1834-1903 *AmBi, ApCAB,*
DcAmB, NatCAB 9, TwCBDA,
WhAm 1
Hurst, Peter F 1910-1969 *WhAm 5*
Hurst, S Grant 1864-1929 *NatCAB 24*
Hurst, Vida 1890-1958 *NatCAB 43*
Hurst, William Henry 1853- *WhAm 4*
Hurston, Zora Neale d1960 *WhAm 3*
Hurt, Huber William 1883-1966 *WhAm 4*
Hurt, John Jeter 1873- *WhAm 5*
Hurt, John Smith 1892-1966 *WhAm 4*
Hurt, Rollin 1860- *WhAm 4*
Hurt, Willson Irby 1903-1963 *NatCAB 55*
Hurtado DeMendoza, Andres 1500?-1561
ApCAB
Hurtado DeMendoza, Garcia 1531-1610?
ApCAB
Hurth, Peter Joseph 1857-1935 *WhAm 1*
Hurty, John Newell 1852-1925 *NatCAB 22,*
WhAm 1
Hurtz, Leonard E 1881- *WhAm 6*
Hurwith, Howard Kenneth 1897-1973
NatCAB 57
Hurwitz, Adolf 1859-1919 *DcScB*
Hurwitz, Henry 1886-1961 *WhAm 4*
Hurwitz, Wallie Abraham 1886-1958 *WhAm 3*
Hus, John 1372?-1415 *McGEWB*
Husain, Zaklr 1897-1969 *WhAm 5*
Husayn, Taha 1889- *McGEWB*
Husband, George Rosewall 1896-1958 *WhAm 3*
Husband, Helene Borgman 1869-
WomWWA 14
Husband, Joseph 1885-1938 *WhAm 1*
Husband, Richard Wellington 1869-1924
WhAm 1
Husband, William Walter 1871-1942
NatCAB 34, WhAm 2
Husbands, Herman 1724-1795 *ApCAB, Drake,*
NatCAB 13
Husbands, Hermon 1724-1795 *DcAmB,*
WhAm H
Husbands, Sam Henry 1891-1955 *WhAm 3*
Huschke, Emil 1797-1858 *DcScB*
Huse, Caleb 1831-1905 *BiDConf, DcAmB*

Huse, Charles Phillips 1883-1958 *WhAm 3*
Huse, Charles Wells 1905-1974 *WhAm 6*
Huse, Harry Pinckney 1858-1942 *NatCAB 30,*
WhAm 2
Huse, John Oldham 1898-1954 *NatCAB 40*
Huse, Raymond Howard 1880-1954 *WhAm 3*
Huse, Sibyl Marvin *ApCAB X, BiCAW*
Huse, William 1898-1958 *WhAm 3*
Huse, William L 1835- *NatCAB 9*
Husein Ibn Ali 1854?-1931 *McGEWB*
Hush, Valentine Goldsmith 1842-1908
NatCAB 33
Husik, Isaac 1876-1939 *NatCAB 31, WhAm 1*
Husing, Edward B 1901-1962 *WhAm 4*
Husk, Charles Ellsworth 1872-1916 *DcAmB*
Huske, Ellis 1700?-1755 *ApCAB, Drake,*
NatCAB 7
Huske, John 1721?-1773 *ApCAB, Drake*
Huskins, C Leonard 1897-1953 *WhAm 3*
Huskins, James Preston 1864-1948 *WhAm 2*
Husmann, George 1827-1902 *DcAmB*
Huson, Florence 1857-1915 *NatCAB 17*
Huss, George Morehouse 1857-1947 *WhAm 2*
Huss, Henry Holden 1862-1953 *ApCAB X,*
NatCAB 8, WhAm 3
Huss, Magnus 1752-1799 *ApCAB*
Hussa, Cora Isabel Warburton *WomWWA 14*
Hussakof, Louis 1881- *WhAm 6*
Hussein, Taha 1889-1973 *WhAm 6*
Husseini, Amin El 1900- *WhWW-II*
Husselman, Roy 1883-1936 *NatCAB 28*
Husserl, Edmond 1859-1938 *WhAm HA,*
WhAm 4
Husserl, Edmund 1859-1938 *McGEWB*
Hussey, Charles Lincoln 1870-1934 *NatCAB 27,*
WhAm 1
Hussey, Cornelia Collins 1827- *AmWom*
Hussey, Curtis Grubb 1802-1893 *ApCAB,*
DcAmB, NatCAB 33, TwCBDA,
WhAm H
Hussey, E C *NewYHSD*
Hussey, Ethel Fountain *WomWWA 14*
Hussey, Franklin Bliss 1859-1930 *NatCAB 22*
Hussey, John 1831-1888 *TwCBDA*
Hussey, John Brennan 1907-1960 *NatCAB 49,*
WhAm 4
Hussey, Nora Large *WomWWA 14*
Hussey, Obed 1791-1859 *NatCAB 11*
Hussey, Obed 1792-1860 *DcAmB, EncAAH,*
WebAB, WhAm H
Hussey, Raymond 1883-1953 *NatCAB 41,*
WhAm 3
Hussey, Roland Dennis 1897-1959 *WhAm 4*
Hussey, Tacitus 1833- *WhAm 4*
Hussey, William Joseph 1862-1926 *DcAmB,*
DcScB, NatCAB 21, WhAm 1
Husslein, Joseph 1873-1952 *WhAm 3*
Hussman, George 1827-1902 *WhAm H*
Husson, Chesley Hayward 1903-1972 *WhAm 5*
Hustead, Ashbel Fairchild 1859-1948
NatCAB 37
Husted, Harvey 1854-1928 *ApCAB X*
Husted, James Delno 1857- *WhAm 1*
Husted, James William 1833-1892 *ApCAB,*
NatCAB 25, TwCBDA
Husted, James William 1870-1925 *BiDrAC,*
NatCAB 25, WhAm 1
Husted, James William 1896-1975 *WhAm 6*
Husted, Ladley 1906-1969 *WhAm 5*
Husted, Thomas C *NewYHSD*
Husting, Berthold Juneau 1878-1948 *WhAm 2*
Husting, Paul Oscar 1866-1917 *BiDrAC,*
DcAmB, NatCAB 15, WhAm 1, WhAmP
Hustis, James Humphrey 1864-1942
NatCAB 31, WhAm 2
Huston, Abraham Francis 1852-1930 *ApCAB X,*
NatCAB 15, WhAm 1
Huston, Charles 1771-1849 *NatCAB 16*
Huston, Charles 1822-1897 *ApCAB X,*
DcAmB, NatCAB 15, WhAm H
Huston, Charles Andrews 1876-1922 *WhAm 1*
Huston, Charles Lukens 1856-1951 *ApCAB X,*
NatCAB 15, NatCAB 39, WhAm 3
Huston, Claudius Hart 1876-1952 *WhAm 3*
Huston, Felix d1857 *NatCAB 12*
Huston, Henry Augustus 1858- *WhAm 5*
Huston, Howard Riggins 1892-1955 *WhAm 3*
Huston, John 1906- *WebAB*

Huston, Joseph Waldo 1833-1905 *NatCAB 5,*
WhAm 1
Huston, Luther Allison 1888-1975 *WhAm 6*
Huston, Ralph Chase 1885-1954 *WhAm 3*
Huston, Ralph Ernest 1902-1969 *WhAm 5*
Huston, S Arthur 1876- *WhAm 5*
Huston, Sarah A *WomWWA 14*
Huston, Stewart 1898-1971 *WhAm 5*
Huston, Thad 1846- *WhAm 1*
Huston, Walter 1884-1950 *DcAmB S4,*
WebAB, WhAm 4
Hutawa, Julius *NewYHSD*
Hutchens, Frank Townsend d1937 *WhAm 1*
Hutcheon, Robert James 1869-1940 *WhAm 1*
Hutcherson, Dudley Robert 1902-1960 *WhAm 4*
Hutcheson, Allen Carrington, Jr. 1912-1962
WhAm 4
Hutcheson, David 1843- *WhAm 4*
Hutcheson, Ernest 1871-1951 *NatCAB 38,*
NatCAB 47
Hutcheson, Grote 1862-1948 *NatCAB 37,*
WhAm 2
Hutcheson, J Morrison 1883-1972 *NatCAB 57*
Hutcheson, John Bell 1860-1939 *WhAm 1*
Hutcheson, John Redd 1886-1962 *WhAm 4*
Hutcheson, Joseph C, Jr. 1879-1973 *WhAm 5*
Hutcheson, Joseph Chappell 1842-1924 *BiDrAC,*
NatCAB 8, TwCBDA, WhAm 4
Hutcheson, Martha Brookes 1871- *WhAm 5*
Hutcheson, Sterling 1894-1969 *NatCAB 56*
Hutcheson, Walter Randolph 1874-1951
NatCAB 39
Hutcheson, William Anderson 1868-1942
WhAm 2
Hutcheson, William Levi 1874-1953 *DcAmB S5,*
WhAm 3
Hutchin, Mary 1875- *WomWWA 14*
Hutchings *NewYHSD*
Hutchings, A B 1828?- *NewYHSD*
Hutchings, Frank Day 1859-1929 *WhAm 1*
Hutchings, George Ernest 1915- *WhAm 6*
Hutchings, John Bacon 1859-1916 *NatCAB 17*
Hutchings, John Henry 1822- *NatCAB 9*
Hutchings, John Richard, Jr. 1893-1958
WhAm 3
Hutchings, Leslie Morton 1915-1959 *WhAm 3,*
WhAm 4
Hutchings, Lester 1896-1951 *NatCAB 40,*
WhAm 3
Hutchings, Richard Henry 1869-1947 *WhAm 2*
Hutchings, Stephen B *NewYHSD*
Hutchings, W H *NewYHSD*
Hutchings, William E *NewYHSD*
Hutchins *NewYHSD*
Hutchins, Amos Francis 1884-1959 *NatCAB 49*
Hutchins, Augustus Schell 1856-1948
NatCAB 37, WhAm 2
Hutchins, Charles Clifford 1858- *WhAm 4*
Hutchins, Charles Franklin 1878- *ApCAB X*
Hutchins, Charles Henry 1847-1922 *WhAm 1*
Hutchins, Charles Lewis 1838- *ApCAB,*
NatCAB 3, TwCBDA, WhAm 4
Hutchins, Charles Pelton 1872-1938 *WhAm 1*
Hutchins, Charles Thomas 1844-1920 *WhAm 1*
Hutchins, Clarence Lisle 1885-1959 *NatCAB 49*
Hutchins, Edward 1890-1937 *NatCAB 30*
Hutchins, Edward Webster 1851-1929
NatCAB 30, WhAm 1
Hutchins, Elliott Holdsworth 1880-1953
NatCAB 41
Hutchins, Fannie *WomWWA 14*
Hutchins, Francis Sessions 1877-1924
ApCAB X
Hutchins, Frank Avery 1851-1914 *DcAmLiB,*
WhAm 3
Hutchins, Frank Frazier 1870-1942 *NatCAB 45,*
WhAm 2
Hutchins, Harry Burns 1847-1930 *DcAmB,*
NatCAB 16, TwCBDA, WhAm 1
Hutchins, Henry Clinton 1820-1894 *NatCAB 30*
Hutchins, Horace Andrews 1839-1914
NatCAB 28
Hutchins, James Calhoun 1857-1921 *WhAm 1*
Hutchins, Jere Chamberlain 1851-1943
WhAm 3
Hutchins, John 1812-1891 *BiAUS, BiDrAC,*
TwCBDA, WhAm H
Hutchins, John Corbin 1864-1938 *WhAm 1*

Hutchins, John Corydon 1840-1932 *NatCAB 2,*
NatCAB 40
Hutchins, John Power 1873-1952 *NatCAB 42*
Hutchins, Joseph 1747-1833 *TwCBDA*
Hutchins, Lee Wilson 1895-1956 *WhAm 3*
Hutchins, Lewis Reid 1905-1952 *NatCAB 41*
Hutchins, Margaret 1884-1961 *DcAmLiB*
Hutchins, Robert Maynard 1899-1977
BiDAmEd, EncAB, McGEWB, WebAB
Hutchins, Stilson 1830-1912 *NatCAB 1,*
WhAm 1
Hutchins, Thomas 1730-1789 *AmBi, ApCAB,*
DcAmB, Drake, NatCAB 9, TwCBDA,
WebAB, WebAMB, WhAm H
Hutchins, Waldo 1822-1891 *ApCAB Sup,*
BiDrAC, TwCBDA, WhAm H
Hutchins, Waldo 1858-1933 *NatCAB 25*
Hutchins, Wells A 1818- *BiAUS*
Hutchins, Wells Andrews 1818-1875 *TwCBDA*
Hutchins, Wells Andrews 1818-1895 *BiDrAC,*
WhAm H
Hutchins, Will 1878-1945 *WhAm 2*
Hutchins, William J 1871-1958 *WhAm 3*
Hutchinson, Aaron 1722-1800 *ApCAB,*
TwCBDA
Hutchinson, Abby 1829-1892 *ApCAB*
Hutchinson, Abigail Jemima 1829-1892 *NotAW*
Hutchinson, Adoniram Judson Joseph 1817-1859
NatCAB 10, WhAm H
Hutchinson, Amory Hare 1885-1964
NatCAB 57
Hutchinson, Anne d1643 *BiCAW*
Hutchinson, Anne 1590?-1643 *ApCAB,*
NatCAB 9, TwCBDA
Hutchinson, Anne 1591-1643 *AmBi, DcAmB,*
DcAmReB, Drake, EncAB, McGEWB,
NotAW, WebAB, WhAm H, WhAmP
Hutchinson, Asa *ApCAB*
Hutchinson, Aubry Vaughan 1896-1960
WhAm 4
Hutchinson, B Edwin 1888-1961 *WhAm 4*
Hutchinson, Benjamin Peters 1829-1899 *DcAmB,*
WhAm H
Hutchinson, Blanche Boyden 1882-
WomWWA 14
Hutchinson, Cary Talcott 1866-1939 *WhAm 1*
Hutchinson, Charles Lawrence 1854-1924
ApCAB Sup, DcAmB, NatCAB 4,
TwCBDA, WhAm 1
Hutchinson, Charles Lorenzo 1862-1944
NatCAB 33
Hutchinson, Charles Lukens 1853-1946
NatCAB 35
Hutchinson, Cyrus *NewYHSD*
Hutchinson, Edith Stotesbury 1877- *WhAm 5*
Hutchinson, Edmund Green 1824- *NatCAB 4*
Hutchinson, Edward 1613-1675 *ApCAB*
Hutchinson, Edward 1914- *BiDrAC*
Hutchinson, Elijah Cubberley 1855-1932
BiDrAC, WhAm 1
Hutchinson, Elizabeth Bartol Dewing 1886-
WomWWA 14
Hutchinson, Elizabeth P 1850-1915 *NatCAB 16*
Hutchinson, Ely Champion 1882-1955 *WhAm 3*
Hutchinson, Emlen 1844-1926 *NatCAB 32,*
WhAm 4
Hutchinson, Enoch 1810-1885 *TwCBDA*
Hutchinson, Forney 1875- *WhAm 5*
Hutchinson, Frederick Lane 1866-1932
WhAm 1
Hutchinson, Gene Creech 1903-1967
NatCAB 54
Hutchinson, George Alexander 1876-1954
WhAm 3
Hutchinson, Israel 1727-1811 *TwCBDA*
Hutchinson, Israel 1728-1811 *ApCAB, Drake*
Hutchinson, J Raymond B 1902-1961 *WhAm 4*
Hutchinson, James 1752-1793 *ApCAB,*
DcAmB, Drake, NatCAB 11, TwCBDA,
WhAm H
Hutchinson, James Thomas 1880-1957
NatCAB 44
Hutchinson, Jesse 1778-1851 *ApCAB*
Hutchinson, Jesse 1813-1853 *ApCAB,*
NatCAB 10
Hutchinson, John 1811-1861 *DcScB*
Hutchinson, John 1860-1941 *ApCAB X,*
WhAm 1

Hutchinson, John Corrin 1849- *WhAm 4*
Hutchinson, John Irwin 1867-1935 *AmBi,*
NatCAB 26, WhAm 1
Hutchinson, John Russell 1807-1878 *ApCAB,*
TwCBDA
Hutchinson, John Thomas 1889-1958
NatCAB 47
Hutchinson, John Wallace 1821-1908 *ApCAB,*
NatCAB 10, TwCBDA, WhAm 1
Hutchinson, Jonas 1840-1903 *NatCAB 20*
Hutchinson, Sir Jonathan 1828-1913 *BiHiMed*
Hutchinson, Joseph Baldwin 1844-1924
WhAm 1
Hutchinson, Judson *ApCAB*
Hutchinson, Knox Thomas 1894-1957 *WhAm 3*
Hutchinson, Mabel Vernon Dixon
WomWWA 14
Hutchinson, Marc Carvel 1887-1958
NatCAB 48
Hutchinson, Mark Eastwood 1889-1968
WhAm 5
Hutchinson, Melvin Tyler 1902-1973 *WhAm 6*
Hutchinson, Minnie Boyer 1871-
WomWWA 14
Hutchinson, Myron Wells, Jr. 1892-1959
WhAm 3
Hutchinson, Norman 1875-1924 *WhAm 1*
Hutchinson, Octavus Nelson 1862- *NatCAB 17*
Hutchinson, Paul 1890-1956 *NatCAB 42,*
WhAm 3
Hutchinson, Ray Coryton 1907-1975 *WhAm 6*
Hutchinson, Robert *NewYHSD*
Hutchinson, Robert George, Jr. 1866-1945
NatCAB 34
Hutchinson, Robert Hamilton 1879-1935
NatCAB 26
Hutchinson, Robert Lee 1867-1942 *NatCAB 33*
Hutchinson, Robert Orland 1889-1950 *WhAm 3*
Hutchinson, S Pemberton 1861-1929
NatCAB 31, WhAm 1
Hutchinson, Sarah Mears *WomWWA 14*
Hutchinson, Thomas 1711-1780 *AmBi, ApCAB,*
DcAmB, Drake, EncAB, McGEWB,
NatCAB 7, TwCBDA, WebAB,
WhAm H
Hutchinson, Titus 1771-1857 *NatCAB 4,*
TwCBDA
Hutchinson, William 1590?-1642 *NatCAB 10*
Hutchinson, William Henry 1911- *REnAW*
Hutchinson, William K 1896-1958 *WhAm 3*
Hutchinson, William Seely 1876-1945
NatCAB 35
Hutchinson, William Spencer 1870- *WhAm 2*
Hutchinson, William Thomas 1895- *EncAAH*
Hutchinson, Winfield Scott 1845-1911
NatCAB 15
Hutchinson, Woods 1862-1930 *AmBi, DcAmB,*
NatCAB 21, WhAm 1
Hutchison, Benjamin Franklin 1868-1927
WhAm 1
Hutchison, D C 1869-1954 *IIBEAAW*
Hutchison, Frances Kinsley 1857- *WhAm 4*
Hutchison, Frederick William 1879-1953
WhAm 3
Hutchison, George Wayland 1886-1945
WhAm 2
Hutchison, Harvey MacLeary 1878- *WhAm 6*
Hutchison, James Brewster 1913- *WhAm 3*
Hutchison, James Edgar 1860- *WhAm 4*
Hutchison, Joseph Chrisman 1822-1887 *ApCAB,*
TwCBDA
Hutchison, Lon Lewis 1877-1947 *NatCAB 37*
Hutchison, Martin Bell 1860-1918 *WhAm 1*
Hutchison, Miller Reese 1876-1944 *ApCAB X,*
WhAm 2
Hutchison, Ralph Cooper 1898-1966
NatCAB 52, WhAm 4
Hutchison, Robert Alden 1862-1937 *WhAm 1*
Hutchison, Stuart Nye 1877-1958 *WhAm 3,*
WhAm 5
Hutchison, Thomas L 1845- *WhAm 4*
Hutchison, William Easton 1860-1952 *WhAm 3*
Hutchman, J Harper *WhAm 5*
Hutenreith, L *NewYHSD*
Hutson, Charles 1840-1935 *NewYHSD*
Hutson, Charles Woodward 1840- *TwCBDA*
Hutson, Charles Woodward 1840-1936
NatCAB 43, WhAm 1

Hutson, Frederick Leroy 1875-1956 *WhAm 3*
Hutson, Harry Ellsworth 1906-1961
NatCAB 49
Hutson, John B 1890-1964 *WhAm 4*
Hutson, Joshua Brown 1844- *WhAm 4*
Hutson, Leander C 1876- *WhAm 5*
Hutson, Richard *BiAUS*
Hutson, Richard 1747-1793 *ApCAB,*
NatCAB 7, TwCBDA
Hutson, Richard 1748-1795 *BiDrAC, DcAmB,*
WhAm H
Hutt, Edith Palmer 1879- *WomWWA 14*
Hutt, Henry 1875-1950 *NatCAB 14,*
WhAm 2A
Hutt, John *NewYHSD*
Hutten, Philip Von d1546 *ApCAB*
Hutten, Ulrich Von 1488-1523 *McGEWB*
Hutter, Edwin Wilson 1813-1873 *ApCAB*
Hutter, Francis 1881-1964 *WhAm 4*
Huttig, Charles Henry d1913 *NatCAB 12*
Huttig, Charles Henry 1861-1913 *WhAm 1*
Huttig, Charles Henry 1864-1913 *NatCAB 25*
Huttig, Charles Musser 1901-1952 *NatCAB 40*
Huttleson, Henry 1798-1849 *ApCAB X*
Hutton, Abraham Bloodgood 1798-1870 *ApCAB*
Hutton, Charles 1737-1823 *DcScB*
Hutton, Colin Osborne 1910-1971 *WhAm 5*
Hutton, Edward F 1877-1962 *WhAm 4*
Hutton, Edward Hyatt 1872-1934 *WhAm 1*
Hutton, Edward Thomas Henry 1848-
ApCAB Sup
Hutton, Frederick Remsen 1853-1918 *DcAmB,*
NatCAB 16, TwCBDA, WhAm 1
Hutton, Hugh McMillen 1897-1976 *WhAm 6*
Hutton, Isaac 1767?-1855 *NewYHSD*
Hutton, James 1726-1797 *AsBiEn, DcScB,*
McGEWB
Hutton, James Buchanan 1866-1940 *WhAm 1*
Hutton, James Morgan 1870-1940 *WhAm 1*
Hutton, John Edward 1828-1893 *BiDrAC,*
WhAm H
Hutton, Joseph 1787-1828 *Drake*
Hutton, Josiah Lawson 1860- *WhAm 5*
Hutton, Laurence 1843-1904 *AmBi, ApCAB,*
DcAmB, NatCAB 7, TwCBDA,
WhAm 1
Hutton, Leon 1914-1965 *WhAm 4*
Hutton, Levi William 1860-1928 *DcAmB,*
WhAm 1
Hutton, Lynn Dewey 1897-1964 *NatCAB 50*
Hutton, Mancius Holmes 1837-1909 *TwCBDA,*
WhAm 1
Hutton, Norman 1876-1935 *WhAm 1*
Hutton, Samuel Reed 1891-1960 *WhAm 4*
Hutton, William Edward 1845-1934
NatCAB 27
Hutton, William Edward 1872-1957
NatCAB 44, WhAm 3
Hutton, William Rich 1826-1901 *IIBEAAW,*
NewYHSD, TwCBDA
Hutty, Alfred 1877-1954 *NatCAB 46,*
WhAm 3
Hutzler, Albert David 1888-1965 *NatCAB 51,*
WhAm 4
Hutzler, Moses 1800-1889 *NatCAB 11*
Huxford, Walter Scott 1892-1958 *WhAm 3*
Huxham, John 1692-1768 *BiHiMed*
Huxley, Aldous Leonard 1894-1963 *McGEWB,*
WhAm 4
Huxley, Andrew Fielding 1917- *AsBiEn*
Huxley, Henry Minor 1880-1954 *NatCAB 43,*
WhAm 3
Huxley, Sir Julian Sorell 1887-1975 *WhAm 6*
Huxley, Thomas Henry 1825-1895 *AsBiEn,*
DcScB, McGEWB
Huxman, Walter A 1887-1972 *WhAm 5*
Huyck, Ansel Brainard 1891-1959 *NatCAB 48*
Huyck, Edmund Niles 1866-1930 *NatCAB 22,*
WhAm 1
Huyck, Francis Conkling 1838-1907
NatCAB 39
Huyck, Frank Conkling 1874-1938 *NatCAB 35*
Huygens, Christiaan 1629-1695 *AsBiEn,*
DcScB, McGEWB
Huyke, Juan Bernardo 1880- *WhAm 6*
Huyler, John 1808-1870 *BiAUS, BiDrAC,*
WhAm H
Huyler, John S 1846-1910 *NatCAB 15*

Huysmans, Camille 1871-1968 *WhAm 4A*
Huysmans, Joris Karl 1848-1907 *McGEWB*
Hyakutake, Haruyoshi *WhWW-II*
Hyam, Leslie Abraham 1901-1963 *WhAm 4*
Hyamson, Moses 1862-1949 *WhAm 2*
Hyatt, Alpheus 1838-1902 *AmBi, ApCAB,*
BiDAmEd, DcAmB, DcScB, NatCAB 3,
NatCAB 23, TwCBDA, WebAB,
WhAm 1
Hyatt, Anna VanKirk 1869- *WomWWA 14*
Hyatt, Anna Vaughn 1876- *BiCAW,*
NatCAB 18, WomWWA 14
Hyatt, Augustus *NewYHSD*
Hyatt, Campbell Carr 1880-1945 *NatCAB 36*
Hyatt, Carl Britt 1893-1969 *WhAm 5*
Hyatt, Charles Eliot 1851-1930 *WhAm 1*
Hyatt, Edward 1858-1919 *WhAm 1*
Hyatt, Francis Marion 1905-1974 *WhAm 6*
Hyatt, Frank Kelso 1885-1958 *WhAm 3*
Hyatt, Frederick Hargrave 1849-1921
NatCAB 19
Hyatt, Jacob *NewYHSD*
Hyatt, James Philip 1909-1972 *WhAm 6*
Hyatt, James William 1837-1893 *NatCAB 28,*
TwCBDA
Hyatt, John Wesley 1837-1920 *AmBi, ApCAB,*
AsBiEn, DcAmB, NatCAB 12, WhAm 1
Hyatt, Jonathan Deuel 1825- *NatCAB 13*
Hyatt, William W 1826?- *NewYHSD*
Hyde, A Lincoln 1863-1949 *NatCAB 38*
Hyde, Abraham Rubin 1870-1935 *NatCAB 36*
Hyde, Albert Alexander 1848-1935 *WhAm 1*
Hyde, Allan Pearson 1878-1952 *NatCAB 41*
Hyde, Alvan 1768-1833 *ApCAB, Drake*
Hyde, Ammi Bradford 1824-1921 *WhAm 1*
Hyde, Ammi Bradford 1826-1921 *TwCBDA*
Hyde, Anne Rhea Bachman *WomWWA 14*
Hyde, Annie Hayden 1841- *WomWWA 14*
Hyde, Arthur Knox 1895-1970 *WhAm 5*
Hyde, Arthur Mastick 1877-1947 *BiDrUSE,*
DcAmB S4, EncAAH, NatCAB 40,
WhAm 2
Hyde, Arthur Sewall 1875-1920 *ApCAB X*
Hyde, B Talbot Babbitt 1872-1933 *NatCAB 26*
Hyde, Charles Cheney 1873-1952 *DcAmB S5,*
WhAm 3
Hyde, Charles Gilman 1874-1971 *NatCAB 57,*
WhAm 6
Hyde, Charles Leavitt 1860-1938 *NatCAB 34,*
WhAm 1
Hyde, Clarence Ludlam 1878-1945 *NatCAB 35,*
WhAm 2
Hyde, Clayton H 1868- *WhAm 4*
Hyde, Cornelius Willet Gillam 1838- *WhAm 4*
Hyde, D Clark 1896-1957 *WhAm 3*
Hyde, DeWitt Stephen 1909- *BiDrAC*
Hyde, Donald Frizell 1909-1966 *WhAm 4*
Hyde, Douglas 1860-1949 *McGEWB*
Hyde, Edward *NewYHSD*
Hyde, Edward 1650?-1712 *ApCAB, DcAmB,*
Drake, TwCBDA, WhAm H
Hyde, Edward 1661-1723 *DcAmB, NatCAB 5,*
WhAm H
Hyde, Edward Pechin 1879- *WhAm 6*
Hyde, Edward Warden 1868- *WhAm 1*
Hyde, Edward Wyllys 1843-1930 *ApCAB,*
TwCBDA, WhAm 1
Hyde, Edwin Francis 1842-1933 *ApCAB X,*
NatCAB 12, NatCAB 24, WhAm 1
Hyde, Elizabeth 1881-1957 *NatCAB 47*
Hyde, Elizabeth A 1876- *WhAm 5,*
WomWWA 14
Hyde, Elwin Rufus 1851-1930 *NatCAB 23*
Hyde, Frederick 1807-1887 *TwCBDA*
Hyde, Frederick 1809-1887 *ApCAB*
Hyde, Frederick Erastus 1844-1936 *NatCAB 30*
Hyde, Frederick Erastus, Jr. 1874-1944
NatCAB 33
Hyde, Frederick William 1858-1943
NatCAB 32
Hyde, Fritz Carleton 1876-1948 *NatCAB 37*
Hyde, George Baxter 1811-1889 *TwCBDA*
Hyde, George Merriam 1865-1899 *WhAm 1*
Hyde, Grant Milnor 1889-1972 *BiDAmEd,*
WhAm 5
Hyde, Helen 1868-1919 *DcAmB, WhAm 1*
Hyde, Henry *NewYHSD*
Hyde, Henry Baldwin 1834-1899 *ApCAB Sup,*

DcAmB, TwCBDA, WhAm H
Hyde, Henry Baldwin 1835-1899 *NatCAB 4*
Hyde, Henry Morrow 1866- *WhAm 5*
Hyde, Herbert Elijah 1887-1954 *NatCAB 42*
Hyde, Howard Elmer 1876- *WhAm 5*
Hyde, Howard Kemper 1911-1970 *WhAm 5*
Hyde, Howard Linton 1900-1972 *WhAm 5*
Hyde, Ida Henrietta 1857-1945 *NotAW,*
WhAm 3A, WomWWA 14
Hyde, Ira Barnes 1838-1926 *BiAUS, BiDrAC*
Hyde, James Francis Clark 1894-1944 *WhAm 2*
Hyde, James Hazen 1876-1959 *WhAm 3*
Hyde, James Macdonald 1873- *WhAm 5*
Hyde, James Nevins 1840-1910 *ApCAB,*
DcAmB, WhAm 1
Hyde, Jeannette Acord *WhAm 5*
Hyde, Jesse Earl 1884-1936 *NatCAB 45,*
WhAm 1
Hyde, Joel Wilbur 1839-1907 *NatCAB 3,*
NatCAB 31, WhAm 1
Hyde, John 1848-1929 *NatCAB 21, WhAm 1*
Hyde, John Bachman 1890-1970 *WhAm 5*
Hyde, John McEwen 1841-1916 *WhAm 1*
Hyde, John Sedgwick 1867-1917 *WhAm 1*
Hyde, Joseph *WhAm H*
Hyde, Joseph Albert 1847-1921 *NatCAB 6*
Hyde, Lavius 1789-1865 *ApCAB*
Hyde, Louis Fiske 1866-1934 *NatCAB 29*
Hyde, Louis Kepler 1865- *WhAm 4*
Hyde, Mary Backus 1869- *WhAm 5*
Hyde, Mary Caroline d1904 *WhAm 1*
Hyde, Mary Kendall d1940 *WhAm 1*
Hyde, Mary Rebecca 1857- *WomWWA 14*
Hyde, Maxwell Charles 1897-1966 *NatCAB 54*
Hyde, Miles Goodyear 1842- *WhAm 4*
Hyde, Nancy Maria 1792-1816 *ApCAB, Drake*
Hyde, Nelson Collingwood 1888-1971 *WhAm 5*
Hyde, Roscoe Raymond 1884-1943 *NatCAB 32,*
WhAm 2
Hyde, Samuel Clarence 1842-1922 *BiDrAC*
Hyde, Sara Gardner *WomWWA 14*
Hyde, Thomas Worcester 1841-1899 *NatCAB 8,*
TwCBDA
Hyde, Walter Woodburn 1870-1966
NatCAB 53, WhAm 6
Hyde, Warren G *NewYHSD*
Hyde, Wesley Warren 1853-1917 *NatCAB 17*
Hyde, William DeWitt 1858-1917 *ApCAB,*
BiDAmEd, DcAmB, NatCAB 1,
TwCBDA, WhAm 1
Hyde, William Henry 1858-1943 *NatCAB 36,*
WhAm 2
Hyde, William Waldo 1854-1915 *WhAm 1*
Hyde, Winifred *WomWWA 14*
Hyde DeNeuville, Baroness Anne-M-H
1779?-1849 *NewYHSD, WhAm H*
Hyder, Frank Marion 1868- *WhoColR*
Hydrick, Daniel Edward 1860-1921 *WhAm 1*
Hydrick, John Lee 1888-1958 *NatCAB 48*
Hyer, Charles Jacob 1887-1948 *NatCAB 37*
Hyer, David Burns, Jr. 1904-1969 *WhAm 5*
Hyer, Frank Sidney 1869-1957 *WhAm 3*
Hyer, George 1819-1872 *ApCAB, TwCBDA*
Hyer, Julien Capers 1894-1974 *WhAm 6*
Hyer, Robert Stewart 1860-1929 *BiDAmEd,*
DcAmB, NatCAB 24, WhAm 1
Hylacomylus *DcScB*
Hylan, John Francis 1868-1936 *DcAmB S2,*
WhAm 1
Hylan, John Perham 1870- *WhAm 5*
Hyland, Edward Marshall 1859-1919
NatCAB 18
Hyland, Francis E 1901-1968 *WhAm 5*
Hyland, Philip David 1899-1958 *WhAm 3*
Hyland, Thomas Raymond 1837-1884 *ApCAB*
Hyland, William A 1892-1966 *WhAm 4*
Hylander, Clarence John 1897-1964
NatCAB 53
Hyle, Michael William 1901-1967 *WhAm 4*
Hyle, N *NewYHSD*
Hylleraas, Egil Andersen 1898-1965 *DcScB*
Hyllested, August Frederick Ferdinand 1858-
WhAm 4
Hylton, John Dunbar 1837- *NatCAB 2,*
WhAm 4
Hylton, Joseph Roy 1883-1946 *WhAm 2*
Hylton-Foster, Harry 1905-1965 *WhAm 4*
Hyman, Abraham 1883-1966 *NatCAB 51*

Hyman, Albert Salisbury 1893-1972 *WhAm 5*
Hyman, George 1873-1959 *NatCAB 44*
Hyman, Harold Melvin 1924- *EncAAH*
Hyman, Irving 1908-1961 *WhAm 4*
Hyman, John Adams 1840-1891 *BiAUS,*
BiDrAC, WhAm H
Hyman, Libbie Henrietta 1888-1969 *WhAm 5*
Hyman, Lillian Phillips 1860- *WomWWA 14*
Hyman, Marion LaRoche Strobel 1909-1970
WhAm 5
Hyman, Mark 1877-1946 *NatCAB 34*
Hyman, Orren Williams 1890-1968 *NatCAB 56*
Hyman, Sarah Minna Chalk *WomWWA 14*
Hyman, Stanley Edgar 1919-1970 *WhAm 5*
Hyman, William Bryan 1814-1884 *NatCAB 12*
Hymans, Max 1900-1961 *WhAm 4*
Hymon, Mary Watson 1918-1974 *WhAm 6*
Hyndman, James Gilmore 1853-1904 *WhAm 1*
Hyndman, James Gilmour 1853-1904
NatCAB 14
Hyndman, Olan Robert 1899-1966 *NatCAB 53*
Hyndman, Peter 1853-1924 *NatCAB 20*
Hynds, Harry Patrick 1860-1933 *NatCAB 24*
Hynds, John Arthur 1870-1941 *WhAm 2*
Hyneman, John M 1771-1816 *BiAUS, BiDrAC,*
WhAm H
Hyneman, Leon 1805-1879 *ApCAB*
Hynes, John B d1970 *WhAm 5*
Hynes, John William 1886-1953 *WhAm 3*
Hynes, William J 1842-1915 *WhAm 1*
Hynes, William Joseph 1843-1915 *BiAUS,*
BiDrAC
Hynicka, Rudolph Kelker 1859-1927
NatCAB 23, WhAm 1
Hynninen, P J 1883-1960 *WhAm 4*
Hynson, Henry Parr 1855-1921 *NatCAB 19*
Hypatia 370?-415 *AsBiEn, DcScB*
Hypes, Benjamin Murray 1846- *NatCAB 12,*
WhAm 1
Hypes, Oran Faville 1862-1915 *WhAm 1*
Hypes, Samuel L 1894-1963 *WhAm 4*
Hypes, William Findley 1861-1935 *WhAm 3*
Hypsicles Of Alexandria *DcScB*
Hyre, Sarah Emma Cadwallader *WhAm 5*
Hyrne, Edmund Massingberd 1748-1783
DcAmB, WhAm H
Hyrtl, Joseph 1810-1894 *BiHiMed, DcScB*
Hyslop, James Augustus 1884-1953 *WhAm 3*
Hyslop, James Hervey 1854-1920 *AmBi,*
DcAmB, NatCAB 10, NatCAB 14,
NatCAB 26, TwCBDA, WhAm 1
Hyvernat, Henri 1858-1941 *DcAmB S3*
Hyvernat, Henry 1858-1941 *WhAm 1*
Hyzer, Edward M 1854-1925 *WhAm 1*
Hyzer, W Edward 1886-1968 *WhAm 5*

Iamblichus 250?-330? *DcScB*
Iams, Franklin Pierce 1852-1917 *NatCAB 8*
Iams, Lucy Virginia Dorsey 1855-1924 *NotAW,*
WomWWA 14
Iardella, Andrew B *NewYHSD*
Iardella, Francisco 1793-1831 *NewYHSD,*
WhAm H
Iardella, Giuseppe *NewYHSD*
Iaukea, Curtis Piehu 1855- *NatCAB 16*
Ibanez, Adolfo 1829- *ApCAB*
Ibanez DelCampo, Carlos 1877-1960 *McGEWB,*
WhAm 4
Ibanez E Ibanez Delbero, Carlos 1825-1891
DcScB
Ibarra, Andres 1807-1875 *ApCAB*
Ibarra, Francisco De d1572 *ApCAB*
Ibarra, Jose 1688-1756 *ApCAB*
Ibaviosa, Alfred Cruz 1927-1973 *WhAm 6*
Ibbetson, Arvah J *NewYHSD*
Ibbotson, James *NewYHSD*
Ibelshauser, John *NewYHSD*
Ibercourt, Henry Louis D' 1771-1818 *ApCAB*
Ibert, Jacques 1890-1962 *WhAm 4*
Iberville, Pierre Lemoine D' 1661-1706 *Drake*
Iberville, Pierre LeMoyne 1661-1706 *ApCAB*
Iberville, Pierre LeMoyne, Sieur D' 1661-1706
AmBi, McGEWB, REnAW, WebAB
Iberville, Pierre LeMoyne, Sieur De 1661-1706
DcAmB
Ibn Al-Arabi, Muhyi Al-Din 1165-1240
McGEWB
Ibn Battuta, Muhammad 1304-1369? *McGEWB*
Ibn Gabirol, Solomon BenJudah 1021?-1058?
McGEWB
Ibn Hazm, Abu Muhammad Ali 994-1064
McGEWB
Ibn Khaldun, Abd Al-Rahman Ibn Muhammad
1332-1406 *McGEWB*
Ibn Saud, King Of Saudi Arabia 1880-1953
WhWW-II
Ibn Saud, Abd Al-Aziz 1880-1953 *McGEWB*
Ibn Tashufin, Yusuf d1106 *McGEWB*
Ibn Tufayl, Abu Bakr Muhammad 1110?-1185
McGEWB
Ibn Tumart, Muhammad 1080?-1130 *McGEWB*
Ibrahim Ibn Sinan Ibn Thabit Ibn Qurra 908-946
DcScB
Ibrahim Ibn Yaqub Al-Israili Al-T *DcScB*
Ibrahim Pasha 1789-1848 *McGEWB*
Ibsen, Heman Lauritz 1886-1955 *WhAm 3*
Ibsen, Henrik 1828-1906 *McGEWB*
Icart, Pierre Nicolas 1594-1633 *ApCAB*
Icazbalceta, Joaquin Garcia 1825- *ApCAB*
Ice, Harry Lawrence 1886-1966 *WhAm 4*
Ichailovitch, Lioubomir 1874- *WhAm 5*
Ichord, Richard Howard, II 1926- *BiDrAC*
Ickelheimer, Henry Rubens 1868-1940
NatCAB 30, WhAm 4
Ickes, Anna Wilmarth Thompson 1873-1935
NotAW
Ickes, Harold 1874-1952 *WhWW-II*
Ickes, Harold L 1874-1952 *WhAm 3*
Ickes, Harold LeClair 1874-1952 *DcAmB S5,*
EncAAH, NatCAB 40, WebAB
Ickes, Harold LeClair 1874-1953 *BiDrUSE*
Ickes, Harold LeClaire 1874-1952 *EncAB,*
McGEWB
Ickler, Louis 1870-1946 *NatCAB 36*
Ictinus *McGEWB*
Iddings, Andrew Sheets 1880- *WhAm 6*
Iddings, Edward John 1879- *WhAm 3*
Iddings, Joseph Paxon 1857-1920 *DcAmB*
Iddings, Joseph Paxson 1857-1920 *DcScB,*
NatCAB 15, TwCBDA, WhAm 1

Iddings, Joseph Paxton 1857-1920 *ApCAB*
Iddings, Lewis Morris 1850-1921 *NatCAB 29,*
WhAm 1
Iddings, Lola Lamont *WomWWA 14*
Ide, Alba M d1933 *WhAm 1*
Ide, Charles Edward 1892-1959 *NatCAB 50,*
WhAm 3
Ide, Fannie Ogden 1853-1927 *BiCAW,*
TwCBDA, WhAm 1, WomWWA 14
Ide, George Barton 1804-1872 *ApCAB*
Ide, George Edward 1860-1919 *WhAm 1*
Ide, George Elmore 1845-1917 *WhAm 1*
Ide, Henry Clay 1844-1921 *AmBi,*
ApCAB Sup, DcAmB, NatCAB 11,
NatCAB 23, TwCBDA, WhAm 1
Ide, John Jay 1890-1962 *NatCAB 46*
Ide, John Jay 1892-1962 *WhAm 4*
Ide, Robert Leonard 1858- *NatCAB 14*
Ide, William B 1794?- *WhAm H*
Ideda, Kano 1886-1960 *NatCAB 48*
Idell, Albert Edward 1901-1958 *WhAm 3*
Idelson, Maurice Aaron 1895-1970 *NatCAB 53*
Idelson, Naum Ilich 1885-1951 *DcScB*
Idema, Henry 1856-1951 *WhAm 3*
Iden, Earl Clifford 1889-1955 *NatCAB 46*
Ideson, Julia Bedford 1880-1945 *DcAmLiB,*
WhAm 2
Idiaquez, Lope De d1550? *ApCAB*
Idleman, Finis Schuyler 1875-1941 *WhAm 1*
Idleman, Silas Ellsworth 1863-1931 *WhAm 1*
Idol, Virgil A J 1879-1961 *NatCAB 49*
Idris I 1889- *McGEWB*
Idrisi, Abu Abd Allah M, Al-Sharif Al-
1100-1166 *DcScB*
Idrisi, Muhammad Ibn Muhammad, Al-
1100-1165? *McGEWB*
Ietersdorf-Klasten, Gustav Von 1609-1669
ApCAB
Iff, Simon Van 1605-1651 *ApCAB*
Ifft, George Nicolas 1865-1947 *WhAm 2*
Igersheimer, Josef 1879-1965 *NatCAB 51*
Iglauer, Samuel 1871-1944 *NatCAB 34,*
WhAm 2
Iglehart, David Stewart 1873-1946 *WhAm 2*
Iglehart, Fanny Chambers Gooch 1851-
WhAm 4, WomWWA 14
Iglehart, Ferdinand Cowle 1845-1922 *WhAm 1*
Iglehart, N E Berry 1867-1936 *NatCAB 30*
Igleheart, John Levi 1862-1933 *NatCAB 25*
Igleheart, Leslie Thring 1848-1930 *NatCAB 32*
Iglesias, Angel 1829-1870 *ApCAB*
Iglesias, Jose Maria 1823- *ApCAB*
Iglesias, Miguel 1822- *ApCAB*
Iglesias, Rafael 1861- *ApCAB Sup*
Iglesias, Santiago 1872-1939 *BiDrAC,*
DcAmB S2, WhAm 1, WhAmP
Ignacio, Jose DeJesu Maria 1721-1780 *ApCAB*
Ignatius Of Antioch, Saint d115? *McGEWB*
Ignatius Of Loyola, Saint 1491-1556 *McGEWB*
Igne-Chivre, Barthelemy D' 1677-1746 *ApCAB*
Igoe, James Thomas 1883-1971 *BiDrAC,*
WhAm 5
Igoe, Michael Lambert 1885-1967 *BiDrAC,*
NatCAB 53, WhAm 4
Igoe, William Leo 1879-1953 *BiDrAC,*
WhAm 3
Igolino, Giuseppe 1759-1833 *ApCAB*
Iguain, Jose Felix 1800-1851 *ApCAB*
Ihering, Mauritius Van 1580-1635 *ApCAB*
Ihlder, John 1876-1958 *WhAm 3*
Ihle, Leo J 1900-1956 *NatCAB 47, WhAm 3*
Ihlseng, Axel Olaf 1855-1934 *WhAm 1*
Ihlseng, Magnus Colbjorn 1852- *WhAm 4*

Ihmsen, Maximilian Frederick 1868-1921
WhAm 1
Ihrie, Peter, Jr. 1796-1871 *BiAUS, BiDrAC,*
TwCBDA, WhAm H
Ihrig, Harry Karl 1898-1960 *WhAm 4*
Iiams, Frank John 1893-1960 *NatCAB 49*
Iiams, Thomas Marion 1898-1959 *WhAm 4*
Ijams, Frank Burch 1886-1966 *WhAm 4*
Ijams, George Edwin 1888-1964 *WhAm 4*
Ijams, William Putnam 1847-1922 *NatCAB 31*
Ik Marvel 1822-1908 *AmBi, DcAmB*
Ikard, Frank Neville 1914- *BiDrAC*
Ikeda, Hayato 1899-1965 *WhAm 4*
Ikert, Mary Holmes *WomWWA 14*
Ikhnaton *McGEWB*
Ikirt, George Pierce 1852-1927 *BiDrAC*
Ilak, Abdul *WhAm 3*
Iles, Elijah 1796- *NatCAB 12*
Iles, George 1852- *WhAm 4*
Iles, Malvern Wells 1852- *ApCAB, TwCBDA,*
WhAm 4
Iles, Orlando Buff 1869-1941 *WhAm 1*
Iley, Harold Randolph 1896-1951 *NatCAB 40*
Ilgenfritz, Carl Allen 1890-1967 *NatCAB 55*
Ilgenfritz, Carl Allen 1890-1968 *WhAm 4*
Ilgenfritz, E K 1890-1958 *WhAm 3*
Iliff, John Wesley 1831-1878 *NatCAB 28,*
REnAW
Iliff, Thomas Corwin 1845-1918 *WhAm 1*
Iliohan, Henrica 1850- *AmWom*
Ill, Edward Joseph 1854-1942 *NatCAB 13,*
WhAm 2
Illatopa d1542 *ApCAB*
Illges, John P 1881-1957 *WhAm 3*
Illiers, Henry Louis 1750-1794 *ApCAB*
Illigen, Andre 1638-1670 *ApCAB*
Illington, Margaret 1879-1934 *DcAmB S1*
Illington, Margaret 1881-1934 *WhAm 1,*
WomWWA 14
Illingworth, Sir Cyril Gordon 1884-1959
WhAm 3
Illius *NewYHSD*
Illman, Charles T 1842?- *NewYHSD*
Illman, Edward 1833?- *NewYHSD*
Illman, George 1824?- *NewYHSD*
Illman, Henry *NewYHSD*
Illman, Thomas d1860? *NewYHSD*
Illman, William *NewYHSD*
Illoway, Henry 1848-1932 *NatCAB 16,*
WhAm 1
Illowy, Bernhardt 1814-1871 *ApCAB*
Ilpendam, Jan Jansen Van 1595?-1647 *DcAmB*
Ilsley, Daniel 1740-1813 *BiAUS, BiDrAC,*
WhAm H
Ilsley, James Keeler 1854-1924 *WhAm 1*
Ilsley, James Lorimer 1894-1967 *WhAm 4*
Ilsley, Marjorie Henry 1885-1961 *NatCAB 52*
Ilsley, Samuel Marshall 1863- *WhAm 4*
Ilsley, William 1873-1945 *NatCAB 34*
Iltis, Hugo 1882-1952 *NatCAB 42*
Ilyushin, Sergei 1894- *WhWW-II*
Imahorn, Albert Peter 1897-1949 *WhAm 3*
Imam, Alhadji Abubakar 1911- *McGEWB*
Imamura, Akitune 1870-1948 *DcScB*
Imber, Naphtali Herz 1856-1909 *DcAmB*
Imbert, Anthony *NewYHSD*
Imbert, Antoine d1835? *DcAmB, WhAm H*
Imbert, John Claude *NewYHSD*
Imboden, Henry Miles 1909-1963 *NatCAB 50*
Imboden, John Daniel 1823-1895 *DcAmB,*
WebAMB, WhAm H
Imbrie, Addison Murray *ApCAB X*
Imbrie, Andrew Clerk 1875-1965 *NatCAB 57*
Imbrie, Hattie Silliman *WomWWA 14*

Imbrie, James 1880- *WhAm 6*
Imbrie, Robert Whitney 1883-1924 *NatCAB 53*
Imecourt, Antoine D' 1503-1550 *ApCAB*
Imes, Birney, Sr. 1889-1947 *WhAm 2*
Imes, Elmer Samuel *WhoColR*
Imfreville-Baudry, Louis 1731-1780 *ApCAB*
Imhof, Irvin W 1901-1962 *NatCAB 51*
Imhof, Joseph A 1871-1955 *IIBEAAW*
Imhoff, Howard Coleman 1894-1972
    NatCAB 57
Imhoff, Lawrence E 1895-1964 *BiDrAC*
Imhoffer, Gustav Melchior 1593-1651 *ApCAB*
Imhotep 2980BC-2950BC *AsBiEn*
Imlay, Gilbert d1828 *Drake*
Imlay, Gilbert 1750?-1828 *ApCAB*
Imlay, Gilbert 1754?-1828 *AmBi, DcAmB,*
    WhAm H
Imlay, James Henderson 1764-1823 *BiAUS,*
    BiDrAC, WhAm H
Imlay, Lorin Everett 1864-1941 *WhAm 1*
Imler, Harper George 1891-1959 *NatCAB 48*
Immel, Ray Keeslar 1885-1945 *BiDAmEd,*
    NatCAB 33
Immel, Ray Kesslar 1885-1945 *WhAm 2*
Immell, Ruth 1879- *WhAm 6*
Immen, Loraine 1840- *AmWom*
Imperatori, Charles Johnstone 1878-1949
    NatCAB 44, WhAm 3
Inama, Francis 1719- *ApCAB*
Inayat Khan, Noor Madeleine 1914-1944
    WhWW-II
Inborden, Thomas Sewell 1865- *WhoColR*
Ince, Charles R 1903-1964 *WhAm 4*
Ince, Thomas Harper 1880-1924 *WhAm 1*
Inch, George Franklin 1873-1938 *NatCAB 30*
Inch, Richard 1843-1911 *WhAm 1*
Inch, Robert Alexander 1873-1961 *WhAm 4*
Inch, Sydney Richard 1878-1964 *NatCAB 52,*
    WhAm 4
Inch, Thomas Turner 1910-1962 *NatCAB 50*
Indarte, Jose Rivera 1810-1845 *ApCAB*
Inderwick *NewYHSD*
Indiana, Robert 1928- *BnEnAmA*
Infante, Hermenegildo d1692? *ApCAB*
Infante, Jose Miguel 1778-1844 *ApCAB*
Infeld, Leopold 1898-1968 *DcScB, WhAm 4*
Ingalls, Albert Stimson 1874-1943 *NatCAB 50*
Ingalls, Anna Louisa Chesebrough 1843-
    WomWWA 14
Ingalls, Beulah Humphrey Scaff *WomWWA 14*
Ingalls, Carrie Crane 1874- *WomWWA 14*
Ingalls, Charles *NewYHSD*
Ingalls, Charles Cleveland 1864-1928
    NatCAB 38
Ingalls, Charles Russell 1819-1908 *ApCAB Sup,*
    NatCAB 1, TwCBDA, WhAm 1
Ingalls, Claude Eugene 1877-1950 *NatCAB 41*
Ingalls, Edwin Warren 1858-1924 *ApCAB X*
Ingalls, Eleanor Caldwell 1879- *WomWWA 14*
Ingalls, Eliza B *AmWom*
Ingalls, Emma A 1860- *WomWWA 14*
Ingalls, Everett Palmer 1894-1962 *NatCAB 50*
Ingalls, Fay 1882-1957 *WhAm 3*
Ingalls, Florence Allin *WomWWA 14*
Ingalls, Francis Theodore 1844-1892
    NatCAB 13, TwCBDA
Ingalls, Frederick A 1855-1938 *NatCAB 30*
Ingalls, Gardner 1800-1874 *NewYHSD*
Ingalls, George Hoadly 1872-1931 *NatCAB 25,*
    WhAm 1
Ingalls, George Sam 1912-1960 *NatCAB 48*
Ingalls, James Monroe 1837-1927 *TwCBDA,*
    WhAm 1
Ingalls, Jeremiah 1764-1838 *WhAm H*
Ingalls, John James 1833-1900 *AmBi, ApCAB,*
    BiAUS, BiDrAC, DcAmB, NatCAB 8,
    TwCBDA, WhAm 1, WhAmP
Ingalls, Marilla Baker 1828-1902 *DcAmB,*
    WhAm H
Ingalls, Melville Ezra 1842-1914 *AmBi,*
    ApCAB Sup, DcAmB, NatCAB 15,
    WhAm 1
Ingalls, N William 1880-1949 *NatCAB 38*
Ingalls, Phineas Henry 1856-1933 *NatCAB 25*
Ingalls, Robert Ingersoll 1882-1951 *WhAm 3*
Ingalls, Roscoe Cunningham 1891-1969
    NatCAB 55, WhAm 5
Ingalls, Rufus 1818-1893 *TwCBDA*

Ingalls, Rufus 1820-1893 *ApCAB, Drake,*
    NatCAB 12
Ingalls, Thomas 1833-1873 *NatCAB 1*
Ingalls, Thomas Russell 1798-1864 *NatCAB 1,*
    TwCBDA
Ingalls, Walter 1805-1874 *NewYHSD*
Ingalls, Walter Renton 1865-1956 *NatCAB 16,*
    WhAm 3
Ingalls, William 1769-1851 *ApCAB, Drake*
Ingals, Ephraim Fletcher 1848-1918 *DcAmB,*
    WhAm 1
Ingalsbe, Grenville Mellen 1846-1918 *WhAm 1*
Ingalsbe, Jabez Norton 1873-1943 *NatCAB 34*
Ingalsbe, James Leonard 1832-1920 *NatCAB 40*
Ingamells, Dwight David 1903-1968 *NatCAB 55*
Inge, Francis Harrison 1902-1959 *WhAm 3*
Inge, John William, Jr. 1897-1961 *NatCAB 49*
Inge, Samuel Williams *BiAUS*
Inge, Samuel Williams d1867 *ApCAB,*
    TwCBDA
Inge, Samuel Williams 1815-1868 *WhAm H*
Inge, Samuel Williams 1817-1868 *BiDrAC,*
    NatCAB 12
Inge, William 1913-1973 *WhAm 5*
Inge, William Marshall 1802-1846 *BiAUS,*
    BiDrAC, WhAm H
Inge, Zebulon Montgomery Pike 1856-1920
    NatCAB 10, WhAm 3
Ingels, Rosa Russell *WomWWA 14*
Ingen-Housz, Jan 1730-1799 *DcScB*
Ingenhous, Jean Simon 1701-1769 *ApCAB*
Ingenhousz, Jan 1730-1799 *AsBiEn, McGEWB*
Inger, Christian *NewYHSD*
Inger, Edmund *NewYHSD*
Inger, Egmont *NewYHSD*
Ingersoll *NewYHSD*
Ingersoll, A C, Jr. 1913-1965 *WhAm 4*
Ingersoll, Andrew Jackson 1818-1893
    NatCAB 29
Ingersoll, Chalmers 1838-1908 *NatCAB 39*
Ingersoll, Charles Anthony 1798-1860 *ApCAB,*
    BiAUS, Drake
Ingersoll, Charles Edward 1860-1932 *WhAm 1*
Ingersoll, Charles Henry 1865-1948 *NatCAB 37,*
    WhAm 2
Ingersoll, Charles Jared 1782-1862 *AmBi,*
    ApCAB, BiAUS, BiDrAC, DcAmB,
    Drake, NatCAB 7, TwCBDA, WhAm H
Ingersoll, Charles Lee 1844-1896 *NatCAB 1,*
    TwCBDA
Ingersoll, Charles Roberts 1820-1903 *BiAUS*
Ingersoll, Charles Roberts 1821-1903 *ApCAB,*
    NatCAB 10, TwCBDA
Ingersoll, Colin Macrae 1819- *ApCAB,*
    TwCBDA
Ingersoll, Colin Macrae 1819-1903 *BiDrAC*
Ingersoll, Colin Macrae 1819-1904 *NatCAB 13*
Ingersoll, Colin Macrae 1820- *BiAUS*
Ingersoll, Colin Macrae 1858-1948 *TwCBDA,*
    WhAm 2
Ingersoll, Ebon Clark 1831-1879 *BiAUS,*
    BiDrAC, TwCBDA, WhAm H
Ingersoll, Edward 1790-1841 *ApCAB,*
    TwCBDA
Ingersoll, Edward 1812-1891 *NatCAB 15*
Ingersoll, Edward 1817-1893 *ApCAB, DcAmB,*
    TwCBDA, WhAm H
Ingersoll, Edward Payson 1834-1907 *NatCAB 4,*
    WhAm 1
Ingersoll, Ernest 1852-1946 *ApCAB,*
    ApCAB X, NatCAB 9, TwCBDA,
    WhAm 2
Ingersoll, George Pratt 1861-1927 *ApCAB X,*
    NatCAB 18, NatCAB 24, WhAm 1
Ingersoll, Henry Hulbert 1844-1915
    NatCAB 12, WhAm 1
Ingersoll, Henry Wallace 1863-1946 *WhAm 2*
Ingersoll, Jared 1722-1781 *AmBi, ApCAB,*
    DcAmB, TwCBDA
Ingersoll, Jared 1749-1822 *AmBi, ApCAB,*
    BiAUS, BiDrAC, DcAmB, Drake,
    NatCAB 2, TwCBDA, WhAm H
Ingersoll, John 1788-1815 *NewYHSD*
Ingersoll, John Gage 1815-1889 *NewYHSD*
Ingersoll, John Marvin 1869-1947 *NatCAB 36*
Ingersoll, Jonathan 1746-1823 *BiAUS, Drake*
Ingersoll, Joseph Reed 1786-1868 *ApCAB,*
    BiAUS, BiDrAC, Drake, NatCAB 7,

    TwCBDA, WhAm H
Ingersoll, Leonard Rose 1880-1958 *WhAm 3*
Ingersoll, Maud Robert *WomWWA 14*
Ingersoll, Oliver Roland 1837-1914 *NatCAB 23*
Ingersoll, R Sturgis 1891-1973 *NatCAB 57*
Ingersoll, Ralph Eugene 1922- *WhAm 6*
Ingersoll, Ralph Isaacs 1788-1872 *ApCAB*
Ingersoll, Ralph Isaacs 1789-1872 *BiDrAC,*
    NatCAB 25, TwCBDA, WhAm H,
    WhAmP
Ingersoll, Ralph J d1872 *BiAUS*
Ingersoll, Randall E *NewYHSD*
Ingersoll, Raymond Vail 1875-1940 *NatCAB 29,*
    WhAm 1
Ingersoll, Robert Green 1833-1899 *AmBi,*
    ApCAB, ApCAB X, DcAmB, DcAmReB,
    EncAB, McGEWB, NatCAB 9,
    TwCBDA, WebAB, WhAm 1, WhAmP
Ingersoll, Robert Hawley 1859-1928 *DcAmB,*
    WebAB, WhAm 1
Ingersoll, Roy Clair 1884-1966 *NatCAB 54*
Ingersoll, Roy Claire 1884-1966 *WhAm 4*
Ingersoll, Royal Eason 1883-1976 *WebAMB*
Ingersoll, Royal Rodney 1847-1931 *DcAmB,*
    WhAm 1
Ingersoll, Simon 1818-1894 *AmBi, DcAmB,*
    WhAm H
Ingersoll, Stephen Abraham 1858-1936
    NatCAB 45
Ingersoll, Tyrrell Meyer 1902-1972 *WhAm 5*
Ingersoll, William Harrison 1880-1946 *WhAm 2*
Ingersoll, Winifred 1890-1960 *NatCAB 46*
Ingersoll, Winthrop 1865-1928 *NatCAB 30*
Ingham, Charles Cromwell 1796-1863 *AmBi,*
    BnEnAmA, DcAmB, NatCAB 5,
    NewYHSD, WhAm H
Ingham, Charles Cromwell 1797-1863 *ApCAB,*
    Drake, TwCBDA
Ingham, Charles Samuel 1867-1949 *NatCAB 38,*
    WhAm 3
Ingham, Charles T 1876- *WhAm 6*
Ingham, Ellery Percy 1856- *NatCAB 5*
Ingham, Harvey 1858-1949 *WhAm 2*
Ingham, John Albertson 1868-1944 *WhAm 2*
Ingham, Lucius Edwin 1892-1957 *WhAm 3*
Ingham, Mary Bigelow 1832- *AmWom*
Ingham, Mary Hall 1866-1937 *NotAW,*
    WomWWA 14
Ingham, Samuel 1793-1881 *ApCAB, BiAUS,*
    BiDrAC, TwCBDA, WhAm H
Ingham, Samuel Delucenna 1773-1860 *Drake*
Ingham, Samuel Delucenna 1779-1860 *AmBi,*
    ApCAB, BiAUS, BiDrAC, BiDrUSE,
    DcAmB, NatCAB 5, TwCBDA,
    WhAm H, WhAmP
Ingham, Sarah Woodward *WomWWA 14*
Ingham, William *NewYHSD*
Ingham, William Armstrong 1827-1913
    WhAm 1
Ingle, Arthur Harold 1876-1954 *NatCAB 45*
Ingle, David 1875-1967 *NatCAB 54, WhAm 6*
Ingle, Edward 1861-1924 *WhAm 1*
Ingle, James Addison 1867-1903 *NatCAB 5,*
    WhAm 1
Ingle, Richard 1609-1653? *AmBi, ApCAB,*
    DcAmB, WhAm H
Ingle, William 1858- *WhAm 4*
Ingles, William 1877-1966 *NatCAB 54*
Ingleson, Robert G 1868- *WhAm 4*
Ingley, Fred 1878-1951 *WhAm 3*
Inglis, Alexander James 1879-1924 *BiDAmEd,*
    DcAmB, NatCAB 23, WhAm 1
Inglis, Charles 1734-1816 *AmBi, ApCAB,*
    DcAmB, Drake, NatCAB 24, TwCBDA,
    WhAm H
Inglis, David 1825-1877 *ApCAB, TwCBDA*
Inglis, James 1777-1820 *ApCAB, Drake*
Inglis, James 1864-1950 *WhAm 2A*
Inglis, John d1850 *ApCAB*
Inglis, John Auchincloss 1813-1878 *ApCAB,*
    TwCBDA
Inglis, John Eardley Wilmot 1814-1862 *ApCAB*
Inglis, Mary 1729-1813 *ApCAB*
Inglis, Richard 1880-1956 *NatCAB 47,*
    WhAm 3
Inglis, William 1804-1863 *NatCAB 9*
Inglis, William Wallace 1871-1953 *NatCAB 41,*
    WhAm 5

Ingmanson, William Leslie 1924-1966 *WhAm 4*
Ingraham, Daniel Phoenix 1800-1881 *TwCBDA*
Ingraham, Daniel Phoenix 1804-1881
  NatCAB 1
Ingraham, Darius Holbrook 1837-1923
  NatCAB 8, WhAm 1
Ingraham, Duncan Nathaniel 1802- *ApCAB*
Ingraham, Duncan Nathaniel 1802-1863 *Drake*
Ingraham, Duncan Nathaniel 1802-1891 *AmBi,
  DcAmB, NatCAB 8, TwCBDA,
  WhAm H*
Ingraham, Edgar Shugert 1876- *WhAm 5*
Ingraham, Edward 1887-1972 *NatCAB 56*
Ingraham, Edward D 1793-1854 *Drake*
Ingraham, Edward Duffield 1793-1854 *DcAmB,
  NatCAB 13, WhAm H*
Ingraham, Edward Duncan 1793-1854 *ApCAB*
Ingraham, Ellen M 1832-1917 *NewYHSD*
Ingraham, Franc Douglas 1898-1965 *WhAm 4*
Ingraham, Frances Adelaide Leverich d1934
  WhAm 1, WomWWA 14
Ingraham, George Hunt 1870-1950 *NatCAB 40*
Ingraham, George Landon 1847-1931 *TwCBDA,
  WhAm 1*
Ingraham, Harold Carlton 1889-1950
  NatCAB 40
Ingraham, Henry A 1878-1962 *WhAm 4*
Ingraham, Henry Cruise Murphy 1838-1911
  WhAm 1
Ingraham, John Phillips Thurston 1817-1906
  TwCBDA, WhAm 1
Ingraham, Joseph 1762-1800 *DcAmB,
  WhAm H*
Ingraham, Joseph H 1809-1866? *Drake*
Ingraham, Joseph Holt 1809-1860 *AmBi,
  ApCAB, DcAmB, NatCAB 7, TwCBDA,
  WebAB, WhAm H*
Ingraham, Mary L *NewYHSD*
Ingraham, Prentiss 1843-1904 *AmBi, ApCAB,
  DcAmB, WebAB, WebAMB, WhAm 1*
Ingraham, Robert Seney 1865- *NatCAB 16*
Ingraham, Thomas *NewYHSD*
Ingraham, William Moulton 1870-1951
  NatCAB 41, WhAm 3
Ingram, Augustus Eugenio 1867- *WhAm 4*
Ingram, Dwight 1894-1967 *WhAm 5*
Ingram, Edgar Waldo 1880-1966 *NatCAB 54*
Ingram, Edward Lovering 1862- *WhAm 4*
Ingram, Eleanor Marie 1886-1921 *WhAm 1*
Ingram, Eleanor Marie 1887-1921
  WomWWA 14
Ingram, Everett Jefferson 1911-1973 *WhAm 6*
Ingram, Frances 1888- *NatCAB 17*
Ingram, Frederick Fremont 1856-1932
  NatCAB 24, WhAm 1
Ingram, Glen Ray 1887-1957 *NatCAB 47*
Ingram, Henry Atlee 1858- *WhAm 4*
Ingram, Ida Nelson 1867- *WomWWA 14*
Ingram, Jonas Howard 1886-1952 *DcAmB S5,
  WebAMB, WhAm 3*
Ingram, Leon John 1899-1965 *WhAm 5*
Ingram, Louis 1870-1941 *NatCAB 31*
Ingram, Marie Letitia 1867- *WomWWA 14*
Ingram, Orrin Henry 1830- *ApCAB X,
  NatCAB 16*
Ingram, Orrin Henry 1904-1963 *NatCAB 51,
  WhAm 4*
Ingram, Porter 1810-1893 *BiDConf*
Ingram, Rex 1892-1950 *NatCAB 41*
Ingram, William *NewYHSD*
Ingrande, Jose Domingo 1759-1817 *ApCAB*
Ingrassia, Giovanni Filippo 1510?-1580 *DcScB*
Ingres, Jean Auguste Dominique 1780-1867
  McGEWB
Ingulf, Rudolf 1727-1785 *ApCAB*
Ingvoldstad, Orlando 1885-1969 *NatCAB 55,
  WhAm 5*
Ingwersen, John Arthur 1898-1952 *WhAm 3*
Inhambupe, Antonio Luiz Pereira DaCunha
  1760-1837 *ApCAB*
Inhauma, Joaquin Jose Ignacio DeBarros
  1808-1868 *ApCAB*
Inigo, Abad Y Lasierra 1730?-1789 *ApCAB*
Ink, Harper Harry 1888-1953 *NatCAB 42*
Inlow, Richard Morehead 1867-1952 *WhAm 3*
Inman, Arthur Charles 1901-1966 *WhAm 4*
Inman, Edward Hamilton 1881-1931 *WhAm 1,
  WhAm 1C*

Inman, George 1755-1789 *ApCAB, DcAmB,
  WhAm H*
Inman, Grace Elizabeth 1874- *WomWWA 14*
Inman, Henry 1801-1846 *AmBi, ApCAB,
  BnEnAmA, DcAmB, Drake, IIBEAAW,
  NatCAB 5, NatCAB 9, NewYHSD,
  TwCBDA, WebAB, WhAm H*
Inman, Henry 1837-1899 *ApCAB Sup,
  DcAmB, NatCAB 9, TwCBDA,
  WhAm 1*
Inman, Henry Arthur 1869- *WhAm 5*
Inman, John 1805-1850 *ApCAB, DcAmB,
  Drake, NatCAB 9, WhAm H*
Inman, John Hamilton 1844-1896 *ApCAB,
  DcAmB, NatCAB 10, WhAm H*
Inman, John O'Brien 1828-1896 *ApCAB,
  NatCAB 9, NewYHSD*
Inman, Samuel Guy 1877-1965 *WhAm 4*
Inman, Samuel Martin 1843-1915 *DcAmB,
  NatCAB 2*
Inman, Walker Patterson 1894-1954 *WhAm 3*
Inman, William 1797-1874 *ApCAB, Drake,
  NatCAB 9, TwCBDA*
Innes, Charles *NewYHSD*
Innes, Charles Hiller 1870-1939 *NatCAB 35*
Innes, Frederick Neil 1858-1927 *WhAm 1*
Innes, George 1873-1953 *WhAm 3*
Innes, George Mignon 1826- *ApCAB*
Innes, Harry 1752-1816 *ApCAB, DcAmB,
  Drake, NatCAB 10*
Innes, Harry 1753-1816 *WhAm H*
Innes, Harry 1762-1816 *BiAUS*
Innes, Hary 1752-1816 *TwCBDA*
Innes, James d1759 *NatCAB 7*
Innes, James 1754-1798 *AmBi, DcAmB,
  WhAm H*
Innes, John 1863-1941 *IIBEAAW*
Innes, Katherine d1929 *WhAm 1*
Innes, Robert Thorburn Ayton 1861-1933 *DcScB*
Innes, Thomas Christie 1909-1967 *WhAm 4*
Inness, George 1825-1894 *AmBi, ApCAB,
  BnEnAmA, DcAmB, Drake, IIBEAAW,
  McGEWB, NatCAB 2, NewYHSD,
  TwCBDA, WebAB, WhAm H*
Inness, George 1853?-1926 *IIBEAAW*
Inness, George 1854-1926 *AmBi, ApCAB,
  NatCAB 22, TwCBDA, WhAm 1*
Innis, George 1822-1903 *NatCAB 31*
Innis, George Swan 1850- *WhAm 4*
Innis, Robert Alexander 1859-1943 *NatCAB 33*
Innis, William Reynolds 1859-1920 *WhAm 1*
Innocent III 1160?-1216 *McGEWB*
Innocenti, Umberto 1895-1968 *NatCAB 54*
Innokentii *DcAmB, WhAm H*
Ino, Tadataka 1745-1818 *DcScB*
Inonu, Ismet 1884-1973 *WhAm 6*
Inonu, Ismet 1884-1974 *WhWW-II*
Inouye, Daniel Ken 1924- *BiDrAC*
Inshtatheamba 1854-1903 *AmBi, DcAmB*
Inskeep, Annie Lucy Dolman d1959 *WhAm 3,
  WomWWA 14*
Inskip, John Swanel 1816-1884 *DcAmB,
  WhAm H*
Inskip, John Swanell 1816-1884 *ApCAB*
Inskipp, E Frank 1903-1953 *NatCAB 40*
Inslee, Charles T *NewYHSD*
Inslee, William *NewYHSD*
Insley, Will 1929- *BnEnAmA*
Insley, William Henry 1870- *WhAm 5*
Insull, Frederick William 1875-1939
  NatCAB 29, WhAm 1
Insull, Martin John 1869- *WhAm 5*
Insull, Samuel 1859-1938 *AmBi, ApCAB X,
  DcAmB S2, EncAB, McGEWB,
  NatCAB 14, WebAB, WhAm 1*
Intemann, Ernest August George 1848-
  NatCAB 15
Intemann, Ernst August George 1848-
  NatCAB 15
Inukai, Tsuyoshi 1855-1932 *McGEWB*
Inverchapel, Lord Archibald J K C Kerr d1951
  WhAm 3
Inverforth, Lord 1865-1955 *WhAm 3*
Invilliers, Edward Vincent D' *WhAm 4*
Ioasaf 1761-1799 *DcAmB, WhAm H*
Ioffe, Abram Fedorovich 1880-1960 *DcScB Sup*
Ionesco, Eugene 1912- *McGEWB*
Ioor, William 1780?-1830? *DcAmB, WhAm H*

Iowa, Marie *NotAW*
Ipatieff, Vladimir Nikolaevich 1867-1952
  AsBiEn, WhAm 5
Ipatiev, Vladimir Nikolaevich 1867-1952 *DcScB*
Ippen, Arthur Thomas 1907-1974 *WhAm 6*
Ippolito, Charles 1880-1953 *NatCAB 41*
Ipsen, Ernest Ludvig 1869-1951 *WhAm 3*
Ipsen, Harold Norregaard 1915-1965
  NatCAB 51
Iqbal, Muhammad 1877?-1938 *McGEWB*
Irala, Domingo Martinez De 1486-1557 *ApCAB*
Iraq, Ibn *DcScB*
Irby, Mrs. Claude 1897- *WomWWA 14*
Irby, John Laurens Manning 1854-1900
  *ApCAB Sup, BiDrAC, NatCAB 2,
  TwCBDA, WhAm 1*
Irby, John Poindexter 1890-1945 *NatCAB 48*
Irby, John St. John 1867-1924 *WhAm 1*
Irby, Nolen Meaders 1887-1958 *WhAm 3*
Irby, Richard 1825- *TwCBDA*
Iredell, Francis Raymond 1894-1972 *WhAm 5*
Iredell, James 1750-1799 *AmBi, ApCAB,
  Drake, NatCAB 1*
Iredell, James 1751-1799 *DcAmB, TwCBDA,
  WebAB, WhAm H*
Iredell, James 1788-1853 *AmBi, ApCAB,
  BiAUS, BiDrAC, Drake, NatCAB 4,
  TwCBDA, WhAm H*
Irelan, Singer B 1889-1956 *WhAm 3*
Ireland, Alleyne 1871- *WhAm 5*
Ireland, Charles Thomas, Jr. 1921-1972
  WhAm 5
Ireland, Clifford Cady 1878-1930 *BiDrAC,
  WhAm 1*
Ireland, James Duane 1878-1921 *NatCAB 43*
Ireland, John 1827-1896 *ApCAB, DcAmB,
  NatCAB 9, TwCBDA, WhAm H,
  WhAmP*
Ireland, John 1838-1918 *AmBi, ApCAB,
  ApCAB X, BiDAmEd, DcAmB,
  DcAmReB, McGEWB, NatCAB 9,
  TwCBDA, WebAB, WhAm 1*
Ireland, John 1879-1962 *WhAm 4*
Ireland, Joseph Norton 1817-1898 *ApCAB,
  DcAmB, TwCBDA, WhAm H*
Ireland, Josias Alexander 1824- *ApCAB,
  WhAm 4*
Ireland, Leroy 1889-1970 *IIBEAAW*
Ireland, Lloyd Owen 1927-1973 *WhAm 5*
Ireland, Margaret Allen 1894-1961 *NatCAB 50*
Ireland, Mary E 1834- *AmWom, WhAm 4,
  WomWWA 14*
Ireland, Mary Nivin Deringer *WomWWA 14*
Ireland, Merritte Weber 1867-1952 *WhAm 3*
Ireland, Oscar Brown 1840- *NatCAB 12,
  WhAm 4*
Ireland, Paul Francis 1860-1932 *NatCAB 41*
Ireland, R W 1892-1968 *WhAm 5*
Ireland, Robert Livingston 1867-1928
  ApCAB X, NatCAB 25, WhAm 1
Ireland, Thomas Saxton 1895-1969 *WhAm 5*
Ireland, William 1880-1935 *WhAm 1*
Ireland, William Dunning 1894-1974 *WhAm 6*
Irene, Sister 1823-1896 *DcAmB, WhAm H*
Ireton, Peter L 1882-1958 *WhAm 3*
Irey, Elmer Lincoln 1888-1948 *WhAm 2*
Ireys, Charles Goodrich 1878-1943 *WhAm 2*
Iribarren, Juan Guillermo 1797-1827 *ApCAB*
Irigoyen, Bernardo De 1823- *ApCAB*
Irigoyen, Hipolito 1850?-1933 *McGEWB*
Irinyi, Janos 1817-1895 *DcScB*
Irion, Alfred Briggs 1833-1903 *BiDrAC*
Irion, Theophil William Henry 1885-1952
  WhAm 3
Irisarri, Antonio Jose De 1786-1868 *ApCAB*
Irisarri, Hermojenes 1819- *ApCAB*
Irish, Charles Frederick 1891-1960 *NatCAB 50*
Irish, Dallas Cadwallader 1832-1899
  NatCAB 18
Irish, Edwin M 1848- *WhAm 4*
Irish, Fred Abbott 1870-1959 *WhAm 3*
Irish, George 1791-1836 *BiAUS*
Irish, John Powell 1843-1923 *NatCAB 12,
  TwCBDA, WhAm 1*
Irish, Lucina Giffin 1869- *WomWWA 14*
Irish, Reuben Hayes 1871-1935 *NatCAB 26*
Irish, Rolland E 1895-1960 *WhAm 4*
Irish, T T *NewYHSD*

Irland, George Allison 1894-1971 *WhAm 5*
Ironquill *WhAm 1*
Irons, Ernest Edward 1877-1959 *WhAm 3*
Irons, Francena Langworthy 1845-
WomWWA 14
Irons, Henry Clay 1898-1962 *WhAm 4*
Irons, James Anderson 1857-1921 *WhAm 1*
Irons, Margaret Hill *WomWWA 14*
Irons, Martin 1832- *ApCAB*
Ironside, Sir Edmund 1880-1959 *WhWW-II,
WhoMilH*
Ironside, Henry Allan 1876-1951 *DcAmB S5,
WhAm 3*
Irvin, Alexander 1800-1874 *BiAUS, BiDrAC,
WhAm H*
Irvin, David *BiAUS*
Irvin, Donald F 1905-1955 *WhAm 3*
Irvin, E Townsend 1875-1957 *NatCAB 43*
Irvin, Isaiah Tucker 1876-1925 *NatCAB 21*
Irvin, James 1800-1862 *ApCAB, BiAUS,
BiDrAC, TwCBDA, WhAm H*
Irvin, Leslie LeRoy 1895-1966 *WhAm 4*
Irvin, Rea 1881-1972 *WhAm 6*
Irvin, William 1805-1865 *ApCAB, TwCBDA*
Irvin, William Adolf 1873-1952 *WhAm 3*
Irvin, William Adolph 1873-1952 *NatCAB 38*
Irvin, William W 1778-1842 *ApCAB, BiAUS,
BiDrAC, Drake, TwCBDA, WhAm H*
Irvine, Acheson Gosford 1837- *ApCAB*
Irvine, Alexander Fitzgerald 1863-1941
WhAm 1
Irvine, Alonzo Blair 1875-1940 *WhAm 1*
Irvine, Andrew d1789 *ApCAB*
Irvine, Armstrong d1817 *ApCAB*
Irvine, Benjamin Franklin d1940 *WhAm 1*
Irvine, Callender 1774-1841 *ApCAB*
Irvine, Christopher d1786 *ApCAB*
Irvine, Clarence 1898-1975 *WhAm 6*
Irvine, Fergus Albert 1901-1968 *WhAm 5*
Irvine, Frank 1858-1931 *NatCAB 34,
WhAm 1*
Irvine, George 1826- *ApCAB*
Irvine, Harry Garfield 1881-1964 *NatCAB 54*
Irvine, Horace Hills 1878-1947 *NatCAB 36*
Irvine, James 1735-1819 *ApCAB, DcAmB,
Drake, TwCBDA, WhAm H*
Irvine, James 1766-1829 *ApCAB*
Irvine, James 1793-1835 *TwCBDA*
Irvine, James 1798?- *NatCAB 4*
Irvine, James 1867- *WhAm 4*
Irvine, James Milton, Jr. 1909-1967 *NatCAB 54*
Irvine, John Duer 1874- *TwCBDA*
Irvine, John George 1802-1871 *ApCAB*
Irvine, Julia Josephine 1848-1930 *NatCAB 12,
TwCBDA, WhAm 1, WomWWA 14*
Irvine, Leigh Hadley 1863-1942 *WhAm 2*
Irvine, Matthew *ApCAB*
Irvine, Matthew Bell 1832- *ApCAB*
Irvine, Robert Tate 1862-1929 *WhAm 1*
Irvine, Thomas 1841-1930 *NatCAB 36*
Irvine, Thomas Edward 1910-1953 *NatCAB 41*
Irvine, William 1741-1804 *AmBi, ApCAB,
BiAUS, BiDrAC, DcAmB, Drake,
NatCAB 1, TwCBDA, WebAMB,
WhAm H*
Irvine, William 1750?-1820 *ApCAB, TwCBDA*
Irvine, William 1820-1882 *BiAUS, BiDrAC,
WhAm H*
Irvine, William 1851-1927 *NatCAB 18,
WhAm 1*
Irvine, William 1906-1964 *WhAm 4*
Irvine, William Bay 1893-1963 *WhAm 4*
Irvine, William Burriss 1866-1940 *WhAm 1*
Irvine, William C 1852-1924 *REnAW*
Irvine, William Mann 1865-1928 *DcAmB,
NatCAB 16, WhAm 1*
Irvine, William N *ApCAB*
Irvine, Wilson Henry 1869-1936 *NatCAB 42,
WhAm 1*
Irving, A Duer, Jr. 1873-1941 *NatCAB 40*
Irving, Ernest Walker 1869- *WhoColR*
Irving, Frederick Carpenter 1883-1957 *WhAm 3*
Irving, George Henry, Jr. 1874-1914 *WhAm 1*
Irving, George Milton 1901-1961 *WhAm 4*
Irving, Sir Henry Brodribb 1838-1905 *WhAm 1*
Irving, Isabel 1871-1944 *WhAm 2,
WomWWA 14*
Irving, J Grant 1907-1972 *NatCAB 57*

Irving, Jacob Aemilius 1797-1856 *ApCAB*
Irving, John Beaufain 1825-1877 *AmBi,
ApCAB, DcAmB, NewYHSD, TwCBDA,
WhAm H*
Irving, John Duer 1874-1918 *DcAmB,
NatCAB 23, WhAm 1*
Irving, John Treat 1778-1838 *ApCAB,
NatCAB 9, TwCBDA*
Irving, John Treat 1810?-1906 *Drake*
Irving, John Treat 1812-1906 *ApCAB, DcAmB,
TwCBDA, WhAm 1*
Irving, Levin Thomas Handy 1828-1892
TwCBDA
Irving, Minna d1940 *WhAm 1*
Irving, Paulus A 1857- *WhAm 4*
Irving, Paulus Aemilius 1714-1796 *ApCAB*
Irving, Paulus Aemilius 1751-1828 *ApCAB,
Drake*
Irving, Peter 1771-1838 *ApCAB, Drake,
TwCBDA*
Irving, Peter 1772-1838 *DcAmB, WhAm H*
Irving, Pierre Munro 1803-1876 *DcAmB,
TwCBDA, WhAm H*
Irving, Pierre Munroe 1803-1876 *ApCAB*
Irving, Roland Duer 1847-1888 *AmBi, ApCAB,
DcAmB, TwCBDA, WhAm H*
Irving, Theodore 1809-1880 *ApCAB, Drake,
TwCBDA*
Irving, Theodore Leonard 1898-1962 *BiDrAC*
Irving, Thomas Patrick 1880-1967 *WhAm 4*
Irving, Walter Edward 1873-1958 *NatCAB 44*
Irving, Washington 1783-1859 *AmBi, ApCAB,
BiAUS, DcAmB, Drake, EncAAH,
EncAB, McGEWB, NatCAB 3,
NewYHSD, REnAW, TwCBDA, WebAB,
WhAm H*
Irving, William 1766-1821 *ApCAB, BiAUS,
BiDrAC, DcAmB, Drake, NatCAB 9,
TwCBDA, WhAm H, WhAmP*
Irwin, Agnes 1841-1914 *NotAW, TwCBDA,
WhAm 1, WomWWA 14*
Irwin, Bernard John Dowling 1830-1917
WhAm 1
Irwin, Charles Walter 1868-1934 *WhAm 1*
Irwin, Clinton Fillmore 1854- *WhAm 4*
Irwin, DeLaCherois Thomas 1843?-1928
IlBEAAW
Irwin, Donald Jay 1926- *BiDrAC*
Irwin, Edith Alice d1971 *WhAm 6*
Irwin, Edna Campbell *WomWWA 14*
Irwin, Edward Michael 1869-1933 *BiDrAC,
WhAm 1*
Irwin, Elisabeth Antoinette 1880-1942
*DcAmB S3, NotAW, WhAm 2,
WomWWA 14*
Irwin, Elizabeth Agnes *WomWWA 14*
Irwin, Frank 1868-1948 *NatCAB 37*
Irwin, Franklin Kilshaw 1859-1931 *NatCAB 24*
Irwin, Frederick Charles 1870- *WhAm 5*
Irwin, George LeRoy 1868-1931 *DcAmB,
WhAm 1*
Irwin, Harry N 1884-1955 *WhAm 3*
Irwin, Harvey Samuel 1844-1916 *BiDrAC,
WhAm 4*
Irwin, Henderson 1884-1958 *NatCAB 45*
Irwin, Henry d1777 *Drake*
Irwin, Inez Haynes 1873- *WhAm 5*
Irwin, James Ellis 1920-1974 *WhAm 6*
Irwin, Jared 1750-1818 *AmBi, ApCAB,
NatCAB 1, TwCBDA*
Irwin, Jared 1751-1818 *BiAUS, Drake*
Irwin, Jared 1768- *BiDrAC, WhAm H*
Irwin, John 1832-1901 *AmBi, ApCAB,
TwCBDA, WhAm 1*
Irwin, John Arthur 1853-1912 *NatCAB 2,
WhAm 4*
Irwin, John Nichol 1845-1905 *NatCAB 12*
Irwin, John Nichol 1847-1905 *TwCBDA,
WhAm 1*
Irwin, John Scull 1825-1901 *ApCAB,
NatCAB 11, WhAm 1*
Irwin, Joseph Ireland 1824-1910 *NatCAB 33*
Irwin, Kilshaw McHenry 1893-1960 *WhAm 4*
Irwin, Mrs. Lee Fearn 1840-1919 *NewYHSD*
Irwin, Lucian James 1867-1914 *NatCAB 17*
Irwin, Mac 1894-1961 *NatCAB 50*
Irwin, Mary Eleanor Barrows 1876-
WomWWA 14

Irwin, Mathew 1740-1800 *ApCAB*
Irwin, May 1862-1938 *AmBi, DcAmB S2,
NotAW, WhAm 1, WomWWA 14*
Irwin, Nathaniel 1756-1812 *ApCAB*
Irwin, Noble Edward 1869-1937 *NatCAB 28,
WhAm 1*
Irwin, Richard William 1857-1932 *WhAm 1*
Irwin, Robert Benjamin 1883-1951 *BiDAmEd,
DcAmB S5, WhAm 3*
Irwin, Robert Forsythe, Jr. 1892-1967 *WhAm 4*
Irwin, Robert Winfred 1869- *WhAm 5*
Irwin, Royal Wentworth 1877-1950 *NatCAB 39*
Irwin, Solden *WhAm H*
Irwin, Staford LeRoy 1893-1955 *WhAm 3*
Irwin, Theodore 1827-1902 *NatCAB 5,
NatCAB 26*
Irwin, Thomas 1785-1870 *ApCAB, BiAUS,
BiDrAC, TwCBDA, WhAm H*
Irwin, Vincent Joseph 1857-1939 *NatCAB 31*
Irwin, W Francis 1866-1932 *WhAm 1*
Irwin, Wallace 1875-1959 *WhAm 3*
Irwin, Wallace 1876-1959 *ApCAB X,
NatCAB 14*
Irwin, Walter McMaster 1872- *WhAm 5*
Irwin, Warren W 1894-1960 *WhAm 4*
Irwin, Will 1873-1948 *NatCAB 35*
Irwin, William 1827-1886 *ApCAB, BiAUS,
NatCAB 4, TwCBDA*
Irwin, William Andrew 1864-1954 *NatCAB 44*
Irwin, William Andrew 1884-1967 *NatCAB 53,
WhAm 4*
Irwin, William George 1844-1914 *NatCAB 25*
Irwin, William Glanton 1866-1943 *NatCAB 33,
WhAm 2*
Irwin, William Henry 1873-1948 *ApCAB X,
DcAmB S4, WhAm 2*
Irwin, William Wallace 1803-1856 *BiAUS,
BiDrAC, NatCAB 7, TwCBDA,
WhAm H*
Irwing, Mary Katie 1678-1721 *ApCAB*
Isaac Israeli *DcScB*
Isaac Judaeus *DcScB*
Isaac, E W D 1863- *WhoColR*
Isaac, Edward John 1896-1954 *NatCAB 42*
Isaac, Hannah M Underhill 1833- *AmWom*
Isaac, Heinrich 1450?-1517 *McGEWB*
Isaac, Joseph Elias 1898- *WhAm 6*
Isaacs, Abraham Samuel 1852-1920
ApCAB Sup
Isaacs, Abram Samuel 1851-1920 *DcAmB,
NatCAB 23, WhAm 1*
Isaacs, Abram Samuel 1852-1920 *TwCBDA*
Isaacs, Andrew 1810?- *IlBEAAW, NewYHSD*
Isaacs, Asher 1902-1963 *WhAm 4*
Isaacs, Charles Applewhite 1881-1937 *WhAm 1*
Isaacs, Charles Edward 1811-1860 *DcScB*
Isaacs, Edith J R 1878-1956 *WhAm 3*
Isaacs, Harry Julius 1894-1971 *NatCAB 56*
Isaacs, Hart 1906- *WhAm 4, WhAm 5*
Isaacs, Henry G 1840-1895 *WhAm H*
Isaacs, John Dove 1848- *WhAm 4*
Isaacs, Jorge 1837-1895 *McGEWB*
Isaacs, Lewis Montefiore 1877-1944 *WhAm 2*
Isaacs, Lucinda Fulton 1841-1916 *BiCAW*
Isaacs, Moses Legis 1899-1970 *WhAm 5*
Isaacs, Myer Samuel 1841-1904 *NatCAB 6,
TwCBDA, WhAm 1*
Isaacs, Nathan 1886-1941 *NatCAB 31,
WhAm 1*
Isaacs, Raphael 1891-1965 *WhAm 4*
Isaacs, Samuel Myer 1804-1878 *ApCAB,
DcAmB, NatCAB 11, TwCBDA,
WhAm H*
Isaacs, Stanley Myer 1882-1962 *WhAm 4*
Isaacson, Charles David 1891-1936 *WhAm 1*
Isaacson, John Olaf 1875-1939 *NatCAB 33*
Isaak, Nicholas 1913-1975 *WhAm 6*
Isabella I 1451-1504 *McGEWB*
Isabella II 1830-1904 *McGEWB*
Isacks, Jacob C *BiAUS, BiDrAC, WhAm H*
Isacson, Leo 1910- *BiDrAC*
Isaiah *McGEWB*
Isaly, Henry William 1905-1961 *NatCAB 46*
Isambert, Henry 1749-1800 *ApCAB*
Isbell, Egbert Raymond 1898-1968 *NatCAB 55,
WhAm 5*
Isbrandtsen, Hans Jeppesen 1891-1953
DcAmB S5, NatCAB 41, WhAm 3

Iselin, Adrian d1935 *WhAm 1*
Iselin, Adrian, II 1885-1961 *NatCAB 48*
Iselin, Adrian George 1818-1905 *NatCAB 26*
Iselin, Charles Oliver 1854-1932 *NatCAB 26,*
WhAm 1
Iselin, Columbus O'Donnell 1851-1933
NatCAB 26, WhAm 1
Iselin, Columbus O'Donnell 1904-1971
WhAm 5
Iselin, Ernest 1876-1954 *WhAm 3*
Iselin, Jacob Christian 1753-1811 *ApCAB*
Iselin, Lewis 1879-1928 *NatCAB 22*
Iselin, Oliver 1887-1963 *NatCAB 50,*
WhAm 4
Iselin, Oliver 1917-1969 *NatCAB 55*
Isely, Frederick B 1873-1947 *WhAm 2*
Iseman, Lawrence Lee 1879-1951 *NatCAB 44*
Isenstead, Joseph Herman 1891-1973 *WhAm 6*
Iserman, Michael 1898-1971 *WhAm 5*
Isert, Paul Edmond 1757-1789 *ApCAB*
Ish, George William Stanley, Jr. 1919-1965
NatCAB 54, WhoColR
Isham, Arthur Smith 1865-1924 *NatCAB 22*
Isham, Asa Brainerd 1844- *WhAm 4*
Isham, Edward Swift 1836- *NatCAB 7*
Isham, Frederic Stewart 1866-1922 *NatCAB 20,*
WhAm 1
Isham, Frederick Asher 1860-1937 *NatCAB 39*
Isham, Helen 1881- *WomWWA 14*
Isham, Henry Porter 1894-1969 *NatCAB 55,*
WhAm 5
Isham, Howard Edwin 1894-1975 *WhAm 6*
Isham, Jirah 1778-1842 *ApCAB, Drake*
Isham, Mary Keyt 1871-1947 *ApCAB X,*
WhAm 2, WomWWA 14
Isham, Norman Morrison 1864-1943
NatCAB 42, WhAm 2
Isham, Pierrepont 1802-1872 *NatCAB 7*
Isham, Pierrepont 1865- *NatCAB 7*
Isham, Ralph 1820?- *NewYHSD*
Isham, Ralph 1865-1937 *NatCAB 33*
Isham, Ralph Heyward 1890-1955 *DcAmB S5,*
WhAm 3
Isham, Samuel 1855-1914 *DcAmB,*
NatCAB 35, WhAm 1
Ishaq Ibn Hunayn, Abu Yaqub d911? *DcScB*
Isherwood, Benjamin Franklin 1822-1915
DcAmB, NatCAB 12, WebAMB,
WhAm 1
Isherwood, Henry *NewYHSD*
Isherwood, John Alexander 1901-1964
NatCAB 52
Ishiwara, Jun 1881-1947 *DcScB*
Isidore Of Seville 560?-636 *AsBiEn, BiHiMed,*
DcScB, McGEWB
Isidorus Of Miletus *DcScB*
Iskowitz, Edward Israel *WebAB*
Isle, Walter Whitfield 1889-1951 *WhAm 3*
Isles, Andre 1530-1565 *ApCAB*
Ismail Pasha 1830-1895 *McGEWB*
Ismay, Lord 1887-1965 *WhAm 4*
Ismay, Sir Hastings 1887-1965 *WhWW-II*
Isnard, Jean Jacques *NewYHSD*
Isoart, Louis 1599-1640 *ApCAB*
Isocrates 436BC-338BC *McGEWB*
Isom, Edward Whitten 1885-1962 *WhAm 4*
Isom, Elbert Chittenden 1896-1970 *NatCAB 55*
Isom, Mary Frances 1865-1920 *DcAmB,*
DcAmLiB, NotAW, WhAm 1,
WomWWA 14
Israel, Arthur, Jr. 1900-1966 *WhAm 4*
Israel, Edward L 1896-1941 *WhAm 1*
Israel, Harold Edward 1899-1961 *NatCAB 50,*
WhAm 4
Israel, Mina W 1875- *WomWWA 14*
Israel, Rogers 1854-1921 *NatCAB 21,*
WhAm 1
Israels, Belle Lindner 1877-1933 *NotAW,*
WomWWA 14
Israels, Carlos Lindner 1904-1969 *WhAm 5*
Isseks, Samuel Shepp 1900-1951 *NatCAB 40,*
WhAm 3
Issel, Arturo 1842-1922 *DcScB*
Isserman, Ferdinand Myron 1898-1972
NatCAB 57, WhAm 5
Issertieux, Diendonne Gabriel Yves 1753-1819
ApCAB
Istel, Andre 1887-1966 *WhAm 4*

Isthuanfi, Nicolas 1742-1806 *ApCAB*
Itaborahy, Joaquim Jose Rodrigues Torres
1802-1873 *ApCAB*
Itamaraca, Antonio Peregrino M Monteiro
1802-1868 *ApCAB*
Itaparica, Manoel DeSanta Rita 1704-1770?
ApCAB
Itauma, Candido Borges Monteiro 1812-1872
ApCAB
Ito, Hirobumi 1841-1909 *McGEWB*
Ittel, George Alfred 1899- *WhAm 4*
Ittleson, Henry d1948 *WhAm 2*
Ittleson, Henry, Jr. 1900-1973 *WhAm 6*
Ittner, Anthony Friday 1837-1931 *BiDrAC*
Ittner, Martin Hill 1870-1945 *NatCAB 35,*
WhAm 2
Ittner, William Butts 1864-1936 *WhAm 1*
Iturbide, Agustin De 1783-1824 *ApCAB,*
McGEWB
Iturbide, Augustin De 1784-1824 *Drake*
Iturri, Francisco Javier 1738-1800? *ApCAB*
Iturriaga, Manuel Mariano De 1728-1814
ApCAB
Iturribalzaga, Antonio De 1656-1728 *ApCAB*
Iturrigaray, Jose De 1760-1815 *ApCAB*
Ivan III 1440-1505 *McGEWB*
Ivan IV 1530-1584 *McGEWB*
Ivan The Terrible 1530-1584 *WhoMilH*
Ivanov, Ilya Ivanovich 1870-1932 *DcScB*
Ivanov, Piotr Pavlovich 1878-1942 *DcScB*
Ivanovsky, Dmitri Iosifovich 1864-1920 *DcScB*
Ivanowski, Sigismond De 1875- *WhAm 5*
Iveagh, The Earl Of 1874-1967 *WhAm 4A*
Iversen, Lorenz 1876-1967 *NatCAB 53,*
WhAm 4, WhAm 6
Iverson, Alfred 1798-1873 *ApCAB, BiAUS,*
BiDrAC, DcAmB, Drake, NatCAB 4,
TwCBDA, WhAm H, WhAmP
Iverson, Alfred, Jr. 1829-1911 *BiDConf*
Iverson, Samuel Gilbert 1859-1928 *WhAm 1*
Ives, Alice Emma *AmWom*
Ives, Ansel Beeman 1852-1922 *NatCAB 6*
Ives, Ansel W 1788-1838 *Drake*
Ives, Augustus Wright 1861- *WhAm 4*
Ives, Brayton 1840-1914 *ApCAB Sup,*
WhAm 1
Ives, Charles Edward 1874-1954 *DcAmB S5,*
EncAB, McGEWB, NatCAB 42, WebAB,
WhAm 3
Ives, Charles John 1831- *WhAm 4*
Ives, Charles Linnaeus 1831-1879 *ApCAB,*
TwCBDA
Ives, Charles Taylor 1864- *WhAm 4*
Ives, Chauncey Bradley 1810-1894 *BnEnAmA,*
DcAmB, NewYHSD, WhAm H
Ives, Clarence Albert 1869- *WhAm 5*
Ives, Edith Wetherill 1869- *WomWWA 14*
Ives, Edward *NewYHSD*
Ives, Eli 1778-1861 *DcAmB, WhAm H*
Ives, Eli 1779-1861 *ApCAB, Drake,*
NatCAB 12, TwCBDA
Ives, F Badger 1858-1914 *NatCAB 16*
Ives, Florence C 1854- *AmWom*
Ives, Frederic Eugene 1856-1937 *AmBi,*
ApCAB X, DcAmB S2, NatCAB 13,
NatCAB 15, WebAB, WhAm 1
Ives, Frederick Augustus 1860-1936 *NatCAB 26*
Ives, Frederick Manley 1880-1960 *WhAm 3*
Ives, George Burnham 1856-1930 *WhAm 1*
Ives, Georgiana Luvanne 1867- *WomWWA 14*
Ives, Halsey Cooley 1846-1911 *TwCBDA,*
WhAm 1
Ives, Halsey Cooley 1847-1911 *DcAmB,*
NatCAB 24
Ives, Herbert Eugene 1882-1953 *DcScB,*
NatCAB 15, NatCAB 41, WhAm 3
Ives, Howard Chapin 1878-1944 *WhAm 2*
Ives, Irving McNeil 1896-1962 *BiDrAC,*
WhAm 4, WhAmP
Ives, J J *NewYHSD*
Ives, James Edmund 1865-1943 *NatCAB 31,*
WhAm 2
Ives, James Merritt 1824-1895 *DcAmB,*
EncAAH, NewYHSD, WebAB,
WhAm H
Ives, James Merritt *see also* Currier And Ives
Ives, Joel Stone 1847-1924 *WhAm 1*
Ives, John Hiett 1906-1965 *WhAm 5*

Ives, John Winsor 1901-1958 *WhAm 3*
Ives, Joseph Christmas 1828-1868 *BiAUS,*
DcAmB, NewYHSD, WhAm H
Ives, Joseph Moss 1876-1939 *NatCAB 29,*
WhAm 1
Ives, L T *NewYHSD*
Ives, Levi 1750-1826 *ApCAB, Drake*
Ives, Levi Silliman 1797-1867 *ApCAB, DcAmB,*
DcAmReB, Drake, NatCAB 5, WhAm H
Ives, Levi Silliman 1797-1876 *TwCBDA*
Ives, Loyal Moss *NewYHSD*
Ives, Mildred Card *WomWWA 14*
Ives, Moses Brown 1794-1857 *TwCBDA*
Ives, Percy 1864-1928 *NatCAB 11, WhAm 1*
Ives, Ralph Burkett 1873-1934 *WhAm 1*
Ives, Robert Hale 1798-1875 *TwCBDA*
Ives, Sarah Noble *WhAm 5, WomWWA 14*
Ives, Sumner Albert 1882-1944 *WhAm 2*
Ives, Susanna Mary 1866- *WomWWA 14*
Ives, Thomas Poynton 1769-1835 *TwCBDA*
Ives, Thomas Poynton 1834-1865 *ApCAB,*
TwCBDA
Ives, Victoria Sires *WomWWA 14*
Ives, Willard 1806-1896 *BiAUS, BiDrAC,*
WhAm H
Ivey, Alphonso Lynn 1884-1949 *WhAm 2*
Ivey, George Melvin 1896-1968 *NatCAB 54,*
WhAm 5
Ivey, Henry Best 1888-1951 *NatCAB 39*
Ivey, Herbert Dee 1885-1966 *WhAm 4*
Ivey, Joseph Benjamin 1864-1958 *NatCAB 46,*
WhAm 3
Ivey, Thomas Neal 1860-1923 *WhAm 1*
Ivie, Benjamin Elliott 1882-1962 *NatCAB 49*
Ivie, John Mark 1933-1975 *WhAm 6*
Ivie, Joseph Henry d1942 *WhAm 2*
Ivie, William Noah 1873- *WhAm 5*
Ivins, Anthony Woodward 1852-1934
DcAmB S1, WhAm 1
Ivins, Antoine Ridgway 1881-1967 *WhAm 5*
Ivins, Benjamin Franklin Price 1884-1962
NatCAB 50, WhAm 4
Ivins, Haddon 1878-1941 *NatCAB 31*
Ivins, Horace Fremont 1856- *NatCAB 3*
Ivins, James S Y 1885-1960 *WhAm 4*
Ivins, Lester Sylvan 1878-1961 *NatCAB 48,*
WhAm 4
Ivins, William Mills 1851-1915 *DcAmB,*
NatCAB 12, NatCAB 30, WhAm 1
Ivinson, Edward 1830- *WhAm 4*
Ivison, David Brinkerhoff 1835-1903
ApCAB Sup, WhAm 1
Ivison, Henry 1808-1884 *ApCAB, NatCAB 3,*
TwCBDA
Ivory, James 1765-1842 *DcScB*
Ivy, Hardy *WhAm H*
Ivy, Robert Henry 1881-1974 *WhAm 6*
Iwabuchi, Sanji *WhWW-II*
Iwakura, Tomomi 1825-1883 *McGEWB*
Iwert, Sebald 1558-1603 *ApCAB*
Iwonski, Carl G Von 1830-1922 *NewYHSD*
Ixtlilcuechahua 734?-825? *ApCAB*
Ixtlilxochitl I d1419 *ApCAB*
Ixtlilxochitl II 1500?-1550? *ApCAB*
Ixtlilxochitl, Fernando DeAlba 1570-1649
ApCAB
Ixtlilxochitl, Fernando DeAlva 1568?-1648?
Drake
Iyenaga, Toyokichi 1862-1936 *WhAm 3*
Izac, Edouard Victor Michel 1891- *BiDrAC*
Izant, Clarence Stephen 1884-1949 *NatCAB 37*
Izard, George 1776-1828 *ApCAB Sup,*
DcAmB, TwCBDA, WebAMB, WhAm H
Izard, George 1777-1828 *AmBi, ApCAB,*
BiAUS, Drake, NatCAB 3, NatCAB 10
Izard, James F 1811-1836 *ApCAB*
Izard, Mark W *BiAUS*
Izard, Ralph d1804 *ApCAB*
Izard, Ralph 1741?-1804 *DcAmB*
Izard, Ralph 1742-1804 *AmBi, ApCAB,*
BiAUS, BiDrAC, Drake, NatCAB 3,
TwCBDA, WhAm H
Izard, Thomas C 1893-1960 *WhAm 4*
Izcohuatl d1436 *ApCAB*
Izlar, James Ferdinand 1832-1912 *BiDrAC,*
NatCAB 4

J

Jabbour, Joseph Mitchell 1902-1970
  NatCAB 56
Jabir, Ibn Hayyan *McGEWB*
Jabir Ibn Aflah Al-Ishbili, Abu Muhammad
  DcScB
Jabir Ibn Hayyan *DcScB*
Jabotinsky, Vladimir Evgenevich 1880-1940
  McGEWB
Jaccard, Auguste 1833-1895 *DcScB*
Jaccard, Walter M 1870- *WhAm 5*
Jacchia, Agide 1875-1932 *WhAm 1*
Jacintha, DoSan Jose 1716-1768 *ApCAB*
Jack, Annie L 1839- *AmWom*
Jack, Captain 1837?-1873 *DcAmB*
Jack, Cecil McKee 1876-1949 *NatCAB 41*
Jack, Charles E 1893-1958 *NatCAB 44*
Jack, Charlotte Briggs Nelson *WomWWA 14*
Jack, D Franklin 1843-1917 *NatCAB 17*
Jack, Frederick Lafayette 1861-1951 *WhAm 3*
Jack, George Whitfield 1875-1924 *NatCAB 20,*
  WhAm 1
Jack, James Robertson 1866-1952 *WhAm 3*
Jack, John George 1861-1949 *WhAm 3*
Jack, Marion Elizabeth *WomWWA 14*
Jack, Summers Melville 1852-1945 *BiDrAC,*
  TwCBDA, WhAm 4
Jack, Theodore Henley 1881-1964 *WhAm 4*
Jack, William 1788-1852 *BiAUS, BiDrAC,*
  WhAm H
Jack, William Blake 1877-1943 *WhAm 2*
Jack, William Saunders 1888-1960 *NatCAB 48*
Jackaway, Zachary Taylor 1874-1956
  NatCAB 47
Jacker, Edward 1830?-1887 *ApCAB*
Jacklin, Edward G 1907-1971 *WhAm 5*
Jackling, Daniel Cowan 1869-1956 *WhAm 3*
Jackman, Alonzo 1809-1879 *NatCAB 16*
Jackman, Charles Lyman 1871-1957 *WhAm 3*
Jackman, Howard Hill 1852- *WhAm 4*
Jackman, Lena *WomWWA 14*
Jackman, Wilbur Samuel 1855-1907 *AmBi,*
  BiDAmEd, DcAmB, NatCAB 27,
  WhAm 1
Jackman, William G *NewYHSD*
Jacks, Allen 1937-1975 *WhAm 6*
Jacks, Horace Leonard 1924-1973 *WhAm 6*
Jacks, Leo Vincent 1896-1972 *WhAm 5*
Jackson *NewYHSD*
Jackson, Abner 1811-1874 *ApCAB,*
  NatCAB 3, TwCBDA
Jackson, Abraham Reeves 1827-1892 *DcAmB,*
  NatCAB 7, WhAm H
Jackson, Abraham Valentine Williams
  1862-1937 *AmBi, DcAmB S2, NatCAB 13,*
  TwCBDA, WhAm 1
Jackson, Abraham Willard 1843-1911 *WhAm 1*
Jackson, Al d1975 *WhAm 6*
Jackson, Albert Atlee 1867-1939 *WhAm 1*
Jackson, Albert Mathews 1860-1919 *WhAm 1*
Jackson, Alexander Young 1882-1976
  IIBEAAW
Jackson, Alfred Metcalf 1860-1924 *BiDrAC*
Jackson, Algernon Brashear 1878-1942
  NatCAB 32, WhoColR
Jackson, Alice Hooker Day 1872-1926
  NatCAB 21, WomWWA 14
Jackson, Allan 1876-1963 *WhAm 4*
Jackson, Amos Henry 1846-1924 *BiDrAC*
Jackson, Amos Henry 1874- *WhAm 3*
Jackson, Amos Wade 1904-1972 *WhAm 5*
Jackson, Andrew 1767-1845 *AmBi, ApCAB,*
  BiAUS, BiDrAC, BiDrUSE, DcAmB,
  Drake, EncAAH, EncAB, McGEWB,
  NatCAB 5, REnAW, TwCBDA, WebAB,

WebAMB, WhAm H, WhAmP,
  WhoMilH
Jackson, Annie Brown *WomWWA 14*
Jackson, Arnold S 1893-1964 *WhAm 4*
Jackson, Arthur C 1858- *WhAm 3*
Jackson, Arthur Conard 1879- *WhAm 6*
Jackson, Arthur Smith 1873- *WhoColR*
Jackson, Benjamin Aborn 1848-1921
  NatCAB 19
Jackson, Bennett Barron 1868- *WhAm 4*
Jackson, Bertha Christine 1872- *WomWWA 14*
Jackson, Burris C 1905-1967 *WhAm 4*
Jackson, Byron Hubbard 1873-1939
  NatCAB 38, NatCAB 47
Jackson, Carl Newell 1875-1946 *WhAm 2*
Jackson, Carlton 1880- *WhAm 6*
Jackson, Caroline Cooke 1855- *WomWWA 14*
Jackson, Charles *NewYHSD*
Jackson, Charles 1775-1855 *ApCAB, BiAUS,*
  DcAmB, Drake, NatCAB 5, TwCBDA,
  WhAm H
Jackson, Charles 1797-1876 *BiAUS,*
  NatCAB 9, TwCBDA
Jackson, Charles 1903-1968 *WhAm 5*
Jackson, Charles Akerman 1857- *TwCBDA,*
  WhAm 4
Jackson, Charles Cabot 1843-1926 *WhAm 1*
Jackson, Charles Davis 1811-1871 *ApCAB,*
  Drake, TwCBDA
Jackson, Charles Douglas 1902-1964
  NatCAB 51, WhAm 4
Jackson, Charles Freeman 1886-1945
  NatCAB 34
Jackson, Charles H Spurgeon 1858- *WhAm 4*
Jackson, Charles Loring 1847-1935 *ApCAB,*
  NatCAB 11, NatCAB 42, TwCBDA,
  WhAm 1, WhAm 1C
Jackson, Charles Samuel 1860-1924 *DcAmB,*
  NatCAB 16, NatCAB 33, WhAm 1,
  WhAm 1C
Jackson, Charles Tenney 1874- *WhAm 5*
Jackson, Charles Thomas 1805-1880 *AmBi,*
  ApCAB, AsBiEn, DcAmB, DcScB, Drake,
  NatCAB 3, NewYHSD, TwCBDA,
  WebAB, WhAm H
Jackson, Charles Warren 1864- *WhAm 1*
Jackson, Chevalier 1865-1958 *WhAm 3*
Jackson, Chevalier L 1900-1961 *WhAm 4*
Jackson, Claiborne Fox 1806-1862 *AmBi,*
  DcAmB, WhAm H, WhAmP
Jackson, Claiborne Fox 1807-1862 *ApCAB,*
  BiAUS, BiDConf, Drake, NatCAB 12,
  TwCBDA
Jackson, Clara Thompson 1857- *WomWWA 14*
Jackson, Clarence Martin 1875-1947
  DcAmB S4, WhAm 2
Jackson, Clifford Linden 1857-1921 *WhAm 1*
Jackson, Conrad Faeger 1813-1862 *ApCAB*
Jackson, Conrad Feger 1813-1862 *Drake,*
  TwCBDA
Jackson, Cora May Brussman 1874-
  WomWWA 14
Jackson, Daniel Dana 1870-1941 *WhAm 1*
Jackson, David d1801 *BiAUS*
Jackson, David 1730?-1801 *BiDrAC*
Jackson, David 1747?-1801 *ApCAB, DcAmB,*
  TwCBDA, WhAm H
Jackson, David E *WhAm H*
Jackson, David Sherwood 1813-1872 *BiAUS,*
  BiDrAC, WhAm H
Jackson, Delbert Linscott 1881-1934
  NatCAB 25
Jackson, Donald Lester 1910- *BiDrAC*
Jackson, Dorothy Branch 1881-1933 *WhAm 1*

Jackson, Dugald Caleb 1865-1951 *DcAmB S5,*
  TwCBDA, WhAm 3
Jackson, Dunham 1888-1946 *DcAmB S4,*
  WhAm 2
Jackson, E Franklin 1911-1975 *WhAm 6*
Jackson, Ebenezer, Jr. 1796-1874 *BiAUS,*
  BiDrAC, WhAm H
Jackson, Ed 1873-1954 *NatCAB 46, WhAm 3*
Jackson, Edward 1759-1828 *REnAW*
Jackson, Edward 1856-1942 *DcAmB S3,*
  NatCAB 12, NatCAB 42, WhAm 2
Jackson, Edward Brake 1793-1826 *BiAUS,*
  BiDrAC, REnAW, TwCBDA, WhAm H,
  WhAmP
Jackson, Edward Payson 1840-1905 *ApCAB,*
  DcAmB, NatCAB 11, TwCBDA,
  WhAm 1
Jackson, Edward Schuyler 1869- *ApCAB X*
Jackson, Edwin Boyd 1877-1951 *NatCAB 40*
Jackson, Edwin W *NewYHSD*
Jackson, Elihu Emory 1836-1907 *NatCAB 9*
Jackson, Elihu Emory 1837-1907 *NatCAB 35,*
  TwCBDA, WhAm 1
Jackson, Elizabeth Noland 1916-1974 *WhAm 6*
Jackson, Ella Jefferson 1888- *WhoColR*
Jackson, Emily d1836 *ApCAB*
Jackson, Ernest Bryan 1896-1965 *WhAm 4*
Jackson, Ernest Hilton 1869-1950 *WhAm 3*
Jackson, Everett Gee 1900- *IIBEAAW*
Jackson, Mrs. Evert Wendell 1883-
  WomWWA 14
Jackson, Fanny Rebecca *WomWWA 14*
Jackson, Florence 1872- *WomWWA 14*
Jackson, Francis 1789-1861 *ApCAB, Drake,*
  NatCAB 2, TwCBDA, WhAm H
Jackson, Francis Aristide 1830-1901
  NatCAB 12
Jackson, Francis Lloyd 1914-1963 *NatCAB 52*
Jackson, Frank Dar 1854-1938 *TwCBDA,*
  WhAm 1
Jackson, Frank Darr 1854-1938 *NatCAB 11*
Jackson, Frank Lee 1882-1971 *WhAm 5*
Jackson, Franklyn John 1895-1918 *NatCAB 17*
Jackson, Fred Dewey 1898-1945 *NatCAB 35*
Jackson, Fred Schuyler 1868-1931 *BiDrAC,*
  WhAm 1
Jackson, Frederic Ellis 1879-1950 *WhAm 2*
Jackson, Frederick Gray 1881-1949 *NatCAB 39*
Jackson, Frederick Harvey 1847-1915
  NatCAB 19
Jackson, Frederick John Foakes 1855-1941
  WhAm 1
Jackson, Frederick Mitchell 1859-1945
  WhAm 3
Jackson, Gabrielle Emilie 1861- *WomWWA 14*
Jackson, Gabrielle Snow 1861- *WhAm 4*
Jackson, George 1757-1831 *BiDrAC, REnAW,*
  TwCBDA, WhAm H, WhAmP
Jackson, George 1809-1885 *ApCAB*
Jackson, George 1878- *WhAm 1*
Jackson, George Anson 1846-1907 *NatCAB 12,*
  TwCBDA, WhAm 1
Jackson, George B 1879-1963 *WhAm 4*
Jackson, George Edwards 1828-1910 *TwCBDA,*
  WhAm 1
Jackson, George Frederick 1844-1933
  NatCAB 33
Jackson, George Henry 1847- *WhoColR A*
Jackson, George K 1758-1822 *DcAmB,*
  WhAm H
Jackson, George Leroy 1875- *WhAm 5*
Jackson, George Pullen 1874-1953 *NatCAB 42,*
  WhAm 3

Jackson, George Somerville 1867-1935 *NatCAB 27, WhAm 1*
Jackson, George Thomas 1852-1916 *DcAmB, NatCAB 11, WhAm 1*
Jackson, George Washington 1856-1922 *WhoColR*
Jackson, George Washington 1861-1922 *ApCAB X, NatCAB 14, WhAm 1*
Jackson, George Whitten 1801-1862 *NatCAB 16*
Jackson, Giles 1733-1810 *TwCBDA*
Jackson, Giles B *WhoColR A*
Jackson, Grant 1869- *ApCAB X*
Jackson, H Clair 1871-1957 *NatCAB 47*
Jackson, H Louis 1879-1947 *NatCAB 37*
Jackson, Hall 1739-1797 *DcAmB, NatCAB 16, WhAm H*
Jackson, Hancock *BiAUS*
Jackson, Hannah 1748-1833 *ApCAB*
Jackson, Harry Andrew 1924- *IIBEAAW*
Jackson, Helen Maria Fiske Hunt 1830-1885 *AmBi, DcAmB, EncAB, McGEWB, NotAW, REnAW, WhAm H*
Jackson, Helen Maria Fiske Hunt 1831-1885 *AmWom, ApCAB, EncAAH, NatCAB 1, TwCBDA, WebAB*
Jackson, Helene E Dunn 1876- *WomWWA 14*
Jackson, Henry *NewYHSD*
Jackson, Henry 1747-1809 *ApCAB*
Jackson, Henry 1748-1809 *Drake*
Jackson, Henry 1778-1840 *ApCAB, BiAUS, Drake, TwCBDA*
Jackson, Henry 1798-1863 *ApCAB, Drake, TwCBDA*
Jackson, Henry 1837- *WhAm 1*
Jackson, Henry 1845-1895 *NatCAB 7*
Jackson, Henry Clay 1838- *NatCAB 14*
Jackson, Henry Ezekiel 1869-1939 *WhAm 1*
Jackson, Henry Godden 1838- *NatCAB 9*
Jackson, Henry Hollister 1884-1955 *WhAm 3*
Jackson, Henry Martin 1912- *BiDrAC*
Jackson, Henry Melville 1849-1900 *ApCAB Sup, NatCAB 3, TwCBDA, WhAm 1*
Jackson, Henry Rootes 1820-1898 *ApCAB, BiAUS, BiDConf, DcAmB, Drake, NatCAB 3, TwCBDA, WhAm H*
Jackson, Henry Rootes 1828-1898 *AmBi*
Jackson, Henry S 1860- *WhAm 1*
Jackson, Herbert Spencer 1883-1951 *WhAm 3*
Jackson, Herbert W, Jr. 1897-1966 *WhAm 4*
Jackson, Herbert Worth 1865-1936 *NatCAB 28, WhAm 1*
Jackson, Holland Taylor 1910-1961 *WhAm 4*
Jackson, Holmes Condict 1875-1927 *WhAm 1*
Jackson, Howard Campbell, Sr. 1892-1961 *WhAm 4*
Jackson, Howell Edmunds 1832-1895 *AmBi, ApCAB, BiDrAC, DcAmB, NatCAB 8, TwCBDA, WebAB, WhAm H, WhAmP*
Jackson, Hugh Parks 1836- *TwCBDA*
Jackson, Ida Joyce 1863- *WhoColR*
Jackson, Isaac Rand d1843 *BiAUS*
Jackson, Isaac Wilber 1804-1877 *TwCBDA*
Jackson, Isaac Wilber 1805-1877 *ApCAB*
Jackson, J *NewYHSD*
Jackson, J Frederick 1871-1945 *NatCAB 36*
Jackson, J Hugh 1891-1962 *WhAm 4*
Jackson, J S *WhoColR*
Jackson, Jabez North 1868-1935 *NatCAB 40, WhAm 1*
Jackson, Jabez Young 1790- *BiAUS, BiDrAC, WhAm H, WhAmP*
Jackson, Jacob Beeson 1829-1893 *NatCAB 12, REnAW*
Jackson, James *NewYHSD*
Jackson, Mrs. James *WomWWA 14*
Jackson, James 1757-1806 *AmBi, ApCAB, BiAUS, BiDrAC, DcAmB, Drake, NatCAB 1, TwCBDA, WhAm H, WhAmP*
Jackson, James 1777-1867 *AmBi, ApCAB, DcAmB, Drake, NatCAB 5, TwCBDA, WhAm H*
Jackson, James 1819-1887 *ApCAB, BiAUS, BiDrAC, DcAmB, WhAm H, WhAmP*
Jackson, James 1820-1887 *NatCAB 2, TwCBDA*

Jackson, James A 1889-1962 *WhAm 4*
Jackson, James Allen 1884-1938 *AmBi*
Jackson, James Arthur 1864-1922 *WhAm 3*
Jackson, James Caleb 1811-1895 *ApCAB, DcAmB, NatCAB 3, TwCBDA, WhAm H*
Jackson, James F 1861-1927 *WhAm 1*
Jackson, James Frederick 1851-1937 *NatCAB 40, WhAm 1*
Jackson, James Hathaway 1841-1928 *NatCAB 7, TwCBDA, WhAm 2*
Jackson, James Houston 1872-1923 *NatCAB 6*
Jackson, James Kirkman 1900-1966 *NatCAB 52, WhAm 4*
Jackson, James M 1866-1924 *NatCAB 28*
Jackson, James Monroe 1825-1901 *BiDrAC*
Jackson, James S d1862 *BiAUS*
Jackson, James S 1822?-1862 *Drake*
Jackson, James Streshley 1823-1862 *ApCAB, NatCAB 5, TwCBDA*
Jackson, James Streshly 1823-1862 *BiDrAC, WhAm H*
Jackson, Jess Hamilton 1888-1957 *NatCAB 48*
Jackson, Jesse Benjamin 1871-1947 *WhAm 2*
Jackson, Jesse Louis 1941- *WebAB*
Jackson, John d1674? *NatCAB 11*
Jackson, John Adams 1822-1879 *TwCBDA*
Jackson, John Adams 1825-1879 *AmBi, ApCAB, BnEnAmA, DcAmB, NatCAB 8, NewYHSD, WhAm H*
Jackson, John Barnard Swett 1806-1879 *TwCBDA*
Jackson, John Beard 1845-1908 *ApCAB X, NatCAB 16*
Jackson, John Bert 1876-1950 *NatCAB 46*
Jackson, John Brinckerhoff 1862-1920 *DcAmB, NatCAB 12, WhAm 1*
Jackson, John David 1834-1875 *TwCBDA*
Jackson, John Davies 1834-1875 *DcAmB, WhAm H*
Jackson, John Davis 1834-1875 *ApCAB*
Jackson, John Day 1868-1961 *NatCAB 47, WhAm 4*
Jackson, John Edward 1898-1971 *WhAm 5*
Jackson, John Edwin 1875- *WhAm 5*
Jackson, John George d1825 *BiAUS, Drake*
Jackson, John George 1774-1825 *ApCAB*
Jackson, John George 1777-1825 *BiDrAC, DcAmB, REnAW, TwCBDA, WhAm H, WhAmP*
Jackson, John Gillespie 1880-1959 *WhAm 3*
Jackson, John Gillespie, Jr. 1909-1973 *WhAm 6*
Jackson, John Henry 1838-1908 *WhAm 1*
Jackson, John Hora 1888-1950 *NatCAB 45*
Jackson, John Hughlings 1834-1911 *BiHiMed*
Jackson, John Hughlings 1835-1911 *DcScB*
Jackson, John J 1 *WhAm 5*
Jackson, John J 1829-1866 *Drake*
Jackson, John Jacob 1868-1940 *NatCAB 31*
Jackson, John Jay, Jr. 1824-1907 *BiAUS, NatCAB 11, REnAW, TwCBDA, WhAm 1*
Jackson, John Jay, Sr. 1800-1877 *REnAW*
Jackson, John King 1828-1866 *ApCAB, BiDConf, TwCBDA*
Jackson, John Long 1884-1948 *NatCAB 37, WhAm 2*
Jackson, John Luther 1866-1945 *NatCAB 36*
Jackson, John Peter 1837-1880 *ApCAB X*
Jackson, John Putnam 1833- *NatCAB 7*
Jackson, Jonathan 1743-1810 *ApCAB, BiAUS, BiDrAC, Drake, TwCBDA, WhAm H*
Jackson, Mrs. Joseph *NewYHSD*
Jackson, Joseph d1850 *NewYHSD*
Jackson, Joseph 1867-1946 *WhAm 2*
Jackson, Joseph Cooke 1835-1913 *ApCAB, TwCBDA, WhAm 1*
Jackson, Joseph Henry 1894-1955 *DcAmB S5, WhAm 2, WhAm 3*
Jackson, Joseph R 1837-1924 *ApCAB X*
Jackson, Joseph Raymond 1880-1969 *WhAm 5*
Jackson, Joseph Webber 1796-1854 *BiAUS, BiDrAC, WhAm H*
Jackson, Josephine Agnes 1865-1945 *WhAm 2*
Jackson, Kate Johnson 1841-1921 *WomWWA 14*
Jackson, Kate Veronica 1857- *WomWWA 14*
Jackson, Katharine Johnson 1841-1921 *AmWom,*

NatCAB 7, WhAm 3
Jackson, Katherine Gauss 1904-1975 *WhAm 6*
Jackson, Lambert Lincoln 1870-1952 *NatCAB 41, WhAm 3*
Jackson, Leonora 1878- *WhAm 6*
Jackson, Leroy Freeman 1881- *WhAm 6*
Jackson, Lewis Beal 1875-1945 *NatCAB 34*
Jackson, Lily Irene *AmWom*
Jackson, Lyle William 1887-1951 *NatCAB 41*
Jackson, Lyman E 1897-1973 *WhAm 6*
Jackson, M D *NewYHSD*
Jackson, M Roy 1876-1944 *NatCAB 39*
Jackson, Mabel Sapho 1884- *WhoColR*
Jackson, Mahalia 1911-1972 *WebAB, WhAm 5*
Jackson, Mallery Raby 1845-1925 *NatCAB 23*
Jackson, Margaret Doyle 1868- *WhAm 4, WomWWA 14*
Jackson, Margaret Weymouth 1895-1974 *WhAm 6*
Jackson, Martha Kellogg 1906-1969 *NatCAB 55, WhAm 5*
Jackson, Mary Anna Morrison d1915 *WhAm 1, WomWWA 14*
Jackson, May Howard 1877- *WhoColR*
Jackson, McStay 1898-1964 *WhAm 4*
Jackson, Mercy Bisbee 1802-1877 *ApCAB*
Jackson, Mercy Ruggles Bisbe 1802-1877 *DcAmB, WhAm H*
Jackson, Michael 1734-1801 *ApCAB, Drake, TwCBDA*
Jackson, Mortimer Melville 1809-1889 *DcAmB, WhAm H*
Jackson, Mortimer Melville 1814-1889 *ApCAB, NatCAB 3, TwCBDA*
Jackson, N Baxter 1890-1973 *WhAm 6*
Jackson, Nathaniel James d1892 *Drake*
Jackson, Nathaniel James 1818-1892 *TwCBDA*
Jackson, Nathaniel James 1825?-1892 *ApCAB*
Jackson, Oliver Howard 1871-1942 *NatCAB 33*
Jackson, Oliver Toussiant 1862- *WhoColR*
Jackson, Orton Porter 1873-1925 *NatCAB 21*
Jackson, Oscar Lawrence 1840-1920 *BiDrAC, NatCAB 3*
Jackson, Oswald 1838-1891 *NatCAB 29*
Jackson, Patrick Tracy 1780-1847 *AmBi, ApCAB, DcAmB, Drake, NatCAB 5, TwCBDA, WhAm H*
Jackson, Paul Rainey 1903-1969 *WhAm 5*
Jackson, Pearl Cashell 1869- *WomWWA 14*
Jackson, Percival E 1891-1970 *WhAm 5*
Jackson, Percy 1863-1941 *WhAm 1*
Jackson, Philip Ludwell 1893-1953 *NatCAB 42, WhAm 3*
Jackson, Rachel Donelson Robards 1767-1828 *AmBi, ApCAB, NatCAB 5, NotAW, TwCBDA, WhAm H*
Jackson, Ralph LeRoy 1888-1952 *WhAm 3*
Jackson, Raymond Thomas 1892-1967 *NatCAB 53, WhAm 5*
Jackson, Reginald Henry 1876-1939 *NatCAB 29, WhAm 1*
Jackson, Reuben Wright 1889-1955 *NatCAB 47*
Jackson, Richard, Jr. 1764-1838 *BiAUS, BiDrAC, TwCBDA, WhAm H, WhAmP*
Jackson, Richard Arbuthnot 1858-1934 *WhAm 1*
Jackson, Richard Harrison 1866-1971 *NatCAB 57, WhAm 5*
Jackson, Richard Henry 1830-1892 *ApCAB Sup*
Jackson, Richard Seymour 1910-1974 *WhAm 6*
Jackson, Richard Webber 1912-1952 *NatCAB 43, WhAm 3*
Jackson, Robert 1880- *WhAm 6*
Jackson, Robert Cornelius 1881- *WhoColR*
Jackson, Robert Houghwout 1892-1954 *BiDrUSE, DcAmB S5, EncAB, McGEWB, WebAB, WhAm 3*
Jackson, Robert Manson 1907-1973 *WhAm 6*
Jackson, Robert Montgomery Smith 1815-1865 *ApCAB, Drake*
Jackson, Robert Raymond 1870-1942 *DcAmB S3, WhoColR*
Jackson, Robert Tracy 1861-1948 *NatCAB 42, WhAm 2*
Jackson, Roscoe Bradbury 1879-1929 *WhAm 1*

Jackson, Russell 1874-1937 *WhAm 1*
Jackson, Samuel *NewYHSD*
Jackson, Samuel 1787-1872 *ApCAB, DcAmB, Drake, NatCAB 11, TwCBDA, WhAm H*
Jackson, Samuel Bartlett 1880-1953 *NatCAB 44*
Jackson, Samuel Dillon 1895-1951 *BiDrAC, WhAm 3, WhAmP*
Jackson, Samuel Macauley 1851-1912 *AmBi, DcAmB, NatCAB 9, TwCBDA, WhAm 1*
Jackson, Samuel McCartney 1833-1907 *NatCAB 6*
Jackson, Samuel Morley 1864-1945 *WhAm 2*
Jackson, Samuel P 1818-1885 *WhAm H*
Jackson, Samuel Spencer 1832-1875 *NatCAB 17*
Jackson, Sarah York 1806-1887 *ApCAB*
Jackson, Sarah Yorke 1806-1887 *TwCBDA*
Jackson, Schuyler Brinckerhoff 1849-1914 *ApCAB X*
Jackson, Schuyler Wood 1904-1964 *WhAm 4*
Jackson, Sheldon 1834-1909 *AmBi, ApCAB, BiDAmEd, DcAmB, DcAmReB, NatCAB 9, REnAW, TwCBDA, WebAB, WhAm 1*
Jackson, Shirley 1919-1965 *WhAm 4*
Jackson, Stella Barnaby *WomWWA 14*
Jackson, Stonewall 1824-1863 *AmBi*
Jackson, Stonewall 1824-1955 *NatCAB 43*
Jackson, T J *NewYHSD*
Jackson, Theodore Fredlinghuysen 1830- *WhAm 4*
Jackson, Theron Skeels 1885-1944 *NatCAB 34*
Jackson, Thomas Birdsall 1797-1881 *BiDrAC, TwCBDA, WhAm H*
Jackson, Thomas Birdsall 1885-1944 *BiAUS*
Jackson, Thomas Broun 1892-1966 *NatCAB 54, WhAm 5*
Jackson, Thomas E 1852- *NatCAB 4*
Jackson, Thomas Herbert 1874-1937 *NatCAB 29, WhAm 1, WhAm 1C*
Jackson, Thomas J d1842 *NewYHSD*
Jackson, Thomas Jonathan 1824-1863 *AmBi, ApCAB, BiDConf, DcAmB, Drake, EncAB, McGEWB, NatCAB 4, REnAW, TwCBDA, WebAB, WebAMB, WhAm H, WhoMilH*
Jackson, Thomas Taylor 1878- *WhoColR*
Jackson, Thomas Wright 1869- *WhAm 5*
Jackson, Timothy d1858 *Drake*
Jackson, V T 1889-1950 *WhAm 3*
Jackson, Victor Hugo 1850-1929 *NatCAB 22*
Jackson, Virgil Thomas, Sr. 1888-1959 *WhAm 4*
Jackson, W T 1794-1882 *BiAUS*
Jackson, W T *see also* Jackson, William Terry
Jackson, W Turrentine 1915- *REnAW*
Jackson, W Turrentine *see also* Jackson, William Turrentine
Jackson, Wilfrid J 1900-1959 *WhAm 3*
Jackson, William 1732-1813 *ApCAB*
Jackson, William 1746-1834 *ApCAB*
Jackson, William 1759-1828 *ApCAB, DcAmB, Drake, NatCAB 3, TwCBDA, WhAm H*
Jackson, William 1768-1842 *Drake*
Jackson, William 1783-1855 *ApCAB, BiAUS, BiDrAC, DcAmB, Drake, NatCAB 13, TwCBDA, WhAm H, WhAmP*
Jackson, William 1848-1910 *WhAm 1*
Jackson, William Alexander 1905-1964 *WhAm 4*
Jackson, William Benjamin 1870-1937 *NatCAB 18, WhAm 1*
Jackson, William Elvin 1904-1972 *NatCAB 57*
Jackson, William F *NewYHSD*
Jackson, William H 1832- *NewYHSD*
Jackson, William H 1901-1971 *WhAm 5*
Jackson, William Henry 1843-1942 *BnEnAmA, DcAmB S3, IIBEAAW, REnAW, WhAm 2*
Jackson, William Henry 1863-1925 *ApCAB X*
Jackson, William Hicks 1835-1903 *ApCAB, BiDConf, DcAmB, NatCAB 9, TwCBDA*
Jackson, William Hicks 1836-1903 *WhAm 1*
Jackson, William Humphreys 1839-1915 *BiDrAC, WhAm 1, WhAmP*
Jackson, William J 1859-1932 *WhAm 1*

Jackson, William Kenneth 1886-1947 *WhAm 2*
Jackson, William Lowther 1825-1890 *ApCAB, BiDConf, REnAW, TwCBDA*
Jackson, William Neil 1928-1972 *WhAm 6*
Jackson, William Nichols 1912-1969 *WhAm 5*
Jackson, William Payne 1868-1945 *NatCAB 42, WhAm 2*
Jackson, William Purnell 1868-1939 *BiDrAC, NatCAB 15, WhAm 1, WhAmP*
Jackson, William Tecumseh Sherman 1866- *WhoColR*
Jackson, William Terry 1794-1882 *BiDrAC, WhAm H*
Jackson, William Terry *see also* Jackson, W T
Jackson, William Trayton 1876-1933 *WhAm 1*
Jackson, William Turrentine 1915- *EncAAH*
Jackson, William Turrentine *see also* Jackson, W Turrentine
Jackson, William Walrond 1810- *ApCAB*
Jackson, William Wirt 1860-1943 *NatCAB 42*
Jackson-Coppin, Fanny *NotAW*
Jackvony, Louis Vincent 1892-1950 *NatCAB 38, WhAm 3*
Jacob, Charles Donald 1838- *NatCAB 7*
Jacob, Edwin 1794-1868 *ApCAB*
Jacob, Francois 1920- *AsBiEn*
Jacob, John Jeremiah 1829-1893 *BiAUS, NatCAB 12*
Jacob, Louis Leon 1768-1854 *ApCAB*
Jacob, Ned 1938- *IIBEAAW*
Jacob, Richard Taylor 1825-1903 *ApCAB, DcAmB, TwCBDA, WhAm 1*
Jacob, Robert Byron 1916-1971 *NatCAB 57, WhAm 5*
Jacob, Rudolph Louis 1884-1956 *NatCAB 45*
Jacob, Stephen d1817 *BiAUS, Drake*
Jacob Ben Mahir Ibn Tibbon *DcScB*
Jacobberger, Francis Benedict 1898-1962 *WhAm 4*
Jacobi, Abraham 1830-1919 *AmBi, ApCAB, ApCAB X, BiHiMed, DcAmB, McGEWB, NatCAB 9, TwCBDA, WebAB, WhAm 1*
Jacobi, Carl Gustav Jacob 1804-1851 *DcScB*
Jacobi, Frederick 1891-1952 *WhAm 3*
Jacobi, Friedrich Heinrich 1743-1819 *McGEWB*
Jacobi, Herbert P 1916- *WhAm 5*
Jacobi, Mary Corinna Putnam 1842-1906 *AmBi, AmWom, ApCAB, BiDAmEd, DcAmB, NatCAB 8, NotAW, TwCBDA, WhAm 1*
Jacobi, Mary Putnam 1834-1906 *McGEWB*
Jacobi, Moritz Hermann Von 1801-1874 *DcScB*
Jacobs, Aaron Jacob 1888-1961 *NatCAB 45*
Jacobs, Andrew, Jr. 1932- *BiDrAC*
Jacobs, Andrew, Sr. 1906- *BiDrAC*
Jacobs, Arthur Irving 1858- *NatCAB 16*
Jacobs, Arthur P 1922-1973 *WhAm 6*
Jacobs, Belle Austin 1867- *WomWWA 14*
Jacobs, Benjamin Franklin 1834-1902 *WhAm 1*
Jacobs, Bernard 1918-1975 *WhAm 6*
Jacobs, Carl Marion 1886-1967 *WhAm 4*
Jacobs, Charles Cook 1862- *WhoColR*
Jacobs, Charles Mattathias 1850-1919 *NatCAB 14, WhAm 1*
Jacobs, Charles Michael 1875-1938 *WhAm 1*
Jacobs, Edmund *NewYHSD*
Jacobs, Edwin Elmore 1877-1953 *WhAm 3*
Jacobs, Elbridge Churchill 1873-1957 *NatCAB 47, WhAm 5*
Jacobs, Elmer Pruett 1887-1970 *NatCAB 56*
Jacobs, Emil *NewYHSD*
Jacobs, Emil 1802-1866 *NewYHSD*
Jacobs, Fenton Stratton 1892-1966 *WhAm 4*
Jacobs, Ferris 1836-1881 *ApCAB*
Jacobs, Ferris, Jr. 1836-1886 *BiDrAC, TwCBDA, WhAm H*
Jacobs, Frances Wisebart 1843-1892 *NotAW*
Jacobs, Francis Edward 1903-1950 *NatCAB 39*
Jacobs, Fred Clinton 1865- *WhAm 4*
Jacobs, Fred Poaque 1880-1957 *NatCAB 48*
Jacobs, Frederic Burnham 1880-1942 *NatCAB 31*
Jacobs, Frederick Phillip 1882-1950 *NatCAB 39*
Jacobs, George 1834- *ApCAB*
Jacobs, George Amidon 1877-1945 *NatCAB 33*
Jacobs, Harold Duane 1890-1959 *WhAm 3*

Jacobs, Harry Allan 1872-1932 *NatCAB 23*
Jacobs, Henry 1801-1874 *NewYHSD*
Jacobs, Henry Barton 1858-1939 *WhAm 1*
Jacobs, Henry Eyster 1844-1932 *ApCAB, DcAmB S1, NatCAB 11, TwCBDA, WhAm 1*
Jacobs, Henry L 1875-1963 *WhAm 4*
Jacobs, Hiram *NewYHSD*
Jacobs, Isaac *NewYHSD*
Jacobs, Israel 1726-1796 *BiAUS, BiDrAC, WhAm H*
Jacobs, J Arthur 1848-1923 *WhAm 1*
Jacobs, Jay Wesley 1898-1968 *WhAm 5*
Jacobs, John Adamson 1806-1869 *ApCAB, TwCBDA*
Jacobs, John Adamson 1839-1878 *ApCAB, TwCBDA*
Jacobs, John Hall 1905-1967 *DcAmLiB, WhAm 4*
Jacobs, John Marshall 1897-1966 *WhAm 4*
Jacobs, Joseph *NewYHSD*
Jacobs, Joseph 1854-1916 *AmBi, DcAmB, NatCAB 24, WhAm 1*
Jacobs, Joseph 1859-1929 *DcAmB, NatCAB 7*
Jacobs, Joseph 1891-1967 *NatCAB 51*
Jacobs, Joseph Earle 1893-1971 *WhAm 5*
Jacobs, Joseph Joshua 1898-1962 *NatCAB 48*
Jacobs, Josephine Chace *WomWWA 14*
Jacobs, Joshua West 1843-1905 *NatCAB 16, WhAm 1*
Jacobs, L R *NewYHSD*
Jacobs, Laura Hewes Downing 1852- *WomWWA 14*
Jacobs, Lawrence Merton 1878- *ApCAB X*
Jacobs, Mary Frick *BiCAW, WomWWA 14*
Jacobs, Melville 1902-1971 *WhAm 5*
Jacobs, Michael 1808-1871 *ApCAB, DcAmB, NatCAB 11, TwCBDA, WhAm H*
Jacobs, Michael Strauss 1880-1953 *DcAmB S5*
Jacobs, Michael William 1850- *ApCAB, WhAm 4*
Jacobs, Michel 1877-1958 *WhAm 3*
Jacobs, Morris Boris 1905-1965 *NatCAB 52*
Jacobs, Myrl Lamont 1885-1948 *WhAm 3*
Jacobs, Nathan Bernd 1891-1956 *NatCAB 50, WhAm 3*
Jacobs, Nehemiah Pitman Mann 1863- *WhAm 4*
Jacobs, Orange 1827-1914 *BiDrAC, WhAmP*
Jacobs, Orange 1829-1914 *ApCAB, BiAUS*
Jacobs, Pattie Ruffner 1875-1935 *NotAW, WhAm 1, WomWWA 14*
Jacobs, Randall 1885-1967 *WhAm 4*
Jacobs, Robert Edmond 1877- *WhoColR*
Jacobs, Rowley *NewYHSD*
Jacobs, S D *BiAUS*
Jacobs, Sarah Sprague 1813- *ApCAB, Drake*
Jacobs, Tevis 1906-1974 *WhAm 6*
Jacobs, Thornwell 1877-1956 *NatCAB 43, WhAm 3*
Jacobs, W C 1840- *NatCAB 1*
Jacobs, Walter Abraham 1883-1967 *DcScB Sup, WhAm 4*
Jacobs, Walter Ballou 1861-1932 *WhAm 1*
Jacobs, Walter Charles 1873-1933 *NatCAB 24*
Jacobs, Whipple 1897-1952 *WhAm 3*
Jacobs, Wilbur S 1918- *REnAW*
Jacobs, William Plumer 1842-1917 *DcAmB*
Jacobs, William Plumer 1893-1948 *NatCAB 38*
Jacobs, William Plummer 1893-1948 *WhAm 2*
Jacobs, William States 1871-1951 *WhAm 3*
Jacobs, Woody Elmer 1885- *WhoColR*
Jacobs-Bond, Carrie 1862-1946 *NatCAB 36, NotAW*
Jacobsen, A P 1879- *WhAm 6*
Jacobsen, Alfred 1890-1967 *WhAm 4*
Jacobsen, Bernhard Martin 1862-1936 *BiDrAC, WhAm 1, WhAmP*
Jacobsen, Carlyle 1902-1974 *WhAm 6*
Jacobsen, Einar A 1906-1972 *WhAm 5*
Jacobsen, Jens Peter 1847-1885 *McGEWB*
Jacobsen, Jerome Vincent 1894-1970 *WhAm 5*
Jacobsen, Norman 1884- *WhAm 6*
Jacobsen, Simon 1624-1679 *ApCAB*
Jacobsen, Sophus Chris 1892-1969 *NatCAB 55*
Jacobsen, William Sebastian 1887-1955 *BiDrAC, WhAmP*

Jacobsohn, Simon Eberhard 1839-1902 *WhAm 1*
Jacobson, Anton Joseph 1869-1914 *NatCAB 16*
Jacobson, Arthur Clarence 1872-1958 *WhAm 3*
Jacobson, Belle Elizabeth 1900-1970 *WhAm 5*
Jacobson, Carl Alfred 1876- *WhAm 5*
Jacobson, Carl Frederick 1877-1946 *WhAm 2*
Jacobson, Christian 1528-1596 *ApCAB*
Jacobson, Conrad 1877-1955 *NatCAB 46*
Jacobson, Fritz 1863- *WhAm 5*
Jacobson, Gabe 1875-1944 *WhAm 2*
Jacobson, John Christian 1795-1870 *ApCAB, DcAmB, Drake, NatCAB 13, TwCBDA, WhAm H*
Jacobson, Morris Lazarev 1868- *WhAm 4*
Jacobson, Moses Abraham 1896-1970 *WhAm 5*
Jacobson, Nettie Catherine *WomWWA 14*
Jacobson, Oscar Brousse 1882- *IIBEAAW*
Jacobson, Peter Nathaniel 1881-1948 *NatCAB 37*
Jacobson, Samuel d1974 *WhAm 6*
Jacobsson, Per 1894-1963 *WhAm 4*
Jacobstein, Meyer 1880-1963 *BiDrAC, WhAm 4*
Jacobus, David Schenck 1862-1955 *NatCAB 44, TwCBDA, WhAm 3*
Jacobus, Melanchthon Williams 1816-1876 *ApCAB*
Jacobus, Melanchthon Williams 1855-1937 *TwCBDA*
Jacobus, Melancthon Williams 1816-1876 *Drake, NatCAB 3, TwCBDA*
Jacobus, Melancthon Williams 1855-1937 *NatCAB 27, WhAm 1*
Jacobus, Peter H 1836?- *NewYHSD*
Jacobus, Philip *NewYHSD*
Jacoby, Douglas Peter Alexander 1873-1945 *NatCAB 34*
Jacoby, Elias J 1855-1935 *NatCAB 30*
Jacoby, George W 1856-1940 *NatCAB 29, WhAm 1*
Jacoby, Hans 1902-1958 *NatCAB 48*
Jacoby, Harold 1865-1932 *AmBi, NatCAB 23, TwCBDA, WhAm 1, WhAm 1C*
Jacoby, Henry Sylvester 1857-1955 *BiDAmEd, TwCBDA, WhAm 3*
Jacoby, J Ralph 1871- *WhAm 6*
Jacoby, James *NewYHSD*
Jacoby, Kurt 1892-1968 *NatCAB 54*
Jacoby, Lois Almy *WomWWA 14*
Jacoby, Ludwig Sigismund 1813-1874 *ApCAB*
Jacoby, Ludwig Sigmund 1813-1874 *DcAmB, WhAm H*
Jacoby, Mark Walton 1893-1957 *NatCAB 48*
Jacoby, Raymond W 1889-1959 *WhAm 4*
Jacoby, Rudolph 1890-1942 *NatCAB 42*
Jacoby, William Lawall 1873-1930 *WhAm 1*
Jacome, Diego d1565 *ApCAB*
Jacopone Da Todi 1236?-1306 *McGEWB*
Jacoway, Henderson Madison 1870-1947 *BiDrAC, WhAm 5, WhAmP*
Jacoway, William Usery 1844-1944 *NatCAB 35*
Jacques, D H 1825?-1877 *ApCAB*
Jacques, Sidney Bennett 1911-1962 *WhAm 4*
Jacques, William White 1855-1932 *AmBi, WhAm 1*
Jacquet, Pierre Armand 1906-1967 *DcScB*
Jacquin, Nicolas Joseph 1727-1817 *ApCAB*
Jacquin, Nikolaus Josef 1727-1817 *DcScB*
Jadassohn, Josef 1863-1936 *BiHiMed*
Jadwin, Cornelius Comegys 1835-1913 *BiDrAC*
Jadwin, Edgar 1865-1931 *AmBi, DcAmB, NatCAB 27, WebAMB, WhAm 1*
Jaeckel, Theodore 1882-1935 *NatCAB 25, WhAm 1*
Jaeger, Alfred Sydenham 1877-1965 *NatCAB 52*
Jaeger, Alphons Otto 1886-1953 *NatCAB 40, WhAm 3*
Jaeger, Ellsworth 1897-1962 *NatCAB 52*
Jaeger, Frans Maurits 1877-1945 *DcScB*
Jaeger, Gebhard d1959 *WhAm 4*
Jaeger, Georg Friedrich 1785-1866 *DcScB*
Jaeger, Herman Joseph 1865-1934 *NatCAB 24*
Jaeger, James Emile 1877-1918 *NatCAB 22*
Jaeger, Werner Wilhelm 1888-1961 *NatCAB 47, WhAm 4*
Jaegers, Albert 1868-1925 *NatCAB 16,*

WhAm 1
Jaegers, Augustine 1878-1952 *NatCAB 39, WhAm 6*
Jaegle, Robert Fulton 1892-1950 *NatCAB 39*
Jaekel, Frederic Blair 1882-1943 *WhAm 2*
Jaekel, Otto 1863-1929 *DcScB*
Jafar Al-Balkhi *DcScB*
Jaffa, Edward Moss 1896-1965 *NatCAB 51*
Jaffa, Myer Edward 1857-1931 *WhAm 1*
Jaffarian, John Paul 1898-1967 *NatCAB 52*
Jaffe, David Lawrence 1913-1975 *WhAm 6*
Jaffe, Louis Isaac 1888-1950 *NatCAB 38, WhAm 2A*
Jaffe, Meyer 1891-1964 *NatCAB 52*
Jaffray, Clive Talbot 1865-1956 *NatCAB 49, WhAm 3*
Jaffrey, George 1682-1749 *ApCAB, Drake, NatCAB 12, TwCBDA*
Jagannatha *DcScB*
Jagemann, Hans Carl Gunther Von 1859-1926 *WhAm 1*
Jagens, William 1818?- *NewYHSD*
Jaggar, Thomas Augustus 1839-1912 *ApCAB, NatCAB 13, TwCBDA*
Jaggar, Thomas Augustus, Jr. 1871-1953 *DcAmB S5, DcScB, WhAm 3*
Jaggard, Edwin Ames 1859-1911 *WhAm 1*
Jahiz, Abu Uthman Amr Ibn Bahr, Al-776?-868? *DcScB*
Jahn, Gunnar 1883-1971 *WhAm 5*
Jahn, Hans Max 1853-1906 *DcScB*
Jahn, Walter J 1918-1970 *WhAm 5*
Jahncke, Ernest Lee 1877-1960 *WhAm 4*
Jahncke, P F, Sr. *WhAm 5*
Jahr, Torstein 1871- *WhAm 5*
Jahraus, J L *NewYHSD*
Jahraus, Jacob 1838?- *NewYHSD*
Jainsen, Wilson Carl 1899-1974 *WhAm 6*
Jaisohn, Philip 1869-1951 *NatCAB 40*
Jakosky, John Jay 1896-1964 *WhAm 4*
Jallade, Louis Eugene 1876-1957 *WhAm 3*
Jamacie, Louis *NewYHSD*
Jamar, Walker 1885-1963 *NatCAB 51*
Jamerson, G H 1869- *WhAm 5*
James *NewYHSD*
James I 1394-1437 *McGEWB*
James I 1566-1625 *McGEWB*
James II 1633-1701 *McGEWB, WhoMilH*
James III 1451-1488 *McGEWB*
James Of Venice d1147? *DcScB*
James, A C *NewYHSD*
James, A R *NewYHSD*
James, Addison Davis 1850-1947 *BiDrAC, WhAm 4, WhAmP*
James, Albert Calder 1888-1960 *WhAm 4*
James, Albert William 1902-1975 *WhAm 6*
James, Alexander 1890-1946 *NatCAB 35, WhAm 2*
James, Alfred Farragut 1868-1959 *WhAm 3*
James, Alice 1848-1892 *NotAW*
James, Alice Archer Sewall 1870-1955 *WhAm 3*
James, Amaziah Bailey 1812-1883 *BiDrAC, WhAm H*
James, Annie Laurie Wilson 1862- *AmWom*
James, Aphie 1869- *WhAm 5, WomWWA 14*
James, Arthur Curtiss 1867-1941 *DcAmB S3, WhAm 1*
James, Arthur Horace 1883-1973 *WhAm 5*
James, Bartlett Burleigh 1866-1953 *NatCAB 42*
James, Bartlett Burleigh 1867-1953 *WhAm 3*
James, Ben 1897-1965 *WhAm 4*
James, Benjamin 1768-1825 *ApCAB*
James, Benjamin Franklin 1885-1961 *BiDrAC, WhAm 4, WhAmP*
James, Bushrod Washington 1836-1903 *NatCAB 3, TwCBDA, WhAm 1*
James, Charles 1880-1928 *DcAmB, NatCAB 26, WhAm 1*
James, Charles Fenton 1844-1902 *TwCBDA, WhAm 1*
James, Charles H 1863- *WhoColR*
James, Charles Henry 1870-1957 *NatCAB 47*
James, Charles Pinckney 1818-1899 *TwCBDA, WhAm 1*
James, Charles Tillinghast 1804-1862 *ApCAB, Drake, NatCAB 28*
James, Charles Tillinghast 1805-1862 *BiDrAC, DcAmB, WhAm H, WhAmP*

James, Charles Tillinghast 1806-1862 *BiAUS, TwCBDA*
James, Daniel, Jr. 1920- *WebAMB*
James, Daniel Willis 1832-1907 *ApCAB X, DcAmB, WhAm 1*
James, Darwin Rush 1834-1908 *BiDrAC, NatCAB 1, NatCAB 23, TwCBDA, WhAm 1*
James, Darwin Rush 1873-1937 *NatCAB 28, WhAm 1*
James, David Bushrod 1874-1933 *WhAm 1*
James, David Bushrod, Jr. 1905-1960 *NatCAB 48*
James, Donald Denny 1900-1968 *WhAm 5*
James, Edmund Janes 1855-1925 *AmBi, ApCAB, BiDAmEd, DcAmB, NatCAB 11, TwCBDA, WhAm 1*
James, Edward Christopher 1841-1901 *DcAmB, NatCAB 9, WhAm H*
James, Edward David 1897-1969 *WhAm 5*
James, Edward Holton 1873-1954 *WhAm 3*
James, Edward Washington 1916-1972 *WhAm 5*
James, Edwin d1862 *Drake*
James, Edwin 1797-1861 *ApCAB, DcAmB, REnAW, TwCBDA, WhAm H*
James, Edwin Leland 1890-1951 *DcAmB S5, WhAm 3*
James, Edwin Warley 1877-1967 *NatCAB 54, WhAm 5*
James, Eldon Revare 1875-1949 *NatCAB 42, WhAm 2*
James, Elias Olan 1879- *WhAm 6*
James, Elizabeth Blakeslee *WomWWA 14*
James, Fleming 1877-1959 *WhAm 3*
James, Francis 1799-1886 *BiAUS, BiDrAC, WhAm H*
James, Francis Bacon 1864- *ApCAB X, WhAm 1*
James, Francis Marion 1873-1953 *NatCAB 40*
James, Frank 1843-1915 *REnAW*
James, Frank Cyril 1903-1972 *WhAm 5*
James, Frank Lowber 1841-1907 *WhAm 1*
James, Frank Lowber 1842-1907 *NatCAB 12*
James, George 1915-1972 *WhAm 5*
James, George Francis 1867-1932 *TwCBDA, WhAm 1*
James, George Oscar 1873-1931 *NatCAB 25, WhAm 1*
James, George Roosa 1866-1937 *WhAm 1*
James, George Wharton 1858-1923 *AmBi, DcAmB, NatCAB 19, WhAm 1*
James, Guy H 1899-1966 *NatCAB 52*
James, Hannah Packard 1835-1903 *DcAmLiB*
James, Harlean 1877- *WhAm 6*
James, Henry *NewYHSD*
James, Henry 1811-1882 *AmBi, ApCAB, DcAmB, Drake, NatCAB 13, TwCBDA, WebAB, WhAm H*
James, Henry 1843-1916 *AmBi, ApCAB, DcAmB, EncAB, McGEWB, NatCAB 1, TwCBDA, WebAB, WhAm HA, WhAm 1, WhAm 4A*
James, Henry 1879-1947 *NatCAB 36, WhAm 2*
James, Henry Ammon 1854- *ApCAB*
James, Herman Brooks 1912-1973 *WhAm 5*
James, Herman Gerlach 1887-1959 *NatCAB 46*
James, Hinton 1884-1948 *BiDrAC*
James, Howard Currie 1906-1960 *NatCAB 48*
James, Howard Meredith 1904-1968 *NatCAB 55*
James, J *NewYHSD*
James, James *NewYHSD*
James, James Alton 1864-1962 *WhAm 4*
James, James Charles 1882-1969 *WhAm 5*
James, Jean Eleanor 1876- *WomWWA 14*
James, Jesse Woodson 1847-1882 *AmBi, DcAmB, EncAAH, McGEWB, REnAW, WebAB, WhAm H*
James, John *NewYHSD*
James, John 1732-1791 *NatCAB 8*
James, John Edwin 1844- *NatCAB 3, TwCBDA, WhAm 4*
James, Joseph Francis 1857-1897 *ApCAB, TwCBDA*
James, Joseph Hidy 1868-1948 *NatCAB 36, WhAm 2*

James, Jules 1885-1957 *NatCAB 46*
James, Julia Bradford Huntington 1810-1897 *TwCBDA*
James, Lina Balis 1864- *WomWWA 14*
James, Louis 1842-1910 *DcAmB, NatCAB 16, WhAm 1*
James, Maria 1793-1868 *ApCAB*
James, Marquis 1891-1955 *DcAmB S5, NatCAB 44, WhAm 3*
James, Mary E 1834-1912 *WhAm 1*
James, Mary Latimer 1883-1963 *NatCAB 51, WomWWA 14*
James, Mary Tootle 1863- *WomWWA 14*
James, May Hall 1889-1972 *WhAm 6*
James, Minnie Kennedy 1874- *WhAm 5*
James, Nathaniel Willis 1852-1911 *NatCAB 26*
James, Oliver Victor 1879-1955 *NatCAB 41*
James, Ollie Murray 1871-1918 *BiDrAC, DcAmB, WhAmP*
James, Ollie Murray 1871-1919 *NatCAB 15, WhAm 1*
James, Ollie Murray 1908-1972 *WhAm 5*
James, Parker Kent 1909-1970 *NatCAB 57*
James, Pauline Sholes 1874- *WomWWA 14*
James, Philip 1890-1975 *WhAm 6*
James, Phillip 1901-1975 *WhAm 6*
James, Rebecca Salsbury 1891-1968 *IIBEAAW*
James, Reese D 1889-1960 *WhAm 4*
James, Richard Sexton 1824- *TwCBDA*
James, Mrs. Robert Darrington *WomWWA 14*
James, Rorer Abraham 1859-1921 *BiDrAC*
James, S C *NewYHSD*
James, Samuel Catlett 1854- *WhAm 4*
James, Samuel Henry 1880-1946 *NatCAB 35*
James, Theodore *NewYHSD*
James, Thomas 1590?- *ApCAB, Drake*
James, Thomas 1592-1678? *ApCAB, Drake*
James, Thomas 1782-1847 *AmBi, DcAmB, WhAm H*
James, Thomas Chalkley 1766-1835 *ApCAB, DcAmB, Drake, NatCAB 11, TwCBDA, WhAm H*
James, Thomas Lemuel 1831-1916 *AmBi, ApCAB, BiDrUSE, DcAmB, NatCAB 4, TwCBDA, WhAm 1*
James, Thomas Potts 1803-1882 *ApCAB, DcAmB, TwCBDA, WhAm H*
James, W Frank 1873-1945 *WhAm 2*
James, Walter Belknap 1858-1927 *ApCAB X, NatCAB 21, WhAm 1*
James, Walter Gilbert 1880-1948 *WhAm 2*
James, Warren William 1884-1945 *NatCAB 35, WhAm 2*
James, Will 1892-1942 *DcAmB S3, IIBEAAW, NatCAB 35, REnAW, WhAm 2*
James, William d1827 *Drake*
James, William 1842-1910 *AmBi, ApCAB, AsBiEn, BiDAmEd, DcAmB, DcAmReB, DcScB, EncAB, McGEWB, NatCAB 18, TwCBDA, WebAB, WhAm 1*
James, William 1882-1961 *WhAm 4*
James, William Carey 1867-1958 *WhAm 3*
James, William Daniel 1885-1947 *NatCAB 50*
James, William David 1893-1951 *NatCAB 40*
James, William Fletcher 1845-1919 *NatCAB 18*
James, William Francis 1873-1945 *BiDrAC, WhAmP*
James, William Hartford 1831-1920 *BiAUS, NatCAB 12, TwCBDA, WhAm 1*
James, William John 1860-1941 *WhAm 1*
James, William Knowles 1852-1927 *WhAm 1*
James, William M 1901-1957 *WhAm 3*
James, William P 1870-1940 *WhAm 1*
James, William Roderick 1892-1942 *EncAAH*
James, William Stubbs 1892-1964 *WhAm 4*
Jameson, Charles Davis 1827-1862 *ApCAB, Drake, TwCBDA*
Jameson, David 1752-1839 *ApCAB, Drake*
Jameson, Edwin Cornell 1864-1945 *NatCAB 37, WhAm 2*
Jameson, Ephraim Orcutt 1832- *TwCBDA*
Jameson, Henry 1848-1924 *NatCAB 10, WhAm 1*
Jameson, Henry Washington 1865- *WhoColR*
Jameson, Horatio Gates 1778-1855 *DcAmB, NatCAB 15, WhAm H*

Jameson, James Drane 1850-1925 *NatCAB 21*
Jameson, John 1802-1857 *BiAUS, BiDrAC, TwCBDA, WhAm H*
Jameson, John Alexander 1824-1890 *ApCAB, DcAmB, Drake, TwCBDA, WhAm H*
Jameson, John Alexander 1868-1937 *NatCAB 27*
Jameson, John Butler 1873-1960 *NatCAB 50, WhAm 5*
Jameson, John Franklin 1859-1937 *AmBi, ApCAB Sup, DcAmB S2, NatCAB 10, TwCBDA, WebAB, WhAm 1*
Jameson, Sir Leander Starr 1853-1917 *McGEWB*
Jameson, Maud Eaton 1866- *WomWWA 14*
Jameson, P Henry 1848- *WhAm 4*
Jameson, Patrick Henry 1824- *ApCAB, NatCAB 9, WhAm 4*
Jameson, Robert 1774-1854 *DcScB*
Jameson, Robert Willis 1875-1953 *WhAm 3*
Jameson, Rose Howe 1865- *WomWWA 14*
Jameson, Russell Parsons 1878-1954 *WhAm 3*
Jameson, Samuel Young 1859-1921 *NatCAB 25*
Jameson, William 1791-1873 *ApCAB, TwCBDA*
Jami 1414-1492 *McGEWB*
Jamieson, Charles Clark 1866-1935 *WhAm 1*
Jamieson, Douglas James 1906-1973 *WhAm 6*
Jamieson, Edmund Scudder 1886-1941 *WhAm 1*
Jamieson, Francis Anthony 1904-1960 *NatCAB 43, WhAm 3*
Jamieson, Guy Arthur 1867- *WhAm 4*
Jamieson, John Quentin 1855-1932 *NatCAB 37*
Jamieson, Louise Campbell 1862- *WomWWA 14*
Jamieson, Mary Scudder 1858- *WomWWA 14*
Jamieson, Robert Cary 1881-1946 *WhAm 2*
Jamieson, Thomas N 1848- *WhAm 4*
Jamieson, Walter Wilson 1857- *NatCAB 14*
Jamieson, William Darius 1873-1949 *BiDrAC, WhAm 2*
Jamieson, William Edward 1907-1962 *WhAm 4*
Jamison, Alcinous Berton 1851- *NatCAB 6*
Jamison, Alice Peyton 1860- *WomWWA 14*
Jamison, Alpha Pierce 1875- *WhAm 5*
Jamison, Atha Thomas 1866-1947 *WhAm 2*
Jamison, Cecelia Viets 1848-1909 *TwCBDA*
Jamison, Cecilia Viets 1848-1909 *WhAm 4*
Jamison, Cecilia Viets Dakin Hamilton 1837-1909 *DcAmB*
Jamison, Charles Laselle 1885-1965 *WhAm 4*
Jamison, David 1660-1739 *DcAmB, NatCAB 12, WhAm H*
Jamison, David Flavel 1810-1864 *DcAmB*
Jamison, David Lee 1867-1947 *WhAm 2*
Jamison, George W d1868 *NewYHSD*
Jamison, John Henry 1892-1954 *NatCAB 43*
Jamison, John P *NewYHSD*
Jamison, Joseph Warren 1868-1940 *WhAm 1*
Jamison, Minnie Lou 1866- *WhAm 4*
Jamison, Monroe Franklin 1849-1918 *WhAm 1, WhoColR*
Jamison, Paul Bailey 1877- *WhAm 5*
Jamison, Robert H 1884-1965 *WhAm 4*
Jamison, Thomas Worth, Jr. 1893-1964 *WhAm 4*
Jamison, William Arbuckle 1863-1928 *WhAm 1*
Jamison, William Jacob 1865-1926 *NatCAB 23*
Jamshid Ibn Mahmud Al-Kashi *DcScB*
Janacek, Leos 1854-1928 *McGEWB*
Janauschek, Francesca Romana Magdalena 1829-1904 *NotAW*
Janauschek, Francesca Romana Magdalena 1830-1904 *NatCAB 10*
Janauschek, Franziska Magdalena Romance 1830-1904 *DcAmB*
Janaushek, Francesca 1830-1904 *WhAm 1*
Jane, Robert Stephen 1898-1958 *WhAm 3*
Janes, Edmund Storer 1807-1876 *ApCAB, Drake, NatCAB 10, TwCBDA*
Janes, Edward Houghton 1820-1893 *ApCAB, NatCAB 8*
Janes, Edwin L 1807-1875 *ApCAB*
Janes, George Milton 1869-1936 *WhAm 1*
Janes, Henry Fisk 1792-1879 *BiAUS, BiDrAC, TwCBDA, WhAm H*
Janes, John Valle 1898-1972 *WhAm 5*

Janes, Lewis George 1844-1901 *DcAmB, NatCAB 12, TwCBDA, WhAm H, WhAm 1*
Janes, Martha Waldron 1832- *AmWom*
Janet, Henry *NewYHSD*
Janet, Pierre Marie Felix 1859-1947 *McGEWB*
Janeway, Edward Gamaliel 1841-1911 *AmBi, ApCAB, DcAmB, NatCAB 13, TwCBDA, WhAm 1*
Janeway, Frank Latimer 1880-1964 *NatCAB 51, WhAm 4*
Janeway, Henry Harrington 1873-1921 *NatCAB 26*
Janeway, Jacob Jones 1774-1858 *ApCAB, NatCAB 13, TwCBDA*
Janeway, Jacob Jones 1776-1858 *Drake*
Janeway, Phineas Allen 1868-1946 *WhAm 4*
Janeway, Theodore Caldwell 1872-1917 *AmBi, DcAmB, NatCAB 17, WhAm 1*
Janeway, Thomas Leiper 1805-1895 *TwCBDA*
Janeway, William Richard 1848-1928 *NatCAB 22*
Janin, Flora Earle 1882- *WomWWA 14*
Janin, Louis 1837-1914 *DcAmB, NatCAB 18*
Janis, Elsie 1889-1956 *WhAm 3, WomWWA 14*
Janisse, Denis R 1898-1962 *WhAm 4*
Janiszewski, Zygmunt 1888-1920 *DcScB*
Janney, Asa Moore 1802-1871 *ApCAB*
Janney, Eli Hamilton 1831-1912 *DcAmB*
Janney, Frances Moale 1882- *WomWWA 14*
Janney, Nelson Wilson 1881-1935 *NatCAB 26*
Janney, Oliver Edward 1856-1930 *DcAmB, NatCAB 33, WhAm 1*
Janney, Russell 1883-1963 *WhAm 4*
Janney, Samuel M 1801-1880 *Drake*
Janney, Samuel Macpherson 1801-1880 *ApCAB*
Janney, Samuel McPherson 1801-1880 *DcAmB, NatCAB 7, TwCBDA, WhAm H*
Janney, Thomas 1634-1696 *ApCAB, Drake*
Janney, Thomas B 1838-1924 *WhAm 1*
Janney, Walter Thompson 1878-1969 *NatCAB 56*
Jannotta, Alfred Vernon 1894-1972 *WhAm 5*
Jannsens, Francis 1847- *ApCAB*
Jansen, Cornelis 1585-1638 *McGEWB*
Jansen, Ernest George d1959 *WhAm 3*
Jansen, Marie 1881-1914 *WhAm 1*
Jansen, Olaus 1714-1778 *ApCAB*
Jansen, Peter 1852- *WhAm 4*
Jansen, Reinier d1705? *TwCBDA*
Jansen, Reinier d1706 *DcAmB, WhAm H*
Jansen, Reynier d1706 *ApCAB*
Jansen, William 1887- *WhAm 4A*
Jansen, Zacharias 1588-1628? *DcScB*
Jansen Van Ilpendam, Jan d1685? *ApCAB*
Jansky, Karl Guthe 1905-1950 *AsBiEn, DcAmB S4, WebAB*
Janson, Christian William 1879-1950 *NatCAB 38*
Janson, Kristofer Nagel 1841-1917 *ApCAB, DcAmB*
Janss, Peter W 1904-1969 *WhAm 5*
Janssen, E C d1946 *WhAm 2*
Janssen, Henry 1866-1948 *NatCAB 35, WhAm 2*
Janssen, John 1835-1913 *ApCAB Sup, NatCAB 12, TwCBDA, WhAm 1*
Janssen, Pierre Jules Cesar 1824-1907 *AsBiEn, DcScB*
Janssens, Francis 1843-1897 *DcAmB, NatCAB 7, TwCBDA, WhAm H*
Jansson, Arthur August 1890- *IIBEAAW*
Jansson, Axel Julius 1885-1963 *NatCAB 52*
Jansson, Edward Fritiof 1894-1963 *WhAm 4*
January, Anna L 1879- *WomWWA 14*
January, Derick A 1813-1879 *NatCAB 16*
January, William Louis 1853-1931 *NatCAB 32, WhAm 4*
Janvier, Albert Wilson *NewYHSD*
Janvier, Caesar A Rodney 1861-1928 *WhAm 1*
Janvier, Catharine Ann d1923 *WhAm 1*
Janvier, Catharine Ann Drinker 1841-1922 *DcAmB*
Janvier, Catherine Drinker *WomWWA 14*
Janvier, Charles 1857-1927 *WhAm 1*
Janvier, Francis DeHaes 1775?-1824 *NewYHSD*
Janvier, Levi 1816-1864 *ApCAB*

Janvier, Margaret Thompson 1844-1913
  WomWWA 14
Janvier, Margaret Thomson 1844-1913 DcAmB,
  NatCAB 12, WhAm 1
Janvier, Thomas Allibone 1849-1913
  ApCAB Sup, DcAmB, NatCAB 12,
  TwCBDA, WhAm 1
Janvrin, Edmund Randolph Peaslee 1884-1973
  NatCAB 57
Janvrin, Joseph Edward 1839-1911 NatCAB 4,
  WhAm 1
Janvrin, Mary W 1830-1870 Drake
Janzen, Assar Gotrik 1904-1971 WhAm 5
Janzen, Danile H 1906-1970 WhAm 5
Jaqua, Albert Roscoe 1893-1957 NatCAB 49,
  WhAm 3
Jaqua, Ernest James 1882-1972 WhAm 5
Jaqua, Robert Erwin 1918-1964 NatCAB 50
Jaques, Alfred 1857-1937 WhAm 1
Jaques, Bertha Evelyn 1863-1941 WhAm 2,
  WomWWA 14
Jaques, Charles Everett 1873-1955 WhAm 3
Jaques, Francis Lee 1887-1969 WhAm 5
Jaques, Herbert 1857-1916 ApCAB X,
  WhAm 1
Jaques, Jabez Robert 1828-1892 TwCBDA
Jaques, Willard Wight 1875-1940 NatCAB 38,
  WhAm 1
Jaques, William Henry 1848-1916 WhAm 1
Jaquess, James Frazier 1819-1898 DcAmB,
  WhAm H
Jaquess, William Thomas 1858- WhAm 4
Jaquet, Augustus NewYHSD
Jaquett, Warren Reed 1881-1960 NatCAB 49
Jaquette, William Alderman 1876-1945
  NatCAB 35
Jaquez, Christoval d1555 ApCAB
Jaquith, Harold Clarence 1888-1943 WhAm 2
Jarauta, Cenobio d1848 ApCAB
Jarava, Manuel 1621-1673 ApCAB
Jaray, Luis De Cespedes d1640 ApCAB
Jarboe, Henry Lee 1874-1961 WhAm 4
Jarcho, Julius 1880-1963 NatCAB 50
Jardella NewYHSD
Jardine, David 1840-1892 WhAm H
Jardine, James Tertius 1881-1954 WhAm 3
Jardine, John Bishop 1914-1963 NatCAB 54
Jardine, John Earle 1871-1956 WhAm 3
Jardine, John Earle, Jr. 1899-1972 WhAm 5
Jardine, Joseph P NewYHSD
Jardine, Robert 1840- ApCAB
Jardine, William Marion 1879-1955 BiDrUSE,
  DcAmB S5, EncAAH, WhAm 3
Jardins, Charles Francois Des 1729-1791
  ApCAB
Jarecki, Charles 1869-1952 NatCAB 39
Jarecki, Frank Joseph 1875-1966 NatCAB 52
Jarecky, Herman 1863- WhAm 4
Jarman, John 1915- BiDrAC
Jarman, Joseph Leonard 1867-1947 WhAm 2
Jarman, Lewis Wilson 1880-1957 WhAm 3
Jarman, Pete 1892-1955 BiDrAC, NatCAB 46,
  WhAm 3, WhAmP
Jarman, Sanderford 1884-1954 NatCAB 40,
  WhAm 3
Jarnac, Gaston Louis De 1758-1818 ApCAB
Jarnagin, Milton Preston 1881- WhAm 6
Jarnagin, Spencer d1851 BiAUS
Jarnagin, Spencer 1792-1853 BiDrAC,
  WhAm H
Jarnagin, Spencer 1793?-1851 ApCAB,
  NatCAB 11
Jarnette, Evelyn Magruder AmWom
Jarnigan, Spencer 1792?-1851 TwCBDA
Jarque, Francisco 1636-1691 ApCAB
Jarratt, Devereaux 1733-1801 WhAm H
Jarratt, Devereux 1733-1801 ApCAB, DcAmB,
  DcAmReB
Jarratt, Hill 1906-1969 WhAm 5
Jarrell, Albert Polk 1907-1967 WhAm 4,
  WhAm 5
Jarrell, Charles Crawford 1874- WhAm 5
Jarrell, Randall 1914-1965 WebAB, WhAm 4
Jarrett, Benjamin 1881-1944 BiDrAC,
  WhAm 2
Jarrett, Cora Hardy 1877- WhAm 5,
  WomWWA 14
Jarrett, Delta Ira 1874-1949 NatCAB 37

Jarrett, Devereux see also Jarratt, Devereux
Jarrett, Edwin Seton 1862-1938 WhAm 1
Jarrett, Harry B 1898-1974 WhAm 6
Jarrett, William Ambrose 1886-1958 WhAm 3
Jarrett, William Paul 1877- WhAm 1
Jarrett, William Paul 1877-1929 BiDrAC,
  WhAmP
Jarrett, William Paul 1877-1930 WhAm 2
Jarric, Louis Etienne 1757-1791 ApCAB
Jarrold, Ernest 1850- WhAm 4
Jars, Antoine Gabriel 1732-1769 DcScB
Jarvass, Jacob NewYHSD
Jarves, Deming 1790-1869 BnEnAmA, DcAmB,
  NatCAB 27
Jarves, James Jackson 1818-1888 AmBi,
  BnEnAmA, DcAmB, Drake, TwCBDA,
  WebAB, WhAm H
Jarves, James Jackson 1820-1888 ApCAB,
  NatCAB 11
Jarvie, James Newbegin 1853-1929 NatCAB 22,
  WhAm 1
Jarvie, William 1841- NatCAB 12
Jarvis, Abraham 1739-1813 ApCAB, DcAmB,
  Drake, NatCAB 3, TwCBDA
Jarvis, Anna WomWWA 14
Jarvis, Charles 1748-1807 ApCAB, Drake
Jarvis, Charles H 1837-1895 DcAmB,
  WhAm H
Jarvis, Charles Maples 1856- NatCAB 11
Jarvis, Charles Wesley 1812-1868 NewYHSD
Jarvis, Chester Deacon 1876-1948 WhAm 2
Jarvis, David Henry 1852- NatCAB 13
Jarvis, David Henry 1881- WhAm 4
Jarvis, DeForest Clinton 1881-1966 NatCAB 53,
  WhAm 4
Jarvis, Deming 1790?-1869 WhAm H
Jarvis, Edward 1803-1884 ApCAB, DcAmB,
  NatCAB 12, WhAm H
Jarvis, George Atwater 1806-1893 ApCAB Sup,
  TwCBDA
Jarvis, George Cyprian 1834- NatCAB 5,
  TwCBDA
Jarvis, George Tibbals 1869- WhAm 5
Jarvis, H Gildersleeve 1885-1968 NatCAB 54
Jarvis, Harry Aydelotte 1909-1972 WhAm 5
Jarvis, Hezekiah 1746-1838 NatCAB 3
Jarvis, Holly Clyde 1893-1967 NatCAB 52
Jarvis, James Armstead 1904-1968 NatCAB 54
Jarvis, John Wesley 1780-1840 ApCAB,
  BnEnAmA, Drake, NewYHSD
Jarvis, John Wesley 1781-1839 AmBi, DcAmB,
  WhAm H
Jarvis, Leonard 1781-1854 BiDrAC, TwCBDA,
  WhAm H, WhAmP
Jarvis, Leonard 1782-1854 BiAUS
Jarvis, Miss M IIBEAAW
Jarvis, Marshall Northam 1886-1962
  NatCAB 50
Jarvis, Mary D WomWWA 14
Jarvis, Noah 1768-1842 NatCAB 3
Jarvis, Robert Edward Lee 1870- WhAm 5
Jarvis, Russell 1791-1853 ApCAB
Jarvis, Samuel NewYHSD
Jarvis, Samuel Farmar 1786-1851 ApCAB,
  NatCAB 3, TwCBDA
Jarvis, Samuel Farmer 1786-1851 Drake
Jarvis, Samuel Miller 1853-1913 NatCAB 15,
  WhAm 1
Jarvis, Samuel Peters 1820- ApCAB Sup
Jarvis, Thomas Jordan 1836-1915 AmBi,
  ApCAB, BiDrAC, DcAmB, NatCAB 4,
  TwCBDA, WhAm 1
Jarvis, Thomas Neilson 1854-1926 WhAm 2
Jarvis, VanZandt 1873-1940 NatCAB 48
Jarvis, W Frederick IIBEAAW
Jarvis, William 1770-1859 ApCAB, DcAmB,
  Drake, NatCAB 12, TwCBDA, WhAm H
Jarvis, William 1796-1871 NatCAB 3
Jarvis, William Chapman 1855-1895 DcAmB,
  WhAm H
Jason, William Charles 1859- TwCBDA
Jasper, William 1750?-1779 AmBi, ApCAB,
  DcAmB, Drake, NatCAB 1, TwCBDA,
  WebAMB, WhAm H
Jaspers, Karl 1883-1969 McGEWB
Jasspon, William Henry 1888-1951 WhAm 3
Jastram, Edward Perkins 1873-1954 WhAm 3
Jastrow, Joseph 1863-1944 DcAmB S3,

NatCAB 11, TwCBDA, WhAm 2
Jastrow, Marcus 1829-1903 AmBi, DcAmB,
  NatCAB 11, WhAm 1
Jastrow, Morris 1861-1921 AmBi, DcAmB,
  NatCAB 11, TwCBDA, WhAm 1
Jastrow, Rachel Szold 1865- WomWWA 14
Jaszi, Oscar 1875-1957 WhAm 3
Jaubert, Edouard Etienne 1629-1698 ApCAB
Jaucourt, Paul De 1754-1793 ApCAB
Jaume, Alexander Charles d1858 NewYHSD
Jaume, J NewYHSD
Jauncey, George Eric MacDonnell 1888-1947
  WhAm 2
Jauregui, Guillermo Patterson Y 1868-1937
  WhAm 1
Jauregui Y Aguilar, Domingo 1705-1758 ApCAB
Jauregui Y Aldecoa, Agustin De 1708-1784
  ApCAB
Jaures, Jean-Leon 1859-1914 McGEWB,
  WhoMilH
Jaureybo I d1514 ApCAB
Jaureybo II ApCAB
Javis, Abraham 1740-1813 WhAm H
Javits, Benjamin Abraham 1894-1973
  NatCAB 57, WhAm 6
Javits, Jacob Koppel 1904- BiDrAC
Jawara, Sir Dauda Kairaba 1924- McGEWB
Jawhari, Al-Abbas Ibn Said, Al- DcScB
Jay, Allen 1831-1910 DcAmB, NatCAB 24
Jay, Clarence Hollingsworth 1886-1957
  WhAm 3
Jay, DeLancey Kane 1881-1941 NatCAB 42
Jay, Sir James 1732-1815 ApCAB, DcAmB,
  Drake, TwCBDA, WhAm H
Jay, John 1745-1829 AmBi, ApCAB, BiAUS,
  BiDrAC, BiDrUSE, DcAmB, Drake,
  EncAAH, EncAB, McGEWB, NatCAB 1,
  TwCBDA, WebAB, WhAm H, WhAmP
Jay, John 1817-1894 AmBi, ApCAB, BiAUS,
  DcAmB, Drake, NatCAB 7, TwCBDA,
  WhAm H
Jay, John Clarkson 1808-1891 ApCAB,
  NatCAB 6, TwCBDA
Jay, John Clarkson 1844-1923 NatCAB 6
Jay, John Clarkson 1880-1941 NatCAB 36,
  WhAm 1
Jay, John Edwin 1868- WhAm 4
Jay, John Henry 1889-1943 NatCAB 32
Jay, Lawrence Merton 1878-1934 ApCAB X,
  WhAm 1
Jay, Mary NewYHSD
Jay, Mary Rutherfurd 1872-1953 WhAm 3
Jay, Milton 1833-1905 WhAm 1
Jay, Nelson Dean 1883-1972 WhAm 5
Jay, Peter Augustus 1776-1843 ApCAB,
  DcAmB, Drake, NatCAB 3, TwCBDA,
  WhAm H
Jay, Peter Augustus 1877-1933 NatCAB 44,
  WhAm 1
Jay, Pierre 1870-1949 WhAm 2
Jay, Robert W NewYHSD
Jay, William 1789-1858 AmBi, ApCAB,
  DcAmB, Drake, McGEWB, NatCAB 8,
  TwCBDA, WhAm H
Jay, William 1792-1837 BnEnAmA
Jay, William 1794-1837 WhAm H
Jay, William 1841-1915 NatCAB 9,
  NatCAB 24, TwCBDA, WhAm 1
Jayasimha 1686-1743 DcScB
Jaycox, Walter Husted 1863-1927 WhAm 1
Jaymes, Sully 1878- WhoColR
Jayne, Anselm Helm 1856- WhAm 4
Jayne, Benaiah Gustin 1831- WhAm 4
Jayne, Caroline Furness 1873-1909 WhAm 1
Jayne, Clarence D 1902-1963 BiDAmEd
Jayne, David 1799-1866 ApCAB
Jayne, E Stanley 1888-1965 NatCAB 52
Jayne, Harry Walker 1857-1910 NatCAB 19
Jayne, Henry LaBarre 1857-1920 NatCAB 19,
  WhAm 1
Jayne, Horace Fort 1859-1913 ApCAB,
  DcAmB, NatCAB 13, TwCBDA,
  WhAm 1
Jayne, Horace Howard Furness 1898-1975
  WhAm 6
Jayne, Joseph Lee 1863-1928 WhAm 1
Jayne, Trafford Newton 1868- NatCAB 6
Jayne, Walter Addison 1853-1929 WhAm 1

Jayne, Wilfred Hudson 1888-1961 *NatCAB 47*
Jayne, William 1826-1916 *BiAUS, BiDrAC*
Jaynes, Allan Brown 1879-1920 *NatCAB 19, WhAm 1*
Jayyani, Abu Abd Allah M Ibn Muadh, Al-989?-1079? *DcScB*
Jazari, Badi Al-Zaman Abul-Izz, Al-*DcScB Sup*
Jazari, Badial-Zaman, Al-Razzaz, Al- *DcScB*
Jean De Meun 1240?-1305 *McGEWB*
Jean, Sister Anne 1910-1973 *WhAm 5*
Jean, Sally Lucas 1878-1971 *WhAm 5*
Jeanes, Anna Thomas 1822-1907 *DcAmB, NotAW*
Jeanes, Jacob 1800-1877 *NatCAB 3*
Jeanmard, Jules Benjamin 1879-1957 *NatCAB 44, WhAm 3*
Jeanneret, Henry A *NewYHSD*
Jeanneret, Ulysses *NewYHSD*
Jeannin, Jean Baptiste 1792?-1863 *NewYHSD*
Jeannin, T B *NewYHSD*
Jeannot, William Eliodore 1866-1938 *NatCAB 29*
Jeans, Sir James Hopwood 1877-1946 *AsBiEn, DcScB, McGEWB*
Jeans, Philip Charles 1883-1952 *WhAm 3*
Jeaurat, Edme-Sebastien 1724-1803 *DcScB*
Jebavy, Ladimer George 1880-1964 *NatCAB 50*
Jebens, Henry Hans 1880-1950 *NatCAB 40*
Jeck, George G 1875- *WhAm 5*
Jeck, Howard Sheffield 1883-1949 *NatCAB 38*
Jefferies, Emily Brown 1921- *WhAm 6*
Jefferies, Richard Manning 1889-1964 *NatCAB 51*
Jefferis, Albert Webb 1868-1942 *BiDrAC, WhAm 4*
Jefferis, Charles Robinson 1879-1965 *NatCAB 51*
Jefferis, Marea Wood *AmWom*
Jefferis, William Walter 1820-1906 *NatCAB 15, WhAm 1*
Jeffers, Clyde G 1881- *WhAm 6*
Jeffers, Eliakim Tupper 1841-1915 *NatCAB 25, TwCBDA, WhAm 1*
Jeffers, Henry William 1871-1953 *WhAm 3*
Jeffers, John Robinson 1887-1962 *McGEWB*
Jeffers, Katharine R 1907-1959 *WhAm 3*
Jeffers, Lamar 1888- *BiDrAC*
Jeffers, LeRoy 1878-1926 *WhAm 1*
Jeffers, Mary 1868- *WomWWA 14*
Jeffers, Paul Eells 1889-1953 *NatCAB 42*
Jeffers, Robinson 1887-1962 *WebAB, WhAm 4*
Jeffers, William Hamilton 1838-1914 *WhAm 1*
Jeffers, William Martin 1876-1953 *DcAmB S5, WhAm 3*
Jeffers, William Nicholson 1824-1883 *ApCAB, DcAmB, NatCAB 4, TwCBDA, WhAm H*
Jefferson, Benjamin Lafayette 1871-1950 *NatCAB 40, WhAm 5*
Jefferson, Bradley Carter 1894-1964 *WhAm 4*
Jefferson, C Frederic 1888-1971 *NatCAB 56*
Jefferson, Charles Edward 1860-1937 *AmBi, DcAmB S2, NatCAB 27, WhAm 1*
Jefferson, Charles William 1888-1959 *NatCAB 46*
Jefferson, Clarence Ernest 1889-1960 *WhAm 4*
Jefferson, Cornelia 1835-1899 *TwCBDA*
Jefferson, Cornelia Burke *WhAm H*
Jefferson, Floyd Wellman 1878-1972 *WhAm 5, WhAm 6*
Jefferson, Floyd Wellman, Jr. 1911-1965 *NatCAB 52, WhAm 4*
Jefferson, J Rupert 1869- *WhoColR*
Jefferson, James Alvin 1871- *WhoColR*
Jefferson, John Percival 1852-1934 *NatCAB 26, WhAm 1*
Jefferson, Joseph 1774-1832 *ApCAB, DcAmB, NewYHSD, TwCBDA, WhAm H*
Jefferson, Joseph 1776-1832 *Drake*
Jefferson, Joseph 1804-1842 *ApCAB, NewYHSD, TwCBDA*
Jefferson, Joseph 1829-1905 *AmBi, ApCAB, DcAmB, Drake, McGEWB, NatCAB 1, NewYHSD, TwCBDA, WebAB, WhAm 1*
Jefferson, Joseph 1869-1919 *WhAm 1*

Jefferson, Lottie Adelia 1885- *WhoColR*
Jefferson, Mark Sylvester William 1863-1949 *BiDAmEd, DcAmB S4, WhAm 4*
Jefferson, Martha Wayles Skelton 1748-1782 *AmWom, ApCAB, NatCAB 3, NotAW, TwCBDA, WhAm H*
Jefferson, Robert 1881-1968 *WhAm 4*
Jefferson, Thomas 1743-1826 *AmBi, ApCAB, AsBiEn, BiAUS, BiDAmEd, BiDrAC, BiDrUSE, BnEnAmA, DcAmB, DcAmLiB, DcAmReB, DcScB, Drake, EncAAH, EncAB, McGEWB, NatCAB 3, REnAW, TwCBDA, WebAB, WhAm H, WhAmP*
Jefferson, Wilson 1879- *WhoColR*
Jeffery, Edward Turner 1843-1927 *ApCAB Sup, DcAmB, WhAm 1*
Jeffery, Edward Turner 1844-1927 *NatCAB 8*
Jeffery, Elmore Berry 1870-1929 *NatCAB 23, WhAm 1, WhAm 1C*
Jeffery, Isadore Gilbert 1840?- *AmWom*
Jeffery, Joseph Arthur 1873-1944 *NatCAB 38*
Jeffery, Robert Emmett 1875-1935 *WhAm 1*
Jeffery, Rosa Griffith Vertner Johnson 1828-1894 *WhAm H*
Jeffery, William Oats 1873-1942 *NatCAB 31*
Jeffery, William Prentiss 1878- *WhAm 3*
Jefferys, Charles William 1869-1951 *IlBEAAW, WhAm 3*
Jefferys, Edward Miller 1865-1946 *WhAm 2*
Jefferys, Thomas R *NewYHSD*
Jefferys, William Hamilton 1871-1945 *WhAm 2*
Jeffords, Elza 1826-1885 *BiDrAC, WhAm H*
Jeffords, Joe Lawrence 1912-1974 *WhAm 6*
Jeffords, Lawrence Suggs 1892-1974 *WhAm 6*
Jeffords, Olin Merrill 1890-1964 *NatCAB 52, WhAm 4*
Jeffords, Thomas J 1832-1914 *REnAW*
Jeffrays *NewYHSD*
Jeffress, Thomas Fox 1859-1938 *NatCAB 29*
Jeffrey, Benjamin *NewYHSD*
Jeffrey, Edward Charles 1866-1952 *DcAmB S5, DcScB, NatCAB 39, WhAm 4*
Jeffrey, Frank Rumer 1889-1940 *WhAm 2*
Jeffrey, Harry Palmer 1901- *BiDrAC*
Jeffrey, Jennette Atwater Street 1872- *WomWWA 14*
Jeffrey, Joseph Andrew 1836-1928 *DcAmB, NatCAB 12, NatCAB 30*
Jeffrey, Max Leroy 1887-1971 *NatCAB 56*
Jeffrey, Robert Hutchins 1873- *WhAm 6*
Jeffrey, Rosa Griffith Vertner Johnson 1828-1894 *DcAmB*
Jeffrey, Rosa Vertner Griffith 1828-1894 *AmWom, ApCAB, NatCAB 11*
Jeffreys, Sir Harold 1891- *AsBiEn, McGEWB*
Jeffreys, Herbert d1678 *NatCAB 13*
Jeffreys, John Gwyn 1809-1885 *DcScB*
Jeffries, Benjamin Joy 1833-1915 *ApCAB, DcAmB, NatCAB 24, TwCBDA, WhAm 1*
Jeffries, Edward J 1900-1950 *WhAm 3*
Jeffries, James Jackson 1875-1953 *DcAmB S5*
Jeffries, John 1744?-1819 *AmBi, DcAmB, NatCAB 24*
Jeffries, John 1745-1819 *ApCAB, Drake, WebAB, WhAm H*
Jeffries, Louis Eugene 1868-1932 *WhAm 1*
Jeffries, Millard Dudley 1855-1936 *WhAm 1*
Jeffries, Noah L 1828- *BiAUS*
Jeffries, Ruben Lee 1902-1964 *NatCAB 51*
Jeffries, Walter Sooy 1893-1954 *BiDrAC, WhAm 3*
Jeffries, Zay 1888-1965 *DcScB, WhAm 4*
Jeffris, Malcolm George 1862-1933 *WhAm 1*
Jeffs, Charles Richardson 1893-1959 *WhAm 3*
Jeidels, Otto 1882-1947 *WhAm 2*
Jelke, F Frazier 1880-1953 *NatCAB 40*
Jelke, Ferdinand Frazier 1886-1953 *WhAm 3*
Jelke, John Faris 1887-1965 *WhAm 4*
Jelks, James Thomas 1849- *NatCAB 7, WhAm 4*
Jelks, John Lemuel 1870-1945 *WhAm 2*
Jelks, William Dorsey 1855-1931 *NatCAB 13, WhAm 1*
Jelleff, Frank Ronaldson 1878-1961 *NatCAB 47*
Jellema, William Harry, Jr. 1933-1975 *WhAm 6*

Jellicoe, John Rushworth Jellicoe, Earl 1859-1935 *McGEWB, WhoMilH*
Jelliff, Horatio F 1844-1892 *WhAm H*
Jelliffe, Smith Ely 1866-1945 *DcAmB S3, NatCAB 33, WhAm 2*
Jellinek, Elvin M 1890-1963 *WhAm 4*
Jellinghaus, C L 1889-1957 *WhAm 3*
Jellison, Walter Fremont 1862- *WhAm 4*
Jelly, George Frederick 1842-1911 *NatCAB 15*
Jemison, David Vivian 1875-1954 *WhAm 3*
Jemison, Mary d1833 *NatCAB 15*
Jemison, Mary 1742?-1833 *ApCAB*
Jemison, Mary 1743-1833 *AmBi, DcAmB, NotAW, WhAm H*
Jemison, Robert 1802-1871 *ApCAB, BiDConf*
Jemison, Robert, Jr. 1878- *WhAm 6*
Jemison, Robert, Sr. 1853-1927 *WhAm 1*
Jenckes, Adaline Louise *WomWWA 14*
Jenckes, Earl Stanton 1872-1956 *NatCAB 45*
Jenckes, George Augustine 1900-1966 *NatCAB 53*
Jenckes, George Washington 1829-1913 *NatCAB 45*
Jenckes, Joseph 1602-1683 *ApCAB, DcAmB, NewYHSD, TwCBDA*
Jenckes, Joseph 1623-1717 *WhAm H*
Jenckes, Joseph 1632-1716 *ApCAB*
Jenckes, Joseph 1632-1717 *DcAmB, TwCBDA*
Jenckes, Joseph 1656-1740 *AmBi, ApCAB, DcAmB, NatCAB 10, TwCBDA, WhAm H*
Jenckes, Joseph Sherburne, Jr. 1908-1970 *WhAm 5*
Jenckes, Lawrence Bates 1867-1922 *NatCAB 19*
Jenckes, Marcien 1900-1971 *WhAm 5*
Jenckes, Sarah Pratt *WomWWA 14*
Jenckes, Thomas Allen 1818-1875 *AmBi, ApCAB, BiAUS, BiDrAC, DcAmB, NatCAB 8, TwCBDA, WhAm H, WhAmP*
Jenckes, Thomas Allen 1856-1928 *NatCAB 27*
Jenckes, Virginia Ellis 1877-1975 *BiDrAC*
Jenckes, Virginia Ellis 1882-1975 *WhAm 6*
Jencks, Andrew Edmund 1871-1928 *NatCAB 21*
Jencks, Francis Mankin 1846-1918 *ApCAB X, NatCAB 18*
Jencks, Millard Henry 1881-1945 *NatCAB 34, WhAm 2*
Jenifer, Daniel 1723-1790 *ApCAB, BiAUS, BiDrAC, Drake, WhAm H, WhAmP*
Jenifer, Daniel 1791-1855 *ApCAB, BiAUS, BiDrAC, Drake, NatCAB 13, TwCBDA, WhAm H, WhAmP*
Jenifer, Daniel Of St. Thomas 1723-1790 *DcAmB, NatCAB 2, TwCBDA*
Jenifer, John Thomas 1835- *WhoColR*
Jenings, Edmund 1659-1727 *NatCAB 13*
Jenison, Austin 1893-1954 *NatCAB 42*
Jenison, Edward Halsey 1907- *BiDrAC*
Jenison, Madge C 1874- *WomWWA 14*
Jenison, Silas H 1791-1849 *BiAUS, Drake, NatCAB 8*
Jenkin, Henry Charles Fleeming 1833-1885 *DcScB*
Jenkins, Ab 1883-1956 *NatCAB 45*
Jenkins, Albert Gallatin 1830-1864 *AmBi, ApCAB, BiAUS, BiDConf, BiDrAC, DcAmB, Drake, NatCAB 5, TwCBDA, WhAm H, WhAmP*
Jenkins, Alfred Alexander, Jr. 1899-1959 *WhAm 3*
Jenkins, Alice Thornton 1857- *WomWWA 14*
Jenkins, Anna Almy 1790-1849 *ApCAB, Drake*
Jenkins, Anna Spalding 1869- *WomWWA 14*
Jenkins, Arthur 1851-1903 *NatCAB 4, NatCAB 25, WhAm 1*
Jenkins, Arthur C, Jr. 1918-1963 *NatCAB 50*
Jenkins, Burris, Jr. 1896-1966 *WhAm 4*
Jenkins, Burris Atkins 1869-1945 *NatCAB 13, WhAm 2*
Jenkins, Charles Francis 1865-1951 *NatCAB 43, WhAm 3*
Jenkins, Charles Francis 1867-1934 *AmBi, WhAm 1*
Jenkins, Charles Jones 1805-1883 *AmBi, ApCAB, BiAUS, BiDConf, DcAmB,*

NatCAB 1, TwCBDA, WhAm H
Jenkins, Charles Milton 1854-1929 NatCAB 21
Jenkins, Charles Rush 1871- WhAm 5
Jenkins, Charles Waldo 1820?- NewYHSD
Jenkins, Claudius Bissell 1865-1940 WhAm 3
Jenkins, Daniel Edwards 1866-1927 NatCAB 21,
  TwCBDA, WhAm 1
Jenkins, Daniel S NewYHSD
Jenkins, David Hibbs 1916-1968 NatCAB 55
Jenkins, David P 1823-1915 NatCAB 17
Jenkins, David Rhys 1865-1949 WhAm 3
Jenkins, Douglas 1880-1961 NatCAB 49,
  WhAm 6
Jenkins, E Fellows 1844-1923 WhAm 1
Jenkins, Edward 1838- ApCAB
Jenkins, Edward Corbin 1875- WhAm 5
Jenkins, Edward Elmer 1873- WhAm 5
Jenkins, Edward Hopkins 1850-1931 DcAmB,
  NatCAB 24, WhAm 1
Jenkins, Farrand Sayre 1884-1959 NatCAB 47
Jenkins, Florence Foster d1944 WhAm 4
Jenkins, Frances 1872- WhAm 5,
  WomWWA 14
Jenkins, Frances C 1826- AmWom
Jenkins, Francis A NewYHSD
Jenkins, Francis A 1899-1960 WhAm 4
Jenkins, Frank Edwin 1854-1934 NatCAB 25,
  WhAm 4
Jenkins, Frederick Warren 1878-1940 WhAm 1
Jenkins, George Carrell 1836-1930 NatCAB 27
Jenkins, George Franklin 1842-1914 WhAm 1
Jenkins, George Washington Allston 1816-1907
  NewYHSD
Jenkins, Gertrude Halbert WomWWA 14
Jenkins, Harry Hibbs 1906-1972 WhAm 6
Jenkins, Harvey NewYHSD
Jenkins, Helen Hartley 1860-1934 BiCAW,
  NotAW
Jenkins, Herbert F 1873- WhAm 5
Jenkins, Herbert Theodore, Jr. 1902-1970
  NatCAB 56, WhAm 5
Jenkins, Hermon Dutilh 1842-1918 WhAm 1
Jenkins, Herschel Vespasian 1871-1960
  NatCAB 47, WhAm 4
Jenkins, Hester Donaldson 1869-
  WomWWA 14
Jenkins, Hilger Perry 1902-1970 NatCAB 55,
  WhAm 5
Jenkins, Howard Malcolm 1842-1902
  ApCAB Sup, DcAmB, NatCAB 25,
  WhAm 1
Jenkins, Irene Fowler Brown 1871-
  WomWWA 14
Jenkins, Isaac William 1875- WhoColR
Jenkins, J Caldwell 1883-1956 WhAm 3
Jenkins, J S, Sr. NewYHSD
Jenkins, James 1764-1847 NatCAB 10
Jenkins, James Alexander 1870-1960 WhAm 4,
  WhAm 5
Jenkins, James Frances 1882- WhoColR
Jenkins, James Graham 1834-1921 DcAmB,
  NatCAB 16, NatCAB 19, TwCBDA,
  WhAm 1
Jenkins, John 1728-1784 ApCAB
Jenkins, John 1728-1785 AmBi, DcAmB,
  NatCAB 24, WhAm H
Jenkins, John 1751-1827 AmBi, ApCAB,
  DcAmB, NatCAB 25, TwCBDA
Jenkins, John James 1843-1911 ApCAB X,
  BiDrAC, TwCBDA, WhAm 1, WhAmP
Jenkins, John Murray 1863-1958 WhAm 3
Jenkins, John S, Jr. 1895-1969 WhAm 5
Jenkins, John Stillwell 1815-1852 TwCBDA
Jenkins, John Stillwell 1818-1852 NatCAB 24
Jenkins, John Stilwell 1818-1852 ApCAB,
  DcAmB, Drake, WhAm H
Jenkins, John Theophilus 1829- ApCAB
Jenkins, Joseph NewYHSD
Jenkins, Joseph Harley 1890-1973 WhAm 6
Jenkins, Joseph J 1861- WhAm 4
Jenkins, Lemuel 1789-1862 BiAUS, BiDrAC,
  WhAm H
Jenkins, Louis William, Jr. 1904-1951
  NatCAB 42
Jenkins, MacGregor 1869-1940 WhAm 1
Jenkins, Mary B WomWWA 14
Jenkins, Mary Emma 1879- WomWWA 14
Jenkins, Mary Otis 1860- WomWWA 14

Jenkins, Micah 1835-1864 BiDConf, DcAmB,
  WhAm H
Jenkins, Micah 1836-1864 ApCAB Sup,
  NatCAB 10, WhAm H
Jenkins, Micah John 1857- NatCAB 10
Jenkins, Michael d1915 WhAm 1
Jenkins, Mitchell 1896- BiDrAC
Jenkins, Nathaniel 1812-1872 DcAmB,
  WhAm H
Jenkins, Newell Sill 1840-1919 NatCAB 19
Jenkins, Oliver Peebles 1850-1935 TwCBDA,
  WhAm 1
Jenkins, P O NewYHSD
Jenkins, Paul Burrill 1872-1936 WhAm 1
Jenkins, Perry Wilson 1867-1955 WhAm 3
Jenkins, Ralph Carlton 1891-1946 WhAm 2
Jenkins, Robert 1769-1848 BiAUS, BiDrAC,
  WhAm H
Jenkins, Robert Burns 1899-1958 NatCAB 46
Jenkins, Robert Edwin 1846-1907 WhAm 1
Jenkins, Romilly James Heald 1907-1969
  WhAm 5
Jenkins, Speight 1894-1970 NatCAB 57
Jenkins, Stella Frances 1862- WomWWA 14
Jenkins, Stephen 1857-1913 WhAm 1
Jenkins, Therese A 1853- AmWom
Jenkins, Thomas 1871- WhAm 5
Jenkins, Thomas Albert 1880-1959 BiDrAC,
  WhAm 3, WhAmP
Jenkins, Thomas Atkinson 1868-1935 WhAm 1
Jenkins, Thomas Christopher 1832-1907
  NatCAB 25
Jenkins, Thomas Nicholas 1892-1962
  NatCAB 51
Jenkins, Thornton Alexander 1811-1893 AmBi,
  ApCAB, DcAmB, Drake, NatCAB 4,
  TwCBDA, WhAm H
Jenkins, Timothy 1799-1859 BiAUS, BiDrAC,
  TwCBDA, WhAm H, WhAmP
Jenkins, Vernon Henry 1887-1952 WhAm 3
Jenkins, Waldo C NewYHSD
Jenkins, Will F 1896-1975 WhAm 6
Jenkins, William Adrian 1879- WhAm 6
Jenkins, William Dunbar d1914 WhAm 1
Jenkins, William Franklin 1876-1961
  NatCAB 51
Jenkins, William J 1873-1953 WhAm 3
Jenkins, William Leroy 1898-1957 WhAm 3
Jenkins, William M 1856-1941 WhAm 1
Jenkins, William Oscar 1878-1963 WhAm 4
Jenkins, William Robert 1902-1969 WhAm 5
Jenkins, William Sylvanus 1860-1949
  NatCAB 39
Jenkinson, George W NewYHSD
Jenkinson, Isaac 1825-1911 WhAm 1
Jenkinson, John Wilfred 1871-1915 DcScB
Jenkinson, Joseph NewYHSD
Jenkinson, Richard C 1853-1930 NatCAB 28,
  WhAm 1, WhAm 1C
Jenks, Agnes M WomWWA 14
Jenks, Albert 1824-1901 NewYHSD
Jenks, Albert Ernest 1869-1953 WhAm 3
Jenks, Almet 1892-1966 WhAm 4
Jenks, Almet Francis 1853-1924 NatCAB 27,
  WhAm 1
Jenks, Anson Brown 1834-1918 NatCAB 19
Jenks, Arthur Byron 1866-1947 BiDrAC,
  WhAm 2
Jenks, Arthur Whipple 1863-1922 WhAm 1
Jenks, B W NewYHSD
Jenks, Benjamin L 1889-1966 WhAm 4
Jenks, Clarence Wilfred 1909-1973 WhAm 6
Jenks, Edward Watrous 1833-1903 ApCAB,
  TwCBDA, WhAm 1
Jenks, Edward Watrous 1838-1903 NatCAB 4
Jenks, Edwin Hart 1862-1927 NatCAB 22,
  WhAm 1
Jenks, Francis Haynes 1812-1888 NatCAB 18
Jenks, George Augustus 1836-1908 BiAUS,
  BiDrAC, NatCAB 13, TwCBDA,
  WhAm 1
Jenks, George Charles 1850-1929 ApCAB X,
  DcAmB, WhAm 1
Jenks, George Walton 1838-1898 NatCAB 16
Jenks, Harry Neville 1893-1965 NatCAB 52
Jenks, Henry Fitch 1842- ApCAB, WhAm 4
Jenks, Horace Howard 1878-1931 NatCAB 24
Jenks, James Lawrence 1858-1940 WhAm 1

Jenks, James Messer 1850-1919 NatCAB 19
Jenks, Jeremiah Whipple 1856-1929 AmBi,
  ApCAB X, DcAmB, NatCAB 14,
  TwCBDA, WhAm 1
Jenks, John Edward 1866-1932 WhAm 1
Jenks, John Stanley 1871-1933 NatCAB 24
Jenks, John Story 1876-1946 WhAm 2
Jenks, John Whipple Potter 1819- ApCAB
Jenks, John Whipple Potter 1819-1894
  TwCBDA
Jenks, John Whipple Potter 1819-1895
  NatCAB 10, WhAm H
Jenks, Joseph 1602-1683 DcAmB, Drake,
  NatCAB 22, TwCBDA, WhAm H
Jenks, Joseph 1656-1740 BiAUS, Drake
Jenks, Joseph William 1808-1884 ApCAB,
  TwCBDA
Jenks, Llywellyn Howard 1862-1939
  NatCAB 31
Jenks, Michael Hutchinson 1795-1867 BiAUS,
  BiDrAC, WhAm H
Jenks, Nathan 1872-1916 ApCAB X
Jenks, Orrin Roe 1868-1951 WhAm 3
Jenks, Phoebe Ann Pickering 1847-1907 ApCAB
  NatCAB 12, TwCBDA, WhAm 1
Jenks, Robert Rice 1888-1946 NatCAB 33
Jenks, Samuel Haynes 1789-1863 Drake
Jenks, Stephen Arnold 1833-1913 NatCAB 40
Jenks, Stephen Moore 1901-1974 WhAm 6
Jenks, Thomas Harry 1869-1941 NatCAB 36
Jenks, Tudor Storrs 1857-1922 DcAmB,
  NatCAB 24, TwCBDA, WhAm 1
Jenks, William 1778-1866 ApCAB, DcAmB,
  Drake, NatCAB 24, TwCBDA, WhAm H
Jenks, William Jackson 1870-1960 WhAm 3
Jenks, William Lee 1856- NatCAB 17
Jenks, William Pearson 1872-1955 NatCAB 44
Jenne, Ida Sherman 1860- WomWWA 14
Jenne, James Nathaniel 1859-1937 BiDAmEd,
  NatCAB 28, WhAm 1
Jenner, Edward 1749-1823 AsBiEn, BiHiMed,
  DcScB, McGEWB
Jenner, William NewYHSD
Jenner, Sir William 1815-1898 BiHiMed
Jenner, William Ezra 1908- BiDrAC
Jenness, Benning Wentworth 1806-1879 ApCAB
  BiAUS, BiDrAC, NatCAB 7, TwCBDA,
  WhAm H
Jenness, Leslie George 1898-1968 NatCAB 54,
  WhAm 5
Jenness, Lyndon Yates 1843- WhAm 4
Jenness, Theodora Robinson 1847- WhAm 4
Jennewein, Paul 1890- BnEnAmA
Jenney, Caroline King 1879- WomWWA 14
Jenney, Charles Albert 1841- NatCAB 11,
  WhAm 4
Jenney, Charles Francis 1860-1923 NatCAB 20,
  WhAm 1
Jenney, Chester Ezekiel 1881- WhAm 6
Jenney, Julie Regula WomWWA 14
Jenney, Marie Regula WomWWA 14
Jenney, Ralph E 1883-1945 WhAm 2
Jenney, Robert 1687-1762 Drake
Jenney, Ruth Marie WomWWA 14
Jenney, William LeBaron 1832-1907 AmBi,
  ApCAB Sup, DcAmB, NatCAB 10,
  TwCBDA, WebAB, WhAm 1
Jenney, William Sherman 1867- WhAm 5
Jennings, Mister NewYHSD
Jennings, Abraham Gould 1821-1904
  NatCAB 2
Jennings, Albert Gould 1870-1946 NatCAB 35
Jennings, Alpheus Felch 1884-1945 NatCAB 45
Jennings, Andrew Jackson 1849-1923
  NatCAB 20, WhAm 1
Jennings, Arthur Bates 1849-1927 NatCAB 32
Jennings, Asa Kent 1877-1933 NatCAB 23
Jennings, B Brewster 1898-1968 NatCAB 54,
  WhAm 5
Jennings, Bryan Sherman 1893- ApCAB X
Jennings, Charles Ellis 1846- NatCAB 18
Jennings, Charles Godwin 1857-1936
  NatCAB 26, WhAm 1
Jennings, Charles Henry 1878-1964 NatCAB 50
Jennings, Charles Howard 1877-1953
  NatCAB 42
Jennings, Cortez Hicks 1855-1920 NatCAB 19

Jennings, Curtis Herman 1876-1934
NatCAB 26
Jennings, David 1787-1834 *BiAUS, BiDrAC,*
WhAm H
Jennings, David 1882-1955 *WhAm 3*
Jennings, Dean Southern 1905-1969 *WhAm 5*
Jennings, Edward Allen 1881-1958 *NatCAB 47*
Jennings, Edward Henry 1852-1923 *NatCAB 11,*
WhAm 1
Jennings, Edwin B 1855- *WhAm 4*
Jennings, Elzy Dee 1880-1938 *WhAm 1*
Jennings, Francis 1808-1891 *ApCAB Sup*
Jennings, Frank E 1877- *WhAm 5*
Jennings, Frederic Beach 1853-1920 *WhAm 1*
Jennings, Frederick Beach 1853-1920 *ApCAB X,*
NatCAB 14
Jennings, George Augustus 1850-1936
NatCAB 27
Jennings, Glenn Edwards 1884-1954
NatCAB 44
Jennings, Hennen 1854-1920 *NatCAB 18,*
WhAm 1
Jennings, Henry Burritt 1883-1927 *NatCAB 43,*
WhAm 1
Jennings, Henry C 1850-1927 *WhAm 1*
Jennings, Herbert Spencer 1868-1947
DcAmB S4, DcScB, NatCAB 47,
WhAm 2
Jennings, Isaac, Jr. *WhAm 5*
Jennings, J S *NewYHSD*
Jennings, James Hennen 1854-1920 *DcAmB*
Jennings, Joe Leslie 1901- *WhAm 5*
Jennings, John 1738?-1802 *DcAmB, WhAm H*
Jennings, John, Jr. 1880-1956 *BiDrAC,*
WhAm 3, WhAmP
Jennings, John Edward 1875-1945 *NatCAB 34*
Jennings, John Edward, Jr. 1906-1973 *WhAm 6*
Jennings, John Gould 1856-1937 *NatCAB 28*
Jennings, John Joseph 1853-1909 *WhAm 1*
Jennings, Jonathan d1834 *BiAUS, Drake*
Jennings, Jonathan 1776?-1834 *ApCAB,*
TwCBDA
Jennings, Jonathan 1784-1834 *BiDrAC,*
DcAmB, NatCAB 13, WhAm H,
WhAmP
Jennings, Judson Toll 1872-1948 *DcAmLiB,*
WhAm 2
Jennings, Kenneth Dinsmore 1895-1952
NatCAB 39
Jennings, Lacy Donoho 1885-1938 *NatCAB 35*
Jennings, Leslie Nelson 1892-1972 *WhAm 5*
Jennings, Louis John 1836-1893 *WhAm H*
Jennings, Lynn Fitch 1895-1958 *NatCAB 47*
Jennings, Maria Croft 1886-1965 *WhAm 4*
Jennings, Martin Luther 1847-1913 *WhAm 1*
Jennings, Mary Kirby 1871- *WomWWA 14*
Jennings, May Austin Mann *ApCAB X*
Jennings, Newell 1883-1965 *NatCAB 52,*
WhAm 4
Jennings, Oliver Burr 1825-1893 *NatCAB 22*
Jennings, Oliver Gould d1936 *WhAm 1*
Jennings, Otto Emery 1877-1964 *NatCAB 52,*
WhAm 4
Jennings, Percy Hall 1881-1951 *NatCAB 39,*
WhAm 6
Jennings, Perry Wells 1884-1959 *NatCAB 47*
Jennings, Phillipena G 1852- *WomWWA 14*
Jennings, Richard 1819-1891 *NatCAB 11*
Jennings, Richard William 1866-1928
NatCAB 23, WhAm 1
Jennings, Robert Emmet 1845-1929 *NatCAB 23*
Jennings, Robert W 1838- *NatCAB 2*
Jennings, Robert William 1864- *WhAm 4*
Jennings, Roscoe G 1833- *WhAm 4*
Jennings, Rudolph D 1852-1916 *WhAm 3*
Jennings, Russell 1800-1888 *ApCAB Sup*
Jennings, Samuel *NewYHSD*
Jennings, Samuel d1708 *ApCAB, NatCAB 16*
Jennings, Samuel Clemens 1867-1952 *WhAm 3*
Jennings, Samuel Kennedy 1771-1854 *ApCAB*
Jennings, Sidney Johnston 1863-1928
NatCAB 26, WhAm 1
Jennings, Stephen Richard 1875- *WhAm 5*
Jennings, T Albert 1865-1917 *WhAm 1*
Jennings, Thomas Reed 1805-1874 *ApCAB*
Jennings, Walter 1858-1933 *NatCAB 24,*
WhAm 1
Jennings, Walter Louis 1866-1944 *WhAm 2*

Jennings, Wesley William 1903-1970 *WhAm 5*
Jennings, William *NewYHSD*
Jennings, William 1823-1886 *REnAW*
Jennings, William Beatty 1859-1935 *WhAm 1*
Jennings, William Pat 1919- *BiDrAC*
Jennings, William Paul 1874-1944 *NatCAB 33*
Jennings, William Sherman 1863-1920
ApCAB X, NatCAB 11, WhAm 1
Jennison, George Birney 1860-1942 *NatCAB 36*
Jennison, Ralph Drury 1885-1956 *NatCAB 46*
Jennison, Samuel 1788-1860 *ApCAB, Drake*
Jennison, Silas Hemenway 1791-1849 *TwCBDA*
Jenny *NewYHSD*
Jenny, Herbert John 1886-1956 *NatCAB 43*
Jenny, Johann Heinrich *NewYHSD*
Jenny, N D *NewYHSD*
Jennys, J William *NewYHSD*
Jennys, Richard *NewYHSD*
Jennys, William *BnEnAmA, NewYHSD*
Jensen, Ben Franklin 1892-1970 *WhAm 5*
Jensen, Benton Franklin 1892-1970 *BiDrAC*
Jensen, Carl Oluf 1864-1934 *DcScB*
Jensen, Charles Frederick 1869-1924
NatCAB 20
Jensen, Christen 1881- *WhAm 6*
Jensen, Christian Nephi 1880- *WhAm 6*
Jensen, Elmer C 1870-1955 *WhAm 3*
Jensen, Frank A 1879-1947 *WhAm 2*
Jensen, Gerard Edward 1884-1970 *NatCAB 56*
Jensen, Harry Lauritz Melanchton 1895-1965
NatCAB 52
Jensen, Howard C d1972 *WhAm 5*
Jensen, J Hans Daniel 1907- *AsBiEn*
Jensen, Jens 1860-1951 *DcAmB S5, WhAm 3*
Jensen, Johan Ludvig William Valdemar
1859-1925 *DcScB*
Jensen, Johannes V 1873-1950 *WhAm 3*
Jensen, John Christian 1880-1957 *WhAm 3*
Jensen, Leslie 1892-1964 *WhAm 4*
Jensen, Ralph Adelbert 1888-1946 *WhAm 2*
Jenson, Andrew 1843-1917 *NatCAB 17*
Jenson, David 1877- *NatCAB 18*
Jent, John William 1877-1941 *WhAm 1*
Jente, Richard 1888-1952 *WhAm 3*
Jenter, Martin 1885-1951 *NatCAB 48*
Jentgen, Charles John 1885-1964 *NatCAB 50*
Jentzsch, Richard Alvin 1892-1974 *WhAm 6*
Jephson, Lady *WomWWA 14*
Jepperson, Samuel Hans 1854?-1931 *IIBEAAW*
Jeppson, George Nathaniel 1873-1962
NatCAB 56, WhAm 4
Jepsen, Glenn Lowell 1903-1974 *WhAm 6*
Jepson, Harry Benjamin 1870-1952 *NatCAB 41,*
WhAm 3
Jepson, Ivar Per 1903-1968 *WhAm 5*
Jepson, Mabel Preston Wyatt 1870-
WomWWA 14
Jepson, Samuel L 1842-1922 *WhAm 1*
Jepson, William 1863-1946 *WhAm 2*
Jepson, Willis Linn 1867-1946 *DcAmB S4,*
DcScB
Jequitinhonha, Francisco GeA DeM 1794-1870
ApCAB
Jeremiah *McGEWB*
Jeremie 1660?-1714? *ApCAB*
Jerez, Francisco De 1504-1570? *ApCAB*
Jerferson, Samuel Mitchell 1849-1914 *WhAm 1*
Jergens, Andrew d1967 *WhAm 4*
Jermain, James Barclay 1809-1897 *NatCAB 16,*
TwCBDA
Jermain, Louis Francis 1867-1935 *WhAm 1*
Jerman, Carnelia 1874- *WomWWA 14*
Jerman, Cornelia Petty 1874- *WhAm 5*
Jerman, Thomas Palmer 1906-1974 *WhAm 6*
Jermane, William Wallace 1862- *WhAm 4*
Jernagin, William Henry 1869- *WhoColR*
Jernberg, Reinert August 1855-1942 *WhAm 2*
Jernegan, Marcus Wilson 1872-1949 *WhAm 2*
Jernegan, Prescott Ford 1866- *WhAm 4*
Jernegan, Ralph Hartwell 1877-1957
NatCAB 46
Jernigan, Charlton C 1904-1953 *WhAm 3*
Jernstrom, Roy Enoch 1896-1959 *NatCAB 48*
Jeroboam I *McGEWB*
Jeroloman, John 1845- *WhAm 4*
Jerolomen, William *NewYHSD*
Jerome, Brother 1896-1959 *WhAm 3*
Jerome, Saint 345?-420 *McGEWB*

Jerome, Amalie Hofer 1864- *WomWWA 14*
Jerome, Chauncey 1793-1868 *DcAmB,*
NatCAB 7, WhAm H
Jerome, David Howell 1829-1896 *NatCAB 5,*
TwCBDA
Jerome, Elizabeth Gilbert 1824-1910
NewYHSD
Jerome, Harry 1886-1938 *WhAm 1*
Jerome, Irene Elizabeth 1858- *ApCAB*
Jerome, Jerome Tyrrell 1899-1961 *NatCAB 50*
Jerome, Leonard Walter 1817-1891 *NatCAB 32*
Jerome, William Travers 1859-1934 *AmBi,*
DcAmB S1, NatCAB 14, NatCAB 26,
WhAm 1
Jerome, William Travers, Jr. 1890-1952
NatCAB 40
Jerrard, George Birch 1804-1863 *DcScB*
Jersild, Arthur Thomas 1902- *BiDAmEd*
Jersild, Marvin A 1897-1967 *WhAm 5*
Jertberg, Gilbert H *WhAm 6*
Jervey, Caroline Howard Gilman 1823-1877
TwCBDA
Jervey, Harold Edward 1894- *WhAm 6*
Jervey, Henry 1866-1942 *WhAm 2*
Jervey, Huger Wilkinson 1878-1949 *WhAm 2*
Jervey, James Postell 1808-1875 *NatCAB 16*
Jervey, James Postell 1869-1947 *WhAm 2*
Jervey, James Wilkinson 1874-1945 *NatCAB 36,*
WhAm 2
Jervis, Sir John 1734-1823 *ApCAB*
Jervis, John Bloomfield 1795-1885 *AmBi,*
ApCAB, DcAmB, NatCAB 9, TwCBDA,
WhAm H
Jervis, William 1818?- *NewYHSD*
Jeschonnek, Hans 1899-1943 *WhWW-II*
Jeserich, Paul Harold 1893-1973 *NatCAB 57*
Jess, Clara Alice 1887- *WomWWA 14*
Jesse, Philip d1858 *Drake*
Jesse, Richard Henry 1853-1921 *BiDAmEd,*
DcAmB, NatCAB 8, TwCBDA,
WhAm 2
Jesse, Richard Henry 1884-1955 *WhAm 3*
Jesse, William Herman 1908-1970 *DcAmLiB,*
WhAm 5
Jessel, George Albert 1898- *WebAB*
Jessen, Karl Detlev 1872-1919 *WhAm 1*
Jessop, Earl Percy 1873-1940 *NatCAB 30*
Jessop, Francis Woodward 1873-1955
NatCAB 45
Jessopp, Dudley Frederick 1901-1964 *WhAm 4*
Jessup, Charles Augustus 1862- *WhAm 4*
Jessup, Ebenezer *NewYHSD*
Jessup, Edgar B 1890-1961 *WhAm 4*
Jessup, Everett Colgate 1887-1968 *WhAm 5*
Jessup, Henry Harris 1832-1910 *AmBi,*
ApCAB, DcAmB, NatCAB 10, TwCBDA,
WhAm 1
Jessup, Henry Wynans 1864-1934 *WhAm 1*
Jessup, Jared *NewYHSD*
Jessup, Joseph John 1856-1957 *WhAm 3*
Jessup, Mary Hay 1866- *WomWWA 14*
Jessup, Philip Caryl 1897- *WebAB*
Jessup, Samuel 1833- *ApCAB, NatCAB 10,*
TwCBDA, WhAm 1
Jessup, Walter Albert 1877-1944 *BiDAmEd,*
DcAmB S3, NatCAB 37, WhAm 2
Jessup, William 1797-1868 *ApCAB, Drake,*
NatCAB 10, TwCBDA
Jessup, William Huntting 1830- *NatCAB 10*
Jester, Beauford Halbert 1893-1949
NatCAB 42, WhAm 5
Jester, John Roberts 1875- *WhAm 5*
Jesup, Henry Griswold 1826-1903 *TwCBDA,*
WhAm 1
Jesup, Morris Ketchum 1830-1908 *AmBi,*
ApCAB, DcAmB, NatCAB 11, TwCBDA,
WhAm 1
Jesup, Thomas Sidney 1788-1860 *ApCAB,*
DcAmB, Drake, NatCAB 12, REnAW,
TwCBDA, WebAMB, WhAm H
Jesus BenSera 170?BC- *McGEWB*
Jesus Of Nazareth 004?BC-030?AD *McGEWB*
Jeter, Frank Hamilton 1891-1955 *WhAm 3*
Jeter, Jeremiah Bell 1802-1880 *ApCAB,*
DcAmB, Drake, TwCBDA, WhAm H
Jeter, Thomas Bothwell 1827-1883 *NatCAB 12,*
TwCBDA
Jett, Ewell Kirk 1893-1965 *WhAm 4*

Jett, Robert Carter 1865- *WhAm 5*
Jett, Shelby Magoffin 1889-1944 *NatCAB 34*
Jett, Thomas Marion 1862-1939 *BiDrAC, NatCAB 45, TwCBDA, WhAm 4*
Jevons, William Stanley 1835-1882 *DcScB, McGEWB*
Jewell, Benson Mundy 1880-1952 *NatCAB 39*
Jewell, Bert Mark 1881- *WhAm 6*
Jewell, Edith Winifred 1879- *WomWWA 14*
Jewell, Edward Alden 1888-1947 *WhAm 2*
Jewell, Frederick Swartz 1821-1903 *TwCBDA, WhAm 1*
Jewell, Harry Sanford 1867-1945 *NatCAB 37*
Jewell, Harvey 1820-1881 *ApCAB, BiAUS, DcAmB, TwCBDA, WhAm H*
Jewell, James Ralph 1878- *WhAm 6*
Jewell, James Stewart 1837-1887 *ApCAB*
Jewell, Jesse Dale 1891-1975 *WhAm 6*
Jewell, John Franklin 1874-1927 *WhAm 1*
Jewell, Louise Pond d1943 *WhAm 2*
Jewell, Marshall 1825-1883 *AmBi, ApCAB, BiAUS, BiDrUSE, DcAmB, Drake, NatCAB 4, TwCBDA, WhAm H*
Jewell, Marshall Henry 1857- *NatCAB 11*
Jewell, Robert Houston 1897-1967 *NatCAB 55*
Jewell, Theodore Frelinghuysen 1844-1932 *ApCAB Sup, NatCAB 13, TwCBDA, WhAm 1*
Jewell, Theodore Frelinhuysen 1844-1932 *ApCAB X*
Jewell, William Henry 1892-1957 *WhAm 3*
Jewett, Albert Gallatin 1802-1885 *NatCAB 12*
Jewett, Arthur Crawford 1878-1957 *WhAm 3*
Jewett, C C *BiAUS*
Jewett, Carlton Rogers 1852-1937 *NatCAB 28*
Jewett, Charles 1839-1910 *WhAm 1*
Jewett, Charles 1842- *NatCAB 13, TwCBDA*
Jewett, Charles A 1816-1878 *NewYHSD*
Jewett, Charles Coffin 1816-1868 *AmBi, ApCAB, BiAUS, DcAmB, DcAmLiB, Drake, NatCAB 5, TwCBDA, WhAm H*
Jewett, Clarence Frederick 1852-1909 *DcAmB*
Jewett, Daniel Tarbox 1807-1906 *BiDrAC, NatCAB 12*
Jewett, David 1772-1842 *DcAmB, NatCAB 30, WhAm H*
Jewett, David Baldwin 1880-1951 *NatCAB 41*
Jewett, Edward Hurtt 1830-1907 *TwCBDA, WhAm 1*
Jewett, Ezekiel 1791-1877 *ApCAB Sup, TwCBDA*
Jewett, Fannie Cornelia Frisbie 1878- *WomWWA 14*
Jewett, Frances Campbell 1863- *WomWWA 14*
Jewett, Frances Gulick 1854- *WhAm 4, WomWWA 14*
Jewett, Frank Baldwin 1879-1949 *DcAmB S4, DcScB, WhAm 2*
Jewett, Frank Fanning 1844-1926 *NatCAB 20, WhAm 3*
Jewett, Frederick A 1859-1906 *NatCAB 24*
Jewett, Frederick Stiles 1819-1864 *NewYHSD, WhAm H*
Jewett, Freeborn Garrettson 1791-1858 *BiAUS, BiDrAC, NatCAB 12, WhAm H*
Jewett, Freeland 1865-1937 *NatCAB 28*
Jewett, George Anson 1847-1934 *ApCAB X, WhAm 1*
Jewett, George Baker 1818-1886 *ApCAB, TwCBDA*
Jewett, George Franklin 1857-1926 *ApCAB X, NatCAB 20*
Jewett, George Franklin 1859-1925 *WhAm 1*
Jewett, George Frederick 1896-1956 *NatCAB 47, WhAm 3*
Jewett, Harry Mulford 1870-1933 *WhAm 1*
Jewett, Harvey C 1863-1937 *WhAm 1*
Jewett, Harvey Chase, Jr. 1895-1953 *WhAm 3*
Jewett, Henry 1862-1930 *NatCAB 22*
Jewett, Henry Clay 1840- *NatCAB 12*
Jewett, Hugh 1907-1975 *WhAm 6*
Jewett, Hugh Judge d1898 *BiAUS*
Jewett, Hugh Judge 1812?-1898 *ApCAB*
Jewett, Hugh Judge 1813-1898 *NatCAB 7*
Jewett, Hugh Judge 1817-1898 *BiDrAC, DcAmB, NatCAB 31, TwCBDA, WhAm H*
Jewett, Hugh Judge 1869-1926 *NatCAB 31*

Jewett, Isaac Appleton 1808-1853 *ApCAB, Drake*
Jewett, James Richard 1862-1943 *NatCAB 35, WhAm 2*
Jewett, John Howard 1843-1925 *NatCAB 13, WhAm 1, WhAm 4*
Jewett, John Punchard 1814-1884 *ApCAB, DcAmB, NatCAB 26, WhAm H*
Jewett, John R d1821 *Drake*
Jewett, Joshua Husband 1812-1861 *BiAUS, TwCBDA*
Jewett, Joshua Husband 1815-1861 *BiDrAC, WhAm H*
Jewett, Luther 1772-1860 *ApCAB, BiAUS, BiDrAC, Drake, TwCBDA, WhAm H*
Jewett, Mary B 1858- *WomWWA 14*
Jewett, Milo Parker 1808-1882 *AmBi, ApCAB, BiDAmEd, DcAmB, Drake, NatCAB 5, TwCBDA, WhAm H*
Jewett, Nannie Hume 1881- *WomWWA 14*
Jewett, Nelson J 1872-1951 *WhAm 3*
Jewett, Richard Dickinson 1857-1917 *NatCAB 30*
Jewett, Rutger Bleecker 1867-1935 *WhAm 1*
Jewett, Sara 1847-1899 *NatCAB 11, TwCBDA*
Jewett, Sarah Orne 1849-1909 *AmBi, AmWom, ApCAB, DcAmB, EncAAH, McGEWB, NatCAB 1, NotAW, TwCBDA, WebAB, WhAm 1*
Jewett, Smith 1812-1873 *NewYHSD*
Jewett, Sophie 1861-1909 *NatCAB 12, WhAm 1*
Jewett, Stephen Perham 1882-1971 *WhAm 5*
Jewett, Stephen Shannon 1858-1932 *WhAm 1*
Jewett, Susan W *ApCAB*
Jewett, Theodore Herman 1815-1878 *ApCAB*
Jewett, Thomas Lightfoot 1810?-1875 *ApCAB, NatCAB 7*
Jewett, William 1789?-1874 *NewYHSD*
Jewett, William 1792-1874 *DcAmB, WhAm H*
Jewett, William 1795-1873 *BnEnAmA, Drake*
Jewett, William Averill 1875-1966 *NatCAB 53*
Jewett, William Cornell 1823-1893 *DcAmB, WhAm H*
Jewett, William Samuel Lyon 1834-1876 *NewYHSD, WhAm H*
Jewett, William Smith 1812-1873 *IlBEAAW, NewYHSD, WhAm H*
Jewitt, Albert G *BiAUS*
Jewitt, W J *NewYHSD*
Jickling, David Saunders 1876-1951 *NatCAB 40*
Jicotencal 1486-1521 *ApCAB*
Jiggits, Louis Meredith 1899-1945 *WhAm 2*
Jimenez, Jesus 1820?- *ApCAB*
Jimenez, Juan Ramon 1881-1958 *McGEWB, WhAm 3*
Jimenez DeQuesada, Gonzalo 1509-1579 *McGEWB*
Jimenez Oreamuno, Ricardo 1859-1945 *WhAm 2*
Jimenez Perez, Manuel 1720-1781 *ApCAB*
Jinnah, Mahomed Ali 1876-1948 *WhAm 2*
Jinnah, Mohammad Ali 1876-1948 *McGEWB*
Jipson, Norton William 1865- *NatCAB 17*
Jirka, Frank Joseph 1886-1963 *NatCAB 52*
Jirka, Irwin Grover 1884-1958 *NatCAB 47*
Jllek, Lubor 1926-1975 *WhAm 6*
Joachim Of Fiore 1132?-1202 *McGEWB*
Joachim, Georg *DcScB*
Joachim, Henry 1883-1941 *NatCAB 30*
Joachim, Jerome 1898-1956 *NatCAB 47*
Joachimsthal, Ferdinand 1818-1861 *DcScB*
Joan Of Arc 1412?-1431 *McGEWB*
Joannes, Francis Y 1876-1952 *WhAm 3*
Job, Frederick William 1862- *WhAm 4*
Job, Herbert Keightley 1864-1933 *WhAm 1*
Job, Leon *NewYHSD*
Job, Robert 1866- *WhAm 4*
Job, Thomas 1900-1947 *WhAm 2*
Jobes, Andrew Cook 1857-1933 *NatCAB 28*
Jobes, Harry C 1877- *WhAm 5*
Jobin, Raoul 1906-1974 *WhAm 6*
Jobling, James Wesley 1876-1961 *WhAm 4*
Joblot, Louis 1645-1723 *DcScB*
Jobst, Conrad 1889-1957 *NatCAB 45*
Jobst, Norbert Raymond 1920-1975 *WhAm 6*

Jocelin, Simeon 1746-1823 *NewYHSD*
Jocelyn, Albert H *NewYHSD*
Jocelyn, George Bemies 1824-1877 *TwCBDA*
Jocelyn, George Beniers 1824-1877 *NatCAB 5*
Jocelyn, Nathaniel 1796-1881 *DcAmB, NatCAB 25, NewYHSD, WhAm H*
Jocelyn, Simeon Smith 1799-1879 *NatCAB 2, NewYHSD, WhAm H*
Jocelyn, Simeon Starr *NewYHSD*
Jocelyn, Stephen Perry 1843-1920 *NatCAB 19, WhAm 1*
Jochem, Anita M 1912-1975 *WhAm 6*
Jochems, William Dennis 1886-1960 *NatCAB 48, WhAm 4*
Jodidi, Samuel Leo 1867-1944 *NatCAB 33*
Jodl, Alfred 1890-1946 *WhoMilH*
Jodl, Alfried 1890-1946 *WhWW-II*
Joeckel, Carleton Bruns 1886-1960 *DcAmLiB*
Joehr, Adolf 1878- *WhAm 4*
Joekel, Samuel Levinson 1893-1954 *WhAm 3*
Joel, George William Freeman 1902-1959 *WhAm 3*
Joelson, Charles Samuel 1916- *BiDrAC*
Joerg, Wolfgang Louis Gottfried 1885-1952 *NatCAB 40, WhAm 3*
Joesting, Harold Carl 1904-1946 *NatCAB 35*
Joesting, Henry Rochambeau 1903-1965 *NatCAB 52, WhAm 4*
Joffee, Jerome Morton 1895-1953 *NatCAB 42*
Joffre, Joseph Jacques Cesaire 1852-1931 *McGEWB, WhoMilH*
Jogues, Isaac 1607-1646 *AmBi, ApCAB, DcAmB, DcAmReB, Drake, McGEWB, REnAW, WhAm H*
Johanan BenZakkai *McGEWB*
Johann, Carl 1849-1930 *WhAm 1*
Johannes IV 1836-1889 *McGEWB*
Johannes Lauratius DeFundis 1428-1473 *DcScB*
Johannes Leo *DcScB*
Johannes, Dana Berry 1910-1972 *NatCAB 57*
Johannes, Francis 1874-1937 *WhAm 1*
Johannessen, Walter 1891-1954 *NatCAB 44*
Johannsen, Albert 1871-1962 *DcScB*
Johannsen, Oskar Augustus 1870-1961 *NatCAB 47, WhAm 4*
Johannsen, Robert Walter 1925- *EncAAH, REnAW*
Johannsen, Wilhelm Ludvig 1857-1927 *DcScB*
Johannsen, Wilhelm Ludwig 1857-1927 *AsBiEn*
Johansen, August Edgar 1905- *BiDrAC, WhAmP*
Johansen, George P 1896-1964 *WhAm 4*
Johansen, Johan 1851-1934 *NatCAB 27*
Johansen, John Christen 1876-1964 *NatCAB 52, WhAm 4*
Johansen, John M 1916- *BnEnAmA*
Johansen, M Jean McLane *WomWWA 14*
Johansing, Harry George 1883-1954 *NatCAB 44*
Johanson, Alvin Roswell 1899-1964 *NatCAB 53*
Johanson, Patricia 1940- *BnEnAmA*
John 1167-1216 *McGEWB*
John II 1319-1364 *McGEWB*
John III 1629-1696 *McGEWB, WhoMilH*
John XXIII 1881-1963 *McGEWB, WhAm 4*
John, Archduke Of Austria 1782-1859 *WhoMilH*
John Buridan *DcScB*
John Chrysostom, Saint 347?-407 *McGEWB*
John Danko Of Saxony *DcScB*
John De'Dondi *DcScB*
John Duns Scotus *DcScB*
John Lichtenberger *DcScB*
John Marliani *DcScB*
John Maurice Of Nassau 1604-1679 *McGEWB*
John Of Damascus, Saint 680?-750? *McGEWB*
John Of Dumbleton d1349? *DcScB*
John Of Gaunt 1340-1399 *McGEWB*
John Of Gmunden 1380?-1442 *DcScB*
John Of Halifax *DcScB*
John Of Holywood *DcScB*
John Of Leiden 1509-1536 *McGEWB*
John Of Ligneres *DcScB*
John Of Murs *DcScB*
John Of Palermo *DcScB*
John Of Piano Carpini 1180?-1252 *McGEWB*
John Of Sacrobosco *DcScB*
John Of Salisbury 1115?-1180 *McGEWB*

John Of Saxony *DcScB*
John Of Sicily *DcScB*
John Of The Cross, Saint 1542-1591 *McGEWB*
John Peckham *DcScB*
John Philoponus *DcScB*
John, Saint *McGEWB*
John Scottus Eriugena *DcScB*
John Simonis Of Selandia *DcScB*
John The Baptist, Saint *McGEWB*
John, Augustus 1821?- *NewYHSD*
John, Augustus Edwin 1878-1961 *McGEWB,*
WhAm 4
John, Ch A *NewYHSD*
John, Grace Spaulding 1890-1972 *IlBEAAW*
John, John Price Durbin 1843-1916 *NatCAB 7,*
WhAm 1
John, Jonathan Blaine 1870-1956 *NatCAB 43*
John, Samuel Will 1845- *WhAm 4*
John, Waldemar Alfred Paul 1895-1964
NatCAB 50, WhAm 4
John, William Mestrezat 1888-1962 *WhAm 4*
John, William Scott 1878-1954 *WhAm 3*
John Francis, Sister Mary 1911-1969 *WhAm 5*
Johnes, Edward Rodolph 1852-1903 *NatCAB 3,*
TwCBDA, WhAm 1
Johnes, Timothy 1717-1794 *Drake*
Johnes, William Foulke 1868-1918 *NatCAB 18*
Johns, Alice Gillette 1863- *WomWWA 14*
Johns, Carl Oscar 1870-1942 *NatCAB 30,*
WhAm 2
Johns, Charles A 1857-1932 *NatCAB 24,*
WhAm 1
Johns, Choate Webster 1903-1965 *WhAm 4*
Johns, Christian *NewYHSD*
Johns, Clarence D 1888-1950 *WhAm 3*
Johns, Clayton 1857-1932 *DcAmB S1,*
NatCAB 13, TwCBDA, WhAm 1
Johns, Cyrus N 1894-1973 *WhAm 5*
Johns, Foster 1893-1970 *WebAB*
Johns, Frank Stoddert 1884-1971 *WhAm 5*
Johns, George Sibley 1857-1941 *WhAm 1*
Johns, Henry VanDyck 1803-1859 *TwCBDA*
Johns, Henry VanDyke 1803-1859 *NatCAB 5*
Johns, James Arnold McGilvray 1830- *ApCAB*
Johns, Jasper 1930- *BnEnAmA, EncAB,*
McGEWB
Johns, John 1796-1876 *ApCAB, DcAmB,*
Drake, NatCAB 3, TwCBDA, WhAm H
Johns, Joseph W *NewYHSD*
Johns, Joshua Leroy 1881-1947 *BiDrAC,*
WhAm 2
Johns, Kensey 1759-1848 *ApCAB, DcAmB,*
Drake, TwCBDA, WhAm H
Johns, Kensey 1759-1849 *NatCAB 5*
Johns, Kensey 1791-1857 *ApCAB, BiAUS,*
BiDrAC, DcAmB, Drake, NatCAB 7,
TwCBDA, WhAm H, WhAmP
Johns, Laura M 1849- *AmWom,*
WomWWA 14
Johns, Mary J V 1851- *WomWWA 14*
Johns, Roy William 1902-1967 *NatCAB 54,*
WhAm 4
Johns, Thomas Richards 1865-1944 *NatCAB 34*
Johns, Walter Robinson 1880-1949 *NatCAB 39*
Johns, William *NewYHSD*
Johns, William Hingston 1868-1944
NatCAB 18, WhAm 2
Johnsen, Erik Kristian 1863-1923 *DcAmB,*
WhAm 1
Johnson *NewYHSD*
Johnson, Mrs. *NewYHSD*
Johnson, A N 1866- *WhoColR*
Johnson, Aben 1884-1966 *WhAm 4*
Johnson, Adam Rankin 1834- *WhAm 4*
Johnson, Adam Rankin 1872-1951 *NatCAB 40*
Johnson, Adelaide *WomWWA 14*
Johnson, Adelaide McFadyen 1905-1960
WhAm 4
Johnson, Adna Romulus 1860-1938 *BiDrAC,*
WhAm 4
Johnson, Al 1885-1949 *NatCAB 38*
Johnson, Alba Boardman 1858-1935
NatCAB 25, WhAm 1
Johnson, Albert 1869-1957 *BiDrAC, WhAm 3,*
WhAmP
Johnson, Albert Henry 1893-1965 *WhAm 5*
Johnson, Albert Mussey 1872-1948 *WebAB,*
WhAm 2

Johnson, Albert Richard 1910-1967 *NatCAB 54,*
WhAm 4
Johnson, Albert Rittenhouse 1880-1960
WhAm 3A
Johnson, Albert Walter 1906- *BiDrAC*
Johnson, Albert Williams 1872-1957
NatCAB 48, WhAm 3
Johnson, Albinus Alonzo 1852- *WhAm 4*
Johnson, Alden Porter 1914-1972 *WhAm 5*
Johnson, Alex Carlton 1861-1938 *WhAm 1*
Johnson, Alexander 1847-1941 *DcAmB S3,*
WhAm 1
Johnson, Alexander Bryan 1786-1867 *ApCAB,*
DcAmB, Drake, WhAm H
Johnson, Alexander Byron *ApCAB*
Johnson, Alexander S 1822- *BiAUS*
Johnson, Alexander Smith 1817-1878 *ApCAB,*
DcAmB, NatCAB 5, TwCBDA,
WhAm H
Johnson, Alfred LeRoy 1881-1967 *WhAm 4*
Johnson, Alfred Remund 1874-1954
NatCAB 44
Johnson, Alfred Sidney 1860-1925 *WhAm 1*
Johnson, Alice Adams 1860- *WomWWA 14*
Johnson, Alice Frein 1900-1973 *WhAm 6*
Johnson, Alice Williams 1870- *WomWWA 14*
Johnson, Allan Chester 1881-1955 *NatCAB 45,*
WhAm 3
Johnson, Allen 1870-1931 *AmBi, DcAmB,*
NatCAB 21, WhAm 1
Johnson, Allen Huggins 1911-1952 *NatCAB 42*
Johnson, Alvin Saunders 1874-1971 *BiDAmEd,*
DcAmLiB, EncAB, McGEWB, WebAB,
WhAm 5
Johnson, Amos Howe 1831-1896 *NatCAB 19*
Johnson, Amos Neill 1908-1975 *WhAm 6*
Johnson, Andrew 1808-1875 *AmBi, ApCAB,*
BiAUS, BiDrAC, BiDrUSE, DcAmB,
Drake, EncAAH, EncAB, McGEWB,
NatCAB 2, TwCBDA, WebAB,
WhAm H, WhAmP
Johnson, Andrew Gustavus 1857-1924 *WhAm 1*
Johnson, Andrew W 1887-1964 *WhAm 4*
Johnson, Andrew Wallace 1826-1887 *ApCAB*
Johnson, Ann *NewYHSD*
Johnson, Anna 1860- *WhAm 3,*
WomWWA 14
Johnson, Anna Hayward *WomWWA 14*
Johnson, Anna Louise 1869- *WomWWA 14*
Johnson, Anna Marilla 1849- *WomWWA 14*
Johnson, Anne 1871- *WomWWA 14*
Johnson, Annie Davis 1847- *WomWWA 14*
Johnson, Anton Joseph 1878-1958 *BiDrAC,*
WhAm 6, WhAmP
Johnson, Arbella d1630 *ApCAB*
Johnson, Armer Eugene 1870-1949 *NatCAB 53*
Johnson, Arnold Burges 1834-1915 *NatCAB 16*
Johnson, Arnold Edwin 1876-1952 *NatCAB 41*
Johnson, Arnold Milton 1907-1960 *WhAm 3*
Johnson, Artemas Nixon 1817- *ApCAB, Drake*
Johnson, Arthur Charles 1874-1950 *WhAm 3*
Johnson, Arthur Cornelius 1891-1967
NatCAB 54
Johnson, Arthur Monrad 1878-1943 *WhAm 2*
Johnson, Arthur Newhall 1870-1940 *WhAm 1*
Johnson, Ashley Sidney 1857-1925 *WhAm 1*
Johnson, Axel Petrus 1878-1952 *WhAm 3*
Johnson, Aymar 1883-1942 *NatCAB 31*
Johnson, Bascom 1878-1954 *WhAm 3*
Johnson, Ben 1858-1950 *BiDrAC, WhAm 3,*
WhAmP
Johnson, Ben 1881-1955 *NatCAB 45,*
WhAm 3
Johnson, Benjamin *BiAUS, NewYHSD*
Johnson, Benjamin Alvin 1887-1943 *WhAm 2*
Johnson, Benjamin Franklin 1856-1921
NatCAB 11, WhAm 1
Johnson, Benjamin Newhall 1856-1932
NatCAB 24, WhAm 1
Johnson, Benjamin Pierce 1793-1869 *ApCAB,*
DcAmB, TwCBDA, WhAm H
Johnson, Bernard Lyman 1883-1947
NatCAB 37, WhAm 2
Johnson, Bolling Arthur 1862-1925 *WhAm 1*
Johnson, Bradley Taylor 1829-1903 *AmBi*
Johnson, Bradley Tyler 1829-1903 *ApCAB,*
DcAmB, NatCAB 4, TwCBDA,
WhAm 1

Johnson, Buford Jeanette 1880- *WhAm 6*
Johnson, Burritt Byron 1874-1939 *NatCAB 29*
Johnson, Burt W 1890-1927 *WhAm 1*
Johnson, Bushrod Rust 1817-1880 *AmBi,*
ApCAB, BiDConf, DcAmB, Drake,
TwCBDA, WhAm H
Johnson, Byron 1865-1921 *WhAm HA,*
WhAm 4
Johnson, Byron Arthur 1886-1960 *WhAm 4*
Johnson, Byron Bancroft 1864-1931 *DcAmB*
Johnson, Byron Bancroft 1865-1931 *WhAm 1*
Johnson, Byron Lindberg 1917- *BiDrAC*
Johnson, C A *NewYHSD*
Johnson, C Fred 1855-1950 *NatCAB 48*
Johnson, Caleb Elliott 1857-1924 *NatCAB 29*
Johnson, Calvin Dean 1898- *BiDrAC*
Johnson, Campbell Carrington 1895-1968
WhAm 5
Johnson, Carl August 1877-1954 *NatCAB 41*
Johnson, Carl Edward 1883-1953 *NatCAB 42*
Johnson, Carl Edward 1898-1970 *WhAm 5*
Johnson, Carl Gunnard 1902-1966 *WhAm 4*
Johnson, Carl W 1886-1956 *WhAm 3*
Johnson, Carolyn Mae Lord 1875-
WomWWA 14
Johnson, Carrie Ashton 1863- *AmWom*
Johnson, Carrie Mabel Dexter 1878-
WomWWA 14
Johnson, Carroll Warren 1907-1971
NatCAB 56
Johnson, Cave 1793-1866 *AmBi, ApCAB,*
BiAUS, BiDrAC, BiDrUSE, DcAmB,
Drake, NatCAB 6, TwCBDA, WhAm H,
WhAmP
Johnson, Chapman 1779-1849 *ApCAB,*
DcAmB, Drake, WhAm H
Johnson, Charles d1802 *BiDrAC, WhAm H*
Johnson, Charles 1858-1948 *NatCAB 38*
Johnson, Charles Arthur 1857- *NatCAB 18*
Johnson, Charles E *NewYHSD*
Johnson, Charles Ellicott 1920-1969 *WhAm 5*
Johnson, Charles Eugene 1880-1936 *WhAm 1*
Johnson, Charles F 1827?- *NewYHSD*
Johnson, Charles F, Jr. 1887-1959 *WhAm 3*
Johnson, Charles Fabian Herman 1880-1952
NatCAB 39, WhAm 3
Johnson, Charles Fletcher 1859-1930 *BiDrAC,*
NatCAB 21, WhAm 1
Johnson, Charles Frederick 1836-1931 *TwCBDA,*
WhAm 1
Johnson, Charles Harmany 1870-1918
ApCAB X
Johnson, Charles Henry 1870-1948 *NatCAB 36,*
WhAm 2
Johnson, Charles Nelson 1860-1938 *NatCAB 16,*
WhAm 1
Johnson, Charles Oscar 1886-1965 *WhAm 4*
Johnson, Charles Philip 1836-1920 *NatCAB 6,*
WhAm 1
Johnson, Charles Price 1914-1965 *WhAm 5*
Johnson, Charles Spurgeon 1893-1956
BiDAmEd, EncAB, McGEWB,
NatCAB 48, WhAm 3
Johnson, Charles Sumner 1854- *WhAm 4*
Johnson, Charles Williamson 1845- *NatCAB 17,*
WhAm 4
Johnson, Charles Willis 1873-1949 *NatCAB 39,*
WhAm 2
Johnson, Charles Willison 1863-1932 *WhAm 1,*
WhAm 1C, WhAm 2
Johnson, Clarence Alexander 1876-1941
NatCAB 39
Johnson, Clarence Hazelton 1906-1973
WhAm 6
Johnson, Clarence Leonard 1910- *WebAMB*
Johnson, Clarence S 1892-1952 *WhAm 3*
Johnson, Clark Moore 1898-1948 *NatCAB 36*
Johnson, Clarke Howard 1851-1930
NatCAB 18, WhAm 1
Johnson, Claude M 1852- *WhAm 4*
Johnson, Clifton 1865-1940 *NatCAB 11,*
NatCAB 40, WhAm 1
Johnson, Clinton Charles 1897-1974 *WhAm 6*
Johnson, Clyde Parker 1871-1940 *NatCAB 31*
Johnson, Cone 1860-1933 *WhAm 4*
Johnson, Constance Fuller Wheeler 1879-
WhAm 6, WomWWA 14

Johnson, Constantine Nicholas 1880-1954
NatCAB 42
Johnson, Content *BiCAW*
Johnson, Crawford Toy 1873-1942 *WhAm 2*
Johnson, Crawford Toy 1898- *WhAm 5*
Johnson, Crockett 1906-1975 *WhAm 6*
Johnson, Curtis Boyd 1875-1950 *NatCAB 41,*
WhAm 3
Johnson, D B *BiAUS*
Johnson, Daniel 1629-1675 *ApCAB*
Johnson, Daniel Harris 1825-1900 *NatCAB 11*
Johnson, David 1782-1855 *ApCAB, BiAUS,*
Drake, NatCAB 12, TwCBDA
Johnson, David 1827-1908 *ApCAB, BnEnAmA,*
NewYHSD, TwCBDA, WhAm 1
Johnson, David Bancroft 1856-1928 *BiDAmEd,*
DcAmB, NatCAB 3, TwCBDA,
WhAm 1
Johnson, David Benoni 1870-1954 *NatCAB 41*
Johnson, David Clayton 1885-1942 *WhAm 2*
Johnson, David Dale 1875-1954 *NatCAB 42*
Johnson, David G *NewYHSD*
Johnson, Dewey William 1899-1941 *BiDrAC*
Johnson, Douglas Wilson 1878-1944 *DcAmB S3,*
DcScB, NatCAB 33, WhAm 2
Johnson, Duncan Starr 1867-1937 *AmBi,*
NatCAB 32, WhAm 1
Johnson, E Fred 1896-1968 *WhAm 5*
Johnson, E Pauline *AmWom*
Johnson, Earl A 1899-1970 *WhAm 5*
Johnson, Earl Shepard 1894- *BiDAmEd*
Johnson, Earle Frederick 1886-1958 *WhAm 3*
Johnson, Earle George 1887-1964 *WhAm 4*
Johnson, Earle Levan 1895-1947 *NatCAB 35*
Johnson, Eastman 1824-1906 *AmBi, ApCAB,*
BnEnAmA, DcAmB, Drake, NatCAB 9,
NewYHSD, REnAW, TwCBDA, WebAB,
WhAm 1
Johnson, Eben Samuel 1866-1939 *WhAm 1*
Johnson, Ebenezer Alfred 1813-1891 *NatCAB 8,*
TwCBDA
Johnson, Edgar Augustus Jerome 1900-1972
WhAm 5
Johnson, Edgar Hutchinson 1873-1944
NatCAB 32, WhAm 2
Johnson, Edgar N 1901-1969 *WhAm 5*
Johnson, Edith Cherry 1879- *WomWWA 14*
Johnson, Edith Christina 1891-1954
NatCAB 41, WhAm 3
Johnson, Edward *NewYHSD*
Johnson, Edward 1598-1672 *DcAmB,*
WhAm H
Johnson, Edward 1599-1672 *ApCAB, Drake,*
NatCAB 8
Johnson, Edward 1816-1873 *ApCAB, BiDConf,*
DcAmB, NatCAB 12, TwCBDA,
WhAm H
Johnson, Edward 1817?-1873 *Drake*
Johnson, Edward Austin 1860-1944 *DcAmB S3,*
WhoColR
Johnson, Edward Bryant 1863-1935 *WhAm 1*
Johnson, Edward Darlington 1873-1943
NatCAB 35
Johnson, Edward Gilpin *WhAm 5*
Johnson, Edward Hibberd 1846-1917
NatCAB 33
Johnson, Edward Hibberd 1846-1919
NatCAB 6
Johnson, Edward Payson 1850-1924 *TwCBDA,*
WhAm 1
Johnson, Edward Roberts 1882-1960 *WhAm 4*
Johnson, Edwin Carl 1884-1970 *BiDrAC,*
WhAm 5
Johnson, Edwin Charles 1897-1969 *NatCAB 55*
Johnson, Edwin Clifford 1882-1960 *WhAm 4*
Johnson, Edwin Ferry 1803-1872 *AmBi,*
DcAmB, NatCAB 17, WhAm H
Johnson, Edwin Stockton 1857-1933 *BiDrAC,*
NatCAB 42, WhAm 1, WhAmP
Johnson, Effie *WhAm 1*
Johnson, Elbert Leland 1863-1949 *WhAm 2*
Johnson, Eldridge Reeves 1867-1945 *DcAmB S3,*
WhAm 2
Johnson, Eleanor Hope *WomWWA 14*
Johnson, Electa Amanda 1838- *AmWom*
Johnson, Elias Finley 1861-1933 *WhAm 1*
Johnson, Elias Henry 1841-1906 *DcAmB,*
WhAm 1

Johnson, Elias Mattison 1856-1935 *NatCAB 25*
Johnson, Elijah 1780?-1849 *DcAmB,*
WhAm H
Johnson, Eliza McCardle 1810-1876 *AmWom,*
ApCAB, NatCAB 2, NotAW, TwCBDA
Johnson, Elizabeth *WhAm H*
Johnson, Elizabeth Ayer 1886- *WomWWA 14*
Johnson, Elizabeth Forrest 1881- *WhAm 6*
Johnson, Elizabeth Hopkins 1874-
WomWWA 14
Johnson, Elizabeth Winthrop 1850- *WhAm 4*
Johnson, Elizabeth Winthrop 1859-
WomWWA 14
Johnson, Ellen *WhAm H*
Johnson, Ellen Cheney 1819-1899 *TwCBDA*
Johnson, Ellen Cheney 1829-1899 *DcAmB,*
NotAW, WhAm H
Johnson, Elliott 1889-1957 *NatCAB 48*
Johnson, Ellis Adolph 1906-1973 *WhAm 6*
Johnson, Elmer Harland 1872-1942 *NatCAB 32*
Johnson, Elmer Herman 1897-1957 *NatCAB 43*
Johnson, Elmer Walter 1892-1959 *NatCAB 46*
Johnson, Elvera Crosby 1912-1973 *WhAm 6*
Johnson, Elza Delno 1870-1950 *NatCAB 40*
Johnson, Emil Fritiof 1864- *WhAm 4*
Johnson, Emory Richard 1864-1950
NatCAB 36, TwCBDA, WhAm 2A
Johnson, Emsley Wright 1878-1950 *WhAm 3*
Johnson, Ernest Amos 1895-1959 *NatCAB 50,*
WhAm 3
Johnson, Evan 1869-1955 *NatCAB 45*
Johnson, Evan Malbone 1791-1865 *ApCAB*
Johnson, Evan Malbone 1861-1923 *WhAm 1*
Johnson, Evangeline Maria *ApCAB*
Johnson, Fenton 1888- *WhoColR*
Johnson, Florence Merriam *WomWWA 14*
Johnson, Frances Adams 1878- *WomWWA 14*
Johnson, Francis 1776-1842 *BiAUS, BiDrAC,*
WhAm H
Johnson, Francis Ellis 1885-1968 *WhAm 5*
Johnson, Francis Godschall 1817-1891
ApCAB Sup
Johnson, Francis Howe 1835-1920 *ApCAB X,*
WhAm 1
Johnson, Francis Kirk 1895-1963 *WhAm 4*
Johnson, Francis Marion 1828-1893
NatCAB 16
Johnson, Francis Rarick 1901-1960 *NatCAB 47,*
WhAm 4
Johnson, Francis Raymond 1895-1965 *WhAm 4*
Johnson, Frank Asbury 1845-1916 *NatCAB 18,*
WhAm 4
Johnson, Frank Donald 1899-1970 *NatCAB 55*
Johnson, Frank Fisk 1862-1937 *WhAm 1*
Johnson, Frank Grant 1835- *ApCAB*
Johnson, Frank H 1869- *WhoColR*
Johnson, Frank James 1856-1935 *NatCAB 44*
Johnson, Frank Pearson 1872- *WhAm 1*
Johnson, Frank Seward 1856-1922 *WhAm 1*
Johnson, Frank Tenney 1874-1939 *IIBEAAW,*
NatCAB 28, REnAW, WhAm 1
Johnson, Frank W 1799-1885 *NatCAB 5*
Johnson, Franklin d1870 *BiAUS*
Johnson, Franklin 1836- *TwCBDA*
Johnson, Franklin 1836-1914 *NatCAB 16*
Johnson, Franklin 1836-1916 *BiDAmEd,*
DcAmB, WhAm 1
Johnson, Franklin Paradise 1888-1943
NatCAB 34, WhAm 2
Johnson, Franklin Russell 1864-1939
NatCAB 41
Johnson, Franklin Winslow 1870-1956
NatCAB 45, WhAm 3
Johnson, Fred Gustus 1876-1951 *BiDrAC,*
WhAm 5
Johnson, Fred Hjalmar 1896-1954 *NatCAB 44*
Johnson, Fred Page 1874-1938 *WhAm 1*
Johnson, Frederic Ayres 1876-1926 *NatCAB 20*
Johnson, Frederic Mortimer 1874-1942
NatCAB 46
Johnson, Frederick 1887-1968 *WhAm 5*
Johnson, Frederick Avery 1833-1893 *BiDrAC,*
WhAm H
Johnson, Frederick Charles 1853- *NatCAB 11*
Johnson, Frederick Ernest 1884-1969 *WhAm 5*
Johnson, Frederick Foote 1866-1943 *WhAm 2*
Johnson, Frederick Green 1890-1941 *WhAm 1*

Johnson, Frederick William 1881-1955
WhAm 3
Johnson, Frost *NewYHSD*
Johnson, Garrison *IIBEAAW*
Johnson, George 1837- *ApCAB Sup*
Johnson, George 1872-1961 *WhAm 4*
Johnson, George 1889-1944 *DcAmB S3,*
WhAm 2
Johnson, George 1897-1966 *NatCAB 53*
Johnson, George C 1894-1965 *WhAm 4*
Johnson, George E Q 1874-1949 *WhAm 2*
Johnson, George Ellsworth 1862-1931 *WhAm 1*
Johnson, George Francis 1857-1948 *DcAmB S4,*
WhAm 2
Johnson, George Henry Martin 1816-1884
ApCAB
Johnson, George Henry Trust 1842-
NatCAB 11
Johnson, George Howard 1885-1959
NatCAB 50, WhAm 3A
Johnson, George Kinney 1822-1908 *NatCAB 8*
Johnson, George Knorr 1848-1923 *NatCAB 36,*
WhAm 1
Johnson, George Stevens 1897-1951 *NatCAB 40*
Johnson, George W 1817-1862 *TwCBDA*
Johnson, George W 1880-1953 *WhAm 3*
Johnson, George Washington 1811-1862
ApCAB Sup, BiDConf
Johnson, George William 1869-1944 *BiDrAC,*
WhAm 2, WhAmP
Johnson, Glen Dale 1911- *BiDrAC*
Johnson, Glover 1900-1973 *WhAm 6*
Johnson, Gove G 1869-1944 *WhAm 2*
Johnson, Grace Allen 1871-1952 *WhAm 3*
Johnson, Grace Mott 1882- *BiCAW*
Johnson, Grafton 1864-1934 *NatCAB 24*
Johnson, Grove Lawrence 1841-1926 *BiDrAC*
Johnson, Gustavus 1856- *WhAm 4*
Johnson, Guy 1740?-1788 *AmBi, ApCAB,*
DcAmB, Drake, NewYHSD, WhAm H
Johnson, H C *BiAUS Sup*
Johnson, Hale 1847- *ApCAB Sup*
Johnson, Hale 1847-1902 *WhAm 1*
Johnson, Hale 1847-1903 *TwCBDA*
Johnson, Hallett 1888-1968 *WhAm 5*
Johnson, Hamlin *NewYHSD*
Johnson, Hansford Duncan 1887-1965 *WhAm 4*
Johnson, Harley Alden 1884-1956 *NatCAB 44*
Johnson, Harold Bowtell 1880-1949 *WhAm 2*
Johnson, Harold Keith 1912- *WebAMB*
Johnson, Harold Terry 1907- *BiDrAC*
Johnson, Harry Fayette 1870-1948 *NatCAB 37*
Johnson, Harry Leonard 1873-1921 *NatCAB 19*
Johnson, Harry McCrindell 1867-1930 *WhAm 1*
Johnson, Harry Miles 1885-1953 *WhAm 3*
Johnson, Harry Thomas 1875-1943 *NatCAB 32*
Johnson, Harvey Hull 1808-1896 *BiAUS,*
BiDrAC, WhAm H
Johnson, Harvey W 1920?- *IIBEAAW*
Johnson, Hayden 1874-1936 *WhAm 1*
Johnson, Helen Louise Kendrick d1917 *ApCAB,*
WomWWA 14
Johnson, Helen Louise Kendrick 1843-1917
TwCBDA
Johnson, Helen Louise Kendrick 1844-1917
DcAmB, NatCAB 2, WhAm 1,
WomWWA 14
Johnson, Helen Ross 1872- *WomWWA 14*
Johnson, Helgi 1904-1974 *WhAm 6*
Johnson, Henderson Lafayette 1861-1918
NatCAB 18
Johnson, Henry *NewYHSD*
Johnson, Sir Henry 1748-1835 *ApCAB, Drake*
Johnson, Henry 1783-1861 *BiAUS*
Johnson, Henry 1783-1864 *ApCAB, BiDrAC,*
Drake, NatCAB 10, TwCBDA, WhAm H,
WhAmP
Johnson, Henry 1855-1918 *DcAmB,*
NatCAB 23, WhAm 1
Johnson, Henry 1867-1953 *BiDAmEd*
Johnson, Henry Abert 1855-1942 *NatCAB 31*
Johnson, Henry Charles 1868-1916 *NatCAB 17*
Johnson, Henry Clark 1851-1904 *NatCAB 2,*
TwCBDA, WhAm 1
Johnson, Henry Herbert 1861-1937 *WhAm 1*
Johnson, Henry Lincoln 1870-1925 *WhAm 1,*
WhoColR
Johnson, Henry Lincoln 1886-1947 *NatCAB 36*

Johnson, Henry Lowry Emilius 1858-1915 *WhAm 1*
Johnson, Henry Mortimer 1878-1950 *WhAm 3*
Johnson, Henry Underwood 1850-1939 *BiDrAC, TwCBDA, WhAm 4*
Johnson, Henry Viley 1852- *WhAm 4*
Johnson, Herbert 1878-1946 *WhAm 2*
Johnson, Herbert Fisk 1868-1928 *WhAm 1*
Johnson, Herbert Morris 1876-1937 *WhAm 1*
Johnson, Herbert Spencer 1866-1942 *NatCAB 32, WhAm 2*
Johnson, Herman E 1913-1972 *WhAm 5*
Johnson, Herman M 1815-1868 *Drake*
Johnson, Herman Merrill 1815-1868 *NatCAB 6, TwCBDA*
Johnson, Herman Merrills 1815-1868 *ApCAB*
Johnson, Herrick 1832-1913 *ApCAB, NatCAB 10, TwCBDA, WhAm 1*
Johnson, Herschel Vespasian 1812-1880 *AmBi, ApCAB, BiDConf, BiDrAC, DcAmB, Drake, NatCAB 1, TwCBDA, WhAm H, WhAmP*
Johnson, Herschel Vespasian 1894-1966 *NatCAB 54, WhAm 4*
Johnson, Herschell V 1812-1880 *BiAUS*
Johnson, Hewlett 1874-1966 *WhAm 4*
Johnson, Hezekiah S 1828- *BiAUS*
Johnson, Hiram Warren 1866-1945 *ApCAB X, BiDrAC, DcAmB S3, EncAB, McGEWB, NatCAB 15, NatCAB 40, REnAW, WebAB, WhAm 2, WhAmP*
Johnson, Hobart Stanley 1873-1942 *NatCAB 33*
Johnson, Homer Hosea 1862-1960 *WhAm 4*
Johnson, Horace 1893-1964 *WhAm 4*
Johnson, Horace Chauncey 1820-1890 *ApCAB, NatCAB 12, NewYHSD, TwCBDA*
Johnson, Hosmer Allen 1822-1891 *NatCAB 12*
Johnson, Howard Albert 1915-1974 *WhAm 6*
Johnson, Howard Cooper 1876-1952 *NatCAB 42, WhAm 3*
Johnson, Howard Deering 1896?-1972 *WebAB, WhAm 5*
Johnson, Hugh McCain 1874-1944 *NatCAB 51, WhAm 2*
Johnson, Hugh Samuel 1882-1942 *DcAmB S3, EncAB, NatCAB 42, WebAB, WebAMB, WhAm 2*
Johnson, Irving Petka 1866-1947 *WhAm 2*
Johnson, Isaac d1630 *ApCAB, Drake, NatCAB 12*
Johnson, Isaac d1853 *BiAUS, Drake, NatCAB 10, TwCBDA*
Johnson, Isaac 1841-1926 *NatCAB 20*
Johnson, Isaac Cureton 1881-1960 *WhAm 3A*
Johnson, Iver 1841-1895 *NatCAB 33*
Johnson, J Allen 1882-1935 *NatCAB 29*
Johnson, J E *NewYHSD*
Johnson, J Ford 1887-1962 *WhAm 4*
Johnson, Mrs. J Lindsay *WomWWA 14*
Johnson, J Neely d1872 *BiAUS*
Johnson, J Neely *see also* Johnson, James Neely
Johnson, J Richard 1879-1956 *NatCAB 45*
Johnson, J Rosamond 1873- *WhoColR, WhoColR A*
Johnson, J Sidney 1890- *WhAm 5*
Johnson, Jack Arthur 1878-1946 *DcAmB S4, WebAB*
Johnson, Jackson 1859-1929 *NatCAB 24, WhAm 1*
Johnson, Jacob 1847-1925 *BiDrAC, WhAm 3, WhAmP*
Johnson, James *NewYHSD*
Johnson, James 1774-1826 *ApCAB, BiAUS, BiDrAC, DcAmB, TwCBDA, WebAMB, WhAm H, WhAmP*
Johnson, James 1795?-1825 *BiAUS, BiDrAC, WhAm H*
Johnson, James 1810-1891 *NatCAB 1, TwCBDA*
Johnson, James 1811-1891 *ApCAB, BiAUS, BiDrAC, WhAm H*
Johnson, James 1886-1952 *NatCAB 42*
Johnson, James 1916- *WhWW-II*
Johnson, James A 1820-1883 *ApCAB*
Johnson, James Augustus 1829- *BiAUS*
Johnson, James Augustus 1829-1896 *BiDrAC*
Johnson, James Augustus 1829-1897 *WhAm H*
Johnson, James Buford 1909-1964 *WhAm 4*

Johnson, James Clarence 1865- *WhAm 4*
Johnson, James Gibson 1839-1905 *WhAm 1*
Johnson, James Grant 1871-1950 *NatCAB 38*
Johnson, James Granville 1857-1936 *WhAm 1*
Johnson, James Hutchins 1802-1887 *BiAUS, BiDrAC, WhAm H*
Johnson, James Leeper 1818-1877 *BiAUS, BiDrAC, WhAm H*
Johnson, James Marcus 1862-1935 *NatCAB 25*
Johnson, James McIntosh 1883-1953 *WhAm 3*
Johnson, James Neely 1825-1872 *TwCBDA*
Johnson, James Neely 1828?-1872 *NatCAB 4*
Johnson, James Neely *see also* Johnson, J Neely
Johnson, James T 1839-1904 *TwCBDA*
Johnson, James T *see also* Johnston, James Thomas
Johnson, James Weldon 1871-1938 *AmBi, DcAmB S2, EncAB, McGEWB, WebAB, WhAm 1, WhAmP, WhoColR A*
Johnson, Jed Joseph 1888-1963 *BiDrAC, WhAm 4*
Johnson, Jed Joseph, Jr. 1939- *BiDrAC*
Johnson, Jefferson Deems, Jr. 1900-1960 *WhAm 4*
Johnson, Jennie Fowler Willing *WomWWA 14*
Johnson, Jeremiah Augustus 1836-1914 *TwCBDA, WhAm 1*
Johnson, Jeromus 1775-1846 *BiAUS, BiDrAC, WhAm H*
Johnson, Jesse 1863-1951 *WhAm 3*
Johnson, John *NewYHSD*
Johnson, John d1856 *Drake*
Johnson, Sir John 1742-1830 *AmBi, ApCAB, DcAmB, Drake, McGEWB, NatCAB 8, WhAm H*
Johnson, John 1771-1842 *NatCAB 17*
Johnson, John 1805-1867 *BiDrAC, WhAm H*
Johnson, John 1808-1867 *BiAUS*
Johnson, John 1829-1907 *NatCAB 8, TwCBDA, WhAm 1*
Johnson, John Albert 1857-1928 *NatCAB 21, WhAm 1, WhoColR*
Johnson, John Albert 1861-1909 *AmBi, DcAmB, NatCAB 14, WhAm 1*
Johnson, John Algot 1876-1960 *NatCAB 48*
Johnson, John Arthur *WebAB*
Johnson, John B 1868- *WhAm 1*
Johnson, John Barent 1769-1803 *ApCAB*
Johnson, John Beauregard 1908-1972 *WhAm 6*
Johnson, John Bertrand 1887-1970 *NatCAB 55*
Johnson, John Bockover, Jr. 1912-1972 *WhAm 5*
Johnson, John Butler 1850-1902 *AmBi, DcAmB, NatCAB 11, TwCBDA, WhAm 1*
Johnson, John David 1881- *WhAm 6*
Johnson, John Davis 1844- *NatCAB 6, WhAm 4*
Johnson, John Edgar 1907-1960 *NatCAB 49*
Johnson, John Edward 1864-1938 *WhAm 1*
Johnson, John Edward 1912-1970 *WhAm 5*
Johnson, John Emil 1870- *ApCAB X*
Johnson, John George 1833-1917 *ApCAB X*
Johnson, John Gilmore 1852-1921 *NatCAB 13, WhAm 1*
Johnson, John Graver 1841-1917 *ApCAB X, DcAmB, NatCAB 16, WhAm 1*
Johnson, John H 1864-1929 *NatCAB 23*
Johnson, John Harold 1918- *EncAB, WebAB*
Johnson, John J 1870- *WhoColR*
Johnson, John Lindsay 1855-1915 *NatCAB 8*
Johnson, John Lipscomb 1869-1932 *WhAm 1*
Johnson, John Lovell 1876- *WhAm 1*
Johnson, John Mercer 1818-1868 *ApCAB*
Johnson, John Milton 1812-1886 *ApCAB, TwCBDA*
Johnson, John Mitchell 1845- *WhAm 4*
Johnson, John Monroe 1878-1964 *WhAm 4*
Johnson, John Quincy 1865- *WhoColR*
Johnson, John R *NewYHSD*
Johnson, John Samuel Adolphus 1878-1931 *WhAm 1*
Johnson, John Smoke 1792-1886 *ApCAB*
Johnson, John T 1788-1856 *ApCAB*
Johnson, John T 1788-1857 *BiAUS*
Johnson, John T 1856- *WhAm 4*
Johnson, John Telemachus 1788-1856 *BiDrAC, WhAm H, WhAmP*
Johnson, John Theodore 1902-1963 *WhAm 4*

Johnson, John Trimble 1788-1856 *TwCBDA*
Johnson, John Wesley 1836-1898 *NatCAB 28, TwCBDA*
Johnson, John William 1872-1933 *NatCAB 24, WhAm 1*
Johnson, Jonathan Eastman 1824-1906 *AmBi, DcAmB, IlBEAAW, McGEWB, NewYHSD, WebAB, WhAm HA, WhAm 4*
Johnson, Joseph 1776-1862 *ApCAB, DcAmB, Drake, NatCAB 8, WhAm H*
Johnson, Joseph 1785-1877 *ApCAB, BiAUS, BiDrAC, NatCAB 5, TwCBDA, WhAm H, WhAmP*
Johnson, Joseph French 1853-1925 *AmBi, BiDAmEd, DcAmB, TwCBDA, WhAm 1*
Johnson, Joseph Hoffman 1821-1890 *NewYHSD*
Johnson, Joseph Horsfall 1847-1928 *NatCAB 12, TwCBDA, WhAm 1*
Johnson, Joseph Lowery 1874- *WhAm 5*
Johnson, Joseph Taber 1845-1921 *ApCAB, WhAm 1*
Johnson, Joseph Tabor 1845-1921 *NatCAB 12*
Johnson, Joseph Travis 1858-1919 *BiDrAC, NatCAB 18, WhAm 1, WhAmP*
Johnson, Joseph Travis 1894-1967 *WhAm 4*
Johnson, Joshua d1802 *Drake*
Johnson, Jotham 1905-1967 *WhAm 4*
Johnson, Julia Macfarlane Carson 1862-1935 *BiCAW, WhAm 1, WomWWA 14*
Johnson, Julia Trippe 1870- *WomWWA 14*
Johnson, Julius 1877-1958 *NatCAB 44*
Johnson, Justin 1903-1962 *WhAm HA, WhAm 4*
Johnson, Justin Leroy 1888-1961 *BiDrAC, WhAmP*
Johnson, Justus Leonard 1879-1956 *NatCAB 47*
Johnson, Kate Burr 1881- *WhAm 6*
Johnson, Katherine Smyth 1856- *WomWWA 14*
Johnson, Keen 1896-1970 *WhAm 5*
Johnson, Kenneth D 1898-1958 *WhAm 3*
Johnson, L Dale 1888-1962 *NatCAB 50*
Johnson, Lambert Dunning 1889-1955 *NatCAB 45, WhAm 3*
Johnson, Laura C *WomWWA 14*
Johnson, Laura Elder *WomWWA 14*
Johnson, Laura Wilson *WomWWA 14*
Johnson, Laurence 1801-1860 *NewYHSD*
Johnson, Laurence 1845-1893 *NatCAB 16*
Johnson, Lawrence 1801-1860 *ApCAB*
Johnson, Lee Payne 1886-1964 *WhAm 4*
Johnson, Leighton Foster 1891-1953 *WhAm 3*
Johnson, Leon H 1908-1969 *WhAm 5*
Johnson, Leonard Victor 1899-1963 *NatCAB 50*
Johnson, Lester Bicknell 1918-1971 *WhAm 5*
Johnson, Lester R 1901-1975 *BiDrAC, WhAm 6, WhAmP*
Johnson, Levi 1786-1871 *DcAmB, NatCAB 25, WhAm H*
Johnson, Lewis Edgar 1860-1948 *WhAm 2*
Johnson, Lewis Jerome 1867-1952 *ApCAB X, WhAm 3*
Johnson, Ligon 1873-1951 *WhAm 3*
Johnson, Lilian Wyckoff 1864- *WhAm 4, WomWWA 14*
Johnson, Lincoln 1893-1957 *WhAm 3*
Johnson, Lindsay Franklin 1907-1974 *WhAm 6*
Johnson, Lionel Hubert 1898-1928 *NatCAB 22*
Johnson, Livingston 1857-1931 *WhAm 1*
Johnson, Loren Bascom Taber 1875-1941 *NatCAB 40, WhAm 2*
Johnson, Lorenzo Medici 1843-1904 *NatCAB 6, WhAm 1*
Johnson, Louis Arthur 1891-1956 *BiDrUSE*
Johnson, Louis Arthur 1891-1966 *NatCAB 51, WhAm 4*
Johnson, Louis R W 1878- *WhoColR*
Johnson, Lucius E 1846-1921 *WhAm 1*
Johnson, Lucius Henry 1863- *WhAm 1*
Johnson, Lucy Amelyne Ferrell *WomWWA 14*
Johnson, Luther Alexander 1875-1965 *BiDrAC, WhAm 4*
Johnson, Luther Appeles 1858-1900 *WhAm 1*
Johnson, Lydia Bernhardina 1875- *WomWWA 14*
Johnson, Lyndon Baines 1908-1973 *BiDrAC,*

BiDrUSE, EncAAH, EncAB, McGEWB,
WebAB, WhAm 5, WhAmP
Johnson, Lytle W *NewYHSD*
Johnson, Mabel Lucretia Prouty 1872-
WomWWA 14
Johnson, Mabel Ruth 1883- *WomWWA 14*
Johnson, Madison Conyers 1806-1886 *ApCAB,*
TwCBDA
Johnson, Maggie Pogue *WhoColR*
Johnson, Magnus 1871-1936 *ApCAB X,*
BiDrAC, DcAmB S2, NatCAB 35,
WhAm 1, WhAmP
Johnson, Malcolm 1902-1958 *WhAm 3*
Johnson, Manuel John 1805-1859 *DcScB*
Johnson, Marcus Morton 1843-1914
NatCAB 16
Johnson, Margaret 1860- *WhAm 4*
Johnson, Margaret Edith Henry *WomWWA 14*
Johnson, Margaret Hill Hilles *WomWWA 14*
Johnson, Margaret Louise 1902-1973 *WhAm 6*
Johnson, Marian Gray 1852- *WomWWA 14*
Johnson, Marietta Louise Pierce 1864-1938
BiDAmEd, WhAm 1
Johnson, Marion Alvin 1901-1964 *NatCAB 51,*
WhAm 4
Johnson, Marmaduke d1674 *DcAmB,*
WhAm H
Johnson, Martha 1828- *ApCAB*
Johnson, Martin Elmer 1884-1937 *AmBi,*
NatCAB 28, WhAm 1
Johnson, Martin Nelson 1850-1909 *BiDrAC,*
NatCAB 14, TwCBDA, WhAm 1,
WhAmP
Johnson, Mary 1832-1883 *ApCAB*
Johnson, Mary Ann 1808-1872 *ApCAB*
Johnson, Mary Ella *WomWWA 14*
Johnson, Mary Hooker 1875- *WomWWA 14*
Johnson, Mary Simonds 1874- *WomWWA 14*
Johnson, Mary Zelene 1887-1955 *NatCAB 44*
Johnson, Max Sherred 1902-1968 *WhAm 4*
Johnson, Melvin Blake 1862-1920 *ApCAB X,*
NatCAB 20
Johnson, Melvin Maynard 1871-1957 *WhAm 3*
Johnson, Melvin Maynard, Jr. 1909-1965
WhAm 4
Johnson, Merle DeVore 1874-1935 *WhAm 1*
Johnson, Milbank 1871-1944 *WhAm 2*
Johnson, Montgomery Hunt 1872-1952
NatCAB 42
Johnson, Mordecai Wyatt 1890-1976 *BiDAmEd*
Johnson, Mortimer Lawrence 1842-1913
TwCBDA, WhAm 1
Johnson, Murrey Levering 1860-1954
NatCAB 43
Johnson, Myrtle Elizabeth 1881-
WomWWA 14
Johnson, N Oscar 1872-1924 *NatCAB 20*
Johnson, Nathan Manly 1891-1959 *NatCAB 46*
Johnson, Sir Nathaniel 1645?-1713 *ApCAB,*
DcAmB, Drake, NatCAB 12, WhAm H
Johnson, Nels G 1896-1958 *WhAm 3*
Johnson, Nelson Trusler 1887-1954 *NatCAB 43,*
WhAm 3
Johnson, Neville 1808?- *NewYHSD*
Johnson, Noadiah 1795-1839 *BiAUS, BiDrAC,*
WhAm H
Johnson, Noble Jacob 1887-1968 *BiDrAC*
Johnson, Oliver 1809-1889 *AmBi, ApCAB,*
DcAmB, NatCAB 2, TwCBDA,
WhAm H
Johnson, Oliver Francis d1936 *WhAm 1,*
WhAm 1C
Johnson, Orson Thomas 1839-1916 *ApCAB X,*
NatCAB 31
Johnson, Osa Helen Leighty 1894-1952
NatCAB 39
Johnson, Osa Helen Leighty 1894-1953
DcAmB S5, WhAm 3
Johnson, Oscar 1864-1916 *NatCAB 24*
Johnson, Oscar John 1870-1946 *WhAm 2*
Johnson, Osgood 1803-1837 *NatCAB 10*
Johnson, Otis Coe 1839-1912 *NatCAB 19,*
WhAm 1
Johnson, Otis R 1887-1957 *WhAm 3*
Johnson, Ovid Frazer 1807-1854 *ApCAB*
Johnson, Owen McMahon 1878-1952
DcAmB S5, NatCAB 41, WhAm 3
Johnson, Palmer Oliver 1891-1960 *BiDAmEd,*

WhAm 3
Johnson, Paul Burney 1880-1943 *BiDrAC,*
WhAm 2
Johnson, Paul Emanuel 1898-1974 *WhAm 6*
Johnson, Paul Franklin 1874-1946 *NatCAB 34*
Johnson, Paul Luther 1917-1972 *WhAm 6*
Johnson, Paul Maurice 1900-1961 *NatCAB 48*
Johnson, Paul Rodgers 1888-1948 *WhAm 2*
Johnson, Perley Brown 1798-1870 *BiAUS,*
BiDrAC, WhAm H
Johnson, Peter d1848 *Drake*
Johnson, Philander Chase 1866-1939 *WhAm 1*
Johnson, Philip 1818-1867 *BiAUS, BiDrAC,*
NatCAB 11, TwCBDA, WhAm H
Johnson, Philip Carrigain 1828-1887 *ApCAB,*
TwCBDA
Johnson, Philip Cortelyou 1906- *BnEnAmA,*
McGEWB, WebAB
Johnson, Philip G 1894-1944 *WhAm 2*
Johnson, Phillip Thomas 1899-1970 *NatCAB 55*
Johnson, R Harold 1899-1964 *NatCAB 51*
Johnson, Ralph Blake 1904-1966 *WhAm 4*
Johnson, Ralph Cross 1843-1923 *NatCAB 25*
Johnson, Randall Edward 1938- *WhAm 6*
Johnson, Ray Prescott 1878-1932 *NatCAB 32*
Johnson, Ray Prescott 1907-1964 *WhAm 4*
Johnson, Rebecca Franks *NotAW*
Johnson, Reginald Davis 1882-1952 *NatCAB 42,*
WhAm 3
Johnson, Reverdy 1796-1876 *AmBi, ApCAB,*
BiAUS, BiAUS Sup, BiDrAC, BiDrUSE,
DcAmB, Drake, NatCAB 4, TwCBDA,
WebAB, WhAm H, WhAmP
Johnson, Richard Allen 1843-1914 *NatCAB 31*
Johnson, Richard Ellis 1909-1974 *WhAm 6*
Johnson, Richard H 1855-1942 *WhAm 3*
Johnson, Richard Harvey 1870-1929 *WhAm 1*
Johnson, Richard Mentor 1780-1850 *AmBi,*
BiAUS, DcAmB, REnAW, WebAB,
WebAMB
Johnson, Richard Mentor 1781-1850 *ApCAB,*
BiDrAC, BiDrUSE, Drake, NatCAB 6,
TwCBDA, WhAm H, WhAmP
Johnson, Richard Newhall 1900-1971
NatCAB 56, WhAm 5
Johnson, Richard W 1827-1897 *AmBi, ApCAB,*
DcAmB, Drake, NatCAB 12,
NatCAB 15, TwCBDA, WhAm H
Johnson, Richard Zina 1837-1913 *WhAm 1*
Johnson, Robert *BiAUS*
Johnson, Robert d1735 *Drake*
Johnson, Robert 1676?-1735 *DcAmB,*
WhAm H
Johnson, Robert 1682-1735 *ApCAB,*
NatCAB 12
Johnson, Robert Davis 1883-1961 *BiDrAC*
Johnson, Robert Livingston 1894-1966 *WhAm 4*
Johnson, Robert Livingston, Jr. 1919-1970
WhAm 5
Johnson, Robert Payne 1854-1948 *NatCAB 37*
Johnson, Robert Rosser 1886-1937 *NatCAB 28*
Johnson, Robert Underwood 1853-1937 *AmBi,*
ApCAB Sup, ApCAB X, DcAmB S2,
NatCAB 1, NatCAB 46, TwCBDA,
WhAm 1
Johnson, Robert V *WhAm 6*
Johnson, Robert W 1888-1963 *WhAm 4*
Johnson, Robert Ward 1814-1879 *ApCAB,*
BiAUS, BiDConf, BiDrAC, DcAmB,
NatCAB 5, REnAW, TwCBDA,
WhAm H, WhAmP
Johnson, Robert Wilkinson 1854-1930
NatCAB 40, WhAm 1
Johnson, Robert Wood 1845-1910 *NatCAB 35*
Johnson, Robert Wood 1893-1968 *WhAm 5*
Johnson, Robert Wood, Jr. 1920-1970 *WhAm 5*
Johnson, Roger Bruce Cash 1867-1946
NatCAB 34, WhAm 3
Johnson, Rosa Vertner d1853 *Drake*
Johnson, Rosamond 1873-1954 *WhAm 3*
Johnson, Rossiter 1840-1931 *AmBi, ApCAB,*
ApCAB X, NatCAB 2, TwCBDA,
WhAm 1
Johnson, Rowland 1816-1886 *ApCAB*
Johnson, Roy Melisander 1881- *WhAm 6*
Johnson, Roy William 1905-1965 *NatCAB 51,*
WhAm 4
Johnson, Royal Cleaves 1882-1939 *BiDrAC,*

WhAm 1, WhAmP
Johnson, S Arthur 1866- *WhAm 4*
Johnson, S D *NewYHSD*
Johnson, S Lloyd 1890-1958 *NatCAB 48*
Johnson, Sallie M Mills 1862- *AmWom*
Johnson, Samuel *NewYHSD*
Johnson, Samuel 1696-1772 *AmBi, ApCAB,*
BiDAmEd, DcAmB, DcAmReB, Drake,
McGEWB, NatCAB 6, TwCBDA,
WhAm H
Johnson, Samuel 1709-1784 *McGEWB*
Johnson, Samuel 1822-1882 *ApCAB, DcAmB,*
Drake, NatCAB 2, WhAm H
Johnson, Samuel, Jr. 1757-1836 *ApCAB Sup*
Johnson, Samuel Ben 1847- *NatCAB 10*
Johnson, Samuel Frost 1835- *ApCAB,*
NatCAB 7, NewYHSD
Johnson, Samuel M 1860- *NatCAB 6*
Johnson, Samuel O 1874- *WhoColR*
Johnson, Samuel R 1830-1915 *NatCAB 27*
Johnson, Samuel Roosevelt 1802-1873 *ApCAB,*
TwCBDA
Johnson, Samuel S 1857-1905 *NatCAB 38*
Johnson, Samuel William 1727-1819 *NatCAB 6*
Johnson, Samuel William 1830-1909 *ApCAB,*
DcAmB, EncAAH, NatCAB 6, TwCBDA,
WhAm 1
Johnson, Sarah Barclay 1837-1885 *ApCAB,*
NatCAB 11
Johnson, Mrs. Seth Albert 1865-
WomWWA 14
Johnson, Seth Whitmore 1811-1907 *DcAmB*
Johnson, Silas 1889-1951 *WhAm 3*
Johnson, Simeon Moses 1859-1957 *WhAm 3*
Johnson, Solomon Charles 1869- *WhoColR*
Johnson, Stanley 1892-1946 *WhAm 2*
Johnson, Stanley H 1872-1926 *WhAm 1*
Johnson, Stephen Olin 1847-1924 *NatCAB 20*
Johnson, Stewart 1880-1926 *NatCAB 36*
Johnson, Susan Rachel Harrison
WomWWA 14
Johnson, Sveinbjorn 1883-1946 *WhAm 2*
Johnson, Sylvanus Elihu 1841-1908 *WhAm 1*
Johnson, Talmage Casey 1896-1964 *WhAm 4*
Johnson, Theodore 1882-1956 *NatCAB 45,*
WhAm 4
Johnson, Theodore Taylor 1818- *ApCAB*
Johnson, Thomas *NewYHSD, WhAm 1*
Johnson, Thomas d1877 *NatCAB 5*
Johnson, Thomas 1600?-1644 *DcScB*
Johnson, Thomas 1732-1819 *AmBi, ApCAB,*
BiAUS, BiDrAC, DcAmB, Drake,
NatCAB 1, NatCAB 9, TwCBDA,
WebAB, WhAmP
Johnson, Thomas 1812-1906 *BiDConf*
Johnson, Thomas Albert 1874-1957 *NatCAB 47*
Johnson, Thomas Cary 1859-1936 *TwCBDA,*
WhAm 1
Johnson, Thomas Crossley 1862-1934
NatCAB 26
Johnson, Thomas Francis 1909- *BiDrAC*
Johnson, Thomas Humrickhouse 1841-1914
WhAm 1
Johnson, Thomas Joseph Allan 1876-1934
WhAm 1
Johnson, Thomas Moore 1851-1919 *WhAm 1*
Johnson, Tillman Davis 1858-1953 *NatCAB 47,*
WhAm 3
Johnson, Tom Loftin 1854-1911 *AmBi,*
BiDrAC, DcAmB, EncAB, McGEWB,
NatCAB 14, TwCBDA, WebAB,
WhAm 1, WhAmP
Johnson, Tracy Ayres 1879-1945 *NatCAB 35*
Johnson, Treat Baldwin 1875-1947 *DcAmB S4,*
NatCAB 35, WhAm 2
Johnson, Trimble 1894-1946 *NatCAB 35*
Johnson, Virgil E 1903-1963 *NatCAB 51*
Johnson, Virgil Lamont 1868- *WhAm 4*
Johnson, Virginia Eshelman 1925- *EncAB*
Johnson, Virginia Wales 1849-1916 *ApCAB,*
DcAmB, NatCAB 13, TwCBDA,
WhAm 1
Johnson, W Ogden 1893-1966 *WhAm 4*
Johnson, Wait Chatterton 1877-1937
NatCAB 28
Johnson, Waldo Paten 1882-1955 *NatCAB 45*
Johnson, Waldo Porter 1817-1885 *ApCAB,*
BiAUS, BiDConf, BiDrAC, NatCAB 12,

TwCBDA, WhAm H

Johnson, Wallace 1867- *WhAm 4*

Johnson, Wallace Clyde 1859-1906 *WhAm 1*

Johnson, Walter Alexander 1876- *WhoColR*

Johnson, Walter Frederick 1899-1948 *NatCAB 35*

Johnson, Walter H 1848- *WhAm 4*

Johnson, Walter Lathrop 1874-1966 *WhAm 4*

Johnson, Walter Lee 1869-1958 *NatCAB 46*

Johnson, Walter Nathan 1875-1952 *WhAm 4*

Johnson, Walter Perry 1887-1946 *DcAmB S4, WebAB, WhAm HA, WhAm 4*

Johnson, Walter Richard 1897-1974 *WhAm 6*

Johnson, Walter Rogers 1794-1852 *ApCAB, Drake, NatCAB 12, TwCBDA*

Johnson, Walter Werston 1875- *WhoColR*

Johnson, Wanda Mae d1969 *WhAm 5*

Johnson, Warren S 1847- *NatCAB 3*

Johnson, Wayne 1892-1947 *NatCAB 37, WhAm 2*

Johnson, Wendell Andrew Leroy 1906-1965 *NatCAB 53, WhAm 4*

Johnson, Willard 1820-1900 *NatCAB 13*

Johnson, Willard Drake 1859-1917 *DcScB*

Johnson, William *NewYHSD*

Johnson, William 1610?-1665 *DcScB*

Johnson, Sir William 1715-1774 *AmBi, ApCAB, DcAmB, Drake, EncAB, McGEWB, NatCAB 5, REnAW, WebAB, WebAMB, WhAm H*

Johnson, William 1742-1818 *NatCAB 8*

Johnson, William 1768-1848 *Drake*

Johnson, William 1769-1848 *DcAmB, WhAm H*

Johnson, William 1770?-1848 *ApCAB*

Johnson, William 1771-1834 *ApCAB, BiAUS, DcAmB, Drake, NatCAB 2, TwCBDA, WebAB, WhAm H*

Johnson, William 1819-1866 *BiAUS*

Johnson, William *see also* Johnston, William

Johnson, William Allen 1833-1909 *WhAm 1*

Johnson, William Arthur 1885-1956 *WhAm 3*

Johnson, William B *NewYHSD*

Johnson, William Bishop 1858- *WhoColR*

Johnson, William Bullein 1782-1862 *DcAmB, WhAm H*

Johnson, William Bullien 1782-1862 *ApCAB, NatCAB 12*

Johnson, William Burdett 1875-1959 *WhAm 3*

Johnson, William C 1902-1951 *WhAm 3*

Johnson, William Christie 1843-1917 *NatCAB 13, WhAm 1*

Johnson, William Clinton 1885-1938 *NatCAB 30*

Johnson, William Colet 1876-1943 *NatCAB 32*

Johnson, William Cost 1806-1860 *BiAUS, BiDrAC, TwCBDA, WhAm H, WhAmP*

Johnson, William Crawford 1856-1943 *NatCAB 32*

Johnson, William Decker 1869- *WhoColR*

Johnson, William Driscoll 1905-1969 *WhAm 5*

Johnson, William Ernest 1858-1931 *DcScB*

Johnson, William Eugene 1862-1945 *NatCAB 35, WhAm 2*

Johnson, William F d1858 *Drake*

Johnson, William F 1838- *WhAm 4*

Johnson, William Franklin 1856- *WhAm 4*

Johnson, William Geary 1879-1949 *WhAm 4*

Johnson, William Hallock 1865-1963 *NatCAB 51, WhAm 4*

Johnson, William Hannibal 1860-1934 *WhAm 1*

Johnson, William Harold 1920-1972 *WhAm 5*

Johnson, William Henry 1845-1907 *WhAm 1*

Johnson, William Henry 1871-1934 *NatCAB 31*

Johnson, William Houston 1879-1964 *WhAm 4*

Johnson, William Howard 1866-1940 *WhAm 1*

Johnson, William Jasper 1860-1942 *NatCAB 31*

Johnson, William Lupton 1800-1870 *ApCAB*

Johnson, William Martin 1771?-1797 *NatCAB 8*

Johnson, William Martin 1862- *WhAm 4*

Johnson, William Mindred 1847-1928 *WhAm 1*

Johnson, William Newton 1898-1957 *NatCAB 43*

Johnson, William Pierce 1859-1926 *NatCAB 33*

Johnson, William Ransom 1782-1849 *DcAmB, WhAm H*

Johnson, William Richard 1875-1938 *BiDrAC*

Johnson, William Samuel 1727-1819 *AmBi, ApCAB, BiAUS, BiDrAC, DcAmB, Drake, TwCBDA, WebAB, WhAm H, WhAmP*

Johnson, William Samuel 1859-1937 *NatCAB 28, WhAm 1*

Johnson, William T *NewYHSD*

Johnson, William Templeton 1877-1957 *NatCAB 46, WhAm 3*

Johnson, William Ward 1892-1963 *BiDrAC*

Johnson, William Woolsey 1841-1927 *BiDAmEd, DcAmB, NatCAB 23, TwCBDA, WhAm 1*

Johnson, Willis Ernest 1869-1951 *WhAm 3*

Johnson, Willis Fletcher 1857-1931 *AmBi, DcAmB, NatCAB 24, WhAm 1*

Johnson, Willis Grant 1866-1908 *WhAm 1*

Johnson, Wingate Memory 1885-1963 *NatCAB 51, WhAm 4*

Johnson, Woolsey 1842-1887 *ApCAB*

Johnston, A Langstaff 1850-1901 *NatCAB 28*

Johnston, A Langstaff, Jr. 1882-1957 *NatCAB 50*

Johnston, Adelia Antoinette Field 1837-1910 *AmWom, WhAm 1*

Johnston, Albert Sidney 1802-1862 *TwCBDA*

Johnston, Albert Sidney 1803-1862 *AmBi, ApCAB, BiDConf, DcAmB, Drake, NatCAB 29, REnAW, WebAMB, WhAm H, WhoMilH*

Johnston, Albert Sydney 1803-1862 *NatCAB 1, WebAB*

Johnston, Alexander 1849-1889 *AmBi, ApCAB, DcAmB, NatCAB 24, WhAm H*

Johnston, Almira Sutton 1859- *WomWWA 14*

Johnston, Alva 1888-1950 *NatCAB 38, WhAm 3*

Johnston, Alvanley 1875-1951 *NatCAB 40, WhAm 3*

Johnston, Amelia *WomWWA 14*

Johnston, Amos Randall 1810-1879 *ApCAB*

Johnston, Anna Harper 1853- *WomWWA 14*

Johnston, Annie Fellows 1863-1931 *DcAmB, NatCAB 13, NotAW, WhAm 1, WomWWA 14*

Johnston, Archibald 1865- *WhAm 4*

Johnston, Augustus 1730?-1790? *DcAmB, WhAm H*

Johnston, Benjamin 1740-1818 *NewYHSD*

Johnston, C Howard, Jr. 1888-1959 *NatCAB 48*

Johnston, Caroline A Dorsey 1860- *WomWWA 14*

Johnston, Cecil Frederick 1904-1958 *NatCAB 45*

Johnston, Charles 1793-1845 *BiAUS, BiDrAC, WhAm H*

Johnston, Charles 1867-1931 *WhAm 1*

Johnston, Charles Clement 1795-1832 *BiAUS, BiDrAC, WhAm H*

Johnston, Charles Eugene 1881-1951 *WhAm 3*

Johnston, Charles G 1899-1960 *WhAm 4*

Johnston, Charles Haven Ladd 1877-1943 *WhAm 2*

Johnston, Charles Hughes 1877-1917 *WhAm 1*

Johnston, Charles Worth 1861-1941 *WhAm 1*

Johnston, Christopher 1822- *ApCAB*

Johnston, Christopher 1856-1914 *WhAm 1*

Johnston, Clarence Howard 1859-1936 *NatCAB 9, WhAm 1*

Johnston, Clarence Thomas 1872- *WhAm 5*

Johnston, Mrs. D *NewYHSD*

Johnston, David Claypole 1797-1865 *Drake*

Johnston, David Claypoole 1797-1865 *ApCAB, NatCAB 8*

Johnston, David Claypoole 1799-1865 *DcAmB, NewYHSD, WhAm H*

Johnston, David Emmons 1845-1917 *BiDrAC, TwCBDA, WhAm 4*

Johnston, David Ira 1876-1958 *WhAm 3*

Johnston, David Lorimer 1872-1932 *NatCAB 36*

Johnston, Douglas T 1887-1962 *WhAm 4*

Johnston, Edgar Clinton 1899-1951 *NatCAB 40*

Johnston, Edgar Francis 1859-1926 *NatCAB 21*

Johnston, Edward Neele 1876-1936 *NatCAB 36*

Johnston, Elizabeth Bryant d1907 *WhAm 1*

Johnston, Ella Bond 1860- *WhAm 4, WomWWA 14*

Johnston, Eric A 1895-1963 *WhAm 4*

Johnston, Eva 1865- *WomWWA 14*

Johnston, Forney 1879-1965 *NatCAB 53, WhAm 4*

Johnston, Frances Benjamin 1864-1952 *DcAmB S5, WhAm 3*

Johnston, Francis 1749-1815 *Drake, TwCBDA*

Johnston, Francis Hans 1888-1948 *IIBEAAW*

Johnston, Francis Wayland 1882-1960 *WhAm 4*

Johnston, Franklin Davis 1900-1971 *WhAm 5*

Johnston, Gabriel 1699-1752 *AmBi, ApCAB, DcAmB, Drake, NatCAB 5, WhAm H*

Johnston, Gabriel *see also* Johnstone, Gabriel

Johnston, George Ben 1853-1916 *DcAmB, WhAm 1*

Johnston, George Benjamin 1853-1916 *NatCAB 13*

Johnston, George Doherty 1832-1910 *BiDConf, WhAm 1*

Johnston, Gordon 1874-1934 *WhAm 1*

Johnston, Gordon 1903-1958 *WhAm 3*

Johnston, Harold Whetstone 1859-1912 *TwCBDA, WhAm 1*

Johnston, Harriet Lane 1830-1903 *NotAW*

Johnston, Harriet Lane 1833-1903 *AmWom, ApCAB, NatCAB 5, TwCBDA*

Johnston, Harry Bauer 1890-1955 *NatCAB 43*

Johnston, Harry Buchanan 1880-1953 *NatCAB 40*

Johnston, Harry Lang 1873-1948 *WhAm 2*

Johnston, Harry Raymond 1922-1975 *WhAm 6*

Johnston, Harvey Pollard 1903-1971 *WhAm 5*

Johnston, Henrietta 1670?- *BnEnAmA*

Johnston, Henrietta 1670?-1728? *DcAmB, NewYHSD, NotAW*

Johnston, Henrietta 1670?-1729 *WhAm H*

Johnston, Henry Alan 1884-1956 *WhAm 3*

Johnston, Henry Donaldson 1905-1964 *WhAm 4*

Johnston, Henry Hamilton 1858-1927 *McGEWB*

Johnston, Henry Phelps 1842-1923 *DcAmB, NatCAB 11, WhAm 1*

Johnston, Herbert Lincoln 1869-1938 *NatCAB 28*

Johnston, Herbert Richard 1895-1967 *NatCAB 54*

Johnston, Herrick Lee 1898-1965 *NatCAB 52, WhAm 4*

Johnston, Howard Agnew 1860-1936 *NatCAB 12, WhAm 1*

Johnston, Hugh 1840-1922 *ApCAB, WhAm 1*

Johnston, Ivan Murray 1898-1960 *WhAm 4*

Johnston, J Thomas 1872- *WhoColR*

Johnston, James 1833- *WhAm 4*

Johnston, James A 1874-1954 *WhAm 3*

Johnston, James Davis 1875-1955 *NatCAB 42*

Johnston, James Martin 1895-1967 *WhAm 4*

Johnston, James Steptoe 1843-1924 *ApCAB Sup, NatCAB 13, TwCBDA, WhAm 1*

Johnston, James Thomas 1839-1904 *BiDrAC*

Johnston, James Thomas *see also* Johnson, James T

Johnston, John d1818 *Drake*

Johnston, John 1752-1818 *ApCAB*

Johnston, John 1753-1818 *NewYHSD*

Johnston, John 1763-1834 *Drake*

Johnston, John 1775-1861 *ApCAB, Drake*

Johnston, John 1778-1855 *Drake*

Johnston, John 1791-1880 *DcAmB, WhAm H*

Johnston, John 1806-1879 *ApCAB, Drake*

Johnston, John 1836-1904 *NatCAB 3, NatCAB 30, WhAm 1*

Johnston, John 1881-1950 *DcAmB S4, WhAm 3*

Johnston, John Alexander 1858-1940 *WhAm 1*

Johnston, John Allen 1884-1944 *NatCAB 35*

Johnston, John Black 1868-1939 *NatCAB 29*

Johnston, John Black 1868-1947 *WhAm 2*

Johnston, John Brown 1882-1960 *BiDrAC*

Johnston, John Humphreys 1857- *NatCAB 13*

Johnston, John Humphreys *see also* Johnstone, John Humphreys

Johnston, John Lawrence 1887-1958 *WhAm 3*

Johnston, John M *NewYHSD*

Johnston, John R *NewYHSD*

Johnston, John T M 1856-1930 *WhAm 1*

Johnston, John Taylor 1820-1893 *ApCAB,
 DcAmB, NatCAB 23, TwCBDA,
 WhAm H*

Johnston, John Warfield 1818-1889 *ApCAB,
 BiAUS, BiDrAC, NatCAB 12, TwCBDA,
 WhAm H*

Johnston, John White 1879- *NatCAB 16*

Johnston, Joseph Eccleston 1807-1891 *Drake*

Johnston, Joseph Eggleston 1807-1891 *AmBi,
 BiDConf, BiDrAC, DcAmB, EncAB,
 McGEWB, NatCAB 5, TwCBDA,
 WebAB, WebAMB, WhAm H, WhoMilH*

Johnston, Joseph Eggleston 1809-1891 *ApCAB*

Johnston, Joseph Forney 1843-1913 *BiDrAC,
 DcAmB, NatCAB 10, TwCBDA,
 WhAm 1*

Johnston, Joshua *BnEnAmA, NewYHSD*

Johnston, Josiah Stoddard 1784-1833 *AmBi,
 ApCAB, BiAUS, BiDrAC, DcAmB,
 Drake, NatCAB 5, TwCBDA, WhAm H,
 WhAmP*

Johnston, Josiah Stoddard 1833-1913 *ApCAB,
 TwCBDA, WhAm 1*

Johnston, Julia Harriette 1849-1919
 NatCAB 20, WhAm 1, WomWWA 14

Johnston, Kilbourne 1907-1972 *WhAm 5*

Johnston, L S 1887-1955 *WhAm 3*

Johnston, Lawrence Albert 1855-1918 *WhAm 1*

Johnston, Leon H 1886-1961 *WhAm 4*

Johnston, Leslie Morgan 1876- *WhAm 5*

Johnston, Lizzie Johnston Evans 1851-1934
 NatCAB 31

Johnston, Lucy Brown 1847- *WomWWA 14*

Johnston, Lucy Browne 1846-1937 *WhAm 1*

Johnston, Marbury 1860-1934 *WhAm 1*

Johnston, Maria Isabella 1835- *AmWom,
 WhAm 5*

Johnston, Marie Decca *AmWom*

Johnston, Mary 1870-1936 *AmBi, DcAmB S2,
 NatCAB 10, NotAW, TwCBDA,
 WhAm 1, WomWWA 14*

Johnston, Mary Beattie 1884- *WomWWA 14*

Johnston, Mary H Stoddard 1865-
 WomWWA 14

Johnston, Mary Virginia DelCastillo 1865-
 WomWWA 14

Johnston, Myrtle Alice Dean d1971 *WhAm 6*

Johnston, Nathan Robinson 1860- *WhAm 4*

Johnston, Norwood 1864-1950 *NatCAB 45*

Johnston, Olin DeWitt Talmadge 1896-1965
 BiDrAC, NatCAB 50, WhAm 4

Johnston, Oliver Martin 1866- *WhAm 4*

Johnston, Oscar Goodbar 1880-1955 *WhAm 3*

Johnston, Percy Hampton 1881-1957 *WhAm 3*

Johnston, Peter 1763-1831 *DcAmB, WhAm H*

Johnston, Peter 1763-1841 *ApCAB*

Johnston, Philip Harbison 1903-1958
 NatCAB 48

Johnston, Richard Hall 1871-1923 *NatCAB 20,
 WhAm 5*

Johnston, Richard Holland 1868-1955 *WhAm 3*

Johnston, Richard Malcolm 1822-1898 *AmBi,
 ApCAB, BiDAmEd, DcAmB, NatCAB 1,
 TwCBDA, WhAm H*

Johnston, Rienzi Melville 1849-1926 *BiDrAC*

Johnston, Rienzi Melville 1850-1926
 NatCAB 20, NatCAB 21, WhAm 1

Johnston, Robert 1818-1885 *BiDConf*

Johnston, Robert Born 1910-1967 *WhAm 5*

Johnston, Robert Daniel 1837-1919 *BiDConf,
 WhAm 4*

Johnston, Robert Matteson 1867-1920 *DcAmB,
 NatCAB 23, WhAm 1*

Johnston, Robert Story 1874-1944 *WhAm 2*

Johnston, Rowland Louis 1872-1939 *BiDrAC,
 WhAm 1*

Johnston, Rufus Perry 1861-1924 *WhAm 1*

Johnston, Rufus Zenas 1874-1959 *NatCAB 48*

Johnston, Russell M 1864- *WhAm 4*

Johnston, Russell Ziebell 1894-1959
 NatCAB 44

Johnston, S Edna *WomWWA 14*

Johnston, Samuel 1733-1816 *AmBi, ApCAB,
 BiAUS, BiDrAC, DcAmB, Drake,
 NatCAB 4, WhAm H*

Johnston, Samuel 1835-1911 *ApCAB, DcAmB,
 NatCAB 13, TwCBDA, WhAm 4*

Johnston, Samuel 1837-1911 *NatCAB 24*

Johnston, Samuel *see also* Johnstone, Samuel

Johnston, Samuel M 1890-1969 *WhAm 5*

Johnston, Sidney Robinson 1902-1968
 NatCAB 54

Johnston, Stanley 1898-1969 *NatCAB 54*

Johnston, Stanley 1900-1962 *WhAm 4*

Johnston, Stewart 1865-1933 *NatCAB 25,
 WhAm 1*

Johnston, Thomas 1708?-1767 *BnEnAmA,
 DcAmB, NewYHSD, WhAm H*

Johnston, Thomas, Jr. 1731- *NewYHSD*

Johnston, Thomas Alexander 1848-1934
 WhAm 1

Johnston, Thomas Dillard 1840-1902 *BiDrAC*

Johnston, Thomas Luckey 1859-1938
 NatCAB 30

Johnston, Thomas Murphy 1834-1869
 NewYHSD, WhAm H

Johnston, Thomas Slater 1845-1915 *NatCAB 16*

Johnston, Thomas William 1862-1917 *WhAm 1*

Johnston, Victor A 1900-1967 *WhAm 4*

Johnston, Walt 1932- *IIBEAAW*

Johnston, Walter R *NewYHSD*

Johnston, Walter Vail 1883-1963 *WhAm 4*

Johnston, Ward Reynold 1897-1961
 NatCAB 49

Johnston, Wayne Andrew 1897-1967 *WhAm 4A*

Johnston, William 1732-1772 *NewYHSD*

Johnston, William 1819-1866 *BiDrAC,
 WhAm H*

Johnston, William *see also* Johnson, William

Johnston, William Agnew 1848-1937 *NatCAB 5,
 WhAm 1*

Johnston, William Allen 1876- *WhAm 5*

Johnston, William Andrew 1871-1929 *DcAmB,
 WhAm 1*

Johnston, William Atkinson 1868-1937
 WhAm 1

Johnston, William Dawson 1861-1933 *WhAm 1*

Johnston, William Dawson 1871-1928 *WhAm 1*

Johnston, William Drumm, Jr. 1899-1972
 WhAm 5

Johnston, William Fenton 1895-1965 *WhAm 4*

Johnston, William Freame 1808-1872 *ApCAB,
 BiAUS, NatCAB 2, TwCBDA*

Johnston, William Greer 1900-1957 *WhAm 3*

Johnston, William Hartshorne 1861-1933
 DcAmB S1

Johnston, William Howard 1885-1963
 NatCAB 51

Johnston, William Hugh 1874-1937 *AmBi,
 DcAmB S2, WhAm 1*

Johnston, William L *NewYHSD*

Johnston, William M 1821-1907 *NewYHSD*

Johnston, William Milton 1867-1938 *WhAm 1*

Johnston, William Pollock 1839-1920 *TwCBDA,
 WhAm 1*

Johnston, William Preston 1831-1899 *ApCAB,
 BiDConf, DcAmB, NatCAB 9, TwCBDA,
 WhAm 1*

Johnston, William Waring 1843-1902 *WhAm 1*

Johnston, Wilson 1867-1943 *NatCAB 35*

Johnston, Wirt 1846-1900 *WhAm 1*

Johnston, Zachariah 1742-1800 *DcAmB,
 NatCAB 24, WhAm H*

Johnston, Zachariah F d1859 *Drake*

Johnstone, Arthur Edward 1860-1944
 NatCAB 32, WhAm 5

Johnstone, Arthur Weir 1853-1905 *NatCAB 15*

Johnstone, Bruce 1876- *WhAm 5*

Johnstone, David *ApCAB Sup*

Johnstone, Edward Ransom 1870-1946
 BiDAmEd, DcAmB S4, WhAm 2A

Johnstone, Edward Robert 1849- *TwCBDA,
 WhAm 1*

Johnstone, Ernest Kinloch 1871-1948
 NatCAB 37, WhAm 2

Johnstone, Francis Upton d1858 *ApCAB Sup*

Johnstone, Gabriel 1699-1752 *TwCBDA*

Johnstone, Gabriel *see also* Johnston, Gabriel

Johnstone, George d1787 *ApCAB, Drake*

Johnstone, George 1846-1921 *BiDrAC*

Johnstone, George Albert 1876-1942
 NatCAB 31

Johnstone, Henry Fraser 1902-1962 *NatCAB 50,
 WhAm 4*

Johnstone, Henry Webb 1892-1971 *WhAm 5*

Johnstone, Herbert George 1903-1958
 NatCAB 47

Johnstone, James Hope Stewart 1861-1916
 NatCAB 17

Johnstone, Job 1793-1862 *ApCAB, DcAmB,
 WhAm H*

Johnstone, John *ApCAB Sup*

Johnstone, John 1662-1732 *ApCAB Sup*

Johnstone, John Francis 1874-1948 *NatCAB 39*

Johnstone, John Humphreys 1857- *WhAm 4*

Johnstone, John Humphreys *see also* Johnston,
 John Humphreys

Johnstone, Mary Margaret Sewall 1870-
 WomWWA 14

Johnstone, Samuel 1733-1816 *TwCBDA*

Johnstone, Samuel *see also* Johnston, Samuel

Johnstone, William Jackson 1867-1939
 WhAm 1

Johnstone, William Souter d1818 *Drake*

Johonnot, James 1823-1888 *ApCAB*

Johonnott, Edwin Sheldon 1868-1925 *WhAm 1*

Joiner, John J *NewYHSD*

Joiner, Otis William 1919-1975 *WhAm 6*

Joiner, William A 1869- *WhoColR*

Joinville, Jean De 1224?-1317 *McGEWB*

Joliet, Louis 1645-1700 *Drake, WhAm H*

Joline, Adrian Hoffman 1850-1912 *DcAmB,
 NatCAB 15, WhAm 1*

Joline, Charles VanDyke 1851-1930
 NatCAB 29

Joliot, Frederic 1900-1958 *DcScB*

Joliot-Curie, Frederic 1900-1958 *AsBiEn,
 WhAm 3*

Joliot-Curie, Irene 1897-1956 *AsBiEn, DcScB,
 WhAm 3*

Joliot-Curie, Jean Frederic 1900-1958
 McGEWB

Jolivet, Andre 1905-1974 *WhAm 6*

Jolles, Otto Jolle Matthijs 1911-1968 *WhAm 5*

Jolley, John Lawlor 1840-1926 *BiDrAC*

Jolliet, Louis 1645-1700 *AmBi, ApCAB,
 DcAmB, McGEWB, NatCAB 5, REnAW,
 WebAB*

Jolliffe, Charles Byron 1894-1970 *WhAm 5*

Jolliffe, Norman Hayhurst 1901-1961
 NatCAB 45, WhAm 4

Jolly, Austin Howell 1852- *WhAm 4*

Jolly, Philipp Johann Gustav Von 1809-1884
 DcScB

Jolly, Robert Garland 1885-1952 *NatCAB 41,
 WhAm 3*

Jolson, Al 1886-1950 *DcAmB S4, WebAB*

Jolson, Al 1888-1950 *WhAm 3*

Joly, Henry Gustave 1829- *ApCAB*

Joly, John 1857-1933 *DcScB*

Jome, Hiram L 1895-1958 *WhAm 3*

Jomini, Antoine Henri 1779-1869 *WhoMilH*

Jonah, Frank Gilbert 1864-1945 *WhAm 2*

Jonas, Anna Isabel 1881- *WomWWA 14*

Jonas, August Frederick 1858-1934 *WhAm 1*

Jonas, Augustus Frederick 1858-1934
 NatCAB 13

Jonas, Benjamin Franklin 1834-1911 *ApCAB,
 BiDrAC, NatCAB 4, TwCBDA,
 WhAm 1*

Jonas, Charles Andrew 1876-1955 *BiDrAC,
 WhAm 5*

Jonas, Charles Raper 1904- *BiDrAC*

Jonas, Edgar Allan 1885-1965 *BiDrAC,
 WhAm 4*

Jonas, Franz 1899-1974 *WhAm 6*

Jonas, Jack Henry 1917-1968 *WhAm 5*

Jonas, Maryla 1911-1959 *WhAm 3*

Jonas, Nathan Solomon 1868-1943 *NatCAB 32,
 WhAm 4*

Jonas, Ralph 1878-1952 *WhAm 3*

Jonas, Russell E 1902-1971 *WhAm 5*

Jonathan, Joseph Leabua 1914- *McGEWB*

Jones *NewYHSD*

Jones, Mother *WebAB*

Jones, A Charles 1913-1966 *NatCAB 52*

Jones, A L *NewYHSD*

Jones, A Marshall 1872-1949 *WhAm 2*

Jones, Aaron 1838- *WhAm 4*

Jones, Abner 1772-1841 *DcAmB, WhAm H*

Jones, Ada 1873-1922 *WhAm 4*

Jones, Adam Leroy 1873-1934 *NatCAB 24,
 WhAm 1*

Jones, Albert Eugene 1902-1962 *NatCAB 48*
Jones, Albert Monmouth 1890-1967 *WhAm 4*
Jones, Albert Norman 1843-1924 *NatCAB 22*
Jones, Albert R 1874- *WhAm 5*
Jones, Alexander 1802?-1863 *AmBi, ApCAB, DcAmB, NatCAB 24, WhAm H*
Jones, Alexander Francis 1891-1966 *NatCAB 53, WhAm 4*
Jones, Alexander Hamilton 1822-1901 *ApCAB, BiAUS, BiDrAC, TwCBDA*
Jones, Alfred 1819-1900 *AmBi, ApCAB, DcAmB, NatCAB 12, NewYHSD, TwCBDA, WhAm 1*
Jones, Alfred 1889-1943 *WhAm 2*
Jones, Alfred B 1874-1965 *WhAm 4*
Jones, Alfred D 1814-1902 *NatCAB 12*
Jones, Alfred Gilpin 1824- *ApCAB*
Jones, Alfred Miles 1837-1910 *WhAm 1*
Jones, Alfred Power 1885-1966 *NatCAB 51*
Jones, Alfred S 1861- *WhoColR*
Jones, Alice *WomWWA 14*
Jones, Allan Dudley 1875-1954 *NatCAB 45*
Jones, Allen 1739- *BiAUS, Drake*
Jones, Allen 1739-1798 *ApCAB, BiDrAC, TwCBDA, WhAmP*
Jones, Allen 1739-1807 *DcAmB, NatCAB 24, WhAm H*
Jones, Allen Arthur 1864-1950 *NatCAB 42*
Jones, Allen Northey 1896-1958 *WhAm 3*
Jones, Amanda Theodosia 1835-1914 *AmWom, ApCAB, DcAmB, NatCAB 7, NotAW, WhAm 1, WomWWA 14*
Jones, Amos Blanch 1841- *NatCAB 1, TwCBDA*
Jones, Andrieus Aristieus 1862-1927 *ApCAB X, BiDrAC, NatCAB 20, WhAm 1, WhAmP*
Jones, Anthony W *NewYHSD*
Jones, Archibald Amos 1860- *TwCBDA, WhAm 4*
Jones, Archie Austin 1898-1952 *NatCAB 41*
Jones, Arthur Edward 1893-1956 *NatCAB 45*
Jones, Arthur Gray 1868-1929 *WhAm 1*
Jones, Arthur Julius 1871-1963 *BiDAmEd, NatCAB 51, WhAm 5*
Jones, Arthur Woodruff 1879-1957 *NatCAB 52, WhAm 6*
Jones, Augustine 1835-1925 *NatCAB 6, TwCBDA, WhAm 1*
Jones, Augustus 1796-1887 *TwCBDA*
Jones, Avonia Stanhope 1839-1867 *Drake*
Jones, Barry Holme 1874-1919 *NatCAB 18*
Jones, Barton Mills 1885-1957 *WhAm 3*
Jones, Bassett 1877-1960 *WhAm 3*
Jones, Benjamin *NewYHSD*
Jones, Benjamin 1787-1861 *BiAUS, BiDrAC, WhAm H*
Jones, Benjamin Francis *WhoColR*
Jones, Benjamin Franklin 1824-1903 *DcAmB, NatCAB 13, WhAm H*
Jones, Benjamin Franklin 1831- *NatCAB 5*
Jones, Benjamin Franklin 1870-1935 *WhAm 1, WhAm 1C*
Jones, Benjamin Franklin, Jr. 1868-1928 *WhAm 1*
Jones, Bob 1883-1968 *WhAm 4*
Jones, Bobby 1902-1971 *WebAB*
Jones, Bradley 1889-1957 *NatCAB 46*
Jones, Breckinridge 1856-1928 *NatCAB 12, WhAm 1*
Jones, Brian d1969 *WhAm 5*
Jones, Bruce Carr 1877-1959 *WhAm 3*
Jones, Buck 1894-1942 *NatCAB 32*
Jones, Buell Fay 1892-1947 *WhAm 2*
Jones, Burr W 1846-1935 *ApCAB X, BiDrAC, NatCAB 10, NatCAB 28, WhAm 1*
Jones, Burton Rensselaer 1845-1933 *WhAm 1*
Jones, Calvin 1775-1846 *DcAmB, WhAm H*
Jones, Carl Allen 1879-1950 *NatCAB 39*
Jones, Carl H 1893-1958 *WhAm 3*
Jones, Carl Waring 1887-1957 *WhAm 3*
Jones, Carlton Allen 1879-1950 *WhAm 3*
Jones, Carroll Sherman 1857-1921 *NatCAB 20*
Jones, Carter Helm 1861-1946 *WhAm 2*
Jones, Casey 1864-1900 *WebAB*

Jones, Catesby ApRoger 1821-1877 *DcAmB, TwCBDA, WebAMB, WhAm H*
Jones, Catesby ApRoger 1830?-1877 *NatCAB 5*
Jones, Catlit 1750?-1829 *Drake*
Jones, Cecil Cain 1892-1963 *NatCAB 50*
Jones, Charles 1804-1859 *NatCAB 17*
Jones, Charles A 1815-1851 *ApCAB, Drake*
Jones, Charles Alfred 1869-1942 *WhAm 2*
Jones, Charles Alvin 1887-1966 *NatCAB 53, WhAm 4*
Jones, Charles Andrews d1958 *WhAm 3*
Jones, Charles Colcock 1804-1863 *ApCAB, TwCBDA*
Jones, Charles Colcock 1831-1893 *AmBi, ApCAB, DcAmB, NatCAB 5, TwCBDA, WhAm H*
Jones, Charles Colcock, III 1865- *WhAm 5*
Jones, Charles Davies 1871-1935 *WhAm 1*
Jones, Charles Edward 1867-1941 *WhAm 1*
Jones, Charles F d1971 *WhAm 5*
Jones, Charles Fremont 1856-1931 *WhAm 1*
Jones, Charles Hampson 1858-1932 *WhAm 1*
Jones, Charles Hebard 1845- *ApCAB X*
Jones, Charles Henry 1837- *ApCAB Sup*
Jones, Charles Henry 1848-1913 *NatCAB 1, WhAm 1*
Jones, Charles Hodge 1878- *WhAm 6*
Jones, Charles Jesse 1844-1918 *WebAB*
Jones, Charles Paul 1878- *WhAm 6*
Jones, Charles Reading 1862-1944 *WhAm 2*
Jones, Charles Reynolds 1886-1967 *NatCAB 53*
Jones, Charles S d1970 *WhAm 5*
Jones, Charles Sumner 1858-1927 *WhAm 1*
Jones, Charles Thomas 1865- *WhoColR*
Jones, Charles William 1834-1897 *ApCAB, BiAUS, BiDrAC, NatCAB 10, TwCBDA, WhAmP*
Jones, Cheney Church 1880-1954 *WhAm 3*
Jones, Chester Lloyd 1881-1941 *WhAm 1*
Jones, Chester Morse 1891-1972 *WhAm 5*
Jones, Clara Louise 1866- *WomWWA 14*
Jones, Claud Ashton 1885-1948 *NatCAB 53, WhAm 2*
Jones, Clement Ross 1871-1939 *WhAm 1*
Jones, Cliff C 1879-1960 *WhAm 4*
Jones, Clyde Edward 1895-1959 *NatCAB 49, WhAm 3*
Jones, Cyril Hamlen 1893-1972 *WhAm 5*
Jones, Daniel Fiske 1868-1937 *NatCAB 28, WhAm 1*
Jones, Daniel Jonathan 1889-1965 *WhAm 4*
Jones, Daniel Lanning 1880-1967 *NatCAB 53*
Jones, Daniel Terryll 1800-1861 *BiAUS, BiDrAC, WhAm H*
Jones, Daniel Webster 1839-1918 *NatCAB 10, TwCBDA, WhAm 1*
Jones, David 1699-1775 *ApCAB, Drake, TwCBDA*
Jones, David 1736-1820 *ApCAB, DcAmB, Drake, NatCAB 8, TwCBDA, WhAm H*
Jones, David 1895-1974 *WhAm 6*
Jones, David C 1921- *WebAMB*
Jones, David Dallas 1887-1956 *NatCAB 48, WhAm 3*
Jones, David Ford 1818- *ApCAB*
Jones, David Hugh 1861- *WhAm 4*
Jones, David Percy 1860-1927 *WhAm 1*
Jones, David Phillips 1841- *TwCBDA*
Jones, David Rump 1825-1863 *ApCAB*
Jones, David Rumph 1824-1863 *BiDConf*
Jones, David Rumph 1825-1863 *AmBi, DcAmB, Drake, WhAm H*
Jones, David Rumple 1825-1863 *TwCBDA*
Jones, David Samuel 1777-1848 *ApCAB, TwCBDA*
Jones, Della A 1866- *WomWWA 14*
Jones, Donald Forsha 1890-1963 *NatCAB 49, WhAm 4*
Jones, Donald Twining 1906-1961 *NatCAB 50*
Jones, Duane 1897-1961 *NatCAB 46*
Jones, Dwight Arven 1854-1913 *NatCAB 26*
Jones, Dwight Bangs 1900-1958 *WhAm 3*
Jones, Dymae J Durling *WomWWA 14*
Jones, E Milton 1874- *WhAm 5*
Jones, Earl J 1893-1957 *NatCAB 43, WhAm 3*
Jones, Ed 1912- *BiDrAC*
Jones, Edgar DeWitt 1876-1956 *WhAm 3*

Jones, Edgar Laroy 1853-1915 *WhAm 1*
Jones, Edgar LeRoy 1903-1969 *NatCAB 54*
Jones, Edith Beatrice *WomWWA 14*
Jones, Edith Kathleen 1868- *WhAm 1*
Jones, Edmund Adams 1842-1926 *WhAm 1*
Jones, Edward *NewYHSD*
Jones, Edward 1762-1841 *TwCBDA*
Jones, Edward Archie 1863-1928 *NatCAB 22*
Jones, Edward C *NewYHSD*
Jones, Edward Campbell 1861-1933 *NatCAB 24, WhAm 1*
Jones, Edward Coffin 1805-1880 *ApCAB X*
Jones, Edward Darlington 1885-1954 *NatCAB 41*
Jones, Edward David 1870-1944 *WhAm 3*
Jones, Edward Dorr Griffin 1824-1904 *NatCAB 31*
Jones, Edward E 1867-1951 *WhAm 3*
Jones, Edward Fairfax Berkley 1874-1957 *NatCAB 45*
Jones, Edward Franc 1828-1913 *WhAm 1*
Jones, Edward Groves 1874-1921 *WhAm 1*
Jones, Edward Hallaran 1885-1956 *NatCAB 50*
Jones, Edward M 1862- *WhoColR*
Jones, Edward Perry 1872- *WhAm 5, WhoColR*
Jones, Edward Raymond 1884- *ApCAB X*
Jones, Edwin 1863-1921 *NatCAB 19*
Jones, Edwin Epes 1890-1969 *NatCAB 54*
Jones, Edwin Frank 1859-1918 *WhAm 1*
Jones, Edwin Lee 1891-1971 *NatCAB 57, WhAm 5*
Jones, Edwin Leslie 1920-1973 *WhAm 6*
Jones, Edwin Whiting 1896-1956 *WhAm 4*
Jones, Eleanor Dwight 1880- *WomWWA 14*
Jones, Eleanor Hooper *WomWWA 14*
Jones, Eleanor Louise 1875- *WhAm 5*
Jones, Eli 1807-1890 *NatCAB 2*
Jones, Eli Stanley 1884-1973 *WhAm 5*
Jones, Eliot 1887-1971 *WhAm 5*
Jones, Elisha Henry 1883- *WhoColR*
Jones, Elizabeth *ApCAB*
Jones, Elizabeth Ann McKey 1850- *WomWWA 14*
Jones, Elizabeth Bartram 1871- *WomWWA 14*
Jones, Elizabeth Dickson 1862- *WhAm 4*
Jones, Elizabeth Howard Blanton 1868- *WomWWA 14*
Jones, Ella Virginia 1865- *WhAm 4*
Jones, Elmer Ellsworth 1866- *WhAm 5*
Jones, Elmer Ray 1874-1961 *WhAm 4*
Jones, Elton B 1908-1963 *WhAm 4*
Jones, Emanuel *NewYHSD*
Jones, Emery *NewYHSD*
Jones, Erastus Beverly 1852-1923 *NatCAB 31*
Jones, Ernest Alfred 1879-1958 *McGEWB*
Jones, Ernest Elwood 1888-1954 *NatCAB 44*
Jones, Ernest Lester 1876-1929 *DcAmB, NatCAB 26, WhAm 1*
Jones, Eugene Kinckle 1885- *WhoColR*
Jones, Eva Linnette Soule 1873- *WomWWA 14*
Jones, Evan Hudson 1881-1955 *NatCAB 45*
Jones, Evan John 1872-1952 *BiDrAC, WhAm 5*
Jones, Evan William 1852-1908 *DcAmB, NatCAB 25*
Jones, Evelyn Tubb d1969 *WhAm 5*
Jones, Everett Foster 1884-1940 *NatCAB 37*
Jones, Everett Starr 1864- *WhAm 4*
Jones, Ezra Albert 1880-1963 *NatCAB 50*
Jones, F P *NewYHSD*
Jones, Fernando 1820-1911 *WhAm 1*
Jones, FitzEdwin *NewYHSD*
Jones, Floyd William 1891-1969 *WhAm 5*
Jones, Forrest Robert 1861- *TwCBDA, WhAm 4*
Jones, Francis *BiAUS, BiDrAC, WhAm H*
Jones, Francis Arthur 1877-1947 *NatCAB 37*
Jones, Francis Coates 1857-1932 *AmBi, NatCAB 13, NatCAB 27, TwCBDA, WhAm 1*
Jones, Francis Ilah 1864- *WhAm 3*
Jones, Francis Wiley 1846- *NatCAB 4*
Jones, Frank 1832-1902 *BiDrAC, DcAmB, NatCAB 23, TwCBDA, WhAm 1*
Jones, Frank Cameron 1873-1952 *NatCAB 41*
Jones, Frank Cazenove 1857-1918 *NatCAB 27*
Jones, Frank Cazenove 1867- *NatCAB 11*

Jones, Frank Cazenove 1887-1949 *WhAm 2*
Jones, Frank Hatch 1854-1931 *NatCAB 23*
Jones, Frank Herbert 1858-1927 *NatCAB 27*
Jones, Frank Johnston 1838-1927 *WhAm 1*
Jones, Frank Leonard 1872-1953 *NatCAB 44,*
WhAm 3
Jones, Frank Morton 1869-1962 *NatCAB 50*
Jones, Frank Pierce 1905-1975 *WhAm 6*
Jones, Frank Smith 1847-1927 *ApCAB X,*
NatCAB 13, NatCAB 25
Jones, Franklin D 1887-1929 *WhAm 1*
Jones, Franklin Elmore 1873- *WhAm 5*
Jones, Fred Goodwin 1883-1951 *NatCAB 42*
Jones, Fred Reuel 1884-1956 *NatCAB 45*
Jones, Frederic Marshall 1874-1946 *WhAm 2*
Jones, Frederic Randolph 1878- *WhAm 6*
Jones, Frederick *NewYHSD*
Jones, Frederick E d1974 *WhAm 6*
Jones, Frederick Ellis 1873-1937 *NatCAB 28*
Jones, Frederick Hall 1867-1947 *NatCAB 35*
Jones, Frederick McKinley 1892-1961
NatCAB 50
Jones, Frederick Robertson 1872-1941 *WhAm 1,*
WhAm 2
Jones, Gabriel 1724-1806 *DcAmB, WhAm H*
Jones, Gabriel L 1858- *WhoColR*
Jones, Gaius J 1843- *NatCAB 11, WhAm 4*
Jones, Gardner Maynard 1850-1941 *NatCAB 6,*
TwCBDA, WhAm 1
Jones, George *NewYHSD*
Jones, George d1838 *BiAUS*
Jones, George 1760?-1838 *NatCAB 5*
Jones, George 1766-1838 *BiDrAC, WhAm H*
Jones, George 1800-1870 *ApCAB, DcAmB,*
Drake, TwCBDA, WhAm H
Jones, George 1810- *Drake*
Jones, George 1811-1891 *DcAmB, NatCAB 1,*
NatCAB 21, TwCBDA, WhAm H
Jones, George 1882-1946 *NatCAB 35*
Jones, George Clark 1829-1914 *NatCAB 16*
Jones, George Edwin 1824-1870 *NewYHSD*
Jones, George G 1872-1946 *NatCAB 35*
Jones, George Heber 1867-1919 *DcAmB,*
NatCAB 18, WhAm 1
Jones, George Henry 1872-1928 *NatCAB 23,*
WhAm 1
Jones, George Herbert 1856-1941 *WhAm 1*
Jones, George Howard 1889-1952 *NatCAB 39*
Jones, George James 1856- *TwCBDA,*
WhAm 4
Jones, George Lewis, Jr. 1907-1971 *WhAm 5*
Jones, George Milton 1866-1970 *NatCAB 56*
Jones, George Salley 1871-1938 *WhAm 1*
Jones, George T 1818?- *NewYHSD*
Jones, George Wallace 1804-1896 *AmBi,*
ApCAB, BiAUS, BiDrAC, DcAmB,
NatCAB 3, TwCBDA, WhAm H
Jones, George Washington 1806-1884 *BiAUS,*
BiDConf, BiDrAC, WhAm H, WhAmP
Jones, George Washington 1828-1903 *BiDrAC*
Jones, George Washington 1865-1930 *WhAm 1*
Jones, George William 1837-1911 *WhAm 1*
Jones, Georgia H Lloyd 1875- *WomWWA 14*
Jones, Gilbert Edward 1888-1925 *NatCAB 20*
Jones, Gilbert Haven 1883-1966 *BiDAmEd*
Jones, Gordon 1862-1917 *NatCAB 17*
Jones, Grace Latimer 1879- *WomWWA 14*
Jones, Grace McHardy *WomWWA 14*
Jones, Grace Morris Allen 1879- *WhoColR*
Jones, Griffith *NatCAB 2*
Jones, Grinnell 1884-1947 *NatCAB 36,*
WhAm 2
Jones, Guernsey 1868-1929 *WhAm 1*
Jones, Hamilton Chamberlain 1884-1957
BiDrAC
Jones, Harold Eldred 1887-1950 *NatCAB 39*
Jones, Harold Ellis 1894-1960 *NatCAB 47,*
WhAm 4
Jones, Harold Houston 1891-1955 *NatCAB 45*
Jones, Sir Harold Spencer 1890-1960 *AsBiEn,*
DcScB
Jones, Harold Wellington 1877-1958 *WhAm 3*
Jones, Harriet B 1856- *AmWom*
Jones, Harriman 1876-1956 *NatCAB 45*
Jones, Harriot Hamblen 1886-1957 *WhAm 3*
Jones, Harrison 1867-1967 *WhAm 4*
Jones, Harry Burnell 1888- *WhAm 5*
Jones, Harry Clary 1865-1916 *DcAmB, DcScB,*

Jones, Harry Lewis 1882- *NatCAB 18*
Jones, Harry Stewart 1864- *WhAm 4*
Jones, Harry Stuart Vedder 1878-1942
WhAm 1
Jones, Harry Wild 1859-1935 *WhAm 1*
Jones, Heber 1848- *WhAm 1*
Jones, Helen Beach 1857- *WomWWA 14*
Jones, Henrietta Ord 1860- *WhAm 4*
Jones, Henry Cox 1821-1913 *BiDConf,*
NatCAB 15
Jones, Henry Craig 1879-1929 *WhAm 1*
Jones, Henry Lawrence 1839- *TwCBDA,*
WhAm 4
Jones, Henry N 1881- *WhAm 6*
Jones, Henry Wilson 1872-1957 *NatCAB 43*
Jones, Herbert Coffin 1880- *WhAm 6*
Jones, Herbert Vincent 1878- *WhAm 2*
Jones, Herschel Vespasian 1861-1928 *DcAmB*
Jones, Herschell V 1861-1928 *WhAm 1*
Jones, Hilary Pollard 1863-1938 *DcAmB S2,*
NatCAB 30, WhAm 1
Jones, Hilton Ira 1882-1955 *WhAm 3*
Jones, Hiram Arthur 1899-1945 *NatCAB 35*
Jones, Homer Raymond 1893-1970 *BiDrAC*
Jones, Horace Conrad 1857-1940 *NatCAB 30,*
WhAm 1
Jones, Horace Croom 1898-1960 *NatCAB 48*
Jones, Horatio *BiAUS*
Jones, Horatio Gates 1777-1853 *ApCAB,*
TwCBDA
Jones, Horatio Gates 1822-1893 *ApCAB,*
TwCBDA
Jones, Howard 1853- *WhAm 4*
Jones, Howard Palfrey 1899-1973 *WhAm 6*
Jones, Howel 1844-1928 *NatCAB 21*
Jones, Hugh d1760 *Drake*
Jones, Hugh 1669-1760 *ApCAB, TwCBDA*
Jones, Hugh 1670?-1760 *DcAmB, NatCAB 24,*
WhAm H
Jones, Hugh 1867-1928 *ApCAB X*
Jones, Hugh Bolton 1848-1927 *AmBi, ApCAB,*
DcAmB, NatCAB 13, NatCAB 27,
TwCBDA, WhAm 1
Jones, Hugh McK 1880-1960 *WhAm 4*
Jones, I Howland 1868- *WhAm 5*
Jones, Ida Irwin 1872- *WomWWA 14*
Jones, Idwal 1888-1964 *WhAm 4*
Jones, Ilion Tingnal 1889- *WhAm 5*
Jones, Inigo 1573-1652 *McGEWB*
Jones, Ira B 1851-1927 *NatCAB 21*
Jones, Irma Theoda 1845- *AmWom*
Jones, Irving Luther 1879-1946 *NatCAB 43*
Jones, Isaac Dashiell 1806-1893 *BiAUS,*
BiDrAC, WhAm H
Jones, Isaac Thomas 1838-1907 *WhAm 1*
Jones, Isham 1894-1956 *WhAm 4A*
Jones, Isham Giggs 1887- *WhoColR*
Jones, J Catron 1889-1934 *WhAm 1*
Jones, J Claude 1877-1932 *WhAm 1*
Jones, J Glancy 1811-1878 *BiAUS, Drake*
Jones, J Glancy *see also* Jones, Jehu Glancy
Jones, J Levering 1851- *WhAm 1*
Jones, J M *BiAUS*
Jones, J Morris 1896-1962 *WhAm 4*
Jones, J Russell 1823-1909 *BiAUS*
Jones, J Russell *see also* Jones, Joseph Russell
Jones, J S William 1866-1944 *WhAm 2*
Jones, J Shirley 1876-1954 *WhAm 3*
Jones, J Wynne 1845-1918 *NatCAB 30*
Jones, Jack Walker 1894-1961 *NatCAB 50*
Jones, Jacob 1768-1850 *AmBi, ApCAB,*
DcAmB, Drake, NatCAB 2, TwCBDA,
WebAMB, WhAm H
Jones, Jacob Paul 1806-1885 *TwCBDA*
Jones, James *NewYHSD*
Jones, James 1740-1801 *BiAUS, BiDrAC,*
WhAm H
Jones, James 1772-1848 *BiAUS, BiDrAC,*
WhAm H
Jones, James 1807-1873 *ApCAB, TwCBDA*
Jones, James Addison 1869-1950 *NatCAB 38*
Jones, James Archibald 1911-1966 *WhAm 4*
Jones, James Athearn 1790-1853 *ApCAB,*
Drake
Jones, James Benson 1879-1938 *NatCAB 28*
Jones, James C *NewYHSD*
Jones, James C 1809-1859 *BiAUS*

Jones, James Chamberlain 1809-1859 *ApCAB,*
BiDrAC, Drake, NatCAB 7, TwCBDA
Jones, James Chamberlayne 1809-1859 *DcAmB,*
WhAm H
Jones, James Coulter 1866-1946 *WhAm 2*
Jones, James Emlyn 1875-1938 *WhAm 1*
Jones, James Hazlitt 1896- *WhAm 5*
Jones, James Henry 1830-1904 *BiDrAC*
Jones, James Kimbrough 1829-1908 *AmBi,*
DcAmB
Jones, James Kimbrough 1839-1908 *ApCAB,*
BiDrAC, NatCAB 1, TwCBDA,
WhAm 1, WhAmP
Jones, James Marion, Jr. 1884-1940 *WhAm 1*
Jones, James Mills 1861- *WhAm 4*
Jones, James Milton 1827-1904 *NatCAB 33*
Jones, James P *NewYHSD*
Jones, James Sumner 1881-1940 *WhAm 1*
Jones, James Taylor 1832-1895 *BiDrAC,*
WhAm H
Jones, Jane Elizabeth Hitchcock 1813-1896
NotAW
Jones, Jefferson 1891-1965 *WhAm 4*
Jones, Jehu Glancy 1811-1878 *BiDrAC,*
DcAmB, NatCAB 7, TwCBDA,
WhAm H, WhAmP
Jones, Jehu Glancy *see also* Jones, John Glancy
Jones, Jenkin Lloyd 1843-1918 *DcAmB,*
NatCAB 14, TwCBDA, WhAm 1
Jones, Jennie E 1833- *AmWom*
Jones, Jennie Wood 1857- *WomWWA 14*
Jones, Jerome 1837-1916 *NatCAB 27,*
WhAm 1
Jones, Jesse Holman 1874-1956 *BiDrUSE,*
EncAB, WhAm 3
Jones, Jesse Lee 1865-1929 *NatCAB 21*
Jones, Jessie Russell 1870- *WomWWA 14*
Jones, Joe 1909-1963 *WhAm 4*
Jones, Joel 1795-1860 *ApCAB, BiAUS,*
DcAmB, Drake, TwCBDA, WhAm H
Jones, Joel 1797-1860 *NatCAB 7*
Jones, John *NewYHSD*
Jones, John 1716-1801 *NatCAB 5*
Jones, John 1729-1791 *AmBi, ApCAB,*
BiHiMed, DcAmB, Drake, NatCAB 5,
TwCBDA, WhAm H
Jones, John 1744-1776 *NatCAB 5*
Jones, John 1796-1861 *ApCAB, NatCAB 11*
Jones, John 1802?- *NewYHSD*
Jones, John Anna 1865- *WomWWA 14*
Jones, John B 1834-1881 *DcAmB, WhAm H*
Jones, John Beauchamp 1810-1866 *AmBi,*
ApCAB, BiDConf, DcAmB, Drake,
WhAm H
Jones, John Carleton 1856-1930 *NatCAB 28,*
WhAm 1
Jones, John Divine 1814- *ApCAB*
Jones, John Edward 1840-1896 *NatCAB 11,*
TwCBDA
Jones, John Edward 1868-1918 *WhAm 1*
Jones, John Emory 1882- *WhoColR*
Jones, John Franklin 1846-1939 *NatCAB 34*
Jones, John George 1869-1956 *WhAm 3*
Jones, John Glancy 1811-1877 *ApCAB*
Jones, John Glancy *see also* Jones, J Glancy
Jones, John Henry 1866- *NatCAB 14*
Jones, John J *NewYHSD*
Jones, John James 1824-1898 *BiAUS, BiDrAC*
Jones, John Logan 1859- *WhAm 4*
Jones, John Luther *WebAB*
Jones, John M 1822-1864 *Drake*
Jones, John Marshall 1820-1864 *ApCAB,*
NatCAB 13, TwCBDA
Jones, John Marvin 1886- *BiDrAC*
Jones, John Mather 1826-1874 *ApCAB*
Jones, John P 1838- *BiAUS*
Jones, John Paul 1742-1792 *AmBi*
Jones, John Paul 1747-1792 *ApCAB, DcAmB,*
Drake, EncAB, McGEWB, NatCAB 2,
TwCBDA, WebAB, WebAMB, WhAm H,
WhoMilH
Jones, John Paul 1890-1970 *NatCAB 56*
Jones, John Paul 1898-1965 *WhAm 4*
Jones, John Paul 1902-1966 *NatCAB 53*
Jones, John Percival 1829-1912 *AmBi, BiDrAC,*
DcAmB, REnAW, WhAm 1, WhAmP
Jones, John Percival 1830- *ApCAB,*
NatCAB 1, TwCBDA

Jones, John Peter 1847-1916 *DcAmB, NatCAB 23*

Jones, John Price 1877-1964 *NatCAB 51, WhAm 4*

Jones, John Pringle 1812-1874 *ApCAB*

Jones, John Rice 1759-1824 *NatCAB 16, TwCBDA*

Jones, John Rice 1792-1845 *TwCBDA*

Jones, John Richter 1803-1863 *ApCAB*

Jones, John Sills 1835-1903 *TwCBDA*

Jones, John Sills 1836-1903 *ApCAB, BiDrAC, WhAm H*

Jones, John Sparhawk 1841-1910 *WhAm 1*

Jones, John Taylor 1802-1851 *ApCAB, DcAmB, Drake, WhAm H*

Jones, John Tecumseh 1800-1872 *TwCBDA*

Jones, John Wesley 1863- *WhAm 4*

Jones, John William 1806- *BiAUS*

Jones, John William 1806-1871 *BiDrAC, WhAm H*

Jones, John William 1806-1872 *ApCAB*

Jones, John William 1836-1909 *DcAmB, WhAm 1*

Jones, John Winston 1791-1848 *AmBi, ApCAB, BiAUS, BiDrAC, DcAmB, Drake, NatCAB 12, TwCBDA, WebAB, WhAm H, WhAmP*

Jones, Johnston Blakeley 1814-1889 *NatCAB 16, TwCBDA*

Jones, Jonathan 1882-1960 *NatCAB 49, WhAm 4*

Jones, Joseph 1727-1805 *ApCAB, BiAUS, BiDrAC, DcAmB, EncAAH, NatCAB 24, TwCBDA, WhAm H*

Jones, Joseph 1749-1824 *TwCBDA*

Jones, Joseph 1833-1896 *ApCAB, BiDConf, DcAmB, NatCAB 10, TwCBDA, WhAm H*

Jones, Joseph Addison 1873-1949 *WhAm 2*

Jones, Joseph Augustus 1860-1927 *NatCAB 24*

Jones, Joseph Huntington 1797-1868 *ApCAB*

Jones, Joseph Lawrence 1868- *WhoColR*

Jones, Joseph Merrick 1903-1963 *WhAm 4*

Jones, Joseph Montgomery 1877-1949 *NatCAB 41*

Jones, Joseph Russell 1823-1909 *NatCAB 1, TwCBDA, WhAm 1*

Jones, Joseph Russell *see also* Jones, J Russell

Jones, Joseph Seawell d1855 *Drake*

Jones, Joseph Seawell 1808?-1855 *NatCAB 7, WhAm H*

Jones, Joseph Seawell 1811?-1855 *ApCAB*

Jones, Joseph Stansbury 1888-1946 *NatCAB 33*

Jones, Joseph Stevens 1809-1877 *DcAmB, WhAm H*

Jones, Joseph Stevens 1811-1877 *ApCAB, TwCBDA*

Jones, Joseph Thomas 1842-1916 *NatCAB 7, NatCAB 22*

Jones, Joshua H 1856-1932 *WhAm 1, WhoColR*

Jones, Joshua Wiestling 1831- *NatCAB 10*

Jones, Kate Emery Sanborn 1860- *TwCBDA, WhAm 4, WomWWA 14*

Jones, Katherine Currier *WomWWA 14*

Jones, L Leroy 1892-1953 *NatCAB 42*

Jones, Lake 1867-1930 *WhAm 1, WhAm 1C*

Jones, Lauder William 1869-1960 *NatCAB 51*

Jones, Laurence Clifton 1884-1975 *WhAm 6*

Jones, Lawrence Clark 1893-1972 *NatCAB 57, WhAm 5*

Jones, Lawrence Clifton 1884-1975 *BiDAmEd, WhoColR*

Jones, Lawrence Donald 1901-1961 *WhAm 4*

Jones, Lawrence E 1888- *WhAm 4*

Jones, Leonard Augustus 1832-1909 *AmBi, ApCAB, DcAmB, NatCAB 11, TwCBDA, WhAm 1*

Jones, Leonard Chester 1886-1933 *NatCAB 25*

Jones, LeRoi *WebAB*

Jones, Lester Forsythe 1877-1972 *NatCAB 57*

Jones, Lester Martin 1884-1954 *WhAm 3*

Jones, Lewis Barrett 1889- *WhAm 4*

Jones, Lewis Henry 1844-1917 *TwCBDA, WhAm 1*

Jones, Lewis Henry 1856-1932 *WhAm 1*

Jones, Lewis Howel 1900-1969 *WhAm 5*

Jones, Lewis Ralph 1864-1945 *DcAmB S3, NatCAB 35, WhAm 2*

Jones, Lewis Webster 1899-1975 *WhAm 6*

Jones, Livingston Erringer 1878-1941 *WhAm 2*

Jones, Livingston French 1865-1928 *WhAm 1*

Jones, Llewellyn 1840- *ApCAB*

Jones, Llewellyn 1884-1961 *WhAm 4*

Jones, Lloyd E 1889-1958 *WhAm 3*

Jones, Louis Cleveland 1870-1945 *ApCAB X, NatCAB 33*

Jones, Louis Davis 1873- *WhoColR*

Jones, Louis R d1973 *WhAm 5*

Jones, Louisa 1868- *WomWWA 14*

Jones, Louise Caldwell *WomWWA 14*

Jones, Louise Tayler 1870- *WhAm 2*

Jones, Loyd Ancile 1884-1954 *NatCAB 41, WhAm 3*

Jones, Lynds 1865-1951 *DcAmB S5, WhAm 3*

Jones, Mabel Cronise 1860- *WhAm 1, WomWWA 14*

Jones, Madison Lafayette 1849-1948 *NatCAB 37*

Jones, Madison Ralph 1872-1929 *NatCAB 43*

Jones, Marcus Eugene 1852-1934 *TwCBDA, WhAm 1*

Jones, Marian Hastings *WomWWA 14*

Jones, Mark Perrin 1902-1959 *NatCAB 48*

Jones, Marvin 1886- *EncAAH*

Jones, Marvin Fisher 1886-1952 *WhAm 3*

Jones, Mary *NewYHSD*

Jones, Mary Elizabeth *WomWWA 14*

Jones, Mary Harris 1830-1930 *DcAmB, EncAB, NatCAB 23, NotAW, WebAB, WhAm HA, WhAm 4*

Jones, Mary Katharine *NotAW*

Jones, Mary Lee Bufkin *WomWWA 14*

Jones, Mary Montford *ApCAB*

Jones, Mary Noyes Tyler 1868- *WomWWA 14*

Jones, Matilda Sissieretta Joyner 1869-1933 *NotAW*

Jones, Matilda Sissierretta 1869-1933 *NatCAB 13*

Jones, Matt Bushnell 1871-1940 *WhAm 1*

Jones, Mattison Boyd 1869-1941 *NatCAB 38, WhAm 2*

Jones, Maude Emily 1884- *WomWWA 14*

Jones, May C 1842- *AmWom*

Jones, May Florence VanAkin 1866- *WomWWA 14*

Jones, May L *WomWWA 14*

Jones, Melodia Blackmarr 1850-1931 *NatCAB 32*

Jones, Melvin 1879-1961 *WhAm 4*

Jones, Meredith Ashby 1868-1947 *WhAm 2*

Jones, Millard Franklin 1891-1950 *WhAm 3*

Jones, Milo T 1881-1945 *NatCAB 41*

Jones, Minetry Leigh 1892-1963 *WhAm 4*

Jones, Mollie E J 1830- *WomWWA 14*

Jones, Montfort 1890-1954 *NatCAB 43, WhAm 3*

Jones, Morgan 1830-1894 *BiDrAC, WhAm H*

Jones, Morgan 1832-1894 *BiAUS*

Jones, Morgan 1864-1945 *NatCAB 34*

Jones, Morton Tebbs 1892-1962 *WhAm 4*

Jones, Nard 1904-1972 *WhAm 5*

Jones, Nathaniel 1788-1866 *BiAUS, BiDrAC, WhAm H*

Jones, Nathaniel Magruder 1850-1936 *NatCAB 32*

Jones, Nellie Sawyer Kedzie 1858-1956 *WhAm 3*

Jones, Nellie Sawyer Kedzie 1859-1956 *WomWWA 14*

Jones, Nelson Edwards 1821-1901 *NatCAB 17, WhAm 1*

Jones, Newell N 1905-1971 *WhAm 5*

Jones, Noble Wimberly 1724-1805 *ApCAB, BiAUS, Drake, NatCAB 11*

Jones, Noble Wymberley 1723-1805 *BiDrAC*

Jones, Noble Wymberley 1724?-1805 *DcAmB, WhAm H*

Jones, Noble Wymberly 1732-1805 *TwCBDA*

Jones, Norman Edward 1904-1972 *WhAm 5*

Jones, Norman L 1870-1940 *WhAm 1*

Jones, O Garfield 1884-1957 *WhAm 3*

Jones, Obadiah *BiAUS*

Jones, Olin McKendree 1885-1966 *WhAm 4*

Jones, Olive Branch 1863- *WomWWA 14*

Jones, Olive M 1871- *WhAm 5*

Jones, Oliver King 1879-1956 *NatCAB 44*

Jones, Ollie E 1892-1975 *WhAm 6*

Jones, Otis Lovejoy 1879-1955 *NatCAB 47*

Jones, Owen 1819-1878 *BiAUS, BiDrAC, WhAm H*

Jones, Owen Elon 1864-1926 *NatCAB 22*

Jones, P N 1865-1923 *NatCAB 31*

Jones, Patrick Henry 1830- *ApCAB Sup*

Jones, Paul 1854- *NatCAB 5*

Jones, Paul 1880-1941 *NatCAB 32, WhAm 6*

Jones, Paul 1880-1965 *WhAm 4*

Jones, Paul Caruthers 1901- *BiDrAC, WhAmP*

Jones, Paul Fouts 1898-1953 *WhAm 3*

Jones, Paul Stanley 1882-1962 *NatCAB 48*

Jones, Pembroke 1858-1919 *NatCAB 32*

Jones, Peter Smith 1906-1972 *WhAm 5*

Jones, Philip Harold 1896-1970 *WhAm 5*

Jones, Philip Lovering 1838-1913 *WhAm 1*

Jones, Philip Mills 1870-1916 *WhAm 1*

Jones, Phineas 1819-1884 *BiDrAC, WhAm H*

Jones, Quill 1875-1954 *WhAm 3*

Jones, R Irl 1891-1957 *NatCAB 48*

Jones, Ralph Beaumont 1893-1965 *WhAm 4*

Jones, Ralph Cowan 1897-1972 *NatCAB 57*

Jones, Ralph McAdam 1886-1946 *NatCAB 35, WhAm 2*

Jones, Rebecca 1739-1818 *ApCAB, NotAW*

Jones, Reginald Lamont 1886-1949 *WhAm 2*

Jones, Richard 1855-1923 *TwCBDA, WhAm 1*

Jones, Richard Channing 1841-1903 *NatCAB 12, TwCBDA, WhAm 1*

Jones, Richard Foster 1886-1965 *NatCAB 51*

Jones, Richard Hugh 1889-1955 *WhAm 3*

Jones, Richard Lee 1893-1975 *WhAm 6*

Jones, Richard Lloyd 1873-1963 *WhAm 4*

Jones, Richard Mott 1843-1917 *NatCAB 2, WhAm 1*

Jones, Richard Saxe 1861-1926 *WhAm 1*

Jones, Richard Uriah 1877-1941 *NatCAB 30, WhAm 1*

Jones, Richard Walter 1864-1951 *NatCAB 39, WhAm 4*

Jones, Richard Watson 1837-1914 *NatCAB 19, TwCBDA, WhAm 1*

Jones, Robert *NewYHSD*

Jones, Robert Edmond 1887-1954 *DcAmB S5, WhAm 3*

Jones, Robert Elijah 1872- *WhoColR*

Jones, Robert Ellis 1858-1929 *NatCAB 13, TwCBDA, WhAm 1*

Jones, Robert Emmett, Jr. 1912- *BiDrAC*

Jones, Robert Franklin 1907-1968 *BiDrAC, WhAm 5*

Jones, Robert Freeman 1847-1939 *NatCAB 29*

Jones, Robert Haydon 1910-1974 *WhAm 6*

Jones, Robert Lee 1867- *WhAm 4*

Jones, Robert Looney 1893-1965 *WhAm 4*

Jones, Robert Louis 1875- *WhoColR*

Jones, Robert Martin 1925-1974 *WhAm 6*

Jones, Robert McDonald 1808-1872 *BiDConf*

Jones, Robert Otis 1894-1960 *WhAm 4*

Jones, Robert S *NewYHSD*

Jones, Robert Taylor 1884-1958 *WhAm 3*

Jones, Robert Tyre, Jr. 1902-1971 *WebAB, WhAm 5*

Jones, Robert Vernon 1901-1973 *WhAm 5*

Jones, Robinson Godfrey 1871-1938 *NatCAB 28, WhAm 1*

Jones, Rodney Wilcox 1876- *WhAm 6*

Jones, Roger 1789-1852 *ApCAB, Drake, NatCAB 12, TwCBDA*

Jones, Roger 1831-1889 *ApCAB Sup, TwCBDA*

Jones, Roland 1813-1869 *BiAUS, BiDrAC, WhAm H*

Jones, Rosa Belle 1888- *WhoColR*

Jones, Roy Bergstresser 1883-1948 *WhAm 3*

Jones, Roy Childs 1885-1963 *WhAm 4*

Jones, Rufus Matthew 1863-1948 *DcAmB S4, DcAmReB, NatCAB 38, WebAB, WhAm 2*

Jones, S *NewYHSD*

Jones, S K 1825- *NewYHSD*

Jones, Sam Dews 1856-1930 *NatCAB 50*

Jones, Samuel d1818 *NewYHSD*

Jones, Samuel 1734-1819 *ApCAB, BiAUS, BiDrAC, DcAmB, NatCAB 11, TwCBDA, WhAm H*

Jones, Samuel 1735-1814 *ApCAB Sup*
Jones, Samuel 1769-1853 *ApCAB, BiAUS, Drake, NatCAB 11, TwCBDA*
Jones, Samuel 1770-1853 *DcAmB, WhAm H*
Jones, Samuel 1819-1887 *BiDConf*
Jones, Samuel 1820-1864 *Drake*
Jones, Samuel 1820-1887 *ApCAB, NatCAB 4, TwCBDA*
Jones, Samuel Augustus 1874- *WhAm 5*
Jones, Samuel B 1827?- *NewYHSD*
Jones, Samuel Benjamin 1874- *WhoColR*
Jones, Samuel Fosdick 1874-1946 *WhAm 2*
Jones, Samuel Goode 1865-1944 *NatCAB 33*
Jones, Samuel J 1836-1901 *NatCAB 10, TwCBDA, WhAm 1*
Jones, Samuel Mansfield 1887-1954 *NatCAB 43*
Jones, Samuel Milton 1846-1904 *AmBi, DcAmB S1, EncAB, McGEWB, NatCAB 10, TwCBDA, WebAB, WhAm 1, WhAmP*
Jones, Samuel Porter 1847-1906 *AmBi, ApCAB, DcAmB, DcAmReB, NatCAB 13, TwCBDA, WhAm 1*
Jones, Samuel Ralph 1878-1928 *NatCAB 22*
Jones, Samuel Rufus 1858-1931 *NatCAB 23*
Jones, Samuel Sheldon 1850-1928 *NatCAB 22*
Jones, Samuel William 1791-1855 *ApCAB*
Jones, Sarah Gibson 1845- *WhoColR*
Jones, Seaborn 1788-1864 *BiDrAC, WhAm H*
Jones, Seaborn 1788-1874 *ApCAB, BiAUS, NatCAB 11, TwCBDA*
Jones, Sebastian Chatham 1863-1929 *WhAm 1*
Jones, Seth Benjamin 1841- *WhAm 4*
Jones, Seward William 1857- *WhAm 4*
Jones, Sibyl 1808-1873 *ApCAB Sup*
Jones, Silas Armistead 1853-1933 *NatCAB 43*
Jones, Singleton Thomas Webster 1825- *ApCAB Sup*
Jones, Sissieretta *NotAW*
Jones, Spencer Cone 1836-1915 *NatCAB 16*
Jones, Spencer Loch 1890-1963 *NatCAB 50*
Jones, Stephen Alfred 1848-1915 *NatCAB 25, TwCBDA, WhAm 1*
Jones, Stephen George 1893-1959 *NatCAB 43*
Jones, Stephen S 1887-1960 *NatCAB 48*
Jones, Sullivan W 1878-1955 *WhAm 3*
Jones, Sybil 1808-1873 *DcAmB, NatCAB 2, NotAW, WhAm H*
Jones, Sydney Tucker, Jr. 1915-1971 *NatCAB 56*
Jones, T P *NewYHSD*
Jones, Tabitha Redman 1861- *WomWWA 14*
Jones, Theodore *NewYHSD*
Jones, Theodore Wellington 1853- *WhoColR*
Jones, Thomas 1665-1713 *ApCAB, TwCBDA*
Jones, Thomas 1731-1792 *ApCAB, DcAmB, NatCAB 9, TwCBDA, WhAm H*
Jones, Thomas Adolphus 1873- *WhoColR*
Jones, Thomas Alban 1880-1958 *NatCAB 46*
Jones, Thomas Albert Dwight 1887-1957 *NatCAB 44*
Jones, Thomas Albert Dwight, Jr. 1913-1958 *NatCAB 44*
Jones, Thomas Alfred 1859-1937 *WhAm 1*
Jones, Thomas ApCatesby 1789-1858 *ApCAB, Drake, TwCBDA*
Jones, Thomas ApCatesby 1790-1858 *AmBi, DcAmB, REnAW, WebAMB, WhAm H*
Jones, Thomas ApCatsby 1789-1858 *NatCAB 12*
Jones, Thomas Clive 1867-1945 *WhAm 2*
Jones, Thomas Davies 1851-1930 *WhAm 1*
Jones, Thomas Dow 1811-1881 *NewYHSD, WhAm H*
Jones, Thomas Dow 1811-1891 *BnEnAmA*
Jones, Thomas Edward *ApCAB X*
Jones, Thomas Elsa 1888-1973 *WhAm 6*
Jones, Thomas Evans 1892-1949 *NatCAB 43*
Jones, Thomas Goode 1844-1914 *DcAmB, NatCAB 1, NatCAB 10, TwCBDA, WhAm 1*
Jones, Thomas Hoyt 1887-1948 *WhAm 2*
Jones, Thomas Hudson 1892-1969 *WhAm 5*
Jones, Thomas Jesse 1873-1950 *BiDAmEd, WhAm 2*
Jones, Thomas Laurens 1819-1887 *BiAUS, BiDrAC, WhAm H*

Jones, Thomas Lucius 1863- *WhoColR*
Jones, Thomas McKissick 1816-1892 *BiDConf*
Jones, Thomas P 1774-1848 *DcAmB, Drake, WhAm H*
Jones, Thomas R *NewYHSD*
Jones, Thomas Robert 1891-1951 *NatCAB 40*
Jones, Thomas Sambola 1859-1933 *WhAm 1*
Jones, Thomas Samuel, Jr. 1882-1932 *WhAm 1*
Jones, Valentine d1815 *Drake*
Jones, Victor Owen 1905-1970 *NatCAB 54, WhAm 5*
Jones, Vincent Lloyd d1963 *WhAm 4*
Jones, Virginia Smith 1827-1906 *TwCBDA, WhAm 1*
Jones, Mrs. W J *WhAm 5*
Jones, W Paul 1901-1955 *WhAm 3*
Jones, Wade Anthony 1874- *WhoColR*
Jones, Walk Claridge 1874-1964 *WhAm 4*
Jones, Wallace Thaxter 1890-1946 *WhAm 2A*
Jones, Walter 1745-1815 *ApCAB, BiAUS, BiDrAC, Drake, NatCAB 2, TwCBDA, WhAm H, WhAmP*
Jones, Walter 1775-1861 *ApCAB Sup, BiAUS*
Jones, Walter 1776-1861 *DcAmB, NatCAB 1, WhAm H*
Jones, Walter 1865-1935 *NatCAB 43, WhAm 1*
Jones, Walter A Fleming 1871-1917 *WhAm 1*
Jones, Walter Beaman 1913- *BiDrAC*
Jones, Walter Burgwyn 1888-1963 *WhAm 4*
Jones, Walter Clinton 1874-1948 *WhAm 2*
Jones, Walter Clyde 1870-1928 *ApCAB X, NatCAB 17, WhAm 1*
Jones, Walter John 1892-1968 *NatCAB 55*
Jones, Walter Parker 1894-1974 *WhAm 6*
Jones, Walter Restored 1793-1855 *ApCAB, NatCAB 11*
Jones, Warren Clinton 1877-1952 *NatCAB 48*
Jones, Warren Francis 1896-1971 *WhAm 5*
Jones, Washington 1822- *WhAm 1*
Jones, Wesley Livsey 1863-1932 *AmBi, ApCAB X, BiDrAC, DcAmB S1, NatCAB 14, TwCBDA, WhAm 1, WhAmP*
Jones, Wharton Stewart 1849-1936 *WhAm 1*
Jones, Wiley Emmet 1856- *WhAm 1*
Jones, Wilie d1801 *Drake*
Jones, Wilie 1850- *WhAm 4*
Jones, Wilie *see also* Jones, Willie
Jones, Will Owen 1862-1928 *WhAm 1*
Jones, William *NewYHSD*
Jones, William 1675-1749 *DcScB*
Jones, William 1753-1822 *DcAmB, NatCAB 9, TwCBDA, WhAm H*
Jones, William 1754-1822 *ApCAB, BiAUS, Drake*
Jones, William 1760-1831 *ApCAB, BiAUS, BiDrAC, BiDrUSE, DcAmB, Drake, NatCAB 5, TwCBDA, WhAm H, WhAmP*
Jones, William 1871-1909 *DcAmB, NatCAB 24*
Jones, William A 1844- *WhAm 4*
Jones, William Albert 1841-1914 *WhAm 1*
Jones, William Alexander 1859-1931 *NatCAB 42, WhAm 1*
Jones, William Alfred 1817-1900 *ApCAB, DcAmB, Drake, NatCAB 12, TwCBDA, WhAm 1*
Jones, William Alton 1891-1962 *WhAm 4*
Jones, William Ambrose 1865-1921 *WhAm 1*
Jones, William Atkinson 1849-1918 *BiDrAC, TwCBDA, WhAm 1, WhAmP*
Jones, William Benjamin 1862-1919 *NatCAB 18*
Jones, William Carey 1854-1923 *NatCAB 20, WhAm 1*
Jones, William Carey 1855-1927 *BiDrAC, WhAm 1, WhAmP*
Jones, William Edmondson 1824-1864 *ApCAB, Drake, TwCBDA*
Jones, William Ewart 1893-1954 *NatCAB 47*
Jones, William Foster 1815?- *NewYHSD*
Jones, William Giles 1808-1883 *BiAUS, BiDConf*
Jones, William H 1845-1916 *NatCAB 18*
Jones, William Jackson 1879- *WhAm 6*
Jones, William James 1901-1973 *WhAm 6*

Jones, William James, Jr. 1870-1917 *WhAm 1*
Jones, William Larimer, Jr. 1891-1954 *WhAm 3*
Jones, William Lewis 1877-1949 *NatCAB 40*
Jones, William Louis 1827- *NatCAB 9*
Jones, William Martin 1841- *NatCAB 5*
Jones, William Otterbein 1874-1938 *WhAm 1*
Jones, William Palmer 1819-1897 *ApCAB, DcAmB, NatCAB 11, WhAm H*
Jones, William Patterson 1831-1886 *DcAmB, NatCAB 24, WhAm H*
Jones, William R *NewYHSD*
Jones, William Ralph 1880- *WhAm 6*
Jones, William Richard 1839-1889 *DcAmB, NatCAB 15, WhAm H*
Jones, William Robert 1873-1925 *NatCAB 23*
Jones, William Russell 1870- *WhAm 5*
Jones, William Steuben 1863-1939 *NatCAB 30*
Jones, William Strother 1852- *TwCBDA*
Jones, William Theopilus 1842-1882 *BiAUS, BiDrAC, WhAm H, WhAmP*
Jones, Willie d1801 *BiAUS*
Jones, Willie 1731-1801 *ApCAB, TwCBDA*
Jones, Willie 1740-1801 *BiDrAC, WhAmP*
Jones, Willie 1741?-1801 *DcAmB, WhAm H*
Jones, Willie *see also* Jones, Wilie
Jones, Woodrow Wilson 1914-1968 *BiDrAC*
Jongers, Alphonse 1872-1945 *WhAm 3*
Jongh, Andree De 1916- *WhWW-II*
Jongh, James De *NewYHSD*
Jonkman, Bartel John 1884-1955 *BiDrAC, NatCAB 46, WhAmP*
Jonquiere, Jaques P DeT, Marquis DeLa 1686-1752 *Drake*
Jonquieres, Ernest Jean P Fauque De 1820-1901 *DcScB*
Jonson, Ben 1572-1637 *McGEWB*
Jonson, Jep C 1833- *WhAm 4*
Jonson, Libby Anne 1944- *WhAm 6*
Jonson, Raymond 1891- *IIBEAAW*
Jonsson, Axel 1888-1950 *WhAm 3*
Jonsson, Sixten 1882-1943 *NatCAB 32*
Jonston, John 1603-1675 *DcScB*
Joplin, Janis d1970 *WhAm 5*
Joplin, Scott 1868-1917 *WebAB*
Jopling, Reginald Furness 1866-1942 *NatCAB 32*
Jopp, Charles B 1874- *WhAm 5*
Jopson, John Howard 1871-1954 *WhAm 3*
Jordaens, Jacob 1593-1678 *McGEWB*
Jordaens, Mauritius 1762-1824 *ApCAB*
Jordaens, Melchior 1751-1829 *ApCAB*
Jordan, Alexis 1814-1897 *DcScB*
Jordan, Ambrose Latting 1789-1865 *NatCAB 11*
Jordan, Ambrose Latting 1791-1865 *ApCAB*
Jordan, Arthur 1855-1934 *WhAm 1*
Jordan, Arthur Wheeler 1878- *WhAm 6*
Jordan, Benjamin Everett 1896-1974 *BiDrAC, WhAm 6*
Jordan, Camille 1838-1921 *DcScB*
Jordan, Charles Bernard 1878-1941 *NatCAB 43, WhAm 2*
Jordan, Charles Edward 1901-1974 *WhAm 6*
Jordan, Chester Bradley 1839-1914 *NatCAB 11, WhAm 1*
Jordan, Clarence Lorin 1877- *WhAm 5*
Jordan, Conrad N 1830-1903 *ApCAB, WhAm 1*
Jordan, Cornelia Jane Matthews 1830- *AmWom, ApCAB*
Jordan, Cornelius Hughes 1877-1944 *NatCAB 33*
Jordan, David Francis 1890-1942 *WhAm 2*
Jordan, David Starr 1851-1931 *AmBi, ApCAB, ApCAB X, BiDAmEd, DcAmB, DcScB, McGEWB, NatCAB 2, NatCAB 22, TwCBDA, WebAB, WhAm 1*
Jordan, Dock Jackson 1866- *WhoColR*
Jordan, Eben Dyer 1822-1895 *NatCAB 2*
Jordan, Eben Dyer 1857-1916 *DcAmB, WhAm 1*
Jordan, Edith Monica 1877- *WomWWA 14*
Jordan, Edward Benedict 1884-1951 *WhAm 3*
Jordan, Edward Stanlaw 1882-1959 *WhAm 3*
Jordan, Edwin Oakes 1866-1936 *AmBi, DcAmB S2, DcScB, NatCAB 42, WhAm 1*
Jordan, Eldridge Elmore 1874-1929 *NatCAB 27*

Jordan, Elizabeth d1947 *BiCAW, WhAm 2*
Jordan, Elizabeth Garver 1865-1947 *NotAW*
Jordan, Elizabeth Garver 1867-1947 *AmWom, NatCAB 40, WomWWA 14*
Jordan, Elsie Medora *WomWWA 14*
Jordan, Ettie Amelia *WomWWA 14*
Jordan, Floyd 1900-1959 *WhAm 4*
Jordan, Francis 1820- *NatCAB 7*
Jordan, Francis, Jr. 1843-1911 *WhAm 1*
Jordan, Frank Craig 1865-1941 *NatCAB 35, WhAm 1*
Jordan, Frank Morrill 1888-1970 *WhAm 5*
Jordan, Frederick Freas d1938 *WhAm 1*
Jordan, G Gunby 1846-1930 *WhAm 1*
Jordan, G Ray 1896-1964 *WhAm 4*
Jordan, Harvey Bryant 1895-1965 *NatCAB 51, WhAm 4*
Jordan, Harvey Ernest 1878- *WhAm 6*
Jordan, Harvey Herbert 1885- *WhAm 5*
Jordan, Harvie 1861- *WhAm 5*
Jordan, Henry *NewYHSD*
Jordan, Henry Donaldson 1897-1972 *WhAm 6*
Jordan, Henry Dowling 1878-1959 *NatCAB 49*
Jordan, Howard William 1887-1964 *WhAm 4*
Jordan, Isaac M 1835-1890 *BiDrAC, WhAm H*
Jordan, J Homer 1856-1948 *NatCAB 42*
Jordan, James Francis 1859-1919 *NatCAB 18*
Jordan, James Henry 1842-1912 *TwCBDA, WhAm 1*
Jordan, James Joseph 1856- *NatCAB 4*
Jordan, Jessie Knight 1866- *WomWWA 14*
Jordan, John 1808- *ApCAB*
Jordan, John H 1848- *WhAm 4*
Jordan, John Woolf 1840-1921 *ApCAB, DcAmB, NatCAB 11, TwCBDA, WhAm 4*
Jordan, Joseph 1695-1735 *ApCAB*
Jordan, Jules 1850-1927 *NatCAB 16, WhAm 1*
Jordan, Kate 1862-1926 *DcAmB, WhAm 1*
Jordan, Leonard Beck 1899- *BiDrAC*
Jordan, Lewis Garnett 1852?- *WhoColR*
Jordan, Lyman Granville 1845-1921 *NatCAB 20, WhAm 1*
Jordan, M Evangeline 1865- *NatCAB 17*
Jordan, Mahlon Kline 1911-1967 *NatCAB 54, WhAm 4*
Jordan, Marian 1898-1961 *WhAm 4*
Jordan, Mary A L Ranken *WomWWA 14*
Jordan, Mary Adela *WomWWA 14*
Jordan, Mary Augusta 1855-1941 *WhAm 1, WomWWA 14*
Jordan, Myra Beach 1863- *WomWWA 14*
Jordan, Ralph Curtis 1882-1966 *NatCAB 52, WhAm 4*
Jordan, Richard 1756-1826 *ApCAB, NatCAB 7*
Jordan, Richard Henry 1877-1971 *WhAm 5*
Jordan, Riverda Harding 1873-1950 *NatCAB 42, WhAm 3*
Jordan, Robert 1693-1742 *ApCAB, Drake*
Jordan, Samuel *NewYHSD*
Jordan, Samuel Martin 1871-1952 *NatCAB 41, WhAm 3*
Jordan, Samuel X 1903-1962 *NatCAB 49*
Jordan, Sara Murray 1884-1959 *WhAm 3*
Jordan, Scipio A 1860- *WhoColR*
Jordan, Thomas 1819-1895 *AmBi, ApCAB, BiDConf, DcAmB, NatCAB 4, TwCBDA, WebAMB, WhAm H*
Jordan, Thomas Walden 1848-1919 *TwCBDA, WhAm 1*
Jordan, Virgil 1892-1965 *WhAm 4*
Jordan, Weymouth Tyree 1912-1968 *EncAAH, NatCAB 57, WhAm 5*
Jordan, Whitman Howard 1851-1931 *WhAm 1*
Jordan, William Conrad 1898-1968 *NatCAB 54*
Jordan, William Frederick 1867- *WhAm 1*
Jordan, William George 1864-1928 *DcAmB, NatCAB 23, WhAm 1*
Jordan, William Mark 1909-1966 *WhAm 4*
Jordan, William Mudd 1873-1951 *NatCAB 40*
Jordanus DeNemore *DcScB*
Jorden, Edward Fletcher 1858-1927 *WhAm 1*
Jorden, Edwin James 1863-1903 *BiDrAC*
Jordon, Dillon *BiAUS*
Jordon, Edward *BiAUS*

Jordon, Edward 1801-1869 *ApCAB*
Jorgensen, Christian 1860-1935 *IIBEAAW*
Jorgensen, Joseph 1844-1888 *BiDrAC, WhAm H*
Jorgensen, Sophus Mads 1837-1914 *DcScB*
Jorgenson, Ralph Enoch 1908-1972 *WhAm 6*
Jorgenson, Theodore 1894-1971 *WhAm 6*
Jorn, Asger 1914-1973 *WhAm 6*
Jorpes, J Erik 1894-1973 *WhAm 6*
Jorquera, Jacinto 1600-1675 *ApCAB*
Jorrin, Jose Silverio 1816- *ApCAB*
Jorrin, Miguel 1902-1965 *NatCAB 52*
Jorstad, Louis Helmar 1896-1972 *NatCAB 57*
Josaphare, Lionel 1876- *WhAm 5*
Josaphare, Maude Josephine Coan 1886- *WomWWA 14*
Jose DeSanta, Theresa 1658-1736 *ApCAB*
Joseffy, Rafael 1852-1915 *ApCAB X, DcAmB*
Josenberger, Mame Stewart 1868- *WhoColR*
Joseph 1840?-1904 *AmBi, DcAmB, McGEWB, WebAB, WebAMB*
Joseph II 1741-1790 *McGEWB*
Joseph, Brother 1843-1931 *AmBi*
Joseph, Chief *REnAW*
Joseph, Chief 1831-1904 *WhoMilH*
Joseph, Chief 1840?-1904 *EncAAH*
Joseph, Sister *NotAW*
Joseph, Antonio 1846-1910 *BiDrAC, NatCAB 6, REnAW, WhAmP*
Joseph, Don Rosco 1881-1928 *WhAm 1*
Joseph, Lawrence Edgar 1896-1954 *WhAm 3*
Joseph, Lazarus 1891-1966 *WhAm 4*
Joseph, Samuel *NewYHSD*
Joseph, William *NatCAB 7*
Joseph-Ferdinand, Archduke 1872-1942 *WhoMilH*
Josephi, Isaac A *WhAm 5*
Josephine 1763-1814 *ApCAB*
Josephson, Aksel Gustav Salomon 1860-1944 *DcAmLiB, NatCAB 18, WhAm 2*
Josephson, Clarence Egbert 1897- *WhAm 5*
Josephus Flavius 037?-100 *McGEWB*
Josephy, Herman 1887-1960 *NatCAB 48*
Joset, Joseph 1810-1900 *REnAW*
Joshi, Samuel Lucas 1874- *WhAm 1*
Joslin, C Loring 1887-1958 *NatCAB 48*
Joslin, Cedric Freeman 1889-1922 *WhAm 1*
Joslin, Elliott Proctor 1869-1962 *NatCAB 46, WhAm 4*
Joslin, Falcon 1866-1928 *WhAm 1*
Joslin, Harold Vincent 1883-1928 *WhAm 1*
Joslin, John Jay 1834-1890 *NatCAB 1*
Joslin, Rebecca Richardson *WomWWA 14*
Joslin, Theodore Goldsmith 1890-1944 *WhAm 2*
Joslin, William Cary 1852-1923 *WhAm 1*
Joslyn, Lee Everett 1864- *NatCAB 17*
Joslyn, Marcellus Lindsey 1873-1963 *WhAm 4*
Josquin Des Prez 1440?-1521 *McGEWB*
Joss, John 1902-1955 *WhAm 3*
Josselyn, Benage S 1858- *WhAm 4*
Josselyn, Charles 1847- *WhAm 4*
Josselyn, Freeman Marshall 1866- *WhAm 1*
Josselyn, Henry *ApCAB*
Josselyn, John *ApCAB, DcAmB, Drake, NatCAB 7, WhAm H*
Josselyn, Livingston Eli 1904-1957 *NatCAB 45*
Josset, Raoul Jean 1892-1957 *WhAm 3*
Jost, Henry Lee 1873-1950 *BiDrAC, WhAm 3*
Jost, Hudson 1912-1963 *WhAm 4*
Josten, Werner Eric 1885-1963 *WhAm 4*
Jostes, Frederick Augustus 1895-1952 *WhAm 3*
Jouannet, Francis Lionel 1895-1961 *NatCAB 49*
Joubert, Antoine Henry 1601-1674 *ApCAB*
Joubert, Pietrus Jacobus 1831-1900 *WhoMilH*
Joubert DeLaFerte, Sir Philip 1897-1965 *WhWW-II*
Joubert DeLaMuraille, James Hector M N 1777-1843 *DcAmB, WhAm H*
Jouet, Matthew 1783-1826 *Drake*
Jouett, Alexander Stuart 1816-1849 *ApCAB*
Jouett, Edward Stockton 1863- *WhAm 5*
Jouett, George Payne 1813-1862 *ApCAB*
Jouett, James Edward 1826-1902 *AmBi, DcAmB, WebAMB*
Jouett, James Edward 1828-1902 *ApCAB, NatCAB 4, TwCBDA, WhAm 1*
Jouett, John 1754-1822 *DcAmB, WhAm H*
Jouett, John Hamilton 1892-1968 *WhAm 5*

Jouett, Matthew Harris 1787-1827 *AmBi, BnEnAmA, DcAmB, NewYHSD, WhAm H*
Jouett, Matthew Harris 1788-1827 *ApCAB, NatCAB 6, TwCBDA*
Jouffroy, Gabriel 1631-1685 *ApCAB*
Jouhaux, Leon 1879-1954 *WhAm 3*
Jouin, Louis 1818-1899 *ApCAB, WhAm 1*
Joule, James Prescott 1818-1889 *AsBiEn, DcScB, McGEWB*
Joullin, Amedee 1862-1917 *IIBEAAW*
Joullin, Lucile 1876-1924 *IIBEAAW*
Jourard, Sidney Marshall 1926-1974 *WhAm 6*
Jourdan, James H d1930 *WhAm 1*
Jourdan, Jean Baptiste 1762-1833 *WhoMilH*
Journet, Marcel 1870-1933 *WhAm 1*
Joutel, Henri 1645-1723 *DcAmB, WhAm H*
Joutel, Henry 1645-1723 *ApCAB*
Jouvenal, Jacques 1829-1905 *NewYHSD, WhAm H*
Jowett, Benjamin 1817-1893 *McGEWB*
Jowett, John Henry 1864-1923 *WhAm 1*
Joy, Agnes Elisabeth Winona Leclercq 1840-1912 *ApCAB X, TwCBDA, WhAm HA, WhAm 4A*
Joy, Agnes Eliza 1840-1912 *DcAmB*
Joy, Charles Arad 1823-1891 *ApCAB, NatCAB 5, TwCBDA*
Joy, Charles Frederick 1849-1921 *BiDrAC, NatCAB 6, TwCBDA, WhAm 4, WhAmP*
Joy, Charles Turner 1895-1956 *NatCAB 45, WebAMB, WhAm 3*
Joy, Clyde Royal 1867- *NatCAB 15*
Joy, Edmund Lewis 1835-1892 *ApCAB X, NatCAB 6, NatCAB 24, TwCBDA*
Joy, Edmund Steele 1864-1931 *NatCAB 24*
Joy, Effie May Beresford *NatCAB 10*
Joy, Helen Hall Newberry 1869- *BiCAW, WomWWA 14*
Joy, Henry Bourne 1864-1936 *DcAmB S2, NatCAB 27, WhAm 1*
Joy, Homer Thrall 1872-1949 *NatCAB 37*
Joy, Ida 1858- *ApCAB*
Joy, James Frederick 1810-1896 *ApCAB, DcAmB, NatCAB 11, NatCAB 18, REnAW, WebAB, WhAm H*
Joy, James Richard 1863-1957 *WhAm 3*
Joy, Richard Pickering 1870-1930 *NatCAB 25, WhAm 5*
Joy, Sylvanus 1833- *ApCAB*
Joy, Thomas 1610-1678 *ApCAB X, DcAmB, NatCAB 7, TwCBDA, WhAm H*
Joyce, Adrian Dwight 1872-1954 *NatCAB 46, WhAm 3*
Joyce, Charles Duane 1863-1921 *NatCAB 19*
Joyce, Charles Herbert 1830-1916 *ApCAB, BiAUS, BiDrAC, NatCAB 11, TwCBDA, WhAm 4*
Joyce, Dwight P 1900-1970 *WhAm 5*
Joyce, Isaac Wilson 1836-1905 *DcAmB, NatCAB 13, TwCBDA, WhAm 1*
Joyce, J Wallace 1907-1970 *NatCAB 55, WhAm 5*
Joyce, James *NewYHSD*
Joyce, James 1870-1931 *BiDrAC, WhAm 3*
Joyce, James 1882-1941 *McGEWB*
Joyce, John Alexander 1840-1915 *WhAm 1*
Joyce, John Francis 1863-1921 *NatCAB 19*
Joyce, John Michael 1884-1964 *WhAm 4*
Joyce, Kenyon Ashe 1879-1960 *WhAm 3*
Joyce, Matthew M 1877- *WhAm 3*
Joyce, Nedra Norton 1937- *WhAm 6*
Joyce, Patrick H d1946 *WhAm 2*
Joyce, R Edwin 1897-1959 *NatCAB 51, WhAm 3*
Joyce, Robert Dwyer 1836-1883 *ApCAB*
Joyce, Thomas Martin 1885-1947 *NatCAB 36, WhAm 2*
Joyce, Walter Eves 1895-1973 *WhAm 5*
Joyce, Walter Frank 1905-1968 *NatCAB 55, WhAm 5*
Joyce, William 1906-1946 *WhWW-II*
Joyce, William Albert 1851-1917 *NatCAB 17*
Joyce, William Barnard 1866-1962 *WhAm 4*
Joyce, William Henry 1868-1941 *WhAm 1*
Joye, John 1790- *NewYHSD*
Joyes, John Warren 1870-1945 *WhAm 2*

Joyner, Fred Bunyan 1895-1965 *NatCAB 51, WhAm 4*
Joyner, James Yadkin 1862-1954 *BiDAmEd*
Joyner, James Yadkin 1862-1956 *WhAm 3*
Joyner, Matilda Sissieretta *NotAW*
Joynes, Edward Southey 1834-1917 *ApCAB, BiDAmEd, DcAmB, NatCAB 11, TwCBDA, WhAm 1*
Joynes, Levin Smith 1819-1881 *ApCAB, NatCAB 11, TwCBDA*
Joynes, William Thomas 1817-1874 *TwCBDA*
Joys, Andrew Marelius 1835-1919 *NatCAB 36*
Juan Of Austria 1545-1578 *WhoMilH*
Juan Y Santacilia, Jorge 1713-1773 *ApCAB*
Juan Y Santacilla, Jorge 1713-1773 *DcScB*
Juana Ines DeLaCruz, Sister 1651-1695 *McGEWB*
Juarez, Benito 1806-1872 *ApCAB, McGEWB, WhAm H, WhoMilH*
Juarez, Benito 1807-1872 *Drake*
Juarez, Jose *ApCAB*
Juarez, Juan *ApCAB*
Juarez, Juan d1528 *ApCAB*
Juarez, Luis d1650? *ApCAB*
Juarez, Nicolas Rodriguez *ApCAB*
Juarez-Celman, Miguel 1844- *ApCAB*
Juarrez, Jose Domingo 1801-1837 *ApCAB*
Juarros, D Domingos d1818? *Drake*
Juarros, Domingo 1752-1820 *ApCAB*
Jube, Albert Riordan 1888-1970 *WhAm 5*
Juch, Emma Antonia Joanna 1863-1939 *WomWWA 14*
Juch, Emma Antonia Joanna 1865-1939 *AmBi, WhAm 1*
Juch, Emma Johanna Antonia 1860-1939 *NotAW*
Juch, Emma Johanna Antonia 1863-1939 *AmWom, NatCAB 6*
Jucherau, Louis 1676-1731? *ApCAB*
Jucherau, Nicholas 1626-1692 *ApCAB*
Juchhoff, Frederick 1884-1953 *WhAm 3*
Judah I 135?-220? *McGEWB*
Judah Halevi 1085?-1150? *McGEWB*
Judah, Henry Moses 1821-1866 *ApCAB, Drake, TwCBDA*
Judah, Joseph Stillson 1882-1956 *NatCAB 43*
Judah, Noble Brandon 1851-1918 *WhAm 1*
Judah, Noble Brandon 1884-1938 *NatCAB 28, WhAm 4*
Judah, Samuel 1798-1869 *DcAmB, NatCAB 24, WhAm H*
Judah, Samuel Benjamin Helbert 1799?-1876 *DcAmB, WhAm H*
Judah, Theodore Dehone 1826-1863 *DcAmB, McGEWB, REnAW, WhAm H*
Judas Maccabeus d160BC *McGEWB*
Juday, Chancey 1871-1944 *DcAmB S3, DcScB, NatCAB 42, WhAm 2*
Judd, Bathel 1776?-1858 *NatCAB 1*
Judd, Bertha Grimmell 1871-1947 *WhAm 2*
Judd, Bethel 1776-1858 *Drake, TwCBDA*
Judd, Charles Hubbard 1873-1946 *BiDAmEd, DcAmB S4, NatCAB 42, WebAB, WhAm 2*
Judd, Charles Sheldon 1881-1939 *NatCAB 36*
Judd, Climena Lyman 1875- *WhAm 5*
Judd, Cornelius Myers 1879-1951 *NatCAB 41*
Judd, David Wright 1838-1888 *ApCAB, TwCBDA*
Judd, Deane Brewster 1900-1972 *NatCAB 56, WhAm 5*
Judd, Donald 1928- *BnEnAmA*
Judd, E Clarence 1882-1946 *NatCAB 36*
Judd, Edward Starr 1878-1935 *DcAmB S1, NatCAB 29, WhAm 1*
Judd, Edwin Young 1862-1942 *NatCAB 31*
Judd, Gerrit Parmalee 1803-1873 *ApCAB*
Judd, Gerrit Parmele 1803-1873 *DcAmB, NatCAB 25, WhAm H*
Judd, Gerrit Parmele, IV 1915-1971 *WhAm 5*
Judd, Herman Sinclair 1872-1944 *NatCAB 35*
Judd, Horace 1868-1945 *NatCAB 34*
Judd, James Robert 1876-1947 *WhAm 2*
Judd, John Thomas 1851-1931 *NatCAB 25*
Judd, John Waltus 1839- *WhAm 4*
Judd, Lawrence McCully 1887-1968 *WhAm 5*
Judd, Norman Buel 1815-1878 *AmBi, ApCAB, BiAUS, BiDrAC, DcAmB, Drake,*

NatCAB 11, TwCBDA, WhAm H, WhAmP
Judd, Orange 1822-1892 *AmBi, ApCAB, DcAmB, EncAAH, NatCAB 8, TwCBDA, WhAm H*
Judd, Orrin Reynolds 1870-1955 *WhAm 3*
Judd, Sylvester 1789-1860 *ApCAB, Drake, TwCBDA*
Judd, Sylvester 1813-1853 *ApCAB, DcAmB, Drake, NatCAB 9, TwCBDA, WhAm H*
Judd, T W 1911-1970 *NatCAB 57*
Judd, Walter Henry 1898- *BiDrAC, WhAmP*
Judd, Willard 1804-1840 *ApCAB*
Judd, William Hawley 1850- *ApCAB X*
Judd, Zebulon d1960 *WhAm 4*
Judge, Thomas Augustine 1868-1933 *DcAmB S1*
Judge, William John 1873- *WhAm 5*
Judge, William Quan 1851-1896 *AmBi, DcAmB, NatCAB 15, WhAm H*
Judge, Winifred E *WomWWA 14*
Judkins, Charles Otis 1868-1934 *WhAm 1*
Judkins, Eliza Maria 1809-1887 *NewYHSD*
Judkins, J Byron 1851-1915 *NatCAB 16*
Judson, Adoniram 1788-1850 *AmBi, ApCAB, DcAmB, DcAmReB, Drake, McGEWB, NatCAB 3, TwCBDA, WebAB, WhAm H*
Judson, Adoniram Brown 1837-1916 *DcAmB, NatCAB 20, WhAm 1*
Judson, Alexander Corbin 1883-1973 *WhAm 6*
Judson, Andrew Thompson 1784-1853 *ApCAB, BiAUS, BiDrAC, TwCBDA, WhAm H*
Judson, Ann Haseltine 1789-1826 *ApCAB*
Judson, Ann Hasseltine 1789-1826 *DcAmB, Drake, NatCAB 3, NotAW, TwCBDA, WebAB, WhAm H*
Judson, Arthur 1881-1975 *WhAm 6*
Judson, Charles N *NewYHSD*
Judson, Charles Wingfield 1909-1972 *WhAm 5*
Judson, Clara Ingram 1879-1960 *WhAm 4*
Judson, Clay 1892-1960 *WhAm 4*
Judson, Edward 1844-1914 *AmBi, ApCAB, DcAmB, NatCAB 12, TwCBDA, WhAm 1*
Judson, Edward B 1814- *NatCAB 7*
Judson, Edward Z C 1822-1886 *ApCAB, NatCAB 13, TwCBDA*
Judson, Edward Zane Carroll 1823-1886 *AmBi, DcAmB, EncAAH, WebAB, WhAm H*
Judson, Egbert Putnam 1812-1893 *DcAmB, NatCAB 24, WhAm H*
Judson, Emily 1817-1854 *TwCBDA*
Judson, Emily Chubbock 1817-1854 *WebAB*
Judson, Emily Chubbuck 1817-1854 *AmBi, ApCAB, DcAmB, Drake, NatCAB 3, NotAW, WhAm H*
Judson, Fletcher Wesley 1868- *WhAm 5*
Judson, Frederick Joseph 1804-1862 *NatCAB 7*
Judson, Frederick Newton 1845-1919 *DcAmB, NatCAB 7, WhAm 1*
Judson, Harry Pratt 1849-1927 *BiDAmEd, DcAmB, NatCAB 11, NatCAB 20, TwCBDA, WhAm 1*
Judson, Jennie S 1859- *AmWom*
Judson, John Charles 1889-1942 *NatCAB 33*
Judson, Katherine Berry *WomWWA 14*
Judson, Margaret 1880- *WomWWA 14*
Judson, Sarah Hall Boardman 1803-1845 *AmBi, ApCAB, DcAmB, NatCAB 3, NotAW, TwCBDA, WebAB, WhAm H*
Judson, Sarah Worrall *WomWWA 14*
Judson, Stiles 1862-1914 *NatCAB 16*
Judson, Wilber 1880-1951 *WhAm 3*
Judson, William Lees 1842-1928 *IIBEAAW, WhAm 1*
Judson, William Pierson 1849-1925 *NatCAB 12, WhAm 1*
Judson, William Voorhees 1865-1923 *NatCAB 28, WhAm 1*
Judy, Arthur Markley 1854- *WhAm 4*
Judy, Clinton Kelly 1879-1955 *NatCAB 45, WhAm 5*
Judy, John Abram 1888-1957 *NatCAB 49*
Juel, Sophus Christian 1855-1935 *DcScB*
Juels, Niels 1729-1793 *ApCAB*
Juengling, Frederick 1846-1889 *AmBi, ApCAB, DcAmB, NatCAB 11, TwCBDA,*

WhAm H
Juergens, Alfred 1866-1934 *WhAm 1*
Juettner, Otto 1865-1922 *WhAm 1*
Jugler, Lorenz 1692-1764 *ApCAB*
Juhan, Frank Alexander 1887-1967 *WhAm 4*
Juhan, William Jefferson 1859-1924 *NatCAB 23*
Juhring, Frances Fisher *WomWWA 14*
Juhring, John Christopher 1850-1932 *NatCAB 11, WhAm 1*
Juhring, William Lewis 1856-1938 *NatCAB 28*
Juilliard, Augustus D d1919 *WhAm 1*
Juilliard, Augustus D 1836-1919 *AmBi, DcAmB, NatCAB 28*
Juilliard, Augustus D 1840-1919 *ApCAB X, NatCAB 14*
Juilliard, Frederic A d1937 *WhAm 1*
Juin, Alphonse Henri 1888-1967 *WhAm 4*
Juin, Alphonse Pierre 1888-1967 *WhWW-II, WhoMilH*
Jukes, Joseph Beete 1811-1869 *DcScB*
Julia, Sister 1827-1901 *DcAmB, NotAW, WhAm H*
Julian Of Norwich 1342-1416? *McGEWB*
Julian The Apostate 331-363 *McGEWB*
Julian, George Washington 1817-1899 *AmBi, ApCAB, BiAUS, BiDrAC, DcAmB, EncAAH, NatCAB 5, TwCBDA, WhAm H, WhAm 1, WhAmP*
Julian, Isaac Hoover 1823- *ApCAB, NatCAB 11, TwCBDA, WhAm 1*
Julian, John Herndon 1886-1965 *WhAm 4*
Julian, Percy Lavon 1899-1975 *WebAB, WhAm 6*
Julian, William Alexander 1861-1949 *NatCAB 45, WhAm 2*
Juliand, Janet *WomWWA 14*
Julien, Alexis Anastay 1840-1919 *ApCAB, NatCAB 18, TwCBDA, WhAm 1*
Julien, Juliette Marie 1894-1972 *WhAm 5*
Julio, E B D Fabrino 1843-1879 *ApCAB*
Julius II 1443-1513 *McGEWB*
Julius, Emanuel *WebAB*
Julius, Willem Henri 1860-1925 *DcScB*
Juljul, Sulayman Ibn Hasan, Ibn 944-994? *DcScB*
Jull, Morley Allan 1885-1959 *WhAm 3*
Juman, H *NewYHSD*
Jumel, Eliza Bowen 1769-1865 *ApCAB*
Jumel, Eliza Bowen 1775-1865 *NotAW*
Jumel, Stephen 1754?-1832 *AmBi, DcAmB, WhAm H*
Jumonville, N Coulon De 1725?-1754 *ApCAB*
Jump, Edward 1831?- *NewYHSD*
Jump, Edward 1838-1883 *IIBEAAW*
Jump, Herbert Atchinson 1875-1934 *WhAm 1*
Jump, William Ashby 1891-1949 *WhAm 2*
Jumpello, Simon *NewYHSD*
Jumper, Carl Everett 1878-1957 *NatCAB 49*
Jumper, Henry Francis 1894-1951 *NatCAB 38*
Jumper, Royal Thiesen 1902-1960 *WhAm 4*
Junayd, Abu Al-Qasim Ibn Muhammad, Al-830?-910 *McGEWB*
Junca, Mousx *NewYHSD*
Juncker, Henry Damian 1809-1868 *TwCBDA*
Juncker, Henry Damian 1810?-1868 *ApCAB, Drake, NatCAB 6, NatCAB 12*
Juncker, Johann 1679-1759 *DcScB*
June, Jennie *DcAmB, NotAW*
Juneau, Laurent Solomon 1793-1856 *ApCAB, NatCAB 6*
Juneau, Solomon Laurent 1793-1856 *AmBi, DcAmB, WebAB, WhAm H*
Junell, John 1886-1949 *WhAm 3*
Jung, Carl Gustav 1875-1955 *WhAm 3*
Jung, Carl Gustav 1875-1961 *AsBiEn, DcScB, McGEWB, WhAm 4*
Jung, Franz August Richard 1869- *WhAm 5*
Jungbluth, Karl 1848-1928 *NatCAB 22*
Jungclaus, William Peter 1849-1924 *NatCAB 35*
Junge, Carl Stephen 1880-1972 *WhAm 5*
Junger, Aegideus 1833-1895 *TwCBDA*
Junger, Aegidius 1833-1895 *ApCAB*
Junger, Aegidius 1843-1895 *NatCAB 13*
Junger, Ernst 1895- *McGEWB*
Junggren, Oscar Frederik 1865-1935 *NatCAB 26*

Jungius, Joachim 1587-1657 *DcScB*
Jungman, John George 1720-1808 *DcAmB,*
  WhAm H
Jungmann, Bernhardt 1671-1747 *ApCAB*
Jungmann, John George 1720-1808 *ApCAB,*
  NatCAB 6
Junipero, Miguel Jose Serra 1713-1784 *AmBi,*
  ApCAB, NatCAB 12
Junjel, Barthol *NewYHSD*
Junkerman, Gustavus S 1859-1931 *WhAm 1*
Junkermann, Charles Franklin 1862- *WhAm 4*
Junkersfeld, Peter 1869-1930 *ApCAB X,*
  NatCAB 22, WhAm 1
Junkin, Benjamin Franklin 1822-1908 *BiDrAC*
Junkin, Benjamin T 1822- *BiAUS*
Junkin, David Favier 1808-1880 *NatCAB 11*
Junkin, David X 1808-1880 *ApCAB, TwCBDA*
Junkin, Francis Thomas Anderson 1864-1928
  NatCAB 22, WhAm 1
Junkin, George 1790-1868 *ApCAB, BiDAmEd,*
  DcAmB, Drake, NatCAB 3, NatCAB 11,
  TwCBDA, WhAm H
Junkin, George 1827- *ApCAB, TwCBDA*
Junkin, Margaret *NotAW*
Junkin, Samuel Presley 1878-1957 *NatCAB 43*
Junod, Henri Pell 1900-1971 *WhAm 6*
Junod, Louis Henri 1861- *ApCAB X*
Junot, Andoche 1771-1813 *WhoMilH*
Jupp, Alfred John 1875-1934 *NatCAB 32*
Jurchak, Peter Paul 1900-1948 *NatCAB 38*
Jurenev, Serge B 1899-1960 *WhAm 4*
Jurgatis, John Paul 1915-1958 *WhAm 3*
Jurgens, Hendrik Joseph 1872-1941 *NatCAB 32*
Jurica, Hilary Stanislaus 1892-1970 *WhAm 5*
Jusserand, Jean Adrien Antoine Jules 1855-1932
  WhAm 1
Jussieu, Adrien Henri Laurent De 1797-1853
  DcScB
Jussieu, Antoine De 1686-1758 *DcScB*
Jussieu, Antoine Laurent De 1748-1836 *AsBiEn,*
  DcScB
Jussieu, Bernard De 1699-1777 *DcScB*
Jussieu, Joseph De 1704-1779 *DcScB*
Just, Ernest Everett 1883-1941 *DcAmB S3,*
  WebAB, WhAm 1
Just, Ernest Everett 1884-1941 *WhoColR*
Just, Theodor Karl 1904-1960 *WhAm 4*
Just, William *NewYHSD*
Juster, Peter Beryl 1887-1957 *NatCAB 43*
Justh *NewYHSD*
Justi, Johann Heinrich Gottlob Von 1720-1771
  DcScB
Justice, Edwin Judson 1867-1917 *WhAm 1*
Justice, Joseph *NewYHSD*
Justice, Michael Hoke 1844-1919 *NatCAB 19*
Justin Martyr, Saint 100?-165? *McGEWB*
Justin, Joel Gilbert 1851- *NatCAB 4*
Justin, Joel Gilbert 1852- *TwCBDA*
Justin, Margaret M 1889-1967 *WhAm 5*
Justinian I 482?-565 *McGEWB*
Justiniano, Bartolome *ApCAB*
Justo, Agustin Pedro 1876-1943 *McGEWB*
Juul, Niels 1859-1929 *BiDrAC, WhAm 1*
Juvara, Filippo 1678-1736 *McGEWB*
Juve, Walter Henry 1890-1944 *NatCAB 35*
Juvenal d127? *McGEWB*

K

Kaminsky, Isaac 1874-1946 *NatCAB 37*
Kamm, Jacob 1823-1912 *NatCAB 16*
Kamman, Gordon Richard 1898-1961
NatCAB 49
Kamman, William Frederick 1885-1960
NatCAB 48, WhAm 4
Kammer, Adolph Gottlieb 1903-1962
NatCAB 48, WhAm 4
Kammer, Alfred Charles 1884- *WhAm 5*
Kammer, Edward Joseph 1908-1975 *WhAm 6*
Kammerer, Herbert Anthony 1905-1966 *WhAm 4*
Kammerer, Frederic 1856-1928 *WhAm 1*
Kammerer, Frederick 1856-1928 *NatCAB 23*
Kammerer, Percy Gamble 1885-1946 *WhAm 3*
Kammerer, Webb Louis 1893-1971 *WhAm 5*
Kammert, Donald Milton 1909-1971 *WhAm 5*
Kammeyer, Julius Ernest 1867-1936 *WhAm 1*
Kammu 737-806 *McGEWB*
Kamp, Byron Aarie 1882-1954 *NatCAB 45*
Kamper, Gary Henry 1902-1961 *NatCAB 48*
Kamper, Louis 1861-1953 *WhAm 3*
Kamperman, George Abel 1880-1961
NatCAB 48
Kamphuisen, Pieter Wilhelmus 1897-1961
WhAm 4
Kampman, Lewis Francis 1817-1884 *NatCAB 2*
Kanaka *DcScB*
Kanaley, Byron Vincent 1882-1960 *WhAm 4*
Kanar, William P 1866-1926 *NatCAB 20*
Kanavel, Allen Buckner 1874-1938 *NatCAB 28,
WhAm 1*
Kandel, Isaac Leon 1881-1965 *BiDAmEd,
NatCAB 51, WhAm 4*
Kander, Allen 1888-1970 *WhAm 5*
Kander, Lizzie Black 1858-1940 *NotAW*
Kandinsky, Vasily 1866-1944 *WhAm 4*
Kandinsky, Wassily 1866-1944 *McGEWB*
Kane, DeLancey Astor 1848-1915 *ApCAB X*
Kane, Elias K 1795?-1835 *BiAUS*
Kane, Elias Kent 1794-1835 *BiDrAC,
WhAm H, WhAmP*
Kane, Elias Kent 1796-1835 *ApCAB,
NatCAB 11, TwCBDA*
Kane, Elisha Kent 1820-1857 *AmBi, ApCAB,
DcAmB, Drake, NatCAB 3, TwCBDA,
WebAB, WebAMB, WhAm H*
Kane, Elisha Kent 1856-1935 *WhAm 1*
Kane, Elizabeth C *WomWWA 14*
Kane, Francis Fisher 1866-1955 *WhAm 3*
Kane, Frank James 1912-1968 *NatCAB 53*
Kane, George Proctor 1817-1878 *ApCAB,
NatCAB 5*
Kane, Grace Miriam Wilson 1879-
WomWWA 14
Kane, Grenville 1854-1943 *ApCAB X,
NatCAB 32, WhAm 2*
Kane, Howard Francis 1887-1946 *WhAm 2*
Kane, James Henry 1878-1935 *NatCAB 38*
Kane, James Johnson 1837-1921 *WhAm 1*
Kane, John 1860-1934 *BnEnAmA, DcAmB S1,
McGEWB*
Kane, John Kent 1873-1937 *NatCAB 28*
Kane, John Kintzing 1795-1858 *AmBi, ApCAB,
BiAUS, DcAmB, NatCAB 11, TwCBDA,
WhAm H*
Kane, John Kintzing 1833-1886 *TwCBDA*
Kane, John Patrick 1849- *NatCAB 12*
Kane, John William 1891-1965 *NatCAB 52*
Kane, Leo Aloysius 1897-1961 *WhAm 4*
Kane, LeRoy Adrian 1903-1958 *NatCAB 48*
Kane, Matthew John 1863-1924 *NatCAB 18,
WhAm 1*
Kane, Nicholas Thomas 1846-1887 *BiDrAC,
WhAm H*
Kane, Paul 1810-1871 *ApCAB, IIBEAAW,
McGEWB, NewYHSD, REnAW*
Kane, Paul 1820?- *Drake*
Kane, Paul Vincent 1892-1959 *NatCAB 51,
WhAm 3*
Kane, Richmond Keith 1900-1974 *WhAm 6*
Kane, Robert John 1809-1890 *DcScB*
Kane, Susan Mary 1866- *WomWWA 14*
Kane, Theodore Porter 1869-1943 *WhAm 2*
Kane, Thomas Franklin 1863- *WhAm 5*
Kane, Thomas Leiper 1822-1883 *AmBi,
ApCAB, DcAmB, TwCBDA, WhAm H*
Kane, Thomas Leo 1888-1959 *WhAm 4*
Kane, William Edward 1866-1945 *NatCAB 34*

Kane, William Patterson 1847-1906 *WhAm 1*
Kane, William T 1880-1946 *WhAm 2*
Kaneko, Josephine Conger *WomWWA 14*
K'ang, Yu-Wei 1858-1927 *McGEWB*
K'ang-Hsi 1654-1722 *McGEWB*
Kangaroo, Captain *WebAB*
Kann, Alexander 1828?- *NewYHSD*
Kann, Gustave Herman 1886-1953 *NatCAB 42*
Kann, Moritz 1826?- *NewYHSD*
Kannegieser, Sigismund 1706-1759 *ApCAB*
Kannel, John William 1868-1951 *NatCAB 38*
Kanner, Abram Otto 1893-1967 *NatCAB 52*
Kanner, Irving F 1913-1974 *WhAm 6*
Kanner, Oscar 1896-1965 *NatCAB 51*
Kanner, Samuel Jacob 1912-1967 *WhAm 5*
Kanouse, Theodore Dwight 1838- *WhAm 4*
Kanski, Francis 1870- *WhAm 5*
Kant, Immanuel 1724-1804 *AsBiEn, DcScB,
McGEWB*
Kant, Rudolph Martin 1902-1951 *NatCAB 40*
Kanter, Aaron E 1893-1967 *WhAm 4,
WhAm 5*
Kanter, Charles Andrew 1887- *WhAm 3*
Kantor, John Leonard 1890-1947 *NatCAB 36*
Kantor, Morris 1896-1974 *BnEnAmA,
WhAm 6*
Kantorowicz, Ernst H 1895-1963 *WhAm 4*
Kantzler, George R 1897-1957 *WhAm 3*
Kanzler, Ernest Carlton 1892-1967 *WhAm 4*
Kanzler, Jacob 1879-1940 *NatCAB 30*
Kao-Tsung 1107-1187 *McGEWB*
Kapell, William 1922-1953 *WhAm 3*
Kapenstein, Ira 1936-1971 *WhAm 5*
Kapiolani 1781?-1841 *NotAW*
Kapitsa, Peter Leonidovich 1894- *McGEWB*
Kapitza, Peter Leonidovich 1894- *AsBiEn*
Kaplan, Abraham David Hannath 1893-1974
WhAm 6
Kaplan, Abraham Gerard 1887-1962
NatCAB 47
Kaplan, Benjamin 1906-1972 *WhAm 5*
Kaplan, Bernard Michael 1874-1941 *WhAm 1*
Kaplan, Charles I 1903-1964 *NatCAB 52*
Kaplan, David Michael 1876-1952 *NatCAB 39*
Kaplan, Ellezer 1891-1952 *WhAm 3*
Kaplan, Frank Raphael Selig 1886-1957
NatCAB 49, WhAm 3
Kaplan, Gabriel Louis 1901-1968 *NatCAB 53,
NatCAB 54*
Kaplan, Harry 1901-1969 *WhAm 5*
Kaplan, Jacob Joseph 1889-1960 *WhAm 4*
Kaplan, Kivie 1904-1975 *WhAm 6*
Kaplan, Louis Simeon 1896-1964 *NatCAB 52*
Kaplan, Milton Lewis 1920-1972 *WhAm 5*
Kaplan, Mordecai Menahem 1881- *McGEWB,
WebAB, WhAm 6*
Kaplan, Morris 1898-1964 *NatCAB 50,
WhAm 4*
Kaplan, Samuel 1907-1970 *WhAm 5*
Kaplan, Stanley Midell 1914-1960 *NatCAB 47*
Kaposi, Moriz 1837-1902 *BiHiMed*
Kapp, Carl Gailard 1903-1962 *NatCAB 47*
Kapp, Frederick *Drake*
Kapp, Friedrich 1824-1884 *ApCAB, DcAmB,
NatCAB 24, WhAm H*
Kapp, Jack 1901-1949 *WhAm 2*
Kapp, Marie F 1843- *WomWWA 14*
Kapp, Roland 1903-1965 *NatCAB 53*
Kapp, Wolfgang 1858-1922 *McGEWB*
Kappel, Gertrude 1893-1971 *WhAm 5*
Kappel, Samuel 1889-1957 *WhAm 3*
Kapper, Isaac M 1864- *WhAm 4*
Kappes, Alfred 1850-1894 *TwCBDA*
Kapteyn, Jacobus Cornelis 1851-1922 *McGEWB*
Kapteyn, Jacobus Cornelius 1851-1922 *AsBiEn,
DcScB*
Karaji, Abu Bakr Ibn M Al Husayn, Al- *DcScB*
Karamzin, Nikolai Mikhailovich 1766-1826
McGEWB
Karapetoff, Vladimir 1876-1948 *WhAm 2*
Karavongse, Phya Prabha 1873- *WhAm 5*
Karch, Charles Adam 1875-1932 *BiDrAC,
WhAm 1*
Karcher, Walter Thompson 1881-1953
NatCAB 43, WhAm 3
Kardatzke, Carl Henry 1904-1959 *NatCAB 50*
Karel, John Connell 1873- *WhAm 5*
Karelitz, George B 1895-1943 *WhAm 2*

Karfiol, Bernard 1886-1952 *DcAmB S5,
WhAm 3*
Karge, Joseph 1815-1892 *NatCAB 7*
Karge, Joseph 1823-1892 *TwCBDA*
Karger, Gustav J 1866-1924 *WhAm 1*
Karig, Walter d1956 *WhAm 3*
Karim, Saied Nasif 1900-1958 *NatCAB 48*
Karim Khan Zand d1779 *McGEWB*
Karkeet, Robert Budd 1884-1960 *NatCAB 50*
Karker, Earl Clarence 1895-1963 *NatCAB 49*
Karker, Maurice Harmon 1886-1951
NatCAB 40, WhAm 3
Karl, Tom 1846- *WhAm 4*
Karlen, Sven Bernhard 1914-1969 *WhAm 5*
Karlin, Isaac William 1897-1962 *NatCAB 46*
Karloff, Boris 1887-1969 *WebAB, WhAm 5*
Karlstadt, Andreas Bodenheim Von 1480?-1541
McGEWB
Karlstrom, Arthur Elof 1902-1951 *NatCAB 41*
Karman, Theodore Von 1881-1963 *DcScB,
McGEWB, WebAB, WebAMB*
Karn, Daniel Earl 1890-1969 *WhAm 5*
Karn, Harry Wendell 1907-1969 *WhAm 5*
Karnes, Henry W d1840 *NatCAB 6*
Karnes, Joseph V C 1841-1911 *WhAm 1*
Karney, Rex Lambert 1914-1966 *WhAm 4*
Karnga, Abayomi Winfred 1882- *WhoColR*
Karns, Emily Sophia 1853- *WomWWA 14*
Karns, John Delano 1863-1932 *NatCAB 25*
Karns, Louise M 1870- *WomWWA 14*
Karolik, Maxim 1894-1966 *WhAm 4*
Karow, Herman Charles 1874-1957 *NatCAB 44*
Karp, Lazarus 1885-1938 *NatCAB 29*
Karpas, Irving David 1889-1971 *NatCAB 55*
Karpen, Michael 1868-1950 *NatCAB 44*
Karpick, John Joseph 1883-1960 *NatCAB 49*
Karpinski, Louis Charles 1878-1956 *DcScB Sup,
WhAm 3*
Karpinsky, Alexandr Petrovich 1847-1936
DcScB
Karpovich, Michael 1888-1959 *WhAm 3*
Karr, Edmund Joseph 1884-1972 *WhAm 5*
Karr, Elizabeth *WhAm 5*
Karr, Frank 1875- *WhAm 5*
Karr, Louise 1857- *WomWWA 14*
Karr, Robert McNary 1878- *WhAm 6*
Karrer, Enoch 1887-1946 *WhAm 2*
Karrer, Paul 1889-1971 *AsBiEn, DcScB Sup,
WhAm 5*
Karrer, Sebastian 1889-1973 *WhAm 6*
Karrick, David Brewer 1893-1960 *WhAm 4*
Karsner, Daniel 1842-1918 *NatCAB 3,
NatCAB 18*
Karsner, Howard Thomas 1879-1970
NatCAB 55, WhAm 5
Karst, John 1836-1922 *NewYHSD*
Karst, Raymond Willard 1902- *BiDrAC*
Karsten, Andrew 1895-1962 *NatCAB 52*
Karsten, Frank Melvin 1913- *BiDrAC,
WhAmP*
Karsten, Gustaf E 1859-1908 *WhAm 1*
Karsten, Gustaf Friedrich 1859-1908 *TwCBDA*
Karsten, Karl Johann Bernhard 1782-1853
DcScB
Kartak, Franz August 1887-1947 *WhAm 3*
Karth, Joseph Edward 1922- *BiDrAC*
Kartheiser, Frank L 1893-1973 *WhAm 6*
Karume, Sheikh Abeid Amani 1905-1972
McGEWB
Karwoski, Theodore F 1896-1957 *WhAm 3*
Kasabach, Harry Yervant 1912-1969
NatCAB 55
Kasanin, Jacob Sergi 1897-1946 *WhAm 2*
Kasavubu, Joseph 1913?-1969 *McGEWB,
WhAm 5*
Kasberg, Karl Gary 1932-1971 *WhAm 5*
Kase, Max 1898-1974 *WhAm 6*
Kasebier, Gertrude Stanton 1852-1934
*BnEnAmA, NotAW, WhAm 1,
WhAm 1C*
Kasem, George Albert 1919- *BiDrAC*
Kaseman, George Ambrose 1868-1938
NatCAB 29
Kashi, Ghiyath Al-Din Jamshid Masud, Al-
d1429 *DcScB*
Kasner, Edward 1878-1955 *NatCAB 16,
NatCAB 41, WhAm 3*
Kassabian, Mihran Krikor 1868-1910 *WhAm 1*

Kassay, Allan Attila 1928-1973 *WhAm 6*
Kassel, Charles 1877-1943 *WhAm 2*
Kassler, Edwin Stebbins 1866-1962 *WhAm 4*
Kassler, Kenneth Stone 1905-1964 *WhAm 4*
Kassner, James Lyle 1894-1970 *NatCAB 56*
Kasson, Frank H 1852- *WhAm 4*
Kasson, John A 1822-1910 *BiAUS*
Kasson, John Adam 1822-1910 *AmBi, BiDrAC,*
DcAmB, NatCAB 4, TwCBDA,
WhAm 1, WhAmP
Kasson, John Adams 1822-1910 *ApCAB*
Kast, Ida G *WomWWA 14*
Kast, Ludwig 1877-1941 *WhAm 1*
Kast, Miller I *WhAm 2*
Kasten, Harry Edward 1888-1968 *WhAm 5*
Kasten, Walter 1880-1950 *WhAm 3*
Kasten, William Henry 1891-1963 *NatCAB 53,*
WhAm 4
Kastenmeier, Robert William 1924- *BiDrAC*
Kaster, John P 1857-1938 *WhAm 1*
Kastle, Joseph Hoeing 1864-1916 *NatCAB 15,*
WhAm 1
Kastler, Alfred 1902- *AsBiEn*
Kastner, Alfred Louis 1878-1953 *NatCAB 44*
Kastner, Erhart 1904-1974 *WhAm 6*
Kastner, Erich 1899-1974 *WhAm 6*
Kastor, Adolph 1856-1946 *NatCAB 14,*
NatCAB 33
Kastor, Alfred Bernard 1889-1963 *NatCAB 50*
Katayama, Sen 1860-1933 *McGEWB*
Katchen, Julius 1926-1969 *WhAm 5*
Katcher, Archie 1914-1974 *WhAm 6*
Katek, Charles 1910-1971 *WhAm 5*
Kater, Henry 1777-1835 *DcScB*
Kathrens, Richard Donland 1866- *WhAm 4*
Katir Al-Farghani, Ibn *DcScB*
Katker, William Cortnum 1893-1961
NatCAB 50
Kato, Frederick 1866-1909 *WhAm 1*
Katte, Edwin Britton 1871-1928 *WhAm 1*
Katte, Walter 1830-1917 *ApCAB, DcAmB,*
NatCAB 16, TwCBDA, WhAm 4
Kattell, Thomas Blaine 1875-1947 *NatCAB 37*
Katterle, Zeno Bernel 1903-1969 *WhAm 5*
Kattwinkel, Egon Emil 1901-1964 *NatCAB 51*
Katukov, Mikhail 1900- *WhWW-II*
Katz, Abner Roland 1898-1964 *WhAm 4*
Katz, Benjamin Samuel 1892-1969 *WhAm 5*
Katz, Frank J 1883-1930 *WhAm 1*
Katz, Joseph 1888-1958 *NatCAB 49,*
WhAm 4
Katz, Label Abraham 1918-1975 *WhAm 6*
Katz, Mark Jacob 1863-1927 *WhAm 1*
Katz, Michael H d1962 *WhAm 4*
Katz-Suchy, Juliusz 1912-1971 *WhAm 5*
Katzenbach, Edward Lawrence 1878-1934
WhAm 1
Katzenbach, Edward Lawrence, Jr. 1919-1974
WhAm 6
Katzenbach, Frank S, Jr. 1868-1929 *WhAm 1*
Katzenbach, Nicholas DeBelleville 1922-
BiDrUSE
Katzenberger, William E 1876- *WhAm 5*
Katzenellenbogen, Adolf 1901-1964 *NatCAB 51,*
WhAm 4
Katzenstein, Martin L 1879-1955 *NatCAB 44*
Katzentine, A Frank 1902-1960 *WhAm 3A*
Katzer, Frederic Xavier 1844-1903 *ApCAB Sup,*
DcAmB, WhAm 1
Katzer, Frederick Xavier 1844-1903
NatCAB 12, TwCBDA
Katzin, Eugene M 1904-1966 *WhAm 4*
Katzman, Morris 1904-1957 *NatCAB 48*
Katzmann, Frederick Gunn 1875-1953
NatCAB 40
Kauba, Carl 1865-1922 *IIBEAAW*
Kaucher, Dorothy Wanita 1892-1972
NatCAB 57
Kauffman, Benjamin Franklin 1874-1948
NatCAB 47, WhAm 2
Kauffman, Calvin Henry 1869-1931 *AmBi,*
DcAmB, NatCAB 22, WhAm 1
Kauffman, Clara Norton 1857- *WomWWA 14*
Kauffman, George Beecher 1855-1921
NatCAB 19
Kauffman, James Laurence 1887-1963
NatCAB 51
Kauffman, James Lee 1886-1968 *WhAm 5*

Kauffman, Lawrence A 1898-1959 *WhAm 4*
Kauffman, Margaret Belle Houston
WomWWA 14
Kauffman, Nelle Dunham *WomWWA 14*
Kauffman, Reginald Wright 1877-1959
NatCAB 13, NatCAB 48
Kauffman, Ruth Wright 1883-1952 *WhAm 3,*
WomWWA 14
Kauffman, Thomas Jacob 1882-1937
NatCAB 32
Kauffman, Treva Erdine 1889-1975 *BiDAmEd,*
WhAm 6
Kauffmann, Alfred Otto 1879-1959 *WhAm 3*
Kauffmann, Rudolph 1853-1927 *WhAm 1*
Kauffmann, Rudolph Max 1882-1956 *WhAm 3*
Kauffmann, Samuel Hay 1829-1906 *NatCAB 13,*
TwCBDA, WhAm 1
Kauffmann, Samuel Hay 1898-1971 *NatCAB 57,*
WhAm 5
Kauffmann, Victor 1868- *WhAm 5*
Kaufman, A Spencer 1882-1958 *NatCAB 46*
Kaufman, Abraham Charles 1839- *NatCAB 11,*
WhAm 4
Kaufman, David E 1883-1962 *WhAm 4,*
WhAm 5
Kaufman, David Spangler 1813-1851 *ApCAB,*
BiAUS, BiDrAC, NatCAB 12, TwCBDA,
WhAm H, WhAmP
Kaufman, George Simon 1889-1961 *McGEWB,*
WebAB, WhAm 4
Kaufman, Gerald Lynton 1893-1968
NatCAB 53
Kaufman, Harold John 1890-1955 *NatCAB 44*
Kaufman, Herbert 1878-1947 *WhAm 2*
Kaufman, Hiram Joseph 1884-1963 *NatCAB 52*
Kaufman, Jay 1918-1971 *NatCAB 56*
Kaufman, Jerome George 1901-1972
NatCAB 57
Kaufman, Kenneth Carlyle 1887-1945 *WhAm 2*
Kaufman, Louis Graveraet 1872-1942 *WhAm 2*
Kaufman, Louis Rene 1881-1964 *NatCAB 51*
Kaufman, Paul D 1899-1952 *WhAm 3*
Kaufman, Pauline 1857- *WomWWA 14*
Kaufman, Ralph Odell 1879-1949 *WhAm 3*
Kaufman, Samuel H 1893-1960 *WhAm 4*
Kaufman, Sigismund 1825-1889 *NatCAB 2*
Kaufman, Theodore 1814- *ApCAB*
Kaufman, Theodore see also Kaufmann, Theodor
Kaufmann, Annie Millington 1867-
WomWWA 14
Kaufmann, Betty Wolf 1861-1942 *NatCAB 32*
Kaufmann, Charles Beecher 1890-1957
NatCAB 49
Kaufmann, Christopher Alphonso 1907-1963
WhAm 4
Kaufmann, Ed 1864- *WhAm 4*
Kaufmann, Edgar Jonas 1885-1955 *WhAm 3*
Kaufmann, Edmund Isador 1886-1950
NatCAB 41, WhAm 3
Kaufmann, Ezekiel 1889-1963 *McGEWB*
Kaufmann, Gordon Bernie 1888-1949 *WhAm 3*
Kaufmann, Henry 1860-1955 *NatCAB 50*
Kaufmann, Herbert Moses 1870-1950
NatCAB 55
Kaufmann, Isaac 1851- *ApCAB X*
Kaufmann, John Heiden 1919-1972 *WhAm 5*
Kaufmann, Morris 1858-1917 *NatCAB 29*
Kaufmann, Nicolaus *DcScB*
Kaufmann, Paul 1862- *WhAm 4*
Kaufmann, Theodor 1814- *NewYHSD*
Kaufmann, Theodor see also Kaufman, Theodore
Kaufmann, Theodore 1814- *IIBEAAW*
Kaufmann, Walter 1871-1947 *DcScB*
Kaufmann, Wilford E 1893-1953 *WhAm 3*
Kaul, John Lanzel 1866-1931 *WhAm 1*
Kaula, William Jurian 1871-1953 *NatCAB 45*
Kaulbach, Charles Edwin 1834- *ApCAB*
Kaulbach, Henry Adolphus Newman 1830-
ApCAB
Kaulback, Frank S 1878-1956 *WhAm 3*
Kaunda, Kenneth David 1924- *McGEWB*
Kauper, Paul Gerhardt 1907-1974 *WhAm 6*
Kauth, Francis *NewYHSD*
Kautilya *McGEWB*
Kautsky, Karl Johann 1854-1938 *McGEWB*
Kautz, Albert 1839-1907 *AmBi, ApCAB,*
NatCAB 14, TwCBDA, WhAm 1
Kautz, August Valentine 1828-1895 *AmBi,*

ApCAB, DcAmB, Drake, NatCAB 14,
TwCBDA, WhAm H
Kautz, John Arthur 1860-1938 *WhAm 1*
Kautzky, Theodore 1896-1953 *WhAm 3*
Kauvar, C E Hillel 1879-1971 *WhAm 5*
Kavana, Rose M *WomWWA 14*
Kavanagh, Edward 1795-1844 *ApCAB, BiAUS,*
BiDrAC, DcAmB, Drake, NatCAB 6,
TwCBDA, WhAm H
Kavanagh, Francis Bernard 1879-1956
NatCAB 48, WhAm 3
Kavanagh, Hubbard Hinde 1802-1884 *TwCBDA*
Kavanagh, James Edward 1871-1957
NatCAB 46, WhAm 3
Kavanagh, Leslie J 1866-1934 *WhAm 1*
Kavanagh, Marcus A 1859-1937 *WhAm 1*
Kavanagh, Robert Vincent 1905-1957 *WhAm 3*
Kavanagh, Thomas Matthew 1909-1975
WhAm 6
Kavanagh, William Francis 1878-1963
NatCAB 49
Kavanaugh, Benjamin Taylor 1805-1888
ApCAB Sup
Kavanaugh, Charles Nicholas 1892-1955
NatCAB 45
Kavanaugh, Hubbard Hinde 1802-1884 *ApCAB,*
NatCAB 9
Kavanaugh, John Michael 1918- *WhAm 5*
Kavanaugh, Luke Joseph 1877-1965 *NatCAB 51*
Kavanaugh, William Harrison 1873-1939
WhAm 1
Kavanaugh, William Kerr 1860-1932 *WhAm 1*
Kavanaugh, William Marmaduke 1866-1915
BiDrAC
Kavanaugh, Williams Marmaduke 1866-1915
NatCAB 19, WhAm 1
Kaveler, Herman Henry 1905-1966 *NatCAB 52,*
WhAm 4A
Kavraysky, Vladimir Vladimirovich 1884-1954
DcScB
Kawabata, Yasunari 1899-1972 *McGEWB,*
WhAm 5
Kawakami, Jotaro 1889-1966 *WhAm 4A*
Kawakami, K K 1875-1949 *WhAm 2*
Kawananakoa, Prince David 1868-1908
NatCAB 49
Kawawa, Rashidi Mfaume 1929- *McGEWB*
Kawden, Henry *NewYHSD*
Kay, Abraham Simon 1899-1963 *NatCAB 50*
Kay, Edgar Boyd 1860-1931 *DcAmB,*
NatCAB 22, WhAm 1
Kay, George Frederick 1873-1943 *DcScB,*
NatCAB 32, WhAm 2
Kay, Gertrude Alice d1939 *WhAm 1*
Kay, James I 1853-1921 *ApCAB X*
Kay, Jane Heartt 1880- *WomWWA 14*
Kay, Jenny Mieville Totten 1856-
WomWWA 14
Kay, Joseph William 1849-1928 *ApCAB X*
Kay, Joseph William 1845-1928 *WhAm 2*
Kay, Marshall 1904-1975 *WhAm 6*
Kay, Thomas 1837-1900 *NatCAB 34*
Kay, Ulysses Simpson 1917- *WebAB*
Kay, William *NewYHSD*
Kay, William Edward 1859-1939 *NatCAB 41,*
WhAm 1
Kay-Scott, Cyril 1879- *WhAm 6*
Kayan, Carl F 1899-1970 *WhAm 5*
Kaye, Danny 1913- *WebAB*
Kaye, Frederick Benjamin 1892-1930 *DcAmB*
Kaye, James Hamilton Barcroft 1862-1932
WhAm 1
Kaye, John William 1846- *TwCBDA,*
WhAm 1
Kaye, Joseph 1912-1961 *WhAm 4*
Kaye-Smith, Sheila 1887-1956 *WhAm 3*
Kayflick, Henry *NewYHSD*
Kayn, Hilde B 1903-1950 *WhAm 3*
Kaynor, William Kirk 1884-1929 *BiDrAC,*
NatCAB 21
Kays, Donald Jackson 1886-1956 *WhAm 3*
Kays, John 1739-1829 *ApCAB X*
Kayser *NewYHSD*
Kayser, Albert Henry 1863-1923 *NatCAB 27*
Kayser, Carl Eberhard 1889-1965 *NatCAB 52*
Kayser, Heinrich Johannes Gustav 1853-1940
DcScB
Kazan, Elia 1909- *WebAB*

WhAm 4

Keeling, Walter Angus 1873-1945 *WhAm 2*
Keelmann, Charles *NewYHSD*
Keelor, Charlotte 1882- *WomWWA 14*
Keely, Isaac H 1817-1891 *NewYHSD*
Keely, John Ernest Worrall 1827-1898
 NatCAB 9
Keely, John Ernst Worrell 1827-1898 *DcAmB,*
 WhAm H
Keely, John Worrall 1837- *ApCAB*
Keely, Patrick Charles 1816-1896 *ApCAB Sup,*
 TwCBDA
Keely, Robert Neff 1860- *WhAm 4*
Keen, Dora 1871- *WomWWA 14*
Keen, Edward Leggett 1870-1943 *WhAm 2*
Keen, George 1620?-1690? *ApCAB*
Keen, Gregory Bernard 1844-1930 *ApCAB,*
 NatCAB 11, TwCBDA, WhAm 1
Keen, J Velma 1899-1963 *NatCAB 51,*
 WhAm 4
Keen, Kennard Garton, Jr. 1908-1966 *WhAm 4*
Keen, Matthias 1667-1714 *ApCAB*
Keen, Morris Longstreth 1820-1883 *ApCAB,*
 DcAmB, NatCAB 11, TwCBDA,
 WhAm H
Keen, Victor 1898-1955 *WhAm 3*
Keen, William C *NewYHSD*
Keen, William Williams 1837-1932 *AmBi,*
 ApCAB, ApCAB X, BiDAmEd, BiHiMed,
 DcAmB S1, NatCAB 11, TwCBDA,
 WhAm 1
Keena, James Trafton 1850-1924 *WhAm 1*
Keena, Leo John 1878- *WhAm 6*
Keena, Martin J 1901-1965 *WhAm 4*
Keenan, Albert Joseph, Jr. 1913-1968 *WhAm 5*
Keenan, Alexander Stanislaus 1872-1958
 NatCAB 48, WhAm 5
Keenan, Frank 1858-1929 *WhAm 1*
Keenan, George 1859- *NatCAB 11*
Keenan, George Mungovan 1891-1962
 NatCAB 49, WhAm 4
Keenan, Henry Francis 1847- *WhAm 4*
Keenan, Henry Francis 1849-1928 *ApCAB,*
 NatCAB 6
Keenan, James Francis 1858-1929 *DcAmB*
Keenan, James Francis 1891-1970 *NatCAB 57*
Keenan, James R 1891-1957 *WhAm 3*
Keenan, John Edward 1897-1957 *NatCAB 48*
Keenan, Joseph Berry 1888-1954 *WhAm 3*
Keenan, Peter 1834-1863 *ApCAB*
Keenan, Thomas Johnson, Jr. 1859-1927
 NatCAB 5
Keenan, Thomas Johnston 1859-1927 *WhAm 1*
Keenan, Thomas Joseph 1873-1948 *NatCAB 37*
Keenan, William 1810?- *NewYHSD*
Keene, Amor Frederick 1879-1940 *NatCAB 30,*
 WhAm 1
Keene, Arthur Samuel 1875- *WhAm 5*
Keene, Carolyn *WebAB*
Keene, Carter Brewster 1868-1938 *WhAm 1*
Keene, Charles Herbert 1875- *WhAm 6*
Keene, David 1820-1893 *NatCAB 16*
Keene, Edward Spencer 1864-1928 *WhAm 1*
Keene, Floyd Elwood 1881-1938 *NatCAB 30,*
 WhAm 1
Keene, James Robert 1832-1913 *NatCAB 15*
Keene, James Robert 1838-1913 *DcAmB,*
 WhAm 1
Keene, Laura 1820?-1873 *ApCAB, NatCAB 8,*
 NotAW, TwCBDA, WebAB
Keene, Laura 1826?-1873 *AmBi, DcAmB,*
 WhAm H
Keene, Laura 1830-1873 *Drake*
Keene, Rodolphus D 1885-1973 *NatCAB 57*
Keene, Thomas Wallace 1840-1898 *DcAmB,*
 NatCAB 8, TwCBDA, WhAm H
Keener, Bruce, Jr. 1891-1969 *NatCAB 55*
Keener, Gladys M d1961 *WhAm 4*
Keener, John Christian 1819- *ApCAB,*
 NatCAB 13, TwCBDA, WhAm 1
Keener, John Ormond 1854-1898 *TwCBDA*
Keener, Walter Ney 1880-1932 *WhAm 1*
Keener, William Albert 1856-1913 *DcAmB,*
 NatCAB 9, TwCBDA, WhAm 1
Keeney, Abner 1826-1884 *NatCAB 1*
Keeney, Albert Lawrence 1900-1963 *WhAm 4*
Keeney, Calvin Noyes 1849-1930 *NatCAB 47*
Keeney, Francis B 1884-1957 *WhAm 3*

Keeney, Frederick Thomas 1863-1952 *WhAm 3*
Keeney, Paul Aloysius 1903-1970 *WhAm 5*
Keeney, Mrs. Ralph D 1889-1959 *WhAm 3*
Keeney, Russell Watson 1897-1958 *BiDrAC,*
 NatCAB 43, WhAm 3
Keeney, Willard Franklin 1862-1946
 NatCAB 37, WhAm 2
Keenon, Rodman W 1883-1966 *NatCAB 53*
Keep, Albert 1826-1907 *WhAm 1*
Keep, Charles Hallam 1861-1941 *WhAm 1*
Keep, Chauncey 1853-1929 *WhAm 1*
Keep, Henry 1818-1869 *ApCAB, DcAmB,*
 NatCAB 23, WhAm H
Keep, Ida Savory 1852- *WomWWA 14*
Keep, John 1781-1870 *ApCAB, Drake,*
 NatCAB 2, TwCBDA
Keep, John Joseph 1892-1947 *NatCAB 36,*
 WhAm 2
Keep, Oliver Davis 1903-1965 *WhAm 4*
Keep, Robert Porter 1844-1904 *DcAmB,*
 TwCBDA, WhAm 1
Keep, William John 1842-1918 *NatCAB 18,*
 WhAm 1
Keers, Walter Frederick 1907-1952 *NatCAB 41*
Kees, Frederick 1852- *NatCAB 7*
Keese, John 1805-1856 *ApCAB, TwCBDA*
Keese, Richard 1794-1883 *BiAUS, BiDrAC,*
 WhAm H
Keese, William Linn 1835-1904 *ApCAB,*
 NatCAB 11, TwCBDA, WhAm 1
Keesecker, Raymond P 1891-1960 *WhAm 4*
Keeshan, Robert James 1927- *WebAB*
Keesing, Felix Maxwell 1902-1961 *WhAm 4*
Keesing, Frans Arnold George 1913-1972
 WhAm 5
Keesling, Francis Valentine 1877-1963 *WhAm 4*
Keesom, Willem Hendrik 1876-1956 *DcScB*
Keeton, Robert Wood 1883-1957 *NatCAB 46,*
 WhAm 2
Keever, Edwin Francis 1864-1949 *NatCAB 39*
Keevil, Charles Samuel 1899-1969 *WhAm 5*
Keezer, Martha Moulton Whittemore 1870-
 AmWom, WomWWA 14
Kefauver, Carey Estes 1903-1963 *BiDrAC,*
 EncAB, WebAB, WhAmP
Kefauver, Cary Estes 1903-1963 *EncAAH*
Kefauver, Clarence Eugene 1894-1968 *WhAm 5*
Kefauver, Estes 1903-1963 *NatCAB 52,*
 WhAm 4
Kefauver, Grayson Neikirk 1900-1946 *BiDAmEd,*
 DcAmB S4, NatCAB 35, WhAm 2
Kefauver, Harry Joshua 1878- *WhAm 2*
Keffer, Charles Albert 1861-1935 *WhAm 1*
Keffer, Frederic 1861-1947 *NatCAB 33*
Keffer, J L *NewYHSD*
Kegel, Arnold Henry 1894- *WhAm 5*
Kehew, Mary Morton Kimball 1859-1918
 DcAmB, NotAW
Kehew, Millo Marie *WomWWA 14*
Kehl, John Elwin 1870- *WhAm 5*
Kehlenbeck, Alfred Paul 1906-1969 *WhAm 5*
Kehoe, Arthur Henry 1889-1969 *WhAm 5*
Kehoe, Harry Patrick 1895-1961 *NatCAB 49*
Kehoe, James Nicholas 1862-1945 *BiDrAC,*
 WhAm 2
Kehoe, James Walter 1870-1938 *BiDrAC*
Kehoe, Joseph W 1890-1959 *WhAm 3*
Kehoe, Walter 1870- *WhAm 5*
Kehr, Cyrus 1856-1941 *NatCAB 30*
Kehr, Edward Charles 1837-1918 *BiAUS,*
 BiDrAC
Kehr, Gustav Herman 1581-1639 *ApCAB*
Kehrlein, Frances Cassandra 1886-
 WomWWA 14
Kehrweider, Charles *NewYHSD*
Kehrweider, Otto *NewYHSD*
Kehrweider, William, Jr. *NewYHSD*
Kehrweider, William, Sr. 1795?- *NewYHSD*
Keidel, George Charles 1868-1942 *WhAm 2*
Keifer, Joseph Warren 1836-1932 *ApCAB,*
 BiDrAC, DcAmB S1, NatCAB 4,
 TwCBDA, WebAB, WhAm 1, WhAmP
Keifer, Martha Steele 1867- *WomWWA 14*
Keightley, Edwin William 1843-1926 *BiDrAC*
Keigwin, A Edwin 1869-1951 *WhAm 3*
Keigwin, Albert Newton 1840-1920 *NatCAB 19*
Keigwin, Charles Albert 1862-1940 *NatCAB 34*
Keil, Doctor 1811- *NatCAB 12*

Keil, Leota Wheeler 1865- *WomWWA 14*
Keil, Valentine *NewYHSD*
Keila, Louis 1882-1954 *NatCAB 43*
Keilberth, Joseph 1908-1968 *WhAm 5*
Keiley, Anthony M 1835-1905 *NatCAB 13*
Keiley, Benjamin Anthony 1873-1943
 NatCAB 32
Keiley, Benjamin J 1847-1925 *NatCAB 12,*
 WhAm 1
Keilin, David 1887-1963 *DcScB*
Keill, James 1673-1719 *DcScB*
Keill, John 1671-1721 *DcScB*
Keiller, William 1861-1931 *NatCAB 22,*
 WhAm 1
Keim, Addison 1890-1957 *NatCAB 48*
Keim, Augusta Morris Madison *WomWWA 14*
Keim, Franklin David 1886-1956 *WhAm 3*
Keim, George DeBenneville 1884-1943 *WhAm 2*
Keim, George May 1805-1861 *BiAUS, BiDrAC,*
 NatCAB 3, WhAm H
Keim, George May 1805-1862 *TwCBDA*
Keim, John *NewYHSD*
Keim, W Franklin, Jr. 1910-1971 *NatCAB 56*
Keim, William H 1843- *NatCAB 3*
Keim, William High 1813-1862 *ApCAB,*
 BiAUS, BiDrAC, Drake, TwCBDA,
 WhAm H
Keimer, Samuel *Drake*
Keimer, Samuel d1738? *ApCAB, TwCBDA*
Keimer, Samuel 1688-1739? *DcAmB*
Keines, Simon *NewYHSD*
Keinhart, Francis *NewYHSD*
Keinley, Augustus *NewYHSD*
Keiper, Henry Brinser 1858-1920 *NatCAB 21*
Keiper, Jacob Daniel 1884-1943 *NatCAB 34*
Keir, James 1735-1820 *DcScB*
Keir, John Sibbit 1892-1959 *WhAm 4*
Keirn, Gideon Isaac 1854- *WhAm 4*
Keisar, Mauritius Van 1663-1725 *ApCAB*
Keiser, Albert 1887-1959 *WhAm 4*
Keiser, Edward Harrison 1861-1940
 NatCAB 30, WhAm 4
Keiser, Elizabeth Harris 1870- *WomWWA 14*
Keiser, George Camp 1900-1956 *WhAm 3*
Keiser, John Pinckney 1833-1901 *NatCAB 28*
Keiser, Laurence Bollon 1895-1969 *WhAm 5*
Keiser, Robert Hough 1872-1928 *NatCAB 23*
Keister, Abraham Lincoln 1852-1917 *BiDrAC,*
 WhAm 1
Keister, Lillie Resler 1851- *AmWom*
Keita, Modibo 1915- *McGEWB*
Keitel, Wilhelm 1882-1946 *WhWW-II*
Keitel, Wilhelm 1892-1946 *WhoMilH*
Keith, Adelphus Bartlett 1855- *NatCAB 12*
Keith, Adelphus Bartlett 1877- *WhAm 5*
Keith, Alexander 1795-1873 *ApCAB*
Keith, Allen Phelps 1872-1947 *WhAm 3*
Keith, Arthur 1864-1944 *DcAmB S3,*
 WhAm 2
Keith, Sir Arthur 1866-1955 *BiHiMed, DcScB*
Keith, Arthur Leslie 1874-1942 *WhAm 2*
Keith, Arthur Monroe 1852-1918 *WhAm 1*
Keith, Ben Ellington 1882-1959 *NatCAB 44*
Keith, Benjamin Franklin 1846-1914 *DcAmB,*
 NatCAB 15, WhAm 1
Keith, Charles Penrose 1854-1939 *ApCAB,*
 TwCBDA, WhAm 1
Keith, Charles S 1873-1945 *WhAm 2*
Keith, Darwin Mills 1867-1929 *NatCAB 27*
Keith, David *NewYHSD*
Keith, David 1847-1918 *WhAm 1*
Keith, David 1895-1948 *WhAm 2*
Keith, Dora Wheeler 1857-1940 *WhAm 1,*
 WomWWA 14
Keith, Edson 1833- *NatCAB 2*
Keith, Edson 1862-1939 *NatCAB 33*
Keith, Elbridge Gerry 1840-1905 *NatCAB 2,*
 WhAm 1
Keith, Eliza D 1854- *AmWom, NatCAB 2*
Keith, Frances Guignard Gibbes *WomWWA 14*
Keith, George d1710? *Drake*
Keith, George 1638?-1716 *AmBi, DcAmB,*
 DcAmReB, WhAm H
Keith, George 1645?-1715 *ApCAB*
Keith, George A *NewYHSD*
Keith, George Eldon 1850-1920 *NatCAB 11,*
 WhAm 1

Keith, George Keith Elphinstone 1746-1823
WhoMilH
Keith, Hardy Lester 1875- *WhoColR*
Keith, Harold Chessman 1884-1961 *WhAm 4*
Keith, Hastings 1915- *BiDrAC*
Keith, Irving Lester 1874-1961 *NatCAB 49*
Keith, Isaac Stockton 1755-1813 *ApCAB,*
Drake
Keith, James 1643-1719 *ApCAB*
Keith, James 1839-1918 *DcAmB, NatCAB 13,*
WhAm 1
Keith, Jehu Frank 1857-1921 *NatCAB 19*
Keith, John Alexander Hull 1869-1931 *WhAm 1*
Keith, Lawrence Massillon 1824-1864 *WhAm H*
Keith, Marie Morrisey d1965 *WhAm 4*
Keith, Minor Cooper 1848-1929 *AmBi,*
ApCAB X, DcAmB, McGEWB,
NatCAB 14, NatCAB 22, WhAm 1
Keith, Nathaniel S 1906-1973 *WhAm 6*
Keith, Nathaniel Shepard 1838-1925 *WhAm 1*
Keith, Reuel 1792-1842 *ApCAB, TwCBDA*
Keith, Reuel 1793-1842 *Drake*
Keith, Reuel 1826- *BiAUS*
Keith, Richard Henry 1842-1905 *NatCAB 9,*
NatCAB 34
Keith, Robert J 1914-1973 *WhAm 6*
Keith, Robert Russell 1879-1937 *NatCAB 31*
Keith, Samuel Jackson 1831-1909 *NatCAB 8*
Keith, Walter Jackson 1861-1934 *NatCAB 26*
Keith, Sir William 1680-1749 *AmBi, ApCAB,*
DcAmB, Drake, NatCAB 2, TwCBDA,
WhAm H
Keith, William 1839-1911 *DcAmB, IIBEAAW,*
NatCAB 13, NewYHSD, REnAW,
WhAm 1
Keith, William Hammond 1911-1965 *WhAm 4*
Keithahn, Edward Linnaeus 1900-1970
WhAm 5
Keitt, George Wannamaker 1889-1969
WhAm 5
Keitt, Laurence Massillon 1824-1864 *ApCAB,*
BiDrAC, NatCAB 4, TwCBDA, WhAmP
Keitt, Lawrence Massillon 1824-1864 *BiAUS,*
BiDConf, DcAmB, Drake
Keitt, William Lawrence 1905-1974 *WhAm 6*
Kekule, Friedrich August 1829-1896 *McGEWB*
Kekule VonStradonitz, Friedrich August
1829-1896 *AsBiEn, DcScB*
Kelby, Charles Hendre 1870-1944 *WhAm 2*
Kelby, James Edward 1862- *WhAm 4*
Kelce, L Russell 1897-1957 *WhAm 3*
Kelce, Merl C 1905- *WhAm 5*
Kelcey, Guy 1889-1973 *WhAm 6*
Kelcey, Herbert 1856-1917 *WhAm 1*
Kelch, Ohmer Eugene 1894-1962 *NatCAB 50*
Keleher, William Aloysius 1886-1972 *REnAW,*
WhAm 5
Keleher, William L 1906-1975 *WhAm 6*
Kelham, George William 1871-1936
NatCAB 27, WhAm 1
Keliher, John 1891-1964 *WhAm 4*
Keliher, John Austin 1866-1938 *BiDrAC,*
WhAm 4
Keliher, Sylvester 1863- *WhAm 4*
Kelker, James Joseph Arthur 1906-1973
WhAm 6
Kelker, Rudolph Frederick, Jr. 1875- *WhAm 5*
Kell, Claude Owen 1893-1955 *NatCAB 46*
Kell, John McIntosh 1823-1900 *BiDConf,*
NatCAB 2, TwCBDA
Kellam, Alphonso George 1837- *NatCAB 13*
Kellam, Floyd Eaton 1894-1958 *NatCAB 44*
Kelland, Clarence Budington 1881-1964
WhAm 4
Kellar, Chambers 1867-1950 *WhAm 3*
Kellar, Ezra 1812-1848 *ApCAB, TwCBDA*
Kellar, Frances Alice 1873- *NatCAB 15*
Kellar, George Currant 1879-1954 *NatCAB 43*
Kellar, Harry 1849-1922 *NatCAB 14,*
WhAm 1
Kellar, Herbert Anthony 1887-1955 *WhAm 3*
Kellas, Eliza 1864-1943 *BiDAmEd, NotAW,*
WhAm 2
Kellaway, Herbert John 1867-1947 *NatCAB 35,*
WhAm 5
Kelleher, Daniel 1864-1929 *WhAm 1*
Kelleher, Louis Francis *WhAm 4*
Kelleher, Michael T 1897-1958 *WhAm 3*

Kellems, Vivien 1896-1975 *WhAm 6*
Kellen, Robert *NewYHSD*
Kellen, William Vail 1852-1942 *NatCAB 32,*
WhAm 4
Kellenberger, Hunter 1904-1975 *WhAm 6*
Keller, Adam *NewYHSD*
Keller, Adolph 1872- *WhAm 5*
Keller, Albert Galloway 1874-1956 *WhAm 3*
Keller, Alexander Sidney 1905-1958
NatCAB 44
Keller, Amelia R 1871- *WhAm 5,*
WomWWA 14
Keller, Arnold B 1881-1964 *WhAm 4*
Keller, Arthur Ignatius 1866?-1924 *IIBEAAW,*
NatCAB 11
Keller, Arthur Ignatius 1867-1924 *DcAmB,*
WhAm 1
Keller, Benjamin Franklin 1857-1921 *WhAm 1*
Keller, Carl Tilden 1872-1955 *WhAm 3*
Keller, Caroline Gould *WomWWA 14*
Keller, Charles 1868-1949 *NatCAB 38*
Keller, Christian Arnold 1711-1790 *ApCAB*
Keller, Clyde Leon 1872- *IIBEAAW*
Keller, David Alexander 1853-1926 *NatCAB 26*
Keller, Dellis Clifton 1869-1950 *NatCAB 38*
Keller, Edith Livingston Mason 1878-
WomWWA 14
Keller, Eleanor 1876- *WomWWA 14*
Keller, Elizabeth Catharine 1837- *AmWom*
Keller, Emil Ernest 1863- *WhAm 4*
Keller, Francis *NewYHSD*
Keller, Frederick 1897-1960 *WhAm 4*
Keller, Gert 1905-1966 *WhAm 4*
Keller, Gottfried 1819-1890 *McGEWB*
Keller, Harry Frederick 1861-1924 *WhAm 1*
Keller, Harry Melick 1866-1933 *NatCAB 25*
Keller, Helen Adams 1880- *ApCAB X,*
NatCAB 15, WomWWA 14
Keller, Helen Adams 1880-1962 *McGEWB*
Keller, Helen Adams 1880-1968 *NatCAB 57,*
WebAB, WhAm 5
Keller, Henry, Jr. 1895-1954 *WhAm 3*
Keller, Henry, Jr. 1922- *WhAm 6*
Keller, Henry George 1869-1949 *NatCAB 43,*
WhAm 2
Keller, Herbert Paist 1875- *NatCAB 15,*
WhAm 5
Keller, Ida Augusta 1866- *WomWWA 14*
Keller, Inez Rice *WomWWA 14*
Keller, Mrs. J *NewYHSD*
Keller, James Albert 1887-1948 *WhAm 2*
Keller, John William 1856-1919 *WhAm 1*
Keller, Joseph Edward 1827-1886 *ApCAB,*
TwCBDA
Keller, Kaufman Thuma 1885-1966 *WhAm 4*
Keller, Keith Koolen 1898-1965 *NatCAB 51*
Keller, Kent Ellsworth 1867-1954 *BiDrAC,*
WhAm 3
Keller, Lewis Henry 1858-1938 *WhAm 1*
Keller, Mathias 1813-1875 *DcAmB,*
NatCAB 24, WhAm H
Keller, May Lansfield 1877-1964 *WhAm 4,*
WomWWA 14
Keller, Mollie V Everett d1969 *WhAm 5*
Keller, Oliver James 1898-1968 *NatCAB 53,*
WhAm 4
Keller, Oscar Edward 1878-1927 *BiDrAC,*
WhAm 1
Keller, Oscar H 1896-1962 *WhAm 4*
Keller, Ralph Edward 1885-1964 *WhAm 4*
Keller, Theodore Christian 1864-1930
NatCAB 29
Keller, Wallace *NewYHSD*
Keller, Walter 1873-1940 *WhAm 1*
Keller, Will E 1868- *ApCAB X, WhAm 4*
Keller, William Huestis 1869-1945 *WhAm 2*
Keller, William J *NewYHSD*
Keller, William Simpson 1874-1925 *WhAm 1*
Kellerman, Karl Frederic 1879-1934 *DcAmB S1,*
NatCAB 26, WhAm 1
Kellerman, Maude 1888- *WomWWA 14*
Kellerman, William Ashbrook 1850-1908
NatCAB 9, NatCAB 26, TwCBDA,
WhAm 1
Kellermann, Francois Christophe 1735-1820
WhoMilH
Kellermann, Francois Etienne 1770-1835
WhoMilH

Kellersberger, Eugene Roland 1888-1966
WhAm 4
Kellert, Ellis 1886-1968 *NatCAB 55*
Kelleter, Paul Delmar 1881-1950 *WhAm 3*
Kellett, Sir Henry 1807-1875 *ApCAB*
Kellett, William Wallace 1891-1951 *DcAmB S5*
Kelley, A Lillian Clark *WomWWA 14*
Kelley, Abby 1810-1887 *NotAW*
Kelley, Abby 1811-1887 *NatCAB 2*
Kelley, Albert Wesley 1853-1916 *WhAm 1*
Kelley, Alfred 1787-1859 *ApCAB*
Kelley, Alfred 1789-1859 *DcAmB, NatCAB 15,*
WhAm H
Kelley, Alfred Kendall 1891-1941 *NatCAB 45,*
WhAm 1
Kelley, Augustine Bernard 1883-1957 *BiDrAC,*
WhAm 3, WhAmP
Kelley, Benjamin Franklin 1807-1891 *ApCAB,*
NatCAB 6, TwCBDA, WebAMB
Kelley, Bethel Bowles 1912-1974 *WhAm 6*
Kelley, Camille McGee d1955 *WhAm 3*
Kelley, Charles Earl 1880-1935 *NatCAB 26*
Kelley, Charles Felix 1882-1941 *NatCAB 31*
Kelley, Charles Sampson 1846- *ApCAB X*
Kelley, Clara Nichols 1873- *WomWWA 14*
Kelley, Clement Earl 1874-1943 *NatCAB 32*
Kelley, Clement Earl, Jr. 1920-1970 *WhAm 5*
Kelley, Cornelius Francis 1875-1957 *WhAm 3*
Kelley, David Campbell 1833-1909 *NatCAB 1,*
TwCBDA, WhAm 1
Kelley, Edgar Stillman 1857-1944 *ApCAB X,*
DcAmB S3, NatCAB 11, TwCBDA,
WhAm 2
Kelley, Edith Summers 1884-1956 *EncAAH*
Kelley, Ella Maynard 1859- *AmWom*
Kelley, Eugene Robert 1882-1925 *WhAm 1*
Kelley, Florence 1859-1932 *AmBi, DcAmB S1,*
EncAB, McGEWB, NatCAB 23, NotAW,
WhAm 1
Kelley, Francis Alphonsus 1888-1931 *WhAm 1*
Kelley, Francis Clement 1870-1948 *NatCAB 40,*
WhAm 2
Kelley, Frank Harrison 1889-1953 *WhAm 3*
Kelley, Hall Jackson 1790-1874 *AmBi, ApCAB,*
DcAmB, EncAAH, McGEWB, REnAW,
TwCBDA, WhAm H
Kelley, Harold Hitchcock 1884-1965 *WhAm 4*
Kelley, Harrison 1835-1897 *WhAm H*
Kelley, Harrison 1836-1897 *BiDrAC*
Kelley, Henry Allen 1866-1945 *NatCAB 36*
Kelley, Hermon Alfred 1859-1925 *NatCAB 15,*
WhAm 1
Kelley, Howard G 1858-1928 *WhAm 1*
Kelley, J Herbert 1875- *WhAm 5*
Kelley, J Thomas 1863-1953 *NatCAB 42*
Kelley, James Douglas Jerrold 1847-1922
DcAmB, NatCAB 24, TwCBDA,
WhAm 1
Kelley, Jay George 1838-1899 *WhAm 1*
Kelley, Jerome Telfair 1899-1963 *WhAm 4*
Kelley, Jessie Stillman d1937 *WhAm 4*
Kelley, Jessie Stillman d1949 *WhAm 2*
Kelley, Joanna R *WomWWA 14*
Kelley, John Bernard 1898-1955 *NatCAB 42*
Kelley, John Edward 1853-1941 *BiDrAC*
Kelley, John Harrison 1882-1950 *NatCAB 41*
Kelley, John S 1853- *WhAm 4*
Kelley, John William 1865-1913 *WhAm 1*
Kelley, Joseph *NewYHSD*
Kelley, Lilla Elizabeth 1872- *BiCAW,*
WhAm 5
Kelley, Louise 1894-1961 *WhAm 4*
Kelley, Nicholas 1885-1965 *WhAm 4*
Kelley, Oliver Hudson 1826-1913 *AmBi,*
DcAmB, EncAAH, McGEWB,
NatCAB 23, WebAB, WhAm HA,
WhAm 4
Kelley, Patrick Henry 1867-1925 *BiDrAC,*
WhAm 1, WhAmP
Kelley, Pearce Clement 1895-1968 *WhAm 5*
Kelley, Phelps 1901-1959 *WhAm 3*
Kelley, Ramon 1939- *IIBEAAW*
Kelley, Robert Hamilton 1888-1966 *WhAm 4*
Kelley, Robert Michael 1877- *WhAm 5*
Kelley, Robert Weeks 1853-1928 *NatCAB 22,*
WhAm 1
Kelley, Samuel Walter 1855-1929 *ApCAB X,*
WhAm 1

Kelley, Selden Dee 1897-1949 *WhAm 2*
Kelley, Solomon John 1866-1956 *NatCAB 47*
Kelley, Truman Lee 1884-1961 *BiDAmEd,*
NatCAB 49, WhAm 4
Kelley, Walter Pearson 1878-1965 *WhAm 4*
Kelley, William Andrew Gresham 1911-1972
WhAm 5
Kelley, William Darrah 1814-1890 *AmBi,*
ApCAB, BiDrAC, DcAmB, Drake,
NatCAB 6, TwCBDA, WhAm H,
WhAmP
Kelley, William Fitch 1864-1916 *NatCAB 31*
Kelley, William Henry 1867-1943 *NatCAB 33*
Kelley, William Valentine 1843-1927 *NatCAB 9,*
TwCBDA, WhAm 2
Kelley, William Vallandigham 1861-1932
WhAm 1
Kelley, William W 1814- *BiAUS*
Kellicott, David Simons 1842-1898 *NatCAB 13,*
TwCBDA
Kellicott, William Erskine 1878-1919 *WhAm 1*
Kellinger, John A *NewYHSD*
Kellner, David *DcScB*
Kellner, Elisabeth Willard Brooks d1916
WhAm 1, WomWWA 14
Kellner, Max 1861-1935 *WhAm 1*
Kellogg, Abraham Lincoln 1860-1946 *WhAm 2*
Kellogg, Albert 1813-1887 *ApCAB, DcAmB,*
DcScB, NatCAB 25, TwCBDA,
WhAm H
Kellogg, Alice Lovell 1882- *WomWWA 14*
Kellogg, Alice Rogers Ropes *WomWWA 14*
Kellogg, Amos Markham 1832-1914 *TwCBDA,*
WhAm 1
Kellogg, Angel Ivey 1922-1974 *WhAm 6*
Kellogg, Arthur Piper 1878-1934 *WhAm 1*
Kellogg, Arthur Remington 1892-1969 *WhAm 5*
Kellogg, Brainerd *WhAm 5*
Kellogg, Charles 1773-1842 *BiAUS, BiDrAC,*
TwCBDA, WhAm H
Kellogg, Charles Collins 1858-1933 *WhAm 1*
Kellogg, Charles Edmund *NewYHSD*
Kellogg, Charles Wetmore 1880-1969
NatCAB 55, WhAm 5
Kellogg, Charles White 1815-1894 *NatCAB 2*
Kellogg, Clara Cook *WomWWA 14*
Kellogg, Clara Louise 1842-1916 *AmBi,*
AmWom, ApCAB, DcAmB, Drake,
NatCAB 2, NotAW, TwCBDA,
WhAm 1, WomWWA 14
Kellogg, Clara N 1870- *WomWWA 14*
Kellogg, Cornelia VanWyck Halsey
WomWWA 14
Kellogg, Daniel 1791-1875 *TwCBDA*
Kellogg, Daniel Fiske 1865-1920 *NatCAB 34,*
WhAm 1
Kellogg, Daniel Wright 1807-1874 *NewYHSD*
Kellogg, David Sherwood 1847- *WhAm 4*
Kellogg, Edgar Romeyn 1842-1914 *TwCBDA,*
WhAm 1
Kellogg, Edmund Burke 1809-1872 *NewYHSD*
Kellogg, Edward 1790-1858 *AmBi, ApCAB,*
DcAmB, Drake, NatCAB 24, TwCBDA,
WhAm H
Kellogg, Edward Brinley 1850- *TwCBDA,*
WhAm 4
Kellogg, Edward Henry 1828-1900 *NatCAB 2*
Kellogg, Edward Leland 1872-1948 *NatCAB 37,*
WhAm 2
Kellogg, Elijah 1813-1901 *AmBi, ApCAB,*
DcAmB, NatCAB 2, TwCBDA,
WhAm H
Kellogg, Elijah Chapman 1811-1881 *NewYHSD,*
WhAm H
Kellogg, Ella Eaton 1853- *WomWWA 14*
Kellogg, Eva Mary Crosby 1860- *WhAm 4*
Kellogg, Florence May Scripps 1870-1958
NatCAB 44
Kellogg, Francis W 1810- *BiAUS*
Kellogg, Francis William 1810-1878 *ApCAB,*
TwCBDA
Kellogg, Francis William 1810-1879 *BiDrAC,*
WhAm H
Kellogg, Frank Billings 1856-1937 *AmBi,*
ApCAB X, BiDrAC, BiDrUSE,
DcAmB S2, EncAB, McGEWB,
NatCAB 12, NatCAB 28, WebAB,
WhAm 1, WhAmP

Kellogg, Frederic Rogers 1867-1935
NatCAB 54, WhAm 1
Kellogg, Frederick Conway 1897-1960 *WhAm 4*
Kellogg, Frederick William 1866-1940
NatCAB 31, WhAm 1
Kellogg, George 1812- *ApCAB, NatCAB 7*
Kellogg, George 1812-1880 *AmBi*
Kellogg, George 1812-1901 *TwCBDA*
Kellogg, George Dwight 1873-1955 *WhAm 3*
Kellogg, George Ward 1822-1899 *TwCBDA*
Kellogg, Gordon Hill 1884-1955 *WhAm 3*
Kellogg, Harold Field 1884-1964 *WhAm 4*
Kellogg, Harry Francis 1878-1955 *NatCAB 45*
Kellogg, Henry Theodore 1869-1942
NatCAB 41, WhAm 2
Kellogg, Howard 1881-1969 *NatCAB 55,*
WhAm 6
Kellogg, Howard, Jr. 1908-1962 *WhAm 4*
Kellogg, James C 1859-1916 *WhAm 1*
Kellogg, James G 1881-1963 *WhAm 4*
Kellogg, James Hull 1912-1967 *NatCAB 53,*
WhAm 5
Kellogg, James Lawrence 1866-1938
NatCAB 29, WhAm 1
Kellogg, Jarvis Griggs 1805-1873 *NewYHSD*
Kellogg, John Harvey 1852- *ApCAB X,*
TwCBDA
Kellogg, John Harvey 1852-1943 *DcAmB S3,*
NatCAB 35, WhAm 2C
Kellogg, John Harvey 1852-1945 *WhAm 2*
Kellogg, John Leonard 1883-1950 *NatCAB 38*
Kellogg, John Morris 1851-1925 *WhAm 1*
Kellogg, John Prescott 1860-1925 *WhAm 1*
Kellogg, Joseph Augustus 1865-1929 *WhAm 1*
Kellogg, Julia Antoinette 1830- *WomWWA 14*
Kellogg, Karl Hugh 1881-1955 *NatCAB 46*
Kellogg, Laura Cornelius 1880- *WhAm 5*
Kellogg, Leroy DeWolf 1877-1933 *NatCAB 33*
Kellogg, Louise Phelps 1862-1942 *NotAW,*
WhAm 3, WomWWA 14
Kellogg, Lucia Hosmer 1829- *WomWWA 14a*
Kellogg, Luther Laflin 1849-1918 *NatCAB 8,*
NatCAB 41, WhAm 1
Kellogg, Martin 1828-1903 *DcAmB,*
NatCAB 7, TwCBDA, WhAm 1
Kellogg, Miner Kilbourne 1814-1889 *NewYHSD*
Kellogg, Morris W 1873-1952 *WhAm 3*
Kellogg, Noah J *NewYHSD*
Kellogg, Olin Clay 1870- *TwCBDA, WhAm 2*
Kellogg, Oliver Dimon 1873-1932 *NatCAB 23*
Kellogg, Oliver Dimon 1878-1932 *WhAm 1*
Kellogg, Orlando 1809-1865 *BiAUS, BiDrAC,*
WhAm H
Kellogg, Orson Chester 1826-1919 *NatCAB 18*
Kellogg, Paul Underwood 1879-1958 *EncAB,*
WhAm 3
Kellogg, Peter Comstock 1841- *WhAm 4*
Kellogg, Ralph Averill 1867- *WhAm 4*
Kellogg, Remington 1892-1969 *NatCAB 54*
Kellogg, Robert James 1869-1951 *WhAm 3*
Kellogg, Samuel Henry 1839-1899 *AmBi,*
ApCAB, DcAmB, TwCBDA, WhAm H
Kellogg, Scott D 1908-1968 *WhAm 5*
Kellogg, Spencer 1851-1922 *NatCAB 20,*
WhAm 1
Kellogg, Spencer, Jr. 1876-1944 *NatCAB 33*
Kellogg, Stephen Wright 1822-1904 *BiAUS,*
BiDrAC, NatCAB 8, TwCBDA,
WhAm 1
Kellogg, Theodore Harvey 1841-1931
NatCAB 26, WhAm 5
Kellogg, Thomas Moore 1862-1935 *NatCAB 26,*
WhAm 1
Kellogg, Vernon Lyman 1867-1937 *AmBi,*
ApCAB X, DcScB, NatCAB 15,
NatCAB 28, TwCBDA, WhAm 1
Kellogg, Walter Guest 1877-1956 *WhAm 3*
Kellogg, Warren Franklin 1860- *WhAm 4*
Kellogg, Wilbur Ralph 1884-1956 *WhAm 3*
Kellogg, Will Keith 1860-1951 *DcAmB S5,*
WebAB, WhAm 3
Kellogg, Willett Harold, Jr. 1886-1966
NatCAB 52
Kellogg, William 1814-1872 *ApCAB, BiAUS,*
BiDrAC, NatCAB 11, TwCBDA,
WhAm H
Kellogg, William Pitt 1830-1918 *BiAUS,*
DcAmB, WhAm 1

Kellogg, William Pitt 1831-1918 *ApCAB,*
BiDrAC, NatCAB 10, TwCBDA,
WhAmP
Kellogg, Winthrop Huntington 1887-1966
NatCAB 57
Kellor, Frances Alice 1873-1952 *DcAmB S5,*
WhAm 3, WomWWA 14
Kells, Clarence Howard 1892-1954 *WhAm 3*
Kellstadt, Charles H 1896-1975 *WhAm 6*
Kellum, John 1809-1871 *ApCAB, TwCBDA*
Kellway, Cedric Vernon 1892-1963 *WhAm 4*
Kelly, Adelaide Skeel *WomWWA 14a*
Kelly, Alfred Hinsey 1907-1976 *WhAm 6*
Kelly, Aloysius Oliver Joseph 1870-1911 *DcAmB,*
WhAm 1
Kelly, Alvin A 1893-1952 *WebAB*
Kelly, Augustus *NewYHSD*
Kelly, Bradley 1894-1969 *WhAm 5*
Kelly, Charles E 1910-1968 *WhAm 5*
Kelly, Chester Young 1881-1956 *NatCAB 48*
Kelly, Clinton 1808-1875 *NatCAB 17*
Kelly, David George 1900-1964 *WhAm 4*
Kelly, Dennis Francis 1868-1938 *NatCAB 36,*
WhAm 1
Kelly, Edmond 1851-1909 *AmBi, DcAmB,*
NatCAB 14
Kelly, Edmund Pirrung 1893-1937 *NatCAB 28*
Kelly, Edna Flannery 1906- *BiDrAC, WhAmP*
Kelly, Edward A 1853-1925 *WhAm 1*
Kelly, Edward Austin 1892-1969 *BiDrAC*
Kelly, Edward Joseph 1875-1950 *NatCAB 47*
Kelly, Edward Joseph 1876-1950 *DcAmB S4,*
WhAm 3
Kelly, Edward Joseph 1890-1956 *WhAm 3*
Kelly, Edward Leo 1901-1942 *NatCAB 33*
Kelly, Edward Wendell, Jr. 1907-1971 *WhAm 6*
Kelly, Eleanor 1879- *WhAm 4*
Kelly, Ellsworth 1923- *BnEnAmA, McGEWB,*
WebAB
Kelly, Emmett 1898- *WebAB*
Kelly, Eric Philbrook 1884-1960 *NatCAB 44,*
WhAm 3
Kelly, Eugene 1808-1894 *DcAmB, WhAm H*
Kelly, Eugene Hill 1887-1948 *WhAm 2*
Kelly, Fanny Wiggins 1845-1904 *NotAW*
Kelly, Florence Finch 1858-1939 *NotAW,*
WhAm 1, WomWWA 14
Kelly, Francis Marmion 1886-1950 *NatCAB 40*
Kelly, Francis Martin 1886-1950 *WhAm 3*
Kelly, Frank A 1880-1943 *NatCAB 35,*
WhAm 2
Kelly, Frank Stephen, Jr. 1904-1965
NatCAB 51
Kelly, Frank V 1880-1946 *WhAm 2*
Kelly, Fred C 1882-1959 *WhAm 3*
Kelly, Frederick James 1880-1959 *WhAm 4*
Kelly, Genevieve Ruth 1927-1975 *WhAm 6*
Kelly, George 1887-1974 *WhAm 6*
Kelly, George Alexander 1905-1967 *WhAm 4A*
Kelly, George Arthur 1886-1958 *WhAm 4*
Kelly, George B 1900-1972 *WhAm 5*
Kelly, George Bradshaw 1900-1971 *BiDrAC*
Kelly, George Henderson 1854-1929 *WhAm 1*
Kelly, George Thomas 1873- *NatCAB 16*
Kelly, Sir Gerald 1879-1972 *WhAm 5*
Kelly, Grace Patricia 1929- *WebAB*
Kelly, Guy Edward 1876-1940 *WhAm 1*
Kelly, Harry Eugene 1870-1936 *NatCAB 16,*
NatCAB 26, WhAm 1
Kelly, Harry Francis 1895-1971 *WhAm 5*
Kelly, Harry Joseph 1893-1964 *WhAm 4*
Kelly, Harry McCormick 1867-1936 *WhAm 1*
Kelly, Harry Raphael Jerome 1899-1947
NatCAB 36
Kelly, Harry Xing 1891-1971 *NatCAB 57*
Kelly, Henry Thomas 1876-1951 *NatCAB 41*
Kelly, Howard Atwood 1858-1943 *BiHiMed,*
DcAmB S3, NatCAB 15, WhAm 2
Kelly, Howard Charles 1887-1952 *WhAm 3*
Kelly, Hugh 1858-1908 *ApCAB X,*
NatCAB 14
Kelly, J Frederick 1888-1947 *NatCAB 36*
Kelly, J Redding d1939 *WhAm 1*
Kelly, James *NewYHSD*
Kelly, James d1819 *BiAUS*
Kelly, James 1760-1819 *BiDrAC, WhAm H*
Kelly, James 1762?-1819 *TwCBDA*
Kelly, James 1829- *NatCAB 5*

Kelly, James Edward 1855-1933 *AmBi,*
ApCAB, NatCAB 11, NatCAB 25, TwCBDA,
WhAm 1
Kelly, James F 1907-1968 *NatCAB 54*
Kelly, James Kerr 1819-1903 *ApCAB, BiAUS,*
BiDrAC, NatCAB 12, TwCBDA,
WhAm 1, WhAmP
Kelly, James Madison 1795-1849 *ApCAB,*
Drake
Kelly, John 1786-1860 *ApCAB, Drake*
Kelly, John 1821-1886 *ApCAB, BiAUS,*
BiDrAC, NatCAB 3, TwCBDA,
WhAm H
Kelly, John 1822-1886 *AmBi, DcAmB*
Kelly, John C 1852-1920 *WhAm 1*
Kelly, John Clarence 1881- *WhAm 6*
Kelly, John Eoghan 1893-1954 *NatCAB 43*
Kelly, John Forrest 1859-1922 *WhAm 1*
Kelly, John Grant 1872-1962 *WhAm 4*
Kelly, John Hedges 1885-1933 *NatCAB 26,*
WhAm 1
Kelly, John Herbert 1838-1864 *BiDConf*
Kelly, John William 1875- *WhAm 5*
Kelly, Jonathan Falconbridge 1818-1854
ApCAB, Drake
Kelly, Joseph *NewYHSD*
Kelly, Joseph Alexander 1854-1932 *NatCAB 27*
Kelly, Joseph James 1897-1963 *WhAm 4*
Kelly, Joseph Luther 1867-1925 *NatCAB 20,*
WhAm 1
Kelly, Judith 1908-1957 *WhAm 3*
Kelly, Junea Wangeman 1886-1969 *NatCAB 55*
Kelly, Lawrence Vincent 1928-1974 *WhAm 6*
Kelly, Lon Hamman 1871-1938 *WhAm 1*
Kelly, Luther Sage 1849-1928 *DcAmB,*
WebAMB, WhAm HA, WhAm 4
Kelly, Machine Gun 1895-1954 *DcAmB S5*
Kelly, Marian E 1869- *WomWWA 14*
Kelly, Mary 1862- *WomWWA 14*
Kelly, Mary Rutledge 1876- *WomWWA 14*
Kelly, Maud McLure *WomWWA 14*
Kelly, Melville Clyde 1883-1935 *BiDrAC,*
WhAm 1, WhAmP
Kelly, Mervin Joseph 1894-1971 *NatCAB 56,*
WhAm 5
Kelly, Michael *NewYHSD*
Kelly, Michael D 1872- *WhAm 5*
Kelly, Michael J 1857-1894 *DcAmB, WhAm H*
Kelly, Milton 1818-1892 *BiAUS, REnAW*
Kelly, Monroe 1886-1956 *WhAm 3*
Kelly, Myra 1875-1910 *DcAmB, NatCAB 24,*
WhAm 2
Kelly, Oliver Hudson 1826-1913 *REnAW*
Kelly, Orie R 1890-1969 *WhAm 5*
Kelly, Patrick 1779-1829 *ApCAB, NatCAB 6,*
TwCBDA
Kelly, Paul 1899-1956 *NatCAB 44, WhAm 3*
Kelly, Percy R 1870-1949 *WhAm 2*
Kelly, Ralph 1888-1962 *WhAm 4*
Kelly, Raymond 1882- *WhAm 5*
Kelly, Richard 1821-1897 *ApCAB X*
Kelly, Richard Busteed 1851-1922 *ApCAB X*
Kelly, Robert 1808-1856 *ApCAB, TwCBDA*
Kelly, Robert 1809-1856 *Drake*
Kelly, Robert James 1877- *WhAm 5*
Kelly, Robert Lincoln 1865-1954 *WhAm 3*
Kelly, Robert Morrison 1836- *ApCAB*
Kelly, Robert Morrow 1836-1913 *NatCAB 11,*
WhAm 1
Kelly, Sherman Lybirna 1869-1952 *NatCAB 41*
Kelly, Shipwreck *WebAB*
Kelly, Stephen 1847- *WhAm 4*
Kelly, Susan M *WomWWA 14*
Kelly, T Howard 1895-1967 *WhAm 5*
Kelly, T J *NewYHSD*
Kelly, Thomas *NewYHSD*
Kelly, Thomas 1795?-1841? *NewYHSD*
Kelly, Virgil Leonidas 1904-1959 *NatCAB 49*
Kelly, Walt 1913-1973 *WhAm 6*
Kelly, Walter Crawford 1913-1973 *WebAB*
Kelly, Walter Frederic 1874-1961 *NatCAB 48*
Kelly, William 1770-1832 *ApCAB, BiAUS,*
BiDrAC, NatCAB 11, TwCBDA,
WhAm H
Kelly, William 1807-1872 *ApCAB, TwCBDA*
Kelly, William 1811-1888 *AmBi, ApCAB,*
DcAmB, EncAB, McGEWB, NatCAB 13,
TwCBDA, WebAB, WhAm H

Kelly, William 1854-1937 *NatCAB 28,*
WhAm 1
Kelly, William A 1850- *WhAm 4*
Kelly, William Albert 1895-1963 *WhAm 4*
Kelly, William Anthony 1900-1963 *WhAm 4*
Kelly, William Arthur 1896-1961 *WhAm 4*
Kelly, William Aultin 1896-1968 *NatCAB 54*
Kelly, William Cody 1849-1933 *NatCAB 27*
Kelly, William Edward 1876-1948 *NatCAB 41*
Kelly, William F *NewYHSD*
Kelly, William Francis 1907-1965 *NatCAB 53,*
WhAm 4
Kelly, William J 1838?- *NewYHSD*
Kelly, William Jarmleh 1899-1955 *NatCAB 45,*
WhAm 3
Kelly, William Joseph 1860-1927 *WhAm 1*
Kelly, William Joseph 1876-1949 *NatCAB 36*
Kelly, William Louis 1837- *WhAm 4*
Kelly, William Powers 1865-1953 *WhAm 3*
Kelly, Willis Frank 1858-1935 *NatCAB 34*
Kelman, John 1864-1929 *WhAm 1*
Kelpius, Johann 1673-1708 *DcAmB, WhAm H*
Kelpius, John 1673-1708 *ApCAB*
Kelsall, Oliver Holt 1878-1957 *NatCAB 48*
Kelsen, Hans 1881-1973 *WebAB, WhAm 5*
Kelser, David M 1906-1975 *WhAm 6*
Kelser, Raymond Alexander 1892-1952
DcAmB S5, DcScB, NatCAB 43,
WhAm 3
Kelsey, Albert 1870-1950 *NatCAB 38,*
WhAm 3
Kelsey, Albert Warren 1840-1921 *NatCAB 18*
Kelsey, C *NewYHSD*
Kelsey, Carl 1870-1953 *NatCAB 45, WhAm 3*
Kelsey, Charles Bert 1863-1935 *NatCAB 27*
Kelsey, Charles Boyd 1850-1917 *WhAm 1*
Kelsey, Charles Edward 1862-1931 *WhAm 1*
Kelsey, Clarence Hill 1856-1930 *NatCAB 22,*
WhAm 1
Kelsey, Corinne Rider *NotAW*
Kelsey, Edward Everett 1840-1927 *NatCAB 21*
Kelsey, Edward Russell 1878-1929 *NatCAB 23*
Kelsey, Francis Willey 1858-1927 *DcAmB,*
NatCAB 14, NatCAB 26, TwCBDA,
WhAm 1
Kelsey, Frederick Trowbridge 1886-1957
WhAm 3
Kelsey, Frederick Wallace 1850-1935 *WhAm 1*
Kelsey, Harlan Page 1872- *WhAm 5*
Kelsey, Harold d1975 *WhAm 6*
Kelsey, Helen Marian 1872- *WomWWA 14*
Kelsey, Henry 1667?-1724 *McGEWB*
Kelsey, Henry Hopkins 1853- *WhAm 1*
Kelsey, Hugh Alexander 1872-1958 *WhAm 3*
Kelsey, Joseph A d1938 *WhAm 1*
Kelsey, Preston Halliday 1903-1971 *NatCAB 57*
Kelsey, Preston Telford 1867-1957 *NatCAB 43,*
WhAm 3
Kelsey, Rayner Wickersham 1879-1934
DcAmB S1, WhAm 1
Kelsey, William Andrews 1851-1932
NatCAB 24
Kelsey, William Henry 1812-1879 *BiAUS,*
BiDrAC, WhAm H
Kelso, James Anderson 1873-1951 *WhAm 3*
Kelso, John Bolton 1875- *WhAm 5*
Kelso, John Russell 1831-1891 *BiAUS,*
BiDrAC, WhAm H
Kelso, Robert Wilson 1880- *WhAm 6*
Kelso, Tessa L *WomWWA 14*
Kelso, Thomas 1784-1878 *ApCAB*
Kelso, Walter Arthur 1892-1964 *NatCAB 57*
Kelter, William J *NewYHSD*
Kelton, Edith Russell Wills *WomWWA 14*
Kelton, John Cuningham 1828-1893 *ApCAB,*
NatCAB 5
Kelton, John Cunningham 1828-1893 *DcAmB,*
NatCAB 32, TwCBDA, WhAm H
Kelton, Josephine Parmly 1852- *WomWWA 14*
Kelton, Robert Hall Campbell 1872-1922
NatCAB 6
Kelton, Samuel *NewYHSD*
Kelton, Stanton Colt 1889-1956 *WhAm 3*
Kelty, Paul Ray 1872-1944 *WhAm 2*
Kelvin 1824-1907 *DcScB*
Kelvin, William Thomson, Baron 1824-1907
AsBiEn, McGEWB
Kem, James Preston 1890-1965 *BiDrAC,*

WhAm 4
Kem, Omer Madison 1855-1942 *BiDrAC,*
TwCBDA, WhAmP
Kemb, Charles *NewYHSD*
Kemble, Charles 1775-1854 *ApCAB*
Kemble, Edward Windsor 1861-1933 *AmBi,*
IlBEAAW, TwCBDA, WhAm 1
Kemble, Fanny 1809-1893 *WebAB*
Kemble, Frances Anne 1809-1893 *AmBi,*
ApCAB, DcAmB, McGEWB, NotAW,
WhAm H
Kemble, Frances Anne 1811-1893 *Drake,*
NatCAB 3
Kemble, Gouverneur 1786-1875 *AmBi, ApCAB,*
BiAUS, BiDrAC, DcAmB, TwCBDA,
WebAB, WebAMB, WhAm H
Kemble, William *NewYHSD*
Kemble, William Penn 1876-1957 *NatCAB 43*
Kemerer, Benjamin Tibbits 1874- *WhAm 5*
Kemeys, Edward 1843-1907 *AmBi, ApCAB,*
DcAmB, IlBEAAW, NatCAB 8,
TwCBDA, WhAm 1
Kemler, Walter James 1903-1963 *WhAm 4*
Kemmelmeyer, Frederick *NewYHSD*
Kemmer, Alva Ernest 1879-1953 *NatCAB 42*
Kemmerer, Edwin Walter 1875-1945
DcAmB S3, WhAm 2
Kemmerer, Frances Ream 1878- *WomWWA 14*
Kemmerer, John Leisenring 1869-1944
NatCAB 32, WhAm 2
Kemmerer, Mahlon Sistie 1843-1925
NatCAB 35
Kemmerer, Mahlon Sistie 1913-1963
NatCAB 50
Kemmler, Edward Albert 1867-1955 *WhAm 3*
Kemp, Agnes Nininger 1823-1908 *AmWom,*
WhAm 1
Kemp, Alexander Nesbitt d1955 *WhAm 3*
Kemp, Bolivar Edwards 1871-1933 *BiDrAC,*
NatCAB 25, WhAm 1
Kemp, Charles 1883-1948 *NatCAB 38*
Kemp, Ellwood Leitheiser 1857- *WhAm 4*
Kemp, Everett 1873- *WhAm 5*
Kemp, George Stevenson 1877-1948 *NatCAB 37*
Kemp, Harold Augustus 1894-1953 *WhAm 3*
Kemp, Harold Francis 1896-1968 *WhAm 5*
Kemp, Harriet 1881- *WomWWA 14*
Kemp, Harry Hibbard 1883-1960 *WhAm 4*
Kemp, James 1764-1827 *ApCAB, DcAmB,*
Drake, NatCAB 6, TwCBDA, WhAm H
Kemp, James Furman 1859-1926 *AmBi,*
DcAmB, NatCAB 5, NatCAB 21,
TwCBDA, WhAm 1
Kemp, Jennie Murray 1858- *WomWWA 14*
Kemp, John 1763-1812 *ApCAB, DcAmB,*
Drake, NatCAB 6, TwCBDA, WhAm H
Kemp, John Arthur 1912-1963 *NatCAB 50*
Kemp, Joseph Alexander 1861-1930 *NatCAB 29*
Kemp, Louis Wiltz 1881-1956 *NatCAB 45,*
WhAm 3
Kemp, Matthew Stanley *WhAm 5*
Kemp, Minta Proctor *WomWWA 14*
Kemp, Philip Claris 1897-1960 *WhAm 4*
Kemp, Robert H 1820-1897 *DcAmB,*
WhAm H
Kemp, Theodore 1868-1937 *WhAm 1*
Kemp, W Lloyd 1896-1961 *NatCAB 49*
Kemp, W Thomas 1877-1925 *WhAm 1*
Kemp, William *NewYHSD*
Kemp, William Miller 1814-1886 *ApCAB*
Kemp, William Paul 1881- *WhoColR*
Kemp, William Webb 1873-1946 *NatCAB 35,*
WhAm 2
Kemp, Wyndham 1845- *WhAm 4*
Kemp, Zachariah Willis 1857- *WhAm 4*
Kempel, Arthur Bushnell 1888-1966
NatCAB 53
Kemper, Arthur Bernard 1912-1972 *WhAm 5*
Kemper, Arthur Thomson 1870-1954
NatCAB 42
Kemper, Charles Pendleton 1860- *WhAm 4*
Kemper, Constantine Faith 1886-1967
NatCAB 54
Kemper, Graham Hawes 1877-1961 *WhAm 4*
Kemper, Henry W *NewYHSD*
Kemper, Jackson 1789-1870 *ApCAB, DcAmB,*
Drake, NatCAB 11, TwCBDA, WhAm H

Kemper, James d1834 *Drake*
Kemper, James Lawson 1823-1895 *AmBi,*
ApCAB, BiDConf, DcAmB, NatCAB 5,
TwCBDA, WhAm H
Kemper, James Lawson 1824-1895 *BiAUS,*
Drake
Kemper, James Madison 1894-1965 *WhAm 4*
Kemper, John Adolph 1913-1970 *NatCAB 55*
Kemper, John Mason 1912-1971 *WhAm 5*
Kemper, Reuben d1827 *AmBi, DcAmB,*
WhAm H
Kemper, Reuben 1770-1826 *ApCAB*
Kemper, Sophia Cornelia 1777-1879 *ApCAB*
Kemper, William Harrison 1839-1927 *WhAm 1*
Kemper, William Mauzy 1881- *WhAm 5*
Kemper, William Thornton 1866-1938 *WhAm 1*
Kempf, Charles Henry 1831-1916 *NatCAB 18*
Kempf, Edward John 1885-1971 *NatCAB 57*
Kempfer, Hannah Jensen 1880-1943 *NotAW*
Kempff, Clarence S 1874-1959 *WhAm 4*
Kempff, Louis 1841-1920 *ApCAB X, DcAmB,*
TwCBDA, WebAMB, WhAm 1
Kempner, Aubrey John 1880- *WhAm 5*
Kempner, Daniel Webster 1877-1956
NatCAB 43
Kempner, Isaac Herbert 1873-1967 *WhAm 5*
Kempner, Isaac Herbert, Jr. 1906-1953
WhAm 3
Kempshall, Thomas 1796?-1865 *BiAUS,*
BiDrAC, WhAm H
Kempson, Julie Beers 1835-1913 *NewYHSD*
Kempster, James Aquila 1864- *WhAm 4*
Kempster, Walter 1841-1918 *DcAmB,*
NatCAB 5, TwCBDA, WhAm 1
Kempster, Walter 1842-1918 *ApCAB*
Kempt, Sir James 1765-1855 *ApCAB, Drake*
Kempton, Charles Walter 1847- *WhAm 4*
Kempton, Willard Hoyt 1878-1951 *NatCAB 43*
Kemsley 1883-1969 *WhAm 5*
Kenan, Augustus Holmes 1805-1865 *BiDConf*
Kenan, Graham 1883-1920 *NatCAB 37*
Kenan, Oren Rand 1804-1887 *BiDConf*
Kenan, Thomas 1771-1843 *BiAUS, BiDrAC,*
TwCBDA, WhAm H
Kenan, William Rand 1845-1903 *NatCAB 43*
Kenan, William Rand 1872-1965 *NatCAB 53,*
WhAm 4
Kendal, Mrs. 1849- *WhAm 4*
Kendal, Samuel 1753-1814 *Drake*
Kendal, William Hunter 1843-1917 *WhAm 1*
Kendall, Ada Davenport 1867- *WomWWA 14*
Kendall, Adela Parker *WomWWA 14*
Kendall, Albert Stearns 1883-1941 *NatCAB 30*
Kendall, Amos d1869 *NatCAB 6*
Kendall, Amos 1787-1869 *TwCBDA*
Kendall, Amos 1789-1869 *AmBi, ApCAB,*
BiAUS, BiDrUSE, DcAmB, Drake,
EncAB, McGEWB, NatCAB 5, WebAB,
WhAm H
Kendall, Arthur Isaac 1877-1959 *NatCAB 49,*
WhAm 6
Kendall, Bion Freeman 1827-1863 *ApCAB*
Kendall, Calvin Noyes 1858-1921 *BiDAmEd,*
WhAm 1
Kendall, Charles Harry 1902-1969 *WhAm 5*
Kendall, Charles Howard 1908-1970 *WhAm 5*
Kendall, Charles Pierce 1873- *WhAm 5*
Kendall, Charles Shilling 1905- *WhAm 5*
Kendall, Charles West 1828-1914 *BiAUS,*
BiDrAC, WhAmP
Kendall, Courts P 1869- *WhAm 5*
Kendall, David Wolcott 1851-1910 *NatCAB 16*
Kendall, Edward Calvin 1886-1972 *AsBiEn,*
DcScB Sup, McGEWB, WebAB,
WhAm 5
Kendall, Edward Hale 1842-1901 *ApCAB,*
NatCAB 12, TwCBDA, WhAm 1
Kendall, Elizabeth Kimball d1952 *WhAm 3*
Kendall, Elva Roscoe 1893-1968 *BiDrAC,*
WhAm 5
Kendall, Ezra Fremont 1861-1910 *WhAm 1*
Kendall, Ezra Otis 1818-1899 *ApCAB Sup,*
NatCAB 2, TwCBDA
Kendall, Frank Alexander 1865-1934
NatCAB 26
Kendall, George R 1882-1969 *WhAm 5*
Kendall, George Valentine 1891-1972 *WhAm 5*
Kendall, George Wilkins 1807-1867 *Drake*

Kendall, George Wilkins 1809-1867 *AmBi,*
ApCAB, DcAmB, NatCAB 12, TwCBDA,
WhAm H
Kendall, Harry R 1876-1958 *WhAm 3*
Kendall, Henry Hubbard 1855-1943
NatCAB 32, WhAm 2
Kendall, Henry Madison 1901-1966 *NatCAB 53,*
WhAm 4
Kendall, Henry Plimpton 1878-1959 *ApCAB X,*
NatCAB 49, WhAm 3
Kendall, Henry Wiseman 1897-1967 *WhAm 4*
Kendall, Ira Hunt 1878-1950 *NatCAB 40*
Kendall, James 1889- *WhAm 5*
Kendall, John C 1886-1951 *WhAm 3*
Kendall, John Chester 1877-1941 *NatCAB 30,*
WhAm 1
Kendall, John Smith 1874- *WhAm 5*
Kendall, John Wilkerson 1834-1892 *BiDrAC,*
WhAm H
Kendall, Jonas 1757-1844 *BiAUS, BiDrAC,*
WhAm H
Kendall, Joseph Gowing 1788-1847 *BiAUS,*
BiDrAC, WhAm H
Kendall, Joseph Morgan 1863-1933 *BiDrAC*
Kendall, Joseph Sutton 1884-1919 *NatCAB 17*
Kendall, Margaret 1871- *WomWWA 14*
Kendall, Margaret 1871-1933 *WhAm 1*
Kendall, Margaret 1871-1935 *WhAm 2*
Kendall, Mary Buzzell 1860- *WomWWA 14*
Kendall, Messmore 1872-1959 *WhAm 3*
Kendall, Myron A 1882-1962 *WhAm 4*
Kendall, Nathan Edward 1868-1936 *BiDrAC,*
NatCAB 29, WhAm 1, WhAmP
Kendall, Nathaniel Wyeth 1848-1921
NatCAB 25
Kendall, Paul 1894-1967 *NatCAB 53*
Kendall, Paul Raymond 1822-1897 *TwCBDA*
Kendall, Ralph Charles 1918-1967 *WhAm 4*
Kendall, Samuel Austin 1859-1933 *BiDrAC,*
WhAm 1, WhAmP
Kendall, Sergeant 1869-1938 *AmBi, WhAm 1*
Kendall, Valerius Horatio 1886-1958 *WhAm 4*
Kendall, William Converse 1861-1939
NatCAB 34, WhAm 1
Kendall, William Mitchell 1856-1941 *WhAm 1*
Kendall, William Morgan 1897-1966 *WhAm 4*
Kendall, William Sergeant 1869-1938
ApCAB X, NatCAB 13
Kendell, Robert Lothar 1900-1970 *WhAm 5*
Kenderdine, Augustus Frederick 1870-1947
IIBEAAW
Kendig, Bess Horton d1973 *WhAm 6*
Kendig, Calvin Miles 1877-1952 *WhAm 3*
Kendig, H Evert 1878-1950 *WhAm 3*
Kendrew, John Cowdery 1917- *AsBiEn*
Kendrick, Adin Ariel 1836- *TwCBDA*
Kendrick, Asahel Clark 1809-1895 *ApCAB,*
BiDAmEd, DcAmB, Drake, NatCAB 12,
TwCBDA, WhAm H
Kendrick, Benjamin Burks 1884-1946 *WhAm 2*
Kendrick, Charles d1970 *WhAm 5*
Kendrick, Charles Mattox 1907-1958
NatCAB 44
Kendrick, Clark 1775-1824 *ApCAB, TwCBDA*
Kendrick, Edmund Peaslee 1849-1923
NatCAB 20
Kendrick, Edward Stillman 1886-1959
NatCAB 48, WhAm 4
Kendrick, Eliza Hall 1863-1940 *WhAm 1*
Kendrick, Ella Bagnell 1849- *AmWom*
Kendrick, Fayette Dwyght 1856- *NatCAB 7*
Kendrick, Georgia A 1848-1922 *WhAm 1,*
WomWWA 14
Kendrick, Helen Fryer *WomWWA 14*
Kendrick, Henry Lane 1811-1891 *ApCAB,*
TwCBDA
Kendrick, James Ryland 1821-1889 *ApCAB,*
NatCAB 5, TwCBDA
Kendrick, John d1800? *Drake*
Kendrick, John 1740?-1794 *AmBi, DcAmB,*
WhAm H
Kendrick, John 1745?-1800 *ApCAB*
Kendrick, John Benjamin 1857-1933 *ApCAB X,*
BiDrAC, DcAmB S1, NatCAB 25,
REnAW, WhAm 1, WhAmP
Kendrick, John Mills 1836-1911 *NatCAB 12,*
TwCBDA, WhAm 1
Kendrick, John William 1853-1924 *WhAm 1*

Kendrick, Nathanael 1777-1848 *TwCBDA*
Kendrick, Nathaniel 1777-1848 *ApCAB, Drake,*
NatCAB 5
Kendrick, Nathaniel Cooper 1900-1969
WhAm 5
Kendrick, Philip Eugene 1899-1975 *WhAm 6*
Kendrick, W Freeland 1874-1953 *WhAm 3*
Kendricks, Edward James 1899-1956 *WhAm 3*
Kene, Joseph Alphonse 1857- *WhAm 4*
Kenealy, Ahmed John 1854- *WhAm 4*
Kenealy, Alexander C 1864- *WhAm 4*
Kenealy, Matthew Henry 1884-1950
NatCAB 38
Kenealy, William James 1904-1974 *WhAm 6*
Kenedy, John Gregory 1856-1931 *NatCAB 39*
Kenedy, John Gregory, Jr. 1886-1948
NatCAB 39
Kenedy, Mifflin 1818-1895 *NatCAB 20,*
REnAW
Kenedy, Patrick John 1843-1906 *DcAmB,*
NatCAB 39
Kenefick, Daniel Joseph 1863-1949 *NatCAB 45,*
WhAm 2
Kenefick, Peter Richard 1902-1965 *NatCAB 51*
Kenerson, Edward Hibbard 1880- *WhAm 6*
Kenerson, William Herbert 1873- *WhAm 6*
Kengla, Hannah M Egan 1891-1949 *WhAm 3*
Kenin, Herman David 1901-1970 *WhAm 5*
Keniston, Hayward 1883-1970 *WhAm 5*
Keniston, James Mortimer 1848-1927 *WhAm 1*
Kenkel, Frederick P 1863-1952 *WhAm 3*
Kenlon, John 1859-1940 *WhAm 1*
Kenly, John Reese 1822-1891 *ApCAB,*
NatCAB 6, TwCBDA
Kenly, John Reese 1847-1928 *WhAm 1*
Kenly, Julie Woodbridge Terry 1869-1943
WhAm 2
Kenly, Ritchie Graham 1866-1939 *WhAm 1*
Kenly, William Lacy 1864-1928 *WhAm 1*
Kenna, Edward Dudley 1861- *ApCAB X,*
NatCAB 6, WhAm 4
Kenna, Frank 1874-1947 *WhAm 2*
Kenna, Howard James 1901-1973 *WhAm 6*
Kenna, John Edward 1848-1893 *ApCAB,*
BiDrAC, DcAmB, NatCAB 1, TwCBDA,
WhAm H, WhAmP
Kenna, Joseph Norris 1888-1950 *NatCAB 39,*
WhAm 3
Kenna, Roger 1909-1959 *WhAm 4*
Kenna, Thomas James 1844- *NatCAB 5*
Kenna, W Thomas 1888-1952 *NatCAB 41*
Kennaday, John 1800-1863 *ApCAB*
Kennamer, Charles Brents 1874-1955 *WhAm 3*
Kennamer, Franklin Elmore 1879- *WhAm 6*
Kennan, George 1845- *ApCAB, ApCAB X,*
NatCAB 1, TwCBDA
Kennan, George 1845-1923 *WhAm 1*
Kennan, George 1845-1924 *AmBi, DcAmB*
Kennan, George Frost 1904- *EncAB, WebAB*
Kennan, Thomas Lathrop 1827-1920
NatCAB 19
Kennard, Beulah Elfrath *WomWWA 14a*
Kennard, Frederic Hedge 1865-1937 *WhAm 1*
Kennard, Joseph Spencer 1859-1944
NatCAB 33, WhAm 1
Kennard, Richard J 1900-1954 *NatCAB 48*
Kennard, Samuel M 1842- *NatCAB 12,*
WhAm 1
Kennard, William Jeffers 1906-1973 *WhAm 6*
Kennebeck, George Robert 1892-1969 *WhAm 5*
Kennebrook, Martha Jane 1869- *WomWWA 14*
Kennedy, Albert Joseph 1879- *WhAm 6*
Kennedy, Alexander Blackie William 1847-1928
DcScB
Kennedy, Alfred Doby 1881-1950 *NatCAB 40*
Kennedy, Alfred L 1818-1896 *ApCAB,*
TwCBDA
Kennedy, Ambrose 1875-1967 *BiDrAC*
Kennedy, Ambrose Jerome 1893-1950 *BiDrAC,*
WhAm 3, WhAmP
Kennedy, Andrew 1810-1847 *BiAUS, BiDrAC,*
TwCBDA, WhAm H
Kennedy, Annie Richardson 1868- *WhAm 3*
Kennedy, Anthony 1810-1892 *BiDrAC,*
WhAm H, WhAmP
Kennedy, Anthony 1811-1892 *ApCAB, BiAUS,*
NatCAB 7, TwCBDA

Kennedy, Anthony Kennedy 1870-1945
  NatCAB 35
Kennedy, Archibald d1794 *Drake*
Kennedy, Archibald 1685-1763 *ApCAB,
  DcAmB, WhAm H*
Kennedy, Arthur Garfield 1880-1954 *WhAm 3*
Kennedy, Barrett 1907-1971 *NatCAB 57*
Kennedy, Benjamin Eli Barnet 1827-1916
  NatCAB 17
Kennedy, Charles Augustus 1869-1951 *BiDrAC,
  WhAm 5, WhAmP*
Kennedy, Charles Ferguson 1880-1951
  NatCAB 41
Kennedy, Charles Rann 1871-1950 *WhAm 2*
Kennedy, Charles Rex 1882-1938 *NatCAB 35*
Kennedy, Charles William 1882-1969 *WhAm 5*
Kennedy, Chase Wilmot 1859-1936 *WhAm 1*
Kennedy, Clarence 1892-1972 *WhAm 5*
Kennedy, Clarence Hamilton 1879-1952
  WhAm 5
Kennedy, Clyde Raymond 1894-1970 *WhAm 5*
Kennedy, Crammond 1842-1918 *ApCAB,
  NatCAB 18, TwCBDA, WhAm 1*
Kennedy, D J *NewYHSD*
Kennedy, Daniel Joseph 1862- *WhAm 1*
Kennedy, David *NewYHSD*
Kennedy, David M 1905- *BiDrUSE*
Kennedy, David Scott 1856-1938 *WhAm 1*
Kennedy, Edmund Pendleton 1780-1844 *Drake*
Kennedy, Edward Anthony 1880-1943
  NatCAB 32
Kennedy, Edward Moore 1932- *BiDrAC,
  WebAB*
Kennedy, Edwin 1833-1913 *NatCAB 16*
Kennedy, Elijah Robinson 1844-1926 *WhAm 1*
Kennedy, Elizabeth Smith 1879- *WhAm 6*
Kennedy, Emma Baker d1930 *WhAm 1*
Kennedy, Foster 1884-1952 *WhAm 3*
Kennedy, Francis Williard 1874-1938 *WhAm 1*
Kennedy, Frank Artemas 1841-1926 *ApCAB X,
  NatCAB 20*
Kennedy, Frank J 1903-1974 *WhAm 6*
Kennedy, Frank Lowell 1870-1937 *WhAm 1*
Kennedy, Fred J 1891-1969 *WhAm 5*
Kennedy, Fred Wilhelm 1870-1953 *NatCAB 42*
Kennedy, Frederick Washington 1875-1952
  NatCAB 45
Kennedy, Gall 1900-1972 *WhAm 5*
Kennedy, George A 1901-1960 *WhAm 4*
Kennedy, Gilbert Falconer 1871-1971
  NatCAB 57, WhAm 5
Kennedy, Grafton Clagett 1859-1909
  NatCAB 25
Kennedy, Harris 1871-1951 *NatCAB 40*
Kennedy, Henry L 1897-1957 *WhAm 3*
Kennedy, Henry VanRensselaer 1863-1912
  NatCAB 25
Kennedy, Howard Samuel 1858-1938
  NatCAB 28, WhAm 1
Kennedy, Howard Samuel 1907-1964 *WhAm 4*
Kennedy, Jacob Martin 1864- *NatCAB 14*
Kennedy, James *NewYHSD*
Kennedy, James 1850-1922 *WhAm 1*
Kennedy, James 1853-1928 *BiDrAC*
Kennedy, James Aloysius Charles 1875-1975
  WhAm 6
Kennedy, James Arthur 1896-1967 *WhAm 4*
Kennedy, James Ferguson 1824- *TwCBDA*
Kennedy, James Francis, Jr. 1924-1973
  WhAm 6
Kennedy, James Henry 1849-1934 *WhAm 1*
Kennedy, James K *BiAUS*
Kennedy, James Lincoln 1862-1923 *NatCAB 22*
Kennedy, James Madison 1865-1930
  NatCAB 22, WhAm 1
Kennedy, James Melvin 1899-1965 *WhAm 4*
Kennedy, Jane McLeod 1876- *WomWWA 14*
Kennedy, John *NewYHSD*
Kennedy, John 1774- *NatCAB 16*
Kennedy, John Alexander 1803-1873 *ApCAB*
Kennedy, John Arthur 1889-1946 *NatCAB 33*
Kennedy, John Bright 1894-1961 *WhAm 4,
  WhAm 5*
Kennedy, John Doby 1840-1896 *DcAmB,
  WhAm H*
Kennedy, John Fitzgerald 1917-1963 *BiDrAC,
  BiDrUSE, EncAAH, EncAB, McGEWB,
  NatCAB 52, WebAB, WhAm 4, WhAmP*

Kennedy, John Lauderdale 1854-1946 *BiDrAC,
  NatCAB 35, WhAm 4, WhAmP*
Kennedy, John Louis 1854- *WhAm 4*
Kennedy, John McCartney 1873- *ApCAB X*
Kennedy, John Pendleton 1795-1870 *AmBi,
  ApCAB, BiAUS, BiDrAC, BiDrUSE,
  DcAmB, Drake, McGEWB, NatCAB 6,
  TwCBDA, WhAm H, WhAmP*
Kennedy, John Pendleton 1871- *WhAm 5*
Kennedy, John Stewart 1830-1909 *DcAmB,
  NatCAB 15, TwCBDA, WhAm 1*
Kennedy, John Thomas 1883-1958 *WhAm 3*
Kennedy, Joseph 1858-1937 *WhAm 1*
Kennedy, Joseph Camp Griffith 1813-1887
  *ApCAB, BiAUS, DcAmB, NatCAB 11,
  NatCAB 16, TwCBDA, WhAm H*
Kennedy, Joseph Conrad 1903-1961 *NatCAB 48*
Kennedy, Joseph Patrick 1888-1969 *WhAm 5,
  WhWW-II*
Kennedy, Joseph William 1916-1957 *WhAm 3*
Kennedy, Josiah Forrest 1834- *ApCAB,
  TwCBDA, WhAm 4*
Kennedy, Julian 1852-1932 *ApCAB X,
  NatCAB 11, NatCAB 24, WhAm 1*
Kennedy, Julian, Jr. 1886-1955 *NatCAB 49*
Kennedy, Kate 1827-1890 *NatCAB 30,
  NotAW*
Kennedy, Leonard 1886-1936 *NatCAB 36*
Kennedy, Lloyd Ellison 1894-1965 *WhAm 4*
Kennedy, Lloyd Weston 1907-1954 *NatCAB 45*
Kennedy, Lorne Edward 1907-1964 *WhAm 4*
Kennedy, Lyle Henry 1889-1958 *NatCAB 49*
Kennedy, Margaret 1896-1967 *WhAm 4,
  WhAm 6*
Kennedy, Martin John 1892-1955 *BiDrAC,
  WhAm 3, WhAmP*
Kennedy, Merton Grant 1890-1963 *NatCAB 50,
  WhAm 4*
Kennedy, Michael Joseph 1897-1949 *BiDrAC,
  WhAm 2*
Kennedy, Miles Coverdale 1893-1965 *WhAm 4*
Kennedy, Millard Bryant 1889-1947
  NatCAB 34
Kennedy, Moorhead Cowell 1862-1936 *WhAm 1*
Kennedy, Nathalie Sieboth *WomWWA 14*
Kennedy, Olin Wood 1874- *WhAm 5*
Kennedy, Paca 1878-1931 *WhAm 1*
Kennedy, Paul Horace 1848- *WhoColR*
Kennedy, Philip Benjamin 1882-1965 *WhAm 4*
Kennedy, Ralph Dale 1897-1965 *WhAm 4*
Kennedy, Raymond 1906-1950 *WhAm 3*
Kennedy, Richard Oakley 1885-1959
  NatCAB 43, WhAm 3
Kennedy, Robert Foster 1884-1952 *DcAmB S5*
Kennedy, Robert Francis 1925-1968 *BiDrAC,
  BiDrUSE, EncAB, McGEWB, WebAB,
  WhAm 5, WhAmP*
Kennedy, Robert Lenox 1822-1887 *NatCAB 5*
Kennedy, Robert Macmillan 1866- *WhAm 5*
Kennedy, Robert Morris 1867-1946 *WhAm 2*
Kennedy, Robert Patterson 1840-1918 *BiDrAC,
  DcAmB, NatCAB 17, TwCBDA,
  WhAm 1*
Kennedy, Roderick Duncan 1878-1941
  NatCAB 31
Kennedy, Roger L J 1897-1966 *WhAm 4*
Kennedy, Rose Walker Fisher *WomWWA 14*
Kennedy, Ruby Jo Reeves 1908-1970 *WhAm 5*
Kennedy, S *NewYHSD*
Kennedy, Samuel 1720-1787 *ApCAB*
Kennedy, Samuel Grant 1865-1941 *NatCAB 31*
Kennedy, Samuel Macaw 1863-1929 *WhAm 1*
Kennedy, Sara Beaumont d1921 *WhAm 1,
  WomWWA 14*
Kennedy, Sidney Robinson 1875- *WhAm 5*
Kennedy, Stanley Carmichael 1890-1968
  WhAm 5
Kennedy, Sylvester Michael 1894-1973 *WhAm 5*
Kennedy, T Blake 1874-1957 *NatCAB 43,
  WhAm 3*
Kennedy, T J *NewYHSD*
Kennedy, Ted *WebAB*
Kennedy, Thomas 1887-1963 *NatCAB 52,
  WhAm 4*
Kennedy, Thomas Francis 1858-1917
  NatCAB 16, WhAm 1
Kennedy, Thomas J 1832- *TwCBDA*
Kennedy, W McNeil 1909-1970 *WhAm 5*

Kennedy, Walker 1857-1909 *WhAm 1*
Kennedy, Walter Ambrose 1880-1960
  NatCAB 48
Kennedy, Willard John 1876-1942 *WhAm 2*
Kennedy, William 1768-1834 *BiAUS, BiDrAC,
  WhAm H*
Kennedy, William 1799-1849 *ApCAB, Drake*
Kennedy, William 1854-1918 *BiDrAC,
  WhAm 1*
Kennedy, William Henry 1888-1934
  NatCAB 26
Kennedy, William Henry Joseph 1888-1948
  WhAm 2
Kennedy, William Megee 1773-1840 *ApCAB*
Kennedy, William Nassau 1839-1885 *ApCAB*
Kennedy, William Parker 1892-1968 *WhAm 5*
Kennedy, William Pierce 1877- *WhAm 5*
Kennedy, William Sloane 1822-1861 *ApCAB*
Kennedy, William Sloane 1850-1929 *DcAmB,
  WhAm 1*
Kennedy, William W 1817?- *NewYHSD*
Kennedy, Wray David 1917-1969 *WhAm 5*
Kennell, Lloyd 1888-1957 *NatCAB 46*
Kennelly, Arthur Edwin 1861-1939 *ApCAB X,
  AsBiEn, DcAmB S2, DcScB, NatCAB 13,
  NatCAB 32, WhAm 1*
Kennelly, Edward F 1904-1966 *WhAm 4*
Kennelly, Marguerite Amy *BiCAW*
Kennelly, Martin H 1887-1961 *WhAm 4*
Kenner, Albert Walton 1889-1959 *WhAm 3*
Kenner, Duncan Farrar 1813-1887 *AmBi,
  ApCAB, BiDConf, DcAmB, TwCBDA,
  WhAm H*
Kenner, Frank Terry 1904-1961 *WhAm 4*
Kenner, Nettie Cox 1861- *WomWWA 14*
Kennerley, Mitchell 1878- *WhAm 6*
Kennerly, John Hanger 1856-1926 *WhAm 1*
Kennerly, Thomas Martin 1874-1962 *WhAm 4*
Kennerly, Wesley Travis 1877-1944 *NatCAB 35,
  WhAm 2*
Kenneson, Taddeus Davis 1859-1924 *WhAm 1*
Kennett, Francis Julian 1847-1911 *NatCAB 36*
Kennett, Frank E 1896-1968 *NatCAB 57*
Kennett, Luther Martin 1807-1873 *BiAUS,
  BiDrAC, NatCAB 52, WhAm H*
Kenney, Benjamin Harris *NewYHSD*
Kenney, Edward Aloysius 1884-1938 *BiDrAC,
  WhAm 1*
Kenney, Elizabeth L 1869- *WomWWA 14*
Kenney, Flora Bate *WomWWA 14*
Kenney, George Churchill 1889-1977 *WebAMB,
  WhWW-II*
Kenney, James Francis 1898-1974 *WhAm 6*
Kenney, John Andrew 1874-1950 *WhAm 2,
  WhoColR*
Kenney, Mabelle King 1884- *WomWWA 14*
Kenney, Mary *DcAmB S3*
Kenney, Richard Rolland 1856-1931
  *ApCAB Sup, BiDrAC, NatCAB 12,
  NatCAB 44, TwCBDA, WhAm 1,
  WhAmP*
Kenney, William Francis d1940 *WhAm 1*
Kenney, William P 1870-1939 *WhAm 1*
Kenngott, George Frederick 1864- *WhAm 4*
Kennicott, Cass 1871- *WhAm 5*
Kennicott, Donald 1881-1965 *WhAm 4*
Kennicott, Mrs. J A *NewYHSD*
Kennicott, Robert 1835-1866 *DcAmB,
  NatCAB 24, WhAm H*
Kennicott, Robert 1836-1866 *AmBi*
Kenniebrew, A H 1875- *WhoColR*
Kennish, John 1857- *WhAm 4*
Kennon, Beverley 1793-1844 *NatCAB 4*
Kennon, Beverly 1793-1844 *Drake*
Kennon, Jack Eccleston 1902-1961 *WhAm 4*
Kennon, Lyman Walter Vere 1858-1918
  WhAm 1
Kennon, William, Jr. 1802-1867 *BiDrAC,
  WhAm H*
Kennon, William, Sr. 1793-1881 *BiAUS,
  BiDrAC, WhAm H*
Kennon, William Lee 1882-1952 *WhAm 3*
Kenny, Albert Sewall 1841-1930 *ApCAB Sup,
  TwCBDA, WhAm 1*
Kenny, Sir Edward 1800- *ApCAB*
Kenny, Elizabeth 1886-1952 *McGEWB,
  WhAm 3*
Kenny, Frederic 1894-1971 *NatCAB 57*

Kern, Edith Kingman *WhAm 5,
WomWWA 14*
Kern, Edward Meyer 1823-1863 *IlBEAAW,
NewYHSD, REnAW, WhAm H*
Kern, Ernst Carl 1875-1948 *NatCAB 36*
Kern, Frank Dunn 1883-1973 *WhAm 6*
Kern, Frederick John 1864-1931 *BiDrAC,
WhAm 1*
Kern, Harold G d1976 *WhAm 6*
Kern, Herbert Arthur 1890-1963 *NatCAB 55,
WhAm 4*
Kern, Howard Lewis 1886-1947 *WhAm 2*
Kern, Jerome David 1885-1945 *DcAmB S3,
McGEWB, NatCAB 34, WebAB,
WhAm 2*
Kern, John *NewYHSD, REnAW*
Kern, John Adam 1846-1926 *NatCAB 20,
NatCAB 42, TwCBDA, WhAm 1*
Kern, John Dwight 1900-1948 *WhAm 2*
Kern, John Worth 1849-1917 *AmBi, BiDrAC,
DcAmB, NatCAB 14, NatCAB 52,
WhAm 1, WhAmP*
Kern, John Worth 1900-1971 *WhAm 5*
Kern, Josiah Quincy 1838-1913 *WhAm 1*
Kern, Maximilian 1890-1964 *WhAm 4*
Kern, Murrel Alvin 1888-1954 *NatCAB 45*
Kern, Olly J 1861- *WhAm 4*
Kern, Paul Bentley 1882-1953 *WhAm 3*
Kern, Richard Hovenden 1821-1853 *IlBEAAW,
NewYHSD, WhAm H*
Kern, Richard Hovenden 1821-1853 *REnAW*
Kern, Robert H 1850- *WhAm 4*
Kern, Walter McCollough 1865- *WhAm 2*
Kern, William Albert 1903-1964 *WhAm 4*
Kernahan, A Earl 1888-1944 *WhAm 2*
Kernan, Francis 1816-1892 *ApCAB, BiAUS,
BiDrAC, DcAmB, NatCAB 8, TwCBDA,
WhAm H, WhAmP*
Kernan, Francis Joseph 1859- *WhAm 2*
Kernan, John Devereux 1878-1961 *WhAm 4*
Kernan, Thomas Jones 1854- *WhAm 4*
Kernan, Walter Avery 1913-1975 *WhAm 6*
Kernan, Walter Gerard 1908-1963 *NatCAB 51*
Kernan, Warnick J 1880- *WhAm 6*
Kernan, Will Hubbard 1845- *WhAm 4*
Kerne, Leo J d1965 *WhAm 4*
Kerner, Otto 1884-1952 *WhAm 3*
Kerner, Otto 1908-1976 *WhAm 6*
Kerner, Robert Joseph 1887-1956 *WhAm 3*
Kerner, Theodore 1854- *NatCAB 17*
Kerney *NewYHSD*
Kerney, James 1873-1934 *DcAmB S1,
WhAm 1*
Kerney, Martin Joseph 1819-1861 *ApCAB,
Drake, TwCBDA*
Kerney, Sarah M 1876-1960 *WhAm 4*
Kerno, Ivan 1891-1961 *WhAm 4*
Kernochan, Joseph Frederick *WhAm 5*
Kernochan, Marshall 1880-1955 *NatCAB 42*
Kernot, Henry 1806-1874 *ApCAB*
Kerns, Frank Walter 1876-1949 *NatCAB 37*
Kerns, Shirley Kendrick 1872-1950 *NatCAB 43,
WhAm 3*
Kernweider, M *NewYHSD*
Kerouac, Jack 1922-1969 *EncAB, WebAB,
WhAm 5*
Keroualle, Eloi Ferdinand Latour De 1772-1831
ApCAB
Kerper, Hazel Bowman d1975 *WhAm 6*
Kerr, Abram Tucker 1873-1938 *WhAm 1*
Kerr, Albert Boardman 1875-1945 *NatCAB 34,
WhAm 2*
Kerr, Alexander 1828-1919 *WhAm 1*
Kerr, Alexander Hewitt 1862-1925 *NatCAB 30*
Kerr, Alexander Taylor 1920-1972 *WhAm 5*
Kerr, Alexander Thomas Warwick 1888-1931
WhAm 1
Kerr, Alfred Fontaine 1875-1966 *NatCAB 53*
Kerr, Alvah Milton 1858-1924 *WhAm 1*
Kerr, Andrew 1878- *WhAm 6*
Kerr, Andrew Affleck 1877-1929 *NatCAB 28*
Kerr, Arthur Neal 1882-1955 *NatCAB 43*
Kerr, Charles 1863-1950 *WhAm 2*
Kerr, Charles Volney 1861-1949 *NatCAB 40,
TwCBDA, WhAm 2*
Kerr, Charles William 1875-1951 *WhAm 3*
Kerr, Clarence D 1878-1957 *WhAm 3*
Kerr, Clark 1911- *BiDAmEd, EncAB*

Kerr, Daniel 1836-1916 *BiDrAC*
Kerr, David Ramsey 1850-1929 *TwCBDA,
WhAm 1*
Kerr, Duncan John 1883-1940 *NatCAB 30,
WhAm 1*
Kerr, Edgar Davis 1881- *WhAm 6*
Kerr, Eugene Wycliff 1874- *WhAm 5*
Kerr, Evelyn Nichols *WomWWA 14*
Kerr, Frank Marion 1869-1941 *WhAm 1*
Kerr, Frank Montgomery 1851-1924
NatCAB 20
Kerr, George Howard 1878- *WhAm 6*
Kerr, George Walker 1864-1930 *NatCAB 23*
Kerr, H Farquharson 1874- *WhAm 5*
Kerr, Harold Carnes 1881-1944 *NatCAB 36*
Kerr, Harold Dabney 1892-1973 *WhAm 6*
Kerr, Harriet Bower *WomWWA 14*
Kerr, Harry Hyland 1881- *WhAm 6*
Kerr, Helen Culver 1870- *BiCAW*
Kerr, Henry H 1892-1959 *WhAm 3*
Kerr, Henry Hampton 1864-1932 *WhAm 1*
Kerr, Henry Scanlan 1866- *NatCAB 10*
Kerr, Howard Ickis 1881- *WhAm 6*
Kerr, Hugh T 1871-1950 *WhAm 3*
Kerr, J W *NewYHSD*
Kerr, James *NewYHSD*
Kerr, James 1764?-1846 *ApCAB*
Kerr, James 1848-1911 *WhAm 1*
Kerr, James 1849-1911 *NatCAB 20*
Kerr, James 1851-1908 *BiDrAC, NatCAB 20*
Kerr, James Bremer 1867-1930 *WhAm 1*
Kerr, James Taggart 1859-1949 *WhAm 2*
Kerr, John *BiAUS*
Kerr, John 1782-1842 *ApCAB, BiDrAC,
TwCBDA, WhAm H*
Kerr, John 1824-1907 *DcScB*
Kerr, John, Jr. 1811-1879 *ApCAB, BiAUS,
BiDrAC, TwCBDA, WhAm H*
Kerr, John Bozman 1809-1878 *ApCAB, BiAUS,
BiDrAC, NatCAB 5, TwCBDA,
WhAm H*
Kerr, John Brown 1847-1928 *WhAm 1*
Kerr, John Brown 1851-1939 *WhAm 1*
Kerr, John Daniel 1895-1965 *WhAm 4*
Kerr, John Davis 1903-1964 *NatCAB 51,
WhAm 4*
Kerr, John Glasgow 1824-1901 *DcAmB,
WhAm H*
Kerr, John Graham 1869-1957 *DcScB*
Kerr, John Henry 1858-1936 *NatCAB 27,
WhAm 1*
Kerr, John Hosea 1873-1958 *BiDrAC,
WhAm 3, WhAmP*
Kerr, John Hubert 1877-1945 *NatCAB 35*
Kerr, John Leeds 1780-1844 *ApCAB, BiAUS,
BiDrAC, NatCAB 7, TwCBDA,
WhAm H*
Kerr, John N 1890- *WhAm 5*
Kerr, John Steele 1847-1925 *NatCAB 42,
WhAm 1*
Kerr, John Walter 1871- *WhAm 5*
Kerr, Joseph d1837 *ApCAB, BiAUS*
Kerr, Joseph 1765-1837 *BiDrAC, WhAm H*
Kerr, Joseph 1770?-1837 *NatCAB 12*
Kerr, Josiah Leeds 1861-1920 *BiDrAC*
Kerr, Legrand 1870- *WhAm 5*
Kerr, Mabel Bushnell 1870- *WomWWA 14*
Kerr, Mark Brickell 1860-1917 *TwCBDA,
WhAm 1*
Kerr, Michael Crawford 1827-1876 *ApCAB,
BiAUS, BiDrAC, NatCAB 8, TwCBDA,
WebAB, WhAm H, WhAmP*
Kerr, Mina 1878- *WomWWA 14*
Kerr, R Kenneth 1898-1953 *NatCAB 43*
Kerr, Robert *NewYHSD*
Kerr, Robert Floyd 1850-1921 *TwCBDA,
WhAm 1*
Kerr, Robert Pollok 1850-1923 *WhAm 1*
Kerr, Robert Samuel 1896-1963 *BiDrAC,
NatCAB 53, REnAW, WhAm 4,
WhAmP*
Kerr, Sophie 1880-1965 *WhAm 4*
Kerr, Walter Craig 1858-1910 *DcAmB,
WhAm 1*
Kerr, Washington Caruthers 1827-1885 *ApCAB,
DcAmB, NatCAB 7, TwCBDA,
WhAm H*
Kerr, William Jasper 1863-1947 *BiDAmEd,

WhAm 2
Kerr, William Melville 1860- *WhAm 4*
Kerr, William Watt 1853- *WhAm 5*
Kerr, Willis Holmes 1880- *WhAm 6*
Kerr, Winfield Scott 1852-1917 *BiDrAC,
TwCBDA, WhAm 5*
Kerrick, Harrison Summers 1873- *WhAm 5*
Kerrigan, Frank Henry 1868-1935 *WhAm 1*
Kerrigan, James E 1828-1899 *BiAUS, BiDrAC*
Kerrigan, James J 1894-1956 *WhAm 3*
Kerrigan, Philip, Jr. 1904-1958 *NatCAB 48*
Kerrigan, Walter C 1892-1957 *WhAm 3*
Kerrison, Philip David 1861-1944 *NatCAB 32,
WhAm 4*
Kerruish, Sheldon Quayle 1861-1938
NatCAB 30
Kersaint, Gui Pierre DeCaetnempreu 1742-1793
ApCAB
Kershaw, Frederick *NewYHSD*
Kershaw, J B 1822-1894 *Drake*
Kershaw, James M *NewYHSD*
Kershaw, John 1765-1829 *BiAUS, BiDrAC,
WhAm H*
Kershaw, Joseph Brevard 1822-1894 *AmBi,
ApCAB, BiDConf, DcAmB, NatCAB 12,
TwCBDA, WhAm H*
Kershner, Frederick Doyle 1875-1953
NatCAB 43
Kershner, Frederick Doyle 1875-1954 *WhAm 3*
Kershner, Jefferson Engel 1854- *TwCBDA*
Kerst, Donald William 1911- *AsBiEn*
Kersten, Armand George 1891-1949
NatCAB 38
Kersten, Charles Joseph 1902- *BiDrAC*
Kersten, George 1853-1934 *NatCAB 27*
Kersten, Harold John 1898-1955 *NatCAB 45*
Kerswill, Roy 1925- *IlBEAAW*
Kerverseau, Antoine Nicolas 1751-1802 *ApCAB*
Kerwin, Hugh Leo 1873-1937 *WhAm 1*
Kerwin, J S d1966 *WhAm 4*
Kerwin, James Charles 1850-1921 *WhAm 1*
Kesava *DcScB*
Keschner, Moses 1876-1956 *WhAm 3*
Kesey, Ken 1935- *REnAW*
Kesler, Frederick *NewYHSD*
Kesler, John Louis 1861-1955 *WhAm 4*
Kesler, Martin Luther 1858-1932 *WhAm 1*
Kessel, Leo 1881-1932 *NatCAB 32*
Kessel, Reuben A 1923-1975 *WhAm 6*
Kesselman, Louis Coleridge 1919-1974 *WhAm 6*
Kesselring, Albert 1885-1960 *McGEWB,
WhoMilH*
Kesselring, Albrecht 1885-1960 *WhWW-II*
Kesselring, Joseph Otto 1902-1967 *NatCAB 53,
WhAm 4*
Kessing, Oliver Owen 1890-1963 *WhAm 4*
Kessinger, Augustus C 1842- *NatCAB 4*
Kessler, Alfred August, Jr. 1898-1956 *WhAm 3*
Kessler, Bernard 1922-1972 *WhAm 5*
Kessler, Bordon Bowne 1879- *WhAm 6*
Kessler, Cora Parsons *BiCAW*
Kessler, Edward John 1897-1969 *NatCAB 56*
Kessler, Ernest H *NewYHSD*
Kessler, Fred Wilfred 1904-1963 *NatCAB 51*
Kessler, George Edward 1862-1923 *NatCAB 20,
WhAm 1*
Kessler, Harry Clay 1844-1907 *NatCAB 12,
WhAm 1*
Kessler, Louis Robert 1909-1961 *NatCAB 50,
WhAm 4*
Kesten, Paul W 1898-1956 *WhAm 3*
Kester, Frederick Edward 1873-1954 *WhAm 3*
Kester, Paul 1870-1933 *DcAmB S1, WhAm 1*
Kester, Reuben P 1869- *WhAm 5*
Kester, Roy Bernard 1882-1965 *WhAm 4*
Kester, Vaughan 1869-1911 *DcAmB,
NatCAB 25, WhAm 1*
Kesterson, M M 1899-1965 *WhAm 4*
Kestnbaum, Meyer 1896-1960 *WhAm 4*
Ketch, Samuel 1851-1899 *NatCAB 22*
Ketcham, Albert Henry 1870-1935 *NatCAB 27*
Ketcham, Charles Burgess 1889-1953
NatCAB 43, WhAm 3
Ketcham, Daniel Warren 1867-1935 *WhAm 1*
Ketcham, Earle Hoyt 1893-1964 *WhAm 4*
Ketcham, Frank Atherton 1875- *WhAm 5*
Ketcham, Harriet Ann 1846-1890 *NatCAB 9*

Ketcham, Heber Dwight 1858-1944 *WhAm 2*
Ketcham, Isaac A 1827-1915 *NatCAB 6*
Ketcham, John Clark 1873-1941 *BiDrAC, EncAAH, WhAm 1, WhAmP*
Ketcham, John Henry 1831-1906 *ApCAB, BiAUS, TwCBDA*
Ketcham, John Henry 1832-1906 *BiDrAC, NatCAB 8, WhAm 1, WhAmP*
Ketcham, Leander Smith 1818-1870 *ApCAB*
Ketcham, Rosemary d1940 *WhAm 1*
Ketcham, Susan M *WomWWA 14*
Ketcham, Tuthill 1894-1955 *NatCAB 42*
Ketcham, Victor Alvin 1883-1947 *WhAm 2*
Ketcham, Victor Alvin 1884-1947 *NatCAB 35*
Ketcham, William Alexander 1846-1921 *NatCAB 9, NatCAB 26, WhAm 1*
Ketcham, William Ezra 1837-1903 *WhAm 1*
Ketcham, William Henry 1868-1921 *WhAm 1*
Ketchum, Alexander Phoenix 1839- *NatCAB 2, WhAm 1*
Ketchum, Annie Chambers 1824- *ApCAB*
Ketchum, Edgar 1840-1905 *NatCAB 4, WhAm 1*
Ketchum, George Augustus 1825-1906 *NatCAB 8*
Ketchum, John Buckhout 1837-1914 *TwCBDA, WhAm 1*
Ketchum, Milo Smith 1872-1934 *WhAm 1*
Ketchum, Omar Bartlett 1898-1963 *WhAm 4*
Ketchum, Richard Bird 1874-1952 *WhAm 4*
Ketchum, Robyna Neilson d1972 *WhAm 6*
Ketchum, William Scott 1813-1871 *ApCAB, Drake, TwCBDA*
Ketchum, Winthrop Welles 1820-1879 *ApCAB, BiAUS, BiDrAC, WhAm H*
Ketel, Henry 1878-1965 *NatCAB 51*
Kethley, William Marion 1894-1964 *WhAm 4*
Ketler, Isaac Conrad 1853-1913 *WhAm 1*
Ketman, Tony Louis 1868- *WhAm 4*
Ketner, Forrest Guy 1888-1967 *WhAm 4*
Ketola, Helen 1915-1974 *WhAm 6*
Kett, Emil 1828?- *NewYHSD*
Kettell *NewYHSD*
Kettell, Samuel 1800-1855 *ApCAB, DcAmB, Drake, TwCBDA, WhAm H*
Ketten, Maurice 1875- *WhAm 6*
Kettering, Charles Franklin 1876-1958 *DcScB, NatCAB 48, WebAB, WhAm 3*
Kettering, Eugene Williams 1908-1969 *WhAm 5*
Ketterlinus, Eugene *NewYHSD*
Kettig, William Henry 1863-1939 *WhAm 1*
Kettle, Edgar Ulf 1868-1933 *WhAm 1*
Kettle, Ronald Harry 1902-1967 *NatCAB 53*
Kettler, Stanton Peter 1907-1971 *WhAm 5*
Kettles, Robert P 1859-1916 *NatCAB 16*
Kettner, William 1864-1930 *BiDrAC, NatCAB 23, WhAm 1*
Ketton-Cremer, Robert Wyndham 1906-1969 *WhAm 5*
Keuchenmeister, Mathilde Brinker 1848- *WomWWA 14*
Keuffel, Jack Warren 1919-1974 *WhAm 6*
Keuffel, Wilhelm Johann Diedrich 1838-1908 *NatCAB 17*
Keuffel, William Gottfried 1875-1942 *NatCAB 31*
Keulen, Ludolph Van *DcScB*
Kew, William S W 1890-1961 *WhAm 4*
Kewell, William Henry 1905-1972 *NatCAB 57*
Kewley, John 1770?-1816? *ApCAB*
Key, Albert Lenoir 1860- *WhAm 4*
Key, Ben Witt 1883-1940 *NatCAB 35*
Key, David McKendree 1824-1900 *AmBi, ApCAB, BiAUS, BiDrAC, BiDrUSE, DcAmB, NatCAB 3, TwCBDA, WhAm 1, WhAmP*
Key, Francis Scott *NewYHSD*
Key, Francis Scott 1779-1843 *AmBi, BiAUS, DcAmB, Drake, EncAB, WebAB, WhAm H*
Key, Francis Scott 1780-1843 *ApCAB, NatCAB 5, TwCBDA*
Key, Frederick C *NewYHSD*
Key, Henry *NewYHSD*
Key, J Albert 1890-1955 *NatCAB 44*
Key, James Biggers 1877- *WhAm 5*
Key, James Lee 1867-1939 *WhAm 1*
Key, John Alexander 1871-1954 *BiDrAC,*

WhAm 5
Key, John Ross 1832-1920 *IlBEAAW, NewYHSD*
Key, John Ross 1837-1920 *ApCAB, TwCBDA*
Key, Joseph Staunton 1829-1920 *TwCBDA, WhAm 1*
Key, Philip 1750-1820 *ApCAB, BiAUS, BiDrAC, NatCAB 11, WhAm H*
Key, Philip Barton 1757-1815 *ApCAB, BiDrAC, DcAmB, NatCAB 11, WhAm H, WhAmP*
Key, Philip Barton 1765-1815 *BiAUS*
Key, Philip Barton 1804-1854 *ApCAB*
Key, Pierre VanRensselaer 1872-1945 *WhAm 2*
Key, Thomas Marshall 1819-1869 *ApCAB*
Key, V O, Jr. 1908-1963 *WhAm 4*
Key, Vladimir Orlando, Jr. 1908-1963 *McGEWB*
Key, William Mercer 1850-1923 *WhAm 1*
Key, William Shaffer 1889-1959 *WhAm 3*
Keyes, Caroline 1810- *NewYHSD*
Keyes, Charles Frederick 1874-1955 *NatCAB 45*
Keyes, Charles Henry 1858-1925 *BiDAmEd, NatCAB 20, WhAm 1*
Keyes, Charles Reuben 1871-1951 *WhAm 3*
Keyes, Charles Rollin 1864-1942 *NatCAB 13, NatCAB 31, WhAm 2*
Keyes, Conrad Saxe 1874-1962 *WhAm 4*
Keyes, Edward Lawrence 1843-1924 *ApCAB, DcAmB, NatCAB 9, TwCBDA, WhAm 1*
Keyes, Edward Loughborough 1873-1949 *WhAm 2*
Keyes, Elias 1758-1844 *BiAUS, BiDrAC, WhAm H*
Keyes, Elisha Williams 1828-1910 *DcAmB, NatCAB 10*
Keyes, Emerson Willard 1828-1897 *ApCAB, TwCBDA*
Keyes, Emma Willard Scudder 1871- *WomWWA 14*
Keyes, Erasmus Darwin 1810-1895 *AmBi, ApCAB, DcAmB, NatCAB 4, TwCBDA, WebAMB, WhAm H*
Keyes, Erasmus Darwin 1811-1895 *Drake*
Keyes, Frances Parkinson Wheeler 1885-1970 *BiCAW, WhAm 5*
Keyes, Geoffrey 1888-1967 *WhAm 4*
Keyes, Geoffrey 1917-1941 *WhWW-II, WhoMilH*
Keyes, Harold Brown 1885-1965 *NatCAB 50*
Keyes, Harold Francis, Jr. 1912- *WhAm 6*
Keyes, Helen Johnson 1874- *WomWWA 14*
Keyes, Henry Wilder 1862-1938 *NatCAB 38*
Keyes, Henry Wilder 1863-1938 *ApCAB X, BiDrAC, WhAm 1, WhAmP*
Keyes, Homer Eaton 1875-1938 *NatCAB 28, WhAm 1*
Keyes, Michael J 1876-1959 *WhAm 3*
Keyes, Regina Flood 1870- *WomWWA 14*
Keyes, Roger John Brownlow 1872-1945 *WhoMilH*
Keyes, Rollin Arthur 1854-1925 *WhAm 1*
Keyes, Thomas Bassett 874-1938 *WhAm 1*
Keyes, Victor Ernest 1879-1927 *NatCAB 21, WhAm 1*
Keyes, Wade, Jr. 1821- *BiDConf*
Keyes, Winfield Scott 1839-1906 *TwCBDA, WhAm 1*
Keyl, Ernst Gerhard Wilhelm 1804-1872 *ApCAB*
Keynes, John Maynard, Baron Of Tilton 1883-1946 *DcScB, McGEWB, WhAm 2*
Keys, Clement Melville 1876-1952 *DcAmB S5, WhAm 3*
Keys, Jane *NewYHSD*
Keys, John *DcScB*
Keys, Noel 1893-1948 *NatCAB 36, WhAm 2*
Keyser, Cassius Jackson 1862-1947 *WhAm 2*
Keyser, Charles Philip 1869- *WhAm 6*
Keyser, Charles Shearer 1825- *TwCBDA, WhAm 1*
Keyser, Constantine *NewYHSD*
Keyser, Earl E 1903-1955 *WhAm 3*
Keyser, Ephraim 1850-1937 *AmBi, ApCAB, TwCBDA, WhAm 1*
Keyser, Ernest Wise 1876-1959 *WhAm 3*

Keyser, Harrietta Amelia 1841- *BiCAW*
Keyser, Harriette A 1841- *WhAm 4, WomWWA 14*
Keyser, Leander Sylvester 1856-1937 *WhAm 1*
Keyser, Peter *NewYHSD*
Keyser, Peter Dirck 1835- *ApCAB*
Keyser, Peter Dirck 1835-1896 *NatCAB 4*
Keyser, Peter Dirck 1835-1897 *TwCBDA*
Keyser, R Brent 1859-1927 *WhAm 1*
Keyser, Stanley Samuel 1900-1974 *WhAm 6*
Keyserling, Alexandr Andreevich 1815-1891 *DcScB*
Keysor, Jennie Ellis 1860- *AmWom*
Keyston, George Noel 1890-1968 *WhAm 5*
Keyt, Alonzo Thrasher 1827-1885 *DcAmB, NatCAB 15, WhAm H*
Keyworth, Maurice Reed 1884-1935 *WhAm 1*
Kezer, Alvin 1877- *WhAm 5*
Khachaturian, Aram Ilich 1903- *McGEWB*
Khair-Ed-Din *WhoMilH*
Khaldun, Ibn 1332-1406 *DcScB*
Khalil, Sayyid Abdullah 1892-1970 *McGEWB*
Khalili, Shams Al-Din Abu Abdallah, Al- *DcScB Sup*
Khama, Sir Seretse 1921- *McGEWB*
Khampan, Tiao d1966 *WhAm 4*
Khan, Mirza Ali Kuli 1879- *WhAm 6*
Kharas, Ralph Earle 1902-1966 *WhAm 4*
Kharasch, Morris Selig 1895-1957 *DcScB, WhAm 3*
Khayyami, Ghiyath Al-Din Abu'l-Fath, Al- 1048?-1131? *DcScB*
Khazin, Abu Jafar M Ibn Al-Hasan, Al- d961? *DcScB*
Khazini, Abu'l-Fath Abd Al-Rahman, Al- *DcScB*
Khinchin, Aleksandr Yakovlevich 1894-1959 *DcScB*
Khorana, Har Gobind 1922- *AsBiEn, McGEWB, WebAB*
Khosrow I 531-576 *McGEWB*
Khouri Bey, Faris El- 1879-1962 *WhAm 4*
Khrushchev, Nikita Sergeevich 1894-1971 *McGEWB*
Khrushchev, Nikita Sergeyevich 1894-1971 *WhAm 5*
Khuen, Richard 1865-1938 *NatCAB 29*
Khufu *McGEWB*
Khujandi, Abu Mahmud Hamid Al-Khidr, Al- d1000 *DcScB*
Khunrath, Conrad d1614? *DcScB*
Khunrath, Heinrich 1560?-1605 *DcScB*
Khurradadhbih, Abul-Qasim Ubayd, Ibn 820?-912? *DcScB*
Khuwarizmi, Abu Abd Allah Muhammad, Al- *DcScB*
Khwarizmi, Abu Jafar M Ibn Musa, Al- 800?-847? *DcScB*
Khwarizmi, Muhammad Ibn Musa, Al- 780?-850? *AsBiEn, McGEWB*
Kiam, Omar 1894-1954 *DcAmB S5*
Kiang, Chiping H C 1908-1968 *WhAm 5*
Kibbe, Flora Harriet D'Auby Jenkins 1872-1943 *NatCAB 37*
Kibbe, Harry Ulysses 1865-1922 *NatCAB 37*
Kibbee, Bon Emerson 1883-1968 *NatCAB 54*
Kibbee, Charles Carroll 1839- *NatCAB 7*
Kibbey, Bessie Juliet *WomWWA 14*
Kibbey, Joseph Henry 1853-1924 *NatCAB 23, WhAm 1*
Kibbey, Minnie Gertrude 1855- *WomWWA 14*
Kibler, A Franklin 1891-1955 *WhAm 3*
Kibler, Charles Samuel 1889-1946 *NatCAB 36*
Kibler, Edward 1887-1946 *NatCAB 35*
Kibler, Raymond Spier 1917-1969 *WhAm 5*
Kibler, Thomas L 1882-1957 *WhAm 3*
Kichlein, Peter 1722-1789 *TwCBDA*
Kicking Bird d1875 *DcAmB, WhAm H*
Kidd *NewYHSD*
Kidd, Elizabeth 1904-1958 *WhAm 3*
Kidd, Herbert A 1895-1961 *WhAm 4*
Kidd, Isaac Campbell 1884-1941 *NatCAB 33, WhAm 2*
Kidd, J *NewYHSD*
Kidd, J B *NewYHSD*
Kidd, John 1775-1851 *AsBiEn, DcScB*
Kidd, John William 1880-1941 *NatCAB 31*
Kidd, Lucy Ann 1839- *AmWom*

Kidd, Paul Hays 1906-1965 *NatCAB 52*
Kidd, Robert L 1901-1972 *WhAm 5*
Kidd, Samuel Elberts 1914-1972 *WhAm 5*
Kidd, Steven R 1911- *IIBEAAW*
Kidd, William 1645?-1701 *AmBi, ApCAB, DcAmB, Drake, WebAB, WhAm H*
Kidd-Key, Lucy Ann 1839-1916 *NatCAB 17*
Kidde, Walter 1877-1943 *NatCAB 31, WhAm 2*
Kidder, Alfred Vincent 1885-1963 *McGEWB, NatCAB 50, REnAW, WhAm 4*
Kidder, Benjamin Harrison 1836-1909 *WhAm 1*
Kidder, Bradley Paige 1901-1973 *WhAm 5*
Kidder, Camillus George 1850-1921 *NatCAB 8*
Kidder, Charles Holland 1846-1927 *NatCAB 21*
Kidder, Daniel Parish 1815-1891 *ApCAB, DcAmB, Drake, TwCBDA, WhAm H*
Kidder, Daniel Parrish 1815-1891 *NatCAB 11*
Kidder, Daniel Selvey 1848-1907 *WhAm 1*
Kidder, David 1787-1860 *BiAUS, BiDrAC, TwCBDA, WhAm H*
Kidder, Frank Eugene 1859- *WhAm 4*
Kidder, Frank Woodman Kinsman 1886-1956 *NatCAB 47*
Kidder, Fred Thomas 1858-1925 *NatCAB 20, WhAm 1*
Kidder, Frederic 1804-1885 *ApCAB, DcAmB, Drake, TwCBDA, WhAm H*
Kidder, Henry Purkitt 1823-1886 *NatCAB 12, TwCBDA*
Kidder, James *NewYHSD*
Kidder, Jefferson Parish 1815-1883 *BiAUS, BiDrAC, WhAm H, WhAmP*
Kidder, Jerome Henry 1842-1889 *ApCAB Sup, NatCAB 15*
Kidder, John C *NewYHSD*
Kidder, Kathryn d1939 *WhAm 1*
Kidder, Nathaniel Thayer 1860-1938 *WhAm 1*
Kidder, Wellington Parker 1853-1924 *NatCAB 3, NatCAB 26, TwCBDA, WhAm 1*
Kidder, William *NewYHSD*
Kiddinu 340?BC- *AsBiEn*
Kiddle, Henry 1824-1891 *ApCAB, BiDAmEd, NatCAB 2, TwCBDA, WhAm H*
Kiddoo, Joseph B 1840?-1880 *ApCAB*
Kiderlen, William Ludwig Joseph 1813-1877 *ApCAB*
Kidner, Frederick Clinton 1879-1950 *NatCAB 42*
Kidney, John Steinfort 1819- *Drake*
Kidney, William F *NewYHSD*
Kido, Koicho 1886- *WhWW-II*
Kidwell, Zedekiah 1814-1872 *ApCAB, BiAUS, BiDrAC, TwCBDA, WhAm H*
Kieb, Raymond Frances Charles 1881-1956 *WhAm 3*
Kieckhefer, Alfred John 1885-1960 *NatCAB 49*
Kieckhefer, Ferdinand A W 1852-1919 *NatCAB 11, WhAm 1*
Kiefer, Andrew Robert 1832-1904 *BiDrAC, WhAm 1*
Kiefer, Andrew Robert 1836-1904 *TwCBDA*
Kiefer, Carl J 1882-1961 *WhAm 4*
Kiefer, Daniel 1856-1923 *WhAm 1*
Kiefer, Dixie 1896-1945 *NatCAB 35, WhAm 2*
Kiefer, Edgar Weber 1880-1964 *WhAm 4*
Kiefer, Emil 1872-1941 *WhAm 1*
Kiefer, Guy Lincoln 1867-1930 *WhAm 1*
Kiefer, Herman 1825-1911 *ApCAB*
Kiefer, Hermann 1825-1911 *NatCAB 11, TwCBDA, WhAm 1*
Kieffer, George Linn 1883-1937 *WhAm 1*
Kieffer, Henry Martyn 1845-1930 *NatCAB 39, WhAm 1, WhAm 1C*
Kieffer, John Spangler 1904-1975 *WhAm 6*
Kieffer, Joseph Spangler 1842-1919 *WhAm 1*
Kieffer, Louis *NewYHSD*
Kieffer, Moses 1814-1888 *ApCAB, TwCBDA*
Kieffer, Paul 1881-1969 *WhAm 5*
Kiefhofer, William Henry 1883-1951 *WhAm 3*
Kiefner, Charles Edward 1869-1942 *BiDrAC, WhAm 5*
Kieft, Wilhelm 1600?-1647 *ApCAB, NatCAB 6*
Kieft, Willem 1597-1647 *AmBi, DcAmB, WhAm H*

Kiehle, David Litchard 1837-1918 *BiDAmEd, TwCBDA, WhAm 4*
Kiehler, Elmer George 1891-1961 *NatCAB 50*
Kiehnel, Richard 1870-1944 *WhAm 2*
Kiekhoefer, H J 1849- *WhAm 4*
Kiel, Emil Charles 1895-1971 *WhAm 5*
Kiel, Henry William 1871-1942 *WhAm 2*
Kieler, Charles Benedict 1908-1971 *WhAm 6*
Kielland, Soren Theodor Munch Bull 1854- *NatCAB 12*
Kielmeyer, Carl Friedrich 1765-1844 *DcScB*
Kielstra, Johannes Coenraad 1878- *WhAm 6*
Kiely, John J d1940 *WhAm 2*
Kienholz, Edward 1927- *BnEnAmA*
Kienle, Roy Herman 1896-1957 *NatCAB 50*
Kientpoos 1837?-1873 *DcAmB*
Kientzle *NewYHSD*
Kienzle, George Jacob 1910-1965 *WhAm 4*
Kiepe, Edward John 1868- *WhAm 4*
Kiepura, Jan d1966 *WhAm 4*
Kier, Samuel M 1813-1874 *DcAmB, NatCAB 11, WhAm H*
Kieran, James Michael 1862-1936 *NatCAB 26*
Kieran, James Michael 1863-1936 *WhAm 1*
Kieran, William A 1897- *WhAm 6*
Kierkegaard, Soren Aabye 1813-1855 *McGEWB*
Kiernan, James George 1852-1923 *WhAm 1*
Kiernan, James Lawlor 1837-1869 *ApCAB, Drake*
Kiernan, Loyd Julian 1895-1972 *WhAm 5*
Kiernan, Peter D 1876-1958 *WhAm 3*
Kiernan, Thomas Joseph 1897-1967 *WhAm 4*
Kiersted, Andrew Jackson 1832-1910 *WhAm 1*
Kiersted, Henry Stevens 1872-1942 *NatCAB 39*
Kiersted, Wynkoop 1857-1934 *NatCAB 25, WhAm 1*
Kies, Benjamin Bernhard 1893-1956 *NatCAB 45*
Kies, William Joseph 1887-1956 *NatCAB 43*
Kies, William Samuel 1877-1950 *NatCAB 17, NatCAB 39, WhAm 2*
Kiesel, Fred J d1919 *WhAm 1*
Kiesel, Fred William 1874- *WhAm 5*
Kiesel, William Frederic, Jr. 1866-1954 *NatCAB 40*
Kiesler, Frederick 1896-1965 *WhAm 4*
Kiesling, Charles *NewYHSD*
Kieslinger, Alois 1900-1975 *WhAm 6*
Kiess, Carl Clarence 1887-1967 *NatCAB 54*
Kiess, Edgar Raymond 1875-1930 *BiDrAC, WhAm 1, WhAmP*
Kiesselbach, T A 1884-1964 *WhAm 4*
Kiessling, Calvin 1874-1956 *NatCAB 43*
Kiessling, Christopher *NewYHSD*
Kiest, Edwin John 1861-1941 *NatCAB 42, WhAm 1*
Kietzman, William Arthur 1888-1961 *NatCAB 46*
Kiev, Isaac Edward 1905-1975 *WhAm 6*
Kievit, Jasper 1893-1950 *NatCAB 39*
Kighley, John *NewYHSD*
Kihn, W Langdon 1898-1957 *NatCAB 53, WhAm 3*
Kihn, William Langdon 1898-1957 *IIBEAAW*
Kiker, Henry A 1881- *WhAm 6*
Kikuchi, Seishi 1902-1974 *WhAm 6*
Kilander, H Frederick 1900-1968 *WhAm 5*
Kilborn, George Darius 1853-1923 *NatCAB 22*
Kilborn, William T 1897-1957 *WhAm 3*
Kilborne, Robert Stewart 1874-1950 *NatCAB 43*
Kilbourn, Arthur Goss 1876-1932 *NatCAB 24*
Kilbourn, James 1770-1850 *BiAUS*
Kilbourn, Judson Giles 1860-1915 *WhAm 1*
Kilbourn, William Douglas 1880- *WhAm 6*
Kilbourne, Charles Evans 1844-1903 *TwCBDA, WhAm 1*
Kilbourne, Charles Evans 1872-1963 *NatCAB 51, WhAm 4*
Kilbourne, Edward Corliss 1856- *NatCAB 11*
Kilbourne, James 1770-1850 *AmBi, ApCAB, BiDrAC, DcAmB, Drake, NatCAB 5, TwCBDA, WhAm H*
Kilbourne, James 1842- *NatCAB 5, WhAm 1*
Kilbourne, John 1787-1831 *ApCAB, Drake*
Kilbourne, John 1787-1833 *TwCBDA*
Kilbourne, Lincoln 1810-1891 *NatCAB 5*
Kilbourne, Payne Kenyon 1815-1859 *ApCAB,*

Drake, TwCBDA
Kilbourne, Samuel A 1836-1881 *NewYHSD*
Kilbreth, John William 1876-1958 *WhAm 3*
Kilburn, Charles Lawrence 1819-1899 *ApCAB, TwCBDA, WhAm 1*
Kilburn, Clarence Evans 1893-1975 *BiDrAC, WhAm 6, WhAmP*
Kilburn, Lawrence 1720-1775 *NewYHSD*
Kilburn, Robert William 1914-1974 *WhAm 6*
Kilburn, Samuel S, Jr. *NewYHSD*
Kilby, Charles Betts 1869-1942 *ApCAB X, NatCAB 32*
Kilby, Christopher 1705-1771 *DcAmB S1, WhAm H*
Kilby, Clinton Maury 1874-1948 *WhAm 2*
Kilby, Quincy 1854-1931 *WhAm 1*
Kilby, Thomas d1746 *Drake*
Kilby, Thomas Erby 1865-1943 *ApCAB X, WhAm 2*
Kilcawley, Edward James 1893-1969 *NatCAB 57*
Kildahl, Johan Nathan 1857-1920 *DcAmB*
Kildahl, John Nathan 1857-1920 *NatCAB 25, TwCBDA, WhAm 1*
Kildare, Owen Frawley 1864-1911 *WhAm 1*
Kilday, Paul Joseph 1900-1968 *BiDrAC, WhAm 5*
Kildea, John *NewYHSD*
Kildow, George Oliver 1894-1962 *WhAm 4*
Kilduff, Edward Jones 1889-1969 *WhAm 5*
Kilenyi, Julio 1885-1959 *NatCAB 45, WhAm 3*
Kiley, James Stephen 1873-1950 *NatCAB 39*
Kiley, John 1908-1952 *WhAm 3*
Kiley, John Coleman 1884-1952 *WhAm 3*
Kiley, Michael H 1861-1923 *WhAm 1*
Kiley, Moses Elias 1876-1953 *NatCAB 40, WhAm 3*
Kiley, Roger Joseph 1900-1974 *WhAm 6*
Kilgallen, Dorothy 1913-1965 *WhAm 4*
Kilgard, Ross Miller 1903-1959 *NatCAB 47*
Kilgen, Charles Christian 1859-1932 *NatCAB 24*
Kilgen, Eugene Robyn 1897-1967 *WhAm 5*
Kilgo, John Carlisle 1861-1922 *NatCAB 13, TwCBDA, WhAm 1*
Kilgore, Benjamin Wesley 1867-1943 *WhAm 2*
Kilgore, Bernard 1908-1967 *WhAm 4*
Kilgore, Caroline Burnham 1838-1909 *NatCAB 5*
Kilgore, Carrie Burnham 1838-1909 *NotAW*
Kilgore, Constantine Buckley 1835-1897 *BiDrAC, TwCBDA, WhAm H, WhAmP*
Kilgore, Daniel d1851 *BiAUS, TwCBDA*
Kilgore, Daniel 1793-1851 *BiDrAC*
Kilgore, Daniel 1804-1851 *WhAm H*
Kilgore, David 1804- *BiAUS*
Kilgore, David 1804-1879 *BiDrAC, WhAm H*
Kilgore, David 1804-1900 *TwCBDA*
Kilgore, Eugene Sterling 1878-1942 *NatCAB 32*
Kilgore, George Lester 1902-1954 *NatCAB 43*
Kilgore, Harley Martin 1893-1956 *BiDrAC, NatCAB 42, WhAm 3, WhAmP*
Kilgore, James 1865- *WhAm 5*
Kilgore, Joe Madison 1918- *BiDrAC*
Kilgour, Bayard Livingston 1869-1935 *NatCAB 27*
Kilgour, David Eckford 1912- *WhAm 6*
Kilgour, Dwight Foster 1863-1935 *NatCAB 26*
Kilgour, John 1834-1914 *NatCAB 27*
Kilham, Walter H 1868-1948 *WhAm 2*
Kiliani, Lilian Bayard Taylor 1858- *WomWWA 14*
Kiliani, Otto George Theobald 1863-1928 *WhAm 1*
Kilker, Michael Ambrose 1870-1935 *NatCAB 36*
Killam, Charles Wilson 1871-1961 *WhAm 4*
Killam, Elson Trask 1900-1968 *NatCAB 54*
Kille, Joseph 1790-1865 *BiAUS, BiDrAC, WhAm H*
Killebrew, Joseph Buckner 1831-1906 *NatCAB 8, TwCBDA, WhAm 1*
Killen, James Sinclair 1908-1972 *WhAm 5*
Killen, William 1722-1803 *NatCAB 4*
Killen, William 1722-1805 *ApCAB, BiAUS, Drake*

Killhour, William Brelsford 1900-1961 *NatCAB 49*
Killian, John Allen 1891-1957 *WhAm 3*
Killian, John Calvin 1870- *WhAm 5*
Killikelly, Sarah Hutchins 1840-1912 *NatCAB 19, WhAm 1*
Killinger, John Weinland 1824-1896 *BiDrAC, TwCBDA, WhAm H, WhAmP*
Killinger, John Weinland 1825-1896 *BiAUS*
Killits, John Milton 1858-1938 *NatCAB 29, WhAm 1*
Killoran, Clair John 1905-1975 *WhAm 6*
Killorin, John Farrell 1870-1941 *NatCAB 30*
Kilman, Leroy Noble 1878- *WhAm 3*
Kilmer, Alfred Joyce 1886-1918 *AmBi, ApCAB X, DcAmB*
Kilmer, Aline 1888-1941 *WhAm 1*
Kilmer, Chauncey 1816- *WhAm 4*
Kilmer, Frederick Barnett 1851-1934 *WhAm 1*
Kilmer, Joyce 1886-1918 *NatCAB 19, WebAB, WebAMB, WhAm 1*
Kilmer, Theron Wendell 1872-1946 *NatCAB 35, WhAm 2*
Kilmer, Willis Sharpe 1869- *NatCAB 17*
Kilmuir, Earl Of 1900-1967 *WhAm 4A*
Kilner, Frederic Richard 1892-1963 *NatCAB 50*
Kilner, Thomas 1777-1862 *Drake*
Kilner, Walter Glenn 1888-1940 *WhAm 1*
Kilpatrick, Armour Kemp 1898-1960 *WhAm 5*
Kilpatrick, Harry Colman 1907-1952 *WhAm 3*
Kilpatrick, Hugh Judson 1836-1881 *AmBi, ApCAB, DcAmB, NatCAB 4, TwCBDA, WebAMB, WhAm H*
Kilpatrick, James Hall Tanner 1788-1869 *TwCBDA*
Kilpatrick, James Hines 1833-1908 *TwCBDA, WhAm 1*
Kilpatrick, John Reed 1889-1960 *WhAm 4*
Kilpatrick, Judson 1836- *BiAUS, Drake*
Kilpatrick, Mana Ruckle Needels *WomWWA 14*
Kilpatrick, Samuel Davenport 1859-1925 *NatCAB 24*
Kilpatrick, Thomas 1841-1916 *WhAm 1*
Kilpatrick, Walter Kenneth 1887-1949 *WhAm 2*
Kilpatrick, Washington Lafayette 1829-1896 *TwCBDA*
Kilpatrick, William D d1950 *WhAm 3*
Kilpatrick, William Heard 1871-1965 *BiDAmEd, WhAm 4*
Kilty, Augustus Henry 1807-1879 *ApCAB, Drake, TwCBDA*
Kilty, William 1757-1821 *BiAUS, DcAmB, NatCAB 24, WhAm H*
Kim, Il-Song 1912- *McGEWB*
Kim, Ok-Kyun 1851-1894 *McGEWB*
Kim, Pusik 1075-1151 *McGEWB*
Kimball *NewYHSD*
Kimball, Mrs. A B 1872- *WomWWA 14*
Kimball, Alanson Mellen 1827-1913 *BiAUS, BiDrAC*
Kimball, Alfred Redington 1848-1929 *WhAm 1*
Kimball, Alfred Sanders 1842-1915 *WhAm 1*
Kimball, Alice 1876- *WomWWA 14*
Kimball, Alonzo 1874-1923 *WhAm 1*
Kimball, Amos Samuel 1840-1909 *TwCBDA, WhAm 1*
Kimball, Arthur Lalanne 1856-1922 *TwCBDA, WhAm 1*
Kimball, Arthur Reed 1855-1933 *NatCAB 47, WhAm 1*
Kimball, Arthur Richmond 1862- *TwCBDA, WhAm 4*
Kimball, Asa F *NewYHSD*
Kimball, Benjamin Ames 1833-1920 *ApCAB X, NatCAB 17*
Kimball, Caleb A 1829-1916 *NatCAB 17*
Kimball, Charles Dean 1859-1930 *ApCAB X, NatCAB 13, NatCAB 25, WhAm 1*
Kimball, Charles Denny 1875-1927 *NatCAB 21*
Kimball, Charles Frederick 1835-1907 *NewYHSD*
Kimball, Charles Nathaniel 1872-1956 *WhAm 3*
Kimball, Clarence Oliver 1868-1934 *WhAm 1*
Kimball, Claude D 1879- *WhAm 6*
Kimball, Clifford 1875-1941 *NatCAB 40*
Kimball, Comer Johnstone 1902-1966 *WhAm 4*
Kimball, Corinne 1873- *AmWom*

Kimball, Curtis Nathaniel 1862-1936 *NatCAB 18, NatCAB 27, WhAm 1*
Kimball, Dan A 1896-1970 *WhAm 5*
Kimball, Daniel d1817 *Drake*
Kimball, David Pulsifer 1833-1923 *NatCAB 14, WhAm 1*
Kimball, Dean Grover 1867-1933 *NatCAB 24*
Kimball, Dexter Simpson 1865-1952 *BiDAmEd, DcAmB S5, NatCAB 42, WhAm 3*
Kimball, Eben Wallace 1828- *NatCAB 7*
Kimball, Edgar Allen 1822-1863 *TwCBDA*
Kimball, Edgar Allison 1821-1863 *ApCAB*
Kimball, Edward Ancel 1845-1909 *NatCAB 31*
Kimball, Edward Partridge 1882-1937 *WhAm 1*
Kimball, Eliphalet Addison 1822-1863 *NatCAB 4*
Kimball, Elizabeth Jeanette Judson 1831-1918 *ApCAB X*
Kimball, Ellen Imogen Hayward *WomWWA 14*
Kimball, Eugene Sue 1849-1919 *ApCAB X*
Kimball, Everett 1873-1948 *WhAm 2*
Kimball, Fiske 1888-1955 *DcAmB S5, NatCAB 47, WhAm 3*
Kimball, Frances Ayers 1842- *WomWWA 14*
Kimball, Francis H 1845- *NatCAB 15*
Kimball, Francis Nelson 1895-1966 *NatCAB 52*
Kimball, Frank Edward 1861-1916 *NatCAB 17*
Kimball, Fred Mason 1861-1930 *NatCAB 22*
Kimball, George Albert 1850-1912 *NatCAB 15, WhAm 1*
Kimball, George Cook 1879-1942 *NatCAB 41, WhAm 1*
Kimball, George Elbert 1906-1967 *WhAm 4*
Kimball, George Henry 1849-1936 *WhAm 1, WhAm 1C*
Kimball, George Selwyn 1846-1909 *WhAm 1*
Kimball, George Turner 1874-1953 *WhAm 3*
Kimball, George Washington 1858-1927 *ApCAB X*
Kimball, Gilman 1804-1892 *ApCAB, DcAmB, NatCAB 5, TwCBDA, WhAm H*
Kimball, Grace *AmWom*
Kimball, Grace Niebuhr 1855- *WomWWA 14*
Kimball, Gustavus Sylvester 1860-1937 *WhAm 1*
Kimball, Hannah Parker 1861- *WhAm 4, WomWWA 14*
Kimball, Hannibal I 1832-1895 *TwCBDA*
Kimball, Harriet McEwen 1834-1917 *AmWom, ApCAB, NatCAB 11, WhAm 1*
Kimball, Harry Gilbert 1870-1945 *NatCAB 34*
Kimball, Harry Grant 1877-1945 *NatCAB 34*
Kimball, Harry Swift 1875-1957 *WhAm 3*
Kimball, Heber Chase 1801-1868 *AmBi, ApCAB, DcAmB, Drake, NatCAB 7, NatCAB 16, TwCBDA, WhAm H*
Kimball, Henry 1829-1890 *NatCAB 2*
Kimball, Henry Dox 1841-1915 *WhAm 1*
Kimball, Henry Mahlon 1878-1935 *BiDrAC*
Kimball, Herbert Harvey 1862- *WhAm 5*
Kimball, Hiram 1845-1899 *NatCAB 44*
Kimball, Mrs. Horace *NewYHSD*
Kimball, Increase 1777-1856 *ApCAB, Drake, NatCAB 4*
Kimball, Ingalls 1874-1933 *NatCAB 30*
Kimball, Jacob, Jr. 1761-1826 *TwCBDA, WhAm H*
Kimball, James Henry 1874-1943 *NatCAB 32, WhAm 2*
Kimball, James Madison 1814- *NatCAB 9*
Kimball, James Putnam 1836-1913 *ApCAB, NatCAB 11, WhAm 1*
Kimball, James William 1812-1885 *ApCAB*
Kimball, Jennie 1851- *AmWom*
Kimball, John 1821-1913 *NatCAB 17*
Kimball, John C 1832-1910 *WhAm 1*
Kimball, John White 1828-1910 *TwCBDA, WhAm 1*
Kimball, Jonathan Golden 1853-1938 *REnAW*
Kimball, Joseph C 1867- *WhAm 4*
Kimball, Joseph Horace 1813-1838 *ApCAB, Drake*
Kimball, Justin Ford 1872-1956 *WhAm 3*
Kimball, Kate Fisher 1860-1917 *WhAm 1, WomWWA 14*
Kimball, Katharine 1866-1949 *WhAm 2*
Kimball, LeRoy Elwood 1888-1962 *NatCAB 50, WhAm 4*

Kimball, Luella D *WomWWA 14*
Kimball, Maria Brace 1852- *WomWWA 14*
Kimball, Maria Porter *AmWom*
Kimball, Marie Goebel d1955 *WhAm 3*
Kimball, Mark 1821-1891 *ApCAB X*
Kimball, Martha Gertrude 1840-1894 *ApCAB Sup*
Kimball, Martha Smith 1870- *WomWWA 14*
Kimball, Mary Ann *NewYHSD*
Kimball, Matie E 1871- *WomWWA 14*
Kimball, Maulsby 1874-1956 *NatCAB 51*
Kimball, Miles 1906-1949 *NatCAB 39*
Kimball, Monte Jay 1862-1943 *NatCAB 31*
Kimball, Moses 1809-1895 *NatCAB 20*
Kimball, Moses 1810-1895 *TwCBDA*
Kimball, Nathan d1898 *ApCAB*
Kimball, Nathan 1822-1898 *NatCAB 6, TwCBDA*
Kimball, Nathan 1823?-1898 *DcAmB, WhAm H*
Kimball, Philip Horatio 1890-1942 *WhAm 2*
Kimball, Ralph Horace 1886-1947 *WhAm 2*
Kimball, Richard Burleigh 1816-1892 *ApCAB, DcAmB, Drake, NatCAB 10, TwCBDA, WhAm H*
Kimball, Richard Huntington 1882-1942 *NatCAB 38*
Kimball, Robert Jackson 1836- *NatCAB 10*
Kimball, Robert Merriman 1909-1963 *WhAm 4*
Kimball, Spofford Harris 1901-1967 *WhAm 4*
Kimball, Stockton 1902-1958 *NatCAB 51, WhAm 3*
Kimball, Sumner Increase 1834-1923 *AmBi, ApCAB, DcAmB, NatCAB 2, TwCBDA, WhAm 1*
Kimball, Thomas Lord 1831-1899 *NatCAB 5*
Kimball, Thomas Rogers 1862-1934 *NatCAB 25, WhAm 1*
Kimball, Ulyra Weston 1875- *WomWWA 14*
Kimball, Walter Gardner 1888-1951 *WhAm 3*
Kimball, Willard 1854- *WhAm 4*
Kimball, William Coggin 1847-1914 *WhAm 1*
Kimball, William Hazen 1817-1892 *NewYHSD*
Kimball, William Preston 1857-1926 *BiDrAC, WhAm 4*
Kimball, William Smith 1837-1895 *NatCAB 4*
Kimball, William Wallace 1828-1904 *NatCAB 9, WhAm 1*
Kimball, William Wirt 1848-1930 *AmBi, DcAmB, WebAMB, WhAm 1*
Kimball, Willis Gove Carleton 1880-1964 *NatCAB 51*
Kimbark, Seneca D 1832-1912 *NatCAB 15*
Kimbel, George William 1903-1968 *NatCAB 54*
Kimbell, Kay 1886-1964 *WhAm 4*
Kimber, Arthur Clifford 1844- *NatCAB 11, TwCBDA, WhAm 4*
Kimber, Harry Goldring 1892-1966 *WhAm 4*
Kimber, T Wyckoff 1868-1957 *NatCAB 47*
Kimberland, Angie Graham 1881- *WomWWA 14*
Kimberly, Denison 1814-1863 *NewYHSD*
Kimberly, James H *NewYHSD*
Kimberly, John 1818-1882 *TwCBDA*
Kimberly, John Alfred 1836-1928 *NatCAB 52*
Kimberly, Joseph A *NewYHSD*
Kimberly, Lewis Ashfield 1830-1902 *ApCAB, NatCAB 10, TwCBDA, WhAm 1*
Kimble, Colby *NewYHSD*
Kimble, Francis Marion 1901-1946 *NatCAB 35*
Kimble, John Haines 1860-1938 *WhAm 1*
Kimble, Joseph Chanslor 1910-1972 *WhAm 5*
Kimbrough, Bradley Thomas 1846- *WhAm 1*
Kimbrough, Carolyn Lowe Vroom 1847- *WomWWA 14*
Kimbrough, Herbert 1876- *WhAm 5*
Kimbrough, J Lloyd 1879-1937 *NatCAB 43*
Kimbrough, Robert Alexander 1869- *WhAm 5*
Kimbrough, Robert Alexander, Jr. 1899-1967 *WhAm 4*
Kimbrough, Thomas Charles 1873-1945 *WhAm 2*
Kimes, Russell A 1912-1963 *WhAm 4*
Kimm, Neal Edwin 1917-1962 *WhAm 4*
Kimmel, Benjamin Bruce 1870-1953 *NatCAB 44*
Kimmel, Christopher 1830?- *NewYHSD*
Kimmel, Frederick K *NewYHSD*

Kimmel, Gustav Bernard 1874-1939 *WhAm 1*
Kimmel, Husband Edward 1882-1968
    NatCAB 54, WebAMB, WhAm 5,
    WhWW-II
Kimmel, John D *NewYHSD*
Kimmel, Lester Franklin 1893-1962 *WhAm 4*
Kimmel, Lu 1905-1973 *IlBEAAW*
Kimmel, P K *NewYHSD*
Kimmel, William 1812-1886 *BiDrAC,*
    WhAm H
Kimmel, William 1835?-1886 *NatCAB 11*
Kimmelstiel, Paul 1900-1970 *WhAm 5*
Kimmett, Marcus Aurelius 1858-1925
    NatCAB 20
Kimura, Hisashi 1870-1943 *DcScB*
Kinard, F Marion 1902-1960 *WhAm 4*
Kinard, James Pinckney 1864-1951 *WhAm 3*
Kincaid, Bess Beardsley 1879- *WomWWA 14*
Kincaid, Charles Easton 1855-1906 *ApCAB*
Kincaid, Charles Euston 1855-1906 *TwCBDA,*
    WhAm 1
Kincaid, Elbert Alvis 1884-1958 *WhAm 3*
Kincaid, Eugenio 1798-1883 *ApCAB*
Kincaid, Harrison Rittenhouse 1836-
    NatCAB 7
Kincaid, James Leslie 1884-1973 *WhAm 6*
Kincaid, John 1791-1873 *ApCAB, BiAUS,*
    BiDrAC, TwCBDA, WhAm H
Kincaid, Robert Lee 1893-1960 *WhAm 4*
Kincaid, Trevor 1872- *WhAm 5*
Kincaid, William A 1859-1922 *WhAm 1*
Kincaid, William Joseph 1841-1923 *NatCAB 6*
Kincaid, William Wallace 1868- *WhAm 2*
Kincaide, Henry Lincoln 1867-1929 *ApCAB X*
Kincannon, Andrew Armstrong 1859-1938
    NatCAB 15, NatCAB 35, WhAm 4
Kincer, Joseph Burton 1874- *WhAm 5*
Kincey, Herbert Furniss 1898-1971 *NatCAB 57*
Kincheloe, David Hayes 1877-1950 *BiDrAC,*
    NatCAB 37, WhAm 3, WhAmP
Kinchen, Elijah Wesley 1874- *WhoColR*
Kind, John Louis 1877-1958 *WhAm 3*
Kindel, George John 1855-1930 *BiDrAC,*
    NatCAB 22, WhAm 1
Kindelberger, James Howard 1895-1962
    WhAm 4
Kinderman, Robert Henry 1913-1974 *WhAm 6*
Kindi, Abu Yusuf Yaqub Ibn, Al- 801?-866?
    DcScB Sup
Kindi, Abu Yusuf Yaqub Ibn Ishaq, Al- d873?
    DcScB, McGEWB
Kindig, James William 1879-1950 *NatCAB 48,*
    WhAm 4
Kindle, Edward Martin 1869-1940 *WhAm 1*
Kindleberger, Charles Poor 1870-1957
    NatCAB 46
Kindleberger, David 1834-1921 *WhAm 1*
Kindleberger, Jacob 1875-1947 *WhAm 3*
Kindler, George *NewYHSD*
Kindler, Hans 1893-1949 *NatCAB 39,*
    WhAm 2
Kindred, Ella Cramer *WomWWA 14*
Kindred, John Joseph 1864-1937 *BiDrAC,*
    WhAm 1, WhAmP
Kinealy, John Henry 1864-1928 *WhAm 1*
Kineon, George Goodhue 1879-1943 *WhAm 2*
King, Adam d1835 *BiAUS*
King, Adam 1785-1835 *TwCBDA*
King, Adam 1790-1835 *BiDrAC, WhAm H,*
    WhAmP
King, Aden J 1897-1971 *WhAm 5*
King, Albert Freeman Africanus 1841-1914
    ApCAB X, DcAmB, NatCAB 24,
    WhAm 1
King, Albion Roy 1895-1972 *WhAm 5*
King, Alexander 1816-1890 *ApCAB X*
King, Alexander 1900-1965 *WhAm 4*
King, Alexander Campbell 1856-1926
    NatCAB 22, WhAm 1
King, Alfred Clinton 1868-1933 *NatCAB 25*
King, Alfred Rufus 1857-1916 *WhAm 1*
King, Alonzo 1796-1835 *ApCAB*
King, Alvin Olin 1890-1958 *WhAm 3*
King, Andrew 1812-1895 *BiAUS, BiDrAC,*
    WhAm H
King, Annie Farrar VanSweringen Barret 1843-
    WomWWA 14
King, Arno Warren 1855-1918 *WhAm 1*

King, Arthur 1841-1917 *NatCAB 17*
King, Arthur Dale 1872-1952 *WhAm 3*
King, Arthur S 1876-1957 *WhAm 3*
King, Austin Augustus 1801-1870 *ApCAB,*
    BiAUS, Drake, NatCAB 12, TwCBDA
King, Austin Augustus 1802-1870 *BiDrAC,*
    DcAmB, WhAm H
King, Basil 1859-1928 *AmBi, DcAmB,*
    NatCAB 21, WhAm 1
King, Benjamin Flint 1830-1868 *ApCAB*
King, Byron Wesley 1859-1924 *NatCAB 20*
King, Campbell 1871-1953 *WhAm 3*
King, Carl 1880-1943 *NatCAB 34*
King, Carleton James 1904- *BiDrAC*
King, Carol Weiss 1895-1952 *DcAmB S5*
King, Caroline B d1947 *WhAm 2*
King, Cecil Rhodes 1898-1974 *BiDrAC,*
    WhAm 6, WhAmP
King, Charles *NewYHSD*
King, Charles 1789-1867 *AmBi, ApCAB,*
    DcAmB, Drake, NatCAB 6, TwCBDA,
    WhAm H
King, Charles 1844-1933 *AmBi, ApCAB,*
    NatCAB 5, NatCAB 25, TwCBDA,
    WhAm 1
King, Charles Banks *WhAm 5*
King, Charles Bird 1785-1862 *ApCAB,*
    BnEnAmA, IlBEAAW, NewYHSD,
    REnAW, WhAm H
King, Charles Bird 1786-1862 *Drake*
King, Charles Brady 1868-1957 *NatCAB 48*
King, Charles Burton 1875- *WhAm 5*
King, Charles D B d1961 *WhAm 4*
King, Charles Edward 1874-1950 *NatCAB 39*
King, Charles Francis 1843-1924 *BiDAmEd,*
    NatCAB 20, WhAm 1
King, Charles Garfield 1873-1945 *NatCAB 35*
King, Charles Glen 1896- *AsBiEn*
King, Charles Gorman 1866-1955 *NatCAB 43*
King, Charles Gregory 1901-1951 *NatCAB 41*
King, Charles Kelley 1867-1952 *WhAm 3*
King, Charles William 1809?-1845 *DcAmB,*
    WhAm H
King, Clarence 1842-1901 *AmBi, ApCAB,*
    DcAmB, DcScB, EncAAH, McGEWB,
    NatCAB 13, TwCBDA, WebAB,
    WhAm 1
King, Clark Whipkey 1907-1962 *NatCAB 48,*
    WhAm 4
King, Clifford William 1882- *WhAm 2*
King, Clyde Lanier 1874-1941 *NatCAB 35*
King, Clyde Lyndon 1879-1937 *WhAm 1*
King, Cora Smith 1867-1939 *WhAm 1,*
    WomWWA 14
King, Cornelia Bonnell Greene 1873-
    WomWWA 14
King, Cyrus 1772-1817 *ApCAB, BiAUS,*
    BiDrAC, Drake, TwCBDA, WhAm H,
    WhAmP
King, Cyrus Murdock 1860-1922 *NatCAB 19*
King, D J 1909-1955 *WhAm 3*
King, Dan 1791-1864 *ApCAB, DcAmB, Drake,*
    TwCBDA, WhAm H
King, Daniel Putnam 1800-1850 *BiAUS*
King, Daniel Putnam 1801-1850 *ApCAB,*
    BiDrAC, Drake, TwCBDA, WhAm H
King, David 1774-1836 *ApCAB*
King, David 1812-1882 *ApCAB*
King, David Bennett 1848- *ApCAB, WhAm 4*
King, David Sjodahl 1917- *BiDrAC*
King, David Ward 1857- *WhAm 4*
King, Dennis 1897-1971 *WhAm 5*
King, Dougall Macdougall 1878-1922 *WhAm 1*
King, Douglass Stone 1907-1971 *WhAm 6*
King, Earl 1885-1948 *NatCAB 41*
King, Earl Beardsley 1906-1957 *NatCAB 46*
King, Edgar 1884-1970 *WhAm 5*
King, Edmund Burritt 1850-1934 *WhAm 1*
King, Edna Elvira Swanson d1969 *WhAm 5*
King, Edward 1794-1873 *ApCAB*
King, Edward 1795-1836 *ApCAB*
King, Edward 1795-1873 *BiAUS*
King, Edward 1833-1908 *ApCAB X,*
    NatCAB 15, WhAm 1
King, Edward 1848-1896 *ApCAB, TwCBDA*
King, Edward Charles 1876-1961 *NatCAB 49*
King, Edward Duncan 1896-1975 *WhAm 6*
King, Edward Jasper 1916-1973 *WhAm 6*

King, Edward John 1867-1929 *BiDrAC,*
    WhAm 1, WhAmP
King, Edward Lacy 1884-1963 *WhAm 4*
King, Edward Leonard 1873-1933 *DcAmB S1,*
    NatCAB 42, WhAm 1
King, Edward Postell, Jr. 1884-1958 *WhAm 3*
King, Edward Skinner 1861-1931 *AmBi,*
    DcAmB, WhAm 1
King, Edward Smith 1848-1896 *DcAmB,*
    NatCAB 24, WhAm H
King, Edwin Burruss 1876- *WhAm 5*
King, Edwin F *NewYHSD*
King, Eldon Paul 1893-1962 *WhAm 4*
King, Eleanor Augusta Frink 1854-
    WomWWA 14
King, Elisha Alonzo 1870- *WhAm 5*
King, Emma B *WomWWA 14*
King, Ernest Joseph 1878-1956 *EncAB,*
    McGEWB, NatCAB 46, WebAB,
    WebAMB, WhAm 3, WhWW-II,
    WhoMilH
King, Esther Howard *WomWWA 14*
King, Everett Edgar 1877-1960 *WhAm 5*
King, Fain White 1892-1972 *WhAm 5*
King, Fannie Bayly 1864- *WomWWA 14*
King, Florence Lord 1872- *WomWWA 14*
King, Florence Rich 1869- *WomWWA 14*
King, Mrs. Francis *NotAW*
King, Francis Boland 1903-1949 *NatCAB 37*
King, Francis Campbell 1861-1946 *NatCAB 35*
King, Francis Scott 1850- *WhAm 1*
King, Frank Ingersoll 1860-1921 *NatCAB 19*
King, Frank Lamar 1909-1970 *WhAm 5*
King, Frank O 1883-1969 *WebAB, WhAm 5*
King, Frank William 1855-1916 *NatCAB 16*
King, Franklin Hiram 1848-1911 *AmBi,*
    DcAmB, NatCAB 19, WhAm 1
King, Frederic Gore 1801-1829 *ApCAB*
King, Frederick *NewYHSD*
King, Frederick Allen 1865-1939 *WhAm 1*
King, Gamaliel 1790?-1865? *ApCAB*
King, George Anderson 1855-1938 *WhAm 1*
King, George B *NewYHSD*
King, George B 1848- *WhAm 4*
King, George C d1870 *BiAUS*
King, George Edwin 1839- *ApCAB Sup*
King, George Elias 1846-1912 *NatCAB 42*
King, George Gordon 1807-1870 *BiDrAC,*
    WhAm H, WhAmP
King, George Gordon 1807-1871 *NatCAB 8,*
    TwCBDA
King, George Lincoln, Jr. 1900-1967
    NatCAB 53
King, Goodman 1848?-1926 *NatCAB 12,*
    NatCAB 24
King, Grace Elizabeth 1851-1932 *DcAmB*
King, Grace Elizabeth 1852-1932 *NatCAB 2,*
    TwCBDA, WhAm 1, WomWWA 14
King, Grace Elizabeth 1853?-1932 *NotAW*
King, Grace Elizabeth 1859-1932 *AmBi*
King, Hamilton 1852-1912 *NatCAB 12,*
    TwCBDA, WhAm 1
King, Harold Davis 1879- *WhAm 6*
King, Harold Joseph 1913-1966 *WhAm 4*
King, Harold William 1899-1962 *WhAm 4*
King, Harry Albert 1901-1974 *WhAm 6*
King, Harry Andrews 1867-1927 *WhAm 1*
King, Harry Clifton 1885-1958 *NatCAB 46*
King, Harry Edwin 1860-1923 *NatCAB 19*
King, Helen Dean 1869-1955 *WhAm 3,*
    WomWWA 14
King, Henrietta Maria Morse Chamberlain
    1832-1925 *NatCAB 20*
King, Henry 1790-1861 *BiAUS, BiDrAC,*
    TwCBDA, WhAm H
King, Henry 1842-1915 *DcAmB, NatCAB 24,*
    WhAm 1
King, Henry Churchill 1858-1934 *AmBi,*
    DcAmB S1, NatCAB 13, TwCBDA,
    WhAm 1
King, Henry Eugene 1870-1950 *NatCAB 39*
King, Henry Lord Page 1831-1862 *ApCAB,*
    NatCAB 2
King, Henry Lord Page 1895-1952 *WhAm 3*
King, Henry Melville 1838-1919 *DcAmB,*
    NatCAB 25, WhAm 1
King, Henry Stouffer 1850-1943 *WhAm 2*
King, Herbert Hiram 1882-1949 *WhAm 2*

King, Hiram Cheatham 1873-1949 *NatCAB 49*
King, Homer C 1892-1965 *WhAm 4*
King, Homer Snodgrass 1841-1919 *NatCAB 33*
King, Horace Williams 1874-1951 *NatCAB 39,*
WhAm 3
King, Horatio 1811-1897 *ApCAB, BiAUS,*
BiDrUSE, DcAmB, NatCAB 5,
TwCBDA, WhAm H
King, Horatio Collins 1837-1918 *ApCAB,*
NatCAB 6, TwCBDA, WhAm 1
King, Howell Atwater 1896-1971 *WhAm 5*
King, Irving 1874- *WhAm 5*
King, J Berre 1854-1913 *NatCAB 14,*
NatCAB 26
King, J Berry 1888-1962 *NatCAB 50*
King, James A d1899 *WhAm 1*
King, James Aloysius 1899-1961 *WhAm 4*
King, James Edward 1874-1947 *NatCAB 42*
King, James G 1819-1867 *BiAUS*
King, James Gore 1791-1853 *AmBi, ApCAB,*
BiAUS, BiDrAC, DcAmB, Drake,
NatCAB 1, TwCBDA, WhAm H,
WhAmP
King, James Gore 1868-1932 *NatCAB 14,*
NatCAB 23
King, James H 1873-1955 *WhAm 3*
King, James Harold 1892-1953 *WhAm 3*
King, James Joseph 1882-1935 *WhAm 1*
King, James L 1850-1919 *NatCAB 6,*
TwCBDA
King, James Marcus 1839-1907 *WhAm 1*
King, James Moore 1867- *WhAm 4*
King, James S *NewYHSD*
King, James W *NewYHSD*
King, James William 1905-1970 *WhAm 5*
King, James Wilson 1818-1905 *WhAm 4*
King, James Wilson 1822-1905 *NatCAB 13,*
TwCBDA
King, John *NewYHSD*
King, John 1750?-1830? *ApCAB*
King, John 1775-1836 *BiAUS, BiDrAC,*
WhAm H
King, John 1813-1893 *DcAmB, NatCAB 15,*
WhAm H
King, John A 1834-1916 *WhAm 1*
King, John Alsop 1788-1867 *AmBi, ApCAB,*
BiAUS, BiDrAC, DcAmB, NatCAB 3,
TwCBDA, WhAm H, WhAmP
King, John Alsop 1788-1868 *Drake*
King, John Alsop 1817-1900 *NatCAB 5*
King, John Cheston 1865- *WhAm 4*
King, John Crookshanks 1806-1882 *ApCAB,*
BnEnAmA, Drake, NatCAB 8,
NewYHSD, TwCBDA, WhAm H
King, John Floyd 1842-1915 *BiDrAC*
King, John Francis 1859-1922 *NatCAB 34*
King, John Glen 1787-1857 *ApCAB*
King, John Haskell d1888 *Drake, TwCBDA*
King, John Haskell 1818-1888 *ApCAB*
King, John Haskell 1820-1888 *NatCAB 30*
King, John Jefferson 1863-1940 *WhAm 1*
King, John Joseph 1922-1975 *WhAm 6*
King, John Lord 1909-1960 *WhAm 4*
King, John Mark 1829-1899 *ApCAB Sup*
King, John Pendleton 1799- *BiAUS*
King, John Pendleton 1799-1887 *NatCAB 2*
King, John Pendleton 1799-1888 *ApCAB,*
BiDrAC, DcAmB, TwCBDA, WhAm H
King, John Rigdon 1844-1934 *WhAm 1*
King, John W *BiAUS*
King, John William *NewYHSD*
King, Jonas 1792-1869 *ApCAB, DcAmB,*
Drake, TwCBDA, WhAm H
King, Joseph Elijah 1823-1913 *NatCAB 1,*
WhAm 1
King, Joseph Melville 1853-1926 *NatCAB 22*
King, Joseph Stanley 1909-1970 *NatCAB 55*
King, Joshua Ingersoll 1801-1887 *ApCAB*
King, Josiah Brown 1831-1889 *NewYHSD*
King, Josias Ridgate 1832- *NatCAB 14*
King, Julie Rive 1857-1937 *AmWom,*
NatCAB 7, NotAW
King, Julie Rive 1859-1937 *WhAm 3*
King, Karl Clarence 1897- *BiDrAC*
King, Karl Lawrence 1891-1971 *NatCAB 56*
King, LeRoy Albert 1886-1942 *WhAm 2*
King, Lida Shaw 1868-1932 *NatCAB 23,*
NotAW, WhAm 1, WomWWA 14

King, Lorenzo H 1878-1946 *WhAm 2*
King, Louisa Boyd Yeomans 1863-1948 *NotAW,*
WhAm 5, WomWWA 14
King, Louise Woodward 1850-1878 *ApCAB*
King, M A *NewYHSD*
King, Margaret Isadora 1879- *WhAm 6*
King, Martin Luther, Jr. 1929-1968 *DcAmReB,*
EncAB, McGEWB, NatCAB 54, WebAB,
WhAm 4A, WhAmP
King, Mary 1769-1819 *ApCAB*
King, Mary Cutts Howard 1865-
WomWWA 14
King, Mary Perry *WhAm 5*
King, Maxwell Clark 1899-1969 *WhAm 5*
King, Melvin L d1946 *WhAm 2*
King, Merrill Bryant 1890-1933 *NatCAB 34*
King, Merrill Jenks 1894-1965 *WhAm 4*
King, Mitchell 1783-1862 *ApCAB, Drake,*
TwCBDA
King, Morland 1881-1958 *NatCAB 49,*
WhAm 6
King, Myron *NewYHSD*
King, Nina Ansley *WomWWA 14*
King, Oliver Kenneth 1897-1960 *NatCAB 48*
King, Oscar A 1851-1921 *WhAm 1*
King, Paul 1867-1947 *NatCAB 36, WhAm 2*
King, Paul Howard 1879-1942 *WhAm 2*
King, Perkins 1784-1875 *BiAUS, BiDrAC*
King, Preston 1806-1865 *ApCAB, BiAUS,*
BiDrAC, DcAmB, Drake, NatCAB 2,
TwCBDA, WhAm H, WhAmP
King, Putnam 1784-1875 *WhAm H*
King, Ralph Thrall 1855-1926 *NatCAB 22*
King, Raymond Thomas 1893-1971 *WhAm 5*
King, Richard 1824-1885 *REnAW*
King, Richard 1825-1885 *DcAmB, EncAAH,*
NatCAB 8, WebAB, WhAm H
King, Richard 1860-1922 *NatCAB 20*
King, Richard Hayne 1878-1941 *WhAm 2*
King, Robert Adolph 1862-1932 *NatCAB 26*
King, Robert Luther 1912-1967 *WhAm 5*
King, Roy Stevenson 1876-1956 *WhAm 3*
King, Rufus 1755-1827 *AmBi, ApCAB,*
BiAUS, BiDrAC, DcAmB, Drake,
McGEWB, NatCAB 6, TwCBDA,
WebAB, WhAm H, WhAmP
King, Rufus 1814-1876 *AmBi, ApCAB,*
BiAUS, DcAmB, Drake, NatCAB 5,
TwCBDA, WhAm H
King, Rufus 1817-1891 *NatCAB 23*
King, Rufus 1893- *WhAm 6*
King, Rufus DeWitt 1883-1952 *NatCAB 38*
King, Rufus Gunn 1879-1944 *NatCAB 34*
King, Rufus H 1784-1867 *ApCAB*
King, Rufus H 1820-1890 *BiAUS, BiDrAC,*
WhAm H
King, Samuel *ApCAB*
King, Samuel 1748?-1819 *DcAmB, NewYHSD,*
WhAm H
King, Samuel 1749-1819 *TwCBDA*
King, Samuel 1749-1820 *ApCAB*
King, Samuel Alexander 1834- *NatCAB 9*
King, Samuel Archer 1828-1914 *ApCAB,*
DcAmB, NatCAB 24, TwCBDA,
WhAm HA, WhAm 4
King, Samuel G 1816-1899 *NatCAB 6*
King, Samuel Ward 1786-1851 *BiAUS,*
DcAmB, NatCAB 9, TwCBDA,
WhAm H
King, Samuel Wilder 1886-1959 *BiDrAC,*
WhAm 3, WhAmP
King, Scott d1975 *WhAm 6*
King, Sibley Paul 1860-1940 *NatCAB 30*
King, Stanley 1883-1951 *DcAmB S5,*
NatCAB 47, WhAm 3
King, Stanton Henry 1867-1939 *WhAm 2*
King, Steve M 1878-1958 *WhAm 3*
King, Stoddard 1889-1933 *WhAm 1*
King, Susan *Drake*
King, Sylvan N 1900-1966 *WhAm 4*
King, T Butler 1804-1864 *BiAUS*
King, Theophilus 1844-1935 *ApCAB X,*
WhAm 1
King, Thomas Brown 1861- *WhAm 4*
King, Thomas Butler 1800-1864 *BiDrAC,*
DcAmB, NatCAB 2, TwCBDA,
WhAm H
King, Thomas Butler 1804-1864 *ApCAB,*

King, Thomas D 1779-1854 *ApCAB*
King, Thomas James 1842-1919 *NatCAB 40*
King, Thomas Luther 1908-1969 *WhAm 5*
King, Thomas Starr 1824-1863 *ApCAB*
King, Thomas Starr 1824-1864 *AmBi, DcAmB,*
Drake, NatCAB 4, TwCBDA, WhAm H
King, Vernon Curtis 1887-1960 *NatCAB 47*
King, Virginia Ann 1856- *WhAm 4*
King, W Grant 1871-1955 *NatCAB 46*
King, Wilburn Hill 1839-1910 *WhAm 1*
King, Wilford Isbell 1880-1962 *WhAm 4*
King, Willard Vinton 1868-1955 *WhAm 3*
King, William *NewYHSD*
King, William d1826 *ApCAB, Drake*
King, William 1768-1852 *ApCAB, BiAUS,*
DcAmB, Drake, NatCAB 6, TwCBDA,
WhAm H, WhAmP
King, William Albert 1855-1937 *WhAm 1*
King, William Benjamin Basil 1859-1928 *AmBi,*
DcAmB
King, William Bulluck 1911-1973 *WhAm 6*
King, William Elisha 1866- *WhoColR*
King, William Fletcher 1830-1921 *BiDAmEd,*
NatCAB 7, TwCBDA, WhAm 1
King, William Frederick 1850-1909 *NatCAB 14,*
WhAm 1
King, William Harold 1868- *WhoColR*
King, William Henry 1862-1949 *NatCAB 39*
King, William Henry 1863-1949 *BiDrAC,*
WhAm 2, WhAmP
King, William Henry 1864-1949 *ApCAB X*
King, William Henry, Jr. 1888-1961
NatCAB 48
King, William J *NewYHSD*
King, William Lyon Mackenzie 1874-1950
McGEWB, WhAm 3, WhWW-II
King, William Montgomery 1796-1882
NatCAB 9
King, William Newton 1882-1945 *NatCAB 35*
King, William Perry 1876-1949 *WhAm 2*
King, William Peter 1871-1957 *WhAm 3*
King, William Reynolds 1869- *WhAm 5*
King, William Robert 1868-1951 *WhAm 3*
King, William Rufus 1864-1934 *ApCAB X,*
WhAm 1
King, William Rufus 1876-1965 *WhAm 4*
King, William Rufus DeVane 1786-1853 *AmBi,*
ApCAB, BiAUS, BiDrAC, BiDrUSE,
DcAmB, Drake, NatCAB 4, TwCBDA,
WebAB, WhAm H, WhAmP
King, William Smith 1828-1900 *BiAUS,*
BiDrAC
King, William Sterling 1818-1882 *ApCAB*
King, William Wirt 1862-1957 *WhAm 3*
King, Willis L 1851-1936 *WhAm 1*
King, Willis Percival 1839- *WhAm 4*
King, Woods 1900-1947 *NatCAB 41*
King, Yelverton P 1794-1868 *BiAUS,*
NatCAB 5
King Of William, James 1822-1856 *DcAmB,*
WhAm H
King Philip 1639?-1676 *EncAAH*
King Philip *see also* Philip And Philip, King
Kingdon, Frank 1894-1972 *WhAm 5*
Kingdon, George 1861-1942 *NatCAB 31*
Kingdon, Hollingsworth Tully 1837- *ApCAB*
Kingery, Hugh Macmaster 1860-1927 *WhAm 1*
Kingfish *EncAAH*
Kingham, John Burton 1902-1964 *NatCAB 50*
Kingman, A Salome 1895-1970 *WhAm 5*
Kingman, Dan Christie 1852-1916 *NatCAB 28*
Kingman, Eugene 1909-1975 *WhAm 6*
Kingman, Eugene Allerton 1880-1961
NatCAB 49, WhAm 4
Kingman, Henry Selden 1893-1968 *WhAm 5*
Kingman, Howard Fithian 1890-1968
NatCAB 55
Kingman, John J d1948 *WhAm 2*
Kingman, Lewis 1845-1912 *WhAm 1*
Kingman, Lucius Collinwood 1878-1958
NatCAB 47
Kingman, Matthew Henry 1890-1946 *WhAm 2*
Kingman, Ralph Clarke 1890-1946 *NatCAB 34*
Kingman, Russell Barclay 1884-1959 *WhAm 3*
Kingman, Samuel Austin 1822- *NatCAB 13*
Kingsborough, Edward King 1795-1837 *ApCAB,*
Drake

Kingsbury, Albert 1862-1943 *DcAmB S3,*
NatCAB 32
Kingsbury, Albert 1863-1943 *WhAm 2*
Kingsbury, Alice Cary Bussing 1872-
WomWWA 14
Kingsbury, Benjamin Freeman 1872-1946
WhAm 2
Kingsbury, Charles People 1818-1879 *ApCAB,*
Drake, TwCBDA
Kingsbury, Cyrus 1786-1870 *ApCAB,*
TwCBDA
Kingsbury, Edward Martin 1854-1946
NatCAB 36
Kingsbury, Frederick Hutchinson 1864-1942
NatCAB 32
Kingsbury, Frederick John 1823-1910
NatCAB 12, WhAm 1
Kingsbury, Jacob 1755-1837 *ApCAB, Drake*
Kingsbury, James 1765?-1820? *NatCAB 5*
Kingsbury, Jerome d1944 *WhAm 2*
Kingsbury, John 1801-1874 *BiDAmEd, DcAmB,*
NatCAB 9, WhAm H
Kingsbury, John A 1876-1956 *WhAm 3*
Kingsbury, Joseph Thomas 1853-1937
NatCAB 28, WhAm 1, WhAm 1C
Kingsbury, Julius Jesse Bronson 1801-1856
ApCAB
Kingsbury, Kenneth Raleigh 1876-1937
NatCAB 29, WhAm 1
Kingsbury, Marguerite Hempstead 1876-
WomWWA 14
Kingsbury, Nathan Corning 1866-1920
NatCAB 18, WhAm 1
Kingsbury, Selden Bingham 1840-1915
WhAm 1
Kingsbury, Susan Myra 1870-1949 *NotAW,*
WhAm 2, WomWWA 14
Kingsbury, Thomas H C 1807-1862 *ApCAB,*
Drake
Kingsbury, William Wallace 1828-1892 *BiAUS,*
BiDrAC, WhAm H
Kingscott, Louis Clifton 1898-1962 *WhAm 4*
Kingsford, Howard Nelson 1871-1950
WhAm 2A
Kingsford, Joan Elizabeth 1930-1971 *WhAm 5*
Kingsford, Thomas 1799-1869 *DcAmB,*
NatCAB 5, WhAm H
Kingsford, Thomson 1828- *NatCAB 5*
Kingsford, William 1819-1898 *ApCAB Sup*
Kingsland, Mrs. Burton *WhAm 1*
Kingsley, Alfred Crosgrove 1876-1949
NatCAB 42
Kingsley, Bessie Cook 1868- *WomWWA 14*
Kingsley, Bruce Gordon 1875- *WhAm 5*
Kingsley, Calvin 1812-1870 *ApCAB, DcAmB,*
Drake, NatCAB 13, TwCBDA, WhAm H
Kingsley, Charles 1819-1875 *McGEWB*
Kingsley, Chester Ward 1824-1904 *TwCBDA,*
WhAm 1
Kingsley, Clarence Darwin 1874-1926 *BiDAmEd,*
NatCAB 20, WhAm 1
Kingsley, Darwin Pearl 1857-1932 *DcAmB S1,*
WhAm 1
Kingsley, Dwight *NewYHSD*
Kingsley, Edward Daniel 1869-1940
NatCAB 37
Kingsley, Elbridge 1842-1918 *DcAmB,*
NatCAB 13, TwCBDA, WhAm 1
Kingsley, Florence Morse 1859-1937
NatCAB 11, WhAm 1, WomWWA 14
Kingsley, Frances Hubbard 1878-
WomWWA 14
Kingsley, George Almon 1872-1953 *NatCAB 39*
Kingsley, Harold Merrybright 1887- *WhoColR*
Kingsley, Hiram Webster 1888-1971 *WhAm 5*
Kingsley, Howard Lamb 1892-1948 *NatCAB 36,*
WhAm 2
Kingsley, J Sterling 1853-1929 *WhAm 1*
Kingsley, James Luce 1778-1852 *ApCAB,*
BiDAmEd, DcAmB, Drake, NatCAB 10,
TwCBDA, WhAm H
Kingsley, John H 1880-1963 *WhAm 4*
Kingsley, John Sterling 1854-1929 *NatCAB 12,*
TwCBDA
Kingsley, Norman William 1829-1913 *DcAmB,*
NatCAB 25, NewYHSD, WhAm 1
Kingsley, Rose 1845-1925 *IIBEAAW*
Kingsley, Sherman Colver 1866- *WhAm 4*

Kingsley, Willey Lyon 1866-1931 *WhAm 1*
Kingsley, William Charles 1833-1885 *ApCAB*
Kingsley, William H d1945 *WhAm 2*
Kingsley, William Lathrop 1824-1896 *TwCBDA*
Kingsley, William Morgan 1863-1942
NatCAB 31, WhAm 2
Kingsmill, Harold *WhAm 2*
Kingsmill, Hugh 1889-1949 *WhAm 2*
Kingsmore, C H *NewYHSD*
Kingston, Elwood Almon 1876-1956
NatCAB 45
Kingston, George Frederick 1889-1950 *WhAm 3*
Kingston, Robert d1794 *Drake*
Kinison, Charles Richard 1889-1965
NatCAB 51
Kinkade, Charles *NewYHSD*
Kinkade, Reynolds Robert 1854-1935 *WhAm 1*
Kinkaid, Mary Holland 1861-1948 *WhAm 2,*
WomWWA 14
Kinkaid, Moses Parsons 1850-1922 *NatCAB 20*
Kinkaid, Moses Pierce 1854-1922 *WhAm 1*
Kinkaid, Moses Pierce 1856-1922 *BiDrAC,*
REnAW, WhAmP
Kinkaid, Thomas Cassin 1888-1972 *WebAMB,*
WhAm 5, WhWW-II
Kinkaid, Thomas Wright 1860-1920 *WhAm 1*
Kinkead, Cleves 1882-1955 *WhAm 3*
Kinkead, Edgar Benton 1862-1930 *WhAm 1*
Kinkead, Edgar Benton 1863-1930 *DcAmB*
Kinkead, Eleanor Talbot *WomWWA 14*
Kinkead, Elizabeth Shelby *WhAm 5,*
WomWWA 14
Kinkead, Eugene Francis 1876-1960 *BiDrAC,*
NatCAB 44, WhAm 4
Kinkead, John Henry 1826-1904 *NatCAB 11,*
TwCBDA
Kinkel, Gustavus Adolphus 1854-1937
NatCAB 28
Kinkeldey, Otto 1878-1966 *DcAmLiB,*
WhAm 4
Kinkhead, John Henry 1826-1904 *WhAm 1*
Kinley, David 1861-1944 *BiDAmEd, TwCBDA,*
WhAm 2
Kinley, John James 1881- *WhAm 6*
Kinloch, Cleland 1759-1823 *ApCAB*
Kinloch, Cleland 1760-1823 *DcAmB,*
WhAm H
Kinloch, Francis 1755-1826 *ApCAB, BiAUS,*
BiDrAC, TwCBDA, WhAm H
Kinloch, Robert Alexander 1826-1891 *ApCAB,*
DcAmB, NatCAB 15, WhAm H
Kinnan, Alexander Phoenix Waldron 1856-1924
WhAm 1
Kinnan, William Asahel 1863- *WhAm 4*
Kinnane, Charles Herman 1898-1954
NatCAB 41, WhAm 3
Kinnane, John E 1862-1936 *WhAm 1*
Kinnane, Raphael Ignatius 1881- *WhAm 6*
Kinnard, George L 1803-1836 *BiDrAC,*
TwCBDA, WhAm H
Kinnard, George L 1803-1838 *BiAUS*
Kinnard, Leonard Hummel 1869- *WhAm 5*
Kinne, Aaron 1744-1824 *NatCAB 6*
Kinne, Aaron 1745-1824 *ApCAB, Drake*
Kinne, Charles Mason 1841-1913 *NatCAB 16*
Kinne, Clarence Evelyn 1869-1950 *NatCAB 39*
Kinne, Edward DeWitt 1842-1921 *WhAm 1*
Kinne, Helen d1917 *WhAm 1*
Kinne, LaVega George 1846-1906 *DcAmB,*
NatCAB 12, TwCBDA, WhAm 1
Kinnear, James Wesley 1859-1922 *WhAm 1*
Kinnear, John 1836-1928 *ApCAB X*
Kinnear, Wilson Sherman 1864-1941
NatCAB 37, WhAm 1
Kinnersley, Augustus F 1822?- *NewYHSD*
Kinnersley, Ebenezer 1711-1778 *ApCAB,*
DcAmB, DcScB, NatCAB 1, TwCBDA,
WhAm H
Kinnersley, Henry *NewYHSD*
Kinnett, William Ennis 1849-1929 *WhAm 1*
Kinney, Abbot 1850-1920 *TwCBDA, WhAm 1*
Kinney, Amory 1791-1859 *NatCAB 18*
Kinney, Ansel McBryde 1898-1969 *NatCAB 54,*
WhAm 5
Kinney, Antoinette Brown d1945 *WhAm 2*
Kinney, Benjamin Harris 1821-1888 *NewYHSD*
Kinney, Bruce 1865-1936 *WhAm 1*
Kinney, Charles Noyes 1879- *WhAm 6*

Kinney, Charlotte Pearl Conkright 1886-
WomWWA 14
Kinney, Clesson Selwyne 1859- *WhAm 4*
Kinney, Coates 1826-1904 *ApCAB, Drake,*
NatCAB 7, TwCBDA, WhAm 1
Kinney, Edmund J 1879- *WhAm 6*
Kinney, Elizabeth C Dodge Stedman 1810-1889
ApCAB, DcAmB, Drake, NatCAB 13,
WhAm H
Kinney, Eunice Draper 1852- *WomWWA 14*
Kinney, Florence Elizabeth *BiCAW*
Kinney, George Alfred 1873-1963 *NatCAB 50*
Kinney, Gilbert 1884-1952 *WhAm 3*
Kinney, H E *NewYHSD*
Kinney, Henry Walsworth *WhAm 5*
Kinney, Jacob Millison 1877-1955 *NatCAB 43*
Kinney, John Clarence 1872-1949 *NatCAB 39*
Kinney, John Fitch 1816-1902 *ApCAB, BiAUS,*
BiDrAC, TwCBDA
Kinney, Jonathan Kendrick 1843- *ApCAB*
Kinney, Laurence Forman 1902-1966 *WhAm 4*
Kinney, Lucien Blair 1895-1971 *WhAm 5*
Kinney, Margaret West 1872- *WhAm 5,*
WomWWA 14
Kinney, Narcissa Edith White 1854- *AmWom*
Kinney, O S d1869? *WhAm H*
Kinney, Sara Thomson 1842- *WomWWA 14*
Kinney, Thomas Tallmadge 1821-1900
NatCAB 6, TwCBDA, WhAm 1
Kinney, Timothy 1846- *WhAm 4*
Kinney, Troy 1871-1938 *NatCAB 28,*
WhAm 1
Kinney, William Aloysius 1907-1973 *WhAm 6*
Kinney, William Burnet 1799-1880 *ApCAB,*
BiAUS, DcAmB, NatCAB 13, TwCBDA,
WhAm H
Kinney, William Burnet 1871-1925 *NatCAB 22*
Kinney, William Morton 1885-1964 *WhAm 4*
Kinney, William Palmer 1860-1922 *NatCAB 22*
Kinney, William Rumsey 1883-1958
NatCAB 47
Kinnicutt, Francis Parker 1846-1913
NatCAB 15, WhAm 1
Kinnicutt, Leonard Parker 1854-1911 *DcAmB,*
NatCAB 25, TwCBDA, WhAm 1
Kinnicutt, Lincoln Newton 1849-1921 *WhAm 1*
Kinnison, David 1736-1851 *ApCAB,*
NatCAB 1
Kinnison, David 1736-1852 *Drake*
Kinnoch, P A 1888-1951 *WhAm 3*
Kinnoch, Peter Arnot 1888-1951 *NatCAB 40*
Kino, Eusebio Francisco 1644?-1711 *WebAB*
Kino, Eusebio Francisco 1645?-1711 *DcAmB,*
DcAmReB, McGEWB, REnAW,
WhAm H
Kinsell, Laurance Wilkie 1908-1968 *WhAm 5*
Kinsella, Thomas 1832-1884 *ApCAB, BiAUS,*
BiDrAC, DcAmB, WhAm H
Kinsella, Thomas James 1895-1969 *NatCAB 55,*
WhAm 5
Kinsella, William J 1846- *NatCAB 12*
Kinsey, Alfred Charles 1894-1956 *EncAB,*
WebAB, WhAm 3
Kinsey, Charles 1773-1849 *BiAUS, BiDrAC,*
WhAm H
Kinsey, E Lee 1903-1961 *WhAm 4*
Kinsey, James 1731-1802 *BiAUS, Drake,*
TwCBDA
Kinsey, James 1731-1803 *ApCAB, BiDrAC,*
NatCAB 12, WhAm H
Kinsey, John 1693-1750 *ApCAB, DcAmB,*
NatCAB 16, TwCBDA, WhAm H
Kinsey, John DeCou 1895-1967 *WhAm 5*
Kinsey, Nathaniel 1829?- *NewYHSD*
Kinsey, Oliver P 1849- *WhAm 4*
Kinsey, William Irvin 1876-1962 *NatCAB 49*
Kinsey, William Medcalf 1846-1931 *BiDrAC*
Kinsler, Alexander *NewYHSD*
Kinsler, James C 1869- *WhAm 5*
Kinsley, Albert Thomas 1877-1941 *WhAm 2*
Kinsley, Carl 1870- *WhAm 5*
Kinsley, Martin 1754-1835 *BiAUS, BiDrAC,*
WhAm H
Kinsley, Philip 1880-1960 *WhAm 4*
Kinsley, William Wirt 1837-1923 *WhAm 1*
Kinsloe, Charles Lambert 1881- *WhAm 6*
Kinsman, Anna Barnard 1866- *WomWWA 14*
Kinsman, David Nathaniel 1834-1911 *WhAm 1*

Kinsman, Delos Oscar 1868-1948 *NatCAB 37, WhAm 2*
Kinsman, Frederick Joseph 1868-1944 *NatCAB 14, WhAm 3*
Kinsman, J Warren 1894-1965 *WhAm 4*
Kinsman, William A 1877- *WhAm 5*
Kinsolving, Arthur Barksdale 1861-1951 *WhAm 3*
Kinsolving, Arthur Barksdale, II 1894-1964 *WhAm 4*
Kinsolving, George Herbert 1849-1928 *NatCAB 12, TwCBDA, WhAm 1*
Kinsolving, Lucien Lee 1862-1929 *ApCAB Sup, NatCAB 28, TwCBDA, WhAm 1*
Kinsolving, Sally Bruce 1876-1962 *WhAm 4, WomWWA 14*
Kinsworthy, Edgar Burton 1859- *WhAm 4*
Kinter, William Lewis 1877-1935 *WhAm 1*
Kintner, Edwin G 1881-1971 *WhAm 5*
Kintner, Robert Chester 1900-1974 *WhAm 6*
Kintner, Samuel Montgomery 1871-1936 *WhAm 1*
Kintpuash *DcAmB, WhAm H*
Kintzing, Pearce 1861-1917 *WhAm 1*
Kintzinger, John W 1870-1946 *WhAm 2*
Kinyon, Claudius Bligh 1851-1924 *NatCAB 20*
Kinyoun, Floyd Homer 1890-1954 *NatCAB 42*
Kinyoun, Joseph James 1860-1919 *NatCAB 23, WhAm 1*
Kinzer, J Roland 1874-1955 *WhAm 3*
Kinzer, John Roland 1874-1955 *BiDrAC, WhAmP*
Kinzie, John 1763-1828 *ApCAB, DcAmB, WhAm H*
Kinzie, John Harris 1803-1865 *ApCAB Sup*
Kinzie, Juliette Augusta Magill 1806-1870 *ApCAB Sup, NotAW*
Kinzie, Robert Allen 1874-1957 *NatCAB 48*
Kiokemeister, Fred Ludwig 1913-1969 *WhAm 5*
Kip, Abraham Lincoln 1865- *WhAm 4*
Kip, Frederic Ellsworth 1862- *WhAm 4*
Kip, Leonard 1826-1906 *ApCAB, NatCAB 11, TwCBDA, WhAm 1*
Kip, Leonard William 1837-1901 *TwCBDA*
Kip, William Ingraham 1811-1893 *ApCAB, DcAmB, Drake, NatCAB 3, TwCBDA, WhAm H*
Kipling, Joseph Rudyard 1865-1936 *McGEWB*
Kipling, Rudyard 1865-1936 *ApCAB Sup*
Kiplinger, Willard Monroe 1891-1967 *WhAm 4A*
Kipp, Charles John 1838-1911 *WhAm 1*
Kipp, George Washington 1847-1911 *BiDrAC, WhAm 1*
Kipp, Josephine 1845- *AmWom*
Kipp, Orin Lansing 1885-1958 *WhAm 3*
Kippax, John R 1849- *WhAm 1*
Kipping, Frederic Stanley 1863-1949 *AsBiEn*
Kipping, Frederick Stanley 1863-1949 *DcScB*
Kipps, Arthur *NewYHSD*
Kirby, Absalom 1837-1924 *WhAm 1*
Kirby, C Valentine 1875-1947 *WhAm 2*
Kirby, Daniel Bartholomew 1891-1953 *WhAm 3*
Kirby, Daniel Noyes 1864-1945 *NatCAB 34, WhAm 2*
Kirby, Edmund 1794-1849 *ApCAB*
Kirby, Edmund 1840-1863 *ApCAB, Drake*
Kirby, Edmund Burgis 1859-1935 *NatCAB 27, WhAm 1, WhAm 1C*
Kirby, Ephraim 1757-1804 *ApCAB, BiAUS, DcAmB, Drake, NatCAB 11, TwCBDA, WhAm H*
Kirby, Frank E 1849-1929 *WhAm 1*
Kirby, Fred Morgan 1861-1940 *NatCAB 41, WhAm 1*
Kirby, George Franklin 1868- *TwCBDA*
Kirby, George Hughes 1875-1935 *DcAmB S1, NatCAB 26, WhAm 1*
Kirby, Grady 1889-1969 *NatCAB 55*
Kirby, Gustavus Town 1874-1956 *ApCAB X, NatCAB 45*
Kirby, Harold, Jr. 1900-1952 *NatCAB 41, WhAm 3*
Kirby, Isaac Minor 1834- *TwCBDA*
Kirby, J Hudson 1819-1848 *ApCAB, DcAmB, WhAm H*
Kirby, Jack Temple 1938- *EncAAH*
Kirby, John, Jr. 1850-1925 *NatCAB 14,*

NatCAB 18, NatCAB 29, WhAm 1
Kirby, John Henry 1860-1940 *WhAm 1*
Kirby, Laverne Howe 1912-1972 *WhAm 6*
Kirby, Philip H 1835-1915 *ApCAB X*
Kirby, R Harper 1861-1928 *WhAm 1*
Kirby, Reynold Marvin 1790-1842 *ApCAB*
Kirby, Robert J 1889-1944 *WhAm 2*
Kirby, Rollin 1875-1952 *DcAmB S5, NatCAB 47, WhAm 3*
Kirby, Stephen Robinson 1876-1955 *NatCAB 42*
Kirby, Thomas E 1846-1924 *ApCAB X*
Kirby, William 1817- *ApCAB*
Kirby, William Fosgate 1867-1934 *BiDrAC, NatCAB 44, WhAm 1, WhAmP*
Kirby, William Gerard 1916-1969 *WhAm 5*
Kirby, William Maurice 1842- *WhAm 4*
Kirby-Smith, Edmund 1824-1893 *AmBi, BiDAmEd, DcAmB, WebAMB, WhAm H, WhoMilH*
Kirby-Smith, Maude Tompkins 1882- *WomWWA 14*
Kirbye, J Edward 1873-1939 *NatCAB 14, WhAm 1*
Kirch *DcScB*
Kirch, Christfried 1694-1740 *DcScB*
Kirch, Christine 1696?-1782 *DcScB*
Kirch, Gottfried 1639-1710 *DcScB*
Kirch, Maria Margarethe Winkelmann 1670-1720 *DcScB*
Kirchbaum, Joseph 1831?-1926 *NewYHSD*
Kircher, Athanasius 1601-1680 *AsBiEn*
Kircher, Athanasius 1602?-1680 *BiHiMed, DcScB*
Kircher, Effie Irene 1871- *WomWWA 14*
Kirchhof, Frank 1865-1949 *NatCAB 39*
Kirchhof, Konstantin Sigizmundovich 1764-1833 *DcScB*
Kirchhoff, Charles William Henry 1853-1916 *ApCAB, DcAmB, NatCAB 10, WhAm 1*
Kirchhoff, Gustav Robert 1824-1887 *AsBiEn, DcScB, McGEWB*
Kirchhoff, Theodor 1828-1899 *NatCAB 11*
Kirchmayer, John 1860?-1930 *DcAmB*
Kirchner, Arthur Adolph 1903-1966 *WhAm 4*
Kirchner, Ernst Ludwig 1880-1938 *McGEWB*
Kirchner, George Henry 1866-1938 *NatCAB 29, WhAm 1*
Kirchner, Henry Paul 1890-1957 *NatCAB 48, WhAm 3*
Kirchner, Otto 1846-1920 *NatCAB 19, WhAm 1*
Kirchner, William Herman 1868-1956 *NatCAB 45*
Kirchoffer, William Gray 1870-1956 *NatCAB 43*
Kirchwey, Freda d1976 *WhAm 6*
Kirchwey, George W 1885-1942 *WhAm 2*
Kirchwey, George Washington 1855-1942 *DcAmB S3, NatCAB 47*
Kirk, Abby 1865- *WomWWA 14*
Kirk, Alan Goodrich 1888-1963 *NatCAB 50, WebAMB, WhAm 4*
Kirk, Albert E 1880- *WhAm 6*
Kirk, Andrew Jackson 1866-1933 *BiDrAC*
Kirk, Arthur Dale 1886-1944 *WhAm 2*
Kirk, Charles Albert 1904-1947 *WhAm 2*
Kirk, Charles Townsend 1876-1945 *WhAm 2*
Kirk, David 1849-1922 *NatCAB 20*
Kirk, Dolly Williams *WhAm 5*
Kirk, Edward Cameron 1856-1933 *NatCAB 36, WhAm 1*
Kirk, Edward N 1828-1863 *ApCAB, Drake, TwCBDA*
Kirk, Edward Norris 1802-1874 *ApCAB, DcAmB, DcAmReB, Drake, NatCAB 6, TwCBDA, WhAm H*
Kirk, Edwin 1884-1955 *NatCAB 45*
Kirk, Ella Boyce 1862- *WomWWA 14*
Kirk, Ellen Warner Olney 1842- *AmWom, ApCAB, NatCAB 1, WhAm 4, WomWWA 14*
Kirk, Ellen Warner Olney 1846- *TwCBDA*
Kirk, Frank C 1898-1963 *WhAm 4*
Kirk, Frank Martin 1863-1952 *NatCAB 42*
Kirk, Harris C 1897-1960 *WhAm 4*
Kirk, Harris Elliott 1872-1953 *WhAm 3*
Kirk, James Smith 1818-1886 *NatCAB 1*

Kirk, John 1823?-1862? *NewYHSD*
Kirk, John Esben 1905-1975 *WhAm 6*
Kirk, John Foster 1820-1904 *Drake*
Kirk, John Foster 1824-1904 *ApCAB, DcAmB, NatCAB 1, TwCBDA, WhAm 1*
Kirk, John Franklin 1873-1934 *WhAm 1*
Kirk, John Robert 1851-1937 *BiDAmEd, WhAm 1*
Kirk, Lester King 1899-1970 *WhAm 5*
Kirk, May 1864- *WhAm 4*
Kirk, Nettie Madora 1854-1880 *NatCAB 6*
Kirk, Norman Thomas 1888-1960 *WhAm 4*
Kirk, Paul Leland 1902-1970 *NatCAB 56*
Kirk, Ralph G 1881- *WhAm 6*
Kirk, Raymond Eller 1890-1957 *NatCAB 47, WhAm 3*
Kirk, Raymond V 1901-1947 *WhAm 2*
Kirk, Robert C 1821- *BiAUS, NatCAB 12*
Kirk, Robert Carey 1877-1955 *NatCAB 45*
Kirk, Robert Horner 1872-1925 *ApCAB X*
Kirk, Samuel 1793-1872 *BnEnAmA, NatCAB 29*
Kirk, Samuel Alexander 1904- *BiDAmEd*
Kirk, Thomas Jefferson 1852- *WhAm 4*
Kirk, Waldorf Tilton 1897-1957 *WhAm 3*
Kirk, William 1880-1961 *WhAm 4*
Kirk, William Frederick 1877-1927 *WhAm 1*
Kirk, William Talbot 1918-1974 *WhAm 6*
Kirkaldy, David 1820-1897 *DcScB*
Kirkbride, Elizabeth Butler *WomWWA 14*
Kirkbride, Franklin Butler 1867-1955 *WhAm 3*
Kirkbride, Thomas Story 1809-1883 *AmBi, ApCAB, DcAmB, NatCAB 6, TwCBDA, WhAm H*
Kirkbride, Walter George 1881- *WhAm 6*
Kirkby, Thomas *NewYHSD*
Kirke, Sir David 1596-1655? *ApCAB*
Kirke, Edmund 1822-1903 *AmBi*
Kirke, Louis *ApCAB*
Kirkeby, Arnold S 1901-1962 *WhAm 4*
Kirkendall, Frederick Charles 1871-1925 *NatCAB 20*
Kirkendall, Henry Laing 1905-1955 *NatCAB 43*
Kirkendall, Richard Stewart 1928- *EncAAH*
Kirker, Nellie Wiles 1864- *WomWWA 14*
Kirker, Thomas *BiAUS*
Kirker, William Bredin 1860- *NatCAB 13*
Kirkes, William Senhouse 1823-1864 *BiHiMed*
Kirkham, Francis Marion 1836-1913 *NatCAB 18*
Kirkham, Harold Laurens Dundas 1887-1949 *WhAm 2*
Kirkham, James Wilson 1850-1927 *NatCAB 22*
Kirkham, John Henry 1865- *WhAm 1*
Kirkham, Ralph Wilson 1821-1893 *ApCAB, TwCBDA*
Kirkham, Reuben 1850-1886 *IIBEAAW*
Kirkham, Samuel R 1833?- *NewYHSD*
Kirkham, Stanton Davis 1868-1944 *WhAm 2*
Kirkham, William Barri 1890-1939 *WhAm 5*
Kirkland, Archie Howard 1873-1931 *NatCAB 14, WhAm 1*
Kirkland, Caroline *WomWWA 14*
Kirkland, Caroline Matilda Stansbury 1801-1864 *ApCAB, DcAmB, Drake, NatCAB 5, NotAW, TwCBDA, WhAm H*
Kirkland, Edward Chase 1894-1975 *WhAm 6*
Kirkland, Elizabeth Stansbury 1828-1896 *ApCAB, TwCBDA*
Kirkland, Forrest 1892-1942 *IIBEAAW*
Kirkland, Henry Bingham 1902-1969 *NatCAB 54*
Kirkland, James Hampton 1859-1939 *AmBi, BiDAmEd, DcAmB S2, NatCAB 8, NatCAB 29, TwCBDA, WhAm 1*
Kirkland, James Robert 1903-1958 *WhAm 3*
Kirkland, John Thornton 1770-1840 *ApCAB, BiDAmEd, DcAmB, Drake, NatCAB 6, TwCBDA, WhAm H*
Kirkland, Joseph 1770-1844 *BiDrAC, NatCAB 5, WhAm H*
Kirkland, Joseph 1771-1844 *BiAUS*
Kirkland, Joseph 1830-1894 *ApCAB, DcAmB, NatCAB 5, TwCBDA, WhAm H*
Kirkland, Samuel 1741-1808 *AmBi, ApCAB, DcAmB, McGEWB, NatCAB 1, NatCAB 7, TwCBDA, WhAm H*
Kirkland, Samuel 1744-1808 *Drake*

Kirkland, Thomas 1835- *ApCAB*
Kirkland, Weymouth 1877-1965 *NatCAB 51, WhAm 4*
Kirkland, William 1800-1846 *ApCAB, TwCBDA*
Kirkland, William Ashe 1836-1898 *ApCAB Sup, TwCBDA*
Kirkland, Winifred Margaretta 1872-1943 *WhAm 2, WomWWA 14*
Kirklin, Byrl Raymond 1888-1957 *NatCAB 45, WhAm 3*
Kirklin, Henry 1858- *WhoColR*
Kirkman, Marshall Monroe 1842-1921 *ApCAB, DcAmB, NatCAB 3, TwCBDA, WhAm 1*
Kirkman, Ralph 1883-1955 *NatCAB 45*
Kirkman, Thomas Penyngton 1806-1895 *DcScB*
Kirkpatrick, Andrew 1756-1831 *ApCAB, ApCAB X, BiAUS, DcAmB, Drake, NatCAB 12, TwCBDA, WhAm H*
Kirkpatrick, Andrew 1844-1904 *ApCAB Sup, TwCBDA, WhAm 1*
Kirkpatrick, Blaine Evron 1887-1959 *WhAm 3*
Kirkpatrick, Carlos Stevens 1881-1957 *WhAm 3*
Kirkpatrick, Clifford 1855-1918 *NatCAB 17*
Kirkpatrick, Clifford 1898-1971 *WhAm 5*
Kirkpatrick, Edwin Asbury 1862-1937 *BiDAmEd, NatCAB 37, WhAm 1*
Kirkpatrick, Elbert Marion 1870-1916 *NatCAB 17*
Kirkpatrick, Elbert W 1844-1924 *WhAm 1*
Kirkpatrick, Florence Wynn 1880- *WomWWA 14*
Kirkpatrick, George Airey 1841- *ApCAB*
Kirkpatrick, George Holland 1880-1968 *WhAm 5*
Kirkpatrick, George Ross 1867-1937 *NatCAB 27*
Kirkpatrick, Ivone Elliott *WhAm 4*
Kirkpatrick, Jane Bayard 1772-1851 *ApCAB*
Kirkpatrick, John Bayard 1872- *NatCAB 10*
Kirkpatrick, John Lycan 1813-1885 *ApCAB, TwCBDA*
Kirkpatrick, John Milton 1825-1898 *NatCAB 8*
Kirkpatrick, Lee 1874-1958 *NatCAB 44*
Kirkpatrick, Leonard Henry 1907-1962 *WhAm 4*
Kirkpatrick, Lex Jackson 1853-1926 *NatCAB 20*
Kirkpatrick, Littleton 1797-1859 *ApCAB, BiAUS, BiDrAC, TwCBDA*
Kirkpatrick, Marion Powers *WomWWA 14*
Kirkpatrick, Mattie Gaston *WomWWA 14*
Kirkpatrick, Richard Llewellyn 1817-1879 *TwCBDA*
Kirkpatrick, Sanford 1842-1932 *BiDrAC, WhAm 4*
Kirkpatrick, Sidney Dale 1894-1973 *WhAm 5*
Kirkpatrick, Snyder Solomon 1848-1909 *BiDrAC*
Kirkpatrick, Thomas LeRoy 1877-1946 *WhAm 2*
Kirkpatrick, Villie Black 1881-1947 *NatCAB 36*
Kirkpatrick, William 1768-1832 *BiAUS*
Kirkpatrick, William 1769-1832 *BiDrAC, WhAm H*
Kirkpatrick, William Dawson 1887-1961 *WhAm 4*
Kirkpatrick, William Huntington 1885-1970 *BiDrAC, WhAm 5*
Kirkpatrick, William James 1838-1921 *WhAm 1*
Kirkpatrick, William Sebring 1844-1932 *ApCAB Sup, BiDrAC, NatCAB 8, TwCBDA, WhAm 1*
Kirkus, William 1830-1907 *WhAm 1*
Kirkwood, Arthur Carter 1900-1970 *WhAm 5*
Kirkwood, Daniel 1814-1895 *AmBi, ApCAB, AsBiEn, DcAmB, DcScB, NatCAB 4, TwCBDA, WhAm H*
Kirkwood, Edith Brown *WomWWA 14*
Kirkwood, Irwin Russell 1878-1927 *NatCAB 22, WhAm 1*
Kirkwood, James Pugh 1807-1877 *ApCAB, NatCAB 9*
Kirkwood, John Gamble 1907-1959 *DcScB, WhAm 3*
Kirkwood, Joseph Edward 1872-1928 *WhAm 1*

Kirkwood, Robert 1730-1791 *ApCAB, Drake*
Kirkwood, Robert 1793-1866 *ApCAB*
Kirkwood, Samuel Jordan 1813-1894 *AmBi, ApCAB, BiAUS, BiDrAC, DcAmB, NatCAB 4, NatCAB 11, TwCBDA, WhAm H, WhAmP*
Kirkwood, Samuel Jordon 1813-1894 *BiDrUSE*
Kirkwood, William Reeside 1837- *TwCBDA, WhAm 4*
Kirlin, Joseph Louis Jerome 1868-1926 *DcAmB*
Kirn, George John 1863- *WhAm 4*
Kirner, Walter Raymond 1895-1972 *NatCAB 57*
Kiroack, Howard 1888-1951 *WhAm 3*
Kirponos, Mikhail 1892-1941 *WhWW-II*
Kirsch, John Nicholas 1903-1964 *NatCAB 51, WhAm 4*
Kirschbaum, Arthur 1910-1958 *WhAm 3*
Kirschbaum, Edward Harry 1888-1969 *NatCAB 55*
Kirschen, Sidney 1909-1959 *NatCAB 47*
Kirschner, Don Stuart 1928- *EncAAH*
Kirshman, John Emmett 1883-1945 *WhAm 2*
Kirshner, Charles Henry 1863-1938 *WhAm 2*
Kirstein, Arthur 1893-1959 *WhAm 4*
Kirstein, Louis Edward 1867-1942 *DcAmB S3, WhAm 2*
Kirstein, Max 1897-1969 *WhAm 5*
Kirtland, Dorrance 1770-1840 *BiAUS, BiDrAC, WhAm H*
Kirtland, Fred Durrell 1892-1972 *WhAm 5*
Kirtland, Mrs. Ira Bushnell 1860- *WomWWA 14*
Kirtland, Jared Potter 1793-1877 *ApCAB, DcAmB, NatCAB 11, TwCBDA, WhAm H*
Kirtland, John Copeland 1870-1951 *WhAm 3*
Kirtland, Lucian Swift 1881-1965 *WhAm 4*
Kirtley, James Addison, Jr. 1905-1968 *NatCAB 55*
Kirtley, James Samuel *WhAm 3*
Kirwan, Albert Dennis 1904-1971 *NatCAB 57, WhAm 5*
Kirwan, Michael Joseph 1886-1970 *BiDrAC, WhAm 5*
Kirwan, Richard 1733?-1812 *DcScB*
Kirwin, Thomas Joseph 1891-1959 *NatCAB 48, WhAm 3*
Kisch, Bruno Zacharias 1890-1966 *NatCAB 55*
Kiselev, Evgeny Dmitrievich 1908-1963 *WhAm 4*
Kiser, Edgar Fayette 1880-1958 *NatCAB 46*
Kiser, George Riley 1828-1910 *ApCAB X*
Kiser, John William 1857-1916 *ApCAB X, NatCAB 17*
Kiser, John William, Jr. 1889- *ApCAB X, NatCAB 17*
Kiser, Louise Venable Kennedy 1895-1954 *NatCAB 42*
Kiser, Samuel Ellsworth d1942 *WhAm 1, WhAm 2*
Kishi, Nobusuke 1896- *McGEWB*
Kiskadden, Maude *WebAB*
Kiskadden, William Sherrill 1894-1969 *NatCAB 55*
Kislingbury, Frederick Foster 1847-1884 *AmBi, ApCAB*
Kisner, Squire Monroe 1883-1960 *NatCAB 47*
Kissam, Henry Snyder 1866-1930 *WhAm 1*
Kissam, Richard Sharpe 1763-1822 *ApCAB, Drake*
Kissel, Eleonora 1891-1966 *IIBEAAW*
Kissel, Gustav Edward 1854-1911 *NatCAB 15*
Kissel, John 1864-1938 *BiDrAC, WhAm 1*
Kissell, Harry Seaman 1875-1946 *WhAm 2*
Kissinger, Henry Alfred 1923- *EncAB, WebAB*
Kissock, John 1851-1918 *NatCAB 17*
Kister, George Raphael 1865- *WhAm 4*
Kistler, John Clinton 1859- *WhAm 1*
Kistler, Raymon M 1891-1965 *WhAm 4*
Kistler, Samuel Stephens 1900-1975 *WhAm 6*
Kistler, Seth Wessner 1873-1946 *NatCAB 35*
Kitaibel, Pal 1757-1817 *DcScB*
Kitasato, Baron Shibasaburo 1852-1931 *DcScB*
Kitasato, Baron Shibasaburo 1856-1931 *AsBiEn*
Kitchel, Aaron 1744-1820 *TwCBDA*
Kitchel, Harvey Denison 1812-1895 *NatCAB 12, TwCBDA*

Kitchel, Horace 1875-1922 *NatCAB 19*
Kitchel, Lloyd 1898-1950 *WhAm 3*
Kitchel, William Lloyd 1869-1947 *WhAm 2*
Kitchell, Aaron 1744-1820 *ApCAB, BiAUS, BiDrAC, NatCAB 11, WhAm H, WhAmP*
Kitchell, John *NewYHSD*
Kitchell, Joseph Gray 1862-1947 *WhAm 2*
Kitchelt, Florence Ledyard Cross 1874- *WomWWA 14*
Kitchen, A Samuel 1875-1946 *NatCAB 40*
Kitchen, Bethuel Middleton 1812-1895 *BiAUS, BiDrAC, WhAm H*
Kitchen, James 1800- *NatCAB 3*
Kitchen, Joseph Ambrose 1878- *WhAm 6*
Kitchen, Karl Kosciusko 1899-1949 *NatCAB 38*
Kitchen, William Gordon 1876-1939 *NatCAB 29*
Kitchener, Horatio Herbert 1850-1916 *McGEWB, WhoMilH*
Kitchens, Wade Hampton 1878-1966 *BiDrAC, WhAm 4*
Kitchin, Alvin Paul 1908- *BiDrAC, WhAmP*
Kitchin, Claude 1869-1923 *BiDrAC, DcAmB, NatCAB 15, WhAm 1, WhAmP*
Kitchin, Thurman Delna 1885-1955 *NatCAB 42, WhAm 3*
Kitchin, William Copeman 1855-1920 *WhAm 1*
Kitchin, William Hodges 1837-1901 *BiDrAC, WhAmP*
Kitchin, William Walton 1866-1924 *BiDrAC, DcAmB, NatCAB 14, TwCBDA, WhAm 1, WhAmP*
Kitching, John Benjamin 1813-1887 *ApCAB*
Kitching, John Howard 1840-1865 *ApCAB, NatCAB 5*
Kite, Edward Everett 1878-1956 *NatCAB 48*
Kite, Elizabeth S 1864- *WomWWA 14*
Kite, Eva Mary 1851- *WomWWA 14*
Kite, William 1810-1900 *TwCBDA*
Kitfield, Philip Hooper 1898-1971 *NatCAB 57*
Kitson, Geoffrey Herbert 1896-1974 *WhAm 6*
Kitson, Harry Dexter 1886-1959 *BiDAmEd, NatCAB 52, WhAm 3*
Kitson, Henry Hudson 1863-1947 *WhAm 2*
Kitson, Henry Hudson 1864-1947 *NatCAB 12*
Kitson, Samuel James 1848-1906 *TwCBDA, WhAm 1*
Kitson, Theo Alice Ruggles 1871-1932 *WhAm 1, WomWWA 14*
Kitt, Randall Reuben 1905-1964 *NatCAB 51*
Kittell, Albert George 1881-1943 *WhAm 2*
Kittell, James Shepard 1873-1937 *WhAm 1*
Kittell, Michael McDonald 1858-1938 *NatCAB 28*
Kittell, Nicholas Biddle 1822-1894 *NewYHSD*
Kittelle, Sumner Ely Wetmore 1867-1950 *NatCAB 44, WhAm 3*
Kittelson, John Henry 1930- *IIBEAAW*
Kittera, John Wilkes d1801 *BiAUS*
Kittera, John Wilkes 1752-1801 *BiDrAC, WhAm H, WhAmP*
Kittera, John Wilkes 1753-1801 *TwCBDA*
Kittera, Thomas 1789-1839 *BiAUS, BiDrAC, TwCBDA, WhAm H, WhAmP*
Kittinger, Harold D 1889-1947 *WhAm 2*
Kittle, Charles Morgan 1880-1928 *WhAm 1*
Kittredge, Abbott Eliot 1834-1912 *WhAm 1*
Kittredge, Alfred Beard 1861-1911 *BiDrAC, NatCAB 12, NatCAB 16, WhAm 1, WhAmP*
Kittredge, Charles James 1893-1944 *NatCAB 34*
Kittredge, Edward Holmes 1888-1943 *NatCAB 33*
Kittredge, Frank Alvah 1883-1954 *WhAm 3*
Kittredge, George Lyman 1860-1941 *DcAmB S3, NatCAB 13, NatCAB 34, WebAB, WhAm 1*
Kittredge, George Washington 1805-1881 *BiAUS, BiDrAC, WhAm H*
Kittredge, George Watson 1856-1947 *NatCAB 15, WhAm 2*
Kittredge, Henry Grattan 1845-1909 *WhAm 1*
Kittredge, Jonathan 1793-1864 *ApCAB*
Kittredge, Josiah Edwards 1836-1913 *NatCAB 7, WhAm 1*
Kittredge, Lewis Harris 1871- *ApCAB X*

Kittredge, Mabel Hyde 1867-1955 *WhAm 3*
Kittredge, Raymond Brown 1886-1956
    NatCAB 45
Kittredge, Thomas 1746-1818 *ApCAB, Drake*
Kittredge, Walter 1834-1905 *WhAm 1*
Kittredge, Wheaton 1882-1936 *WhAm 1*
Kittrell, Norman Goree 1849- *WhAm 1*
Kittrell, Thomas Fleming 1870-1951
    NatCAB 38
Kittridge, Walter 1834- *ApCAB Sup*
Kitts, Harriet Elizabeth Walrath
    WomWWA 14
Kitts, Joseph Arthur 1881-1947 *WhAm 2*
Kitts, Willard Augustus, III 1894-1964
    WhAm 4
Kittson, Norman Wolfred 1814-1888 *DcAmB,
    REnAW, WhAm H*
Kivel, John 1855-1924 *WhAm 1*
Kivette, Frederick Norman 1902-1975 *WhAm 6*
Kivlin, Vincent Earl 1896-1967 *WhAm 5*
Kiwanuka, Benedicto Kagima Mugumba 1922-
    McGEWB
Kixmiller, Edgar Byron 1885-1974 *WhAm 6*
KixMiller, William 1885-1945 *WhAm 2*
Kizer, Benjamin Hamilton 1878- *WhAm 6*
Kizer, Charles Graham 1867-1944 *NatCAB 33*
Kjeldahl, Johann Gustav Christoffer 1849-1900
    DcScB
Kjellgren, Bengt Ragnar Fritiof 1894-1968
    NatCAB 55, WhAm 5
Kjerstad, Conrad Lund 1883-1967 *WhAm 6*
Kjoeping, Olaus 1741-1809 *ApCAB*
Klaber, Eugene Henry 1883-1971 *WhAm 5*
Klabunde, Earl Horace 1909-1968 *WhAm 5*
Klaeber, Frederick 1863- *WhAm 4*
Klaebisch, Louis *NewYHSD*
Klaerner, Richard Albert 1908-1966 *WhAm 4*
Klaestad, Helge 1885-1965 *WhAm 4*
Klaffenbach, Arthur O 1880-1963 *WhAm 4*
Klain, Zora 1884-1952 *WhAm 3*
Klak, John James 1900-1966 *NatCAB 51*
Klammer, Aloysius A 1889-1953 *WhAm 3*
Klapp, Elinor Evans 1848- *WomWWA 14*
Klapp, Eugene 1867-1938 *NatCAB 28*
Klapp, Lyman 1827- *NatCAB 13*
Klapp, William Henry 1849-1924 *WhAm 1*
Klapper, Paul 1885-1952 *BiDAmEd, WhAm 3*
Klaproth, Martin Heinrich 1743-1817 *AsBiEn,
    DcScB*
Klare, Robert Edward 1905-1966 *WhAm 4*
Klaren, John Hugo 1867-1929 *NatCAB 22*
Klarmann, Adolf D 1904-1975 *WhAm 6*
Klath, Thormod Oscar 1890-1943 *WhAm 2*
Klauber, Adolph 1869-1933 *WhAm 1*
Klauber, Edward 1887-1954 *WhAm 3*
Klauber, Laurence Monroe 1883-1968
    NatCAB 54, WhAm 5
Klauder, Charles Zeller 1872-1938 *DcAmB S2,
    NatCAB 29, WhAm 1*
Klauder, Jacob *NewYHSD*
Klaus, Irving Goncer 1900-1969 *WhAm 5*
Klauser, Karl 1823-1905 *NatCAB 7, WhAm 1*
Klausmeyer, David Michael 1902-1970
    WhAm 5
Klauss, William George 1877-1940 *NatCAB 30*
Klaw, Marc 1858-1936 *AmBi, DcAmB S2,
    WhAm 1*
Klawans, Arthur Herman 1902-1973 *WhAm 6*
Klebenov, Louis H 1901-1974 *WhAm 6*
Kleber, Jean Baptiste 1753-1800 *WhoMilH*
Kleber, Luther Aaron 1897-1966 *NatCAB 52*
Kleberg, Edward Robert 1877-1957 *WhAm 3*
Kleberg, Richard Mifflin, Sr. 1887-1955 *BiDrAC,
    WhAm 3, WhAmP*
Kleberg, Robert Justus, Jr. 1896-1974 *WhAm 6*
Kleberg, Rudolph 1847-1924 *BiDrAC,
    TwCBDA, WhAm 1, WhAmP*
Klebs, Arnold Carl 1870-1943 *WhAm 2*
Klebs, Edwin 1834-1913 *AmBi, BiHiMed*
Klebs, Georg Albrecht 1857-1918 *DcScB*
Klecki, Paul 1900-1973 *WhAm 6*
Kleckner, Martin Seler 1890-1958 *WhAm 3*
Kleczka, John Casimir 1885-1959 *BiDrAC*
Klee, Paul 1879-1940 *McGEWB*
Kleeberg, Minna 1841-1878 *ApCAB*
Kleegman, Sophia Josephine 1901-1971
    WhAm 5
Kleeman, Arthur S 1889-1965 *WhAm 4*

Kleeman, Benton Frederick 1869-1934
    NatCAB 26
Kleene, Gustav Adolph 1868-1946 *WhAm 2*
Kleiber, Hans 1887-1967 *IIBEAAW*
Klein, Arthur George 1904-1968 *BiDrAC,
    WhAm 4A*
Klein, Arthur Warner 1880- *WhAm 6*
Klein, August *NewYHSD*
Klein, August Clarence 1887-1948 *DcAmB S4*
Klein, Bruno Oscar 1858-1911 *DcAmB,
    WhAm 1*
Klein, Charles 1867-1915 *AmBi, DcAmB,
    NatCAB 24, WhAm 1*
Klein, Christian Felix 1849-1925 *DcScB*
Klein, Clarence Charles 1899-1954 *NatCAB 40*
Klein, Eugene S 1876- *WhAm 2*
Klein, Francis Joseph 1911-1968 *WhAm 5*
Klein, Fred 1859-1943 *NatCAB 33*
Klein, Frederick Benjamin 1886-1950
    NatCAB 39, WhAm 3
Klein, Frederick Charles 1857-1926 *WhAm 1*
Klein, George H 1880- *WhAm 6*
Klein, Gerald Brown 1902-1968 *WhAm 5*
Klein, Gustav Frederic 1708-1771 *ApCAB*
Klein, Harry Martin John 1873-1965
    NatCAB 51, WhAm 5
Klein, Harry Thomas 1886-1965 *WhAm 4*
Klein, Henry Weber 1918-1969 *WhAm 5*
Klein, Herman William 1889-1956 *WhAm 3*
Klein, Hermann 1856- *WhAm 4*
Klein, Hermann Joseph 1844-1914 *DcScB*
Klein, Horace C 1876-1963 *WhAm 4*
Klein, Jacob 1845-1910 *WhAm 1*
Klein, Jacob Theodor 1685-1759 *DcScB*
Klein, John Warren 1872-1957 *WhAm 3*
Klein, Joseph Frederic 1849-1918 *DcAmB,
    NatCAB 18, WhAm 1*
Klein, Joseph J d1975 *WhAm 6*
Klein, Julius 1886-1961 *WhAm 4*
Klein, Manuel 1876-1919 *WhAm 1*
Klein, Mathias Anthony 1905-1966 *NatCAB 53*
Klein, Melanie 1882-1960 *McGEWB,
    WhAm 5*
Klein, Murray 1891-1950 *NatCAB 38*
Klein, Oscar Peter 1894-1950 *NatCAB 42*
Klein, Samuel 1855-1950 *NatCAB 39*
Klein, Sandor Sidney 1906-1970 *WhAm 5*
Klein, Simon Robert 1868- *WhAm 4*
Klein, William 1884-1954 *NatCAB 47*
Klein, William, Jr. 1917-1971 *NatCAB 57,
    WhAm 5*
Klein, William M 1878-1965 *WhAm 4*
Kleinenberg, Nicolaus 1842-1897 *DcScB*
Kleiner, Charles 1854-1943 *NatCAB 33*
Kleiner, Hugo Gustav 1897-1963 *WhAm 5*
Kleiner, Israel S 1885-1966 *WhAm 4*
Kleiner, John Jay 1845-1911 *BiDrAC*
Kleinofen, Henry *NewYHSD*
Kleinpell, William Darwin 1898-1959 *WhAm 3*
Kleinschmidt, Edward Ernst 1875- *WhAm 6*
Kleinschmidt, Rudolph August 1878-1947
    NatCAB 38, WhAm 2
Kleinsmid, Rufus Bernard Von 1875-1964
    WhAm 4
Kleinstuck, Caroline I Hubbard 1855-
    WomWWA 14
Kleiser, George William 1874-1952 *WhAm 3*
Kleiser, Grenville 1868-1953 *WhAm 3*
Kleiser, Lorentz 1879-1963 *WhAm 4*
Kleist, Ewald Georg Von 1700?-1748 *DcScB*
Kleist, Heinrich Von 1777-1811 *McGEWB*
Kleist, James Aloysius 1873-1949 *WhAm 3*
Kleist, Paul Ewald Von 1881-1954 *WhWW-II,
    WhoMilH*
Kleitz, William L 1894-1957 *WhAm 3*
Klem, William J 1874-1951 *DcAmB S5*
Klemin, Alexander 1888-1950 *WhAm 3*
Klemm, Louis Richard 1845-1916 *WhAm 1*
Klemme, Edward Julius 1875- *WhAm 5*
Klemme, Gottlieb Dietrich 1861-1941
    NatCAB 33
Klemme, Maurice Gottlieb 1888-1952
    NatCAB 41
Klemme, Randall Telford 1911- *WhAm 6*
Klemme, Roland Metzler 1896-1957
    NatCAB 50, WhAm 3
Klemperer, Otto 1885-1973 *WhAm 5*
Klendshoj, Niels Christian 1902-1975 *WhAm 6*

Klenk, Sophie Gottliebe *WomWWA 14*
Klenke, William Walter 1888-1961 *WhAm 4*
Klenner, Richard Matthew 1911-1966
    NatCAB 53
Klepetko, Frank 1856- *WhAm 4*
Kleppe, Thomas Savig 1919- *BiDrAC*
Klepper, Frank B 1864-1933 *BiDrAC,
    WhAm 3*
Klepper, Frank Earl 1890- *IIBEAAW*
Klepper, Max Francis 1861-1907 *NatCAB 12,
    WhAm 1*
Klett, George Washington 1874-1926
    NatCAB 6
Kletting, Richard Karl August 1858-1943
    NatCAB 33
Kletzki, Paul 1900-1973 *WhAm 5*
Kletzsch, Gustave Adolph 1857- *NatCAB 10*
Kleymeyer, Henry Charles 1872-1950
    NatCAB 42
Klibanow, William J 1900-1969 *WhAm 5*
Klieforth, Ralph George 1901-1966 *WhAm 4*
Kliegl, Anton Tiberius 1872-1927 *ApCAB X*
Klien, Arthur Jay 1884-1957 *WhAm 3*
Klies, Ed 1890-1950 *NatCAB 50*
Kliewer, John Walter 1869-1938 *WhAm 1*
Klika, Ervin Robert 1905-1962 *WhAm 4*
Klimas, John Edward 1927-1975 *WhAm 6*
Klimm, Lester E 1902-1960 *WhAm 4*
Klinck, Arthur William 1900-1959 *WhAm 3*
Klinck, Leonard Silvanus 1877- *WhAm 5*
Klinckowstrom, Axel Leonhard 1775-1837
    NewYHSD
Klindworth, Edward Claus 1897-1966
    NatCAB 53
Kline, Allan Blair 1895-1968 *WhAm 5*
Kline, Allen Marshall 1881- *WhAm 6*
Kline, Ardolph Loges 1858-1930 *BiDrAC,
    WhAm 1*
Kline, Barton Leeorie 1901-1975 *WhAm 6*
Kline, C Mahlon 1880-1967 *NatCAB 53,
    WhAm 4*
Kline, Charles Demarest 1866-1937 *NatCAB 34*
Kline, Charles H 1870-1933 *WhAm 1*
Kline, Effie Ober 1843- *WomWWA 14*
Kline, Elmer Merle 1897-1967 *NatCAB 54*
Kline, Fannie Talbot Littleton 1869-
    WomWWA 14
Kline, Frances Talbot Littleton 1869- *BiCAW*
Kline, Franz 1910-1962 *BnEnAmA, McGEWB*
Kline, Franz Josef 1910-1962 *EncAB*
Kline, Franz Joseph 1919-1962 *WebAB*
Kline, George 1757?-1800 *WhAm H*
Kline, George 1757?-1820 *DcAmB*
Kline, George Milton 1878- *WhAm 1*
Kline, George Washington 1864-1922 *WhAm 1*
Kline, I Clinton 1858-1947 *WhAm 3*
Kline, Ira M 1880- *WhAm 6*
Kline, Isaac Clinton 1858-1947 *BiDrAC*
Kline, Jacob 1840-1908 *ApCAB Sup,
    TwCBDA, WhAm 1*
Kline, John Robert 1891-1955 *NatCAB 45,
    WhAm 3*
Kline, Marcus Charles Lawrence 1855-1911
    BiDrAC, WhAm 1
Kline, Marion Justus 1871-1934 *WhAm 1*
Kline, Mary Frances 1842- *WomWWA 14*
Kline, Paul Robert 1907-1970 *WhAm 5*
Kline, Quentin McKay 1900- *WhAm 6*
Kline, Raymond Albright 1886-1948
    NatCAB 40
Kline, Virgil Philip 1844-1917 *WhAm 1*
Kline, Walter Winter 1899-1975 *WhAm 6*
Kline, Webster Harnish 1881-1951 *NatCAB 42*
Kline, Whorten Albert 1864-1946 *WhAm 2*
Kline, William Fair 1870-1931 *NatCAB 13,
    WhAm 1*
Kline, William Jay 1848-1930 *WhAm 1*
Klinefelter, Howard Emanuel 1902-1956
    WhAm 3
Kling, Catherine A *WomWWA 14*
Kling, Charles Fergus 1913-1972 *WhAm 6*
Kling, Philip *NewYHSD*
Klingaman, Orie Erb 1874-1941 *WhAm 1*
Klingbiel, Ray I 1901-1973 *WhAm 5*
Klinge, Ernest F 1889-1952 *WhAm 3*
Klingelsmith, Margaret Center 1859-1931
    DcAmB, WomWWA 14
Klingensmith, John, Jr. 1785- *BiAUS, BiDrAC,*

WhAm H
Klingenstein, Henry Selly 1907-1960
NatCAB 48
Klingenstierna, Samuel 1698-1765 DcScB
Klinger, William August 1888-1971 NatCAB 56
Klinginsmith, John Glenn 1890-1947
NatCAB 41
Klingler, Harry J 1889-1966 WhAm 4
Klingman, William 1880- WhAm 6
Klingsohr, John Augustus 1746-1798 ApCAB
Klink, Jane Seymour 1855- WomWWA 14
Klinker, Orpha 1895?-1964 IIBEAAW
Klippart, John Hancock 1823-1878 DcAmB,
NatCAB 17, WhAm H
Klipstein, Ernest Carl 1866-1931 WhAm 1
Klipstein, Louis Frederick 1813-1878 DcAmB,
WhAm H
Klock, John Nellis 1865-1938 NatCAB 32
Klock, Mabie Crouse 1880-1955 NatCAB 41,
WhAm 3
Kloeb, Frank LeBlond 1890-1975 BiDrAC
Kloeber, Charles Edward 1869-1933 WhAm 1
Kloeffler, Royce Gerald 1890-1975 WhAm 6
Kloman, Erasmus Helm 1884-1957 NatCAB 47
Kloman, William Christopher 1876-1951
NatCAB 38
Klopman, William 1900-1974 WhAm 6
Klopp, Edward Jonathan 1880-1936 WhAm 1
Klopp, Henry Irwin 1870-1945 WhAm 2
Klopsch, Louis 1852-1910 AmBi, DcAmB,
WhAm 1
Klopstock, Friedrich Gottlieb 1724-1803
McGEWB
Klose, Nelson 1914- EncAAH
Kloss, Charles Luther 1862-1931 WhAm 1
Kloss, Gene 1903- IIBEAAW
Klossner, Howard Jacob 1889-1965 WhAm 4
Klots, Allen Trafford 1889-1965 WhAm 4
Klots, Henry Durell 1863-1914 NatCAB 33
Klotz, Hermann Gustav 1844-1928 NatCAB 22
Klotz, Oskar 1878-1936 WhAm 1
Klotz, Robert 1819-1895 BiDrAC, NatCAB 3,
TwCBDA, WhAm H
Klotzburger, Edwin Carl 1906-1966 WhAm 4
Kluber, Melchior 1713-1764 ApCAB
Klubertanz, George Peter 1912-1972 WhAm 5
Kluck, Alexander Von 1846-1934 WhoMilH
Kluckhohn, Clyde Kay Maben 1905-1960
McGEWB, REnAW, WhAm 4
Kluckholn, Frank Louis 1907-1970 WhAm 5
Kluczynski, John Carl 1896-1975 BiDrAC,
WhAm 6
Klug, Norman Robert 1905-1966 NatCAB 53,
WhAm 4
Kluge, Albert Carl 1892-1956 NatCAB 42
Kluge, Gunther Von 1882-1944 WhWW-II,
WhoMilH
Klugel, Georg Simon 1739-1812 DcScB
Klugescheid, Richard Charles 1889-1968
WhAm 5
Klugh, Paul Brown 1878-1941 NatCAB 30
Klugherz, John Anthony 1900-1953 WhAm 3
Klumpke, Anna Elizabeth 1856-1942
NatCAB 31
Klumpke, Dorothea 1861- NatCAB 13
Klumpke, John Gerard 1825-1916 NatCAB 31
Klumpkey, Julia NatCAB 31
Klumpp, Carl Spannagel 1883-1947 NatCAB 35
Klumpp, John Bartleman 1871-1955
NatCAB 44
Klumpp, William 1828?- NewYHSD
Kluss, Charles LaVerne 1912-1967 WhAm 4
Kluttz, Theodore Franklin 1848-1918 BiDrAC,
TwCBDA, WhAm 1
Kluttz, Whitehead 1881- WhAm 6
Kluyver, Albert Jan 1888-1956 DcScB,
WhAm 3
Klyce, Scudder 1879-1933 NatCAB 25,
WhAm 1
Klyuchevsky, Vasily Osipovich 1841-1911
McGEWB
Klyver, Henry Peter 1860- WhAm 4
Knab, Frederick 1865-1918 DcAmB,
NatCAB 24
Knabe, Lula Cates WomWWA 14
Knabe, Valentine Wilhelm Ludwig 1803-1864
DcAmB, WhAm H
Knabe, William 1803-1864 NatCAB 11

Knabenshue, Paul 1883-1942 WhAm 1,
WhAm 2
Knabenshue, Roy 1876-1960 WhAm 3
Knabenshue, Samuel S 1845-1926 WhAm 1
Knaebel, Ernest 1872-1947 WhAm 2
Knap, Joseph Moss 1837- NatCAB 10
Knaplund, Paul Alexander 1885-1964 WhAm 4
Knapp, A Blair 1905-1968 WhAm 5
Knapp, Adeline 1860- WhAm 1
Knapp, Andrew Stephen 1892-1961 WhAm 4
Knapp, Annie Miller 1867- WomWWA 14
Knapp, Anthony Lausett 1828-1881 BiAUS,
BiDrAC, WhAm H
Knapp, Arnold Herman 1869-1956 WhAm 3
Knapp, Arthur Mason 1839-1898 TwCBDA
Knapp, Arthur May 1841- WhAm 4
Knapp, Bliss d1958 WhAm 3
Knapp, Bradford 1870-1938 DcAmB S2,
NatCAB 29, NatCAB 34, WhAm 1
Knapp, Charles 1797-1880 BiAUS, BiDrAC,
WhAm H
Knapp, Charles 1868-1936 AmBi, WhAm 1
Knapp, Charles Junius 1845-1916 BiDrAC
Knapp, Charles Luman 1847-1929 BiDrAC,
WhAm 1
Knapp, Charles W 1823-1900 NewYHSD
Knapp, Charles Welbourne 1848-1916
NatCAB 12, NatCAB 18, TwCBDA,
WhAm 1
Knapp, Charles Whittemore 1885-1953
NatCAB 44
Knapp, Chauncey Langdon 1809-1898 BiAUS,
BiDrAC, NatCAB 11, TwCBDA,
WhAm H
Knapp, Clarence Albert 1846-1918 NatCAB 18
Knapp, Cleon Talboys 1882-1953 WhAm 3
Knapp, Ella Adelaide 1861- WomWWA 14
Knapp, Elwin Duane 1887-1969 NatCAB 55
Knapp, Francis 1672-1715? ApCAB
Knapp, Francis Atherton 1907-1969 WhAm 5
Knapp, Frank Averill 1901-1963 WhAm 4
Knapp, Frank Norris 1891-1962 NatCAB 49
Knapp, Fred Church 1865-1943 WhAm 2
Knapp, George 1814-1883 DcAmB,
NatCAB 19, WhAm H
Knapp, George Kasson 1833-1910 NewYHSD
Knapp, George Leonard 1872- WhAm 5
Knapp, George Nelson 1867-1948 NatCAB 39
Knapp, George Selick 1884-1965 NatCAB 51
Knapp, Gertrude Allen WomWWA 14
Knapp, Grace Higley 1870- WhAm 5
Knapp, Harold Everard 1867- WhAm 4
Knapp, Harold Jennings 1887-1955 NatCAB 45
Knapp, Harry Shepard 1856-1923 NatCAB 20,
WhAm 1
Knapp, Henry Alonzo 1851-1931 NatCAB 10,
NatCAB 25, WhAm 1
Knapp, Herman 1832-1911 DcAmB, WhAm 1
Knapp, Herman 1863-1935 WhAm 1
Knapp, Isaac 1804-1843 NatCAB 2
Knapp, Jacob 1799-1874 ApCAB
Knapp, Jacob Hermann 1832- ApCAB
Knapp, John 1816-1888 NatCAB 12
Knapp, John Joseph 1857-1915 WhAm 1
Knapp, John Rudolph 1869-1959 NatCAB 50
Knapp, Joseph F NewYHSD
Knapp, Joseph Fairchild 1832-1891 ApCAB X,
NatCAB 24
Knapp, Joseph G BiAUS
Knapp, Joseph Palmer 1864-1951 DcAmB S5,
NatCAB 39, WhAm 3
Knapp, Kemper K 1860-1944 WhAm 2
Knapp, Lyman Enos 1837-1904 NatCAB 12,
TwCBDA, WhAm 1
Knapp, Martha Severance 1827-1928 IIBEAAW
Knapp, Martin Augustine 1843-1923 DcAmB,
NatCAB 4, WhAm 1
Knapp, Mathias 1752-1814 ApCAB
Knapp, Patricia L Bryan 1914-1972 DcAmLiB
Knapp, Philip Coombs 1858-1920 DcAmB,
NatCAB 24, WhAm 1
Knapp, Phoebe Palmer 1839- AmWom
Knapp, Robert Hampden 1915-1974 WhAm 6
Knapp, Robert McCarty 1831-1889 BiAUS,
BiDrAC
Knapp, Robert Talbot 1899-1957 NatCAB 50,
WhAm 3
Knapp, Samuel Lorenzo 1774-1838 NatCAB 7

Knapp, Samuel Lorenzo 1783-1838 AmBi,
ApCAB, DcAmB, Drake, TwCBDA,
WhAm H
Knapp, Seaman Asahel 1833-1911 AmBi,
BiDAmEd, DcAmB, EncAAH, McGEWB,
NatCAB 28, TwCBDA, WhAm 1
Knapp, Shepherd 1873-1946 WhAm 2
Knapp, Stanley Merrill 1894-1965 WhAm 4
Knapp, Thad Johnson 1876-1933 WhAm 1
Knapp, Thomas McCartan 1890-1965 WhAm 4
Knapp, Walter I 1899-1971 WhAm 5
Knapp, Willard A 1885-1964 WhAm 4
Knapp, William, Jr. NewYHSD
Knapp, William Ireland 1835-1908 DcAmB,
NatCAB 24, WhAm 1
Knappe, Adolph Herman 1888-1964
NatCAB 50
Knappen, Loyal Edwin 1854-1930 NatCAB 28,
WhAm 1
Knappen, Theodore Macfarlane 1871-1938
WhAm 1
Knappen, Theodore Temple 1900-1951
DcAmB S5
Knappenberg, Charles William 1885-1952
NatCAB 42
Knappenberger, J William 1848- WhAm 4
Knappertsbusch, Hans 1888-1965 WhAm 4
Knaths, Karl 1891-1971 BnEnAmA, WhAm 5
Knaths, Otto Karl 1891-1971 IIBEAAW
Knauer, Guy Waldo 1889-1963 NatCAB 49
Knauer, Philip Sheridan 1870-1952 NatCAB 42
Knauf, Arthur John 1885-1963 NatCAB 50
Knauf, Arthur Raymond 1890-1965 NatCAB 51
Knauff, Christian 1841-1916 NatCAB 18
Knaufft, Ernest 1864- WhAm 4
Knauss, Francis Jacob 1884-1968 NatCAB 54
Knauss, Harold Paul 1900-1963 WhAm 4
Knauss, William 1869-1951 NatCAB 41
Knauth, Arnold Whitman 1890-1960
NatCAB 45, WhAm 4
Knauth, Oswald Whitman 1887-1962 WhAm 4
Knauth, Percival 1851-1900 NatCAB 26
Knauth, Theodore Whitman 1885-1962
NatCAB 49
Kneass, George Bryan 1897-1971 WhAm 5
Kneass, Samuel Honeyman 1806-1858 DcAmB,
NatCAB 25, NewYHSD, WhAm H
Kneass, Strickland 1821-1884 ApCAB, DcAmB,
WhAm H
Kneass, Strickland Landis 1861-1928
NatCAB 39, WhAm 1
Kneass, William 1780-1840 DcAmB,
NatCAB 25, NewYHSD, WhAm H
Knecht, Andrew Wilson 1907-1973 WhAm 6
Knecht, Karl Kae 1883-1972 WhAm 5
Knee, Gina 1898- IIBEAAW
Kneedler, William L 1856- WhAm 4
Kneeland, Abner 1774-1844 ApCAB, DcAmB,
Drake, NatCAB 24, TwCBDA, WhAm H
Kneeland, George Jackson 1872- WhAm 5
Kneeland, Horace 1808?-1860? NewYHSD
Kneeland, Robert Shepherd 1883-1971 WhAm 5
Kneeland, Samuel 1696-1769 ApCAB, Drake
Kneeland, Samuel 1697-1769 DcAmB,
NatCAB 25
Kneeland, Samuel 1698-1769 WhAm H
Kneeland, Samuel 1821-1888 AmBi, ApCAB,
DcAmB, Drake, NatCAB 26, TwCBDA,
WhAm H
Kneeland, Stillman Foster 1845-1926 DcAmB,
NatCAB 7, WhAm 1
Kneeland, Yale 1901-1970 WhAm 5
Knefler, Cynthelia Isgrig 1872- WomWWA 14
Kneifel, Lulu Phelps 1875- WomWWA 14
Kneil, Caroline 1860- WomWWA 14
Kneil, Robert Chipman 1892-1966 WhAm 4
Kneip, Herbert Joseph 1888-1955 WhAm 3
Kneipp, G NewYHSD
Kneisel, Franz 1865-1926 AmBi, ApCAB X,
DcAmB, NatCAB 14, WhAm 1
Kneiss, Gilbert Harold 1899-1964 WhAm 4
Kneivih, Ot NewYHSD
Knelzow, Minnie L 1872- WomWWA 14
Knepper, Edwin Garfield 1886-1962
NatCAB 48, WhAm 4
Knerr, Calvin Brobst 1847-1940 NatCAB 30
Knerr, Harold Hering 1882-1949 NatCAB 40,
NatCAB 47

Kneser, Adolf 1862-1930 *DcScB*
Knevels, Gertrude 1881-1962 *WhAm 4*
Knibbs, Harry Herbert 1874-1945 *WhAm 2*
Knickerbacker, David Buel 1833-1894
  NatCAB 3, TwCBDA
Knickerbocker, Charles E *NewYHSD*
Knickerbocker, David Buel 1833-1894 *ApCAB*
Knickerbocker, Fred Hugh 1875-1955 *WhAm 3*
Knickerbocker, Harmen Jansen 1650?-1720?
  WhAm H
Knickerbocker, Herman 1779-1855 *BiDrAC,*
  DcAmB, WhAm H
Knickerbocker, Herman 1780-1855 *BiAUS*
Knickerbocker, Herman 1782-1855 *ApCAB,*
  NatCAB 11, TwCBDA
Knickerbocker, Herman Jansen 1650?-1716?
  AmBi
Knickerbocker, Hubert Renfro 1898-1949
  WhAm 2
Knickerbocker, Johannes 1749-1827? *ApCAB*
Knickerbocker, William E 1885-1960 *WhAm 4*
Knickerbocker, William Herrick 1853-1937
  NatCAB 27
Knickerbocker, William Skinkle 1892-1972
  WhAm 5
Kniess, Lydia Hebron *WomWWA 14*
Kniffin, Frank Charles 1894-1968 *BiDrAC*
Kniffin, William Henry 1874-1951 *NatCAB 40,*
  WhAm 3
Knight, Madam 1666-1727 *AmBi*
Knight, Abner Richard 1885-1957 *NatCAB 46*
Knight, Adele Ferguson 1867- *WhAm 4*
Knight, Albion Williamson 1859-1936
  NatCAB 16, WhAm 1
Knight, Alfred 1874- *WhAm 6*
Knight, Arthur Merrill, Jr. 1914-1971 *WhAm 6*
Knight, Augustus Charles 1877-1958
  NatCAB 48
Knight, Augustus Smith 1864-1948 *NatCAB 36,*
  WhAm 2
Knight, Austin Melvin 1854-1927 *DcAmB,*
  NatCAB 20, NatCAB 24, WebAMB,
  WhAm 1
Knight, Benjamin Brayton 1813-1898 *TwCBDA*
Knight, Charles *NewYHSD*
Knight, Charles 1877- *WhAm 5*
Knight, Charles A *NewYHSD*
Knight, Charles Asher 1864-1924 *NatCAB 6*
Knight, Charles Huntoon 1849-1913
  NatCAB 25
Knight, Charles Landon 1867-1933 *ApCAB X,*
  BiDrAC, NatCAB 18, WhAm 1
Knight, Charles Mellen 1848-1941 *NatCAB 32,*
  WhAm 2
Knight, Charles Prescott 1861- *ApCAB X*
Knight, Charles Robert 1874-1953 *NatCAB 39,*
  WhAm 3
Knight, Clarence A 1853-1911 *NatCAB 11,*
  NatCAB 15, WhAm 1
Knight, Cyrus Frederic 1831-1891 *ApCAB Sup*
Knight, Cyrus Frederick 1831-1891 *NatCAB 11,*
  TwCBDA
Knight, Daniel Ridgeway 1845?-1924 *ApCAB*
Knight, Daniel Ridgway 1840-1924 *AmBi,*
  DcAmB, NewYHSD
Knight, Daniel Ridgway 1845-1924 *NatCAB 13*
Knight, Daniel Ridgway *see also* Knight, Ridgway
Knight, Edgar Wallace 1885-1953 *NatCAB 40*
Knight, Edgar Wallace 1886-1953 *BiDAmEd,*
  WhAm 3
Knight, Edward *NewYHSD*
Knight, Edward Collings 1813-1892 *ApCAB,*
  DcAmB, NatCAB 6, TwCBDA,
  WhAm H
Knight, Edward Henry 1824-1883 *ApCAB,*
  DcAmB, TwCBDA, WhAm H
Knight, Edward Hooker 1854-1948 *WhAm 2*
Knight, Edward Jennings 1864-1908
  NatCAB 14
Knight, Edward Wallace 1866-1939 *WhAm 1*
Knight, Erastus Cole 1857-1923 *NatCAB 12,*
  WhAm 2
Knight, Eric 1897-1943 *NatCAB 40, WhAm 2*
Knight, Ernest Otto 1873-1961 *NatCAB 49*
Knight, Eugene Herbert 1884-1971 *WhAm 5*
Knight, Felix Harrison 1878- *WhAm 6*
Knight, Francis McMaster 1890-1958 *WhAm 3*
Knight, Frank A 1907-1956 *WhAm 3*

Knight, Frank Henry 1877-1962 *NatCAB 51*
Knight, Frank Hyneman 1885-1972 *McGEWB,*
  WhAm 5
Knight, Frederic Butterfield 1891-1948
  WhAm 2
Knight, Frederic Harrison 1859-1922 *WhAm 1*
Knight, Frederick 1791-1849 *ApCAB*
Knight, Frederick Irving 1841-1909 *DcAmB,*
  NatCAB 14, WhAm 1
Knight, Galen Victor 1897-1950 *NatCAB 39*
Knight, George *NewYHSD*
Knight, George Alexander 1851-1916 *WhAm 1*
Knight, George Henry 1855-1912 *NatCAB 15*
Knight, George Laurence 1878-1948 *WhAm 2*
Knight, George Thomson 1850-1911 *WhAm 1*
Knight, George Wells 1858-1932 *NatCAB 12,*
  NatCAB 24, TwCBDA, WhAm 1
Knight, Goodwin 1896-1970 *WhAm 5*
Knight, Grant Cochran 1893-1956 *NatCAB 43,*
  WhAm 3
Knight, Harold Audas 1890-1954 *WhAm 3*
Knight, Harry Clifford 1876-1949 *WhAm 2*
Knight, Harry Edward 1876- *WhAm 5*
Knight, Harry S 1868-1957 *WhAm 3*
Knight, Henry 1830?- *NewYHSD*
Knight, Henry Cogswell 1788?-1835 *ApCAB,*
  Drake
Knight, Henry Cogswell 1789-1835 *DcAmB,*
  WhAm H
Knight, Henry Francis 1874-1948 *NatCAB 37*
Knight, Henry Granger 1878-1942 *WhAm 2*
Knight, Henry Martyn 1827-1880 *NatCAB 15*
Knight, Herbert Miller 1865-1948 *NatCAB 37*
Knight, Horatio Gates 1817-1895 *NatCAB 16*
Knight, Howard Lawton 1881- *WhAm 6*
Knight, Howard Roscoe 1889-1947 *WhAm 2*
Knight, J Lee *NewYHSD*
Knight, J Oliver 1884-1951 *NatCAB 40*
Knight, James 1810-1887 *ApCAB*
Knight, James Ernest 1890-1972 *WhAm 5*
Knight, Jesse 1845-1921 *NatCAB 19*
Knight, Jesse 1850-1905 *NatCAB 14,*
  WhAm 1
Knight, Jesse William 1874-1956 *WhAm 3*
Knight, John 1802?- *NewYHSD*
Knight, John 1871-1955 *WhAm 3*
Knight, John A 1825?- *NewYHSD*
Knight, John George David 1846-1919 *WhAm 1*
Knight, John Thornton 1861-1930 *WhAm 1*
Knight, Jonathan 1777-1858 *NatCAB 11*
Knight, Jonathan 1787-1858 *BiAUS, BiDrAC,*
  DcAmB, WhAm H
Knight, Jonathan 1789-1864 *ApCAB, DcAmB,*
  Drake, NatCAB 12, TwCBDA, WhAm H
Knight, Katharine B *WomWWA 14*
Knight, L Aston 1873-1948 *NatCAB 36,*
  WhAm 2
Knight, Leona Kaiser d1960 *WhAm 4*
Knight, Lucian Lamar 1868-1933 *DcAmB S1,*
  WhAm 1
Knight, Margaret E 1838-1914 *NotAW*
Knight, Mariette Amanda Barnes 1858-
  WomWWA 14
Knight, Milton 1906-1971 *WhAm 5*
Knight, Montgomery 1901-1943 *WhAm 2*
Knight, Nehemiah 1746-1808 *BiAUS, BiDrAC,*
  TwCBDA, WhAm H
Knight, Nehemiah Rice 1780-1854 *ApCAB,*
  BiAUS, BiDrAC, Drake, NatCAB 9,
  TwCBDA, WhAm H, WhAmP
Knight, Nicholas 1861- *WhAm 4*
Knight, Ora Willis 1874-1913 *WhAm 1*
Knight, Otis D 1898-1964 *WhAm 4*
Knight, Paul Kenneth 1893-1957 *NatCAB 46*
Knight, Peter Oliphant 1865-1946 *WhAm 2*
Knight, Rachel 1878- *WomWWA 14*
Knight, Richard 1771-1863 *NatCAB 8*
Knight, Ridgway 1840-1924 *DcAmB,*
  NatCAB 27, WhAm 1
Knight, Robert 1826-1912 *TwCBDA, WhAm 1*
Knight, Robert Palmer 1902-1966 *WhAm 4*
Knight, Robert T 1827?- *NewYHSD*
Knight, Ryland 1876-1955 *WhAm 3*
Knight, Samuel 1730?-1804 *NatCAB 4*
Knight, Samuel 1863-1943 *NatCAB 31,*
  WhAm 2
Knight, Sarah Kemble 1666-1727 *AmBi,*
  ApCAB, DcAmB, Drake, NotAW,

Knight, Stephen Albert 1828-1907 *TwCBDA,*
  WhAm 1
Knight, T *NewYHSD*
Knight, Thomas Andrew 1759-1838 *DcScB*
Knight, Thomas Edmund 1868-1943 *WhAm 2*
Knight, Thomas Edmund, Jr. 1898-1937
  WhAm 1
Knight, Walter David 1891-1959 *WhAm 3*
Knight, Webster 1854-1933 *NatCAB 39,*
  WhAm 1
Knight, Wilbur Clinton 1858-1903 *TwCBDA,*
  WhAm 1
Knight, William Allen 1863-1957 *WhAm 3*
Knight, William Asher 1873-1943 *NatCAB 33*
Knight, William D 1886-1959 *NatCAB 51,*
  WhAm 4
Knight, William Henry 1835-1925 *WhAm 1*
Knighton, Frederick 1812-1888 *NatCAB 6*
Knipe, Alden Arthur 1870-1950 *WhAm 4*
Knipe, Emilie Benson 1870-1958 *WhAm 3*
Knipe, Joseph Farmer 1823- *ApCAB*
Knipers, W *NewYHSD*
Knipling, Edward Fred 1909- *McGEWB*
Knipp, Charles Tobias 1869-1948 *WhAm 2*
Knippenberg, Henry 1843-1924 *NatCAB 23*
Knirsch, Otto *NewYHSD*
Kniskern, Leslie Albert 1900-1961 *WhAm 4*
Kniskern, Philip Wheeler 1889-1961 *WhAm 4*
Kniskern, Warren B 1851-1931 *WhAm 1*
Knobe, Bertha Damaris *WomWWA 14*
Knoblauch, Mary Bookstaver 1873-
  WomWWA 14
Knobloch, Henry F J 1877- *WhAm 5*
Knode, Oliver M d1962 *WhAm 4*
Knode, Ralph Howard 1893-1963 *WhAm 4*
Knoedler, Cyriak *NewYHSD*
Knoizen, Arthur Samuel 1897-1950 *NatCAB 39*
Knoles, Tully Cleon 1876-1959 *WhAm 3*
Knoll, Florence 1917- *BnEnAmA*
Knoll, Hans G 1914-1955 *BnEnAmA,*
  WhAm 3
Knollenberg, Bernhard 1892-1973 *NatCAB 57,*
  WhAm 6
Knollin, Albert Jason 1862-1949 *NatCAB 38*
Knollys, Edward George William Tyrwhitt
  1895-1966 *WhAm 4*
Knollys, Hansard 1598?-1691 *ApCAB*
Knollys, Hanserd 1598-1691 *Drake*
Knoop, Frederic Barnes 1908-1969 *WhAm 5*
Knoote, Josephine Phoebe Eva *WomWWA 14*
Knopf, Adolph 1882-1966 *NatCAB 53,*
  WhAm 4
Knopf, Alfred Abraham 1892- *WebAB*
Knopf, Blanche 1894-1966 *WhAm 4, WhAm 5*
Knopf, Carl Sumner 1889-1942 *WhAm 2*
Knopf, Philip 1847-1920 *BiDrAC, WhAm 4*
Knopf, S Adolphus 1857-1940 *NatCAB 29,*
  WhAm 1
Knopf, William Cleveland, Jr. 1910-1970
  WhAm 5
Knoph, Aden 1843-1917 *NatCAB 17*
Knopp, Herbert William, Sr. 1907-1963
  WhAm 4
Knopp, Konrad 1882-1957 *DcScB*
Knorr, Fred August 1913-1960 *WhAm 4*
Knorr, Frederick August 1913-1960 *NatCAB 47*
Knorr, Georg Wolfgang 1705-1761 *DcScB*
Knorr, George *NewYHSD*
Knorr, Walter Herbert 1908-1973 *WhAm 6*
Knortz, Karl 1841- *ApCAB, NatCAB 10,*
  WhAm 4
Knott, A Leo d1918 *WhAm 1*
Knott, Aloysius Leo 1829-1918 *DcAmB*
Knott, Aloysius Leo 1835-1918 *NatCAB 11*
Knott, Cargill Gilston 1856-1922 *DcScB*
Knott, David H 1879-1954 *WhAm 3*
Knott, Emmet Kennard 1897-1961 *WhAm 4*
Knott, Heber Adelbert 1860-1923 *NatCAB 24*
Knott, J C 1893-1975 *WhAm 6*
Knott, J Proctor 1830-1911 *BiAUS*
Knott, James E 1891-1963 *WhAm 4*
Knott, James Proctor 1830-1911 *AmBi,*
  ApCAB, BiDrAC, DcAmB, NatCAB 13,
  TwCBDA, WhAm 1, WhAmP
Knott, Jane Gillmore 1862- *WomWWA 14*

Knott, John Francis 1878-1963 *WhAm 4*
Knott, Lester R 1895-1962 *WhAm 4*
Knott, Minerva *WomWWA 14*
Knott, Richard Wilson 1849-1917 *WhAm 1*
Knott, Stuart R 1859- *WhAm 4*
Knott, Thomas Albert 1880-1945 *WhAm 2*
Knott, VanBuren 1871- *WhAm 5*
Knott, William John 1882-1951 *NatCAB 40*
Knotts, Armanis F 1856-1937 *WhAm 1*
Knotts, E Paul 1895-1962 *NatCAB 47*
Knotts, Edward C 1863-1933 *WhAm 1*
Knotts, Howard C 1895-1942 *WhAm 2*
Knotts, J Owen 1892-1949 *NatCAB 47*
Knotts, Raymond 1893-1968 *WhAm 5*
Knouff, Ralph Albert 1890-1966 *WhAm 4*
Knous, John 1833-1929 *NatCAB 23*
Knous, William Lee 1889-1959 *WhAm 3*
Knower, Henry McElderry 1868-1940 *WhAm 1*
Knowland, Joseph Russell 1873-1966 *BiDrAC,*
 WhAm 4, WhAmP
Knowland, William Fife 1908-1974 *BiDrAC,*
 WhAm 6
Knowles, Archibald Campbell 1865-1951
 NatCAB 43, WhAm 5
Knowles, Burt LeRoy 1879-1967 *NatCAB 53*
Knowles, Chester Lewis 1894-1972 *NatCAB 57*
Knowles, Daniel Clark 1836-1913 *WhAm 1*
Knowles, Edward Gillett 1892-1969 *WhAm 5*
Knowles, Edward Randall 1861- *WhAm 4*
Knowles, Edwin Blackwell 1903-1967 *WhAm 5*
Knowles, Elizabeth A McGillivray 1866-
 WomWWA 14
Knowles, Ella L 1870- *AmWom*
Knowles, Ellin J 1834-1929 *WhAm 1*
Knowles, Francis Bangs 1823-1890 *NatCAB 29*
Knowles, Frederic Lawrence 1869-1905
 NatCAB 18, TwCBDA, WhAm 1
Knowles, Frederick Milton 1877- *WhAm 5*
Knowles, Freeman Tulley 1846-1910 *BiDrAC*
Knowles, Hiram 1834-1911 *BiAUS, NatCAB 4,*
 WhAm 1
Knowles, Horace Greeley 1863-1913
 NatCAB 14, WhAm 1
Knowles, James Davis 1798-1838 *ApCAB,*
 Drake, NatCAB 8, TwCBDA
Knowles, John d1685 *Drake*
Knowles, John P *BiAUS*
Knowles, Lucius James 1819-1884 *AmBi,*
 ApCAB, DcAmB, NatCAB 5, TwCBDA,
 WhAm H
Knowles, Lucius James 1879-1920 *ApCAB X*
Knowles, Mary Henrietta 1845-1926
 NatCAB 22
Knowles, Melita 1875- *WhAm 5*
Knowles, Morris 1869-1932 *NatCAB 26,*
 WhAm 1
Knowles, Nathaniel 1899-1972 *WhAm 5*
Knowles, Richard George 1858- *NatCAB 14*
Knowles, Robert Bell d1958 *WhAm 3*
Knowles, W L *NewYHSD*
Knowlson, James S 1883-1959 *WhAm 3*
Knowlton, Ansel Alphonse 1875-1957 *WhAm 3*
Knowlton, Archer Eben 1886-1962 *NatCAB 48*
Knowlton, Charles 1800-1850 *DcAmB, EncAB,*
 WhAm H
Knowlton, Charles 1801-1850 *TwCBDA*
Knowlton, Charles Davison 1867-1945
 NatCAB 34
Knowlton, Charles Osmond 1895-1962 *WhAm 4,*
 WhAm 5
Knowlton, Daniel Chauncey 1876- *WhAm 5*
Knowlton, Daniel Waldo 1881-1969 *NatCAB 55*
Knowlton, Ebenezer 1815-1874 *BiAUS,*
 BiDrAC, WhAm H
Knowlton, Eliot A 1844-1927 *WhAm 1*
Knowlton, Frank Hall 1860-1926 *AmBi,*
 DcAmB, NatCAB 10, NatCAB 47,
 TwCBDA, WhAm 1
Knowlton, Frank P 1875- *WhAm 5*
Knowlton, Frederic Kirk 1879-1939 *NatCAB 35*
Knowlton, George Willard 1839-1931 *WhAm 1*
Knowlton, Helen Mary 1832-1918 *ApCAB,*
 NewYHSD, NotAW, TwCBDA,
 WhAm 1, WomWWA 14
Knowlton, Hosea Morrill 1847-1902 *WhAm 1*
Knowlton, Ida Mann 1855- *WomWWA 14*
Knowlton, Ida P 1855- *WomWWA 14*
Knowlton, J H *NewYHSD*

Knowlton, John Stocker Coffin 1798-1871
 Drake Sup, TwCBDA
Knowlton, Julius William 1838-1921 *NatCAB 7,*
 NatCAB 19
Knowlton, Luke 1738-1810 *NatCAB 8*
Knowlton, Marcus Perrin 1839-1918 *DcAmB,*
 NatCAB 13, TwCBDA, WhAm 1
Knowlton, Mark Dean 1840-1906 *NatCAB 35*
Knowlton, Miles Justin 1825-1874 *ApCAB,*
 TwCBDA
Knowlton, Miner 1804-1870 *ApCAB, Drake*
Knowlton, P Clarke 1892-1930 *WhAm 1*
Knowlton, Paul Howard 1787-1863 *ApCAB*
Knowlton, Philip Arnold 1887-1959 *WhAm 3*
Knowlton, Robert Henry 1882-1961 *NatCAB 49,*
 WhAm 4
Knowlton, Theodore Ely 1872-1953 *NatCAB 48*
Knowlton, Thomas 1740-1776 *AmBi, ApCAB,*
 DcAmB, Drake, NatCAB 2, WebAMB,
 WhAm H
Knowlton, Willis Taylor 1848-1925 *NatCAB 20*
Knox, Adeline Trafton 1842- *WhAm 4,*
 WomWWA 14
Knox, Adeline Trafton 1845- *AmWom*
Knox, Alice Adelaide 1876- *WomWWA 14*
Knox, Mrs. Charles B 1857-1950 *WhAm 3*
Knox, Charles Edwin 1865-1925 *NatCAB 20*
Knox, Charles Eugene 1833-1900 *TwCBDA*
Knox, Dudley Wright 1877-1960 *WhAm 4*
Knox, Edna Doughty 1872- *WomWWA 14*
Knox, Ellen Mary *WomWWA 14*
Knox, Frank 1857- *NatCAB 7*
Knox, Frank 1874-1944 *DcAmB S3,*
 NatCAB 37
Knox, Mrs. Frank 1875- *WhAm 5*
Knox, Frank *see also* Knox, W Frank And Knox,
 William Franklin
Knox, Franklin 1874-1944 *WhAm 2*
Knox, George William 1829-1892 *NatCAB 3*
Knox, George William 1853-1912 *ApCAB,*
 DcAmB, NatCAB 23, TwCBDA,
 WhAm 1
Knox, Harry 1848-1923 *WhAm 1*
Knox, Harry Austin 1875-1957 *NatCAB 45*
Knox, Helen May 1862- *WomWWA 14*
Knox, Henry 1750-1802 *TwCBDA*
Knox, Henry 1750-1806 *AmBi, ApCAB,*
 BiAUS, BiDrUSE, DcAmB, Drake,
 McGEWB, NatCAB 1, WebAB,
 WebAMB, WhAm H
Knox, Henry Danforth 1876-1934 *NatCAB 25*
Knox, Henry Martyn 1830-1904 *NatCAB 6*
Knox, Hugh 1733-1790 *ApCAB*
Knox, J H Mason, Jr. 1872-1951 *NatCAB 41*
Knox, James *ApCAB*
Knox, James 1807-1876 *ApCAB, BiAUS,*
 BiDrAC, TwCBDA, WhAm H
Knox, James E 1892-1958 *WhAm 3*
Knox, James Hall Mason 1824-1903
 NatCAB 11, TwCBDA
Knox, Janette Hill 1845- *AmWom,*
 WomWWA 14
Knox, Jessie Juliet Daily *WhAm 5,*
 WomWWA 14
Knox, John d1790 *Drake*
Knox, John 1505?-1572 *McGEWB*
Knox, John 1790-1858 *ApCAB, NatCAB 6,*
 TwCBDA
Knox, John Armoy 1851- *ApCAB Sup*
Knox, John Barnett 1857-1935 *WhAm 1*
Knox, John Clark 1881-1966 *WhAm 4*
Knox, John J 1791-1876 *ApCAB*
Knox, John Jay 1828-1892 *AmBi, ApCAB,*
 BiAUS, DcAmB, NatCAB 3, TwCBDA,
 WhAm H
Knox, Joseph B *NewYHSD*
Knox, Louis 1874- *WhAm 2*
Knox, Lucy 1754-1824 *ApCAB*
Knox, Martin VanBuren 1841- *TwCBDA,*
 WhAm 4
Knox, Mary Alice 1851-1911 *WhAm 1*
Knox, Philander Chase 1853-1921 *AmBi,*
 ApCAB X, BiDrAC, BiDrUSE, DcAmB,
 EncAB, McGEWB, NatCAB 11,
 NatCAB 14, NatCAB 24, TwCBDA,
 WebAB, WhAm 1, WhAmP
Knox, Raymond Collyer 1876-1952 *NatCAB 41,*
 WhAm 5

Knox, Reuben 1850-1930 *NatCAB 23*
Knox, Robert 1793-1862 *DcScB*
Knox, Robert White 1859-1942 *WhAm 3*
Knox, Rose Markward 1857-1950 *DcAmB S4,*
 NotAW
Knox, Rush Hightower 1879-1946 *WhAm 3*
Knox, Samuel 1756-1832 *BiAUS, BiDAmEd,*
 DcAmB, NatCAB 24, WhAm H
Knox, Samuel 1815-1905 *BiDrAC*
Knox, Samuel Lippincott Griswold 1870-1947
 WhAm 2
Knox, Samuel McIlhenny 1857-1924
 NatCAB 33
Knox, Samuel Richardson 1811-1883 *ApCAB,*
 TwCBDA
Knox, Sara Cecelia *WomWWA 14*
Knox, Susan Ricker *IIBEAAW,*
 WomWWA 14
Knox, Thomas Wallace 1835-1896 *ApCAB,*
 DcAmB, NatCAB 7, TwCBDA,
 WhAm H
Knox, Victor Alfred 1899- *BiDrAC, WhAmP*
Knox, W Frank 1874-1944 *WhWW-II*
Knox, W Frank *see also* Knox, Frank
Knox, W P *NewYHSD*
Knox, William 1732-1810 *ApCAB, Drake*
Knox, William Eaton 1820-1883 *TwCBDA*
Knox, William Elliott 1862-1927 *NatCAB 26,*
 WhAm 1
Knox, William Franklin 1874-1944 *BiDrUSE,*
 EncAB
Knox, William Russell 1879- *WhAm 6*
Knox, William Shadrach 1843-1914 *BiDrAC,*
 NatCAB 37, TwCBDA, WhAm 4
Knox, William White 1842-1929 *WhAm 1*
Knubel, Frederick Hermann 1870-1945
 NatCAB 49, WhAm 2
Knubel, Frederick Ritscher 1897-1957
 NatCAB 49, WhAm 3
Knudsen, Charles William 1890-1951 *WhAm 3*
Knudsen, Eigil Carlos 1890-1953 *NatCAB 41*
Knudsen, Martin Hans Christian 1871-1949
 DcScB
Knudsen, Morris Hans 1862-1943 *NatCAB 35*
Knudsen, Thorkild Rostgaard 1890-1965
 NatCAB 53, WhAm 4
Knudsen, Vern O 1893-1974 *WhAm 6*
Knudsen, William S 1879-1948 *DcAmB S4,*
 EncAB, WhAm 2
Knudson, Albert Cornelius 1873-1953
 DcAmReB, WhAm 3
Knudson, Bennett Olin 1890-1964 *WhAm 4*
Knudson, James K 1906-1963 *WhAm 4*
Knudson, John Immanuel 1888-1959 *WhAm 3*
Knudson, Lewis 1884-1958 *NatCAB 47*
Knudson, Robert 1929- *IIBEAAW*
Knupfer, Charles 1877-1949 *NatCAB 38*
Knuppe, Belle Crouch 1865- *WomWWA 14*
Knuth, Paul Erich Otto Wilhelm 1854-1900
 DcScB
Knutson, Coya Gjesdal 1912- *BiDrAC*
Knutson, Harold 1880-1953 *BiDrAC,*
 DcAmB S5, WhAm 3, WhAmP
Knutson, Kent Siguart 1924-1973 *WhAm 5*
Knyphausen, Dodo Henry 1730-1789 *Drake*
Knyphausen, Baron Wilhelm Von 1716-1800
 AmBi, ApCAB
Kobak, Alfred Julian 1898-1972 *WhAm 6*
Kobak, Edgar 1895-1962 *NatCAB 52,*
 WhAm 4
Kobbe, Carolyn Wheeler 1862- *WomWWA 14*
Kobbe, Gustav 1857-1918 *DcAmB,*
 NatCAB 10, NatCAB 35, WhAm 1
Kobbe, William August 1840-1931 *ApCAB Sup,*
 WhAm 1
Kobe, Kenneth Albert 1905-1958 *WhAm 4*
Kobel, Jacob 1460?-1533 *DcScB*
Kobelt, Karl 1891-1968 *WhAm 4*
Kober, Alice Elizabeth 1906-1950 *NotAW*
Kober, Arthur 1900-1975 *WhAm 6*
Kober, George Martin 1850-1931 *DcAmB,*
 WhAm 1
Kobes, Herbert Richard 1904-1959 *NatCAB 48*
Kobrak, Heinrich 1905-1957 *NatCAB 46*
Koch, Alfred 1879-1951 *WhAm 3*
Koch, August William 1852-1932 *NatCAB 24*
Koch, Carl Allinger 1902-1966 *NatCAB 53*
Koch, Carleton Spaythe 1875-1938 *NatCAB 32*

Koch, Charles Rudolph Edward 1844-1916
  NatCAB 19, WhAm 1
Koch, Edward Irving 1924- BiDrAC
Koch, Edward William 1882-1946 WhAm 2
Koch, Elers 1880-1954 WhAm 3
Koch, Felix John 1882-1933 WhAm 1
Koch, Fred Chase 1900-1967 NatCAB 57,
  WhAm 5
Koch, Fred Conrad 1876-1948 DcAmB S4,
  NatCAB 46, WhAm 2
Koch, Frederick Henry 1877-1944 DcAmB S3,
  WebAB, WhAm 2
Koch, G Ashburn 1907-1959 NatCAB 47
Koch, George NewYHSD
Koch, George Price 1910-1972 WhAm 5
Koch, Heinrich Hermann Robert 1843-1910
  DcScB, McGEWB
Koch, Helge Von 1870-1924 DcScB
Koch, Henry C 1841- NatCAB 2
Koch, Henry Francis 1881-1953 NatCAB 45
Koch, Henry G 1840- WhAm H
Koch, Herbert Frank 1894-1971 NatCAB 57
Koch, Joseph 1844- NatCAB 5
Koch, Julius Arnold 1864-1956 WhAm 3
Koch, Otto d1948 WhAm 3
Koch, Robert 1843-1910 AsBiEn, BiHiMed
Koch, Theodore Wesley 1871-1941 DcAmLiB,
  NatCAB 30, WhAm 1
Koch, Thomas Jacob 1859-1915 NatCAB 16
Koch, William John 1912-1970 NatCAB 55
Kochan, Edward John 1922-1969 WhAm 5
Kocher, A Lawrence 1885-1969 WhAm 5
Kocher, Theodor 1841-1917 BiHiMed
Kochersperger, Edmund Stanley 1883-1952
  NatCAB 39
Kochersperger, Hiram Miller 1856- WhAm 4
Kochersperger, Stephen Morris 1872-1916
  NatCAB 17
Kocherthal, Josua Von 1669-1719 DcAmB,
  WhAm H
Kochin, Louis Mordecai 1898-1971 WhAm 5
Kochin, Nikolai Yevgrafovich 1901-1944 DcScB
Kochs, August 1871-1960 NatCAB 47,
  WhAm 4
Kocialkowski, Leo Paul 1882-1958 BiDrAC,
  WhAm 3, WhAmP
Kock, J C NewYHSD
Kockerthal, Joshua 1669?-1719 NatCAB 12
Kockritz, Ewald 1876-1931 WhAm 1
Kocourek, Albert 1875- WhAm 5
Kocsis, Ann d1972 WhAm 6
Kocyan, Joseph James 1884-1973 NatCAB 57
Kodaly, Zoltan 1882-1967 McGEWB,
  WhAm 4
Koebel, Ralph Francis 1911-1966 WhAm 4
Koeberle, John Eugene 1866- ApCAB X
Koebig, Adolf Helidor 1852-1944 NatCAB 33
Koeckert, Frederick William 1879-1962
  NatCAB 46
Koegel, Otto Erwin 1891-1975 WhAm 6
Koehler NewYHSD
Koehler, Alexander Daniel 1762-1828 ApCAB
Koehler, Francis X 1818-1886 NewYHSD
Koehler, George Richard 1883-1949
  NatCAB 38
Koehler, John Daniel 1737-1805 ApCAB,
  NatCAB 13, TwCBDA
Koehler, Joseph NewYHSD
Koehler, LeRoy Jennings 1896-1971
  NatCAB 56
Koehler, Otto NewYHSD
Koehler, Otto A 1893-1969 WhAm 5
Koehler, Robert 1850-1917 ApCAB, DcAmB,
  NatCAB 17, WhAm 1
Koehler, Sylvester Rosa 1837-1900 ApCAB,
  DcAmB, NatCAB 25, TwCBDA,
  WhAm 1
Koehler, Wilhelm Reinhold Walter 1884-1959
  WhAm 3
Koehler, William Carl 1862-1953 NatCAB 43
Koehring, William J 1872- WhAm 5
Koehrman, John William 1875-1959
  NatCAB 47
Koelbel, Arthur William 1903-1966 NatCAB 53
Koelliker, Herman Michael 1891-1951
  NatCAB 38
Koelliker, Rudolf Albert Von 1817-1905 DcScB
Koelreuter. Joseph Gottlieb 1733-1806 DcScB

Koemmenich, Louis 1866-1922 DcAmB
Koempel, Henry NewYHSD
Koenig, Adolph 1855-1932 NatCAB 12,
  NatCAB 23, WhAm 1
Koenig, Charles Albert 1884-1958 NatCAB 47
Koenig, Egmont Francis 1892-1974 WhAm 6
Koenig, George August 1844-1913 NatCAB 17
Koenig, George Augustus 1844-1913 DcAmB,
  WhAm 1
Koenig, George Augustus 1845?-1913 ApCAB
Koenig, Ivan Jacob 1894-1964 NatCAB 50
Koenig, Johann Samuel 1712-1757 DcScB
Koenig, Joseph Pierre d1970 WhAm 5
Koenig, Juan Ramon 1623-1709 ApCAB
Koenig, Julius 1849-1914 DcScB
Koenig, Karl Rudolph 1832-1901 DcScB
Koenig, Louis F 1885-1963 WhAm 4
Koenig, M Glenn 1931-1972 WhAm 6
Koenig, Marie Pierre Joseph Francois 1898-1970
  WhWW-II, WhoMilH
Koenig, Myron L 1910-1971 WhAm 5
Koenigs, Gabriel 1858-1931 DcScB
Koenigsberg, Moses 1878-1945 DcAmB S3,
  WhAm 2
Koepel, Norbert Francis 1897-1967 WhAm 4
Koepfli, Joseph Otto 1866-1942 NatCAB 32
Koepke, Charles Augustus 1893-1966
  NatCAB 53
Koeppen, Adolphus Louis 1804-1873 ApCAB
Koerber, Leila WebAB
Koerble, Charles Edward 1914-1975 WhAm 6
Koerner, Andrew 1894-1964 WhAm 4
Koerner, Gustav 1809-1896 ApCAB
Koerner, Gustave Philip 1809-1896 DcAmB,
  NatCAB 8, WhAm H
Koerner, Gustavius 1809-1896 BiAUS
Koerner, Gustavus 1809-1896 TwCBDA
Koerner, H T 1855?-1927 IIBEAAW
Koerner, Theodor 1873-1957 WhAm 3,
  WhAm 5
Koerner, William 1886-1940 NatCAB 30,
  WhAm 1
Koerner, William Henry David 1878-1938
  IIBEAAW
Koerner, William Henry Dethlep 1878-1938
  WhAm 1
Koert-Kronold, Selma NotAW
Koester, Frank 1876-1927 WhAm 1
Koester, George Arthur 1912-1974 WhAm 6
Koeth, Theo NewYHSD
Koff, Sidney Carton 1895-1950 NatCAB 39
Koffka, Kurt 1886-1941 DcAmB S3, WhAm 1
Koffner, J NewYHSD
Koffsky, Samuel 1902-1953 NatCAB 41
Kofoid, Charles Atwood 1865-1947 DcAmB S4,
  DcScB, WhAm 2
Kofron, Joseph Vaclav 1869-1946 NatCAB 34
Koga, Mineichi 1885-1943 WhWW-II
Kohl, Carl Clarence, Jr. 1916-1955 NatCAB 47
Kohl, Edwin Phillips 1891-1968 WhAm 4
Kohl, Henry 1870-1937 NatCAB 31
Kohl, John George 1808-1871 Drake
Kohl, John George 1808-1878 ApCAB
Kohl, Ortelia NewYHSD
Kohlbeck, Peter NewYHSD
Kohlbeck, Valentine 1864-1937 WhAm 1
Kohlberg, Olga 1864- WomWWA 14
Kohler, August Karl Johann Valentin 1866-1948
  DcScB
Kohler, Carl James 1905-1960 NatCAB 50
Kohler, Elmer Peter 1865-1938 DcAmB S2,
  WhAm 1
Kohler, Eric Louis 1892-1976 WhAm 6
Kohler, Fred 1864-1934 WhAm 1
Kohler, G A Edward 1864-1932 WhAm 1
Kohler, Gustavus Adolphus Edward 1864-1932
  NatCAB 23
Kohler, Henry 1891-1943 NatCAB 31
Kohler, Herbert Calvin 1891-1953 WhAm 3
Kohler, Herbert Vollrath 1891-1968 WhAm 5
Kohler, John Michael 1902-1968 NatCAB 54
Kohler, Karl NewYHSD
Kohler, Kaufman 1843-1926 NatCAB 13
Kohler, Kaufmann 1843-1926 AmBi, DcAmB,
  DcAmReB, WhAm 1
Kohler, Max James 1871-1934 DcAmB S1,
  NatCAB 26, WhAm 1
Kohler, Robert NewYHSD

Kohler, Rose 1873- BiCAW
Kohler, Ruth DeYoung 1906-1953 WhAm 3
Kohler, Walter Jodok 1875-1940 ApCAB X,
  DcAmB S2, NatCAB 35, WhAm 1
Kohler, Wolfgang 1887-1967 AsBiEn,
  NatCAB 55, WhAm 4, WhAm 5
Kohlhaas, Frank John 1876-1943 NatCAB 33
Kohlhepp, Charles E 1896-1972 WhAm 5
Kohlmann, Anthony 1771-1836 DcAmB,
  NatCAB 24, WhAm H
Kohlmann, Anthony 1771-1838 ApCAB,
  TwCBDA
Kohlmann, William 1863-1921 NatCAB 19
Kohlmeier, Albert L 1883-1964 WhAm 4
Kohlmer, Fred 1905-1969 WhAm 5
Kohlmeyer, Frederick William 1920- EncAAH
Kohlrausch, Friedrich Wilhelm Georg 1840-1910
  DcScB
Kohlrausch, Rudolph Herrmann Arndt
  1809-1858 DcScB
Kohlsaat, Amy M 1870- WomWWA 14
Kohlsaat, Christian Cecil 1844-1918
  NatCAB 28, WhAm 1
Kohlsaat, Frances 1870- WomWWA 14
Kohlsaat, Herman Henry 1853-1924 DcAmB,
  NatCAB 19, TwCBDA, WhAm 1
Kohlstedt, Donald Winston 1909-1971 WhAm 5
Kohlstedt, Edward Delor 1874-1963 WhAm 4
Kohn, August 1868- WhAm 1
Kohn, Gabriel 1910-1975 BnEnAmA,
  WhAm 6
Kohn, Henry H 1868-1944 WhAm 2
Kohn, Irene Goldsmith 1868- WomWWA 14
Kohn, Isidore 1882-1964 NatCAB 50
Kohn, Jacob 1881-1968 WhAm 5
Kohn, Julius NewYHSD
Kohn, Louis A 1907-1971 WhAm 6
Kohn, Philippe NewYHSD
Kohn, Robert David 1870-1953 NatCAB 46,
  WhAm 3
Kohne, Frederick 1757-1829 ApCAB, Drake
Kohner, William 1816-1876 NewYHSD
Kohns, Lee 1864-1927 WhAm 1
Kohnstamm, Frank Rayfield 1896-1959
  NatCAB 47, WhAm 3
Kohnstamm, Lothair Setta 1881-1950
  NatCAB 38
Kohut, Alexander 1842-1894 ApCAB Sup,
  DcAmB, NatCAB 4, WhAm H
Kohut, George Alexander 1874-1933
  DcAmB S1, NatCAB 26
Kohut, Rebekah Bettelheim 1864-1951
  NatCAB 41, WomWWA 14
Koiner, C Wellington 1870-1947 WhAm 3
Koiso, Kuniaki 1880-1950 WhWW-II
Kojong 1852-1919 McGEWB
Kokatnur, Vaman Ramachandra 1886-1950
  WhAm 3
Kokeritz, K A Helge 1902-1964 WhAm 4
Kokernot, Herbert Lee 1867-1949 NatCAB 40,
  WhAm 5
Kokes, Richard Joseph 1927-1973 WhAm 6
Kokoschka, Oskar 1886- McGEWB
Kolar, Victor 1888-1957 NatCAB 43,
  WhAm 3
Kolb, Allie Carl 1886-1959 NatCAB 49
Kolb, Charles August 1895-1961 WhAm 4
Kolb, Charles Ellsworth 1864-1921 NatCAB 19
Kolb, Dielman 1691-1756 DcAmB, WhAm H
Kolb, Ellsworth Leonardson 1876- WhAm 5
Kolb, James Monroe 1904-1969 WhAm 6
Kolb, John Harrison 1888-1963 WhAm 4
Kolb, Louis John 1865-1941 WhAm 1
Kolb, Reuben Francis 1839-1918 DcAmB
Kolbe, Adolf Wilhelm Hermann 1818-1884
  DcScB
Kolbe, Adolph Wilhelm Hermann 1818-1884
  AsBiEn
Kolbe, Parke Rexford 1881-1942 NatCAB 32,
  WhAm 2
Kolchak, Aleksandr Vasilievich 1873-1920
  McGEWB
Kolchak, Alexander Vasilievich 1875-1920
  WhoMilH
Kole, Leon Robert 1914-1970 NatCAB 56
Kole, Lessing Lawrence 1894-1969 WhAm 5
Kolinski, Maximillian Charles 1894-1958
  NatCAB 49

Kolker, Henry d1947 *WhAm 2*
Kolkey, Eugene Louis 1927-1975 *WhAm 6*
Koll, Milton Lee 1894-1951 *NatCAB 40*
Kolle, Frederick Strange 1871-1929 *WhAm 1*
Kolle, Frederick Strange 1872-1929 *DcAmB*
Kollen, George Edward 1871-1919 *NatCAB 17*
Kollen, Gerrit John 1843-1915 *TwCBDA, WhAm 1*
Koller, Carl 1857-1944 *AsBiEn, DcAmB S3, WhAm 2*
Koller, John J *ApCAB X*
Koller, Paul Warren 1872-1937 *WhAm 1*
Kolliker, Rudolf Albert Von 1817-1905 *AsBiEn*
Kollmer, Huber *NewYHSD*
Kollmorgen, Frederick Ludwig George 1871-1961 *NatCAB 46*
Kollner *NewYHSD*
Kollner, Augustus 1813- *NewYHSD*
Kollock, Charles Wilson 1857-1931 *WhAm 1*
Kollock, Florence E 1848- *AmWom*
Kollock, Henry 1778-1819 *ApCAB, Drake, TwCBDA*
Kollock, Mary 1832-1911 *NatCAB 10, TwCBDA, WhAm 4*
Kollock, Mary 1840-1911 *ApCAB, NewYHSD*
Kollock, Shepard 1750-1839 *ApCAB, DcAmB, NatCAB 10, TwCBDA, WhAm H*
Kollock, Shepard Kosciusko 1795-1865 *TwCBDA*
Kollock, Shepard Kosciuszko 1795-1865 *ApCAB*
Kollock, Shepherd 1750-1839 *Drake*
Kollock, Sheppard Kosciusko 1795-1865 *Drake*
Kollontai, Aleksandra Mikhailovna 1872-1952 *McGEWB*
Kollwitz, Kathe Schmidt 1867-1945 *WhAm 4*
Kolman, Burton A d1967 *WhAm 5*
Kolmer, John Albert 1886-1962 *WhAm 4*
Kolodny, Anatole 1892-1948 *NatCAB 36*
Kolosov, Gury Vasilievich 1867-1936 *DcScB*
Kolowich, George Jerome 1897-1955 *NatCAB 46, WhAm 3*
Kolseth, J Harold 1904-1972 *WhAm 5*
Kolster, Frederick August 1883-1950 *NatCAB 41*
Koltes, John A 1823-1862 *ApCAB*
Koltzoff, Nikolai Konstantinovich 1872-1940 *DcScB*
Koluwsky, Herminias *NewYHSD*
Komarewsky, Vasili Ilyich 1895-1957 *WhAm 3*
Komarov, Vladimir 1927-1967 *WhAm 4*
Komensky, Jan Amos *DcScB*
Kominsky, David Daniel *WebAB*
Kommers, William John 1872- *WhAm 5*
Komora, Paul O 1891-1950 *WhAm 3*
Komp, William H Wood 1893-1955 *NatCAB 48, WhAm 3*
Komroff, Manuel 1890-1974 *WhAm 6*
Kondakov, Ivan Lavrentievich 1857-1931 *DcScB*
Kondiaronk d1701 *ApCAB*
Kondo, Nobutake *WhWW-II*
Kone, Edward Reeves 1848- *WhAm 4*
Konenkov, Sergei Timopheevitch 1874-1971 *WhAm 5*
Konev, Ivan 1897-1973 *WhWW-II*
Konev, Ivan Stefanovich 1897-1973 *McGEWB*
Konev, Ivan Stepanovich 1897-1973 *WhoMilH*
Konger, Henry *NewYHSD*
Konheim, Vladimir M 1893-1959 *NatCAB 47*
Konig, Arthur 1856-1901 *DcScB*
Konig, Emanuel 1658-1731 *DcScB*
Konig, George 1856-1913 *WhAm 1*
Konig, George 1865-1913 *BiDrAC*
Konigsberger, Leo 1837-1921 *DcScB*
Konikow, Antoinette F 1869- *WomWWA 14*
Koninck, Laurent-Guillaume De 1809-1887 *DcScB*
Konings, Anthony 1821-1884 *WhAm H*
Konjovic, Petar 1883-1970 *WhAm 5*
Konkel, E Vernon 1923-1970 *NatCAB 57*
Konkle, Burton Alva 1861-1944 *WhAm 2*
Konkle, Laura Louisa Allen 1877- *WomWWA 14*
Konkoly Thege, Miklos Von 1842-1916 *DcScB*
Konoe, Prince Fumimaro 1891-1945 *McGEWB*
Konop, Thomas Frank 1879-1964 *BiDrAC, WhAm 4*
Konovalov, Dmitry Petrovich 1856-1929 *DcScB*
Konoye, Prince Fumimaro 1891-1945 *WhWW-II*

Konschak, Count Ferdinand 1703-1760 *ApCAB*
Konta, Alexander 1862-1933 *WhAm 1*
Konta, Annie Lemp 1867- *WhAm 5*
Konta, Geoffrey 1887-1942 *WhAm 2*
Konti, Isidore 1862-1938 *AmBi, NatCAB 14, WhAm 1*
Kontz, Anton Louis 1851- *NatCAB 7*
Kontz, Ernest Charles 1865-1945 *WhAm 2*
Konwin, Robert Benedict 1902-1965 *NatCAB 52*
Kooistra, Henry P 1904-1965 *NatCAB 51*
Koon, E L 1832-1892 *NatCAB 31*
Koon, Martin B 1841-1912 *WhAm 1*
Koons, Charles Alfred 1908-1968 *NatCAB 54, WhAm 4A, WhAm 5*
Koons, Henry Haynes 1867-1929 *NatCAB 27*
Koons, James *NewYHSD*
Koons, John Cornelius 1873-1937 *WhAm 1*
Koons, Tilghman Benjamin 1852- *WhAm 4*
Koontz, Amos Ralph 1890-1965 *NatCAB 52*
Koontz, Arthur Burke 1885-1963 *WhAm 4*
Koontz, Frederick Bowers 1889-1953 *WhAm 3*
Koontz, James R 1868- *WhAm 4*
Koontz, Louis Knott 1890-1951 *WhAm 3*
Koontz, William Henry 1830-1911 *BiAUS, BiDrAC, TwCBDA*
Koop, William H d1952 *WhAm 3*
Koopman, Augustus 1869-1914 *DcAmB, NatCAB 24, WhAm 1*
Koopman, Harry Lyman 1860-1937 *DcAmLiB, NatCAB 11, NatCAB 29, TwCBDA, WhAm 1*
Koos, Frank Hermann 1884-1966 *NatCAB 54*
Koos, Leonard Vincent 1881- *BiDAmEd, WhAm 6*
Kooweskoowe 1790-1866 *WebAB*
Kooweskowe 1790?-1866 *AmBi, DcAmB*
Kooyman, Frank Iemke 1880-1963 *NatCAB 51*
Kopald, Louis Joseph 1885-1931 *NatCAB 26, WhAm 1*
Kopetzky, Samuel Joseph 1876-1950 *WhAm 3*
Kopf, Carl Heath 1902-1958 *WhAm 3*
Kopf, Howard Elsworth 1897-1960 *NatCAB 50*
Kopke, Ernst 1854- *NatCAB 16*
Koplar, Sam 1888-1961 *WhAm 4*
Koplik, Henry 1858-1927 *WhAm 1*
Kopman, Benjamin 1887-1965 *WhAm 4*
Kopp, Arthur William 1874-1967 *BiDrAC, WhAm 4, WhAm 5*
Kopp, Arthur William 1875-1967 *NatCAB 54*
Kopp, George A 1900-1968 *WhAm 5*
Kopp, Hermann Franz Moritz 1817-1892 *AsBiEn, DcScB*
Kopp, Otto 1896-1961 *WhAm 4*
Kopp, William Frederick 1869-1938 *BiDrAC, WhAm 1, WhAmP*
Koppel, Charles *IlBEAAW, NewYHSD*
Kopper, Samuel Keene Claggett 1914-1957 *WhAm 3*
Kopperud, Andrew 1924-1973 *WhAm 6*
Koppius, O T 1889-1965 *WhAm 4*
Kopplemann, Herman Paul 1880-1957 *BiDrAC, WhAm 3*
Koprulu, Ahmed 1635-1676 *McGEWB*
Koprulu, Fazil Ahmed 1635-1676 *WhoMilH*
Koprulu, Mehmed Pasha 1583-1661 *WhoMilH*
Koquethagachton d1778 *ApCAB*
Korbel, Mario 1882-1954 *WhAm 3*
Korbly, Charles Alexander 1871-1937 *BiDrAC, WhAm 1*
Korda, Sir Alexander 1893-1956 *WhAm 3*
Korell, Franklin Frederick 1889-1965 *BiDrAC*
Koren, John 1861-1923 *DcAmB, NatCAB 19, WhAm 1*
Koren, Ulrik Vilhelm 1826-1910 *DcAmB*
Koren, Ulrik Vilhelm 1826-1911 *WhAm 1*
Koren, William, Jr. 1909-1956 *WhAm 3*
Korey, Saul Roy 1918-1963 *NatCAB 49*
Korf, Earnie Orville 1889-1949 *NatCAB 41*
Korff, Baroness Alletta VanReypen 1878- *WomWWA 14*
Korff, Herman *NewYHSD*
Korff, Louis *NewYHSD*
Korff, Sergius Alexander 1876-1924 *WhAm 1*
Korfmacher, Edwin Stanley 1904-1960 *NatCAB 49*
Korin, Pavel Dmitrievich 1892-1967 *WhAm 5*
Korn, Chester Frederick 1871-1954 *NatCAB 41*

Korn, Clara A 1866- *NatCAB 7*
Korn, George *NewYHSD*
Korn, Joseph *NewYHSD*
Korn, Peter George 1903-1972 *WhAm 5*
Kornberg, Arthur 1918- *AsBiEn, WebAB*
Kornblueh, Igho Hart 1898-1973 *NatCAB 57*
Korndoerfer, Augustus 1843- *NatCAB 3*
Kornegay, Horace Robinson 1924- *BiDrAC*
Kornegay, Wade Hampton 1865-1939 *WhAm 1*
Korner, Alice Dore 1890- *WomWWA 14*
Korner, Alice Masten 1859- *WomWWA 14*
Korner, Gustav Philipp 1809-1896 *DcAmB, WhAm H*
Korner, Jules Gilmer, Jr. 1888-1967 *NatCAB 51, WhAm 4*
Korner, Theodor 1873- *WhAm 5*
Kornfeld, Albert 1901-1962 *WhAm 4*
Kornfeld, Murray d1972 *WhAm 5*
Korngold, Eric Wolfgang 1897-1957 *WhAm 3*
Korngold, Janet Fenimore 1888- *WomWWA 14*
Kornhauser, Sidney Isaac 1887-1959 *WhAm 3*
Kornilov, Lavr Georgievich 1870-1918 *McGEWB*
Kornilov, Lavrenti Georgievich 1870-1918 *WhoMilH*
Kornitzer, Joseph 1824- *NatCAB 7*
Korolev, Sergey Pavlovich 1907-1966 *DcScB*
Korsakov, Aleksander Mikhailovich 1753-1840 *WhoMilH*
Korsakov, Sergei Sergeivich 1853-1900 *BiHiMed*
Korsmeyer, Frederick August 1877-1961 *WhAm 4*
Korsmo, Carl Thurston 1916-1965 *NatCAB 51*
Korstian, Clarence Ferdinand 1889-1968 *WhAm 4A*
Korteweg, Diederik Johannes 1848-1941 *DcScB*
Korzybski, Alfred Habdank 1879-1950 *WebAB, WhAm 2A*
Kosa, Emil Jean, Jr. 1903-1968 *WhAm 5*
Kosanovitch, Sava N 1894-1956 *WhAm 3*
Kosciatowski, Napoleon *NewYHSD*
Koscinski, Arthur A 1887-1957 *WhAm 3*
Kosciusko, Thaddeus 1746-1817 *WebAB*
Kosciuszko, Tadeus A B 1746-1817 *NewYHSD*
Kosciuszko, Tadeusz 1746-1817 *ApCAB, TwCBDA, WebAMB*
Kosciuszko, Tadeusz 1756-1817 *Drake*
Kosciuszko, Tadeusz Andrzej Bonaventura 1746-1817 *WhoMilH*
Kosciuszko, Tadeusz Andrzej Bonaventura 1746-1817 *DcAmB, McGEWB, WhAm H*
Kosciuszko, Thaddeus 1746-1817 *AmBi, NatCAB 1*
Koser, Ralph B 1909-1969 *WhAm 5*
Koser, Stewart Arment 1894-1971 *WhAm 5*
Kosky, Purre *NewYHSD*
Kosmak, George William 1873-1954 *NatCAB 44, WhAm 3*
Kosolapoff, Gennady Michael 1909-1976 *WhAm 6*
Koss, David 1905-1960 *NatCAB 45*
Kossel, Albrecht 1853-1927 *AsBiEn*
Kossel, Karl Martin Leonhard Albrecht 1853-1927 *DcScB*
Kossel, Walther 1888-1956 *DcScB*
Kossin, J W 1900-1961 *WhAm 4*
Kossuth, Lajos 1802-1894 *McGEWB, WhAm H*
Kossuth, Louis 1802-1894 *McGEWB*
Kost, Frederick W 1861-1923 *WhAm 1*
Kost, John 1819-1904 *WhAm 1*
Kostalek, John Anton 1885-1937 *WhAm 1*
Kostanecki, Stanislaw 1860-1910 *DcScB*
Kostellow, Alexander Jusserand 1897-1954 *WhAm 3*
Koster, Frederick Jacob 1868-1958 *NatCAB 49, WhAm 3*
Koster, Henry 1793-1820 *ApCAB*
Koster, John S 1841- *NatCAB 10*
Koster, Willem 1911-1975 *WhAm 6*
Kostinsky, Sergey Konstantinovich 1867-1936 *DcScB*
Kostka, William James 1905-1974 *WhAm 6*
Kostrzewski, Jozef Wiadyslaw 1885-1969 *WhAm 6*
Koszalka, Michael Francis 1911-1970 *NatCAB 56, WhAm 5*
Kotany, Ludwig 1860-1930 *WhAm 1*

Kotelnikov, Aleksandr Petrovich 1865-1944
  DcScB
Koth, Arthur William 1907-1966 *WhAm 4*
Koto, Bunjiro 1856-1935 *DcScB*
Kotz, Adam Lovine 1856-1940 *NatCAB 29*
Kotzebue, Otto Von 1787-1846 *ApCAB,
  McGEWB*
Kotzschmar, Hermann 1829-1908 *NatCAB 15*
Koudelka, Joseph Maria 1852-1921 *NatCAB 15,
  WhAm 1*
Koues, Helen d1960 *WhAm 4*
Koufax, Sanford 1935- *WebAB*
Kouns, Charles Wesley 1854-1916 *NatCAB 17*
Kouns, Nathan Chapman 1833- *ApCAB*
Kountz, George McClellan 1870-1942
  NatCAB 39
Kountz, John S 1846-1909 *ApCAB, NatCAB 4,
  WhAm 1*
Kountz, William Bryan 1896-1962 *NatCAB 50*
Kountze, Augustus Frederick 1870-1927
  NatCAB 24, WhAm 1
Kountze, Charles Thomas 1871- *WhAm 5*
Kountze, DeLancey 1878-1946 *ApCAB X,
  WhAm 2*
Kountze, Harold 1885-1965 *WhAm 4*
Kountze, Herman 1833-1906 *NatCAB 18*
Kountze, Luther 1841-1918 *ApCAB X,
  NatCAB 20*
Koussevitsky, Serge 1874-1951 *WebAB*
Koussevitzky, Serge Alexandrovich 1874-1951
  DcAmB S5, NatCAB 39
Koussevitzky, Sergei 1874-1951 *WhAm 3*
Koutensky, William Edward 1901-1971
  NatCAB 57
Koutzen, Boris 1901-1966 *WhAm 4*
Kouwenhoven, William Bennett 1886-1975
  WhAm 6
Kouwenhoven, William Williamson 1846-1928
  ApCAB X
Kovach, George Stephen 1904-1960 *WhAm 4*
Kovacs, Ernie 1919-1962 *WhAm 4*
Kovacs, Richard 1884-1950 *NatCAB 45,
  WhAm 3*
Kovalevski, Alexander Onufriyevich 1840-1901
  AsBiEn
Kovalevsky, Aleksandr Onufrievich 1840-1901
  DcScB
Kovalevsky, Sonya 1850-1891 *DcScB*
Kovalevsky, Vladimir Onufrievich 1842-1883
  DcScB
Kovalsky, Marian Albertovich 1821-1884 *DcScB*
Kovarik, Alois Francis 1880- *WhAm 6*
Kowal, Chester *WhAm 4*
Kowalewsky *DcScB*
Kowalski, Frank 1907-1974 *BiDrAC, WhAm 6,
  WhAmP*
Kownatzki, Hans 1866- *WhAm 4*
Koyl, Charles Herschel 1855-1931 *DcAmB,
  NatCAB 27, WhAm 1*
Koyre, Alexandre 1892-1964 *DcScB, WhAm 5*
Kozlov, Frol Romanovich 1908-1965 *WhAm 4*
Kozlowski, Edward 1860-1915 *NatCAB 15*
Kozyrev, Nikolai Alexandrovich 1908- *AsBiEn*
Kraby, Peter Darra 1859- *NatCAB 5*
Kracauer, Siegfried d1966 *WhAm 4*
Kracke, Frederick J H 1868-1952 *WhAm 3*
Kracke, Roy Rachford 1897-1950 *WhAm 3*
Krackowizer, Ernest 1822-1875 *ApCAB*
Kraeling, Carl H 1897-1966 *WhAm 4*
Kraemer, Casper John, Jr. 1895-1958 *WhAm 3*
Kraemer, Elmer Otto 1898-1943 *NatCAB 32*
Kraemer, Harry Michael 1946- *NatCAB 34*
Kraemer, Henry 1868-1924 *DcAmB,
  NatCAB 26, WhAm 1*
Kraemer, Peter *NewYHSD*
Kraepelin, Emil 1856-1926 *BiHiMed*
Kraetzer, Arthur Furman 1891-1940 *WhAm 1*
Kraetzer, Gustav *NewYHSD*
Krafft, Carl R 1884-1938 *WhAm 1*
Krafft, Walter A 1889-1959 *WhAm 3*
Krafft, Walter E 1890-1963 *WhAm 4*
Krafft-Ebing, Baron Richard Von 1840-1902
  AsBiEn
Krafka, Joseph, Jr. 1890-1946 *WhAm 2*
Kraft, Charles Herbert 1880-1952 *NatCAB 41*
Kraft, Edwin Arthur 1883-1962 *NatCAB 50,
  WhAm 4*
Kraft, James Lewis 1874-1953 *DcAmB S5,*

Kraft, Jens 1720-1765 *DcScB*
Kraft, John H d1972 *WhAm 5*
Kraft, Lewis *NewYHSD*
Kraft, Louis 1891-1975 *WhAm 6*
Krafve, Richard Ernest 1907-1974 *WhAm 6*
Krag, Leona Alford 1878- *ApCAB X*
Krahleng, Charles *NewYHSD*
Krahn, George Washington 1888-1951
  NatCAB 40
Kraitsir *NewYHSD*
Kraitsir, Charles 1804-1860 *ApCAB*
Kral, Josef Jiri 1870- *WhAm 5*
Kramer, A Walter 1890-1969 *NatCAB 55,
  WhAm 5*
Kramer, Adele Jackson Pickel *WomWWA 14*
Kramer, Albert Ludlow 1878-1948 *WhAm 2*
Kramer, Andrew Anthony 1867- *WhAm 5*
Kramer, Benjamin 1888-1972 *NatCAB 57,
  WhAm 6*
Kramer, Charles *NewYHSD*
Kramer, Charles 1879-1943 *BiDrAC, WhAmP*
Kramer, Edwin Weed 1877-1941 *WhAm 2*
Kramer, Ella Wilson 1859- *WomWWA 14*
Kramer, Flora Cornelia Fitch 1879-
  WomWWA 14
Kramer, Frederick Ferdinand 1861-1946
  WhAm 2
Kramer, George Washington 1847-1938
  NatCAB 9, WhAm 1
Kramer, Hans 1894-1957 *WhAm 3*
Kramer, Harold Morton 1873-1930 *WhAm 1*
Kramer, Herman Frederick 1892-1964 *WhAm 4*
Kramer, John Franklin 1869-1956 *NatCAB 18,
  NatCAB 47, WhAm 5*
Kramer, John Matthias *NewYHSD*
Kramer, Joseph 1896-1951 *NatCAB 43*
Kramer, Peter 1823-1907 *NewYHSD*
Kramer, Raymond Charles 1901-1957 *WhAm 3*
Kramer, Rudolph Jesse 1872-1954 *WhAm 3*
Kramer, Samuel Edmond 1878-1960 *WhAm 4*
Kramer, Simon Gad 1903-1970 *WhAm 5*
Kramer, Simon Pendleton 1868-1940
  NatCAB 29, WhAm 4
Kramer, Stephanie Shambaugh 1908-1973
  WhAm 6
Kramer, Verle V 1905-1968 *NatCAB 55*
Kramer, Xavier Alexis 1879-1943 *NatCAB 39*
Kramers, Hendrik Anthony 1894-1952 *DcScB*
Kramm, Gustavus *NewYHSD*
Kramm, Max 1874- *NatCAB 17*
Krammes, Emma Ruess 1864-1956 *WhAm 3*
Kramp, Chretien 1760-1826 *DcScB*
Kramp, William C *NewYHSD*
Krank, Alfred Jacob 1866-1928 *NatCAB 30*
Krannert, Herman C 1887-1972 *WhAm 5*
Krans, Horatio Sheafe 1872-1952 *NatCAB 39,
  WhAm 5*
Krans, Olaf 1838-1916 *BnEnAmA, IIBEAAW,
  NewYHSD, WhAm HA, WhAm 4*
Krantz, Arthur James 1874-1960 *NatCAB 48*
Krantz, Hubert Francis 1863-1942 *NatCAB 33*
Krantz, Philip 1858-1922 *DcAmB*
Kranz, Leon George 1895-1956 *WhAm 3*
Krapp, George Philip 1872-1934 *AmBi,
  DcAmB S1, WhAm 1*
Kraschel, Nelson George 1889-1957
  NatCAB 45, WhAm 3
Krasheninnikov, Stepan Petrovich 1711-1755
  DcScB
Krasik, Sidney 1911-1965 *NatCAB 51,
  WhAm 4*
Krasnov, Andrey Nikolaevich 1862-1915 *DcScB*
Krasnow, Albert 1911-1972 *NatCAB 56*
Krasovsky, Theodosy Nicolaevich 1878-1948
  DcScB
Krass, Nathan d1949 *WhAm 3*
Krathwohl, William Charles 1882-1969
  WhAm 5
Kratt, Theodore 1897-1962 *WhAm 4*
Kratz, Alonzo Plumsted 1885-1970 *WhAm 5*
Kratz, Henry Elton 1849-1929 *WhAm 1*
Kraus, Adolf 1850-1928 *WhAm 1*
Kraus, Charles August 1875-1967 *DcScB,
  WhAm 4*
Kraus, Edward Henry 1875-1973 *WhAm 5*
Kraus, John 1815-1896 *BiDAmEd, DcAmB,
  NatCAB 13, WhAm H*

Kraus, Mother M Seraphine 1854-1954
  BiDAmEd
Kraus, Milton 1866-1942 *BiDrAC, WhAm 4*
Kraus, Rene Raoul 1902-1947 *WhAm 2*
Kraus, Walter Max 1889-1944 *NatCAB 34,
  WhAm 2*
Kraus, William 1823- *NatCAB 3*
Kraus, William Christopher 1863-1909
  NatCAB 12
Kraus, William Christopher *see also* Krauss,
  William C
Kraus-Boelte, Maria 1836-1918 *BiDAmEd,
  DcAmB, NatCAB 13, NotAW,
  WomWWA 14*
Kraus-Boelte, Maria *see also* Krauss-Boelte,
  Maria
Krause, Allen Kramer 1881-1941 *DcAmB S3,
  WhAm 1*
Krause, Carl Albert 1872-1929 *WhAm 1*
Krause, Charles Schurz 1876-1951 *NatCAB 38*
Krause, Chester T 1899-1966 *WhAm 4*
Krause, Ernest William 1877-1953 *NatCAB 43*
Krause, Ernst Ludwig 1839-1903 *DcScB*
Krause, Harry Theodore 1894- *WhAm 5*
Krause, Henry 1820?- *NewYHSD*
Krause, Louise B *WhAm 5*
Krause, Lyda Farrington 1864-1939 *WhAm 1*
Krause, Lydia Farrington 1864-1939
  WomWWA 14
Krause, Otto Adolph 1877-1950 *NatCAB 47*
Krause, Rudolph 1863- *NatCAB 16, WhAm 4*
Krause, Sydney 1901-1969 *NatCAB 54*
Krauskopf, Joseph 1858-1923 *AmBi, DcAmB,
  NatCAB 3, WhAm 1*
Krauss, Blanche Youngblood 1884-
  WomWWA 14
Krauss, Elmer Frederick 1862-1946 *WhAm 2*
Krauss, James 1866- *NatCAB 18*
Krauss, Lee 1885-1955 *NatCAB 42*
Krauss, Stephen *NewYHSD*
Krauss, William 1861-1935 *WhAm 1*
Krauss, William Christopher 1863-1909
  WhAm 1
Krauss, William Christopher *see also* Kraus,
  William C
Krauss-Boelte, Maria 1836-1918 *WhAm 4*
Krauss-Boelte, Maria *see also* Kraus-Boelte,
  Maria
Kraut, Hans Baptiste 1881-1947 *NatCAB 44*
Krautbauer, Francis Xavier 1824-1885 *ApCAB,
  NatCAB 12, TwCBDA*
Krautbauer, Franz Xaver 1824-1885 *WhAm H*
Krauth, Charles Philip 1796-1867 *Drake*
Krauth, Charles Philip 1797-1867 *ApCAB,
  DcAmB, TwCBDA, WhAm H*
Krauth, Charles Porterfield 1823-1883 *ApCAB,
  DcAmB, DcAmReB, Drake, NatCAB 1,
  TwCBDA, WhAm H*
Krauthoff, Charles Rieseck 1863-1936 *WhAm 1*
Krauthoff, Louis Charles 1858-1918
  NatCAB 18, WhAm 1
Kravchenko, Victor A 1905-1966 *WhAm 4*
Kraybill, Henry Reist 1891-1956 *NatCAB 48,
  WhAm 3*
Kraybill, William Gress 1914-1961 *NatCAB 49*
Krayenhoff, Cornelis Rudolphus Theodorus
  1758-1840 *DcScB*
Krebs, Adolph K *NewYHSD*
Krebs, Sir Hans Adolf 1900- *AsBiEn,
  McGEWB*
Krebs, Henrik Johannes 1847-1929 *NatCAB 31*
Krebs, Jacob 1782-1847 *BiAUS, BiDrAC,
  WhAm H*
Krebs, John Michael 1804-1867 *ApCAB, Drake,
  TwCBDA*
Krebs, Paul Joseph 1912- *BiDrAC*
Krebs, Stanley LeFevre 1864-1935 *WhAm 1*
Krebs, Walter Winston 1894-1974 *WhAm 6*
Krebs, William Samuel 1889-1958 *WhAm 3*
Krech, Alvin Wilhelm 1858-1928 *ApCAB X*
Krech, Alvin William 1858-1928 *NatCAB 21,
  WhAm 1*
Krech, Shepard 1891-1968 *NatCAB 54*
Krecker, Ada May *WomWWA 14*
Krecker, Frederick H 1881- *WhAm 6*
Krecker, Marguerite 1874- *WomWWA 14*
Kreeger, Morris Harold 1910-1975 *WhAm 6*
Kreel, John *NewYHSD*

Krefeld, William John 1892-1965 *NatCAB 51,
WhAm 4*
Kreger, Clarence W 1896-1960 *WhAm 4*
Kreger, Edward Albert 1868-1955 *NatCAB 42,
WhAm 3*
Kreger, Henry Ludwig Flood 1892-1966
NatCAB 53, WhAm 4
Krehbiel, Christian 1832-1909 *DcAmB,
WhAm HA, WhAm 4*
Krehbiel, Christian Emanuel 1869-1948
WhAm 2
Krehbiel, Edward 1878-1950 *WhAm 3*
Krehbiel, Frank William 1897- *ApCAB X*
Krehbiel, Helen Virginia Osborne 1846-1894
TwCBDA
Krehbiel, Henry Edward 1854-1923 *AmBi,
ApCAB, ApCAB X, DcAmB,
NatCAB 12, TwCBDA, WebAB,
WhAm 1*
Krehl, Ludolf Von 1861-1937 *BiHiMed*
Kreicker, William Henri 1904-1968 *NatCAB 54*
Kreider, Aaron Shenk 1863-1929 *BiDrAC,
NatCAB 21, WhAm 1, WhAmP*
Kreider, Charles Daniel 1867-1953 *WhAm 3*
Kreider, Louis S 1886-1961 *NatCAB 49*
Kreinheder, Oscar Carl 1877-1946 *WhAm 2*
Kreis, Henry 1899-1963 *WhAm 4*
Kreiser, Edward Franklin 1869-1917 *WhAm 1*
Kreisinger, Henry 1876-1946 *NatCAB 38,
WhAm 2*
Kreisler, Fritz 1875-1962 *ApCAB X, WebAB,
WhAm 4*
Kreismann, Frederick Herman 1869- *WhAm 5*
Kreismann, Pauline W 1867- *WomWWA 14*
Kreitser, H *NewYHSD*
Kreitzer, John William 1852- *ApCAB X*
Krejci, Milo William 1876-1963 *WhAm 4*
Krekel, Arnold 1815-1888 *ApCAB Sup,
BiAUS*
Kremer, Charles Edward 1850- *WhAm 4*
Kremer, Charles S 1875-1964 *WhAm 4*
Kremer, George 1775-1854 *BiAUS, BiDrAC,
TwCBDA, WhAm H*
Kremer, J Bruce 1878-1940 *WhAm 1*
Kremer, Walter Wall 1900-1968 *WhAm 4*
Kremers, Edward 1865-1941 *DcAmB S3,
NatCAB 30, WhAm 1*
Kremers, J H 1898-1962 *WhAm 4*
Krempel, John P 1861- *WhAm 1*
Krenek, Ernst 1900- *McGEWB*
Krenson, William Day 1857- *ApCAB X*
Kreps, Ida Belle *WomWWA 14*
Kresel, Isidor Jacob 1878-1957 *WhAm 3*
Kresevich, Joseph 1905-1965 *NatCAB 51*
Kresge, Sebastian Spering 1867-1966 *ApCAB X,
NatCAB 52, WhAm 4*
Kress, Albert Leland 1894-1973 *WhAm 6*
Kress, C Adam 1879-1955 *WhAm 3*
Kress, Claude Washington 1876-1940
ApCAB X, NatCAB 31, WhAm 1
Kress, Daniel H 1862- *WhAm 4*
Kress, George Henry 1874-1954 *NatCAB 16,
NatCAB 41, WhAm 3*
Kress, John Alexander 1839-1933 *NatCAB 25,
WhAm 1*
Kress, Palmer John 1870-1936 *NatCAB 27*
Kress, Rush Harrison 1877-1963 *NatCAB 47,
WhAm 4*
Kress, Samuel Henry 1863-1955 *DcAmB S5,
NatCAB 41, WebAB, WhAm 3*
Kress, Walter Jay 1893-1968 *WhAm 5*
Kressman, Mabel A Gridley 1887-1970
WhAm 5
Kretschmer, Ernst 1888-1964 *BiHiMed*
Kretschmer, Herman Louis 1879-1951
NatCAB 40, WhAm 3
Kretschmer, Otto 1912- *WhWW-II*
Kretzinger, Clara Jeannette Wilson 1851-
WomWWA 14
Kretzinger, George Washington 1844-1913
NatCAB 12
Kretzinger, George Washington 1846-1913
WhAm 1
Kretzmann, M F 1878- *WhAm 6*
Kretzmann, Otto Paul 1901-1975 *WhAm 6*
Kreuder, Ernst 1903-1972 *WhAm 6*
Kreuscher, Philip Heinrich 1885-1943 *WhAm 2*
Kreusi, John 1843-1899 *TwCBDA*

Kreuter, Adam 1860-1931 *NatCAB 23*
Kreutzmann, Henry Adolph Robert 1890-1953
NatCAB 45
Krewson, Charles Fleming 1905-1968
NatCAB 54
Krey, August Charles 1887-1961 *BiDAmEd,
WhAm 4*
Kreyche, Robert Joseph 1920-1974 *WhAm 6*
Kreymborg, Alfred 1883-1966 *WhAm 4*
Krez, John Julius 1893-1955 *NatCAB 45*
Krez, Konrad 1828-1897 *DcAmB, WhAm H*
Kribben, Earl 1903-1959 *WhAm 3*
Kribbs, George Frederic 1846-1938 *BiDrAC,
TwCBDA*
Krichamer, Arnold Henry 1900-1966
NatCAB 53
Krick, Charles Shalter 1866-1943 *WhAm 2*
Krick, Edwin Vernon 1881-1952 *WhAm 3*
Kridel, Samuel 1868- *ApCAB X*
Kridl, Manfred 1882-1957 *WhAm 3*
Kriebel, Oscar Schultz 1863-1932 *WhAm 1*
Kriebel, William F 1890-1956 *WhAm 3*
Krieble, Vernon Kriebel 1885-1964 *WhAm 4*
Krieg, Laurel Lee 1907- *WhAm 6*
Kriege, Herbert Frick 1895-1965 *NatCAB 54*
Kriege, Otto Edward 1865- *WhAm 5*
Krieger, Knut Axel 1911-1975 *WhAm 6*
Krieghoff, Cornelius David 1812-1872
NewYHSD
Krieghoff, Cornelius David 1815-1872
IlBEAAW, McGEWB
Kriegshaber, Adeline Mayer *WomWWA 14*
Kriehn, George 1868- *TwCBDA, WhAm 4*
Kriendler, Maxwell Arnold 1908-1973 *WhAm 6*
Krigbaum, Roy Edmund 1893-1951 *NatCAB 44*
Krill, Alex Eugene 1928-1972 *WhAm 5*
Krimbill, Walter Michael 1876-1952
NatCAB 40
Krimmel, John Lewis 1787-1821 *ApCAB,
BnEnAmA, TwCBDA*
Krimmel, John Lewis 1789-1821 *DcAmB,
NewYHSD, WhAm H*
Kriner, Harry L 1894-1973 *WhAm 6*
Krinsky, Alexander 1916-1964 *NatCAB 50*
Krips, Henry Joseph 1902-1974 *WhAm 6*
Krishna, Menon Vengalil Krishman 1897-1974
WhAm 6
Krishnamurti, Jiddu 1895- *McGEWB*
Krishnan, Sir Kariamanikkam Srinivasa
1898-1961 *WhAm 4*
Kristjanson, Hjorleifur Trausti 1876-1954
NatCAB 42
Kristoffersen, Magnus K 1898-1960 *WhAm 4*
Kritz, Karl d1969 *WhAm 5*
Kriz, Frank H 1886-1965 *NatCAB 51*
Kriza, John 1919-1975 *WhAm 6*
Krochmal, Nachman Kohen 1785-1840
McGEWB
Krock, Arthur 1886-1974 *EncAB*
Krock, Arthur 1886-1974 *WhAm 6*
Kroeber, Alfred L 1875-1960 *NatCAB 14*
Kroeber, Alfred Louis 1876-1960 *McGEWB,
NatCAB 49, REnAW, WebAB, WhAm 4*
Kroeck, Louis Samuel 1872- *WhAm 5*
Kroeger, Adolph Ernst 1837-1882 *ApCAB,
DcAmB, NatCAB 3, TwCBDA,
WhAm H*
Kroeger, Alice Bertha 1864-1909 *DcAmLiB,
NotAW*
Kroeger, Ernest Richard 1862-1934 *DcAmB S1,
NatCAB 6, TwCBDA, WhAm 1*
Kroeger, Frederick Charles 1888-1944 *WhAm 2*
Kroeger, Laura Clark 1872- *WomWWA 14*
Kroeger, William John 1906-1966 *NatCAB 51*
Kroeh, Charles Frederick 1846-1928 *NatCAB 4,
TwCBDA, WhAm 2*
Kroehle, Ralph 1892-1970 *NatCAB 56*
Kroehler, Peter Edward 1872-1950 *WhAm 3*
Kroeze, Barend Herman 1868- *WhAm 5*
Kroger, Bernard Henry 1860-1938 *DcAmB S2,
NatCAB 32, WhAm 1*
Krogh, August 1874-1949 *BiHiMed*
Krogh, Schack August Steenberg 1874-1949
DcScB, McGEWB
Krogstrupp, Otto Christian 1714-1785 *ApCAB*
Kroh, Aldine Resley 1877-1927 *NatCAB 21*
Kroha, Jiri 1893-1974 *WhAm 6*
Krohn, Joseph Hyacinthe 1766-1823 *ApCAB*

Krohn, William Otterbein 1868-1927 *WhAm 1*
Krol, Bastiaen Jansen 1595-1674 *DcAmB,
WhAm H*
Kroll, Jack 1885-1971 *WhAm 5*
Kroll, Leon 1884-1974 *BnEnAmA, IlBEAAW,
WhAm 6*
Kromer, Leon Benjamin 1876-1966 *WhAm 4*
Kron, Joseph 1912- *WhAm 6*
Kronberg, Louis 1872-1965 *WhAm 4*
Krone, Max Thomas 1901-1970 *WhAm 5*
Kronecker, Hugo 1839-1914 *BiHiMed, DcScB*
Kronecker, Leopold 1823-1891 *AsBiEn, DcScB*
Kronenberg, Max 1894-1972 *NatCAB 57*
Kronig, August Karl 1822-1879 *DcScB*
Kronmiller, John 1858-1928 *BiDrAC, WhAm 4*
Kronold, Selma 1861-1920 *NotAW*
Kronshage, Theodore 1869-1934 *NatCAB 24,
WhAm 5*
Kronwall, Konstantin 1900-1966 *WhAm 4*
Kroos, Oscar August 1880-1957 *WhAm 3*
Krooss, Herman Edward 1912-1975 *WhAm 6*
Kropa, Edward L 1907-1965 *NatCAB 51*
Kropotkin, Peter Alekseevich 1842-1921
McGEWB
Kropotkin, Petr Alekseevich 1842-1921 *DcScB*
Krotel, Gottlob Frederick 1826-1907 *ApCAB,
TwCBDA, WhAm 1*
Krouse, Charles *NewYHSD*
Krout, Caroline Virginia *WomWWA 14*
Krout, Mary H 1852-1927 *AmWom*
Krout, Mary Hannah 1853-1927 *WomWWA 14*
Krout, Mary Hannah 1857-1927 *WhAm 1*
Kroyt, Boris 1897-1969 *WhAm 5*
Krsna *DcScB*
Kruber, Aleksandr Aleksandrovich 1871-1941
DcScB
Kruckemeyer, Edward Herman 1886-1965
NatCAB 52
Kruckman, Arnold 1880-1959 *WhAm 3*
Krueger, Allison Ferdinand 1913-1967
NatCAB 54
Krueger, Ernest Theodore 1885-1945 *WhAm 2*
Krueger, John Frederick 1881-1935 *WhAm 1*
Krueger, Otto 1890-1963 *BiDrAC, WhAm 4*
Krueger, Walter 1881-1967 *WebAMB,
WhAm 4, WhWW-II*
Krueger, William Conrad 1888- *WhAm 3*
Kruell, Gustav 1843-1907 *DcAmB,
NatCAB 11, WhAm 1*
Kruesi, Frank E 1885-1949 *WhAm 2*
Kruesi, John 1843-1899 *DcAmB, NatCAB 26,
WhAm 1*
Kruesi, Paul John 1878-1965 *WhAm 4*
Kruesi, Walter Edison 1881- *WhAm 6*
Kruetgen, Ernest J 1868-1948 *WhAm 2*
Krug, Frederick 1893-1970 *NatCAB 55*
Krug, Henry, Jr. 1861-1946 *WhAm 2*
Krug, Julius Albert 1907-1970 *BiDrUSE,
EncAAH, NatCAB 56, WhAm 5*
Kruger, Ferdinand *NewYHSD*
Kruger, Frederick Konrad 1887-1953 *WhAm 3*
Kruger, Minna Nicola Kruger d1975 *WhAm 6*
Kruger, Otto 1885-1974 *WhAm 6*
Kruger, Stephanus Johannes Paulus 1825-1904
McGEWB, WhoMilH
Krugler, Joseph Anthony 1899-1950
NatCAB 39
Krulish, Emil 1878- *WhAm 6*
Krum, Charles Lyon 1852-1937 *NatCAB 28*
Krum, Chester Harding 1840-1923 *NatCAB 8,
NatCAB 26, WhAm 1*
Krum, Howard Lewis 1883-1961 *WhAm 4*
Krum, Octavia L 1861- *WomWWA 14*
Krumb, Henry 1875-1958 *NatCAB 44,
WhAm 4*
Krumbein, Paul Otto 1875-1949 *WhAm 2*
Krumbhaar, E B 1882-1966 *WhAm 4*
Krumm, Tahlman 1912-1969 *NatCAB 56*
Krummacher, Friedrich Wilhelm 1796-1868
ApCAB
Krummrich, William Gustav 1895-1951
NatCAB 39
Krumrei, Walter Ernest 1890-1966 *NatCAB 55*
Krumreig, Edward Ludwig 1861- *WhAm 4*
Krumwiede, Charles 1879-1930 *NatCAB 30,
WhAm 1, WhAm 1C*
Krupa, Gene 1909-1973 *WhAm 6*

Krupp, Alfried VonBohlen Und Halbach 1907-1967 *WhAm 4*
Krupp Family *McGEWB*
Krupp VonBohlen Und Halbach, Alfried 1907-1967 *WhWW-II*
Krupsaw, David Loeb 1911-1960 *WhAm 4*
Kruse, E T d1947 *WhAm 3*
Kruse, Edward H 1918- *BiDrAC*
Kruse, Frederick William 1852-1938 *NatCAB 41*
Kruse, Frederick William 1852-1939 *WhAm 1*
Kruse, Otto Von 1886-1941 *NatCAB 30*
Kruse, Peter 1874-1951 *NatCAB 39*
Krusen, Frank Hammond 1898-1973 *WhAm 6*
Krusen, Ursula Leden 1921-1973 *WhAm 6*
Krusen, Wilmer 1869-1943 *WhAm 2*
Krusenstern, Adam Johann Von 1770-1846 *ApCAB*
Krush, Thaddeus Paul 1915-1965 *NatCAB 52*
Krushchev, Nikita 1894-1973 *WhWW-II*
Krushenick, Nicholas 1929- *BnEnAmA*
Krusi, Johann Heinrich Hermann 1817-1903 *BiDAmEd, DcAmB*
Krutch, Joseph Wood 1893-1970 *EncAAH, WebAB, WhAm 5*
Kruttschnitt, Ernest Benjamin 1852-1906 *NatCAB 10, WhAm 1*
Kruttschnitt, Julius 1854-1925 *NatCAB 25, REnAW, WhAm 1*
Krych, Felix Joseph 1882-1945 *NatCAB 34*
Kryl, Bohumir 1875- *WhAm 5*
Krylov, Aleksei Nikolaevich 1863-1945 *DcScB*
Krylov, Nikolai Mitrofanovich 1879-1955 *DcScB*
Kryn d1690 *ApCAB*
Kryszak, Mary Olszewski 1875-1945 *NotAW*
Kryter, Charles Conrad 1873-1944 *NatCAB 33*
Krzyzanowski, Wladimir 1824-1887 *TwCBDA*
Ku, Chieh-Kang 1895- *McGEWB*
Ku, K'ai-Chih 345?-406? *McGEWB*
Kuang-Hsu 1871-1908 *McGEWB*
Kuang-Wu-Ti 006BC-057AD *McGEWB*
Kubanek, Joseph Louis 1896-1970 *NatCAB 56*
Kubat, Jerald Richard 1928-1969 *WhAm 5*
Kubel, Stephen Joseph 1858-1936 *WhAm 1*
Kubelik, Jan 1880-1940 *WhAm 1*
Kubelsky, Benjamin 1894- *WebAB*
Kubert, Joseph Mandel 1917-1974 *WhAm 6*
Kubie, Lawrence S 1896-1973 *WhAm 6*
Kubie, Matilda Steinam 1869- *ApCAB X*
Kubitschek DeOliveira, Juscelino 1902- *McGEWB*
Kublai Khan 1215-1294 *McGEWB*
Kubrick, Stanley 1928- *WebAB*
Kucera, Louis Benedict 1888-1957 *NatCAB 45, WhAm 3*
Kucharo, William Frederick 1885-1949 *NatCAB 40*
Kuchel, Charles Conrad 1820- *IIBEAAW, NewYHSD*
Kuchel, Jacob *NewYHSD*
Kuchel, Thomas Henry 1910- *BiDrAC*
Kuckro, William Emil 1877-1951 *NatCAB 39*
Kuczynski, Robert Rene 1876-1947 *WhAm 2*
Kuder, Blanche Allyn Bane 1882- *WomWWA 14*
Kudlich, Hans 1823-1917 *NatCAB 31*
Kudner, Arthur Henry 1890-1944 *NatCAB 32, WhAm 2*
Kuebler, Clark George 1908-1974 *WhAm 6*
Kuebler, John R 1890-1967 *WhAm 4*
Kuechenmeister, Alvin August 1881-1958 *NatCAB 48*
Kuechenmeister, Henry William 1877-1932 *NatCAB 27*
Kuehn, Louis 1867-1948 *NatCAB 39*
Kuehne, Hugo Franz 1884-1963 *NatCAB 52, WhAm 4*
Kuehner, Quincy Adams 1879- *WhAm 6*
Kuellmer, Fay L *WomWWA 14*
Kuemmerle, Gustave Albert 1847-1927 *NatCAB 22*
Kuenen, Johannes Petrus 1866-1922 *DcScB*
Kuersteiner, Albert Frederick 1865-1917 *WhAm 1*
Kuester, Clarence Otto 1876-1948 *WhAm 2*
Kuether, Frederick William 1922-1969 *WhAm 5*
Kuflewski, Wladyslaw Augustyn 1870-1945 *NatCAB 35*

Kugeler, Henry Behrent Albert 1870-1914 *NatCAB 17*
Kugelman, Frederick Benjamin 1892-1930 *DcAmB*
Kugler, Anna Sarah 1856-1930 *NotAW*
Kuh, Sydney 1866-1934 *WhAm 1*
Kuhl, Ernest Peter 1881- *WhAm 6*
Kuhl, Frederick *NewYHSD*
Kuhler, Otto 1894- *IIBEAAW*
Kuhlman, Kathryn 1910-1976 *WhAm 6*
Kuhn, Adam 1741-1817 *ApCAB, DcAmB, Drake, NatCAB 7, NatCAB 21, WhAm H*
Kuhn, Alfred 1885-1968 *DcScB*
Kuhn, Arthur K 1876-1954 *WhAm 3*
Kuhn, C John 1897-1960 *WhAm 4*
Kuhn, Charles Francis 1870-1935 *NatCAB 27*
Kuhn, Eusebius Francis 1650?-1711 *ApCAB*
Kuhn, Ferd William 1893-1957 *WhAm 3*
Kuhn, Franz Christian 1872-1926 *NatCAB 29, WhAm 1*
Kuhn, Harry Waldo 1873-1965 *WhAm 4*
Kuhn, Joseph Ernst 1864-1935 *DcAmB S1, WhAm 1*
Kuhn, Justus Engelhardt 1708-1717 *BnEnAmA*
Kuhn, Justus Englehardt 1708-1717 *NewYHSD*
Kuhn, Oliver Owen 1886-1937 *WhAm 1*
Kuhn, Paul R 1889-1951 *NatCAB 38*
Kuhn, R Parker 1894-1963 *NatCAB 51*
Kuhn, Richard 1900-1967 *AsBiEn, DcScB*
Kuhn, Robert *NewYHSD*
Kuhn, Robert F 1920- *IIBEAAW*
Kuhn, Walt 1877-1949 *DcAmB S4*
Kuhn, Walt 1880?-1949 *BnEnAmA, IIBEAAW, WhAm 2*
Kuhn, Werner 1899-1963 *DcScB*
Kuhn, William Frederick 1849-1924 *WhAm 1*
Kuhn, William Speer 1855-1944 *NatCAB 33*
Kuhne, Percival 1861- *NatCAB 9*
Kuhne, Wilhelm Friedrich 1837-1900 *DcScB*
Kuhne, Willy 1837-1900 *AsBiEn, BiHiMed*
Kuhns, Austin Hubbert 1894-1962 *NatCAB 49, WhAm 4*
Kuhns, Edward Louis 1859-1917 *NatCAB 18*
Kuhns, Harold Samuel 1905-1965 *WhAm 4*
Kuhns, Joseph Henry 1800-1883 *BiAUS, BiDrAC, WhAm H*
Kuhns, Luther Melanchthon 1861-1939 *WhAm 1*
Kuhns, Oscar 1856-1929 *NatCAB 22, WhAm 1*
Kuhns, William Rodney 1897-1972 *WhAm 5*
Kuichling, Emil 1848-1914 *NatCAB 16, WhAm 1*
Kuiper, Edward 1897-1959 *NatCAB 48*
Kuiper, Gerard Peter 1905-1973 *AsBiEn, WhAm 6*
Kuist, Howard Tillman 1895-1964 *WhAm 4*
Kuizenga, John E 1876-1949 *WhAm 3*
Kujoth, Jean Spealman 1935-1975 *WhAm 6*
Kuk, Abraham Isaac 1865-1935 *McGEWB*
Kukai 774-835 *McGEWB*
Kulas, Elroy John 1880-1952 *NatCAB 41, WhAm 3*
Kuldell, Rudolph Charles 1889-1973 *WhAm 6*
Kuler, Fritz 1914-1971 *WhAm 5*
Kulikowski, Adam 1890-1966 *WhAm 4, WhAm 5*
Kuljian, Harry A 1893-1974 *WhAm 6*
Kullman, Harold John Frederick 1901-1972 *NatCAB 57, WhAm 5*
Kullmer, Charles Julius 1879-1942 *NatCAB 31*
Kulp, Albert Guido 1910-1965 *NatCAB 52*
Kulp, Clarence Arthur 1895-1957 *WhAm 3*
Kulp, Harry Wolf 1889-1962 *NatCAB 49*
Kulp, Monroe Henry 1858-1911 *BiDrAC, TwCBDA*
Kulp, Victor Henry 1881-1967 *WhAm 4*
Kulp, William 1826-1870 *NatCAB 7*
Kumarajiva 344?-413? *McGEWB*
Kumler, Franklin Abia Zeller 1854-1942 *NatCAB 31, TwCBDA*
Kumler, Henry 1775-1854 *DcAmB, WhAm H*
Kumler, John A 1838- *WhAm 4*
Kumm, Einar Axel 1901-1952 *WhAm 3*
Kumm, H Karl William 1874-1930 *WhAm 1*
Kumm, Herman Karl William 1874-1930 *NatCAB 23*

Kumm, Ward Confarr 1893-1966 *NatCAB 51*
Kummel, Henry Barnard 1867-1945 *NatCAB 14, NatCAB 34, WhAm 2*
Kummer, Ernst Eduard 1810-1893 *DcScB*
Kummer, Frederic Arnold 1873-1943 *WhAm 2*
Kummer, Julius Hermann 1817-1869? *IIBEAAW, NewYHSD*
Kump, Albert Barker 1908-1958 *NatCAB 47*
Kump, Herman Guy 1877-1962 *WhAm 4*
Kunckel, Johann 1630?-1702? *DcScB*
Kundt, August Adolph Eduard Eberhard 1839-1894 *AsBiEn, DcScB*
Kuner, Albert 1819-1906 *NewYHSD*
Kunesh, Joseph Francis 1890-1959 *WhAm 4*
Kung, H H 1881-1967 *WhAm 4*
Kung, Hans 1928- *McGEWB*
Kunhardt, Henry Rudolph 1860-1923 *NatCAB 32*
Kunhardt, Kingsley 1897-1959 *NatCAB 47, WhAm 3*
Kunhardt, Wheaton Bradish 1859-1933 *NatCAB 30*
Kuniansky, Max 1899-1953 *NatCAB 42, WhAm 3*
Kunitzer, Robert 1865-1924 *NatCAB 15*
Kunitzer, Robert 1866-1924 *WhAm 1*
Kuniyoshi, Yasuo 1893-1953 *BnEnAmA, DcAmB S5, IIBEAAW, NatCAB 39, WhAm 3*
Kunkel, A William 1925-1972 *WhAm 5*
Kunkel, Beverly Waugh 1881-1969 *NatCAB 55, WhAm 5*
Kunkel, Frank Henry 1874-1950 *WhAm 3*
Kunkel, Jacob M 1822-1870 *BiAUS*
Kunkel, Jacob Michael 1822-1870 *BiDrAC, WhAm H*
Kunkel, Jacob Michel 1822-1870 *TwCBDA*
Kunkel, John Atley 1835-1921 *NatCAB 19*
Kunkel, John Christian 1816-1870 *ApCAB, BiAUS, BiDrAC, Drake, NatCAB 11, TwCBDA, WhAm H*
Kunkel, John Crain 1898-1970 *BiDrAC, WhAm 5, WhAmP*
Kunkel, Louis Otto 1884-1960 *WhAm 3A*
Kunkel, William Albert, Jr. 1895-1948 *WhAm 2*
Kunkel VonLowenstern *DcScB*
Kunkely, Julius *NewYHSD*
Kunkerley, Edward *NewYHSD*
Kunkle, Albert Henry 1860-1935 *NatCAB 26*
Kunkle, Bayard Dickenson 1882-1953 *WhAm 3*
Kunkle, George Ray 1881-1965 *NatCAB 55*
Kuno, Hisashi 1910-1969 *WhAm 5*
Kunsmiller, Adolph *WhAm 6*
Kunst, George Henry Augustus 1873-1955 *NatCAB 43*
Kunstadter, Albert 1872-1965 *WhAm 4*
Kunstadter, Ralph Hess 1905-1965 *WhAm 4*
Kunstler, Morton 1931- *IIBEAAW*
Kunth, Carl Sigismund 1788-1850 *DcScB Sup*
Kunth, Charles Sigismund 1788-1850 *ApCAB*
Kuntz, Albert 1879-1957 *WhAm 3*
Kuntz, Henry 1830-1905 *NatCAB 29*
Kuntz, Werner Hinrich 1898-1973 *WhAm 6*
Kuntze, Carl Ernst Otto 1843-1907 *DcScB Sup*
Kuntze, Edward J 1826-1870 *ApCAB, NewYHSD*
Kunwald, Ernst 1868- *WhAm 4*
Kunz, Adolf Henry d1966 *WhAm 5*
Kunz, George Frederick 1856-1932 *AmBi, ApCAB, DcAmB S1, NatCAB 4, TwCBDA, WhAm 1*
Kunz, Jakob 1874-1939 *WhAm 1*
Kunz, Josef L 1890-1970 *WhAm 5*
Kunz, Stanley Henry 1864-1946 *BiDrAC, WhAm 4, WhAmP*
Kunze, Edward J 1826-1870 *Drake*
Kunze, John Christopher 1744-1807 *ApCAB, DcAmB, Drake, NatCAB 6, TwCBDA, WhAm H*
Kunze, Richard Ernest 1838-1919 *ApCAB, DcAmB, NatCAB 3, WhAm 1*
Kunze, William Frederick 1872- *WhAm 5*
Kunzel, Fred 1901-1969 *WhAm 5*
Kunzig, Louis A 1882-1956 *WhAm 3*
Kunzmann, Jacob Christoph 1852- *WhAm 5*
Kuo, Mo-Jo *McGEWB*
Kuo, Ping Wen 1880-1969 *WhAm 5*
Kuony, Victor *NewYHSD*

Kuony, Victor, Jr. *NewYHSD*
Kupferman, Theodore Roosevelt 1920- *BiDrAC*
Kuplic, J L 1911-1968 *WhAm 5*
Kuplic, James Leslie 1911-1968 *NatCAB 54*
Kuppenheimer, Jonas 1854-1921 *NatCAB 20*
Kurchatov, Igor V 1903-1960 *WhAm 3*
Kurchatov, Igor Vasilevich 1903-1960 *AsBiEn*
Kurchatov, Igor Vasilievich 1903-1960 *DcScB*
Kuribayashi, Tadamichi 1885-1945 *WhWW-II,*
  WhoMilH
Kurita, Takeo *WhWW-II*
Kurland, Nancy Jamie 1938-1972 *WhAm 6*
Kurlbaum, Ferdinand 1857-1927 *DcScB*
Kurn, James M 1870-1945 *WhAm 2*
Kurnakov, Nikolai Semyonovich 1860-1941
  DcScB
Kurochkin, Pavel 1900- *WhWW-II*
Kuroki, Baron Jamemoto 1844-1923 *WhoMilH*
Kuropatkin, Alexei Nikolaievich 1848-1925
  WhoMilH
Kurosawa, Akira 1910- *McGEWB*
Kurrelmeyer, William 1874-1957 *WhAm 3*
Kurrie, Harry Rushworth d1938 *WhAm 1*
Kurschak, Jozsef 1864-1933 *DcScB*
Kurt, Franklin Thomas 1872-1947 *WhAm 2*
Kurt, Katherine 1852- *AmWom*
Kurth, Ernest Lynn 1885-1960 *WhAm 4*
Kurth, Joseph Hubert, Jr. 1883-1967
  NatCAB 53
Kurth, Wilfred 1875-1959 *WhAm 3*
Kurtz, Benjamin 1795-1865 *ApCAB, DcAmB,*
  NatCAB 24, TwCBDA, WhAm H
Kurtz, Benjamin Putnam 1878-1950 *WhAm 3*
Kurtz, Charles Jewett 1885-1963 *NatCAB 50*
Kurtz, Charles Lindley 1854-1929 *NatCAB 22,*
  WhAm 1
Kurtz, Charles M 1855-1909 *WhAm 1*
Kurtz, Charles Theodore 1874-1956 *NatCAB 45*
Kurtz, Daniel Webster 1879- *WhAm 6*
Kurtz, Eugene E 1914-1964 *NatCAB 52*
Kurtz, Ford 1885-1956 *WhAm 3*
Kurtz, Henry 1822?- *NewYHSD*
Kurtz, Horatio J *NewYHSD*
Kurtz, Jacob Banks 1867-1960 *BiDrAC,*
  WhAm 4, WhAmP
Kurtz, John D 1822?-1877 *ApCAB*
Kurtz, John Daniel 1763-1856 *ApCAB,*
  TwCBDA
Kurtz, John Nicholas 1720?-1794 *ApCAB*
Kurtz, Louis Charles 1867- *WhAm 5*
Kurtz, Robert Merrill 1871-1941 *NatCAB 30,*
  WhAm 1
Kurtz, Thomas Richardson 1881-1956 *WhAm 3*
Kurtz, Wilbur George 1882-1967 *NatCAB 52*
Kurtz, William 1833-1904 *NewYHSD*
Kurtz, William Henry 1804-1868 *BiAUS,*
  BiDrAC, WhAm H
Kurz, Emil *NewYHSD*
Kurz, Friedrich 1818-1871 *NewYHSD*
Kurz, Louis 1833-1921 *NewYHSD,*
  WhAm HA, WhAm 4
Kurz, Louis Frederick 1891-1965 *WhAm 4*
Kurz, Rudolph Friedrich 1818-1871 *IlBEAAW,*
  REnAW
Kurz, Walter Charles 1908-1971 *WhAm 5*
Kurzman, Harold Phillip 1902-1972 *WhAm 5*
Kusch, Polycarp 1911- *WebAB*
Kuschner, Beatrice Barbara Katz 1913-1969
  WhAm 5
Kuser, Anthony Rudolph 1862-1929
  NatCAB 26
Kuser, John Louis 1862-1937 *NatCAB 34*
Kuser, Rudolph Victor 1865-1931 *NatCAB 34*
Kush, Gustave 1857-1946 *NatCAB 35*
Kushner, Daniel Stephen 1922-1974 *WhAm 6*
Kushyar Ibn Labban Bashahri, Al-Jili *DcScB*
Kuskov, Ivan Aleksandrovich 1765-1823 *DcAmB,*
  WhAm H
Kussevitsky, Sergei Alexandrovitch 1874-1951
  WebAB
Kussmaul, Adolf 1822-1902 *BiHiMed*
Kussy, Nathan 1872- *WhAm 5*
Kusterer, Arthur Emil 1883-1951 *NatCAB 38*
Kustermann, Gustav 1850-1919 *BiDrAC,*
  WhAm 4
Kusworm, Sidney Grover 1885-1969 *WhAm 5*
Kutak, Robert I 1899-1959 *WhAm 3*
Kutchin, Mary Kimball 1874- *WomWWA 14*

Kutts, John *NewYHSD*
Kutusov, Mikhail L Golenishchev 1745-1813
  WhoMilH
Kutuzov, Mikhail Ilarionovich 1745-1813
  McGEWB
Kutz, Charles Willauer 1870- *WhAm 5*
Kutz, George Fink 1835-1921 *WhAm 1*
Kutzing, Friedrich Traugott 1807-1893 *DcScB*
Kuwatly, Shukri Al 1891-1967 *WhAm 4*
Kuykendall, Andrew Jackson 1815-1891 *BiDrAC,*
  WhAm H
Kuykendall, Andrew Z 1815-1891 *BiAUS*
Kuykendall, Dan Heflin 1924- *BiDrAC*
Kuypers, Gerardus Arentse 1766-1833 *ApCAB,*
  NatCAB 12
Kuypers, Warmuldus 1732-1797 *ApCAB*
Kuzell, Charles Raphael 1889-1971 *NatCAB 56*
Kuznets, Simon Smith 1901- *EncAB, WebAB*
Kuznetsov, Nikolay 1902- *WhWW-II*
Kuznetsov, Vasiliy 1894-1964 *WhWW-II*
Kvale, O J 1869-1929 *WhAm 1*
Kvale, Ole Juulson 1868-1929 *NatCAB 22*
Kvale, Ole Juulson 1869-1929 *BiDrAC,*
  WhAmP
Kvale, Paul John 1896-1960 *BiDrAC, WhAmP*
Kvale, Walter Frederick 1907-1970 *WhAm 5*
Kwanggaet'o 375-413 *McGEWB*
Kwangjong 925-975 *McGEWB*
Kyan, John H 1775-1850 *ApCAB, Drake*
Kyd, Thomas 1558-1594 *McGEWB*
Kyes, Lafayette Martin 1879-1954 *NatCAB 43*
Kyes, Preston 1875-1949 *NatCAB 39,*
  WhAm 2
Kyes, Roger Martin 1906-1971 *NatCAB 56,*
  WhAm 5
Kyker, Benjamin Franklin 1893-1960 *WhAm 4*
Kyl, John Henry 1919- *BiDrAC*
Kyle, Alice James Aunspaugh 1868-
  WomWWA 14
Kyle, D Braden 1863-1916 *WhAm 1*
Kyle, David Braden 1863-1916 *DcAmB,*
  NatCAB 26
Kyle, Edwin Dewees 1869- *WhAm 5*
Kyle, Edwin Jackson 1876- *WhAm 5*
Kyle, Hugh Graham 1849-1927 *NatCAB 37,*
  WhAm 1
Kyle, James Henderson 1854-1901 *ApCAB Sup,*
  BiDrAC, DcAmB, NatCAB 1, REnAW,
  TwCBDA, WhAm 1, WhAmP
Kyle, John *NewYHSD*
Kyle, John Curtis 1851-1913 *BiDrAC,*
  TwCBDA
Kyle, John Johnson 1869-1920 *NatCAB 24,*
  WhAm 1
Kyle, John Merrill 1856-1918 *WhAm 1*
Kyle, John William 1891-1965 *WhAm 5*
Kyle, Joseph 1815-1863 *NewYHSD*
Kyle, Joseph 1849- *WhAm 1*
Kyle, Joseph Blair 1890-1961 *WhAm 4*
Kyle, Laurence Harwood 1916- *WhAm 5*
Kyle, Mary Elizabeth Chambers 1866-
  WomWWA 14
Kyle, Melvin Grove 1858-1933 *WhAm 1*
Kyle, Thomas Barton 1856-1915 *BiDrAC,*
  WhAm 4
Kyle, Willard Hugh 1903-1961 *WhAm 4*
Kyle, William S 1851-1931 *WhAm 1,*
  WhAm 1C
Kyles, Linwood W 1874- *WhoColR*
Kyles, Lynwood Westinghouse 1874- *WhAm 5*
Kylin, Johann Harald 1879-1949 *DcScB*
Kyne, Peter Bernard 1880-1957 *WhAm 3*
Kynett, Alpha Gilruth 1858-1939 *WhAm 1*
Kynett, Alpha Jefferson 1829-1899 *DcAmB,*
  NatCAB 4, TwCBDA, WhAm H
Kynett, Harold Havelock 1889-1973 *WhAm 6*
Kyrk, Hazel 1886-1957 *WhAm 3*
Kyros, Peter Nicholas 1925- *BiDrAC*
Kyser, Kathryn Belle 1882- *WomWWA 14*
Kyser, William D 1882-1932 *WhAm 1*
Kyster, Olaf Helgesen, Jr. 1903-1959 *WhAm 4*
Kyster, Olaf Helgeson, Jr. 1903-1959
  NatCAB 49

L

L A *NewYHSD*

LaBach, James Oscar 1871-1922 *WhAm 1*

Labagh, Isaac Peter 1804-1879 *ApCAB,*
TwCBDA

Labagh, Peter 1773-1858 *ApCAB*

Labarbinais LeGentil, Etienne Marcel 1685-1731
ApCAB

Labaree, Benjamin 1801-1883 *ApCAB, Drake,*
NatCAB 12, TwCBDA

Labaree, Benjamin 1834-1906 *WhAm 1*

Labaree, Mary Schauffler 1868-1954 *WhAm 3*

LaBarge, Joseph 1815-1899 *DcAmB, REnAW,*
WhAm H

Labarte, John B *NewYHSD*

Labarthe, Jules 1874-1951 *NatCAB 39*

Labarthe, Pedro Juan 1910-1966 *WhAm 4A*

Labaste, John B *NewYHSD*

Labastida Y Davalos, Pelagio Antonio De 1815-
ApCAB

Labat, John Baptist 1663-1738 *ApCAB, Drake*

Labat, Leon 1803-1847 *ApCAB*

Labatut, Isador *NewYHSD*

Labatut, J *NewYHSD*

Labatut, T *NewYHSD*

Labbe, Antoine G 1881-1936 *WhAm 1*

Labberton, John Madison 1893-1953
NatCAB 41, WhAm 3

LaBeaume, Louis 1873-1961 *WhAm 4*

Labelle, J Edouard 1883-1957 *WhAm 3*

Laberge, Charles Joseph 1827-1874 *ApCAB*

Labezares, Guido De 1510-1580 *ApCAB*

Labino, Dominick 1910- *BnEnAmA*

Lablanche, Alcee *BiAUS*

Labom, Adolphe *NewYHSD*

LaBorde *ApCAB*

LaBorde, Maximilian 1804-1873 *ApCAB,*
DcAmB, Drake, NatCAB 11, WhAm H

Laborn, Adolphe *NewYHSD*

Laboulaye, Edouard Rene Lefevre 1811-1883
ApCAB

LaBoyteaux, William Harvell 1872-1947
NatCAB 35

Labra, Rafael M De 1841- *ApCAB*

LaBranche, Alcee Louis 1806-1861 *BiDrAC,*
WhAm H

LaBranche, George Michel Lucien 1875-1961
NatCAB 46

Labreque, Michael Thomas 1849- *ApCAB Sup*

Labrie, James 1783-1831 *ApCAB*

LaBrosse, Guy De 1586?-1641 *DcScB*

Labrouste, Pierre Francois Henri 1801-1875
McGEWB

LaBruere, Pierre Boucher De 1837- *ApCAB*

Labrum, J Harry *WhAm 5*

LaBruyere, Jean De 1645-1696 *McGEWB*

Labunski, Wiktor 1895-1974 *WhAm 6*

LaBuy, Walter J 1889-1967 *WhAm 4*

LaBuy, Walter Jacob 1888-1967 *NatCAB 54*

Lacaille, Nicolas Louis De 1713-1762 *AsBiEn,*
DcScB

LaCamera, Joseph 1896-1957 *NatCAB 47*

Lacascade, Etienne Theodore Mondesir 1841-
ApCAB Sup

Lacasse, Gustave 1890-1953 *WhAm 3*

LaCauza, Frank Emilio 1900-1964 *WhAm 4*

LaCava, Gregory 1892-1952 *NatCAB 40,*
WhAm 3

Lacaze-Duthiers, Felix-Joseph Henri De
1821-1901 *DcScB*

Lacepede, Bernard-G-Etienne, Comte De
1756-1825 *DcScB*

Lacerda Y Almeida, Francisco Jose De
1750?-1798? *ApCAB*

Lacey, Douglas Raymond 1913-1973 *WhAm 6*

Lacey, Edward Samuel 1835-1916 *BiDrAC,*
NatCAB 17, TwCBDA, WhAm 1

Lacey, James D 1849-1932 *WhAm 1*

Lacey, John 1755-1814 *ApCAB, DcAmB,*
Drake, NatCAB 1, TwCBDA, WhAm H

Lacey, John Fletcher 1841-1913 *BiDrAC,*
DcAmB, NatCAB 25, TwCBDA,
WhAm 1, WhAmP

Lacey, John Wesley 1848-1936 *WhAm 1*

Lacey, Lila Henry Patterson *WomWWA 14*

Lacey, Raymond Henry 1876- *WhAm 5*

Lacey, Robert Alexander 1878- *WhAm 6*

Lacey, William Brittainham 1781-1866 *ApCAB*

Lachaise, Gaston 1882-1935 *BnEnAmA,*
DcAmB S1, McGEWB, WebAB,
WhAm 1, WhAm 4

LaChance, Leander Hanscom 1874- *WhAm 5*

Lacher *IlBEAAW*

Lachman, Arthur 1873- *WhAm 5*

Lachman, Harry 1886-1975 *WhAm 6*

Lachmund, Carl Valentine 1853-1928
NatCAB 21

Laciar, Elizabeth Tremper Darrow 1878-
WomWWA 14

Lackaye, Wilton 1862-1932 *DcAmB S1,*
NatCAB 3, WhAm 1

Lackey, Frank Ross 1880-1944 *NatCAB 34*

Lackey, Henry Ellis 1876- *WhAm 3*

Lackey, John Newton 1875-1942 *WhAm 2*

Lackey, Vinson 1889-1959 *IlBEAAW*

Lackland, Frank Dorwin 1884-1943 *WhAm 2*

Lackner, Julius Ernest 1887-1945 *NatCAB 37*

Laclede, Pierre 1729-1778 *REnAW*

Laclede, Pierre Ligueste 1724?-1778 *AmBi,*
ApCAB, DcAmB, TwCBDA, WebAB,
WhAm H

Laclotte, Hyacinthe *NewYHSD*

Lacock, Abner 1770-1837 *ApCAB, BiAUS,*
BiDrAC, DcAmB, NatCAB 10, TwCBDA,
WhAm H

Lacock, Ira J 1831-1900 *NatCAB 12*

Lacombe, Albert 1827-1916 *McGEWB*

Lacombe, Emile Henry 1846-1924 *ApCAB X,*
TwCBDA, WhAm 1

LaCondamine, Charles Marie De 1701-1774
AsBiEn, DcScB, DcScB Sup

Lacordaire, Jean Baptiste Henri 1802-1861
McGEWB

Lacordaire, Jean Theodore 1801-1870 *ApCAB*

LaCorne, Pierre *ApCAB, Drake*

LaCoss, Louis 1890-1966 *WhAm 4*

LaCossitt, Henry 1901-1962 *WhAm 4*

Lacoste, Alexander 1842- *ApCAB*

Lacoste, Etienne Philippe, Baron De 1730-1820
ApCAB

Lacour, Auguste 1795-1866 *ApCAB*

LaCour, Paul Louis 1859?- *WhoColR*

Lacour, Peter *NewYHSD*

Lacour-Gayet, Jacques 1883-1953 *WhAm 3*

Lacroix, Alfred 1863-1948 *DcScB*

Lacroix, Baron Jean Baptiste Raymond
1776-1803 *ApCAB*

Lacroix, Joseph F Pamphile, Viscount De
1774-1841 *ApCAB*

LaCroix, Morris Felten 1888-1955 *WhAm 3*

Lacroix, Paul *NewYHSD*

Lacroix, Sylvestre Francois 1765-1843 *DcScB*

Lacrosse, Jean Baptiste Raymond 1765-1829
ApCAB

Lacunza, Jose Maria 1809-1869 *ApCAB, Drake*

Lacunza, Juan N 1812-1843 *ApCAB*

Lacunza, Manuel 1731-1801 *ApCAB*

Lacy, Arthur Jay 1876- *WhAm 6*

Lacy, Daniel George 1882-1950 *NatCAB 38*

Lacy, Drury 1758-1815 *DcAmB, NatCAB 2,*
TwCBDA

Lacy, Ernest 1863-1916 *DcAmB, NatCAB 20,*
WhAm 1

Lacy, Franz Moritz, Graf Von 1725-1801
WhoMilH

Lacy, George Carleton 1888-1951 *WhAm 3*

Lacy, Howard John, II 1906-1959 *NatCAB 44*

Lacy, James Horace 1865- *WhAm 4*

Lacy, Paul B 1890-1965 *WhAm 4*

Lacy, Thomas J *BiAUS*

Lacy, Thomas Norman 1885-1954 *NatCAB 42,*
WhAm 3

Lacy, Walter Garner 1877-1960 *WhAm 4*

Lacy, William Henry 1858-1925 *WhAm 1*

Lacy, William Stokes 1874-1943 *WhAm 2*

Lada-Mocarski, Valerian 1898-1971 *WhAm 5*

Ladd, Adoniram Judson 1861- *WhAm 4*

Ladd, Alan Walbridge 1913-1964 *WhAm 4*

Ladd, Anna Coleman 1878-1939 *WhAm 1,*
WomWWA 14

Ladd, Azel Parkhurst 1811-1854 *BiDAmEd*

Ladd, Mrs. B F *NewYHSD*

Ladd, B F *NewYHSD*

Ladd, Carl Edwin 1888-1943 *DcAmB S3,*
NatCAB 34, WhAm 2

Ladd, Catherine 1808-1899 *DcAmB, WhAm H*

Ladd, Catherine 1809-1899 *ApCAB,*
NatCAB 24, TwCBDA

Ladd, Edwin Freemont 1859-1925 *BiDrAC,*
WhAmP

Ladd, Edwin Fremont 1859-1925 *AmBi,*
ApCAB X, DcAmB, EncAAH,
NatCAB 19, REnAW, WhAm 1

Ladd, Eugene F 1859-1927 *WhAm 1*

Ladd, Franklin Bacon 1815-1898 *NewYHSD*

Ladd, George Dutton 1850-1913 *NatCAB 9,*
NatCAB 16

Ladd, George Edgar 1864-1940 *WhAm 1*

Ladd, George Tallman 1871-1943 *NatCAB 51,*
WhAm 2

Ladd, George Trumbull 1842-1921 *AmBi,*
ApCAB, ApCAB X, BiDAmEd, DcAmB,
NatCAB 13, NatCAB 33, TwCBDA,
WhAm 1

Ladd, George Washington 1818-1892 *BiDrAC,*
WhAm H

Ladd, Herbert Warren 1843-1913 *NatCAB 9,*
NatCAB 18, WhAm 1, WhAm 1C

Ladd, Horatio Oliver 1839-1932 *TwCBDA,*
WhAm 1

Ladd, James M *NewYHSD*

Ladd, Jesse A 1887-1957 *WhAm 3*

Ladd, John William 1877-1951 *NatCAB 40,*
WhAm 3

Ladd, Joseph Brown 1764-1786 *ApCAB,*
DcAmB, Drake, NatCAB 7, WhAm H

Ladd, Kate Everit Macy 1863-1945 *DcAmB S3,*
NatCAB 32, NotAW

Ladd, Mary Babbott 1887-1964 *NatCAB 51*

Ladd, Mary Louise Gregory 1878-
WomWWA 14

Ladd, Maynard 1873-1942 *WhAm 2*

Ladd, Niel Morrow 1877-1940 *WhAm 1*

Ladd, Prudence Hyman 1864- *WomWWA 14*

Ladd, Sanford Burritt 1844-1936 *WhAm 1*

Ladd, Scott M 1855-1931 *NatCAB 12,*
WhAm 1

Ladd, William 1778-1841 *AmBi, ApCAB,*
DcAmB, Drake, McGEWB, NatCAB 13,
TwCBDA, WebAB, WhAm H

Ladd, William Edwards 1880-1967 *NatCAB 53,*
WhAm 4A

Ladd, William Mead 1855-1931 *NatCAB 24,*

WhAm 1

Ladd, William Palmer 1870-1941 *NatCAB 30, WhAm 1*

Ladd, William Sargeant 1887-1949 *WhAm 2*

Ladd, William Sargent 1826-1893 *DcAmB, NatCAB 7, WhAm H*

Ladd, William Sargent 1887-1949 *NatCAB 38*

Ladd-Franklin, Christine 1847-1930 *AmBi, DcAmB, NatCAB 26, NotAW, WhAm 1*

Laddey, Clara Schlee 1856- *WomWWA 14*

Laddon, Isaac Machlin 1894-1976 *WhAm 6*

Ladds, Herbert Preston 1896-1963 *WhAm 4*

Ladehoff, Arthur Detlef 1894-1953 *NatCAB 45*

Ladenburg, Albert 1842-1911 *DcScB*

Ladenburg, Rudolf Walter 1882-1952 *WhAm 3*

Ladenburg, Rudolf Walther 1882-1952 *DcScB*

Ladew, Edward R 1855-1905 *NatCAB 14, WhAm 1*

Ladner, Albert H 1882- *WhAm 3*

Ladner, Grover C 1885-1954 *WhAm 3*

LaDow, George Augustus 1826-1875 *BiDrAC, WhAm H*

LaDow, George Augustus 1828-1875 *BiAUS*

Ladreyt, Casimir 1797-1877 *ApCAB*

Ladrilleros, Juan *ApCAB*

LaDu, Dwight B 1876-1954 *WhAm 3*

Ladue, Laurence Knight 1903-1951 *WhAm 3*

Ladue, Pomeroy 1868- *TwCBDA, WhAm 4*

Lady, Joseph Emerson 1907-1961 *NatCAB 49*

Laemmle, Carl 1867-1939 *AmBi, DcAmB S2, NatCAB 15, NatCAB 30, WebAB, WhAm 1*

Laennec, Rene Theophile Hyacinthe 1781-1826 *AsBiEn, BiHiMed*

Laennec, Theophile-Rene-Hyacinthe 1781-1826 *DcScB*

Laer, Ferdinand Von *NewYHSD*

Laessle, Albert 1877-1954 *NatCAB 40, WhAm 3*

Laet, Jan d1649 *ApCAB*

Laet, John De d1649 *Drake*

Laetsch, Theodore 1877- *WhAm 5*

LaFaille, Charles De 1597-1652 *DcScB*

LaFarge, Bancel 1865-1938 *NatCAB 28, WhAm 1*

LaFarge, Christopher 1897-1956 *NatCAB 42, WhAm 3*

LaFarge, Christopher Grant 1862-1938 *DcAmB S2, NatCAB 28, TwCBDA, WhAm 1*

LaFarge, John 1835-1910 *AmBi, ApCAB, BnEnAmA, DcAmB, EncAB, McGEWB, NatCAB 9, NewYHSD, TwCBDA, WebAB, WhAm 1*

LaFarge, John 1880-1963 *DcAmReB, NatCAB 49, WhAm 4*

LaFarge, Oliver 1901-1963 *REnAW, WhAm 4*

Lafargue, John Baptist 1864- *WhoColR*

Lafayette, George Washington 1779-1849 *ApCAB*

Lafayette, M J P Y DuMotier, Marquis De 1757-1834 *AmBi, ApCAB, DcAmB, Drake, McGEWB, NatCAB 1, TwCBDA, WebAB, WebAMB, WhAm H, WhoMilH*

LaFayette, M M P DeLaV, Comtesse De 1634-1693 *McGEWB*

Lafean, Daniel Franklin 1861-1922 *BiDrAC, WhAm 1*

LaFetra, Linnaeus Edford 1868-1965 *NatCAB 52, WhAm 4*

LaFetra, Sarah Doan 1843- *AmWom*

Lafever, Minard 1798-1854 *BnEnAmA, DcAmB S1, WhAm H*

Laffan, William Mackay 1848-1909 *AmBi, DcAmB, NatCAB 30, WhAm 1*

Lafferty, Abraham Walter 1875-1964 *BiDrAC, WhAm 4, WhAm 5*

Lafferty, Alma V 1857- *WhAm 4, WomWWA 14*

Lafferty, John James 1837-1909 *WhAm 1*

Lafferty, Louise M DeG Taylor *WomWWA 14*

Lafferty, William Thornton 1856-1922 *WhAm 1*

Laffey, John Paul 1862-1937 *NatCAB 28*

Laffey, Thomas Joseph, Jr. 1913-1968 *NatCAB 54*

Laffite, Jean *AmBi*

Laffite, Jean 1779?-1825? *WhAm H*

Laffite, Jean 1780?-1821? *DcAmB*

Laffite, Jean 1780?-1825? *WebAB, WebAMB*

Laffoon, Carthrae Merrette 1888-1957 *NatCAB 50*

Laffoon, Polk 1844-1906 *BiDrAC*

Laffoon, Ruby 1869-1941 *NatCAB 30, WhAm 1*

Lafitau, Joseph Francis d1740 *ApCAB*

Lafiteau, Joseph Francis 1670-1740 *Drake*

Lafitte, Jean 1780?-1826? *ApCAB, Drake*

Laflamme, Toussaint Antoine Radolphe 1827- *ApCAB*

LaFleche, Leo Richer 1888-1956 *WhAm 3*

Lafleche, Louis Francois Richer 1818- *ApCAB*

LaFlesche, Francis 1857-1932 *REnAW*

LaFlesche, Francis 1860?-1932 *AmBi, WhAm 1*

LaFlesche, Susan *NotAW*

LaFlesche, Susette 1854-1903 *AmBi, DcAmB, NotAW, WhAm H*

Laflin, Addison Henry 1823-1878 *BiAUS, BiDrAC, TwCBDA, WhAm H*

Laflin, Lewis Eugene 1895-1956 *NatCAB 45*

Laflin, Matthew 1803-1897 *NatCAB 21*

LaFollette, Belle Case 1859-1931 *AmWom, NotAW, WhAm 1*

LaFollette, Charles Marion 1898- *BiDrAC*

LaFollette, Fola d1970 *WhAm 5, WomWWA 14*

LaFollette, Grant A 1862-1951 *NatCAB 40*

LaFollette, Harvey Marion 1858-1929 *WhAm 1*

LaFollette, Philip Fox 1897-1965 *NatCAB 52, WhAm 4*

LaFollette, Robert Marion 1855-1925 *AmBi, ApCAB X, BiDrAC, DcAmB, EncAAH, EncAB, McGEWB, NatCAB 12, NatCAB 19, TwCBDA, WebAB, WhAm 1, WhAmP*

LaFollette, Robert Marion, Jr. 1895-1953 *BiDrAC, DcAmB S5, EncAB, NatCAB 40, WhAm 3, WhAmP*

LaFollette, Robert Russell 1894-1967 *WhAm 4*

LaFollette, William Leroy 1860-1934 *BiDrAC, WhAm 1, WhAmP*

Lafon, Barthelemy d1820 *Drake*

Lafon, Thomy 1810-1893 *DcAmB, WhAm H*

LaFond, William Ernest 1890-1956 *NatCAB 45*

Lafond DeLurcy, Gabriel 1802-1876 *ApCAB*

LaFontaine, Jean De 1621-1695 *McGEWB*

Lafontaine, Sir Louis-Hippolyte 1807-1864 *McGEWB*

Lafontaine, Sir Louis Hypolite 1807-1864 *ApCAB, Drake*

LaFontaine, Rachel Adelaide 1845- *WhAm 1*

Lafonte, Aunet 1812-1875 *ApCAB*

LaForce, Carolina Bousquet *WomWWA 14*

Lafore, John Armand, Jr. 1905- *BiDrAC*

LaForest, Antoine Mathurin, Comte De 1756-1846 *ApCAB, Drake*

Laforey, Sir Francis 1760?-1835 *ApCAB*

LaForge, Laurence 1871-1954 *NatCAB 41, WhAm 3*

LaForge, Margaret Getchell 1841-1880 *NotAW*

Laforgue, Jules 1860-1887 *McGEWB*

Lafount, Harold Arundel 1880-1952 *WhAm 3*

Lafragua, Jose Maria 1813-1875 *ApCAB*

Lafrentz, Ferdinand Wilhelm 1859-1954 *NatCAB 44*

Lafrentz, Ferdinand William 1859-1954 *WhAm 3*

LaFuente Y Alcantara, Miguel 1817-1850 *ApCAB*

LaGallissonniere, Roland M B, Count De d1756 *ApCAB*

Lagan, Matthew D 1830-1901 *NatCAB 10*

Lagan, Matthew Diamond 1829-1901 *BiDrAC*

LaGarde, Fannie D *WomWWA 14*

LaGarde, Louis Anatole 1849-1920 *WhAm 1*

Lagen, Mary Huneker *WhAm 5*

Lager, Eric W 1900-1974 *WhAm 6*

Lagercrantz, Ava De *WomWWA 14*

Lagercrantz, Herman Ludvig, Fabian De 1859- *WhAm 4*

Lagergren, Carl Gustaf 1846-1941 *WhAm 1*

Lagerkvist, Par Fabian 1891-1974 *McGEWB, WhAm 6*

Lagerloef, Hans 1880-1952 *NatCAB 42*

Lagerlof, Selma Ottiliana Lovisa 1858-1940 *McGEWB*

Lagerquist, Walter Edwards 1881-1944 *WhAm 2*

Lages, Joao Vieira DeCarvalho 1781-1847 *ApCAB*

Lagny, Thomas Fantet De 1660-1734 *DcScB*

LaGorce, John Oliver 1880-1959 *WhAm 3*

Lagos, Manoel Ferreira 1816-1867 *ApCAB*

Lagos, Pedro 1827-1884 *ApCAB*

Lagrandiere, Charles Marie De 1729-1812 *ApCAB*

LaGrange, Frank Crawford 1893-1964 *WhAm 4*

Lagrange, Joseph Louis, Comte De 1736-1813 *AsBiEn, DcScB, McGEWB*

LaGrange, Magdalene Isadora 1864- *AmWom*

Lagraviere, Jurien Pierre Roch De 1772-1849 *ApCAB*

LaGuardia, Fiorello Henry 1882-1947 *BiDrAC, DcAmB S4, EncAB, McGEWB, NatCAB 36, WebAB, WhAm 2, WhAmP*

LaGuerra, Pablo De d1874 *ApCAB*

Laguerre, Edmond Nicolas 1834-1886 *DcScB*

Laguna, Theodore DeLeo De 1876-1930 *DcAmB, WhAm 1*

Lagurane, John *NewYHSD*

Lagurane, Peter *NewYHSD*

Lagurane, Santonio *NewYHSD*

LaHailandiere, Celestine R L G De 1798-1882 *ApCAB*

Lahee, Henry Charles 1856- *TwCBDA, WhAm 4*

Lahey, Edward Vincent 1893-1964 *NatCAB 52*

Lahey, Edwin A 1902-1969 *WhAm 5*

Lahey, Frank Howard 1880-1953 *DcAmB S5, WhAm 3*

LaHire, Gabriel-Philippe De 1677-1719 *DcScB*

LaHire, Philippe De 1640-1718 *DcScB*

Lahm, Frank Purdy 1877-1963 *NatCAB 51, WebAMB, WhAm 4, WhAm 5*

Lahm, Frank Samuel 1846-1931 *NatCAB 33*

Lahm, Samuel 1812-1876 *BiAUS, BiDrAC, TwCBDA, WhAm H*

LaHontan 1667?- *Drake*

Lahontan, Baron De *WhAm H*

LaHontan, Armand Louis DeD, Baron De 1667?-1715 *ApCAB*

Lahontan, Louis-A DeL D'Arce, Baron De 1666-1713? *AmBi, DcAmB*

Lahontan, Louis-Armand De 1666?-1715? *REnAW*

Lahr, Bert 1895-1967 *WebAB, WhAm 4*

Lahr, Nicholas Francis 1893-1967 *NatCAB 54*

Lahr, Raymond Merrill 1914-1973 *WhAm 6*

Lahrheim, Irving *WebAB*

Lai, Chia-Chiu 1922-1969 *WhAm 5*

Laidlaw, Alexander Hamilton 1828-1908 *NatCAB 7, WhAm 1*

Laidlaw, Alexander Hamilton, Jr. 1869-1908 *WhAm 1*

Laidlaw, Harriet Burton 1873-1949 *NatCAB 38, NotAW, WhAm 2*

Laidlaw, Harriet Burton 1874-1949 *BiCAW, WomWWA 14*

Laidlaw, James B 1822?-1854 *NewYHSD*

Laidlaw, James Lees 1868-1932 *NatCAB 38*

Laidlaw, John Blake 1901-1974 *WhAm 6*

Laidlaw, Walter 1861-1936 *WhAm 1*

Laidlaw, William Grant 1840-1908 *BiDrAC, TwCBDA*

Laidler, Harry Wellington 1884-1970 *WhAm 5*

Laidler, Thomas *NewYHSD*

Laidley, Roy Russell 1904-1968 *WhAm 5*

Laidley, Theodore Thaddeus Sobieski 1822-1886 *ApCAB, NatCAB 7, TwCBDA*

Laidlie, Archibald 1720-1779 *Drake*

Laidlie, Archibald 1727-1779 *ApCAB, NatCAB 13*

Laighton, Albert 1829-1887 *ApCAB*

Laimbeer, George Morgan 1905-1962 *WhAm 4*

Laimbeer, Nathalie Schenck 1882-1929 *DcAmB*

Laine, Damaso Theodore 1866-1938 *NatCAB 30*

Laing, Allen Blackwell 1874-1961 *NatCAB 49*

Laing, Chester William 1910-1967 *WhAm 4*

Laing, George Stuart 1878-1948 *NatCAB 45*

Laing, Gordon Jennings 1869-1945 *WhAm 2*

Laing, John 1865-1943 *NatCAB 36, WhAm 2*

Laing, John Albert 1883-1953 *WhAm 3*
Laing, Mary Elizabeth 1854- *WomWWA 14*
Laing, Samuel McPherson 1892-1944 *WhAm 2*
Lainhart, Spencer Toll 1886-1957 *NatCAB 47*
Laipply, Thomas Charles 1910-1968 *WhAm 5*
Laird, A Wilson 1900-1966 *NatCAB 51*
Laird, Alexander 1798-1873 *ApCAB*
Laird, Allison White 1863-1931 *WhAm 1*
Laird, David 1833- *ApCAB*
Laird, Edmund Cody 1906-1961 *WhAm 4*
Laird, Elizabeth Rebecca 1874- *WomWWA 14*
Laird, Frank Foster 1856- *NatCAB 7*
Laird, Gertrude S J 1862- *WomWWA 14*
Laird, J Packard 1876-1927 *NatCAB 28*
Laird, James 1845-1889 *TwCBDA*
Laird, James 1849-1889 *BiDrAC, WhAm H*
Laird, John Baker 1866- *WhAm 5*
Laird, John Kenneth, Jr. 1903-1973 *WhAm 6*
Laird, Melvin Robert 1922- *BiDrAC,
BiDrUSE*
Laird, Nellie Hazeltine Andrews 1884-
WomWWA 14
Laird, Philip Dandridge 1846-1920 *NatCAB 18*
Laird, Philip Dandridge 1888-1947 *NatCAB 38*
Laird, Samuel 1835-1913 *WhAm 1*
Laird, Warren Powers 1861-1948 *BiDAmEd,
WhAm 2*
Laird, William Henry 1871-1919 *NatCAB 39*
Laird, William Ramsey, III 1916-1974 *BiDrAC,
WhAm 6*
Laird, William Winder 1878-1927 *NatCAB 28*
Lairy, Moses Barnett 1859-1927 *WhAm 1*
Laist, Frederick 1878-1963 *NatCAB 52*
Laist, Theodore Frederick 1869- *WhAm 1*
Laistner, Max Ludwig Wolfram 1890-1959
WhAm 3
Lait, Jacquin Leonard 1883-1954 *DcAmB S5,
WhAm 3*
Lajoie, Antoine Gerin 1824-1879 *ApCAB*
Lajoie, Marie Gerin 1867- *WomWWA 14*
LaJonquiere, Jacques P DeT, Marquis De
1686?-1752 *ApCAB*
Lakanal, Joseph 1762-1845 *AmBi, ApCAB,
WhAm H*
Lake, Mother *WebAB*
Lake, Bert Melvin 1875-1925 *NatCAB 20*
Lake, Charles H 1879-1958 *WhAm 4*
Lake, Devereux 1876- *WhAm 5*
Lake, Everett John 1871-1948 *NatCAB 37,
WhAm 2*
Lake, Fred Wrightman 1888-1955 *NatCAB 42,
WhAm 3*
Lake, George Baker 1827- *NatCAB 5*
Lake, George Burt 1880-1943 *NatCAB 33,
WhAm 2*
Lake, Gerard 1744-1808 *ApCAB, Drake,
WhoMilH*
Lake, Harriet Isadora *WomWWA 14*
Lake, Harry Beaston 1886-1969 *WhAm 5*
Lake, Ira 1863-1954 *NatCAB 44*
Lake, James K 1835-1917 *NatCAB 17*
Lake, Jesse S 1825-1896 *NatCAB 20*
Lake, John 1870- *WhAm 3*
Lake, Kirsopp 1872-1946 *DcAmB S4,
WhAm 2*
Lake, Leonora Marie Barry 1849- *NotAW,
WhAm 4, WomWWA 14*
Lake, Mack Clayton 1890-1954 *WhAm 3*
Lake, Marguerite Brunelle 1882-
WomWWA 14
Lake, Marshall E 1900-1958 *WhAm 3*
Lake, Richard Conover 1846-1919 *NatCAB 18*
Lake, Richard Pinkney 1848-1921 *NatCAB 8*
Lake, Simon 1866-1945 *ApCAB X,
DcAmB S3, NatCAB 15, WebAB,
WebAMB, WhAm 2*
Lake, Stuart Nathaniel 1889-1964 *NatCAB 51*
Lake, William 1787-1805 *Drake*
Lake, William Augustus 1808-1861 *BiAUS,
BiDrAC, WhAm H*
Lakeman, Mary Ropes 1870- *WomWWA 14*
Lakeman, Nathaniel 1756-1830? *NewYHSD*
Lakes, Arthur 1844- *WhAm 4*
Lakey, Alice 1857-1935 *NotAW, WhAm 1,
WomWWA 14*
Lakey, Emily Jane 1831-1896 *TwCBDA*
Lakey, Emily Jane 1837-1896 *ApCAB Sup,
NewYHSD*

Lakin, Herbert Conrad 1872-1952 *NatCAB 44,
WhAm 5*
Lakin, James Sansome 1864-1934 *WhAm 1*
Lalande, Joseph-Jerome Lefrancais De 1732-1807
DcScB
Lalande, Joseph Jerome LeFrancois De
1732-1807 *AsBiEn*
LaLandelle, Guillaume Joseph Gabriel De 1812-
ApCAB
LaLanne, Frank Dale 1849-1913 *WhAm 1*
LaLanne, Mary E *NewYHSD*
Lalemant, Gabriel 1610-1649 *ApCAB*
Lalemant, Jerome 1593-1673 *ApCAB*
Lalement, Charles 1587-1674 *ApCAB Sup*
Lalibela *McGEWB*
LaLiberte, Henry 1885-1963 *NatCAB 52*
Lall, James *NewYHSD*
Lalla *DcScB*
Lallemand, Charles Francois Antoine 1774-1839
ApCAB
Lallemand, Charles Frederick Antoine 1774-1839
Drake
Lallemand, Henri Dominique 1777-1823 *ApCAB*
Lally, Thomas Arthur, Comte De 1702-1766
WhoMilH
Lalone, Emerson Hugh 1899-1960 *WhAm 4*
Lalor, Alice 1766-1846 *DcAmB, WhAm H*
Lalor, Mother Teresa 1766-1846 *AmBi,
ApCAB, TwCBDA*
LaLoutre, Louis Joseph De 1690?-1770?
ApCAB
Lalouvere, Antoine De 1600-1664 *DcScB*
Lalumier, Edward Louis 1887- *WhAm 6*
Lamade, Dietrick 1859-1938 *WhAm 1*
Lamade, George R 1894-1965 *WhAm 4*
Lamade, Howard John 1891-1958 *WhAm 3*
LaMadrid, Gregorio Araos De 1796-1870
ApCAB
Lamar, Andrew Jackson 1847-1933 *WhAm 1*
Lamar, Clarinda Huntington Pendleton
1856-1943 *ApCAB X, NatCAB 32,
WhAm 2*
Lamar, Gazaway Bugg 1798-1874 *ApCAB,
BiDConf, DcAmB, WhAm H*
Lamar, George Holt 1867-1945 *NatCAB 35*
Lamar, Henry Gazaway *TwCBDA*
Lamar, Henry Graybill 1798-1861 *BiAUS,
BiDrAC, WhAm H*
Lamar, James Robert 1866-1923 *BiDrAC*
Lamar, James Sanford 1829- *WhAm 4*
Lamar, John Basil 1812-1862 *BiDrAC,
WhAm H*
Lamar, Jose 1778-1830 *ApCAB, Drake*
Lamar, Joseph Rucker 1857-1916 *AmBi,
ApCAB X, DcAmB, NatCAB 15,
WebAB, WhAm 1*
Lamar, Lucius Q C 1825-1893 *BiAUS*
Lamar, Lucius Quintius Cincinnatus 1825-1893
NatCAB 1
Lamar, Lucius Quintus Cincinnatus 1797-1834
ApCAB, TwCBDA
Lamar, Lucius Quintus Cincinnatus 1825-1893
*AmBi, ApCAB, BiDConf, BiDrAC,
BiDrUSE, DcAmB, EncAAH, McGEWB,
TwCBDA, WebAB, WhAm H, WhAmP*
Lamar, Mirabeau Buonaparte 1798-1859 *AmBi,
ApCAB, BiAUS, DcAmB, Drake,
NatCAB 9, REnAW, TwCBDA, WebAB,
WebAMB, WhAm H, WhAmP*
LaMar, Norvelle Chappell 1897-1964
NatCAB 51
Lamar, Philip Rucker 1880-1938 *NatCAB 28*
Lamar, William Bailey 1853-1928 *BiDrAC,
NatCAB 25, WhAmP*
Lamar, William Harmong 1859-1928 *WhAm 1*
Lamarck, Jean Baptiste P A DeMonet De
1744-1829 *AsBiEn, DcScB, McGEWB*
LaMardelle, Guillaume Francois De 1732-1813
ApCAB
Lamare-Picquot, N 1785?-1835? *ApCAB*
LaMarmora, Alberto 1789-1863 *WhoMilH*
LaMarmora, Alfonso Ferrero, Marchese
1804-1878 *WhoMilH*
LaMarmora, Alessandro 1799-1855 *WhoMilH*
LaMarr, Esther Bernice Randall 1916-1967
WhAm 5
Lamartine, Alphonse Marie Louis De 1790-1869
McGEWB

Lamartis *NewYHSD*
Lamas, Andres 1817- *ApCAB*
Lamb, Albert Eugene 1843-1928 *ApCAB X*
Lamb, Albert Richard 1881-1959 *WhAm 3*
Lamb, Alfred William 1824-1888 *BiAUS,
BiDrAC, WhAm H*
Lamb, Arthur Becket 1880-1952 *DcAmB S5,
NatCAB 46, WhAm 3*
Lamb, Charles 1775-1834 *McGEWB*
Lamb, Charles Rollinson d1942 *WhAm 2*
Lamb, Clarence Joseph 1894-1955 *NatCAB 45*
Lamb, Daniel Smith 1843-1929 *NatCAB 27,
TwCBDA, WhAm 1*
Lamb, Edward 1828-1887 *ApCAB*
Lamb, Edwin Travis 1863-1919 *WhAm 1*
Lamb, Ella Condie d1936 *WhAm 3,
WomWWA 14*
Lamb, Frank Heady 1877-1947 *NatCAB 36*
Lamb, Frank Joseph 1877-1949 *NatCAB 37*
Lamb, Frederick Stymetz 1863-1928 *ApCAB X,
NatCAB 11, WhAm 4*
Lamb, Frederick William 1874-1928
NatCAB 26
Lamb, George Benedict 1896-1956 *NatCAB 45*
Lamb, Harold Albert 1892-1962 *NatCAB 52,
WhAm 4*
Lamb, Harry Hayes 1876-1953 *NatCAB 43*
Lamb, Harvey Densmore 1883-1950
NatCAB 39
Lamb, Henry Whitney 1853-1926 *WhAm 1*
Lamb, Horace 1849-1934 *DcScB*
Lamb, Hugh Louis 1890-1959 *WhAm 3*
Lamb, Isaac Wixan 1840-1906 *ApCAB*
Lamb, Isaac Wixom 1840-1906 *DcAmB,
NatCAB 7, TwCBDA, WhAm 1*
Lamb, Isabel Haslup 1864- *WomWWA 14*
Lamb, James Gibson 1889-1929 *WhAm 5*
Lamb, James Hazard 1841- *TwCBDA*
Lamb, John *NewYHSD*
Lamb, John 1735-1800 *AmBi, ApCAB,
DcAmB, Drake, NatCAB 1, TwCBDA,
WhAm H*
Lamb, John 1840-1924 *BiDrAC, TwCBDA,
WhAm 4, WhAmP*
Lamb, John Edward 1852-1914 *BiDrAC,
WhAm 1*
Lamb, John Henderson 1905-1961 *NatCAB 48*
Lamb, Joseph 1831-1898 *NatCAB 11*
Lamb, Joseph 1833-1898 *NewYHSD*
Lamb, Joseph F 1892-1964 *WhAm 4*
Lamb, K A *NewYHSD*
Lamb, Martha Joanna Reade Nash 1826-1893
NotAW
Lamb, Martha Joanna Reade Nash 1829-1893
*AmBi, AmWom, ApCAB, DcAmB,
NatCAB 1, TwCBDA, WhAm H*
Lamb, Martin Thomas *ApCAB*
Lamb, Mary Elizabeth 1839- *WomWWA 14*
Lamb, Nellie A 1865- *WomWWA 14*
Lamb, Owen Pirl 1873-1959 *NatCAB 48*
Lamb, Peter Oswald 1890-1935 *WhAm 1*
Lamb, Ralph John 1860-1937 *NatCAB 27*
Lamb, Richard Hubbert 1916-1959 *WhAm 4*
Lamb, Robert Keen 1905-1952 *NatCAB 42*
Lamb, Robert Scott 1876-1956 *NatCAB 42,
WhAm 3*
Lamb, Roger 1756-1830 *AmBi, ApCAB*
Lamb, Roland Olmstead 1850-1921 *ApCAB X,
WhAm 1*
Lamb, William 1835-1909 *NatCAB 1,
WhAm 1*
Lamb, William Frederick 1883-1952 *DcAmB S5,
WhAm 3*
Lamb, Willis Eugene, Jr. 1913- *WebAB*
Lambdin, Alfred Cochran 1846- *ApCAB,
TwCBDA*
Lambdin, George Cochran 1830-1896 *ApCAB,
BnEnAmA, NewYHSD, TwCBDA*
Lambdin, J Harrison 1841?- *NewYHSD*
Lambdin, James Reid 1807-1889 *ApCAB,
DcAmB, NewYHSD, TwCBDA,
WhAm H*
Lambdin, Jerry Elmer 1889-1960 *WhAm 4*
Lambdin, Milton Bennett 1850-1940 *WhAm 1*
Lambdin, Robert Lynn 1886- *IlBEAAW*
Lambdin, William Wallace 1861- *WhAm 1*
Lambe, Sir Charles Edward 1900-1960
WhAm 4

Lamberson, Ray Guernsey 1886-1974 *WhAm 6*
Lambert, Adrian VanSinderen 1872- *WhAm 5*
Lambert, Albert Bond 1875-1946 *NatCAB 36,*
WhAm 2
Lambert, Alexander 1861-1939 *WhAm 1*
Lambert, Alexander 1862- *NatCAB 7*
Lambert, Alexander 1862-1929 *ApCAB X*
Lambert, Avery Eldorus 1873- *WhAm 5*
Lambert, Belle Short *WomWWA 14*
Lambert, Byron James 1874-1952 *NatCAB 41,*
WhAm 3
Lambert, Catholina 1834- *NatCAB 16*
Lambert, Charles 1816-1892 *NewYHSD,*
WhAm H
Lambert, Charles Irwin 1877-1954 *WhAm 3*
Lambert, Edith B Lowry *WomWWA 14*
Lambert, Edward Wilberforce 1831-
NatCAB 10
Lambert, Francis Eddy 1860-1924 *NatCAB 21*
Lambert, Fred Dayton 1871-1931 *WhAm 1*
Lambert, George Charles 1867-1934
NatCAB 25
Lambert, Gerard Barnes 1886-1967 *NatCAB 52,*
WhAm 4
Lambert, Hubert Cottrell 1916-1973 *WhAm 6*
Lambert, Jack Lincoln 1892-1967 *WhAm 4*
Lambert, Johann Heinrich 1728-1777 *AsBiEn,*
DcScB
Lambert, John d1823 *BiAUS, Drake*
Lambert, John 1746-1823 *BiDrAC, WhAm H,*
WhAmP
Lambert, John 1748-1823 *ApCAB,*
NatCAB 11, TwCBDA
Lambert, Sir John 1772-1847 *ApCAB, Drake*
Lambert, John 1775?- *ApCAB, NewYHSD*
Lambert, John 1847-1922 *NatCAB 19,*
WhAm 1
Lambert, John Henry 1875-1949 *NatCAB 37*
Lambert, John Raymond 1870-1927
NatCAB 21
Lambert, John S 1851-1936 *WhAm 3*
Lambert, Lillian Vitalique *WomWWA 14*
Lambert, Louis Aloisius 1835-1910 *DcAmB,*
NatCAB 24, TwCBDA, WhAm 1
Lambert, Lydia Newsom 1871- *WomWWA 14*
Lambert, Oscar Doane 1888-1959 *WhAm 4*
Lambert, Robert Archibald 1883-1960
NatCAB 48, WhAm 4
Lambert, Robert Eugene 1869- *WhAm 5*
Lambert, Samuel Waldron 1859-1942
NatCAB 37, WhAm 2
Lambert, Sterling 1870- *WhoColR*
Lambert, Sylvanus Elmer 1867-1954
NatCAB 42
Lambert, Sylvester Maxwell 1882-1947
NatCAB 38
Lambert, T Arthur 1891-1964 *WhAm 4*
Lambert, Tallmadge Augustine 1842- *WhAm 4*
Lambert, W V 1897-1973 *WhAm 6*
Lambert, Walter Davis 1879-1968 *NatCAB 54,*
WhAm 6
Lambert, Walter Eyre 1859-1930 *NatCAB 24*
Lambert, William Harrison 1842-1912
NatCAB 10, WhAm 1
Lambert, Wilton John 1871-1935 *WhAm 1*
Lamberton, Benjamin Paulding 1878-1938
NatCAB 34
Lamberton, Benjamin Peffer d1912 *TwCBDA*
Lamberton, Benjamin Peffer 1843-1912
ApCAB Sup
Lamberton, Benjamin Peffer 1844-1912 *DcAmB,*
NatCAB 34, WhAm 1
Lamberton, Chess 1877- *WhAm 5*
Lamberton, Genio Madison 1850-1902 *WhAm 1*
Lamberton, Harry Clabaugh 1906-1961
NatCAB 49
Lamberton, James McCormick 1856-1915
NatCAB 16, WhAm 1
Lamberton, John A 1873-1946 *WhAm 2*
Lamberton, John Porter 1839-1917 *TwCBDA,*
WhAm 1
Lamberton, Robert Alexander 1824-1893
NatCAB 7, TwCBDA
Lamberton, Robert Eneas 1886-1941 *WhAm 1*
Lamberton, William Alexander 1848-1910
TwCBDA, WhAm 1
Lamberton, William Purnell 1880-1957
BiDrAC, WhAm 3, WhAmP

Lambertus, Paul Theodore 1909-1970
NatCAB 55
Lambertus, Peter 1890-1953 *NatCAB 43*
Lamberville, James d1706? *ApCAB*
Lamberville, Jean De 1633-1714 *AmBi*
Lamberville, John De d1699 *ApCAB*
Lambeth, James Erwin 1885-1947 *NatCAB 36*
Lambeth, John Walter 1896-1961 *BiDrAC*
Lambeth, William Alexander 1867-1944
NatCAB 34, WhAm 2
Lambeth, William Arnold 1879-1952 *WhAm 3*
Lambie, Frank Dalton 1865- *NatCAB 15*
Lambing, Andrew Arnold 1842-1918 *DcAmB,*
NatCAB 6
Lamble, John W 1897-1969 *WhAm 5*
Lamble, John Walter 1898-1969 *NatCAB 55*
Lamborn, Charles William 1867-1952
NatCAB 40
Lambourne, Alfred 1850-1926 *IIBEAAW*
Lambright, Edwin Dart 1874-1959 *WhAm 3*
Lambrix, Joseph H 1896-1971 *WhAm 5*
Lambuth, David Kelley 1879-1948 *NatCAB 37*
Lambuth, James William 1830-1892 *DcAmB,*
WhAm H
Lambuth, Walter Russell 1854-1921 *DcAmB,*
NatCAB 19, WhAm 1
Lamdin, Alfred Cochran 1846-1911 *WhAm 1*
Lamdrum, William Warren 1853- *WhAm 1*
Lame, Gabriel 1795-1870 *DcScB*
Lamennais, Hugues Felicite Robert De 1782-1854
McGEWB
LaMer, Victor Kuhn 1895-1966 *NatCAB 52,*
WhAm 4
Lameth, Alexander 1760-1829 *Drake*
Lameth, Alexandre 1760-1829 *ApCAB*
Lameth, Charles Malo Francis, Count De
1757-1832 *Drake*
Lameth, Charles Malo Francois 1757-1832
ApCAB
Lameth, Count Theodore 1756-1854 *ApCAB*
Lametherie, Jean-Claude De 1743-1817 *DcScB*
LaMettrie, Julien Offray De 1709-1751 *DcScB,*
McGEWB
Lamey, Arthur Francis 1892-1963 *WhAm 4*
Lamison, Charles N 1820-1896 *BiAUS*
Lamison, Charles Nelson 1826-1896 *BiDrAC*
Lamith, Joseph *NewYHSD*
Lamkin, Daisye Buck 1877- *WomWWA 14*
Lamkin, John Tillman 1811-1870 *BiDConf*
Lamkin, Nina Belle 1873- *NatCAB 18*
Lamm, Emile 1834-1873 *ApCAB, TwCBDA*
Lamm, Henry 1846-1926 *NatCAB 18,*
NatCAB 21, WhAm 4
Lamm, Lynne M 1890-1949 *WhAm 3*
Lamme, Benjamin Garver 1864-1924 *DcAmB,*
NatCAB 20, NatCAB 28, WhAm 1
Lamneck, Arthur Philip 1880-1944 *BiDrAC*
Lamon, Ward Hill 1828-1893 *DcAmB,*
WhAm H
Lamont, Austin 1905-1969 *NatCAB 55*
Lamont, Daniel G *NewYHSD*
Lamont, Daniel Scott 1851-1905 *AmBi,*
ApCAB Sup, BiDrUSE, DcAmB,
NatCAB 3, TwCBDA, WhAm 1
Lamont, Florence Haskell Corliss
WomWWA 14
Lamont, Forrest 1885-1937 *WhAm 1*
Lamont, Frederick *NewYHSD*
Lamont, George D 1823-1876 *BiAUS*
Lamont, Hammond 1864-1909 *DcAmB,*
NatCAB 25, WhAm 1
Lamont, Johann Von 1805-1879 *AsBiEn,*
DcScB
Lamont, Peter T 1900-1970 *WhAm 5*
Lamont, Robert Patterson 1867-1948 *BiDrUSE,*
WhAm 2
Lamont, Thomas Stilwell 1899-1967
NatCAB 53, WhAm 4
Lamont, Thomas William 1870-1948 *ApCAB X,*
DcAmB S4, NatCAB 41, WhAm 2
LaMontagne, Walter E 1839-1915 *NewYHSD*
LaMontague, Walter E 1839-1915 *NewYHSD*
LaMonte, John Life 1902-1949 *WhAm 3*
Lamor, Antony 1824?- *NewYHSD*
Lamoreaux, Peter Gaius 1831-1913 *NatCAB 16*
Lamoriciere, Louis Christophe Leon J De
1806-1865 *WhoMilH*
Lamorisse, Albert 1922-1970 *WhAm 5*

Lamoroux, Wendell 1825- *TwCBDA*
LaMothe, John Dominique 1868-1928 *WhAm 1*
LaMotte, Ellen Newbold 1873-1961 *WhAm 4*
LaMountain, John 1830-1870 *DcAmB, Drake,*
WhAm H
LaMountain, John 1830-1878 *ApCAB,*
TwCBDA
L'Amour, Louis Dearborn 1908- *REnAW*
LaMoure, Howard Alexander 1875- *WhAm 5*
Lamoureux, Andrew Jackson 1850-1928 *DcAmB,*
NatCAB 21
Lamoureux, Silas Wright 1843-1909 *WhAm 1*
Lamouroux, Jean Vincent Felix 1776-1825
DcScB
Lampe, Joseph Joachim 1837-1920 *WhAm 1*
Lampe, William Edmund 1875-1950 *WhAm 3*
Lampen, Albert Eugene 1887-1963 *WhAm 4*
Lampert, Floran d1930 *WhAm 1*
Lampert, Florian 1863-1930 *BiDrAC*
Lampert, Nelson Norman 1872-1918
NatCAB 17
Lamphear, Amos Stuart 1868-1957 *NatCAB 43*
Lampkin, Clifton Wallace 1884-1959
NatCAB 49
Lampland, Arthur Orlando 1911-1963
NatCAB 51
Lampland, Carl Otto 1873-1951 *WhAm 3*
Lampman, Archibald 1861-1899 *McGEWB*
Lampman, Ben Hur 1886-1954 *WhAm 3*
Lampman, Lewis 1843- *WhAm 4*
Lamport, Alexander 1886-1961 *NatCAB 50*
Lamport, Arthur Matthew 1883-1940
NatCAB 29
Lamport, Harold 1908-1975 *WhAm 6*
Lamport, Samuel Charles 1880-1941
NatCAB 41
Lamport, William Henry 1811-1891 *BiAUS,*
BiDrAC, WhAm H
Lamprecht, Karl 1856-1915 *McGEWB*
Lamprecht, Sterling Power 1890-1973 *WhAm 6*
Lamprey, Estella Loomis 1862- *WomWWA 14*
Lamprey, Eva Blanche *WomWWA 14*
Lamprey, Louise 1869-1951 *WhAm 3*
Lampson, Sir Curtis Miranda 1806-1885
ApCAB, DcAmB, Drake, WhAm H
Lampson, William 1840-1897 *TwCBDA*
Lampton, Thaddeus Booth 1867-1938 *WhAm 1*
Lampton, Walter M 1850- *WhAm 4*
Lampton, William James d1917 *WhAm 1*
Lamson, Alvan 1792-1864 *ApCAB, Drake*
Lamson, Armene Tashjian 1883-1970
NatCAB 56
Lamson, Charles Henry 1847-1930 *WhAm 1*
Lamson, Charles Marion 1843-1899
ApCAB Sup, NatCAB 7, TwCBDA,
WhAm 1
Lamson, Daniel Lowell 1834- *ApCAB*
Lamson, Fred Mason 1862-1940 *WhAm 1*
Lamson, George Herbert, Jr. 1882-1931
WhAm 1
Lamson, Guy Caleb 1875- *WhAm 5*
Lamson, Isaac Porter 1832-1912 *NatCAB 21*
Lamson, J 1825?- *IIBEAAW, NewYHSD*
Lamson, Joseph *NewYHSD*
Lamson, Julius Gustavus 1853-1942 *WhAm 2*
Lamson, Kate Glidden *WomWWA 14*
Lamson, Lucy Stedman 1857- *AmWom*
Lamson, Otis Floyd 1876-1956 *NatCAB 44*
Lamson, Paul Dudley 1884-1962 *NatCAB 50,*
WhAm 4
Lamson-Scribner, Frank 1851-1938 *AmBi,*
NatCAB 40, TwCBDA, WhAm 1
Lamy, Bernard 1640-1715 *DcScB*
Lamy, Guillaume *DcScB*
Lamy, Jean Baptiste 1814-1888 *DcAmReB,*
McGEWB, REnAW, WebAB
Lamy, John Baptist 1814-1888 *ApCAB,*
DcAmB, NatCAB 12, TwCBDA,
WhAm H
Lamy, Juan Bautista 1814-1888 *AmBi*
Lanahan, Annie Snowden *WomWWA 14*
Lanahan, Francis H, Jr. 1897-1975 *WhAm 6*
Lanahan, Henry 1873-1963 *WhAm 4*
Lanahan, William Wallace 1884-1948 *WhAm 2*
Lanaux, Louis Adrien 1874-1956 *NatCAB 46*
Lancashire, James Henry 1858-1936
ApCAB X, NatCAB 32

Lancashire, Ammi Wright 1887-1918
ApCAB X
Lancaster, Bruce 1896-1963 NatCAB 48,
WhAm 4
Lancaster, Charles Bartlett 1837-1913
NatCAB 39
Lancaster, Chester L 1904-1957 WhAm 3
Lancaster, Columbia 1803-1893 BiAUS,
BiDrAC, WhAm H
Lancaster, Dabney Stewart 1889-1975 WhAm 6
Lancaster, Edward Lee 1898-1958 NatCAB 48
Lancaster, Edward Moulton 1832-1919
NatCAB 20
Lancaster, Ellsworth Gage 1861-1934 WhAm 3
Lancaster, Henry Carrington 1882-1954
DcAmB S5, NatCAB 40, WhAm 3
Lancaster, Hewes 1871-1933 WhAm H
Lancaster, Sir James 1550?-1620 ApCAB,
Drake
Lancaster, John Edward 1863-1905 NatCAB 28
Lancaster, John Herrold 1898-1969 WhAm 5
Lancaster, John Lynch 1869-1962 WhAm 4
Lancaster, Joseph 1771-1838 Drake
Lancaster, Joseph 1778-1838 ApCAB,
McGEWB, TwCBDA
Lancaster, Joseph Robert 1876-1962
NatCAB 50
Lancaster, Lydia 1684-1761 ApCAB
Lancaster, R Hilary 1876-1944 NatCAB 33
Lancaster, Richard Venable 1863- WhAm 4
Lancaster, W Emery 1875-1957 NatCAB 47
Lancaster, Walter Brackett 1863-1951
NatCAB 42, WhAm 3
Lancastro Y Abreu, Maria Ursula 1682-1730
ApCAB
Lance, Richard Oliver 1869-1954 NatCAB 43
Lance, William 1791-1840 ApCAB
Lancelin, John L d1822 NewYHSD
Lanchero, Luis d1562 ApCAB
Lanchester, Frederick William 1868-1946
DcScB
Lancisi, Giovanni Maria 1654-1720 BiHiMed,
DcScB
Lancour, Adlore Harold 1908- BiDAmEd
Lancret, Michel Ange 1774-1807 DcScB
Land, Alfred Dillingham 1842- WhAm 1
Land, Charles Henry 1847-1922 NatCAB 14,
WhAm 1
Land, Edwin Herbert 1909- AsBiEn, EncAB,
McGEWB, WebAB
Land, Emory Scott 1879-1971 WhAm 5
Land, Fort Elmo 1878-1927 WhAm 1
Land, Frank Sherman 1890-1959 WhAm 3,
WhAm 4
Land, William Jesse Goad 1865-1942 WhAm 2
Landa, Diego De 1524-1579 ApCAB
Landacre, Francis Leroy 1867-1933 WhAm 1
Landacre, Paul Hambleton 1893-1963 WhAm 4
Landahl, Carl William 1870- WhAm 5
Landais, Pierre 1731?-1820 DcAmB,
WhAm H
Landais, Pierre De 1734-1820 Drake
Landau, Edmund 1877-1938 DcScB
Landau, H Sidney 1898-1965 NatCAB 51
Landau, Jacob 1900-1966 WhAm 5
Landau, Lev Davidovich 1908-1968 AsBiEn,
DcScB, McGEWB, WhAm 5
Landberg, Edwin Carl 1894-1962 NatCAB 50
Landee, Franc Arthur 1911-1968 NatCAB 54
Landegger, Karl Francis 1905-1976 WhAm 6
Landen, John 1719-1790 DcScB
Lander, Benjamin 1844- NatCAB 9
Lander, Edward 1816-1907 BiAUS, DcAmB,
TwCBDA, WhAm 1
Lander, Frederic West 1822-1862 Drake
Lander, Frederick West 1821-1862 AmBi,
DcAmB, EncAAH, TwCBDA, WhAm H
Lander, Frederick William 1821-1862 ApCAB
Lander, Frederick William 1822-1862
NatCAB 8
Lander, Jean Margaret Davenport 1829-1903
ApCAB, DcAmB, Drake, NatCAB 8,
TwCBDA, WhAm 1
Lander, Louisa 1826-1923 ApCAB, NewYHSD,
TwCBDA, WhAm 4
Lander, Louisa 1835?-1923 Drake
Lander, Sarah West 1819-1872 ApCAB
Lander, William 1817-1868 BiDConf

Landerholm, Edwin Francis 1898-1961 WhAm 4
Landers, Ann WebAB
Landers, Franklin 1825-1901 ApCAB, BiAUS,
BiDrAC, TwCBDA
Landers, G M 1813-1895 BiAUS
Landers, George Foreman 1865-1939 WhAm 1
Landers, George Marcellus 1813-1895 BiDrAC,
WhAm H
Landers, Howe Stone 1885-1943 WhAm 2
Landers, Janie Dean 1876- WomWWA 14
Landers, John Joseph 1888-1932 NatCAB 25
Landers, Joseph Samuel 1863- WhAm 4
Landers, Julia Ethel WomWWA 14
Landers, Warren Prince 1869-1946 WhAm 2
Landers, Wilbur Nelson 1902-1965 WhAm 4
Landers, William John 1851-1908 NatCAB 16
Landes, Bertha Ethel Knight 1868-1943 BiCAW,
NotAW, WhAm 2
Landes, Henry 1867-1936 NatCAB 14,
WhAm 1
Landes, Herbert Ellis 1894-1959 WhAm 3
Landes, Silas Zephaniah 1842-1910 BiDrAC
Landes, William Grant 1865- WhAm 5
Landfield, Jerome Barker 1871-1954
NatCAB 44, WhAm 3
Landgrebe, Earl Fredrick 1916- BiDrAC
Landini, Francesco 1335?-1397 McGEWB
Landis, Benson Young 1897-1966 WhAm 4
Landis, Carney 1897-1962 WhAm 4
Landis, Cary Dayton 1873-1938 NatCAB 29,
WhAm 1
Landis, Charles Beary 1858-1922 BiDrAC,
TwCBDA, WhAm 1, WhAmP
Landis, Charles Israel 1856-1932 NatCAB 23,
WhAm 1
Landis, Charles William 1877- WhAm 5
Landis, Eva May 1868- WomWWA 14
Landis, Franklin Frick 1845-1932 NatCAB 25
Landis, Frederick 1872-1934 BiDrAC,
WhAm 1, WhAmP
Landis, Gerald Wayne 1895-1971 BiDrAC,
WhAm 5
Landis, Harry DeWitt 1878-1956 WhAm 3
Landis, Henry Robert Murray 1872-1937
DcAmB S2, WhAm 1
Landis, James McCauley 1899-1964 WhAm 4
Landis, Jessie Royce d1972 WhAm 5
Landis, John 1805- NewYHSD
Landis, John Herr 1853- NatCAB 5
Landis, John Howard 1860-1918 WhAm 1
Landis, Josiah Pennabecker 1843-1937 WhAm 1
Landis, Kenesaw Mountain 1866-1944
ApCAB X, DcAmB S3, EncAB,
NatCAB 33, WebAB, WhAm 2
Landis, Kenesaw Mountain, II 1910-1949
WhAm 2
Landis, Mary Green 1906-1973 WhAm 6
Landis, Paul Nissley 1893-1970 WhAm 5
Landis, Robert Kumler 1885-1961 WhAm 4
Landis, Walter Savage 1881-1944 DcAmB S3,
NatCAB 33
Landis, William Weldman 1869-1942 WhAm 2
Landivar, Raphael 1731-1795 ApCAB
Landman, Isaac 1880-1946 WhAm 2
Landman, J Henry 1898-1961 NatCAB 48,
WhAm 4
Landman, Louis W 1869-1952 WhAm 3
Landmann NewYHSD
Landmann, Barbara NotAW
Lando, Francisco Manuel De d1539 ApCAB
Landolphe, John Francis 1747-1825 ApCAB
Landolt, Hans Heinrich 1831-1910 DcScB
Landolt, Percy Edward 1891-1970 NatCAB 55
Landon, Alfred Mossman 1887- EncAAH,
EncAB, WebAB
Landon, Charles Griswold 1818-1893
NatCAB 29
Landon, Charles Raeburne 1900-1970 WhAm 5
Landon, Emily Augusta Pierce 1835-
WomWWA 14
Landon, George Washington 1847-1929
NatCAB 36
Landon, Hal D 1862- WhAm 4
Landon, Howard Fitch 1869-1950 NatCAB 39
Landon, Hugh McKennan 1867-1947
NatCAB 36, WhAm 2
Landon, Judson Stuart 1832-1905 NatCAB 37,
TwCBDA, WhAm 1

Landon, Mary Hornor 1874- WomWWA 14
Landon, Melville DeLancey 1839-1910 DcAmB,
NatCAB 6, WhAm 1
Landon, Sydney Wellington 1880-1953
NatCAB 41
Landon, Thomas Durland 1865-1934
NatCAB 42, WhAm 1
Landon, Thompson Hoadley 1830-1917
WhAm 1
Landon, Warren Hall 1851-1928 WhAm 1
Landone, Leon Elbert 1857- WhAm 4
Landor, Walter Savage 1775-1864 McGEWB
Landowska, Wanda 1879-1959 WhAm 3
Landram, John James 1826- ApCAB
Landreth, Burnet 1842-1928 NatCAB 24,
WhAm 1
Landreth, David 1802-1880 ApCAB, DcAmB,
TwCBDA, WhAm H
Landreth, Earl 1893-1967 WhAm 5
Landreth, Olin Henry 1852-1931 ApCAB,
NatCAB 9, TwCBDA, WhAm 1
Landreth, Symington Phillips 1908-1973
WhAm 6
Landreth, William Barker 1857- NatCAB 12,
WhAm 4
Landriani, Marsilio 1751?-1816? DcScB
Landrigan, Charles Raymond 1894-1962
NatCAB 49, WhAm 4
Landrith, Ira 1865-1941 WhAm 1
Landrum, Clarence Underwood 1889-1963
NatCAB 50
Landrum, John Morgan 1815-1861 BiAUS,
BiDrAC, WhAm H
Landrum, Phillip Mitchell 1909- BiDrAC
Landrum, Robert D 1882- WhAm 2
Landry, Aubrey Edward 1880-1972 WhAm 5
Landry, Auguste Charles Phillipe Robert 1846-
ApCAB
Landry, Lord Beaconsfield 1878- WhoColR
Landry, Eldrige Percival 1881- WhoColR
Landry, George A 1889-1961 WhAm 4
Landry, J Aristide 1817-1881 BiAUS
Landry, Jerome Emanuel 1881-1951
NatCAB 47
Landry, Joseph Aristide 1817-1881 BiDrAC,
WhAm H
Landry, Pierre Armand 1846- ApCAB,
WhoColR
Landsberg, Georg 1865-1912 DcScB
Landsberg, Grigory Samuilovich 1890-1957
DcScB
Landsberg, Max 1845-1927 WhAm 1
Landsiedel, Harry 1883-1965 NatCAB 53
Landsiedel, Harry 1883-1966 WhAm 4
Landsteiner, Karl 1868-1943 AsBiEn,
DcAmB S3, DcScB, McGEWB, WebAB,
WhAm 2
Landstreet, Fairfax Stuart 1861-1931 WhAm 1
Landstrom, Oscar Emil 1878-1952 NatCAB 41
Landy, James 1813-1875 BiAUS, BiDrAC,
WhAm H
Landye, James Thomas 1910-1956 NatCAB 46
Lane, Albert Grannis 1841-1906 NatCAB 12,
WhAm 1
Lane, Alfred Church 1863-1948 NatCAB 13,
NatCAB 36, WhAm 2
Lane, Sir Allen 1902-1970 WhAm 5
Lane, Alonzo NewYHSD
Lane, Amos d1850 BiAUS
Lane, Amos 1778-1849 ApCAB, BiDrAC,
TwCBDA, WhAm H, WhAmP
Lane, Anna Eichberg King 1856- WhAm 4
Lane, Annie Eichberg WomWWA 14
Lane, Arthur Bliss 1894-1956 NatCAB 45,
WhAm 3
Lane, Arthur Sherman 1864- ApCAB X
Lane, B Elizabeth 1876- WomWWA 14
Lane, Charles 1790-1854 NewYHSD
Lane, Charles Elmaar 1864- WhAm 5
Lane, Charles Franklin 1893- WhoColR A
Lane, Charles Homer 1877-1944 WhAm 1,
WhAm 2
Lane, Charles Stoddard 1860-1938 WhAm 1,
WhAm 1C
Lane, Chester Tevis 1905-1959 NatCAB 47,
WhAm 3
Lane, Clarence Guy 1882-1954 NatCAB 42,
WhAm 3

Lane, Clement Quirk 1897-1958 *WhAm 3*
Lane, Ebenezer 1793- *BiAUS*
Lane, Ebenezer 1793-1866 *ApCAB, Drake, NatCAB 4, TwCBDA*
Lane, Ebenezer 1793-1870 *Drake*
Lane, Edward 1842-1912 *BiDrAC, TwCBDA*
Lane, Edward Binney 1860-1941 *NatCAB 31, WhAm 1*
Lane, Edward Hudson 1891-1973 *WhAm 6*
Lane, Edward Wood 1869-1942 *WhAm 2*
Lane, Elbert Clarence 1870-1950 *WhAm 3*
Lane, Elinor Macartney d1909 *WhAm 1*
Lane, Elisha Frederick 1826-1921 *NatCAB 19*
Lane, Emory Wilson 1891-1963 *NatCAB 51*
Lane, Etta Freeman 1868- *WomWWA 14*
Lane, Everett Hale 1904-1974 *WhAm 6*
Lane, Fitz Hugh 1804-1865 *BnEnAmA, McGEWB, NewYHSD*
Lane, Frances Margaret *WomWWA 14*
Lane, Francis Ransom 1858- *WhAm 4*
Lane, Frank Hardy 1870- *WhAm 5*
Lane, Franklin Knight 1864-1921 *AmBi, BiDrUSE, DcAmB, NatCAB 19, WhAm 1*
Lane, Freeman Parker 1853-1927 *NatCAB 22*
Lane, Gardiner Martin 1859-1914 *WhAm 1*
Lane, George 1784-1859 *ApCAB, NatCAB 5*
Lane, George Martin 1823-1897 *AmBi, ApCAB Sup, DcAmB, TwCBDA, WhAm H*
Lane, George W d1863 *BiAUS*
Lane, George Washington 1815-1848 *ApCAB*
Lane, George William 1818-1883 *NatCAB 1*
Lane, Gertrude Battles 1874-1941 *DcAmB S3, NotAW, WhAm 2, WomWWA 14*
Lane, Harriet *NotAW*
Lane, Harry 1855-1917 *BiDrAC, NatCAB 18, WhAm 1, WhAmP*
Lane, Harvey Bradburn 1813-1888 *ApCAB Sup, TwCBDA*
Lane, Henry Higgins 1878- *WhAm 6*
Lane, Henry Marcus 1854-1929 *WhAm 1*
Lane, Henry Smith 1811-1881 *AmBi, ApCAB, BiAUS, BiDrAC, DcAmB, Drake, NatCAB 13, TwCBDA, WhAm H, WhAmP*
Lane, Horace M 1837-1912 *DcAmB*
Lane, Isaac d1833 *Drake*
Lane, Isaac 1834-1937 *WhAm 1, WhoColR*
Lane, James Crandall 1823-1888 *ApCAB Sup, NatCAB 4, TwCBDA*
Lane, James Franklin 1874-1944 *WhAm 2*
Lane, James Franklin 1878-1944 *WhoColR*
Lane, James Henry 1814-1866 *AmBi, ApCAB, BiAUS, BiDrAC, DcAmB, Drake, NatCAB 4, REnAW, TwCBDA, WebAB, WebAMB, WhAm H, WhAmP*
Lane, James Henry 1833-1907 *ApCAB Sup, BiDConf, DcAmB, NatCAB 27, TwCBDA, WhAm 1*
Lane, James Warren 1864-1927 *NatCAB 22*
Lane, Joel 1740-1795 *ApCAB*
Lane, John *NewYHSD*
Lane, John 1789-1855 *ApCAB, DcAmB, TwCBDA, WhAm H*
Lane, John Edward 1857-1930 *NatCAB 42*
Lane, John Edward 1872-1933 *WhAm 1*
Lane, Jonathan 1855-1916 *WhAm 1*
Lane, Jonathan Abbot 1822-1898 *NatCAB 10, TwCBDA*
Lane, Jonathan Homer 1819-1880 *ApCAB, DcScB, NatCAB 3, TwCBDA*
Lane, Joseph 1801-1881 *AmBi, ApCAB, BiAUS, BiDrAC, DcAmB, Drake, NatCAB 8, REnAW, TwCBDA, WhAm H, WhAmP*
Lane, Joseph Reed 1858-1931 *BiDrAC*
Lane, Josie Ivey *WomWWA 14*
Lane, Katharine Jane 1866- *WomWWA 14*
Lane, LaFayette 1842-1896 *ApCAB, BiAUS, BiDrAC, NatCAB 11, TwCBDA, WhAm H, WhAmP*
Lane, Laurence William 1890-1967 *NatCAB 53, WhAm 4*
Lane, Levi Cooper 1830-1902 *DcAmB, NatCAB 14, WhAm 1*
Lane, Loras Thomas 1910-1968 *NatCAB 54, WhAm 5*

Lane, Mary Blanche 1873- *WomWWA 14*
Lane, Merritt 1881-1939 *WhAm 1*
Lane, Mills Bee 1860-1945 *WhAm 2*
Lane, Moses 1823-1882 *NatCAB 9*
Lane, Otho Evans 1880-1961 *WhAm 4*
Lane, Peter Henry 1875-1920 *NatCAB 18*
Lane, Sir Ralph 1530?-1603 *AmBi, DcAmB, WhAm H*
Lane, Sir Ralph 1530?-1604 *ApCAB, Drake*
Lane, Raymond A 1894-1974 *WhAm 6*
Lane, Remington W *IIBEAAW*
Lane, Robert Porter 1891-1953 *WhAm 3*
Lane, Robert Ripley 1880-1959 *WhAm 4*
Lane, Rose Wilder 1886-1968 *NatCAB 54*
Lane, Rose Wilder 1887-1968 *WhAm 5*
Lane, Rufus Herman 1870-1948 *WhAm 2*
Lane, Samuel *BiAUS*
Lane, Samuel 1850-1923 *NatCAB 23*
Lane, Samuel Morse 1909- *WhAm 5*
Lane, Smith Edward 1829- *NatCAB 4, WhAm 1*
Lane, Stoddard 1887-1943 *WhAm 2*
Lane, Susan Minot 1832-1893 *NewYHSD*
Lane, Thomas Alphonsus 1906-1975 *WhAm 6*
Lane, Thomas Henry 1815-1900 *NewYHSD*
Lane, Thomas Joseph 1898- *BiDrAC, WhAmP*
Lane, Thomas Welsh 1855-1927 *WhAm 1*
Lane, Tidence 1724-1806 *DcAmB, WhAm H*
Lane, Victor Hugo 1852-1930 *WhAm 1*
Lane, Wallace Rutherford 1876-1946 *NatCAB 47, NatCAB 35, WhAm 2*
Lane, Walter Appleton 1873-1940 *NatCAB 29*
Lane, Walter Paye 1817-1892 *DcAmB, NatCAB 8, WhAm H*
Lane, Warren Zeph 1917-1969 *NatCAB 56*
Lane, Wilfred Gayton 1885-1949 *NatCAB 51*
Lane, William Carr 1789-1863 *DcAmB, WhAm H, WhAmP*
Lane, William Carr 1789-1864 *NatCAB 5*
Lane, William Channing 1847- *NatCAB 18*
Lane, William Coolidge 1859-1931 *ApCAB Sup, DcAmLiB, NatCAB 12, TwCBDA, WhAm 1*
Lane, William Dennis 1885-1965 *NatCAB 51*
Lane, William Jared 1789-1867 *NewYHSD*
Lane, William Preston 1851-1938 *NatCAB 29*
Lane, William Preston, Jr. 1892-1967 *WhAm 4*
Lane, William Thomas 1905-1971 *WhAm 5*
Lane, Winthrop Bent 1893-1969 *NatCAB 55*
Lane, Zephaniah 1857-1925 *NatCAB 22*
Laney, Francis Baker 1875-1938 *WhAm 1*
Laney, Lucy Craft 1854-1933 *BiDAmEd, NotAW*
Lanford, John Alexander 1881-1940 *WhAm 1*
Lanfranc 1010-1089 *McGEWB*
Lang, Albert Ray 1885-1971 *NatCAB 57*
Lang, Albion Earl 1849-1938 *NatCAB 29*
Lang, Arnold 1855-1914 *DcScB*
Lang, Arthur H 1909-1972 *WhAm 5*
Lang, Benjamin Johnson 1837-1909 *DcAmB, NatCAB 7, TwCBDA, WhAm 1*
Lang, C Thompson 1912-1971 *WhAm 5*
Lang, Charles *NewYHSD*
Lang, Charles Albert 1875-1959 *NatCAB 47*
Lang, Charles B 1887-1958 *WhAm 3*
Lang, Charles H, Jr. 1850- *WhAm 1*
Lang, Charles Michael Angelo 1860-1934 *WhAm 1*
Lang, Chester Henry 1893-1961 *WhAm 4*
Lang, Currier 1883-1964 *NatCAB 54*
Lang, Donald Buzick 1898-1967 *WhAm 4*
Lang, Florence Osgood Rand 1861-1943 *NatCAB 32*
Lang, Frank Silas 1855-1936 *NatCAB 33*
Lang, Gavin 1835- *ApCAB*
Lang, George *NewYHSD*
Lang, George 1879- *WhAm 6*
Lang, George S 1799- *NewYHSD*
Lang, George Washington 1888-1959 *NatCAB 47*
Lang, Henry 1864-1930 *NatCAB 26*
Lang, Henry Albert 1854- *WhAm 4*
Lang, Henry Roseman 1853-1934 *DcAmB S1, WhAm 1*
Lang, Herbert 1879- *WhAm 6*
Lang, John 1841-1926 *NatCAB 21*
Lang, John Albert, Jr. 1910-1974 *WhAm 6*
Lang, John Thomas 1876- *McGEWB*

Lang, Karl 1871- *WhAm 5*
Lang, Karl Nikolaus 1670-1741 *DcScB*
Lang, Leonard Dwight 1888- *WhoColR*
Lang, Louis 1812-1893 *ApCAB, TwCBDA*
Lang, Louis 1814-1893 *Drake, NewYHSD*
Lang, Louis 1866-1932 *NatCAB 26*
Lang, Louis LaCourse 1880- *WhAm 6*
Lang, Margaret Ruthven 1867- *BiCAW, NatCAB 7, TwCBDA, WomWWA 14*
Lang, Merle Howie 1921-1972 *WhAm 5*
Lang, Oscar Theodore 1888-1960 *WhAm 4*
Lang, Ph *NewYHSD*
Lang, Valorus Frederick 1905-1957 *NatCAB 47*
Lang, Walter Barnes 1890-1973 *NatCAB 57*
Lang, William 1825?- *NewYHSD*
Lang, William Henry 1874-1960 *DcScB*
Lang, William Peter 1879-1955 *NatCAB 45*
Langan, William Bernard 1860-1944 *NatCAB 33*
Langbehn, F Milton 1894-1949 *NatCAB 38*
Langdale, John William 1874-1940 *WhAm 1*
Langdell, Christopher Columbus 1826-1906 *AmBi, ApCAB, BiDAmEd, DcAmB, NatCAB 6, TwCBDA, WebAB, WhAm 1*
Langdell, Giles *NewYHSD*
Langdon, Andrew d1919 *WhAm 1*
Langdon, Charles Carter 1805-1889 *NatCAB 18*
Langdon, Charles Jervis 1849-1916 *NatCAB 16*
Langdon, Chauncey *NewYHSD*
Langdon, Chauncey 1763-1830 *BiAUS, BiDrAC, TwCBDA, WhAm H*
Langdon, Courtney 1861-1924 *DcAmB, NatCAB 20, WhAm 1*
Langdon, Frank Warren 1852-1933 *WhAm 1*
Langdon, George Dorland 1933- *EncAAH*
Langdon, H Maxwell 1876-1948 *NatCAB 36*
Langdon, Harry Philmore 1884-1944 *DcAmB S3*
Langdon, John d1819 *BiAUS*
Langdon, John 1739-1819 *ApCAB, Drake*
Langdon, John 1741-1819 *AmBi, BiDrAC, DcAmB, NatCAB 1, NatCAB 11, TwCBDA, WhAm H, WhAmP*
Langdon, Loomis Lyman 1830-1910 *NatCAB 52, WhAm 1*
Langdon, Marie Geraldine 1869- *WomWWA 14*
Langdon, Mary *NotAW*
Langdon, Oliver Monroe 1817-1878 *ApCAB, TwCBDA*
Langdon, Russell Creamer 1872-1963 *NatCAB 52, WhAm 5*
Langdon, Samuel 1723-1797 *AmBi, ApCAB, DcAmB, Drake, NatCAB 6, TwCBDA, WhAm H*
Langdon, Stephen Herbert 1876-1937 *WhAm 1*
Langdon, William Chauncey 1831-1895 *TwCBDA*
Langdon, William Chauncey 1871-1947 *WhAm 2*
Langdon, William Chauncy 1831-1895 *ApCAB, DcAmB, NatCAB 8, WhAm H*
Langdon, William Henry 1873-1939 *WhAm 1*
Langdon, Woodbury d1805 *BiAUS*
Langdon, Woodbury 1738?-1805 *DcAmB, NatCAB 10*
Langdon, Woodbury 1739-1805 *ApCAB, BiDrAC, Drake, TwCBDA, WhAmP*
Langdon, Woodbury 1836-1921 *NatCAB 13, WhAm 1*
Langdon, Woodbury Gersdorf 1849-1919 *NatCAB 2*
Lange, Alexis Frederick 1862-1924 *BiDAmEd, DcAmB, NatCAB 25, WhAm 1*
Lange, Carl Georg 1834-1900 *DcScB*
Lange, Caroline Penny 1867- *WomWWA 14*
Lange, Dietrich 1863-1940 *WhAm 2*
Lange, Dorothea 1895-1965 *BnEnAmA, WebAB, WhAm HA, WhAm 4*
Lange, Frederick Edward 1920-1974 *WhAm 6*
Lange, Halvard Manthey 1902-1970 *WhAm 5*
Lange, Hans 1884-1960 *WhAm 4*
Lange, Linda Bartels *WomWWA 14*
Lange, Louis 1829-1893 *DcAmB, WhAm H*
Lange, Mary T 1848- *AmWom*
Lange, Norbert Adolph 1892-1970 *NatCAB 55*
Lange, Oscar Richard 1904-1965 *WhAm 4*

Lansing, Elfleda Haecker *WomWWA 14*
Lansing, Frederick 1838-1894 *BiDrAC,*
WhAm H
Lansing, Garret *NewYHSD*
Lansing, Gerit Yates 1783-1862 *BiAUS,*
WhAm H
Lansing, Gerret *NewYHSD*
Lansing, Gerrit Yates 1783-1862 *BiDrAC,*
TwCBDA
Lansing, Gulian 1825-1892 *DcAmB, WhAm H*
Lansing, J Townsend 1844-1919 *NatCAB 19*
Lansing, John 1754-1829 *AmBi, ApCAB,*
BiAUS, BiDrAC, DcAmB, Drake,
NatCAB 4, TwCBDA, WhAm H
Lansing, John 1832-1907 *NatCAB 20*
Lansing, John Belcher 1919-1970 *WhAm 5*
Lansing, John Ernest 1878-1958 *NatCAB 46,*
WhAm 3
Lansing, Marion Florence 1883- *WomWWA 14*
Lansing, Nicholas 1748-1835 *ApCAB*
Lansing, Robert 1864-1928 *AmBi, ApCAB X,*
BiDrUSE, DcAmB, EncAB, McGEWB,
NatCAB 20, WebAB, WhAm 1
Lansing, Sarah Treadway 1861- *WomWWA 14*
Lansing, Stuart Douglas 1866-1927 *NatCAB 39*
Lansing, William E 1822-1883 *BiAUS*
Lansing, William Esselstyne 1821-1883 *BiDrAC,*
WhAm H
Lansingh, VanRensselaer 1873- *WhAm 5*
Lansot, A D *NewYHSD*
Lansot, L *NewYHSD*
Lanston, Tolbert 1844-1913 *AmBi, DcAmB,*
NatCAB 13
Lanstrum, Oscar Monroe 1869-1928 *WhAm 1*
Lantaff, William Courtland 1913-1970 *BiDrAC,*
WhAm 5
Lanter, Fred Merrill 1900-1960 *WhAm 4*
Lantz, A *NewYHSD*
Lantz, David Ernest 1855-1918 *WhAm 1*
Lantz, Eleanor 1881- *WomWWA 14*
Lanza, Anthony Joseph 1884-1964 *WhAm 4*
Lanza, Clara 1859- *AmWom, WhAm 4*
Lanza, Conrad Hammond 1878- *WhAm 6*
Lanza, Gaetano 1848-1928 *WhAm 1*
Lanza, Mario 1921-1959 *WhAm 3*
Lanza DiBrolo, Clara, Marquise 1859-
WomWWA 14
Lanzetta, James Joseph 1894-1956 *BiDrAC,*
WhAm 3
Lao, She 1899-1966 *McGEWB*
Lao, Tzu *McGEWB*
Lapa, Jose DeA V S E Carvallo, Count Of d1782
ApCAB
LaPage, Gertrude 1871- *WomWWA 14*
LaPeltrie, Marie Madeleine De 1603-1671
ApCAB
LaPerouse, Jean Francois DeGalaup 1741-1788
ApCAB
LaPerouse, John Francis Galoup De 1741-1788
Drake
Lapham, Edward Burnham 1887-1962
NatCAB 50
Lapham, Elbridge Gerry 1814-1890 *ApCAB,*
BiAUS, BiDrAC, NatCAB 11, TwCBDA,
WhAm H
Lapham, Increase Allen 1811-1875 *ApCAB,*
DcAmB, Drake, NatCAB 8, TwCBDA,
WhAm H
Lapham, J H 1885-1956 *WhAm 3*
Lapham, J M *IIBEAAW, NewYHSD*
Lapham, John Raymond 1886-1939 *WhAm 1*
Lapham, Kathleen Helena Mary Boddy 1870-
WomWWA 14
Lapham, Lewis Henry 1858-1934 *NatCAB 52*
Lapham, Mary E 1860- *WomWWA 14*
Lapham, Oscar 1837-1926 *BiDrAC, TwCBDA,*
WhAm 1
Lapham, Roger Dearborn 1883-1966 *WhAm 4*
Lapham, Samuel 1892-1972 *WhAm 5*
Lapham, William Berry 1828-1894 *ApCAB,*
DcAmB, TwCBDA, WhAm H
Laphame, J P *NewYHSD*
LaPiana, George 1879-1971 *WhAm 5*
Lapicque, Louis 1866-1952 *DcScB*
Laplace, Cyrille Pierre Theodore 1793-1875
IIBEAAW, NewYHSD
Laplace, Ernest 1861-1924 *WhAm 1*

Laplace, Pierre Simon, Marquis De 1749-1827
AsBiEn, DcScB, DcScB Sup, McGEWB
Lapointe, Francis Jerome 1885-1953
NatCAB 40
Laporte, Alphonse A 1902-1962 *WhAm 4*
Laporte, Cloyd 1892-1974 *WhAm 6*
Laporte, John 1798-1862 *BiAUS, BiDrAC,*
WhAm H
Laporte, Otto 1902-1971 *WhAm 5*
Laporte, Raymond 1911-1970 *WhAm 5*
LaPorte, William Ralph 1889-1955 *WhAm 3*
Lapp, Claude Jerome 1892-1973 *WhAm 6*
Lapp, John A 1880-1960 *WhAm 4*
Lapparent, Albert-Auguste Cochon De
1839-1908 *DcScB*
Lappin, Warren Curtis 1900-1975 *WhAm 6*
Lappington, Myrtle Parke *WomWWA 14*
LaPrade, Arthur Thornton 1895-1957
NatCAB 43, WhAm 3
Laprade, Lloyd Stone 1902-1953 *WhAm 3*
Laprade, William Thomas 1883-1975 *WhAm 6*
Lapsley, Robert Alberti 1858-1934 *WhAm 1*
Lapsley, Robert McKee 1870-1943 *NatCAB 35*
LaPuerta, Luis 1811- *ApCAB*
Lapworth, Arthur 1872-1941 *DcScB*
Lapworth, Charles 1842-1920 *DcScB*
Larabee, Frank Sheridan 1864-1921
NatCAB 19, WhAm 1
Larabee, Lottie B d1975 *WhAm 6*
Larabee, William Clarke 1802-1859 *NatCAB 3*
LaRamee, Pierre De *DcScB*
Laramie, Jacques d1821 *DcAmB, WhAm H*
LaRavardiere, Daniel DeLa Tousche
1570?-1631? *ApCAB*
Larca, Joseph Bennett 1900-1945 *NatCAB 34*
Larcade, Henry Dominique, Jr. 1890-1966.
BiDrAC
L'Archeveque, Jean De d1720 *ApCAB Sup*
Larco Herrera, Rafael 1872- *WhAm 5*
Larcom, Lucy 1824-1893 *AmBi, DcAmB,*
NotAW, TwCBDA, WhAm H
Larcom, Lucy 1826-1893 *AmWom, ApCAB,*
Drake, NatCAB 1
Lard, Moses E 1818-1880 *DcAmB, WhAm H*
Lardner, Dionysius 1793-1859 *ApCAB*
Lardner, Henry Ackley 1871-1952 *WhAm 3*
Lardner, James Lawrence 1802-1881 *ApCAB,*
DcAmB, Drake, NatCAB 4, TwCBDA,
WebAMB, WhAm H
Lardner, James Lawrence 1873- *WhAm 5*
Lardner, John 1912-1960 *WhAm 3*
Lardner, John J 1893-1948 *WhAm 2*
Lardner, Lena Bogardus 1843- *WhAm 4,*
WomWWA 14
Lardner, Ring W 1885-1933 *AmBi,*
NatCAB 32, WebAB, WhAm 1
Lardner, Ringgold Wilmer 1885-1933
DcAmB S1, McGEWB
Lardner, William J 1858- *NatCAB 7*
Lareau, Edmond 1848- *ApCAB*
Large, George Elwyn 1899-1973 *WhAm 6*
Large, George Knowles 1879-1958 *NatCAB 44*
Large, John J 1875-1928 *WhAm 1*
Large, Virginia 1914- *IIBEAAW*
Largey, Morris Sellers 1880- *NatCAB 5*
Largey, Patrick Albert 1836-1898 *NatCAB 13*
Largey, Patrick Albert 1838-1898 *ApCAB X*
Larghi, Bernardino 1812-1877 *DcScB*
LaRibourde, Gabriel De 1610-1680 *ApCAB*
LaRichardie, Armand De *WhAm H*
Larimer, Edgar Brown 1876- *WhAm 5*
Larimer, Loyal Herbert 1869- *WhAm 5*
Larimer, William, Jr. 1809-1875 *ApCAB,*
NatCAB 4
Larimore, Joseph William 1887-1971 *WhAm 5*
Larimore, Louise Doddridge 1889-1948
WhAm 2
Larimore, N Greene 1835-1913 *WhAm 1*
LaRive, Arthur-Auguste De 1801-1873 *DcScB*
LaRive, Charles-Gaspard De 1770-1834 *DcScB*
LaRiviere, Alphonse Alfred Clement 1842-
ApCAB
Lark-Horovitz, Karl 1892-1958 *WhAm 3*
Larkey, Sanford Vincent 1898-1969
NatCAB 55
Larkin, Adrian Hoffman 1865-1942
NatCAB 31, WhAm 2
Larkin, Charles Henry *NewYHSD*

Larkin, Charles Lewis 1889-1967 *NatCAB 53*
Larkin, Edgar Lucien 1847-1924 *NatCAB 20,*
WhAm 1
Larkin, Edna Crate 1880- *WomWWA 14*
Larkin, Francis Marion 1861-1933 *WhAm 1*
Larkin, Fred Viall 1883-1954 *WhAm 3*
Larkin, John 1801-1858 *DcAmB, NatCAB 2,*
TwCBDA, WhAm H
Larkin, John 1833?-1890 *NatCAB 2*
Larkin, John Adrian 1891-1948 *NatCAB 39,*
WhAm 2
Larkin, John Durrant 1845-1926 *NatCAB 23*
Larkin, Joseph Maurice 1888-1970 *WhAm 5*
Larkin, Katherine B S *WomWWA 14*
Larkin, Maurice Daniel 1878- *ApCAB X*
Larkin, Oliver Waterman 1896-1971 *WhAm 5*
Larkin, Rosemary Rita 1922-1972 *WhAm 6*
Larkin, Thomas B 1890-1968 *WhAm 5*
Larkin, Thomas Oliver 1802-1858 *AmBi,*
DcAmB, McGEWB, REnAW, WhAm H
Larkin, William Harrison 1902-1969 *WhAm 5*
Larmande, Leo J *NewYHSD*
Larmando, Leo J *NewYHSD*
Larmon, Russell Raymond 1897-1973
NatCAB 57, WhAm 5
Larmor, Joseph 1857-1942 *DcScB*
Larmour, William Gardham 1871-1943
NatCAB 34
Larned, Augusta 1835- *ApCAB, NatCAB 13,*
TwCBDA, WhAm 4, WomWWA 14
Larned, Benjamin Franklin 1794-1862 *ApCAB*
Larned, Charles William 1850-1911
NatCAB 38, TwCBDA, WhAm 1
Larned, Ebenezer 1728-1801 *ApCAB,*
NatCAB 1, TwCBDA
Larned, Edwin Channing 1820-1884 *ApCAB*
Larned, Ellen Douglas 1825- *ApCAB,*
WhAm 4
Larned, John Insley Blair 1883-1955 *WhAm 3*
Larned, Joseph Gay Eaton 1819-1870 *ApCAB,*
DcAmB, NatCAB 24, TwCBDA,
WhAm H
Larned, Josephus Nelson 1836-1913 *AmBi,*
DcAmB, DcAmLiB, NatCAB 12,
NatCAB 16, WhAm 1
Larned, Linda Hull 1853-1939 *WhAm 1,*
WomWWA 14
Larned, Samuel *BiAUS, NatCAB 12*
Larned, Simon d1817 *BiAUS*
Larned, Simon 1753-1817 *ApCAB, BiDrAC,*
WhAm H
Larned, Simon 1754-1817 *Drake*
Larned, Sylvester 1796-1820 *ApCAB, Drake*
Larned, Trowbridge d1928 *WhAm 1*
Larned, Walter Cranston 1850-1914 *WhAm 1*
Larned, William Augustus 1806-1862 *ApCAB,*
TwCBDA
Larned, William Augustus 1872-1926 *DcAmB*
Larner, Edward Atkins 1897-1970 *NatCAB 56,*
WhAm 5
Larner, John Bell 1858-1931 *NatCAB 5,*
NatCAB 22, WhAm 1
Larner, Noble Danforth 1830- *NatCAB 5*
Larner, Robert Martin 1856-1906 *WhAm 1*
Laroche, Antoine De *ApCAB*
LaRoche, Estienne De *DcScB*
LaRoche, Rene 1755-1819 *ApCAB*
LaRoche, Rene 1795-1872 *ApCAB, DcAmB,*
WhAm H
LaRochefoucauld, Francois, Duc De 1613-1680
McGEWB
LaRochelle, Philippe De 1871- *WhAm 5*
Larocque, Joseph 1831-1908 *WhAm 1*
LaRoe, Wilbur, Jr. 1888-1957 *WhAm 3*
Larom, Elizabeth Elmira Shute 1867-
WomWWA 14
LaRonde, Louis Denis, Sieur De 1675-1741
DcAmB
LaRoque, George Paul 1876-1934 *WhAm 1,*
WhAm 1C
LaRoque, O K 1883-1956 *WhAm 3*
Laroque, Paul Stanislaus 1846- *ApCAB Sup*
Larose, J Henry 1909-1962 *NatCAB 50*
Larose, John Jacob 1755-1844 *ApCAB*
Larpenteur, Auguste Louis 1823-1919
NatCAB 17
Larpenteur, Charles 1807-1872 *DcAmB,*
REnAW, WhAm H

Larrabee, Anna Matilda 1842- *AmWom*
Larrabee, Anna Pratt 1872- *WomWWA 14*
Larrabee, C R 1898-1964 *WhAm 4*
Larrabee, Charles Hathaway 1820-1883 *ApCAB,*
BiAUS, BiDrAC, DcAmB, NatCAB 25,
TwCBDA, WhAm H
Larrabee, Charles William 1870-1957
NatCAB 46
Larrabee, Edward Allan 1852-1924 *WhAm 1*
Larrabee, William 1832-1912 *ApCAB Sup,*
DcAmB, NatCAB 11, TwCBDA,
WhAm 1
Larrabee, William Clark 1802-1859 *ApCAB,*
BiDAmEd, DcAmB, NatCAB 25,
TwCBDA, WhAm H
Larrabee, William Henry 1829-1913 *TwCBDA,*
WhAm 1
Larrabee, William Henry 1870-1960 *BiDrAC,*
WhAmP
Larrazolo, Octaviano Ambrosio 1859-1930
BiDrAC, DcAmB, REnAW, WhAm 1,
WhAmP
Larremore, Richard Ludlow 1830-1893 *ApCAB,*
TwCBDA
Larremore, Wilbur 1855-1918 *WhAm 1*
Larreta, Enrique 1875-1961 *WhAm 4*
Larrey, Dominique Jean 1766-1842 *BiHiMed,*
WhoMilH
Larrick, George Potter 1901-1968 *NatCAB 54,*
WhAm 5
Larrimore, Francine *WhAm 6*
Larrinaga, Tulio 1847-1917 *BiDrAC, DcAmB,*
WhAm HA, WhAm 4, WhAmP
Larsen, Alfred 1877-1949 *WhAm 2*
Larsen, Bent Franklin 1882-1970 *IIBEAAW*
Larsen, Christian 1874-1948 *WhAm 2*
Larsen, Ellouise Baker 1877-1967 *WhAm 4*
Larsen, Esper Signius, Jr. 1879-1961 *DcScB,*
NatCAB 45, WhAm 4
Larsen, Finn Jacob 1915-1971 *WhAm 5*
Larsen, Hanna Astrup 1873-1945 *WhAm 2*
Larsen, Harold D 1904-1961 *WhAm 4*
Larsen, Henning 1889-1971 *NatCAB 56,*
WhAm 5
Larsen, Henry Louis 1890-1962 *NatCAB 52,*
WhAm 4
Larsen, Herbert J 1896-1953 *NatCAB 40*
Larsen, Jens Willard 1901-1972 *WhAm 6*
Larsen, Laur 1833-1915 *NatCAB 25*
Larsen, Lauritz 1882-1923 *WhAm 1*
Larsen, Lewis A 1875-1954 *WhAm 3*
Larsen, Lewis P d1955 *WhAm 3*
Larsen, Merwin John 1909-1965 *NatCAB 51,*
WhAm 4
Larsen, Peter Laurentius 1833-1915 *AmBi,*
BiDAmEd, DcAmB, TwCBDA, WhAm 1,
WhAm 1C
Larsen, William 1909-1971 *WhAm 5*
Larsen, William Washington 1871-1938 *BiDrAC,*
WhAm 1, WhAmP
Larson, Agnes 1875- *WomWWA 14*
Larson, Agnes M 1892-1967 *WhAm 5*
Larson, Algot J E 1881- *WhAm 6*
Larson, Carl W 1881-1954 *WhAm 3*
Larson, Carrel Blaine 1896-1958 *NatCAB 48*
Larson, Charles Henry 1868-1950 *NatCAB 37*
Larson, Christian Daa 1874- *WhAm 5*
Larson, Cora Gunn 1859-1906 *WhAm 1*
Larson, Frank Oscar 1880- *WhAm 6*
Larson, George Victor 1895-1952 *WhAm 3*
Larson, Gustus Ludwig 1881-1953 *WhAm 3*
Larson, John Albert 1884-1949 *NatCAB 42*
Larson, John Augustus 1892-1965 *AsBiEn,*
WhAm 4
Larson, Lars Moore 1856-1931 *BiDAmEd,*
NatCAB 3, WhAm 3
Larson, Laurence Marcellus 1868-1938
DcAmB S2, WhAm 1
Larson, Leonard W 1898-1974 *WhAm 6*
Larson, Martin Magnuss 1885-1961
NatCAB 49
Larson, Morgan Foster 1882-1961 *NatCAB 46*
Larson, O T 1904-1966 *WhAm 4*
Larson, Oscar John 1871-1957 *BiDrAC*
Larson, Ralph Norman 1904-1973 *WhAm 6*
Larson, Randell 1893-1966 *WhAm 4*
Larson, Roy Frank 1893-1973 *NatCAB 57,*
WhAm 6

Larson, T A 1910- *REnAW*
Larson, Winford Porter 1880-1947 *WhAm 2*
Larsson, C G Emil 1864-1936 *NatCAB 28*
Larsson, Gustaf 1861-1919 *WhAm 1*
Lartet, Edouard Amant Isidore Hippolyte
1801-1871 *DcScB*
Lartet, Edouard Armand Isidore Hippolyte
1801-1871 *AsBiEn*
Lartet, Louis 1840-1899 *DcScB*
Lartigue, James 1777-1840 *ApCAB, Drake*
LaRue, Carl Downey 1888-1955 *WhAm 3*
LaRue, Daniel Wolford 1878-1969 *WhAm 5*
LaRue, George Roger 1882-1967 *NatCAB 53*
LaRue, John W *WhAm 3*
LaRue, Mabel Guinnip 1880-1971 *WhAm 5*
LaRue, Walt 1925?- *IIBEAAW*
LaRue, William Earl 1876- *WhAm 5*
Larus, Charles Dunning 1849-1908 *NatCAB 33*
Larus, Charles Dunning, Jr. 1881-1946
NatCAB 41
Larus, Lewis Griffin 1887-1966 *NatCAB 51*
LaSalle, Sieur De 1643-1687 *WebAB,*
WhAm H
Lasalle, Antoine Charles Louis 1775-1809
WhoMilH
LaSalle, Charles 1894-1958 *IIBEAAW*
LaSalle, Rene Robert Cavelier, Sieur De
1643-1687 *AmBi, McGEWB, REnAW*
LaSalle, Robert Cavalier, Sieur De 1643-1687
NatCAB 3
LaSalle, Robert Cavelier 1635?-1687 *Drake*
LaSalle, Robert Cavelier, Sieur De 1643-1687
ApCAB, DcAmB
Lasansky, Mauricio 1914- *BnEnAmA*
Lasater, Edward Cunningham 1860-1930
DcAmB, NatCAB 28, WhAm 1
Lasater, Robert Edward 1867-1954 *NatCAB 43*
Lasby, William Frederick 1876- *WhAm 5*
Lascari, Salvatore 1884-1967 *WhAm 4*
LasCasas 1474-1566 *Drake*
LasCasas, Bartolome De 1474-1566 *McGEWB*
LasCasas, Gonzalo 1543-1601 *ApCAB*
Lascoff, J Leon 1867-1943 *NatCAB 33*
Lasell, Chester Whitin 1861-1932 *NatCAB 32*
Lasell, John Whitin 1897-1943 *NatCAB 38*
Lasell, Josiah Manning 1863-1939 *NatCAB 30*
Laselle, Mary Augusta 1860- *WhAm 4*
LaSere, Emile 1802-1882 *BiAUS, BiDrAC,*
WhAm H
Lash, Bertha Beatrice *WomWWA 14*
Lash, Israel George 1810-1878 *BiAUS,*
BiDrAC, WhAm H
Lash, James Hamilton 1872-1949 *WhAm 3*
Lashanska, Hulda 1890-1974 *NatCAB 57*
Lashar, Walter Benjamin 1870-1955
NatCAB 45, WhAm 3
LaShelle, Kirke 1862-1905 *NatCAB 12,*
WhAm 1
Lasher, George Starr 1885-1964 *WhAm 4*
Lasher, George William 1831-1920 *WhAm 1*
Lasher, Susan Elizabeth *WomWWA 14*
LasHeras, Juan Gregorio De 1780-1866 *ApCAB*
Lashley, Karl Spencer 1890-1958 *DcScB,*
McGEWB, NatCAB 44, WebAB,
WhAm 3
Lashly, Arthur Valentine 1880-1957 *WhAm 3*
Lashly, Jacob Mark 1882-1967 *WhAm 4*
Lasker, Albert Davis 1880-1952 *DcAmB S5,*
NatCAB 42, WebAB, WhAm 3
Lasker, Bruno 1880-1965 *WhAm 4*
Lasker, Loula Davis 1888-1961 *NatCAB 48,*
WhAm 4
Laskey, John Ellsworth 1868-1945 *NatCAB 35,*
WhAm 2
Laski, Harold Joseph 1893-1950 *McGEWB,*
WhAm 2A
Laskoske, Aloysius William 1901-1969
WhAm 5
Lasky, Jesse Louis 1880- *ApCAB X,*
NatCAB 18
Lasky, Jesse Louis 1880-1956 *WhAm 3*
Lasky, Jesse Louis 1880-1958 *WebAB*
Lasky, Wayne Edward 1902-1968 *WhAm 5*
Laso DeLaVega, Jose Silvester 1779-1842
ApCAB
LaSpisa, Jake Anthony 1909-1972 *WhAm 5*
Lassalle, Charles 1817-1888 *ApCAB Sup*
Lassalle, Ferdinand 1825-1864 *McGEWB*

Lassalle, Leo Joseph 1886-1970 *NatCAB 56*
Lassar-Cohn *DcScB*
Lassaw, Ibram 1913- *BnEnAmA*
Lassell, William 1799-1880 *AsBiEn, DcScB*
Lassen, Ben 1904-1968 *NatCAB 56*
Lassen, Helene Siverine 1840- *WomWWA 14*
Lassen, Henry 1861-1919 *NatCAB 18*
Lassen, Peter 1800- *WhAm H*
Lasser, Jacob Kay 1896-1954 *DcAmB S5,*
NatCAB 42, WhAm 3
Lasserre, Charles Louis 1762-1826 *ApCAB*
Lassinger, Larry Wayne 1937-1973 *WhAm 6*
Lassiter, Daniel William 1827- *NatCAB 10*
Lassiter, Francis Rives 1866-1909 *BiDrAC,*
WhAm 1
Lassiter, Herbert Carlyle d1950 *WhAm 3*
Lassiter, Newton Hance 1860- *WhAm 5*
Lassiter, Robert 1877- *WhAm 5*
Lassiter, William 1867-1959 *WhAm 3*
Lassus, Roland De 1532-1594 *McGEWB*
Lasswell, Harold Dwight 1902- *McGEWB,*
WebAB
Last, Murray A 1901-1953 *NatCAB 45*
Lastarria, Jose Victorino 1812- *ApCAB*
Lastinger, John Williams 1902-1972 *WhAm 5*
Lastra, Francisco DeLa 1777-1852 *ApCAB*
Laszlo, Daniel 1902-1958 *NatCAB 43*
Latadeva *DcScB*
Latane, James Allen 1831-1902 *ApCAB,*
NatCAB 36, TwCBDA, WhAm 1
Latane, John Holladay 1869-1932 *AmBi,*
DcAmB S1, NatCAB 13, NatCAB 23,
WhAm 1
Latch, Edward Biddle 1833-1911 *TwCBDA,*
WhAm 1
Latchaw, D Austin 1861-1948 *WhAm 2*
Latchaw, John Roland Harris 1851-1928
TwCBDA, WhAm 3
Latham, Barbara 1896- *IIBEAAW*
Latham, Carl Ray 1872-1962 *WhAm 4*
Latham, Charles Kellogg 1847-1926
NatCAB 20
Latham, Charles Louis 1877- *WhAm 5*
Latham, Dana 1898-1974 *WhAm 6*
Latham, Elsie Gaylord 1879- *WomWWA 14*
Latham, George Henry 1895-1964 *NatCAB 51*
Latham, George Robert 1832-1917 *BiAUS,*
BiDrAC
Latham, Harold Strong 1887-1969 *WhAm 5*
Latham, Henry Jepson 1908- *BiDrAC*
Latham, James Edwin 1866-1946 *NatCAB 33*
Latham, John *NewYHSD*
Latham, John Campbell 1844- *NatCAB 9*
Latham, Louis Charles 1840-1895 *BiDrAC,*
WhAm H
Latham, Milton S 1827-1882 *BiAUS, Drake*
Latham, Milton Scott 1827-1882 *ApCAB,*
NatCAB 4
Latham, Milton Slocum 1827-1882 *BiDrAC,*
DcAmB, TwCBDA, WhAm H
Latham, Orval Ray 1890-1940 *WhAm 1*
Latham, Rex Knight 1883-1938 *WhAm 1*
Latham, Vida Annette 1866-1958 *NatCAB 44,*
WhAm 4
Lathan, Robert 1881-1837 *WhAm 1*
Lathbury, Albert Augustus 1849- *WhAm 4*
Lathbury, Clarence 1854-1939 *WhAm 1*
Lathbury, Mary Artemisia 1841-1913 *DcAmB,*
NatCAB 10, WhAm 1
Lathe, Herbert William 1851-1932 *WhAm 1*
Lathem, Abraham Lance 1866-1955 *WhAm 3*
Lathers, Richard 1820-1903 *ApCAB Sup,*
WhAm 1
Lathrap, Mary Torrans 1838- *AmWom*
Lathrop, Alanson Peckham 1861-1950
NatCAB 38, WhAm 3
Lathrop, Austin Eugene 1865-1950 *WhAm 3*
Lathrop, Betsy B *NewYHSD*
Lathrop, Bryan 1844-1916 *WhAm 1*
Lathrop, Cap 1865-1950 *REnAW*
Lathrop, Charles Gardner 1849-1914
NatCAB 23
Lathrop, Charles Newton 1871-1931 *WhAm 1*
Lathrop, Clarissa Caldwell 1892- *AmWom*
Lathrop, Cyrus Clark 1862-1931 *NatCAB 26*
Lathrop, Edward Potter 1863-1940 *NatCAB 31*
Lathrop, Francis Augustus 1849-1909 *AmBi,*
ApCAB, DcAmB, NatCAB 11, TwCBDA,

WhAm 1

Lathrop, Frank Holland 1851-1936 *NatCAB 27*
Lathrop, Gardiner 1850-1938 *ApCAB X,
NatCAB 17, NatCAB 34, WhAm 1*
Lathrop, George Parsons 1851-1898 *AmBi,
ApCAB, DcAmB, NatCAB 9, TwCBDA,
WhAm H*
Lathrop, Henry Burrowes 1867-1936 *WhAm 1,
WhAm 1C*
Lathrop, Ida Pulis 1859- *WomWWA 14*
Lathrop, Isabel Stevens *WomWWA 14*
Lathrop, John 1740-1816 *ApCAB, Drake*
Lathrop, John 1772-1820 *ApCAB, DcAmB,
Drake, NatCAB 7, WhAm H*
Lathrop, John 1835-1910 *TwCBDA, WhAm 1*
Lathrop, John Carroll 1871- *WhAm 1*
Lathrop, John D *NewYHSD*
Lathrop, John Hiram 1799-1866 *ApCAB,
ApCAB X, BiDAmEd, DcAmB, Drake,
NatCAB 5, NatCAB 8, TwCBDA,
WhAm H*
Lathrop, John Howland 1880-1967 *WhAm 4*
Lathrop, Joseph 1731-1820 *ApCAB, Drake,
TwCBDA*
Lathrop, Julia Clifford 1858-1932 *AmBi,
DcAmB S1, NatCAB 24, NotAW,
WhAm 1, WomWWA 14*
Lathrop, Mary Alinda 1868- *WomWWA 14*
Lathrop, Mother Mary Alphonsa 1851-1926
NotAW
Lathrop, Palmer Jadwin 1909-1953 *WhAm 3*
Lathrop, Robert 1870-1943 *NatCAB 33*
Lathrop, Rose Hawthorne 1851-1926 *AmBi,
AmWom, ApCAB, DcAmB, NatCAB 9,
NotAW, TwCBDA, WhAm 1*
Lathrop, Rose Hawthorne 1854-1926
WomWWA 14
Lathrop, Samuel 1771-1846 *BiAUS*
Lathrop, Samuel 1772-1846 *BiDRAC,
TwCBDA, WhAm H*
Lathrop, Thomas d1675 *Drake*
Lathrop, Walter W 1903-1973 *WhAm 6*
Lathrop, William 1825-1907 *BiDRAC,
NatCAB 32*
Lathrop, William Arthur 1854-1912
NatCAB 18
Lathrop, William Gerard 1841-1896
NatCAB 39
Lathrop, William Langson 1859-1938 *WhAm 1*
Lathrop, William Whiting 1862-1949
NatCAB 39
Latil, Alexandre 1816-1851 *DcAmB,
WhAm H*
Latilla, Eugenio Honorius 1808-1861
NewYHSD
Latimer, Asbury Churchill 1851-1908
NatCAB 12
Latimer, Asbury Churchwell 1851-1908 *BiDRAC,
TwCBDA, WhAm 1, WhAmP*
Latimer, Caroline Wormeley *WomWWA 14*
Latimer, Charles 1827-1888 *ApCAB,
TwCBDA*
Latimer, Claiborne Green 1893-1960 *WhAm 4*
Latimer, Clyde Burney 1890-1952 *WhAm 3*
Latimer, Elizabeth Wormeley 1822-1904
AmWom, TwCBDA, WhAm 1
Latimer, Frederick Palmer 1875-1940
NatCAB 30
Latimer, George 1750-1825 *ApCAB, TwCBDA*
Latimer, George Washington 1821-1896
ApCAB Sup
Latimer, Henry 1752-1819 *BiDRAC, TwCBDA,
WhAm H*
Latimer, Henry *see also* Lattimer, Henry
Latimer, Bishop Hugh 1492?-1555 *McGEWB*
Latimer, James Elijah 1826-1884 *ApCAB,
NatCAB 11, TwCBDA*
Latimer, James M *NewYHSD*
Latimer, John Austin 1891-1973 *WhAm 6*
Latimer, John Newton Franklin 1877- *WhoColR*
Latimer, Julian Lane 1868-1939 *NatCAB 31,
WhAm 1*
Latimer, Lewis Howard 1848- *WhoColR*
Latimer, Lilian Emmeline 1875- *WomWWA 14*
Latimer, Lorenzo Palmer 1857-1941 *IIBEAAW*
Latimer, M Gregg 1877-1942 *NatCAB 31*
Latimer, Margery Bodine 1899-1932 *WhAm 1*

Latimer, Mary Elizabeth Wormeley 1822-1904
DcAmB, NatCAB 9
Latimer, Mary Elizabeth Wormeley *see also*
Latimer, Elizabeth W
Latimer, Rodney Amos 1891-1965 *NatCAB 52*
Latimer, Samuel Lowry, Jr. 1891-1975 *WhAm 6*
Latimer, Thomas Erwin 1879-1937 *WhAm 1*
Latimer, Thomas Sargent 1839-1906 *WhAm 1*
Latimer, Wendell Mitchell 1893-1955
*DcAmB S5, DcScB, NatCAB 43,
WhAm 3*
Latimer, William K 1809- *Drake*
Latimer, William Kay 1794-1873 *ApCAB*
Latimer, William Key 1794-1873 *TwCBDA*
Latimer, William T *NewYHSD*
Latizar, Ferdinand *NewYHSD*
Latoix, Gaspard *IIBEAAW*
Latorre, Juan Jose 1843- *ApCAB*
LaTouche Treville, Louis Rene Vassor 1745-1804
ApCAB
Latour, Arsene Lacarriere *NewYHSD*
LaTour, Georges De 1593-1652 *McGEWB*
LaTour, LeBlond De d1723 *DcAmB*
LaTour, LeBlonde De d1723 *WhAm H*
Latourette, Earl C 1889-1956 *WhAm 3*
Latourette, Howard Fenton 1883-1957 *WhAm 3*
Latourette, Kenneth Scott 1884-1968 *DcAmReB*
Latreille, Pierre-Andre 1762-1833 *DcScB*
Latrobe, Benjamin H d1820 *BiAUS*
Latrobe, Benjamin Henry 1764-1820 *AmBi,
ApCAB, BnEnAmA, DcAmB, EncAB,
McGEWB, NatCAB 9, NewYHSD,
TwCBDA, WebAB, WhAm H*
Latrobe, Benjamin Henry 1767-1820 *Drake*
Latrobe, Benjamin Henry 1806-1878 *AmBi,
DcAmB, WhAm H*
Latrobe, Benjamin Henry 1807-1878 *ApCAB,
NatCAB 9, TwCBDA*
Latrobe, Charles Hazelhurst 1834-1902
WhAm 4
Latrobe, Charles Hazlehurst 1833-1902 *ApCAB,
NatCAB 9, TwCBDA*
Latrobe, Charles Hazlehurst 1834-1902 *DcAmB*
Latrobe, Charles Joseph 1801-1875 *ApCAB*
Latrobe, Ferdinand Claiborne 1833-1911
ApCAB, NatCAB 9, TwCBDA, WhAm 1
Latrobe, John Hazlehurst Boneval 1803-1891
*AmBi, ApCAB, DcAmB, NewYHSD,
TwCBDA, WhAm H*
Latrobe, John Hazlehurst Bonval 1803-1891
NatCAB 9
Latrobe, Mary *NewYHSD*
Latshaw, David 1835-1892 *NatCAB 32*
Latshaw, David Gardner 1869- *WhAm 5*
Latshaw, William Hart 1855-1911 *NatCAB 18*
Latson, Harvey Harrelson 1889-1970
NatCAB 55
Latta, A B 1821-1865 *Drake*
Latta, Alexander Bonner 1821-1865 *ApCAB,
DcAmB, NatCAB 13, TwCBDA,
WhAm H*
Latta, Delbert Leroy 1920- *BiDRAC*
Latta, Edward Dilworth 1851-1925 *NatCAB 20*
Latta, James 1732-1801 *ApCAB, TwCBDA*
Latta, James Polk 1844-1911 *BiDRAC,
WhAm 1*
Latta, Robert Edward 1894-1956 *WhAm 3*
Latta, Samuel Arminius 1804-1852 *ApCAB*
Latta, Samuel Whitehill 1848- *WhAm 4*
Latta, Thomas Albert 1872-1931 *WhAm 1*
Lattig, Herbert Elmer 1892-1953 *WhAm 3*
Lattimer, George W 1856-1920 *WhAm 1*
Lattimer, Henry 1752-1819 *ApCAB, BiAUS,
Drake, NatCAB 2*
Lattimer, Henry *see also* Latimer, Henry
Lattimore, Eleanor Larrabee *WomWWA 14*
Lattimore, John Aaron Cicero 1876- *WhAm 5*
Lattimore, John Compere 1862-1915 *TwCBDA,
WhAm 1*
Lattimore, John Lee 1894-1967 *NatCAB 54*
Lattimore, Offa Shivers 1865- *WhAm 1*
Lattimore, Samuel Allan 1828-1913 *ApCAB,
NatCAB 12, TwCBDA, WhAm 1*
Lattimore, Sarah Catherine Shivers 1841-
WomWWA 14
Lattimore, William 1774-1843 *BiAUS,
BiDRAC, DcAmB, NatCAB 25, TwCBDA,
WhAm H*

Lattin, Leroy Emory 1896-1974 *WhAm 6*
Lattman, Morris 1896-1962 *NatCAB 51*
Lattman, Walter 1899-1965 *WhAm 4*
Latto, Thomas Carstairs 1818- *ApCAB*
Lattre DeTassigny, Jean J M Gabriel De
1889-1952 *WhAm 3, WhoMilH*
Latus, Grace Druitt *WomWWA 14*
Laty, Michael 1826-1848 *NewYHSD*
Latz, G Irving 1888-1947 *NatCAB 36*
Latzer, John Albert 1876-1952 *NatCAB 41,
WhAm 3*
Latzer, Louis 1848-1924 *NatCAB 19*
Lau, Hans Emil 1879-1918 *DcScB*
Lau, Robert Frederick 1885-1943 *WhAm 2*
Laubach, Charles 1836-1904 *WhAm 1*
Laubach, Frank Charles 1884-1970 *BiDAmEd,
WhAm 5*
Laubach, Howard L 1870- *WhAm 5*
Laubaugh, Ernest Ellsworth 1887-1936
NatCAB 28
Laubender, Ruth Elizabeth 1864-
WomWWA 14
Laubengayer, Richard August 1902-1966
WhAm 4
Laubengayer, Robert J 1884-1958 *WhAm 3*
Laubenheimer, Rudolph *NewYHSD*
Lauber, Joseph 1855-1948 *NatCAB 36,
WhAm 2*
L'Auberiviere, Francis L DePourroy De
1711-1741 *ApCAB*
Lauchheimer, Charles Henry 1859-1920
WhAm 1
Lauck, John *NewYHSD*
Lauck, W Jett 1879-1949 *WhAm 2*
Laucks, S Forry 1870-1942 *NatCAB 34*
Laucks, Wilson Charles 1898-1950 *NatCAB 39*
Laud, Henry S *NewYHSD*
Laud, Sam 1896-1963 *WhAm 4*
Laud, William 1573-1645 *McGEWB*
Lauder, Charles *NewYHSD*
Lauder, Ella Louise 1863- *WomWWA 14*
Lauder, Harry 1870-1950 *WhAm 4*
Lauder, Isaac 1830?- *NewYHSD*
Lauder, James 1825?- *NewYHSD*
Lauder, John *NewYHSD*
Lauder, John, Jr. *NewYHSD*
Lauder, Maria Elise Turner *AmWom*
Lauder, William *NewYHSD*
Lauderbach *NewYHSD*
Lauderdale, James 1780?-1814 *ApCAB, Drake*
Lauderdale, Josephine Lane *WomWWA 14*
Lauderdale, Ursula 1880?- *IIBEAAW*
Laudon, Gideon Ernst, Freiherr Von 1717-1790
WhoMilH
Laudonniere, Rene Goulaine De *AmBi,
ApCAB, DcAmB, Drake*
Laue, Max Theodor Felix Von 1879-1960
AsBiEn, DcScB
Lauer, Conrad Newton 1869-1943 *NatCAB 32,
WhAm 2*
Lauer, Stewart Ellwood 1890-1962 *WhAm 4*
Lauer, Walter Ernst 1893-1966 *WhAm 4*
Lauer-Leonardi, Boris 1905-1971 *NatCAB 57*
Lauf, Hubert Peter 1894-1954 *NatCAB 44*
Laufer, Berthold 1874-1934 *DcAmB S1,
WhAm 1*
Laufer, Calvin Weiss 1874-1938 *NatCAB 29,
WhAm 1*
Laufer, Harold Edward 1897-1952 *NatCAB 43*
Laufman, Philip Harrington 1822- *NatCAB 11*
Laugel, Raymond William 1922-1973 *WhAm 6*
Laughinghouse, Charles O'Hagan 1871-1930
NatCAB 22, WhAm 1
Laughlin, Ada Mabelle 1850- *WomWWA 14*
Laughlin, Alexander 1866-1943 *NatCAB 32*
Laughlin, Alexander, Jr. 1889-1926 *NatCAB 20*
Laughlin, Alice Denniston 1895-1952
NatCAB 42
Laughlin, Clara Elizabeth 1873-1941 *WhAm 1,
WomWWA 14*
Laughlin, Frank C 1859-1943 *WhAm 2*
Laughlin, Gail 1868-1952 *WhAm 3,
WomWWA 14*
Laughlin, George Ashton 1862-1936
NatCAB 27, WhAm 1
Laughlin, George Mark 1872-1948 *WhAm 2*
Laughlin, George McCully, Jr. 1873-1946
NatCAB 50, WhAm 2

Laughlin, Harry Hamilton 1880-1943
DcAmB S3, WhAm 2
Laughlin, Homer 1843-1913 *NatCAB 9,
NatCAB 16*
Laughlin, Hugh C 1904-1973 *WhAm 6*
Laughlin, Irwin 1871-1941 *NatCAB 30,
WhAm 1*
Laughlin, James 1806-1882 *ApCAB*
Laughlin, James, Jr. 1847-1919 *NatCAB 29*
Laughlin, James Benn 1864-1928 *NatCAB 28*
Laughlin, James Laurence 1850-1933 *AmBi,
ApCAB, DcAmB S1, NatCAB 11,
NatCAB 24, TwCBDA, WhAm 1*
Laughlin, John 1856-1905 *NatCAB 6*
Laughlin, John Edward, Jr. 1908-1970
NatCAB 55, WhAm 5
Laughlin, Julian 1852- *NatCAB 17, WhAm 1*
Laughlin, Kate Kimbrough 1857-
WomWWA 14
Laughlin, Napoleon Bonaparte 1844- *WhAm 4*
Laughlin, Samuel Ott, Jr. 1891-1957 *WhAm 3*
Laughlin, Sceva Bright 1881-1947 *WhAm 2*
Laughlin, T Cowden 1870- *WhAm 5*
Laughon, Absalom Barr 1870-1944 *NatCAB 32*
Laughon, Albert J 1873-1943 *NatCAB 35*
Laughton, Charles 1899-1962 *WhAm 4*
Laughton, George 1875-1941 *WhAm 1*
Laughton, Sarah Elizabeth 1852- *WhAm 4*
Lauman, Jacob Gartner 1813-1867 *ApCAB,
TwCBDA*
Launitz, Robert Eberhard Schmidt VonDer
1806-1870 *ApCAB, DcAmB, Drake,
NewYHSD, TwCBDA*
Launt, Francis Albemarle Delbretons 1864-
WhAm 1
Laurance, John 1750-1810 *AmBi, BiAUS Sup,
BiDrAC, DcAmB, NatCAB 2, WhAm H,
WhAmP*
Laurance, John *see also* Lawrance, John
Laurel, Stan 1890-1965 *WebAB*
Lauren, Bertus Clark 1868-1953 *NatCAB 46*
Laurence, Daniel 1873-1961 *NatCAB 49*
Laurence, John *NewYHSD*
Laurence, Samuel 1812-1884 *NewYHSD*
Laurence, William Beach 1800-1881 *NatCAB 9*
Laurence, William Beach *see also* Lawrence,
William Beach
Laurens, Andre Du 1558-1609 *DcScB*
Laurens, Henry 1724-1792 *AmBi, ApCAB,
BiAUS, BiDrAC, BiDrUSE, DcAmB,
Drake, EncAB, McGEWB, NatCAB 3,
TwCBDA, WebAB, WhAm H, WhAmP*
Laurens, John 1753-1782 *Drake, NatCAB 1,
TwCBDA*
Laurens, John 1754-1782 *AmBi, DcAmB,
WhAm H*
Laurens, John 1756-1782 *ApCAB*
Laurent, Auguste 1807-1853 *AsBiEn, DcScB*
Laurent, Cornelius Baldran *ApCAB*
Laurent, Matthieu Paul Hermann 1841-1908
DcScB
Laurent, Pierre Alphonse 1813-1854 *DcScB*
Laurent, Robert 1890-1970 *BnEnAmA,
WhAm 5*
Laurenti, Mario d1922 *WhAm 1*
Laurey, James Richard 1907-1964 *NatCAB 51*
Laurgaard, Olaf 1880-1945 *WhAm 2*
Lauriat, Charles Emelius 1842-1920 *WhAm 1*
Lauriat, Harriet Fidelia 1847- *WomWWA 14*
Laurie, A *NewYHSD*
Laurie, Annie *NotAW*
Laurie, James 1778-1853 *ApCAB*
Laurie, James 1811-1875 *ApCAB, DcAmB,
NatCAB 9, WhAm H*
Laurie, James Woodin 1903-1970 *WhAm 5*
Laurie, John Wimburn 1835- *ApCAB*
Laurie, Thomas 1821-1897 *ApCAB, TwCBDA*
Laurie, Wilfrid Rhodes 1898-1973 *WhAm 6*
Laurie, William 1832-1908 *WhAm 1*
Laurier *NewYHSD*
Laurier, Sir Wilfrid 1841-1919 *ApCAB,
McGEWB*
Lauritsen, Catherine Grollman 1938- *EncAAH*
Lauritsen, Charles Christian 1892-1968
NatCAB 54, WhAm 5
Lauritz, Paul 1889- *IIBEAAW*
Lauritzen, Ivar 1900-1974 *WhAm 6*
Laursen, Laurits Aksel 1881-1941 *NatCAB 35*

Laurvik, J Nilsen 1877- *WhAm 5*
Lauryssen, Gaston 1898-1962 *WhAm 4*
Lausche, Frank John 1895- *BiDrAC*
Laussat, Antony 1806-1833 *ApCAB*
Laussedat, Aime 1819-1907 *DcScB*
Laut, Agnes C 1871-1936 *WhAm 1,
WomWWA 14*
Lautaro 1535?-1557 *McGEWB*
Lautaro 1537-1556 *ApCAB*
Lauterbach, Amanda Friedman *WomWWA 14*
Lauterbach, Edward 1844-1923 *NatCAB 1,
NatCAB 14, NatCAB 26, WhAm 1*
Lauterbach, Jacob Zallel 1873-1942 *WhAm 2*
Lauterbach, Richard E 1914-1950 *WhAm 3*
Lauterpacht, Hersch 1897-1960 *WhAm 4*
Lautmann, Herbert Moses 1891-1970 *WhAm 5*
Lautz, Frederick Christopher Martin 1846-1905
NatCAB 24
Lautz, Henry B 1876- *WhAm 5*
Lautz, William 1838-1915 *NewYHSD*
Laux, August 1847-1921 *NatCAB 7, WhAm 1*
Lauzon, Jean De 1582- *ApCAB*
Lauzun, Armand Louis DeGontaut, Duc De
1747-1793 *ApCAB, Drake*
Lavake, Rae Thornton 1883-1975 *WhAm 6*
Laval, Antony J De d1758 *ApCAB*
Laval, Francois DeMontmorency 1622-1708
Drake
Laval, Francois Xavier De 1623-1708 *McGEWB*
Laval, Jacint 1762?-1822 *ApCAB, Drake*
Laval, Jean M 1854-1937 *WhAm 1*
Laval, Mathieu J F Laval Montmorency d1826
Drake
Laval, Montmorency Mathieu Paul Louis
1748-1817 *Drake*
Laval, Pierre 1883-1945 *McGEWB, WhWW-II*
Laval-Montmorency, Francis Xavier De
1623-1708 *ApCAB*
Laval-Montmorency, Mathieu Jean Felicite
1767-1826 *ApCAB*
Laval-Montmorency, Mathieu P L, Duc De
1748-1809 *ApCAB*
Lavalette, Antoine De 1707- *ApCAB*
LaValette, Elie A F 1789-1862 *Drake*
LaValette, Elie A F 1790?-1862 *ApCAB*
Lavalle, John 1896-1971 *WhAm 5*
LaValle, Juan 1797-1841 *ApCAB*
Lavallee, Calixa 1842-1891 *WhAm H*
Lavallee, Joseph Aime 1895-1965 *NatCAB 52*
Lavalleja, Juan Antonio 1778-1853 *McGEWB*
Lavalleja, Juan Antonio 1795-1853 *ApCAB*
Lavanha, Joao Baptista 1550?-1624 *DcScB*
Laveille, Joseph d1842 *WhAm H*
Lavell, Cecil Fairfield 1872-1948 *WhAm 2*
Lavelle, Michael J 1856-1939 *WhAm 1*
Lavely, Henry Alexander 1831- *WhAm 4*
Lavender, Mrs. Charles 1817-1898 *NewYHSD*
Lavender, Christ *NewYHSD*
Lavender, David 1910- *REnAW*
Lavender, Eugenie Aubanel 1817-1898
IIBEAAW
Lavender, Harrison Morton 1890-1952 *WhAm 3*
Lavenson, Jay 1889-1968 *NatCAB 54*
Laveran, Charles Louis Alphonse 1845-1922
AsBiEn, DcScB
Laverdiere, Charles Honore 1826-1873 *ApCAB*
LaVerendrye, Pierre G DeV, Sieur De 1685-1749
*AmBi, DcAmB, McGEWB, REnAW,
WhAm H*
Lavergne, Antoine *NewYHSD*
Laverty, Roger Montgomery 1890-1968
NatCAB 54
Lavery, Urban A 1885-1959 *WhAm 3*
Laves, Kurt 1866-1944 *WhAm 2*
Lavialle, Peter Joseph 1820-1867 *ApCAB,
NatCAB 12, TwCBDA, WhAm H*
Lavialle, Pierre Joseph 1820-1867 *Drake*
Lavidge, A W 1888-1964 *WhAm 4*
Lavigerie, Charles Martel Allemand 1825-1892
McGEWB
Lavigne *NewYHSD*
Lavinder, Claude Hervey 1872- *WhAm 5*
Lavington, Leon Edward 1889-1961 *NatCAB 51*
LaViolette, William Alfred 1900-1955
NatCAB 44
Lavis, Fred 1871- *WhAm 5*
Lavisse, Ernest 1842-1922 *McGEWB*
Lavoisier, Antoine Laurent 1743-1794 *AsBiEn,*

BiHiMed, DcScB, McGEWB
Lavradio, Antonio DeA S E P, Marquis De
1729-1790 *ApCAB*
Lavrentiev, Boris Innokentievich 1892-1944
DcScB
Lavretta, Constantine Lawrence 1858-
NatCAB 7
Law, Mrs. *NewYHSD*
Law, Andrew 1748-1821 *AmBi, ApCAB,
DcAmB, Drake, NatCAB 25*
Law, Andrew 1749-1821 *WhAm H*
Law, Arthur Ayer 1872-1930 *WhAm 1*
Law, Charles Blakeslee 1872-1929 *BiDrAC,
WhAm 1*
Law, Evander McIver 1836-1920 *WhAm 1*
Law, Evander McIvor 1836-1920 *BiDConf,
DcAmB*
Law, Francis Marion 1877-1970 *WhAm 5*
Law, Frank Fidelis 1894-1950 *NatCAB 41*
Law, Fred Hayes 1876-1942 *WhAm 2*
Law, Frederick Houk 1871-1957 *WhAm 3*
Law, George 1806-1881 *ApCAB, DcAmB,
NatCAB 3, TwCBDA, WhAm H*
Law, Glen Ramsey 1897-1961 *NatCAB 48*
Law, Herbert Edward 1864- *WhAm 5*
Law, Homer Lycurgus 1846-1909 *NatCAB 29*
Law, James 1838-1921 *NatCAB 38, WhAm 1*
Law, James Richard 1865-1952 *WhAm 3*
Law, John 1671-1729 *ApCAB, McGEWB*
Law, John 1796-1873 *ApCAB, BiAUS,
BiDrAC, DcAmB, NatCAB 11, TwCBDA,
WhAm H*
Law, John Adger 1869-1949 *WhAm 2*
Law, Jonathan 1672-1750 *NatCAB 10*
Law, Jonathan 1674-1750 *ApCAB, BiAUS,
DcAmB, Drake, TwCBDA, WhAm H*
Law, Lizzie Woodbury *WomWWA 14*
Law, Lyman 1770-1842 *ApCAB, BiAUS,
BiDrAC, NatCAB 11, TwCBDA,
WhAm H*
Law, Marion 1867-1930 *NatCAB 23*
Law, Richard 1733-1806 *ApCAB, BiAUS,
BiDrAC, DcAmB, Drake, NatCAB 4,
TwCBDA, WhAm H*
Law, Robert 1874-1932 *WhAm 1*
Law, Robert 1874-1933 *NatCAB 34*
Law, Robert Adger 1879-1961 *WhAm 4*
Law, Robert Oswald, Jr. 1897-1960 *NatCAB 49*
Law, Russell 1882-1942 *NatCAB 32,
WhAm 2*
Law, Sallie Chapman Gordon 1805-1894
*ApCAB Sup, DcAmB, NatCAB 25,
WhAm H*
Law, Thomas Cassels 1880-1962 *NatCAB 52*
Law, Thomas Hart 1838-1923 *NatCAB 47,
WhAm 1*
Law, Walter William 1837-1924 *NatCAB 31*
Law, William 1686-1761 *McGEWB*
Law, William Adger 1864-1936 *WhAm 1*
Law, Willie 1867-1940 *NatCAB 30*
Lawall, Charles Elmer 1891-1973 *WhAm 5*
LaWall, Charles Herbert 1871-1937
NatCAB 27, WhAm 1
Lawder, Henry Miller 1901-1966 *WhAm 4*
Lawes, Sir John Bennett 1814-1900 *AsBiEn,
DcScB*
Lawes, Lewis Edward 1883-1947 *DcAmB S4,
WebAB, WhAm 2*
Lawes And Gilbert *DcScB*
Lawhead, Lydia D 1859- *WomWWA 14*
Lawler, Francis Xavier 1822-1900 *TwCBDA*
Lawler, Frank 1842-1896 *BiDrAC, TwCBDA,
WhAm H*
Lawler, Joab 1796-1838 *ApCAB, BiAUS,
BiDrAC, TwCBDA, WhAm H*
Lawler, John Joseph 1862-1948 *NatCAB 15,
WhAm 2*
Lawler, Michael K 1820?- *ApCAB*
Lawler, Thomas Bonaventure 1864-1945
NatCAB 35, WhAm 2
Lawler, Thomas G 1844-1908 *NatCAB 4,
WhAm 1*
Lawless, Alfred, Jr. 1873- *WhoColR*
Lawless, John T 1885-1960 *WhAm 4*
Lawless, Margaret Wynne 1847- *AmWom*
Lawless, Michael Joseph 1881-1961 *NatCAB 50*
Lawless, Theodore Kenneth 1893-1971
WhAm 5

Lawless, Thomas Jefferson 1875-1944
NatCAB 33
Lawley, Brace Irving 1879-1958 *NatCAB 49*
Lawley, George Frederick 1848-1928 *DcAmB*
Lawlor, Daniel Joseph 1875-1950 *NatCAB 38,*
WhAm 3
Lawlor, Lillie 1874- *WomWWA 14*
Lawlor, William F d1959 *WhAm 3*
Lawlor, William Patrick 1854- *WhAm 1*
Lawman, Jasper Holman 1825-1906 *NewYHSD*
Lawrance, Charles Lanier 1882-1950 *ApCAB X,*
DcAmB S4, NatCAB 38, WhAm 3
Lawrance, James Peyton Stuart 1852- *TwCBDA*
Lawrance, James Peyton Stuart *see also*
Lawrence, James Peyton S
Lawrance, John 1750-1810 *ApCAB, DcAmB,*
Drake
Lawrance, John *see also* Lawrence, John
Lawrance, Marion 1850-1924 *WhAm 1*
Lawrance, Uriah Marion 1850-1924 *DcAmB*
Lawrance, William Irvin 1853-1935 *WhAm 1*
Lawrence, A A *NewYHSD*
Lawrence, Abbott 1792-1855 *AmBi, ApCAB,*
BiAUS, BiDrAC, DcAmB, Drake,
McGEWB, NatCAB 3, TwCBDA,
WebAB, WhAm H
Lawrence, Abraham Riker 1932-1917 *WhAm 1*
Lawrence, Albert Gallatin 1834-1887 *ApCAB*
Lawrence, Albert Gallatin 1836-1887
NatCAB 11, TwCBDA
Lawrence, Albert Lathrop 1865- *WhAm 4*
Lawrence, Alberta 1864- *ApCAB X*
Lawrence, Amory Appleton 1848-1912 *WhAm 1*
Lawrence, Amos 1786-1852 *AmBi, ApCAB,*
DcAmB, Drake, EncAB, NatCAB 3,
TwCBDA, WhAm H
Lawrence, Amos Adams 1814-1886 *AmBi,*
ApCAB, DcAmB, TwCBDA, WebAB,
WhAm H
Lawrence, Andrew Middleton d1942 *WhAm 2*
Lawrence, Armon Jay 1897-1965 *WhAm 4*
Lawrence, Arthur 1842- *TwCBDA*
Lawrence, Arthur Clarence 1849-1922
NatCAB 20
Lawrence, Benjamin Franklin 1877-1965
WhAm 4
Lawrence, Carl Gustavus 1871-1954 *WhAm 3*
Lawrence, Carrie Craft 1859- *WomWWA 14*
Lawrence, Charles d1760 *ApCAB, Drake*
Lawrence, Charles B *NewYHSD*
Lawrence, Charles Brush 1820-1883
ApCAB Sup, NatCAB 5
Lawrence, Charles Drummond 1878-1975
WhAm 6
Lawrence, Charles Edward 1862-1924
NatCAB 28
Lawrence, Charles Kennedy 1856-1942
WhAm 2
Lawrence, Charles Solomon 1878-1930
WhAm 1
Lawrence, Chester Ripley 1870-1920 *ApCAB X*
Lawrence, Cornelius VanWyck 1791-1861
ApCAB, BiAUS, BiDrAC, NatCAB 8,
TwCBDA, WhAm H
Lawrence, Daniel Warren 1830-1921 *ApCAB X*
Lawrence, David 1888-1973 *NatCAB 57,*
WhAm 5
Lawrence, David Herbert 1885-1930 *McGEWB*
Lawrence, David Leo 1889-1966 *WhAm 4*
Lawrence, E George 1908-1974 *WhAm 6*
Lawrence, Edwin Alonzo 1910-1956
NatCAB 45
Lawrence, Edwin Gordon 1859-1950 *WhAm 3*
Lawrence, Edwin Winship 1881- *WhAm 6*
Lawrence, Effingham 1820-1878 *BiDrAC,*
WhAm H
Lawrence, Effingham 1878-1956 *NatCAB 50*
Lawrence, Egbert Charles 1845-1916 *TwCBDA,*
WhAm 1
Lawrence, Ella Park *WomWWA 14*
Lawrence, Ellis Fuller 1879-1946 *WhAm 2*
Lawrence, Ernest Orlando 1901-1958 *AsBiEn,*
DcScB, EncAB, McGEWB, NatCAB 48,
WebAB, WhAm 3
Lawrence, Eugene 1823-1894 *ApCAB,*
TwCBDA
Lawrence, Florence 1886-1938 *NotAW*
Lawrence, Florus Fremont 1863- *WhAm 4*

Lawrence, Frank Pell 1886-1957 *WhAm 3*
Lawrence, George 1846-1928 *NatCAB 21*
Lawrence, George Andrew 1914-1975 *WhAm 6*
Lawrence, George Edwin 1844-1921
NatCAB 19
Lawrence, George Newbold 1806-1895 *DcAmB,*
NatCAB 2, TwCBDA, WhAm H
Lawrence, George Pelton 1859-1917 *BiDrAC,*
TwCBDA, WhAm 1, WhAmP
Lawrence, George VanEman 1818-1904 *BiAUS,*
BiDrAC, TwCBDA
Lawrence, George Warren 1875-1939
NatCAB 31, WhAm 1
Lawrence, George Washington 1823- *ApCAB*
Lawrence, Gertrude 1898-1952 *DcAmB S5*
Lawrence, Gertrude 1902-1952 *WhAm 3*
Lawrence, Henry *NewYHSD*
Lawrence, Henry Corbin 1859-1919 *NatCAB 17*
Lawrence, Henry Franklin 1868-1950 *BiDrAC,*
WhAm 4
Lawrence, Sir Henry Montgomery 1806-1857
WhoMilH
Lawrence, Henry Wells 1879-1942 *WhAm 1*
Lawrence, Hollie Middleton 1868-1941
NatCAB 32
Lawrence, Howard Cyrus 1890-1961
NatCAB 49, WhAm 4
Lawrence, Ida 1864- *NatCAB 4*
Lawrence, Isaac 1828-1919 *WhAm 1*
Lawrence, Isabel 1853- *WomWWA 14*
Lawrence, J Custis 1867-1944 *NatCAB 33*
Lawrence, J Don, Jr. 1904-1972 *NatCAB 56*
Lawrence, Jacob 1917- *BnEnAmA, McGEWB*
Lawrence, James 1781-1813 *AmBi, ApCAB,*
DcAmB, Drake, McGEWB, NatCAB 8,
TwCBDA, WebAB, WebAMB, WhAm H
Lawrence, James Cooper 1890-1932 *WhAm 1,*
WhAm 1C
Lawrence, James Earnest 1889-1957 *WhAm 3*
Lawrence, James Peyton Stuart 1852- *WhAm 4*
Lawrence, James Peyton Stuart *see also*
Lawrance, James Peyton S
Lawrence, Jason Valentine O'Brien 1791-1823
NatCAB 15
Lawrence, John *NewYHSD*
Lawrence, John 1724-1799 *NatCAB 16*
Lawrence, John 1750-1810 *AmBi, BiAUS,*
TwCBDA
Lawrence, John 1811-1879 *WhoMilH*
Lawrence, John 1861-1926 *ApCAB X*
Lawrence, John Benjamin 1873- *WhAm 6*
Lawrence, John Marshall 1895-1972 *WhAm 6*
Lawrence, John Silsbee 1878- *WhAm 6*
Lawrence, John Strachan 1849- *WhAm 1*
Lawrence, John Watson 1800-1888 *BiAUS,*
BiDrAC, WhAm H
Lawrence, John William 1923-1971 *WhAm 5*
Lawrence, Jonathan 1807-1833 *ApCAB, Drake*
Lawrence, Joseph 1786-1842 *BiDrAC,*
WhAm H
Lawrence, Joseph 1788-1842 *BiAUS, TwCBDA*
Lawrence, Joseph 1797-1865 *ApCAB X*
Lawrence, Joseph Joshua 1836- *NatCAB 12*
Lawrence, Joseph Sell 1877-1965 *NatCAB 51*
Lawrence, Joseph Stagg 1896-1950 *WhAm 3*
Lawrence, Joseph Wilson 1818- *ApCAB*
Lawrence, Lina *WomWWA 14*
Lawrence, Margaret 1889-1929 *WhAm 1*
Lawrence, Margaret Stanton 1852-
WomWWA 14
Lawrence, Mary Dahlgren *WomWWA 14*
Lawrence, Mortimer James 1843-1922
NatCAB 6
Lawrence, Newbold Trotter 1893-1968
WhAm 5
Lawrence, Osa Alonzo 1878- *WhoColR*
Lawrence, Philip K *BiAUS*
Lawrence, Ralph Restieaux 1873- *WhAm 5*
Lawrence, Ray Ellsworth 1903-1970 *WhAm 6*
Lawrence, Richard Smith 1817-1892 *DcAmB,*
NatCAB 24, WhAm H
Lawrence, Richard Wesley 1878-1948
NatCAB 37, WhAm 2
Lawrence, Robert H, Jr. 1935-1967 *WhAm 4,*
WhAm 1
Lawrence, Robert Means 1847-1935 *ApCAB X,*
NatCAB 42, WhAm 1

Lawrence, Russell Ellsworth 1889-1934
NatCAB 25
Lawrence, Ruth *WomWWA 14*
Lawrence, Samuel *NewYHSD*
Lawrence, Samuel 1759-1827 *TwCBDA*
Lawrence, Samuel 1773-1837 *BiAUS, BiDrAC,*
WhAm H
Lawrence, Samuel Crocker 1832-1911
NatCAB 16, TwCBDA, WhAm 1
Lawrence, Sidney 1801-1892 *BiAUS, BiDrAC,*
WhAm H
Lawrence, Stringer 1697-1775 *WhoMilH*
Lawrence, Sydney M 1865?-1940 *IIBEAAW*
Lawrence, Sir Thomas 1769-1830 *McGEWB*
Lawrence, Thomas 1832- *TwCBDA, WhAm 4*
Lawrence, Thomas Edward 1888-1935
McGEWB, WhoMilH
Lawrence, Timothy Bigelow 1826-1869 *Drake*
Lawrence, Victor H 1897-1958 *WhAm 3*
Lawrence, W S *NewYHSD*
Lawrence, Warrington Gillette 1861-1938
NatCAB 41
Lawrence, Washington Herbert 1840-1900
NatCAB 22
Lawrence, William d1841 *Drake*
Lawrence, William 1783-1848 *DcAmB,*
NatCAB 5, WhAm H
Lawrence, William 1783-1867 *DcScB*
Lawrence, William 1814-1895 *BiAUS, BiDrAC,*
TwCBDA, WhAm H
Lawrence, William 1819-1899 *AmBi, ApCAB,*
BiAUS, BiDrAC, DcAmB, Drake,
NatCAB 24, TwCBDA, WhAm 1,
WhAmP
Lawrence, William 1850-1941 *ApCAB Sup,*
ApCAB X, DcAmB S3, TwCBDA,
WhAm 1
Lawrence, William Appleton 1889-1968
WhAm 5
Lawrence, William Badger 1856-1928
NatCAB 10, NatCAB 22
Lawrence, William Beach 1800-1881 *AmBi,*
ApCAB, BiAUS, DcAmB, Drake,
TwCBDA, WhAm H
Lawrence, William Beach *see also* Laurence,
William Beach
Lawrence, William Henry 1868-1958 *WhAm 3*
Lawrence, William Hereford 1877- *WhAm 5*
Lawrence, William Howard 1916-1972
WhAm 5
Lawrence, William Joseph 1891-1941
NatCAB 41
Lawrence, William Mangam 1848-1934
NatCAB 13, WhAm 1
Lawrence, William Richards 1812-1885 *ApCAB*
Lawrence, William Roderick 1829-1856
NewYHSD
Lawrence, William Thomas 1788-1859 *BiAUS,*
BiDrAC, WhAm H
Lawrence, William VanDuzer 1842-1927
NatCAB 12, NatCAB 21, WhAm 1
Lawrence, William W *BiAUS*
Lawrence, William Witherle 1876-1958
WhAm 3
Lawrie, Alexander 1828-1917 *ApCAB, DcAmB,*
NatCAB 25, NewYHSD
Lawrie, Alvah Kittredge 1852-1936 *NatCAB 31*
Lawrie, Lee 1877-1961 *WhAm 4*
Lawrie, Lee 1877-1963 *BnEnAmA,*
NatCAB 50
Lawrie, Ritchie 1890-1962 *NatCAB 50,*
WhAm 4
Laws, Annie 1855-1927 *NatCAB 22, NotAW,*
WhAm 1, WomWWA 14
Laws, Bolitha James 1891-1958 *WhAm 3*
Laws, Curtis Lee 1868-1946 *WhAm 2*
Laws, Elijah 1833-1926 *WhAm 1*
Laws, Frank Arthur 1867-1936 *NatCAB 28,*
WhAm 1, WhAm 1C
Laws, George William 1870-1945 *WhAm 1,*
WhAm 2
Laws, Gilbert Lafayette 1838-1907 *BiDrAC*
Laws, H Langdon 1880-1955 *NatCAB 45*
Laws, Samuel Spahr 1824-1921 *BiDAmEd,*
DcAmB, NatCAB 8, TwCBDA, WebAB,
WhAm 1
Lawshe, Abraham Lincoln 1860-1919 *WhAm 1*
Lawson, Albert Gallatin 1842-1929 *WhAm 1*

Lawson, Albert Thomas 1898-1963 *NatCAB 51,*
WhAm 4
Lawson, Alexander 1772-1846 *ApCAB,*
TwCBDA
Lawson, Alexander 1773-1846 *DcAmB,*
NewYHSD, WhAm H
Lawson, Alfred William 1869-1954 *WhAm 3*
Lawson, Andrew Cowper 1861-1952 *BiDAmEd,*
DcAmB S5, DcScB, NatCAB 41,
WhAm 3
Lawson, Anna Meredith *WomWWA 14*
Lawson, Ben Hill 1882-1955 *NatCAB 44*
Lawson, Claude Sims 1895-1964 *NatCAB 50,*
WhAm 4
Lawson, David A 1923-1975 *WhAm 6*
Lawson, Douglas E 1903-1961 *WhAm 4*
Lawson, Edward Burnett 1895-1962 *WhAm 4*
Lawson, Ernest 1873-1939 *BnEnAmA,*
DcAmB S2, IlBEAAW, NatCAB 31,
WhAm 1
Lawson, Eugene B 1871-1931 *NatCAB 48*
Lawson, Evald Benjamin 1904-1965
NatCAB 51, WhAm 4
Lawson, George 1827- *ApCAB*
Lawson, George 1898-1951 *WhAm 3*
Lawson, George Benedict 1867-1952 *WhAm 3*
Lawson, George Bilton 1879-1967 *NatCAB 54*
Lawson, Hampden Clisby 1904-1961
NatCAB 48
Lawson, Harry Leland, Jr. 1907-1962
NatCAB 49
Lawson, Helen E *NewYHSD*
Lawson, Henry 1867-1922 *McGEWB*
Lawson, Huron Willis 1873-1949 *NatCAB 37,*
WhAm 5
Lawson, James 1799-1880 *ApCAB, DcAmB,*
Drake, NatCAB 25, WhAm H
Lawson, James Gilchrist 1874-1946 *WhAm 2*
Lawson, James Joseph 1888-1962 *WhAm 4*
Lawson, Jesse 1856- *WhoColR*
Lawson, John *NatCAB 7*
Lawson, John d1711 *AmBi, DcAmB,*
WhAm H
Lawson, John d1712 *ApCAB, Drake*
Lawson, John Daniel 1816-1896 *BiAUS,*
BiDrAC, WhAm H
Lawson, John Davison 1852-1921 *NatCAB 22,*
WhAm 1
Lawson, John William 1837-1905 *BiDrAC*
Lawson, Joseph Albert 1859- *WhAm 4*
Lawson, Joseph Warren 1900-1974 *WhAm 6*
Lawson, Laurin Leonard 1876-1938 *WhAm 3*
Lawson, Lawrence James 1896-1961
NatCAB 48
Lawson, Leonidas Merion 1812-1864 *DcAmB,*
WhAm H
Lawson, Leonidas Moreau 1812-1864 *ApCAB,*
TwCBDA
Lawson, Leonidas Moreau 1836-1909
NatCAB 2
Lawson, Louise 1861- *AmWom, ApCAB*
Lawson, Maria 1852- *WomWWA 14*
Lawson, Martin Emert 1867-1957 *NatCAB 47,*
WhAm 3
Lawson, Mary J 1828-1890 *AmWom*
Lawson, Mary Lockhart *ApCAB*
Lawson, Oscar A 1813-1854 *ApCAB,*
NewYHSD, TwCBDA
Lawson, Paul Bowen 1888-1954 *WhAm 3*
Lawson, Percival P 1815?- *NewYHSD*
Lawson, Publius Virgilius 1853-1920
NatCAB 19, WhAm 1
Lawson, Raymond Augusta 1875- *WhoColR*
Lawson, Reuben Ernest 1920-1963 *NatCAB 50*
Lawson, Robert d1805 *ApCAB, Drake,*
NatCAB 1
Lawson, Robert 1892-1957 *IlBEAAW,*
WhAm 3
Lawson, Robert Hemphill 1900-1965
NatCAB 52
Lawson, Roberta Campbell 1878-1940
NatCAB 36, NotAW, WhAm 1
Lawson, Thomas *NewYHSD*
Lawson, Thomas d1861 *Drake*
Lawson, Thomas 1781?-1861 *ApCAB, DcAmB,*
WhAm H
Lawson, Thomas 1789-1861 *NatCAB 4,*
TwCBDA

Lawson, Thomas Bayley 1807-1888 *NewYHSD*
Lawson, Thomas Goodwin 1835-1912
NatCAB 2, TwCBDA, WhAm 1
Lawson, Thomas Graves 1835-1912 *BiDrAC*
Lawson, Thomas William 1857-1925 *DcAmB,*
McGEWB, NatCAB 26, WhAm 1
Lawson, Victor Freemont 1850-1925 *DcAmB*
Lawson, Victor Fremont 1850-1925 *AmBi,*
ApCAB X, NatCAB 13, NatCAB 26,
WhAm 1
Lawson, W Elsworth 1868- *WhAm 4*
Lawson, Walter Carson 1901-1975 *WhAm 6*
Lawson, Warner *WhAm 5*
Lawson, William C 1903-1954 *WhAm 3*
Lawther, Harry Preston 1859-1942 *WhAm 2*
Lawther, William 1847-1928 *NatCAB 47*
Lawton, Alexander Robert 1818-1896 *ApCAB,*
BiDConf, DcAmB, NatCAB 2, TwCBDA,
WhAm H
Lawton, Alexander Robert 1820?- *Drake*
Lawton, Alexander Robert 1884-1963 *WhAm 5*
Lawton, Alexander Rudolf 1858-1936 *WhAm 1*
Lawton, Alice Maude *WomWWA 14*
Lawton, Bessie Eliza Boyd *WomWWA 14*
Lawton, Charles Augustus 1844-1917
NatCAB 44
Lawton, Edwin Franklin 1870-1936 *NatCAB 28*
Lawton, Ezra Mills 1864-1931 *WhAm 1*
Lawton, Francis *NewYHSD*
Lawton, Frederick 1852-1941 *WhAm 3*
Lawton, Frederick Joseph 1900-1975 *WhAm 6*
Lawton, Henrietta Beebe 1844- *AmWom*
Lawton, Henry Ware 1843-1899 *AmBi,*
ApCAB Sup, DcAmB, NatCAB 10,
TwCBDA, WebAM, WhAm 1
Lawton, Jeannie Lathrop *WomWWA 14*
Lawton, Joseph James 1861-1941 *NatCAB 30*
Lawton, Louis Bowen 1872- *WhAm 5*
Lawton, Maria Coles 1864- *WhoColR*
Lawton, Mary Agnes 1876- *WomWWA 14*
Lawton, Richard C *NewYHSD*
Lawton, Samuel Tilden 1884-1961 *WhAm 4*
Lawton, Shailer Emery 1853-1923 *NatCAB 20*
Lawton, Shailer Upton 1894-1966 *NatCAB 51,*
WhAm 4
Lawton, William Cranston 1853- *TwCBDA,*
WhAm 4
Lawton, William Henry 1853- *WhAm 4*
Lawton, William Rufus 1860- *WhoColR*
Lawwill, Stewart 1892-1967 *WhAm 5*
Lawyer, George 1865-1927 *WhAm 1*
Lawyer, Jay 1866- *WhAm 4*
Lawyer, Thomas 1785-1868 *BiAUS, BiDrAC,*
WhAm H
Lax, Gaspar 1487-1560 *DcScB*
Lay, A W *NewYHSD*
Lay, Albert Tracy 1825-1918 *NatCAB 19*
Lay, Alfred Morrison 1836-1879 *BiDrAC,*
WhAm H
Lay, Benjamin 1677-1759 *AmBi, DcAmB,*
NatCAB 25, WhAm H
Lay, Benjamin 1681-1760 *ApCAB, Drake*
Lay, Charles Downing 1877-1956 *WhAm 3*
Lay, Chester Frederic 1895-1973 *WhAm 6*
Lay, Frank Morrill 1869-1957 *NatCAB 44,*
WhAm 3
Lay, Fred L 1836?- *NewYHSD*
Lay, George Washington 1798-1860 *BiAUS,*
BiDrAC, NatCAB 12, TwCBDA,
WhAm H
Lay, George William 1860- *WhAm 4*
Lay, Henry Champlin 1823-1885 *ApCAB,*
DcAmB, NatCAB 13, TwCBDA,
WhAm H
Lay, John L 1832-1899 *ApCAB*
Lay, John Lewis 1832-1899 *NatCAB 7*
Lay, John Louis 1832-1899 *AmBi, DcAmB,*
TwCBDA, WhAm H
Lay, Julius Gareche 1872-1939 *NatCAB 45,*
WhAm 1
Lay, Oliver Ingraham 1845-1890 *ApCAB,*
TwCBDA
Lay, Robert Dwight 1875-1940 *WhAm 1*
Lay, Wilfrid 1872- *WhAm 5*
Layamon *McGEWB*
Laybourne, Lawrence Eugene 1913-1976
WhAm 6

Laycock, Charles Wilbur 1860-1940 *WhAm 1*
Laycock, Craven 1866- *WhAm 4*
Laycock, Robert Lucky 1907-1968 *WhWW-II*
Laycock, Thomas 1812-1876 *BiHiMed*
Layden, Elmer Francis 1903-1973 *WhAm 6*
Laye, Camara 1928- *McGEWB*
Laye, Francis 1753?-1828 *ApCAB, Drake*
Laylin, Lewis Cass d1923 *WhAm 1*
Layman, E *NewYHSD*
Layman, James H *NewYHSD*
Layman, Waldo Arnold 1869-1950 *WhAm 3*
Laymon, Herman Basil 1888-1968 *NatCAB 54*
Layne, Charles 1700-1821 *Drake*
Layne, J Gregg 1885-1952 *WhAm 3*
Layng, James Dawson 1833-1908 *NatCAB 14,*
WhAm 1
Layte, Ralph R 1893-1965 *WhAm 4*
Layton, Caleb Rodney 1851-1930 *BiDrAC,*
WhAm 1
Layton, Fernando Coello 1847-1926 *BiDrAC,*
TwCBDA
Layton, Frank Davis 1879-1956 *NatCAB 46,*
WhAm 3
Layton, Frederick 1827-1919 *WhAm 1*
Layton, Joseph Evert 1908-1964 *NatCAB 51,*
WhAm 4
Layton, Olivia Higgins 1897-1975 *WhAm 6*
Layton, Walter Thomas 1884-1966 *WhAm 4*
Lazan, Benjamin J 1917-1966 *WhAm 4*
Lazar, Benedict Joseph 1884-1955 *WhAm 3*
Lazard, Marie VonUnschuld *WomWWA 14*
Lazaree, Joseph d1851? *NewYHSD*
Lazarev, Mikhail Petrovich 1788-1851 *DcScB*
Lazarev, Petr Petrovich 1878-1942 *DcScB*
Lazaro, Hipolito 1889-1974 *WhAm 6*
Lazaro, Ladislas 1872-1927 *BiDrAC, WhAm 1,*
WhAmP
Lazarovich-Hrebelianovich, Princess d1957
WhAm 3
Lazarovich-Hrebelianovich, Eleanor Hulda
d1957 *WomWWA 14*
Lazarow, Arnold 1916-1975 *WhAm 6*
Lazarsfeld, Paul Felix 1901- *EncAB*
Lazarus, Eldon Spencer 1883-1955 *NatCAB 48*
Lazarus, Emma 1849-1887 *AmBi, AmWom,*
ApCAB, DcAmB, McGEWB, NatCAB 3,
NotAW, TwCBDA, WebAB, WhAm H
Lazarus, Fred, Jr. 1884-1973 *WhAm 6*
Lazarus, Henry Lawrence 1853- *NatCAB 9*
Lazarus, Hyman 1871-1924 *NatCAB 20*
Lazarus, Jacob Hart 1822-1891 *NewYHSD*
LaZarus, Jennie Harrison *WomWWA 14*
Lazarus, Lewis *NewYHSD*
Lazarus, Reuben Avis 1895-1971 *WhAm 5*
Lazarus, Robert 1890-1973 *WhAm 5*
Lazarus, Simon 1882-1947 *WhAm 2*
Lazcano, Francis Xavier 1702-1762 *ApCAB*
Lazear, Jesse 1804-1877 *BiAUS, BiDrAC,*
WhAm H
Lazear, Jesse William 1866-1900 *AsBiEn,*
DcAmB, NatCAB 15, WhAm H
Lazelle, Henry Martyn 1832-1917 *ApCAB,*
TwCBDA, WhAm 1
Lazenby, Albert 1852- *WhAm 4*
Lazenby, Laura *WomWWA 14*
Lazenby, Maurice 1877-1928 *NatCAB 29*
Lazenby, Ralph Manlius 1893-1958 *NatCAB 44*
Lazenby, William Rane 1850- *WhAm 1*
Lazenby, William Rane 1852- *ApCAB,*
NatCAB 10, TwCBDA
Lazo, Hector 1899-1965 *WhAm 4*
Lazonby, J Lance 1909-1969 *NatCAB 57*
Lazrus, S Ralph 1898-1959 *WhAm 3*
Lazzaree, Joseph d1851? *NewYHSD*
Lazzari, Carolina 1891-1946 *WhAm 2*
Lazzelle, I Grant 1862-1936 *NatCAB 28*
Lea, Benjamin James 1833-1894 *NatCAB 13,*
TwCBDA
Lea, Clarence Frederick 1874-1964 *BiDrAC,*
WhAm 4
Lea, Fanny Heaslip 1883-1955 *NatCAB 42*
Lea, Fanny Heaslip 1884-1955 *WhAm 3*
Lea, Henry Carey 1825-1909 *Drake*
Lea, Henry Charles 1825-1909 *AmBi, ApCAB,*
ApCAB X, DcAmB, McGEWB,
NatCAB 5, NatCAB 23, TwCBDA,
WhAm 1
Lea, Homer 1876-1912 *AmBi, DcAmB,*

NatCAB 2, WebAB, WebAMB, WhAm 1

Lea, Isaac 1792-1886 *AmBi, ApCAB, DcScB, Drake, NatCAB 6, TwCBDA, WhAm H*

Lea, John McCormick 1818- *ApCAB, BiAUS, NatCAB 10, TwCBDA, WhAm 1*

Lea, Joseph Tatnall 1840-1916 *NatCAB 17*

Lea, Luke 1782-1851 *ApCAB, BiAUS, TwCBDA*

Lea, Luke 1783-1851 *BiDrAC, WhAm H*

Lea, Luke 1810-1898 *BiAUS, TwCBDA*

Lea, Luke 1879-1945 *BiDrAC, DcAmB S3, NatCAB 15, WhAm 2*

Lea, Mathew Carey 1823-1897 *AmBi, ApCAB, DcAmB, NatCAB 10, WhAm H, WhAm 4*

Lea, Preston 1841-1916 *NatCAB 13, WhAm 1*

Lea, Pryor 1794- *BiAUS*

Lea, Pryor 1794-1879 *BiDrAC, WhAm H*

Lea, Pryor 1794-1880 *TwCBDA*

Lea, Robert Brooke 1891-1968 *NatCAB 56*

Lea, Robert Wentworth 1886-1956 *WhAm 3*

Lea, Sydney Longstreth Wright 1909-1966 *NatCAB 52*

Lea, Thomas Gibson 1785-1844 *ApCAB, Drake*

Lea, Tom 1907- *IIBEAAW, REnAW*

Lea, Wallace Bruce 1892-1966 *NatCAB 52*

Leach, A *NewYHSD*

Leach, Abby 1855-1918 *DcAmB, NatCAB 12, NotAW, WhAm 1, WomWWA 14*

Leach, Albert Ernest 1864-1910 *NatCAB 19, WhAm 1*

Leach, Antoinette D 1859- *WomWWA 14*

Leach, Archibald Alexander *WebAB*

Leach, Arthur Burtis 1863-1939 *WhAm 1*

Leach, Charles Nelson 1884-1971 *WhAm 5*

Leach, Daniel Dyer 1806-1891 *BiDAmEd, DcAmB, NatCAB 8, WhAm H*

Leach, DeWitt Clinton 1822-1909 *ApCAB, BiAUS, BiDrAC, NatCAB 17, TwCBDA, WhAm 4, WhAmP*

Leach, Douglas Edward 1920- *EncAAH*

Leach, Edmund C 1894-1963 *WhAm 4*

Leach, Edward Giles 1849-1928 *WhAm 1*

Leach, Elizabeth Dwight 1863- *WomWWA 14*

Leach, Ellis 1906-1971 *WhAm 5*

Leach, Eugene Walter 1857- *WhAm 1*

Leach, Frank Aleamon 1846- *NatCAB 14, WhAm 4*

Leach, Frank Aleamon, Jr. 1871- *WhAm 5*

Leach, Frank Willing 1855- *ApCAB, TwCBDA*

Leach, George Emerson 1876-1955 *NatCAB 46, WhAm 3*

Leach, Giles *ApCAB*

Leach, Henry Goddard 1880-1970 *NatCAB 56, WhAm 5*

Leach, Howard Seavoy 1887-1948 *WhAm 3*

Leach, Hugh 1894-1971 *WhAm 5*

Leach, James Madison 1815-1891 *ApCAB, BiAUS, BiDConf, BiDrAC, TwCBDA, WhAm H*

Leach, James Thomas 1805-1883 *BiDConf*

Leach, John 1743?-1804 *ApCAB Sup*

Leach, John Enfield 1907-1974 *WhAm 6*

Leach, John Sayles 1891-1964 *WhAm 4*

Leach, Josiah Granville 1842-1922 *ApCAB, NatCAB 19, WhAm 1*

Leach, Lawrence 1589-1662 *ApCAB*

Leach, MacEdward 1896-1967 *WhAm 4*

Leach, Margaret Kernochan 1893-1974 *WhAm 6*

Leach, Neal McCann 1869-1934 *NatCAB 26*

Leach, Ralph Waldo Emerson 1874- *WhAm 5*

Leach, Raymond Hotchkiss 1883-1942 *WhAm 2*

Leach, Robert *ApCAB*

Leach, Robert Milton 1879-1952 *BiDrAC, NatCAB 41*

Leach, S W *NewYHSD*

Leach, Samuel *NewYHSD*

Leach, Sheperd 1778-1832 *ApCAB*

Leach, Shepherd 1778-1832 *DcAmB, NatCAB 25, WhAm H*

Leach, Thomas Witt 1896-1966 *NatCAB 52*

Leach, W Barton 1900-1971 *WhAm 5*

Leach, Walter Cowles 1862-1940 *NatCAB 31*

Leach, William Fillmore 1894-1968 *WhAm 5*

Leach, William Herman 1888-1962 *WhAm 4*

Leach, William Turnbull 1805-1886 *ApCAB*

Leach, Wilmon Whilldin 1870-1926 *NatCAB 20*

Leacock, Arthur Gordner 1868-1947 *NatCAB 38, WhAm 2*

Leacock, Hamble James 1795-1856 *ApCAB*

Leacock, Stephen Butler 1869-1944 *WhAm 2*

Leadbelly *EncAAH, WebAB*

Leadbetter, Caroline Pittock 1875- *WhAm 5*

Leadbetter, D P 1797-1870 *BiAUS*

Leadbetter, Daniel Parkhurst 1797-1870 *BiDrAC, WhAm H*

Leadbetter, Frederick William 1875-1948 *WhAm 2*

Leadbetter, Guy Whitman 1893-1945 *NatCAB 35*

Leadbetter, Wyland F 1907-1974 *WhAm 6*

Leader, Benjamin 1884-1961 *NatCAB 46*

Leader, Henry John 1909-1972 *NatCAB 56*

Leader, Olive Moorman 1852- *AmWom*

Leadingham, Roy Samuel 1882-1966 *NatCAB 51*

Leadley, David *NewYHSD*

Leaf, Elizabeth Trenchard 1866- *WomWWA 14*

Leaf, Frank George 1889-1942 *NatCAB 31*

Leahey, Thomas Francis 1885-1940 *NatCAB 31*

Leahy, Edward Laurence 1886-1953 *BiDrAC*

Leahy, Edward Lawrence 1886-1953 *NatCAB 42, WhAm 3*

Leahy, Frank 1908-1973 *WhAm 5*

Leahy, Lamar Richard 1880-1958 *WhAm 3*

Leahy, Louise Harrington *WomWWA 14*

Leahy, Paul 1904-1966 *WhAm 4*

Leahy, Timothy John 1868-1934 *WhAm 1*

Leahy, William Augustine 1867-1941 *WhAm 1*

Leahy, William Daniel 1875-1959 *WebAB, WebAMB, WhAm 3, WhWW-II*

Leahy, William Edward 1886-1956 *NatCAB 43, WhAm 3*

Leak, C Elmer 1882-1967 *NatCAB 54*

Leak, Herbert Poe 1885-1952 *NatCAB 40*

Leak, James Alexander 1855-1934 *NatCAB 25*

Leak, John F *NewYHSD*

Leak, Roy Lathen 1875-1967 *NatCAB 54*

Leake, Eugene Walter 1877-1959 *BiDrAC, WhAm 3*

Leake, Frank 1856- *WhAm 4*

Leake, Hunter Collins 1859-1946 *NatCAB 35*

Leake, James Miller 1879- *WhAm 6*

Leake, James Payton 1881-1973 *WhAm 5*

Leake, Joseph Bloomfield 1828-1913 *TwCBDA, WhAm 1*

Leake, Mrs. S C *NewYHSD*

Leake, Shelton Farrar 1812-1884 *BiAUS, BiDrAC, NatCAB 13, TwCBDA, WhAm H*

Leake, Walter d1825 *BiAUS, Drake*

Leake, Walter 1760?-1825 *ApCAB, TwCBDA*

Leake, Walter 1762-1825 *BiDrAC, NatCAB 13, WhAm H*

Leakey, Jeannie Clara Drake *WomWWA 14*

Leakey, Louis Seymour Bazett 1903-1972 *DcScB, McGEWB, WhAm 5*

Leakin, George Armistead 1818- *TwCBDA*

Leakin, Sheppard Church 1790-1867 *TwCBDA*

Leale, Charles Augustus 1842-1932 *ApCAB X, NatCAB 2, WhAm 1*

Leale, Medwin 1873-1934 *WhAm 1*

Leaman, William Gilmore, Jr. 1898-1973 *WhAm 6*

Leaming, Charlotte 1878- *IIBEAAW*

Leaming, Edmund Bennett 1857-1932 *NatCAB 24, WhAm 1*

Leaming, Jacob Spicer 1815-1858 *AmBi*

Leaming, Jacob Spicer 1815-1885 *DcAmB, NatCAB 25, WhAm H*

Leaming, Jeremiah d1804 *NatCAB 25*

Leaming, Jeremiah 1717-1804 *ApCAB, DcAmB, TwCBDA, WhAm H*

Leaming, Jeremiah 1719-1804 *Drake*

Leaming, R W *NewYHSD*

Leaming, Thomas 1748-1797 *ApCAB, DcAmB, TwCBDA, WhAm H*

Leaming, Thomas 1858-1911 *NatCAB 15*

Leaming, Thomas Harold 1893-1925 *NatCAB 20*

Leamy, Frank Ashton 1900-1966 *WhAm 4*

Leamy, Frederick Walter 1886-1951 *WhAm 3*

Leamy, Hugh 1899-1935 *WhAm 1*

Leamy, James Patrick 1892-1949 *WhAm 2*

Leander, Hugo Austin 1894-1970 *NatCAB 55, WhAm 5*

Leandro DoSacramento 1762-1809 *ApCAB*

Leans, Martin 1817?- *NewYHSD*

Lear, Ben 1879-1966 *WhAm 4*

Lear, Edward 1812-1888 *McGEWB*

Lear, Fred Roy 1882-1950 *WhAm 3*

Lear, Harry Bonnell 1881-1967 *WhAm 4*

Lear, John Emery 1879-1948 *NatCAB 49*

Lear, Tobias 1762-1816 *ApCAB, BiAUS, DcAmB, Drake, NatCAB 13, TwCBDA, WhAm H*

Lear, William Powell 1902- *WebAB*

Lear, Wilson Henry 1864-1938 *NatCAB 45*

Learnard, George Edward 1874- *WhAm 5*

Learnard, Henry Grant 1867-1937 *WhAm 1*

Learnard, Henry Heath 1871-1953 *NatCAB 40*

Learned, Albert Preisach 1888-1968 *NatCAB 54*

Learned, Amasa 1750-1825 *BiAUS, BiDrAC, TwCBDA, WhAm H*

Learned, Andrew Brown 1869-1961 *NatCAB 49*

Learned, Arthur Garfield 1872-1959 *WhAm 3*

Learned, Dwight Whitney 1848- *WhAm 4*

Learned, Ebenezer 1728-1801 *DcAmB, Drake, WhAm H*

Learned, Ellin Craven d1940 *BiCAW, WhAm 1, WomWWA 14*

Learned, Harry *IIBEAAW*

Learned, Henry Barrett 1868-1931 *NatCAB 31, WhAm 1*

Learned, John George 1879-1943 *NatCAB 33*

Learned, Marion Dexter 1857-1917 *DcAmB, NatCAB 4, TwCBDA, WhAm 1*

Learned, Mary Poppleton 1873- *WomWWA 14*

Learned, Samuel Julius 1823-1892 *NatCAB 16*

Learned, Victorine Upshur *WomWWA 14*

Learned, Walter 1847-1915 *NatCAB 8, TwCBDA, WhAm 1*

Learned, William Law 1821-1904 *ApCAB, NatCAB 2, TwCBDA, WhAm 1*

Learned, William Setchel 1876-1950 *DcAmLiB, NatCAB 38, WhAm 2*

Learoyd, Mabel Woodbury 1870- *WomWWA 14*

Learsi, Rufus 1889-1964 *WhAm 4*

Leary, Annie d1919 *BiCAW*

Leary, Cornelius Lawrence Ludlow 1813-1893 *BiAUS, BiDrAC, WhAm H*

Leary, Daniel Bell 1886-1946 *WhAm 2*

Leary, Francis Thomas 1914-1968 *WhAm 5*

Leary, Frederick 1882-1953 *WhAm 3*

Leary, Herbert Fairfax 1885-1957 *NatCAB 43, WhAm 3*

Leary, John 1837-1905 *ApCAB X, DcAmB, NatCAB 25*

Leary, John Digney 1911-1974 *WhAm 6*

Leary, John Joseph, Jr. 1874-1944 *WhAm 2*

Leary, Julia May Crofton *BiCAW*

Leary, Leo H 1883-1966 *WhAm 4*

Leary, Lewis Gaston 1877-1951 *WhAm 3*

Leary, Michael *NewYHSD*

Leary, Montgomery Elihu 1868- *WhAm 5*

Leary, Nicholas *NewYHSD*

Leary, Olga Cushing 1878- *WomWWA 14*

Leary, Peter, Jr. 1840-1911 *WhAm 1*

Leary, Richard Phillips 1842-1901 *TwCBDA, WhAm 1*

Leary, Timothy 1870-1954 *WhAm 3*

Leary, William Henry 1881-1957 *WhAm 3*

Leas, David Porter 1842-1916 *NatCAB 28*

Leas, Leroy Porter 1875-1954 *NatCAB 44*

Lease, Emory Bair 1863-1931 *NatCAB 22, WhAm 1*

Lease, Mary Elizabeth Clyens 1850-1933 *NotAW*

Lease, Mary Elizabeth Clyens 1853-1933 *DcAmB S1, McGEWB, REnAW, WhAm 1, WhAmP, WomWWA 14*

Lease, Mary Elizabeth Cylens 1853-1933 *WebAB*

Leasure, Lida Powers *WomWWA 14*

Leatherbee, Andrew Faden 1842-1920
ApCAB X
Leatherbee, Frances Crane 1887-
WomWWA 14
Leatherman, Minnie Wells *WomWWA 14*
Leatherock, Wesley Kenneth 1897-1949
NatCAB 43
Leathers, Waller Smith 1874-1946 *DcAmB S4,*
NatCAB 42, WhAm 2
Leathers Of Purfleet, Baron 1883-1965
WhAm 4
Leatherwood, Elmer O 1872-1929 *BiDrAC,*
WhAm 1, WhAmP
Leatherwood, Nancy Albaugh 1873-
WomWWA 14
Leavell, Frank Hartwell 1884-1949 *WhAm 2*
Leavell, James Berry 1880-1933 *WhAm 1*
Leavell, James Reader 1884-1974 *WhAm 6*
Leavell, Landrum Pinson 1874-1929 *WhAm 1*
Leavell, Richard Marion 1838-1918 *TwCBDA,*
WhAm 3
Leavell, Ullin Whitney 1894-1960 *WhAm 4*
Leavell, William Hayne 1850-1930 *NatCAB 44,*
WhAm 1, WhAmP
Leavelle, Arnaud Bruce 1914-1956 *WhAm 3*
Leavelle, Robert Bryan 1916-1969 *WhAm 5*
Leavens, Dickson Hammond 1887-1955
NatCAB 45
Leavens, Robert French 1878-1961 *NatCAB 49,*
WhAm 6
Leavens, William *ApCAB X*
Leavenworth, Abner Johnson 1803-1869 *ApCAB*
Leavenworth, Elias Warner 1803-1887 *ApCAB,*
BiAUS, BiDrAC, TwCBDA, WhAm H
Leavenworth, Emma E Gifford 1860-
WomWWA 14
Leavenworth, Francis Preserved 1858-
NatCAB 8
Leavenworth, Francis Preserved 1858-1928
DcAmB
Leavenworth, Francis Preserved 1858-1929
WhAm 1
Leavenworth, Henry 1783-1834 *ApCAB,*
DcAmB, Drake, TwCBDA, WebAB,
WebAMB, WhAm H
Leavenworth, Sarah Theodosia Allen
WomWWA 14
Leavitt, Amy Clement 1858- *WomWWA 14*
Leavitt, Ashley Day 1877-1959 *WhAm 3*
Leavitt, Burke Fay 1844- *WhAm 4*
Leavitt, Charles Wellford 1871-1928
NatCAB 24, WhAm 1
Leavitt, Charlotte Mendell 1867-
WomWWA 14
Leavitt, Dudley 1772-1851 *ApCAB, DcAmB,*
Drake, NatCAB 25, WhAm H
Leavitt, Erasmus Darwin 1836-1916 *DcAmB,*
NatCAB 12, NatCAB 24, WhAm 1
Leavitt, Florence Pennock 1855- *WomWWA 14*
Leavitt, Frank McDowell 1856-1928 *ApCAB X,*
DcAmB, NatCAB 15, WhAm 1
Leavitt, Frank Simmons 1889-1953 *DcAmB S5*
Leavitt, Frank Simmons 1891-1953 *WebAB*
Leavitt, George H *NewYHSD*
Leavitt, Halsey B 1878-1960 *WhAm 4*
Leavitt, Henrietta Swan 1868-1921 *AsBiEn,*
DcAmB, DcScB, NatCAB 25, NotAW
Leavitt, Humphrey Howe 1796-1873 *ApCAB,*
BiAUS, BiDrAC, DcAmB, NatCAB 24,
TwCBDA, WhAm H, WhAmP
Leavitt, John McDowell 1824- *ApCAB,*
NatCAB 1, TwCBDA, WhAm H
Leavitt, Joseph *NewYHSD*
Leavitt, Joseph Warren 1804-1838 *NewYHSD*
Leavitt, Joshua 1794-1873 *ApCAB, DcAmB,*
Drake, NatCAB 2, TwCBDA, WhAm H
Leavitt, Julia White 1852- *WomWWA 14*
Leavitt, Julius Adelbert 1852-1925 *TwCBDA,*
WhAm 1
Leavitt, Mary Augusta 1876- *BiCAW*
Leavitt, Mary Greenleaf Clement 1830-1912
AmWom, DcAmB, NatCAB 5, NotAW,
TwCBDA, WhAm 1
Leavitt, Roger 1860- *WhAm 3*
Leavitt, Scott 1879-1966 *BiDrAC, WhAm 4*
Leavitt, Sheldon 1848-1933 *NatCAB 23,*
WhAm 1
Leavitt, V Russell 1891-1946 *NatCAB 35*

Leavitt, William 1887-1974 *NatCAB 57*
Leavy, Charles Henry 1884-1952 *BiDrAC,*
NatCAB 42, WhAm 3, WhAmP
Leaycraft, Charles Russell 1852-1913
NatCAB 39
Leaycraft, J Edgar 1849-1916 *WhAm 1*
Leaycraft, Julia Searing 1885- *WomWWA 14a*
LeBaron, John Francis 1847-1935 *WhAm 1*
LeBaron, John Kittredge 1855- *WhAm 4*
LeBaron, William d1958 *WhAm 3*
Lebay, Theodore Constant 1795-1849 *ApCAB*
Lebcke, Charles *NewYHSD*
Lebedev, Petr Nikolaevich 1866-1912 *DcScB*
Lebedev, Pyotr Nicolaievich 1866-1912 *AsBiEn*
Lebedev, Sergei Vasilievich 1874-1934 *DcScB*
Lebedinsky, Vyacheslav Vasilievich 1888-1956
DcScB
Lebeke, Charles *NewYHSD*
LeBel, Joseph Achille 1847-1930 *AsBiEn,*
DcScB
Leber, Charles Tudor 1898-1959 *NatCAB 47,*
WhAm 4
Lebesgue, Henri Leon 1875-1941 *DcScB*
Lebhar, Godfrey Montague 1882-1963 *WhAm 4*
LeBlanc, Max Julius Louis 1865-1943 *DcScB*
Leblanc, Nicolas 1742-1806 *AsBiEn, DcScB*
LeBlanc, Thomas John 1894-1948 *WhAm 2*
Leblanc, William *NewYHSD*
LeBlond, Charles Hubert 1883-1958 *WhAm 3*
LeBlond, Francis *NewYHSD*
LeBlond, Francis C 1821-1902 *BiAUS*
LeBlond, Francis Celeste 1821-1902 *BiDrAC*
LeBlond, Francis Celestian 1821-1902 *TwCBDA*
LeBlond, Harold Robson 1896-1968
NatCAB 56, WhAm 5
Leblond, Jean Baptiste 1747-1815 *ApCAB*
LeBlond, Richard Knight 1864-1953
NatCAB 42
LeBlond, Robert 1816-1863 *NewYHSD*
Lebo, Thomas Coverley 1842-1910 *WhAm 1*
LeBoeuf, Edmond 1809-1888 *WhoMilH*
LeBoeuf, Randall James 1870-1939 *NatCAB 37,*
WhAm 1
LeBoeuf, Randall James, Jr. 1897-1975
WhAm 6
Lebold, Foreman M 1895-1953 *WhAm 3*
LeBon, Gustave 1841-1931 *McGEWB*
Leborgne DeBoigne, Claude Pierre J 1764-1822
ApCAB
LeBouteux, Jean-Michel *NewYHSD*
LeBoutillier, George 1876-1952 *NatCAB 42,*
WhAm 3
LeBoutillier, Philip 1880- *ApCAB X*
LeBouyer DeFontenelle, Bernard *DcScB*
LeBreton, Prescott 1872-1956 *NatCAB 44*
LeBreton, Tomas Alberto 1868- *WhAm 5*
LeBreton, William *NewYHSD*
Lebretton, Jules *NewYHSD*
LeBrun, Charles 1619-1690 *McGEWB*
LeBrun, Napoleon Eugene Henry Charles
1821-1901 *DcAmB, NatCAB 9, WhAm H*
Lebrun, Rico 1900-1964 *BnEnAmA, WhAm 4*
LeCaron, Joseph d1632 *ApCAB*
LeCat, Claude-Nicolas 1700-1768 *DcScB*
LeChatelier, Henri Louis 1850-1936 *AsBiEn*
LeChatelier, Henry Louis 1850-1936 *DcScB*
Leche, Paul 1857- *WhAm 4*
Leche, Richard Webster 1898-1965 *NatCAB 54,*
WhAm 4
Lecher, Louis Arthur 1880-1948 *NatCAB 39,*
WhAm 2
Lechford, Thomas 1590?-1644? *ApCAB,*
DcAmB, Drake, WhAm H
Lechner, Carl Bernard 1908-1970 *NatCAB 56,*
WhAm 5
Leckert, Edmund Lawrence 1882-1962
NatCAB 50
Leckie, Adam Edward Lloyd 1868-1919
WhAm 1
Leckie, Frederick Lawrence 1874-1950
NatCAB 44
Leckie, Katherine d1930 *WhAm 1,*
WomWWA 14
Leckrone, Milton Emanuel 1901-1945
NatCAB 35
Leckrone, Walter 1897-1964 *WhAm 4*
Leckwijck, William Peter Edward Van 1902-1975
WhAm 6

Lecky, Prescott 1892-1941 *NatCAB 30*
Lecky, William Edward Hartpole 1838-1903
McGEWB
Leclair, Edward E, Jr. 1922-1969 *WhAm 5*
Leclair, Titus G 1899-1968 *WhAm 5*
LeClaire, Antoine 1797-1861 *NatCAB 12*
Leclaire, Berthelot Adrian 1905-1958
NatCAB 47
LeClear, Thomas 1818-1882 *ApCAB, DcAmB,*
Drake, NatCAB 8, NewYHSD, TwCBDA,
WhAm H
Leclerc *DcScB*
LeClerc 1750?-1817 *ApCAB*
Leclerc, Charles Victor Emmanuel 1722-1802
WhoMilH
LeClerc, Daniel 1652-1728 *BiHiMed*
LeClerc, J Arthur 1873-1956 *WhAm 3*
Leclerc, Jacques Philippe 1902-1947 *McGEWB*
Leclerc, Philippe Francois Marie 1902-1947
WhWW-II, WhoMilH
Leclerc, Victor Emmanuel 1779-1802 *ApCAB*
LeClercq, Charles 1823-1895 *ApCAB Sup,*
TwCBDA
Leclercq, Chretien 1630?-1695? *Drake*
LeClere, J Burk 1892-1967 *NatCAB 53*
Leclerq, Chretien 1630?-1695? *ApCAB*
L'Ecluse, Charles De 1526-1609 *DcScB*
L'Ecluse, Julia Manley Weeks 1876-
WomWWA 14
Lecompte, Irville Charles 1872- *WhAm 5*
Lecompte, Joseph 1797-1851 *BiAUS, BiDrAC,*
WhAm H
LeCompte, Karl Miles 1887-1972 *BiDrAC,*
WhAm 5
LeCompte, Samuel Dexter 1814-1888 *BiAUS,*
TwCBDA
Lecomte DuNouy, Pierre 1883-1947 *NatCAB 36*
LeConte, John 1818-1891 *ApCAB, DcAmB,*
DcScB, NatCAB 7, TwCBDA, WhAm H
LeConte, John Eaton 1784-1860 *Drake*
LeConte, John Eatton 1784-1860 *ApCAB,*
TwCBDA
LeConte, John Lawrence 1825-1883 *ApCAB,*
DcAmB, Drake, NatCAB 11, TwCBDA,
WhAm H
LeConte, Joseph 1823-1901 *AmBi, ApCAB,*
DcAmB, DcScB, Drake, NatCAB 7,
TwCBDA, WhAm 1
LeConte, Joseph Nisbet 1870-1950 *WhAm 2*
LeConte, Lewis 1782-1835 *NatCAB 11*
LeConte, Lewis 1782-1838 *ApCAB, TwCBDA*
LeConte, Robert Grier 1865-1924 *NatCAB 20,*
WhAm 1
LeConte, William 1738-1788 *TwCBDA*
Leconte DeLisle, Charles Marie Rene 1818-1894
McGEWB
Lecoq DeBoisbaudran *DcScB*
Lecoq DeBoisbaudran, Paul Emile 1838-1912
AsBiEn
Lecor, Carlos Federico 1765?-1836 *ApCAB*
LeCorbusier 1887-1965 *McGEWB*
LeCorbusier, Charles-Edouard 1887-1965
WhAm 4
Lecornu, Leon Francois Alfred 1854-1940
DcScB
LeCount, Edwin Raymond 1868-1935 *WhAm 1*
Lecuona, Ernesto d1963 *WhAm 4*
LeDantec, Felix 1869-1917 *DcScB*
Ledbetter, Allison Woodville 1901-1964
WhAm 4
Ledbetter, Huddie 1885-1949 *DcAmB S4*
Ledbetter, Huddie 1888-1949 *WebAB,*
WhAm 4
Ledbetter, Huddie 1888-1951 *EncAAH*
Ledbetter, Thomas *NewYHSD*
Ledbetter, Walter A 1863-1934 *WhAm 1*
Leddy, Bernard Joseph 1910-1972 *NatCAB 56,*
WhAm 5
Leddy, Eugene Thomas 1892-1958 *NatCAB 46*
Lederberg, Joshua 1925- *AsBiEn, EncAB,*
WebAB
Lederer, Charles 1856-1925 *WhAm 1*
Lederer, Charles 1877-1954 *WhAm 3*
Lederer, Erwin Reginald 1882-1943 *WhAm 2*
Lederer, Francis Loeffler 1898-1973 *WhAm 5*
Lederer, George W 1861-1938 *WhAm 1*
Lederer, John *ApCAB, DcAmB, Drake,*
WhAm H

Lederer, Norbert Lewis 1888-1955 *WhAm 3*
Lederer, Richard M 1887-1952 *WhAm 3*
Lederle, Ernst Joseph 1865-1921 *WhAm 1*
Ledford, Henry Pender 1889-1947 *NatCAB 34*
Ledleton, T *NewYHSD*
Ledlie, George 1861-1927 *WhAm 1*
Ledlie, James Hewett 1832-1882 *ApCAB*
Lednicki, Waclaw 1891-1967 *WhAm 4*,
  WhAm 5
Ledo, Joaquim Goncalves 1771-1847 *ApCAB*
LeDouble, Anatole Felix 1848-1913 *DcScB*
Ledoux, Albert Reid 1852-1923 *NatCAB 12*,
  WhAm 1
Ledoux, Claude Nicolas 1736-1806 *McGEWB*
Ledoux, John Walter 1860-1932 *NatCAB 23*,
  WhAm 1
Ledoux, Louis Vernon 1880-1948 *NatCAB 36*,
  WhAm 2
Ledru, Andre Pierre 1761-1825 *ApCAB*
Ledru, Hector Priam 1726-1775 *ApCAB*
LeDuc, Ernest 1869-1918 *NatCAB 17*
LeDuc, William Gates 1823-1917 *ApCAB Sup*,
  DcAmB, EncAAH, NatCAB 24,
  TwCBDA, WhAm 1
Ledvina, Emmanuel B 1868- *WhAm 5*
Ledwith, William Laurence 1850-1904 *WhAm 1*
Ledyard, Benjamin 1753-1803 *ApCAB X*
Ledyard, Benjamin, II 1779-1812 *ApCAB X*
Ledyard, Erwin d1902 *WhAm 1*
Ledyard, Henry 1812-1880 *ApCAB X,*
  NatCAB 13, NatCAB 22
Ledyard, Henry 1875-1932 *WhAm 1*
Ledyard, Henry Brockholst 1844-1921
  ApCAB X, NatCAB 22, WhAm 1
Ledyard, John 1751-1789 *AmBi, ApCAB,*
  DcAmB, Drake, NatCAB 5, WebAB,
  WhAm H
Ledyard, Joshua Heard 1875- *WhAm 5*
Ledyard, Lewis Cass 1851-1932 *ApCAB X,*
  NatCAB 22, WhAm 1
Ledyard, Lewis Cass, Jr. 1879-1936 *NatCAB 28,*
  WhAm 1
Ledyard, William 1738-1781 *AmBi, DcAmB,*
  Drake, NatCAB 5, WebAMB, WhAm H
Ledyard, William 1750?-1781 *ApCAB,*
  TwCBDA
Lee, Agnes d1939 *WhAm 1, WomWWA 14*
Lee, Albert 1868-1946 *NatCAB 36, TwCBDA,*
  WhAm 2
Lee, Albert Elmer 1879-1956 *NatCAB 44*
Lee, Albert Lindley 1834-1907 *ApCAB,*
  TwCBDA, WhAm 1
Lee, Albert R 1874- *WhoColR*
Lee, Alexander Edmund 1913-1974 *WhAm 6*
Lee, Alfred 1807-1887 *ApCAB, DcAmB,*
  Drake, NatCAB 11, TwCBDA, WhAm H
Lee, Alfred Emory 1838-1905 *ApCAB Sup,*
  NatCAB 8, TwCBDA, WhAm 4
Lee, Algernon 1873-1954 *WhAm 3*
Lee, Alice 1854- *WomWWA 14*
Lee, Alice Louise 1868- *WhAm 4,*
  WomWWA 14
Lee, Alonzo Hester 1903-1974 *WhAm 6*
Lee, Andrew 1745-1832 *ApCAB*
Lee, Andrew Erickson 1847-1934 *NatCAB 13,*
  REnAW
Lee, Andrew Ericson 1847-1934 *TwCBDA,*
  WhAm 1
Lee, Ann 1736-1784 *AmBi, ApCAB, DcAmB,*
  DcAmReB, Drake, EncAB, NatCAB 5,
  NotAW, REnAW, TwCBDA, WebAB,
  WhAm H
Lee, Archie Laney 1888-1951 *WhAm 3*
Lee, Arthur 1740-1792 *AmBi, ApCAB,*
  BiAUS, BiDrAC, DcAmB, Drake,
  McGEWB, NatCAB 8, TwCBDA,
  WebAB, WhAm H, WhAmP
Lee, Arthur 1881-1961 *BnEnAmA,*
  NatCAB 54, WhAm 4
Lee, Arthur Louis 1876- *ApCAB X*
Lee, Bee Virginia 1902- *WhAm 4*
Lee, Benjamin 1765-1828 *ApCAB*
Lee, Benjamin 1833-1913 *ApCAB,*
  NatCAB 11, TwCBDA, WhAm 1
Lee, Benjamin Fisler 1828-1909 *WhAm 1*
Lee, Benjamin Franklin 1841- *ApCAB,*
  NatCAB 5, TwCBDA, WhAm 1,
  WhoColR

Lee, Blair 1857-1944 *BiDrAC, WhAm 2*
Lee, Blair 1867-1944 *NatCAB 35*
Lee, Blewett 1867- *TwCBDA, WhAm 4*
Lee, Bradner Wells 1850-1925 *ApCAB X,*
  NatCAB 8, WhAm 1
Lee, Burton James 1874-1933 *WhAm 1*
Lee, Canada 1907-1952 *DcAmB S5, WhAm 3*
Lee, Charles 1731-1782 *AmBi, ApCAB,*
  DcAmB, Drake, EncAB, NatCAB 1,
  NatCAB 8, TwCBDA, WebAB,
  WebAMB, WhAm H
Lee, Charles 1758-1815 *AmBi, ApCAB,*
  BiAUS, BiDrUSE, DcAmB, Drake,
  NatCAB 1, TwCBDA, WhAm H,
  WhAmP
Lee, Charles Alfred 1801-1872 *ApCAB,*
  DcAmB, NatCAB 15, WhAm H
Lee, Charles Arnold 1845- *NatCAB 6*
Lee, Charles Benjamin 1867-1925 *NatCAB 23*
Lee, Charles Carroll 1839-1893 *NatCAB 31*
Lee, Charles Hamilton 1883-1967 *WhAm 4*
Lee, Charles O'Donnell, Jr. 1883-1918
  NatCAB 20
Lee, Charlie 1926- *IlBEAAW*
Lee, Chauncey 1763-1842 *ApCAB, Drake,*
  TwCBDA
Lee, D Collins 1888-1949 *NatCAB 38*
Lee, Daniel 1802-1890 *EncAAH*
Lee, David Aaron 1932-1974 *WhAm 6*
Lee, David B 1907-1968 *WhAm 5*
Lee, David Russell 1869-1933 *WhAm 1*
Lee, Day Kellogg 1816-1869 *ApCAB*
Lee, Delia Foreacre 1871- *WhAm 5*
Lee, Doris 1905- *BnEnAmA*
Lee, Edgar Desmond 1880- *WhAm 6*
Lee, Edward Brown 1875-1956 *NatCAB 48*
Lee, Edward Edson 1884-1944 *WhAm 2*
Lee, Edward Hervey 1863-1937 *WhAm 1*
Lee, Edward Michael 1885-1955 *NatCAB 42*
Lee, Edward Thomas 1861-1943 *NatCAB 42,*
  WhAm 2
Lee, Edward Trumbull 1855-1913 *WhAm 1*
Lee, Edwin Augustus 1888-1966 *WhAm 4*
Lee, Edwin F 1884-1948 *WhAm 2*
Lee, Eleanor Percy 1820?-1850? *Drake*
Lee, Elijah *NewYHSD*
Lee, Elisha 1870-1933 *WhAm 1*
Lee, Eliza Buckminster 1788?-1864 *DcAmB,*
  WhAm H
Lee, Eliza Buckminster 1789-1864 *NatCAB 25*
Lee, Eliza Buckminster 1794?-1864 *ApCAB,*
  Drake
Lee, Elizabeth Leighton 1864- *WomWWA 14*
Lee, Elmer 1856- *WhAm 4*
Lee, Elmina Bennett 1821-1908 *NewYHSD*
Lee, Elmo Pearce 1882-1949 *WhAm 2*
Lee, Elva *WomWWA 14*
Lee, Ethel Pollock 1880- *WomWWA 14*
Lee, Ezra 1749-1821 *ApCAB, WebAMB*
Lee, Fitzhugh 1835-1905 *AmBi, ApCAB,*
  ApCAB Sup, ApCAB X, BiDConf,
  DcAmB, NatCAB 9, TwCBDA, WebAB,
  WebAMB, WhAm 1, WhAmP
Lee, Francis 1803-1859 *Drake*
Lee, Francis Bazley 1869-1914 *WhAm 1*
Lee, Francis D 1826-1885 *WhAm H*
Lee, Francis Lightfoot 1734-1797 *AmBi,*
  ApCAB, BiAUS, BiDrAC, DcAmB,
  Drake, NatCAB 5, TwCBDA, WhAm H,
  WhAmP
Lee, Francis Loring 1823-1886 *ApCAB Sup*
Lee, Mrs. Frank 1849- *WomWWA 14*
Lee, Frank 1861-1930 *WhAm 1*
Lee, Frank Augustus 1852- *NatCAB 12,*
  WhAm 4
Lee, Frank Hood 1873-1952 *BiDrAC*
Lee, Frank Hood 1873-1953 *WhAm 3*
Lee, Frank Theodosius 1847-1934 *WhAm 2*
Lee, Franklin Pierce 1853-1941 *NatCAB 31*
Lee, Frederic Edward 1886-1952 *WhAm 3*
Lee, Frederic Girard 1873-1923 *WhAm 1*
Lee, Frederic Paddock 1893-1968 *WhAm 5*
Lee, Frederic Schiller 1859-1939 *DcAmB S2,*
  NatCAB 29, TwCBDA, WhAm 1
Lee, Frederick Crosby 1878- *WhAm 6*
Lee, G M *NewYHSD*
Lee, Gentry 1903-1965 *WhAm 4*
Lee, George Bolling 1872-1948 *NatCAB 40,*

  WhAm 2
Lee, George Cabot 1871-1950 *WhAm 3*
Lee, George Hugh 1881- *ApCAB X*
Lee, George Washington Custis 1832-1913
  AmBi, ApCAB, BiDConf, DcAmB,
  NatCAB 3, TwCBDA, WhAm 1
Lee, George Winthrop 1867-1948 *WhAm 2A*
Lee, Gerald Stanley 1862-1944 *WhAm 2*
Lee, Gertrude Adams 1869-1959 *WomWWA 14*
Lee, Gertrude Adams 1871-1959 *WhAm 3*
Lee, Gideon 1777-1841 *BiAUS*
Lee, Gideon 1778-1841 *ApCAB, BiDrAC,*
  NatCAB 5
Lee, Gordon 1859-1927 *BiDrAC, WhAm 1,*
  WhAmP
Lee, Gordon Canfield 1916-1972 *WhAm 5*
Lee, Graham 1861-1916 *WhAm 3*
Lee, Guy Carleton 1862-1936 *WhAm 1*
Lee, Guy Carleton 1867- *TwCBDA*
Lee, Gypsy Rose 1914-1970 *WebAB, WhAm 5*
Lee, Halfdan 1888-1975 *WhAm 6*
Lee, Hannah Farnham Sawyer 1780-1865
  ApCAB, DcAmB, Drake, NatCAB 25,
  WhAm H
Lee, Harold B 1899-1973 *WhAm 6*
Lee, Harry 1872-1935 *WhAm 1*
Lee, Harry Winfield 1894-1964 *WhAm 4*
Lee, Helen Evans Williams 1887- *WhoColR*
Lee, Helena Crumett 1867- *WomWWA 14*
Lee, Henry 1756-1818 *AmBi, ApCAB, BiAUS,*
  BiDrAC, DcAmB, Drake, NatCAB 3,
  TwCBDA, WebAB, WebAMB, WhAm H,
  WhAmP, WhoMilH
Lee, Henry 1758-1846 *ApCAB*
Lee, Henry 1782-1867 *ApCAB Sup, DcAmB,*
  NatCAB 13, TwCBDA, WhAm H
Lee, Henry 1787-1837 *ApCAB, DcAmB,*
  Drake, NatCAB 25, TwCBDA, WhAm H
Lee, Henry 1817-1898 *ApCAB Sup, TwCBDA,*
  WhAm 4
Lee, Henry B *BiAUS*
Lee, Henry Charles 1864-1930 *NatCAB 28*
Lee, Henry Haworth 1880-1941 *WhAm 1*
Lee, Henry Thomas 1840- *WhAm 4*
Lee, Henry Washington 1815-1874 *ApCAB,*
  NatCAB 3, TwCBDA
Lee, Hildegarde Langsdorf 1868-1922 *WhAm 1,*
  WomWWA 14
Lee, Homer 1856-1923 *NatCAB 5, WhAm 1*
Lee, Horatio Shumway 1867-1925 *NatCAB 20*
Lee, Howard Johnson 1851-1915 *NatCAB 17*
Lee, Hugh Bertram 1888-1964 *NatCAB 51*
Lee, Hugh Johnson 1871-1944 *WhAm 2*
Lee, Ivy Ledbetter 1877-1934 *DcAmB S1,*
  EncAB, WebAB, WhAm 1
Lee, J Beveridge 1865-1944 *WhAm 2*
Lee, J Edgar 1866-1958 *NatCAB 49*
Lee, J Gordon 1902-1959 *NatCAB 48*
Lee, J Wesley 1892-1966 *NatCAB 51*
Lee, James 1795-1874 *ApCAB*
Lee, James Bainbridge 1916-1964 *NatCAB 52*
Lee, James D, Jr. *NewYHSD*
Lee, James Grafton Carleton 1836-1916
  WhAm 1
Lee, James J 1900-1972 *WhAm 5*
Lee, James Melvin 1878-1929 *BiDAmEd,*
  DcAmB, NatCAB 23, WhAm 1
Lee, James P d1955 *WhAm 3*
Lee, James Paris 1831-1904 *WhAm 1*
Lee, James Thomas 1877-1968 *NatCAB 54,*
  WhAm 4
Lee, James Wideman 1849-1919 *DcAmB,*
  NatCAB 9, WhAm 1
Lee, Jason 1803-1845 *AmBi, DcAmB,*
  NatCAB 25, REnAW, WebAB,
  WhAm H
Lee, Jennette 1860-1951 *WhAm 3, WhAm 4,*
  WomWWA 14
Lee, Jesse 1758-1816 *AmBi, ApCAB, DcAmB,*
  DcAmReB, Drake, NatCAB 13,
  TwCBDA, WhAm H
Lee, Jesse Matlock 1843-1926 *NatCAB 30,*
  WhAm 1
Lee, John 1788-1871 *BiAUS, BiDrAC,*
  WhAm H
Lee, John Abbott Independence 1839-
  NatCAB 5
Lee, John Clarence 1856-1940 *NatCAB 10,*

TwCBDA, WhAm 1
Lee, John Clifford Hodges 1887-1958 *WebAMB, WhAm 3*
Lee, John Doyle 1812-1877 *AmBi, DcAmB, WhAm H*
Lee, John Mallory 1852-1925 *WhAm 1*
Lee, John Mallory 1852-1926 *NatCAB 20*
Lee, John Martin 1888-1946 *NatCAB 36*
Lee, John N *NewYHSD*
Lee, John Penn 1867- *WhAm 4*
Lee, John Stebbins 1820-1902 *NatCAB 10, TwCBDA, WhAm 1*
Lee, John W 1884- *WhoColR*
Lee, Jordan G, Jr. 1885-1956 *WhAm 3*
Lee, Joseph d1819 *Drake*
Lee, Joseph 1828-1880 *IIBEAAW*
Lee, Joseph 1862-1937 *DcAmB S2, NatCAB 33, WhAm 1*
Lee, Joseph 1864-1927 *NatCAB 22*
Lee, Joseph 1908-1960 *WhAm 4*
Lee, Joseph Daniel 1848- *NatCAB 16*
Lee, Joseph Wilcox Jenkins 1870- *NatCAB 14, WhAm 5*
Lee, Josh 1892-1967 *NatCAB 53*
Lee, Joshua 1783-1842 *BiAUS, BiDrAC, WhAm H*
Lee, Joshua Bryan 1892-1967 *BiDrAC, WhAm 4*
Lee, L Lyons 1882-1962 *NatCAB 50*
Lee, Lansing Burrows 1887-1944 *NatCAB 33, WhAm 2*
Lee, Laura 1867- *WomWWA 14*
Lee, Laura Billings 1864- *WomWWA 14*
Lee, Laurence Frederick 1888-1961 *WhAm 4*
Lee, Leroy Madison 1808-1882 *ApCAB, Drake*
Lee, Leslie Alexander 1852-1908 *NatCAB 20, WhAm 1*
Lee, Light-Horse Harry *WebAB*
Lee, Luther 1800- *ApCAB, Drake*
Lee, Luther 1800-1877 *WhAm H*
Lee, Luther 1800-1889 *DcAmB, NatCAB 25*
Lee, Luther James, Jr. 1912-1961 *WhAm 4*
Lee, M D *WhoColR A*
Lee, M Lindley 1805-1876 *BiAUS*
Lee, Mabel 1886- *BiDAmEd*
Lee, Manfred Bennington 1905-1971 *WebAB, WhAm 5*
Lee, Margaret 1840-1914 *NatCAB 15, WhAm 1, WomWWA 14*
Lee, Marguerite Thouron 1871- *WomWWA 14*
Lee, Mary Ann 1824?-1899 *NotAW*
Lee, Mary C Skeel 1849- *WhAm 4*
Lee, Mary Catherine *WhAm 5*
Lee, Mary Elizabeth 1813-1849 *ApCAB, Drake, NatCAB 6*
Lee, Mary Randolph Custis 1806-1873 *ApCAB*
Lee, Melicent Humason 1889-1943 *WhAm 2*
Lee, Minnie Mary *NotAW*
Lee, Moses Lindley 1805-1876 *BiDrAC, WhAm H*
Lee, Muna 1895-1965 *WhAm 4*
Lee, Oliver Justin 1881-1964 *WhAm 4*
Lee, Oscar Grant 1863- *WhAm 4*
Lee, Otho Scott 1840-1918 *NatCAB 17*
Lee, Otis 1902-1948 *WhAm 2*
Lee, Paul Wayne 1876-1954 *WhAm 3*
Lee, Peter Martinus 1879-1935 *WhAm 1*
Lee, Porter Raymond 1879-1939 *DcAmB S2, WhAm 1*
Lee, Ralph C 1876-1963 *NatCAB 51*
Lee, Ray Elmer 1878-1963 *WhAm 4*
Lee, Raymond Eliot 1886-1958 *WhAm 3*
Lee, Richard d1690? *ApCAB*
Lee, Richard 1590?-1660? *ApCAB*
Lee, Richard 1590?-1664 *AmBi, DcAmB, WhAm H*
Lee, Richard Bland 1761-1827 *BiAUS, BiDrAC, DcAmB, Drake, NatCAB 25, TwCBDA, WhAm H, WhAmP*
Lee, Richard Edwin 1876-1936 *NatCAB 30, WhAm 1*
Lee, Richard Everett 1915-1972 *NatCAB 57*
Lee, Richard Henry 1732-1794 *AmBi, ApCAB, BiAUS, BiDrAC, BiDrUSE, DcAmB, Drake, EncAAH, EncAB, McGEWB, NatCAB 3, TwCBDA, WebAB, WhAm H, WhAmP*
Lee, Richard Henry 1794-1865 *ApCAB,*

TwCBDA
Lee, Richard Henry 1877-1934 *NatCAB 28*
Lee, Richard Henry 1887- *WhoColR*
Lee, Robert C 1892-1951 *WhAm 3*
Lee, Robert Corwin 1888-1971 *WhAm 5*
Lee, Robert Edmund 1807-1870 *Drake*
Lee, Robert Edward 1807-1870 *AmBi, ApCAB, BiDConf, DcAmB, EncAB, McGEWB, NatCAB 3, NatCAB 4, TwCBDA, WebAB, WebAMB, WhAm H, WhoMilH*
Lee, Robert Edward 1843-1914 *WhAm 1*
Lee, Robert Edward 1893-1966 *NatCAB 53*
Lee, Robert Edward 1900-1963 *NatCAB 50*
Lee, Robert Emmett 1868-1916 *BiDrAC, WhAm 1*
Lee, Robert Emmons 1878-1925 *NatCAB 22*
Lee, Robert Erwin 1868-1954 *NatCAB 44*
Lee, Robert H 1904-1956 *WhAm 3*
Lee, Robert M 1933- *IIBEAAW*
Lee, Robert Quincy 1869-1930 *BiDrAC*
Lee, Roger Irving 1881-1965 *NatCAB 52, WhAm 4*
Lee, Ronald Freeman 1905-1972 *NatCAB 57*
Lee, Rose Hum 1904-1964 *WhAm 4*
Lee, Samuel 1625-1691 *ApCAB*
Lee, Samuel Edward 1858- *NatCAB 5*
Lee, Samuel Henry 1832-1918 *WhAm 1*
Lee, Samuel Hunt, Jr. 1918-1975 *WhAm 6*
Lee, Samuel M d1841 *NewYHSD*
Lee, Samuel Phillips 1811-1897 *Drake*
Lee, Samuel Phillips 1812-1897 *ApCAB, DcAmB, NatCAB 11, TwCBDA, WebAMB, WhAm H*
Lee, Samuel Todd 1876-1958 *WhAm 3*
Lee, Silas 1760-1814 *BiAUS, BiDrAC, TwCBDA, WhAm H*
Lee, Simeon Lemuel 1844-1927 *NatCAB 21*
Lee, Stephen Dill 1833-1908 *AmBi, ApCAB Sup, BiDAmEd, BiDConf, DcAmB, NatCAB 5, TwCBDA, WebAMB, WhAm 1*
Lee, Sydney Smith 1802-1869 *TwCBDA*
Lee, Thomas d1750 *ApCAB*
Lee, Thomas d1855 *BiAUS*
Lee, Thomas 1690?-1750 *NatCAB 7, NatCAB 13*
Lee, Thomas 1702?-1750 *TwCBDA*
Lee, Thomas 1769-1839 *ApCAB, BiAUS, DcAmB, Drake, TwCBDA, WhAm H*
Lee, Thomas 1780-1856 *BiDrAC, WhAm H*
Lee, Thomas Bailey 1873- *WhAm 2*
Lee, Thomas Fitzhugh 1877- *WhAm 5*
Lee, Thomas George 1860-1932 *NatCAB 26, WhAm 1*
Lee, Thomas George 1878-1934 *WhAm 1*
Lee, Thomas Leslie 1901-1949 *NatCAB 39*
Lee, Thomas Ludwell 1730?-1777 *ApCAB, Drake, TwCBDA*
Lee, Thomas Ludwill 1730?-1777 *BiAUS*
Lee, Thomas Sim d1819 *Drake*
Lee, Thomas Sim 1743-1810 *BiAUS*
Lee, Thomas Sim 1744-1819 *ApCAB*
Lee, Thomas Sim 1745-1819 *BiDrAC, DcAmB, NatCAB 9, TwCBDA, WhAm H*
Lee, Thomas Sim 1866-1966 *NatCAB 51*
Lee, Thomas Zanslaur 1866-1931 *NatCAB 29, WhAm 1*
Lee, Thurman 1895-1960 *NatCAB 48*
Lee, Tsung-Dao 1926- *AsBiEn, WebAB*
Lee, Umphrey 1893-1958 *NatCAB 45, WhAm 3*
Lee, Voyd Frank 1911-1973 *WhAm 6*
Lee, Wallace Howe 1861-1936 *WhAm 1*
Lee, Wallace Rodgers 1879- *WhAm 6*
Lee, Walter Estell 1879- *WhAm 6*
Lee, Walter John 1866-1924 *NatCAB 20*
Lee, Warren Isbell 1876-1955 *BiDrAC, WhAm 3*
Lee, Wesley T 1872- *WhAm 5*
Lee, William *BiAUS, WebAB*
Lee, William 1737?-1795 *ApCAB, BiAUS, Drake, TwCBDA*
Lee, William 1739-1795 *AmBi, DcAmB, NatCAB 25, WhAm H*
Lee, William 1826-1906 *NatCAB 11, TwCBDA, WhAm 1*
Lee, William 1841-1893 *ApCAB Sup*
Lee, William Amalphus 1859-1926 *NatCAB 20*

Lee, William Carey 1895-1948 *NatCAB 38, WhAm 2*
Lee, William Erwin 1882-1955 *NatCAB 42, WhAm 3*
Lee, William Granville 1859-1929 *DcAmB, WhAm 1*
Lee, William H d1929 *NatCAB 12, WhAm 1*
Lee, William Henry Fitzhugh 1837-1891 *AmBi, ApCAB, BiDConf, BiDrAC, DcAmB, NatCAB 4, TwCBDA, WhAm H, WhAmP*
Lee, William L 1866- *WhAm 4*
Lee, William Little 1821-1857 *ApCAB, DcAmB, NatCAB 12, WhAm H*
Lee, William States 1872-1934 *NatCAB 24, WhAm 1*
Lee, Willis Augustus, Jr. 1888-1945 *DcAmB S3, NatCAB 36, WhAm 2*
Lee, Willis Thomas 1864-1926 *WhAm 1*
Lee, Wilson 1761-1804 *ApCAB*
Lee, Z Collins 1805-1859 *BiAUS, Drake*
Leeb, Wilhelm Ritter Von 1876-1956 *WhWW-II, WhoMilH*
Leebrick, Kate 1842- *WomWWA 14*
Leece, Bennett Major 1876-1948 *NatCAB 37*
Leech, Caroline Apperson 1859- *WomWWA 14*
Leech, Daniel D Tompkins 1810-1869 *ApCAB*
Leech, Edward Owen 1850-1900 *NatCAB 13*
Leech, Edward Towner 1892-1949 *WhAm 2*
Leech, Grover Cleveland 1884-1956 *NatCAB 48*
Leech, Harper 1885-1951 *WhAm 3*
Leech, J Russell 1888-1952 *WhAm 3*
Leech, James Anderson 1843-1919 *NatCAB 18*
Leech, James Russell 1888-1952 *BiDrAC*
Leech, Paul Nicholas 1889-1941 *WhAm 1*
Leech, Samuel VanDerlip 1837- *ApCAB*
Leech, Thomas *NewYHSD*
Leeder, Frederick Saskatoon 1904-1961 *NatCAB 48*
Leedom, Boyd Stewart 1906-1969 *WhAm 5*
Leedom, John Peter 1847-1895 *BiDrAC, WhAm H*
Leeds, Charles Tileston 1879-1960 *NatCAB 48, WhAm 4*
Leeds, Daniel 1652-1720 *ApCAB, DcAmB, NatCAB 18, WhAm H*
Leeds, Edmund Ingersoll 1873-1958 *NatCAB 46*
Leeds, John 1705-1780 *ApCAB*
Leeds, John 1705-1790 *DcAmB, Drake, NatCAB 25, WhAm H*
Leeds, John Wattey *NewYHSD*
Leeds, Jules C 1872-1952 *WhAm 3*
Leeds, Morris Evans 1869-1952 *NatCAB 42, WhAm 3*
Leeds, Paul 1869-1958 *WhAm 3*
Leeds, Rudolph Gaar 1886-1964 *WhAm 4*
Leeds, Samuel Penniman 1824-1910 *WhAm 1*
Leeds, Samuel Pharo 1872-1946 *NatCAB 35*
Leeds, Warner Mifflin, II 1868-1925 *NatCAB 21*
Leeds, William B 1861-1908 *NatCAB 14*
Leeds, William Bateman 1822-1894 *NatCAB 16*
Leedy, Charles Denoe 1900-1964 *WhAm 4*
Leedy, John Whitnah 1849-1935 *NatCAB 8, TwCBDA, WhAm 1*
Leedy, Robert Franklin 1863-1924 *NatCAB 20*
Leedy, William Hart 1855-1922 *NatCAB 19*
Leefe, George E *NewYHSD*
Leefe, Julius *NewYHSD*
Leek, Elizabeth Austin 1866- *WomWWA 14*
Leek, John Halvor 1896-1967 *WhAm 5*
Leeman, Paul James 1883-1934 *WhAm 1*
Leeming, Mrs. Thomas L *WomWWA 14*
Leeming, Thomas Lonsdale 1872-1925 *NatCAB 6*
Leeming, Tom 1896-1953 *NatCAB 42, WhAm 3*
Leeming, Woodruff 1870- *NatCAB 16*
Leeper, James Daniel 1862-1936 *NatCAB 27*
Leeper, John Milton 1872-1935 *NatCAB 27*
Leeper, Laura Ferguson *WomWWA 14*
Leermakers, Peter Anthony 1937-1971 *WhAm 5*
Lees, Ann 1736-1784 *AmBi, DcAmB*
Lees, George Cooper 1881-1954 *NatCAB 44*
Lees, James Thomas 1859-1926 *NatCAB 21, WhAm 1*
Lees, John Walter 1863-1932 *NatCAB 25*

Leese, Sir Oliver 1894- *WhWW-II*
Leeser, Isaac 1806-1868 *ApCAB, BiDAmEd, DcAmB, DcAmReB, Drake, NatCAB 10, WhAm H*
Leesman, Elmer Martin 1884-1959 *WhAm 3*
Leeson, Joseph Robert 1844-1930 *NatCAB 36*
Leeson, Robert Ainsworth 1877-1953 *WhAm 3*
Leet, H Halbert 1911-1959 *NatCAB 47*
Leet, Isaac 1801-1844 *BiDrAC, WhAm H*
Leet, Isaac 1802-1844 *BiAUS*
Leet, Lewis Don 1901-1974 *WhAm 6*
Leet, Mary Garrett 1877- *WomWWA 14*
Leet, Russell Joseph 1897-1956 *NatCAB 45*
Leetch, Henry Winship 1894-1970 *NatCAB 55*
Leete, Charles Henry 1857-1936 *WhAm 1*
Leete, Frederick DeLand 1866-1958 *WhAm 3*
Leete, John Hopkin 1868-1929 *WhAm 1*
Leete, William d1683 *Drake*
Leete, William 1603?-1683 *ApCAB*
Leete, William 1613?-1683 *DcAmB, NatCAB 10, WhAm H*
Leete, William White 1854-1946 *WhAm 2*
Leeuwenhoek, Anton Van 1632-1723 *AsBiEn, McGEWB*
Leeuwenhoek, Antoni Van 1632-1723 *DcScB*
Lefavour, Henry 1862-1946 *WhAm 2*
Lefebvre, Francois Joseph 1755-1820 *WhoMilH*
Lefebvre, Georges 1874-1959 *McGEWB*
Lefebvre, Gordon 1889-1957 *WhAm 3*
LeFebvre, Nicaise 1610?-1669 *DcScB*
Lefebvre-Desnouettes, Charles 1773-1822 *ApCAB*
LeFever, Jacob 1830-1905 *BiDrAC, TwCBDA*
Lefever, Joseph 1760-1826 *BiDrAC, WhAm H*
Lefever, Peter Paul d1869 *WhAm H*
Lefevere, Peter Paul 1804-1869 *DcAmB*
Lefevre, Albert 1873- *WhAm 5*
LeFevre, Alice Louise 1898-1963 *DcAmLiB*
LeFevre, Arthur 1863-1929 *WhAm 1*
LeFevre, Benjamin F 1838-1922 *BiDrAC, TwCBDA*
Lefevre, Clement Fall 1797-1882 *NatCAB 16*
Lefevre, Edwin 1871-1943 *NatCAB 32, WhAm 1, WhAm 2*
LeFevre, Egbert 1858-1914 *WhAm 1*
LeFevre, Frank Jacob 1874-1941 *BiDrAC, NatCAB 30, WhAm 5*
Lefevre, George 1869-1923 *NatCAB 20, WhAm 1*
LeFevre, James 1828- *TwCBDA*
LeFevre, Jay 1893-1970 *BiDrAC, WhAm 5*
LeFevre, Jean 1652?-1706 *DcScB*
Lefevre, Joseph *BiAUS*
LeFevre, Lily Alice *WomWWA 14*
LeFevre, Owen Edgar 1848-1921 *NatCAB 19*
Lefevre, Peter Paul 1804-1869 *ApCAB, Drake, NatCAB 5, TwCBDA*
Lefevre, Theodore-Joseph Alberic-Marie 1914-1973 *WhAm 6*
Leffel, James 1806-1866 *DcAmB, WhAm H*
Lefferts, George Morewood 1846-1920 *ApCAB, DcAmB, NatCAB 23, WhAm 1*
Lefferts, John 1785-1829 *BiAUS, BiDrAC, WhAm H*
Lefferts, Marshall 1821-1876 *ApCAB, DcAmB, NatCAB 10, TwCBDA, WhAm H*
Lefferts, Marshall Clifford 1848- *NatCAB 10*
Lefferts, Sara Tawney *WomWWA 14*
Leffingwell, Albert 1845-1917 *WhAm 1*
Leffingwell, Charles Wesley 1840-1928 *ApCAB, NatCAB 5, TwCBDA, WhAm 1*
Leffingwell, Elisha Dyer 1849-1916 *NatCAB 17*
Leffingwell, Forrest Emmett 1904-1919 *WhAm 5*
Leffingwell, Russell Cornell 1878-1960 *NatCAB 48, WhAm 4*
Leffingwell, William Elderkin 1855-1927 *WhAm 1*
Leffingwell, William Henry 1876-1934 *BiDAmEd, WhAm 1*
Leffler, Charles Doyle 1868-1939 *NatCAB 41, WhAm 1*
Leffler, Charles Doyle 1897-1961 *NatCAB 49, WhAm 5*
Leffler, George Leland 1899-1958 *WhAm 3*
Leffler, Isaac 1788-1866 *BiAUS, BiDrAC, DcAmB, NatCAB 25, WhAm H, WhAmP*

Leffler, Ray Victor 1892-1941 *WhAm 1*
Leffler, Ross Lillie 1886-1964 *NatCAB 51, WhAm 4*
Leffler, Shepherd 1811-1879 *BiAUS, BiDrAC, DcAmB, WhAm H, WhAmP*
Leffler, William Skilling 1894-1964 *WhAm 4*
Leffmann, Henry 1847-1930 *DcAmB, NatCAB 25, WhAm 1*
Lefkin, Philip 1909-1955 *NatCAB 44*
LeFlore, Basil 1811-1886 *ApCAB Sup*
Leflore, Greenwood 1800-1865 *DcAmB, WhAm H*
LeForgee, Charles Chambers 1867-1951 *NatCAB 41, WhAm 5*
Lefranc, Margaret 1907- *IIBEAAW*
Lefroy, Sallie Watson *WomWWA 14*
Lefschetz, Solomon 1884-1972 *NatCAB 56, WhAm 5*
Leftowich, Bill *IIBEAAW*
Leftwich, Jabez d1855 *BiAUS*
Leftwich, Jabez 1765-1855 *BiDrAC, WhAm H*
Leftwich, Jabez 1766-1855 *TwCBDA*
Leftwich, Joel 1759-1846 *ApCAB, Drake, TwCBDA*
Leftwich, John William 1826-1870 *BiAUS, BiDrAC, WhAm H*
Leftwich, John William 1826-1871 *TwCBDA*
LeGallais, Hugues 1896-1964 *WhAm 4*
LeGallienne, Eva 1899- *WebAB*
LeGallienne, Richard 1866-1947 *ApCAB X, WhAm 2*
Legallois, Julien Jean Cesar 1770-1814 *DcScB*
Legarda, Benito 1853- *WhAm 4*
Legarda Y Tuason, Benito 1853-1915 *BiDrAC*
Legare, George S 1870-1913 *WhAm 1*
Legare, George Swinton 1869-1913 *BiDrAC, WhAmP*
Legare, Hugh Swinton 1789-1843 *ApCAB*
Legare, Hugh Swinton 1797-1843 *AmBi, BiAUS, BiDrAC, BiDrUSE, DcAmB, Drake, NatCAB 6, TwCBDA, WebAB, WhAm H, WhAmP*
Legare, James Mathewes 1823-1859 *NewYHSD, WhAm H*
Legare, James Matthews 1823-1859 *NatCAB 12*
Legare, Mary S 1792- *NewYHSD*
Legaspi, Miguel Lopez De 1524-1572 *ApCAB*
Legendre, Adrien-Marie 1752-1833 *DcScB*
LeGendre, Charles William 1829?-1899 *TwCBDA*
LeGendre, Charles William 1830-1899 *DcAmB, NatCAB 25*
Legendre, Napoleon Narcisse Gabriel 1841- *ApCAB*
LeGendre, William Charles 1856-1926 *NatCAB 25*
LeGentil DeLaGalaisiere, Guillaume 1725-1792 *DcScB*
Leger, Fernand 1881-1955 *McGEWB*
Leger, Jacques Nicolas 1859- *ApCAB Sup, WhAm 4*
Leger, Urbain-Louis-Eugene 1866-1948 *DcScB*
Legg, Frederick 1885-1957 *NatCAB 48*
Leggat, Alexander 1876-1961 *NatCAB 49*
Legge, Alexander 1866-1933 *DcAmB S1, NatCAB 26, WhAm 1*
Legge, Barnwell R 1891-1949 *WhAm 3*
Legge, Charlotte M 1838- *WomWWA 14*
Legge, Francis d1783 *Drake*
Legge, Lionel Kennedy 1889-1970 *NatCAB 56, WhAm 5*
Legge, Robert Thomas 1872- *WhAm 5*
Legge, William 1731-1801 *ApCAB*
Leggett, Albert Earle 1887-1972 *NatCAB 57*
Leggett, Benjamin Franklin 1834-1924 *WhAm 1*
Leggett, Catharine S *NewYHSD*
Leggett, Eugene Sheldon 1902-1939 *AmBi, WhAm 1*
Leggett, Francis H 1840-1909 *NatCAB 2*
Leggett, Henry Theodore 1873- *NatCAB 14*
Leggett, Joseph A 1860-1922 *NatCAB 43*
Leggett, Joseph Palmer 1856-1921 *NatCAB 20*
Leggett, Lillian Ketcham *WomWWA 14*
Leggett, Lucille 1896- *IIBEAAW*
Leggett, Mary Lydia 1852- *AmWom, WomWWA 14*

Leggett, Mortimer D d1896 *BiAUS*
Leggett, Mortimer Dormer 1821-1896 *AmBi, DcAmB, NatCAB 2, TwCBDA, WhAm H*
Leggett, Mortimer Dormer 1831-1896 *ApCAB, Drake*
Leggett, Robert 1826?- *NewYHSD*
Leggett, Robert Louis 1926- *BiDrAC*
Leggett, William 1801-1839 *AmBi, DcAmB, WhAm H*
Leggett, William 1802-1839 *ApCAB, Drake, NatCAB 6*
Leggett, William Henry 1816-1882 *ApCAB, NatCAB 6*
Leggette, Lubin Poe 1912-1968 *WhAm 5*
Legh-Jones, Sir George 1890-1960 *WhAm 4*
Legier, John 1878-1973 *WhAm 5*
Legler, Henry Edouard 1861-1917 *NatCAB 24*
Legler, Henry Eduard 1861-1917 *DcAmB, DcAmLiB, WhAm 1*
LeGrand *NewYHSD*
LeGrand, Abraham 1869- *WhAm 3*
LeGrand, Henry *NewYHSD*
LeGrand, John Carroll 1814-1861 *NatCAB 12*
LeGrand, John Quince 1905-1967 *NatCAB 54*
Legrand, Jules *NewYHSD*
Legrand, Pierre 1620?-1670 *ApCAB*
LeGrand, W *NewYHSD*
LeGrande, J *NewYHSD*
Legrange, Vincent *NewYHSD*
LeGras, Gustave 1858-1912 *WhAm 1*
Leguia Y Salcedo, Augusto Bernardino 1863-1932 *McGEWB*
LeHardy, C *NewYHSD*
LeHardy DeBeaulieu, Julius-Caesar L V 1831- *NatCAB 10*
Lehlbach, Frederick Reimold 1876-1937 *BiDrAC, WhAm 1, WhAmP*
Lehlbach, Herman 1845-1904 *BiDrAC, WhAmP*
Lehman, Albert Carl 1878-1935 *NatCAB 30, WhAm 1*
Lehman, Alcuin Williams 1897-1970 *WhAm 5*
Lehman, Allan Sigmund 1885-1952 *NatCAB 41, WhAm 3*
Lehman, Ambrose Edwin 1851-1917 *WhAm 1*
Lehman, Arthur 1873-1936 *DcAmB S2, WhAm 1*
Lehman, B B *NewYHSD*
Lehman, Clarence O 1892-1945 *WhAm 2*
Lehman, Edwin Partridge 1888-1954 *WhAm 3*
Lehman, Emanuel 1827-1907 *NatCAB 25*
Lehman, Eugene Heitler 1879-1972 *WhAm 5*
Lehman, Ezra 1871-1931 *WhAm 1*
Lehman, Frank Alfred 1871- *WhAm 5*
Lehman, George d1870 *NewYHSD*
Lehman, George Mustin 1863- *WhAm 5*
Lehman, Harry J 1883-1959 *NatCAB 49*
Lehman, Harvey Christian 1889-1965 *NatCAB 52*
Lehman, Herbert Henry 1878-1963 *ApCAB X, BiDrAC, EncAAH, McGEWB, WebAB, WhAm 4, WhAmP*
Lehman, I Howard 1880-1969 *NatCAB 54*
Lehman, Irvin Frank 1877-1936 *NatCAB 30*
Lehman, Irving 1876-1945 *DcAmB S3, NatCAB 37, WhAm 2*
Lehman, Japhet F 1860-1932 *NatCAB 25*
Lehman, Leo 1880-1948 *NatCAB 36*
Lehman, Linwood 1895-1953 *WhAm 3*
Lehman, Louis Oliver 1877-1923 *WhAm 1*
Lehman, Paul 1889-1945 *NatCAB 35*
Lehman, Philip 1861-1947 *WhAm 2*
Lehman, Robert 1891-1969 *WhAm 5*
Lehman, Thomas E *NewYHSD*
Lehman, Thomas F *NewYHSD*
Lehman, William 1779-1829 *NatCAB 5*
Lehman, William E 1822-1895 *BiAUS*
Lehman, William Eckart 1821-1895 *BiDrAC, WhAm H*
Lehmann, Carl Blayney 1884-1949 *NatCAB 38*
Lehmann, Emil Wilhelm 1887-1972 *WhAm 5*
Lehmann, Frederick William 1853-1931 *DcAmB, NatCAB 12, WhAm 1*
Lehmann, Frederick William, Jr. 1883-1961 *WhAm 4*
Lehmann, Johann Gottlob 1719-1767 *DcScB*
Lehmann, John Stark 1886-1967 *NatCAB 54*

Lehmann, Karl 1894-1960 *WhAm 4*
Lehmann, Katharine 1876-1960 *WhAm 4*
Lehmann, Lilli 1848- *ApCAB Sup*
Lehmann, Otto 1855-1922 *DcScB*
Lehmann, Robert Edmund 1921-1974 *NatCAB 57*
Lehmann, Timothy 1881- *WhAm 6*
Lehmbruck, Wilhelm 1881-1919 *McGEWB*
Lehmer, Derrick Norman 1867-1938 *NatCAB 28, WhAm 1*
Lehnert, F *IIBEAAW*
Lehnerts, Edward M 1873-1953 *WhAm 3*
Lehoczky, Paul Nicholas 1905-1974 *WhAm 6*
Lehotsky, Koloman 1906-1975 *WhAm 6*
Lehr, Arthur 1906-1960 *WhAm 4*
Lehr, Charles *NewYHSD*
Lehr, Henry Solomon 1838-1923 *NatCAB 20, WhAm 1*
Lehr, John Camillus 1878-1958 *BiDrAC, WhAm 3*
Lehr, John H d1841 *NewYHSD*
Lehrbas, Lloyd Allan 1896-1964 *WhAm 4*
Lehrman, Daniel Sanford 1919-1972 *WhAm 5*
Lehrman, Jacob 1911-1974 *WhAm 6*
Lehtinen, Artturl August 1896-1966 *WhAm 4*
Lehy, John Francis 1850-1919 *TwCBDA, WhAm 1*
Leib, George Carr 1890-1974 *NatCAB 57, WhAm 6*
Leib, Michael d1822 *BiAUS*
Leib, Michael 1759-1822 *ApCAB, NatCAB 4, TwCBDA*
Leib, Michael 1760-1822 *AmBi, BiDrAC, DcAmB, Drake, WhAm H, WhAmP*
Leib, Owen D d1848 *BiAUS, BiDrAC, WhAm H*
Leib, Samuel Franklin 1848-1924 *WhAm 1*
Leibenson, Leonid S *DcScB*
Leibensperger, George Franklin 1892-1965 *NatCAB 53*
Leiber, Fritz 1882-1949 *DcAmB S4*
Leibert, Morris William 1855- *WhAm 1*
Leibniz, Gottfried Wilhelm 1646-1716 *AsBiEn, DcScB, McGEWB*
Leibold, Paul Francis 1914-1972 *WhAm 5*
Leibowitz, Rene 1913-1972 *WhAm 5*
Leiby, Adrian Coulter 1904-1976 *WhAm 6*
Leicester, Robert Dudley, Earl Of 1532?-1588 *McGEWB*
Leichliter, Gould A 1891-1971 *WhAm 5*
Leichterkost, Martin *NewYHSD*
Leichtman, Jacob 1896-1975 *WhAm 6*
Leichtweis, Louis 1824?- *NewYHSD*
Leidesdorf, Samuel David 1881-1968 *WhAm 5*
Leidesdorff, Alexander *REnAW*
Leidigh, Arthur Henry 1880- *WhAm 6*
Leiding, Harriette Kershaw 1878-1948 *WhAm 3, WomWWA 14*
Leidy, Clarence Fontaine Maury 1873-1926 *NatCAB 24*
Leidy, Joseph 1823-1891 *AmBi, ApCAB, BiDAmEd, BiHiMed, DcAmB, DcScB, Drake, EncAB, NatCAB 5, TwCBDA, WebAB, WhAm H*
Leidy, Joseph, II 1866-1932 *WhAm 1*
Leidy, Paul 1813-1877 *BiAUS, BiDrAC, WhAm H*
Leidy, Thomas H 1845-1921 *NatCAB 19*
Leidy, Thomas Kemmerer 1873-1953 *NatCAB 43*
Leidy, William B *NewYHSD*
Leif Ericson 971-1015? *McGEWB*
Leif Ericsson *AmBi, WebAB*
Leigh, Benjamin Watkins 1781-1849 *ApCAB, BiDrAC, DcAmB, Drake, NatCAB 11, TwCBDA, WhAm H, WhAmP*
Leigh, Benjamin Watkins 1782-1849 *BiAUS*
Leigh, Charles d1815 *Drake*
Leigh, Edward Baker 1853-1932 *NatCAB 26*
Leigh, Edwin 1815-1890 *BiDAmEd, NatCAB 20*
Leigh, Hezekiah Gilbert 1795-1853 *NatCAB 13*
Leigh, Hezekiah Gilbert 1795-1858 *ApCAB, TwCBDA*
Leigh, Horace 1906-1958 *NatCAB 44*
Leigh, Mercedes *AmWom*
Leigh, Randolph 1891-1953 *WhAm 3*
Leigh, Richard Henry 1870-1946 *NatCAB 35,*

WhAm 2
Leigh, Robert Devore 1890-1961 *BiDAmEd, DcAmLiB, NatCAB 51, WhAm 4*
Leigh, Southgate 1864-1936 *NatCAB 42*
Leigh, Southgate 1866-1936 *WhAm 1*
Leigh, Townes Randolph 1880-1949 *WhAm 2*
Leigh, Vivien 1913-1967 *WhAm 4*
Leigh, William Robinson 1866-1955 *DcAmB S5, IIBEAAW, NatCAB 41, REnAW, WhAm 3*
Leigh-Mallory, Sir Trafford 1892-1944 *WhWW-II, WhoMilH*
Leight, Angelina 1875- *BiCAW*
Leighton, Alfred Crocker 1901-1965 *IIBEAAW*
Leighton, Benjamin Farnsworth 1847-1921 *NatCAB 19*
Leighton, Benjamin Franklin d1921 *WhAm 1*
Leighton, Delmar 1897-1966 *WhAm 4*
Leighton, Etta Veronica 1880- *WomWWA 14*
Leighton, Frank Thomson 1885-1943 *WhAm 2*
Leighton, Frederick 1884-1948 *NatCAB 36*
Leighton, George A *NewYHSD*
Leighton, George Eliot 1835-1901 *NatCAB 4, WhAm 1*
Leighton, George William 1863- *NatCAB 26*
Leighton, Joseph Alexander 1870-1954 *WhAm 3*
Leighton, Kathryn Woodman 1876-1952 *IIBEAAW, WhAm 3*
Leighton, Margaret 1922-1976 *WhAm 6*
Leighton, Marshall Ora d1958 *WhAm 3*
Leighton, Mary *NatCAB 26*
Leighton, Morris Morgan 1887-1971 *WhAm 5*
Leighton, Nicholas Winfield Scott d1898 *TwCBDA*
Leighton, Thomas 1786-1849 *NatCAB 26*
Leighton, William *DcAmB*
Leighton, William 1808-1891 *NatCAB 26*
Leighton, William 1810?-1868 *WhAm H*
Leighton, William 1833-1911 *ApCAB, NatCAB 1, NatCAB 26, TwCBDA*
Leighty, George Earle 1897-1973 *WhAm 6*
Leighty, Jacob D 1839-1912 *BiDrAC*
Leimbach, Alfred T 1901-1971 *WhAm 5*
Leinbach, Gary Earl 1933-1973 *WhAm 6*
Leinbach, Paul Seibert 1874-1941 *WhAm 1*
Leindecker, John Philip 1889-1958 *WhAm 3*
Leinen, Raymond F 1890-1951 *WhAm 3*
Leininger, William Grill 1863-1938 *NatCAB 27*
Leiper, George Gray 1786-1868 *ApCAB, BiAUS, BiDrAC, WhAm H*
Leiper, Henry Smith 1891-1975 *WhAm 6*
Leiper, Macon Anderson 1879-1936 *WhAm 1*
Leiper, Thomas 1745-1825 *ApCAB, DcAmB, NatCAB 11, WhAm H*
Leipheimer, Edwin George 1880- *WhAm 6*
Leipzig, Nate 1873-1939 *DcAmB S2*
Leipziger, Henry Marcus 1853-1917 *NatCAB 14*
Leipziger, Henry Marcus 1854-1917 *BiDAmEd, DcAmB, WhAm 1*
Leisen, Mitchell 1898-1972 *WhAm 5*
Leisenring, Edward B, Jr. 1926-1968 *WhAm 5*
Leisenring, Edward Barnes 1895-1952 *WhAm 3*
Leisenring, John 1853-1901 *BiDrAC*
Leisenring, Luther Morris 1875-1965 *WhAm 4*
Leiser, Christian *NewYHSD*
Leiserson, William Morris 1883-1957 *NatCAB 52, WhAm 3*
Leisewitz, Julia Margaret 1856- *WomWWA 14*
Leishman, John G A 1857-1924 *AmBi, DcAmB, NatCAB 13, WhAm 1*
Leishman, Sir William Boog 1865-1926 *AsBiEn*
Leisk, Ross Dudley 1891-1964 *NatCAB 51*
Leisler, Jacob 1640-1691 *AmBi, ApCAB, DcAmB, Drake, McGEWB, NatCAB 13, TwCBDA, WebAB, WhAm H, WhAmP*
Leisser, Martin B 1845- *NatCAB 14*
Leist, Henry Gottlieb 1871-1937 *WhAm 1*
Leister, Claude Willard 1893-1963 *NatCAB 51*
Leisy, Ernest Erwin 1887-1968 *WhAm 5*
Leitch, Joseph Dugald 1864-1938 *WhAm 1*
Leitch, Mary Sinton 1876-1954 *WhAm 3*
Leitch, Richard P *IIBEAAW*
Leitch, William 1814-1864 *ApCAB*
Leite Ferreira DeMello, Jose Bento 1785-1844 *ApCAB*
Leiter, Benjamin Franklin 1813-1866 *BiAUS,*

BiDrAC, TwCBDA, WhAm H
Leiter, H Evans 1906-1958 *NatCAB 46*
Leiter, Joseph 1868-1932 *ApCAB Sup, DcAmB S1, NatCAB 36, WhAm 1*
Leiter, Levi Zeigler 1834-1904 *ApCAB Sup, DcAmB, NatCAB 12, WhAm 1*
Leiter, Mary Victoria *ApCAB Sup*
Leith, Charles Kenneth 1875-1956 *NatCAB 47, WhAm 3*
Leith, Dorothy Louise 1910-1973 *WhAm 6*
Leith, Sir James 1763-1816 *ApCAB*
Leithead, Barry T 1907-1974 *WhAm 6*
Leitman, Max 1894-1960 *NatCAB 49*
Leitz, Louis *NewYHSD*
Leitzel, Lillian 1892-1931 *NotAW*
Leitzell, Charles Wilson 1870-1950 *NatCAB 39, WhAm 3*
Leiva, Andres Diaz Venero De 1523-1585 *ApCAB*
Leiva, Carlos 1879- *WhAm 6*
Leix, Frederick 1865-1921 *NatCAB 19*
LeJau, Francis 1665-1717 *DcAmB, WhAm H*
LeJeune, Claude 1530?-1600 *McGEWB*
Lejeune, John Archer 1867-1942 *DcAmB S3, WebAMB, WhAm 2*
LeJeune, Paul 1592-1664 *ApCAB*
Lejwa, Arthur 1895-1972 *NatCAB 57*
Leland, Miss *NewYHSD*
Leland, Aaron 1761-1833 *ApCAB*
Leland, Abby Porter 1879- *WomWWA 14*
Leland, Alonzo 1817-1891 *REnAW*
Leland, Caroline Weaver 1840- *AmWom*
Leland, Charles A 1859- *WhAm 1*
Leland, Charles Godfrey 1824-1903 *AmBi, ApCAB, DcAmB, Drake, NatCAB 5, TwCBDA, WhAm 1*
Leland, Cyrus Austin 1887-1949 *WhAm 2*
Leland, Forrest LeRoy 1880-1948 *NatCAB 38*
Leland, Frank Bruce 1857-1926 *NatCAB 32, WhAm 5*
Leland, George Adams 1850-1924 *DcAmB*
Leland, George Adams, Jr. 1886-1943 *WhAm 2*
Leland, Henry 1850-1877 *ApCAB*
Leland, Henry Martyn 1843-1932 *NatCAB 40, WhAm 1*
Leland, Henry Perry 1828-1868 *ApCAB, Drake, TwCBDA*
Leland, John 1754-1841 *ApCAB, DcAmB, DcAmReB, Drake, NatCAB 5, WhAm H*
Leland, Joseph Daniels 1885-1968 *WhAm 5*
Leland, Lester 1864-1933 *NatCAB 14, WhAm 1*
Leland, Oliver Shepard d1870 *Drake*
Leland, Ora Miner 1876- *WhAm 5*
Leland, Rosco Genung 1885-1949 *NatCAB 42*
Leland, Samuel Phelps 1837- *WhAm 4*
Leland, Waldo Gifford 1879-1966 *NatCAB 54, WhAm 4*
Leland, William Emmons 1870-1945 *NatCAB 34*
LeLanne *NewYHSD*
LeLong, Lucien 1889-1958 *WhAm 3*
Lely, Nicholas George 1887-1958 *WhAm 3*
Lely, Sir Peter 1618-1680 *McGEWB*
LeLyonnet, Charles 1767-1826 *ApCAB*
LeMaire, Amy Dandrow 1907-1972 *WhAm 6*
Lemaire, Jacques *DcScB*
LeMaire, James 1565?-1616 *ApCAB*
Lemaire, Pierre *DcScB*
Lemaitre, Georges Edouard 1894-1966 *AsBiEn, McGEWB*
Lemaitre, Georges Edouard Etienne 1898-1972 *WhAm 6*
Leman, Beaudry 1878-1951 *WhAm 3*
Leman, Gerard Mathieu 1851-1920 *WhoMilH*
Lemann, Isaac Ivan 1877-1937 *NatCAB 39*
Lemann, Isaac Ivan 1877-1938 *WhAm 1*
Lemann, Monte M 1884-1959 *WhAm 3A*
LeMarchant, John Gaspard 1766-1812 *WhoMilH*
Lemare, Edwin Henry 1866-1934 *WhAm 1*
Lemass, Sean Francis 1899-1971 *WhAm 5*
LeMaster, Josiah Patterson 1890-1968 *NatCAB 54*
LeMay, Alan 1899-1964 *WhAm 4*
LeMay, Curtis Emerson 1906- *WebAB, WebAMB, WhWW-II*
Lemay, Leon Pamphile 1837- *ApCAB*

Lembke, Francis Christian 1704-1785 *ApCAB, NatCAB 5*
Lemcke, Gesine 1841-1904 *WhAm 1*
Lemcke, Henry 1796-1882 *ApCAB*
Leme, Antonio Pires DaSilva Pontes 1756?-1807 *ApCAB*
Lemelin, Emile 1899-1967 *NatCAB 53*
Lemen, Lewis Erastus 1849-1920 *NatCAB 6*
LeMercier, Andrew 1692-1763 *ApCAB, Drake*
LeMercier, Francis d1690 *ApCAB*
Lemere, Alexis *NewYHSD*
Lemerle, Augustus E, Jr. *NewYHSD*
Lemert, Charles Clarence 1874-1958 *NatCAB 49*
Lemery, Louis 1677-1743 *DcScB*
Lemery, Nicolas 1645-1715 *DcScB*
Lemet, Louis 1779?-1832 *NewYHSD*
Lemkau, Hudson Bardon 1910-1974 *WhAm 6*
Lemke, Peter Henry 1796-1882 *DcAmB, WhAm H*
Lemke, William 1878-1950 *BiDrAC, DcAmB S4, EncAAH, NatCAB 38, REnAW, WhAm 3, WhAmP*
Lemkin, Raphael 1900-1959 *WhAm 3*
Lemley, Harry Jacob 1883-1965 *NatCAB 53, WhAm 4*
Lemly, Elizabeth Cary 1871- *WomWWA 14*
Lemly, Henry Rowan 1851-1925 *ApCAB Sup, WhAm 1*
Lemly, Samuel Conrad 1853-1909 *WhAm 1*
Lemme, William *NewYHSD*
Lemmel, William Hugo 1896-1953 *WhAm 3*
Lemmens, John Nicholas 1850- *ApCAB Sup*
Lemmon, Dal Millington 1887-1958 *WhAm 3*
Lemmon, Guy Morrison 1889-1959 *NatCAB 48, NatCAB 49*
Lemmon, John Gill 1832-1908 *ApCAB Sup, DcAmB, WhAm 1*
Lemmon, Reuben C 1825-1905 *WhAm 1*
Lemmon, Robert Stell 1885-1964 *WhAm 4*
Lemmon, Sara Allen Plummer 1836- *WhAm 5*
Lemmon, Sarah Allen Plummer 1836- *ApCAB Sup*
Lemmon, Walter Stedecker 1896-1967 *NatCAB 53, WhAm 4*
Lemnitzer, Lyman L 1899- *WebAMB*
Lemoine, Albert Napoleon 1884-1957 *NatCAB 48*
Lemoine, Antoine 1683-1730? *Drake*
Lemoine, Charles 1656-1729 *Drake*
Lemoine, Emile Michel Hyacinthe 1840-1912 *DcScB*
LeMoine, James MacPherson 1825- *ApCAB*
Lemoine, Joseph 1668-1734 *Drake*
Lemoine, Louis Rice 1858-1926 *NatCAB 28*
Lemoine, Paul 1663-1702? *Drake*
Lemoine, Sanvolle 1671-1701 *Drake*
LeMoine, Sauvolle 1671?-1701 *ApCAB*
Lemon, Allan Clark 1889-1948 *WhAm 2*
Lemon, Edward Rivers 1855-1919 *ApCAB X*
Lemon, Frank Kyle 1875-1946 *WhAm 2*
Lemon, Harvey B 1885-1965 *WhAm 4*
Lemon, James Garfield *WhoColR*
Lemon, Luther Orange 1900-1957 *WhAm 3*
Lemon, William C *NewYHSD*
Lemon, Willis Storrs 1878- *WhAm 3*
Lemond, James S 1851- *WhAm 4*
LeMone, David 1904-1948 *NatCAB 36*
Lemonnier, Andre 1896-1963 *WhAm 4*
LeMonnier, Louis-Guillaume 1717-1799 *DcScB*
LeMonnier, Pierre-Charles 1715-1799 *DcScB*
Lemos Mesa, Manoel De 1670-1744 *ApCAB*
Lemosey, Francis William *NewYHSD*
Lemosy, Francis William *NewYHSD*
LeMoyne, Antoine 1683-1747 *ApCAB*
LeMoyne, Charles 1626-1683 *ApCAB*
LeMoyne, Charles 1656-1729 *ApCAB*
LeMoyne, Charles 1687-1755 *ApCAB*
LeMoyne, Francis Julius 1798-1879 *ApCAB, DcAmB, NatCAB 15, TwCBDA, WhAm H*
LeMoyne, J Baptiste, Sieur DeBienville 1680-1768 *TwCBDA*
LeMoyne, Jacques DeMorgues d1588 *IIBEAAW, NewYHSD, WhAm H*
LeMoyne, James 1659-1690 *ApCAB*
LeMoyne, Jean B, Sieur DeBienville 1680-1765 *NatCAB 5*

LeMoyne, Jean Baptiste 1680-1767 *WhAm H*
LeMoyne, Jean Baptiste 1680-1768 *AmBi, DcAmB, WebAB*
LeMoyne, John Valcoulon 1828-1918 *BiDrAC, TwCBDA*
LeMoyne, Joseph 1668-1734 *ApCAB*
LeMoyne, Joseph Dominick Emanuel 1807- *ApCAB*
LeMoyne, Louis Valcoulon 1860-1928 *WhAm 1*
LeMoyne, Paul 1663-1704 *ApCAB*
LeMoyne, Paul-Joseph 1701-1778 *ApCAB*
LeMoyne, Peter, Sieur D'Iberville 1661-1706 *NatCAB 5*
LeMoyne, Pierre 1661-1706 *DcAmB, WebAB, WhAm H*
LeMoyne, Sarah 1859- *NatCAB 13*
LeMoyne, Simon 1604-1665 *ApCAB*
LeMoyne, William J 1831-1905 *DcAmB, NatCAB 5, WhAm 1*
Lemp, William J 1836- *NatCAB 12*
Lempe, George Gustave 1865-1915 *NatCAB 18*
Lempereur, Glenn Nestor 1914-1965 *NatCAB 51*
Lempereur, Jeannot 1763-1791 *ApCAB*
Lempira d1537 *ApCAB*
Lena, Hugh Francis 1888-1948 *NatCAB 40*
Lenahan, James Lawrence 1906-1965 *WhAm 4*
Lenahan, John Thomas 1852-1920 *BiDrAC, NatCAB 19, WhAm 4*
LeNain, Antoine 1588-1648 *McGEWB*
LeNain, Louis 1593-1648 *McGEWB*
LeNain, Mathieu 1607-1677 *McGEWB*
Lenard, Philipp Eduard Anton Von 1862-1947 *AsBiEn, DcScB*
Lendall, Harry N 1878- *WhAm 6*
Lenders, Emil W d1934 *IIBEAAW*
Leney, William Satchwell 1769-1831 *DcAmB, NewYHSD, WhAm H*
L'Enfant, Peter Charles 1755-1825 *ApCAB, Drake*
L'Enfant, Pierre Charles 1754-1825 *AmBi, BnEnAmA, DcAmB, EncAB, McGEWB, NatCAB 16, WebAB, WhAm H*
Lenfestey, Nathan Coggeshall 1890-1954 *NatCAB 43, WhAm 3*
Lengel, William C d1965 *WhAm 4, WhAm 5*
Lengfeld, Felix 1863-1938 *WhAm 1*
Lenghi, Moses G *NewYHSD*
L'Engle, Claude 1868-1919 *BiDrAC, WhAm 4*
L'Engle, Edward McCrady 1878-1947 *NatCAB 36*
L'Engle, William Johnson 1884-1957 *WhAm 4*
Lenhard, Augustus *NewYHSD*
Lenher, Victor 1873-1927 *NatCAB 21, WhAm 1*
Lenihan, Bernard James 1902-1960 *WhAm 4*
Lenihan, Ernest Patrick 1873-1936 *NatCAB 28*
Lenihan, Mathias Clement 1854- *NatCAB 13, WhAm 3*
Lenihan, Michael Joseph 1865-1944 *WhAm 2*
Lenihan, Michael Joseph 1865-1958 *WhAm 3*
Lenihan, Thomas Mathias 1845-1901 *ApCAB Sup, NatCAB 12, WhAm 1*
Lenihan, Thomas Matthias 1845-1901 *TwCBDA*
Lenin, Vladimir Ilich 1870-1924 *McGEWB*
Lenin, Vladimir Ilyich 1870-1924 *DcScB*
Lenker, Jesse Luther 1882-1942 *NatCAB 32*
Lenker, John Luther 1908-1964 *WhAm 4*
Lenker, John Nicholas 1858-1929 *DcAmB, NatCAB 21, WhAm 1*
Lenna, Oscar Anrep 1876-1951 *NatCAB 41*
Lennard-Jones, John Edward 1894-1954 *DcScB*
Lenneberg, Eric Heinz 1921-1975 *WhAm 6*
Lennen, Philip Weiting 1887-1955 *WhAm 3*
Lennihan, Richard 1893-1961 *NatCAB 51*
Lennon, Alton Asa 1906- *BiDrAC*
Lennon, John 1940- *McGEWB*
Lennon, John Brown 1849-1923 *NatCAB 25*
Lennon, John Brown 1850-1923 *DcAmB, WhAm 1*
Lennon, Thomas J 1866-1926 *WhAm 1*
Lennox, Charlotte 1720-1804 *AmBi*
Lennox, Charlotte Ramsay 1720-1804 *ApCAB, DcAmB, NatCAB 6, WhAm H*
Lennox, Charlotte Ramsey 1720-1804 *TwCBDA*
Lennox, Edwin 1878-1956 *WhAm 3*
Lennox, Patrick Joseph 1862-1943 *WhAm 2*
Lennox, William 1850-1936 *NatCAB 40, WhAm 1*

Lennox, William Gordon 1884-1960 *WhAm 4*
Lenoir, Jean Joseph Etienne 1822-1900 *AsBiEn*
Lenoir, Joseph 1822-1861 *ApCAB Sup*
Lenoir, William 1751-1839 *ApCAB, Drake, NatCAB 7, TwCBDA*
LeNotre, Andre 1613-1700 *McGEWB*
Lenox, James 1800-1880 *AmBi, ApCAB, DcAmB, NatCAB 3, TwCBDA, WhAm H*
Lenox, John Powell 1851-1926 *WhAm 1*
Lenox, Robert 1759-1839 *NatCAB 1*
Lenroot, Irvine Luther 1869-1949 *ApCAB X, BiDrAC, DcAmB S4, NatCAB 37, WhAm 2, WhAmP*
Lensen, Serge 1893-1961 *NatCAB 46*
Lensing, William Bernard 1872-1951 *NatCAB 40*
Lenski, Lois 1893-1974 *WhAm 6*
Lenski, Richard Charles Henry 1864-1936 *NatCAB 27, WhAm 1, WhAm 1C*
Lent, Abraham E *NewYHSD*
Lent, Frank T *IIBEAAW*
Lent, Frederick 1872-1942 *WhAm 2*
Lent, James 1782-1833 *BiAUS, BiDrAC, WhAm H*
Lent, Louis P 1820?- *NewYHSD*
Lent, Mary Simons 1865- *WomWWA 14*
Lent, Norman Frederick 1905-1956 *NatCAB 46*
Lente, Ellen Kemble *WomWWA 14*
Lente, Frederick Divoux 1823-1883 *ApCAB, NatCAB 7*
Lentelli, Leo 1879-1961 *WhAm 4*
Lenthall, John 1807-1882 *DcAmB, NatCAB 26, WhAm H*
Lentine, Joseph 1906-1970 *WhAm 5*
Lentz, Arthur George d1974 *WhAm 6*
Lentz, Bernard 1881-1961 *WhAm 4*
Lentz, John Jacob 1856-1931 *BiDrAC, TwCBDA, WhAm 1*
Lentz, Max Carl Guenther 1857-1924 *WhAm 1*
Lentz, Oscar Hubert 1919-1963 *NatCAB 52*
Lenygon, Francis Henry 1877-1943 *NatCAB 31, WhAm 2*
Lenz, Charles Otto 1868-1955 *NatCAB 43*
Lenz, Emil Khristianovich 1804-1865 *DcScB*
Lenz, Heinrich Friedrich Emil 1804-1865 *AsBiEn*
Lenz, Maurice 1890-1974 *WhAm 6*
Lenz, Oscar Louis 1873-1912 *NatCAB 17*
Lenz, Sidney S 1873-1960 *WhAm 3A*
Leo *DcScB*
Leo I 400?-461 *McGEWB*
Leo III 680?-741 *McGEWB*
Leo IX 1002-1054 *McGEWB*
Leo X 1475-1521 *McGEWB*
Leo XIII 1810-1903 *McGEWB*
Leo Suavius *DcScB*
Leo The African 1485?-1554? *DcScB*
Leo The Mathematician 790?-869? *DcScB*
Leo, Brother Z 1881- *WhAm 6*
Leodamas Of Thasos *DcScB*
Leon, Alonso De 1640?- *ApCAB*
Leon, Antonio 1794-1847 *ApCAB*
Leon, Harry Joshua 1896-1967 *WhAm 5*
Leon, Juan Velazquez De d1520 *ApCAB*
Leon, Maurice 1880-1952 *WhAm 4*
Leon, Moses De 1250?-1305 *McGEWB*
Leon, Rene 1882-1965 *NatCAB 51*
Leonard, Abiel 1797-1863 *TwCBDA*
Leonard, Abiel 1848-1903 *ApCAB Sup, NatCAB 12, TwCBDA, WhAm 1*
Leonard, Adna B 1837-1916 *WhAm 1*
Leonard, Adna Wright 1874-1943 *NatCAB 33, WhAm 2*
Leonard, Agnes 1842- *ApCAB*
Leonard, Albert 1857-1931 *WhAm 1, WhAm 1C*
Leonard, Alexander Thomas 1858-1939 *WhAm 1*
Leonard, Alton William 1873-1959 *WhAm 3*
Leonard, Anna Byford 1843- *AmWom*
Leonard, Anton *NewYHSD*
Leonard, Arthur Gray 1865-1932 *WhAm 1*
Leonard, Arthur Newton 1870-1950 *NatCAB 39*
Leonard, Arthur Thomas 1894-1968 *WhAm 5*
Leonard, Carrie Boyd 1856- *WomWWA 14*

Leonard, Charles Hall 1822-1918 *WhAm 1*
Leonard, Charles Henri 1850-1925 *WhAm 1*
Leonard, Charles Leslie 1864- *WhAm 4*
Leonard, Charles Lester 1861-1913 *DcAmB*
Leonard, Charles Ransom 1860- *WhAm 4*
Leonard, Clifford Milton 1879-1956 *WhAm 3*
Leonard, Cynthia H VanName 1828- *AmWom*
Leonard, Daniel 1740-1829 *ApCAB, DcAmB, Drake, McGEWB, NatCAB 25, WhAm H*
Leonard, Delavan Levant 1834-1917 *WhAm 1*
Leonard, Donald William 1903-1950 *NatCAB 38*
Leonard, Fred Churchill 1856-1921 *BiDrAC*
Leonard, Fred Eugene 1866-1922 *WhAm 1*
Leonard, Frederick Charles 1896-1960 *NatCAB 45, WhAm 4*
Leonard, George 1698-1778 *ApCAB, TwCBDA*
Leonard, George 1729-1819 *ApCAB, BiAUS, BiDrAC, Drake, TwCBDA, WhAm H*
Leonard, George 1742-1826 *DcAmB, WhAm H*
Leonard, George Alexander 1886-1956 *NatCAB 45*
Leonard, George Bement 1838-1914 *NatCAB 17*
Leonard, George M *NewYHSD*
Leonard, Harry Ward 1861-1915 *DcAmB*
Leonard, Helen Louise 1861-1922 *AmBi, DcAmB, WebAB*
Leonard, Henry 1876-1945 *WhAm 2*
Leonard, Henry S 1905-1967 *WhAm 4*
Leonard, Henry Sylvester 1874-1963 *NatCAB 51*
Leonard, Herbert Henry 1880- *WhAm 6*
Leonard, Hermon Camp 1823-1916 *NatCAB 24*
Leonard, Hiram James 1881-1948 *NatCAB 40*
Leonard, Jack E 1911-1973 *WhAm 5*
Leonard, James *NewYHSD*
Leonard, James Abraham 1854-1918 *NatCAB 19*
Leonard, James Dennis 1896-1963 *NatCAB 50*
Leonard, James Herron 1842-1915 *NatCAB 17*
Leonard, James T d1832 *Drake*
Leonard, Jane Elizabeth 1840-1924 *WhAm 1*
Leonard, Joel Marvin 1852-1916 *WhAm 1*
Leonard, John Charles 1903-1966 *WhAm 4*
Leonard, John Edwards 1845-1878 *ApCAB, BiDrAC, NatCAB 5, WhAm H*
Leonard, John Ireson 1886-1961 *NatCAB 54*
Leonard, John Walter 1868-1938 *WhAm 1*
Leonard, Jonah FitzRandolph 1832- *WhAm 1*
Leonard, Jonathan Norton 1903-1975 *WhAm 6*
Leonard, Joseph 1751-1842 *NatCAB 12*
Leonard, Joseph Alexander 1830- *WhAm 1*
Leonard, Levi Washburn 1773-1864 *ApCAB*
Leonard, Levi Washburn 1790-1864 *BiDAmEd, DcAmB, Drake, NatCAB 26, WhAm H*
Leonard, Mary Cleavland Johnston 1857- *WomWWA 14*
Leonard, Mary Finley 1862- *WhAm 4, WomWWA 14*
Leonard, Mary Hall 1847-1921 *NatCAB 20, WhAm 1*
Leonard, Merrill Dana 1863-1953 *NatCAB 43*
Leonard, Moses Gage 1809-1899 *BiAUS, BiDrAC, NatCAB 8*
Leonard, Nathan Ransom 1832-1917 *NatCAB 25*
Leonard, Neil 1898-1968 *NatCAB 55, WhAm 5*
Leonard, Nellie Mabel 1875-1956 *WhAm 3*
Leonard, Nicholas Germain 1744-1793 *ApCAB*
Leonard, Orville R 1834- *NatCAB 12*
Leonard, Paul Holland 1889-1963 *NatCAB 52*
Leonard, Pauline Wiggin 1869- *WomWWA 14*
Leonard, Priscilla *NotAW*
Leonard, Richard 1780-1833 *ApCAB*
Leonard, Robert Bruce 1910-1973 *WhAm 6*
Leonard, Robert Josselyn 1885-1929 *BiDAmEd, DcAmB, NatCAB 25, WhAm 1*
Leonard, Robert Walton 1910-1967 *WhAm 5*
Leonard, Russell Henry 1888-1949 *WhAm 3*
Leonard, Stephen Banks 1793-1876 *BiAUS, BiDrAC, TwCBDA, WhAm H*
Leonard, Sterling Andrus 1888-1931 *BiDAmEd, DcAmB, NatCAB 26, WhAm 1*
Leonard, Thomas 1877-1954 *NatCAB 42*

Leonard, Thomas Dimock 1872-1957 *NatCAB 45*
Leonard, Veader 1888-1947 *NatCAB 36*
Leonard, Walter Anderson 1880- *WhAm 6*
Leonard, Ward 1861-1915 *NatCAB 15*
Leonard, Warren Henry 1900-1966 *NatCAB 52, WhAm 5*
Leonard, William Andrew 1848-1930 *DcAmB, NatCAB 7, NatCAB 24, TwCBDA, WhAm 1*
Leonard, William Andrews 1848-1930 *ApCAB*
Leonard, William Ellery 1876-1944 *DcAmB S3, NatCAB 33, WhAm 2*
Leonard, William Ezekiel 1865- *WhAm 4*
Leonard, William Henry 1873-1947 *NatCAB 37, WhAm 2*
Leonard, William Henry 1874-1954 *NatCAB 42*
Leonard, William Samuel 1856- *WhAm 4*
Leonard, Zenas 1809-1857 *DcAmB, REnAW, WhAm H*
Leonardo DaVinci 1452-1519 *AsBiEn, DcScB, McGEWB*
Leonardo DaVinci *see also* DaVinci, Leonardo
Leonardo Of Pisa *DcScB*
Leonardo, Richard Anthony 1894-1959 *NatCAB 48*
Leonhard, Charles *NewYHSD*
Leonhard, Karl Casar Von 1779-1862 *DcScB*
Leonhardi, Johann Gottfried 1746-1823 *DcScB*
Leonhardt, Frederick Henry 1873-1956 *NatCAB 44*
Leonhardt, Theodore 1818-1877 *NewYHSD*
Leonhardt, Thomas *NewYHSD*
Leoni, Raul 1905-1972 *WhAm 5*
Leoniceno, Nicolo 1428-1524 *DcScB*
Leonin *McGEWB*
Leonori, R G L *NewYHSD*
Leonowens, Anna Hariette Crawford 1834- *WhAm 4*
Leonowens, Anna Harriette Crawford 1834- *ApCAB*
Leontief, Wassily W 1906- *WebAB*
Leonty, Metropolitan 1876-1965 *WhAm 4*
Leopardi, Giacomo 1798-1837 *McGEWB*
Leopold I 1790-1865 *McGEWB*
Leopold II 1747-1792 *McGEWB*
Leopold II 1835-1909 *McGEWB*
Leopold III 1901- *McGEWB, WhWW-II*
Leopold I, Prince Of Anhalt Dessau 1676-1747 *WhoMilH*
Leopold, Aldo 1886-1948 *DcAmB S4, EncAAH, REnAW, WhAm HA, WhAm 2, WhAm 4A*
Leopold, Aldo 1887-1948 *WebAB*
Leopold, Charles Stein 1896-1960 *NatCAB 48, WhAm 4*
Leopold, Francis *NewYHSD*
Leopold, Isaiah Edwin *WebAB*
Leotti, George *NewYHSD*
Leovy, Frank Adair 1870-1949 *NatCAB 39*
Leovy, Henry Jefferson 1826- *NatCAB 9*
Leovy, Victor 1867-1942 *WhAm 2*
Lepage, Michel *NewYHSD*
LePage DuPratz *NewYHSD*
LePage DuPratz, Antoine Simon *DcAmB*
LePaige, Constantin 1852-1929 *DcScB*
Lepekhin, Ivan Ivanovich 1740-1802 *DcScB*
Lepelletier, Michael *NewYHSD*
LePere, John Gardner 1869-1949 *NatCAB 36*
LePlay, Pierre Guillaume Frederic 1806-1882 *McGEWB*
LePlongeon, Alice D 1851- *AmWom*
LePoivre, Jacques-Francois *DcScB*
Lepoutre, Jacques 1893-1956 *NatCAB 44*
Leppard, Benjamin Arnold 1921-1966 *NatCAB 54*
Leppart, John Culver 1898-1968 *NatCAB 55, WhAm 5*
LePrince, Joseph Augustin 1875- *WhAm 5*
Leprohon, Jean Lukin 1822- *ApCAB*
Leprohon, Rosanna Eleanor 1832-1879 *AmWom*
Leprohon, Rosanna Elenora 1832-1879 *ApCAB*
Leray, Francis Xavier 1825-1887 *ApCAB, NatCAB 5, TwCBDA, WhAm H*
Lerch, Alice Hollister d1951 *WhAm 3*
Lerch, Archer Lynn 1894-1947 *NatCAB 37, WhAm 2*
Lerch, Mathias 1860-1922 *DcScB*

Lerdan, Nicolas Etienne 1761-1826 *ApCAB*
Lerdo DeTejada, Miguel 1812-1861 *McGEWB*
Lerdo DeTejada, Miguel 1814-1861 *ApCAB*
Lerdo DeTejada, Sebastian 1825-1889 *ApCAB*
Lereboullet, Dominique-Auguste 1804-1865 *DcScB*
Leri, Jean De 1534-1611 *Drake*
Lermontov, Mikhail Yurievich 1814-1841 *McGEWB*
Lerner, Joseph J 1887-1954 *WhAm 3*
Lerner, Joseph Solomon 1898-1971 *NatCAB 56, WhAm 5*
Lerner, Leo Alfred 1907-1965 *WhAm 4*
Lerner, Samuel A d1956 *WhAm 3*
LeRossignol, James Edward 1866- *NatCAB 13, WhAm 5*
LeRoux, Bartholomew 1665?-1713 *DcAmB, WhAm H*
LeRoux, Charles *NewYHSD*
LeRoux, Charles 1689-1745 *DcAmB, WhAm H*
Leroux, L *NewYHSD*
LeRow, Caroline Bigelow 1843- *WhAm 4*
LeRoy, Charles 1726-1779 *DcScB*
LeRoy, Edouard 1870-1954 *DcScB*
Leroy, Elizabeth Emmet 1794-1878 *NewYHSD*
LeRoy, Fanny Wayne 1863- *WomWWA 14*
LeRoy, Herman *NatCAB 3*
LeRoy, Howard Sanderson 1891-1949 *NatCAB 38, WhAm 5*
LeRoy, Jean-Baptiste 1720-1800 *DcScB*
Leroy, Louis 1874-1944 *WhAm 2*
Leroy, Paul Eugene Holcombe 1892-1963 *WhAm 4*
LeRoy, Robert 1885-1946 *NatCAB 36*
LeRoy, William Edgar 1817-1888 *ApCAB, Drake*
LeRoy, William Edgar 1818-1888 *NatCAB 4, TwCBDA*
Lerrigo, Charles Henry 1872-1955 *WhAm 3*
Lerrigo, Marion Olive 1898-1968 *WhAm 5*
Lerrigo, Peter Hugh James 1875-1958 *WhAm 3*
Lersner, Victor Alexander 1864-1949 *NatCAB 37, WhAm 3*
Lery, Vicomte De 1754-1824 *ApCAB, Drake*
Lery, Jean De 1534-1611 *ApCAB*
Lery, Joseph Gaspard Chausse-Gros De 1721-1797 *DcAmB*
Lesage, Alain Rene 1668-1747 *McGEWB*
Lesage, George-Louis 1724-1803 *DcScB*
Lescallier, Daniel 1743-1822 *ApCAB*
Lescan, Agnes Francois 1728-1794 *ApCAB*
L'Escarbot, Marc 1590-1630? *ApCAB, Drake*
Lescarboura, Austin Celestin 1891-1962 *NatCAB 49, WhAm 4*
Lescaze, William Edmond 1896-1969 *BnEnAmA, NatCAB 54*
Leschi d1858 *DcAmB, WhAm H*
Lescohier, Alexander William 1885-1951 *WhAm 3*
Lescot, Elle 1883-1974 *WhAm 6*
Lescot, Pierre 1500?-1578 *McGEWB*
Lesem, Alex Mark 1879-1957 *NatCAB 47*
Lesem, Isaac Henry 1847-1928 *ApCAB X*
Lesemann, Louis Frederick William 1869-1941 *WhAm 1*
LeSerrurier, Madame Jacques *NewYHSD*
Lesh, Charles Perry 1859-1927 *NatCAB 21*
Lesh, John Andrew 1879-1939 *WhAm 1*
Lesh, Paul Edgar 1886-1944 *NatCAB 33*
Lesh, Ulysses Samuel 1868- *WhAm 5*
Lesher, Arthur Lawrence 1862-1931 *NatCAB 22*
Lesher, John Vandling 1866-1932 *BiDrAC, WhAm 1*
Lesieur-Desaulniers, Isaac 1811-1868 *ApCAB*
Lesinski, John 1885-1950 *BiDrAC, NatCAB 38, WhAm 3, WhAmP*
Lesinski, John, Jr. 1914- *BiDrAC, WhAmP*
Lesley, Everett Parker 1874-1945 *NatCAB 34*
Lesley, J Peter 1819-1903 *DcAmB, DcScB, NatCAB 8, WhAm 1*
Lesley, John Thomas 1835- *NatCAB 5*
Lesley, Peter 1819-1903 *AmBi, ApCAB, DcAmB, TwCBDA*
Lesley, Robert Whitman 1853-1935 *NatCAB 15, WhAm 1*

Lesley, Susan Inches *ApCAB, WhAm 1*
Leslie, Alexander 1740?-1794 *ApCAB, Drake*
Leslie, Alfred 1927- *BnEnAmA*
Leslie, Amy *WomWWA 14*
Leslie, Amy 1855-1939 *NotAW*
Leslie, Amy 1860- *WhAm 4*
Leslie, Anne 1792-1860? *NewYHSD*
Leslie, Annie Louise 1870-1948 *WhAm 2*
Leslie, Annie Louise Brown 1869-1948 *NotAW*
Leslie, Charles Robert 1794-1859 *ApCAB, DcAmB, Drake, NatCAB 5, NewYHSD, TwCBDA, WhAm H*
Leslie, Eliza 1787-1858 *ApCAB, DcAmB, Drake, NatCAB 7, NewYHSD, NotAW, WhAm H*
Leslie, Elmer Archibald 1888-1965 *WhAm 4*
Leslie, Frank 1821-1880 *AmBi, ApCAB, DcAmB, EncAB, NatCAB 3, NewYHSD, TwCBDA, WebAB, WhAm H*
Leslie, Frank 1842- *REnAW*
Leslie, Mrs. Frank 1851-1914 *AmWom, WhAm 1*
Leslie, Mrs. Frank 1861- *WomWWA 14*
Leslie, Frank Elliott 1873-1951 *WhAm 3*
Leslie, Gaylard Millard 1878-1943 *NatCAB 32*
Leslie, Harry Braham 1904-1973 *WhAm 6*
Leslie, Harry Guyer 1878-1937 *NatCAB 29, WhAm 1*
Leslie, James 1786-1873 *ApCAB*
Leslie, John *NewYHSD*
Leslie, John 1766-1832 *DcScB*
Leslie, John Douglass 1860-1935 *WhAm 1*
Leslie, John L *NewYHSD*
Leslie, Joseph Alexander, Jr. 1894-1972 *WhAm 5*
Leslie, Mary *WomWWA 14*
Leslie, Miriam Florence Folline 1836?-1914 *ApCAB, DcAmB, NatCAB 25, NotAW, TwCBDA, WebAB*
Leslie, Norman Henry 1898- *WhAm 3*
Leslie, Preston Hopkins 1819-1907 *ApCAB, BiAUS, NatCAB 11, NatCAB 13, TwCBDA, WhAm 1*
Leslie, R C *NewYHSD*
Leslie, S Inglis 1880-1967 *NatCAB 52*
Leslie, Thomas Jefferson 1796-1874 *ApCAB*
Leslie, Warren 1871-1952 *NatCAB 41*
Lesniewski, Stanislaw 1886-1939 *DcScB*
Lesourd, Howard Marion 1889-1972 *WhAm 5*
L'Esperance, Elise Strang d1959 *WhAm 3*
L'Esperance, Elsie Strang *WomWWA 14*
Lespinasse, Victor Darwin 1878-1946 *WhAm 2*
Lesquereux, Leo 1806-1889 *AmBi, ApCAB, DcAmB, DcScB, NatCAB 9, TwCBDA, WhAm H*
Less, William L, II d1964 *WhAm 4*
Lessells, John Moyes 1888-1961 *WhAm 4*
Lessen, Ferdinand *NewYHSD*
Lessenberry, David Daniel 1896- *BiDAmEd*
Lessenger, Waldo Emerson 1898- *WhAm 3*
Lesseps, Ferdinand Marie, Vicomte De 1805-1894 *McGEWB*
Lesseps, Ferdinand Marie, Viscount De 1805-1894 *ApCAB*
Lesser, Myer 1874-1954 *NatCAB 46*
Lessing, Gotthold Ephraim 1729-1781 *McGEWB*
Lessing, Gunther R 1887-1965 *WhAm 4*
Lessing, Otto Eduard 1875- *WhAm 5*
Lessler, Montague 1869-1938 *BiDrAC, WhAm 5*
Lessley, Eliza Popjoy *WomWWA 14*
Lessley, William James *NewYHSD*
Lesslie, James 1802-1885 *ApCAB*
Lessner, Frederick *NewYHSD*
Lesson, Rene-Primevere 1794-1849 *DcScB*
Lester, Bernadotte Perrin 1896-1974 *WhAm 6*
Lester, Charles Cooke 1850- *WhAm 4*
Lester, Charles Edward 1815-1890 *WhAm H*
Lester, Charles Edwards 1815-1890 *ApCAB, DcAmB, Drake, NatCAB 13, TwCBDA*
Lester, Charles Smith 1824-1903 *ApCAB, WhAm 1*
Lester, Clarence Brown 1877-1951 *WhAm 3*
Lester, E F 1871- *WhAm 1*
Lester, Fanny Boggs 1858- *WomWWA 14*
Lester, George Nelson 1824-1892 *BiDConf*
Lester, James Allen 1891-1958 *NatCAB 46,*

WhAm 3
Lester, James Westcott 1859-1932 *NatCAB 23, WhAm 1*
Lester, John Angelo 1864- *WhoColR*
Lester, John Crego 1856-1937 *NatCAB 28*
Lester, Oliver Clarence 1873-1951 *WhAm 3*
Lester, Orrin Clifford 1878-1958 *WhAm 3*
Lester, Posey Green 1850-1929 *BiDrAC, TwCBDA*
Lester, Robert MacDonald 1889-1969 *DcAmLiB, NatCAB 55, WhAm 5*
Lester, Rufus Ezekiel 1837-1906 *BiDrAC, NatCAB 16, TwCBDA, WhAm 1, WhAmP*
Lester, Thomas Bryan 1824-1888 *ApCAB Sup*
Lester, William 1889-1956 *WhAm 3*
LeSueur *ApCAB*
LeSueur, Arthur 1867- *WhAm 4*
Lesueur, Charles Alexandre 1778-1846 *DcScB*
Lesueur, Charles Alexander 1778-1846 *NatCAB 8, TwCBDA*
Lesueur, Charles Alexandre 1778-1846 *DcAmB, NewYHSD, WhAm H*
LeSueur, Pierre Charles 1657?-1705? *AmBi, DcAmB, WhAm H*
Letcher, John 1812-1884 *BiDConf*
Letcher, John 1813-1884 *AmBi, ApCAB, BiAUS, BiDrAC, DcAmB, Drake, McGEWB, NatCAB 5, TwCBDA, WhAm H, WhAmP*
Letcher, John Talbert 1881- *WhAm 1*
Letcher, Marion 1872-1948 *WhAm 2*
Letcher, Robert Perkins 1788-1861 *ApCAB, BiAUS, BiDrAC, DcAmB, Drake, NatCAB 13, TwCBDA, WhAm H, WhAmP*
Letchworth, Edward Hance 1881-1958 *WhAm 3*
Letchworth, Josiah 1836-1913 *NatCAB 15*
Letchworth, Ogden Pearl 1851-1939 *NatCAB 31*
Letchworth, William Pryor 1823-1910 *DcAmB, NatCAB 15, WhAm 1*
LeTenneur, Jacques-Alexandre d1652? *DcScB*
Lethiere, Guillaume Guillon 1760-1832 *ApCAB*
Letmate, Frederick W *NewYHSD*
LeTonnelier DeBreteuil *DcScB*
LeTourneau, Robert Gilmour 1888-1969 *WhAm 5*
Letourneau, Severin 1871- *WhAm 5*
Lett, Sherwood 1895-1961 *WhAm 4*
Lettenberger, Joseph 1873-1955 *NatCAB 42*
Letterman, Jonathan 1824-1872 *DcAmB, NatCAB 18, WebAMB, WhAm H*
Letton, Charles Blair 1853- *WhAm 1*
Letton, Ralph *NewYHSD*
Lettow-Vorbeck, Paul Emil Von 1870-1964 *WhoMilH*
Letts, Arthur 1862-1923 *NatCAB 13, NatCAB 38, WhAm 1*
Letts, Cora Perkins 1874- *WomWWA 14*
Letts, F Dickinson 1875-1965 *NatCAB 50, WhAm 4*
Letts, Frank Crawford 1861- *NatCAB 14*
Letts, Fred Dickinson 1875-1965 *BiDrAC*
Letts, Ira Lloyd 1889-1947 *WhAm 2*
Letts, John Cowen 1861-1935 *NatCAB 47*
Lettsom, John Coakley 1744-1815 *BiHiMed*
Leuba, James Henry 1868-1946 *WhAm 2*
Leucippus 490?BC- *AsBiEn, DcScB*
Leuckart, Karl Georg Friedrich Rudolf 1822-1898 *AsBiEn, DcScB*
Leupp, Francis Ellington 1849-1918 *DcAmB, NatCAB 15, WhAm 1*
Leupp, Harold Lewis 1877-1952 *WhAm 3*
Leurechon, Jean 1591?-1670 *DcScB*
Leuret, Francois 1797-1851 *DcScB*
Leuschner, Armin Otto 1868-1953 *WhAm 3*
Leutner, Winfred George 1879-1961 *WhAm 4*
Leutwiler, Oscar Adolph 1877-1953 *WhAm 3*
Leutze, Emanuel Gottlieb 1816-1868 *AmBi, ApCAB, BiAUS, BnEnAmA, DcAmB, Drake, IlBEAAW, NatCAB 12, NewYHSD, TwCBDA, WebAB, WhAm H*
Leutze, Eugene Henry Cozzens 1847-1931 *ApCAB, NatCAB 16, TwCBDA, WhAm 1*
Leutze, Trevor William 1877- *WhAm 5*

Lev, Ray d1968 *WhAm 5*
Lev, Saul Nathan 1910-1974 *WhAm 6*
Levaditi, Constantin 1874-1953 *DcScB*
Levadoux, Michael 1746-1815 *WhAm H*
Levaillant, Francois 1753-1824 *DcScB*
LeValley, Laura A Woodin *AmWom, WomWWA 14*
LeVan, Daniel Hayden 1890-1961 *NatCAB 50*
LeVan, William Barnet 1829- *ApCAB, TwCBDA*
Levand, Louis 1887-1953 *WhAm 3*
Levand, Max M 1892-1960 *WhAm 3, WhAm 4*
Levant, Oscar 1906-1972 *WhAm 5*
LeVau, Louis 1612-1670 *McGEWB*
Leveck, John Herbert 1866-1958 *NatCAB 48*
LeVee, Raymond Nathaniel 1903-1968 *NatCAB 54*
Leven, Alexander Leslie, Earl Of 1580-1661 *WhoMilH*
Levene, Alexander 1885-1967 *NatCAB 51*
Levene, Phoebus Aaron Theodor 1869-1940 *AsBiEn, DcScB*
Levene, Phoebus Aaron Theodore 1869-1940 *DcAmB S2, WhAm 1*
Levengood, Claude Anderson 1910-1975 *WhAm 6*
Levenson, Joseph Richmond 1920-1969 *NatCAB 55, WhAm 5*
Levenson, Walter Sabin 1897-1950 *NatCAB 39*
Leventhal, Albert Rice 1907-1976 *WhAm 6*
Leventhal, Jules 1889-1949 *NatCAB 38*
Leventhal, Michael Leo 1901-1971 *NatCAB 56*
Leventhorpe, Collett 1815-1889 *NatCAB 7*
Leventhorpe, Collett 1816-1889 *ApCAB Sup*
Leventritt, David 1845-1926 *NatCAB 14, NatCAB 24, WhAm 1*
Leventritt, M Victor 1914-1968 *NatCAB 53*
Leveque, Joseph Mark 1868-1911 *WhAm 1*
Lever, Asbury Francis 1875-1940 *BiDrAC, DcAmB S2, EncAAH, WhAm 1, WhAmP*
Lever, Hayley 1876-1958 *WhAm 3*
Lever, John C W 1811-1858 *BiHiMed*
Lever, Michael 1908-1972 *NatCAB 57*
Levere, William C 1872-1927 *WhAm 1*
Leverett, Frank 1859-1943 *DcAmB S3, NatCAB 10, NatCAB 32, WhAm 2*
Leverett, Frederic Percival 1803-1836 *Drake*
Leverett, Frederick Percival 1803-1836 *ApCAB*
Leverett, George Vasmer 1846-1917 *ApCAB X, WhAm 1*
Leverett, Sir John 1616-1679 *AmBi, ApCAB, DcAmB, Drake, NatCAB 3, WhAm H*
Leverett, John 1662-1724 *ApCAB, DcAmB, Drake, NatCAB 6, TwCBDA, WhAm H*
Leverett, Warren Hamilton 1886-1971 *NatCAB 56*
Leverhulme, Viscount 1888-1949 *WhAm 2*
Leverich, Henry Priestley 1907-1959 *WhAm 3*
Leverich, William d1677 *Drake*
Leveridge, John 1792-1886 *ApCAB*
Leveridge, Phyllis Mayer 1868- *WomWWA 14*
Levering, Albert 1869-1929 *WhAm 1*
Levering, Eugene, Jr. 1845-1928 *NatCAB 21, WhAm 1*
Levering, Grace Wade 1883- *WomWWA 14*
Levering, Griffith George 1900-1955 *NatCAB 45*
Levering, Joseph Mortimer 1849-1908 *DcAmB, NatCAB 24*
Levering, Joshua 1845-1935 *ApCAB Sup, NatCAB 29, TwCBDA, WhAm 1*
Levering, Julia Henderson 1851- *WomWWA 14*
Levering, Robert Woodrow 1914- *BiDrAC*
Levermore, Charles Herbert 1856-1927 *DcAmB, NatCAB 5, NatCAB 33, TwCBDA, WhAm 1*
Leverone, Louis Edward 1880-1957 *WhAm 3*
Leverone, Nathaniel 1884-1969 *NatCAB 55, WhAm 5*
Leveroni, Frank 1879-1948 *NatCAB 36, WhAm 2*
Leverrier, Urbain Jean Joseph 1811-1877 *AsBiEn, DcScB, McGEWB*
Leverson, Montague R 1830- *WhAm 4*
LeVert *NewYHSD*

LeVert, Octavia Celeste Walton 1811-1877 *NotAW*
LeVert, Octavia Walton 1810?-1877 *ApCAB, NatCAB 6, TwCBDA*
LeVert, Octavia Walton 1820?- *Drake*
Leveson Gower, William Spencer 1880-1953 *WhAm 3*
Levesque, Eugene d1852 *Drake*
Levett, Benjamin Arthur 1873- *WhAm 5*
Levett, David Maurice 1844-1914 *WhAm 1*
Levett, David Morris 1844-1914 *NatCAB 7*
Levey, Charles Mack 1858-1929 *WhAm 1*
Levey, Edgar Coleman 1881-1962 *NatCAB 50, WhAm 4*
Levey, Harold Alvin 1889-1967 *NatCAB 53*
Levey, Martin 1913-1970 *NatCAB 56, WhAm 5*
Levey, Stanley 1915-1967 *NatCAB 54*
Levi BenGershon 1288-1344? *McGEWB*
Levi BenGerson 1288-1344? *DcScB*
Levi, Carlo 1902-1975 *McGEWB, WhAm 6*
Levi, Gerson Baruch 1878-1939 *AmBi, WhAm 1*
Levi, Giuseppe 1872-1965 *DcScB*
Levi, Harry 1875- *WhAm 5*
Levi, Isaac *NewYHSD*
Levi, Julian Clarence 1874-1971 *WhAm 5*
Levi, Kate Everest 1859- *WomWWA 14*
Levi, Moritz 1857- *WhAm 4*
Levi-Civita, Tullio 1873-1941 *DcScB*
Levi-Strauss, Claude Gustave 1908- *McGEWB*
Levick, James Jones 1824-1893 *NatCAB 9*
Levie, John E *NewYHSD*
Levien, Sara A 1888- *WomWWA 14*
Leviero, Anthony Harry 1905-1956 *WhAm 3*
Levin, Isaac 1866-1945 *WhAm 2*
Levin, Jack 1898-1974 *WhAm 6*
Levin, Joseph Jay 1897-1972 *WhAm 5*
Levin, Leonard S 1874-1952 *WhAm 3*
Levin, Lewis Charles 1808-1860 *ApCAB, BiAUS, BiDrAC, DcAmB, NatCAB 25, TwCBDA, WhAm H, WhAmP*
Levin, Louis 1897-1947 *NatCAB 34*
Levin, Theodore 1897-1970 *WhAm 5*
Levine, Harry Harvey 1919-1969 *WhAm 5*
Levine, Jack 1915- *BnEnAmA, WebAB*
Levine, Les 1935- *BnEnAmA*
Levine, Manuel 1881- *WhAm 1*
Levine, Marks 1890-1971 *WhAm 5*
Levine, Maurice 1902-1971 *NatCAB 57, WhAm 5*
Levine, Max 1889-1967 *WhAm 4*
Levine, Michael 1886-1952 *NatCAB 39*
Levine, Morris 1900-1972 *WhAm 5*
Levine, Samuel Albert 1891-1966 *WhAm 4*
Levine, Victor Emanuel 1891-1963 *NatCAB 54*
Levine, Victor Emanuel 1892-1963 *WhAm 4*
Levinge, Sir Richard George Augustus 1811-1884 *NewYHSD*
Levinger, David 1887-1956 *WhAm 3*
Levinger, Elma Ehrlich 1887-1958 *WhAm 3*
Levinger, Lee Joseph 1890-1966 *WhAm 4*
Levings, Alfred Hamilton 1847-1918 *NatCAB 17*
Levings, Miriam Fairbank 1900-1969 *WhAm 5*
Levings, Noah 1796-1849 *ApCAB*
Levins, Thomas C 1789-1843 *DcAmB, WhAm H*
LeVinsen, Florenza D'Arona *WhAm 5*
Levinson, Abraham 1888-1955 *WhAm 3*
Levinson, David 1884-1964 *NatCAB 50*
Levinson, David 1889-1973 *WhAm 6*
Levinson, Edwin David 1875-1954 *NatCAB 43*
Levinson, Norman 1912-1975 *WhAm 6*
Levinson, Salmon Oliver 1865-1941 *ApCAB X, DcAmB S3, NatCAB 31, WhAm 1*
Levinson-Lessing, Franz Yulevich 1861-1939 *DcScB*
Levinthal, Bernard Louis 1865-1952 *WhAm 3*
Levis, Francois Gaston, Duc De 1720-1787 *ApCAB, Drake*
Levis, George McClellan 1854-1933 *NatCAB 40*
Levis, J Preston 1901-1973 *WhAm 6*
Levis, William Edward 1890-1962 *NatCAB 50, WhAm 4*
Levison, Jacob Bertha 1862-1947 *WhAm 2*
Levison, Wallace Goold 1846-1924 *NatCAB 19*

Levitan, Solomon 1862-1940 *WhAm 1*
Levitas, Arnold 1879-1934 *WhAm 1*
Levitas, Samuel M 1894-1961 *WhAm 4*
Levitsky, Louis Moses 1897-1975 *WhAm 6*
Levitt, Albert 1887-1968 *WhAm 5*
Levitt, Robert Daniels 1910-1958 *WhAm 3*
Levitt, Thomas J 1890-1953 *NatCAB 40*
Levitzki, Mischa 1898-1941 *WhAm 1*
Levly, Morris *NewYHSD*
Levorsen, Arville Irving 1894-1965 *NatCAB 50*
Levowitz, David 1908-1967 *NatCAB 54*
Levy, Adele Rosenwald 1892-1960 *WhAm 3A*
Levy, Alexander Oscar 1881-1947 *WhAm 2*
Levy, Arthur Joseph 1897-1972 *NatCAB 57*
Levy, Austin Theodore 1880-1951 *NatCAB 45, WhAm 3*
Levy, Beatrice A 1890- *WomWWA 14*
Levy, Clifton Harby 1867- *WhAm 5*
Levy, Daniel Frederick 1893-1959 *NatCAB 47*
Levy, David *BiDrAC, TwCBDA, WhAm H*
Levy, Edgar M 1822-1906 *WhAm 1*
Levy, Edward Dailey 1879-1966 *WhAm 4*
Levy, Ernest Coleman 1868-1938 *WhAm 1*
Levy, Felix Alexander 1884-1963 *WhAm 4*
Levy, Florence Nightingale 1870-1947 *BiDAmEd, NotAW, WomWWA 14*
Levy, Harriet Mooney *WomWWA 14*
Levy, Henrietta Platnauer 1868- *WomWWA 14*
Levy, Henry Titche 1887-1954 *NatCAB 42*
Levy, Herbert 1897-1966 *WhAm 4*
Levy, I Montefiore 1881-1960 *NatCAB 46*
Levy, Irving J 1904-1951 *WhAm 3*
Levy, Isaac D 1892-1975 *WhAm 6*
Levy, Jefferson Monroe 1852-1924 *BiDrAC, NatCAB 17, WhAm 1, WhAmP*
Levy, John *NewYHSD*
Levy, Joseph Leonard 1865-1917 *ApCAB X, DcAmB, NatCAB 14, WhAm 1*
Levy, Leo S 1886-1961 *WhAm 4*
Levy, Louis 1889-1952 *NatCAB 42*
Levy, Louis Edward 1846-1919 *DcAmB, NatCAB 13, WhAm 1*
Levy, Marx Meyer 1869-1951 *NatCAB 40*
Levy, Matthew Malltz 1899-1971 *WhAm 5*
Levy, Maurice 1838-1910 *DcScB*
Levy, Maurice Ambrose 1874-1939 *WhAm 1*
Levy, Max 1857-1926 *DcAmB, WhAm 1*
Levy, Moses *NewYHSD*
Levy, Nathan 1909- *WhAm 6*
Levy, Newman 1888-1966 *WhAm 4*
Levy, Raphael 1900-1969 *WhAm 5*
Levy, Richard Butt 1866-1949 *NatCAB 38*
Levy, Robert 1864-1945 *NatCAB 37, WhAm 2*
Levy, Robert J 1902-1974 *WhAm 6*
Levy, Robert Louis 1888-1974 *WhAm 6*
Levy, Robert Michael 1916-1974 *WhAm 6*
Levy, Russell David 1903-1966 *WhAm 4*
Levy, Samuel D 1860-1940 *WhAm 1*
Levy, Samuel Henry 1860-1953 *NatCAB 40*
Levy, Samuel Maurice 1883-1947 *NatCAB 36*
Levy, Samuel Morris 1872-1941 *NatCAB 33*
Levy, Saul 1891-1964 *WhAm 4*
Levy, Serve-Dieu Abailard 1795-1841 *DcScB*
Levy, Uriah Phillips d1862 *Drake*
Levy, Uriah Phillips 1792-1862 *DcAmB, WebAB, WebAMB, WhAm H*
Levy, Uriah Phillips 1795?-1862 *ApCAB*
Levy, William Mallory 1827-1882 *BiAUS, BiDrAC, WhAm H*
Levy-Bruhl, Lucien 1857-1939 *McGEWB*
LeWald, Leon Theodore 1874-1962 *NatCAB 50, WhAm 5*
Lewandowska, Maidelle De 1876- *WomWWA 14*
Lewars, Elsie Singmaster 1879- *WomWWA 14*
Lewelling, Henderson 1809-1878 *DcAmB*
Lewelling, Lorenzo Dow 1846-1900 *DcAmB, NatCAB 8, TwCBDA, WhAm 1, WhAmP*
Lewers, Robert 1862-1922 *WhAm 1*
Lewers, Samuel *NewYHSD*
Lewey, Matthew McFarland 1844- *WhoColR*
Lewi, Emily 1867- *WomWWA 14*
Lewi, Isidor 1850-1939 *WhAm 1*
Lewi, Maurice J 1857-1957 *NatCAB 45*
Lewin, Adolph Leo 1871-1953 *NatCAB 42*
Lewin, C L *NewYHSD*

Lewin, Charles J 1902-1965 *WhAm 4*
Lewin, James M 1836-1877 *NewYHSD*
Lewin, Kurt 1890-1947 *DcAmB S4, McGEWB, WhAm 2*
Lewin, Philip 1888-1960 *WhAm 4*
Lewin, Raphael DeCordova 1844-1886 *ApCAB*
Lewine, Jerome 1885-1962 *WhAm 4*
Lewing, Adele 1866- *WhAm 4*
Lewing, Adele 1868- *AmWom*
Lewinhoff, Theodore *NewYHSD*
Lewinthal, Isidore 1849-1922 *WhAm 1*
Lewis, A Dennie 1889-1962 *NatCAB 50*
Lewis, Aaron Dennison 1865- *WhAm 4*
Lewis, Abner *BiAUS, BiDrAC, WhAm H*
Lewis, Abram Herbert 1836- *ApCAB Sup, TwCBDA, WhAm 1*
Lewis, Addison 1889-1971 *NatCAB 56*
Lewis, Albert Buell 1867-1940 *WhAm 1*
Lewis, Alexander 1864-1912 *WhAm 1*
Lewis, Alfred Henry d1914 *WhAm 1*
Lewis, Alfred Henry 1855-1914 *NatCAB 25*
Lewis, Alfred Henry 1858?-1914 *AmBi, DcAmB*
Lewis, Alice G *WomWWA 14*
Lewis, Allen 1873-1957 *WhAm 3*
Lewis, Alma Dennie 1889-1962 *WhAm 4*
Lewis, Alonzo 1794-1861 *ApCAB, Drake*
Lewis, Alvin Fayette 1861- *WhAm 4*
Lewis, Amanda Kerr *WomWWA 14*
Lewis, Amelia C 1801?-1820 *NewYHSD*
Lewis, Andrew 1720?-1781 *AmBi, ApCAB, DcAmB, McGEWB, NatCAB 1, REnAW, TwCBDA, WebAMB, WhAm H*
Lewis, Andrew 1730?-1780 *Drake*
Lewis, Arthur 1846-1930 *DcAmB*
Lewis, Arthur 1873- *WhAm 5*
Lewis, Arthur Gardner 1874-1948 *NatCAB 36*
Lewis, Arthur R, Jr. 1909-1954 *WhAm 3*
Lewis, Augusta *NotAW*
Lewis, Austin Warren 1910-1974 *WhAm 6*
Lewis, B Palmer 1874-1949 *WhAm 2*
Lewis, Barbour 1818-1893 *BiDrAC, WhAm H*
Lewis, Barbour 1824-1893 *BiAUS*
Lewis, Bessie Hastings Williams *WomWWA 14*
Lewis, Bill 1895-1961 *NatCAB 48*
Lewis, Bransford 1862-1941 *NatCAB 38, WhAm 1*
Lewis, Burdett Gibson 1882-1966 *WhAm 4*
Lewis, Burwell Boykin 1837-1885 *NatCAB 12*
Lewis, Burwell Boykin 1838-1885 *BiAUS, BiDrAC, TwCBDA, WhAm H*
Lewis, C E *NewYHSD*
Lewis, Calvin Leslie 1868-1935 *WhAm 1*
Lewis, Carolyn Trowbridge 1877- *WomWWA 14*
Lewis, Carrie Bullard 1865- *WomWWA 14*
Lewis, Cecil Day 1904-1972 *McGEWB*
Lewis, Cecil Day *see also* Day-Lewis, Cecil
Lewis, Ceylon Harris 1849-1939 *WhAm 1*
Lewis, Charles d1774 *ApCAB, Drake*
Lewis, Charles 1853-1912 *NatCAB 18*
Lewis, Charles Bertrand 1842-1924 *DcAmB, NatCAB 6, TwCBDA, WhAm 1*
Lewis, Charles Clarke 1857- *WhAm 4*
Lewis, Charles Hance 1816- *BiAUS, NatCAB 12*
Lewis, Charles Henry 1839-1904 *NatCAB 6*
Lewis, Charles Hildreth 1837-1906 *NatCAB 18*
Lewis, Charles Levin 1808-1860 *WhAm H*
Lewis, Charles Lundy 1852- *WhAm 4*
Lewis, Charles McLeod 1894-1955 *NatCAB 42*
Lewis, Charles Swearinger 1821-1878 *BiDrAC, WhAm H*
Lewis, Charles Willard 1860-1904 *TwCBDA, WhAm 1*
Lewis, Charlton Miner 1866-1923 *WhAm 1*
Lewis, Charlton Thomas 1834-1904 *ApCAB, DcAmB, NatCAB 11, NatCAB 38, TwCBDA, WhAm 1*
Lewis, Clarence Irving 1883-1964 *McGEWB, WhAm 4*
Lewis, Clark 1840-1896 *TwCBDA*
Lewis, Clarke 1840-1896 *BiDrAC, WhAm H*
Lewis, Claude Bernard 1878-1957 *NatCAB 42*
Lewis, Claude Isaac 1880-1924 *NatCAB 20, WhAm 1*
Lewis, Clive Staples 1898-1963 *WhAm 4*
Lewis, Cora Gilbert 1866- *WomWWA 14*
Lewis, D B Wyndham 1891-1969 *WhAm 5*

Lewis, Daniel 1846-1919 *NatCAB 7, WhAm 1*
Lewis, Daniel F 1849- *NatCAB 3, WhAm 4*
Lewis, Dave 1870- *WhAm 5*
Lewis, David *NewYHSD*
Lewis, David John 1869-1952 *BiDrAC, NatCAB 39, WhAm 3, WhAmP*
Lewis, David Peter 1820-1884 *BiAUS, BiDConf, NatCAB 10, TwCBDA*
Lewis, David W 1815-1885 *BiDConf*
Lewis, Dean DeWitt 1874-1941 *DcAmB S3, NatCAB 31, WhAm 1*
Lewis, Dio 1823-1886 *ApCAB, NatCAB 10, TwCBDA*
Lewis, Diocesian 1823-1886 *WhAm H*
Lewis, Dioclesian 1823-1886 *AmBi, BiDAmEd, DcAmB*
Lewis, Dixon Hall 1802-1848 *ApCAB, BiAUS, BiDrAC, DcAmB, Drake, NatCAB 4, TwCBDA, WhAm H, WhAmP*
Lewis, Earl Ramage 1887-1956 *BiDrAC*
Lewis, Ebenezer Ellesville 1841-1919 *NatCAB 19, WhAm 1*
Lewis, Edith Rannells 1885- *WomWWA 14*
Lewis, Edmonia 1843?-1909? *IIBEAAW*
Lewis, Edmonia 1845-1909? *ApCAB, NatCAB 5, NotAW, TwCBDA, WhoColR*
Lewis, Edmund Darch 1835-1910 *DcAmB, NatCAB 26, NewYHSD*
Lewis, Edmund Darch 1837-1910 *ApCAB, TwCBDA*
Lewis, Edmund Harris 1884-1972 *WhAm 5*
Lewis, Edward *NewYHSD*
Lewis, Edward D *NewYHSD*
Lewis, Edward Gardner 1869- *WhAm 5*
Lewis, Edward Mann 1863-1949 *NatCAB 38, WhAm 2*
Lewis, Edward McElhiney 1884-1954 *WhAm 3*
Lewis, Edward Morgan 1872-1936 *NatCAB 30, WhAm 1*
Lewis, Edward Parke Custis 1837-1892 *ApCAB, NatCAB 13, TwCBDA*
Lewis, Edward Samuel 1855-1934 *WhAm 1*
Lewis, Edward Taylor 1834-1927 *BiDrAC*
Lewis, Edwin Herbert 1866-1938 *WhAm 1*
Lewis, Edwin James, Jr. 1859-1937 *WhAm 1*
Lewis, Edwin Owen 1879- *WhAm 6*
Lewis, Edwin Seelye 1868-1935 *WhAm 1*
Lewis, Eleanor Parke Custis 1779-1852 *ApCAB*
Lewis, Elias, Jr. 1820-1894 *NatCAB 2*
Lewis, Elijah Banks 1854-1920 *BiDrAC, TwCBDA, WhAm 3, WhAmP*
Lewis, Elijah P *NewYHSD*
Lewis, Elise Lathrop 1874- *WomWWA 14*
Lewis, Elisha Joseph 1820- *ApCAB, Drake*
Lewis, Elizabeth *WomWWA 14*
Lewis, Elizabeth Dabney Langhorne 1851- *WomWWA 14*
Lewis, Elizabeth Foreman 1892-1958 *WhAm 3*
Lewis, Ella Louise Hatch 1865- *WomWWA 14*
Lewis, Ellis 1798-1871 *ApCAB, BiAUS, DcAmB, Drake, NatCAB 10, WhAm H*
Lewis, Ellis Smyser 1870-1941 *NatCAB 30*
Lewis, Emily Augusta Westwood 1877- *WomWWA 14*
Lewis, Emily Sargent 1866- *WomWWA 14*
Lewis, Enoch 1776-1856 *ApCAB, BiDAmEd, DcAmB, Drake, NatCAB 10, WhAm H*
Lewis, Ernest Irving 1873-1947 *NatCAB 43, WhAm 2*
Lewis, Ernest Sidney 1840-1935 *WhAm 1*
Lewis, Ernest Sydney 1840-1935 *NatCAB 11*
Lewis, Ernest William 1875-1927 *NatCAB 34, WhAm 1*
Lewis, Essington 1881-1961 *WhAm 4*
Lewis, Estelle Anna Blanche Robinson 1824-1880 *ApCAB, DcAmB, Drake, NatCAB 10, WhAm H*
Lewis, Eugene Castner 1845-1917 *NatCAB 8, NatCAB 42*
Lewis, Eugene Howard 1852- *WhAm 1*
Lewis, Eugene Richards 1877-1953 *NatCAB 41*
Lewis, Eugene W 1870-1954 *WhAm 3*
Lewis, Eva Jane 1882- *WhoColR*
Lewis, Exum Percival 1863-1926 *DcAmB, NatCAB 20, NatCAB 22, WhAm 1*
Lewis, F Park 1855-1940 *NatCAB 32, WhAm 1*

Lewis, Fielding 1725-1781 *TwCBDA*
Lewis, Fielding 1725-1782? *DcAmB, WhAm H*
Lewis, Fielding 1726-1781 *ApCAB*
Lewis, Fletcher 1869-1955 *WhAm 3*
Lewis, Frances Graham Hoyt 1874- *WomWWA 14*
Lewis, Francis 1713-1802 *AmBi, ApCAB, DcAmB, TwCBDA, WhAm H*
Lewis, Francis 1713-1803 *BiAUS, BiDrAC, Drake, NatCAB 5, WhAmP*
Lewis, Francis Albert 1857- *WhAm 4*
Lewis, Francis Park 1855-1940 *DcAmB S2*
Lewis, Frank Grant 1865-1945 *WhAm 2*
Lewis, Frank J 1842-1916 *NatCAB 16*
Lewis, Frank James 1867-1960 *NatCAB 47, WhAm 4*
Lewis, Frank Stuart 1879-1947 *NatCAB 39*
Lewis, Frank Tapp 1884-1947 *NatCAB 36*
Lewis, Franklin Allan 1904-1958 *WhAm 3*
Lewis, Franklin Crocker 1877-1930 *WhAm 1*
Lewis, Franklin Fillmore 1877-1957 *WhAm 3*
Lewis, Fred 1888-1970 *WhAm 5*
Lewis, Fred B 1878- *WhAm 6*
Lewis, Fred Ewing 1865-1949 *BiDrAC, NatCAB 43, WhAm 2, WhAmP*
Lewis, Fred Justin 1890-1959 *NatCAB 49, WhAm 3*
Lewis, Frederic Thomas 1875-1951 *WhAm 3*
Lewis, Frederick Wheeler 1873-1968 *NatCAB 54, WhAm 5*
Lewis, Fulton, Jr. 1903-1966 *WhAm 4*
Lewis, G Griffin 1865- *WhAm 4*
Lewis, George Albert 1829-1915 *WhAm 1*
Lewis, George Charles 1874-1938 *NatCAB 29*
Lewis, George Chase 1876-1943 *NatCAB 33*
Lewis, George Francis 1885-1953 *WhAm 3*
Lewis, George Henry 1842-1913 *NatCAB 29*
Lewis, George Kenneth 1902-1967 *NatCAB 53*
Lewis, George Lester 1857-1932 *NatCAB 24*
Lewis, George Morris 1899-1966 *WhAm 4*
Lewis, George W *NewYHSD*
Lewis, George William 1882-1948 *DcAmB S4, NatCAB 36, WhAm 2*
Lewis, Gilbert Newton 1875-1946 *AsBiEn, DcAmB S4, DcScB, McGEWB, NatCAB 36, WebAB, WhAm 2*
Lewis, Grace Robbins 1877- *WomWWA 14*
Lewis, Graceanna 1821- *AmWom, NatCAB 9, TwCBDA*
Lewis, Grant Kirkland 1868-1937 *WhAm 1*
Lewis, H Edgar 1882-1948 *WhAm 2*
Lewis, Han *NewYHSD*
Lewis, Harold C 1887-1946 *WhAm 2*
Lewis, Harold M 1889-1973 *WhAm 6*
Lewis, Harold Wilcox 1896-1964 *NatCAB 54*
Lewis, Harry Herbert 1891- *WhAm 3*
Lewis, Harry Sinclair 1885-1951 *DcAmB S5, EncAB*
Lewis, Harry Slocum 1882-1950 *NatCAB 51*
Lewis, Henry 1819-1904 *IIBEAAW, NewYHSD, WhAm H*
Lewis, Henry 1871-1932 *WhAm 1, WhAm 1C*
Lewis, Henry Carleton 1873- *WhAm 5*
Lewis, Henry Carvill 1853-1888 *AmBi, ApCAB, NatCAB 5, TwCBDA*
Lewis, Henry Gould 1820-1891 *NatCAB 5*
Lewis, Henry Harrison 1863- *WhAm 4*
Lewis, Henry Latane 1876-1943 *NatCAB 34*
Lewis, Henry Llewellyn Daingerfield 1843-1893 *TwCBDA*
Lewis, Henry Steele 1900-1954 *WhAm 3*
Lewis, Henry Thomas 1847-1903 *WhAm 1*
Lewis, Herbert Lefkovitz 1898-1971 *WhAm 5*
Lewis, Herbert Wesley 1859- *WhAm 4*
Lewis, Homer Pierce 1849- *WhAm 4*
Lewis, Howard 1877-1950 *WhAm 3*
Lewis, Howard Augustus 1890-1963 *WhAm 4*
Lewis, Howard Bishop 1887-1954 *NatCAB 41, WhAm 3*
Lewis, Howard Bradbury 1900-1957 *NatCAB 46*
Lewis, Howard Corwin 1890-1952 *WhAm 3*
Lewis, Howard Worthington 1855-1940 *NatCAB 30*
Lewis, Hugh Alban 1893-1964 *WhAm 4*
Lewis, I B *NewYHSD*
Lewis, Ida d1911 *WhAm 1*

Lewis, Ida 1841-1911 *AmBi, AmWom, ApCAB, NatCAB 5*
Lewis, Ida 1842-1911 *NotAW*
Lewis, Irving Jefferson d1927 *WhAm 1*
Lewis, Irving Stanton 1919-1971 *WhAm 5*
Lewis, Isaac d1854 *ApCAB*
Lewis, Isaac Chauncey 1812- *NatCAB 10*
Lewis, Isaac Newton 1848-1931 *ApCAB X*
Lewis, Isaac Newton 1858-1931 *AmBi, DcAmB, NatCAB 16, WebAMB, WhAm 1*
Lewis, Isabel Eleanor Martin 1881- *WomWWA 14*
Lewis, Ivy Foreman 1882-1964 *WhAm 4*
Lewis, J Edward, Jr. 1909-1966 *NatCAB 51*
Lewis, J Volney 1869-1969 *WhAm 5*
Lewis, J Wilbur 1892-1959 *WhAm 3*
Lewis, James 1837-1896 *DcAmB, WhAm H*
Lewis, James 1840-1896 *ApCAB Sup, NatCAB 1*
Lewis, James Artemus 1890-1958 *NatCAB 43*
Lewis, James Edward 1873-1939 *NatCAB 29*
Lewis, James Hamilton d1939 *WhAm 1*
Lewis, James Hamilton 1863-1939 *BiDrAC, DcAmB S2, WhAmP*
Lewis, James Hamilton 1864-1939 *NatCAB 28*
Lewis, James Hamilton 1866-1939 *NatCAB 15*
Lewis, James M 1827-1907 *WhAm 1*
Lewis, James Malcolm 1898-1954 *WhAm 3*
Lewis, James Ogier 1886-1954 *WhAm 3*
Lewis, James Otto 1799-1858 *IIBEAAW, NewYHSD, WhAm H*
Lewis, James Polk 1845-1912 *NatCAB 51*
Lewis, James Taylor 1819- *BiAUS, NatCAB 12, TwCBDA*
Lewis, James Taylor 1865-1935 *NatCAB 27*
Lewis, Janet Cook *BiCAW, WomWWA 14*
Lewis, Jay Whittington 1847-1925 *NatCAB 21*
Lewis, Jesse Willard 1880-1957 *WhAm 3*
Lewis, John Beavens 1841-1923 *NatCAB 20, WhAm 1*
Lewis, John Beavins 1841-1923 *ApCAB X*
Lewis, John Benjamin 1832-1914 *NatCAB 5, NatCAB 16*
Lewis, John Calhoun 1857- *WhoColR*
Lewis, John Francis 1818-1895 *ApCAB, BiAUS, BiDrAC, DcAmB, NatCAB 13, TwCBDA, WhAm H, WhAmP*
Lewis, John Frederick 1860-1932 *WhAm 1*
Lewis, John Frederick, Jr. 1899-1965 *NatCAB 51, WhAm 4*
Lewis, John Henry 1830-1929 *BiDrAC*
Lewis, John Henry 1884-1958 *WhAm 3*
Lewis, John Kent 1897-1961 *NatCAB 49, WhAm 4*
Lewis, John L 1858-1913 *WhAm 1*
Lewis, John Lawson 1800-1886 *ApCAB, TwCBDA*
Lewis, John Llewellyn 1880-1969 *EncAB, McGEWB, NatCAB 57, WebAB*
Lewis, John Milligan 1889-1972 *WhAm 6*
Lewis, John Neher 1869-1940 *NatCAB 31, WhAm 5*
Lewis, John Philip 1903-1961 *WhAm 4*
Lewis, John Travers 1825- *ApCAB*
Lewis, John Travers 1827- *Drake*
Lewis, John W 1801-1865 *BiDConf*
Lewis, John William 1841-1913 *BiDrAC*
Lewis, Joseph *NewYHSD*
Lewis, Joseph 1906-1970 *WhAm 5*
Lewis, Joseph, Jr. 1772-1834 *BiAUS, BiDrAC, WhAm H, WhAmP*
Lewis, Joseph Horace 1824-1904 *BiAUS, BiDConf, BiDrAC, DcAmB, NatCAB 12, TwCBDA, WhAm 1*
Lewis, Joseph Jackson 1801-1883 *BiAUS, NatCAB 27*
Lewis, Joseph L *NewYHSD*
Lewis, Joseph R *BiAUS*
Lewis, Joseph William 1868-1936 *WhAm 1*
Lewis, Joshua 1774-1833 *ApCAB, BiAUS*
Lewis, Josiah 1839-1885 *TwCBDA*
Lewis, Judd Mortimer 1867-1945 *WhAm 2*
Lewis, Kathryn 1911-1962 *WhAm 4*
Lewis, Kemp Plummer 1880-1952 *WhAm 3*
Lewis, L *NewYHSD*
Lewis, Lafayette Arthur 1888-1966 *WhAm 4*
Lewis, Lawrence 1767-1839 *TwCBDA*
Lewis, Lawrence 1856-1890 *DcAmB,*

WhAm H
Lewis, Lawrence 1857- *ApCAB*
Lewis, Lawrence 1879-1943 *BiDrAC, WhAm 2, WhAmP*
Lewis, Lee Rich 1865-1945 *WhAm 2*
Lewis, Leicester Crosby 1887-1949 *WhAm 2*
Lewis, Lena Morrow *WomWWA 14*
Lewis, Leo Logan 1887-1965 *WhAm 4*
Lewis, Leon Lawrence 1888-1954 *NatCAB 43*
Lewis, Leon Patteson 1878-1932 *WhAm 1*
Lewis, Leonard William 1874- *WhoColR*
Lewis, Lillian d1899 *WhAm 1*
Lewis, Lina Redwood 1850- *WomWWA 14*
Lewis, Llewellyn Roy 1890-1948 *NatCAB 40*
Lewis, Lloyd Downs 1891-1949 *DcAmB S4, WhAm 2*
Lewis, Lloyd Griffith 1902-1959 *WhAm 3*
Lewis, Loran Ludowick 1825-1916 *NatCAB 11, WhAm 1*
Lewis, Lorie Mackey 1871- *WomWWA 14*
Lewis, Lowery Lamon 1869-1922 *WhAm 1*
Lewis, Lucy May 1879-1951 *WhAm 3*
Lewis, Lunsford Lomax 1846- *ApCAB Sup, NatCAB 12, WhAm 4*
Lewis, M *NewYHSD*
Lewis, Madison Horton 1896-1969 *NatCAB 54*
Lewis, Mahlon Everett 1901-1960 *WhAm 4*
Lewis, Margaret A Reed 1881- *WomWWA 14*
Lewis, Margaret Cameron 1867- *BiCAW, WomWWA 14*
Lewis, Marion L d1951 *WhAm 3*
Lewis, Martin 1883-1962 *BnEnAmA*
Lewis, Marvin Harrison 1873- *WhAm 5*
Lewis, Mary Ann *NewYHSD*
Lewis, Mary Delia *WomWWA 14*
Lewis, Mary Sybil 1900-1941 *WhAm 1, WhAm 2*
Lewis, Mason Avery 1887-1963 *WhAm 4*
Lewis, Mathew Gregory 1775-1818 *ApCAB*
Lewis, Matthew *NewYHSD*
Lewis, Matthew Gregory 1775-1818 *McGEWB*
Lewis, Melissa Ann 1848- *WomWWA 14*
Lewis, Melvin S 1881-1969 *WhAm 5*
Lewis, Meriwether 1774-1809 *AmBi, ApCAB, BiAUS, DcAmB, Drake, EncAAH, EncAB, McGEWB, NatCAB 5, REnAW, TwCBDA, WebAB, WebAMB, WhAm H*
Lewis, Merton Elmer 1861-1937 *WhAm 1*
Lewis, Merton Harry 1902-1969 *WhAm 5*
Lewis, Minard 1812?- *IIBEAAW, NewYHSD*
Lewis, Morgan 1754-1844 *AmBi, ApCAB, DcAmB, Drake, NatCAB 3, TwCBDA, WebAMB, WhAm H, WhAmP*
Lewis, Morgan 1754-1854 *BiAUS*
Lewis, Morris James 1852-1928 *WhAm 1*
Lewis, Nancy Duke 1910-1961 *WhAm 4*
Lewis, Nelson Peter 1856-1924 *WhAm 1*
Lewis, Norman Stanley 1864-1926 *NatCAB 21*
Lewis, Oborn Garrett Levis 1877-1948 *NatCAB 36*
Lewis, Olin Bailey 1861- *WhAm 4*
Lewis, Orlando Faulkland 1873-1922 *DcAmB, NatCAB 25, WhAm 1*
Lewis, Oscar 1914-1970 *WhAm 5*
Lewis, Paul A 1879-1929 *WhAm 1*
Lewis, Reuben Alexander, Jr. 1895-1948 *WhAm 2*
Lewis, Richard Hanna 1887- *WhoColR*
Lewis, Richard Henry 1850-1926 *WhAm 1*
Lewis, Richard James 1851- *NatCAB 1*
Lewis, Richard Welborne 1861- *WhAm 4*
Lewis, Robert 1862-1939 *WhAm 1*
Lewis, Robert Curtis 1888-1969 *NatCAB 55*
Lewis, Robert E 1857-1941 *WhAm 1*
Lewis, Robert Jacob 1864-1933 *BiDrAC*
Lewis, Robert Leech 1882-1968 *NatCAB 54*
Lewis, Robert Steele 1856-1956 *NatCAB 43*
Lewis, Roger Kenneth 1903-1951 *NatCAB 40*
Lewis, Samuel *NewYHSD*
Lewis, Samuel 1799-1854 *ApCAB, BiDAmEd, DcAmB, Drake, NatCAB 25, WhAm H*
Lewis, Sarah Borden Durfee 1851- *WomWWA 14*
Lewis, Seth *BiAUS*
Lewis, Sinclair 1884-1951 *WhAm 3*
Lewis, Sinclair 1885-1951 *DcAmB S5, EncAAH, McGEWB, NatCAB 57, WebAB*

Lewis, Spearman 1879-1954 *WhAm 3*
Lewis, Spencer Jay 1895-1957 *NatCAB 49*
Lewis, Spencer Steen 1888- *WhAm 3*
Lewis, Tayler 1802-1877 *ApCAB, DcAmB, Drake, NatCAB 10, TwCBDA*
Lewis, Ted 1891-1971 *WhAm 5*
Lewis, Theodore Leonard 1903-1959 *WhAm 3*
Lewis, Thomas *BiAUS, BiDrAC, WhAm H*
Lewis, Thomas 1718-1790 *ApCAB, BiAUS, Drake, NatCAB 4, TwCBDA*
Lewis, Sir Thomas 1881-1945 *BiHiMed, DcScB*
Lewis, Thomas H 1836-1914 *NatCAB 16*
Lewis, Thomas Hamilton 1852-1929 *TwCBDA, WhAm 1*
Lewis, Thomas Jenkins 1875-1970 *NatCAB 56*
Lewis, Thomas L 1907- *IIBEAAW*
Lewis, Timothy Richards 1841-1886 *DcScB*
Lewis, Tracy Hammond 1890-1951 *NatCAB 40*
Lewis, Verner Moore 1872-1954 *NatCAB 44*
Lewis, Virgil Anson 1848-1912 *WhAm 1*
Lewis, Vivian Murchison 1869-1950 *NatCAB 38, WhAm 2A*
Lewis, W D, Jr. *NewYHSD*
Lewis, Walker 1847- *WhAm 1*
Lewis, Walter Oliver 1877-1965 *WhAm 4*
Lewis, Warren Harmon 1870-1964 *WhAm 4*
Lewis, Warren Kendall 1882-1975 *WhAm 6*
Lewis, Wilfred 1854-1929 *DcAmB S1, WhAm 1*
Lewis, William *BiAUS, NewYHSD*
Lewis, William 1708-1781 *DcScB*
Lewis, William 1724-1811 *ApCAB, TwCBDA*
Lewis, William 1750?-1819 *ApCAB Sup*
Lewis, William 1751-1819 *DcAmB, NatCAB 16*
Lewis, William 1752-1819 *WhAm H*
Lewis, William 1764-1825 *TwCBDA*
Lewis, William 1765-1825 *ApCAB*
Lewis, William 1767-1825 *Drake*
Lewis, William 1788- *NewYHSD*
Lewis, William 1868-1959 *BiDrAC*
Lewis, William Alexander 1876-1933 *WhAm 1*
Lewis, William Bennett 1904-1975 *WhAm 6*
Lewis, William Berkeley 1784-1866 *AmBi, ApCAB, DcAmB, NatCAB 7, WhAm H*
Lewis, William David 1792-1881 *ApCAB, DcAmB, WhAm H*
Lewis, William David 1828-1872 *ApCAB*
Lewis, William Dodge 1870-1960 *NatCAB 47, WhAm 4*
Lewis, William Draper 1867-1949 *DcAmB S4, WhAm 2*
Lewis, William Eugene 1860-1924 *NatCAB 20, WhAm 1*
Lewis, William Fisher 1902-1964 *WhAm 4*
Lewis, William Gaston 1835-1901 *DcAmB, TwCBDA*
Lewis, William Gatson 1835-1901 *NatCAB 24*
Lewis, William Henry 1803- *Drake*
Lewis, William Henry 1868-1949 *DcAmB S4, WhAm 4, WhoColR*
Lewis, William J 1766-1828 *BiAUS, BiDrAC, WhAm H*
Lewis, William J 1843- *NatCAB 5*
Lewis, William Jerauld 1856- *NatCAB 13*
Lewis, William Luther 1884-1952 *NatCAB 42, WhAm 3*
Lewis, William Mather 1878-1945 *NatCAB 34, WhAm 2*
Lewis, William Stanley 1876- *WhAm 5*
Lewis, Sir Willmott Harsant 1877-1950 *WhAm 2*
Lewis, Wilson Seeley 1857-1921 *WhAm 1*
Lewis, Winford Lee 1878-1943 *WhAm 2*
Lewis, Winslow 1770-1850 *ApCAB, DcAmB, NatCAB 25, WhAm H*
Lewis, Winslow 1799-1875 *ApCAB, Drake*
Lewis, Yancey 1861-1915 *WhAm 1*
Lewis, Yardley *NewYHSD*
Lewis, Zachariah 1773-1840 *ApCAB, Drake, NatCAB 11*
Lewisohn, Adolph 1849-1938 *ApCAB X, DcAmB S2, NatCAB 33, WhAm 1*
Lewisohn, Irene 1892-1944 *NotAW*
Lewisohn, Leonard 1847-1902 *NatCAB 27*
Lewisohn, Ludwig 1882-1955 *DcAmB S5*
Lewisohn, Ludwig 1883-1955 *NatCAB 42,*

WhAm 3
Lewisohn, Margaret Seligman 1895-1954 *NatCAB 44, WhAm 3*
Lewisohn, Sam Adolph 1884-1951 *DcAmB S5, NatCAB 40, WhAm 3*
Lewitt, Sol 1928- *BnEnAmA*
Lewman, Frank C 1890-1964 *WhAm 4*
Lewman, Harry Lucesco 1866-1917 *NatCAB 17*
Lewton, Frederick Lewis 1874-1959 *WhAm 3*
Lewy, Ted 1912-1963 *NatCAB 50*
Lex, Charles E 1812-1872 *WhAm H*
Lexell, Anders Johan 1740-1784 *DcScB*
Lexow, Caroline 1882- *WomWWA 14*
Lexow, Clarence 1852-1910 *DcAmB, NatCAB 5, WhAm 1*
Ley, Fred Theodore 1872-1958 *NatCAB 43*
Ley, Frederick Theodore 1872-1958 *WhAm 3*
Ley, Harold Alexander 1874-1956 *ApCAB X, NatCAB 15, NatCAB 46, WhAm 3*
Ley, Willy 1906-1969 *AsBiEn, WhAm 5*
Leybenzon, Leonid Samuilovich 1879-1951 *DcScB*
Leyburn, John 1814- *ApCAB*
Leyburn, John 1814-1893 *NatCAB 2*
Leyburn, John 1814-1894 *TwCBDA*
Leydig, Franz Von 1821-1908 *DcScB*
Leydon, John Koebig 1916-1971 *WhAm 5*
Leydt, Johannes 1718-1783 *ApCAB, TwCBDA*
Leyendecker, Frank X 1879-1924 *WhAm 1*
Leyendecker, Joseph Christian 1874-1951 *DcAmB S5, WhAm 3*
Leyman, Harry Stoll 1873- *WhAm 5*
Leyner, John George 1860-1920 *DcAmB, NatCAB 25*
Leypoldt, Frederick 1835-1884 *ApCAB, DcAmB, DcAmLiB, NatCAB 7, WebAB, WhAm H*
Leys, James Farquharson 1867-1938 *WhAm 1*
Leys, Wayne Albert Risser 1905-1973 *WhAm 5*
Leysen, Ralph J 1888-1951 *WhAm 3*
Leyshon, Hal Irwin 1900-1967 *WhAm 4*
L'Halle, Constantin De d1706 *DcAmB, WhAm H*
L'Heritier DeBrutelle, Charles Louis 1746-1800 *DcScB*
Lherminier, Felix Louis 1779-1833 *ApCAB*
Lhermitte, Jean Marthe Adrien 1766-1826 *ApCAB*
L'Heureux, Camille 1898-1964 *WhAm 4*
L'Heureux, Herve Joseph 1899-1957 *WhAm 3*
Lhevinne, Josef 1874-1944 *DcAmB S3, WhAm 2*
L'Hommedieu, Ezra 1734-1811 *AmBi, ApCAB, BiAUS, BiDrAC, DcAmB, Drake, NatCAB 12, TwCBDA, WhAm H, WhAmP*
L'Hommedieu, James Howard 1884-1950 *NatCAB 39*
L'Hospital, Guillaume-F-Antoine De 1661-1704 *DcScB*
Lhote, Andre 1885-1962 *WhAm 4*
L'Huillier, Simon-Antoine-Jean 1750-1840 *DcScB*
Lhwyd, Edward 1660-1709 *DcScB*
Li, Chih 1192-1279 *DcScB*
Li, Choh Hao 1913- *AsBiEn*
Li, Hung-Chang 1823-1901 *McGEWB*
Li, Kuo-Ching 1892-1961 *WhAm 4*
Li, Po 701-762 *McGEWB*
Li, Shih-Chen 1518-1593 *DcScB*
Li, Ssu 280?BC-208BC *McGEWB*
Li, Ta-Chao 1889-1927 *McGEWB*
Li, Tzu-Ch'eng 1606?-1645 *McGEWB*
Li, Yeh *DcScB*
Liang, Ch'i-Ch'ao 1873-1929 *McGEWB*
Liang, Wu-Ti 464-549 *McGEWB*
Liaquat Ali Khan 1896-1951 *McGEWB*
Liautaud, Andre 1906-1951 *WhAm 3*
Liautaud, B A *NewYHSD*
Libavius 1540?-1616 *AsBiEn*
Libavius, Andreas 1560?-1616 *DcScB*
Libbey, Edward Drummond 1854-1925 *DcAmB, NatCAB 13, WhAm 1*
Libbey, George Albert 1851-1922 *NatCAB 19*
Libbey, Grace E *WomWWA 14*
Libbey, Harry 1843-1913 *BiDrAC*
Libbey, Hosea Waite 1834-1900 *NatCAB 12*
Libbey, James Addison 1846- *NatCAB 12*

Libbey, Jonas Marsh 1857-1922 *WhAm 1*
Libbey, Laura Jean *WomWWA 14*
Libbey, Laura Jean d1924 *WhAm 1*
Libbey, Laura Jean 1862-1924 *NatCAB 19*
Libbey, Laura Jean 1862-1925 *NotAW*
Libbey, Mary Elizabeth Green 1859-
WomWWA 14
Libbey, Walter *NewYHSD*
Libbey, William 1855-1927 *NatCAB 10,*
TwCBDA, WhAm 1
Libby, Arthur Albion 1831-1899 *ApCAB X*
Libby, Arthur Stephen 1877-1948 *WhAm 2,*
WhAm 5
Libby, Charles Freeman 1844-1915 *NatCAB 14,*
NatCAB 37, WhAm 1
Libby, Edward Norton 1868-1929 *WhAm 1*
Libby, Edward W *NewYHSD*
Libby, Frederick Joseph 1874-1970 *WhAm 5*
Libby, Harriet Martin 1881- *WomWWA 14*
Libby, Harry Cummings 1895-1960 *NatCAB 50*
Libby, Hattie Payson Brazier 1888-
WomWWA 14
Libby, Herbert Carlyle 1878-1965 *NatCAB 50*
Libby, Lawrence Richards 1865-1927
NatCAB 21
Libby, Mary Stokes 1879- *WomWWA 14*
Libby, Melanchthon Fennessy 1864-1921
WhAm 1
Libby, Orin Grant 1864-1952 *DcAmB S5,*
REnAW, WhAm 3
Libby, Samuel Hammonds 1864- *WhAm 5*
Libby, Warren Edgar 1888-1955 *WhAm 3*
Libby, Willard Frank 1908- *AsBiEn,*
McGEWB, WebAB
Libenau *NewYHSD*
Liberati, Alessandro 1847- *NatCAB 14*
Liberman, Alexander 1912- *BnEnAmA*
Liberman, Samuel Halpern 1895-1966 *WhAm 5*
Liberson, Frank 1888-1947 *NatCAB 45*
Liberte, Jean 1896-1965 *WhAm 4*
Libhart, John Jay 1806- *NewYHSD*
Libman, Emanuel 1872-1946 *DcAmB S4,*
WhAm 2
Libolt, Mrs. S H *NewYHSD*
Libonati, Roland Victor 1900- *BiDrAC,*
WhAmP
Libramento, Joaquim Francisco Do 1761-1829
ApCAB
Liceaga, Eduardo 1839-1920 *DcScB*
Lich, Charles Albert 1888-1949 *NatCAB 38*
Lichford, Lewis Edmund 1882-1952
NatCAB 41
Lichiter, McIlyar Hamilton 1877-1961
WhAm 4
Licht, George Augustus 1878- *WhAm 6*
Lichten, Robert Lyon 1921-1971 *WhAm 6*
Lichtenberg, Bernard 1892-1944 *WhAm 2*
Lichtenberg, Georg Christoph 1742-1799 *DcScB*
Lichtenberg, Joseph Stanly 1869-1933
NatCAB 24
Lichtenberg, Leopold 1861-1935 *WhAm 1*
Lichtenberger, Arthur Carl 1900-1968
NatCAB 54, WhAm 5
Lichtenberger, James Buchanan 1876-1949
NatCAB 37
Lichtenberger, James Pendleton 1870-1953
NatCAB 41, WhAm 3
Lichtenstein, Alfred Ferdinand 1876-1947
NatCAB 35
Lichtenstein, Clara *WomWWA 14*
Lichtenstein, Joseph 1892-1970 *NatCAB 55*
Lichtenstein, Joy 1873- *WhAm 5*
Lichtenstein, Morris Levy 1901-1970
NatCAB 56
Lichtenstein, Roy 1923- *BnEnAmA,*
McGEWB, WebAB
Lichtenstein, Walter 1880-1964 *WhAm 4*
Lichtentag, Alexander 1868-1938 *WhAm 1*
Lichtenwalner, Norton Lewis 1889-1960
BiDrAC
Lichtenwalter, Franklin Herbert 1910-1973
BiDrAC, WhAm 5
Lichter, Adolph Harry 1887-1967 *NatCAB 54*
Lichter, Jacob 1897-1968 *NatCAB 54*
Lichtman, A E 1889-1965 *NatCAB 43*
Lichtman, Al 1888-1958 *NatCAB 43*
Lichty, John Alden 1866-1932 *WhAm 1*
Lichty, John Alden 1866-1934 *NatCAB 51*

Lichty, L 1891-1972 *WhAm 5*
Lick, Charles Jacob 1882-1971 *NatCAB 56*
Lick, James 1796-1876 *ApCAB, DcAmB,*
NatCAB 3, TwCBDA, WhAm H
Lick, Maxwell John 1884-1946 *NatCAB 36,*
WhAm 2
Licks, Frederick Charles 1905-1957 *NatCAB 50*
Lidbury, Frank Austin 1879- *WhAm 6*
Liddell, Donald Macy 1879-1958 *WhAm 3*
Liddell, Eva Louise d1937 *WhAm 1*
Liddell, Frank Austin 1892-1964 *WhAm 4*
Liddell, Henry 1843- *WhAm 4*
Liddell, Howard Scott 1895-1962 *WhAm 4*
Liddell, Mark Harvey 1866-1936 *NatCAB 27,*
TwCBDA, WhAm 1
Liddell, Vinton 1859-1915 *NatCAB 17*
Liddell Hart, Sir Basil Henry 1895-1970
WhWW-II, WhoMilH
Liddle, Charles Allen 1877-1961 *WhAm 4*
Liddle, James W *NewYHSD*
Liddle, Leonard Merritt 1885-1920 *NatCAB 18*
Liddon, Benjamin Sullivan 1853-1909
NatCAB 12, WhAm 1
Lie, Jonas 1880-1940 *AmBi, BnEnAmA,*
DcAmB S2, NatCAB 30, WhAm 1
Lie, Marius Sophus 1842-1899 *DcScB*
Lie, Trygve Halvdan 1896-1968 *McGEWB*
Lieb, Charles 1852-1928 *BiDrAC, WhAm 3*
Lieb, Charles Christian 1880-1956 *WhAm 3*
Lieb, Clarence William 1885-1967 *NatCAB 54*
Lieb, John William 1860-1929 *ApCAB X,*
DcAmB, NatCAB 13, WhAm 1
Lieb, Joseph Patrick 1901-1971 *WhAm 6*
Liebel, Michael, Jr. 1870-1927 *BiDrAC,*
WhAm 5
Liebel, Willard Koehler 1901-1961 *WhAm 4*
Liebeler, Wilbert Ashton 1897-1954
NatCAB 42
Liebenau, Henry 1802?- *NewYHSD*
Lieber, B Franklin 1853-1915 *WhAm 1*
Lieber, Eugene 1907-1965 *WhAm 4*
Lieber, Francis 1798?-1872 *McGEWB*
Lieber, Francis 1800-1872 *AmBi, ApCAB,*
BiDAmEd, DcAmB, Drake, EncAB,
NatCAB 5, TwCBDA, WebAB,
WebAMB, WhAm H
Lieber, Guido Norman 1837-1923 *ApCAB,*
NatCAB 28, TwCBDA, WhAm 1
Lieber, Hamilton 1835-1876 *ApCAB*
Lieber, Hugh Gray 1896-1961 *WhAm 4*
Lieber, Oscar Montgomery 1830-1862 *ApCAB,*
Drake, NatCAB 13, TwCBDA
Lieber, Richard 1869-1944 *WhAm 2*
Lieber, Thomas *DcScB*
Lieberkuhn, Johannes Nathanael 1711-1756
DcScB
Lieberman, Clarence 1900-1967 *NatCAB 55*
Lieberman, Elias 1883-1969 *WhAm 5*
Lieberman, Elias 1888-1969 *NatCAB 56*
Liebermann, Carl Theodore 1842-1914 *DcScB*
Liebermann, Max 1847-1935 *McGEWB*
Liebers, Otto Hugo 1881-1968 *WhAm 5*
Liebes, Dorothy Wright 1899-1972 *WhAm 5*
Liebhart *NewYHSD*
Liebig, Baron Justus Von 1803-1873 *AsBiEn,*
DcScB, McGEWB
Liebler, Theodore August 1830-1890 *NewYHSD*
Liebling, Abbott Joseph 1904-1963 *WhAm 4*
Liebling, Emil 1851-1914 *DcAmB, NatCAB 24,*
WhAm 1
Liebling, George 1865- *WhAm 4*
Liebling, Leonard 1880-1945 *WhAm 2*
Liebman, Charles Joseph 1877-1957
NatCAB 43
Liebman, Joshua Loth 1907-1948 *DcAmB S4,*
NatCAB 38, WhAm 2
Liebman, Julius d1937 *WhAm 1*
Liebmann, Joseph 1831-1913 *NatCAB 46*
Liebmann, Philip 1915- *WhAm 5*
Liecty, Austin N 1866- *WhAm 5*
Lieder, Frederick William Charles 1881-1953
NatCAB 42, WhAm 3
Lieder, Paul Robert 1889-1956 *WhAm 3*
Liefeld, Albert 1831-1907 *WhAm 1*
Lieghley, Perlee Alvin 1872-1962 *NatCAB 50*
Lien, Arnold Johnson 1886-1963 *WhAm 4*
Lien, Elias Johnson 1868- *WhAm 4*
Lien, Robert Cowles 1926-1969 *WhAm 6*

Lienau, Detlef 1818-1887 *BnEnAmA,*
DcAmB S1, NatCAB 29, WhAm H
Lies, Eugene Theodore 1876- *WhAm 5*
Liesganig, Joseph Xaver 1719-1799 *DcScB*
Lieurance, Artemas Floyd 1882-1955
NatCAB 41
Lieurance, Thurlow 1878-1963 *NatCAB 51,*
WhAm 4
Lieutaud, Joseph 1703-1780 *DcScB*
Life, Andrew Creamor 1869-1933 *WhAm 1*
Life, Frank Mann 1870-1933 *WhAm 1*
Liff, Nathan 1889-1963 *NatCAB 50*
Lifschey, Samuel 1889-1961 *WhAm 4*
Liggett, Anna Coates Wardle *WomWWA 14*
Liggett, Ella Mary *WomWWA 14*
Liggett, Gertrude Irwin 1881- *WomWWA 14*
Liggett, Hunter 1857-1935 *AmBi, ApCAB X,*
DcAmB S1, WebAMB, WhAm 1
Liggett, Louis Kroh 1875-1946 *ApCAB X,*
DcAmB S4, NatCAB 14, WhAm 2
Liggett, Luther Mayne 1869-1949 *NatCAB 39*
Liggett, Thomas 1857-1942 *NatCAB 35*
Liggett, Walter William 1886-1935 *DcAmB S1,*
WhAm 1
Liggins, John 1829-1912 *WhAm 1*
Light, Alexander Luder 1822- *ApCAB*
Light, Charles 1860-1919 *NatCAB 18*
Light, Charles Porterfield 1871-1955 *WhAm 3*
Light, Evelyn 1904-1958 *WhAm 3*
Light, George W 1810-1868 *Drake*
Light, George Washington 1809-1868 *ApCAB*
Light, Gilson Don 1883-1941 *NatCAB 30*
Light, Israel 1915-1975 *WhAm 6*
Light, Richard D 1848-1914 *NatCAB 17*
Light, Roderick Hudson 1898-1955 *NatCAB 49*
Light, Rudolph Alvin 1909-1970 *WhAm 5*
Lightburn, George William 1899-1964 *WhAm 4*
Lightburn, Joseph Andrew Jackson 1824-1901
ApCAB, DcAmB, TwCBDA, WhAm 1
Lightcap, Harrison Barksdale 1884-1949
NatCAB 41
Lightfoot, James A Garfield 1882- *WhoColR*
Lightfoot, Mary Washington Minor
WomWWA 14
Lighthall, William Douw 1857- *ApCAB Sup*
Lighthipe, Charles Francis 1853-1928
ApCAB X
Lightner, Adam Mortimer *NewYHSD*
Lightner, Clarence Ashley 1862-1938 *WhAm 1*
Lightner, Ezra Wilberforce *WhAm 5*
Lightner, Letitia Catherine 1849-
WomWWA 14
Lightner, Milton Clarkson 1890-1968
NatCAB 55, WhAm 5
Lighton, William Rheem 1866- *WhAm 4*
Lignier, Elie Antoine Octave 1855-1916 *DcScB*
Ligon, Charles Worthington Dorsey 1856-1917
NatCAB 34
Ligon, Cora Sarah Reed *WomWWA 14*
Ligon, Ellen Lee Barret 1864- *WomWWA 14*
Ligon, Elvin Seth 1878- *WhAm 6*
Ligon, Elvin Seth, Jr. 1911-1975 *WhAm 6*
Ligon, P Garland 1883-1968 *NatCAB 54*
Ligon, Richard *ApCAB*
Ligon, Robert Fulwood 1823-1901 *BiDrAC*
Ligon, Robert Fulwood 1863-1939 *NatCAB 29*
Ligon, Thomas Watkins *ApCAB, BiAUS,*
Drake
Ligon, Thomas Watkins 1810-1881 *BiDrAC,*
DcAmB, WhAm H, WhAmP
Ligon, Thomas Watkins 1812-1881 *NatCAB 9,*
TwCBDA
Liguest, Pierre Laclede 1724?-1778 *Drake,*
NatCAB 13, WebAB
Lihme, C Bai 1866-1946 *WhAm 2*
Likly, Henry 1870-1922 *NatCAB 20*
Likly, William F 1864- *WhAm 4*
Lilburne, John 1615-1657 *McGEWB*
Lile, William Minor 1859-1935 *DcAmB S1,*
WhAm 1
Liles, Luther Brooks 1890-1947 *WhAm 2*
Lilienthal, David Eli 1899- *EncAB, McGEWB,*
WebAB
Lilienthal, Howard 1861-1946 *WhAm 2*
Lilienthal, Jesse Warren 1855-1919 *NatCAB 20,*
WhAm 1
Lilienthal, Joseph Leo, Jr. 1911-1955 *WhAm 3*
Lilienthal, Max 1815-1882 *ApCAB, DcAmB,*

NatCAB 11, WhAm H

Lilienthal, Otto 1848-1896 *AsBiEn*

Lilienthal, Samuel 1884-1957 *WhAm 3*

Liliuokalani 1838-1917 *NotAW, WhAm HA, WhAm 4*

Liliuokalani, Lydia Kamakaeha 1838-1917 *McGEWB*

Liliuokalani, Lydia Kamekeha 1828-1917 *AmBi*

Liljencrantz, Ottilie Adaline 1876-1910 *WhAm 1*

Liljestrand, Goran 1886-1968 *WhAm 5*

Lill, Joseph Charles 1893-1945 *NatCAB 43*

Lillard, Benjamin 1847- *WhAm 4*

Lillard, Walter Huston 1881-1967 *WhAm 4, WhAm 5*

Lilley, Charles Sumner 1851-1921 *WhAm 1*

Lilley, George Leavens 1859-1909 *BiDrAC, NatCAB 14, WhAm 1*

Lilley, George Washington 1854-1904 *NatCAB 25, WhAm 1*

Lilley, Mial Eben 1850-1915 *BiDrAC, WhAm 4*

Lilley, Robert 1839- *WhAm 4*

Lillibridge, Francis Marion 1848-1916 *NatCAB 18*

Lillibridge, William Otis 1877-1909 *WhAm 1*

Lillick, Ira S 1877-1967 *WhAm 4*

Lillie, Abraham Bruyn Hasbrouck d1905 *WhAm 1*

Lillie, Charles A 1880-1964 *WhAm 4*

Lillie, Frank Rattray 1870-1947 *BiDAmEd, DcAmB S4, DcScB, NatCAB 14, NatCAB 36, WhAm 2*

Lillie, Gordon William 1860-1942 *DcAmB S3, WhAm 1, WhAm 2*

Lillie, Harold Irving 1888-1957 *WhAm 3*

Lillie, Helen Eva Makepeace 1876- *WomWWA 14*

Lillie, Howard Russell 1902-1961 *WhAm 4*

Lillie, John 1812-1867 *ApCAB, TwCBDA*

Lillie, John 1867-1942 *NatCAB 32*

Lillie, John Hoyt 1813- *NatCAB 9*

Lillie, Lucy Cecil 1855- *WhAm 1*

Lillie, Ralph Stayner 1875-1952 *WhAm 3*

Lillie, Samuel Morris 1851- *WhAm 4*

Lilliefors, Katharine Fackenthal 1867- *WomWWA 14*

Lillington, John *ApCAB*

Lillington, John Alexander 1725?-1786 *ApCAB, Drake, TwCBDA*

Lillis, Ant *NewYHSD*

Lillis, Donald Chace 1901-1968 *NatCAB 54, WhAm 5*

Lillis, James F 1908-1963 *WhAm 4*

Lillis, Thomas F 1861-1938 *WhAm 1*

Lillis, Thomas Francis 1862- *NatCAB 5, NatCAB 16*

Lillo, Eusebio 1826- *ApCAB*

Lilly, Charles Hervey 1860-1930 *NatCAB 29*

Lilly, D Clay 1870-1939 *NatCAB 29, WhAm 1*

Lilly, Eli 1838-1898 *NatCAB 9*

Lilly, George Raysor 1905-1969 *NatCAB 57*

Lilly, Henry Walter 1856-1938 *NatCAB 31*

Lilly, Josiah Kirby 1861-1948 *DcAmB S4, NatCAB 42, WhAm 2*

Lilly, Josiah Kirby 1893-1966 *NatCAB 53, WhAm 4*

Lilly, Lillian Augusta Armstrong *WomWWA 14*

Lilly, Linus Augustine 1876-1943 *WhAm 2*

Lilly, Richard C 1884-1959 *WhAm 3*

Lilly, Samuel 1815-1880 *ApCAB, BiAUS, BiDrAC, WhAm H*

Lilly, Thomas Jefferson 1878-1955 *WhAm 3*

Lilly, Thomas Jefferson 1878-1956 *BiDrAC*

Lilly, William 1821-1893 *BiDrAC, WhAm H*

Lillywhite, Raphael 1891-1958 *IIBEAAW*

Lim, Pilar Hidalgo 1893-1973 *WhAm 6*

Lima, Francisco d1704 *ApCAB*

Lima, Joao DeBrito 1671-1747 *ApCAB*

Lima, Jose Ignacio De Abreu De 1796-1869 *ApCAB*

Lima, Jose Ignacio Ribeiro Abreu De 1770?-1817 *ApCAB*

Lima, Manoel De 1685-1750 *ApCAB*

Lima, Manoel DeOliveira 1867-1928 *WhAm 1*

Lima E Silva, Francisco De 1785-1853 *ApCAB*

Lima E Silva, Luis Alves 1803- *ApCAB*

Liman VonSanders, Otto 1855-1929 *WhoMilH*

Limantour, Jose Ives 1854- *ApCAB Sup*

Limbach, Russell Theodore 1904-1971 *WhAm 5*

Limbert, George Brown 1862-1920 *NatCAB 6*

Limbert, Lee Middleton 1897-1966 *WhAm 4*

Limbourg Brothers *McGEWB*

Limburg, Francis *NewYHSD*

Limerick, Earl *WhAm H*

Limoelan *NewYHSD*

Limoges, Joseph Eugene 1879- *WhAm 6*

Limon, Jose Arcadio 1908-1972 *WhAm 5*

Limpert, Gregory Henry 1890-1969 *NatCAB 55*

Lin, Piao 1906-1971 *WhAm 5*

Lin, Piao 1907-1971 *McGEWB*

Lin, Piao 1908-1971? *WhoMilH*

Lin, Tse-Hsu 1785-1850 *McGEWB*

Linacre, Thomas 1460?-1524 *BiHiMed, DcScB*

Linan Y Cisneros, Melchor De 1629-1708 *ApCAB*

Linares, Jose Maria 1810-1861 *ApCAB*

Linburg, Watson Harrison 1839-1916 *NatCAB 18*

L'Incarnation, Marie De 1599-1672 *ApCAB*

Lincecum, Gideon 1793-1874 *ApCAB, DcAmB, NatCAB 25, TwCBDA, WhAm H*

Lincoln, Abraham 1809-1865 *AmBi, ApCAB, BiAUS, BiDrAC, BiDrUSE, DcAmB, DcAmReB, Drake, EncAAH, EncAB, McGEWB, NatCAB 2, REnAW, TwCBDA, WebAB, WhAm H, WhAmP*

Lincoln, Allen B 1858-1941 *WhAm 1*

Lincoln, Almira Hart *BiDAmEd, NotAW*

Lincoln, Arba Nelson 1849-1922 *NatCAB 20*

Lincoln, Arleigh Leon 1910-1966 *WhAm 4*

Lincoln, Asa Liggett 1891-1974 *WhAm 6*

Lincoln, Azariah Thomas 1868-1956 *WhAm 3*

Lincoln, Benjamin 1733-1810 *AmBi, ApCAB, DcAmB, Drake, McGEWB, NatCAB 1, TwCBDA, WebAB, WebAMB, WhAm H, WhoMilH*

Lincoln, Charles Clark 1866-1928 *WhAm 1*

Lincoln, Charles Monroe 1866-1950 *WhAm 3*

Lincoln, Charles Perez 1843-1911 *NatCAB 8, WhAm 1*

Lincoln, Charles Sherman 1875-1941 *WhAm 1*

Lincoln, Charles Zebina 1848- *WhAm 4*

Lincoln, Cicero Lee 1886-1956 *NatCAB 44*

Lincoln, Daniel Waldo 1882-1971 *NatCAB 56, WhAm 5*

Lincoln, David Francis 1841-1916 *ApCAB, TwCBDA, WhAm 1*

Lincoln, Edmond E 1888-1958 *WhAm 3*

Lincoln, Enoch 1788-1829 *ApCAB, BiAUS, BiDrAC, DcAmB, Drake, NatCAB 6, TwCBDA, WhAm H, WhAmP*

Lincoln, Francis Church 1877- *WhAm 5*

Lincoln, Gatewood Sanders 1875-1957 *WhAm 3*

Lincoln, George Arthur 1907-1975 *WhAm 6*

Lincoln, George Gould 1880-1974 *WhAm 6*

Lincoln, Heman 1821-1887 *ApCAB, TwCBDA*

Lincoln, Henry *NewYHSD*

Lincoln, James Claiborne 1862-1923 *WhAm 1*

Lincoln, James Finney 1883-1965 *NatCAB 56, WhAm 4*

Lincoln, James Rush 1845- *ApCAB Sup, WhAm 4*

Lincoln, James Sullivan 1811-1887 *ApCAB Sup*

Lincoln, James Sullivan 1811-1888 *NewYHSD, WhAm H*

Lincoln, Jane Elizabeth 1829- *ApCAB*

Lincoln, Jeanie Gould d1921 *WhAm 1*

Lincoln, Jeanie Gould 1853-1921 *TwCBDA*

Lincoln, Jeanie Thomas Gould 1846-1921 *WomWWA 14*

Lincoln, John Cromwell 1866-1959 *NatCAB 47, WhAm 3*

Lincoln, John Larkin 1817-1891 *ApCAB, DcAmB, NatCAB 8, TwCBDA, WhAm H*

Lincoln, John Leonard 1859-1914 *ApCAB X*

Lincoln, Jonathan Thayer 1869-1942 *WhAm 2*

Lincoln, Joseph Bates 1836-1895 *NatCAB 14*

Lincoln, Joseph Crosby 1870-1944 *DcAmB S3, NatCAB 14, WhAm 2*

Lincoln, Joseph Freeman 1900-1962 *WhAm 4*

Lincoln, Julius 1872-1954 *WhAm 3*

Lincoln, Leontine 1846-1923 *WhAm 1*

Lincoln, Leroy Alton 1880-1957 *NatCAB 47, WhAm 3*

Lincoln, Levi 1749-1820 *AmBi, ApCAB, BiAUS, BiDrAC, BiDrUSE, DcAmB, Drake, NatCAB 1, NatCAB 3, TwCBDA, WhAm H, WhAmP*

Lincoln, Levi 1782-1868 *AmBi, ApCAB, BiAUS, BiDrAC, DcAmB, Drake, NatCAB 1, TwCBDA, WhAm H, WhAmP*

Lincoln, Lowell 1836- *NatCAB 10*

Lincoln, Martha D 1838- *AmWom*

Lincoln, Mary Johnson Bailey 1844-1921 *DcAmB, NatCAB 24, NotAW, WhAm 1, WomWWA 14*

Lincoln, Mary Todd 1818-1882 *AmBi, AmWom, ApCAB, DcAmB, NatCAB 2, NotAW, TwCBDA, WhAm H*

Lincoln, Murray Danforth 1892-1966 *WhAm 4*

Lincoln, Natalie Sumner d1935 *WhAm 1, WomWWA 14*

Lincoln, Nathan Smith 1828- *NatCAB 3*

Lincoln, Paul Martyn 1870-1944 *WhAm 2*

Lincoln, Robert Todd 1843-1926 *AmBi, ApCAB, BiDrUSE, DcAmB, EncAB, NatCAB 4, NatCAB 21, TwCBDA, WhAm 1, WhAmP*

Lincoln, Rufus Pratt 1840-1900 *DcAmB, WhAm H*

Lincoln, Rufus Pratt 1841-1900 *ApCAB X, NatCAB 15*

Lincoln, Sarah Bush 1785?-1869 *NatCAB 2*

Lincoln, Solomon 1838-1907 *NatCAB 14, WhAm 1*

Lincoln, Sumner H 1840-1928 *WhAm 1*

Lincoln, Thomas Waterman 1862-1934 *NatCAB 25*

Lincoln, Waldo 1849-1933 *NatCAB 14, NatCAB 42, WhAm 1*

Lincoln, William 1801-1843 *ApCAB, Drake*

Lincoln, William Addison 1857-1920 *NatCAB 41*

Lincoln, William Ensign 1847- *WhAm 4*

Lincoln, William Henry 1835-1925 *NatCAB 21, WhAm 1*

Lincoln, William Shattuck 1837- *NatCAB 5*

Lincoln, William Slosson 1813-1893 *BiAUS, BiDrAC, WhAm H*

Lincoyan 1519?-1560 *ApCAB*

Lind, Alice Adele 1859- *WomWWA 14*

Lind, Ethel C 1910-1970 *WhAm 5*

Lind, James 1716-1794 *AsBiEn, BiHiMed, DcScB*

Lind, James Francis 1900- *BiDrAC*

Lind, Jenny 1820-1887 *AmBi*

Lind, Jenny 1821-1887 *NatCAB 3, WhAm H*

Lind, John 1854-1930 *AmBi, BiDrAC, DcAmB, NatCAB 10, TwCBDA, WhAm 1, WhAmP*

Lind, Lewis *NewYHSD*

Lind, Ralph Armond 1897-1955 *NatCAB 46*

Lind, Samuel Colville 1879-1965 *NatCAB 51, WhAm 4*

Lind-Goldschmidt, Jenny 1821-1887 *ApCAB*

Lindabury, Irvin L 1880- *WhAm 6*

Lindabury, Richard Vliet 1850-1925 *DcAmB, NatCAB 33, WhAm 1*

Lindabury, Richard Vliet 1900-1975 *WhAm 6*

Lindahl, Johan Harald Josua 1844- *NatCAB 13*

Lindahl, Josua 1844-1912 *WhAm 1*

Lindahl, Oscar Nathanael 1884-1952 *NatCAB 42, WhAm 3*

Lindbeck, John M H 1915-1971 *WhAm 5*

Lindberg, Abram Frank 1881-1934 *WhAm 1*

Lindberg, Axel Nathaniel 1875-1942 *NatCAB 43*

Lindberg, Carl Otto 1879-1960 *NatCAB 45, WhAm 6*

Lindberg, Charles August 1860-1924 *WhAm 1*

Lindberg, Charles Augustus 1859-1924 *WhAmP*

Lindberg, Charles Augustus 1902-1974 *EncAB*

Lindberg, Conrad Emil 1852-1930 *DcAmB, WhAm 1*

Lindberg, David Oscar Nathaniel 1891-1964 *WhAm 4*

Lindberg, Irving Augustus 1887-1957 *WhAm 3*

Lindbergh, Charles Augustus 1859-1924 *AmBi, BiDrAC, DcAmB, EncAAH, NatCAB 25*

Lindbergh, Charles Augustus 1902-1974 *AsBiEn, McGEWB, WebAB, WebAMB, WhAm 6*
Lindblad, Bertil 1895-1965 *AsBiEn, DcScB, WhAm 4*
Lindbloom, Pauline Funk 1911-1975 *WhAm 6*
Linde, Carl Von 1842-1934 *DcScB*
Linde, Christian 1817-1887 *DcAmB, WhAm H*
Linde, Karl Von 1842-1934 *AsBiEn*
Lindeberg, Carl *IlBEAAW*
Lindeberg, Harrie Thomas 1880-1959 *NatCAB 47, WhAm 3*
Lindegren, Alina M 1887-1957 *WhAm 3*
Lindeke, William 1835-1892 *NatCAB 28*
Lindelof, Ernst Leonhard 1870-1946 *DcScB*
Lindeman, Charles Bernard 1891-1969 *WhAm 5*
Lindeman, Eduard Christian 1885-1953 *DcAmB S5, WhAm 3*
Lindeman, Frank, Jr. 1909-1963 *WhAm 4*
Lindemann, Carl Louis Ferdinand 1852-1939 *DcScB*
Lindemann, Erich 1900-1974 *WhAm 6*
Lindemann, Ferdinand 1852-1939 *AsBiEn*
Lindemann, Frederick Alexander 1886-1957 *DcScB*
Linden, Frank Cutler 1860- *NatCAB 17*
Lindenau, Bernhard August Von 1779-1854 *DcScB*
Lindenkohl, Adolph 1833-1904 *DcAmB, NatCAB 26, WhAm 1*
Lindenmeyr, Philip *NewYHSD*
Lindenthal, Gustav 1850-1935 *DcAmB S1, NatCAB 14, NatCAB 16, WhAm 1*
Lindenthal, Gustave 1850-1935 *AmBi*
Linder, Fred E 1888-1949 *NatCAB 40*
Linder, Frederick M 1892-1956 *WhAm 3*
Linder, Oliver Anderson 1862-1939 *WhAm 1*
Linderfelt, Klas August 1847-1900 *DcAmLiB*
Linderman, Fannie Beatrice *BiCAW*
Linderman, Frank Bird 1869-1938 *NatCAB 40, WhAm 1*
Linderman, Garrett Brodhead 1829-1885 *NatCAB 5*
Linderman, Henry Richard 1825-1879 *ApCAB, DcAmB, NatCAB 4, TwCBDA, WhAm H*
Linderman, Robert Packer 1863-1903 *NatCAB 5, WhAm 1*
Linderstrom-Lang, Kaj 1896-1959 *WhAm 3*
Lindgren, Waldemar 1860-1939 *DcAmB S2, DcScB, NatCAB 30, WebAB, WhAm 1*
Lindheimer, Ferdinand Jacob 1801-1879 *DcAmB, NatCAB 24, WhAm H*
Lindley, Albert 1864- *WhAm 4*
Lindley, Curtis Holbrook 1850-1920 *DcAmB, NatCAB 25, WhAm 1*
Lindley, Daniel 1801-1880 *DcAmB S1, WhAm H*
Lindley, Erasmus Christopher 1870-1957 *WhAm 3*
Lindley, Ernest Hiram 1869-1940 *BiDAmEd, NatCAB 42, WhAm 1*
Lindley, Harlow 1875- *WhAm 5*
Lindley, Harold Ferguson 1888-1944 *NatCAB 34*
Lindley, Hervey 1854-1929 *WhAm 1*
Lindley, Jacob 1774-1857 *DcAmB, NatCAB 9, WhAm H*
Lindley, James Johnson 1822-1891 *BiAUS, BiDrAC, WhAm H*
Lindley, John 1799-1865 *DcScB*
Lindley, John Franklin 1918-1971 *WhAm 6*
Lindley, Paul Cameron 1877-1933 *WhAm 1*
Lindley, Walter 1852-1922 *NatCAB 13, NatCAB 21, WhAm 1*
Lindley, Walter C 1880-1958 *WhAm 3*
Lindly, William Alden 1846-1932 *NatCAB 23*
Lindmark, Winter *NewYHSD*
Lindner, Clarence Richard 1890-1952 *NatCAB 40, WhAm 3*
Lindner, Richard 1901- *BnEnAmA*
Lindner, Robert M 1915-1956 *WhAm 4*
Lindneux, Robert Ottokar 1871-1970 *IlBEAAW*
Lindquist, Clarence Gustav 1895-1964 *NatCAB 50*
Lindquist, Erick Gunnard 1885-1952 *NatCAB 42*
Lindquist, Everet Franklin 1901- *BiDAmEd*
Lindquist, Francis Oscar 1869-1924 *BiDrAC,*

WhAm 1
Lindquist, Robert John 1902-1951 *WhAm 3*
Lindquist, Rudolph Daniel 1888-1949 *WhAm 2*
Lindsay, Alexander, Jr. 1871-1926 *WhAm 1*
Lindsay, Alexander M 1841-1920 *NatCAB 19*
Lindsay, Andrew Jackson 1820?-1895 *IlBEAAW, NewYHSD*
Lindsay, Anna Laura *WhoColR*
Lindsay, Anna Robertson Brown 1864-1948 *NatCAB 36, WhAm 2, WomWWA 14*
Lindsay, Arthur Hawes 1862-1949 *WhAm 2*
Lindsay, Arthur Oliver 1877-1956 *NatCAB 47*
Lindsay, Arthur Oliver 1878-1956 *WhAm 3*
Lindsay, Charles 1820- *Drake*
Lindsay, Charles *see also* Lindsey, Charles
Lindsay, D Moore 1862- *WhAm 4*
Lindsay, Edmond James 1838- *NatCAB 2*
Lindsay, Edwin Parker 1869-1925 *NatCAB 22*
Lindsay, F M 1879-1972 *WhAm 5*
Lindsay, George David 1862-1946 *NatCAB 38*
Lindsay, George Henry 1837-1916 *BiDrAC, WhAm 1, WhAmP*
Lindsay, George LeRoy 1888-1943 *WhAm 2*
Lindsay, George Washington 1865-1938 *BiDrAC, WhAm 1, WhAmP*
Lindsay, Hal 1891-1965 *NatCAB 51, WhAm 4*
Lindsay, Hamilton Lawson 1866-1932 *NatCAB 39*
Lindsay, Henry Drennan 1859-1914 *WhAm 1*
Lindsay, Howard 1889-1968 *NatCAB 54, WhAm 4A*
Lindsay, James Edwin 1826-1915 *ApCAB X*
Lindsay, James Gordon 1892-1965 *NatCAB 53*
Lindsay, James Hubert 1862-1933 *WhAm 1*
Lindsay, James Menesse 1835- *NatCAB 11*
Lindsay, John Douglas 1865-1932 *ApCAB X, NatCAB 15, NatCAB 26, WhAm 1*
Lindsay, John Summerfield 1842-1903 *ApCAB, NatCAB 6, TwCBDA, WhAm 1*
Lindsay, John Vliet 1921- *BiDrAC, EncAB*
Lindsay, John Wesley 1820- *NatCAB 11, TwCBDA, WhAm 1*
Lindsay, Joseph Coppliss 1868- *WhoColR*
Lindsay, Kenneth 1890-1964 *NatCAB 51*
Lindsay, Lizzie *NewYHSD*
Lindsay, Lynn Grout 1893-1968 *WhAm 5*
Lindsay, Marrill Kirk 1884-1960 *WhAm 4*
Lindsay, Mary Ann Batson 1839-1918 *BiCAW*
Lindsay, Maud McKnight 1874-1941 *WhAm 2*
Lindsay, Nicholas Vachel 1879-1931 *DcAmB*
Lindsay, Robert Burns 1824-1902 *BiAUS, NatCAB 10, TwCBDA, WhAm 1*
Lindsay, Sir Ronald 1877- *WhAm 5*
Lindsay, Roy Wallace 1886-1964 *WhAm 4*
Lindsay, Samuel McCune 1869-1959 *NatCAB 12, WhAm 3*
Lindsay, T C 1845-1907 *IlBEAAW*
Lindsay, Thomas Bond 1853-1909 *WhAm 1*
Lindsay, Thomas Corwin 1845-1907 *NewYHSD, WhAm 1*
Lindsay, Vachel 1879-1931 *AmBi, ApCAB X, DcAmB, McGEWB, NatCAB 23, WebAB, WhAm 1*
Lindsay, William *NewYHSD*
Lindsay, William 1835-1909 *BiDrAC, DcAmB, NatCAB 11, TwCBDA, WhAm 1*
Lindsay, William *see also* Lindsey, William
Lindsay, William Sharp 1852- *WhAm 4*
Lindsay-Wynekoop, Alice Lois *WomWWA 14*
Lindsey, Ben Barr 1869-1943 *NatCAB 32, WhAm 2*
Lindsey, Benjamin Barr 1869-1943 *ApCAB X, DcAmB S3, EncAB, McGEWB, NatCAB 15, WebAB*
Lindsey, Charles 1820- *ApCAB*
Lindsey, Charles *see also* Lindsay, Charles
Lindsey, Daniel Weisiger 1835-1917 *ApCAB, WhAm 1*
Lindsey, Edward Allen 1871- *WhAm 5*
Lindsey, Edward Sherman 1872-1943 *WhAm 2*
Lindsey, Harry W, Jr. 1889-1959 *WhAm 3*
Lindsey, Joseph Bridgeo 1862-1939 *WhAm 1*
Lindsey, Julian Robert 1871-1948 *WhAm 2*
Lindsey, Kenneth Lovell 1888-1969 *WhAm 5*
Lindsey, Louis 1877- *WhAm 5*
Lindsey, Louise M 1872- *WomWWA 14*
Lindsey, Malcolm F 1891-1975 *WhAm 6*

Lindsey, Stephen Decatur 1828-1884 *BiDrAC, WhAm H*
Lindsey, Sterling Paul, Jr. 1902-1950 *WhAm 3*
Lindsey, Therese Kayser 1870- *WhAm 5*
Lindsey, Mrs. Washington E *WomWWA 14*
Lindsey, Washington Ellsworth 1862-1926 *NatCAB 23, WhAm 1*
Lindsey, William 1835-1909 *ApCAB*
Lindsey, William 1858-1922 *DcAmB, NatCAB 14, NatCAB 21, WhAm 1*
Lindsey, William *see also* Lindsay, William
Lindsey, William Henry 1879-1940 *WhAm 1*
Lindsley, Charles Augustus 1826-1906 *NatCAB 8, NatCAB 26, TwCBDA, WhAm 1*
Lindsley, Charles Frederick 1894-1960 *WhAm 4*
Lindsley, Dorlissa Johnston *WomWWA 14*
Lindsley, Harvey 1804-1889 *NatCAB 12*
Lindsley, Henry Dickinson 1872-1938 *WhAm 1*
Lindsley, Henry Dickinson 1873-1938 *ApCAB X*
Lindsley, Herbert Kitchel 1874-1951 *WhAm 3*
Lindsley, James Girard 1819-1898 *BiDrAC*
Lindsley, John Berrien 1822-1897 *ApCAB, BiDAmEd, DcAmB, NatCAB 8, TwCBDA, WhAm H*
Lindsley, Nathaniel Lawrence 1816-1868 *ApCAB, NatCAB 3*
Lindsley, Philip 1786-1855 *ApCAB, BiDAmEd, DcAmB, Drake, NatCAB 8, TwCBDA, WhAm H*
Lindsley, Smith M 1847-1909 *WhAm 1*
Lindsley, Stuart 1849-1942 *NatCAB 31*
Lindsley, William Dell 1812-1890 *BiAUS, BiDrAC, WhAm H*
Lindstrand, Frans Albin 1847- *NatCAB 11*
Lindstrom, Carl E 1896-1969 *WhAm 5*
Lindstrom, Ernest W 1891-1948 *WhAm 2*
Lineaweaver, Thomas Harbaugh 1896-1955 *NatCAB 43*
Linebarger, Charles Elijah 1867-1937 *WhAm 1*
Linebarger, Paul Myron Anthony 1913-1966 *WhAm 4*
Linebarger, Paul Myron Wentworth 1871-1939 *AmBi, NatCAB 38, WhAm 1*
Linebaugh, Daniel Haden 1878-1940 *WhAm 1*
Lineberger, Abel Caleb 1857-1947 *NatCAB 37*
Lineberger, Archibald Caleb 1900-1951 *NatCAB 40*
Lineberger, Walter Franklin 1883-1943 *BiDrAC, WhAm 2*
Lineberger, William Munday 1886-1936 *NatCAB 35*
Linehan, Daniel Francis 1869-1928 *ApCAB X*
Linehan, John C 1840-1905 *WhAm 1*
Linehan, Neil Joseph 1895-1967 *BiDrAC, WhAm 4*
Linen, George 1802-1888 *NewYHSD*
Linen, Herbert Murray 1877-1922 *ApCAB X*
Linen, James 1808-1873 *ApCAB*
Linen, James A, Jr. 1884-1957 *WhAm 3*
Linen, James Alexander 1840-1918 *NatCAB 5, NatCAB 32*
Linen, John 1800?- *NewYHSD*
Linen, Robert Walker 1841-1919 *ApCAB X*
Lines, Augustus E 1823?- *NewYHSD*
Lines, Edwin Stevens 1845-1927 *NatCAB 13, WhAm 1*
Lines, George 1853-1929 *NatCAB 22, WhAm 1*
Lines, H Wales 1838-1927 *WhAm 1*
Lines, Harvey Klopp 1873-1928 *ApCAB X*
Lines, Mary Louise 1859- *NatCAB 16, WomWWA 14*
Lineweaver, Goodrich Wilson 1887-1961 *WhAm 4*
Linfield, Adolphus 1880- *WhAm 6*
Linfield, Frances Eleanor Ross 1852-1890 *ApCAB X, NatCAB 19, WhAm 4*
Linfield, Frederick Bloomfield 1866-1948 *WhAm 3*
Linfield, George Fisher 1846-1890 *ApCAB X, NatCAB 19*
Linford, James Henry 1863- *WhAm 4*
Linford, Leon Blood 1904-1957 *WhAm 3*
Linford, Maurice Blood 1901-1960 *NatCAB 48*
Linforth, Ivan Mortimer 1879- *WhAm 6*
Ling, Charles Joseph 1867- *WhAm 5*

Ling, David W d1965 *WhAm 4*
Ling, James Joseph 1922- *EncAB*
Ling, Reese M 1868- *WhAm 4*
Lingan, James Maccubin 1752?-1812 *ApCAB, Drake*
Lingard, James W *WhAm H*
Lingelbach, Anna Lane 1873-1954 *DcAmB S5, NatCAB 44, WhAm 3*
Lingelbach, William E 1871-1962 *WhAm 4*
Lingeman, Edward Laurel 1887-1950 *NatCAB 38*
Lingenfelter, Mary Rebecca 1893-1953 *WhAm 3*
Lingham, Fred J 1875-1954 *WhAm 3*
Lingle, Bowman Church 1876-1959 *WhAm 3*
Lingle, David Judson 1863- *WhAm 4*
Lingle, Elmore Yokum 1910-1974 *WhAm 6*
Lingle, Thomas Wilson 1871-1937 *NatCAB 29, WhAm 1*
Lingle, Walter Lee 1868-1956 *WhAm 3*
Lingley, Charles Ramsdell 1877-1934 *WhAm 1*
Linhart, Samuel Black 1865-1936 *WhAm 1*
Liniers, Bremont, Don Santiago 1760?-1809 *Drake*
Lining, John 1708-1760 *ApCAB, DcAmB, Drake, NatCAB 25, WhAm H*
Lininger, Frederick Fouse 1892-1974 *WhAm 6*
Link, Arthur 1920- *EncAAH*
Link, B Lillian 1880- *WomWWA 14*
Link, Harvey 1824- *ApCAB*
Link, Heinrich Friedrich 1767-1851 *DcScB*
Link, Henry Charles 1889-1952 *DcAmB S5, WhAm 3*
Link, J William 1866-1933 *NatCAB 27*
Link, John Ephraim 1839- *WhAm 4*
Link, Margaret C Schott 1910-1972 *WhAm 6*
Link, Samuel Albert 1848- *ApCAB Sup, TwCBDA, WhAm 3*
Link, Theodore Carl 1850- *NatCAB 12, WhAm 4*
Link, William Walter 1884-1950 *BiDrAC, WhAm 3*
Linklater, Eric 1899-1974 *WhAm 6*
Linn, Alonzo 1827-1901 *WhAm 1*
Linn, Alvin Frank 1864-1939 *WhAm 1*
Linn, Archibald L 1802-1857 *BiAUS*
Linn, Archibald Ladley 1802-1857 *BiDrAC, WhAm H*
Linn, Archibald Laidlie 1802-1857 *ApCAB*
Linn, Clarence Andrew 1893-1967 *NatCAB 54*
Linn, Edith Lenore Willis 1865- *AmWom, WomWWA 14*
Linn, Henry W 1904-1969 *WhAm 5*
Linn, James d1820 *BiAUS*
Linn, James 1749-1821 *BiDrAC, WhAm H*
Linn, James 1750-1820 *ApCAB, TwCBDA*
Linn, James Weber 1876-1939 *NatCAB 38, NatCAB 47, WhAm 1*
Linn, John 1763-1821 *BiAUS, BiDrAC, TwCBDA, WhAm H*
Linn, John Blair 1777-1804 *ApCAB, DcAmB, Drake, NatCAB 13, TwCBDA, WhAm H*
Linn, John Blair 1831-1899 *ApCAB, TwCBDA*
Linn, Lewis Fields 1795-1843 *ApCAB, DcAmB, Drake, NatCAB 4, REnAW, TwCBDA*
Linn, Lewis Fields 1796-1843 *BiAUS, BiDrAC, WhAm H*
Linn, Mary Hunter *WomWWA 14*
Linn, Paul Hinkle 1873-1924 *NatCAB 25, WhAm 1*
Linn, Robert A 1904-1963 *WhAm 4*
Linn, William d1781 *ApCAB Sup*
Linn, William 1752-1808 *ApCAB, Drake, NatCAB 3, TwCBDA*
Linn, William 1790-1867 *ApCAB, TwCBDA*
Linn, William Alexander 1846-1917 *DcAmB, NatCAB 26, WhAm 3*
Linn, William Bomberger 1871-1950 *WhAm 3*
Linnaeus, Carl 1707-1778 *DcScB, McGEWB*
Linnaeus, Carolus 1707-1778 *AsBiEn, BiHiMed*
Linnard, Joseph Hamilton 1860-1935 *WhAm 1*
Linnell, Irving Nelson 1881-1954 *NatCAB 41*
Linnell, William Shepherd 1885-1968 *NatCAB 55, WhAm 4*
Linneman, Herbert F 1914-1971 *WhAm 5*
Linnen, Edward Bangs 1864-1928 *WhAm 1*
Linnes, Lowell Claude 1931-1974 *WhAm 6*

Linney, Frank Armfield 1874-1928 *WhAm 1*
Linney, Robert Joseph 1908-1971 *NatCAB 57, WhAm 5*
Linney, Romulus Zachariah 1841-1910 *BiDrAC, TwCBDA*
Linnik, Iuril Vladimirovich 1915-1975 *WhAm 6*
Linoff, Joseph Louis 1898-1950 *NatCAB 39*
Linscheid, Adolph 1879-1949 *WhAm 3*
Linscott, Robert Newton 1886-1964 *WhAm 4*
Linsey, Jay Wood 1885-1957 *NatCAB 46*
Linsley, Daniel Chipman 1827-1889 *NatCAB 16*
Linsley, Duncan Robertson 1900-1972 *WhAm 5*
Linsley, James Harvey 1787-1843 *ApCAB, Drake, NatCAB 4, TwCBDA*
Linsley, Joel Harvey 1790-1868 *Drake, TwCBDA*
Linsley, Joel Hervey 1790-1868 *ApCAB*
Linsley, John Hatch 1859-1901 *NatCAB 15*
Linsley, Joseph Hatch 1859- *ApCAB Sup*
Linsly, Jared 1803-1887 *ApCAB, TwCBDA*
Linson, Corwin Knapp 1864- *WhAm 5*
Linthicum, Charles Clarence 1857-1916 *WhAm 1*
Linthicum, George Milton 1870-1935 *NatCAB 29, WhAm 1*
Linthicum, John Charles 1867-1932 *BiDrAC, WhAm 1, WhAmP*
Linthicum, Richard 1859-1934 *WhAm 1*
Lintner, Joseph Albert 1822-1898 *ApCAB, DcAmB, NatCAB 5, TwCBDA, WhAm H*
Linton, Arthur Wilson 1878-1922 *NatCAB 19*
Linton, Edwin 1855-1939 *NatCAB 29, TwCBDA, WhAm 1*
Linton, Eliza Lynn 1822- *ApCAB*
Linton, Frank B A 1871-1943 *WhAm 2*
Linton, Laura Alberta 1853- *AmWom, NatCAB 12*
Linton, Morris Albert 1887-1966 *NatCAB 53, WhAm 4*
Linton, Ralph 1893-1953 *DcAmB S5, McGEWB, WebAB, WhAm 3*
Linton, Robert 1870-1942 *NatCAB 31, WhAm 2*
Linton, William James 1812-1897 *AmBi, ApCAB, DcAmB, NatCAB 8, TwCBDA, WhAm H*
Linton, William Seelye 1856-1927 *BiDrAC, TwCBDA, WhAm 1*
Lintott, Edward Barnard 1875-1951 *WhAm 3*
Linville, Clarence Philander 1879- *WhAm 6*
Linville, Henry Richardson 1866-1941 *BiDAmEd, WhAm 2*
Linz, Paul Francis 1899-1974 *WhAm 6*
Lion, Henry 1900-1966 *IIBEAAW*
Lion, Jules 1816?- *NewYHSD*
Lion, P P *NewYHSD*
Lionberger, Isaac H 1854-1948 *WhAm 3*
Liouville, Joseph 1809-1882 *AsBiEn, DcScB*
Lipchitz, Jacques 1891-1973 *BnEnAmA, McGEWB, WhAm 5*
Lipe, George Oehler 1874-1950 *NatCAB 42*
Lipe, W Charles 1901-1929 *NatCAB 25*
Lipe, W Coughtry 1861-1924 *NatCAB 25*
Lipe, Walter Hudson 1860-1921 *NatCAB 23*
Liper, John *NewYHSD*
Lipka, Joseph 1883-1924 *AmBi*
Lipman, Charles Bernard 1883-1944 *WhAm 2*
Lipman, Clara 1872-1952 *WhAm 3, WomWWA 14*
Lipman, Frederick Lockwood 1866-1950 *WhAm 3*
Lipman, George Simon 1908-1962 *NatCAB 49*
Lipman, Jacob Goodale 1874-1939 *DcAmB S2, WhAm 1*
Lipman, Louis *NewYHSD*
Lipmann, Fritz Albert 1899- *AsBiEn, WebAB*
Lippard, George 1822-1854 *ApCAB, DcAmB, Drake, WhAm H*
Lippe, Adolph 1812-1888 *ApCAB Sup*
Lippencott, Edward *NewYHSD*
Lippershey, Hans 1587-1619 *AsBiEn*
Lippett, Sara Wiches 1789-1847 *NewYHSD*
Lipphard, William Benjamin 1886-1971 *WhAm 5*
Lippi, Filippo 1406?-1469 *McGEWB*
Lippiatt, Thomas 1832?- *NewYHSD*

Lippincott, C H 1860- *AmWom*
Lippincott, Charles Augustus 1865-1929 *WhAm 1*
Lippincott, Craige 1846-1911 *NatCAB 29, WhAm 1*
Lippincott, Ellis Ridgeway, Jr. 1920-1974 *WhAm 6*
Lippincott, Esther J Trimble 1838-1888 *AmWom*
Lippincott, Horace Mather 1877-1967 *WhAm 4*
Lippincott, James 1864-1936 *NatCAB 27, WhAm 1*
Lippincott, James Aubrey 1847- *NatCAB 10*
Lippincott, James Starr 1819-1885 *ApCAB, DcAmB, TwCBDA, WhAm H*
Lippincott, Job H 1842-1900 *WhAm 1*
Lippincott, Joseph Barlow 1864-1942 *NatCAB 36, WhAm 2*
Lippincott, Joshua Allan 1835- *TwCBDA*
Lippincott, Joshua Allen 1835- *NatCAB 9*
Lippincott, Joshua Ballinger 1813-1886 *AmBi, DcAmB, NatCAB 26, TwCBDA, WhAm H*
Lippincott, Joshua Ballinger 1816-1886 *ApCAB, NatCAB 4*
Lippincott, Joshua Bertram 1857-1940 *NatCAB 36, WhAm 1*
Lippincott, Leon Stanley 1888-1950 *NatCAB 39*
Lippincott, Martha Shepard d1949 *WhAm 2, WomWWA 14*
Lippincott, Mary Woodward 1881- *WomWWA 14*
Lippincott, Richard H 1901-1957 *WhAm 3*
Lippincott, Sara Jane Clarke 1823-1904 *AmBi, AmWom, ApCAB, DcAmB, Drake, NatCAB 4, NotAW, TwCBDA, WhAm 1*
Lippincott, William Adams 1882-1931 *WhAm 1*
Lippincott, William Dunton 1871-1944 *NatCAB 41*
Lippincott, William Henry 1849-1920 *ApCAB, NatCAB 6, TwCBDA, WhAm 1*
Lippitt, Charles Warren 1846-1924 *ApCAB X, NatCAB 9, TwCBDA, WhAm 1*
Lippitt, Charles Warren 1894-1970 *WhAm 5*
Lippitt, Christopher 1744-1824 *ApCAB, Drake, TwCBDA*
Lippitt, Flora K *WomWWA 14*
Lippitt, Francis James 1812-1902 *WhAm 1*
Lippitt, Henry 1818-1891 *BiAUS, DcAmB, NatCAB 9, TwCBDA, WhAm H*
Lippitt, Henry Frederick 1856-1933 *BiDrAC, NatCAB 25, WhAm 1*
Lippitt, S Herman 1886-1934 *NatCAB 26*
Lippitt, William Donald 1885-1935 *NatCAB 40, WhAm 1*
Lippman, Benjamin Melvin 1876-1948 *NatCAB 37*
Lippman, Hyman Shalit 1896-1972 *WhAm 6*
Lippman, Leonard Bing 1907-1974 *WhAm 6*
Lippmann, Gabriel Jonas 1845-1921 *DcScB*
Lippmann, Julie Mathilde 1864-1952 *TwCBDA, WhAm 3, WomWWA 14*
Lippmann, Robert Korn 1898-1969 *NatCAB 54, WhAm 5*
Lippmann, Walter 1889-1974 *ApCAB X, EncAB, McGEWB, WebAB, WhAm 6*
Lippold, Richard 1915- *BnEnAmA*
Lipps, Oscar Hiram 1872- *WhAm 5*
Lipschitz, Rudolf Otto Sigismund 1832-1903 *DcScB*
Lipschultz, Samuel 1894-1960 *WhAm 4*
Lipscomb, Abner Smith 1789-1856 *DcAmB, WhAm H*
Lipscomb, Abner Smith 1789-1857 *ApCAB, Drake, TwCBDA*
Lipscomb, Abner Smith 1789-1858 *NatCAB 5*
Lipscomb, Andrew Adgate 1816-1890 *ApCAB, DcAmB, NatCAB 6, NatCAB 9, TwCBDA, WhAm H*
Lipscomb, David 1831-1917 *DcAmReB*
Lipscomb, David 1831-1918 *WhAm 1*
Lipscomb, Glenard Paul 1915-1970 *BiDrAC, WhAm 5*
Lipscomb, Guy Fleming 1884-1958 *NatCAB 48*
Lipscomb, Mary Ann 1848- *TwCBDA*
Lipscomb, William 1896-1960 *NatCAB 47*
Lipscomb, William H 1888-1957 *WhAm 3*

Lipset, Seymour Martin 1922- *WebAB*
Lipsey, Plautus Iberus 1865-1947 *WhAm 2*
Lipsey, Plautus Iberus, Jr. 1893-1970 *WhAm 5*
Lipsitz, Louis 1872-1927 *WhAm 1*
Lipsky, Louis 1876-1963 *WhAm 4, WhAm 5*
Lipton, Barbara 1928-1974 *WhAm 6*
Lipton, Maurice Frank 1906-1964 *NatCAB 51*
Lipton, Seymour 1903- *BnEnAmA*
Lipton, Sir Thomas Johnstone d1933 *WhAm 3*
Lira, Maximo Rafael 1845- *ApCAB*
Lisa, Manuel 1772-1820 *AmBi, DcAmB, REnAW, WebAB, WhAm H*
Lisboa, Balthazar 1761-1840 *ApCAB*
Lisboa, Bento DaSilva 1793-1864 *ApCAB*
Lisboa, Joao De *DcScB*
Lisboa, Joao Francisco 1812-1863 *ApCAB*
Lisboa, Jose Antonio 1777-1850 *ApCAB*
Lisboa, Jose DaSilva 1756-1835 *ApCAB*
Lisboa Serra, Joao Duarte 1818-1855 *ApCAB*
Lischer, Benno Edward 1876-1959 *WhAm 3*
Liscum, Emerson Hamilton 1841-1900 *TwCBDA, WhAm 1*
Liskey, Dan Dale 1888-1952 *NatCAB 42*
Lisle, Arthur Beymer 1871-1949 *NatCAB 37, WhAm 2*
Lisle, Henry M d1814 *Drake*
Lisle, Marcus Claiborne 1862-1894 *BiDrAC, WhAm H*
Lisle, Robert Patton 1842-1911 *WhAm 1*
Lisman, Frederick J 1865-1940 *WhAm 1*
Lispenard, George *NewYHSD*
Lispenard, Leonard 1716-1790 *ApCAB, BiAUS, NatCAB 5, TwCBDA*
Liss, Edward 1890-1967 *NatCAB 53*
Lissajous, Jules Antoine 1822-1880 *DcScB*
Lissak, Ormond Mitchell 1861-1912 *NatCAB 25*
Lissaute, Pierre *NewYHSD*
Lisser, Louis 1850-1919 *NatCAB 27, WhAm 1*
Lissner, Herbert Richard 1908-1965 *NatCAB 51*
Lissner, Meyer 1871-1930 *WhAm 1*
List, Ambrose Shaw 1854-1938 *WhAm 1*
List, Carl F 1902-1968 *WhAm 5*
List, Emanuel 1891-1967 *WhAm 4*
List, Frederick 1789-1846 *Drake*
List, Friedrich 1789-1846 *ApCAB*
List, Georg Friedrich 1789-1846 *DcAmB, McGEWB, WhAm H*
List, Harriet Winslow 1819- *Drake*
List, Kurt 1913-1970 *WhAm 5*
List, Wilhelm 1880-1971 *WhWW-II, WhoMilH*
Listemann, Bernhard 1841-1917 *DcAmB, WhAm 1*
Listemann, Fritz 1839-1909 *WhAm 1*
Lister, Charles Baynard 1898-1951 *WhAm 3*
Lister, Edwin 1829- *NatCAB 5*
Lister, Ernest 1870-1918 *NatCAB 15, WhAm 1*
Lister, Lord Joseph 1827-1912 *AsBiEn, BiHiMed, DcScB, McGEWB*
Lister, Joseph Jackson 1786-1869 *AsBiEn, DcScB*
Lister, Martin 1639-1712 *DcScB*
Lister, Walter Bartlett 1899-1967 *WhAm 4*
Listle, Alice Ingersoll 1876- *WomWWA 14*
Listoe, Soren 1846- *WhAm 4*
Liston, H, Sr. 1889-1956 *WhAm 3*
Liston, Robert 1794-1847 *BiHiMed*
Liszt, Franz 1811-1886 *McGEWB*
Litch, Ernest Wheeler 1897-1967 *WhAm 4*
Litchfield, Edward Harold 1914-1968 *WhAm 5*
Litchfield, Electus Backus 1813-1889 *DcAmB, NatCAB 28, WhAm H*
Litchfield, Electus Darwin 1872-1952 *NatCAB 50, WhAm 3*
Litchfield, Elisha 1785-1859 *BiDrAC, WhAm H*
Litchfield, Elisha 1795-1859 *BiAUS, TwCBDA*
Litchfield, Grace Denio 1849-1944 *AmWom, NatCAB 12, NatCAB 43, WhAm 2, WomWWA 14*
Litchfield, Lawrence 1861-1930 *NatCAB 22, WhAm 1*
Litchfield, Lawrence, Jr. 1900-1967 *WhAm 4*
Litchfield, Mary Elizabeth 1854- *WhAm 4,*

WomWWA 14
Litchfield, Paul Weeks 1875-1959 *WhAm 3*
Litchfield, William Elias 1861-1921 *ApCAB X, WhAm 1*
Litchman, Charles Henry 1849-1902 *WhAm 1*
Lithgow, David Cunningham 1868- *IIBEAAW*
Lithgow, James Smith 1812- *NatCAB 11*
Lithgow, William 1750-1796 *Drake*
Litin, Edward Mortimer 1921-1972 *WhAm 6*
Litke, Fyodor Petrovich 1797-1882 *DcScB*
Litman, Simon 1873- *WhAm 5*
Litsey, Edwin Carlile 1874-1970 *WhAm 5*
Litsinger, Edward Robert 1874- *WhAm 5*
Litt, Jacob 1860-1905 *WhAm 1*
Litta, Marie 1856-1883 *NatCAB 3*
Littauer, Lucius Nathan 1859-1944 *BiDrAC, DcAmB S3, NatCAB 32, TwCBDA, WhAm 2, WhAmP*
Littauer, William 1865-1953 *NatCAB 41*
Littel, Emlyn T 1840-1891 *WhAm H*
Littell, Clair Francis 1887-1966 *WhAm 4*
Littell, Clarence Guy 1882-1958 *WhAm 3*
Littell, Eliakim 1797-1870 *ApCAB, DcAmB, Drake, NatCAB 24, TwCBDA, WhAm H*
Littell, Frank Bowers 1869-1951 *WhAm 3*
Littell, Isaac William 1857-1924 *NatCAB 20, WhAm 1*
Littell, John Stockton 1806-1875 *ApCAB, NatCAB 5*
Littell, Philip 1868-1943 *NatCAB 32, WhAm 2*
Littell, Robert 1896-1963 *NatCAB 50, WhAm 4*
Littell, Samuel Harrington 1873-1967 *WhAm 4*
Littell, Squier 1803-1886 *ApCAB, DcAmB, NatCAB 25, WhAm H*
Littell, William 1768-1824 *DcAmB, Drake, NatCAB 24, WhAm H*
Littell, William 1780?-1825 *ApCAB*
Litten, Frederic Nelson 1885-1951 *WhAm 3*
Littick, Orville Beck 1890-1953 *WhAm 3*
Littick, William Oliver 1867-1941 *NatCAB 38*
Littig, Lawrence William 1858-1918 *WhAm 1*
Littinov, Maxim Maximovich 1876-1952 *WhWW-II*
Little, Alden Howe 1881-1964 *WhAm 4*
Little, Alice Cowles 1865- *WomWWA 14*
Little, Ann *NewYHSD*
Little, Archibald Alexander 1860- *WhAm 4*
Little, Arthur 1837-1915 *WhAm 1*
Little, Arthur Dehon 1863-1935 *AmBi, DcAmB S1, NatCAB 15, WhAm 1*
Little, Arthur Mitchell 1865- *WhAm 5*
Little, Arthur W 1873-1943 *WhAm 2*
Little, Arthur Wilde 1856-1910 *WhAm 1*
Little, Bascom 1879-1940 *WhAm 1*
Little, Caroline Frances *WomWWA 14*
Little, Charles 1845-1921 *WhAm 1*
Little, Charles Coffin 1799-1869 *ApCAB, DcAmB, NatCAB 25, TwCBDA, WhAm H*
Little, Charles Eugene 1838- *WhAm 4*
Little, Charles Henry 1874-1947 *NatCAB 36*
Little, Charles Joseph 1840-1911 *ApCAB Sup, DcAmB, NatCAB 25, TwCBDA, WhAm 1*
Little, Charles Newton 1858-1923 *WhAm 1*
Little, Charles Sherman 1869-1936 *DcAmB S2*
Little, Chauncey Bundy 1877-1952 *BiDrAC, WhAm 3*
Little, Clarence Belden 1857- *WhAm 2*
Little, Clarence C 1888-1971 *WhAm 5*
Little, Clinton Egbert 1876-1965 *NatCAB 51*
Little, David Mason 1896-1954 *NatCAB 41, WhAm 3*
Little, Dillon Alva 1887-1950 *NatCAB 39*
Little, E H 1881- *WhAm 6*
Little, Edward Campbell 1858-1924 *BiDrAC, WhAm 1*
Little, Edward Preble 1788-1875 *BiAUS*
Little, Edward Preble 1791-1875 *BiDrAC, WhAm H*
Little, Ernest 1888-1973 *NatCAB 57, WhAm 6*
Little, Frances *WhAm 4*
Little, Francis 1886-1933 *NatCAB 25*
Little, Fred Albert 1893-1945 *NatCAB 36*
Little, George 1754-1809 *ApCAB, DcAmB,*

Drake, NatCAB 25, TwCBDA, WebAMB, WhAm H
Little, George 1838-1924 *WhAm 1*
Little, George E 1880- *WhAm 6*
Little, George French 1865-1925 *ApCAB X*
Little, George Obadiah 1839- *WhAm 4*
Little, George Thomas 1857-1915 *TwCBDA, WhAm 1*
Little, Gilbert Francis 1845- *WhAm 4*
Little, Harry Britton 1882-1944 *NatCAB 38, WhAm 2*
Little, Harvey D 1803-1833 *ApCAB, Drake*
Little, Henry G 1901-1974 *WhAm 6*
Little, Herbert Satterthwaite 1902-1972 *WhAm 5*
Little, Homer Payson 1884-1966 *WhAm 4*
Little, James Laurence 1836-1885 *ApCAB*
Little, James Lawrence 1836-1885 *NatCAB 13, TwCBDA*
Little, James Lovell 1874-1948 *WhAm 2*
Little, John 1837-1900 *BiDrAC, TwCBDA*
Little, John Dozier 1871-1934 *WhAm 1*
Little, John Goulding 1880-1955 *NatCAB 44*
Little, John Lowery 1872-1913 *NatCAB 17*
Little, John Pat 1909-1974 *WhAm 6*
Little, John Russell 1903-1968 *NatCAB 56*
Little, John Sebastian 1851-1916 *NatCAB 23*
Little, John Sebastian 1853-1916 *BiDrAC, TwCBDA, WhAm 1, WhAmP*
Little, John Wesley 1867-1923 *WhAm 1*
Little, John Wesley 1890-1969 *NatCAB 55*
Little, Joseph James 1841-1913 *BiDrAC, NatCAB 4, WhAm 1*
Little, Julia Eveline Lockhart 1856- *WomWWA 14*
Little, Kenneth Buxton 1897-1966 *WhAm 4*
Little, Lewis Henry 1818-1862 *ApCAB, Drake, TwCBDA*
Little, Louis McCarty 1878-1960 *WhAm 4*
Little, Lucius Freeman 1869-1946 *WhAm 2*
Little, Malcolm *EncAB, WebAB, WhAmP*
Little, Marou Brown *WomWWA 14*
Little, Martha H Neal 1851- *WomWWA 14*
Little, Mitchell Stuart 1885-1969 *WhAm 5*
Little, Moses 1724-1798 *ApCAB, Drake, TwCBDA*
Little, Peter 1775-1830 *ApCAB, BiAUS, BiDrAC, TwCBDA, WhAm H, WhAmP*
Little, Philip 1857-1942 *NatCAB 31, WhAm 2*
Little, Richard 1898-1973 *NatCAB 57*
Little, Richard Henry d1946 *WhAm 2*
Little, Riley McMillan 1865-1939 *WhAm 1*
Little, Robbins 1832- *ApCAB, TwCBDA, WhAm 4*
Little, Robert Rice 1881-1948 *WhAm 2*
Little, Russell A 1849-1922 *WhAm 1*
Little, S George 1903-1974 *WhAm 6*
Little, Sarah F Cowles 1838- *AmWom*
Little, Sidney Wahl 1904-1972 *WhAm 5*
Little, Sophia Louise 1799- *ApCAB, Drake*
Little, Tom 1898-1972 *WhAm 5*
Little, William 1692-1734 *NatCAB 8*
Little, William Augustus 1838-1924 *NatCAB 5, WhAm 3*
Little, William Cyrus 1849-1912 *NatCAB 16*
Little, William Myers 1867- *NatCAB 9*
Little, William Nelson 1852-1925 *NatCAB 6, WhAm 1*
Little Crow d1863 *ApCAB*
Little Crow 1810?-1863 *REnAW*
Little Crow V 1803?-1863 *DcAmB, WebAMB, WhAm H*
Little Turtle 1752?-1812 *AmBi, ApCAB, DcAmB, Drake, EncAAH, NatCAB 10, REnAW, WebAMB, WhAm H*
Little Wolf d1904 *REnAW*
Littledale, Clara Savage 1891-1956 *WhAm 3*
Littlefield, Alfred Henry 1829-1893 *NatCAB 9, TwCBDA*
Littlefield, Arthur Stevens 1864-1924 *NatCAB 20*
Littlefield, Charles Edgar 1851-1915 *BiDrAC, NatCAB 37, TwCBDA, WhAm 1, WhAmP*
Littlefield, Charles H *NewYHSD*
Littlefield, Charles William 1880-1961 *WhAm 4*
Littlefield, Eben Northup 1854-1935 *WhAm 1,*

WhAm 1C

Littlefield, Francis A *NewYHSD*

Littlefield, George Emery 1844-1915 *WhAm 1*

Littlefield, George Henry 1848-1939
NatCAB 30

Littlefield, George Washington 1842-1920
DcAmB, NatCAB 28, WhAm 4

Littlefield, Horace Robert 1846-1910
NatCAB 17

Littlefield, Jesse Braxton 1898-1959
NatCAB 47

Littlefield, Milton Smith 1832-1899
ApCAB Sup, TwCBDA

Littlefield, Milton Smith 1864-1934 *WhAm 1,
WhAm 1C*

Littlefield, Minnie Ella 1867- *WomWWA 14*

Littlefield, Nahum *NewYHSD*

Littlefield, Nathan Whitman 1846-1929
WhAm 1

Littlefield, Nathaniel Swett 1804-1882 *BiAUS,
BiDrAC, TwCBDA, WhAm H*

Littlefield, Walter 1867-1948 *NatCAB 37,
WhAm 2*

Littlehales, George Washington 1860-1943
ApCAB X, NatCAB 10, WhAm 2

Littlejohn, Abraham Newkirk 1824-1901
WhAm 1

Littlejohn, Abram Newkirk 1824-1901 *AmBi,
ApCAB, DcAmB, Drake, NatCAB 3,
TwCBDA*

Littlejohn, David 1876-1955 *NatCAB 43*

Littlejohn, DeWitt Clinton 1818-1892
*ApCAB Sup, BiAUS, BiDrAC,
NatCAB 11, TwCBDA, WhAm H*

Littlejohn, Elbridge Gerry 1862-1935 *WhAm 1*

Littlejohn, Frank Leslie 1868-1935 *WhAm 1*

Littlejohn, Jesse Matlock 1867-1923 *WhAm 1*

Littlejohn, John Martin 1867- *WhAm 4*

Littlejohn, Rebecca Bolling 1873-
WomWWA 14

Littlepage, Adam Brown 1859-1921 *BiDrAC,
WhAm 4, WhAmP*

Littlepage, Lewis 1762-1802 *ApCAB, DcAmB,
Drake, WhAm H*

Littlepage, Thomas Price 1873-1942 *WhAm 2*

Littler, Carl William 1880-1947 *NatCAB 49*

Littleton, Annie S 1843- *WomWWA 14*

Littleton, Arthur 1895-1973 *WhAm 6*

Littleton, Benjamin H 1889-1966 *WhAm 4*

Littleton, Harvey 1922- *BnEnAmA*

Littleton, J T 1887-1966 *WhAm 4*

Littleton, Jesse Matlock 1867-1923 *NatCAB 19*

Littleton, Jesse Talbot 1856-1929 *WhAm 1*

Littleton, Martin Wiley 1872-1934 *BiDrAC,
DcAmB S1, WhAm 1*

Littleton, William Graham 1868-1937 *WhAm 1*

Littlewood, William 1898-1967 *WhAm 4*

Littmann, Max 1846-1921 *NatCAB 19*

Litton, Abram 1814- *NatCAB 10*

Litvinov, Maxim Maximovich 1876-1951
McGEWB

Litz, Alma Zarah 1869-1940 *NatCAB 30*

Litz, George William 1872-1916 *NatCAB 17*

Litz, Moroni Orson 1874-1955 *NatCAB 50*

Litzenberg, Homer Laurence 1903-1963
WhAm 4

Litzenberg, Jennings Crawford 1870-1948
NatCAB 38, WhAm 2

Litzinger, Marie 1899-1952 *WhAm 3*

Liu, Hsieh 465?-522 *McGEWB*

Liu, Hui *DcScB*

Liu, Shao-Ch'i 1900-1974 *McGEWB*

Liu, Shao-Chi 1905-1974 *WhAm 6*

Liu, Ta-Chung 1914-1975 *WhAm 6*

Liu, Tsung-Yuan 773-819 *McGEWB*

Liva, Arcangelo 1887-1953 *NatCAB 44*

Livasse, William *NewYHSD*

Lively, Charles Elson 1890-1969 *WhAm 5*

Lively, Chauncy Clinton 1883-1949 *NatCAB 38*

Lively, Daniel O'Connell 1868-1933 *WhAm 1*

Lively, Frank 1864-1947 *WhAm 2*

Lively, John Jefferson 1879-1966 *NatCAB 53*

Lively, Robert Alexander 1922-1973 *WhAm 6*

Lively, Robert Maclin 1855-1929 *BiDrAC*

Livengood, Baxter Alphonso 1899-1956
NatCAB 53

Liveright, Horace Brisbin 1886-1933 *DcAmB S1,
WhAm 1*

Liverman, Harry d1961 *WhAm 4*

Livermore, Abiel Abbot 1811-1892 *ApCAB,
DcAmB, Drake, NatCAB 15, TwCBDA,
WhAm H*

Livermore, Arthur 1766-1853 *BiDrAC, DcAmB,
Drake, NatCAB 12, TwCBDA, WhAm H,
WhAmP*

Livermore, Arthur 1776-1853 *ApCAB, BiAUS*

Livermore, Caroline Sealy 1883- *WomWWA 14*

Livermore, Edward St. Joe 1762-1832 *TwCBDA*

Livermore, Edward St. Loe 1762-1832 *ApCAB,
BiAUS, BiDrAC, DcAmB, Drake,
NatCAB 20, NatCAB 24, WhAm H,
WhAmP*

Livermore, George 1809-1865 *ApCAB, DcAmB,
Drake, NatCAB 6, TwCBDA, WhAm H*

Livermore, George Robertson 1878-1962
WhAm 4

Livermore, Harriet 1788-1868 *NotAW,
TwCBDA*

Livermore, Henrietta J Wells 1864- *BiCAW,
WomWWA 14*

Livermore, Jesse Lauriston 1877-1940
NatCAB 47

Livermore, John Robert McDowell 1838-1925
NatCAB 22

Livermore, Mary Ashton Rice 1820-1905 *AmBi,
DcAmB, NotAW, TwCBDA, WebAB,
WhAm 1*

Livermore, Mary Ashton Rice 1821-1905
*AmWom, ApCAB, DcAmReB, Drake,
NatCAB 3*

Livermore, Mary Spear 1806- *NewYHSD*

Livermore, Norman Banks 1872-1953
NatCAB 40, WhAm 5

Livermore, Russell B 1894-1958 *WhAm 3*

Livermore, Samuel 1732-1803 *ApCAB, BiAUS,
BiDrAC, DcAmB, Drake, NatCAB 2,
TwCBDA, WhAm H, WhAmP*

Livermore, Samuel 1786-1833 *ApCAB,
DcAmB, Drake, WhAm H*

Livermore, William Roscoe 1843-1919 *WhAm 1*

Livernash, Edward James 1866-1938 *BiDrAC,
WhAm 4*

Liverpool, Robert B Jenkinson, Earl Of
1770-1828 *McGEWB*

Liversidge, Horace Preston 1878-1955 *WhAm 3*

Livesey, Frederick 1886-1961 *NatCAB 49*

Livesey, Sydney 1880-1947 *NatCAB 37*

Livingood, Charles Jacob 1866- *WhAm 5*

Livingston, Alice Delafield 1872-
WomWWA 14

Livingston, Arthur 1883-1944 *NatCAB 33,
WhAm 2*

Livingston, Bettie Phipps *WomWWA 14*

Livingston, Brockholst 1757-1823 *BiAUS,
Drake*

Livingston, Burton Edward 1875-1948
*DcAmB S4, DcScB, NatCAB 36,
WhAm 2*

Livingston, Charlotte Lucia *WomWWA 14*

Livingston, Clara Dudley 1875- *WomWWA 14*

Livingston, Crawford 1848-1925 *ApCAB X,
NatCAB 42, WhAm 1*

Livingston, Douglas Clermont 1877- *WhAm 5*

Livingston, Edward *NewYHSD*

Livingston, Edward 1764-1836 *AmBi, ApCAB,
BiAUS, BiDrAC, BiDrUSE, DcAmB,
Drake, McGEWB, NatCAB 5, REnAW,
TwCBDA, WebAB, WhAm H, WhAmP*

Livingston, George 1886-1954 *WhAm 3*

Livingston, Gerald Moncrieffe 1883- *ApCAB X*

Livingston, Goodhue 1867-1951 *NatCAB 39,
WhAm 3*

Livingston, Harriet 1786-1824 *NewYHSD*

Livingston, Henry *NewYHSD*

Livingston, Henry 1752-1823 *Drake*

Livingston, Henry Beekman 1750-1831 *ApCAB,
Drake, TwCBDA*

Livingston, Henry Brockholst 1757-1823 *AmBi,
ApCAB, DcAmB, NatCAB 2, TwCBDA,
WebAB, WhAm H*

Livingston, Henry Walter 1764-1810 *BiAUS,
Drake*

Livingston, Henry Walter 1768-1810 *ApCAB,
BiDrAC, TwCBDA, WhAm H, WhAmP*

Livingston, Homer J 1903-1970 *WhAm 5*

Livingston, James 1747-1832 *ApCAB, DcAmB,*

Drake, TwCBDA, WhAm H

Livingston, James Duane 1859-1936 *WhAm 1*

Livingston, Jesse Elsmer 1909-1961 *NatCAB 55,
WhAm 4*

Livingston, John Henry 1746-1825 *ApCAB,
DcAmB, DcAmReB, Drake, NatCAB 3,
TwCBDA, WhAm H*

Livingston, John Henry 1848-1927 *NatCAB 20*

Livingston, John White 1889-1962 *NatCAB 50*

Livingston, John William 1804-1885 *ApCAB,
DcAmB, NatCAB 25, TwCBDA,
WhAm H*

Livingston, Leonidas Felix 1832-1912 *BiDrAC,
NatCAB 2, TwCBDA, WhAm 1,
WhAmP*

Livingston, Marjorie M Johnson 1884-
WomWWA 14

Livingston, Montgomery 1816- *NewYHSD*

Livingston, Olga Theodora 1884-
WomWWA 14

Livingston, Paul Yount 1893-1963 *WhAm 4*

Livingston, Peter R 1766-1847 *NatCAB 3*

Livingston, Peter VanBrugh 1710-1792 *AmBi,
ApCAB, DcAmB, TwCBDA, WhAm H*

Livingston, Philip 1686-1749 *ApCAB,
TwCBDA*

Livingston, Philip 1716-1778 *AmBi, ApCAB,
BiAUS, BiDrAC, DcAmB, Drake,
NatCAB 3, TwCBDA, WhAm H,
WhAmP*

Livingston, Philip 1861-1938 *WhAm 1*

Livingston, Robert 1654-1725 *ApCAB,
TwCBDA*

Livingston, Robert 1654-1728 *AmBi, DcAmB,
McGEWB, NatCAB 24, WhAm H*

Livingston, Robert Francis 1871-1955
NatCAB 44

Livingston, Robert Irvin 1914-1967 *NatCAB 55,
WhAm 4*

Livingston, Robert LeRoy *BiAUS, BiDrAC,
WhAm H*

Livingston, Robert R 1718-1775 *ApCAB,
DcAmB, NatCAB 2, TwCBDA,
WhAm H*

Livingston, Robert R 1719-1775 *Drake*

Livingston, Robert R 1746-1813 *AmBi, ApCAB,
BiDrAC, DcAmB, EncAB, McGEWB,
NatCAB 2, TwCBDA, WebAB,
WhAm H, WhAmP*

Livingston, Robert R 1747-1813 *BiAUS, Drake*

Livingston, Robert Teviot 1896-1968 *WhAm 4*

Livingston, Rose Florence *WomWWA 14*

Livingston, Sigmund 1872-1946 *NatCAB 35,
WhAm 2*

Livingston, Solomon Bernheimer 1852-
NatCAB 13

Livingston, VanBrugh 1792-1868 *BiAUS,
NatCAB 13*

Livingston, Walter 1740-1797 *ApCAB, BiAUS,
BiDrAC, TwCBDA, WhAm H, WhAmP*

Livingston, William 1723-1790 *AmBi, ApCAB,
BiAUS, BiDrAC, DcAmB, Drake,
NatCAB 5, TwCBDA, WebAB,
WhAm H, WhAmP*

Livingston, William 1815-1879 *TwCBDA*

Livingston, William Henry 1898-1965
NatCAB 51, WhAm 4

Livingston, William Reinhardt 1870-1952
NatCAB 45

Livingstone, Colin Hamilton 1863-1943
WhAm 2

Livingstone, David 1813-1873 *McGEWB*

Livingstone, John Alexander 1885-1937
WhAm 1

Livingstone, Lemuel W *WhoColR*

Livingstone, M L *NewYHSD*

Livingstone, Seabourn Rome 1888-1961
NatCAB 51

Livingstone, William 1844-1925 *DcAmB,
NatCAB 25, WhAm 1*

Livius, Peter 1727-1795 *ApCAB, Drake*

Livy 064?BC-012?AD *McGEWB*

Lizana Y Beaumont, Francisco Javier De
1750-1811 *ApCAB*

Lizarraga, Reginaldo De 1545-1615 *ApCAB*

Lizars, Kathleen Macfarlane *WomWWA 14*

Lizars, Rawson Goodsir 1900-1969 *NatCAB 57,
WhAm 5*

Lleras Camargo, Alberto 1906- *McGEWB*
Llewellyn, A Stanley 1887-1960 *NatCAB 50*
Llewellyn, David Edgar 1874-1963 *NatCAB 50*
Llewellyn, Fred Warde 1878-1955 *NatCAB 44,*
WhAm 6
Llewellyn, Frederick Britton 1897-1971
WhAm 5
Llewellyn, Joseph Corson 1855-1932
NatCAB 44, WhAm 1
Llewellyn, Karl Nickerson 1893-1962 *WhAm 4*
Llewellyn, Maxwell Bowler 1914-1972 *WhAm 6*
Llewellyn, Morgan 1846-1920 *NatCAB 26*
Llewellyn, Silas James 1860-1925 *WhAm 1*
Llewellyn, William H H 1854- *WhAm 3*
Llewellyn ApGruffydd, Prince Of Wales d1282
McGEWB
Lloyd, Alfred Henry 1864-1927 *DcAmB,*
NatCAB 23, WhAm 1
Lloyd, Alice Crocker 1893-1950 *WhAm 2A*
Lloyd, Arthur Selden 1857-1936 *ApCAB X,*
NatCAB 30, TwCBDA, WhAm 1
Lloyd, Bolivar Jones 1872-1955 *WhAm 3*
Lloyd, Caroline Alma 1875-1945 *NatCAB 33*
Lloyd, Caroline Augusta 1859- *WomWWA 14*
Lloyd, Curtis Gates 1859-1926 *NatCAB 25,*
WhAm 1
Lloyd, David 1656-1731 *ApCAB, DcAmB,*
Drake, NatCAB 16, WhAm H
Lloyd, David Demarest 1851-1889 *TwCBDA*
Lloyd, David Demarest 1911-1962 *WhAm 4*
Lloyd, Demarest 1883-1937 *NatCAB 28,*
WhAm 1
Lloyd, E Russell 1882- *WhAm 3*
Lloyd, Edmund Grindal Rawson 1903-1966
WhAm 4
Lloyd, Edward d1695 *NatCAB 11*
Lloyd, Edward 1668-1719 *NatCAB 9*
Lloyd, Edward 1744-1796 *BiDrAC, DcAmB,*
WhAm H, WhAmP
Lloyd, Edward 1779-1834 *ApCAB, BiAUS,*
BiDrAC, DcAmB, Drake, NatCAB 9,
TwCBDA, WhAm H, WhAmP
Lloyd, Edward, VIII 1857-1948 *WhAm 2,*
WhAm 3
Lloyd, Edward Lester 1903-1959 *NatCAB 47,*
WhAm 3
Lloyd, Edward Read 1867- *WhAm 4*
Lloyd, Edward William 1872-1940 *ApCAB X,*
NatCAB 30
Lloyd, Ella Stryker Mapes 1870- *WhAm 5*
Lloyd, Francis Ernest 1868-1947 *WhAm 2*
Lloyd, Francis Guerin 1848-1920 *NatCAB 22*
Lloyd, Frank S 1900-1957 *WhAm 3*
Lloyd, Frank T 1859-1951 *WhAm 3*
Lloyd, Frederic Ebenezer John 1859-1933
WhAm 1
Lloyd, Frederick Ebenezer John 1859-1933
ApCAB X
Lloyd, Glen Alfred 1895-1975 *WhAm 6*
Lloyd, Harold Clayton 1894-1971 *WebAB,*
WhAm 5
Lloyd, Henry 1852-1932 *ApCAB, NatCAB 9,*
TwCBDA, WhAm 1
Lloyd, Henry Demarest 1847-1903 *AmBi,*
DcAmB, EncAB, McGEWB, NatCAB 12,
NatCAB 28, TwCBDA, WebAB,
WhAm 1, WhAmP
Lloyd, Henry Demarest 1907-1970 *WhAm 5*
Lloyd, Hinton Summerfield 1833-1918
WhAm 1
Lloyd, Horatio Gates 1867-1937 *WhAm 1*
Lloyd, Howard Bird 1897-1970 *NatCAB 57*
Lloyd, Humphrey 1800-1881 *DcScB*
Lloyd, James 1728-1810 *ApCAB, DcAmB,*
Drake, WhAm H
Lloyd, James 1745-1820 *ApCAB, BiAUS,*
BiDrAC, NatCAB 4, WhAm H
Lloyd, James 1769-1831 *ApCAB, BiAUS,*
BiDrAC, Drake, NatCAB 4, TwCBDA,
WhAm H
Lloyd, James Hendrie 1853-1932 *NatCAB 28*
Lloyd, James Tighman 1857-1944 *WhAm 2*
Lloyd, James Tilghman 1857-1944 *BiDrAC,*
TwCBDA, WhAm H
Lloyd, John 1876-1946 *NatCAB 38*
Lloyd, John Elwy 1848- *NatCAB 11*
Lloyd, John Uri 1849-1936 *DcAmB S2, DcScB,*
NatCAB 13, TwCBDA, WhAm 1

Lloyd, John W *NewYHSD*
Lloyd, L Duncan 1899-1972 *WhAm 5*
Lloyd, Lola Maverick 1875-1944 *NatCAB 33,*
WomWWA 14
Lloyd, Louis 1841-1924 *NatCAB 34*
Lloyd, Malcolm, Jr. 1874-1949 *NatCAB 38*
Lloyd, Marshall Burns 1858-1927 *DcAmB,*
WhAm 1
Lloyd, Marshall Burns 1881-1927 *NatCAB 25*
Lloyd, Mary Helen Wingate 1868-
WomWWA 14
Lloyd, Mary Sybil 1867- *WomWWA 14*
Lloyd, Milton Sills 1893-1954 *NatCAB 42*
Lloyd, Morton Githens 1874-1941 *NatCAB 30,*
WhAm 1
Lloyd, Nelson McAllister 1872-1933 *WhAm 1*
Lloyd, Oliver Schaefer 1884-1956 *NatCAB 47*
Lloyd, Ralph Bramel 1875-1953 *WhAm 3*
Lloyd, Ralph Irving 1875- *WhAm 5*
Lloyd, Robert McAllister 1864-1927
NatCAB 18, NatCAB 32
Lloyd, Samuel 1860-1926 *NatCAB 23,*
WhAm 1
Lloyd, Samuel 1897-1959 *NatCAB 47,*
WhAm 3
Lloyd, Sherman Parkinson 1914- *BiDrAC*
Lloyd, Stacy Barcroft 1876-1941 *WhAm 1*
Lloyd, Stewart Joseph 1881-1959 *WhAm 3*
Lloyd, Thomas 1640-1694 *ApCAB, DcAmB,*
NatCAB 5, WhAm H
Lloyd, Thomas 1649-1694 *Drake*
Lloyd, Thomas Spencer 1830-1883 *NatCAB 22*
Lloyd, Walter Hamilton, Jr. 1896- *WhAm 3*
Lloyd, Warren Estel 1869-1922 *NatCAB 33*
Lloyd, Wesley 1883-1936 *BiDrAC, WhAm 1*
Lloyd, William Allison 1870-1946 *WhAm 2*
Lloyd, Mrs. William H *NewYHSD*
Lloyd, William Henry 1870-1936 *NatCAB 27,*
WhAm 1
Lloyd, Woodrow Stanley 1913-1972 *WhAm 5*
Lloyd George, David 1863-1945 *McGEWB*
Lloyd-Jones, Esther McDonald 1901- *BiDAmEd*
Lloyd-Smith, Walter 1856-1928 *NatCAB 24*
Lloyd-Smith, Wilton 1894-1940 *NatCAB 30*
Llwyd, Edward *DcScB*
Loan, Benjamin Franklin 1819-1881 *BiAUS,*
BiDrAC, TwCBDA, WhAm H, WhAmP
Loar, James Leazure 1864-1927 *WhAm 1*
Loasby, Arthur William 1876-1936 *WhAm 1*
Loayza, Jeronimo De 1500?-1575 *ApCAB*
Lobachevski, Nikolai Ivanovich 1793-1856
AsBiEn
Lobachevskii, Nikolai Ivanovich 1792-1856
McGEWB
Lobachevsky, Nikolai Ivanovich 1792-1856
DcScB
Lobdell, Charles E 1861-1949 *WhAm 2*
Lobdell, Edwin Lyman 1857-1936 *NatCAB 27*
Lobdell, Effie L *WhAm 5*
Lobdell, Harold E 1896-1963 *WhAm 4*
Lobeck, Armin Kohl 1886-1958 *NatCAB 50,*
WhAm 3
Lobeck, Charles Otto 1852-1920 *BiDrAC,*
WhAm 1, WhAmP
Lobeck, Justus Florian d1869 *ApCAB*
L'Obel, Mathias De 1538-1616 *DcScB*
Lobengula d1894? *McGEWB*
Lobenstine, Edwin Carlyle 1872-1958 *WhAm 3*
Lober, Georg John d1961 *WhAm 4*
Loberg, Harry John 1905-1965 *NatCAB 51,*
WhAm 4
Lobingier, Andrew Stewart 1862-1939
NatCAB 13, WhAm 1
Lobingier, Charles Sumner 1866-1956
NatCAB 43
Lobingier, Elizabeth Miller 1889- *WhAm 6*
Lobingier, Kate Reynolds *WomWWA 14*
Lobo, Arthur 1882-1960 *NatCAB 45*
Lobo, Fernando 1896-1966 *WhAm 4*
Lobo, Martin 1580?-1642 *ApCAB*
Lobrano, Gustave S 1902-1956 *WhAm 3*
Locatelli, Ercole Hermano 1881-1949
NatCAB 37
Locher, Casper William 1866-1934 *WhAm 1*
Locher, Cyrus 1877-1929 *NatCAB 22*
Locher, Cyrus 1878-1929 *BiDrAC, WhAm 1*
Locher, John Joseph 1912-1967 *NatCAB 53*
Lochman, Augustus Herman 1802- *ApCAB*

Lochman, John George 1773-1826 *ApCAB,*
DcAmB, WhAm H
Lochner, G Emory 1867-1947 *NatCAB 35*
Lochner, Louis Paul 1887-1975 *WhAm 6*
Lochner, Stephan 1410?-1451 *McGEWB*
Lochrane, Osborne Augustus 1829-1887 *ApCAB,*
NatCAB 1, TwCBDA
Lochren, William 1832-1912 *NatCAB 12,*
TwCBDA, WhAm 1
Lochridge, P D 1863-1935 *WhAm 1*
Lochrie, Elizabeth Davey 1890- *IIBEAAW*
Lock, F W *NewYHSD*
Locke, Alain LeRoy 1886-1954 *BiDAmEd,*
DcAmB S5, EncAB, WebAB, WhAm 3,
WhoColR
Locke, Alfred Hamilton 1922-1972 *WhAm 6*
Locke, Annette Elizabeth Philbrick 1875-
WomWWA 14
Locke, Bessie 1865-1952 *BiCAW, DcAmB S5,*
NatCAB 39, WhAm 3
Locke, Charles E 1874-1948 *WhAm 2*
Locke, Charles Edward 1858-1940 *WhAm 1*
Locke, Clinton 1829- *TwCBDA*
Locke, David Ross 1833-1888 *AmBi, ApCAB,*
DcAmB, Drake, NatCAB 6, TwCBDA,
WebAB, WhAm H, WhAmP
Locke, Edward 1869-1945 *WhAm 2*
Locke, Edwin 1857-1918 *WhAm 1*
Locke, Etta Ober 1873- *WomWWA 14*
Locke, Eugene Murphy 1918-1972 *WhAm 5*
Locke, Eugene Perry 1883-1946 *WhAm 2*
Locke, Eva M 1874- *WomWWA 14*
Locke, Francis 1766-1823 *BiAUS, NatCAB 7,*
TwCBDA
Locke, Francis 1776-1823 *BiDrAC, WhAm H*
Locke, Frank Lovering 1865-1934 *WhAm 1*
Locke, Franklin Day 1843-1927 *NatCAB 23,*
WhAm 1
Locke, George Herbert 1870-1937 *DcAmLiB,*
WhAm 1
Locke, Grace Perley 1875- *WomWWA 14*
Locke, Harry Leslie Franklin 1886-1968
WhAm 5
Locke, Ione Eddy *WomWWA 14*
Locke, James 1869-1928 *WhAm 1*
Locke, James Dewitt Clinton 1829-1904
WhAm 1
Locke, James Kelsey 1861-1924 *NatCAB 20*
Locke, James William 1837-1922 *BiAUS,*
WhAm 1
Locke, Jane Ermina 1805-1859 *ApCAB, Drake,*
TwCBDA
Locke, John 1632-1704 *DcScB, McGEWB,*
WhAm H
Locke, John 1764-1855 *BiAUS, BiDrAC,*
TwCBDA, WhAm H
Locke, John 1792-1856 *ApCAB, DcAmB,*
NatCAB 15, TwCBDA, WhAm H
Locke, John Staples 1836-1906 *WhAm 1*
Locke, L Leland 1880-1943 *NatCAB 31*
Locke, M Katherine d1936 *WhAm 1*
Locke, Mary Stoughton 1856- *WomWWA 14*
Locke, Mathew 1730-1801 *Drake*
Locke, Matthew 1730-1801 *ApCAB, BiAUS,*
BiDrAC, DcAmB, NatCAB 2, TwCBDA,
WhAm H, WhAmP
Locke, Powhattan B *BiAUS*
Locke, Preston Erie Saint Clair 1888-1938
NatCAB 34
Locke, Richard Adams 1800-1871 *ApCAB,*
DcAmB, NatCAB 13, WhAm H
Locke, Robert Wynter 1926-1971 *WhAm 5*
Locke, Robinson 1856-1920 *NatCAB 13,*
WhAm 1
Locke, Samuel 1731-1778 *TwCBDA*
Locke, Samuel 1732-1778 *ApCAB, Drake,*
NatCAB 6
Locke, Sidney Eri 1866-1925 *NatCAB 20*
Locke, Victor Murat, Jr. 1876- *WhAm 5*
Locke, W Taz 1910-1951 *NatCAB 39*
Locke, Walter 1875-1957 *WhAm 3*
Locke, Warren Andrew 1847-1920 *NatCAB 19*
Locker, Jesse Dwight 1891-1955 *NatCAB 44*
Locker, William Henry 1870- *NatCAB 17*
Lockerby, Frank McCarthy 1899-1969
NatCAB 54, WhAm 5
Lockett, Andrew M 1865- *WhAm 3*
Lockett, James 1855- *WhAm 4*

Lockette, John Anderson 1877- *WhoColR*
Lockey, Joseph Byrne 1877-1946 *WhAm 2*
Lockey, Mary Ishbel d1939 *WhAm 1*
Lockey, Richard 1845- *NatCAB 7*
Lockhart, Arthur John 1850-1926 *ApCAB Sup*,
  NatCAB 8, WhAm 1
Lockhart, Burton Wellesley 1855-1937
  WhAm 3
Lockhart, Caroline 1875- *WhAm 5*
Lockhart, Charles 1818-1905 *DcAmB*
Lockhart, Charles 1906-1963 *WhAm 4*
Lockhart, Clinton 1858-1951 *NatCAB 42*,
  TwCBDA, WhAm 3
Lockhart, Earl Granger 1879- *WhAm 6*
Lockhart, Ernest Ray 1911-1971 *WhAm 5*
Lockhart, Frank P 1881-1949 *WhAm 2*
Lockhart, Gene d1957 *WhAm 3*
Lockhart, Henry, Jr. 1877-1943 *WhAm 2*
Lockhart, James 1806-1857 *BiAUS, BiDrAC*,
  WhAm H
Lockhart, James Alexander 1850-1905 *BiDrAC*
Lockhart, James Henry d1938 *WhAm 1*
Lockhart, Joseph Smith 1855-1927 *NatCAB 20*
Lockhart, Lizzie Marion 1874- *WomWWA 14*
Lockhart, Malcolm Mabry 1877-1940 *WhAm 1*
Lockhart, Oliver Cary 1879-1975 *WhAm 6*
Lockhart, Walter Samuel 1874- *WhAm 1*
Lockheed, Allan Haines 1889-1969 *WhAm 5*
Lockley, Fred 1871-1958 *WhAm 3*
Lockley, Lawrence Campbell 1899-1969
  WhAm 5
Lockling, H David 1904-1960 *NatCAB 48*
Lockman, DeWitt McClellan 1870-1957
  WhAm 3
Lockman, John Thomas 1834-1912 *WhAm 1*
Lockrey, Sarah Hunt 1863-1929 *DcAmB*
Lockridge, Frances Louise Davis 1896-1963
  NatCAB 47, WhAm 4
Lockridge, Ross Franklin 1877-1952 *WhAm 3*
Lockridge, Ross Franklin, Jr. 1914-1948
  NatCAB 39, WhAm 2
Lockrow, David Mount 1869-1925 *NatCAB 20*
Lockwood, Albert 1871-1933 *WhAm 1*
Lockwood, Alfred Collins 1875- *WhAm 5*
Lockwood, Belva Ann Bennett 1830-1917 *AmBi*,
  AmWom, ApCAB, DcAmB, NatCAB 2,
  NotAW, TwCBDA, WebAB, WhAm 1,
  WhAmP, WomWWA 14
Lockwood, Benjamin Curtis 1844-1926
  WhAm 1
Lockwood, Bertha Greene 1863- *WomWWA 14*
Lockwood, Charles Andrews, Jr. 1890-1967
  NatCAB 53, WhAm 4
Lockwood, Charles Clapp 1877-1958 *WhAm 3*
Lockwood, Charles Daniel 1868-1932 *WhAm 1*
Lockwood, Charles Davenport 1877-1949
  WhAm 3
Lockwood, Daniel Newton 1844-1906 *BiDrAC*,
  TwCBDA, WhAm 1
Lockwood, Daniel Wright 1845- *WhAm 4*
Lockwood, David Benjamin 1827- *NatCAB 5*
Lockwood, Edward *NewYHSD*
Lockwood, Edward Kenton 1870-1960
  NatCAB 47
Lockwood, Edward T 1904-1963 *WhAm 4*
Lockwood, Francis Cummins 1864-1948
  NatCAB 38, WhAm 2
Lockwood, Frank 1865-1936 *NatCAB 26*
Lockwood, Frank C 1864-1948 *REnAW*
Lockwood, Frederick St. John 1825-1907
  NatCAB 6
Lockwood, George Browning 1872-1932
  WhAm 1
Lockwood, George Rae 1861-1931 *WhAm 1*
Lockwood, George Roe 1861-1931 *NatCAB 22*
Lockwood, George Roe 1862-1931 *ApCAB X*
Lockwood, H H 1814-1899 *BiAUS Sup*
Lockwood, Harold J 1890-1960 *WhAm 4*
Lockwood, Harold Paul 1902-1969 *WhAm 5*
Lockwood, Helen Drusilla 1891-1971 *WhAm 5*
Lockwood, Henry 1869-1932 *WhAm 1*
Lockwood, Henry A *BiAUS*
Lockwood, Henry Hall 1814-1899 *Drake*
Lockwood, Henry Hayes 1814-1899 *AmBi*,
  ApCAB, TwCBDA, WhAm 1
Lockwood, Henry Roswell 1843-1905 *TwCBDA*,
  WhAm 1
Lockwood, Homer Nichols 1833-1913 *ApCAB*,

Lockwood, Howard 1846-1892 *NatCAB 3*
Lockwood, Ingersoll 1841- *WhAm 4*
Lockwood, Ira Hiram 1885-1957 *WhAm 3*
Lockwood, James 1714-1772 *Drake*
Lockwood, James Booth 1852-1884 *AmBi*,
  ApCAB, DcAmB, NatCAB 3, TwCBDA,
  WhAm H
Lockwood, John Alexander 1856- *WhAm 1*
Lockwood, John Salem 1907-1950 *WhAm 3*
Lockwood, John Ward 1894-1963 *IIBEAAW*
Lockwood, Joshua *NewYHSD*
Lockwood, Katharine Read 1843-
  WomWWA 14
Lockwood, Laura Emma 1863- *WhAm 4*,
  WomWWA 14
Lockwood, Luke Burnell 1901-1975 *WhAm 6*
Lockwood, Luke Vincent 1872-1951
  NatCAB 44, WhAm 3
Lockwood, Mary Smith 1831- *NatCAB 3*,
  WhAm 4
Lockwood, Preston 1891-1951 *WhAm 3*
Lockwood, Ralph Ingersoll 1798-1858 *DcAmB*,
  WhAm H
Lockwood, Rembrandt *NewYHSD*
Lockwood, Richard John 1882-1963 *WhAm 4*
Lockwood, Robert Wilton 1861-1914 *DcAmB*,
  TwCBDA
Lockwood, Rufus A 1811-1857 *NatCAB 18*
Lockwood, Samuel 1803-1893 *ApCAB*,
  TwCBDA
Lockwood, Samuel 1819- *ApCAB*
Lockwood, Samuel 1820- *Drake*
Lockwood, Samuel Drake 1789-1874
  ApCAB Sup, DcAmB, NatCAB 25,
  WhAm H
Lockwood, Sara Elizabeth Husted 1854-
  WhAm 4, WomWWA 14
Lockwood, Stephen Timothy 1874- *WhAm 5*
Lockwood, Thomas B 1873-1947 *WhAm 2*
Lockwood, Thomas Dixon 1848-1927
  NatCAB 22, WhAm 3
Lockwood, Ward 1894-1963 *NatCAB 53*
Lockwood, William F *BiAUS*
Lockwood, William Penn Bignell 1875-
  NatCAB 16
Lockwood, Wilton 1861-1914 *AmBi, DcAmB*,
  NatCAB 24, WhAm 1
Lockyer, Sir Joseph Norman 1836-1920 *AsBiEn*,
  DcScB
Locquist *NewYHSD*
Locraft, Thomas Hall 1903-1959 *WhAm 4*
Locy, William Albert 1857-1924 *DcAmB*,
  NatCAB 18, WhAm 1
Loder, Nina S 1880- *WomWWA 14*
Lodge, Edmund Anderson 1889-1972 *WhAm 6*
Lodge, George Cabot 1873-1909 *DcAmB*,
  NatCAB 24
Lodge, Giles Henry 1805- *ApCAB*
Lodge, Gonzalez 1863-1942 *BiDAmEd*,
  NatCAB 31, WhAm 4
Lodge, Henry Cabot 1850-1924 *AmBi, ApCAB*,
  ApCAB X, BiDrAC, DcAmB, EncAB,
  McGEWB, NatCAB 1, NatCAB 19,
  TwCBDA, WebAB, WhAm 1, WhAmP
Lodge, Henry Cabot, Jr. 1902- *BiDrAC*,
  WebAB
Lodge, James Llewellyn 1840-1907 *NatCAB 6*
Lodge, John Christian 1862-1950 *NatCAB 37*,
  WhAm 2
Lodge, John Davis 1903- *BiDrAC*
Lodge, John Ellerton 1876-1942 *DcAmB S3*,
  NatCAB 32
Lodge, John Ellerton 1878-1942 *WhAm 2*
Lodge, John Friend 1870-1944 *NatCAB 34*
Lodge, Lee Davis 1865-1923 *NatCAB 2*,
  WhAm 1
Lodge, Sir Oliver Joseph 1851-1940 *AsBiEn*,
  DcScB
Lodge, Susan C *WomWWA 14*
Lodge, Sydney Johnston 1887-1952 *NatCAB 41*
Lodian, L 1866- *WhAm 4*
Lodor, Richard 1832-1917 *WhAm 1*
Loe, Adolph 1871-1935 *NatCAB 27*
Loeb, Anne Leonard 1862- *WomWWA 14*
Loeb, Arthur 1872-1940 *NatCAB 30*
Loeb, Arthur Joseph 1914-1968 *WhAm 5*
Loeb, Benjamin M 1902-1965 *WhAm 4*

Loeb, Carl Morris 1875-1955 *NatCAB 43*,
  WhAm 3
Loeb, Charlotte *WomWWA 14*
Loeb, G M 1899-1974 *WhAm 6*
Loeb, Hanau Wolf 1865-1927 *NatCAB 25*,
  WhAm 1
Loeb, Howard A 1873-1955 *WhAm 3*
Loeb, Isidor 1868-1954 *WhAm 3*
Loeb, Jacob Moritz 1875-1944 *NatCAB 33*,
  WhAm 2
Loeb, Jacques 1859-1924 *AmBi, AsBiEn*,
  DcAmB, DcScB, EncAB, NatCAB 11,
  WebAB, WhAm 1
Loeb, James Morris 1867-1933 *AmBi*,
  DcAMB S1, WebAB, WhAm 1
Loeb, Leo 1869-1959 *DcScB, NatCAB 44*,
  WhAm 3
Loeb, Louis 1866-1909 *AmBi, DcAmB*,
  NatCAB 14, TwCBDA, WhAm 1
Loeb, Milton B 1889-1972 *WhAm 5*
Loeb, Morris 1863-1912 *DcAmB, NatCAB 26*,
  WhAm 1
Loeb, Robert Frederick 1895-1973 *WhAm 6*
Loeb, Sara *WomWWA 14*
Loeb, Sophie Irene Simon 1876-1929 *DcAmB*,
  EncAB, NatCAB 24, NotAW, WhAm 1
Loeb, Willard Eugene 1896-1958 *NatCAB 48*
Loeb, William 1866-1937 *AmBi, NatCAB 18*,
  WhAm 1
Loeffel, William John 1894-1962 *NatCAB 50*,
  WhAm 4
Loeffler, Carl August 1873-1968 *WhAm 5*
Loeffler, Charles *NewYHSD*
Loeffler, Charles Martin Tornov 1861-1935
  AmBi, DcAmB S1, WhAm 1
Loeffler, Friedrich August Johannes 1852-1915
  BiHiMed, DcScB
Loeffler, Friedrich August Johannes see also
  Loffler, Friedrich
Loeffler, Gisella 1900- *IIBEAAW*
Loefler, Charles Martin 1861- *ApCAB X*
Loefling, Peter 1729-1756 *ApCAB*
Loehr, Leon Lee 1864-1934 *NatCAB 27*
Loehr, Rodney Clement 1907- *EncAAH*
Loehrke, Leah Marie 1918-1971 *NatCAB 57*
Loehwing, Walter Ferdinand 1896-1960
  WhAm 4
Loekle, Charles *NewYHSD*
Loemans, Alexander F *IIBEAAW*
Loesch, Frank Joseph 1852-1944 *ApCAB X*,
  NatCAB 32, WhAm 2
Loeser, Nathan 1869-1953 *NatCAB 42*
Loesser, Frank Henry 1910-1969 *WebAB*,
  WhAm 6
Loetscher, Frederick William 1875-1966
  WhAm 4
Loevenhart, Arthur Solomon 1878-1929
  WhAm 1
Loevy, Frank Adair 1870-1949 *WhAm 3*
Loew, Charles E 1827-1886 *NatCAB 7*
Loew, E Victor 1873-1950 *NatCAB 38*
Loew, Edward Victor 1839- *NatCAB 7*,
  WhAm 4
Loew, Fred Aaron 1874-1950 *NatCAB 40*
Loew, Frederick William 1834- *NatCAB 7*
Loew, Marcus 1870-1927 *DcAmB*,
  NatCAB 23, WhAm 1
Loewe, Dietrich Eduard 1852-1935 *NatCAB 15*,
  WhAm 1
Loewenberg, Bert James 1905-1974 *WhAm 6*
Loewenberg, Henry *NewYHSD*
Loewenberg, Kurt 1900-1966 *NatCAB 53*
Loewenstein, Karl 1891-1973 *WhAm 6*
Loewenstern, Isidore 1807-1856 *ApCAB*,
  ApCAB Sup
Loewenthal, Isidor 1826-1864 *ApCAB*
Loewenthal, Isidor 1827?-1864 *DcAmB*,
  WhAm H
Loewi, Otto 1873-1961 *AsBiEn, DcScB*,
  McGEWB, WhAm 4
Loewinson-Lessing *DcScB*
Loewner, Charles 1893-1968 *DcScB*
Loewy, Alfred 1873-1935 *DcScB*
Loewy, Edwin 1893- *WhAm 3*
Loewy, Erwin 1897-1959 *WhAm 3*
Loewy, Raymond Fernand 1893- *WebAB*
Lofberg, Grace Ethel Ward *WomWWA 14*

Loffler, Friedrich August Johannes 1852-1915 *AsBiEn*
Loffler, Friedrich August Johannes *see also* Loeffler, Friedrich
Loffredo, Louis 1894-1964 *NatCAB 50*
Lofland, James Rush 1823-1894 *BiAUS, BiDrAC, WhAm H*
Loft, George William 1865-1943 *BiDrAC, WhAm 4, WhAmP*
Loft, P *IIBEAAW, NewYHSD*
Loftin, James Otis 1887-1955 *WhAm 3*
Loftin, Scott Marion 1878-1953 *BiDrAC, NatCAB 46, WhAm 3*
Lofting, Hugh 1886-1947 *WhAm 2*
Lofton, George Augustus 1839-1914 *NatCAB 10, NatCAB 16, WhAm 1*
Loftus, Cissie 1876-1943 *NotAW*
Loftus, Clarence James 1886-1953 *NatCAB 40*
Loftus, Clarence James 1887-1953 *WhAm 3*
Loftus, John Thomas 1908-1969 *WhAm 5*
Logan 1725?-1780 *AmBi, Drake*
Logan, Albert J 1857-1934 *NatCAB 8, WhAm 1*
Logan, Archibald Hodge 1877-1958 *NatCAB 47*
Logan, Archie Francis 1892-1970 *WhAm 5*
Logan, Arthur Courtney 1909-1973 *NatCAB 57*
Logan, Benjamin 1742?-1802 *Drake*
Logan, Benjamin 1743?-1802 *AmBi, DcAmB, TwCBDA, WhAm H*
Logan, Benjamin 1752?-1802 *ApCAB*
Logan, Bertha Allen *WomWWA 14*
Logan, C *NewYHSD*
Logan, Celia *NotAW*
Logan, Celia 1837- *TwCBDA*
Logan, Celia 1839- *ApCAB*
Logan, Celia 1840- *AmWom*
Logan, Charles Alexander 1874- *WhAm 5*
Logan, Cornelius A 1800-1853 *Drake*
Logan, Cornelius Ambrose d1899 *BiAUS*
Logan, Cornelius Ambrose 1832-1899 *DcAmB, TwCBDA, WhAm H*
Logan, Cornelius Ambrose 1836-1899 *ApCAB, NatCAB 5*
Logan, Cornelius Ambrosius 1806-1853 *ApCAB, DcAmB, NatCAB 12, TwCBDA, WhAm H*
Logan, Deborah Norris 1761-1839 *DcAmB, NatCAB 25, NotAW*
Logan, Edward Lawrence 1875-1939 *NatCAB 31*
Logan, Eliza d1872 *NotAW*
Logan, Eliza 1827-1872 *TwCBDA*
Logan, Eliza 1829-1872 *ApCAB*
Logan, Eliza 1830-1872 *Drake*
Logan, Frank G 1851-1937 *WhAm 1*
Logan, George 1753-1821 *AmBi, ApCAB, BiAUS, BiDrAC, DcAmB, Drake, EncAB, NatCAB 8, TwCBDA, WebAB, WhAm H, WhAmP*
Logan, George 1778-1861 *ApCAB*
Logan, George W 1815-1899 *BiDConf*
Logan, George Wood 1868-1915 *NatCAB 6, NatCAB 25*
Logan, Grace Redfield Boynton *WomWWA 14*
Logan, Harley A 1864-1927 *NatCAB 22*
Logan, Harry Lambert, Jr. 1907-1965 *NatCAB 51*
Logan, Henry 1784-1866 *BiAUS, BiDrAC, TwCBDA, WhAm H*
Logan, James *NewYHSD*
Logan, James 1674-1751 *AmBi, ApCAB, DcAmB, DcScB, Drake, McGEWB, NatCAB 2, REnAW, TwCBDA, WebAB, WhAm H*
Logan, James 1725?-1780 *AmBi, DcAmB, REnAW, WebAB, WebAMB, WhAm H*
Logan, James 1852-1929 *WhAm 1*
Logan, James Addison 1879-1930 *AmBi, WhAm 1, WhAm 1C*
Logan, James Elmore 1861- *WhAm 1*
Logan, James Harvey 1841-1928 *DcAmB, NatCAB 21*
Logan, James Jackson 1876-1957 *NatCAB 47*
Logan, James Parmelee 1857-1938 *WhAm 1*
Logan, James Venable 1835- *ApCAB, TwCBDA*
Logan, John 1725?-1780 *AmBi, ApCAB,*

Logan, John 1735?-1780 *NatCAB 10*
Logan, Mrs. John A 1838-1923 *NotAW, WhAm 1*
Logan, John Alexander 1826-1886 *AmBi, ApCAB, BiAUS, BiDrAC, DcAmB, Drake, NatCAB 4, NatCAB 27, TwCBDA, WebAB, WebAMB, WhAm H, WhAmP*
Logan, John Alexander, Jr. 1865-1899 *NatCAB 37, WhAm 1*
Logan, John Daniel 1869- *WhAm 5*
Logan, John Henry 1822-1885 *ApCAB, NatCAB 10, WhAm H*
Logan, John Hubbard 1876-1936 *WhAm 1*
Logan, John Thomas 1865-1929 *NatCAB 21*
Logan, John Wesley 1810?-1872 *ApCAB*
Logan, Josephine Hancock 1862-1943 *NatCAB 35, WhAm 2*
Logan, Leavitt Curtis 1846-1921 *WhAm 1*
Logan, Martha Daniell 1704-1779 *NotAW*
Logan, Marvel Mills 1874-1939 *WhAm 1*
Logan, Marvel Mills 1875-1939 *BiDrAC, NatCAB 46*
Logan, Mary Simmerson Cunningham 1838-1923 *AmWom, ApCAB, NatCAB 4, NotAW, WomWWA 14*
Logan, Mercer Patton 1856-1928 *WhAm 1*
Logan, Milburn Hill 1855-1905 *NatCAB 8, WhAm 4*
Logan, Olive 1839-1909 *DcAmB, NotAW, TwCBDA, WhAm 1*
Logan, Olive 1841-1909 *ApCAB, Drake, NatCAB 6*
Logan, Patton Lyon 1874-1928 *NatCAB 37*
Logan, Richard Dougherty 1884-1949 *NatCAB 38*
Logan, Robert Fulton d1959 *WhAm 3*
Logan, Robert Henry 1874-1942 *NatCAB 30*
Logan, Stephen Trigg 1800-1880 *AmBi, ApCAB, DcAmB, NatCAB 7, TwCBDA, WhAm H*
Logan, Thomas Dale 1851-1921 *WhAm 3*
Logan, Thomas Francis 1881-1928 *WhAm 1*
Logan, Thomas Moldrup 1808-1876 *WhAm H*
Logan, Thomas Muldrup 1808-1876 *ApCAB, DcAmB, NatCAB 12*
Logan, Thomas Muldrup 1840-1914 *DcAmB, NatCAB 1, WhAm 1*
Logan, Walter Seth 1847-1906 *NatCAB 2, WhAm 1*
Logan, William 1718-1776 *ApCAB*
Logan, William 1776-1822 *ApCAB, BiAUS, BiDrAC, NatCAB 4, TwCBDA, WhAm H*
Logan, Sir William Edmond 1798-1875 *ApCAB, DcScB, Drake, McGEWB*
Logan, William Hoffman Gardiner 1872-1943 *NatCAB 32, WhAm 2*
Logan, William Newton 1869- *WhAm 2*
Logan, William Richard 1856-1912 *NatCAB 16*
Logan, William Turner 1874-1941 *BiDrAC, WhAm 5*
Logasa, Hannah 1879-1967 *DcAmLiB*
Loggins, Vernon 1893-1968 *WhAm 5*
Loghuer, Henry *NewYHSD*
LoGrasso, Horace 1881-1956 *NatCAB 44*
Logue, Emily 1879- *WomWWA 14*
Logue, J Washington 1863-1925 *WhAm 1*
Logue, James Washington 1863-1925 *BiDrAC*
Logue, John James 1810?- *NewYHSD*
Logue, John Terrell 1888-1947 *WhAm 2*
Logue, Kate 1825?- *NewYHSD*
Loguen, Jermain Wesley 1813?-1872 *DcAmB, WhAm H, WhAmP*
Loher, Franz Von 1818- *ApCAB*
Lohest, Marie Joseph Maximin 1857-1926 *DcScB*
Lohman, Ann Trow 1812-1878 *NotAW*
Lohman, Joseph D 1910-1968 *WhAm 5*
Lohman, Maurice Rosenthal 1889-1948 *NatCAB 39*
Lohman, William Henry 1881-1943 *NatCAB 32*
Lohmann, Carl Albert 1887-1957 *NatCAB 43, WhAm 4*
Lohmann, Karl Baptiste 1887-1963 *NatCAB 51*
Lohnes, Horace L 1897-1954 *WhAm 3*

Lohneyss, Georg Engelhardt Von 1552-1625? *DcScB*
Lohr, Lenox Riley 1891-1968 *WhAm 5*
Lohr, Oliver Willison 1894-1967 *NatCAB 54*
Lohre, Nels J 1873-1933 *WhAm 1*
Lohse, Wilhelm Oswald 1845-1915 *DcScB*
Loichot, Raymond William 1891-1957 *WhAm 3*
Loines, Elma 1882- *WomWWA 14*
Loines, Hilda 1878- *WhAm 6*
Loiseau, John Elmer 1891-1966 *NatCAB 52, WhAm 4*
Loisy, Alfred Firmin 1857-1940 *McGEWB*
Loizeaux, Charles Edward 1889-1947 *NatCAB 40*
Lokey, Eugene 1892-1956 *WhAm 3*
Lokhtin, Vladimir Mikhaylovich 1849-1919 *DcScB*
Lokken, Roscoe Leonard 1904-1974 *WhAm 6*
Lokrantz, Sven 1892-1940 *NatCAB 40, WhAm 1*
Lollar, Myron E 1878-1956 *NatCAB 45*
Lomas, Alfred Jackson 1886-1954 *WhAm 3*
Lomax, Alan 1915- *WebAB*
Lomax, Edward Lloyd 1852-1916 *WhAm 1*
Lomax, John Avery 1867-1948 *DcAmB S4, NatCAB 38, REnAW, WebAB, WhAm 2*
Lomax, John Tayloe 1781-1862 *ApCAB, DcAmB, Drake, TwCBDA, WhAm H*
Lomax, John Taylor 1781-1862 *NatCAB 5*
Lomax, Joseph 1809- *NatCAB 14*
Lomax, Lindsay Lunsford 1835- *ApCAB Sup*
Lomax, Louis Emanuel 1922-1970 *WhAm 5*
Lomax, Lunsford Lindsay 1835-1913 *BiDConf, DcAmB, NatCAB 6, TwCBDA, WhAm 1*
Lomax, Paul Sanford 1890-1975 *BiDAmEd, WhAm 6*
Lomax, Tennent 1820-1862 *NatCAB 18, TwCBDA*
Lomax, Tennent 1858- *NatCAB 7, WhAm 1*
Lomax, Thomas Henry 1832- *ApCAB Sup*
Lomax, William 1813-1893 *NatCAB 6*
Lomb, Henry 1828-1908 *NatCAB 23*
Lomb, Henry Charles 1872-1936 *NatCAB 28*
Lombard d1744? *ApCAB*
Lombard, Alvin Orlando 1856-1937 *NatCAB 35*
Lombard, Carole 1908-1942 *DcAmB S3, NotAW, WhAm 1*
Lombard, Catherine B 1810?- *NewYHSD*
Lombard, Frank Alanson 1872- *WhAm 5*
Lombard, Louis 1861-1927 *ApCAB X, NatCAB 21, WhAm 4*
Lombard, Percival Hall 1872-1932 *NatCAB 42*
Lombard, Percy Newman Hall 1880-1925 *NatCAB 20*
Lombard, Peter 1095?-1160 *McGEWB*
Lombard, Walter Edwin 1861-1942 *NatCAB 32*
Lombard, Warren Plimpton 1855-1939 *DcAmB S2, WhAm 1*
Lombardi, C 1845-1919 *WhAm 1*
Lombardi, Cornelius Ennis 1888-1956 *NatCAB 42, WhAm 3*
Lombardi, Ethel Peck 1881- *WomWWA 14*
Lombardi, Vincent Thomas 1913-1970 *WebAB, WhAm 5*
Lombardini, Manuel Maria 1802-1853 *ApCAB*
Lombardo, Guy Albert 1902- *WebAB*
Lombroso, Cesare 1835-1909 *McGEWB*
Lome, Enrique Dupuy De 1851- *ApCAB Sup*
Lomen, Carl Joys 1880-1965 *NatCAB 54*
Lomen, Gudbrand J 1854-1934 *WhAm 1*
Lommen, Christian Peter 1865-1926 *WhAm 1*
Lomonosov, Mikhail Vasilevich 1711-1765 *McGEWB*
Lomonosov, Mikhail Vasilievich 1711-1765 *AsBiEn, DcScB*
Lonabaugh, Ellsworth Eugene 1861-1938 *NatCAB 49*
Lonardi, Eduardo 1896-1956 *WhAm 3*
Lonati, Nichola *NewYHSD*
London, Alexander Troy 1847-1908 *NatCAB 34, WhAm 1*
London, Daniel Edwin 1905-1974 *WhAm 6*
London, Frank 1876-1945 *NatCAB 34*
London, Fritz 1900-1954 *DcScB, NatCAB 40, NatCAB 47*
London, Heinz 1907-1970 *DcScB*
London, Hoyt Hobson 1900- *BiDAmEd*

London, Jack 1876-1916 *AmBi, ApCAB X, DcAmB, EncAB, McGEWB, NatCAB 13, NatCAB 57, WebAB, WhAm 1*
London, Meyer 1871-1926 *BiDrAC, DcAmB, NatCAB 22, WebAB, WhAm 1, WhAmP*
Lone Wolf 1882-1965? *IlBEAAW*
Lonergan, Augustine 1874-1947 *BiDrAC, NatCAB 36, WhAm 2, WhAmP*
Lonergan, James *NewYHSD*
Lonergan, William Ignatius 1884-1936 *WhAm 1*
Lonesome Charley 1842?-1876 *DcAmB*
Long, Albert Limerick 1832-1901 *WhAm 1*
Long, Alexander 1816-1886 *BiAUS, BiDrAC, NatCAB 5, WhAm H*
Long, Andrew Theodore 1866-1946 *NatCAB 38, WhAm 2*
Long, Armistead L 1826-1864 *Drake*
Long, Armistead Lindsay 1825?-1891 *BiDConf, DcAmB, NatCAB 26, WhAm H*
Long, Armistead Lindsay 1827-1891 *ApCAB, TwCBDA*
Long, Arthur *NewYHSD*
Long, Augustine J 1903-1969 *WhAm 5*
Long, Augustine V 1877-1955 *WhAm 3*
Long, Augustus White 1862- *WhAm 4*
Long, Boaz Walton 1876-1962 *NatCAB 50, WhAm 4*
Long, Breckinridge 1881-1958 *NatCAB 44, WhAm 3*
Long, Catherine Stoneman 1862- *WomWWA 14*
Long, Charles Chaille 1842-1917 *AmBi, ApCAB, DcAmB*
Long, Charles D 1841-1902 *NatCAB 5, WhAm 1*
Long, Charles Franklin 1869-1931 *NatCAB 22*
Long, Charles Grant 1869-1943 *WhAm 2*
Long, Charles Leonard 1851-1929 *NatCAB 32*
Long, Charles Philip 1866-1940 *NatCAB 31*
Long, Charles Ramsay 1872-1946 *WhAm 2*
Long, Chester Isaiah 1860-1934 *BiDrAC, NatCAB 13, TwCBDA, WhAm 1, WhAmP*
Long, Clarence Dickinson 1908- *BiDrAC*
Long, Clement 1806-1861 *ApCAB, TwCBDA*
Long, Crawford Williamson 1815-1878 *AmBi, ApCAB, AsBiEn, BiHiMed, DcAmB, McGEWB, NatCAB 13, TwCBDA, WebAB, WhAm H*
Long, Cyril Norman Hugh 1901-1970 *WhAm 5*
Long, Daniel Albright 1844- *NatCAB 12, TwCBDA, WhAm 4*
Long, E D *NewYHSD*
Long, Earl Albert 1909-1968 *WhAm 5*
Long, Earl Kemp 1895-1960 *WhAm 4*
Long, Edgar Allen 1871- *WhoColR*
Long, Edgar William 1876-1948 *NatCAB 40*
Long, Edward 1734-1813 *ApCAB*
Long, Edward Harvey 1898-1959 *WhAm 4*
Long, Edward Henry 1838-1911 *NatCAB 5, WhAm 1*
Long, Edward Henry Carroll 1808-1865 *BiAUS, BiDrAC, WhAm H*
Long, Edward Vaughan 1908-1972 *WhAm 5*
Long, Edward Vaughn 1908-1972 *BiDrAC*
Long, Eli 1836-1903 *Drake*
Long, Eli 1837-1903 *ApCAB, NatCAB 12, TwCBDA, WhAm 1*
Long, Eli 1871-1948 *NatCAB 36*
Long, Elizabeth Ballard *WomWWA 14*
Long, Ellen Call 1825-1905 *REnAW*
Long, Ernest D 1872- *WhAm 5*
Long, Eugene Rufus 1862-1931 *TwCBDA, WhAm 1*
Long, Frank Cornelius 1860- *WhoColR*
Long, Franklin Bidwell 1842-1912 *NatCAB 15*
Long, Frederick *NewYHSD*
Long, Frederick Able 1908-1965 *WhAm 4*
Long, Gabriel 1751-1827 *ApCAB, Drake*
Long, George Baker 1901-1961 *NatCAB 50*
Long, George C, Jr. d1958 *WhAm 3*
Long, George Durward 1883-1944 *NatCAB 41*
Long, George Edward 1856-1957 *WhAm 3*
Long, George Shannon 1883-1958 *BiDrAC, WhAm 3, WhAmP*
Long, Gillis William 1923- *BiDrAC*
Long, Haniel 1888-1956 *WhAm 3*
Long, Harold 1898-1968 *NatCAB 54*

Long, Harold Joseph 1894-1971 *NatCAB 56*
Long, Harriet Catherine 1887-1941 *WhAm 2*
Long, Harry 1881-1962 *NatCAB 50*
Long, Harvey Clayton 1869-1948 *NatCAB 37*
Long, Henry Fletcher 1869-1939 *WhAm 1*
Long, Henry Follansbee 1883-1956 *NatCAB 45*
Long, Howard Hale 1888-1957 *WhAm 3*
Long, Huey Pierce 1893-1935 *AmBi, BiDrAC, DcAmB S1, EncAAH, EncAB, McGEWB, NatCAB 30, REnAW, WebAB, WhAm 1, WhAmP*
Long, Hugh W d1964 *WhAm 4*
Long, Isaac Jasper 1831-1891 *TwCBDA*
Long, James 1793?-1822 *DcAmB, WhAm H*
Long, James Parker d1970 *WhAm 5*
Long, James Walter 1900-1952 *NatCAB 39*
Long, Jefferson Franklin 1836-1900 *BiDrAC, WhAmP*
Long, John 1785-1857 *BiAUS, BiDrAC, WhAm H*
Long, John Benjamin 1843-1924 *BiDrAC*
Long, John Budd 1894-1962 *NatCAB 49*
Long, John Chenault 1908-1972 *NatCAB 56*
Long, John Collins 1795-1865 *ApCAB, Drake, TwCBDA*
Long, Mrs. John D *AmWom*
Long, John D 1874-1949 *WhAm 2*
Long, John Davis 1838-1915 *AmBi, ApCAB, BiDrAC, BiDrUSE, DcAmB, NatCAB 1, NatCAB 11, TwCBDA, WhAm 1, WhAmP*
Long, John Dietrich 1858- *WhAm 4*
Long, John G 1846-1903 *WhAm 1*
Long, John Harper 1856-1918 *DcAmB, NatCAB 13, NatCAB 19, WhAm 1*
Long, John Luther 1861-1927 *AmBi, DcAmB, WhAm 1*
Long, John Wesley 1859-1926 *NatCAB 21*
Long, John Wesley 1859-1927 *WhAm 1*
Long, Joseph Harvey 1863-1958 *NatCAB 52, WhAm 3*
Long, Joseph Ragland 1870-1932 *DcAmB S1, WhAm 1*
Long, LeRoy 1869-1940 *WhAm 1*
Long, LeRoy Downing 1897-1970 *WhAm 5*
Long, Lewis Marshall 1883-1957 *BiDrAC, NatCAB 47, WhAm 3*
Long, Lily Augusta d1927 *WhAm 1*
Long, Lois 1901-1974 *WhAm 6*
Long, Louis Francis 1899-1969 *NatCAB 57*
Long, Luman Harrison 1907-1971 *WhAm 5*
Long, Margaret *WomWWA 14*
Long, Mason 1892-1964 *WhAm 4*
Long, Maurice Alvin 1875-1938 *NatCAB 27, WhAm 1*
Long, Medora Welch 1853- *WomWWA 14*
Long, Minnie Wilson *WomWWA 14*
Long, Mitchell 1889-1953 *NatCAB 41, WhAm 3*
Long, Nicholas d1819 *Drake*
Long, Omera Floyd 1870-1945 *WhAm 2*
Long, Oren Ethelbirt 1889-1965 *BiDAmEd, BiDrAC, WhAm 4*
Long, Orie William 1882-1955 *NatCAB 44, WhAm 3*
Long, Oscar Fitzalan 1852-1928 *WhAm 1*
Long, Percy Vincent 1870-1953 *NatCAB 48*
Long, Percy Waldron 1876-1952 *NatCAB 41, WhAm 3*
Long, Perrin Hamilton 1899-1965 *WhAm 4*
Long, Pierce 1739-1789 *BiAUS*
Long, Pierse 1739-1789 *ApCAB, BiDrAC, Drake, TwCBDA, WhAm H*
Long, Princess Clark 1862- *WomWWA 14*
Long, Ralph Herman 1882-1948 *WhAm 2*
Long, Ray 1878-1935 *WhAm 1*
Long, Richard Henry 1865- *ApCAB X*
Long, Robert Alexander 1850-1934 *NatCAB 15, NatCAB 32, WhAm 1*
Long, Robert Carey 1770-1833 *WhAm H*
Long, Robert Carey 1819-1849 *ApCAB*
Long, Robert Cary 1819-1849 *Drake*
Long, Robert Cary, Sr. 1770-1833 *BnEnAmA*
Long, Robert Franklin 1920-1970 *WhAm 5*
Long, Robert William 1843-1915 *NatCAB 18*
Long, Rose McConnell 1892-1970 *BiDrAC, WhAm 5*
Long, Russell Billiu 1918- *BiDrAC*

Long, Samuel Arthur 1879- *WhoColR*
Long, Samuel Dismukes 1859- *WhAm 4*
Long, Samuel P *NewYHSD*
Long, Seely Frederick 1855-1921 *WhAm 1*
Long, Simon Cameron 1857-1917 *WhAm 1*
Long, Simon Peter 1860-1929 *NatCAB 22, WhAm 1*
Long, Speedy Oteria 1928- *BiDrAC*
Long, Stanley M 1892-1972 *IlBEAAW*
Long, Stephen Harriman 1784-1864 *AmBi, ApCAB, BiAUS, DcAmB, Drake, NatCAB 11, REnAW, TwCBDA, WebAMB, WhAm H*
Long, Theodore Kepner 1856-1947 *WhAm 2*
Long, Theodore Kepner 1857-1947 *NatCAB 16*
Long, Thomas Alexander *WhoColR*
Long, Thomas George 1883-1973 *WhAm 6*
Long, Thomas John 1852- *NatCAB 10*
Long, Thomas Johnathan 1874-1943 *NatCAB 34*
Long, Thomas Williams Mason 1886-1941 *NatCAB 36*
Long, Veldon Oscar 1907-1973 *WhAm 6*
Long, Walker 1896-1961 *NatCAB 46, WhAm 4*
Long, Walter E d1961 *WhAm 4*
Long, Wendell McLean 1899-1946 *WhAm 2*
Long, Westray Battle 1901-1972 *NatCAB 57*
Long, William Edgar 1873-1961 *NatCAB 48*
Long, William H 1888-1963 *NatCAB 50*
Long, William Henry 1867- *WhAm 4*
Long, William Joseph 1866-1952 *NatCAB 42, WhAm 3*
Long, William Joseph 1867- *NatCAB 13*
Long, William Lunsford 1890-1964 *NatCAB 51, WhAm 4*
Longacre, Andrew 1831?- *NewYHSD*
Longacre, Charles Smull 1871-1956 *WhAm 3*
Longacre, Jacob Elias 1870-1934 *NatCAB 26*
Longacre, James Barton 1794-1869 *ApCAB, DcAmB, Drake, NatCAB 25, NewYHSD, WhAm H*
Longacre, Lindsay Bartholomew 1870- *WhAm 5*
Longacre, Matthias Reiff 1836- *NewYHSD*
Longan, Edward Everett 1865- *WhAm 4*
Longan, Emma Lard 1854- *WomWWA 14*
Longan, George Baker 1879-1942 *WhAm 1*
Longaxe *NewYHSD*
Longbrake, Gertrude Brandsmark *WomWWA 14*
Longcope, Warfield Theobald 1877-1953 *DcAmB S5, WhAm 3*
Longden, Aladine Cummings 1857-1941 *WhAm 1*
Longden, Henry Boyer 1860-1948 *WhAm 2*
Longdon, Harriet Ruger 1871- *WomWWA 14*
Longenecker, G William 1899-1969 *NatCAB 55*
Longest, Christopher 1874-1962 *WhAm 4, WhAm 5*
Longfellow, A Wadsworth 1854-1934 *WhAm 1*
Longfellow, Ernest Wadsworth 1845-1921 *ApCAB, DcAmB, Drake, NatCAB 21, TwCBDA, WhAm 1*
Longfellow, Frederick William 1870-1938 *NatCAB 29*
Longfellow, Henry Wadsworth 1807-1882 *AmBi, ApCAB, DcAmB, Drake, EncAAH, EncAB, McGEWB, NatCAB 2, TwCBDA, WebAB, WhAm H*
Longfellow, Julia Livingston Delafield *BiCAW, WomWWA 14*
Longfellow, Marian Adele 1849- *WomWWA 14*
Longfellow, Samuel 1819-1892 *AmBi, ApCAB, DcAmB, Drake, NatCAB 8, TwCBDA, WhAm H*
Longfellow, Stephen 1775-1849 *ApCAB, BiAUS, BiDrAC, Drake, WhAm H, WhAmP*
Longfellow, Stephen 1776-1849 *DcAmB, NatCAB 10, TwCBDA*
Longfellow, Thomas 1900-1962 *NatCAB 47, WhAm 4*
Longfellow, William Pitt Preble 1836-1913 *DcAmB, NatCAB 23, NewYHSD, WhAm 1*

Longino, Andrew Houston 1855-1942
NatCAB 13, WhAm 2
Longino, Olin Harrington 1887-1955 *WhAm 3*
Longinos, Jose 1750?-1803 *ApCAB*
Longinus *McGEWB*
Longley, Alcander 1832-1918 *DcAmB*
Longley, Clifford Boles 1888-1954 *WhAm 3*
Longley, Edmund Waters 1863-1941 *WhAm 1*
Longley, Francis Fielding 1879- *WhAm 6*
Longley, Harry Sherman 1868-1944
NatCAB 37, WhAm 2
Longley, James Wilberforce 1849- *ApCAB Sup*
Longley, W H 1881-1937 *WhAm 1*
Longley, William Preston 1851-1878 *REnAW*
Longley, William Raymond 1880- *WhAm 6*
Longmaid, Sydney Esterbrook 1905-1967
WhAm 4
Longman, Evelyn Beatrice 1874-1954 *BiCAW,
NatCAB 40, WhAm 3, WomWWA 14*
Longmire, Victor Melton 1889-1953
NatCAB 42
Longmire, William Marcellus 1870-1953
NatCAB 41
Longnecker, Edwin 1844-1923 *WhAm 1*
Longnecker, Elisabeth Dye *WomWWA 14*
Longnecker, Henry C 1825-1871 *BiAUS*
Longnecker, Henry Clay 1820-1871 *ApCAB,
BiDrAC, TwCBDA, WhAm H*
Longomontanus *DcScB*
Longshore, Hannah E Myers 1819-1901
*AmWom, BiCAW, NatCAB 5, NotAW,
WhAm 1*
Longshore, Joseph Skelton 1809-1879
NatCAB 5
Longshore, Thomas Ellwood 1812-1898
NatCAB 26
Longstreet, Augustus Baldwin 1790-1870 *AmBi,
ApCAB, DcAmB, Drake, NatCAB 1,
TwCBDA, WebAB, WhAm H*
Longstreet, Cornelius Tyler 1814-1881
NatCAB 5
Longstreet, Helen Dortch d1962 *WhAm 4,
WomWWA 14*
Longstreet, James 1820-1904 *Drake*
Longstreet, James 1821-1904 *AmBi, ApCAB,
BiDConf, DcAmB, EncAB, NatCAB 4,
TwCBDA, WebAB, WebAMB, WhAm 1,
WhoMilH*
Longstreet, William 1759-1814 *DcAmB,
NatCAB 9, TwCBDA, WhAm H*
Longstreet, William 1760?-1814 *ApCAB,
Drake*
Longstreth, Benjamin Taylor 1849-1912
NatCAB 24
Longstreth, Bevis 1893-1944 *NatCAB 33*
Longstreth, Charles 1868-1948 *WhAm 2*
Longstreth, Clyde Marion 1898-1972 *WhAm 6*
Longstreth, Edward 1839-1905 *NewYHSD,
WhAm H*
Longstreth, Miers Fisher 1819- *ApCAB*
Longstreth, Morris 1846- *WhAm 4*
Longstreth, William Morris 1853-1918
NatCAB 45
Longsworth, Walter Ira 1885-1959 *WhAm 4*
Longua, Paul J 1881- *WhAm 6*
Longueuil, Paul Joseph De d1778 *Drake*
Longwell, Benton Elkins 1874-1938 *NatCAB 30*
Longwell, Chester Ray 1887-1975 *WhAm 6*
Longwell, Daniel 1899-1968 *WhAm 5*
Longwell, Oliver Henry 1855-1921 *WhAm 3*
Longwell, Robson Nathan 1881-1952
NatCAB 40
Longwell, William Howard 1839-1921
NatCAB 19
Longworth, Langdon Rives 1846-1879
NatCAB 15
Longworth, Montreville *NewYHSD*
Longworth, Nicholas 1782-1863 *AmBi, DcAmB,
Drake, NatCAB 11, WhAm H*
Longworth, Nicholas 1844-1890 *NatCAB 29*
Longworth, Nicholas 1869-1931 *AmBi,
BiDrAC, DcAmB, NatCAB 23, WebAB,
WhAm 1, WhAmP*
Longworth, Nicholas Murray 1913-1963
NatCAB 50
Longworth, Nicholas Murray 1913-1964
WhAm 4
Longworth, Nicolas 1782-1863 *ApCAB*

Longworth, Raymond A *WhAm 6*
Longworthy, John 1814-1885 *ApCAB*
Longyear, Edmund Joseph 1864-1954 *WhAm 3*
Longyear, John Munro 1850-1922 *ApCAB X,
NatCAB 15, WhAm 1*
Longyear, John Munroe 1850-1922 *DcAmB*
Longyear, John Wesley 1820-1875 *ApCAB,
BiAUS, BiDrAC, NatCAB 11, TwCBDA,
WhAm H*
Longyear, Robert Davis 1892-1970 *WhAm 5*
Lonicerus, Adam 1528-1586 *DcScB*
Lonn, E Julius 1869- *ApCAB X*
Lonn, Ella 1878- *WhAm 6*
Lonnquist, Carl Adolph 1869-1937 *WhAm 1*
Lonsdale, Charles William 1871-1930
NatCAB 23
Lonsdale, John Gerdes 1872-1943 *NatCAB 13,
WhAm 2*
Lonsdale, John Tipton 1895-1960 *WhAm 4*
Lonsdale, Kathleen Yardley 1903-1971 *DcScB*
Lonsdale, William 1794-1871 *DcScB*
Lontz, John Milton 1862-1933 *NatCAB 27*
Loof, A *NewYHSD*
Loofbourow, Frederick Charles 1874-1949
BiDrAC, NatCAB 37, WhAmP
Loofbourow, John Robert 1902-1951 *WhAm 3*
Look, David Millard 1863-1945 *NatCAB 34*
Looker, Cloyd Delson 1889-1965 *NatCAB 52*
Looker, Othniel 1757-1845 *BiAUS, Drake*
Looker, Silas *NewYHSD*
Looker, Thomas Henry 1829-1910 *WhAm 1*
Loomis, Alfred Fullerton 1890-1968
NatCAB 54, WhAm 5
Loomis, Alfred Lebbeus 1831-1895 *AmBi,
ApCAB, NatCAB 8, TwCBDA*
Loomis, Alfred Lee 1887-1975 *WhAm 6*
Loomis, Andrew 1892-1959 *NatCAB 47*
Loomis, Andrew Williams 1797-1873 *BiDrAC,
WhAm H*
Loomis, Archibald Gilbert 1848-1927 *WhAm 1*
Loomis, Arphaxad 1798-1885 *BiAUS,
NatCAB 25, TwCBDA*
Loomis, Arphaxed 1798-1885 *ApCAB,
BiDrAC, DcAmB, WhAm H*
Loomis, Arthur Pope 1919-1965 *WhAm 4*
Loomis, Augustus Ward 1816-1891
ApCAB Sup
Loomis, Benjamin Bloomfield 1836-1917
WhAm 1
Loomis, C Grant 1901-1963 *NatCAB 50,
WhAm 4*
Loomis, Caspar *NewYHSD*
Loomis, Charles Battell 1861-1911 *DcAmB,
NatCAB 14, WhAm 1*
Loomis, Charles Wheeler 1891-1957 *WhAm 3*
Loomis, Chester 1852-1924 *IIBEAAW,
WhAm 1*
Loomis, Clara Denison 1887- *WomWWA 14*
Loomis, Dwight 1821-1903 *ApCAB, BiAUS,
BiDrAC, DcAmB, NatCAB 11,
NatCAB 30, TwCBDA, WhAm 1*
Loomis, Eben Jencks 1828-1912 *WhAm 1*
Loomis, Eben Jenks 1828-1912 *NatCAB 40*
Loomis, Edward Eugene d1937 *WhAm 1*
Loomis, Edward Eugene 1864-1937 *NatCAB 36*
Loomis, Edward Eugene 1865-1937 *ApCAB X*
Loomis, Edwin Cooley 1865-1925 *NatCAB 21*
Loomis, Elias 1811-1889 *AmBi, ApCAB,
DcAmB, DcScB, Drake, NatCAB 7,
TwCBDA*
Loomis, Elisha Scott 1852- *NatCAB 15*
Loomis, Ellen Seymour Hanson 1860-
WomWWA 14
Loomis, Elmer Howard 1861-1931 *DcAmB,
NatCAB 25, WhAm 1*
Loomis, Francis Butler 1861-1948 *NatCAB 12,
NatCAB 37, TwCBDA, WhAm 2*
Loomis, Francis Wheeler 1889-1976 *WhAm 6*
Loomis, Frederic Brewster 1873-1937
NatCAB 30, WhAm 1
Loomis, Frederic Morris 1877-1949 *WhAm 2*
Loomis, George 1817-1886 *TwCBDA*
Loomis, Gustavus 1789-1872 *ApCAB, Drake*
Loomis, Harold Francis 1890-1970 *WhAm 5*
Loomis, Harvey Worthington 1865-1930
NatCAB 23, WhAm 1
Loomis, Helen Augusta 1875- *WhAm 5*

Loomis, Henry M 1875- *WhAm 5*
Loomis, Henry Patterson 1859-1907
NatCAB 23, WhAm 1
Loomis, James Lee 1878- *WhAm 6*
Loomis, James M *NewYHSD*
Loomis, Jennie 1871- *WomWWA 14*
Loomis, John 1875- *WhAm 5*
Loomis, John Mason 1825-1900 *NatCAB 6*
Loomis, Julia Stimson *BiCAW*
Loomis, Justin 1810-1888 *NatCAB 12*
Loomis, Justin R 1810- *Drake*
Loomis, Justin Rolph 1810-1898 *TwCBDA*
Loomis, Justin Rudolph 1810- *ApCAB*
Loomis, Kenneth Bradley 1900-1974 *WhAm 6*
Loomis, Lafayette Charles 1824-1906 *ApCAB,
TwCBDA, WhAm 1*
Loomis, Lee Pierson 1884-1964 *WhAm 4*
Loomis, Leverett Mills 1857-1928 *WhAm 1*
Loomis, Louise Ropes 1874-1958 *WhAm 3,
WomWWA 14*
Loomis, Madeleine Seymour d1950 *WhAm 3*
Loomis, Mahlon 1826-1884 *TwCBDA*
Loomis, Mahlon 1826-1886 *AmBi, DcAmB,
NatCAB 25, WhAm H*
Loomis, Mary Trask 1877- *WomWWA 14*
Loomis, Milton Early 1887-1973 *WhAm 6*
Loomis, Nelson Henry 1862-1933 *WhAm 1*
Loomis, Noel Miller 1905-1969 *WhAm 5*
Loomis, Orland Steen 1893-1942 *NatCAB 33,
WhAm 2*
Loomis, Osbert Burr 1813- *NewYHSD*
Loomis, Pascal 1826-1878 *IIBEAAW,
NewYHSD*
Loomis, Robert Herbert 1890-1964 *NatCAB 50,
WhAm 4*
Loomis, Roger Sherman 1887-1966 *NatCAB 53,
WhAm 4*
Loomis, Ruth 1864-1957 *WhAm 3*
Loomis, Samuel Lane 1856-1938 *WhAm 1,
WhAm 1C*
Loomis, Seymour Crane 1861-1921 *WhAm 1*
Loomis, Silas Laurence 1822-1896 *ApCAB*
Loomis, Silas Lawrence 1822-1896 *TwCBDA*
Loomis, Wesley Horace 1831-1920 *NatCAB 28*
Loomis, Wesley Horace, Jr. 1884-1946
NatCAB 36
Loomis, William Farnsworth 1914-1973
WhAm 6
Loomis, William Stiles 1840-1914 *NatCAB 15*
Loomis, Willis Henry 1870-1944 *NatCAB 35*
Looms, George 1886-1926 *NatCAB 21,
WhAm 1*
Looney, Marion A 1886-1965 *WhAm 4A*
Loop, Augustus Henry 1831-1895 *WhAm H*
Loop, Henry Augustus 1831-1895 *ApCAB,
DcAmB, NatCAB 13, NewYHSD,
TwCBDA*
Loop, Jennette Shephard Harrison 1840-1909
AmWom
Loop, Jennette Shepherd Harrison 1840-1909
ApCAB, NewYHSD, TwCBDA, WhAm 1
Looper, Edward Anderson 1888-1953 *WhAm 3*
Loos, Augustus Jacob 1853-1926 *NatCAB 21*
Loos, Charles Louis 1823-1912 *ApCAB,
DcAmB, NatCAB 4, TwCBDA,
WhAm 4*
Loos, Charles Louis 1849-1917 *NatCAB 17*
Loos, Isaac Althaus 1856-1919 *TwCBDA,
WhAm 1*
Looscan, Michael 1838-1897 *NatCAB 8*
Loose, Jacob Leander 1850-1923 *NatCAB 19*
Loose, Katharine Riegel 1877- *WhAm 5,
WomWWA 14*
Loot, Gerard Van 1705-1761 *ApCAB*
Lootens, Louis 1825-1898 *ApCAB*
Lootens, Louis 1827-1898 *TwCBDA*
Lopaze, D *NewYHSD*
Lope De Vega 1562-1635 *McGEWB*
Loper, Don 1906-1972 *WhAm 5*
Loper, Ruth Rust 1886- *WomWWA 14*
Lopes, Caetano 1780-1860 *ApCAB*
Lopez *NewYHSD*
Lopez, Aaron 1731-1782 *DcAmB, WhAm H*
Lopez, Carlos Antonio 1790-1862 *ApCAB*
Lopez, Carlos Antonio 1792-1862 *McGEWB*
Lopez, Charles Albert 1869-1906 *WhAm 1*
Lopez, DeZuniga Y Velasco, Diego 1510-1564
ApCAB

Lopez, Don Francisco Solano 1831-1870 *Drake*
Lopez, Estanislao 1786-1838 *ApCAB*
Lopez, Francisco Solano 1826-1870 *McGEWB*
Lopez, Francisco Solano 1827-1870 *ApCAB*
Lopez, Juan Francisco 1699-1778 *WhAm H*
Lopez, Maria DeG E 1881- *WomWWA 14*
Lopez, Martin *ApCAB*
Lopez, Narciso 1798-1851 *McGEWB*
Lopez, Narciso 1799-1851 *ApCAB, Drake*
Lopez, Pumarejo Alfonso 1886-1959 *WhAm 3*
Lopez DeAyala, Pedro 1332-1407 *McGEWB*
Lopez-Mateos, Adolfo 1910-1969 *WhAm 5*
Lopez Y Planes, Vicente 1784-1856 *ApCAB*
Lopp, Harry Leonard 1888- *IIBEAAW*
Lopp, William Thomas 1864-1939 *WhAm 1*
Loquillo 1478?-1525? *ApCAB*
Lorain, Lorenzo 1831-1882 *ApCAB, NatCAB 4*
Loram, Charles Templeman 1879-1940 *WhAm 1*
Lorance, George Toel 1898-1973 *WhAm 6*
Loranger, Albert Joseph 1905-1955 *NatCAB 46*
Loranger, Louis Onesime 1837- *ApCAB*
Loranger, Thomas Jean Jacques 1823-1885 *ApCAB*
Loras, Jean Mathias Pierre 1792-1858 *DcAmB, WhAm H*
Loras, Mathias 1792-1858 *ApCAB, Drake, NatCAB 12*
Loras, Pierre Jean Mathias 1792-1858 *TwCBDA*
Lorber, Herbert James 1892-1964 *WhAm 4*
Lorch, Emil 1870- *WhAm 1*
Lord, Arthur 1850-1925 *NatCAB 28, WhAm 1*
Lord, Arthur Evarts 1883-1947 *NatCAB 45*
Lord, Asa Dearborn 1816-1874 *NatCAB 12*
Lord, Asa Dearborn 1816-1875 *BiDAmEd, DcAmB, WhAm H*
Lord, Augustus Mendon 1861-1941 *NatCAB 31, WhAm 1*
Lord, Austin Willard 1860-1922 *NatCAB 11, WhAm 1*
Lord, Benjamin 1694-1784 *ApCAB, Drake*
Lord, Bert 1869-1939 *BiDrAC, WhAm 1*
Lord, Charles Bachus 1810-1868 *ApCAB*
Lord, Charles Boyne 1902-1967 *WhAm 4*
Lord, Charles Edward 1875- *NatCAB 17*
Lord, Charles Edwin 1865-1942 *ApCAB X, NatCAB 31*
Lord, Charles King 1848- *WhAm 4*
Lord, Charles M *NewYHSD*
Lord, Chester Bradford 1875-1958 *WhAm 3*
Lord, Chester Sanders 1850-1933 *DcAmB S1, NatCAB 13, NatCAB 25, TwCBDA, WhAm 1*
Lord, Clarence Jefferson 1863-1937 *NatCAB 27*
Lord, Daniel 1794-1868 *Drake*
Lord, Daniel 1795-1868 *ApCAB, DcAmB, WhAm H*
Lord, Daniel Aloysius 1888-1955 *WhAm 3*
Lord, Daniel Miner 1844-1930 *NatCAB 22, WhAm 1*
Lord, Daniel Minor 1800-1861 *ApCAB*
Lord, David Nevins 1792-1880 *ApCAB, DcAmB, TwCBDA, WhAm H*
Lord, Edward Thomas Sumner 1871- *WhAm 5*
Lord, Eleanor Louisa 1866- *WhAm 4, WomWWA 14*
Lord, Eleazar 1788-1871 *ApCAB, DcAmB, Drake, TwCBDA, WhAm H*
Lord, Elizabeth W Russell 1819- *AmWom*
Lord, Everett William 1871-1965 *WhAm 4*
Lord, Franklin Butler 1850-1908 *NatCAB 14*
Lord, Franklin Butler, Jr. 1911-1971 *NatCAB 56*
Lord, Fred Townley 1893-1962 *WhAm 4*
Lord, Frederic Pomeroy 1876-1970 *NatCAB 57*
Lord, Frederic W 1871-1951 *WhAm 3*
Lord, Frederick Taylor 1875-1941 *NatCAB 34, WhAm 1*
Lord, Frederick William 1800-1860 *BiAUS, BiDrAC, WhAm H*
Lord, George DeForest 1891-1950 *WhAm 2*
Lord, Henry 1847- *WhAm 1*
Lord, Henry Curwen 1866-1925 *DcAmB, WhAm 1*
Lord, Henry Gardner 1865-1961 *NatCAB 46, WhAm 4*

Lord, Henry William 1821-1891 *BiDrAC, WhAm H*
Lord, Herbert Gardiner 1849-1930 *NatCAB 21, NatCAB 23, WhAm 1*
Lord, Herbert Gardiner 1889-1966 *NatCAB 53*
Lord, Herbert Mayhew 1859-1930 *AmBi, DcAmB, NatCAB 21, WhAm 1*
Lord, Hugh Compton 1867-1952 *NatCAB 46*
Lord, Isaac Wilson 1836-1917 *NatCAB 30*
Lord, Isabel Ely 1871- *WhAm 5, WomWWA 14*
Lord, James Brown 1858-1902 *WhAm 1*
Lord, James Couper 1825-1869 *ApCAB*
Lord, James Osborn 1891-1958 *NatCAB 47*
Lord, James Revell 1878- *WhAm 6*
Lord, Jere Williams 1864-1933 *WhAm 1*
Lord, John 1810-1894 *DcAmB, NatCAB 25, TwCBDA, WhAm H*
Lord, John 1812-1894 *ApCAB*
Lord, John 1879-1949 *WhAm 2*
Lord, John Chase 1805-1877 *ApCAB*
Lord, John Foley 1909-1970 *WhAm 5*
Lord, John King 1819-1849 *ApCAB*
Lord, John King 1848-1926 *NatCAB 20, WhAm 1*
Lord, John Norton 1910-1962 *WhAm 4*
Lord, John Prentiss 1860-1940 *NatCAB 12, NatCAB 16, WhAm 1*
Lord, John W, Jr. 1901-1972 *WhAm 5*
Lord, John Walter 1875-1920 *NatCAB 19*
Lord, Katharine *WomWWA 14*
Lord, Kenneth Prince 1888-1957 *WhAm 3*
Lord, Lillos Montgomery d1970 *WhAm 5*
Lord, Livingston Chester 1851-1933 *BiDAmEd*
Lord, Livingston G 1851-1933 *WhAm 1*
Lord, Louis Eleazer 1875-1956 *WhAm 3*
Lord, Louis Eleazer 1875-1957 *NatCAB 47*
Lord, Mary *NewYHSD*
Lord, Nathan 1792-1870 *BiDAmEd, DcAmB, NatCAB 9, TwCBDA, WhAm H*
Lord, Nathan 1793-1870 *ApCAB, Drake*
Lord, Nathaniel Wright 1854-1911 *WhAm 1*
Lord, Otis Phillips 1812-1884 *ApCAB, DcAmB, NatCAB 25, WhAm H*
Lord, Pauline 1890-1950 *DcAmB S4, NotAW, WhAm 3*
Lord, Philip 1814-1888 *NewYHSD*
Lord, Phillips H 1902-1975 *WhAm 6*
Lord, Phoebe Griffin 1831-1875 *NewYHSD*
Lord, Rivington David 1858-1938 *WhAm 1*
Lord, Robert Howard 1885-1954 *NatCAB 41, WhAm 3*
Lord, Robert Mendon 1893-1963 *NatCAB 50*
Lord, Robert Waterston 1828-1923 *NatCAB 31*
Lord, Royal Bertram 1899-1963 *WhAm 4*
Lord, Scott 1820-1885 *ApCAB, BiAUS, BiDrAC, TwCBDA, WhAm H*
Lord, Thomas *NewYHSD*
Lord, William Freeman 1848-1927 *NatCAB 22*
Lord, William Paine 1838-1911 *NatCAB 38, WhAm 1*
Lord, William Paine 1839-1911 *DcAmB, NatCAB 8, TwCBDA*
Lord, William Sinclair 1863-1925 *WhAm 1*
Lord, William W 1818?-1907 *Drake*
Lord, William Wilberforce 1819-1907 *ApCAB, DcAmB, NatCAB 3, WhAm 1*
Lord, Willis 1809-1888 *ApCAB, TwCBDA*
Lore, Charles Brown 1831-1911 *BiDrAC, NatCAB 7, TwCBDA, WhAm 1*
Lore, Emma Maria Theresa 1868- *WomWWA 14*
Loree, Ira Dean 1869-1936 *NatCAB 27*
Loree, James Taber 1888-1973 *WhAm 5*
Loree, Leonor Fresnel 1858-1940 *ApCAB X, DcAmB S2, NatCAB 18, WhAm 1*
Lorencez, Charles Ferdinand Latrille 1814- *ApCAB*
Lorentz, Hendrik Antoon 1853-1928 *AsBiEn, DcScB, McGEWB*
Lorentz, Pare 1906- *EncAAH*
Lorenz, Alexander 1808?- *NewYHSD*
Lorenz, Daniel Edward 1862- *WhAm 4*
Lorenz, Edmund Simon 1854-1942 *NatCAB 32*
Lorenz, Egon 1891-1954 *NatCAB 41*
Lorenz, Hans 1865-1940 *DcScB*
Lorenz, Henry William Frederick 1871- *WhAm 5*

Lorenz, Joseph 1893-1958 *WhAm 3*
Lorenz, Julius 1862- *NatCAB 14, WhAm 4*
Lorenz, Keith 1890-1952 *WhAm 3*
Lorenz, Ludwig Valentin 1829-1891 *DcScB*
Lorenz, Max Otto 1876-1959 *NatCAB 47, WhAm 5*
Lorenz, Richard 1858-1915 *IIBEAAW, REnAW, WhAm 1*
Lorenz, Richard 1863-1929 *DcScB*
Lorenz, Rolland Carl 1907-1965 *WhAm 4*
Lorenz, William Frederick 1882-1958 *WhAm 3*
Lorenzana Y Butron, Francisco Antonio 1722-1804 *ApCAB*
Lorenzen, Ernest Gustav 1876-1951 *NatCAB 39*
Lorenzen, Ernest Gustav 1876-1952 *WhAm 3*
Lorenzetti, Ambrogio *McGEWB*
Lorenzetti, Pietro *McGEWB*
Lorenzoni, Giuseppe 1843-1914 *DcScB*
Lorge, Irving 1905-1961 *WhAm 4*
Loria, Gino 1862-1954 *DcScB*
Loria, Sam F *NewYHSD*
Lorigan, William George 1855- *WhAm 1*
Lorillard, Jacob 1774-1838 *ApCAB*
Lorillard, Pierre 1833-1901 *ApCAB, DcAmB, WhAm H*
Lorillard, Pierre 1860-1940 *WhAm 1*
Lorimer, George Claud 1838-1904 *ApCAB*
Lorimer, George Claude 1838-1904 *DcAmB, NatCAB 11, TwCBDA, WhAm 1*
Lorimer, George Horace 1867-1937 *DcAmB S2, NatCAB 13, NatCAB 27, WebAB*
Lorimer, George Horace 1868-1937 *AmBi, TwCBDA, WhAm 1*
Lorimer, John Hewetson 1846-1918 *NatCAB 19*
Lorimer, John Wightman 1865-1947 *NatCAB 44*
Lorimer, William 1861-1934 *BiDrAC, DcAmB S1, NatCAB 14, WhAm 1, WhAmP*
Lorimer, Wright 1874-1911 *WhAm 1*
Lorimier, Mary-Thomas Chevalier De 1805-1839 *ApCAB*
Lorimier, Pierre Louis 1748-1812 *DcAmB, WhAm H*
Loring, Albert Carpenter d1932 *WhAm 1*
Loring, Anna S *WomWWA 14*
Loring, Augustus Peabody 1856-1938 *WhAm 1*
Loring, Augustus Peabody, Jr. 1885-1951 *WhAm 3*
Loring, Bertha Darrow 1872- *WomWWA 14*
Loring, Caleb William 1819-1897 *NatCAB 27*
Loring, Charles 1873-1961 *WhAm 4*
Loring, Charles Greeley 1794-1867 *Drake*
Loring, Charles Greeley 1794-1868 *ApCAB*
Loring, Charles Greely 1794-1867 *NatCAB 22*
Loring, Charles Greely 1828-1902 *NatCAB 25, WhAm 1*
Loring, Charles Harding 1828-1907 *DcAmB, NatCAB 12, WhAm 1*
Loring, Charles Morgridge 1832-1922 *DcAmB*
Loring, Edward G 1802- *BiAUS*
Loring, Edward Greely 1837-1888 *ApCAB Sup, DcAmB, WhAm H*
Loring, Ellis Gray 1803-1858 *ApCAB, DcAmB, Drake, NatCAB 2, TwCBDA, WhAm H*
Loring, Emilie d1951 *WhAm 3*
Loring, Florence Barton *WomWWA 14*
Loring, Frances Norma 1887- *WomWWA 14*
Loring, Francis William 1838-1905 *NewYHSD*
Loring, Frederick Wadsworth 1848-1871 *ApCAB, DcAmB, Drake Sup, NatCAB 8, WhAm H*
Loring, George Bailey 1817-1891 *ApCAB, BiDrAC, DcAmB, EncAAH, NatCAB 4, NatCAB 15, TwCBDA, WhAm H, WhAmP*
Loring, George Fullington 1851- *NatCAB 11*
Loring, Hannibal Hamlin 1862-1936 *NatCAB 34*
Loring, Henry Delano 1884-1957 *NatCAB 46*
Loring, Homer 1875- *WhAm 5*
Loring, Israel 1682-1772 *ApCAB, Drake*
Loring, J Brown 1857-1942 *NatCAB 33*
Loring, James Spear 1799-1884 *ApCAB, Drake*
Loring, John Alden 1871-1947 *WhAm 2*
Loring, Joseph Holland 1882-1912 *NatCAB 16*
Loring, Joshua 1716-1781 *ApCAB, DcAmB, Drake, WhAm H*

Loring, Joshua 1737-1789 *ApCAB*
Loring, Joshua 1744-1789 *DcAmB, WhAm H*
Loring, Paule Stetson 1899-1968 *WhAm 5*
Loring, Ralph Alden 1897-1952 *WhAm 3*
Loring, Richard Tuttle 1900-1948 *WhAm 2*
Loring, Victor Joseph 1859-1947 *NatCAB 15, WhAm 2*
Loring, William Caleb 1851-1930 *NatCAB 22, WhAm 1*
Loring, William Cushing 1879-1959 *NatCAB 44*
Loring, William W 1815?- *Drake*
Loring, William Wing 1818-1886 *AmBi, ApCAB, BiDConf, DcAmB, NatCAB 4, TwCBDA, WebAMB, WhAm H*
Lorini, Louise Chase 1875- *WomWWA 14*
Lorini, Virginia d1865 *Drake*
Lorio, Peter *NewYHSD*
Lorne, John G H D S Campbell, Marquis Of 1845- *ApCAB*
Lorne, Marion 1888-1968 *WhAm 5*
Lorquet, Louis Michael Polemon 1825-1876 *ApCAB*
Lorraine, Narcisse Zephrin 1842- *ApCAB*
Lorre, Peter 1904-1964 *WhAm 4*
Lorry, Anne Charles 1726-1783 *DcScB*
Lorton, Eugene 1869-1949 *NatCAB 40, WhAm 2*
Lorton, Richard *NewYHSD*
Lorwin, Lewis L 1883-1970 *WhAm 5*
Lory, Carrie Richards 1873- *WomWWA 14*
Lory, Charles Alfred 1872-1970 *WhAm 5*
Losada, Diego 1519-1569 *Drake*
Losada, Diego De 1519-1569 *ApCAB*
Losada, Manuel 1825?-1873 *ApCAB*
Loschi, Augustus 1885-1966 *NatCAB 52*
Loschmidt, Johann Joseph 1821-1895 *DcScB*
Lose, George William 1852- *WhAm 4*
Lose, Rebecca Justina 1857- *WomWWA 14*
Loser, Joseph Carlton 1892- *BiDrAC, WhAmP*
Losey, Frederick Douglas 1866-1932 *WhAm 1*
Losey, Frederick Douglas 1868-1932 *NatCAB 23*
Losey, John Clark 1883-1948 *NatCAB 37*
Loshe, Lillie Deming 1877- *WomWWA 14*
Loskiel, George Henry 1740-1814 *ApCAB, DcAmB, Drake, NatCAB 13, TwCBDA, WhAm H*
Loss, Lewis Homri 1803-1865 *ApCAB*
LosSantos, Thomas De 1826-1868 *ApCAB*
Lossberg, Fritz Von 1868-1943 *WhoMilH*
Lossen, Karl August 1841-1893 *DcScB*
Lossing, Benson John 1813-1891 *AmBi, ApCAB, DcAmB, Drake, NatCAB 4, NewYHSD, TwCBDA, WhAm H*
Lossing, Helen S 1834- *WhAm 4*
Lostine, Henry *NewYHSD*
Lotave, Carl G 1872-1924 *IIBEAAW*
Lotbiniere, Eustace G M Chartier De d1821 *ApCAB*
Lotbiniere, Michael E G, Marquis De 1723-1799 *ApCAB*
Lothian, Marquess Of 1882-1940 *WhAm 1*
Lothringer, Alfred Otto 1897-1960 *NatCAB 48*
Lothrop, Alice Louise Higgins 1870-1920 *DcAmB, NotAW*
Lothrop, Amy *AmBi, WhAm 1*
Lothrop, Charles Henry 1831- *ApCAB*
Lothrop, Daniel 1831-1892 *DcAmB, NatCAB 8, TwCBDA, WhAm H*
Lothrop, Fannie Mack *WhAm 5*
Lothrop, Fanny Mack *WomWWA 14*
Lothrop, George VanNess 1817-1897 *ApCAB, DcAmB, NatCAB 5, TwCBDA, WhAm H*
Lothrop, Harriet Mulford Stone 1844-1924 *TwCBDA, WomWWA 14*
Lothrop, Harriett Mulford Stone 1844-1924 *AmWom, ApCAB, DcAmB, NatCAB 8, NotAW, WhAm 1*
Lothrop, Howard Augustus 1864-1928 *ApCAB X, WhAm 1*
Lothrop, Marcus Thompson 1884-1935 *NatCAB 32, WhAm 1*
Lothrop, Samuel Kirkland 1804-1886 *ApCAB, Drake, NatCAB 12, TwCBDA*
Lothrop, Samuel Kirkland 1892-1965 *WhAm 4*
Lothrop, Thomas d1675 *ApCAB, NatCAB 11*

Lothrop, Thornton Kirkland 1830-1913 *NatCAB 14, WhAm 1*
Lothrop, William Kirkpatrick 1810- *NatCAB 4*
Lothropp, John 1584-1653 *DcAmB, WhAm H*
Loti, Pierre 1850-1923 *McGEWB*
Lotichius, Ernest *NewYHSD*
Lotka, Alfred James 1880-1949 *DcAmB S4, DcScB, WhAm 2*
Lotspeich, Claude Meek 1880-1966 *NatCAB 51*
Lotspeich, Ethel Moore 1886-1962 *WhAm 4*
Lotspeich, Roy Nicholas 1882-1951 *NatCAB 44, WhAm 3*
Lotspeich, William Douglas 1920-1968 *WhAm 5*
Lotsy, Jan Paulus 1867-1931 *DcScB*
Lott, Abraham Grant 1871- *WhAm 5*
Lott, Charles H 1876- *WhAm 3*
Lott, Edson Schuyler 1856-1945 *WhAm 2*
Lott, Henry DeWitt 1864-1928 *ApCAB X*
Lott, James H *WhoColR*
Lott, John A 1805-1878 *ApCAB*
Lott, John Abraham 1806-1878 *TwCBDA*
Lotta 1847-1924 *AmBi, DcAmB, NotAW, WhAm 1*
Lotta, L *NewYHSD*
Lotte, Edward F L 1868-1931 *WhAm 1*
Lottenschiold, Mathias 1729-1782 *ApCAB*
Lotter, Frederic August 1741-1806 *ApCAB*
Lotter, Matthew Albert *NewYHSD*
Lottier, Sarah Peyton 1887- *WhoColR*
Lottinville, Savoie 1906- *REnAW*
Lotto, Lorenzo 1480?-1556 *McGEWB*
Lottridge, Silas A 1863-1940 *WhAm 1*
Lotz, Frederick *NewYHSD*
Lotz, George 1868-1958 *NatCAB 48*
Lotz, John 1913-1973 *WhAm 6*
Lotz, John R d1965 *WhAm 4*
Lotz, Matilda 1861- *WomWWA 14*
Lotz, Oscar 1880-1953 *NatCAB 41, WhAm 3*
Lotze, Hermann Rudolph 1817-1881 *DcScB*
Lotze, Rudolf Hermann 1817-1881 *McGEWB*
Loubat, Joseph Florimund Duc De 1831- *WhAm 1*
Loubois, Chevalier De *ApCAB*
Louchheim, Walter Clinton, Jr. 1899-1973 *WhAm 5*
Loucks, Charles Olney 1877-1967 *WhAm 4*
Loucks, Elton Crocker 1892-1969 *WhAm 5*
Loucks, Henry Langford 1846-1928 *DcAmB, NatCAB 26, REnAW, WhAmP*
Loucks, Philip G 1899-1965 *WhAm 4*
Loucks, William Dewey 1879-1957 *WhAm 3*
Loud, Annie Frances 1856- *NatCAB 8, WhAm 4, WomWWA 14*
Loud, Bessie Alberta 1880- *WomWWA 14*
Loud, Eugene Francis 1847-1908 *BiDrAC, TwCBDA, WhAm 1, WhAmP*
Loud, Frank Herbert 1852-1927 *NatCAB 31, TwCBDA, WhAm 1*
Loud, George Alvin 1852-1925 *BiDrAC, NatCAB 25, WhAm 1, WhAmP*
Loud, Mrs. H C *NewYHSD*
Loud, Henry Martin 1824-1905 *WhAm 1*
Loud, Hulda Barker 1844- *AmWom*
Loud, John Hermann 1873- *WhAm 5*
Loud, Marguerite St. Leon 1800?- *ApCAB*
Loud, Norman Wiley 1892-1967 *NatCAB 54*
Louden, Elizabeth Valentine 1877- *WomWWA 14*
Louden, Frederic Allc 1897-1964 *WhAm 4*
Louden, William 1841-1931 *NatCAB 41, WhAm 1*
Loudenslager, Henry Clay 1852-1911 *BiDrAC, TwCBDA, WhAm 1, WhAmP*
Louderbach, James W *NewYHSD*
Louderback, DeLancey Horton 1849-1914 *NatCAB 16*
Louderback, George Davis 1874-1957 *NatCAB 17, WhAm 3*
Louderback, Harold 1881-1941 *NatCAB 31, WhAm 1*
Louderback, William Johnson 1864-1926 *WhAm 1*
Louderbough, Harry Cox 1873-1939 *NatCAB 33*
Loudon, A 1892-1953 *WhAm •3*
Loudon, Anne Louise 1884- *WomWWA 14*
Loudon, James Arlington *NatCAB 8*

Loudon, John 1800-1884 *NatCAB 8*
Loudon, John Campbell 1705-1782 *Drake*
Loudon, Jonkheer John 1866- *WhAm 4*
Loudon, Samuel 1727?-1813 *DcAmB, NatCAB 25, WhAm H*
Loudoun, Earl *WhAm H*
Loudoun, John Campbell, Earl Of 1705-1782 *ApCAB, DcAmB*
Loudy, Flavius Earl 1891-1953 *NatCAB 42*
Lougee, Francis Eaton 1923-1972 *WhAm 6*
Lougee, Richard Jewett 1905-1960 *NatCAB 48*
Lougee, Willis Eugene 1857-1935 *WhAm 1*
Lough, James Edwin 1871-1952 *WhAm 3*
Lough, Samuel Alexander 1864- *WhAm 4*
Lough, William Henry 1881- *WhAm 6*
Loughan, Katherine O'Neil 1881- *WhAm 6*
Loughborough, James Fairfax 1873-1945 *NatCAB 41, WhAm 2*
Loughborough, James Moore 1833-1876 *ApCAB*
Loughborough, Mary Webster 1836-1887 *ApCAB*
Loughead, Flora Haines 1855- *AmWom, NatCAB 11, WhAm 4*
Loughead, Isaac Marselis 1861-1922 *NatCAB 19*
Lougheed, Robert Elmer 1910- *IIBEAAW*
Lougheed, William Foster 1910-1962 *WhAm 4*
Loughin, Charles A 1897-1963 *WhAm 4*
Loughlin, Gerald Francis 1880-1946 *NatCAB 36, WhAm 2*
Loughlin, John 1816- *ApCAB*
Loughlin, John 1817-1891 *NatCAB 3, TwCBDA, WhAm H*
Loughran, John Thomas 1889-1953 *NatCAB 40, WhAm 3*
Loughridge, Robert Hills 1843- *WhAm 4*
Loughridge, Robert McGill 1809-1900 *BiDAmEd, DcAmB, NatCAB 19, WhAm H*
Loughridge, William 1827-1889 *BiAUS, BiDrAC, TwCBDA, WhAm H, WhAmP*
Louis I 778-840 *McGEWB*
Louis VI 1081-1137 *McGEWB*
Louis VII 1120?-1180 *McGEWB*
Louis IX 1214-1270 *McGEWB*
Louis XI 1423-1483 *McGEWB*
Louis XII 1462-1515 *McGEWB, WhoMilH*
Louis XIII 1601-1643 *McGEWB*
Louis XIV 1638-1715 *McGEWB, WhoMilH*
Louis XV 1710-1774 *McGEWB*
Louis XVI 1754-1793 *McGEWB*
Louis XVIII 1755-1824 *McGEWB*
Louis Philippe 1773-1850 *McGEWB*
Louis, Andrew 1907-1967 *WhAm 5*
Louis, C *NewYHSD*
Louis, Joe 1914- *EncAB, McGEWB, WebAB*
Louis, John F *NewYHSD*
Louis, John Jeffry 1895-1959 *WhAm 3*
Louis, Father M *WebAB*
Louis, Max C 1897-1962 *WhAm 4*
Louis, Minnie Dessau 1841- *NatCAB 18, WomWWA 14*
Louis, Morris 1912-1962 *BnEnAmA*
Louis, Pierre-Charles Alexandre 1787-1872 *BiHiMed, McGEWB*
Lounsberry, Alice 1873- *WomWWA 14*
Lounsberry, Frank Burton 1890-1963 *NatCAB 50, WhAm 4*
Lounsbery, Harriet Camp 1856- *WomWWA 14*
Lounsbery, William 1831-1905 *BiDrAC*
Lounsbury, Charles Edwin 1898-1952 *WhAm 3*
Lounsbury, George Edward 1838-1904 *NatCAB 12, TwCBDA, WhAm 1*
Lounsbury, George Fenner 1872-1958 *WhAm 3*
Lounsbury, James Breckinridge 1909-1974 *WhAm 6*
Lounsbury, Nellie E *WomWWA 14*
Lounsbury, Phineas Chapman 1841-1925 *NatCAB 10, TwCBDA*
Lounsbury, Phineas Chapman 1844-1925 *WhAm 1*
Lounsbury, Ralph Reed 1871-1933 *WhAm 1*
Lounsbury, Thomas Raynesford 1838-1915 *AmBi, ApCAB Sup, DcAmB, NatCAB 8, TwCBDA, WhAm 1*
Lourat, Joseph Florimund Duc De 1831- *ApCAB Sup*
Lourie, Alexander *NewYHSD*

Lourie, Arthur 1892-1966 *WhAm 4*
Lourie, David Abraham 1878-1930 *NatCAB 23,
WhAm 1, WhAm 1C*
Louterburg, W *NewYHSD*
Loutfi, Omar 1908-1963 *WhAm 4*
Louthan, Florence S 1860- *WomWWA 14*
Louthan, Hattie Horner 1865- *WhAm 5,
WomWWA 14*
Louthan, Henry Thompson 1866-1953 *WhAm 3*
Loutherbourg, Annibale Christian H De
1765-1813 *NewYHSD, WhAm H*
Loutre, Louis Joseph DeLa *Drake*
Louttit, Chauncey McKinley 1901-1956
WhAm 3
Louttit, George William 1868- *WhAm 4*
Louttit, James Alexander 1848-1906 *BiDrAC*
Louttit, William Easton, Jr. 1904-1973
NatCAB 57, WhAm 5
Loutzenheiser, Joe L 1899-1945 *WhAm 2*
L'Ouverture, Pierre Dominique 1743-1803
WhoMilH
Louvigny, Louis DeLaPorte 1654?-1725 *ApCAB*
Louvois, Francois LeTellier, Marquis De
1641-1691 *WhoMilH*
Louw, Eric Hendrik 1890-1968 *WhAm 5*
Lovatt, George Ignatius 1872- *WhAm 5*
Love, Albert Gallatin 1877- *WhAm 5*
Love, Albert Irving 1905-1971 *WhAm 5*
Love, Alfred Henry 1830-1913 *AmBi, DcAmB,
NatCAB 16, WhAm 1*
Love, Andrew Leo 1902-1965 *WhAm 4*
Love, Anita Hemmings 1872- *WomWWA 14*
Love, Archibald Longworth 1854-1931
NatCAB 32
Love, Augustus Edward Hough 1863-1940
DcScB
Love, Charles Everts 1910-1955 *WhAm 3*
Love, Clyde Elton 1882-1960 *NatCAB 47*
Love, Cornelius Ruxton, Jr. 1903-1971 *WhAm 5*
Love, Don Lathrop 1863-1940 *WhAm 1*
Love, Edgar Amos 1891-1974 *WhAm 6*
Love, Edward Bainbridge 1906-1972 *WhAm 5*
Love, Emanuel King 1850-1900 *DcAmB,
NatCAB 7, WhAm H*
Love, Francis Johnson 1901- *BiDrAC*
Love, Frank Samuel 1874-1933 *WhAm 1*
Love, G *NewYHSD*
Love, George Maltby 1831-1887 *ApCAB,
TwCBDA*
Love, George Willard Kirkland 1880- *WhoColR*
Love, Harry Houser 1880-1966 *WhAm 4*
Love, Hattie Frank 1884- *WomWWA 14*
Love, Isaac Newton 1853-1903 *NatCAB 6*
Love, J Mack 1851- *WhAm 4*
Love, James 1795-1874 *BiAUS, BiDrAC,
WhAm H*
Love, James Jay 1898-1961 *WhAm 4*
Love, James Lee 1860-1950 *NatCAB 38,
WhAm 3*
Love, James Madison 1820-1891 *BiAUS,
TwCBDA*
Love, James Sanford, Jr. 1910-1972 *WhAm 5*
Love, James Spencer 1896-1962 *WhAm 4*
Love, John d1822 *BiAUS, BiDrAC,
WhAm H*
Love, John W 1892-1958 *WhAm 3*
Love, Julian Price 1894-1969 *WhAm 5*
Love, Lonnie Adam 1893-1969 *NatCAB 54*
Love, Nat 1854-1921 *McGEWB*
Love, Peter Early 1818-1866 *BiAUS, BiDrAC,
WhAm H*
Love, Robertus Donnell 1867-1930 *DcAmB,
NatCAB 24, WhAm 1*
Love, Rodney Marvin 1908- *BiDrAC*
Love, Samuel G 1821-1893 *NatCAB 12*
Love, Smoloff Palace 1826-1903 *ApCAB,
WhAm 1*
Love, Stephen Hunter 1865-1937 *WhAm 1*
Love, Thomas Bell 1870-1948 *WhAm 2*
Love, Thomas Cutting 1789-1853 *BiAUS,
BiDrAC, WhAm H*
Love, Thomas J 1891-1955 *WhAm 3*
Love, Tracy Robinson 1878-1961 *NatCAB 50*
Love, William Carter 1784-1835 *BiAUS,
BiDrAC, WhAm H*
Love, William DeLoss 1819-1898 *NatCAB 11*
Love, William DeLoss 1851-1918 *WhAm 1*
Love, William Franklin 1850-1898 *BiDrAC*

Lovecraft, Howard Phillips 1890-1937 *WebAB*
Lovejoy, A L 1811-1882 *NatCAB 12*
Lovejoy, Arthur Oncken 1873-1962 *DcScB,
McGEWB, WhAm 4*
Lovejoy, Arthur Oncken 1873-1963 *WebAB*
Lovejoy, Asa Lawrence 1808-1882 *DcAmB,
WhAm H*
Lovejoy, Clarence Earle 1894-1974 *WhAm 6*
Lovejoy, Debora Eliza *WomWWA 14*
Lovejoy, Elijah Parish 1802-1837 *AmBi,
ApCAB, DcAmB, Drake, EncAAH,
EncAB, McGEWB, NatCAB 2,
TwCBDA, WebAB, WhAm H, WhAmP*
Lovejoy, Ellis 1860-1946 *NatCAB 34*
Lovejoy, Esther Pohl d1967 *WhAm 4A,
WomWWA 14*
Lovejoy, Francis Thomas Fletcher 1854-1932
NatCAB 10, NatCAB 41, WhAm 1
Lovejoy, Frank William 1871-1945 *NatCAB 49,
WhAm 2*
Lovejoy, Fred Prescott 1874-1940 *NatCAB 31*
Lovejoy, George Edwards 1843-1916 *WhAm 1*
Lovejoy, George Newell 1844- *WhAm 4*
Lovejoy, Hatton 1877-1964 *NatCAB 53,
WhAm 6*
Lovejoy, J Robert 1863-1945 *WhAm 2*
Lovejoy, John H *NewYHSD*
Lovejoy, John Meston 1889-1968 *NatCAB 54,
WhAm 5*
Lovejoy, Kildow 1906-1955 *NatCAB 46*
Lovejoy, Laura Armstrong 1884-
WomWWA 14
Lovejoy, Lillian *WomWWA 14*
Lovejoy, Mary Evelyn Wood 1847-
WomWWA 14
Lovejoy, Owen 1811-1864 *AmBi, ApCAB,
BiAUS, BiDrAC, DcAmB, Drake,
EncAAH, NatCAB 2, TwCBDA,
WhAm H, WhAmP*
Lovejoy, Owen Reed 1866-1961 *WhAm 4*
Lovejoy, Philip 1894-1966 *WhAm 4*
Lovejoy, Prescott Richardson 1902-1947
NatCAB 36
Lovejoy, Thomas E 1875-1939 *WhAm 1*
Lovelace, Benjamin Franklin 1876-1923
NatCAB 31
Lovelace, Curtis M 1890-1960 *WhAm 4*
Lovelace, Delos Wheeler 1894-1967 *WhAm 4*
Lovelace, Francis 1618?-1709 *Drake,
NatCAB 13*
Lovelace, Francis 1621?-1675 *AmBi, DcAmB,
WhAm H*
Lovelace, Francis 1630?- *ApCAB*
Lovelace, Richard 1618?-1657? *McGEWB*
Lovelace, William Randolph, II 1907-1965
NatCAB 53, WhAm 4
Loveland, Abner 1796-1879 *NatCAB 5*
Loveland, Albert J 1893-1961 *WhAm 4*
Loveland, Charles Asa 1881-1951 *NatCAB 39*
Loveland, Edward Rutherford 1893-1960
WhAm 4
Loveland, Ernest Kilborn 1871-1955
NatCAB 45
Loveland, Francis Augustus 1859- *NatCAB 16*
Loveland, Francis William 1857-1921
NatCAB 22
Loveland, Francis William 1859-1921
NatCAB 13, WhAm 1
Loveland, Frank Clarence 1839- *NatCAB 5*
Loveland, George Andrew 1863-1940
NatCAB 31
Loveland, Gilbert 1892-1956 *WhAm 3*
Loveland, Hansell William 1886-1963 *WhAm 4*
Loveland, Seymour 1859- *WhAm 4*
Loveland, William Austin Hamilton 1826-1894
DcAmB, NatCAB 8, WhAm H
Loveless, Clyde John 1871-1946 *NatCAB 34*
Lovell, Sir Alfred Charles Bernard 1913-
AsBiEn, McGEWB
Lovell, Alfred Henry 1884-1960 *WhAm 4*
Lovell, Antona *NewYHSD*
Lovell, Carleton Woodward 1892-1965
NatCAB 50
Lovell, Charles Swain 1811-1871 *ApCAB,
Drake, TwCBDA*
Lovell, Earl B 1869-1948 *WhAm 2*
Lovell, Ernest James, Jr. 1918-1975 *WhAm 6*
Lovell, Frederick Solon 1814-1878 *ApCAB*

Lovell, George Blakeman 1878- *WhAm 6*
Lovell, J Barton *NatCAB 18*
Lovell, James 1737-1814 *AmBi, ApCAB,
BiAUS, BiDrAC, DcAmB, Drake,
NatCAB 12, TwCBDA, WhAm H*
Lovell, James 1758-1850 *ApCAB, TwCBDA*
Lovell, James Arthur, Jr. 1928- *WebAMB*
Lovell, John 1710-1778 *ApCAB, DcAmB,
Drake, NatCAB 12, TwCBDA, WhAm H*
Lovell, John Epy 1795-1892 *BiDAmEd,
DcAmB, WhAm H*
Lovell, John Harvey 1860-1939 *DcScB,
NatCAB 37, WhAm 1*
Lovell, John Prince 1820-1897 *TwCBDA*
Lovell, Joseph 1788-1836 *ApCAB, BiHiMed,
DcAmB, Drake, NatCAB 4, WebAMB,
WhAm H*
Lovell, Leander Newton 1835-1912 *NatCAB 6*
Lovell, Louis S 1816- *BiAUS*
Lovell, Malcolm R d1975 *WhAm 6*
Lovell, Mansfield 1822-1884 *AmBi, ApCAB,
BiDConf, DcAmB, Drake, NatCAB 4,
TwCBDA, WebAMB, WhAm H*
Lovell, Moses Richardson 1895-1944 *WhAm 2*
Lovell, Ralph L 1865-1945 *WhAm 2*
Lovell, Tom 1909- *IlBEAAW*
Lovell, Walter Raleigh 1890-1968 *WhAm 5*
Lovely, John A 1843-1907 *WhAm 1*
Loveman, Amy 1881-1955 *DcAmB S5,
NatCAB 44, WhAm 3*
Loveman, Robert 1864-1923 *NatCAB 13,
WhAm 1*
Loveman, William Harvey 1893-1972
NatCAB 57
Loven, Sven 1809-1895 *DcScB*
Loveridge, Blanche Grosbec 1871- *WhAm 5*
Loveridge, C *NewYHSD*
Loveridge, Earl W 1890-1959 *WhAm 3*
Lovering, Charles T 1879-1961 *WhAm 4*
Lovering, Henry Bacon 1841-1911 *BiDrAC,
TwCBDA, WhAm 1*
Lovering, Joseph 1813-1892 *ApCAB, DcAmB,
NatCAB 6, TwCBDA, WhAm H*
Lovering, Joseph Amon 1876-1959 *NatCAB 49*
Lovering, Leonard Austin 1854-1914
NatCAB 16
Lovering, William Croad 1835-1910 *BiDrAC,
NatCAB 26, TwCBDA, WhAmP*
Lovering, William Croad 1837-1910 *WhAm 1*
Lovet-Lorski, Boris 1894-1973 *WhAm 5*
Lovett, Archibald Battle 1884-1945 *WhAm 2*
Lovett, Edgar Odell 1871-1957 *NatCAB 50,
WhAm 3*
Lovett, Fremont Leslie 1889-1953 *NatCAB 47*
Lovett, George H 1824-1894 *NewYHSD*
Lovett, John d1818 *BiAUS*
Lovett, John 1760?-1818 *TwCBDA*
Lovett, John 1761-1818 *BiDrAC, WhAm H*
Lovett, John D *NewYHSD*
Lovett, Robert 1796?- *NewYHSD*
Lovett, Robert, Jr. 1817?- *NewYHSD*
Lovett, Robert Abercrombie 1895- *BiDrUSE*
Lovett, Robert Harry 1860-1926 *NatCAB 21,
WhAm 1*
Lovett, Robert K 1841?- *NewYHSD*
Lovett, Robert Morss 1870-1956 *NatCAB 44,
WhAm 3*
Lovett, Robert Scott 1860-1932 *ApCAB X,
DcAmB S1, NatCAB 28, WhAm 1*
Lovett, Robert Williamson 1859-1924 *DcAmB,
NatCAB 20, NatCAB 28, WhAm 1*
Lovett, Thomas 1820?-1856 *NewYHSD*
Lovett, Thomas Lamar 1904-1966 *NatCAB 54*
Lovett, William 1773-1801 *NewYHSD*
Lovett, William Cuyler 1852-1940 *WhAm 1*
Lovette, Joyce Metz 1924-1968 *WhAm 5*
Lovette, Leland Pearson 1897-1967 *WhAm 4,
WhAm 5*
Lovette, Oscar Byrd 1871-1934 *BiDrAC,
WhAm 1*
Lovewell, John 1634?-1754? *ApCAB*
Lovewell, John 1691-1725 *ApCAB, DcAmB,
Drake, NatCAB 10, WebAMB,
WhAm H*
Lovewell, Jonathan 1713-1792 *ApCAB*
Lovewell, Joseph Taplin 1833-1918 *WhAm 1*
Lovewell, Nehemiah 1726-1800? *NatCAB 16*
Lovewell, Samuel Harrison 1865- *WhAm 4*

Lovewell, Zaccheus 1701-1772 *ApCAB*
Lovie, Henri *NewYHSD*
Loving, James Carroll 1836- *NatCAB 11*
Loving, Joseph *NewYHSD*
Loving, Lucas Powell 1871-1947 *NatCAB 35*
Loving, Oliver 1812-1867 *REnAW*
Loving, Starling 1827-1911 *WhAm 1*
Loving, Taylor Abbitt 1899-1947 *NatCAB 37*
Lovins, William Thomas 1887-1957 *WhAm 4*
Lovis, C *NewYHSD*
Lovits, Johann Tobias 1757-1804 *DcScB*
Lovitt, John Valentine 1898-1966 *NatCAB 53*
Lovitt, William Vernon 1881- *WhAm 6*
Lovre, Harold Orrin 1904-1972 *BiDrAC,*
   WhAm 5
Lovvorn, James Lewis 1862-1926 *NatCAB 20*
Low *NewYHSD*
Low, A Augustus 1889-1963 *WhAm 4*
Low, Sir A Maurice 1860-1929 *WhAm 1*
Low, Abiel Abbot 1811-1893 *ApCAB, DcAmB,*
   TwCBDA, WhAm H
Low, Abiel Abbott 1811-1893 *NatCAB 1*
Low, Abraham Adolph 1891-1954 *NatCAB 45,*
   WhAm 3
Low, Albert Howard 1855-1936 *WhAm 1,*
   WhAm 1C
Low, Andrew *NewYHSD*
Low, Benjamin Robbins Curtis 1880-1941
   NatCAB 42, WhAm 1
Low, Berthe Julienne 1853-1909 *WhAm 1*
Low, Sir David 1891-1963 *WhAm 4*
Low, Edward d1724 *ApCAB*
Low, Emile 1854-1927 *NatCAB 25*
Low, Ethelbert Ide 1880-1946 *WhAm 2*
Low, Fletcher 1893-1973 *NatCAB 57*
Low, Francis Stuart 1894-1964 *NatCAB 51,*
   WhAm 4
Low, Frederick F d1894 *BiAUS*
Low, Frederick Ferdinand 1820-1894
   NatCAB 4
Low, Frederick Ferdinand 1828-1894 *ApCAB,*
   BiDrAC, DcAmB, Drake Sup, TwCBDA,
   WhAm H
Low, Frederick Rollins 1860-1936 *WhAm 1*
Low, Harold Townsend 1885-1962 *NatCAB 48*
Low, Isaac d1791 *BiAUS, Drake*
Low, Isaac 1731-1791 *TwCBDA*
Low, Isaac 1735-1791 *ApCAB, BiDrAC,*
   DcAmB, NatCAB 1, WhAm H, WhAmP
Low, J Herbert 1868- *ApCAB X*
Low, James E 1837- *NatCAB 2*
Low, John Gardner 1835-1907 *DcAmB,*
   NatCAB 14
Low, Juliette Gordon 1860-1927 *DcAmB,*
   NatCAB 24, NotAW, WebAB,
   WhAm HA, WhAm 4
Low, Marcus A 1842-1921 *WhAm 1*
Low, Marie Dickson d1953 *WhAm 3*
Low, Mary Fairchild 1858- *WhAm 2,*
   WomWWA 14
Low, May Austin 1863- *WomWWA 14*
Low, Nicholas 1739-1826 *ApCAB, DcAmB,*
   WhAm H
Low, Philip Burrill 1836-1912 *BiDrAC,*
   TwCBDA
Low, Samuel 1765- *ApCAB, Drake,*
   NatCAB 8
Low, Sanford Ballard Dole 1905-1964
   NatCAB 53
Low, Seth 1850-1916 *AmBi, ApCAB,*
   ApCAB X, DcAmB, EncAB, McGEWB,
   NatCAB 6, TwCBDA, WebAB, WhAm 1,
   WhAmP
Low, Will Hicok 1853-1932 *AmBi, ApCAB,*
   ApCAB X, DcAmB S1, NatCAB 6,
   TwCBDA, WhAm 1
Low, William Edgar, Jr. 1888-1954 *NatCAB 41*
Low, William Gilman 1844-1936 *ApCAB X,*
   NatCAB 26, WhAm 1
Low, William Gilman 1875-1945 *NatCAB 35*
Low-Beer, Bertram Vojtech Adelbert 1900-1955
   NatCAB 45
Lowater, Frances *WomWWA 14*
Lowber, J B S *NewYHSD*
Lowber, James William 1847-1930 *NatCAB 6,*
   WhAm 4
Lowden, Frank Oren 1861-1943 *EncAAH*
Lowden, Frank Orren 1861-1943 *BiDrAC,*

Lowell, Amy 1874-1925 *AmBi, ApCAB X,*
   DcAmB S3, NatCAB 10, NatCAB 31,
   WebAB, WhAm 2
Lowden, Isabel d1957 *WhAm 3*
Lowden, Thomas Scott 1863-1937 *NatCAB 28*
Lowdermilk, Patricia Cannales d1928 *WhAm 1*
Lowdermilk, Walter Clay 1888-1974 *WhAm 6*
Lowdermilk, William Harrison 1839-1897
   ApCAB Sup
Lowe, Arthur Houghton 1853-1932 *NatCAB 24,*
   WhAm 1
Lowe, Betsey Barker 1881- *WomWWA 14*
Lowe, Charles 1828-1874 *DcAmB, WhAm H*
Lowe, Charles Frederic 1867-1928 *NatCAB 22*
Lowe, Clarence George 1897-1965 *WhAm 4*
Lowe, Clement Belton 1846- *WhAm 4*
Lowe, Clifton Dunkel 1883-1955 *NatCAB 44*
Lowe, Clowney Oswald 1906-1972 *WhAm 6*
Lowe, David P 1823-1882 *BiAUS*
Lowe, David Pearly 1823-1882 *ApCAB*
Lowe, David Perley 1823-1882 *BiDrAC,*
   WhAm H
Lowe, Donald Vaughn 1891-1969 *NatCAB 55,*
   WhAm 5
Lowe, Edward *NewYHSD*
Lowe, Elias Avery 1879-1969 *WhAm 5*
Lowe, Emily Lynch d1966 *WhAm 4*
Lowe, Enoch Louis 1820-1892 *BiAUS,*
   NatCAB 9, TwCBDA
Lowe, Ephraim Noble 1864-1933 *WhAm 1*
Lowe, F *NewYHSD*
Lowe, Frank E 1885-1968 *WhAm 5*
Lowe, George Hale 1855- *WhAm 4*
Lowe, Herman A 1905-1961 *WhAm 4*
Lowe, Houston 1849-1920 *NatCAB 18*
Lowe, J *NewYHSD*
Lowe, Jacob Israel *WhoColR*
Lowe, Joe 1883-1969 *WhAm 5*
Lowe, John *NewYHSD*
Lowe, John 1750-1798 *ApCAB*
Lowe, John 1838-1930 *WhAm 1*
Lowe, John Smith 1878-1954 *WhAm 3*
Lowe, John William 1868-1948 *WhAm 2*
Lowe, John Williamson 1809-1861 *ApCAB,*
   Drake
Lowe, John Zollicoffer 1887-1950 *NatCAB 40*
Lowe, Joseph 1846?-1899 *REnAW*
Lowe, Louis Robert 1906-1968 *WhAm 5*
Lowe, Louise 1905-1969 *WhAm 5*
Lowe, Malcolm Branson 1892-1971 *WhAm 5*
Lowe, Martha Ann Perry 1829-1902 *AmWom,*
   ApCAB, NatCAB 10, TwCBDA,
   WhAm 1
Lowe, Perley 1845-1924 *NatCAB 51*
Lowe, Peter 1550?-1610 *BiHiMed*
Lowe, Peter Perlee 1801-1886 *TwCBDA*
Lowe, Ralph Phillips 1805-1883 *BiAUS,*
   DcAmB, NatCAB 11, TwCBDA,
   WhAm H
Lowe, Richard Barrett 1902-1972 *WhAm 5*
Lowe, Robert *NewYHSD*
Lowe, Robert Joseph 1903-1951 *NatCAB 40*
Lowe, Samuel W *NewYHSD*
Lowe, Stanley 1903-1969 *WhAm 5*
Lowe, Thaddeus Sobieski Coulincourt 1832-1913
   ApCAB, DcAmB, TwCBDA, WebAB,
   WebAMB, WhAm 1
Lowe, Thomas Francis 1880-1941 *NatCAB 36*
Lowe, Thomas Merritt 1901-1962 *NatCAB 51,*
   WhAm 4
Lowe, Titus 1877-1959 *NatCAB 43, WhAm 3*
Lowe, Walter Irenaeus 1867-1929 *WhAm 1*
Lowe, William Baird 1871-1946 *WhAm 2*
Lowe, William Bell 1839- *NatCAB 7*
Lowe, William Herbert 1862-1933 *NatCAB 26*
Lowe, William Herman 1881- *WhAm 6*
Lowe, William Manning 1842-1881 *TwCBDA*
Lowe, William Manning 1842-1882 *BiDrAC*
Lowe, William Warren 1831-1898 *ApCAB,*
   TwCBDA
Lowe, William Webb 1887-1961 *NatCAB 48,*
   WhAm 4
Lowell, Abbott Lawrence 1856-1943 *ApCAB X,*
   BiDAmEd, DcAmB S3, EncAB,
   McGEWB, NatCAB 14, NatCAB 31,
   WebAB, WhAm 2
Lowell, Albert Fay 1875-1939 *NatCAB 29*
Lowell, Alfred Putnam 1890-1954 *NatCAB 46*
Lowell, Amy 1874-1925 *AmBi, ApCAB X,*

Lowell, Charles Russell 1835-1864 *ApCAB,*
   DcAmB, EncAB, McGEWB, NatCAB 19,
   NotAW, WebAB, WhAm 1,
   WomWWA 14
Lowell, Anna C d1874 *Drake*
Lowell, Anna Cabot 1811-1874 *TwCBDA*
Lowell, Anna Cabot 1819-1874 *ApCAB*
Lowell, Charles 1782-1861 *ApCAB, Drake,*
   TwCBDA
Lowell, Charles 1782-1864 *NatCAB 11*
Lowell, Charles Russell 1835-1864 *ApCAB,*
   Drake, TwCBDA
Lowell, Daniel Ozro Smith 1851-1928 *WhAm 1*
Lowell, Delmar Rial 1844-1912 *WhAm 1*
Lowell, Edith Allen 1872- *WomWWA 14*
Lowell, Edward Jackson 1845-1894 *AmBi,*
   ApCAB, DcAmB, NatCAB 26, TwCBDA,
   WhAm H
Lowell, Ettie Lois 1869- *NatCAB 14*
Lowell, Francis Cabot 1775-1817 *AmBi,*
   ApCAB, DcAmB, Drake, EncAB,
   McGEWB, NatCAB 7, TwCBDA,
   WebAB, WhAm H
Lowell, Francis Cabot 1855-1911 *NatCAB 21,*
   TwCBDA, WhAm 1
Lowell, Guy 1870-1927 *DcAmB, NatCAB 15,*
   NatCAB 21, WhAm 1
Lowell, James Arnold 1869-1933 *WhAm 1*
Lowell, James Burnett 1873-1947 *NatCAB 35*
Lowell, James Harrison 1860-1944 *WhAm 2*
Lowell, James Jackson d1862 *ApCAB, Drake*
Lowell, James Russell 1819-1891 *AmBi,*
   ApCAB, DcAmB, Drake, EncAB,
   McGEWB, NatCAB 1, NatCAB 2,
   TwCBDA, WebAB, WhAm H
Lowell, Joan 1902-1967 *WhAm 4*
Lowell, John 1743-1802 *AmBi, ApCAB,*
   BiDrAC, DcAmB, Drake, TwCBDA,
   WhAm H
Lowell, John 1744-1802 *BiAUS, NatCAB 7*
Lowell, John 1769-1840 *AmBi, ApCAB,*
   DcAmB, Drake, TwCBDA, WhAm H
Lowell, John 1799-1836 *AmBi, ApCAB,*
   DcAmB, Drake, NatCAB 7, TwCBDA,
   WhAm H
Lowell, John 1824-1897 *AmBi, ApCAB,*
   BiAUS, DcAmB, NatCAB 11, TwCBDA,
   WhAm H
Lowell, John 1856- *WhAm 1*
Lowell, John Adams *NewYHSD*
Lowell, John Amory 1798-1881 *TwCBDA*
Lowell, Josephine Shaw 1843-1905 *AmBi,*
   ApCAB, DcAmB, McGEWB, NatCAB 8,
   NotAW, TwCBDA, WhAm 1
Lowell, Joshua Adams 1801-1873 *TwCBDA*
Lowell, Joshua Adams 1801-1874 *BiAUS,*
   BiDrAC, WhAm H
Lowell, Maria White 1821-1853 *ApCAB,*
   Drake, NatCAB 8, NotAW
Lowell, Mary Chandler *WomWWA 14*
Lowell, Mary Ella Purington 1858-
   WomWWA 14
Lowell, Orson Byron 1871-1956 *IIBEAAW,*
   WhAm 3
Lowell, Percival 1855-1916 *AmBi,*
   ApCAB Sup, ApCAB X, AsBiEn,
   DcAmB, DcScB, NatCAB 8, TwCBDA,
   WebAB, WhAm 1
Lowell, Robert Trail Spence, Jr. 1917-
   McGEWB
Lowell, Robert Traill Spence 1816-1891 *ApCAB,*
   DcAmB, Drake, NatCAB 8, TwCBDA,
   WhAm H
Lowell, Robert Traill Spence, Jr. 1917- *EncAB,*
   WebAB
Lowell, Sherman James 1858-1940 *WhAm 1*
Lowen, Charles Jules, Jr. 1915-1956 *WhAm 3*
Lowenberg, Bettie 1845- *WhAm 4*
Lowenberg, Victor *NewYHSD*
Lowengrund, Ernest 1858-1949 *NatCAB 36*
Lowenstein, Alice Moritz 1869- *WomWWA 14*
Lowenstein, Allard Kenneth 1929- *BiDrAC*
Lowenstein, Bernard Benjamin 1881-1953
   NatCAB 43
Lowenstein, Gabriel Abraham 1889-1965
   NatCAB 52
Lowenstein, Harriet B *WomWWA 14*
Lowenstein, Henry Polk 1859-1946 *WhAm 4*
Lowenstein, Lloyd L 1902-1967 *WhAm 4*

Lowenstein, Melvyn Gordon 1892-1971
WhAm 5
Lowenstein, Otto 1889-1965 *NatCAB 56*
Lowenstein, Solomon 1877-1942 *WhAm 1*
Lowenstine, Mandel 1882-1957 *WhAm 3*
Lowenthal, John Jacob 1810- *ApCAB*
Lower, Christian 1740-1806 *BiAUS, BiDrAC,
WhAm H*
Lower, Richard 1631-1691 *AsBiEn, BiHiMed,
DcScB*
Lower, William Edgar 1867-1948 *DcAmB S4,
WhAm 2*
Loweree, F Harold 1898-1962 *WhAm 4*
Lowery, Ellin Prince *NotAW*
Lowery, John Francis 1841-1904 *NatCAB 2*
Lowery, Woodbury 1853-1906 *DcAmB,
NatCAB 18*
Lowes, John Livingston 1867-1945 *DcAmB S3,
WhAm 2*
Loweth, Charles Frederick 1857-1935
NatCAB 29, WhAm 1
Lowie, Robert Harry 1883-1957 *McGEWB,
NatCAB 46, REnAW, WebAB, WhAm 3*
Lowinson, Louis 1874-1952 *NatCAB 39*
Lowitz, J T *DcScB*
Lowman, Arthur Ames 1878- *WhAm 6*
Lowman, Charles LeRoy 1879- *WhAm 6*
Lowman, Guy Sumner 1877-1943 *NatCAB 33*
Lowman, Guy Sumner 1909-1941 *NatCAB 33*
Lowman, Harmon 1894- *WhAm 5*
Lowman, John Bodine 1873-1953 *NatCAB 44*
Lowman, Mary D 1842- *AmWom*
Lowman, Seymour 1868-1940 *WhAm 1*
Lowman, Webster B 1841-1904 *WhAm 1*
Lowndes, Arthur 1858-1917 *TwCBDA,
WhAm 1*
Lowndes, Charles 1798-1885 *ApCAB,
TwCBDA*
Lowndes, Charles Henry Tilghman 1866-
WhAm 5
Lowndes, Charles Lucien Baker 1903-1967
WhAm 4
Lowndes, Lloyd 1845-1905 *BiAUS, BiDrAC,
DcAmB, NatCAB 9, NatCAB 41,
TwCBDA, WhAm 1*
Lowndes, Mary Elizabeth 1864-1947 *WhAm 2*
Lowndes, Rawlins 1721-1800 *AmBi, DcAmB,
NatCAB 12, TwCBDA, WhAm H*
Lowndes, Rawlins 1722-1800 *ApCAB, Drake*
Lowndes, Stanley Howard 1857-1914
NatCAB 16
Lowndes, Tasker Gantt 1883-1952 *NatCAB 41*
Lowndes, Thomas 1765-1843 *ApCAB, BiAUS,
Drake*
Lowndes, Thomas 1766-1843 *BiDrAC,
TwCBDA, WhAm H, WhAmP*
Lowndes, William Jones 1782-1822 *AmBi,
ApCAB, BiAUS, BiDrAC, DcAmB,
Drake, NatCAB 13, TwCBDA, WhAm H,
WhAmP*
Lownes, Caleb *NewYHSD*
Lownes, E John 1900-1965 *NatCAB 51*
Lowney, Walter McPherson 1855-1921
ApCAB X, WhAm 1
Lownsbery, Charles Hatch 1910-1969 *WhAm 5*
Lowrance, John Witherspoon 1886-1934
NatCAB 26
Lowrance, William B 1859-1946 *NatCAB 36*
Lowrey, B G 1862-1947 *TwCBDA*
Lowrey, Bill Green 1862-1947 *BiDrAC,
WhAm 2*
Lowrey, Frederick Jewett 1858-1948
NatCAB 48, WhAm 4
Lowrey, George 1770?-1852 *ApCAB, Drake*
Lowrey, Harvey H 1878-1961 *WhAm 4*
Lowrey, Lawson Gentry 1890-1957 *ApCAB X,
WhAm 3*
Lowrey, Mark Perrin 1828-1885 *BiDConf,
DcAmB, TwCBDA, WhAm H*
Lowrey, William Tyndale 1858-1944
NatCAB 34, TwCBDA
Lowria, Rebecca Lawrence 1891-1975 *WhAm 6*
Lowrie, Albert Bruckner 1870-1957 *NatCAB 46*
Lowrie, Charles Nassau 1869-1939 *NatCAB 33*
Lowrie, Frederic Low 1878-1948 *NatCAB 38*
Lowrie, James Walter 1856-1930 *DcAmB,
WhAm 4*
Lowrie, John Cameron 1808-1900 *ApCAB,*

NatCAB 12, TwCBDA, WhAm 1
Lowrie, John Marshall 1817-1867 *ApCAB,
TwCBDA*
Lowrie, Jonathan Roberts 1823-1885 *ApCAB,
TwCBDA*
Lowrie, Randolph Washington 1839- *TwCBDA*
Lowrie, Reuben Post 1827-1860 *ApCAB,
TwCBDA*
Lowrie, Samuel Thompson 1835-1924 *ApCAB,
TwCBDA, WhAm 1*
Lowrie, Walter 1784-1868 *ApCAB, BiDrAC,
DcAmB, Drake, NatCAB 11, TwCBDA,
WhAm H, WhAmP*
Lowrie, Walter 1785-1863 *BiAUS*
Lowrie, Walter 1868- *WhAm 5*
Lowrie, Walter Hoge 1807-1876 *ApCAB,
BiAUS, NatCAB 13, TwCBDA*
Lowrie, Walter Macon 1819-1847 *ApCAB,
Drake, TwCBDA*
Lowrie, Will Leonard 1869-1944 *NatCAB 33,
WhAm 2*
Lowry, Charles Frederick 1903-1964
NatCAB 51
Lowry, D R d1955 *WhAm 3*
Lowry, Edith Belle 1878-1945 *WhAm 2,
WomWWA 14*
Lowry, Edith C d1970 *WhAm 5*
Lowry, Edward George 1875-1943 *NatCAB 32*
Lowry, Edward George 1876-1943 *WhAm 2*
Lowry, Erwin Foster 1891-1957 *NatCAB 46*
Lowry, Fesington Carlyle 1885-1962 *WhAm 4*
Lowry, Forrest Ellsworth 1903-1971
NatCAB 57
Lowry, Frank Clifford 1878-1968 *WhAm 5*
Lowry, Frank J 1888-1955 *WhAm 3*
Lowry, Frank Wagner 1895-1962 *NatCAB 50*
Lowry, H H 1898-1971 *WhAm 5*
Lowry, Hiram Harrison 1843-1924 *DcAmB,
WhAm 4*
Lowry, Horace 1880-1931 *WhAm 1*
Lowry, Howard Foster 1901-1967 *WhAm 4*
Lowry, Howard James 1894-1967 *WhAm 5*
Lowry, James Barnett 1868-1951 *NatCAB 41*
Lowry, John 1882-1962 *WhAm 4*
Lowry, Joseph E 1899- *WhAm 4*
Lowry, Joseph Edmond 1868- *TwCBDA*
Lowry, Malcolm 1909-1957 *WhAm 4*
Lowry, Reigart B 1826-1880 *NatCAB 11*
Lowry, Robert 1822- *TwCBDA*
Lowry, Robert 1824-1904 *BiDrAC*
Lowry, Robert 1826-1899 *ApCAB, TwCBDA,
WhAm 1*
Lowry, Robert 1829- *TwCBDA*
Lowry, Robert 1830-1910 *DcAmB, WhAm 1*
Lowry, Robert 1831- *NatCAB 13*
Lowry, Robert James 1840- *NatCAB 12*
Lowry, Thomas 1843-1909 *DcAmB,
NatCAB 2, WhAm 1*
Lowry, Thomas 1910-1968 *NatCAB 55*
Lowry, Thomas Claude d1945 *WhAm 2*
Lowsley, Oswald Swinney 1884-1955
NatCAB 46, WhAm 3
Lowstuter, William Jackson d1957 *WhAm 3*
Lowstuter, William Jackson 1871-1958
WhAm 3
Lowth, Frank James 1872- *WhAm 5*
Lowther, George d1722 *ApCAB*
Lowther, Granville 1848-1933 *NatCAB 28,
WhAm 1*
Lowther, Hugh Sears 1877-1959 *WhAm 3*
Lowthorp, Fannie Willets 1860- *WomWWA 14*
Lowy, Alexander 1889-1941 *NatCAB 37,
WhAm 1*
Loy, Matthias 1828-1915 *ApCAB, DcAmB,
NatCAB 12, TwCBDA, WhAm 1*
Loy, Sylvester K 1879- *WhAm 3*
Loyall, George 1789-1868 *BiAUS, BiDrAC,
WhAm H*
Loyall, George Robert 1863-1941 *NatCAB 36*
Loyall, George Robert 1867-1941 *WhAm 1*
Loyall, L George 1789-1868 *TwCBDA*
Loyaute, Anne Philippe Dieudonne De
1750-1830? *ApCAB, Drake*
Loyd, Samuel 1841-1911 *DcAmB*
Loyhed, Frances Ames 1861- *WomWWA 14*
Loyola, Martin Garcia Onez De 1553-1598
ApCAB

Loyzance, Joseph Marie Rene 1820-1897
NatCAB 4, TwCBDA
Loza, Jose Manuel 1799-1862 *ApCAB*
Lozano, Francisco Ruiz 1607-1677 *ApCAB*
Lozano, Pedro *ApCAB*
Lozier, Charlotte Irene 1844-1870 *ApCAB*
Lozier, Clemence Sophia Harned 1812-1888
ApCAB, TwCBDA
Lozier, Clemence Sophia Harned 1813-1888
*AmBi, BiDAmEd, DcAmB, NatCAB 25,
NotAW, WhAm H*
Lozier, Jeanne DeLaMontagnie 1850?-
WomWWA 14
Lozier, Jennie DeLaMontagnie 1850?- *AmWom,
NatCAB 13*
Lozier, Ralph Fulton 1866-1945 *BiDrAC,
NatCAB 42, WhAm 2, WhAmP*
Lozner, Joseph 1905-1973 *WhAm 6*
Lozowick, Louis 1892-1973 *WhAm 6*
Lu, Chi 261-303 *McGEWB*
Lu, Chiu-Yuan 1139-1193 *McGEWB*
Lu, Hsun 1881-1936 *McGEWB*
Luaces, Joaquin Lorenzo 1826-1867 *ApCAB*
Luard, Richard George Amherst 1829- *ApCAB*
Lubbeck, F R 1815-1905 *BiAUS*
Lubbers, T C *NewYHSD*
Lubbock, Francis Richard 1815-1905 *ApCAB,
BiDConf, DcAmB, NatCAB 9, TwCBDA,
WhAm 1*
Lubbock, Sir John 1834-1913 *DcScB*
Lubbock, John William 1803-1865 *DcScB*
Lubbock, Richard 1759?-1808 *DcScB*
Lubeck, Henry 1856-1933 *WhAm 1*
Luben, Raymond Raphael 1888-1965
NatCAB 51
Luberoff, George 1879- *WhAm 6*
Lubin, David 1849-1919 *AmBi, DcAmB,
EncAAH, NatCAB 19, WhAm 1*
Lubin, Simon Julius 1876-1936 *NatCAB 27,
WhAm 1*
Lubitsch, Ernst 1892-1947 *DcAmB S4,
McGEWB, WhAm 2*
Lubke, Carl Heinrich 1894-1972 *WhAm 5*
Lubke, George William 1845- *NatCAB 5*
Lubomirski, Prince Casimir 1869-1930 *WhAm 1*
Lubschez, Ben Judah 1881- *WhAm 6*
Luby, James 1856-1925 *NatCAB 6, WhAm 1*
Luby, Sylvester Daniel 1902-1965 *WhAm 4*
Lucan, George Charles Bingham, Earl Of
1800-1885 *WhoMilH*
Lucaris, Cyril 1572-1637 *McGEWB*
Lucas VanLeyden 1494-1533 *McGEWB*
Lucas, Albert Hawley 1894-1973 *WhAm 6*
Lucas, Albert Pike d1945 *WhAm 2*
Lucas, Anthony Francis 1855-1921 *DcAmB,
NatCAB 29, WhAm 1*
Lucas, Arthur 1859- *WhAm 4*
Lucas, Arthur Fletcher 1896-1953 *NatCAB 42,
WhAm 3*
Lucas, Arthur Melville 1881-1943 *NatCAB 33,
WhAm 2*
Lucas, Bertha June Richardson *WomWWA 14*
Lucas, Charles 1792-1817 *NatCAB 13*
Lucas, Clarence Edward 1886- *WhoColR*
Lucas, Daniel Bedinger 1836-1909 *ApCAB,
DcAmB, NatCAB 6, TwCBDA,
WhAm 1*
Lucas, Douglas P 1881- *WhAm 6*
Lucas, Edward 1780-1858 *BiAUS, BiDrAC,
WhAm H*
Lucas, Eliza 1722-1793 *DcAmB, NotAW*
Lucas, Francis Ferdinand 1884-1961 *WhAm 4*
Lucas, Francois-Edouard-Anatole 1842-1891
DcScB
Lucas, Frederic Augustus 1852-1929 *DcAmB,
NatCAB 13, WhAm 1*
Lucas, Frederick William 1894-1966
NatCAB 52
Lucas, George Washington 1800-1880? *ApCAB*
Lucas, Harry Percy 1876-1955 *NatCAB 49*
Lucas, J *NewYHSD*
Lucas, J Lynn 1898-1974 *WhAm 6*
Lucas, James Clarence Merryman 1873-1943
NatCAB 32, WhAm 6
Lucas, James H 1800-1873 *DcAmB, WhAm H*
Lucas, Jean *NewYHSD*
Lucas, Jim Griffing 1914-1970 *WhAm 5*

Lucas, John Baptiste Charles 1758-1842
   BiDrAC, DcAmB, WhAm H
Lucas, John Baptiste Charles 1762-1842 ApCAB,
   BiAUS, Drake, NatCAB 11, TwCBDA
Lucas, John Henry 1861-1919 WhAm 1
Lucas, John Porter 1890-1949 NatCAB 39,
   WebAMB, WhAm 2
Lucas, Johnathan 1754-1821 WhAm H
Lucas, Jonathan 1754-1821 DcAmB, EncAAH
Lucas, Jonathan 1775-1832 DcAmB,
   WhAm H
Lucas, Keith 1879-1916 DcScB
Lucas, Leo Sherman 1894-1961 WhAm 4
Lucas, Mattie Davis 1869- WomWWA 14
Lucas, Noah 1887-1956 WhAm 3
Lucas, Oliver G d1950 WhAm 3
Lucas, Robert 1781-1853 ApCAB, BiAUS,
   DcAmB, Drake, NatCAB 3, NatCAB 11,
   TwCBDA, WhAm H
Lucas, Robert Hendry 1888-1947 NatCAB 34,
   WhAm 2
Lucas, Scott Wike 1892-1968 BiDrAC,
   WhAm 4A
Lucas, Simons Ravenel 1885-1946 NatCAB 34
Lucas, Thomas John 1826- ApCAB, TwCBDA,
   WhAm 1
Lucas, W W WhoColR A
Lucas, Ward 1892-1961 NatCAB 50
Lucas, William 1800-1877 BiAUS, BiDrAC,
   WhAm H
Lucas, William B NewYHSD
Lucas, William Cardwell 1877-1954 WhAm 3
Lucas, William Palmer 1880-1960 WhAm 4
Lucas, William Vincent 1835-1921 BiDrAC
Lucas, William Walter 1870- WhoColR
Lucas, Wingate Hezekiah 1908- BiDrAC
Luccearini, Andrew NewYHSD
Luccearini, John NewYHSD
Lucchesi, Pascal Francis 1903-1973 WhAm 6
Luccock, Emory Wylie 1894-1960 WhAm 4
Luccock, George Naphtali 1857-1943 WhAm 1,
   WhAm 1C, WhAm 2
Luccock, Halford Edward 1885-1960
   NatCAB 47, WhAm 4
Luccock, Naphtali 1853-1916 WhAm 1
Luce, Alice Hanson 1861- TwCBDA,
   WhAm 4
Luce, Barnard Coffin 1879-1956 NatCAB 42
Luce, Clare Boothe 1903- BiDrAC, WebAB
Luce, Cyrus Gray 1824-1905 NatCAB 5,
   TwCBDA, WhAm 1
Luce, Dean Sherwood 1876-1953 NatCAB 42
Luce, Edgar Augustine 1881-1958 NatCAB 49,
   WhAm 3
Luce, Francis Cathcart 1897-1943 NatCAB 37
Luce, Harry James 1861-1929 NatCAB 14,
   WhAm 1
Luce, Harvey Gardner 1900-1955 WhAm 3
Luce, Henry Robinson 1898-1967 EncAB,
   McGEWB, WebAB, WhAm 4
Luce, Henry Winters 1868-1941 DcAmB S3,
   NatCAB 34
Luce, Moses Augustine 1842-1933 NatCAB 45
Luce, Robert 1862-1946 BiDrAC, NatCAB 46,
   WhAm 2, WhAmP
Luce, Roscoe Rudolph 1889-1962 NatCAB 49
Luce, Stephen Bleecker 1827-1917 AmBi,
   ApCAB, DcAmB, NatCAB 4, TwCBDA,
   WebAMB, WhAm 1
Luceck, G NewYHSD
Lucey, Dennis Benedict 1860-1929 WhAm 1
Lucey, Patrick Joseph 1873-1947 WhAm 2
Lucey, Patrick Joseph 1891-1960 WhAm 4
Lucey, Thomas Elmore 1874-1947 WhAm 3
Luchsinger, Benjamin Franklin 1879-1940
   NatCAB 30
Luchsinger, John 1839-1922 NatCAB 6
Lucian 120?-200? McGEWB
Luciani, Luigi 1840-1919 DcScB
Lucier, Phillip Joseph 1921-1970 WhAm 5
Lucio, Rafael 1819-1886 ApCAB
Lucke, Balduin 1889-1954 NatCAB 44,
   WhAm 3
Lucke, Charles Edward 1876-1951 NatCAB 15,
   WhAm 3
Lucke, Henry John 1876-1948 NatCAB 34

Lucke, Marion Hague Rea 1885-1946
   NatCAB 36
Luckenbach, Abraham 1777-1854 ApCAB
Luckenbach, Edgar Frederick 1868-1943
   NatCAB 35, WhAm 2
Luckenbach, Edgar Frederick, Jr. 1925-1974
   WhAm 6
Luckenbach, John Lewis 1883-1951 DcAmB S5,
   WhAm 3
Luckenbach, Reuben O 1818-1880 NewYHSD
Luckenbill, Daniel David 1881-1927
   NatCAB 21, WhAm 1
Luckey, David Franklin 1869-1956 NatCAB 47,
   WhAm 5
Luckey, George Washington Andrew 1855-1933
   BiDAmEd, WhAm 1
Luckey, Henry Carl 1868-1956 BiDrAC,
   WhAm 3
Luckey, James S 1867-1937 WhAm 1
Luckey, Robert Burneston 1905-1974 WhAm 6
Luckey, Samuel 1791-1869 ApCAB, TwCBDA
Luckhardt, Arno Benedict 1885-1957
   NatCAB 42, WhAm 3
Luckie, Kenneth Earle 1903-1958 NatCAB 48
Luckiesh, Matthew 1889-1967 WhAm 4
Lucking, Alfred 1856-1929 BiDrAC,
   NatCAB 26, WhAm 1
Lucking, William Alfred 1882-1960 WhAm 4
Luckner, Nicolas 1722-1794 WhoMilH
Luckstone, Isidore 1861-1941 NatCAB 30
Lucretius 094?BC-055?BC McGEWB
Lucretius 095?BC-055?BC AsBiEn, DcScB
Ludden, Patrick Anthony 1836-1912
   NatCAB 13, TwCBDA, WhAm 1
Ludden, Patrick Anthony 1838-1912 ApCAB
Luddy, Michael G 1893-1967 WhAm 5
Ludekens, Fred 1900- IlBEAAW
Ludeling, John Theodore 1824-1890 NatCAB 13
Ludeling, John Theodore 1827-1891 DcAmB,
   WhAm H
Luden, William H 1859- ApCAB X
Ludendorff, Erich Friedrich Wilhelm 1865-1937
   McGEWB, WhoMilH
Ludendorff, F W Hans 1873-1941 DcScB
Luders, Gustav Carl 1865-1912 WhAm 1
Ludewig, Herman Ernst 1809-1856 Drake
Ludewig, Hermann Ernst 1809-1856 ApCAB
Ludewig, Joseph W 1904-1958 WhAm 3
Ludin, Mohammed Kahir d1966 WhAm 4
Ludington, Arthur Crosby 1880-1914 WhAm 1
Ludington, C Townsend 1896-1968 NatCAB 55
Ludington, Charles Henry 1866-1927
   NatCAB 41, WhAm 1
Ludington, Elliot Kingman 1876-1958
   NatCAB 50
Ludington, Flora Belle 1898-1967 DcAmLiB
Ludington, Francis Henry 1836-1910
   NatCAB 16
Ludington, G Franklin 1895-1949 NatCAB 39
Ludington, Harrison 1812-1891 NatCAB 12,
   TwCBDA
Ludington, Marshall Independence 1839-1919
   ApCAB Sup, NatCAB 18, WhAm 1
Ludington, Mildred Wilson 1879-
   WomWWA 14
Ludington, Sybil 1761-1839 WebAMB
Ludins, Ryah 1896-1957 NatCAB 50
Ludlam, Charles Stewart 1866-1934
   NatCAB 25
Ludlam, Reuben 1831-1899 ApCAB Sup,
   NatCAB 12, WhAm 1
Ludlow, Arabut 1818-1896 NatCAB 19
Ludlow, Arthur Clyde 1861-1927 WhAm 1
Ludlow, Benjamin Chambers 1831-1898
   ApCAB Sup, TwCBDA
Ludlow, C A NewYHSD
Ludlow, Clara Southmayd 1852- BiCAW,
   WomWWA 14
Ludlow, Daniel 1750-1814 DcAmB, WhAm H
Ludlow, David Hunt 1857-1945 NatCAB 34
Ludlow, Edward Hunter 1810-1884 NewYHSD
Ludlow, Edwin 1858-1924 NatCAB 23,
   WhAm 1
Ludlow, F Milton 1896-1959 WhAm 3
Ludlow, FitzHugh 1836-1870 AmBi, ApCAB,
   DcAmB, NatCAB 13, TwCBDA,
   WhAm H
Ludlow, FitzHugh 1837-1870 Drake

Ludlow, Gabriel Augustus 1800-1838
   NewYHSD
Ludlow, Gabriel George 1736-1808 ApCAB,
   DcAmB, Drake, WhAm H
Ludlow, George Craig 1830-1900 NatCAB 5,
   TwCBDA
Ludlow, George Duncan 1734-1808 ApCAB,
   DcAmB, Drake, WhAm H
Ludlow, Gulian 1764-1826 NewYHSD
Ludlow, Henry 1848-1923 NatCAB 19
Ludlow, Henry Gilbert 1823-1904 WhAm 1
Ludlow, Henry Hunt 1854- WhAm 2
Ludlow, Henry Shattuck 1870-1938 NatCAB 28
Ludlow, Jacob Lott 1862-1930 WhAm 1
Ludlow, James Meeker 1841-1932 ApCAB Sup,
   NatCAB 8, TwCBDA, WhAm 1
Ludlow, James Minor 1917-1974 WhAm 6
Ludlow, James Reily 1825-1886 ApCAB
Ludlow, James Ryley 1825-1886 TwCBDA
Ludlow, John 1793-1857 ApCAB, Drake,
   NatCAB 1, TwCBDA
Ludlow, John Livingston 1819-1888 NatCAB 3
Ludlow, Louis Leon 1873-1950 BiDrAC,
   WhAm 3, WhAmP
Ludlow, Nicoll 1842-1915 ApCAB Sup,
   NatCAB 17, TwCBDA, WhAm 1
Ludlow, Noah Miller 1795-1886 ApCAB,
   DcAmB, NatCAB 28, WhAm H
Ludlow, Roger DcAmB, Drake
Ludlow, Roger 1590-1664 WhAm H
Ludlow, Roger 1590?-1665? ApCAB
Ludlow, Roger 1590-1668? NatCAB 12
Ludlow, Theodore Russell 1883-1961 WhAm 4
Ludlow, Thomas William 1795-1878 DcAmB,
   NatCAB 13, WhAm H
Ludlow, Thomas William 1881-1929
   NatCAB 21
Ludlow, William 1843-1901 ApCAB Sup,
   DcAmB, NatCAB 9, TwCBDA,
   WebAMB, WhAm 1
Ludlow, William Orr 1870-1954 WhAm 3
Ludlowe, Roger DcAmB
Ludlum, Clarence Allen 1865-1948 NatCAB 36,
   WhAm 4
Ludlum, Seymour DeWitt 1876-1956
   NatCAB 43, WhAm 3
Ludlum, Walter Denton, Jr. 1903-1970
   NatCAB 56
Ludovici, Alice E 1871- WomWWA 14
Ludovici, Alice Emelie 1872- WhAm 5
Ludwell, Philip 1660?-1704? DcAmB,
   NatCAB 12, WhAm H
Ludwick, Christopher 1720-1801 ApCAB,
   DcAmB, WebAB, WebAMB, WhAm H
Ludwig, August Henry 1882-1948 NatCAB 36
Ludwig, Carl 1816-1895 BiHiMed
Ludwig, Carl Friedrich Wilhelm 1816-1895
   DcScB
Ludwig, Charles H 1921-1970 WhAm 5
Ludwig, Charles L NewYHSD
Ludwig, Emil 1881-1948 WhAm 2
Ludwig, Henry NewYHSD
Ludwig, Karl Friedrich Wilhelm 1816-1895
   AsBiEn, McGEWB
Ludwig, Sylvester Theodore 1903-1964
   WhAm 4
Ludwig, Theodore Henry 1873-1946
   NatCAB 36
Ludwig, William NewYHSD
Ludy, Llewellyn V 1875-1952 WhAm 3
Ludy, Robert Borneman 1870-1936 NatCAB 28
Luebke, Frederick Carl 1927- EncAAH
Luebke, Melvin William 1924-1972 WhAm 6
Lueck, Martin Lawrence 1872-1926
   NatCAB 21, WhAm 1
Luecke, John Frederick 1889-1952 BiDrAC,
   WhAm 3
Luecke, Martin 1859-1926 WhAm 1
Luedde, William Henry d1952 WhAm 3
Luedecke, Henry Herman 1883-1971
   NatCAB 57
Luedeking, Robert 1853-1908 NatCAB 15,
   WhAm 1
Lueder, Arthur Charles 1876-1957 NatCAB 47,
   WhAm 3
Lueders, William Herman 1865-1939
   NatCAB 29
Luedke, August J 1884-1954 WhAm 3

Luelling, Henderson 1809-1878 *DcAmB,*
WhAm H
Lueroth, Jakob 1844-1910 *DcScB*
Luers, Fred Herman 1885-1957 *NatCAB 46*
Luers, John Henry 1819-1871 *ApCAB,*
NatCAB 13, TwCBDA, WhAm H
Luerssen, George Vandegrift 1890-1964
NatCAB 53
Luette, Eleanor d1970 *WhAm 5*
Lufbery, Raoul Gervais Victor 1885-1918
DcAmB, WebAMB
Luff, Ralph Gordon 1894-1961 *WhAm 4*
Luffman, John *NewYHSD*
Lufkin, Chauncey Forbush 1834-1918
NatCAB 26
Lufkin, Elgood Chauncey 1864-1935 *WhAm 1*
Lufkin, Garland 1896-1950 *WhAm 3*
Lufkin, Richard Henry 1851-1922 *NatCAB 20*
Lufkin, Wilfred W 1879-1934 *WhAm 1*
Lufkin, Willfred Weymouth 1879-1934 *BiDrAC*
Lufkin, Willfred Weymouth, Jr. 1903-1957
WhAm 3
Lugard, Baron John Dealtry Lugard 1858-1945
McGEWB
Lugenbush, Julius L *NewYHSD*
Lugeon, Maurice 1870-1953 *DcScB*
Lugg, Charles Henry 1862- *WhAm 4*
Lugg, Thomas Bransford 1889-1967 *WhAm 5*
Luginin, Vladimir Fedorovich 1834-1911 *DcScB*
Lugo, Bernardo De *ApCAB*
Lugo, Francisco De 1580-1652 *ApCAB*
Lugosi, Bela 1884-1956 *WebAB*
Luhan, Mabel Dodge 1879-1962 *REnAW,*
WhAm 4
Luhn, Hans Peter 1896-1964 *DcAmLiB,*
WhAm 4
Luhring, Oscar Raymond 1879-1944 *BiDrAC,*
WhAm 2
Luhrs, Henry Ernst 1901-1962 *NatCAB 50,*
WhAm 4
Luhrs, Jennie McLellan Patterson
WomWWA 14
Luhrsen, Julius G 1877-1956 *WhAm 3*
Luick, David James 1904-1963 *NatCAB 50*
Luitwieler, Clarence Seward 1861-1948
ApCAB X, NatCAB 37
Lujan, Manuel, Jr. 1928- *BiDrAC*
Luka, Milo 1890- *WhAm 3*
Lukacs, Gyorgy 1885-1971 *McGEWB*
Lukas, Edwin Jay 1902-1973 *WhAm 6*
Lukas, Paul 1895-1971 *WhAm 5*
Lukasiewicz, Jan 1878-1956 *DcScB*
Luke, Saint *McGEWB*
Luke, Allan 1881-1948 *NatCAB 40*
Luke, Arthur Fuller 1853-1917 *WhAm 1*
Luke, Edmon G 1903-1968 *WhAm 5*
Luke, Frank, Jr. 1897-1918 *NatCAB 19,*
WebAMB
Luke, John Guthrie 1857-1921 *NatCAB 32*
Luke, Mary Bailey 1859- *WomWWA 14*
Luke, Thomas d1948 *WhAm 2*
Luke, William 1790- *NewYHSD*
Lukeman, Augustus 1871-1935 *NatCAB 32,*
WhAm 1
Lukeman, Henry Augustus 1871-1935 *AmBi,*
DcAmB S1
Luken, Martin Girard 1882-1968 *WhAm 5*
Lukens, Anna 1844- *AmWom*
Lukens, Donald Edgar 1931- *BiDrAC*
Lukens, Glen 1887-1967 *BnEnAmA*
Lukens, Henry Clay 1838- *ApCAB,*
NatCAB 13
Lukens, Herman Tyson 1865-1949 *WhAm 2*
Lukens, Rebecca Webb Pennock 1794-1854
ApCAB X, BiCAW, DcAmB, NatCAB 15,
NotAW, WhAm H
Lukens, Rinaldo Abram 1894-1961 *NatCAB 49*
Lukens, Theodore Parker 1849-1918
NatCAB 18
Lukin, Charles James 1859- *WhAm 4*
Luks, George Benjamin 1867-1933 *AmBi,*
BnEnAmA, DcAmB S1, McGEWB,
WhAm 1
Lulek, Ralph Norbert 1901-1970 *NatCAB 56,*
WhAm 5
Lull, Cabot 1874- *WhAm 5*
Lull, Edward Phelps 1836-1887 *ApCAB,*
DcAmB, TwCBDA, WhAm H

Lull, Gerard Bramley 1877- *WhAm 5*
Lull, Henry Morris 1875-1949 *WhAm 2*
Lull, Herbert Galen 1874- *WhAm 5*
Lull, Ramon 1232?-1316 *DcScB*
Lull, Raymond 1232?-1316 *McGEWB*
Lull, Richard Swann 1867-1957 *WhAm 3*
Lully, Jean Baptiste 1632-1687 *McGEWB*
Lum, Charles M *NewYHSD*
Lum, David Walker 1855- *WhAm 4*
Lum, Frederick Harvey 1848-1905 *NatCAB 31*
Lum, Ralph Emerson 1877-1952 *WhAm 3*
Lum, Ralph Emerson, Jr. 1905-1974 *WhAm 6*
Luman, Clark McEwen 1878-1943 *NatCAB 34*
Lumas, Parker *NewYHSD*
Lumb, George Haigh 1861-1946 *NatCAB 35*
Lumbrozo, Jacob d1666? *DcAmB,*
NatCAB 11, WhAm H
Lumley, Arthur 1837?-1912 *NewYHSD*
Lumley, Frederick Elmore 1880-1954 *WhAm 3*
Lummer, Otto Richard 1860-1925 *DcScB*
Lummis, Charles Fletcher 1859-1928 *AmBi,*
ApCAB Sup, DcAmB, DcAmLiB,
NatCAB 11, NatCAB 42, REnAW,
TwCBDA, WhAm 1
Lummis, Dorothea 1860- *AmWom*
Lummis, George Deardorff 1863-1940
NatCAB 35
Lummus, Ezra Franklin 1855-1921 *NatCAB 36*
Lummus, F Edward 1879-1947 *NatCAB 36*
Lummus, Henry Tilton 1876-1960 *NatCAB 48,*
WhAm 4
Lumpkin, Alva Moore 1886-1941 *BiDrAC,*
NatCAB 35, WhAm 1
Lumpkin, John Henry 1812-1860 *ApCAB,*
BiAUS, BiDrAC, NatCAB 1, TwCBDA,
WhAm H, WhAmP
Lumpkin, Joseph Henry 1799-1867 *AmBi,*
ApCAB, DcAmB, Drake, NatCAB 10,
TwCBDA, WhAm H
Lumpkin, Joseph Henry 1856-1916 *WhAm 1*
Lumpkin, Sam Edgerton 1909-1964 *NatCAB 52*
Lumpkin, Samuel 1848-1903 *NatCAB 3,*
TwCBDA, WhAm 1
Lumpkin, Wilson 1783- *BiAUS*
Lumpkin, Wilson 1783-1870 *AmBi, ApCAB,*
BiDrAC, DcAmB, NatCAB 1, TwCBDA,
WhAm H, WhAmP
Lumpkin, Wilson 1783-1871 *Drake*
Lumsden, Francis Asbury d1860 *NatCAB 13*
Lumsden, Leslie Leon 1875-1946 *NatCAB 36,*
WhAm 2
Lumsdon, Christine Marie d1937 *WhAm 1*
Lumumba, Patrice Emery 1925-1961 *McGEWB*
Luna, Emerico 1882-1963 *DcScB*
Luna, Solomon 1858-1912 *REnAW, WhAm 1*
Luna, Tranquilino 1849-1892 *BiDrAC,*
WhAm H, WhAmP
Luna Y Arellano, Tristan De 1519-1571 *ApCAB,*
DcAmB, WhAm H
Lunceford, James Melvin 1902-1947 *DcAmB S4*
Lund, Andrew Boardo 1877-1959 *NatCAB 47*
Lund, Anthon Henrik 1844- *NatCAB 16*
Lund, Charles Carroll 1895-1972 *NatCAB 57,*
WhAm 5
Lund, Chester Benford 1901-1965 *WhAm 4*
Lund, Emil 1850- *WhAm 4*
Lund, Frank Joel 1876-1966 *NatCAB 53*
Lund, Franze Edward 1909-1973 *WhAm 6*
Lund, Fred Bates 1865-1950 *NatCAB 46,*
WhAm 5
Lund, Frederick Hansen 1894-1965 *NatCAB 52,*
WhAm 4
Lund, J Thomsen 1903-1957 *NatCAB 46*
Lund, Lawrence Henry 1897-1949 *WhAm 3*
Lund, Robert Leathan 1875-1957 *NatCAB 53,*
WhAm 3
Lund, Theodore *NewYHSD*
Lund-Quist, Carl E 1908-1965 *WhAm 4*
Lunday, Charles G 1872- *WhAm 5*
Lundbeck, G Hilmer 1870-1949 *WhAm 2*
Lundberg, Alfred J 1890-1956 *WhAm 3*
Lundberg, Charles J d1949 *WhAm 2*
Lundberg, Clarence Harry 1907-1968 *WhAm 5*
Lundberg, Frank A 1875- *WhAm 5*
Lundberg, Hugo Balzaar 1877-1967 *NatCAB 54*
Lundbery, Peter *NewYHSD*
Lundblad, Claus David 1883-1962 *NatCAB 50*
Lundbom, Oscar Franz 1878-1955 *NatCAB 47*

Lundborg, Florence 1880?-1949 *IIBEAAW,*
WhAm 2
Lundeberg, Harry 1901-1957 *WhAm 3*
Lundeen, Ernest 1878-1940 *BiDrAC,*
DcAmB S2, EncAAH, NatCAB 40,
WhAm 1, WhAmP
Lundell, Gustav Ernst Frederick 1881-1950
WhAm 3
Lundell, Gustav Ernst Fredrik 1881-1950
NatCAB 40
Lundell, Otto Amandus 1879-1940 *NatCAB 30*
Lunderman, Charles Johnson, Jr. 1922-1973
WhAm 6
Lundgren, Arnold Alinder 1895-1962
NatCAB 47
Lundgren, Eric 1906-1971 *NatCAB 56*
Lundgren, Maude Cohoon 1879- *WomWWA 14*
Lundie *NewYHSD*
Lundie, Edwin Hugh 1886-1972 *WhAm 5*
Lundie, John 1857-1931 *DcAmB, NatCAB 24,*
WhAm 1
Lundigan, William 1914-1975 *WhAm 6*
Lundin, Carl Axel Robert 1851-1915 *DcAmB,*
WhAm 1
Lundin, Frederick 1868-1947 *BiDrAC,*
WhAm 4
Lundquist, Albert G 1874-1915 *NatCAB 17*
Lundquist, Harold Leonard 1894-1959 *WhAm 3*
Lundstrom, Carl Brynolf 1899-1956 *NatCAB 48*
Lundstrum, Allan Winston 1902-1972 *WhAm 5*
Lundy, Ayres Derby 1861- *WhAm 4*
Lundy, Benjamin 1789-1839 *AmBi, ApCAB,*
DcAmB, Drake, EncAB, McGEWB,
NatCAB 2, TwCBDA, WebAB,
WhAm H
Lundy, Elmer Johnston 1880-1944 *WhAm 2*
Lundy, Frank Arthur 1905-1975 *WhAm 6*
Lundy, James Andrew 1905-1973 *WhAm 6*
Lundy, John Patterson 1823- *ApCAB*
Lundy, Wilson Thomas 1884-1963 *WhAm 4*
Lunenschloss, Leo L 1886-1968 *NatCAB 53*
Lung, George Augustus 1862-1921 *WhAm 1*
Lunge, George 1839-1923 *DcScB*
Lunger, John B 1864-1919 *WhAm 1*
Lungkwitz, Carl Hermann Frederick 1813-1891
IIBEAAW, REnAW
Lungkwitz, Hermann 1813-1891 *NewYHSD*
Lungren, Charles Marshall 1853- *ApCAB*
Lungren, Ferdinand Harvey 1857- *ApCAB*
Lungren, Fernand Harvey 1859?-1932
IIBEAAW, WhAm 4
Lungren, Samuel Smith 1827- *ApCAB*
Luning, Henry Herman 1898-1975 *WhAm 6*
Lunken, Edmund H 1861-1944 *NatCAB 15,*
WhAm 2
Lunken, Eshelby F 1890-1949 *WhAm 3*
Lunkenheimer, Frederick 1825-1889
NatCAB 15
Lunn, Arthur Constant 1877-1949 *WhAm 2*
Lunn, Ernest 1874-1942 *NatCAB 32*
Lunn, George Richard 1873-1948 *BiDrAC,*
DcAmB S4, NatCAB 36, WhAm 2
Lunsford, William 1859-1927 *NatCAB 21,*
WhAm 1
Lunt, Alfred 1893- *WebAB*
Lunt, George 1803-1885 *ApCAB, DcAmB,*
Drake, NatCAB 6, TwCBDA, WhAm H
Lunt, Horace Gray 1847-1923 *NatCAB 24*
Lunt, Horace Gray 1847-1928 *WhAm 1,*
WhAm 1C
Lunt, Orrington 1815-1897 *ApCAB Sup,*
DcAmB, NatCAB 2, TwCBDA,
WhAm H
Lunt, William Edward 1882-1956 *NatCAB 46,*
WhAm 3
Lunt, William Parsons 1805-1857 *ApCAB,*
Drake
Luntz, Samuel 1867-1960 *NatCAB 45*
Luolie, Peter *NewYHSD*
Lupton, Charles Thomas 1878-1935 *NatCAB 26,*
WhAm 1, WhAm 1C
Lupton, Frances Platt Townsend *NewYHSD*
Lupton, John Thomas 1862-1933 *WhAm 1*
Lupton, Nathaniel Thomas 1830-1893 *ApCAB,*
NatCAB 12, TwCBDA
Luque, Fernando De 1484-1531 *ApCAB*
Luque, Hernando De d1532 *Drake*
Luquer, Lea McIlvaine 1864-1930 *NatCAB 23,*

WhAm 1
Luquiens, Frederick Bliss 1875-1940
NatCAB 29, WhAm 1
Luquiens, Jules 1845-1899 *NatCAB 29,
TwCBDA*
Lurcat, Jean-Marie 1892-1966 *WhAm 4*
Luria, Alexander Levi 1880-1951 *NatCAB 55*
Luria, Isaac BenSolomon Ashkenazi 1534-1572
McGEWB
Luria, Salvador Edward 1912- *WebAB*
Lurie, Harry Lawrence 1892-1973 *WhAm 6*
Lurie, Louis Robert 1888-1972 *NatCAB 57,
WhAm 5*
Lurie, Ted R 1909-1974 *WhAm 6*
Lurton, Douglas Ellsworth 1897-1956 *WhAm 3*
Lurton, Horace Harmon 1844-1914 *AmBi,
ApCAB Sup, ApCAB X, DcAmB,
NatCAB 8, TwCBDA, WebAB, WhAm 1*
Lusby, James *NewYHSD*
Luscomb, Arthur Fielden 1878-1925
NatCAB 23
Luscomb, Fred A 1860-1924 *NatCAB 21*
Luscomb, William Henry 1805-1866 *NewYHSD*
Luscombe, Walter Otis 1851-1939 *NatCAB 30*
Luse, Claude Zeph 1879-1932 *WhAm 1*
Lush, Charles Keeler 1861- *WhAm 4*
Lusignan, Jean Baptiste Alphonse 1843- *ApCAB*
Lusitanus, Amatus 1511-1568 *DcScB*
Lusk, Clayton Riley 1872-1959 *WhAm 3*
Lusk, Frank Stillman 1857-1930 *WhAm 1*
Lusk, Georgia Lee 1893-1971 *BiDrAC,
WhAm 5*
Lusk, Graham 1866-1932 *AmBi, BiHiMed,
DcAmB S1, DcScB, NatCAB 15,
WhAm 1*
Lusk, Hall Stoner 1883- *BiDrAC*
Lusk, James Loring 1855-1906 *WhAm 1*
Lusk, James W 1841- *WhAm 4*
Lusk, John 1734-1838 *ApCAB, Drake*
Lusk, Leila Lee Fearn 1863- *WomWWA 14*
Lusk, Robert Davies 1902-1962 *NatCAB 52*
Lusk, Robert Emmett 1902-1971 *NatCAB 55*
Lusk, Willard Clayton 1869-1940 *WhAm 1*
Lusk, William Chittenden 1868-1934
NatCAB 27
Lusk, William Foster 1874- *WhAm 5*
Lusk, William Thompson 1838-1897 *ApCAB,
DcAmB, NatCAB 9, NatCAB 27,
WhAm H*
Lussan, August *NewYHSD*
Lussan, Raveneau De 1663- *ApCAB*
Lussan, Zelie De *NotAW*
Lust, Adeline Cohnfeld 1860- *WhAm 4*
Lust, Benedict 1872-1945 *NatCAB 32*
Lust, Herbert Confield 1885- *NatCAB 18*
Lustig, Alessandro 1857-1937 *DcScB*
Lustig, Alvin 1915-1955 *WhAm 3*
Lustman, Seymour Leonard 1920-1971
WhAm 5
Lustrat, Joseph 1858-1927 *WhAm 1*
Luten, Daniel Benjamin 1869-1946 *WhAm 2*
Lutes, Della Thompson d1942 *WhAm 2*
Luther, Agnes Vinton *WomWWA 14*
Luther, C Robert 1822-1900 *DcScB*
Luther, Clara M 1859- *WomWWA 14*
Luther, Edward Staats 1876- *NatCAB 17*
Luther, Edwin Cornelius 1878-1935 *WhAm 1*
Luther, Flavel Sweeten 1850-1928 *NatCAB 13,
WhAm 1*
Luther, George Benjamin 1870-1951
NatCAB 40
Luther, George Martin 1849-1913 *NatCAB 17*
Luther, Hans 1879-1963 *WhAm 4*
Luther, John Carlyle 1910- *WhAm 5*
Luther, John Hill 1824- *TwCBDA*
Luther, Margaret E 1875- *WomWWA 14*
Luther, Mark Lee 1872- *WhAm 5*
Luther, Martin 1483-1546 *McGEWB*
Luther, Seth 1790?-1850? *DcAmB, WebAB,
WhAm H*
Luther, Willard Blackinton 1879-1962 *WhAm 4*
Luthringer, George Francis 1904-1955 *WhAm 3*
Luthule, Albert John 1899-1967 *WhAm 4*
Luthuli, Albert John 1898-1967 *McGEWB*
Luthy, Fred 1894-1963 *NatCAB 50, WhAm 4*
Luthy, Max 1898-1967 *NatCAB 53*
Lutkin, Harris Carman 1886-1961 *NatCAB 49*
Lutkin, Peter Christian 1858-1931 *BiDAmEd,*

DcAmB, NatCAB 26, WhAm 1
Lutoslawski, Witold 1913- *McGEWB*
Lutrell, Estelle *WomWWA 14a*
Lutterbeck, Eugene Feistmann 1909-1973
WhAm 6
Lutterloh, Charles Hartzell 1897-1953
NatCAB 51
Luttrell, Estelle *WomWWA 14*
Luttrell, John E 1889-1969 *WhAm 5*
Luttrell, John King 1831-1893 *BiAUS, BiDrAC,
WhAm H*
Lutz, Adelia Armstrong 1859- *AmWom*
Lutz, Alma 1890-1973 *WhAm 6*
Lutz, Brenton Reid 1890-1960 *WhAm 4*
Lutz, Charles Abner 1871-1947 *WhAm 2*
Lutz, Conrad *NewYHSD*
Lutz, E Russell 1902-1970 *WhAm 5*
Lutz, Edwin George 1868- *WhAm 4*
Lutz, Frank Eugene 1879-1943 *DcAmB S3,
NatCAB 42, WhAm 2*
Lutz, Frank Joseph 1855-1916 *NatCAB 12,
WhAm 1*
Lutz, Frederick 1850- *NatCAB 5*
Lutz, George Washington 1855- *WhAm 4*
Lutz, Grace Livingston Hill 1865-1947 *WhAm 2,
WomWWA 14*
Lutz, Harley Leist 1882-1975 *WhAm 6*
Lutz, Helen Howland 1876- *WomWWA 14,
WomWWA 14a*
Lutz, J Fletcher 1872-1948 *NatCAB 38*
Lutz, Jacob *NewYHSD*
Lutz, Jacob 1831?- *NewYHSD*
Lutz, Nicholas 1740-1807 *ApCAB*
Lutz, Parke Henry 1896-1975 *WhAm 6*
Lutz, Philip 1888-1947 *WhAm 2*
Lutz, Ralph Haswell 1886-1968 *WhAm 5*
Lutz, Samuel G 1868-1956 *WhAm 3*
Lutz, William A 1850- *WhAm 4*
Lux, Frederick 1893-1958 *NatCAB 45*
Lux, Rudolph *NewYHSD*
Luxembourg, Francois H DeM-B, Duc De
1628-1695 *WhoMilH*
Luxemburg, Rosa 1870-1919 *McGEWB*
Luxford, Ansel F 1911-1971 *WhAm 5*
Luxford, G A 1880- *WhAm 6*
Luykx, Nicolaas Godfried Maria 1865-1930
ApCAB X
Luyties, Carl Johann 1860-1916 *WhAm 1*
Luz, Arturo Rogerio 1926- *McGEWB*
Luz, Kadish 1895-1972 *WhAm 6*
Luz-Caballero, Jose DeLa 1800-1862 *ApCAB*
Luzada, Samuel *NewYHSD*
Luzenberg, Charles Aloysius 1805-1848 *ApCAB,
Drake*
Luzerne, Anne Caesar DeLa 1741-1791 *Drake*
Luzin, Nikolai Nikolaievich 1883-1950 *DcScB*
Luzuriaga, Toribio 1770-1837 *ApCAB*
Luzzato, Moses Hayyim 1707-1747 *McGEWB*
Lwoff, Andre Michael 1902- *AsBiEn,
McGEWB*
Ly, Abdoulaye 1919- *McGEWB*
Lyall, David 1910-1972 *NatCAB 57*
Lyall, James 1836-1901 *ApCAB, ApCAB Sup,
DcAmB, NatCAB 7, WhAm 1*
Lyall, Toni Owen 1911-1968 *WhAm 5*
Lyapunov, Aleksandr Mikhailovich 1857-1918
DcScB
Lyautey, Louis Hubert Gonzalve 1854-1934
McGEWB, WhoMilH
Lybarger, Donald Fisher 1896-1970 *WhAm 5*
Lybarger, Lee Francis 1865- *WhAm 4*
Lybrand, Archibald 1840-1910 *ApCAB Sup,
BiDrAC, TwCBDA, WhAm 1*
Lybrand, Jacob *NewYHSD*
Lybrand, Joseph 1793-1845 *ApCAB*
Lybrand, Walter Archibald 1879-1964
NatCAB 50, WhAm 6
Lybyer, Albert Howe 1876-1949 *WhAm 2*
Lyctston, F A *NewYHSD*
Lyda, E Roscoe 1885-1949 *NatCAB 38*
Lydecker, Charles Edward 1851-1920 *WhAm 1*
Lydecker, F A 1885-1961 *WhAm 4*
Lydecker, Garrett J 1843-1914 *WhAm 1*
Lydecker, Garrit Abraham 1901-1967 *WhAm 4*
Lydenberg, Harry Miller 1874-1960 *DcAmLiB,
NatCAB 49, WhAm 3A, WhAm 4*
Lyder, Jay W 1868- *WhAm 5*

Lyders, Elizabeth Mary Perkins 1879-
WomWWA 14
Lydgate, John 1370?-1450? *McGEWB*
Lydick, Jesse Dean 1876-1944 *WhAm 2*
Lydius, Johannes d1709 *ApCAB*
Lydius, John Henry 1693-1791 *ApCAB*
Lydon, Eugene Keeley 1903-1963 *NatCAB 50,
WhAm 4*
Lydon, Richard Paul 1868-1946 *NatCAB 35,
WhAm 2*
Lydston, Francis A 1819- *NewYHSD*
Lydston, G Frank 1858-1923 *ApCAB X,
NatCAB 24*
Lydston, George Frank 1857-1923 *DcAmB*
Lydston, George Frank 1858-1923 *WhAm 1*
Lydston, William, Jr. *NewYHSD*
Lye, Len 1901- *BnEnAmA*
Lyell, Sir Charles 1797-1875 *ApCAB, AsBiEn,
DcScB, Drake, McGEWB*
Lyell, Thomas 1775-1848 *ApCAB, TwCBDA*
Lyerly, Jacob Martin Luther 1862-1923
NatCAB 20
Lyeth, J M Richardson 1886-1957 *WhAm 3*
Lyford, Charles Albert 1882-1953 *NatCAB 45*
Lyford, James Otis 1853-1924 *WhAm 1*
Lyford, Oliver Smith 1823-1914 *WhAm 1*
Lyford, Oliver Smith 1870-1952 *NatCAB 41,
WhAm 3*
Lyford, Will Hartwell 1858-1934 *WhAm 1*
Lyie, Eliphalet Oram 1842-1913 *WhAm 1*
Lykes, Frederick Eugene 1877-1951
NatCAB 40
Lykes, James McKay 1880-1943 *NatCAB 32*
Lykes, John Wall 1887-1957 *NatCAB 47*
Lykes, Joseph T 1888-1967 *WhAm 4*
Lykken, Henry Gilman 1880-1958 *NatCAB 44*
Lylburn, William Henry Chamberlain 1861-1930
NatCAB 24
Lyle, Aaron 1759-1825 *BiAUS, BiDrAC,
TwCBDA, WhAm H*
Lyle, Benjamin Franklin 1861-1939 *WhAm 1*
Lyle, Clay 1894-1971 *WhAm 5*
Lyle, David Alexander 1845-1937 *NatCAB 28*
Lyle, Eugene P, Jr. 1873- *WhAm 5*
Lyle, Frances Douglas 1876- *WomWWA 14*
Lyle, Henry Hamilton Moore 1874-1947
WhAm 2
Lyle, Hubert Samuel 1873-1931 *WhAm 1*
Lyle, J Irvine 1874-1942 *NatCAB 31*
Lyle, John 1769-1825 *ApCAB*
Lyle, John Emmett, Jr. 1910- *BiDrAC*
Lyle, William 1822- *ApCAB*
Lyle, William Thomas 1875-1933 *WhAm 1*
Lyman *NewYHSD*
Lyman, Albert *NewYHSD*
Lyman, Albert Josiah 1845-1915 *DcAmB,
NatCAB 25, WhAm 1*
Lyman, Alexander Steele 1860-1930 *WhAm 1*
Lyman, Amy Brown 1872-1959 *WhAm 4*
Lyman, Arthur 1861-1933 *NatCAB 33*
Lyman, Arthur Theodore 1832-1915
NatCAB 16, WhAm 1
Lyman, Benjamin Smith 1835-1920 *ApCAB,
DcAmB, DcScB, NatCAB 9, TwCBDA,
WhAm 1*
Lyman, Bertha Burton Thayer 1875-
WomWWA 14
Lyman, Carl Morris 1903-1969 *NatCAB 56*
Lyman, Charles 1843-1913 *NatCAB 13,
WhAm 1*
Lyman, Charles Baldwin 1863-1927 *WhAm 1*
Lyman, Charles Elihu 1894-1970 *NatCAB 55*
Lyman, Charles Huntington 1875-1945
WhAm 2
Lyman, Charles Huntington, III 1903-1972
WhAm 5
Lyman, Chester Smith 1814-1890 *AmBi,
ApCAB, DcAmB, DcScB, NatCAB 25,
TwCBDA, WhAm H*
Lyman, Chester Wolcott 1861-1926 *ApCAB X,
NatCAB 21, WhAm 1*
Lyman, Daniel 1756-1830 *NatCAB 10,
TwCBDA*
Lyman, Daniel Wanton 1844-1886 *ApCAB*
Lyman, David Belden 1803-1884 *ApCAB*
Lyman, David Belden 1803-1885 *TwCBDA*
Lyman, David Brainerd 1840-1914 *NatCAB 11,
WhAm 1*

Lyman, David Russell 1876-1956 *NatCAB 45, WhAm 3*
Lyman, Edith Alice Evelyn 1870- *WomWWA 14*
Lyman, Edna D Steward 1881- *WomWWA 14*
Lyman, Edward Branch 1876- *WhAm 5*
Lyman, Edward Brandon 1904-1973 *WhAm 6*
Lyman, Edward Dean 1881-1962 *WhAm 4*
Lyman, Elias 1849-1923 *WhAm 1*
Lyman, Elmer Adelbert 1861-1934 *WhAm 1*
Lyman, Emily Stewart *WomWWA 14*
Lyman, Eugene William 1872-1948 *DcAmB S4, NatCAB 36, WhAm 2*
Lyman, Evelyn May 1910-1973 *WhAm 6*
Lyman, Francis Marion 1840- *NatCAB 5*
Lyman, Frank 1852- *WhAm 4*
Lyman, Frank Hubbard 1863-1957 *WhAm 3*
Lyman, Frederic A 1864- *NatCAB 4*
Lyman, Frederick Schwartz 1837-1918 *NatCAB 40*
Lyman, Frederick Sylvester 1853-1933 *NatCAB 25*
Lyman, Frederick Wolcott 1849-1931 *WhAm 1*
Lyman, George Dunlap 1882-1949 *NatCAB 37, WhAm 3*
Lyman, George Richard 1871-1926 *WhAm 1*
Lyman, George Richards 1844-1935 *WhAm 1*
Lyman, H *NewYHSD*
Lyman, Hannah Willard 1816-1871 *ApCAB*
Lyman, Harry Webster 1873- *WhAm 5*
Lyman, Hart 1851-1927 *WhAm 1*
Lyman, Henrietta Crane *WomWWA 14*
Lyman, Henry 1809-1834 *ApCAB*
Lyman, Henry 1810-1834 *Drake*
Lyman, Henry Darius 1852-1921 *NatCAB 14, WhAm 1*
Lyman, Henry Gilman 1880-1955 *NatCAB 44*
Lyman, Henry Munson 1835-1904 *ApCAB, NatCAB 12, TwCBDA, WhAm 1*
Lyman, Herbert 1864-1941 *NatCAB 31*
Lyman, Homer Childs 1861- *WhAm 4*
Lyman, James 1862-1934 *NatCAB 28, WhAm 1*
Lyman, Jesse Philyer 1862-1931 *ApCAB X, NatCAB 27*
Lyman, John VanReed 1857- *ApCAB X*
Lyman, Joseph 1749-1828 *ApCAB, NatCAB 7*
Lyman, Joseph 1750-1828 *Drake*
Lyman, Joseph 1840-1890 *BiDrAC, TwCBDA, WhAm H*
Lyman, Joseph 1843-1913 *ApCAB, TwCBDA, WhAm 1*
Lyman, Joseph Bardwell 1829-1872 *ApCAB, DcAmB, NatCAB 11, TwCBDA, WhAm H*
Lyman, Joseph Stebbins 1785-1821 *BiAUS, BiDrAC, WhAm H*
Lyman, Laura Elizabeth Baker 1831- *ApCAB*
Lyman, Lauren Dwight 1891-1971 *WhAm 5*
Lyman, Levi Chamberlain 1866-1948 *NatCAB 40*
Lyman, Mary Ely 1887-1975 *WhAm 6*
Lyman, Phineas 1715-1774 *AmBi, DcAmB, NatCAB 25, WhAm H*
Lyman, Phineas 1716-1774 *ApCAB, TwCBDA*
Lyman, Phineas 1716-1775 *Drake*
Lyman, Richard Eldredge 1869-1943 *NatCAB 41*
Lyman, Richard Roswell 1870-1963 *NatCAB 51, WhAm 4*
Lyman, Richard Sherman 1891-1959 *NatCAB 48*
Lyman, Robert Hunt 1864-1937 *NatCAB 28, WhAm 1*
Lyman, Ronald Theodore 1879-1962 *NatCAB 51, WhAm 6*
Lyman, Rose Clarissa 1869- *WomWWA 14*
Lyman, Rufus Ashley 1875-1957 *WhAm 3*
Lyman, Samuel 1749-1802 *BiAUS, BiDrAC, TwCBDA, WhAm H*
Lyman, Sarah E *WhAm 1*
Lyman, Sarah Joiner 1805-1885 *ApCAB*
Lyman, Susan Chester 1867- *WomWWA 14*
Lyman, Sylvester S 1813-1878? *NewYHSD*
Lyman, Theodore 1792-1849 *ApCAB, DcAmB, Drake, TwCBDA, WhAm H*
Lyman, Theodore 1833-1897 *AmBi, ApCAB, BiDrAC, DcAmB, NatCAB 24, TwCBDA,*

Lyman, *WhAm H*
Lyman, Theodore 1874-1954 *DcAmB S5, DcScB, WhAm 3*
Lyman, Theodore Benedict 1815-1893 *ApCAB, NatCAB 6, TwCBDA*
Lyman, William d1811 *BiAUS*
Lyman, William d1833 *Drake*
Lyman, William 1753-1811 *ApCAB, Drake*
Lyman, William 1755-1811 *BiDrAC, TwCBDA, WhAm H*
Lyman, William Denison 1852-1920 *WhAm 1*
Lyman, William Henry 1852-1930 *NatCAB 32*
Lymburner, Adam 1746-1836 *ApCAB*
Lymer, Elmer E 1862- *WhAm 1*
Lymer, William Barker 1882- *WhAm 1*
Lynah, James 1881-1956 *NatCAB 47*
Lynch, Anna *NewYHSD*
Lynch, Anna d1946 *WhAm 2*
Lynch, Anna Charlotte 1815-1891 *DcAmB*
Lynch, Anne Charlotte 1815-1891 *AmBi, NotAW*
Lynch, Brandon *IlBEAAW*
Lynch, C Arthur 1903-1963 *WhAm 4*
Lynch, Caroline Vinia *WomWWA 14*
Lynch, Cecil Shannon 1883-1958 *NatCAB 47*
Lynch, Charles d1783 *Drake*
Lynch, Charles d1785? *ApCAB, TwCBDA*
Lynch, Charles d1853 *ApCAB, BiAUS, NatCAB 13, TwCBDA*
Lynch, Charles 1699-1753 *NatCAB 11*
Lynch, Charles 1736-1796 *AmBi, DcAmB, NatCAB 11, WebAB, WhAm H*
Lynch, Charles 1868- *WhAm 4*
Lynch, Charles F 1884-1942 *WhAm 2*
Lynch, Charles Wesley 1851- *WhAm 1*
Lynch, Clyde Alvin 1891-1950 *WhAm 3*
Lynch, Dolly Suite 1858- *WomWWA 14*
Lynch, Edward James 1884-1968 *WhAm 4A*
Lynch, Ella Frances 1882-1945 *WhAm 2, WomWWA 14*
Lynch, Florence 1891-1953 *WhAm 3*
Lynch, Francis 1880-1945 *NatCAB 37*
Lynch, Frank Worthington 1871-1945 *NatCAB 34, WhAm 2*
Lynch, Frederick 1867-1934 *WhAm 1*
Lynch, Frederick Becknell 1896- *ApCAB X*
Lynch, Frederick Bicknell 1866- *WhAm 4*
Lynch, Frederick J 1889-1957 *WhAm 3*
Lynch, George Arthur 1880-1962 *WhAm 4*
Lynch, Gertrude *WomWWA 14*
Lynch, Harriet Powe 1864- *WomWWA 14*
Lynch, Howard Eldridge 1900-1955 *NatCAB 47*
Lynch, Humphrey James 1880-1938 *NatCAB 30*
Lynch, Isabel Purdon 1868- *WomWWA 14*
Lynch, Isidore De 1755-1821 *Drake*
Lynch, Isidore De 1755-1841 *ApCAB*
Lynch, J Harold 1902-1962 *NatCAB 50*
Lynch, James Daniel 1836-1903 *ApCAB, DcAmB, TwCBDA, WhAm 4*
Lynch, James Jeremiah 1910-1962 *NatCAB 51*
Lynch, James Kennedy 1857-1919 *WhAm 1*
Lynch, James Mathew 1867-1930 *DcAmB, WhAm 1*
Lynch, James William 1865- *WhAm 4*
Lynch, Jeremiah 1849- *WhAm 1*
Lynch, Jerome Morley d1951 *WhAm 3*
Lynch, John 1825-1892 *BiAUS, BiDrAC, WhAm H*
Lynch, John 1843-1910 *BiDrAC*
Lynch, John A 1853-1938 *NatCAB 17, WhAm 1*
Lynch, John David 1890-1946 *WhAm 2*
Lynch, John Emmet 1914-1971 *NatCAB 56*
Lynch, John Fairfield 1845-1923 *WhAm 1*
Lynch, John Joseph 1816-1888 *ApCAB, WhAm H*
Lynch, John Roy 1847-1939 *ApCAB, BiAUS, BiDrAC, DcAmB S2, NatCAB 3, TwCBDA, WhAm 1, WhAmP, WhoColR*
Lynch, Joseph Bertram 1893-1961 *NatCAB 49, WhAm 4*
Lynch, Joseph Patrick 1872-1954 *NatCAB 15, WhAm 3*
Lynch, Junius F 1865- *NatCAB 4*
Lynch, Kenneth Merrill 1887-1974 *WhAm 6*
Lynch, Mary Atkins *NotAW*
Lynch, Mary Virginia 1863- *WomWWA 14*

Lynch, Matthew Christopher 1882-1931 *WhAm 1*
Lynch, Mercer Genin 1908-1960 *NatCAB 47*
Lynch, Patricio 1825-1886 *ApCAB*
Lynch, Patrick Neeson 1817-1882 *DcAmB, TwCBDA, WhAm H*
Lynch, Patrick Niesen 1817-1882 *ApCAB, NatCAB 12*
Lynch, Patrick Nieson 1817-1882 *BiDConf*
Lynch, Rachel Ann Cartwright *WomWWA 14*
Lynch, Raymond A 1913- *WhAm 5*
Lynch, Robert Clyde 1880-1931 *DcAmB, NatCAB 24*
Lynch, Robert Newton 1875-1931 *WhAm 1*
Lynch, Thomas d1776 *BiAUS*
Lynch, Thomas 1720?-1776 *ApCAB, NatCAB 5, TwCBDA*
Lynch, Thomas 1727-1776 *AmBi, BiDrAC, DcAmB, WhAm H, WhAmP*
Lynch, Thomas 1749-1779 *AmBi, ApCAB, BiAUS, BiDrAC, DcAmB, Drake, NatCAB 10, TwCBDA, WhAm H, WhAmP*
Lynch, Thomas 1844-1898 *BiDrAC, TwCBDA*
Lynch, Thomas 1903-1914 *NatCAB 16*
Lynch, Thomas Francis 1900-1968 *WhAm 5*
Lynch, Walter Aloysius 1894-1957 *BiDrAC, WhAm 3, WhAmP*
Lynch, Walton D 1897-1962 *WhAm 4*
Lynch, Warren J d1950 *WhAm 3*
Lynch, Willard A 1893- *WhAm 3*
Lynch, William Francis 1801-1865 *AmBi, ApCAB, DcAmB, Drake, NatCAB 13, TwCBDA, WebAMB, WhAm H*
Lynch, William Henry 1847- *ApCAB Sup*
Lynch, William Orlando 1870-1957 *WhAm 3*
Lynch, William Warren 1845- *ApCAB*
Lynd, Robert Staughton 1892-1970 *McGEWB, NatCAB 55, WebAB, WhAm 5*
Lynd, William Elmer 1893-1968 *NatCAB 55*
Lynde, Benjamin 1666-1745 *ApCAB, Drake, TwCBDA*
Lynde, Benjamin 1700-1781 *ApCAB, DcAmB, Drake, NatCAB 4, TwCBDA, WhAm H*
Lynde, Carleton John 1872- *WhAm 5*
Lynde, Francis 1856-1930 *DcAmB, NatCAB 13, NatCAB 41, TwCBDA, WhAm 1*
Lynde, Helen Eldred Storke 1879- *WomWWA 14*
Lynde, Mary Elizabeth Blanchard 1819- *AmWom*
Lynde, Samuel Adams 1855-1930 *WhAm 1*
Lynde, William Pitt 1817-1885 *ApCAB, BiAUS, BiDrAC, NatCAB 10, TwCBDA, WhAm H, WhAmP*
Lyndon, Dennis Charles 1913-1967 *NatCAB 53*
Lyndon, Josiah 1704-1778 *ApCAB*
Lyndon, Josiah 1721-1778 *BiAUS, Drake*
Lyndon, Josias 1704-1778 *NatCAB 10, TwCBDA*
Lyndon, Lamar 1871-1940 *WhAm 1*
Lynds, Elam 1784-1855 *DcAmB, WhAm H*
Lynds, Joseph Edward 1854-1924 *NatCAB 28*
Lyndsay, Sir David 1485?-1555 *McGEWB*
Lyne, Daniel Joseph 1889-1957 *NatCAB 51, WhAm 3*
Lyne, James Garnett 1898-1966 *WhAm 4*
Lyne, Wickliffe Campbell 1850-1933 *NatCAB 6, WhAm 1*
Lynen, Feodor 1911- *AsBiEn*
Lynes, Frank 1858- *NatCAB 8*
Lynes, J Colton 1844-1936 *NatCAB 27*
Lynett, Edward James 1856-1943 *WhAm 2*
Lynett, Edward James 1906-1966 *WhAm 4*
Lynett, Elizabeth Ruddy 1902-1959 *WhAm 3*
Lynk, Beebe Steven 1872- *WhoColR*
Lynk, Miles Vandahurst 1871- *WhoColR*
Lynn, Benjamin *ApCAB*
Lynn, Charles J 1874-1958 *WhAm 3*
Lynn, David 1873-1961 *WhAm 4*
Lynn, Eldin Verne 1886-1955 *NatCAB 44*
Lynn, Frank Sidle 1884-1938 *NatCAB 29*
Lynn, Harry Hudson 1885-1956 *WhAm 3*
Lynn, James Jesse 1892-1955 *NatCAB 43*
Lynn, John 1852-1933 *NatCAB 31*
Lynn, Marion *WomWWA 14*
Lynn, Robert Henry 1892-1949 *WhAm 3*

Lynn, Robert Marshall 1871-1944 *WhAm 2*
Lynn, Thomas Edward 1925-1971 *WhAm 6*
Lynn, William *NewYHSD*
Lyon, A Maynard 1818-1916 *NatCAB 17, WhAm 1*
Lyon, Adrian 1869-1950 *NatCAB 16, NatCAB 41, WhAm 5*
Lyon, Alexander Parker 1829-1861 *ApCAB X*
Lyon, Alfred *NewYHSD*
Lyon, Alfred Emanuel 1886-1967 *NatCAB 53, WhAm 4*
Lyon, Andrew Hutchinson 1890-1961 *WhAm 4*
Lyon, Anne Bozeman 1860- *AmWom, WhAm 4*
Lyon, Annie Bozeman 1860- *WomWWA 14*
Lyon, Asa 1763-1841 *ApCAB, BiAUS, BiDrAC, Drake, TwCBDA, WhAm H*
Lyon, B B Vincent 1880- *WhAm 6*
Lyon, Bertrand 1880- *WhAm 6*
Lyon, Caleb 1821-1875 *DcAmB, WhAm H*
Lyon, Caleb 1822-1875 *ApCAB, BiAUS, BiDrAC, TwCBDA, WhAmP*
Lyon, Cecil Andrew 1869-1916 *WhAm 1*
Lyon, Charles Gershom 1912-1973 *WhAm 6*
Lyon, Charles Wesley 1887-1960 *NatCAB 50*
Lyon, Chittenden d1842 *Drake*
Lyon, Chittenden 1786-1842 *ApCAB, BiAUS, TwCBDA*
Lyon, Chittenden 1787-1842 *BiDrAC, WhAmP*
Lyon, Clifford Stanley 1888-1946 *NatCAB 35*
Lyon, Clyde Laten 1880- *WhAm 6*
Lyon, David Gordon 1852-1935 *DcAmB S1, TwCBDA, WhAm 1*
Lyon, David Willard 1870-1949 *DcAmB S4*
Lyon, Dorsey Alfred 1871-1945 *WhAm 2*
Lyon, Edmund 1855-1920 *NatCAB 19, WhAm 1*
Lyon, Edmund Daniel 1862-1942 *WhAm 2*
Lyon, Edwin *NewYHSD*
Lyon, Edwin Bowman 1892-1971 *WhAm 5*
Lyon, Eldridge Merick 1853-1935 *WhAm 1*
Lyon, Elias Potter 1867-1937 *WhAm 1*
Lyon, Ellen Chynoweth 1850- *WomWWA 14*
Lyon, Ernest 1860-1938 *NatCAB 14, WhAm 2, WhoColR*
Lyon, Ernest Neal 1873- *WhAm 1*
Lyon, F Emory 1864-1943 *NatCAB 35, WhAm 2*
Lyon, Frances Dimmick 1881- *WomWWA 14*
Lyon, Francis Strother 1800-1882 *BiAUS, BiDConf, BiDrAC, DcAmB, TwCBDA, WhAm H*
Lyon, Frank *WhAm 3*
Lyon, Frank Almon 1855-1921 *NatCAB 19*
Lyon, Frank Randolph 1871-1933 *NatCAB 24*
Lyon, Franklin Smith 1819- *NatCAB 1*
Lyon, Frederick Saxton 1873-1948 *WhAm 2*
Lyon, G Albert 1881-1961 *NatCAB 49*
Lyon, George Armstrong 1837-1914 *WhAm 1*
Lyon, George Francis 1795-1832 *ApCAB*
Lyon, George Frederick 1849-1940 *NatCAB 30, WhAm 1*
Lyon, George Harry 1890-1971 *WhAm 5*
Lyon, Gideon Allen 1867-1951 *WhAm 3*
Lyon, Harris Merton 1883-1916 *DcAmB, NatCAB 25*
Lyon, Harrison Armstrong 1815-1900 *NatCAB 23*
Lyon, Hastings 1876-1953 *NatCAB 40, WhAm 3*
Lyon, Henry Ware d1929 *WhAm 1*
Lyon, Herb 1918-1968 *WhAm 5*
Lyon, Homer LeGrand 1879-1956 *BiDrAC, NatCAB 48, WhAm 6*
Lyon, Howard 1860-1926 *NatCAB 20*
Lyon, J Adair 1876- *WhAm 5*
Lyon, J B *NewYHSD*
Lyon, James 1735-1794 *DcAmB, WhAm H*
Lyon, James Alexander 1882-1955 *WhAm 3*
Lyon, James Benjamin 1821-1909 *DcAmB, NatCAB 23*
Lyon, James Bertram 1858-1929 *NatCAB 23*
Lyon, John d1780 *ApCAB X*
Lyon, John Christian 1802-1868 *ApCAB*
Lyon, John Denniston 1861-1939 *ApCAB X, NatCAB 29, WhAm 1*
Lyon, John Stanley 1861- *WhAm 4*
Lyon, Jules *NewYHSD*

Lyon, Leonard Saxton 1896-1964 *WhAm 4*
Lyon, LeRoy Springs 1866-1920 *WhAm 1*
Lyon, Leverett Samuel 1885-1959 *NatCAB 48, WhAm 3*
Lyon, Lucius 1800-1851 *ApCAB, BiAUS, BiDrAC, NatCAB 11, TwCBDA, WhAm H*
Lyon, M W *NewYHSD*
Lyon, Marcus Ward, Jr. 1875-1942 *WhAm 2*
Lyon, Mary Mason 1797-1849 *AmBi, AmWom, ApCAB, BiDAmEd, DcAmB, Drake, EncAB, NatCAB 4, NotAW, TwCBDA, WebAB, WhAm H*
Lyon, Mathew 1746-1822 *BiAUS, Drake*
Lyon, Matthew 1746-1822 *ApCAB, BiDrAC, NatCAB 2, WhAmP*
Lyon, Matthew 1750-1822 *AmBi, DcAmB, TwCBDA, WhAm H*
Lyon, Merrick 1815-1888 *NatCAB 8*
Lyon, Milford Hall 1868- *WhAm 5*
Lyon, Nathaniel 1818-1861 *AmBi, ApCAB, DcAmB, NatCAB 4, TwCBDA, WebAMB, WhAm H*
Lyon, Nathaniel 1819-1861 *Drake*
Lyon, Nelson Reed 1905-1972 *WhAm 5*
Lyon, Philip Henry 1872-1956 *NatCAB 46*
Lyon, Pritchett Alfred 1868- *WhAm 4*
Lyon, Richard *ApCAB, Drake*
Lyon, Sanford Gifford 1866-1936 *NatCAB 27*
Lyon, Scott Cary 1884-1942 *WhAm 2*
Lyon, Simon 1870-1946 *NatCAB 34*
Lyon, T Lyttleton 1869-1938 *NatCAB 29, WhAm 1*
Lyon, Theodatus Timothy 1813-1900 *DcAmB*
Lyon, Waldo Vinton 1881-1958 *NatCAB 47*
Lyon, Wallace Chittenden 1863-1954 *NatCAB 52*
Lyon, Walter Jefferson 1883-1962 *WhAm 4*
Lyon, William 1729-1809 *ApCAB X*
Lyon, William Alexander 1902-1975 *WhAm 6*
Lyon, William Henry 1846-1915 *WhAm 1*
Lyon, William Penn 1822-1913 *DcAmB, NatCAB 13, WhAm 1*
Lyonet, Pierre 1706-1789 *DcScB*
Lyons, Albert Brown 1841-1926 *ApCAB, NatCAB 16, TwCBDA, WhAm 1*
Lyons, Chalmers J 1874-1935 *WhAm 1*
Lyons, Champ 1907-1965 *WhAm 4*
Lyons, Charles William 1868-1939 *WhAm 1*
Lyons, Charlton Havard 1894-1973 *WhAm 6*
Lyons, Coleburke 1899-1967 *WhAm 5*
Lyons, Dennis Francis 1880-1937 *WhAm 1*
Lyons, Gerald Edward 1892-1943 *WhAm 2*
Lyons, H A *BiAUS*
Lyons, James 1801-1882 *BiDConf*
Lyons, James 1857-1913 *NatCAB 18*
Lyons, James Gilborne d1868 *ApCAB, Drake*
Lyons, James J 1890-1966 *WhAm 4*
Lyons, John Andrew 1896-1950 *NatCAB 39*
Lyons, John Frederick 1878- *WhAm 6*
Lyons, John Sprole 1861-1942 *WhAm 2*
Lyons, Joseph Aloysius 1879-1939 *McGEWB*
Lyons, Joseph Henry 1874- *WhAm 6*
Lyons, Judson Whitlock 1858-1924 *TwCBDA*
Lyons, Judson Whitlocke 1858-1924 *ApCAB Sup*
Lyons, Judson Whitlocke 1860-1924 *WhAm 1*
Lyons, Julius J 1843-1920 *WhAm 1*
Lyons, Katharine 1889-1933 *WhAm 1*
Lyons, Lucile Manning 1879-1958 *WhAm 3, WomWWA 14*
Lyons, Maritcha Remond 1848- *WhoColR*
Lyons, Minnie Leora Bartlett 1879- *WomWWA 14*
Lyons, Peter 1734?-1809 *DcAmB, WhAm H*
Lyons, Richard Bickerton Pemell 1817-1887 *ApCAB, Drake*
Lyons, Robert Edward 1869-1946 *WhAm 2*
Lyons, Samuel Ross 1849- *ApCAB Sup, TwCBDA, WhAm 4*
Lyons, Sidney S *NewYHSD*
Lyons, Thomas Richard 1867-1941 *WhAm 1*
Lyons, Timothy Augustine 1845-1919 *WhAm 1*
Lyot, Bernard Ferdinand 1897-1952 *AsBiEn, DcScB*
Lysander d395BC *McGEWB* •
Lysenko, Trofim Denisovich 1898- *AsBiEn, McGEWB*

Lyster, Henry Francis LeHunte 1837-1894 *DcAmB, NatCAB 16, WhAm H*
Lyster, Theodore Charles 1875-1933 *WhAm 1*
Lyster, William John LeHunte 1869-1947 *NatCAB 37*
Lyte, Eliphalet Oram 1842-1913 *ApCAB Sup, BiDAmEd, NatCAB 5, TwCBDA*
Lytell, Bert 1865-1954 *NatCAB 43*
Lytell, Bert 1885-1954 *ApCAB X*
Lytell, Bert 1887-1954 *WhAm 3*
Lyter, Jean Curtis 1883-1937 *WhAm 1*
Lytle, Almon Wheeler 1876-1964 *WhAm 4*
Lytle, J Horace 1884-1961 *WhAm 4*
Lytle, John T 1844-1907 *REnAW*
Lytle, John Wesley 1836- *NatCAB 10*
Lytle, Peregrine Marion 1840-1931 *NatCAB 23*
Lytle, Robert Todd 1804-1839 *BiAUS, BiDrAC, NatCAB 4, TwCBDA, WhAm H*
Lytle, William Haines 1826-1863 *AmBi, ApCAB, DcAmB, Drake, NatCAB 4, TwCBDA, WhAm H*
Lyttelton, Oliver 1893-1972 *WhAm 5*
Lyttelton, William Henry 1724-1808 *DcAmB*
Lyttlelton, William Henry 1724-1808 *WhAm H*
Lyttleton, William Henry d1808 *Drake*
Lyttleton, William Henry 1720?-1808 *ApCAB*
Lyttleton, William Henry 1724-1808 *NatCAB 12*
Lytton, Bart 1912-1969 *WhAm 5*
Lytton, Henry Charles 1846- *NatCAB 9*

M

M J *NewYHSD*
M P J *NewYHSD*
Ma, Yuan *McGEWB*
Ma-Ka-Tai-Me-She-Kia-Kiak 1767-1838 *DcAmB*
Maag, Oscar Lewis 1890-1956 *NatCAB 49*
Maag, William Frederick, Jr. 1883-1968 *WhAm 5*
Maanen, Adriaan Van 1884-1946 *DcScB*
Maar, Maria Peterson *WomWWA 14*
Maas *NewYHSD*
Maas, Anthony J 1858-1927 *DcAmB, WhAm 1*
Maas, Carlos J 1897-1972 *WhAm 5*
Maas, Charles E 1827?- *NewYHSD*
Maas, Elizabeth Catherine 1866- *WomWWA 14*
Maas, George Louis 1866-1925 *NatCAB 6*
Maas, Jacob 1800?- *NewYHSD*
Maas, Melvin Joseph 1898-1964 *BiDrAC, WhAm 4*
Maas, William A *NewYHSD*
Maaske, Roben J 1903-1955 *WhAm 3*
Maass, Herbert Halsey 1878- *WhAm 3*
Maass, Otto 1890-1961 *WhAm 4*
Mabbott, J Milton 1862-1938 *NatCAB 28*
Mabbott, Thomas Ollive 1898-1968 *NatCAB 54, WhAm 5*
Mabee, Frank Petrie 1881-1948 *NatCAB 37*
Mabee, George W 1878-1948 *WhAm 2*
Mabery, Charles Frederic 1850-1927 *AmBi, ApCAB, DcAmB, NatCAB 10, WhAm 1*
Mabey, Charles R 1877- *WhAm 5*
Mabie, Charles Elias 1855- *NatCAB 9*
Mabie, Edward Charles 1892-1956 *WhAm 3*
Mabie, Hamilton Wright 1845-1916 *AmBi, ApCAB Sup, DcAmB*
Mabie, Hamilton Wright 1846-1916 *NatCAB 10, TwCBDA, WhAm 1*
Mabie, Henry Clay 1847-1918 *WhAm 1*
Mabie, Louise Kennedy d1957 *WhAm 3*
Mabie, Mary E *WomWWA 14*
Mabillon, Jean 1632-1707 *McGEWB*
Mabini, Apolinario 1864-1903 *McGEWB*
Mabley, Jackie d1975 *WhAm 6*
Mably, Gabriel Bonnot De 1709-1785 *ApCAB, Drake*
Mabon, James Brown 1865-1941 *NatCAB 30*
Mabon, John Steele 1856-1915 *NatCAB 29*
Mabon, Thomas McCance 1890-1958 *WhAm 3*
Mabry, Jane *IIBEAAW*
Mabry, Joseph Alexander 1826-1882 *NatCAB 11*
Mabry, Milton Harvey 1851- *NatCAB 5, WhAm 4*
Mabuchi, Kamo 1697-1769 *McGEWB*
Mabury, Margaret Ellis d1909 *WhAm 1*
Macadam, Carrie Farrant *WomWWA 14*
MacAdam, George Hartley 1865- *WhAm 4*
Macadam, John 1868-1927 *NatCAB 20*
Macadam, John Loudoun 1756-1836 *ApCAB*
Macadam, John Loudoun *see also* McAdam, John Loudon
MacAfee, John Blair 1861-1921 *WhAm 1*
MacAgy, Douglas Guernsey 1913-1973 *WhAm 6*
MacAlarney, Robert Emmet 1873-1945 *WhAm 2*
Macalester, Charles 1765-1832 *ApCAB, DcAmB, WhAm H*
Macalester, Charles 1798-1873 *ApCAB, DcAmB, WhAm H*
MacAlister, Sir Ian 1878-1957 *WhAm 3*
MacAlister, James 1840-1913 *ApCAB,*

BiDAmEd, DcAmB, NatCAB 13, TwCBDA, WhAm 1
MacAllister, Archibald Thomas, Jr. 1905-1966 *NatCAB 52, WhAm 4*
Macallum, Archibald Byron 1858-1934 *DcScB*
MacAlpine, John Campbell, Jr. 1903-1965 *NatCAB 51*
Macalpine, John Henry 1859-1927 *NatCAB 20*
MacAlpine, Robert John 1874-1926 *WhAm 1*
Macanally, David Rice 1810-1895 *Drake*
Macanally, David Rice *see also* McAnally, David Rice
MacAnally, James R 1908- *WhAm 5*
Macapagal, Diosdado 1910- *McGEWB*
MacArthur, Alfred 1885-1967 *WhAm 4*
MacArthur, Archibald 1834-1908 *WhAm 1*
MacArthur, Arthur 1815-1896 *ApCAB, NatCAB 13, TwCBDA*
MacArthur, Arthur 1845-1912 *AmBi, DcAmB S1, NatCAB 14, TwCBDA, WebAB, WebAMB, WhAm 1, WhoMilH*
MacArthur, Arthur 1850-1914 *WhAm 1*
MacArthur, Arthur Frederic 1860-1926 *WhAm 1*
MacArthur, Arthur Frederick 1860-1926 *ApCAB X, NatCAB 22*
MacArthur, Charles 1895-1956 *WhAm 3*
MacArthur, Charles Lafayette 1824-1898 *ApCAB, NatCAB 4, TwCBDA*
MacArthur, Douglas 1880-1964 *EncAB, McGEWB, WebAB, WebAMB, WhAm 4, WhWW-II, WhoMilH*
MacArthur, Harry d1973 *WhAm 6*
MacArthur, James 1866-1909 *WhAm 1*
Macarthur, John 1767?-1834 *McGEWB*
MacArthur, John 1823-1890 *ApCAB*
MacArthur, John *see also* McArthur, John
MacArthur, John R 1862- *WhAm 1*
Macarthur, John R 1874-1960 *WhAm 3*
MacArthur, Mary 1858- *WomWWA 14*
MacArthur, Mildred Sherwood 1886- *WomWWA 14*
MacArthur, Robert Dougall 1843-1922 *ApCAB X*
MacArthur, Robert Helmer 1930-1972 *WhAm 5*
MacArthur, Robert Stuart 1841-1923 *ApCAB Sup, ApCAB X, DcAmB, NatCAB 5, TwCBDA, WhAm 1*
MacArthur, Ruth Alberta Brown 1881- *WhAm 6*
MacArthur, Walter 1862- *WhAm 4*
Macarthy, J *NewYHSD*
Macartney, Clarence Edward Noble 1879-1957 *NatCAB 46, WhAm 3*
Macartney, John W d1966 *WhAm 5*
Macartney, Thomas Benton, Jr. 1875-1929 *NatCAB 22, WhAm 1*
Macaulay, Fannie Caldwell 1863-1941 *WhAm 2, WhAm 4*
Macaulay, Frances Caldwell *WomWWA 14*
Macaulay, Francis Sowerby 1862-1937 *DcScB*
Macaulay, Herbert 1864-1945 *McGEWB*
Macaulay, Sir James Buchanan 1793-1859 *ApCAB*
MacAulay, Malcolm George 1926-1974 *WhAm 6*
Macaulay, Peter Stewart 1901-1966 *WhAm 4*
Macaulay, Thomas Babington 1800-1859 *McGEWB*
Macauley, Alvan 1872-1952 *NatCAB 41, WhAm 3*
Macauley, Charles Raymond 1871-1934 *WhAm 1, WhAm 5*

Macauley, Edward 1875-1964 *WhAm 4*
Macauley, Edward Yorke 1827-1894 *DcAmB*
Macauley, Frederick Robertson 1882-1970 *WhAm 5*
Macauley, Irving P 1890-1966 *WhAm 4*
Macauly, John *NewYHSD*
MacAusland, William Russell 1882-1965 *NatCAB 51*
Macavoy, Clarissa Harben *WomWWA 14*
MacBean, William Munro 1852-1924 *NatCAB 6*
Macbeth d1057 *McGEWB*
Macbeth, Alexander Barksdale 1873-1945 *WhAm 2*
Macbeth, Arthur Laidler 1864- *WhoColR*
Macbeth, Florence 1891-1966 *WhAm 4*
Macbeth, George Alexander 1845-1916 *NatCAB 13, WhAm 1*
Macbeth, George Duff 1892-1968 *NatCAB 54, WhAm 5*
Macbeth, George Trenholm 1879-1952 *NatCAB 41*
Macbeth, Hazel Adrienne 1891- *WhoColR*
Macbeth, Henry 1858- *WhAm 4*
Macbeth, Hugh Ellwood 1884- *WhoColR*
MacBoyle, Errol 1880-1949 *NatCAB 40*
MacBrair, Archibald *NewYHSD*
MacBrayer, Reuben Adolphus 1891-1948 *NatCAB 40*
MacBrayne, Lewis E 1871-1954 *WhAm 3*
MacBrayne, Sarah Thurlow 1876- *WomWWA 14*
MacBride, D S 1893-1959 *WhAm 3*
Macbride, David 1726-1778 *DcScB*
MacBride, Donald Swan 1893-1959 *NatCAB 49*
MacBride, Ernest William 1866-1940 *DcScB*
Macbride, James 1784-1817 *ApCAB*
Macbride, James *see also* McBride, James
Macbride, Philip Douglas 1887-1965 *NatCAB 51, WhAm 4*
Macbride, Thomas Huston 1848-1934 *ApCAB X, NatCAB 11, TwCBDA, WhAm 1*
MacCabe, John Alexander 1842- *ApCAB Sup*
MacCalla, Clifford Sherron 1876-1935 *WhAm 1*
MacCallum, Emily *WomWWA 14*
MacCallum, George Alexander 1843-1936 *NatCAB 32*
MacCallum, John Archibald 1874-1946 *WhAm 2*
MacCallum, John Bruce 1876-1906 *NatCAB 15, WhAm 5*
MacCallum, William George 1874-1944 *DcAmB S3, NatCAB 15, NatCAB 32, WhAm 2*
MacCameron, Robert Lee 1866-1912 *DcAmB, NatCAB 15, WhAm 1*
MacCardle, Ross Clayton 1901-1964 *NatCAB 52*
MacCarthy, Gerald R 1897-1974 *WhAm 6*
MacCartney, Washington 1812-1856 *ApCAB, TwCBDA*
MacCartney, Washington *see also* McCartney, Washington
MacCarty, William Carpenter 1880-1964 *WhAm 4*
Maccaud, Francis William *WhAm 5*
MacCaughey, Vaughan 1887-1954 *BiDAmEd, WhAm 3*
MacCauley, Clay 1843-1925 *DcAmB, WhAm 1*
MacChesney, Charles Eugene 1861- *NatCAB 3*

MacChesney, Chester MacKenzie 1887-1967
NatCAB 53, WhAm 4
MacChesney, Clara Taggart 1861-1928 *AmBi,
WhAm 5, WomWWA 14*
MacChesney, Lena Frost *WomWWA 14*
MacChesney, Nathan William 1878-1954
ApCAB X, NatCAB 44, WhAm 3
MacClintock, Paul 1891-1970 *WhAm 5*
Macclintock, Samuel 1732-1804 *ApCAB*
Macclintock, Samuel 1872- *WhAm 5*
Macclintock, Samuel *see also* McClintock,
Samuel
MacClintock, William Darnall 1858-1936
NatCAB 11, WhAm 1
MacCloskey, James Edward, Jr. 1876-
WhAm 5
MacClure, Sir Robert John LeMesurier
1807-1873 *Drake*
MacClure, Sir Robert John LeMesurier *see also*
McClure, Sir R
MacColl, Alexander 1866- *WhAm 5*
MacColl, Evan 1808- *ApCAB*
MacColl, Evan *see also* McColl, Evan
MacColl, James Roberton 1856-1931
NatCAB 22, WhAm 1
MacColl, Mary Jemima 1847- *ApCAB*
MacColl, William Bogle 1886-1941 *WhAm 1*
MacColl, William Hamilton 1873-1937
WhAm 1
MacConnell, Charles Jenkins 1837-1909
WhAm 1
Macconnell, John L 1826- *Drake*
MacConnell, John Wilson 1878-1950 *WhAm 3*
MacCord, Charles William 1836-1915 *WhAm 1*
Maccord, David J 1797-1855 *Drake*
Maccord, David J *see also* McCord, David James
Maccord, Louisa S 1810- *Drake*
Maccord, Louisa S *see also* McCord, Louisa S
Cheves
MacCorkle, Emmett Wallace 1855-1938
WhAm 1
MacCorkle, William Alexander 1857-1930
NatCAB 12, TwCBDA, WhAm 1
MacCormack, Daniel William 1880-1937
NatCAB 28, WhAm 1
MacCornack, Walter Roy 1877-1961
NatCAB 45
MacCornack, Walter Roy 1879-1961 *WhAm 4*
MacCorry, P J 1868- *WhAm 4*
MacCoull, Kari P Gamble 1865-
WomWWA 14
MacCoun, Townsend 1845- *WhAm 4*
MacCoy, Alexander Watt 1847-1924
NatCAB 38
MacCoy, William Edward 1875-1944
NatCAB 33
MacCoy, William Logan 1885-1948 *WhAm 2*
MacCracken, Henry Mitchell 1840-1918
*ApCAB Sup, BiDAmEd, DcAmB,
NatCAB 6, TwCBDA, WhAm 1*
MacCracken, Henry Mitchell *see also*
McCracken, Henry Mitchell
MacCracken, Henry Noble 1880-1970
NatCAB 15, NatCAB 55, WhAm 5
MacCracken, John Henry 1875-1948
NatCAB 15, TwCBDA, WhAm 2
MacCracken, William Benjamin 1907-1960
NatCAB 48
MacCracken, William Patterson, Jr. 1888-1969
WhAm 5
MacCrate, John 1885- *BiDrAC*
Maccrea, Jane 1754-1777 *Drake*
Maccrea, Jane *see also* McCrea, Jane
MacCullagh, James 1809-1847 *DcScB*
Macculloch, John 1773-1835 *DcScB*
MacCullough, Gleason Harvey 1895-1956
WhAm 3
MacCurdy, George Grant 1863-1947
DcAmB S4, NatCAB 17, WhAm 2
MacCutcheon, Aleck 1881-1954 *WhAm 3*
MacDade, Albert Dutton 1871-1954
NatCAB 41
MacDaniel, Frank 1872-1932 *WhAm 1*
MacDaniel, Robert D 1895-1961 *WhAm 4*
MacDermott, Charles Thomas 1884-1953
NatCAB 41
Macdermott, William A 1845?- *NatCAB 11*
MacDill, David 1826-1903 *WhAm 1*

MacDill, David *see also* McDill, David
Macdonald, Albert James 1889-1924 *ApCAB X*
Macdonald, Alexander 1867- *WhAm 1*
Macdonald, Alexander Black 1861-1942
WhAm 2
Macdonald, Andrew Archibald 1829- *ApCAB*
Macdonald, Angus Lewis 1890-1954 *WhAm 3*
Macdonald, Angus Snead 1883-1961 *DcAmLiB*
Macdonald, Anna Addams 1871- *WhAm 5*
Macdonald, Annie Caroline *WomWWA 14*
Macdonald, Archibald Arnott 1876- *WhAm 5*
MacDonald, Arthur 1856-1936 *AmBi,
BiDAmEd, NatCAB 26, WhAm 1*
Macdonald, Arthur Jay 1861- *WhAm 4*
Macdonald, Augustin Sylvester 1865- *WhAm 5*
Macdonald, Austin Faulks 1898-1962
NatCAB 47
Macdonald, Belle Jeanne 1866- *WomWWA 14*
MacDonald, Bernard Callaghan 1897-1967
WhAm 4
Macdonald, Betty 1908-1958 *WhAm 3*
Macdonald, Byrnes 1908-1959 *WhAm 3*
Macdonald, Carlos Frederick 1845-1926
NatCAB 20, WhAm 1
Macdonald, Charles 1837-1928 *NatCAB 11,
NatCAB 42, WhAm 1*
Macdonald, Charles Blair 1856-1939
DcAmB S2
Macdonald, Chisholm Nicholson 1900-1952
NatCAB 42
MacDonald, Christie 1877-1962 *NatCAB 50*
Macdonald, Cordelia Howard *NotAW*
MacDonald, David James 1875-1959
NatCAB 45
Macdonald, Donald 1712-1784 *ApCAB*
Macdonald, Donald Alexander 1817- *ApCAB*
Macdonald, Duncan Black 1863-1943 *WhAm 2*
MacDonald, Edward 1844-1919 *ApCAB X*
MacDonald, Edwina Levin 1878- *WhAm 6*
MacDonald, Flora 1720-1790 *Drake*
MacDonald, Flora *see also* McDonald, Flora
MacDonald, George 1875-1961 *WhAm 4*
Macdonald, George Alexander 1869-1936
WhAm 1
Macdonald, George Everett 1857-1944 *WhAm 3*
Macdonald, George Saxe 1866-1945
NatCAB 34, WhAm 2
Macdonald, Godfrey 1899-1967 *WhAm 4*
Macdonald, Gordon 1856-1908 *WhAm 1*
MacDonald, Henry 1890-1956 *WhAm 3*
Macdonald, Herbert Stone 1842- *ApCAB*
MacDonald, Hugh 1827- *ApCAB*
Macdonald, Hugh 1893-1957 *NatCAB 43*
Macdonald, Hugh John 1850- *ApCAB Sup*
Macdonald, Ian 1903-1968 *WhAm 5*
Macdonald, Jacques Etienne J Alexandre
1765-1840 *WhoMilH*
Macdonald, James 1803-1849 *Drake*
Macdonald, James *see also* McDonald, James
Macdonald, James Allan d1929 *WhAm 1*
MacDonald, James Davis 1866-1925
NatCAB 20
MacDonald, James Edward Hervey 1873-1932
IlBEAAW
MacDonald, James Madison 1812-1876 *ApCAB,
Drake, TwCBDA*
MacDonald, James Ramsay 1866-1937
McGEWB
MacDonald, James Reliance 1903-1966
NatCAB 52, WhAm 4
MacDonald, James Williamson Galloway
1897-1960 *IlBEAAW*
MacDonald, James Wilson Alexander 1824-1908
*AmBi, ApCAB, DcAmB, NatCAB 25,
NewYHSD, WhAm HA, WhAm 4*
Macdonald, Jeanette 1907-1965 *WhAm 4*
Macdonald, Jesse Juan *WhAm 5*
Macdonald, John *NewYHSD*
Macdonald, John 1787-1860 *ApCAB*
Macdonald, John 1824- *ApCAB*
Macdonald, Sir John Alexander 1814-1891
Drake
Macdonald, Sir John Alexander 1815-1891
ApCAB, McGEWB
MacDonald, John Alexander 1879-1947
NatCAB 34, WhAm 2
MacDonald, John H 1881-1965 *WhAm 4*
MacDonald, John Lewis 1838-1903 *BiDrAC*

MacDonald, John Louis 1838-1903 *NatCAB 6,
TwCBDA*
Macdonald, John Sandfield 1812-1872 *ApCAB*
Macdonald, John William 1844-1913 *WhAm 1*
MacDonald, Katherine Cunningham d1973
WhAm 6
MacDonald, L W *IlBEAAW*
Macdonald, Lucy Maud Montgomery 1874-
WomWWA 14
MacDonald, Maie Tucker *WomWWA 14*
MacDonald, Margaret Baxter *WomWWA 14*
MacDonald, Margaret Chisholm 1878-
WomWWA 14
MacDonald, Marshall 1835-1895 *NatCAB 13*
Macdonald, Mary Bartlett 1850-
WomWWA 14
Macdonald, Mary Catharine VanV Hopkins
WomWWA 14
MacDonald, Milton Tenny 1895-1967 *WhAm 4*
MacDonald, Milton Theodore 1905-1973
WhAm 6
MacDonald, Moses 1814-1869 *ApCAB*
MacDonald, Moses 1815-1869 *BiAUS,
BiDrAC, WhAm H*
MacDonald, Moses *see also* McDonald, Moses
MacDonald, Muriel Irwin 1867- *WomWWA 14*
Macdonald, Neil Carnot 1876-1923 *WhAm 1*
MacDonald, Peter 1928- *REnAW*
MacDonald, Pirie 1867-1942 *WhAm 2*
MacDonald, Ranald 1824-1894 *DcAmB,
WhAm H*
Macdonald, Robert 1861- *WhAm 4*
MacDonald, Thomas Harris 1881-1957
WhAm 3
Macdonald, Torbert Hart 1917- *BiDrAC*
Macdonald, William 1863-1938 *TwCBDA,
WhAm 1*
MacDonald, William Alexander 1895-1961
WhAm 4
Macdonald, William H d1906 *WhAm 1*
Macdonald, William J 1874-1946 *WhAm 5*
MacDonald, William Josiah 1873-1946 *BiDrAC*
Macdonald, Willis Goss 1863-1910 *WhAm 1*
MacDonald-Wright, Stanton 1890-1973
BnEnAmA, WhAm 6
Macdonall, Angus 1876-1927 *WhAm 1*
Macdonall, Angus Peter 1875-1927 *NatCAB 21*
Macdonell, Alexander 1762-1840 *ApCAB*
Macdonell, Allan 1808- *ApCAB*
Macdonell, Miles 1767-1828 *ApCAB*
MacDonell, Tochie Williams 1861-
WomWWA 14
Macdonnell, Daniel James 1843- *ApCAB*
MacDonnell, James Francis Carlin 1881-
WhAm 6
Macdonnell, James Smellie 1877-1958
NatCAB 46
MacDonnell, Ronald Macalister 1909-1973
WhAm 6
Macdonough, Thomas 1783-1825 *AmBi,
ApCAB, DcAmB, Drake, NatCAB 7,
TwCBDA, WebAB, WebAMB, WhAm H*
MacDouall, Robert 1780?-1848 *ApCAB*
MacDougal, Daniel Trembly 1865-1958
NatCAB 13, WhAm 3
MacDougal, David D 1809-1882 *Drake*
MacDougal, David D *see also* McDougal, David
MacDougal, W H *NewYHSD*
MacDougald, Dan 1883-1953 *WhAm 3*
MacDougald, Daniel 1883-1953 *NatCAB 42*
MacDougall, A Edward 1896-1957 *NatCAB 46*
Macdougall, Alexander 1731-1786 *ApCAB,
NatCAB 1, TwCBDA*
Macdougall, Alexander *see also* McDougall,
Alexander
MacDougall, Alice Foote 1867- *WhAm 4*
MacDougall, Charles 1804-1885 *ApCAB*
MacDougall, Charles 1807?-1885 *TwCBDA*
MacDougall, Charlotte Sackett Stone 1873-
WomWWA 14
MacDougall, Clinton Dugald 1839-1914 *BiAUS,
BiDrAC, TwCBDA, WhAm 1*
MacDougall, Clinton Dugald *see also* McDougal,
Clinton Dugald
MacDougall, Edward Archibald 1874-1944
NatCAB 32, WhAm 4
Macdougall, Elizabeth *ApCAB*
MacDougall, Frank Henry 1883-1974 *WhAm 6*

Macdougall, Hamilton Crawford 1858-
WhAm 2
Macdougall, John Lorn 1838- *ApCAB*
Macdougall, Joseph Easton 1846- *ApCAB*
MacDougall, Sir Patrick Leonard 1819- *ApCAB*
MacDougall, Ranald 1915-1973 *WhAm 6*
MacDougall, Robert 1866-1939 *WhAm 1*
MacDougall, Robert Leak 1901-1960
NatCAB 50
Macdougall, William 1822- *ApCAB*
Macdougall, William *see also* McDougall,
William
MacDougall, William Dugald 1868-1943
WhAm 2
MacDowell, Charles Henry 1867-1954
ApCAB X, NatCAB 44, WhAm 3
MacDowell, Mrs. Edward 1857-1956 *WhAm 3*
MacDowell, Edward Alexander 1861-1908 *AmBi,
ApCAB X, DcAmB, EncAAH, EncAB,
McGEWB, NatCAB 11, TwCBDA,
WebAB, WhAm 1*
MacDowell, Katherine Sherwood Bonner
1849-1883 *DcAmB, WhAm H*
MacDowell, Katherine Sherwood Bonner *see also*
McDowell, K S B
MacDowell, Thain Wendell 1890-1960 *WhAm 4*
Macduff, R Bruce 1892-1951 *NatCAB 40*
MacDuffee, Cyrus Colton 1895-1961
NatCAB 49, WhAm 4
Macduffie, George 1788?-1851 *Drake*
Macduffie, George *see also* McDuffie, George
Macduffie, John 1861-1941 *WhAm 1*
Mace, A Wilbur 1882-1961 *NatCAB 50*
Mace, Daniel 1811-1867 *BiAUS, BiDrAC,
TwCBDA, WhAm H*
Mace, Frances Laughton 1836-1899 *AmWom,
ApCAB, NatCAB 10, WhAm 1*
Mace, Frank William 1906-1962 *WhAm 4*
Mace, Harold Loring 1907-1946 *WhAm 2*
Mace, William Harrison 1852-1938 *BiDAmEd,
NatCAB 4, TwCBDA, WhAm 1*
MacEachern, Bernard Angus 1780?-1835
ApCAB
MacEachern, Malcolm T 1881-1956 *WhAm 3*
Macedo, Joaquim Manoel De 1820- *ApCAB*
Macedo, Sergio Teixeira De 1809-1865 *ApCAB*
Macedo Soares, Jose Carlos 1883-1968
WhAm 5
Macellama *DcScB*
MacElree, Wilmer W 1859- *WhAm 4*
MacElroy, Andrew Jackson 1875-1963
WhAm 4, WhAm 5
Macelwane, Geraldine Frances 1909-1974
WhAm 6
Macelwane, James B 1883-1956 *WhAm 3*
Macelwane, John Patrick 1896-1970 *WhAm 5*
MacElwee, Roy Samuel 1883-1944 *NatCAB 45,
WhAm 2*
Macenulty, John Forrest 1880- *WhAm 6*
Maceo, Antonio 1845-1896 *McGEWB*
Maceo, Antonio 1848-1896 *ApCAB Sup*
Maceo, Jose 1846-1896 *ApCAB Sup*
MacEuen, Mary Carnell 1865- *WomWWA 14*
MacEvoy, Clifford Frank 1886-1960
NatCAB 49
MacEwen, Ewen Murchison 1885-1947
NatCAB 35, WhAm 2
MacEwen, Walter 1860-1943 *NatCAB 15,
WhAm 2*
Macfadden, Bernarr 1868-1955 *DcAmB S5,
NatCAB 45, WebAB, WhAm 3*
MacFadyen, Alexander 1879-1936 *WhAm 1*
Macfarlan, Will C 1870-1945 *WhAm 2*
Macfarland, Charles Stedman 1866-1956
NatCAB 52, WhAm 3
MacFarland, Erwin Golly 1885-1937
NatCAB 28
MacFarland, Finlay Leroy 1862-1937 *WhAm 1*
MacFarland, Frank Mace 1869-1951 *WhAm 3*
MacFarland, Hays 1890-1975 *WhAm 6*
Macfarland, Henry Brown Floyd 1861-1921
NatCAB 19, WhAm 1
Macfarland, Horace Greeley 1872-1915
NatCAB 17
Macfarland, Lanning 1898-1971 *WhAm 5*
Macfarland, Mary Perley 1875- *WomWWA 14*
MacFarland, Robert *NewYHSD*
MacFarland, Robert Alfred d1960 *WhAm 3A*

MacFarland, William H 1799-1872 *BiDConf*
Macfarlane, Alexander 1818- *ApCAB*
Macfarlane, Alexander 1851- *TwCBDA,
WhAm 4*
Macfarlane, Alice O'Rear 1842- *WomWWA 14*
Macfarlane, Catharine 1877-1969 *WhAm 5*
Macfarlane, Charles William 1850-1931 *AmBi,
DcAmB, NatCAB 22, WhAm 5*
MacFarlane, David Laing 1893-1953 *WhAm 3*
Macfarlane, George Walter 1847- *NatCAB 12*
Macfarlane, Howard Pettingill 1888- *WhAm 5*
Macfarlane, Hugh Campbell 1851- *NatCAB 11*
MacFarlane, J Hutton 1887-1954 *NatCAB 41*
MacFarlane, James 1873- *WhAm 6*
Macfarlane, James Rieman 1858-1938
NatCAB 30
Macfarlane, John C 1889-1954 *WhAm 3*
Macfarlane, John Muirhead 1855- *WhAm 4*
MacFarlane, Joseph Arthur 1893-1966
WhAm 4
MacFarlane, Peter 1884-1958 *WhAm 3*
Macfarlane, Peter Clark 1871-1924 *WhAm 1*
Macfarlane, Robert 1815-1883 *ApCAB,
DcAmB, WhAm H*
Macfarlane, Robert Forgie 1842-1930
ApCAB X
Macfarlane, W E d1944 *WhAm 2*
MacFarlane, Warren Courtland 1883-1965
NatCAB 52
Macfarlane, Will C 1870- *NatCAB 15*
MacFarlane, William d1974 *WhAm 6*
MacFarren, John *NewYHSD*
Macfee, Anna Maria *WomWWA 14*
Macfee, Janet Donalda *WomWWA 14*
Macfeely, Robert 1820-1901 *TwCBDA*
Macfeely, Robert 1828?-1901 *ApCAB,
WhAm 1*
Macferron, David 1817- *NatCAB 7*
MacGahan, Barbara 1852-1904 *AmWom,
WhAm 1*
MacGahan, Janarius Aloysius 1844-1878
NatCAB 6
MacGahan, Januarius Alousius 1844-1878
WhAm H
MacGahan, Januarius Aloysius 1844-1878 *AmBi,
ApCAB, DcAmB, TwCBDA*
Macgeorge, Robert Jackson 1811- *ApCAB*
MacGill, Helen Gregory *WomWWA 14*
MacGillivray, Alexander 1740?-1793 *Drake*
MacGillivray, Alexander *see also* McGillivray,
Alexander
MacGillivray, Alexander Dyer 1868-1924
WhAm 1
MacGillivray, William *WhAm H*
MacGilvary, Norwood 1874-1949 *WhAm 2*
MacGilvary, Paton 1896-1921 *WhAm 1*
MacGinley, John Bernard 1871- *WhAm 5*
MacGinniss, John 1867-1936 *WhAm 1*
MacGlashan, David Pollock 1914- *WhAm 6*
MacGowan, Alice 1858- *WhAm 4,
WomWWA 14*
Macgowan, David Bell 1870- *WhAm 5*
MacGowan, Edward *NewYHSD*
MacGowan, Gault 1894-1970 *WhAm 5*
MacGowan, Granville 1857-1935 *ApCAB X,
WhAm 1*
MacGowan, John Encil 1831-1903 *NatCAB 1,
WhAm 1*
MacGowan, John Kee 1878-1942 *WhAm 2*
Macgowan, Kenneth 1888-1963 *WhAm 4*
MacGrath, Harold 1871-1932 *NatCAB 14,
WhAm 1*
MacGreggor, David 1710-1777 *ApCAB*
MacGreggor, David *see also* McGregor, David
MacGreggor, James 1677-1729 *ApCAB*
MacGregor, Alma Follansbee 1879-
WomWWA 14
MacGregor, Charles Peter 1871- *WhAm 5*
MacGregor, Clarence 1872-1952 *BiDrAC,
NatCAB 44, WhAm 3, WhAmP*
MacGregor, Clark 1922- *BiDrAC*
Macgregor, David Hutchison 1877-1953
WhAm 3, WhAm 5
MacGregor, Fanny 1863- *WomWWA 14*
MacGregor, Frank Silver 1897-1971 *WhAm 5*
MacGregor, Henry Frederick 1855-1923
WhAm 1
MacGregor, John 1797-1857 *ApCAB, Drake*

MacGregor, John 1873-1933 *NatCAB 27*
MacGregor, Mary Esther Miller *WomWWA 14*
MacGregor, Theodore Douglas 1879- *WhAm 6*
MacGregor, Wallace Forrest 1874-1939
NatCAB 47
MacGuffie, Robert Nichol 1888-1949
NatCAB 37
Mach, Ernst 1838-1916 *AsBiEn, DcScB,
McGEWB*
Machado DeAssis, Joaquim Maria 1839-1908
McGEWB
Machado Y Morales, Gerardo 1871-1939
McGEWB
Machar, Agnes Maule *WomWWA 14*
MacHarg, John Brainerd 1873-1954 *WhAm 3*
MacHarg, William 1872-1951 *WhAm 3*
Machaut, Guillaume De 1300?-1377 *McGEWB*
Machebeuf, Joseph Projectus 1812-1889 *AmBi,
DcAmB, TwCBDA, WhAm H*
Macheboeuf, Joseph Projectus 1812-1889
ApCAB, NatCAB 12
Macheboeuf, Michel 1900-1953 *DcScB*
Machen, Arthur Webster 1877-1950 *WhAm 3*
Machen, Hervey Gilbert 1916- *BiDrAC*
Machen, John Gresham 1881-1937 *DcAmB S2,
DcAmReB, WebAB, WhAm 1*
Machen, Willis Benson 1810-1893 *ApCAB,
BiAUS, BiDConf, BiDrAC, NatCAB 12,
TwCBDA, WhAm H*
Machiavelli, Niccolo 1469-1527 *McGEWB*
Machin, Thomas 1744-1816 *ApCAB*
Machin, Thomas 1796-1875 *ApCAB*
Machir, James d1827 *BiAUS, BiDrAC,
WhAm H*
Machlett, Raymond R 1900-1955 *WhAm 3*
Machlett, Robert Herman 1872-1926
NatCAB 30
Machmer, William Lawson 1883-1953 *WhAm 3*
Machold, Earle John 1903-1973 *WhAm 6*
Machold, Henry Edmund 1880-1967 *WhAm 4*
Machray, Robert 1832- *ApCAB*
Machrowicz, Thaddeus Michael 1899-1970
BiDrAC, WhAm 5
Maciejewski, Anton Frank 1893-1949 *BiDrAC,
WhAm 3*
Macilvaine, Charles Pettit 1798-1873 *Drake*
Macilvaine, Charles Pettit *see also* McIlvaine,
Charles Pettit
MacIlvaine, Francis Shippen 1884-1967
NatCAB 53
MacInnes, Donald 1824- *ApCAB*
MacInnes, Duncan Arthur 1885-1965 *WhAm 4*
MacInnis, John Murdoch 1871-1940 *WhAm 1*
Macintosh, Douglas Clyde 1877-1948
DcAmB S4, DcAmReB, WhAm 2
MacIntosh, John Alexander 1868-1927
WhAm 1
Macintyre, Angus Dugald 1877-1948
NatCAB 37
Macintyre, Archibald James 1908-1969
WhAm 5
MacIntyre, Archibald Thompson 1822-1900
BiDrAC
MacIntyre, Archibald Thompson *see also*
McIntyre, Archibald T
MacIntyre, Burnett Clinton 1848-1927
NatCAB 22
MacIntyre, Edward Campbell 1882-1947
NatCAB 36
Macintyre, Sheila Scott 1910-1960 *NatCAB 48*
Macintyre, William Arthur 1881- *WhoColR*
Maciora, Lucien John 1902- *BiDrAC*
MacIsaac, Fred 1886-1940 *WhAm 1*
MacIver, Robert Morrison 1882-1970 *McGEWB,
WebAB, WhAm 5*
MacIvor, John William 1878- *WhAm 6*
Mack, Mister *NewYHSD*
Mack, A B 1884-1954 *WhAm 3*
Mack, Andrew 1863-1931 *WhAm 1*
Mack, Anna DeWolf 1869- *WomWWA 14*
Mack, Augustus Frederick 1873-1940
NatCAB 31
Mack, Augustus Frederick, Jr. 1907-1967
WhAm 4
Mack, Carl Theodore 1896-1971 *WhAm 5*
Mack, Clifford Wilmot 1884-1948 *NatCAB 37*
Mack, Connie 1862-1956 *WebAB, WhAm 3*
Mack, Ebenezer *NewYHSD*

Mack, Edgar M 1877- *WhAm 2*
Mack, Edward 1868-1951 *NatCAB 43,*
WhAm 3
Mack, Edward, Jr. 1893-1956 *NatCAB 43*
Mack, Edward Lawrence 1890-1952
NatCAB 41
Mack, Edwin S 1869-1942 *WhAm 2*
Mack, Elisha Hutchinson 1858-1952
NatCAB 39
Mack, Flora Alice Davenport 1849-
WomWWA 14
Mack, George Herbert 1874- *WhAm 5*
Mack, Harry Claude 1875-1968 *NatCAB 54*
Mack, Harvey Flemming 1878-1956
NatCAB 44
Mack, Henry Whitcomb 1903-1964 *WhAm 4*
Mack, Howard 1907-1967 *WhAm 4*
Mack, Isaac Foster 1837-1912 *WhAm 1*
Mack, J S 1914-1968 *WhAm 5*
Mack, John E 1874-1958 *WhAm 3*
Mack, John Givan Davis 1867-1924 *WhAm 1*
Mack, John M 1852-1915 *WhAm 1*
Mack, John Martin 1715-1784 *ApCAB,*
NatCAB 11
Mack, John Sephus 1880-1940 *WhAm 1*
Mack, John Talman 1846-1914 *NatCAB 43*
Mack, Joseph Sanford 1870-1953 *NatCAB 41*
Mack, Julian Ellis 1903-1966 *NatCAB 51,*
WhAm 4
Mack, Julian William 1866-1943 *DcAmB S3,*
NatCAB 32, WhAm 2
Mack, Karl Freiherr VonLeiberich 1752-1828
WhoMilH
Mack, Leal 1892-1962 *IIBEAAW*
Mack, Mabel Waller *WomWWA 14*
Mack, Norman Edward 1855-1932 *NatCAB 4*
Mack, Norman Edward 1858-1932 *WhAm 1*
Mack, Norman Eugene 1858-1932 *NatCAB 26*
Mack, Pauline Beery 1891-1974 *WhAm 6*
Mack, Peter Francis, Jr. 1916- *BiDrAC*
Mack, Rebecca Robins 1879- *WomWWA 14*
Mack, Richard Alfred 1909-1963 *WhAm 4*
Mack, Russell Vernon 1891-1960 *BiDrAC,*
WhAm 3, WhAmP
Mack, Warren Bryan 1896-1952 *WhAm 3*
Mack, William 1865-1941 *NatCAB 35,*
WhAm 2
Mackall, Lawton 1888-1968 *WhAm 5*
Mackall, Leonard Leopold 1879-1937 *WhAm 1*
Mackall, Louis 1831-1906 *NatCAB 20*
Mackall, Louis, Jr. 1867-1930 *NatCAB 22,*
WhAm 1
Mackall, Paul 1886-1954 *NatCAB 43,*
WhAm 3
Mackall, William Whann 1817-1871
NatCAB 11
Mackall, William Whann 1817-1891 *BiDConf*
Mackall, William Whann 1818-1891 *ApCAB,*
TwCBDA
Mackau, Ange Rene Armand, Baron De
1788-1855 *ApCAB*
Mackauer, Christian Wilhelm 1897-1970
NatCAB 55
Mackay, Albert Edward 1863-1952 *NatCAB 42*
Mackay, Alexander 1808-1849 *ApCAB*
Mackay, Charles 1814- *ApCAB*
Mackay, Clarence Hungerford 1874-1938 *AmBi,*
DcAmB S2, NatCAB 14, NatCAB 31,
WebAB, WhAm 1
Mackay, Constance D'Arcy d1966 *WhAm 4,*
WomWWA 14
Mackay, Donald 1840-1912 *NatCAB 16*
MacKay, Donald Dundas 1862- *WhAm 4*
Mackay, Donald Sage 1863-1908 *NatCAB 12,*
WhAm 1
Mackay, Frank Findley 1832-1923 *NatCAB 17*
Mackay, G M Johnstone 1883-1938 *NatCAB 28*
Mackay, George Devereux 1854- *NatCAB 14*
Mackay, Helen 1876-1966 *WhAm 4,*
WhAm 5
MacKay, Henry Squarebriggs, Jr. 1891-1954
WhAm 3
Mackay, Isabel Ecclestone 1875-
WomWWA 14
Mackay, James 1759?-1822 *DcAmB,*
WhAm H
Mackay, John Keiller 1888-1970 *WhAm 5*
Mackay, John William 1831-1902 *AmBi,*

ApCAB, DcAmB, McGEWB, NatCAB 4,
REnAW, TwCBDA, WhAm 1
Mackay, Katherine Alexander Duer 1878-
WomWWA 14
MacKay, Katherine Joanna *WomWWA 14*
Mackay, Malcolm Sutherland 1881-1932
NatCAB 25
Mackay, Margaret 1907-1968 *WhAm 5*
Mackay, Robert 1816-1888 *ApCAB*
Mackay, Robert 1871- *WhAm 5*
Mackay, Roland Parks 1900-1968 *NatCAB 54,*
WhAm 4
MacKay, Simon 1869-1956 *NatCAB 45*
Mackay, Stanley French 1888-1956 *NatCAB 44*
Mackay, William Andrew 1876-1939 *WhAm 1*
Mackay, William Eshorne 1865-1935
NatCAB 35, WhAm 1
Mackay Of Scourie, Hugh 1640-1692 *WhoMilH*
Mackay-Smith, Alexander 1850-1911 *ApCAB,*
TwCBDA, WhAm 1
Mackaye, Arthur Loring 1863- *WhAm 4*
MacKaye, Benton 1879- *WebAB, WhAm 6*
Mackaye, Harold Steele 1866-1928 *WhAm 1*
MacKaye, James 1872-1935 *NatCAB 14,*
WhAm 1
MacKaye, James Morrison Steele 1842-1894
DcAmB, WebAB, WhAm H
Mackaye, James Steele 1844-1894 *TwCBDA*
MacKaye, Percy 1875-1956 *ApCAB X,*
NatCAB 14, WhAm 3
MacKaye, Steele 1842-1894 *AmBi, DcAmB,*
NatCAB 14, WebAB
MacKeachie, Douglas Cornell 1900-1943
WhAm 2
MacKechnie, Hugh Neil 1874-1962 *NatCAB 50,*
WhAm 4
MacKee, George Miller 1878-1955 *NatCAB 48,*
WhAm 3
Mackeever, Isaac 1793-1856 *Drake*
Mackeever, Isaac *see also* McKeever, Isaac
MacKeever, John Charles 1885-1956
NatCAB 46, WhAm 3
Mackellar, Gertrude Elizabeth *WomWWA 14*
MacKellar, James 1864-1918 *NatCAB 17*
Mackellar, Patrick 1717-1778 *DcAmB,*
WhAm H
MacKellar, Thomas 1812-1899 *AmBi, ApCAB,*
DcAmB, Drake, NatCAB 3, TwCBDA,
WhAm H, WhAm 4
Mackellar, William Henry Howard 1863-1946
WhAm 2
MacKelvie, Neil Bruce 1879-1918 *ApCAB X*
Macken, Walter 1915-1967 *WhAm 4*
Mackenna, Juan 1771-1814 *ApCAB*
MacKenna, Kenneth 1899-1962 *NatCAB 48*
Mackensen, August Von 1849-1944 *WhoMilH*
Mackensen, Eberhard Von 1889- *WhoMilH*
MacKenty, John Edmund 1869-1931
NatCAB 23
Mackenzie, Alastair St. Clair 1875- *WhAm 5*
Mackenzie, Sir Alexander d1820 *Drake*
Mackenzie, Sir Alexander 1755?-1820 *ApCAB*
Mackenzie, Sir Alexander 1764?-1820
McGEWB
Mackenzie, Alexander 1822-1892 *ApCAB,*
McGEWB
Mackenzie, Alexander 1844-1921 *NatCAB 14,*
WhAm 1
MacKenzie, Alexander Cameron 1850-1915
NatCAB 17, WhAm 1
Mackenzie, Alexander Slidell 1803-1848 *AmBi,*
ApCAB, DcAmB, Drake, NatCAB 4,
TwCBDA, WebAMB, WhAm H
Mackenzie, Alexander Slidell 1842-1867
ApCAB, TwCBDA
MacKenzie, Angus Howard 1865-1937
NatCAB 31
Mackenzie, Arthur 1869- *WhAm 5*
MacKenzie, Arthur Stanley 1865- *WhAm 4*
MacKenzie, Augus Gilvary 1849-1917
NatCAB 18
Mackenzie, Cameron 1882-1921 *WhAm 1*
Mackenzie, Charles Kenneth 1788-1862 *ApCAB,*
Drake
Mackenzie, Donald 1783-1851 *ApCAB,*
DcAmB, REnAW, WhAm H
Mackenzie, Donald 1882-1941 *WhAm 2*
Mackenzie, Donald Hector 1901-1955 *WhAm 3*

MacKenzie, E *NewYHSD*
Mackenzie, Frank Simmons 1845-1920
NatCAB 20
MacKenzie, Frederick William 1883-1928
WhAm 1
Mackenzie, George Henry 1837-1891 *ApCAB,*
DcAmB, NatCAB 4, WhAm H
Mackenzie, Hettie 1810?-1845 *ApCAB*
MacKenzie, Ian 1903-1953 *NatCAB 41*
Mackenzie, J Gazzam 1870-1931 *WhAm 5*
Mackenzie, Sir James 1853-1925 *BiHiMed*
MacKenzie, James A 1840-1904 *TwCBDA*
MacKenzie, James A *see also* McKenzie, James
Andrew
Mackenzie, James Cameron 1852-1931
BiDAmEd, DcAmB, NatCAB 14,
NatCAB 43, TwCBDA, WhAm 1
Mackenzie, James Cameron 1887-1963
NatCAB 56
MacKenzie, James Henry 1881-1956
NatCAB 43
Mackenzie, Jean Kenyon 1874-1936
NatCAB 28, NotAW, WhAm 1
MacKenzie, John Douglas 1897-1973 *WhAm 6*
Mackenzie, John Joseph 1865-1922 *NatCAB 19*
Mackenzie, John Noland 1853-1925
ApCAB Sup, DcAmB, NatCAB 25,
WhAm 1
Mackenzie, Joseph Gazzam 1870-1931
NatCAB 23
Mackenzie, Joseph William 1882-1944
NatCAB 33
Mackenzie, Kenneth 1797-1861 *AmBi, DcAmB,*
REnAW, WhAm H
Mackenzie, Kenneth 1804-1883 *ApCAB*
Mackenzie, Kenneth Alexander J 1859-1920
WhAm 1
Mackenzie, Kenneth Gerard 1887-1967
WhAm 5
Mackenzie, Mary Elizabeth Forwood
WomWWA 14
Mackenzie, Sir Morell 1837-1892 *BiHiMed*
Mackenzie, Morris Robinson Slidell d1915
WhAm 1
Mackenzie, Murdo 1850-1939 *DcAmB S2,*
WhAm 1
Mackenzie, Philip Edward 1872-1946 *WhAm 2*
Mackenzie, Ranald Slidell 1840-1889 *AmBi,*
ApCAB, DcAmB, Drake, NatCAB 12,
REnAW, TwCBDA, WebAB, WebAMB,
WhAm H
MacKenzie, Robert 1845-1925 *NatCAB 14,*
WhAm 1
Mackenzie, Robert Shelton 1809-1880 *ApCAB,*
Drake, TwCBDA
Mackenzie, Robert Shelton 1809-1881 *DcAmB,*
WhAm H
Mackenzie, Roderick Dempster 1865- *WhAm 1*
Mackenzie, Tandy 1892-1963 *WhAm 4*
Mackenzie, Thomas Hanna 1867-1942 *WhAm 2*
Mackenzie, William 1758-1828 *ApCAB,*
DcAmB, WhAm H
Mackenzie, William Adams 1870-1943
WhAm 2
Mackenzie, William Douglas 1859-1936
WhAm 1
Mackenzie, William Lyon 1795-1861 *ApCAB,*
Drake, McGEWB
MacKenzie, William Ross 1885-1960 *WhAm 3*
Mackenzie, William Roy 1883-1957 *WhAm 3*
Mackeown, Samuel Stuart 1895-1952
NatCAB 42, WhAm 3
Mackerrow, Horace Gilford 1879- *WhoColR*
Mackey, Absalom Weever 1869-1925
NatCAB 23
Mackey, Albert Gallatin 1807-1881 *ApCAB,*
DcAmB, Drake, TwCBDA, WhAm H
Mackey, Ansel Elliott 1836- *NatCAB 2*
Mackey, Charles Osborn 1903-1965 *WhAm 4*
Mackey, Charles William 1842-1917 *NatCAB 7,*
NatCAB 40, WhAm 1
Mackey, Cyrus Fay 1872-1940 *NatCAB 37*
Mackey, David Ray 1917-1975 *WhAm 6*
Mackey, Edmund William McGregor 1846-1884
BiAUS, BiDrAC, WhAm H
Mackey, Edward W M 1846-1884 *TwCBDA*
Mackey, Eugene Joseph 1911-1968 *NatCAB 55*
Mackey, Harry A 1873-1938 *WhAm 1*

Mackey, James *NewYHSD*
Mackey, James, Jr. *NewYHSD*
Mackey, John 1765-1831 *ApCAB*
Mackey, Joseph 1822-1879 *NatCAB 25*
Mackey, Joseph T 1879-1961 *WhAm 4*
Mackey, L A 1819-1889 *BiAUS*
Mackey, Levi Augustus 1819-1889 *BiDrAC, TwCBDA, WhAm H*
Mackey, Maryette Goodwin 1865- *WomWWA 14*
Mackey, Matthew *NewYHSD*
Mackey, Russell Anderson 1889-1964 *NatCAB 54*
Mackey, William *NewYHSD*
Mackey, William Fleming 1858- *WhAm 4*
Mackie, Alexander 1885-1966 *NatCAB 51, WhAm 4*
Mackie, David Ives 1903-1966 *NatCAB 51, WhAm 4*
Mackie, Ernest Lloyd 1893-1972 *WhAm 5*
Mackie, George Goodwin 1909-1956 *NatCAB 47*
Mackie, John C 1920- *BiDrAC*
Mackie, John Milton 1813-1894 *ApCAB, Drake, NatCAB 12, TwCBDA*
Mackie, Joseph Bolton Cooper 1882-1942 *WhAm 2*
Mackie, Josias d1716 *ApCAB*
Mackie, Laura V Gustin 1852- *WomWWA 14*
Mackie, Matthew *NewYHSD*
Mackie, Pauline Bradford 1874- *WhAm 5*
Mackie, Thomas Turlay 1895-1955 *WhAm 3*
Mackie, William Arthur 1851-1921 *NatCAB 6*
Mackimmie, A Anderson 1878-1950 *NatCAB 39*
Mackin, Joseph Hoover 1906-1968 *WhAm 5*
MacKinney, Loren Carey 1891-1963 *WhAm 4*
MacKinnie, Adelaide Orff *WomWWA 14*
Mackinnon, Allan P 1880- *WhAm 1*
MacKinnon, Eugene 1898-1951 *WhAm 3*
MacKinnon, George Edward 1906- *BiDrAC*
MacKinnon, George Valentine 1882-1939 *NatCAB 29, WhAm 1*
MacKinnon, Harold Alexander 1902-1972 *WhAm 5*
MacKinnon, James Angus 1881-1958 *WhAm 3*
MacKinnon, John Charles 1907-1973 *NatCAB 57, WhAm 6*
MacKinnon, Lee Warner 1878-1935 *WhAm 1*
Mackintire, George Winthrop 1855-1946 *NatCAB 36*
Mackintosh, Alexander 1861-1945 *WhAm 2*
Mackintosh, Charles Herbert 1843- *ApCAB*
Mackintosh, George Lewes 1860-1932 *NatCAB 23*
Mackintosh, George Lewis 1860-1932 *WhAm 1*
Mackintosh, Harold Vincent 1891-1964 *WhAm 4*
Mackintosh, Hugh 1907-1974 *WhAm 6*
Mackintosh, Kenneth 1875- *WhAm 5*
MacKintosh, Peter Grant 1888-1965 *NatCAB 54*
Mackintosh, Miss S B *NewYHSD*
Mackintosh, William Archibald 1895-1970 *WhAm 5*
Macklanburg, Louis August 1888-1965 *NatCAB 51*
Macklem, Heloise 1879- *WomWWA 14*
Macklin, James Edgar 1846-1925 *WhAm 1*
Macklin, John Farrell 1883-1949 *NatCAB 40*
Macklin, Justin Wilford d1963 *WhAm 4*
Macklin, W A Stewart 1897-1957 *WhAm 3*
Macklow, J *NewYHSD*
MacKnight, Dodge 1860- *WhAm 3*
Macksey, Kenneth William 1894-1958 *NatCAB 45*
Mackubin, Florence 1861-1918 *DcAmB, NatCAB 15, WhAm 1, WomWWA 14*
MacKusick, Mary Alcott 1865- *WomWWA 14*
Mackwitz, William 1831-1919 *NewYHSD*
Macky, Eric Spencer 1880-1958 *WhAm 3*
Maclachan, David Cathcart 1869- *WhAm 1*
MacLachlan, Daniel A 1852-1938 *WhAm 1*
MacLachlan, James Angell 1891-1967 *NatCAB 53*
Maclachlan, John Miller 1905-1959 *NatCAB 48, WhAm 3*
MacLachlan, Lachlan 1874- *WhAm 1*

MacLachlan, Margery Jean 1900-1963 *WhAm 4*
MacLafferty, James Henry 1871-1937 *BiDrAC, WhAm 1*
Maclanahan, James X 1809-1864? *BiAUS*
Maclanahan, James X *see also* McLanahan, James Xavier
MacLane, Gerald Robinson 1919-1972 *WhAm 5*
MacLane, Jean 1878-1964 *NatCAB 52*
MacLane, M Jean 1878-1964 *WhAm 4*
MacLane, Mary 1881-1929 *WhAm 2*
MacLane, Mary 1883-1929 *WhAm 1*
MacLaren, Archibald 1858-1924 *NatCAB 20, WhAm 1*
MacLaren, Archibald Waters 1879-1950 *NatCAB 39*
Maclaren, John James 1842- *ApCAB*
MacLaren, Katherine Dean 1868- *WomWWA 14*
MacLaren, Malcolm 1869-1945 *WhAm 2*
MacLauchlan, James Angell 1891-1967 *WhAm 4*
Maclaurin, Colin 1698-1746 *DcScB*
Maclaurin, Richard Cockburn 1870-1920 *DcAmB, NatCAB 14, WhAm 1*
Maclaurin, William Rupert 1907-1959 *WhAm 3*
Maclay, Archibald 1776-1860 *ApCAB, TwCBDA*
Maclay, Arthur Collins 1853-1930 *NatCAB 25*
Maclay, Edgar Stanton 1863-1919 *DcAmB, NatCAB 10, TwCBDA, WhAm 4*
Maclay, Isaac Walker 1841-1909 *WhAm 1*
Maclay, James 1864-1919 *WhAm 1*
Maclay, Otis Hardy 1873-1936 *NatCAB 28, WhAm 1*
Maclay, Robert 1834- *NatCAB 4*
Maclay, Robert Samuel 1824-1907 *DcAmB, TwCBDA, WhAm 1*
Maclay, Samuel 1741-1811 *ApCAB, BiAUS, BiDrAC, DcAmB, NatCAB 12, TwCBDA, WhAm H, WhAmP*
Maclay, William d1804 *BiAUS*
Maclay, William 1734-1804 *AmBi, DcAmB, WhAm H*
Maclay, William 1737-1804 *ApCAB, BiDrAC, NatCAB 5, TwCBDA, WhAmP*
Maclay, William 1765-1825 *BiAUS, BiDrAC, TwCBDA, WhAm H*
Maclay, William Brown 1812-1882 *ApCAB, BiDrAC, DcAmB, NatCAB 13, TwCBDA, WhAm H, WhAmP*
Maclay, William Brown 1815-1882 *BiAUS*
Maclay, William Plunkett 1774-1842 *ApCAB, BiAUS, BiDrAC, TwCBDA, WhAm H, WhAmP*
Maclay, William Walter 1846- *ApCAB, NatCAB 13, WhAm 3*
MacLean, Adelaine Lockwood 1866- *WomWWA 14*
Maclean, Alexander Tweedie 1887-1950 *NatCAB 38, WhAm 3*
MacLean, Sir Allan 1725?-1784 *ApCAB, Drake*
MacLean, Angus Dhu 1877-1937 *WhAm 1*
MacLean, Annie Marion d1934 *WhAm 1, WomWWA 14*
MacLean, Arthur Winfield 1880-1943 *NatCAB 31, WhAm 2*
MacLean, Basil Clarendon 1895-1963 *WhAm 4*
Maclean, Charles Fraser d1924 *WhAm 1*
MacLean, Charles Thomas Agnew 1880-1928 *WhAm 1*
MacLean, Clara Victoria Dargan 1841- *ApCAB Sup, NatCAB 7, WhAm 4*
Maclean, Daniel 1843- *WhAm 4*
MacLean, Donald 1839-1903 *NatCAB 5*
Maclean, Eda W 1860- *WomWWA 14*
Maclean, Fitzroy 1911- *WhWW-II*
MacLean, Francis 1727?-1781 *ApCAB*
Maclean, George 1801-1847 *McGEWB*
MacLean, George Edwin 1850-1938 *ApCAB Sup, DcAmB S2, NatCAB 8, TwCBDA, WhAm 1*
MacLean, George Everett 1900-1957 *NatCAB 47*
MacLean, Henry Coit 1881-1968 *WhAm 4*
MacLean, Iona M 1873- *WomWWA 14*

MacLean, James Alexander 1868-1945 *TwCBDA, WhAm 2*
Maclean, John 1771-1814 *ApCAB, BiDAmEd, DcAmB, DcScB, Drake, TwCBDA, WhAm H*
Maclean, John 1800-1886 *ApCAB, BiDAmEd, DcAmB, NatCAB 5, TwCBDA, WhAm H*
Maclean, John Norman 1862-1941 *WhAm 2*
MacLean, Malcolm Shaw, Jr. 1920-1974 *WhAm 6*
MacLean, Munroe Deacon 1907-1969 *WhAm 5*
MacLean, Paul Robert 1902-1971 *WhAm 5*
MacLean, Ray Butts 1873-1947 *WhAm 2*
MacLean, Richard Earle 1864-1920 *NatCAB 40*
Maclean, Samuel Richter 1842- *WhAm 4*
Maclean, Stuart 1872- *WhAm 5*
MacLean, William Swan 1842- *NatCAB 11*
MacLear, Anne Bush d1938 *WhAm 1*
Maclear, Thomas 1794-1879 *DcScB*
MacLeary, Bonnie *WhAm 6*
Macleay, Donald 1834-1897 *NatCAB 17*
Macleay, Lachlan 1879-1952 *NatCAB 41*
MacLeish, Andrew 1838-1928 *NatCAB 13, NatCAB 24, WhAm 1*
MacLeish, Archibald 1892- *McGEWB, WebAB*
MacLeish, Bruce 1882-1973 *WhAm 6*
MacLeish, John E 1879- *WhAm 5*
MacLeish, Martha Hillard 1856-1947 *NotAW, WomWWA 14*
MacLellan, Isaac, Jr. 1810-1899 *Drake*
MacLellan, Isaac, Jr. *see also* McLellan, Isaac
Maclellan, Kenneth F d1971 *WhAm 5*
Maclellan, Robert Jardine 1874-1956 *NatCAB 44, WhAm 3*
Maclellan, Robert Llewellyn 1906-1971 *WhAm 5*
Maclennan, Francis 1879-1935 *WhAm 1*
Maclennan, Francis William 1876-1947 *NatCAB 33, WhAm 2*
MacLennan, Frank Pitts 1855-1933 *NatCAB 11, WhAm 1*
MacLennan, Hugh 1907- *McGEWB*
MacLennan, Simon Fraser 1870- *WhAm 5*
MacLeod, Bruce Hamilton 1913-1966 *WhAm 4*
MacLeod, Clair Whitman 1909-1968 *NatCAB 57*
MacLeod, Colin Munro 1909-1972 *WhAm 5*
MacLeod, Della Campbell *WomWWA 14*
MacLeod, Donald 1821-1865 *NatCAB 5*
MacLeod, Donald Campbell 1868-1942 *WhAm 2*
Macleod, Elizabeth S 1848- *WomWWA 14*
MacLeod, Frank Norman 1866-1933 *NatCAB 35*
Macleod, Frederick Joseph 1870-1935 *WhAm 1*
MacLeod, Grace 1878-1962 *NatCAB 50*
Macleod, Iain Norman 1913-1970 *WhAm 5*
Macleod, John James Rickard 1876-1935 *DcScB, WhAm 1*
MacLeod, Malcolm James 1865-1940 *NatCAB 30, WhAm 1*
MacLeod, Norman Douglas 1891-1963 *NatCAB 52*
MacLeod, Pegi Nicol 1904-1949 *IIBEAAW*
Macleod, Robert Brodie 1907-1972 *WhAm 5*
Macleod, William Alexander 1856-1913 *NatCAB 30*
Macleod, Xavier Donald 1821-1865 *Drake*
Macleod, Xavier Donald *see also* McLeod, Xavier Donald
MacLeod-Thorp, Mrs. L E G d1944 *WhAm 2*
Maclin, Benoit *NewYHSD*
Macloskie, George 1834-1920 *ApCAB, NatCAB 19, WhAm 1*
Maclure, William 1763-1840 *AmBi, ApCAB, DcAmB, DcScB, Drake, NatCAB 13, WhAm H*
Maclure, William *see also* MClure, William
MacIver, Loren 1909- *BnEnAmA*
MacMahon, Bernard 1775?-1816 *ApCAB*
MacMahon, Bernard *see also* McMahon, Bernard
MacMahon, Marie Edme Patrice Maurice 1808-1893 *WhoMilH*
MacMahon, Percy Alexander 1854-1929 *DcScB*
MacManus, Seumas 1869-1960 *WhAm 4,*

WhAm 5
MacMartin, Mary 1864- *WomWWA 14*
Macmaster, Donald 1846- *ApCAB*
MacMechen, T Rutherford 1869- *NatCAB 16*
MacMichael, Morton 1807-1879 *Drake*
MacMichael, Morton *see also* McMichael, Morton
MacMillan, Cargill 1900-1968 *WhAm 5*
MacMillan, Conway 1867-1929 *TwCBDA, WhAm 2*
Macmillan, Cyrus 1882-1953 *WhAm 3*
MacMillan, Donald Baxter 1874-1970 *ApCAB X, McGEWB, WhAm 6*
MacMillan, Dougald, III 1897-1975 *WhAm 6*
MacMillan, Duncan D 1837-1908 *NatCAB 16*
MacMillan, Sir Ernest Campbell 1893-1973 *WhAm 5*
MacMillan, George Whitfield 1827- *TwCBDA, WhAm 5*
Macmillan, Harold 1894- *McGEWB*
MacMillan, Harvey Reginald 1885- *WhAm 6*
MacMillan, Hugh R 1903-1957 *WhAm 3*
Macmillan, Isabel *WomWWA 14*
MacMillan, James 1838-1902 *TwCBDA*
MacMillan, Jason Leon 1882-1959 *WhAm 4*
MacMillan, John Alwyn d1952 *WhAm 3*
MacMillan, John Hugh, Jr. 1895-1960 *NatCAB 49, WhAm 4*
Macmillan, Kerr Duncan 1871-1938 *WhAm 1*
MacMillan, Lucy Hayes 1868- *WhAm 4, WomWWA 14*
MacMillan, Mary 1870- *WomWWA 14*
MacMillan, Richard F 1912-1973 *WhAm 6*
MacMillan, Thomas C 1850-1935 *WhAm 1*
MacMillan, Webster Charles 1896-1951 *NatCAB 40*
MacMillan, William Duncan 1871-1948 *DcScB, WhAm 2*
Macmillen, Francis 1885- *NatCAB 14*
MacMinn, Clarence Alfred 1872-1946 *NatCAB 35*
MacMonnies, Alice Jones *WomWWA 14*
MacMonnies, Frederick 1863-1937 *AmBi, ApCAB Sup, ApCAB X, BnEnAmA, DcAmB S2, IlBEAAW, NatCAB 8, WhAm 1*
MacMonnies, Frederick 1865-1937 *TwCBDA*
MacMullan, Ralph A 1917-1972 *WhAm 5*
MacMullen, Wallace 1860-1943 *WhAm 2*
MacMurchy, Helen *WomWWA 14*
MacMurchy, Marjory *WomWWA 14*
MacMurphy, Mary Stuart *WomWWA 14*
MacMurray, James E 1862-1943 *WhAm 2*
MacMurray, John VanAntwerp 1881-1960 *WhAm 4*
MacNab, Sir Alan Napier 1798-1862 *Drake*
MacNab, Sir Allan Napier 1798-1862 *ApCAB*
MacNair, Florence Wheelock Ayscough d1942 *WhAm 2*
MacNair, Harley Farnsworth 1891-1947 *DcAmB S4, NatCAB 42, WhAm 2*
MacNair, James Duncan 1874-1946 *WhAm 2*
MacNair, John Donald 1912-1971 *NatCAB 57*
MacNamara, Arthur James 1885-1962 *WhAm 4*
Macnaughtan, Myra Kelly 1875-1910 *DcAmB*
MacNaughton, Edgar 1887-1971 *NatCAB 57, WhAm 5*
MacNaughton, Ernest Boyd 1880-1960 *NatCAB 48, WhAm 4*
MacNaughton, James 1864-1949 *NatCAB 44, WhAm 2*
MacNaughton, Lewis Winslow 1902-1969 *NatCAB 55, WhAm 5*
Macnaughton, Moray Fraser 1899-1962 *WhAm 4*
MacNeal, Robert E 1903-1967 *WhAm 4*
MacNeal, Ward J 1881-1946 *WhAm 2*
Macneice, Louis 1907- *WhAm 4*
MacNeil, Carol Brooks 1871- *WhAm 5*
MacNeil, Hermon Atkins 1866-1947 *BnEnAmA, DcAmB S4, IlBEAAW, NatCAB 13, NatCAB 34, WhAm 2*
MacNeil, Neil 1891-1969 *WhAm 5*
Macneil, Sayre 1886-1961 *WhAm 4*
MacNeil, Virginia Allen Bagby 1920- *WhAm 6*
MacNeill, Charles Mather 1871-1923 *WhAm 1*

MacNeill, Clara Norwood 1888- *WomWWA 14*
Macneill, Hector 1746-1818 *ApCAB*
MacNeille, Holbrook Mann 1907-1973 *WhAm 6*
MacNeille, Martin Benjamin 1887-1960 *NatCAB 50*
MacNeille, Stephen Mann 1912-1972 *WhAm 6*
MacNeir, Andrew E 1828?- *NewYHSD*
Macneish, Noel Stones 1900-1964 *WhAm 4*
MacNeven, William James 1763-1841 *DcAmB, NatCAB 9, TwCBDA, WhAm H*
MacNeven, William James *see also* McNeven, William James
MacNevin, William 1906-1961 *NatCAB 50*
MacNevin, William James 1763-1841 *ApCAB*
MacNicol, Roy Vincent 1889-1970 *WhAm 5*
MacNider, Hanford 1889-1968 *NatCAB 54, WhAm 4, WhAm 5*
MacNider, William DeBerniere 1881-1951 *NatCAB 40, WhAm 3*
MacNiff, Robert 1877-1928 *ApCAB X*
MacNulty, William K 1892-1964 *WhAm 4*
Macomb, Alexander 1748-1832 *ApCAB*
Macomb, Alexander 1782-1841 *AmBi, ApCAB, DcAmB, Drake, NatCAB 2, TwCBDA, WebAMB, WhAm H*
Macomb, Augustus Canfield 1854- *WhAm 4*
Macomb, David Betton 1827-1911 *WhAm 1*
Macomb, Montgomery Meigs 1852-1924 *NatCAB 20, WhAm 1*
Macomb, William Henry 1818-1872 *ApCAB, Drake, NatCAB 2, TwCBDA*
Macomber, Alexander 1885-1956 *NatCAB 42, WhAm 3*
Macomber, Eleanor 1801-1840 *ApCAB*
Macomber, Frank Gair, Jr. 1883-1929 *NatCAB 24*
Macomber, Herbert Holland 1872-1939 *NatCAB 30*
Macomber, Jennie 1850- *WomWWA 14*
Macomber, John R 1875-1955 *WhAm 3*
Macomber, Mabel E 1876- *WomWWA 14*
Macomber, Mary Elizabeth 1861-1916 *WomWWA 14*
Macomber, Mary Lizzie 1861-1916 *DcAmB, NatCAB 24*
Macomber, Stanley 1887-1967 *NatCAB 53*
Macomber, William *NewYHSD*
Macomber, William 1857-1920 *WhAm 1*
Macon, John Alfred 1851-1891 *NatCAB 8*
Macon, Nathaniel 1757-1837 *ApCAB, BiAUS, BiDrAC, Drake, NatCAB 5, TwCBDA, WhAmP*
Macon, Nathaniel 1758?-1837 *AmBi, DcAmB, McGEWB, WebAB, WhAm H*
Macon, Robert Bruce 1859-1925 *BiDrAC, NatCAB 26, WhAm 1, WhAmP*
Macondray, Atherton 1900-1950 *NatCAB 40*
Macougtry, James *NewYHSD*
Macoun, John 1831- *ApCAB Sup*
MacPhail, Leland Stanford 1890-1975 *WhAm 6*
MacPhail, William 1881-1962 *WhAm 4*
Macpherson, Sir David Lewis 1818- *ApCAB*
Macpherson, David Murdoch 1847- *ApCAB*
MacPherson, Earle Steele 1891-1960 *WhAm 3*
MacPherson, Ford John 1913-1969 *NatCAB 55*
MacPherson, Harriet Dorothea 1892-1967 *DcAmLiB*
Macpherson, James 1738-1796 *Drake*
MacPherson, Leslie Coombs, Jr. 1886-1975 *WhAm 6*
Macpherson, Margaret Campbell *WomWWA 14*
Macpherson, Walter Henry 1877-1955 *NatCAB 42, WhAm 3*
Macpherson, William 1756-1813 *Drake*
Macpherson, William *see also* McPherson, William
MacPhie, Elmore I 1888-1955 *WhAm 3*
MacPhie, John Peter 1854- *WhAm 4*
Macquarie, Lachlan 1762-1824 *McGEWB*
MacQueary, Thomas Howard 1861-1930 *NatCAB 6, WhAm 1, WhAm 2*
MacQueary, Thomas Howard *see also* McQueary, Thomas Howard
MacQueen, Donald Bruce 1876- *WhAm 5*
MacQueen, Peter 1865-1924 *WhAm 1*

Macquer, Pierre Joseph 1718-1784 *DcScB*
MacQuigg, Charles Ellison 1885-1952 *WhAm 3*
MacQuillin, Lillian Gertrude 1876- *WomWWA 14*
MacQuoid, Charles Wight 1862-1931 *NatCAB 24*
Macrae, Donald 1870-1932 *NatCAB 28*
Macrae, Elliott Beach 1900-1967 *WhAm 4*
MacRae, Elmer Livingston 1875-1953 *WhAm 3*
MacRae, Floyd Willcox 1861-1921 *WhAm 4*
MacRae, Floyd Willcox *see also* McRae, Floyd Willcox
Macrae, Frederick Thomas 1893-1943 *NatCAB 32*
Macrae, George Wythe 1838- *NatCAB 9, WhAm 4*
MacRae, Harry B 1891-1958 *WhAm 3*
MacRae, Henry 1874-1944 *NatCAB 33*
MacRae, Hugh 1865-1951 *NatCAB 45, WhAm 5*
MacRae, James Cameron 1838-1909 *WhAm 1*
Macrae, John 1866-1944 *DcAmB S3, WhAm 2*
MacRae, William 1834-1882 *NatCAB 7*
MacRae, William Alexander 1856-1927 *WhAm 1*
MacRea, William 1767-1832 *ApCAB, Drake*
Macready, Charles Foster 1879-1950 *NatCAB 43*
Macready, William Charles 1793-1873 *ApCAB*
Macristy, William 1897-1965 *NatCAB 51*
Macrobius, Ambrosius Theodosius *DcScB*
MacSherry, Charles Whitman 1911-1973 *WhAm 6*
MacSparran, James 1693-1757 *DcAmB, WhAm H*
MacTavish, William Caruth 1893-1968 *WhAm 5*
Macteer, Kenneth Sutherland 1862-1943 *NatCAB 32*
Macune, Charles William 1851-1940 *DcAmB S2*
Macurdy, Grace Harriet 1866-1946 *NotAW, WomWWA 14*
MacVane, Edith 1880- *WhAm 6, WomWWA 14*
Macvane, Silas Marcus 1842-1914 *WhAm 3*
MacVane, William Leslie 1875-1949 *NatCAB 38*
MacVeagh, Charles 1860-1931 *DcAmB S1, NatCAB 23, WhAm 1*
MacVeagh, Charlton 1901-1963 *NatCAB 50*
MacVeagh, Ewen Cameron 1895-1971 *NatCAB 55, WhAm 5*
MacVeagh, Franklin 1837-1934 *AmBi, BiDrUSE, DcAmB S1, NatCAB 14, WhAm 1*
MacVeagh, Isaac Wayne 1833-1917 *DcAmB*
MacVeagh, Lincoln 1858-1927 *ApCAB X*
MacVeagh, Lincoln 1890-1972 *WhAm 5*
MacVeagh, Wayne 1833-1917 *AmBi, ApCAB, ApCAB X, BiAUS, BiDrUSE, NatCAB 4, TwCBDA, WhAm 1*
MacVey, William Pitt 1873- *WhAm 5*
MacVicar, Donald Harvey 1831- *ApCAB*
MacVicar, John 1859- *NatCAB 15, WhAm 4*
MacVicar, John George d1945 *WhAm 2*
MacVicar, Malcolm 1829-1904 *ApCAB, BiDAmEd, DcAmB, NatCAB 4, TwCBDA*
MacVickar, John 1787-1868 *Drake*
MacVickar, John *see also* McVickar, John
MacVitty, Karl DeG 1883-1959 *WhAm 3*
MacWhorter, Alexander 1734-1807 *DcAmB, Drake*
MacWhorter, Alexander 1735-1807 *WhAm H*
MacWhorter, Alexander *see also* McWhorter, Alexander
MacWilliam, John Alexander 1857-1937 *BiHiMed*
MacWillie, Malcolm H *BiDConf*
Macy, Anne Mansfield Sullivan 1866-1936 *AmBi, NotAW, WebAB, WhAm 4*
Macy, Arthur 1842-1904 *WhAm 1*
Macy, C Ward 1899-1962 *WhAm 4*
Macy, Carleton 1872-1949 *NatCAB 39, WhAm 3*
Macy, Edith Brander 1875- *WomWWA 14*

Macy, Edith Dewing d1967 *WhAm 4*
Macy, Edward Warren 1893-1958 *WhAm 3*
Macy, Elizabeth Wise 1887- *WomWWA 14*
Macy, George 1900-1956 *WhAm 3*
Macy, Jesse 1842-1919 *DcAmB, NatCAB 21, TwCBDA, WhAm 1*
Macy, John Albert 1877-1932 *AmBi, DcAmB, NatCAB 23, WhAm 1*
Macy, John B *BiAUS*
Macy, John B 1799-1856 *BiDrAC, WhAm H*
Macy, John B 1799-1857 *TwCBDA*
Macy, Josiah 1785-1872 *ApCAB, DcAmB, NatCAB 22, WhAm H*
Macy, Josiah, Jr. 1838-1876 *NatCAB 22*
Macy, Josiah, Jr. 1910-1972 *WhAm 5*
Macy, Josiah Henry 1840-1917 *NatCAB 25*
Macy, Nelson 1869-1957 *WhAm 3*
Macy, Paul Griswold 1888-1960 *NatCAB 51, WhAm 4*
Macy, Reuben *NewYHSD*
Macy, Valentine E., Jr. 1898-1970 *WhAm 5*
Macy, Valentine Everit 1871-1930 *DcAmB, NatCAB 22, WhAm 1*
Macy, William Austin 1862-1918 *NatCAB 18*
Macy, William Henry 1805-1887 *ApCAB, NatCAB 22*
Macy, William Kingsland 1889-1961 *BiDrAC, NatCAB 47, WhAm 4, WhAmP*
Macy, William Starbuck 1853- *ApCAB*
Macy, William Starbuck 1854- *NatCAB 3, TwCBDA*
Madan, Frederic C 1885- *IIBEAAW*
Madaule, L *NewYHSD*
Madden, Edward *NewYHSD*
Madden, Edwin Charles 1907- *WhAm 4*
Madden, Eva Anne 1863- *WhAm 4, WomWWA 14*
Madden, George Albert 1850- *NatCAB 5*
Madden, James Loomis 1892-1972 *WhAm 5*
Madden, John 1900-1969 *WhAm 5*
Madden, John Edward 1856-1929 *DcAmB*
Madden, John Fitz 1870-1946 *WhAm 2*
Madden, John Griffith 1900-1961 *WhAm 4*
Madden, John Joseph 1902-1962 *NatCAB 49, WhAm 4*
Madden, John Thomas 1882-1948 *NatCAB 41, WhAm 2*
Madden, Joseph Warren 1890-1972 *WhAm 5*
Madden, Lillian Gertrude 1898- *WhAm 6*
Madden, M Lester 1866-1961 *NatCAB 50, WhAm 4*
Madden, Martin Barnaby 1855-1928 *BiDrAC, DcAmB, NatCAB 34, WhAm 1, WhAmP*
Madden, Maude Whitmore 1867- *WhAm 4*
Madden, Paul Eugene 1897-1958 *NatCAB 46*
Madden, Ray John 1892- *BiDrAC*
Madden, Richard Robert 1798-1886 *ApCAB*
Madden, Wales Hendrix 1896-1951 *NatCAB 40*
Maddin, Percy Downs 1860-1941 *WhAm 2*
Maddin, Thomas Lafayette 1826-1908 *NatCAB 8*
Maddison, Isabel *WomWWA 14*
Maddock, Catharine Young Glen 1872- *WhAm 5*
Maddock, Catherine Young Glen 1872- *WomWWA 14*
Maddock, George C *NewYHSD*
Maddock, Thomas 1818- *NatCAB 4*
Maddock, Walter Grierson 1901-1962 *NatCAB 50, WhAm 4*
Maddock, Walter Jeremiah 1880-1951 *NatCAB 39, NatCAB 47*
Maddock, William A 1830?- *NewYHSD*
Maddock, William Eli 1868- *WhAm 5*
Maddocks, Caroline Shaw 1866- *WomWWA 14*
Maddon, John W 1848-1922 *WhAm 3*
Maddox, Dwayne D 1897- *WhAm 2*
Maddox, Emily Christy 1883- *WomWWA 14*
Maddox, Fletcher 1860-1931 *WhAm 1*
Maddox, Florence Spring 1870- *WomWWA 14*
Maddox, Hugh Garth 1884-1951 *NatCAB 40*
Maddox, James Gray 1907-1973 *WhAm 6*
Maddox, John J 1876-1945 *WhAm 2*
Maddox, John W 1848-1922 *BiDrAC, TwCBDA, WhAmP*
Maddox, Louis Wilson 1891-1956 *WhAm 3*
Maddox, Robert Charles 1930-1974 *WhAm 6*

Maddox, Robert Daniel 1876-1955 *NatCAB 46*
Maddox, Robert Flournoy 1829-1899 *NatCAB 2*
Maddox, Robert Foster 1870- *WhAm 5*
Maddox, Samuel T d1916 *WhAm 1*
Maddox, William Arthur 1883-1933 *NatCAB 25, WhAm 1*
Maddox, William Hedrick 1872-1950 *NatCAB 39*
Maddox, William Percy 1901-1972 *NatCAB 57, WhAm 5*
Maddry, Charles Edward 1876-1962 *WhAm 4*
Maddux, Charles Jenkins 1861-1919 *NatCAB 19*
Maddux, Jared 1911-1971 *WhAm 5*
Maddux, Parker Simmons 1880-1953 *WhAm 3*
Maddy, Joseph Edgar 1891-1966 *BiDAmEd, WhAm 4*
Madeira, Daniel *NewYHSD*
Madeira, Jean Browning 1924-1972 *WhAm 5*
Madeira, Louis Childs 1853-1930 *WhAm 1*
Madeira, Lucy *WomWWA 14*
Madeira, Marie Louise Ireland *WomWWA 14*
Madeira, Percy Child 1862-1942 *WhAm 2*
Madeira, Percy Childs, Jr. 1889-1967 *NatCAB 53*
Madeleva, Sister Mary 1887-1964 *BiDAmEd, NatCAB 51, WhAm 4*
Maderna, Bruno 1920-1973 *WhAm 6*
Maderno, Carlo 1556-1629 *McGEWB*
Madero, Francisco Indalecio 1873-1913 *McGEWB*
Madigan, LaVerne d1962 *WhAm 4*
Madill, Grant Charles 1864-1943 *NatCAB 33, WhAm 2*
Madisen, Erik Levanger 1893-1960 *NatCAB 48*
Madison, Charles C 1878-1957 *WhAm 3*
Madison, Dolley Payne Todd 1768-1849 *NotAW*
Madison, Dolly Payne Todd 1768-1849 *AmBi, DcAmB*
Madison, Dorothea Payne Todd 1772-1849 *WhAm H*
Madison, Dorothy Payne Todd 1767-1849 *TwCBDA*
Madison, Dorothy Payne Todd 1772-1849 *AmWom, ApCAB, NatCAB 5*
Madison, Edmond Haggard 1865-1911 *BiDrAC, WhAm 1*
Madison, Frank Delino 1867-1941 *NatCAB 32, WhAm 2*
Madison, George 1763-1816 *ApCAB, BiAUS, Drake, NatCAB 13, TwCBDA*
Madison, Harold Lester 1878-1950 *NatCAB 45, WhAm 3*
Madison, Henry Flood 1864-1926 *NatCAB 21*
Madison, James 1749-1812 *ApCAB, DcAmB, Drake, NatCAB 3, NatCAB 7, TwCBDA, WhAm H*
Madison, James 1750?-1836 *DcAmB*
Madison, James 1751-1836 *AmBi, ApCAB, BiAUS, BiDrAC, BiDrUSE, Drake, EncAAH, EncAB, McGEWB, NatCAB 5, TwCBDA, WebAB, WhAm H, WhAmP*
Madison, Lucy Foster 1865-1932 *WhAm 1, WomWWA 14*
Madler, Johann Heinrich 1794-1874 *DcScB*
Madockawando 1630?-1698 *ApCAB, Drake, NatCAB 9*
Madole, Ross 1912-1966 *NatCAB 51*
Madrid, Jose Fernandez De 1789-1830 *Drake*
Madry, Buford Gregory 1899-1962 *NatCAB 57*
Madsen, Sern 1885-1943 *NatCAB 32*
Madson, Norman Arthur 1886-1962 *WhAm 4*
Maeder, Clara Fisher 1811-1898 *DcAmB, NatCAB 10, NotAW*
Maeder, Frederick George 1840-1891 *NatCAB 6, TwCBDA*
Maeder, Leroy M A 1898-1968 *WhAm 6*
Maegli, Hallo 1924-1972 *WhAm 6*
Maelzl, John Nepomuk 1772-1838 *ApCAB*
Maenchen, Otto John 1894-1969 *NatCAB 54*
Maenner, Theodore Henry 1891-1958 *WhAm 3*
Maentel, Jacob 1763-1863 *BnEnAmA*
Maentle, Jacob 1763-1863 *BnEnAmA, NewYHSD*
Maertz, Louise 1837- *WomWWA 14*
Maes, Camillus Paul 1846-1915 *ApCAB, DcAmB, NatCAB 12, TwCBDA,*

WhAm 1
Maes, Urban 1878-1954 *NatCAB 43, WhAm 6*
Maescher, John Victor 1891-1964 *NatCAB 50*
Maestlin, Michael *DcScB*
Maestre, Sidney 1891-1965 *WhAm 4*
Maestri, Robert S 1889-1974 *WhAm 6*
Maeterlinck, Maurice 1862-1949 *WhAm 2*
Maeterlinck, Count Maurice 1863-1949 *McGEWB*
Maffett, James Thompson 1837-1912 *BiDrAC*
Maffey, NewYHSD
Maffitt, David 1819-1838 *DcAmB, WhAm H*
Maffitt, John Newland 1794-1850 *Drake, TwCBDA*
Maffitt, John Newland 1795-1850 *ApCAB*
Maffitt, John Newland 1819-1886 *ApCAB, BiDConf, DcAmB, TwCBDA, WebAMB*
Maffitt, P Chouteau 1845-1919 *NatCAB 31*
Maffittz, John Newland 1819-1886 *WhAm H*
Magafan, Ethel 1916- *IIBEAAW*
Magalhaens, Domingo Jose Goncalves De 1811- *ApCAB*
Magalhaens DeGandavo, Pedro De 1540- *ApCAB*
Magalhaes *DcScB*
Magalotti, Lorenzo 1637-1712 *DcScB*
Magan, Percy Tilson 1867-1947 *NatCAB 36, WhAm 2*
Magary, Alvin Edwin 1879-1964 *WhAm 4*
Magati, Cesare 1579-1647 *DcScB*
Magavern, Willard John 1900-1968 *NatCAB 54*
Magaw, Charles Albert 1872- *WhAm 5*
Magaw, Robert d1789 *Drake*
Magaw, Samuel 1735-1812 *TwCBDA*
Magaw, Samuel 1739-1812 *NatCAB 1*
Magaw, Samuel 1740?-1812 *ApCAB*
Magaziner, Louis 1878-1956 *NatCAB 50*
Magee, Bell Mhoon 1875- *WomWWA 14*
Magee, Carlton Cole 1873-1946 *WhAm 2*
Magee, Charles Lohr 1876- *WhAm 5*
Magee, Christopher 1829-1909 *NatCAB 14*
Magee, Christopher Lyman 1848-1901 *DcAmB, NatCAB 5, WhAm 1*
Magee, Clare 1899-1969 *BiDrAC, WhAm 5*
Magee, Edward Fifer 1878-1949 *NatCAB 40*
Magee, J Ralph 1880-1970 *WhAm 5*
Magee, James 1862-1919 *NatCAB 6*
Magee, James Carre 1883-1975 *WhAm 6*
Magee, James Dysart 1881-1948 *NatCAB 43, WhAm 2*
Magee, James McDevitt 1877-1949 *BiDrAC, WhAm 2*
Magee, John 1794-1868 *BiAUS, BiDrAC, TwCBDA, WhAm H*
Magee, John 1867- *WhAm 4*
Magee, John Alexander 1827-1903 *BiAUS, BiDrAC*
Magee, John Benjamin 1887-1943 *NatCAB 32, WhAm 2*
Magee, John Fackenthal 1892-1960 *NatCAB 48, WhAm 4*
Magee, John L *NewYHSD*
Magee, Rena Tucker 1880- *WhAm 6*
Magee, Richard *NewYHSD*
Magee, Rufus 1845- *NatCAB 12*
Magee, Thomas 1840-1902 *NatCAB 33*
Magee, Walter Warren 1861-1927 *BiDrAC, WhAm 1, WhAmP*
Magee, Wayland Wells 1881- *WhAm 6*
Magee, William Addison 1873-1938 *WhAm 1*
Magee, William Frank 1866-1952 *NatCAB 47*
Magee, William Michael 1885-1965 *WhAm 4*
Magellan, Ferdinand 1470-1521 *Drake, NatCAB 6*
Magellan, Ferdinand 1480?-1521 *AsBiEn, McGEWB, WhAm H*
Magellan, Fernando 1470-1521 *ApCAB*
Magellan, Jean-Hyacinthe 1722-1790 *DcScB*
Magelssen, William Christian 1873-1919 *WhAm 1*
Magendie, Francois 1783-1855 *AsBiEn, BiHiMed, DcScB*
Magenis, H *NewYHSD*
Magens, Joachim Melchoir 1715?-1783 *ApCAB*
Mager, Charles Augustus 1878-1956 *WhAm 3*
Mager, Daniel *NewYHSD*
Magers, John Elias 1847-1919 *NatCAB 18*

Magevney, Eugene A 1855- *WhAm 4*
Maggard, Edward Harris 1875- *WhAm 5*
Maggi, Bartolomeo 1477-1552 *DcScB*
Magginni, Joseph *NewYHSD*
Maggiolo, Henry Louis 1905-1962 *NatCAB 50*
Maggs, Douglas Blount 1899-1962 *WhAm 4*
Magie, David 1795-1865 *ApCAB*
Magie, David 1877-1960 *NatCAB 48,*
  WhAm 5
Magie, Margaret McCosh 1852-
  WomWWA 14
Magie, William Ashley 1861-1941 *NatCAB 33*
Magie, William Francis 1858-1943 *NatCAB 12,*
  TwCBDA, WhAm 2
Magie, William Jay 1832-1917 *DcAmB,*
  NatCAB 12, TwCBDA, WhAm 1
Magil, Mary Ellen Ryan d1968 *WhAm 5*
Magill, Charles *BiAUS*
Magill, Edmund Charles 1889-1940 *WhAm 1*
Magill, Edward Hicks 1825-1907 *ApCAB,*
  BiDAmEd, DcAmB, NatCAB 6,
  TwCBDA, WhAm 1
Magill, Frank Stockton 1875-1952 *WhAm 3*
Magill, George Paull 1867-1954 *WhAm 3*
Magill, H Kelvin 1909-1956 *NatCAB 47*
Magill, Helen *NotAW*
Magill, Hugh Stewart 1868-1958 *WhAm 3*
Magill, James Phineas 1885-1974 *WhAm 6*
Magill, Mary Tucker 1832-1899 *ApCAB,*
  TwCBDA
Magill, Robert Edward 1861-1939 *WhAm 1*
Magill, Roswell 1895-1963 *NatCAB 50,*
  WhAm 4
Magill, Samuel Edward 1861-1913 *WhAm 1*
Magill, William Seagrove 1866- *WhAm 5*
Magilligan, Donald James 1903-1968 *WhAm 5*
Magin, Francis W 1883-1965 *WhAm 4*
Magini, Giovanni Antonio 1555-1617 *DcScB*
Maginnes, Albert Bristol 1897-1966 *WhAm 4*
Maginnis, Arthur Ambrose 1815-1877
  NatCAB 9
Maginnis, Arthur Ambrose, II 1848- *NatCAB 9*
Maginnis, Charles Donagh 1867-1955
  DcAmB S5, NatCAB 43, WhAm 3
Maginnis, John 1814-1863 *Drake*
Maginnis, John Sharp 1805-1852 *ApCAB*
Maginnis, Martin 1840-1919 *BiAUS*
Maginnis, Martin 1841-1919 *BiDrAC, DcAmB,*
  NatCAB 24, TwCBDA, WhAm 1,
  WhAmP
Maginnis, Samuel Abbot 1885-1941 *WhAm 1*
Maginot, Andre 1877-1932 *WhoMilH*
Magiotti, Raffaello 1597-1656 *DcScB*
Magistad, Oscar Conrad 1900-1953 *WhAm 3*
Maglin, William Henry 1898-1958 *NatCAB 47,*
  WhAm 3
Magna, Edith Scott 1885-1960 *NatCAB 49*
Magnani, Anna 1918-1973 *WhAm 6*
Magnasco, Alessandro 1667-1749 *McGEWB*
Magnenus, Johann Chrysostom 1590?-1679?
  DcScB
Magner, David *NewYHSD*
Magner, F J 1887-1947 *WhAm 2*
Magner, Francis Joseph 1887-1947 *NatCAB 36*
Magner, James Joseph 1891-1969 *WhAm 5*
Magner, John F 1855-1907 *WhAm 1*
Magner, Thomas Francis 1860-1945 *BiDrAC,*
  TwCBDA, WhAm 2
Magnes, Judah Leon 1877-1948 *DcAmB S4,*
  NatCAB 35, WebAB, WhAm 2
Magni, Valeriano 1586-1661 *DcScB*
Magnier, Anthony Aloysius 1898-1959 *WhAm 3*
Magnin, Grover Arnold 1885-1969 *NatCAB 54*
Magnitsky, Leonty Filippovich 1669-1739
  DcScB
Magnol, Pierre 1638-1715 *DcScB*
Magnus, Charles *NewYHSD*
Magnus, Edward 1885-1950 *NatCAB 38*
Magnus, Eugene William 1891-1968
  NatCAB 55
Magnus, Heinrich Gustav 1802-1870 *DcScB*
Magnus, Joseph Emil 1891-1965 *WhAm 4*
Magnus, Leonard *NewYHSD*
Magnus, Olaus *DcScB*
Magnus, Rudolf 1873-1927 *BiHiMed, DcScB*
Magnus, Valerianus *DcScB*
Magnuson, Donald Hammer 1911- *BiDrAC,*
  WhAmP

Magnuson, Paul Budd 1884-1968 *NatCAB 54*
Magnuson, Warren Grant 1905- *BiDrAC*
Magnusson, Carl Edward 1872-1941
  NatCAB 30, WhAm 1
Magnusson, Magnus Vignir 1910-1971
  WhAm 5
Magnusson, Peter Magnus 1865- *WhAm 4*
Magny, Risso 1798-1850 *NewYHSD*
Magny, Xavier *NewYHSD*
Magoffin, Beriah 1815-1885 *AmBi, ApCAB,*
  BiAUS, DcAmB, NatCAB 13, TwCBDA,
  WhAm H, WhAmP
Magoffin, James Wiley 1799-1868 *DcAmB,*
  REnAW, WhAm H
Magoffin, Ralph VanDeman 1874-1942
  WhAm 2
Magone, Daniel 1829-1904 *ApCAB Sup,*
  WhAm 1
Magonigle, Edith Marian Day 1877-1949
  NatCAB 37
Magonigle, Edith Marion Day 1877-1949
  WhAm 5
Magonigle, Harold VanBuren 1867-1935
  ApCAB X, DcAmB S1, NatCAB 15,
  NatCAB 27, WhAm 1
Magoon, Charles Edward 1861-1920 *AmBi,*
  DcAmB, NatCAB 14, WhAm 1
Magoon, Elias Lyman 1810-1886 *ApCAB,*
  TwCBDA
Magoon, Elisha L 1810-1886 *Drake*
Magoon, Henry Sterling 1832-1889 *BiAUS,*
  BiDrAC, WhAm H, WhAmP
Magor, S F 1888-1957 *WhAm 3*
Magoun, George Frederic 1821-1896 *DcAmB,*
  TwCBDA, WhAm H
Magoun, George Frederick 1821-1896
  NatCAB 24
Magoun, Henry Albert 1863-1931 *NatCAB 26,*
  WhAm 1
Magoun, Herbert William 1856-1956 *TwCBDA,*
  WhAm 3
Magoun, Jeanne Bartholow 1870- *WhAm 5*
Magoun, Martha Roberts 1861- *TwCBDA*
Magowan, Sir John Hall 1893-1951 *WhAm 3*
Magrady, Frederick William 1863-1954 *BiDrAC,*
  WhAm 3
Magragh, George *NewYHSD*
Magrath, A G 1813-1893 *BiAUS*
Magrath, Andrew Gordon 1813-1893
  ApCAB Sup, BiDConf, DcAmB,
  NatCAB 12, TwCBDA, WhAm H
Magrath, George Burgess 1870-1938 *WhAm 1*
Magrath, William 1838-1918 *AmBi, ApCAB,*
  NewYHSD, TwCBDA, WhAm 3
Magraw, Lester Andrew 1883-1949 *WhAm 2*
Magri, Lavinia Warren *NotAW*
Magrish, James Lee 1901-1972 *NatCAB 57*
Magritte, Rene 1898-1967 *WhAm 4*
Magruder, Allan Bowie 1775?-1822 *ApCAB,*
  BiAUS, BiDrAC, Drake, NatCAB 4,
  TwCBDA, WhAm H
Magruder, Belle Burns *WomWWA 14*
Magruder, Benjamin Drake 1838-1910
  NatCAB 12, WhAm 1
Magruder, Bruce 1882-1953 *WhAm 3*
Magruder, Calvert 1893-1968 *NatCAB 56,*
  WhAm 5
Magruder, David Lynn 1825-1910 *WhAm 1*
Magruder, Frank Abbott 1882-1949 *BiDAmEd,*
  WhAm 2
Magruder, George Lloyd 1848-1914 *DcAmB,*
  WhAm 1
Magruder, Hampton 1876-1962 *NatCAB 53*
Magruder, John 1887-1958 *WhAm 3*
Magruder, John Bankhead 1810-1871 *AmBi,*
  ApCAB, BiDConf, DcAmB, Drake,
  NatCAB 4, TwCBDA, WebAMB,
  WhAm H, WhoMilH
Magruder, John H, Jr. 1889-1963 *WhAm 4*
Magruder, Julia 1854-1907 *ApCAB, DcAmB,*
  NatCAB 8, NotAW, TwCBDA,
  WhAm 1
Magruder, Patrick 1768-1819 *BiDrAC,*
  DcAmLiB, WhAm H
Magruder, Patrick 1768-1820? *•BiAUS*
Magruder, Richard B d1844 *BiAUS*
Magruder, Thomas Pickett 1867-1938
  NatCAB 39, WhAm 1

Magruder, William Thomas 1861-1935
  TwCBDA, WhAm 1
Magsaysay, Ramon 1907-1957 *McGEWB,*
  WhAm 3
Maguire, Charles Bonaventure 1768-1833
  DcAmB
Maguire, Hamilton Ewing 1891-1971 *WhAm 5*
Maguire, James George 1853-1920 *BiDrAC,*
  TwCBDA, WhAm 4
Maguire, James Herbert 1853-1928 *ApCAB X*
Maguire, Jeremiah DeSmet 1877-1959 *WhAm 4*
Maguire, Jeremiah DeSmet 1879-1959
  ApCAB X
Maguire, John Arthur 1870-1939 *BiDrAC*
Maguire, John Arthur 1872-1939 *WhAm 5*
MaGuire, Marie E A 1891- *WomWWA 14*
Maguire, Mary M d1910 *NewYHSD*
Maguire, Matthew 1850- *ApCAB Sup,*
  WhAm 4
Maguire, Philip Francis, Jr. 1905-1973 *WhAm 6*
Maguire, Raymer Francis 1890-1960 *WhAm 4*
Maguire, Russell 1897-1966 *WhAm 4*
Maguire, Thomas 1776?-1854 *ApCAB*
Maguire, Walter Norman 1893-1967
  NatCAB 51, WhAm 4
Maguire, Walter Richmond 1890-1962
  NatCAB 49
Maguire, William George 1868-1965 *WhAm 4*
Maguire, William George 1886-1965
  NatCAB 51
Mahadeva *DcScB*
Mahaffey, Birch Oliver 1877-1958 *NatCAB 47*
Mahaffey, Jesse Lynn 1879-1948 *WhAm 2*
Mahaffey, John Quincy 1866- *WhAm 4*
Mahaffie, Charles Delahunt 1884-1969
  NatCAB 54, WhAm 5
Maham, Hezekiah 1739-1789 *ApCAB, Drake*
Mahan, Alfred Thayer 1840-1914 *AmBi,*
  ApCAB Sup, DcAmB, EncAB, McGEWB,
  NatCAB 10, TwCBDA, WebAB,
  WebAMB, WhAm 1, WhoMilH
Mahan, Asa 1799-1889 *BiDAmEd, DcAmB,*
  WhAm H
Mahan, Asa 1800-1889 *ApCAB, NatCAB 2,*
  TwCBDA
Mahan, Bryan Francis 1856-1923 *BiDrAC,*
  WhAm 3
Mahan, Dennis Hart 1802-1871 *ApCAB,*
  BiDAmEd, DcAmB, Drake, NatCAB 10,
  TwCBDA, WebAMB, WhAm H,
  WhoMilH
Mahan, Dennis Hart 1849-1925 *WhAm 1*
Mahan, Edgar Clyde 1879-1948 *NatCAB 42,*
  WhAm 2
Mahan, Frances Israel 1869- *WomWWA 14*
Mahan, Francis *NewYHSD*
Mahan, Frederick Augustus 1847- *ApCAB,*
  NatCAB 10
Mahan, George Addison 1851-1936 *WhAm 1*
Mahan, Lawrence Elmer 1891-1946 *WhAm 2*
Mahan, Milo 1819-1870 *ApCAB, DcAmB,*
  Drake, NatCAB 10, TwCBDA, WhAm H
Mahan, Patrick Joseph 1880-1938 *WhAm 1*
Mahana, George Shaw 1870- *WhAm 5*
Mahaney, C R 1898-1973 *WhAm 6*
Mahani, Abu Abd Allah M Ibn Isa, Al- *DcScB*
Mahany, Rowland Blennerhassett 1864-1937
  BiDrAC, NatCAB 9, TwCBDA, WhAm 1
Mahar, Edward Albert 1900-1973 *WhAm 5*
Mahavira *DcScB*
Mahdi, The 1843-1885 *WhoMilH*
Mahdi, The 1844?-1885 *McGEWB*
Mahendra Bir Bikram Shah Deva 1920-1972
  WhAm 5
Mahendra Suri *DcScB*
Maher, Aldea 1892-1959 *NatCAB 51,*
  WhAm 3
Maher, Aly Pacha d1960 *WhAm 4*
Maher, Chauncey Carter 1897-1970
  NatCAB 55, WhAm 5
Maher, Dale Wilford 1897-1948 *WhAm 2*
Maher, George Washington 1864-1926
  WhAm 1
Maher, James Denis 1854-1921 *WhAm 1*
Maher, James Paul 1865-1946 *BiDrAC,*
  WhAm 4
Maher, Stephen John 1860-1939 *NatCAB 33,*
  WhAm 1

Maheshwari, Panchanan 1904-1966 *WhAm 4*
Maheu, Rene Gabriel Eugene 1905-1975 *WhAm 6*
Mahier, Edith 1892- *IIBEAAW*
Mahin, Edward Garfield 1876-1952 *NatCAB 48, WhAm 3*
Mahin, Frank Cadle 1887-1942 *WhAm 2*
Mahin, Frank Webster 1851-1936 *NatCAB 27, WhAm 1*
Mahin, John Lee 1869-1930 *WhAm 1*
Mahl, Max *NewYHSD*
Mahl, William 1843-1918 *ApCAB X, WhAm 1*
Mahle, Arthur Edwin 1893-1962 *NatCAB 49, WhAm 4*
Mahler, Ernst 1887-1967 *NatCAB 54, WhAm 4*
Mahler, Fritz 1901-1973 *WhAm 6*
Mahler, Gustav 1860-1911 *McGEWB, WhAm HA, WhAm 4*
Mahmud II 1785-1839 *McGEWB*
Mahmud Of Ghazni 971-1030 *McGEWB*
Mahmud Ibn Masud Al-Shirazi *DcScB*
Mahon, David W *BiAUS*
Mahon, Gabriel Heyward, Jr. 1889-1962 *BiDrAC*
Mahon, George Herman 1900- *BiDrAC*
Mahon, John Joseph 1895-1956 *NatCAB 44*
Mahon, Russell Clay 1890-1956 *NatCAB 45, WhAm 3*
Mahon, Ruth Ferguson *WomWWA 14*
Mahon, Stephen Keith 1877- *WhAm 5*
Mahon, Thaddeus Maclay 1840-1916 *BiDrAC, TwCBDA, WhAm 4, WhAmP*
Mahon, Wilfred John 1880-1933 *NatCAB 25, WhAm 1*
Mahon, William D 1861-1949 *WhAm 2*
Mahone, William 1826-1895 *AmBi, ApCAB, BiDConf, BiDrAC, DcAmB, McGEWB, NatCAB 5, TwCBDA, WhAm H, WhAmP*
Mahone, William 1827?-1895 *Drake Sup*
Mahoney, Bernard Joseph 1875-1939 *WhAm 1*
Mahoney, Caroline Smith d1909 *WhAm 1*
Mahoney, Charles H 1886-1966 *WhAm 4*
Mahoney, Charles Harold 1901-1967 *NatCAB 53*
Mahoney, Daniel Joseph 1889-1963 *WhAm 4*
Mahoney, Edward R 1881-1937 *WhAm 1*
Mahoney, Francis Xavier 1871-1936 *NatCAB 26*
Mahoney, George William 1860- *WhAm 3*
Mahoney, Jeremiah T 1878-1970 *WhAm 5*
Mahoney, John C 1881-1946 *WhAm 2*
Mahoney, John Dennis 1876- *WhAm 5*
Mahoney, John Friend 1889-1957 *NatCAB 47, WhAm 3*
Mahoney, John Joseph 1880-1964 *BiDAmEd, NatCAB 52, WhAm 4*
Mahoney, John Patrick Shields 1869-1935 *NatCAB 26*
Mahoney, Joseph Nathaniel 1878-1946 *WhAm 2*
Mahoney, Joseph P 1864- *NatCAB 9*
Mahoney, Mary Eliza 1845-1926 *NotAW*
Mahoney, Paul Leo 1894-1967 *NatCAB 56*
Mahoney, Peter Paul 1848-1889 *BiDrAC, WhAm H*
Mahoney, Roy Bernard 1897-1956 *NatCAB 45*
Mahoney, William Edward 1891-1948 *NatCAB 42*
Mahoney, William Frank 1856-1904 *BiDrAC, WhAm 1*
Mahoney, William J 1896-1947 *WhAm 2*
Mahony, Emogene 1876- *WomWWA 14*
Mahony, Emon Ossian 1874-1920 *NatCAB 19, WhAm 1*
Mahony, Michael Joseph 1860-1936 *WhAm 1*
Mahony, Thomas Harrison 1885-1969 *WhAm 5*
Mahony, Walter Butler 1877-1954 *NatCAB 39, WhAm 3*
Mahood, Alexander Maitland 1900-1947 *NatCAB 36*
Mahood, J W 1864- *WhAm 4*
Mahool, John Barry 1870-1935 *WhAm 1*
Mahpiua Luta *WebAB*
Mahuran, Stuart Ansala 1892-1953 *WhAm 3*
Mahurin, Guy Marshall 1877-1942 *NatCAB 32*

Mahy, George Gordon 1865- *WhAm 4*
Maiden, Robert King 1858- *WhAm 4*
Maier, Alois 1888- *ApCAB X*
Maier, Andrew Cornelius 1882-1964 *NatCAB 52*
Maier, Frederick Hurst 1871-1946 *NatCAB 37*
Maier, Guy d1956 *WhAm 3*
Maier, J *NewYHSD*
Maier, Michael 1568?-1662 *DcScB*
Maier, Paul David Irvin 1874-1936 *NatCAB 27*
Maier, Roe Johnson 1894-1961 *NatCAB 49*
Maier, Walter Arthur 1893-1950 *DcAmB S4, NatCAB 42, WhAm 2*
Maige, Albert 1872-1943 *DcScB*
Maignan, Emanuel 1601?-1676 *DcScB*
Maijgren, Henry Thorvald 1909-1971 *NatCAB 57*
Mailer, Norman Kingsley 1923- *EncAB, McGEWB, WebAB*
Mailhouse, Max 1857-1941 *WhAm 2*
Maillard, Abbe d1768 *ApCAB*
Mailler, William Henry 1823-1903 *NatCAB 3, WhAm 1*
Maillet, Benoit De 1656-1738 *DcScB*
Mailliard, John Ward 1862-1936 *NatCAB 39*
Mailliard, John Ward, Jr. 1891-1954 *NatCAB 43, WhAm 3*
Mailliard, William Somers 1917- *BiDrAC*
Maillol, Aristide 1861-1944 *McGEWB*
Mailloux, Cyprien Odilon 1857-1932 *NatCAB 26*
Mailly, Bertha Howell 1869- *WomWWA 14*
Mailly, William 1871-1912 *DcAmB, WhAm 1*
Mails, Thomas E 1920?- *IIBEAAW*
Maiman, Theodore Harold 1927- *AsBiEn*
Maimonides 1135-1204 *AsBiEn, McGEWB*
Maimonides, Moses BenMaimon 1135-1204 *BiHiMed, DcScB*
Main, Archibald M 1870-1961 *WhAm 4*
Main, Arthur Elwin 1846-1933 *WhAm 1*
Main, Charles Thomas 1856-1943 *ApCAB X, DcAmB S3, NatCAB 15, NatCAB 33, WhAm 2*
Main, Charlotte Emerson *WomWWA 14*
Main, David John 1882-1955 *NatCAB 46*
Main, Frank Wilbur 1879-1954 *NatCAB 43*
Main, Hanford 1889-1959 *NatCAB 47, WhAm 4*
Main, Herschel 1845-1909 *WhAm 1*
Main, Hubert Platt 1839-1925 *WhAm 1*
Main, John *WebAB*
Main, John Fleming 1864-1942 *WhAm 2*
Main, John Hanson Thomas 1859-1931 *DcAmB S1, NatCAB 23, WhAm 1*
Main, Marjorie 1890-1975 *WhAm 6*
Main, Verner Wright 1885-1965 *BiDrAC*
Main, William 1796-1876 *NewYHSD, WhAm H*
Main, William Holloway 1862-1933 *WhAm 1*
Maine, Clara Horton 1858- *WomWWA 14*
Maine, George DeL *NewYHSD*
Maine, Sir Henry James Sumner 1822-1888 *McGEWB*
Maine, Mary Talulah 1869- *WhAm 5, WomWWA 14*
Mainelli, John Peter 1894-1971 *NatCAB 57*
Maines, William Ripley 1874-1943 *NatCAB 33*
Mains, Edwin Butterworth 1890-1968 *NatCAB 55*
Mains, George Preston 1844-1930 *NatCAB 12, WhAm 1*
Mains, J R *NewYHSD*
Mains, Kathryn Pauline d1970 *WhAm 5*
Mainus, Polly *WomWWA 14*
Mainwaring, William Bernard 1897-1957 *NatCAB 48, WhAm 3*
Maior, John 1469-1550 *DcScB*
Mair, C H *NewYHSD*
Mair, Charles 1840- *ApCAB*
Mair, Edmand Findlay 1895-1953 *NatCAB 43*
Mair, Hugh 1797-1854 *ApCAB*
Mair, Simon *DcScB*
Mair, William J 1900-1965 *WhAm 4*
Mairan, Jean Jacques D'Ortous De 1678-1771 *DcScB*
Maire, Rene-Charles-Joseph-Ernest 1878-1949 *DcScB*
Mairs, Elwood Donald 1905-1972 *WhAm 5*

Mairs, John Dows 1827-1881 *NatCAB 31*
Mairs, Samuel 1879- *WhAm 3*
Mairs, Thomas Isaiah 1871- *WhAm 5*
Mairs, William Henry 1834-1913 *NatCAB 36*
Maisch, Henry Charles Christian 1862-1901 *WhAm 1*
Maisch, John Michael 1831-1893 *ApCAB, DcAmB, NatCAB 5, WhAm H*
Maish, Levi 1837-1899 *BiAUS, BiDrAC, TwCBDA*
Maisky, Ivan 1884-1975 *WhWW-II*
Maisoneuve, Paul DeChomedey, Sieur De 1612-1676 *McGEWB*
Maisonneuve, Paul DeChomedey 1612-1676 *ApCAB*
Maistral, Desire Marie 1764-1842 *ApCAB*
Maistral, Ernest Trauquille 1763-1815 *ApCAB*
Maistre, Joseph De 1753-1821 *McGEWB*
Maita Capac *ApCAB*
Maitin, Jose Antonio 1798-1874 *ApCAB*
Maitland, Alexander 1866-1926 *NatCAB 20*
Maitland, Frederic William 1850-1906 *McGEWB*
Maitland, George H d1965 *WhAm 4*
Maitland, James Dreher 1883-1964 *WhAm 4*
Maitland, John d1779 *Drake*
Maitland, John 1789-1839 *ApCAB*
Maitland, Sir Peregrine 1777-1854 *ApCAB*
Maitland, Royal Lethington 1889-1946 *WhAm 2*
Maitz DeGoimpy, F L E G, Count Du 1729-1792 *ApCAB*
Majali, Hazaa 1916-1960 *WhAm 4*
Majeski, John F 1892-1971 *WhAm 5*
Majid, Shihab Al-Din A Ibn Majid, Ibn *DcScB*
Majocchi, Domenico 1849-1929 *BiHiMed*
Major, Alfred Job 1861- *WhAm 4*
Major, Cedric Aylwin 1891-1961 *NatCAB 46, WhAm 4*
Major, Charles 1856-1913 *AmBi, DcAmB, NatCAB 13, TwCBDA, WhAm 1*
Major, Daniel 1815?- *NewYHSD*
Major, David R 1866- *WhAm 1*
Major, Duncan Kennedy, Jr. 1876-1947 *WhAm 2*
Major, Elliott Woolfolk 1864-1949 *NatCAB 15, NatCAB 43, WhAm 2*
Major, Guy Gebhart 1859-1912 *NatCAB 31*
Major, Henry B *NewYHSD*
Major, James Earl 1887-1972 *BiDrAC, WhAm 5*
Major, James Parsons 1818-1900 *NewYHSD*
Major, John *NewYHSD*
Major, Julian Neville 1887-1953 *NatCAB 40*
Major, Richard C *NewYHSD*
Major, Samuel Collier 1869-1931 *BiDrAC, WhAm 1*
Major, Samuel Glenn 1900-1942 *NatCAB 32*
Major, William Warner 1804-1854 *IIBEAAW, NewYHSD, WhAm H*
Majorana, Ettore 1906-1938 *DcScB*
Majors, Alexander 1814-1900 *DcAmB, EncAAH, REnAW*
Majors, Monroe Alphus 1864- *WhoColR*
Majors, Thomas Jefferson 1841-1932 *BiDrAC*
Majriti, Abu 'l-Qasim M Ibn Ahmad, Al- d1007? *DcScB*
Majusi, Abul-Hasan Ali Ibn Abbas, Al- d994 *DcScB*
Makaranda *DcScB*
Makarov, Stepan Osipovich 1848-1904 *WhoMilH*
Makarov, Stepan Osipovich 1849-1904 *DcScB*
Makataimeshekiakiak *WebAB*
Makemie, Francis 1658?-1708 *AmBi, ApCAB, DcAmB, DcAmReB, Drake, McGEWB, NatCAB 11, WebAB, WhAm H*
Makepeace, Charles Denison 1875-1960 *NatCAB 47, WhAm 4*
Makepeace, Colin MacRae 1890-1967 *WhAm 4*
Makibi, Kibi-No 693-775 *McGEWB*
Makin, Thomas 1665?-1733 *ApCAB*
Makin, Thomas 1665?-1735 *Drake*
Makinson, George Albert 1887- *WhAm 1*
Makita, Yolchiro d1972 *WhAm 5*
Makonnen Endalkacaw 1892-1963 *McGEWB*
Maksimov, Nikolay Aleksandrovich 1880-1952 *DcScB*

Maksutov, Dmitry Dmitrievich 1896-1964 *DcScB*
Makuen, George Hudson 1855-1917 *NatCAB 12, NatCAB 19, WhAm 1*
Malakis, Emile 1897-1954 *WhAm 3*
Malambre, John A *NewYHSD*
Malamud, Bernard 1914- *WebAB*
Malan, Clement Timothy 1883-1961 *WhAm 4*
Malan, Daniel Francois 1874-1959 *McGEWB, WhAm 3*
Maland, Talfourd Abbot 1909-1974 *WhAm 6*
Malarkey, James Alfred 1872-1948 *NatCAB 38*
Malartie, Anne J Hyppolite, Count De 1730-1800 *ApCAB*
Malaspina, Alejandro 1750?-1810? *ApCAB*
Malaver, Antonio E 1835- *ApCAB*
Malbone, Edward Greene 1777-1807 *AmBi, ApCAB, BnEnAmA, DcAmB, Drake, NatCAB 9, NewYHSD, TwCBDA, WebAB, WhAm H*
Malbone, Francis d1809 *BiAUS, NatCAB 8*
Malbone, Francis 1757-1809 *ApCAB, TwCBDA*
Malbone, Francis 1759-1809 *BiDrAC, WhAm H*
Malburn, William Peabody d1945 *WhAm 2*
Malby, George Roland 1857-1912 *BiDrAC, WhAm 1*
Malcarney, Arthur Leno 1913-1968 *WhAm 5*
Malchow, Stella Wellington *WomWWA 14*
Malcolm III d1093 *McGEWB*
Malcolm X 1925-1965 *DcAmReB, EncAB, McGEWB, WebAB, WhAm 4, WhAmP*
Malcolm, Alexander d1763 *Drake*
Malcolm, D O 1877-1955 *WhAm 3*
Malcolm, Daniel 1725-1769 *DcAmB, WhAm H*
Malcolm, George Arthur 1881-1961 *NatCAB 49, WhAm 4*
Malcolm, Gilbert 1892-1965 *WhAm 4*
Malcolm, Harold Ray 1894-1967 *NatCAB 53*
Malcolm, Howard 1799-1879 *NatCAB 12*
Malcolm, James Peller 1767-1815 *ApCAB, DcAmB, Drake, NewYHSD, WhAm H*
Malcolm, Robert Bruce 1934-1972 *WhAm 6*
Malcolm, Roy 1881-1959 *NatCAB 47, WhAm 4*
Malcolm, Russell Laing 1906-1967 *WhAm 5*
Malcolm, William 1823-1890 *NatCAB 13*
Malcolm, William Lindsay 1884-1948 *WhAm 2*
Malcolmson, Charles Tousley 1874-1922 *WhAm 1*
Malcolmson, James W 1866-1917 *WhAm 1*
Malcolmson, Margaret Ewing 1878- *WomWWA 14*
Malcom, Daniel 1725-1769 *DcAmB*
Malcom, Howard 1799-1879 *ApCAB, DcAmB, Drake, TwCBDA, WhAm H*
Malcom, James Peller 1767-1815 *DcAmB*
Malcom, Thomas Shields 1821-1886 *ApCAB*
Malcom, William 1823-1890 *TwCBDA*
Malcomson, Alexander Young 1865-1923 *NatCAB 22*
Maldarelli, Oronzio 1892-1963 *WhAm 4*
Maldeis, Howard James 1879-1949 *NatCAB 37*
Maldonado, Diego d1564 *ApCAB*
Male, Job 1808- *ApCAB*
Malebranche, Nicolas 1638-1715 *DcScB, McGEWB*
Malenkov, Georgy 1902- *WhWW-II*
Malesherbes, Chretien-G DeLamoignon De 1721-1794 *DcScB*
Malevich, Kasimir 1878-1935 *McGEWB*
Maley, Anna Agnes *WomWWA 14*
Maley, Rose Anna Bird 1884- *WomWWA 14*
Malfatti, Gian Francesco 1731-1807 *DcScB*
Malgaigne, Joseph-Francois 1806-1865 *BiHiMed*
Malherbe, Francois De 1555-1628 *McGEWB*
Malibran, Maria Felicia 1808-1836 *ApCAB*
Malick, Clay Packer 1901-1965 *NatCAB 52*
Malick, Simon Peter 1848-1920 *NatCAB 19*
Malin, James Claude 1893- *EncAAH, REnAW*
Malin, Patrick Murphy 1903-1964 *NatCAB 51, WhAm 4*
Malincourt, Hector Charles 1703-1750 *ApCAB*
Malinovsky, Rodion Yakovlevich 1898-1967 *WhAm 4, WhWW-II*

Malinowski, Bronislaw Kasper 1884-1942 *WhAm 2*
Malinowski, Kaspar Bronislaw 1884-1942 *McGEWB*
Malipiero, G Francesco 1882-1973 *WhAm 6*
Malipiero, Gian Francesco 1882-1973 *McGEWB*
Malisoff, William Marias 1895-1947 *WhAm 2*
Malitz, Lester M 1907-1965 *WhAm 4*
Malka, Ibn *DcScB*
Malkam Khan, Mirza 1831-1908 *McGEWB*
Malkiel, Leon Andrew 1866- *WhAm 1*
Malkin, Morris 1891-1951 *NatCAB 41*
Malko, Nicolai 1888-1961 *WhAm 4*
Mall, Franklin Paine 1862-1917 *DcAmB, DcScB, NatCAB 14, WhAm 1*
Mallalieu, Wilbur V 1876-1943 *WhAm 2*
Mallalieu, Willard Francis 1828-1911 *NatCAB 7, TwCBDA, WhAm 1*
Mallalieu, Williard Francis 1828-1911 *ApCAB*
Mallard, Ernest 1833-1894 *DcScB*
Mallarme, Stephane 1842-1898 *McGEWB*
Mallary, Charles Daniel 1801-1864 *Drake*
Mallary, Charles Dutton 1801-1864 *ApCAB, TwCBDA*
Mallary, R DeWitt 1851- *WhAm 1*
Mallary, Rollin C 1784-1831 *BiAUS*
Mallary, Rollin Carlos 1784-1831 *Drake*
Mallary, Rollin Carolas 1784-1831 *BiDrAC, DcAmB, WhAm H, WhAmP*
Mallary, Rollin Carolos 1784-1831 *TwCBDA*
Mallary, Rollin Carolus 1784-1831 *ApCAB, NatCAB 12*
Mallery, Earl Dean 1889-1952 *WhAm 3*
Mallery, Garrick 1784-1866 *ApCAB, Drake*
Mallery, Garrick 1831-1894 *ApCAB, DcAmB, NatCAB 7, TwCBDA, WhAm H*
Mallery, Otto Tod 1881-1956 *NatCAB 44, WhAm 3*
Mallet, F *NewYHSD*
Mallet, John William 1832-1912 *ApCAB, DcAmB, NatCAB 13, TwCBDA, WhAm 1*
Mallet, John William 1835-1912 *BiDConf*
Mallet, Robert 1810-1881 *DcScB*
Mallet-Prevost, Severo 1860-1948 *ApCAB Sup, WhAm 2*
Mallett, Charles William 1846-1921 *NatCAB 19*
Mallett, Daniel Trowbridge 1862- *WhAm 4*
Mallett, Donald Roger 1910-1971 *WhAm 5*
Mallett, Frank J 1858- *NatCAB 4*
Mallett, Reginald 1893-1965 *WhAm 4*
Mallett, Wilbert Grant 1867-1942 *WhAm 1*
Mallian, Julien De 1805-1851 *ApCAB*
Mallin, Morris Charles 1888-1953 *NatCAB 40*
Mallina, Rudolph Frederic 1892-1970 *NatCAB 56*
Mallinckrodt, Edward 1845-1928 *AmBi, DcAmB, WhAm 1*
Mallinckrodt, Edward, Jr. 1878-1967 *NatCAB 54, WhAm 4*
Mallinckrodt, Laurence Edward 1909-1975 *WhAm 6*
Mallinckrodt, Pauline 1817-1881 *WhAm H*
Mallinson, Herbert 1894-1941 *NatCAB 33*
Mallinson, Hiram Royal 1873-1931 *NatCAB 28*
Mallison, Richard Speight 1908-1971 *WhAm 5*
Malloch, Douglas 1877-1938 *NatCAB 28, WhAm 1*
Mallon, Alfred Edward 1892-1947 *WhAm 2*
Mallon, Guy Ward 1864- *WhAm 4*
Mallon, Mary 1870?-1938 *WebAB*
Mallon, Paul 1901-1950 *WhAm 3*
Mallon, Winifred 1879-1954 *WhAm 3*
Mallory, Colonel d1780 *Drake*
Mallory, C C 1890-1959 *WhAm 3*
Mallory, Charles Arthur 1850-1935 *NatCAB 15, NatCAB 26*
Mallory, Charles K d1820 *Drake*
Mallory, Clifford Day 1881-1941 *DcAmB S3, WhAm 1*
Mallory, Ezra Andrews 1820-1902 *NatCAB 15, NatCAB 26*
Mallory, Francis 1807-1860 *BiAUS, BiDrAC, TwCBDA, WhAm H*
Mallory, Frank Burr 1862-1941 *DcAmB S3, NatCAB 33, WhAm 2*
Mallory, George Scovill 1838-1897 *ApCAB,*

TwCBDA
Mallory, Hannah Jane *WhoColR*
Mallory, Helen Newberry Ladue 1872- *WomWWA 14*
Mallory, Henry Reed 1892-1970 *NatCAB 57*
Mallory, Hervey Foster 1866-1943 *NatCAB 32*
Mallory, Hugh 1874-1937 *WhAm 1*
Mallory, Hugh Shepherd Darby 1848- *WhAm 1*
Mallory, Kathleen Moore 1879- *WhAm 6*
Mallory, Leila Fish 1875- *WomWWA 14*
Mallory, Lucy A 1846- *AmWom*
Mallory, Meredith *BiAUS, BiDrAC, WhAm H*
Mallory, Philip Rogers 1885-1975 *WhAm 6*
Mallory, Richard P *NewYHSD*
Mallory, Robert 1815-1885 *BiAUS, BiDrAC, TwCBDA, WhAm H*
Mallory, Rufus 1831-1914 *BiAUS, BiDrAC, WhAm 4*
Mallory, Stephen Russell 1810?-1873 *BiAUS, Drake*
Mallory, Stephen Russell 1812?-1873 *BiDConf, BiDrAC, WhAm H, WhAmP*
Mallory, Stephen Russell 1813?-1873 *AmBi, ApCAB, DcAmB, NatCAB 4, TwCBDA*
Mallory, Stephen Russell 1848-1907 *ApCAB Sup, BiDrAC, NatCAB 12, TwCBDA, WhAm 1, WhAmP*
Mallory, Tracy Burr 1896-1951 *NatCAB 39, WhAm 3*
Mallory, William Ezra 1856-1938 *NatCAB 32*
Malloy, John Anthony 1896-1943 *WhAm 2*
Malluk, Antonio Michel 1870-1920 *ApCAB X*
Mally, Frederick William 1868- *WhAm 4*
Malm, Arthur Theodore 1884-1959 *NatCAB 47*
Malm, Gustav Nathanael 1869-1928 *WhAm 1*
Malmberg, John George 1880-1951 *NatCAB 41*
Malmfeldt, Carl John 1891-1949 *NatCAB 38*
Malmgren, George Erland 1902-1949 *NatCAB 38*
Malmore, John *NewYHSD*
Malo, Oscar Louis 1877-1964 *NatCAB 52*
Malone, Booth M 1854- *WhAm 4*
Malone, Clarence M 1885-1960 *WhAm 4*
Malone, Clifton J 1904-1959 *WhAm 4*
Malone, Dana 1857-1917 *NatCAB 28, WhAm 1*
Malone, Dudley Field 1882-1950 *DcAmB S4, WhAm 3*
Malone, Dumas 1892- *EncAAH, McGEWB*
Malone, George Wilson 1890-1961 *BiDrAC, WhAm 4, WhAmP*
Malone, J Walter 1857-1935 *WhAm 1*
Malone, James Comer 1890-1960 *NatCAB 48, WhAm 4*
Malone, James Henry 1851- *NatCAB 18*
Malone, James Thomas 1865-1920 *ApCAB X, WhAm 1*
Malone, John Lee 1923-1975 *WhAm 6*
Malone, John Walter, Jr. 1888-1962 *WhAm 4*
Malone, John Wesley 1856-1930 *WhAm 1*
Malone, Kemp 1889-1971 *WhAm 5*
Malone, Maud 1877- *WomWWA 14*
Malone, Noel H 1903-1965 *WhAm 4*
Malone, Paul Bernard 1872-1960 *WhAm 4*
Malone, Richard Harwell 1857-1937 *WhAm 1*
Malone, Rosser Lynn 1910-1974 *WhAm 6*
Malone, Sarah Francis 1865- *WhoColR*
Malone, Sylvester 1821-1899 *DcAmB, NatCAB 9, TwCBDA*
Malone, Thomas Henry 1872-1941 *WhAm 1*
Malone, Walter 1866-1915 *DcAmB, NatCAB 13, WhAm 1*
Malone, Walter Yancey 1877-1950 *NatCAB 39*
Malone, William Battle 1874-1939 *WhAm 1*
Maloney, Francis Thomas 1894-1945 *BiDrAC, NatCAB 40, WhAm 2, WhAmP*
Maloney, Franklin John 1899-1958 *BiDrAC*
Maloney, James Henry 1856-1926 *NatCAB 23*
Maloney, John Philip 1881-1950 *WhAm 3*
Maloney, Joseph F 1865- *WhAm 4*
Maloney, Martin 1846-1929 *ApCAB X, NatCAB 23*
Maloney, Martin 1847-1929 *DcAmB*
Maloney, Maurice 1812?-1872 *ApCAB*
Maloney, Morris William 1895-1963 *NatCAB 50*
Maloney, Paul Herbert 1876-1967 *BiDrAC,*

WhAm 5
Maloney, Richard Clogher 1904- *WhAm 6*
Maloney, Richard Leo 1905-1962 *WhAm 4*
Maloney, Robert Sarsfield 1881-1934 *BiDrAC,
WhAm 6*
Maloney, Russell 1895-1957 *NatCAB 44*
Maloney, Walter H 1885-1967 *WhAm 5*
Maloney, William J M A 1882-1952 *WhAm 3*
Maloney, William M 1815?- *NewYHSD*
Malony, Harry James 1889-1971 *NatCAB 56,
WhAm 5*
Maloof, Sam 1916- *BnEnAmA*
Malory, Sir Thomas *McGEWB*
Malot, Francois Paul 1770-1832 *ApCAB*
Malott, Clyde A 1887-1950 *WhAm 3*
Malouet, Pierre Victor 1740-1814 *ApCAB*
Malouin, Paul-Jacques 1701-1778 *DcScB*
Maloy, Wayland Hoyt 1895-1957 *NatCAB 51*
Malpass, Frank Page 1884-1957 *NatCAB 45*
Malpighi, Marcello 1628-1694 *AsBiEn,
BiHiMed, DcScB, McGEWB*
Malraux, Andre 1901- *McGEWB*
Malsbary, George Elmer 1873- *WhAm 5*
Maltbie, Milo Roy 1871- *WhAm 5*
Maltbie, William Henry 1867-1926 *WhAm 1*
Maltbie, William Mills 1880-1961 *WhAm 4*
Maltby, Edith Frances 1874- *WomWWA 14*
Maltby, Isaac 1767-1819 *ApCAB, Drake*
Maltby, Jasper Adalmorn 1826-1867 *ApCAB*
Maltby, Margaret Eliza 1860-1944 *NotAW,
WhAm 4, WomWWA 14*
Maltby, Ralph B d1952 *WhAm 3*
Maltby, Virginia Minerva 1849- *WomWWA 14*
Malter, Henry 1864-1925 *DcAmB*
Malter, Henry 1867-1925 *WhAm 1*
Malthus, Thomas Robert 1766-1834 *AsBiEn,
DcScB, McGEWB*
Maltsev, Anatoly Ivanovich 1909-1967 *DcScB*
Maltz, George L 1842- *WhAm 4*
Maltzan, Adolf Georg Otto Freiherr Von
1877-1927 *WhAm 1*
Maltzeff, Alexis George 1896-1961 *NatCAB 47*
Malus, Alex *NewYHSD*
Malus, Etienne Louis 1775-1812 *AsBiEn,
DcScB*
Malvern, Viscount 1883-1971 *WhAm 5*
Malzberg, Benjamin 1893-1975 *WhAm 6*
Mambertou, Henry 1506?-1611 *ApCAB*
Mambre, Zenobius 1645-1687 *ApCAB*
Mammen, Ernest 1855-1937 *NatCAB 27*
Mamun, Abdallah, Al- 786-833 *McGEWB*
Man, Alrick Hubbell 1858- *WhAm 1*
Man, Ernest A 1849-1917 *WhAm 1*
Managan, William Henry 1864-1934 *WhAm 1*
Manahan, James 1866-1932 *BiDrAC,
NatCAB 23, WhAm 1*
Manahan, John Levi 1887-1966 *NatCAB 53*
Manardo, Giovanni 1462-1536 *DcScB*
Manasco, Carter 1902- *BiDrAC*
Manasseh *DcScB*
Manasseh BenIsrael 1604-1657 *McGEWB*
Manatt, James Irving 1845-1915 *DcAmB,
NatCAB 8, TwCBDA, WhAm 1*
Mance, Grover Cleveland 1883-1955 *WhAm 3*
Mance, Jeanne 1606-1673 *ApCAB*
Mance, Robert Weston, II 1903-1968 *WhAm 5*
Manchee, Arthur Leavens 1899-1970 *WhAm 5*
Manchester, Albertine 1832-1889 *NatCAB 9*
Manchester, Arthur Livingston 1862-1947
WhAm 2
Manchester, Charles 1858- *TwCBDA*
Manchester, Charles Howard 1865-1930
NatCAB 35, WhAm 1
Manchester, Earl Northup 1881-1954 *WhAm 3*
Manchester, Edward Montagu, Earl Of
1602-1671 *WhoMilH*
Manchester, Herbert A 1859-1943 *WhAm 2*
Manchester, M M *NewYHSD*
Manchester, Margaret MacGregor 1874-
WomWWA 14
Mancini, John *NewYHSD*
Manco Capac 1500?-1544 *Drake*
Manco Capac 1500?-1545 *McGEWB*
Manco Capac I d1107? *ApCAB, Drake*
Manco Inca Yupanqui 1516-1544 *ApCAB*
Mancuso, Francis X 1888-1970 *WhAm 5*
Mandel, Edwin Frank 1875-1963 *WhAm 4*
Mandel, Frederick Leon 1870-1930 *NatCAB 23*

Mandel, John Alfred 1865-1929 *WhAm 1*
Mandel, Leon 1841-1911 *NatCAB 16*
Mandel, Leon 1902-1974 *WhAm 6*
Mandel, Robert 1871- *WhAm 5*
Mandela, Nelson Rolihlahla 1918- *McGEWB*
Mandelbaum, Samuel d1946 *WhAm 2*
Mandell, George Snell 1867-1934 *NatCAB 25,
WhAm 1*
Mandell, Henry Addison 1861-1928 *NatCAB 21*
Mandell, Kaufman 1840- *WhAm 4*
Mandell, Samuel Pierce 1833-1920 *NatCAB 28*
Mandelman, Beatrice 1912- *IIBEAAW*
Mandelshtam, Leonid Isaakovich 1879-1944
DcScB
Mandelstam, Osip Emilyevich 1891-1938
McGEWB
Manderson, Charles Frederick 1837-1911
*ApCAB, BiDrAC, DcAmB, NatCAB 1,
TwCBDA, WhAm 1, WhAmP*
Mandeville, Bernard 1670?-1733 *McGEWB*
Mandeville, Charles Henry Wesley 1876-1947
NatCAB 34
Mandeville, Giles Henry 1825-1904 *TwCBDA,
WhAm 1*
Mandeville, Henry 1804-1858 *ApCAB*
Mandeville, Hubert Carpenter 1867-1943
NatCAB 40, WhAm 2
Mandeville, Sir John *McGEWB*
Mandeville, John Appleton 1882-1941 *WhAm 1*
Mandeville, William Howard 1841-1911
NatCAB 17
Mandeville, William Hubert 1893-1954
NatCAB 41, WhAm 3
Mandl, Emma B 1843- *WomWWA 14*
Mandrillon, Joseph 1742-1794 *Drake*
Mandrillon, Joseph 1743-1794 *ApCAB*
Maneiro, Juan Luis 1744-1802 *ApCAB*
Manes, Alfred 1877-1963 *WhAm 4*
Manet, Edouard 1832-1883 *McGEWB*
Maney, Clement Joseph 1885-1954 *NatCAB 41*
Maney, George Alfred 1888-1947 *NatCAB 34,
WhAm 2*
Maney, George Earl 1826-1901 *BiDConf,
DcAmB, NatCAB 5, TwCBDA*
Maney, Richard 1892-1968 *WhAm 5*
Manfred, Frederick 1912- *REnAW*
Manfredi, Eustachio 1674-1739 *DcScB*
Mangan, Thomas J 1872-1947 *WhAm 2*
Mangas Coloradas 1795?-1863 *REnAW*
Mangasarian, Mangasar Mugurditch 1859-
WhAm 4
Mangel, Sol d1972 *WhAm 5*
Mangels, Hermann N 1897-1961 *WhAm 4*
Manger, Charles *NewYHSD*
Manger, Charles Christian 1871-1923
NatCAB 20
Manger, Heinrich 1833- *NewYHSD*
Manger, Julius 1867-1937 *NatCAB 27*
Manges, Morris 1865-1944 *WhAm 2*
Manges, Willis Fastnacht 1876-1936
NatCAB 29
Manghum, Mason 1885-1960 *NatCAB 53*
Mangin, Charles Marie Emmanuel 1866-1925
WhoMilH
Mangin, Joseph Francois *DcAmB,
NatCAB 25, WhAm H*
Mangin, Louis Alexandre 1852-1937 *DcScB*
Mangold, George Benjamin 1876- *WhAm 5*
Mangore 1480?-1532 *ApCAB*
Mangum, Charles Staples 1870-1939 *WhAm 1*
Mangum, Clare Perkins 1885- *WomWWA 14*
Mangum, Josiah Thomas 1876- *WhAm 5*
Mangum, Willie Person 1792-1861 *ApCAB,
BiAUS, BiDrAC, DcAmB, Drake,
NatCAB 4, TwCBDA, WhAm H,
WhAmP*
Mangum, Willis Lester 1873-1949 *WhAm 3*
Mangurian, Armen Stephen 1877-1951
NatCAB 41
Manhart, Franklin Pierce 1852-1933
NatCAB 42, WhAm 1
Manheimer, Arthur Emanuel 1888-1957
NatCAB 47
Manheimer, Wallace Aaron 1887-1949
NatCAB 36
Manhoff, Bill 1919-1974 *WhAm 6*
Mani 216-277? *McGEWB*
Manic, Peter *NewYHSD*

Manicaotex *ApCAB*
Manice, Edward Augustus 1870-1925
ApCAB X, NatCAB 32
Manice, William DeForest 1889-1961 *WhAm 4*
Manierre, Alfred Lee 1861-1911 *WhAm 1*
Manierre, Eleanor Mason 1884- *WomWWA 14*
Manierre, John Foster 1902-1947 *NatCAB 34*
Manierre, John Thompson 1870-1945
NatCAB 34
Manierre, William Reid 1847-1925 *NatCAB 37*
Manigault, Arthur Middleton 1824-1886
*ApCAB, BiDConf, DcAmB, TwCBDA,
WhAm H*
Manigault, Charles 1795-1874 *ApCAB*
Manigault, Gabriel 1704-1781 *ApCAB,
DcAmB, Drake, TwCBDA, WhAm H*
Manigault, Gabriel 1758-1809 *WhAm H*
Manigault, Gabriel Edward 1833-1899 *ApCAB,
NatCAB 10, TwCBDA, WhAm 1*
Manigault, Gabriel Henry 1788-1834 *ApCAB*
Manigault, Peter 1731-1773 *DcAmB,
WhAm H*
Manigault, Pierre d1729 *DcAmB, WhAm H*
Manigault, R S d1945 *WhAm 2*
Manilius, Marcus *DcScB*
Manim, Sr. *NewYHSD*
Manin, Daniele 1804-1857 *McGEWB*
Manion, Edward J 1872- *WhAm 5*
Manion, William Cecil 1916-1970 *WhAm 5*
Manis, Hubert Clyde 1909-1968 *WhAm 5*
Mankiewicz, Herman Jacob 1897-1953
DcAmB S5, WhAm 3
Mankin, Edward 1873-1951 *NatCAB 41*
Mankin, Helen Douglas 1896-1956 *BiDrAC,
WhAmP*
Mankins, Elvin Orland 1911-1974 *WhAm 6*
Manley, Charles Thomas 1891-1946
NatCAB 34
Manley, F Nason 1894-1965 *WhAm 4*
Manley, Frederick Willis 1881- *WhAm 6*
Manley, George Leroy 1892-1971 *NatCAB 56*
Manley, Henry DeHaven 1839- *ApCAB*
Manley, Jane Helena *NewYHSD*
Manley, John 1733-1793 *ApCAB*
Manley, John 1734?-1793 *AmBi, DcAmB,
WebAMB, WhAm H*
Manley, John Ellis 1879- *WhAm 3*
Manley, John Michael 1868-1958 *NatCAB 47*
Manley, Joseph Homan 1842-1905 *DcAmB,
NatCAB 6, WhAm 1*
Manley, Norman Washington 1893-1969
WhAm 5
Manley, Thomas Henry 1851-1905 *WhAm 1*
Manley, Thomas Rathbone 1853-1938
NatCAB 44
Manley, William T *NewYHSD*
Manlove, Gilbert Beebe 1850-1909 *NatCAB 14*
Manlove, Joe Jonathan 1876-1956 *BiDrAC,
WhAmP*
Manly *NewYHSD*
Manly, Basil 1798-1868 *ApCAB, BiDConf,
DcAmB, Drake, NatCAB 12, TwCBDA,
WhAm H*
Manly, Basil 1825-1892 *ApCAB, DcAmB,
NatCAB 25, TwCBDA, WhAm H*
Manly, Basil Maxwell 1886-1950 *DcAmB S4,
NatCAB 38, WhAm 3*
Manly, Charles 1795-1871 *ApCAB, BiAUS,
NatCAB 4, TwCBDA*
Manly, Charles 1837-1924 *NatCAB 25,
TwCBDA, WhAm 1*
Manly, Charles Matthews 1876-1927 *DcAmB,
NatCAB 21, WhAm 1*
Manly, Chesly 1905-1970 *WhAm 5*
Manly, Fanny Louisa 1857- *TwCBDA*
Manly, George C 1863-1936 *WhAm 1,
WhAm 1C*
Manly, James *NewYHSD*
Manly, John 1733-1793 *Drake, NatCAB 5,
TwCBDA*
Manly, John Matthews 1865-1940 *BiDAmEd,
DcAmB S2, NatCAB 48, TwCBDA,
WhAm 1*
Manly, Lewis Frederick 1903-1970 *WhAm 5*
Manly, Matthias Evans 1800-1881 *ApCAB,
NatCAB 7, TwCBDA*
Manly, Robert Emmet 1869- *WhAm 3*
Manly, William Hester 1875-1938 *WhAm 1*

Mann, A Dudley 1805-1889 *BiAUS, Drake*
Mann, Abijah, Jr. 1793-1868 *ApCAB, BiAUS, BiDrAC, TwCBDA, WhAm H*
Mann, Alan Newhall 1886-1963 *WhAm 4*
Mann, Albert 1853-1935 *NatCAB 25, WhAm 1*
Mann, Albert Clinton 1881-1948 *WhAm 2*
Mann, Albert Russell 1880-1947 *NatCAB 36, WhAm 2*
Mann, Albert Zachariah 1887-1962 *WhAm 4*
Mann, Alden T 1895-1966 *WhAm 4*
Mann, Alexander 1860-1948 *NatCAB 42, WhAm 2*
Mann, Ambrose Dudley 1801-1889 *ApCAB, BiDConf, DcAmB, NatCAB 25, TwCBDA, WhAm H*
Mann, Anthony 1906-1967 *WhAm 4*
Mann, Arthur 1901-1963 *WhAm 4*
Mann, Arthur Robert 1877-1968 *WhAm 5*
Mann, Arthur Teall 1866-1935 *WhAm 1*
Mann, B Pickman 1848-1922 *WhAm 1*
Mann, Cameron 1851-1932 *NatCAB 13, WhAm 1*
Mann, Caroline Whallon Judd 1885- *WomWWA 14*
Mann, Carrie Foote *WomWWA 14*
Mann, Charles August 1886-1949 *WhAm 2*
Mann, Charles Holbrook 1839-1918 *WhAm 1*
Mann, Charles Riborg 1869-1942 *WhAm 2*
Mann, Charles William 1879-1943 *WhAm 2*
Mann, Conrad Henry 1871- *WhAm 3*
Mann, Cynthia Pease 1853- *WomWWA 14*
Mann, Cyrus 1785-1859 *ApCAB, Drake*
Mann, Edward Ames 1867-1915 *WhAm 1*
Mann, Edward Coke 1880-1931 *BiDrAC*
Mann, Edward Garnett Batson 1863- *WhAm 4*
Mann, Edwin Jonathan 1878-1954 *NatCAB 42*
Mann, Ellery Wilson 1890-1956 *WhAm 3*
Mann, Emma *WomWWA 14*
Mann, Erika d1969 *WhAm 5*
Mann, Estes Wilson 1894-1958 *NatCAB 47*
Mann, Floris Janette Perkins 1885- *WomWWA 14*
Mann, Frank Charles 1887-1962 *WhAm 4*
Mann, Frank Hurt 1883-1954 *WhAm 3*
Mann, Frank Irving 1854-1937 *WhAm 1*
Mann, Fred Parker 1870- *WhAm 5*
Mann, Frederick Maynard 1868- *WhAm 5*
Mann, George Douglas 1879-1936 *WhAm 1*
Mann, Gustav 1864- *WhAm 4*
Mann, Heinrich Ludwig 1871-1950 *McGEWB, WhAm 3*
Mann, Henry 1848-1915 *WhAm 1*
Mann, Henry 1890-1968 *WhAm 5*
Mann, Horace 1796-1859 *AmBi, ApCAB, BiAUS, BiDAmEd, BiDrAC, DcAmB, DcAmReB, Drake, EncAB, McGEWB, NatCAB 3, TwCBDA, WebAB, WhAm H, WhAmP*
Mann, Horace Borchsenius 1868-1937 *WhAm 1*
Mann, Horace L 1872-1942 *WhAm 4*
Mann, Isaac Thomas 1863-1932 *NatCAB 15*
Mann, Isaac Thomas 1864-1932 *WhAm 1*
Mann, James 1759-1832 *ApCAB, DcAmB, Drake, WhAm H*
Mann, James 1822-1868 *BiDrAC, WhAm H*
Mann, James Robert 1856-1922 *AmBi, BiDrAC, DcAmB, EncAAH, TwCBDA, WhAm 1, WhAmP*
Mann, James Robert 1920- *BiDrAC*
Mann, James Walter 1872-1930 *WhAm 1*
Mann, Job 1795-1873 *BiAUS, BiDrAC, TwCBDA, WhAm H*
Mann, Joel Keith 1780-1857 *BiAUS, BiDrAC, TwCBDA, WhAm H*
Mann, John Joseph 1907-1975 *WhAm 6*
Mann, Joseph F 1890-1951 *WhAm 3*
Mann, Klaus 1906-1949 *WhAm 3*
Mann, Kristine 1873-1945 *BiCAW, NatCAB 34, WhAm 2, WomWWA 14*
Mann, Lester Bradwell 1886-1954 *WhAm 3*
Mann, Lewis Merritt 1848-1923 *NatCAB 21*
Mann, Louis 1865-1931 *DcAmB, WhAm 1*
Mann, Louis Leopold 1890-1966 *NatCAB 51, WhAm 4*
Mann, Manly Glenwood 1889-1958 *NatCAB 49*
Mann, Margaret 1873-1960 *DcAmLiB, WhAm 5*

Mann, Martha Elizabeth Foss 1848- *WomWWA 14*
Mann, Mary Adeline 1862- *WomWWA 14*
Mann, Mary Ridpath 1867- *WhAm 4*
Mann, Mary Tyler Peabody 1806-1887 *ApCAB, DcAmB, NotAW, TwCBDA, WhAm H*
Mann, Matthew Derbyshire 1845-1921 *NatCAB 10, WhAm 1*
Mann, Millicent E 1863- *WhAm 4*
Mann, Nancy Murray *WhAm 5*
Mann, Newton 1836-1926 *DcAmB, NatCAB 20, WhAm 1*
Mann, Parker 1852-1918 *NatCAB 19, WhAm 1*
Mann, Paul Blakeslee 1876-1943 *NatCAB 42, WhAm 2*
Mann, Rowena Morse 1870-1958 *WhAm 3, WomWWA 14*
Mann, Seth 1860-1935 *WhAm 1*
Mann, Stanley 1876-1958 *WhAm 3*
Mann, Thomas 1875-1955 *McGEWB, WhAm 3*
Mann, William Abram 1854-1934 *WhAm 1*
Mann, William Alfred 1898-1971 *NatCAB 56, WhAm 5*
Mann, William Benson 1816- *ApCAB, NatCAB 1*
Mann, William D'Alton 1839-1920 *NatCAB 11, WhAm 1*
Mann, William Hodges 1843-1927 *NatCAB 14, WhAm 1*
Mann, William Julius 1819-1892 *ApCAB, DcAmB, TwCBDA, WhAm H*
Mann, William M 1886-1960 *NatCAB 47, WhAm 4*
Mann, William Orris 1869-1915 *NatCAB 19*
Manner, Jane d1943 *WhAm 2*
Mannerheim, Baron Carl Gustav Emil Von 1867-1951 *McGEWB, WhWW-II, WhoMilH*
Mannering, Mary 1876-1953 *NatCAB 42, WomWWA 14*
Manners, Frances Louise Whittlesey 1861- *WomWWA 14*
Manners, George d1853 *Drake*
Manners, John Hartley 1870-1928 *DcAmB, NatCAB 25, WhAm 1*
Mannes, Clara Damrosch 1869-1948 *BiDAmEd, DcAmB S4, NotAW, WomWWA 14*
Mannes, David 1866-1959 *BiDAmEd, NatCAB 47, WhAm 3*
Mannes, Glenn Jay 1910-1958 *NatCAB 45*
Mannes, Leopold Damrosch 1899-1964 *NatCAB 52, WhAm 4*
Manney, Charles Fonteyn 1872-1951 *WhAm 3*
Manney, Henry Newman 1844-1915 *WhAm 1*
Mannheim, Hermann 1889-1974 *WhAm 6*
Mannheim, Jean d1945 *WhAm 2*
Mannheim, Karl 1893-1947 *McGEWB*
Mannheim, Victor Mayer Amedee 1831-1906 *DcScB*
Mannheimer, Jennie *WomWWA 14*
Manning, Alan Monroe 1903-1965 *NatCAB 52*
Manning, Andrew Adger 1880-1962 *NatCAB 50*
Manning, Charles Henry 1844-1919 *WhAm 1*
Manning, Charles N 1875-1947 *WhAm 2*
Manning, Clarence Augustus 1893-1972 *NatCAB 57, WhAm 5*
Manning, Daniel 1831-1887 *AmBi, ApCAB, ApCAB X, BiDrUSE, DcAmB, NatCAB 2, TwCBDA, WhAm H*
Manning, Edward Betts 1874-1948 *WhAm 2*
Manning, Edward McClure 1872-1956 *NatCAB 46*
Manning, Estelle Hempstead 1879- *WhAm 6*
Manning, Fowler 1879-1948 *NatCAB 37*
Manning, Frank Leary 1873- *ApCAB X*
Manning, George Charles 1892-1964 *WhAm 4*
Manning, George H 1883-1934 *WhAm 1*
Manning, Harry 1897-1974 *WhAm 6*
Manning, Cardinal Henry Edward 1808-1892 *McGEWB*
Manning, Henry Parker 1859-1956 *NatCAB 45, WhAm 4*
Manning, Herbert Alan 1875-1959 *NatCAB 47*
Manning, Isaac A 1864- *WhAm 4*
Manning, Isaac Hall 1866-1946 *WhAm 2*

Manning, Jacob Merrill 1824-1882 *ApCAB, TwCBDA*
Manning, James d1791 *BiAUS*
Manning, James 1735-1791 *WhAm H*
Manning, James 1738-1791 *ApCAB, BiDAmEd, BiDrAC, DcAmB, DcAmReB, Drake, NatCAB 1, NatCAB 8, TwCBDA*
Manning, James Hilton 1854-1925 *NatCAB 1, TwCBDA, WhAm 1*
Manning, James Smith 1859-1938 *WhAm 1*
Manning, Jeremiah Lordan 1878-1922 *ApCAB X*
Manning, Jessie Wilson 1855- *AmWom*
Manning, Jewel Evangeline Berger 1910-1973 *WhAm 6*
Manning, John d1686? *ApCAB*
Manning, John, Jr. 1830-1899 *BiAUS, BiDrAC, NatCAB 3, TwCBDA*
Manning, John Alexander 1838- *NatCAB 3*
Manning, John Alexander 1869-1938 *NatCAB 37*
Manning, John B, II 1869- *ApCAB X*
Manning, John Bernard 1833-1918 *ApCAB X, NatCAB 31*
Manning, John Charles 1893-1967 *WhAm 4*
Manning, John H *NewYHSD*
Manning, John Joseph d1962 *WhAm 4*
Manning, John L 1816-1889 *BiAUS*
Manning, John Laurence 1816-1889 *NatCAB 12*
Manning, John Lawrence 1816-1889 *ApCAB, TwCBDA*
Manning, Joseph J 1862-1926 *ApCAB X*
Manning, Joseph Patrick 1866-1944 *NatCAB 32, WhAm 2*
Manning, Joseph Thruston, III 1917-1970 *WhAm 5*
Manning, Lucius Bass 1894-1944 *NatCAB 33, WhAm 2*
Manning, Maria Potter 1860- *WomWWA 14*
Manning, Marie 1873?-1945 *DcAmB S3, NotAW, WhAm 2*
Manning, Mary Margaret Fryer 1845-1928 *WomWWA 14*
Manning, Mary Margaretta Fryer 1845-1928 *NatCAB 12, NatCAB 26, WhAm 1, WhAm 1C*
Manning, Mary O'Leary 1836-1906 *ApCAB X*
Manning, Pierre *NewYHSD*
Manning, Randolph 1804-1864 *ApCAB*
Manning, Richard Henry 1809-1887 *NatCAB 14*
Manning, Richard Irvine 1789-1836 *ApCAB, BiAUS, BiDrAC, DcAmB, Drake, NatCAB 12, TwCBDA, WhAm H*
Manning, Richard Irvine 1859-1931 *DcAmB, NatCAB 23, WhAm 1*
Manning, Robert 1784-1842 *ApCAB, DcAmB, EncAAH, TwCBDA, WhAm H*
Manning, Thomas Courtland 1825-1887 *DcAmB, TwCBDA, WhAm H*
Manning, Thomas Courtland 1831-1887 *ApCAB, NatCAB 4*
Manning, Van H 1839-1892 *TwCBDA*
Manning, Vannoy Hartrog 1839-1892 *BiDrAC, WhAm H*
Manning, Vannoy Hartrog 1861-1932 *DcAmB, WhAm 1*
Manning, Walter Webster 1875-1931 *WhAm 1*
Manning, Warren Henry 1860-1938 *NatCAB 33, WhAm 1*
Manning, William 1616?-1692 *ApCAB*
Manning, William Albert 1876-1972 *WhAm 5*
Manning, William Ray 1871-1942 *WhAm 2*
Manning, William T 1865-1908 *WhAm 1*
Manning, William Thomas 1866-1949 *DcAmB S4, NatCAB 38, WhAm 2*
Manning, William W 1873-1954 *NatCAB 44*
Mannix, Archbishop Daniel 1864-1963 *McGEWB*
Mannock, Edward 1887-1918 *WhoMilH*
Mannon, Floyd Ralph 1898-1964 *NatCAB 53, WhAm 4*
Manny, Frank Addison 1868- *WhAm 5*
Manny, John H 1825-1856 *NatCAB 11*
Manogue, Patrick 1831-1895 *ApCAB, TwCBDA*
Manoog, John M *NewYHSD*

Manosalvas, Hernan Venegas Carillo d1583
  ApCAB
Manouvrier, Jules *NewYHSD*
Manrique, Jorge 1440?-1478 *McGEWB*
Manrique, Jose Angel 1777-1822 *ApCAB*
Manross, Newton Spalding 1825-1862
  NatCAB 11
Manross, Newton Spaulding 1825-1862 *ApCAB*
Mansan, Mrs. *NewYHSD*
Mansart, Francois 1598-1666 *McGEWB*
Mansart, Jules Hardouin 1646-1708 *McGEWB*
Mansell, O S 1896-1963 *WhAm 4*
Mansell, William Albert 1864-1913 *DcAmB*
Manser, Clarence Adelbert 1901-1959
  NatCAB 50
Manser, Frances Mary *WomWWA 14*
Manser, Harry 1874-1955 *WhAm 4*
Mansergh, Robert 1900-1970 *WhAm 5*
Mansfeld, Ernst, Graf Von 1580-1626 *WhoMilH*
Mansfield, Adelaide Claflin 1874-
  WomWWA 14
Mansfield, Arabella 1846-1911 *NotAW*
Mansfield, Archibald Romaine 1871-1934
  WhAm 1
Mansfield, Beatrice Cameron 1868- *WhAm 4*
Mansfield, Blanche McManus 1869-
  WomWWA 14
Mansfield, Burton 1856-1932 *WhAm 1*
Mansfield, Charles B 1819-1855 *ApCAB*
Mansfield, Edward Deering 1801-1880 *ApCAB,*
  DcAmB, Drake, NatCAB 11, TwCBDA,
  WhAm H
Mansfield, Frederick William 1877-1958
  WhAm 3
Mansfield, George Rogers 1875-1947
  NatCAB 35, WhAm 5
Mansfield, Helen Coolidge 1860-
  WomWWA 14
Mansfield, Henry Buckingham 1846-1918
  NatCAB 17, WhAm 1
Mansfield, Howard 1849-1938 *WhAm 1*
Mansfield, Ira Franklin 1842- *WhAm 4*
Mansfield, Jared 1759-1830 *ApCAB, DcAmB,*
  NatCAB 3, TwCBDA, WhAm H
Mansfield, Jared 1875-1947 *Drake*
Mansfield, Jayne 1937-1967 *WhAm 4*
Mansfield, John Brainard 1826-1886 *ApCAB*
Mansfield, Joseph Jefferson 1861-1947 *BiDrAC,*
  NatCAB 37, WhAm 2, WhAmP
Mansfield, Joseph King Fenno 1803-1862 *AmBi,*
  ApCAB, DcAmB, Drake, NatCAB 4,
  TwCBDA, WebAMB, WhAm H
Mansfield, Mary Allen *WomWWA 14*
Mansfield, Michael Joseph 1903- *BiDrAC*
Mansfield, Myrtle Gibson *WomWWA 14*
Mansfield, Orlando Augustine 1865- *WhAm 4*
Mansfield, Richard 1723-1820 *ApCAB,*
  DcAmB, NatCAB 12, WhAm H
Mansfield, Richard 1851?-1907 *TwCBDA*
Mansfield, Richard 1854?-1907 *AmBi, DcAmB,*
  WebAB
Mansfield, Richard 1857?-1907 *ApCAB Sup,*
  NatCAB 9, WhAm 1
Mansfield, Robert E 1866-1925 *WhAm 1*
Mansfield, Samuel Mather 1839-1928 *WhAm 1*
Mansfield, Susan Hegeman 1868-
  WomWWA 14
Mansfield, Thomas Robert 1891-1973
  NatCAB 57
Mansfield, William Douglass 1878-1952
  NatCAB 41, WhAm 3
Manship, Andrew 1824- *ApCAB*
Manship, Charles Phelps 1881-1947 *WhAm 2*
Manship, Paul 1885-1966 *BnEnAmA,*
  WhAm 4
Mansion, Paul 1844-1919 *DcScB*
Manske, Walter Earl 1928-1973 *WhAm 6*
Manso, Alonso 1470?-1540 *ApCAB*
Manso DeVelasco, Jose Antonio d1770? *ApCAB*
Manson, Daniel Edgar 1870-1942 *NatCAB 32,*
  WhAm 2
Manson, Edward Charles 1865-1941
  NatCAB 30
Manson, Frederic E 1860- *WhAm 4*
Manson, John Thomas 1861-1944 *WhAm 2*
Manson, Louise Hutcheson *WomWWA 14*
Manson, Mahlon Dickerson 1820-1895 *ApCAB,*
  BiAUS, BiDrAC, TwCBDA, WhAm H

Manson, Marsden 1850-1931 *NatCAB 41,*
  WhAm 1
Manson, Otis Frederick 1822-1888 *ApCAB Sup,*
  DcAmB, NatCAB 15, WhAm H
Manson, Sir Patrick 1844-1922 *AsBiEn,*
  BiHiMed, DcScB
Manson, Philip 1877-1941 *NatCAB 31*
Manson, Ray H 1877-1961 *WhAm 4*
Manson, Richard 1901-1954 *WhAm 3*
Manss, Harvey McKnight 1886-1959 *WhAm 3*
Manss, William Henry 1866-1941 *NatCAB 31*
Manstein, Erich VonLewinski Von 1887-1973
  WhWW-II, WhoMilH
Mansur, Abu Jafar Ibn Muhammad, Al- 712-775
  McGEWB
Mansur, Charles Harley 1835-1895 *BiDrAC,*
  WhAm H
Mansur, Charles Harvey 1835-1895 *TwCBDA*
Mansur, Zophar M 1843-1914 *WhAm 1*
Mansur Ibn Ali Ibn Iraq, Abu Nasr d1036?
  DcScB
Mansure, Charles 1832?- *NewYHSD*
Mansure, Edmund Lionel 1860-1935
  NatCAB 27
Mansure, Edmund Lionel 1862-1935 *ApCAB X*
Mansure, John J 1834?- *NewYHSD*
Mansure, Robert *NewYHSD*
Mantani, Walter 1918-1963 *NatCAB 48*
Mante, Thomas *Drake*
Mantegazza, Paolo 1831-1910 *DcScB*
Mantegna, Andrea 1430?-1506 *McGEWB*
Mantell, Gideon Algernon 1790-1852 *DcScB*
Mantell, Robert Bruce 1854-1928 *AmBi,*
  DcAmB, NatCAB 10, NatCAB 14,
  WhAm 1
Manter, Harold W 1898-1971 *WhAm 5*
Manteuffel, Edwin Hans K Freiherr Von
  1809-1885 *WhoMilH*
Manteuffel, Hasso Von 1897- *WhoMilH*
Manteuffel, Tadeusz 1902-1970 *WhAm 6*
Mantilla, Luis Felipe 1833-1878 *ApCAB*
Mantle, Burns 1873-1948 *DcAmB S4,*
  NatCAB 37, WhAm 2
Mantle, Gladys Ann Doyle 1896-1969 *WhAm 5*
Mantle, Lee 1851-1934 *ApCAB Sup,*
  ApCAB X, BiDrAC, NatCAB 11,
  NatCAB 44, TwCBDA, WhAm 1,
  WhAmP
Mantle, Mickey Charles 1931- *WebAB*
Manton, Benjamin Dyer 1829-1911 *NatCAB 8*
Manton, Frank Stead 1838-1909 *ApCAB X*
Manton, Martin Thomas 1880-1946 *WhAm 2A*
Manton, Walter Porter 1858-1925 *WhAm 1*
Mantynband, Louis M 1897-1971 *WhAm 5*
Mantz, H J 1877- *WhAm 5*
Mantz, Herbert Leslie 1896-1953 *NatCAB 43*
Manucy, Dominic 1823-1885 *ApCAB,*
  NatCAB 13, TwCBDA, WhAm H
Manuel I 1469-1521 *McGEWB*
Manuel I, Comnenus 1123?-1180 *McGEWB*
Manuel, W A 1891-1970 *WhAm 5*
Manuilsky, Dmitry Zakharavish 1883-1959
  WhAm 3
Manville, Charles Brayton 1834-1927
  NatCAB 24
Manville, Charles Rollins 1866-1920
  NatCAB 24
Manville, Edward Britton 1879-1944 *WhAm 2*
Manville, H Edward 1872-1944 *NatCAB 56,*
  WhAm 2
Manville, H Estelle 1878-1947 *NatCAB 56*
Manville, Helen Adelia 1839- *AmWom,*
  NatCAB 24
Manville, T Franklyn 1862-1925 *NatCAB 24*
Manwaring, A Homer, II 1912-1956 *WhAm 3*
Manwaring, Elizabeth Wheeler 1879-1949
  WhAm 2, WomWWA 14
Manwaring, Wilfred Hamilton 1871- *WhAm 5*
Manypenny, George W *BiAUS*
Manzanares, Francisco Antonio 1843-1904
  BiDrAC, REnAW, WhAm 1, WhAmP
Manzano, Juan Francisco 1797-1854 *ApCAB*
Manzer, Adaline Brower 1870- *WomWWA 14*
Manzo, Jose 1789-1840? *ApCAB*
Manzoni, Alessandro 1785-1873 *McGEWB*
Manzu, Giacomo 1908- *McGEWB*
Mao, Tse-Tung 1893-1976 *McGEWB,*
  WhAm 6, WhWW-II, WhoMilH

Mapes, Carl Edgar 1874-1939 *BiDrAC,*
  NatCAB 30, WhAm 1, WhAmP
Mapes, Carl Herbert 1900-1966 *WhAm 4*
Mapes, Charles Halsted 1864- *NatCAB 3*
Mapes, Charles Victor 1836-1916 *ApCAB,*
  DcAmB, NatCAB 3, TwCBDA,
  WhAm 1
Mapes, Charles Whitcraft 1879-1937
  NatCAB 38
Mapes, Clarel Bowman 1902-1967 *WhAm 5*
Mapes, Eugene Edward 1861-1947 *NatCAB 36*
Mapes, George Washington 1833-1923
  NatCAB 38
Mapes, James Jay 1806-1866 *AmBi, ApCAB,*
  DcAmB, Drake, EncAAH, NatCAB 3,
  NewYHSD, TwCBDA, WhAm H
Mapes, Milton Crawford 1888-1968
  NatCAB 54
Mapes, Victor 1870-1943 *NatCAB 43,*
  WhAm 5
Maphis, Charles Gilmore 1865-1938 *WhAm 1*
Maple, Frank Fulton 1886-1965 *NatCAB 51*
Maples, Harold E 1890-1950 *WhAm 2A*
Maples, Thomas 1803?- *NewYHSD*
Mapother, Dillon H *NewYHSD*
Mapother, Wible Lawrence 1872-1926 *WhAm 1*
Mapow, Abraham B 1907-1969 *WhAm 6*
Mapp, G Walter 1873-1941 *NatCAB 39*
Mappa, Adam Gerard 1754-1828 *DcAmB,*
  WhAm H
Mappin, Lillian M *WomWWA 14*
Maqdisi, Shams Al-Din Abu Abdallah, Al- 946?-
  DcScB
Mar, Juan Manuel Del 1806-1862 *ApCAB*
Marable, Fate 1890-1947 *WhAm 4*
Marable, John Hartwell 1786-1844 *BiAUS,*
  BiDrAC, WhAm H
Maraldi, Giacomo Filippo 1665-1729 *DcScB*
Maraldi, Giovanni Domenico 1709-1788 *DcScB*
Maranhao, Jeronimo DeAlburquerque 1548-1618
  ApCAB
Maranville, Walter James Vincent 1891-1954
  DcAmB S5
Maras *NewYHSD*
Marat, Jean Paul 1743-1793 *McGEWB*
Marbau, Pedro De 1630?-1706? *ApCAB*
Marble, Albert Prescott 1836-1906 *BiDAmEd,*
  DcAmB, NatCAB 13
Marble, Anna Warren 1815- *ApCAB*
Marble, Annie Russell 1864-1936 *NatCAB 27,*
  WhAm 1, WomWWA 14
Marble, Arthur H 1870-1945 *WhAm 2*
Marble, Callie Bonney *AmWom*
Marble, Charles Baldwin 1875-1927 *WhAm 1*
Marble, Charles Francis 1865-1947 *NatCAB 35*
Marble, Danford 1807-1849 *ApCAB*
Marble, Danforth 1807-1849 *Drake*
Marble, Danforth 1810-1849 *DcAmB,*
  WhAm H
Marble, Edgar Martin 1838-1908 *NatCAB 13,*
  WhAm 1
Marble, Elizabeth Dana *WomWWA 14*
Marble, Ella M S 1850- *AmWom*
Marble, Fred Elmer 1861- *WhAm 1*
Marble, George Watson 1870-1930 *WhAm 1*
Marble, Harriet Fuller 1874- *WomWWA 14*
Marble, Harriett Beecher Stowe 1885-
  WhoColR
Marble, J Russel 1852-1920 *NatCAB 19*
Marble, John Hobart 1868-1913 *NatCAB 16*
Marble, John Hobart 1869-1913 *WhAm 1*
Marble, John Putnam 1897-1955 *WhAm 3*
Marble, Manton 1834-1917 *TwCBDA,*
  WhAm 1
Marble, Manton Malone 1835-1917 *AmBi,*
  ApCAB, DcAmB, Drake
Marble, Mitchell Stewart 1854- *WhAm 4*
Marble, Sebastian Streeter 1817-1902
  NatCAB 5
Marble, Sebastien Streeter 1817-1902 *TwCBDA*
Marble, Thomas Littlefield 1876-1952
  NatCAB 41, WhAm 3
Marble, William Allen 1849-1930 *NatCAB 15,*
  WhAm 1, WhAm 1C
Marble, William Edward 1877-1940
  NatCAB 30
Marbois, Francois DeBarbe, Marquis De
  1745-1837 *ApCAB, Drake*

Marbourg, Dolores *WomWWA 14*
Marburg, Edgar 1864-1918 *NatCAB 42, WhAm 1*
Marburg, Fanny Dulany Moncure 1868- *WomWWA 14*
Marburg, Otto 1874-1948 *NatCAB 36, WhAm 2*
Marburg, Theodore 1862-1946 *DcAmB S4, NatCAB 15, NatCAB 34, WhAm 2*
Marburg, Theodore Herman 1873-1944 *NatCAB 33*
Marburger, Ralph E 1894-1954 *WhAm 3*
Marbury, Elisabeth 1856-1933 *DcAmB S1, NotAW, WhAm 1, WomWWA 14*
Marbury, William G 1912-1971 *WhAm 5*
Marbury, William L 1858-1935 *WhAm 1*
Marbut, Curtis Fletcher 1863-1935 *AmBi, DcAmB S1, EncAAH, NatCAB 33, WhAm 1*
Marby, Giddings Edlon 1877- *WhAm 6*
Marc, Franz 1880-1916 *McGEWB*
Marc, Henri Michel 1900-1962 *NatCAB 50, WhAm 4*
Marca-Relli, Conrad 1913- *BnEnAmA*
Marcadet, Etienne Edouard 1773-1838 *ApCAB*
Marcantonio, Vito Anthony 1902-1954 *BiDrAC, DcAmB S5, WhAm 3, WhAmP*
Marceau, Francois Severin 1769-1796 *WhoMilH*
Marceau, Henri 1896-1969 *WhAm 5*
Marcel, Gabriel Honore 1889-1973 *McGEWB, WhAm 6*
Marcelle, Vito *NewYHSD*
Marcey, William *NewYHSD*
Marcgraf, Georg *DcScB*
March, Abraham Wolf 1909-1969 *NatCAB 57, WhAm 5*
March, Alden 1795-1869 *ApCAB, DcAmB, Drake, NatCAB 2, WhAm H*
March, Alden 1869-1942 *WhAm 2*
March, Anthony 1912-1973 *WhAm 6*
March, Charles Hoyt 1870-1945 *NatCAB 36, WhAm 2*
March, Charles Wainwright 1815-1864 *ApCAB, Drake*
March, Daniel 1816-1909 *ApCAB, TwCBDA, WhAm 1*
March, Francis Andrew 1825-1911 *AmBi, ApCAB, BiDAmEd, DcAmB, NatCAB 11, TwCBDA, WebAB, WhAm 1*
March, Francis Andrew, Jr. 1863-1928 *DcAmB, WhAm 1*
March, Frank Morrison 1863- *ApCAB X*
March, Fredric 1897-1975 *WhAm 6*
March, Giovanni *NewYHSD*
March, H W 1878- *WhAm 6*
March, Hal 1920-1970 *WhAm 5*
March, Harry Addison 1875-1940 *NatCAB 31*
March, John 1658-1725 *TwCBDA*
March, John Lewis 1873- *WhAm 5*
March, Peyton Conway 1864-1955 *ApCAB X, DcAmB S5, NatCAB 41, WebAMB, WhAm 3*
March, Thomas Stone 1868-1939 *WhAm 1*
March, William Edward 1893-1954 *DcAmB S5*
Marchais, Etienne Renaud 1683-1728 *ApCAB*
Marchais DesGentils, Jules *NewYHSD*
Marchal, Nicolas 1731-1802 *ApCAB*
Marchand, Albert Gallatin 1811-1848 *BiAUS, BiDrAC, WhAm H*
Marchand, David *NewYHSD*
Marchand, David 1776-1832 *BiAUS, BiDrAC, WhAm H*
Marchand, Etienne 1755-1793 *ApCAB*
Marchand, Felix Gabriel 1832- *ApCAB*
Marchand, Jean Baptiste 1863-1934 *WhoMilH*
Marchand, John Bonnett 1808-1875 *ApCAB, DcAmB, Drake, TwCBDA, WhAm H*
Marchand, John Norval 1875-1921 *IIBEAAW*
Marchand, Jules *NewYHSD*
Marchand, Richard Felix 1813-1850 *DcScB*
Marchant, Dalton Edward 1806-1887 *ApCAB*
Marchant, Edward Dalton 1806-1887 *NewYHSD, WhAm H*
Marchant, G W *NewYHSD*
Marchant, Henry 1741-1796 *ApCAB, BiAUS, BiDrAC, DcAmB, Drake, NatCAB 9, TwCBDA, WhAm H, WhAmP*

Marchant, Henry A 1839?- *NewYHSD*
Marchant, Jean 1650-1738 *DcScB*
Marchant, Nicolas d1678 *DcScB*
Marchant, Trelawney E 1887-1950 *WhAm 3*
Marchase, Joseph Anthony 1911-1965 *NatCAB 53*
Marchbanks, Andrew J d1867 *BiAUS*
Marchbanks, Stanton Sanders 1882-1970 *NatCAB 57*
Marchbanks, Tom Earl 1922-1975 *WhAm 6*
Marchegiano, Rocco Francis *WebAB*
Marchetti, Andrew A 1901-1970 *WhAm 5*
Marchev, Alfred 1896-1947 *WhAm 2*
Marchi, Vittorio 1851-1908 *DcScB*
Marchiafava, Ettore 1847-1935 *DcScB*
Marchino, Frederick *NewYHSD*
Marchlewski, Leon Pawel Teodor 1869-1946 *DcScB*
Marci Of Kronland, Johannes Marcus 1595-1667 *DcScB*
Marcial-Dorado, Carolina 1889-1941 *WhAm 1*
Marciano, Rocky 1924-1969 *WebAB*
Marcin, Max 1879- *WhAm 6*
Marcion *McGEWB*
Marck, Siegfried 1889-1957 *NatCAB 43*
Marckwardt, Albert Henry 1903-1975 *WhAm 6*
Marco, Herbert Francis 1907-1969 *WhAm 5*
Marco, Salvatore Michael 1907-1973 *WhAm 6*
Marcon, Lucien *NewYHSD*
Marconi, Guglielmo 1874-1937 *AsBiEn, DcScB, McGEWB*
Marconi, William 1874-1937 *WhAm 1*
Marcos De Niza 1500?-1558 *McGEWB*
Marcos, Ferdinand 1917- *McGEWB*
Marcosson, Isaac Frederick 1877-1961 *WhAm 4*
Marcosson, Sol 1869-1940 *WhAm 1*
Marcotte, Henry 1870-1955 *WhAm 3*
Marcou, John Belknap 1855- *WhAm 4*
Marcou, Jules 1824-1898 *ApCAB, ApCAB Sup, DcAmB, DcScB, IIBEAAW, NatCAB 25, TwCBDA, WhAm H*
Marcou, Lucien *NewYHSD*
Marcoux, Joseph 1770?-1855 *ApCAB*
Marcoux, Vanni 1879- *WhAm 6*
Marcum, Thomas 1843- *WhAm 4*
Marcus Aurelius Antoninus 121-180 *McGEWB*
Marcus, Bernard Kent 1890?-1954 *DcAmB S5*
Marcus, Johannes *DcScB*
Marcus, Joseph Anthony 1894-1960 *NatCAB 47, WhAm 4*
Marcus, Louis 1880-1936 *WhAm 1*
Marcus, Louis William 1863-1923 *WhAm 1*
Marcus, Ralph 1900-1956 *WhAm 3*
Marcuse, Herbert 1898- *EncAB, McGEWB, WebAB*
Marcuse, Milton E 1869-1946 *NatCAB 35, WhAm 2*
Marcy, Daniel 1809-1893 *BiAUS, BiDrAC, WhAm H*
Marcy, E E 1815-1900 *Drake*
Marcy, Erastus Edgerton 1815-1900 *ApCAB, TwCBDA, WhAm 1*
Marcy, Frank Earl 1872-1959 *NatCAB 49*
Marcy, George Edward 1863-1939 *WhAm 1*
Marcy, Henry Orlando 1837-1924 *BiHiMed, DcAmB, NatCAB 6, WhAm 1*
Marcy, Mary Elizabeth Smith 1847- *WomWWA 14*
Marcy, Oliver 1820-1899 *ApCAB, NatCAB 13, TwCBDA, WhAm 1*
Marcy, Randolph Barnes 1811?-1887 *BiAUS, Drake*
Marcy, Randolph Barnes 1812-1887 *ApCAB, DcAmB, NatCAB 4, REnAW, TwCBDA, WebAMB, WhAm H*
Marcy, William Larned 1786-1857 *BiAUS*
Marcy, William Learned 1786-1857 *AmBi, ApCAB, BiDrAC, BiDrUSE, DcAmB, Drake, EncAB, McGEWB, NatCAB 6, TwCBDA, WebAB, WhAm H, WhAmP*
Marden, Charles Carroll 1867-1932 *DcAmB, WhAm 1*
Marden, Clare Evans 1878- *WomWWA 14*
Marden, Elizabeth M 1878- *WomWWA 14*
Marden, George Augustus 1839-1906 *NatCAB 6, TwCBDA, WhAm 1*
Marden, Jesse Krekore 1872- *WhAm 5*

Marden, Orison Swett 1848?-1924 *NatCAB 14*
Marden, Orison Swett 1850-1924 *DcAmB, TwCBDA, WhAm 1*
Marden, Orison Swett 1906-1975 *WhAm 6*
Marden, Oscar Avery 1853-1932 *ApCAB X, WhAm 1*
Marden, Philip Sanford 1874-1963 *WhAm 4*
Marden, Robert Fiske 1876-1935 *WhAm 1*
Mardis, Samuel Wright 1800-1836 *BiDrAC, WhAm H*
Mardis, Samuel Wright 1801-1836 *BiAUS, TwCBDA*
Mare *NewYHSD*
Mare, John 1739?- *NewYHSD*
Marean, Elizabeth Richards *WomWWA 14*
Marean, Emma Endicott 1854-1936 *WhAm 1, WomWWA 14*
Marean, Josiah Taylor 1842-1922 *WhAm 1*
Marean, Willis Adams 1853-1939 *NatCAB 12, WhAm 1*
Marechal, Ambroise 1769-1828 *Drake*
Marechal, Ambrose 1764-1828 *DcAmB, DcAmReB, TwCBDA, WhAm H*
Marechal, Ambroise 1768-1828 *ApCAB, NatCAB 1*
Marechal, Edwin Lesley 1850-1909 *NatCAB 8*
Marek, Kurt W 1915-1972 *WhAm 5*
Mareno, Francisco Ildefonse *WhAm H*
Marenzio, Luca 1553?-1599 *McGEWB*
Mares, Lumir Martin 1901-1967 *WhAm 5*
Maresca, Virginia Keller 1923-1975 *WhAm 6*
Marest, Gabriel d1715 *ApCAB*
Marest, Pierre Gabriel 1662-1714 *DcAmB, WhAm H*
Maret, Gabriel d1715 *ApCAB*
Marett, Philip 1792-1869 *TwCBDA*
Maretzek, Max 1821-1897 *ApCAB, DcAmB, NatCAB 8, WhAm H*
Mareuil, Peter De d1742 *ApCAB*
Marey, Etienne-Jules 1830-1904 *DcScB*
Marford, Mirible 1814-1827 *NewYHSD*
Margai, Sir Milton Augustus Striery 1895-1964 *McGEWB*
Margaret Of Anjou 1430-1482 *McGEWB*
Margaret Of Scotland, Saint 1045-1093 *McGEWB*
Margerie, Emmanuel Marie P M Jacquin De 1862-1953 *DcScB*
Margesson, Helen Pearson *WomWWA 14*
Marget, Arthur William 1899-1962 *WhAm 4*
Marggraf, Andreas Sigismund 1709-1782 *DcScB*
Marggraf, George 1610-1644 *ApCAB*
Margil, Antonio 1657-1726 *WhAm H*
Margil, Jesus De 1657-1726 *Drake*
Margil Of Jesus, Anthony 1655-1726 *ApCAB*
Margiotti, Charles Joseph d1956 *WhAm 3*
Margold, Nathan Ross 1899-1947 *WhAm 2*
Margolis, Max Leopold 1866-1932 *AmBi, DcAmB, NatCAB 23, WhAm 1*
Margot, Augustus P *NewYHSD*
Margoulies, Vladimir De 1897-1962 *WhAm 4*
Margraf, Gustav Bernhard 1915-1969 *NatCAB 55, WhAm 5*
Margraff, Francis *NewYHSD*
Marguerittes, Julie De 1814-1866 *ApCAB, Drake*
Marguerittes, Noemie *ApCAB*
Margules, Max 1856-1920 *DcScB*
Margulois, David *WebAB*
Maria Theresa 1717-1780 *McGEWB*
Mariana, Juan De 1536-1624 *McGEWB*
Mariani, Nicola 1868- *NatCAB 17*
Marianna Of Jesus 1618-1645 *ApCAB*
Mariano, Jacopo *DcScB*
Mariategui, Jose Carlos 1895-1930 *McGEWB*
Marie Antoinette 1755-1793 *McGEWB*
Marie De France *McGEWB*
Marie, Pierre 1853-1940 *BiHiMed, DcScB*
Marienthal, George Edward 1909-1972 *WhAm 5*
Marietta, Shelley Uriah 1881-1974 *WhAm 6*
Mariette, Ernest Sidney 1888-1950 *NatCAB 39*
Marignac, Jean Charles Galissard De 1817-1894 *DcScB*
Marigny, Bernard 1785-1868 *DcAmB, WhAm H*
Marigny, Charles Rene Louis, Viscount De 1740-1815 *ApCAB*

Marin, Fredrik 1898-1973 *NatCAB 57*
Marin, John 1870-1951 *DcAmB S5*
Marin, John 1870-1953 *BnEnAmA, EncAB, IlBEAAW, McGEWB*
Marin, John 1872-1953 *EncAAH, WebAB, WhAm 3*
Marin, Jose Gaspar 1772-1839 *ApCAB*
Marin, Joseph 1905-1966 *NatCAB 54, WhAm 4*
Marina *ApCAB*
Marindin, Henri Louis Francois 1843- *WhAm 1*
Marine, Harriet Perkins *WomWWA 14*
Marine, William Matthew 1843-1904 *NatCAB 31*
Marinho, Jose Antonio 1803-1853 *ApCAB*
Marini, Marino 1901- *McGEWB*
Marino, Frank C 1894-1965 *NatCAB 51*
Marino, Santiago 1788-1854 *ApCAB*
Marinoni, Antonio 1879-1944 *WhAm 2*
Marinus *DcScB*
Mario, Alessandro E *NewYHSD*
Mario, Giuseppe 1810-1883 *ApCAB*
Mario, Queena 1896-1951 *WhAm 3*
Marion, Alonzo Weaver 1904-1962 *NatCAB 50*
Marion, Antoine Fortune 1846-1900 *DcScB*
Marion, Frances 1890-1973 *ApCAB X, WhAm 6*
Marion, Francis 1732-1795 *AmBi, ApCAB, DcAmB, Drake, McGEWB, NatCAB 1, TwCBDA, WebAB, WebAMB, WhAm H, WhoMilH*
Marion, Horace Eugene 1843-1914 *NatCAB 16*
Marion, John Hardin 1874-1944 *WhAm 2*
Marion, Otis Humphry 1847-1906 *NatCAB 15*
Marion, Robert *BiAUS, BiDrAC, TwCBDA, WhAm H*
Mariotte, Edme 1620-1684 *AsBiEn, DcScB*
Maris, Anna M 1845- *WomWWA 14*
Mariscal, Ignacio 1829- *ApCAB*
Marisol Escobar 1930- *BnEnAmA*
Maritain, Jacques 1882-1973 *McGEWB, WhAm 5*
Marius, Gaius 157?BC-086BC *McGEWB*
Marius, Simon 1570-1624 *AsBiEn, DcScB*
Marivaux, Pierre Carlet DeChamblain De 1688-1763 *McGEWB*
Marix, Adolph 1848-1919 *WhAm 1*
Marjerison, Howard Mitchell 1895-1955 *WhAm 3*
Mark, Saint *McGEWB*
Mark, Clarence 1882-1955 *WhAm 3*
Mark, Clayton 1858-1936 *NatCAB 27, WhAm 1*
Mark, Edgar H 1852- *WhAm 4*
Mark, Edward Laurens 1847-1946 *NatCAB 9, TwCBDA, WhAm 2*
Mark, George Washington d1879 *NewYHSD*
Mark, Irving 1908- *EncAAH*
Mark, James *NewYHSD*
Mark, Joseph George 1905-1971 *NatCAB 55*
Mark, Kenneth Lamartine 1874-1958 *WhAm 3*
Mark, Louis 1892-1954 *NatCAB 46*
Mark, Mary Louise 1878-1975 *WhAm 6, WomWWA 14*
Mark, Nellie Virginia 1857- *AmWom, WomWWA 14*
Markbreit, Leopold 1842-1909 *BiAUS, NatCAB 12, WhAm 1*
Markee, Joseph Eldridge 1903-1970 *NatCAB 56, WhAm 5*
Markel, Samuel A 1885-1954 *WhAm 3*
Markeley, Philip Swenk 1789-1834 *WhAm H*
Markell, Catherine Sue 1828- *ApCAB Sup*
Markell, Charles 1882-1955 *NatCAB 49, WhAm 3*
Markell, Charles Frederick 1855-1941 *ApCAB Sup, NatCAB 31, WhAm 1*
Markell, Frank Eugene 1853-1960 *NatCAB 48*
Markell, Henry 1792-1831 *BiAUS, BiDrAC, WhAm H*
Markell, Jacob 1770-1852 *BiAUS, BiDrAC, WhAm H*
Markell, William Ody 1886-1953 *NatCAB 41*
Markens, Isaac 1846-1928 *WhAm 1*
Markert, Frederic Schaefer 1901-1954 *WhAm 3*
Markey, Daniel Peter 1857- *WhAm 4*
Markey, John Clifton 1889-1968 *WhAm 5*
Markey, Lawrence Morris 1899-1950 *WhAm 3*

Markgraf, Georg 1610-1644 *DcScB*
Markham, Anna Catherine *WomWWA 14*
Markham, Charles Cole 1837-1907 *NatCAB 8, NewYHSD*
Markham, Charles Henry 1861-1930 *DcAmB, NatCAB 25, WhAm 1*
Markham, Clements Robert 1830-1916 *ApCAB, DcScB*
Markham, Edward M 1877-1950 *WhAm 3*
Markham, Edwin 1852-1940 *AmBi, DcAmB S2, EncAB, McGEWB, NatCAB 9, TwCBDA, WebAB, WhAm 1*
Markham, Edwin C 1902-1966 *WhAm 4*
Markham, George C *WhAm 5*
Markham, George Dickson 1859-1947 *NatCAB 12, WhAm 2*
Markham, Henry Harrison 1840-1923 *BiDrAC, TwCBDA, WhAm 1*
Markham, Henry Harrison 1841-1923 *NatCAB 2, NatCAB 4*
Markham, Herbert Ira 1882-1960 *WhAm 4*
Markham, James Walter 1910-1972 *NatCAB 57, WhAm 5*
Markham, Jared Clark 1816- *ApCAB, WhAm 4*
Markham, John Raymond 1895-1971 *WhAm 5*
Markham, Leonard Bailey 1878-1955 *NatCAB 42*
Markham, Osmon Grant 1865-1943 *WhAm 2*
Markham, Reuben Henry 1887-1949 *NatCAB 39, WhAm 3*
Markham, Reuel Finney 1891-1957 *NatCAB 43, WhAm 3*
Markham, Samuel Shepherd 1891-1940 *NatCAB 30*
Markham, Thomas F 1891-1952 *WhAm 3*
Markham, Walter Tipton 1885-1946 *BiDAmEd, WhAm 2*
Markham, William 1635?-1704 *AmBi, ApCAB, DcAmB, NatCAB 5, WhAm H*
Markham, William 1811-1890 *NatCAB 2*
Markham, William Colfax 1868-1961 *NatCAB 50*
Markham, William Guy 1836-1922 *WhAm 1*
Markham, William Hugh 1888-1958 *WhAm 3*
Markin, Morris 1893-1970 *WhAm 5*
Markino, Yoshio 1874- *WhAm 5*
Markland, Absolom Hanks 1825-1888 *ApCAB Sup*
Markland, James *NewYHSD*
Markle, Alvan 1861-1931 *NatCAB 54, WhAm 1*
Markle, Bessie *WomWWA 14*
Markle, George Bushar 1827-1888 *ApCAB X, NatCAB 24*
Markle, George Busher 1827-1888 *NatCAB 7*
Markle, John 1858-1933 *ApCAB X, NatCAB 18, WhAm 1*
Markley, Alfred Collins 1843-1926 *WhAm 1*
Markley, Edward Anthony 1891-1952 *WhAm 3*
Markley, Joseph Lybrand 1859-1930 *WhAm 1*
Markley, Klare S 1895-1973 *WhAm 6*
Markley, Philip Swenk d1834 *BiAUS*
Markley, Philip Swenk 1788?-1834 *TwCBDA*
Markley, Philip Swenk 1789-1834 *BiDrAC*
Markley, Stephen Charles 1872-1943 *NatCAB 34*
Markoe, Abraham 1727-1806 *DcAmB, WhAm H*
Markoe, Abram 1729-1806 *ApCAB, NatCAB 13*
Markoe, Francis, Jr. *NewYHSD*
Markoe, Peter d1792 *Drake*
Markoe, Peter 1752?-1792 *DcAmB, WhAm H*
Markoe, Peter 1753?-1792? *ApCAB*
Markoe, Rupert Clarence Laurberg 1898-1971 *NatCAB 56*
Markoe, Stephen Caldwell 1885-1939 *NatCAB 31*
Markoe, Thomas Masters 1819-1901 *ApCAB, NatCAB 11, WhAm 1*
Markoff, Samuel Tobias 1902-1959 *NatCAB 48*
Markov, Andrei Andreevich 1856-1922 *DcScB*
Markovnikov, Vladimir Vasilevich 1837?-1904 *DcScB*
Marks *NewYHSD*
Marks, Albert Smith 1836-1891 *NatCAB 7, TwCBDA*

Marks, Amasa Abraham 1825-1905 *DcAmB, NatCAB 11*
Marks, Avery C, Jr. 1887-1935 *WhAm 1*
Marks, Bernard 1833-1915 *WhAm 1*
Marks, Bradley Cornelius 1883-1964 *NatCAB 51, WhAm 4*
Marks, Carl 1898-1961 *WhAm 4*
Marks, Edward Bennett 1865-1945 *NatCAB 34, WhAm 2*
Marks, Edwin I 1888-1970 *WhAm 5*
Marks, Elias 1790-1886 *ApCAB, DcAmB, NatCAB 25, WhAm H*
Marks, George B 1923- *IlBEAAW*
Marks, George S 1895-1956 *NatCAB 46*
Marks, Henry Kingdon d1942 *WhAm 2*
Marks, Herbert S 1907-1960 *WhAm 4*
Marks, J Christopher 1863- *WhAm 5*
Marks, Jeannette 1875-1964 *WhAm 4, WomWWA 14*
Marks, Josephine Preston Peabody *NotAW, WomWWA 14*
Marks, Mrs. L S *WhAm 1*
Marks, Laurence Mandeville 1892-1958 *WhAm 3*
Marks, Leon John 1898-1972 *WhAm 5*
Marks, Lionel Simeon 1871-1955 *NatCAB 43, WhAm 3*
Marks, Louis Benedict 1869-1939 *NatCAB 15, NatCAB 52*
Marks, Marcus M 1858-1934 *WhAm 1*
Marks, Percy 1891-1956 *NatCAB 46, WhAm 3*
Marks, Sidney Jerome 1904- *WhAm 5*
Marks, Solon 1827-1914 *NatCAB 2, WhAm 1*
Marks, Willard Leighton 1883-1947 *NatCAB 36, WhAm 2*
Marks, William 1778-1858 *ApCAB, BiAUS, BiDrAC, NatCAB 11, TwCBDA, WhAm H*
Marks, William Dennis 1849-1914 *TwCBDA, WhAm 1*
Marks, Wirt Peebles, Jr. 1893-1963 *WhAm 4*
Markscheffel, Louise 1857- *AmWom*
Markus, Henry Alkanay 1899-1972 *NatCAB 57*
Markus, Roy Charles 1904-1965 *NatCAB 51*
Markward, Joseph Bradley 1869-1933 *WhAm 1*
Markwart, Arthur Hermann 1880-1940 *WhAm 1*
Markwell, Lulu Alice 1864- *WomWWA 14*
Markwood, Michael Edward 1914-1957 *WhAm 3*
Marland, Ernest Whitworth 1874-1941 *BiDrAC, DcAmB S3, NatCAB 34, WhAm 2*
Marland, William C 1918-1965 *WhAm 4*
Marlatt, Abby Lillian 1869-1943 *BiDAmEd, DcAmB S3, NotAW, WhAm 5, WomWWA 14*
Marlatt, Charles Lester 1863-1954 *NatCAB 13, NatCAB 49, WhAm 3*
Marlatt, H Irving d1929 *IlBEAAW*
Marlborough, John Churchill, Duke Of 1650-1722 *McGEWB, WhoMilH*
Marler, Herbert Meredith 1876-1940 *WhAm 1*
Marley, James Preston 1882-1952 *NatCAB 41, WhAm 3*
Marley, Joseph Alexander 1883- *WhoColR*
Marliani, Giovanni d1483 *DcScB*
Marlin, Harry Halpine 1869-1939 *WhAm 1*
Marlin, Wenona *WomWWA 14*
Marling, Alfred Erskine 1858-1935 *DcAmB S1, WhAm 1*
Marling, Mrs. Jacob *NewYHSD*
Marling, Jacob 1774-1833 *NewYHSD*
Marling, James H 1857-1895 *WhAm H*
Marling, John Leake 1825-1856 *BiAUS, DcAmB, NatCAB 13, WhAm H*
Marlio, Louis 1878- *WhAm 6*
Marlor, Henry S 1890-1960 *WhAm 4*
Marlow, Frank William 1858-1942 *WhAm 2*
Marlow, Thomas A 1861-1938 *WhAm 1*
Marlowe, Christopher 1564-1593 *McGEWB*
Marlowe, Julia d1950 *TwCBDA*
Marlowe, Julia 1865-1950 *AmWom, WomWWA 14*
Marlowe, Julia 1866-1950 *DcAmB S4, NotAW, WhAm 3*
Marlowe, Julia 1870-1950 *ApCAB X, NatCAB 13*

Marmaduke, Henry Hungerford 1842-
    NatCAB 13
Marmaduke, John Sappington 1833-1887 AmBi,
    ApCAB, BiDConf, DcAmB, NatCAB 12,
    TwCBDA, WhAm H
Marmaduke, Meredith Miles 1791-1864 ApCAB,
    NatCAB 12, TwCBDA
Marmer, Harry Aaron 1885- WhAm 3
Marmer, Milton Jacob 1913-1970 WhAm 5
Marmette, Joseph 1844- ApCAB
Marmier, Pierre Edouard 1922-1973 WhAm 6
Marmier, Xavier 1809- ApCAB
Marmion, Keith Robert 1927-1968 WhAm 5
Marmion, Robert Augustine 1844-1907
    WhAm 1
Marmol, Jose 1817-1871 McGEWB
Marmol, Jose 1818-1871 ApCAB
Marmon, Howard C 1876-1943 WhAm 2
Marmon, Jeff Berry 1861-1933 WhAm 1
Marmont, August Frederic Louis Viesse De
    1774-1852 WhoMilH
Marmorstein, Max 1895-1961 NatCAB 50
Marmur, Jacland 1901-1970 WhAm 5
Marnell, Robert Overton 1869-1933 WhAm 1
Maron, Samuel Herbert 1908-1975 WhAm 6
Maroney, Frederick William 1884-1958
    WhAm 3
Marot, Helen 1865-1940 NotAW, WhAm 1,
    WomWWA 14
Marot, Mary Louise 1870- WhAm 5,
    WomWWA 14
Marot, Samuel 1835?- NewYHSD
Maroto, Rafael 1780-1853 ApCAB
Maroto, Rafael 1785-1847 WhoMilH
Marott, George Joseph 1858-1946 NatCAB 34
Marple, Festus Oval 1885-1952 NatCAB 38
Marple, Florence Alice WomWWA 14
Marple, Joseph 1877-1958 NatCAB 48
Marple, William L 1827-1910 IIBEAAW
Marquand, Allan 1853-1924 ApCAB, DcAmB,
    NatCAB 37, TwCBDA, WhAm 1
Marquand, Frederick 1799-1882 ApCAB,
    NatCAB 19
Marquand, Henry Gurdon 1819-1902 AmBi,
    ApCAB, DcAmB, NatCAB 8, TwCBDA,
    WhAm 1
Marquand, John Phillips 1893-1960 NatCAB 47,
    WebAB, WhAm 4
Marquard, Frank Frederick 1875-1948
    NatCAB 38
Marquardt, Carl Eugene 1884-1968 WhAm 5
Marquardt, Edward William 1876-1958
    NatCAB 43
Marquardt, Gilbert Henry 1903-1965
    NatCAB 52
Marquardt, Oswald Frederick 1884-1952
    NatCAB 40
Marquardt, Walter William 1878- WhAm 6
Marquart, Edward John 1880-1954 WhAm 3
Marquat, William Frederic 1894-1960 WhAm 4
Marques, Thomas 1753-1827 ApCAB
Marques Perdigao, Joao DaPurificacao d1864
    ApCAB
Marquess, John Miller 1882- WhoColR
Marquess, William Hoge 1854-1921 WhAm 1
Marquett, Turner Masten 1831-1894 NatCAB 8
Marquett, Turner Mastin 1829-1894 DcAmB,
    WhAm H
Marquette, Jacques 1637-1675 AmBi, DcAmB,
    DcAmReB, Drake, McGEWB,
    NatCAB 12, REnAW, WebAB,
    WhAm H
Marquette, James 1637-1675 ApCAB
Marquette, T M d1894 BiAUS
Marquette, Turner Mastin 1831-1894 BiDrAC
Marquez, Leonardo 1820?- ApCAB
Marquez, Pedro Jose 1741-1820 ApCAB
Marquis, Albert Nelson 1855-1943 DcAmB S3,
    WhAm 2
Marquis, Alexander 1811-1884 NewYHSD
Marquis, David Calhoun 1834-1912 WhAm 1
Marquis, Don 1878-1937 AmBi, DcAmB S2,
    NatCAB 30, WhAm 1
Marquis, Donald George 1908-1973
    NatCAB 57, WhAm 5
Marquis, Donald Robert Perry 1878-1937
    WebAB
Marquis, Frank Henry 1868-1945 NatCAB 34

Marquis, George 1820- WhAm 4
Marquis, George Paull 1868-1933 WhAm 1
Marquis, John Abner 1861-1931 DcAmB,
    NatCAB 22, WhAm 1
Marquis, Karl McDonald 1891-1964
    NatCAB 51
Marquis, Robert Lincoln 1880-1934 WhAm 1
Marquis, Rollin Ruthwin 1853-1935 WhAm 1
Marquis, Samuel Simpson 1866-1948 WhAm 2
Marquis, Vivienne 1921-1966 WhAm 4
Marquis, William Stevenson 1853-1929
    WhAm 1
Marquis, William Vance 1828-1899 WhAm 1
Marr, Alem 1787-1843 BiAUS, BiDrAC,
    WhAm H
Marr, Carl 1858-1936 AmBi, NatCAB 11,
    WhAm 1
Marr, Charles David 1856-1924 NatCAB 6
Marr, Charles Edward 1880-1946 NatCAB 35
Marr, Frances Harrison 1835- TwCBDA
Marr, George Washington Lent 1779-1856
    BiAUS, BiDrAC, WhAm H
Marr, Isabelle WomWWA 14
Marr, Jane Barron Hope 1859- TwCBDA
Marr, Jennie Louise Estes WomWWA 14
Marr, John Quincy 1825-1861 TwCBDA
Marr, Robert Athelstan, Jr. 1856- TwCBDA
Marr, Thomas Elmer 1891-1952 NatCAB 40
Marras, John NewYHSD
Marriage, E Charles D 1881-1950 WhAm 3
Marrias NewYHSD
Marriner, Robie D 1901-1956 WhAm 3
Marriner, Theodore 1892-1937 WhAm 1
Marriott, Abraham Robert 1860-1931 WhAm 1
Marriott, Arthur C d1957 WhAm 3
Marriott, Crittenden 1867- WhAm 4
Marriott, Lucretia E Williams WomWWA 14
Marriott, Ross W 1882-1955 WhAm 3
Marriott, Williams McKim 1885-1936
    DcAmB S2, NatCAB 36, WhAm 1
Marrolim, S NewYHSD
Marron, Adrian Raphael 1892-1964 WhAm 4
Marron, John BiAUS
Marrone, Joseph 1891-1961 WhAm 4
Marroquin, Francisco 1503-1563 ApCAB
Marroquin, Jose Manuel 1827- ApCAB
Marrow, John BiAUS
Marrs, Starlin Marion Newberry 1862-1932
    NatCAB 28, WhAm 1
Marrs, Wyatt 1893-1963 WhAm 4
Marryat, Florence 1837- ApCAB
Marryat, Francis Samuel 1826-1855 IIBEAAW,
    NewYHSD
Marryat, Frederick 1792-1848 ApCAB, Drake
Marryat, Samuel Francis 1826-1855 ApCAB
Marsac, Harvey NewYHSD
Marsalis, John Henry 1904- BiDrAC
Marsch, Wolf Dieter 1928-1972 WhAm 6
Marschall, Frederic William Von 1721-1802
    NatCAB 2
Marschall, Frederick William Von 1721-1802
    ApCAB
Marschall, Nicola 1829-1917 NatCAB 17,
    NewYHSD, WhAm HA, WhAm 4
Marsden, Raymond Robb 1884-1942 WhAm 2
Marsden, Robert Samuel 1905-1960 WhAm 4
Marsden, Theodore NewYHSD
Marsden, William 1807-1885 ApCAB
Marseilles, Charles 1846- NatCAB 11
Marsel, Charles Joseph 1921-1964 NatCAB 51
Marsellus, John 1846-1941 NatCAB 30
Marselus, Nicholas John 1792-1876 ApCAB
Marsh, Alice Esty AmWom
Marsh, Annie NewYHSD
Marsh, Arthur Merwin 1870-1942 WhAm 2
Marsh, Ben R 1887-1967 WhAm 4
Marsh, Benjamin Clarke 1877- WhAm 5
Marsh, Benjamin Franklin 1839-1905 BiDrAC,
    TwCBDA, WhAm 1, WhAmP
Marsh, C Arthur 1883-1961 NatCAB 49
Marsh, Caroline Crane 1816- ApCAB, Drake
Marsh, Charles 1765-1849 ApCAB, BiAUS,
    BiDrAC, Drake, NatCAB 2, TwCBDA,
    WhAm H
Marsh, Charles Dwight 1855-1932 NatCAB 27,
    TwCBDA, WhAm 1
Marsh, Charles Edward 1887-1964 WhAm 4
Marsh, Charles Wesley 1834-1918 AmBi,

DcAmB, NatCAB 11
Marsh, Charles Wyatt 1871-1943 NatCAB 33
Marsh, Cleta McGinn 1906-1973 WhAm 6
Marsh, Daniel L 1880-1968 NatCAB 54
Marsh, David Fielding 1919-1957 NatCAB 46
Marsh, Dexter 1806-1853 ApCAB, Drake
Marsh, Edward Clark 1875-1922 WhAm 1
Marsh, Edward Williams 1836-1913
    NatCAB 17
Marsh, Egbert 1873-1945 WhAm 2
Marsh, Eleanor Blake 1884- WomWWA 14
Marsh, Eli J 1833- NatCAB 1
Marsh, Ella Sherman 1852- WomWWA 14
Marsh, Ellen J F Bennett 1866- WomWWA 14
Marsh, Ernest Sterling 1903-1975 WhAm 6
Marsh, Frances Wellock 1876- WomWWA 14
Marsh, Francis Hedley 1874-1949 WhAm 2
Marsh, Frank Burr 1880-1940 DcAmB S2,
    WhAm 1
Marsh, Frank Earl, Jr. 1895-1961 WhAm 4
Marsh, Frank Edward 1901-1962 WhAm 4
Marsh, Fred Dana 1872-1961 NatCAB 49,
    WhAm 4
Marsh, Genevieve WomWWA 14
Marsh, Genevieve Cutler 1881- WomWWA 14
Marsh, George NewYHSD
Marsh, George Havens 1918-1975 WhAm 6
Marsh, George Perkins 1801-1882 AmBi,
    ApCAB, BiAUS, BiDrAC, DcAmB,
    Drake, EncAAH, EncAB, NatCAB 2,
    TwCBDA, WebAB, WhAm H, WhAmP
Marsh, George T 1876-1945 WhAm 2
Marsh, Gerald E 1900-1975 WhAm 6
Marsh, Grant Prince 1834-1916 DcAmB,
    REnAW
Marsh, Henry NewYHSD
Marsh, Herbert Eugene 1874-1948 WhAm 2
Marsh, Howard Daniel 1871-1945 NatCAB 46
Marsh, James d1804 Drake
Marsh, James 1794-1842 ApCAB, DcAmB,
    DcAmReB, Drake, NatCAB 2, TwCBDA,
    WhAm H
Marsh, James A 1879-1946 WhAm 2
Marsh, James Prentiss 1862-1941 WhAm 2
Marsh, John NewYHSD
Marsh, John 1788-1864 ApCAB
Marsh, John 1788-1868 DcAmB, Drake,
    TwCBDA, WhAm H
Marsh, John 1799-1856 DcAmB, REnAW,
    WhAm H
Marsh, John Bigelow 1887-1967 WhAm 4
Marsh, John Edward 1846-1914 ApCAB X
Marsh, John Otho, Jr. 1926- BiDrAC
Marsh, John Porter 1874-1957 NatCAB 47
Marsh, John Rollin 1863-1949 NatCAB 38
Marsh, Joseph 1726-1811 TwCBDA
Marsh, Joseph Franklin 1877-1949 WhAm 3
Marsh, Joseph Walker 1836-1915 NatCAB 16
Marsh, Joseph William 1858-1936 NatCAB 13,
    NatCAB 27, WhAm 1
Marsh, Joseph Y NewYHSD
Marsh, Juliet Garvin Hamill WomWWA 14
Marsh, Luther Rawson 1813-1902 ApCAB,
    NatCAB 3, TwCBDA
Marsh, Mae 1895-1968 WhAm 4A
Marsh, Mary Louise Montgomery
    WomWWA 14
Marsh, Mary McWilliams 1876-
    WomWWA 14
Marsh, Myron Maurice 1860- WhAm 4
Marsh, Othniel Charles 1831-1899 AmBi,
    ApCAB, AsBiEn, DcAmB, DcScB,
    EncAB, McGEWB, NatCAB 9,
    TwCBDA, WebAB, WhAm H
Marsh, Raymond E 1885-1971 WhAm 5
Marsh, Reginald 1898-1954 BnEnAmA,
    DcAmB S5, McGEWB, WebAB,
    WhAm 3
Marsh, Richard Oglesby 1883-1953 NatCAB 40
Marsh, Robert McCurdy 1878-1958
    NatCAB 48, WhAm 3
Marsh, Samuel 1796-1874 ApCAB
Marsh, Sidney Harper 1825-1879 TwCBDA
Marsh, Simeon Butler 1798-1875 AmBi
Marsh, Spencer Scott d1944 WhAm 2
Marsh, Susan Louise Cotton 1890- WhAm 5
Marsh, Sylvester 1803-1884 AmBi, ApCAB,
    DcAmB, TwCBDA, WhAm H

Marsh, Tamerlane Pliny 1845-1903 *TwCBDA, WhAm 1*
Marsh, Theodore McCurdy 1883-1964 *NatCAB 51*
Marsh, Walter Randall 1867-1947 *WhAm 2*
Marsh, William *NewYHSD*
Marsh, William John 1880- *WhAm 6*
Marsh, William R 1810?- *NewYHSD*
Marsh, William Wallace 1836-1918 *DcAmB*
Marshall *NewYHSD*
Marshall, Albert Brainerd 1849-1931 *WhAm 1*
Marshall, Albert Edward 1884-1951 *WhAm 3*
Marshall, Albert Ware 1874-1958 *NatCAB 48, WhAm 5*
Marshall, Alexander Keith 1770-1825 *ApCAB, Drake*
Marshall, Alexander Keith 1808-1884 *BiAUS, BiDrAC, WhAm H*
Marshall, Alfred 1797?-1868 *BiAUS, BiDrAC, WhAm H*
Marshall, Alfred 1842-1924 *McGEWB*
Marshall, Alfred 1868- *WhAm 1*
Marshall, Alfred C 1872- *WhAm 2*
Marshall, Andrew 1755?-1856 *ApCAB*
Marshall, Arthur Lawrence 1900-1956 *WhAm 3*
Marshall, Benjamin 1782-1858 *DcAmB, WhAm H*
Marshall, Benjamin Howard 1874-1944 *NatCAB 35, WhAm 2*
Marshall, Benjamin Tinkham 1872-1946 *WhAm 2*
Marshall, Bernard Gay 1875-1945 *WhAm 3*
Marshall, Buena Vista 1852-1929 *NatCAB 38*
Marshall, C Morgan 1881-1945 *NatCAB 34*
Marshall, Caleb Howard 1840-1910 *NatCAB 16*
Marshall, Carl 1884-1950 *NatCAB 38*
Marshall, Caroline Louise 1849- *WhAm 4*
Marshall, Carrington Tanner 1869-1958 *WhAm 3*
Marshall, Charles 1744-1825 *ApCAB, BiDAmEd, NatCAB 5*
Marshall, Charles 1830-1902 *ApCAB, TwCBDA, WhAm 1*
Marshall, Charles Alexander 1809- *ApCAB*
Marshall, Charles Clinton 1860-1938 *WhAm 1*
Marshall, Charles D 1888-1945 *WhAm 2*
Marshall, Charles Edward 1866-1927 *NatCAB 23, WhAm 1*
Marshall, Charles Henry 1792-1865 *ApCAB, DcAmB, NatCAB 5, TwCBDA, WhAm H*
Marshall, Christopher 1709-1797 *ApCAB, BiAUS, DcAmB, Drake, WhAm H*
Marshall, Clara d1931 *WhAm 5, WomWWA 14*
Marshall, Clara 1847-1931 *NotAW*
Marshall, Clara 1848?-1931 *DcAmB*
Marshall, Clarence James 1864-1938 *WhAm 1*
Marshall, Daniel 1706-1784 *DcAmB, DcAmReB, WhAm H*
Marshall, E Kennerly, Jr. 1889-1966 *WhAm 4*
Marshall, Edison 1894-1967 *WhAm 4*
Marshall, Edmund Aaron 1896-1958 *NatCAB 45*
Marshall, Edward 1869-1933 *WhAm 1*
Marshall, Edward Asaph 1866- *WhAm 4*
Marshall, Edward Carrington 1877-1953 *NatCAB 42*
Marshall, Edward Chauncey 1821-1893 *BiAUS, BiDrAC, WhAm H*
Marshall, Edward Chauncey 1824-1898 *ApCAB, Drake, TwCBDA*
Marshall, Edward Colston 1820- *ApCAB*
Marshall, Edwin Jessop 1860-1937 *ApCAB X, NatCAB 15, WhAm 1*
Marshall, Elder Watson 1883-1968 *WhAm 5*
Marshall, Elijah D *NewYHSD*
Marshall, Elisha Gaylord 1829-1883 *ApCAB, TwCBDA*
Marshall, Ella Ormsby 1857- *WomWWA 14*
Marshall, Elton Lewis 1887-1970 *WhAm 5*
Marshall, Emily *NewYHSD*
Marshall, Emily 1807-1836 *ApCAB*
Marshall, Eugene 1858-1917 *NatCAB 17*
Marshall, Finnis E 1860- *NatCAB 12*
Marshall, Florence M *BiCAW*
Marshall, Francis Cutler 1867- *WhAm 4*

Marshall, Frank Anton 1905-1972 *WhAm 6*
Marshall, Frank James 1877-1944 *DcAmB S3, WhAm 2*
Marshall, Fred 1906- *BiDrAC, WhAmP*
Marshall, Frederick Rupert 1877-1953 *WhAm 4*
Marshall, George Alexander 1851-1899 *BiDrAC*
Marshall, George Anthony 1892-1958 *WhAm 3*
Marshall, George Catlett 1880-1959 *BiDrUSE, EncAB, McGEWB, NatCAB 45, WebAB, WebAMB, WhAm 3, WhWW-II, WhoMilH*
Marshall, George Morley 1858-1935 *NatCAB 26*
Marshall, H Snowden 1870-1931 *NatCAB 27*
Marshall, Harold 1866-1932 *WhAm 1*
Marshall, Harold Joseph 1905-1964 *WhAm 4*
Marshall, Harry Taylor 1875-1929 *NatCAB 34*
Marshall, Henry 1805-1864 *BiDConf*
Marshall, Henry Rutgers 1852-1927 *DcAmB, NatCAB 11, WhAm 1*
Marshall, Henry Wright 1865-1951 *NatCAB 45, WhAm 3*
Marshall, Henry Wright, Jr. 1892-1952 *NatCAB 45*
Marshall, Herbert 1890-1966 *WhAm 4*
Marshall, Herbert Camp 1871- *WhAm 5*
Marshall, Howard Drake 1924-1972 *WhAm 5*
Marshall, Humphrey d1841 *BiAUS, Drake*
Marshall, Humphrey 1722-1801 *ApCAB, Drake, EncAAH, WhAm H*
Marshall, Humphrey 1756-1841 *ApCAB, NatCAB 2, TwCBDA*
Marshall, Humphrey 1760-1841 *AmBi, BiDrAC, DcAmB, WhAm H, WhAmP*
Marshall, Humphrey 1812-1872 *AmBi, ApCAB, BiAUS, BiDConf, BiDrAC, DcAmB, Drake, TwCBDA, WhAm H, WhAmP*
Marshall, Humphry 1722-1801 *DcAmB*
Marshall, Isaac Holmes 1821-1895 *NatCAB 29*
Marshall, J Warren 1881-1953 *NatCAB 42*
Marshall, James *BiAUS*
Marshall, James 1834-1896 *NatCAB 5, TwCBDA*
Marshall, James A K 1890-1951 *WhAm 3*
Marshall, James Fowle Baldwin 1818-1891 *DcAmB*
Marshall, James Markham 1764-1848 *ApCAB, DcAmB, WhAm H*
Marshall, James Rush 1851-1927 *WhAm 1*
Marshall, James William 1822-1910 *BiDrUSE, NatCAB 4, TwCBDA*
Marshall, James William 1844-1911 *BiDrAC*
Marshall, James Wilson 1810-1885 *DcAmB, WebAB, WhAm H*
Marshall, James Wilson 1812-1855 *NatCAB 5*
Marshall, James Wilson 1812-1885 *ApCAB, TwCBDA*
Marshall, Jessie Ames 1882- *WomWWA 14*
Marshall, Joanna 1822- *AmWom*
Marshall, John 1755-1835 *AmBi, ApCAB, BiDrUSE, DcAmB, Drake, EncAAH, EncAB, McGEWB, NatCAB 1, TwCBDA, WebAB, WhAm H, WhAmP*
Marshall, John 1755-1836 *BiAUS*
Marshall, John 1855-1925 *WhAm 1*
Marshall, John 1858-1931 *NatCAB 46, WhAm 1*
Marshall, John 1881-1966 *NatCAB 51, WhAm 4*
Marshall, John, Jr. 1867-1932 *NatCAB 41*
Marshall, John Albert 1884-1941 *WhAm 2*
Marshall, John Augustine 1854-1941 *NatCAB 30, WhAm 4*
Marshall, John Daniel 1885-1960 *WhAm 4*
Marshall, John Edward 1855-1917 *NatCAB 18*
Marshall, John James 1785-1846 *BiAUS, Drake*
Marshall, John Jay 1785-1846 *ApCAB*
Marshall, John Noble 1897-1958 *WhAm 3*
Marshall, John Patten 1877-1941 *WhAm 1*
Marshall, Josephus C 1856-1926 *NatCAB 20*
Marshall, Josiah 1771-1848 *ApCAB*
Marshall, Josiah 1773-1841 *ApCAB X*
Marshall, Julian Franklin 1847- *WhoColR*
Marshall, Lenore Guinzburg 1897-1971 *NatCAB 55*

Marshall, Lenore Guinzburg 1899-1971 *WhAm 5*
Marshall, Leon Carroll 1879-1966 *BiDAmEd, WhAm 4*
Marshall, Leroy Tate 1883-1950 *BiDrAC*
Marshall, Louis 1773-1866 *ApCAB, DcAmB, NatCAB 3, TwCBDA, WhAm 1*
Marshall, Louis 1856-1929 *DcAmB, NatCAB 26, WebAB, WhAm 1*
Marshall, Lycurgus Luther 1888-1958 *BiDrAC*
Marshall, M Lee 1884-1950 *WhAm 3*
Marshall, Madison Lincoln 1906-1956 *NatCAB 49*
Marshall, Marguerite Mooers 1887-1964 *WhAm 4, WomWWA 14*
Marshall, Martin 1777-1853 *ApCAB*
Marshall, Marvin Gene 1927-1972 *WhAm 6*
Marshall, Mary Ellen C *WomWWA 14*
Marshall, Mary Louise Donnell *WomWWA 14*
Marshall, Matthew *NewYHSD*
Marshall, Moses 1758-1813 *NatCAB 20*
Marshall, Nelly Nichol 1844-1898 *TwCBDA*
Marshall, Nelly Nichol 1845-1898 *ApCAB*
Marshall, Nicholas Taliaferro 1810-1858 *ApCAB*
Marshall, Nina Lovering 1861- *WomWWA 14*
Marshall, Nira Lovering 1861- *WhAm 4*
Marshall, O Dixon 1906-1962 *NatCAB 50*
Marshall, Orsamus Holmes 1813-1884 *ApCAB, TwCBDA*
Marshall, Peter 1902-1949 *WhAm 2*
Marshall, Ray Gifford 1881-1946 *WhAm 2*
Marshall, Raymond Willett 1885-1966 *WhAm 4*
Marshall, Rembert 1892-1957 *WhAm 3*
Marshall, Richard Coke, Jr. 1879-1961 *ApCAB X, WhAm 4*
Marshall, Richard Jacquelin 1895-1973 *WhAm 6*
Marshall, Richard Mather 1890-1970 *NatCAB 55*
Marshall, Robert Bradford 1867-1949 *NatCAB 37, WhAm 4*
Marshall, Robert Edward 1912-1964 *WhAm 4*
Marshall, Robert Eliot 1883-1937 *WhAm 1*
Marshall, Rosamond VanDerZee 1902-1957 *WhAm 3*
Marshall, Ross Smiley 1880-1960 *WhAm 4*
Marshall, Roujet DeLisle 1847-1922 *WhAm 1*
Marshall, Roy E 1890-1966 *WhAm 4, WhAm 5*
Marshall, Samuel Scott 1821-1890 *BiAUS, BiDrAC, TwCBDA, WhAm H, WhAmP*
Marshall, Stewart M 1879-1965 *WhAm 4*
Marshall, Thomas 1655?-1704 *ApCAB*
Marshall, Thomas 1718-1800 *ApCAB, Drake*
Marshall, Thomas 1730-1802 *ApCAB, DcAmB, TwCBDA, WhAm H*
Marshall, Thomas 1761-1817 *ApCAB*
Marshall, Thomas 1793-1853 *ApCAB, NatCAB 12, TwCBDA*
Marshall, Thomas 1831-1903 *NatCAB 11, WhAm 1*
Marshall, Thomas 1834-1903 *WhAm 1*
Marshall, Thomas Alexander 1794-1871 *AmBi, ApCAB, BiAUS, BiDrAC, DcAmB, Drake, NatCAB 4, TwCBDA, WhAm H, WhAmP*
Marshall, Thomas Alexander 1812- *ApCAB*
Marshall, Thomas Alfred, Jr. 1911-1970 *NatCAB 55, WhAm 5*
Marshall, Thomas Chalmers 1868- *WhAm 5*
Marshall, Thomas Francis d1864 *Drake*
Marshall, Thomas Francis 1800-1864 *BiAUS*
Marshall, Thomas Francis 1801-1864 *ApCAB, BiDrAC, NatCAB 8, WhAm H*
Marshall, Thomas Frank 1854-1921 *BiDrAC, WhAm 1, WhAmP*
Marshall, Thomas Franklin 1871- *WhAm 5*
Marshall, Thomas Linder 1890-1964 *NatCAB 51, WhAm 4*
Marshall, Thomas Maitland 1876-1936 *WhAm 1*
Marshall, Thomas Riley 1854-1925 *AmBi, BiDrAC, BiDrUSE, DcAmB, NatCAB 19, WebAB, WhAm 1, WhAmP*
Marshall, Thomas Worth 1872-1952 *WhAm 3*
Marshall, Thornton Francis 1819- *ApCAB*

Marshall, Thurgood 1908- *EncAB, McGEWB, WebAB*
Marshall, Tully 1864-1943 *WhAm 2*
Marshall, Verne 1889-1965 *WhAm 4*
Marshall, Wade Hampton 1907-1972 *WhAm 5*
Marshall, Waldo Hall 1864-1923 *NatCAB 37, WhAm 1*
Marshall, Walter P 1901-1969 *WhAm 5*
Marshall, William 1735-1809 *ApCAB*
Marshall, William 1827- *ApCAB*
Marshall, William 1848- *NatCAB 5*
Marshall, William A 1847-1931 *WhAm 1, WhAm 1C*
Marshall, William Alexander 1849-1926 *WhAm 1*
Marshall, William Champe 1807-1873 *ApCAB*
Marshall, William Champe 1849- *WhAm 4*
Marshall, William Edgar 1837-1906 *AmBi, ApCAB, DcAmB, NatCAB 7, NewYHSD, TwCBDA*
Marshall, William Gilbert 1888-1957 *WhAm 3*
Marshall, William Henderson 1874-1948 *NatCAB 36*
Marshall, William Henry 1864-1928 *NatCAB 22*
Marshall, William Kennedy 1835- *WhAm 4*
Marshall, William Legramd 1907- *WhAm 5*
Marshall, William Louis 1846-1920 *DcAmB, NatCAB 11, WhAm 1*
Marshall, William R 1825- *BiAUS*
Marshall, William Rainey 1825- *ApCAB*
Marshall, William Rainey 1825-1895 *TwCBDA*
Marshall, William Rainey 1825-1896 *DcAmB, WhAm H*
Marshall, William Rogerson 1825-1896 *NatCAB 10*
Marshall, William Stanley 1866-1947 *WhAm 2*
Marshall, William Worton 1911-1971 *WhAm 6*
Marshburn, Joseph Hancock 1890-1975 *WhAm 6*
Marshman, John Tryon 1874-1962 *WhAm 4*
Marshutz, Elmer Glenville 1895-1961 *WhAm 4*
Marshutz, Joseph H 1877-1956 *WhAm 3*
Marsiglia, Gherlando 1792-1850 *NewYHSD, WhAm H*
Marsiglia, M *NewYHSD*
Marsili, Luigi Ferdinando 1658-1730 *DcScB*
Marsilius Of Inghen d1396 *DcScB*
Marsilius Of Padua 1275?-1342 *McGEWB*
Marsland, Cora 1859- *WhAm 4, WomWWA 14*
Marsteller, Ross Perry 1882-1954 *NatCAB 45*
Marsten, Francis Edward 1855-1915 *WhAm 1*
Marston, Anson 1864-1949 *NatCAB 44, WhAm 3*
Marston, Edgar Lewis 1860- *ApCAB X, WhAm 1*
Marston, George Washington 1840-1901 *NatCAB 7, TwCBDA, WhAm 1*
Marston, George White 1850-1946 *WhAm 2*
Marston, Gilman 1811-1890 *ApCAB, BiAUS, BiDrAC, Drake, NatCAB 5, TwCBDA, WhAm H*
Marston, Isaac 1839-1891 *NatCAB 4*
Marston, J B *NewYHSD*
Marston, John 1795-1885 *ApCAB*
Marston, John 1796-1885 *TwCBDA*
Marston, John 1847-1957 *NatCAB 49*
Marston, Mary Alice Day 1865- *WomWWA 14*
Marston, Percival Freeman 1863-1916 *WhAm 1*
Marston, Russell 1882-1948 *NatCAB 55*
Marston, Sylvanus Boardman 1883-1946 *WhAm 2*
Marston, William Moulton 1893-1947 *NatCAB 35, WhAm 2*
Mart, Leon Thomas 1891-1959 *NatCAB 48, WhAm 4*
Martel, Charles 1860-1945 *DcAmB S3, DcAmLiB, WhAm 2*
Martel, Leon Charles 1902-1966 *NatCAB 53*
Martel, Romeo Raoul 1890-1965 *WhAm 4*
Martell, Eldred Roland 1901-1957 *WhAm 3*
Martell, Forrest Hartwell 1896-1953 *NatCAB 42*
Marten *NewYHSD*
Marten, Albert Segar 1845- *NatCAB 14*
Martens, Adolf 1850-1914 *DcScB*
Martens, Clarence Gerd 1896-1958 *NatCAB 44*

Martens, Frederic 1635-1699 *ApCAB*
Martens, Frederick Herman 1874-1932 *AmBi, WhAm 1*
Martens, G *NewYHSD*
Martens, John W *NewYHSD*
Martens, Vestina Gladys 1872- *WomWWA 14*
Martens, Walter Frederic 1890-1969 *WhAm 5*
Marter, John *NewYHSD*
Marti, Jose Julian 1853-1895 *ApCAB Sup, McGEWB*
Marti Franques, Antonio De 1750-1832 *DcScB*
Marti-Ibanez, Felix d1972 *WhAm 5*
Martial 038?-104? *McGEWB*
Martianus Capella *DcScB*
Martien, William Stockton 1798-1861 *ApCAB*
Martin V 1368-1431 *McGEWB*
Martin, A C 1835-1879 *WhAm H*
Martin, Abe *WebAB, WhAm 1*
Martin, Adam 1835- *ApCAB*
Martin, Agnes 1921- *BnEnAmA*
Martin, Albert Thompson 1927-1966 *WhAm 4*
Martin, Alexander 1740-1807 *ApCAB, BiAUS, BiDrAC, DcAmB, Drake, NatCAB 4, TwCBDA, WhAm H, WhAmP*
Martin, Alexander 1822-1893 *BiDAmEd, NatCAB 7*
Martin, Alexander Tertius 1886-1968 *NatCAB 55*
Martin, Alfred Wilhelm 1862-1932 *NatCAB 23, WhAm 1*
Martin, Allie Beth Dent 1914-1976 *DcAmLiB*
Martin, Alvah Howard 1858-1918 *WhAm 1*
Martin, Alvah Howard 1890-1957 *NatCAB 46*
Martin, Andrew Bennett 1836- *WhAm 4*
Martin, Angelique Marie *NewYHSD*
Martin, Anne Henrietta 1875-1951 *BiCAW, DcAmB S5, REnAW, WhAm 3, WomWWA 14*
Martin, Archer John Porter 1910- *AsBiEn*
Martin, Artemas 1835-1918 *DcAmB, NatCAB 2, TwCBDA, WhAm 1*
Martin, Arthur Coe 1883-1956 *NatCAB 49*
Martin, Arthur T 1902-1946 *WhAm 2*
Martin, Asa Earl 1885-1962 *NatCAB 49, WhAm 4*
Martin, Attwood Reading 1861-1944 *NatCAB 33*
Martin, Auguste Marie 1803-1875 *WhAm H*
Martin, Auguste Marie 1820?-1875 *ApCAB*
Martin, Augustus Marie 1803-1875 *NatCAB 5*
Martin, Augustus Mary 1803-1875 *TwCBDA*
Martin, Augustus Mary 1803-1879 *BiDConf*
Martin, Augustus Newton 1847-1901 *BiDrAC, TwCBDA, WhAmP*
Martin, Barclay 1802-1890 *BiAUS, BiDrAC, WhAm H*
Martin, Benjamin 1704?-1782 *DcScB*
Martin, Benjamin Ellis d1909 *WhAm 1*
Martin, Benjamin Franklin 1828-1895 *BiDrAC, WhAm H*
Martin, Benjamin Nicholas 1816-1883 *ApCAB, TwCBDA*
Martin, Bernard Francis 1843-1914 *ApCAB X*
Martin, Bradley 1841-1913 *WhAm 1*
Martin, Bradley, Jr. 1873-1963 *NatCAB 14, WhAm 4*
Martin, Burton McMahan 1866- *WhAm 1*
Martin, C Hugh 1890-1959 *NatCAB 50*
Martin, Carey 1894-1965 *WhAm 4*
Martin, Carl Neidhard 1874- *WhAm 5*
Martin, Catharine *WomWWA 14*
Martin, Catherine E Dodge 1859- *WomWWA 14*
Martin, Celora E 1834-1909 *WhAm 1*
Martin, Chalmers 1859-1934 *TwCBDA, WhAm 1*
Martin, Charles *NewYHSD*
Martin, Charles 1820-1906 *NewYHSD*
Martin, Charles 1856-1917 *BiDrAC*
Martin, Charles Cyril 1831-1903 *ApCAB, NatCAB 14, TwCBDA, WhAm 1*
Martin, Charles Douglass *WhoColR*
Martin, Charles Drake 1829-1911 *BiAUS, BiDrAC*
Martin, Charles Fletcher 1876-1949 *WhAm 3*
Martin, Charles Henry 1848-1931 *BiDrAC*
Martin, Charles Henry 1863-1946 *BiDrAC, NatCAB 35, WhAm 2, WhAmP*

Martin, Charles Irving 1871-1953 *WhAm 3*
Martin, Chester W 1853- *WhAm 4*
Martin, Clara Brett *WomWWA 14*
Martin, Clara Davis *WomWWA 14*
Martin, Clarence 1868- *WhAm 4*
Martin, Clarence Augustine 1862-1944 *NatCAB 33, WhAm 2*
Martin, Clarence Eugene 1880-1955 *WhAm 3*
Martin, Clarence Reuben 1886-1972 *NatCAB 57*
Martin, Claude Alexander 1882-1956 *NatCAB 45*
Martin, Clyde Sayers 1884-1963 *NatCAB 50*
Martin, Crawford Collins 1916-1972 *WhAm 5*
Martin, Daniel d1830 *BiAUS*
Martin, Daniel 1780-1831 *NatCAB 9, TwCBDA*
Martin, Daniel J 1902-1970 *WhAm 5*
Martin, Daniel Strobel 1842-1925 *WhAm 1*
Martin, Daniel Webster 1878-1961 *NatCAB 49*
Martin, David *NewYHSD*
Martin, David d1856 *Drake*
Martin, David 1839-1901 *NatCAB 12*
Martin, David B d1909 *WhAm 1*
Martin, David Grier 1910-1974 *WhAm 6*
Martin, David Herron 1849- *WhAm 4*
Martin, David Thomas 1907- *BiDrAC*
Martin, Dempster Disbrow 1862-1935 *WhAm 1*
Martin, Douglas DeVeny 1885-1963 *WhAm 4*
Martin, E *NewYHSD*
Martin, E Hall *NewYHSD*
Martin, E O *NewYHSD*
Martin, Earle 1874-1938 *WhAm 1*
Martin, Earle D 1890-1969 *WhAm 5*
Martin, Eben Wever 1855-1932 *BiDrAC, WhAm 1, WhAmP*
Martin, Edgar 1871-1951 *WhAm 3*
Martin, Edgar Stanley 1873-1940 *WhAm 1*
Martin, Edith Copeland 1865- *WomWWA 14*
Martin, Edmund Denegre 1863-1933 *NatCAB 24*
Martin, Edward 1858-1938 *NatCAB 33*
Martin, Edward 1859-1938 *WhAm 1*
Martin, Edward 1879-1967 *BiDrAC, WhAm 4*
Martin, Edward Gillette 1880-1951 *NatCAB 39*
Martin, Edward Hamilton 1865-1921 *WhAm 1*
Martin, Edward Livingston 1837-1897 *BiDrAC, WhAm H*
Martin, Edward Sandford 1856-1939 *AmBi, DcAmB S2, NatCAB 10, WhAm 1*
Martin, Edwin Manton 1902-1956 *WhAm 3*
Martin, Edwin Moore 1872-1935 *WhAm 1*
Martin, Elbert Sevier 1829?-1876 *BiAUS, BiDrAC, WhAm H*
Martin, Eliza Gathright 1847- *WomWWA 14*
Martin, Elizabeth Price 1864-1932 *DcAmB S1*
Martin, Ellen Annette 1847- *WomWWA 14*
Martin, Ellis *WhAm 4*
Martin, Elsie Stark *WhAm 6*
Martin, Emilie Norton 1869- *WomWWA 14*
Martin, Ernest F *NewYHSD*
Martin, Ernest Gale 1876-1934 *WhAm 1*
Martin, Ernest Gale 1877-1934 *NatCAB 32*
Martin, Everett Dean 1880-1941 *DcAmB S3, WhAm 1*
Martin, F O 1871-1951 *WhAm 3*
Martin, Felix 1804- *ApCAB*
Martin, Ferdinand *NewYHSD*
Martin, Fernando Wood 1863-1933 *WhAm 1*
Martin, Fletcher 1904- *IIBEAAW*
Martin, Mrs. Fletcher Burr 1866- *WomWWA 14*
Martin, Florence Arminta Delong 1864- *WhAm 5*
Martin, Floyd A 1888-1954 *WhAm 3*
Martin, Frances McG *WomWWA 14*
Martin, Francois-Xavier 1762-1846 *AmBi, BiAUS, DcAmB, Drake, WhAm H*
Martin, Francois Xavier 1764-1846 *ApCAB, NatCAB 5, TwCBDA*
Martin, Frank 1863-1920 *NatCAB 19*
Martin, Frank 1864-1943 *WhAm 3*
Martin, Frank 1890-1974 *WhAm 6*
Martin, Mrs. Frank A 1858- *WomWWA 14*
Martin, Frank Joseph 1865-1929 *WhAm 1*
Martin, Frank Lee 1881-1941 *WhAm 1*
Martin, Frank Leslie 1887-1958 *NatCAB 48*
Martin, Frank Lorin 1908-1962 *NatCAB 51*

Martin, Frank White 1894-1959 *NatCAB 48*
Martin, Franklin Henry 1857-1935 *DcAmB S1, WhAm 1*
Martin, Fred Collins 1882-1945 *NatCAB 34*
Martin, Fred James 1904-1972 *WhAm 6*
Martin, Frederick LeRoy 1882-1954 *NatCAB 42, WhAm 3*
Martin, Frederick Oskar 1871-1951 *NatCAB 39*
Martin, Frederick Roy 1871-1952 *NatCAB 41, WhAm 3*
Martin, Frederick Stanley 1794-1865 *BiAUS, BiDrAC, WhAm H*
Martin, Frederick Townsend 1849-1914 *DcAmB, WhAm 1*
Martin, George 1805-1867 *BiAUS*
Martin, George 1815-1867 *ApCAB, Drake, NatCAB 12*
Martin, George 1826-1886 *NatCAB 15*
Martin, George 1889-1938 *WhAm 1*
Martin, George Abraham 1865-1944 *WhAm 2*
Martin, George Brown 1876-1945 *BiDrAC, NatCAB 44, WhAm 2*
Martin, George Curtis 1875- *WhAm 5*
Martin, George E 1857-1948 *WhAm 2*
Martin, George Ellsworth 1872-1936 *WhAm 1*
Martin, George Elmer 1896-1962 *NatCAB 50*
Martin, George Ernest 1894-1968 *NatCAB 54*
Martin, George Forrest 1862-1934 *WhAm 1*
Martin, George Henry 1841-1917 *WhAm 1*
Martin, George Henry 1859- *NatCAB 7*
Martin, George Madden 1866-1946 *NatCAB 33, NotAW, WhAm 2, WomWWA 14*
Martin, George Marshall 1897-1965 *WhAm 4*
Martin, George R 1897-1975 *WhAm 6*
Martin, George Riley 1864-1938 *WhAm 1*
Martin, George Washington 1841-1914 *NatCAB 15, WhAm 1*
Martin, George Wesley 1905-1963 *NatCAB 51*
Martin, George Whitney 1887-1959 *NatCAB 46, WhAm 3*
Martin, George William 1854- *WhAm 4*
Martin, Gertrude Shorb 1869-1962 *WhAm 4, WhAm 5, WomWWA 14*
Martin, Glenn Luther 1886-1955 *DcAmB S5, WebAB, WhAm 3*
Martin, Gustav Julius 1910-1967 *WhAm 4*
Martin, Guy H 1866-1933 *WhAm 1*
Martin, H Warner 1882-1945 *NatCAB 34*
Martin, Harold Montgomery 1896-1972 *WhAm 5*
Martin, Harry Brownlow 1873-1959 *WhAm 3*
Martin, Harry Leland 1908-1958 *WhAm 3*
Martin, Helen Reimensnyder 1868-1939 *WhAm 1, WomWWA 14*
Martin, Henry Austin 1824-1884 *ApCAB, DcAmB, WhAm H*
Martin, Henry Newell 1848-1896 *ApCAB, DcAmB, DcScB, NatCAB 12, TwCBDA, WhAm H*
Martin, Herbert Spencer 1882-1929 *ApCAB X*
Martin, Herbert Spencer 1882-1930 *WhAm 1*
Martin, Homer Dodge 1836-1897 *AmBi, ApCAB, BnEnAmA, DcAmB, EncAAH, NatCAB 9, NewYHSD, TwCBDA, WebAB, WhAm H*
Martin, Horace Hawes 1855-1925 *NatCAB 20*
Martin, Hugh 1874- *WhAm 5*
Martin, Hugh Ellis 1902-1973 *NatCAB 57*
Martin, Hugh Krepps 1889-1974 *WhAm 6*
Martin, Hutson 1892-1965 *NatCAB 52*
Martin, Ida Shaw 1867- *WomWWA 14*
Martin, Irving 1865-1952 *NatCAB 53*
Martin, Irving Lewthwaite 1918-1967 *NatCAB 53*
Martin, Isaac Jack 1908-1966 *WhAm 4*
Martin, Isabel Eleanor 1881- *WomWWA 14*
Martin, J A *NewYHSD*
Martin, J H Thayer 1875-1958 *WhAm 3*
Martin, James *ApCAB, NewYHSD*
Martin, James 1796-1846 *ApCAB, TwCBDA*
Martin, James 1862-1910 *WhAm 1*
Martin, James Aloyisius 1881-1958 *NatCAB 47*
Martin, James Arthur 1876- *WhoColR*
Martin, James Douglas 1918- *BiDrAC*
Martin, James Green 1819-1878 *ApCAB, BiDConf, DcAmB, TwCBDA, WhAm H*
Martin, James L 1880- *WhoColR*
Martin, James Lawrence 1878-1954 *WhAm 3*

Martin, James Loren 1846-1915 *WhAm 1*
Martin, James MacDonald 1875-1956 *WhAm 3*
Martin, James Royal 1881- *WhAm 6*
Martin, James Sankey 1861- *WhAm 4*
Martin, James Stewart 1826-1907 *ApCAB, BiAUS, BiDrAC*
Martin, John 1730?- *ApCAB, BiAUS, Drake, NatCAB 2*
Martin, John 1833-1913 *ApCAB Sup, BiDrAC, NatCAB 7, TwCBDA, WhAm 1*
Martin, John 1864-1956 *WhAm 3*
Martin, John 1884-1949 *WhAm 2*
Martin, John A Lee *NewYHSD*
Martin, John Alexander 1839-1889 *ApCAB, DcAmB, NatCAB 8, TwCBDA, WhAm H*
Martin, John Andrew 1868-1939 *BiDrAC, WhAm 1, WhAmP*
Martin, John Blennerhasset 1797-1857 *WhAm H*
Martin, John Blennerhassett 1797-1857 *NewYHSD*
Martin, John Breckinridge 1857- *IIBEAAW*
Martin, John Calvin 1845-1912 *WhAm 1*
Martin, John Cunningham 1880-1952 *BiDrAC*
Martin, John Cunningham 1880-1852 *WhAm 3*
Martin, John Donelson 1883-1962 *WhAm 4*
Martin, John Hill 1823-1906 *ApCAB, DcAmB*
Martin, John Irwin 1848-1923 *WhAm 1*
Martin, John Jacob 1826- *BiAUS*
Martin, John James 1870-1934 *WhAm 1*
Martin, John Marshall 1832-1921 *BiDConf*
Martin, John Mason 1837-1898 *ApCAB, BiDrAC, NatCAB 11*
Martin, John Nicholas 1725?-1795 *ApCAB*
Martin, John Preston 1811-1862 *BiAUS, BiDrAC, WhAm H*
Martin, John Ross 1856-1923 *NatCAB 6*
Martin, John Thomas 1816-1897 *NatCAB 8*
Martin, John Wellborn 1884-1958 *WhAm 3*
Martin, Joseph 1740-1808 *NatCAB 7*
Martin, Joseph 1878- *WhAm 2*
Martin, Joseph C 1866- *WhoColR*
Martin, Joseph Hamilton 1825-1887 *ApCAB*
Martin, Joseph I 1894-1957 *WhAm 3*
Martin, Joseph John 1833-1900 *BiDrAC*
Martin, Joseph P 1760-1850 *Drake*
Martin, Joseph William, Jr. 1884-1968 *BiDrAC, NatCAB 57, WebAB, WhAm 4A, WhAmP*
Martin, Joshua Lanier 1799-1856 *ApCAB, BiAUS, BiDrAC, Drake, NatCAB 10, TwCBDA, WhAm H*
Martin, Josiah 1737-1786 *AmBi, ApCAB, BiAUS, DcAmB, Drake, NatCAB 13, WhAm H*
Martin, Juliet *NewYHSD*
Martin, Julius C 1861-1949 *WhAm 2*
Martin, Kingsley Leverich 1869-1947 *NatCAB 36, WhAm 2*
Martin, Kirk 1906- *IIBEAAW*
Martin, Larkin Morris 1853-1909 *WhAm 1*
Martin, Lawrence 1880-1955 *NatCAB 44, WhAm 6*
Martin, Lawrence Crawford 1887-1970 *WhAm 5*
Martin, Lee Roy 1911-1960 *NatCAB 47*
Martin, Leila Moss 1873- *WomWWA 14*
Martin, Leonora Monteiro *WomWWA 14*
Martin, Leroy Albert 1901-1972 *WhAm 5*
Martin, Lester 1907-1959 *WhAm 3*
Martin, Lester Francis 1895-1955 *NatCAB 45*
Martin, Lewis J 1844-1913 *BiDrAC*
Martin, Lillian Jane 1851-1943 *TwCBDA*
Martin, Lillien Jane 1851-1943 *NatCAB 16, NotAW, WhAm 2, WomWWA 14*
Martin, Lilly *NewYHSD*
Martin, Louis Adolphe, Jr. 1880-1938 *NatCAB 28, WhAm 1*
Martin, Louisa 1852- *WomWWA 14*
Martin, Luther 1744-1826 *BiAUS, BiDrAC, Drake, TwCBDA, WhAm H, WhAmP*
Martin, Luther 1748?-1826 *AmBi, ApCAB, DcAmB, McGEWB, NatCAB 3, WebAB*
Martin, Luther, III 1873-1962 *WhAm 4*
Martin, Mabel Agnes 1881-1957 *NatCAB 46*
Martin, Mabel Wood d1956 *WhAm 3*
Martin, Margaret Maxwell 1807- *ApCAB*

Martin, Maria 1796-1863 *NewYHSD, NotAW*
Martin, Martha Evans d1925 *WhAm 1, WomWWA 14*
Martin, Mary Augusta Ricker *WomWWA 14*
Martin, Mary Etta *WomWWA 14*
Martin, Mary Tredick *WomWWA 14*
Martin, Matilda Work 1848- *WomWWA 14*
Martin, Mellen Chamberlain 1886-1952 *NatCAB 43, WhAm 3*
Martin, Melvin Albert 1871-1936 *WhAm 1*
Martin, Miles Macon 1850- *WhAm 4*
Martin, Milward Wyatt 1895-1974 *WhAm 6*
Martin, Morgan Lewis 1805-1887 *BiAUS, BiDrAC, WhAm H*
Martin, Motte 1879-1946 *WhAm 3*
Martin, Myra Belle 1861- *NatCAB 14, WomWWA 14*
Martin, Nellie B Barton *WomWWA 14*
Martin, Noah 1801-1863 *BiAUS, NatCAB 11, TwCBDA*
Martin, Oliver Curtis 1873-1942 *NatCAB 32*
Martin, Orel Francis 1892-1957 *NatCAB 47*
Martin, Patrick Minor 1924-1968 *BiDrAC, WhAm 5*
Martin, Paul Alexander 1886-1965 *WhAm 4*
Martin, Paul Curtis 1876-1939 *WhAm 1*
Martin, Paul Gordon 1896-1967 *NatCAB 54*
Martin, Paul Leo 1881-1962 *WhAm 4*
Martin, Paul Sidney 1899-1974 *WhAm 6*
Martin, Percy Alvin 1879-1942 *WhAm 2*
Martin, Ralph Andrew 1907-1967 *WhAm 5*
Martin, Raymond George 1927-1970 *WhAm 6*
Martin, Reginald Wesley d1963 *WhAm 4*
Martin, Renwick Harper 1872-1958 *NatCAB 47, WhAm 5*
Martin, Riccardo 1881-1952 *WhAm 3*
Martin, Robert *NewYHSD*
Martin, Robert Grant 1883-1931 *WhAm 1*
Martin, Robert Hugh 1858-1939 *WhAm 1*
Martin, Robert M 1798-1870 *Drake*
Martin, Robert Nicols 1798-1870 *ApCAB, BiAUS, BiDrAC, TwCBDA, WhAm H*
Martin, Robert William 1915-1975 *WhAm 6*
Martin, Roscoe Coleman 1903-1972 *NatCAB 56, WhAm 5*
Martin, Roy David 1885-1957 *NatCAB 47*
Martin, Royce George 1884-1954 *WhAm 3*
Martin, Rudolf 1864-1925 *DcScB*
Martin, Rufus Winfield 1828-1892 *NatCAB 12*
Martin, Samuel Albert 1853-1921 *NatCAB 25, TwCBDA, WhAm 1*
Martin, Santford 1886-1957 *WhAm 3*
Martin, Selden Osgood 1881-1942 *WhAm 2*
Martin, Simeon d1819 *Drake*
Martin, Solomon *NewYHSD*
Martin, Sylvester Mitchell 1857-1937 *WhAm 1*
Martin, Thomas *NewYHSD*
Martin, Thomas Commerford 1856-1924 *DcAmB, NatCAB 13, WhAm 1*
Martin, Thomas Ellsworth 1893-1971 *BiDrAC, WhAm 5*
Martin, Thomas Joseph 1898-1968 *WhAm 5*
Martin, Thomas Mower 1838-1934 *ApCAB, IIBEAAW*
Martin, Thomas Paul 1864- *WhAm 3*
Martin, Thomas Powderly 1887-1963 *NatCAB 49, WhAm 4*
Martin, Thomas Staples 1847-1919 *ApCAB Sup, BiDrAC, DcAmB, NatCAB 11, TwCBDA, WhAm 1, WhAmP*
Martin, Thomas T 1862-1939 *WhAm 3*
Martin, Thomas Walter 1882-1951 *NatCAB 42*
Martin, Thomas Wesley 1881-1964 *WhAm 4*
Martin, Truman J 1857-1930 *NatCAB 22*
Martin, V G 1891-1936 *WhAm 3*
Martin, Victoria Claflin Woodhull 1838-1927 *AmBi, DcAmB, WhAm 1, WomWWA 14*
Martin, W Worth 1907-1964 *NatCAB 50*
Martin, Wallace Harold 1894-1972 *NatCAB 57, WhAm 5*
Martin, Walter Bramblette 1888-1966 *NatCAB 52, WhAm 4*
Martin, Walter Frederick 1875-1940 *NatCAB 31*
Martin, Walton 1869-1949 *WhAm 3*
Martin, Warren Frederic 1878- *WhAm 6*
Martin, Whitmell Pugh 1867-1929 *BiDrAC, WhAm 1, WhAmP*

Martin, William 1765-1846 *Drake,* *NatCAB 7*
Martin, William 1807-1889 *NatCAB 6*
Martin, William 1848- *WhAm 4*
Martin, William A K 1817-1867 *NewYHSD*
Martin, William Alexander Parsons 1827-1916
ApCAB, DcAmB, TwCBDA, WhAm 1
Martin, William D *NewYHSD*
Martin, William D 1789-1833 *BiAUS,* *Drake*
Martin, William Dickinson 1789-1833 *BiDrAC*
Martin, William Dobbin 1789-1833 *ApCAB,*
TwCBDA, WhAm H
Martin, William Elejius 1874- *WhAm 5*
Martin, William Franklin 1863-1942 *WhAm 2*
Martin, William H 1889-1974 *WhAm 6*
Martin, William Harrison 1823-1898 *BiDrAC*
Martin, William Hope 1890-1962 *WhAm 4*
Martin, William Joseph 1830-1896 *TwCBDA*
Martin, William Joseph 1868-1943 *NatCAB 44,*
WhAm 2
Martin, William Joseph 1918-1970 *WhAm 5*
Martin, William Leslie 1854- *WhAm 4*
Martin, William Logan 1850- *NatCAB 7*
Martin, William Logan 1883-1959 *NatCAB 49,*
WhAm 3, WhAm 4
Martin, William McChesney 1874-1955
NatCAB 48, WhAm 3
Martin, William Mulford 1813-1898 *TwCBDA*
Martin, William Oliver 1903-1975 *WhAm 6*
Martin, William Parmenter 1871- *ApCAB X,*
NatCAB 18
Martin, William Thomas 1910-1966 *WhAm 4*
Martin, William Thompson 1823-1910 *BiDConf,*
DcAmB, TwCBDA, WhAm 3
Martin, Winfred Robert 1852-1915 *NatCAB 15,*
WhAm 1
Martin, Woods Hibbard 1882-1960 *NatCAB 48*
Martin DeMoussy, Jean Antoine Victor
1810-1869 *ApCAB*
Martin DeMoyville, Edouard Nicolas H
1715-1779 *ApCAB*
Martin DuGard, Roger 1881-1958 *McGEWB,*
WhAm 3
Martinays, Edouard Simon 1739-1796 *ApCAB*
Martindale, Charles 1857-1936 *NatCAB 27*
Martindale, Earl Henry 1885-1964 *WhAm 4*
Martindale, Elijah Bishop 1828-1910
NatCAB 30
Martindale, Elijah Bishop 1903-1967
NatCAB 53
Martindale, F Carew 1889-1961 *WhAm 4*
Martindale, Henry Clinton 1780-1860 *ApCAB,*
BiAUS, BiDrAC, TwCBDA, WhAm H
Martindale, John Henry 1815-1881 *ApCAB,*
DcAmB, Drake, NatCAB 2, TwCBDA,
WhAm H
Martindale, John Taylor 1868-1938 *NatCAB 30*
Martindale, Thomas 1845-1916 *NatCAB 3,*
WhAm 1
Martine, James Edgar 1849-1925 *NatCAB 15*
Martine, James Edgar 1850-1925 *BiDrAC,*
WhAm 1
Martineau, Harriet 1802-1876 *ApCAB, Drake,*
McGEWB, WhAm H
Martineau, John B 1901-1956 *NatCAB 45*
Martineau, John Ellis 1873-1937 *WhAm 1*
Martineau, John Ellis 1873-1947 *NatCAB 36*
Martineau, Roland Guy 1932-1974 *WhAm 6*
Martinek, Frank V 1895-1971 *WhAm 5*
Martinelli, Giovanni 1885-1969 *WhAm 5*
Martinelli, Raymond Constantine 1914-1949
NatCAB 39
Martinelli, Sebastian 1848- *ApCAB Sup*
Martines, Domingo Jose 1780-1817 *ApCAB*
Martinez, Crescencio d1918 *IlBEAAW*
Martinez, Crisostomo 1638-1694 *DcScB*
Martinez, Enrique 1570?-1632 *ApCAB*
Martinez, Felipe Andres 1902-1962 *NatCAB 49*
Martinez, Felix 1857-1916 *WhAm 1*
Martinez, Jose Antonio 1793-1867 *REnAW*
Martinez, Julian 1897-1943? *IlBEAAW*
Martinez, Maria Montoya 1881?- *IlBEAAW,*
REnAW
Martinez, Pedro 1523-1565 *ApCAB*
Martinez, Pete 1894- *IlBEAAW*
Martinez, Xavier 1869-1943 *IlBEAAW,*
WhAm 2
Martinez-Campos, Arsenio 1831- *ApCAB*

Martinez DeAldunate, Jose Antonio 1730-1811
ApCAB
Martinez DeRozas, Juan 1759-1813 *ApCAB*
Martinez Y Corres, Cristobal 1823-1842 *ApCAB*
Martini *NewYHSD*
Martini, Eugene Richard 1915-1965
NatCAB 53
Martini, Francesco DiGiorgio 1439-1501 *DcScB*
Martini, Pietro *NewYHSD*
Martini, Roland 1903-1966 *WhAm 4*
Martini, Simone *McGEWB*
Martino, Gaetano 1900-1967 *WhAm 4*
Martinon, Jean 1910-1976 *WhAm 6*
Martinot, Sadie 1861- *NatCAB 12, WhAm 4*
Martinovics, Ignac 1755-1795 *DcScB*
Martins, Maria Alves 1900-1973 *WhAm 5*
Martinu, Bohuslav 1890-1959 *McGEWB,*
WhAm 3
Martiny, Philip 1858-1927 *AmBi, DcAmB,*
NatCAB 24, WhAm 1
Martius, Charles Frederic Philip De 1794-1869
ApCAB
Martius, Karl Friedrich Philipp Von 1794-1868
DcScB
Martland, Harrison Stanford 1883-1954
NatCAB 44
Martonne, Emmanuel-Louis-Eugene De
1873-1955 *DcScB*
Marts, Arnaud Cartwright 1888-1970
NatCAB 54, WhAm 5
Marts, Carroll Hartman 1907-1961 *WhAm 4*
Martwick, William Lorimer 1894-1968
WhAm 5
Marty, Aletta Elise *WomWWA 14*
Marty, Benjamin *NewYHSD*
Marty, Martin 1834-1896 *ApCAB, DcAmB,*
NatCAB 12, WhAm H
Marty, Martin 1835-1896 *TwCBDA*
Martyn, Anna Thompson 1873- *WomWWA 14*
Martyn, Carlos 1841-1917 *WhAm 1*
Martyn, Chauncey White 1865-1939 *ApCAB X,*
WhAm 1
Martyn, Sarah Towne Smith 1805-1879 *ApCAB,*
DcAmB, TwCBDA, WhAm H
Martyn, William Carlos 1841- *ApCAB,*
TwCBDA
Martz, Hyman Scher 1909-1969 *WhAm 5*
Martz, Velorus 1880- *WhAm 6*
Marum, Martin Van 1750-1837 *DcScB*
Marure, Alejandro 1803-1866 *ApCAB*
Maruszewski, Mariusz 1932-1973 *WhAm 6*
Marvel, David Thomas 1851-1931 *NatCAB 18,*
NatCAB 29
Marvel, Ik 1822-1908 *AmBi, DcAmB,*
WhAm 1
Marvel, Josiah 1866-1930 *NatCAB 18,*
NatCAB 29
Marvel, Josiah 1904-1955 *NatCAB 45,*
WhAm 3
Marvel, Mary Jackson 1875- *WomWWA 14*
Marvel, Robert 1805-1889 *NatCAB 2*
Marvel, Robert Wiley 1918-1974 *WhAm 6*
Marvell, Andrew 1621-1678 *McGEWB*
Marvell, George Ralph 1869-1941 *WhAm 2*
Marvell, Mary Brayton 1880- *WomWWA 14*
Marvil, Joshua Hopkins 1825-1895 *NatCAB 11,*
TwCBDA
Marvin, Adelaide Hoffman 1877-
WomWWA 14
Marvin, Arba Bryan 1878-1960 *NatCAB 47*
Marvin, C *NewYHSD*
Marvin, Charles Dinsmore 1855-1932
NatCAB 24
Marvin, Charles Frederick 1858-1943
DcAmB S3, NatCAB 16, NatCAB 40,
TwCBDA, WhAm 2
Marvin, Cloyd Heck 1889-1969 *WhAm 5*
Marvin, Dudley 1786-1852 *BiAUS, DcAmB,*
NatCAB 26, WhAm H
Marvin, Dudley 1786-1856 *ApCAB, BiDrAC,*
TwCBDA
Marvin, Dwight 1880-1972 *WhAm 5*
Marvin, Dwight Edwards 1851-1940 *WhAm 1*
Marvin, Enoch Mather 1823-1877 *ApCAB,*
DcAmB, NatCAB 13, TwCBDA,
WhAm H
Marvin, Francis 1828-1905 *BiDrAC,*
NatCAB 16

Marvin, Frank Olin 1852-1915 *WhAm 1*
Marvin, Fred Richard 1868-1939 *WhAm 1*
Marvin, Frederic Rowland 1847-1919
NatCAB 12, TwCBDA, WhAm 1
Marvin, George 1873-1955 *WhAm 3*
Marvin, Henry Howard 1884-1954 *WhAm 3*
Marvin, Hubert Burns 1879-1944 *NatCAB 45*
Marvin, J L *NewYHSD*
Marvin, James 1820- *NatCAB 9, TwCBDA*
Marvin, James Arthur 1888-1964 *WhAm 4*
Marvin, James Madison 1809-1901 *BiAUS,*
BiDrAC, NatCAB 5, TwCBDA
Marvin, John Gage 1815-1857 *BiDAmEd*
Marvin, John Miles 1854-1941 *NatCAB 33*
Marvin, Joseph Benson 1852-1913 *WhAm 1*
Marvin, Joseph Dana 1839-1877 *ApCAB*
Marvin, L P Waldo 1870-1930 *NatCAB 28*
Marvin, Langdon Parker 1876-1957 *NatCAB 43,*
WhAm 3
Marvin, Richard Pratt 1803-1892 *BiAUS,*
BiDrAC, TwCBDA, WhAm H
Marvin, Selden Erastus 1835-1899 *NatCAB 28*
Marvin, Thomas O 1867-1952 *WhAm 3*
Marvin, Walter Sands 1889-1971 *NatCAB 56,*
WhAm 5
Marvin, Walter Taylor 1872-1944 *NatCAB 33,*
WhAm 2
Marvin, William 1808-1892 *BiAUS,*
NatCAB 11
Marvin, William Glenn 1892-1932 *NatCAB 30,*
WhAm 1
Marvin, Winthrop Lippitt 1863-1926 *WhAm 1*
Marwazi, Al- *DcScB*
Marwedel, Emma Jacobina Christiana 1818-1893
BiDAmEd, DcAmB, NotAW, WhAm H
Marwitz, Georg VonDer 1856-1929 *WhoMilH*
Marx, Alexander 1878-1953 *WhAm 3*
Marx, Charles David 1857-1939 *NatCAB 32,*
WhAm 1
Marx, Frederick Zero 1876-1956 *NatCAB 47*
Marx, Fredrick William 1893-1958 *NatCAB 46*
Marx, Groucho 1895- *WebAB*
Marx, Guido Hugo 1871-1949 *NatCAB 38,*
WhAm 3
Marx, Harry S 1878-1948 *WhAm 2*
Marx, Joseph *NewYHSD*
Marx, Karl Heinrich 1818-1883 *DcScB,*
DcScB Sup, McGEWB, WhAm H
Marx, Lawrence 1886-1938 *NatCAB 28*
Marx, Oscar B 1866-1923 *WhAm 1*
Marx, Otto 1869-1963 *WhAm 4*
Marx, Robert S 1889-1960 *WhAm 4*
Marx, Samuel Abraham 1885-1964 *WhAm 4*
Marx Brothers *McGEWB*
Mary *McGEWB*
Mary I 1516-1558 *McGEWB*
Mary II 1662-1694 *McGEWB*
Mary, Queen Of Scots 1542-1587 *McGEWB*
Marye, George Thomas 1849-1933 *WhAm 1*
Marye, George Thomas 1857-1933 *NatCAB 30*
Marzall, John Adams 1896-1959 *WhAm 3*
Marzo, Eduardo 1852-1929 *DcAmB, WhAm 1*
Masaccio 1401-1428 *McGEWB*
Masaryk, Jan 1886-1946 *WhWW-II*
Masaryk, Jan 1886-1948 *WhAm 2*
Masaryk, Tomas Garrigue 1850-1937 *McGEWB*
Mascagni, Paolo 1755-1815 *DcScB*
Mascarene, Jean Paul 1684-1760 *ApCAB,*
Drake
Mascarenhas DeCastello Branco, Jose J
1731-1805 *ApCAB*
Mascart, Eleuthere Elie Nicolas 1837-1908
DcScB
Mascheroni, Lorenzo 1750-1800 *DcScB*
Maschke, Alfred Samuel 1874-1964
NatCAB 50
Maschke, Heinrich 1853-1908 *DcAmB*
Maschke, Maurice 1868-1936 *NatCAB 27,*
WhAm 1
Maschmedt, Flora Huntley *WomWWA 14*
Mascolo, Edward Gregory 1889-1947
NatCAB 34
Mascuch, John Thomas 1899-1951 *WhAm 3*
Mase, Stanley Wilson 1918-1964 *WhAm 4*
Masefield, John 1878-1967 *WhAm 4*
Maseng, Sigurd 1889-1952 *WhAm 3*
Maseres, Francis 1731-1824 *ApCAB, DcScB*
Mashaallah *DcScB*

Mashburn, Gray 1873- *WhAm 5*
Mashburn, Lloyd Abner 1897-1963 *NatCAB 56, WhAm 4*
Masias, Beato Juan 1585-1645 *ApCAB*
Maskelyne, Nevil 1732-1811 *DcScB*
Masland, John W, Jr. 1912-1968 *WhAm 5*
Masland, Mary Elizabeth 1878- *WomWWA 14*
Maslenikov, Oleg Alexander 1907-1972 *NatCAB 57*
Masliansky, Zvi Hirsch 1856-1943 *DcAmB S3*
Maslow, Abraham Harold 1908-1970 *BiDAmEd, WhAm 5*
Maso, Bartolome Y Marquez 1834- *ApCAB Sup*
Mason, A Lawrence 1842- *WhAm 4*
Mason, Abraham John 1794- *NewYHSD, WhAm H*
Mason, Alby Walker *WomWWA 14*
Mason, Alexander Macomb 1841-1897 *ApCAB Sup*
Mason, Alexander Taylor 1859-1920 *ApCAB X*
Mason, Alfred Bishop 1851-1933 *WhAm 1*
Mason, Alfred DeWitt 1855-1923 *WhAm 1*
Mason, Alva *NewYHSD*
Mason, Alvin Hughlett 1905-1974 *WhAm 6*
Mason, Amelia Ruth Gere d1923 *WhAm 1, WomWWA 14*
Mason, Amos Lawrence 1842- *NatCAB 2, TwCBDA*
Mason, Armistead Thomson 1785-1819 *BiAUS*
Mason, Armistead Thomson 1787-1819 *ApCAB, BiDrAC, Drake, NatCAB 4, TwCBDA, WhAm H*
Mason, Arthur Ellery 1865-1943 *NatCAB 32, WhAm 4*
Mason, Arthur John 1857-1933 *DcAmB S1, NatCAB 29*
Mason, Asa *NewYHSD*
Mason, Augustus Lynch 1859-1939 *WhAm 1*
Mason, Benjamin Franklin 1804-1871 *NewYHSD*
Mason, Bernard Sterling 1896-1953 *WhAm 3*
Mason, C Avery 1904-1970 *WhAm 5*
Mason, C D 1830-1915 *NewYHSD*
Mason, Cara Pratt 1855- *WomWWA 14*
Mason, Carlile 1817-1901 *NatCAB 17*
Mason, Caroline Atherton 1823- *ApCAB*
Mason, Caroline Atwater 1853-1939 *NatCAB 4, TwCBDA, WhAm 1, WomWWA 14*
Mason, Cassity E d1933 *WhAm 1*
Mason, Charles *NewYHSD*
Mason, Charles d1786 *DcScB*
Mason, Charles 1730?-1787 *ApCAB, Drake, NatCAB 10, WebAB*
Mason, Charles 1804-1882 *ApCAB, DcAmB, NatCAB 3, TwCBDA, WhAm H*
Mason, Charles 1808?-1882 *BiAUS, Drake*
Mason, Charles Frederick 1882-1967 *WhAm 4*
Mason, Charles Harrison 1866-1961 *DcAmReB, WhAm 4*
Mason, Charles Noble 1869- *WhAm 5*
Mason, Claibourne Rice 1800-1885 *DcAmB, WhAm H*
Mason, Conie Bear 1875- *WomWWA 14*
Mason, Daniel Gregory 1873-1953 *DcAmB S5, NatCAB 15, WhAm 3*
Mason, David 1758- *NewYHSD*
Mason, David H *NewYHSD*
Mason, David Hastings 1828-1903 *ApCAB*
Mason, David Hastings 1829-1903 *NatCAB 10, TwCBDA, WhAm 1*
Mason, Dean d1928 *NatCAB 23*
Mason, Donald Bentley 1898-1969 *NatCAB 54*
Mason, Ebenezer Porter 1819-1840 *ApCAB, Drake, NatCAB 19*
Mason, Edith 1893-1973 *WhAm 6*
Mason, Edward Campbell 1864-1937 *NatCAB 27, WhAm 1*
Mason, Edward Gay 1839-1898 *ApCAB, ApCAB Sup, TwCBDA*
Mason, Edward Halton 1855-1948 *NatCAB 38*
Mason, Edward Tuckerman 1847-1911 *WhAm 1*
Mason, Edward Wilson 1877-1947 *WhAm 2*
Mason, Edwin Cooley 1831-1898 *NatCAB 8, TwCBDA*
Mason, Elizabeth Spaulding *WomWWA 14*
Mason, Emily Virginia 1815-1909 *ApCAB,*

NatCAB 5, WhAm 1
Mason, Erskine 1805-1851 *ApCAB, Drake, NatCAB 33, TwCBDA*
Mason, Erskine 1837-1882 *ApCAB, NatCAB 32, TwCBDA*
Mason, Eva Cordelia Child 1859- *WomWWA 14*
Mason, Fanny Peabody *BiCAW*
Mason, Flora L 1871- *WomWWA 14*
Mason, Frances Bell 1877- *WomWWA 14*
Mason, Frances Fay Calhoun *WomWWA 14*
Mason, Francis 1799-1874 *ApCAB, DcAmB, Drake, WhAm H*
Mason, Frank Henry 1879-1948 *NatCAB 37*
Mason, Frank Holcomb 1840-1916 *TwCBDA, WhAm 1*
Mason, Frank Stuart 1883-1929 *AmBi, DcAmB, WhAm 1*
Mason, Fred 1867-1948 *NatCAB 36*
Mason, Frederick Clark 1877-1953 *NatCAB 40*
Mason, Frederick Hamilton 1854- *NatCAB 7*
Mason, Frederick Robert 1859-1927 *NatCAB 21*
Mason, G Grant, Jr. 1904-1970 *WhAm 5*
Mason, George d1773 *NewYHSD*
Mason, George 1629?-1686? *ApCAB, DcAmB, WhAm H*
Mason, George 1670?-1716 *ApCAB*
Mason, George 1690?-1735 *ApCAB*
Mason, George 1725-1792 *AmBi, ApCAB, DcAmB, EncAAH, EncAB, McGEWB, WebAB, WhAm H*
Mason, George 1726-1792 *BiAUS, Drake, NatCAB 3, TwCBDA*
Mason, George 1840- *NatCAB 17*
Mason, George Allen 1870- *WhAm 3*
Mason, George Champlin 1820-1894 *ApCAB, Drake, NewYHSD, TwCBDA, WhAm H*
Mason, George Dewitt 1856- *WhAm 5*
Mason, George Grant 1868-1955 *NatCAB 44, WhAm 3*
Mason, George Jefferson d1963 *WhAm 4*
Mason, George W 1891-1954 *WhAm 3*
Mason, Grace Sartwell 1877- *WomWWA 14*
Mason, Gregory 1889-1968 *NatCAB 54*
Mason, Guy 1880-1955 *WhAm 3*
Mason, Harold Whitney 1895-1944 *WhAm 2*
Mason, Harriet Lawrence 1862- *TwCBDA, WhAm 4, WomWWA 14*
Mason, Harry Howland 1873-1946 *BiDrAC, WhAm 2*
Mason, Helen Jackson 1851- *WomWWA 14*
Mason, Henry 1831-1890 *DcAmB, NatCAB 13, WhAm H*
Mason, Henry Freeman 1860-1927 *WhAm 1*
Mason, Henry James 1884- *WhoColR*
Mason, Henry Lowell 1864-1957 *NatCAB 14, NatCAB 48*
Mason, Herbert Delavan 1878-1947 *WhAm 2*
Mason, Horatio Pleasants 1840-1906 *NatCAB 31*
Mason, Isaac Mason 1831-1909 *NatCAB 8*
Mason, Israel B 1832- *NatCAB 3*
Mason, J Alden 1885-1967 *WhAm 4*
Mason, J Rupert 1886- *ApCAB X*
Mason, James Brown d1819 *BiAUS*
Mason, James Brown 1774-1819 *TwCBDA*
Mason, James Brown 1775-1819 *BiDrAC, WhAm H*
Mason, James Edward 1859- *WhoColR A*
Mason, James L *NewYHSD*
Mason, James Louis 1817-1853 *ApCAB, Drake*
Mason, James Monroe 1871- *WhAm 5*
Mason, James Murray 1798-1871 *AmBi, ApCAB, BiAUS, BiDConf, BiDrAC, DcAmB, Drake, McGEWB, NatCAB 2, TwCBDA, WebAB, WhAm H, WhAmP*
Mason, James Orley 1883-1958 *WhAm 3*
Mason, James Otis 1846-1912 *ApCAB X*
Mason, James Tate 1882-1936 *NatCAB 26, WhAm 1*
Mason, James Weir 1836-1905 *WhAm 1*
Mason, Jeremiah 1768-1848 *AmBi, ApCAB, BiAUS, BiDrAC, DcAmB, Drake, NatCAB 2, TwCBDA, WhAm H*
Mason, Jesse Henry 1889- *WhAm 2*
Mason, John 1586-1635 *AmBi, ApCAB, Drake*

Mason, John 1600?-1672 *AmBi, ApCAB, DcAmB, Drake, NatCAB 4, WebAMB, WhAm H*
Mason, John 1601-1672 *TwCBDA*
Mason, John 1734-1792 *ApCAB, Drake, TwCBDA*
Mason, John 1773-1839 *NatCAB 13*
Mason, John 1858-1919 *DcAmB, NatCAB 15, WhAm 1*
Mason, John Calvin 1802-1865 *BiAUS, BiDrAC, WhAm H*
Mason, John Henry 1850-1928 *WhAm 1*
Mason, John Mitchell 1770-1829 *ApCAB, BiDAmEd, DcAmB, Drake, NatCAB 6, TwCBDA, WhAm H*
Mason, John Sanford 1824-1897 *ApCAB, NatCAB 12, TwCBDA*
Mason, John Thomson 1764-1824 *ApCAB*
Mason, John Thomson 1815-1873 *BiAUS, BiDrAC, WhAm H*
Mason, John W *NewYHSD*
Mason, John William 1842-1919 *WhAm 1*
Mason, John William 1862-1941 *NatCAB 30*
Mason, John Young 1799-1859 *AmBi, ApCAB, BiAUS, BiDrAC, BiDrUSE, DcAmB, Drake, NatCAB 6, TwCBDA, WhAm H, WhAmP*
Mason, Jonathan 1752-1831 *ApCAB, BiDrAC, Drake, NatCAB 2, TwCBDA*
Mason, Jonathan 1756-1831 *DcAmB, WhAm H*
Mason, Jonathan 1757-1831 *BiAUS*
Mason, Jonathan, Jr. 1795-1884 *NewYHSD*
Mason, Joseph 1828-1914 *BiDrAC, TwCBDA*
Mason, Joseph R 1808-1842 *NewYHSD*
Mason, Joseph Rogers 1918-1971 *NatCAB 55*
Mason, Joseph Warren Teets 1879-1941 *WhAm 1*
Mason, Julian Starkweather 1876-1954 *NatCAB 48, WhAm 3*
Mason, L Walter 1861- *WhAm 1*
Mason, Leslie Fenton 1903-1964 *WhAm 5*
Mason, Lewis Duncan 1843-1927 *WhAm 1*
Mason, Lowell 1792-1872 *AmBi, ApCAB, BiDAmEd, DcAmB, Drake, McGEWB, NatCAB 7, TwCBDA, WebAB, WhAm H*
Mason, Luther Whiting 1821-1896 *TwCBDA*
Mason, Luther Whiting 1828-1896 *BiDAmEd, DcAmB, WhAm H*
Mason, Madison Charles Butler 1859-1915 *WhAm 1*
Mason, Madison Charles Butler 1861-1915 *WhoColR*
Mason, Marion Houghton 1882- *BiCAW, WomWWA 14*
Mason, Mary Augusta 1861- *NatCAB 4, WhAm 5*
Mason, Mary Knight Wood 1857- *WhAm 4*
Mason, Mary Louisa 1864- *WomWWA 14*
Mason, Mary Lyman *WomWWA 14*
Mason, Mary Quaife Smith 1872- *WomWWA 14*
Mason, Maud M 1867-1956 *WhAm 3*
Mason, Maud M 1870-1956 *WomWWA 14*
Mason, Max 1877-1961 *WhAm 4*
Mason, Melancthon Wells 1805-1875 *ApCAB*
Mason, Michael Livingood 1895-1963 *NatCAB 52, WhAm 4*
Mason, Miriam Evangeline 1900-1973 *WhAm 6*
Mason, Moses 1789-1866 *BiAUS, BiDrAC, TwCBDA, WhAm H*
Mason, Nathaniel Robert 1876-1948 *NatCAB 36*
Mason, Newton Eliphalet 1850-1945 *WhAm 2*
Mason, Noah Morgan 1882-1965 *BiDrAC, NatCAB 52, WhAm 4, WhAmP*
Mason, Oliver P 1829-1891 *NatCAB 5*
Mason, Oscar Gleason 1830-1921 *ApCAB X*
Mason, Otis Tufton 1838-1908 *ApCAB, DcAmB, NatCAB 10, TwCBDA, WhAm 1*
Mason, Paul Hooker 1895-1954 *NatCAB 43*
Mason, Phillips 1876- *WhAm 5*
Mason, Rebecca P Stevenson *WomWWA 14*
Mason, Richard *NewYHSD*
Mason, Richard Barnes 1797-1850 *ApCAB, DcAmB, Drake, NatCAB 7, WhAm H*

Mason, Richard Sharp 1795-1875 *ApCAB,*
NatCAB 12
Mason, Richard Sharpe 1795-1874 *TwCBDA*
Mason, Roy Martell 1886-1972 *WhAm 5*
Mason, Rufus Osgood 1830-1903 *NatCAB 27,*
TwCBDA, WhAm 1
Mason, Samson 1793-1869 *BiAUS, BiDrAC,*
TwCBDA, WhAm H, WhAmP
Mason, Samuel *NewYHSD*
Mason, Samuel 1750?-1803 *DcAmB,*
WhAm H
Mason, Sanford 1798?-1862? *NewYHSD*
Mason, Silas Boxley 1879-1936 *NatCAB 36,*
WhAm 1
Mason, Silas Cheever 1857-1935 *AmBi,*
NatCAB 29, WhAm 1
Mason, Stevens Thompson 1811-1843 *Drake*
Mason, Stevens Thomson 1760-1803 *ApCAB,*
BiAUS, BiDrAC, DcAmB, Drake,
NatCAB 2, TwCBDA, WhAm H
Mason, Stevens Thomson 1811-1843 *ApCAB,*
DcAmB, TwCBDA, WhAm H, WhAmP
Mason, Stevens Thomson 1812-1843 *NatCAB 5*
Mason, Susan Hinke 1861- *WomWWA 14*
Mason, Theodore Bailey Myers 1848-1899
ApCAB Sup
Mason, Theodore Lewis 1803-1882 *ApCAB,*
TwCBDA
Mason, Thomas Crisp 1882-1949 *NatCAB 38*
Mason, Thomson 1730-1785 *BiAUS, Drake*
Mason, Thomson 1733-1785 *ApCAB, DcAmB,*
WhAm H
Mason, Ulysses Grant 1872- *WhoColR*
Mason, Verne Rheem 1889-1965 *NatCAB 51*
Mason, Victor Louis 1870-1912 *WhAm 1*
Mason, Virginia Murdoch Wilson
WomWWA 14
Mason, Wallace Edward 1861-1944 *WhAm 2*
Mason, Walt 1862-1939 *DcAmB S2,*
NatCAB 30, WhAm 1
Mason, Walter G *NewYHSD*
Mason, Wilbur Nesbitt 1867- *WhAm 5*
Mason, William *NewYHSD*
Mason, William 1786-1860 *BiAUS, BiDrAC,*
WhAm H
Mason, William 1808-1883 *DcAmB,*
NatCAB 10, WhAm H
Mason, William 1829-1908 *ApCAB, BiDAmEd,*
DcAmB, NatCAB 7, TwCBDA,
WhAm 1
Mason, William Albert 1854-1923 *NatCAB 6*
Mason, William Ambrose 1847- *NatCAB 13*
Mason, William Beverley 1874-1949
NatCAB 38
Mason, William Clarke d1957 *WhAm 3*
Mason, William Ernest 1850-1921 *ApCAB Sup,*
BiDrAC, DcAmB, NatCAB 12, TwCBDA,
WhAm 1, WhAmP
Mason, William G *NewYHSD*
Mason, William Horatio 1877-1940 *NatCAB 37*
Mason, William Madison 1877- *WhAm 5*
Mason, William Pitt 1853-1937 *NatCAB 27,*
WhAm 1, WhAm 1C
Mason, William Powell 1791-1867 *ApCAB,*
NatCAB 30
Mason, William Powell 1835-1901 *NatCAB 26*
Mason, William Sanford 1824-1864 *NewYHSD,*
WhAm H
Mason, William Smith 1866-1961 *NatCAB 50,*
WhAm 4
Mason, William Spencer 1832- *NatCAB 7*
Mason, William Waldo 1846-1914 *NatCAB 17*
Mason, William Woodman 1851-1938 *WhAm 1*
Maspero, Pierre Antoine d1822 *NewYHSD*
Masqueray, Emmanuel Louis 1861-1917
NatCAB 10, WhAm 1
Masquerier, Lewis 1802- *DcAmB, WhAm H*
Mass, Charles *NewYHSD*
Mass, Godfrey *NewYHSD*
Mass, Gotfried *NewYHSD*
Mass, Jacob *NewYHSD*
Massa, Niccolo 1485-1569 *DcScB*
Massabo, Justin *NewYHSD*
Massaglia, Joseph, Jr. 1908-1969 *WhAm 5*
Massard, Victor *NewYHSD*
Massaro, Victor *NewYHSD*
Massasoit d1661 *Drake*
Massasoit 1580?-1660 *ApCAB*

Massasoit 1580?-1661 *AmBi*
Massasoit 1590?-1661 *WebAB*
Massassoit d1661 *DcAmB, WhAm H*
Masse, Enemond 1574-1646 *ApCAB*
Masse, Mathilde Marie VonEschenbach 1880-
WomWWA 14
Massee, Edward Kingsley 1871-1960 *WhAm 3*
Massee, Jasper Cortenus 1871- *WhAm 5*
Massee, May 1881-1966 *WhAm 4*
Massee, W Wellington 1873-1942 *NatCAB 31,*
WhAm 2
Massena, Andre 1756-1817 *WhoMilH*
Massengill, Samuel Evans 1871-1946
NatCAB 34
Massett, J W *NewYHSD*
Massey, Albert 1837?- *NewYHSD*
Massey, Augustus *NewYHSD*
Massey, Evan 1897-1962 *NatCAB 49*
Massey, Eyre 1719-1804 *ApCAB, Drake*
Massey, G Hubard 1893-1964 *NatCAB 51*
Massey, George Betton 1856-1927 *DcAmB,*
NatCAB 25, WhAm 1
Massey, George Valentine 1841-1924 *WhAm 1*
Massey, Hart Almerrin 1823- *ApCAB*
Massey, John 1834- *WhAm 4*
Massey, John Edward 1819-1901 *DcAmB,*
NatCAB 19, TwCBDA
Massey, Joseph *NewYHSD*
Massey, Lucius Saunders 1865- *WhAm 4*
Massey, Luther M 1895-1974 *WhAm 6*
Massey, Marie L *NewYHSD*
Massey, Mary Elizabeth 1915- *WhAm 6*
Massey, Richard W d1949 *WhAm 3*
Massey, Vincent 1887-1967 *WhAm 4*
Massey, Wilbur Fisk 1839-1923 *WhAm 1*
Massey, William Alexander 1856-1914 *BiDrAC,*
WhAm 1
Massey, William Ferguson 1856-1925
McGEWB
Massey, Zachary David 1864-1923 *BiDrAC*
Massie, David Meade 1859-1927 *WhAm 1*
Massie, Eugene Carter 1861- *WhAm 1*
Massie, James William 1799-1869 *ApCAB*
Massie, Nathaniel 1763-1813 *ApCAB, Drake,*
NatCAB 2, TwCBDA
Massie, Robert Kinloch 1864-1932 *WhAm 1*
Massie, Robert Kinloch, Jr. 1892-1930 *WhAm 1*
Massingale, Sam Chapman 1870-1941 *WhAm 1*
Massingale, Samuel Chapman 1870-1941
BiDrAC, WhAmP
Massinger, Philip 1583-1640 *McGEWB*
Massingham, Agnes Boyce 1873-
WomWWA 14
Masslenson, T W G *NewYHSD*
Masslich, Chester Bentley 1872-1933 *WhAm 1*
Massmann, Frederick H 1876- *WhAm 5*
Masson, Antoine-Philibert 1806-1860 *DcScB*
Masson, Clement Buchanan 1898-1946
NatCAB 39
Masson, Emile *NewYHSD*
Masson, Henry James 1891-1973 *WhAm 6*
Masson, Louis Francois Roderique 1833-
ApCAB
Masson, Robert Louis 1891-1970 *WhAm 5*
Masson, Thomas Lansing 1866-1934
DcAmB S1, NatCAB 17, WhAm 1
Massover, Alfred Jacob 1912-1956 *NatCAB 45*
Massue, Louis Huet 1828- *ApCAB*
Massy *NewYHSD*
Massys, Quentin 1465?-1530 *McGEWB*
Mast, Burdette Pond 1891-1964 *WhAm 4*
Mast, Phineas Price 1825-1898 *DcAmB,*
WhAm H
Mast, Samuel Ottmar 1871-1947 *DcScB,*
NatCAB 33, WhAm 2
Masten, Alvin Emmett 1863-1921 *ApCAB X,*
NatCAB 19
Master, Arthur Matthew 1895-1973 *WhAm 6*
Master, Henry Buck 1871-1955 *WhAm 3*
Masterman, Stillman 1831-1863 *Drake*
Masters, Benjamin Franklin 1859- *NatCAB 18*
Masters, Edgar Lee 1868-1950 *NatCAB 37*
Masters, Edgar Lee 1869-1950 *DcAmB S4,*
EncAAH, McGEWB, WebAB,
WhAm 2A
Masters, Edna Crocker 1888- *WomWWA 14*
Masters, Frank Meriro 1870-1959 *WhAm 3*
Masters, Harris Kennedy 1873- *WhAm 5*

Masters, Helen Jenkins *WomWWA 14*
Masters, Henry Hamilton 1869-1924
NatCAB 6
Masters, Howard Russell 1894-1959
NatCAB 49, WhAm 3
Masters, J Edward 1873-1952 *NatCAB 42*
Masters, John Lewis 1859-1916 *NatCAB 17*
Masters, John Volney 1884-1954 *WhAm 3*
Masters, Josiah 1763-1822 *BiAUS, BiDrAC,*
NatCAB 12, TwCBDA, WhAm H
Masters, Keith 1903-1973 *NatCAB 57,*
WhAm 5
Masters, Sybilla d1720 *NotAW*
Masters, Thomas d1723 *NatCAB 17*
Masters, Victor Irvine 1867-1954 *WhAm 3*
Masters, William 1915- *EncAB*
Masterson, Bat 1853-1921 *REnAW*
Masterson, James W 1894- *IIBEAAW*
Masterson, John Joseph 1881-1962 *WhAm 4*
Masterson, Kate 1870- *WhAm 5,*
WomWWA 14
Masterson, Louis 1935- *REnAW*
Masterson, Patrick J 1910- *WhAm 3*
Masterson, William Barclay 1853-1921 *DcAmB,*
WebAB, WhAm HA, WhAm 4
Masterson, William Edward 1889-1967
NatCAB 54, WhAm 5
Masterson, William Wesley 1861-1922
WhAm 1
Mastick, Josephine Hinchman *WomWWA 14*
Mastick, Seabury Cone 1871-1969 *NatCAB 56,*
WhAm 5
Mastin, Charles Robert 1878-1950 *NatCAB 39*
Mastin, Claudius Henry 1826-1898 *ApCAB,*
DcAmB, NatCAB 10, WhAm H
Mastin, Flora Williams 1864- *WomWWA 14*
Mastin, William McDowell 1853-1933
NatCAB 10, NatCAB 25, WhAm 1
Mastini, Silvain *NewYHSD*
Mastlin, Michael 1550-1631 *DcScB*
Maston, Robert H 1897-1957 *WhAm 3*
Mastriani, Frank Paul 1877-1942 *NatCAB 31*
Mastrilli, Nicolas 1570-1653 *ApCAB*
Masudi, Abu L-Hasan Ali I Al-Husayn, Al-
d957? *DcScB*
Masudi, Ali Ibn Al-Husayn, Al- d956
McGEWB
Masur, Jack 1908-1969 *NatCAB 54, WhAm 5*
Masury, John Wesley 1820-1895 *DcAmB,*
NatCAB 5, WhAm H
Matamoros, Mariano 1770-1814 *ApCAB,*
McGEWB
Matas, Rodolphe 1860-1957 *BiHiMed*
Matas, Rudolph 1860-1957 *NatCAB 10,*
NatCAB 47, WhAm 3
Match, Augustus *NewYHSD*
Matchett, Charles Horatio 1843-1919
ApCAB Sup, WhAm 1
Matchett, David Fleming 1867-1946
NatCAB 37, WhAm 2
Matchette, Franklin James 1863-1943
NatCAB 32
Mateer, Calvin Wilson 1836-1908 *DcAmB,*
WhAm 1
Mateer, John Gaston 1890-1966 *NatCAB 52*
Matel, Adolph *NewYHSD*
Mateliger, Jan Ernst 1852-1889 *WhAm H*
Materna, Amalie 1847- *ApCAB*
Mateson *NewYHSD*
Mathedi, Angelo *NewYHSD*
Matheny, Albert Ralston 1874-1922
NatCAB 19
Matheny, Ezra Stacy 1870- *WhAm 5*
Mather, Alonzo Clark d1941 *WhAm 1*
Mather, Amasa Stone 1884-1920 *NatCAB 22*
Mather, Arthur 1868-1944 *WhAm 2*
Mather, Cotton 1662?-1727? *DcAmB*
Mather, Cotton 1663-1728 *AmBi, ApCAB,*
DcAmReB, Drake, EncAAH, EncAB,
McGEWB, NatCAB 4, TwCBDA,
WebAB, WhAm H
Mather, David 1845- *REnAW*
Mather, Eleazer 1637-1669 *ApCAB*
Mather, Elizabeth Ring Ireland 1891-1957
NatCAB 43
Mather, Elmer James 1889-1958 *WhAm 3*
Mather, Flora Stone 1852-1909 *NatCAB 44*
Mather, Frank Jewett, Jr. 1868-1953 *BiDAmEd,*

DcAmB S5, WhAm 3

Mather, Fred 1833-1900 *ApCAB, DcAmB, WhAm 1*

Mather, Frederic Gregory 1844-1925 *ApCAB, NatCAB 20, WhAm 1*

Mather, Frederick 1833-1900 *NatCAB 13*

Mather, Fredrick 1833-1900 *TwCBDA*

Mather, Gordon Macdonald 1868- *WhAm 3*

Mather, Increase 1639-1723 *AmBi, ApCAB, BiDAmEd, DcAmB, DcAmReB, Drake, EncAB, McGEWB, NatCAB 6, TwCBDA, WebAB, WhAm H*

Mather, John Waterhouse 1899-1961 *WhAm 4*

Mather, Margaret 1859-1898 *NatCAB 9, TwCBDA*

Mather, Margaret 1862-1898 *AmWom*

Mather, Margaret Morgan Herbert d1900 *WhAm 1*

Mather, Moses 1719-1806 *ApCAB, Drake*

Mather, Nathaniel 1630-1697 *ApCAB*

Mather, Nathaniel 1669-1688 *ApCAB*

Mather, Richard 1596-1669 *AmBi, ApCAB, DcAmB, Drake, NatCAB 5, TwCBDA, WebAB, WhAm H*

Mather, Richard Henry 1835-1890 *ApCAB, NatCAB 5, TwCBDA*

Mather, Robert 1859-1911 *NatCAB 17, WhAm 1*

Mather, Roland 1809-1897 *TwCBDA*

Mather, Rufus Graves 1874-1952 *NatCAB 44, WhAm 3*

Mather, S Livingston 1882-1960 *NatCAB 50*

Mather, S Livington 1882-1960 *WhAm 4*

Mather, Samuel 1626-1671 *ApCAB, Drake*

Mather, Samuel 1650-1728 *ApCAB*

Mather, Samuel 1674- *ApCAB*

Mather, Samuel 1706-1785 *ApCAB, DcAmB, Drake, NatCAB 6, WhAm H*

Mather, Samuel 1851-1931 *DcAmB, NatCAB 14, NatCAB 44, WhAm 1*

Mather, Samuel Holmes 1813-1894 *ApCAB, DcAmB, WhAm H*

Mather, Samuel Livingston 1817-1890 *ApCAB X, DcAmB, NatCAB 14, WhAm H*

Mather, Samuel Livingstone 1817-1890 *REnAW*

Mather, Sarah Ann 1820- *AmWom*

Mather, Stephen Tyng 1867-1930 *DcAmB, EncAAH, NatCAB 26, WebAB, WhAm 1*

Mather, Thomas Ray 1890-1947 *WhAm 2*

Mather, William *NewYHSD*

Mather, William Allan 1885-1961 *WhAm 4*

Mather, William Gwinn 1857-1951 *ApCAB X, NatCAB 41, WhAm 3*

Mather, William Tyler 1864-1937 *WhAm 1*

Mather, William Williams 1804-1859 *ApCAB, DcAmB, DcScB, Drake, NatCAB 8, TwCBDA, WhAm H*

Mather, Winifred Holt 1874-1945 *ApCAB X, DcAmB S3, NatCAB 34, NotAW*

Matherly, Walter Jeffries 1888-1954 *WhAm 3*

Mathers, Frank C 1881-1973 *WhAm 5*

Mathers, Hugh Thompson 1866- *WhAm 4*

Mathes, James Harvey 1841-1902 *NatCAB 12*

Mathes, James Monroe 1889-1957 *WhAm 3*

Mathes, Robert *NewYHSD*

Mathes, William C 1899-1967 *WhAm 4*

Mathesius, Walther Emil Ludwig 1886-1966 *WhAm 4*

Matheson, Alexander E 1868-1931 *WhAm 1*

Matheson, George Wilson 1894-1957 *NatCAB 45, WhAm 3*

Matheson, James Pleasant 1879-1937 *WhAm 1*

Matheson, John Flood 1906-1965 *NatCAB 52, WhAm 4*

Matheson, Kenneth Gordon 1864-1931 *NatCAB 23, WhAm 1*

Matheson, Martin 1895-1972 *WhAm 5*

Matheson, Robert 1881-1958 *WhAm 3*

Matheson, Roderick 1792?-1872 *ApCAB*

Matheson, William John 1856-1930 *ApCAB X, DcAmB, NatCAB 27, WhAm 1*

Mathew, Edward 1729-1805 *ApCAB, Drake*

Mathew, Theobald 1790-1856 *ApCAB*

Mathews *NewYHSD*

Mathews, Albert 1820-1903 *ApCAB, DcAmB, NatCAB 8, TwCBDA, WhAm 1*

Mathews, Albert Prescott 1871-1957 *WhAm 3*

Mathews, Alfred 1852-1904 *WhAm 1*

Mathews, Alfred Edward 1831-1874 *IIBEAAW, NewYHSD, REnAW, WhAm H*

Mathews, Ann Teresa 1732-1800 *NotAW*

Mathews, Arthur Frank 1860-1945 *IIBEAAW, WhAm 2*

Mathews, Basil Joseph 1879-1951 *WhAm 3*

Mathews, Blanche Dingley 1873- *WomWWA 14*

Mathews, Charles *NewYHSD*

Mathews, Charles 1776-1835 *ApCAB*

Mathews, Charles Erwin 1909-1960 *NatCAB 49*

Mathews, Charles James 1803-1878 *ApCAB*

Mathews, Charles Stewart 1853-1923 *NatCAB 20*

Mathews, Charles Thompson 1863-1934 *NatCAB 29*

Mathews, Charles Thompson 1865-1934 *TwCBDA*

Mathews, Charles Thomson 1863-1934 *WhAm 1*

Mathews, Clarence Wentworth 1861-1928 *WhAm 1*

Mathews, Clifton 1880-1962 *WhAm 4*

Mathews, Cornelius 1817-1889 *ApCAB, DcAmB, Drake, NatCAB 13, TwCBDA, WhAm H*

Mathews, Daniel F 1904-1967 *NatCAB 53*

Mathews, David Oscar 1903-1973 *WhAm 6*

Mathews, Delancey North 1849-1935 *WhAm 1*

Mathews, E P *NewYHSD*

Mathews, Edward Bennett 1869-1944 *NatCAB 32, WhAm 2*

Mathews, Ferdinand Schuyler 1854-1938 *TwCBDA, WhAm 1*

Mathews, Frances Aymar d1923 *WhAm 2, WomWWA 14*

Mathews, Frank Asbury, Jr. 1890-1964 *BiDrAC, WhAm 4*

Mathews, Frank Stuart 1869-1936 *WhAm 1*

Mathews, George 1739-1812 *ApCAB, BiDrAC, DcAmB, NatCAB 1, TwCBDA, WhAm H, WhAmP*

Mathews, George 1774-1836 *ApCAB, Drake, NatCAB 5*

Mathews, George *see also* Matthews, George

Mathews, George Arthur 1852-1941 *BiDrAC*

Mathews, George Ballard 1861-1922 *DcScB*

Mathews, George Brewster 1847-1942 *NatCAB 31*

Mathews, George C 1886-1946 *WhAm 2*

Mathews, George H *NewYHSD*

Mathews, George Martin 1848-1921 *WhAm 1*

Mathews, Helen Whitman 1876- *WomWWA 14*

Mathews, Henry Mason 1834-1884 *DcAmB, NatCAB 12, WhAm H*

Mathews, James 1805-1887 *BiAUS, BiDrAC, WhAm H*

Mathews, James Abram 1881-1933 *WhAm 1*

Mathews, James Edward 1876-1935 *NatCAB 28, WhAm 1*

Mathews, James Harold 1895-1945 *NatCAB 37*

Mathews, James Macfarlane 1785-1870 *NatCAB 6, TwCBDA*

Mathews, James McFarlane 1785-1870 *ApCAB*

Mathews, James Thomas 1891-1947 *WhAm 2*

Mathews, Joanna Hooe 1849-1901 *WhAm 1*

Mathews, John 1744-1802 *ApCAB, BiDrAC, DcAmB, NatCAB 12, TwCBDA, WhAm H, WhAmP*

Mathews, John *see also* Matthews, John

Mathews, John Alexander 1872-1935 *DcAmB S1, NatCAB 16, WhAm 1*

Mathews, John Elie 1892-1955 *WhAm 3*

Mathews, John Lathrop 1874-1916 *WhAm 1*

Mathews, Joseph Howard 1881-1970 *WhAm 5*

Mathews, Joseph McDowell 1847- *NatCAB 13, WhAm 4*

Mathews, Rachel Ellicott 1870- *WomWWA 14*

Mathews, Robert T 1851-1900 *NatCAB 40*

Mathews, S Sherberne 1847-1910 *WhAm 1*

Mathews, Samuel *NewYHSD*

Mathews, Samuel 1600?-1660 *DcAmB, WhAm H*

Mathews, Samuel *see also* Matthews, Samuel

Mathews, Shailer 1863-1941 *DcAmB S3,*

DcAmReB, NatCAB 11, TwCBDA, WhAm 2

Mathews, Vincent 1766-1846 *ApCAB, BiAUS, BiDrAC, WhAm H*

Mathews, Vincent *see also* Matthews, Vincent

Mathews, Walter J 1850-1947 *NatCAB 48*

Mathews, William 1818-1909 *ApCAB, DcAmB, NatCAB 11, TwCBDA, WhAm 1*

Mathews, William Beaufort 1883-1955 *NatCAB 46*

Mathews, William Burdette 1866-1943 *NatCAB 32, WhAm 2*

Mathews, William Gordon 1877-1923 *NatCAB 20*

Mathews, William Hooker 1890-1959 *NatCAB 47, WhAm 3*

Mathews, William Rankin 1893-1969 *WhAm 5*

Mathews, William Smith Babcock 1837-1912 *NatCAB 10, WhAm 1*

Mathews, William Smythe Babcock 1837-1912 *DcAmB, TwCBDA*

Mathews, William T 1821-1905 *NewYHSD, WhAm H*

Mathewson, Champion Herbert 1881- *WhAm 6*

Mathewson, Charles Frederick 1860-1915 *NatCAB 14, WhAm 1*

Mathewson, Christopher 1880-1925 *DcAmB, WebAB, WhAm HA, WhAm 4*

Mathewson, Earl Jerome 1882-1965 *NatCAB 51*

Mathewson, Edward Payson 1864-1948 *DcAmB S4, WhAm 5*

Mathewson, Elisha 1767-1853 *ApCAB, BiAUS, BiDrAC, NatCAB 4, TwCBDA, WhAm H*

Mathewson, Frank Elliott 1869-1930 *NatCAB 23*

Mathewson, George Bowen 1804-1877 *NewYHSD*

Mathewson, George Lawrence 1889-1943 *NatCAB 32*

Mathewson, Ozias Danforth 1864-1944 *NatCAB 34, WhAm 2*

Mathewson, Park, II 1872-1930 *NatCAB 23*

Mathewson, Stanley Bernard 1884-1943 *WhAm 2*

Mathewson, Thomas 1815?-1862 *NewYHSD*

Mathewson, William Kirk 1889-1937 *NatCAB 39*

Mathey, Dean 1890-1972 *WhAm 5*

Mathias, Charles McCurdy, Jr. 1922- *BiDrAC*

Mathias, Henry Edwin 1901-1966 *WhAm 4*

Mathias, Robert Bruce 1930- *BiDrAC, WebAB*

Mathias, Robert David 1897-1953 *WhAm 3*

Mathiasen, Karl 1860-1920 *NatCAB 19*

Mathie, David Robert 1902-1958 *NatCAB 47*

Mathie, Karl 1866-1938 *NatCAB 29*

Mathies, J L D *IIBEAAW, NewYHSD*

Mathies, Wharton 1902-1969 *WhAm 5*

Mathieson, Samuel James d1945 *WhAm 2*

Mathieu, Antoine *NewYHSD*

Mathieu, Beltran 1853- *WhAm 4*

Mathieu, Emile Leonard 1835-1890 *DcScB*

Mathieu, J B *NewYHSD*

Mathieu, Pierre 1804?- *NewYHSD*

Mathiez, Albert 1874-1932 *McGEWB*

Mathiot, Joshua 1800-1849 *BiAUS, BiDrAC, WhAm H*

Mathis, Harry R 1908-1967 *WhAm 4*

Mathis, Wallace Brigham 1877-1965 *NatCAB 54*

Mathison, Edward Thomson 1870-1930 *WhAm 1*

Mathison, John Kelly 1916-1974 *WhAm 6*

Mathot, Alice Croly *WomWWA 14*

Mathuranatha Sarman *DcScB*

Mathus *NewYHSD*

Matignon, Francis Anthony 1753-1818 *ApCAB, DcAmB, WhAm H*

Matile, George Auguste 1807-1881 *ApCAB*

Matile, Leon Albert 1844-1938 *WhAm 1*

Matis, Francisco Javier 1774-1851 *ApCAB*

Matisse, Henri 1869-1954 *McGEWB, WhAm 3, WhAm 4*

Matlack, Mrs. George S *WomWWA 14*

Matlack, James 1775-1840 *BiAUS, BiDrAC, WhAm H*

Matlack, Timothy 1730-1829 *ApCAB, BiAUS, BiDrAC, Drake, NatCAB 10, TwCBDA, WhAmP*
Matlack, Timothy 1733?-1829 *WhAm H*
Matlack, Timothy 1734-1829 *DcAmB*
Matlick, William *NewYHSD*
Matoaka *WebAB*
Matrat, J B *NewYHSD*
Matre, Joseph Boucard 1888-1966 *NatCAB 52*
Matrone, Gennard 1914-1975 *WhAm 6*
Matros, Nathaniel Hamilton 1903-1968 *NatCAB 56*
Matruchot, Louis 1863-1921 *DcScB*
Matsch, Franz 1899-1973 *WhAm 6*
Matsell, George Washington 1811-1877 *ApCAB*
Matson, Aaron 1770-1855 *BiAUS, BiDrAC, WhAm H*
Matson, Anna Glover 1851- *WomWWA 14*
Matson, Carlton Kingsbury 1890-1948 *WhAm 2*
Matson, Caroline Ruby 1867- *WhAm 4*
Matson, Clarence Henry 1872-1943 *WhAm 2*
Matson, Courtland Cushing 1841-1915 *BiDrAC, NatCAB 11, TwCBDA, WhAm 1, WhAmP*
Matson, Donald Darrow 1913-1969 *WhAm 5*
Matson, Frederick Eugene 1869-1941 *NatCAB 30, WhAm 1*
Matson, George Charlton 1873-1940 *WhAm 1*
Matson, Henry 1829-1901 *WhAm 1*
Matson, Kathleen Connor 1877- *WomWWA 14*
Matson, Leroy Edison 1896-1960 *NatCAB 47, WhAm 4*
Matson, Max M 1900-1970 *WhAm 5*
Matson, Ralph Charles 1880-1945 *WhAm 2*
Matson, Robert H 1897-1957 *WhAm 3*
Matson, Roderick Nathaniel 1871-1933 *NatCAB 36, WhAm 1*
Matson, Roy Lee 1908-1960 *WhAm 4*
Matson, Smith Corbin 1872-1936 *WhAm 1*
Matson, Theodore Malvin 1903-1954 *WhAm 3*
Matson, William 1849-1917 *NatCAB 40, WhAm 1*
Matsudaira, Tsuneo 1877-1949 *WhAm 2*
Matsunaga, Spark Masayuki 1916- *BiDrAC*
Matsuoka, Yosuke 1880-1946 *WhWW-II*
Matta, Guillermo 1829- *ApCAB*
Matta, Manuel Antonio 1826- *ApCAB*
Mattacks, John 1777-1847 *ApCAB, Drake*
Mattei, Albert Chester 1895-1969 *WhAm 5*
Mattei, Mattis *NewYHSD*
Mattell *NewYHSD*
Matter, Charles Martin 1875-1942 *NatCAB 31*
Matter, Martin 1850-1908 *NatCAB 31*
Matter, Milton 1887-1947 *NatCAB 36*
Matter, Philip 1842-1928 *NatCAB 33*
Matter, Robert 1891-1950 *NatCAB 41*
Mattern, David Earl 1890- *WhAm 3*
Mattern, Gertrude Lewis 1873- *WomWWA 14*
Matterson, Clarence H 1908-1967 *WhAm 4*
Matteson, Charles 1840-1925 *NatCAB 12, TwCBDA, WhAm 1*
Matteson, Frank Willington 1869-1933 *NatCAB 34, WhAm 1*
Matteson, Herman Howard 1875-1951 *WhAm 3*
Matteson, Joel A d1874 *BiAUS*
Matteson, Joel Aldrich 1808-1873 *DcAmB, NatCAB 11, WhAm H*
Matteson, Joel Aldrich 1808-1883 *ApCAB, TwCBDA*
Matteson, Leonard Jerome 1891-1967 *WhAm 4*
Matteson, Orsamus Benajah 1805-1889 *BiAUS, BiDrAC, TwCBDA, WhAm H*
Matteson, Thompkins Harrison 1813-1884 *NatCAB 12*
Matteson, Tompkins Harrison 1813-1884 *AmBi, ApCAB, DcAmB, Drake, NewYHSD, TwCBDA, WhAm H*
Matteson, Victor Andre 1872- *WhAm 5*
Matteucci, Carlo 1811-1868 *DcScB*
Mattfeld, Julius 1893-1968 *NatCAB 54*
Mattfeld, Marie *WhAm 5*
Matthaei, Frederick Carl 1892-1973 *WhAm 5*
Matthaei, William Peter 1886-1967 *NatCAB 54*
Matthai, Joseph Fleming 1889-1955 *NatCAB 46, WhAm 3*
Matthai, William Henry 1856- *WhAm 4*
Matthes, Francois Emile 1874-1948 *DcAmB S4, NatCAB 36, WebAB, WhAm 2*
Matthes, Gerard Hendrik 1874-1959 *NatCAB 43, WhAm 3*
Matthew Paris 1200?-1259 *McGEWB*
Matthew, Saint *McGEWB*
Matthew, Allan Pomeroy 1881-1965 *WhAm 4*
Matthew, Robert Hogg 1906-1975 *WhAm 6*
Matthew, Robert John 1907-1975 *WhAm 6*
Matthew, William Diller 1871-1930 *DcAmB, WhAm 1*
Matthew, Winfield Scott 1848-1932 *NatCAB 24*
Matthewman, Lisle DeVaux 1867- *WhAm 1*
Matthews *NewYHSD*
Matthews, Agnes Rounds *WomWWA 14*
Matthews, Albert 1860-1946 *WhAm 2*
Matthews, Albert 1873-1949 *WhAm 2*
Matthews, Albert Franklin 1858- *TwCBDA*
Matthews, Armstrong R 1902-1960 *WhAm 3A*
Matthews, Arthur John 1859-1942 *WhAm 2*
Matthews, Brander 1852-1929 *AmBi, ApCAB, DcAmB, NatCAB 26, TwCBDA, WhAm 1*
Matthews, Brander *see also* Matthews, James Brander
Matthews, Burrows 1893-1954 *WhAm 3*
Matthews, Charles 1856-1932 *BiDrAC*
Matthews, Charles Herbert 1897-1963 *WhAm 4*
Matthews, Charles Samuel 1914-1970 *WhAm 5*
Matthews, Claude 1845-1898 *ApCAB Sup, DcAmB, NatCAB 13, TwCBDA, WhAm H*
Matthews, Donald Ray 1907- *BiDrAC, WhAmP*
Matthews, Edmund Orville 1836-1911 *ApCAB Sup, TwCBDA, WhAm 1*
Matthews, Ernest Crawford, III 1927-1973 *WhAm 6*
Matthews, Eugene Alexander 1908-1972 *WhAm 5*
Matthews, Florence B 1857- *WomWWA 14*
Matthews, Francis Patrick 1887-1952 *DcAmB S5, NatCAB 52, WhAm 3*
Matthews, Franklin 1858-1917 *DcAmB, WhAm 1*
Matthews, Fred Elwood 1875-1942 *NatCAB 31*
Matthews, Fred Vivian 1865-1946 *NatCAB 36*
Matthews, George 1739-1812 *BiAUS, Drake*
Matthews, George, Jr. 1774-1836 *BiAUS*
Matthews, George *see also* Mathews, George
Matthews, George Adelman 1852-1914 *NatCAB 18*
Matthews, George Edward 1855-1911 *NatCAB 12, WhAm 1*
Matthews, George H *NewYHSD*
Matthews, George Henry 1808-1869 *NatCAB 8*
Matthews, H Alexander 1879- *WhAm 6*
Matthews, Harlan Julius 1877-1942 *WhAm 2*
Matthews, Harry S, Jr. 1902-1954 *WhAm 3*
Matthews, Henry P *NewYHSD*
Matthews, Hugh 1876-1943 *WhAm 2*
Matthews, Irma Blanchard 1872- *WomWWA 14*
Matthews, Isaac George 1871-1959 *NatCAB 48, WhAm 4*
Matthews, J Houston 1884-1950 *NatCAB 40*
Matthews, James Brander 1852-1929 *BiDAmEd, DcAmB*
Matthews, James Brander *see also* Matthews, Brander
Matthews, James Green 1881-1962 *NatCAB 50*
Matthews, James Newson 1828-1888 *NatCAB 12*
Matthews, Jane Skinker 1886- *WomWWA 14*
Matthews, John 1772-1848 *ApCAB, TwCBDA*
Matthews, John 1774-1802 *BiAUS, Drake*
Matthews, John 1808-1870 *DcAmB, WhAm H*
Matthews, John *see also* Mathews, John
Matthews, John Harold 1890-1947 *NatCAB 35*
Matthews, John L L *NewYHSD*
Matthews, Joseph Merritt 1874-1931 *DcAmB, NatCAB 15, WhAm 1*
Matthews, Joseph W d1863? *NatCAB 13*
Matthews, Mark Allison 1867-1940 *WhAm 1*
Matthews, Marmaduke 1837-1913 *IIBEAAW*
Matthews, Matthew Clement 1862-1921 *NatCAB 19*
Matthews, Murrell O 1893-1964 *NatCAB 51, WhAm 4*
Matthews, Nathan 1854-1927 *DcAmB, NatCAB 25, WhAm 1*
Matthews, Nelson Edwin 1852-1917 *BiDrAC, WhAm 1*
Matthews, Orus Jones 1900-1964 *WhAm 4*
Matthews, Oscar Homer 1878-1952 *NatCAB 42*
Matthews, Paul Clement 1866-1954 *NatCAB 50, WhAm 3*
Matthews, Peter B *NewYHSD*
Matthews, Peter V *NewYHSD*
Matthews, Robert David 1886-1943 *WhAm 2*
Matthews, Robert Orville 1878-1934 *WhAm 2*
Matthews, Sir Ronald Wilfred 1885-1959 *WhAm 4*
Matthews, Samuel 1600?-1659 *ApCAB Sup*
Matthews, Samuel 1600?-1660 *NatCAB 13*
Matthews, Samuel *see also* Mathews, Samuel
Matthews, Stanley 1824-1889 *AmBi, ApCAB, BiDrAC, DcAmB, NatCAB 2, TwCBDA, WebAB, WhAm H, WhAmP*
Matthews, Stephen Johnson 1912- *WhAm 5*
Matthews, Vann Marshall 1890-1954 *NatCAB 45*
Matthews, Velma Dare 1904-1958 *WhAm 3*
Matthews, Victoria Earle 1861-1907 *NotAW*
Matthews, Vincent 1766-1846 *TwCBDA*
Matthews, Vincent *see also* Mathews, Vincent
Matthews, Walter Robert 1881- *WhAm 6*
Matthews, Washington 1843-1905 *AmBi, DcAmB, NatCAB 13, TwCBDA, WhAm 1*
Matthews, William 1755- *BiAUS, BiDrAC, WhAm H*
Matthews, William 1822-1896 *DcAmB, WhAm H*
Matthews, William 1905-1975 *WhAm 6*
Matthews, William Albert 1868- *WhAm 5*
Matthews, William Arthur 1911-1972 *NatCAB 57*
Matthews, William Baxter 1864- *WhoColR*
Matthews, William Baynham 1850- *WhAm 1*
Matthews, William Clarence 1877- *WhoColR*
Matthews, William Frederick 1898-1963 *NatCAB 50*
Matthews, William Henry 1868-1946 *WhAm 2, WhAm 5*
Matthews, William Robinson 1874-1951 *NatCAB 39*
Matthews, Zachariah Keodirelang 1901-1968 *WhAm 5*
Matthias 1790?-1840 *ApCAB, Drake*
Matthias, Benjamin *NewYHSD*
Matthias, Edward Shiloh 1873-1953 *WhAm 3*
Matthias, Gwynn John 1888-1951 *NatCAB 48*
Matthias, John Marshall 1903-1973 *WhAm 5*
Matthies, George Erastus 1863-1922 *NatCAB 24*
Matthies, William Hugo 1879-1946 *NatCAB 38*
Matthiessen, Augustus 1831-1870 *DcScB*
Matthiessen, Francis Otto 1902-1950 *DcAmB S4, NatCAB 41, WhAm 3*
Matthiessen, Frederick William 1835-1918 *DcAmB*
Matthiessen, Ralph H d1975 *WhAm 6*
Matthison, Edith Wynne d1955 *WhAm 3*
Mattia, Virginius Dante, Jr. 1923-1971 *NatCAB 56, WhAm 5*
Mattice, Asa Martines 1853-1925 *DcAmB*
Mattice, Burr 1856- *WhAm 1*
Mattiello, Joseph J 1900-1948 *WhAm 2*
Mattill, Henry Albright 1883-1953 *NatCAB 41, WhAm 3*
Mattill, Peter Milton 1887-1958 *NatCAB 47*
Mattimore, John Clarke 1916-1975 *WhAm 6*
Mattingly, Barak Thomas 1901-1957 *WhAm 3*
Mattingly, Frederick Browning 1901-1969 *WhAm 5*
Mattingly, Garrett 1900-1962 *NatCAB 47, WhAm 4*
Mattingly, Marie *NotAW*
Mattingly, Robert Edgar 1868-1948 *NatCAB 37, WhAm 3*
Mattingly, Sarah Irwin 1852-1934 *NatCAB 30, NotAW*
Mattingly, William Francis 1837-1918 *WhAm 1*
Mattioli, Lino 1853- *WhAm 4*

Mattioli, Pietro Andrea Gregorio 1501-1577 *DcScB*
Mattis, Elsie Curtis 1881- *WomWWA 14*
Mattison, Donald Magnus 1905-1975 *WhAm 6*
Mattison, Evan Axford 1904-1958 *NatCAB 53*
Mattison, Fitch Champlin Edmonds 1861-1932 *WhAm 1, WhAm 1C*
Mattison, H B d1871 *Drake*
Mattison, Hiram 1811-1868 *ApCAB, DcAmB, Drake, NatCAB 12, WhAm H*
Mattison, Richard Vanselous 1851-1936 *WhAm 1*
Mattison, Richard VanZeelust 1851-1936 *NatCAB 27*
Mattlin, A Homer 1912-1960 *WhAm 4*
Mattocks, Charles Porter 1840-1910 *ApCAB Sup, TwCBDA, WhAm 1*
Mattocks, John 1776-1847 *BiAUS*
Mattocks, John 1777-1847 *BiDrAC, DcAmB, NatCAB 8, TwCBDA, WhAm H, WhAmP*
Mattocks, John 1839-1889 *NatCAB 11*
Mattoon, Arthur Martyn 1855-1924 *WhAm 1*
Mattoon, Ebenezer 1755-1842 *TwCBDA*
Mattoon, Ebenezer 1755-1843 *ApCAB, BiAUS, BiDrAC, Drake, NatCAB 5, WhAm H*
Mattoon, Harold Frank 1894-1964 *NatCAB 51*
Mattoon, Stephen 1816-1889 *ApCAB, DcAmB, TwCBDA, WhAm H*
Mattos, Euzebio 1629-1690 *ApCAB*
Mattos, Gregorio De 1613-1696 *ApCAB*
Mattox, Norman Thomas 1910-1960 *NatCAB 48*
Mattox, William Earl 1906-1967 *WhAm 5*
Mattson, Bernard Gause 1866- *WhAm 4*
Mattson, Hans 1832-1893 *DcAmB, TwCBDA, WhAm 4*
Mattson, Karl Evald 1905-1964 *WhAm 4*
Mattson, Peter August 1865-1944 *WhAm 2*
Matulka, Jan 1890- *IIBEAAW*
Maturana, Marcos 1802-1871 *ApCAB*
Maturin, Edward 1812-1881 *ApCAB, Drake*
Matuyama, Motonori 1884-1958 *DcScB*
Matz, Israel 1869-1950 *NatCAB 40*
Matz, Myron Harold 1913-1973 *WhAm 6*
Matz, Nicholas Chrysostom 1850-1917 *ApCAB, NatCAB 12, TwCBDA, WhAm 1*
Matz, Philip Benjamin 1885-1938 *WhAm 1*
Matz, Rudolph 1860-1917 *WhAm 1*
Matzeliger, Jan Ernest 1852-1889 *WebAB*
Matzeliger, Jan Ernst 1852-1889 *DcAmB*
Matzen, Herman Nicolai 1861-1938 *IIBEAAW, NatCAB 44, WhAm 1*
Matzenauer, Margaret 1881-1963 *NatCAB 51*
Matzenauer, Margarete 1881-1963 *WhAm 4*
Matzke, Edwin Bernard 1902-1969 *NatCAB 54, WhAm 5*
Matzke, John Ernst 1862-1910 *WhAm 1*
Mauborgne, Joseph Oswald 1881-1971 *WhAm 5*
Mauch, Max d1864 *NewYHSD*
Mauchly, Sebastian Jacob 1878-1928 *WhAm 1*
Mauck, Joseph William 1852-1937 *NatCAB 33, TwCBDA, WhAm 1*
Mauck, Victor 1873-1956 *NatCAB 43*
Mauck, Wilfred Otto 1899-1975 *WhAm 6*
Maude, Cyril Francis 1862-1951 *WhAm 3*
Maude, John *Drake, NewYHSD*
Maude, William L 1894-1966 *WhAm 4*
Maudsley, Sutcliffe *NewYHSD*
Mauduit, Israel 1708-1787 *ApCAB, Drake*
Mauduit, Jasper *ApCAB*
Mauduit DuPlessis, Thomas Antoine 1752-1791 *ApCAB*
Mauduit Duplessis, Thomas Antoine 1753-1791 *Drake*
Maugh, Lawrence C 1901-1971 *WhAm 5*
Maugham, W Somerset 1874-1965 *WhAm 4*
Maugham, William Somerset 1874-1965 *BiHiMed, McGEWB*
Mauguin, Charles Victor 1878-1958 *DcScB*
Mauk, Charlotte E 1907-1973 *WhAm 6*
Maul, Joseph *BiAUS*
Maul, William G *ApCAB X*
Maulbertsch, Franz Anton 1724-1796 *McGEWB*
Mauldin, Frank Gratin 1864-1940 *WhAm 1*
Mauldin, Ivy Milton 1875-1927 *NatCAB 21*
Mauldin, William Henry 1921- *WebAB, WebAMB*

Maule, Frances 1889-1966 *WhAm 4*
Maule, Harry Edward 1886-1971 *WhAm 5*
Maule, Mary Katherine 1861- *WomWWA 14*
Maule, Tallie Burton 1917-1974 *WhAm 6*
Maulevrier *NewYHSD*
Maull, Millicent Howell 1868- *WomWWA 14*
Maumus, Achilles J 1861- *WhAm 4*
Maunder, Edward Walter 1851-1928 *DcScB*
Mauney, Dorris Carl 1881-1956 *NatCAB 49, NatCAB 50*
Mauney, Jacob Simra 1846-1936 *NatCAB 37*
Mauney, Lawrence 1876-1958 *NatCAB 47*
Mauney, William Andrew 1841-1929 *NatCAB 22*
Maunoury, Michel Joseph 1847-1923 *WhoMilH*
Maupas, Francois Emile 1842-1916 *DcScB*
Maupassant, Henri Rene Albert Guy De 1850-1893 *McGEWB*
Maupertuis, Pierre Louis Moreau De 1698-1759 *AsBiEn, DcScB*
Mauphin, Socrates 1808-1871 *TwCBDA*
Maupin, Socrates 1808-1871 *BiDAmEd*
Maupin, Socrates 1809-1871 *NatCAB 13*
Maupin, William Austin 1869-1954 *NatCAB 41*
Maupin, William Gabriel 1890-1951 *NatCAB 39*
Mauran, John Lawrence 1866-1933 *DcAmB S1, WhAm 1*
Mauran, Joseph 1796-1873 *NatCAB 10*
Maurepas, Jean F Phelypeaux, Comte De 1701-1781 *ApCAB*
Maurepas, Jean F Phelypeaux, Count De 1701-1781 *Drake*
Maurer, Alfred Henry 1868-1932 *BnEnAmA, NatCAB 25*
Maurer, Edward Rose 1869-1948 *WhAm 2*
Maurer, Henry 1830- *NatCAB 5*
Maurer, Irving 1879-1942 *WhAm 2*
Maurer, James Hudson 1864-1944 *DcAmB S3, WhAm 2, WhAm 5*
Maurer, Julius Maximilian 1857-1938 *DcScB*
Maurer, Louis 1832-1932 *AmBi, IIBEAAW, NatCAB 25, NewYHSD*
Maurer, Oscar Edward 1878-1950 *NatCAB 39, WhAm 3*
Maurer, Oscar Valentine 1881-1946 *NatCAB 35*
Maurer, Robert Adam 1879- *WhAm 6*
Maurer, William Allen 1872-1929 *WhAm 1*
Mauriac, Francois 1885-1970 *McGEWB, WhAm 5*
Maurice Of Nassau 1567-1625 *McGEWB, WhoMilH*
Maurice, Arthur Bartlett 1873-1946 *WhAm 2*
Maurice, James 1814-1884 *BiAUS, BiDrAC, WhAm H*
Maurice, John Frederick Denison 1805-1872 *McGEWB*
Mauriceau, Francois 1637-1709 *BiHiMed*
Maurillo, Dominick Francis 1898-1975 *WhAm 6*
Maurin, Aristide Peter 1877-1949 *DcAmReB*
Maurin, Frank Daniel 1905-1960 *NatCAB 49*
Maurin, Peter Aristide 1877-1949 *DcAmB S4*
Mauritson, Mayne H 1890-1967 *NatCAB 54*
Mauritzson, Jules Gote Ultimus 1868-1930 *WhAm 1*
Mauro, Fra d1459? *DcScB*
Mauro, Philip 1859-1952 *WhAm 3*
Mauro-Cottone, Melchiorre 1886- *ApCAB X*
Maurois, Andre 1885-1967 *WhAm 4*
Maurolico, Francesco 1494-1575 *DcScB*
Maurras, Charles Marie Photius 1868-1952 *McGEWB*
Maurville, Louis C J, Count Bide De 1752-1840 *ApCAB*
Maury, Abraham P d1848 *BiAUS*
Maury, Abram Poindexter 1801-1848 *BiDrAC, TwCBDA*
Maury, Ann 1803-1876 *ApCAB, Drake, TwCBDA*
Maury, Antonia Caetana DePaiva Pereira 1866-1952 *DcScB, WhAm 3*
Maury, Antonia Coetana 1866-1952 *WomWWA 14*
Maury, Carlotta Joaquina 1874-1938 *NatCAB 28, WhAm 1, WomWWA 14*
Maury, Dabney H 1824?-1900 *Drake*

Maury, Dabney Herndon 1822-1900 *AmBi, ApCAB, BiDConf, DcAmB, NatCAB 4, TwCBDA, WhAm 1*
Maury, Dabney Herndon 1863-1933 *WhAm 1*
Maury, Edward *NewYHSD*
Maury, Francis Fontaine 1840-1879 *ApCAB, DcAmB, WhAm H*
Maury, John Minor 1795-1823 *ApCAB*
Maury, John Minor 1795-1825 *TwCBDA*
Maury, John William Draper 1871- *WhAm 5*
Maury, Magruder Gordon 1878-1948 *NatCAB 36, WhAm 2*
Maury, Matthew Fontaine 1806-1873 *AmBi, ApCAB, AsBiEn, BiAUS, BiDConf, DcAmB, DcScB, Drake, EncAB, McGEWB, NatCAB 6, TwCBDA, WebAB, WebAMB, WhAm H*
Maury, Mytton 1839-1919 *WhAm 1*
Maury, Richard Brooke 1834-1919 *NatCAB 14, WhAm 1*
Maury, Sarah Mytton d1848 *Drake*
Maury, Sarah Mytton 1803-1849 *ApCAB*
Maury, William Arden d1918 *WhAm 1*
Maus, Casper 1816-1876 *NatCAB 37*
Maus, L Mervin 1851-1939 *WhAm 1*
Maus, Marion Perry 1850-1930 *DcAmB, NatCAB 24, WebAMB, WhAm 1*
Maus, Mattie Lindsay Poor 1875- *WomWWA 14*
Maus, William Donald 1893-1960 *WhAm 4*
Mauss, Marcel 1872-1950 *McGEWB*
Mauthe, James Lester 1890-1967 *NatCAB 56, WhAm 4*
Mauvais, A *NewYHSD*
Mauze, Jean 1903-1973 *WhAm 6*
Mauze, Joseph Layton 1873-1937 *WhAm 1*
Mauzey, Merritt 1897?-1975 *IIBEAAW*
Mauzy, Anna J Ross 1885- *WomWWA 14*
Maveety, Patrick John 1855-1946 *WhAm 2*
Maver, William, Jr. 1851-1928 *ApCAB X, WhAm 1*
Maverick, Aaron Howell 1809-1846 *NewYHSD*
Maverick, Andrew 1782-1826 *NewYHSD*
Maverick, Andrew Rushton 1809?-1835? *NewYHSD*
Maverick, Ann 1810?-1863 *NewYHSD*
Maverick, Brewster 1830?-1898 *NewYHSD*
Maverick, Catharine 1811-1887 *NewYHSD*
Maverick, Emily 1803-1850 *NewYHSD*
Maverick, Fontaine Maury 1895-1954 *BiDrAC, WhAmP*
Maverick, Maria Ann 1805-1832 *NewYHSD*
Maverick, Maury 1895-1954 *DcAmB S5, NatCAB 42, WhAm 3*
Maverick, Octavia 1814-1882 *NewYHSD*
Maverick, Peter 1780-1831 *ApCAB, DcAmB, NewYHSD, TwCBDA, WhAm H*
Maverick, Peter, Jr. 1809-1845 *NewYHSD*
Maverick, Peter Rushton 1755-1811 *NewYHSD*
Maverick, Samuel 1602- *NatCAB 8*
Maverick, Samuel 1602?-1667 *Drake*
Maverick, Samuel 1602?-1670? *ApCAB*
Maverick, Samuel 1602?-1676? *DcAmB, WhAm H*
Maverick, Samuel 1789-1845 *NewYHSD*
Maverick, Samuel Augustus 1803-1870 *NatCAB 6, TwCBDA, WebAB*
Maverick, Samuel R 1812-1839 *NewYHSD*
Maverick, W *NewYHSD*
Mavor, James Watt 1883-1963 *NatCAB 52*
Mawe, John 1764-1829 *ApCAB*
Mawer, Colin Drummond 1875-1965 *NatCAB 50*
Mawhinney, Robert James 1859-1954 *WhAm 3*
Mawson, Christopher Orlando Sylvester 1870-1938 *NatCAB 29*
Mawson, Sir Douglas 1882-1958 *DcScB, McGEWB*
Maxcy, Carroll Lewis 1865-1936 *WhAm 1*
Maxcy, Charles Josiah 1887-1966 *WhAm 4*
Maxcy, Gardiner Josiah 1913-1971 *WhAm 5*
Maxcy, Jonathan 1768-1820 *ApCAB, BiDAmEd, DcAmB, Drake, NatCAB 1, NatCAB 8, NatCAB 11, TwCBDA, WhAm H*
Maxcy, Kenneth Fuller 1889-1966 *WhAm 4*
Maxcy, Virgil 1785-1844 *ApCAB, DcAmB, Drake, NatCAB 4, WhAm H*

Maxey, Edward Ernest 1867-1934 *WhAm 1*
Maxey, Edwin 1869- *WhAm 5*
Maxey, George Wendell 1878-1950 *NatCAB 38, WhAm 2A*
Maxey, S B 1825-1895 *BiAUS*
Maxey, Samuel Bell 1825-1895 *ApCAB, BiDConf, BiDRAC, DcAmB, NatCAB 4, TwCBDA, WebAMB, WhAm H, WhAmP*
Maxey, Thomas S 1846-1921 *WhAm 1*
Maxey, Virgil d1844 *BiAUS*
Maxfield, Ezra Kempton 1881-1941 *WhAm 1*
Maxfield, Francis N 1877-1945 *WhAm 2*
Maxfield, James Robert 1871-1958 *NatCAB 45*
Maxfield, William Maupin 1899-1962 *NatCAB 50*
Maxim, Florence 1873- *WomWWA 14*
Maxim, Hiram Percy 1869-1936 *AmBi, DcAmB S2, NatCAB 15, WebAB, WhAm 1*
Maxim, Sir Hiram Stevens 1840-1916 *AmBi, ApCAB Sup, AsBiEn, DcAmB, McGEWB, NatCAB 6, TwCBDA, WebAB, WebAMB, WhAm 1*
Maxim, Hudson 1853-1927 *AmBi, ApCAB X, DcAmB, NatCAB 13, WebAB, WebAMB, WhAm 1*
Maximilian 1832-1867 *ApCAB, McGEWB, WhAm H*
Maximilian I 1459-1519 *McGEWB, WhoMilH*
Maximilian II 1527-1576 *McGEWB*
Maximilian, Charlotte Marie Amelie 1840- *ApCAB*
Maximilian, Ferdinand Joseph 1832-1867 *Drake*
Maximos, Demetrios 1873-1955 *WhAm 3*
Maximov *DcScB*
Maxon, Charles *NewYHSD*
Maxon, Dudley Wendle 1892-1964 *NatCAB 50*
Maxon, James Matthew 1875-1948 *NatCAB 42, WhAm 2*
Maxon, Lou Russell 1900-1971 *WhAm 5*
Maxon, William Densmore 1857-1940 *WhAm 1*
Maxon, William Ralph 1877-1948 *NatCAB 38, WhAm 2*
Maxson, John Haviland 1906-1966 *NatCAB 53*
Maxson, Ralph Nelson 1879-1943 *NatCAB 32, WhAm 2*
Maxson, Willis Edward 1864-1952 *WhAm 3*
Maxtla d1430 *ApCAB*
Maxwell, Allison 1848-1915 *WhAm 1*
Maxwell, Anna Caroline 1851-1929 *BiCAW, NotAW, WomWWA 14*
Maxwell, Archibald McIntyre 1895-1949 *WhAm 2*
Maxwell, Arthur Freeman 1899-1972 *WhAm 5*
Maxwell, Arthur Stanley 1896-1970 *WhAm 5, WhAm 6*
Maxwell, Augustus E 1820-1903 *BiAUS*
Maxwell, Augustus Emmet 1820-1903 *ApCAB*
Maxwell, Augustus Emmett 1820-1903 *BiDConf, BiDRAC, DcAmB, NatCAB 7, TwCBDA, WhAm 1, WhAmP*
Maxwell, Bertram Wayburn 1891-1972 *NatCAB 56*
Maxwell, Carrie Estelle 1863- *WomWWA 14*
Maxwell, Charles Augustus 1854- *WhAm 4*
Maxwell, Charles Robert 1878-1939 *WhAm 1*
Maxwell, Clara M Barry *WomWWA 14*
Maxwell, David Hervey 1786-1854 *DcAmB, WhAm H*
Maxwell, David Lander 1892-1953 *NatCAB 40*
Maxwell, Ellen Blackmar *WomWWA 14*
Maxwell, Ellen Blackmer *TwCBDA*
Maxwell, Elmer Stephens 1888-1959 *NatCAB 47*
Maxwell, Elsa 1883-1963 *WebAB, WhAm 4*
Maxwell, Emma Eliza *WomWWA 14*
Maxwell, Ernestine McDaniel *WomWWA 14*
Maxwell, Evelyn Croom 1863- *WhAm 3*
Maxwell, Francis Taylor 1861-1943 *ApCAB X, WhAm 2*
Maxwell, French Thornhill 1872-1946 *NatCAB 34*
Maxwell, Gavin 1914-1969 *WhAm 5*
Maxwell, George Clifford 1771-1816 *BiAUS, BiDRAC, WhAm H*
Maxwell, George Hebard 1860-1946 *DcAmB S4, WhAm 2*

Maxwell, George Holmes 1864-1932 *NatCAB 32, WhAm 1*
Maxwell, George Lawrence 1896-1947 *WhAm 2*
Maxwell, George Troup 1827-1897 *DcAmB, TwCBDA, WhAm H*
Maxwell, George Troupe 1827-1897 *ApCAB*
Maxwell, Gertrude Appleget Wyckoff 1840- *WomWWA 14*
Maxwell, Glenn Nicholas 1896-1946 *NatCAB 36*
Maxwell, Guy Everett 1870-1939 *WhAm 1*
Maxwell, Haymond 1879-1958 *WhAm 4*
Maxwell, Hugh 1733-1799 *ApCAB, Drake, NatCAB 2*
Maxwell, Hugh 1787-1873 *ApCAB, DcAmB, NatCAB 2, WhAm H*
Maxwell, J P B 1805-1845 *BiAUS*
Maxwell, James Angus 1862- *WhAm 4*
Maxwell, James Clerk 1831-1879 *AsBiEn, DcScB, McGEWB*
Maxwell, James Hoyt 1901-1960 *NatCAB 44, WhAm 4*
Maxwell, John Henry 1899-1967 *NatCAB 53*
Maxwell, John Mills 1849- *WhAm 4*
Maxwell, John Milo 1866- *WhAm 4*
Maxwell, John Paterson Bryant 1804-1845 *TwCBDA*
Maxwell, John Patterson Bryan 1804-1845 *BiDRAC, WhAm H*
Maxwell, John Rogers 1846-1910 *ApCAB X, WhAm 1*
Maxwell, Jonathan Dixon 1864-1928 *NatCAB 25*
Maxwell, Joseph Raymond Nonnatus 1899-1971 *WhAm 5*
Maxwell, Laura 1858- *WomWWA 14*
Maxwell, Lawrence 1853-1927 *NatCAB 13, NatCAB 23, WhAm 1*
Maxwell, Lee Wilder 1881-1948 *WhAm 2*
Maxwell, Leon Ryder 1883-1956 *WhAm 4*
Maxwell, Lewis 1790-1862 *BiAUS, BiDRAC, WhAm H*
Maxwell, Lucien Bonaparte 1818-1875 *DcAmB, REnAW, WhAm H*
Maxwell, Margery 1895-1966 *WhAm 4*
Maxwell, Nathaniel Hamilton 1880-1943 *NatCAB 39*
Maxwell, Nathaniel Van 1809-1886 *TwCBDA*
Maxwell, Ralph Lester 1905-1956 *WhAm 3*
Maxwell, Robert Moore 1865-1933 *NatCAB 24*
Maxwell, Russell Lamonte 1890-1968 *NatCAB 54, WhAm 5*
Maxwell, Samuel 1825-1901 *BiDRAC, DcAmB, NatCAB 12, WhAmP*
Maxwell, Samuel 1826-1901 *WhAm 1*
Maxwell, Samuel Steen 1860- *WhAm 4*
Maxwell, Sidney Denise 1831- *ApCAB, NatCAB 7, TwCBDA*
Maxwell, Thomas 1792-1864 *BiAUS, BiDRAC, WhAm H*
Maxwell, Thomas Andrew 1891-1950 *NatCAB 39*
Maxwell, Thompson 1742-1825 *ApCAB*
Maxwell, Thompson 1742-1835 *NatCAB 2*
Maxwell, William 1733?-1796 *DcAmB, TwCBDA, WebAMB, WhAm H*
Maxwell, William 1733?-1798 *ApCAB, Drake, NatCAB 1*
Maxwell, William 1755?-1809 *DcAmB, WhAm H*
Maxwell, William 1784-1857 *ApCAB, DcAmB, Drake, NatCAB 2, TwCBDA, WhAm H*
Maxwell, William 1852-1925 *NatCAB 20*
Maxwell, William Allison, Jr. 1879-1946 *WhAm 2*
Maxwell, William Clarence 1871-1942 *NatCAB 32*
Maxwell, William Cochrane 1865-1936 *WhAm 1*
Maxwell, William Donald 1900-1975 *WhAm 6*
Maxwell, William Henry 1852-1920 *ApCAB, BiDAmEd, DcAmB, NatCAB 13, TwCBDA, WhAm 1*
Maxwell, William John 1859- *WhAm 4*
May, A Wilfred 1900-1969 *WhAm 5*
May, Abigail Williams 1829-1888 *NotAW, TwCBDA*
May, Alonzo Beryl 1906-1968 *WhAm 5*

May, Andrew Jackson 1875-1959 *BiDRAC, WhAm 3, WhAmP*
May, Arthur James 1899-1968 *NatCAB 55, WhAm 5*
May, Ben Ernest 1889-1972 *NatCAB 57*
May, Benjamin Mackall 1884-1952 *NatCAB 40*
May, Benjamin Victor 1880-1945 *NatCAB 34*
May, Caroline *NewYHSD*
May, Caroline 1820?- *ApCAB*
May, Catherine Dean 1914- *BiDRAC*
May, Charles Augustus 1817-1864 *ApCAB, TwCBDA, WebAMB*
May, Charles Augustus 1819-1864 *NatCAB 4*
May, Charles Henry 1861-1943 *NatCAB 14, WhAm 2*
May, David 1848- *ApCAB X*
May, David 1865- *WhAm 4*
May, David William 1868-1937 *WhAm 1*
May, Earl Chapin 1873-1960 *WhAm 4*
May, Edna 1878-1917 *WhAm 1*
May, Edward *NewYHSD*
May, Edward 1838-1917 *WhAm 1*
May, Edward Harrison 1824-1887 *ApCAB, DcAmB, NewYHSD, TwCBDA, WhAm H*
May, Edwin 1824-1880 *WhAm H*
May, Edwin Hyland, Jr. 1924- *BiDRAC*
May, Ernest H 1859-1935 *WhAm 1*
May, Frederick 1773-1847 *ApCAB, Drake, NatCAB 5*
May, Frederick John 1812-1891 *NatCAB 15*
May, Geoffrey 1900-1964 *WhAm 4*
May, George Henry 1869-1945 *NatCAB 34*
May, George Oliver 1875-1961 *WhAm 4*
May, George Storr 1890-1962 *WhAm 4*
May, George W *NewYHSD*
May, Geraldine Pratt 1895- *WebAMB*
May, Harry Kenneth 1927-1972 *NatCAB 57*
May, Henry d1863 *BiAUS*
May, Henry 1816-1866 *ApCAB, BiDRAC, TwCBDA, WhAm H*
May, Henry 1861-1944 *NatCAB 43*
May, Herbert Arthur 1892-1966 *NatCAB 52, WhAm 4*
May, Herbert Louis 1877-1966 *WhAm 4*
May, Irving 1891-1964 *WhAm 4*
May, Isaac 1862-1953 *NatCAB 41*
May, Jacques Meyer 1896-1975 *WhAm 6*
May, James Vance 1873-1947 *WhAm 2*
May, John 1748-1812 *ApCAB, TwCBDA*
May, John Wilder 1819-1883 *ApCAB*
May, Joseph 1836-1918 *NatCAB 17*
May, Julia Harris 1833-1912 *WhAm 1*
May, Karl Friedrich 1842-1912 *REnAW*
May, Lewis 1823-1897 *ApCAB Sup, NatCAB 4*
May, Luke S 1886-1955 *WhAm 4*
May, Maria B *NewYHSD*
May, Max 1861- *WhAm 1*
May, Max Benjamin 1866-1929 *WhAm 1*
May, Michael *NewYHSD*
May, Mitchell 1870-1961 *BiDRAC*
May, Mortimer 1892-1974 *WhAm 6*
May, Morton J d1968 *WhAm 5*
May, Otto Bernard 1880-1952 *NatCAB 39*
May, Philip William 1864-1903 *IIBEAAW*
May, Samuel 1810-1899 *NatCAB 19*
May, Samuel Chester 1887-1955 *NatCAB 44, WhAm 3*
May, Samuel Joseph 1797-1871 *AmBi, ApCAB, DcAmB, Drake, NatCAB 2, TwCBDA, WhAm H*
May, Samuel Passmore 1828- *ApCAB*
May, Siegmund Henry 1897-1970 *NatCAB 55*
May, Sophie 1833-1906 *DcAmB, NotAW, TwCBDA*
May, Stella Burke d1961 *WhAm 4*
May, Thomas d1968 *WhAm 5*
May, Thomas 1860-1927 *WhAm 1*
May, William Andrew 1850-1923 *NatCAB 19, WhAm 1*
May, William H *NewYHSD*
May, William Henry 1875- *WhAm 5*
May, William L 1793?-1849 *BiAUS, BiDRAC, WhAm H*
May, Winifred Martin 1869- *WomWWA 14*
Mayakovsky, Vladimir Vladimirovich 1893-1930 *McGEWB*

Mayall, Eliza McLellan 1822- *NewYHSD*
Mayall, Samuel 1816-1892 *BiAUS, BiDrAC, WhAm H*
Mayall, Thomas Jefferson 1826-1888 *ApCAB Sup, NatCAB 5*
Maybank, Burnet Rhett 1899-1954 *BiDrAC, DcAmB S5, NatCAB 44, WhAm 3, WhAmP*
Maybaum, Jacob Lewis 1884-1951 *NatCAB 38*
Maybe, Emmeline *NewYHSD*
Maybeck, Bernard Ralph 1862-1957 *BnEnAmA, NatCAB 43, WhAm 5*
Maybell, Claude 1872- *WhAm 5*
Mayberry, Charles 1876-1944 *NatCAB 34*
Mayberry, James 1841?- *NewYHSD*
Mayborn, Ward Carlton 1879-1958 *NatCAB 47*
Maybury, William Cotter 1848-1909 *BiDrAC, TwCBDA*
Maybury, William Cotter 1849-1909 *WhAm 1*
Maycall, John 1842?- *NewYHSD*
Maycann, John Anthony 1892-1950 *NatCAB 39*
Maychick, Edward John 1901-1961 *NatCAB 46*
Mayer, Albert J, Jr. 1906-1960 *NatCAB 47, WhAm 4*
Mayer, Alfred Goldsborough 1868-1922 *DcAmB*
Mayer, Alfred Marshall 1836-1897 *ApCAB, DcAmB, DcScB, NatCAB 13, TwCBDA, WhAm H*
Mayer, Andre 1875-1956 *WhAm 3*
Mayer, Belle Falck *WomWWA 14*
Mayer, Brantz 1809-1879 *ApCAB, DcAmB, Drake, NatCAB 10, TwCBDA, WhAm H*
Mayer, C W *NewYHSD*
Mayer, Caspar 1871- *NatCAB 10*
Mayer, Charles F d1864 *BiAUS*
Mayer, Charles Frederick 1832-1904 *NatCAB 18*
Mayer, Charles Herbert 1903-1966 *WhAm 4*
Mayer, Charles Holt 1876-1958 *NatCAB 47, WhAm 5*
Mayer, Charles Raphael 1860- *WhAm 4*
Mayer, Christian 1719-1783 *DcScB*
Mayer, Christian Gustav Adolph 1839-1908 *DcScB*
Mayer, Constant 1829-1911 *DcAmB, NewYHSD*
Mayer, Constant 1832- *ApCAB, TwCBDA*
Mayer, Constant 1832-1901 *WhAm 1*
Mayer, Edgar 1889-1975 *WhAm 6*
Mayer, Edward Everett 1876- *WhAm 5*
Mayer, Elias 1877-1945 *WhAm 2*
Mayer, Emil 1854-1931 *DcAmB, NatCAB 25, WhAm 1*
Mayer, Ernest DeW 1903-1968 *WhAm 5*
Mayer, Ferdinand 1817?- *NewYHSD*
Mayer, Francis Blackwell 1827-1899 *NewYHSD, TwCBDA, WhAm H*
Mayer, Francis VonRossdell 1874-1946 *NatCAB 35*
Mayer, Frank Blackwell 1827-1899 *ApCAB, IIBEAAW*
Mayer, George John 1861-1950 *NatCAB 40*
Mayer, Gottfried Oscar 1908-1969 *WhAm 5*
Mayer, Harry Hubert 1874- *WhAm 5*
Mayer, Henrik Martin 1908-1973 *WhAm 5*
Mayer, Hy 1868-1954 *WhAm 3*
Mayer, Isaac Henry 1864-1967 *WhAm 4*
Mayer, Jerry Gershon 1891-1947 *NatCAB 36*
Mayer, Johann Tobias 1723-1762 *DcScB*
Mayer, John Ignatius 1907-1974 *WhAm 6*
Mayer, Joseph *NewYHSD, WebAB*
Mayer, Joseph 1887-1975 *WhAm 6*
Mayer, Joseph Bell 1849-1951 *WhAm 3*
Mayer, Joseph Edward 1871-1957 *NatCAB 45*
Mayer, Joseph Ralph 1897-1961 *NatCAB 47*
Mayer, Julius *NewYHSD*
Mayer, Julius Marshuetz 1865-1925 *NatCAB 20, WhAm 1*
Mayer, Julius Robert 1814-1878 *AsBiEn, DcScB*
Mayer, Karl Kuner 1879-1946 *NatCAB 34*
Mayer, Levy 1858-1922 *NatCAB 6, WhAm 1*
Mayer, Lewis 1783-1849 *ApCAB Sup, DcAmB, WhAm H*
Mayer, Louis Burt 1885-1957 *EncAB, WebAB, WhAm 3*
Mayer, Lucius W 1882-1947 *WhAm 2*
Mayer, Maria Goeppert 1906-1972 *WebAB,*

WhAm 5
Mayer, Mary Hicks 1876- *WomWWA 14*
Mayer, Mrs. Max 1872- *WomWWA 14*
Mayer, Oscar Ferdinand 1859-1955 *NatCAB 45, WhAm 3*
Mayer, Oscar Gottfried 1888-1965 *NatCAB 54, WhAm 4*
Mayer, Philip Frederick 1781-1857 *TwCBDA*
Mayer, Philip Frederick 1781-1858 *ApCAB, DcAmB, WhAm H*
Mayer, Rene 1895-1972 *WhAm 5*
Mayer, Richard 1898-1967 *WhAm 4*
Mayer, Robert B d1974 *WhAm 6*
Mayer, Rudolph Leopold 1895-1962 *NatCAB 47*
Mayer, Walter Ralph 1885-1941 *NatCAB 30*
Mayer-Eymar, Karl 1826-1907 *DcScB*
Mayerberg, Emil R 1892-1960 *NatCAB 46*
Mayers, Andrew *NewYHSD*
Mayers, Chauncey Maurice 1892-1961 *NatCAB 52*
Mayers, Lawrence Seymour 1890-1956 *WhAm 3*
Mayers, Lewis 1890-1975 *WhAm 6*
Mayers, Richard 1852- *WhoColR*
Mayes, Edward 1846-1917 *DcAmB, NatCAB 13, TwCBDA, WhAm 1*
Mayes, Joel Bryan 1833-1891 *ApCAB, DcAmB, NatCAB 25, WhAm H*
Mayes, Robert Burns 1867-1921 *NatCAB 17, WhAm 1*
Mayes, William Harding 1861-1939 *WhAm 1*
Mayfield, Earle Bradford 1881-1964 *ApCAB X, BiDrAC, WhAm 4*
Mayfield, Irving Hall 1885-1963 *WhAm 4*
Mayfield, James Jefferson 1861-1927 *WhAm 1*
Mayfield, Pearson Blythe 1877-1936 *NatCAB 41*
Mayfield, Reuben Newton 1859- *NatCAB 11*
Mayfield, Robert Lee 1870- *WhoColR*
Mayfield, William Henderson 1852- *NatCAB 12*
Mayginnes, Patrick Henry 1871-1954 *NatCAB 43*
Mayhall, William Franklin 1854-1917 *NatCAB 18*
Mayham, Ray Edwin 1882-1952 *WhAm 3*
Mayham, S L 1825-1908 *BiAUS*
Mayham, Stephen Lorenzo 1826-1908 *BiDrAC*
Mayhew, Experience 1673-1758 *ApCAB, DcAmB, Drake, NatCAB 5, WhAm H*
Mayhew, George Noel 1897-1965 *NatCAB 51, WhAm 4*
Mayhew, Ira 1814-1894 *Drake, NatCAB 5*
Mayhew, John d1689 *ApCAB*
Mayhew, Jonathan 1720-1766 *ApCAB, DcAmB, DcAmReB, Drake, NatCAB 7, TwCBDA, WebAB, WhAm H*
Mayhew, Mathew d1710 *ApCAB*
Mayhew, Thomas *ApCAB*
Mayhew, Thomas 1592-1682 *ApCAB, Drake, NatCAB 7, WhAm H*
Mayhew, Thomas 1593-1682 *DcAmB*
Mayhew, Thomas 1621?-1657 *ApCAB, DcAmB, Drake, NatCAB 7, WhAm H*
Mayhew, William C *NewYHSD*
Mayhew, Zecharia 1717-1806 *ApCAB*
Maylath, Heinrich 1827-1883 *WhAm H*
Maylem, John 1691-1715 *Drake*
Maylender, William Henry 1868-1941 *NatCAB 30*
Maynadier, Gustavus Howard 1867-1960 *WhAm 4*
Maynadier, William 1806-1871 *ApCAB*
Maynadier, William 1807-1871 *NatCAB 28*
Maynard, Charles Johnson 1845-1929 *ApCAB X, DcAmB, TwCBDA, WhAm 1*
Maynard, Edward 1813-1891 *AmBi, ApCAB, DcAmB, NatCAB 11, TwCBDA, WhAm H*
Maynard, Edward Washburn 1875-1966 *NatCAB 54, NatCAB 56*
Maynard, Edwin Post 1864-1949 *WhAm 2*
Maynard, Fred Augustus 1852- *WhAm 4*
Maynard, George Colton 1838-1918 *NatCAB 25*
Maynard, George Colton 1839-1918 *NatCAB 17, WhAm 1*

Maynard, George William 1839-1913 *ApCAB Sup, DcAmB, WhAm 1*
Maynard, George Willoughby 1843-1923 *AmBi, ApCAB, DcAmB, NatCAB 11, TwCBDA, WhAm 1*
Maynard, Harold Howard 1889-1957 *WhAm 3*
Maynard, Harry Lee 1861-1922 *BiDrAC, WhAm 4*
Maynard, Horace 1814-1882 *AmBi, ApCAB, BiAUS, BiDrAC, BiDrUSE, DcAmB, NatCAB 9, TwCBDA, WhAm H, WhAmP*
Maynard, James 1853-1926 *NatCAB 35, WhAm 1*
Maynard, John d1850 *BiAUS, BiDrAC, WhAm H*
Maynard, John Albert 1884-1962 *WhAm 4*
Maynard, John Blackwell 1887-1945 *WhAm 2*
Maynard, John Fernando 1846-1937 *NatCAB 28*
Maynard, John Frederick 1884-1945 *NatCAB 39*
Maynard, John Walter 1859-1939 *NatCAB 36, WhAm 1*
Maynard, John William 1877-1957 *WhAm 3*
Maynard, LaSalle Almeron 1857-1906 *WhAm 1*
Maynard, Laurens 1866- *WhAm 4*
Maynard, Leonard Amby 1887-1972 *WhAm 5*
Maynard, Lester 1877- *WhAm 5*
Maynard, Lucy Julia Warner 1852- *WomWWA 14*
Maynard, Margaret Ryerson 1885- *WomWWA 14*
Maynard, Mila Tupper 1864- *WhAm 4, WomWWA 14*
Maynard, Poole 1883-1952 *WhAm 3*
Maynard, Reuben Leslie 1862-1945 *WhAm 2*
Maynard, Rezin Augustus 1852- *WhAm 4*
Maynard, Richard Field 1875-1964 *WhAm 4*
Maynard, Robert Washburn 1879-1969 *NatCAB 56, WhAm 5*
Maynard, Roger 1914-1968 *WhAm 5*
Maynard, Samuel Taylor 1844-1923 *TwCBDA, WhAm 1*
Maynard, Theodore 1890-1956 *WhAm 3*
Maynard, Walter 1906-1971 *WhAm 5*
Maynard, Walter Effingham 1871-1925 *WhAm 1*
Maynard, Washburn 1844-1913 *TwCBDA, WhAm 1*
Maynard, William Hale 1835- *WhAm 4*
Mayne, Arthur Ferdinand d1972 *WhAm 5*
Mayne, Dexter Dwight 1863- *WhAm 1*
Mayne, Wiley 1917- *BiDrAC*
Mayo, Amory Dwight 1823-1907 *ApCAB, BiDAmEd, DcAmB, Drake, NatCAB 25, TwCBDA, WhAm 1*
Mayo, Caswell Armstrong 1862-1928 *NatCAB 22*
Mayo, Charles Horace 1865-1939 *AmBi, ApCAB X, DcAmB S2, EncAB, NatCAB 30, WebAB, WhAm 1*
Mayo, Chester Garst 1881- *WhAm 6*
Mayo, Earl Williams 1873-1957 *WhAm 3*
Mayo, Edmund Cooper 1885-1972 *WhAm 5*
Mayo, Frank Maguire 1839-1896 *DcAmB, NatCAB 23, TwCBDA, WhAm H*
Mayo, Frederick Joseph 1906-1972 *WhAm 5*
Mayo, George Elton 1880-1949 *DcAmB S4, WhAm 2*
Mayo, Hamilton *ApCAB X*
Mayo, Henry Thomas 1856-1937 *AmBi, DcAmB S2, NatCAB 15, NatCAB 27, WebAMB, WhAm 1*
Mayo, Herbert 1796-1852 *BiHiMed, DcScB*
Mayo, J E *NewYHSD*
Mayo, John 1737-1780 *ApCAB*
Mayo, John 1760-1818 *ApCAB*
Mayo, John Caldwell Calhoun 1864-1914 *NatCAB 45*
Mayo, Joseph 1795-1872 *ApCAB*
Mayo, Katherine 1867-1940 *NatCAB 30, NotAW, WhAm 1*
Mayo, Mary Anne Bryant 1845-1903 *DcAmB*
Mayo, Nelson Slater 1866-1958 *WhAm 3*
Mayo, Paul Thoburn 1894-1940 *NatCAB 36*
Mayo, Robert 1784-1864 *ApCAB, NatCAB 10, TwCBDA, WhAm H*

Mayo, Robert Murphy 1836-1896 *BiDrAC,*
WhAm H
Mayo, Robert William Bainbridge 1883-1937
WhAm 1
Mayo, Sara Tew 1869-1930 *NotAW*
Mayo, Sarah Carter Edgarton 1819-1848
ApCAB, DcAmB, Drake, NatCAB 2,
TwCBDA, WhAm H
Mayo, William 1684?-1744 *DcAmB,*
WhAm H
Mayo, William 1685?-1744 *ApCAB*
Mayo, William Barnabas 1854-1930
NatCAB 22
Mayo, William Benson 1866-1944 *NatCAB 39,*
WhAm 2
Mayo, William Henry 1843- *NatCAB 7*
Mayo, William James 1861-1939 *AmBi,*
ApCAB X, DcAmB S2, EncAB,
NatCAB 14, NatCAB 30, WebAB,
WhAm 1
Mayo, William Kennon 1829-1900 *DcAmB,*
NatCAB 26, TwCBDA, WhAm H,
WhAm 1
Mayo, William Starbuck 1811-1895 *DcAmB,*
WhAm H
Mayo, William Starbuck 1812-1895 *ApCAB,*
Drake, NatCAB 8, TwCBDA
Mayo, William Worrall 1819-1911 *DcAmB*
Mayo, William Worrall 1819-1911 *NatCAB 19*
Mayo-Smith, Mabel 1863- *WomWWA 14*
Mayo-Smith, Richmond 1854-1901 *AmBi,*
DcAmB, McGEWB, NatCAB 29,
WhAm 1
Mayo-Smith, Richmond 1888-1950 *NatCAB 38*
Mayobanex d1498 *ApCAB*
Mayor, Alfred Goldsborough 1868-1922 *DcAmB,*
NatCAB 19, WhAm 1
Mayorga, Martin De d1783 *ApCAB*
Mayow, John 1640-1679 *AsBiEn*
Mayow, John 1641?-1679 *BiHiMed, DcScB*
Mayr, Christian 1805?-1851 *NewYHSD*
Mayr, Simon 1573-1624 *DcScB*
Mayrant, William *BiAUS, BiDrAC,*
WhAm H
Mayrhofer, Albert Vincent 1889-1948
NatCAB 37
Mays, A S *WhoColR*
Mays, Benjamin Elijah 1895- *BiDAmEd*
Mays, Calhoun Allen 1884-1967 *WhAm 5*
Mays, Dannite Hill 1852-1930 *BiDrAC*
Mays, Dannite Hill 1852-1930 *WhAm 4*
Mays, David John 1896-1971 *WhAm 5*
Mays, Floyd Rosenbaum 1879-1953 *WhAm 3*
Mays, Franklin Pierce 1855-1932 *NatCAB 25*
Mays, James Henry 1868-1926 *BiDrAC,*
WhAm 4, WhAmP
Mays, Paul Kirtland 1887-1961 *IIBEAAW,*
WhAm 4
Mays, Percy Joseph 1909-1974 *WhAm 6*
Mays, Samuel Edward 1864-1932 *NatCAB 23*
Mays, Willie Howard, Jr. 1931- *WebAB*
Maytag, Elmer Henry 1883-1940 *NatCAB 52*
Maytag, Fred, II 1911-1962 *NatCAB 49,*
WhAm 4
Maytag, Frederick Louis 1857-1927 *WhAm 1*
Maytag, Frederick Louis 1857-1937 *DcAmB S2,*
NatCAB 27
Maytag, Lewis B 1888-1967 *WhAm 4*
Maytag, Theodore Henry 1864-1931
NatCAB 24
Maywald, Frederick John 1870-1937
NatCAB 28
Maywood, Augusta 1825-1876 *NotAW*
Maza, Jose 1889-1964 *WhAm 4*
Mazarin, John *NewYHSD*
Mazarin, Jules 1602-1661 *McGEWB*
Maze, Matthew T 1857-1940 *WhAm 1*
Mazella, Camillus 1833- *ApCAB*
Mazepa, Ivan Stepanovich 1644?-1709
McGEWB
Mazer, Abraham 1876-1953 *NatCAB 43*
Mazer, Jacob 1885-1954 *NatCAB 43*
Mazer, Jacob 1898-1968 *WhAm 5*
Mazet, Robert 1857-1945 *ApCAB Sup,*
WhAm 2
Maziel, Juan Baltasar 1727-1788 *ApCAB*
Mazini, Al- *DcScB*

Mazique, Douglas Wilkerson 1909-1964
NatCAB 50
Mazureau, Etienne 1777-1849 *DcAmB,*
WhAm H
Mazurkiewicz, Stefan 1888-1945 *DcScB*
Mazyck, Isaac *NewYHSD*
Mazyck, William Gaillard 1846-1942 *WhAm 2*
Mazzanovich, Lawrence 1871-1959 *WhAm 4*
Mazzara *NewYHSD*
Mazzara, Francis *NewYHSD*
Mazzei, Philip 1730-1816 *ApCAB, DcAmB,*
Drake, WebAB, WhAm H
Mazzilli, Ranieri 1910-1975 *WhAm 6*
Mazzini, Giuseppe 1805-1872 *McGEWB*
Mazzuchelli, Samuel Charles 1806-1864 *AmBi,*
DcAmB, NatCAB 25, WhAm H
M'ba, Leon 1902-1967 *WhAm 4*
Mboya, Thomas Joseph 1930-1969 *McGEWB*
McAbee, John W *NewYHSD*
McAchran, Flora J Clayton 1854-
WomWWA 14
McAdam, David 1838-1901 *NatCAB 13,*
WhAm 1
McAdam, Dunlap Jamison 1843-1925 *WhAm 1*
McAdam, Edward Lippincott, Jr. 1905-1969
WhAm 5
McAdam, George Harrison 1854-1925 *WhAm 1*
McAdam, John Loudon 1756-1836 *AsBiEn*
McAdam, John Loudoun 1756-1836 *Drake*
McAdam, John Loudoun *see also* Macadam, John
Loudoun
McAdams, Charles Rupert 1882-1963
NatCAB 50
McAdams, Clark 1874-1935 *DcAmB S1,*
WhAm 1
McAdams, James Carlin 1899-1954 *NatCAB 47*
McAdams, John Pope 1872-1960 *WhAm 4*
McAdams, John Quincy 1884-1968 *NatCAB 57*
McAdams, Joseph Edward 1880- *WhAm 6*
McAdams, Thomas Branch 1879-1957
NatCAB 44, WhAm 3
McAdams, William Ross 1898-1967
NatCAB 55
McAden, Hugh d1751 *NatCAB 9*
McAdie, Alexander George 1863-1943
DcAmB S3, NatCAB 35, WhAm 2
McAdoo, Henry Molseed 1880-1951 *WhAm 3*
McAdoo, Mary Faith Floyd 1832- *ApCAB,*
WhAm 5, WomWWA 14
McAdoo, William 1853-1930 *AmBi, BiDrAC,*
TwCBDA, WhAm 1, WhAmP
McAdoo, William Gibbs 1820- *ApCAB*
McAdoo, William Gibbs 1863-1941 *ApCAB X,*
BiDrAC, BiDrUSE, DcAmB S3,
EncAAH, EncAB, McGEWB,
NatCAB 14, WebAB, WhAm 1, WhAmP
McAfee, Cleland Boyd 1866-1944 *WhAm 2*
McAfee, Effie Lynch Danforth 1873-
WomWWA 14
McAfee, Helen 1884-1956 *NatCAB 43*
McAfee, Ila Mae 1897?- *IIBEAAW*
McAfee, James 1736-1811 *NatCAB 3*
McAfee, John Armstrong 1831-1890 *DcAmB,*
NatCAB 26, WhAm H
McAfee, Joseph Ernest 1870-1947 *DcAmReB,*
WhAm 2
McAfee, Lapsley Armstrong 1864-1935
WhAm 1
McAfee, Lowell Mason 1860- *WhAm 1*
McAfee, Mary Jane 1842- *WomWWA 14*
McAfee, Ralph Canfield 1888-1963 *WhAm 4*
McAfee, Robert Breckinridge 1784-1849
ApCAB, DcAmB, NatCAB 5, TwCBDA,
WhAm H
McAfee, Robert William 1881- *WhAm 6*
McAfee, W Keith 1893-1950 *NatCAB 39*
McAfee, William A 1890-1971 *WhAm 5*
McAffe, Robert Breckinridge 1784-1849 *BiAUS,*
Drake
McAleenan, Clifford Charles 1908-1973
NatCAB 57
McAleer, William 1838-1912 *BiDrAC,*
TwCBDA, WhAm 4
McAlester, Andrew Walker 1841-1922
WhAm 1
McAlester, Andrew Walker, Jr. 1876-1954
WhAm 3
McAlester, Miles D 1834-1869 *Drake*

McAlester, Miles Daniel 1833-1869 *ApCAB*
McAlexander, Ulysses Grant 1864-1936
DcAmB S2, WebAMB, WhAm 1
McAliley, R George 1879-1945 *NatCAB 34*
McAlister, Alexander Worth 1862-1946
WhAm 3
McAlister, Charles Bishop 1905-1966
NatCAB 51
McAlister, Heber Lowrey 1882-1956 *WhAm 3*
McAlister, Hill 1875-1959 *NatCAB 47,*
WhAm 3
McAlister, John Barr 1864-1948 *WhAm 2*
McAlister, Lottie 1868- *WomWWA 14*
McAlister, Samuel Bertran 1898-1963 *WhAm 4*
McAlister, William King 1850-1923
NatCAB 42, WhAm 1
McAll, Reginald Ley 1878-1954 *WhAm 3*
McAllester, Samuel Jackson 1884-1957
WhAm 3
McAllister, Addams Stratton 1875-1946
NatCAB 15, WhAm 2
McAllister, Alan H d1967 *WhAm 5*
McAllister, Archibald 1813-1883 *BiDrAC,*
WhAm H
McAllister, Archibald 1814-1883 *BiAUS*
McAllister, Charles Albert 1867-1932 *DcAmB,*
NatCAB 25, WhAm 1
McAllister, Charles Eldridge 1893-1952
WhAm 3
McAllister, Clifton Lopez 1886- *WhoColR*
McAllister, David 1835-1907 *WhAm 1*
McAllister, Elliott 1898-1973 *NatCAB 57,*
WhAm 5
McAllister, Elliott Ward 1862-1931 *NatCAB 24*
McAllister, Frank Winton 1873-1948 *WhAm 2*
McAllister, G Stanley 1900-1970 *NatCAB 56*
McAllister, George Franklin 1874- *WhAm 5*
McAllister, Hall 1826-1888 *DcAmB,*
WhAm H
McAllister, Harry Lee 1899-1975 *WhAm 6*
McAllister, Henry 1872-1954 *WhAm 3*
McAllister, Hugh N 1809-1873 *NatCAB 10,*
NatCAB 11
McAllister, James C *NewYHSD*
McAllister, James Gray 1872-1970 *NatCAB 14,*
WhAm 5
McAllister, John *NewYHSD*
McAllister, John Craig 1861-1938 *NatCAB 30*
McAllister, Joseph Thompson 1866-1927
WhAm 1
McAllister, Julia Gabriella 1853-
WomWWA 14
McAllister, Julian 1823-1887 *ApCAB*
McAllister, Matthew Hall 1800-1865 *ApCAB,*
BiAUS, DcAmB, Drake, NatCAB 11,
TwCBDA, WhAm H
McAllister, Robert 1813-1891 *NatCAB 2,*
TwCBDA
McAllister, Samuel Ward 1827-1895 *DcAmB,*
WhAm H
McAllister, Sydney G d1946 *WhAm 2*
McAllister, Ward 1827-1895 *NatCAB 6,*
WebAB
McAllister, Ward 1855-1908 *ApCAB,*
WhAm 1
McAloney, Thomas Simpson 1869-1932
WhAm 1
McAlpin, Benjamin Brandreth 1871-1931
WhAm 1
McAlpin, David Hunter 1816-1901 *NatCAB 6,*
NatCAB 33
McAlpin, David Hunter 1862-1934 *NatCAB 33*
McAlpin, David Hunter 1880-1932 *NatCAB 36*
McAlpin, Edwin Augustus 1848-1917
NatCAB 14, NatCAB 28
McAlpin, Edwin Augustus, Jr. 1874-1936
NatCAB 42, WhAm 1
McAlpin, George Lodowick 1856-1922
NatCAB 30
McAlpin, Margaret Johnston 1868-1924
NatCAB 20
McAlpine, Archibald Duncan 1882-1949
NatCAB 37
McAlpine, Charles Alonzo 1874-1945 *WhAm 2*
McAlpine, Kenneth 1860- *WhAm 4*
McAlpine, William H 1874-1956 *WhAm 3*
McAlpine, William Jarvis 1812-1890 *AmBi,*
ApCAB, DcAmB, NatCAB 10, TwCBDA,

WhAm H

McAlvay, Aaron Vance 1847-1915 *NatCAB 20,*
WhAm 1

McAnally, Arthur Monroe 1911-1972 *DcAmLiB,*
WhAm 5

McAnally, David Rice 1810-1895 *ApCAB,*
DcAmB, WhAm H

McAnally, David Rice *see also* Macanally, David
Rice

McAnany, Edwin Sebast 1871- *WhAm 5*

McAndless, Alva John 1890-1954 *WhAm 3*

McAndrew, James William 1862-1922
NatCAB 19, WhAm 1

McAndrew, William 1863-1937 *DcAmB S2,*
NatCAB 27, WhAm 1

McAndrew, William Robert 1914-1968
WhAm 5

McAndrews, James 1862-1942 *BiDrAC,*
WhAm 2, WhAmP

McAndrews, Richard Aloysius 1851-
NatCAB 5

McAneeny, William Joseph 1872-1935 *WhAm 1*

McAneny, George 1869-1953 *WhAm 3*

McAnney, B O 1891-1962 *WhAm 4*

McArdle, Harry Arthur 1836-1908 *NewYHSD*

McArdle, Henry Arthur 1836-1908 *IlBEAAW*

McArdle, James *NewYHSD*

McArdle, John H *ApCAB X*

McArdle, Joseph A 1903-1967 *BiDrAC,*
WhAm 4

McArdle, Montrose Pallen 1868- *WhAm 4*

McArdle, Thomas Eugene 1852- *WhAm 4*

McArthur, Albert Chase 1881-1951 *NatCAB 39*

McArthur, Arthur *BiAUS*

McArthur, C L 1881-1960 *NatCAB 52*

McArthur, Charles Mortimer 1937-1973
WhAm 6

McArthur, Clifton Nesmith 1879-1923 *BiDrAC,*
WhAm 1, WhAmP

McArthur, Duncan 1772- *BiAUS*

McArthur, Duncan 1772-1839 *AmBi, ApCAB,*
BiDrAC, DcAmB, Drake, TwCBDA,
WhAm H, WhAmP

McArthur, Duncan 1772-1840 *NatCAB 3*

McArthur, Fred Mellon 1882-1945 *NatCAB 36*

McArthur, Harold Sheldon 1902-1961
NatCAB 49

McArthur, James Neville 1892-1972
NatCAB 57

McArthur, John 1823-1890 *DcAmB, TwCBDA,*
WhAm H

McArthur, John 1826-1906 *ApCAB, DcAmB,*
Drake, TwCBDA, WhAm 1

McArthur, John *see also* MacArthur, John

McArthur, Lewis Linn 1843-1897 *NatCAB 33*

McArthur, Lewis Linn 1858-1934 *NatCAB 30,*
WhAm 1

McArthur, Lewis Linn, Jr. 1898-1960 *WhAm 3*

McArthur, Richard Norment 1882-1956
NatCAB 45

McArthur, Robert 1838-1914 *NatCAB 18*

McArthur, Selim Walker 1888-1961
NatCAB 50

McArthur, William Pope 1814-1850 *DcAmB,*
NatCAB 25, WebAMB, WhAm H

McArthur, William Taylor 1866-1930
NatCAB 24, WhAm 1

M'Carthy, Edward *NewYHSD*

McAskill, James Ernest 1888-1956 *NatCAB 46*

McAtee, John Lind d1904 *WhAm 1*

McAtee, Lloyd Wesley 1882-1946 *ApCAB X,*
NatCAB 35

McAulay, George Frederick 1870-1941
NatCAB 34

McAuley, Jeremiah 1839?-1884 *ApCAB,*
DcAmB

McAuley, Jerry 1840?-1884 *NatCAB 11*

McAuley, Thomas 1777-1862 *NatCAB 7*

McAuley, Thomas 1778-1862 *DcAmB,*
WhAm H

McAuley, Thomas 1780-1842 *TwCBDA*

McAuliff, Cornelius 1850-1911 *WhAm 1*

McAuliffe, Anthony Clement 1898-1975 *WebAB,*
WebAMB, WhAm 6

McAuliffe, Daniel J 1874-1957 *WhAm 3*

McAuliffe, Eugene 1866-1959 *WhAm 3*

McAuliffe, Eugene 1867-1959 *NatCAB 48*

McAuliffe, J *NewYHSD*

McAuliffe, John 1879-1960 *WhAm 4*

McAuliffe, Joseph John d1942 *WhAm 2*

McAuliffe, Maurice Francis 1875-1944
NatCAB 34, WhAm 2

McAvity, Malcolm 1889-1944 *NatCAB 33,*
WhAm 2

McAvoy, Charles D 1878-1937 *WhAm 1*

McAvoy, Emma 1841- *AmWom*

McAvoy, John Vincent 1878-1937 *WhAm 1*

McAvoy, Thomas Bell 1881-1955 *NatCAB 45*

McAvoy, Thomas D 1905-1966 *WhAm 4*

McAvoy, Thomas Timothy 1903-1969 *WhAm 5*

McBain, Howard Lee 1880-1936 *AmBi,*
DcAmB S2, WhAm 1

McBain, James William 1882-1953 *NatCAB 42,*
WhAm 3

McBaine, James Patterson 1882-1961 *WhAm 4*

McBean, Atholl 1879-1968 *NatCAB 55,*
WhAm 6

McBean, Jane Virginia *WomWWA 14*

McBean, Thomas *WhAm H*

McBeath, James Mark 1865- *WhAm 4*

McBee, Earl Thurston 1906-1973 *WhAm 5*

McBee, Mary Vardrine 1879-1965 *WhAm 4*

McBee, Silas 1853-1924 *WhAm 1*

McBeth, Susan Law 1830-1893 *NotAW*

McBlair, Mary Tayloe Key 1857-
WomWWA 14

McBrayer, Louis Burgin 1868-1938 *WhAm 1*

McBride, Allan Clay 1885-1944 *WhAm 2*

McBride, Andrew Francis 1869-1946
NatCAB 35

McBride, Andrew Jay 1836- *NatCAB 1,*
WhAm 4

McBride, Donald 1884-1927 *NatCAB 23*

McBride, F Scott 1872-1955 *DcAmB S5,*
NatCAB 45, WhAm 3

McBride, George McCutchen 1876- *WhAm 5*

McBride, George Wickliffe 1854-1911
ApCAB Sup, NatCAB 11, TwCBDA,
WhAm 1

McBride, George Wycliffe 1854-1911 *BiDrAC,*
WhAmP

McBride, Harold Herkimer 1894-1960 *WhAm 4*

McBride, Harry Alexander 1887-1961 *WhAm 4*

McBride, Henry 1856-1937 *NatCAB 14,*
WhAm 1

McBride, James 1784-1817 *NatCAB 11*

McBride, James 1802-1875 *BiAUS,*
NatCAB 13

McBride, James *see also* Macbride, James

McBride, James Harvey 1849- *WhAm 1*

McBride, James Henry 1815?-1862 *ApCAB*

McBride, John Rogers 1832-1904 *BiAUS,*
BiDrAC, WhAmP

McBride, Karl R, Sr. d1957 *WhAm 3*

McBride, Lucia McCurdy 1880-1970
NatCAB 57

McBride, Malcolm Lee 1878-1941 *NatCAB 31,*
WhAm 2

McBride, N Craig 1879-1960 *NatCAB 48*

McBride, Robert Edwin 1873-1947 *WhAm 2*

McBride, Robert Wesley 1842-1926
NatCAB 17, WhAm 1

McBride, Thomas Allen 1847-1930 *WhAm 1*

McBride, Thomas Canning 1868-1955
NatCAB 49

McBride, Wilbert George 1879- *WhAm 6*

McBride, William Manley 1894-1960
WhAm 3A

McBrien, Dean Depew 1892-1964 *WhAm 4*

McBrien, Jasper Leonidas 1867-1935 *WhAm 1*

McBroom, Charles Emmett 1864- *WhAm 4*

McBroom, David Edward 1883-1955
NatCAB 45

McBryde, Archibald 1766-1816 *BiDrAC,*
WhAm H

McBryde, Charles Neil 1872- *WhAm 5*

McBryde, James Bolton 1866-1925 *WhAm 1*

McBryde, John McLaren 1841-1923 *DcAmB,*
EncAAH, NatCAB 11, TwCBDA,
WhAm 1

McBryde, John McLaren 1846-1923 *NatCAB 3*

McBryde, Warren Horton 1876- *WhAm 5*

McBurney, Benjamin Thomas 1882-1937
NatCAB 27

McBurney, Catharine Watson 1866-
WomWWA 14

McBurney, Charles 1845-1913 *AmBi, BiHiMed,*
DcAmB, NatCAB 13, NatCAB 14,
NatCAB 26, WhAm 1

McBurney, James Edwin 1868-1955
NatCAB 42

McBurney, John White 1890-1961 *NatCAB 49,*
WhAm 4

McBurney, Ralph 1883-1964 *WhAm 4*

McBurney, Robert Ross 1837-1898 *AmBi,*
DcAmB, WhAm H

McCaa, David Galen 1882-1954 *NatCAB 42*

McCabe, Charles B 1899-1970 *WhAm 5*

McCabe, Charles Cardwell 1836-1906 *DcAmB,*
DcAmReB, NatCAB 13, TwCBDA,
WhAm 1

McCabe, Charles Martin 1870- *WhAm 5*

McCabe, Daniel Trigg 1849-1931 *NatCAB 37*

McCabe, David Aloysius 1883-1974 *WhAm 6*

McCabe, E *NewYHSD*

McCabe, Edward Raynsford Warner 1876-
WhAm 5

McCabe, Francis Xavier 1872-1948 *NatCAB 41,*
WhAm 5

McCabe, Harriet Calista Clark 1827-1919
AmWom, WhAm 1, WomWWA 14

McCabe, Ira Emmett 1894-1957 *NatCAB 43*

McCabe, James Dabney 1808-1875 *ApCAB,*
NatCAB 7, WhAm H

McCabe, James Dabney 1842-1883 *ApCAB,*
Drake Sup, NatCAB 7, TwCBDA

McCabe, James Joseph 1858-1930 *NatCAB 24*

McCabe, John Collins 1810-1875 *ApCAB,*
DcAmB, NatCAB 12, TwCBDA,
WhAm H

McCabe, Lida Rose 1865-1938 *AmWom,*
WhAm 1, WomWWA 14

McCabe, Lorenzo Dow 1817-1897 *TwCBDA*

McCabe, Ross 1891-1959 *NatCAB 45*

McCabe, William Gordon 1841-1920 *ApCAB,*
DcAmB, NatCAB 8, TwCBDA,
WhAm 1

McCabe, William Hugh 1893-1962 *WhAm 4*

McCadden, John Edward 1885-1964 *WhAm 4*

McCafferty, Don 1921-1974 *WhAm 6*

McCafferty, Henry *NewYHSD*

McCafferty, Thomas Bowles 1898-1954
WhAm 3

McCaffery, Joseph James 1872-1949
NatCAB 52

McCaffery, Richard Stanislaus 1874-1945
WhAm 2

McCaffrey, John 1806-1881 *DcAmB,*
WhAm H

McCaffrey, John 1806-1882 *ApCAB,*
NatCAB 11, TwCBDA

McCagg, Ezra Butler 1825-1908 *ApCAB,*
NatCAB 20, WhAm 1

McCague, James Alexander 1871-1933
NatCAB 24

McCahan, Belle Travers *WomWWA 14*

McCahan, David 1897-1954 *WhAm 3*

McCahey, James B 1890-1976 *WhAm 6*

McCaig, William Dougal 1874-1951 *WhAm 3*

McCain, C Curtice 1856-1942 *WhAm 2*

McCain, Charles Simonton 1884-1957 *WhAm 3*

McCain, Dewey Marven 1899-1966 *WhAm 4*

McCain, George Nox 1856-1934 *WhAm 1*

McCain, Henry Pinckney 1861-1941 *WhAm 1*

McCain, James Ross 1881-1965 *WhAm 4*

McCain, John Sidney 1884-1945 *NatCAB 41,*
WhAm 2

McCain, Mary V Overholt *WomWWA 14*

McCain, Paul Pressly 1884-1946 *WhAm 2*

McCain, Samuel Adams 1906-1964 *NatCAB 51,*
WhAm 4

McCain, William Alexander 1878- *WhAm 6*

McCain, William Dwight 1913-1974 *WhAm 6*

McCain, William Ross 1878-1972 *NatCAB 57,*
WhAm 6

McCaine, Alexander 1768?-1856 *DcAmB,*
WhAm H

McCaine, Alexander 1775?-1856 *ApCAB*

McCaine, Helen J *WomWWA 14*

McCaleb, Albert Gilbert 1893-1951 *NatCAB 38*

McCaleb, Edwin Howard 1843-1909
NatCAB 11, NatCAB 26

McCaleb, Ella 1856-1933 *WhAm 1,*
WomWWA 14

McCaleb, John Bell 1856-1931 *WhAm 1*
McCaleb, Theodore Howard 1810-1864 *BiAUS, DcAmB, NatCAB 26, TwCBDA, WhAm H*
McCaleb, Thomas Farrar 1795-1832 *TwCBDA*
McCaleb, Walter Flavius 1873-1967 *WhAm 5*
McCall, Alvin Clay 1889-1948 *NatCAB 36*
McCall, Arthur G 1874- *WhAm 3*
McCall, Daniel Thompson 1869-1955 *NatCAB 46*
McCall, Edward Everett 1863-1924 *WhAm 1*
McCall, Edward R 1790-1853 *ApCAB, Drake, TwCBDA*
McCall, Edward Rutledge 1790-1853 *DcAmB, WhAm H*
McCall, Edward Rutley 1790-1853 *NatCAB 12*
McCall, Florence Mabel 1867- *WomWWA 14*
McCall, Fred B 1893-1973 *WhAm 5*
McCall, George 1858-1938 *NatCAB 33*
McCall, George Archibald 1802-1868 *ApCAB, Drake, TwCBDA*
McCall, Harry 1887-1965 *WhAm 4*
McCall, Henry 1847- *NatCAB 9*
McCall, Hugh 1767-1824 *ApCAB, Drake*
McCall, John Augustine 1849-1906 *DcAmB, NatCAB 11, WhAm 1*
McCall, John Cadwalader 1793-1846 *ApCAB*
McCall, John Etheridge 1859-1920 *NatCAB 19, WhAm 1*
McCall, John Ethridge 1859-1920 *BiDrAC*
McCall, John Gordon 1876-1959 *NatCAB 49*
McCall, John Oppie 1879- *WhAm 6*
McCall, Joseph Benton 1870-1926 *NatCAB 21*
McCall, Milton Lawrence 1911-1963 *WhAm 4*
McCall, Oswald Walter Samuel d1959 *WhAm 3*
McCall, Peter 1809-1880 *ApCAB, NatCAB 4, TwCBDA, WhAm H*
McCall, Robert Theodore 1919- *IIBEAAW*
McCall, Samuel Walker 1851-1923 *AmBi, BiDrAC, DcAmB, NatCAB 20, TwCBDA, WhAm 1, WhAmP*
McCall, Thomas 1889-1946 *WhAm 2*
McCall, Thomas Montgomery 1887-1965 *WhAm 4*
McCall, Willard 1900-1961 *NatCAB 50*
McCalla, Albert 1846-1918 *NatCAB 13, WhAm 1*
McCalla, Bowman Hendry 1844-1910 *DcAmB, NatCAB 24, TwCBDA, WebAMB, WhAm 1*
McCalla, Daniel 1748-1809 *ApCAB, Drake, NatCAB 25*
McCalla, Elizabeth Hazard Sargent 1850- *WhAm 4*
McCalla, John *BiAUS*
McCalla, William Latta 1788-1859 *ApCAB, DcAmB, NatCAB 24, WhAm H*
McCallam, James Alexander 1894-1969 *WhAm 5*
McCalley, Henry 1852-1904 *WhAm 1*
McCallie, Robert Lewis 1911-1965 *WhAm 4*
McCallie, Samuel Washington 1856-1933 *WhAm 1*
McCallie, Spencer Jarnagin 1875-1949 *WhAm 2*
McCallie, Thomas Spencer 1869-1936 *WhAm 1*
McCallum, Angus 1911- *WhAm 5*
McCallum, Charles Ray 1894-1946 *NatCAB 47*
McCallum, Daniel Craig 1815-1878 *ApCAB, DcAmB, NatCAB 7, WebAMB, WhAm H*
McCallum, Francis Marion 1867- *WhAm 2*
McCallum, George Porterfield 1871-1952 *NatCAB 47*
McCallum, George Porterfield, Jr. 1902-1969 *NatCAB 55*
McCallum, Gilbert *NewYHSD*
McCallum, James 1806-1889 *BiDConf*
McCallum, James Dow 1893-1971 *NatCAB 56*
McCallum, Lachlan 1823- *ApCAB*
McCalmont, Alfred Brunsen 1825-1874 *ApCAB, BiAUS, NatCAB 5*
McCalmont, David Burnett 1876-1947 *NatCAB 37*
McCamant, Catherine 1862- *WomWWA 14*
McCamant, Wallace 1867-1944 *NatCAB 34, WhAm 2*

McCambridge, William John 1889-1964 *NatCAB 51, WhAm 4*
McCamey, Harold Emerson 1894-1967 *WhAm 4*
McCamic, Charles d1957 *WhAm 3*
McCammon, Anna Estelle 1881- *WomWWA 14*
McCammon, George Edward 1867- *WhAm 4*
McCammon, Joseph Kay 1845-1907 *WhAm 1*
McCammon, Milo Franklin 1908-1967 *WhAm 4*
McCammon, Robert McMullen 1842-1922 *NatCAB 19*
McCampbell, Charles Wilbur 1882-1962 *WhAm 4*
McCampbell, Eugene Franklin 1880-1937 *WhAm 1*
McCampbell, Eugene Franklin 1883-1937 *NatCAB 27*
McCampbell, Leavelle 1879-1946 *NatCAB 34, WhAm 2*
McCan, Martha Nelson 1867- *WomWWA 14*
McCance, Pressly Hodge 1893-1965 *WhAm 4*
McCandless, Alice 1864- *WomWWA 14*
McCandless, Boyd Bowden 1915-1975 *WhAm 6*
McCandless, Bruce 1911-1968 *WhAm 5*
McCandless, Byron 1881- *WhAm 6*
McCandless, Clay 1859-1951 *NatCAB 39*
McCandless, David Alexander 1865-1939 *WhAm 1*
McCandless, James W 1908-1964 *WhAm 4*
McCandless, John Andrew 1853-1930 *WhAm 1*
McCandless, Lincoln Loy 1859-1940 *BiDrAC, NatCAB 37, WhAm 1*
McCandless, Robert Buchanan 1855-1958 *WhAm 3*
McCandless, Wilson 1810-1882 *ApCAB, TwCBDA*
McCandless, Wilson 1811-1882 *BiAUS*
McCandlish, Benjamin Vaughan 1886- *WhAm 6*
McCandlish, Howard Sheild 1891-1955 *NatCAB 43*
McCandliss, Lester Chipman 1886-1945 *WhAm 2*
McCanliss, Lee 1883-1968 *NatCAB 55*
McCann, Alfred Watterson 1879-1931 *DcAmB, NatCAB 24, WhAm 1*
McCann, Benjamin Franklin 1861-1924 *NatCAB 20*
McCann, Charles Edward Francis 1876-1941 *NatCAB 31*
McCann, Charles Mallette 1893-1959 *WhAm 3*
McCann, George 1864-1932 *NatCAB 24, WhAm 1*
McCann, H D G *NewYHSD*
McCann, Harold Gilman 1916-1969 *WhAm 5*
McCann, Harrison King 1880-1962 *WhAm 4*
McCann, Henry G 1808?- *NewYHSD*
McCann, Horace Ferdinand 1851-1918 *NatCAB 18*
McCann, J *NewYHSD*
McCann, James 1837-1893 *NatCAB 15*
McCann, James J 1887-1961 *WhAm 4*
McCann, Mary A *NewYHSD*
McCann, R L 1896-1971 *WhAm 5*
McCann, Rebecca d1927 *WhAm 1*
McCann, Robert Caldwell 1901-1965 *WhAm 4*
McCann, T Addison 1858-1943 *WhAm 2*
McCann, William *NewYHSD*
McCann, William Penn 1830-1906 *ApCAB, DcAmB, NatCAB 10, TwCBDA, WhAm 1*
McCann, William Sharp 1889-1971 *NatCAB 57, WhAm 5*
McCanna, Henry Anthony 1923-1974 *WhAm 6*
McCannel, Archibald Duncan 1879-1959 *NatCAB 47*
McCants, E Crayton 1865-1953 *WhAm 3*
McCard, William G 1871- *WhoColR*
McCardell, Claire 1905-1958 *WhAm 3*
McCardell, Lee Adrian 1901-1963 *WhAm 4*
McCardell, Roy Larcom 1870- *WhAm 5*
McCardle, Battle 1872-1941 *NatCAB 31*
McCardle, Carl Wesley 1904-1972 *NatCAB 57, WhAm 5*
McCarey, Leo 1898-1969 *WhAm 5*
McCarl, John Raymond 1879-1940 *WhAm 1*
McCarn, Jeff 1861-1942 *WhAm 2*

McCarran, Patrick Anthony 1876-1954 *BiDrAC, DcAmB S5, REnAW, WhAm 3, WhAmP*
McCarrell, Samuel John Milton 1842-1920 *NatCAB 19*
McCarren, Patrick Henry 1847-1909 *DcAmB, WhAm 1*
McCarrens, John Sylvester 1869-1943 *NatCAB 32, WhAm 2*
McCarroll, Henry Relton 1905-1972 *WhAm 5*
McCarroll, James 1814-1892 *ApCAB, DcAmB, WhAm H*
McCarroll, Russell Hudson 1890-1948 *WhAm 2*
McCarroll, William 1851-1933 *WhAm 1*
McCartan, Edward 1879-1947 *WhAm 2*
McCartee, Divie Bethune 1820-1900 *ApCAB, DcAmB, NatCAB 24, TwCBDA, WhAm H*
McCartee, Jessie Graham 1796-1855 *ApCAB*
McCartee, Robert 1790-1865 *TwCBDA*
McCartee, Robert 1791-1865 *ApCAB*
McCarten, John 1916-1974 *WhAm 6*
McCarter, George William Childs 1887-1951 *NatCAB 41*
McCarter, Henry 1864-1942 *WhAm 2*
McCarter, Henry 1865-1942 *TwCBDA*
McCarter, James W 1872-1939 *WhAm 1*
McCarter, Margaret Hill d1938 *WhAm 1, WomWWA 14*
McCarter, Richard Farrell 1935-1974 *WhAm 6*
McCarter, Robert Harris 1859-1941 *ApCAB X, NatCAB 31, WhAm 1*
McCarter, Thomas Nesbitt 1824-1901 *NatCAB 19*
McCarter, Thomas Nesbitt 1824-1902 *WhAm 1*
McCarter, Thomas Nesbitt 1867-1955 *NatCAB 44, WhAm 3*
McCarter, Thomas Nesbitt, Jr. 1899-1959 *NatCAB 44, WhAm 4*
McCarter, Uzal Haggerty 1861-1931 *NatCAB 23, WhAm 1*
McCarter, William *NewYHSD*
McCartheyn, Mary Elizabeth Maxwell 1814-1893 *NewYHSD*
McCarthy *NewYHSD*
McCarthy, Alphonsus Martin 1897-1962 *NatCAB 50*
McCarthy, Carlton 1847- *WhAm 4*
McCarthy, Charles 1873-1921 *DcAmB, DcAmLiB, NatCAB 19, WhAm 1*
McCarthy, Charles Hallan 1860-1941 *WhAm 2*
McCarthy, Charles James 1861-1929 *NatCAB 22, WhAm 1*
McCarthy, Charles Penderghast 1881-1950 *NatCAB 38, NatCAB 47*
McCarthy, Daniel Edward 1859-1922 *WhAm 1*
McCarthy, Daniel Justin 1874-1958 *NatCAB 45*
McCarthy, Denis Aloysius 1870-1931 *WhAm 1*
McCarthy, Dennis 1814-1886 *BiAUS, BiDrAC, TwCBDA, WhAm H*
McCarthy, Edward 1857- *NatCAB 10, WhAm 4*
McCarthy, Edward 1893-1967 *WhAm 5*
McCarthy, Edwin 1876-1935 *NatCAB 42*
McCarthy, Ellen S *WomWWA 14*
McCarthy, Eugene 1857-1903 *WhAm 1*
McCarthy, Eugene Joseph 1916- *BiDrAC, EncAB, McGEWB, WebAB*
McCarthy, Eugene Ross 1882-1971 *WhAm 5*
McCarthy, Frank C 1924- *IIBEAAW*
McCarthy, Frank Charles 1897-1956 *NatCAB 46*
McCarthy, Frank Jeremiah 1905- *WhAm 3*
McCarthy, Henry Francis 1906-1961 *WhAm 4*
McCarthy, Henry Jefferson 1845-1903 *NatCAB 12*
McCarthy, J A 1879- *WhAm 6*
McCarthy, James Anthony Joseph 1895-1964 *WhAm 4*
McCarthy, James E 1896-1958 *WhAm 3*
McCarthy, James Frederick 1867-1940 *NatCAB 51, WhAm 1*
McCarthy, John Daly 1886-1928 *NatCAB 21*
McCarthy, John Edward 1894-1960 *NatCAB 45, WhAm 4*
McCarthy, John Francis 1857-1923 *NatCAB 31*
McCarthy, John Henry 1850-1908 *BiDrAC*
McCarthy, John Humphrey 1840- *NatCAB 7*

McCarthy, John Jay 1857-1943 *BiDrAC*
McCarthy, John Ralph 1897-1963 *WhAm 4*
McCarthy, Joseph Edward 1876-1955
  NatCAB 41, *WhAm 3*
McCarthy, Joseph Francis 1874-1965 *WhAm 4*
McCarthy, Joseph Raymond 1908-1957 *BiDrAC*,
  EncAAH, *McGEWB*, *WebAB*, *WhAm 3*,
  WhAmP
McCarthy, Joseph Raymond 1909-1957 *EncAB*
McCarthy, Justin 1830- *ApCAB*
McCarthy, Justin Howard 1894-1968 *WhAm 5*
McCarthy, Kathryn O'Loughlin 1894-1952
  BiDrAC, *WhAm 3*
McCarthy, Kenneth Cecil 1902-1964 *WhAm 4*
McCarthy, Leighton Goldie 1869-1952
  WhAm 3
McCarthy, Leon Edward 1902-1962
  NatCAB 49
McCarthy, Louise Roblee 1888-1970 *WhAm 5*
McCarthy, Mary Therese 1912- *WebAB*
McCarthy, Michael Henry 1853-1920 *WhAm 1*
McCarthy, P H 1863-1933 *WhAm 1*
McCarthy, Patrick Henry 1869-1955
  NatCAB 45
McCarthy, Patrick Joseph 1848-1921
  NatCAB 6
McCarthy, Raymond Gerald 1901-1964
  NatCAB 51
McCarthy, Richard Dean 1927- *BiDrAC*
McCarthy, Walter Raymond 1887-1952
  NatCAB 40
McCarthy, William Henry 1877-1958
  NatCAB 48, *WhAm 5*
McCarthy, Wilson 1884-1956 *WhAm 3*
McCartney, Albert Joseph d1965 *WhAm 4*
McCartney, Frank Maxwell 1875-1927
  NatCAB 22
McCartney, Henry *NewYHSD*
McCartney, Herbert Swift Greenwood 1865-1943
  NatCAB 47
McCartney, James Lincoln 1898-1969 *WhAm 5*
McCartney, James Robert 1897-1963
  NatCAB 51
McCartney, James S 1851- *WhAm 4*
McCartney, Mary Elizabeth Maxwell 1814-1893
  WhAm H
McCartney, Napoleon *NewYHSD*
McCartney, Washington 1812-1856 *DcAmB*,
  NatCAB 11, *WhAm H*
McCartney, Washington *see also* MacCartney,
  Washington
McCarty, Alexander E *NewYHSD*
McCarty, Andrew Zimmerman 1808-1879
  BiAUS, *BiDrAC*, *WhAm H*
McCarty, C Walter 1892-1965 *WhAm 4*
McCarty, Charles Paschal 1920-1974 *WhAm 6*
McCarty, Dan 1912-1953 *NatCAB 42*,
  WhAm 3
McCarty, Daniel *NewYHSD*
McCarty, Daniel Justin 1874-1958 *WhAm 3*
McCarty, Dwight Gaylord 1878- *WhAm 6*
McCarty, E Prosper 1873- *WhAm 5*
McCarty, Earl Hauser 1886-1942 *NatCAB 31*
McCarty, Edward *NewYHSD*
McCarty, Franklin Bennett 1888-1972 *WhAm 6*
McCarty, Henry *REnAW*
McCarty, J J *NewYHSD*
McCarty, James 1820?- *NewYHSD*
McCarty, John Charles 1840- *NatCAB 12*
McCarty, Johnathan 1795-1852 *BiDrAC*,
  WhAm H
McCarty, Jonathan d1855 *BiAUS*
McCarty, Jonathan 1800?-1855 *TwCBDA*
McCarty, Lea Franklin 1905- *IIBEAAW*
McCarty, Milburn 1881-1959 *NatCAB 43*
McCarty, Milburn, IV 1912-1963 *NatCAB 55*,
  WhAm 4
McCarty, Nicholas 1834-1915 *NatCAB 16*
McCarty, Orin Philip 1848-1925 *WhAm 1*
McCarty, Ray Bardwell 1899-1950 *NatCAB 39*
McCarty, Richard 1780-1844 *BiAUS*, *BiDrAC*,
  WhAm H
McCarty, Richard Justin 1851-1934
  /NatCAB 17, *NatCAB 24*, *WhAm 3*
McCarty, Sidney Louis 1874- *WhAm 5*
McCarty, Thomas J 1863-1933 *WhAm 1*
McCarty, William Mason 1789?-1863 *BiAUS*,
  BiDrAC, *WhAm H*

McCarty, William Monroe 1816- *ApCAB*
McCarty, William Murdock 1859-1918
  NatCAB 19
McCarty, William Murdock 1859-1919
  WhAm 1
McCarty, William T 1889-1972 *WhAm 5*
McCarver, Morton Matthew 1807-1875 *AmBi*,
  NatCAB 4
McCash, Isaac Newton 1861- *NatCAB 12*,
  WhAm 5
McCaskey, Charles Irving 1877-1954 *WhAm 3*
McCaskey, Hiram Dryer 1871-1936 *WhAm 1*
McCaskey, John Piersol 1837-1935 *WhAm 3*
McCaskey, William Spencer 1843-1914
  WhAm 1
McCaskill, James Lane 1901-1974 *WhAm 6*
McCaskill, Oliver LeRoy 1877-1953 *WhAm 3*
McCaskill, Virgil Everett 1866-1922 *WhAm 1*
McCasland, S Vernon 1896-1970 *WhAm 6*
McCaslin, Albert Andrew 1876-1958
  NatCAB 47
McCaslin, Frank Erwin 1897-1973 *WhAm 6*
McCaslin, Harvey 1878-1955 *NatCAB 49*
McCaslin, Robert Horace d1958 *WhAm 3*
McCaughan, Russell Craig 1889-1957 *WhAm 3*
McCaughan, William John 1859-1910 *WhAm 1*
McCaughey, William John 1882-1962
  NatCAB 50
McCaughrin, James Nance 1879-1927
  NatCAB 22
McCaul, Helen *WomWWA 14*
McCaul, J 1810?- *Drake*
McCaul, John 1807- *ApCAB*
McCaul, Verne James 1903-1968 *NatCAB 54*
McCauley, Calvin Hudson 1850-1910 *WhAm 1*
McCauley, Charles Adam Hoke 1847- *ApCAB*,
  WhAm 4
McCauley, Charles Adams Hoke 1847-
  TwCBDA
McCauley, Charles Stewart 1793-1869 *ApCAB*,
  DcAmB, *Drake*, *NatCAB 11*, *TwCBDA*,
  WebAMB, *WhAm H*
McCauley, Clayton M 1876-1957 *WhAm 3*
McCauley, David Vincent 1895-1950
  WhAm 2A
McCauley, Edward Yorke 1826-1894 *ApCAB*
McCauley, Edward Yorke 1827-1894 *DcAmB*,
  NatCAB 13, *TwCBDA*, *WhAm H*
McCauley, Herbert James 1882-1960
  NatCAB 48
McCauley, James Andrew 1822-1896
  NatCAB 6, *TwCBDA*
McCauley, James Wayne 1902-1958 *WhAm 3*
McCauley, Jeremiah 1839?-1884 *WhAm H*
McCauley, Lena May 1859-1940 *WhAm 1*,
  WomWWA 14
McCauley, Mary E Mendenhall 1853-
  WomWWA 14
McCauley, Mary Ludwig Hays 1744-1823
  TwCBDA
McCauley, Mary Ludwig Hays 1754-1832 *AmBi*,
  DcAmB, *NotAW*, *WebAB*, *WebAMB*,
  WhAm H
McCauley, William Fletcher 1858-1915
  WhAm 1
McCauley, William James 1900-1964
  NatCAB 51
McCaulle, Thomas Harris d1800? *Drake*
McCausland, John 1836-1927 *BiDConf*,
  DcAmB, *WebAMB*
McCausland, Thomas Wilton 1869-1948
  NatCAB 36
McCausland, W Clifton 1861-1935 *NatCAB 29*
McCauslen, William Cochran 1796-1863 *BiAUS*,
  BiDrAC, *WhAm H*
McCaustland, Elmer James 1864- *WhAm 5*
McCaw, Henry 1893-1952 *NatCAB 39*,
  WhAm 3
McCaw, James Brown 1772-1846 *ApCAB*
McCaw, James Brown 1823-1906 *BiDConf*,
  DcAmB
McCaw, Walter Drew 1863-1939 *WhAm 1*
McCawley, Alfred L 1876-1966 *WhAm 4*
McCawley, Charles Grymes 1827-1891 *ApCAB*,
  DcAmB, *WebAMB*, *WhAm H*
McCawley, Charles Laurie 1865-1935
  DcAmB S1, *WhAm 1*
McCay, Bruce Benjamin 1878-1954 *WhAm 4*

McCay, Charles Francis 1810-1889 *DcAmB*,
  NatCAB 11, *TwCBDA*, *WhAm H*
McCay, Henry Kent 1820-1886 *DcAmB*,
  NatCAB 4
McCay, Leroy Wiley 1857-1937 *WhAm 1*
McCay, Ora Lee 1878-1947 *NatCAB 41*
McCheney, William J 1796-1864 *NatCAB 11*
McChesney, Calvin Stewart 1857-1924
  NatCAB 21, *WhAm 1*
McChesney, Dora Greenwell 1871-1912
  WhAm 1
McChesney, Elizabeth Studdiford 1841-1906
  WhAm 1
McChesney, Frank Marks 1883-1967
  NatCAB 52
McChesney, May Louise 1875- *WhAm 5*
McChesney, Robert Watson 1831- *NatCAB 11*
McChesney, Wilbert Renwick 1871-1944
  WhAm 2
McChesney, William J *NewYHSD*
McChord, Charles Caldwell 1859-1937
  NatCAB 28, *WhAm 1*, *WhAm 1C*
McClain *NewYHSD*
McClain, Dayton Ernest 1879-1971 *WhAm 5*
McClain, Edward Lee 1861-1934 *NatCAB 16*,
  WhAm 1
McClain, Emlin 1851-1915 *ApCAB X*,
  DcAmB, *NatCAB 14*, *NatCAB 16*,
  WhAm 1
McClain, Francis *NewYHSD*
McClain, Francis Bernard 1864-1925
  NatCAB 20
McClain, John Wilcox 1904-1967 *WhAm 4*
McClain, Joseph Adolphus, Jr. 1903-1970
  NatCAB 57, *WhAm 5*
McClain, Josiah 1843- *WhAm 4*
McClain, Louise Bowman 1841- *AmWom*
McClain, Thomas Ernest 1876- *WhoColR*
McClammy, Charles Washington 1839-1896
  BiDrAC, *NatCAB 9*, *TwCBDA*, *WhAm H*
McClanahan, Ellis Joshua 1894-1964 *WhAm 4*
McClanahan, Harry Monroe 1857-1929
  WhAm 1
McClaran, John Walter 1887-1948 *WhAm 3*
McClary, Nelson Alvin 1856-1936 *WhAm 1*
McClaskey, Henry Morrison, Jr. 1919-1970
  WhAm 5
McClatchey, Robert J 1836-1883 *NatCAB 3*
McClatchy, Carlos Kelly 1891-1933 *WhAm 1*
McClatchy, Charles Kenny 1858-1936
  DcAmB S2, *WhAm 1*
McClatchy, Valentine Stuart 1857-1938
  WhAm 1
McClaughry, Robert Wilson 1839-1920
  NatCAB 26, *WhAm 1*
McClave, Charles Rowley 1873-1956 *WhAm 3*
McClean *NewYHSD*
McClean, Harry J 1891-1963 *WhAm 4*
McClean, J A *NewYHSD*
McClean, John *NewYHSD*
McClean, Moses 1804-1870 *BiAUS*, *BiDrAC*,
  WhAm H
McClean, Samuel Neal 1857-1930 *NatCAB 26*
McCleary, Elmer Theodore 1878-1930
  NatCAB 23
McCleary, George Deardorff 1846-1915
  WhAm 1
McCleary, Glenn Avann 1895-1967 *NatCAB 54*
McCleary, James Thompson 1853-1924 *BiDrAC*,
  TwCBDA, *WhAm 1*, *WhAmP*
McCleary, Jesse Earl 1905-1972 *WhAm 6*
McCleary, Robert Altwig 1923-1973 *WhAm 5*
McCleave, Robert 1874- *WhAm 5*
McCleery, James 1837-1871 *BiDrAC*,
  WhAm H
McCleery, James 1840-1871 *ApCAB*
McClelan, Abner Reid 1831- *ApCAB*
McCleland, Thomas *NewYHSD*
McClellan, Abraham 1789-1866 *BiAUS*,
  BiDrAC, *WhAm H*
McClellan, Bryon Charles 1869-1946 *WhAm 2*
McClellan, Carswell 1835-1892 *ApCAB*,
  NatCAB 4, *TwCBDA*, *WhAm H*
McClellan, Charles A O 1835-1898 *BiDrAC*,
  TwCBDA
McClellan, Charles L 1866- *NatCAB 5*
McClellan, Edwin 1861-1924 *NatCAB 25*
McClellan, Elisabeth 1851-1920 *WhAm 1*,

McClellan, Ely 1834-1893 *ApCAB Sup,*
TwCBDA
McClellan, George 1796-1847 *AmBi, ApCAB,*
BiHiMed, DcAmB, Drake, NatCAB 4,
TwCBDA, WhAm H
McClellan, George 1849-1913 *AmBi, DcAmB,*
NatCAB 15
McClellan, George 1856-1927 *BiDrAC*
McClellan, George Armstrong 1870-1924
NatCAB 20
McClellan, George Brinton 1826-1885 *AmBi,*
ApCAB, BiAUS, DcAmB, Drake, EncAB,
McGEWB, NatCAB 4, TwCBDA,
WebAB, WebAMB, WhAm H, WhoMilH
McClellan, George Brinton 1865-1940 *BiDrAC,*
DcAmB S2, NatCAB 4, TwCBDA,
WhAm 1, WhAmP
McClellan, George Marion 1860- *WhoColR*
McClellan, Henry Brainerd 1840-1904 *ApCAB,*
BiDAmEd, DcAmB, NatCAB 4,
TwCBDA, WhAm 1
McClellan, Irene Moulton Ward 1881-1967
NatCAB 53
McClellan, John 1847-1928 *NatCAB 21,*
WhAm 1
McClellan, John Hill Brinton 1823-1874 *ApCAB,*
NatCAB 4
McClellan, John Jasper 1874-1926 *WhAm 1*
McClellan, John Little 1896- *BiDrAC*
McClellan, Maria Rabb *WhoColR*
McClellan, Robert 1770-1815 *DcAmB,*
WhAm H
McClellan, Robert 1806-1860 *BiAUS, BiDrAC,*
TwCBDA, WhAm H
McClellan, Robert 1867-1924 *NatCAB 31*
McClellan, Samuel 1730-1807 *ApCAB,*
NatCAB 4, TwCBDA
McClellan, Samuel 1800-1853 *ApCAB,*
NatCAB 4
McClellan, Thomas Cowan 1873-1929 *WhAm 1*
McClellan, Thomas Nicholas 1853-1906
NatCAB 12, TwCBDA, WhAm 1
McClellan, William 1872-1950 *NatCAB 40,*
WhAm 3
McClelland *NewYHSD*
McClelland, Alexander 1794-1864 *TwCBDA*
McClelland, Alexander 1796-1864 *ApCAB,*
NatCAB 4
McClelland, Charles Paul 1854-1944
NatCAB 36, WhAm 2
McClelland, Charles Samuel 1852-1933
WhAm 1
McClelland, David *NewYHSD*
McClelland, Ella Gale *WomWWA 14*
McClelland, George William 1880-1955
WhAm 3
McClelland, Harold Mark 1893-1965 *WhAm 4*
McClelland, Henry Thom 1849- *WhAm 4*
McClelland, James Farley 1878-1955 *WhAm 3*
McClelland, James Henderson 1845-1913
ApCAB, ApCAB X, WhAm 4
McClelland, Mary Greenway 1853-1895
NatCAB 2
McClelland, Milo Adams 1837- *ApCAB*
McClelland, Nancy Vincent *WomWWA 14*
McClelland, Robert 1807-1880 *AmBi, ApCAB,*
BiAUS, BiDrAC, BiDrUSE, DcAmB,
Drake, NatCAB 4, TwCBDA, WhAm H,
WhAmP
McClelland, Ross St. John 1878- *WhAm 5*
McClelland, Silas Edward 1860-1953 *WhAm 3*
McClelland, Thomas 1846-1926 *NatCAB 20,*
TwCBDA, WhAm 1
McClelland, Thomas Calvin 1869-1917
WhAm 1
McClelland, William 1842-1892 *BiAUS,*
BiDrAC, WhAm H
McClelland, William 1883-1949 *NatCAB 38,*
NatCAB 47, WhAm 2
McClelland, William Craig 1852- *WhAm 4*
McClement, John Hall 1862-1924 *NatCAB 14,*
WhAm 1
McClenachan, Blair d1812 *BiAUS, BiDrAC,*
WhAm H
McClenachan, Charles Thomson 1829-1896
ApCAB, NatCAB 3

McClenaghan, George Pinckney 1897-1961
NatCAB 48, WhAm 4
McClenahan, Daniel Henry 1876-1959
NatCAB 48
McClenahan, David A 1853- *WhAm 4*
McClenahan, Howard 1872-1935 *DcAmB S1,*
NatCAB 26, WhAm 1
McClenahan, Perry Eugene 1873- *WhAm 5*
McClenahan, Robert Stewart 1871- *WhAm 5*
McClench, Katharine Hill 1858-
WomWWA 14
McClench, William Wallace 1854-1928
WhAm 1
McClendon, Caesar P *WhoColR A*
McClendon, James Wooten 1873-1972
NatCAB 57, WhAm 6
McClendon, Rose 1884-1936 *NotAW*
McClene, James 1730-1806 *BiAUS, BiDrAC,*
WhAm H
McClennen, Edward Francis 1874-1948
WhAm 2
McClenny, George L d1947 *WhAm 2*
McClenon, Mary Adeline White *WomWWA 14*
McClernand, Edward John 1848-1926 *WhAm 1*
McClernand, John Alexander 1812-1900 *AmBi,*
ApCAB, BiAUS, BiDrAC, DcAmB,
Drake, NatCAB 4, TwCBDA, WebAMB,
WhAm 1, WhAmP, WhoMilH
McCleuen, David *NewYHSD*
McCleuen, James *NewYHSD*
McClintic, George Warwick 1866-1942
WhAm 2
McClintic, Guthrie 1893-1961 *WhAm 4*
McClintic, Howard Hale 1867-1938
NatCAB 29, WhAm 1
McClintic, James V 1878-1948 *WhAm 2*
McClintic, James Vernon 1878-1948 *BiDrAC,*
WhAmP
McClintic, James Vernor 1878-1948
NatCAB 40
McClintic, Olive Leaman *WomWWA 14*
McClintic, Robert Hofferd 1901-1970
NatCAB 55, WhAm 5
McClintock, Andrew Hamilton 1852-1919
NatCAB 33, WhAm 1
McClintock, Charles Blaine 1886-1965 *BiDrAC*
McClintock, Earl Irvine 1889-1963 *WhAm 4*
McClintock, Edward Buck 1874-1943
NatCAB 37
McClintock, Emory 1840-1916 *ApCAB X,*
DcAmB, NatCAB 12, WhAm 1
McClintock, Euphemia E *WhAm 5*
McClintock, Sir Francis Leopold 1819-1907
ApCAB, Drake, McGEWB
McClintock, Franklin Trunkey 1904-1972
WhAm 6
McClintock, Gilbert Stuart 1886- *WhAm 4*
McClintock, Harry Winfred 1907-1969
WhAm 5
McClintock, Harvey Childs 1882- *ApCAB X*
McClintock, Helen Elizabeth 1883-
WomWWA 14
McClintock, J O 1887-1962 *WhAm 4*
McClintock, James Harvey 1864-1934
DcAmB S1, REnAW, WhAm 1
McClintock, John 1814-1870 *AmBi, ApCAB,*
NatCAB 6, TwCBDA
McClintock, John Calvin 1843-1903 *WhAm 1*
McClintock, John Calvin 1906-1969 *WhAm 5*
McClintock, John Thomas 1873-1955
NatCAB 45
McClintock, John Thomas 1874-1939
NatCAB 29
McClintock, Mary Law d1925 *WhAm 1*
McClintock, Miller 1894-1960 *NatCAB 44,*
WhAm 3
McClintock, Norman 1868-1938 *ApCAB X,*
WhAm 1
McClintock, Oliver 1839-1922 *ApCAB X,*
DcAmB, NatCAB 12, WhAm 1
McClintock, Samuel 1732-1804 *Drake,*
NatCAB 4, TwCBDA
McClintock, Samuel *see also* Macclintock,
Samuel
McClintock, Walter 1870-1949 *ApCAB X,*
WhAm 2
McClintock, Washington 1814-1870 *ApCAB X*
McClish, Eli 1846-1918 *TwCBDA, WhAm 1*

McClory, Peter *NewYHSD*
McClory, Robert 1908- *BiDrAC*
McCloskey, Alice Gertrude 1870-
WomWWA 14
McCloskey, Augustus 1878-1950 *BiDrAC,*
WhAm 6
McCloskey, Francis Augustine 1860-1927
NatCAB 21
McCloskey, George V A 1883-1933 *WhAm 1*
McCloskey, Henry Bernard 1884-1948
NatCAB 37
McCloskey, James Paul 1870-1945 *WhAm 2*
McCloskey, John *Drake*
McCloskey, John 1810-1885 *AmBi, ApCAB,*
DcAmB, McGEWB, NatCAB 1,
TwCBDA, WebAB, WhAm H
McCloskey, John 1815-1880 *TwCBDA*
McCloskey, John 1817-1880 *ApCAB*
McCloskey, John Francis 1894-1957 *WhAm 3*
McCloskey, Manus 1874-1963 *NatCAB 52,*
WhAm 5
McCloskey, Matthew H 1893-1973 *WhAm 5*
McCloskey, Paul Norton, Jr. 1927- *BiDrAC*
McCloskey, Robert Green 1916-1969 *WhAm 5*
McCloskey, Thomas David 1873- *WhAm 5*
McCloskey, William George 1823-1909 *ApCAB,*
DcAmB, NatCAB 12, TwCBDA,
WhAm 1
McClosky, B Martin 1901-1958 *NatCAB 47*
McCloud, Bentley Grimes 1884-1956 *WhAm 3*
McCloud, Charles A 1860-1937 *WhAm 1*
McCloud, Earl d1949 *WhAm 3*
McCloud, Lucy Carter *WomWWA 14*
McClow, Lloyd L 1896-1962 *WhAm 4*
McCloy, Charles Harold 1886-1959 *BiDAmEd,*
WhAm 3
McCloy, Joseph Francis 1880-1965 *NatCAB 52*
McCluan, Malcolm Joseph 1912-1960
NatCAB 49
McCluer, James Steele 1877-1961 *NatCAB 52*
McCluney, Mabel McKeighan 1883-
WomWWA 14
McCluney, William J 1796-1864 *ApCAB,*
Drake, TwCBDA
McClung, Alexander K 1812?-1855 *ApCAB,*
BiAUS, Drake, NatCAB 3
McClung, Calvin Morgan 1855-1919
NatCAB 20, WhAm 1
McClung, Clarence Erwin 1870-1946
DcAmB S4, DcScB, NatCAB 34,
WhAm 2
McClung, Donald Riley 1898-1966 *NatCAB 53*
McClung, Florence Elliott 1896- *IlBEAAW*
McClung, Frank Arthur 1882-1954 *NatCAB 49*
McClung, George Harlan 1879-1952 *WhAm 3*
McClung, Herbert James 1869-1934
NatCAB 31
McClung, Hugh Lawson 1858-1936 *NatCAB 34,*
WhAm 1
McClung, John Alexander 1804-1859 *ApCAB,*
NatCAB 11
McClung, Lee 1870-1914 *NatCAB 20,*
WhAm 1
McClung, Nellie Letitia Mooney 1873-
WomWWA 14
McClung, O Hunter 1879-1947 *NatCAB 36*
McClung, Reid Lage 1885-1961 *WhAm 4*
McClung, Robert Gardner 1868- *NatCAB 16*
McClung, Will Clinton 1886-1937 *WhAm 3*
McClung, William *BiAUS*
McClung, William H 1854-1936 *WhAm 3*
McClure, Abbot 1879- *WhAm 6*
McClure, Addison Smith 1839-1903 *BiDrAC,*
TwCBDA
McClure, Alexander Kelly 1828-1909 *AmBi,*
ApCAB, DcAmB, NatCAB 1, TwCBDA,
WhAm 1
McClure, Alexander Wilson 1808-1865 *ApCAB,*
DcAmB, Drake, NatCAB 11, WhAm H
McClure, Alfred James Pollock 1854- *WhAm 4*
McClure, Charles 1804-1846 *BiDrAC,*
WhAm H
McClure, Charles Franklin 1828-1914
NatCAB 15
McClure, Charles Freeman Williams 1865-1955
NatCAB 15, WhAm 3
McClure, Charles Wylie 1866- *WhAm 4*
McClure, Daniel E 1854- *WhAm 4*

McClure, David 1748-1820 *ApCAB*
McClure, David 1749-1820 *Drake*
McClure, David 1848-1912 *NatCAB 26*
McClure, Frank David 1872-1950 *NatCAB 42*
McClure, Frank Trelford 1916-1973
NatCAB 57
McClure, George 1770?-1851 *DcAmB,*
WebAMB, WhAm H
McClure, George 1771-1851 *ApCAB, Drake*
McClure, George Henry 1897-1961 *WhAm 4*
McClure, Grace Latimer Jones 1879- *WhAm 6*
McClure, Harry Bell 1903-1975 *WhAm 6*
McClure, Howard 1865- *WhAm 5*
McClure, Jake 1903-1940 *REnAW*
McClure, James Albertus 1924- *BiDrAC*
McClure, James Gore King 1848-1932 *TwCBDA,*
WhAm 1
McClure, James Gore King 1884-1956 *WhAm 3*
McClure, John 1730?-1780 *ApCAB*
McClure, John 1834-1915 *NatCAB 19*
McClure, John Clarence 1865- *WhAm 4*
McClure, Marjorie Barkley d1967 *WhAm 4*
McClure, Martha d1945 *WhAm 2*
McClure, Mary Alice 1855- *WomWWA 14*
McClure, Matthew Thompson, Jr. 1883-1964
WhAm 4
McClure, Meade Lowrie 1863-1934 *NatCAB 25,*
WhAm 1
McClure, Nathaniel Fish 1865-1942 *WhAm 2*
McClure, Norman Egbert 1893-1962 *WhAm 4*
McClure, Robert A 1897-1957 *WhAm 3*
McClure, Sir Robert John LeMesurier 1807-1873
ApCAB
McClure, Sir Robert John LeMesurier *see also*
MacClure, Sir R
McClure, Robert Owen 1885- *WhAm 3*
McClure, Roy Donaldson 1882-1951
NatCAB 44, WhAm 3
McClure, Russell Everett 1906-1974 *WhAm 6*
McClure, Samuel 1839-1922 *NatCAB 19*
McClure, Samuel Grant 1863-1948 *WhAm 2*
McClure, Samuel Sidney 1857-1949 *DcAmB S4,*
EncAB, McGEWB, NatCAB 12, WebAB,
WhAm 2
McClure, W Frank 1877-1951 *WhAm 3*
McClure, Walter Tennant 1856- *WhAm 4*
McClure, William Leander 1880-1949
NatCAB 42, WhAm 3
McClure, Worth 1886-1962 *NatCAB 49,*
WhAm 4
McClurg, Alexander Caldwell 1832-1901 *AmBi,*
DcAmB, TwCBDA
McClurg, Alexander Caldwell 1834?-1901
WhAm 1
McClurg, Alexander Caldwell 1835?-1901
ApCAB, NatCAB 4
McClurg, James 1746?-1823 *DcAmB,*
WhAm H
McClurg, James 1747-1825 *ApCAB, Drake,*
NatCAB 3
McClurg, Joseph Washington 1818-1900
ApCAB, BiAUS, BiDrAC, DcAmB, Drake,
NatCAB 12, TwCBDA, WhAm H,
WhAmP
McClurg, Ogden Trevor 1878-1926 *NatCAB 20*
McClurg, Trevor 1816-1893 *IIBEAAW,*
NewYHSD
McClurg, Walter Audubon 1852-1917
NatCAB 18, WhAm 1
McClurkin, John Knox 1853-1923 *WhAm 1*
McClurkin, Robert d1949 *WhAm 3*
McClurkin, Robert J G 1891-1956 *WhAm 3*
McCluskey, Edmund Roberts 1900-1962
WhAm 4
McCluskey, Thomas Joseph 1857-1937
NatCAB 14, WhAm 1
McCluskey, William *NewYHSD*
McClusky, Mrs. O W 1884- *WomWWA 14*
McClymonds, James Walter 1842-1912
NatCAB 17
McClymont, John I 1858-1934 *IIBEAAW*
McCoach, David, Jr. 1887-1951 *WhAm 3*
McCobb, Paul 1917-1969 *BnEnAmA,*
WhAm 5
McCoid, Moses Ayers 1840-1904 *BiDrAC,*
TwCBDA
McColl, Edith Pusey Durand 1883-
WomWWA 14

McColl, Evan 1808- *Drake*
McColl, Evan *see also* MacColl, Evan
McColl, Hugh 1837-1909 *DcScB*
McColl, James Macpherson 1885-1968
NatCAB 54
McColl, Jay Robert 1867-1936 *WhAm 1*
McColl, Robert Boyd 1882-1972 *WhAm 5*
McCollester, Lee Sullivan 1859-1943 *WhAm 2*
McCollester, Parker 1890-1954 *WhAm 3*
McCollester, Sullivan Holman 1826-1921
TwCBDA, WhAm 1
McCollestre, Sullivan Holman 1826-1921
ApCAB
McCollin, Frances 1892-1960 *NatCAB 46*
McColloch, Frank Cleveland 1892- *WhAm 5*
McColloch, James Walker 1889-1929
NatCAB 23
McCollom, John Hildreth 1843-1915
NatCAB 16, WhAm 1
McCollom, Vivian C 1902-1959 *WhAm 4*
McCollum, Earl 1889-1947 *WhAm 2*
McCollum, Elmer Verner 1879-1967 *AsBiEn,*
DcScB, EncAB, WhAm 4
McCollum, Fenelon 1841-1925 *NatCAB 20*
McCollum, J Brewster 1832-1903 *NatCAB 12*
McComas, Alice Moore 1850- *AmWom,*
WomWWA 14
McComas, Arthur Rochford 1868-1956
NatCAB 49
McComas, Francis John 1874-1938 *IIBEAAW,*
NatCAB 29, WhAm 1
McComas, Henry Clay 1875- *WhAm 5*
McComas, Louis Emory 1846-1907
ApCAB Sup, BiDrAC, DcAmB,
NatCAB 12, TwCBDA, WhAm 1,
WhAmP
McComas, O Parker 1895-1957 *WhAm 3*
McComas, William 1795-1865 *BiAUS,*
BiDrAC, WhAm H
McComb, Arthur James 1880-1958 *WhAm 3*
McComb, Edgar 1881-1956 *WhAm 3*
McComb, Eleazer d1798 *BiAUS, BiDrAC,*
WhAm H
McComb, John d1811 *WhAm H*
McComb, John 1763-1853 *AmBi, BnEnAmA,*
DcAmB, NewYHSD, WhAm H
McComb, Samuel 1864- *WhAm 4*
McComb, Samuel Deems 1879-1944
NatCAB 17, NatCAB 33
McComb, William 1828- *WhAm 4*
McComb, William Andrew 1860-1939 *WhAm 1*
McComb, William Randolph 1892-1957
WhAm 3
McCombs, Carl Esselstyn 1883-1949
NatCAB 42, WhAm 2
McCombs, Georgette *WomWWA 14*
McCombs, Solomon 1913- *IIBEAAW*
McCombs, Vernon Monroe 1875-1951 *WhAm 3*
McCombs, William Frank 1875-1921 *WhAm 1*
McConachie, Harry Steele 1900-1967 *WhAm 4*
McConachie, Lauros Grant 1866- *WhAm 5*
McConachy, John *NewYHSD*
McConathy, Osbourne 1875-1947 *BiDAmEd,*
NatCAB 39, WhAm 2
McConaughy, David 1775-1852 *ApCAB, Drake,*
TwCBDA
McConaughy, James 1857-1934 *NatCAB 25,*
WhAm 1
McConaughy, James Lukens 1887-1948
NatCAB 38, WhAm 2
McConaughy, Robert 1852-1923 *WhAm 1*
McConihe, Isaac 1787-1867 *BiAUS*
McConihe, Malcolm Stuart 1872- *WhAm 5*
McConkey, Benjamin M 1821?- *NewYHSD*
McConkey, Bertha M *WomWWA 14*
McConkey, Mack 1893-1958 *NatCAB 47*
McConkey, William *NewYHSD*
McConkey, William Arthur 1871-1945
NatCAB 34
McConn, Charles Maxwell 1881-1953
NatCAB 44, WhAm 3
McConnaughey, George Carlton 1896-1966
NatCAB 52, WhAm 4
McConnaughey, Robert Kendall 1904-1966
WhAm 4
McConnel, John Ludlum 1826-1862 *ApCAB,*
DcAmB, NatCAB 5, WhAm H
McConnel, Mervin Gilbert 1882-1948 *WhAm 3*

McConnel, Murray 1895-1961 *WhAm 4*
McConnel, Roger Harmon 1908-1971 *WhAm 5*
McConnell, Adelaide Dorn 1869-1942
NatCAB 31
McConnell, Andrew M 1873- *WhAm 5*
McConnell, Charles Melvin 1886-1957 *WhAm 3*
McConnell, David Hall 1858-1937 *NatCAB 33*
McConnell, David Hall 1901-1944 *NatCAB 33*
McConnell, Ella Mead 1859- *WomWWA 14*
McConnell, Evan 1890-1949 *NatCAB 38*
McConnell, Felix Grundy 1809-1846 *BiAUS,*
BiDrAC, TwCBDA, WhAm H
McConnell, Fernando Coello 1856-1929
WhAm 1
McConnell, Fowler Beery 1894-1961
NatCAB 50, WhAm 4
McConnell, Francis John 1871-1953 *DcAmB S5,*
DcAmReB, NatCAB 15, WhAm 3
McConnell, Franz Marshall 1862- *WhAm 5*
McConnell, Genevieve Knapp 1876-
WomWWA 14
McConnell, H Hugh 1908-1960 *NatCAB 47,*
WhAm 3A
McConnell, H S 1893-1958 *WhAm 3*
McConnell, Henry 1879- *WhAm 6*
McConnell, Herbert S 1905-1971 *WhAm 5*
McConnell, Ira Welch 1871-1933 *DcAmB S1,*
WhAm 1
McConnell, James *NewYHSD*
McConnell, James 1829-1914 *NatCAB 18*
McConnell, James Eli 1860-1928 *WhAm 1,*
WhAm 1C
McConnell, James Moore 1868-1933 *WhAm 1*
McConnell, John Griffith 1911-1974 *WhAm 6*
McConnell, John Lorenzo 1881-1971
NatCAB 56
McConnell, John Paul 1908- *WebAMB*
McConnell, John Preston 1866- *WhAm 4*
McConnell, Joseph Moore 1875-1935
NatCAB 34, WhAm 1
McConnell, Joseph William 1877-1918
NatCAB 18
McConnell, Lincoln 1867-1930 *WhAm 1*
McConnell, Luther Graham 1885-1961
NatCAB 48, WhAm 4
McConnell, Marion Vincent Ellis 1865-
WomWWA 14
McConnell, Maude Wells *WomWWA 14*
McConnell, Murray *BiAUS*
McConnell, Newton W *NatCAB 12*
McConnell, Richard Brumby 1867- *NatCAB 3*
McConnell, Robert Darll 1891-1971 *WhAm 5*
McConnell, Robert Perche 1895-1973 *WhAm 5*
McConnell, Roy F 1884-1962 *WhAm 4*
McConnell, Samuel *NewYHSD*
McConnell, Samuel David 1845-1939 *WhAm 1*
McConnell, Samuel David 1846-1939
NatCAB 10, TwCBDA
McConnell, Samuel Kerns, Jr. 1901- *BiDrAC*
McConnell, Samuel Parsons 1850-1935
WhAm 1
McConnell, Thomas 1865-1938 *NatCAB 28*
McConnell, Thomas Raymond 1901- *BiDAmEd*
McConnell, W Joseph 1883-1955 *NatCAB 45,*
WhAm 3
McConnell, Wallace Robert 1881-1960
BiDAmEd, NatCAB 51, WhAm 4
McConnell, William John 1839-1925 *BiDrAC,*
NatCAB 12, TwCBDA, WhAm 1,
WhAmP
McConnico, Andrew Jackson 1875- *WhAm 5*
McConway, William 1842-1925 *WhAm 1*
McCooey, John Henry 1864-1934 *NatCAB 25*
McCook, Alexander McDowell 1831-1903 *AmBi,*
ApCAB, DcAmB, Drake, NatCAB 4,
TwCBDA, WebAMB, WhAm 1
McCook, Anson George 1835-1917 *AmBi,*
ApCAB, ApCAB X, BiDrAC, DcAmB,
NatCAB 4, TwCBDA, WhAm 1,
WhAmP
McCook, Anson Theodore 1881-1966
NatCAB 53
McCook, Charles Morris 1843-1861 *ApCAB,*
NatCAB 4
McCook, Dan 1834-1864 *Drake*
McCook, Daniel 1798-1863 *ApCAB,*
NatCAB 4, TwCBDA
McCook, Daniel 1834-1864 *ApCAB,*

NatCAB 4, TwCBDA

McCook, Edward M 1834- *BiAUS, Drake Sup*

McCook, Edward Moody 1833- *ApCAB, NatCAB 4, TwCBDA*

McCook, Edward Moody 1833-1909 *DcAmB, WebAMB, WhAm 1*

McCook, Edward Moody 1835-1919 *NatCAB 6*

McCook, Edwin Stanton 1837-1873 *ApCAB, NatCAB 4, TwCBDA*

McCook, George 1792-1873 *TwCBDA*

McCook, George Wythe 1821-1877 *ApCAB, NatCAB 4, TwCBDA*

McCook, Henry Christopher 1837-1911 *AmBi, ApCAB, DcAmB, NatCAB 4, TwCBDA, WhAm 1*

McCook, John 1806-1865 *ApCAB, NatCAB 4, TwCBDA*

McCook, John James 1823-1842 *NatCAB 4*

McCook, John James 1843-1927 *AmBi, ApCAB, DcAmB, NatCAB 4, TwCBDA, WhAm 1*

McCook, John James 1845-1911 *ApCAB, NatCAB 4, TwCBDA, WhAm 1*

McCook, Latimer A 1820-1869 *NatCAB 4, TwCBDA*

McCook, Philip James 1873-1963 *NatCAB 48*

McCook, Rhoderick Sheldon 1839-1886 *NatCAB 4*

McCook, Robert Latimer 1827-1862 *ApCAB, Drake, NatCAB 4, TwCBDA*

McCook, Roderick Sheldon 1839-1886 *ApCAB, TwCBDA*

McCook, Willis Fisher 1851-1923 *NatCAB 33, WhAm 1*

McCooks, The *NatCAB 4*

McCool, Daniel 1853-1916 *NatCAB 17*

McCool, William Allen 1850-1923 *NatCAB 33*

McCoole, Joseph Raphael 1879-1940 *NatCAB 30*

McCoole, Michael *NewYHSD*

McCord, Alvin Carr 1867-1956 *NatCAB 42, WhAm 3*

McCord, Andrew 1754?-1808 *BiAUS, BiDrAC, WhAm H*

McCord, Andrew King 1904-1974 *WhAm 6*

McCord, Annie Elizabeth 1878- *WomWWA 14*

McCord, Charles Wallace 1865-1927 *NatCAB 21*

McCord, Clinton Preston 1881-1953 *NatCAB 48*

McCord, David James 1797-1855 *ApCAB, DcAmB, TwCBDA, WhAm H*

McCord, David James *see also* Maccord, David J

McCord, Eugene Woodworth 1854-1913 *NatCAB 16*

McCord, George Herbert 1848-1909 *AmBi, ApCAB, TwCBDA, WhAm 1*

McCord, Henry Darius 1836- *NatCAB 7*

McCord, J S 1801-1865 *Drake*

McCord, James 1826- *NatCAB 11*

McCord, James Bennett 1870-1950 *DcAmB S4*

McCord, James Benney 1878-1936 *NatCAB 27*

McCord, James Nance 1879-1968 *WhAm 5*

McCord, Jim Nance 1879-1968 *BiDrAC*

McCord, John 1711-1793 *ApCAB*

McCord, John Samuel 1801-1865 *ApCAB*

McCord, Joseph 1880-1943 *WhAm 2*

McCord, Joseph Alexander 1857- *WhAm 4*

McCord, Leon 1878-1952 *WhAm 4*

McCord, Louisa Susanna Cheves 1810-1879 *DcAmB, WhAm H*

McCord, Louisa Susannah 1810-1880 *ApCAB, NatCAB 9, TwCBDA*

McCord, Louisa Susannah Cheves 1810-1879 *NotAW*

McCord, Louisa Susannah Cheves *see also* Maccord, Louisa S

McCord, May Kennedy 1880- *WhAm 6*

McCord, Myron Hawley 1840-1908 *BiDrAC, TwCBDA*

McCord, Myron Hawley 1844-1908 *WhAm 1*

McCord, Robert D 1885-1961 *WhAm 4*

McCord, Sidney Pearson, Jr. 1912-1970 *NatCAB 55*

McCord, William Clay 1905-1961 *NatCAB 51, WhAm 4*

McCord, William Hewlett 1846- *NatCAB 4, WhAm 4*

McCorkle, Graham K 1887-1964 *WhAm 4*

McCorkle, Joseph Walker 1819-1884 *BiAUS, BiDrAC, WhAm H*

McCorkle, Paul Grier 1863-1934 *BiDrAC*

McCorkle, Samuel Eusebius 1746-1811 *ApCAB, BiDAmEd, NatCAB 7*

McCorkle, Thomas Smith 1898-1955 *WhAm 3*

McCorkle, William Foster 1855-1927 *NatCAB 22*

McCormac, Eugene Irving 1872-1943 *NatCAB 32, WhAm 2*

McCormack, Alfred 1901-1956 *WhAm 3*

McCormack, Arthur Thomas 1872-1943 *NatCAB 32, WhAm 2*

McCormack, Buren H 1909-1972 *WhAm 5*

McCormack, Christopher Joseph 1904-1950 *NatCAB 39*

McCormack, Emmet John 1880-1965 *NatCAB 52, WhAm 4*

McCormack, George Bryant 1859-1925 *NatCAB 32, WhAm 1*

McCormack, James 1910-1975 *WhAm 6*

McCormack, John Francis 1884-1945 *DcAmB S3, NatCAB 33, WhAm 2*

McCormack, John William 1891- *BiDrAC, WebAB*

McCormack, Joseph Nathaniel 1847-1922 *DcAmB, WhAm 1*

McCormack, M Harriet Joyce d1971 *WhAm 5*

McCormack, Thomas Joseph 1865-1932 *WhAm 1*

McCormick, Albert Edward 1895-1961 *WhAm 4*

McCormick, Albert M D 1866-1932 *WhAm 1*

McCormick, Alexander A *NewYHSD*

McCormick, Alexander Agnew 1863-1925 *NatCAB 26, WhAm 1*

McCormick, Alexander Hugh 1842-1915 *TwCBDA, WhAm 1*

McCormick, Andrew Phelps 1832-1916 *NatCAB 19, WhAm 1*

McCormick, Anne Elizabeth O'Hare 1882-1954 *DcAmB S5, WhAm 3*

McCormick, Arch Gerald 1874-1943 *NatCAB 33*

McCormick, Bradley Thomas 1880-1945 *WhAm 3*

McCormick, Charles Augustus 1873-1935 *NatCAB 29*

McCormick, Charles Owen 1886-1957 *NatCAB 49*

McCormick, Charles Perry 1896-1970 *NatCAB 55, WhAm 5*

McCormick, Charles Renton 1870-1955 *NatCAB 45*

McCormick, Charles Tilford 1889-1963 *WhAm 4*

McCormick, Charles Wesley 1856-1920 *WhAm 1*

McCormick, Chauncey 1884-1954 *WhAm 3*

McCormick, Cyrus 1890-1970 *NatCAB 54, WhAm 5*

McCormick, Cyrus Hall 1809-1884 *AmBi, ApCAB, ApCAB X, DcAmB, Drake, EncAAH, EncAB, McGEWB, NatCAB 5, NatCAB 21, TwCBDA, WebAB, WhAm H*

McCormick, Mrs. Cyrus Hall 1835-1923 *NatCAB 21*

McCormick, Cyrus Hall 1859-1936 *DcAmB S2, EncAAH, WhAm 1*

McCormick, David 1864- *WhAm 4*

McCormick, David Cummings 1832-1910 *NatCAB 15*

McCormick, Donald 1868-1945 *WhAm 2*

McCormick, Edith Rockefeller 1872-1932 *BiCAW, NotAW, WhAm 1, WomWWA 14*

McCormick, Edmund Burke 1870-1926 *WhAm 1*

McCormick, Edward James 1891-1975 *WhAm 6*

McCormick, Ernest O d1923 *WhAm 1*

McCormick, Fowler 1898-1973 *WhAm 5*

McCormick, Frederick d1951 *WhAm 3*

McCormick, George Chalmers 1872-1968 *WhAm 5*

McCormick, George Wellesley 1871-1950 *WhAm 3*

McCormick, George Winford 1903-1973 *WhAm 6*

McCormick, Gertrude Howard 1874-1953 *WhAm 3, WhAm 5*

McCormick, Harold Fowler 1872-1941 *NatCAB 35, WhAm 1*

McCormick, Harriet Bradley Hammond 1862-1921 *BiCAW, NatCAB 21, WhAm 1, WomWWA 14*

McCormick, Henry Buehler 1869-1941 *WhAm 1*

McCormick, Henry Clay 1844-1902 *BiDrAC, NatCAB 37, TwCBDA*

McCormick, Howard 1875-1943 *IIBEAAW, WhAm 2*

McCormick, Ida May 1863- *WomWWA 14*

McCormick, J Jett 1868-1939 *NatCAB 29*

McCormick, J Rossa 1877-1947 *NatCAB 36*

McCormick, James *NewYHSD*

McCormick, James 1858-1930 *NatCAB 21*

McCormick, James Robinson 1824-1897 *BiAUS, BiDrAC, TwCBDA, WhAm H*

McCormick, James Thomas 1876-1950 *WhAm 3*

McCormick, John Dale 1877-1961 *WhAm 4*

McCormick, John Francis 1874-1943 *WhAm 2*

McCormick, John Henry 1870- *WhAm 5*

McCormick, John Newton 1863-1939 *WhAm 1*

McCormick, John Vincent 1891-1971 *WhAm 5*

McCormick, John Watts 1831-1917 *BiDrAC*

McCormick, Joseph Medill 1876-1925 *ApCAB X*

McCormick, Joseph Medill 1877-1925 *AmBi, DcAmB, NatCAB 19, WhAmP*

McCormick, Katherine Dexter 1876- *WomWWA 14*

McCormick, Langdon d1954 *WhAm 3*

McCormick, Leander Hamilton 1859-1934 *WhAm 1*

McCormick, Leander James 1819-1900 *DcAmB, NatCAB 1, TwCBDA, WhAm 1*

McCormick, Lynde Dupuy 1895-1956 *NatCAB 45, WhAm 3*

McCormick, Marshall 1849-1918 *WhAm 1*

McCormick, Medill 1877-1925 *BiDrAC, DcAmB, WhAm 1*

McCormick, Myron 1907-1962 *WhAm 4*

McCormick, Nelson B 1847-1914 *BiDrAC, WhAmP*

McCormick, Nettie Fowler 1835-1923 *NotAW*

McCormick, Patrick Joseph 1880- *WhAm 3*

McCormick, Paul 1845-1921 *NatCAB 11, WhAm 1*

McCormick, Paul John 1879-1960 *WhAm 4*

McCormick, Richard Cunningham 1832-1901 *ApCAB, BiAUS, BiDrAC, DcAmB, NatCAB 24, REnAW, TwCBDA, WhAm 1, WhAmP*

McCormick, Robert 1780-1846 *DcAmB, NatCAB 1, NatCAB 24, TwCBDA, WhAm H*

McCormick, Robert Elliott 1903-1969 *WhAm 5*

McCormick, Robert Hall 1847-1917 *NatCAB 21, WhAm 1*

McCormick, Robert Hall 1878-1963 *NatCAB 51, WhAm 4*

McCormick, Robert Laird 1847-1911 *ApCAB X, NatCAB 10, NatCAB 31, WhAm 1*

McCormick, Robert Louis Laing 1917-1975 *WhAm 6*

McCormick, Robert Rutherford 1880-1955 *DcAmB S5, McGEWB, NatCAB 41, WebAB, WhAm 3*

McCormick, Robert Sanderson 1849-1919 *DcAmB, NatCAB 13, WhAm 1*

McCormick, Ruth Hanna d1944 *DcAmB S3, NotAW*

McCormick, Ruth Hanna 1880-1944 *BiCAW, BiDrAC, WhAmP*

McCormick, Ruth Hanna 1887-1944 *WomWWA 14*

McCormick, S Frederick 1877-1953 *NatCAB 50*

McCormick, Samuel Black 1858-1928 *BiDAmEd, DcAmB, NatCAB 15,*

NatCAB 24, TwCBDA, WhAm 1

McCormick, Sophia Grant 1869-
WomWWA 14

McCormick, Stephen 1784-1875 *DcAmB,
NatCAB 25, WhAm H*

McCormick, Thomas Carson 1892-1954
WhAm 3

McCormick, Thomas Gerard 1908-1961
WhAm 4

McCormick, Vance Criswell 1872-1946
NatCAB 35, WhAm 2

McCormick, Washington Jay 1884-1949
BiDrAC, WhAmP

McCormick, William 1866-1923 *WhAm 1*

McCormick, William Bernard 1868- *WhAm 5*

McCormick, William Laird 1876-1953
NatCAB 50, WhAm 3

McCormick, Willoughby Madden 1864-1932
NatCAB 24, WhAm 1

McCornack, John Knox 1863-1937 *WhAm 1*

McCornick, William Sylvester 1837-
NatCAB 7

McCornock, Edward Ray 1886-1971
NatCAB 57

McCort, John J 1860-1936 *NatCAB 16,
WhAm 1*

McCorvey, Gessner Tutwiler 1882-1965
WhAm 4

McCorvey, Thomas Chalmers 1851-1932
TwCBDA, WhAm 1

McCosh, Andrew James 1858-1908 *DcAmB,
NatCAB 24, WhAm 1*

McCosh, James 1811-1894 *AmBi, ApCAB,
BiDAmEd, DcAmB, DcAmReB, Drake,
McGEWB, NatCAB 5, TwCBDA,
WhAm H*

McCosker, Alfred Justin 1886-1959 *WhAm 3*

McCoskey, Samuel Allen 1804-1886 *Drake*

McCoskry, Samuel Allen 1804-1886 *ApCAB,
NatCAB 5, TwCBDA*

McCotter, Cyrus Rawson 1883-1959 *WhAm 4*

McCouch, Gordon Mallett 1885-1962 *IlBEAAW*

McCourt, Walter Edward 1884-1943 *WhAm 2*

McCowen, Edward Oscar 1877-1953 *BiDrAC,
WhAm 3*

McCown, Albert 1890-1953 *WhAm 3*

McCown, Ben 1870- *WhoColR*

McCown, Chester Charlton 1877- *WhAm 5*

McCown, Edward C 1875-1946 *WhAm 2*

McCown, John Porter 1815-1879 *BiDConf,
TwCBDA*

McCown, John Porter 1820?-1879 *ApCAB*

McCown, Theodore Doney 1908-1969 *WhAm 5*

McCoy, Albert Clarence 1913-1972 *NatCAB 57*

McCoy, Archie 1853-1924 *NatCAB 22*

McCoy, Bernice *WhAm 5*

McCoy, Camilla Harrison 1861-
WomWWA 14

McCoy, Clifford Benson 1867-1919 *NatCAB 17*

McCoy, Daniel 1845-1908 *WhAm 1*

McCoy, David Oren 1911-1960 *NatCAB 48*

McCoy, Donald Richard 1928- *EncAAH*

McCoy, Elijah 1843-1929 *DcAmB,
WhAm HA, WhAm 4*

McCoy, Emma Augusta *WomWWA 14*

McCoy, Etta Joe 1874- *WomWWA 14*

McCoy, Frank Ross 1874-1954 *NatCAB 44,
WebAMB, WhAm 3*

McCoy, George Loren 1872-1921 *NatCAB 19*

McCoy, George Walter 1876- *WhAm 5*

McCoy, George Washington 1871-1932
NatCAB 41

McCoy, Henry Bayard 1866-1923 *WhAm 1*

McCoy, Henry Kent 1820-1886 *WhAm H*

McCoy, Herbert Newby 1870-1945 *WhAm 2*

McCoy, Horace Lyman 1888-1946 *WhAm 2*

McCoy, Isaac 1784-1846 *AmBi, ApCAB,
DcAmB, EncAAH, McGEWB,
NatCAB 18, TwCBDA, WhAm H,
WhAmP*

McCoy, James H 1855- *NatCAB 17*

McCoy, James Henry 1868-1919 *NatCAB 25,
WhAm 1*

McCoy, John Hall 1887-1958 *WhAm 3*

McCoy, John Willard 1882-1961 *WhAm 4*

McCoy, Joseph G 1837-1915 *REnAW*

McCoy, Joseph Geating 1837-1915 *AmBi,*

DcAmB, EncAAH, WebAB

McCoy, Joseph Geiting 1837-1915 *McGEWB*

McCoy, Joseph L *WhoColR*

McCoy, Joseph Sylvester 1863-1931
NatCAB 24

McCoy, Lee Marcus 1882- *WhoColR*

McCoy, Leeta Myrtle *WomWWA 14*

McCoy, Lester 1877-1942 *NatCAB 40*

McCoy, Mary Elenora Delaney 1846- *WhoColR*

McCoy, Philbrick 1897-1973 *WhAm 6*

McCoy, Robert d1849 *BiAUS, BiDrAC,
WhAm H*

McCoy, Samuel Duff 1882-1964 *WhAm 4*

McCoy, Thomas Francis 1824-1899
ApCAB Sup

McCoy, Walter Irving 1859-1933 *BiDrAC,
NatCAB 25, WhAm 1*

McCoy, Whitley Peterson 1894-1971 *WhAm 5*

McCoy, William d1864 *BiAUS, BiDrAC,
WhAm H, WhAmP*

McCoy, William Charles 1892-1969
NatCAB 54

McCoy, William D 1853-1893 *NatCAB 14*

McCoy, William Daniel 1896-1967 *WhAm 5*

McCoy, William Edward 1840-1919 *NatCAB 2*

McCrackan, William Denison 1864-1923
ApCAB Sup, NatCAB 19, WhAm 1

McCracken, Annie Virginia 1868- *AmWom*

McCracken, Charles Chester 1882-1957
NatCAB 43, WhAm 3

McCracken, Elizabeth 1876- *WomWWA 14*

McCracken, Frederic Calvin 1880-1958
NatCAB 47

McCracken, Harlan Linneus 1889-1961
WhAm 4

McCracken, Henry Mitchell 1840-1918 *AmBi*

McCracken, Henry Mitchell *see also*
MacCracken, Henry Mitchell

McCracken, James DeWitt 1859-1936
NatCAB 28

McCracken, John 1934- *BnEnAmA*

McCracken, John Rufus 1874-1949 *NatCAB 38*

McCracken, Mary Unger 1879- *WomWWA 14*

McCracken, Robert James 1904- *WhAm 5*

McCracken, Robert McDowell 1874-1934
BiDrAC, WhAm 5, WhAmP

McCracken, Samuel 1876-1951 *WhAm 3*

McCracken, Thomas Cooke 1876-1961
NatCAB 50, WhAm 4

McCrackin, Belle Fitzhugh McPherson 1870-
WomWWA 14

McCrackin, Josephine Woempner Clifford
1838-1920 *NotAW, WhAm 1,
WomWWA 14*

McCrady, Edward 1803-1892 *TwCBDA*

McCrady, Edward 1833-1903 *DcAmB,
NatCAB 11, TwCBDA, WhAm 1*

McCrady, John 1831-1881 *NatCAB 11,
TwCBDA*

McCrady, John 1911-1968 *WhAm 5*

McCrae, Thomas 1870-1935 *DcAmB S1,
WhAm 1*

McCrae, William 1810- *ApCAB*

McCraken, Tracy Stephenson 1894-1960
REnAW, WhAm 4

McCrary, Alvin Jasper 1844- *WhAm 4*

McCrary, George Washington 1835-1890 *AmBi,
ApCAB, BiAUS, BiDrAC, BiDrUSE,
DcAmB, NatCAB 3, TwCBDA,
WhAm H, WhAmP*

McCrary, Isaac Newton 1886-1949 *NatCAB 42*

McCrary, John Alva 1871- *WhAm 5*

McCrary, John Raymond 1872-1951 *WhAm 3*

McCrate, John Dennis 1800?-1879 *BiAUS*

McCrate, John Dennis 1802-1879 *BiDrAC,
WhAm H*

McCraw, William 1896-1955 *WhAm 3*

McCray, Elmer Ellsworth d1937 *NatCAB 30*

McCray, Warren Terry 1865-1938 *NatCAB 31,
WhAm 1*

McCrea, Annette E d1928 *WhAm 1*

McCrea, Archie Elbert 1880-1950 *WhAm 3*

McCrea, Charles Harold 1890-1946 *WhAm 2*

McCrea, James 1848-1913 *NatCAB 14,
WhAm 1*

McCrea, James Alexander 1875-1923
NatCAB 21, WhAm 1

McCrea, James Birney 1875-1943 *NatCAB 34*

McCrea, Jane 1752?-1777 *NotAW*

McCrea, Jane 1753-1777 *ApCAB, NatCAB 10*

McCrea, Jane *see also* Maccrea, Jane

McCrea, Nelson Glenn 1863-1944 *NatCAB 33,
WhAm 2*

McCrea, Roswell Cheney 1876-1951
NatCAB 43, WhAm 3

McCrea, Tully 1839-1918 *WhAm 1*

McCready, Benjamin William 1813-1892
NatCAB 9

McCready, John Hollis 1879-1949 *NatCAB 38*

McCready, Margaret Merkley 1865-
WomWWA 14

McCready, Robert Thompson Miller d1942
WhAm 2

McCready, William Wick 1908-1962
NatCAB 51

McCreary, George Boone 1875- *WhAm 5*

McCreary, George Deardorff 1846-1915
BiDrAC, NatCAB 19

McCreary, Irvin 1896-1961 *NatCAB 51*

McCreary, James Bennett 1835-1918 *BiAUS*

McCreary, James Bennett 1838-1918 *BiDrAC,
DcAmB, NatCAB 3, NatCAB 13,
TwCBDA, WhAm 1, WhAmP*

McCreary, John 1761-1833 *BiAUS, BiDrAC,
WhAm H*

McCreary, Pitt L 1851-1885 *TwCBDA*

McCreary, Thomas Clay 1817-1890 *TwCBDA*

McCreary, William *BiAUS*

McCreath, Andrew S 1849- *WhAm 4*

McCreath, Lesley 1881-1957 *NatCAB 47*

McCredie, Marion MacMaster 1863- *WhAm 4,
WomWWA 14*

McCredie, William Wallace 1862-1935 *BiDrAC*

McCreedy, Jo Ann 1924-1972 *WhAm 6*

McCreedy, William *BiAUS*

McCreery, Andrew Buchanan 1830-1913
NatCAB 28

McCreery, Charles 1785-1826 *DcAmB,
NatCAB 3, WhAm H*

McCreery, Donald Chalmers 1886-1962
WhAm 4

McCreery, Elbert L 1877-1955 *WhAm 3*

McCreery, Fenton Reuben 1866-1940
NatCAB 14, WhAm 1

McCreery, Hugh Pete 1900-1974 *WhAm 6*

McCreery, James Thomas 1844-1925
NatCAB 31

McCreery, James Work 1849-1923 *DcAmB,
WhAm 1*

McCreery, Janie Cole 1875- *WomWWA 14*

McCreery, John Alexander 1850-1899
NatCAB 35

McCreery, Maria Maud Leonard 1883-1938
NotAW

McCreery, Sir Richard 1898-1967 *WhWW-II,
WhoMilH*

McCreery, Samuel 1886-1965 *NatCAB 51*

McCreery, Thomas Clay 1816-1890 *BiDrAC,
WhAm H*

McCreery, Thomas Clay 1817-1890 *ApCAB,
BiAUS, NatCAB 4*

McCreery, William 1750-1814 *BiDrAC,
WhAm H, WhAmP*

McCreery, William 1786-1841 *BiDrAC,
WhAm H*

McCreight, George Artemus 1883-1966
WhAm 4

McCreight, Patrick 1825?- *NewYHSD*

McCrillis, Mary F 1856- *WomWWA 14*

McCrorey, Henry Lawrence 1863-1951
BiDAmEd, NatCAB 42, WhAm 3

McCrory, John Raymond 1894-1937
NatCAB 30

McCrory, Samuel Henry 1879-1949 *WhAm 3*

McCrory, Wilton Wade 1873- *WhAm 5*

McCrosky, Theodore Tremain 1902-1968
WhAm 5

McCrossin, Edward Francis 1887-1962
WhAm 4

McCrossin, William Patrick, Jr. 1890-1960
NatCAB 50, WhAm 4

McCruden, Donald Breslin 1896-1961
NatCAB 50

McCrum, Blanche Prichard 1887-1969 *WhAm 5*

McCrumb, Fred Rodgers, Jr. 1925-1976
WhAm 6

McCrummen, Thomas Dodson 1898-1954
NatCAB 45
McCue, C A 1879-1942 WhAm 1
McCue, Frank Love 1863- WhAm 4
McCuen, Charles Leroy 1892-1975 WhAm 6
McCuen, Leslie Eugene 1886-1942 NatCAB 31
McCuish, John Berridge 1906-1962 NatCAB 50,
WhAm 4
McCullagh, George C 1905-1952 WhAm 3
McCullagh, John 1811- ApCAB
McCullagh, John 1845- WhAm 4
McCullagh, Joseph Burbridge 1842-1896
DcAmB, WhAm H
McCullagh, Joseph Burbridge 1843-1896
NatCAB 1
McCullers, Carson Smith 1917-1967 WebAB,
WhAm 4
McCulley, Bruce 1873- WhAm 5
McCulley, Johnston 1883-1958 WhAm 3
McCulloch, Ben 1811-1862 AmBi, ApCAB,
DcAmB, NatCAB 4, WebAMB,
WhAm H
McCulloch, Ben 1814-1862 Drake
McCulloch, Benjamin 1811-1862 TwCBDA
McCulloch, Catharine Gouger Waugh 1862-1945
AmWom, NotAW, WhAm 2,
WomWWA 14
McCulloch, Catherine Gouger Waugh 1862-1945
BiCAW
McCulloch, Champe Carter, Jr. 1869-1928
WhAm 1
McCulloch, Charles Alexander 1875-1946
WhAm 2
McCulloch, Duncan 1853-1932 WhAm 1
McCulloch, Edgar Allen 1861-1933 NatCAB 15,
WhAm 1
McCulloch, Frank Hathorn 1863-1947 WhAm 2
McCulloch, George 1792-1861 BiAUS,
BiDrAC, WhAm H
McCulloch, Harriet Ellen Mize 1842-
WomWWA 14
McCulloch, Henry Eustace 1816- TwCBDA
McCulloch, Hugh 1808-1895 AmBi, ApCAB,
BiAUS, BiDrUSE, DcAmB, Drake,
EncAB, McGEWB, NatCAB 4,
TwCBDA, WhAm H
McCulloch, Hugh 1888-1974 WhAm 6
McCulloch, James Edward 1873-1939 WhAm 1
McCulloch, John 1806-1879 BiAUS, BiDrAC,
WhAm H
McCulloch, John Wellington 1860- WhAm 4
McCulloch, Joseph Flavius 1856- TwCBDA
McCulloch, Margaret WomWWA 14
McCulloch, Oscar Carleton 1843-1891 DcAmB,
NatCAB 19, WhAm H
McCulloch, Philip Doddridge, Jr. 1851-1928
BiDrAC, TwCBDA, WhAm 4, WhAmP
McCulloch, Richard 1869-1940 NatCAB 30,
WhAm 1
McCulloch, Robert 1820-1905 WhAm 1
McCulloch, Roscoe Conkling 1880-1958
BiDrAC, NatCAB 48, WhAm 3
McCulloch, Thomas G BiAUS
McCulloch, Walter Fraser 1905-1973 WhAm 5
McCulloch, William Alexander 1889-1959
WhAm 3
McCulloch, William Edward 1869-1952
WhAm 3
McCulloch, William Moore 1901- BiDrAC
McCullogh, Thomas Grubb 1785-1848
WhAm H
McCullogh, Welty 1847-1889 BiDrAC,
WhAm H
McCulloh, Allan 1858-1932 WhAm 1
McCulloh, Charles Sears 1856-1940 WhAm 1
McCulloh, James Haines 1781-1869 NewYHSD
McCulloh, James Haines 1793?-1869 ApCAB
McCulloh, James Sears 1868-1957 NatCAB 45,
WhAm 5
McCullough, Campbell Rogers 1900-1970
NatCAB 55, WhAm 5
McCullough, Conde Balcom 1887-1946
NatCAB 35
McCullough, Davis NewYHSD
McCullough, Ernest 1867-1931 AmBi, DcAmB,
WhAm 1
McCullough, Hall Park 1872-1966 NatCAB 53,
WhAm 4

McCullough, Hiram 1813-1885 BiAUS,
BiDrAC, TwCBDA, WhAm H
McCullough, Hiram R 1850-1932 WhAm 1
McCullough, Hugh NatCAB 2
McCullough, James E 1847- WhAm 4
McCullough, John Edward 1832-1885 AmBi,
DcAmB, NatCAB 9, TwCBDA,
WhAm H
McCullough, John Edward 1837-1885 ApCAB
McCullough, John Fife 1883-1963 NatCAB 51
McCullough, John Griffith 1835-1915 DcAmB,
NatCAB 14, TwCBDA, WhAm 1
McCullough, John Russell 1905-1957
NatCAB 45
McCullough, Joseph Allen 1865- WhAm 1
McCullough, Matthew Pearce 1878- WhAm 6
McCullough, Myrtle Reed 1874-1911
NatCAB 15, NotAW, WhAm 1, WhAm 2,
WhAm 5
McCullough, Richard Philip 1881-1966
WhAm 4
McCullough, Theodore Wilson 1861-1937
WhAm 1
McCullough, Thomas Grubb 1785-1848 BiDrAC
McCullough, William Davis 1886-1940
NatCAB 43
McCullough, Willis d1948 WhAm 2
McCully, Henry NewYHSD
McCully, Jonathan 1809-1877 ApCAB
McCumber, Porter James 1856-1933
ApCAB Sup
McCumber, Porter James 1858-1933 AmBi,
BiDrAC, DcAmB S1, EncAAH,
NatCAB 13, REnAW, TwCBDA,
WhAm 1, WhAmP
McCune, Charles Nathaniel 1885-1964
WhAm 4
McCune, Charles William 1851-1940 EncAAH
McCune, George Shannon 1873-1941
NatCAB 42, WhAm 2
McCune, Henry Long 1862-943 WhAm 2
McCune, Lilian May 1856- WomWWA 14
McCune, Margaret Elizabeth 1879- WhoColR
McCune, Samuel L 1875-1936 WhAm 1
McCunn, John Niven 1858- WhAm 4
McCunniff, William Barlow 1920-1967
WhAm 5
McCurdy, Allan Anderson 1894-1965
NatCAB 51
McCurdy, Arthur Williams 1856- WhAm 4
McCurdy, Charles Johnson 1797-1891 ApCAB,
BiAUS, Drake, NatCAB 4, TwCBDA
McCurdy, Charles William 1856- TwCBDA,
WhAm 4
McCurdy, Fleming Blanchard 1875-1952
WhAm 1
McCurdy, Frederick Everett 1879-1954
NatCAB 47
McCurdy, Irwin Pounds 1856- TwCBDA,
WhAm 1
McCurdy, James Frederick 1847- ApCAB
McCurdy, James Huff 1866-1940 BiDAmEd,
NatCAB 30, WhAm 1
McCurdy, Laurence 1897-1956 WhAm 3
McCurdy, Merle M 1912-1968 WhAm 5
McCurdy, Richard Aldrich 1835-1916 DcAmB,
NatCAB 18, WhAm 1
McCurdy, Robert Morrill 1878- WhAm 6
McCurdy, S P BiAUS
McCurdy, Sidney Morrill 1881-1944
NatCAB 33
McCurdy, Stewart LeRoy 1859-1931
NatCAB 12, WhAm 1
McCurdy, Theodore Edward Alexis 1877-
WhoColR
McCurdy, Thomas Alexander 1839-1915
WhAm 1
McCurdy, Wesley 1881- WhAm 6
McCurdy, William Edward 1893-1967
NatCAB 53, WhAm 4
McCusker, Hubert Joseph 1893-1967 WhAm 4
McCusker, Thomas 1858-1926 NatCAB 21
McCutchan, Robert Guy 1877-1958 WhAm 3,
WhAm 5
McCutchen, Charles Walter 1845-1930
NatCAB 23
McCutchen, Cicero Decatur 1824- NatCAB 1

McCutchen, Edward Johnson 1857-1933
WhAm 1
McCutchen, George 1876-1951 WhAm 3
McCutchen, George Thomas 1909-1967
NatCAB 53
McCutchen, Robert Othello 1880-1954
NatCAB 44
McCutchen, Samford Brown 1834- NatCAB 10
McCutchen, Samuel Proctor 1901-1966
WhAm 4
McCutcheon, Ben Frederick 1875-1934
WhAm 1
McCutcheon, George Barr 1866-1928 AmBi,
DcAmB, NatCAB 14, WhAm 1
McCutcheon, Hattie Louise WomWWA 14
McCutcheon, James 1843-1914 NatCAB 18
McCutcheon, John Lindsay 1857-1905
NatCAB 16
McCutcheon, John Tinney 1870-1949 WebAB,
WhAm 2
McCutcheon, Keith Barr 1915-1971 WhAm 5
McCutcheon, Leona WomWWA 14
McCutcheon, Malcolm Wallace 1906-1969
WhAm 5
McCutcheon, Otis Eddy 1845-1926 WhAm 1
McCutcheon, Roger Philip 1889-1965 WhAm 4
McCutcheon, Stanley James 1917-1975
WhAm 6
McDade, Joseph Michael 1931- BiDrAC
McDaniel, Agnes M McLaughlin 1907-1975
WhAm 6
McDaniel, Arthur Bee 1895-1943 NatCAB 32,
WhAm 2
McDaniel, Edward Davies 1822- ApCAB,
WhAm 4
McDaniel, George White 1875-1927 WhAm 1
McDaniel, Giles 1885-1955 NatCAB 44
McDaniel, Hattie 1898-1952 DcAmB S5
McDaniel, Henry Bonner 1903-1972 WhAm 5
McDaniel, Henry Dickerson 1836-1926 DcAmB,
NatCAB 26, WhAm 1
McDaniel, Henry Dickerson 1837-1926 ApCAB,
NatCAB 1, TwCBDA
McDaniel, Leon Sayre 1887-1963 NatCAB 50
McDaniel, Lock 1847- WhAm 4
McDaniel, Lowry Harold 1898-1965
NatCAB 52
McDaniel, Martha Douglass Scarborough
WomWWA 14
McDaniel, Reuben E 1846-1920 WhAm 1
McDaniel, Sanders 1867-1934 WhAm 1
McDaniel, Walton Brooks 1871- WhAm 5
McDaniel, William d1854? BiDrAC,
WhAm H
McDaniels, Joseph Hetherington 1840-1938
WhAm 1
McDannald, Alexander H 1877-1957 WhAm 3
McDannald, Clyde Elliott 1876-1949 WhAm 2
McDannold, John James 1851-1904 BiDrAC
McDavid, Charles William 1914-1972 WhAm 6
McDavid, Constance Louise Webb 1896-1973
WhAm 6
McDavitt, Thomas 1857-1926 WhAm 1
McDearmon, James Calvin 1844-1902 BiDrAC,
TwCBDA, WhAm H
McDermaid, John 1842-1918 NatCAB 18
McDermott, Allan Langdon 1854-1908 BiDrAC,
WhAm 1
McDermott, Arthur Vincent 1888-1949
WhAm 2
McDermott, Bernard NewYHSD
McDermott, Charles Edward 1901-1961
NatCAB 49
McDermott, Charles J 1867-1941 WhAm 1
McDermott, Edward John 1852-1926 WhAm 1
McDermott, Eugene 1899-1973 WhAm 6
McDermott, Frank 1877-1930 WhAm 1,
WhAm 1C
McDermott, George Robert 1860-1937
WhAm 1
McDermott, George Thomas 1886-1937
WhAm 1
McDermott, Harrison John 1891-1956
NatCAB 47
McDermott, J Francis 1894-1953 NatCAB 44
McDermott, Jack Chipman 1905-1966 WhAm 4
McDermott, James Thomas 1872-1938 BiDrAC,
WhAm 5

McDermott, John *New YHSD*
McDermott, John Francis 1902- *REnAW*
McDermott, John R 1919- *IlBEAAW*
McDermott, Michael James 1894-1955
   NatCAB 46, *WhAm 3*
McDermott, Neil Thomas 1905-1959
   NatCAB 47
McDermott, R Thomas 1899-1970 *NatCAB 57*,
   WhAm 5
McDermott, William F 1891-1958 *WhAm 3*
McDevitt, Charles Joseph 1887-1950
   NatCAB 39
McDevitt, George Edwin 1910-1971 *WhAm 5*
McDevitt, James Lawrence 1898-1963 *WhAm 4*
McDevitt, Patrick *New YHSD*
McDevitt, Philip Richard 1858-1935
   NatCAB 25, *WhAm 1*
McDiarmid, Errett Weir 1877-1937 *NatCAB 42*,
   WhAm 1
McDill, Alexander Stuart 1822-1875 *ApCAB*,
   BiAUS, *BiDrAC*, *NatCAB 4*, *TwCBDA*,
   WhAm H
McDill, David 1826-1903 *TwCBDA*
McDill, David *see also* MacDill, David
McDill, James Wilson 1834-1894 *ApCAB*,
   BiAUS, *BiDrAC*, *DcAmB*, *NatCAB 11*,
   TwCBDA, *WhAm H*
McDill, John Rich 1860-1934 *WhAm 1*
McDoel, William Henry 1841-1916 *WhAm 1*
McDonald, Alexander 1827?-1897 *NatCAB 13*
McDonald, Alexander 1832-1903 *ApCAB*,
   BiAUS, *BiDrAC*, *NatCAB 12*
McDonald, Alexander 1833-1910 *NatCAB 10*,
   WhAm 1
McDonald, Alexander Roderick 1862- *WhAm 4*
McDonald, Allen Colfax 1876-1942 *WhAm 2*
McDonald, Angus D 1878-1941 *WhAm 2*
McDonald, Archibald Leete 1879- *WhAm 6*
McDonald, Bill 1909-1969 *WhAm 5*
McDonald, Carlos John 1880- *WhAm 6*
McDonald, Charles Henry 1872- *WhAm 5*
McDonald, Charles Howard 1913-1953
   NatCAB 41
McDonald, Charles James 1793-1860 *ApCAB*,
   BiAUS, *DcAmB*, *NatCAB 1*, *TwCBDA*,
   WhAm H
McDonald, Charles Sanford 1879-1934
   WhAm 1
McDonald, Chester Bernard 1895-1948
   NatCAB 39
McDonald, Clara Bird 1874- *WomWWA 14*
McDonald, Daniel 1785-1830 *TwCBDA*
McDonald, Daniel 1822-1885 *ApCAB*
McDonald, David 1803-1869 *BiAUS*,
   TwCBDA
McDonald, David Lamar 1906- *WebAMB*
McDonald, Donald 1712-1784? *ApCAB*, *Drake*
McDonald, Donald 1816-1879 *ApCAB*
McDonald, Donald 1869-1937 *NatCAB 29*
McDonald, Edward Francis 1844-1892 *BiDrAC*,
   NatCAB 6, *WhAm H*
McDonald, Edwin C 1897-1972 *WhAm 5*
McDonald, Ellice 1876-1955 *WhAm 3*
McDonald, Etta Austin Blaisdell 1872-
   WhAm 5, *WomWWA 14*
McDonald, Eugene F, Jr. 1890-1958 *WhAm 3*
McDonald, Flora 1720-1790 *ApCAB*
McDonald, Flora *see also* MacDonald, Flora
McDonald, Florin Lee 1906-1967 *WhAm 4*
McDonald, Frederick 1877-1958 *NatCAB 48*
McDonald, Frederick Honour 1892-1972
   WhAm 5
McDonald, Harl 1899-1955 *NatCAB 44*,
   WhAm 3
McDonald, Harry Alexander 1894-1964
   NatCAB 50, *WhAm 4*
McDonald, Henry Dearborn 1847-1925
   NatCAB 29
McDonald, Henry Temple 1872-1951
   NatCAB 40
McDonald, Howard 1876-1927 *WhAm 1*
McDonald, Hunter 1860-1937 *NatCAB 15*,
   WhAm 1
McDonald, J E 1819-1891 *BiAUS*
McDonald, J E *see also* McDonald, Joseph Ewing
McDonald, J Frank 1850- *WhoColR*
McDonald, Jack H 1932- *BiDrAC*

McDonald, James 1803-1849 *ApCAB*
McDonald, James 1828- *ApCAB*
McDonald, James 1875-1957 *WhAm 3*
McDonald, James *see also* Macdonald, James
McDonald, James Erdis 1904-1960 *NatCAB 48*
McDonald, James Eric 1881- *WhAm 6*
McDonald, James Gailard 1865-1940
   NatCAB 33
McDonald, James Grover 1886-1964 *WhAm 4*
McDonald, James Madden 1881-1956
   NatCAB 46
McDonald, James Richard 1867-1933 *WhAm 1*
McDonald, James Walton 1869- *WhAm 3*
McDonald, James William 1858- *NatCAB 12*
McDonald, Jesse Fuller 1858-1942 *NatCAB 14*,
   WhAm 2
McDonald, Jessie Claire 1869-1928 *WhAm 1*
McDonald, John 1837-1917 *BiDrAC*
McDonald, John B 1844-1911 *WhAm 1*
McDonald, John Bacon 1859-1926 *WhAm 1*
McDonald, John Bart 1844-1911 *NatCAB 5*
McDonald, John Bartholomew 1844-1911
   DcAmB
McDonald, John D *New YHSD*
McDonald, John Daniel 1863-1952 *WhAm 3*
McDonald, John Samuel 1865-1941 *NatCAB 37*,
   WhAm 1
McDonald, Joseph Albert 1903-1963 *WhAm 4*
McDonald, Joseph Ewing 1819-1891 *ApCAB*,
   BiDrAC, *DcAmB*, *NatCAB 11*, *TwCBDA*,
   WhAm H, *WhAmP*
McDonald, Joseph Ewing *see also* McDonald, J E
McDonald, Joseph John 1913-1967 *WhAm 5*
McDonald, Karola Jenny 1920-1970 *WhAm 5*
McDonald, Lillie Ann Neal 1884-1966
   NatCAB 53
McDonald, Lloyd Davison 1894-1954 *WhAm 3*
McDonald, Margaret Puth d1968 *WhAm 5*
McDonald, Marshall 1835- *ApCAB Sup*
McDonald, Marshall Franklin 1854- *NatCAB 5*
McDonald, Morris 1865-1938 *WhAm 1*
McDonald, Moses 1814-1869 *TwCBDA*
McDonald, Moses *see also* MacDonald, Moses
McDonald, Patrick Joseph 1863-1941
   NatCAB 40
McDonald, Robert A F 1878- *WhAm 6*
McDonald, Robert C 1881- *WhAm 6*
McDonald, Ronald 1835- *ApCAB*
McDonald, Roy William 1905-1972 *WhAm 5*
McDonald, Samuel F 1871- *WhAm 5*
McDonald, Stella Breyfogle *WomWWA 14*
McDonald, Stewart d1957 *WhAm 3*
McDonald, T Morton 1882-1951 *NatCAB 40*
McDonald, Thaddeus John 1866-1937
   NatCAB 30
McDonald, Thomas Edward 1893-1939
   WhAm 1
McDonald, William 1820-1901 *WhAm 1*
McDonald, William C 1858-1918 *NatCAB 17*,
   WhAm 1
McDonald, William Douglas d1961 *WhAm 4*
McDonald, William Henry 1861-1961
   NatCAB 50
McDonald, William James 1870-1948 *WhAm 2*
McDonald, William Jesse 1852-1918 *WhAm 1*
McDonald, William Johnson 1844-1926
   NatCAB 29
McDonald, William Madison 1866- *WhoColR*
McDonald, William Naylor 1834-1898
   NatCAB 19
McDonald, Willis Stewart 1901-1967 *WhAm 4*
McDonald, Witten 1846-1910 *WhAm 1*
McDonell, Alexander Angus 1882-1936
   NatCAB 28
McDonell, Alexander B 1840-1913 *NatCAB 15*
McDonnell, Charles Edward 1854-1921
   ApCAB Sup, *NatCAB 12*, *TwCBDA*,
   WhAm 1
McDonnell, Donald N 1899-1969 *WhAm 5*
McDonnell, E *New YHSD*
McDonnell, Edward Orrick 1891-1960 *WhAm 4*
McDonnell, Nannie Chilton 1860-
   WomWWA 14
McDonnell, Nicholas Silvester 1842-1914
   NatCAB 18
McDonnell, Thomas Francis Irving 1868-1939
   WhAm 1
McDonnell, Thomas John 1894-1961 *WhAm 4*

McDonnold, Benjamin Wilburn 1827-1889
   TwCBDA
McDonnough, James *New YHSD*, *WhAm H*
McDonnough, James Martin 1893-1965
   NatCAB 51
McDonogh, John 1778-1850 *Drake*
McDonogh, John 1779-1850 *AmBi*, *ApCAB*,
   DcAmB, *NatCAB 9*, *TwCBDA*,
   WhAm H
McDonough, C Edward 1916-1971 *NatCAB 56*
McDonough, Frank Wheatley 1905-1950
   WhAm 2
McDonough, Gordon Leo 1895-1968 *BiDrAC*,
   WhAm 5, *WhAmP*
McDonough, Henry *New YHSD*
McDonough, James Aloysius 1885-1941
   NatCAB 30
McDonough, James Buchanan 1865- *WhAm 5*
McDonough, John Henry 1858-1938 *WhAm 1*
McDonough, John James 1857-1912 *WhAm 1*
McDonough, John Justin 1907-1961 *WhAm 4*
McDonough, John Thomas 1843- *WhAm 4*
McDonough, Roger Ignatius 1892-1966
   WhAm 4
McDonough, Thomas Francis 1900-1964
   WhAm 4
McDougal, Clinton Dugald 1839-1914 *ApCAB*
McDougal, Clinton Dugald *see also* MacDougall,
   Clinton Dugald
McDougal, David Stockton 1809-1882 *ApCAB*,
   DcAmB, *NatCAB 13*, *WebAMB*,
   WhAm H
McDougal, David Stockton *see also* McDougall,
   David
McDougal, Douglas Cassel 1876-1964 *WhAm 4*
McDougal, James Alexander *New YHSD*
McDougal, James Barton 1866- *ApCAB X*,
   WhAm 4
McDougal, John 1827?- *New YHSD*
McDougal, Joseph Wesley 1900-1966
   NatCAB 53
McDougal, Luther Love 1878-1948 *NatCAB 41*
McDougal, Mary Carmack 1891-
   WomWWA 14
McDougal, Myrtle Archer *WhAm 5*,
   WomWWA 14
McDougall, Alexander 1731-1786 *BiAUS*,
   BiDrAC, *Drake*, *WhAmP*
McDougall, Alexander 1732-1786 *AmBi*,
   DcAmB, *NatCAB 11*, *WebAMB*,
   WhAm H
McDougall, Alexander 1845-1923 *AmBi*,
   DcAmB, *REnAW*, *WhAm 1*
McDougall, Alexander *see also* Macdougall,
   Alexander
McDougall, Alexander Miller 1884-1951
   NatCAB 42, *WhAm 3*
McDougall, David 1809-1882 *TwCBDA*
McDougall, David *see also* MacDougall, David D
McDougall, Edward George 1875- *WhAm 5*
McDougall, Frances Harriet 1805-1878 *DcAmB*
McDougall, George Francis 1882-1959
   WhAm 3
McDougall, James Alexander 1817-1867
   ApCAB, *BiAUS*, *BiDrAC*, *Drake*,
   NatCAB 11, *TwCBDA*, *WhAm H*,
   WhAmP
McDougall, John 1818-1866 *BiAUS*,
   NatCAB 4, *TwCBDA*
McDougall, John Alexander 1810?-1894
   New YHSD, *WhAm H*
McDougall, Marion Eliza 1851- *WomWWA 14*
McDougall, Walter Hugh 1858- *WhAm 4*
McDougall, William 1822- *Drake*
McDougall, William 1871-1938 *AmBi*,
   BiDAmEd, *DcAmB S2*, *WebAB*,
   WhAm 1
McDougall, William *see also* Macdougall,
   William
McDougle, Ernest Clifton 1867- *WhAm 5*
McDougle, Herbert Irwin 1901-1961 *WhAm 4*
McDougle, Ivan Eugene 1892-1955 *WhAm 3*
McDowall, Robert Edward 1927-1968 *WhAm 5*
McDowell, Alexander 1845-1913 *BiDrAC*,
   NatCAB 15, *WhAm 1*, *WhAmP*
McDowell, Alfred Henderson, Jr. 1907-1967
   NatCAB 54, *WhAm 4*
McDowell, Anne Elizabeth 1826-1901 *NotAW*

McDowell, Arthur Roscoe 1890-1938 *WhAm 1*
McDowell, Caroline Dent 1879- *WhAm 6*
McDowell, Cecile Rebecca 1880-
WomWWA 14
McDowell, Charles 1743-1815 *ApCAB,*
DcAmB, Drake, TwCBDA, WhAm H
McDowell, Charles 1857-1945 *NatCAB 34*
McDowell, Charles 1868-1942 *NatCAB 31*
McDowell, Charles Samuel, Jr. 1871-1943
WhAm 2
McDowell, Clotilda Lyon 1858-1930 *WhAm 3,*
WomWWA 14
McDowell, Cyrus R 1864- *WhoColR*
McDowell, E G *NewYHSD*
McDowell, Edmond Andrews 1857-1924
NatCAB 21
McDowell, Edmund Wilson 1857- *WhAm 4*
McDowell, Elizabeth Estill 1873-
WomWWA 14
McDowell, Emma M Scott 1857-
WomWWA 14
McDowell, Ephraim 1771-1830 *ApCAB,*
BiHiMed, DcAmB, Drake, NatCAB 5,
REnAW, TwCBDA, WebAB, WhAm H
McDowell, George Stanley 1855-1932 *WhAm 1*
McDowell, Grace Greenlee *ApCAB*
McDowell, Harris Brown, Jr. 1906- *BiDrAC,*
WhAmP
McDowell, Harry Bleakley 1882-1947
NatCAB 36
McDowell, Henry Burden 1857-1928 *WhAm 1*
McDowell, Henry Clay 1861-1933 *WhAm 1*
McDowell, Irvin 1818-1885 *AmBi, ApCAB,*
DcAmB, Drake, TwCBDA, WebAMB,
WhAm H, WhoMilH
McDowell, Irwin 1818-1885 *NatCAB 4*
McDowell, James *NewYHSD*
McDowell, James 1795-1851 *AmBi, DcAmB,*
NatCAB 5, TwCBDA
McDowell, James 1796-1851 *ApCAB, BiAUS,*
BiDrAC, Drake, WhAm H
McDowell, James Foster 1825-1887 *BiAUS,*
BiDrAC, WhAm H
McDowell, John 1751-1820 *DcAmB, Drake,*
NatCAB 1, TwCBDA, WhAm H
McDowell, John 1771-1820 *NatCAB 1*
McDowell, John 1780-1863 *ApCAB, DcAmB,*
NatCAB 13, TwCBDA, WhAm H
McDowell, John 1870-1937 *AmBi, WhAm 1*
McDowell, John 1909-1974 *WhAm 6*
McDowell, John Anderson 1853-1927 *BiDrAC,*
TwCBDA, WhAm 3
McDowell, John Ralph 1902-1957 *BiDrAC,*
WhAm 3
McDowell, John Sherman 1868-1931 *WhAm 1*
McDowell, Joseph 1756-1801 *ApCAB, BiAUS,*
BiDrAC, DcAmB, NatCAB 2, TwCBDA,
WebAMB, WhAm H
McDowell, Joseph 1758-1799 *BiDrAC,*
WhAm H
McDowell, Joseph 1758-1801 *Drake*
McDowell, Joseph Jefferson 1800-1877 *ApCAB,*
BiAUS, BiDrAC, TwCBDA, WhAm H
McDowell, Katharine Sherwood Bonner
1849-1883 *NotAW*
McDowell, Katharine Sherwood Bonner
1849-1884 *TwCBDA*
McDowell, Katherine Sherwood Bonner
1849-1883 *NatCAB 11*
McDowell, Katherine Sherwood Bonner
1849-1884 *ApCAB*
McDowell, Katherine Sherwood Bonner *see also*
MacDowell, K S B
McDowell, Louise Sherwood 1876-1966
WhAm 4, WomWWA 14
McDowell, Mary Eliza 1854-1936 *DcAmB S2,*
NotAW, WhAm 1, WomWWA 14
McDowell, Pauline 1874- *WomWWA 14*
McDowell, Philetus H 1873- *WhAm 5*
McDowell, Pierce Hubert 1902-1975 *WhAm 6*
McDowell, Rachel Kollock 1880-1949 *WhAm 2*
McDowell, Ralph Walker 1883-1935 *WhAm 1*
McDowell, Samuel 1735-1817 *ApCAB, Drake,*
TwCBDA

McDowell, Silas 1795-1879 *ApCAB*
McDowell, Thomas David 1823-1898 *BiDConf*
McDowell, Tremaine 1893-1959 *WhAm 3*
McDowell, William Adair 1795-1853 *ApCAB*
McDowell, William Fraser 1858-1937
DcAmB S2, NatCAB 13, TwCBDA,
WhAm 1
McDowell, William George 1882-1938 *WhAm 1*
McDowell, William Osborne 1848- *NatCAB 3,*
WhAm 4
McDowell, William Wallace 1867-1934
NatCAB 29
McDuffee, Charles Henry 1868-1927
NatCAB 20
McDuffie, Charles Dennett 1894-1964
NatCAB 51
McDuffie, Duncan 1877-1951 *NatCAB 40,*
WhAm 3
McDuffie, George 1788?-1851 *ApCAB, BiAUS*
McDuffie, George 1790-1851 *AmBi, BiDrAC,*
DcAmB, McGEWB, NatCAB 12,
TwCBDA, WebAB, WhAm H, WhAmP
McDuffie, George *see also* Macduffie, George
McDuffie, John 1883-1950 *BiDrAC,*
NatCAB 50, WhAm 3, WhAmP
McDuffie, John Van 1841-1896 *BiDrAC,*
WhAm H
McDuffie, William C 1886-1963 *WhAm 4*
McEachern, Daniel Victor 1879-1971 *WhAm 5*
McEachern, John Newton 1899-1950 *WhAm 3*
McEachron, Duncan Lendrum 1863-1937
WhAm 1
McEachron, Karl Boyer 1889-1954 *NatCAB 46,*
WhAm 3
McEglaw *NewYHSD*
McEldowney, Charles Roy 1894-1959 *WhAm 3*
McEldowney, Henry Clay 1868-1935
NatCAB 29, WhAm 1
McElduff, John Vincent 1898-1959 *WhAm 3*
McElfatrick, George Charles 1881-1940
NatCAB 30
McElfresh, William Edward 1867-1943
WhAm 2
McElhany, J L d1959 *WhAm 3*
McElhenney, Jane *NotAW*
McElhenney, Thomas Jefferson 1897-1968
NatCAB 54
McElhinney, John H 1888-1955 *WhAm 3*
McElhinney, John William 1851-1928
NatCAB 27
McElhinney, Philip Paul Bliss 1893-1951
NatCAB 45
McEllerow, Charles *NewYHSD*
McElligott, James Napoleon 1812-1866 *ApCAB,*
Drake, NatCAB 3, TwCBDA
McElmell, Jackson 1834-1908 *WhAm 1*
McElrath, Thomas 1807-1888 *ApCAB,*
DcAmB, NatCAB 3, TwCBDA,
WhAm H
McElreath, Walter 1867-1951 *NatCAB 42,*
WhAm 3
McElroy, Benjamin Lincoln 1860-1948
WhAm 3
McElroy, Clarence Underwood 1847- *WhAm 1*
McElroy, Frank D 1878- *WhAm 6*
McElroy, George Beamish 1824- *TwCBDA*
McElroy, George Wightman 1858-1931
WhAm 1
McElroy, Henry F 1865-1939 *WhAm 1*
McElroy, James Finney 1852-1915 *NatCAB 40*
McElroy, James W 1892-1971 *WhAm 5*
McElroy, John 1782-1877 *ApCAB, DcAmB,*
TwCBDA, WhAm H
McElroy, John 1846-1929 *DcAmB,*
NatCAB 22, WhAm 1
McElroy, John George Repplier 1842-1890
TwCBDA
McElroy, Mary Arthur 1841-1917
WomWWA 14
McElroy, Mary Arthur 1842-1917 *AmWom,*
ApCAB, WhAm 1
McElroy, Neil Hosler 1904-1972 *BiDrUSE,*
WhAm 5
McElroy, Robert 1872-1959 *WhAm 3*
McElroy, Warren Finley 1865-1948
NatCAB 36
McElroy, William H *WhAm 1*
McElroy, William Thomas 1889-1963 *WhAm 4*

McElveen, William Thomas 1867-1933
WhAm 1
McElvenny, Robert Talbot 1904-1965 *WhAm 4*
McElwain, Charles Church 1872- *WhAm 5*
McElwain, Edwin 1908-1960 *WhAm 4*
McElwain, Frank Arthur 1875-1957
NatCAB 43, WhAm 3
McElwain, Henry Ely, Jr. 1891- *WhAm 4*
McElwain, J Franklin 1874-1958 *WhAm 3*
McElwain, William Henry 1904-1972 *WhAm 5*
McElwain, William Howe 1867-1908 *DcAmB,*
NatCAB 14
McEnary, Dale Robert 1890-1964 *WhAm 4*
McEnerney, Garret William 1865-1942
NatCAB 31, WhAm 2
McEnerny, Harry 1860-1941 *NatCAB 31*
McEnerny, Harry, Jr. 1897-1972 *NatCAB 57*
McEnery, John 1833-1891 *ApCAB Sup,*
NatCAB 10, TwCBDA
McEnery, Samuel Douglas 1837-1910
ApCAB Sup, BiDrAC, DcAmB,
NatCAB 10, TwCBDA, WhAm 1,
WhAmP
McEniry, William Hugh, Jr. 1916-1974
WhAm 6
McEntee, Girard Lindsley 1880-1957
NatCAB 44
McEntee, Jervis 1828-1891 *AmBi, ApCAB,*
DcAmB, Drake, NatCAB 5, NewYHSD,
TwCBDA, WhAm H
McEntegart, Bryan Joseph 1893-1968
NatCAB 55, WhAm 5
McEntire, Richard Brooke 1911-1958 *WhAm 3*
McEntire, Walter Francis 1861- *ApCAB X*
McEttrick, Michael Joseph 1848-1921 *BiDrAC*
McEuen, Anne Middleton *NewYHSD*
McEvoy, Harry 1828-1914 *NewYHSD*
McEvoy, Henry N 1828-1914 *NewYHSD*
McEvoy, James 1874-1941 *NatCAB 30,*
WhAm 1
McEvoy, John Halpin 1879-1955 *NatCAB 46*
McEvoy, Joseph Patrick 1895-1958 *WhAm 3*
McEvoy, Reginald 1881- *WhAm 6*
McEwan, Alexander Fraser 1862-1945
NatCAB 35
McEwan, Arthur 1872-1943 *NatCAB 32*
McEwan, Thomas, Jr. 1854-1926 *BiDrAC,*
TwCBDA
McEwan, William *NewYHSD*
McEwan, William Leonard 1859-1937 *WhAm 1*
McEwen, James Henry 1894-1946 *NatCAB 35,*
WhAm 2
McEwen, Katherine 1875- *IIBEAAW*
McEwen, Mary Gilruth 1872- *WomWWA 14*
McEwen, Merrill Clyde 1900-1957 *WhAm 3*
McEwen, Robert Cameron 1920- *BiDrAC*
McEwen, Robert Ward 1906-1967 *WhAm 4*
McFadden, Edgar Sharp 1891-1956 *NatCAB 44*
McFadden, Effie Belle 1872- *WhAm 5*
McFadden, Elizabeth Apthorp *WomWWA 14*
McFadden, George 1873-1931 *NatCAB 44,*
WhAm 1
McFadden, George Henry 1847-1926
NatCAB 44
McFadden, J Franklin 1862-1936 *NatCAB 27*
McFadden, James Augustine 1880-1952
WhAm 3
McFadden, John B *NewYHSD*
McFadden, John Francis d1957 *WhAm 3*
McFadden, Joseph A d1971 *WhAm 6*
McFadden, Louis Thomas 1876-1936 *BiDrAC,*
DcAmB S2, WhAm 1, WhAmP
McFadden, Manus 1888-1955 *WhAm 3*
McFadden, Obadiah Benton 1815-1875 *BiDrAC,*
WhAm H
McFadden, Obadiah Benton 1817-1875 *ApCAB,*
BiAUS, NatCAB 5, TwCBDA
McFadden, Paul Webb 1866-1946 *NatCAB 36*
McFadden, Philip Grandin 1878-1949
NatCAB 39
McFadden, S Willis 1864- *WhAm 4*
McFadden, Theodore Francis 1898-1966
NatCAB 53
McFadden, William Hartman 1869-1956
WhAm 3
McFadden George Henry 1847-1926 *WhAm 1*
McFaden, Frank Talbot 1864-1933 *WhAm 1*

McFadyen, Bernice Musgrove 1896-1954
WhAm 3
McFall, John Joseph 1918- *BiDrAC*
McFall, John Monteith 1885-1958 *WhAm 3*
McFall, Merrill Borden 1906- *WhAm 6*
McFall, Robert James 1887-1963 *NatCAB 53*
McFall, Thurlow Elwin 1888-1959 *NatCAB 51*
McFarlan, Duncan d1816 *BiAUS, BiDrAC,*
WhAm H
McFarland, Amanda R 1837?- *ApCAB*
McFarland, Andrew 1817-1891 *ApCAB Sup*
McFarland, Archie J 1883-1950 *WhAm 3*
McFarland, Asa 1769-1827 *ApCAB Sup,*
Drake
McFarland, Asa 1804-1879 *ApCAB Sup*
McFarland, David Ford 1878-1955 *NatCAB 44,*
WhAm 3
McFarland, Earl 1883-1972 *WhAm 5*
McFarland, Elizabeth Kneeland *ApCAB Sup*
McFarland, Ernest William 1894- *BiDrAC*
McFarland, Eugene James 1908-1955 *WhAm 3*
McFarland, Francis Patrick 1819-1874 *ApCAB,*
NatCAB 10, TwCBDA, WhAm H
McFarland, Gary 1933-1971 *WhAm 5*
McFarland, George Austin 1858-1938 *WhAm 1*
McFarland, George Bradley 1886-1942
DcAmB S3
McFarland, George Eldric 1863-1925
NatCAB 29
McFarland, Greyble Lewis, Jr. 1919-1971
WhAm 5
McFarland, Guy Ernest 1908-1964 *NatCAB 51*
McFarland, James Franklin 1847-1917
NatCAB 17
McFarland, Jean Henderson 1907-1966
WhAm 4
McFarland, John Clemson 1877- *WhAm 5*
McFarland, John Horace 1859-1948 *DcAmB S4,*
WhAm 2
McFarland, John Thomas 1851-1913 *DcAmB,*
WhAm 1
McFarland, Joseph 1868-1945 *WhAm 2*
McFarland, Julian Ecwart 1902-1969
NatCAB 56
McFarland, Kermit 1905-1972 *WhAm 5*
McFarland, Lucy *NewYHSD*
McFarland, Raymond 1872- *WhAm 5*
McFarland, Reginald Adams 1900-1958
NatCAB 47
McFarland, Robert White 1825-1910 *TwCBDA,*
WhAm 1
McFarland, Russell S 1893-1968 *WhAm 5*
McFarland, Samuel Gamble 1830-1897 *DcAmB,*
WhAm H
McFarland, Silas Clark 1859-1908 *WhAm 1*
McFarland, Thomas Bard 1828-1908 *DcAmB,*
NatCAB 18, WhAm 1
McFarland, Thomas C 1893-1954 *WhAm 3*
McFarland, Walter Martin 1859-1935 *WhAm 1*
McFarland, Wilfred Myers 1898-1963 *WhAm 4*
McFarland, William 1821-1900 *BiAUS,*
BiDrAC
McFarlane, Arthur Emerson 1876-1945
WhAm 2
McFarlane, Charles T 1872- *WhAm 5*
McFarlane, D *NewYHSD*
McFarlane, Flora *WomWWA 14*
McFarlane, Frederick 1882-1962 *NatCAB 50*
McFarlane, Ida Grace Kruse *WomWWA 14*
McFarlane, R *NewYHSD*
McFarlane, William Doddridge 1894- *BiDrAC*
McFaul, James Augustine 1850-1917
ApCAB Sup, DcAmB, NatCAB 12,
TwCBDA, WhAm 1
McFayden, Donald 1876-1951 *NatCAB 41,*
WhAm 5
McFee, Henry Lee 1886-1953 *BnEnAmA,*
WhAm 3
McFee, William 1881-1966 *NatCAB 52,*
WhAm 4
McFee, William David 1874-1949 *NatCAB 37*
McFeely, Richard Harding 1904-1966
NatCAB 56, WhAm 4
McFeely, Wilbur Morris 1908-1974 *WhAm 6*
McFerran, John Courts 1831-1872 *ApCAB*
McFerrin, Andersen Purdy 1818- *ApCAB*
McFerrin, James 1784-1840 *ApCAB*
McFerrin, John Berry 1807-1887 *ApCAB,*

DcAmB, NatCAB 8, TwCBDA,
WhAm H
McFetridge, William Lane 1893-1969 *WhAm 5*
McFie, John Robert 1848-1930 *WhAm 1*
McGaffey, Ernest 1867- *WhAm 4*
McGaffin, Alexander 1870-1929 *WhAm 1*
McGaffin, William 1910-1975 *WhAm 6*
McGahan, Paul James 1888-1972 *WhAm 5*
McGann, John C *NewYHSD*
McGann, Lawrence Edward 1852-1928 *BiDrAC,*
TwCBDA
McGann, Marion Eudora Hotchkiss d1969
WhAm 5
McGannon, Matthew Charles 1857- *NatCAB 9,*
WhAm 4
McGarity, Charles Benjamin 1883-1966
NatCAB 53
McGarraghy, Joseph C 1897-1975 *WhAm 6*
McGarrah, Albert Franklin 1878-1962 *WhAm 4*
McGarrah, Gates White 1863-1940 *DcAmB S2,*
NatCAB 30, WhAm 1
McGarrell, James 1930- *BnEnAmA*
McGarry, Edmund Daniels 1891-1973 *WhAm 6*
McGarry, William James 1894-1941 *WhAm 1*
McGarry, William Robert 1917-1970
NatCAB 57
McGarry, William Rutledge 1872-1942
NatCAB 39, WhAm 5
McGarvey, John William 1829-1911 *ApCAB,*
DcAmB, DcAmReB, NatCAB 4,
TwCBDA, WhAm 1
McGarvey, Robert Neill 1888-1952 *BiDrAC,*
WhAm 3
McGarvey, William 1861-1924 *WhAm 1*
McGaugh, Elmer Thomas 1872- *WhAm 1*
McGaughey, Dean Smith 1882-1964
NatCAB 51
McGaughey, Edward Wilson 1817-1852 *BiAUS,*
BiDrAC, TwCBDA, WhAm H
McGaughey, William Ray 1879-1955
NatCAB 45, WhAm 4
McGaughy, James Ralph 1888-1954 *WhAm 3*
McGauran, John Baptist 1872- *WhAm 5*
McGauran, Patrick *NewYHSD*
McGavack, Thomas Hodge 1898-1973 *WhAm 6*
McGavick, Alexander Joseph 1863-1948
NatCAB 40, NatCAB 47, TwCBDA,
WhAm 2
McGavin, Charles 1874-1940 *BiDrAC,*
WhAm 5
McGavin, Peter Murphy 1908-1975 *WhAm 6*
McGavran, Edward Grafton 1902-1972
NatCAB 57, WhAm 5
McGaw, Alex James 1909- *WhAm 5*
McGaw, Francis Alexander 1857-1944
NatCAB 42
McGaw, George Keen 1850-1919 *NatCAB 31,*
WhAm 1
McGaw, John 1865-1948 *NatCAB 36*
McGeachin, George 1871-1949 *NatCAB 38*
McGeachy, Archibald Alexander 1869-1928
WhAm 1
McGee, Alice G 1869- *AmWom*
McGee, Anita Newcomb 1864-1940
ApCAB Sup, NatCAB 10, NotAW,
TwCBDA, WhAm 4, WomWWA 14
McGee, Charles Augustus Anson 1874-1955
NatCAB 41
McGee, Clifford W 1873-1958 *WhAm 3*
McGee, Cushman d1962 *WhAm 4*
McGee, Frank 1921-1974 *WhAm 6*
McGee, Gale William 1915- *BiDrAC*
McGee, Homer Edgar 1885-1963 *WhAm 4*
McGee, Hugh Henry 1885-1947 *NatCAB 36*
McGee, James Ellington 1868-1925 *WhAm 1*
McGee, John Bernard 1853-1923 *WhAm 1*
McGee, John Franklin 1861-1925 *WhAm 1*
McGee, Julia *NewYHSD*
McGee, Mark 1889-1953 *NatCAB 44*
McGee, Milton *WhAm H*
McGee, Reginald Everett 1916-1974 *WhAm 6*
McGee, Thomas D'Arcy 1825-1868 *ApCAB,*
Drake, WhAm H
McGee, W J 1853-1912 *ApCAB, NatCAB 10,*
WhAm 1
McGee, William John 1853-1912 *DcAmB*
McGeehan, William O'Connell 1879-1933
DcAmB S1, WhAm 1

McGeehee, Edward 1786-1880 *BiDConf*
McGeever, John F 1912-1969 *WhAm 5*
McGehee, Daniel Rayford 1883-1962 *BiDrAC*
McGehee, Harvey 1887-1965 *WhAm 4,*
WhAm 5
McGehee, Lucius Polk 1868-1923 *WhAm 1*
McGehee, Micijah C, Jr. 1903-1960 *WhAm 4*
McGeoch, John Alexander 1897-1942 *WhAm 2*
McGeoch, Peter 1833-1895 *NatCAB 7*
McGeorge, Thomas *NewYHSD*
McGeorge, William, Jr. 1841- *WhAm 4*
McGettigan, Charles Dominic 1873-1931
ApCAB X, NatCAB 50
McGettigan, Margaret Mary 1929-1974
WhAm 6
McGhee, Charles McClung 1828-1907 *DcAmB,*
NatCAB 12
McGhee, James E 1896-1964 *WhAm 4*
McGhee, Paul Ansley 1900-1964 *WhAm 4*
McGibbon, James *NewYHSD*
McGiffert, Arthur Cushman 1861-1933 *AmBi,*
ApCAB Sup, DcAmB S1, DcAmReB,
NatCAB 24, TwCBDA, WhAm 1
McGiffert, Gertrude Huntington Boyce
1869-1962 *NatCAB 51, WomWWA 14*
McGiffert, James 1863-1943 *WhAm 2*
McGiffert, John Rutherford 1869-1949
NatCAB 37
McGiffert, Julian Esselstyn 1885-1947 *WhAm 2*
McGiffin, Malcolm 1872-1934 *ApCAB X,*
WhAm 1, WhAm 1C
McGiffin, Philo Norton 1860-1897 *ApCAB Sup,*
DcAmB, NatCAB 25, WebAMB,
WhAm H
McGiffin, William J 1893-1955 *WhAm 3*
McGill, Alexander Taggart 1807-1889 *ApCAB,*
NatCAB 12, TwCBDA
McGill, Alexander Taggart 1843-1900 *ApCAB,*
NatCAB 12, TwCBDA
McGill, Andrew Ryan 1840-1905 *NatCAB 10,*
TwCBDA, WhAm 1
McGill, C H 1892-1966 *WhAm 4*
McGill, David Frazier 1857-1931 *WhAm 1*
McGill, George 1879-1963 *BiDrAC, WhAm 4*
McGill, George McCulloch 1838-1867 *ApCAB,*
NatCAB 12
McGill, Grace Collins 1885- *WomWWA 14*
McGill, J Nota 1867-1915 *WhAm 1*
McGill, James 1744-1813 *ApCAB, Drake*
McGill, James Henry 1848-1948 *WhAm 2*
McGill, John 1752-1834 *ApCAB*
McGill, John 1809-1872 *ApCAB, DcAmB,*
Drake Sup, NatCAB 10, TwCBDA,
WhAm H
McGill, John Dale 1846-1912 *WhAm 1*
McGill, John Thomas 1851-1946 *WhAm 2*
McGill, Mary E Wilson 1853- *WomWWA 14*
McGill, Peter 1789-1860 *ApCAB*
McGill, Ralph Emerson 1898-1969 *WhAm 5*
McGill, Stephenson Waters 1870- *WhAm 5*
McGill, Thomas Julian 1876-1936 *WhAm 1*
McGill, William L 1899-1959 *WhAm 3*
McGillicuddy, Cornelius *WebAB*
McGillicuddy, Daniel John 1859-1936 *BiDrAC,*
WhAm 1
McGillicuddy, Robert James 1908-1967
NatCAB 53
McGillivray, A C *NewYHSD*
McGillivray, Alexander 1739-1793 *EncAAH*
McGillivray, Alexander 1740-1793 *ApCAB*
McGillivray, Alexander 1746-1793 *NatCAB 18*
McGillivray, Alexander 1759?-1793 *AmBi,*
DcAmB, McGEWB, REnAW, WebAB,
WebAMB, WhAm H
McGillivray, Alexander *see also* MacGillivray,
Alexander
McGillycuddy, Valentine T O'Connell 1849-
WhAm 4
McGilton, Edmund George Burke 1859-1933
NatCAB 25
McGilvary, Daniel 1828-1911 *DcAmB*
McGilvary, Evander Bradley 1864-1953
WhAm 3
McGilvery, Freeman 1823-1864 *ApCAB,*
NatCAB 4
McGilvia, Edith Jennette 1855- *WomWWA 14*
McGilvra, John Jay 1827-1903 *NatCAB 14*
McGilvra, Ralph Donald 1913-1962 *NatCAB 51*

McGilvrey, John Edward 1867-1945 *WhAm 3*
McGimsey, Benjamin Brooks 1888-1971
 NatCAB 57
McGinley, Anna Mathilda Agnes 1868-
 WhAm 4
McGinley, Charles Calvin 1866- *WhAm 4*
McGinley, Daniel Eugene 1846-1904 *WhAm 1*
McGinley, Donald Francis 1920- *BiDrAC*
McGinley, John Rainey 1851-1926 *NatCAB 22*
McGinley, Paul Anthony 1915-1964
 NatCAB 52
McGinley, Thomas Atterbury 1880-1940
 NatCAB 29
McGinn, John Labbe 1871-1959 *NatCAB 47*
McGinness, John Randolph 1840-1918 *WhAm 1*
McGinnies, Joseph A 1861-1945 *WhAm 2*
McGinnis, Alan Ross 1897-1960 *WhAm 4*
McGinnis, Clara Buchanan 1859-
 WomWWA 14
McGinnis, Edward Francis 1897-1973 *WhAm 6*
McGinnis, Edwin 1877-1933 *WhAm 1*
McGinnis, Felix Signoret 1883-1945 *WhAm 2*
McGinnis, George 1858- *WhAm 4*
McGinnis, George Francis 1826- *ApCAB,*
 NatCAB 4, TwCBDA
McGinnis, Mary Bladen 1877- *WomWWA 14*
McGinnis, Orville Webster 1869-1934
 NatCAB 37
McGinnis, Patrick Benedict 1904-1973 *WhAm 5*
McGinnis, William F 1867-1932 *WhAm 1*
McGinnis, William Hereford 1855-1930
 WhAm 1
McGinty, Abner Crawford 1872-1962
 NatCAB 49
McGinty, Francis Patrick 1888-1949 *WhAm 3*
McGinty, George Banks 1878-1937 *WhAm 1*
McGirk, Matthias 1790- *NatCAB 12*
McGirth, Daniel d1789 *ApCAB*
McGittergan, Thomas, Jr. *NewYHSD*
McGiveran, Stanley James 1904-1967 *WhAm 4*
McGiveran, Stanley James 1905-1967
 NatCAB 54
McGivney, Michael Joseph 1852-1890 *DcAmB,*
 WhAm H
McGlachlin, Edward Fenton 1868-1946
 WhAm 2
McGlachlin, Elizabeth Gardiner 1868-
 WomWWA 14
McGlannan, Alexius 1872-1940 *NatCAB 29,*
 WhAm 1
McGlannan, Sally Porter Law *WomWWA 14*
McGlauflin, William Henry 1856-1927
 WhAm 1
McGlennon, Cornelius Augustine 1878-1931
 BiDrAC, NatCAB 23, WhAm 1
McGlinchey, Herbert Joseph 1904- *BiDrAC*
McGlinchey, John 1838-1916 *NatCAB 19*
McGlinn, John Alexander, Jr. 1911-1974
 WhAm 6
McGlothlan, Arthur B 1873-1961 *NatCAB 50*
McGlothlin, William Joseph 1867-1933
 DcAmB S1, WhAm 1
McGlynn, Edward 1837- *ApCAB, NatCAB 9*
McGlynn, Edward 1837-1899 *WhAm 1*
McGlynn, Edward 1837-1900 *AmBi, DcAmB,*
 DcAmReB, TwCBDA
McGlynn, Frank 1866-1951 *WhAm 3*
McGlynn, James Vincent 1919-1973 *WhAm 6*
McGoey, Thomas *NewYHSD*
McGoffin, John 1813- *NewYHSD*
McGohey, John F X d1972 *WhAm 5*
McGoldrick, Edward Joseph 1871-1951
 NatCAB 42
McGoldrick, James Patrick 1859-1939
 NatCAB 34
McGoldrick, John Kenneth 1879-1952
 NatCAB 44
McGoldrick, Thomas Aloysius 1874-1956
 WhAm 3
McGolrick, James 1841-1918 *NatCAB 19,*
 WhAm 1
McGolrick, James 1844-1918 *ApCAB Sup*
McGonagle, William Albert 1861-1930
 NatCAB 22, WhAm 1
McGonigal, George John 1892-1953
 NatCAB 46
McGonigle, William, Jr. *NewYHSD*
McGoodwin, Henry Kerr 1871- *WhAm 1*

McGoodwin, Preston 1880- *WhAm 6*
McGoorty, John P d1953 *WhAm 3*
McGovern, Francis Edward 1866-1946
 NatCAB 17, WhAm 2
McGovern, George Stanley 1922- *BiDrAC,*
 EncAAH, EncAB, McGEWB, WebAB
McGovern, J Raymond 1898-1974 *WhAm 6*
McGovern, James Lawrence 1869-1952
 WhAm 3
McGovern, John 1850-1917 *DcAmB, WhAm 1*
McGovern, John Joseph 1864- *NatCAB 16*
McGovern, John Terence 1876-1960 *WhAm 4*
McGovern, John W d1975 *WhAm 6*
McGovern, Patrick Alphonsus 1872-1951
 NatCAB 15, WhAm 3
McGovern, Philip Patrick 1901-1971
 NatCAB 55, WhAm 6
McGovern, Thomas 1832-1898 *ApCAB Sup,*
 NatCAB 13, TwCBDA
McGovern, Thomas Arnold 1908-1971
 NatCAB 56
McGovern, William Montgomery 1897-1964
 WhAm 4
McGovern, William Robbins d1964 *WhAm 4*
McGovney, Dudley Odell 1877-1947 *WhAm 2*
McGowan, Lord d1961 *WhAm 4*
McGowan, Arthur C 1892-1958 *WhAm 3*
McGowan, Edwin W 1894-1955 *WhAm 3*
McGowan, Emmett Daniel 1859-1944
 NatCAB 38
McGowan, Hugh Joseph 1857-1911 *NatCAB 5,*
 NatCAB 27
McGowan, James, Jr. 1886-1961 *WhAm 4*
McGowan, John 1805-1891 *TwCBDA*
McGowan, John 1843-1915 *WhAm 1*
McGowan, John Denis 1853-1946 *NatCAB 35*
McGowan, Jonas Hartzell 1837-1909 *BiDrAC,*
 TwCBDA
McGowan, Samuel 1819-1897 *ApCAB Sup,*
 BiDConf, DcAmB, NatCAB 25,
 TwCBDA, WhAm H
McGowan, Samuel 1870-1934 *WhAm 1*
McGowen, James Greer 1870-1941 *WhAm 2*
McGowen, Norris Cochran 1890-1969
 NatCAB 55
McGown, Chester Stowe 1870- *WhAm 5*
McGown, Floyd 1862-1921 *NatCAB 6*
McGowran *NewYHSD*
McGrady, Edward Francis 1872-1960 *WhAm 4*
McGrady, Thomas 1863- *WhAm 1*
McGraft, Newcomb Farwell 1840-1904
 NatCAB 27
McGrail, John 1891-1945 *NatCAB 38*
McGranahan, James 1840-1907 *WhAm 1*
McGranahan, Ralph Wilson 1862-1936
 WhAm 1
McGranahan, Raymond Depue 1914-1970
 WhAm 5
McGrane, Miles Ambrose 1877-1947
 NatCAB 35
McGranery, James Patrick 1895-1962 *BiDrAC,*
 BiDrUSE, WhAm 4
McGrann, William Hugh 1870-1945
 NatCAB 35
McGrath, A G *BiAUS*
McGrath, Benjamin R 1873-1940 *WhAm 1*
McGrath, Bonnie Hill 1877- *WomWWA 14*
McGrath, Christopher Columbus 1902- *BiDrAC*
McGrath, Earl James 1902- *BiDAmEd*
McGrath, James *NewYHSD*
McGrath, James 1835-1898 *DcAmB,*
 WhAm H
McGrath, James Howard 1903-1966 *BiDrAC,*
 BiDrUSE, NatCAB 52, WhAm 4
McGrath, John Joseph 1868-1953 *WhAm 3*
McGrath, John Joseph 1872-1951 *BiDrAC*
McGrath, John Wesley 1842- *NatCAB 5*
McGrath, Joseph F d1950 *WhAm 3*
McGrath, Justin 1867-1931 *WhAm 1*
McGrath, Sister Mary 1896-1970 *WhAm 5*
McGrath, Mary Carson *WomWWA 14*
McGrath, Matthew J 1876-1941 *DcAmB S3*
McGrath, Raymond Dyer 1890-1971 *WhAm 5*
McGrath, Thomas Charles, Jr. 1927- *BiDrAC*
McGrath, William H 1879-1954 *WhAm 3*
McGrath, William Louis 1885-1947 *NatCAB 40*
McGraw, Curtis Whittlesey 1895-1953
 WhAm 3

McGraw, Donald C 1897-1974 *WhAm 6*
McGraw, Edward Walker 1837-1921
 NatCAB 20
McGraw, Frank 1893-1949 *NatCAB 37*
McGraw, Frank H 1871- *WhAm 6*
McGraw, James Henry, Jr. 1893-1970
 NatCAB 56, WhAm 5
McGraw, James Herbert 1860-1948 *DcAmB S4,*
 WhAm 2
McGraw, James J 1874-1928 *WhAm 1*
McGraw, Jennie *ApCAB*
McGraw, John 1815-1877 *ApCAB, TwCBDA*
McGraw, John Harte 1850-1910 *DcAmB,*
 NatCAB 12, WhAm 38, WhAm 1
McGraw, John Joseph 1873-1934 *DcAmB S1,*
 WebAB, WhAm HA, WhAm 4
McGraw, John Thomas 1856-1920 *WhAm 1*
McGraw, Maria Loraine Dickinson 1843-
 WomWWA 14
McGraw, Max 1883-1964 *WhAm 4*
McGraw, Robert Bush 1896-1960 *WhAm 4*
McGraw, Theodore Alexander 1875-1924
 NatCAB 20
McGraw, Theodore Andrews 1839-1921
 NatCAB 20, WhAm 1
McGready, James 1758?-1817 *AmBi, ApCAB,*
 DcAmB, DcAmReB, WhAm H
McGregor, Alexander Grant 1880-1949
 WhAm 3
McGregor, Archie James 1904-1962
 NatCAB 50
McGregor, David 1710-1777 *Drake*
McGregor, David *see also* MacGregor, David
McGregor, Douglas Murray 1906-1964
 NatCAB 52, WhAm 4
McGregor, Edward *NewYHSD*
McGregor, George Wilbur 1853- *WhAm 4*
McGregor, Gordon Roy 1901-1971 *WhAm 5*
McGregor, J Harry 1896-1958 *BiDrAC,*
 WhAm 3, WhAmP
McGregor, James Clyde 1883-1940 *WhAm 1*
McGregor, James Howard 1872-1954 *WhAm 3*
McGregor, Robert Gardner 1870- *WhAm 2*
McGregor, Stuart Malcolm 1892-1963 *WhAm 4*
McGregor, Thomas 1837-1921 *WhAm 1*
McGregor, Thomas Burnett 1881-1965
 NatCAB 51, WhAm 4
McGregor, Tracy William 1869-1936
 NatCAB 34, WhAm 1
McGregor, W Eugene 1869-1939 *NatCAB 30*
McGregor, William Morrell 1869- *WhAm 5*
McGregory, Joseph Frank 1855-1934 *TwCBDA,*
 WhAm 1
McGrew, Clarence Alan 1875- *WhAm 5*
McGrew, Dallas Dayton Lore 1881- *WhAm 6*
McGrew, Donald Cargill 1904-1962 *WhAm 4*
McGrew, George Harrison 1846-1917 *WhAm 1*
McGrew, George Smith 1851- *NatCAB 9*
McGrew, Henry Edwin 1868- *WhAm 5*
McGrew, J M *BiAUS*
McGrew, James Clark 1813-1910 *BiAUS,*
 BiDrAC, TwCBDA
McGrew, John Gilbert 1910-1968 *WhAm 5*
McGrew, Julia Bird 1862- *WomWWA 14*
McGrew, Ralph Brownell 1916- *IIBEAAW*
McGrigor, Sir James 1771-1858 *BiHiMed*
McGrigor, Sir Rhoderick 1893-1959 *WhAm 3*
McGroarty, John Steven 1862-1944 *BiDrAC,*
 WhAm 2, WhAmP
McGroarty, Sister Julia 1827-1901 *NotAW*
McGroarty, Stephen Joseph 1830-1870 *ApCAB*
McGroarty, Susan 1827-1901 *BiDAmEd,*
 DcAmB, WhAm H
McGuffey, Margaret D *WomWWA 14*
McGuffey, William Holmes 1800-1873 *AmBi,*
 ApCAB, BiDAmEd, DcAmB, EncAAH,
 EncAB, McGEWB, NatCAB 4,
 TwCBDA, WebAB, WhAm H
McGugin, Dan E 1879-1936 *WhAm 1*
McGugin, Harold Clement 1893-1946 *BiDrAC,*
 WhAm 2
McGuigan, F H *WhAm 3*
McGuigan, Henry Thomas 1875-1958
 NatCAB 48
McGuigan, Hugh 1874-1964 *WhAm 4,*
 WhAm 5
McGuigan, James 1819?- *NewYHSD*
McGuigan, James Charles 1894-1974 *WhAm 6*

McGuigan, Joseph J 1876- *WhAm 5*
McGuiness, James John 1903-1966 *NatCAB 53*
McGuinn, Warner T 1863- *WhoColR*
McGuinness, Eugene Joseph 1889-1957
 NatCAB 45, WhAm 3
McGuire, Alice Rebecca Brooks 1902-1975
 DcAmLiB, WhAm 6
McGuire, Andrew Thomas 1911-1975 *WhAm 6*
McGuire, Bird Segle 1865-1930 *BiDrAC,
 WhAm 4, WhAmP*
McGuire, Charles Bonaventure 1768-1833
 DcAmB, WhAm H
McGuire, Edgar Robinson 1877-1931 *WhAm 1*
McGuire, Edna Leona 1878- *WomWWA 14*
McGuire, Floyd Edward 1902-1964 *NatCAB 53*
McGuire, Frank Augustine 1851-1921
 NatCAB 6
McGuire, Frederick Thomas, Jr. 1905-1966
 NatCAB 52
McGuire, George Alexander 1866-1934
 WhAm 1
McGuire, Hunter Holmes 1835-1900 *ApCAB,
 ApCAB Sup, BiDConf, DcAmB,
 NatCAB 5, NatCAB 27, TwCBDA,
 WhAm 1*
McGuire, Hunter Holmes 1875-1949
 NatCAB 42
McGuire, James Clark 1867-1930 *WhAm 1*
McGuire, James Kennedy 1868-1923 *NatCAB 7,
 WhAm 3*
McGuire, John *NewYHSD*
McGuire, John 1858- *WhAm 4*
McGuire, John A 1869-1942 *WhAm 2*
McGuire, John Andrew 1906- *BiDrAC*
McGuire, John Francis 1864-1932 *NatCAB 27*
McGuire, John Peyton 1866-1948 *NatCAB 38*
McGuire, Joseph Deakins 1842-1916 *DcAmB,
 WhAm 1*
McGuire, Joseph Hubert 1865-1947 *WhAm 2*
McGuire, Lee Wesley 1883-1959 *NatCAB 48*
McGuire, Lloyd Horace 1904-1964 *NatCAB 53*
McGuire, Louis David 1893-1955 *WhAm 3*
McGuire, Martin Rawson Patrick 1897-1969
 WhAm 5
McGuire, Michael Francis 1886-1951 *WhAm 3*
McGuire, Michael Francis 1887-1951
 NatCAB 40
McGuire, Murray Mason 1872-1945
 NatCAB 34, WhAm 2
McGuire, Ollie Roscoe 1892-1963 *WhAm 4*
McGuire, Stuart 1867-1948 *ApCAB X,
 NatCAB 37, WhAm 2*
McGuire, Thomas B, Jr. 1920-1945 *WebAMB*
McGuire, Ulysses Melville 1856-1939 *WhAm 1*
McGuire, William *BiAUS*
McGuire, William Anthony 1887-1940 *WhAm 1*
McGunnegle, George Kennedy 1854- *WhAm 4*
McGurk, Edward A 1841-1896 *TwCBDA*
McGurk, Joseph F 1892-1962 *WhAm 4*
McGus *NewYHSD*
McHale, Frank Martin 1891-1975 *WhAm 6*
McHale, Kathryn 1889-1956 *NatCAB 45,
 WhAm 3*
McHaney, Edgar LaFayette 1876-1948
 WhAm 2
McHaney, Powell B 1905-1957 *WhAm 3*
McHarg, Henry King 1851-1941 *NatCAB 29,
 WhAm 1*
McHarg, Ormsby 1871- *WhAm 5*
McHattie, William Alexander 1902-1972
 WhAm 5
McHatton, Henry 1856-1917 *NatCAB 18*
McHatton, Robert Lytle 1788-1835 *BiAUS,
 BiDrAC, WhAm H*
McHendrie, Andrew Watson 1874- *WhAm 5*
McHenry, Carl Holbrook 1887-1960 *WhAm 4*
McHenry, Donald Edward 1895- *WhAm 5*
McHenry, Edwin Harrison 1859-1931
 NatCAB 24, WhAm 4
McHenry, Henry Davis 1826-1890 *BiAUS,
 BiDrAC, WhAm H*
McHenry, Isaac *NewYHSD*
McHenry, James 1753-1816 *AmBi, ApCAB,
 BiDrAC, BiDrUSE, DcAmB, Drake,
 NatCAB 1, TwCBDA, WhAm H,
 WhAmP*
McHenry, James 1755?-1816 *BiAUS*
McHenry, James 1785-1845 *ApCAB, DcAmB,*

TwCBDA, WhAm H
McHenry, James 1817- *ApCAB*
McHenry, John Geiser 1868-1912 *BiDrAC,
 WhAm 1*
McHenry, John Hardin 1797-1871 *BiAUS,
 BiDrAC, TwCBDA, WhAm H*
McHenry, Junius Hardin 1876-1953 *ApCAB X,
 NatCAB 42*
McHenry, Mary *ApCAB*
McHenry, Mary Sears 1834- *AmWom*
McHenry, Troy Lee 1912-1956 *NatCAB 44*
McHenry, William Harrison, Jr. 1860-1925
 NatCAB 20
McHugh, Anna 1873-1944 *BiDAmEd*
McHugh, Daniel Joseph 1877-1965 *WhAm 4*
McHugh, Isaac *NewYHSD*
McHugh, James F 1894-1969 *WhAm 5*
McHugh, John *NewYHSD*
McHugh, John 1865-1948 *WhAm 2*
McHugh, Kate A 1855- *WomWWA 14*
McHugh, Keith Stratton 1895-1975 *WhAm 6*
McHugh, Lerah G *WomWWA 14*
McHugh, Olivia Henderson 1881-
 WomWWA 14
McHugh, Rose John 1881-1952 *DcAmB S5*
McHugh, William Douglas 1859-1923 *WhAm 1*
McIlhenney, Charles Morgan 1858-1904
 ApCAB, TwCBDA, WhAm 1
McIlhenny, Edward Avery 1872-1949 *WhAm 2*
McIlhenny, Francis Salisbury 1873-1927
 WhAm 1
McIlhenny, John Avery 1867- *WhAm 4*
McIlhenny, John D 1866-1925 *WhAm 1*
McIlhiney, Parker Cairns 1870-1923 *WhAm 1*
McIlroy, Carol 1924- *IlBEAAW*
McIlroy, Malcolm Strong 1902-1956 *WhAm 3*
McIlvain, J Gibson 1845-1920 *NatCAB 27*
McIlvain, Robert Wallace 1875-1959
 NatCAB 48, WhAm 3
McIlvaine, Abraham Robinson 1804-1863
 BiAUS, BiDrAC, TwCBDA, WhAm H
McIlvaine, Caroline Margaret *BiCAW*
McIlvaine, Charles 1840-1909 *WhAm 1*
McIlvaine, Charles Pettit 1799-1873 *ApCAB,
 DcAmB, DcAmReB, NatCAB 7,
 TwCBDA, WhAm H*
McIlvaine, Charles Pettit *see also* Macilvaine,
 Charles Pettit
McIlvaine, George W *NatCAB 12*
McIlvaine, Harold Ralph Clair 1912-1962
 WhAm 4
McIlvaine, James Hall 1846-1921 *WhAm 1*
McIlvaine, John Wilson 1907-1963 *WhAm 4*
McIlvaine, Joseph 1765-1826 *TwCBDA*
McIlvaine, Joseph 1768-1826 *ApCAB, BiAUS,
 Drake, NatCAB 11*
McIlvaine, Joseph 1769-1826 *BiDrAC,
 WhAm H*
McIlvaine, Joshua Hall 1815-1897 *ApCAB,
 NatCAB 5, TwCBDA*
McIlvaine, William, Jr. 1813-1867 *IlBEAAW,
 NewYHSD, WhAm H*
McIlvaine, William Brown d1943 *WhAm 2*
McIlwain, Charles Howard 1871- *WhAm 6*
McIlwaine, Henry Read 1864-1934 *WhAm 1*
McIlwaine, Richard 1834-1913 *ApCAB,
 DcAmB, NatCAB 2, TwCBDA,
 WhAm 4*
McIlwaine, William Baird 1854-1930
 NatCAB 10, NatCAB 23, WhAm 1
McIlworth, Thomas *NewYHSD*
McIlwraith, Jean Newton *WomWWA 14*
McIlwraith, William Forsythe 1867-1940
 IlBEAAW
McIlwrath, William 1834-1910 *NatCAB 6*
McInally, William Keith 1905-1964 *WhAm 4*
McIndoe, Archibald 1900- *WhWW-II*
McIndoe, Walter Duncan 1819-1872 *BiAUS,
 BiDrAC, TwCBDA, WhAm H*
McInerney, Francis Xavier 1899-1956
 NatCAB 46, WhAm 3
McInerney, James Lawrence 1888-1968
 WhAm 5
McInerney, Michael Joseph 1905-1967
 NatCAB 53
McInerny, John Joseph 1895-1966 *WhAm 4*
McInerny, Timothy A 1902-1965 *WhAm 4*
McInnerney, Thomas H 1867-1952 *WhAm 3*

McInnes, Thomas Robert 1840- *ApCAB*
McInnis, Charles Ballard 1899-1970 *WhAm 5*
McInnis, Edgar Wardwell 1899-1973 *WhAm 6*
McIntire, Albert Washington 1853-1935
 NatCAB 6, WhAm 1, WhAm 1C
McIntire, Charles 1847- *NatCAB 12,
 WhAm 1*
McIntire, Charles John 1842-1927 *NatCAB 14,
 NatCAB 22*
McIntire, Clifford Guy 1908-1974 *BiDrAC,
 WhAm 6, WhAmP*
McIntire, Homer Marlatte 1885-1956
 NatCAB 43
McIntire, Ida Noyes 1859- *WomWWA 14*
McIntire, James Franklin 1882-1951
 NatCAB 41
McIntire, John *NewYHSD*
McIntire, Paul Goodloe 1860-1952 *NatCAB 41,
 WhAm 3*
McIntire, Ross T 1889-1959 *NatCAB 48,
 WhAm 3*
McIntire, Rufus 1784-1866 *BiDrAC, TwCBDA*
McIntire, Rufus *see also* McIntyre, Rufus
McIntire, Samuel 1757-1811 *AmBi, BnEnAmA,
 DcAmB, McGEWB, NewYHSD, WebAB,
 WhAm H*
McIntire, Samuel Field 1780-1819 *NewYHSD*
McIntire, Virlon Willard 1889-1963
 NatCAB 50
McIntire, Walter Oscar 1875- *WhAm 5*
McIntire, Warren Wallace 1869-1922 *WhAm 1*
McIntire, William Watson 1850-1912 *BiDrAC*
McIntosh, Alexander Angus 1874-1950
 WhAm 3
McIntosh, Alexander Ennis 1899-1964 *WhAm 4*
McIntosh, Arthur Tuttle 1877-1955 *WhAm 3*
McIntosh, Bella Marcuse *WomWWA 14*
McIntosh, Benjamin Harrison 1881- *WhAm 6*
McIntosh, Bruce 1874-1966 *NatCAB 52*
McIntosh, Burr 1862-1942 *WhAm 2*
McIntosh, Charles Herbert 1875- *WhAm 5*
McIntosh, Charles Kenneth 1867-1950
 NatCAB 44, WhAm 3
McIntosh, David Gregg 1836-1916 *NatCAB 29*
McIntosh, David Gregg, Jr. 1877-1940
 NatCAB 29
McIntosh, Donald d1915 *WhAm 3*
McIntosh, Donald Alexander 1843-1915
 ApCAB X
McIntosh, Duncan d1820 *Drake*
McIntosh, Elizabeth E *WomWWA 14*
McIntosh, Franklin Gray 1875-1940
 NatCAB 29
McIntosh, Harry Milne 1856-1932 *NatCAB 25*
McIntosh, Henry Payne 1846-1935 *WhAm 1*
McIntosh, Henry Thomas 1874-1965 *WhAm 4*
McIntosh, Horace Parker 1852-1929
 NatCAB 28
McIntosh, James Alexander 1845-1916
 ApCAB X
McIntosh, James Henry 1858-1941 *WhAm 1*
McIntosh, James McKay 1792-1860 *ApCAB,
 Drake, TwCBDA*
McIntosh, James McQueen 1828-1862 *ApCAB,
 TwCBDA*
McIntosh, James Simmons 1787-1847 *ApCAB,
 Drake, TwCBDA*
McIntosh, John 1755-1826 *ApCAB, Drake,
 TwCBDA*
McIntosh, John Alexander 1878-1965
 NatCAB 52
McIntosh, John Baillie 1829-1888 *ApCAB,
 DcAmB, Drake, TwCBDA, WhAm H*
McIntosh, Joseph Wallace 1873-1952 *WhAm 3*
McIntosh, Kate Hamilton Pier 1868-
 WomWWA 14
McIntosh, Lachlan 1725-1806 *AmBi, ApCAB,
 BiDrAC, DcAmB, Drake, NatCAB 1,
 TwCBDA, WebAMB, WhAm H*
McIntosh, Loy N 1890-1973 *WhAm 6*
McIntosh, Maria Jane 1803-1878 *ApCAB,
 Drake, NatCAB 6, NotAW, TwCBDA*
McIntosh, Minnie Dixson 1867- *WomWWA 14*
McIntosh, Robert John 1922- *BiDrAC*
McIntosh, Walter Kenneth 1878- *WhAm 2*
McIntosh, William 1775?-1825 *AmBi, ApCAB,
 DcAmB, Drake, EncAAH, NatCAB 9,
 WebAMB, WhAm H*

McIntosh, William Arthur 1860-1951
NatCAB 40

McIntosh, William M 1876-1946 *WhAm 2*

McIntyre, Albert Washington 1853- *TwCBDA*

McIntyre, Alexander Fraser 1847- *ApCAB*

McIntyre, Alfred Robert 1886-1948 *DcAmB S4,*
WhAm 2

McIntyre, Archibald Thompson 1822-1900
BiAUS

McIntyre, Archibald Thompson *see also*
MacIntyre, Archibald T

McIntyre, Augustine 1876-1954 *WhAm 3*

McIntyre, Brouwer Davis 1905- *WhAm 4*

McIntyre, Daniel Eugene 1812- *ApCAB*

McIntyre, Florence Percy *WomWWA 14*

McIntyre, Frank 1865-1944 *NatCAB 32,*
WhAm 2

McIntyre, Frank 1877-1949 *NatCAB 38*

McIntyre, Frederick W 1887-1959 *WhAm 4*

McIntyre, Glenn Smith 1884-1962 *NatCAB 48*

McIntyre, Hugh Henry 1844-1906 *WhAm 1*

McIntyre, James 1857-1937 *DcAmB S2*

McIntyre, John Francis 1855- *WhAm 4*

McIntyre, John Joseph 1904- *BiDrAC*

McIntyre, John T 1871-1951 *WhAm 3*

McIntyre, Louise L LeVerenz 1862-
WomWWA 14

McIntyre, Lydia Fletcher 1876- *WomWWA 14*

McIntyre, Marvin Hunter 1878-1943 *WhAm 2*

McIntyre, Oscar Odd 1884-1938 *AmBi,*
DcAmB S2, NatCAB 36, WhAm 1

McIntyre, Peter 1818- *ApCAB*

McIntyre, Peter Adolphus 1840- *ApCAB*

McIntyre, Robert 1851-1914 *NatCAB 14,*
NatCAB 16, WhAm 1

McIntyre, Robert Allen 1899-1967 *NatCAB 54*

McIntyre, Robson Duncan 1899-1971 *WhAm 5*

McIntyre, Ross 1847-1947 *NatCAB 35*

McIntyre, Rufus 1784-1866 *BiAUS, WhAm H*

McIntyre, Rufus *see also* McIntire, Rufus

McIntyre, Thomas Alexander 1855- *NatCAB 4*

McIntyre, Thomas James 1915- *BiDrAC*

McIntyre, William Davis 1906-1964
NatCAB 50, WhAm 4

McIntyre, William H 1865-1947 *WhAm 2*

McIntyre, William Howell 1887-1947
NatCAB 40

McIsaac, Archibald MacDonald 1903-1960
WhAm 3

McIver, Alexander 1822- *TwCBDA*

McIver, Angus Vaughn 1892-1974 *WhAm 6*

McIver, Charles Duncan 1860-1906 *BiDAmEd,*
DcAmB, NatCAB 25, TwCBDA,
WhAm 1

McIver, George Willcox 1858-1947 *WhAm 3*

McIver, Henry 1826-1903 *NatCAB 7,*
TwCBDA, WhAm 1

McIver, John McMillan 1838-1923 *NatCAB 6*

McIver, Joseph 1886-1940 *WhAm 1*

McIver, Milo Kenneth 1897-1962 *NatCAB 51,*
WhAm 4

McIvor, Donald Guy 1890-1961 *NatCAB 50*

McIvor, Nicholas Williams 1860-1915 *WhAm 1*

McIvor-Tyndall, Alexander James d1940
WhAm 1

McJunkin, Ebenezer 1819-1907 *BiAUS,*
BiDrAC, TwCBDA

McKaig, William McMahon 1845-1907 *BiDrAC,*
TwCBDA

McKain, Arthur Albert 1851- *NatCAB 10*

McKamy, David Knox 1893-1957 *WhAm 3*

McKay *NewYHSD*

McKay, Alexander 1886-1953 *NatCAB 42*

McKay, Ambrose Noble 1868-1924 *WhAm 1*

McKay, Archibald 1879-1948 *NatCAB 37*

McKay, Claude d1948 *WhAm 5*

McKay, Claude 1889-1948 *DcAmB S4,*
WebAB

McKay, Claude 1890-1948 *McGEWB,*
WhAm 2

McKay, David 1860-1918 *NatCAB 42*

McKay, David Oman 1873-1970 *NatCAB 56,*
REnAW, WhAm 5

McKay, Donald 1809-1880 *Drake*

McKay, Donald 1810-1880 *AmBi, ApCAB,*
DcAmB, EncAB, McGEWB, NatCAB 2,
TwCBDA, WebAB, WhAm H

McKay, Donald Cope 1902-1959 *WhAm 3*

McKay, Douglas James 1893-1959 *BiDrUSE,*
EncAAH, NatCAB 50, WhAm 3

McKay, Florence Lucinda 1882-
WomWWA 14

McKay, Frederick Sumner 1874-1959 *WhAm 3*

McKay, George William 1899-1946 *NatCAB 36*

McKay, Gordon 1821-1903 *DcAmB,*
NatCAB 10

McKay, Horace 1841-1914 *NatCAB 16*

McKay, James 1815?-1879 *ApCAB*

McKay, James Iver 1792-1853 *DcAmB,*
WhAm H

McKay, James Iver 1793-1853 *BiDrAC,*
WhAmP

McKay, James J 1793-1853 *BiAUS,*
NatCAB 11, TwCBDA

McKay, John Angus 1864-1928 *NatCAB 26*

McKay, John Sophronus 1850-1917 *NatCAB 17*

McKay, Kenneth Ivor 1881-1945 *WhAm 2*

McKay, Llewelyn R 1904-1975 *WhAm 6*

McKay, Martha K 1848- *WomWWA 14*

McKay, Neal H 1896-1951 *WhAm 3*

McKay, Neil S 1898-1965 *WhAm 4*

McKay, Oscar Reed 1861-1942 *WhAm 2*

McKay, Paul Leonard 1917-1971 *WhAm 5*

McKay, Robert Stephenson 1871-1946
NatCAB 36

McKay, Seth Shepard 1888-1969 *WhAm 5*

McKay, Stanley Albert 1850- *WhAm 4*

McKay, Thomas Clayton 1922-1971 *WhAm 5*

McKay, Thomas Jefferson 1877-1956
NatCAB 50

McKay, William M 1887-1947 *WhAm 2*

McKay, William O 1889- *WhAm 3*

McKeag, Anna Jane 1864-1947 *WhAm 2,*
WomWWA 14

McKean, Andrew Porter 1870-1954 *NatCAB 40*

McKean, Frank Chalmers 1874-1958 *WhAm 3*

McKean, George Edwin 1868-1934 *NatCAB 26*

McKean, Horace Grant 1864-1927 *WhAm 1*

McKean, Hugh Kiefer 1904-1964 *WhAm 4*

McKean, James Bedell 1821-1879 *BiAUS,*
BiDrAC, TwCBDA, WhAm H

McKean, James William 1860-1949 *DcAmB S4,*
NatCAB 37

McKean, Joseph 1776-1818 *ApCAB, Drake,*
TwCBDA

McKean, Joseph Borden 1764-1826 *ApCAB,*
DcAmB, WhAm H

McKean, Josiah Slutts 1864-1951 *WhAm 3*

McKean, Richard Moore 1896-1961
NatCAB 49

McKean, Samuel d1840 *BiAUS*

McKean, Samuel 1787-1841 *BiDrAC, DcAmB,*
WhAm H, WhAmP

McKean, Samuel 1790-1840 *ApCAB,*
NatCAB 11, TwCBDA

McKean, Thomas 1734-1817 *AmBi, ApCAB,*
BiAUS, BiDrAC, BiDrUSE, DcAmB,
Drake, NatCAB 2, TwCBDA, WebAB,
WhAmP

McKean, Thomas 1735-1817 *WhAm H*

McKean, Thomas 1869-1942 *WhAm 1,*
WhAm 2

McKean, Thomas Jefferson 1810-1870 *ApCAB,*
TwCBDA

McKean, William Vincent 1820- *TwCBDA*

McKean, William Vincent 1820-1902 *WhAm 1*

McKean, William Vincent 1820-1903
NatCAB 8

McKean, William Wister 1800-1865 *ApCAB,*
DcAmB, TwCBDA, WebAMB, WhAm H

McKean, William Wister 1801-1865 *Drake*

McKechnie, Neil Kenneth 1873- *WhAm 5*

McKechnie, Robert Edward 1861-1944
WhAm 2

McKechnie, William Hobart 1867-1941
NatCAB 34

McKee, Alexander Ellsworth 1862-1934
WhAm 1

McKee, Andrew Irwin 1896-1976 *WhAm 6*

McKee, Arthur Glenn 1871-1956 *NatCAB 45,*
WhAm 5

McKee, Charles James 1892-1957 *NatCAB 46*

McKee, David Harris 1868- *WhAm 4*

McKee, David Ritchie 1842-1924 *WhAm 1*

McKee, Florence Cutcheon 1860-
WomWWA 14

McKee, Forest E 1893-1951 *NatCAB 41*

McKee, Frederick Chadwick 1891-1961
NatCAB 49, WhAm 4

McKee, Garnet 1877-1944 *NatCAB 34*

McKee, George Colin 1836?-1890 *ApCAB,*
TwCBDA

McKee, George Colin 1837-1890 *BiAUS,*
BiDrAC, WhAm H

McKee, George Wilson 1842-1891 *NatCAB 28*

McKee, Henry S 1868-1956 *WhAm 3*

McKee, James 1844- *TwCBDA*

McKee, James Robert 1857-1942 *NatCAB 33*

McKee, James S 1865-1927 *NatCAB 41*

McKee, Jesse Lynne 1881- *WhAm 6*

McKee, John 1771- *BiAUS*

McKee, John 1771-1832 *BiDrAC, DcAmB,*
WhAm H

McKee, John 1771-1834? *TwCBDA*

McKee, John 1851- *ApCAB X*

McKee, John Dempster 1865-1948 *WhAm 2*

McKee, Joseph V d1956 *WhAm 3*

McKee, Kenneth Newton 1903-1972
NatCAB 54

McKee, Oliver, Jr. 1893-1948 *WhAm 2*

McKee, Paul Boole 1891-1968 *WhAm 4A*

McKee, Paul Gordon 1897-1974 *WhAm 6*

McKee, Ralph Harper 1874- *WhAm 5*

McKee, Rose d1971 *WhAm 5*

McKee, Ruth Karr 1874-1951 *WhAm 3,*
WomWWA 14

McKee, Samuel 1774-1826 *BiAUS, BiDrAC,*
WhAm H

McKee, Samuel 1833-1898 *BiAUS, BiDrAC,*
TwCBDA

McKee, Sarah Galt Elwood 1842-
WomWWA 14

McKee, Sarah Hughes 1860- *WomWWA 14*

McKee, Sol Reid 1864- *WhAm 4*

McKee, William 1895-1974 *WhAm 6*

McKee, William James 1853-1925 *TwCBDA,*
WhAm 1

McKee, William James 1875-1957 *NatCAB 43*

McKee, William Meek 1877-1967 *NatCAB 53*

McKee, William Parker 1862-1933 *WhAm 1*

McKee, William R 1808-1847 *Drake*

McKeefry, Cardinal Peter 1899-1973 *WhAm 6*

McKeeghan, William Arthur 1842- *TwCBDA*

McKeehan, Charles Louis 1876-1925 *WhAm 1*

McKeehan, Hobart Deitrich 1897-1953
WhAm 3

McKeehan, Homer Hudson 1870-1938
NatCAB 29

McKeehan, Joseph Parker 1876-1950 *WhAm 3*

McKeehan, Louis Williams 1887-1975 *WhAm 6*

McKeel, Ben S 1898-1948 *WhAm 2*

McKeel, John Francis 1866-1954 *NatCAB 45*

McKeen, Benjamin 1864-1947 *WhAm 2*

McKeen, Helen Josephine *WomWWA 14*

McKeen, James 1797-1873 *NatCAB 15*

McKeen, James 1844-1910 *WhAm 1*

McKeen, James 1844-1911 *NatCAB 29*

McKeen, Joseph 1757-1807 *ApCAB, DcAmB,*
Drake, NatCAB 1, TwCBDA, WhAm H

McKeen, Stanley Stewart 1897-1966 *WhAm 4*

McKeen, William *NewYHSD*

McKeen, William Malcolm 1869-1938
NatCAB 29

McKeen, William Riley 1869- *WhAm 5*

McKeever, Arthur Garfield 1881-1949
NatCAB 40

McKeever, Chauncey 1828?-1901 *ApCAB,*
WhAm 1

McKeever, Chauncey 1829-1901 *TwCBDA*

McKeever, Duncan Clark 1905-1959
NatCAB 48, WhAm 4

McKeever, Emmet G d1947 *WhAm 2*

McKeever, Francis Michael 1901-1973 *WhAm 5*

McKeever, Franklin Garrett 1852-1922
WhAm 1

McKeever, Harriet Burn 1807-1886 *ApCAB*

McKeever, Isaac 1793-1856 *ApCAB*

McKeever, Isaac 1794-1856 *NatCAB 3,*
NatCAB 11, TwCBDA

McKeever, Isaac *see also* Mackeever, Isaac

McKeever, William Arch 1868-1940
NatCAB 40, NatCAB 47, WhAm 1

McKeighan, John Elmore 1841- *NatCAB 5*

McKeighan, William Arthur 1842-1895 *BiDrAC,*

WhAm H

McKeith, David, Jr. 1896-1961 *WhAm 4*

McKeldin, Theodore Roosevelt 1900-1974
WhAm 6

McKell, William E 1887-1964 *WhAm 4*

McKellar, Archibald 1816- *ApCAB*

McKellar, Kenneth Douglas 1869-1957
ApCAB X, BiDrAC, WhAm 3, WhAmP

McKellar, Margaret 1861- *WomWWA 14*

McKelvey, Gilbert Johnston 1906-1951
NatCAB 39

McKelvey, Graham Norton 1907-1972 *WhAm 5*

McKelvey, John Jay 1863- *WhAm 2*

McKelvey, Mary Mattocks 1862-
WomWWA 14

McKelvey, S Willis 1869- *WhAm 5*

McKelvie, Samuel Roy 1881-1956 *WhAm 3*

McKelvy, Blanche L 1858- *WomWWA 14*

McKelvy, David 1842-1918 *NatCAB 30*

McKelvy, Francis Graham 1883-1952 *WhAm 3*

McKelvy, J D 1892-1963 *WhAm 4*

McKelvy, John H 1837-1896 *NatCAB 12*

McKelvy, Robert 1875-1937 *NatCAB 27*

McKelvy, William Henry 1843-1909
NatCAB 39

McKelvy, William Rush 1904-1972 *WhAm 6*

McKelway, Alexander Jeffrey 1866-1918
WhAm 1

McKelway, St. Clair 1845-1915 *ApCAB Sup,
DcAmB, NatCAB 4, NatCAB 17,
TwCBDA, WhAm 1*

McKendree, William 1757-1835 *AmBi, ApCAB,
DcAmB, DcAmReB, Drake, NatCAB 10,
TwCBDA, WhAm H*

McKendrick, Edward John 1899-1968 *WhAm 5*

McKendry, John Joseph 1933-1975 *WhAm 6*

McKendry, William 1798- *ApCAB*

McKenna, Charles Francis 1861-1930 *WhAm 1*

McKenna, Charles Hyacinth 1835-1917 *DcAmB*

McKenna, Charles Morgan 1879-1945
NatCAB 34

McKenna, Edward William 1848- *WhAm 1*

McKenna, Henry Joseph 1885-1958 *NatCAB 45*

McKenna, James 1878-1955 *NatCAB 43*

McKenna, Joseph 1843-1926 *ApCAB Sup,
BiDrAC, BiDrUSE, DcAmB, NatCAB 11,
TwCBDA, WebAB, WhAm 1, WhAmP*

McKenna, Mrs. Joseph E *AmWom*

McKenna, Brother Joseph G 1922-1973
WhAm 6

McKenna, Norbert Augustine 1902-1964
WhAm 4

McKenna, Patrick Joseph 1897-1956
NatCAB 43

McKenna, Philip M 1897-1969 *WhAm 5*

McKenna, Roy Carnegie 1883-1958 *ApCAB X,
NatCAB 50, WhAm 3*

McKenna, William Joseph 1881-1950
NatCAB 40

McKennan, Thomas McKean Thompson
1794-1852 *ApCAB, BiAUS, BiDrAC,
BiDrUSE, DcAmB, NatCAB 29,
TwCBDA, WhAm H*

McKennan, Thomas McKean Thompson
1859-1935 *WhAm 1*

McKennan, William 1816- *BiAUS*

McKenney, A Carlton 1873-1950 *WhAm 3*

McKenney, Descum Clayton 1872-1947
NatCAB 36

McKenney, Frederic Duncan 1863-1949
WhAm 2

McKenney, Henrietta Foxhall 1825-1887
NewYHSD

McKenney, James Hall 1837-1913 *TwCBDA,
WhAm 1*

McKenney, Robert Lee 1865-1947 *WhAm 2*

McKenney, Ruth 1911-1972 *WhAm 5*

McKenney, Thomas Loraine 1785-1859 *DcAmB,
WhAm H*

McKenney, Thomas Lorraine 1785-1858 *BiAUS,
Drake*

McKenney, Thomas Lorraine 1785-1859 *ApCAB,
TwCBDA*

McKenney, William Robertson 1851-1916
BiDrAC, NatCAB 16

McKenny, Charles 1860-1933 *WhAm 1*

McKenny, Francis Xavier 1860- *WhAm 4*

McKenty, Jacob Kerlin 1827-1866 *BiAUS,*

BiDrAC, WhAm H

McKenzie, Alexander 1830-1914 *ApCAB,
DcAmB, NatCAB 11, TwCBDA,
WhAm 1*

McKenzie, Alexander John 1851-1922
NatCAB 32, REnAW

McKenzie, Aline 1882-1948 *WhAm 2*

McKenzie, Caleb *NewYHSD*

McKenzie, Carlton Dietly 1895-1960
NatCAB 48

McKenzie, Charles Edgar 1896-1956 *BiDrAC*

McKenzie, Donald *NewYHSD*

McKenzie, Ethel O'Neil 1880- *WomWWA 14*

McKenzie, Fayette Avery 1872-1957
NatCAB 44, WhAm 3

McKenzie, George 1871-1924 *WhAm 1*

McKenzie, Harry Carroll 1906-1963 *WhAm 4*

McKenzie, James Andrew 1840-1904 *BiDrAC,
NatCAB 13, WhAm 1*

McKenzie, James Andrew *see also* MacKenzie,
James A

McKenzie, John Charles 1860-1941 *BiDrAC,
WhAm 1, WhAmP*

McKenzie, John Cummings 1913-1962 *WhAm 4*

McKenzie, John Heyward 1862-1920 *WhAm 1*

McKenzie, Kenneth 1870-1949 *WhAm 2*

McKenzie, Lewis 1810-1895 *BiAUS, BiDrAC,
WhAm H*

McKenzie, Margaret McLeod Ross
WomWWA 14

McKenzie, Robert Tait 1867-1938 *AmBi,
BiDAmEd, DcAmB S2, WhAm 1*

McKenzie, Roderick Duncan 1885-1940
WhAm 1

McKenzie, Ronald 1898-1945 *NatCAB 35*

McKenzie, Vernon 1887-1963 *WhAm 4*

McKenzie, W Raymond 1890-1966 *NatCAB 53*

McKenzie, William 1841-1914 *NatCAB 15*

McKenzie, William Dexter 1873- *WhAm 5*

McKenzie, William Patrick 1861-1942
NatCAB 31, WhAm 1

McKenzie, William White 1869- *WhAm 5*

McKeogh, Arthur 1890-1937 *WhAm 1*

McKeon, Elsie McVitty 1880- *WomWWA 14*

McKeon, John d1883 *BiAUS*

McKeon, John 1804-1883 *NatCAB 6*

McKeon, John 1807-1883 *TwCBDA*

McKeon, John 1808-1883 *ApCAB, BiDrAC,
NatCAB 3, WhAm H*

McKeon, John J 1877-1948 *WhAm 2*

McKeon, Thomas *NewYHSD*

McKeon, Thomas James 1867-1938 *NatCAB 33*

McKeon, William *NewYHSD*

McKeough, Raymond Stephen 1888- *BiDrAC*

McKeown, Elmer Eason 1879-1947 *NatCAB 36*

McKeown, Hugh Spencer 1895-1944
NatCAB 34

McKeown, J L G *NatCAB 5*

McKeown, Thomas Deitz 1878-1951 *BiDrAC,
WhAm H*

McKeown, Tom D 1878-1951 *WhAm 3*

McKernan, Maureen 1893-1968 *WhAm 5*

McKernon, Edward d1943 *WhAm 2*

McKerr, George Joseph 1893-1963 *WhAm 4*

McKerroll, Mary Catharine 1877-
WomWWA 14

McKesson, Claude Leon 1881-1952 *NatCAB 41*

McKesson, Elmer Isaac 1881-1935 *NatCAB 25*

McKesson, Irving 1872-1958 *NatCAB 43*

McKesson, John 1807- *NatCAB 3*

McKey, Martin *NewYHSD*

McKibben, Frank Pape 1871-1936 *WhAm 1*

McKibben, George Fitch 1851- *TwCBDA*

McKibben, James A 1868- *WhAm 4*

McKibben, Paul Stilwell 1886-1941 *WhAm 1*

McKibben, William Watson 1874-1968
NatCAB 54

McKibbin, Chambers 1841-1919 *ApCAB Sup,
TwCBDA, WhAm 1*

McKibbin, George Baldwin 1888-1960
NatCAB 49, WhAm 4

McKibbin, John 1836- *WhAm 4*

McKibbin, Joseph Chambers 1824-1896 *BiAUS,
BiDrAC, WhAm H*

McKibbin, William 1850-1931 *WhAm 1*

McKillican, Janet *WomWWA 14*

McKim, Alexander 1748-1832 *BiAUS, BiDrAC,
TwCBDA, WhAm H, WhAmP*

McKim, Baltimore 1775-1838 *WhAm H*

McKim, Charles Follen 1847-1909 *AmBi,
ApCAB, ApCAB X, BnEnAmA, DcAmB,
DcAmLiB, McGEWB, NatCAB 11,
NatCAB 23, TwCBDA, WebAB,
WhAm 1*

McKim, Henrietta 1868- *WomWWA 14*

McKim, Isaac 1775-1838 *BiAUS, BiDrAC,
DcAmB, TwCBDA, WhAm H, WhAmP*

McKim, James Miller 1810-1874 *ApCAB,
DcAmB, NatCAB 2, TwCBDA,
WhAm H*

McKim, John 1852-1936 *NatCAB 13,
TwCBDA, WhAm 1*

McKim, Judson J 1877-1948 *WhAm 2*

McKim, Randolph Harrison 1842- *TwCBDA*

McKim, Randolph Harrison 1842-1920
ApCAB X

McKim, Randolph Harrison 1842-1921
WhAm 1

McKim, Robert 1816-1887 *ApCAB*

McKim, Robert James 1895-1973 *WhAm 6*

McKim, William Duncan 1855-1935
NatCAB 34, WhAm 1

McKim, William Julian Albert 1870-1932
NatCAB 23

McKimmon, Jane Simpson 1869- *WhAm 5*

McKiniry, Richard Francis 1878-1950 *BiDrAC,
WhAm 6*

McKinlay, Arthur Patch 1871-1958 *NatCAB 47,
WhAm 3*

McKinlay, Chauncey Angus 1890-1969
NatCAB 55, WhAm 5

McKinlay, Duncan E 1862-1914 *BiDrAC,
WhAm 4*

McKinlay, John 1874-1953 *NatCAB 42,
WhAm 3*

McKinlay, Leland Murray 1893-1973
NatCAB 57

McKinley, Abner d1904 *WhAm 1*

McKinley, Albert Edward 1870-1936
DcAmB S2, WhAm 1

McKinley, Benjamin Louis 1874-1950
NatCAB 39

McKinley, Carlyle 1847-1904 *DcAmB,
WhAm 1*

McKinley, Charles Ethelbert 1870- *WhAm 5*

McKinley, Earl Baldwin 1894-1938 *WhAm 1*

McKinley, Ida Saxton 1847-1907 *AmWom,
NatCAB 11, NotAW, TwCBDA,
WhAm 1*

McKinley, J Charnley 1891-1950 *NatCAB 42,
WhAm 3*

McKinley, James F 1880-1941 *WhAm 1*

McKinley, James Wilfred 1857-1918
NatCAB 18

McKinley, James Wilfred 1891-1957 *WhAm 3*

McKinley, John 1780-1852 *AmBi, ApCAB,
BiAUS, BiDrAC, DcAmB, Drake,
NatCAB 2, TwCBDA, WebAB,
WhAm H, WhAmP*

McKinley, John Milton 1882-1940 *NatCAB 38*

McKinley, John William 1866-1935 *NatCAB 27*

McKinley, Johnson Camden 1877-1927
NatCAB 22

McKinley, Lloyd 1895-1961 *WhAm 4*

McKinley, William *BiAUS, BiDrAC,
WhAm H*

McKinley, William 1834-1918 *NatCAB 6*

McKinley, William 1843-1901 *AmBi,
ApCAB Sup, BiDrAC, BiDrUSE,
DcAmB, EncAAH, EncAB, McGEWB,
NatCAB 11, TwCBDA, WebAB,
WhAm 1, WhAmP*

McKinley, William Brown 1856-1926
*ApCAB X, BiDrAC, DcAmB S1,
NatCAB 15, WhAm 1, WhAmP*

McKinlock, George Alexander 1857-1936
NatCAB 31, WhAm 1

McKinly, John 1721-1796 *DcAmB, NatCAB 5,
TwCBDA, WhAm H*

McKinly, John 1724-1796 *ApCAB, Drake*

McKinney, Alexander Harris 1858-1941
WhAm 1

McKinney, Annie Booth *WhAm 5*

McKinney, Arthur Wesley 1895-1963 *WhAm 4*

McKinney, Buckner Abernathy 1872-1939
WhAm 1

McKinney, Colin Pierson 1873-1944 *WhAm 2*
McKinney, Corvell 1890-1973 *WhAm 6*
McKinney, David 1860-1934 *WhAm 1*
McKinney, Frank Cowan 1878-1950
NatCAB 38
McKinney, Frank Cowen 1878-1950 *WhAm 3*
McKinney, Frank E 1904-1974 *WhAm 6*
McKinney, Henry Crawford 1872-1952
NatCAB 42
McKinney, Henry Nelson 1849-1918
NatCAB 21
McKinney, Ida Scott Taylor *WhAm 5*
McKinney, James 1825-1907 *NatCAB 18*
McKinney, James 1852-1934 *BiDrAC,*
WhAm 1
McKinney, James Polk 1848-1917 *ApCAB X*
McKinney, James William 1872-1938
NatCAB 27
McKinney, Jane Amy 1832- *AmWom*
McKinney, John F 1827-1903 *BiAUS*
McKinney, John Frank 1827-1903 *TwCBDA*
McKinney, John Franklin 1827-1903 *BiDrAC,*
WhAmP
McKinney, John Luke 1842-1937 *NatCAB 30*
McKinney, Kate Slaughter 1857- *AmWom,*
WhAm 4
McKinney, Laurence 1891-1968 *WhAm 5*
McKinney, Louis Curtis 1871-1954 *NatCAB 48*
McKinney, Luther Franklin 1841-1922 *BiDrAC,*
NatCAB 12, TwCBDA, WhAm 3
McKinney, Madge M 1893-1956 *WhAm 3*
McKinney, May Mourning Faris 1874-
WomWWA 14
McKinney, Mayela Genevieve 1882-
WomWWA 14
McKinney, Mordecai 1796?-1867 *ApCAB,*
TwCBDA
McKinney, Philip Watkins 1832-1899
NatCAB 2, TwCBDA, WhAm 1
McKinney, Robert Cochran 1852-1916
NatCAB 24, WhAm 1
McKinney, Robert J *NatCAB 5*
McKinney, Roberta Montgomery
WomWWA 14
McKinney, Sarah Gertrude 1874-
WomWWA 14
McKinney, Theophilus Elisha 1899-1962
WhAm 4
McKinney, Thomas Emery 1864-1930 *WhAm 1*
McKinney, Walter H 1889-1952 *WhAm 3*
McKinney, William Mark 1865-1955 *WhAm 3*
McKinnie, James Renwick 1846- *WhAm 4*
McKinnis, George E, Sr. d1959 *WhAm 3*
McKinnon, Clinton Dotson 1906- *BiDrAC*
McKinnon, Colin F 1810-1879 *ApCAB*
McKinnon, James 1843-1920 *NatCAB 23*
McKinnon, John 1808- *ApCAB*
McKinnon, Luther 1840- *TwCBDA*
McKinnon, Neil John 1911-1975 *WhAm 6*
McKinsey, Folger 1866-1950 *WhAm 3*
McKinsey, J C C 1908-1953 *WhAm 3*
McKinsey, James O 1889-1937 *WhAm 1*
McKinstry, Addis Emmett 1870-1941 *WhAm 1*
McKinstry, Alexander 1822-1879 *DcAmB,*
WhAm H
McKinstry, Charles Hedges 1866- *WhAm 4*
McKinstry, Elisha Williams 1825-1901 *DcAmB,*
NatCAB 16, WhAm H
McKinstry, Grace E d1936 *WhAm 1*
McKinstry, Guy Hale 1884-1957 *NatCAB 45*
McKinstry, Helen 1878-1949 *NatCAB 37,*
WhAm 2
McKinstry, James Paterson 1807-1873 *ApCAB,*
Drake, TwCBDA
McKinstry, Justus 1820?- *NatCAB 4*
McKinstry, Justus 1821?- *ApCAB*
McKinstry, Karl Virgil 1909-1971 *NatCAB 57*
McKinstry, Ross Waldron 1896-1948
NatCAB 42
McKisick, Lewis 1866-1942 *WhAm 2*
McKissack, E H 1860- *WhoColR*
McKissick, Anthony Foster 1869-1938
NatCAB 32, WhAm 1
McKissick, J Rion 1884-1944 *NatCAB 33,*
WhAm 2
McKissick, Margaret Adger Smyth 1870-
WomWWA 14
McKissock, Thomas 1790-1866 *BiDrAC,*

WhAm H
McKissock, Thomas 1798-1866 *BiAUS*
McKisson, Robert Erastus 1863- *WhAm 4*
McKittrick, Frank George Wellington 1875-1946
NatCAB 45
McKittrick, John *NewYHSD*
McKittrick, Roy 1888-1961 *NatCAB 48,*
WhAm 4
McKittrick, Thomas H 1864- *NatCAB 12*
McKittrick, Thomas Harrington 1889-1970
WhAm 5
McKittrick, William James 1854-1916
NatCAB 20, WhAm 1
McKneally, Martin Boswell 1914- *BiDrAC*
McKnight, Alexander 1823?- *ApCAB*
McKnight, Alexander G 1878-1950 *WhAm 3*
McKnight, Alexander Hearne 1874-1929
WhAm 1
McKnight, Anna Caulfield 1866-1947 *WhAm 2,*
WomWWA 14
McKnight, Charles 1750-1791 *ApCAB, Drake,*
NatCAB 9, TwCBDA
McKnight, Charles 1826-1881 *NatCAB 22*
McKnight, Charles 1863-1926 *NatCAB 20,*
WhAm 1
McKnight, David *NewYHSD*
McKnight, Douglas 1895-1974 *WhAm 6*
McKnight, George 1840- *ApCAB*
McKnight, George Harley 1871- *WhAm 5*
McKnight, Harvey Washington 1843-1914
ApCAB, NatCAB 25, TwCBDA,
WhAm 1
McKnight, Henry Turney 1913-1972 *WhAm 5*
McKnight, James Rankin 1878-1951 *WhAm 3*
McKnight, John *NewYHSD*
McKnight, Robert 1789?-1846 *DcAmB,*
WhAm H
McKnight, Robert 1820-1885 *BiAUS, BiDrAC,*
TwCBDA, WhAm H
McKnight, Robert James George 1878-
WhAm 6
McKnight, Roy Jerome 1897-1967 *WhAm 4*
McKnight, William F 1863-1919 *NatCAB 17*
McKnight, William Hodges 1894-1969
WhAm 6
McKone, Don Townsend 1896- *WhAm 4*
McKoon, Dennis Daniel 1827- *NatCAB 7*
McKowen, John Clay 1842- *NatCAB 4,*
WhAm 4
McKown, Edgar M 1896-1973 *WhAm 6*
McKown, Harry Charles 1892-1963 *BiDAmEd,*
NatCAB 52, WhAm 4
McKowne, Frank A 1889-1948 *WhAm 2*
McKoy, Robert *NewYHSD*
McKuen, Rod Marvin 1933- *WebAB*
McKusick, Marshall Noah 1879-1950 *WhAm 3*
McLachlan, Alexander 1818- *ApCAB*
McLachlan, Archibald C 1858- *WhAm 4*
McLachlan, James 1852-1940 *BiDrAC,*
NatCAB 29, TwCBDA, WhAm 1,
WhAmP
McLachlen, Archibald Malcolm 1857-
WhAm 4
McLagan, Sara Anne 1855- *WomWWA 14*
McLaglen, Victor 1886-1959 *WhAm 3*
McLain, Mrs. Arthur Horace 1869-
WomWWA 14
McLain, Bernard Francis 1891-1968
NatCAB 56
McLain, Bobby Maurice 1925-1973 *WhAm 6*
McLain, Chester Alden 1891-1953 *NatCAB 42,*
WhAm 3
McLain, Ernest Simms 1864-1958 *NatCAB 46*
McLain, Frank Alexander 1852-1920 *BiDrAC,*
WhAmP
McLain, Frank Alexander 1853-1920 *TwCBDA,*
WhAm 4
McLain, John Scudder 1853-1931 *WhAm 1*
McLain, John Speed 1848-1907 *WhAm 1*
McLain, Nelson Wylie 1844-1918 *NatCAB 17*
McLain, Raymond S 1890-1954 *WhAm 3*
McLallen, Walter Field 1868- *WhAm 4*
McLanahan, Austin 1871-1946 *WhAm 2*
McLanahan, Duer 1899-1962 *NatCAB 50*
McLanahan, James Xavier 1809-1861 *ApCAB,*
BiDrAC, TwCBDA, WhAm H
McLanahan, James Xavier *see also* Maclanahan,
James Xavier

McLanahan, Nettie Paskell 1873-
WomWWA 14
McLandburgh, Florence 1850- *ApCAB*
McLandress, Robert John 1870-1942
NatCAB 31
McLane, A V 1874- *WhAm 5*
McLane, Allan 1746-1829 *ApCAB, DcAmB,*
WhAm H
McLane, Allan 1822-1891 *ApCAB X*
McLane, Allan 1823-1897 *NatCAB 16*
McLane, Allan 1864-1940 *NatCAB 35*
McLane, Allen 1746-1829 *Drake*
McLane, Catherine Milligan 1850-
WomWWA 14
McLane, Charles Keith 1921-1974 *WhAm 6*
McLane, Charles Lourie 1862- *WhAm 5*
McLane, James Woods 1839-1912 *WhAm 1*
McLane, Jeremiah 1767-1837 *BiAUS, Drake*
McLane, John 1852-1911 *NatCAB 14,*
WhAm 1
McLane, John Roy 1886-1969 *NatCAB 55,*
WhAm 5
McLane, Louis 1776-1857 *NatCAB 5*
McLane, Louis 1784-1857 *BiAUS*
McLane, Louis 1786-1857 *AmBi, ApCAB,*
BiDrAC, BiDrUSE, DcAmB, Drake,
TwCBDA, WhAm H, WhAmP
McLane, Patrick 1875-1946 *BiDrAC,*
WhAm 5
McLane, Robert Milligan 1815-1898 *ApCAB,*
BiAUS, BiDrAC, DcAmB, Drake,
NatCAB 9, TwCBDA, WhAm H,
WhAmP
McLane, Ruby Roach 1880- *WhAm 6*
McLane, William *NewYHSD*
McLane, William Ward 1846-1931 *WhAm 1*
McLaren, Alice Day 1884- *WomWWA 14*
McLaren, Daniel *WebAB*
McLaren, Donald 1834-1920 *TwCBDA,*
WhAm 1
McLaren, Donald Campbell 1794-1882 *ApCAB,*
TwCBDA
McLaren, Jennette M 1857- *WomWWA 14*
McLaren, John 1846-1943 *DcAmB S3*
McLaren, John Finlay 1803-1883 *TwCBDA*
McLaren, Malcolm 1865-1922 *NatCAB 19*
McLaren, Peter Lawrence 1858-1955
NatCAB 42
McLaren, Richard Wellington 1918-1976
WhAm 6
McLaren, Robert Neil 1828-1886 *ApCAB,*
TwCBDA
McLaren, Walter Wallace 1877- *WhAm 5*
McLaren, William Edward 1831-1905 *ApCAB,*
DcAmB, NatCAB 11, TwCBDA,
WhAm 1
McLaren, William Gardner 1875- *WhAm 5*
McLaren, William Pratt 1834- *NatCAB 1*
McLarin, Howard Marion 1887-1942
NatCAB 32
McLarty, Norman Alexander 1889-1945
WhAm 2
McLauchlan, Jay Chandler 1874-1929
NatCAB 24
McLauchlin, Dugald Neil 1863-1932
NatCAB 25
McLaughlen, Napoleon Bonaparte 1823-1887
ApCAB, TwCBDA
McLaughlin, Allan Joseph 1872-1961
NatCAB 50, WhAm 5
McLaughlin, Andrew Cunningham 1861-1947
DcAmB S4, NatCAB 13, NatCAB 36,
TwCBDA, WhAm 2
McLaughlin, Charles Francis 1887-1976
BiDrAC, WhAm 6
McLaughlin, Charles V 1875- *WhAm 5*
McLaughlin, Chester Bentine 1856-1929
WhAm 1
McLaughlin, Chester Bond 1895-1952 *WhAm 3*
McLaughlin, Dean Benjamin 1901-1965
NatCAB 51, WhAm 4
McLaughlin, Dorsey Elmer 1863-1945 *WhAm 2*
McLaughlin, Edward Aloysius 1893-1972
WhAm 6
McLaughlin, Edward Augustus 1798-1861
ApCAB, Drake
McLaughlin, Edward H 1895-1962 *WhAm 4*

McLaughlin, Emma Moffat 1880-1968
WhAm 5
McLaughlin, Frank 1828-1897 *NatCAB 8*
McLaughlin, George *NewYHSD*
McLaughlin, George Asbury 1851-1933
WhAm 1
McLaughlin, George Dunlap 1887-1945
WhAm 2
McLaughlin, Harold Newell 1896-1967
WhAm 5
McLaughlin, Henry Woods 1869-1950 *WhAm 3*
McLaughlin, Hugh 1826-1904 *DcAmB,*
NatCAB 14
McLaughlin, Hugh 1827-1904 *ApCAB Sup,*
WhAm 1
McLaughlin, J Frank 1908-1962 *WhAm 4*
McLaughlin, James 1842-1923 *DcAmB,*
REnAW, WhAm 1
McLaughlin, James Campbell 1858-1932
BiDrAC, WhAm 1, WhAmP
McLaughlin, James Matthew 1857- *WhAm 4*
McLaughlin, James W 1834-1923 *WhAm 1*
McLaughlin, James Wharton 1840-1909
NatCAB 8
McLaughlin, Joseph 1867-1926 *BiDrAC,*
WhAm 1
McLaughlin, Mary Louise 1847-1939 *WhAm 1,*
WomWWA 14
McLaughlin, Melvin Orlando 1876-1928
BiDrAC, WhAm 1, WhAmP
McLaughlin, Napoleon Bonaparte 1823-1887
NatCAB 12
McLaughlin, Paul 1900-1971 *WhAm 5*
McLaughlin, Robert Emmet 1889-1968
NatCAB 54
McLaughlin, Robert Samuel 1871- *WhAm 5*
McLaughlin, Robert William 1866-1936
WhAm 1
McLaughlin, Roland Rusk 1901-1970 *WhAm 5*
McLaughlin, Stuart Watts 1905-1967 *WhAm 5*
McLaughlin, Theodora North *WomWWA 14*
McLaughlin, Thomas Henry 1881-1947
NatCAB 40, WhAm 2
McLaughlin, Thomas Notley 1861-1922
NatCAB 23
McLaughlin, William Blair 1853-1914
NatCAB 19
McLaughlin, William F 1827-1905 *NatCAB 17*
McLaughry, Margaret 1854- *WomWWA 14*
McLaurin, Anselm Joseph 1848-1909 *BiDrAC,*
DcAmB, NatCAB 13, TwCBDA,
WhAm 1, WhAmP
McLaurin, John Loundes 1860-1934 *TwCBDA*
McLaurin, John Lowndes 1860-1934
ApCAB Sup, BiDrAC, NatCAB 37,
WhAm 1, WhAmP
McLaurin, John Lownies 1860-1934
NatCAB 13
McLauthlin, Herbert Weston 1854-1939
NatCAB 17, WhAm 1
McLauthlin, Martin Bernard 1871-1947
NatCAB 34
McLaws, Emily Lafayette *WomWWA 14*
McLaws, Lafayette 1821-1897 *AmBi, ApCAB,*
BiDConf, DcAmB, Drake, NatCAB 4,
TwCBDA, WhAm H
McLeaish, Robert Burns 1898-1962 *WhAm 4*
McLean *NewYHSD*
McLean 1791-1865 *Drake*
McLean, A Neil 1885-1967 *WhAm 4*
McLean, Addie L 1860- *WomWWA 14*
McLean, Adelaide Lare *WomWWA 14*
McLean, Alexander 1823?- *NewYHSD*
McLean, Alexander C *NewYHSD*
McLean, Alney 1779-1841 *BiAUS, BiDrAC,*
TwCBDA, WhAm H
McLean, Andrew 1848-1922 *NatCAB 13,*
WhAm 1
McLean, Angus 1862-1939 *WhAm 1*
McLean, Angus Wilton 1870-1935 *DcAmB S1,*
NatCAB 26, WhAm 1
McLean, Archibald 1791-1865 *ApCAB*
McLean, Archibald 1849-1920 *DcAmB*
McLean, Archibald 1850-1920 *WhAm 1*
McLean, Arthur Edward 1891-1961 *WhAm 4*
McLean, Avriett Alexander 1858-1927
NatCAB 30
McLean, Carl Hugh 1875-1946 *NatCAB 35*

McLean, Clara Clementine Chamberlain 1861-
WomWWA 14
McLean, Daniel Veech 1801-1869 *ApCAB,*
NatCAB 11, TwCBDA
McLean, Daniel Verch 1801-1869 *Drake*
McLean, David J 1879- *WhAm 6*
McLean, Donald 1852- *WhAm 1*
McLean, Donald Holman 1884- *BiDrAC*
McLean, Edward Beale 1886-1941 *DcAmB S3,*
WhAm 1
McLean, Edward Cochrane 1903-1972 *WhAm 5*
McLean, Ella Louise *WomWWA 14*
McLean, Emily Nelson Ritchie 1859-1916
TwCBDA, WhAm 1, WomWWA 14
McLean, Evalyn Walsh 1886-1947 *NotAW*
McLean, Fannie Williams 1863-
WomWWA 14
McLean, Finis Ewing 1806-1881 *BiAUS,*
BiDrAC, WhAm H
McLean, Floyd Dana 1885-1946 *NatCAB 34*
McLean, Franklin Chambers 1888-1968
NatCAB 54, WhAm 5
McLean, Fred 1878- *WhAm 6*
McLean, George Payne 1857-1932 *ApCAB X,*
BiDrAC, NatCAB 13, NatCAB 29,
TwCBDA, WhAm 1, WhAmP
McLean, George Roberts 1873-1933
NatCAB 26
McLean, Georgiana Grant *WomWWA 14*
McLean, Heber Hampton 1899-1971 *WhAm 5*
McLean, Helena Chapin *WomWWA 14*
McLean, James Henry 1829-1886 *BiDrAC,*
NatCAB 7, WhAm H
McLean, James Robert 1823-1870 *BiDConf*
McLean, James Stanley 1876-1955 *WhAm 3*
McLean, Jay 1890-1957 *BiHiMed*
McLean, John 1759-1823 *Drake*
McLean, John 1761-1823 *ApCAB*
McLean, John 1785-1861 *AmBi, ApCAB,*
BiAUS, BiDrAC, BiDrUSE, DcAmB,
Drake, McGEWB, NatCAB 2, TwCBDA,
WebAB, WhAm H, WhAmP
McLean, John 1791-1830 *ApCAB, BiAUS,*
BiDrAC, NatCAB 5, TwCBDA,
WhAm H
McLean, John 1828- *ApCAB*
McLean, John 1852- *ApCAB Sup*
McLean, John Emery 1865- *WhAm 4*
McLean, John Godfrey 1917-1974 *WhAm 6*
McLean, John Knox 1834-1914 *WhAm 1*
McLean, John M 1909-1968 *WhAm 5*
McLean, John Ray 1849- *NatCAB 1*
McLean, John Roll 1848-1916 *TwCBDA,*
WhAm 1
McLean, Marrs 1883-1953 *NatCAB 42*
McLean, Mary Hancock 1861- *WomWWA 14*
McLean, Milton Robbins 1874-1951 *WhAm 3*
McLean, Nathaniel Collins 1815- *ApCAB,*
TwCBDA
McLean, Newton Esic 1879- *WhoColR*
McLean, Ridley 1872-1933 *NatCAB 25,*
WhAm 1
McLean, Robert Norris 1882-1964 *WhAm 4*
McLean, Samuel 1826-1877 *BiAUS, BiDrAC,*
TwCBDA, WhAm H
McLean, Sarah Pratt d1935 *NotAW,*
TwCBDA
McLean, Sarah Pratt 1856-1935 *AmBi*
McLean, Sarah Pratt 1858-1935 *ApCAB*
McLean, Simon James 1871-1946 *WhAm 3*
McLean, Stafford 1886-1932 *NatCAB 24*
McLean, Thomas Chalmers 1847-1919
NatCAB 18, WhAm 1
McLean, Wallace Donald 1873- *WhAm 6*
McLean, Walter 1855-1930 *DcAmB,*
NatCAB 24, WhAm 1
McLean, William d1839 *ApCAB, BiAUS*
McLean, William 1788?-1839 *TwCBDA*
McLean, William 1794-1829 *WhAm H*
McLean, William 1794-1839 *BiDrAC*
McLean, William Campbell 1896-1965
NatCAB 51
McLean, William L, Jr. 1895-1954 *WhAm 3*
McLean, William Lippard 1852-1931 *DcAmB,*
NatCAB 23, WhAm 1
McLean, William Pinkney 1836-1925 *BiAUS,*
BiDrAC

McLean, William Swan, Jr. 1877-1938
NatCAB 32, WhAm 1
McLearn, Frank Cecil 1901-1969 *WhAm 6*
McLeary, James Harvey 1845-1914 *WhAm 1*
McLeary, M *IlBEAAW*
McLeer, James 1840- *NatCAB 5*
McLees, Archibald 1817?-1890 *NewYHSD,*
WhAm H
McLees, Daniel *NewYHSD*
McLees, Daniel 1836?- *NewYHSD*
McLees, James *NewYHSD*
McLees, James 1830?- *NewYHSD*
McLees, John *NewYHSD*
McLees, John 1790?- *NewYHSD*
McLees, Michael 1833?- *NewYHSD*
McLeish, Elizabeth Jane Moore 1882-
WomWWA 14
McLeister, Ira Ford 1879- *WhAm 6*
McLelan, Archibald Woodbury 1824- *ApCAB*
McLellan, Archibald 1857-1917 *WhAm 1*
McLellan, Asahel Walker 1868-1943
NatCAB 33, WhAm 2
McLellan, David *NewYHSD*
McLellan, David 1825?- *NewYHSD*
McLellan, Douglas Hull 1897-1959 *NatCAB 45*
McLellan, George W *BiAUS*
McLellan, H B *NewYHSD*
McLellan, Hugh Dean 1876-1953 *NatCAB 39,*
WhAm 5
McLellan, Isaac 1806-1899 *ApCAB, DcAmB,*
NatCAB 6, TwCBDA, WhAm 1
McLellan, Isaac *see also* MacLellan, Isaac, Jr.
McLellan, James 1798?- *NewYHSD*
McLellan, James, Jr. 1828?- *NewYHSD*
McLellan, John 1841?- *NewYHSD*
McLellan, Robert 1843?- *NewYHSD*
McLellan, Thomas George 1898-1969 *WhAm 5*
M'Clement, Alexander *NewYHSD*
M'Clement, George *NewYHSD*
McLemore, Albert Sydney 1869- *WhAm 5*
McLemore, Atkins Jefferson 1857-1929 *BiDrAC*
McLemore, Jeff 1857-1929 *WhAm 1*
McLenan, John 1827-1866 *NewYHSD*
McLendon, Lennox Polk 1890-1968 *WhAm 5*
McLendon, Robert Burns 1937-1974 *WhAm 6*
McLendon, Sol Brown 1905-1967 *WhAm 4*
McLene, James 1730-1806 *ApCAB, TwCBDA*
McLene, Jeremiah 1767-1837 *ApCAB,*
BiDrAC, TwCBDA, WhAm H
McLenegan, Charles Edward 1858-1920
WhAm 1
McLennan, Donald Roderick 1873-1944
WhAm 2
McLennan, Grace Tytus 1875-1928 *WhAm 1*
McLennan, J C Earle 1891-1965 *NatCAB 51*
McLennan, Peter Baillie 1850-1913 *WhAm 1*
McLeod, Alexander 1774-1833 *ApCAB,*
DcAmB, Drake, NatCAB 11, TwCBDA,
WhAm H
McLeod, Arthur Brundage 1871-1941
NatCAB 35
McLeod, Augus Archibald 1847-1902
NatCAB 13
McLeod, Clarence John 1895-1959 *BiDrAC,*
WhAm 3, WhAmP
McLeod, Duncan Allen 1907-1975 *WhAm 6*
McLeod, Frank Hilton 1868-1944 *WhAm 2*
McLeod, Hugh 1814-1862 *ApCAB, DcAmB,*
WhAm H
McLeod, Hugh 1867-1927 *NatCAB 23*
McLeod, Hugh Carroll 1895-1958 *NatCAB 47*
McLeod, James Carlisle 1897-1947 *NatCAB 36*
McLeod, James Farquharson 1836- *ApCAB*
McLeod, John 1788-1849 *ApCAB*
McLeod, John Gordon 1867-1929 *NatCAB 23*
McLeod, John Niel 1806-1874 *ApCAB,*
NatCAB 11
McLeod, Malcolm 1821- *ApCAB*
McLeod, Malcolm 1818-1966 *WhAm 4*
McLeod, Martin 1813-1860 *DcAmB,*
WhAm H
McLeod, Mary Louise DeMarco 1914-1968
WhAm 5
McLeod, Murdoch 1868-1957 *WhAm 3*
McLeod, N H F 1875-1948 *WhAm 5*
McLeod, Nelson Wesley 1860- *WhAm 4*
McLeod, Norman Hugh Finley 1875-1948
NatCAB 37

McLeod, Pearl Monk 1883- *WomWWA 14*
McLeod, Samuel Brown Wylie 1831-1899
NatCAB 13
McLeod, Scott 1914-1961 *WhAm 4*
McLeod, Thomas Gordon 1868-1932 *WhAm 1*
McLeod, Walter Herbert 1887-1965 *WhAm 4*
McLeod, William *NewYHSD*
McLeod, Xavier Donald 1821-1865 *ApCAB,*
NatCAB 11
McLeod, Xavier Donald *see also* Macleod, Xavier
Donald
McLeskey, Waymon B 1893-1964 *WhAm 4*
McLester, Amelia *WomWWA 14*
McLester, James Somerville 1877-1954
WhAm 3
McLester, Judson Cole, Jr. 1908-1965 *WhAm 4*
McLevy, Jasper 1878-1962 *NatCAB 49,*
WhAm 4
McLin, Anna Eva d1970 *WhAm 5*
McLin, James *NatCAB 7*
M'Clintock, John 1814-1870 *DcAmB, Drake,*
WhAm H
McLoghlin, John Joseph 1855- *NatCAB 7*
McLoskey, Robert Thaddeus 1907- *BiDrAC*
M'Cloud *NewYHSD*
McLoughlin, John 1784-1857 *AmBi, DcAmB,*
McGEWB, NatCAB 6, REnAW, WebAB,
WhAm H
McLoughlin, William Gerald 1922- *EncAAH*
McLouth, Donald B 1901-1954 *WhAm 3*
McLouth, Lawrence Amos 1863-1927 *WhAm 1*
McLucas, Walter Scott 1875-1953 *NatCAB 42,*
WhAm 3
McLure, Charles Derickson 1844- *WhAm 4*
McLure, Elizabeth Meriwether 1888-
WomWWA 14
McLure, William 1763-1840 *TwCBDA*
McLure, William *see also* Maclure, William
McMahan, Anna Benneson 1846-1919 *WhAm 1,*
WomWWA 14
McMahan, Arthur Knight 1892-1945
NatCAB 34
McMahan, George Thomas 1901-1967 *WhAm 5*
McMahan, Matthew Bogle 1827-1915
NatCAB 16
McMahon, Alphonse 1895- *WhAm 5*
McMahon, Amos Philip 1890-1947 *WhAm 2*
McMahon, Arthur Laurence 1863- *WhAm 5*
McMahon, Barnard 1775-1816 *Drake*
McMahon, Bernard 1775-1816 *DcAmB,*
WhAm H
McMahon, Bernard *see also* MacMahon, Bernard
McMahon, Brien 1903-1952 *DcAmB S5,*
NatCAB 40, WhAm 3
McMahon, Gregory 1915- *BiDrAC*
McMahon, Henry George 1900-1966 *WhAm 5*
McMahon, James 1817-1901 *TwCBDA*
McMahon, James 1831-1913 *NatCAB 15*
McMahon, James 1856-1922 *WhAm 1*
McMahon, James Joseph 1897-1972
NatCAB 57
McMahon, James O'Brien 1903-1952 *BiDrAC*
McMahon, John A 1833-1923 *BiAUS, BiDrAC,*
TwCBDA, WhAm 1
McMahon, John Daniel 1859-1923 *NatCAB 28*
McMahon, John Eugene 1860-1920 *WhAm 1*
McMahon, John Henry 1893-1963 *NatCAB 50*
McMahon, John Joseph 1875-1932 *NatCAB 23,*
WhAm 1
McMahon, John Robert 1875-1956 *WhAm 3*
McMahon, John VanLaer 1800-1871
NatCAB 11
McMahon, John VanLear 1800-1871 *ApCAB,*
DcAmB, WhAm H
McMahon, Johnson Daniel 1887-1963
NatCAB 53
McMahon, Joseph H 1862-1939 *WhAm 1*
McMahon, Karl Cornelius 1897-1955
NatCAB 43
McMahon, Laurence Stephen 1835-1893
ApCAB, NatCAB 10
McMahon, Laurence Stephen 1835-1893
TwCBDA, WhAm H
McMahon, Martin F *BiAUS*
McMahon, Martin Thomas 1838-1906 *AmBi,*
ApCAB, NatCAB 4, TwCBDA, WhAm 1
McMahon, Patrick Julius 1863-1916
NatCAB 17

McMahon, Raymond John 1890-1966
NatCAB 53
McMahon, Stephen John 1881-1960 *WhAm 3*
McMahon, Thomas F 1870-1944 *WhAm 2*
McMahon, Thomas J 1909-1956 *WhAm 3*
McMahon, William 1786-1870 *NatCAB 10*
McMain, Eleanor Laura 1866-1934 *NotAW*
McMain, Eleanor Laura 1868-1934 *WhAm 2,*
WomWWA 14
McManaman, Edward Peter 1900-1964
WhAm 4
McManamon, James Emmett 1905-1954
WhAm 3
McManamy, Frank 1870-1944 *NatCAB 33,*
WhAm 2
McManes, James 1822-1899 *DcAmB,*
WhAm H, WhAmP
McManes, Kenmore Mathew 1900-1973
WhAm 5
McManis, Fred 1879-1952 *NatCAB 39*
McManis, John Thomas 1870- *WhAm 5*
McMannus, James *NewYHSD*
McManus, Blanche *WomWWA 14*
McManus, Charles Edward 1881-1946
NatCAB 39, WhAm 2
McManus, Emily Julian 1865- *AmWom,*
WomWWA 14
McManus, George 1883-1954 *NatCAB 45*
McManus, George 1884?-1954 *DcAmB S5,*
WhAm 3
McManus, George Henry 1867- *WhAm 5*
McManus, Howard Norbert, Jr. 1921-1974
WhAm 6
McManus, Jane *NotAW*
McManus, John Joseph 1897-1958 *WhAm 4*
McManus, Richard George 1919-1965
NatCAB 52
McManus, Samuel Martin 1886-1953
NatCAB 42
McManus, Terence Joseph 1871-1950
NatCAB 37
McManus, Thomas 1834-1914 *NatCAB 27*
McManus, William 1780-1835 *BiAUS,*
BiDrAC, WhAm H
McMarlin, John Gilmore 1870-1954
NatCAB 43
McMartin, Charles 1880-1954 *WhAm 3*
McMartin, J L d1848 *BiAUS*
McMartin, William Joseph 1904-1971 *WhAm 5*
McMaster, Erasmus Darwin 1806-1866 *ApCAB,*
Drake, NatCAB 2, TwCBDA
McMaster, Fitz Hugh 1867- *WhAm 5*
McMaster, Florence R 1916-1973 *WhAm 6*
McMaster, Gilbert 1778-1854 *ApCAB, Drake,*
TwCBDA
McMaster, Guy Humphrey 1829-1887 *ApCAB,*
NatCAB 11
McMaster, Guy Humphreys 1829-1887 *DcAmB,*
WhAm H
McMaster, James Alphonsus 1820-1886 *ApCAB,*
DcAmB, NatCAB 24, TwCBDA,
WhAm H
McMaster, John Bach 1852-1932 *AmBi,*
ApCAB, BiDAmEd, DcAmB, EncAAH,
McGEWB, NatCAB 11, TwCBDA,
WebAB, WhAm 1
McMaster, John Stevenson 1859- *WhAm 1*
McMaster, LeRoy 1879-1946 *NatCAB 34,*
WhAm 2
McMaster, Philip Duryee 1891-1973 *WhAm 5*
McMaster, Ross Huntington 1880-1962
WhAm 4
McMaster, William 1811-1887 *ApCAB*
McMaster, William E 1823-1860? *NewYHSD*
McMaster, William Henry 1875-1962
NatCAB 47, WhAm 4, WhAm 5
McMaster, William Henry 1877-1968 *BiDrAC,*
EncAAH, NatCAB 55, WhAm 5
McMath, Francis Charles 1867-1938
NatCAB 29, WhAm 1
McMath, Robert Edwin 1886-1968 *WhAm 5*
McMath, Robert Emmet 1833-1918 *DcAmB*
McMath, Robert Emmett 1833-1918
NatCAB 26, WhAm 4
McMath, Robert Raynolds 1891-1962
NatCAB 50, WhAm 4
McMeans, George Beale 1913-1967 *WhAm 4*

McMechan, Francis Hoeffer 1879-1939
WhAm 1
McMeen, Samuel Groenendyke 1864-1934
WhAm 1
McMein, Neysa d1949 *WhAm 2*
McMein, Neysa 1888-1949 *NotAW*
McMein, Neysa 1890-1949 *NatCAB 36*
McMenamin, Hugh L 1871-1947 *WhAm 2*
McMenamy, Francis Xavier 1872-1949
WhAm 2
McMenimen, William V d1965 *WhAm 4*
McMichael, Charles Bannesley 1850-
ApCAB X
McMichael, Clayton 1844-1906 *ApCAB,*
NatCAB 2, TwCBDA, WhAm 1
McMichael, Morton 1807-1879 *ApCAB,*
DcAmB, NatCAB 2, TwCBDA,
WhAm H
McMichael, Morton, Jr. 1836-1904 *NatCAB 14*
McMichael, Morton *see also* MacMichael,
Morton
McMichael, Stanley Livingston 1878-1950
NatCAB 39
McMichael, Thomas Hanna 1863-1938
WhAm 1
McMichael, William 1841-1893 *ApCAB,*
BiAUS, TwCBDA
McMicken, Frances Marsh 1865-
WomWWA 14
McMicken, Gilbert 1813- *ApCAB*
McMillan, Alexander d1817 *BiDrAC,*
WhAm H
McMillan, Alexander 1859- *WhAm 4*
McMillan, Alfred E 1900-1972 *WhAm 5*
McMillan, Benton 1845-1933 *WhAmP*
McMillan, Charles 1841-1927 *ApCAB Sup,*
WhAm 1
McMillan, Charles VanVechten 1851-1923
NatCAB 20
McMillan, Clara Gooding 1894- *BiDrAC*
McMillan, Claude Richelieu 1899-1961
WhAm 4
McMillan, Daniel Hugh 1846-1908 *NatCAB 8*
McMillan, Daniel Hugh 1848-1908 *WhAm 4*
McMillan, Duncan James 1846-1939
NatCAB 11, NatCAB 29, WhAm 1
McMillan, Edward John 1890-1964 *NatCAB 51,*
WhAm 4
McMillan, Edwin Mattison 1907- *AsBiEn,*
WebAB
McMillan, Fred Orville 1890-1956 *WhAm 3*
McMillan, George Scholefield 1895- *WhAm 5*
McMillan, Homer 1873-1958 *WhAm 3*
McMillan, Howard Ives 1897-1960 *NatCAB 50*
McMillan, James 1838-1902 *ApCAB, BiDrAC,*
DcAmB, NatCAB 2, WhAm 1, WhAmP
McMillan, James Thayer 1885-1946
NatCAB 35, WhAm 2
McMillan, James Winning 1825-1903 *DcAmB,*
TwCBDA, WhAm 1
McMillan, John 1752-1833 *ApCAB,*
NatCAB 5, TwCBDA
McMillan, John Gilmore 1851-1935
NatCAB 42
McMillan, John Lanneau *BiDrAC*
McMillan, John Loudon 1859-1946 *NatCAB 35*
McMillan, Neil Alexander d1927 *WhAm 5*
McMillan, Philip Hamilton 1872-1919 *WhAm 1*
McMillan, Putnam Dana 1881-1961 *WhAm 4*
McMillan, Robert Johnston 1885-1941
WhAm 2
McMillan, Samuel 1850-1924 *BiDrAC,*
WhAm 4
McMillan, Samuel James Renwick 1826-1897
ApCAB, BiAUS, BiDrAC, NatCAB 4,
TwCBDA, WhAm H, WhAmP
McMillan, Thomas Ellwood 1887-1962
NatCAB 51
McMillan, Thomas Sanders 1888-1939 *BiDrAC,*
WhAm 1, WhAmP
McMillan, Wheeler 1893- *EncAAH*
McMillan, William 1764-1804 *BiDrAC,*
WhAm H
McMillan, William 1777-1832 *TwCBDA*
McMillan, William Charles 1861-1907
WhAm 1
McMillan, William H 1837-1911 *WhAm 1*
McMillan, William Joshua 1870- *WhAm 5*

McMillan, William Linn 1829-1902 *WhAm 1*
McMillen, Alonzo Bertram 1861-1927 *WhAm 1*
McMillen, Dale Wilmore 1880-1971
  NatCAB 56, WhAm 5
McMillen, Fred Ewing 1882-1959 *WhAm 3*
McMillen, James Adelbert 1889-1953 *WhAm 3*
McMillen, Rolla Coral 1880-1961 *BiDrAC*
McMillen, Verne 1886-1960 *NatCAB 51*
McMillen, William Linn 1829-1902 *ApCAB,
  TwCBDA*
McMillin, Alvin Nugent 1895-1952 *DcAmB S5*
McMillin, Alvin Nugent 1899-1952 *WhAm 3*
McMillin, Mrs. Benton *WomWWA 14*
McMillin, Benton 1845-1933 *BiDrAC,
  DcAmB S1, NatCAB 13, TwCBDA,
  WhAm 1*
McMillin, Emerson 1844-1922 *NatCAB 10,
  NatCAB 24, WhAm 1*
McMillin, Francis Briggs 1868-1938 *WhAm 1*
McMillin, Frederick Nelson 1872-1937
  NatCAB 27, WhAm 1
McMillin, John Harold 1895-1970 *NatCAB 55*
McMillin, John Milton 1883-1951 *WhAm 3*
McMillin, Lucille Foster d1949 *WhAm 2*
McMillin, Ruth Strong 1880- *WomWWA 14*
McMillin, Stewart Earl 1889-1952 *WhAm 3*
McMillin, Walter Fraser 1879-1952
  NatCAB 45
McMin, Joseph 1758-1824 *BiAUS, Drake*
McMinn, Joseph 1758-1824 *DcAmB,
  NatCAB 7, TwCBDA, WhAm H*
McMoran, George Andrew 1909-1975 *WhAm 6*
McMorran, Henry Gordon 1841-1929 *WhAm 3*
McMorran, Henry Gordon 1844-1929 *BiDrAC,
  NatCAB 37*
McMorris, Charles H 1890-1954 *WhAm 3*
McMorrow, Francis Joseph 1910-1963 *WhAm 4*
McMorrow, Thomas 1886-1957 *WhAm 3*
McMullan, Harry 1884-1955 *WhAm 3*
McMullan, Joseph Vincent 1896-1973
  NatCAB 57
McMullan, Oscar 1856- *WhAm 4*
McMullen, Adam 1874- *WhAm 5*
McMullen, Charles Bell 1871- *WhAm 5*
McMullen, Chester Bartow 1902-1953 *BiDrAC,
  WhAm 3*
McMullen, Clements 1892-1959 *WhAm 3*
McMullen, Donald Bard 1903-1967 *NatCAB 53*
McMullen, Fayette d1880 *BiAUS*
McMullen, Fayette 1805-1880 *BiDConf,
  BiDrAC, WhAm H*
McMullen, Fayette 1810-1880 *TwCBDA*
McMullen, Hugh Aloysius 1859-1937 *WhAm 1*
McMullen, John 1832-1883 *NatCAB 12,
  TwCBDA*
McMullen, John 1832-1885 *WhAm H*
McMullen, John 1833-1883 *ApCAB*
McMullen, John Joseph 1901-1970 *WhAm 5*
McMullen, John Lawrence 1873-1935
  NatCAB 26
McMullen, Justus Clarke 1851-1888
  ApCAB Sup
McMullen, Lynn Banks 1875-1963 *WhAm 4*
McMullen, Richard Cann 1868-1944
  NatCAB 33, WhAm 2
McMullen, Roswell Silas 1882-1942
  NatCAB 31
McMullin, Jessica Genevieve Lake
  WomWWA 14
McMullin, Samuel Hildeburn 1831-1892
  TwCBDA
McMullin, Virginia McNulty *WomWWA 14*
McMurchy, Wilton George 1872-1923
  NatCAB 6
McMurdie, Henry 1822-1880 *ApCAB,
  TwCBDA*
McMurdo, Katharine Albert *AmWom*
McMurdy, Robert 1819-1892 *TwCBDA*
McMurdy, Robert 1860-1941 *WhAm 2*
McMurran, Stockton Mosby 1887-1920
  NatCAB 20
McMurray, Charles Backman 1865-1940
  NatCAB 30, WhAm 1
McMurray, DeWitt 1866- *WhAm 4*
McMurray, Eugene Augustus 1872-1949
  NatCAB 38
McMurray, Howard Johnstone 1901-1961
  BiDrAC, WhAm 4

McMurray, James Donald 1911-1969 *WhAm 5*
McMurray, James Henry 1871-1938 *WhAm 1*
McMurray, John 1873- *WhAm 5*
McMurray, Lida Brown 1853- *WomWWA 14*
McMurray, Orrin Kip 1869- *WhAm 2*
McMurray, Walter Earl 1887-1964 *NatCAB 53*
McMurray, William 1810- *ApCAB*
McMurray, William Josiah 1842-1905
  NatCAB 8, WhAm 1
McMurrich, James Playfair 1859-1939
  *DcAmB S2, NatCAB 14, TwCBDA,
  WhAm HA, WhAm 4, WhAm 4*
McMurrich, John 1804-1883 *ApCAB*
McMurrin, Sterling Moss 1914- *BiDAmEd*
McMurry, Charles Alexander 1857-1929
  BiDAmEd, TwCBDA, WhAm 1
McMurry, Frank Morton 1862-1936 *BiDAmEd,
  DcAmB S2, WhAm 1*
McMurry, Leonard 1913- *IIBEAAW*
McMurry, Lida Brown 1853- *WhAm 2*
McMurry, William Fletcher 1864-1934
  WhAm 1
McMurtie, William Birch 1816-1872
  NewYHSD
McMurtrie, Douglas Crawford 1888-1944
  DcAmB S3, DcAmLiB, WhAm 2
McMurtrie, Henry 1793-1865 *ApCAB, Drake*
McMurtrie, James, Jr. *NewYHSD*
McMurtrie, Richard Coxe 1819- *ApCAB*
McMurtrie, Uz 1884-1960 *NatCAB 48,
  WhAm 4*
McMurtrie, William 1851-1913 *ApCAB,
  DcAmB, NatCAB 12, TwCBDA,
  WhAm 1*
McMurtrie, William Birch 1816-1872
  IIBEAAW
McMurtry, George G 1838-1915 *ApCAB X*
McMurtry, George Gibson, Jr. 1876-1958
  ApCAB X, NatCAB 47
McMurtry, James Gilmer 1870-1954 *WhAm 3*
McMurtry, John 1812-1890 *WhAm H*
McMurtry, John Gibson 1870-1919 *NatCAB 18*
McMurtry, Larry 1936- *REnAW*
McMurtry, Lewis Samuel 1850-1924
  NatCAB 13, WhAm 1
McMurtry, William John 1859- *WhAm 4*
McMynn, John Gibson 1824-1900 *BiDAmEd*
McNab, Alexander J 1877-1956 *WhAm 3*
McNab, Anson Stuart 1863- *NatCAB 5*
McNab, Archibald Peter 1864-1945 *WhAm 2*
McNab, Joseph Lowe 1872-1946 *NatCAB 34*
McNab, Richard *NewYHSD*
McNabb, Joe Hector 1887-1949 *WhAm 2*
McNabb, Joseph Hector 1887-1949 *NatCAB 37*
McNabb, Richard *NewYHSD*
McNabb, Samuel W 1868-1940 *WhAm 1*
McNagny, Phil McClellan 1886-1969 *WhAm 5*
McNagny, William Forgy 1850-1923 *BiDrAC*
McNair *NewYHSD*
McNair, Alexander d1826 *BiAUS, Drake*
McNair, Alexander 1774-1826 *ApCAB,
  NatCAB 12, TwCBDA*
McNair, Alexander 1775-1826 *DcAmB,
  WhAm H*
McNair, Antoine Reilhe 1839- *ApCAB*
McNair, Douglas G 1893-1960 *NatCAB 49*
McNair, Frank 1881- *WhAm 6*
McNair, Fred Walter 1862-1924 *DcAmB,
  WhAm 1*
McNair, Frederick Vallette 1839-1900 *ApCAB,
  DcAmB, NatCAB 10, TwCBDA,
  WhAm 1*
McNair, Grace Elizabeth *WomWWA 14*
McNair, James Birtley 1889-1967 *WhAm 5*
McNair, Jean Ferguson *WomWWA 14*
McNair, John 1800-1861 *BiAUS, BiDrAC,
  TwCBDA, WhAm H*
McNair, John Babbitt 1889-1968 *WhAm 5*
McNair, Lesley James 1883-1944 *DcAmB S3,
  NatCAB 33, WebAMB, WhAm 2,
  WhWW-II*
McNair, William Sharp 1868-1936 *WhAm 1*
McNairy, John 1762-1837 *BiAUS*
McNall, Neil Adams 1913- *EncAAH*
McNally, Andrew 1886-1954 *WhAm 3*
McNally, Frederick George 1865-1907 *WhAm 1*
McNally, George Frederick 1878- *WhAm 6*
McNally, James Clifford 1865-1920 *WhAm 1*

McNally, Joseph Thomas 1869- *WhAm 5*
McNally, Paul Aloysius 1890-1955 *WhAm 3*
McNally, Robert Emmett 1885-1951
  NatCAB 45
McNally, William Duncan 1882-1961
  NatCAB 50, WhAm 4
McNally, William James 1891-1967
  NatCAB 54, WhAm 4
McNamara, Adelaide Luisita *WomWWA 14*
McNamara, Francis Thomas 1896-1969
  NatCAB 55
McNamara, Harley Vincent 1894-1966
  WhAm 4
McNamara, John 1824-1885 *ApCAB,
  TwCBDA*
McNamara, John Gerard 1894-1958
  NatCAB 47
McNamara, John Michael 1878-1960
  NatCAB 45, WhAm 4
McNamara, Joseph Augustine 1892-1972
  WhAm 5
McNamara, Martin D 1898-1966 *WhAm 4*
McNamara, Patrick Vincent 1894-1966 *BiDrAC,
  NatCAB 52, WhAm 4, WhAmP*
McNamara, R Reid 1903-1964 *NatCAB 50*
McNamara, Robert Charles 1881-1967
  WhAm 4, WhAm 5
McNamara, Robert Strange 1916- *BiDrUSE,
  EncAB, WebAMB*
McNamara, Sylvester James 1869-1943
  NatCAB 37
McNamee, C Declan 1890-1964 *WhAm 4*
McNamee, Charles Joseph 1890-1965 *WhAm 4*
McNamee, Graham 1888-1942 *DcAmB S3,
  NatCAB 31, WhAm 2*
McNamee, John 1842-1914 *NatCAB 16*
McNamee, Luke 1871- *WhAm 5*
McNamee, Theodore 1813-1871 *NatCAB 8*
McNamee, William John, Jr. 1912-1949
  WhAm 2
McNarney, Joseph Taggart 1893-1972
  WebAMB, WhAm 5
McNary, Charles Linza 1874-1944 *ApCAB X,
  BiDrAC, DcAmB S3, EncAAH,
  NatCAB 32, WhAm 2, WhAmP*
McNary, Henrietta Williamson 1905-1962
  WhAm 4
McNary, James Graham 1877-1962 *WhAm 4*
McNary, William Sarsfield 1863-1930 *BiDrAC,
  WhAm 4*
McNatt, John Harding 1905-1964 *NatCAB 51*
McNaugher, John 1857-1947 *NatCAB 40,
  WhAm 2*
McNaught, Francis Hector 1854-1940 *WhAm 1*
McNaught, Francis Hector 1856-1940
  NatCAB 12
McNaught, James 1842- *WhAm 4*
McNaught, James Bernard 1894-1959
  NatCAB 48, WhAm 3
McNaughton *NewYHSD*
McNaughton, Andrew George Latta 1887-1966
  WhAm 4
McNaughton, Donald *NewYHSD*
McNaughton, James 1796-1874 *ApCAB*
McNaughton, John Hugh 1829- *WhAm 1*
McNaughton, John Theodore 1921-1967
  WhAm 4
McNaughton, William Francis 1875-1965
  WhAm 4
McNaughton, William Francis 1876-1965
  WhAm 5
McNeal, Alice 1897-1964 *WhAm 4*
McNeal, Donald Hamlin 1901-1965 *WhAm 4*
McNeal, Edgar Holmes 1874-1955 *WhAm 3*
McNeal, Joshua Vansant 1846-1917 *WhAm 1*
McNeal, Thomas Allen 1853-1942 *NatCAB 11,
  WhAm 2*
McNeal, William Horton 1878- *WhAm 6*
McNealy, Raymond William 1886-1958
  WhAm 3
McNear, George Plummer, Jr. 1891-1947
  WhAm 2
McNear, George Washington 1837-1909
  NatCAB 7, NatCAB 42
McNeely, Eugene J 1900-1973 *WhAm 6*
McNeely, Frances Carlisle Jones 1889-
  WomWWA 14

McNeely, Harry Gregory 1887-1968
NatCAB 53, *WhAm 5*
McNeely, James 1861-1918 *NatCAB 18*
McNeely, Robert Whitehead 1873- *WhAm 5*
McNeely, Thompson Ware 1835-1921 *BiAUS,*
BiDrAC
McNees, Sterling G 1887-1959 *WhAm 3*
McNeil, Edwin Colyer 1882-1965 *NatCAB 52,*
WhAm 4
McNeil, Elton Burbank 1924-1974 *WhAm 6*
McNeil, Everett 1862-1929 *WhAm 1*
McNeil, George 1906- *BnEnAmA*
McNeil, George Elroy 1891-1953 *NatCAB 40*
McNeil, Hiram Colver 1866-1937 *WhAm 1*
McNeil, John 1784-1850 *Drake, NatCAB 13*
McNeil, John 1813-1891 *ApCAB, NatCAB 5,*
TwCBDA
McNeil, John 1820?- *Drake*
McNeil, John 1853-1940 *NatCAB 32*
McNeil, Kenneth Gordon 1902-1970 *WhAm 5*
McNeil, Sister Mary Donald 1899-1969
WhAm 5
McNeil, Robert Lincoln 1883-1968 *WhAm 5*
McNeil, Roderick Clanranald, II 1914-1969
NatCAB 54
McNeil, William Gibbs 1802-1853 *Drake*
McNeill, Archibald d1849 *BiDrAC, WhAm H*
McNeill, Clyde 1894-1957 *NatCAB 46*
McNeill, Daniel 1748-1833 *DcAmB, WhAm H*
McNeill, Edwin 1822-1875 *NatCAB 18*
McNeill, Edwin Ruthven 1880-1962 *WhAm 5*
McNeill, George 1827-1861 *TwCBDA*
McNeill, George Edwin 1837-1906 *DcAmB,*
NatCAB 25, TwCBDA, WhAm 1
McNeill, George Rockwell 1854-1901 *TwCBDA,*
WhAm 1
McNeill, Hector 1728-1785 *DcAmB,*
WhAm H
McNeill, I C 1855- *WhAm 4*
McNeill, John Charles 1874-1907 *WhAm 1*
McNeill, John Hanson 1815-1864 *DcAmB,*
WhAm H
McNeill, John Thomas 1885-1975 *WhAm 6*
McNeill, Lawrence 1849-1915 *NatCAB 16*
McNeill, Neal Edward 1875-1958 *WhAm 3*
McNeill, Rivers 1858-1918 *NatCAB 18*
McNeill, Robert Hayes 1877- *WhAm 6*
McNeill, Thomas W 1900-1958 *WhAm 3*
McNeill, William Gibbs 1800-1853 *ApCAB*
McNeill, William Gibbs 1801-1853 *DcAmB,*
NatCAB 9, TwCBDA, WhAm H
McNeir, George 1860-1941 *ApCAB X,*
WhAm 1
McNeir, William 1864- *WhAm 4*
McNeirny, Francis 1828-1894 *WhAm H*
McNellis, Frank 1880- *NatCAB 18*
McNelly, Leander H 1844-1877 *REnAW*
McNeven, William James 1763-1841 *Drake*
McNeven, William James *see also* MacNeven,
William James
McNevin, John *NewYHSD*
McNew, John Thomas Lamar 1895-1946
WhAm 2
McNich, Frank Ramsay 1873-1950 *WhAm 3*
McNichol, Paul John 1908-1971 *WhAm 5*
McNicholas, John Timothy 1877-1950
DcAmB S4, NatCAB 39, WhAm 3
McNichols, John Patrick 1875-1932 *WhAm 1*
McNider, Alexander *NewYHSD*
McNiece, Harold Francis 1923-1972 *WhAm 5*
McNiece, Robert Gibson 1839-1913 *WhAm 1*
McNiel, Archibald *BiAUS*
McNiel, John 1784-1850 *ApCAB, TwCBDA*
McNierney, Francis 1828-1894 *ApCAB,*
NatCAB 3, TwCBDA
McNinch, Frank Ramsay 1873-1950
NatCAB 39
McNish, George 1660?-1722 *ApCAB*
McNulta, John 1837-1900 *BiAUS, BiDrAC,*
WhAm 1, WhAm 4
McNulty, Anna 1864- *WomWWA 14*
McNulty, Caleb J *BiAUS*
McNulty, Chester Hugh 1889-1957 *NatCAB 46,*
WhAm 3
McNulty, Frank Joseph 1872-1926 *BiDrAC,*
DcAmB, WhAm 5
McNulty, George Albert 1900-1964 *WhAm 4*
McNulty, James 1900-1972 *WhAm 5*

McNulty, John Laurence 1898-1959 *WhAm 3*
McNulty, P M *NewYHSD*
McNulty, Robert Wilkinson 1897-1966
WhAm 4
McNutt, Alexander 1725?-1811? *DcAmB,*
WhAm H
McNutt, Alexander Gallatin 1801-1848 *ApCAB,*
BiAUS, Drake, TwCBDA
McNutt, Alexander Gallatin 1802-1848
NatCAB 13
McNutt, Anna Mary d1969 *WhAm 5*
McNutt, Patterson 1833-1886 *TwCBDA*
McNutt, Paul Vories 1891-1955 *DcAmB S5,*
WhAm 3
McNutt, Sarah Jane *NatCAB 15*
McNutt, Thomas Ford 1902-1963 *NatCAB 51*
McNutt, William Fletcher 1839- *NatCAB 7,*
WhAm 4
McNutt, William Roy 1879- *WhAm 6*
McOrmond, Raymond Richards 1886-1943
NatCAB 32
McOuat, Mary Elizabeth *WomWWA 14*
McParlan, James 1844-1919 *WebAB*
McParlan, Thomas Francis 1869-1928
ApCAB X
McPeak, William Wallace 1908-1964 *WhAm 4*
McPhail, George Wilson 1816-1871
NatCAB 11, TwCBDA
McPhee, Eugene Roderick 1902-1975 *WhAm 6*
McPhee, Julian A 1896-1967 *WhAm 4*
McPheeters, Chester Amos 1895-1961 *WhAm 4*
McPheeters, J D Laurance 1887-1956
NatCAB 48
McPheeters, John William 1908-1944
NatCAB 34
McPheeters, William Emmett 1884-1962
WhAm 4
McPheeters, William Marcellus 1815- *ApCAB,*
TwCBDA
McPheeters, William Marcellus 1854-1935
WhAm 1
McPherren, Charles Elmo 1875- *WhAm 5*
McPherrin, John Weitz 1897-1974 *WhAm 6*
McPherson, Aimee Semple 1890-1944
DcAmB S3, DcAmReB, EncAAH,
McGEWB, NatCAB 35, NotAW,
WebAB, WhAm HA, WhAm 2,
WhAm 4A
McPherson, Alexander 1836- *NatCAB 18*
McPherson, Charles 1873-1945 *WhAm 2*
McPherson, Donald Fraser 1884-1944
NatCAB 32
McPherson, Edward 1830-1895 *AmBi, ApCAB,*
BiAUS, BiDrAC, DcAmB, Drake,
NatCAB 4, TwCBDA, WhAm H,
WhAmP
McPherson, George Edwin 1876-1945
NatCAB 35
McPherson, Harry Wright 1879-1957
NatCAB 43, WhAm 3
McPherson, Hobart M 1896-1955 *WhAm 3*
McPherson, Isaac V 1868- *WhAm 4*
McPherson, Isaac V 1868-1932 *WhAm 2*
McPherson, Isaac Vanbert 1868-1931 *BiDrAC*
McPherson, James Birdseye 1828-1864 *AmBi,*
ApCAB, DcAmB, Drake, NatCAB 4,
TwCBDA, WebAMB, WhAm H
McPherson, John *NewYHSD*
McPherson, John Bayard 1846-1919 *WhAm 1*
McPherson, John Edward 1872-1937 *WhAm 1*
McPherson, John Hanson Thomas 1865-1953
NatCAB 13, TwCBDA, WhAm 3
McPherson, John Rhoderic 1833-1897 *BiDrAC,*
WhAm H, WhAmP
McPherson, John Rhoderick 1833-1897
NatCAB 3
McPherson, John Roderic 1833-1897 *ApCAB,*
TwCBDA
McPherson, Logan Grant 1863-1925 *DcAmB,*
NatCAB 25, WhAm 1
McPherson, Lucy Belle Harmon 1855-
WomWWA 14
McPherson, Lydia Starr *AmWom*
McPherson, R Bruce 1870-1956 *NatCAB 47*
McPherson, Robert 1880-1950 *NatCAB 40*
McPherson, Robert A 1812?-• *NewYHSD*
McPherson, Ross 1876-1935 *WhAm 1*
McPherson, Samuel Dace 1873-1953 *WhAm 3*

McPherson, Sherman Tecumseh 1864-
WhAm 4
McPherson, Simon John 1850-1919 *NatCAB 14,*
NatCAB 51, WhAm 1
McPherson, Smith 1848-1915 *BiDrAC,*
DcAmB, NatCAB 25, TwCBDA,
WhAm 1
McPherson, W J *NewYHSD*
McPherson, William 1751-1813 *ApCAB*
McPherson, William 1813-1872 *ApCAB*
McPherson, William 1864-1951 *NatCAB 41,*
WhAm 3
McPherson, William, Jr. 1834-1915 *NatCAB 17*
McPherson, William *see also* Macpherson,
William
McPherson, William Lenhart 1865-1930
WhAm 1
McPhillips, James 1872-1949 *NatCAB 42*
McPike, Henry H d1940 *WhAm 1*
McQuade, Eugene Thomas 1898-1965
NatCAB 52
McQuade, James 1829-1885 *ApCAB,*
NatCAB 7, TwCBDA
McQuade, Vincent Augustine 1909-1971
WhAm 5
McQuaid, Bernard John 1823-1909 *ApCAB,*
BiDAmEd, DcAmB, DcAmReB,
NatCAB 12, TwCBDA, WhAm 1
McQuaid, William Ravenel 1881-1965 *WhAm 4*
McQuarrie, Irvine 1891-1961 *WhAm 4*
McQuay, William *NewYHSD*
McQueary, Thomas Howard 1861-1930
TwCBDA
McQueary, Thomas Howard *see also* MacQueary,
Thomas Howard
McQueen, Elizabeth Lippincott 1879- *WhAm 6*
McQueen, Frederick Emil 1891-1963 *WhAm 4*
McQueen, Henry Clay 1846-1935 *WhAm 1*
McQueen, John 1804-1867 *BiDConf, BiDrAC,*
WhAm H, WhAmP
McQueen, John 1808-1867 *ApCAB, BiAUS,*
TwCBDA
McQueen, John Walter 1875-1953 *NatCAB 46*
McQueen, Katherine Margaret *WomWWA 14*
McQueen, L A 1893-1971 *WhAm 5*
McQueen, McIntosh *BiAUS*
McQueen, Stewart 1857-1923 *WhAm 1*
McQueen, Thomas 1803-1861 *ApCAB*
McQuesten, Frederick 1857-1923 *ApCAB X*
McQuide, Sarah Tappin 1868- *WomWWA 14*
McQuigg, John Rea 1865-1928 *WhAm 1*
McQuigg, Martin V B 1861- *ApCAB X*
McQuilkin, Robert Crawford 1886-1952
WhAm 3
McQuillen, John Hugh 1826-1879 *ApCAB,*
DcAmB, TwCBDA, WhAm H
McQuillin, Eugene 1860-1937 *WhAm 1*
McRae, Austin Lee 1861-1922 *WhAm 1*
McRae, Bruce 1867-1927 *WhAm 1*
McRae, Colin John 1812-1877 *BiDConf*
McRae, Duncan Kirkland 1820-1888 *DcAmB,*
WhAm H
McRae, Emma Montgomery 1848-
WomWWA 14
McRae, Fannie Collier *WomWWA 14*
McRae, Floyd Willcox 1861-1921 *NatCAB 19*
McRae, Floyd Willcox *see also* MacRae, Floyd
Willcox
McRae, George W 1888-1950 *WhAm 3*
McRae, James Henry 1863-1940 *NatCAB 46,*
WhAm 1
McRae, James Wilson 1910-1960 *WhAm 3*
McRae, John Albert 1875-1962 *NatCAB 46*
McRae, John C *NewYHSD*
McRae, John J d1868 *BiAUS*
McRae, John J 1810?-1868 *ApCAB, Drake,*
TwCBDA
McRae, John Jones 1815-1861 *WhAm H*
McRae, John Jones 1815-1868 *BiDConf,*
BiDrAC, NatCAB 13, WhAmP
McRae, Milton Alexander 1858-1930 *DcAmB,*
NatCAB 16, WhAm 1
McRae, Norman Howard 1895-1957
NatCAB 48
McRae, Roderick 1906-1960 *WhAm 4*
McRae, Thomas Chipman 1851-1929 *BiDrAC,*
DcAmB, NatCAB 17, TwCBDA,
WhAm 1, WhAmP

McRae, William Allan, Jr. 1909-1973 *WhAm 6*
McRary, Robert Baxter *WhoColR*
McRaven, Hortense McMorries 1886-
  WomWWA 14
McReady, James *BiAUS*
McRee, Griffith John 1758-1801 *ApCAB*
McRee, Griffith John 1820-1872 *ApCAB,*
  Drake, NatCAB 7
McRee, Samuel 1801-1849 *ApCAB*
McRee, William 1787-1832 *Drake*
McRee, William 1787-1833 *ApCAB*
McReynolds, Andrew Thomas 1806-1898
  NatCAB 6
McReynolds, Andrew Thomas 1808-1898
  ApCAB Sup
McReynolds, Frederick Wilson 1872- *WhAm 5*
McReynolds, George Edgar 1910-1954 *WhAm 3*
McReynolds, James Clark 1862-1946 *ApCAB X,*
  BiDrUSE, DcAmB S4, NatCAB 33,
  WebAB, WhAm 2
McReynolds, Jennie Elizabeth Davis
  WomWWA 14
McReynolds, John Oliver 1865-1942
  NatCAB 32, WhAm 2
McReynolds, Peter Wesley 1872-1917 *WhAm 1*
McReynolds, Samuel Davis 1872-1939 *BiDrAC,*
  DcAmB S2, NatCAB 32, WhAm 1,
  WhAmP
McReynolds, William Henry 1880-1951
  WhAm 3
McRill, Albert Leroy 1880-1956 *WhAm 3*
McRoberts, Harriet Skinner d1946 *WhAm 2*
McRoberts, Samuel d1843 *BiAUS*
McRoberts, Samuel 1799-1843 *BiDrAC,*
  TwCBDA, WhAm H
McRoberts, Samuel 1800?-1843 *ApCAB,*
  NatCAB 5
McRoberts, Samuel 1868-1947 *NatCAB 36*
McRoberts, Samuel 1869-1947 *ApCAB X*
McRuer, Donald Campbell 1826-1898 *BiAUS,*
  BiDrAC
McShane, Andrew James 1864-1936 *WhAm 1*
McShane, Augustus 1861-1923 *NatCAB 17*
McShane, Henry 1830-1889 *NatCAB 3*
McShane, John Albert 1850-1923 *BiDrAC,*
  NatCAB 20
McShane, John James 1878-1943 *NatCAB 32*
McSherry, James 1776-1849 *BiAUS, BiDrAC,*
  WhAm H
McSherry, James 1819-1869 *ApCAB,*
  TwCBDA
McSherry, James 1842- *NatCAB 13*
McSherry, Jennie Emma 1880- *WomWWA 14*
McSherry, Richard 1817-1885 *ApCAB,*
  TwCBDA, WhAm H
McSherry, William 1799-1839 *ApCAB Sup*
McSkimmon, William Bingham 1872-1953
  NatCAB 45, WhAm 5
McSoley, Raymond Joseph 1897-1959 *WhAm 3*
McSorley, Edward 1902-1966 *WhAm 4*
McSorley, G Franklin 1903-1966 *NatCAB 53*
McSorley, Joseph 1874-1963 *WhAm 4*
McSpadden, Joseph Walker 1874-1960
  WhAm 4
McSparran, James 1680?-1757 *ApCAB, Drake*
McSparran, John Aldus 1873- *WhAm 5*
McSurely, William Harvey 1865-1943 *WhAm 2*
McSwain, John Jackson 1875-1936 *BiDrAC,*
  WhAm 1, WhAmP
McSween, Alexander *REnAW*
McSween, Harold Barnett 1926- *BiDrAC*
McSweeney, Henry 1855-1946 *NatCAB 35,*
  WhAm 2
McSweeney, John 1890-1969 *BiDrAC,*
  WhAm 5
McSweeney, Miles Benjamin 1855-1909
  NatCAB 12, TwCBDA, WhAm 1
McTague, Charles Patrick 1890-1966 *WhAm 4*
McTammany, John 1845-1915 *DcAmB,*
  WebAB, WhAm HA, WhAm 4
McTarnahan, William Chamberlin 1882-1951
  WhAm 3
McTavish, Donald 1755?-1815 *ApCAB*
McTyeire, Holland Nimmons 1824-1889
  ApCAB, BiDConf, DcAmB, NatCAB 8,
  TwCBDA, WhAm H
McVay, Anna Pearl 1871- *WomWWA 14*

McVay, Charles Butler, Jr. 1868-1949
  NatCAB 45, WhAm 2
McVay, Hugh 1788-1851 *TwCBDA*
McVea, Emilie Watts 1867-1928 *NatCAB 21,*
  WhAm 1, WomWWA 14
McVean, Charles 1802-1848 *BiAUS, BiDrAC,*
  WhAm H
McVean, David Bowie 1903-1959 *NatCAB 48*
McVeigh, Charles Senff 1883-1962 *NatCAB 47*
McVeigh, John Newburn 1912-1959 *WhAm 3*
McVeigh, Sherman 1864-1951 *NatCAB 42*
McVeigh, Thomas Michael 1868-1935
  NatCAB 26
McVey, Frank LeRond 1869-1953 *BiDAmEd,*
  DcAmB S5, NatCAB 13, TwCBDA,
  WhAm 3
McVey, Mabel Sawyer 1875- *WomWWA 14*
McVey, Walter Lewis, Jr. 1922- *BiDrAC*
McVey, William E 1864-1931 *WhAm 1*
McVey, William Estus 1885-1958 *BiDrAC,*
  WhAm 3
McVicar, Nelson 1871-1960 *NatCAB 47,*
  WhAm 4
McVicar, Peter 1829-1903 *BiDAmEd,*
  TwCBDA
McVickar, Estelle R *WomWWA 14*
McVickar, John 1787-1868 *ApCAB, DcAmB,*
  NatCAB 6, TwCBDA, WhAm H
McVickar, John see also MacVickar, John
McVickar, William Augustus 1827-1877
  ApCAB
McVickar, William Neilson 1843-1910
  ApCAB Sup, DcAmB, NatCAB 11,
  TwCBDA, WhAm 1
McVicker, James Hubert 1822-1896 *ApCAB,*
  DcAmB, NatCAB 6, WhAm H
McVicker, Mary Frances d1881 *ApCAB*
McVicker, Roy Harrison 1924- *BiDrAC*
McVinney, Russell J 1898-1971 *WhAm 5*
McVitty, Albert Elliott 1876-1948 *NatCAB 36*
McWade, Robert Malachi 1857- *TwCBDA,*
  WhAm 1
McWane, Arthur Thomas 1884-1954
  NatCAB 43
McWane, Henry Edward 1859-1914
  NatCAB 30
McWane, James Ransom 1869-1933 *WhAm 1*
McWhinney, Thomas Martin 1823-1909
  WhAm 1
McWhirter, Felix Tyree 1853-1915 *ApCAB X,*
  WhAm 1
McWhirter, Luella Frances Smith 1859-1952
  WhAm 3, WomWWA 14
McWhirter, William Allan 1890-1955 *WhAm 4*
McWhorter, Alexander 1734-1807 *ApCAB,*
  TwCBDA
McWhorter, Alexander 1822-1880 *ApCAB*
McWhorter, Alexander see also MacWhorter,
  Alexander
McWhorter, Ashton Waugh 1877-1938
  WhAm 1
McWhorter, Ernest D 1884-1950 *WhAm 2*
McWhorter, George G 1833-1891 *NatCAB 12*
McWhorter, Golder Lewis 1888-1938
  NatCAB 29
McWhorter, Henry Clay 1836-1913
  NatCAB 20, WhAm 1
McWhorter, William Breese 1887-1958
  NatCAB 48
McWilliam, John R 1889-1966 *WhAm 4*
McWilliams, Alexander 1775-1850 *NatCAB 15*
McWilliams, Clarence Arthur 1870-1927
  ApCAB X, WhAm 1
McWilliams, Daniel Wilkin 1837-1919
  NatCAB 19
McWilliams, John 1880-1962 *NatCAB 50*
McWilliams, John Dacher 1891- *BiDrAC*
McWilliams, John Probasco 1891-1972
  NatCAB 57, WhAm 5
McWilliams, Margaret Stovel 1875-
  WomWWA 14
McWilliams, Roland Fairbairn 1874-1957
  WhAm 3
McWilliams, Thomas Samuel 1865-1936
  NatCAB 28
McWilliams, Thomas Samuel 1865-1937
  WhAm 1

McWilliams, William John 1896-1957
  NatCAB 46
McWillie, Thomas Anderson 1849-1911
  WhAm 1
McWillie, William 1795-1869 *ApCAB, BiAUS,*
  BiDrAC, Drake, NatCAB 13, TwCBDA,
  WhAm H
M'Dougall, John *NewYHSD*
M'Dowell, William H *NewYHSD*
Meacham, Franklin Adams 1862-1902
  NatCAB 15
Meacham, Henry Clay 1869-1929 *NatCAB 44*
Meacham, James 1810-1856 *ApCAB, BiAUS,*
  BiDrAC, Drake, TwCBDA, WhAm H,
  WhAmP
Meacham, W Banks 1873- *WhAm 5*
Meachem, John Goldesbrough 1823-1896
  NatCAB 16
Meachem, John Goldesbrough 1846-
  NatCAB 16
Meachem, John Goldesbrough, III 1873-
  NatCAB 16
Meachum, McDonald 1876-1957 *NatCAB 43*
Mead, Aaron Benedict 1838-1925 *NatCAB 20*
Mead, Ada Wing *WomWWA 14*
Mead, Albert Davis 1869-1946 *NatCAB 36,*
  WhAm 2
Mead, Albert Edward 1861-1913 *NatCAB 14,*
  WhAm 1
Mead, Arthur Emett 1902-1963 *WhAm 4*
Mead, Arthur Raymond 1880- *WhAm 6*
Mead, Ben Carlton 1902- *IIBEAAW*
Mead, Charles Larew 1868-1941 *NatCAB 33,*
  WhAm 1
Mead, Charles Marsh 1836-1911 *ApCAB,*
  DcAmB, NatCAB 10, TwCBDA,
  WhAm 1
Mead, Charles Wilbur 1887-1956 *NatCAB 48*
Mead, Cowles 1776-1844 *BiAUS, BiDrAC,*
  WhAm H
Mead, Cyrus DeWitt 1875-1943 *NatCAB 32*
Mead, D Irving 1875-1951 *NatCAB 39,*
  WhAm 3
Mead, Daniel Webster 1862-1948 *NatCAB 41,*
  WhAm 2
Mead, Edward Campbell 1837-1908 *TwCBDA,*
  WhAm 1
Mead, Edward Sherwood 1874-1956
  NatCAB 43, WhAm 5
Mead, Edward Spencer 1847-1894 *TwCBDA*
Mead, Edwin Doak 1849-1937 *ApCAB,*
  DcAmB S2, NatCAB 11, NatCAB 28,
  TwCBDA, WhAm 1
Mead, Edwin H 1822- *NatCAB 3*
Mead, Elinor Gertrude 1837-1910 *NewYHSD*
Mead, Elizabeth Manning Cleveland 1876-1946
  NatCAB 38
Mead, Elizabeth Storrs Billings 1832-1917
  NotAW, TwCBDA, WhAm 1,
  WomWWA 14
Mead, Elizabeth Storrs Billings 1835?-1917
  NatCAB 4
Mead, Elwood 1858-1936 *AmBi, DcAmB S2,*
  NatCAB 18, NatCAB 26, REnAW,
  WhAm 1
Mead, Emily Fogg 1871- *WomWWA 14*
Mead, Frederick Sumner 1866-1935
  NatCAB 28, WhAm 1
Mead, George Herbert 1863-1931 *DcAmB S1,*
  McGEWB, WebAB, WhAm 1
Mead, George Houk 1877-1963 *NatCAB 53,*
  WhAm 4
Mead, George Jackson 1891-1949 *NatCAB 37,*
  WhAm 2
Mead, George Whitefield d1946 *WhAm 2*
Mead, George Wilson 1871-1961 *NatCAB 51,*
  WhAm 4
Mead, Gilbert Wilcox 1889-1949 *NatCAB 37,*
  WhAm 2
Mead, Harry Leighton 1883-1965 *NatCAB 51,*
  WhAm 4
Mead, Henry E 1832?- *NewYHSD*
Mead, James Michael 1885-1964 *BiDrAC,*
  NatCAB 51, WhAm 4
Mead, John Abner 1841-1920 *NatCAB 19,*
  WhAm 1
Mead, Julian Augustus 1856-1913 *NatCAB 16*

Mead, Kate Campbell Hurd 1867-1941
*NatCAB 38, NotAW, WhAm 1,
WomWWA 14*
Mead, Larkin Goldsmith 1835-1910 *AmBi,
ApCAB, BnEnAmA, DcAmB, NatCAB 1,
NewYHSD, TwCBDA, WhAm 1*
Mead, Leon 1861- *WhAm 4*
Mead, Leonard Charles 1856-1920 *WhAm 1*
Mead, Lucia True Ames 1856-1936 *BiCAW,
NatCAB 28, NotAW, TwCBDA,
WhAm 1, WomWWA 14*
Mead, Margaret 1901- *EncAB, McGEWB,
WebAB*
Mead, Nelson Prentiss 1878-1967 *WhAm 4*
Mead, Richard 1673-1754 *BiHiMed*
Mead, Robert Gillespie 1871-1947 *NatCAB 38*
Mead, Roderick Fletcher 1900-1971
NatCAB 56
Mead, Solomon Cristy 1867- *WhAm 5*
Mead, Sterling V 1888-1972 *WhAm 5*
Mead, Theodore Hoe 1837-1909 *NatCAB 25,
WhAm 4*
Mead, Warren Hewitt 1836-1910 *NatCAB 6*
Mead, Warren Judson 1883-1960 *WhAm 4*
Mead, William Edward 1860- *NatCAB 16,
WhAm 5*
Mead, William Henry 1921-1974 *WhAm 6*
Mead, William Leon 1861- *TwCBDA*
Mead, William Rutherford 1846-1928 *AmBi,
ApCAB, DcAmB, NatCAB 23, TwCBDA,
WhAm 1*
Mead, William Whitman 1845-1930 *WhAm 1*
Meaddough, Ray James 1869- *WhoColR*
Meade, Edwin Ruthven 1836-1889 *BiAUS,
BiDrAC, WhAm H*
Meade, Eleanore Hussey 1884-1969 *WhAm 5*
Meade, Francis 1814?- *NewYHSD*
Meade, Francis Louis 1894-1958 *WhAm 3*
Meade, Frank B 1867-1947 *WhAm 2*
Meade, George 1741-1808 *ApCAB, DcAmB,
NatCAB 4, WhAm H*
Meade, George 1843- *ApCAB*
Meade, George Edward 1914-1972 *WhAm 5*
Meade, George Gordon 1815-1872 *AmBi,
ApCAB, DcAmB, EncAB, McGEWB,
NatCAB 4, TwCBDA, WebAB,
WebAMB, WhAm H, WhoMilH*
Meade, George Gordon 1816-1872 *Drake*
Meade, George Peterkin 1883-1975 *WhAm 6*
Meade, Hugh Allen 1907-1949 *BiDrAC*
Meade, James J 1882-1949 *WhAm 3*
Meade, Janifer Dewitt 1868- *WhAm 4*
Meade, Larkin G *Drake*
Meade, Richard Kidder d1862 *BiAUS*
Meade, Richard Kidder 1746-1805 *ApCAB,
DcAmB, NatCAB 10, TwCBDA,
WhAm H*
Meade, Richard Kidder 1795?-1862 *ApCAB,
TwCBDA*
Meade, Richard Kidder 1801-1862 *NatCAB 10*
Meade, Richard Kidder 1803-1862 *BiDrAC,
WhAm H*
Meade, Richard Kidder 1874-1930 *NatCAB 10,
WhAm 1*
Meade, Richard Worsam 1778-1828 *ApCAB,
DcAmB*
Meade, Richard Worsam 1807-1870 *ApCAB,
DcAmB, NatCAB 4, TwCBDA,
WhAm H*
Meade, Richard Worsam 1837-1897 *ApCAB,
DcAmB, TwCBDA, WhAm H*
Meade, Richard Worsam 1870-1933
NatCAB 41, WhAm 1
Meade, Robert Douthat 1903-1974 *WhAm 6*
Meade, Robert Leamy 1841-1910 *DcAmB,
WhAm 1*
Meade, Wendell Howes 1912- *BiDrAC*
Meade, William d1833 *Drake*
Meade, William 1789-1862 *DcAmB, Drake,
NatCAB 7, TwCBDA, WhAm H*
Meade, William Kidder 1851- *NatCAB 9*
Meader, George 1907- *BiDrAC, WhAmP*
Meader, Lucie Claflin 1876- *WomWWA 14*
Meador, Chastain Clark d1905 *NatCAB 3,
WhAm 1*
Meador, Elihu Newton 1878-1959 *NatCAB 44*
Meadowcroft, William Henry 1853-1937
WhAm 1

Meadows, Christian 1814?- *NewYHSD*
Meadows, Clarence Watson 1904-1961
WhAm 4
Meadows, James Allen 1884-1970 *WhAm 5*
Meadows, R M *NewYHSD*
Meagher, James Francis 1858-1917 *WhAm 1*
Meagher, James Luke 1848-1920 *WhAm 1*
Meagher, Jennie Elizabeth *WomWWA 14*
Meagher, John 1844?- *REnAW*
Meagher, Joseph Aloysius 1880-1947
NatCAB 36
Meagher, Michael 1844?-1881 *REnAW*
Meagher, Raymond 1872-1954 *WhAm 3*
Meagher, Thomas Francis 1823-1867 *AmBi,
ApCAB, DcAmB, Drake, NatCAB 5,
TwCBDA, WhAm H*
Meaker, Isabelle Jackson 1874- *WomWWA 14*
Meakin, Louis Henry 1850?-1917 *IIBEAAW,
WhAm 1*
Mealey, Carroll Edward 1893-1963 *WhAm 4*
Meals, Samuel Wilbur 1869-1939 *NatCAB 30*
Meance, Miss *NewYHSD*
Meance, Peter I *NewYHSD*
Meance, Peter J *NewYHSD*
Meanes, Lenna Leota *WomWWA 14*
Meaney, Thomas Francis 1888-1968 *WhAm 5*
Means, Alexander 1801-1883 *ApCAB, Drake,
NatCAB 1, TwCBDA*
Means, Charles Streamer 1865-1930
NatCAB 25
Means, David MacGregor 1847-1931 *WhAm 1*
Means, Earl A 1877-1952 *WhAm 3*
Means, Eldred Kurtz 1878-1957 *WhAm 3*
Means, Elliott Anderson 1905-1962 *IIBEAAW*
Means, Emily Adams *WhAm 5*
Means, Frank Wilson 1879- *WhAm 3*
Means, Gaston Bullock 1879-1938 *DcAmB S2,
WebAB, WhAm HA, WhAm 4*
Means, George Hamilton 1886-1941 *WhAm 2*
Means, Howard Chester 1875-1951 *NatCAB 42*
Means, James Howard 1885-1967 *NatCAB 53,
WhAm 4*
Means, John Hugh 1812-1862 *ApCAB, BiAUS,
Drake, NatCAB 12, TwCBDA*
Means, Philip Ainsworth 1892-1944 *WhAm 2*
Means, Rice William 1877-1949 *BiDrAC,
NatCAB 36, WhAm 2*
Means, Russel Garrett 1895-1970 *NatCAB 55*
Means, Stewart 1852-1940 *WhAm 2*
Means, Thomas Herbert 1875- *WhAm 5*
Means, William Alfred 1867-1939 *NatCAB 34*
Meanwell, Walter E 1884-1953 *WhAm 3*
Meany, Edmond Stephen 1862-1935 *DcAmB S1,
WhAm 1*
Meany, Edward P 1854-1938 *NatCAB 14,
WhAm 1*
Meany, George 1894- *EncAB, McGEWB,
WebAB*
Meara, Frank S 1866- *WhAm 1*
Meares, John 1746-1801 *ApCAB*
Meares, John 1756?-1809 *NewYHSD*
Mearns, Edgar Alexander 1856-1916 *DcAmB,
NatCAB 25, WhAm H, WhAm 1*
Mearns, Hughes 1875-1965 *WhAm 4*
Mearns, Robert Walter 1866-1949 *NatCAB 38*
Mearns, William Hughes 1875-1965 *BiDAmEd*
Mears, Brainerd 1881- *WhAm 6*
Mears, Catharine *NewYHSD*
Mears, David Otis 1842-1915 *DcAmB,
NatCAB 12, NatCAB 21, WhAm 1*
Mears, Edgar Howard 1895-1966 *NatCAB 53*
Mears, Eliot Grinnell 1889-1946 *NatCAB 35,
WhAm 2*
Mears, Frederick 1878-1939 *NatCAB 29,
WhAm 1*
Mears, Helen Farnsworth 1872-1916 *DcAmB,
NatCAB 25, NotAW*
Mears, Helen Farnsworth 1878-1916 *WhAm 1,
WomWWA 14*
Mears, Howard Reber, Jr. 1904-1962
NatCAB 50
Mears, J Ewing 1838- *WhAm 4*
Mears, John William 1825-1881 *ApCAB,
DcAmB, TwCBDA, WhAm H*
Mears, Leverett 1850-1917 *WhAm 1*
Mears, Louise Wilhelmina 1874- *WhAm 5*
Mears, Mary 1876- *WhAm 5, WomWWA 14*
Mears, Mary Grinnell 1857-1935 *NatCAB 31*

Mears, Otto 1840-1931 *DcAmB, REnAW*
Mease, James 1771-1846 *ApCAB, DcAmB,
Drake, WhAm H*
Mease, John 1746-1826 *ApCAB, NatCAB 5*
Mease, Matthew d1787 *ApCAB*
Meason, Isaac 1742-1818 *DcAmB, WhAm H*
Mebane, Albert Leonidas 1880- *WhoColR*
Mebane, Alexander 1744-1795 *ApCAB, BiAUS,
BiDrAC, WhAm H*
Mebane, Alexander Duff 1855-1923
NatCAB 20
Mebane, B Frank 1865- *WhAm 4*
Mebane, Daniel 1894-1956 *WhAm 3*
Mebane, George Allen 1863-1921 *NatCAB 29*
Mebane, Harry Bartlett, Jr. 1909-1967 *WhAm 5*
Mebane, James *ApCAB*
Mebane, Robert Sloan 1868-1934 *NatCAB 26,
WhAm 1*
Mebus, George Brinker 1903-1972 *NatCAB 57*
Mecartney, Malcolm 1899-1958 *NatCAB 44*
Mech, Stephen John 1909-1968 *WhAm 5*
Mechain, Pierre-Francois-Andre 1744-1804
DcScB
Mechau *NewYHSD*
Mechau, Frank, Jr. 1904-1946 *WhAm 2*
Mechau, Frank Albert, Jr. 1903?-1946
IIBEAAW
Mechem, Edwin Leard 1912- *BiDrAC*
Mechem, Floyd Russell 1858-1928 *BiDAmEd,
DcAmB, NatCAB 23, WhAm 1*
Mechem, Merritt Cramer 1870-1946
NatCAB 33, WhAm 2
Mechem, Philip 1892-1969 *WhAm 5*
Mecherle, George Jacob 1877-1951 *WhAm 3*
Mecherle, Ramond Perry 1904-1954
NatCAB 45, WhAm 3
Mechesi *NewYHSD*
Mechlin, Leila 1874-1949 *NotAW, WhAm 2,
WomWWA 14*
Mechnikov, Ilya Ilich 1845-1916 *AsBiEn,
DcScB*
Meckel, Johann Friedrich 1724-1774 *BiHiMed*
Meckel, Johann Friedrich 1781-1833 *BiHiMed,
DcScB*
Meckel, Max *NewYHSD*
Mecklin, John Martin 1918-1971 *NatCAB 57,
WhAm 5*
Mecklin, John Moffatt 1871-1956 *NatCAB 44,
WhAm 3*
Mecom, Benjamin 1732-1776? *DcAmB,
WhAm H*
Mecom, Jane Franklin 1712-1794? *NotAW*
Mecord, Henry E *NewYHSD*
Medairy, Alexander R *NewYHSD*
Medairy, Charles E 1834?- *NewYHSD*
Medairy, John 1798?- *NewYHSD*
Medalie, George Zerdin 1883-1946 *WhAm 2*
Medary, Milton Bennett 1874-1929 *DcAmB,
NatCAB 24, WhAm 1*
Medary, Samuel 1801-1864 *AmBi, ApCAB,
BiAUS, DcAmB, Drake, NatCAB 8,
TwCBDA, WhAm H, WhAmP*
Medawar, Peter Brian 1915- *AsBiEn,
McGEWB*
Medbery, Chauncey Joseph 1851-1918
NatCAB 18
Medbery, Rebecca B 1808-1868 *ApCAB*
Medbury, Charles Sanderson 1865-1932
WhAm 1
Medearis, T W 1889-1970 *WhAm 5*
Meder, Florence Fashauer 1879-
WomWWA 14
Medford, William 1909-1969 *WhAm 5*
Medhurst, Sir Charles E H 1896-1954 *WhAm 3*
Medici, Cosimo De 1389-1464 *McGEWB*
Medici, Cosmo *NewYHSD*
Medici, Lorenzo De 1449-1492 *McGEWB*
Medicus, Friedrich Casimir 1736-1808 *DcScB*
Medill, Joseph 1823-1899 *AmBi, ApCAB,
DcAmB, McGEWB, NatCAB 1,
TwCBDA, WebAB, WhAm H, WhAmP*
Medill, Monica Morgan 1866- *WomWWA 14*
Medill, William d1865 *BiAUS*
Medill, William 1801-1865 *NatCAB 3*
Medill, William 1802-1865 *BiDrAC, WhAm H*
Medill, William 1805-1865 *ApCAB, Drake,
TwCBDA*
Medina, Antonio 1824-1884 *ApCAB*

Medina, Pedro De 1493-1576 *DcScB*
Medlar, Adele Bishop 1880- *WomWWA 14*
Medley, John 1804- *ApCAB, Drake*
Medley, Mat *WhAm H*
Medlicott, Mary 1845- *WomWWA 14*
Medows, Sir William 1738-1813 *Drake*
Medsger, Oliver Perry 1870- *WhAm 5*
Meduna, Ladislas Joseph 1896-1964
    NatCAB 50
Mee, Cassie Ward 1848- *AmWom*
Mee, Emma L Gilmore 1869- *WomWWA 14*
Mee, William 1861-1931 *NatCAB 42*
Mee, William 1861-1932 *WhAm 1*
Meech, Ezra 1773-1856 *BiAUS, BiDrAC,
    TwCBDA, WhAm H*
Meech, Jeannette DuBois 1835- *AmWom*
Meeds, Lloyd 1927- *BiDrAC*
Meehan, John S 1793-1861 *BiAUS,
    NatCAB 13*
Meehan, John Silva 1790-1863 *DcAmLiB*
Meehan, Joseph *NewYHSD*
Meehan, M Joseph 1901-1963 *WhAm 4*
Meehan, Thomas 1826-1901 *AmBi, ApCAB,
    DcAmB, NatCAB 11, TwCBDA,
    WhAm 1*
Meehan, Thomas A 1907-1965 *WhAm 4*
Meehan, William Edward 1853- *NatCAB 16*
Meek, Alexander Beaufort 1814-1865 *AmBi,
    ApCAB, DcAmB, Drake, NatCAB 11,
    TwCBDA, WhAm H*
Meek, Annie Winfrey 1862- *WomWWA 14*
Meek, B B 1883-1937 *NatCAB 27*
Meek, Benjamin Franklin 1836-1899 *WhAm 1*
Meek, Channing Frank 1855-1912 *NatCAB 15*
Meek, Charles Simpson 1870-1952 *WhAm 3*
Meek, Edward Roscoe 1865- *WhAm 5*
Meek, Fielding Bradford 1817-1876 *AmBi,
    ApCAB, DcAmB, DcScB, NatCAB 11,
    TwCBDA, WhAm H*
Meek, Howard Bagnall 1893-1969 *NatCAB 55,
    WhAm 5*
Meek, John Henry 1877-1940 *WhAm 1*
Meek, Joseph A 1904-1971 *WhAm 5*
Meek, Joseph L 1810-1875 *DcAmB, REnAW,
    WhAm H*
Meek, Robert Abner 1867-1949 *WhAm 3*
Meek, Samuel Mills 1835-1901 *NatCAB 20*
Meek, Seth Eugene 1859-1914 *WhAm 1*
Meek, Sterner St. Paul 1894-1972 *WhAm 5*
Meek, Theophile James 1881- *WhAm 6*
Meek, Walter Joseph 1878- *WhAm 6*
Meeker, Arthur 1866-1946 *WhAm 2*
Meeker, Arthur 1902-1971 *WhAm 5*
Meeker, Benjamin B *BiAUS*
Meeker, Charles Augustus 1846-1913
    NatCAB 15
Meeker, Clara Ella *WomWWA 14*
Meeker, Claude 1861-1929 *WhAm 1*
Meeker, Ezra 1830-1928 *AmBi, DcAmB,
    NatCAB 21, WhAm 1*
Meeker, Frank Leroy 1869-1944 *WhAm 2*
Meeker, George Herbert 1871-1945 *WhAm 2*
Meeker, Harold Denman 1875-1945
    NatCAB 34
Meeker, Jacob Edwin 1878-1918 *BiDrAC,
    WhAm 1*
Meeker, James Rusling 1827-1887 *WhAm H*
Meeker, Jonathan Magie 1850-1917 *WhAm 1*
Meeker, Joseph Rusling 1827-1889? *ApCAB,
    IIBEAAW, NatCAB 12, NewYHSD*
Meeker, Jotham 1804-1855 *DcAmB,
    WhAm H*
Meeker, Moses 1790-1865 *ApCAB, DcAmB,
    WhAm H*
Meeker, Nathan Cook 1817-1879 *DcAmB,
    EncAAH, NatCAB 8, WebAB,
    WhAm H*
Meeker, Ralph 1845-1921 *NatCAB 19*
Meeker, Ralph Inman 1878- *WhAm 6*
Meeker, Royal 1873-1953 *WhAm 3*
Meeker, Sidney 1870-1937 *NatCAB 27*
Meeker, Stephen Jones 1843- *NatCAB 3*
Meekins, Isaac Melson 1875-1946 *NatCAB 39,
    WhAm 2*
Meekins, Katherine Webster 1862-
    WomWWA 14
Meekins, Lynn Roby 1862-1933 *WhAm 1*
Meekison, David Stewart 1849-1915 *BiDrAC,*

NatCAB 17, TwCBDA, WhAm 4
Meeks, Benjamin Wiltshire 1879- *WhAm 6*
Meeks, Carroll Louis Vanderslice 1907-1966
    NatCAB 52, WhAm 4
Meeks, Clarence Gardner 1880-1954 *WhAm 3*
Meeks, Edward *BnEnAmA*
Meeks, Eugene 1843- *ApCAB*
Meeks, Everett Victor 1879-1954 *NatCAB 47,
    WhAm 3*
Meeks, Frances Rebecca Pearson 1870-
    WomWWA 14
Meeks, J R *NewYHSD*
Meeks, James Andrew 1864-1946 *BiDrAC,
    NatCAB 41, WhAm 3*
Meeks, James Leonard 1877-1941 *NatCAB 31*
Meeks, Joseph 1771-1868 *BnEnAmA*
Meem, Harry Grant 1870-1949 *NatCAB 37,
    WhAm 2*
Meem, James Cowan 1866-1936 *NatCAB 27*
Meeman, Edward John 1889-1966 *NatCAB 53,
    WhAm 4*
Meenes, Max 1901-1974 *WhAm 6*
Meer, John, Jr. *NewYHSD*
Meer, John, Sr. *NewYHSD*
Meerbach *NewYHSD*
Meerbach, Philip *NewYHSD*
Meerschaert, Theophile 1847-1924 *ApCAB Sup,
    DcAmB, NatCAB 15, WhAm 1*
Mees, Arthur 1850-1923 *DcAmB, TwCBDA,
    WhAm 1*
Mees, C E Kenneth 1882-1960 *NatCAB 52*
Mees, Carl Leo 1853-1932 *ApCAB,
    NatCAB 26, TwCBDA, WhAm 1*
Mees, Charles Edward Kenneth 1882-1960
    WhAm 4
Mees, Graham Charles 1910-1965 *NatCAB 52*
Mees, Otto 1859-1958 *NatCAB 45, WhAm 3*
Mees, Theophilus 1848-1923 *WhAm 1*
Meese, Alfred Hall 1887-1961 *WhAm 4*
Meese, William August 1856-1920 *NatCAB 19*
Meese, William Henry 1883-1939 *NatCAB 29,
    WhAm 1*
Meeser, Spenser Byron 1859-1939 *WhAm 1*
Meessen, Hubert Joseph 1911-1962 *WhAm 4*
Meeteer, Henrietta Josephine 1857-
    WomWWA 14
Meffert, J B *NewYHSD*
Meftah, Davood Khan 1873- *WhAm 5*
Megan, Charles P 1876-1947 *WhAm 2*
Megan, Graydon 1910-1962 *WhAm 4*
Megapolensis, Johannes 1603-1670 *ApCAB,
    DcAmB, DcAmReB, NatCAB 12,
    WhAm H*
Megapolensis, John, Jr. d1669? *Drake*
Megapolensis, Samuel 1634-1700? *ApCAB*
Megarey, Henry J 1818-1845 *NewYHSD*
Megarey, John 1818-1845 *NewYHSD*
Megargee, Alonzo 1883?-1960 *IIBEAAW*
Megargee, Edwin d1958 *WhAm 3*
Megargee, Gilbert 1900-1960 *NatCAB 49,
    NatCAB 50*
Megaro, Gaudens 1903-1958 *WhAm 3*
Megaw, Elmer Earle 1880-1955 *NatCAB 47*
Megeath, Samuel Addison 1870-1932
    NatCAB 25
Meggee, Rowland Fay 1894-1948 *NatCAB 37*
Meggers, William Frederick 1888-1966 *DcScB,
    NatCAB 53, WhAm 4*
Megginson, William 1869- *WhAm 5*
Megilp *IIBEAAW*
Meginness, John Franklin 1827-1899
    NatCAB 10
Megler, Joseph George 1838-1915 *NatCAB 17*
Megowen, Carl Robert 1898-1962 *NatCAB 46,
    WhAm 4*
Megran, Herbert Brown 1888-1958 *NatCAB 48,
    WhAm 3*
Megraw, Herbert Ashton 1876-1951 *WhAm 3*
Megrue, Roi Cooper 1883-1927 *DcAmB,
    NatCAB 20, WhAm 1*
Mehaffy, Tom Miller 1859-1944 *WhAm 2*
Mehan, John Dennis *WhAm 4*
Mehan, Mona Catharine 1909-1973 *WhAm 6*
Mehemet Ali 1769-1849 *WhoMilH*
Mehl, Robert Franklin 1898-1976 *WhAm 6*
Mehlberg, Josephine J Bednarski Spinner
    1915-1969 *WhAm 5*
Mehler, John Sauter 1917-1966 *WhAm 4*

Mehlin, Theodore Grefe 1906-1971 *WhAm 5*
Mehling, Theodore John 1906-1961 *WhAm 4*
Mehornay, Robert Lee 1888-1951 *NatCAB 42,
    WhAm 3*
Mehornay, Robert Lee 1912-1963 *NatCAB 51*
Mehrbach, Philip *NewYHSD*
Mehren, Edward J 1881-1963 *WhAm 4*
Mehta, Gaganvihari L 1900-1974 *WhAm 6*
Mehta, Sir Pherozeshah 1845-1915 *McGEWB*
Meidell, Harold M 1910-1968 *WhAm 5*
Meier, Edward Clarence 1868-1918 *NatCAB 17*
Meier, Edward Daniel 1841-1914 *NatCAB 15,
    NatCAB 23*
Meier, Fabian Allan 1922-1963 *WhAm 4*
Meier, Fred Campbell 1893-1938 *WhAm 1*
Meier, Gertrude Gibbs 1870- *WomWWA 14*
Meier, Henry Albert 1850-1927 *NatCAB 20*
Meier, Julius L 1874-1937 *NatCAB 29,
    WhAm 1*
Meier, Norman Charles 1893-1967 *NatCAB 54,
    WhAm 4*
Meier, Walter Frederick 1879-1940 *WhAm 1*
Meiere, M Hildreth d1961 *WhAm 4*
Meiggs, Henry 1811-1877 *AmBi, ApCAB,
    DcAmB, McGEWB, NatCAB 13,
    WebAB, WhAm H*
Meighan, Thomas 1879-1936 *WhAm 1*
Meighen, Arthur 1874-1960 *McGEWB,
    WhAm 4*
Meighen, John Felix Dryden 1877-1957
    WhAm 3
Meignelle, James *NewYHSD*
Meigs, Arthur Ingersoll 1882-1956 *WhAm 3*
Meigs, Arthur Vincent 1850-1912 *DcAmB,
    NatCAB 15, NatCAB 25, WhAm 1*
Meigs, Charles Delucena 1792-1869 *ApCAB,
    DcAmB, Drake, NatCAB 6, WhAm H*
Meigs, Charles Edward 1872-1925 *NatCAB 37*
Meigs, Cornelia Lynde 1884-1973 *WhAm 6*
Meigs, Edward Browning 1879-1940
    NatCAB 30
Meigs, Ferris Jacobs 1868-1943 *NatCAB 31*
Meigs, Grace Lynde 1881- *WhAm 6,
    WomWWA 14*
Meigs, Henry 1782-1861 *BiAUS, BiDrAC,
    WhAm H*
Meigs, James Aitken 1829-1879 *ApCAB,
    DcAmB, NatCAB 8, WhAm H*
Meigs, John 1852-1911 *DcAmB, NatCAB 26,
    WhAm 1*
Meigs, John Forsyth 1818-1882 *ApCAB,
    DcAmB, NatCAB 25, WhAm H*
Meigs, John Liggett 1916- *IIBEAAW*
Meigs, John Rodgers 1842-1864 *ApCAB,
    NatCAB 4*
Meigs, Josiah 1757-1822 *ApCAB, BiAUS,
    DcAmB, NatCAB 9, TwCBDA, WebAB,
    WhAm H*
Meigs, Katharine H *WomWWA 14*
Meigs, Louise Lawrence 1871- *WomWWA 14*
Meigs, Matthew Kughler 1812-1889
    NatCAB 26
Meigs, Merrill Church 1883-1968 *WhAm 4*
Meigs, Montgomery 1847-1931 *WhAm 1*
Meigs, Montgomery Cunningham 1816-1892
    *AmBi, ApCAB, DcAmB, Drake,
    NatCAB 4, TwCBDA, WebAMB,
    WhAm H*
Meigs, Return J d1825 *BiAUS*
Meigs, Return Johnathan, Jr. 1764-1825
    WhAmP
Meigs, Return Jonathan 1734-1823 *ApCAB,
    NatCAB 1*
Meigs, Return Jonathan 1740-1823 *AmBi,
    DcAmB, Drake, TwCBDA, WhAm H*
Meigs, Return Jonathan 1764-1824 *AmBi,
    BiDrUSE, DcAmB, TwCBDA, WhAm H*
Meigs, Return Jonathan 1764-1825 *BiDrAC*
Meigs, Return Jonathan 1765-1825 *ApCAB,
    Drake*
Meigs, Return Jonathan 1766-1825 *NatCAB 3*
Meigs, Return Jonathan 1801-1891 *ApCAB,
    DcAmB, TwCBDA, WhAm H*
Meigs, Robert Van 1873- *WhAm 5*
Meigs, William Montgomery 1852-1929 *DcAmB,
    TwCBDA, WhAm 1*
Meiji, Tenno 1852-1912 *McGEWB*
Meikle, George Stanley 1886-1960 *WhAm 3A*

Meikle, Stephen Mack 1897-1960 *NatCAB 49*
Meiklejohn, Alexander 1872-1964 *ApCAB X,
BiDAmEd, NatCAB 51, WebAB,
WhAm 4*
Meiklejohn, George DeRue 1857-1929
*ApCAB Sup, BiDrAC, TwCBDA,
WhAm 1*
Meiks, Lyman Thompson 1902-1972 *WhAm 5*
Meilink, John Girard 1889-1957 *WhAm 3*
Meilleur, Jean Baptiste 1795-1878 *ApCAB*
Mein, John Gordon 1913-1968 *NatCAB 54,
WhAm 5*
Mein, William Wallace 1873-1964 *ApCAB X,
WhAm 4*
Meine, Franklin Julius 1896-1968 *WhAm 5*
Meinecke, Emilio Pepe Michael 1869-1957
WhAm 3
Meinecke, Friedrich 1862-1954 *McGEWB*
Meinel, William John 1893-1961 *NatCAB 52,
WhAm 4*
Meinell, William *NewYHSD*
Meinesz, F A Vening *DcScB*
Meinhold, H E d1971 *WhAm 5, WhAm 6*
Meinholtz, Frederick E 1890-1961 *WhAm 4*
Meinong, Alexius 1853-1920 *McGEWB*
Meinrath, Joseph 1857-1941 *WhAm 1*
Meins, Carroll Leach 1892-1953 *WhAm 3*
Meinung, A *NewYHSD*
Meinzer, Oscar Edward 1876-1948 *DcAmB S4,
DcScB, WhAm 2*
Meir, Golda 1898- *McGEWB*
Meirelles, Joaquim Candido Soares De
1777-1868 *ApCAB*
Meisburger, Louis 1867-1927 *NatCAB 25*
Meisel, Augustus *NewYHSD*
Meisel, Berthold *NewYHSD*
Meisel, Francis 1846-1916 *NatCAB 33*
Meisel, Sam 1887-1944 *NatCAB 32*
Meisenhelder, Edmund Webster 1876-1952
NatCAB 44, WhAm 3
Meisenhelter, L R 1880- *WhAm 6*
Meiser, Edward A 1865-1951 *NatCAB 40*
Meisle, Kathryn 1899-1970 *WhAm 5*
Meisnest, Darwin 1896-1952 *NatCAB 42*
Meiss, Millard 1904-1975 *WhAm 6*
Meissner, Alvin Richard 1875-1949 *NatCAB 38*
Meissner, Carl August 1859-1930 *NatCAB 31*
Meissner, Edwin Benjamin 1884-1956 *WhAm 3*
Meissner, Georg 1829-1905 *DcScB*
Meissner, K W 1891-1959 *WhAm 3*
Meisten, John Nicholas 1909-1971 *WhAm 5*
Meister, Fred *NewYHSD*
Meister, John William 1916-1974 *WhAm 6*
Meiter, Edward George 1898-1968 *NatCAB 54*
Meitner, Lise 1878-1968 *AsBiEn, DcScB,
WhAm 5*
Mejia, Federico 1861- *WhAm 4*
Mejia, Tomas 1815?-1867 *ApCAB*
Mekeel, Isaac A 1870-1913 *NatCAB 15*
Mekeel, Scudder 1902-1947 *WhAm 2*
Mela, Pomponius 005?BC- *AsBiEn, DcScB*
Melamid, Michael 1882-1950 *NatCAB 37*
Melancthon, Philip 1497-1560 *McGEWB*
Melander, A L 1878-1962 *WhAm 4*
Melander, George Harold 1906-1974 *WhAm 6*
Melas, Michael Friedrich B Freiherr Von
1729-1806 *WhoMilH*
Melba, Helen Porter 1865- *ApCAB Sup*
Melba, Nellie 1866-1931 *WhAm 1*
Melbert, James *NewYHSD*
Melbourne, C *NewYHSD*
Melbourne, William Lamb, Viscount 1779-1848
McGEWB
Melby, Benedik 1877-1959 *NatCAB 47*
Melby, Ernest Oscar 1891- *BiDAmEd*
Melcher, Bertha L Corbett 1872-
WomWWA 14
Melcher, Carl A 1889-1954 *WhAm 3*
Melcher, Columbus Rudolph 1863-1947
WhAm 2
Melcher, Frank Otis 1864-1912 *WhAm 1*
Melcher, Frederic Gershom 1879-1963
DcAmLiB, WhAm 4
Melcher, George 1868- *WhAm 4*
Melcher, George B 1880-1963 *WhAm 4*
Melcher, John 1924- *BiDrAC*
Melcher, Joseph 1806-1873 *TwCBDA,
WhAm H*

Melcher, Joseph 1807-1873 *ApCAB,
NatCAB 12*
Melchers, Gari 1860-1932 *AmBi, ApCAB X,
BnEnAmA, DcAmB, NatCAB 13,
WhAm 1*
Melchers, Julius Theodore 1830-1903
NewYHSD
Melchers, Leo Edward 1887-1974 *WhAm 6*
Melchert, James 1930- *BnEnAmA*
Melchett, Julian Edward Alfred 1925-1973
WhAm 6
Melchior, George Sally 1870-1948 *NatCAB 37*
Melchior, Lauritz Lebrecht Hommel 1890-1973
WhAm 5
Melchor, Oliver Hoffman 1848-1928 *WhAm 1*
Melden, Charles A 1853- *TwCBDA*
Melden, Charles Manly 1853- *WhAm 4*
Meldrim, Peter Wiltberger 1848-1933
NatCAB 2, NatCAB 24, WhAm 1
Meldrum, A Mackenzie 1876- *WhAm 5*
Meldrum, Andrew Barclay 1857-1928 *WhAm 1*
Meldrum, Herbert Alexander 1870- *WhAm 5*
Meldrum, John William 1843-1936 *NatCAB 27*
Meldrum, Norman Sackett 1859-1936
NatCAB 36
Meldrum, William Buell 1887-1956 *NatCAB 46,
WhAm 3*
Melear, James Melville d1955 *WhAm 3*
Melekian, Yervant 1888-1966 *NatCAB 53*
Melencio, Jose P 1894-1952 *WhAm 3*
Melendy, Jesse George 1877-1954 *NatCAB 42*
Melendy, Mary Ries 1841- *WhAm 4*
Meleney, Carolyn Coit 1858-1934 *NatCAB 29*
Meleney, Carolyn Cort 1858-1934
WomWWA 14
Meleney, Clarence Edmund 1853-1938
NatCAB 29, WhAm 1
Meleney, Frank Lamont 1889-1963 *NatCAB 53,
WhAm 4*
Meleney, Henry Edmund 1887-1970
NatCAB 57
Melette, Arthur C *NatCAB 13*
Melgar, Mariano 1791-1815 *ApCAB*
Melgarejo, Mariano 1818-1871 *ApCAB*
Melhado, Vernon Kenric 1889-1938 *NatCAB 42*
Melhase, John 1885-1938 *NatCAB 28*
Melhorn, Donald Franklin 1889-1974 *WhAm 6*
Melhorn, Nathan R 1871- *WhAm 5*
Melhus, Irving E 1881- *WhAm 6*
Melick, Clark Owen 1886-1961 *NatCAB 48*
Melin, George Cornelius 1902-1968 *NatCAB 54*
Meline, Frank Louis 1875-1944 *NatCAB 33,
WhAm 2*
Meline, James Florant 1811-1873 *ApCAB,
NatCAB 8*
Meline, James Florant 1813-1873 *TwCBDA*
Meline, James Florant 1841-1908 *WhAm 1*
Meliodon, Jules Andre 1867- *WhAm 5*
Melish, John 1771-1822 *ApCAB, DcAmB,
Drake, WhAm H*
Melish, John Howard 1874- *WhAm 5*
Melish, William Bromwell 1852- *WhAm 4*
Melius, L Malcolm 1887-1962 *WhAm 4*
Melko, Matthew Francis 1898-1958
NatCAB 46
Mell, Patrick Hues 1814-1888 *ApCAB,
DcAmB, NatCAB 9, TwCBDA,
WhAm H*
Mell, Patrick Hues 1850-1918 *DcAmB,
NatCAB 15, TwCBDA, WhAm 1*
Mella, Hugo 1888-1969 *NatCAB 54*
Mellanby, Edward 1884-1955 *DcScB,
DcScB Sup*
Melle, Rosine 1860- *WhAm 4*
Mellen, Charles Sanger 1851-1927 *DcAmB,
NatCAB 29, WhAm 1*
Mellen, Chase 1863-1939 *WhAm 1*
Mellen, Dan 1889-1957 *NatCAB 48*
Mellen, Edward d1875 *BiAUS*
Mellen, Ellen Johnson 1863- *WomWWA 14*
Mellen, F *NewYHSD*
Mellen, George Frederick 1859-1927 *TwCBDA,
WhAm 1*
Mellen, Grenville 1799-1841 *ApCAB, DcAmB,
Drake, NatCAB 7, TwCBDA, WhAm H*
Mellen, Henry 1757-1809 *ApCAB, Drake*
Mellen, Ida M 1877- *WhAm 6*
Mellen, John 1722-1807 *ApCAB*

Mellen, John 1752-1828 *ApCAB*
Mellen, Prentiss 1764-1840 *ApCAB, BiAUS,
BiDrAC, DcAmB, Drake, NatCAB 11,
TwCBDA, WhAm H*
Mellen, Seth Smith 1821-1893 *NatCAB 18*
Mellenthin, Herman Edward 1888-1942
NatCAB 31
Meller, Harry Bertine 1878-1943 *WhAm 2*
Mellett, Donald Ring 1891-1926 *NatCAB 20*
Mellett, Lowell 1884-1960 *WhAm 3A*
Mellette, Arthur Calvin 1842-1896 *DcAmB,
NatCAB 2, TwCBDA, WhAm H*
Melley, William Henry 1903-1959 *NatCAB 44*
Mellick, George Phelps 1862-1925 *NatCAB 24*
Mellier, Kennedy Duncan 1849-1926
NatCAB 20
Mellin, Carl Johan 1851-1924 *WhAm 1*
Mellinger, Aubrey Hugo 1881-1960 *WhAm 4*
Mellinger, Samuel 1914-1966 *WhAm 4*
Mellinger, William Jesse 1886-1948 *NatCAB 37*
Mellis, Mister *NewYHSD*
Mellis, Isaac *NewYHSD*
Mellish, David Batcheller 1831-1874 *BiAUS,
BiDrAC, WhAm H*
Mellish, Mary 1890- *WhAm 3*
Melliss, David Ernest 1848-1913 *WhAm 1*
Mellmann, Fred Bohle 1892-1958 *NatCAB 48*
Mello, Antonio Joaquim De 1791-1861 *ApCAB*
Mello, Francisco De 1490-1536 *DcScB*
Mello, Francisco Manoel 1611-1665 *ApCAB*
Mellon, Andrew William 1855-1937 *AmBi,
ApCAB X, BiDrUSE, DcAmB S2,
EncAB, McGEWB, NatCAB 28, WebAB,
WhAm 1*
Mellon, James Ross 1846-1934 *ApCAB X,
NatCAB 28, WhAm 1*
Mellon, Jennie King *WomWWA 14*
Mellon, Richard Beatty 1858-1933 *ApCAB X,
NatCAB 24, WhAm 1*
Mellon, Richard King 1899-1970 *WhAm 5*
Mellon, Thomas 1813-1908 *NatCAB 28,
WhAm 1*
Mellon, Thomas Alexander 1873-1948 *WhAm 2*
Mellon, William Larimer 1868-1949 *DcAmB S4,
WhAm 2*
Melloni, Macedonio 1798-1854 *AsBiEn, DcScB*
Mellor, Barry Stephen 1883-1956 *NatCAB 43*
Mellor, Charles Chauncey 1836-1909 *WhAm 1*
Mellor, George *NewYHSD*
Mellor, Laura Reinhart *WomWWA 14*
Mellor, Lewis LeRoy 1889-1961 *NatCAB 50*
Mellor, Norman 1869-1951 *NatCAB 40*
Mellor, Walter 1880-1940 *WhAm 1*
Mellott, Arthur Johnson 1888-1957 *NatCAB 48,
WhAm 3*
Melluish, James George 1870- *WhAm 5*
Melmoth, Mrs. d1823 *Drake*
Melo, Francisco Manuel De 1608-1666
WhoMilH
Melogan, Alexander *NewYHSD*
Meloney, Agatha P 1863- *WomWWA 14*
Meloney, Marie Mattingly 1878-1943 *NotAW,
WhAm 2*
Meloney, William Brown 1878-1925
NatCAB 21, WhAm 1
Meloney, William Brown 1905-1971 *WhAm 5*
Meloy, Luella Price *WomWWA 14*
Melrose, Andrew W 1836-1901 *IIBEAAW,
NewYHSD*
Melrose, Kenneth *NewYHSD*
Mels, Edgar 1867- *WhAm 4*
Melsheimer, Frederick Valentine 1749-1814
ApCAB
Melsheimer, Friedrich Valentin 1749-1814
DcAmB, WhAm H
Melton, Charles Lewis 1865- *WhAm 3*
Melton, Elijah Stephen *WhoColR*
Melton, James 1904-1961 *WhAm 4*
Melton, Julia Ferguson 1888- *WhoColR*
Melton, LeRoy 1881-1950 *WhAm 2*
Melton, Wightman Fletcher 1867-1944
WhAm 2
Melton, William Davis 1868-1926 *NatCAB 29,
WhAm 1*
Melton, William Walter 1879- *WhAm 6*
Meltzer, Charles Henry 1853-1936 *NatCAB 27,
WhAm 1*
Meltzer, Philip Edward 1895-1967 *NatCAB 53*

Meltzer, Samuel James 1851-1920 *DcAmB, DcScB, NatCAB 15, WhAm 1*
Melvain, Janet Frederica 1883- *WomWWA 14*
Melvil-Bloncourt, Sainte Suzanne 1825- *ApCAB*
Melvill, Thomas 1726-1753 *DcScB*
Melvill, Thomas 1751-1832 *NatCAB 11*
Melville, Andrew Hutton 1872-1946 *NatCAB 35*
Melville, C Glennon 1896-1962 *NatCAB 50*
Melville, David 1773-1856 *DcAmB, WhAm H*
Melville, Frank, Jr. 1860-1935 *NatCAB 29, WhAm 1*
Melville, George Wallace 1841-1912 *AmBi, ApCAB, DcAmB, McGEWB, NatCAB 3, TwCBDA, WebAB, WebAMB, WhAm 1*
Melville, Henry 1858-1930 *NatCAB 16, WhAm 1*
Melville, Herman 1819-1891 *AmBi, ApCAB, DcAmB, Drake, EncAB, McGEWB, NatCAB 4, TwCBDA, WebAB, WhAm H*
Melville, K I 1902-1975 *WhAm 6*
Melville, Robert 1723-1809 *ApCAB*
Melville, Rose 1873-1946 *WhAm 2*
Melville, Thomas 1751-1832 *Drake*
Melville, Velma Caldwell 1858- *AmWom*
Melvin, Alonzo Dorus 1862-1917 *WhAm 1*
Melvin, Bradford Morse 1894-1961 *WhAm 4*
Melvin, Frank Worthington 1884-1962 *WhAm 4*
Melvin, Henry Alexander 1865-1920 *WhAm 1*
Melvin, Marion Edmund 1876- *WhAm 5*
Melvin, Myron Soule 1885-1966 *NatCAB 53, WhAm 4*
Melvin, Parker Laney 1895-1945 *NatCAB 41*
Melvin, Ridgely Prentiss 1881-1945 *WhAm 2*
Melyn, Cornelis 1602?-1674 *NatCAB 10*
Membertou, Henry 1510?-1611 *ApCAB*
Membre, Zenobie 1645-1687 *ApCAB*
Membre, Zenobius 1645-1687? *DcAmB, WhAm H*
Membreno, Alberto 1859- *WhAm 4*
Memhard, Allen Raymond 1884-1957 *NatCAB 46*
Memin *NewYHSD*
Meminger, James Wilbert 1859- *NatCAB 7, WhAm 3*
Memling, Hans 1440?-1494 *McGEWB*
Memminger, Allard 1854-1936 *WhAm 1*
Memminger, Charles Gustavus 1803-1888 *ApCAB, Drake*
Memminger, Christopher Gustavus 1803-1888 *AmBi, BiDAmEd, BiDConf, DcAmB, McGEWB, NatCAB 4, WhAm H*
Memminger, Christopher Gustavus 1865-1930 *WhAm 1*
Memminger, Lucien 1879- *WhAm 6*
Memringer, Charles Gustavius 1803-1888 *TwCBDA*
Men DeSaa d1572 *ApCAB*
Mena, Carlos De 1560?-1633 *ApCAB*
Menabrea, Luigi Federico 1809-1896 *DcScB*
Menacho, Juan Perez De 1565-1626 *ApCAB*
Menaechmus *DcScB*
Menagh, Frank Robert 1890-1967 *NatCAB 53*
Menagh, Louis Randolph, Jr. 1892-1973 *WhAm 6*
Menander 342BC-291BC *McGEWB*
Menapace, Robert Bernard 1893-1968 *NatCAB 54*
Menard, Berenice 1801-1888 *ApCAB Sup*
Menard, Michel Branamour 1805-1856 *ApCAB, DcAmB, WebAB, WhAm H*
Menard, Pierre 1766-1844 *DcAmB, REnAW, WebAB, WhAm H*
Menard, Pierre 1767-1845 *ApCAB Sup*
Menard, Rene 1604-1661 *ApCAB*
Menard, Rene 1605-1661 *DcAmB, WhAm H*
Menchilli, George G *NewYHSD*
Mencius 371?BC-289?BC *McGEWB*
Mencken, August 1889-1967 *WhAm 4*
Mencken, Henry Louis 1880-1956 *DcAmReB, EncAAH, EncAB, McGEWB, WebAB, WhAm 3*
Mencken, Sara Powell Haardt 1898-1935 *WhAm 1*
Menconi, Ralph Joseph 1915-1972 *WhAm 6*
Mendana DeNeyra, Alvaro 1541-1596 *ApCAB*

Mendana DeNeyra, Alvaro De 1541-1595 *McGEWB*
Mendel, Edward *NewYHSD*
Mendel, Gregor Johann 1822-1884 *AsBiEn, EncAAH*
Mendel, James Harold 1894-1958 *NatCAB 44*
Mendel, Johann Gregor 1822-1884 *DcScB, McGEWB*
Mendel, Lafayette Benedict 1872-1935 *DcAmB S1, DcScB, NatCAB 26, WhAm 1*
Mendel, Warner H 1906-1967 *WhAm 5*
Mendeleev, Dmitri Ivanovich 1834-1907 *AsBiEn*
Mendeleev, Dmitrii Ivanovich 1834-1907 *McGEWB*
Mendeleev, Dmitry Ivanovich 1834-1907 *DcScB*
Mendell, Clarence Whittlesey 1883-1970 *WhAm 5*
Mendell, Seth 1845-1922 *ApCAB X, WhAm 1*
Mendelsohn, Charles Jastrow 1880-1939 *NatCAB 43, WhAm 1*
Mendelsohn, Erich 1887-1953 *DcAmB S5, McGEWB, WhAm HA, WhAm 4*
Mendelsohn, Samuel 1850-1922 *WhAm 1*
Mendelsohn, Samuel 1895-1966 *NatCAB 53*
Mendelson, Ethel Morrison *WomWWA 14*
Mendelson, Ralph Waldo 1888-1968 *NatCAB 54*
Mendelssohn, Louis 1854-1935 *WhAm 1*
Mendelssohn, Moses 1729-1786 *McGEWB*
Mendelssohn-Bartholdy, Felix Jakob L 1809-1847 *McGEWB*
Mendenhall, Alice Ann *WomWWA 14*
Mendenhall, Charles Elwood 1872-1935 *DcAmB S1, WhAm 1*
Mendenhall, Dorothy Reed 1874- *WomWWA 14*
Mendenhall, George 1814-1874 *ApCAB, NatCAB 12*
Mendenhall, George Newton 1878- *WhAm 6*
Mendenhall, Harlan George 1851-1940 *NatCAB 43, WhAm 1*
Mendenhall, J Z *NewYHSD*
Mendenhall, Richard Junius 1828-1906 *NatCAB 6*
Mendenhall, Thomas Corwin 1841-1924 *AmBi, ApCAB, DcAmB, NatCAB 10, TwCBDA, WhAm 1*
Mendenhall, Walter Curran 1871-1957 *NatCAB 47, WhAm 3*
Mendenhall, Walter Hill 1877-1927 *NatCAB 20*
Mendenhall, William Orville 1879-1958 *NatCAB 47, WhAm 6*
Menderes, Adnan 1899-1961 *WhAm 4*
Mendes, Frederic DeSola 1850-1927 *DcAmB*
Mendes, Frederick DeSola 1850-1927 *NatCAB 21, WhAm 1*
Mendes, Grace P 1854- *WomWWA 14*
Mendes, Henry Pereira 1852-1937 *DcAmB S2, DcAmReB, NatCAB 39, WhAm 1*
Mendes, Manoel Odorico 1799-1864 *ApCAB*
Mendes, Murilo Monteiro 1901-1975 *WhAm 6*
Mendes, Pedro 1558-1643 *ApCAB*
Mendes, Valentim 1689-1747 *ApCAB*
Mendez, Charles E 1914-1967 *NatCAB 53*
Mendez, Joaquin 1862- *WhAm 4*
Mendez Y LaBarta, Ramon Ignacio 1784-1839 *ApCAB*
Mendive, Rafael Maria De 1821-1886 *ApCAB*
Mendl, Elsie DeWolfe *NotAW*
Mendleson, Alan N 1904-1956 *WhAm 3*
Mendleson, Jerome 1874-1940 *NatCAB 29*
Mendonca, Augusto Netto De 1834-1868 *ApCAB*
Mendoza, Antonio De 1480?-1552 *ApCAB*
Mendoza, Antonio De 1490-1552 *McGEWB*
Mendoza, Gumesindo 1829-1886 *ApCAB Sup*
Mendoza, Juan 1540?-1619 *ApCAB*
Mendoza, Juan Suarez De d1681 *ApCAB*
Mendoza, Lorenzo Suarez d1583 *ApCAB*
Mendoza, Pedro De 1487?-1535 *Drake*
Mendoza, Pedro De 1487?-1536 *ApCAB*
Mendoza Y Luna, Juan De 1560?-1625? *ApCAB*
Meneely, A Howard 1899-1961 *NatCAB 47, WhAm 4*
Meneely, Andrew 1802-1851 *DcAmB, WhAm H*
Meneely, Clinton Hanks 1839-1923 *NatCAB 39*

Menees, Thomas 1823-1905 *ApCAB, BiDConf, WhAm 1*
Menefee, Arthur Burley 1886-1950 *NatCAB 39*
Menefee, F N 1886-1973 *WhAm 5*
Menefee, Richard Hickman 1809-1841 *BiDrAC, NatCAB 9, WhAm H*
Meneghetti, Egidio 1892-1961 *DcScB*
Menelaus Of Alexandria *DcScB, DcScB Sup*
Menendez, Pedro DeAviles 1519-1574 *NatCAB 11, WhAm H*
Menendez DeAviles, Pedro 1519-1574 *AmBi, DcAmB, Drake, McGEWB, REnAW, WebAB*
Menetrey, Joseph 1812-1891 *DcAmB, WhAm H*
Menetry, Joseph 1812-1891 *NatCAB 6*
Menewa 1766?-1835 *DcAmB, WhAm H*
Meng, John 1734-1754? *NewYHSD*
Mengarini, Gregory 1811-1886 *DcAmB, WhAm H*
Menge, Edward John VonKomorowski 1882-1941 *NatCAB 45*
Menge, Frederick 1869-1951 *WhAm 3*
Mengel, Levi Walter Scott 1868-1941 *NatCAB 45, WhAm 1*
Menger, Edward 1832?- *NewYHSD*
Menges, Franklin 1858-1956 *BiDrAC, WhAm 3*
Menghini, Vincenzo Antonio 1704-1759 *DcScB*
Mengle, Glenn Arthur 1897-1968 *NatCAB 55, WhAm 4*
Mengoli, Pietro 1625-1686 *DcScB*
Mengs, Anton Raphael 1728-1779 *McGEWB*
Menier, Joseph Henry 1590-1671 *ApCAB*
Meniere, Prosper 1799-1862 *BiHiMed*
Menifee, Richard H d1841 *BiAUS*
Menilek II 1844-1913 *McGEWB*
Menjou, Adolphe Jean 1890-1963 *WhAm 4*
Menke, Henry Charles 1877-1953 *NatCAB 48*
Menken, Adah Isaacs 1835-1868 *AmBi, ApCAB, DcAmB, Drake, NatCAB 5, NotAW, WebAB, WhAm H*
Menken, Alice Davis 1870- *BiCAW*
Menken, Helen 1901-1966 *WhAm 4*
Menken, Jacob Stanwood 1838- *NatCAB 8*
Menken, S Stanwood 1870-1954 *WhAm 3*
Menker, Samuel 1820?- *NewYHSD*
Menlowe, Patterson Morris 1899-1958 *NatCAB 52*
Menna Barreto, Joao Propicio 1809-1867 *ApCAB*
Menne, Frank Raymond 1888-1971 *NatCAB 57*
Mennen, Gerhard 1857-1902 *NatCAB 5*
Mennen, William Gerhard 1884-1968 *WhAm 4*
Menner, Horace Twitchell 1845-1921 *NatCAB 6*
Menner, Robert James 1892-1951 *WhAm 3*
Menninger, Charles Frederick 1862-1953 *DcAmB S5*
Menninger, Karl Augustus 1893- *WebAB*
Menninger, William Claire 1899-1966 *WhAm 4*
Menno Simons 1496?-1561 *McGEWB*
Menocal, Aniceto Garcia 1836-1908 *NatCAB 12*
Menocal, Aniceto Garcia 1836-1908 *DcAmB, NatCAB 14, TwCBDA, WhAm 1*
Menocal, Mario Garcia 1866-1941 *McGEWB*
Menoher, Charles Thomas 1862-1930 *DcAmB, NatCAB 27, WebAMB, WhAm 1*
Menoher, Pearson 1892-1958 *WhAm 3*
Menon, Maniketh Gopala 1900-1967 *WhAm 4*
Menon, Vengalil Krishnan Krishna 1897- *McGEWB*
Menotti, Gian Carlo 1911- *McGEWB, WebAB*
Mensel, Ernst Edmund 1891-1959 *WhAm 4*
Mensel, Ernst Heinrich 1865-1942 *WhAm 2*
Menshekov, Prince Alexander Sergeivich 1787-1869 *WhoMilH*
Menshutkin, Nikolay Aleksandrovich 1842-1907 *DcScB*
Mentelle, Francois Simon 1731-1799 *ApCAB*
Menton, A Paul 1901-1969 *WhAm 5*
Mentz, George Francis Millen 1896-1957 *WhAm 3*
Mentzer, John Franklin 1862-1958 *NatCAB 47*
Mentzer, William Cyrus 1907-1971 *NatCAB 56, WhAm 5*
Menuhin, Yehudi 1916- *WebAB*

Menuret DeChambaud, Jean Jacques 1733-1815
DcScB
Menville, Leon Jean 1882-1955 *NatCAB 44,*
WhAm 3
Menville, Raoul Louis 1885-1946 *WhAm 2*
Menzel, Adolphus *NewYHSD*
Menzel, Charles 1822?- *NewYHSD*
Menzel, Donald Howard 1901- *AsBiEn*
Menzel, Gustavus A *NewYHSD*
Menzel, Herman G *NewYHSD*
Menzel, William *NewYHSD*
Menzies, Alan Wilfrid Cranbrook 1877-1966
WhAm 4, WhAm 5
Menzies, John Thomson 1891-1965 *WhAm 4*
Menzies, John William 1819-1897 *BiAUS,*
BiDrAC, WhAm H
Menzies, Kenneth Campbell 1871-1957
NatCAB 43
Menzies, Percival Keith 1886-1971 *WhAm 6*
Menzies, Sir Robert Gordon 1894- *McGEWB,*
WhWW-II
Meores, George *NewYHSD*
Meras, Albert Amedee 1880-1926 *WhAm 1*
Meray, Hugues Charles Robert 1835-1911
DcScB
Mercado, Jose Maria 1770?-1811 *ApCAB*
Mercado, Tomas d1575 *ApCAB*
Mercati, Michele 1541-1593 *DcScB*
Mercator, Gerardus 1512-1594 *AsBiEn, DcScB*
Mercator, Gerhardus 1512-1594 *McGEWB*
Mercator, Nicolaus 1619?-1687 *DcScB*
Mercein, Thomas Fitz Randolph 1825-1856
ApCAB
Mercer, Alfred Clifford 1855-1927 *NatCAB 12,*
WhAm 1
Mercer, Ann Jane 1817-1886 *ApCAB*
Mercer, Archibald 1848- *WhAm 4*
Mercer, Augustus White 1867- *WhoColR*
Mercer, Beverly Howard 1894-1975 *WhAm 6*
Mercer, Carroll 1855-1917 *NatCAB 27*
Mercer, Charles Fenton 1778-1858 *ApCAB,*
BiAUS, BiDrAC, DcAmB, Drake,
NatCAB 13, TwCBDA, WhAm H,
WhAmP
Mercer, David Henry 1857-1919 *BiDrAC,*
TwCBDA, WhAm 1, WhAmP
Mercer, Edward W 1859- *NatCAB 3*
Mercer, Eugene LeRoy 1888-1957 *WhAm 3*
Mercer, Frederick Olen 1901-1966 *NatCAB 52*
Mercer, Frederick Olin 1901-1966 *WhAm 4*
Mercer, George 1733-1784 *TwCBDA*
Mercer, George Anderson 1835-1907
NatCAB 2
Mercer, George Gluyas 1853- *NatCAB 10*
Mercer, Henry Chapman 1856-1930 *AmBi,*
ApCAB X, DcAmB, NatCAB 21,
TwCBDA, WhAm 1
Mercer, Hugh 1720?-1777 *ApCAB, TwCBDA*
Mercer, Hugh 1721?-1777 *Drake, NatCAB 10,*
WhAm H
Mercer, Hugh 1725?-1777 *AmBi, DcAmB,*
WebAMB
Mercer, Hugh Victor 1869- *WhAm 5*
Mercer, Hugh Weedon 1808-1877 *TwCBDA*
Mercer, James d1793 *BiAUS, Drake*
Mercer, James 1736-1793 *BiDrAC, DcAmB,*
NatCAB 25, TwCBDA, WhAmP
Mercer, James 1737-1793 *WhAm H*
Mercer, James 1747-1793 *ApCAB*
Mercer, James Sidney 1880-1945 *NatCAB 34*
Mercer, Jesse 1769-1841 *ApCAB, DcAmB,*
Drake, NatCAB 6, TwCBDA, WhAm H
Mercer, John 1704-1768 *TwCBDA*
Mercer, John Francis d1821 *BiAUS*
Mercer, John Francis 1758-1821 *Drake*
Mercer, John Francis 1759-1821 *ApCAB,*
BiDrAC, DcAmB, NatCAB 9, TwCBDA,
WhAm H, WhAmP
Mercer, John Walter 1864-1949 *NatCAB 38*
Mercer, Lauron W *WhAm 4*
Mercer, Lewis Pyle 1847-1906 *DcAmB,*
NatCAB 12
Mercer, Margaret 1791-1846 *DcAmB,*
NatCAB 4, WhAm H
Mercer, Margaret 1792-1846 *ApCAB*
Mercer, Mary Elizabeth 1880- *WomWWA 14*
Mercer, Samuel 1800-1862 *Drake*
Mercer, Samuel Alfred Browne 1880- *WhAm 6*

Mercer, Saul Erastus 1868- *WhAm 4*
Mercer, Warren Charles 1871-1954 *NatCAB 44*
Mercer, William 1773-1850 *NewYHSD*
Mercer, William Fairfield 1864-1929 *WhAm 1*
Merchant, Alexander 1872-1952 *NatCAB 41*
Merchant, Biddle *NewYHSD*
Merchant, Charles George 1821-1855 *ApCAB*
Merchant, Charles Spencer 1795-1879 *ApCAB*
Merchant, Clarke 1836- *ApCAB, NatCAB 12*
Merchant, Frank Ivan 1855- *WhAm 3*
Merchant, George W *NewYHSD*
Merchant, Jesse 1878- *WhoColR*
Mercier, Armand Theodore 1881-1957
NatCAB 47, WhAm 3
Mercier, Charles Alfred 1816-1894 *DcAmB,*
WhAm H
Mercier, Honore 1840- *ApCAB*
Mercier, Louis Charles Antoine 1744-1812
ApCAB
Mercier, Louis Joseph Alexandre 1880-1953
NatCAB 46
Merck, George 1867-1926 *NatCAB 37*
Merck, George Wilhelm 1894-1957 *NatCAB 57,*
WhAm 3
Mercur, James 1842-1896 *TwCBDA*
Mercur, Rodney Augustus 1851- *WhAm 1*
Mercur, Ulysses 1818-1887 *ApCAB, BiAUS,*
BiDrAC, DcAmB, NatCAB 13, TwCBDA,
WhAm H
Mercur, William Henry 1861-1933 *NatCAB 25*
Mercy, Claudius Florimund, Graf Von 1666-1734
WhoMilH
Mercy, Franz, Freiherr Von 1590-1645
WhoMilH
Meredith, Albert Barrett 1871-1946 *WhAm 2*
Meredith, Edna Elliott 1879- *WhAm 6*
Meredith, Edwin Thomas 1876-1928 *AmBi,*
BiDrUSE, DcAmB, EncAAH,
NatCAB 21, WhAm 1
Meredith, Edwin Thomas, Jr. 1906-1966
WhAm 4
Meredith, Elisabeth Gray 1858- *WomWWA 14*
Meredith, Elisha Edward 1848-1900 *BiDrAC*
Meredith, Ellis *WomWWA 14*
Meredith, Ernest Sidney 1879- *WhAm 6*
Meredith, Florence Lyndon 1883-1951
NatCAB 46
Meredith, George 1828-1909 *McGEWB*
Meredith, James Alva 1875-1942 *WhAm 2*
Meredith, James Howard 1933- *WebAB*
Meredith, John Moyer 1905-1962 *NatCAB 52*
Meredith, Joseph Carroll 1856-1909 *WhAm 1*
Meredith, Samuel 1740-1817 *ApCAB, Drake*
Meredith, Samuel 1741-1817 *BiDrAC, DcAmB,*
TwCBDA, WhAm H
Meredith, Samuel 1750-1817 *BiAUS*
Meredith, Solomon 1810-1875 *AmBi, ApCAB,*
NatCAB 5, TwCBDA
Meredith, Sullivan Amory 1816-1874 *ApCAB*
Meredith, Virginia Claypool 1848-1936
WhAm 1, WomWWA 14
Meredith, Sir William Collis 1812- *ApCAB*
Meredith, William Farragut 1872-1943
NatCAB 38
Meredith, William Henry 1844-1911 *WhAm 1*
Meredith, William Morris 1799- *Drake*
Meredith, William Morris 1799-1872 *BiAUS*
Meredith, William Morris 1799-1873 *AmBi,*
ApCAB, BiDrUSE, DcAmB, NatCAB 4,
TwCBDA, WhAm H
Meredith, William Morton 1835- *TwCBDA,*
WhAm 4
Meredith, William Ralph 1840- *ApCAB*
Meredith, Wyndham Robertson 1859-1940
NatCAB 29
Meredith, Wynn 1868-1950 *NatCAB 42*
Meretskov, Kirill 1897- *WhWW-II*
Merezhkovsky, Dmitry Sergeyevich 1865-1941
McGEWB
Mergenthaler, Ottmar 1854-1899 *AmBi,*
DcAmB, EncAB, McGEWB, NatCAB 9,
TwCBDA, WebAB, WhAm H
Mergler, Marie Josepha 1851-1901 *DcAmB,*
NotAW, WhAm H
Meriam, Ebenezer 1794-1864 *ApCAB, Drake*
Meriam, Junius Lathrop 1872-1960 *BiDAmEd,*
NatCAB 47
Merian, Marie Sibylle 1647-1717 *ApCAB*

Merica, Charles Oliver 1864-1918 *NatCAB 17,*
WhAm 1
Merica, Paul Dyer 1889-1957 *DcScB,*
NatCAB 46, WhAm 3
Mericka, William John 1898-1965 *WhAm 5*
Merigold, Benjamin Shores 1873- *WhAm 5*
Merilh, Edmond L 1898-1964 *WhAm 4*
Merillat, Louis Adolph 1868- *WhAm 6*
Merimee, Prosper 1803-1870 *McGEWB*
Merine, A *NewYHSD*
Merine, J C *NewYHSD*
Merington, Marguerite d1951 *WhAm 3*
Merino, Ignacio 1819- *ApCAB*
Merinsky, S *NewYHSD*
Meritt, Edgar Briant 1874- *WhAm 5*
Merivale, Philip 1886-1946 *WhAm 2*
Meriwether, Colyer d1920 *TwCBDA,*
WhAm 1
Meriwether, David 1755-1822 *ApCAB, BiAUS,*
BiDrAC, Drake, TwCBDA, WhAm H
Meriwether, David 1800-1893 *ApCAB, BiAUS,*
BiDrAC, NatCAB 12, TwCBDA,
WhAm H
Meriwether, Elizabeth Avery 1824-1917
WhAm 1, WomWWA 14
Meriwether, I A 1806-1852 *BiAUS*
Meriwether, James 1789-1854 *BiAUS, BiDrAC,*
WhAm H
Meriwether, James A 1806-1852 *BiDrAC,*
WhAm H
Meriwether, Lee 1862-1966 *ApCAB,*
NatCAB 10, TwCBDA, WhAm 4
Meriwether, Lide 1829- *AmWom*
Meriwether, Lucy Underwood Western 1868-
WomWWA 14
Merk, Frederick 1887- *REnAW*
Merk, Frederick 1897- *EncAAH*
Merk, Hugo 1905-1969 *NatCAB 54*
Merker, Harvey Milton 1888-1970 *WhAm 5*
Merkert, Charles Earl 1896-1966 *NatCAB 52*
Merkle, Augustus *NewYHSD*
Merklin, Leon Charles 1740-1797 *ApCAB*
Merkt, Gustav Adolf 1878-1938 *NatCAB 31*
Merle-Smith, VanSantvoord 1889-1943
NatCAB 32, WhAm 2
Merle-Smith, Wilton 1856-1923 *NatCAB 21,*
WhAm 1
Merleau-Ponty, Maurice 1908-1961 *McGEWB,*
WhAm 4
Merlini, G *NewYHSD*
Merman, Ethel 1909- *WebAB*
Mermey, Maurice 1901-1974 *WhAm 6*
Mermilliod, Charles *NewYHSD*
Merner, Garfield David d1972 *WhAm 5*
Merola, Gaetano 1881- *WhAm 6*
Meroney, William Penn 1881-1938 *WhAm 1*
Merory, Joseph 1895-1970 *WhAm 5*
Merrell, B S *NewYHSD*
Merrell, Edgar Sanford Keen 1865-1942
NatCAB 34, WhAm 2
Merrell, Edward Huntington 1835- *TwCBDA*
Merrell, George R 1898-1962 *WhAm 4*
Merrell, Herman Stroup 1908-1966 *WhAm 4*
Merrell, Irvin Seward 1875-1959 *WhAm 3*
Merrell, J M *NewYHSD*
Merrell, John Hastings 1875-1958 *WhAm 3*
Merrell, John Porter 1846-1916 *NatCAB 6,*
WhAm 1
Merrell, William Dayton 1869-1954
NatCAB 48
Merrell, William Dayton 1869-1955 *WhAm 3*
Merrem, Daniel Karl Theodor 1790-1859
BiHiMed
Merrett, Christopher 1614-1695 *DcScB*
Merrett, Susan *NewYHSD*
Merriam, Adolphus 1820-1888 *NatCAB 32*
Merriam, Alexander Ross 1849-1928 *WhAm 1*
Merriam, Ann Page *NewYHSD*
Merriam, Augustus Chapman 1843-1895
ApCAB Sup, DcAmB, NatCAB 8,
TwCBDA, WhAm H
Merriam, Carroll Burnham 1870-1941 *WhAm 1*
Merriam, Charles 1806-1887 *ApCAB, DcAmB,*
TwCBDA, WebAB, WhAm H
Merriam, Charles Edward 1874-1953 *BiDAmEd,*
DcAmB S5, EncAB, McGEWB,
WhAm 3
Merriam, Clinton Hart 1855-1942 *ApCAB Sup,*

DcAmB S3, DcScB, NatCAB 13,
TwCBDA, WhAm 2
Merriam, Clinton Levi 1824-1900 *BiAUS,*
BiDrAC, TwCBDA
Merriam, Cyrus Knapp 1848- *NatCAB 8*
Merriam, Edmund Franklin 1847-1930
NatCAB 22, WhAm 1
Merriam, Edwin Garrald 1851-1927
NatCAB 21
Merriam, Elizabeth 1865- *WomWWA 14*
Merriam, Everet Brooks 1835-1915 *NatCAB 17*
Merriam, Florence Augusta *NotAW*
Merriam, Frank Dillingham 1865-1937
NatCAB 28
Merriam, Frank Finley 1865-1955 *NatCAB 42,*
WhAm 3
Merriam, George 1803-1880 *ApCAB,*
TwCBDA
Merriam, George Spring 1843-1914 *NatCAB 33,*
TwCBDA, WhAm 1
Merriam, Henry Clay 1837-1912 *ApCAB Sup,*
DcAmB, NatCAB 13, TwCBDA,
WebAMB, WhAm 1
Merriam, Henry M 1865-1952 *WhAm 3*
Merriam, James Arthur 1880-1951 *NatCAB 39*
Merriam, John Campbell 1869-1945 *BiDAmEd,*
DcAmB S3, DcScB, WhAm 2
Merriam, John Everett 1900-1961 *NatCAB 49,*
WhAm 4
Merriam, Nellie Bronson *WomWWA 14*
Merriam, William Rush 1849-1931 *DcAmB,*
NatCAB 10, TwCBDA, WhAm 1
Merrick, Benjamin Paul 1877-1946 *NatCAB 36*
Merrick, Caroline Elizabeth Thomas 1825-1908
AmWom, NatCAB 10, NotAW, TwCBDA
Merrick, Clinton 1886-1944 *NatCAB 34*
Merrick, David 1912- *WebAB*
Merrick, David Andrew 1833- *NatCAB 4,*
TwCBDA
Merrick, Edward Steele 1904-1968 *WhAm 5*
Merrick, Edwin Thomas 1808-1897 *DcAmB*
Merrick, Edwin Thomas 1809-1897 *BiDConf,*
NatCAB 10, TwCBDA
Merrick, Edwin Thomas 1859-1935 *NatCAB 10,*
NatCAB 26, WhAm 1
Merrick, Eliza Johnson 1857- *WomWWA 14*
Merrick, Frank Anderson d1944 *WhAm 2*
Merrick, Frederick 1810-1894 *DcAmB,*
NatCAB 4, TwCBDA, WhAm H
Merrick, George Edgar 1886-1942 *WhAm 2*
Merrick, George Peck 1862-1938 *WhAm 1*
Merrick, Harry Hopkins 1873- *WhAm 5*
Merrick, Harry L 1859-1903 *WhAm 1*
Merrick, Herbert Lansing 1873-1938
NatCAB 28
Merrick, J Hartley 1869- *WhAm 3*
Merrick, James Lyman 1803-1866 *ApCAB,*
Drake, TwCBDA
Merrick, John Vaughan 1828-1906 *WhAm 1*
Merrick, Mary George Seavey 1867-
WomWWA 14
Merrick, Pliny 1794-1867 *ApCAB, DcAmB,*
Drake, NatCAB 10, WhAm H
Merrick, Richard Thomas 1826-1885 *ApCAB*
Merrick, Samuel Vaughan 1801-1870 *ApCAB,*
DcAmB, NatCAB 13, TwCBDA,
WhAm H
Merrick, Sarah Newcomb 1844- *AmWom*
Merrick, Walter Chapman 1872-1960 *WhAm 4*
Merrick, William Duhurst 1793-1857 *ApCAB,*
BiAUS, BiDrAC, NatCAB 7, TwCBDA,
WhAm H
Merrick, William M 1818-1889 *BiAUS*
Merrick, William Marshall 1833- *IlBEAAW*
Merrick, William Matthew 1818-1889 *BiDrAC,*
WhAm H
Merrick, William Matthews 1818-1889 *ApCAB,*
TwCBDA

Merrifield, Fred 1874-1935 *WhAm 1*
Merrifield, Frederick William 1887-1958
NatCAB 47
Merrifield, Izola L Forrester 1878-
WomWWA 14
Merrifield, Webster 1852-1916 *BiDAmEd,*
NatCAB 17, WhAm 1
Merrifield, William Trowbridge 1807-1895
NatCAB 19

Merriken, Francis M *NewYHSD*
Merrild, Knud 1894-1954 *IlBEAAW*
Merrill, Aaron Stanton 1890-1961 *WhAm 4*
Merrill, Abner Hopkins 1843-1923 *WhAm 1*
Merrill, Albert B 1888-1960 *WhAm 3*
Merrill, Alfred Ellsworth 1845-1909
NatCAB 17
Merrill, Allyne Litchfield 1864- *WhAm 4*
Merrill, Alma Lowell 1886-1961 *NatCAB 53,*
WhAm 4
Merrill, Alonzo *NewYHSD*
Merrill, Amos Newlove 1875- *WhAm 5*
Merrill, Ayres Phillips 1793-1873 *ApCAB*
Merrill, Ayres Phillips 1826-1882 *NatCAB 12*
Merrill, Ayres Phillips 1826-1883 *NatCAB 10*
Merrill, Barzille Winfred 1864-1954 *WhAm 3*
Merrill, Beardslee Bliss 1904-1962 *WhAm 4*
Merrill, Cassius Exum 1838- *WhAm 4*
Merrill, Catharine 1824-1900 *NatCAB 19*
Merrill, Charles Clarkson 1872-1961 *WhAm 4*
Merrill, Charles Edward 1885-1956 *NatCAB 53,*
WhAm 3
Merrill, Charles Washington 1861-1956
NatCAB 15
Merrill, Charles Washington 1869-1956
WhAm 3
Merrill, Charles White 1861-1920 *WhAm 1*
Merrill, Charles White 1900-1972 *WhAm 5*
Merrill, Cyrus Strong 1847-1926 *ApCAB Sup,*
WhAm 1
Merrill, D Bailey 1912- *BiDrAC*
Merrill, Dana True 1876-1957 *NatCAB 45,*
WhAm 3
Merrill, Daniel 1765-1833 *ApCAB, DcAmB,*
TwCBDA, WhAm H
Merrill, David 1798-1850 *ApCAB, Drake*
Merrill, Dora Ellen 1877- *WomWWA 14*
Merrill, Dora Estella *WomWWA 14*
Merrill, Earl Stephen 1895-1941 *NatCAB 31*
Merrill, Edward Bagley 1835-1920 *WhAm 1*
Merrill, Edward Folsom 1883-1962 *WhAm 4*
Merrill, Edwin Godfrey 1873-1950 *ApCAB X,*
WhAm 2
Merrill, Edwin Katte 1902-1963 *WhAm 4*
Merrill, Ellen Byrne 1849- *WomWWA 14*
Merrill, Elmer Drew 1876-1956 *DcScB Sup,*
NatCAB 45, WhAm 3
Merrill, Elmer Truesdell 1860-1936 *DcAmB S2,*
NatCAB 14, TwCBDA, WhAm 1
Merrill, Everett Frank 1898-1955 *NatCAB 44*
Merrill, F C *NewYHSD*
Merrill, Francis Ellsworth 1904-1969 *WhAm 5*
Merrill, Frank 1903-1950 *WhWW-II*
Merrill, Frank Dow 1903-1955 *DcAmB S5,*
NatCAB 46, WebAMB, WhAm 3
Merrill, Frank Thayer 1848- *NatCAB 6,*
TwCBDA, WhAm 4
Merrill, Frederick Augustus 1875- *WhAm 5*
Merrill, Frederick James Hamilton 1861-1916
NatCAB 13, TwCBDA, WhAm 1
Merrill, Gardner B *NewYHSD*
Merrill, George Arthur 1866-1944 *BiDAmEd,*
WhAm 4
Merrill, George Earnest 1870-1933 *WhAm 1*
Merrill, George Edmands 1846-1908 *DcAmB,*
NatCAB 13, TwCBDA, WhAm 1
Merrill, George Perkins 1854-1929 *AmBi,*
DcAmB, DcScB, NatCAB 8, TwCBDA,
WhAm 1
Merrill, George Robert 1845-1925 *NatCAB 6*
Merrill, George Sargent 1837- *NatCAB 7*
Merrill, George W 1837- *NatCAB 12*
Merrill, Helen Abbot 1864-1949 *BiDAmEd,*
NatCAB 42, WomWWA 14
Merrill, Helen M *WomWWA 14*
Merrill, Helen Maud 1865- *AmWom*
Merrill, Henry Ferdinand 1853-1935 *WhAm 1*
Merrill, Henry Foster 1864-1956 *NatCAB 44*
Merrill, Herbert Woodruff 1874-1919
NatCAB 18
Merrill, Hugh Davis 1877-1954 *WhAm 3*
Merrill, James 1790-1841 *ApCAB*
Merrill, James Andrew 1861-1938 *WhAm 1*
Merrill, James Cushing 1853-1902 *DcAmB,*
NatCAB 15, WhAm 1
Merrill, James Griswold 1840-1920 *DcAmB,*
TwCBDA, WhAm 1
Merrill, James Milford 1847- *WhAm 4*

Merrill, Jane Summerside 1849- *WomWWA 14*
Merrill, Jenny Biggs *WomWWA 14*
Merrill, John Buxton 1910-1955 *WhAm 3*
Merrill, John Charles Fremont 1850-1917
NatCAB 18
Merrill, John Fuller Appleton 1866-1944
NatCAB 32, WhAm 2
Merrill, John Lenord 1866-1949 *WhAm 2*
Merrill, John Lisgar 1903-1969 *WhAm 5*
Merrill, John Ogden 1896-1975 *WhAm 6*
Merrill, John P *NewYHSD*
Merrill, John Wesley 1808-1900 *TwCBDA*
Merrill, Joseph Francis 1868-1952 *NatCAB 41,*
WhAm 3
Merrill, Joseph Hansell 1862-1925 *NatCAB 17*
Merrill, Joseph L 1899-1970 *WhAm 5*
Merrill, Joseph Warren 1819-1889 *NatCAB 13*
Merrill, Joshua 1820-1904 *DcAmB*
Merrill, Joshua 1828-1904 *NatCAB 13*
Merrill, Julia Wright 1881-1961 *DcAmLiB,*
WhAm 6
Merrill, Kate Pomeroy 1855- *WomWWA 14*
Merrill, Katherine L Yancey *WomWWA 14*
Merrill, Keith 1887-1959 *NatCAB 50*
Merrill, Kenneth Griggs 1891-1963 *NatCAB 51*
Merrill, Leon Stephen 1864-1933 *WhAm 1*
Merrill, Lewis 1834-1896 *ApCAB, TwCBDA*
Merrill, Lillie McDonald 1868- *WomWWA 14*
Merrill, Louis Taylor 1896-1960 *WhAm 4*
Merrill, Lucius Herbert 1857-1935 *WhAm 1*
Merrill, M W *NewYHSD*
Merrill, Margaret Manton 1859-1893 *AmWom*
Merrill, Mary Sroufe *WomWWA 14*
Merrill, Moody 1836- *NatCAB 4*
Merrill, Moses Emery 1803-1847 *ApCAB*
Merrill, Olin 1854-1928 *NatCAB 33*
Merrill, Orsamus Cook 1775-1865 *BiDrAC,*
WhAm H
Merrill, Orsamus Cook 1776-1865 *BiAUS*
Merrill, Oscar Charles 1874-1951 *WhAm 3*
Merrill, Paul Willard 1887-1961 *NatCAB 49,*
WhAm 4
Merrill, Payson 1842-1933 *WhAm 1*
Merrill, Richard Nye 1881- *WhAm 6*
Merrill, Robert Valentine 1892-1951
NatCAB 40, WhAm 3
Merrill, Sam Riley 1876-1957 *NatCAB 44*
Merrill, Samuel 1792-1855 *DcAmB, WhAm H*
Merrill, Samuel 1822-1899 *BiAUS,*
NatCAB 11, TwCBDA
Merrill, Samuel 1831-1924 *NatCAB 24,*
WhAm 1
Merrill, Samuel 1855-1932 *WhAm 1*
Merrill, Sara Ann Louise Taylor 1850-
WomWWA 14
Merrill, Sarah *NewYHSD*
Merrill, Selah 1837-1909 *AmBi, ApCAB,*
DcAmB, NatCAB 13, TwCBDA,
WhAm 1
Merrill, Sherburn Sanborn 1818-1885
NatCAB 18
Merrill, Stephen Mason 1825-1905 *ApCAB,*
DcAmB, NatCAB 5, TwCBDA,
WhAm 1
Merrill, Stuart Fitzrandolph 1863-1915 *DcAmB*
Merrill, Thais A 1908-1964 *WhAm 4*
Merrill, Thomas Abbot 1780-1855 *ApCAB,*
Drake
Merrill, Thomas Emery 1875-1943 *WhAm 2*
Merrill, Walter Hibbard 1873-1952 *NatCAB 41*
Merrill, William Augustus 1860- *WhAm 4*
Merrill, William Bradford 1861-1928 *DcAmB,*
NatCAB 1, WhAm 1
Merrill, William Emery 1837-1891 *AmBi,*
ApCAB, DcAmB, WhAm H
Merrill, William Emory 1837-1891 *NatCAB 10*
Merrill, William Fessenden 1842-1922 *WhAm 1*
Merrill, William Fessenden 1877-1933
NatCAB 42, WhAm 1
Merrill, William Henry 1840-1907 *TwCBDA,*
WhAm 1
Merrill, William J 1859- *WhAm 4*
Merrill, William Orville 1885-1959 *NatCAB 44*
Merrill, William Pierson 1867-1954 *WhAm 3*
Merrill, William Stetson 1866-1969 *DcAmLiB*
Merrill, William Wesley 1873- *ApCAB X*
Merrill, Winifred Edgerton 1862-1951
NatCAB 41

Merriman, Daniel 1838-1912 *NatCAB 18,* *TwCBDA,* *WhAm 1*
Merriman, Effie Woodward *WomWWA 14*
Merriman, George Benjamin 1834- *TwCBDA*
Merriman, Harold Thurston 1870-1941 *NatCAB 31*
Merriman, Harry Morton 1874-1954 *ApCAB X,* *WhAm 3*
Merriman, Helen Bigelow 1844- *TwCBDA,* *WhAm 4, WomWWA 14*
Merriman, Henry Payson 1838-1911 *NatCAB 16*
Merriman, Mabel Lillian *WomWWA 14*
Merriman, Mansfield 1848-1925 *AmBi,* *ApCAB, NatCAB 23, TwCBDA,* *WhAm 1*
Merriman, Margaret Mather 1880- *WomWWA 14*
Merriman, Myra Hunt Kingman 1873-1922 *WhAm 1, WhAm 5*
Merriman, Roger Bigelow 1876-1945 *WhAm 2*
Merriman, SanLorenzo 1869-1950 *WhAm 3*
Merriman, Thaddeus 1876-1939 *NatCAB 29,* *WhAm 1*
Merriman, Truman Adams 1839-1892 *BiDrAC,* *TwCBDA, WhAm H*
Merriman, William Edward 1825-1892 *TwCBDA*
Merrimon, Augustus Summerfield 1830-1892 *ApCAB, BiAUS, BiDrAC, DcAmB,* *NatCAB 9, TwCBDA, WhAm H*
Merritt, A Haywood 1832-1913 *NatCAB 16*
Merritt, Abraham 1884-1943 *NatCAB 32,* *WhAm 2*
Merritt, Anna Iea 1844-1930 *WhAm 4*
Merritt, Anna Lea 1844-1930 *AmBi, ApCAB,* *DcAmB, TwCBDA*
Merritt, Arthur Hastings 1870-1961 *NatCAB 46, WhAm 4*
Merritt, Dixon Lanier 1879-1972 *WhAm 5*
Merritt, Douglas 1847-1927 *NatCAB 22*
Merritt, E *NewYHSD*
Merritt, Edward Lester 1894-1956 *NatCAB 45*
Merritt, Edwin Albert 1860-1914 *BiDrAC,* *NatCAB 17*
Merritt, Edwin Atkins 1828-1916 *ApCAB,* *NatCAB 17, TwCBDA, WhAm 1*
Merritt, Emma Laura Sutro *WhAm 5,* *WomWWA 14*
Merritt, Ernest George 1865-1948 *NatCAB 15,* *WhAm 2*
Merritt, Ethel Moore 1882- *WomWWA 14*
Merritt, Frank 1856-1930 *WhAm 1*
Merritt, George Washington 1855-1928 *NatCAB 21*
Merritt, Hulett Clinton 1872-1956 *WhAm 3*
Merritt, Israel John 1829-1911 *DcAmB,* *NatCAB 5*
Merritt, James White 1886-1972 *WhAm 6*
Merritt, Leonidas 1844-1926 *DcAmB,* *WhAm 1*
Merritt, LeRoy Charles 1912-1970 *DcAmLiB,* *WhAm 6*
Merritt, Matthew Joseph 1895-1946 *BiDrAC,* *WhAm 2, WhAmP*
Merritt, Percival 1860-1932 *WhAm 1*
Merritt, Robert Clarence d1927 *WhAm 1*
Merritt, Samuel Augustus 1827-1910 *BiDrAC,* *WhAmP*
Merritt, Samuel Augustus 1828-1910 *BiAUS*
Merritt, Schuyler 1853-1953 *BiDrAC,* *NatCAB 42, WhAm 3, WhAmP*
Merritt, Thomas Wright 1902-1971 *NatCAB 57*
Merritt, Timothy 1775-1845 *ApCAB, Drake*
Merritt, Walter Gordon 1880-1968 *WhAm 5*
Merritt, Wesley 1834-1910 *AmBi, DcAmB,* *WebAMB*
Merritt, Wesley 1836-1910 *ApCAB, Drake,* *NatCAB 9, TwCBDA, WhAm 1*
Merritt, William 1640?-1708 *ApCAB*
Merrow, Chester Earl 1906-1974 *BiDrAC,* *WhAm 6, WhAmP*
Merrow, George Woodbridge 1852-1943 *NatCAB 39*
Merrow, Harriet Lathrop 1858- *WomWWA 14*
Merry, Ann Brunton 1769-1808 *ApCAB,* *DcAmB, NotAW, WhAm H*
Merry, Anna Wall 1872- *WomWWA 14*

Merry, Henry Raymond 1885- *WhoColR*
Merry, John Fairfield 1840-1916 *WhAm 1*
Merry, Joseph James 1901-1968 *WhAm 5*
Merry, Robert 1756-1798 *Drake*
Merry, Robert Watson 1913-1973 *WhAm 6*
Merry, William Lawrence 1834-1911 *NatCAB 12*
Merry, William Lawrence 1835-1911 *NatCAB 42*
Merry, William Lawrence 1842-1911 *DcAmB,* *WhAm 1*
Merryfield, Mary Ainsworth 1911-1974 *WhAm 6*
Merryman, Andrew Curtis 1831-1909 *WhAm 1*
Merryman, Benjamin Kelcier 1887-1940 *NatCAB 30*
Merryman, William Curtis 1861-1941 *NatCAB 33*
Merryweather, George Edmund 1872-1930 *NatCAB 42,* *WhAm 1*
Merseles, Theodore Frelinghuysen 1863-1929 *ApCAB X, WhAm 1*
Mersenne, Marin 1588-1648 *AsBiEn,* *DcScB*
Mersereau, Eugene Leavens 1884-1943 *NatCAB 41*
Mersereau, George Jefferson 1875-1947 *WhAm 2*
Mersereau, John Daniel 1854-1915 *NatCAB 16*
Mersereau, Nellie Colman *WomWWA 14*
Mersereau, William Bradford 1852-1914 *NatCAB 35*
Merseth, Sidney Ingmar 1913-1968 *WhAm 5*
Mershon, James 1865-1917 *NatCAB 18*
Mershon, Martin Luther 1891-1968 *WhAm 5*
Mershon, Oliver Francis 1873-1953 *NatCAB 41*
Mershon, Ralph Davenport 1868-1952 *NatCAB 15, WhAm 3*
Mershon, Stephen Lyon 1859-1938 *NatCAB 41*
Mershon, William Butts 1856-1943 *WhAm 2*
Mersman, Edward Henry 1872-1940 *NatCAB 46*
Merson, Alexander J 1905-1971 *WhAm 5*
Mertens, George William 1878- *WhAm 6*
Mertins, Gustave Frederick 1872- *WhAm 5*
Mertins, Louis 1885-1973 *WhAm 6*
Mertins, Marshall Louis 1885-1973 *WhAm 5*
Merton, Holmes Whittier 1860-1948 *WhAm 2*
Merton, Robert King 1910- *EncAB, WebAB*
Merton, Thomas 1915-1968 *DcAmReB,* *WebAB, WhAm 5*
Mertz, Albert 1851-1936 *WhAm 1*
Mertz, Augustus Schaefer 1887-1968 *NatCAB 56*
Mertzke, Emma Virginia 1854- *WomWWA 14*
Merulo, Claudio 1533-1604 *McGEWB*
Mervin, Orange *BiAUS*
Mervine, Graydon Duncan 1878-1954 *NatCAB 47*
Mervine, William 1790-1868 *ApCAB, Drake,* *TwCBDA*
Mervine, William 1791-1868 *DcAmB,* *WebAMB, WhAm H*
Merving, Christopher *NewYHSD*
Mervis, Meyer Bernard 1893-1959 *WhAm 3*
Merwin, Frederic Eaton 1907-1975 *WhAm 6*
Merwin, Henry Childs 1853-1929 *WhAm 1*
Merwin, Herbert Eugene 1878-1963 *NatCAB 50, WhAm 4*
Merwin, Loring Chase 1906-1972 *WhAm 5*
Merwin, Marcus Gaylord 1883-1936 *NatCAB 35*
Merwin, Milton Hervey 1832-1916 *NatCAB 7,* *NatCAB 28, WhAm 1*
Merwin, Orange 1777-1853 *BiDrAC, TwCBDA,* *WhAm H*
Merwin, Orange Fowler 1871-1952 *NatCAB 41*
Merwin, Samuel 1874-1936 *AmBi, WhAm 1*
Merwin, Samuel Edwin 1831-1907 *WhAm 1*
Merwin, Timothy Dwight 1850- *WhAm 4*
Mery, Gaston Etienne 1793-1844 *ApCAB*
Mery, Jean 1645-1722 *DcScB*
Meryman, Richard Sumner 1882-1963 *WhAm 4*
Meryweather, Mary Benson 1883- *WomWWA 14*
Merz, August 1873-1970 *NatCAB 56*
Merz, Charles Cleveland 1888-1952 *NatCAB 40*
Merz, Eugene 1869- *NatCAB 18*

Merz, Henry 1833-1905 *NatCAB 18*
Merz, Karl 1836-1890 *DcAmB*
Meschter, Wayne Clemmer 1883-1963 *NatCAB 51*
Meserole, Clinton V, Jr. 1918-1974 *WhAm 6*
Meserole, Clinton Vanderbilt 1876-1951 *WhAm 3*
Meserole, Katherine Louise Maltby 1853- *WomWWA 14*
Meserve, Charles Francis 1850-1936 *BiDAmEd,* *NatCAB 26, TwCBDA, WhAm 1*
Meserve, Frederic Hill 1865-1962 *WhAm 4*
Meserve, Frederick Hill 1865-1962 *ApCAB X*
Meserve, Harry Chamberlain 1868- *WhAm 1*
Meserve, Harry Fessenden 1867-1941 *NatCAB 31*
Meserve, John Bartlett 1869-1943 *WhAm 2*
Meserve, Nathaniel 1705?-1758 *DcAmB,* *NatCAB 32, WhAm H*
Meservey, Arthur Bond 1884-1952 *NatCAB 41*
Meservey, Edwin Clement 1861-1935 *NatCAB 34*
Meshchersky, Ivan Vsevolodovich 1859-1935 *DcScB*
Mesick, Jane Louise 1884-1967 *WhAm 4*
Mesick, William Smith 1856-1942 *BiDrAC,* *WhAm 4*
Mesier, Edward S *NewYHSD*
Mesier, Peter *NewYHSD*
Mesker, Bernard Theodore 1851-1936 *NatCAB 29*
Mesker, Frank 1861-1952 *NatCAB 44*
Mesker, George Luke 1857-1936 *NatCAB 30*
Meskill, Thomas Joseph 1928- *BiDrAC*
Meslin, Etienne Edouard 1751-1812 *ApCAB*
Mesmer, Franz Anton 1734-1815 *AsBiEn,* *DcScB, McGEWB*
Mesnard, Henry Etienne 1603-1663 *ApCAB*
Mesnil, Felix 1868-1938 *DcScB*
Mesquita, Jose Francisco De 1790-1872 *ApCAB*
Mesquita, Salvador De 1646- *ApCAB*
Mess, Otto 1879-1958 *WhAm 3*
Messahala *DcScB*
Messein, Charles Francis Bailly De 1741-1794 *ApCAB*
Messenbaugh, Joseph Fife 1873-1928 *NatCAB 38*
Messenger, Ivan 1895- *IIBEAAW*
Messenger, J Franklin 1872-1952 *WhAm 3*
Messenger, Lillian Rozell 1844- *AmWom,* *TwCBDA, WomWWA 14*
Messenger, North Overton 1865-1925 *WhAm 1*
Messenger, Robert Pocock 1888-1964 *NatCAB 53, WhAm 4*
Messenger, Ruth Ellis 1884-1964 *NatCAB 51*
Messer, Alpha 1842-1902 *WhAm 1*
Messer, Asa 1760-1836 *NatCAB 1*
Messer, Asa 1769-1836 *ApCAB, BiDAmEd,* *DcAmB, Drake, NatCAB 8, TwCBDA,* *WhAm H*
Messer, Edmund Clarence 1842-1919 *WhAm 1*
Messer, Elizabeth Walcott Lyman 1875- *WomWWA 14*
Messer, L Wilbur 1856-1923 *WhAm 1*
Messer, Samuel d1963 *WhAm 4*
Messer, William Stuart 1882-1960 *WhAm 4*
Messersmith, George Strausser 1883-1960 *NatCAB 47, WhAm 3, WhAm 4*
Messerve, Frederic W 1860- *NatCAB 3*
Messerve, Nathaniel d1758 *Drake*
Messervy, George Passarow 1856-1934 *NatCAB 26*
Messheimer, Frederick V d1814? *Drake*
Messiaen, Olivier 1908- *McGEWB*
Messier, Charles 1730-1817 *AsBiEn, DcScB*
Messina, Angelina Rose 1910-1968 *WhAm 5*
Messing, Abraham Joseph 1873- *WhAm 5*
Messinger, Charles Raymond 1883-1941 *WhAm 1*
Messinger, Edwin John 1907-1965 *WhAm 4*
Messinger, Harry Carleton 1881-1950 *NatCAB 38*
Messinger, Robert Hinckley 1811-1874 *ApCAB,* *NatCAB 8*
Messiter, Arthur Henry 1834-1916 *WhAm 1*
Messler, Abraham 1800-1882 *ApCAB,* *TwCBDA*
Messler, Eugene Lawrence 1873- *WhAm 5*

Messler, Thomas Doremus 1833-1893 *DcAmB,*
WhAm H
Messmer, Clemens 1881-1958 *NatCAB 48*
Messmer, Sebastian Gebhard 1847-1930
ApCAB Sup, DcAmB, NatCAB 12,
TwCBDA, WhAm 1
Messmore, George Harold 1884-1961
NatCAB 46
Messner, Julian 1890-1948 *WhAm 2*
Messner, Kathryn G 1902-1964 *WhAm 4*
Messo, Dominick *NewYHSD*
Mesta, Frank Albert 1894-1963 *WhAm 4*
Mesta, L W d1953 *WhAm 3*
Mesta, Perle d1975 *WhAm 6*
Mestern, H Edward 1909-1968 *WhAm 5*
Mestre, Harold DeVilla Urrutia 1884-1939
NatCAB 29
Mestrezat, Stephen Leslie 1848-1918 *WhAm 1*
Mestrovic, Ivan 1883-1962 *WhAm 4*
Mesy, Augustin DeSaffray De d1665 *ApCAB*
Mesyatsev, Ivan Illarionovich 1885-1940 *DcScB*
Metacomet *AmBi, WebAB, WebAMB*
Metaxas, Joannis 1871-1941 *WhWW-II*
Metcalf, Anna 1840- *TwCBDA*
Metcalf, Arunah 1771-1848 *BiAUS, BiDrAC,*
WhAm H
Metcalf, Caleb B 1814-1891 *NatCAB 2*
Metcalf, Caroline Graham Soule
WomWWA 14
Metcalf, Clarence Sheridan 1878- *WhAm 6*
Metcalf, Clell Lee 1888-1948 *NatCAB 42,*
WhAm 2
Metcalf, Edward Potter 1859- *WhAm 4*
Metcalf, Edwin Dickinson 1848-1915
NatCAB 18
Metcalf, Edwin Flint 1876-1949 *NatCAB 38*
Metcalf, Eliab 1785-1834 *BnEnAmA,*
NewYHSD
Metcalf, Frank Arthur 1873-1939 *WhAm 1*
Metcalf, George P d1957 *WhAm 3*
Metcalf, George Wallace 1855- *WhAm 4*
Metcalf, Haven 1875-1940 *WhAm 2*
Metcalf, Henry Brewer 1829-1904 *WhAm 1*
Metcalf, Henry Harrison 1841-1932 *DcAmB,*
NatCAB 22, WhAm 1
Metcalf, Irving Wight 1855-1938 *WhAm 1*
Metcalf, Jesse 1887-1945 *NatCAB 35*
Metcalf, Jesse Houghton 1860-1942 *BiDrAC,*
NatCAB 38, WhAm 2, WhAmP
Metcalf, Joel Hastings 1866-1925 *DcAmB,*
NatCAB 25, WhAm 1
Metcalf, John *NewYHSD*
Metcalf, John Calvin 1865-1949 *NatCAB 36,*
WhAm 2
Metcalf, John Milton Putnam 1864- *WhAm 4*
Metcalf, John Richards 1889-1966 *NatCAB 53*
Metcalf, Lee 1911- *BiDrAC*
Metcalf, Lee Grant 1861-1921 *NatCAB 19*
Metcalf, Leonard 1870-1926 *WhAm 1*
Metcalf, Lorettus Sutton 1837-1920 *ApCAB,*
NatCAB 1, TwCBDA, WhAm 1
Metcalf, Manton Bradley 1864-1923
NatCAB 21
Metcalf, Martin Kellogg 1881- *WhAm 6*
Metcalf, Mason Jerome 1807-1883 *ApCAB,*
NatCAB 12, TwCBDA
Metcalf, Maynard Mayo 1868-1940 *WhAm 1*
Metcalf, Ralph 1798-1858 *ApCAB, BiAUS,*
Drake, NatCAB 11, TwCBDA
Metcalf, Ralph 1861-1939 *NatCAB 37,*
WhAm 1
Metcalf, Richard 1829-1881 *ApCAB*
Metcalf, Robert Mitchell 1881-1962
NatCAB 50
Metcalf, Stephen Olney 1857-1950 *NatCAB 41,*
WhAm 3
Metcalf, Theron 1784-1875 *ApCAB, DcAmB,*
Drake, TwCBDA, WhAm H
Metcalf, Victor Howard 1853-1936 *AmBi,*
BiDrAC, BiDrUSE, NatCAB 13,
NatCAB 14, TwCBDA, WhAm 1,
WhAmP
Metcalf, Walter Bradford 1867-1956
NatCAB 44
Metcalf, Wilder Stevens 1855-1935 *NatCAB 11,*
WhAm 1
Metcalf, Willard Leroy 1853-1925 *BnEnAmA*
Metcalf, Willard Leroy 1858-1925 *AmBi,*

DcAmB, IIBEAAW, NatCAB 13,
NatCAB 31, WhAm 1
Metcalf, William 1838-1909 *DcAmB,*
NatCAB 12, WhAm 1
Metcalf, William H 1821-1892 *NatCAB 3*
Metcalf, Zeno Payne 1885-1956 *NatCAB 44,*
WhAm 3
Metcalfe, Anne H *WomWWA 14*
Metcalfe, Baron Charles Theophilus 1785-1846
ApCAB, Drake, McGEWB
Metcalfe, George Richmond 1865-1938
WhAm 1
Metcalfe, Henry 1847-1927 *ApCAB,*
NatCAB 22, TwCBDA, WhAm 4
Metcalfe, Henry Bleecker 1805-1881 *BiAUS,*
BiDrAC, WhAm H
Metcalfe, James Stetson 1858-1927 *WhAm 1*
Metcalfe, John T 1818- *TwCBDA*
Metcalfe, Lyne Shackelford 1822-1906 *BiDrAC*
Metcalfe, Richard Lee 1861-1954 *WhAm 3*
Metcalfe, Samuel Lytler 1798-1856 *ApCAB,*
DcAmB, Drake, NatCAB 5, WhAm H
Metcalfe, Thomas 1780-1855 *ApCAB, BiAUS,*
BiDrAC, DcAmB, Drake, NatCAB 13,
TwCBDA, WhAm H, WhAmP
Metcalfe, Tristram Walker 1880-1952 *WhAm 3*
Metchnikoff, Elie 1845-1916 *BiHiMed, DcScB,*
McGEWB
Meteyard, Thomas Buford 1865-1928 *WhAm 1*
Metford, Samuel 1810-1896 *NewYHSD*
Methodius, Saint *see* Cyril And Methodius, Saints
Methuen, Baron Paul Sandford 1845-1932
WhoMilH
Metius, Adriaen 1571-1635 *DcScB*
Metius, Adriaen Anthonisz 1543?-1620 *DcScB*
Metius, Jacob d1628 *DcScB*
Meton 440?BC- *AsBiEn, DcScB*
Mettauer, John Peter 1787-1875 *BiHiMed,*
DcAmB, NatCAB 15, WhAm H
Metten, John Farrell 1873-1968 *WhAm 5*
Metten, William F 1871- *WhAm 5*
Mettenius, Georg Heinrich 1823-1866 *DcScB*
Metternich, Prince Clemens W N L Von
1773-1859 *McGEWB*
Mettler, John Wyckoff 1878-1952 *WhAm 3*
Mettler, L Harrison 1863- *WhAm 4*
Metts, John VanBokkelen 1876-1959 *WhAm 5*
Metts, John VanBokkelen 1878-1959
NatCAB 47
Metz, A F *NewYHSD*
Metz, Abraham Louis 1864- *WhAm 4*
Metz, Albert Frederick 1893-1967 *WhAm 4*
Metz, Arthur Ray 1887-1963 *NatCAB 52,*
WhAm 4
Metz, Charles William 1889-1975 *WhAm 6*
Metz, Christian 1794-1867 *AmBi, DcAmB,*
NatCAB 13, WebAB, WhAm H
Metz, George 1839-1918 *NatCAB 17*
Metz, Herman August 1867-1934 *ApCAB X,*
BiDrAC, NatCAB 14, WhAm 1
Metz, William Payne 1888-1950 *NatCAB 39*
Metzdorf, Robert Frederick 1912-1975
WhAm 6
Metzelaar, Jan 1891-1929 *NatCAB 21*
Metzenbaum, Myron Firth 1876-1944 *WhAm 2*
Metzgar, Charles Watson 1860- *WhAm 4*
Metzgar, Robert Henry 1904-1962 *NatCAB 49*
Metzger, Albert Elbracht 1865-1931
NatCAB 23
Metzger, Delbert Everner 1875-1967 *WhAm 4*
Metzger, Fraser 1872-1954 *NatCAB 44,*
WhAm 3
Metzger, Frederick Elder 1868-1952 *WhAm 3*
Metzger, Helene 1889-1944 *DcScB*
Metzger, Herman Arthur 1900-1974 *WhAm 6*
Metzger, Hutzel 1894-1951 *WhAm 3*
Metzger, Irvin Dilling 1873-1947 *WhAm 2*
Metzger, Joe 1883-1965 *NatCAB 50*
Metzger, Kern Delos 1902-1955 *NatCAB 42*
Metzger, Lewis Pow 1873-1939 *NatCAB 44*
Metzger, Owen William 1882-1960 *NatCAB 48*
Metzger, Ralph Alfred 1897-1972 *WhAm 5*
Metzger, Robert William 1909-1965
NatCAB 51
Metzger, T Warren 1887-1949 *NatCAB 37*
Metzler, William Henry 1863- *WhAm 4*
Metzman, Gustav 1886-1960 *WhAm 3A,*
WhAm 4

Meucci, Anthony *NewYHSD*
Meucci, Nina *NewYHSD*
Meuser, Edwin Henry 1897-1949 *WhAm 2*
Meusnier DeLaPlace, Jean-Baptiste 1754-1793
DcScB
Meuttman, W *IIBEAAW*
Mewhinney, Ella Koepke 1891- *IIBEAAW*
Mewse, Thomas *NewYHSD*
Mexia, Ynes Enriquetta Julietta 1870-1938
NotAW
Mey, Cornelius Jacobsen *WhAm H*
Meyen, Franz Julius Ferdinand 1804-1840
DcScB
Meyenberg, Johann Baptist 1847-1914
NatCAB 41
Meyer *NewYHSD*
Meyer, Adele 1873- *WomWWA 14*
Meyer, Adolf 1866-1950 *BiDAmEd,*
DcAmB S4, NatCAB 38, WhAm 2
Meyer, Adolph 1842-1908 *BiDrAC,*
NatCAB 16, TwCBDA, WhAm 1,
WhAmP
Meyer, Adolph Frederick 1880-1962
NatCAB 50
Meyer, Adolphe Erich 1897- *BiDAmEd*
Meyer, Adolphus William 1860-1937 *WhAm 1*
Meyer, Agnes Ernst 1887-1970 *NatCAB 56*
Meyer, Albert Gregory 1903-1965 *WhAm 4*
Meyer, Alfred 1854-1950 *WhAm 3*
Meyer, Alfred Henry 1888-1944 *WhAm 2*
Meyer, Alfred Reuben 1888-1962 *WhAm 4*
Meyer, Andrew Harry 1913-1964 *NatCAB 51*
Meyer, Annie Florance Nathan 1867-1951
AmWom, BiCAW, DcAmB S5,
NatCAB 42, TwCBDA, WhAm 3,
WomWWA 14
Meyer, Arthur John 1878-1930 *WhAm 1*
Meyer, Arthur Simon 1880-1955 *WhAm 3*
Meyer, Arthur William 1873-1966 *WhAm 4*
Meyer, August Robert 1851-1905 *NatCAB 16*
Meyer, B G 1882-1949 *WhAm 2*
Meyer, Balthasar Henry 1866-1954 *NatCAB 42,*
WhAm 5
Meyer, Ben R 1879-1957 *WhAm 3*
Meyer, Bernhard 1537-1609 *ApCAB*
Meyer, C Louis 1886-1953 *NatCAB 40*
Meyer, Carleton Wiepking 1903-1953
NatCAB 41
Meyer, Charles F 1864-1948 *WhAm 2*
Meyer, Charles Garrison 1879-1950 *WhAm 3*
Meyer, Charles Harrison 1892-1962 *WhAm 4*
Meyer, Charles Zachary 1895-1971 *WhAm 5*
Meyer, Christian 1838-1907 *NewYHSD*
Meyer, Christian Erich Hermann Von 1801-1869
DcScB
Meyer, Christian Frederick Godlove 1830-1905
NatCAB 12
Meyer, Christian Frederick Gottlieb 1830-1905
WhAm 1
Meyer, Clarence Earle 1891-1965 *NatCAB 51,*
WhAm 4
Meyer, Cord 1854-1910 *NatCAB 16*
Meyer, Edward Barnard 1882-1937 *NatCAB 41,*
WhAm 1
Meyer, Elizabeth *NewYHSD*
Meyer, Ely 1890-1971 *WhAm 5*
Meyer, Estelle Reel 1862- *WhAm 5*
Meyer, Estelle Reel 1865- *WomWWA 14*
Meyer, Eugene 1875-1959 *WhAm 3*
Meyer, Ferdinand *NewYHSD*
Meyer, Ferdinand 1817?- *NewYHSD*
Meyer, Ferdinand August 1863-1936
NatCAB 27
Meyer, Frank Nicholas 1875-1918 *EncAAH,*
NatCAB 20
Meyer, Frank Straus 1909-1972 *WhAm 5*
Meyer, Frederick Henry 1872-1961 *WhAm 4,*
WhAm 5
Meyer, Fredrik 1898-1972 *WhAm 5*
Meyer, Fritz *NewYHSD*
Meyer, George A d1974 *WhAm 6*
Meyer, George Homer 1858-1926 *WhAm 1*
Meyer, George John 1871-1945 *NatCAB 34*
Meyer, George Joseph 1864-1919 *NatCAB 18*
Meyer, George VonLengerke 1858-1918 *AmBi,*
BiDrUSE, DcAmB, NatCAB 11,
NatCAB 14, TwCBDA, WhAm 1

Meyer, George VonLengerke 1891-1950
NatCAB 41

Meyer, George W 1912-1967 *WhAm 4*

Meyer, George William 1884-1959 *WhAm 3*

Meyer, Gottlieb *NewYHSD*

Meyer, Grover Cleveland 1892-1949
NatCAB 38

Meyer, H E *NewYHSD*

Meyer, H Kenneth 1906-1964 *WhAm 4*

Meyer, Henry 1848- *NatCAB 7*

Meyer, Henry Coddington 1844-1935
DcAmB S1, NatCAB 13, NatCAB 25

Meyer, Henry Coddington, Jr. 1870-1957
WhAm 3

Meyer, Henry Herman 1874-1951 *NatCAB 42,
WhAm 3*

Meyer, Henry Hoppner 1782?-1847 *NewYHSD*

Meyer, Herbert Alton 1886-1950 *BiDrAC,
WhAm 3, WhAmP*

Meyer, Herbert Alton, Jr. 1912-1971 *WhAm 5*

Meyer, Herbert Willy 1896-1973 *WhAm 5*

Meyer, Herman Henry Bernard 1864-1937
DcAmLiB, NatCAB 27, WhAm 1

Meyer, Hermanus 1733-1791 *ApCAB*

Meyer, Hoppner *NewYHSD*

Meyer, Hugo Richard 1866- *WhAm 4*

Meyer, J Franklin 1875-1944 *WhAm 2*

Meyer, Jacob Gibble 1884-1951 *NatCAB 40*

Meyer, Johann Friedrich 1705-1765 *DcScB*

Meyer, John *NewYHSD*

Meyer, John Ambrose 1899-1969 *BiDrAC*

Meyer, John Charles 1919-1975 *WhAm 6*

Meyer, John DaCosta 1878- *WhAm 6*

Meyer, John Jacob 1870- *WhAm 5*

Meyer, John Philip 1899-1960 *NatCAB 48*

Meyer, Joseph *NewYHSD*

Meyer, Joseph Francis 1851-1935 *NatCAB 9,
WhAm 1*

Meyer, Julian Erdreich 1894-1956 *NatCAB 48*

Meyer, Julius Eduard 1822-1899 *WhAm H*

Meyer, Julius Lothar 1830-1895 *AsBiEn,
DcScB*

Meyer, Julius Paul 1871-1945 *WhAm 2*

Meyer, Karl Albert 1886-1972 *WhAm 5*

Meyer, Karl Friedrich 1884-1974 *WhAm 6*

Meyer, Keith Thomas 1899-1957 *NatCAB 47*

Meyer, Kurt Heinrich 1883-1952 *DcScB*

Meyer, Lothar 1906-1971 *WhAm 5*

Meyer, Lucy Jane Rider 1849-1922 *BiCAW,
NotAW, WhAm 1, WomWWA 14*

Meyer, Marie Florence Baird *WomWWA 14*

Meyer, Martin Abraham 1879-1923 *DcAmB,
WhAm 1*

Meyer, Max F 1873- *WhAm 5*

Meyer, Maximilian Courtland 1883- *WhAm 3*

Meyer, Paul D 1935-1966 *WhAm 6*

Meyer, Richard 1877-1951 *NatCAB 46*

Meyer, Richard Max *IlBEAAW*

Meyer, Rudolph J 1841-1912 *WhAm 1*

Meyer, Samuel Bernhard 1887-1951
NatCAB 47

Meyer, Schuyler Merritt 1885-1970 *WhAm 5*

Meyer, Solomon L 1893-1963 *NatCAB 51*

Meyer, Theodore Frederick 1857-1916 *WhAm 1*

Meyer, Theodore Robert 1902-1973
NatCAB 57, WhAm 6

Meyer, Victor 1848-1897 *DcScB*

Meyer, Viktor 1848-1897 *AsBiEn*

Meyer, Wallace 1888-1971 *WhAm 5*

Meyer, Wilhelm Franz 1856-1934 *DcScB*

Meyer, William 1891-1960 *NatCAB 49*

Meyer, William Briggs 1910-1968 *WhAm 4*

Meyer, William H *NewYHSD*

Meyer, William Henry 1914- *BiDrAC*

Meyer, Willy 1858-1932 *NatCAB 13,
WhAm 1*

Meyer, Wilson 1896-1973 *WhAm 6*

Meyerbeer, Giacomo 1791-1864 *McGEWB*

Meyercord, George Rudolph 1875-1941
WhAm 1

Meyerding, Henry William 1884-1969 *WhAm 5*

Meyerheim, Paul Friedrich 1842-1915
IlBEAAW

Meyerhof, Otto Fritz 1884-1951 *AsBiEn,
BiHiMed, DcAmB S5, DcScB, McGEWB,
WhAm 3*

Meyerhold, Vsevolod Emilievich 1874-1942?
McGEWB

Meyerholz, Charles Henry *WhAm 5*

Meyers *NewYHSD*

Meyers, A Lincoln 1898-1947 *NatCAB 36*

Meyers, Alice Hanford 1878- *WomWWA 14*

Meyers, Arthur DuBois 1891-1949 *NatCAB 38*

Meyers, Benjamin Franklin 1833-1918 *BiAUS,
BiDrAC, NatCAB 5*

Meyers, Carl W 1891-1960 *WhAm 3A*

Meyers, Carlisle Paul 1915-1972 *WhAm 5*

Meyers, Charles Bradford 1875-1958
NatCAB 53

Meyers, Clarence L 1886-1961 *NatCAB 50*

Meyers, Erwin A 1888-1965 *WhAm 4*

Meyers, George Julian 1881-1939 *NatCAB 29,
WhAm 1*

Meyers, J Edward 1862- *WhAm 4*

Meyers, Joseph 1898-1957 *WhAm 3*

Meyers, Joseph Hugh 1904-1972 *WhAm 5*

Meyers, Milton Kayton 1882-1954 *NatCAB 42*

Meyers, Robert C V 1858- *WhAm 1*

Meyers, Robert William 1919-1970 *IlBEAAW*

Meyers, Sidney Stuyvesant 1876- *NatCAB 15,
WhAm 5*

Meyers, Solomon George 1897-1965
NatCAB 52

Meyers, Willard Franklin 1861-1929
NatCAB 38

Meyers, William Henry *IlBEAAW,
NewYHSD*

Meyers, William John 1869-1928 *WhAm 1*

Meyersburg, Harry 1884-1962 *NatCAB 50*

Meyerson, Émile 1859-1933 *DcScB,
DcScB Sup*

Meyerstein, Benjamin *NewYHSD*

Meyher, John *NewYHSD*

Meylan, George Louis 1873-1960 *WhAm 3*

Meylan, Paul Julien 1882-1961 *WhAm 4*

Meyler, James Joseph 1866-1901 *NatCAB 35*

Meyn, Antoinette Affeld 1879- *WomWWA 14*

Meyne, Gerhardt 1880-1966 *WhAm 5*

Meynell, Sir Francis d1975 *WhAm 6*

Meyniac, Mrs. M R *NewYHSD*

Meyr *NewYHSD*

Meyre *NewYHSD*

Meyrick, Richard *NewYHSD*

Meyrowitz, Emil B 1851- *WhAm 4*

Mezarra, Francis *NewYHSD*

Mezes, Sidney Edward 1863-1931 *AmBi,
BiDAmEd, DcAmB, NatCAB 15,
NatCAB 30, WhAm 1*

Mezzara, Angelica d1868 *NewYHSD*

Mezzera, Francis *NewYHSD*

Mezzera, M *NewYHSD*

Mezzerer, Peter *NewYHSD*

Mezzrow, Mezz 1899-1972 *WhAm 5*

M'Farlan, Thomas *NewYHSD*

M'Gahey *NewYHSD*

M'Gee, John L *NewYHSD*

M'Ginnis *NewYHSD*

Mi, Fei 1051-1107 *McGEWB*

Miantonomo 1565?-1643 *AmBi, ApCAB,
DcAmB, Drake, WhAm H*

Miantunnomoh *NatCAB 10*

Mibelli, Vittorio 1860-1910 *BiHiMed*

Micah *McGEWB*

Micconopy 1786?-1849 *ApCAB, Drake*

Mich, Daniel D 1905-1965 *WhAm 4*

Michael 1892-1954 *WhAm 3*

Michael, King Of Rumania 1921- *WhWW-II*

Michael VIII, Palaeologus 1224?-1282
McGEWB

Michael Psellus *DcScB*

Michael Scot 1200?-1235? *DcScB*

Michael, Arthur 1853-1942 *ApCAB Sup,
DcAmB S3, DcScB, NatCAB 15,
WhAm 1, WhAm 2*

Michael, Charles Edwin 1871-1938 *NatCAB 29*

Michael, Elias 1854-1913 *NatCAB 12,
NatCAB 17, WhAm 1*

Michael, Helen Abbott d1904 *WhAm 1*

Michael, Jerome 1890-1953 *WhAm 3*

Michael, Max 1884-1949 *WhAm 3*

Michael, Moina Belle 1869-1944 *WhAm 2*

Michael, Morris 1883-1943 *NatCAB 32*

Michael, Rachel Stix 1866- *WomWWA 14*

Michael, William Henry 1845-1916 *WhAm 1*

Michaelides, George Peter 1892-1963 *WhAm 4*

Michaelis, George V S 1873- *WhAm 5*

Michaelis, Leonor 1875-1949 *AsBiEn,
DcAmB S4, WhAm 2*

Michaelis, Richard C 1839-1909 *WhAm 1*

Michaelius, Jonas 1577-1638 *ApCAB,
NatCAB 12*

Michaelius, Jonas 1584- *DcAmB*

Michaelius, Jonas 1584-1637? *WhAm H*

Michaels, Charles Frederick 1869-1944
WhAm 2

Michaels, Ernest Edwin 1897-1970 *WhAm 5*

Michaels, Henry 1909-1951 *WhAm 3*

Michaels, Hunter 1889-1962 *WhAm 4*

Michaelson, M Alfred 1878-1949 *WhAm 2*

Michaelson, Magne Alfred 1878-1949 *BiDrAC,
WhAmP*

Michal, Aristotle Demetrius 1899-1953
NatCAB 42, WhAm 3

Michalek, Anthony 1878-1916 *BiDrAC,
WhAm 6*

Michalson, Carl 1915-1965 *WhAm 4*

Michaud, Gustave 1860- *WhAm 4*

Michaud, John Stephen 1843-1908 *ApCAB Sup,
NatCAB 5, TwCBDA, WhAm 1*

Michaud, Regis 1880-1939 *WhAm 1*

Michaux, Andre 1746-1802 *AmBi, ApCAB,
DcAmB, DcScB, Drake, WhAm H*

Michaux, Francois Andre 1770-1855 *ApCAB,
DcAmB, WhAm H*

Michaux, Stuart Neville 1878-1950 *NatCAB 41*

Micheaux, Oscar 1884-1951 *DcAmB S5*

Michel, Carl 1890-1946 *NatCAB 35*

Michel, Charles E 1875- *WhAm 5*

Michel, Dieudonne Gabriel Lucien 1605-1669
ApCAB

Michel, Ernest A 1887-1947 *WhAm 2*

Michel, Jacques Leonard 1620-1677 *ApCAB*

Michel, Lincoln Mattheus 1911-1972 *WhAm 5*

Michel, Nettie Leila 1863- *AmWom*

Michel, Richard Fraser 1827-1907 *TwCBDA,
WhAm 1*

Michel, Robert Henry 1923- *BiDrAC*

Michel, Virgil George 1890-1938 *DcAmB S2,
DcAmReB, WhAm HA, WhAm 4*

Michel, William 1866- *WhAm 4*

Michel, William C 1894-1970 *WhAm 5*

Michel, William Middleton 1822-1894 *ApCAB,
DcAmB, NatCAB 24, TwCBDA,
WhAm H*

Michel-Levy, Auguste 1844-1911 *DcScB*

Michelangelo Buonarroti 1475-1564 *McGEWB*

Michelet, Jules 1798-1874 *McGEWB*

Michelfelder, Sylvester Clarence 1889-1951
WhAm 3

Micheli, Pier Antonio 1679-1737 *DcScB*

Michelin, Francis *NewYHSD*

Michelin, Henry Etienne 1726-1795 *ApCAB*

Michelini, Famiano 1604-1665 *DcScB*

Michell, John 1724?-1793 *AsBiEn, DcScB*

Michelozzo 1396?-1472 *McGEWB*

Michels, Nicholas Aloysius 1891-1969
NatCAB 55, WhAm 5

Michels, Robert 1876-1936 *McGEWB*

Michels, Walter Christian 1906-1975 *WhAm 6*

Michelson, Albert Abraham 1851-1931 *AmBi*

Michelson, Albert Abraham 1852-1931 *ApCAB,
AsBiEn, DcAmB, DcScB, EncAB,
McGEWB, NatCAB 12, NatCAB 33,
TwCBDA, WebAB, WhAm 1*

Michelson, Albert Heminway 1878-1915
WhAm 1

Michelson, Albert Sidney 1895-1974 *WhAm 6*

Michelson, Arnold 1893-1969 *WhAm 5*

Michelson, Charles 1868-1947 *WhAm 2*

Michelson, Charles 1868-1948 *DcAmB S4*

Michelson, Halvor 1838-1923 *REnAW*

Michelson, Henry E 1888-1972 *WhAm 5*

Michelson, Miriam 1870-1942 *WhAm 2,
WomWWA 14*

Michelson, Truman 1879-1938 *WhAm 1,
WhAm 1C*

Michener, Carroll Kinsey 1885-1970
NatCAB 56

Michener, Earl Cory 1876-1957 *BiDrAC,
WhAm 3, WhAmP*

Michener, Ezra 1794-1857 *NatCAB 15*

Michener, Ezra 1794-1887 *DcAmB, WhAm H*

Michener, James Albert 1907- *WebAB*

Michener, Louis Theodore 1848-1928 *WhAm 1*

Michener, William Ernest 1881-1955
  NatCAB 41
Michi Kini Kwa 1752?-1812 *WhAm H*
Michie, A Hewson 1897-1957 *WhAm 3*
Michie, H Stuart 1871- *WhAm 5*
Michie, James Newton 1879-1958 *WhAm 3*
Michie, Peter Smith 1839-1901 *ApCAB,*
  DcAmB, TwCBDA, WhAm 1
Michie, Robert Edward Lee 1864-1918
  WhAm 1
Michie, Thomas Johnson 1896-1973 *WhAm 5*
Michikinikwa 1752?-1812 *AmBi, DcAmB*
Michinard, Frank 1855- *WhAm 4*
Michler, Francis *WhAm 5*
Michler, Nathaniel 1827-1881 *ApCAB,*
  DcAmB S1, WhAm H
Michurin, Ivan Vladimirovich 1855-1935 *DcScB,*
  DcScB Sup
Mickelsen, Antone Otto 1890-1948 *NatCAB 37*
Mickelsen, Stanley R 1895-1966 *WhAm 4*
Mickelson, George Theodore 1903-1965
  NatCAB 50, WhAm 4
Mickey, Harold Chandler 1908-1968 *WhAm 5*
Mickey, J Ross 1856-1928 *BiDrAC*
Mickey, John Hopwood 1845-1910 *NatCAB 12,*
  WhAm 1
Mickle, Joe J 1898-1965 *WhAm 4*
Mickle, William English 1846-1920 *WhAm 1*
Mickler, William Felix 1836-1927 *NatCAB 21*
Mickley, Minnie Fogel *WomWWA 14*
Micou, Richard Wilde 1848-1912 *NatCAB 15,*
  WhAm 1
Middelschulte, Wilhelm 1863-1943 *WhAm 2*
Middelton, J Ira 1880-1941 *NatCAB 31*
Middendorf, Aleksandr Fedorovich 1815-1894
  DcScB
Middendorf, Henry Stump 1893-1972
  NatCAB 57
Middendorf, John William 1849-1928
  NatCAB 42
Middlebrook, Louis Francis 1866-1937 *WhAm 1*
Middlebrook, Louis Nathaniel 1825-1908
  NatCAB 16
Middlebrook, Walter Clark 1886-1955
  NatCAB 44
Middlebrook, William Theophilus 1891-1974
  WhAm 6
Middlebrooks, Audy Jefferson 1897-1965
  WhAm 4
Middlebush, Frederick Arnold 1890-1971
  WhAm 5
Middlekauff, Peter Downey 1858-1939
  NatCAB 30
Middleswart, Belle Otis 1873- *WomWWA 14*
Middleswarth, Ner d1865 *BiAUS*
Middleswarth, Ner 1780?-1865 *ApCAB*
Middleswarth, Ner 1783-1865 *BiDrAC,*
  WhAm H
Middleton, Arthur 1681-1737 *ApCAB, DcAmB,*
  Drake, NatCAB 12, TwCBDA, WhAm H
Middleton, Arthur 1742-1787 *AmBi, ApCAB,*
  BiDrAC, DcAmB, NatCAB 5, TwCBDA,
  WhAm H, WhAmP
Middleton, Arthur 1743-1788 *BiAUS, Drake*
Middleton, Arthur 1795-1853 *ApCAB*
Middleton, Arthur D 1880-1929 *WhAm 1*
Middleton, Austin Dickinson 1845- *ApCAB X*
Middleton, Austin Ralph 1881-1956 *WhAm 3*
Middleton, Caleb Scattergood 1839- *NatCAB 4*
Middleton, Charles Gibson 1883-1956 *WhAm 3*
Middleton, Christopher d1770 *ApCAB, Drake*
Middleton, Cornelius W 1893-1966 *WhAm 4*
Middleton, E R 1885-1938 *NatCAB 29*
Middleton, Edward d1685? *ApCAB*
Middleton, Edward 1810-1883 *ApCAB,*
  NatCAB 7, TwCBDA
Middleton, Elijah C *NewYHSD*
Middleton, Sir Frederick Dobson 1825- *ApCAB*
Middleton, George *NewYHSD*
Middleton, George 1800-1888 *BiDrAC,*
  WhAm H
Middleton, George 1811- *BiAUS*
Middleton, George 1880-1967 *WhAm 4*
Middleton, Henry d1846 *BiAUS*
Middleton, Henry 1717-1784 *AmBi, ApCAB,*
  BiDrAC, BiDrUSE, DcAmB, NatCAB 5,
  TwCBDA, WhAm H, WhAmP
Middleton, Henry 1770-1846 *AmBi, BiDrAC,*

DcAmB, NatCAB 12, TwCBDA,
  WhAm H, WhAmP
Middleton, Henry 1771-1846 *ApCAB, BiAUS,*
  Drake
Middleton, Henry 1797-1876 *ApCAB,*
  NatCAB 9, TwCBDA
Middleton, John *ApCAB*
Middleton, John Albert 1914-1975 *WhAm 6*
Middleton, John Cavarly 1833-1888
  ApCAB Sup
Middleton, John Izard 1785-1849 *ApCAB,*
  DcAmB, Drake, NewYHSD, WhAm H
Middleton, John Izard 1800-1877 *ApCAB*
Middleton, Mrs. Joseph M *WomWWA 14*
Middleton, Melbourne F 1842- *NatCAB 3*
Middleton, Nathan Atherton 1887-1931
  NatCAB 24
Middleton, Nathaniel Russell 1810-1890
  DcAmB, WhAm H
Middleton, Peter d1781 *ApCAB, DcAmB,*
  Drake, WhAm H
Middleton, Stanley Grant 1852-1942 *WhAm 2*
Middleton, Thomas 1580-1627 *McGEWB*
Middleton, Thomas 1719-1766 *ApCAB,*
  NatCAB 7
Middleton, Thomas 1797-1863 *NewYHSD*
Middleton, Thomas Cooke 1842-1923 *DcAmB,*
  NatCAB 25, WhAm 4
Middleton, Washington Irving 1870-1934
  NatCAB 24
Middleton, Sir William *ApCAB*
Middleton, William *ApCAB*
Middleton, William 1710- *ApCAB*
Middleton, William Shainline 1890-1975
  WhAm 6
Middleton, William Vernon 1902-1965 *WhAm 4*
Middour, Emory J 1890- *WhAm 3*
Midgley, Albert Leonard 1878- *WhAm 6*
Midgley, Harry Clegg 1886-1952 *NatCAB 42*
Midgley, John William 1843-1922 *WhAm 1*
Midgley, Thomas, Jr. 1889-1944 *AsBiEn,*
  DcAmB S3, DcScB, NatCAB 34,
  WhAm 2
Mie, Gustav 1868-1957 *DcScB*
Miedel, Robert Eugene 1920-1969 *WhAm 5*
Miege, John Baptist 1815-1884 *ApCAB,*
  TwCBDA
Miel, Charles Jan 1898-1956 *NatCAB 47*
Mielatz, Charles Frederic William 1860-1919
  NatCAB 25
Mielatz, Charles Frederick William 1860-1919
  DcAmB, WhAm 1
Mieli, Aldo 1879-1950 *DcScB*
Mielziner, Jo 1901-1976 *WhAm 6*
Mielziner, Leo 1869-1935 *NatCAB 32,*
  WhAm 1
Mielziner, Moses 1828-1903 *DcAmB,*
  NatCAB 7, TwCBDA, WhAm 1
Miers, Earl Schenck 1910-1972 *WhAm 5*
Miers, Henry Alexander 1858-1942 *DcScB*
Miers, Henry Virgil 1925-1967 *WhAm 5*
Miers, John 1789-1879 *ApCAB*
Miers, Robert Walter 1848-1930 *BiDrAC,*
  TwCBDA, WhAm 1
Miersch, Ella E *WomWWA 14*
Miersch, Paul Frederic Theodore 1868-
  WhAm 4
Mies VanDerRohe, Ludwig 1886-1969
  BiDAmEd, BnEnAmA, EncAB, McGEWB,
  WebAB, WhAm 5
Miescher, Johann Friedrich, II 1844-1895
  AsBiEn, DcScB
Miesse, Gabriel 1807- *NewYHSD*
Miesse, Kate DeWitt *WomWWA 14*
Miessner, W Otto 1880- *WhAm 6*
Mietus, Conrad Alexander 1900-1967
  NatCAB 54
Mifflin, George Harrison 1845-1921 *ApCAB X,*
  WhAm 1
Mifflin, John Houston 1807-1888 *NewYHSD*
Mifflin, Lloyd 1846-1921 *DcAmB,*
  NatCAB 18, WhAm 1
Mifflin, Thomas 1744-1800 *AmBi, ApCAB,*
  BiAUS, BiDrAC, BiDrUSE, DcAmB,
  Drake, NatCAB 2, TwCBDA, WebAMB,
  WhAmP
Mifflin, Thomas 1745-1800 *WhAm H*
Mifflin, Warner 1745-1798 *AmBi, ApCAB,*

DcAmB
Miflin, Thomas 1744-1800 *WebAB*
Migatz, Marshall d1973 *WhAm 6*
Migel, Julius A 1878-1976 *WhAm 6*
Mighels, Ella Sterling 1853-1934 *WhAm 2,*
  WhAm 4
Mighels, Henry *NewYHSD*
Mighels, Philip Verrill 1869-1911 *WhAm 1*
Mignone, Albert Edmund 1914- *WhAm 5*
Mignot, Louis Remy 1831-1870 *ApCAB,*
  DcAmB, Drake, NewYHSD
Mihailovic, Draza 1893-1946 *WhoMilH*
Mihajlovic, Draza 1893-1946 *WhWW-II*
Mihalyfi, Erno 1898-1972 *WhAm 6*
Mihills, Carrie Sizer 1861- *WomWWA 14*
Mihills, Mildred 1886- *WomWWA 14*
Mijares, Jacobo 1695-1751 *ApCAB*
Mikawa, Gunichi *WhWW-II*
Mikell, Henry Judah 1873-1942 *WhAm 2*
Mikell, William Ephraim 1868-1944
  NatCAB 33
Mikell, William Ephraim 1868-1945 *WhAm 2*
Mikesell, Doyle 1915-1958 *WhAm 3*
Mikesell, Jerome Byron 1901-1968 *WhAm 5*
Mikesell, William Henry d1969 *WhAm 5*
Mikhalapov, George Sergei 1906-1971 *WhAm 5*
Mikkelsen, Michael Andreas 1865-1941
  NatCAB 30
Miklukho-Maklay, Mikhail Nikolaevich
  1857-1927 *DcScB Sup*
Mikolajczyk, Stanislaw 1901-1967 *WhWW-II*
Mikoyan, Artem 1905- *WhWW-II*
Mikules, T Leonard 1909-1972 *WhAm 6*
Mikva, Abner Joseph 1926- *BiDrAC*
Milam, Arthur Yeager 1889-1956 *WhAm 3*
Milam, Avis Sanders 1860- *WomWWA 14*
Milam, Carl Hastings 1884-1963 *DcAmLiB,*
  NatCAB 51, WhAm 4
Milan, Luis 1500?-1561? *McGEWB*
Milanes, Jose Jacinto 1814-1863 *ApCAB*
Milas, Nicholas Althanasius 1897-1971
  WhAm 5
Milbank, Albert Goodsell 1873-1949 *WhAm 2*
Milbank, Charles Albert 1879-1967 *NatCAB 53*
Milbank, Dunlevy 1878-1959 *NatCAB 49,*
  WhAm 3
Milbank, Jeremiah 1887-1972 *NatCAB 57,*
  WhAm 5
Milbank, Thomas Powell Fowler 1913-1974
  WhAm 6
Milbank, William Edward 1841- *NatCAB 13*
Milbert, Jacques Gerard 1766-1840 *ApCAB,*
  NewYHSD, WhAm H
Milbourn, Charles C *NewYHSD*
Milbourn, Frank William 1882-1957
  NatCAB 47
Milbourne, C *NewYHSD*
Milbourne, Cotton *NewYHSD*
Milbourne, Harvey Lee 1895-1966 *WhAm 4*
Milbourne, Manfull Stephen 1851-1940
  NatCAB 32
Milburn, Arthur W d1937 *WhAm 1*
Milburn, Edward Garland 1919-1971 *WhAm 5*
Milburn, Frank Pierce 1868- *NatCAB 12*
Milburn, George 1906-1966 *WhAm 4*
Milburn, George Roszelle 1850-1910 *WhAm 1*
Milburn, John *NewYHSD*
Milburn, John George 1851-1930 *NatCAB 32,*
  WhAm 1
Milburn, William Henry 1823-1903 *ApCAB,*
  DcAmB, Drake, NatCAB 7, TwCBDA,
  WhAm 1
Milch, Erhard 1892-1972 *WhWW-II*
Milden, Alfred William 1868-1944 *WhAm 2*
Mildon, Henry Hill 1836-1916 *NatCAB 18*
Mildon, Reginald Brind 1877-1952 *NatCAB 41*
Milen, Frederick Blumenthal 1835- *WhAm 4*
Miles, Basil 1877-1928 *NatCAB 21, WhAm 1*
Miles, Benjamin Clarkson 1865-1939
  NatCAB 38
Miles, C Edwin 1830- *WhAm 4*
Miles, Carlton Wright 1884- *WhAm 3*
Miles, Clarence Paul 1879-1966 *WhAm 4*
Miles, Daniel Curtis 1827-1912 *WhAm 1*
Miles, Dixon S 1803-1862 *Drake*
Miles, Dixon Stansbury 1804-1862 *ApCAB,*
  TwCBDA
Miles, Dudley 1881-1954 *WhAm 3*

Miles, Edson Russell 1875-1958 *WhAm 3*
Miles, Edward 1752-1828 *DcAmB, NewYHSD*
Miles, Ellen E 1834- *WhAm 4*
Miles, Emma Bell 1879-1919 *WhAm 2, WomWWA 14*
Miles, Evan 1838-1908 *WhAm 1*
Miles, Francis Turquand 1827-1903 *NatCAB 20*
Miles, Frederick 1815-1896 *BiDrAC, TwCBDA, WhAm H*
Miles, George Carpenter 1904-1975 *WhAm 6*
Miles, George D 1827?-1881 *NewYHSD*
Miles, George Henry 1824-1871 *ApCAB, DcAmB*
Miles, George Henry 1824-1872 *NatCAB 6*
Miles, George Wellington 1868-1939 *NatCAB 29*
Miles, Gilbert Frazer 1893-1954 *NatCAB 44*
Miles, Henry Adolphus 1809-1895 *ApCAB, DcAmB, Drake*
Miles, Henry Dixon 1864-1945 *NatCAB 40*
Miles, Henry Shillingford 1866-1957 *NatCAB 44*
Miles, Herbert Delahaye 1866-1958 *NatCAB 49*
Miles, Hooper Steele 1895-1964 *WhAm 4*
Miles, James Browning 1822-1875 *ApCAB*
Miles, James Warley 1818-1875 *ApCAB*
Miles, James Warley 1819?-1875 *Drake*
Miles, John 1621?-1683 *DcAmB*
Miles, John 1859- *NatCAB 11*
Miles, John Esten 1884- *BiDrAC*
Miles, Joshua Weldon 1858-1929 *BiDrAC, WhAm 1*
Miles, L Wardlaw 1873-1944 *WhAm 2*
Miles, Lee Lewis 1878-1948 *NatCAB 37*
Miles, Lovick Pierce 1871-1953 *WhAm 3*
Miles, Manly 1826-1898 *BiDAmEd, DcAmB, EncAAH, NatCAB 15*
Miles, Martin Bernard 1904-1960 *NatCAB 49*
Miles, Milton Edward 1900-1961 *WhAm 4*
Miles, Nelson Appleton 1839-1925 *AmBi, ApCAB, DcAmB, Drake, McGEWB, NatCAB 4, NatCAB 9, REnAW, TwCBDA, WebAB, WebAMB, WhAm 1, WhoMilH*
Miles, Perry Lester 1873- *WhAm 5*
Miles, Pliny 1818-1865 *ApCAB, Drake, NatCAB 5*
Miles, Richard Pius 1791-1860 *ApCAB, DcAmB, Drake, NatCAB 12, TwCBDA*
Miles, Robert Parker 1866-1940 *WhAm 1*
Miles, Robert Whitfield 1890-1952 *WhAm 3*
Miles, Rufus Lawson 1872-1950 *NatCAB 38*
Miles, Samuel 1740-1805 *ApCAB, TwCBDA*
Miles, Vincent Morgan 1885-1947 *WhAm 2*
Miles, Waldo Garland 1911-1973 *WhAm 6*
Miles, Willard Wesbery 1845-1926 *WhAm 1*
Miles, William Henry 1828-1892 *NatCAB 14*
Miles, William Porcher 1822-1899 *BiDConf, BiDrAC, DcAmB, NatCAB 11, TwCBDA, WhAm 1*
Miles, William Raphael 1817- *NatCAB 9*
Milet, Peter 1708- *ApCAB*
Milewski, Leo A 1910-1969 *NatCAB 54*
Miley, Jess Wells 1878-1952 *WhAm 3*
Miley, John 1814-1896 *TwCBDA*
Miley, John David 1862-1899 *ApCAB Sup, NatCAB 28*
Miley, John Henry 1878-1944 *WhAm 2*
Milford, Morton Marshall 1883-1938 *WhAm 1*
Milfort, LeClerc *Drake*
Milham, Frank Hickman 1864-1921 *NatCAB 19*
Milham, Willis Isbister 1874-1957 *NatCAB 14, NatCAB 45, WhAm 3*
Milhau, John J De 1828-1891 *NatCAB 2*
Milhau, John Tiburce Gregoire Francis De 1796-1874 *NatCAB 2*
Milhau, Zella De 1870- *BiCAW, WomWWA 14*
Milhaud, Darius 1892-1974 *McGEWB, WhAm 6*
Milhaud, Gaston 1858-1918 *DcScB*
Milholland, Inez 1886-1916 *DcAmB, NotAW*
Milholland, John Elmer 1860-1925 *ApCAB X, WhAm 1*

Milholland, Sara Agnes 1871- *WomWWA 14*
Milholland, Vida *BiCAW*
Milholland-Boissevain, Inez 1886-1916 *WomWWA 14*
Milinowski, Harriot Ransom 1857- *WomWWA 14*
Milinowski, Marta 1885- *WomWWA 14*
Militz, Annie Rix 1855-1924 *NatCAB 21, WomWWA 14*
Miliukov, Pavel Nikolayevich 1859-1943 *McGEWB*
Milk, Arthur Leslie 1905-1962 *WhAm 4*
Milkman, Louis Arthur 1895-1951 *BiHiMed*
Milkowski, Antoni 1935- *BnEnAmA*
Milks, Howard Jay 1879-1954 *WhAm 3*
Mill, James 1773-1836 *McGEWB*
Mill, John Stuart 1806-1873 *DcScB, McGEWB*
Millais, Sir John Everett 1829-1896 *McGEWB*
Millar, Addison Thomas 1860- *NatCAB 11*
Millar, Alexander Copeland 1861-1940 *TwCBDA, WhAm 1*
Millar, Branford Price 1914-1975 *WhAm 6*
Millar, Clara Smart 1852- *AmWom*
Millar, Earl Bruce 1837-1916 *NatCAB 27*
Millar, Edward Alexander 1860-1934 *WhAm 1*
Millar, Ellen Maud Graham 1876- *WomWWA 14*
Millar, John Rutherford 1887-1959 *NatCAB 48*
Millar, Preston Strong 1880-1949 *NatCAB 37, WhAm 2*
Millar, Robert Cameron 1900-1971 *WhAm 5*
Millar, Robert Wyness 1876-1959 *WhAm 3*
Millar, Ronald 1890-1946 *WhAm 2*
Millar, William Bell d1930 *WhAm 1*
Millard, Alice Welch Kellogg 1871- *WomWWA 14*
Millard, Bailey 1859-1941 *WhAm 1*
Millard, Cecil Vernon 1898-1959 *NatCAB 47*
Millard, Charles Dunsmore 1873-1944 *BiDrAC, WhAm 2*
Millard, Charles Dunsmore 1873-1945 *NatCAB 34*
Millard, Charles Sterling 1874-1942 *WhAm 2*
Millard, Clifford 1861- *WhAm 4*
Millard, D Ralph 1883-1965 *NatCAB 51*
Millard, David 1794-1873 *ApCAB, Drake*
Millard, Douglas 1879-1946 *WhAm 2*
Millard, Earl 1905-1970 *WhAm 5*
Millard, Everett Lee 1877-1933 *WhAm 1*
Millard, Floyd Hays 1888-1955 *WhAm 3*
Millard, Frank Ashley 1861- *WhAm 4*
Millard, Frank Bailey 1859- *NatCAB 10*
Millard, Gertrude Binney 1872- *WomWWA 14*
Millard, Harrison 1829-1895 *ApCAB, NatCAB 7*
Millard, Harrison 1830-1895 *WhAm H*
Millard, Joseph Hopkins 1836-1922 *BiDrAC, NatCAB 13, TwCBDA, WhAm 1*
Millard, Paul Adsworth 1892-1945 *WhAm 2*
Millard, Stephen Columbus 1841-1914 *BiDrAC, NatCAB 8*
Millard, Thomas Franklin Fairfax 1868-1942 *WhAm 2*
Millard, Willard B, Jr. 1900-1969 *WhAm 5*
Millard, William Barrett 1867- *WhAm 4*
Millay, Edna St. Vincent 1892-1950 *ApCAB X, DcAmB S4, McGEWB, NatCAB 38, NotAW, WebAB, WhAm 3*
Millay, Kathleen d1943 *WhAm 2*
Millberry, Guy Stillman 1872- *WhAm 5*
Milledge, John 1757-1818 *AmBi, ApCAB, BiAUS, BiDrAC, DcAmB, Drake, NatCAB 1, TwCBDA, WhAm H, WhAmP*
Milledoler, Philip 1775-1852 *ApCAB, DcAmB, Drake, NatCAB 3, TwCBDA, WhAm H*
Milleken *NewYHSD*
Millen, Edmund 1848-1927 *NatCAB 20*
Millen, John 1804-1843 *BiAUS, BiDrAC, WhAm H*
Millener, John A 1885-1948 *WhAm 4*
Miller, A *NewYHSD*
Miller, A Blanchard 1878-1941 *NatCAB 41, WhAm 1, WhAm 2*
Miller, Aaron Benjamin 1859-1925 *NatCAB 20*
Miller, Addie Dickman 1859- *AmWom*
Miller, Adolph Caspar 1866-1953 *NatCAB 42, WhAm 3*

Miller, Albert 1828-1900 *NatCAB 18*
Miller, Albert Edward 1861-1939 *WhAm 1*
Miller, Albert Fullerton 1910-1973 *WhAm 6*
Miller, Albert L d1958 *WhAm 3*
Miller, Albion Kendall 1835- *NatCAB 9*
Miller, Alden Holmes 1906-1965 *WhAm 4*
Miller, Alexander 1856-1941 *NatCAB 31*
Miller, Alexander Macomb d1904 *WhAm 1*
Miller, Alfred Brashear 1829-1902 *TwCBDA, WhAm 1*
Miller, Alfred Jacob 1810-1874 *ApCAB, IlBEAAW, NewYHSD, REnAW, WhAm H*
Miller, Alfred Jameson 1846-1904 *ApCAB X*
Miller, Alfred Parkin 1894-1963 *WhAm 4*
Miller, Alfred Stanley 1856-1928 *WhAm 1*
Miller, Alice Duer 1874-1942 *NotAW, WhAm 2, WomWWA 14*
Miller, Alten Sidney 1868-1967 *NatCAB 53*
Miller, Alvah 1855- *ApCAB X*
Miller, Alvah Lawrence 1894-1950 *NatCAB 42*
Miller, Amos Calvin 1866-1949 *WhAm 2*
Miller, Andreas Mitchell 1838-1917 *NatCAB 17*
Miller, Andrew 1870- *WhAm 5*
Miller, Andrew Galbraith 1801-1874 *BiAUS, NatCAB 16*
Miller, Andrew Jackson 1806-1856 *NatCAB 2*
Miller, Andrew Jackson, Jr. 1906-1959 *WhAm 3*
Miller, Andrew James 1855- *WhAm 4*
Miller, Andrew Joyce 1867-1937 *NatCAB 28, WhAm 1*
Miller, Anna Jenness 1859- *WhAm 5*
Miller, Anna Virginia *WomWWA 14*
Miller, Annie Jenness 1859- *AmWom*
Miller, Antha Lucy Knowlton *WomWWA 14*
Miller, Arthur 1910-1967 *WhAm 4*
Miller, Arthur 1915- *EncAB, McGEWB, WebAB*
Miller, Arthur Korschgen 1902-1963 *NatCAB 50, WhAm 4*
Miller, Arthur Lewis 1892-1967 *BiDrAC, NatCAB 53, WhAm 4*
Miller, Arthur McQuiston 1861-1929 *WhAm 1*
Miller, Arthur Merkel 1894-1959 *NatCAB 47*
Miller, Arthur W 1876- *WhAm 5*
Miller, Athol Morton 1874-1912 *NatCAB 17*
Miller, Augustus Samuel 1847-1905 *WhAm 1*
Miller, Austin Vicente 1877-1955 *WhAm 3*
Miller, Barnette *WomWWA 14*
Miller, Barse 1904-1973 *WhAm 5*
Miller, Benjamin 1845-1914 *NatCAB 16*
Miller, Benjamin Kurtz 1830-1898 *NatCAB 16*
Miller, Benjamin Kurtz 1857-1929 *WhAm 1*
Miller, Benjamin LeRoy 1874-1944 *WhAm 2*
Miller, Benjamin Meek 1864-1944 *NatCAB 33, WhAm 2*
Miller, Benjamin Orville 1898-1965 *WhAm 4*
Miller, Benjamin Warren 1892-1945 *NatCAB 36*
Miller, Bert Henry 1879-1949 *BiDrAC, WhAm 2*
Miller, Bertha Everett Mahony 1882-1969 *WhAm 5*
Miller, Bina West 1867-1954 *NatCAB 44, WhAm 3*
Miller, Bloomfield Jackson 1849-1905 *NatCAB 12, WhAm 1*
Miller, Branch Knox 1857-1906 *NatCAB 24*
Miller, Byron E 1855-1925 *ApCAB X, WhAm 1*
Miller, C G 1800?- *NewYHSD*
Miller, Carl A 1891-1953 *WhAm 3*
Miller, Carl Gustave 1904-1955 *NatCAB 42*
Miller, Carl Wallace 1893-1975 *WhAm 6*
Miller, Carroll 1875-1949 *WhAm 2*
Miller, Charles *NewYHSD*
Miller, Charles 1820?- *NewYHSD*
Miller, Charles 1843-1927 *NatCAB 31, WhAm 1*
Miller, Charles Addison 1867-1944 *WhAm 2*
Miller, Charles Archer d1955 *NatCAB 44*
Miller, Charles Armand 1864-1917 *WhAm 1*
Miller, Charles Brookshire 1882-1961 *NatCAB 51*
Miller, Charles C 1831-1920 *WhAm 1*
Miller, Charles Edwin 1852-1939 *NatCAB 29*

Miller, Charles Ervine 1867-1939 *NatCAB 28,*
WhAm 1
Miller, Charles F *NewYHSD*
Miller, Charles Franklin 1875- *WhAm 5*
Miller, Charles Henry 1842-1922 *AmBi,*
ApCAB, DcAmB, NatCAB 8, NewYHSD,
TwCBDA, WhAm 1
Miller, Charles Henry 1866-1925 *NatCAB 20*
Miller, Charles Jeff 1874-1936 *NatCAB 29,*
WhAm 1
Miller, Charles Lewis 1861- *WhAm 4*
Miller, Charles Mosher 1906-1974 *WhAm 6*
Miller, Charles R 1857-1927 *NatCAB 20,*
WhAm 1
Miller, Charles R D 1899-1964 *WhAm 4*
Miller, Charles Ransom 1849-1922 *DcAmB,*
NatCAB 1, TwCBDA, WhAm 1
Miller, Charles Russel 1858-1916 *WhAm 1*
Miller, Charles Wesley 1863-1923 *WhAm 1*
Miller, Charles Wilbur 1879-1955 *WhAm 3*
Miller, Charles William Emil 1863-1934
WhAm 1
Miller, Charles Y 1892-1954 *NatCAB 42*
Miller, Chester Franklin 1860-1924 *NatCAB 20*
Miller, Christian Otto Gerberding 1865-1952
NatCAB 46, WhAm 3
Miller, Christie Poppenheim 1874-
WomWWA 14
Miller, Christine 1884- *WomWWA 14*
Miller, Christopher Chaffe 1897-1955
NatCAB 45
Miller, Cincinnatus Heine 1841-1913 *ApCAB X,*
NatCAB 7, WhAm 1
Miller, Cincinnatus Hiner d1913 *Drake,*
WebAB
Miller, Cincinnatus Hiner 1839-1913 *DcAmB*
Miller, Cincinnatus Hiner 1841-1913 *AmBi,*
ApCAB
Miller, Clara E Skinner 1860- *WomWWA 14*
Miller, Clarence A 1890-1953 *WhAm 3*
Miller, Clarence Benjamin 1872-1922 *BiDrAC,*
NatCAB 21, WhAm 1
Miller, Clarence E 1917- *BiDrAC*
Miller, Clarence Lee 1905-1965 *NatCAB 51*
Miller, Clem 1916-1962 *NatCAB 52*
Miller, Clement Woodnutt 1916-1962 *BiDrAC,*
WhAm 4
Miller, Cleo Maurice 1903-1973 *NatCAB 57*
Miller, Clifford Leonard 1880- *WhoColR*
Miller, Clifton Meredith 1873-1943 *NatCAB 31*
Miller, Clyde Winwood 1875-1940 *WhAm 1*
Miller, Cora Wise 1864- *WomWWA 14*
Miller, Crosby Parke 1843-1927 *WhAm 1*
Miller, Cynthia Hawes Fisher *WomWWA 14*
Miller, Daniel 1812-1870 *ApCAB Sup*
Miller, Daniel 1849-1898 *NatCAB 8*
Miller, Daniel Fry 1814-1895 *BiAUS, BiDrAC,*
WhAm H
Miller, Daniel H d1846 *BiAUS, BiDrAC,*
WhAm H
Miller, Daniel Long 1841-1921 *NatCAB 19,*
WhAm 1
Miller, Darius 1859-1914 *NatCAB 18,*
WhAm 1
Miller, David Aaron 1869-1958 *NatCAB 47,*
WhAm 3
Miller, David Lewis 1904-1970 *WhAm 5*
Miller, David Martin 1860-1950 *NatCAB 40*
Miller, Dayton Clarence 1866-1941 *AsBiEn,*
DcAmB S3, DcScB, NatCAB 30,
WhAm 1
Miller, Dewitt 1857-1911 *WhAm 1*
Miller, Dick 1871- *WhAm 5*
Miller, Dickinson Sergeant 1868-1963
NatCAB 51, WhAm 4
Miller, Don Clark 1914-1970 *WhAm 5*
Miller, Don Hugo 1909-1968 *WhAm 5*
Miller, Dora Richards *AmWom*
Miller, Dudley Livingston 1921-1969 *WhAm 5*
Miller, E K 1890-1968 *WhAm 5*
Miller, Earl Burns 1894-1968 *NatCAB 56*
Miller, Earle Brenneman 1891-1962
NatCAB 49
Miller, Edgar Calvin Leroy 1867- *WhAm 5*
Miller, Edgar Grim, Jr. 1893-1955 *WhAm 3*
Miller, Edith Jane *WomWWA 14*
Miller, Edmund Howd 1869-1906 *NatCAB 20,*
WhAm 1

Miller, Edmund Thornton 1878-1952 *WhAm 3*
Miller, Edmund W 1872-1960 *WhAm 4*
Miller, Edward *NewYHSD*
Miller, Edward 1760-1812 *ApCAB, DcAmB,*
Drake, NatCAB 10
Miller, Edward A *NewYHSD*
Miller, Edward Alanson 1866- *WhAm 4*
Miller, Edward Edwin 1880-1946 *BiDrAC*
Miller, Mrs. Edward F 1840- *WomWWA 14*
Miller, Edward Furber 1866-1933 *NatCAB 24,*
WhAm 1
Miller, Edward Godfrey, Jr. 1911-1968
WhAm 5
Miller, Edward Terhune 1870-1938 *NatCAB 38,*
WhAm 1
Miller, Edward Tylor 1895-1968 *BiDrAC,*
WhAm 5
Miller, Edward Waite 1865-1939 *WhAm 1*
Miller, Edward Whitney 1880- *WhAm 6*
Miller, Edwin Child 1857-1920 *ApCAB X*
Miller, Edwin Lang 1887-1971 *NatCAB 56*
Miller, Edwin Lee 1887-1943 *WhAm 2*
Miller, Edwin Lillie 1868-1934 *BiDAmEd,*
NatCAB 25, WhAm 1
Miller, Edwin Morton 1888-1972 *WhAm 6*
Miller, Eleazer Hutchinson 1831-1921
NatCAB 5, NewYHSD
Miller, Elihu Spencer 1817-1879 *ApCAB,*
Drake, NatCAB 10, WhAm H
Miller, Eliza Thurston 1851- *WomWWA 14*
Miller, Elizabeth 1836- *AmWom*
Miller, Elizabeth C North *WomWWA 14*
Miller, Elizabeth Cravath 1868- *WomWWA 14*
Miller, Elizabeth Smith 1822-1911 *NotAW,*
WhAm 1
Miller, Ellen Robertson 1859- *WomWWA 14*
Miller, Elmer 1916-1962 *NatCAB 50*
Miller, Emerson R 1862- *WhAm 1*
Miller, Emil *NewYHSD*
Miller, Emil Charles 1875-1938 *NatCAB 28*
Miller, Emily Clark Huntington 1833-1913
AmWom, DcAmB, NatCAB 10, NotAW,
TwCBDA, WhAm 1, WomWWA 14,
WomWWA 14a
Miller, Emily VanDorn *WomWWA 14*
Miller, Emma Guffey 1874-1970 *NatCAB 55,*
WhAm 5
Miller, Emma P Smith *WhAm 1*
Miller, Ephraim 1833-1930 *WhAm 1*
Miller, Erie Henry 1870- *WomWWA 14*
Miller, Ernest B 1898-1959 *WhAm 3*
Miller, Ernest Henry 1888-1932 *WhAm 1*
Miller, Ernest Ivan 1907-1972 *WhAm 5*
Miller, Ernest J 1885-1961 *NatCAB 51*
Miller, Ernest Wilson 1881-1966 *NatCAB 53*
Miller, Ethel Hull 1889-1962 *WhAm 4*
Miller, Etta Laura *WomWWA 14*
Miller, Eugene Harper 1869-1940 *WhAm 1*
Miller, Eugene Walter 1877-1951 *WhAm 3*
Miller, Ezra 1812-1885 *ApCAB, DcAmB,*
NatCAB 7, WhAm H
Miller, F Harvey 1867-1945 *NatCAB 35*
Miller, Flo Jamison 1859- *WomWWA 14*
Miller, Francis Garner 1866-1934 *WhAm 1*
Miller, Francis Hegan 1874-1950 *NatCAB 39*
Miller, Francis Trevelyn 1877-1959 *WhAm 3*
Miller, Frank Allen 1886-1963 *NatCAB 51,*
WhAm 4
Miller, Frank Augustus 1857-1935 *NatCAB 33,*
WhAm 1
Miller, Frank Ebenezer 1859-1932 *NatCAB 14,*
NatCAB 26, WhAm 1
Miller, Frank Harvey 1836-1908 *WhAm 1*
Miller, Frank Joseph 1872-1939 *NatCAB 29*
Miller, Frank Justus 1858-1938 *WhAm 1*
Miller, Frank O'Hara 1875- *WhoColR*
Miller, Frank Theodore 1873-1948 *NatCAB 36*
Miller, Frank Theron 1874-1922 *NatCAB 19*
Miller, Frank Wallace 1871-1937 *NatCAB 28*
Miller, Frank William 1866- *WhAm 4*
Miller, Franklin 1878-1952 *NatCAB 41*
Miller, Franklin Thomas 1873-1940 *WhAm 1*
Miller, Fred Augustus 1868-1938 *NatCAB 31*
Miller, Fred John 1857-1939 *NatCAB 30,*
WhAm 1
Miller, Fred Merle 1891-1956 *NatCAB 46*
Miller, Fred W 1891- *WhAm 2*
Miller, Frederic Howell 1903-1964 *NatCAB 50,*

WhAm 4
Miller, Frederic K 1908-1975 *WhAm 6*
Miller, Frederic Magoun 1896-1958 *WhAm 3*
Miller, Frederick A 1879-1948 *WhAm 3*
Miller, Frederick Alfred 1868-1954 *NatCAB 44,*
WhAm 3
Miller, Frederick Samuel 1869-1951
NatCAB 41
Miller, Freeman Edwin 1864- *WhAm 4*
Miller, Frieda Segelke 1889-1973 *WhAm 6,*
WhAmP
Miller, G F 1911- *WhAm 6*
Miller, Galen 1895- *WhAm 5*
Miller, Garfield Lankard 1882- *ApCAB X*
Miller, George *NewYHSD*
Miller, George 1774-1816 *DcAmB*
Miller, George 1889-1950 *WhAm 3*
Miller, George 1898-1966 *WhAm 4*
Miller, George Abram 1863-1951 *DcAmB S5,*
DcScB, NatCAB 16, WhAm 5
Miller, George Carter 1878-1939 *WhAm 1*
Miller, George E d1934 *WhAm 1*
Miller, George Frazier *WhoColR*
Miller, George Frederick 1880-1960 *WhAm 4*
Miller, George Funston 1809-1885 *BiAUS,*
BiDrAC, TwCBDA, WhAm H
Miller, George H 1844?- *NewYHSD*
Miller, George Henry 1871- *WhAm 5*
Miller, George Henry 1887-1972 *WhAm 6*
Miller, George Heyn 1878-1949 *NatCAB 38*
Miller, George LaForest 1829-1920 *NatCAB 19*
Miller, George LaForest 1831-1920 *REnAW*
Miller, George Lee 1881-1929 *WhAm 1*
Miller, George M d1819 *NewYHSD,*
WhAm H
Miller, George Macculloch 1832-1917
NatCAB 4, NatCAB 28, WhAm 1
Miller, George McAnelly 1858- *WhAm 4*
Miller, George Morey 1868-1937 *WhAm 1*
Miller, George Noyes 1845-1904 *WhAm 1*
Miller, George Paul 1891- *BiDrAC*
Miller, George Peckham 1858-1931 *NatCAB 16,*
NatCAB 23
Miller, George Stewart 1884-1971 *WhAm 5*
Miller, Gerrit Smith 1845-1937 *NatCAB 42,*
WhAm 1
Miller, Gerrit Smith, Jr. 1869-1956 *WhAm 3*
Miller, Gilbert Heron 1884-1969 *NatCAB 54,*
WhAm 5
Miller, Giles Henry 1875-1964 *NatCAB 51*
Miller, Glenn 1904-1944 *DcAmB S3, WebAB,*
WhAm 2
Miller, Gottfried *NewYHSD*
Miller, Grace Moncrieff 1875-1933 *WhAm 1*
Miller, Gray d1947 *WhAm 2*
Miller, Gustavus Hindman 1857-1929 *WhAm 1*
Miller, H Eugene 1885-1964 *NatCAB 50*
Miller, Hammond *NewYHSD*
Miller, Harlan d1968 *WhAm 5*
Miller, Harlan Dewey 1880-1926 *NatCAB 21*
Miller, Harold Abiud 1891-1949 *NatCAB 37*
Miller, Harold C 1889-1955 *WhAm 3*
Miller, Harriet F Huffman 1878-
WomWWA 14
Miller, Harriet Mann 1831-1918 *DcAmB,*
NatCAB 9, NotAW, TwCBDA,
WhAm 1, WomWWA 14
Miller, Harry 1903-1969 *WhAm 5*
Miller, Harry Donald 1885-1957 *NatCAB 48*
Miller, Harry Edward 1878-1952 *NatCAB 42*
Miller, Harry Edward 1897-1937 *WhAm 1*
Miller, Harry Irving 1862-1930 *NatCAB 12,*
WhAm 1
Miller, Harvey H 1883-1950 *WhAm 3*
Miller, Hazel Belle 1912-1975 *WhAm 6*
Miller, Heinrich 1702-1782 *DcAmB*
Miller, Helen Richards Guthrie 1862-1949
WhAm 2, WomWWA 14
Miller, Helen Topping 1884-1960 *WhAm 3,*
WhAm 4
Miller, Henry *NewYHSD*
Miller, Henry 1751-1824 *ApCAB, Drake,*
NatCAB 3
Miller, Henry 1800-1874 *ApCAB, DcAmB,*
NatCAB 12
Miller, Henry 1827-1916 *REnAW, WhAm 1*
Miller, Henry 1863-1926 *WhAm 1*
Miller, Henry 1893-1964 *WhAm 4*

Miller, Henry Alexander 1877-1948 *NatCAB 38*
Miller, Henry B 1854-1921 *NatCAB 19, WhAm 1*
Miller, Henry Carleton 1828-1899 *NatCAB 4*
Miller, Henry John 1860-1926 *AmBi, DcAmB, NatCAB 38, WebAB, WhAm 1*
Miller, Henry Russell 1880-1955 *NatCAB 46, WhAm 3*
Miller, Henry Valentine 1891- *McGEWB, WebAB*
Miller, Henry Watkins 1868-1933 *WhAm 1*
Miller, Herbert Adolphus 1875-1951 *NatCAB 41, WhAm 5*
Miller, Herbert Cecil 1864-1947 *NatCAB 42*
Miller, Herman Albert 1890-1954 *NatCAB 43*
Miller, Hilliard Eve 1893-1945 *NatCAB 42, WhAm 2*
Miller, Homer Martin Virgil 1814-1896 *ApCAB*
Miller, Homer Virgil Milton 1814-1896 *BiDrAC, NatCAB 12, TwCBDA, WhAm H*
Miller, Horace Alden 1872-1941 *WhAm 1*
Miller, Horace H *BiAUS*
Miller, Howard 1911-1971 *NatCAB 57*
Miller, Howard Shultz 1879-1970 *BiDrAC, WhAm 6*
Miller, Hugh 1802-1856 *DcScB*
Miller, Hugh 1881- *WhAm 6*
Miller, Hugo Eugene 1903-1973 *WhAm 6*
Miller, Humphreys Henry Clay 1845-1910 *WhAm 1*
Miller, Ida Farr *WomWWA 14*
Miller, Irving Elgar 1869- *WhAm 5*
Miller, Isaac *NewYHSD*
Miller, Isaac Eugene 1879-1955 *WhAm 3*
Miller, Israel 1866-1929 *NatCAB 24*
Miller, Ivan 1895-1957 *NatCAB 47*
Miller, J *NewYHSD*
Miller, J Allen 1866-1935 *NatCAB 40*
Miller, J C *NewYHSD*
Miller, J Clifford 1871-1927 *NatCAB 45*
Miller, J M C 1855- *WhAm 4*
Miller, J Martin 1859- *WhAm 4*
Miller, Jack Richard 1916- *BiDrAC*
Miller, Jacob F 1837-1906 *NatCAB 4, WhAm 1*
Miller, Jacob Jay 1857-1929 *WhAm 1*
Miller, Jacob Welsh 1800-1862 *ApCAB, BiDrAC, NatCAB 4, TwCBDA, WhAm H, WhAmP*
Miller, Jacob Welsh 1802-1862 *BiAUS*
Miller, Jacob William 1847-1918 *NatCAB 25, WhAm 1*
Miller, Jacques Francis Albert Pierre 1931- *AsBiEn*
Miller, James 1776-1851 *ApCAB, BiAUS, Drake, NatCAB 10, TwCBDA, WebAMB*
Miller, James 1844-1916 *WhAm 1*
Miller, James Alexander 1874-1948 *DcAmB S4, WhAm 2*
Miller, James Collins 1880-1940 *WhAm 1*
Miller, James Conelese 1891-1956 *WhAm 3*
Miller, James Decatur, Jr. 1897-1969 *WhAm 5*
Miller, James Ely 1883-1918 *NatCAB 18*
Miller, James Ferguson 1803-1868 *Drake*
Miller, James Ferguson 1805-1868 *ApCAB*
Miller, James Francis 1830-1902 *BiDrAC*
Miller, James Kenneth 1904-1971 *WhAm 5*
Miller, James Monroe 1852-1926 *BiDrAC, WhAm 4, WhAmP*
Miller, James P 1866-1909 *REnAW*
Miller, James Raglan 1886-1971 *NatCAB 57*
Miller, James Russell 1840-1912 *DcAmB, NatCAB 10, TwCBDA, WhAm 1*
Miller, James William d1829 *Drake*
Miller, Janet Goucher 1880- *WomWWA 14*
Miller, Jason G 1818-1891 *NatCAB 8*
Miller, Jesse 1800-1850 *BiAUS, BiDrAC, WhAm H*
Miller, Jesse A 1869-1941 *NatCAB 31*
Miller, Jesse I 1891-1949 *WhAm 2*
Miller, Joaquin d1913 *ApCAB Sup, WhAm 1*
Miller, Joaquin 1837-1913 *McGEWB, WebAB*
Miller, Joaquin 1839-1913 *DcAmB, REnAW*
Miller, Joaquin 1841-1913 *AmBi*
Miller, Joaquin 1842-1913 *TwCBDA*
Miller, Joel Drury 1837-1919 *NatCAB 19*
Miller, John *ApCAB, Drake, NewYHSD*

Miller, John d1846 *BiAUS, Drake*
Miller, John 1722-1791 *ApCAB*
Miller, John 1774-1862 *BiAUS, BiDrAC, WhAm H*
Miller, John 1780-1846 *ApCAB, NatCAB 12, TwCBDA*
Miller, John 1781-1846 *BiDrAC, DcAmB, WhAm H, WhAmP*
Miller, John 1819-1895 *ApCAB, DcAmB, NatCAB 10, TwCBDA, WhAm H*
Miller, John 1843-1908 *NatCAB 13, TwCBDA, WhAm 1*
Miller, John Anthony 1859- *WhAm 5*
Miller, John Barnes 1869-1932 *ApCAB X, WhAm 1*
Miller, John Bleecker 1856- *WhAm 4*
Miller, John Briggs 1908-1962 *WhAm 4*
Miller, John Calvin 1844-1923 *TwCBDA, WhAm 1*
Miller, John Chapman 1831-1901 *NatCAB 33*
Miller, John D 1856-1946 *WhAm 2*
Miller, John Elvis 1888- *BiDrAC*
Miller, John Eschelman 1857-1938 *WhAm 1*
Miller, John Fisher Garr 1877-1939 *NatCAB 29*
Miller, John Ford 1830- *WhAm 4*
Miller, John Franklin 1831-1886 *ApCAB, BiDrAC, DcAmB, NatCAB 8, TwCBDA, WhAm H, WhAmP*
Miller, John Franklin 1859-1939 *NatCAB 31, WhAm 1*
Miller, John Franklin 1862-1936 *BiDrAC, WhAm 1, WhAmP*
Miller, John Gaines 1812-1856 *BiAUS, BiDrAC, WhAm H*
Miller, John Hampton 1906-1971 *NatCAB 56*
Miller, John Harold 1859-1926 *NatCAB 22*
Miller, John Hearst 1858-1919 *NatCAB 30*
Miller, John Henderson 1845-1923 *WhAm 1*
Miller, John Henry 1702-1782 *ApCAB, DcAmB, NatCAB 24*
Miller, John Henry 1854-1935 *NatCAB 16, NatCAB 26, WhAm 1*
Miller, John Joseph 1869-1948 *NatCAB 39*
Miller, John King 1906-1972 *WhAm 6*
Miller, John King 1906-1973 *NatCAB 57*
Miller, John Krepps 1819-1863 *BiAUS, BiDrAC, TwCBDA, WhAm H*
Miller, John Lewis 1917-1963 *NatCAB 51*
Miller, John Maffit, Jr. 1868-1948 *WhAm 2*
Miller, John Oliver 1874-1962 *NatCAB 50*
Miller, John Oliver 1875-1963 *NatCAB 50*
Miller, John Peter 1709-1796 *DcAmB*
Miller, John Richard 1894-1949 *NatCAB 40*
Miller, John Richardson 1890-1966 *WhAm 4*
Miller, John Rulon, Jr. 1883-1931 *WhAm 1*
Miller, John Stocker 1847-1922 *NatCAB 16, WhAm 1*
Miller, John Stocker 1888-1965 *NatCAB 52, WhAm 4*
Miller, Jonathan P 1797-1847 *ApCAB*
Miller, Jonathan Peckham 1796-1847 *DcAmB, NatCAB 25, WhAm H*
Miller, Joseph *NewYHSD*
Miller, Joseph 1819-1862 *BiAUS, BiDrAC, WhAm H*
Miller, Joseph Dana 1864-1939 *WhAm 1*
Miller, Joseph Henry 1890-1955 *NatCAB 44, WhAm 3*
Miller, Joseph Hillis 1899-1953 *NatCAB 40, WhAm 3*
Miller, Joseph Leggett 1867-1937 *NatCAB 27, WhAm 1, WhAm 2C*
Miller, Joseph Maxwell 1877-1933 *WhAm 1*
Miller, Joseph Nelson 1836-1909 *ApCAB, TwCBDA, WhAm 1*
Miller, Joseph Torrence 1871-1938 *WhAm 1*
Miller, Joseph Zachary, Jr. 1863-1951 *NatCAB 47*
Miller, Josiah 1828-1870 *WhAm H*
Miller, Julian Creighton 1895-1971 *WhAm 5*
Miller, Julian Howell 1890-1961 *NatCAB 47, WhAm 4*
Miller, Julian Sidney 1886-1946 *WhAm 2*
Miller, Justin 1888-1973 *WhAm 5*
Miller, K F 1841- *WomWWA 14*
Miller, Karl 1884-1959 *NatCAB 49*
Miller, Kelly 1863-1939 *BiDAmEd, DcAmB S2, EncAB, WhAm 2, WhoColR*

Miller, Kelton Bedell 1860-1941 *NatCAB 33*
Miller, Kempster Blanchard 1870-1933 *DcAmB S1, NatCAB 41, WhAm 1*
Miller, Kenneth Hayes 1876-1952 *BnEnAmA, DcAmB S5, NatCAB 40, WhAm 3*
Miller, Kenneth S 1906-1974 *WhAm 6*
Miller, Killian 1785-1859 *BiAUS, BiDrAC*
Miller, Knox Emerson 1886-1969 *WhAm 5*
Miller, Lawrence William 1897-1961 *NatCAB 49, WhAm 4*
Miller, Lee Graham 1902-1961 *WhAm 4*
Miller, Lee P 1891-1962 *WhAm 4*
Miller, Leo Edward 1887-1952 *NatCAB 40, WhAm 3*
Miller, Leo L 1901-1969 *WhAm 5*
Miller, Leslie Andrew 1886-1970 *WhAm 5*
Miller, Leslie Freeland 1883-1958 *WhAm 3*
Miller, Leslie William 1848-1931 *BiDAmEd, DcAmB, WhAm 1*
Miller, Leverett Saltonstall 1865-1931 *WhAm 1*
Miller, Lewis 1795-1882 *NewYHSD*
Miller, Lewis 1829-1899 *DcAmB, NatCAB 6, NatCAB 31, TwCBDA, WhAm H*
Miller, Lewis Bennett 1861- *WhAm 4*
Miller, Linton Ossman 1860-1917 *NatCAB 47*
Miller, Logan C 1887-1958 *WhAm 3*
Miller, Loren 1903-1967 *WhAm 4*
Miller, Loren Barker 1906-1958 *WhAm 3*
Miller, Louis Ebenezer 1899-1952 *BiDrAC, NatCAB 41*
Miller, Louisa F *NewYHSD*
Miller, Louise Klein 1854-1943 *WhAm 2, WomWWA 14*
Miller, Loye Holmes 1874-1970 *WhAm 5*
Miller, Lucas Miltiades 1824-1902 *BiDrAC*
Miller, Lucia Edna Wood *WomWWA 14*
Miller, Lucius Hopkins 1876-1949 *WhAm 2*
Miller, Luther Deck 1890-1972 *WhAm 5*
Miller, Lynn Thomas 1886-1958 *NatCAB 48*
Miller, M V d1951 *WhAm 3*
Miller, Madison 1811- *ApCAB*
Miller, Mahlon Frederick 1906-1969 *NatCAB 54*
Miller, Malcolm E 1909-1960 *WhAm 4*
Miller, Marcus Peter 1835-1906 *TwCBDA, WhAm 1*
Miller, Marilyn 1898-1936 *AmBi, NotAW*
Miller, Marion Mills 1864- *WhAm 4*
Miller, Mary A *AmWom*
Miller, Mary Belle Field 1850- *WomWWA 14*
Miller, Mary Britton 1883-1975 *WhAm 6*
Miller, Mary Elizabeth Critcherson *WomWWA 14*
Miller, Mary Elizabeth White *WomWWA 14*
Miller, Mary Farrand Rogers 1868- *WhAm 4, WomWWA 14*
Miller, Mary Jean 1866- *WomWWA 14*
Miller, Maude Murray d1935 *WhAm 1*
Miller, Maurice Strasburger 1877-1957 *NatCAB 47*
Miller, Max 1899-1967 *WhAm 4, WhAm 5*
Miller, Max Emmett 1893-1950 *NatCAB 41*
Miller, Maxwell Martin, Jr. 1916-1960 *NatCAB 47*
Miller, Melville Winans 1856- *WhAm 4*
Miller, Merrill 1842-1914 *WhAm 1*
Miller, Merrill 1847-1914 *TwCBDA*
Miller, Merritt Finley 1875- *WhAm 5*
Miller, Michael A d1960 *WhAm 4*
Miller, Mike Anthony 1908-1968 *NatCAB 54*
Miller, Milton 1911-1969 *WhAm 5*
Miller, Milton A 1862- *WhAm 1*
Miller, Minnie Willis Baines 1845- *AmWom*
Miller, Morris Smith 1779-1824 *BiAUS, BiDrAC, WhAm H*
Miller, Morris Smith 1814-1870 *ApCAB*
Miller, Mortimer Craig 1856-1933 *NatCAB 31*
Miller, Myron Henry 1894-1951 *NatCAB 40*
Miller, N M *BiAUS*
Miller, Nathan 1743-1790 *BiAUS, BiDrAC, NatCAB 8, TwCBDA, WhAm H*
Miller, Nathan 1750?-1787? *ApCAB*
Miller, Nathan Lewis 1868-1953 *DcAmB S5, NatCAB 43, WhAm 3*
Miller, Nellie Burget 1875-1952 *WhAm 3*
Miller, Newton 1879-1961 *NatCAB 54, WhAm 4*
Miller, Niels Christian 1898-1962 *NatCAB 53*

Miller, Olive Beaupre 1883-1968 *NatCAB 54*
Miller, Olive Thorne 1831-1918 *AmWom,*
DcAmB, NotAW, TwCBDA, WhAm 1
Miller, Oliver 1824-1892 *DcAmB*
Miller, Orrin Larrabee 1856-1926 *BiDrAC*
Miller, Orville Rae 1893-1948 *NatCAB 37*
Miller, Oscar Phineas 1850-1928 *WhAm 1*
Miller, Otto 1874-1950 *WhAm 3*
Miller, Park Hays 1879- *WhAm 6*
Miller, Paul Duryea 1899-1965 *WhAm 4*
Miller, Paul E 1888-1954 *WhAm 3*
Miller, Paul Gerard 1875-1952 *BiDAmEd,*
WhAm 3
Miller, Paul Wright 1897-1968 *NatCAB 57*
Miller, Perl Simpson 1890-1945 *NatCAB 33*
Miller, Perry B 1867-1939 *WhAm 1*
Miller, Perry Gilbert Eddy 1905-1963 *EncAB,*
WebAB, WhAm 4
Miller, Peter *NewYHSD*
Miller, Peter 1709-1796 *DcAmB*
Miller, Philip 1691-1771 *DcScB*
Miller, Pleasant Moorman d1849 *BiAUS,*
BiDrAC, WhAm H
Miller, Pleasant Thomas 1875- *WhAm 5*
Miller, Polk 1844-1914 *NatCAB 18*
Miller, R T, Jr. 1867-1958 *WhAm 3*
Miller, Rachel H McMasters 1861-
WomWWA 14
Miller, Ralph Davison 1858-1945 *IlBEAAW,*
NatCAB 36
Miller, Ralph English 1899-1959 *NatCAB 49,*
WhAm 3
Miller, Ralph Horace 1871-1945 *NatCAB 36*
Miller, Ransford Stevens 1867-1932 *WhAm 1*
Miller, Ray Edward 1895-1954 *NatCAB 42*
Miller, Ray Haggard 1912-1973 *WhAm 6*
Miller, Ray Thomas 1893-1966 *NatCAB 53,*
WhAm 4
Miller, Raymond Louis 1913-1973 *NatCAB 57*
Miller, Reed 1880-1923 *WhAm 1*
Miller, Reuben, III 1839-1916 *ApCAB X*
Miller, Reuben, Jr. 1805-1890 *ApCAB X*
Miller, Richard Edward 1875-1943 *WhAm 1,*
WhAm 2
Miller, Richard Edward 1876-1943 *NatCAB 35*
Miller, Richard Henry 1884-1953 *WhAm 3*
Miller, Richard Paul 1894-1962 *WhAm 4*
Miller, Richard Thompson 1845- *NatCAB 5,*
WhAm 4
Miller, Robert *NewYHSD*
Miller, Robert Frederick 1929-1972 *WhAm 5*
Miller, Robert Johnson 1853- *WhAm 1*
Miller, Robert Loren, Jr. 1911-1972
NatCAB 57
Miller, Robert Netherland 1879-1968 *WhAm 4*
Miller, Robert Rowland 1903-1971 *WhAm 5*
Miller, Robert Talbott 1834-1914 *WhAm 1*
Miller, Robert Talbott, Jr. 1878-1960 *WhAm 4*
Miller, Robert Walter 1896-1954 *WhAm 3*
Miller, Robert Warren 1917-1974 *WhAm 6*
Miller, Robert Watt 1899-1970 *NatCAB 57,*
WhAm 5
Miller, Roger 1886-1944 *WhAm 2*
Miller, Roland Eugene 1912-1957 *NatCAB 50*
Miller, Rome 1855-1941 *NatCAB 30*
Miller, Roshier Welsh 1870-1950 *NatCAB 39*
Miller, Roswell 1843-1913 *NatCAB 29,*
WhAm 1
Miller, Roy Ben 1877-1950 *NatCAB 38*
Miller, Rufus Wilder 1862-1925 *WhAm 1*
Miller, Russell 1894-1959 *WhAm 4*
Miller, Russell Benjamin 1867- *WhAm 4*
Miller, Russell Cooper 1901-1974 *WhAm 6*
Miller, Russell King 1871-1939 *WhAm 1*
Miller, Rutger Bleecker 1805-1877 *BiAUS,*
BiDrAC, WhAm H
Miller, Samuel 1769-1850 *ApCAB, DcAmB,*
DcAmReB, Drake, NatCAB 7, TwCBDA
Miller, Samuel 1816-1883 *ApCAB,*
NatCAB 10, TwCBDA
Miller, Samuel 1820-1901 *DcAmB*
Miller, Samuel A 1836-1897 *TwCBDA*
Miller, Samuel Augustine 1819-1890 *BiDConf*
Miller, Samuel Charles 1903-1958 *WhAm 3*
Miller, Samuel Duncan 1869-1939 *WhAm 1*
Miller, Samuel Franklin 1827-1892 *BiAUS,*
BiDrAC, WhAm H
Miller, Samuel Freeman 1816-1890 *AmBi,*

ApCAB, BiAUS, DcAmB, McGEWB,
NatCAB 2, TwCBDA, WebAB,
WhAm H
Miller, Samuel H 1816-1890 *Drake*
Miller, Samuel Haas 1869-1929 *WhAm 1*
Miller, Samuel Henry 1840-1918 *BiDrAC*
Miller, Samuel Howard 1900-1968 *WhAm 5*
Miller, Samuel Warren 1857-1940 *WhAm 1*
Miller, Samuel William 1904-1967 *NatCAB 53,*
WhAm 4
Miller, Seton Ingersoll 1902-1974 *WhAm 6*
Miller, Seward Albert 1877-1952 *NatCAB 41*
Miller, Shackelford 1856-1924 *NatCAB 16,*
WhAm 1
Miller, Sidney Lincoln 1890-1957 *WhAm 3*
Miller, Sidney Trowbridge 1864-1940 *WhAm 1*
Miller, Smith 1804-1872 *BiAUS, BiDrAC,*
WhAm H
Miller, Spencer 1859-1953 *NatCAB 15,*
NatCAB 45, WhAm 3
Miller, Stanley Lloyd 1930- *AsBiEn*
Miller, Stephen 1816-1881 *ApCAB, BiAUS,*
NatCAB 10, TwCBDA
Miller, Stephen Decatur 1787-1838 *ApCAB,*
BiAUS, BiDrAC, DcAmB, Drake,
NatCAB 12, TwCBDA, WhAm H,
WhAmP
Miller, Stephen Franks d1867 *Drake*
Miller, Stephen Franks 1805-1867 *NatCAB 9*
Miller, Stephen Franks 1810?-1867 *ApCAB*
Miller, Stephen Ivan 1876- *WhAm 5*
Miller, Sydney Robotham 1883-1949 *WhAm 2*
Miller, Theodore 1816- *ApCAB*
Miller, Theodore Joseph 1901-1959 *WhAm 3*
Miller, Thomas 1806-1873 *NatCAB 2*
Miller, Thomas, Jr. *NewYHSD*
Miller, Thomas Byron 1896- *BiDrAC*
Miller, Thomas Condit 1848- *WhAm 4*
Miller, Thomas Ezekiel 1849-1938 *BiDrAC,*
WhAmP
Miller, Thomas Marshall 1847-1920 *WhAm 1*
Miller, Thomas Richard 1843-1914 *NatCAB 40*
Miller, Thomas Root 1903-1966 *WhAm 4*
Miller, Thomas William 1875-1945 *NatCAB 35*
Miller, Thomas Woodnutt 1886- *BiDrAC,*
NatCAB 16
Miller, Troup 1879-1957 *WhAm 3*
Miller, Vaughn 1892-1964 *WhAm 4*
Miller, Victor Arthur 1898-1963 *NatCAB 52*
Miller, Viola D Waite 1852- *WomWWA 14*
Miller, Virginia *WomWWA 14*
Miller, W Leslie 1890-1948 *WhAm 2*
Miller, Walter 1864-1949 *NatCAB 40,*
WhAm 2
Miller, Walter 1881-1949 *WhAm 3*
Miller, Walter John 1904-1973 *WhAm 6*
Miller, Walter McNab 1859- *WhAm 4*
Miller, Walter Pawson 1867-1935 *NatCAB 27*
Miller, Ward MacLaughlin 1902- *BiDrAC*
Miller, Warner 1838-1918 *ApCAB, BiDrAC,*
DcAmB, NatCAB 4, TwCBDA,
WhAm 1, WhAmP
Miller, Warren 1847-1920 *BiDrAC, TwCBDA*
Miller, Warren Hastings 1876-1960 *NatCAB 48,*
WhAm 4
Miller, Watson B 1878-1961 *WhAm 4*
Miller, Watson John 1849- *NatCAB 9*
Miller, Webb 1892-1940 *DcAmB S2,*
WhAm 1
Miller, Wendell Zerbe 1892-1958 *NatCAB 43*
Miller, Westley Thomas 1896-1964 *NatCAB 50*
Miller, Wilbur K 1892-1976 *WhAm 6*
Miller, Wilhelm 1869- *WhAm 5*
Miller, William *NewYHSD*
Miller, William 1770-1825 *BiAUS, NatCAB 4,*
TwCBDA
Miller, William 1775-1845 *ApCAB Sup*
Miller, William 1781-1849 *Drake*
Miller, William 1782-1849 *AmBi, ApCAB,*
DcAmB, DcAmReB, McGEWB,
NatCAB 6, TwCBDA, WebAB,
WhAm H
Miller, William 1795-1861 *ApCAB*
Miller, William 1835?-1907 *ApCAB,*
NewYHSD
Miller, William 1850-1923 *WhAm 1*
Miller, William Allen 1817-1870 *DcScB*

Miller, William Augustus 1857-1921
NatCAB 34
Miller, William Davis 1887-1959 *WhAm 4*
Miller, William E 1889-1956 *WhAm 3*
Miller, William Edward 1823-1896 *NatCAB 12*
Miller, William Edward 1914- *BiDrAC*
Miller, William H 1820?- *NewYHSD*
Miller, William H 1828- *BiAUS*
Miller, William Hallowes 1801-1880 *DcScB*
Miller, William Henry 1829-1870 *BiDrAC,*
WhAm H
Miller, William Henry Harrison 1840- *ApCAB,*
NatCAB 1, TwCBDA
Miller, William Henry Harrison 1840-1913
NatCAB 16
Miller, William Henry Harrison 1840-1917
AmBi, BiDrUSE, DcAmB, NatCAB 18,
WhAm 1
Miller, William J *NewYHSD*
Miller, William Jasper 1893-1962 *WhAm 4*
Miller, William Jennings 1899-1950 *BiDrAC,*
WhAm 3, WhAmP
Miller, William Lash 1866-1940 *DcScB*
Miller, William M *NewYHSD*
Miller, William Morrison 1886-1967 *WhAm 4*
Miller, William Niswonger 1855-1928 *WhAm 1*
Miller, William Otto 1877-1931 *NatCAB 25*
Miller, William Read 1823-1887 *NatCAB 10,*
TwCBDA
Miller, William Rickarby 1818-1893 *NewYHSD,*
WhAm H
Miller, William Smith 1843-1926 *NatCAB 36*
Miller, William Snow 1858-1939 *DcAmB S2,*
NatCAB 38, WhAm 1
Miller, William Starr 1793-1854 *BiAUS,*
BiDrAC, WhAm H
Miller, William Todd 1888-1962 *WhAm 4*
Miller, William Wilson 1870-1941 *WhAm 1*
Miller, Willis Dance 1893-1960 *WhAm 4*
Miller, Willoughby Dayton 1853-1907 *DcAmB*
Miller, Wilson 1829-1908 *ApCAB X*
Millerd, Clara Elizabeth 1873- *WomWWA 14*
Milles, Carl Wilhelm Emil 1875-1955
BnEnAmA, NatCAB 43, WhAm 3
Millet, Baudouin Henry 1583-1651 *ApCAB*
Millet, Clarence 1897-1959 *WhAm 3*
Millet, Francis Davis 1846-1912 *AmBi, ApCAB,*
BnEnAmA, DcAmB, IlBEAAW,
NatCAB 15, TwCBDA, WhAm 1
Millet, Jean Francois 1814-1875 *IlBEAAW,*
McGEWB
Millet, John Alfred Parsons 1888-1976 *WhAm 6*
Millet, Josiah Byram 1853-1938 *NatCAB 28*
Millet, Pierre 1631-1711 *ApCAB*
Millett, Fred Benjamin 1890-1976 *WhAm 6*
Millett, George Van 1864- *WhAm 5*
Millett, Paul Ford 1900-1951 *NatCAB 39*
Millett, Stephen Caldwell 1840-1874 *ApCAB X,*
NatCAB 34
Millett, Thomas F 1845-1927 *NatCAB 20*
Millette, John W 1869-1943 *WhAm 2*
Millhauser, DeWitt 1884-1946 *WhAm 2*
Millican, Carl Fenton 1885-1943 *NatCAB 34*
Milligan, Alexander Reed 1842-1913 *WhAm 1*
Milligan, Edward 1862-1937 *NatCAB 27,*
WhAm 1
Milligan, Elizabeth *NewYHSD*
Milligan, Elizabeth May Bolger 1882-
WomWWA 14
Milligan, Ezra McLeod 1858-1935 *WhAm 1*
Milligan, Harold Vincent 1883-1951
NatCAB 38, WhAm 3
Milligan, Harry Joseph 1854-1916 *NatCAB 24*
Milligan, Henry Coggill 1851-1940 *NatCAB 30*
Milligan, Jacob LeRoy 1889-1951 *BiDrAC,*
NatCAB 38, WhAm 3, WhAmP
Milligan, John Jones 1795-1875 *BiAUS,*
BiDrAC, NatCAB 15, TwCBDA,
WhAm H, WhAmP
Milligan, Josephine Ewing *WomWWA 14*
Milligan, Lucy Richardson 1887-1967
NatCAB 53
Milligan, Maurice Morton 1884-1959
NatCAB 50
Milligan, Melvin Lee 1860- *WhAm 4*
Milligan, Orlando Howard 1873-1954 *WhAm 3*
Milligan, Robert 1814-1875 *ApCAB, DcAmB,*

NatCAB 4, TwCBDA
Milligan, Robert Wiley 1843-1909 DcAmB, WhAm 1
Milligan, Samuel BiAUS
Milligan, Samuel 1820?-1874 NatCAB 5
Milligan, Samuel 1887-1965 NatCAB 51, WhAm 4
Milligan, William Edwin 1867-1930 WhAm 1
Millikan, Charles English 1890-1949 NatCAB 38
Millikan, Clark Blanchard 1903-1966 WhAm 4
Millikan, George Lee 1912- WhAm 3
Millikan, Lynn Boyd 1860-1940 NatCAB 30
Millikan, Max Franklin 1913-1969 WhAm 5
Millikan, Rhoda Houghton 1838-1903 NewYHSD
Millikan, Robert Andrews 1868-1953 AsBiEn, BiDAmEd, DcAmB S5, DcScB, EncAB, McGEWB, NatCAB 42, WebAB, WhAm 3
Milliken, Arnold White 1899-1964 WhAm 4
Milliken, Benjamin Love 1851-1916 WhAm 1
Milliken, Carl Elias 1877-1961 NatCAB 49, WhAm 4
Milliken, Charles William 1827-1915 BiDrAC
Milliken, Edward Redington 1881-1956 NatCAB 43
Milliken, Edwin C 1851- WhAm 4
Milliken, Foster 1865-1945 NatCAB 33
Milliken, Frank Albion 1854-1944 NatCAB 35
Milliken, George NewYHSD
Milliken, Gerrish Hill 1877-1947 NatCAB 36, WhAm 2
Milliken, Henry Oothout 1884-1945 NatCAB 34
Milliken, John David 1848- WhAm 4
Milliken, Joseph Knowles 1875-1938 WhAm 1
Milliken, Joseph Knowles 1875-1961 NatCAB 52, WhAm 4
Milliken, Orris John 1861- NatCAB 18
Milliken, Richard Allen 1817-1896 NatCAB 11
Milliken, Seth Llewellyn 1831-1897 BiDrAC, NatCAB 8, TwCBDA, WhAm H, WhAmP
Milliken, Seth Mellen 1836-1920 NatCAB 37, WhAm 1
Milliken, Seth Minot 1875-1957 NatCAB 46
Milliken, William H, Jr. 1897-1969 BiDrAC
Milliken, William Thomas 1871- WhAm 6
Millikin, Benjamin Love 1851-1916 NatCAB 44
Millikin, Charles W 1827- BiAUS
Millikin, Eugene Donald 1891-1958 BiDrAC, WhAm 3, WhAmP
Millikin, James 1827-1909 NatCAB 18
Milliman, Elmer Edward 1890-1946 WhAm 2
Millin, Sarah Gertrude d1968 WhAm 5
Milling, Robert Edward 1861-1947 NatCAB 44, WhAm 2
Milling, Robert Edward, Jr. 1898-1960 WhAm 4
Milling, Roberts Clay 1885-1973 NatCAB 57
Millington, Charles Stephen 1855-1913 BiDrAC, WhAm 1
Millington, Ernest John Oldknow 1871-1958 WhAm 3
Millington, John 1779-1868 DcAmB
Millington, Thomas 1628-1704 DcScB
Millington, Thomas Charles NewYHSD
Millington, William 1879-1962 NatCAB 53
Million, Helen Louisa Lovell 1865- WomWWA 14
Million, John Wilson 1863-1941 WhAm 1
Millis, Fred 1892-1951 NatCAB 39
Millis, Harry Alvin 1873-1948 DcAmB S4, NatCAB 41, WhAm 2
Millis, Harry Lee 1888-1942 WhAm 2
Millis, John 1858-1952 ApCAB X, WhAm 3
Millis, Wade 1868-1939 WhAm 1
Millis, Walter 1899-1968 WhAm 5
Millis, William Alfred 1868- NatCAB 14, WhAm 2
Millison, David G 1837-1928 NatCAB 22
Millman, Edward 1907-1964 WhAm 4
Millner, Walker LeRoy 1897-1964 WhAm 4
Millon, Auguste-Nicolas-Eugene 1812-1867 DcScB
Millon, Solidor NewYHSD
Milloy, James S 1895-1971 WhAm 5

Mills, Abbot Low 1858-1927 NatCAB 26, WhAm 1
Mills, Abraham 1796-1867 ApCAB, Drake
Mills, Adelbert Marion 1903-1970 NatCAB 56
Mills, Adelbert Philo 1883-1918 NatCAB 18
Mills, Albert Leopold 1854-1916 ApCAB Sup, NatCAB 11, TwCBDA, WhAm 1
Mills, Alfred Elmer 1858-1929 WhAm 1
Mills, Andrew 1848- NatCAB 5
Mills, Anson 1834-1924 DcAmB, NatCAB 10, WhAm 1
Mills, Augustus K, III 1902-1954 WhAm 3
Mills, Ballinger 1879-1947 NatCAB 40
Mills, Belle Chase 1871- WomWWA 14
Mills, Benjamin 1779-1831 DcAmB, NatCAB 25, WhAm H
Mills, Benjamin 1739-1785 NatCAB 10
Mills, Benjamin Fay 1857-1916 DcAmB, DcAmReB, NatCAB 14, WhAm 1
Mills, Blake David 1867-1949 WhAm 3
Mills, C Wright 1916-1962 McGEWB, WhAm 4
Mills, Caleb 1806-1879 BiDAmEd, NatCAB 38
Mills, Caroline Marsh Hungerford WomWWA 14
Mills, Charles NewYHSD
Mills, Charles Burdick 1868- WhAm 4
Mills, Charles Francis 1843-1915 WhAm 1
Mills, Charles Henry 1873-1937 WhAm 1
Mills, Charles Karsner 1845-1931 AmBi, DcAmB, WhAm 1
Mills, Charles Smith 1861-1942 WhAm 2
Mills, Charles Wilson 1879-1945 WhAm 2
Mills, Charles Winfred 1923-1975 WhAm 6
Mills, Charles Wright 1916-1962 EncAB
Mills, Clara McOmber 1871- WomWWA 14
Mills, Clark 1810-1883 AmBi, BnEnAmA, DcAmB, NewYHSD, WhAm H
Mills, Clark 1815-1883 ApCAB, BiAUS, Drake, NatCAB 5, TwCBDA
Mills, Clyde Marvin 1900-1960 WhAm 4
Mills, Cyrus Taggart 1819-1884 DcAmB, NatCAB 25, TwCBDA, WhAm H
Mills, Daniel Webster 1838-1904 BiDrAC
Mills, Darius Ogden 1825-1910 AmBi, ApCAB, ApCAB X, DcAmB, NatCAB 1, NatCAB 18, TwCBDA, WhAm 1
Mills, David 1831- ApCAB Sup
Mills, Dwight M 1901-1969 WhAm 5
Mills, Earl Cuthbert 1870-1947 WhAm 2
Mills, Earle Watkins 1896-1968 NatCAB 53, WhAm 5
Mills, Edmund Mead 1848-1933 WhAm 1
Mills, Edward Coe 1863-1928 ApCAB X, NatCAB 21
Mills, Edward Kirkpatrick 1874-1938 NatCAB 28
Mills, Edward Kirkpatrick, Jr. 1906-1964 WhAm 4
Mills, Edwin Claude 1881-1959 NatCAB 43, WhAm 3
Mills, Edwin Stanton 1870-1951 NatCAB 45
Mills, Elden 1908-1965 NatCAB 51
Mills, Elijah H 1778-1829 BiAUS
Mills, Elijah Hunt 1776-1829 ApCAB, BiDrAC, DcAmB, NatCAB 10, TwCBDA, WhAm H
Mills, Enos Abijah 1870-1922 DcAmB S1, NatCAB 20, WhAm 1
Mills, Florence 1895-1927 NotAW
Mills, Florence Gertrude 1851- WomWWA 14
Mills, Frank Moody 1831- WhAm 4
Mills, Frederick Cecil 1892-1964 WhAm 4
Mills, Frederick John 1865-1953 NatCAB 40
Mills, George Henry 1895-1975 WhAm 6
Mills, George W NewYHSD
Mills, Hanson Fowler 1887-1938 NatCAB 29
Mills, Harriet May 1857- NatCAB 15, WhAm 4, WomWWA 14
Mills, Harriette Melissa d1929 WhAm 1
Mills, Henry Edmund 1850-1920 NatCAB 6, WhAm 4
Mills, Herbert Elmer 1861-1946 NatCAB 35, TwCBDA, WhAm 3
Mills, Herbert Hagerman 1910-1972 WhAm 5
Mills, Hillis 1907-1965 WhAm 4
Mills, Hiram Francis 1836-1921 ApCAB X,

DcAmB, NatCAB 12, WhAm 1
Mills, Isaac Newton 1851-1929 WhAm 1
Mills, J Warner 1852-1907 WhAm 1
Mills, James Edward 1876-1950 NatCAB 45, WhAm 3
Mills, James McVicar 1857-1948 NatCAB 36
Mills, James Theodore 1900-1974 WhAm 6
Mills, Jesse T 1883-1962 WhAm 4
Mills, Job Smith 1848-1909 TwCBDA, WhAm 1
Mills, John d1796 NatCAB 12
Mills, John 1880-1948 WhAm 2
Mills, John Gootee 1857-1943 NatCAB 32
Mills, John Harrison 1842-1916 IlBEAAW
Mills, John Nelson 1856-1922 NatCAB 26
Mills, John Proctor 1879- NatCAB 16
Mills, John Sedwick 1856-1928 WhAm 1
Mills, Joseph John 1847- TwCBDA, WhAm 4
Mills, Lawrence 1881-1956 NatCAB 46
Mills, Lawrence Heyworth 1837-1918 DcAmB
Mills, Lennox A 1896-1968 WhAm 5
Mills, Luther Laflin 1848-1909 WhAm 1
Mills, Madison 1810-1873 ApCAB Sup
Mills, Mark Muir 1917-1958 NatCAB 48
Mills, Mary Russell 1859- WomWWA 14
Mills, Matthew 1877- WhAm 5
Mills, Newt Virgus 1899- BiDrAC
Mills, Ogden 1856-1929 WhAm 1, WhAm 1C
Mills, Ogden Livingston 1884-1937 AmBi, BiDrAC, BiDrUSE, DcAmB S2, NatCAB 32, WhAm 1, WhAmP
Mills, Ralph Garfield 1881-1944 NatCAB 35
Mills, Ralph Walter 1877-1924 NatCAB 20
Mills, Robert 1781-1855 AmBi, ApCAB, BiAUS, BnEnAmA, DcAmB, Drake, McGEWB, NatCAB 18, NewYHSD, TwCBDA, WebAB, WhAm H
Mills, Robert 1809-1888 ApCAB Sup, DcAmB, WhAm H
Mills, Robert Hilliard 1883-1965 NatCAB 52
Mills, Robert Q BiAUS
Mills, Roger Quarles 1832-1911 AmBi, ApCAB Sup, BiDrAC, DcAmB, NatCAB 8, TwCBDA, WhAm 1, WhAmP
Mills, Russell 1892-1959 NatCAB 49
Mills, Samuel John 1743-1833 ApCAB
Mills, Samuel John 1783-1818 ApCAB, DcAmB, DcAmReB, Drake, NatCAB 13, TwCBDA, WhAm H
Mills, Samuel Myers 1843-1907 WhAm 1
Mills, Sebastian Bach 1839-1898 ApCAB Sup, WhAm 1
Mills, Stephen Crosby 1854-1914 WhAm 1
Mills, Susan Lincoln Tolman 1825-1912 BiDAmEd, NatCAB 19, NotAW, TwCBDA
Mills, Susan Lincoln Tolman 1826-1912 DcAmB, WhAm 1
Mills, Theodore Augustus 1839-1916 NewYHSD
Mills, Theophilus 1842?- NewYHSD
Mills, Thomas Brooks 1857-1930 WhAm 1
Mills, Thomas Wesley 1847- ApCAB
Mills, Thornton Allen 1855-1922 WhAm 1
Mills, Thornton Anthony 1881-1929 WhAm 1
Mills, Walker Hill 1893-1962 NatCAB 50
Mills, Weymer Jay 1880-1938 WhAm 2
Mills, Wilbur Daigh 1909- BiDrAC
Mills, Wiley Wright 1869-1943 NatCAB 39
Mills, William Corless 1860-1928 NatCAB 22, WhAm 1
Mills, William FitzRandolph 1856-1942 NatCAB 18, WhAm 2
Mills, William Hayne 1872-1942 WhAm 2
Mills, William Hobson 1873-1959 DcScB
Mills, William Hough 1851-1928 NatCAB 23
Mills, William Howard 1839-1904 WhAm 1
Mills, William Joseph 1849-1915 NatCAB 19, WhAm 1
Mills, William McMaster 1860-1949 NatCAB 37, WhAm 4
Mills, William Merrill 1883-1958 NatCAB 48, WhAm 4
Mills, William O 1925-1973 WhAm 6
Mills, William Webster 1852-1931 WhAm 1
Mills, Wilson Waddingham 1888-1968 NatCAB 55

Millsaps, Reuben Webster 1833-1916
NatCAB 18, *WhAm 1*
Millson, John Singleton 1808-1873 *TwCBDA*
Millson, John Singleton 1808-1874 *BiAUS,*
BiDrAC, WhAm H, WhAmP
Millsop, Thomas E 1898-1967 *WhAm 4*
Millspaugh, Arthur Chester 1883-1955
WhAm 3
Millspaugh, Charles Frederick 1854-1923
DcAmB, NatCAB 25, WhAm 1
Millspaugh, E T *NewYHSD*
Millspaugh, Edward Judson 1861-1922
NatCAB 6
Millspaugh, Frank Crenshaw 1872-1947 *BiDrAC,*
WhAm 3
Millspaugh, Frank Rosebrook 1848-1916
NatCAB 12, TwCBDA, WhAm 1
Millspaugh, Jesse Fonda 1855-1919 *WhAm 1*
Millspaugh, M Laurence 1884-1964 *NatCAB 51*
Millspaugh, Willard Pierrepont 1872-1937
NatCAB 29
Millspaugh, William Hulse 1868-1959 *WhAm 3*
Millward, John *BiAUS*
Millward, Russell Hastings 1877- *WhAm 5*
Millward, William 1822-1871 *BiAUS, BiDrAC,*
WhAm H
Milmoe, Margaret Mooney 1865-
WomWWA 14
Milmoe, Michael Joseph 1870-1938 *NatCAB 36*
Milmore, Joseph 1841-1886 *NatCAB 8*
Milmore, Joseph 1842-1886 *ApCAB, TwCBDA*
Milmore, Martin 1844-1883 *AmBi, ApCAB,*
DcAmB, NatCAB 1, NatCAB 8,
TwCBDA, WhAm H
Milmore, Martin 1845-1883 *Drake*
Milne, A *NewYHSD*
Milne, Alan Alexander 1882-1956 *WhAm 3*
Milne, Alma Eliza Tuttle *WomWWA 14*
Milne, Caleb Jones, Jr. 1861-1941 *NatCAB 32,*
WhAm 1
Milne, Colin R 1817?- *NewYHSD*
Milne, Sir David 1763-1845 *ApCAB*
Milne, David 1859-1929 *WhAm 1*
Milne, David Brown 1882-1953 *McGEWB*
Milne, Edward Arthur 1896-1950 *DcScB*
Milne, Frances Margaret 1846- *AmWom,*
WhAm 5
Milne, J Scott 1898-1955 *WhAm 3*
Milne, James M 1850-1904 *WhAm 1*
Milne, John 1850-1913 *AsBiEn, DcScB*
Milne, John 1880-1956 *WhAm 3*
Milne, Joseph Davis 1855-1926 *NatCAB 20*
Milne, Sir Robert Shore 1746-1836? *ApCAB*
Milne, William James 1843- *WhAm 4*
Milne-Edwards, Henri 1800-1885 *DcScB*
Milner, Alfred, Viscount 1854-1925 *McGEWB*
Milner, Duncan Chambers 1841-1928 *WhAm 1*
Milner, Henry Key 1866-1939 *WhAm 1*
Milner, John 1886-1937 *NatCAB 33*
Milner, John Turner 1826-1898 *DcAmB,*
NatCAB 19, WhAm H
Milner, Joseph 1890-1972 *NatCAB 56*
Milner, Moses Embree 1829-1876 *AmBi,*
DcAmB, WebAMB, WhAm H
Milner, Robert Teague *WhAm 5*
Milner, Thomas Picton 1822-1891 *DcAmB*
Milner, Willis Justus, Jr. 1892-1960 *WhAm 4*
Milnes, Alfred 1844-1916 *BiDrAC*
Milnes, William, Jr. 1827-1889 *BiAUS,*
BiDrAC, WhAm H
Milnor, Frank Richmond 1846-1938
NatCAB 41
Milnor, George Sparks 1880-1959 *WhAm 3*
Milnor, J Willard 1889-1949 *NatCAB 37*
Milnor, James 1773-1844 *ApCAB, BiDrAC,*
NatCAB 8, TwCBDA, WhAm H
Milnor, James 1773-1845 *BiAUS, Drake*
Milnor, Leland Topping 1874-1949 *NatCAB 38*
Milnor, Nathaniel Funston 1882-1956
NatCAB 46
Milnor, William 1769-1848 *BiAUS, BiDrAC,*
WhAm H
Milnor, William 1785-1843 *TwCBDA*
Milns, William d1801 *Drake*
Milofsky, Allan Henry 1933-1971 *WhAm 5*
Milot, Arthur Charles 1861-1921 *NatCAB 19*
Milroy, Charles Martin 1867-1931 *NatCAB 16,*
WhAm 1

Milroy, Robert Arthur 1915-1967 *WhAm 6*
Milroy, Robert H 1814-1890 *Drake*
Milroy, Robert Houston 1816-1890 *TwCBDA*
Milroy, Robert Huston 1816-1890 *ApCAB,*
DcAmB, NatCAB 4, WhAm H
Milroy, William Forsyth 1855-1942 *BiHiMed,*
NatCAB 31, WhAm 2
Milroy, William McCracken 1855- *WhAm 4*
Milstead, William Bryan 1896-1954
NatCAB 44
Miltenberger, George Warner 1819-1905
ApCAB, WhAm 1
Miltiades 549?BC-488BC *McGEWB*
Miltner, Charles Christopher 1886-1966
WhAm 4
Milton, George Fort 1869-1924 *NatCAB 10,*
WhAm 1
Milton, George Fort 1894-1955 *DcAmB S5,*
WhAm 3
Milton, Homer Virgil 1781-1822 *Drake,*
TwCBDA
Milton, John 1608-1674 *McGEWB*
Milton, John 1740?-1804? *ApCAB, NatCAB 4,*
TwCBDA
Milton, John 1807-1865 *BiAUS, BiDConf,*
DcAmB, NatCAB 11, TwCBDA,
WhAm H
Milton, John Brown 1848-1931 *NatCAB 45,*
WhAm 1
Milton, John Gerald 1881- *BiDrAC*
Milton, William Hall 1864-1942 *BiDrAC,*
NatCAB 14, TwCBDA, WhAm 1,
WhAm 2, WhAm 4
Milton, William Hammond 1868- *WhAm 4*
Milton, William Henry 1829-1900 *TwCBDA*
Miltoun, Francis 1871- *WhAm 5*
Mimee, E W *NewYHSD*
Mimeure, Victor Emmanuel Leon De 1723-1791
ApCAB
Mims, Edwin 1872-1959 *NatCAB 49,*
WhAm 3
Mims, Henry L 1874- *WhoColR*
Mims, Joseph Starke 1883-1955 *NatCAB 47*
Mims, Livingston 1833-1906 *WhAm 1*
Mims, Stewart Lea 1880-1961 *WhAm 4*
Mims, Sue Harper 1842- *AmWom*
Min, Queen 1851-1895 *McGEWB*
Mina, Francisco Espozy 1784-1836 *WhoMilH*
Mina, Francisco Javier 1789-1817 *ApCAB*
Mina, Xavier 1789-1817 *Drake*
Minahan, Daniel Francis 1877-1947 *BiDrAC,*
WhAm 5
Minahan, Patrick Robert 1875-1953
NatCAB 43
Minahan, Thomas Boromea 1853-1917
NatCAB 17
Minahan, Victor Ivan 1881-1954 *WhAm 3*
Minamoto Yoritomo 1147-1199 *McGEWB*
Minard, Abel 1814-1871 *ApCAB*
Minard, Archibald Ellsworth 1878-1950
WhAm 3
Minard, Duane Elmer 1880- *WhAm 6*
Minard, Florence 1886- *WomWWA 14*
Minary, Thomas Jay 1850-1935 *WhAm 1*
Minas, Edward Conrad 1863-1949 *NatCAB 43*
Minchin, George H 1882-1961 *WhAm 4*
Minchin, Nina Mesirow d1972 *WhAm 5*
Minckler, Robert Lee 1898-1963 *NatCAB 52,*
WhAm 4
Minding, Ernst Ferdinand Adolf 1806-1885
DcScB
Mindon Min *McGEWB*
Mindszenty, Cardinal Jozsef 1892-1975
WhAm 6
Mineo, Sal 1939-1976 *WhAm 6*
Miner, Mrs. *NewYHSD*
Miner, Ahiman Louis 1804-1886 *BiAUS,*
BiDrAC, WhAm H
Miner, Alice Trainer 1863-1950 *NatCAB 40*
Miner, Alonzo Ames 1814-1895 *AmBi, ApCAB,*
DcAmB, Drake, NatCAB 1, TwCBDA,
WhAm H
Miner, Asher 1860-1924 *WhAm 1*
Miner, Carl Shelley 1878- *WhAm 6*
Miner, Caroline Ida Doane 1867-
WomWWA 14
Miner, Charles 1778?-1865 *BiAUS*
Miner, Charles 1780-1865 *ApCAB, BiDrAC,*

DcAmB, Drake, NatCAB 5, TwCBDA,
WhAm H
Miner, Charles Wright 1840- *WhAm 4*
Miner, Edward Griffith 1863-1955 *WhAm 3*
Miner, Frederick Bingham 1876-1945
NatCAB 34
Miner, Frederick Roland 1876- *IIBEAAW*
Miner, George Roberts 1862-1918 *WhAm 1*
Miner, H C d1950 *WhAm 3*
Miner, Harlan Sherman 1864-1938 *NatCAB 29,*
WhAm 1, WhAm 1C
Miner, Henry Clay 1842-1900 *BiDrAC*
Miner, Jack 1865- *WhAm 4*
Miner, James Alvin 1842-1907 *NatCAB 13,*
WhAm 1
Miner, James Burt 1873-1943 *WhAm 2*
Miner, Jean Pond 1866- *AmWom*
Miner, Julius Francis 1823-1886 *NatCAB 16*
Miner, Julius Howard 1896-1963 *NatCAB 49,*
WhAm 4
Miner, Luella 1861-1935 *WhAm 1*
Miner, Maude E *BiCAW, WomWWA 14*
Miner, Myrtilla 1815-1864 *ApCAB, BiDAmEd,*
DcAmB, NatCAB 12, NotAW,
WhAm H
Miner, Phineas 1777-1839 *BiAUS, BiDrAC,*
WhAm H
Miner, Robert Bradford 1916-1971 *WhAm 5*
Miner, Roy Waldo 1875-1955 *WhAm 3*
Miner, Sarah Luella 1861-1935 *NotAW*
Miner, Thomas 1777-1841 *ApCAB, Drake,*
NatCAB 15
Miner, William Harvey 1877-1934 *WhAm 1*
Miner, William Henry 1862-1930 *NatCAB 40*
Mines, Flavel Scott 1811-1852 *ApCAB*
Mines, Flavel Scott 1843-1878 *ApCAB*
Mines, James H 1825?- *NewYHSD*
Mines, John Flavel 1835- *ApCAB*
Mineur, Henri 1899-1954 *DcScB*
Minford, Levis Waln 1850-1926 *ApCAB X,*
NatCAB 32
Ming, John Joseph 1838-1910 *DcAmB*
Ming, William Robert, Jr. 1911-1973 *WhAm 6*
Mingay, Gordon Edmund 1923- *EncAAH*
Mingeau, Francois *NewYHSD*
Mingenback, Eugene Carl 1888- *WhAm 5*
Mingle, Elizabeth 1835?- *NewYHSD*
Mingle, Harry Bowers 1876- *NatCAB 16*
Mingle, Joseph 1839-1903 *NewYHSD*
Mingos, Howard L 1891-1955 *WhAm 3*
Minich, Henry Dudley 1889-1952 *NatCAB 41*
Minich, Verne Elwood 1867-1958 *NatCAB 52,*
WhAm 3
Minick, James William 1898-1949 *WhAm 2*
Minier, George Washington 1813-1902
NatCAB 12, WhAm 1
Minifie, William 1805-1880 *ApCAB,*
NewYHSD
Minifie, William Charles 1869- *WhAm 5*
Miniger, Clement Orville 1874-1944
NatCAB 37, WhAm 2
Minihan, Jeremiah Francis 1903-1973 *WhAm 6*
Minish, Joseph George 1916- *BiDrAC*
Miniter, Edith May Dowe 1869- *WhAm 5,*
WomWWA 14
Mink, Joseph Cortland 1911-1972 *NatCAB 56*
Mink, Patsy Takemoto 1927- *BiDrAC*
Minkowski, Hermann 1864-1909 *AsBiEn,*
DcScB
Minkowski, Oskar 1858-1931 *BiHiMed*
Minkowski, Rudolph Leo B 1895-1976 *AsBiEn,*
WhAm 6
Minnaert, Marcel Gilles Jozef 1893-1970 *DcScB,*
WhAm 5 ,
Minnewit, Peter *WebAB*
Minnich, Dwight Elmer 1890-1965 *WhAm 4*
Minnich, Harvey C 1861-1952 *WhAm 3*
Minnick, John Harrison 1877- *WhAm 5*
Minnigerode, C Powell 1876-1951 *WhAm 3*
Minnigerode, Lucy 1871-1935 *DcAmB S1,*
WhAm 1
Minnigerode, Meade 1887-1967 *NatCAB 54,*
WhAm 4
Minns, Thomas d1836 *Drake*
Minor, Anne Rogers d1947 *WhAm 2,*
WomWWA 14
Minor, Benjamin Blake 1818- *Drake,*
TwCBDA

Minor, Benjamin Blake 1818-1904 *WhAm 1*
Minor, Benjamin Blake 1818-1905 *DcAmB,*
NatCAB 8
Minor, Benjamin Saunders 1865-1946 *WhAm 2*
Minor, Berkeley, Jr. 1879-1959 *WhAm 4*
Minor, Charles Lancelot 1897-1950 *NatCAB 40*
Minor, Charles Launcelot 1865-1928
NatCAB 18, NatCAB 24, WhAm 1
Minor, Clark Haynes 1878-1967 *ApCAB X,*
NatCAB 53, WhAm 4
Minor, Edward Sloman 1840-1924 *BiDrAC,*
TwCBDA, WhAm 1, WhAmP
Minor, George Henry 1866-1937 *WhAm 1*
Minor, H Dent 1868- *WhAm 2*
Minor, John Barbee 1813-1895 *ApCAB,*
BiDAmEd, DcAmB, NatCAB 20,
TwCBDA, WhAm H
Minor, John Barbee 1866-1952 *NatCAB 39*
Minor, Lucian 1802-1858 *ApCAB, DcAmB,*
Drake, NatCAB 21, TwCBDA, WhAm H
Minor, Milton Carlisle 1892-1974 *WhAm 6*
Minor, Raleigh Colston 1869-1923 *DcAmB,*
NatCAB 26, WhAm 1
Minor, Robert 1884-1952 *DcAmB S5,*
WhAm 3
Minor, Robert Crannell 1839-1904 *AmBi,*
DcAmB, NatCAB 12, NewYHSD,
TwCBDA
Minor, Robert Crannell 1840-1904 *ApCAB,*
WhAm 1
Minor, Stanley Nelson 1891-1970 *NatCAB 57*
Minor, Thomas Chalmers 1846-1912 *WhAm 1*
Minor, Virginia Louisa 1824-1894 *AmBi,*
ApCAB, DcAmB, NotAW, TwCBDA,
WhAm H
Minor, Virginia Louise 1824-1894 *NatCAB 25*
Minor, William Thomas 1815-1889 *ApCAB,*
BiAUS, Drake, NatCAB 10, TwCBDA
Minot *NewYHSD*
Minot, Charles 1810-1866 *ApCAB, TwCBDA*
Minot, Charles Sedgwick 1852-1914 *AmBi,*
ApCAB, BiDAmEd, DcAmB, DcScB,
NatCAB 6, TwCBDA, WhAm 1
Minot, Fanny Elizabeth Pickering
WomWWA 14
Minot, Francis 1821-1899 *ApCAB,*
NatCAB 12
Minot, George 1817-1856 *ApCAB*
Minot, George 1817-1858 *Drake*
Minot, George Evans 1898-1976 *WhAm 6*
Minot, George Richards 1758-1802 *ApCAB,*
DcAmB, Drake, NatCAB 7, TwCBDA,
WhAm H
Minot, George Richards 1813-1883 *NatCAB 20*
Minot, George Richards 1885-1950 *AsBiEn,*
BiHiMed, DcAmB S4, DcScB,
NatCAB 38, WebAB, WhAm 2
Minot, John Clair 1872-1941 *WhAm 2*
Minot, Joseph Grafton 1858-1939 *NatCAB 30,*
WhAm 2
Minot, Josiah *BiAUS*
Minot, Lawrence *ApCAB X*
Minot, Lucy Woodworth 1888- *WomWWA 14*
Minot, William 1849-1900 *NatCAB 33,*
WhAm 1
Minot, William 1885-1937 *NatCAB 33,*
WhAm 1
Minott *NewYHSD*
Minsch, William J 1884- *WhAm 3*
Minshall, Robert J 1898-1954 *WhAm 3*
Minshall, Thaddeus Armstrong 1834-
NatCAB 12, WhAm 4
Minshall, William Edwin 1877-1952
NatCAB 46
Minshall, William Edwin, Jr. 1911- *BiDrAC*
Minskoff, Sam 1884-1950 *NatCAB 38*
Minsky, Abraham Bennett 1881-1949
NatCAB 37
Minter, Mary Miles 1902- *WhAm 4*
Minter, William Ramseur 1873-1943 *WhAm 2*
Minto, Gilbert John Murray Kynynmond E 1845-
ApCAB Sup
Minto, Walter 1753-1796 *ApCAB, DcAmB,*
Drake, WhAm H
Minton, Henry Collin 1855-1924 *TwCBDA,*
WhAm 1
Minton, Henry McKee 1871- *WhoColR*
Minton, John *NewYHSD*

Minton, Maurice Meyer 1859- *WhAm 4*
Minton, Melville 1885-1955 *WhAm 3*
Minton, Ollie Francis 1879- *WhAm 6*
Minton, Sherman 1890-1965 *BiDrAC,*
NatCAB 53, WebAB, WhAm 4
M'Intosh, William Carmichael 1838-1931
DcScB
Minturn, James Francis 1860-1934 *WhAm 1*
Minturn, Robert Bowne 1805-1866 *ApCAB,*
DcAmB, Drake, NatCAB 9, WhAm H
Minturn, Robert Bowne 1836-1889 *ApCAB*
Minty, Frederick Walter 1882-1945 *NatCAB 36*
Minty, Robert Horatio George 1831-1906
ApCAB, DcAmB, Drake
Mintzer, Ida Jessica 1893-1970 *NatCAB 55*
Minuit, Peter 1580?- *Drake*
Minuit, Peter 1580?-1638 *AmBi, DcAmB,*
EncAAH, McGEWB, WebAB, WhAm H
Minuit, Peter 1580?-1641 *ApCAB,*
NatCAB 12
Minzie, Helene M *WomWWA 14*
Miquel, Friedrich Anton Wilhelm 1811-1871
DcScB
Mirabeau, Boniface Riquetti, Vicomte De
1754-1792 *ApCAB, Drake*
Mirabeau, Honore Gabriel DeR, Comte De
1749-1791 *McGEWB*
Mirabel, Vicente 1918-1945 *IIBEAAW*
Miracle, John Herbert 1901-1974 *WhAm 6*
Miramon, Miguel 1830-1867 *Drake*
Miramon, Miguel 1832-1867 *ApCAB*
Miranda, Carmen 1909-1955 *DcAmB S5*
Miranda, Francisco De d1816 *WhAm H*
Miranda, Francisco De 1750?-1816 *Drake,*
McGEWB, WhoMilH
Miranda, Francisco De 1756-1816 *ApCAB*
Miranda, Heber Isaac 1906-1973 *WhAm 6*
Miranda, Pedro De 1510?-1569 *ApCAB*
Miranda-Ribeiro, Jose Cesario 1792-1856
ApCAB
Mirbel, Charles Francois Brisseau De 1776-1854
DcScB
Mireil, Jules Cesar 1699-1763 *ApCAB*
Mirick, George Alonzo 1863-1938 *NatCAB 28,*
WhAm 4
Mirick, Henry Dustin 1836- *NatCAB 12*
Mirisch, Harold Joseph 1907-1968 *WhAm 5*
Mirkine-Guetzevitch, Boris 1892-1955 *WhAm 3*
Miro, Esteban Rodriguez 1744-1795 *DcAmB,*
WhAm H
Miro, Joan 1893- *McGEWB*
Miro Ferrer, Gabriel 1879-1930 *McGEWB*
Mirovitch, Alfred 1884-1959 *NatCAB 45*
Mirrielees, Edith Ronald 1878-1962 *WhAm 4*
Mirsky, Alfred Ezra 1900-1974 *WhAm 6*
Mirsky, I Arthur 1907-1974 *WhAm 6*
Mirza, Iskander 1899-1969 *WhAm 5*
Mirza, Youel Benjamin 1888-1947 *WhAm 2*
Misbach, Lorenz 1901-1958 *NatCAB 47,*
WhAm 3
Misener, Geneva *WomWWA 14*
Misener, John Isaac 1875-1941 *NatCAB 34*
Miser, Hugh Dinsmore 1884-1969 *WhAm 5*
Mises, Ludwig Von 1881- *McGEWB*
Mises, Richard Von 1883-1953 *DcScB*
Mishima, Yukio 1925-1970 *WhAm 5*
Miskell, Edward Wesley 1863-1953 *NatCAB 44*
Missiessy, Edouard T Burgues, Comte De
1754-1832 *ApCAB*
Missroon, John Stoney 1810-1865 *ApCAB,*
Drake
Mistral, Gabriela 1889-1957 *McGEWB*
Mistral, Gabriela 1899-1957 *WhAm 3*
Mitcham, Orin Burlingame 1853-1934 *WhAm 1*
Mitchel, Charles Burton 1815-1864 *ApCAB,*
BiDConf, BiDrAC, TwCBDA, WhAm H
Mitchel, Edwin Kent 1901-1972 *WhAm 5*
Mitchel, Frederick Augustus 1839- *WhAm 1*
Mitchel, John 1815-1875 *AmBi, ApCAB,*
DcAmB, Drake
Mitchel, John Purroy 1879-1918 *AmBi,*
DcAmB, NatCAB 18, WhAm 1
Mitchel, Ormsby MacKnight 1809-1862 *AmBi,*
ApCAB, DcAmB, WebAMB, WhAm H
Mitchel, Ormsby MacKnight 1810-1862 *Drake*
Mitchel, Ormsby McKnight 1809-1862
NatCAB 3, TwCBDA
Mitchell, Agnes *NewYHSD*

Mitchell, Albert 1893-1954 *WhAm 3*
Mitchell, Albert Graeme 1889-1941 *DcAmB S3,*
NatCAB 42, WhAm 1
Mitchell, Albert Melvin 1889-1952 *NatCAB 41*
Mitchell, Albert Roscoe 1856-1933 *WhAm 1*
Mitchell, Alexander 1817-1887 *ApCAB,*
BiAUS, BiDrAC, DcAmB, NatCAB 1,
TwCBDA, WhAm H
Mitchell, Alexander Clark 1860-1911 *BiDrAC*
Mitchell, Alexander Ireland 1866-1932
NatCAB 32
Mitchell, Alfred *IIBEAAW*
Mitchell, Alfred 1837-1915 *WhAm 1*
Mitchell, Alfred Newton 1876- *WhAm 5*
Mitchell, Alfred R 1888?-1972 *IIBEAAW*
Mitchell, Allan Charles Gray 1902-1963
WhAm 4
Mitchell, Allister Stewart 1880-1962
NatCAB 49
Mitchell, Anderson 1800-1876 *BiAUS, BiDrAC,*
WhAm H
Mitchell, Andrew 1831-1923 *NatCAB 19*
Mitchell, Arthur 1889- *IIBEAAW*
Mitchell, Arthur Evan 1883-1956 *WhAm 3*
Mitchell, Arthur Wergs 1883-1968 *BiDrAC,*
WhAm 5
Mitchell, Benjamin T 1816-1880 *NewYHSD*
Mitchell, Bert Jones 1908-1965 *NatCAB 51*
Mitchell, Bruce 1908-1963 *NatCAB 47,*
WhAm 4
Mitchell, C Lionel 1917- *WhAm 6*
Mitchell, Carrie Burks 1858- *WomWWA 14*
Mitchell, Charles Anderson 1864-1948 *WhAm 3*
Mitchell, Charles Andrews 1857-1921 *WhAm 1*
Mitchell, Charles Bayard 1857-1941 *WhAm 2*
Mitchell, Charles Burton 1815-1864 *BiAUS,*
NatCAB 4
Mitchell, Charles Dennis 1866-1941 *WhAm 1*
Mitchell, Charles Edward 1870-1937 *WhAm 1,*
WhAm 1C
Mitchell, Charles Edwin 1877-1955 *ApCAB X,*
NatCAB 44, WhAm 3
Mitchell, Charles Eliot 1837-1911 *NatCAB 1*
Mitchell, Charles Elliott 1837-1911 *WhAm 1*
Mitchell, Charles F 1808?- *BiAUS, BiDrAC,*
WhAm H
Mitchell, Charles Franklin 1875- *WhAm 5*
Mitchell, Charles LeMoyne 1844-1890 *BiDrAC,*
TwCBDA, WhAm H
Mitchell, Charles S 1876-1943 *NatCAB 32*
Mitchell, Charles Scott 1909-1972 *WhAm 5*
Mitchell, Charles Tennant 1880-1948 *WhAm 2*
Mitchell, Charles William 1882-1958
NatCAB 43
Mitchell, Clarence Blair 1865- *WhAm 5*
Mitchell, Clifford 1854-1939 *WhAm 1*
Mitchell, Curtis 1900- *WhAm 4*
Mitchell, David 1742-1818 *ApCAB, Drake*
Mitchell, David 1884-1956 *WhAm 3*
Mitchell, David Bradie 1737-1837 *BiAUS*
Mitchell, David Bradie 1766-1837 *ApCAB,*
Drake, NatCAB 1, TwCBDA
Mitchell, David Brydie 1766-1837 *DcAmB,*
WhAm H
Mitchell, David Dawson 1806-1861 *DcAmB,*
WhAm H
Mitchell, David Farrar 1918-1975 *WhAm 6*
Mitchell, David Ray 1898-1972 *WhAm 5*
Mitchell, Donald Grant 1822-1908 *AmBi,*
ApCAB, DcAmB, Drake, NatCAB 6,
TwCBDA, WhAm 1
Mitchell, E *NewYHSD*
Mitchell, Edmund 1861-1917 *WhAm 1*
Mitchell, Edward 1769-1834 *ApCAB Sup*
Mitchell, Edward Archibald 1910- *BiDrAC*
Mitchell, Edward Clay 1882-1955 *NatCAB 45*
Mitchell, Edward Coppee 1836-1887 *ApCAB*
Mitchell, Edward Cushing 1829-1900 *ApCAB,*
DcAmB, NatCAB 25, TwCBDA,
WhAm 1
Mitchell, Edward Dana 1876-1953 *NatCAB 46*
Mitchell, Edward Page 1852-1927 *DcAmB,*
NatCAB 4, WhAm 1
Mitchell, Edwin Knox 1853-1934 *DcAmB S1,*
WhAm 1
Mitchell, Edwin Thomas 1886-1953 *WhAm 3*
Mitchell, Elisha 1793-1857 *AmBi, ApCAB,*
DcAmB, DcScB, Drake, NatCAB 7,

Mitchell, *TwCBDA, WhAm H*
Mitchell, Elizabeth Roberts 1858-
WomWWA 14
Mitchell, Ellen M 1842- *WomWWA 14*
Mitchell, Elmer Dayton 1889- *BiDAmEd*
Mitchell, Emory Forrest 1864- *WhAm 5*
Mitchell, Eugene Muse 1866-1944 *NatCAB 54*
Mitchell, Evelyn Groesbeek *WomWWA 14*
Mitchell, F Edward 1871- *WhAm 5*
Mitchell, Frances Pearle 1863- *WomWWA 14*
Mitchell, Francis N *NewYHSD*
Mitchell, Frank *NewYHSD*
Mitchell, G P 1856-1943 *WhAm 2*
Mitchell, George 1820?- *NewYHSD*
Mitchell, George 1864- *NatCAB 13, WhAm 4*
Mitchell, George Bertrand 1872?-1966
IIBEAAW
Mitchell, George DePui 1866-1950 *NatCAB 38*
Mitchell, George Edward 1781-1832 *BiAUS,
BiDrAC, DcAmB, NatCAB 26, TwCBDA,
WhAm H, WhAmP*
Mitchell, George Franklin 1888- *WhAm 3*
Mitchell, George Frederick 1881-1973 *WhAm 6*
Mitchell, George Henry 1875- *WhoColR*
Mitchell, George T 1874-1945 *WhAm 2*
Mitchell, George Washington 1842- *TwCBDA,
WhAm 4*
Mitchell, Geraldine E *WomWWA 14*
Mitchell, Giles Sandy 1852-1904 *NatCAB 13*
Mitchell, Guy Bateman 1878-1956 *NatCAB 46*
Mitchell, Guy Elliott 1870-1939 *WhAm 1*
Mitchell, Hal E 1869-1947 *WhAm 2*
Mitchell, Harlan Erwin 1924- *BiDrAC*
Mitchell, Harold E 1901-1950 *WhAm 3*
Mitchell, Harold Hubbard 1888-1964
NatCAB 51
Mitchell, Harriet Post 1866- *WomWWA 14*
Mitchell, Harry Aloysius 1883-1958
NatCAB 47
Mitchell, Harry B d1955 *WhAm 3*
Mitchell, Harry Dawson 1863-1926 *NatCAB 20,
WhAm 1*
Mitchell, Harry Luzerne 1883-1948 *WhAm 2*
Mitchell, Harry Walter 1867-1933 *WhAm 1*
Mitchell, Harvey 1801?-1864? *NewYHSD*
Mitchell, Hattie Moore 1866- *WomWWA 14*
Mitchell, Hazel Haynes d1970 *WhAm 5*
Mitchell, Helen Codman 1905-1966 *WhAm 4*
Mitchell, Henry *NewYHSD*
Mitchell, Henry 1784-1856 *BiDrAC,
WhAm H*
Mitchell, Henry 1784-1858 *BiAUS*
Mitchell, Henry 1810-1893 *NatCAB 4*
Mitchell, Henry 1830-1902 *AmBi, ApCAB,
DcAmB, NatCAB 8, TwCBDA,
WhAm 1*
Mitchell, Henry 1845-1919 *NatCAB 13,
WhAm 1*
Mitchell, Henry Bedinger 1874-1956 *WhAm 3*
Mitchell, Henry Clay 1855-1930 *NatCAB 29*
Mitchell, Henry Lawrence 1831-1903
NatCAB 11
Mitchell, Henry Lyman 1845-1926 *NatCAB 17*
Mitchell, Henry Post 1840-1929 *NatCAB 24*
Mitchell, Henry Sewall d1958 *WhAm 3*
Mitchell, Henry Zehring 1884-1965 *NatCAB 51*
Mitchell, Hinckley Gilbert Thomas 1846-1920
*ApCAB, DcAmB, NatCAB 11, TwCBDA,
WhAm 1*
Mitchell, Homer Rawlins 1871-1956 *WhAm 3*
Mitchell, Horace Franklin 1864- *WhoColR*
Mitchell, Howard Hawks 1885-1943 *WhAm 2*
Mitchell, Howard Holmes 1879-1933
NatCAB 25
Mitchell, Howard Walton 1867-1943
NatCAB 35, WhAm 2
Mitchell, Hugh Burnton 1907- *BiDrAC*
Mitchell, Hugh Chester 1877-1956 *WhAm 3*
Mitchell, Hugh Gordon 1902-1972 *WhAm 5*
Mitchell, Humphrey 1894-1950 *WhAm 3*
Mitchell, Isaac 1759?-1812 *DcAmB, WhAm H*
Mitchell, J *NewYHSD*
Mitchell, J Douglas 1876-1951 *NatCAB 39*
Mitchell, J Murray 1898-1973 *WhAm 6*
Mitchell, James 1833-1902 *NatCAB 4,
WhAm 1*
Mitchell, James 1866-1920 *ApCAB X*
Mitchell, James Alfred d1902 *WhAm 1*

Mitchell, James C d1843 *BiAUS*
Mitchell, James C 1790?-1843 *ApCAB*
Mitchell, James Coffield 1786-1843 *BiDrAC,
WhAm H*
Mitchell, James Farnandis 1871-1961 *WhAm 4*
Mitchell, James George 1847-1919 *NatCAB 18*
Mitchell, James George 1877-1964 *WhAm 4*
Mitchell, James Herbert 1889-1964 *WhAm 4*
Mitchell, James McCormick 1873-1948
WhAm 2
Mitchell, James Paul 1900-1964 *BiDrUSE,
EncAAH, WhAm 4*
Mitchell, James S 1784-1844 *BiAUS, BiDrAC,
TwCBDA, WhAm H*
Mitchell, James Tyndale 1834-1915 *ApCAB,
DcAmB, NatCAB 11, TwCBDA,
WhAm 1*
Mitchell, Joan 1926- *BnEnAmA*
Mitchell, John d1768 *ApCAB, DcAmB,
Drake, WebAB, WhAm H*
Mitchell, John 1781-1849 *BiAUS, BiDrAC,
WhAm H*
Mitchell, John 1794-1870 *ApCAB, Drake,
NatCAB 5*
Mitchell, John 1811-1866 *NewYHSD*
Mitchell, John 1815-1875 *WhAm H*
Mitchell, John 1870-1919 *AmBi, DcAmB,
EncAB, McGEWB, NatCAB 15,
NatCAB 24, WhAm 1*
Mitchell, John, Jr. 1863- *WhoColR*
Mitchell, John Ames 1845-1918 *AmBi, DcAmB,
NatCAB 1, TwCBDA, WhAm 1*
Mitchell, John Blanton 1917-1968 *NatCAB 53,
WhAm 5*
Mitchell, John Doyle 1936- *WhAm 5*
Mitchell, John Elvin 1871-1938 *NatCAB 29*
Mitchell, John Elvin, Jr. 1896-1972 *NatCAB 56*
Mitchell, John Fulton Berrien 1878-1956
WhAm 3
Mitchell, John Gordon 1878- *WhAm 6*
Mitchell, John Grant 1838- *ApCAB Sup*
Mitchell, John Harrington 1904-1972 *WhAm 6*
Mitchell, John Hipple 1835-1905 *ApCAB,
BiAUS, BiDrAC, DcAmB, NatCAB 2,
REnAW, TwCBDA, WhAm 1, WhAmP*
Mitchell, John Inscho 1838-1907 *ApCAB,
BiDrAC, NatCAB 12, NatCAB 39,
TwCBDA, WhAm 1*
Mitchell, John James 1853-1927 *NatCAB 21,
WhAm 1*
Mitchell, John Joseph 1873-1925 *BiDrAC,
WhAm 1*
Mitchell, John Kearsley 1793-1858 *DcAmB,
WhAm H*
Mitchell, John Kearsley 1796-1858 *Drake*
Mitchell, John Kearsley 1798-1858 *ApCAB,
NatCAB 9, TwCBDA*
Mitchell, John Kearsley 1859-1917 *WhAm 1*
Mitchell, John Lendrum 1842-1904
*ApCAB Sup, BiDrAC, NatCAB 2,
TwCBDA, WhAm 1*
Mitchell, John Marvin 1908-1972 *WhAm 5*
Mitchell, John McKenney 1895-1969 *WhAm 5*
Mitchell, John Murray 1858-1905 *ApCAB Sup,
BiDrAC, NatCAB 10, WhAm 1*
Mitchell, John Newton 1913- *BiDrUSE*
Mitchell, John Nicholas 1847- *NatCAB 3,
WhAm 4*
Mitchell, John R 1861-1939 *WhAm 1*
Mitchell, John Raymond 1868-1933
NatCAB 25, WhAm 1
Mitchell, John Raymond 1869- *ApCAB X*
Mitchell, John Ridley 1877-1962 *BiDrAC*
Mitchell, John Roberts 1873-1950 *NatCAB 39*
Mitchell, John Waite 1848-1919 *NatCAB 6*
Mitchell, John William 1869-1933 *WhAm 1*
Mitchell, Jonathan 1624-1668 *ApCAB,
DcAmB, Drake, NatCAB 8, WhAm H*
Mitchell, Joseph Alfred 1904-1956 *NatCAB 45*
Mitchell, Judith 1793-1837 *NewYHSD*
Mitchell, Julia M 1859- *WomWWA 14*
Mitchell, Julian 1867- *WhAm 5*
Mitchell, Julius Linoble 1867- *WhoColR*
Mitchell, Lang Allen 1881-1950 *NatCAB 40*
Mitchell, Langdon Elwyn 1862-1935 *AmBi,
DcAmB S1, NatCAB 4, WhAm 1,
WhAm 1C*
Mitchell, Leander Perry 1849-1912 *WhAm 1*

Mitchell, Lebbeus 1879- *WhAm 6*
Mitchell, Leeds 1877-1957 *WhAm 3*
Mitchell, Lucy Myers Wright 1845-1888
*ApCAB Sup, DcAmB, NatCAB 6,
TwCBDA, WhAm H*
Mitchell, Lucy Sprague 1878-1967 *NatCAB 53,
WomWWA 14*
Mitchell, Lynn Boal 1881- *WhAm 6*
Mitchell, Mabel Stebbins 1876- *WomWWA 14*
Mitchell, Maggie 1832-1918 *NotAW,
WhAm 1*
Mitchell, Mance Randolph 1902-1970
NatCAB 55
Mitchell, Margaret Johnes 1869- *WhAm 5,
WomWWA 14*
Mitchell, Margaret Julia 1832-1918 *ApCAB,
TwCBDA*
Mitchell, Margaret Julia 1837-1918 *AmBi,
DcAmB, NatCAB 25*
Mitchell, Margaret Munnerlyn 1900-1949
*DcAmB S4, NatCAB 38, NotAW,
WebAB, WhAm 2*
Mitchell, Maria 1818-1889 *AmBi, AmWom,
ApCAB, BiDAmEd, DcAmB, DcScB,
Drake, EncAB, McGEWB, NatCAB 5,
NotAW, TwCBDA, WebAB, WhAm H*
Mitchell, Marian 1840-1885 *NewYHSD*
Mitchell, Marion Juliet 1836- *AmWom*
Mitchell, Marion Sheffield *WomWWA 14*
Mitchell, Martha Elizabeth B Jennings
1918-1976 *WhAm 6*
Mitchell, Martha Reed 1818- *AmWom*
Mitchell, Mary Annie Clark *WomWWA 14*
Mitchell, Mary Greening 1867- *WomWWA 14*
Mitchell, Mary Paulsell 1870- *WomWWA 14*
Mitchell, Mary Warren Otey *WomWWA 14*
Mitchell, Mason 1859-1930 *WhAm 1*
Mitchell, Mayme Katherine 1892- *WhoColR*
Mitchell, Mina *NewYHSD*
Mitchell, Minnie Belle 1860- *WomWWA 14*
Mitchell, Nahum 1769-1853 *ApCAB, BiAUS,
BiDrAC, DcAmB, Drake, NatCAB 25,
TwCBDA, WhAm H*
Mitchell, Nathaniel 1753-1814 *BiAUS,
BiDrAC, DcAmB, NatCAB 11, TwCBDA,
WhAm H, WhAmP*
Mitchell, Nathaniel McDonald 1889-1965
WhAm 4
Mitchell, Neal 1855- *NatCAB 11*
Mitchell, Nellie Louise *WomWWA 14*
Mitchell, O W H 1886-1948 *WhAm 3*
Mitchell, Oscar 1863-1937 *WhAm 1*
Mitchell, Percy VanGelder 1876-1967
NatCAB 54
Mitchell, Peter 1824- *ApCAB*
Mitchell, Philip Henry 1883-1955 *WhAm 3*
Mitchell, Philip Sidney 1854- *NatCAB 12*
Mitchell, Phoebe *NewYHSD*
Mitchell, R Verne 1885-1955 *NatCAB 43,
WhAm 3*
Mitchell, Ralph Clinton, Jr. 1913-1972
WhAm 5
Mitchell, Rexford Samuel 1896-1973 *WhAm 6*
Mitchell, Richard Bland 1887-1961 *WhAm 4*
Mitchell, Richard F 1889-1969 *WhAm 5*
Mitchell, Robert 1778-1848 *BiAUS, BiDrAC,
WhAm H*
Mitchell, Robert 1811-1899 *NatCAB 7,
WhAm 1*
Mitchell, Robert 1864- *WhoColR*
Mitchell, Robert Byington 1823-1882 *ApCAB,
DcAmB, NatCAB 25, TwCBDA,
WhAm H*
Mitchell, Robert Byington 1828-1882 *BiAUS,
Drake*
Mitchell, Robert Goodwin 1843- *NatCAB 2*
Mitchell, Robert McBurney 1879-1956
NatCAB 43
Mitchell, Roland Burnell 1910-1974 *WhAm 6*
Mitchell, Rosalie Leonard *WomWWA 14*
Mitchell, Roscoe Lee 1877- *WhAm 5*
Mitchell, Roscoe Rowland 1883-1932
NatCAB 27
Mitchell, Ruth Comfort 1882-1953 *WhAm 3*
Mitchell, Ruth Comfort 1882-1954 *NatCAB 44*
Mitchell, S Weir 1829-1914 *Drake*
Mitchell, S Weir *see also* Mitchell, Silas Weir
Mitchell, Samuel Alfred 1874-1960 *WhAm 3*

Mitchell, Samuel Alfred 1883-1966 *WhAm 4*
Mitchell, Samuel Augustus 1792-1868 *ApCAB,*
BiDAmEd, DcAmB, Drake, WhAm H
Mitchell, Samuel Chiles 1864-1948 *BiDAmEd,*
NatCAB 14, WhAm 2
Mitchell, Samuel Latham 1763-1831 *BiAUS*
Mitchell, Samuel Latham *see also* Mitchill,
Samuel Latham
Mitchell, Samuel Phillips 1864- *WhAm 4*
Mitchell, Samuel S 1839-1919 *WhAm 1*
Mitchell, Samuel Thomas 1851-1901 *ApCAB,*
NatCAB 5, TwCBDA, WhAm 1
Mitchell, Sara Patterson Snowden
WomWWA 14
Mitchell, Sidney 1876-1938 *WhAm 1*
Mitchell, Sidney Alexander 1895-1966 *WhAm 4*
Mitchell, Sidney Zollicoffer 1862-1944
DcAmB S3
Mitchell, Sidney Zollicoffer 1862-1949
WhAm 2
Mitchell, Silas Weir 1829-1914 *AmBi, ApCAB,*
ApCAB X, BiHiMed, DcAmB, DcScB,
NatCAB 9, TwCBDA, WebAB, WhAm 1
Mitchell, Silas Weir *see also* Mitchell, S Weir
Mitchell, Sollace 1858- *NatCAB 11*
Mitchell, Steele d1940 *WhAm 2*
Mitchell, Stephen Arnold 1903-1974 *WhAm 6*
Mitchell, Stephen Mix 1743-1835 *ApCAB,*
BiAUS, BiDrAC, DcAmB, Drake,
NatCAB 3, TwCBDA, WhAm H
Mitchell, Stewart 1892-1957 *WhAm 3*
Mitchell, Sydney Bancroft 1878-1948 *WhAm 2*
Mitchell, Sydney Bancroft 1878-1951 *DcAmLiB,*
NatCAB 41, WhAm 3
Mitchell, Sydney Knox 1875-1948 *NatCAB 37,*
WhAm 5
Mitchell, Thomas 1892-1962 *NatCAB 51*
Mitchell, Thomas 1895-1962 *WhAm 4*
Mitchell, Thomas A 1892- *WhAm 5*
Mitchell, Thomas Dache 1791-1865 *WhAm H*
Mitchell, Thomas Duche 1791-1865 *DcAmB*
Mitchell, Thomas Edward 1874-1959 *WhAm 4*
Mitchell, Thomas Edward 1901-1965 *WhAm 3*
Mitchell, Thomas John 1875- *IlBEAAW*
Mitchell, Thomas R 1783-1837 *BiAUS*
Mitchell, Thomas Rothmahler 1783?-1837
TwCBDA
Mitchell, Thomas Rothmaler 1783-1837
BiDrAC, WhAm H
Mitchell, Thompson Hampton 1901-1973
WhAm 6
Mitchell, Viola 1911- *WhAm 4*
Mitchell, W M Parker 1883-1962 *NatCAB 50*
Mitchell, W Norman 1891-1970 *NatCAB 55*
Mitchell, Walter 1826-1908 *WhAm 1*
Mitchell, Walter Howard 1878-1955
NatCAB 45
Mitchell, Walter Jenifer 1871-1955 *NatCAB 45,*
WhAm 3
Mitchell, Walter Lee 1915-1968 *WhAm 5*
Mitchell, Walter Scott 1857-1930 *NatCAB 26,*
WhAm 1
Mitchell, Wesley Clair 1874-1948 *DcAmB S4,*
EncAB, McGEWB, WebAB, WhAm 2
Mitchell, Willard A 1868-1942 *WhAm 2*
Mitchell, William 1791-1868 *ApCAB,*
NatCAB 11, TwCBDA
Mitchell, William 1791-1869 *DcAmB,*
WhAm H
Mitchell, William 1793-1867 *ApCAB*
Mitchell, William 1798-1856 *ApCAB, DcAmB,*
NatCAB 8, WhAm H
Mitchell, William 1801-1886 *ApCAB Sup,*
DcAmB, NatCAB 10, TwCBDA,
WhAm H
Mitchell, William 1807-1865 *BiAUS, BiDrAC,*
WhAm H
Mitchell, William 1832-1900 *DcAmB,*
NatCAB 25, WhAm 1
Mitchell, William 1879-1936 *AmBi,*
DcAmB S2, EncAB, NatCAB 26,
WebAB, WebAMB, WhAm 1, WhoMilH
Mitchell, William Bell 1843-1930 *NatCAB 22*
Mitchell, William Bilbo 1850-1913 *NatCAB 17*
Mitchell, William Carl 1896-1962 *WhAm 4*
Mitchell, William DeWitt 1874-1955 *BiDrUSE,*
DcAmB S5, WhAm 3

Mitchell, William Edward 1882-1960
NatCAB 53, WhAm 4
Mitchell, William Henry 1891-1958
NatCAB 47, WhAm 3
Mitchell, William Isaac 1855- *WhoColR*
Mitchell, William J *NewYHSD*
Mitchell, William John 1906-1972 *WhAm 5*
Mitchell, William Ledyard 1881-1964 *WhAm 4*
Mitchell, William Samuel 1877-1936 *WhAm 1*
Mitchell, William Thomas 1817-1916
NatCAB 17
Mitchell, William Thomas, Jr. 1890-1949
NatCAB 38
Mitchell, William Whittier 1854-1915 *WhAm 1*
Mitchell, Wilmot Brookings 1867- *WhAm 5*
Mitchell, Z W William 1867- *WhoColR A*
Mitchill, Samuel Latham 1764-1831 *AmBi,*
ApCAB, BiDrAC, DcAmB, Drake,
NatCAB 4, TwCBDA, WhAm H,
WhAmP
Mitchill, Samuel Latham *see also* Mitchell,
Samuel Latham
Mitchill, Theodore Clarence 1866- *WhAm 4*
Mitchner, Lillian M 1862- *WomWWA 14*
Mitford, Nancy 1904-1973 *WhAm 6*
Mitke, Charles A 1881-1970 *WhAm 5*
Mitre, Bartholomew 1821-1906 *Drake*
Mitre, Bartolome 1821-1906 *ApCAB,*
McGEWB
Mitre, Don Luis 1869-1950 *WhAm 3*
Mitropoulos, Dimitri 1896-1960 *WhAm 4*
Mitscher, Marc Andrew 1887-1947 *DcAmB S4,*
NatCAB 36, WebAMB, WhAm 2,
WhWW-II, WhoMilH
Mitscherlich, Eilhard 1794-1863 *DcScB*
Mitscherlich, Eilhardt 1794-1863 *AsBiEn*
Mittag-Leffler, Magnus Gustaf 1846-1927
DcScB
Mittasch, Alwin 1869-1953 *DcScB*
Mittelman, Edward 1903-1960 *WhAm 4*
Mittelstaed, Gustav Adolphus 1890-1958
NatCAB 47
Mitten, Thomas Eugene 1864-1929 *DcAmB,*
WhAm 1
Mittenthal, Abraham 1877-1954 *NatCAB 43*
Mitton, George W d1947 *WhAm 2*
Mitty, John Joseph 1884-1961 *NatCAB 45,*
WhAm 4
Mitzscherling, Gustave 1823?- *NewYHSD*
Mivart, St. George Jackson 1827-1900 *DcScB*
Mix, Arthur Jackson 1888-1956 *WhAm 3*
Mix, Charles E *BiAUS*
Mix, Charles Louis 1869-1935 *WhAm 1*
Mix, Charles Melvin 1873-1930 *NatCAB 30*
Mix, Edward Townsend 1831-1890 *NatCAB 2,*
WhAm H
Mix, Frank Englemann 1860-1918 *NatCAB 18*
Mix, Loraine 1877-1952 *NatCAB 41*
Mix, Lucius C *NewYHSD*
Mix, Melville Walter 1865- *WhAm 4*
Mix, Thomas E 1880-1940 *ApCAB X*
Mix, Tom 1880-1940 *DcAmB S2, WebAB,*
WhAm 1
Mix, William Winter 1857- *WhAm 4*
Mixer, Albert Harrison 1822-1908 *WhAm 1*
Mixsell, Harold Ruckman 1885-1958
NatCAB 47
Mixsell, Raymond Boileau 1882-1949
NatCAB 41
Mixter, Charles Galloupe 1882-1965
NatCAB 51
Mixter, Charles Whitney 1867- *WhAm 4*
Mixter, George 1889-1968 *WhAm 5*
Mixter, Samuel Jason 1855-1926 *DcAmB,*
WhAm 1
Mixter, William Gilbert 1846-1936 *WhAm 1*
Mixter, William Jason 1880-1958 *NatCAB 45*
Mize, Chester Louis 1917- *BiDrAC*
Mize, Robert Herbert 1870-1956 *WhAm 3*
Mize, Sidney Carr 1888-1965 *NatCAB 55,*
WhAm 4
Mizell, Wilmer David 1930- *BiDrAC*
Mizen, Frederic Kimball 1888-1964? *IlBEAAW*
Mizner, Addison 1872-1933 *DcAmB S1,*
WebAB
Mizner, Henry Rutgeras 1827-1915 *WhAm 1*
Mizner, John Kemp 1837-1898 *ApCAB Sup,*
TwCBDA

Mizner, Lansing Bond 1825- *NatCAB 5*
Mizner, Wilson 1876-1933 *WebAB, WhAm 1*
M'Kenzie, J *NewYHSD*
Moak, Nathaniel Cleveland 1833-1892 *ApCAB,*
NatCAB 11, TwCBDA
Moale, Edward 1840-1913 *WhAm 1*
Moale, John 1731-1798 *NewYHSD*
Mobius, August Ferdinand 1790-1868 *AsBiEn,*
DcScB
Mobius, Karl August 1825-1908 *DcScB*
Mobley, Eleanor Smith 1906-1964 *NatCAB 51*
Mobley, Ernest Cramer 1878- *WhAm 6*
Mobley, John Elmer 1871-1926 *NatCAB 20*
Mobley, Lawrence Eugene 1925-1974 *WhAm 6*
Mobley, Mayor Dennis 1899-1967 *NatCAB 53,*
WhAm 4
Mobley, Radford E 1905-1969 *WhAm 5*
Mobley, William Carlton 1906- *BiDrAC*
Mobutu Sese Seko 1930- *McGEWB*
Mochel, Maude McKinney 1882-
WomWWA 14
Mocino, Jose 1760?-1819 *ApCAB*
Mocino, Jose Mariano 1757-1820 *DcScB*
Mock, Charles Adolphus 1873- *WhAm 5*
Mock, Fred McKinley 1901-1963 *WhAm 4*
Mock, Harry Edgar 1880-1959 *WhAm 3*
Mockmore, Charles Arthur 1891-1953
NatCAB 46, WhAm 3
Mockridge, John Charles Hillier 1872-
WhAm 5
Mod, Aladar 1908-1973 *WhAm 6*
Modarelli, Alfred E 1898-1957 *WhAm 3*
Modder, Montagu Frank 1891-1958 *WhAm 3*
Model, Jean 1915-1955 *NatCAB 44, WhAm 3*
Model, Walther 1891-1945 *WhWW-II,*
WhoMilH
Modell, Clarion d1970 *WhAm 5*
Moderwell, Charles McClellan 1868-1955
WhAm 3
Modigliani, Amedeo 1884-1920 *McGEWB*
Modjeska, Helena 1840-1909 *AmBi, DcAmB,*
NotAW
Modjeska, Helena 1844-1909 *AmWom,*
ApCAB, NatCAB 10, WhAm 1
Modjeski, Ralph 1861-1940 *DcAmB S2,*
NatCAB 15, WhAm 1
Modzelewski, Zymunt 1900- *WhAm 3*
Moe, Alfred Kean 1874- *WhAm 5*
Moe, Henry Allen 1894-1975 *WhAm 6*
Moehlenpah, Henry A 1867-1944 *WhAm 2*
Moehlman, Arthur Bernard 1889-1952
BiDAmEd, NatCAB 42, WhAm 3
Moehlman, Conrad Henry 1879- *WhAm 6*
Moekle, Herman Liveright 1885-1957 *WhAm 3*
Moeller, Charles *NewYHSD*
Moeller, Edith 1916-1975 *WhAm 6*
Moeller, Harold Frederick 1904-1967 *WhAm 5*
Moeller, Henry 1843-1924 *NatCAB 23*
Moeller, Henry 1849-1925 *DcAmB,*
NatCAB 13, TwCBDA, WhAm 1
Moeller, Louis Frederick Charles 1855-1930
TwCBDA, WhAm 1
Moeller, Louis Frederick Charles 1856-1930
ApCAB
Moeller, Paul Gunther 1892-1967 *NatCAB 54*
Moeller, Philip 1880-1958 *WhAm 3*
Moeller, Walter Henry 1910- *BiDrAC*
Moellmann, Albert 1904-1969 *WhAm 5*
Moellring, George H 1878-1935 *WhAm 1*
Moelmann, John Matthew 1911-1974 *WhAm 6*
Moen, Philip Louis 1824-1890 *NatCAB 6*
Moen, Reuben O 1892-1966 *WhAm 4*
Moench, Charles L 1855-1927 *WhAm 1*
Moench, Conrad 1744-1805 *DcScB*
Moenkhaus, William J 1871-1947 *WhAm 2,*
WhAm 5
Moerbeke, William Of 1220?-1286 *DcScB*
Moerdyke, Peter 1845-1923 *TwCBDA,*
WhAm 1
Moerk, Frank Xavier 1863-1945 *NatCAB 35,*
WhAm 2
Moeur, Benjamin Baker 1869-1937 *NatCAB 28,*
WhAm 1
Moffat, Barclay Wellington 1890-1942
NatCAB 33
Moffat, David Halliday 1839-1910 *NatCAB 6*
Moffat, David Halliday 1839-1911 *DcAmB,*
REnAW, WhAm 1

Moffat, David William 1870-1944 *NatCAB 34,*
WhAm 2
Moffat, Dean Alexander 1907-1967 *NatCAB 53*
Moffat, Donald 1894-1958 *WhAm 3*
Moffat, Douglas Maxwell 1881-1956
NatCAB 42, WhAm 3
Moffat, Edgar Vietor 1856-1930 *NatCAB 35*
Moffat, Edward Stewart 1844-1893 *ApCAB,*
TwCBDA
Moffat, Frederick G 1861-1930 *WhAm 1*
Moffat, Henry 1840-1913 *NatCAB 32*
Moffat, James Clement 1811-1890 *ApCAB,*
DcAmB, TwCBDA, WhAm H
Moffat, James David 1846-1916 *ApCAB,*
NatCAB 20, NatCAB 21, TwCBDA,
WhAm 1
Moffat, James E 1883-1957 *WhAm 3*
Moffat, Jay Pierrepont 1896-1943 *DcAmB S3,*
NatCAB 32, WhAm 2
Moffat, Jessie Emerson 1883- *WomWWA 14*
Moffat, John Little 1853-1917 *WhAm 1*
Moffat, R Burnham *ApCAB X*
Moffat, William Henry 1875-1963 *NatCAB 53*
Moffatt, Fred Cushing 1889-1940 *WhAm 2*
Moffatt, James 1870-1944 *DcAmB S3,*
WhAm 2
Moffatt, James Hugh 1878-1929 *WhAm 3*
Moffatt, James Strong 1860- *WhAm 4*
Moffatt, Lucius Gaston 1899-1971 *WhAm 5*
Moffatt, Seth Crittenden 1841-1887 *BiDrAC,*
WhAm H
Moffet, John 1831-1884 *BiDrAC, WhAm H*
Moffet, John 1832-1884 *BiAUS*
Moffet, Thomas *NewYHSD*
Moffet, Thomas 1553-1604 *BiHiMed*
Moffett, Charles Alexander 1864-1949
NatCAB 36, WhAm 3
Moffett, Cleveland Langston 1863-1926 *DcAmB,*
NatCAB 14, NatCAB 24, WhAm 1
Moffett, Donovan Clifford 1900-1963
NatCAB 51, WhAm 4
Moffett, Edna Virginia *WomWWA 14*
Moffett, Elwood Stewart 1908- *WhAm 5*
Moffett, George Monroe 1883-1951 *WhAm 3*
Moffett, Guy 1882-1963 *NatCAB 51*
Moffett, Henry Lee 1915-1972 *NatCAB 57*
Moffett, James Andrew 1851-1913 *NatCAB 24*
Moffett, James Andrew 1886-1953 *WhAm 3*
Moffett, James William 1908-1967 *WhAm 4*
Moffett, Louis Burdelle 1874- *WhAm 5*
Moffett, Paul Gayland 1899-1948 *NatCAB 36*
Moffett, Ross E 1888-1971 *WhAm 6*
Moffett, Rudolph Duryea 1886-1962
NatCAB 47
Moffett, Samuel Austin 1864-1939 *WhAm 1*
Moffett, Samuel Erasmus 1860-1908 *WhAm 1*
Moffett, Thomas 1553-1604 *DcScB*
Moffett, Thomas Clinton 1869-1945 *WhAm 2*
Moffett, William Adger 1869-1933 *DcAmB S1,*
EncAB, NatCAB 25, WebAMB,
WhAm 1
Moffett, William Walter 1854-1926 *WhAm 1*
Moffit, Alexander 1902-1969 *WhAm 5*
Moffit, Hosea 1757-1825 *BiAUS*
Moffit, S P d1950 *WhAm 3*
Moffitt, Edward Richard 1853-1921
NatCAB 19
Moffitt, Herbert Charles 1867- *WhAm 5*
Moffitt, Hosea 1757-1825 *BiDrAC, WhAm H*
Moffitt, James Kennedy d1955 *WhAm 3*
Moffitt, John Henry 1843-1926 *BiDrAC*
Moffitt, John M 1837-1887 *ApCAB,*
NewYHSD
Moffitt, Joseph Vestal 1883-1948 *NatCAB 36*
Moffitt, Louis Moseley 1890-1952 *NatCAB 42*
Moffitt, Walter Volentine 1905-1968 *WhAm 5*
Moffly, Charles K 1906-1967 *WhAm 4*
Mofolo, Thomas 1876-1948 *McGEWB*
Mofras, Eugene Duflot De 1810-1851 *ApCAB*
Mogavero, Francesco 1902-1956 *NatCAB 47*
Mogensen, Walter Alexander 1897-1965
WhAm 4
Mogila, Peter 1596?-1646 *McGEWB*
Moguer, Andres De 1505-1577 *ApCAB*
Mohamed, Duce *WhoColR*
Mohammad Reza Shah Pahlavi 1919- *McGEWB*
Mohammed 570?-632 *McGEWB*
Mohammed II 1432-1481 *McGEWB*

Mohammed V 1909-1961 *WhAm 4*
Mohammed V 1911-1961 *McGEWB*
Mohammed Ali 1769-1849 *McGEWB*
Mohl, Hugo Von 1805-1872 *AsBiEn, DcScB*
Mohler, A L 1850-1930 *WhAm 1*
Mohler, Adam Leon 1849-1930 *ApCAB X*
Mohler, Adam Leon 1850-1930 *NatCAB 33*
Mohler, Bruce Monroe 1881-1967 *NatCAB 53*
Mohler, Daniel Nathan 1892-1951 *WhAm 3*
Mohler, Francis 1903-1956 *NatCAB 49*
Mohler, Henry Keller 1887-1941 *NatCAB 35,*
WhAm 1
Mohler, Jacob Christian 1875-1953 *WhAm 3*
Mohler, John Frederick 1864-1930 *AmBi,*
NatCAB 42, WhAm 1
Mohler, John Robbins 1875- *WhAm 5*
Mohler, Roy William 1892-1964 *NatCAB 50*
Mohler, Samuel Loomis 1895- *WhAm 5*
Mohler, William Edward 1852-1935
NatCAB 41
Mohn, Henrik 1835-1916 *DcScB*
Mohn, Thorbjorn Nilson 1844-1899 *WhAm 1*
Moholy-Nagy, Laszlo George 1895-1946
DcAmB S4, McGEWB, WebAB,
WhAm 2
Mohorovicic, Andrija 1857-1936 *AsBiEn,*
DcScB
Mohr, Carl Friedrich 1806-1879 *DcScB*
Mohr, Charles 1844-1907 *NatCAB 3,*
WhAm 1
Mohr, Charles Adam 1869- *WhAm 5*
Mohr, Charles Theodor 1824-1901 *NatCAB 26,*
TwCBDA, WhAm 1
Mohr, Charles Theodore 1824-1901 *DcAmB*
Mohr, Christian Otto 1835-1918 *DcScB*
Mohr, Georg 1640-1697 *DcScB*
Mohr, Wesley George 1925-1975 *WhAm 6*
Mohs, Friedrich 1773-1839 *AsBiEn, DcScB*
Mohun, Barry 1873-1931 *NatCAB 34,*
WhAm 1
Moidel, Isadore 1904-1960 *NatCAB 51*
Moinet, Edward Julien 1873-1952 *WhAm 3*
Moir, Henry 1871-1937 *NatCAB 35,*
WhAm 1
Moir, John Troup 1859-1933 *NatCAB 39,*
WhAm 1
Moire, Thomas *NewYHSD*
Moise, Charles W *NewYHSD*
Moise, Edwin Warren 1811-1868 *NatCAB 9*
Moise, Edwin Warren 1889-1961 *WhAm 4*
Moise, Harold A 1879-1958 *WhAm 3*
Moise, Penina 1797-1880 *ApCAB, DcAmB,*
NotAW
Moise, Pennina 1797-1880 *WhAm H*
Moise, Theodore Sydney 1806-1883 *NewYHSD*
Moiseev, Nikolay Dmitrievich 1902-1955 *DcScB*
Moiseiwitsch, Benno 1890-1963 *WhAm 4*
Moissan, Ferdinand Frederic Henri 1852-1907
AsBiEn, DcScB
Moisseiff, Leon Solomon 1872-1943 *DcAmB S3,*
NatCAB 40, WhAm 2
Moivre, Abraham De 1667-1754? *DcScB*
Mojica, Jose 1899-1974 *WhAm 6*
Mola, Emilio 1887-1937 *WhoMilH*
Mold, Harry James 1881-1942 *NatCAB 31*
Moldavsky, Leon Frank 1911-1970 *NatCAB 56*
Moldehnke, Edward Frederick 1836-1904
DcAmB, WhAm 1
Moldenhawer, Johann Jacob Paul 1766-1827
DcScB
Moldenhawer, Julius Valdemar 1877-1948
NatCAB 42, WhAm 2
Moldenke, Charles Edward 1860-1935 *ApCAB,*
NatCAB 28, TwCBDA, WhAm 1
Moldenke, Edward Frederick 1836- *ApCAB,*
TwCBDA
Moldenke, Richard George Gottlob 1864-1930
DcAmB, NatCAB 28, WhAm 1
Molders, Oberst Werner 1913-1941 *WhWW-II*
Moldveen-Geronimus, Miriam Esther 1925-1970
WhAm 5
Mole, Harvey E 1869-1957 *WhAm 3*
Moleen, George Arnold 1876- *WhAm 5*
Moleschott, Jacob 1822-1893 *DcScB*
Moley, Raymond 1886-1975 *WhAm 6*
Moliere 1622-1673 *McGEWB*
Molieres, Joseph Privat De *DcScB*
Molin, Fedor Eduardovich 1861-1941 *DcScB*

Molina, Alonso De 1510?-1584 *ApCAB*
Molina, Edward Charles Dixon 1877- *WhAm 6*
Molina, Felipe 1812-1855 *ApCAB, Drake*
Molina, Giovanni Ignazio 1740-1829 *Drake*
Molina, Juan Ignacio 1740-1829 *ApCAB,*
DcScB
Molina, Pedro 1777-1850? *ApCAB, Drake*
Molinare, Anthony William 1901-1974
WhAm 6
Molineux, Edward Leslie 1833-1915 *ApCAB,*
NatCAB 2, TwCBDA, WhAm 1
Molineux, Marie Ada 1760- *TwCBDA,*
WhAm 5, WomWWA 14
Molineux, Roland Burnham 1866- *WhAm 4*
Molini, Raffael 1814?- *NewYHSD*
Molinos, Miguel De 1628-1696 *McGEWB*
Molitor, David Albert 1866-1939 *NatCAB 15,*
WhAm 2
Molitor, Frederic Albert 1868-1938 *WhAm 1*
Molitor, Hans 1895-1970 *WhAm 5*
Moll, Friedrich Rudolf Heinrich Carl 1882-1951
DcScB
Moll, Gerard 1785-1838 *DcScB*
Moll, Theophilus John 1872-1930 *NatCAB 23*
Mollenhauer, Emil 1855-1927 *DcAmB,*
WhAm 1
Mollenhauer, Henry 1825-1889 *NatCAB 13,*
WhAm H
Mollenhauer, Louis 1863- *NatCAB 13*
Mollenkopf, Jack Kenneth Webster 1903-1975
WhAm 6
Moller, Charles *NewYHSD*
Moller, Didrik Magnus Axel 1830-1896 *DcScB*
Moller, Henry 1749-1829 *ApCAB*
Moller, Knud Ove 1896-1973 *WhAm 6*
Moller, Mathias Peter 1855-1937 *WhAm 1*
Moller, Mathias Peter, Jr. 1902-1961 *WhAm 4*
Moller, Sarah Isabel Towle *WomWWA 14*
Mollet, Guy 1905-1975 *WhAm 6*
Mollhausen, Balduin 1825-1905 *ApCAB*
Mollhausen, Heinrich Balduin 1825-1905
DcAmB, IlBEAAW, NewYHSD
Molliard, Marin 1866-1944 *DcScB*
Mollier, Richard 1863-1935 *DcScB*
Mollin, Fernand E 1887- *WhAm 3*
Mollinari, John 1814?- *NewYHSD*
Mollinari, Joseph *NewYHSD*
Mollison, Irvin Charles 1898-1962 *NatCAB 50,*
WhAm 4
Mollison, James Alexander 1897-1970 *WhAm 5*
Mollison, Willis E 1859- *WhoColR*
Mollohan, Robert Homer 1909- *BiDrAC*
Molloy, Daniel Murrah 1882-1944 *NatCAB 32*
Molloy, Sister Mary Aloysia 1880-1954
WomWWA 14
Molloy, Sister Mary Aloysius 1880-1954
BiDAmEd, WhAm 3
Molloy, Thomas Marcus 1874-1945 *WhAm 2*
Mollweide, Karl Brandan 1774-1825 *DcScB*
Molly, Captain 1756?-1789? *ApCAB Sup*
Molnar, Ferenc d1952 *WhAm 3*
Molnar, Ferenc d1969 *WhAm 4*
Molnar, Julius Paul d1973 *WhAm 5*
Molohon, Albin D 1900-1970 *WhAm 5*
Moloney, George Hale 1885-1965 *WhAm 4*
Moloney, Herbert William 1895-1967 *WhAm 4*
Moloney, Raymond Thomas 1900-1958
NatCAB 47
Moloney, Thomas W 1862- *WhAm 4*
Moloney, William Curry 1907-1972 *WhAm 5*
Molony, Richard Sheppard 1811-1891 *BiAUS,*
BiDrAC, WhAm H
Molony, William *NewYHSD*
Molony, William Hayes 1884- *WhAm 3*
Molotov, Viachislav M 1890- *WhWW-II*
Molotov, Vyacheslav Mikhailovich 1890-
McGEWB
Moloy, Howard Carman 1903-1953 *NatCAB 41*
Molson, John 1764-1836 *ApCAB*
Molson, John 1787-1860 *ApCAB*
Molson, William 1793-1875 *ApCAB*
Molt, William Franklin 1876-1958 *NatCAB 48*
Molter, Harold d1959 *WhAm 3*
Molthan, Emil Henry 1894-1952 *NatCAB 40*
Moltke, Count Helmuth Karl Bernard Von
1800-1891 *McGEWB, WhoMilH*
Molton, Thomas Hunter 1853-1932 *NatCAB 38*
Molyneaux, Joseph West 1863-1940 *WhAm 1*

Molyneux *NewYHSD*
Molyneux, Richard 1696-1766 *ApCAB*
Molyneux, Robert 1738-1808 *DcAmB,*
  WhAm H
Molyneux, Samuel 1689-1728 *DcScB*
Molyneux, William 1656-1698 *DcScB*
Momaday, Alfred Morris 1913- *IlBEAAW*
Momaday, N Scott 1934- *REnAW*
Momberger, William 1829- *ApCAB, Drake,*
  NewYHSD
Mombert, Jacob Isidor 1829-1913 *ApCAB,*
  DcAmB, TwCBDA, WhAm 1
Moment, John James 1875-1959 *WhAm 3*
Mommer, Peter Paul 1899-1963 *WhAm 4*
Mommsen, Theodore 1817-1903 *McGEWB*
Mompesson, Roger d1715 *ApCAB,*
  NatCAB 13
Momsen, Charles B d1967 *WhAm 4*
Momsen, Richard Paul 1890-1964 *WhAm 4*
Monachaise *NewYHSD*
Monachesi, Elio David 1905-1971 *WhAm 5*
Monachesi, F *NewYHSD*
Monachesi, Nocola 1795-1851 *NewYHSD*
Monachise *NewYHSD*
Monaelesser, Adolph 1855-1936 *WhAm 1*
Monagan, Charles Andrew 1872-1931
  NatCAB 24
Monagan, John Stephen 1911- *BiDrAC*
Monagas, Jacinto 1785-1819 *ApCAB*
Monagas, Jose Gregorio 1795-1858 *ApCAB*
Monagas, Jose Tadeo 1784-1868 *ApCAB*
Monagas, Jose Tadeo 1786?-1868 *Drake*
Monaghan, Anna Jackson *WomWWA 14*
Monaghan, Eileen *IlBEAAW*
Monaghan, Frank 1904-1969 *NatCAB 56*
Monaghan, Frank J 1890-1942 *WhAm 2*
Monaghan, J F 1863- *WhAm 4*
Monaghan, James 1854-1949 *WhAm 2*
Monaghan, James Charles 1857-1917
  NatCAB 27, TwCBDA, WhAm 1
Monaghan, Jay 1891- *REnAW*
Monaghan, John Henry 1895-1957 *NatCAB 44*
Monaghan, John James 1856-1935 *ApCAB Sup,*
  NatCAB 15, NatCAB 42, TwCBDA,
  WhAm 1
Monaghan, Joseph Patrick 1906- *BiDrAC*
Monaghan, Noel 1890-1964 *NatCAB 51*
Monaghan, Peter Joseph 1881-1942 *WhAm 2*
Monahan, Arthur Coleman 1877- *WhAm 5*
Monahan, James Gideon 1855-1923 *BiDrAC,*
  WhAm H
Monahan, Louis John 1876-1920 *NatCAB 19*
Monahan, Michael 1865-1933 *NatCAB 44,*
  WhAm 1
Monarch, Richard 1838-1915 *NatCAB 17*
Monardes, Nicolas Bautista 1493?-1588 *DcScB*
Monast, Louis 1863-1936 *BiDrAC, WhAm 4*
Moncabrie DePeytes, Joseph S, Comte De
  1741-1819 *ApCAB*
Monceau *NewYHSD*
Monceau, P H *NewYHSD*
Moncey, BonAdrien Jeannot De 1754-1842
  WhoMilH
Moncheur, Baron Ludovic 1857- *WhAm 4*
Monck, Charles Stanley 1819- *ApCAB, Drake*
Monck, George, Duke Of Albemarle 1608-1670
  McGEWB, WhoMilH
Monckton, Henry 1740-1778 *ApCAB*
Monckton, Robert 1726-1782 *AmBi, ApCAB,*
  DcAmB, Drake, NatCAB 13, WhAm H
Monckton, Sir Walter Turner 1891-1965
  WhAm 4
Moncrief, John Wildman 1850-1936 *WhAm 1*
Moncrieff, Ernest VanDyke 1890-1950
  NatCAB 38
Moncrieff, James d1793 *Drake*
Moncrieffe, James d1793 *ApCAB*
Moncure, Philip St. Leger 1867-1955
  NatCAB 49
Moncure, Richard Cassius Lee 1805-1882
  DcAmB, WhAm H
Moncure, Richard L C 1805-1882 *NatCAB 7*
Mond, Ludwig 1839-1909 *DcScB*
Mondale, Walter Frederick 1928- *BiDrAC*
Mondelet, Charles Joseph Elzear 1801-1877
  ApCAB
Mondell, Frank Wheeler 1860-1939 *DcAmB S2,*
  NatCAB 30, REnAW, TwCBDA,

WhAm 1
Mondell, Franklin Wheeler 1860-1939 *BiDrAC,*
  WhAmP
Mondelli, Antoine *NewYHSD*
Mondesir, Charles Stanislas 1750-1817 *ApCAB*
Mondeville *DcScB*
Mondino De'Luzzi 1265?-1326 *McGEWB*
Mondino De'Luzzi 1275?-1326 *AsBiEn, DcScB*
Mondlane, Eduardo Chivambo 1920-1969
  McGEWB
Mondrian, Piet 1872-1944 *McGEWB,*
  WhAm 4
Mone, Francis Daniel 1905-1962 *NatCAB 50*
Monell, Ambrose d1921 *WhAm 1*
Monell, Claudius L 1815-1876 *ApCAB*
Monell, Frances Wallach 1852- *WomWWA 14*
Monell, Robert 1786-1860 *BiAUS, BiDrAC,*
  WhAm H
Monet, Claude 1840-1926 *McGEWB*
Monette, John Wesley 1803-1851 *ApCAB Sup,*
  DcAmB, Drake, NatCAB 15, WhAm H
Money, H D 1839-1912 *BiAUS*
Money, Hernando DeSoto 1839-1912
  ApCAB Sup, BiDrAC, DcAmB,
  NatCAB 11, TwCBDA, WhAm 1,
  WhAmP
Monfils, Napoleon Arthur 1870-1954
  NatCAB 47
Monfort, Adele Harwood Bloss 1884-
  WomWWA 14
Monfort, Elias Riggs 1842-1920 *WhAm 1*
Monfort, Francis Cassatt 1844-1928
  NatCAB 24, TwCBDA, WhAm 4
Monfort, Francis Cassatte 1844-1928 *ApCAB*
Monfort, Joseph Glass 1810-1906 *ApCAB,*
  TwCBDA, WhAm 1
Monge, Gaspard 1746-1818 *DcScB*
Monges, Gordon 1832-1907 *NatCAB 17*
Monges, Josephine DeTeisseire 1863-
  WomWWA 14
Mongkut 1804-1868 *McGEWB*
Monhelm, Leonard Myers 1911-1971 *WhAm 5*
Monigan, John James, Jr. 1913-1972
  NatCAB 56
Monihon, J Davidson 1836-1904 *NatCAB 26*
Monin, Louis Celestin 1857-1931 *WhAm 1*
Monino Y Redondo, Jose *WhAm H*
Monis, Judah 1683-1764 *ApCAB, DcAmB,*
  Drake, WhAm H
Moniz, Antonio Caetano De Abreu Freire E
  1874-1955 *AsBiEn*
Moniz, Antonio Egas 1874-1955 *BiHiMed*
Moniz, Egas 1874-1955 *DcScB, WhAm 3*
Monjo, Ferdinand Nicolas 1875-1929
  NatCAB 34
Monk, Dudley Connor 1887-1966 *NatCAB 54*
Monk, Maria 1816-1849 *NotAW*
Monk, Maria 1817?-1850? *ApCAB*
Monk, Wesley Elias 1874-1958 *NatCAB 46,*
  WhAm 3
Monkiewicz, Boleslaus Joseph 1898- *BiDrAC*
Monks, Charles *NewYHSD*
Monks, George Howard 1853-1933 *NatCAB 27,*
  WhAm 4
Monks, John Austin Sands 1850-1917 *WhAm 1*
Monks, Leander John 1848-1919 *WhAm 1*
Monks, Lester Hawthorne 1870-1927 *WhAm 1*
Monks, Robert Hatton 1856-1923 *ApCAB X*
Monks, Sarah Preston *WomWWA 14*
Monmonier, William B *NewYHSD*
Monmouth, James Scott, Duke Of 1649-1685
  McGEWB, WhoMilH
Monnet, Antoine-Grimoald 1734-1817 *DcScB*
Monnet, Jean 1888- *McGEWB*
Monnet, Julien Charles 1868-1951 *NatCAB 40,*
  WhAm 4
Monnett, Francis Sylvester *WhAm 3*
Monnett, Mary Zouck 1876- *WomWWA 14*
Monnett, Victor 1889-1972 *WhAm 5*
Monnette, Mervin Jeremiah 1847-1931
  WhAm 1
Monnette, Orra Eugene 1873-1936 *NatCAB 27,*
  WhAm 1, WhAm 1C
Monnier, France X 1831-1912 *NewYHSD*
Monnot, Edward Louis 1896-1947 *NatCAB 37*
Monnot, John Ferreol 1864- *NatCAB 14*
Monod, Jacques Lucien 1910- *AsBiEn*
Monod, Theodore 1836- *ApCAB*

Monohan, Edward Sheehan, III 1910-1965
  WhAm 4
Monohan, John McKiernan 1881-1931
  NatCAB 26, WhAm 1
Monosmith, Olney Benton 1871-1957
  NatCAB 46
Monrad, Anna Marie *WomWWA 14*
Monrad, Margaret *WomWWA 14*
Monro, Alexander 1697-1767 *BiHiMed, DcScB*
Monro, Alexander 1733-1817 *BiHiMed, DcScB*
Monro, Alexander, III *BiHiMed*
Monro, Charles Bedell 1901-1972 *WhAm 5*
Monro, Hugh Reginald 1871-1954 *WhAm 3*
Monro, William Loftus 1866-1945 *WhAm 2*
Monroe, Andrew 1792-1871 *ApCAB*
Monroe, Andrew Perrine 1890-1965 *WhAm 4*
Monroe, Anna Hamill 1869- *BiCAW,*
  WomWWA 14
Monroe, Anne Shannon 1877-1942 *NatCAB 45,*
  WhAm 2
Monroe, Arthur 1874-1956 *NatCAB 45*
Monroe, Arthur Eli 1885-1965 *WhAm 4*
Monroe, Charles 1849-1937 *NatCAB 43,*
  WhAm 4
Monroe, Charles Fraser 1884-1935 *WhAm 1*
Monroe, Daniel L d1973 *WhAm 5*
Monroe, Edwin Paul 1885-1964 *WhAm 4*
Monroe, Elizabeth Kortright 1763?-1830
  NotAW
Monroe, Elizabeth Kortright 1768-1830 *AmBi,*
  AmWom, ApCAB, NatCAB 6, TwCBDA
Monroe, Frank 1873-1959 *NatCAB 44*
Monroe, Frank Adair 1844-1927 *NatCAB 12,*
  WhAm 1
Monroe, Harriet 1860-1936 *AmBi, DcAmB S2,*
  NatCAB 28, NotAW, WebAB, WhAm 1,
  WomWWA 14
Monroe, Harriet Earhart 1842-1927 *AmWom,*
  WhAm 1, WomWWA 14
Monroe, J Blanc 1880-1960 *WhAm 4*
Monroe, J Raburn 1909-1961 *NatCAB 51,*
  WhAm 4
Monroe, James 1758-1831 *AmBi, ApCAB,*
  BiAUS, BiDrAC, BiDrUSE, DcAmB,
  Drake, EncAAH, EncAB, McGEWB,
  NatCAB 6, TwCBDA, WebAB,
  WhAm H, WhAmP
Monroe, James 1799-1870 *ApCAB, BiDrAC,*
  WhAm H
Monroe, James 1821-1898 *ApCAB, BiAUS,*
  BiDrAC, TwCBDA
Monroe, Jay Randolph 1883-1937 *NatCAB 16,*
  NatCAB 27, WhAm 1
Monroe, Lawrence Alexander 1912-1969
  WhAm 5
Monroe, Lilla Day *WomWWA 14*
Monroe, Marilyn 1926-1962 *WebAB,*
  WhAm 4
Monroe, Paul 1869-1947 *BiDAmEd,*
  DcAmB S4, NatCAB 36, WhAm 2
Monroe, Pleasant Edgar 1875-1954 *WhAm 3*
Monroe, R Grier 1860-1924 *NatCAB 29*
Monroe, Samuel Yorke 1816-1867 *ApCAB*
Monroe, Thomas 1899-1959 *WhAm 3*
Monroe, Thomas Bell 1791-1865 *BiAUS,*
  BiDConf
Monroe, V *BiAUS*
Monroe, Vaughn 1911-1973 *WhAm 6*
Monroe, Walter Dillman 1889-1948
  NatCAB 42
Monroe, Walter Scott 1882-1961 *BiDAmEd,*
  NatCAB 53
Monroe, Will Seymour 1863-1939 *BiDAmEd,*
  NatCAB 42, WhAm 1
Monroe, William Stanton 1868- *WhAm 3*
Monroney, Almer Stillwell Mike 1902- *BiDrAC*
Monroy, Antonio 1634-1715 *ApCAB*
Monsarrat, Nicholas 1839-1910 *NatCAB 18,*
  WhAm 1
Monsell, Edwin Moreland 1883-1940
  NatCAB 31
Monsen, Frederick Imman 1865-1929 *WhAm 1*
Monser, John Watson 1838- *TwCBDA*
Monserrat, Joaquin De 1710?-1770? *ApCAB*
Monsky, Henry 1890-1947 *DcAmB S4,*
  WhAm 2
Monsman, Gerald 1899-1970 *WhAm 5*
Monson, George S 1869-1933 *WhAm 1*

Monsseau, P H *NewYHSD*
Montagu, Ashley 1905- *WebAB*
Montagu, Lord Charles Greville 1741-1784
 NatCAB 12
Montagu, George 1750-1829 *ApCAB, Drake*
Montague, Abraham 1892-1961 *WhAm 4*
Montague, Amy Angell Collier *WomWWA 14*
Montague, Andrew Jackson 1862-1937 *BiDrAC,
 DcAmB S2, NatCAB 13, NatCAB 38,
 TwCBDA, WhAm 1, WhAmP*
Montague, Andrew Philip 1854-1928
 NatCAB 25, TwCBDA, WhAm 1
Montague, Charles Elbert 1866-1953
 NatCAB 40
Montague, David Thompson 1864-1945
 NatCAB 45
Montague, Dwight Preston 1853-1921 *WhAm 1*
Montague, Elizabeth Lyne Hoskins 1868-
 WomWWA 14
Montague, Fairfax Eubank 1925-1971 *WhAm 5*
Montague, George Prescott 1849-1936
 NatCAB 27
Montague, Gilbert Holland 1880-1961 *WhAm 4*
Montague, Helen Weymouth 1876- *WhAm 5*
Montague, Henry James 1843-1878 *DcAmB,
 NatCAB 11, WhAm H*
Montague, James Edward, Jr. 1903-1966
 WhAm 5
Montague, James Jackson 1873-1941 *WhAm 1,
 WhAm 2*
Montague, Joseph Franklin 1895-1974 *WhAm 6*
Montague, Margaret Prescott *WomWWA 14*
Montague, Richard Ward 1862-1935
 NatCAB 42, WhAm 1
Montague, Robert Latane 1819-1880 *ApCAB,
 BiDConf, TwCBDA*
Montague, Robert Latane 1897-1972 *WhAm 5*
Montague, Robert Miller 1899-1958 *WhAm 3*
Montague, Theodore Giles 1898-1967 *WhAm 4*
Montague, Theodore Langdon 1877-1948
 NatCAB 39
Montague, Wallace Tenney 1889-1952 *WhAm 3*
Montague, William Lewis 1831-1908 *ApCAB,
 NatCAB 10, TwCBDA, WhAm 1*
Montague, William Pepperell 1873-1953
 DcAmB S5, NatCAB 43, WhAm 3
Montaigne, Michel Eyquem De 1533-1592
 McGEWB
Montaigne DeNogaret, Charles Stanislas
 1667-1742 *ApCAB*
Montalambert, Marc Rene, Marquis De
 1714-1800 *WhoMilH*
Montalant, Julius O *NewYHSD*
Montale, Eugenio 1896- *McGEWB*
Montalembert, Charles Forbes, Comte De
 1810-1870 *McGEWB*
Montalvo, Juan Maria 1832-1889 *McGEWB*
Montalvo Y Ambulodi, Francisco 1754-1832
 ApCAB
Montana, Bob 1920-1975 *WhAm 6*
Montanari, Geminiano 1633-1687 *DcScB*
Montani, Nicola Aloysius 1880-1948
 NatCAB 43
Montanus *McGEWB*
Montanus, Edward Sidney 1886-1947
 NatCAB 48
Montanya, J D L *BiAUS*
Montauband 1650?-1700 *ApCAB*
Montavon, William Frederick 1874- *WhAm 5*
Montbars 1645?- *ApCAB*
Montcalm, Louis, Saint Veran, Marquis De
 1712-1759 *Drake*
Montcalm, Louis Joseph, Marquis De 1712-1759
 WhoMilH
Montcalm, Paul Francois Joseph 1756-1812
 ApCAB
Montcalm DeSaint-Veran, L J, Marquis De
 1712-1759 *McGEWB*
Montcalm Gozon DeSaint Veran, Louis J
 1712-1759 *ApCAB*
Monte, Guidobaldo, Marchese Del 1545-1607
 DcScB
Monte-Sano, Vincent d1955 *WhAm 3*
Monteagudo, Bernardo 1787-1825 *ApCAB*
Montecuccoli, Raimundo 1609-1680 *WhoMilH*
Montefiore, Joshua 1752-1843 *Drake*
Montefiore, Joshua 1762-1843 *ApCAB,
 DcAmB, WhAm H*

Monteil, Nicolas Antoine 1771-1833 *ApCAB*
Monteiro, Candido Borges 1812-1872 *ApCAB*
Monteith, John 1833-1918 *NatCAB 19*
Monteith, Walter E 1877- *WhAm 5*
Montejo, Francisco 1502-1560 *ApCAB*
Montejo, Francisco De 1479-1549 *ApCAB*
Montelatici, Ferruccio L 1859-1914 *NatCAB 16*
Montelius, George Dunton 1872-1914
 NatCAB 16
Montelius, Gustav Oscar 1843-1921 *DcScB*
Montemayor, Alonso De d1552 *ApCAB*
Monten, William Andrew 1879-1958
 NatCAB 47
Montenegro, Alfonso De d1553 *ApCAB*
Montenier, Jules Bernard 1895-1962
 NatCAB 52, WhAm 4
Monterde, Mariano 1789-1861 *ApCAB*
Montero, Lizardo 1832- *ApCAB*
Montes DeOca, Ignacio 1840- *ApCAB*
Montes DeOca, Luis d1958 *WhAm 3*
Montesinos, Antonio De *ApCAB*
Montesinos, Fernando 1593-1655 *ApCAB*
Montesquieu, Charles-Louis, Baron De
 1689-1755 *DcScB, McGEWB*
Montesquiou-Fezensac, P A F, Comte De
 1753-1833 *ApCAB*
Montessori, Maria 1870-1952 *McGEWB*
Montet, Numa Francois 1892- *BiDrAC*
Monteux, Pierre 1875-1964 *WhAm 4*
Monteverde, Juan Domingo 1772?-1820 *ApCAB*
Monteverdi, Claudio Giovanni Antonio
 1567-1643 *McGEWB*
Montez, Lola 1818-1861 *NotAW, REnAW,
 WebAB, WhAm H*
Montez, Lola 1824-1861 *ApCAB, Drake*
Montezuma I d1471 *Drake*
Montezuma I 1390-1464 *ApCAB*
Montezuma II 1466-1520 *ApCAB, McGEWB,
 WhAm H*
Montezuma II 1480?-1520 *Drake*
Montezuma, Carlos 1867-1923 *WhAm 1*
Montfort, Simon De, Earl Of Leicester
 1208-1265 *McGEWB*
Montgery, Jacques-Philippe Merigon De
 1781-1839 *DcScB*
Montgolfier, Etienne Jacques De 1745-1799
 DcScB
Montgolfier, Jacques Etienne 1745-1799 *AsBiEn,
 McGEWB*
Montgolfier, Joseph Michel 1740-1810 *AsBiEn,
 McGEWB*
Montgolfier, Michel Joseph De 1740-1810
 DcScB
Montgomerie, John d1731 *Drake, NatCAB 13,
 WhAm H*
Montgomery *NewYHSD*
Montgomery Of Alamein, Viscount 1887-1976
 WhAm 6
Montgomery, A E d1971 *WhAm 5*
Montgomery, Albert Horr 1882-1948
 NatCAB 37
Montgomery, Alexander Brooks 1837-1910
 BiDrAC, NatCAB 13, TwCBDA
Montgomery, Alfred E 1891-1961 *WhAm 4*
Montgomery, Benjamin F *WhAm 5*
Montgomery, Bernard Law, Viscount 1887-1976
 McGEWB, WhWW-II, WhoMilH
Montgomery, Caroline W 1865- *WomWWA 14*
Montgomery, Carrie Frances Judd 1858-
 AmWom
Montgomery, Charles Carroll 1876-1943
 WhAm 2
Montgomery, Charles Wesley 1880-1958
 NatCAB 43
Montgomery, Charlotte Elizabeth Wood 1867-
 WomWWA 14
Montgomery, Cora *NotAW*
Montgomery, Daniel, Jr. 1765-1831 *BiAUS,
 BiDrAC, WhAm H*
Montgomery, David Henry 1837-1928 *DcAmB,
 NatCAB 24*
Montgomery, Douglass William 1859-1941
 NatCAB 31, WhAm 4
Montgomery, Edmund Duncan 1835-1911
 DcAmB, DcScB, WhAm 1
Montgomery, Edna Morley 1896-1970 *WhAm 5*

Montgomery, Edward Emmet 1849-1927
 NatCAB 13, WhAm 1
Montgomery, Edward Gerrard 1878- *WhAm 6*
Montgomery, Edward Louis 1874- *WhAm 1*
Montgomery, Emily P 1897-1971 *WhAm 5*
Montgomery, Eugene Emmett, Jr. 1900-1926
 NatCAB 20
Montgomery, Fletcher H 1880-1948 *WhAm 2*
Montgomery, Francis S *ApCAB X*
Montgomery, Frank Hugh 1862-1908 *WhAm 1*
Montgomery, George 1847-1907 *NatCAB 12,
 TwCBDA, WhAm 1*
Montgomery, George 1867-1938 *NatCAB 28*
Montgomery, George Granville 1894-1974
 WhAm 6
Montgomery, George Hugh Alexander 1874-1951
 WhAm 3
Montgomery, George Redington 1870-1945
 WhAm 2
Montgomery, George Washington 1804-1841
 *ApCAB, DcAmB, Drake, NatCAB 18,
 WhAm H*
Montgomery, George Washington 1810-
 ApCAB
Montgomery, Gillespie V 1920- *BiDrAC*
Montgomery, Guy 1886-1951 *NatCAB 40,
 WhAm 3*
Montgomery, Helen Barrett 1861-1934 *NotAW,
 WhAm 1*
Montgomery, Henry Arthur 1887-1957
 WhAm 3
Montgomery, Henry Eglinton 1820-1874
 ApCAB, TwCBDA
Montgomery, Hortense Hoban *WomWWA 14*
Montgomery, J Hugh 1902-1953 *NatCAB 42*
Montgomery, Jack Percival 1877- *WhAm 5*
Montgomery, James 1814-1871 *ApCAB,
 DcAmB, NatCAB 8, WhAm H*
Montgomery, James Alan 1866-1949
 DcAmB S4, WhAm 5
Montgomery, James Boyce 1832-1900
 ApCAB X
Montgomery, James Edward 1884-1960
 NatCAB 48
Montgomery, James Eglinton d1909 *WhAm 1*
Montgomery, James Harvey 1856-1933
 NatCAB 25
Montgomery, James Llewellyn 1869- *WhAm 5*
Montgomery, James Shera d1952 *WhAm 3*
Montgomery, Job Herrick 1851-1941
 NatCAB 31
Montgomery, John 1722-1808 *ApCAB,
 BiDrAC*
Montgomery, John 1764-1828 *ApCAB, BiAUS,
 BiDrAC, WhAm H*
Montgomery, John Berrien 1794-1873 *AmBi,
 ApCAB, DcAmB, Drake, NatCAB 10,
 TwCBDA, WhAm H*
Montgomery, John Flournoy 1878-1954
 NatCAB 45, WhAm 3
Montgomery, John Gallagher 1805-1857 *BiAUS,
 BiDrAC, WhAm H*
Montgomery, John Harold 1874-1929 *WhAm 1*
Montgomery, John Joseph 1858-1911
 NatCAB 15
Montgomery, John Knox 1861-1931
 NatCAB 23, WhAm 1
Montgomery, John Rhea 1892-1973 *WhAm 6*
Montgomery, John Rogerson 1866-1937
 WhAm 1
Montgomery, Joseph 1733-1794 *ApCAB,
 BiAUS, BiDrAC, TwCBDA, WhAm H*
Montgomery, Lemuel Purnell 1786-1814
 NatCAB 12
Montgomery, Mack Allen 1854- *WhAm 4*
Montgomery, Martin VanBuren 1840-1898
 ApCAB, NatCAB 8
Montgomery, Mary Phelps 1846- *ApCAB X*
Montgomery, Mary Williams 1874- *WhAm 5,
 WomWWA 14*
Montgomery, Morris Carpenter 1907-1969
 WhAm 5
Montgomery, Oscar Hilton 1859-1936 *WhAm 1*
Montgomery, R Ames 1870-1950 *WhAm 3*
Montgomery, Richard 1736-1775 *ApCAB,
 Drake, McGEWB, NatCAB 1, TwCBDA*
Montgomery, Richard 1738-1775 *AmBi,
 DcAmB, WebAMB, WhAm H*

Montgomery, Richard D 1889-1952 *WhAm 3*
Montgomery, Richard Malcolm 1853- *NatCAB 3*
Montgomery, Sir Robert 1680?-1731 *ApCAB*
Montgomery, Robert 1872-1936 *WhAm 1*
Montgomery, Robert Hiester 1872-1953 *ApCAB X, WhAm 3*
Montgomery, Robert M 1849-1920 *NatCAB 12, WhAm 1*
Montgomery, Robert Nathaniel 1900-1967 *WhAm 4*
Montgomery, Roselle Mercier 1874-1933 *NatCAB 24, WhAm 1*
Montgomery, S A 1896-1961 *WhAm 4*
Montgomery, Samuel James 1896-1957 *BiDrAC*
Montgomery, Samuel Thomas 1860-1938 *WhAm 1*
Montgomery, Thomas d1828 *BiAUS*
Montgomery, Thomas 1778?-1828 *TwCBDA*
Montgomery, Thomas 1779-1828 *BiDrAC, WhAm H*
Montgomery, Thomas Harrison, Jr. 1873-1912 *DcAmB, DcScB, NatCAB 15, WhAm 1*
Montgomery, Thomas Lynch 1862-1929 *DcAmLiB, NatCAB 24, WhAm 1*
Montgomery, Thomas Stuart 1909-1970 *NatCAB 56*
Montgomery, Valda Stewart 1888-1959 *WhAm 3*
Montgomery, Victor 1891-1960 *NatCAB 50, WhAm 4*
Montgomery, Walter Alexander 1872-1949 *NatCAB 37*
Montgomery, Whitney Maxwell 1877-1966 *WhAm 4*
Montgomery, William 1736-1816 *BiAUS, BiDrAC, WhAm H*
Montgomery, William 1789-1843 *TwCBDA*
Montgomery, William 1789-1844 *BiAUS, BiDrAC, WhAm H*
Montgomery, William 1818-1870 *BiDrAC, TwCBDA, WhAm H*
Montgomery, William 1819-1870 *ApCAB, BiAUS*
Montgomery, William 1869-1955 *WhAm 3*
Montgomery, William Alvin 1854-1930 *NatCAB 23*
Montgomery, William B 1790?-1834 *ApCAB*
Montgomery, William Bell 1829-1904 *DcAmB*
Montgomery, William Coons 1866-1934 *WhAm 1*
Montgomery, William Reading 1801-1871 *ApCAB*
Montgomery, William Watts 1827-1897 *NatCAB 2*
Montgomery, William Woodrow, Jr. 1877-1950 *WhAm 3*
Montgomery-Marsh, Mary Louise *WomWWA 14*
Montherlant, Henry De 1896-1972 *WhAm 5*
Monti, Luigi 1830- *ApCAB*
Montigny, Casimir Amable Testard De 1787-1863 *ApCAB*
Montigny, Francis Joliet De 1661-1725 *ApCAB*
Montigny, Jacques Testard De 1662?-1737 *ApCAB*
Montigny, Jean Baptiste Testard 1724-1786 *ApCAB*
Montilla, Mariano 1782-1851 *ApCAB*
Montilla, Tomas 1778-1822 *ApCAB*
Montmagny, Charles Jacques Huault De d1649 *ApCAB*
Montmor, Henri Louis Habert De 1600?-1679 *DcScB*
Montmorency, Anne, Duc De 1493-1567 *WhoMilH*
Montmorency, Henri, Duc De 1595-1632 *ApCAB*
Montmort, Pierre Remond De 1678-1719 *DcScB*
Montonna, Ralph E 1894-1952 *WhAm 3*
Montour, Madame 1684?-1752? *NotAW*
Montour, Catherine 1684?-1752? *ApCAB*
Montour, Esther *ApCAB*
Montoya, Alfredo d1913 *IIBEAAW*
Montoya, Antonio Ruiz De 1585-1652 *ApCAB*
Montoya, Atanasio 1875-1935 *WhAm 1*
Montoya, Geronima Cruz 1915- *IIBEAAW*
Montoya, Joseph Manuel 1915- *BiDrAC*

Montoya, Nestor 1862-1923 *BiDrAC, WhAm 1, WhAmP*
Montpensier, Antoine P D'O, Duc De 1775-1807 *NewYHSD*
Montpreville, Cyrille 1819?- *NewYHSD*
Montpreville, Cyrus De 1819?- *NewYHSD*
Montresor, James Gabriel 1702-1776 *DcAmB, WhAm H*
Montresor, John 1736-1799 *DcAmB, WhAm H*
Montreuil, Gaetane De *WomWWA 14*
Montreuil, Pierre De *McGEWB*
Montreville, Cyrille 1819?- *NewYHSD*
Montreville, Cyrus De 1819?- *NewYHSD*
Montrose, James Graham, Marquis Of 1612-1650 *WhoMilH*
Montrueil, Desire Amable Ferdinand 1709-1760 *ApCAB*
Monts, Pierre DuGuast, Comte De 1560?-1611 *ApCAB, Drake*
Montt, Manuel 1809-1881 *ApCAB*
Montt Torres, Manuel 1809-1880 *McGEWB*
Montucla, Jean Etienne 1725-1799 *DcScB*
Montufar, Lorenzo 1823- *ApCAB*
Montule, Edouard De *NewYHSD*
Montzheimer, Arthur 1869- *WhAm 5*
Monypeny, William 1829-1900 *NatCAB 3*
Monzani, John Teobaldo 1919-1969 *NatCAB 55*
Mooar, George 1830-1904 *ApCAB, TwCBDA, WhAm 1*
Mood, Francis Asbury 1830-1884 *DcAmB, WhAm H*
Mood, Orlando Clarendon 1899-1953 *NatCAB 44, WhAm 3*
Moodie, Campbell 1908-1970 *WhAm 5*
Moodie, John Wedderbar Dunbar 1797-1869 *ApCAB*
Moodie, Roy Lee 1880-1934 *WhAm 1*
Moodie, Susanna 1803-1885 *ApCAB, McGEWB*
Moody, Agnes Claypole *WomWWA 14*
Moody, Arthur Edson Blair 1902-1954 *BiDrAC*
Moody, Arthur Winfield 1912-1959 *NatCAB 49*
Moody, Benjamin 1841-1914 *NatCAB 16*
Moody, Blair 1902-1954 *DcAmB S5, NatCAB 47, WhAm 3*
Moody, Clara Amalia 1879- *WomWWA 14*
Moody, Dan 1893-1966 *NatCAB 53, WhAm 4*
Moody, David William *NewYHSD*
Moody, Lady Deborah d1659? *NotAW*
Moody, Dexter 1812-1896 *NatCAB 2*
Moody, Dwight Lyman 1837-1899 *AmBi, ApCAB, DcAmB, DcAmReB, EncAAH, EncAB, McGEWB, NatCAB 7, TwCBDA, WebAB, WhAm 1*
Moody, Edwin *IIBEAAW, NewYHSD*
Moody, Elizabeth Eddy 1856- *WomWWA 14*
Moody, Ernest Addison 1903-1975 *WhAm 6*
Moody, Frank Sims 1849-1920 *WhAm 1*
Moody, Gideon Curtis 1832-1904 *ApCAB Sup, BiDrAC, NatCAB 2, TwCBDA, WhAm 1, WhAmP*
Moody, Granville 1812-1887 *ApCAB*
Moody, H W 1877-1949 *WhAm 3*
Moody, Harry Anson 1858-1926 *NatCAB 24*
Moody, Helen Watterson d1928 *AmWom*
Moody, Helen Watterson 1859-1928 *NatCAB 22*
Moody, Helen Watterson 1860-1928 *WomWWA 14*
Moody, Helen Wills *WebAB*
Moody, Herbert Raymond 1869-1947 *NatCAB 36, WhAm 2*
Moody, Isaac I 1874-1918 *NatCAB 18*
Moody, James 1744-1809 *AmBi, ApCAB, DcAmB, Drake, NatCAB 7, WhAm H*
Moody, James Montraville 1858-1903 *BiDrAC*
Moody, John 1759-1781 *ApCAB*
Moody, John E *NewYHSD*
Moody, Joseph Burnley 1838-1931 *WhAm 1*
Moody, Joshua 1633-1697 *ApCAB, Drake*
Moody, Julia Eleanor 1869- *WomWWA 14*
Moody, Lewis Ferry 1880-1953 *NatCAB 47, WhAm 3*
Moody, Malcolm Adelbert 1854-1925 *BiDrAC, WhAm 4*
Moody, Mary Blair 1837- *AmWom*

Moody, Mary Noel 1864- *WomWWA 14*
Moody, Nelson Kingsland 1877-1944 *WhAm 2*
Moody, Paul 1779-1831 *ApCAB, DcAmB, Drake, NatCAB 25, WhAm H*
Moody, Paul Dwight 1879-1947 *WhAm 2*
Moody, Robert Orton 1864-1948 *NatCAB 36*
Moody, Samuel 1676-1747 *ApCAB, Drake*
Moody, Samuel 1725-1795 *Drake*
Moody, Shearn 1895-1936 *NatCAB 27*
Moody, Sidney Clarke 1895-1974 *WhAm 6*
Moody, Virginia Green 1881-1955 *WhAm 3*
Moody, Volney Delos 1829-1901 *NatCAB 16*
Moody, Walter Dwight 1874-1920 *NatCAB 18, WhAm 1*
Moody, Walter Sherman 1864-1938 *WhAm 1*
Moody, William Henry 1853-1917 *AmBi, BiDrAC, BiDrUSE, DcAmB, NatCAB 13, NatCAB 14, TwCBDA, WebAB, WhAm 1, WhAmP*
Moody, William Lewis, Jr. 1865-1954 *NatCAB 41, WhAm 3*
Moody, William Revell 1869-1933 *NatCAB 40, NatCAB 47, WhAm 1*
Moody, William Vaughan 1869-1910 *NatCAB 11*
Moody, William Vaughn 1869-1910 *AmBi, DcAmB, TwCBDA, WebAB, WhAm 1*
Moody, Winfield Scott 1856- *WhAm 4*
Moody, Zenas Ferry 1832-1917 *NatCAB 8, TwCBDA, WhAm 1*
Mooers, Benjamin 1758-1838 *ApCAB, Drake*
Mooers, Jacob B *NewYHSD*
Moog, Wilson Townsend 1881-1953 *WhAm 3*
Moon, Carl 1879-1948 *IIBEAAW, NatCAB 42, WhAm 2*
Moon, Charles Franklin 1890-1970 *NatCAB 56*
Moon, Don Pardee 1894-1944 *NatCAB 34, WhAm 2*
Moon, Edwin G 1870-1939 *WhAm 1*
Moon, Franklin 1880-1929 *WhAm 1*
Moon, Grace d1947 *WhAm 2*
Moon, Henry Dukso 1914-1974 *WhAm 6*
Moon, John Austin 1855-1921 *BiDrAC, TwCBDA, WhAm 1, WhAmP*
Moon, John Barclay 1849-1915 *NatCAB 18*
Moon, John Wesley 1836-1898 *BiDrAC*
Moon, Lottie Digges 1840-1912 *NotAW*
Moon, Merl Perrott 1891-1958 *NatCAB 46*
Moon, Owen 1872-1947 *NatCAB 35*
Moon, Parker Thomas 1892-1936 *DcAmB S2, NatCAB 28, WhAm 1*
Moon, Reuben Osborne 1847-1919 *BiDrAC, WhAm 4, WhAmP*
Moon, Samuel 1805-1860 *NewYHSD*
Moon, Truman Jesse 1879-1946 *WhAm 3*
Moon, Virgil Holland 1879- *WhAm 6*
Moon, William *NewYHSD*
Mooney, Charles Anthony 1879-1931 *BiDrAC, WhAm 1, WhAmP*
Mooney, Charles Patrick Joseph 1865-1926 *NatCAB 23, WhAm 1*
Mooney, Daniel Francis 1865-1930 *NatCAB 33, WhAm 1*
Mooney, Edmund L 1865-1933 *WhAm 1*
Mooney, Cardinal Edward A 1882-1958 *NatCAB 44, WhAm 3*
Mooney, Edward Ludlow 1813-1887 *ApCAB, NewYHSD, TwCBDA*
Mooney, Eugene Francis 1907-1971 *WhAm 5*
Mooney, Fletcher Dines 1856-1897 *NatCAB 8*
Mooney, Franklin D 1873-1966 *WhAm 4*
Mooney, Guy 1899-1965 *WhAm 4*
Mooney, Henry 1874-1927 *NatCAB 21*
Mooney, James 1830?- *NatCAB 7*
Mooney, James 1861-1921 *AmBi, DcAmB, NatCAB 25, REnAW, TwCBDA, WebAB, WhAm 1*
Mooney, James David 1884-1957 *WhAm 3*
Mooney, James Edmund 1832-1919 *NatCAB 23*
Mooney, James Elliott 1901-1968 *WhAm 5*
Mooney, James Garth 1921-1971 *WhAm 5*
Mooney, John Henry 1848- *NatCAB 4*
Mooney, Joseph Francis 1848-1923 *TwCBDA, WhAm 1*
Mooney, Joseph W 1900-1965 *WhAm 4*
Mooney, Lawrence *NewYHSD*
Mooney, Robert Johnstone d1937 *WhAm 1*
Mooney, Robert Lee 1911-1960 *WhAm 4*

Mooney, Thomas Joseph 1882-1942 *DcAmB S3*
Mooney, Urban Drening 1878- *WhAm 1*
Mooney, Voigt 1894-1948 *NatCAB 39*
Mooney, William 1756-1831 *DcAmB,*
NatCAB 3, TwCBDA, WhAm H,
WhAmP
Mooney, William Crittenden 1855-1918 *BiDrAC,*
WhAm 4
Mooney, William Henley 1888-1966
NatCAB 51
Mooney, William M 1870-1960 *WhAm 3A*
Mooney, William Roberts 1884-1963
NatCAB 51
Moonlight, Thomas 1833-1899 *NatCAB 12,*
WhAm 1
Moor, Elizabeth I d1965 *WhAm 4*
Moor, Henry Britt 1888-1966 *NatCAB 51*
Moor, Wyman B S 1814-1869 *BiAUS*
Moor, Wyman Bradbury Seavy 1811-1869
BiDrAC, WhAm H
Moor, Wyman Bradbury Seuvey 1811-1869
NatCAB 5
Moor, Wyman Bradbury Sevey 1811-1869
TwCBDA
Moor, Wyman Bradbury Sevey 1814-1869
ApCAB
Moora, Robert L 1912-1971 *WhAm 5*
Moore, A E *NewYHSD*
Moore, A M 1863- *WhoColR*
Moore, Abel Buel 1806-1879 *NewYHSD*
Moore, Addison 1868-1936 *NatCAB 27*
Moore, Addison Webster 1866-1930 *DcAmB,*
NatCAB 33, WhAm 1
Moore, Agnes Lawrence Hall *WomWWA 14*
Moore, Albert Burton 1887-1967 *NatCAB 53,*
WhAm 4
Moore, Albert Voorhis 1880-1953 *NatCAB 45,*
WhAm 3
Moore, Albert Weston 1842- *WhAm 4*
Moore, Alexander George Montgomery 1833-
ApCAB Sup
Moore, Alexander Pollock 1867-1930
NatCAB 24, WhAm 1
Moore, Alfred 1755-1810 *ApCAB, BiAUS,*
DcAmB, Drake, NatCAB 2, TwCBDA,
WebAB, WhAm H
Moore, Alfred 1783-1837 *ApCAB, Drake*
Moore, Alfred Stibbs 1846-1920 *WhAm 1*
Moore, Alice Medora Rogers 1857-
NatCAB 16, WhAm 1, WomWWA 14
Moore, Alice Ruth *NotAW*
Moore, Allen, II 1886-1945 *WhAm 2*
Moore, Allen Francis 1869-1945 *BiDrAC,*
WhAm 5
Moore, Andrew 1752-1821 *ApCAB, BiAUS,*
BiDrAC, DcAmB, Drake, NatCAB 5,
TwCBDA, WhAm H, WhAmP
Moore, Andrew Barry d1873 *BiAUS*
Moore, Andrew Barry 1806-1873 *ApCAB,*
TwCBDA
Moore, Andrew Barry 1807-1873 *BiDConf,*
NatCAB 10
Moore, Andrew Charles 1866- *WhAm 1*
Moore, Andrew Given Tobias 1889-1961
NatCAB 50
Moore, Andrew Lewis 1870-1935 *NatCAB 27*
Moore, Anna Lewis *WomWWA 14*
Moore, Anne *WomWWA 14*
Moore, Anne Carroll 1871-1961 *DcAmLiB,*
WhAm 4
Moore, Annette 1874- *WomWWA 14*
Moore, Annie Aubertine Woodward 1841-1929
DcAmB, NotAW
Moore, Ansley Cunningham 1903-1973
WhAm 5
Moore, Arch Alfred, Jr. 1923- *BiDrAC*
Moore, Arthur Harry 1879-1952 *BiDrAC,*
WhAm 3, WhAmP
Moore, Arthur James 1888-1974 *WhAm 6*
Moore, Aubertine Woodward 1841-1929
AmWom, TwCBDA, WhAm 1
Moore, Aubrey Shannon 1883-1955 *WhAm 3*
Moore, Austin Talley 1899-1963 *WhAm 4*
Moore, Barrington 1883- *ApCAB X,*
NatCAB 18
Moore, Bartholomew Figures 1801-1878
ApCAB, DcAmB, NatCAB 9, TwCBDA,
WhAm H

Moore, Ben Wheeler 1891-1958 *WhAm 3*
Moore, Benjamin *NewYHSD*
Moore, Benjamin 1748-1816 *ApCAB,*
ApCAB X, DcAmB, Drake, NatCAB 1,
NatCAB 6, TwCBDA, WhAm H
Moore, Bertha Pearl 1894-1925 *WhAm 1*
Moore, Blaine Free 1879-1941 *WhAm 1*
Moore, Bob 1910-1950 *WhAm 3*
Moore, Bryant Edward 1894-1951 *NatCAB 39,*
WhAm 3
Moore, Burton Evans 1866-1925 *WhAm 1*
Moore, Byron Leander 1886-1958 *NatCAB 48*
Moore, C Ellis 1884-1941 *WhAm 1*
Moore, C Ellis *see also* Moore, Charles Ellis
Moore, C Ulysses 1877-1937 *NatCAB 35*
Moore, Carl Allphin 1911-1973 *WhAm 6*
Moore, Carl Richard 1892-1955 *WhAm 3*
Moore, Carl Vernon 1908-1972 *NatCAB 57,*
WhAm 5
Moore, Carlyle 1875-1924 *NatCAB 20*
Moore, Charles 1855-1942 *DcAmB S3,*
WhAm 2
Moore, Charles Albert 1864- *WhAm 4*
Moore, Charles Alexander 1901-1967 *WhAm 4*
Moore, Charles Arthur d1914 *WhAm 1*
Moore, Charles Arthur 1845-1914 *ApCAB X*
Moore, Charles Arthur 1846-1914 *NatCAB 25*
Moore, Charles Arthur 1880-1949 *ApCAB X,*
WhAm 3
Moore, Charles Beatty 1881-1951 *NatCAB 51*
Moore, Charles Brainard Taylor 1853-1923
WhAm 1
Moore, Charles Cadwell 1868-1932 *WhAm 1*
Moore, Charles Calvin 1866-1958 *WhAm 3*
Moore, Charles Ellis 1884-1941 *BiDrAC,*
WhAmP
Moore, Charles Ellis *see also* Moore, C Ellis
Moore, Charles Forrest 1863- *WhAm 4*
Moore, Charles Gillingham 1876-1951
NatCAB 40
Moore, Charles Herbert 1840-1930 *DcAmB,*
NatCAB 27, NewYHSD, WhAm 1
Moore, Charles I D 1865-1944 *ApCAB X,*
NatCAB 45
Moore, Charles James 1875-1950 *NatCAB 39,*
WhAm 2
Moore, Charles Leonard 1854- *ApCAB,*
NatCAB 11, WhAm 1
Moore, Charles Lothrop 1915-1972 *WhAm 5*
Moore, Charles Sumner 1857-1915 *NatCAB 16*
Moore, Charles Ulysses 1877- *WhAm 1*
Moore, Charles W 1925- *BnEnAmA*
Moore, Charles Whitlock 1801- *Drake*
Moore, Chester Biven 1881-1962 *NatCAB 50*
Moore, Clara Sophia Jessup 1824-1899 *AmWom,*
ApCAB, NatCAB 9, NotAW, TwCBDA
Moore, Clarence Bloomfield 1852- *WhAm 1*
Moore, Clarence King 1873- *WhAm 5*
Moore, Clarence Lemuel Elisha 1876-1931
DcAmB, WhAm 1
Moore, Clement Clarke 1779-1863 *AmBi,*
ApCAB, DcAmB, Drake, NatCAB 7,
TwCBDA, WebAB, WhAm H
Moore, Clement Clarke 1847-1910 *ApCAB X*
Moore, Clifford Herschel 1866-1931 *DcAmB,*
NatCAB 24, WhAm 1
Moore, Clyde B 1886-1973 *WhAm 6*
Moore, Cornelius 1806- *Drake*
Moore, Daniel *ApCAB*
Moore, Daniel David Tompkins 1820-1892
TwCBDA
Moore, Daniel Decatur 1869-1938 *WhAm 1*
Moore, Daniel McFarlan 1869-1936 *AmBi,*
NatCAB 13, WhAm 1
Moore, David 1787-1856 *ApCAB*
Moore, David 1822- *NatCAB 7*
Moore, David Albert 1814- *ApCAB*
Moore, David Hastings 1838-1915 *NatCAB 12,*
NatCAB 19, TwCBDA, WhAm 1
Moore, David Richard 1877-1951 *WhAm 3*
Moore, Dewitt VanDeusen 1874- *WhAm 5*
Moore, Donald Bernard 1905-1957 *NatCAB 47*
Moore, Douglas Stuart 1893-1969 *WhAm 5*
Moore, Dunlop 1830-1905 *ApCAB, WhAm 1*
Moore, E *NewYHSD*
Moore, Edmond H 1862-1925 *WhAm 1*
Moore, Edmund Joseph 1897-1963 *NatCAB 50,*
WhAm 4

Moore, Edward *WhoColR*
Moore, Edward, Jr. 1906-1959 *WhAm 3*
Moore, Edward Bruce 1851-1915 *NatCAB 30,*
WhAm 1
Moore, Edward Caldwell 1857-1943
NatCAB 32, WhAm 2
Moore, Edward Charles 1827-1891 *ApCAB Sup*
Moore, Edward Charles 1835?-1891 *BnEnAmA*
Moore, Edward Colman 1877-1935 *WhAm 1*
Moore, Edward Hall 1871-1950 *BiDrAC,*
NatCAB 40, WhAm 3
Moore, Edward James 1873-1948 *WhAm 2*
Moore, Edward Jay 1861-1935 *WhAm 1*
Moore, Edward Mott 1814-1902 *ApCAB,*
DcAmB, Drake, NatCAB 12, TwCBDA,
WhAm 1
Moore, Edward Roberts 1894-1952 *WhAm 3*
Moore, Edward Small 1881-1948 *WhAm 2*
Moore, Edward William 1864-1928 *NatCAB 22,*
WhAm 1
Moore, Edwin E 1894-1965 *WhAm 4*
Moore, Edwin King 1847-1931 *WhAm 1*
Moore, Edwin Ward 1810-1865 *DcAmB,*
WebAMB, WhAm H
Moore, Edwin Ward 1811-1865 *ApCAB, Drake*
Moore, Elbert Edmund 1897-1962 *WhAm 4*
Moore, Eleanor M Hiestand *WomWWA 14*
Moore, Eliakim Hastings 1812-1900 *BiAUS,*
BiDrAC
Moore, Eliakim Hastings 1862-1932 *DcAmB S1,*
DcScB, NatCAB 12, TwCBDA, WhAm 1
Moore, Elizabeth *ApCAB*
Moore, Ella Maude 1849-1922 *WhAm 1,*
WomWWA 14
Moore, Elon Howard 1894-1953 *WhAm 3*
Moore, Ely 1798-1860 *BiAUS, DcAmB,*
WhAm H
Moore, Ely 1798-1861 *BiDrAC, NatCAB 25*
Moore, Emery N 1816-1890 *NewYHSD*
Moore, Emily Dungan 1878- *WomWWA 14*
Moore, Emily S *NewYHSD*
Moore, Emmeline 1872- *WomWWA 14*
Moore, Erasmus Darwin 1802- *ApCAB*
Moore, Ernest Carroll 1871-1955 *BiDAmEd,*
NatCAB 40, WhAm 5
Moore, Ernest Carroll, Jr. 1913-1972 *WhAm 5*
Moore, Escum Lionel 1907-1973 *WhAm 6*
Moore, Ethelbert Allen 1864-1956 *NatCAB 45,*
WhAm 3
Moore, Eva Perry 1852-1931 *WhAm 1,*
WomWWA 14
Moore, Fillmore 1856- *WhAm 4*
Moore, Floyd Wayne 1889-1966 *NatCAB 52*
Moore, Forris Jewett 1867-1926 *WhAm 1*
Moore, Francis 1841-1928 *WhAm 1*
Moore, Francis Cruger 1842- *WhAm 4*
Moore, Francis Lee 1886-1946 *NatCAB 35*
Moore, Frank 1828-1904 *AmBi, ApCAB,*
DcAmB, Drake, TwCBDA
Moore, Frank A 1844- *WhAm 1*
Moore, Frank Donaldson 1870-1931
NatCAB 25
Moore, Frank Ernest 1877-1954 *NatCAB 41*
Moore, Frank Gardner 1865-1955 *WhAm 3*
Moore, Frank Horace 1872- *WhAm 5*
Moore, Frank Lincoln 1866-1935 *WhAm 1*
Moore, Frank Martin 1906-1964 *NatCAB 51*
Moore, Frank R 1897- *WhAm 4*
Moore, Franklin Benjamin 1874-1934 *WhAm 1*
Moore, Fred Atkins 1882-1951 *WhAm 3*
Moore, Fred Randolph 1857- *WhoColR*
Moore, Frederick Ferdinand 1877- *WhAm 5*
Moore, Frederick Randolph 1857-1943
DcAmB S3
Moore, Frederick Wightman 1863-1911
WhAm 1
Moore, G Bedell 1840-1908 *WhAm 1*
Moore, Gabriel d1844 *BiAUS, Drake*
Moore, Gabriel 1785?-1844 *TwCBDA*
Moore, Gabriel 1785-1845 *BiDrAC, DcAmB,*
NatCAB 10, WhAm H, WhAmP
Moore, Gabriel 1790?-1844 *ApCAB*
Moore, George *NewYHSD*
Moore, George Andrew 1871-1945 *NatCAB 39,*
WhAm 2
Moore, George Charles 1855-1931 *NatCAB 24*
Moore, George Curtis 1925-1973 *WhAm 5*
Moore, George Edward 1873-1958 *McGEWB,*

WhAm 4

Moore, George F 1887-1949 *WhAm 2*
Moore, George Fleming 1822-1883 *DcAmB, NatCAB 5, WhAm H*
Moore, George Foot 1851-1931 *AmBi, DcAmB, NatCAB 10, NatCAB 42, TwCBDA, WhAm 1*
Moore, George Gail 1889- *WhAm 5*
Moore, George Godfrey 1872-1939 *WhAm 1*
Moore, George Gordon 1876- *ApCAB X*
Moore, George Gordon 1878- *WhAm 6*
Moore, George Henry 1823-1892 *ApCAB, DcAmB, Drake, NatCAB 4, TwCBDA, WhAm H*
Moore, George Herbert 1878-1962 *WhAm 4*
Moore, George Nelson 1878-1950 *NatCAB 43*
Moore, George Sheppard 1883- *WhoColR*
Moore, George Thomas 1871-1956 *NatCAB 13, NatCAB 47, WhAm 3*
Moore, George Thomas 1898-1966 *WhAm 4*
Moore, George Washington 1854- *WhoColR*
Moore, Grace 1898-1947 *NotAW*
Moore, Grace 1901-1947 *DcAmB S4, NatCAB 38, WhAm 2*
Moore, Miss H N *NewYHSD*
Moore, Harold Alexander 1897-1947 *NatCAB 36*
Moore, Harold Emerson 1903-1974 *WhAm 6*
Moore, Harrie G 1864-1939 *WhAm 1*
Moore, Harrison Bray *NatCAB 3, WhAm 5*
Moore, Harrison Sherman 1849-1928 *NatCAB 23*
Moore, Harry H *WhAm 3*
Moore, Harry Hascall 1881-1949 *WhAm 2*
Moore, Harry Humphrey 1844- *ApCAB*
Moore, Harry Humphrey 1844-1923 *AmBi*
Moore, Harry Humphrey 1844-1926 *WhAm 1*
Moore, Harry Tunis 1874- *WhAm 5*
Moore, Harry William 1891- *WhAm 6*
Moore, Helen 1894-1963 *WhAm 4*
Moore, Heman Allen 1809-1844 *BiDrAC, WhAm H*
Moore, Heman Allen 1810-1844 *BiAUS*
Moore, Henrietta Greer d1940 *AmWom, WhAm 1, WomWWA 14*
Moore, Sir Henry 1713-1769 *AmBi, ApCAB, DcAmB, Drake, NatCAB 5, WhAm H*
Moore, Henry 1898- *McGEWB*
Moore, Henry Dunning 1817-1887 *BiAUS, BiDrAC, WhAm H*
Moore, Henry Dyer 1842-1930 *NatCAB 41*
Moore, Henry Eaton 1803-1831 *ApCAB, TwCBDA*
Moore, Henry Eaton 1803-1841 *Drake*
Moore, Henry Frank 1867-1948 *WhAm 2*
Moore, Henry Hoyt 1860- *WhAm 4*
Moore, Henry J 1802-1875 *NatCAB 9*
Moore, Henry Lynn 1854-1928 *WhAm 1*
Moore, Henry Trumbull 1903-1974 *WhAm 6*
Moore, Herbert Fisher 1875-1960 *NatCAB 47*
Moore, Herbert McComb 1876-1942 *NatCAB 33, WhAm 2*
Moore, Herman Aubrey 1902-1948 *NatCAB 36*
Moore, Hight C 1871-1957 *WhAm 3*
Moore, Homer 1863- *NatCAB 12*
Moore, Horace Ladd 1837-1914 *BiDrAC, NatCAB 11*
Moore, Horatio Newton 1814-1859 *ApCAB, Drake*
Moore, Houston Burger 1879-1953 *WhAm 3*
Moore, Hoyt Augustus 1870-1958 *WhAm 3*
Moore, Hugh 1887-1972 *WhAm 5*
Moore, Hugh Benton 1874-1944 *NatCAB 36, WhAm 3*
Moore, Hugh Kelsea 1872-1939 *NatCAB 29, WhAm 1*
Moore, Inez Macondray *WomWWA 14*
Moore, Irwin L 1896-1972 *WhAm 5*
Moore, Isaac Sadler 1870- *WhAm 5*
Moore, Isaac W *NewYHSD*
Moore, Isabel 1872- *WomWWA 14*
Moore, J Herbert 1861-1921 *NatCAB 19*
Moore, J W E *WhAm 5*
Moore, Jackson Tenbrook 1865-1944 *NatCAB 36*
Moore, Jacob Bailey 1772-1813 *ApCAB, Drake*
Moore, Jacob Bailey 1797-1853 *ApCAB, DcAmB, Drake, NatCAB 4, TwCBDA,*

WhAm H

Moore, Jacob Bailey 1815-1893 *NewYHSD*
Moore, James *NewYHSD*
Moore, James d1706 *DcAmB, NatCAB 12, WhAm H*
Moore, James d1723 *NatCAB 12*
Moore, James d1776 *Drake*
Moore, James 1640?-1729 *ApCAB, Drake*
Moore, James 1667-1740 *ApCAB, TwCBDA*
Moore, James 1729?-1777 *NatCAB 10*
Moore, James 1737-1777 *ApCAB, DcAmB, TwCBDA, WebAMB, WhAm H*
Moore, James 1764-1814 *BiDAmEd, DcAmB, NatCAB 4, WhAm H*
Moore, James 1813-1897 *NatCAB 18*
Moore, James Alexander 1861-1929 *NatCAB 26*
Moore, James Edward 1852-1918 *DcAmB, NatCAB 6, WhAm 1*
Moore, James Gregory 1870- *WhAm 5*
Moore, James Henry 1867-1954 *NatCAB 42*
Moore, James Hobart 1852-1916 *WhAm 1*
Moore, James Leonard 1875-1924 *NatCAB 22*
Moore, James Miles 1837-1905 *WhAm 1*
Moore, James Monroe 1886-1942 *NatCAB 32*
Moore, James W 1844-1909 *ApCAB, NatCAB 11, TwCBDA, WhAm 1*
Moore, James William 1818-1877 *BiDConf*
Moore, Jared Sparks 1879-1951 *NatCAB 41, WhAm 3*
Moore, Jere 1845- *TwCBDA*
Moore, Jere 1883-1946 *WhAm 2*
Moore, Jesse Cameron 1868-1957 *NatCAB 47*
Moore, Jesse Hale 1817-1883 *ApCAB, BiAUS, BiDrAC, TwCBDA, WhAm H*
Moore, Joanna Patterson 1832- *WomWWA 14*
Moore, John *ApCAB, NewYHSD*
Moore, John 1658?-1732? *ApCAB*
Moore, John 1659?-1732 *DcAmB, WhAm H*
Moore, John 1686-1749 *ApCAB*
Moore, Sir John 1761-1809 *WhoMilH*
Moore, John 1788-1867 *BiAUS, BiDrAC, TwCBDA, WhAm H*
Moore, John 1810?- *NewYHSD*
Moore, John 1826-1907 *ApCAB, NatCAB 12, TwCBDA, WhAm 1*
Moore, John 1834-1901 *DcAmB, TwCBDA*
Moore, John 1835-1901 *ApCAB, WhAm 1*
Moore, John Augustus 1878-1947 *NatCAB 36*
Moore, John Basset 1860-1947 *NatCAB 11*
Moore, John Bassett 1860-1947 *ApCAB Sup, ApCAB X, DcAmB S4, TwCBDA, WhAm 2*
Moore, John Beverly 1884-1965 *NatCAB 50*
Moore, John C d1946 *WhAm 2*
Moore, John Cecil 1907-1967 *WhAm 5*
Moore, John Creed 1824-1919 *BiDConf*
Moore, John Cunningham 1892-1963 *WhAm 4*
Moore, John D 1874-1940 *WhAm 1*
Moore, John Ferguson 1868- *WhAm 5*
Moore, John G 1848- *WhAm 4*
Moore, John Godfrey 1847-1899 *NatCAB 5, NatCAB 22*
Moore, John Hebron 1920- *EncAAH*
Moore, John Henry 1876- *WhoColR*
Moore, John Howard 1862-1916 *WhAm 1*
Moore, John Jamison 1814- *ApCAB Sup*
Moore, John Langlois 1885-1952 *NatCAB 41*
Moore, John Leverett 1859- *TwCBDA, WhAm 4*
Moore, John M d1924 *WhAm 1*
Moore, John Matthew 1862-1940 *BiDrAC*
Moore, John Mayhew 1827-1901 *NatCAB 24*
Moore, John Merrick 1880-1954 *WhAm 3*
Moore, John Milton 1871-1947 *WhAm 2*
Moore, John Monroe 1867-1948 *WhAm 2*
Moore, John Peabody 1879- *WhAm 6*
Moore, John Percy 1869-1965 *WhAm 4*
Moore, John Small 1876- *WhAm 5*
Moore, John Trotwood 1858-1929 *DcAmB, NatCAB 13, WhAm 1*
Moore, Mrs. John Trotwood 1875-1957 *WhAm 3*
Moore, John W 1861-1925 *WhAm 1*
Moore, John W 1865- *IIBEAAW*
Moore, John Walker 1884-1952 *WhAm 3*
Moore, John Weeks 1807-1889 *ApCAB, DcAmB, Drake, TwCBDA, WhAm H*

Moore, John Wheeler 1833-1906 *NatCAB 8*
Moore, John White 1832-1913 *TwCBDA, WhAm H*
Moore, John William 1837-1893 *NatCAB 8*
Moore, John William 1877-1941 *BiDrAC, WhAm 2*
Moore, Joseph 1832- *TwCBDA*
Moore, Joseph 1870-1923 *WhAm 1*
Moore, Joseph Arthur 1879-1937 *WhAm 1*
Moore, Joseph B 1845-1930 *NatCAB 7, WhAm 1*
Moore, Joseph Earle 1892-1957 *WhAm 3*
Moore, Joseph Haines 1878-1949 *DcAmB S4, DcScB, NatCAB 37, WhAm 2*
Moore, Joseph Hampton 1864-1950 *BiDrAC, WhAm 5, WhAmP*
Moore, Joseph Thoits 1796-1854 *NewYHSD*
Moore, Joseph Waldron 1879- *WhAm 6*
Moore, Josiah John 1886-1964 *NatCAB 51, WhAm 4*
Moore, Josiah Staunton 1843- *WhAm 4*
Moore, Julia Augusta 1878- *WhoColR*
Moore, Julia Katherine DeClercq *WomWWA 14*
Moore, Julian Alison 1896-1959 *NatCAB 48*
Moore, Julian H 1882-1933 *WhAm 1*
Moore, Kenneth W 1902-1971 *WhAm 5*
Moore, Kirke Tonner 1882-1938 *NatCAB 48*
Moore, Laban Theodore 1829-1892 *BiAUS, BiDrAC, WhAm H*
Moore, Lammie Lamar 1880-1962 *NatCAB 50*
Moore, Lawrence Berac 1898-1971 *NatCAB 56*
Moore, Lewis Baxter 1866- *TwCBDA, WhAm 4, WhoColR*
Moore, Lillian 1911-1967 *WhAm 4*
Moore, Lillian Russell *WhAm 1*
Moore, Littleton Wilde 1835-1911 *BiDrAC, TwCBDA, WhAmP*
Moore, Louis Herbert 1860-1918 *WhAm 1*
Moore, Lyle Stickley 1885-1954 *WhAm 3*
Moore, Lyman Sweet 1910-1952 *WhAm 3*
Moore, Margaret King *WomWWA 14*
Moore, Marguerite 1849- *AmWom*
Moore, Marianne Craig 1887-1972 *EncAB, McGEWB, NatCAB 57, WebAB, WhAm 5*
Moore, Mark Egbert 1871- *WhAm 5*
Moore, Marshal F *BiAUS*
Moore, Martin 1790-1866 *ApCAB, Drake*
Moore, Mary Carr 1873-1957 *WhAm 3, WomWWA 14*
Moore, Mary Norman 1874- *WhAm 5, WomWWA 14*
Moore, Matthew Coleman 1874-1952 *NatCAB 41*
Moore, Maurice 1670?-1740 *ApCAB*
Moore, Maurice 1670?-1745? *NatCAB 10*
Moore, Maurice 1735-1776 *Drake*
Moore, Maurice 1735-1777 *ApCAB, DcAmB, NatCAB 10, TwCBDA, WhAm H*
Moore, Maurice Malcolm 1884-1961 *WhAm 4*
Moore, Merrill 1903-1957 *WhAm 3*
Moore, Miles Conway 1845-1919 *NatCAB 23*
Moore, Miles Conway 1845-1920 *WhAm 1*
Moore, Milton Harvey 1879- *WhAm 5*
Moore, Minor Lee 1876-1958 *NatCAB 48*
Moore, Mollie Evelyn *NotAW*
Moore, Morris *NewYHSD*
Moore, Myra Drake 1856- *WomWWA 14*
Moore, N Hudson d1927 *WhAm 1, WomWWA 14*
Moore, Nathan Grier 1853-1946 *NatCAB 42, WhAm 2*
Moore, Nathaniel Drummond 1880-1940 *WhAm 1*
Moore, Nathaniel Fish 1782-1872 *ApCAB, DcAmB, Drake, NatCAB 6, TwCBDA, WhAm H*
Moore, Neil Sewell 1887-1958 *NatCAB 43*
Moore, Nelson Augustus 1824-1902 *NewYHSD*
Moore, Nicholas d1689 *AmBi, DcAmB, NatCAB 16*
Moore, Nicholas Ruxton 1756-1816 *BiAUS, BiDrAC, WhAmP*
Moore, Sir Norman 1847-1922 *BiHiMed*
Moore, Orren Cheney 1839-1893 *BiDrAC, WhAm H*
Moore, Orval Floyd 1889-1958 *WhAm 3*

Moore, Oscar Fitzallen 1817-1885 *BiAUS,*
BiDrAC, WhAm H
Moore, Paul 1885-1959 *WhAm 3*
Moore, Paul H 1898-1964 *WhAm 4*
Moore, Paul John 1868-1938 *BiDrAC,*
WhAm 4
Moore, Peter Wredick 1859- *WhoColR*
Moore, Philip North 1849-1930 *DcAmB,*
WhAm 1
Moore, Philip Wyatt 1880- *WhAm 6*
Moore, Randle T 1875- *WhAm 5*
Moore, Ransom Asa 1861-1941 *NatCAB 37,*
WhAm 1
Moore, Raymond Cecil 1892-1974 *WhAm 6*
Moore, Rebecca Deming 1877- *WomWWA 14*
Moore, Richard Bishop 1871-1931 *AmBi,*
ApCAB X, DcAmB, NatCAB 40,
WhAm 1
Moore, Richard Channing 1762-1841 *ApCAB,*
DcAmB, Drake, NatCAB 7, TwCBDA,
WhAm H
Moore, Richard Curtis 1880-1966 *WhAm 4*
Moore, Richard Lawson 1875-1944 *NatCAB 35*
Moore, Robert 1778-1831 *BiAUS, BiDrAC,*
WhAm H
Moore, Robert 1838-1922 *NatCAB 12,*
WhAm 1
Moore, Robert Allan 1901-1971 *WhAm 5*
Moore, Robert Allen 1901-1971 *NatCAB 57*
Moore, Robert Emmett 1849- *NatCAB 18*
Moore, Robert Foster 1902-1964 *WhAm 4*
Moore, Robert H 1886-1962 *NatCAB 51*
Moore, Robert H 1907-1972 *WhAm 5*
Moore, Robert Lee 1867-1940 *BiDrAC,*
WhAm 4
Moore, Robert Lee 1870- *WhAm 5*
Moore, Robert Lee 1882-1974 *WhAm 6*
Moore, Robert Martin 1884-1952 *WhAm 3*
Moore, Robert McDonald 1907-1961
NatCAB 49, WhAm 4
Moore, Robert Murray 1901-1964 *WhAm 4*
Moore, Robert S 1857-1930 *WhAm 1*
Moore, Robert Thomas 1882-1958 *WhAm 3*
Moore, Robert Walton 1859-1941 *BiDrAC,*
WhAm 1
Moore, Robert Webber 1862- *WhAm 4*
Moore, Roberts Cosby 1905-1969 *WhAm 5*
Moore, Ronald Prinz 1897-1968 *NatCAB 56*
Moore, Roy 1887-1954 *NatCAB 41, WhAm 3*
Moore, Roy W 1891-1971 *WhAm 5*
Moore, Roy Webb 1884-1958 *NatCAB 48*
Moore, Rufus Scudder 1855- *NatCAB 17*
Moore, Rupert Eastmer 1872- *WhAm 5*
Moore, S McD 1796-1875 *BiAUS*
Moore, Samuel 1774-1861 *BiAUS, BiDrAC,*
NatCAB 12, TwCBDA, WhAm H
Moore, Samuel 1877-1934 *NatCAB 42,*
WhAm 1
Moore, Samuel B 1789-1846 *NatCAB 10*
Moore, Samuel Campbell 1872-1953
NatCAB 42
Moore, Samuel McDowell 1796-1875 *ApCAB,*
BiDrAC, WhAm H
Moore, Samuel Preston 1813-1889 *BiDConf,*
DcAmB, NatCAB 18, TwCBDA,
WhAm H
Moore, Samuel Wallace 1862-1938 *NatCAB 28,*
WhAm 1
Moore, Sarah Wool 1846- *AmWom*
Moore, Sherwood 1880-1963 *WhAm 4*
Moore, Stanford 1913- *WebAB*
Moore, Stephen 1835-1920 *WhAm 1*
Moore, Susanne Vandegrift 1848- *AmWom*
Moore, Sydenham 1817-1862 *BiAUS, BiDrAC,*
TwCBDA, WhAm H
Moore, Thomas *NewYHSD*
Moore, Thomas 1689- *ApCAB*
Moore, Thomas 1759-1822 *BiAUS, BiDrAC,*
WhAm H, WhAmP
Moore, Thomas 1849-1917 *NatCAB 17*
Moore, Thomas Channing 1872- *ApCAB X*
Moore, Thomas Clay 1882- *WhoColR*
Moore, Thomas Jefferson 1840-1898
NatCAB 16
Moore, Thomas Joseph 1864- *WhAm 4*
Moore, Thomas Justin 1890-1958 *NatCAB 47,*
WhAm 3
Moore, Thomas Love d1862 *BiDrAC,*

Moore, *WhAm H*
Moore, Thomas Morrell 1856- *WhAm 4*
Moore, Thomas Overton d1876 *BiAUS*
Moore, Thomas Overton 1804-1876 *BiDConf,*
DcAmB, WhAm H
Moore, Thomas Overton 1805-1876 *NatCAB 10,*
TwCBDA
Moore, Thomas Patrick 1795-1853 *BiAUS,*
Drake
Moore, Thomas Patrick 1796?-1853 *DcAmB*
Moore, Thomas Patrick 1797-1853 *ApCAB,*
BiDrAC, NatCAB 5, TwCBDA
Moore, Thomas Robinson 1870-1937
NatCAB 27
Moore, Thomas S *BiAUS*
Moore, Thomas Verner 1818-1871 *NatCAB 19,*
TwCBDA
Moore, Thomas Verner 1877-1926 *WhAm 1*
Moore, Thomas Verner 1877-1969 *WhAm 5*
Moore, Thomas Vernon 1818-1871 *ApCAB*
Moore, Thomas Waterman 1866- *WhAm 5*
Moore, Tom James 1892- *IlBEAAW*
Moore, Underhill 1879-1949 *WhAm 2*
Moore, Veranus Alva 1859-1931 *DcAmB,*
NatCAB 22, WhAm 1
Moore, Victor F 1876-1962 *WhAm 4,*
WhAm 5
Moore, Vida Frank d1915 *WhAm 1*
Moore, W Bedford, Jr. 1886-1953 *NatCAB 40*
Moore, W Cabell 1879-1960 *NatCAB 50*
Moore, Walter Bedford 1863-1947 *WhAm 2*
Moore, Walter Burritt 1836- *ApCAB*
Moore, Walter Harvey 1887-1961 *NatCAB 49*
Moore, Walter Howard 1844-1917 *NatCAB 18*
Moore, Walter William 1857-1926 *NatCAB 27,*
WhAm 1
Moore, Walton Norwood 1864- *WhAm 4*
Moore, Warren G, Sr. 1906-1964 *WhAm 4*
Moore, William *DcScB, NewYHSD*
Moore, William 1699-1783 *ApCAB, DcAmB,*
TwCBDA, WhAm H
Moore, William 1734-1793 *NatCAB 2,*
TwCBDA
Moore, William 1735?-1793 *ApCAB, DcAmB,*
WhAm H
Moore, William 1754-1824 *ApCAB*
Moore, William 1790-1851 *NewYHSD*
Moore, William 1810-1878 *BiAUS, BiDrAC,*
WhAm H
Moore, William 1827-1904 *NatCAB 15*
Moore, William Adolphus 1819-1891
NatCAB 2
Moore, William Augustus 1864-1925
NatCAB 20
Moore, William Austin 1823- *NatCAB 9*
Moore, William Carric 1844-1915 *NatCAB 38*
Moore, William Charles 1864- *WhAm 4*
Moore, William Davis 1882-1950 *NatCAB 39*
Moore, William Emmet d1941 *WhAm 1,*
WhAm 2
Moore, William Eves 1823-1899 *ApCAB,*
WhAm 1
Moore, William F 1855-1927 *ApCAB X*
Moore, William F 1899-1975 *WhAm 6*
Moore, William Garrett 1874-1944 *WhAm 2*
Moore, William George 1934-1970 *WhAm 5*
Moore, William Graham 1868-1917
NatCAB 17
Moore, William Henry 1848-1923 *DcAmB,*
NatCAB 14, NatCAB 23, WebAB,
WhAm 1
Moore, William Henry Helme 1824- *NatCAB 5*
Moore, William Preston 1873- *WhoColR*
Moore, William Robert 1830-1909 *BiDrAC,*
NatCAB 8, TwCBDA
Moore, William Sturtevant 1846-1914
NatCAB 16, WhAm 1
Moore, William Sutton 1822-1877 *BiAUS,*
BiDrAC, WhAm H
Moore, William Thomas 1832-1926 *DcAmB,*
WhAm 4
Moore, Willis Luther 1856-1927 *AmBi,*
ApCAB Sup, NatCAB 13, NatCAB 21,
TwCBDA, WhAm 1
Moore, Wilmer Lee 1868- *WhAm 4*
Moore, Zephaniah Swift 1770-1823 *ApCAB,*
DcAmB, Drake, NatCAB 5, TwCBDA,
WhAm H

Moorehead, Agnes Robertson 1900-1974
WhAm 6
Moorehead, Frederick Brown 1878-1944
WhAm 2
Moorehead, Scipio *NewYHSD*
Moorehead, Singleton Peabody 1900-1964
NatCAB 54, WhAm 4
Moorehead, Tom VanHorn 1898- *BiDrAC*
Moorehead, Warren King 1866-1939
NatCAB 10, NatCAB 36, WhAm 1
Moorehead, William Gallogly 1836-1914
DcAmB, WhAm 1
Moorer, Thomas Hinman 1912- *WebAMB*
Moores, Charles Bruce 1849- *WhAm 1*
Moores, Charles Washington 1862-1923
WhAm 1
Moores, Elizabeth Nichols *WomWWA 14*
Moores, Harry C 1881-1965 *NatCAB 50*
Moores, James Henry 1846-1918 *WhAm 1*
Moores, Merrill 1856-1929 *BiDrAC, WhAm 1,*
WhAmP
Moorhead, Dudley Thomas 1913-1972 *WhAm 5*
Moorhead, Frank Graham 1876- *WhAm 3*
Moorhead, Harley G 1876-1944 *WhAm 2*
Moorhead, Helen Armstrong Howell 1882-
WomWWA 14
Moorhead, Hugh McKee 1879-1961
NatCAB 50
Moorhead, James Kennedy 1806-1884 *ApCAB,*
BiAUS, BiDrAC, DcAmB, NatCAB 4,
TwCBDA, WhAm H
Moorhead, John U *ApCAB X*
Moorhead, Louis David 1892-1928 *WhAm 1*
Moorhead, Louis David 1892-1951 *WhAm 3*
Moorhead, Maxwell K 1877- *WhAm 5*
Moorhead, Robert Lowry 1875- *WhAm 5*
Moorhead, William Alexander 1886-1948
NatCAB 37
Moorhead, William Singer 1883-1952
NatCAB 41, WhAm 3
Moorhead, William Singer 1923- *BiDrAC*
Moorhouse, Glen Erle 1908-1963 *NatCAB 50*
Moorhouse, Harold Roy 1903-1961 *WhAm 4*
Moorhouse, William Russell 1873-1925
NatCAB 23
Moorland, Jesse Edward 1863- *WhoColR*
Moorman, Charles Harwood 1875-1938
NatCAB 33
Moorman, Charles Harwood 1876-1938
WhAm 1
Moorman, Henry DeHaven 1880-1939 *BiDrAC,*
WhAm 6
Moorman, Robert Burrus Buckner 1904-1974
WhAm 6
Moorman, Robert Wardlaw 1919-1974
WhAm 6
Moors, John Farwell 1861-1953 *NatCAB 41*
Moorshead, Alfred John 1853-1939 *NatCAB 36*
Moos, Charles J 1880- *WhAm 6*
Moosbrugger, Frederick 1900-1974 *WhAm 6*
Mooser, William 1834-1896 *WhAm H*
Moosmuller, Oswald William 1832-1901
DcAmB, WhAm H
Moot, Adelbert 1854-1929 *NatCAB 24,*
WhAm 1
Moot, Carrie A VanNess 1861- *WomWWA 14*
Moots, Cornelia Moore Chillson 1843- *AmWom*
Mootz, Herman Edwin 1870-1949 *NatCAB 37*
Mopope, Stephen 1898- *IlBEAAW*
Moque, Alice Lee 1865-1919 *WhAm 1*
Moquihuix 1420?-1470 *ApCAB*
Mora, Antonio Maximo 1818-1897 *ApCAB Sup*
Mora, Diego De 1494?-1555? *ApCAB*
Mora, Francis 1827- *ApCAB, NatCAB 12,*
TwCBDA
Mora, Francis Luis 1874-1940 *IlBEAAW,*
NatCAB 30, WhAm 1
Mora, Jose Antonio 1897-1975 *WhAm 6*
Mora, Jose Joaquin 1784-1848? *ApCAB*
Mora, Joseph Jacinto 1876-1947 *IlBEAAW,*
WhAm 2
Mora Miranda, Marcial 1895-1972 *WhAm 5*
Moraes, E Silva, Antonio De 1756-1825 *ApCAB*
Moraes-Barros, Prudente Jose De 1841-
ApCAB Sup
Morairty, Albert Francis 1888-1948
NatCAB 36
Morais, Sabato 1823-1897 *DcAmB, DcAmReB,*

NatCAB 10, TwCBDA, WhAm H
Morais, Sabato 1824-1897 *ApCAB*
Morales, Agustin 1810-1872 *ApCAB*
Morales, Juan Bautista 1788-1856 *ApCAB*
Morales, Luis De 1519?-1586 *McGEWB*
Morales, Pedro 1537-1614 *ApCAB*
Morales, Sanchez 1867-1934 *WhAm 1*
Morales, Sebastian A De 1823- *ApCAB*
Morales-Lemus, Jose 1808-1870 *ApCAB*
Moran, Mr. *NewYHSD*
Moran, Alfred E 1928-1973 *WhAm 6*
Moran, Annette 1835- *WhAm 1*
Moran, Benjamin 1820-1886 *ApCAB, BiAUS,*
DcAmB, Drake, NatCAB 10, TwCBDA,
WhAm H
Moran, Bernard James 1911-1965 *NatCAB 54*
Moran, C *NewYHSD*
Moran, Daniel Edward 1864-1937 *DcAmB S2,*
WhAm 1
Moran, Daniel James 1888-1948 *WhAm 2*
Moran, Edward 1829-1901 *AmBi, ApCAB,*
DcAmB, IIBEAAW, NatCAB 11,
NewYHSD, TwCBDA, WhAm H
Moran, Edward Carleton, Jr. 1894-1967
BiDrAC, NatCAB 53, WhAm 4
Moran, Edward Joseph 1893-1957 *NatCAB 44*
Moran, Edward Percy 1862-1935 *AmBi,*
NatCAB 10
Moran, Eugene Francis 1872-1961 *NatCAB 53,*
WhAm 4
Moran, Francis Thomas 1865-1929 *WhAm 1*
Moran, Fred T 1855- *WhAm 4*
Moran, J *NewYHSD*
Moran, James Thomas 1864-1936 *WhAm 1,*
WhAm 1C
Moran, Jeannie Blackburn 1850- *ApCAB X*
Moran, John *NewYHSD*
Moran, John Henry 1890-1954 *WhAm 3*
Moran, John Joseph 1915-1969 *WhAm 5*
Moran, John Vallee 1846-1920 *NatCAB 42*
Moran, Julia Porcelli 1917-1974 *WhAm 6*
Moran, Leon 1863-1941 *ApCAB*
Moran, Leon 1864-1941 *NatCAB 11,*
NatCAB 30, TwCBDA, WhAm 1
Moran, Mary Nimmo 1842-1899 *ApCAB,*
NatCAB 22, NotAW, TwCBDA
Moran, Michael Moses 1901-1955 *NatCAB 43*
Moran, Percy 1862-1935 *ApCAB, TwCBDA,*
WhAm 1
Moran, Peter 1841-1914 *AmBi, DcAmB,*
IIBEAAW, NewYHSD, WhAm 1
Moran, Peter 1842-1914 *ApCAB, NatCAB 11,*
TwCBDA
Moran, Richard Bartholomew 1895-1972
WhAm 5
Moran, Robert 1857- *NatCAB 18, WhAm 4*
Moran, Thomas 1837-1926 *AmBi, ApCAB,*
DcAmB, EncAAH, IIBEAAW, McGEWB,
NatCAB 3, NatCAB 22, NewYHSD,
REnAW, TwCBDA, WhAm HA,
WhAm 1, WhAm 4
Moran, Thomas A 1839-1904 *WhAm 1*
Moran, Thomas Francis 1866-1928 *WhAm 1*
Moran, Thomas Lawrence 1899-1963
NatCAB 50
Moran, W H 1889-1975 *WhAm 6*
Moran, William Edward, Jr. 1916-1970
WhAm 5
Moran, William Gerard 1896-1967 *NatCAB 53*
Moran, William Joseph 1859- *WhAm 4*
Morandi, Giorgio 1890-1964 *WhAm 4*
Morang, Alfred Gwynne 1901-1958 *IIBEAAW*
Morang, Dorothy 1906- *IIBEAAW*
Morange, Etienne *NewYHSD*
Moranges, Etienne *NewYHSD*
Morano, Albert Paul 1908- *BiDrAC*
Moranville, John Francis 1760-1824 *ApCAB*
Morard DeGalle, Justin Bonaventure 1741-1809
ApCAB
Moras, Ferdinand 1821-1908 *NewYHSD*
Morat, Jean-Pierre 1846-1920 *DcScB*
Moraud, Dieudonne Gabriel Charles Henry
1503?-1572 *ApCAB*
Moravia, Alberto 1907- *McGEWB*
Morawetz, Albert Richard 1856- *WhAm 4*
Morawetz, Victor 1859-1938 *ApCAB X,*
DcAmB S2, NatCAB 28, WhAm 1
Moray, Sir Robert 1608?-1673 *DcScB*

Morazan, Francisco 1799-1842 *ApCAB, Drake*
Morazan, Jose Francisco 1792-1842 *McGEWB*
Morcom, Clifford Bawden 1885-1951 *WhAm 3*
Morcombe, Katherine Elizabeth 1876-
WomWWA 14
Morde, Theodore A 1911-1954 *WhAm 3*
Mordecai, Alfred 1804-1887 *ApCAB, DcAmB,*
Drake, NatCAB 10, WhAm H
Mordecai, Alfred 1840-1920 *NatCAB 10,*
WhAm 1
Mordecai, George 1801-1871 *NatCAB 10*
Mordecai, Jacob 1762-1838 *NatCAB 10*
Mordecai, Moses Cohen 1804-1888 *DcAmB,*
WhAm H
Mordecai, Samuel Fox 1852-1927 *NatCAB 35,*
WhAm 1
Mordecai, T Moultrie 1855- *WhAm 4*
Morden, Charles Whitney 1888-1951
NatCAB 42
Morden, William J 1886-1958 *WhAm 3*
Mordvinoff, Nicolas 1911-1973 *WhAm 6*
More, Brookes 1859-1942 *WhAm 2*
More, Charles Church 1875-1949 *NatCAB 38,*
WhAm 3
More, Enoch Anson 1854-1932 *WhAm 1*
More, Henry 1614-1687 *DcScB*
More, Herman 1887-1968 *WhAm 5*
More, Herman 1887-1968 *WhAm 5*
More, J Marion 1827?-1868 *REnAW*
More, John Herron 1903-1970 *WhAm 5*
More, Louis Trenchard 1870-1944 *WhAm 2*
More, Louise Bolard 1876- *WomWWA 14*
More, Nicholas d1689 *AmBi, ApCAB,*
DcAmB, NatCAB 25, WhAm H
More, Paul Elmer 1864-1937 *AmBi,*
DcAmB S2, NatCAB 27, TwCBDA,
WebAB, WhAm 1
More, Thomas *NewYHSD*
More, Sir Thomas 1478-1535 *McGEWB*
Moreau, Arthur Edmond 1885-1951 *WhAm 3*
Moreau, Daniel Howard 1898-1963 *NatCAB 53*
Moreau, Jean Victor 1763-1813 *ApCAB,*
WhoMilH
Moreau, Louis Zepherin 1824- *ApCAB*
Moreau-Christophe, Louis Mathurin 1799-1883
ApCAB
Moreau DeSaint-Mery, Mederic-Louis-Elie
1750-1819 *AmBi, ApCAB, DcAmB,*
WhAm H
Moreau-Lislet, Louis Casimir Elisabeth
1767-1832 *DcAmB, WhAm H*
Moreaux, Amable Oli 1874-1942 *WhAm 2*
Moredock, Austin Lane 1870-1954 *NatCAB 43*
Moreell, Ben 1892- *WebAMB*
Morehead, Albert Hodges 1909-1966 *WhAm 4*
Morehead, Carl Edgar 1906-1960 *NatCAB 50*
Morehead, Charles Allen 1901-1957 *WhAm 3*
Morehead, Charles Robert 1836-1921
NatCAB 8
Morehead, Charles Slaughter 1802-1868
ApCAB, BiAUS, BiDrAC, DcAmB, Drake,
NatCAB 13, TwCBDA, WhAm H,
WhAmP
Morehead, French Hugh 1883-1949 *WhAm 3*
Morehead, I T *BiAUS*
Morehead, James Turner 1797-1854 *ApCAB,*
BiAUS, BiDrAC, DcAmB, Drake,
NatCAB 13, TwCBDA, WhAm H
Morehead, James Turner 1799-1875 *BiDrAC,*
WhAm H
Morehead, John Alfred 1867-1936 *NatCAB 13,*
WhAm 1
Morehead, John Henry 1861-1942 *BiDrAC,*
NatCAB 15, WhAm 2, WhAmP
Morehead, John Lindsay 1894-1964 *WhAm 4*
Morehead, John Motley 1796-1866 *ApCAB,*
BiDConf, DcAmB, Drake, NatCAB 4,
TwCBDA, WhAm H
Morehead, John Motley 1866-1923 *BiDrAC,*
WhAm 1
Morehead, John Motley 1870-1965 *WhAm 4*
Morehead, Turner 1757- *NatCAB 13*
Morehous, Philo 1812-1881 *ApCAB X,*
NatCAB 17
Morehouse, Albert Kellogg 1900-1955
NatCAB 45, WhAm 3
Morehouse, Albert Pricket 1835-1891 *TwCBDA*
Morehouse, Daniel Walter 1876-1941
NatCAB 33, WhAm 1

Morehouse, Frances M I d1945 *WhAm 2*
Morehouse, Frederic Cook 1868-1932 *WhAm 1*
Morehouse, George Pierson 1859- *WhAm 4*
Morehouse, George Read 1829-1905 *ApCAB,*
WhAm 1
Morehouse, Henry Lyman 1834-1917 *DcAmB,*
TwCBDA, WhAm 1
Morehouse, Julius Stanley 1894-1961 *WhAm 4*
Morehouse, Linden Husted 1842-1915 *WhAm 1*
Morehouse, Linden Husted 1900-1967 *WhAm 4*
Morehouse, Lyman Foote 1874- *WhAm 5*
Morehouse, Max 1865-1923 *NatCAB 6*
Morehouse, P Gad Bryan 1893-1962 *WhAm 5*
Morehouse, Ward 1901-1966 *WhAm 4*
Morehouse, William Russell 1879-1937
NatCAB 27, WhAm 1
Morein, J Augustus 1810?- *NewYHSD*
Moreira, Luiz DaCunha 1777-1865 *ApCAB*
Morel *NewYHSD*
Morel, Jean 1903-1975 *WhAm 6*
Moreland, Augustus *NewYHSD*
Moreland, Edward Leyburn 1885-1951
NatCAB 40, WhAm 3
Moreland, James Rogers 1879-1955 *NatCAB 45*
Moreland, John F *WhoColR*
Moreland, John Richard 1880-1947 *WhAm 2*
Moreland, Mary Leona 1859- *AmWom,*
WomWWA 14
Moreland, William Hall 1861-1946 *ApCAB Sup,*
NatCAB 13, TwCBDA, WhAm 2
Moreland, William Haywood 1879-1944
WhAm 2
Moreley, James *NewYHSD*
Morell, Anthony Urban 1875-1924 *NatCAB 20*
Morell, George 1786-1845 *ApCAB, Drake,*
NatCAB 5, TwCBDA
Morell, George Webb 1815-1883 *ApCAB,*
DcAmB, NatCAB 4, TwCBDA,
WhAm H
Morell, Parker 1906-1943 *WhAm 2*
Morell, Rosa Blanca Ortiz 1902-1972 *WhAm 6*
Morell, William *ApCAB, NatCAB 7*
Morell, William Nelson 1898-1971 *NatCAB 56,*
WhAm 5
Morell DeSanta Cruz, Pedro Agustin 1694-1768
ApCAB
Morelock, George Leslie 1880- *WhAm 6*
Morelock, Horace Wilson 1873- *WhAm 5*
Morelock, Maurice Melvin 1886-1957
NatCAB 47
Morelos, Jose Maria 1765-1815 *ApCAB,*
McGEWB
Morelos, Jose Maria 1780-1815 *Drake*
Morency, Paul Wilfrid 1899-1974 *WhAm 6*
Moreno, Arthur Alphonse 1883-1950 *WhAm 3*
Moreno, Francis Garcia Drigo S d1846
NatCAB 12
Moreno, Francisco 1827- *ApCAB*
Moreno, Jacob L 1889-1974 *WhAm 6*
Moreno, Manuel 1781-1857 *ApCAB*
Moreno, Mariano 1778-1811 *ApCAB*
Moreno-Lacalle, Julian 1881- *WhAm 6*
Mores, Antoine A M V M DeV, Marquis De
1858-1896 *REnAW*
Mores, S *NewYHSD*
Moreschi, Joseph V d1970 *WhAm 5*
Moresi, Harry James, Jr. 1932-1971 *WhAm 6*
Moreton, Clara *NotAW*
Moretz, Joseph Alfred 1880-1942 *NatCAB 32*
Morewood, George *NewYHSD*
Morey, Agnes Hosmer *BiCAW*
Morey, Anna Riordan 1859- *WomWWA 14*
Morey, Arthur Thornton 1875-1936 *WhAm 1*
Morey, Charles Rufus 1877-1955 *WhAm 3*
Morey, Charles William 1875-1961 *WhAm 4*
Morey, Chester S 1847- *WhAm 1*
Morey, Edward *NewYHSD*
Morey, Frank 1840- *BiAUS*
Morey, Frank 1840-1889 *BiDrAC, WhAm H*
Morey, Frank 1840-1890 *TwCBDA*
Morey, George Washington 1888-1965
NatCAB 53
Morey, Henry Lee 1841-1902 *BiDrAC,*
TwCBDA
Morey, Henry Martyn 1837- *WhAm 3*
Morey, Jeannette Metcalf 1855- *WomWWA 14*
Morey, John William 1878-1956 *NatCAB 47,*
WhAm 3

Morey, Lee B 1894-1973 *WhAm 6*
Morey, Lloyd 1886-1965 *WhAm 4*
Morey, Samuel 1762-1843 *AmBi, ApCAB, DcAmB, NatCAB 11, TwCBDA, WhAm H*
Morey, Sylvester Marvin 1896-1975 *WhAm 6*
Morey, Victor Pinkerton 1905-1951 *WhAm 3*
Morey, William Carey 1843-1925 *TwCBDA, WhAm 1*
Morfa, Raymond J 1894-1952 *WhAm 3*
Morfit, Campbell 1820-1897 *ApCAB, DcAmB, Drake, TwCBDA, WhAm H*
Morfit, Clarence 1828- *ApCAB*
Morford, Henry 1823-1881 *ApCAB, DcAmB, WhAm H*
Morford, James Richard 1898-1959 *WhAm 4*
Morford, Kenneth James 1897-1961 *NatCAB 50*
Morgagni, Giovanni Battista 1682-1771 *AsBiEn, BiHiMed, DcScB, McGEWB*
Morgan, A W *NewYHSD*
Morgan, Abel 1637-1722 *Drake*
Morgan, Abel 1673-1722 *ApCAB, DcAmB, WhAm H*
Morgan, Abel 1713-1785 *ApCAB*
Morgan, Abner 1746-1837 *NatCAB 6, TwCBDA*
Morgan, Adelia A 1845- *WomWWA 14*
Morgan, Albert Thomas 1872-1944 *NatCAB 35*
Morgan, Alexander Perry 1900-1968 *NatCAB 55*
Morgan, Alfred Kenneth 1901-1969 *NatCAB 55*
Morgan, Alfred Powell 1889-1972 *WhAm 5*
Morgan, Algernon Sidney Mountain 1831-1914 *NatCAB 16*
Morgan, Alice M Hill *WomWWA 14*
Morgan, Allie Dexter 1886-1964 *NatCAB 51*
Morgan, Angela d1957 *WhAm 3*
Morgan, Ann Haven 1882-1966 *WhAm 4*
Morgan, Anna 1851-1936 *NatCAB 17, NotAW, WhAm 1, WomWWA 14*
Morgan, Anne 1873-1952 *DcAmB S5, WhAm 3*
Morgan, Anne Eugenia Felicia 1845-1909 *AmWom, WhAm 1*
Morgan, Appleton 1845-1928 *WhAm 1*
Morgan, Appleton 1846-1928 *NatCAB 9, TwCBDA*
Morgan, Arthur Ernest 1878-1975 *BiDAmEd, WhAm 6*
Morgan, Arthur James, Sr 1893-1973 *NatCAB 57*
Morgan, Barbara Spofford 1887-1971 *NatCAB 56*
Morgan, Bayard Quincy 1883-1967 *WhAm 4*
Morgan, Benjamin Stephen 1854-1945 *NatCAB 37*
Morgan, Brooks Sanderson 1877- *WhAm 5*
Morgan, Carey E 1860-1925 *WhAm 1*
Morgan, Caroline Starr *WhAm 5*
Morgan, Carrie E *WomWWA 14*
Morgan, Casey Bruce 1867-1933 *WhAm 1*
Morgan, Charles 1795-1878 *ApCAB, DcAmB, TwCBDA, WhAm H*
Morgan, Charles 1894-1958 *WhAm 3*
Morgan, Charles Carroll 1832-1918 *WhAm 1*
Morgan, Charles Edgar 1900-1960 *NatCAB 48*
Morgan, Charles Eldridge, III 1876-1947 *WhAm 2*
Morgan, Charles Hale 1834-1875 *ApCAB, NatCAB 5, TwCBDA*
Morgan, Charles Henry 1842-1912 *BiAUS, BiDrAC, WhAmP*
Morgan, Charles Henry 1843-1912 *TwCBDA, WhAm 1*
Morgan, Charles Herbert 1852-1939 *WhAm 1*
Morgan, Charles Hill 1831-1911 *DcAmB, NatCAB 13, NatCAB 23, WhAm 1*
Morgan, Charles L 1878- *WhoColR*
Morgan, Charles Stillman 1891-1969 *NatCAB 54*
Morgan, Charles W 1790-1853 *ApCAB, Drake, TwCBDA*
Morgan, Christopher 1808-1877 *ApCAB, BiAUS, BiDrAC, TwCBDA, WhAm H*
Morgan, Clarence 1869-1937 *NatCAB 28*
Morgan, Clarence Hall 1879-1956 *NatCAB 52*

Morgan, Clement Garnett *WhoColR*
Morgan, Clifford Thomas 1915-1976 *WhAm 6*
Morgan, Clifford Veryl 1901-1954 *WhAm 3*
Morgan, Clinton Emory 1882-1956 *WhAm 3*
Morgan, Conway Lloyd 1852-1936 *McGEWB*
Morgan, Conwy Lloyd 1852-1936 *DcScB*
Morgan, D Parker 1843-1915 *NatCAB 2*
Morgan, Dale L 1914-1971 *REnAW*
Morgan, Daniel d1802 *BiAUS*
Morgan, Daniel 1733?-1802 *TwCBDA*
Morgan, Daniel 1735?-1802 *McGEWB*
Morgan, Daniel 1736-1802 *AmBi, ApCAB, BiDrAC, DcAmB, Drake, NatCAB 1, WebAB, WebAMB, WhAm H, WhoMilH*
Morgan, Daniel Davies 1881-1960 *NatCAB 48*
Morgan, Daniel Edgar 1877-1949 *NatCAB 37, WhAm 2*
Morgan, Daniel Nash 1844-1931 *AmBi, NatCAB 28, WhAm 1*
Morgan, David Banister 1773-1848 *ApCAB, Drake*
Morgan, David Bruce 1869-1943 *NatCAB 33*
Morgan, David E 1849-1912 *NatCAB 14, WhAm 1*
Morgan, David P *NewYHSD*
Morgan, David Percy 1894-1974 *WhAm 6*
Morgan, David Pierce 1831-1886 *NatCAB 16*
Morgan, Dayton Samuel 1819-1890 *NatCAB 22*
Morgan, DeWitt Farmer 1868-1940 *NatCAB 42*
Morgan, DeWitt Schuyler 1890-1944 *WhAm 2*
Morgan, Dick Thompson 1853-1920 *BiDrAC, WhAmP*
Morgan, Dick Thompson 1854-1920 *NatCAB 12, WhAm 1*
Morgan, Edith Galt 1915-1968 *NatCAB 55*
Morgan, Edmund Morris, Jr. 1878-1966 *WhAm 4*
Morgan, Edward Barber 1806-1881 *ApCAB*
Morgan, Edward Broadbent 1862-1935 *WhAm 1*
Morgan, Edward M 1855-1925 *WhAm 1*
Morgan, Edwin B 1806-1881 *BiAUS*
Morgan, Edwin Barber 1806-1881 *DcAmB, NatCAB 13, WhAm H*
Morgan, Edwin Barbour 1806-1881 *BiDrAC*
Morgan, Edwin Border 1806-1881 *TwCBDA*
Morgan, Edwin D 1811-1883 *BiAUS*
Morgan, Edwin Denison 1811-1883 *AmBi, DcAmB, WhAm H*
Morgan, Edwin Denison 1854-1933 *NatCAB 44*
Morgan, Edwin Dennison 1811-1883 *ApCAB, BiDrAC, Drake, NatCAB 3, TwCBDA, WhAmP*
Morgan, Edwin Franklin Abell 1892-1965 *WhAm 4*
Morgan, Edwin Lee 1855-1920 *NatCAB 19, WhAm 4*
Morgan, Edwin Vernon 1865-1934 *AmBi, DcAmB S1, NatCAB 14, NatCAB 39, WhAm 1*
Morgan, Edwin Wright 1814-1869 *ApCAB, TwCBDA*
Morgan, Elford C 1905-1962 *WhAm 5*
Morgan, Eliot S N 1832-1894 *WhAm H*
Morgan, Elizabeth Wetmore *WomWWA 14*
Morgan, Elonzo Tell 1875-1956 *NatCAB 49*
Morgan, Enoch 1676-1740 *ApCAB*
Morgan, Ephraim Franklin 1869-1950 *NatCAB 37, WhAm 2*
Morgan, Ezra Leonidas 1879-1937 *WhAm 1*
Morgan, F Corlies 1875-1939 *WhAm 1*
Morgan, Flora A Hower 1855- *WomWWA 14*
Morgan, Forrest 1852-1924 *WhAm 1*
Morgan, Frances Biddle Williams 1884- *WomWWA 14*
Morgan, Francis Patterson 1867- *WhAm 4*
Morgan, Frank 1890-1949 *NatCAB 57, WhAm 3*
Morgan, Frank Millett 1886-1966 *WhAm 4*
Morgan, Fred Bogardus 1874-1950 *WhAm 3*
Morgan, Fred Bruce, Jr. 1919-1975 *WhAm 6*
Morgan, Fred William 1854-1921 *NatCAB 19*
Morgan, Frederic Lindley 1889-1970 *WhAm 5*
Morgan, Sir Frederick 1894-1967 *WhWW-II*
Morgan, Frederick Charles 1884-1948 *NatCAB 36*
Morgan, G Campbell 1863- *WhAm 4*

Morgan, Garrett Agusta 1879- *WhoColR*
Morgan, Geoffrey Francis 1882-1952 *WhAm 3*
Morgan, George 1742-1810 *TwCBDA*
Morgan, George 1743-1810 *AmBi, DcAmB, WhAm H*
Morgan, George 1854-1936 *WhAm 1*
Morgan, George Allen *WhAm 5*
Morgan, George Dayton 1864-1937 *NatCAB 27*
Morgan, George Frederick 1846-1925 *NatCAB 27*
Morgan, George Hagar 1838-1911 *WhAm 1*
Morgan, George Horace 1855- *WhAm 4*
Morgan, George Nelson 1825-1866 *ApCAB*
Morgan, George O 1890-1958 *WhAm 3*
Morgan, George Wagner 1884-1957 *WhAm 3*
Morgan, George Washbourne 1822-1892 *ApCAB, TwCBDA*
Morgan, George Washbourne 1823-1892 *WhAm H*
Morgan, George Washington 1820-1893 *AmBi, ApCAB, BiAUS, BiDrAC, DcAmB, Drake, NatCAB 4, TwCBDA, WhAm H*
Morgan, George Wilson 1875-1931 *WhAm 1*
Morgan, George Wilson 1907-1969 *WhAm 5*
Morgan, Griffith 1819?- *NewYHSD*
Morgan, H Arnold 1903-1967 *NatCAB 54*
Morgan, Harcourt Alexander 1867-1950 *WhAm 3*
Morgan, Harry Dale 1885-1956 *WhAm 3*
Morgan, Harry Hays 1860-1933 *WhAm 1*
Morgan, Helen 1900?-1941 *DcAmB S3, NotAW*
Morgan, Helen Clarissa 1845- *ApCAB*
Morgan, Sir Henry 1637-1690 *ApCAB, Drake*
Morgan, Henry 1825-1884 *ApCAB*
Morgan, Henry Alfred 1861-1942 *NatCAB 34, WhAm 4*
Morgan, Henry James 1842- *ApCAB*
Morgan, Henry William 1853-1920 *NatCAB 8, WhAm 1*
Morgan, Henry Williams, Sr. 1881- *WhAm 6*
Morgan, Herbert Rollo 1875-1957 *DcScB, WhAm 3*
Morgan, Hugh Jackson 1893-1961 *WhAm 4*
Morgan, Ike 1871- *WhAm 5*
Morgan, Isaac B 1862-1945 *WhAm 3*
Morgan, Jacob L 1872- *WhAm 5*
Morgan, James 1756-1822 *BiAUS, BiDrAC, WhAm H*
Morgan, James 1861-1955 *WhAm 3*
Morgan, James Albert 1877-1951 *NatCAB 40*
Morgan, James Appleton 1845-1928 *AmBi*
Morgan, James Appleton 1850-1928 *ApCAB*
Morgan, James Bright 1833-1892 *BiDrAC, WhAm H*
Morgan, James Bright 1835-1892 *TwCBDA*
Morgan, James D 1810-1896 *Drake*
Morgan, James Dada 1810-1896 *DcAmB, WhAm H*
Morgan, James Dady 1810-1896 *ApCAB, TwCBDA*
Morgan, James Dudley 1862-1919 *ApCAB X, NatCAB 22, WhAm 1*
Morgan, James Francis 1862-1912 *NatCAB 40*
Morgan, James Henry 1857-1939 *WhAm 1*
Morgan, James Lafayette 1854-1938 *NatCAB 36*
Morgan, James Morris 1845-1928 *DcAmB, TwCBDA*
Morgan, James Norris 1839-1925 *WhAm 1*
Morgan, James W 1900-1957 *WhAm 3*
Morgan, Jerome J 1880-1967 *WhAm 4*
Morgan, Jesse Robert 1880- *WhAm 6*
Morgan, John 1725-1789 *ApCAB*
Morgan, John 1735-1789 *AmBi, BiDAmEd, BiHiMed, DcAmB, Drake, McGEWB, NatCAB 10, TwCBDA, WebAB, WhAm H*
Morgan, John 1803?-1884 *NatCAB 2*
Morgan, John 1845-1920 *NatCAB 19*
Morgan, John B, Jr. *NewYHSD*
Morgan, John Harcourt Alexander 1867-1950 *DcAmB S4, NatCAB 14*
Morgan, John Heath 1901-1971 *WhAm 5*
Morgan, John Hill 1870-1945 *WhAm 2*
Morgan, John Hunt 1825-1864 *AmBi, BiDConf, DcAmB, WebAB, WebAMB, WhAm H*
Morgan, John Hunt 1826-1864 *ApCAB, Drake,*

NatCAB 4, TwCBDA
Morgan, John Jacob Brooke 1888-1945
WhAm 2
Morgan, John Jordan d1849 *BiAUS*
Morgan, John Jordan 1768-1849 *TwCBDA*
Morgan, John Jordan 1770-1849 *BiDrAC,*
WhAm H
Morgan, John Livingston Rutgers 1872-1935
WhAm 1
Morgan, John Paul 1841-1879 *WhAm H*
Morgan, John Pierpont 1837-1913 *AmBi,*
ApCAB, ApCAB X, DcAmB, EncAB,
McGEWB, NatCAB 10, NatCAB 14,
TwCBDA, WebAB, WhAm 1
Morgan, John Pierpont 1867-1943 *ApCAB X,*
DcAmB S3, EncAB, McGEWB,
NatCAB 15, WhAm 2
Morgan, John Thoburn 1889-1970 *WhAm 5*
Morgan, John Titus 1831- *NatCAB 13*
Morgan, John Tyler 1824-1907 *AmBi, ApCAB,*
BiDConf, BiDrAC, DcAmB, NatCAB 1,
NatCAB 46, TwCBDA, WhAm 1,
WhAmP
Morgan, John Williams 1895-1964 *NatCAB 52*
Morgan, Joseph 1674-1740 *ApCAB*
Morgan, Joseph Richard 1868-1951 *NatCAB 40*
Morgan, Junius Spencer 1813-1890 *AmBi,*
ApCAB, DcAmB, McGEWB, TwCBDA,
WhAm H
Morgan, Junius Spencer 1867-1932 *NatCAB 30*
Morgan, Junius Spencer 1892-1960 *WhAm 4*
Morgan, Justin 1747-1798 *DcAmB, EncAAH,*
WhAm H
Morgan, Justin Colfax 1900-1959 *WhAm 3*
Morgan, Laura Dana 1874- *WomWWA 14*
Morgan, Letitia 1868- *WomWWA 14*
Morgan, Lewis Henry 1818-1881 *AmBi,*
ApCAB, BiDAmEd, DcAmB, EncAAH,
EncAB, McGEWB, NatCAB 6, REnAW,
TwCBDA, WebAB, WhAm H
Morgan, Lewis Lovering 1876-1950 *BiDrAC,*
WhAm 5
Morgan, Lillian Vaughan Sampson
WomWWA 14
Morgan, Louis M 1814-1852 *NewYHSD,*
WhAm H
Morgan, Louise 1886- *WomWWA 14*
Morgan, Sister M Sylvia d1964 *WhAm 4*
Morgan, Maria 1828-1892 *AmWom*
Morgan, Marian Baird 1875- *WomWWA 14*
Morgan, Marshall Shapleigh 1881- *WhAm 6*
Morgan, Mary Aull 1880- *WomWWA 14*
Morgan, Mary Curran 1867- *WomWWA 14*
Morgan, Mary Holmes *WomWWA 14*
Morgan, Mary Kimball 1861-1948 *NotAW*
Morgan, Matthew Somerville 1839-1890 *AmBi,*
ApCAB, DcAmB, NatCAB 5, TwCBDA,
WhAm H
Morgan, Maud 1860-1941 *NatCAB 32*
Morgan, Maud 1864-1941 *AmWom, ApCAB,*
WhAm 1, WomWWA 14
Morgan, Michael Ryan 1833-1911 *ApCAB,*
TwCBDA, WhAm 1
Morgan, Miles 1616-1699 *ApCAB, NatCAB 6,*
TwCBDA
Morgan, Minot Canfield 1876-1955 *NatCAB 49,*
WhAm 5
Morgan, Monta B, Sr. 1890-1958 *WhAm 3*
Morgan, Morris Hicky 1859-1910 *DcAmB,*
WhAm 1
Morgan, Newton 1840-1921 *NatCAB 19*
Morgan, Octavius 1850-1922 *NatCAB 8,*
NatCAB 16, WhAm 1
Morgan, Ora Sherman 1877-1961 *NatCAB 50,*
WhAm 4
Morgan, Otho Herron 1838-1923 *NatCAB 27*
Morgan, Paul Beagary 1869-1952 *WhAm 3*
Morgan, Percy Jaxon 1879-1943 *NatCAB 34*
Morgan, Percy Tredegar 1862- *WhAm 4*
Morgan, Peto Whittaker 1862-1953 *WhAm 4*
Morgan, Philip Hickey 1825-1900 *NatCAB 13*
Morgan, Philip Hicky 1825-1900 *ApCAB,*
DcAmB, TwCBDA, WhAm H
Morgan, Philip M 1896-1965 *WhAm 4*
Morgan, Ralph 1884-1965 *WhAm 4*
Morgan, Raymond A 1903-1964 *WhAm 4*
Morgan, Reed Augustus 1866-1959 *NatCAB 48*

Morgan, Robert Churchman 1873-1947
NatCAB 35
Morgan, Robert F 1929- *IIBEAAW*
Morgan, Robert Kenneth 1864- *WhAm 4*
Morgan, Robert M 1877-1959 *WhAm 3*
Morgan, Russell VanDyke 1893-1952 *WhAm 3*
Morgan, Samuel Asa Leland 1885-1954
NatCAB 45
Morgan, Samuel Tate 1857-1920 *ApCAB X,*
NatCAB 18, WhAm 1
Morgan, Shepard Ashman 1884-1968
NatCAB 56
Morgan, Simpson Harris 1821-1864 *BiDConf*
Morgan, Stephen 1854-1928 *BiDrAC,*
WhAm 4
Morgan, Stokeley Williams 1893-1963 *WhAm 4*
Morgan, Tali Esen 1858-1941 *WhAm 1*
Morgan, Tarquato *NewYHSD*
Morgan, Theophilous John 1872- *WhAm 5*
Morgan, Thomas *WhAm H*
Morgan, Thomas Alfred 1887-1967 *WhAm 4*
Morgan, Thomas Ellsworth 1906- *BiDrAC*
Morgan, Thomas Francis, Jr. 1895-1970
WhAm 5
Morgan, Thomas Henry 1857-1940 *NatCAB 30*
Morgan, Thomas Henry 1868-1926 *NatCAB 29*
Morgan, Thomas Hunt 1866-1945 *AsBiEn,*
DcAmB S3, DcScB, EncAAH, EncAB,
McGEWB, NatCAB 12, NatCAB 35,
WebAB, WhAm 2
Morgan, Thomas Jefferson 1839-1902
BiDAmEd, DcAmB, NatCAB 2, TwCBDA,
WhAm 1
Morgan, Thomas John 1847-1912 *WhAm 1*
Morgan, Thomas W *NewYHSD*
Morgan, Thomas W 1862- *WhAm 1*
Morgan, Tom P 1864-1929 *WhAm 1*
Morgan, Truman Spencer 1868-1940
NatCAB 37
Morgan, Wallace 1873-1948 *NatCAB 36,*
WhAm 2
Morgan, Walter Piety 1871-1958 *WhAm 3*
Morgan, Walter Sydney 1886-1954 *WhAm 3*
Morgan, William *NewYHSD*
Morgan, William 1774?-1826? *AmBi, DcAmB,*
WebAB, WhAm H
Morgan, William 1775?-1826? *ApCAB, Drake,*
NatCAB 7
Morgan, William 1826-1900 *ApCAB,*
NewYHSD
Morgan, William 1828-1900 *TwCBDA*
Morgan, William 1830-1900 *WhAm 1*
Morgan, William Berry 1858- *WhAm 4*
Morgan, William Conger 1874- *WhAm 5*
Morgan, William Edgar, II 1893-1961 *WhAm 4*
Morgan, William Fellowes 1860-1943
ApCAB X, NatCAB 16, NatCAB 32,
WhAm 2
Morgan, William Ferdinand 1815-1888
NatCAB 13
Morgan, William Ferdinand 1816-1888
TwCBDA
Morgan, William Ferdinand 1817-1888 *ApCAB*
Morgan, William Forbes 1879-1937 *WhAm 1*
Morgan, William Gerry 1868-1949 *NatCAB 38,*
WhAm 2
Morgan, William Henry 1818-1901 *BiDAmEd,*
NatCAB 8, WhAm 1
Morgan, William Henry 1865-1928 *WhAm 1*
Morgan, William John 1838-1904 *NatCAB 8*
Morgan, William Manning 1891-1957
NatCAB 46
Morgan, William McKendree 1869-1942
WhAm 2
Morgan, William Mitchell 1870-1935 *BiDrAC,*
WhAm 1
Morgan, William P *NewYHSD*
Morgan, William Pitt 1846-1914 *NatCAB 16*
Morgan, William Rufus 1898-1950 *NatCAB 39*
Morgan, William Sacheus 1864- *WhAm 5*
Morgan, William Stephen 1801- *BiAUS*
Morgan, William Stephen 1801-1876 *TwCBDA*
Morgan, William Stephen 1801-1878 *BiDrAC,*
WhAm H
Morgan, William Thomas 1883-1946 *WhAm 2*
Morgan, William Wilson 1906- *AsBiEn*
Morgan, William Yoast 1866-1932 *NatCAB 23*
Morgan, William Yost 1866-1932 *WhAm 1*

Morganstern, Louis 1896-1972 *NatCAB 57*
Morgenstern, Julian 1881- *WhAm 6*
Morgenstierne, Wilhelm Thorleif Munthe
1887-1963 *WhAm 4*
Morgenthau, Henry 1856-1946 *ApCAB X,*
DcAmB S4, NatCAB 15, NatCAB 36,
WebAB, WhAm 2
Morgenthau, Henry, Jr. 1891-1967 *BiDrUSE,*
EncAB, McGEWB, WebAB, WhAm 4,
WhWW-II
Morgenthau, Julius Caesar 1858-1929
NatCAB 23
Morgulis, Sergius 1885-1971 *WhAm 5*
Morhard, Jeanne Emma *WomWWA 14*
Morhart, Adam 1819?- *NewYHSD*
Moriarity, Patrick Eugene 1804-1875 *DcAmB,*
WhAm H
Moriarty, Albert P *NewYHSD*
Moriarty, Charles Patrick 1895-1966 *WhAm 4*
Moriarty, Eugene d1970 *WhAm 5*
Moriarty, James Joseph 1843-1887 *ApCAB*
Moriarty, John Helenbeck 1903-1971 *DcAmLiB*
Moriarty, John J *NewYHSD*
Moriarty, Patrick Eugene 1804-1875 *ApCAB*
Moriarty, Rose 1882- *WomWWA 14*
Moriarty, William Daniel 1877-1936 *WhAm 1*
Moribecha, Melchior Dias 1689-1741 *ApCAB*
Morichini, Domenico Lino 1773-1836 *DcScB*
Morillo, Pablo 1777-1838 *ApCAB, Drake*
Morin, Alexander C *NewYHSD*
Morin, Alexandre Etienne 1776-1831 *ApCAB*
Morin, Anthony C *NewYHSD*
Morin, Augustin Norbert 1803-1865 *ApCAB*
Morin, Jean-Baptiste 1583-1656 *DcScB*
Morin, John F *NewYHSD*
Morin, John Mary 1868-1942 *BiDrAC,*
WhAm 2, WhAmP
Morin, Paul 1889-1963 *McGEWB*
Morin, Relman 1907-1973 *WhAm 6*
Morine, Henry *NewYHSD*
Morine, William *NewYHSD*
Morini, Austin John 1826-1909 *DcAmB*
Morini, Erika 1906- *WhAm 4*
Morinigo, Higinio 1897- *McGEWB*
Morino, Samuel Milton 1893-1953 *NatCAB 40*
Morison, George Abbot 1879-1966 *WhAm 4*
Morison, George Shattuck 1842-1903 *DcAmB,*
NatCAB 10, TwCBDA, WhAm 1
Morison, Hugh Graham 1878-1925 *NatCAB 20*
Morison, James Henderson Stuart 1864-1952
WhAm 3
Morison, John Hopkins 1808- *ApCAB, Drake*
Morison, Nathaniel Holmes 1815-1890 *ApCAB*
Morison, Robert 1620-1683 *DcScB*
Morison, Robert Brown 1851- *ApCAB*
Morison, Samuel Eliot 1887-1976 *EncAB,*
McGEWB, WebAB, WebAMB, WhAm 6
Morisse, Richard Diehm 1914-1968 *WhAm 5*
Moritz, Adrianus Johannes Leonard 1883-1952
WhAm 4
Moritz, John A 1890-1952 *WhAm 3*
Moritz, Richard Daniel 1872- *WhAm 5*
Moritz, Robert Edouard 1868-1940 *WhAm 1*
Moritz, Theodore Leo 1892- *BiDrAC*
Moritzen, Julius 1863- *WhAm 4*
Mork, P Ralph 1883-1958 *WhAm 3*
Morlacchi, Giuseppina 1836-1886 *NotAW*
Morlan, Albert Edmund 1850- *NatCAB 8*
Morlan, Webster Smith 1848-1915 *NatCAB 17,*
WhAm 1
Morland, Samuel 1625-1695 *DcScB*
Morley, Albert Healey 1856-1937 *NatCAB 30*
Morley, Christopher Darlington 1890-1957
ApCAB X, WhAm 3
Morley, Clarence Joseph 1869- *WhAm 5*
Morley, Edward Williams 1838-1923 *AmBi,*
ApCAB, AsBiEn, DcAmB, DcScB,
NatCAB 4, TwCBDA, WebAB, WhAm 1
Morley, Frank 1860-1937 *DcAmB S2,*
NatCAB 15, NatCAB 28, TwCBDA,
WhAm 1
Morley, George Bidwell 1857-1935 *WhAm 1*
Morley, John, Viscount 1838-1923 *McGEWB*
Morley, John Chapman Biddle 1868-1921
NatCAB 18
Morley, John Henry 1840-1923 *TwCBDA,*
WhAm 1
Morley, Linda Huckel 1881-1972 *DcAmLiB*

Morley, Margaret Warner 1858-1923 *DcAmB,*
WhAm 1, WomWWA 14
Morley, Sylvanus Griswold 1883-1948
DcAmB S4, NatCAB 38, NatCAB 47,
WhAm 2
Morley, Thomas 1557?-1608? *McGEWB*
Morley, William Howard 1894-1970
NatCAB 55
Morling, Edgar Alfred 1864-1932 *WhAm 1*
Morman, James Bale 1866-1930 *WhAm 1*
Morningstar, Thomas Wood 1926-1964
WhAm 4
Morns, F *NewYHSD*
Moro, Antonio-Lazzaro 1687-1764 *DcScB*
Moron, Alonzo Graseano 1909-1971 *WhAm 5*
Moron, J *NewYHSD*
Moroney, Carl Joseph 1886-1951 *NatCAB 42,*
WhAm 3
Moroney, James McQueen 1894-1968 *WhAm 5*
Morosco, Oliver 1876- *WhAm 5*
Morosini, Francisco 1618-1694 *WhoMilH*
Moroso, John Antonio 1874-1957 *WhAm 3*
Morozov, Georgy Fedorovich 1867-1920 *DcScB*
Morphet, Edgar Leroy 1895- *BiDAmEd*
Morphis, Joseph Lewis 1831-1913 *BiAUS,*
BiDrAC, TwCBDA
Morphy, Paul Charles 1837-1884 *AmBi,*
ApCAB, DcAmB, Drake, NatCAB 13,
WebAB, WhAm H
Morrel, William Griffin 1908-1975 *WhAm 6*
Morrell, Benjamin *NewYHSD*
Morrell, Benjamin 1795-1839 *ApCAB, DcAmB,*
Drake, WhAm H
Morrell, Daniel Johnson 1821-1885 *ApCAB Sup,*
BiAUS, BiDrAC, NatCAB 13, TwCBDA,
WhAm H
Morrell, Daniel Silver 1866-1946 *NatCAB 35*
Morrell, Edward DeVeaux 1862-1917 *WhAm 4*
Morrell, Edward DeVeaux 1863-1917 *BiDrAC*
Morrell, Fred 1880- *WhAm 6*
Morrell, George 1786-1845 *BiAUS*
Morrell, George 1881-1966 *NatCAB 52*
Morrell, Imogene Robinson d1908 *ApCAB,*
TwCBDA, WhAm 1
Morrell, John Watson 1864-1936 *NatCAB 34*
Morrell, Thomas 1747-1838 *ApCAB*
Morrell, W D *NewYHSD*
Morrell, Willett H *NewYHSD*
Morrell, William *Drake, NatCAB 8,*
NewYHSD
Morrey, Charles Bradfield 1869-1954 *WhAm 3*
Morrey, Grace Hamilton *WomWWA 14*
Morrey, Humphrey 1650?-1716 *ApCAB*
Morrice, David 1829- *ApCAB*
Morrice, James Wilson 1865-1924 *McGEWB*
Morril, David Lawrence 1772-1849 *ApCAB,*
BiAUS, BiDrAC, DcAmB, NatCAB 11,
TwCBDA, WhAm H, WhAmP
Morrill, Albert Harrison 1891-1963 *NatCAB 50*
Morrill, Albert Henry 1875-1942 *NatCAB 32,*
WhAm 2
Morrill, Albro David 1854-1943 *WhAm 2*
Morrill, Amos 1809-1884 *BiAUS, NatCAB 13*
Morrill, Anson Peaslee 1803-1887 *ApCAB,*
BiAUS, BiDrAC, DcAmB, Drake,
NatCAB 6, TwCBDA, WhAm H,
WhAmP
Morrill, Arthur Putnam 1876-1935 *NatCAB 26*
Morrill, Charles Henry 1842-1928 *WhAm 1*
Morrill, Charles Henry 1878-1946 *NatCAB 35*
Morrill, Charles Sumner 1900-1961 *NatCAB 50*
Morrill, D *NewYHSD*
Morrill, David Lawrence 1772-1849 *Drake*
Morrill, Donald Littlefield 1860-1923
ApCAB X
Morrill, Edmund Needham 1834-1909 *BiDrAC,*
DcAmB, NatCAB 8, TwCBDA,
WhAm 1, WhAmP
Morrill, George Burnham 1867-1934
NatCAB 37
Morrill, George Henry 1829-1909 *NatCAB 24*
Morrill, George Henry, Jr. 1855-1932
NatCAB 24
Morrill, Georgiana Lea *WomWWA 14*
Morrill, Harley Winslow 1872-1943
NatCAB 32
Morrill, Henry Albert 1835- *WhAm 4*
Morrill, Henry Leighton 1836-1904 *NatCAB 35*

Morrill, John Adams 1855-1945 *NatCAB 35,*
WhAm 2
Morrill, Justin Smith 1810-1898 *AmBi,*
ApCAB, BiAUS, BiDrAC, DcAmB,
Drake, EncAAH, EncAB, McGEWB,
NatCAB 1, TwCBDA, WebAB,
WhAm H, WhAmP
Morrill, Katherine Carleton 1865-
WomWWA 14
Morrill, Lot Myrick 1812-1883 *AmBi,*
BiDrUSE, DcAmB, WhAm H
Morrill, Lot Myrick 1813-1883 *ApCAB,*
BiDrAC, Drake, NatCAB 6, TwCBDA,
WhAmP
Morrill, Lot Myrick 1815-1883 *BiAUS,*
BiAUS Sup
Morrill, Mendon d1961 *WhAm 4*
Morrill, Penelope Patten *WomWWA 14*
Morrill, Samuel 1804-1878 *NatCAB 24*
Morrill, Samuel Plummer 1816-1892 *BiAUS,*
BiDrAC, WhAm H
Morrill, W De *NewYHSD*
Morrill, Warren Pearl 1877-1947 *NatCAB 41,*
WhAm 2
Morrill, William Kelso 1903-1968 *WhAm 5*
Morrin, Joseph 1792?-1861 *ApCAB*
Morris, Mrs. *NewYHSD*
Morris, Agnes L 1865- *WomWWA 14*
Morris, Albert Wood 1880-1954 *NatCAB 43*
Morris, Alexander 1826- *ApCAB*
Morris, Alfred Hennen 1864-1959 *NatCAB 48*
Morris, Alice A Parmelee *WhAm 5*
Morris, Alpheus Kaspar 1878- *WhAm 6*
Morris, Andrew *NewYHSD*
Morris, Anna P *WomWWA 14*
Morris, Anthony 1654-1721 *ApCAB, DcAmB,*
NatCAB 17, WhAm H
Morris, Anthony 1682-1763 *ApCAB*
Morris, Anthony 1766-1860 *ApCAB, DcAmB,*
WhAm H
Morris, Anthony James 1739-1831 *ApCAB*
Morris, Araminta Hynson 1867-
WomWWA 14
Morris, Arthur J 1880-1973 *ApCAB X*
Morris, Arthur J 1881-1973 *WhAm 6*
Morris, Benjamin Franklin 1810-1867 *TwCBDA*
Morris, Benjamin Wistar 1819-1906 *ApCAB,*
NatCAB 5, TwCBDA, WhAm 1
Morris, Benjamin Wistar, III 1870-1944
WhAm 2
Morris, Bert Miller 1916-1975 *WhAm 6*
Morris, Cadwalader 1741-1795 *ApCAB,*
BiDrAC, DcAmB, TwCBDA, WhAm H
Morris, Calvary 1798-1871 *BiAUS, BiDrAC,*
TwCBDA, WhAm H
Morris, Calvary 1851-1912 *NatCAB 21*
Morris, Carlyle 1894-1958 *NatCAB 48*
Morris, Caspar 1805-1884 *ApCAB, DcAmB,*
TwCBDA, WhAm H
Morris, Charles *BiAUS*
Morris, Charles 1784-1856 *AmBi, ApCAB,*
DcAmB, Drake, NatCAB 9, TwCBDA,
WebAMB, WhAm H
Morris, Charles 1833-1922 *TwCBDA,*
WhAm 1
Morris, Charles 1844-1912 *WhAm 1*
Morris, Charles Dexter 1883-1954 *NatCAB 45*
Morris, Charles D'Urban 1827-1886 *ApCAB*
Morris, Charles Gould 1871-1961 *WhAm 4*
Morris, Charles Harwood 1871- *WhAm 5*
Morris, Charles John Augustus 1850-1918
NatCAB 18
Morris, Charles Robert 1875-1942 *NatCAB 32*
Morris, Charles Shoemaker 1887-1952
WhAm 3
Morris, Charles Wendel 1892-1961 *WhAm 4*
Morris, Chester 1901-1970 *WhAm 5*
Morris, Clara 1846?-1925 *ApCAB*
Morris, Clara 1847-1925 *NotAW*
Morris, Clara 1848-1925 *AmBi, DcAmB,*
NatCAB 11, TwCBDA, WomWWA 14
Morris, Clara 1849-1925 *WhAm 1*
Morris, Clara 1850-1925 *AmWom*
Morris, Claude Frank 1869- *WhAm 5*
Morris, Claudius Stedman 1869-1958
NatCAB 46
Morris, Clyde Tucker 1877-1965 *NatCAB 52,*
WhAm 5

Morris, Constance Lily d1954 *WhAm 3*
Morris, Daniel 1812-1889 *BiAUS, BiDrAC,*
TwCBDA, WhAm H, WhAmP
Morris, Daniel C *NewYHSD*
Morris, Dave Hennen 1872-1944 *NatCAB 37,*
WhAm 2
Morris, Dave Hennen, Jr. 1900-1975 *WhAm 6*
Morris, David *NewYHSD*
Morris, David Alexander Blair 1826-1882
NatCAB 31
Morris, David Hampton 1884-1943 *NatCAB 36*
Morris, Don 1906-1962 *WhAm 4*
Morris, Don Heath 1902-1974 *WhAm 6*
Morris, Donald Florence 1901-1963 *WhAm 4*
Morris, Douglas 1861-1928 *WhAm 1*
Morris, Dudley 1912-1966 *NatCAB 52*
Morris, Earl Halstead 1889-1956 *WhAm 3*
Morris, Edgar 1889-1968 *NatCAB 54*
Morris, Edgar Leslie 1886-1963 *WhAm 4*
Morris, Edmund 1804-1874 *ApCAB, DcAmB,*
NatCAB 26, WhAm H
Morris, Edmund Montague 1871-1913
IIBEAAW
Morris, Edward 1866-1913 *NatCAB 34,*
WhAm 1
Morris, Edward Dafydd 1825-1915 *ApCAB,*
DcAmB, TwCBDA, WhAm 1
Morris, Edward H 1860- *WhoColR*
Morris, Edward Joy 1815-1881 *AmBi, ApCAB,*
BiDrAC, DcAmB, Drake, NatCAB 13,
TwCBDA, WhAm H
Morris, Edward Joy 1817-1881 *BiAUS*
Morris, Edward Parmelee 1853-1938 *ApCAB,*
NatCAB 28, TwCBDA, WhAm 1
Morris, Edwin Bateman 1881-1971 *WhAm 5*
Morris, Effingham Buckley 1856-1937
NatCAB 27, WhAm 1
Morris, Elias Camp 1855-1922 *WhAm 1,*
WhoColR
Morris, Elisabeth Woodbridge 1870- *WhAm 5,*
WomWWA 14
Morris, Elizabeth 1753?-1826 *DcAmB,*
WhAm H
Morris, Ellen Douglas 1846- *AmWom*
Morris, Emmet 1876-1955 *NatCAB 44*
Morris, Emory William 1905-1974 *WhAm 6*
Morris, Ernest 1927- *IIBEAAW*
Morris, Ernest Melvin 1882-1951 *NatCAB 39,*
WhAm 3
Morris, Esther Hobart McQuigg Slack
1813-1902 *AmWom*
Morris, Esther Hobart McQuigg Slack
1814-1902 *NotAW, REnAW*
Morris, Evangeline Hall 1899-1958 *WhAm 3*
Morris, Felix William James 1845-1900
NatCAB 11, WhAm 1
Morris, Florance Ann 1876-1947 *WhAm 2*
Morris, Florence Ann 1876-1947 *IIBEAAW*
Morris, Florence Ward *WomWWA 14*
Morris, Francis 1842?-1883 *NatCAB 4*
Morris, Frank Edward 1889-1963 *WhAm 4*
Morris, Frank Hubbard 1851-1900 *WhAm 1*
Morris, Frank R 1885-1956 *WhAm 3*
Morris, Frederick Kuhne 1885-1962 *WhAm 4*
Morris, Frederick Wistar, III 1905-1971
WhAm 5
Morris, Froome 1870-1939 *NatCAB 29*
Morris, George 1865-1928 *ApCAB X,*
NatCAB 21
Morris, George 1886-1944 *WhAm 2*
Morris, George Davis 1864- *WhAm 4*
Morris, George Edward 1862- *WhAm 1*
Morris, George Ford d1960 *WhAm 4*
Morris, George Kenneth 1837-1918 *WhAm 1*
Morris, George Lovett Kingsland 1905-1975
IIBEAAW, WhAm 6
Morris, George Maurice 1889-1954 *NatCAB 41,*
WhAm 3
Morris, George Perry 1864-1921 *WhAm 1*
Morris, George Pope 1802-1864 *AmBi, ApCAB,*
DcAmB, Drake, NatCAB 5, TwCBDA,
WhAm H
Morris, George Sylvester 1840-1889 *ApCAB,*
DcAmB, TwCBDA, WhAm H
Morris, George Upham 1830-1875 *AmBi,*
ApCAB, NatCAB 4, TwCBDA,
WebAMB

Morris, George VanDerveer 1867-1928
WhAm 1

Morris, Glenn Kleckner 1897-1953 NatCAB 41

Morris, Gouverneur 1752-1816 AmBi, ApCAB,
BiAUS, BiDrAC, DcAmB, Drake,
EncAB, McGEWB, NatCAB 2,
TwCBDA, WebAB, WhAm H, WhAmP

Morris, Gouverneur 1813-1888 ApCAB Sup

Morris, Gouverneur 1876-1953 WhAm 3

Morris, Hale Dickinson 1903-1957 NatCAB 43

Morris, Harold Cecil 1890-1964 WhAm 4

Morris, Harrison Smith 1856-1948 NatCAB 10,
NatCAB 55, TwCBDA, WhAm 2

Morris, Henry NewYHSD

Morris, Henry 1814-1888 ApCAB Sup

Morris, Henry Crittenden 1868-1948 ApCAB X,
NatCAB 11, NatCAB 39, WhAm 2

Morris, Henry W 1806-1863 ApCAB, Drake,
TwCBDA

Morris, Herbert William 1818-1897 ApCAB,
TwCBDA

Morris, Homer Lawrence 1886-1951 WhAm 3

Morris, Howard 1856-1922 WhAm 1

Morris, Hugh Martin 1878-1966 WhAm 4

Morris, Ira Nelson 1875-1942 NatCAB 31,
WhAm 1

Morris, Isaac Newton 1812-1879 ApCAB,
BiAUS, BiDrAC, TwCBDA, WhAm H

Morris, Jack Sidney 1906-1974 WhAm 6

Morris, Jacob 1755-1844 ApCAB

Morris, James 1798-1865 ApCAB

Morris, James Charlton 1838- WhAm 4

Morris, James Cheston 1831-1923 ApCAB,
TwCBDA, WhAm 1

Morris, James Craik 1870-1944 WhAm 2

Morris, James Flack 1871- ApCAB X

Morris, James Lucien 1885-1926 NatCAB 20

Morris, James Montgomery 1867- WhoColR

Morris, James R 1820- BiAUS

Morris, James Remley 1819-1899 BiDrAC

Morris, James Walter 1858- TwCBDA

Morris, James Ward 1890-1960 WhAm 4

Morris, John 1739?-1785 ApCAB

Morris, John 1803- Drake

Morris, John 1863-1955 WhAm 3

Morris, John Albert 1836-1895 NatCAB 22

Morris, John Baptist 1866-1947 NatCAB 15,
WhAm 2

Morris, John Godlove 1803-1895 NatCAB 3

Morris, John Gottlieb 1803-1895 ApCAB,
DcAmB, TwCBDA, WhAm H

Morris, John Henry 1826- NatCAB 1

Morris, John Norfolk 1872-1935 NatCAB 26

Morris, John Richard 1882-1951 NatCAB 42

Morris, Jonathan NewYHSD

Morris, Jonathan David 1804-1875 ApCAB,
BiAUS, BiDrAC, WhAm H

Morris, Jonathan Flynt 1822-1899 NatCAB 25

Morris, Jones Fawson NewYHSD

Morris, Joseph 1795-1854 BiAUS, BiDrAC,
WhAm H

Morris, Joseph Chandler 1827- NatCAB 9

Morris, Joseph Chandler 1902-1970 WhAm 5

Morris, Joseph E d1961 WhAm 4

Morris, Joseph Watkins 1879-1937 BiDrAC

Morris, Kyle 1918- BnEnAmA

Morris, L E 1850- WomWWA 14

Morris, L W d1961 WhAm 4

Morris, Lawrence 1903-1967 NatCAB 53

Morris, Leland Burnette 1886-1950 NatCAB 39,
WhAm 3

Morris, Lewis ApCAB, NewYHSD

Morris, Lewis 1671-1746 AmBi, ApCAB,
DcAmB, Drake, McGEWB, NatCAB 3,
TwCBDA, WhAm H

Morris, Lewis 1726-1798 AmBi, ApCAB,
BiAUS, BiDrAC, DcAmB, Drake,
NatCAB 3, TwCBDA, WhAm H,
WhAmP

Morris, Lewis 1867-1940 NatCAB 30

Morris, Lewis Coleman 1872-1923 WhAm 1

Morris, Lewis Nelson 1800-1846 ApCAB

Morris, Lewis Owen 1824-1864 ApCAB

Morris, Lewis R 1760-1825 BiAUS, TwCBDA

Morris, Lewis Richard 1760-1825 DcAmB,
WhAm H

Morris, Lewis Robert 1760-1825 BiDrAC,
WhAmP

Morris, Lewis Rutherfurd 1862-1936
NatCAB 26

Morris, Lewis Spencer 1884-1944 WhAm 2

Morris, Lloyd 1893-1954 WhAm 3

Morris, Luzon Burritt 1827-1895 DcAmB,
NatCAB 10, TwCBDA, WhAm H

Morris, Maria NewYHSD

Morris, Martin Ferdinand 1834-1909 WhAm 1

Morris, Martin Ferdinand 1836-1909 TwCBDA

Morris, Mary ApCAB

Morris, Mary Philipse 1730-1825 AmBi,
ApCAB, DcAmB, NatCAB 4

Morris, Mathias 1787-1839 BiAUS, BiDrAC,
WhAm H

Morris, Morgan James Reginald 1893-1961
NatCAB 49

Morris, Moses 1799-1855 NatCAB 7

Morris, Nelson 1838-1907 DcAmB

Morris, Nelson 1839-1907 WhAm 1

Morris, Nephi Lowell 1870-1943 NatCAB 33

Morris, Newbold 1868-1928 ApCAB X,
WhAm 1

Morris, Newbold 1902-1966 WhAm 4

Morris, Nora Jane Smith 1876- WomWWA 14

Morris, Oscar Matison 1874-1943 WhAm 2

Morris, Mrs. Owen 1753?-1826 DcAmB

Morris, Page 1853-1924 NatCAB 38,
TwCBDA, WhAm 1

Morris, Pat G 1898-1967 WhAm 4

Morris, Percy Amos 1899-1969 WhAm 5

Morris, Phineas Pemberton 1817-1888 ApCAB,
TwCBDA

Morris, Richard NewYHSD

Morris, Richard 1730-1810 DcAmB,
NatCAB 12, WhAm H

Morris, Richard Lewis 1875- WhAm 3

Morris, Richard Valentine 1768-1815 ApCAB,
DcAmB, Drake, WebAMB, WhAm H

Morris, Robert d1806 BiAUS

Morris, Robert d1815 Drake

Morris, Robert 1733-1806 Drake

Morris, Robert 1734-1806 AmBi, ApCAB,
BiDrAC, DcAmB, EncAB, McGEWB,
NatCAB 2, TwCBDA, WebAB,
WhAm H, WhAmP

Morris, Robert 1735-1815 BiAUS

Morris, Robert 1745?-1815 ApCAB, DcAmB,
NatCAB 12, WhAm H

Morris, Robert 1818-1888 ApCAB, DcAmB,
NatCAB 25, WhAm H

Morris, Robert 1931- BnEnAmA

Morris, Robert Clark 1869-1938 WhAm 1

Morris, Robert Eugene 1930-1967 WhAm 5

Morris, Robert Hugh 1876-1942 WhAm 2

Morris, Robert Hunter 1700?-1764 ApCAB,
DcAmB, Drake, NatCAB 12, TwCBDA,
WhAm H

Morris, Robert Murray 1824- NatCAB 4

Morris, Robert Nelson 1860- WhAm 4

Morris, Robert Page Walter 1853-1924 BiDrAC

Morris, Robert Seymour 1893-1971 WhAm 5

Morris, Robert Tuttle 1857-1945 NatCAB 1,
NatCAB 39, WhAm 2

Morris, Roger 1717-1794 ApCAB, Drake

Morris, Roger 1727-1794 AmBi, DcAmB,
WhAm H

Morris, Roger Sylvester 1877-1934 WhAm 1

Morris, Roland Sletor 1874-1945 NatCAB 43,
WhAm 2

Morris, Samuel 1700?-1770? ApCAB,
NatCAB 5

Morris, Samuel 1711-1782 ApCAB

Morris, Samuel 1711-1812 ApCAB

Morris, Samuel 1896-1947 NatCAB 54

Morris, Samuel Brooks 1890-1962 WhAm 4

Morris, Samuel Cadwalader 1743-1820 ApCAB

Morris, Samuel Henry 1886-1967 WhAm 4

Morris, Samuel Leslie 1854-1937 WhAm 1

Morris, Samuel Solomon 1878- WhoColR

Morris, Samuel W 1788-1847 BiAUS

Morris, Samuel Wells 1786-1847 ApCAB,
BiDrAC, TwCBDA, WhAm H

Morris, Sarah 1704-1775 ApCAB, Drake

Morris, Sarah Roberts WomWWA 14

Morris, Staats Long 1728-1800 ApCAB, Drake

Morris, Stuyvesant Fish 1843-1928 NatCAB 36

Morris, Stuyvesant Fish, Jr. 1877-1925
NatCAB 36

Morris, Susanna 1683-1755 Drake

Morris, Thomas 1771-1849 BiAUS, BiDrAC,
WhAm H, WhAmP

Morris, Thomas 1776-1844 AmBi, ApCAB,
BiAUS, BiDrAC, DcAmB, Drake,
NatCAB 11, TwCBDA, WhAm H

Morris, Thomas A 1794-1874 Drake

Morris, Thomas Armstrong 1811-1904 ApCAB,
DcAmB, NatCAB 10, WhAm 1

Morris, Thomas Asbury 1794-1874 ApCAB,
TwCBDA

Morris, Thomas Ashury 1794-1874 NatCAB 5

Morris, Thomas Gayle 1919- BiDrAC

Morris, Thomas John 1837-1912 NatCAB 29,
WhAm 1

Morris, Toby 1899- BiDrAC

Morris, Victor Pierpont 1891-1974 WhAm 6

Morris, Watson Budlong 1878-1956
NatCAB 46

Morris, William 1786-1858 ApCAB

Morris, William 1834-1896 McGEWB

Morris, William 1861-1936 WhAm 1

Morris, William Alfred 1875-1946 NatCAB 35,
WhAm 2

Morris, William Carloss 1877-1950 NatCAB 39

Morris, William Charles 1834-1940 WhAm 1

Morris, William Henry Harrison 1890-1971
WhAm 5

Morris, William Hicks 1916-1969 WhAm 5

Morris, William Hopkins 1826-1900 ApCAB,
TwCBDA

Morris, William Hopkins 1827-1900 DcAmB,
NatCAB 4, WhAm H

Morris, William Richard 1859- WhoColR

Morris, William Robert 1880-1965 NatCAB 53,
WhAm 4

Morris, William S BiDConf

Morris, William Shivers 1903-1967 WhAm 4

Morris, William Sylvanus 1855- WhAm 4

Morris, William Thomas 1884-1946 WhAm 2

Morris, William Torrey 1853- WhAm 4

Morris, William V d1887? NewYHSD,
WhAm H

Morris, William Walton 1801-1865 ApCAB,
Drake, TwCBDA

Morris, Windsor 1871-1935 NatCAB 28

Morrish, Will Francis 1883-1955 NatCAB 43

Morrison, A Cressy 1884-1951 WhAm 3

Morrison, Abby Putnam BiCAW

Morrison, Albert Alexander 1862-1931
WhAm 1

Morrison, Alexander Francis 1856-1921
NatCAB 19, NatCAB 25, WhAm 1

Morrison, Angus 1822- ApCAB

Morrison, Angus Washburn 1883-1949
NatCAB 46

Morrison, Cameron A 1869-1953 BiDrAC,
NatCAB 49, WhAm 3

Morrison, Caroline Baldwin 1869-
WomWWA 14

Morrison, Caroline Wood WomWWA 14

Morrison, Charles B 1853-1932 WhAm 1

Morrison, Charles Clayton 1874-1966
DcAmReB, NatCAB 52, WhAm 4

Morrison, Charles Munro 1881-1950 WhAm 2

Morrison, Charles Robert 1819-1893 ApCAB,
TwCBDA

Morrison, Charles Samuel 1919-1967 WhAm 5

Morrison, Charles Walthall 1856-1927
WhAm 1

Morrison, Chester Beaver 1886-1959
NatCAB 47

Morrison, Clayton Wesley 1883-1951
NatCAB 45

Morrison, Clinton 1842-1913 WhAm 1

Morrison, DeLesseps S 1912-1964 WhAm 4

Morrison, Donald Harvard 1914-1959 WhAm 3

Morrison, Edward Lester 1900-1961 WhAm 4

Morrison, Edward Lloyd 1879-1945
NatCAB 34

Morrison, Edwin John 1867-1936 NatCAB 27

Morrison, Edwin Rees 1878-1965 WhAm 4

Morrison, Elizabeth Gearhart 1875-
WomWWA 14

Morrison, Florence Roberts 1871-
WomWWA 14

Morrison, Frank 1859-1949 DcAmB S4,
WhAm 2

Morrison, Frank Ambrose 1889-1947
NatCAB 34
Morrison, Frank Barron 1887-1958 *NatCAB 43,*
WhAm 3
Morrison, Frederick Douglas 1837-1904
WhAm 1
Morrison, George Austin 1832-1916 *WhAm 1*
Morrison, George Douglas 1897-1957
NatCAB 43
Morrison, George Francis 1867-1943
NatCAB 35
Morrison, George Harvey 1854-1932
NatCAB 24
Morrison, George W 1820-1893 *NewYHSD*
Morrison, George Washington 1809-1888
ApCAB, BiAUS, BiDrAC, TwCBDA,
WhAm H
Morrison, Harley James 1866-1950 *NatCAB 39*
Morrison, Harry Steele 1880- *WhAm 6*
Morrison, Harry Winford 1885-1971 *WhAm 5*
Morrison, Harvey Arch 1879-1963 *NatCAB 50,*
WhAm 6
Morrison, Henry Clay 1842-1921 *ApCAB Sup,*
NatCAB 1, TwCBDA, WhAm 1
Morrison, Henry Clay 1857-1942 *NatCAB 33,*
WhAm 2
Morrison, Henry Clinton 1871-1945 *BiDAmEd,*
WhAm 2
Morrison, Herbert 1888-1965 *WhWW-II*
Morrison, Ivan 1893-1957 *WhAm 3*
Morrison, Jack Harold 1911-1969 *WhAm 5*
Morrison, James 1755-1823 *ApCAB*
Morrison, James B 1901-1975 *WhAm 6*
Morrison, James Dalton 1893-1950 *WhAm 3*
Morrison, James Dow 1844-1934 *NatCAB 11,*
TwCBDA, WhAm 1
Morrison, James Frank 1841- *ApCAB,*
WhAm 4
Morrison, James Hobson 1908- *BiDrAC,*
WhAmP
Morrison, James Homer 1892-1949 *NatCAB 38*
Morrison, James L D *BiAUS*
Morrison, James Low 1874-1959 *NatCAB 45*
Morrison, James Lowery Donaldson 1816-1888
BiDrAC, WhAm H
Morrison, James Lowry Donaldson 1814-1888
NatCAB 7
Morrison, James McFarland 1850-1923
NatCAB 6
Morrison, Jasper Newton 1849-1902 *WhAm 1*
Morrison, Jim 1944-1971 *WhAm 5*
Morrison, John Alexander 1814-1904 *BiAUS,*
BiDrAC
Morrison, John Arch 1893-1965 *WhAm 4*
Morrison, John Frank 1857-1932 *NatCAB 23,*
WhAm 1
Morrison, John Irwin 1806-1882 *BiDAmEd,*
DcAmB, TwCBDA, WhAm H
Morrison, John Oliver 1886- *WhoColR*
Morrison, John Taylor 1899-1962 *NatCAB 49*
Morrison, John Tracy 1860- *NatCAB 12,*
WhAm 4
Morrison, Joseph 1848- *WhAm 4*
Morrison, Joseph Curran 1816-1885 *ApCAB*
Morrison, Joseph L 1918-1970 *WhAm 5*
Morrison, Joseph M *NewYHSD*
Morrison, Joseph Peter 1894-1957 *WhAm 3*
Morrison, Joseph Wanton 1783-1826 *ApCAB,*
Drake
Morrison, Julian Knox 1895-1949 *NatCAB 38*
Morrison, Leonard Allison 1843- *ApCAB,*
NatCAB 10
Morrison, Leonard William 1907-1963
NatCAB 52
Morrison, Levi 1839-1917 *WhAm 1*
Morrison, Lewis 1845-1906 *WhAm 1*
Morrison, Lewis Francis 1899-1956 *NatCAB 43*
Morrison, M *NewYHSD*
Morrison, Margaret L 1874- *WomWWA 14*
Morrison, Marshall Lee 1873- *WhoColR*
Morrison, Martin Andrew 1862-1944 *BiDrAC*
Morrison, Mary J Whitney 1832-1904 *WhAm 1*
Morrison, May Treat 1858-1939 *NatCAB 31,*
WhAm 1
Morrison, Nathan Jackson 1828-1907 *DcAmB,*
NatCAB 13, TwCBDA, WhAm 1
Morrison, Ocie Butler, Jr. 1896-1969 *WhAm 5*
Morrison, Paul Cross 1906-1969 *NatCAB 54*

Morrison, Phoebe 1902-1968 *WhAm 5*
Morrison, Pitcairn 1795-1887 *ApCAB*
Morrison, Ralph Waldo 1878-1948 *WhAm 2*
Morrison, Richard R *ApCAB X*
Morrison, Robert Fletcher 1896-1943
NatCAB 32
Morrison, Robert Francis 1826-1887
NatCAB 12, TwCBDA
Morrison, Robert Hall 1798-1889 *TwCBDA*
Morrison, Robert Hugh 1893-1973 *WhAm 5*
Morrison, Robert John 1857-1942 *WhAm 2*
Morrison, Robert Stewart 1843- *WhAm 4*
Morrison, Roger Leroy 1883-1952 *NatCAB 39,*
WhAm 3
Morrison, Sarah Elizabeth *WhAm 5*
Morrison, Sarah Parke 1833- *TwCBDA*
Morrison, Stanley 1892-1955 *WhAm 4*
Morrison, Theodore Neven 1850-1929 *TwCBDA*
Morrison, Theodore Nevin 1850-1929
ApCAB Sup, NatCAB 13, WhAm 1
Morrison, Thomas 1861-1946 *NatCAB 40,*
WhAm 2
Morrison, Thomas Faulkner 1808-1886 *ApCAB*
Morrison, Wayland Augustus 1888-1950
NatCAB 38, WhAm 3
Morrison, Wellman *NewYHSD*
Morrison, Whitelaw Reid 1886-1958
NatCAB 46
Morrison, Willard Langdon 1892-1965
WhAm 4
Morrison, William *NewYHSD*
Morrison, William 1763-1837 *DcAmB,*
WhAm H
Morrison, William 1785-1866 *ApCAB, Drake*
Morrison, William Barrett 1863-1949
NatCAB 38, WhAm 4
Morrison, William Brown 1877-1944 *WhAm 2*
Morrison, William Byrne 1885-1962
NatCAB 49
Morrison, William McCutchan 1867-1918
DcAmB
Morrison, William Ralls 1824?-1909 *DcAmB,*
NatCAB 13
Morrison, William Ralls 1825-1909 *ApCAB,*
BiAUS, BiDrAC, TwCBDA, WhAm 1,
WhAmP
Morrison, William Shepherd 1893-1961
WhAm 4
Morrison, Zaidee Lincoln 1872- *WhAm 5*
Morrison, Zelma Reeves *WhAm 5*
Morriss, Elizabeth Cleveland *WhAm 5*
Morriss, Margaret Shove 1884- *WomWWA 14*
Morrissey, Andrew 1860-1921 *NatCAB 13,*
WhAm 1
Morrissey, Andrew Marcus 1871-1933
NatCAB 17, WhAm 1
Morrissey, Bernard Delbert 1907-1975
WhAm 6
Morrissey, James Peter 1872- *WhAm 5*
Morrissey, John 1831-1878 *BiAUS, BiDrAC,*
DcAmB, WhAm H
Morrissey, John Anthony 1893-1952
NatCAB 45
Morrissey, Mary H Bradley 1861-
WomWWA 14
Morrissey, Michael A 1885-1964 *WhAm 4*
Morrissey, Patrick Henry 1862- *WhAm 4*
Morrisson, James William 1872-1950
NatCAB 40
Morrisson, Mary Foulke 1879-1971 *BiCAW,*
NatCAB 17, NatCAB 56, WomWWA 14
Morron, John Reynolds 1867-1950 *NatCAB 38,*
WhAm 3
Morrow, Albert Sidney 1878-1960 *NatCAB 48*
Morrow, Albert Sydney 1878-1960 *WhAm 4*
Morrow, Chester Fogelman 1886-1943
NatCAB 32
Morrow, Cornelius Wortendyke 1855-1923
WhAm 1
Morrow, Mrs. Dwight Whitney d1955 *WhAm 3*
Morrow, Dwight Whitney 1873-1931 *AmBi,*
BiDrAC, DcAmB, EncAB, McGEWB,
NatCAB 23, WebAB, WhAm 1
Morrow, Edwin P 1878-1935 *WhAm 1*
Morrow, Edwin Porch 1877-1935 *DcAmB S1*
Morrow, Frederick Keenan 1886-1953 *WhAm 3*
Morrow, George Keenan 1873-1941 *WhAm 1*

Morrow, George Washington 1863-1934
WhAm 1
Morrow, Glenn R 1895-1973 *WhAm 5*
Morrow, Henry A 1829-1891 *TwCBDA*
Morrow, Honore Bryant Willsie 1880-1940
NatCAB 29, WhAm 1
Morrow, Hubert T 1881-1951 *WhAm 3*
Morrow, Hugh 1873-1960 *WhAm 4*
Morrow, James Binckley 1855-1924 *TwCBDA*
Morrow, James Binkley 1855-1924 *WhAm 1*
Morrow, James E 1837-1904 *WhAm 1*
Morrow, Jay Johnson 1870-1937 *NatCAB 28,*
WhAm 1
Morrow, Jeremiah 1770-1852 *BiAUS,*
NatCAB 3
Morrow, Jeremiah 1771-1852 *ApCAB,*
BiDrAC, DcAmB, Drake, TwCBDA,
WhAm H, WhAmP
Morrow, John *BiDrAC, WhAm H*
Morrow, John 1865-1935 *BiDrAC, WhAm 1,*
WhAmP
Morrow, John D A 1881-1971 *WhAm 5*
Morrow, John Hague Harcourt 1905-1957
NatCAB 43
Morrow, Lester William Wallace 1888-1942
WhAm 2
Morrow, Libbie Luttrell *WomWWA 14*
Morrow, Marco 1869- *WhAm 5*
Morrow, McKeen Fitch 1887-1941 *NatCAB 37*
Morrow, Nancy Clarissa 1866- *WomWWA 14*
Morrow, Prince Albert 1846-1913 *DcAmB,*
NatCAB 21, WhAm 1
Morrow, Rising Lake 1901-1944 *NatCAB 35*
Morrow, Theodore F 1902-1964 *WhAm 4*
Morrow, Thomas Robert 1857-1921
NatCAB 19, WhAm 1
Morrow, Thomas Vaughan 1804-1850 *DcAmB,*
WhAm H
Morrow, Thomas Vaughn 1804-1850 *ApCAB*
Morrow, W K 1867-1938 *WhAm 1*
Morrow, Walter Alexander 1894-1949 *WhAm 2*
Morrow, William 1872-1931 *NatCAB 34*
Morrow, William Carr 1876-1935 *WhAm 1*
Morrow, William Chambers d1923 *WhAm 1*
Morrow, William Lawrence 1911-1956
NatCAB 47
Morrow, William W 1843-1929 *BiDrAC,*
DcAmB, TwCBDA, WhAm 1
Morrow, Winston Vaughan 1886-1972 *WhAm 5*
Morrow, Wright Chalfant 1858- *WhAm 5*
Morsch, Lucile M 1906-1972 *DcAmLiB,*
WhAm 5
Morschauser, Joseph 1863-1947 *WhAm 2*
Morse, Abbie Fish 1860- *WomWWA 14*
Morse, Abner 1793-1865 *ApCAB, Drake,*
TwCBDA
Morse, Albert Laverne 1919-1972 *WhAm 5*
Morse, Albert Pitts 1863-1936 *NatCAB 27*
Morse, Alexander Porter 1842-1921 *WhAm 1*
Morse, Alice Cordelia 1862- *AmWom*
Morse, Allen Benton 1839- *NatCAB 12*
Morse, Alpheus Carey 1818-1893 *NewYHSD,*
WhAm H
Morse, Anson Daniel 1846-1916 *DcAmB,*
NatCAB 13, TwCBDA, WhAm 1
Morse, Anson Ely 1879-1966 *WhAm 4*
Morse, Arthur David 1920-1971 *WhAm 5*
Morse, Arthur Henry 1880-1950 *WhAm 2*
Morse, Benjamin Clarke 1859-1933 *WhAm 1*
Morse, Benjamin Franklin 1867-1948
NatCAB 37
Morse, Bertha Glaspell 1868- *WomWWA 14*
Morse, Blanche 1870- *WomWWA 14*
Morse, Blanche Leonard *WomWWA 14*
Morse, Bleecker Lansing 1900-1955
NatCAB 43
Morse, Carlton Errol 1901- *WebAB*
Morse, Charles Adelbert 1859- *WhAm 4*
Morse, Charles Frederic 1881- *WhAm 6*
Morse, Charles Henry 1853-1927 *TwCBDA,*
WhAm 1
Morse, Charles Hosmer 1833-1921 *ApCAB X,*
NatCAB 18, WhAm 1
Morse, Charles Hosmer 1873-1959 *WhAm 3*
Morse, Charles Wyman 1856-1933 *DcAmB,*
WebAB, WhAm HA, WhAm 2,
WhAm 4
Morse, Chester James 1891-1962 *NatCAB 51*

Morse, Clark T 1888- *WhAm 3*
Morse, David Appleton 1840- *ApCAB*
Morse, David Sherman 1892-1969 *WhAm 5*
Morse, E Rollins 1845- *WhAm 4*
Morse, Ednah Anne Rich 1871-1945
NatCAB 38
Morse, Edward Leland Clark 1855- *WhAm 4*
Morse, Edward Lind 1857-1923 *WhAm 1*
Morse, Edward Peck 1891-1961 *WhAm 4*
Morse, Edward Sylvester 1838-1925 *AmBi,
ApCAB, DcAmB, DcScB, NatCAB 3,
NatCAB 24, TwCBDA, WhAm 1*
Morse, Edwin Kirtland 1856-1942 *WhAm 2*
Morse, Edwin Wilson 1855-1924 *NatCAB 30,
WhAm 4*
Morse, Effie Dallas Custeed *WomWWA 14*
Morse, Elijah Adams 1841-1898 *BiDrAC,
TwCBDA*
Morse, Elmer Addison 1870-1945 *BiDrAC,
WhAm 5*
Morse, Everett Fleet 1857-1913 *NatCAB 24*
Morse, Frank Bradford 1921- *BiDrAC*
Morse, Frank Lincoln 1864-1935 *WhAm 1*
Morse, Frank Rogers 1839- *NatCAB 5*
Morse, Frank W 1864-1929 *ApCAB X*
Morse, Freeman Harlow 1807-1891 *BiAUS,
BiDrAC, DcAmB, WhAm H*
Morse, Fremont 1857-1936 *WhAm 1*
Morse, George Frederic 1834-1926 *NatCAB 39*
Morse, George Frederick 1834-1926 *NewYHSD*
Morse, George Hazen 1821-1885 *NewYHSD*
Morse, George W 1883-1970 *NatCAB 56*
Morse, George Wray 1912-1967 *NatCAB 54*
Morse, Glenn Tilley 1870-1950 *WhAm 3*
Morse, Godfrey 1846-1911 *WhAm 1*
Morse, Harmon Northrop 1848-1920 *DcAmB,
NatCAB 16, NatCAB 19, WhAm 1*
Morse, Harmon Northrup 1848-1920 *ApCAB*
Morse, Harold M 1892-1966 *WhAm 4*
Morse, Harry Wheeler 1873-1936 *WhAm 1*
Morse, Hazen *NewYHSD*
Morse, Henry Bagg 1836-1874 *ApCAB*
Morse, Henry Dutton 1826-1888 *ApCAB,
DcAmB, NewYHSD, WhAm H*
Morse, Henry Grant 1850-1903 *NatCAB 29*
Morse, Henry Grant 1876-1934 *NatCAB 29*
Morse, Henry Lee 1852-1929 *NatCAB 23*
Morse, Henry Woolson 1858-1897 *TwCBDA*
Morse, Horace Taylor 1905-1966 *WhAm 4*
Morse, Hosea Ballou 1855-1934 *AmBi,
WhAm 1*
Morse, Ira Herbert 1875- *WhAm 5*
Morse, Irving Haskell 1868- *WhAm 5*
Morse, Isaac Edward 1809-1866 *BiDrAC,
TwCBDA, WhAm H*
Morse, Isaac Edwards 1809-1866 *ApCAB,
BiAUS*
Morse, James H *NewYHSD*
Morse, James Herbert 1841- *NatCAB 10,
WhAm 1*
Morse, Jedediah 1761-1826 *Drake*
Morse, Jedidiah 1761-1826 *AmBi, ApCAB,
BiDAmEd, DcAmB, DcAmReB, DcScB,
McGEWB, NatCAB 13, TwCBDA,
WebAB, WhAm H*
Morse, Jerome Edward 1846- *WhAm 4*
Morse, John Lovett 1865-1940 *DcAmB S2,
WhAm 1*
Morse, John Torrey 1840-1937 *AmBi, ApCAB,
DcAmB S2, NatCAB 12, NatCAB 28,
TwCBDA, WhAm 1*
Morse, Joseph W *NewYHSD*
Morse, Josiah 1879-1946 *WhAm 2*
Morse, Leon Jeremiah 1880-1958 *WhAm 3*
Morse, Leonice Brockway 1873- *WomWWA 14*
Morse, Leopold 1831-1892 *BiDrAC, TwCBDA,
WhAm H*
Morse, Lester Langford 1870-1953 *NatCAB 42*
Morse, Lester Samuel 1897-1970 *WhAm 5*
Morse, Lewis Kennedy 1869-1930 *NatCAB 24*
Morse, Lucy Gibbons 1839-1936 *NatCAB 26,
WhAm 1*
Morse, Margaret Fessenden 1877- *WhAm 5,
WomWWA 14*
Morse, Merrill Salisbury 1902-1964 *WhAm 4*
Morse, Moses *NewYHSD*
Morse, Nathan 1848-1923 *NatCAB 20*
Morse, Nathaniel 1688-1748 *NewYHSD*

Morse, O A 1815-1870 *BiAUS*
Morse, Oliver Andrew 1815-1870 *BiDrAC,
WhAm H*
Morse, Paul Franklin 1897-1929 *NatCAB 22*
Morse, Perley 1869-1942 *WhAm 2*
Morse, Plinn Frederick 1885-1962 *NatCAB 50*
Morse, Rebecca A 1821- *AmWom*
Morse, Richard Cary 1795-1868 *ApCAB*
Morse, Richard Cary 1841-1926 *NatCAB 21,
WhAm 1*
Morse, Richard Cary 1882-1963 *WhAm 4*
Morse, Robert Hosmer 1878-1964 *WhAm 4*
Morse, Robert Hosmer 1899-1973 *WhAm 6*
Morse, Robert McNeil 1837-1920 *NatCAB 32,
WhAm 1*
Morse, Roy L 1870-1927 *WhAm 1*
Morse, Samuel Finley Breese 1791-1872 *AmBi,
ApCAB, AsBiEn, BnEnAmA, DcAmB,
Drake, EncAB, McGEWB, NatCAB 4,
NewYHSD, TwCBDA, WebAB,
WhAm H*
Morse, Samuel Finley Brown 1885-1969
WhAm 5
Morse, Sidney 1874-1939 *WhAm 1*
Morse, Sidney Edwards 1794-1871 *AmBi,
ApCAB, DcAmB, Drake, TwCBDA,
WhAm H*
Morse, Sidney Edwards 1835- *NatCAB 13*
Morse, T Vernette 1852- *WomWWA 14*
Morse, Tenney 1864-1921 *NatCAB 20*
Morse, W H *NewYHSD*
Morse, Waldo Grant 1859-1934 *ApCAB X,
WhAm 1, WhAm 1C*
Morse, Walter Levi 1874-1954 *NatCAB 44*
Morse, Warner Jackson 1872-1931 *WhAm 1*
Morse, Wayne Lyman 1900-1974 *BiDrAC,
EncAB, WhAm 6*
Morse, Wilbur, Jr. 1903-1955 *WhAm 3*
Morse, Willard Samuel 1856-1935 *NatCAB 26*
Morse, William Clifford 1874-1962 *NatCAB 52*
Morse, William Inglis 1874-1952 *NatCAB 43*
Morse, William Reginald 1874-1939
NatCAB 29
Morse, Withrow 1880-1951 *WhAm 3*
Morsell, James S 1775-1870 *BiAUS*
Morsell, John Albert 1912- *WhAm 6*
Morsell, Samuel Richard 1874- *WhoColR*
Morsey, Chase 1883-1951 *NatCAB 41*
Morshead, Sir Leslie 1889-1959 *WhWW-II*
Morss, Charles Anthony 1857-1927 *ApCAB X,
NatCAB 27, WhAm 1*
Morss, Everett 1865-1933 *NatCAB 27,
WhAm 1*
Morss, Henry Adams 1871-1936 *NatCAB 27*
Morss, Samuel E 1852-1903 *NatCAB 1,
WhAm 1*
Morstein Marx, Fritz 1900-1969 *WhAm 5*
Mort, Paul R 1894-1962 *BiDAmEd, WhAm 4*
Mortemart, V H E DeR, Viscount De 1757-1783
ApCAB
Mortensen, Crawford Jay 1891-1959
NatCAB 48
Mortensen, Martin 1872- *WhAm 5*
Mortensen, Oscar Nicholas 1886-1937
NatCAB 41
Mortensen, Soren Hansen 1879- *WhAm 6*
Mortenson, Ernest Dawson 1895-1968 *WhAm 5*
Mortenson, Norma Jean *WebAB*
Mortenson, Peter Alvin 1869-1937 *WhAm 1*
Morteza 1866- *WhAm 4*
Morthland, David Vernon 1880- *WhAm 6*
Mortier, Edouard Adolphe Casimir Joseph
1768-1835 *WhoMilH*
Mortier, Edouard Louis 1801-1852 *ApCAB*
Mortillet, Louis-Laurent Gabriel De 1821-1898
DcScB
Mortimer, Alfred Garnett 1848- *WhAm 4*
Mortimer, Edith Beale 1878- *WomWWA 14*
Mortimer, Frank Cogswell 1876- *WhAm 3*
Mortimer, Frederick Craig 1857-1936
NatCAB 26
Mortimer, George D *NewYHSD*
Mortimer, George F *NewYHSD*
Mortimer, George T *NewYHSD*
Mortimer, James Daniel 1879-1950 *WhAm 3*
Mortimer, Lee d1963 *WhAm 4*
Mortimer, Mary 1816-1877 *AmWom,
BiDAmEd, DcAmB, NatCAB 7, NotAW,*

WhAm H
Mortimer, Stanley Grafton 1888-1947
NatCAB 36
Morton, Alexander 1820-1869 *ApCAB*
Morton, Alexander Logan 1846-1917
NatCAB 17
Morton, Alfred Hammond 1897-1974 *WhAm 6*
Morton, Anna Dierfeld 1889- *WomWWA 14*
Morton, Anna Livingston Street 1846- *AmWom*
Morton, Asa Henry 1861- *WhAm 4*
Morton, Brayton 1898-1952 *NatCAB 42*
Morton, Charles 1626-1698 *ApCAB, DcAmB,
Drake*
Morton, Charles 1627-1698 *WhAm H*
Morton, Charles 1846-1914 *WhAm 1*
Morton, Charles Adams 1839- *WhAm 4*
Morton, Charles Gould 1861-1933 *DcAmB S1,
NatCAB 31, WhAm 1*
Morton, Charles W 1899-1967 *WhAm 4*
Morton, Charles William 1876-1963
NatCAB 50
Morton, Conrad Vernon 1905-1972 *WhAm 5*
Morton, David 1886-1957 *WhAm 3*
Morton, Edmund *NewYHSD*
Morton, Eliza Happy 1852-1916 *AmWom,
WhAm 1, WomWWA 14*
Morton, Elizabeth Lee *WomWWA 14*
Morton, Ferdinand Joseph LaMenthe 1885-1941
DcAmB S3, WhAm HA, WhAm 4
Morton, Ferdinand Quintin 1881-1949
DcAmB S4
Morton, Frances Comstock *WomWWA 14*
Morton, Frank Roy 1880-1934 *WhAm 1*
Morton, Frederick William 1859- *WhAm 4*
Morton, George 1585-1624 *DcAmB, EncAAH,
WhAm H*
Morton, George 1585-1628? *ApCAB*
Morton, George 1790-1865 *WhAm H*
Morton, George Carpenter 1868-1930 *WhAm 1*
Morton, George Edwin 1879-1939 *WhAm 1*
Morton, Goodridge Venable 1873-1952
NatCAB 39
Morton, Harold Arthur 1890-1958 *NatCAB 48*
Morton, Henry 1836-1902 *AmBi, ApCAB,
DcAmB, NatCAB 11, NatCAB 24,
TwCBDA*
Morton, Henry 1837-1902 *WhAm 1*
Morton, Henry H 1861-1940 *WhAm 1*
Morton, Henry Jackson *NewYHSD*
Morton, Henry Jackson 1807-1890 *ApCAB,
TwCBDA*
Morton, Henry Samuel 1874-1931 *NatCAB 24*
Morton, Howard McIlvain 1868-1939 *WhAm 2*
Morton, Hudson Throck, Jr. 1902-1973
NatCAB 57
Morton, Ira Abbott 1876-1950 *WhAm 3*
Morton, Irene Elder *WomWWA 14*
Morton, Isaac Wyman 1847-1903 *NatCAB 12*
Morton, J N *NewYHSD*
Morton, Jack A 1913-1971 *WhAm 5*
Morton, Jackson 1794-1874 *ApCAB, BiAUS,
BiDConf, BiDrAC, NatCAB 5, TwCBDA,
WhAm H, WhAmP*
Morton, Jacob 1761-1836 *TwCBDA*
Morton, James Ferdinand 1870-1941 *WhAm 1*
Morton, James Geary 1916-1973 *WhAm 5*
Morton, James Madison 1837-1923 *ApCAB X,
NatCAB 29*
Morton, James Madison 1869-1940 *NatCAB 30,
WhAm 1*
Morton, James Proctor 1874- *WhAm 5*
Morton, James St. Clair 1829-1864 *AmBi,
ApCAB, DcAmB, Drake, TwCBDA,
WhAm H*
Morton, Jelly Roll 1885-1941 *DcAmB S3,
WebAB*
Morton, Jennie Chinn d1920 *WhAm 1,
WomWWA 14*
Morton, Jeremiah 1799-1878 *BiAUS, BiDrAC,
WhAm H, WhAmP*
Morton, Jeremiah Rogers 1842- *WhAm 1*
Morton, John 1670?-1726 *DcScB*
Morton, John 1724-1777 *AmBi, ApCAB,
BiAUS, BiDrAC, DcAmB, Drake,
NatCAB 10, TwCBDA, WhAm H,
WhAmP*
Morton, John 1889-1962 *WhAm 4*
Morton, John Ludlow 1792-1871 *NewYHSD*

Morton, John P 1807-1889 *TwCBDA*
Morton, Joseph d1721 *NatCAB 12*
Morton, Joseph 1911-1945 *WhAm 2*
Morton, Joy 1855-1934 *NatCAB 17, WhAm 1*
Morton, Julius Sterling 1832-1902 *AmBi, ApCAB Sup, BiDrUSE, DcAmB, EncAAH, NatCAB 6, REnAW, TwCBDA, WebAB, WhAm 1*
Morton, Levi Parsons 1824-1920 *AmBi, ApCAB, ApCAB X, BiDrAC, BiDrUSE, DcAmB, NatCAB 1, TwCBDA, WebAB, WhAm 1, WhAmP*
Morton, Louis 1913-1976 *WhAm 6*
Morton, Marcus 1784-1864 *ApCAB, BiAUS, BiDrAC, DcAmB, Drake, NatCAB 1, TwCBDA, WhAm H, WhAmP*
Morton, Marcus 1819-1891 *ApCAB, DcAmB, NatCAB 2, TwCBDA, WhAm H*
Morton, Mark 1859-1951 *NatCAB 41*
Morton, Martha 1865- *AmWom*
Morton, Mary Alpha Hanmer 1875- *WomWWA 14*
Morton, Meyer 1889-1948 *NatCAB 37*
Morton, Nancy Jarrette Brayton *WomWWA 14*
Morton, Nathaniel 1613-1685 *ApCAB, DcAmB, Drake, NatCAB 7, TwCBDA, WhAm H*
Morton, Oliver Hazard Perry Throck 1823-1877 *AmBi, ApCAB, BiAUS, BiDrAC, DcAmB, Drake, McGEWB, NatCAB 13, TwCBDA, WebAB, WhAm H, WhAmP*
Morton, Oliver Perry 1874-1948 *NatCAB 36*
Morton, Oren Frederic 1857-1926 *WhAm 1*
Morton, Paul 1857-1911 *BiDrUSE, DcAmB, NatCAB 13, NatCAB 14, WhAm 1*
Morton, Perez 1751-1837 *ApCAB*
Morton, Perry William 1907-1967 *WhAm 4*
Morton, Richard 1637-1698 *BiHiMed*
Morton, Richard Albert Dunlap 1890-1954 *WhAm 3*
Morton, Richard Lee 1889-1974 *WhAm 6*
Morton, Robert 1760-1786 *ApCAB*
Morton, Rogers Clark Ballard 1914- *BiDrAC, BiDrUSE*
Morton, Rosalie Slaughter 1876- *WhAm 5, WomWWA 14*
Morton, Samuel George 1799-1851 *ApCAB, DcAmB, DcScB, Drake, NatCAB 10, TwCBDA, WhAm H*
Morton, Samuel Packwood, Jr. 1870-1946 *NatCAB 37*
Morton, Samuel Walker 1861-1931 *WhAm 1*
Morton, Sarah Wentworth Apthorp 1759-1846 *ApCAB, DcAmB, Drake, NotAW*
Morton, Sarah Wentworth Apthorpe 1759-1846 *NatCAB 8, WhAm H*
Morton, Sterling 1885-1961 *WhAm 4*
Morton, Thomas *AmBi, DcAmB, WhAm H*
Morton, Thomas d1646? *Drake*
Morton, Thomas 1575?-1646 *ApCAB, NatCAB 7*
Morton, Thomas 1579?-1647 *EncAB*
Morton, Thomas 1590?-1647? *WebAB*
Morton, Thomas George 1835- *ApCAB, TwCBDA, WhAm 4*
Morton, Thruston Ballard 1907- *BiDrAC*
Morton, William Henry Stephenson 1882-1965 *WhAm 4*
Morton, William James 1845-1920 *ApCAB X, DcAmB, NatCAB 8*
Morton, William Thomas Green 1819-1868 *AmBi, ApCAB, ApCAB X, AsBiEn, BiHiMed, DcAmB, Drake, McGEWB, NatCAB 8, TwCBDA, WebAB, WhAm H*
Morton, Woolridge Brown 1882-1967 *WhAm 4*
Morville, Robert W *NewYHSD*
Morviller, Joseph *NewYHSD*
Morwitz, Edward 1815-1893 *ApCAB, DcAmB, NatCAB 8, WhAm H*
Morwitz, Samuel Mordecai 1886-1972 *WhAm 6*
Mory, E Lawrence 1880- *WhAm 6*
Moryson, Francis *NatCAB 13*
Mosander, Carl Gustaf 1797-1858 *DcScB*
Mosander, Carl Gustav 1797-1858 *AsBiEn*
Mosby, Benjamin Harrison 1886- *WhoColR*
Mosby, Charles Virgil 1876-1942 *WhAm 2*

Mosby, John Singleton 1833-1916 *AmBi, ApCAB, DcAmB, NatCAB 4, TwCBDA, WebAB, WebAMB, WhAm 1*
Mosby, Mary Webster 1791-1844 *ApCAB*
Mosby, Thomas Speed 1874-1954 *NatCAB 45*
Moschcowitz, Alexis Victor 1865-1933 *WhAm 1*
Moschcowitz, Paul 1875-1942 *WhAm 2*
Moschel, Louis Conrad 1878-1940 *NatCAB 31*
Moscona, Nicola 1907-1975 *WhAm 6*
Moscoso, Luis Alvarado De 1505-1561 *ApCAB*
Moscoso DeAlvarado, Luis De *DcAmB, WhAm H*
Moscowitz, Grover M 1886-1947 *WhAm 2*
Moscrip, William Smith 1878- *WhAm 6*
Moseley, Beauregard Fritz 1868- *WhoColR*
Moseley, Ben. Perley Poore 1881-1963 *WhAm 4*
Moseley, Benjamin 1739?-1819 *ApCAB*
Moseley, Charles West 1865-1937 *WhAm 3*
Moseley, Douglas 1860-1924 *NatCAB 20*
Moseley, Edward d1749 *NatCAB 7*
Moseley, Edward Augustus 1846-1911 *DcAmB, NatCAB 10, TwCBDA, WhAm 1*
Moseley, Edward Buckland 1846-1923 *WhAm 1*
Moseley, Edwin Lincoln 1865-1948 *NatCAB 41*
Moseley, Ella Lowery *WomWWA 14*
Moseley, Frederick S, Jr. d1972 *WhAm 5*
Moseley, George VanHorn 1874-1960 *WhAm 4*
Moseley, Hal Walters 1888-1941 *WhAm 2*
Moseley, Hal Waters 1888-1941 *NatCAB 30*
Moseley, Hartwell Robert 1863-1926 *NatCAB 20*
Moseley, Henry Gwyn Jeffreys 1887-1915 *AsBiEn, DcScB*
Moseley, John Ohleyer 1893-1955 *NatCAB 46, WhAm 3*
Moseley, Jonathan Ogden 1762-1838 *BiDrAC, WhAm H, WhAmP*
Moseley, Jonathan Ogden 1762-1839 *BiAUS, TwCBDA*
Moseley, Lonzo B 1852- *WhAm 4*
Moseley, Martha Alger 1858- *WomWWA 14*
Moseley, Mercer Pamplin 1872-1928 *WhAm 1*
Moseley, William Abbott d1873 *BiAUS*
Moseley, William Abbott 1798-1873 *BiDrAC, WhAm H*
Moseley, William Abbott 1799-1873 *TwCBDA*
Moseley, William Dunn 1795-1863 *ApCAB, BiAUS, NatCAB 11, TwCBDA*
Mosely, Edward *NewYHSD*
Mosely, Mary Webster d1844 *Drake*
Mosely, Philip Edward 1905-1972 *NatCAB 56, WhAm 5*
Moseman, Clyde Kenneth 1900-1961 *NatCAB 50*
Mosenthal, Herman Otto 1878-1954 *NatCAB 40, WhAm 3*
Mosenthal, Johanna Kroeber *WomWWA 14*
Mosenthal, Joseph 1834-1896 *ApCAB, WhAm H*
Moser, Alfred A 1873- *WhAm 5*
Moser, Charles Kroth 1877- *WhAm 5*
Moser, Christopher Otto 1885-1935 *DcAmB S1, WhAm 1*
Moser, Clarence Patten 1876- *WhAm 5*
Moser, Ellsworth 1895-1965 *WhAm 4*
Moser, Frank H 1886-1964 *NatCAB 52*
Moser, Guy Louis 1886-1961 *BiDrAC, WhAm 4*
Moser, Henry S 1900-1971 *WhAm 5*
Moser, Jefferson Franklin 1848-1934 *NatCAB 26, WhAm 1*
Moser, John Henri 1876-1951 *IIBEAAW*
Moser, Joseph Casper 1891-1964 *NatCAB 50*
Moser, William 1868- *WhAm 1*
Moses 1392?BC-1272?BC *McGEWB*
Moses, Alfred Geiger 1878- *NatCAB 13, WhAm 6*
Moses, Alfred Joseph 1859-1920 *NatCAB 47, WhAm 1*
Moses, Andrew 1874-1946 *NatCAB 41, WhAm 2*
Moses, Anna Mary Robertson 1860-1961 *BnEnAmA, EncAAH, McGEWB, NatCAB 46, WebAB, WhAm 4*
Moses, Annahay Sneed *WomWWA 14*
Moses, B *NewYHSD*
Moses, Belle *WomWWA 14*
Moses, Bernard 1846-1930 *AmBi, DcAmB,*

NatCAB 26, TwCBDA, WhAm 1
Moses, C A 1895-1964 *WhAm 4*
Moses, Charles Leavell 1856-1910 *BiDrAC, NatCAB 2, TwCBDA*
Moses, Charles Malcolm 1851- *NatCAB 14*
Moses, Colter Hamilton 1887-1966 *NatCAB 52, WhAm 4*
Moses, Elbert Raymond 1879- *WhAm 6*
Moses, Ellen Allen 1853- *WomWWA 14*
Moses, Emile Phillips 1880- *WhAm 6*
Moses, F J, Jr. 1838?-1906 *BiAUS*
Moses, Frank Rae 1883-1944 *NatCAB 34*
Moses, Franklin J 1838?-1906 *DcAmB, NatCAB 12*
Moses, Frederick Taft 1885-1959 *WhAm 3*
Moses, G *NewYHSD*
Moses, George Higgins 1869-1944 *ApCAB X, BiDrAC, DcAmB S3, NatCAB 14, NatCAB 43, WhAm 2, WhAmP*
Moses, Harriet Roberts 1881- *WomWWA 14*
Moses, Harry 1882-1958 *NatCAB 49*
Moses, Harry Morgan 1896-1956 *NatCAB 45, WhAm 3*
Moses, Henry L 1879-1961 *WhAm 4*
Moses, Horace Augustus 1862-1947 *WhAm 2*
Moses, John 1825- *ApCAB Sup*
Moses, John 1885-1945 *BiDrAC, NatCAB 35, WhAm 2, WhAmP*
Moses, Lincoln Ellsworth 1860-1928 *NatCAB 23*
Moses, Louis Augustus 1876-1952 *NatCAB 41*
Moses, Lydia Theresa *WomWWA 14*
Moses, Mary Edith *WomWWA 14*
Moses, Mary Frances Goddard 1875- *WomWWA 14*
Moses, Montrose Jonas 1878-1934 *DcAmB S1, WhAm 1*
Moses, Morris *NewYHSD*
Moses, Nicholas Peter 1869-1952 *NatCAB 42*
Moses, Phoebe Ann *REnAW*
Moses, Robert 1888- *WebAB*
Moses, Samuel C 1818?- *NewYHSD*
Moses, Siegfried 1887-1974 *WhAm 6*
Moses, Thomas 1869-1948 *WhAm 3*
Moses, Thomas Freeman 1836-1917 *ApCAB, TwCBDA, WhAm 1*
Moses, Thomas P 1774?- *NewYHSD*
Moses, Walter H 1898-1973 *WhAm 6*
Mosessohn, David Nehemiah 1883-1930 *DcAmB, WhAm 1*
Mosessohn, Moses Dayyan 1884-1940 *NatCAB 30, WhAm 1*
Mosessohn, Nehemiah 1853-1926 *NatCAB 20, WhAm 1*
Mosgrove, James 1821-1900 *BiDrAC*
Mosher, Aaron Alexander Roland 1881-1959 *WhAm 3*
Mosher, Charles Adams 1906- *BiDrAC*
Mosher, Clelia Duel 1863- *WhAm 1, WomWWA 14*
Mosher, Edna *WomWWA 14*
Mosher, Eliza Maria 1846-1928 *ApCAB X, DcAmB, NatCAB 15, NotAW, TwCBDA, WhAm 1, WomWWA 14*
Mosher, Esek Ray 1882-1944 *WhAm 2*
Mosher, Frances Stewart 1845-1926 *ApCAB X*
Mosher, George Clark 1858-1929 *WhAm 1, WhAm 1C*
Mosher, George Frank 1844-1929 *ApCAB X, NatCAB 21, TwCBDA, WhAm 1*
Mosher, Gouverneur Frank 1871-1941 *WhAm 1*
Mosher, Harris Peyton 1867-1954 *WhAm 3*
Mosher, Howard Townsend 1868-1919 *WhAm 1*
Mosher, Ira 1887-1968 *NatCAB 55, WhAm 4A*
Mosher, J Montgomery 1864-1922 *NatCAB 36*
Mosher, Jacob Simmons 1834-1883 *ApCAB, TwCBDA*
Mosher, Mary E *BiCAW*
Mosher, Raymond Mylar 1894-1956 *NatCAB 46, WhAm 3*
Mosher, Robert Brent 1856-1927 *WhAm 1*
Mosher, Samuel Barlow 1892-1970 *WhAm 5*
Mosher, Thomas Bird 1852-1923 *DcAmB, NatCAB 20, WhAm 1*
Mosher, William Allison 1912-1972 *WhAm 5*

Mosher, William Eugene 1877-1945
NatCAB 34, WhAm 2
Moshweshwe 1787?-1868 *McGEWB*
Mosier, Harold Gerard 1889-1971 *BiDrAC,*
WhAm 5
Mosier, J *NewYHSD*
Mosier, Jeremiah George 1862-1922 *WhAm 1*
Mosier, Martin Henry 1856- *ApCAB X*
Mosier, Orval McKinley 1897-1967 *WhAm 4*
Mosiman, Samuel K 1867-1940 *WhAm 1*
Moskowitz, Belle Lindner Israel 1877-1933
BiCAW
Moskowitz, Belle Lindner Israels 1877-1933
DcAmB S1, NotAW, WhAm 1
Mosle, Heinrich 1864-1921 *NatCAB 19*
Mosler, Edwin H 1875-1952 *WhAm 3*
Mosler, Gustavus *NewYHSD*
Mosler, Henry 1841-1920 *AmBi, ApCAB,*
ApCAB X, DcAmB, IIBEAAW,
NatCAB 9, TwCBDA, WhAm 1
Mosler, Henry, Jr. *NewYHSD*
Mosquera, Ruy Garcia 1501-1555 *ApCAB,*
Drake
Mosquera, Tomas Cipriano De 1798-1878
ApCAB, McGEWB
Moss, Albert Bartlett 1849-1914 *WhAm 1*
Moss, Charles McCord 1902-1971 *WhAm 5*
Moss, Charles Melville 1853- *WhAm 4*
Moss, Chase 1912-1974 *WhAm 6*
Moss, Edward *NewYHSD*
Moss, Elizabeth Wilson 1872- *WomWWA 14*
Moss, Emma Sadler 1898-1970 *WhAm 5*
Moss, Eugene Grissom 1877-1949 *NatCAB 39*
Moss, Frank 1838-1905? *NewYHSD*
Moss, Frank 1860-1920 *ApCAB Sup, DcAmB,*
NatCAB 9, WhAm 1
Moss, Frank Edward 1911- *BiDrAC*
Moss, Frank Hazlett 1869-1953 *NatCAB 44*
Moss, Frank John 1863-1943 *NatCAB 44,*
WhAm 5
Moss, Fred August 1893-1966 *NatCAB 52,*
WhAm 4
Moss, George French 1871-1940 *NatCAB 29*
Moss, Herbert James 1910-1955 *WhAm 3*
Moss, Hunter Holmes, Jr. 1874-1916 *BiDrAC,*
WhAm 1
Moss, James Alfred 1872-1941 *NatCAB 30,*
WhAm 1
Moss, Jesse Lathrop 1847- *NatCAB 16*
Moss, John Calvin 1838-1892 *ApCAB, DcAmB,*
NatCAB 11, WhAm H
Moss, John Emerson 1913- *BiDrAC*
Moss, John McKenzie 1868-1929 *BiDrAC*
Moss, Joseph 1886-1955 *WhAm 3*
Moss, Lemuel 1829-1904 *ApCAB, DcAmB,*
NatCAB 11, TwCBDA, WhAm 1
Moss, Leslie Bates 1889-1949 *WhAm 2*
Moss, Louis John 1884-1948 *WhAm 2*
Moss, Mary *WebAB*
Moss, Mary 1864-1914 *WhAm 1,*
WomWWA 14
Moss, Maximilian 1896-1964 *NatCAB 50,*
WhAm 4
Moss, Mildred Emily 1874- *WomWWA 14*
Moss, Nathaniel Peter 1864-1941 *NatCAB 30*
Moss, Ralph Wilbur 1862-1919 *BiDrAC,*
WhAm 4
Moss, Robert Edward 1871-1950 *NatCAB 38*
Moss, Sanford Alexander 1872-1946
DcAmB S4
Moss, Thomas 1836-1881 *ApCAB*
Moss, William Lorenzo 1876-1957 *DcScB,*
WhAm 3
Moss, William Ray 1867- *ApCAB X*
Moss, William Washburn 1872-1949
NatCAB 40, WhAm 2
Moss, Woodson 1852-1920 *WhAm 1*
Mossadegh, Mohammed 1880?-1967 *WhAm 4*
Mossbauer, Rudolf Ludwig 1929- *AsBiEn*
Mossell, Gertrude E H Bustill 1855- *WhoColR*
Mossell, Nathan F 1856- *WhoColR*
Mosser, Charles Marcel 1908-1972 *WhAm 5*
Mossman, B Paul 1870- *WhAm 5*
Mossman, Burton C 1867-1956 *REnAW*
Mossman, Frank E 1873-1945 *WhAm 2*
Mossotti, Angelo 1846-1910 *DcScB*
Mossotti, Ottaviano Fabrizio 1791-1863 *DcScB*
Most, Johann Joseph 1846-1906 *AmBi,*

DcAmB, WhAm HA, WhAm 4
Mosteller, L Karlton 1895-1966 *WhAm 5*
Mostyn, Martin Joseph 1903-1968 *NatCAB 54*
Mota, Alonso DeLa 1550?-1625 *ApCAB*
Mota-Padilla, Matias DeLa 1688-1776 *ApCAB*
Motamed, Hossein 1893-1955 *NatCAB 45*
Motch, Edwin Raymond 1901-1953 *NatCAB 46*
Motchan, Louis A 1908-1973 *WhAm 6*
Mote, Alden 1840-1917 *NewYHSD*
Mote, Carl Henry 1884-1946 *WhAm 2*
Mote, Donald Roosevelt 1900-1968 *NatCAB 54,*
WhAm 5
Mote, Marcus 1817-1898 *NewYHSD*
Moten, Bennie 1894-1935 *WhAm 4*
Moten, Lucy Ella 1851-1933 *BiDAmEd,*
NotAW
Moten, Roger Henwood 1879-1951 *WhAm 3*
Mothe Cadillac, Antoine DeLa 1660?-1717?
Drake
Mothershead, James Frank Hume 1877-1963
NatCAB 50
Motherwell, Hiram 1888-1945 *NatCAB 34*
Motherwell, Robert Burns, II 1884-1944
WhAm 2
Motherwell, Robert Burns, III 1915- *BnEnAmA,*
EncAB, McGEWB
Motley, Edward 1879-1949 *NatCAB 38*
Motley, Emery Tyler 1889-1952 *WhAm 3*
Motley, Ethel Levering 1878- *WomWWA 14*
Motley, J Lothrop 1889-1959 *NatCAB 47*
Motley, John Lothrop 1814-1877 *AmBi,*
ApCAB, BiAUS, DcAmB, Drake,
McGEWB, NatCAB 5, TwCBDA,
WebAB, WhAm H
Motley, Katherine Lincoln *WomWWA 14*
Motley, Warren 1883-1971 *WhAm 5*
Motley, Willard Francis 1912-1965 *WhAm 4*
Motolinia, Toribio De d1568 *ApCAB*
Moton, Robert Russa 1867-1940 *BiDAmEd,*
DcAmB S2, WhAm 1
Moton, Robert Russo 1867-1940 *WhoColR*
Motross, Lynn 1895-1961 *WhAm 4*
Motry, Hubert Louis d1952 *WhAm 3*
Mott, Alexander Brown 1826-1889 *ApCAB,*
NatCAB 9, TwCBDA
Mott, B H *NewYHSD*
Mott, Charles Stewart 1875- *WhAm 5*
Mott, Edward Harold 1845-1920 *NatCAB 18*
Mott, Elliott Bostick 1861-1957 *NatCAB 49*
Mott, Estes B 1907-1951 *NatCAB 40*
Mott, Francis Edward 1904-1973 *WhAm 6*
Mott, Frank Luther 1886-1964 *NatCAB 52,*
WhAm 4
Mott, George Scudder 1829- *ApCAB*
Mott, George Scudder 1829-1891 *NatCAB 14*
Mott, George Scudder 1829-1901 *WhAm 1*
Mott, Gershom 1822-1884 *ApCAB, DcAmB,*
Drake, NatCAB 5, TwCBDA, WhAm H
Mott, Gorden Newell 1812-1887 *BiAUS*
Mott, Gordon Newell 1812-1887 *BiDrAC,*
WhAm H, WhAmP
Mott, Henry Augustus 1852-1896 *ApCAB,*
NatCAB 3, TwCBDA
Mott, James 1739-1823 *BiAUS, BiDrAC,*
WhAm H
Mott, James 1788-1868 *AmBi, ApCAB,*
DcAmB, NatCAB 6, TwCBDA,
WhAm H
Mott, James Wheaton 1883-1945 *BiDrAC,*
WhAm 2, WhAmP
Mott, John Griffin 1874-1942 *NatCAB 31,*
WhAm 2
Mott, John Raleigh 1865-1955 *DcAmB S5,*
DcAmReB, McGEWB, NatCAB 44,
WebAB, WhAm 3
Mott, Jordan Lawrence 1829-1915 *NatCAB 7,*
WhAm 1
Mott, Lewis Freeman 1863-1941 *NatCAB 13,*
NatCAB 31, WhAm 1
Mott, Lucrecia Coffin 1793-1880 *WhAmP*
Mott, Lucretia Coffin 1793-1880 *AmBi,*
AmWom, ApCAB, DcAmB, DcAmReB,
Drake, EncAB, McGEWB, NatCAB 2,
NotAW, TwCBDA, WebAB, WhAm H
Mott, Luther Wright 1874-1923 *BiDrAC,*
WhAm 1, WhAmP
Mott, Marcus Fulton 1837-1906 *NatCAB 6*
Mott, Omer Hillman 1891- *WhAm 2*

Mott, Richard 1804-1888 *ApCAB Sup, BiAUS,*
BiDrAC, TwCBDA, WhAm H
Mott, Rodney Loomer 1896-1971 *WhAm 5*
Mott, Seward Hamilton 1888-1965 *NatCAB 52*
Mott, Stanton 1888-1969 *NatCAB 54*
Mott, T Bentley 1865-1952 *WhAm 3*
Mott, Thaddeus Phelps 1831- *ApCAB*
Mott, Valentine 1785-1865 *AmBi, ApCAB,*
BiHiMed, DcAmB, Drake, NatCAB 6,
TwCBDA, WhAm H
Mott, Valentine 1822-1854 *ApCAB*
Mott, Valentine 1852-1918 *ApCAB, TwCBDA,*
WhAm 1
Mott, William Elton 1868-1945 *NatCAB 34,*
WhAm 2
Mott, William Franklin 1785-1867 *ApCAB*
Mott, William Roy 1880-1929 *NatCAB 22*
Motta Feo E Torres, Luiz De 1769-1823 *ApCAB*
Motte, E A LeC, Comte Du Boys DeLa
1683-1764 *ApCAB*
Motte, Guillaume T, Comte Piquet DeLa
1720-1791 *ApCAB*
Motte, Isaac 1738-1795 *ApCAB, BiAUS,*
BiDrAC, TwCBDA, WhAm H
Motte, Rebecca Brewton 1739-1815 *ApCAB,*
Drake
Motter, Edwin Cameron 1884-1961 *NatCAB 50*
Motter, Orton B 1904-1953 *WhAm 3*
Mottet, Henry 1845-1929 *NatCAB 23,*
WhAm 1
Mottet, Jeanie Gallup *WhAm 5*
Mottey, Joseph 1756-1821 *NatCAB 7*
Mottier, David Myers 1864-1940 *NatCAB 15,*
WhAm 1
Motto, M Paul 1886-1967 *NatCAB 54*
Mottram, C *NewYHSD*
Mottram, James Cecil 1879-1945 *DcScB*
Motzkin, Theodore S 1908-1970 *WhAm 5*
Mouchez, Ernest Barthelemy 1821- *DcScB*
Moudry, Frank William 1895-1971 *NatCAB 56*
Moudy, Alfred L 1879- *WhAm 6*
Moudy, Walter Frank 1929-1973 *WhAm 5*
Mouhtar Bey, Ahmed 1871- *WhAm 5*
Moulac, Vincent Marie 1780-1836 *ApCAB*
Mould, Elmer Wallace King 1886-1950
WhAm 3
Mould, J B *NewYHSD*
Mould, Jacob Wray 1825-1884 *WhAm H*
Mould, Jacob Wrey 1825-1886 *ApCAB,*
NatCAB 3
Moulder, Morgan Moore 1904- *BiDrAC,*
WhAmP
Moulds, George Henry 1915-1973 *WhAm 6*
Moulin, Jean 1899-1943 *WhWW-II*
Moulson, Deborah *NewYHSD*
Moulthrop, Reuben 1763-1814 *BnEnAmA,*
NewYHSD
Moulton, Allen King 1883-1952 *NatCAB 41*
Moulton, Arthur Julian 1883-1951 *NatCAB 41*
Moulton, Arthur Wheelock 1873-1962 *WhAm 4*
Moulton, Augustus Freedom 1848- *NatCAB 14*
Moulton, Charles Robert 1884-1949 *WhAm 2*
Moulton, Charles Wells 1859-1913 *WhAm 1*
Moulton, Charles William 1859-1924
NatCAB 20, WhAm 1
Moulton, Daisy Adkins *WomWWA 14*
Moulton, David Edward 1871-1951 *NatCAB 40*
Moulton, Dudley 1879- *WhAm 6*
Moulton, Earl L 1878-1958 *WhAm 3*
Moulton, Edwin F 1835-1919 *WhAm 1*
Moulton, Elizabeth Armington 1877-
WomWWA 14
Moulton, Ellen Louise Chandler 1835-1908
AmBi, DcAmB, Drake
Moulton, Forest Ray 1872-1952 *AsBiEn,*
DcAmB S5, DcScB, NatCAB 43,
WhAm 3
Moulton, Frances Estelle 1861-1919
NatCAB 22
Moulton, Frank Prescott 1851- *NatCAB 4,*
WhAm 4
Moulton, Fred Hammond 1878-1932
NatCAB 24
Moulton, George Mayhew 1851-1927 *WhAm 1*
Moulton, Gertrude Evelyn 1880- *WhAm 6*
Moulton, Harold Glen 1883-1966 *WhAm 4*
Moulton, Helen Winifred Shute *WomWWA 14*
Moulton, Jeremiah 1688-1765 *ApCAB, Drake*

Moulton, Joseph White 1789-1875 *ApCAB, Drake*
Moulton, Lewis Fenno 1854-1938 *NatCAB 41*
Moulton, Louise Chandler 1835-1908 *AmWom, ApCAB, NatCAB 3, NotAW, TwCBDA, WhAm 1*
Moulton, Mace 1796-1867 *BiAUS, BiDrAC, WhAm H*
Moulton, Manning Cole 1893-1956 *NatCAB 45*
Moulton, Martha Dever 1885- *WomWWA 14*
Moulton, Mary Kennington 1913-1972 *WhAm 6*
Moulton, Olivia Woodburn 1870- *WomWWA 14*
Moulton, Richard Green 1849-1924 *AmBi, DcAmB, WhAm 1*
Moulton, Robert Hurt 1880- *WhAm 6*
Moulton, Robert Taylor 1907-1963 *NatCAB 51*
Moulton, Samuel Wheeler 1821-1905 *BiDrAC, TwCBDA*
Moulton, Samuel Wheeler 1822-1905 *BiAUS*
Moulton, Sherman Roberts 1876-1949 *WhAm 2*
Moulton, Vern 1880-1959 *WhAm 3*
Moulton, Warren Joseph 1865-1947 *WhAm 2*
Moulton, William Clarence 1873-1927 *NatCAB 21*
Moulton, William Horace 1870-1961 *WhAm 4*
Moulton, Willis Bryant 1862-1938 *WhAm 1*
Moultons, Abel 1784-1840? *BnEnAmA*
Moultons, Ebenezer 1768-1824 *BnEnAmA*
Moultons, Enoch 1780-1815 *BnEnAmA*
Moultons, Joseph 1694-1756 *BnEnAmA*
Moultons, Joseph 1744-1816 *BnEnAmA*
Moultons, Joseph 1814-1903 *BnEnAmA*
Moultons, William 1720-1793? *BnEnAmA*
Moultons, William 1772-1861 *BnEnAmA*
Moultrie, James 1793-1869 *ApCAB, NatCAB 12*
Moultrie, John 1729-1798 *ApCAB, DcAmB, WhAm H*
Moultrie, Lloyd Walker 1868-1950 *NatCAB 38*
Moultrie, William 1730-1805 *AmBi, DcAmB, WebAB, WebAMB, WhAm H, WhoMilH*
Moultrie, William 1731-1805 *ApCAB, BiAUS, Drake, NatCAB 1, TwCBDA*
Moultrop, Irving Edwin 1865- *WhAm 4*
Mounger, W M 1901-1957 *WhAm 3*
Mount, Arnold John 1884-1942 *NatCAB 32, WhAm 2*
Mount, Finley Pogue 1866-1938 *WhAm 1*
Mount, George Haines 1879- *WhAm 6*
Mount, Henry Smith 1802-1841 *ApCAB, NewYHSD*
Mount, James Atwell 1843-1901 *NatCAB 13, NatCAB 30, TwCBDA, WhAm 1*
Mount, Mary W Miller 1874- *WomWWA 14*
Mount, Oliver Erskine 1892-1965 *WhAm 4*
Mount, Russell Theodore 1881- *WhAm 6*
Mount, Shepard Alonzo 1804-1868 *ApCAB, NewYHSD*
Mount, Sheppard Alonzo 1804-1868 *TwCBDA*
Mount, Wallace 1859-1921 *NatCAB 14, WhAm 1*
Mount, William Sidney 1807-1868 *AmBi, ApCAB, BnEnAmA, DcAmB, Drake, EncAB, McGEWB, NatCAB 14, NewYHSD, TwCBDA, WebAB, WhAm H*
Mountain, Armine Simcoe Henry 1797-1854 *ApCAB*
Mountain, Armine Wale 1823-1885 *ApCAB*
Mountain, George Jehoshaphat 1789-1863 *ApCAB, Drake*
Mountain, Harry Montgomery 1901-1973 *WhAm 6*
Mountain, Jacob 1750-1825 *ApCAB, Drake*
Mountain, Worrall Frederick 1877-1935 *NatCAB 27*
Mountbatten, Lord Louis 1900- *WhWW-II*
Mountcastle, Clara H 1837- *AmWom, ApCAB*
Mountcastle, George Williams 1871- *WhAm 5*
Mountcastle, Robert Edward Lee 1865-1913 *WhAm 1*
Mountford, William 1816-1885 *ApCAB, Drake*
Mountfort, John 1789-1851 *Drake*
Mountin, Joseph Walter 1891-1952 *NatCAB 41, WhAm 3*
Mountjoy, Baron Charles Blount 1562-1606 *WhoMilH*

Mountz, George Edward 1908-1951 *NatCAB 40*
Moura, Francisco De 1580-1657 *ApCAB*
Mouraille, Theodore Gustave 1594-1651 *ApCAB*
Moursund, Andrew Fleming, Jr. 1901-1972 *WhAm 5*
Moursund, Walter Henrik 1884-1959 *WhAm 3A*
Mourt, G 1585-1624 *Drake*
Mourt, George 1585-1624 *DcAmB*
Mousel, Lloyd Harvey 1903-1970 *WhAm 5*
Mouser, Grant Earl 1868-1949 *BiDrAC, NatCAB 39*
Mouser, Grant Earl, Jr. 1895-1943 *BiDrAC, WhAm 2*
Mousse, John DeLa *ApCAB*
Mousseau, Joseph Alfred 1838- *ApCAB*
Moutard, Theodore Florentin 1827-1901 *DcScB*
Mouton, Alexander d1864 *BiAUS*
Mouton, Alexander 1804-1885 *ApCAB, BiDrAC, DcAmB, WhAm H, WhAmP*
Mouton, Alexandre 1804-1882 *NatCAB 10*
Mouton, Alexandre 1804-1885 *TwCBDA*
Mouton, Alfred 1829-1864 *Drake, TwCBDA*
Mouton, Gabriel 1618-1694 *DcScB*
Mouton, Jean Jacques Alexandre Alfred 1829-1864 *ApCAB*
Mouton, Robert Louis 1892-1956 *BiDrAC*
Mouzon, Edwin DuBose 1869-1937 *NatCAB 29, WhAm 1*
Mouzon, James Carlisle 1907-1975 *WhAm 6*
Movius, John Henry 1860- *NatCAB 17*
Mowat, John Bower 1825- *ApCAB*
Mowat, Magnus 1875- *WhAm 5*
Mowat, Oliver 1820- *ApCAB*
Mowatt, Anna Cara Ogden 1819-1870 *WebAB*
Mowatt, Anna Cora Ogden 1819-1870 *AmBi, ApCAB, DcAmB, Drake, NotAW, TwCBDA, WhAm H*
Mowatt, Henry d1797 *Drake*
Mowbray, Albert H 1881-1949 *WhAm 2*
Mowbray, George Mordey 1814-1891 *DcAmB, NatCAB 23, WhAm H*
Mowbray, George W 1815-1891 *TwCBDA*
Mowbray, Harry Siddons 1858-1928 *AmBi, ApCAB Sup, NatCAB 23, WhAm 1*
Mowbray, Henry Siddons 1858-1928 *DcAmB, NatCAB 12, TwCBDA*
Mowbray-Clarke, John Frederick 1869-1953 *NatCAB 15, WhAm 3*
Mowell, Ada Sprague *WomWWA 14*
Mower, Charles Drown 1875-1942 *WhAm 1, WhAm 2*
Mower, Donald Roger 1910-1964 *NatCAB 51*
Mower, Horace *BiAUS*
Mower, Joseph Anthony 1827-1870 *ApCAB, DcAmB, NatCAB 12, TwCBDA, WebAMB, WhAm H*
Mower, Joseph Anthony 1830?-1870 *Drake*
Mower, Sarah Brown *WomWWA 14*
Mowery, Edward Joseph 1906-1970 *NatCAB 56*
Mowery, William Byron 1899-1957 *WhAm 3*
Mowrer, Frank Roger 1870- *WhAm 5*
Mowrer, Paul Scott 1887-1971 *WhAm 5*
Mowris, William Silas 1867-1936 *NatCAB 27*
Mowry, Blanche Swett 1870- *WomWWA 14*
Mowry, Daniel 1729-1806 *ApCAB, BiAUS, BiDrAC, NatCAB 8, TwCBDA, WhAm H*
Mowry, Harold 1894-1958 *NatCAB 47, WhAm 3*
Mowry, Martha H 1818- *AmWom*
Mowry, Minnie Winsor 1864- *WomWWA 14*
Mowry, Ross Rutledge 1882-1957 *WhAm 3*
Mowry, Sylvester 1830?-1871 *ApCAB, Drake*
Mowry, William Augustus 1829-1917 *BiDAmEd, DcAmB, NatCAB 25, TwCBDA, WhAm 1*
Mowry, William Cary 1850- *NatCAB 7*
Moxey, Albert Frankish 1884-1953 *NatCAB 41*
Moxey, Louis White, Jr. 1877-1956 *NatCAB 46*
Moxham, Arthur James 1854-1931 *DcAmB*
Moxley, William James 1851-1938 *BiDrAC, WhAm 4*
Moxom, Philip Stafford 1848-1923 *DcAmB, NatCAB 19, TwCBDA, WhAm 1*
Moya DeContreras, Pedro 1520?-1591 *ApCAB*
Moyar, Charles Clinton 1881-1943 *NatCAB 37*
Moyer, Albert Weer 1873-1919 *NatCAB 18*

Moyer, Andrew Jackson 1899-1959 *WhAm 3*
Moyer, Benton Leslie 1889-1964 *WhAm 4*
Moyer, Burton Jones d1973 *WhAm 5*
Moyer, Charles H *WhAm 4*
Moyer, David Gurstelle 1900-1971 *WhAm 5*
Moyer, Fayette Elmer 1865-1942 *NatCAB 36*
Moyer, Gabriel Hocker 1873-1939 *WhAm 1*
Moyer, Harold Nicholas 1858-1923 *WhAm 1*
Moyer, Harriet Wheeler 1864- *WomWWA 14*
Moyer, Harvey Allen 1855-1935 *NatCAB 28*
Moyer, Harvey Vernon 1894-1959 *WhAm 3*
Moyer, James Ambrose 1877-1945 *WhAm 2*
Moyer, Joseph Kearney 1890-1969 *WhAm 5*
Moyer, Sarah J Atlee 1831- *WomWWA 14*
Moyer, William Henry 1860-1923 *WhAm 1*
Moyers, William 1916- *IlBEAAW*
Moyerstein *NewYHSD*
Moyerstein, Benjamin *NewYHSD*
Moylan, Lloyd 1893- *IlBEAAW*
Moylan, Stephen 1734-1811 *ApCAB, Drake, NatCAB 1, TwCBDA, WhAm H*
Moylan, Stephen 1737-1811 *DcAmB*
Moylan, William 1822-1891 *NatCAB 2, TwCBDA*
Moyle, Edward Henry 1870- *NatCAB 16*
Moyle, Henry Dinwoodey 1889-1963 *WhAm 4*
Moyle, James Henry 1858-1946 *NatCAB 46, WhAm 2*
Moyle, Walter Gladstone 1895-1970 *WhAm 5*
Moynahan, John Raymond 1891-1952 *NatCAB 41*
Moynelo, Andres Eusebio 1845-1912 *NatCAB 30*
Moynihan, Lord 1865-1936 *BiHiMed*
Moynihan, Charles Joseph 1883-1956 *NatCAB 48*
Moynihan, James Humphrey 1882-1959 *WhAm 4*
Moynihan, P H 1869-1946 *WhAm 2*
Moynihan, Patrick Henry 1869-1946 *BiDrAC*
Moyse, Alphonse, Jr. 1898-1973 *NatCAB 57*
Moyse, Charles Ebenezer 1852- *ApCAB*
Moyse, Hyacinthe 1769-1801 *ApCAB*
Mozart, Wolfgang Amadeus 1756-1791 *McGEWB*
Mozee, Phoebe Anne Oakley 1860-1926 *WebAB, WhAm HA, WhAm 4*
Mozier, Joseph 1812-1870 *AmBi, ApCAB, DcAmB, Drake, NatCAB 8, NewYHSD, WhAm H*
Mozley, Loren Norman 1905- *IlBEAAW*
Mozley, Norman Adolphus 1865-1922 *BiDrAC*
Mqhayi, Samuel Edward Krune 1875-1945 *McGEWB*
Mrak, Ignatius 1810-1901 *ApCAB*
Mrak, Ignatius 1816-1901 *NatCAB 12, TwCBDA, WhAm 1*
Mroz, Rudolph John 1897-1956 *NatCAB 47*
Mruk, Joseph 1903- *BiDrAC*
Mruk, Walter 1883-1942 *IlBEAAW*
Muawiya Ibn Abu Sufyan d680 *McGEWB*
Muchlen, Thomas *NewYHSD*
Muchmore, Minnie Sweet *WomWWA 14*
Muckenfuss, Anthony Moultrie 1869-1941 *WhAm 1*
Muckey, Floyd Summer 1858-1930 *WhAm 1*
Muckle, John Seiser 1862-1929 *NatCAB 18, WhAm 1*
Muckle, Mark Richards 1825-1915 *ApCAB X, WhAm 1*
Mudd, Eugene J 1879- *WhAm 6*
Mudd, Francis DeSales 1909-1972 *NatCAB 57*
Mudd, Harvey Gilmer 1857-1933 *NatCAB 24, WhAm 1*
Mudd, Harvey Seeley 1888-1955 *WhAm 3*
Mudd, Ignatius *BiAUS*
Mudd, Mildred Esterbrook 1891-1958 *WhAm 3*
Mudd, Seeley G 1895-1968 *WhAm 4A*
Mudd, Seeley Wintersmith 1861-1926 *WhAm 1*
Mudd, Stuart 1893-1975 *WhAm 6*
Mudd, Sydney Emanuel 1858-1911 *BiDrAC, WhAm 1, WhAmP*
Mudd, Sydney Emanuel 1885-1924 *BiDrAC, WhAm 1, WhAmP*
Mudd, William Swearingen 1885-1942 *NatCAB 31, WhAm 2*
Mudge, Alfred 1809-1882 *ApCAB*
Mudge, Alfred Eugene 1882-1945 *WhAm 2*

Mudge, Benjamin Franklin 1817-1879 *ApCAB, TwCBDA*
Mudge, Claire Ruskin 1879-1959 *NatCAB 49, WhAm 4*
Mudge, Courtland Sawin 1888-1965 *WhAm 4*
Mudge, Edmund Webster 1870-1949 *NatCAB 49, WhAm 2*
Mudge, Enoch 1776-1850 *ApCAB, DcAmB, TwCBDA, WhAm H*
Mudge, Enoch Redington 1812-1881 *ApCAB*
Mudge, Henry Uri 1856-1920 *NatCAB 11, WhAm 1*
Mudge, Isadore Gilbert 1875-1957 *DcAmLiB, WhAm 3*
Mudge, James 1844-1918 *DcAmB, TwCBDA, WhAm 1*
Mudge, Joseph B *NewYHSD*
Mudge, Lewis Seymour 1868-1945 *WhAm 2*
Mudge, Thomas Hicks 1815-1862 *ApCAB, TwCBDA*
Mudge, Verne Donald 1898-1957 *NatCAB 46, WhAm 3*
Mudge, William Leroy 1872-1956 *NatCAB 46, WhAm 3*
Mudge, Zachariah Atwell 1813-1888 *ApCAB, NewYHSD, TwCBDA*
Muehlberger, Clarence Weinert 1896-1966 *WhAm 4*
Muehlebach, George 1833-1905 *NatCAB 16*
Muehlebach, George Edward 1881- *NatCAB 16*
Muehleisen, Eugene Frederick 1903-1973 *WhAm 6*
Muehling, John Adam 1862-1944 *NatCAB 32, WhAm 2*
Muehlstein, Herman 1879-1962 *NatCAB 50*
Mueller *NewYHSD*
Mueller, Adolph 1866-1944 *NatCAB 33, WhAm 2*
Mueller, Alfred 1853-1896 *WhAm H*
Mueller, Arthur E A 1907-1965 *WhAm 4*
Mueller, Christian Frederick 1839-1926 *NatCAB 34*
Mueller, Edward 1883-1954 *WhAm 3*
Mueller, Edward William 1880-1946 *NatCAB 35*
Mueller, Erwin Wilhelm 1911- *AsBiEn*
Mueller, Fred William 1871- *WhAm 5*
Mueller, Frederick *NewYHSD*
Mueller, Frederick Henry 1893- *BiDrUSE*
Mueller, George Wilheim 1863-1914 *NatCAB 16*
Mueller, Gerhardt *NewYHSD*
Mueller, Hans 1900-1965 *WhAm 4*
Mueller, Hans Alexander 1888-1962 *WhAm 4*
Mueller, Henry Richard 1887-1937 *NatCAB 29*
Mueller, Hermann 1860-1909 *WhAm 1*
Mueller, John *NewYHSD*
Mueller, John Henry 1895-1965 *WhAm 4*
Mueller, John Howard 1891-1954 *WhAm 3*
Mueller, John Jacob d1781 *NewYHSD*
Mueller, John Victor 1893-1963 *WhAm 4*
Mueller, Karl Anton 1867- *WhAm 5*
Mueller, Lucien Wilbur 1895-1953 *NatCAB 44*
Mueller, Michael J 1893-1931 *IIBEAAW*
Mueller, Oscar Bernhardt 1871-1941 *NatCAB 30*
Mueller, Oscar Charles 1876- *NatCAB 13*
Mueller, Paul 1899-1965 *WhAm 4*
Mueller, Paul Albert 1897-1956 *WhAm 3*
Mueller, Paul Ferdinand 1857-1931 *WhAm 1*
Mueller, Paul John 1892-1964 *WhAm 4*
Mueller, Ralph Scott 1877-1966 *NatCAB 52*
Mueller, Robert 1864-1940 *NatCAB 30*
Mueller, Samuel 1876-1957 *NatCAB 43*
Mueller, Theodore Edward 1885-1957 *WhAm 3*
Mueller, Theodore Frederick 1899-1958 *WhAm 3*
Mueller, Theophil Herbert 1897-1961 *WhAm 4*
Mueller, Werner 1892-1964 *WhAm 4*
Mueller, William Everett 1894-1947 *NatCAB 36*
Muench, Aloislus Joseph 1889-1962 *WhAm 4*
Muench, Hugo, Jr. 1894-1972 *WhAm 5, WhAm 6*
Muennich, Ferenc 1886-1967 *WhAm 4*
Muenscher, Walter C 1891-1963 *WhAm 4*
Muenster, Paul 1716-1792 *ApCAB*
Mugford, James 1725-1778 *Drake*

Mugford, William *NewYHSD*
Muggeridge, Edward James *WebAB*
Muhammad, Elijah 1897-1975 *DcAmReB, EncAB, WebAB*
Muhammad Ali *WebAB*
Muhammad Bin Tughluq *McGEWB*
Muhammad Ture, Askia 1443?-1538 *McGEWB*
Muhammed, Elijah 1897-1975 *WhAm 6*
Muhleman, George Washington 1871- *WhAm 5*
Muhleman, Maurice Louis 1852-1913 *WhAm 1*
Muhlenberg, Francis Samuel 1795-1832 *ApCAB, BiAUS*
Muhlenberg, Francis Swaine 1795-1831 *BiDrAC, WhAm H*
Muhlenberg, Frederick Augustus 1818-1901 *ApCAB, DcAmB, NatCAB 5, TwCBDA*
Muhlenberg, Frederick Augustus 1887- *BiDrAC*
Muhlenberg, Frederick Augustus Conrad 1750-1801 *AmBi, ApCAB, BiAUS, BiDrAC, DcAmB, Drake, NatCAB 1, TwCBDA, WebAB, WhAm H, WhAmP*
Muhlenberg, Georgeine Kurtz 1858- *WomWWA 14*
Muhlenberg, Gotthilf Heinrich Ernst 1753-1815 *NatCAB 9, TwCBDA*
Muhlenberg, Gotthilf Henry Ernest 1753-1815 *ApCAB, DcAmB, WhAm H*
Muhlenberg, Gotthilf Henry Ernst 1753-1815 *Drake*
Muhlenberg, Heinrich Melchior 1711-1787 *McGEWB*
Muhlenberg, Henry Augustus 1823-1854 *BiAUS, BiDrAC, WhAm H, WhAmP*
Muhlenberg, Henry Augustus Philip 1782-1844 *ApCAB, BiAUS, BiDrAC, DcAmB, Drake, TwCBDA, WhAm H, WhAmP*
Muhlenberg, Henry Melchior 1711-1787 *AmBi, ApCAB, BiAUS, DcAmReB, Drake, NatCAB 5, TwCBDA, WebAB, WhAm H*
Muhlenberg, Hiester Henry 1885-1956 *NatCAB 45*
Muhlenberg, John Peter Gabriel 1746-1807 *AmBi, ApCAB, BiAUS, BiDrAC, DcAmB, Drake, NatCAB 1, TwCBDA, WebAB, WebAMB, WhAm H, WhAmP*
Muhlenberg, William Augustus 1796-1877 *AmBi, ApCAB, DcAmB, DcAmReB, Drake, McGEWB, NatCAB 9, TwCBDA, WhAm H*
Muhlenberg, William Frederick 1852- *NatCAB 10*
Muhlfeld, George Oscar 1875-1948 *NatCAB 37, WhAm 2*
Muhlhauser, George Philip 1877-1963 *NatCAB 50*
Muhlhofer, Elizabeth 1878-1950 *NatCAB 38*
Muhlmann, Adolf 1867- *WhAm 4*
Muhse, Albert Charles 1866-1953 *NatCAB 42*
Muhse, Albert Charles 1867-1953 *WhAm 4*
Muhse, Effa Funk 1877- *WomWWA 14*
Muhyi 'l-Din Al-Maghribi *DcScB*
Muilenburg, James 1896-1974 *WhAm 6*
Muir, Andrew Forest 1916-1969 *WhAm 5*
Muir, Arthur Trench 1881-1935 *NatCAB 27*
Muir, Charles Henry 1860-1933 *ApCAB X, DcAmB S1, NatCAB 40, WebAMB, WhAm 1*
Muir, Downie Davidson, Jr. 1884-1937 *WhAm 1*
Muir, E Stanton 1863- *WhAm 4*
Muir, Edward Oliver 1899-1967 *NatCAB 54*
Muir, Edwin Hawley 1892-1959 *NatCAB 43*
Muir, James d1960 *WhAm 3A, WhAm 4*
Muir, James 1757-1820 *ApCAB*
Muir, James Irvin 1888-1964 *WhAm 4*
Muir, Jere Taylor *TwCBDA, WhAm 5*
Muir, John 1838-1914 *AmBi, ApCAB Sup, ApCAB X, DcAmB, EncAAH, McGEWB, NatCAB 9, REnAW, TwCBDA, WebAB, WhAm 1*
Muir, John 1847-1935 *ApCAB X, WhAm 1*
Muir, Joseph Johnstone 1847-1927 *NatCAB 2, WhAm 1*
Muir, Laura Findley 1868- *WomWWA 14*
Muir, Margaret Purdum *WomWWA 14*
Muir, Matthew Moncrieff Pattison 1848-1931 *DcScB*
Muir, Roy Cummings 1881-1973 *WhAm 6*

Muir, Samuel C 1785?-1832? *ApCAB*
Muir, William Horace 1902-1964 *NatCAB 53, WhAm 4*
Muir, William Wallace 1851-1954 *NatCAB 47*
Muirhead, James Fullarton 1853-1934 *WhAm 1*
Mukasa, Ham 1870- *WhoColR*
Mukerji, Dhan Gopal 1890-1936 *WhAm 1*
Mukhtar, Ahmed 1839-1899 *WhoMilH*
Mulcahy, Francis Patrick 1894-1973 *WhAm 6*
Mulcaster, Sir William Howe 1785-1837 *ApCAB*
Muldener, Marie Louise 1858- *WomWWA 14*
Mulder, Gerardus Johannes 1802-1880 *DcScB*
Mulder, John 1906-1966 *WhAm 4*
Muldoon, Hugh Cornelius d1956 *WhAm 3*
Muldoon, Michael 1836- *NatCAB 11*
Muldoon, Peter James 1863-1927 *NatCAB 16, TwCBDA, WhAm 1*
Muldoon, William 1845-1933 *NatCAB 26*
Muldoon, William 1852-1933 *DcAmB S1, WhAm HA, WhAm 4*
Muldowney, Michael Joseph 1889-1947 *BiDrAC*
Muldrow, Henry Lowndes 1837-1905 *BiDrAC, TwCBDA*
Muler, Hector B *NewYHSD*
Muley Hacen d1484 *WhoMilH*
Muley Soliman *WhAm H*
Mulfinger, George Abraham 1865-1935 *WhAm 1*
Mulford, Anna Isabella *WomWWA 14*
Mulford, Clarence Edward 1883-1956 *WhAm 3*
Mulford, Elisha 1833-1885 *ApCAB, DcAmB, TwCBDA, WhAm H*
Mulford, John Willett 1902-1964 *WhAm 4*
Mulford, Lewis James 1835-1927 *NatCAB 20*
Mulford, Margaret Biddle Guest Blackwell 1879- *WomWWA 14*
Mulford, Prentice 1834-1891 *AmBi, DcAmB, NatCAB 1, WhAm H*
Mulford, Raymon Howard 1909-1973 *WhAm 5*
Mulford, Roland Jessup 1871- *WhAm 5*
Mulford, Stockton *IIBEAAW*
Mulford, Vincent Strong 1872-1960 *NatCAB 49*
Mulford, Walter 1877-1955 *NatCAB 46, WhAm 5*
Mulgrave, Constantine Henry 1797-1863 *ApCAB*
Mulgrave, Constantine John Phipps 1744-1792 *ApCAB*
Mulgrave, George A Constantine Phipps 1819- *ApCAB*
Mulgrave, Henry Phipps 1755-1831 *ApCAB*
Mulgrew, John Elliott 1886- *NatCAB 19*
Mulhaupt, Frederick J 1871-1938 *WhAm 1*
Mulhauser, Frank A 1887-1946 *NatCAB 33*
Mulhauser, Frederick Ludwig 1911-1974 *WhAm 6*
Mulherin, William Anthony 1872-1945 *NatCAB 37, WhAm 2*
Mulheron, Anne Morton 1883- *WhAm 2*
Mulholland, Everett Samuel 1893-1962 *NatCAB 48*
Mulholland, Frank L 1875-1949 *WhAm 2*
Mulholland, Henry Bearden 1892-1966 *WhAm 4*
Mulholland, John 1898-1970 *WhAm 5*
Mulholland, John Hugh 1900-1974 *WhAm 6*
Mulholland, St. Clair *NewYHSD*
Mulholland, St. Clair Augustin 1839-1910 *DcAmB*
Mulholland, William 1855-1935 *DcAmB S1, WhAm 1*
Mulkey, Frederick William 1874-1923 *NatCAB 23*
Mulkey, Frederick William 1874-1924 *BiDrAC, WhAm 1*
Mulkey, John H *NatCAB 5*
Mulkey, William Oscar 1871-1943 *BiDrAC*
Mulky, Carl 1877-1954 *NatCAB 43*
Mull, George Fulmer 1851-1935 *WhAm 1*
Mull, J Harry 1864-1936 *WhAm 1*
Mull, John Wesley 1887- *WhAm 5*
Mullally, Thornwell d1943 *WhAm 2*
Mullaly, Arthur Lawrence 1888-1949 *NatCAB 41*
Mullaly, Charles J 1877-1949 *WhAm 2*
Mullaly, John 1835- *WhAm 1*
Mullan, Eugene Hagan 1879- *WhAm 6*

Mullan, George Vincent 1872-1931 *NatCAB 24,*
WhAm 1
Mullan, Helen St. Clair 1877- *WomWWA 14*
Mullan, James McElwane 1869-1933 *WhAm 1*
Mullan, John 1830-1909 *AmBi, DcAmB,*
WebAMB
Mullan, W G Read 1860-1910 *WhAm 1*
Mullane, Daniel Francis 1892-1954 *NatCAB 43*
Mullaney, Bernard J *ApCAB X*
Mullaney, Eugene L 1890-1973 *WhAm 6*
Mullaney, J R Madison 1816- *Drake*
Mullaney, James Vincent 1915-1963 *WhAm 4*
Mullaney, John Barry 1900-1971 *WhAm 5*
Mullanphy, John 1758-1833 *WhAm H*
Mullany, James Robert Madison 1818-1887
AmBi, ApCAB, DcAmB, NatCAB 4,
TwCBDA, WhAm H
Mullany, John Francis 1853-1916 *WhAm 1*
Mullany, Patrick Francis 1847-1893 *ApCAB,*
ApCAB X, BiDAmEd, DcAmB,
NatCAB 7, WhAm H
Mullany, Patrick John 1847-1893 *TwCBDA*
Mullen, Arthur Francis 1873-1938 *NatCAB 31,*
WhAm 1
Mullen, Charles Ward 1858-1928 *NatCAB 23*
Mullen, E F *NewYHSD*
Mullen, E J *NewYHSD*
Mullen, F E *IIBEAAW*
Mullen, James 1876-1967 *NatCAB 53,*
WhAm 4
Mullen, James William 1875-1931 *WhAm 1*
Mullen, John Kernan 1847-1929 *NatCAB 21*
Mullen, Joseph 1875- *WhAm 6*
Mullen, Ruth Ackerman d1969 *WhAm 5*
Mullen, Thomas Richard 1893-1958 *WhAm 3*
Mullen, Tobias 1818-1900 *ApCAB, TwCBDA,*
WhAm 1
Mullen, William E 1866- *WhAm 5*
Mullenbach, James 1870-1935 *WhAm 1*
Mullenix, Charles A 1887-1953 *WhAm 3*
Mullenix, Rollin Clarke 1869-1949 *WhAm 2*
Mullens, Priscilla 1604?-1680 *AmBi*
Muller *NewYHSD*
Muller, Adolf Lancken 1898-1972 *WhAm 5*
Muller, Albert A 1800?- *ApCAB*
Muller, Amelia A 1887-1952 *WhAm 3*
Muller, Carl 1900- *WhAm 4*
Muller, Carl Christian 1831-1914 *NatCAB 7,*
WhAm 1
Muller, Charles 1820?- *NewYHSD*
Muller, Dan 1888- *IIBEAAW*
Muller, Edouard 1885-1948 *NatCAB 42,*
WhAm 2
Muller, Edward Alexander 1861-1919
NatCAB 6
Muller, Edward Emil 1883-1954 *NatCAB 44*
Muller, Franz Joseph 1740-1825 *AsBiEn,*
DcScB
Muller, Fritz 1822-1897 *DcScB*
Muller, Georg Elias 1850-1934 *DcScB*
Muller, George Paul 1877-1947 *NatCAB 37,*
WhAm 2
Muller, Geza 1888-1947 *NatCAB 37*
Muller, Gustav 1851-1925 *DcScB*
Muller, Harold Powers 1901-1962 *NatCAB 51*
Muller, Henry *NewYHSD*
Muller, Henry Nicholas, Jr. 1914-1974
WhAm 6
Muller, Herman Edwin 1899-1965 *WhAm 4*
Muller, Hermann Joseph 1890-1967 *AsBiEn,*
DcScB, McGEWB, WebAB, WhAm 4
Muller, James Arthur 1884-1945 *WhAm 2*
Muller, Johann *DcScB*
Muller, Johann Heinrich Jacob 1809-1875
DcScB
Muller, Johann Michael Enzing *NewYHSD*
Muller, Johannes Peter 1801-1858 *AsBiEn,*
BiHiMed, DcScB, McGEWB
Muller, John *NewYHSD*
Muller, Jonas Norman 1920-1969 *WhAm 5*
Muller, Margarethe 1862-1934 *WhAm 3,*
WomWWA 14
Muller, Nicholas 1836-1917 *BiDrAC, WhAmP*
Muller, Nichols 1836-1917 *WhAm 4*
Muller, Nikolaus 1809-1875 *ApCAB*
Muller, Otto Frederik 1730-1784 *DcScB*
Muller, Otto Friedrich 1730-1784 *AsBiEn*
Muller, Paul Hermann 1899-1965 *AsBiEn,*

DcScB, McGEWB
Muller, Robert Anthony 1895-1959 *NatCAB 43*
Muller, Siegfried Hermann 1902-1965 *WhAm 4*
Muller, Siemon William 1900-1970 *WhAm 5*
Muller, W Max 1862-1919 *WhAm 1*
Muller, Walter J 1895-1967 *WhAm 4*
Muller, Wilhelm Max 1862-1919 *DcAmB,*
NatCAB 30
Muller, William Augustus 1867-1941
NatCAB 30
Muller-Breslau, Heinrich 1851-1925 *DcScB*
Muller-Ury, Adolfo 1864-1947 *WhAm 2*
Muller-Ury, Adolph Felix 1862- *NatCAB 6*
Mullett, Alfred Bult 1834-1893 *NatCAB 27*
Mullett, James 1784-1858 *ApCAB, BiAUS*
Mullett, Mary B d1932 *WhAm 1*
Mullett, Thomas Augustine 1868-1935
NatCAB 27
Mullgardt, Louis Christian 1866- *WhAm 4*
Mullgardt, William Oscar 1878- *WhAm 6*
Mulligan, Catharine A 1875- *WhAm 5*
Mulligan, Charles James 1866-1916 *DcAmB,*
NatCAB 26
Mulligan, Charles James 1867-1916 *WhAm 1*
Mulligan, Charles Wise 1905-1969 *WhAm 5*
Mulligan, David B *WhAm 3*
Mulligan, James A 1830-1864 *ApCAB, Drake,*
NatCAB 5, TwCBDA
Mulligan, James Hilary 1844-1916 *WhAm 1*
Mulligan, Minna Rawson 1861- *WomWWA 14*
Mulligan, Richard Thomas 1856-1917 *WhAm 1*
Mulligan, William G 1862-1930 *ApCAB X*
Mulligan, William Joseph 1881- *WhAm 6*
Mulliken, Alfred Henry d1931 *WhAm 1*
Mulliken, Jonathan 1746-1782 *NewYHSD*
Mulliken, Otis E 1907-1972 *WhAm 5*
Mulliken, Robert Sanderson 1896- *AsBiEn,*
WebAB
Mulliken, Samuel Parsons 1864-1934
DcAmB S1, NatCAB 25, WhAm 1
Mullikin, Sidney Albert 1871-1923 *NatCAB 6,*
NatCAB 20, WhAm 1
Mullin, Charles Earl 1890-1953 *NatCAB 41*
Mullin, Francis Anthony 1892-1947 *WhAm 2*
Mullin, Joseph 1811-1882 *BiAUS, BiDrAC,*
WhAm H
Mullin, Patrick *NewYHSD*
Mullin, Sam S 1914-1969 *WhAm 5*
Mullin, William Valentine 1884-1935
NatCAB 26, WhAm 1
Mulliner, Gabrielle Stewart 1872-
WomWWA 14
Mulliner, Mary Rees *WomWWA 14*
Mullinnix, Henry Maston 1892-1943 *WhAm 2*
Mullins, D Frank, Jr. 1915-1973 *WhAm 6*
Mullins, Edgar Young 1860-1928 *DcAmB,*
DcAmReB, NatCAB 21, TwCBDA,
WhAm 1
Mullins, George Walker 1881-1956 *WhAm 3*
Mullins, Isla May 1859-1936 *WhAm 1*
Mullins, James 1807-1873 *BiAUS, BiDrAC,*
WhAm H
Mullins, James Carleton 1891-1942 *NatCAB 33*
Mullins, Thomas C 1922-1971 *WhAm 5*
Mullins, Thomas Clinton 1885-1954
NatCAB 41
Mullins, William 1899-1955 *NatCAB 47*
Mullins, William Harold 1856-1932 *NatCAB 34*
Mullock, John Thomas 1806-1869 *ApCAB*
Mullowney, John James 1878-1952 *WhAm 3*
Mulloy, William Theodore 1892-1959 *WhAm 3*
Muloch, William 1843- *ApCAB*
Mulock, Edwin Hulbert 1882-1964 *NatCAB 51*
Mulock, Marjorie Crissy 1881- *WomWWA 14*
Mulrooney, Edward Pierce *WhAm 5*
Mulry, Joseph Aloysius 1874-1921 *NatCAB 25,*
WhAm 1
Mulry, Thomas Maurice 1855-1916 *DcAmB,*
NatCAB 25
Mulryan, Henry 1898-1972 *NatCAB 57*
Multer, Abraham Jacob 1900- *BiDrAC,*
WhAmP
Multer, Smith Lewis 1874-1952 *WhAm 3*
Mulvane, David Winfield 1863-1932 *WhAm 1*
Mulvania, Maurice 1878- *WhAm 6*
Mulvany, Charles Pelham 1835-1885 *ApCAB*
Mulvany, John 1844-1906? *IIBEAAW*

Mulvehill, Edward Leslie 1901-1961
NatCAB 47
Mulvihill, Michael Joseph 1855-1935 *WhAm 1*
Mumaugh, Frances Miller 1860- *AmWom*
Mumford *NewYHSD*
Mumford, Charles 1840- *WhAm 4*
Mumford, Charles Carney 1860-1918 *WhAm 1*
Mumford, Edward William 1812-1858
NewYHSD
Mumford, Ethel Watts d1940 *WhAm 1*
Mumford, Frederick Blackman 1868-1946
BiDAmEd
Mumford, Frederick Blackmar 1868-1946
WhAm 3
Mumford, George d1818 *BiAUS, BiDrAC,*
WhAm H
Mumford, George Elihu 1831-1892 *NatCAB 4*
Mumford, George Saltonstall 1866-1946
WhAm 2
Mumford, Gurdon Saltonstall 1764-1831 *BiAUS,*
BiDrAC, WhAm H
Mumford, Herbert Windsor 1871-1938
NatCAB 44, WhAm 1
Mumford, James Gregory 1863-1914 *DcAmB,*
WhAm 1
Mumford, John Kimberly 1863-1926 *WhAm 1*
Mumford, Lewis 1895- *EncAB, McGEWB,*
WebAB
Mumford, Mary Eno Bassett 1842-1935 *NotAW,*
WhAm 4, WomWWA 14
Mumford, Paul 1734-1805 *NatCAB 9,*
TwCBDA
Mumford, Philip G d1951 *WhAm 3*
Mumford, Samuel Cranage 1872-1939 *WhAm 1*
Mumford, Thomas Howland 1816- *NewYHSD*
Mumford, Thomas Jefferson 1843-1924
NatCAB 27
Mumler, Andrew C *NewYHSD*
Mumler, William H 1832-1884 *NewYHSD*
Mumma, Harlan L 1894-1972 *WhAm 5*
Mumma, James Hebron 1915-1971 *WhAm 5*
Mumma, Morton Claire, Jr. 1904-1968
WhAm 5
Mumma, Walter Mann 1890-1961 *BiDrAC,*
WhAm 4
Mummart, Clarence Allen 1874-1959 *WhAm 3*
Mummert, Elmer 1863-1917 *NatCAB 17*
Mumper, Norris McAllister 1891-1948
WhAm 2
Mumper, William Norris 1858- *WhAm 4*
Muncaster, Walter James 1850-1934
NatCAB 28
Munce, Lelia Gilliam *WomWWA 14*
Munce, Robert J 1895-1975 *WhAm 6*
Munch, Edward 1863-1944 *McGEWB,*
WhAm 4
Munch, Friedrich 1799-1881 *NatCAB 11*
Muncie, Curtis Hamilton 1887-1963 *ApCAB X,*
WhAm 4
Muncie, J H 1890-1954 *WhAm 3*
Muncke, Georg Wilhelm 1772-1847 *DcScB*
Munday, Richard 1690?-1739 *BnEnAmA*
Munde, Paul Fortunatus 1846-1902 *ApCAB,*
DcAmB, NatCAB 12, WhAm 1
Mundelein, Cardinal George William 1872-1939
AmBi, DcAmB S2, McGEWB,
NatCAB 15, WhAm 1
Munden, Kenneth White 1912-1974 *WhAm 6*
Mundheim, Samuel 1871-1940 *WhAm 1*
Mundie, William Bryce 1863-1939 *WhAm 1*
Mundsen, Sarah H *NewYHSD*
Mundt, G Henry 1886-1962 *WhAm 4*
Mundt, Karl Earl 1900-1974 *BiDrAC,*
WhAm 6
Mundt, Walter J d1971 *WhAm 5*
Mundy, Carll Seymour 1889-1967 *NatCAB 53*
Mundy, Ethel Frances d1964 *WhAm 4*
Mundy, Ezekiel Wilson 1833-1916 *TwCBDA,*
WhAm 1
Mundy, Johnson Marchant 1831-1897
NewYHSD, WhAm H
Mundy, Johnson Marchant 1832-1897
ApCAB Sup, NatCAB 8, TwCBDA
Mundy, Joseph Scudder 1847-1915 *NatCAB 2*
Mundy, Leo Clement 1887-1944 *NatCAB 33*
Mundy, Talbot 1879-1940 *WhAm 1*
Mundy, William Nelson 1860-1946 *NatCAB 35,*
WhAm 2

Munecas, Ildefonso DeLas 1776-1816 *ApCAB*
Munford, George Wythe 1803-1882 *NatCAB 19*
Munford, Mary Cooke Branch 1865-1938
  *BiDAmEd, NotAW, WhAm 1,
  WomWWA 14*
Munford, Morrison 1842-1892 *NatCAB 6*
Munford, Robert d1784 *DcAmB, WhAm H*
Munford, Walter F 1900-1959 *WhAm 3*
Munford, William 1775-1825 *ApCAB, DcAmB,
  Drake, NatCAB 9, WhAm H*
Mungen, William 1821-1887 *BiAUS, BiDRAC,
  TwCBDA, WhAm H*
Munger, Caroline 1808-1892 *NewYHSD*
Munger, Clarissa 1806-1889 *NewYHSD*
Munger, Claude Worrell 1892-1950 *NatCAB 37,
  WhAm 3*
Munger, Dell H 1862- *WhAm 4*
Munger, Earl Arthur 1892-1946 *NatCAB 34*
Munger, Edith C 1865- *WomWWA 14*
Munger, Edwin Thomas 1870-1915 *NatCAB 16*
Munger, Ellwood James 1883-1954 *NatCAB 43*
Munger, Flora Garrett *WomWWA 14*
Munger, George 1781-1825 *NewYHSD*
Munger, George Nicholas 1803-1882
  NewYHSD
Munger, Gilbert Davis 1837?-1903 *IlBEAAW,
  NewYHSD*
Munger, Harold Henry 1890-1970 *WhAm 5*
Munger, Harry Loomis 1868-1952 *NatCAB 41*
Munger, Henry Jairus 1883-1950 *NatCAB 39*
Munger, Robert Sylvester 1854-1923 *DcAmB,
  NatCAB 25*
Munger, Royal F 1894-1944 *WhAm 2*
Munger, Theodore Thornton 1830-1910 *ApCAB,
  DcAmB, DcAmReB, NatCAB 1,
  NatCAB 31, TwCBDA, WhAm 1*
Munger, Thomas Charles 1861-1941 *WhAm 1*
Munger, William Henry 1845-1915 *WhAm 1*
Munhall, Leander Whitcomb 1843-1934
  WhAm 1
Munhall, Michael 1835-1901 *NatCAB 13*
Munholland, John Earl 1907-1966 *NatCAB 53*
Munier-Chalmas, Ernest Charles P Auguste
  1843-1903 *DcScB*
Munisvara Visvarupa 1603- *DcScB*
Muniz, Joao Carlos 1893-1960 *WhAm 4*
Munjala *DcScB*
Munk, Hans 1589-1628 *ApCAB*
Munk, Joseph Amasa 1847-1927 *WhAm 1*
Munkittrick, Richard Kendall 1853-1911
  NatCAB 9, TwCBDA, WhAm 1
Munn, Charles Allen d1924 *WhAm 1*
Munn, Charles Clark 1848-1917 *WhAm 1*
Munn, Frank Benjamin 1860-1929 *NatCAB 23*
Munn, George F 1852-1907 *ApCAB*
Munn, George Frederick 1851-1907 *NatCAB 16*
Munn, Hiram H 1838- *NatCAB 3, WhAm 4*
Munn, James Buell 1890-1967 *WhAm 4*
Munn, John D *NewYHSD*
Munn, John Pixley 1847-1931 *WhAm 1*
Munn, Loyal Levi 1869-1959 *NatCAB 50*
Munn, Margaret Crosby *WomWWA 14*
Munn, Orson Desaix 1824-1907 *AmBi, ApCAB,
  DcAmB, NatCAB 7, TwCBDA,
  WhAm 1*
Munn, Orson Desaix 1883-1958 *WhAm 3*
Munn, Ralph 1894-1975 *DcAmLiB, WhAm 6*
Munn, Wayne Alonzo 1881-1953 *NatCAB 45*
Munn, Wilbur 1868-1943 *NatCAB 42*
Munn, William Phipps 1864-1903 *WhAm 1*
Munnerlyn, Charles James 1822-1898 *BiDConf*
Munnerlyn, Joseph Francis 1888-1923
  NatCAB 20
Munnich, Burkhard Christoph, Graf Von
  1683-1767 *WhoMilH*
Munnikhuysen, Walter Farnandis 1893-1964
  WhAm 4
Munns, Margaret Cairns 1870-1957 *WhAm 3*
Munoz, John Baptist 1745-1800 *Drake*
Munoz, Jorge 1857-1906 *WhAm 1*
Munoz, Juan Bautista 1745-1799 *ApCAB*
Munoz-Cabrera, Ramon 1819-1869 *ApCAB*
Munoz DeCollantes, Juan Miguel Lopez
  1499-1542 *ApCAB*
Munoz-Gamero, Benjamin 1820-1851 *ApCAB*
Munoz Grandes, Agustin 1896-1970 *WhAm 5*
Munoz Marin, Jose Luis Alberto 1898-
  McGEWB

Munoz Marin, Luis 1898- *WebAB*
Munoz-Rivera, Luis 1859-1916 *DcAmB,
  McGEWB*
Munro, Annette Gardner d1955 *WhAm 3*
Munro, Dana Carleton 1866-1933 *AmBi,
  DcAmB, NatCAB 23, WhAm 1*
Munro, David Alexander d1910 *WhAm 1*
Munro, Donald 1889-1973 *WhAm 5*
Munro, Emily Gardner d1924 *WhAm 1*
Munro, George 1825-1896 *DcAmB, NatCAB 7,
  WebAB, WhAm H*
Munro, H G 1905-1957 *WhAm 3*
Munro, Henry 1730-1801 *ApCAB, DcAmB,
  WhAm H*
Munro, James Alan 1898-1972 *WhAm 5*
Munro, John Cummings 1858-1910 *WhAm 1*
Munro, Leslie Knox 1901-1974 *WhAm 6*
Munro, Margaret 1864- *WomWWA 14*
Munro, Peter Jay 1767-1833 *ApCAB*
Munro, Peter Simcoe Morton 1842-
  NatCAB 14
Munro, Robert Frater *WhAm 5*
Munro, Thomas 1897-1974 *WhAm 6*
Munro, Walter J d1958 *WhAm 3*
Munro, Walter Lee 1857-1939 *NatCAB 29,
  WhAm 1*
Munro, Wilfred Harold 1849-1934 *AmBi,
  TwCBDA, WhAm 1*
Munro, William Bennett 1875-1957 *BiDAmEd,
  WhAm 3*
Munroe, Charles Andrews 1875-1957 *WhAm 3*
Munroe, Charles Edward 1849-1938 *ApCAB,
  DcAmB S2, NatCAB 9, NatCAB 29,
  TwCBDA, WhAm 1*
Munroe, Charles Kirk 1856- *ApCAB Sup*
Munroe, Harold Simonds 1883-1948
  NatCAB 37
Munroe, Henry Smith 1850-1933 *WhAm 1*
Munroe, Hersey 1868-1935 *WhAm 1*
Munroe, James d1870 *BiAUS*
Munroe, James Phinney 1862-1929 *NatCAB 16,
  WhAm 1*
Munroe, Jennie L 1848- *WomWWA 14*
Munroe, John 1796?-1861 *ApCAB, Drake*
Munroe, John Alexander 1853- *WhAm 5*
Munroe, Kirk 1850-1930 *AmBi, TwCBDA,
  WhAm 1*
Munroe, Kirk 1856-1930 *NatCAB 11*
Munroe, Mary Barr 1853- *WomWWA 14*
Munroe, Nathan Winship 1789- *NewYHSD*
Munroe, Robert 1866-1943 *NatCAB 32*
Munroe, Robert Clifford 1880-1959 *WhAm 4*
Munroe, Thomas *BiAUS*
Munroe, William Adams 1843-1905 *WhAm 1*
Munroe, William Robert 1886-1966 *WhAm 4*
Munsell, Albert Henry 1858-1918 *NatCAB 12,
  NatCAB 36, WhAm 1*
Munsell, Charles Edward 1858-1918 *WhAm 1*
Munsell, Frank 1857- *WhAm 4*
Munsell, Grace Husted 1880- *WomWWA 14*
Munsell, Harriett Edith 1878- *WomWWA 14*
Munsell, Harry B 1905-1961 *WhAm 4*
Munsell, Harvey May 1843- *NatCAB 3*
Munsell, Joel 1808-1880 *AmBi, ApCAB,
  DcAmB, Drake, TwCBDA, WhAm H*
Munsell, William Oliver 1870- *WhAm 6*
Munsey, Frank Andrew 1854-1925 *AmBi,
  ApCAB X, DcAmB, EncAB, McGEWB,
  NatCAB 20, TwCBDA, WebAB,
  WhAm 1*
Munsn, John Maurice 1878-1950 *WhAm 3*
Munson, Aeneas 1734-1826 *ApCAB, Drake,
  NatCAB 13*
Munson, Agnes McNamara 1883-
  WomWWA 14
Munson, Arley *WomWWA 14*
Munson, C LaRue 1854-1922 *NatCAB 18,
  WhAm 1*
Munson, Edgar 1881-1930 *NatCAB 23*
Munson, Edward Lyman 1868-1947 *WhAm 2*
Munson, Edwin Sterling 1870-1958 *NatCAB 46,
  WhAm 5*
Munson, Florence Averill Seeley 1856-
  WomWWA 14
Munson, Frank C 1876-1936 *WhAm 1*
Munson, Gorham B 1896-1969 *WhAm 5*
Munson, James Decker 1848-1929 *WhAm 1*
Munson, James Eugene 1835- *ApCAB,*

  NatCAB 12, WhAm 1
Munson, James H *NewYHSD*
Munson, John B 1864- *WhAm 4*
Munson, John G 1885-1952 *WhAm 3*
Munson, John Mitchell 1893-1965 *NatCAB 57*
Munson, John P 1860-1928 *WhAm 1*
Munson, Lewis S, Jr. d1971 *WhAm 5*
Munson, Loveland 1843-1921 *NatCAB 17,
  WhAm 1*
Munson, Lucius 1796-1823 *NewYHSD*
Munson, Lyman E *BiAUS*
Munson, Magdalen B 1869- *WomWWA 14*
Munson, Myron Andrews 1835-1922 *WhAm 1*
Munson, Orlie J 1891-1957 *NatCAB 48*
Munson, Samuel B 1806-1880 *NewYHSD*
Munson, Samuel Edgar 1866- *WhAm 5*
Munson, Samuel Lyman 1844-1930 *WhAm 1*
Munson, Thomas Volney 1843-1913 *DcAmB,
  EncAAH, NatCAB 18, TwCBDA,
  WhAm 1*
Munson, Walter David 1843-1908 *ApCAB X,
  DcAmB*
Munson, Welton Marks 1866- *WhAm 1*
Munson, William Benjamin 1846-1930
  NatCAB 22, WhAm 1
Munson, William Giles 1801-1878 *NewYHSD*
Munson, William Howes 1886-1968 *NatCAB 55*
Munster, August W 1882-1958 *WhAm 3*
Munster, Sebastian 1489-1552 *DcScB*
Munsterberg, Hugo 1863-1916 *AmBi,
  ApCAB X, DcAmB, NatCAB 13,
  WebAB, WhAm 1*
Munsterberg, Margarete 1889- *WomWWA 14*
Munsterberg, Selma Oppler 1867-
  WomWWA 14
Munter, Evelyn Lavon 1928-1973 *WhAm 6*
Munter, Richard Strobach 1893-1973 *WhAm 6*
Muntz, Earl Edward 1894-1965 *WhAm 4*
Muntz, Laura *WomWWA 14*
Munz, Friedrich 1865-1916 *NatCAB 18,
  WhAm 1*
Munz, Philip Alexander 1892-1974 *WhAm 6*
Munzer, Thomas 1489?-1525 *McGEWB*
Munzig, George Chickering 1859-1908
  WhAm 1
Murad 1750-1801 *WhoMilH*
Muralt, Carl Leonard De 1873- *WhAm 5*
Muralt, Johannes Von 1645-1733 *DcScB*
Murane, Cornelius Daniel 1867-1951 *WhAm 4*
Murane, Cornelius Daniel 1869-1951
  NatCAB 44
Murasaki, Shikibu 976?-1031? *McGEWB*
Murat, Achille Napoleon 1801-1847 *DcAmB,
  WhAm H*
Murat, Prince Charles L Napoleon Achille
  1801-1847 *Drake*
Murat, Prince Joachim 1767-1815 *McGEWB,
  WhoMilH*
Murat, Napoleon Achille 1801-1847 *ApCAB*
Murat, Napoleon Lucien C J Francois 1803-1878
  ApCAB
Muratore, Lucien d1954 *WhAm 3*
Muratori, Lodovico Antonio 1672-1750
  McGEWB
Muraviev, Mikhail 1795-1866 *WhoMilH*
Muraviev, Nicholas 1810-1881 *WhoMilH*
Muraviev, Prince Nicholas Nikolaievich
  1794-1867 *WhoMilH*
Murch, Chauncey 1856-1907 *WhAm 1*
Murch, James Deforest 1892-1973 *WhAm 6*
Murch, Maynard Hale 1874-1966 *WhAm 4*
Murch, Thompson Henry 1838-1886 *BiDRAC,
  WhAm H, WhAmP*
Murch, Walter Tandy 1907-1967 *WhAm 4*
Murchie, Alexander 1887-1949 *WhAm 3*
Murchie, Harold Hale 1888-1953 *NatCAB 45,
  WhAm 4*
Murchie, Robert Charles 1885-1947 *WhAm 2*
Murchison, Carl Allanmore 1887-1961
  BiDAmEd, WhAm 4
Murchison, Charles 1830-1879 *BiHiMed*
Murchison, Claudius Temple 1889-1968
  WhAm 5
Murchison, Clinton Williams 1895-1969
  WhAm 5
Murchison, Kenneth Mackenzie 1872-1938
  NatCAB 42, WhAm 1

Murchison, Sir Roderick Impey 1792-1871
AsBiEn, DcScB, McGEWB
Murchison, William *NewYHSD*
Murdoch, Cecilia Cunningham Jones 1847-
WomWWA 14
Murdoch, Dora L *WomWWA 14*
Murdoch, Esther R 1855- *WomWWA 14*
Murdoch, Frank Hitchcock 1843-1872 *DcAmB,
WhAm H*
Murdoch, J Clifford 1898-1970 *NatCAB 57*
Murdoch, James Edward 1811-1893 *AmBi,
ApCAB, DcAmB, Drake, NatCAB 6,
TwCBDA, WhAm H*
Murdoch, James Vesey 1906-1974 *WhAm 6*
Murdoch, James Y 1890-1962 *WhAm 4*
Murdoch, Jean Iris 1919- *McGEWB*
Murdoch, John 1836-1923 *NewYHSD*
Murdoch, John 1852-1925 *TwCBDA,
WhAm 1*
Murdoch, John Gormley 1861-1917 *WhAm 1*
Murdoch, Marion 1849- *AmWom*
Murdoch, Marion 1853- *WomWWA 14*
Murdoch, Nellie Kimball 1870- *WomWWA 14*
Murdoch, Thomas 1829-1909 *WhAm 1*
Murdoch, William 1823-1887 *ApCAB*
Murdock, Charles Albert 1841- *WhAm 1*
Murdock, George 1742-1805 *ApCAB*
Murdock, George John 1858-1942 *WhAm 2*
Murdock, Harold 1862-1934 *WhAm 1*
Murdock, Harris H 1879-1959 *WhAm 3*
Murdock, Henry Taylor 1902-1971 *WhAm 5*
Murdock, James 1776-1856 *ApCAB, DcAmB,
Drake, NatCAB 7, WhAm H*
Murdock, John *NewYHSD*
Murdock, John 1835-1924 *IIBEAAW*
Murdock, John Nelson 1820- *ApCAB*
Murdock, John Robert 1885-1972 *BiDrAC,
WhAm 5*
Murdock, John Samuel 1871-1946 *WhAm 2*
Murdock, Joseph Ballard 1851-1931 *DcAmB,
NatCAB 24, WhAm 1*
Murdock, Kenneth Ballard 1895-1975 *WhAm 6*
Murdock, Louise Caldwell 1858-1915 *NotAW*
Murdock, Marcellus Marion 1883-1970
WhAm 5
Murdock, Mary Alice 1869- *WomWWA 14*
Murdock, Melvin J 1917-1971 *NatCAB 57*
Murdock, Orrice Abram, Jr. 1893- *BiDrAC*
Murdock, Thomas Patrick 1888-1957 *WhAm 3*
Murdock, Victor 1871-1945 *BiDrAC,
DcAmB S3, NatCAB 35, WhAm 2,
WhAmP*
Murdock, William 1720?-1775? *ApCAB,
NatCAB 13*
Murdock, William 1754-1839 *AsBiEn*
Murdock, William Edwards 1844- *NatCAB 14*
Murdock, William Lorrain 1870-1941
NatCAB 30
Murel, John A *DcAmB, WebAB*
Murfee, Edward Hunter 1845-1932 *NatCAB 30*
Murfee, Hopson Owen 1874- *WhAm 3*
Murfee, James Thomas 1833-1912 *DcAmB,
WhAm 1*
Murfey, Rose L Richardson *WomWWA 14*
Murfin, James Orin 1875-1940 *NatCAB 32,
WhAm 1*
Murfin, Josephine Hurd Smith 1854-
WomWWA 14
Murfin, Orin Gould 1876-1956 *NatCAB 43,
WhAm 3*
Murfree, Hardy 1752-1809 *ApCAB, TwCBDA*
Murfree, Mary Noailles 1850-1922 *AmBi,
AmWom, ApCAB, DcAmB, NatCAB 2,
NotAW, TwCBDA, WhAm 1,
WomWWA 14*
Murfree, Walter Lee 1880-1954 *WhAm 3*
Murfree, William Hardy 1781-1827 *BiAUS,
BiDrAC, TwCBDA, WhAm H*
Murfree, William Law 1817-1892 *NatCAB 7,
TwCBDA*
Murie, Olaus Johan 1889-1963 *WhAm 4*
Murieta, Joaquin d1853? *WebAB*
Murieta, Joaquin 1830?-1878? *REnAW*
Murietta, Joaquin 1832?-1853 *AmBi, DcAmB*
Murillo, Bartolome Esteban 1617-1682
McGEWB
Murillo-Toro, Manuel 1815-1880 *ApCAB*
Murin *NewYHSD*

Muringer, Caspar *NewYHSD*
Muringer, Lydie Virgenie *WomWWA 14*
Murke, Franz 1869-1923 *NatCAB 20*
Murkland, Charles Sumner 1856-1926 *WhAm 1*
Murkland, Charlotte Marie *WomWWA 14*
Murlin, John Raymond 1874-1960 *NatCAB 47,
WhAm 5*
Murlin, Lemuel Herbert 1861-1935 *BiDAmEd,
NatCAB 15, NatCAB 26, TwCBDA,
WhAm 1*
Murlless, Frederic Thomas, Jr. 1866-1948
NatCAB 37
Murnane, George 1887-1969 *WhAm 5*
Muro Y Salazar, Salvador De 1754-1813
ApCAB
Murph, Daniel Shuford 1879-1958 *WhAm 3*
Murphey *see also* Murphy
Murphey, Archibald DeBow 1777-1832 *ApCAB,
DcAmB, NatCAB 7, WhAm H*
Murphey, Charles 1799-1861 *BiDrAC,
WhAm H*
Murphey, Robert Joseph 1898-1970 *WhAm 5*
Murphree, Albert Alexander 1870-1927
BiDAmEd, WhAm 1
Murphree, Dennis 1886-1949 *NatCAB 37*
Murphree, Eger V 1898-1962 *WhAm 4*
Murphree, Thomas Alexander 1883-1945
WhAm 2
Murphy *see also* Murphey
Murphy, A Stanwood 1892-1963 *NatCAB 51*
Murphy, Agatha 1862- *WomWWA 14*
Murphy, Albert S 1892-1963 *WhAm 4*
Murphy, Alfred J 1868-1931 *WhAm 1*
Murphy, Alice 1871-1909 *NatCAB 55*
Murphy, Alice Harold 1896-1966 *WhAm 4*
Murphy, Anna Elizabeth 1866- *WomWWA 14*
Murphy, Archibald DeBow 1777-1832 *TwCBDA*
Murphy, Arthur Alban 1886-1953 *NatCAB 44,
WhAm 3*
Murphy, Arthur Edward 1901-1962 *WhAm 4*
Murphy, Arthur M 1899-1964 *WhAm 4*
Murphy, Arthur Phillips 1870-1914 *BiDrAC,
WhAm 1*
Murphy, Audie 1924-1971 *WebAB, WebAMB*
Murphy, Benjamin Franklin 1867-1938 *BiDrAC,
WhAmP*
Murphy, Bernard 1847-1918 *NatCAB 18*
Murphy, Blanche Elizabeth M A Noel
1850?-1881 *ApCAB*
Murphy, Blanche Elizabeth Mary A Noel
1845?-1881 *NatCAB 11*
Murphy, Carl James 1889-1967 *WhAm 4,
WhoColR*
Murphy, Charles *BiAUS*
Murphy, Charles Francis 1858-1924 *AmBi,
DcAmB, EncAB, McGEWB, NatCAB 13,
WhAm 1*
Murphy, Charles J 1890-1968 *NatCAB 55*
Murphy, Charles Joseph 1832- *WhAm 4*
Murphy, Charles Stuart 1883-1965 *NatCAB 52*
Murphy, Charlton Lewis, Jr. 1908-1961
NatCAB 51
Murphy, Claudia Quigley 1863- *AmWom*
Murphy, D Hayes 1877- *WhAm 5*
Murphy, Daniel D 1862-1931 *WhAm 1*
Murphy, Daniel J d1957 *WhAm 3*
Murphy, Daniel Joseph 1896-1970 *NatCAB 55,
WhAm 5*
Murphy, Daniel Stephen 1879-1952 *NatCAB 39*
Murphy, Daniel V 1864-1914 *NatCAB 16*
Murphy, Dominic Ignatius 1847-1930 *DcAmB,
NatCAB 13, WhAm 1*
Murphy, Edgar Gardner 1869-1913 *DcAmB,
NatCAB 25, WhAm 1*
Murphy, Edmond George 1910-1973 *WhAm 5*
Murphy, Edmund Albert 1861-1932 *WhAm 1*
Murphy, Edward 1818- *ApCAB*
Murphy, Edward, Jr. 1834-1911 *WhAm 1*
Murphy, Edward, Jr. 1836-1911 *ApCAB Sup,
BiDrAC, NatCAB 13, TwCBDA*
Murphy, Edward Charles 1880-1967
NatCAB 54
Murphy, Edward Francis 1892-1967 *WhAm 4*
Murphy, Edward H *NewYHSD*
Murphy, Edward Thomas 1880-1951 *WhAm 3*
Murphy, Edward Vincent 1870-1939
NatCAB 35

Murphy, Edward William 1868-1950
NatCAB 40
Murphy, Emily *WomWWA 14*
Murphy, Ernest *WhAm 3*
Murphy, Eugene Edward 1903-1965 *WhAm 4*
Murphy, Eva Morley 1856- *WhAm 4,
WomWWA 14*
Murphy, Everett Jerome 1852-1922 *BiDrAC*
Murphy, Evert James 1860-1929 *WhAm 1*
Murphy, Farmer 1871- *WhAm 5*
Murphy, Felix Tone 1857-1900 *NatCAB 17*
Murphy, Francis 1836-1907 *DcAmB, WhAm 1*
Murphy, Francis Daniel 1895-1968 *WhAm 5*
Murphy, Francis P 1896-1973 *WhAm 6*
Murphy, Francis Parnell 1877-1958 *WhAm 3*
Murphy, Francis Stephen 1882-1971
NatCAB 56, WhAm 5
Murphy, Frank 1890-1949 *BiDrUSE,
DcAmB S4, EncAB, McGEWB,
NatCAB 37, WebAB, WhAm 2*
Murphy, Frank Morrill 1854-1917 *WhAm 1*
Murphy, Franklin 1846-1920 *DcAmB,
NatCAB 13, TwCBDA, WhAm 1*
Murphy, Franklin William 1869-1940 *WhAm 1*
Murphy, Fred Towsley 1872-1948 *NatCAB 36,
WhAm 2*
Murphy, Frederick E 1872-1940 *DcAmB S2,
NatCAB 47, WhAm 2*
Murphy, Frederick Vernon 1879-1958 *WhAm 3*
Murphy, George H 1860-1924 *WhAm 1*
Murphy, George Jeremiah 1883-1936 *ApCAB X*
Murphy, George Lloyd 1902- *BiDrAC*
Murphy, George Moseley 1903-1968
NatCAB 54
Murphy, Gerald 1888-1964 *WhAm 4*
Murphy, Gleeson 1910-1951 *NatCAB 40*
Murphy, Grayson M-P 1878-1937 *WhAm 1*
Murphy, Harry C 1892-1967 *WhAm 4*
Murphy, Henry C 1810-1882 *BiAUS*
Murphy, Henry Cloyd 1863-1948 *NatCAB 42*
Murphy, Henry Constant 1873-1947 *WhAm 2*
Murphy, Henry Crude 1810-1882 *Drake*
Murphy, Henry Cruse 1810-1882 *AmBi,
ApCAB, BiDrAC, DcAmB, NatCAB 10,
TwCBDA, WhAm H, WhAmP*
Murphy, Henry Killam 1877-1954 *NatCAB 42,
WhAm 5*
Murphy, Henry Vincent 1888-1960 *NatCAB 46*
Murphy, Herbert Francis 1894-1963 *WhAm 4*
Murphy, Hermann Dudley 1867-1945 *IIBEAAW,
NatCAB 36, WhAm 2*
Murphy, Herschel Stratton 1902-1965
NatCAB 52, WhAm 4
Murphy, Horace Greeley 1865-1946
NatCAB 35
Murphy, Howard Ansley 1896-1962 *WhAm 4*
Murphy, Howard James 1901-1961 *NatCAB 51*
Murphy, Ignatius Joseph 1884-1949
NatCAB 38
Murphy, Isaac 1802-1882 *BiAUS, DcAmB,
NatCAB 10, TwCBDA, WhAm H*
Murphy, J Edwin 1876-1943 *WhAm 2*
Murphy, J Francis 1853-1921 *BnEnAmA*
Murphy, J Francis *see also* Murphy, John Francis
Murphy, J Harvey 1882-1941 *NatCAB 30,
WhAm 1*
Murphy, James *NewYHSD*
Murphy, James A 1895-1955 *WhAm 3*
Murphy, James Augustine 1904-1951
NatCAB 40
Murphy, James Bumgardner 1884-1950
*ApCAB X, DcAmB S4, DcScB,
NatCAB 38, WhAm 3*
Murphy, James Cornelius 1864-1935 *WhAm 1*
Murphy, James Douglas 1895-1964 *NatCAB 52*
Murphy, James Joseph 1898-1962 *BiDrAC*
Murphy, James R 1853- *WhAm 4*
Murphy, James Shields 1870- *WhAm 5*
Murphy, James Smiley 1849- *ApCAB X*
Murphy, James William 1858-1927 *BiDrAC,
WhAm 3*
Murphy, Jeremiah Henry 1835-1893 *BiDrAC,
NatCAB 12, TwCBDA, WhAm H*
Murphy, Jimmy 1892-1965 *WhAm 4*
Murphy, John d1841 *BiAUS*
Murphy, John 1785-1841 *NatCAB 10*
Murphy, John 1786-1841 *ApCAB, BiDrAC,
Drake, TwCBDA, WhAm H*

Murphy, John 1812-1880 *ApCAB, DcAmB, TwCBDA, WhAm H*
Murphy, John A *NewYHSD*
Murphy, John Andrew 1880-1939 *NatCAB 29*
Murphy, John B *NewYHSD*
Murphy, John Benjamin 1857-1916 *AmBi, BiDAmEd, BiHiMed, DcAmB, NatCAB 13, WhAm 1*
Murphy, John Donahoe 1885-1949 *WhAm 2*
Murphy, John Edward 1857-1930 *NatCAB 26*
Murphy, John Francis 1853-1921 *AmBi, ApCAB, DcAmB, NatCAB 13, TwCBDA, WhAm 1*
Murphy, John Francis *see also* Murphy, J Francis
Murphy, John H 1912-1961 *WhAm 4*
Murphy, John Henry 1840- *WhoColR*
Murphy, John J 1844-1892 *NatCAB 4, TwCBDA*
Murphy, John L *BiAUS*
Murphy, John M *NewYHSD*
Murphy, John McLeod 1827-1871 *ApCAB*
Murphy, John Michael 1926- *BiDrAC*
Murphy, John Patrick 1887-1969 *WhAm 5*
Murphy, John R *NewYHSD*
Murphy, John T 1860-1932 *WhAm 1*
Murphy, John Thomas 1885-1944 *NatCAB 33, WhAm 2*
Murphy, John Vernon 1893-1949 *WhAm 3*
Murphy, John William 1902-1962 *BiDrAC, WhAm 4*
Murphy, John Wilson 1828-1874 *ApCAB Sup, DcAmB*
Murphy, Joseph Aloysius Charles 1857-1939 *WhAm 1*
Murphy, Joseph B 1881-1956 *WhAm 3*
Murphy, Joseph Dudley d1969 *WhAm 5*
Murphy, Joseph Nathaniel 1905-1966 *WhAm 4*
Murphy, Katherine Ward *WomWWA 14*
Murphy, Lambert 1885-1954 *WhAm 3*
Murphy, Laurence A 1900-1960 *WhAm 4*
Murphy, Lawrence William 1895-1969 *WhAm 5*
Murphy, Leo Thomas 1892-1957 *NatCAB 44*
Murphy, Loren Edgar 1882-1963 *WhAm 4*
Murphy, Louis 1875-1936 *NatCAB 30*
Murphy, Louis Edward 1874-1940 *NatCAB 32*
Murphy, Mabel Ansley 1870- *WhAm 5*
Murphy, Marvin 1897-1963 *WhAm 4*
Murphy, Maurice J, Jr. 1927- *BiDrAC*
Murphy, Michael *NewYHSD*
Murphy, Michael A 1837- *NatCAB 12*
Murphy, Michael Charles 1861-1913 *DcAmB, WebAB, WhAm HA, WhAm 4*
Murphy, Michael Thomas 1867- *WhAm 4*
Murphy, Morgan 1903-1971 *WhAm 5*
Murphy, Moyes Joseph 1894-1955 *NatCAB 45*
Murphy, N Barnard 1898-1957 *WhAm 3*
Murphy, Nathan Oakes 1849-1908 *BiDrAC, NatCAB 4, TwCBDA, WhAm 1*
Murphy, Nettie Seeley 1857- *WhAm 4*
Murphy, Peter *NewYHSD*
Murphy, Ray Dickinson 1887-1964 *NatCAB 52, WhAm 4*
Murphy, Richard Josephus 1861- *NatCAB 3*
Murphy, Richard Louis 1875-1936 *BiDrAC, WhAm 1*
Murphy, Robert 1894-1958 *WhWW-II*
Murphy, Robert Cushman 1887-1973 *WhAm 5*
Murphy, Robert Donald 1915-1959 *NatCAB 51*
Murphy, Robert F 1899-1976 *WhAm 6*
Murphy, Rosemary Ann 1906-1969 *NatCAB 54*
Murphy, Ross Dale 1882-1962 *NatCAB 50*
Murphy, Samuel Silenus 1867-1926 *WhAm 1*
Murphy, Samuel Wilson 1892-1944 *WhAm 2*
Murphy, Simon Jones 1815-1905 *NatCAB 39*
Murphy, Stanwood d1972 *WhAm 5*
Murphy, Starr Jocelyn 1860-1921 *WhAm 1*
Murphy, Thomas 1823-1900 *ApCAB, WhAm 1*
Murphy, Thomas 1824-1900 *TwCBDA*
Murphy, Thomas Dowler 1866-1928 *NatCAB 16, WhAm 1*
Murphy, Thomas Edward 1856-1933 *NatCAB 13, TwCBDA, WhAm 1*
Murphy, Thomas Francis 1896-1961 *WhAm 4*
Murphy, Thomas J *NewYHSD*
Murphy, Timothy 1844- *NatCAB 5*
Murphy, Timothy Francis 1875- *WhAm 5*

Murphy, Timothy Robert 1918-1961 *NatCAB 50*
Murphy, Vincent R 1896-1974 *WhAm 6*
Murphy, W Leo 1903- *WhAm 5*
Murphy, Walter 1872-1946 *WhAm 2*
Murphy, Walter J 1899-1959 *WhAm 3*
Murphy, Walter Patton 1873-1942 *WhAm 2*
Murphy, William *NewYHSD*
Murphy, William 1885-1950 *NatCAB 37*
Murphy, William Bailey 1877-1937 *NatCAB 36*
Murphy, William Charles, Jr. 1898-1949 *WhAm 2*
Murphy, William D 1834- *NewYHSD*
Murphy, William Dennis Town 1859- *ApCAB X*
Murphy, William F 1885-1950 *WhAm 2*
Murphy, William Gordon 1885-1954 *WhAm 3*
Murphy, William Herbert 1855-1929 *NatCAB 21*
Murphy, William James 1859-1918 *NatCAB 20*
Murphy, William John 1839-1923 *NatCAB 26*
Murphy, William Larkin 1877-1954 *NatCAB 44, WhAm 3*
Murphy, William Mansuetus 1878-1943 *WhAm 2*
Murphy, William Parry 1892- *AsBiEn, WebAB*
Murphy, William Robert 1885-1936 *WhAm 1*
Murphy, William Sumter 1796?-1844 *BiAUS, DcAmB, WhAm H*
Murphy, William Thomas 1899- *BiDrAC*
Murphy, William Walton 1816-1886 *DcAmB, WhAm H*
Murphy, Zela M 1877- *WomWWA 14*
Murrah, Alfred Paul 1904-1975 *WhAm 6*
Murrah, Beulah Fitzhugh 1864- *WomWWA 14*
Murrah, Pendleton 1820?-1865 *BiAUS, BiDConf, Drake, NatCAB 9*
Murrah, William Belton 1851-1925 *NatCAB 29, WhAm 1*
Murrah, William Belton 1852-1925 *TwCBDA*
Murray, A N 1894-1961 *WhAm 4*
Murray, Alexander 1754?-1821 *DcAmB, WhAm H*
Murray, Alexander 1755-1821 *AmBi, ApCAB, Drake, NatCAB 2, TwCBDA*
Murray, Alexander 1811-1885 *ApCAB*
Murray, Alexander 1816-1884 *ApCAB, TwCBDA*
Murray, Alexander 1818-1884 *Drake*
Murray, Alexina E Milton *WhoColR*
Murray, Alfred Lefurgy 1900-1965 *WhAm 4*
Murray, Allen Watts 1894-1964 *NatCAB 51*
Murray, Almey Constance *WomWWA 14*
Murray, Ambrose Spencer 1807-1885 *BiAUS, BiDrAC, WhAm H*
Murray, Arthur 1851-1925 *WhAm 1*
Murray, Arthur Frederic 1884-1961 *NatCAB 48*
Murray, Arthur T 1883- *ApCAB X*
Murray, Arthur T 1890-1949 *WhAm 3*
Murray, Augustus Taber 1866-1940 *NatCAB 30, WhAm 1*
Murray, Benjamin Franklin 1853- *WhAm 4*
Murray, Bredett Corydon 1837-1924 *NatCAB 6*
Murray, Charles 1876- *WhAm 5*
Murray, Charles Bernard 1866-1939 *WhAm 1*
Murray, Charles Burleigh 1837-1918 *WhAm 1*
Murray, Charles H 1855-1916 *WhAm 1*
Murray, Charles Theodore 1843- *WhAm 4*
Murray, Clay Ray 1890-1947 *NatCAB 36*
Murray, Daniel Alexander Payne 1852-1925 *DcAmLiB, WhoColR*
Murray, David 1830-1905 *ApCAB, DcAmB, TwCBDA, WhAm 1*
Murray, David Ambrose 1861-1949 *WhAm 2*
Murray, Donn Piatt 1870-1943 *NatCAB 33*
Murray, Dwight Harrison 1888-1974 *WhAm 6*
Murray, Dwight Henderson 1861-1921 *NatCAB 19*
Murray, Earle d1951 *WhAm 3*
Murray, Edward James 1888-1957 *NatCAB 46*
Murray, Elenor *NewYHSD*
Murray, Eli Houston 1843-1896 *TwCBDA*
Murray, Eli Houston 1844-1896 *ApCAB*
Murray, Eliza *NewYHSD*
Murray, Elizabeth Heaphy 1815-1882 *NewYHSD*
Murray, Ella Maud *WomWWA 14*

Murray, Ella Rush 1876- *BiCAW, WomWWA 14*
Murray, Elsie 1878-1965 *NatCAB 53*
Murray, Eugene d1948 *WhAm 2*
Murray, Francis King 1895-1929 *NatCAB 24*
Murray, Francis Wisner 1855-1929 *NatCAB 27*
Murray, Frank 1893-1951 *NatCAB 42*
Murray, Frank Huron 1889-1974 *WhAm 6*
Murray, George d1822 *NewYHSD*
Murray, Lord George 1694-1760 *WhoMilH*
Murray, George Dominic 1889-1956 *NatCAB 43, WhAm 3*
Murray, George J *NewYHSD*
Murray, George Mosley 1853-1919 *NatCAB 18*
Murray, George R 1865-1939 *BiHiMed*
Murray, George Robert Milne 1858-1911 *DcScB*
Murray, George Washington 1853-1926 *BiDrAC, WhAmP*
Murray, George Welwood 1856-1943 *ApCAB X, NatCAB 31, WhAm 2*
Murray, Gilbert 1866-1957 *WhAm 3*
Murray, Grace Peckham 1848- *NatCAB 12, WhAm 4, WomWWA 14*
Murray, Grant Simpson *WhoColR*
Murray, Hannah Lindley 1777-1836 *ApCAB*
Murray, Howell Worth 1890-1958 *WhAm 3*
Murray, Hugh Campbell 1825-1857 *BiAUS, NatCAB 12*
Murray, James *NewYHSD*
Murray, James d1782 *Drake*
Murray, James d1794 *Drake*
Murray, James 1712?-1794 *ApCAB*
Murray, James 1721-1794 *McGEWB, WhoMilH*
Murray, James 1765?-1806 *ApCAB, Drake, NatCAB 8*
Murray, James Burch 1886-1918 *NatCAB 19*
Murray, James Cunningham 1917- *BiDrAC*
Murray, James Edward 1876-1961 *BiDrAC, WhAm 4, WhAmP*
Murray, James Lee 1887-1957 *NatCAB 45*
Murray, James Ormsbee 1827-1899 *DcAmB, NatCAB 10, TwCBDA, WhAm H*
Murray, James P 1892-1972 *WhAm 5*
Murray, James T 1897-1968 *WhAm 5*
Murray, Jared 1823-1902 *NatCAB 16*
Murray, Jennie Scudder 1874- *WhAm 5*
Murray, John *NewYHSD*
Murray, John 1720- *NatCAB 1*
Murray, John 1731-1798 *ApCAB*
Murray, John 1732-1809 *NatCAB 13, WhAm H*
Murray, John 1737-1808 *DcAmB, WhAm H*
Murray, John 1741-1815 *AmBi, ApCAB, DcAmB, Drake, NatCAB 13, TwCBDA, WhAm H*
Murray, John 1742-1793 *ApCAB, Drake*
Murray, John 1768-1834 *BiAUS, BiDrAC, WhAm H*
Murray, John 1774?-1862 *ApCAB*
Murray, John 1789-1870 *NatCAB 16*
Murray, John 1841-1914 *DcScB*
Murray, John Clark 1836- *ApCAB*
Murray, John Courtney 1904-1967 *DcAmReB, WebAB, WhAm 4*
Murray, John Francis 1899-1937 *NatCAB 39*
Murray, John Gardner 1857-1929 *DcAmB, NatCAB 25, WhAm 1*
Murray, John Gregory 1877-1956 *NatCAB 47, WhAm 3*
Murray, John Gwennap 1906-1961 *WhAm 4*
Murray, John L 1806-1842 *BiAUS, BiDrAC, WhAm H*
Murray, John M'Kane 1847-1885 *TwCBDA*
Murray, John O'Kane 1847-1885 *ApCAB, WhAm H*
Murray, John P 1872-1933 *NatCAB 24*
Murray, John Porry 1830-1895 *BiDConf*
Murray, John Robert 1774-1851 *NewYHSD*
Murray, John Scott 1857-1930 *WhAm 1*
Murray, John Tucker 1877- *WhAm 5*
Murray, Johnston 1902-1974 *WhAm 6*
Murray, Joseph 1693?-1757 *NatCAB 13*
Murray, Joseph 1694?-1757 *DcAmB, WhAm H*
Murray, Joseph Wilson 1879-1958 *WhAm 3*
Murray, Judith Sargent Stevens 1751-1820 *ApCAB, DcAmB, NotAW, WhAm H*

Murray, Lawrence N 1894-1971 *WhAm 5*
Murray, Lawrence Owen 1864-1926
  NatCAB 26, WhAm 1
Murray, Leo Tildon 1902-1958 *WhAm 3*
Murray, Lindley 1745-1826 *AmBi, ApCAB,
  BiDAmEd, DcAmB, Drake, NatCAB 7,
  TwCBDA, WebAB, WhAm H*
Murray, Logan Crittenden 1845- *NatCAB 12*
Murray, Louise Shipman Welles 1854-1931
  DcAmB
Murray, Sister M Reparata 1889-1954 *WhAm 3*
Murray, Mabel 1876-1904 *NatCAB 16*
Murray, Margaret Polson 1844- *BiCAW,
  WomWWA 14*
Murray, Mary *NewYHSD*
Murray, Maxwell 1885-1948 *WhAm 2*
Murray, Nathaniel Carleton 1872-1952
  WhAm 3
Murray, Nicholas 1802-1861 *ApCAB, Drake,
  NatCAB 7, TwCBDA, WhAm H*
Murray, O Willard 1914-1973 *WhAm 5*
Murray, Orlando Dana 1818- *NatCAB 3*
Murray, Oscar G 1847-1917 *NatCAB 18,
  WhAm 1*
Murray, Owen Meredith 1885-1958 *WhAm 3*
Murray, Perry Earl 1899-1955 *NatCAB 50*
Murray, Peter 1867-1941 *WhAm 1*
Murray, Philip 1886-1952 *DcAmB S5, EncAB,
  McGEWB, WebAB, WhAm 3*
Murray, Reid Fred 1887-1952 *BiDrAC,
  WhAm 3, WhAmP*
Murray, Robert 1721-1786 *DcAmB, WhAm H*
Murray, Robert 1822-1913 *ApCAB,
  NatCAB 13, TwCBDA, WhAm 1*
Murray, Robert B, Jr. 1911-1969 *WhAm 5*
Murray, Robert Drake 1845-1903 *WhAm 1*
Murray, Robert Heffron 1881-1972 *NatCAB 57*
Murray, Robert Maynard 1841-1913 *BiDrAC*
Murray, Roy Irving 1882- *WhAm 3*
Murray, Samuel 1870-1941 *WhAm 1*
Murray, Samuel Aloysius 1869-1941
  NatCAB 37
Murray, Sidney Charles 1883-1954 *NatCAB 45,
  WhAm 3*
Murray, Sidney Eugene 1875-1941 *NatCAB 31,
  WhAm 2*
Murray, Stephen Douglas 1854-1938
  NatCAB 28
Murray, Thomas, Jr. 1770-1823 *BiAUS,
  BiDrAC, WhAm H*
Murray, Thomas Edward 1860-1929 *DcAmB*
Murray, Thomas Edward 1891-1961
  NatCAB 49, WhAm 4
Murray, Thomas Hamilton 1857- *TwCBDA,
  WhAm 4*
Murray, Thomas Jefferson 1891-1961 *WhAm 4*
Murray, Thomas Jefferson 1894-1971 *BiDrAC,
  WhAmP*
Murray, Tom 1894-1971 *WhAm 5*
Murray, Virginia M 1876- *WomWWA 14*
Murray, Wallace 1887-1965 *WhAm 4*
Murray, William 1803-1875 *BiAUS, BiDrAC,
  WhAm H*
Murray, William 1820-1895 *NatCAB 7*
Murray, William Andrew 1889-1953
  NatCAB 42
Murray, William D 1858-1939 *WhAm 1*
Murray, William Foley 1893-1959 *NatCAB 44*
Murray, William Francis 1881-1918 *BiDrAC,
  WhAm 1*
Murray, William Henry 1869-1956 *BiDrAC,
  EncAAH, NatCAB 43, WhAm 3,
  WhAmP*
Murray, William Henry 1878-1943 *NatCAB 32*
Murray, William Henry Harrison 1840-1904
  ApCAB, Drake, NatCAB 10, WhAm 1
Murray, William Henry Harrison 1841-1904
  TwCBDA
Murray, William Hilary 1883-1950 *WhAm 3*
Murray, William Parmelee 1854-1918
  NatCAB 16, NatCAB 47
Murray, William Spencer 1873-1942 *WhAm 1*
Murray, William Vans 1760-1803 *BiDrAC,
  DcAmB, WhAm H*
Murray, William Vans 1761?-1803 *BiAUS*
Murray, William Vans 1762-1803 *ApCAB,
  Drake, NatCAB 11, TwCBDA*
Murray, William Walter 1859- *NatCAB 7*

Murray-Aaron, Eugene 1852- *WhAm 4*
Murray-Jacoby, H 1892-1955 *NatCAB 46,
  WhAm 3*
Murrell, John A 1804- *REnAW*
Murrell, John A 1804-1844 *DcAmB*
Murrell, John A 1804-1846? *WhAm H*
Murrell, John A 1804?-1850? *WebAB*
Murrell, William 1853-1912 *BiHiMed*
Murrey, J Alexander 1889-1957 *NatCAB 44*
Murrie, William F R d1950 *WhAm 3*
Murrieta, Joaquin 1830?-1878? *REnAW*
Murrieta, Joaquin 1832?-1853 *DcAmB,
  WhAm H*
Murrietta, Joaquin *WebAB*
Murrill, William Alphonso 1869-1957 *WhAm 3*
Murrin, John 1918-1971 *NatCAB 57*
Murrow, Edward Roscoe 1908-1965 *EncAB,
  McGEWB, NatCAB 52, WebAB,
  WhAm 4*
Murrow, Joseph Samuel 1835-1929 *DcAmB*
Murry, John Middleton 1889-1957 *WhAm 3*
Murry, T *NewYHSD*
Mursell, James Lockhart 1893- *BiDAmEd*
Murtagh, John Martin 1911-1976 *WhAm 6*
Murtaugh, Joseph Stuart 1912-1973 *WhAm 6*
Murtfeldt, Augusta C *WomWWA 14*
Murtfeldt, Edward Warden 1907-1964 *WhAm 4*
Murtfeldt, Mary Esther *WomWWA 14*
Murty, Frank *NewYHSD*
Musa, Mansa d1337 *McGEWB*
Musa Ibn Muhammad Ibn M Al-Rumi Q *DcScB*
Musa Ibn Shakir, Sons Of *DcScB*
Muscat, Victor 1919-1975 *WhAm 6*
Muschamp, George Morris 1908-1969 *WhAm 5*
Muschenheim, Frederick Augustus 1871-1956
  NatCAB 47, WhAm 3
Muse, Aaron *NewYHSD*
Muse, Charles Segret 1869- *WhoColR*
Muse, Vance 1890-1950 *WhAm 3*
Muse, William Foster 1860-1931 *WhAm 1*
Muse, William Sulivane 1842-1911 *WhAm 1*
Muse, William Taylor 1906-1971 *WhAm 5*
Musenbrock, J Richard 1904-1968 *NatCAB 57*
Musgrave, Sir Anthony 1828- *ApCAB*
Musgrave, Fanny Wood *WomWWA 14*
Musgrave, George Clarke 1873- *WhAm 1*
Musgrave, George Washington 1804-1882
  ApCAB, TwCBDA
Musgrave, Harrison 1860-1921 *WhAm 1*
Musgrave, Sir Thomas 1738-1812 *ApCAB,
  Drake*
Musgrave, Walter Emmett 1880-1950 *WhAm 3*
Musgrave, William 1655-1721 *BiHiMed*
Musgrave, William Everett 1869-1927 *WhAm 1*
Musgrove, Mary 1700?-1763? *NotAW*
Mushet, David 1772-1847 *DcScB*
Mushketov, Ivan Vasilievich 1850-1902 *DcScB*
Musial, Stanley Frank 1920- *WebAB*
Musica, Philip Mariano Fausto 1884-1938
  DcAmB S2
Musick, Charles Elvon 1890-1968 *WhAm 5*
Musick, Edwin C 1894-1938 *AmBi*
Musick, John Roy 1849-1901 *ApCAB Sup,
  TwCBDA, WhAm 1*
Musil, Robert Edler Von 1880-1942 *McGEWB*
Musin, Ovide 1854-1929 *DcAmB, WhAm 1*
Muskie, Edmund Sixtus 1914- *BiDrAC*
Musmanno, Michael Angelo 1897-1968
  WhAm 5
Muspratt, Susan Webb 1822-1859 *Drake*
Muss-Arnolt, William 1860- *WhAm 4*
Musschenbroek, Petrus Van 1692-1761 *DcScB*
Musselman, Christian High 1880-1944
  NatCAB 34
Musselman, Clarence Alfred 1872-1946
  WhAm 2
Musselman, Emma Good Sweigert 1880-1966
  NatCAB 52
Musselman, Fren 1882-1964 *WhAm 4*
Musselman, J Rogers 1890-1968 *WhAm 5*
Musselwhite, Harry Webster 1868-1955 *BiDrAC,
  WhAm 3*
Musser, Boyd Anspach 1869-1942 *NatCAB 31*
Musser, Clifton Robert 1869-1956 *NatCAB 46*
Musser, George Washington 1862-1921
  NatCAB 17, NatCAB 19, WhAm 1
Musser, John 1887-1949 *NatCAB 38,
  WhAm 2*

Musser, John Herr 1856-1912 *NatCAB 13,
  WhAm 1*
Musser, John Herr 1883-1947 *NatCAB 42,
  WhAm 2*
Musser, Paul Howard 1892-1951 *WhAm 3*
Musset, Louis Charles Alfred De 1810-1857
  McGEWB
Mussey, Ellen Spencer 1850-1936 *BiCAW,
  DcAmB S2, NatCAB 47, NotAW,
  TwCBDA, WhAm 1, WomWWA 14*
Mussey, Henry Raymond 1875-1940 *WhAm 2*
Mussey, I Osgood 1818?- *NewYHSD*
Mussey, J Osgood 1818?- *NewYHSD*
Mussey, Mabel Hay Barrows 1873-
  WomWWA 14
Mussey, Reuben Dimond 1780-1866 *ApCAB,
  DcAmB, Drake, NatCAB 9, TwCBDA,
  WhAm H*
Mussey, Robert Daniel 1884-1958 *NatCAB 47*
Mussey, William Heberdon 1818-1882 *ApCAB*
Mussolini, Benito 1883-1945 *McGEWB,
  WhAm 4, WhWW-II*
Mussorgsky, Modest Petrovich 1839-1881
  McGEWB
Mussun, William George 1882-1952
  NatCAB 41
Mustapha II d1805 *WhAm H*
Mustard, Harry Stoll 1898-1966 *WhAm 4*
Mustard, Horace Ransom 1909-1966 *WhAm 4*
Mustard, John Archibald 1884-1964
  NatCAB 51
Mustard, Wilfred Pirt 1864-1932 *WhAm 1*
Muste, Abraham Johannes 1885-1967
  McGEWB
Mustin, Henry Schuyler 1854-1918 *NatCAB 18*
Mustin, William Irwin 1860- *NatCAB 11*
Muston, Ronald C G 1905-1974 *WhAm 6*
Musulin, Boris 1929-1973 *WhAm 6*
Musurillo, Herbert 1917-1974 *WhAm 6*
Mutch, Annie Elizabeth *WomWWA 14*
Mutch, William James 1858-1947 *WhAm 2*
Mutchler, Howard 1859-1916 *BiDrAC,
  WhAmP*
Mutchler, William 1831-1893 *BiAUS, BiDrAC,
  TwCBDA, WhAm H, WhAmP*
Mutchmore, Samuel Alexander 1830-1898
  NatCAB 3, TwCBDA
Muter, George d1811 *BiAUS, Drake,
  NatCAB 12*
Muter, Leslie Frederick 1894-1965 *WhAm 4*
Mutesa I 1838?-1884 *McGEWB*
Mutesa, Edward Frederick W M L, II 1924-1969
  McGEWB, WhAm 5
Mutin DePresles, Saturnin Amable 1721-1779
  ApCAB
Mutis, Jose Celestino 1732-1808 *ApCAB,
  Drake, McGEWB*
Mutis Y Bossio, Jose Celestino Bruno 1732-1808
  DcScB Sup
Muto, Anthony 1903-1964 *WhAm 4*
Mutschel, Anna Elizabeth 1872-
  WomWWA 14
Mutter, Thomas Dent 1811-1859 *ApCAB*
Mutzel, Gustav 1839-1893 *IIBEAAW*
Muy, Jean B L P DeF-S-Maime, Comte Du
  1755-1820 *ApCAB*
Muy, Jean Baptiste L Philippe DeFelix
  1751-1820 *Drake*
Muy, Nicholas, Daneaux De 1651-1708 *ApCAB*
Muybridge, Eadweard 1830-1904 *AmBi,
  BnEnAmA, DcAmB, NatCAB 19,
  WebAB, WhAm H*
Muzio, Claudia 1892-1936 *WhAm 1*
Muzquiz, Melchor 1790?-1844 *ApCAB*
Muzzall, Ernest Linwood 1897-1966 *WhAm 4*
Muzzarelli, Antoine J C V Ermanigilde 1847-
  ApCAB, WhAm 1
Muzzey, Artemas Bowers 1802-1892 *ApCAB,
  TwCBDA*
Muzzey, David Saville 1870-1965 *BiDAmEd,
  WhAm 4*
Muzzy, C B *NewYHSD*
Muzzy, Florence Emlyn Downs *WomWWA 14*
Muzzy, H Earle 1890-1972 *WhAm 5*
Muzzy, Howard Gray 1895-1969 *NatCAB 56*
Mwanga 1866?-1901 *McGEWB*
Mydorge, Claude 1585-1647 *DcScB*
Myer *NewYHSD*

Myer, Albert James 1827-1880 *ApCAB, NatCAB 24, TwCBDA*
Myer, Albert James 1828-1880 *NatCAB 4*
Myer, Albert James 1829-1880 *DcAmB, WebAMB, WhAm H*
Myer, Albert Lee 1846-1914 *WhAm 1*
Myer, Edmund John 1846- *WhAm 4*
Myer, Elizabeth Rachel Gillett 1855- *WomWWA 14*
Myer, Erskine Reed 1892-1956 *NatCAB 42*
Myer, Felix *NewYHSD*
Myer, H Ed *NewYHSD*
Myer, Henry *NewYHSD*
Myer, Henry 1837-1881 *WhAm H*
Myer, Isaac 1836-1902 *ApCAB Sup, TwCBDA, WhAm 1*
Myer, Jesse Shire 1873-1913 *WhAm 1*
Myer, John Walden 1901-1972 *NatCAB 57, WhAm 5*
Myer, Joseph Charles 1893-1934 *WhAm 1*
Myer, Sewall 1884-1967 *WhAm 5*
Myer, Walter Evert 1889-1955 *WhAm 3*
Myerberg, Michael 1906-1974 *WhAm 6*
Myers *NewYHSD*
Myers, Abraham Charles 1811-1888 *BiDConf*
Myers, Abraham Charles 1811-1889 *DcAmB, WhAm H*
Myers, Albert Cook 1874-1960 *NatCAB 44, WhAm 5*
Myers, Albert G 1880- *WhAm 6*
Myers, Albert J *Drake*
Myers, Alonzo Franklin 1895-1970 *NatCAB 56, WhAm 5*
Myers, Alvah Newton 1862-1937 *NatCAB 32*
Myers, Amos 1824-1893 *BiAUS, BiDrAC, WhAm H*
Myers, Angie Martin *WomWWA 14*
Myers, Barton 1853-1927 *NatCAB 20, WhAm 1*
Myers, Burton Dorr 1870-1951 *NatCAB 43, WhAm 3*
Myers, Carl Edgar 1842- *TwCBDA*
Myers, Charles Augustus 1889-1955 *WhAm 3*
Myers, Charles Franklin 1876-1948 *WhAm 3*
Myers, Charles Myer 1869-1940 *NatCAB 31*
Myers, Chester Graham 1887-1960 *NatCAB 45*
Myers, Clara Louise 1866- *WomWWA 14*
Myers, Clarence Garland 1890-1954 *NatCAB 42*
Myers, Clifford R 1886-1936 *WhAm 1*
Myers, Clyde Hadley 1883-1944 *WhAm 2*
Myers, Cortland 1864-1941 *WhAm 1*
Myers, Curtis Clark 1879-1954 *WhAm 3*
Myers, David Albert 1859-1955 *WhAm 3*
Myers, David Jackson Duke 1877- *WhAm 5*
Myers, David Moffat 1879-1954 *WhAm 3*
Myers, Dean Wentworth 1874-1955 *WhAm 3*
Myers, Diller S 1887-1947 *WhAm 2*
Myers, Edward Charles 1912-1975 *WhAm 6*
Myers, Edward Delos 1907-1969 *WhAm 5*
Myers, Edward Howell 1816-1876 *NatCAB 5, TwCBDA*
Myers, Edward James 1882-1961 *NatCAB 49*
Myers, Eli Perkins 1871-1940 *NatCAB 35*
Myers, Elizabeth Lehman 1869- *WhAm 5*
Myers, Ernest Edgar 1898-1954 *NatCAB 43*
Myers, Francis E 1849-1923 *NatCAB 20*
Myers, Francis John 1901-1956 *BiDrAC, WhAm 3, WhAmP*
Myers, Frank Clayton 1883-1950 *WhAm 3*
Myers, Frank Harmon 1899-1956 *IlBEAAW*
Myers, Frank Kerchner 1874-1940 *WhAm 1*
Myers, Fred Edward, Jr. 1921-1973 *WhAm 6*
Myers, Frederick Merchant 1888-1963 *NatCAB 49*
Myers, Garry Cleveland 1884-1971 *BiDAmEd, WhAm 5*
Myers, George Boggan 1881- *WhAm 6*
Myers, George Edmund 1871- *WhAm 5*
Myers, George Hewitt 1875-1957 *NatCAB 49, WhAm 3*
Myers, George Smith 1832-1910 *NatCAB 15*
Myers, George Sylvester 1881-1940 *WhAm 1*
Myers, George William 1864-1931 *BiDAmEd, WhAm 1*
Myers, Glenn Edwin 1886-1950 *NatCAB 41*
Myers, Gordon Bennett 1904-1960 *NatCAB 48*
Myers, Gustavus 1872-1942 *DcAmB S3,*

NatCAB 31, WhAm 2
Myers, Guy Charles 1890-1960 *NatCAB 53*
Myers, Guy Chase 1881-1934 *NatCAB 27*
Myers, Harold B 1896-1973 *WhAm 6*
Myers, Harry White 1874- *WhAm 5*
Myers, Henry Alonzo 1906-1955 *WhAm 3*
Myers, Henry Clay 1848-1917 *NatCAB 17*
Myers, Henry Guy 1873-1960 *WhAm 4*
Myers, Henry Lee 1862-1943 *BiDrAC, NatCAB 15, WhAm 2, WhAmP*
Myers, Henry VanSchoonhoven 1842- *TwCBDA*
Myers, Herman 1847- *NatCAB 13*
Myers, Howard 1894-1947 *WhAm 2*
Myers, Howard Barton 1901-1956 *WhAm 3*
Myers, Irene T *WomWWA 14*
Myers, Isaac Louis 1898-1960 *NatCAB 48*
Myers, Jack Allen 1927-1971 *WhAm 5*
Myers, James 1882-1967 *WhAm 4*
Myers, James Jefferson 1842-1915 *NatCAB 17, WhAm 1*
Myers, Jefferson 1863-1943 *WhAm 2*
Myers, Jerome 1867-1940 *BnEnAmA, DcAmB S2, NatCAB 46, WhAm 1*
Myers, John Dashiell 1888-1964 *WhAm 4*
Myers, John Gillespy 1832-1901 *NatCAB 16*
Myers, John J *WhAm H*
Myers, John Llewellyn 1872- *WhAm 5*
Myers, John Platt 1886-1966 *WhAm 4*
Myers, John Quincy 1877-1944 *WhAm 2*
Myers, John Sherman 1897-1969 *NatCAB 53, WhAm 5*
Myers, John Thomas 1927- *BiDrAC*
Myers, John Twiggs 1871-1952 *WebAMB, WhAm 5*
Myers, Johnston 1859-1935 *WhAm 1*
Myers, Joseph Lee 1889- *WhoColR*
Myers, Joseph Simmons 1867-1953 *WhAm 3*
Myers, Junior Winfred 1913-1966 *NatCAB 53*
Myers, Leonard 1827-1905 *BiAUS, BiDrAC, TwCBDA*
Myers, Leslie William 1894-1969 *NatCAB 55*
Myers, Lewis Edward 1863-1945 *WhAm 2*
Myers, Louis Guerineau 1874-1932 *NatCAB 27*
Myers, Louis Robert 1902- *WhAm 5*
Myers, Louis Wescott 1872-1960 *WhAm 3*
Myers, Lucille Walker 1893- *WhoColR*
Myers, M Lorton 1886-1962 *WhAm 4*
Myers, May Ethel Klinck 1881-1960 *NatCAB 46*
Myers, Minnie Walter 1852- *WhAm 4*
Myers, Myer 1723-1795 *BnEnAmA*
Myers, Paul Noxon 1878-1929 *NatCAB 52, WhAm 1*
Myers, Peter Hamilton 1812-1878 *ApCAB, Drake, NatCAB 10*
Myers, Philip Andrew 1853-1932 *NatCAB 27*
Myers, Philip VanNess 1846-1937 *NatCAB 12, TwCBDA, WhAm 1*
Myers, Phillip VanNess 1846-1937 *BiDAmEd*
Myers, Quincy Alden 1853-1921 *NatCAB 19, WhAm 1*
Myers, Ralph Emerson 1888-1945 *NatCAB 37*
Myers, Robert Ellsworth 1886-1953 *NatCAB 45*
Myers, Robert Holtby 1867- *WhAm 4*
Myers, Samuel Rockwell 1829-1915 *NatCAB 16*
Myers, Sarah Ann 1800-1876 *ApCAB*
Myers, Sumner B 1910-1955 *WhAm 4*
Myers, T Halsted 1859-1925 *NatCAB 21*
Myers, Theodore Walter 1844-1918 *WhAm 1*
Myers, Victor Caryl 1883-1948 *WhAm 2*
Myers, W *NewYHSD*
Myers, Walter, Jr. 1914-1967 *WhAm 4*
Myers, Weldon Thomas 1879- *WhAm 6*
Myers, Will Martin 1911-1970 *WhAm 5*
Myers, William 1830-1887 *ApCAB*
Myers, William Barksdale *NewYHSD*
Myers, William Henry 1815- *IlBEAAW, NewYHSD*
Myers, William Henry 1852- *NatCAB 10*
Myers, William Heyward 1856- *WhAm 4*
Myers, William Kurtz 1883-1953 *WhAm 3*
Myers, William Morris 1872-1945 *NatCAB 36*
Myers, William Ralph 1836-1907 *BiDrAC*
Myers, William Raymond 1866-1924 *NatCAB 33*

Myers, William Shields 1866-1945 *NatCAB 17, TwCBDA, WhAm 2*
Myers, William Starr 1877-1956 *WhAm 3*
Myerson, Abraham 1881-1948 *DcAmB S4, NatCAB 46, WhAm 2*
Mygatt, Gerald d1955 *WhAm 3*
Mygatt, Kenneth 1879-1965 *NatCAB 51*
Mygatt, Roland Faxon 1882-1959 *NatCAB 47*
Mygatt, Tracy Dickinson 1885- *BiCAW*
Myhrman, Othelia 1859-1936 *WhAm 1*
Myler, Joseph James 1893-1965 *WhAm 4*
Myler, Joseph Larkin 1905-1973 *WhAm 6*
Myler, William Albert 1851-1918 *NatCAB 27*
Myles, Beverly Russell 1895-1951 *WhAm 3*
Myles, John 1621?-1683 *ApCAB, DcAmB, WhAm H*
Myles, Samuel 1664-1728 *ApCAB, TwCBDA*
Mylks, Gordon Wright 1904-1973 *WhAm 6*
Mylon, Claude 1618?-1660? *DcScB*
Mynarts, H *NewYHSD*
Mynatt, Pryor L 1829-1900 *NatCAB 2*
Mynders, Alfred D 1888-1969 *WhAm 5*
Mynderse, Barent Aaron 1829-1887 *NatCAB 25*
Mynderse, Wilhelmus 1849-1906 *NatCAB 15, WhAm 1*
Mynerts, W E *NewYHSD*
Mynter, Agnes 1877- *WomWWA 14*
Mynter, Harriet Buell 1849- *WomWWA 14*
Myrdal, Karl Gunnar 1898- *McGEWB*
Myrddin-Evans, Sir Guildhaume 1894-1964 *WhAm 4*
Myrick, Arthur Beckwith 1875- *WhAm 5*
Myrick, Eugene Calvin 1868-1945 *NatCAB 35*
Myrick, Franklin Beckwith 1908-1969 *NatCAB 54*
Myrick, Hannah Glidden *WomWWA 14*
Myrick, Harry Pierce 1857-1916 *WhAm 1*
Myrick, Herbert 1860-1927 *DcAmB, NatCAB 25, WhAm 1*
Myrick, John Rencklin 1841-1909 *WhAm 1*
Myrick, Julian Southall 1880-1969 *WhAm 5*
Myrick, Shelby 1878-1965 *WhAm 4*
Myrin, Mabel Pew 1889-1972 *NatCAB 57*
Myron *McGEWB*
Myron, Paul *WhAm 1*
Mzilikazi 1795?-1868 *McGEWB*

N

Naar, David 1800-1880 *ApCAB*
Naar, Joseph L 1843-1905 *NatCAB 13*
Nabers, Benjamin Duke 1812-1878 *BiAUS, BiDrAC, WhAm H*
Nabers, Jane Porter 1913-1973 *WhAm 6*
Nabeshime, Isunatoshi 1910-1969 *WhAm 6*
Nabokov, Vladimir Vladimirovich 1899- *McGEWB, WebAB*
Nabors, Eugene Augustus 1905-1959 *WhAm 4*
Nabours, Robert Kirkland 1875- *WhAm 5*
Nabuco, Joaquim 1849-1910 *WhAm 1*
Nabuco DeAraujo, Joaquim Aurelio 1849-1910 *McGEWB*
Nabuco DeAraujo, Jose Tito 1836- *ApCAB*
Nacht, Osias 1895-1974 *WhAm 6*
Nachtrieb, Henry Francis 1857-1942 *WhAm 2*
Nachtrieb, Michael Strieby 1835-1916 *NewYHSD*
Nack, James M 1807?-1879 *Drake*
Nack, James M 1809-1879 *ApCAB, DcAmB, NatCAB 19, WhAm H*
Nacy, Richard Robert 1895-1961 *NatCAB 48, WhAm 4*
Nadal, Bernard Harrison 1812-1870 *ApCAB*
Nadal, Bernard Harrison 1815-1870 *Drake*
Nadal, Charles Coleman 1855-1931 *NatCAB 28, WhAm 1*
Nadal, Ehrman Syme 1843-1922 *ApCAB, DcAmB, NatCAB 11, WhAm 1*
Nadal, Emmanuel Victurnien, Comte De 1759-1793 *ApCAB*
Nadal, Thomas William 1875-1958 *NatCAB 43, WhAm 4*
Nadeau, Ira Alfred 1856- *WhAm 4*
Nadelman, Elie 1882-1946 *BnEnAmA, DcAmB S4, McGEWB*
Nader Shah Afshar 1688-1747 *McGEWB*
Nader, Ralph 1934- *EncAB, McGEWB, WebAB*
Nadir Shah 1688-1747 *WhoMilH*
Nadler, Carl S 1892-1953 *WhAm 3*
Nadler, Charles Elihu 1892-1962 *NatCAB 50*
Nadler, Marcus 1895-1965 *WhAm 4*
Naeckel, Erwin George 1897-1954 *NatCAB 45, WhAm 3*
Naegele, Charles Frederick 1857-1944 *NatCAB 12, WhAm 2*
Naegeli, Carl Wilhelm Von 1817-1891 *DcScB*
Nafe, Cleon A 1892-1961 *WhAm 4*
Naff, George Tipton 1900-1968 *WhAm 5*
Naffziger, Howard Christian 1884-1961 *NatCAB 51, WhAm 4*
Nafis, Ala Al-Din Abu 'l-Hasan, Ibn Al- d1288 *DcScB*
Nafis, Louis Firth 1874-1955 *NatCAB 41*
Nafziger, Ralph LeRoy 1886-1965 *WhAm 4*
Nafziger, Ralph Otto 1896-1973 *WhAm 6*
Nagaoka, Hantaro 1865-1950 *DcScB*
Nagel, Anne Shepley 1866- *WomWWA 14*
Nagel, Charles 1849-1940 *BiDrUSE, NatCAB 14, NatCAB 16, WhAm 1*
Nagel, Conrad 1897-1970 *WhAm 5*
Nagel, Conrad F, Jr. 1891-1957 *WhAm 3*
Nagel, Ernest 1901- *McGEWB*
Nagel, Joseph Darwin 1867- *WhAm 5*
Nagel, Louis 1817?- *NewYHSD*
Nagel, Stina 1918-1969 *WhAm 5*
Nageli, Karl Wilhelm Von 1817-1891 *AsBiEn*
Nager, Rudolf Felix 1911-1970 *WhAm 5*
Nagesa *DcScB*
Nagle *NewYHSD*
Nagle, Charles Francis 1841-1914 *WhAm 1*
Nagle, Clarence Floyd 1882-1957 *WhAm 3*
Nagle, James 1822-1866 *ApCAB, TwCBDA*

Nagle, James C 1865-1927 *WhAm 1*
Nagle, James Frederick 1833?- *NewYHSD*
Nagle, John Joseph 1892-1961 *WhAm 4*
Nagle, Patrick Sarsfield 1858- *WhAm 1*
Nagle, Raymond Thomas 1897-1951 *WhAm 3*
Nagle, Urban 1905-1965 *WhAm 4*
Naglee, Henry Morris 1815-1886 *ApCAB, Drake, NatCAB 5, TwCBDA*
Naglee, James d1866 *Drake*
Nagler, Ellen Torelle *WomWWA 14*
Nagler, Floyd August 1892-1933 *WhAm 1, WhAm 1C*
Nagler, Forrest 1885-1952 *WhAm 3*
Nagley, Frank Alvin 1880- *WhAm 6*
Nagot, Francis Charles 1734-1816 *ApCAB*
Nagumo, Chuichi 1886-1944 *WhWW-II, WhoMilH*
Nagurski, Bronco 1908- *WebAB*
Nagy, Imre 1896-1958 *WhAm 3*
Naha, Raymond 1933-1976 *IIBEAAW*
Nahl, Arthur *NewYHSD*
Nahl, Charles Christian 1818-1878 *IIBEAAW, NewYHSD, REnAW, WhAm H*
Nahl, Hugo Wilhelm Arthur d1881 *WhAm H*
Nahl, Hugo Wilhelm Arthur 1820-1889 *NewYHSD*
Nahl, Hugo Wilhelm Arthur 1833-1889 *IIBEAAW*
Nahm, Max Brunswick 1865-1958 *NatCAB 47, WhAm 3*
Nahmanides 1194-1270 *McGEWB*
Nahum, Louis Herman 1892-1972 *NatCAB 57*
Naiden, Earl L 1894- *WhAm 2*
Naidu, Sarojini 1879-1949 *McGEWB*
Nail, James H 1856-1928 *WhAm 1*
Nail, John E *WhoColR*
Nailor, Gerald A 1917-1952 *IIBEAAW*
Nair, John Henry, Jr. 1893-1971 *WhAm 5*
Nairizi, Al- *DcScB*
Nairn, Mrs. *NewYHSD*
Nairn, Sir Michael 1874-1952 *WhAm 3*
Nairne, Charles Murray 1808-1882 *ApCAB*
Nairne, Edward 1726-1806 *DcScB*
Nairne, Thomas d1715 *DcAmB, WhAm H*
Naismith, James A 1861-1939 *DcAmB S2, NatCAB 33, WebAB, WhAm 1*
Najib Al-Din *DcScB*
Nakahama, Manjiro 1824?- *ApCAB*
Nakai, Raymond 1918- *REnAW*
Nakashima, George 1905- *BnEnAmA*
Nakdimen, Hiram Spiro 1901-1955 *NatCAB 47*
Nakian, Reuben 1897- *BnEnAmA*
Nalder, Frank Fielding 1876-1937 *WhAm 1*
Nall, Cora Ermina Smith 1872- *WomWWA 14*
Nall, Edwin Henry 1871-1928 *ApCAB X*
Nall, Edwin Henry 1872-1928 *NatCAB 31*
Nall, Mrs. Richard H *WomWWA 14*
Nally, Edward Julian 1859-1953 *ApCAB X, NatCAB 40, WhAm 3*
Nally, Francis Ignatius 1908-1975 *WhAm 6*
Namara, Marguerite 1893-1975 *WhAm 6*
Namath, Joseph William 1943- *WebAB*
Nametkin, Sergey Semenovich 1876-1950 *DcScB*
Namier, Sir Lewis Bernstein 1888-1960 *McGEWB, WhAm 4*
Namm, Benjamin Harrison 1888-1969 *WhAm 5*
Nammack, Charles Edward 1856-1926 *WhAm 1*
Nana Sahib 1825-1859? *WhoMilH*
Nanak 1469-1538 *McGEWB*
Nancarrow, Albert George 1891-1964 *NatCAB 51*
Nance, Albinus 1848-1911 *NatCAB 12, TwCBDA, WhAm 1*
Nance, Earl Francis 1878-1943 *NatCAB 39*

Nance, Ellwood Cecil 1900-1965 *WhAm 4*
Nance, Walter Buckner 1868- *WhAm 4*
Nance, Willis Dean 1896-1968 *WhAm 5*
Nancrede, Charles Beylard Guerard De 1847-1921 *DcAmB, WhAm 1*
Nancrede, Charles Beylard Gureard De 1847-1921 *NatCAB 14*
Nancrede, Joseph Guerard 1793-1857 *ApCAB*
Nancrede, Paul Joseph Guerard De d1841 *WhAm H*
Nancrede, Paul Joseph Guerard De 1760-1841 *ApCAB*
Nancrede, Paul Joseph Guerard De 1761-1841 *DcAmB*
Nangle, John Joseph 1891-1960 *WhAm 4*
Nankivell, Frank Arthur 1869- *WhAm 5*
Nanney, James Philip 1884-1959 *NatCAB 48*
Nanon, Louis *NewYHSD*
Nansen, Fridtjof 1861-1930 *DcScB, DcScB Sup, McGEWB*
Nantel, Antonin 1839- *ApCAB*
Nantel, Guillaume Alphonse 1852- *ApCAB*
Nanuntenoo d1676 *DcAmB*
Nanz, Robert Hamilton 1885-1957 *WhAm 3*
Naon, Romulo S 1875- *WhAm 5*
Naoroji, Dadabhai 1825-1917 *McGEWB*
Naphen, Henry Francis 1847-1905 *WhAm 1*
Naphen, Henry Francis 1852-1905 *BiDrAC, TwCBDA*
Napier, Barnette Turner 1857-1919 *NatCAB 18*
Napier, Sir Charles 1786-1860 *ApCAB, WhoMilH*
Napier, Sir Charles James 1782-1853 *WhoMilH*
Napier, George *NewYHSD*
Napier, George Moultrie 1863-1932 *WhAm 1*
Napier, J Patton 1908-1974 *WhAm 6*
Napier, James C *WhoColR*
Napier, John 1550-1617 *AsBiEn, DcScB, McGEWB*
Napier, Robert Cornelis 1810-1890 *WhoMilH*
Napier, Thomas Hewell 1881-1961 *WhAm 4*
Napier, Walter Pharo 1881- *WhAm 6*
Napier, Sir William Francis Patrick 1785-1860 *WhoMilH*
Napione, Carlo Antonio Galeami 1750?-1814 *ApCAB*
Napoleon I 1769-1821 *McGEWB, WhoMilH*
Napoleon III 1808-1873 *McGEWB*
Napoli, Alexander J 1905-1972 *WhAm 5*
Napolitan, Louis 1895-1950 *NatCAB 38*
Nappenbach, Henry 1862-1931 *IIBEAAW*
Napton, William Barclay 1808-1883 *DcAmB, NatCAB 12, WhAm H*
Narayan, Jayaprakash 1902- *McGEWB*
Narayan, R K 1906- *McGEWB*
Narayana *DcScB*
Narayanan, Teralandur Gopalacharya 1911-1962 *WhAm 4*
Narbonne, Charles Henry 1627?-1681 *ApCAB*
Narbonne, Peter Remi 1806-1839 *ApCAB*
Narborough, Sir John 1637-1688 *ApCAB*
Nardin, Frances Louise 1878- *WhAm 6*
Nardin, William Thompson 1874-1954 *NatCAB 44, WhAm 3*
Nardini, Frank J 1914-1968 *NatCAB 54*
Nares, Sir George Strong 1831- *ApCAB*
Narey, Harry Elsworth 1885-1962 *BiDrAC*
Narine, James *NewYHSD*
Narino, Antonio 1765-1823 *ApCAB, McGEWB*
Narjot, Erneste Etienne DeFrancheville 1827?-1898 *IIBEAAW, NewYHSD*
Narrin, Elgin Edwin 1903-1973 *WhAm 6*
Narten, Lyman Foote 1885-1966 *NatCAB 52*

Narvaez, Pamphilo De d1528 *Drake*
Narvaez, Panfilo De d1528 *WhAm H*
Narvaez, Panfilo De 1470-1528 *ApCAB*
Narvaez, Panfilo De 1478?-1528 *AmBi,*
DcAmB, McGEWB, REnAW
Narvaez, Ramon Maria 1800-1868 *WhoMilH*
Nasatir, Azor Victor 1898-1949 *NatCAB 42*
Nasawi, Abu 'l-Hasan, Ali Ibn Ahmad, Al-
DcScB
Nasby, Petroleum Vesuvius 1833-1888 *AmBi,*
DcAmB, WebAB
Nascher, Friedrich Wilhelm 1702-1764 *ApCAB*
Nash, Abner d1786 *BiAUS, Drake*
Nash, Abner 1716-1786 *ApCAB, NatCAB 4,*
TwCBDA
Nash, Abner 1740?-1786 *AmBi, BiDrAC,*
DcAmB, WhAm H, WhAmP
Nash, Albert C 1826-1890 *WhAm H*
Nash, Archie Lyman 1875-1950 *NatCAB 42*
Nash, Arthur 1870-1927 *DcAmB, WhAm 1*
Nash, Bert Allen 1898-1947 *WhAm 2*
Nash, C E 1844-1913 *BiAUS*
Nash, C Stewart 1893-1971 *WhAm 5*
Nash, Charles Dexter 1843-1913 *NatCAB 15*
Nash, Charles Edmund 1844-1913 *BiDrAC,*
WhAmP
Nash, Charles Ellwood 1855-1932 *NatCAB 24,*
TwCBDA, WhAm 1
Nash, Charles Sumner 1856-1926 *DcAmB,*
WhAm 2
Nash, Charles W 1864-1948 *WhAm 2*
Nash, Charles William 1864-1948 *NatCAB 36*
Nash, Charles Williams 1864-1948 *DcAmB S4*
Nash, Clara Holmes Hapgood 1839- *AmWom*
Nash, Clara Hosmer Hapgood 1839-
WomWWA 14
Nash, Clinton Armstrong 1892-1958
NatCAB 47
Nash, Daniel 1763-1836 *ApCAB, DcAmB,*
WhAm H
Nash, Edgar Smiley 1872-1935 *WhAm 1*
Nash, Edward Myron 1891-1957 *NatCAB 43*
Nash, Edward Watrous 1846-1905 *ApCAB X*
Nash, Edwin A 1836-1911 *WhAm 1*
Nash, Elliott E 1870- *WhAm 5*
Nash, Ethel Miller Hughes 1909-1973 *WhAm 6*
Nash, Francis d1777 *Drake*
Nash, Francis 1720-1777 *ApCAB, NatCAB 1,*
TwCBDA
Nash, Francis 1742?-1777 *AmBi, DcAmB,*
WebAMB, WhAm H
Nash, Francis Phillip d1911 *WhAm 1*
Nash, Frank C 1910-1957 *WhAm 3*
Nash, Fred Chaffee 1878-1967 *NatCAB 53*
Nash, Frederick 1781-1858 *ApCAB, BiAUS,*
DcAmB, Drake, NatCAB 7, TwCBDA,
WhAm H
Nash, George Kilbon 1842-1904 *ApCAB Sup,*
NatCAB 5, WhAm 1
Nash, George Kilburn 1842-1904 *TwCBDA*
Nash, George Williston 1868-1944 *BiDAmEd,*
NatCAB 39, WhAm 2
Nash, Harriet A 1867-1907 *WhAm 1*
Nash, Henry Sylvester 1854-1912 *DcAmB,*
WhAm 1
Nash, Herbert Charles 1857-1902 *WhAm 1*
Nash, Herbert Milton 1831-1911 *NatCAB 8*
Nash, Isaac H 1872- *WhAm 5*
Nash, J Cheshire 1880-1954 *NatCAB 43*
Nash, J F *NewYHSD*
Nash, J Newton 1899-1959 *WhAm 3*
Nash, Jay Bryan 1886-1965 *BiDAmEd,*
NatCAB 53, WhAm 4
Nash, John 1752-1835 *McGEWB*
Nash, John Fiske 1824-1913 *NatCAB 30*
Nash, John Henry 1871-1947 *DcAmB S4,*
NatCAB 35, WhAm 2
Nash, John W d1859 *BiAUS*
Nash, Leo Axel 1910-1964 *NatCAB 52*
Nash, Leonidas Lydwell 1846-1917 *WhAm 1*
Nash, Lewis Hallock 1852-1923 *NatCAB 20*
Nash, Louis Rogers 1907-1968 *WhAm 5*
Nash, Luther Roberts 1871- *WhAm 5*
Nash, Lyman Junius 1845-1930 *WhAm 1*
Nash, Mary Louise 1826- *AmWom*
Nash, Mell Achilles 1890- *BiDAmEd*
Nash, Nina May *WomWWA 14*
Nash, Ogden 1902-1971 *WebAB, WhAm 5*

Nash, Patrick Austin 1863-1943 *NatCAB 33*
Nash, Paul Cleveland Bennett 1877-1913
WhAm 1
Nash, Philip Curtis 1890-1947 *WhAm 2*
Nash, R H *NewYHSD*
Nash, Simeon 1804-1879 *ApCAB, DcAmB,*
Drake, WhAm H
Nash, Stephen Payne 1821-1898 *ApCAB,*
NatCAB 11
Nash, Stevonia Evans 1863- *WomWWA 14*
Nash, Walter 1882-1968 *WhAm 5*
Nash, Willard Ayer 1898-1943 *IIBEAAW*
Nash, William Alexander 1840-1922 *WhAm 1*
Nash, William Holt 1834-1902 *WhAm 1*
Nasimben, Pedro 1703-1755 *ApCAB*
Nasir Al-Din Al-Tusi *DcScB*
Nasiter, Abraham 1904- *EncAAH*
Nasmyth, George William 1882-1920
NatCAB 18, WhAm 1
Nasmyth, James 1808-1890 *DcScB*
Nason, Albert John 1878-1934 *WhAm 1*
Nason, Arthur Huntington 1877-1944
NatCAB 34, WhAm 2
Nason, Daniel W 1825?- *IIBEAAW,*
NewYHSD
Nason, Elias 1811-1887 *ApCAB, DcAmB,*
Drake, TwCBDA, WhAm H
Nason, Emma Huntington 1845- *AmWom,*
WomWWA 14
Nason, Frank Lewis 1856-1928 *WhAm 1*
Nason, Harry Baxter, Jr. 1895-1974 *WhAm 6*
Nason, Henry Bradford 1831-1895 *ApCAB,*
DcAmB, NatCAB 2, WhAm H
Nason, Joseph 1815-1872 *NatCAB 24*
Nason, Leonard Hastings 1895-1970 *WhAm 5*
Nason, Thomas Willoughby 1889-1971
WhAm 5
Nason, Walton Hooker 1886-1964 *NatCAB 50*
Nassau, Charles Francis 1868-1940 *NatCAB 31*
Nassau, Charles William 1804-1878
NatCAB 11, TwCBDA
Nassau, Jason John 1892-1965 *WhAm 4*
Nassau, Jason John 1893-1965 *NatCAB 57*
Nassau, Robert Hamill 1835-1921 *DcAmB,*
WhAm 1
Nassau-Siegen, John Maurice 1604-1679
ApCAB
Nasser, Gamal Abdel 1918-1970 *McGEWB,*
WhAm 5
Nassour, Abraham 1869-1945 *NatCAB 34*
Nast, Albert Julius 1846-1936 *WhAm 1*
Nast, Conde Montrose 1873-1942 *DcAmB S3*
Nast, Conde Montrose 1874-1942 *NatCAB 15,*
WhAm 2
Nast, Thomas 1840-1902 *AmBi, ApCAB,*
DcAmB, Drake, EncAB, IIBEAAW,
McGEWB, NatCAB 7, NewYHSD,
TwCBDA, WhAm HA, WhAm 1,
WhAm 4A, WhAmP
Nast, William 1807-1899 *ApCAB, DcAmB,*
NatCAB 10, TwCBDA, WhAm H
Natalis, Stephanus *DcScB*
Natanson, Wladyslaw 1864-1937 *DcScB*
Natcher, William Huston 1909- *BiDrAC*
Nate, Joseph Cookman 1868-1933 *WhAm 1*
Natelson, Morris 1904-1972 *WhAm 5*
Nathan, Adolph 1844- *NatCAB 11*
Nathan, Alfred 1866- *WhAm 4*
Nathan, Edgar Joshua 1860-1929 *WhAm 1*
Nathan, Edward Isaac 1878- *WhAm 6*
Nathan, George Jean 1882-1958 *WebAB,*
WhAm 3
Nathan, Harold 1865-1941 *NatCAB 30*
Nathan, J Philip 1905-1970 *WhAm 5*
Nathan, Maud 1862-1946 *BiCAW, DcAmB S4,*
NatCAB 15, NotAW, WhAm 2,
WomWWA 14
Nathans, Joseph *NewYHSD*
Nathanson, Ira Theodore 1904-1954 *WhAm 3*
Nathorst, Alfred Gabriel 1850-1921 *DcScB*
Nation, Carry Amelia Moore 1846-1911 *AmBi,*
DcAmB, EncAAH, McGEWB, NotAW,
WebAB, WhAm HA, WhAm 4
Nations, Gilbert Owen 1866- *WhAm 5*
Natividade, Jose Da 1669-1715 *ApCAB*
Natsume, Soseki 1867-1916 *McGEWB*
Natt, Joseph S *NewYHSD*
Natt, Phebe Davis 1848-1899 *NatCAB 12*

Natt, Thomas J *NewYHSD*
Natta, Giulio 1903- *AsBiEn*
Natzler, Gertrud Amon 1908-1971 *BnEnAmA,*
WhAm 6
Natzler, Otto 1908- *BnEnAmA*
Nau, Jacques Jean David 1634?-1671 *ApCAB*
Nau, Maria Dolores Benedicta Josephine 1818-
NatCAB 5
Naudain, Arnold 1790-1872 *ApCAB, BiAUS,*
BiDrAC, NatCAB 11, TwCBDA,
WhAm H
Naudin, Charles 1815-1899 *DcScB*
Naujoks, Herbert Hugh 1902-1961 *WhAm 4*
Nauman, Bruce 1941- *BnEnAmA*
Nauman, George 1802-1863 *Drake*
Naumann, Alexander 1837-1922 *DcScB*
Naumann, Karl Friedrich 1797-1873 *DcScB*
Naumburg, Elsie Margaret Binger 1880-1953
NatCAB 41
Naumburg, George Washington 1876-1970
WhAm 5
Naumburg, Walter Wehle 1867-1959
NatCAB 48, WhAm 3
Naunyn, Bernhard 1839-1925 *BiHiMed*
Nauss, Henry G d1971 *WhAm 5*
Navagh, James Johnston 1901-1965 *WhAm 4*
Navailles, Charles 1270?-1330? *ApCAB*
Navarra Y Rocafull, Melchor De 1625?-1691
ApCAB
Navarre, Bisynthe *NewYHSD*
Navarre, Henri Eugene 1898- *WhoMilH*
Navarre, Pierre 1790?-1874 *DcAmB*
Navarrete, Domingo Fernando 1610-1689
ApCAB
Navarrete, Manuel Maria De 1768-1809 *ApCAB*
Navarrete, Martin Fernandez De 1765-1844
ApCAB
Navarro, Jose Antonio 1795-1870 *NatCAB 5,*
WhAm H
Navarro, Madame Antonio *AmWom*
Navarro, Mary Anderson De *TwCBDA,*
WomWWA 14
Navarro Y Prado, Antonio 1527-1598 *ApCAB*
Navarro Y Prado, Jose Francisco DeN 1823-
ApCAB
Navashin, Sergey Gavrilovich 1857-1930 *DcScB*
Nave, Anna Eliza Semans 1848- *WhAm 4*
Nave, Frederick Solomon 1873-1912
NatCAB 39, WhAm 1
Nave, John Albert 1910-1964 *NatCAB 52*
Nave, Orville James 1841-1917 *WhAm 1*
Navier, Claude-Louis-Marie-Henri 1785-1836
DcScB
Navin, Frank Joseph 1871-1935 *NatCAB 29*
Navin, Robert B 1895-1970 *WhAm 5*
Nawn, Hugh 1888-1973 *WhAm 6*
Nay, Ernest Omar 1892-1971 *NatCAB 57*
Naylon, Edmund Barry 1900-1972 *WhAm 5*
Naylor, Addison Wood 1841- *WhAm 4*
Naylor, Charles 1806-1872 *BiAUS, BiDrAC,*
WhAm H
Naylor, Charles J *NewYHSD*
Naylor, E E 1897-1962 *WhAm 4*
Naylor, Emmett Hay 1885-1938 *WhAm 1*
Naylor, Fannie Comstock *WomWWA 14*
Naylor, Henry L *NewYHSD*
Naylor, James Ball 1860-1945 *WhAm 3*
Naylor, John Calvin 1893-1967 *NatCAB 54,*
WhAm 4
Naylor, John Lewis 1901-1965 *WhAm 4*
Naylor, Joseph Randolph 1878-1948 *WhAm 2*
Naylor, William Keith 1874-1942 *WhAm 2*
Naylor, William Rigby *NewYHSD*
Naylor, Wilson Samuel 1864- *WhAm 4*
Nayrizi, Abu'l-Abbas Al-Fadl Ibn H, Al- *DcScB*
Nazimova, Alla 1878-1945 *DcAmB S3,*
NotAW
Nazimova, Alla 1879-1945 *NatCAB 36,*
WhAm 2
Nazimuddin, Al-Haj Khwaja 1894-1964
WhAm 4
Nazrez, Willis 1820-1875 *ApCAB*
Nazzam, Ibrahim Ibn Sayyar, Al- d840?
McGEWB
Ne, Win 1911- *McGEWB*
Nead, Benjamin Matthias 1847-1923 *ApCAB,*
WhAm 1
Neagle *NewYHSD*

Neagle, David 1847?-1926 *REnAW*
Neagle, Miss E *NewYHSD*
Neagle, James 1769?-1822 *NewYHSD*
Neagle, John 1796-1865 *AmBi*, *ApCAB*, *BnEnAmA*, *DcAmB*, *IlBEAAW*, *NatCAB 5*, *NewYHSD*, *TwCBDA*, *WhAm H*
Neagle, John 1799-1865 *Drake*
Neagle, John B 1796?-1866 *NewYHSD*
Neagle, Lewis 1837?- *NewYHSD*
Neagle, Pickens 1861- *WhAm 2*
Neal, Alfred Gorman 1886-1971 *NatCAB 56*
Neal, Alice B *NotAW*
Neal, Alva Otis 1870-1925 *WhAm 1*
Neal, Clarence Adkins 1880-1943 *NatCAB 34*
Neal, Crawford Chambers 1869- *WhoColR*
Neal, Daniel 1678-1742 *ApCAB*
Neal, Daniel 1678-1743 *Drake*
Neal, David Dalhoff 1838-1915 *AmBi*, *DcAmB*, *IlBEAAW*, *NatCAB 9*, *NewYHSD*, *TwCBDA*, *WhAm 1*
Neal, David Dolloff 1837-1915 *ApCAB*
Neal, E Virgil *ApCAB X*
Neal, Ernest Eugene 1911-1972 *WhAm 5*
Neal, George Franklin 1879- *WhAm 6*
Neal, George Ira 1868-1946 *NatCAB 35*, *WhAm 2*
Neal, Henry Safford 1828-1906 *BiDrAC*, *TwCBDA*
Neal, Herbert Vincent 1869-1940 *NatCAB 30*, *WhAm 1*
Neal, James Arthur 1866-1930 *WhAm 1*
Neal, James Henry 1872-1935 *NatCAB 28*, *WhAm 1*
Neal, John 1793-1876 *ApCAB*, *BnEnAmA*, *DcAmB*, *Drake*, *NatCAB 11*, *NewYHSD*, *TwCBDA*, *WebAB*, *WhAm H*
Neal, John Randolph 1836-1889 *BiDrAC*, *WhAm H*
Neal, John Randolph 1838-1889 *NatCAB 5*
Neal, John Randolph 1876-1959 *WhAm 3*
Neal, John Ross 1880-1941 *NatCAB 31*
Neal, John William 1859-1944 *NatCAB 49*
Neal, Joseph Clay 1807-1847 *ApCAB*, *DcAmB*, *Drake*, *NatCAB 6*, *TwCBDA*, *WhAm H*
Neal, Josephine Bicknell 1880-1955 *DcAmB S5*, *WhAm 3*, *WomWWA 14*
Neal, Lawrence T 1844-1905 *BiAUS*
Neal, Lawrence Talbot 1844-1905 *BiDrAC*
Neal, Lawrence Talbott 1844-1905 *TwCBDA*, *WhAm 4*
Neal, Lucinda *NewYHSD*
Neal, Mary Hester 1883- *WomWWA 14*
Neal, Mills Ferrell 1893-1972 *WhAm 5*
Neal, Minnie Elnora *WomWWA 14*
Neal, Paul Ardeen 1901-1952 *NatCAB 41*, *WhAm 3*
Neal, Phil Hudson 1894-1972 *WhAm 5*
Neal, Robert Wilson 1871-1939 *NatCAB 30*, *WhAm 1*
Neal, Stephen 1817-1905 *NatCAB 8*
Neal, Thomas 1858-1940 *WhAm 1*
Neal, Will E 1875-1959 *WhAm 3*
Neal, William *NewYHSD*
Neal, William Elmer 1875-1959 *BiDrAC*
Neal, William Joseph 1905-1949 *WhAm 2*
Neal, William M 1900-1958 *WhAm 3*
Neal, William Watt 1908-1970 *WhAm 5*
Neal, William Weaver 1874-1952 *WhAm 3*
Neale, Charles *NewYHSD*
Neale, Eugenia Fowler *WomWWA 14*
Neale, H Mary Gillespie *WomWWA 14*
Neale, James Brown 1837-1903 *NatCAB 6*
Neale, James Brown 1872-1943 *NatCAB 32*
Neale, John *NewYHSD*
Neale, John Ernest 1890-1975 *WhAm 6*
Neale, Laurance Irving 1885-1956 *WhAm 3*
Neale, Leonard 1746-1817 *ApCAB*, *DcAmB*, *Drake*, *NatCAB 1*, *TwCBDA*
Neale, Leonard 1746-1819 *WhAm H*
Neale, M Gordon 1887-1963 *WhAm 4*
Neale, Raphael d1833 *BiAUS*, *BiDrAC*, *WhAm H*
Neale, Rollin Heber 1808-1879 *ApCAB*, *Drake*, *NatCAB 5*
Neale, Thomas 1826?- *NewYHSD*
Neale, Walter 1873-1933 *WhAm 1*
Neaman, Pearson Ellis 1903-1961 *NatCAB 48*,

WhAm 4
Neander, Michael 1529-1581 *DcScB*
Nearing, Nellie Marguerite Seeds 1886- *WomWWA 14*
Neary, James Thomas 1883-1962 *NatCAB 47*
Neary, John Stuart 1903-1963 *WhAm 4*
Neary, William Herrmann 1905-1975 *WhAm 6*
Neath, Jasper Arthur 1896-1957 *WhAm 3*
Neave, Maud Killam *WomWWA 14*
Nebe, Artur 1896-1945 *WhWW-II*
Nebeker, Frank Knowlton 1870- *WhAm 5*
Nebel, Berthold 1889-1964 *WhAm 4*
Nebel, Carl *NewYHSD*
Nebel, Ferd Theodore 1882-1950 *NatCAB 39*
Nebinger, Andrew 1819-1886 *ApCAB*
Nebinger, George Washington 1824-1868 *ApCAB*
Nebinger, Robert 1828-1888 *ApCAB*
Neblett, Ann Viola 1842- *AmWom*
Neblett, Charles 1875-1963 *NatCAB 51*
Neblett, Robert Scott 1855-1918 *NatCAB 17*
Nebuchadnezzar *McGEWB*
Nechtow, Mitchell Joseph 1909-1968 *NatCAB 54*
Neckam, Alexander 1157-1217 *AsBiEn*
Necker DeSaussure 1786-1861 *DcScB*
Necker, Jacques 1732-1804 *McGEWB*
Necker, Louis-Albert 1786-1861 *DcScB*
Neckere, Leo Raymond De 1800-1833 *ApCAB*, *Drake*, *NatCAB 5*, *TwCBDA*, *WhAm H*
Necochea, Eugenio 1797-1867 *ApCAB*
Necochea, Mariano 1790-1849 *ApCAB*
Ned *NewYHSD*
Nederkorn, Leonhard Wilhelm 1904-1969 *NatCAB 55*
Nedved, Elizabeth Kimball 1897-1969 *WhAm 5*
Nedzi, Lucien Norbert 1925- *BiDrAC*
Nee, Isidore Charles Sigismond 1784-1837 *ApCAB*
Nee, Maurice Lyden 1915-1964 *WhAm 4*
Neeb, Harry Adolph 1850-1934 *NatCAB 27*
Neeb, John Nicholas 1851-1893 *NatCAB 6*, *NatCAB 7*
Neece, William Henry 1831-1909 *BiDrAC*
Needham, Bessie Pierce 1872- *WomWWA 14*
Needham, Charles Austin 1844- *TwCBDA*
Needham, Charles Austin 1844-1922 *NatCAB 6*
Needham, Charles Austin 1844-1923 *WhAm 1*
Needham, Charles Willis 1848-1935 *NatCAB 14*, *TwCBDA*, *WhAm 2*
Needham, Claude Ervin 1894-1950 *WhAm 3*
Needham, D *NewYHSD*
Needham, Daniel 1891-1971 *WhAm 5*
Needham, Elias Parkman 1812-1889 *NatCAB 5*, *TwCBDA*
Needham, Florian Berle 1900-1973 *WhAm 6*
Needham, Francis Jack 1748-1832 *ApCAB*, *Drake*
Needham, Henry Beach 1871-1915 *WhAm 1*
Needham, James d1663 *REnAW*
Needham, James d1673 *DcAmB*, *WhAm H*
Needham, James Carson 1864-1942 *BiDrAC*, *TwCBDA*, *WhAm 2*, *WhAmP*
Needham, Janet Grant *WomWWA 14*
Needham, John Turberville 1713-1781 *AsBiEn*, *DcScB*
Needham, Lloyd Leonard 1907-1966 *NatCAB 55*
Needham, Maurice Henshaw 1889-1966 *NatCAB 52*, *WhAm 4*
Needham, William Reuel 1899-1939 *NatCAB 29*
Needles, Arthur Chase 1867-1936 *WhAm 1*
Needles, Enoch Ray 1888-1972 *WhAm 5*
Neef, Francis Joseph Nicholas 1770-1854 *BiDAmEd*, *DcAmB*, *WhAm H*
Neef, Frederick Emil 1872- *WhAm 5*
Neel, Harry Campbell 1882-1968 *NatCAB 54*
Neel, Henri Charles 1889-1957 *NatCAB 46*
Neel, Percy Landreth 1876-1926 *NatCAB 20*
Neel, William D 1851- *WhAm 4*
Neelands, Thomas D, Jr. 1902-1972 *WhAm 5*
Neeley, George Arthur 1879-1919 *BiDrAC*, *WhAm 1*
Neeley, John Lawton 1877- *WhAm 5*
Neeley, Matthew Mansfield 1874-1958 *ApCAB X*, *WhAm 3*
Neeley, O *NewYHSD*

Neelley, John Haven 1892-1964 *WhAm 4*
Neely, C *NewYHSD*
Neely, Carrie Blair *WomWWA 14*
Neely, Charles Gracchus 1855-1930 *WhAm 3*
Neely, Charles Lea 1888-1963 *NatCAB 51*
Neely, Henry Adams 1830-1899 *ApCAB*, *Drake*, *NatCAB 12*, *TwCBDA*, *WhAm 1*
Neely, Hugh McDowell 1833-1919 *NatCAB 8*
Neely, J Howard 1858-1921 *NatCAB 19*
Neely, John Marshall, III 1904-1969 *WhAm 5*
Neely, Matthew Mansfield 1874-1958 *BiDrAC*, *WhAmP*
Neely, Thomas Benjamin 1841-1925 *DcAmB*, *WhAm 1*
Ne'eman, Yuval 1925- *AsBiEn*
Nees VonEsenbeck, Christian Gottfried 1776-1858 *DcScB*
Neese, Elbert Haven 1886-1961 *NatCAB 50*
Neese, Laura Janvrin Aldrich 1889-1967 *NatCAB 53*
Neet, George W 1863-1957 *WhAm 3*
Nef, John Ulric 1862-1915 *AsBiEn*, *DcAmB*, *DcScB*, *NatCAB 21*, *WhAm 1*
Neff, Andrew Love 1878-1936 *NatCAB 27*
Neff, Charles Thompson, Jr. 1899-1953 *WhAm 3*
Neff, Edward Williams Stephens 1878-1961 *NatCAB 49*
Neff, Elizabeth Hyer *WhAm 5*, *WomWWA 14*
Neff, Elmer Hartshorn 1866-1946 *NatCAB 34*, *WhAm 2*
Neff, Frank Amandus 1879- *WhAm 6*
Neff, Frank Chaffee d1947 *WhAm 2*
Neff, Frank Howard 1865-1936 *NatCAB 45*, *WhAm 1*
Neff, George N 1861-1933 *WhAm 1*, *WhAm 1C*
Neff, Grover Cleveland 1886-1970 *WhAm 5*
Neff, Harold Hopkins 1891-1971 *WhAm 5*
Neff, J Louis 1894-1963 *WhAm 5*
Neff, Jay H 1854- *WhAm 4*
Neff, John Henry 1887-1938 *WhAm 1*, *WhAm 1C*
Neff, Joseph A 1900-1969 *WhAm 5*
Neff, Joseph Seal 1854-1930 *WhAm 1*, *WhAm 1C*
Neff, Mary Lawson 1862- *WomWWA 14*
Neff, Pat Morris 1871-1952 *NatCAB 41*, *WhAm 3*
Neff, Paul Joseph 1884-1957 *NatCAB 47*, *WhAm 3*
Neff, Peter 1827-1903 *NatCAB 13*
Neff, Peter Rudolph 1832-1912 *NatCAB 25*
Neff, Robert Emery 1887-1969 *NatCAB 56*
Neff, Silas S 1853-1937 *WhAm 1*
Neff, Theodore Lee 1858-1936 *NatCAB 41*
Neff, Ward Andrew 1891-1959 *NatCAB 49*, *WhAm 3*
Neffensperger, J D *NewYHSD*
Nefflen, P *NewYHSD*
Neftel, William B 1830- *WhAm 4*
Neghle, William *NewYHSD*
Negley, Daniel 1802-1867 *WhAm H*
Negley, Georgina G *WomWWA 14*
Negley, James Casper 1883-1951 *NatCAB 38*
Negley, James Scott 1826-1901 *ApCAB*, *BiAUS*, *BiDrAC*, *DcAmB*, *Drake*, *NatCAB 4*, *TwCBDA*, *WhAm 1*
Negley, M Alice *WomWWA 14*
Negreiros, Andre Vidal De d1681 *ApCAB*
Negri, Adelchi 1876-1912 *DcScB*
Negrier, Francois Oscar De 1839-1913 *WhoMilH*
Negrier, Jules Cesar Antonin 1516-1571 *ApCAB*
Negus, Caroline 1814-1867 *NewYHSD*
Negus, Joel *NewYHSD*
Negus, Joseph d1823 *NewYHSD*
Negus, Nathan 1801-1825 *NewYHSD*
Negus, Sidney Stevens 1892-1963 *WhAm 4*
Neher, Fred 1867-1929 *WhAm 1*
Neher, John Hutchins 1899-1973 *NatCAB 57*
Nehlig, Victor 1830-1909 *ApCAB*, *IlBEAAW*, *NewYHSD*, *TwCBDA*, *WhAm 1*
Nehring, Alfred 1845-1904 *DcScB*
Nehring, Millard J 1898-1961 *WhAm 4*
Nehrling, Arno Herbert 1886-1974 *WhAm 6*
Nehrling, Henry 1853-1929 *AmBi*, *DcAmB*,

WhAm 1

Nehru, Jawaharlal 1889-1964 *McGEWB, WhAm 4*

Nehru, Motilal 1861-1931 *McGEWB*

Neideg, William Jonathan d1955 *WhAm 3*

Neider, Gustave *NewYHSD*

Neidhard, Charles 1809-1895 *DcAmB, NatCAB 3, WhAm H*

Neidhold, Carl David 1897-1973 *NatCAB 57*

Neidle, Marks 1891-1954 *NatCAB 41*

Neidlinger, Emily Hartwell 1870- *WomWWA 14*

Neidlinger, William Harold 1863-1924 *WhAm 1*

Neier, Charles Everett 1874-1949 *NatCAB 39*

Neifert, Ira Edward 1891- *WhAm 3*

Neighbors, Robert Simpson 1815-1859 *DcAmB, NatCAB 19, WhAm H*

Neihardt, John G 1881-1973 *REnAW*

Neihardt, John Gneisenau 1881-1973 *WebAB*

Neihardt, John Gneisenau 1881-1975 *WhAm 6*

Neihardt, Mona 1884- *WomWWA 14*

Neil, Albert Bramlett 1873-1966 *NatCAB 53, WhAm 4*

Neil, Edward Wallace d1908 *WhAm 1*

Neil, George M 1907-1957 *WhAm 3*

Neil, Matt Marshall 1849-1925 *WhAm 1*

Neil, Matthew Marshall 1849-1925 *NatCAB 13*

Neil, Thomas Franklin 1877-1952 *NatCAB 41*

Neild, Edward Fairfax 1884-1955 *WhAm 3*

Neiler, Samuel Graham 1866- *WhAm 2*

Neill, Alexander Sutherland 1883-1973 *McGEWB, WhAm 6*

Neill, Charles Patrick 1865-1942 *NatCAB 33, WhAm 2*

Neill, Edward Duffield 1823-1893 *AmBi, ApCAB, BiDAmEd, DcAmB, Drake, NatCAB 9, TwCBDA, WhAm H*

Neill, Harvey Gordon *NewYHSD*

Neill, James Lincoln *WhoColR*

Neill, James Maffett 1894-1964 *WhAm 4*

Neill, John 1819-1880 *ApCAB, DcAmB, TwCBDA, WhAm H*

Neill, John Selby Martin d1912 *WhAm 1*

Neill, Joseph C d1844 *NatCAB 5*

Neill, Lelia Winslow Bray 1892-1969 *WhAm 5*

Neill, Paul 1892-1940 *WhAm 2*

Neill, Reginald King 1863-1948 *NatCAB 36*

Neill, Richard *NewYHSD*

Neill, Richard Renshaw 1845- *NatCAB 5, WhAm 4*

Neill, Robert 1838-1907 *BiDrAC, TwCBDA*

Neill, Thomas Hewson 1826-1885 *ApCAB, DcAmB, NatCAB 13, TwCBDA, WhAm H*

Neill, William 1778-1860 *ApCAB, DcAmB, NatCAB 6, TwCBDA, WhAm H*

Neill, William 1779-1860 *Drake*

Neils, Julius Frederick Bernhard 1855-1933 *NatCAB 36*

Neilson, Anita *WomWWA 14*

Neilson, Charles Hugh 1871-1958 *WhAm 3*

Neilson, Edwin Lee 1875-1950 *NatCAB 40*

Neilson, Francis 1867-1961 *WhAm 4*

Neilson, Harry Rosengarten 1893-1949 *WhAm 2A*

Neilson, J *NewYHSD*

Neilson, James 1784-1862 *NatCAB 26*

Neilson, James 1844-1937 *NatCAB 26*

Neilson, Jason Andrew 1872- *WhAm 5*

Neilson, John 1745-1833 *ApCAB, BiAUS, BiDrAC, DcAmB, Drake, NatCAB 3, NatCAB 26, TwCBDA, WhAm H*

Neilson, John 1776-1848 *ApCAB*

Neilson, Lewis 1860- *WhAm 4*

Neilson, Lillian Adelaide 1850-1880 *ApCAB*

Neilson, Nellie 1873-1947 *NatCAB 36, NotAW, WhAm 2, WomWWA 14*

Neilson, Nevin Paul 1915-1971 *WhAm 5*

Neilson, Nicholas Bayard 1856-1937 *NatCAB 28*

Neilson, Raymond Perry Rodgers 1881-1964 *NatCAB 50, WhAm 4*

Neilson, Sarah Claypoole Lewis *WomWWA 14*

Neilson, Thomas Hall 1844- *WhAm 4*

Neilson, Thomas Rundle 1857-1939 *WhAm 1*

Neilson, Walter Hopper 1857- *NatCAB 16*

Neilson, William Allan 1869-1946 *BiDAmEd, DcAmB S4, NatCAB 33, WhAm 2*

Neilson, William George 1842- *ApCAB*

Neilson, William George 1842-1906 *DcAmB, NatCAB 26*

Neilson, William George 1842-1907 *WhAm 1*

Neilson, William Hude 1816-1887 *ApCAB*

Neilson, William LaCoste 1879-1957 *NatCAB 45, WhAm 3*

Neimeyer, John H *NewYHSD*

Neinken, Jacob 1873-1957 *NatCAB 43*

Neisler, Charles Eugene, Jr. 1895-1966 *NatCAB 54*

Neisser, Albert Ludwig Sigesmund 1855-1916 *DcScB*

Neisser, George 1715-1784 *ApCAB, NatCAB 5*

Neisser, Hans Philip 1895-1975 *WhAm 6*

Neisser, Rittenhouse 1873-1949 *NatCAB 37*

Neiswanger, David 1892-1963 *WhAm 4*

Nekrasov, Aleksandr Ivanovich 1883-1957 *DcScB*

Nel, Louis Taylor 1895-1968 *WhAm 5*

Nelan, Charles 1859-1904 *WhAm 1*

Nelaton, Hector Marie Louis 1775-1827 *ApCAB*

Nelder, A *NewYHSD*

Neligan, William d1880 *ApCAB*

Nell, Louis 1842- *WhAm 4*

Nell, Raymond Boyd 1891-1973 *WhAm 6*

Nell, William Cooper 1816-1874 *ApCAB, DcAmB, NatCAB 14, WhAm H, WhAmP*

Nellany, Michael 1837-1916 *NatCAB 18*

Nelles, Percy W 1892-1951 *WhAm 3*

Nelles, Samuel Sobieski 1823-1887 *ApCAB*

Nelligan, Howard Paul 1903-1952 *WhAm 3*

Nellis, Emma Virginia McAfee 1855- *WomWWA 14*

Nellis, Saunders K G *NewYHSD*

Nelms, William Lewis 1858- *WhAm 4*

Nelsen, Ancher 1904- *BiDrAC*

Nelson *NewYHSD*

Nelson, Miss *NewYHSD*

Nelson, Mrs. *NewYHSD*

Nelson, Adolphus Peter 1872-1927 *BiDrAC, NatCAB 21, WhAm 1*

Nelson, Albert Hobart 1812-1858 *BiAUS, Drake*

Nelson, Alexander Lockhart 1827-1910 *WhAm 1*

Nelson, Alfred Brierley 1844- *WhAm 3*

Nelson, Alfred Erwin 1916-1960 *NatCAB 47*

Nelson, Alfred L 1891-1959 *WhAm 4*

Nelson, Alice Dunbar 1875-1935 *NotAW*

Nelson, Allen Henry 1879-1944 *NatCAB 33*

Nelson, Arthur Emanuel 1892-1955 *BiDrAC, WhAm 3*

Nelson, Aven 1859-1952 *REnAW*

Nelson, Benjamin Franklin 1843-1928 *NatCAB 7, WhAm 1*

Nelson, Bertram Griffith 1876-1938 *WhAm 1*

Nelson, Burton Edsal 1867- *WhAm 5*

Nelson, C Ferdinand 1882-1950 *WhAm 3*

Nelson, Candis Jane *WomWWA 14*

Nelson, Carl K 1899-1961 *WhAm 4*

Nelson, Charles 1881-1960 *NatCAB 47*

Nelson, Charles Alexander 1839-1933 *ApCAB, DcAmB, DcAmLiB, NatCAB 24, TwCBDA, WhAm 1*

Nelson, Charles Donald 1927-1968 *WhAm 5*

Nelson, Charles Eugene 1837- *ApCAB*

Nelson, Charles Pembroke 1907-1962 *BiDrAC, WhAm 4, WhAmP*

Nelson, Clara Albertine 1852-1931 *WhAm 3, WomWWA 14*

Nelson, Clarence 1900-1971 *WhAm 5*

Nelson, Cleland Kinloch 1852-1917 *NatCAB 13, TwCBDA, WhAm 1*

Nelson, Cleland Kinlock 1814-1890 *NatCAB 1*

Nelson, Cleland Kinlock 1852-1917 *ApCAB Sup*

Nelson, Daniel Thurber 1839-1923 *ApCAB, WhAm 1*

Nelson, David 1793-1844 *ApCAB, DcAmB, Drake, TwCBDA, WhAm H*

Nelson, Donald Marr 1888-1959 *WhAm 3*

Nelson, Dotson McGinnis 1880- *WhAm 6*

Nelson, Edgar Andrew 1882-1959 *WhAm 3*

Nelson, Edward Beverly 1850- *ApCAB Sup, WhAm 4*

Nelson, Edward D d1871 *NewYHSD*

Nelson, Edward William 1855-1934 *DcAmB S1, EncAAH, NatCAB 26, WhAm 1*

Nelson, Elmer Frederick 1894-1967 *NatCAB 53*

Nelson, Elmer Martin 1892-1958 *WhAm 3*

Nelson, Elnathan Kemper 1870-1940 *NatCAB 30, WhAm 1*

Nelson, Elsie Coates 1872- *WomWWA 14*

Nelson, Erland Nels Peter 1897-1973 *WhAm 6*

Nelson, Ezra Thayer 1823-1914 *NatCAB 16*

Nelson, Frank 1865- *WhAm 4*

Nelson, Frank Howard 1869-1939 *WhAm 1*

Nelson, Fritz 1890-1958 *NatCAB 48*

Nelson, G Arthur 1885-1946 *NatCAB 36*

Nelson, Gaylord Anton 1916- *BiDrAC, EncAAH*

Nelson, George 1867-1955 *NatCAB 45*

Nelson, George 1908- *BnEnAmA*

Nelson, George Bliss 1876-1943 *WhAm 2*

Nelson, George Francis 1842-1932 *WhAm 1*

Nelson, George Herbert 1902-1965 *NatCAB 52, WhAm 4*

Nelson, Godfrey Nicholas 1878-1954 *WhAm 3*

Nelson, Harold Hayden 1878-1954 *WhAm 3*

Nelson, Harold Raymond 1904-1960 *NatCAB 45*

Nelson, Harry Ord 1884-1958 *NatCAB 44*

Nelson, Helen Stearns 1885- *WomWWA 14*

Nelson, Henry Addison 1820-1906 *ApCAB, WhAm 1*

Nelson, Henry Loomis 1846-1908 *DcAmB, NatCAB 13, WhAm 1*

Nelson, Henry Wade 1886-1961 *NatCAB 47*

Nelson, Herbert Undeen 1886-1956 *WhAm 3*

Nelson, Homer Augustus 1829-1891 *BiAUS, BiDrAC, WhAm H*

Nelson, Horatio, Viscount 1758-1805 *McGEWB, WhoMilH*

Nelson, Horatio Whiteway 1867-1934 *NatCAB 26*

Nelson, Hugh 1768-1836 *ApCAB, BiAUS, BiDrAC, DcAmB, Drake, NatCAB 7, TwCBDA, WhAm H, WhAmP*

Nelson, Hugh 1830- *ApCAB*

Nelson, Irving Robert 1921-1972 *WhAm 6*

Nelson, J Raleigh 1873-1961 *NatCAB 47*

Nelson, Jabez Curry 1884-1952 *WhAm 3*

Nelson, James Augustus 1878-1942 *NatCAB 31*

Nelson, James Boyd 1897-1956 *WhAm 3*

Nelson, James Richard 1897-1956 *NatCAB 42*

Nelson, Jeremiah 1768-1838 *NatCAB 19, TwCBDA*

Nelson, Jeremiah 1769-1838 *BiAUS, BiDrAC, WhAm H, WhAmP*

Nelson, John 1654-1734 *DcAmB, WhAm H*

Nelson, John 1660?-1721 *ApCAB, Drake*

Nelson, John 1791-1860 *AmBi, ApCAB, BiAUS, Drake, NatCAB 6, TwCBDA*

Nelson, John 1794-1860 *BiDrAC, BiDrUSE, WhAm H*

Nelson, John Edward 1874-1955 *BiDrAC, WhAm 3, WhAmP*

Nelson, John Evon 1879-1951 *WhAm 3*

Nelson, John Mandt 1870-1955 *BiDrAC, NatCAB 42, WhAm 5, WhAmP*

Nelson, John Marbury, Jr. 1883-1965 *WhAm 4*

Nelson, John Richard 1858-1924 *NatCAB 20*

Nelson, John Thackeray 1877-1946 *NatCAB 47*

Nelson, Joseph d1830 *Drake*

Nelson, Joseph David, Jr. 1918-1965 *WhAm 4*

Nelson, Joseph E 1897-1960 *WhAm 4*

Nelson, Julia Bullard 1842-1914 *WhAm 1*

Nelson, Julius 1858-1916 *DcAmB, NatCAB 18, WhAm 1*

Nelson, Knute 1843-1923 *AmBi, ApCAB Sup, BiDrAC, DcAmB, NatCAB 10, NatCAB 19, TwCBDA, WhAm 1, WhAmP*

Nelson, Mack Barnabas 1872-1950 *NatCAB 38, WhAm 3*

Nelson, Martin 1871- *WhAm 5*

Nelson, Martin Johan 1894-1970 *WhAm 5*

Nelson, Merab Josephine 1857- *WomWWA 14*

Nelson, Mortimer *NewYHSD*

Nelson, Nellie Cynthia Chase 1860- *WomWWA 14*

Nelson, Nels Christian 1875-1964 *WhAm 4*

Nelson, Nelson Olsen 1844-1922 *DcAmB,*

Neumann, Ernst Valentine 1879-1945
NatCAB 39
Neumann, F Wight 1851-1924 *WhAm 1*
Neumann, Frank 1892-1964 *WhAm 4*
Neumann, Franz Ernst 1798-1895 *DcScB*
Neumann, Franz Leopold 1900-1954 *DcAmB S5*
Neumann, Henry 1882-1960 *WhAm 4*
Neumann, John Nepomucene 1811-1860 *ApCAB,*
BiDAmEd, DcAmB, NatCAB 5,
TwCBDA, WebAB, WhAm H
Neumann, John Nepomucene *see also* Neuman,
John Nepomucene
Neumann, John Von 1903-1957 *AsBiEn,*
WebAB
Neumann, Joseph 1647-1732 *ApCAB*
Neumann, Julie Wurzburger 1875-
WomWWA 14
Neumann, Robert 1897-1975 *WhAm 6*
Neumann, Sigmund 1904-1962 *NatCAB 49,*
WhAm 4
Neumann, Theodore William 1892-1958
NatCAB 44
Neumann, William Louis 1915-1971 *WhAm 5*
Neumark, Arthur Jay 1897-1966 *NatCAB 51,*
WhAm 4
Neumark, David 1866-1924 *DcAmB, WhAm 1*
Neumayr, Melchior 1845-1890 *DcScB*
Neumeyer, Albert Gustave 1910-1970 *WhAm 5*
Neumeyer, Carl Melvin 1911-1972 *WhAm 6*
Neun, Henry Phillip 1869-1922 *NatCAB 45*
Neunaber *NewYHSD*
Neupert, Carl Nicholas 1897-1968 *NatCAB 54,*
WhAm 5
Neupert, Charles *NewYHSD*
Neupert, Edmund 1842-1888 *WhAm H*
Neurath, Konstantin Von 1873-1956 *WhWW-II*
Neuschaefer, Helen Ahrens 1903-1961
NatCAB 45
Neuser, L A W 1837-1902 *NewYHSD*
Neusteter, Meyer 1878-1965 *NatCAB 55*
Neutra, Richard J 1892-1970 *BnEnAmA*
Neutra, Richard Josef 1892-1970 *WebAB*
Neutra, Richard Joseph 1892-1970 *EncAB,*
McGEWB, NatCAB 57, WhAm 5
Neuville *NewYHSD*
Neuville, Chevalier DeLa 1740?-1800? *ApCAB*
Neuville, Jean Guillaume, Baron Hyde De
1776-1847 *ApCAB*
Neuville, Jean Nicolas 1741-1825 *ApCAB*
Neuville, Normiont *ApCAB*
Neuville, Philippe Buache DeLa 1700-1773
ApCAB
Neuwied, Maximilian Alexander Philippe 1782-
Drake
Neuwirth, Isaac 1894-1972 *WhAm 5*
Neuymin, Grigory Nikolaevich 1886-1946
DcScB
Nevada, Emma d1940 *WhAm 5*
Nevada, Emma 1859-1940 *DcAmB S2,*
NotAW
Nevada, Emma 1861-1940 *TwCBDA*
Nevada, Emma Wixom 1861-1940 *ApCAB*
Nevada, Emma Wixon 1861-1940 *AmWom*
Neve, Juergen Ludwig 1865-1943 *WhAm 2*
Nevelson, Louise 1899- *EncAB*
Nevelson, Louise 1900- *BnEnAmA, McGEWB*
Nevers, Roderick *NewYHSD*
Neves, Jose Joaquim DeAndrade 1807-1869
ApCAB
Neville, Donald Weston 1912-1971 *WhAm 5*
Neville, Edgar N *NewYHSD*
Neville, Edmund 1840- *Drake*
Neville, Edwin Lowe 1884-1944 *WhAm 2*
Neville, Glenn 1906-1965 *WhAm 4*
Neville, James *NewYHSD*
Neville, John 1731-1803 *ApCAB, DcAmB,*
Drake, WhAm H
Neville, Joseph 1730-1819 *BiAUS, BiDrAC,*
Drake, WhAm H
Neville, Keith 1884-1959 *NatCAB 51,*
WhAm 3
Neville, Linda 1873- *WomWWA 14*
Neville, Morgan 1786-1839 *ApCAB, Drake*
Neville, Paul Edwin 1919-1969 *WhAm 5*
Neville, Philip 1909-1974 *WhAm 6*
Neville, Presley 1756-1818 *ApCAB, Drake*
Neville, Robert 1905-1970 *WhAm 5*
Neville, Robert Henry 1858- *WhAm 2*

Neville, Wendell Cushing 1870-1930 *AmBi,*
DcAmB, NatCAB 22, WebAMB,
WhAm 1
Neville, William 1843-1909 *BiDrAC, TwCBDA,*
WhAm 1
Nevils, W Coleman 1878-1955 *WhAm 3*
Nevin, Alfred 1816-1890 *ApCAB, DcAmB,*
Drake, TwCBDA, WhAm H
Nevin, Anne Paul *WomWWA 14*
Nevin, Arthur Finley 1871-1943 *WhAm 2*
Nevin, Blanche 1841- *ApCAB, TwCBDA*
Nevin, Charles Merrick 1892-1975 *WhAm 6*
Nevin, David Robert Bruce 1828- *ApCAB*
Nevin, Edwin Henry 1814-1889 *ApCAB,*
DcAmB, TwCBDA, WhAm H
Nevin, Eleanor Hawes 1852- *WomWWA 14*
Nevin, Elizabeth Booth Miller 1875-
WomWWA 14
Nevin, Ethelbert Woodbridge 1862-1901 *AmBi,*
ApCAB X, DcAmB, NatCAB 7,
TwCBDA, WhAm 1
Nevin, George Balch 1859-1933 *DcAmB,*
NatCAB 7, TwCBDA, WhAm 1
Nevin, Gordon Balch 1892-1943 *WhAm 2*
Nevin, Harriet Middleton Ogden 1859-
WomWWA 14
Nevin, James 1854-1921 *NatCAB 6*
Nevin, James Banks 1873-1931 *WhAm 1*
Nevin, John Williamson 1803-1886 *AmBi,*
ApCAB, DcAmB, DcAmReB, Drake,
McGEWB, NatCAB 5, TwCBDA,
WhAm H
Nevin, Joseph Campbell 1870-1934 *NatCAB 25*
Nevin, Robert Jenkins 1839-1906 *ApCAB,*
TwCBDA, WhAm 1
Nevin, Robert Murphy 1850-1912 *BiDrAC,*
WhAm 4
Nevin, Robert Peebles 1820-1908 *DcAmB,*
WhAm 1
Nevin, Robert Reasoner 1875-1952 *WhAm 3*
Nevin, Theodore M 1854-1918 *TwCBDA*
Nevin, Theodore Williamson 1854-1918
WhAm 1
Nevin, William Channing 1844- *ApCAB,*
TwCBDA, WhAm 4
Nevin, William George 1855-1902 *NatCAB 14*
Nevin, William Latta *WhAm 5*
Nevin, William Marvel 1806-1892 *TwCBDA*
Nevin, William Wilberforce 1836- *ApCAB*
Nevins, Allan 1890-1971 *BiDAmEd, EncAAH,*
EncAB, WebAB, WhAm 5
Nevins, Bert 1910-1966 *WhAm 4*
Nevins, Ralph Griffith, Jr 1925-1974 *WhAm 6*
Nevins, William 1797-1835 *ApCAB*
Nevins, Winfield Scott 1850-1921 *NatCAB 19*
Nevius, Albert Carr 1875-1960 *NatCAB 47*
Nevius, Elbert 1808-1897 *TwCBDA*
Nevius, Henry Martin 1841-1911 *NatCAB 14,*
WhAm 1
Nevius, John Livingston 1829-1893 *DcAmB,*
NatCAB 10, TwCBDA, WhAm H
New, Alexander 1861-1931 *NatCAB 23*
New, Anthony 1747-1833 *ApCAB, BiAUS,*
BiDrAC, Drake, NatCAB 2, TwCBDA,
WhAm H, WhAmP
New, Catherine McLaen 1870- *WhAm 5*
New, Catherine McLean 1870- *WomWWA 14*
New, Clarence Herbert 1862-1933 *WhAm 1*
New, George Edward 1894-1962 *WhAm 4*
New, Gordon Balgarnie 1885-1954 *NatCAB 44,*
WhAm 3
New, Harry Stewart 1858-1937 *AmBi,*
ApCAB X, BiDrAC, BiDrUSE,
DcAmB S2, NatCAB 38, WhAm 1,
WhAmP
New, J D 1830-1892 *BiAUS*
New, Jeptha Dudley 1830-1892 *BiDrAC,*
TwCBDA, WhAm H
New, John C 1831-1906 *BiAUS*
New, John Chalfant 1831-1906 *AmBi, ApCAB,*
TwCBDA, WhAm 1
New, John Chalfont 1831-1906 *NatCAB 13*
New, Norman Roman 1875-1942 *NatCAB 42*
New, William Lafayette 1901-1973 *WhAm 6*
Newall, Hugh Frank 1857-1944 *DcScB*
Newbaker, Bryce Atwood 1896-1962
NatCAB 50

Newbegin, James Gifford 1875-1947
NatCAB 37
Newbell, Rhoades Vincent 1909-1969
NatCAB 55
Newberger, Monroe 1894-1938 *NatCAB 29*
Newberne, Robert Edward Lee 1872-1926
WhAm 1
Newberry, Charles Todd 1879-1939 *NatCAB 55*
Newberry, Edgar Andrew 1886-1962
NatCAB 47, WhAm 4
Newberry, Farrar 1887-1968 *WhAm 5*
Newberry, Helen Parmelee Handy 1835-1912
NatCAB 41
Newberry, J S 1822-1892 *Drake*
Newberry, John Josiah 1877-1954 *WhAm 3*
Newberry, John Stoughton 1826-1887 *ApCAB,*
BiDrAC, DcAmB, NatCAB 12,
NatCAB 41, WhAm H
Newberry, John Stoughton 1866-1937
NatCAB 34
Newberry, John Strong 1822-1892 *AmBi,*
ApCAB, DcAmB, DcScB, IlBEAAW,
NatCAB 9, NewYHSD, TwCBDA,
WhAm H
Newberry, Mary Wheeler 1861- *WhAm 3,*
WomWWA 14
Newberry, Oliver 1789-1860 *AmBi, ApCAB,*
DcAmB, REnAW, WhAm H
Newberry, Oliver Perry 1890-1957 *NatCAB 48*
Newberry, Paige Eells 1857- *WomWWA 14*
Newberry, Perry 1870-1938 *WhAm 1*
Newberry, Roger Wolcott 1891-1959 *WhAm 4*
Newberry, Spencer Baird 1857-1922 *ApCAB X,*
NatCAB 20
Newberry, Truman Handy 1864-1945 *BiDrAC,*
BiDrUSE, DcAmB S3, NatCAB 14,
NatCAB 34, WhAm 2
Newberry, Walter Cass 1835-1912 *ApCAB Sup,*
BiDrAC, TwCBDA, WhAm 1
Newberry, Walter Loomis 1804-1868 *AmBi,*
ApCAB, DcAmB, NatCAB 24, TwCBDA,
WhAm H
Newberry, William Belknap 1867- *WhAm 4*
Newbery, Edward *NewYHSD*
Newbery, Rose *NewYHSD*
Newbill, Willard Douglas 1874- *WhAm 3*
Newbold, Ethel Packard 1875- *WomWWA 14*
Newbold, F Eugene 1893-1967 *NatCAB 52*
Newbold, Fleming 1873-1949 *WhAm 2*
Newbold, Joshua G 1830- *NatCAB 11*
Newbold, Thomas 1760-1823 *BiAUS, BiDrAC,*
WhAm H, WhAmP
Newbold, William Henry 1849-1917
NatCAB 17
Newbold, William Romaine 1865-1926 *DcAmB,*
NatCAB 22, WhAm 1
Newborg, Joseph L 1864-1927 *ApCAB X*
Newborg, Leonard David 1894-1972 *WhAm 5*
Newbranch, Harvey Ellsworth 1875-1959
NatCAB 44, WhAm 3
Newbro, Dupont M 1865-1924 *ApCAB X*
Newbrough, John Ballou 1828-1891 *DcAmB,*
WhAm H
Newburger, Frank Lieberman 1873-1946
NatCAB 39
Newburger, Joseph 1858-1926 *WhAm 1*
Newburger, Joseph Emanuel 1853-1931
WhAm 1
Newburger, Morris 1906-1968 *WhAm 6*
Newburger, Samuel Meade 1863-1944
NatCAB 32
Newburn, Harry Kenneth 1906-1974 *WhAm 6*
Newbury, Frank Davies 1880-1969 *WhAm 5*
Newbury, Michael d1970 *WhAm 5*
Newbury, Mollie Netcher d1954 *WhAm 3*
Newby, Leonidas Perry 1856- *WhAm 4*
Newby, Nathan 1868-1951 *WhAm 3*
Newcastle, Thomas Pelham Clinton 1752-1795
ApCAB, Drake
Newcomb, Arthur Thurston 1871-1938
WhAm 1
Newcomb, C A 1830-1902 *BiAUS*
Newcomb, Carman Adam 1830-1902 *BiDrAC*
Newcomb, Charles Benjamin 1845-1922
WhAm 1
Newcomb, Charles Leonard 1854-1930 *DcAmB,*
NatCAB 22, WhAm 1

Newman, Jacob Kiefer 1872-1943 *NatCAB 33,* *WhAm 2*
Newman, James Joseph 1889-1971 *WhAm 5*
Newman, James R 1907-1966 *NatCAB 53,* *WhAm 4*
Newman, Jared Treman 1855-1937 *NatCAB 29,* *WhAm 1*
Newman, Jeanie Stevens *WomWWA 14*
Newman, John *NewYHSD*
Newman, John Grant 1862-1956 *WhAm 3*
Newman, Cardinal John Henry 1801-1890 *McGEWB*
Newman, John Philip 1826-1899 *ApCAB,* *DcAmB, NatCAB 6, TwCBDA,* *WhAm H, WhAm 1*
Newman, John Urquhart 1860- *WhAm 4*
Newman, Louis Israel 1893-1972 *WhAm 5*
Newman, Mark 1772-1859 *NatCAB 10*
Newman, Mary 1872- *WomWWA 14*
Newman, Milton Grant 1865-1937 *NatCAB 29*
Newman, Oliver Peck 1877- *WhAm 5*
Newman, Robert *WhAm 1*
Newman, Robert Loftin 1827-1912 *DcAmB,* *NatCAB 13, NewYHSD*
Newman, Robert Pettit 1857-1921 *ApCAB X*
Newman, Samuel 1601?-1663 *NatCAB 8*
Newman, Samuel 1602-1663 *ApCAB, Drake*
Newman, Samuel Phillips 1796-1842 *ApCAB,* *Drake*
Newman, Samuel Phillips 1797-1842 *BiDAmEd,* *DcAmB, NatCAB 10, TwCBDA,* *WhAm H*
Newman, Stephen Morrell 1845-1924 *WhAm 1*
Newman, William Henry 1820-1883 *ApCAB*
Newman, William Henry 1847-1918 *DcAmB S1,* *NatCAB 14, WhAm 1*
Newman, William Henry Harrison 1826-1912 *NatCAB 8*
Newman, William Truslow 1843-1920 *DcAmB,* *NatCAB 3, WhAm 1*
Newman, Willie Betty 1864- *WhAm 4,* *WomWWA 14*
Newmark, Nathan 1853- *WhAm 4*
Newmark, Harris 1834-1916 *ApCAB X,* *NatCAB 18, WhAm 1*
Newmark, Marco Ross 1878-1959 *NatCAB 51,* *WhAm 6*
Newmark, Maurice Harris 1859-1929 *NatCAB 18, WhAm 1*
Newmyer, Alvin Leroy 1884-1973 *WhAm 6*
Newmyer, Arthur Grover d1955 *WhAm 3*
Newnan, Daniel 1780?-1851 *ApCAB, BiDrAC,* *Drake, WhAm H*
Newnan, Daniel *see also* Newman, Daniel
Newnham, Letitia Agnes 1865- *WomWWA 14*
Newport, Christopher 1565?-1617 *AmBi,* *ApCAB, DcAmB, Drake, WhAm H*
Newport, Elfreda Louise 1866- *AmWom*
Newport, George 1803-1854 *DcScB*
Newport, James W *NewYHSD*
Newport, Reece Marshall 1833-1912 *ApCAB X*
Newquist, Melvin Nathaniel 1897-1972 *NatCAB 57*
Newsalt, Adolph 1853-1927 *NatCAB 23*
Newsam, Albert 1809-1864 *ApCAB, DcAmB,* *IIBEAAW, NewYHSD, WhAm H*
Newsham, Joseph Parkinson 1837-1919 *ApCAB,* *BiDrAC, TwCBDA, WhAm 3*
Newsham, Joseph Parkinson 1837-1919 *BiAUS*
Newsom, Arthur Sumner 1875- *WhoColR*
Newsom, Curtis Bishop d1954 *WhAm 3*
Newsom, Edwin Earl 1897-1973 *WhAm 6*
Newsom, Ella King *NotAW*
Newsom, Ella King 183-?-1913? *BiDConf*
Newsom, Ernest 1883-1954 *NatCAB 45*
Newsom, Herschel D 1905-1970 *WhAm 5*
Newsom, John Flesher 1869-1928 *WhAm 1*
Newsom, Marion Eugene 1884-1948 *NatCAB 37*
Newsom, Reeves 1893-1967 *NatCAB 53*
Newsom, Vida *WomWWA 14*
Newsom, William Monypeny 1887-1942 *WhAm 1, WhAm 2*
Newsome, Albert Ray 1894-1951 *WhAm 3*
Newsome, John Parks 1893-1961 *BiDrAC*
Newsome, William 1869-1930 *NatCAB 26*
Newson, Henry Byron 1860-1910 *WhAm 1*

Newson, Mary Frances Winston 1869- *WomWWA 14*
Newswanger, George *NewYHSD*
Newton, Mrs. *NewYHSD*
Newton, Alfred Edward 1863-1940 *WhAm 1*
Newton, Alfred Edward 1864-1940 *NatCAB 31*
Newton, Arthur William 1868-1963 *WhAm 4*
Newton, Byron R 1861-1938 *WhAm 1*
Newton, Charles Bertram 1871- *WhAm 5*
Newton, Charles Damon 1861-1930 *WhAm 1*
Newton, Charles Howard 1930-1975 *WhAm 6*
Newton, Cherubusco 1848-1910 *BiDrAC*
Newton, Clara Pease 1860- *WomWWA 14*
Newton, Clarence Lucian 1877-1958 *WhAm 3*
Newton, Cleveland Alexander 1873-1945 *BiDrAC, WhAm 2*
Newton, Cosette Faust 1889-1975 *WhAm 6*
Newton, Eben 1795-1885 *BiAUS, BiDrAC,* *WhAm H*
Newton, Edith 1878- *WhAm 6*
Newton, Edwin Meade 1895-1957 *NatCAB 46*
Newton, Edwin Tulley 1840-1930 *DcScB*
Newton, Elbridge Ward 1864- *WhAm 4*
Newton, Elsie Eaton 1871- *WomWWA 14*
Newton, Emily Norcross 1859- *WomWWA 14*
Newton, Francis Chandler 1893-1967 *NatCAB 54*
Newton, Francis Clement 1874-1946 *NatCAB 35*
Newton, Frank Buzzell 1877-1928 *ApCAB X*
Newton, G S *NewYHSD*
Newton, George Durfee 1897-1965 *NatCAB 51*
Newton, Georgiana S 1868- *WomWWA 14*
Newton, Gilbert Stuart 1794-1835 *NewYHSD*
Newton, Gilbert Stuart 1795-1835 *Drake*
Newton, Gilbert Stuart 1797-1835 *ApCAB,* *NatCAB 5*
Newton, Glenn D 1902-1969 *WhAm 5*
Newton, Harry Birk 1888-1970 *NatCAB 56*
Newton, Henry 1845-1877 *ApCAB, NatCAB 4,* *TwCBDA*
Newton, Henry Gleason 1843-1914 *NatCAB 16*
Newton, Henry Jotham 1823-1895 *DcAmB,* *NatCAB 7, WhAm H*
Newton, Herbert Boyden 1874-1958 *NatCAB 44*
Newton, Homer Curtis 1879-1957 *WhAm 3*
Newton, Howard Chamberlain 1892-1964 *NatCAB 50, WhAm 4*
Newton, Hubert Anson 1830-1896 *AmBi,* *ApCAB, DcAmB, DcScB, NatCAB 9,* *TwCBDA, WhAm H*
Newton, Sir Isaac 1642-1727 *AsBiEn, DcScB,* *McGEWB*
Newton, Isaac 1794-1858 *ApCAB, DcAmB,* *Drake, NatCAB 5, TwCBDA, WhAm H*
Newton, Isaac 1800-1867 *ApCAB, BiAUS,* *DcAmB, EncAAH, NatCAB 26,* *TwCBDA, WhAm H*
Newton, Isaac 1837-1884 *ApCAB, NatCAB 4,* *TwCBDA*
Newton, Isaac Burkett 1861-1934 *ApCAB X,* *WhAm 1*
Newton, James Hale 1832-1921 *NatCAB 21*
Newton, James Thornwell 1861-1935 *NatCAB 42, WhAm 1*
Newton, John 1820?-1895 *Drake*
Newton, John 1823-1895 *AmBi, ApCAB,* *DcAmB, NatCAB 4, TwCBDA,* *WhAm H*
Newton, John Brockenbrough 1839-1897 *NatCAB 11, TwCBDA*
Newton, John Caldwell Calhoun 1848-1931 *NatCAB 23*
Newton, John Henry 1881-1948 *WhAm 2*
Newton, John O *NewYHSD*
Newton, John Orpheus 1905-1949 *NatCAB 38*
Newton, John Orville 1864- *WhAm 4*
Newton, John Thomas 1793-1857 *ApCAB,* *Drake, TwCBDA*
Newton, John Wharton 1892-1972 *WhAm 5*
Newton, Joseph Fort 1876-1950 *DcAmB S4,* *NatCAB 38*
Newton, Joseph Fort 1880-1950 *WhAm 2*
Newton, Joseph Lyman 1854-1919 *ApCAB X*
Newton, Mark *NewYHSD*
Newton, Mark Trafton 1855-1922 *NatCAB 19*
Newton, Martin *NewYHSD*

Newton, Maurice 1892-1968 *WhAm 5*
Newton, McGuire 1876-1923 *WhAm 1*
Newton, Oscar 1877-1939 *WhAm 1*
Newton, P Stewart *NewYHSD*
Newton, Richard 1812-1887 *DcAmB,* *WhAm H*
Newton, Richard 1813-1887 *ApCAB,* *TwCBDA*
Newton, Richard Heber 1840-1914 *AmBi,* *ApCAB, DcAmB, NatCAB 3, TwCBDA,* *WhAm 1*
Newton, Robert Crittenden 1840-1887 *ApCAB,* *TwCBDA*
Newton, Robert Safford 1818-1881 *ApCAB,* *DcAmB, NatCAB 2, TwCBDA,* *WhAm H*
Newton, Robert Safford 1855- *ApCAB*
Newton, Roger 1685-1771 *ApCAB, BiAUS,* *Drake*
Newton, Thomas 1660-1721 *DcAmB,* *WhAm H*
Newton, Thomas 1661-1721 *ApCAB, Drake*
Newton, Thomas 1768-1847 *BiDrAC, DcAmB,* *WhAm H, WhAmP*
Newton, Thomas 1769-1847 *BiAUS, TwCBDA*
Newton, Thomas Willoughby 1804-1853 *BiAUS,* *BiDrAC, WhAm H*
Newton, Walter Hughes 1880-1941 *BiDrAC,* *WhAm 1, WhAmP*
Newton, Walter Russell 1855- *WhAm 4*
Newton, Watson J 1848-1913 *WhAm 1*
Newton, William G 1817?- *NewYHSD*
Newton, William J 1817?- *NewYHSD*
Newton, William Wilberforce 1843-1914 *ApCAB, DcAmB, NatCAB 25, TwCBDA,* *WhAm 1*
Newton, Willoughby 1802-1874 *BiAUS,* *BiDrAC, WhAm H*
Nexo, Martin Andersen 1869-1954 *McGEWB*
Ney, Christopher William 1869-1927 *NatCAB 21*
Ney, Elisabet 1830-1907 *IIBEAAW*
Ney, Elisabet 1833-1907 *DcAmB, NotAW*
Ney, Elizabet 1845?-1907 *NatCAB 13*
Ney, Michel 1769-1815 *McGEWB, WhoMilH*
Neyal, Vincent *NewYHSD*
Neylan, John Francis 1885-1960 *WhAm 4*
Neyland, Harry 1877-1958 *WhAm 3*
Neyland, Robert Reese, Jr. 1892-1962 *NatCAB 50, WhAm 4*
Neymann, Clarence Adolph 1887-1951 *NatCAB 41, WhAm 3*
Neynabor, Augustus d1887 *NewYHSD*
Neyra, Domingo 1689?-1748? *ApCAB*
Nez Coupe *WhAm H*
Ng, Poon Chew 1866-1931 *AmBi, DcAmB*
Ngala, Ronald Gideon 1923- *McGEWB*
Ngata, Sir Apirana Turupa 1874-1950 *McGEWB*
Ngo Dinh Diem 1901-1963 *WhAm 4*
Ni, Tsan 1301-1374 *McGEWB*
Nias, Henry 1879-1955 *WhAm 3*
Nibecker, Karl 1886-1957 *NatCAB 48*
Niblack, Albert Parker 1859-1929 *DcAmB,* *NatCAB 28, WhAm 1*
Niblack, Silas Leslie 1825-1883 *BiDrAC,* *WhAm H*
Niblack, Silas N 1825-1883 *BiAUS*
Niblack, William Ellis 1822-1893 *BiAUS,* *BiDrAC, DcAmB, TwCBDA, WhAm H,* *WhAmP*
Nibley, Charles Wilson 1849-1931 *WhAm 1*
Niblo, Fred 1874-1948 *NatCAB 38*
Niblo, Urban 1897-1957 *WhAm 3*
Niblo, William 1789-1875 *ApCAB*
Niblo, William 1789-1878 *DcAmB,* *NatCAB 25, WhAm H*
Niblo, William, Jr. *NewYHSD*
Niboyer, Baudoin Simon 1779-1834 *ApCAB*
Niccolls, Samuel Jack 1838-1915 *NatCAB 5,* *NatCAB 27, WhAm 1*
Niccum, Elmo Everett 1904-1956 *NatCAB 48*
Nice, Harry Whinna 1877-1941 *NatCAB 32,* *WhAm 1*
Nice, Margaret Morse 1883-1974 *WhAm 6*
Nicely, Harold Elliott 1900-1954 *NatCAB 46,* *WhAm 3*
Nicely, James Mount 1899-1964 *NatCAB 50,*

WhAm 4
Niceron, Jean-Francois 1613-1646 *DcScB*
Nichiren 1222-1282 *McGEWB*
Nichol, Archibald Jamieson 1897-1955
   NatCAB 45
Nichol, Edward Sterling 1894-1970 *WhAm 5*
Nichol, Francis David 1897-1966 *WhAm 4*
Nichol, Frederick William 1892-1955 *WhAm 3*
Nichol, Henry H *NewYHSD*
Nichol, William Lytle 1828-1901 *NatCAB 8*
Nichola, Lewis 1717-1807 *ApCAB, TwCBDA*
Nicholas I 1796-1855 *McGEWB*
Nicholas II 1868-1918 *McGEWB*
Nicholas Chuquet *DcScB*
Nicholas, General 1724-1807 *Drake*
Nicholas Nicholaievich, Grand Duke 1856-1929
   WhoMilH
Nicholas Of Cusa 1401-1464 *AsBiEn, DcScB,*
   McGEWB
Nicholas Of Damascus *DcScB*
Nicholas Of Oresme 1320?-1382 *McGEWB*
Nicholas Oresme 1320?-1382 *DcScB*
Nicholas, Anna d1929 *WhAm 1*
Nicholas, Edwin August 1893-1953 *WhAm 3*
Nicholas, Francis Child 1862-1938 *NatCAB 27*
Nicholas, Francis Tillou 1834-1912 *AmBi,*
   DcAmB, WhAmP
Nicholas, George d1799 *BiAUS, Drake*
Nicholas, George 1754?-1799 *DcAmB*
Nicholas, George 1755?-1799 *ApCAB,*
   NatCAB 5, WhAm H
Nicholas, John d1821 *BiAUS*
Nicholas, John 1756?-1819 *DcAmB, WhAm H*
Nicholas, John 1757?-1819 *BiDrAC, WhAmP*
Nicholas, John 1761-1819 *ApCAB, NatCAB 2,*
   NatCAB 4, TwCBDA
Nicholas, John Spangler 1895-1963 *DcScB,*
   NatCAB 48, WhAm 4
Nicholas, Lindsley Vincent 1879- *WhAm 6*
Nicholas, Philip Norborne 1773-1849 *ApCAB*
Nicholas, Philip Norborne 1775?-1849 *DcAmB,*
   WhAm H
Nicholas, Richard Ulysses 1890-1953 *WhAm 3*
Nicholas, Robert Carter d1857 *BiAUS, Drake*
Nicholas, Robert Carter 1715-1780 *ApCAB,*
   BiAUS, Drake, NatCAB 13, TwCBDA
Nicholas, Robert Carter 1728-1780 *DcAmB,*
   WhAm H
Nicholas, Robert Carter 1790-1857 *TwCBDA*
Nicholas, Robert Carter 1793?-1857 *ApCAB,*
   BiDrAC, NatCAB 5, WhAm H, WhAmP
Nicholas, Robert Carter 1875-1941 *NatCAB 35*
Nicholas, Samuel 1744?-1790 *WebAMB*
Nicholas, Samuel Smith 1796-1869 *ApCAB,*
   BiAUS, Drake, TwCBDA
Nicholas, William Gardiner 1853-1915
   WhAm 1
Nicholas, William Oliver 1913- *WhAm 5*
Nicholas, Wilson Cary d1820 *BiAUS, Drake*
Nicholas, Wilson Cary 1757?-1820 *ApCAB,*
   NatCAB 5, TwCBDA
Nicholas, Wilson Cary 1761-1820 *BiDrAC,*
   DcAmB, WhAm H, WhAmP
Nicholes, Anna E 1865- *WomWWA 14*
Nicholes, S Grace 1875- *WomWWA 14*
Nicholl, Horace Wadham 1848-1922 *WhAm 1*
Nicholl, John 1822-1914 *NatCAB 18*
Nicholls, C W DeLyon 1854- *WhAm 1*
Nicholls, Francis Redding 1834-1912 *BiDConf*
Nicholls, Francis Tillon 1834-1912 *ApCAB,*
   WhAm H
Nicholls, Francis Tillou 1834-1912 *NatCAB 10,*
   TwCBDA
Nicholls, George Heaton 1876- *WhAm 5*
Nicholls, John Calhoun 1834-1893 *BiDrAC,*
   WhAm H
Nicholls, John Henry 1867-1925 *NatCAB 20*
Nicholls, Rhoda Holmes 1854-1930 *AmWom,*
   BiCAW, DcAmB, NatCAB 7, WhAm 1,
   WhAm 1C, WomWWA 14
Nicholls, Richard 1624-1672 *WhAm H*
Nicholls, Richard *see also* Nichols, Richard
Nicholls, Samuel Jones 1885-1937 *BiDrAC,*
   WhAm 1
Nicholls, Thomas David 1870-1931 *BiDrAC,*
   WhAm 5
Nicholls, William Durrett 1885-1952 *WhAm 3*
Nichols, Abel 1815-1860 *NewYHSD*

Nichols, Acosta 1872-1945 *NatCAB 40*
Nichols, Mrs. Andrew *NewYHSD*
Nichols, Anne 1891-1966 *WhAm 4*
Nichols, Arthur Angus 1906-1968 *NatCAB 54*
Nichols, Arthur Burr 1876- *WhAm 5*
Nichols, Arthur Howard 1840-1923 *NatCAB 20*
Nichols, Caroline Burgess 1864- *WomWWA 14*
Nichols, Charles *NewYHSD*
Nichols, Charles, Jr. 1903-1961 *NatCAB 54*
Nichols, Charles Archibald 1876-1920 *BiDrAC,*
   WhAm 1
Nichols, Charles Fessenden 1846- *NatCAB 14*
Nichols, Charles Gerry 1903-1963 *WhAm 4*
Nichols, Charles Henry 1820-1889 *ApCAB,*
   DcAmB, WhAm H
Nichols, Charles Henry 1864-1927 *WhAm 1*
Nichols, Charles Lemuel 1851-1929 *DcAmB,*
   NatCAB 24, WhAm 1
Nichols, Charles Leslie 1899-1958 *NatCAB 47*
Nichols, Charles Walter 1875-1963 *NatCAB 52,*
   WhAm 4
Nichols, Claribel 1878- *BiCAW*
Nichols, Clarina Irene Howard 1810-1885 *AmBi,*
   DcAmB, NotAW, WhAm H
Nichols, Clarinda Howard 1810-1885 *ApCAB,*
   NatCAB 5
Nichols, Clark Asahel 1875- *WhAm 5*
Nichols, Clay Lloyd 1882-1959 *NatCAB 46*
Nichols, David 1829-1911 *NewYHSD*
Nichols, Dudley 1895-1960 *NatCAB 45*
Nichols, Edward 1847-1923 *NatCAB 20*
Nichols, Edward Hall 1864-1922 *ApCAB X,*
   WhAm 1
Nichols, Edward Leamington 1854-1937 *AmBi,*
   DcAmB S2, NatCAB 4, TwCBDA,
   WhAm 1
Nichols, Edward T 1822-1886 *Drake*
Nichols, Edward Tatchaln 1823-1886
   NatCAB 4
Nichols, Edward Tatnall 1823-1886 *ApCAB,*
   TwCBDA
Nichols, Edward Tattnall 1852-1934 *WhAm 1*
Nichols, Edward W 1819-1871 *NewYHSD*
Nichols, Edward W 1820-1871 *Drake,*
   NatCAB 5
Nichols, Edward West 1858-1927 *NatCAB 25,*
   WhAm 1
Nichols, Egbert Ray 1884-1958 *WhAm 3*
Nichols, Eleanor *NewYHSD*
Nichols, Ernest Fox 1869-1924 *DcAmB, DcScB,*
   NatCAB 13, NatCAB 21, WhAm 1
Nichols, Ernest Reuben 1858- *TwCBDA*
Nichols, Francis 1737-1812 *ApCAB, TwCBDA*
Nichols, Francis Henry 1868-1904 *WhAm 1*
Nichols, Frank Rudolph 1912-1963 *NatCAB 52,*
   WhAm 4
Nichols, Frederick B 1824-1906? *NewYHSD*
Nichols, Frederick Day 1870- *WhAm 5*
Nichols, Frederick George 1878-1954 *BiDAmEd,*
   WhAm 3
Nichols, George 1809-1882 *ApCAB*
Nichols, George 1827-1907 *NatCAB 18,*
   TwCBDA
Nichols, George A *NewYHSD*
Nichols, George Elwood 1882-1939 *NatCAB 29,*
   WhAm 1
Nichols, George L, Jr. 1860- *NatCAB 3*
Nichols, George Little 1830-1892 *NatCAB 3*
Nichols, George Ward 1831-1885 *DcAmB,*
   WhAm H
Nichols, George Ward 1837-1885 *ApCAB,*
   NatCAB 5
Nichols, Harry Peirce 1850-1940 *WhAm 1*
Nichols, Helen Mae Colegrove 1873-
   WomWWA 14
Nichols, Henry 1816?- *NewYHSD*
Nichols, Henry Drew 1873-1963 *WhAm 4*
Nichols, Henry Hobart 1869-1962 *IIBEAAW*
Nichols, Henry James 1877-1927 *NatCAB 23*
Nichols, Henry Joseph 1877- *WhAm 6*
Nichols, Henry Sargent Prentiss 1858-1936
   WhAm 1
Nichols, Henry Windsor 1866- *WhAm 4*
Nichols, Herbert 1852-1936 *TwCBDA,*
   WhAm 1
Nichols, Herbert L 1886-1964 *WhAm 4*
Nichols, Hester Deane 1862- *WomWWA 14*
Nichols, Hettie M 1843- *WomWWA 14*

Nichols, Hobart, Jr. 1869-1962 *NatCAB 50,*
   WhAm 4
Nichols, Hugh Llewellyn 1865-1942
   NatCAB 34
Nichols, Ichabod 1784-1859 *ApCAB, Drake,*
   NatCAB 10, WhAm H
Nichols, Ida Preston 1853- *WomWWA 14*
Nichols, Isaac 1748-1835 *NatCAB 3*
Nichols, Isabel McIlhenny d1941 *WhAm 2*
Nichols, Jack 1896-1945 *NatCAB 36*
Nichols, James 1830-1916 *NatCAB 6,*
   WhAm 1
Nichols, James Calvin 1883-1962 *NatCAB 50*
Nichols, James Edwin 1845- *NatCAB 14*
Nichols, James Robinson 1819-1888 *ApCAB,*
   DcAmB, NatCAB 5, WhAm H
Nichols, James Walter 1927-1973 *WhAm 6*
Nichols, Jesse Clyde 1880-1950 *WhAm 2*
Nichols, John 1834-1917 *BiDrAC*
Nichols, John Benjamin 1867-1954 *NatCAB 42,*
   WhAm 3
Nichols, John Francis 1873- *WhAm 5*
Nichols, John Conover 1896-1945 *BiDrAC,*
   WhAm 2, WhAmP
Nichols, John Grayson 1892-1941 *WhAm 2*
Nichols, John Hammel 1873-1941 *NatCAB 30*
Nichols, John Richard 1854-1932 *WhAm 1*
Nichols, John Wesley 1897-1974 *WhAm 6*
Nichols, Joseph Longworth 1870-1918
   NatCAB 17
Nichols, Josephine Ralston 1838- *AmWom*
Nichols, Lawrence Ayer, Jr. 1908-1969
   NatCAB 55
Nichols, Lewis 1790?-1859 *NatCAB 3*
Nichols, Lucius Tombes 1858-1942 *NatCAB 33*
Nichols, Malcolm E 1876-1950 *WhAm 3*
Nichols, Maria Longworth *NotAW*
Nichols, Mark Lovel 1888-1971 *WhAm 5*
Nichols, Martha Stewart 1867- *WomWWA 14*
Nichols, Marvin Curtis 1896-1969 *WhAm 6*
Nichols, Mary Holyoke Ward *NewYHSD*
Nichols, Mary Josephine Genung 1876-
   WomWWA 14
Nichols, Mary Louise 1873- *WomWWA 14*
Nichols, Mary P 1836-1905? *NewYHSD*
Nichols, Mary Sargeant Neal Gove 1810-1884
   ApCAB, DcAmB, NatCAB 13, NotAW,
   WhAm H
Nichols, Mary Sargeant Gove 1810-1884 *Drake*
Nichols, Mary Schofield 1875- *WomWWA 14*
Nichols, Matthias H 1824-1862 *BiAUS,*
   BiDrAC, TwCBDA, WhAm H
Nichols, Maud Kenney 1878- *WomWWA 14*
Nichols, May Louise *WomWWA 14*
Nichols, Mike 1931- *WebAB*
Nichols, Minerva Parker 1861-1949 *NotAW*
Nichols, Minerva Parker 1863-1949 *AmWom*
Nichols, Minnie Bowen 1869- *WomWWA 14*
Nichols, Moses 1759-1790 *ApCAB, Drake*
Nichols, Neil Ernest 1879- *WhAm 3*
Nichols, Nicholas *NewYHSD*
Nichols, Othniel Foster 1845-1908 *NatCAB 9,*
   TwCBDA, WhAm 1
Nichols, Pierrepont Herrick 1893-1951
   WhAm 3
Nichols, Rebecca S Reed 1820- *ApCAB, Drake*
Nichols, Richard 1624-1672 *Drake*
Nichols, Richard *see also* Nicholls, Richard
Nichols, Robert 1908-1958 *NatCAB 46*
Nichols, Robert Hastings 1873-1955
   NatCAB 42, WhAm 3
Nichols, Rose Standish *WomWWA 14*
Nichols, Roy Franklin 1896-1973 *WhAm 5*
Nichols, Ruth Rowland 1901-1960 *WhAm 4*
Nichols, Sarah *NewYHSD*
Nichols, Spencer Baird 1875-1950 *WhAm 3*
Nichols, Spencer VanBokkelen 1882-1946
   WhAm 2
Nichols, Spencer VanBokkelen 1892-1947
   NatCAB 35
Nichols, Susan Percival 1873- *WomWWA 14*
Nichols, Thomas Flint 1870- *WhAm 5*
Nichols, Thomas Low 1815-1901 *DcAmB*
Nichols, W D *NewYHSD*
Nichols, Walter Edmond 1875- *WhAm 5*
Nichols, Walter Edmond 1889-1954
   NatCAB 42
Nichols, Walter Franklin 1882-1946 *WhAm 2*

Nichols, Walter Hammond 1866-1935 *WhAm 1*
Nichols, William 1754-1804 *ApCAB*
Nichols, William A 1817-1869 *Drake*
Nichols, William Augustus 1818-1869 *ApCAB,*
TwCBDA
Nichols, William Flynt 1918- *BiDrAC*
Nichols, William Ford 1849-1924 *ApCAB Sup,*
DcAmB, NatCAB 12, TwCBDA,
WhAm 1
Nichols, William Henry 1852-1930 *NatCAB 14,*
NatCAB 24, WhAm 1
Nichols, William LeRoy 1905-1958 *WhAm 3*
Nichols, William Morse 1881-1957 *NatCAB 46*
Nichols, William Ripley 1847-1886 *ApCAB,*
TwCBDA
Nichols, William Theophilus 1863-1931
WhAm 1
Nichols, William Wallace 1860-1948 *ApCAB X,*
WhAm 2
Nicholson *NewYHSD*
Nicholson, Alfred Osborn Pope 1801-1876
TwCBDA
Nicholson, Alfred Osborn Pope 1808-1876
ApCAB, BiAUS, BiDrAC, Drake,
NatCAB 11, WhAm H
Nicholson, Alfred Osborne Pope 1808-1876
DcAmB
Nicholson, Ben 1894- *McGEWB*
Nicholson, Clarence Maurice 1868-1957
NatCAB 48
Nicholson, Donald William 1888-1968 *BiDrAC,*
WhAm 4A
Nicholson, Edward Everett 1873- *WhAm 5*
Nicholson, Eliza Jane Poitevent Holbrook
1849-1896 *AmWom, DcAmB, NatCAB 1,*
NotAW, TwCBDA, WhAm H
Nicholson, Elizabeth 1833-1926 *NewYHSD*
Nicholson, Eugenie Kountze 1867-
WomWWA 14
Nicholson, Sir Francis 1655-1728 *AmBi,*
ApCAB, DcAmB, Drake, McGEWB,
NatCAB 7, NatCAB 12, NatCAB 13,
WhAm H
Nicholson, Frank Lee 1868-1954 *WhAm 3*
Nicholson, Frank Walter 1864- *WhAm 4*
Nicholson, G J Guthrie 1871-1950 *NatCAB 40*
Nicholson, George Edward 1861- *WhAm 1*
Nicholson, George Mansel 1874- *WhAm 5*
Nicholson, George Robert Henderson 1885-1947
WhAm 2
Nicholson, George T 1856-1913 *WhAm 1*
Nicholson, George W 1832-1912 *NewYHSD*
Nicholson, Hammond Burke 1895-1961
WhAm 4
Nicholson, Harold George 1886-1968 *WhAm 5*
Nicholson, Henry Hudson 1850-1940
NatCAB 48, WhAm 1
Nicholson, Henry S *NewYHSD*
Nicholson, Hugh Gideon 1871- *NatCAB 17*
Nicholson, Isaac Lea 1844-1906 *NatCAB 11,*
TwCBDA, WhAm 1
Nicholson, J W A 1821-1887 *Drake*
Nicholson, James 1736?-1804 *AmBi, DcAmB*
Nicholson, James 1737?-1804 *ApCAB, Drake,*
NatCAB 2, TwCBDA, WhAm H
Nicholson, James Bartram 1820-1901 *ApCAB,*
DcAmB, NatCAB 25, WhAm H,
WhAm 4
Nicholson, James Thomas 1893-1969 *WhAm 5*
Nicholson, James William 1844- *NatCAB 13,*
WhAm 1
Nicholson, James William Augustus 1821-1887
AmBi, ApCAB, DcAmB, NatCAB 2,
TwCBDA, WhAm H
Nicholson, Jerome Lee 1863- *WhAm 4*
Nicholson, John *ApCAB*
Nicholson, John d1800 *DcAmB, WhAm H*
Nicholson, John 1765-1820 *BiAUS, BiDrAC,*
WhAm H
Nicholson, John 1822-1857 *WhoMilH*
Nicholson, John 1825-1893 *NewYHSD*
Nicholson, John Anthony 1827-1906 *BiAUS,*
BiDrAC, TwCBDA, WhAmP
Nicholson, John B 1783-1846 *ApCAB, Drake,*
TwCBDA
Nicholson, John Frederick 1878- *WhAm 6*
Nicholson, John Hancock 1867-1937
NatCAB 28

Nicholson, John Page 1842-1922 *WhAm 1*
Nicholson, John Reed 1849-1937 *NatCAB 12,*
TwCBDA, WhAm 1, WhAm 1C
Nicholson, John Rutherford 1887-1965
WhAm 4
Nicholson, John William 1881-1955 *DcScB*
Nicholson, Joseph Hopper 1770-1817 *ApCAB,*
BiAUS, BiDrAC, DcAmB, Drake,
NatCAB 5, TwCBDA, WhAm H,
WhAmP
Nicholson, Joseph J d1838 *Drake*
Nicholson, Katherine Leonard Lea 1878-
WomWWA 14
Nicholson, Leonard Kimball 1881-1952
WhAm 3
Nicholson, Meredith 1866-1947 *DcAmB S4,*
WhAm 2
Nicholson, Nollie Davis 1879- *WhAm 6*
Nicholson, Norman Edwin 1923-1972 *WhAm 5*
Nicholson, Paul Coe 1888-1956 *WhAm 3*
Nicholson, Ralph 1899-1972 *NatCAB 57,*
WhAm 5
Nicholson, Reginald Fairfax 1852-1939
WhAm 1
Nicholson, Rex Lee 1902-1974 *WhAm 6*
Nicholson, Robert Harvey 1889-1969 *WhAm 5*
Nicholson, Samuel 1743-1811 *AmBi, DcAmB,*
Drake, WebAMB, WhAm H
Nicholson, Samuel 1743-1813 *ApCAB,*
NatCAB 4, TwCBDA
Nicholson, Samuel Danford 1859-1923 *BiDrAC,*
DcAmB, NatCAB 23, WhAm 1, WhAmP
Nicholson, Samuel Edgar 1862- *WhAm 1*
Nicholson, Samuel M 1861-1939 *ApCAB X,*
WhAm 1
Nicholson, Samuel Thompson 1867-1948
NatCAB 37
Nicholson, Samuel Thorne *WhAm 5*
Nicholson, Seth Barnes 1891-1963 *AsBiEn,*
DcScB, WhAm 4
Nicholson, Somerville 1822-1905 *TwCBDA,*
WhAm 1
Nicholson, Soterios 1885- *WhAm 3*
Nicholson, Susan Fauntleroy Quarles
NewYHSD
Nicholson, Thomas 1862-1944 *NatCAB 40,*
WhAm 2
Nicholson, Timothy 1828-1924 *DcAmB,*
WhAm 4
Nicholson, Vincent DeWitt 1890-1945 *WhAm 2*
Nicholson, Walter Wick 1867- *WhAm 4*
Nicholson, Watson 1866-1951 *WhAm 3*
Nicholson, William 1753-1815 *AsBiEn, DcScB*
Nicholson, William Calvin 1883-1926
NatCAB 20
Nicholson, William Carmichael 1800-1872
ApCAB, Drake, NatCAB 4, TwCBDA
Nicholson, William Jones 1856-1931 *DcAmB,*
WhAm 1
Nicholson, William McNeal 1905-1974
WhAm 6
Nicholson, William Ramsey, Jr. 1879- *WhAm 6*
Nicholson, William Rufus 1822-1901 *ApCAB,*
TwCBDA, WhAm 1
Nicholson, William Thomas 1834-1893
ApCAB X, DcAmB, NatCAB 8,
WhAm H
Nicholsons *NewYHSD*
Nichter, Frank Henry 1877-1950 *NatCAB 40*
Nickel, Don Frederick 1899-1969 *NatCAB 55*
Nickels, Frances Jacobs *WomWWA 14*
Nickels, John Augustine Heard 1849-1910
WhAm 1
Nickels, Mervyn Millard 1898-1971 *WhAm 5*
Nickerson, Arno Wilbur 1891-1953 *NatCAB 44*
Nickerson, Frank Stillman 1826- *ApCAB,*
WhAm 4
Nickerson, Hiram Robert 1853-1915 *WhAm 1*
Nickerson, Hoffman 1888-1965 *WhAm 4*
Nickerson, John 1852-1956 *WhAm 3*
Nickerson, John Peter 1876-1950 *NatCAB 39*
Nickerson, Kingsbury Smith 1908-1967
NatCAB 57, WhAm 4
Nickerson, Palmer Rice 1898-1969 *NatCAB 55*
Nickerson, Reuben *NewYHSD*
Nickerson, Samuel Mayo 1830- *ApCAB Sup*
Nickerson, Thomas White 1858- *NatCAB 16*

Nickerson, William Emery 1853-1930
NatCAB 24
Nickeus, Johnson 1850-1901 *WhAm 1*
Nicklas, Charles Aubrey 1886-1942 *WhAm 2*
Nicklaus, Jack William 1940- *WebAB*
Nickles, LaMarquis Deal 1911-1959
NatCAB 50
Nicklin, John *NewYHSD*
Nicklin, Philip Holbrook 1786-1842 *ApCAB,*
Drake, TwCBDA
Nicklin, Philip Houlbrouke 1786-1842
NatCAB 4
Nickol, John Peter 1888-1959 *NatCAB 47*
Nicks, F William 1906-1972 *WhAm 5*
Nicodemus, Frank Courtney, Jr. 1881-1957
WhAm 3
Nicol, Alexander R 1862- *WhAm 4*
Nicol, Charles Edgar 1854-1924 *WhAm 1*
Nicol, Jacob 1876- *WhAm 5*
Nicol, Pegi *IIBEAAW*
Nicol, Robert 1833-1879 *NatCAB 16*
Nicol, William 1768-1851 *AsBiEn, DcScB*
Nicola Pisano 1220?-1284? *McGEWB*
Nicola, Lewis 1717-1807 *DcAmB, WhAm H*
Nicolai, A T *NewYHSD*
Nicolai, Friedrich Bernhard Gottfried 1793-1846
DcScB
Nicolai, Harry T 1881-1957 *WhAm 3*
Nicolassen, George Frederick 1857- *WhAm 5*
Nicolaus Of Damascus 064BC- *DcScB*
Nicolay, Helen 1866-1954 *WhAm 3,*
WomWWA 14
Nicolay, John George 1832-1901 *AmBi,*
ApCAB, DcAmB, NatCAB 8, TwCBDA,
WhAm 1, WhAmP
Nicole, Francois Leon Etienne 1731-1773
ApCAB
Nicole, Pierre d1784 *NewYHSD*
Nicolet, Jean 1598-1642 *AmBi, ApCAB,*
DcAmB, REnAW, WebAB, WhAm H
Nicolini, Ernesto 1834-1898 *ApCAB Sup*
Nicoll, DeLancey 1854-1931 *DcAmB,*
NatCAB 14, WhAm 1
Nicoll, Edith Travers 1861- *WomWWA 14*
Nicoll, Henry 1812-1879 *BiAUS, BiDrAC,*
WhAm H
Nicoll, James Craig 1846-1918 *ApCAB,*
NatCAB 7, TwCBDA
Nicoll, James Craig 1847-1918 *AmBi, DcAmB,*
WhAm 1
Nicoll, John C *BiAUS*
Nicoll, Matthias, Jr. 1868-1941 *WhAm 1*
Nicolle, Charles Jules Henri 1866-1936 *AsBiEn,*
BiHiMed, DcScB, DcScB Sup
Nicollet, Jean Nicholas 1786?-1843 *ApCAB,*
BiAUS
Nicollet, Joseph Nicolas 1786-1843 *AmBi,*
DcAmB, REnAW, WebAB, WhAm H
Nicollet, Joseph Nicolas 1795?-1843 *Drake*
Nicolls, Mathias 1630?-1687 *ApCAB*
Nicolls, Matthias 1626-1687? *AmBi, DcAmB*
Nicolls, Matthias 1626-1688? *WhAm H*
Nicolls, Sir Richard 1624-1672 *AmBi, ApCAB,*
DcAmB, NatCAB 13, WhAm H,
WhAmP
Nicolls, William 1657-1723 *ApCAB, DcAmB,*
WhAm H
Nicolls, William 1702-1768 *ApCAB*
Nicolls, William 1715-1780 *ApCAB*
Nicolls, William 1863-1922 *NatCAB 19*
Nicolls, William Jasper 1854-1916 *WhAm 1*
Nicols, Audley Dean *IIBEAAW*
Nicols, John 1812-1873 *ApCAB X*
Nicolson, Alexander McLean 1880-1950
NatCAB 37
Nicolson, George Llewellyn 1864-1952
NatCAB 37
Nicolson, Samuel 1791-1868 *ApCAB, Drake*
Nicomachus Of Gerasa *DcScB*
Nicomedes *DcScB*
Nicot, Jean 1530?-1604 *DcScB*
Nicoud, Henry E *NewYHSD*
Nicuesa, Diego De 1464-1511 *ApCAB*
Nicum, John 1851-1909 *ApCAB, TwCBDA,*
WhAm 1
Niebuhr, Barthold Georg 1776-1831 *McGEWB*
Niebuhr, Carsten 1733-1815 *DcScB*
Niebuhr, Helmut Richard 1894-1962 *DcAmReB,*

McGEWB, NatCAB 47, WhAm 4
Niebuhr, Karl Paul Reinhold 1892-1971
DcAmReB
Niebuhr, Reinhold 1892-1971 *EncAB,*
McGEWB, WebAB, WhAm 5
Niebuhr, Sigismund 1631-1699 *ApCAB*
Niedermeyer, Frederick David 1881-1951
WhAm 3
Niedringhaus, Albert William 1869-1944
NatCAB 36
Niedringhaus, Frederick Gottlieb 1837-1922
BiDrAC, DcAmB, NatCAB 3,
NatCAB 12, WhAm 1
Niedringhaus, George W 1864-1928 *WhAm 1*
Niedringhaus, Hayward 1891-1949 *WhAm 2*
Niedringhaus, Henry Frederick 1864-1941
BiDrAC, WhAm 1
Niedringhaus, J P Erwin 1903-1965 *WhAm 4*
Niedringhaus, Thomas Key 1860-1924 *WhAm 1*
Niehaus, Charles Henry 1855-1935 *AmBi,*
ApCAB Sup, BnEnAmA, DcAmB S1,
NatCAB 9, TwCBDA, WhAm 1
Niehaus, Fredrich Wilhelm 1889-1969 *WhAm 5*
Niehaus, Friedrich Wilhelm 1889-1969
NatCAB 55
Niehaus, John Michael 1855-1934 *NatCAB 41*
Niehaus, Regina Armstrong *WomWWA 14*
Niel, Adolphe 1802-1869 *WhoMilH*
Niel, Frederic Guillaume A Ferdinand 1729-1791
ApCAB
Nields, John Pierce 1868-1943 *NatCAB 32,*
WhAm 2
Nields, Mary Craven *WomWWA 14*
Nielsen, Alice d1943 *WomWWA 14*
Nielsen, Alice 1868?-1943 *NotAW*
Nielsen, Alice 1870?-1943 *DcAmB S3*
Nielsen, Alice 1876-1943 *WhAm 2*
Nielsen, Carl August 1865-1931 *McGEWB*
Nielsen, Elker Rosehill 1892-1956 *NatCAB 44*
Nielsen, Elmer Lawrence 1895-1954
NatCAB 43
Nielsen, Etlar Lester 1905-1969 *NatCAB 54*
Nielsen, Fred Kenelm 1879-1963 *NatCAB 50,*
WhAm 4
Nielsen, Harald Herborg 1903-1973
NatCAB 57, WhAm 5
Nielsen, Johannes Maagaard 1890-1969
WhAm 5
Nielsen, Morris 1875-1955 *NatCAB 44*
Nielsen, Niels 1865-1931 *DcScB*
Nielson, Minnie Jean *WomWWA 14*
Nieman, L W 1857-1935 *NatCAB 1*
Nieman, Lucius William 1857-1935 *DcAmB S1,*
NatCAB 27, WhAm 1
Niemann, Carl George 1908-1964 *NatCAB 50,*
WhAm 4
Niemcewicz, Julian Ursin 1757-1841 *ApCAB*
Niemeyer, Conrade Jacob De 1788-1862 *ApCAB*
Niemeyer, John Henry 1839-1932 *AmBi,*
ApCAB, DcAmB, NewYHSD, TwCBDA,
WhAm 1
Niemeyer Soares Filho, Oscar 1907- *McGEWB*
Niemi, Robert Alvin 1916-1962 *NatCAB 50*
Niepce, Joseph Nicephore 1765-1833 *AsBiEn,*
DcScB
Nier, George Joseph 1895-1959 *NatCAB 47*
Nierensee, John R 1831-1885 *WhAm H*
Nieriker, Ernest, Madame 1840-1879
NewYHSD
Nieriker, May Alcott 1840-1879 *AmWom*
Nierman, John L 1887-1950 *WhAm 3*
Nies, Abby Huntington Ware *WomWWA 14*
Nies, James Buchanan 1856-1922 *DcAmB,*
NatCAB 20, WhAm 1
Nies, Konrad 1861-1921 *DcAmB*
Nieset, Robert Thomas 1912-1975 *WhAm 6*
Niessen-Stone, Matja Von 1870- *NatCAB 14*
Niesten, Jean Louis Nicolas 1844-1920 *DcScB*
Niesz, Homer E 1868-1931 *WhAm 1*
Nietert, Herman Lewis 1866- *NatCAB 12*
Nieto, Jose Apolinario 1810-1873 *ApCAB*
Nieto, Vicente 1753-1810 *ApCAB*
Nieto DelRio, Felix 1888-1953 *WhAm 3*
Nietzsche, Friedrich 1844-1900 *McGEWB*
Nieuwentijt, Bernard 1654-1718 *DcScB*
Nieuwhof, Johann Jacob 1610-1672 *ApCAB*
Nieuwland, Julius Arthur 1878-1936 *AmBi,*
AsBiEn, DcAmB S2, DcScB, NatCAB 26,

WhAm 1
Niezer, Charles M 1877-1941 *WhAm 1*
Nifflin, P *NewYHSD*
Nifo, Agostino 1470?-1538 *DcScB*
Nifong, Frank Gosney 1867- *WhAm 4*
Niggeman, Louis William 1915-1974 *WhAm 6*
Niggli, Paul 1888-1953 *DcScB*
Nigh, William Henshaw 1903-1952 *NatCAB 41*
Nightingale, Augustus Frederick 1843-1925
TwCBDA, WhAm 1
Nightingale, Florence 1820-1910 *BiHiMed,*
McGEWB
Nightingale, John Trowbridge 1888-1954
NatCAB 41
Nightingale, William Thomas 1897-1964
NatCAB 51, WhAm 4
Nihart, Benjamin Franklin 1854-1945 *WhAm 3*
Nihizer, Adonis Hugh 1897-1950 *NatCAB 39*
Nijinsky, Vaslav 1890-1950 *WhAm 4*
Nikander, John Kustaa 1855-1919 *WhAm 1*
Nikirk, Frank Austin 1881-1959 *NatCAB 47*
Nikitin, Sergey Nikolaevich 1851-1909 *DcScB*
Nikolsky, Alexander A 1902-1963 *WhAm 4*
Nikon, Nikita Minov 1605-1681 *McGEWB*
Nilakantha 1444?-1501? *DcScB*
Nilan, John Joseph 1855-1934 *NatCAB 15,*
WhAm 1
Niles, Alfred Salem 1860-1926 *WhAm 1*
Niles, Alva Joseph 1882-1950 *WhAm 2*
Niles, Blair d1959 *WhAm 3*
Niles, David K 1892-1952 *DcAmB S5*
Niles, Edward Cullen 1865-1927 *NatCAB 40*
Niles, Edward Hulbert 1882-1958 *WhAm 3*
Niles, George McCallum 1864-1932 *WhAm 1*
Niles, Henry Carpenter 1858- *WhAm 3*
Niles, Henry Clay 1850-1918 *WhAm 1*
Niles, Henry Clay 1920-1975 *WhAm 6*
Niles, Hezekiah 1777-1839 *AmBi, ApCAB,*
DcAmB, Drake, NatCAB 10, TwCBDA,
WebAB, WhAm H
Niles, J Carroll 1886-1943 *NatCAB 33*
Niles, Jason 1814-1894 *BiAUS, BiDrAC,*
WhAm H
Niles, John Milton 1787-1856 *AmBi, ApCAB,*
BiAUS, BiDrAC, BiDrUSE, DcAmB,
Drake, NatCAB 6, TwCBDA, WhAm H,
WhAmP
Niles, Kossuth 1849-1913 *WhAm 1*
Niles, Louville Varanas 1839-1928 *ApCAB X*
Niles, Mary Blair Rice 1880-1959 *NatCAB 45*
Niles, Nathan Erie 1847-1930 *WhAm 1*
Niles, Nathanael 1741-1828 *Drake*
Niles, Nathaniel 1741-1828 *ApCAB, BiAUS,*
BiDrAC, DcAmB, NatCAB 5, TwCBDA,
WhAm H
Niles, Nathaniel 1791-1869 *DcAmB,*
WhAm H
Niles, Nathaniel 1835-1917 *ApCAB, WhAm 1*
Niles, Philip Bradford 1901-1958 *WhAm 3*
Niles, Samuel 1674-1762 *ApCAB, DcAmB,*
Drake, NatCAB 8, TwCBDA, WhAm H
Niles, Samuel 1711-1804 *ApCAB*
Niles, Samuel 1744-1814 *ApCAB*
Niles, Walter Lindsay 1878-1941 *NatCAB 30,*
WhAm 2
Niles, William Harmon 1838-1910 *NatCAB 12,*
TwCBDA, WhAm 1
Niles, William Henry 1839- *WhAm 4*
Niles, William White 1860-1935 *WhAm 1*
Niles, William Woodruff 1832-1914 *ApCAB,*
NatCAB 5, TwCBDA, WhAm 1
Nilis, Pierre *NewYHSD*
Nilles, Herbert George 1894-1962 *WhAm 4*
Nilson, Axel Hilmer 1849-1927 *NatCAB 26*
Nilson, Lars Fredrik 1840-1899 *AsBiEn*
Nilsson, Christine 1843- *ApCAB*
Nilsson, Fritiof 1895-1972 *WhAm 6*
Nilsson, Hjalmar 1860-1936 *WhAm 1*
Nilsson, Victor 1867-1942 *WhAm 2*
Nilsson-Ehle, Herman 1873-1949 *DcScB*
Nimbs, Areuna B *NewYHSD*
Nimitz, Chester 1885-1966 *WhWW-II*
Nimitz, Chester William 1885-1966 *EncAB,*
McGEWB, WebAB, WebAMB, WhAm 4
Nimitz, Chester Williams 1885-1966 *WhoMilH*
Nimkoff, Meyer F 1904-1965 *WhAm 4*
Nimmo, Ray Everett 1882-1946 *NatCAB 35*
Nimmons, George Croll 1865-1947 *WhAm 2*

Nims, Eugene Dutton 1865-1954 *NatCAB 43,*
WhAm 3
Nims, Harry Dwight 1875-1968 *NatCAB 53,*
WhAm 4
Nims, Jeremiah d1842 *NewYHSD*
Nims, Mary Altha *NewYHSD*
Nims, Theodore S *NewYHSD*
Nims, Thomas Lathrop 1904-1965 *NatCAB 51*
Nimtz, F Jay 1915- *BiDrAC*
Nina, Joao Estevam Miguel DaSilva 1770?-1813
ApCAB
Nincheri, Guido 1885-1973 *NatCAB 57*
Ninde, Edward Summerfield 1866-1935
WhAm 1
Ninde, Henry Summerfield 1835-1931
NatCAB 23
Ninde, William Xavier 1832-1901 *ApCAB,*
NatCAB 13, TwCBDA, WhAm 1
Nindemann, William Friedrich Carl 1850-
ApCAB, NatCAB 3
Ninegret *ApCAB*
Ninigret *Drake, NatCAB 9*
Ninnis, Frederick Charles 1880- *WhAm 6*
Nino, Andres 1475-1530? *ApCAB*
Nino, Pedro Alonso 1468-1505? *ApCAB*
Nino, Pedro Alonzo 1468-1505? *Drake*
Nipher, Francis Eugene 1847- *ApCAB,*
NatCAB 11
Nipher, Francis Eugene 1847-1926 *AmBi,*
DcAmB, NatCAB 22
Nipher, Francis Eugene 1847-1927 *WhAm 1*
Nippert, Alfred Kuno 1872-1956 *NatCAB 46*
Nirenberg, Marshall Warren 1927- *AsBiEn,*
WebAB
Nisbet, Charles 1736-1804 *ApCAB, DcAmB,*
Drake, NatCAB 6, TwCBDA, WhAm H
Nisbet, Charles Richard 1871-1943 *WhAm 2*
Nisbet, E A *BiAUS*
Nisbet, Eugenius Aristides 1803-1871 *AmBi,*
ApCAB, BiAUS, BiDConf, BiDrAC,
DcAmB, NatCAB 5, TwCBDA,
WhAm H
Nisbet, James 1800?-1865 *Drake*
Nisbet, James Douglas 1861-1933 *WhAm 1*
Nisbet, Minnie Jean *WomWWA 14*
Nisbet, Robert Hogg 1879-1961 *WhAm 4*
Nisbet, Walter Olin, Jr. 1906-1969 *WhAm 5*
Nisley, Harold A 1892-1965 *WhAm 4*
Nisonger, Herschel Ward 1890-1969 *WhAm 5*
Nissen, Harry Archibald 1891-1956 *WhAm 3*
Nissen, Hartvig 1855- *WhAm 4*
Nissen, Henry W 1901-1958 *WhAm 3*
Nissen, Ludwig 1855-1924 *ApCAB X,*
NatCAB 4, WhAm 1
Nissl, Franz 1860-1919 *BiHiMed, DcScB*
Nissler, Christian William 1888-1953
NatCAB 40
Nitchie, Edward Bartlett 1876-1917 *DcAmB,*
NatCAB 28
Nitchie, Joseph Howard 1851-1927 *NatCAB 25*
Nitschmann, David 1696-1772 *ApCAB,*
DcAmB, NatCAB 5, TwCBDA,
WhAm H
Nitschmann, John 1703-1772 *ApCAB,*
NatCAB 5, TwCBDA
Nitze, William Albert 1876-1957 *WhAm 3*
Nitzsche, Elsa Koenig 1880-1952 *NatCAB 47,*
WhAm 3
Nitzsche, George E 1874-1961 *WhAm 4*
Nivelle, Robert Georges 1856-1924 *WhoMilH*
Nivelles, Charles Etienne De 1665?-1711
ApCAB
Niven, Archibald Campbell 1803-1882 *BiAUS,*
BiDrAC, WhAm H
Niven, John Ballantine 1871-1954 *WhAm 3*
Niven, William 1850-1937 *WhAm 1*
Nivert, Desire Amable Christian 1605?-1661
ApCAB
Nivison, Robert 1879- *WhAm 6*
Nivola, Constantino 1911- *BnEnAmA*
Nix, Abit 1888-1959 *NatCAB 50*
Nix, James Thomas 1852-1912 *NatCAB 28*
Nix, James Thomas 1887-1945 *WhAm 2*
Nix, John Darling 1870-1940 *NatCAB 30*
Nix, Milton Arthur 1882-1957 *NatCAB 45*
Nix, Robert Nelson Cornelius, Sr. 1905-
BiDrAC
Nixon, Brevard 1866-1937 *WhAm 1*

Nixon, Burnett Roy 1880-1960 *NatCAB 50*
Nixon, Charles Elston 1860- *WhAm 4*
Nixon, Charles L *NewYHSD*
Nixon, Cleveland Ford 1901-1962 *NatCAB 50*
Nixon, Courtland 1874-1934 *NatCAB 26*
Nixon, D *NewYHSD*
Nixon, Don Morrison 1880-1934 *NatCAB 26*
Nixon, Edgar Burkhart 1902- *EncAAH*
Nixon, Edward Adams 1858-1939 *NatCAB 29*
Nixon, Eugene White 1885-1969 *WhAm 5*
Nixon, George Felton 1868-1947 *WhAm 3*
Nixon, George Stuart 1860-1912 *BiDrAC,*
  NatCAB 14, WhAm 1, WhAmP
Nixon, George Washington 1854-1933
  NatCAB 26
Nixon, Henry Barber 1857-1916 *NatCAB 17*
Nixon, Howard Kenneth 1895-1963 *WhAm 4*
Nixon, James M *NewYHSD*
Nixon, James Oscar, Jr. 1849-1888 *NatCAB 25*
Nixon, Jennie Caldwell 1839- *AmWom*
Nixon, John 1725-1815 *ApCAB, Drake*
Nixon, John 1727-1815 *DcAmB, TwCBDA,*
  WebAMB, WhAm H
Nixon, John 1733-1808 *ApCAB, DcAmB,*
  NatCAB 1, TwCBDA, WhAm H
Nixon, John 1733-1809 *Drake*
Nixon, John B *NewYHSD*
Nixon, John Thompson 1820-1889 *ApCAB,*
  BiAUS, BiDrAC, DcAmB, TwCBDA,
  WhAm H
Nixon, Justin Wroe 1886-1958 *WhAm 3*
Nixon, Lewis 1861-1940 *NatCAB 13,*
  TwCBDA, WhAm 1
Nixon, Mary Stites *WomWWA 14*
Nixon, Oliver Woodson 1825-1905 *NatCAB 20,*
  TwCBDA, WhAm 1
Nixon, Pat Ireland 1883-1965 *WhAm 4*
Nixon, Paul 1882-1956 *NatCAB 47, WhAm 3*
Nixon, Richard Milhous 1913- *BiDrAC,*
  BiDrUSE, EncAAH, EncAB, McGEWB,
  WebAB
Nixon, Samuel F 1848- *WhAm 4*
Nixon, T *NewYHSD*
Nixon, Thomas 1736-1800 *ApCAB, Drake*
Nixon, Thomas Carlyle 1890-1967 *WhAm 5*
Nixon, William C 1858-1916 *WhAm 1*
Nixon, William Penn 1833-1912 *DcAmB,*
  NatCAB 9, TwCBDA, WhAm 1
Niza, Marcos De *WhAm H*
Niza, Marcos De d1542 *ApCAB*
Niza, Marcos De d1558 *DcAmB*
Niza, Tadeo De 1500?-1561 *ApCAB*
Nizer, Louis 1902- *WebAB*
Nkrumah, Kwame 1909-1972 *McGEWB,*
  WhAm 5
Noa, Ernestine 1871- *WhAm 5*
Noah, Andrew Hale 1858- *ApCAB X*
Noah, Joseph William 1917-1972 *NatCAB 57*
Noah, Mordecai Manuel 1785-1851 *ApCAB,*
  DcAmB, Drake, NatCAB 9, TwCBDA,
  WhAm H
Noah, Mordecas Manuel 1785-1851 *WhAmP*
Noah, Samuel 1779-1871 *NatCAB 20*
Noailles, Louis Marie, Vicomte De 1756-1804
  AmBi, DcAmB
Noailles, Louis Marie, Viscomte De 1756-1804
  Drake, WhAm H
Noailles, Louis Marie, Viscount De 1756-1804
  ApCAB
Noakes, Edward Bruce 1902-1958 *WhAm 3*
Noakes, Frank Leroy 1903-1971 *WhAm 5*
Noback, Gustave J 1890-1955 *WhAm 3*
Nobel, Alfred Bernhard 1833-1896 *AsBiEn,*
  DcScB, McGEWB
Nobert, Friedrich Adolph 1806-1881 *DcScB*
Nobile, Umberto 1885- *McGEWB*
Nobili, John 1812-1856 *ApCAB, DcAmB,*
  WhAm H
Nobili, Leopoldo 1784-1835 *DcScB*
Noble, Miss *NewYHSD*
Noble, Albert Morris 1884-1962 *NatCAB 48*
Noble, Alfred 1844-1914 *DcAmB, NatCAB 9,*
  WhAm 1
Noble, Annette Lucile 1844-1932 *ApCAB,*
  TwCBDA, WhAm 1, WomWWA 14
Noble, Auguste Emile 1771-1827 *ApCAB*
Noble, Charles 1847- *WhAm 4*
Noble, Charles C 1898-1968 *WhAm 5*

Noble, Charles F 1833?- *NewYHSD*
Noble, Charles Franklin 1872-1931 *WhAm 1*
Noble, Charles Henry 1843-1916 *WhAm 1*
Noble, Charles P 1863-1935 *WhAm 1*
Noble, David Addison 1802-1876 *BiAUS,*
  BiDrAC, WhAm H
Noble, David Watson 1925- *EncAAH*
Noble, Edmund 1853-1937 *NatCAB 12,*
  WhAm 1
Noble, Edna Jane Chaffee 1846-1919 *AmWom,*
  ApCAB X
Noble, Edward John 1882-1958 *NatCAB 43,*
  WhAm 3
Noble, Esther Frothingham 1839-
  WomWWA 14
Noble, Eugene Allen 1868-1948 *NatCAB 18,*
  NatCAB 49, WhAm 2
Noble, Frederic Perry 1863-1945 *NatCAB 35*
Noble, Frederick Alphonso 1832-1917 *DcAmB,*
  NatCAB 12, TwCBDA, WhAm 1
Noble, G Kingsley 1894-1940 *NatCAB 31,*
  WhAm 1
Noble, George Bernard 1892-1972 *WhAm 5*
Noble, George Lawrence 1886- *WhAm 4*
Noble, Gladwyn Kingsley 1894-1940 *DcAmB S2*
Noble, Harold Joyce 1903-1953 *WhAm 3*
Noble, Harriet 1851- *WomWWA 14*
Noble, Henry Smith 1845-1915 *WhAm 1*
Noble, Herbert 1867-1934 *NatCAB 26*
Noble, Howard Scott 1893-1964 *WhAm 4*
Noble, James d1831 *BiAUS*
Noble, James 1783-1831 *DcAmB, WhAm H*
Noble, James 1785-1831 *BiDrAC, TwCBDA,*
  WhAmP
Noble, James 1790?-1831 *ApCAB,*
  NatCAB 11
Noble, John 1874-1934 *IlBEAAW, WhAm 1*
Noble, John 1908-1964 *WhAm 4*
Noble, John Avery 1892-1944 *NatCAB 40*
Noble, John Martin 1869- *WhAm 5*
Noble, John Willcox 1831-1912 *TwCBDA*
Noble, John Willock 1831-1912 *AmBi, ApCAB,*
  BiDrUSE, DcAmB, NatCAB 1, WhAm 1
Noble, Louis Legrand 1811-1882 *TwCBDA*
Noble, Louis Legrand 1812-1882 *Drake*
Noble, Louis Legrand 1813-1882 *ApCAB*
Noble, Lucy 1853- *NatCAB 17*
Noble, Marcus Cicero Stephens 1855-1942
  WhAm 2
Noble, Marietta Josephine Edmand
  WomWWA 14
Noble, Merrill Emmett 1896-1969 *WhAm 5*
Noble, Nelle Sparks 1878- *WhAm 6*
Noble, Noah 1794-1844 *BiAUS, Drake,*
  NatCAB 13, TwCBDA
Noble, Oliver 1757-1792 *Drake*
Noble, Patrick 1787-1840 *ApCAB, BiAUS,*
  Drake, NatCAB 12, TwCBDA
Noble, Sir Percy Lockhart Harnam 1880-1955
  WhAm 3
Noble, Ralph Edward 1899-1972 *NatCAB 57,*
  WhAm 5
Noble, Raymond Goodman 1873-1945
  NatCAB 35, WhAm 2
Noble, Robert Ernest 1870-1956 *WhAm 3*
Noble, Robert Houston 1861-1939 *WhAm 1*
Noble, Robert Peckham 1880-1973 *WhAm 5*
Noble, Samuel 1834-1888 *ApCAB Sup,*
  DcAmB, WhAm H
Noble, Thomas Benjamin, Jr. 1895-1958
  NatCAB 50
Noble, Thomas Satterwhite 1835-1907
  NewYHSD, WhAm HA, WhAm 4
Noble, Thomas Tertius 1867-1953 *WhAm 3*
Noble, Urbane Alexander 1877-1946
  NatCAB 34, WhAm 2
Noble, Warren Perry 1820-1903 *BiDrAC*
Noble, Warren Perry 1821-1903 *BiAUS*
Noble, William Brown 1841-1915 *WhAm 1*
Noble, William Clark 1858-1938 *NatCAB 8,*
  NatCAB 30, WhAm 1
Noble, William Henry 1788-1850 *BiAUS,*
  BiDrAC, WhAm H
Noble, William Lincoln 1860-1937 *WhAm 1*
Noble, Worden Payne 1847-1914 *NatCAB 16*
Nobles, Catharine *AmWom* •
Nobles, Ella Margaret *WomWWA 14*
Nobles, Milton 1847-1924 *WhAm 1*

Noblit, Emma Ewing 1862- *WomWWA 14*
Noblitt, Quintin G 1882-1954 *NatCAB 41,*
  WhAm 3
Noboa, Diego 1789-1870 *ApCAB*
Noboa, Manuel Vasquez De 1783-1855 *ApCAB*
Nobrega, Manoel De 1517-1570 *ApCAB*
Nobs, Ernest 1886-1957 *WhAm 3*
Noce, Daniel 1894- *WhAm 6*
Nock, Albert Jay 1870-1945 *DcAmB S3,*
  WebAB, WhAm 2
Nock, Arthur Darby 1902-1963 *WhAm 4*
Nock, Frederic Stephen 1871-1925 *NatCAB 17*
Noda, Tranquilino S De 1808-1867 *ApCAB*
Nodal, Bartolome Garcia *ApCAB*
Nodal, Gonzalo *ApCAB*
Nodar, Robert Joseph, Jr. 1916- *BiDrAC*
Noddack, Ida Eva Tacke 1896- *AsBiEn*
Noddack, Walter Karl Friedrich 1893-1960
  AsBiEn, DcScB
Noe, Adolf Carl 1873-1939 *WhAm 1*
Noe, Carl Abraham 1904-1960 *NatCAB 49*
Noe, James Thomas Cotton 1864-1953
  NatCAB 41, WhAm 4
Noe, Samuel Vanarsdale 1910-1972 *WhAm 6*
Noeggerath, Emil Oscar Jacob Bruno 1827-1895
  DcAmB, WhAm H
Noehren, Alfred Henry 1879-1959 *NatCAB 47*
Noel, Auguste Louis 1884-1964 *NatCAB 51*
Noel, Cleo Allen, Jr. 1918-1973 *WhAm 5*
Noel, Edmund Favor 1856-1927 *NatCAB 14,*
  WhAm 1
Noel, Etienne 1581-1659 *DcScB*
Noel, F Regis 1891-1952 *WhAm 3*
Noel, James Kingsley 1885-1955 *NatCAB 48*
Noel, James William 1867-1944 *NatCAB 16,*
  WhAm 2
Noel, Joseph Roberts 1872-1940 *NatCAB 18,*
  WhAm 1
Noel, Julia McAlmont 1856- *WomWWA 14*
Noel, Nicolas 1746-1832 *ApCAB, Drake*
Noel, Richard C 1891-1956 *WhAm 3*
Noell, James Turpin, Jr. 1863-1958 *NatCAB 47*
Noell, John William 1816-1863 *BiAUS,*
  BiDrAC, TwCBDA, WhAm H
Noell, Thomas Estes 1839-1867 *BiAUS,*
  BiDrAC, WhAm H
Noelle *NewYHSD*
Noelle, Frederick *NewYHSD*
Noelte, Albert 1885-1946 *WhAm 2*
Noelting, Bernhardt Henry 1851-1941
  NatCAB 33
Noest, Jan Izaak 1895-1955 *WhAm 3*
Noether, Amalie Emmy 1882-1935 *DcScB*
Noether, Max 1844-1921 *DcScB*
Noetzli, Fred Adolph 1887-1933 *NatCAB 29*
Nofer, Edward John 1886-1958 *WhAm 3*
Noffsinger, Hugh Godwin 1873- *WhAm 5*
Noffsinger, John Samuel 1886-1966 *WhAm 4*
Nofftz, Halie Isabel *WomWWA 14*
Nogaret, Stanislas Henry Lucien De 1682-1759
  ApCAB
Noggle, David 1809-1878 *BiAUS, NatCAB 19*
Noggle, William Henry 1866-1950 *NatCAB 38*
Nogi, Maresuke 1849-1912 *WhoMilH*
Nogre, Vincent De 1629-1694 *ApCAB*
Noguchi, Hideyo 1876-1928 *AmBi, BiHiMed,*
  DcAmB, DcScB, WebAB, WhAm 1
Noguchi, Isamu 1904- *BnEnAmA, McGEWB,*
  WebAB
Noirclerc, Albert Paul Charles De 1721-1779
  ApCAB
Nolan, Charles Paul 1909-1973 *WhAm 6*
Nolan, Dennis Edward 1872-1953 *WhAm 3*
Nolan, Edward James 1888-1957 *WhAm 3*
Nolan, J Bennett 1877-1964 *NatCAB 51*
Nolan, James Bennett 1879-1964 *WhAm 4*
Nolan, Jeannette Covert 1896-1974 *WhAm 6*
Nolan, John Henry 1892-1950 *NatCAB 38,*
  WhAm 3
Nolan, John Ignatius 1874-1922 *BiDrAC,*
  WhAm 1, WhAmP
Nolan, John J, Jr. 1892-1959 *WhAm 3*
Nolan, Mae Ella 1886-1973 *BiDrAC, WhAm 6,*
  WhAmP
Nolan, Mark 1901-1967 *NatCAB 54*
Nolan, Michael Nicholas 1833-1905 *BiDrAC*
Nolan, Philip 1771?-1801 *DcAmB, WhAm H*
Nolan, Preston M 1875-1931 *WhAm 1*

Nolan, Ralph Peter 1892-1973 *WhAm 6*
Nolan, S Frank 1874-1957 *NatCAB 46*
Nolan, Sidney Robert 1917- *McGEWB*
Nolan, Thomas 1857-1926 *WhAm 1*
Nolan, Val 1892-1940 *WhAm 1*
Nolan, William Ignatius 1874-1943 *BiDrAC,*
WhAm 5
Noland, Charles Fenton Mercer 1810-1858
REnAW
Noland, Edgar Smith 1902-1971 *WhAm 5*
Noland, Hampton 1886-1960 *NatCAB 48*
Noland, Iveson B 1916-1975 *WhAm 6*
Noland, James Ellsworth 1920- *BiDrAC*
Noland, Kenneth 1924- *BnEnAmA, McGEWB*
Noland, Leon Maxwell 1882-1926 *NatCAB 43*
Noland, Lloyd 1880-1949 *NatCAB 40,*
WhAm 2
Noland, Lowell E 1896-1972 *WhAm 5*
Noland, Stephen Croan 1887-1962 *WhAm 4*
Noland, William Churchill 1865-1951
NatCAB 40, WhAm 3
Nolde, Emil 1867-1956 *McGEWB, WhAm 4*
Nolde, H William 1873-1958 *NatCAB 43*
Nolde, O Frederick 1899-1972 *WhAm 5*
Nolen, Henry S *NewYHSD*
Nolen, John 1869-1937 *DcAmB S2,*
NatCAB 27, WhAm 1
Nolen, William Edward 1901-1963 *NatCAB 49*
Nolen, William Whiting 1860-1923 *WhAm 1*
Noli, Fan Stylian 1882-1965 *WhAm 4*
Nolker, William F 1840- *NatCAB 12*
Noll, A Robert 1906-1968 *NatCAB 54*
Noll, Arthur Howard 1855-1930 *WhAm 1*
Noll, Charles Franklin 1878- *WhAm 6*
Noll, Edward Angus August 1867-1939
WhAm 3
Noll, John Francis 1875-1956 *WhAm 3*
Noll, Raymond Rundell 1881- *WhAm 6*
Nollen, Gerard Scholte 1880-1965 *WhAm 4*
Nollen, Henry Scholte 1866-1942 *WhAm 2*
Nollen, John 1828-1914 *NatCAB 28*
Nollen, John Scholte 1869-1952 *WhAm 3*
Nollet, Jean-Antoine 1700-1770 *DcScB*
Nolte, Albert Ernst 1882-1959 *NatCAB 48*
Nolte, Charles Beach 1885-1941 *NatCAB 44,*
WhAm 2
Nolte, Emil F *NewYHSD*
Nolte, Frank Otto 1894-1962 *WhAm 4*
Nolte, Julius Mosher 1894-1965 *WhAm 4*
Nolte, Louis Gustavus 1862-1942 *WhAm 2*
Nolte, Vincent 1779-1852? *ApCAB*
Nolting, William Greaner 1866-1940 *WhAm 1*
Nomland, Ruben 1899-1960 *WhAm 3A*
Nomura, Kochisaburo 1877-1964 *WhWW-II*
Nones, Robert Hodgson 1864-1936 *WhAm 1*
Nones, Walter Mark 1874-1942 *NatCAB 31*
Nonnast, Paul E 1918- *IlBEAAW*
Nono, Luigi 1924- *McGEWB*
Nooe, Robert Sharpe d1973 *WhAm 6*
Nooe, Roger Theophilus 1881- *WhAm 6*
Noojin, Balpha Lonnie 1885-1950 *WhAm 3*
Noon, Malik Firoz Khan 1893-1970 *WhAm 5*
Noon, Paul A T 1901-1971 *WhAm 5*
Noon, T F *NewYHSD*
Noonan, Edward J 1874- *WhAm 5*
Noonan, Edward Thomas 1861-1923 *BiDrAC,*
WhAm 4
Noonan, George Henry 1828-1907 *BiDrAC*
Noonan, Gregory Francis 1906-1964 *WhAm 4*
Noonan, Herbert C 1875-1956 *WhAm 3*
Noonan, James Patrick 1878-1929 *DcAmB,*
WhAm HA, WhAm 4
Noonan, John A d1955 *WhAm 3*
Noonan, Joseph Francis 1892-1965 *NatCAB 51*
Noonan, Joseph Michael 1892-1959 *WhAm 3*
Noonan, Thomas Hazard 1865-1957 *WhAm 3*
Noonan, William T 1874-1952 *WhAm 3*
Noone, Charles Ashton 1888-1959 *NatCAB 51*
Noone, Michael Joseph 1883-1948 *NatCAB 37*
Noort, Olivier Van 1568-1621? *ApCAB*
Nora, Joseph J 1901-1968 *WhAm 5*
Norbeck, Kermit George 1909-1970 *WhAm 5*
Norbeck, Peter 1870-1936 *ApCAB X, BiDrAC,*
DcAmB S2, EncAAH, NatCAB 38,
REnAW, WhAm 1, WhAmP
Norberg, Barbara Drew Collins d1972 *WhAm 6*
Norberg, Carl F 1898-1959 *WhAm 3*
Norberg, Rudolph Carl 1881-1958 *NatCAB 50,*

WhAm 3
Norblad, Albin Walter, Jr. 1908-1964 *BiDrAC,*
WhAmP
Norblad, Walter 1908-1964 *NatCAB 52,*
WhAm 4
Norbury, Frank Parson 1863-1939 *WhAm 1*
Norby, Joseph Gerhard 1883-1965 *WhAm 4*
Norcross, Amasa 1824-1898 *BiDrAC,*
TwCBDA
Norcross, Bernard Mallon 1915-1975 *WhAm 6*
Norcross, Cellissa Brown 1874- *WomWWA 14*
Norcross, Cleveland 1912-1949 *WhAm 2*
Norcross, Frank Herbert 1869- *NatCAB 18,*
WhAm 5
Norcross, George 1838-1915 *WhAm 1*
Norcross, Grenville Howland 1854-1937
WhAm 1
Norcross, J Arnold 1869-1940 *NatCAB 30*
Norcross, Jonathan 1808- *NatCAB 2*
Norcross, Leonard 1798-1864 *NatCAB 13*
Norcross, Orlando Whitney 1839-1920
ApCAB X, DcAmB, NatCAB 25,
WhAm 1
Norcross, Pliny 1838-1915 *ApCAB X*
Norcross, Simon Allen 1858-1921 *ApCAB X*
Norcross, Wilbur Harrington 1882-1941
WhAm 1
Norcross, William Colburn 1856-1928
NatCAB 22
Nord, Herman Joel 1877-1939 *NatCAB 31*
Nord, James Garesche 1886-1960 *WhAm 3A*
Nord, Walter Godfrey 1884-1967 *NatCAB 56,*
WhAm 5
Nordahl, Edwilda 1868- *WomWWA 14*
Nordberg, Bruno Victor 1857-1924 *DcAmB*
Nordberg, Bruno Victor 1857-1925 *WhAm 1*
Nordberg, Bruno Victor Edward 1884-1946
NatCAB 34
Nordberg, Gustav Severin 1882-1956
NatCAB 47
Nordberg, Harry Malcolm 1905-1963 *WhAm 4*
Nordburg, William Sigurd 1887-1960
NatCAB 47
Nordby, Jorgen 1852-1926 *WhAm 3*
Nordell, Philip Augustus 1846-1930 *NatCAB 21,*
WhAm 1
Nordeman, Jacques Coleman 1892-1953
NatCAB 40
Norden, Carl Lucas 1880-1965 *NatCAB 52*
Norden, Carl Lukas 1880-1965 *WebAMB*
Norden, Fred Washington 1895-1972 *WhAm 5*
Norden, N Lindsay d1956 *WhAm 3*
Nordenhaug, Josef 1903-1969 *WhAm 5*
Nordenskiold, Adolf Erik 1832-1901 *DcScB*
Nordenskiold, Nils Erik 1872-1933 *DcScB*
Nordenskjold, Baron Nils Adolf Erik 1832-1901
McGEWB
Nordenskold, Nils Otto Gustaf 1869-1928
McGEWB
Nordfeldt, Bror Julius Olsson 1878-1955
IlBEAAW, WhAm 3
Nordheimer, Edith Louise *WomWWA 14*
Nordheimer, Isaac 1809-1842 *ApCAB, DcAmB,*
Drake
Nordhoff, Charles 1830-1901 *AmBi, ApCAB,*
DcAmB, Drake, NatCAB 11, TwCBDA,
WhAm 1
Nordhoff, Charles Bernard 1887-1947
DcAmB S5, WhAm 2
Nordhoff, Heinrich 1899-1968 *WhAm 5*
Nordhoff-Jung, Sofie Amalie 1867- *WhAm 4,*
WomWWA 14
Nordica, Lillian 1857-1914 *NotAW*
Nordica, Lillian 1858?-1914 *ApCAB Sup*
Nordica, Lillian 1859-1914 *AmBi, ApCAB X,*
DcAmB, TwCBDA, WebAB, WhAm 1,
WomWWA 14
Nordin, Dennis Sven 1942- *EncAAH*
Nordlund, J Peter 1897-1968 *NatCAB 56*
Nordmark, Godfrey 1907-1973 *WhAm 6*
Nordstrom, Lloyd Walter 1910-1976 *WhAm 6*
Nordstrom, Sven Johan 1881-1951 *WhAm 3*
Norelius, Eric 1833-1916 *DcAmB, WhAm 5*
Norell, Norman 1900-1972 *WhAm 5*
Nores, Simon De 1581-1643 *ApCAB*
Norfleet, Charles Millner 1881-1957
NatCAB 48
Norfleet, Helen Lucile 1891- *WomWWA 14*

Norfolk, Duke Of d1975 *WhAm 6*
Norfolk, Thomas Howard, Duke Of 1473-1554
McGEWB
Norgren, Carl August 1890-1968 *WhAm 5*
Norheimer, Isaac 1809-1842 *WhAm H*
Norlie, Olaf Morgan 1876-1962 *WhAm 4*
Norlin, George 1871-1942 *NatCAB 41,*
WhAm 2
Norling-Christensen, O 1906-1963 *NatCAB 51*
Norman, Misses *NewYHSD*
Norman, Anne d1970 *WhAm 5*
Norman, Benjamin Moore 1809-1860 *ApCAB,*
Drake, NatCAB 18
Norman, Bradford, Jr. 1896-1951 *WhAm 3*
Norman, Carl Adolph 1879- *WhAm 6*
Norman, Charles Reed Adair 1851-
NatCAB 16
Norman, Clyde Churchill 1884-1966
NatCAB 51
Norman, Edward A 1900-1954 *WhAm 3*
Norman, Estella Gertrude 1872-1959
NatCAB 48
Norman, Fred Barthold 1882-1947 *BiDrAC,*
WhAm 2
Norman, Gerald Fitzherbert 1882- *WhoColR*
Norman, John 1748?-1817 *DcAmB,*
NewYHSD, WhAm H
Norman, Jonathan VanDyke 1877-1952
NatCAB 41, WhAm 3
Norman, Mark Wilber 1878-1951 *WhAm 3*
Norman, Montagu Collet 1871-1950 *WhAm 2*
Norman, Robert 1560?- *AsBiEn, DcScB*
Norman, Robert Claude 1875-1932 *WhAm 1*
Norman, S Guy 1889-1951 *NatCAB 44*
Norman, Theodore Arvid 1881-1958
NatCAB 43
Norman, William Sheppard 1858-1954
NatCAB 47
Norman, William T *NewYHSD*
Norman-Wilcox, Gregor 1905-1969 *WhAm 5*
Normand, Jacques Etienne 1809-1867 *ApCAB*
Normand, Mabel Ethelreid 1893?-1930 *NotAW*
Normandin, Fortunat Ernest 1890-1967
WhAm 4
Normoyle, James Edward 1866-1916
NatCAB 17
Norquay, John 1841-1889 *ApCAB*
Norquist, Emanuel Elliot 1874-1948
NatCAB 37
Norraikow, Countess Ella 1853- *AmWom*
Norrell, Catherine Dorris 1901- *BiDrAC*
Norrell, William Frank 1896-1961 *BiDrAC,*
WhAm 4, WhAmP
Norris, Alexander Wilson 1841-1888 *NatCAB 7*
Norris, Alexander Wilson 1872- *NatCAB 7*
Norris, Alfred Edward 1862-1946 *NatCAB 35*
Norris, Benjamin Franklin 1870-1902 *DcAmB,*
EncAAH, EncAB, McGEWB, WebAB
Norris, Benjamin White 1819-1873 *BiAUS,*
BiDrAC, WhAm H
Norris, Charles 1867-1935 *WhAm 1*
Norris, Charles Camblos 1876- *WhAm 5*
Norris, Charles E 1876-1941 *WhAm 1*
Norris, Charles Gilman Smith 1881-1945
DcAmB S3, WhAm 2
Norris, Charles Sumner 1856-1929 *ApCAB X,*
NatCAB 22
Norris, Clara Maud *WomWWA 14*
Norris, Earle Bertram 1882-1966 *WhAm 5*
Norris, Edgar Hughes 1893-1955 *WhAm 4*
Norris, Edgar William 1897-1962 *NatCAB 50*
Norris, Edward d1819? *NewYHSD*
Norris, Edward 1584?-1659 *DcAmB,*
WhAm H
Norris, Edward 1589-1640 *ApCAB*
Norris, Edward 1589?-1659 *Drake*
Norris, Edwin Lee 1865-1924 *NatCAB 14,*
WhAm 1
Norris, Ernest Eden 1882-1958 *WhAm 3*
Norris, Ethelbert *NewYHSD*
Norris, Frank 1870-1902 *AmBi, DcAmB,*
EncAAH, NatCAB 14, NatCAB 15,
REnAW, TwCBDA, WebAB, WhAm 1
Norris, Frank Callan 1907-1967 *WhAm 4*
Norris, George Washington 1808-1875 *ApCAB,*
DcAmB, WhAm H
Norris, George Washington 1864-1942 *WhAm 2*
Norris, George William 1861-1944 *ApCAB X,*

BiDrAC, DcAmB S3, EncAAH, EncAB,
McGEWB, NatCAB 33, REnAW,
WebAB, WhAm 2, WhAmP
Norris, George William 1875-1948 *WhAm 2*
Norris, Grace Mabel *WomWWA 14*
Norris, Hannon Edwards 1898-1962
NatCAB 48
Norris, Harriette Bronson Holbrook
WomWWA 14
Norris, Harry Waldo 1862-1946 *WhAm 2*
Norris, Henry 1875-1941 *WhAm 1*
Norris, Henry Hutchinson 1873-1940 *WhAm 1*
Norris, Henry McCoy 1868-1925 *NatCAB 20,
WhAm 1*
Norris, Herbert T 1904-1952 *WhAm 3*
Norris, Homer Albert 1860-1920 *WhAm 1*
Norris, Isaac 1671-1735 *ApCAB, BiAUS,
DcAmB, Drake, TwCBDA, WhAm H*
Norris, Isaac 1701-1766 *ApCAB, DcAmB,
NatCAB 5, WhAm H, WhAmP*
Norris, Isaac 1707-1766 *TwCBDA*
Norris, Isaac 1834- *WhAm 4*
Norris, James 1878-1952 *NatCAB 42,
WhAm 3*
Norris, James Dougan 1906-1966 *NatCAB 52,
WhAm 4*
Norris, James Flack 1871-1940 *DcAmB S2,
NatCAB 30, WhAm 1*
Norris, James Lawson 1845-1910 *WhAm 1*
Norris, Jean Hortense 1877- *WomWWA 14*
Norris, John 1748-1808 *ApCAB, Drake,
NatCAB 6*
Norris, John Franklyn 1877-1952 *DcAmB S5,
WhAm 3*
Norris, Katharine Hosmer 1869-
WomWWA 14
Norris, Kathleen Thompson 1880-1966
WhAm 4, WomWWA 14
Norris, Kenneth True 1899-1972 *WhAm 5*
Norris, Lester J, Jr. 1925-1967 *WhAm 4*
Norris, Lillian Horsey 1882- *WomWWA 14*
Norris, Mary Harriott 1848-1919 *DcAmB,
TwCBDA, WhAm 1, WomWWA 14*
Norris, Mary Hoge 1887- *WomWWA 14*
Norris, Matthew Tyson 1849-1915 *NatCAB 16*
Norris, Moses 1799-1855 *ApCAB, BiAUS,
BiDrAC, NatCAB 12, TwCBDA,
WhAm H, WhAmP*
Norris, Philip Ashton 1863-1942 *WhAm 2*
Norris, Richard A 1904-1974 *WhAm 6*
Norris, Richard Cooper 1863-1937 *WhAm 2*
Norris, Robert Stewart 1869-1945 *NatCAB 37*
Norris, Rollin 1863-1951 *NatCAB 40*
Norris, Samuel Royall 1897-1950 *NatCAB 40*
Norris, Sarah Dobson *WomWWA 14*
Norris, Scott A 1890-1963 *WhAm 4*
Norris, Thaddeus 1811-1877 *ApCAB*
Norris, True Livingston 1848-1920 *NatCAB 20,
WhAm 1*
Norris, Walter Blake 1879- *WhAm 6*
Norris, William 1802-1867 *DcAmB, WhAm H*
Norris, William 1872-1929 *WhAm 1*
Norris, William Arthur, Jr. 1925-1973 *WhAm 5*
Norris, William Fisher 1839-1901 *DcAmB,
NatCAB 12, NatCAB 18, TwCBDA,
WhAm 1*
Norris, William Francis 1839- *ApCAB*
Norris, William Henry, Jr. 1832- *NatCAB 5*
Norris, William Kibby 1875-1951 *WhAm 3*
Norris, Zoe Anderson *WomWWA 14*
Norrish, Ronald George Wreyford 1897-
AsBiEn
Norstad, Lauris 1907- *WebAMB*
Norsworthy, Naomi 1877-1916 *BiDAmEd,
DcAmB, WhAm 1, WomWWA 14*
North, Arthur A 1907-1966 *WhAm 4*
North, Arthur Walbridge 1874-1943
NatCAB 32
North, Caleb 1753-1840 *ApCAB, Drake,
TwCBDA*
North, Cecil Clare 1878-1961 *WhAm 4*
North, Charles Edward 1869-1961 *WhAm 4*
North, Charles H 1868-1917 *WhAm 1*
North, Dora Briggs 1852- *WomWWA 14*
North, Edward 1820-1903 *ApCAB, BiDAmEd,
DcAmB, NatCAB 4, TwCBDA,
WhAm 1*
North, Elisha 1768-1843 *TwCBDA*

North, Elisha 1771-1843 *ApCAB, DcAmB,
WhAm H*
North, Emmett Pipkin 1877-1935 *WhAm 1*
North, Erasmus Darwin 1806-1856 *TwCBDA*
North, Francis Reid 1876- *WhAm 5*
North, Francis Stanley 1875-1930 *NatCAB 22*
North, Frank Joshua 1840-1885 *DcAmB,
EncAAH, WebAB, WebAMB, WhAm H*
North, Frank Mason 1850-1935 *DcAmB S1,
NatCAB 26, WhAm 1*
North, Baron Frederick 1732-1792 *Drake,
McGEWB*
North, Baron Frederick 1733-1792 *ApCAB*
North, Harold Diodate 1883-1956 *NatCAB 45*
North, Harry B 1872- *WhAm 5*
North, Henry Briggs 1879-1956 *NatCAB 45*
North, Henry Emerson 1889-1962 *WhAm 4*
North, Isaac Franklin 1851- *WhAm 4*
North, James Mortimer 1886-1956 *WhAm 3*
North, James Stanley 1874-1942 *NatCAB 32*
North, John Alden 1901-1971 *NatCAB 56,
WhAm 5*
North, John W *BiAUS*
North, Lila Verplanck *WomWWA 14*
North, Louise McCoy 1859- *WomWWA 14*
North, Ludlow Frey 1901-1964 *WhAm 4*
North, Mary *NewYHSD*
North, Mary Myers *WomWWA 14*
North, Noah *NewYHSD*
North, Orlando d1896 *WhAm H*
North, Simeon 1763-1852 *WhAm H*
North, Simeon 1765-1852 *DcAmB*
North, Simeon 1802-1884 *ApCAB, DcAmB,
NatCAB 7, TwCBDA, WhAm H*
North, Simeon 1825- *Drake*
North, Simon Newton Dexter 1848-1924
DcAmB, NatCAB 44
North, Simon Newton Dexter 1849-1924
NatCAB 13, WhAm 1
North, Solomon Taylor 1853-1917 *BiDrAC,
WhAm 4*
North, Sterling 1906-1974 *WhAm 6*
North, Walter Harper 1871-1952 *NatCAB 41,
WhAm 3*
North, William d1854 *Drake*
North, William 1755-1836 *ApCAB, BiAUS,
BiDrAC, DcAmB, Drake, NatCAB 1,
NatCAB 2, TwCBDA, WhAm H*
North, William B *NewYHSD*
North, William Burrous 1861-1931 *NatCAB 24*
North, William Stanley 1846-1908 *NatCAB 20*
Northcote, Henry *NewYHSD*
Northcote, James 1822-1904 *NewYHSD*
Northcote, Stafford Mantle 1869- *WhAm 5*
Northcott, Elliott 1869-1946 *NatCAB 14,
NatCAB 47, WhAm 2*
Northcott, John A, Jr. 1897-1956 *WhAm 3*
Northcott, William Allen 1854-1917 *WhAm 1*
Northcott, William Newton 1874-1950
WhAm 3
Northcross, Daisy Hill 1881- *WhoColR*
Northcross, David Caneen 1876- *WhoColR*
Northen, Edwin Clyde 1873-1954 *NatCAB 51,
WhAm 3*
Northen, William Ezra 1819-1897 *WhAm H*
Northen, William Jonathan 1835-1913 *DcAmB,
NatCAB 1, TwCBDA, WhAm 1*
Northend, Charles 1814-1895 *ApCAB,
BiDAmEd, DcAmB, Drake, WhAm H*
Northend, Mary Harrod 1850- *WhAm 1*
Northend, William Dummer 1823-1903 *ApCAB,
WhAm 1*
Northerman, George *NewYHSD*
Northey, H Maud Richardson 1868-
WomWWA 14
Northington, James Montgomery 1885-1964
NatCAB 50, WhAm 4
Northington, Merrill Pratt 1875-1938
NatCAB 31
Northington, Page 1892-1962 *NatCAB 50*
Northrop, Aaron Lockwood 1834-1908
NatCAB 17
Northrop, Anna Leiseuring *WomWWA 14*
Northrop, Birdsey Grant 1817-1898 *BiDAmEd,
DcAmB, NatCAB 10, WhAm H*
Northrop, Birdsey Grant *see also* Northrup,
Birdsey Grant
Northrop, Celestia Joslin 1856- *AmWom*

Northrop, Claudian Bellinger 1864-1942
NatCAB 37
Northrop, Cyrus 1834-1922 *AmBi, ApCAB,
BiDAmEd, DcAmB, NatCAB 13,
TwCBDA, WhAm 1*
Northrop, David Ward 1844-1918 *WhAm 1*
Northrop, Edwin Canfield 1882-1960
NatCAB 45
Northrop, Eugene P 1908-1969 *WhAm 5*
Northrop, George Norton 1880-1964 *WhAm 4*
Northrop, Harry Pinckney 1842- *ApCAB,
WhAm 1*
Northrop, Henry Davenport 1836- *WhAm 1*
Northrop, Henry Pinckney 1842- *NatCAB 12,
TwCBDA*
Northrop, Herbert L 1866-1936 *WhAm 1*
Northrop, John DeWolf 1886-1954 *NatCAB 42*
Northrop, John Howard 1891- *AsBiEn,
McGEWB, WebAB*
Northrop, John Knudsen 1895- *WebAMB*
Northrop, Lucius Bellinger 1811-1894 *ApCAB,
BiDConf, DcAmB, TwCBDA, WhAm H*
Northrop, Stephen Abbott 1852-1918 *WhAm 1*
Northrup, Ansel Judd 1833- *ApCAB,
NatCAB 10, TwCBDA, WhAm 1*
Northrup, Birdsey Grant 1817-1898
ApCAB Sup, TwCBDA
Northrup, Birdsey Grant *see also* Northrop,
Birdsey Grant
Northrup, Edwin Fitch 1866-1940 *NatCAB 38,
WhAm 1*
Northrup, Elliott Judd 1870-1950 *WhAm 3*
Northrup, Frederic B 1899-1959 *WhAm 4*
Northrup, George Washington 1826-1900
*ApCAB, NatCAB 12, TwCBDA,
WhAm 1*
Northrup, Jeremiah 1815- *ApCAB*
Northrup, Jesse E 1857-1915 *NatCAB 16*
Northrup, Seaman Francis 1876-1935
NatCAB 27
Northrup, William Perry 1851-1935 *ApCAB X,
WhAm 1*
Northumberland, John Dudley, Duke Of
1502?-1553 *McGEWB*
Northup, Carrie Myers 1874- *WomWWA 14*
Northup, Clark Sutherland 1872-1952 *WhAm 4*
Northup, David Wilmarth 1906-1973 *WhAm 6*
Northup, George Tyler 1874-1964 *WhAm 4*
Northup, John Eldridge 1868-1940 *WhAm 1*
Northup, William Guile 1851-1929 *WhAm 1*
Northwall, Theodore Gustave 1863-1916
NatCAB 18
Northway, Stephen Asa 1833-1898 *BiDrAC,
NatCAB 15, TwCBDA*
Northway, William Herrick 1903-1960
NatCAB 46
Norton, A Warren 1896-1970 *WhAm 5*
Norton, Alice Peloubet 1860-1928 *DcAmB,
NotAW, WhAm 1, WomWWA 14*
Norton, Andrews 1786-1852 *ApCAB,
NatCAB 7, TwCBDA*
Norton, Andrews 1786-1853 *DcAmB,
DcAmReB, Drake, WhAm H*
Norton, Arthur Brigham 1856-1919 *NatCAB 18,
WhAm 1*
Norton, Arthur Edwin 1877-1940 *NatCAB 30*
Norton, Arthur Henry 1870-1939 *WhAm 1*
Norton, Asahel Strong 1765-1853 *ApCAB,
Drake, TwCBDA*
Norton, Augustus Theodore 1808-1884 *ApCAB*
Norton, Carol 1869-1904 *NatCAB 20*
Norton, Chapple 1746-1818 *ApCAB, Drake*
Norton, Charles Benjamin 1825-1891 *DcAmLiB,
TwCBDA*
Norton, Charles Dyer 1871-1922 *WhAm 1*
Norton, Charles Dyer 1871-1923 *NatCAB 6*
Norton, Charles Eliot 1827-1908 *AmBi,
ApCAB, BiDAmEd, DcAmB, EncAB,
NatCAB 6, TwCBDA, WebAB, WhAm 1*
Norton, Charles Hotchkiss 1851-1942
DcAmB S3, NatCAB 31, WhAm 3
Norton, Charles Ladd 1870-1939 *WhAm 1*
Norton, Charles Ledyard 1837-1909 *ApCAB,
TwCBDA, WhAm 1*
Norton, Charles Phelps 1858-1922 *WhAm 1*
Norton, Charles Stuart 1836-1911 *ApCAB Sup,
TwCBDA, WhAm 1*
Norton, Charles Willis 1861-1918 *NatCAB 17*

Norton, Daniel Field 1894-1956 *WhAm 3*
Norton, Daniel Sheldon 1829-1870 *ApCAB,*
BiAUS, BiDrAC, NatCAB 11, TwCBDA,
WhAm H
Norton, David Z 1851-1928 *NatCAB 21,*
WhAm 1
Norton, Della Whitney 1840- *AmWom*
Norton, Ebenezer Foote 1774-1851 *BiAUS,*
BiDrAC, WhAm H
Norton, Eckstein 1831-1893 *NatCAB 3*
Norton, Edith Eliza Ames 1864-1929 *WhAm 1*
Norton, Edward Lee 1892-1966 *WhAm 4*
Norton, Edwin 1845-1914 *NatCAB 15,*
NatCAB 26
Norton, Edwin 1845-1916 *WhAm 1*
Norton, Edwin Clarence 1856-1943 *WhAm 2*
Norton, Elijah Hise 1821-1914 *BiAUS,*
BiDrAC, DcAmB, NatCAB 5
Norton, Eliot 1863-1932 *WhAm 1*
Norton, Eugene Levering 1880-1960
NatCAB 45, WhAm 4
Norton, Evermont Hope 1873-1961 *NatCAB 47,*
WhAm 4
Norton, Frank Henry 1836- *ApCAB,*
NatCAB 9, TwCBDA
Norton, Frederick Owen 1868-1924 *WhAm 1*
Norton, George Chester 1836-1915 *NatCAB 16*
Norton, George Harvey 1863-1930 *NatCAB 22*
Norton, George Hatley 1824-1893 *ApCAB,*
TwCBDA
Norton, George Howison 1896-1971
NatCAB 56
Norton, George Lowell 1837-1923 *WhAm 1*
Norton, George W 1855-1920 *WhAm 1*
Norton, George Washington 1865-1924
WhAm 1
Norton, Grace 1834-1926 *WhAm 1*
Norton, Grace Fallow 1876- *WhAm 5,*
WomWWA 14
Norton, Guy Payne 1880-1952 *NatCAB 41*
Norton, Harold Percival 1855-1933 *WhAm 1*
Norton, Henry Kittredge 1884-1965 *WhAm 4*
Norton, Herman 1799-1850 *ApCAB*
Norton, Hermon 1902-1965 *NatCAB 51*
Norton, Howard Magruder 1894-1963 *WhAm 4*
Norton, J Pease 1877-1952 *WhAm 3*
Norton, James 1843-1920 *BiDrAC, TwCBDA,*
WhAm 4
Norton, James Albert 1843-1912 *BiDrAC,*
TwCBDA, WhAm 4
Norton, James Arthur 1876-1950 *NatCAB 40*
Norton, James Edward 1857-1926 *NatCAB 20*
Norton, Jeanie 1855- *WomWWA 14*
Norton, Jesse Olds 1812-1875 *BiAUS, BiDrAC,*
TwCBDA, WhAm H
Norton, John *ApCAB, Drake*
Norton, John 1606-1663 *ApCAB, DcAmB,*
Drake, NatCAB 7, TwCBDA, WhAm H
Norton, John 1651-1716 *ApCAB*
Norton, John 1716-1778 *ApCAB, Drake*
Norton, John H 1847- *NatCAB 5*
Norton, John Nathaniel 1878-1960 *BiDrAC,*
WhAm 6
Norton, John Nicholas 1820-1881 *ApCAB,*
DcAmB, Drake, NatCAB 15, TwCBDA,
WhAm H
Norton, John Pitkin 1822-1852 *ApCAB,*
BiDAmEd, DcAmB, DcScB, Drake,
NatCAB 8, WhAm H
Norton, John Schade 1893-1946 *NatCAB 34*
Norton, John Warner 1876-1934 *WhAm 1*
Norton, John William Roy 1898-1974 *WhAm 6*
Norton, Laurence Harper 1888-1960
NatCAB 47, WhAm 4
Norton, Laurence J 1896-1956 *WhAm 3*
Norton, Lewis Mills 1783-1860 *NatCAB 4*
Norton, Lewis Mills 1855- *ApCAB*
Norton, Lillian *WebAB*
Norton, Lottie Elouise Gove *WomWWA 14*
Norton, Lucy King *NewYHSD*
Norton, Mabel Gardner White *WomWWA 14*
Norton, Mary Alice Peloubet 1860-1928
BiDAmEd, DcAmB
Norton, Mary Blanche 1875- *BiCAW*
Norton, Mary Castle 1854- *WomWWA 14*
Norton, Mary Louise 1864- *WomWWA 14*
Norton, Mary Teresa Hopkins 1875-1959
BiDrAC, NatCAB 46, WhAm 3, WhAmP

Norton, Merritt Jones 1884-1932 *NatCAB 26*
Norton, Miner Gibbs 1857-1926 *BiDrAC,*
WhAm H
Norton, Minerva Brace 1837- *AmWom*
Norton, Morilla M 1865- *AmWom*
Norton, Nathaniel Willis 1853-1920 *NatCAB 8*
Norton, Nelson Ira 1820-1887 *BiDrAC,*
WhAm H
Norton, Nelson J 1820- *BiAUS*
Norton, Nimrod Lindsay 1830-1903 *BiDConf*
Norton, Oliver Willcox 1839-1920 *NatCAB 19*
Norton, Patrick Daniel 1876-1953 *BiDrAC,*
WhAm 5, WhAmP
Norton, Paul Willard 1883-1969 *NatCAB 55*
Norton, Porter 1853-1918 *WhAm 1*
Norton, Ralph Hubbard 1875-1953 *WhAm 3*
Norton, Richard 1872-1918 *AmBi, WhAm 1*
Norton, Richard Henry 1849-1918 *BiDrAC*
Norton, Richard William 1886-1940
NatCAB 33
Norton, Robert Castle 1879-1959 *NatCAB 47,*
WhAm 3
Norton, Roy 1869-1942 *WhAm 2*
Norton, S Mary *WomWWA 14*
Norton, Sidney Augustus 1835-1918 *ApCAB,*
NatCAB 12, TwCBDA, WhAm 1
Norton, Stephen Alison 1854-1930 *WhAm 1*
Norton, Susan Whittlesey *WomWWA 14*
Norton, Thomas Herbert 1851-1941 *ApCAB,*
ApCAB X, NatCAB 13, TwCBDA,
WhAm 2
Norton, W H *NewYHSD*
Norton, Wilbur H 1903-1963 *WhAm 4*
Norton, William Augustus 1810-1883 *ApCAB,*
Drake, NatCAB 9, TwCBDA
Norton, William Bernard 1857-1936
NatCAB 28, WhAm 1
Norton, William Edward 1843-1916 *DcAmB,*
Drake, NatCAB 6, WhAm 1
Norton, William Harmon 1856-1944 *WhAm 2*
Norton, William Harrison 1888-1952
NatCAB 40
Norton, William Warder 1891-1945 *DcAmB S3,*
WhAm 2
Nortoni, Albert Dexter 1867-1938 *NatCAB 16,*
WhAm 1, WhAm 2
Norval, Theophilas Lincoln 1847-1942
NatCAB 13
Norval, Theophilus Lincoln 1847-1942 *WhAm 2*
Norvell, George Wilhelm 1885-1957
NatCAB 45
Norvell, Ida Wood 1877- *WomWWA 14*
Norvell, John d1850 *BiAUS*
Norvell, John 1789-1850 *BiDrAC, NatCAB 11,*
TwCBDA, WhAm H
Norvell, John 1790-1850 *ApCAB, NatCAB 11*
Norvell, Saunders 1864- *WhAm 5*
Norvell, William Edwin 1883-1958 *NatCAB 50*
Norwich, Viscount 1890-1954 *WhAm 3*
Norwood, C Augustus 1880-1940 *NatCAB 30,*
WhAm 1
Norwood, Charles Joseph 1853-1927 *WhAm 1*
Norwood, Edwin P 1881-1940 *WhAm 1*
Norwood, Elisabeth Fessenden Gragg 1879-
WhAm 6
Norwood, George 1892-1949 *NatCAB 42,*
WhAm 3
Norwood, Guy Earle 1876- *ApCAB X*
Norwood, John Nelson 1879-1965 *WhAm 4*
Norwood, John Wilkins 1865-1945 *WhAm 2*
Norwood, Kittie Maxwell 1876- *WomWWA 14*
Norwood, Maxwell C 1908-1965 *WhAm 4*
Norwood, Richard 1590-1665 *DcScB*
Norwood, Robert Winkworth 1874-1932 *DcAmB,*
NatCAB 25, WhAm 1
Norwood, Thomas Manson 1830-1913 *BiAUS,*
BiDrAC, NatCAB 13, TwCBDA,
WhAm 1
Norwood, Thomas Mason 1830-1913 *ApCAB*
Norwood, William 1767-1840 *BiAUS*
Norworth, Jack 1879-1959 *NatCAB 48*
Noss, Mary Graham 1862- *WomWWA 14*
Noss, Theodore Bland 1852-1909 *DcAmB,*
WhAm 1
Nostradamus, Michael 1503-1566 *DcScB*
Nostrand, Peter Elbert 1856- *NatCAB 12,*
WhAm 4

Nosworthy, Thomas Arthur 1883-1967
WhAm 4
Notaire, Joseph Dessaux *NewYHSD*
Notestein, Ada Louise Comstock *BiDAmEd*
Notestein, Jonas O 1849-1928 *WhAm 1*
Notestein, Wallace 1878-1969 *WhAm 5*
Notestein, William Lee 1859- *WhAm 4*
Nothstein, Ira Oliver 1874- *WhAm 5*
Notker Balbulus 840?-912 *McGEWB*
Notley, Thomas *NatCAB 7*
Notman, Arthur 1883-1961 *NatCAB 46,*
WhAm 4
Notman, James Geoffrey 1901-1974 *WhAm 6*
Notman, John 1810-1865 *BnEnAmA, Drake,*
WhAm H
Notman, John 1851-1907 *NatCAB 15*
Notnagel, Leland Hascall 1903-1958 *WhAm 3*
Notopoulos, James A 1905-1967 *WhAm 4*
Nott, Abner Kingman 1834-1859 *ApCAB*
Nott, Abraham d1830 *BiAUS*
Nott, Abraham 1696-1756 *ApCAB*
Nott, Abraham 1767-1830 *Drake*
Nott, Abraham 1768-1830 *ApCAB, BiDrAC,*
DcAmB, NatCAB 11, WhAm H
Nott, Charles *NewYHSD*
Nott, Charles Cooper 1827-1916 *ApCAB Sup,*
BiAUS, DcAmB, NatCAB 12,
NatCAB 28, TwCBDA, WhAm 1
Nott, Edward 1657-1706 *BiAUS, Drake,*
NatCAB 13
Nott, Eliphalet 1773-1866 *AmBi, ApCAB,*
BiDAmEd, DcAmB, Drake, NatCAB 7,
TwCBDA, WhAm H
Nott, Henry Junius 1797-1837 *ApCAB,*
DcAmB, Drake, NatCAB 11, TwCBDA,
WhAm H
Nott, Joel Benedict 1797-1878 *TwCBDA*
Nott, John 1801-1878 *TwCBDA*
Nott, Josiah Clark 1804-1873 *ApCAB, DcAmB,*
Drake, NatCAB 19, TwCBDA, WhAm H
Nott, Otis Fessenden 1825-1900 *WhAm H*
Nott, Richard Means 1831-1880 *ApCAB*
Nott, Samuel 1754-1852 *ApCAB, DcAmB,*
Drake, WhAm H
Nott, Samuel 1788-1869 *ApCAB, Drake,*
TwCBDA
Nott, Stanley Charles 1902-1957 *WhAm 3*
Nott, Thomas J *NewYHSD*
Notter, Harley A 1903-1950 *WhAm 3*
Nottingham, Gardiner Rodman 1880-1949
NatCAB 42
Nottingham, Severn Marcellus 1879-1954
NatCAB 48
Nottingham, Walter 1930- *BnEnAmA*
Nottingham, Wayne B 1899-1964 *WhAm 4*
Nottingham, William 1853-1921 *NatCAB 19,*
WhAm 1
Notz, Frederick William Augustus 1841-1921
DcAmB
Notz, Frederick William Augustus 1841-1922
WhAm 1
Notz, William Frederick 1879-1935 *WhAm 1*
Noue, Charles Edouard DeLa 1624-1691
ApCAB
Nourrisson, Guy Leon 1575?-1629 *ApCAB*
Nourse, Amos 1794-1877 *ApCAB, BiAUS,*
BiDrAC, NatCAB 11, WhAm H
Nourse, Charles Joseph 1888-1974 *WhAm 6*
Nourse, Dorothy Quincy 1885- *WomWWA 14*
Nourse, Edward Everett 1863-1929 *WhAm 1*
Nourse, Edwin Griswold 1883-1974 *WhAm 6*
Nourse, Elizabeth 1860-1938 *NatCAB 11,*
TwCBDA, WhAm 1, WomWWA 14
Nourse, Henry Stedman 1831-1903 *TwCBDA,*
WhAm 1
Nourse, Henry Stedman 1832-1903 *NatCAB 19*
Nourse, J E 1819-1889 *BiAUS*
Nourse, Jack 1885-1940 *NatCAB 30*
Nourse, James Duncan 1816-1854 *Drake*
Nourse, James Duncan 1817-1854 *ApCAB*
Nourse, John Thomas, Jr. 1877-1958 *WhAm 3*
Nourse, Joseph 1754-1841 *ApCAB, BiAUS,*
Drake, NatCAB 3, TwCBDA
Nourse, Joseph Everett 1819-1889 *ApCAB,*
TwCBDA
Nourse, Joseph Pomeroy d1954 *WhAm 3*
Nourse, Laura A Sunderlin 1836- *AmWom*

Nuthead, William 1654?-1695 *DcAmB,*
WhAm H
Nutt, Clifford Cameron 1896- *WhAm 3*
Nutt, Cyrus 1814-1875 *ApCAB, NatCAB 13,*
TwCBDA
Nutt, George Washington Morrison 1844-1881
ApCAB
Nutt, Henry Curtis 1863-1942 *NatCAB 32*
Nutt, Hubert Wilbur 1873- *WhAm 3*
Nutt, John Budd 1885-1958 *NatCAB 47*
Nutt, Joseph Randolph 1869-1945 *NatCAB 35,*
WhAm 2
Nutt, Robert Lee 1873-1943 *WhAm 2*
Nuttall, Enos 1842- *ApCAB*
Nuttall, George Henry Falkiner 1862-1937
WhAm 1
Nuttall, Leonard John, Jr. 1887-1944 *WhAm 2*
Nuttall, Thomas 1786-1859 *AmBi, ApCAB,*
DcAmB, DcScB, Drake, NatCAB 8,
NewYHSD, TwCBDA, WhAm H
Nuttall, Zelia Maria Magdalena d1933
WhAm 1, WomWWA 14
Nuttall, Zelia Maria Magdalena 1857-1933
NotAW
Nuttall, Zelia Maria Magdalena 1858-1933
TwCBDA
Nutter, Donald Grant 1915-1962 *WhAm 4*
Nutter, Edmondson John Masters 1879-1953
WhAm 3
Nutter, Edward Hoit 1876-1960 *NatCAB 48,*
WhAm 5
Nutter, George Read 1863-1937 *WhAm 1*
Nutter, Isaac Henry 1878- *WhoColR*
Nutter, P David 1908-1963 *NatCAB 49*
Nutter, Roscoe James 1886-1951 *NatCAB 41*
Nutter, Wesley Irving 1860-1926 *NatCAB 23*
Nutting, Abi L Preston 1853- *WomWWA 14*
Nutting, Benjamin F d1887 *NewYHSD*
Nutting, Charles Cleveland 1858-1927 *DcAmB,*
NatCAB 21, WhAm 1
Nutting, Emily *NewYHSD*
Nutting, George Edward 1866- *WhAm 4*
Nutting, Harold Judd 1902-1962 *NatCAB 52,*
WhAm 4
Nutting, Herbert Chester 1872-1934 *WhAm 1*
Nutting, John Danforth 1854-1949 *WhAm 3*
Nutting, Margaret Ogden 1901-1970 *WhAm 5*
Nutting, Mary Adelaide 1858-1948 *BiDAmEd,*
DcAmB S4, NotAW, WhAm 2,
WomWWA 14
Nutting, Mary Olivia 1831-1910 *WhAm 1*
Nutting, Newton Wright 1840-1889 *BiDrAC,*
TwCBDA, WhAm H
Nutting, Perley Gilman 1873-1949 *NatCAB 38,*
WhAm 2
Nutting, Wallace 1861-1941 *DcAmB S3,*
NatCAB 30, WhAm 1
Nuttle, Harry 1885-1973 *WhAm 5*
Nuttman, Louis Meredith 1874- *WhAm 5*
Nuveen, John 1864-1948 *WhAm 2*
Nuveen, John 1896-1968 *WhAm 5*
Nuyttens, Pierre d1960 *WhAm 3*
Nuzum, John Weston 1890-1953 *NatCAB 42*
Nyburg, Sidney Lauer 1880-1957 *NatCAB 47,*
WhAm 3
Nyce, Benjamin Markley 1869-1934 *WhAm 3*
Nyce, Peter Quick 1889-1954 *NatCAB 45*
Nydegger, James Archibald 1864-1934
WhAm 1
Nyden, John Augustus 1878-1932 *NatCAB 24,*
WhAm 1
Nye, Sir Archibald 1895-1967 *WhAm 4,*
WhWW-II
Nye, Bill Edgar Wilson 1850-1896 *AmBi,*
EncAAH, REnAW
Nye, Carl Merryman 1874-1952 *NatCAB 40*
Nye, Clark Henry 1868-1925 *NatCAB 21*
Nye, E *NewYHSD*
Nye, Edgar Hewitt 1879-1943 *WhAm 2*
Nye, Edgar Wilson 1850-1896 *AmBi, ApCAB,*
DcAmB, NatCAB 6, TwCBDA,
WhAm H
Nye, Frank E *WhAm 1*
Nye, Frank Mellen 1852-1935 *BiDrAC,*
NatCAB 7, NatCAB 31, WhAm 4
Nye, George Finley 1864-1947 *NatCAB 36*
Nye, George Hoxie 1894-1952 *NatCAB 41*
Nye, Gerald Prentice 1892-1971 *BiDrAC,*

Nye, Gerald Prentice 1892-1972 *REnAW*
Nye, Irene 1874- *WhAm 5, WomWWA 14*
Nye, James Gordon 1891-1967 *NatCAB 53*
Nye, James Warren 1814-1876 *ApCAB,*
DcAmB, REnAW
Nye, James Warren 1815-1876 *BiAUS,*
BiDrAC, Drake Sup, NatCAB 11,
TwCBDA, WhAm H, WhAmP
Nye, John Hooper 1890-1966 *WhAm 4*
Nye, Martha Waldo 1866- *WomWWA 14*
Nye, Myra Sturtevant 1879- *WomWWA 14*
Nye, Reuben Lovell 1867-1956 *WhAm 3*
Nye, Wallace George 1859- *WhAm 4*
Nye, Ward Higley 1872- *WhAm 5*
Nyel, Louis Isidore *ApCAB*
Nyerere, Julius Kamberage 1922- *McGEWB*
Nygaard, Harlan Kenneth 1899-1965 *WhAm 4*
Nygaard, Hjalmar Carl 1906-1963 *BiDrAC,*
WhAm 4
Nygren, Henning Harold 1890-1944
NatCAB 37
Nyhart, Howard Eldwin 1900-1969 *NatCAB 54*
Nylander, Fredrik 1820-1880 *DcScB*
Nylander, Lennart 1901-1966 *WhAm 4*
Nylander, William 1822-1899 *DcScB*
Nyquist, Carl 1877-1959 *WhAm 3*
Nyquist, Edna Elvera d1969 *WhAm 5*
Nystrom, Albert John 1873-1956 *NatCAB 48*
Nystrom, Charles 1882-1950 *NatCAB 38*
Nystrom, Paul Henry 1878-1969 *WhAm 5*
Nystrom, Wendell Clarence 1892-1971
WhAm 5
Nystrum, Conrad Esadore 1869- *NatCAB 17*
Nyswander, Reuben Edson, Jr. 1878-1941
WhAm 1
Nzinga Nkuwu d1506 *McGEWB*

O

Oace, John Arndt 1879-1957 *NatCAB 47*
Oak, Calvin 1882-1952 *NatCAB 40*
Oakely, Frank F *NewYHSD*
Oakes, Mrs. A T *NewYHSD*
Oakes, Carrie Baker 1865- *WomWWA 14*
Oakes, Clarence Perry 1900-1973 *WhAm 6*
Oakes, David 1869-1947 *NatCAB 36*
Oakes, Frederick Warren 1860- *WhAm 4*
Oakes, George Washington 1909-1965
    NatCAB 53
Oakes, George Washington Ochs 1861-1931
    DcAmB, WhAm 1
Oakes, Herbert King 1873-1933 *NatCAB 25*
Oakes, James 1826-1910 *ApCAB, Drake,*
    WhAm 1
Oakes, John Calvin 1871-1950 *NatCAB 50*
Oakes, Luther Stevens 1877-1955 *NatCAB 45*
Oakes, Robert A 1909-1973 *WhAm 6*
Oakes, Thomas 1644-1719 *ApCAB, Drake*
Oakes, Thomas Fletcher 1843-1919 *DcAmB,*
    NatCAB 1, NatCAB 19, WhAm 4
Oakes, Thomas Fletcher 1900-1966 *WhAm 4*
Oakes, Urian 1631-1681 *ApCAB, DcAmB,*
    Drake, NatCAB 6, TwCBDA, WhAm H
Oakey, Emily Sullivan 1829-1883 *ApCAB*
Oakey, Francis 1883-1950 *NatCAB 39*
Oakey, P Davis 1860-1920 *WhAm 4*
Oakey, Peter Davis 1861-1920 *BiDrAC*
Oakleaf, Joseph Benjamin 1858-1930 *WhAm 1*
Oakley, Amy 1882-1963 *WhAm 4*
Oakley, Annie 1860-1926 *DcAmB, EncAAH,*
    McGEWB, NotAW, REnAW, WebAB,
    WhAm HA, WhAm 4
Oakley, Edward *NewYHSD*
Oakley, Francis Clark 1907-1967 *WhAm 4*
Oakley, George 1793-1869 *NewYHSD*
Oakley, Georgina *NewYHSD*
Oakley, Henry Augustus 1827- *ApCAB,*
    WhAm 4
Oakley, Horace Sweeney 1861-1929
    NatCAB 22, WhAm 1
Oakley, Imogen Brashear 1854-1933 *WhAm 1,*
    WomWWA 14
Oakley, Juliana *NewYHSD*
Oakley, Octavius 1800-1867 *NewYHSD*
Oakley, Seymour Adams 1869-1933 *WhAm 1*
Oakley, Thomas Jackson 1783-1857 *ApCAB,*
    BiAUS, BiDrAC, DcAmB, Drake,
    NatCAB 11, TwCBDA, WhAm H
Oakley, Thomas Pollock 1884-1943 *NatCAB 33*
Oakley, Thornton 1881-1953 *NatCAB 42,*
    WhAm 3
Oakley, Violet 1874-1961 *BiCAW, WhAm 4,*
    WomWWA 14
Oakman, Charles Gibb 1903- *BiDrAC*
Oakman, Walter George 1845-1922 *NatCAB 3,*
    WhAm 1
Oaks *NewYHSD*
Oaksey, Geoffrey Lawrence 1880-1971
    WhAm 5, WhAm 6
Oare, Lenn Jesse 1887-1964 *NatCAB 51*
Oare, Robert Lenn 1912-1960 *WhAm 4*
Oates, Alice 1849-1887 *NatCAB 6*
Oates, James Franklin 1870- *WhAm 3*
Oates, John Alexander 1870-1958 *NatCAB 47*
Oates, Titus 1649-1705 *McGEWB*
Oates, Whitney J 1904-1973 *WhAm 6*
Oates, William Calvin 1835-1910 *BiDrAC,*
    DcAmB, NatCAB 2, TwCBDA,
    WhAm 1, WhAmP
Oates, William Calvin 1837-1910 *ApCAB Sup*
Oatman, Johnson 1856-1922 *DcAmB*
Oatman, Olive Ann 1838?-1903 *NotAW*
Obaldia, Jose Doming De 1845- *WhAm 4*

Obando, Jose Maria 1797-1861 *ApCAB*
O'Bannon, A J *BiAUS*
O'Bannon, Presley Neville 1776-1850 *WebAMB*
O'Banyoun, Ernest Ganson 1884- *WhoColR*
Obe *NewYHSD*
Obear, Hugh Harris 1882-1971 *WhAm 5*
Obee, Charles Walter 1879- *WhAm 6*
O'Beirne, James Rowan 1840-1914 *ApCAB X*
O'Beirne, Thomas Lewis 1748-1823 *ApCAB,*
    Drake
Obenauer, Marie Louise d1947 *WhAm 2*
Obenchain, Eliza Calvert Hall 1856-
    WomWWA 14
Obenchain, William Alexander 1841-1916
    NatCAB 3, TwCBDA, WhAm 1
Obeno *NewYHSD*
Obenshain, Wiley S 1894-1972 *WhAm 5*
Ober, Caroline Haven 1866- *WomWWA 14*
Ober, Charles Kellogg 1856-1948 *NatCAB 37*
Ober, Frank Roberts 1881-1960 *WhAm 4*
Ober, Frank Willis 1860-1949 *NatCAB 37*
Ober, Frederic Albion 1849-1913 *ApCAB*
Ober, Frederick Albion 1849-1913 *DcAmB,*
    NatCAB 13, NatCAB 54, TwCBDA,
    WhAm 1
Ober, Henry Kulp 1878-1939 *WhAm 1*
Ober, J Hambleton 1887-1965 *NatCAB 51*
Ober, Josephine Robb *WomWWA 14*
Ober, Sarah Endicott 1854- *WhAm 4,*
    WomWWA 14
Oberfell, George Grover 1885-1965 *NatCAB 53,*
    WhAm 4
Oberg, Erik 1881-1951 *WhAm 3*
Oberg, Kalervo 1901-1973 *WhAm 6*
Oberg, Stanford Wilbur 1892-1964 *NatCAB 52*
Oberge, Ullericka Hendrietta *WomWWA 14*
Oberhansley, Henry Ernest 1885-1945 *WhAm 2*
Oberhardt, William 1882-1958 *IIBEAAW,*
    WhAm 3
Oberhoffer, Emil Johann 1867-1933 *DcAmB S1,*
    NatCAB 25, WhAm 1
Oberholser, Harry Church 1870-1963 *WhAm 4*
Oberholtzer, Ellis Paxson 1868-1936 *DcAmB S2,*
    WhAm 1
Oberholtzer, Sara Louisa Vickers 1841-1930
    AmWom, ApCAB, DcAmB, NatCAB 7,
    WhAm HA, WhAm 4, WomWWA 14
Oberlaender, Gustav 1867-1936 *NatCAB 27,*
    WhAm 1
Oberlander, Alexander 1834- *NatCAB 5*
Oberlies, Louis Clark 1872-1956 *NatCAB 44*
Oberlin, Thomas William 1875-1941
    NatCAB 31
Oberlink, Boyd Stevenson 1910-1972 *WhAm 5*
Oberly, Eunice Rockwood *WomWWA 14*
Oberly, Henry Sherman 1898-1967 *WhAm 4*
Oberly, Robert Shimer 1885-1923 *NatCAB 21*
Obermann, George Jacob 1844- *NatCAB 5*
Obermann, Julian J 1888-1956 *WhAm 3*
Obermayer, Charles Joseph 1869-1925
    NatCAB 26
Oberndorf, Clarence Paul 1882-1954 *DcAmB S5,*
    NatCAB 49, WhAm 3
Oberndorfer, Anne Shaw Faulkner 1877-
    WhAm 5, WomWWA 14
O'Berry, John E 1919-1965 *WhAm 4*
Oberschmidt, Charles McCormick 1902-1952
    NatCAB 39
Oberteuffer, Delbert 1901- *BiDAmEd*
Oberteuffer, George 1878-1940 *NatCAB 29,*
    WhAm 3
Obertubbesing, Herman 1871-1947 *NatCAB 36*
Oberweiser, Edward Andrew 1879-1954
    NatCAB 42

Oberwortmann, Nugent Robert 1896-1965
    WhAm 4
Obetz, Henry Lorenz 1851-1913 *NatCAB 16*
Obey, David Ross 1938- *BiDrAC*
Obici, Amedeo 1877-1947 *NatCAB 36,*
    WhAm 2
Oblinger, Daniel Beers 1859-1945 *NatCAB 36*
Obookiah, Henry 1792-1818 *ApCAB, Drake*
Obote, Apolo Milton 1925- *McGEWB*
O'Boyle, Francis Joseph 1870-1949 *WhAm 2*
O'Boyle, Michael *NewYHSD*
Obrecht, Jacob 1450-1505 *McGEWB*
Obregon, Alvaro 1880-1928 *McGEWB*
O'Brian, Alma White 1876- *WomWWA 14*
O'Brian, John Lord 1874-1973 *WhAm 5,*
    WhAm 6
O'Brien, Abigail Adaline *WomWWA 14*
O'Brien, Arthur Aloysius 1884-1942
    NatCAB 47
O'Brien, Charles Francis Xavier 1879-1940
    BiDrAC, WhAm 1
O'Brien, Christopher Dillon 1848- *NatCAB 7*
O'Brien, Christopher W *NewYHSD*
O'Brien, Cornelius 1843- *ApCAB*
O'Brien, Daniel *NewYHSD*
O'Brien, Denis 1837-1909 *WhAm 1*
O'Brien, Denis Augustine 1906- *WhAm 3*
O'Brien, Dennis Francis 1876-1946 *WhAm 2*
O'Brien, Edgar David 1898-1968 *WhAm 5*
O'Brien, Edward Charles 1860-1927 *DcAmB,*
    NatCAB 14, WhAm 1
O'Brien, Edward Francis 1876-1945 *WhAm 2*
O'Brien, Edward James 1887-1959 *WhAm 3*
O'Brien, Edward Joseph Harrington 1890-1941
    WhAm 1
O'Brien, Edward Louis 1894-1965 *NatCAB 51*
O'Brien, Ernest Aloysius 1880-1948 *WhAm 2*
O'Brien, Fitz-James 1828?-1862 *AmBi,*
    ApCAB, DcAmB, NatCAB 6, TwCBDA,
    WhAm H
O'Brien, Fitzjames 1829-1862 *Drake*
O'Brien, Francis Patrick 1844- *WhAm 4*
O'Brien, Frank A 1851-1921 *WhAm 1*
O'Brien, Frank Cornelius 1915-1970 *WhAm 5*
O'Brien, Frank James 1888-1964 *WhAm 4*
O'Brien, Frank Michael 1875-1943 *NatCAB 32,*
    WhAm 2
O'Brien, Frank P 1844- *NatCAB 1*
O'Brien, Frederick 1869-1932 *DcAmB,*
    WhAm 1
O'Brien, Frederick William 1881-1965 *WhAm 4*
O'Brien, George Donoghue 1900-1957 *BiDrAC,*
    WhAm 3, WhAmP
O'Brien, Henry Rust 1891-1970 *WhAm 5*
O'Brien, Howard Vincent 1888-1947 *WhAm 2*
O'Brien, Hugh 1827- *ApCAB*
O'Brien, J Emmett 1892-1962 *NatCAB 48*
O'Brien, James *NewYHSD*
O'Brien, James 1841-1907 *BiDrAC*
O'Brien, James Henry 1860-1924 *BiDrAC,*
    WhAm 4
O'Brien, James Patrick 1891-1967 *NatCAB 53*
O'Brien, James Patrick 1913-1963 *WhAm 4*
O'Brien, James Putnam 1861-1931 *WhAm 1*
O'Brien, Jeremiah d1818 *Drake*
O'Brien, Jeremiah 1740-1818 *ApCAB*
O'Brien, Jeremiah 1744-1818 *AmBi, DcAmB,*
    NatCAB 11, WebAMB, WhAm H
O'Brien, Jeremiah 1768-1858 *BiAUS*
O'Brien, Jeremiah 1778-1858 *BiDrAC,*
    WhAm H
O'Brien, John 1750- *NatCAB 11*
O'Brien, John 1829-1879 *ApCAB*
O'Brien, John 1834-1904 *NewYHSD*

O'Brien, John 1836-1887 *NatCAB 10,*
WhAm H
O'Brien, John 1838- *WhAm 1*
O'Brien, John A 1897-1963 *WhAm 4*
O'Brien, John Cornelius 1894-1967 *WhAm 4*
O'Brien, John D 1853-1913 *NatCAB 16*
O'Brien, John Francis 1874-1939 *NatCAB 42,*
WhAm 1
O'Brien, John Joseph 1869-1936 *WhAm 1*
O'Brien, John Patrick 1873-1951 *NatCAB 39,*
WhAm 3
O'Brien, John Paul Jones 1817-1850 *ApCAB,*
Drake
O'Brien, John W *NewYHSD*
O'Brien, Joseph John 1897-1953 *BiDrAC,*
WhAm 3
O'Brien, Justin McCortney 1906-1968 *WhAm 5*
O'Brien, Kenneth 1895-1954 *ApCAB X,*
WhAm 3
O'Brien, Landis P 1902-1968 *NatCAB 54*
O'Brien, Lawrence Francis 1917- *BiDrUSE*
O'Brien, Leo Frederick 1924-1968 *WhAm 5*
O'Brien, Leo William 1900- *BiDrAC, WhAmP*
O'Brien, Lucius Richard 1832-1899 *ApCAB,*
IIBEAAW
O'Brien, Sister M Raphael 1857-1923 *WhAm 3*
O'Brien, Martin *NewYHSD*
O'Brien, Mary Heaton-Vorse *WomWWA 14*
O'Brien, Matthew Anthony 1804-1871 *DcAmB,*
WhAm H
O'Brien, Michael William 1835-1912
NatCAB 16
O'Brien, Miles M 1852- *WhAm 4*
O'Brien, Morgan Joseph 1852-1937 *DcAmB S2,*
NatCAB 14, NatCAB 28, WhAm 1
O'Brien, Patrick Henry 1868-1959 *WhAm 3*
O'Brien, Paul Thomas 1906-1956 *NatCAB 45*
O'Brien, Philip Raymond 1892-1953
NatCAB 41
O'Brien, Reuben Faulkner 1870-1951
NatCAB 45
O'Brien, Richard 1758-1824 *ApCAB, DcAmB,*
Drake, WhAm H
O'Brien, Richard 1839-1923 *NatCAB 20*
O'Brien, Robert *NewYHSD*
O'Brien, Robert Lincoln 1865-1955 *DcAmB S5,*
WhAm 3
O'Brien, S Weldon 1904-1967 *WhAm 4*
O'Brien, Sara Redempta 1875- *WhAm 5,*
WomWWA 14
O'Brien, Seumas 1880- *WhAm 6*
O'Brien, Thomas Charles 1887-1951
NatCAB 41, WhAm 3
O'Brien, Thomas Daniel 1863-1928 *NatCAB 21*
O'Brien, Thomas Dillon 1859-1935 *WhAm 1*
O'Brien, Thomas George 1874- *WhAm 5*
O'Brien, Thomas Henry 1869-1947 *NatCAB 39,*
WhAm 3
O'Brien, Thomas James 1842-1933 *DcAmB S1,*
NatCAB 14, NatCAB 25, WhAm 1
O'Brien, Thomas Joseph 1878-1964 *BiDrAC,*
WhAm 4
O'Brien, Thomas L 1870-1920 *NatCAB 21*
O'Brien, Vincent 1897-1958 *WhAm 3*
O'Brien, William Augustine 1903-1973
WhAm 6
O'Brien, William Austin 1893-1947 *NatCAB 36,*
WhAm 2
O'Brien, William Claire 1904-1971 *NatCAB 55,*
WhAm 5
O'Brien, William David 1878-1962 *WhAm 4*
O'Brien, William James 1836-1905 *BiAUS,*
BiDrAC
O'Brien, William James 1888-1960 *WhAm 4*
O'Brien, William Shoney 1825?-1878 *ApCAB,*
TwCBDA
O'Brien, William Shoney 1826?-1878 *DcAmB,*
WhAm H
O'Brien, William Smith 1862-1948 *BiDrAC,*
WhAm 2
O'Brien, William V O 1900-1958 *WhAm 3*
Obrig, Theo Ernst 1894-1967 *NatCAB 54*
O'Brine, David 1849- *WhAm 4*
Obruchev, Vladimir Afanasievich 1863-1956
DcScB
O'Bryen, Roland Feely 1901-1955 *NatCAB 42*
O'Bryen, William *BiDrAC*

O'Bryne, Michael Edward, Jr. 1911-1972
WhAm 5
Oburg, Oscar 1833-1919 *NatCAB 17*
O'Byrne, John J 1876- *WhAm 5*
Ocagne, Philbert Maurice D' 1862-1938 *DcScB*
O'Callaghan, Edmund Bailey 1797-1880 *ApCAB,*
DcAmB, Drake, EncAAH
O'Callaghan, Edmund Bailey 1797-1880
WhAm H
O'Callaghan, Jeremiah 1780-1861 *DcAmB,*
WhAm H
O'Callaghan, Peter Joseph 1866-1931 *WhAm 1*
Ocampo, Gonzalo De 1572?-1626 *ApCAB*
Ocampo, Melchor 1815?-1861 *ApCAB*
Ocampo, Pablo 1853-1925 *BiDrAC*
Ocampos, Bernardo 1898-1953 *WhAm 3*
O'Casey, Sean 1880-1964 *McGEWB,*
WhAm 4
Occidente, Maria Del 1794?-1845 *AmBi,*
DcAmB, NotAW
Occom, Samson 1723-1792 *ApCAB, DcAmB,*
DcAmReB, WhAm H
Occonostota d1785 *DcAmB*
Occum, Sampson 1723?-1792 *Drake*
Ochiltree, Thomas P 1839-1902 *NatCAB 2*
Ochiltree, Thomas Peck 1837-1903 *BiDrAC*
Ochiltree, Thomas Peck 1842-1902 *TwCBDA*
Ochiltree, Thomas Peck 1845-1902 *ApCAB Sup*
Ochiltree, William Beck 1811-1867 *BiDConf,*
NatCAB 2, TwCBDA
Ochlewski, Tadeusz 1894-1975 *WhAm 6*
Ochoa, Esteban 1831-1888 *REnAW*
Ochoa, Severo 1905- *AsBiEn, WebAB*
Ochoa Y Acuna, Antonio 1783-1833 *ApCAB*
Ochs, Adolph Simon 1858-1935 *AmBi,*
ApCAB X, DcAmB S1, EncAB,
McGEWB, NatCAB 1, TwCBDA,
WebAB, WhAm 1
Ochs, Arthur, Jr. 1919-1969 *WhAm 5*
Ochs, Benjamin Franklin 1862-1933
NatCAB 33
Ochs, Clarence L *WhAm 5*
Ochs, George, Jr. *NewYHSD*
Ochs, Julius 1826-1888 *DcAmB, WhAm H*
Ochs, Milton Barlow 1864- *WhAm 3*
Ochsenius, Carl 1830-1906 *DcScB*
Ochsner, Albert John 1858-1925 *BiHiMed,*
DcAmB, NatCAB 20, WhAm 1
Ochsner, Edward H 1868-1956 *WhAm 3*
Ochterlony, Sir David 1758-1825 *ApCAB,*
Drake
Ochtman, Dorothy 1892-1971 *NatCAB 56,*
WhAm 5
Ochtman, Leonard 1854-1934 *AmBi,*
NatCAB 6, NatCAB 26, TwCBDA,
WhAm 1
Ockeghem, Johannes 1425?-1495 *McGEWB*
Ockenden, Ina Marie Porter 184- *WhAm 5*
Ockenfuss, Lorenz *DcScB*
Ockerblad, Nelse Frederick 1881-1954 *WhAm 3*
Ockerson, John Augustus 1848-1924 *DcAmB,*
NatCAB 25, WhAm HA, WhAm 2,
WhAm 4
Ockham, William Of 1280?-1349 *AsBiEn*
Ockham, William Of 1285?-1349 *DcScB*
O'Connell, Ambrose 1881-1962 *WhAm 4*
O'Connell, Sister Anthony 1814-1897 *NotAW*
O'Connell, C Leonard 1890-1958 *WhAm 3*
O'Connell, Daniel 1775-1847 *McGEWB*
O'Connell, Daniel Theodore 1878-1964
WhAm 4
O'Connell, David Joseph 1868-1930 *AmBi,*
BiDrAC, WhAm 1, WhAmP
O'Connell, Denis Joseph 1849-1927 *DcAmReB,*
NatCAB 15
O'Connell, Dennis Joseph 1849-1927 *WhAm 1*
O'Connell, Desmond Henry 1906-1973 *WhAm 5*
O'Connell, Eugene 1815-1891 *TwCBDA,*
WhAm H
O'Connell, Eugene 1818?-1891 *ApCAB*
O'Connell, Harold J 1896-1964 *WhAm 4*
O'Connell, James 1858-1936 *WhAm 1*
O'Connell, James Timothy 1906-1966 *WhAm 4*
O'Connell, Jeremiah Edward 1883-1964 *BiDrAC,*
NatCAB 51
O'Connell, Jeremiah Joseph 1821-1894 *ApCAB,*
NatCAB 11
O'Connell, Jerry Joseph 1909-1956 *BiDrAC*

O'Connell, John Francis 1892-1945 *NatCAB 35*
O'Connell, John Henry 1915-1970 *WhAm 5*
O'Connell, John Joseph 1840-1927 *WhAm 1*
O'Connell, John Joseph 1894-1949 *WhAm 2*
O'Connell, John Matthew 1872-1941 *BiDrAC,*
WhAm 1, WhAmP
O'Connell, John Michael, Jr. 1895-1955
WhAm 3
O'Connell, Joseph E 1891-1960 *WhAm 4*
O'Connell, Joseph Francis 1872-1942 *BiDrAC,*
NatCAB 32, WhAm 2
O'Connell, Joseph Francis, Jr. 1912-1966
NatCAB 53, WhAm 4
O'Connell, Mary *WhAm H*
O'Connell, Maurice D 1839- *WhAm 4*
O'Connell, Michael John 1898-1958 *WhAm 3*
O'Connell, Patrick Augustin 1871-1958
WhAm 3
O'Connell, Percy Douglas 1895-1960 *WhAm 4*
O'Connell, William Henry 1843-1928 *WhAm 1*
O'Connell, William Henry 1859-1944
DcAmB S3, NatCAB 12, NatCAB 15,
NatCAB 33, WhAm 2
O'Connell, William Lawrence 1871-1936
NatCAB 27
O'Conner, William Douglas 1832-1889
WhAm H
O'Connor *NewYHSD*
O'Connor, Agnes 1854- *WomWWA 14*
O'Connor, Alice Marion Smith *WomWWA 14*
O'Connor, Alice Stanislaus Kelly 1873-
WomWWA 14
O'Connor, Andrew 1874-1941 *WhAm 1*
O'Connor, Basil 1892-1972 *WhAm 5*
O'Connor, Bernard Francis *WhAm 5*
O'Connor, Charles 1878-1940 *BiDrAC,*
WhAm 6
O'Connor, Denis 1841- *ApCAB Sup*
O'Connor, Denis Stanislaus 1893-1971
NatCAB 56, WhAm 5
O'Connor, Edwin 1918-1968 *WhAm 5*
O'Connor, Evangeline M *WhAm 5,*
WomWWA 14
O'Connor, Flannery 1925-1964 *NatCAB 55,*
WhAm 4
O'Connor, Frank 1903-1966 *WhAm 4*
O'Connor, Frank Aloysius 1875-1954 *WhAm 3*
O'Connor, Fred James 1898-1963 *NatCAB 50*
O'Connor, George Bligh 1883-1957 *WhAm 3*
O'Connor, George Gray 1914-1971 *WhAm 6*
O'Connor, George H 1873-1946 *WhAm 2*
O'Connor, Gerald Brown 1900-1972 *WhAm 6*
O'Connor, J F T 1884-1949 *WhAm 2*
O'Connor, James 1823-1890 *ApCAB, DcAmB,*
NatCAB 13, TwCBDA, WhAm H
O'Connor, James 1870-1941 *BiDrAC,*
WhAm 1, WhAmP
O'Connor, James Francis 1878-1945 *BiDrAC,*
WhAm 2, WhAmP
O'Connor, James Francis 1892-1963 *WhAm 4*
O'Connor, James Francis Thaddeus 1884-1949
NatCAB 53
O'Connor, James Frederick 1902-1971 *WhAm 5*
O'Connor, James Vincent 1902-1968
NatCAB 53
O'Connor, Jeremiah J 1913-1964 *WhAm 4*
O'Connor, John 1824-1887 *ApCAB*
O'Connor, John B 1897-1965 *WhAm 4*
O'Connor, John Christopher 1878-1922
NatCAB 19
O'Connor, John J 1896-1962 *WhAm 4*
O'Connor, John Joseph 1855-1927 *NatCAB 12,*
WhAm 1
O'Connor, John Joseph 1885-1960 *BiDrAC,*
WhAm 3, WhAmP
O'Connor, John Lawrence 1875- *WhAm 5*
O'Connor, Johnson 1891-1973 *WhAm 6*
O'Connor, Joseph 1841-1908 *NatCAB 13,*
TwCBDA, WhAm 1
O'Connor, Leslie Michael 1889-1966 *WhAm 4*
O'Connor, Martin Francis 1891-1963
NatCAB 50
O'Connor, Martin Patrick 1878-1946
NatCAB 33
O'Connor, Michael 1810-1872 *ApCAB,*
DcAmB, NatCAB 6, TwCBDA,
WhAm H
O'Connor, Michael Patrick 1831-1881 *BiDrAC,*

WhAm H

O'Connor, Nellie Johnson *WomWWA 14*

O'Connor, Paul Lynch 1909-1974 *WhAm 6*

O'Connor, Sir Richard 1782-1855 *ApCAB*

O'Connor, Richard 1915-1975 *WhAm 6*

O'Connor, Richard Alphonsus 1838-
ApCAB Sup

O'Connor, Sir Richard Nugent 1889-
WhWW-II, WhoMilH

O'Connor, Robert Daniel 1924-1969 *WhAm 5*

O'Connor, T V 1870-1935 *WhAm 1*

O'Connor, Thomas Ventry 1870-1935
NatCAB 42

O'Connor, William Douglas 1832-1889 *DcAmB*

O'Connor, William Douglas 1833-1889 *ApCAB,
NatCAB 2, TwCBDA*

O'Connor, William Roderick 1902-1969
NatCAB 55

O'Connor, William Van 1915-1966 *NatCAB 53,
WhAm 4*

O'Conor, Charles 1804-1884 *AmBi, ApCAB,
BiAUS, DcAmB, Drake, NatCAB 3,
TwCBDA, WhAm H*

O'Conor, Daniel Joseph 1882-1968 *WhAm 5*

O'Conor, Daniel Joseph, Jr. 1916-1974 *WhAm 6*

O'Conor, Herbert Romulus 1896-1959 *WhAm 3*

O'Conor, Herbert Romulus 1896-1960 *BiDrAC,
NatCAB 45, WhAmP*

O'Conor, John Francis Xavier 1852-
ApCAB Sup, TwCBDA, WhAm 4

O'Conor, Norreys Jephson 1885-1958
NatCAB 47, WhAm 3

O'Conor, Patrick Henry 1852-1938 *NatCAB 28*

O'Conor, Thomas 1770-1855 *ApCAB*

O'Conor, Vincent John 1893-1963 *NatCAB 50,
WhAm 4*

Oconostota d1785 *ApCAB, DcAmB,
EncAAH, WhAm H*

Ocvirk, Fred William 1913-1967 *NatCAB 53*

Oda, Nobunaga 1534-1582 *McGEWB*

O'Daniel, Edgar Vaughn 1884-1943 *NatCAB 32*

O'Daniel, John Wilson 1894-1975 *WhAm 6*

O'Daniel, Lillie *WomWWA 14*

O'Daniel, W Lee 1890-1969 *EncAAH,
WhAm 5*

O'Daniel, Wilbert Lee 1890-1969 *BiDrAC,
WhAm 5*

O'Day, Caroline Love Goodwin 1869?-1943
NotAW

O'Day, Caroline Love Goodwin 1875-1943
BiDrAC, WhAm 2, WhAmP

O'Day, Daniel 1844-1906 *NatCAB 14,
WhAm 1*

O'Day, Francis 1881-1932 *NatCAB 25*

O'Day, Thomas 1852-1915 *NatCAB 18*

Oddi, Ruggero 1864-1913 *DcScB*

Oddie, Tasker Lowndes 1870-1950 *ApCAB X,
BiDrAC, NatCAB 39, REnAW,
WhAm 2, WhAmP*

Oddie, Walter M 1808?-1865 *NewYHSD,
WhAm H*

O'Dea, Edward John 1856-1932 *NatCAB 14,
WhAm 1*

O'Dea, James 1871-1914 *WhAm 1*

Odegard, Peter H 1901-1966 *WhAm 4*

Odell, Albert Grove 1878-1947 *NatCAB 35,
WhAm 2*

Odell, Anna *WomWWA 14*

Odell, Arthur Lee 1877-1956 *WhAm 3*

Odell, Benjamin Baker, Jr. 1854-1926 *BiDrAC,
WhAmP*

Odell, Benjamin Barker, Jr. 1854-1926 *DcAmB,
NatCAB 14, TwCBDA, WhAm 1*

Odell, Caleb Herbert 1879-1944 *NatCAB 33*

Odell, Daniel Ingalls 1852- *WhAm 4*

O'Dell, DeForest 1898-1958 *NatCAB 48,
WhAm 3*

Odell, Frank Glenn 1864- *WhAm 4*

Odell, George Clinton Densmore 1866-1949
DcAmB S4, WhAm 2

O'Dell, George Edward 1874- *WhAm 5*

Odell, George Thomas 1848- *WhAm 4*

Odell, George Washington 1857- *NatCAB 14*

Odell, Herbert Leroy 1859-1940 *NatCAB 30*

Odell, Jackson 1792-1849 *ApCAB*

Odell, Jacob 1756-1845 *TwCBDA*

Odell, Jacob 1756-1846 *ApCAB*

Odell, John 1756-1835 *ApCAB*

Odell, John J P 1847- *NatCAB 13*

Odell, Jonathan 1730-1818 *TwCBDA*

Odell, Jonathan 1737-1818 *ApCAB, DcAmB,
NatCAB 25, WhAm H*

Odell, Joseph Henry 1871-1929 *WhAm 1*

Odell, Lillian Atherton 1871- *WomWWA 14*

Odell, Marguerite Twila 1916-1973 *WhAm 6*

Odell, Moses Fowler 1818-1866 *ApCAB,
BiAUS, BiDrAC, TwCBDA, WhAm H*

Odell, N Holmes 1828-1904 *BiAUS*

Odell, Nathaniel Holmes 1828-1904 *BiDrAC*

Odell, Paul Edwin 1870- *WhAm 5*

Odell, Rozeltha Ingram *WomWWA 14*

Odell, T J d1849 *NewYHSD*

Odell, Thomas *NewYHSD*

Odell, William Franklin 1774-1844 *ApCAB*

Odell, William Herrick Lovett 1863-1920
ApCAB X

Odell, William Hunter 1811- *ApCAB*

Odell, William R 1906-1971 *WhAm 5*

Odell, William Robert 1855-1938 *NatCAB 29,
WhAm 1*

Odell, Willis Patterson 1855-1931 *NatCAB 12,
WhAm 1*

Odell, Willmot Mitchell 1878-1932 *WhAm 1*

Odem, Brian Sylvester 1895-1963 *WhAm 4*

Oden, Joshua 1880- *WhAm 6*

Oden, Robert 1882-1964 *NatCAB 50,
WhAm 4*

Odenbach, Frederick Louis 1857-1933 *AmBi,
DcAmB S1, WhAm 1*

Odenheimer, Cordelia Powell 1867- *WhAm 5,
WomWWA 14*

Odenheimer, William Henry 1817-1879 *ApCAB,
DcAmB, Drake, NatCAB 3, TwCBDA,
WhAm H*

Odenweller, Charles J, Jr. 1903-1968 *WhAm 5*

Odermatt, Gotthard 1902-1970 *WhAm 6*

Odets, Clifford 1906-1963 *McGEWB, WebAB,
WhAm 4*

Odgers, Joseph H 1863- *WhAm 4*

Odierna, Gioanbatista 1597-1660 *DcScB*

Odin, John Mary d1870 *Drake*

Odin, John Mary 1801-1870 *ApCAB, DcAmB,
NatCAB 7, TwCBDA*

Odin, John Mary 1807-1870 *WhAm H*

Odinga, Ajuma Jaramogi Oginga 1912-
McGEWB

Odington *DcScB*

Odiorne, Thomas 1769-1851 *ApCAB, Drake,
WhAm H*

Odland, Martin Wendell 1875- *WhAm 5*

Odlin, Arthur Fuller 1860-1926 *NatCAB 20,
WhAm 1*

Odlin, James Edwin 1857-1920 *NatCAB 19*

Odlin, William 1865-1929 *ApCAB X*

Odling, William 1829-1921 *DcScB*

Odlozilik, Otakar 1899-1973 *WhAm 6*

Odlum, Hortense McQuarrie d1970 *WhAm 5*

Odoacer 433-493 *McGEWB*

O'Doherty, Mathew 1854-1928 *NatCAB 22*

Odom, Frederick Marion 1871- *WhAm 5*

Odom, Jamie McClatchy 1902-1972
NatCAB 56

Odom, William 1884-1942 *WhAm 1*

O'Donaghue, Denis 1848-1925 *NatCAB 15,
WhAm 1*

O'Donel, Charles M 1860-1933 *REnAW*

O'Donnel, James Louis 1737-1811 *ApCAB*

O'Donnel, Richard Lincoln 1860-1920
NatCAB 23

O'Donnell, Alfred 1873-1956 *NatCAB 46*

O'Donnell, Bernard 1846-1916 *NatCAB 17*

O'Donnell, Charles Leo 1884-1934 *NatCAB 25,
WhAm 1*

O'Donnell, Daniel Kane 1838-1871 *ApCAB*

O'Donnell, Emmett, Jr. 1906-1971 *WhAm 5*

O'Donnell, Eugene Edward 1883-1933
NatCAB 27

O'Donnell, George Anthony 1899-1952
WhAm 3

O'Donnell, J Hugh 1895-1947 *NatCAB 36,
WhAm 2*

O'Donnell, James 1840-1915 *BiDrAC, WhAmP*

O'Donnell, James 1842-1915 *TwCBDA*

O'Donnell, Jessie Fremont *AmWom*

O'Donnell, John *NewYHSD*

O'Donnell, John 1870-1954 *NatCAB 40*

O'Donnell, John Joseph 1881-1952 *NatCAB 43*

O'Donnell, John Parsons 1896-1961 *WhAm 4*

O'Donnell, Josef 1769-1834 *WhoMilH*

O'Donnell, Leopold 1809-1867 *WhoMilH*

O'Donnell, Martha 1837- *AmWom*

O'Donnell, Mary Eleanor 1882-1913 *WhAm 1,
WomWWA 14*

O'Donnell, Nellie 1867- *AmWom*

O'Donnell, Thomas Edward 1885-1964
NatCAB 50

O'Donnell, Thomas Jefferson 1856-1925 *DcAmB,
NatCAB 16, WhAm 1*

O'Donnell, William Emmett 1907-1974
WhAm 6

O'Donnell, William Francis 1890-1974 *WhAm 6*

O'Donnell, William Francis 1892-1957
NatCAB 50

O'Donoghue, Daniel William 1876-1949
NatCAB 37, WhAm 5

O'Donoghue, John Brennan 1896-1967 *WhAm 4*

O'Donohoe, John 1824- *ApCAB*

O'Donohue, Joseph John 1834- *NatCAB 7*

O'Donohue, Teresa Mary Jerome 1838-1918
BiCAW

O'Donoju, Juan d1821 *ApCAB*

O'Donovan, Charles 1860-1930 *WhAm 1*

O'Donovan, Charles 1902-1964 *NatCAB 51*

O'Donovan, William Rudolf 1844-1920 *ApCAB,
DcAmB, TwCBDA, WhAm 1*

O'Donovan, William Rudolph 1844-1920
NatCAB 20

Odria, Manuel A 1897-1974 *WhAm 6*

Odum, Howard Washington 1884-1954
*BiDAmEd, DcAmB S5, NatCAB 44,
WhAm 3*

O'Dwyer, Joseph 1841-1898 *DcAmB,
WhAm H*

O'Dwyer, William 1890-1964 *WhAm 4*

Oefele, Felix Von 1861- *WhAm 4*

Oehlert, Lewis H 1902-1971 *WhAm 5*

Oehmler, Leo Carl Martin 1867-1930 *DcAmB,
WhAm 1*

Oeland, Isaac Raymond 1862-1941 *NatCAB 30*

Oelrichs, Blanche *NotAW*

Oelrichs, Herman 1850-1906 *NatCAB 3*

Oelrichs, Hermann 1850-1906 *WhAm 1*

Oelschlager, Gustavus *NewYHSD*

Oemler, Arminius 1827-1897 *DcAmB,
EncAAH*

Oemler, Arminus 1827-1897 *WhAm H*

Oemler, Marie Conway 1879-1932 *WhAm 1*

Oenopides Of Chios *DcScB*

Oenslager, Donald Mitchell 1902-1975 *WhAm 6*

Oenslager, George 1873-1956 *NatCAB 50,
WhAm 3*

Oersted, Anders Sandoe 1816-1872 *ApCAB*

Oersted, Hans Christian 1777-1851 *AsBiEn,
DcScB, McGEWB*

Oertel, Hanns 1868- *WhAm 4*

Oertel, Horst 1873- *WhAm 5*

Oertel, Johannes Adam Simon 1823-1909
*ApCAB, DcAmB, IlBEAAW, NatCAB 7,
NewYHSD, TwCBDA, WhAm 1*

Oertel, John James Maximilian 1811-1882
WhAm H

Oeschger, William 1868- *WhAm 4*

Oesinger, Mrs. S *NewYHSD*

Oesterle, Joseph Francis 1888-1943 *WhAm 2*

Oestreich, Otto Albert 1875-1962 *WhAm 4*

Oestreicher, John C 1905-1951 *WhAm 3*

Oettinger, Jonas 1857-1936 *NatCAB 36*

Oexmelin, Alexander Oliver *Drake*

O'Fallon, Benjamin 1793-1842 *DcAmB,
REnAW, WhAm H*

O'Fallon, James 1749-1794? *DcAmB,
WhAm H*

O'Fallon, John 1791-1865 *ApCAB, DcAmB,
Drake, WhAm H*

O'Farrell, Michael Joseph 1832-1894 *ApCAB,
NatCAB 12, TwCBDA, WhAm H*

O'Farrell, Patrick 1832-1902 *WhAm 1*

O'Fearna, Sean Aloysius *EncAB, WebAB*

O'Feeney, Sean Aloysius *WebAB*

O'Ferrall, Charles Triplett 1840-1905 *BiDrAC,
DcAmB, NatCAB 5, TwCBDA,
WhAm 1, WhAmP*

Offenbach, Jacques 1819-1880 *McGEWB*

Offenhauer, Roy Ernest 1881-1938 *WhAm 1*

Offermann, Henry F 1866-1953 *WhAm 3*

Officer, Julia E *WomWWA 14*
Officer, Morris 1823-1874 *ApCAB*
Officer, Thomas 1822-1900 *TwCBDA*
Officer, Thomas S d1860 *ApCAB*
Officer, Thomas S 1810?-1859 *NewYHSD*
Officer, Thomas Sterling 1876- *WhoColR*
Offield, Charles Kirkpatrick 1845-1918
WhAm 1
Offield, James R 1880-1964 *NatCAB 51,*
WhAm 4
Offield, Mary Evelyn 1869- *WomWWA 14*
Offik, Wolfgang George 1913-1973 *WhAm 6*
Offley, Cleland Nelson 1869-1935 *WhAm 1*
Offley, David d1838 *BiAUS, DcAmB,*
WhAm H
Offley, Margaret Agnew 1870- *WomWWA 14*
Offner, Richard 1889-1965 *NatCAB 53,*
WhAm 4
Offray, Claude Victor 1896-1962 *NatCAB 47*
Offutt, Harry Corydon 1882-1957 *NatCAB 48*
Offutt, Nanniene Norton Thomasson 1881-
WomWWA 14
Offutt, Thiemann Scott 1872-1943 *NatCAB 32,*
WhAm 5
O'Flaherty, Hal 1890-1972 *WhAm 5*
O'Flanagan, Dermot 1901-1973 *WhAm 5*
O'Flynn, Edward *NewYHSD*
Ofstie, Ralph Andrew 1897-1956 *NatCAB 43,*
WhAm 3
Oftedal, Sven 1844-1911 *DcAmB*
O'Gaban Y Guerra, Juan Bernardo 1782-1838
ApCAB
O'Gara, Alfred 1893-1968 *WhAm 5*
O'Gara, Cuthbert Martin 1886-1968 *WhAm 5*
O'Gara, John Edward 1895-1973 *WhAm 5*
O'Gara, Mantin 1836- *ApCAB Sup*
Ogborn, Richard Eugene 1920-1967
NatCAB 54
Ogburn, Charlton 1882-1962 *WhAm 4*
Ogburn, William Fielding 1886-1959 *McGEWB,*
WhAm 3
Ogden, Aaron 1756-1839 *AmBi, ApCAB,*
BiAUS, BiDrAC, DcAmB, Drake,
NatCAB 5, TwCBDA, WhAm H
Ogden, Abraham 1743-1798 *ApCAB,*
NatCAB 5
Ogden, Arthur E 1922- *WhAm 6*
Ogden, Charles Franklin d1933 *BiDrAC,*
WhAm 1
Ogden, David 1707-1798 *DcAmB, WhAm H*
Ogden, David 1707-1800 *ApCAB, Drake,*
TwCBDA
Ogden, David A 1770-1829 *BiAUS, BiDrAC,*
WhAm H
Ogden, David B 1769-1849 *Drake*
Ogden, David Bayard 1775-1849 *DcAmB,*
WhAm H
Ogden, Dunbar Hunt 1878-1952 *WhAm 3*
Ogden, Edward William 1870-1946 *NatCAB 35,*
WhAm 2
Ogden, Elias Bailey Dayton 1799-1865 *ApCAB*
Ogden, Elise Lucy *WomWWA 14*
Ogden, Francis Barber 1783-1857 *ApCAB,*
DcAmB, NatCAB 11, WhAm H
Ogden, Frederick Nash 1837-1886 *ApCAB*
Ogden, George Dickie 1868-1936 *WhAm 1*
Ogden, George Washington 1871-1966 *WhAm 4*
Ogden, Henry Alexander 1856-1936 *IIBEAAW,*
WhAm 1
Ogden, Henry Neely 1868-1947 *NatCAB 36,*
WhAm 2
Ogden, Henry W d1860 *Drake*
Ogden, Henry Warren 1842-1905 *BiDrAC,*
TwCBDA, WhAm 1
Ogden, Herbert Gouverneur 1846-1906 *DcAmB,*
WhAm 1
Ogden, Herbert Gouverneur 1873- *NatCAB 14*
Ogden, Herschel Coombs 1869-1943
NatCAB 32, WhAm 2
Ogden, Howard Newton 1864-1915 *NatCAB 16*
Ogden, Hugh Walker 1871-1938 *NatCAB 46*
Ogden, Jacob 1721-1779 *Drake*
Ogden, Jacob 1721-1780 *ApCAB*
Ogden, James DePeyster 1790?-1870 *NatCAB 1*
Ogden, James Matlock 1870- *WhAm 5*
Ogden, Jay Bergen 1868-1927 *NatCAB 20,*
WhAm 4
Ogden, John Cosens 1740?-1800 *ApCAB*

Ogden, John Cosins d1800 *Drake*
Ogden, Lee 1888-1953 *NatCAB 42*
Ogden, Matthias d1791 *Drake*
Ogden, Matthias 1754-1791 *ApCAB*
Ogden, Matthias 1755-1791 *NatCAB 4,*
TwCBDA
Ogden, Peter Skene 1794-1854 *AmBi, DcAmB,*
EncAAH, McGEWB, REnAW,
WhAm H
Ogden, Robert 1716-1787 *ApCAB, BiAUS,*
TwCBDA
Ogden, Robert 1746-1826 *NatCAB 5*
Ogden, Robert Curtis 1836-1913 *BiDAmEd,*
DcAmB, NatCAB 14, WhAm 1
Ogden, Robert Morris 1877-1959 *NatCAB 43,*
WhAm 5
Ogden, Rollo 1856-1937 *AmBi, DcAmB S2,*
WhAm 1
Ogden, Samuel 1746-1810 *DcAmB, WhAm H*
Ogden, Thomas Ludlow 1773-1844 *ApCAB,*
DcAmB, TwCBDA, WhAm H
Ogden, Uzal 1744-1822 *ApCAB, DcAmB,*
Drake, TwCBDA, WhAm H
Ogden, Wesley 1818- *ApCAB*
Ogden, William Butler 1805-1877 *AmBi,*
ApCAB, DcAmB, NatCAB 13, WebAB,
WhAm H
Ogdon, Ina Duley 1872-1964 *WhAm 4,*
WhAm 5
Oge, Jacques Vincent 1750-1791 *ApCAB*
Oge, Vincent 1750?-1791 *Drake*
Ogelsby, Warwick Miller 1866- *WhAm 4*
Ogeron DeLaBouere, Bertrand Denis D'
1615-1675 *ApCAB*
Ogg, Frederic Austin 1878-1951 *DcAmB S5,*
WhAm 3
Ogier, Isaac S K *BiAUS*
Ogilby, Charles FitzRandolph 1879-1962
WhAm 4
Ogilby, Frederick 1813-1878 *ApCAB*
Ogilby, Frederick Darley 1905-1970 *WhAm 5*
Ogilby, John 1600-1676 *Drake*
Ogilby, John David 1810-1851 *ApCAB, Drake,*
TwCBDA
Ogilby, R E *NewYHSD*
Ogilby, Remsen Brinckerhoff 1881-1943
NatCAB 32, WhAm 2
Ogilvie, Clarence Cooper 1874-1959 *WhAm 3*
Ogilvie, Clinton 1838-1900 *ApCAB,*
NatCAB 16, NewYHSD, TwCBDA,
WhAm 4
Ogilvie, Ida Helen 1874- *ApCAB X, BiCAW,*
NatCAB 16, WomWWA 14
Ogilvie, James 1760?-1820 *DcAmB, Drake,*
WhAm H
Ogilvie, John d1774 *Drake*
Ogilvie, John 1722-1774 *ApCAB*
Ogilvie, John 1724-1774 *DcAmB, WhAm H*
Ogilvie, Noel John 1880- *WhAm 6*
Ogilvie, Norman John 1916-1973 *WhAm 6*
Ogilvie, Walter Ellsworth 1864-1956 *WhAm 3*
Ogle, Alexander 1765?-1852 *BiAUS*
Ogle, Alexander 1766-1832 *BiDrAC,*
WhAm H
Ogle, Andrew Jackson 1822-1852 *BiAUS,*
BiDrAC, WhAm H
Ogle, Arthur Hook 1892-1972 *NatCAB 57,*
WhAm 5
Ogle, Ben Caswell 1878-1958 *NatCAB 44*
Ogle, Benjamin 1746-1808 *ApCAB*
Ogle, Benjamin 1746-1809 *NatCAB 9,*
TwCBDA
Ogle, Benjamin 1749-1809 *Drake*
Ogle, Benjamin 1751-1809 *BiAUS*
Ogle, Charles 1789-1841 *WhAm H*
Ogle, Charles 1798-1841 *BiAUS, BiDrAC,*
TwCBDA
Ogle, John Garland 1851-1938 *NatCAB 28*
Ogle, Kenneth Neil 1902-1968 *WhAm 5*
Ogle, Marbury Bladen 1879- *WhAm 6*
Ogle, Samuel d1751 *ApCAB, Drake*
Ogle, Samuel d1752 *NatCAB 7*
Ogle, Samuel 1694?-1752 *TwCBDA*
Ogle, Samuel 1702?-1752 *DcAmB, WhAm H*
Oglebay, Crispin 1876-1949 *NatCAB 44,*
WhAm 2
Oglebay, Earl W 1849-1926 *NatCAB 20*
Oglesby, Mabry Chestly 1870- *WhoColR*

Oglesby, Nicholas Ewing 1892-1957 *WhAm 3*
Oglesby, Richard James 1824-1899 *AmBi,*
ApCAB, BiAUS, BiDrAC, DcAmB,
Drake, NatCAB 11, TwCBDA, WhAm H,
WhAmP
Oglesby, William Thomas 1903-1967 *WhAm 5*
Oglesby, Woodson Ratcliffe 1867-1955 *BiDrAC,*
NatCAB 43, WhAm 3
Oglethorpe, James Edward 1688-1785 *TwCBDA*
Oglethorpe, James Edward 1689-1785
NatCAB 1
Oglethorpe, James Edward 1696-1785 *AmBi,*
DcAmB, EncAAH, McGEWB, WebAB,
WhAm H
Oglethorpe, James Edward 1698-1785 *ApCAB,*
Drake
Ogleton, James *NewYHSD*
Ogletree, George Royden 1878-1949
NatCAB 38
Ogood, Henry Broadwell 1869- *WhAm 5*
O'Gorman, Francis Michael 1877-1934
NatCAB 25
O'Gorman, James Aloysius 1860-1943 *BiDrAC,*
NatCAB 15, NatCAB 32, WhAm 2
O'Gorman, James Michael 1804-1874 *TwCBDA*
O'Gorman, James Michael 1809-1874 *ApCAB*
O'Gorman, James Myles 1811-1874 *NatCAB 13*
O'Gorman, Thomas 1843-1921 *ApCAB Sup,*
BiDAmEd, DcAmB, NatCAB 12,
TwCBDA, WhAm 1
O'Grady, James Mary Early 1863-1928 *BiDrAC,*
NatCAB 21
O'Grady, John 1886-1966 *WhAm 4*
O'Grady, Patrick *NewYHSD*
O'Grady, W H *NewYHSD*
Ogsbury, Charles R 1892-1971 *WhAm 5*
O'Hagan, Anne 1869- *WhAm 5*
O'Hagan, Joseph Bernard 1826-1878 *TwCBDA*
O'Hagan, Thomas 1855-1939 *ApCAB X,*
WhAm 1
O'Hair, Frank Trimble 1870-1932 *BiDrAC,*
WhAm 1
O'Hair, Mary McClellan *WomWWA 14*
O'Halloran, Cornelius Hawkins 1890-1963
WhAm 4
O'Halloran, John Francis 1905-1968
NatCAB 54
O'Halloran, Patrick *NewYHSD*
O'Halloran, William Timothy 1899-1947
NatCAB 36
O'Hanlon, Thomas 1832-1912 *WhAm 1*
O'Hanrahan, Inka Irene d1970 *WhAm 5*
O'Hara, Barratt 1882-1969 *BiDrAC, WhAm 5,*
WhAmP
O'Hara, Charles 1730?-1802 *ApCAB, Drake*
O'Hara, Dwight 1892-1961 *NatCAB 52*
O'Hara, Edward Arthur 1888-1972 *WhAm 5*
O'Hara, Edward H 1853-1936 *WhAm 1*
O'Hara, Edwin Vincent 1881-1956 *DcAmReB,*
NatCAB 43, WhAm 3
O'Hara, Eliot 1890-1969 *WhAm 5*
O'Hara, Frank 1876-1938 *WhAm 1*
O'Hara, Frank 1926-1966 *WhAm 4*
O'Hara, Frank Hurburt 1888-1965 *WhAm 4*
O'Hara, Geoffrey 1882-1967 *WhAm 4*
O'Hara, Gerald Patrick 1895-1963 *WhAm 4*
O'Hara, James 1752-1819 *DcAmB,*
NatCAB 17, TwCBDA, WhAm H
O'Hara, James 1825-1900 *NatCAB 8*
O'Hara, James Edward 1844-1905 *BiDrAC,*
WhAmP
O'Hara, James Frederick 1904- *IIBEAAW*
O'Hara, James Grant 1925- *BiDrAC*
O'Hara, John 1905-1970 *McGEWB,*
NatCAB 55, WhAm 5
O'Hara, John Bernard 1884-1961 *WhAm 4*
O'Hara, John Francis 1888-1960 *NatCAB 45,*
WhAm 4
O'Hara, John Henry 1905-1970 *WebAB*
O'Hara, Joseph Aloysius 1869-1948 *NatCAB 42*
O'Hara, Joseph Alphonsus 1869-1948 *WhAm 2*
O'Hara, Joseph Patrick 1895-1975 *BiDrAC,*
WhAm 6
O'Hara, Neal 1893-1962 *WhAm 4*
O'Hara, Susan *NewYHSD*
O'Hara, Theodore 1820-1867 *ApCAB, DcAmB,*
TwCBDA, WebAMB, WhAm H
O'Hara, Theodore 1822-1867 *NatCAB 4*

O'Hara, Thomas 1856-1919 *NatCAB 18*
O'Hara, Thomas Andrew 1879-1960 *WhAm 4*
O'Hara, William 1816?-1899 *ApCAB, TwCBDA*
O'Hara, William 1817-1899 *NatCAB 12*
O'Hara, William L *WhAm 5*
O'Hara, William T S, Sr. 1864- *WhAm 4*
O'Hare, Edward Henry 1914-1943 *WebAMB*
O'Hare, Kate Cunningham 1877-1948 *DcAmB S4*
O'Hare, Kate Richards *NotAW*
O'Hare, Thomas C *WhAm 3*
O'Harra, Cleophas Cisney 1866-1935 *BiDAmEd, WhAm 1*
O'Harra, M Glenn 1884-1955 *NatCAB 44*
O'Harra, Margaret Tustin 1866-1942 *WhAm 2*
O'Harrow, Dennis 1908-1967 *WhAm 4A*
O'Hearn, James Ambrose 1890-1963 *WhAm 4*
O'Hearne, John 1850-1928 *NatCAB 21*
O'Hern, Charles A 1881-1925 *WhAm 1*
O'Hern, Jennie Margaret 1893-1970 *WhAm 5*
O'Hern, Lewis Jerome 1878-1930 *WhAm 1*
O'Higgins, Ambrosio 1720?-1801 *ApCAB*
O'Higgins, Bernard 1778-1842 *WhoMilH*
O'Higgins, Bernardo 1778-1842 *McGEWB, WhAm H*
O'Higgins, Bernardo 1780-1846 *ApCAB*
O'Higgins, Harvey Jerrold 1876-1929 *DcAmB, NatCAB 25, WhAm 1*
Ohl, Edwin Newton 1850-1922 *NatCAB 19*
Ohl, Henry, Jr. 1873-1940 *WhAm 1*
Ohl, Jeremiah Franklin 1850-1941 *WhAm 1*
Ohl, Josiah Kingsley d1920 *WhAm 1*
Ohl, Maude Andrews 1862- *AmWom*
Ohl, Robert Austin 1917-1970 *WhAm 5*
Ohliger, Lewis Philip 1843-1923 *BiDrAC*
Ohlin, Roy Percival 1897-1971 *NatCAB 56, WhAm 5*
Ohlinger, Gustavus 1877-1972 *WhAm 5*
Ohlmacher, Albert Philip 1865-1916 *DcAmB, NatCAB 26, WhAm 1*
Ohlmacher, Joseph Christian 1874- *WhAm 5*
Ohlson, Algoth 1880- *WhAm 6*
Ohlson, Doug 1936- *BnEnAmA*
Ohlson, Otto Frederick 1870- *WhAm 5*
Ohm, Georg Simon 1787-1854 *AsBiEn*
Ohm, Georg Simon 1789-1854 *DcScB, McGEWB*
Ohm, Robert Ervin 1917-1973 *WhAm 6*
Ohmann-Dumesnil, Amant Henry 1857- *NatCAB 12, WhAm 4*
Ohmart, Philip Edwin 1916-1964 *NatCAB 52*
Ohmer, Charles Thomas 1857-1942 *NatCAB 32*
Ohmer, John Francis 1856-1938 *NatCAB 33*
Ohmer, John Francis, Jr. 1891-1950 *NatCAB 37*
Ohrbach, Nathan M 1885-1972 *WhAm 5*
Ohrn, Arnold Theodore 1889-1963 *WhAm 4*
Ohrstrom, George Lewis 1894-1955 *NatCAB 46, WhAm 3*
Oiouhaton, Teresa 1627- *ApCAB*
Oistrakh, David 1908-1974 *WhAm 6*
Oivermore, Thomas Leonard d1918 *WhAm 1*
Ojeda, Alonso d1550? *ApCAB*
Ojeda, Alonso De 1465-1515 *ApCAB*
Ojeda, Alonzo De 1465?- *Drake*
Ojeda, Diego De 1560-1619 *ApCAB*
Ojeda, Emilio De *WhAm 5*
Ojemann, Ralph Henry 1901-1975 *WhAm 6*
Okakura, Kakuzo 1862-1913 *WhAm 1*
O'Kane, Michael Aloysius 1849- *TwCBDA*
O'Kane, Walter Collins 1877- *WhAm 5*
O'Keefe, Abbie Mabel 1881- *WhAm 6*
O'Keefe, Anna *WhAm 5*
O'Keefe, Arthur Joseph 1876-1943 *WhAm 2*
O'Keefe, Dennis 1910-1968 *WhAm 5*
O'Keefe, Edward Scott 1886-1970 *NatCAB 57*
O'Keefe, Georgia 1887- *IIBEAAW*
O'Keefe, John Aloysius 1916- *AsBiEn*
O'Keefe, Richard Bernard 1914-1973 *WhAm 6*
O'Keefe, William Joseph 1889-1967 *NatCAB 54*
O'Keeffe, Arthur 1899-1948 *WhAm 2*
O'Keeffe, Georgia 1887- *BnEnAmA, EncAB, McGEWB, WebAB*
O'Keeffe, John 1847-1923 *NatCAB 6*
O'Keeffe, Katharine A *AmWom*
O'Keeffe, Mary Catherine *NewYHSD*
O'Kelley, Thomas Washington 1861-1927 *WhAm 1*

O'Kelly, Cadd Grant 1865- *WhoColR*
O'Kelly, James 1735?-1826 *ApCAB, DcAmB, DcAmReB, NatCAB 13, TwCBDA, WhAm H*
O'Kelly, Richard Mary 1915-1975 *WhAm 6*
O'Kelly, Sean Thomas 1882-1966 *WhAm 4*
Okely, John 1721-1792 *NatCAB 8*
Okemos 1780?-1886 *ApCAB*
Oken, Lorenz 1779-1851 *AsBiEn, DcScB*
Okeson, Walter Raleigh 1875-1943 *NatCAB 33*
Okey, John Waterman 1827-1885 *DcAmB, NatCAB 12, WhAm H*
Okey, Samuel *NewYHSD*
Okie, John Brognard 1864- *NatCAB 17*
Okie, R Brognard 1875-1945 *WhAm 2*
Okkelberg, Peter Olaus 1880-1960 *NatCAB 48, WhAm 6*
Oko, Adolph Sigmund 1883-1944 *NatCAB 33*
O'Konski, Alvin Edward 1904- *BiDrAC*
Oku, Yasukata 1846-1930 *WhoMilH*
Okubo, Toshimichi 1830-1878 *McGEWB*
Okuma, Shigenobu 1838-1922 *McGEWB*
Olaf II Haroldsson 990?-1030 *McGEWB*
Olafsson, Olaf J 1882-1957 *NatCAB 47*
Oland, Charles *NewYHSD*
Olander, Milton M F 1899-1961 *NatCAB 51*
Olander, Victor A 1873-1949 *WhAm 2*
Olaneta, Pedro Antonio De 1770?-1825 *ApCAB*
O'Laughlin, John Callan 1873-1949 *WhAm 2*
O'Laughlin, Mabel Hudson 1876- *WomWWA 14*
Olaus Magnus 1490-1557 *DcScB*
Olavide, Pablo Antonio Jose 1725-1803 *ApCAB*
Olaya, Enrique 1882-1937 *WhAm 1*
Olberg, Charles Real 1875-1938 *NatCAB 28*
Olbers, Heinrich Wilhelm Matthaus 1758-1840 *AsBiEn*
Olbers, Heinrich Wilhelm Matthias 1758-1840 *DcScB*
Olbrich, Michael B 1881-1929 *WhAm 1*
Olbricht, Friedrich 1886-1944 *WhWW-II*
Olcott, Alfred VanSantvoord 1886-1961 *NatCAB 46*
Olcott, Ben Wilson 1872-1952 *NatCAB 40, WhAm 5*
Olcott, Chancellor John 1859-1932 *NatCAB 11*
Olcott, Chancellor John 1860-1932 *DcAmB*
Olcott, Charles Sumner 1864-1935 *WhAm 1*
Olcott, Chauncey 1860-1932 *AmBi, DcAmB, WhAm 1*
Olcott, Eben Erskine 1854-1929 *ApCAB X, DcAmB, NatCAB 5, WhAm 1*
Olcott, Frances Jenkins 1872-1963 *DcAmLiB*
Olcott, Frederic P 1841-1909 *WhAm 1*
Olcott, George N 1869-1912 *NatCAB 16, WhAm 1*
Olcott, Henry Steel 1832-1907 *AmBi, DcAmB, DcAmReB, NatCAB 8, WhAm 1*
Olcott, Hiram Wallace 1842-1933 *NatCAB 25*
Olcott, Jacob VanVechten 1856-1940 *BiDrAC, NatCAB 14, WhAm 1*
Olcott, Ralph Thrall 1861-1932 *NatCAB 25*
Olcott, Richard Morgan 1861- *NatCAB 14*
Olcott, Simeon 1735-1815 *ApCAB, BiDrAC, NatCAB 1, TwCBDA, WhAm H*
Olcott, Simeon 1737-1815 *BiAUS, Drake*
Olcott, Thomas Worth 1795-1880 *NatCAB 18*
Olcott, William James 1862- *WhAm 4*
Olcott, William Morrow Knox 1862-1933 *WhAm 1*
Olcott, William Tyler 1873-1936 *WhAm 1*
Old, Francis Paxton 1897-1963 *WhAm 4*
Old, Howard Norman 1890-1953 *WhAm 3*
Old, William D 1901-1965 *WhAm 4*
Old Hickory *EncAAH*
Old Rough And Ready *EncAAH*
Old Stager *WebAB*
Oldacre, William Albert 1932- *WhAm 6*
Oldberg, Arne 1874-1962 *NatCAB 46, WhAm 4*
Oldberg, Oscar 1846-1913 *BiDAmEd, WhAm 1*
Oldberg, Oscar 1846-1923 *NatCAB 20*
Olden, Charles C 1797- *BiAUS*
Olden, Charles Smith 1799-1876 *ApCAB, DcAmB, NatCAB 5, TwCBDA, WhAm H*
Olden, Harry Louis 1881-1965 *NatCAB 50*

Oldenbarnevelt, Johan Van 1547-1619 *McGEWB*
Oldenburg, Claes Thure 1929- *BnEnAmA, WebAB*
Oldenburg, Henry 1618?-1677 *DcScB*
Oldendorf, Jesse *WhWW-II*
Oldendorp, Christian Georg Andreas 1721-1787 *ApCAB*
Older, Clifford 1876-1943 *NatCAB 32, WhAm 2*
Older, Cora Miranda *WhAm 5, WomWWA 14*
Older, Fremont 1856-1935 *AmBi, DcAmB, WhAm 1, WhAmP*
Oldfather, William Abbott 1880-1945 *DcAmB S3, NatCAB 35, WhAm 2*
Oldfield, Barney 1878-1946 *WebAB*
Oldfield, Berna Eli 1878-1946 *DcAmB S4*
Oldfield, Pearl Peden 1876-1962 *BiDrAC, WhAmP*
Oldfield, William Allan 1874-1928 *BiDrAC, WhAm 1, WhAmP*
Oldfield, William Allen 1874-1928 *NatCAB 21*
Oldham, Francis Fox 1849-1912 *NatCAB 45*
Oldham, G Ashton 1877-1963 *NatCAB 50, WhAm 4*
Oldham, John 1600?-1636 *AmBi, ApCAB, DcAmB, Drake, WhAm H*
Oldham, Lemuel E 1870- *WhAm 5*
Oldham, Marie Augusta 1857- *AmWom*
Oldham, Richard Dixon 1858-1936 *DcScB*
Oldham, Robert Pollard 1877-1941 *WhAm 2*
Oldham, Thomas 1816-1878 *DcScB*
Oldham, William 1745?-1791 *ApCAB, Drake*
Oldham, William Fitzjames 1854-1937 *DcAmB S2, NatCAB 14, WhAm 1*
Oldham, William K 1865-1938 *WhAm 1*
Oldham, Williamson Simpson 1813-1868 *BiDConf, DcAmB, TwCBDA, WhAm H*
Oldknow, Oscar Stuart 1899-1951 *NatCAB 40*
Oldmixon, John 1673-1742 *ApCAB, Drake*
Oldmixon, Mary d1835 *Drake*
Oldroyd, Tom Shaw 1853-1932 *NatCAB 24*
Olds, Edson B d1869 *BiAUS*
Olds, Edson Baldwin 1802-1869 *BiDrAC, WhAm H, WhAmP*
Olds, Edson Baldwin 1819-1869 *NatCAB 6, TwCBDA*
Olds, Edwin Glenn 1898-1961 *WhAm 4*
Olds, Emil 1914-1964 *NatCAB 50*
Olds, Gamaliel Smith 1777-1848 *ApCAB, Drake, TwCBDA*
Olds, George 1832- *WhAm 4*
Olds, George Daniel 1853-1931 *NatCAB 24, WhAm 1*
Olds, Henry Worthington 1859-1925 *NatCAB 32*
Olds, Inez Edna 1884- *WomWWA 14*
Olds, Irving S 1887-1963 *WhAm 4*
Olds, Leland 1890-1960 *WhAm 4*
Olds, Mary Augusta Johnson 1862- *WomWWA 14*
Olds, Ransom Eli 1864-1950 *DcAmB S4, NatCAB 39, WebAB*
Olds, Ransom Ell 1864-1950 *WhAm 3*
Olds, Robert 1896-1943 *WhAm 2*
Olds, Robert Edwin 1875-1932 *DcAmB S1, WhAm 1*
Olds, Schuyler Seager 1847-1920 *NatCAB 19*
Olds, Thomas Hartman 1883-1932 *NatCAB 24*
Olds, Walter 1846-1925 *WhAm 1*
Olds, William Benjamin 1874-1948 *NatCAB 35*
Olds, William Henry 1886-1957 *NatCAB 47*
Oldschool, Oliver *WebAB*
Oldschool, Oliver 1794-1875 *DcAmB, WhAm H*
O'Leary, Cornelius M 1840?- *ApCAB, WhAm 1*
O'Leary, Daniel 1846?-1933 *DcAmB S1, WhAm HA, WhAm 4*
O'Leary, Denis 1863-1943 *BiDrAC, WhAm 4*
O'Leary, Edmund Bernard 1900-1968 *NatCAB 54, WhAm 4A*
O'Leary, James Aloysius 1889-1944 *BiDrAC, WhAm 2, WhAmP*
O'Leary, James Lee 1904-1975 *WhAm 6*
O'Leary, John William 1875-1946 *WhAm 2*
O'Leary, Paul Arthur 1891-1955 *NatCAB 46, WhAm 3*

O'Leary, Thomas Lawrence 1885-1964
NatCAB 53
O'Leary, Thomas Mary 1875-1949 NatCAB 40,
WhAm 2
O'Leary, Wesley A 1873-1937 WhAm 1
O'Leary, William Doris 1895-1955 WhAm 3
Olen, Walter A 1875- WhAm 5
Olena, Alfred Douglas 1886-1949 NatCAB 38
Oler, Wesley Marion 1856- WhAm 1
Olesha, Yuri Karlovich 1899-1960 WhAm 4
Oleson, John Prince 1873-1952 WhAm 3
Oleson, Mary Zabriskie 1886- WomWWA 14
Oleson, Wilhelmina Geis 1869- WomWWA 14
Olid, Christoval De 1492?-1524 Drake
Olid, Cristobal De 1492-1542 ApCAB
Olier DeVerneuil, Jean Jacques 1608-1657
ApCAB
Olin, Abraham Baldwin 1812-1879 BiAUS,
NatCAB 4, TwCBDA
Olin, Abram Baldwin 1808-1879 ApCAB,
BiDrAC, WhAm H
Olin, Arvin Solomon 1855-1935 WhAm 1
Olin, Franklin Walter 1860-1951 NatCAB 41,
WhAm 3
Olin, Gideon d1822 BiAUS
Olin, Gideon 1743-1822 NatCAB 11
Olin, Gideon 1743-1823 BiDrAC, TwCBDA,
WhAm H
Olin, Gideon 1750?-1822 ApCAB
Olin, Helen Remington 1854- WomWWA 14
Olin, Henry d1837 BiAUS, Drake
Olin, Henry 1767-1837 ApCAB
Olin, Henry 1768-1837 BiDrAC, NatCAB 4,
TwCBDA, WhAm H
Olin, Hubert Leonard 1880-1964 WhAm 4
Olin, John Myers 1851-1924 WhAm 1
Olin, Julia Matilda 1814-1879 ApCAB,
TwCBDA
Olin, Richard M 1875-1938 WhAm 1
Olin, Stephen 1791-1851 NatCAB 9
Olin, Stephen 1797-1851 ApCAB, BiDAmEd,
DcAmB, Drake, TwCBDA, WhAm H
Olin, Stephen Henry 1847-1925 WhAm 1
Olin, Walter Herbert 1862-1933 WhAm 1
Olin, William Milo 1845-1911 WhAm 1
Olinda, Pedro DeAranjo Lima 1790-1870 Drake
Olinda, Pedro DeAraujo Lima 1793-1870
ApCAB
Olinger, Henri Cesar 1887-1963 WhAm 4
O'Linn, Frances Maria Brainard 1848-
WomWWA 14
Olinsky, Ivan Gregorewitch 1878-1962 WhAm 4
Oliphant, A Dayton 1887-1963 NatCAB 48,
WhAm 4
Oliphant, Charles Lawrence 1889-1970
WhAm 5
Oliphant, David, Jr. NewYHSD
Oliphant, E P BiAUS
Oliphant, Ernest Henry Clark 1862- WhAm 4
Oliphant, Harold Duncan 1882-1970 WhAm 5
Oliphant, Herman 1884-1939 DcAmB S2,
WhAm 1
Oliphant, James Orin 1894- EncAAH
Oliphant, Laurence 1829-1888 ApCAB,
NatCAB 6
Oliphant, Marcus Laurence Elwin 1901- AsBiEn
Oliphant, Nelson Bowman 1857- NatCAB 7
Olitski, Jules 1922- BnEnAmA
Olitsky, Peter Kosciusko 1886-1964 WhAm 4
Oliva, Anello 1593-1642 ApCAB
Olivares, Jose De 1867- WhAm 5
Olivares, Miguel De 1675-1768? ApCAB
Olive, Charles 1630?-1673 ApCAB
Olive, Edgar William 1870- WhAm 5
Olive, George Scott 1881-1962 NatCAB 50,
WhAm 4
Olive, John Ritter 1916-1974 WhAm 6
Olive, Print 1840-1886 REnAW
Oliveira, Candido Baptista De 1801-1865
ApCAB
Oliveira, Manoel Antonio Vital De 1829-1867
ApCAB
Oliveira, Manoel Botelho De 1636-1711 ApCAB
Oliveira, Nathan 1928- BnEnAmA
Oliver, Addison 1833- BiAUS
Oliver, Allen Laws 1886-1970 WhAm 5
Oliver, Andrew 1706-1774 AmBi, ApCAB,
DcAmB, Drake, NatCAB 7, WhAm H

Oliver, Andrew 1731-1799 ApCAB, DcAmB,
Drake, WhAm H
Oliver, Andrew 1815-1889 BiDrAC, TwCBDA,
WhAm H
Oliver, Andrew 1819- BiAUS
Oliver, Andrew 1824- ApCAB
Oliver, Arthur L 1879-1928 WhAm 1
Oliver, Augustus Kountze 1881-1954 WhAm 3
Oliver, Belle Chone WomWWA 14
Oliver, Benjamin Lynde 1788-1843 ApCAB,
Drake
Oliver, Charles Augustus 1853-1911 DcAmB,
WhAm 1
Oliver, Daniel 1787-1842 ApCAB, Drake,
NatCAB 9
Oliver, Daniel Charles 1865-1924 BiDrAC,
WhAm 1
Oliver, David Brown 1834-1934 NatCAB 51
Oliver, Doc Berry 1867-1951 NatCAB 42
Oliver, Edd Charles 1873-1946 NatCAB 37
Oliver, Edna May 1883-1942 WhAm 2
Oliver, Edward Allen 1883-1957 NatCAB 46,
WhAm 3
Oliver, Edwin Austin 1855-1924 WhAm 1
Oliver, Edwin Letts 1878-1955 NatCAB 43,
WhAm 3, WhAm 4
Oliver, Emma Sophia 1819-1885 NewYHSD
Oliver, Etta A 1859- WomWWA 14
Oliver, Fitch Edward 1819-1892 ApCAB,
DcAmB, NatCAB 25, WhAm H
Oliver, Frank 1883-1968 BiDrAC
Oliver, George NewYHSD
Oliver, George 1841-1915 BiHiMed, DcScB
Oliver, George Jeffries 1898-1973 WhAm 6
Oliver, George Melville 1878- WhoColR
Oliver, George Sturges 1878-1963 NatCAB 52,
WhAm 4
Oliver, George Tener 1848-1919 BiDrAC,
DcAmB, NatCAB 7, NatCAB 22,
WhAm 1
Oliver, Grace Atkinson 1844-1899 AmWom,
ApCAB, TwCBDA, WhAm 1
Oliver, Henry 1836?- NewYHSD
Oliver, Henry Kemble 1800-1885 AmBi,
ApCAB, DcAmB, NatCAB 13, TwCBDA,
WhAm H
Oliver, Henry Kemble 1829-1919 NatCAB 19
Oliver, Henry Madison, Jr. 1912-1970 WhAm 5
Oliver, Henry William 1840-1904 ApCAB X,
DcAmB, NatCAB 22, WhAm 1
Oliver, James 1823-1908 ApCAB X, DcAmB,
McGEWB, NatCAB 12, WhAm 1
Oliver, James Brown 1844-1905 NatCAB 16
Oliver, James Churchill 1895- BiDrAC
Oliver, James Edward 1829-1895 ApCAB,
NatCAB 14
Oliver, James Harrison 1857-1928 WhAm 1
Oliver, Jean Nutting WomWWA 14
Oliver, John 1807?- NewYHSD
Oliver, John Chadwick 1862-1946 NatCAB 35,
WhAm 4
Oliver, John Harvey 1870-1940 NatCAB 41
Oliver, John Morrison 1827-1872 ApCAB
Oliver, John Morrison 1828-1872 TwCBDA
Oliver, John Rathbone 1872-1943 WhAm 2
Oliver, Joseph 1885?-1938 DcAmB S2,
WebAB, WhAm HA, WhAm 4
Oliver, Joseph Doty 1850-1933 ApCAB X,
WhAm 1
Oliver, Joseph Whipple 1864-1936 NatCAB 36
Oliver, L NewYHSD
Oliver, L Stauffer 1879-1966 WhAm 4
Oliver, Marion WomWWA 14
Oliver, Martha Capps 1845- AmWom,
WhAm 1, WomWWA 14
Oliver, Mordecai 1819-1898 BiAUS, BiDrAC
Oliver, Oren Austin 1887-1965 NatCAB 52
Oliver, Paul Ambrose 1830-1912 ApCAB,
DcAmB
Oliver, Paul Ambrose 1831-1912 NatCAB 5,
WhAm 1
Oliver, Peter 1713-1791 AmBi, ApCAB,
DcAmB, Drake, NatCAB 4, TwCBDA,
WhAm H
Oliver, Peter 1741-1822 ApCAB
Oliver, Peter 1821-1855 Drake
Oliver, Peter 1822-1855 ApCAB
Oliver, Ralph Addison 1886-1968 NatCAB 55

Oliver, Robert 1738-1810 ApCAB, BiAUS,
Drake
Oliver, Robert Shaw 1847-1935 WhAm 1
Oliver, Robert W 1815-1899 TwCBDA
Oliver, Robin NewYHSD
Oliver, Samuel Addison 1833-1912 BiDrAC
Oliver, Temple WomWWA 14
Oliver, Thomas 1734-1815 ApCAB, Drake
Oliver, Thomas Edward 1871-1946 WhAm 2
Oliver, Wade Wright 1890-1964 NatCAB 53
Oliver, Webster J 1888-1969 WhAm 5
Oliver, William NewYHSD
Oliver, William Bacon 1867-1948 BiDrAC,
WhAm 4, WhAmP
Oliver, William Burns 1911-1974 WhAm 6
Oliver, William F 1914-1971 WhAm 5
Oliver, William J 1867-1925 NatCAB 20
Oliver, William Morrison 1792-1863 BiAUS,
BiDrAC, WhAm H
Oliver, William Sandford 1748-1813 ApCAB
Olivetti, Adriano 1901-1960 WhAm 4
Olivier, Charles Pollard 1884-1975 WhAm 6
Olivier, Stuart 1880- WhAm 6
Ollantai ApCAB
Ollendorp, Christian George Andreas 1721-1787
NatCAB 2
Ollenhauer, Erich 1901-1963 WhAm 4
Ollesheimer, Henry 1856-1933 WhAm 1
Olliffe, Lewis William 1904-1966 NatCAB 52
Ollmann, Loyal Frank 1905-1966 WhAm 4
Olmedo, Jose Joaquin 1781-1847 ApCAB
Olmos, Francisco Andres De d1571 ApCAB
Olmstead, Albert TenEyck 1880-1945
DcAmB S3, WhAm 2
Olmstead, Frank Robert 1904-1958 WhAm 3
Olmstead, James Munson 1794-1870 ApCAB,
Drake
Olmstead, John A NewYHSD
Olmstead, John Wesley 1816-1891 ApCAB,
NatCAB 1, TwCBDA
Olmsted, Alexander Fisher 1822-1853 ApCAB
Olmsted, Allen Seymour 1856-1942 NatCAB 33
Olmsted, C Henry 1873-1955 NatCAB 47
Olmsted, Charles Sanford 1853-1918
NatCAB 12, TwCBDA, WhAm 1
Olmsted, Charles Tyler 1842-1924 NatCAB 13,
TwCBDA, WhAm 1
Olmsted, Denison 1791-1859 AmBi, ApCAB,
BiDAmEd, DcAmB, Drake, NatCAB 8,
TwCBDA, WhAm H
Olmsted, E Stanley 1877- WhAm 5
Olmsted, Elizabeth Martha 1825- AmWom
Olmsted, Elmer Devando 1848-1918 NatCAB 8
Olmsted, Everett Ward 1869-1943 WhAm 2
Olmsted, Francis Allyn 1819-1844 ApCAB,
Drake
Olmsted, Frederick Law 1822-1903 AmBi,
ApCAB, BnEnAmA, DcAmB, Drake,
EncAAH, EncAB, McGEWB, NatCAB 2,
REnAW, TwCBDA, WebAB, WhAm 1
Olmsted, Frederick Law 1870-1957 WhAm 3
Olmsted, George Henry 1843- NatCAB 16
Olmsted, George Welch 1874-1940 NatCAB 30,
WhAm 1
Olmsted, Gideon 1749-1845 DcAmB,
WhAm H
Olmsted, Harry Aborn 1873-1941 NatCAB 31
Olmsted, James Frederic 1859-1914 WhAm 1
Olmsted, James Greeley 1857-1937 WhAm 1
Olmsted, James Montrose Duncan 1886-1956
NatCAB 43, WhAm 3
Olmsted, John Bartow 1854- WhAm 4
Olmsted, John Charles 1852-1920 ApCAB X,
DcAmB, NatCAB 13, TwCBDA,
WhAm 1
Olmsted, Marguerite Prescott 1880-
WomWWA 14
Olmsted, Marlin Edgar d1913 TwCBDA,
WhAm 1
Olmsted, Marlin Edgar 1847-1913 BiDrAC,
DcAmB, NatCAB 8, WhAmP
Olmsted, Marlin Edgar 1853-1913 ApCAB Sup
Olmsted, Millicent d1939 WhAm 1,
WomWWA 14
Olmsted, Robert Ward 1868-1958 NatCAB 44
Olmsted, Victor Hugo 1853- WhAm 4
Olmsted, William Beach 1864-1929 NatCAB 26,
WhAm 1

Olney, Albert J 1888-1958 *WhAm 3*
Olney, Charles Fayette 1831-1903 *NatCAB 6*
Olney, Cyrus *BiAUS*
Olney, Edward 1827-1887 *ApCAB, TwCBDA*
Olney, Elizabeth Williams 1868-
　WomWWA 14
Olney, George Washington 1835-1916 *TwCBDA,*
　WhAm 1
Olney, James P 1856-1928 *NatCAB 22*
Olney, Jeremiah 1750-1812 *ApCAB, Drake*
Olney, Jesse 1798-1872 *AmBi, ApCAB,*
　BiDAmEd, DcAmB, WhAm H
Olney, Louis Atwell 1874-1949 *NatCAB 38,*
　WhAm 2
Olney, Peter Butler 1843-1922 *WhAm 1*
Olney, Richard 1835-1917 *AmBi, ApCAB Sup,*
　ApCAB X, BiDrUSE, DcAmB, EncAB,
　McGEWB, NatCAB 7, TwCBDA,
　WebAB, WhAm 1
Olney, Richard 1871-1939 *BiDrAC, WhAm 1*
Olney, Stephen 1755-1832 *ApCAB, Drake,*
　NatCAB 8
Olney, Stephen Thayer 1812-1878 *NatCAB 13*
Olney, Warren 1841-1921 *WhAm 1*
Olney, Warren, Jr. 1870-1939 *NatCAB 28,*
　WhAm 1
Olotoraca 1548-1573 *ApCAB*
O'Loughlin, John M 1895-1964 *WhAm 5*
O'Loughlin, Kathryn Ellen 1894-1952 *BiDrAC*
Olp, Ernest Everett 1874-1928 *WhAm 1*
Olpp, Archibald Ernest 1882-1949 *BiDrAC*
Olrich, Ernest Louis 1889-1962 *WhAm 4*
Olsen, Arnold 1916- *BiDrAC*
Olsen, Clarence Edward 1899-1971 *NatCAB 57,*
　WhAm 5
Olsen, Forrest Bernell 1887-1966 *NatCAB 53*
Olsen, Herb 1905-1973 *WhAm 6*
Olsen, Herluf Vagn 1899-1966 *WhAm 4*
Olsen, Ingerval M 1861- *WhAm 4*
Olsen, John Charles 1869-1948 *WhAm 2*
Olsen, Julius 1873-1942 *WhAm 2*
Olsen, Leif Ericson 1892-1962 *WhAm 4*
Olsen, Nils Andreas 1886-1940 *WhAm 1*
Olsen, Sigurd 1883-1958 *NatCAB 47*
Olsen, Thomas Siegfried 1884-1956 *WhAm 3*
Olsen, Tinius 1845-1932 *NatCAB 23*
Olsen, William Anderson 1896-1974 *WhAm 6*
Olson, A Warren 1923-1963 *NatCAB 50*
Olson, Albert Eric 1896-1965 *NatCAB 51*
Olson, Alec Gehard 1930- *BiDrAC*
Olson, Axel Ragnar 1889-1954 *NatCAB 43,*
　WhAm 3
Olson, Carl Theodore 1893-1960 *NatCAB 49*
Olson, Carl Walter 1898-1953 *WhAm 3*
Olson, Charles 1910-1970 *WhAm 5*
Olson, Chresten 1876-1926 *NatCAB 20*
Olson, Culbert L 1876-1962 *WhAm 4*
Olson, Edwin August 1868-1947 *WhAm 2*
Olson, Ernest Sivereen 1901-1972 *NatCAB 56*
Olson, Ernst William 1870-1958 *WhAm 3*
Olson, Floyd Bjerstjerne 1891-1936 *AmBi,*
　DcAmB S2, EncAAH, WhAm 1,
　WhAmP
Olson, Floyd Bjornstjerne 1891-1936
　NatCAB 33
Olson, George Edgar 1891-1946 *WhAm 2*
Olson, Grant Franklin 1905-1954 *WhAm 3*
Olson, Harry 1867-1935 *WhAm 1*
Olson, Henry 1893-1963 *WhAm 4*
Olson, Henry Edwin 1894-1966 *WhAm 4*
Olson, J Olaf 1894- *IIBEAAW*
Olson, James Edward 1914-1968 *WhAm 5*
Olson, John Frederick 1919-1969 *WhAm 5*
Olson, Julius Emil 1858- *WhAm 4*
Olson, Julius Johann 1875- *WhAm 5*
Olson, Kenneth Eugene 1895-1967 *WhAm 4*
Olson, Merle 1910- *IIBEAAW*
Olson, Norman O d1974 *WhAm 6*
Olson, Oscar Ludvig 1872-1956 *WhAm 3*
Olson, Oscar Thomas 1887-1964 *WhAm 4*
Olson, Oscar William 1889-1959 *WhAm 3*
Olson, Ralph J 1904-1969 *WhAm 5*
Olson, Ralph O 1902-1955 *WhAm 3*
Olson, Raymond 1904-1974 *WhAm 6*
Olson, Raymond Ferdinand 1891-1965 *WhAm 4*
Olson, Roy Howard 1896-1974 *WhAm 6*
Olssen, William Whittingham 1827- *ApCAB,*
　NatCAB 10, TwCBDA, WhAm 4

Olsson, Alexander 1868-1952 *WhAm 3*
Olsson, Carl Arne 1916-1961 *NatCAB 49*
Olsson, Elis 1880-1959 *NatCAB 49, WhAm 3*
Olsson, Olof 1841-1900 *ApCAB, TwCBDA,*
　WhAm 1
Olstad, Einar Hanson 1876- *IIBEAAW*
Olston, Albert B 1868- *WhAm 4*
Olszewski, Karol Stanislaw 1846-1915 *DcScB*
Olt, George Russell 1895-1958 *WhAm 3*
Olufsen, Christian Friis Rottboll 1802-1855
　DcScB
Olympio, Sylvanus E 1902-1963 *McGEWB*
Olympiodorus 360?-425? *DcScB*
Olyphant, David Washington Cincinnatus
　1789-1851 *DcAmB, WhAm H*
Olyphant, John Kensett, Jr. 1895-1973 *WhAm 6*
Olyphant, Robert 1853-1928 *WhAm 1*
Olyphant, Robert Morrison 1824-1917 *WhAm 1*
Olyphant, Robert Morrison 1824-1918 *DcAmB*
O'Mahoney, Joseph Christopher 1884-1962
　BiDrAC, NatCAB 52, REnAW, WhAm 4
O'Mahoney, Joseph Michael 1884-1959
　WhAm 4
O'Mahoney, Katharine A O'Keeffe
　WomWWA 14
O'Mahony, John Francis 1816-1877 *AmBi,*
　ApCAB, DcAmB, WhAm H
Omalius D'Halloy, Jean Baptiste J D' 1783-1875
　DcScB
O'Malley, Austin 1858-1932 *NatCAB 23,*
　WhAm 1
O'Malley, Charles P 1870- *WhAm 5*
O'Malley, Edward Lawrence 1873-1947
　NatCAB 40
O'Malley, Francis Joseph 1911-1974 *WhAm 6*
O'Malley, Frank Charles 1883-1941
　NatCAB 31
O'Malley, Frank Ward 1875-1932 *AmBi,*
　DcAmB, WhAm 1
O'Malley, Henry 1876-1936 *WhAm 1*
O'Malley, James *NewYHSD*
O'Malley, John Francis 1911-1971 *WhAm 5*
O'Malley, John Gerald 1877-1958 *NatCAB 47*
O'Malley, Joseph Edward 1923-1973 *WhAm 6*
O'Malley, Matthew Vincent 1878-1931 *BiDrAC*
O'Malley, Thomas David Patrick 1903- *BiDrAC*
O'Malley, Thomas F 1872- *WhAm 5*
Oman, Charles Malden 1878-1948 *WhAm 2*
Oman, James *NewYHSD*
Oman, Joseph Wallace 1864-1941 *WhAm 1*
Oman, Samuel Solon 1897-1943 *NatCAB 32*
Omar d1817 *WhAm H*
Omar Ibn Al-Khattab d644 *McGEWB*
Omar Ibn Said Tal, Al-Hajj 1797?-1864
　McGEWB
Omar Khayyam *DcScB*
Omar Khayyam 1048-1132? *McGEWB*
Omar Khayyam 1050?-1123? *AsBiEn*
Omar Pasha 1806-1871 *WhoMilH*
O'Mara, Daniel James 1893-1973 *NatCAB 56*
O'Marr, Louis John 1882-1966 *NatCAB 53*
O'Mealia, E Leo 1884-1960 *WhAm 4*
O'Meara, James *NewYHSD*
O'Meara, John William 1892-1966 *NatCAB 52*
O'Meara, Mark 1874-1937 *NatCAB 28,*
　WhAm 1, WhAm 1C
O'Meara, Patrick *NewYHSD*
O'Meara, Stephen 1854-1918 *TwCBDA,*
　WhAm 1
O'Melia, Albert Joseph 1889-1964 *NatCAB 54*
O'Melveny, Henry William 1859-1941
　NatCAB 44, WhAm 1
Omori, Fusakichi 1868-1923 *DcScB*
O'Mullin, William *NewYHSD*
Omwake, George L 1871-1937 *WhAm 1*
Omwake, Howard Rufus 1878-1942 *WhAm 2*
Omwake, John d1939 *WhAm 1*
Ona, Pedro De 1560?-1620? *ApCAB*
Onahan, William James d1919 *WhAm 1*
Onan, David Warren 1886-1958 *WhAm 3*
Onassis, Aristotle Socrates 1906-1975 *WhAm 6*
Onate, Juan De *WhAm H*
Onate, Juan De 1549?-1624? *DcAmB,*
　McGEWB, REnAW
Onate, Juan De 1550?-1625? *WebAB*
Onate, Juan De 1555?-1615? *AmBi*
Onckelbag, Gerrit 1670-1732 *BnEnAmA*
Ondegardo, Polo 1500?-1570? *ApCAB*

Onderdonk, Adrian Holmes 1877- *WhAm 5*
Onderdonk, Benjamin Treadwell 1791-1861
　Drake, NatCAB 1
Onderdonk, Benjamin Tredwell 1791-1861
　ApCAB, DcAmB, TwCBDA, WhAm H
Onderdonk, Frank Scovill 1871-1936 *WhAm 1*
Onderdonk, Gilbert 1829- *WhAm 4*
Onderdonk, Henry 1804-1886 *ApCAB, DcAmB,*
　Drake, TwCBDA, WhAm H
Onderdonk, Henry Ustic 1789-1858 *Drake*
Onderdonk, Henry Ustick 1789-1858 *ApCAB,*
　DcAmB, NatCAB 3, TwCBDA,
　WhAm H
Onderdonk, Julian 1882-1922 *IIBEAAW*
Onderdonk, Robert Jenkins 1852-1917
　IIBEAAW
Ondrak, Ambrose Leo 1892-1961 *WhAm 4*
O'Neal, Annie Todd *WhoColR*
Oneal, Ben Grady 1874-1960 *NatCAB 44*
O'Neal, Charles Thomas 1873-1950 *NatCAB 39,*
　WhAm 3
O'Neal, Claude E 1884-1971 *WhAm 5*
O'Neal, Edward Asbury 1818-1890 *DcAmB,*
　NatCAB 10, TwCBDA
O'Neal, Edward Asbury 1875-1958 *EncAAH,*
　NatCAB 52, WhAm 3
O'Neal, Edward Ashbury 1818-1890 *BiDConf,*
　WhAm H
O'Neal, Emmet 1853-1922 *NatCAB 15,*
　WhAm 1
O'Neal, Emmet 1887-1967 *BiDrAC,*
　NatCAB 54, WhAm 4
O'Neal, James *NewYHSD*
O'Neal, James 1875- *WhAm 5*
O'Neal, John Belton 1793- *BiAUS*
O'Neal, Maston Emmett, Jr. 1907- *BiDrAC*
O'Neal, Samuel Amos 1899-1956 *WhAm 3*
O'Neal, Samuel Andrew 1865- *WhoColR*
O'Neal, William Russell 1864-1946 *WhAm 2*
O'Neale, Margaret L 1796-1879 *AmBi,*
　DcAmB, WhAm H, WhAmP
O'Neale, Margaret L *see also* O'Neill, Margaret
　L
O'Neale, Peggy *NotAW, WebAB*
O'Neall, John Belton 1793-1863 *ApCAB,*
　DcAmB, Drake, NatCAB 6, TwCBDA,
　WhAm H
O'Neall, John Henry 1837-1907 *TwCBDA*
O'Neall, John Henry 1838-1907 *BiDrAC*
O'Neel, Albert C 1865-1943 *NatCAB 42*
O'Neel, John *NewYHSD*
O'Neil *NewYHSD*
O'Neil, Arthur Samuel 1879-1926 *NatCAB 20*
O'Neil, Barbara Blackman 1880-
　WomWWA 14
O'Neil, Charles 1842-1927 *ApCAB Sup,*
　NatCAB 24, TwCBDA, WhAm 1
O'Neil, Charles Edward 1892-1953 *NatCAB 47*
O'Neil, Daniel Edwin 1847-1925 *NatCAB 6*
O'Neil, Frank R 1851-1908 *WhAm 1*
O'Neil, George F 1863- *WhAm 5*
O'Neil, Hugh Roe 1909-1972 *WhAm 5*
O'Neil, James 1847-1920 *WhAm 1*
O'Neil, James *see also* O'Neill, James
O'Neil, James Charles 1884-1958 *NatCAB 46*
O'Neil, James Julian 1919-1974 *WhAm 6*
O'Neil, John 1849- *NatCAB 6*
O'Neil, John 1915- *IIBEAAW*
O'Neil, John Francis 1857-1926 *WhAm 1*
O'Neil, Joseph Henry 1853-1935 *BiDrAC,*
　TwCBDA, WhAm 1
O'Neil, Joseph Patrick 1863-1938 *NatCAB 29*
O'Neil, Lew Drew 1881- *WhAm 6*
O'Neil, Patrick Henry 1866- *WhAm 4*
O'Neil, Ralph Thomas 1888-1940 *WhAm 1*
O'Neil, William *NewYHSD*
O'Neil, William A *NewYHSD*
O'Neil, William Francis 1885-1960 *NatCAB 46,*
　WhAm 4
O'Neil, William W *NewYHSD*
O'Neil, William Woods 1830-1902 *NatCAB 12*
O'Neill, Albert T 1885-1959 *WhAm 3*
O'Neill, Anne Wade *WomWWA 14*
O'Neill, Bernard Joseph 1876-1959 *NatCAB 39*
O'Neill, Buckey 1860-1898 *REnAW*
O'Neill, Burke 1897-1960 *WhAm 4*
O'Neill, Charles 1821-1893 *BiAUS, BiDrAC,*
　TwCBDA, WhAm H, WhAmP

O'Neill, Charles 1887-1949 *NatCAB 37,*
WhAm 2
O'Neill, Edmond 1859-1933 *WhAm 1*
O'Neill, Edward 1820-1890 *NatCAB 3*
O'Neill, Edward Emerson 1893-1951
NatCAB 39, WhAm 3
O'Neill, Edward Leo 1903-1948 *BiDrAC,*
WhAm 2
O'Neill, Eugene Gladstone 1888-1953
ApCAB X, DcAmB S5, EncAB,
McGEWB, NatCAB 55, WebAB,
WhAm 3
O'Neill, Eugene M 1850-1926 *NatCAB 5,*
WhAm 1
O'Neill, Florence 1868- *WhAm 4*
O'Neill, Francis Aloysius 1880-1941
NatCAB 33
O'Neill, Frank J 1876- *WhAm 5*
O'Neill, Grover 1890-1972 *NatCAB 57*
O'Neill, Harry P 1891-1953 *WhAm 3*
O'Neill, Harry Patrick 1889-1953 *BiDrAC*
O'Neill, Henry 1832-1918 *NatCAB 19*
O'Neill, Hugh 1882- *WhAm 1*
O'Neill, J Henry 1893-1965 *NatCAB 51,*
WhAm 4
O'Neill, James *NewYHSD*
O'Neill, James 1847-1920 *NatCAB 11*
O'Neill, James 1847-1929 *NatCAB 28*
O'Neill, James 1849-1920 *DcAmB*
O'Neill, James see also O'Neil, James
O'Neill, James Albert 1917-1973 *NatCAB 57,*
WhAm 6
O'Neill, James Lewis 1881-1945 *WhAm 2*
O'Neill, James Michael 1879-1941 *NatCAB 30*
O'Neill, James Milton 1881-1970 *WhAm 5*
O'Neill, John *NewYHSD*
O'Neill, John 1821-1905 *BiAUS*
O'Neill, John 1822-1905 *BiDrAC*
O'Neill, John 1834-1878 *ApCAB, DcAmB,*
WhAm H
O'Neill, John A *NewYHSD*
O'Neill, John Edward 1893-1961 *WhAm 4*
O'Neill, John J 1889-1953 *WhAm 3*
O'Neill, John Joseph 1846-1898 *BiDrAC,*
TwCBDA, WhAmP
O'Neill, John Vincent 1903-1968 *WhAm 4*
O'Neill, Laura Holtz *WomWWA 14*
O'Neill, Lewis Patrick 1905-1972 *NatCAB 57,*
WhAm 5
O'Neill, Margaret L 1796-1879 *DcAmB*
O'Neill, Patrick 1851-1919 *NatCAB 18*
O'Neill, Peggy *WebAB*
O'Neill, Robert J *NewYHSD*
O'Neill, Rose Cecil 1874-1944 *DcAmB S3,*
NotAW, WebAB
O'Neill, Susan Cecilia *WomWWA 14*
O'Neill, Thomas Phillip, Jr. 1912- *BiDrAC*
O'Neill DeTyrone, Arthur 1736-1814 *ApCAB*
Onen, Bernard James 1878-1939 *NatCAB 49*
Onesime, Charles Stanislas DeMontigny
1641-1699 *ApCAB*
Ong, Eugene Walter 1877- *ApCAB X*
O'Niell, Charles Austin 1869-1951 *NatCAB 42,*
WhAm 3
Onis, Luis De 1769-1830? *ApCAB*
Onishi, Takijiro *WhWW-II*
Onken, Otto 1815?- *NewYHSD*
Onken, William Henry, Jr. 1876- *WhAm 5*
Onnes, Heike Kamerlingh *DcScB*
Onsager, Lars 1903- *AsBiEn, WebAB*
Onthank, Nahum Ball 1823-1888 *NewYHSD*
Ontra, Buddy 1900-1960 *NatCAB 46*
Ooms, Casper W 1902-1961 *WhAm 4*
Oort, Jan Hendrik 1900- *AsBiEn, McGEWB*
Oort, Piet Van 1615?-1663 *ApCAB*
Oostermeyer, Jan 1897-1967 *WhAm 4*
Oosting, Henry J 1903-1968 *WhAm 5*
Oparin, Alexander Ivanovich 1894- *AsBiEn*
Opdale, Nellie Mann 1860- *WomWWA 14*
Opdycke, Emerson 1830-1884 *ApCAB,*
TwCBDA
Opdycke, John Baker d1956 *WhAm 3*
Opdycke, Leonard Eckstein 1858-1915
NatCAB 16, WhAm 1
Opdyke, George 1805-1880 *ApCAB, DcAmB,*
WhAm H
Opdyke, George 1807-1880 *NatCAB 11*
Opdyke, William Stryker 1836-1922 *WhAm 1*

Opechancanough 1545?-1644 *REnAW*
Openshaw, Clarence Roy 1885-1955
NatCAB 45
Operti, Albert 1852-1927 *WhAm 1*
Opheim, Leonard Bertinius 1901-1968 *WhAm 5*
Ophols, William 1871-1933 *WhAm 1*
Opie, Eugene Lindsay 1873-1971 *BiHiMed,*
NatCAB 57, WhAm 5
Opie, Hierome Lindsay 1880-1943 *NatCAB 33*
Opie, Thomas 1840?- *NatCAB 12*
Opie, Thomas 1842- *WhAm 4*
Opp, Frederick 1863-1916 *NatCAB 8*
Opp, Julie 1871-1921 *WhAm 1,*
WomWWA 14
Oppe, Charles 1885-1967 *NatCAB 53*
Oppel, Albert 1831-1865 *DcScB*
Oppelt, Wolfgang Walter 1933-1974 *WhAm 6*
Oppenheim, Adolf Leo 1904-1974 *WhAm 6*
Oppenheim, Amy Schwartz 1878-1955 *WhAm 3*
Oppenheim, Ansel 1847-1916 *NatCAB 8,*
WhAm 1
Oppenheim, E Phillips 1866-1946 *WhAm 2*
Oppenheim, James 1882-1932 *DcAmB,*
WhAm 1
Oppenheim, Josie Greve *WomWWA 14*
Oppenheim, Nathan 1865-1916 *WhAm 1*
Oppenheim, Samuel 1857-1928 *DcScB*
Oppenheim, Samuel 1859-1928 *WhAm 1*
Oppenheimer, Adele 1874- *WomWWA 14*
Oppenheimer, Arthur 1894-1959 *NatCAB 46*
Oppenheimer, Arthur Cleveland 1884-1950
NatCAB 42
Oppenheimer, Bernard Sutro 1876-1958
NatCAB 48
Oppenheimer, Carol Purse 1884- *WomWWA 14*
Oppenheimer, Edgar Davidson 1883-1946
NatCAB 33
Oppenheimer, Sir Ernest 1880-1957 *WhAm 3*
Oppenheimer, Sir Ernest 1901-1956 *WhAm 3*
Oppenheimer, Francis J 1881- *WhAm 6*
Oppenheimer, Fritz Ernest 1898-1968 *WhAm 5*
Oppenheimer, Henry 1865-1958 *NatCAB 48*
Oppenheimer, Henry Semon 1844- *NatCAB 2*
Oppenheimer, J Robert 1904-1967 *AsBiEn,*
BiDAmEd, DcScB, McGEWB, WebAB,
WhWW-II
Oppenheimer, Jesse Daniel 1870-1964
NatCAB 52
Oppenheimer, Julius Robert 1904-1967 *EncAB*
Oppenheimer, Mary Stoyell *WomWWA 14*
Oppenheimer, Robert 1904-1967 *WhAm 4*
Opper, Clarence Victor 1897-1964 *WhAm 4*
Opper, Frederick Burr 1857-1937 *AmBi,*
DcAmB S2, NatCAB 6, NatCAB 44,
TwCBDA, WhAm 1
Opperman, August *NewYHSD*
Oppert, Charles Etienne D' 1749-1819 *ApCAB*
Oppice, Harold Whinery 1895-1976 *WhAm 6*
Oppitz, William *NewYHSD*
Oppolzer, Theodor Ritter Von 1841-1886 *DcScB*
Optic, Oliver 1822-1897 *AmBi, DcAmB,*
WebAB, WhAm H
Oqwa Pi 1899?- *IIBEAAW*
Orahood, Harper M 1841-1914 *NatCAB 13,*
WhAm 1
Oram, Elizabeth *NewYHSD*
Oram, Joseph Hubbard 1876-1957 *NatCAB 43*
Orbeck, Anders 1891-1962 *NatCAB 49*
Orbegozo, Luis Jose 1795-1847 *ApCAB*
Orbeli, Leon Abgarovich 1882-1958 *DcScB*
Orbigny, Alcide Charles V Dessalines D'
1802-1857 *ApCAB, DcScB, WhAm H*
Orbison, Thomas James 1866-1938 *WhAm 1*
Orcagna 1308?-1368? *McGEWB*
Orchard, John Ewing 1893-1962 *WhAm 4*
Orcott, Samuel 1824-1893 *ApCAB Sup,*
TwCBDA
Orcutt, Calvin B 1847-1911 *WhAm 1*
Orcutt, Emily Louise *WomWWA 14*
Orcutt, Hiram 1815-1899 *BiDAmEd, DcAmB,*
NatCAB 7, WhAm H
Orcutt, Hortense May 1874- *WomWWA 14*
Orcutt, William Dana 1870-1953 *NatCAB 40,*
WhAm 3
Orcutt, William Warren 1869-1942 *NatCAB 40,*
WhAm 2
Ord, Edward Otho Cresap 1818-1883 *AmBi,*
ApCAB, DcAmB, Drake, NatCAB 4,

TwCBDA, WebAMB, WhAm H
Ord, Edward Otho Cresap, II 1858-1923
NatCAB 25
Ord, George 1781-1866 *ApCAB, DcAmB,*
Drake, NatCAB 13, TwCBDA, WhAm H
Ord, Joseph Biays 1805-1865 *NewYHSD*
Ord, P *NewYHSD*
Ordal, Ola Johannessen 1870-1936 *WhAm 1*
Ordal, Zakarias J 1875-1949 *WhAm 3*
Ordaz, Diego 1485-1533 *Drake*
Ordaz, Diego De 1485-1533 *ApCAB*
Ordean, Albert LeGrand 1856-1928 *WhAm 1*
Ordonez, Castor 1880-1938 *WhAm 1*
Ordonez, Diego 1491-1608 *ApCAB*
Ordonez Y Cevallos, Pedro d1620? *ApCAB*
Ordronaux, John 1830-1908 *DcAmB,*
NatCAB 12, WhAm 1
Ordway, Albert 1843-1897 *ApCAB Sup*
Ordway, Alfred 1821-1897 *ApCAB Sup,*
TwCBDA
Ordway, Alfred T 1819-1897 *NewYHSD*
Ordway, Charlotte Partridge 1887-
WomWWA 14
Ordway, Edward Warren 1864- *WhAm 4*
Ordway, John 1775?-1817? *DcAmB, WhAm H*
Ordway, John Gilman 1886-1966 *NatCAB 52,*
WhAm 4
Ordway, John Morse 1823-1909 *ApCAB,*
NatCAB 7, TwCBDA, WhAm 1
Ordway, Lucius Pond 1862-1948 *NatCAB 34*
Ordway, Lucius Pond 1890-1964 *NatCAB 51*
Ordway, Nehemiah 1829-1907 *REnAW*
Ordway, Samuel Gilman 1887-1942 *NatCAB 31*
Ordway, Samuel Hanson 1860-1934 *WhAm 1*
Ordway, Samuel Hanson 1900-1971 *WhAm 5*
Ordway, Thomas 1877-1952 *NatCAB 41,*
WhAm 3
Ore, Luis Jeronimo De d1628 *ApCAB*
Ore, Oystein 1899-1968 *WhAm 5*
O'Rear, Edward Clay 1863-1961 *NatCAB 18,*
NatCAB 49, WhAm 5
Orear, Edward Thomas 1857-1919 *NatCAB 18*
O'Rear, John Davis 1868-1918 *NatCAB 19*
O'Rear, John Davis 1870-1918 *WhAm 1*
O'Regan, Anthony 1809-1866 *ApCAB,*
NatCAB 9, TwCBDA, WhAm H
O'Regan, C *NewYHSD*
O'Regan, James *NewYHSD*
O'Reilly, Alejandro 1725-1794 *REnAW*
O'Reilly, Alexander 1722-1794 *DcAmB,*
WhAm H
O'Reilly, Alexander 1725-1794 *NatCAB 10*
O'Reilly, Count Alexander 1730?-1794 *ApCAB*
O'Reilly, Andrew John Goldsmith 1863-1943
WhAm 2
O'Reilly, Bernard 1803-1856 *ApCAB, Drake,*
NatCAB 10, TwCBDA, WhAm H
O'Reilly, Bernard 1820- *TwCBDA*
O'Reilly, Bernard 1823- *ApCAB*
O'Reilly, Bernard Patrick 1874-1932 *WhAm 1*
O'Reilly, Charles J 1860-1923 *NatCAB 15,*
WhAm 1
O'Reilly, Daniel 1838-1911 *BiDrAC*
O'Reilly, Edward Synnott 1880- *WhAm 6*
O'Reilly, Gabriel Ambrose 1872- *WhAm 5*
O'Reilly, Henry 1806-1886 *ApCAB, DcAmB,*
WhAm H
O'Reilly, James 1850?-1887 *ApCAB*
O'Reilly, James 1856-1934 *NatCAB 15,*
WhAm 1
O'Reilly, James Thomas 1851- *WhAm 4*
O'Reilly, John 1797-1862 *ApCAB*
O'Reilly, John Boyle 1844-1890 *AmBi, ApCAB,*
DcAmB, DcAmReB, EncAB, NatCAB 1,
TwCBDA, WebAB, WhAm H
O'Reilly, Leonora 1870-1927 *NotAW*
O'Reilly, Mary Boyle 1873-1939 *WhAm 1,*
WomWWA 14
O'Reilly, Miles 1829-1868 *AmBi*
O'Reilly, Patrick *NewYHSD*
O'Reilly, Patrick Thomas 1833-1892 *ApCAB,*
NatCAB 13, TwCBDA
O'Reilly, Peter J *WhAm 4*
O'Reilly, Robert Maitland 1845-1912 *DcAmB,*
NatCAB 18, WhAm 1
O'Reilly, Thomas Charles 1873-1938
NatCAB 33, WhAm 1
Orelie Antoine I 1820-1878 *ApCAB*

Orellana, Francisco 1500?-1545 *ApCAB*
Orellana, Francisco 1500?-1549 *Drake*
Orellana, Francisco De 1511?-1546 *McGEWB*
Orendorff, Alfred 1845-1909 *WhAm 1*
Orendorff, Ulysses Grant 1865-1943 *NatCAB 32*
Oresme, Nicole 1320?-1382 *DcScB*
Orff, Annie L Y *AmWom*
Orgaz, Francisco 1815-1873 *ApCAB*
Orgonez, Rodrigo 1490?-1538 *ApCAB*
Oribasius *DcScB*
O'Rielly, Henry 1806-1886 *DcAmB*
Origen 185?-254? *McGEWB*
Orlady, George Boal 1850-1926 *WhAm 1*
Orlando, Giuseppe Alberoni D' 1709-1781 *ApCAB*
Orlando, Vittorio Emmanuele 1860-1952 *McGEWB*
Orleans, Antoine Philippe D' *NewYHSD*
Orleans, Charles, Duc D' 1394-1465 *McGEWB*
Orleans, Ferdinand Philippe L H, Duc D' 1810-1842 *WhoMilH*
Orleans, Francois F Philippe Louis Marie 1818- *ApCAB*
Orleans, Louis Albert Philippe 1838- *ApCAB*
Orleans, Louis Charles D' *NewYHSD*
Orleans, Louis Philippe D' 1773-1850 *ApCAB*
Orleans, Louis Philippe Marie F Gaston 1842- *ApCAB*
Orleans, Philippe, II, Duc D' 1674-1723 *McGEWB*
Orleans, Pierre Philippe Jean Marie 1845- *ApCAB*
Orleans, Robert Philippe L E Ferdinand 1840- *ApCAB*
Orleman, E Louise *WomWWA 14*
Orlov, Aleksandr Yakovlevich 1880-1954 *DcScB*
Orlov, Count Aleksey Grigoryevich 1737-1808 *WhoMilH*
Orlov, Sergey Vladimirovich 1880-1958 *DcScB*
Orman, James Bradley 1849- *NatCAB 3, TwCBDA, WhAm 4*
Ormandy, Eugene 1899- *WebAB*
Orme, James Booth Lockwood 1884-1973 *WhAm 6*
Orme, John Pinckney 1852-1936 *WhAm 1*
Orme, Lindley Bell 1872-1953 *NatCAB 42*
Orme, Mary Phillips 1883- *WomWWA 14*
Orme, William Ward 1832-1866 *ApCAB*
Ormes, Mrs. Manly D 1865?- *IIBEAAW*
Ormiston, William 1821-1899 *NatCAB 13*
Ormond, Alexander Thomas 1847-1915 *NatCAB 34, WhAm 1*
Ormond, Alice 1887- *WomWWA 14*
Ormond, Cesar Venceslas D' 1689-1741 *ApCAB*
Ormond, Jesse Marvin 1878- *WhAm 6*
Ormonde, James Butler, Duke Of 1665-1745 *WhoMilH*
Ormrod, George 1839-1915 *NatCAB 18*
Ormsbee, Ebenezer Jolls 1834-1924 *NatCAB 8, TwCBDA, WhAm 1*
Ormsbee, Thomas Hamilton 1890-1969 *WhAm 5*
Ormsby, Fred Russell 1877-1945 *NatCAB 33*
Ormsby, Mary Frost 1852?- *AmWom*
Ormsby, Oliver Samuel 1874-1954 *WhAm 3*
Ormsby, Robert *NewYHSD*
Ormsby, Stephen *BiAUS*
Ormsby, Stephen d1846 *Drake*
Ormsby, Stephen 1759-1844 *BiDrAC, WhAm H*
Ormsby, Stephen 1765-1846 *ApCAB, TwCBDA*
Ormsby, Waterman Lilly 1809-1883 *ApCAB, DcAmB, NewYHSD, TwCBDA, WhAm H*
Ormston, Mark D 1890-1960 *WhAm 4*
Orndoff, Benjamin Harry 1881-1971 *WhAm 5*
Orndorff, William Ridgely 1862-1927 *WhAm 1*
Ornduff, William Wilmer 1904-1964 *WhAm 5*
Orne, Azor 1731-1796 *ApCAB, TwCBDA*
Orne, Azor 1732-1796 *Drake*
Orne, Caroline Frances 1818-1905 *WhAm 1*
Orne, Caroline Francis 1818-1906 *NatCAB 6*
Orne, Frank Edward 1893-1965 *NatCAB 51*
Orne, John 1834-1911 *DcAmB, WhAm 1*
Orne, Joseph 1747-1786 *Drake*
Orner, Irvin Melvin 1901-1964 *WhAm 4*

Ornitz, Samuel 1890-1957 *WhAm 3*
Ornstein, Leonard Salomon 1880-1941 *DcScB*
Ornstein, Martha *WomWWA 14*
Oro, Justo DeSanta Maria De 1771-1836 *ApCAB*
Oronhyatekha 1841- *ApCAB Sup*
O'Rooke, Michael *NewYHSD*
O'Rorke, Patrick Henry 1837-1863 *ApCAB*
Orosz, Ladislas 1697- *ApCAB*
O'Rourke, Charles Edward 1896-1947 *WhAm 2*
O'Rourke, Fidelis 1902-1971 *WhAm 5*
O'Rourke, John T 1888-1948 *WhAm 2*
O'Rourke, Lawrence James 1892-1965 *WhAm 4*
O'Rourke, Patrick Ira d1948 *WhAm 2*
O'Rourke, William Thomas 1903-1957 *WhAm 3*
Orozco, Jose Clemente 1883-1949 *McGEWB, WhAm 2*
Orozco Y Berra, Fernando 1822-1851 *ApCAB*
Orozco Y Berra, Manuel 1816-1881 *ApCAB*
Orr *NewYHSD*
Orr, Alexander D d1835 *BiAUS*
Orr, Alexander Dalrymple 1761-1835 *BiDrAC, WhAm H*
Orr, Alexander Dalrymple 1765-1835 *TwCBDA*
Orr, Alexander Ector 1831-1914 *ApCAB Sup, DcAmB, NatCAB 13, NatCAB 23, WhAm 1*
Orr, Benjamin 1772-1828 *ApCAB, BiAUS, BiDrAC, Drake, WhAm H*
Orr, Carey 1890-1967 *WhAm 4*
Orr, Charles 1862- *WhAm 4*
Orr, Charles Prentiss 1858-1922 *NatCAB 30, WhAm 1*
Orr, Charles Sumner 1858- *NatCAB 13*
Orr, Douglas William 1892-1966 *NatCAB 54, WhAm 5*
Orr, Eliza A 1854- *WomWWA 14*
Orr, Flora Gracia d1953 *WhAm 3*
Orr, Frances Morris 1880- *WomWWA 14*
Orr, George 1886-1937 *WhAm 1*
Orr, George Deffenbaugh 1849-1917 *NatCAB 17*
Orr, Gustavus John 1819-1887 *BiDAmEd, DcAmB, WhAm H*
Orr, H Winnett 1877-1956 *WhAm 3*
Orr, Hector *NewYHSD*
Orr, Hector 1770-1855 *Drake*
Orr, Hugh 1715-1798 *DcAmB, WhAm H*
Orr, Hugh 1717-1798 *ApCAB, Drake, NatCAB 2*
Orr, Isaac 1793-1844 *ApCAB, Drake*
Orr, Isaac Henry 1862-1954 *NatCAB 44, WhAm 3*
Orr, Jackson 1832-1926 *BiAUS, BiDrAC*
Orr, James Fergus 1883-1947 *NatCAB 38*
Orr, James Lawrence 1822-1873 *AmBi, ApCAB, BiAUS, BiDConf, BiDrAC, DcAmB, Drake, NatCAB 12, TwCBDA, WebAB, WhAm H, WhAmP*
Orr, James Lawrence 1852-1905 *WhAm 1*
Orr, James Washington 1855-1927 *WhAm 1*
Orr, James Wellington 1857-1917 *NatCAB 19*
Orr, Jehu Amaziah 1828-1921 *BiDConf, DcAmB*
Orr, John 1747-1822 *ApCAB, Drake*
Orr, John 1820-1883 *TwCBDA*
Orr, John Alvin 1874-1957 *WhAm 3*
Orr, John Boyd, Baron Of Brechin 1880-1971 *McGEWB, WhAm 5*
Orr, John William 1815-1887 *ApCAB, NewYHSD, TwCBDA, WhAm H*
Orr, Joseph Kyle 1857-1938 *WhAm 1*
Orr, Louis 1879-1966 *WhAm 4*
Orr, Louis McDonald 1899-1961 *NatCAB 50, WhAm 4*
Orr, Louis Thomas 1871- *WhAm 5*
Orr, Marshall Pinckney 1886-1944 *NatCAB 35*
Orr, Nathaniel 1822- *NatCAB 11, NewYHSD*
Orr, Robert *ApCAB*
Orr, Robert 1814-1873 *WhAm H*
Orr, Robert, Jr. 1786-1876 *BiAUS, BiDrAC, WhAm H*
Orr, Robert Hall 1873- *WhAm 5*
Orr, Robert McDaniel 1913-1973 *WhAm 6*
Orr, Robert William 1905-1972 *WhAm 5*
Orr, Robert Williamson 1897-1957 *WhAm 3*
Orr, Stephen Torrance 1888-1969 *NatCAB 55*
Orr, Thomas E 1894-1952 *WhAm 3*

Orr, Thomas Grover 1884-1955 *WhAm 3*
Orr, Thomas L 1895-1961 *WhAm 4*
Orr, Walter Stuart 1891-1961 *WhAm 4*
Orr, Warren Henry 1886-1962 *WhAm 4*
Orr, Wilbur Ray 1891-1956 *NatCAB 42*
Orr, William 1808-1891 *NatCAB 3*
Orr, William 1860-1939 *WhAm 1*
Orr, William Anderson 1883-1950 *WhAm 3*
Orr, William Black 1891-1947 *NatCAB 36*
Orrick, John Cromwell 1840- *NatCAB 5*
Orris, Mae M 1870- *WomWWA 14*
Orris, S Stanhope 1838-1905 *WhAm 1*
Orrok, Douglas Hall 1906-1975 *WhAm 6*
Orrok, George Alexander 1867-1944 *WhAm 2*
Orrok, Jessie Waldo 1859- *WomWWA 14*
Orry, Louis Victor 1642-1691 *ApCAB*
Orry-Kelly 1897-1964 *WhAm 4*
Orsollini, Theodore *NewYHSD*
Ort, Samuel Alfred 1843-1911 *TwCBDA, WhAm 1*
Orta, Garcia D' 1500?-1568? *DcScB*
Orta, Garcia Da 1501?-1568 *BiHiMed*
Ortega, Jose 1700-1754? *ApCAB*
Ortega, Juan De 1480?-1568? *DcScB*
Ortega Y Gasset, Jose 1883-1955 *McGEWB, WhAm 3, WhAm 4*
Ortega Y Montanes, Juan 1627-1708 *ApCAB*
Orteig, Raymond 1870-1939 *NatCAB 42, WhAm 1*
Ortelius, Abraham 1527-1598 *DcScB, McGEWB*
Orth, Bertrand 1848- *WhAm 4*
Orth, Charles J d1921 *WhAm 1*
Orth, Godlove S 1817-1882 *BiAUS, BiAUS Sup*
Orth, Godlove Stein 1817-1882 *BiDrAC, DcAmB, WhAm H, WhAmP*
Orth, Godlove Steiner 1817-1882 *TwCBDA*
Orth, Godlove Stoner 1817-1882 *ApCAB, NatCAB 5*
Orth, Herbert Denny 1885-1965 *NatCAB 51*
Orth, John 1850-1932 *WhAm 1*
Orth, Lizette Emma 1858-1913 *WhAm 1*
Orth, O Sidney 1906-1964 *NatCAB 50, WhAm 4*
Orth, Samuel Peter 1873-1922 *WhAm 1*
Orthwein, Charles F 1839-1898 *DcAmB, WhAm H*
Orthwein, Nina Baldwin 1882- *WomWWA 14*
Orthwein, Percy James 1888-1957 *WhAm 3*
Orthwine, Rudolf Adolf 1893-1970 *WhAm 5*
Ortiz, John F 1798-1858 *ApCAB*
Ortiz, Tomas d1538 *ApCAB*
Ortloff, Henry Stuart 1896-1970 *WhAm 5*
Ortmann, Arnold Edward 1863-1927 *WhAm 1*
Ortmeyer, Daniel Herman 1880-1939 *NatCAB 31*
Orton, Azariah Giles 1789-1864 *ApCAB, Drake*
Orton, Clayton Roberts 1885-1955 *WhAm 3*
Orton, Dwayne 1903-1971 *NatCAB 56, WhAm 5*
Orton, Edward, Jr. 1863-1932 *AmBi, BiDAmEd, NatCAB 13, NatCAB 24, WhAm 1*
Orton, Edward Francis Baxter 1829-1899 *AmBi, ApCAB, BiDAmEd, DcAmB, NatCAB 7, NatCAB 24, TwCBDA, WhAm 1*
Orton, Forrest Hoy 1867-1933 *NatCAB 26*
Orton, Harlow South 1817-1895 *DcAmB, NatCAB 13, WhAm H*
Orton, Helen Fuller 1872-1955 *DcAmB S5, WhAm 3*
Orton, Henry Boylan 1886-1957 *NatCAB 47*
Orton, James 1830-1877 *ApCAB, BiDAmEd, DcAmB, DcScB, NatCAB 11, TwCBDA, WhAm H*
Orton, Jason Rockwood 1806-1867 *ApCAB, Drake*
Orton, Samuel Torrey 1879-1948 *NatCAB 37, WhAm 2*
Orton, William 1826-1878 *ApCAB, BiAUS, DcAmB, NatCAB 7, TwCBDA, WhAm H*
Orton, William Allen 1877-1930 *NatCAB 21, WhAm 1*
Orton, William Aylott 1889-1952 *WhAm 3*
Ortynsky, Stephen Soter 1866-1916 *DcAmB*

Orum, Julia Anna 1844- *AmWom*
Orville, Howard Thomas 1901-1960 *NatCAB 46,*
WhAm 4
Orvilliers, Louis Guillouet 1708-1792 *ApCAB*
Orvin, Jesse Wright 1893-1967 *NatCAB 53*
Orvis, Arthur Emerton 1888-1965 *NatCAB 52*
Orvis, Carrie Emerton 1860- *WomWWA 14*
Orvis, Edwin Waitstill 1853-1939 *NatCAB 30*
Orvis, Ellis Lewis 1857- *WhAm 4*
Orvis, Georgia Sizer *WomWWA 14*
Orvis, Gertrude Swift *WomWWA 14*
Orvis, Julia Swift 1872- *WomWWA 14*
Orvis, Warner Dayton 1886-1967 *NatCAB 54*
Orwell, George 1903-1950 *McGEWB,*
WhAm 4
Ory, Edward Kid 1886-1973 *WhAm 5*
O'Ryan, John F 1874-1961 *WhAm 4*
O'Ryan, William Francis 1861- *WhAm 4*
Osbeck, Peter 1723-1805 *ApCAB*
Osbon, Bradley Sillick 1828-1912 *TwCBDA,*
WhAm 1
Osborn, Abraham Coles 1831-1916 *NatCAB 13,*
WhAm 1
Osborn, Albert Dunbar 1896-1972 *WhAm 5*
Osborn, Albert Sherman 1858-1946 *WhAm 2*
Osborn, Alexander Faickney 1888-1966
NatCAB 53, WhAm 4
Osborn, Alexander Perry 1884-1951 *WhAm 3*
Osborn, Andrew Rule 1875-1949 *NatCAB 38*
Osborn, Anna Brabham 1868- *WomWWA 14*
Osborn, Charles 1775-1850 *AmBi, DcAmB,*
WhAm H
Osborn, Chase Salmon 1860-1949 *DcAmB S4,*
NatCAB 17, NatCAB 38, WhAm 2
Osborn, Cyrus Richard 1897-1968 *WhAm 5*
Osborn, Edwin Faxon 1859-1937 *WhAm 1*
Osborn, Erastus William 1860-1930 *WhAm 1*
Osborn, Ethan 1758-1858 *ApCAB*
Osborn, Ethan *see also* Osborne, Ethan
Osborn, Eugene Ernest 1854-1914 *WhAm 1*
Osborn, Fairfield 1887-1969 *WebAB, WhAm 5*
Osborn, Florence Viola 1879- *WomWWA 14*
Osborn, Frank Chittenden 1857-1922
NatCAB 14, WhAm 1
Osborn, Frank Curtis 1873-1924 *ApCAB X*
Osborn, Frank Henry 1873-1924 *NatCAB 22*
Osborn, Frederick Arthur 1871-1942 *WhAm 2*
Osborn, George Augustus 1884-1972 *WhAm 5*
Osborn, George Wakeman 1860-1921
NatCAB 19
Osborn, Henry Chisholm 1878-1961 *WhAm 4*
Osborn, Henry Fairfield 1857-1935 *AmBi,*
ApCAB X, BiDAmEd, DcAmB S1,
DcScB, NatCAB 11, NatCAB 26,
TwCBDA, WebAB, WhAm 1
Osborn, Henry Leslie 1857-1940 *NatCAB 30,*
WhAm 1
Osborn, Henry Stafford 1823-1894 *ApCAB,*
DcAmB, NatCAB 11, TwCBDA,
WhAm H
Osborn, Herbert 1856-1954 *NatCAB 13,*
TwCBDA, WhAm 3
Osborn, Hervey James 1880-1961 *WhAm 4*
Osborn, James *NewYHSD*
Osborn, James Edward 1858-1940 *NatCAB 30*
Osborn, John *NewYHSD*
Osborn, John 1713-1753 *ApCAB, Drake,*
NatCAB 7
Osborn, John 1741-1825 *ApCAB*
Osborn, John *see also* Osborne, John
Osborn, John Churchill 1766-1819 *ApCAB*
Osborn, John Wilson 1794-1866 *NatCAB 18*
Osborn, Kenneth Howard 1886-1949
NatCAB 37
Osborn, Laughton 1809?-1878 *ApCAB,*
DcAmB, WhAm H
Osborn, Laughton *see also* Osborne, Laughton
Osborn, Loran David 1863-1954 *WhAm 3*
Osborn, Luther W d1901 *WhAm 1*
Osborn, M *NewYHSD*
Osborn, Marvin Griffing 1885-1958 *WhAm 3*
Osborn, Merritt J 1879-1960 *NatCAB 45,*
WhAm 3
Osborn, Milo 1810?- *NewYHSD*
Osborn, Monroe 1887-1947 *WhAm 2*
Osborn, Nathaniel B *NewYHSD*
Osborn, Norris Galpin 1858-1932 *DcAmB,*
NatCAB 25, WhAm 1

Osborn, Richard 1891-1950 *NatCAB 39*
Osborn, Samuel 1690?-1785? *ApCAB, Drake*
Osborn, Selleck 1782?-1826 *DcAmB,*
WhAm H
Osborn, Selleck 1783-1826 *ApCAB, Drake*
Osborn, Sherard 1822-1875 *ApCAB*
Osborn, Sidney Preston 1884-1948 *WhAm 2*
Osborn, Stewart Patrick 1912-1966 *WhAm 4*
Osborn, T W 1836-1898 *BiAUS*
Osborn, Thomas Andrew 1836-1898 *DcAmB,*
NatCAB 8, TwCBDA, WhAm H
Osborn, Thomas Ogden 1832-1904 *DcAmB,*
NatCAB 10, TwCBDA, WhAm 1
Osborn, Thomas Ogden *see also* Osborne, Thomas
O
Osborn, Thomas Q *BiAUS*
Osborn, Thomas Ward 1836-1898 *ApCAB,*
BiDrAC, NatCAB 12, TwCBDA
Osborn, William Church 1862-1951 *NatCAB 39,*
WhAm 3
Osborn, William Henry 1820-1894 *DcAmB,*
WhAm H
Osborn, William Henry 1825-1894 *NatCAB 11*
Osborn, William Henry 1856-1921 *NatCAB 19,*
WhAm 4
Osborn-Hannah, Jane d1943 *WhAm 3*
Osborne *NewYHSD*
Osborne, Antrim Edgar 1857- *WhAm 4*
Osborne, Arthur Dimon 1828-1920 *WhAm 1*
Osborne, Carrie Morton 1878- *WomWWA 14*
Osborne, Charles Devens 1888-1961 *WhAm 4*
Osborne, Duffield 1858-1917 *TwCBDA,*
WhAm 1
Osborne, Earl Dorland 1895-1960 *WhAm 4*
Osborne, Edmund Burke 1865-1917 *NatCAB 18*
Osborne, Edward William 1845-1926
NatCAB 21, WhAm 1
Osborne, Edwin Sylvanus 1839-1900 *BiDrAC,*
NatCAB 4, TwCBDA, WhAm 1
Osborne, Ernest G 1903-1963 *WhAm 4*
Osborne, Ernest Leslie 1889-1973 *WhAm 6*
Osborne, Estelle Massey Riddle 1903-
BiDAmEd
Osborne, Ethan 1758-1858 *Drake*
Osborne, Ethan *see also* Osborn, Ethan
Osborne, Frank Wellman 1878- *WhAm 6*
Osborne, George Abbott 1839-1927 *WhAm 1*
Osborne, Henry *BiDrAC*
Osborne, Henry Zenas 1848-1923 *BiDrAC,*
NatCAB 19, WhAm 1
Osborne, J O *NewYHSD*
Osborne, James Insley 1887-1952 *WhAm 3*
Osborne, James VanWyck 1897-1940 *WhAm 1*
Osborne, James Walker 1859-1919 *DcAmB*
Osborne, John 1713-1753 *WhAm H*
Osborne, John 1929- *McGEWB*
Osborne, John *see also* Osborn, John
Osborne, John Ball 1868- *WhAm 5*
Osborne, John Eugene 1858-1943 *BiDrAC,*
NatCAB 11, WhAmP
Osborne, John Eugene 1860-1943 *TwCBDA*
Osborne, John Eugene 1864-1943 *WhAm 4*
Osborne, John Hogarth 1856-1942 *NatCAB 31*
Osborne, John Stuart 1903-1965 *WhAm 4*
Osborne, Joseph Alexander 1860-1948
NatCAB 38
Osborne, Laughton 1809?-1874 *Drake*
Osborne, Laughton *see also* Osborn, Laughton
Osborne, Leila Grey *WomWWA 14*
Osborne, Loyall Allen 1870-1944 *NatCAB 34,*
WhAm 2
Osborne, Margherita Osborn 1878- *WhAm 6,*
WomWWA 14
Osborne, Milo 1810?- *NewYHSD*
Osborne, Milton Smith 1897-1972 *WhAm 5*
Osborne, Oliver Thomas 1862-1940 *NatCAB 30,*
WhAm 1
Osborne, Phoebe Ann Sayre 1812-1897
TwCBDA
Osborne, Raymond Gaylord 1885-1955
NatCAB 45
Osborne, Reginald Stanley 1889-1967
NatCAB 53
Osborne, Reginald Stanley 1892-1967 *WhAm 5*
Osborne, Samuel Duffield 1858- *NatCAB 10*
Osborne, Thomas Burr 1798-1869 *BiDrAC,*
WhAm H
Osborne, Thomas Burr 1859-1929 *AmBi,*

ApCAB X, BiAUS, DcAmB, DcScB,
EncAAH, NatCAB 15, NatCAB 21,
WhAm 1
Osborne, Thomas Mott 1859-1926 *AmBi,*
ApCAB X, DcAmB, McGEWB,
NatCAB 21, WhAm 1
Osborne, Thomas O 1832-1904 *ApCAB, Drake,*
NatCAB 8
Osborne, Thomas O *see also* Osborn, Thomas
Ogden
Osborne, W Irving 1859-1933 *NatCAB 25*
Osborne, William Hamilton 1873-1942
WhAm 2
Osborne, William McKinley 1842-1902
TwCBDA, WhAm 1
Osbourn, Samuel Edmund 1875- *WhAm 5*
Osbourne, Alfred Slack 1886-1960 *WhAm 4*
Osbourne, George 1852-1916 *NatCAB 17*
Osbourne, Lloyd 1868-1947 *NatCAB 14,*
WhAm 2
Osburn, Raymond Carroll 1872-1955
NatCAB 46
Osburn, Worth James 1882-1956 *WhAm 3*
Oscanyan, Ellen Clifford Stone 1874-
WomWWA 14
Oscanyan, Hatchik 1818- *ApCAB*
Oscar, Stephen A 1875-1949 *WhAm 3*
Osceola 1800?-1838 *DcAmB, McGEWB,*
REnAW, WhAm H
Osceola 1804-1838 *AmBi, ApCAB,*
NatCAB 9, WebAB, WebAMB
Osculati, Gaetano 1808- *ApCAB*
Osenbaugh, Charles Merril 1870-1930 *WhAm 1*
Oseola 1804-1838 *Drake*
Oseroff, Abraham 1891-1960 *WhAm 4*
Osgood, Alfred Townsend 1872-1959 *WhAm 3*
Osgood, Charles 1809-1890 *NewYHSD*
Osgood, Charles Grosvenor 1871-1964 *WhAm 4*
Osgood, David 1747-1822 *ApCAB, Drake*
Osgood, Edward Holyoke 1882-1952
NatCAB 49
Osgood, Edward Louis 1844-1911 *ApCAB X*
Osgood, Edwin Eugene 1899-1969 *NatCAB 57,*
WhAm 5
Osgood, Ellis Carlton 1909-1970 *WhAm 5*
Osgood, Emma Aline 1852?- *ApCAB*
Osgood, Ernest Staples 1888- *EncAAH,*
REnAW
Osgood, Ethel Lewis 1880- *WomWWA 14*
Osgood, Etta Haley 1853- *WhAm 4,*
WomWWA 14
Osgood, Farley 1874-1933 *WhAm 1*
Osgood, Frances Sargent Locke 1811-1850
AmBi, ApCAB, DcAmB, Drake,
NatCAB 2, NotAW, TwCBDA,
WhAm H
Osgood, Gayton Pickman 1797-1861 *BiAUS,*
BiDrAC, WhAm H
Osgood, George Laurie 1844-1922 *DcAmB,*
NatCAB 7, WhAm 4
Osgood, Gilman 1863-1934 *NatCAB 27*
Osgood, Helen Louise 1835?-1868 *Drake*
Osgood, Helen Louise Gibson 1835?-1868
ApCAB
Osgood, Helen Louise Gilson 1835-1868 *NotAW*
Osgood, Henry Brown 1843-1909 *WhAm 1*
Osgood, Henry H 1813- *NewYHSD*
Osgood, Henry Osborne 1879-1927 *WhAm 1*
Osgood, Herbert Levi 1855-1918 *AmBi,*
DcAmB, McGEWB, NatCAB 33,
WhAm 1
Osgood, Howard 1831-1911 *ApCAB, DcAmB,*
NatCAB 6, NatCAB 24, TwCBDA,
WhAm 1
Osgood, Hugh Henry 1821-1899 *NatCAB 16*
Osgood, Irene 1875- *WhAm 1,*
WomWWA 14
Osgood, Jacob 1777-1844 *DcAmB, NatCAB 4,*
WhAm H
Osgood, James Ripley 1836-1892 *TwCBDA*
Osgood, Jason C 1804-1875 *NatCAB 6*
Osgood, John B 1806- *NewYHSD*
Osgood, John Cleveland 1851-1926 *WhAm 1*
Osgood, Joseph 1815- *ApCAB Sup*
Osgood, Kate Putnam 1841- *ApCAB*
Osgood, Margaret Chapin 1871-
WomWWA 14
Osgood, Marion *AmWom*

Osgood, Nellie Thorne 1879- *WomWWA 14*
Osgood, Phillips Endecott 1882-1956 *NatCAB 45, WhAm 3*
Osgood, Robert Bayley 1873-1956 *NatCAB 47, WhAm 3*
Osgood, Robert William 1920-1973 *WhAm 6*
Osgood, Roy Clifton 1876-1958 *NatCAB 48, WhAm 3*
Osgood, Samuel d1813 *BiAUS*
Osgood, Samuel 1747?-1813 *DcAmB*
Osgood, Samuel 1748-1813 *AmBi, ApCAB, BiDrAC, BiDrUSE, Drake, NatCAB 1, TwCBDA, WhAm H, WhAmP*
Osgood, Samuel 1784-1862 *Drake*
Osgood, Samuel 1812-1880 *ApCAB, Drake, NatCAB 9, TwCBDA*
Osgood, Samuel Maurice 1920-1975 *WhAm 6*
Osgood, Samuel Stillman 1808-1885 *IIBEAAW, NewYHSD, WhAm H*
Osgood, Samuel Walter 1876-1921 *WhAm 1*
Osgood, Thaddeus 1775-1852 *ApCAB, Drake*
Osgood, Wilfred Hudson 1875-1946 *NatCAB 36*
Osgood, Wilfred Hudson 1875-1947 *WhAm 2*
Osgood, Willard Sumner 1913-1974 *WhAm 6*
Osgood, William Fogg 1864-1943 *DcAmB S3, DcScB, NatCAB 13, WhAm 2*
Osgoode, William 1754-1824 *ApCAB*
O'Shannessy, J J *NewYHSD*
O'Shaughnessy, Edith Coues d1939 *WhAm 1*
O'Shaughnessy, Elim 1907-1966 *WhAm 4*
O'Shaughnessy, Ignatius Aloysius 1885-1973 *WhAm 6*
O'Shaughnessy, John K 1887-1958 *WhAm 3*
O'Shaughnessy, Louis 1877-1958 *NatCAB 48*
O'Shaughnessy, M M 1864-1934 *WhAm 1*
O'Shaughnessy, Michael Maurice 1864-1934 *DcAmB S1, NatCAB 24*
O'Shaughnessy, Nelson Jarvis Waterbury 1876-1932 *DcAmB S1, WhAm 1*
O'Shaunessy, George Francis 1868-1934 *BiDrAC, WhAm 1, WhAmP*
O'Shea, Benjamin d1952 *WhAm 3*
O'Shea, John Augustine 1864-1939 *NatCAB 29, WhAm 1*
O'Shea, John J 1841-1920 *WhAm 1*
O'Shea, Maurice Culmer 1903-1972 *NatCAB 57*
O'Shea, Michael Vincent 1866-1932 *AmBi, BiDAmEd, DcAmB, WhAm 1*
O'Shea, William James 1863-1939 *NatCAB 27, WhAm 1*
O'Shea, William Joseph 1899-1957 *WhAm 3*
Osiander, Andreas 1498-1552 *DcScB*
Osias, Camilo 1889- *BiDrAC*
Osincup, Gilbert Seymour 1894-1947 *NatCAB 42*
Osius, Frederick Jay 1879-1939 *NatCAB 38*
Osk, Roselle H 1884-1954 *WhAm 3*
Oskison, John Milton 1874- *WhAm 5*
Osland, Birger 1870-1963 *WhAm 4*
Osler, Wilbur *NewYHSD*
Osler, Sir William 1849-1919 *AmBi, ApCAB, BiHiMed, DcAmB, McGEWB, WebAB, WhAm 1*
Osler, Sir William 1850-1919 *NatCAB 12*
Osma-Jaraycejo, Pedro De *ApCAB*
Osman, Pasha 1837-1900 *WhoMilH*
Osmena, Sergio 1878-1961 *McGEWB, WhAm 4, WhWW-II*
Osmer, James H 1832-1912- *BiDrAC*
Osmers, Frank Charles, Jr. 1907- *BiDrAC, WhAmP*
Osmond, Antoine Eustache 1754-1823 *ApCAB*
Osmond, Desire Gaston Rene 1763-1819 *ApCAB*
Osmond, Floris 1849-1912 *DcScB*
Osmond, I Thornton d1939 *WhAm 1*
Osmond, Marie Joseph E, Viscount D' 1756-1839 *ApCAB*
Osmond, Rene Eustache, Marquis De 1751-1838 *ApCAB*
Osmun, A Vincent 1880-1955 *WhAm 3*
Osmun, Russell A 1887-1954 *WhAm 3*
Osmun, Thomas Embley 1834-1902 *NatCAB 9, TwCBDA, WhAm 1*
Osmun, Thomas Embly 1826-1902 *ApCAB*
Osorio, Manuel 1770-1830? *ApCAB*
Osorio, Oscar 1910-1969 *WhAm 5*

Osorio Lizarazo, Jose Antonio 1899-1964 *WhAm 4*
Ospina, Manuel 1803-1885 *ApCAB*
Osserman, Kermit Edward 1909-1972 *WhAm 6*
Ossoli 1810-1850 *Drake*
Ossoli, Marchioness 1810-1850 *WebAB*
Ossoli, Margaret Fuller 1810-1850 *DcAmB, NotAW*
Ossoli, Sarah Margaret Fuller 1810-1850 *AmBi, AmWom, TwCBDA*
Ostaade, Piet Van 1670?-1711 *ApCAB*
Osten Sacken, Carl R Romanovich VonDer 1828-1906 *DcAmB*
Ostenaco *DcAmB, WhAm H*
Ostenso, Martha 1900-1963 *WhAm 4*
Oster, Henry Richard 1895-1949 *WhAm 2*
Osterberg, Max 1869-1904 *WhAm 1*
Osterburg, Herman *NewYHSD*
Osterhaus, Hugo 1851-1927 *NatCAB 43, WhAm 1*
Osterhaus, Hugo Wilson 1878-1972 *WhAm 5*
Osterhaus, Peter Joseph d1917 *Drake*
Osterhaus, Peter Joseph 1820?-1917 *ApCAB*
Osterhaus, Peter Joseph 1823-1917 *AmBi, DcAmB, TwCBDA, WhAm 1*
Osterheld, Hettie Faber *WomWWA 14*
Osterholm, Martin 1863-1927 *WhAm 1*
Osterhout, Winthrop John Vanleuven 1871-1964 *WhAm 4*
Osterman, Henry 1882-1955 *NatCAB 44*
Ostertag, Blanche *WhAm 5*
Ostertag, Harold Charles 1896- *BiDrAC, WhAmP*
Osthagen, Clarence Hilmann 1904-1975 *WhAm 6*
Osthaus, Carl Wilhelm Ferdinand 1862- *WhAm 4*
Osthaus, Edmund 1858-1928 *NatCAB 44, WhAm 4*
Ostinelle, L *NewYHSD*
Ostner, Charles Hinkley *NewYHSD*
Ostrand, James Adolph 1871-1937 *NatCAB 29, WhAm 1*
Ostrander, Dempster 1834-1907 *NatCAB 11, WhAm 1*
Ostrander, Don Richard 1914-1972 *WhAm 5*
Ostrander, Fannie Eliza d1921 *WhAm 1, WomWWA 14*
Ostrander, George Nelson 1869-1944 *NatCAB 33*
Ostrander, Henry 1781-1872 *ApCAB*
Ostrander, Isabel 1885-1924 *WhAm 1*
Ostrander, John Edwin 1865-1938 *WhAm 1*
Ostrander, Lee H d1975 *WhAm 6*
Ostrander, Leroy Farrington 1872-1926 *NatCAB 22*
Ostrander, Philip *NewYHSD*
Ostrander, Russell Cowles 1851-1919 *NatCAB 17, WhAm 1*
Ostrogradsky, Mikhail Vasilievich 1801-1862 *DcScB*
Ostrolenk, Bernhard 1887-1944 *WhAm 2*
Ostrom, George Edgar 1893-1964 *NatCAB 51*
Ostrom, Henry 1862-1941 *WhAm 1*
Ostrom, Homer Irvin 1852-1925 *NatCAB 6*
Ostrom, Kurre Wilhelm 1865- *WhAm 4*
Ostromislensky, Iwan Iwanowich 1880-1939 *DcAmB S2, WhAm HA, WhAm 4*
Ostrowsky, Abbo 1889-1975 *WhAm 6*
Ostwald, Carl Wilhelm Wolfgang 1883-1943 *DcScB*
Ostwald, Friedrich Wilhelm 1853-1932 *AsBiEn, DcScB, DcScB Sup*
O'Sullivan, Curtis D 1894-1967 *WhAm 4*
O'Sullivan, Denis Joseph 1850-1888 *ApCAB Sup*
O'Sullivan, Emma 1862- *WomWWA 14*
O'Sullivan, Eugene Daniel 1883-1968 *BiDrAC*
O'Sullivan, Frank *WhAm 2*
O'Sullivan, Jeremiah 1842-1896 *NatCAB 13, WhAm H*
O'Sullivan, John Louis 1813-1895 *BiAUS, DcAmB, EncAB, NatCAB 12, TwCBDA, WhAm H*
O'Sullivan, Mary Kenney 1864-1943 *DcAmB S3, NotAW*
O'Sullivan, Patrick Brett 1887- *BiDrAC*
O'Sullivan, Timothy H 1840-1882 *BnEnAmA,*

WebAB
O'Sullivan, Vincent 1872- *WhAm 5*
O'Sullivan, William Joseph 1855- *NatCAB 10*
Osuna, Juan Jose 1884-1950 *BiDAmEd, WhAm 3*
Oswald, Eleazer 1755?-1795 *AmBi, ApCAB, Drake, TwCBDA*
Oswald, Felix Leopold 1845-1906 *ApCAB, WhAm 1*
Oswald, John Clyde 1872-1938 *WhAm 1*
Oswald, John Holt *BiAUS*
Oswald, John Isaac 1853-1936 *NatCAB 29*
Oswald, Richard 1705-1784 *ApCAB, Drake*
Otacite *DcAmB*
Otermen, Antonio De *WhAm H*
Otermin, Antonio De *DcAmB*
Otero, Mariano Sabino 1844-1904 *BiDrAC, WhAmP*
Otero, Miguel Antonio 1829-1882 *BiAUS, BiDrAC, REnAW, TwCBDA, WhAm H, WhAmP*
Otero, Miguel Antonio 1859-1944 *REnAW, TwCBDA, WhAm 2*
Otero, Rafael 1827-1876 *ApCAB*
Otetiani *WebAB*
Otey, Elizabeth Dabney Langhorne Lewis 1880- *WomWWA 14*
Otey, Ernest Glenwood 1895-1966 *NatCAB 53, WhAm 4*
Otey, James Harvey 1800-1863 *NatCAB 5*
Otey, James Hervey 1800-1863 *ApCAB, DcAmB, Drake, WhAm H*
Otey, James Hervy 1800-1863 *TwCBDA*
Otey, Peter Johnston 1840-1902 *ApCAB Sup, BiDrAC, NatCAB 19, TwCBDA, WhAm 1*
Othman, Frederick C 1905-1958 *WhAm 3*
Otis, Alfred G 1827- *NatCAB 11*
Otis, Alphonse Elmer Spencer 1864- *WhAm 4*
Otis, Amy *WomWWA 14*
Otis, Arthur Hamilton 1885-1946 *NatCAB 39*
Otis, Arthur Sinton 1886-1964 *WhAm 4*
Otis, Ashton M 1880- *WhAm 6*
Otis, Bass 1784-1861 *AmBi, ApCAB, DcAmB, NatCAB 21, NewYHSD, WhAm H*
Otis, Blanche Heely 1871- *WomWWA 14*
Otis, Charles 1872-1944 *WhAm 2*
Otis, Charles Eugene 1846-1917 *DcAmB, NatCAB 19*
Otis, Charles Rollin 1835-1927 *DcAmB, NatCAB 11*
Otis, Edward Osgood 1848-1933 *ApCAB X, NatCAB 14, WhAm 1*
Otis, Elisha Graves 1811-1861 *AmBi, ApCAB, AsBiEn, DcAmB, McGEWB, NatCAB 11, WebAB, WhAm H*
Otis, Elita Proctor *WomWWA 14*
Otis, Eliza Ann 1833-1904 *AmWom, NatCAB 14*
Otis, Eliza Henderson 1796-1873 *ApCAB, TwCBDA*
Otis, Elwell Stephen 1838-1909 *AmBi, ApCAB, DcAmB, NatCAB 9, NatCAB 33, TwCBDA, WebAMB, WhAm 1*
Otis, Fessenden Nott 1825-1900 *AmBi, ApCAB, DcAmB, IIBEAAW, NatCAB 10, NewYHSD, TwCBDA*
Otis, Fred Alleyne 1881-1959 *NatCAB 43*
Otis, George 1797-1828 *ApCAB*
Otis, George Alexander 1830-1881 *ApCAB, DcAmB, NatCAB 10, TwCBDA, WhAm H*
Otis, George Demont 1879-1962 *NatCAB 51*
Otis, Harold 1883-1958 *WhAm 3*
Otis, Harrison Gray 1765-1838 *NatCAB 7*
Otis, Harrison Gray 1765-1848 *AmBi, ApCAB, BiAUS, BiDrAC, DcAmB, Drake, McGEWB, TwCBDA, WhAm H, WhAmP*
Otis, Harrison Gray 1837- *ApCAB Sup, NatCAB 12, TwCBDA*
Otis, Harrison Gray 1837-1916 *ApCAB X*
Otis, Harrison Gray 1837-1917 *AmBi, DcAmB, WebAB, WhAm 1*
Otis, James *TwCBDA*
Otis, James 1702-1778 *Drake*
Otis, James 1725-1783 *AmBi, ApCAB, BiAUS, DcAmB, Drake, EncAB,*

*McGEWB, NatCAB 1, TwCBDA,
WebAB, WhAm H*
Otis, James 1818-1895 *NatCAB 8,
NatCAB 10*
Otis, James 1863-1942 *NatCAB 31*
Otis, John 1657-1727 *Drake*
Otis, John 1801-1856 *BiAUS, BiDrAC,
WhAm H*
Otis, John Grant 1838-1916 *BiDrAC*
Otis, John Sidney 1858-1928 *NatCAB 21*
Otis, Joseph Edward 1867-1959 *WhAm 3*
Otis, Joseph Edward, Jr. 1892-1963 *NatCAB 53,
WhAm 4*
Otis, Lewis W *NewYHSD*
Otis, Lyman Morris 1831-1906 *NatCAB 18*
Otis, Merrill E 1884-1944 *WhAm 2*
Otis, Norton Prentiss 1840-1905 *BiDrAC,
NatCAB 34, WhAm 1*
Otis, Norton Prentiss 1840-1906 *NatCAB 11*
Otis, Philo Adams 1846-1930 *NatCAB 16,
WhAm 1*
Otis, Samuel Alleyne 1740-1814 *ApCAB,
Drake*
Otis, Samuel Allyne 1740-1814 *BiAUS,
BiDrAC, NatCAB 2, TwCBDA,
WhAm H, WhAmP*
Otis, Spencer 1858- *WhAm 4*
Otis, Susan Gorham *WomWWA 14*
Otis, William Augustus 1794-1868 *NatCAB 26*
Otis, William Augustus 1855-1929 *NatCAB 22,
WhAm 1*
Otis, William Kelly 1860-1906 *WhAm 1*
Otjen, Theobald 1851-1924 *BiDrAC, WhAm 4,
WhAmP*
Otjen, Theobold 1851-1924 *ApCAB Sup,
TwCBDA*
Otjen, William John 1880-1973 *WhAm 6*
Otnes, Fred 1925- *IIBEAAW*
O'Toole, Donald Lawrence 1902-1964 *BiDrAC,
WhAm 4*
O'Toole, John Joseph 1871-1951 *NatCAB 40*
O'Toole, Lawrence J *NewYHSD*
O'Toole, William Joseph 1894-1928 *WhAm 1*
Otsuka, Raymond M 1910-1965 *WhAm 5*
Ott, Charles Henry 1861-1909 *NatCAB 19*
Ott, Edgar Francis 1886-1954 *NatCAB 43*
Ott, Edward Amherst 1867- *WhAm 4*
Ott, Eliza Gutmann *WomWWA 14*
Ott, Emil 1902-1963 *WhAm 4*
Ott, George 1852-1926 *WhAm 1*
Ott, Harvey Newton 1868- *WhAm 5*
Ott, Isaac 1847-1916 *ApCAB, DcAmB,
DcScB, NatCAB 20, WhAm 1*
Ott, Lambert, Jr. 1888-1955 *NatCAB 45*
Ott, Martin Daniel 1890-1947 *NatCAB 37*
Ott, Peter Karl, Freiherr Von 1738-1809
WhoMilH
Ott, Philip *NewYHSD*
Ott, Samuel Jacob 1878-1951 *NatCAB 39*
Ott, William Pinkerton 1876- *WhAm 2*
Ottassite *DcAmB*
Ottaway, Elmer James 1871-1934 *WhAm 1*
Ottaway, Myrtle Redfield *WomWWA 14*
Otte, Hugo Emil 1872-1942 *WhAm 2*
Otte, Louis Edward 1905-1951 *WhAm 3*
Ottemiller, John H 1916-1968 *WhAm 5*
Ottenberg, Reuben 1882-1959 *NatCAB 50*
Ottendorfer, Anna 1815-1884 *ApCAB,
TwCBDA*
Ottendorfer, Anna Behr Uhl 1815-1884 *DcAmB,
NatCAB 8, WhAm H*
Ottendorfer, Anna Sartorius Uhl 1815-1884
NotAW
Ottendorfer, Oswald 1826-1900 *ApCAB,
DcAmB, NatCAB 3, TwCBDA,
WhAm 1*
Ottenheimer, Edward Joseph 1898-1963
NatCAB 52
Otter, John M 1907-1965 *WhAm 4*
Otter, T J *NewYHSD*
Otter, Thomas *WhAm H*
Otter, Thomas P *IIBEAAW, NewYHSD*
Otter, William Dillon 1843- *ApCAB*
Otterbein, H C *WhAm 3*
Otterbein, Philip Wilhelm 1726-1813 *DcAmReB*
Otterbein, Philip William 1726-1813 *AmBi,
ApCAB, DcAmB, Drake, McGEWB,
NatCAB 10, WhAm H*

Otterbourg, Edwin M 1885-1967 *WhAm 4*
Otterbourg, Marius *BiAUS*
Otterson, John Edward 1881-1964 *WhAm 4*
Ottigny, Charles D' 1524-1565 *ApCAB*
Otting, Bernard John 1859- *WhAm 3*
Otting, Leonard Henry 1890-1960 *WhAm 3*
Ottinger, Albert 1878-1938 *WhAm 1*
Ottinger, George Morton 1833-1917 *IIBEAAW*
Ottinger, Lawrence 1884-1954 *WhAm 3*
Ottinger, Richard Lawrence 1929- *BiDrAC*
Ottinger, Simon 1884-1974 *WhAm 6*
Ottis, Francis Joseph 1871-1935 *NatCAB 41*
Ottley, James Henry 1851-1922 *NatCAB 24*
Ottley, John King 1868-1945 *NatCAB 34,
WhAm 2*
Ottley, Passie Fenton d1940 *WhAm 1,
WomWWA 14*
Ottley, Roi 1906-1960 *WhAm 4*
Ottman, Ford Cyrinde 1859-1929 *NatCAB 22,
WhAm 1*
Ottmann, William d1954 *WhAm 3*
Otto I 912-973 *McGEWB*
Otto III 980-1002 *McGEWB*
Otto Of Freising 1114?-1158 *McGEWB*
Otto, Benjamin 1862-1945 *WhAm 2*
Otto, Bodo 1711-1787 *AmBi, DcAmB,
WhAm H*
Otto, Charles 1795-1879 *ApCAB*
Otto, Eberhard 1913-1974 *WhAm 6*
Otto, Frank Wesley 1892-1959 *NatCAB 48*
Otto, Henry J 1901-1975 *WhAm 6*
Otto, John Conrad 1774-1844 *ApCAB,
BiHiMed, DcAmB, WhAm H*
Otto, John Conrad 1775-1845 *Drake*
Otto, Louis William, Count DeMosloy 1754-1817
Drake
Otto, Max Carl 1876-1968 *WhAm 5*
Otto, Nikolaus August 1832-1891 *AsBiEn*
Otto, Raymond Herman 1905-1970 *NatCAB 56*
Otto, William *NewYHSD*
Otto, William Tod 1816-1905 *DcAmB,
TwCBDA*
Otto, William Tod 1817-1905 *ApCAB, BiAUS*
Ottoerbourg, Edwin M 1885-1968 *WhAm 5*
Ottofy, Ladialaus Michael 1865-1942 *WhAm 2*
Ottofy, Louis 1860- *WhAm 5*
Ottoni, Theophilo Benedicto 1807-1869 *ApCAB*
Otts, Cornelius 1869- *NatCAB 17*
Otts, John Martin Philip 1838-1901 *ApCAB,
WhAm 1*
Ou-Yang, Hsiu 1007-1072 *McGEWB*
Ouasakeurat 1845-1881 *ApCAB Sup*
Ouchterloney, James Delgarens 1893-1963
WhAm 4
Ouchterlony, John Arvid 1838-1905 *WhAm 1*
Ouconnastote d1785 *DcAmB*
Oud, Jacobus Johannes Pieter 1890-1963
McGEWB
Oudemans, Corneille Antoine Jean Abram
1825-1906 *DcScB*
Oudin, Christian Jules 1681-1741 *ApCAB*
Oudin, Maurice Agnus 1866-1929 *WhAm 1*
Oudinot, Charles Victor 1791-1863 *WhoMilH*
Oudinot, Nicolas Charles 1767-1847 *WhoMilH*
Oughterson, Ashley W 1895-1956 *WhAm 3*
Oughterson, William Alexander 1872-1930
NatCAB 22
Oughtred, William 1575-1660 *AsBiEn, DcScB*
Ouimet, Francis DeSales 1893-1967 *NatCAB 53*
Ouimet, Gedeon 1823- *ApCAB*
Ouimet, Joseph Alderic 1848- *ApCAB*
Ouimet, Joseph Alfonse 1845- *ApCAB Sup*
Oukrainsky, Serge 1885- *WhAm 6*
Oulahan, Richard Victor 1867-1931 *NatCAB 27,
WhAm 1*
Ould, Robert 1820-1881 *NatCAB 19*
Ould, Robert 1820-1882 *BiDConf*
Ouray 1820-1880 *ApCAB*
Ouray 1833?-1880 *DcAmB, WhAm H*
Ourdan, Joseph James Prosper 1803-1874
NewYHSD
Ourdan, Joseph Prosper 1828-1881 *NewYHSD*
Oureouhare 1697- *ApCAB*
Ourlac, Jean Nicolas 1789-1821 *ApCAB,
NewYHSD*
Oursler, Fulton 1893-1952 *DcAmB S5,
NatCAB 45, WhAm 3*
Oursler, Grace Perkins d1955 *WhAm 3*

Oursler, John Spearman 1868-1948 *NatCAB 40*
Oury, Granville Henderson 1825-1891 *BiDConf,
BiDrAC, WhAm H, WhAmP*
Oury, William Sanders 1817-1887 *REnAW*
Ousamequin *WebAB*
Ousdal, Ashjorn Pedersen 1879- *WhAm 6*
Ouseley, Sir William Gore 1797-1866 *Drake*
Ousley, Benjamin Forsyth 1855- *WhoColR*
Ousley, Clarence 1863-1948 *WhAm 2*
Ousley, James Whitman 1873-1925 *NatCAB 20*
Ousley, Sir William Gore 1791-1866 *ApCAB*
Ousmane, Sembene 1923- *McGEWB*
Outacity d1777? *DcAmB, WhAm H*
Outcault, Richard Felton 1863-1928 *DcAmB,
NatCAB 22, WebAB, WhAm 1*
Outerbridge, Albert Albony 1841-1917 *ApCAB*
Outerbridge, Albert Albouy 1841-1917 *WhAm 1*
Outerbridge, Alexander Ewing, Jr. 1850-1928
DcAmB, NatCAB 13, WhAm 1
Outerbridge, B 1902-1971 *NatCAB 57*
Outerbridge, Eugene Harvey 1860-1932
WhAm 1
Outerbridge, Eugenius Harvey 1860-1932
DcAmB S1
Outhier, Reginald 1694-1774 *DcScB*
Outhouse, Mary Prather 1862- *WomWWA 14*
Outhwaite, Joseph H 1841-1907 *NatCAB 11,
WhAm 1*
Outhwaite, Joseph Hodson 1841-1907 *BiDrAC,
WhAmP*
Outhwaite, Joseph Hudson 1841-1907 *TwCBDA*
Outland, Ethel Grimes *WomWWA 14*
Outland, George Elmer 1906- *BiDrAC*
Outlaw, David 1806-1868 *BiAUS, BiDrAC*
Outlaw, George C d1825 *BiDrAC*
Outlaw, George C d1836 *BiAUS*
Outlaw, John Sutton 1863- *WhoColR*
Outram, Sir James 1803-1863 *WhoMilH*
Outten, Warren B 1844- *NatCAB 7*
Outwater, John Ogden 1894-1949 *NatCAB 38*
Ouvrard, Leon Francois 1767-1826 *ApCAB*
Ouvrier, Pierre Gustave 1765-1822 *ApCAB*
Ovalle, Alfonso De 1601-1651 *ApCAB*
Ovando, Nicolas De 1460-1518 *ApCAB, Drake*
Ovenshine, Alexander Thompson 1873-
WhAm 5
Ovenshine, Samuel 1840-1932 *ApCAB Sup*
Ovenshine, Samuel 1843-1932 *WhAm 1*
Overall, John Wesley 1855-1923 *WhAm 1*
Overbaugh, Abram W *NewYHSD*
Overbeck, Reynolds Covel 1918-1971 *WhAm 5*
Overby, Oscar Rudolph 1892-1964 *WhAm 4*
Overesch, Harvey E 1893-1973 *WhAm 5*
Overfield, Chauncey Percival 1872- *WhAm 5*
Overfield, Peter D 1875- *WhAm 5*
Overholser, Earle Long 1888-1949 *WhAm 2*
Overholser, Edward 1869-1931 *WhAm 1*
Overholser, Henry 1846-1915 *NatCAB 17*
Overholser, Winfred 1892-1964 *NatCAB 52,
WhAm 4*
Overholts, Lee Oras 1890-1946 *NatCAB 48*
Overland, Martha Uboe *WomWWA 14*
Overman, Frederick d1852 *Drake*
Overman, Frederick 1803?-1852 *DcAmB,
WhAm H*
Overman, Frederick 1810?-1852 *ApCAB*
Overman, John Reagan 1921-1967 *NatCAB 53*
Overman, Lee Slater 1854-1930 *AmBi, BiDrAC,
DcAmB, NatCAB 13, WhAm 1, WhAmP*
Overmyer, Arthur Warren 1879-1952 *BiDrAC*
Overmyer, David 1847-1907 *NatCAB 8*
Overmyer, John 1844-1919 *NatCAB 18*
Overpeck, Areli Charles 1879- *WhAm 6*
Overr, Oscar Olen 1876- *WhoColR*
Overs, Walter Henry 1870-1934 *WhAm 1*
Overstolz, Philippine E Von *AmWom*
Overstreet, Alan Burr 1915-1975 *WhAm 6*
Overstreet, Harry Allen 1875-1970 *NatCAB 55,
WhAm 5*
Overstreet, James 1773-1822 *BiAUS, BiDrAC,
WhAm H*
Overstreet, James Whetstone 1866-1938 *BiDrAC,
WhAm 4, WhAmP*
Overstreet, Jesse 1859-1910 *BiDrAC,
TwCBDA, WhAm 1, WhAmP*
Overstreet, Lee-Carl 1898-1955 *NatCAB 43,
WhAm 3*
Overstreet, Roy 1903-1968 *NatCAB 54*

Overton, Anthony 1865-1946 *NatCAB 47*
Overton, Charles Ernest 1865-1933 *DcScB*
Overton, Daniel Hawkins 1862-1920 *WhAm 1*
Overton, Edward, Jr. 1836-1903 *BiDrAC, TwCBDA*
Overton, Eugene 1880- *WhAm 6*
Overton, Frank 1867-1953 *WhAm 3*
Overton, Grant 1887-1930 *AmBi, WhAm 1*
Overton, Gwendolen 1874- *WomWWA 14*
Overton, Gwendolen 1876- *WhAm 5*
Overton, Helen Eliza Canfield *WomWWA 14*
Overton, James Bertram 1868-1937 *WhAm 1*
Overton, Jesse Maxwell 1863-1922 *NatCAB 21*
Overton, John 1766-1833 *ApCAB, DcAmB, NatCAB 4, TwCBDA, WhAm H*
Overton, John Holmes 1875-1948 *BiDrAC, NatCAB 36, WhAm 2, WhAmP*
Overton, John Williams 1894-1918 *NatCAB 21*
Overton, Paul 1879- *WhAm 6*
Overton, Richard Cleghorn 1907- *EncAAH*
Overton, S Watkins 1894-1958 *NatCAB 47*
Overton, Walter Hampden 1788-1845 *BiAUS, BiDrAC, WhAm H*
Overton, Watkins 1894-1958 *WhAm 3*
Overton, Winston 1870-1934 *NatCAB 25, WhAm 1*
Oveson, Raymond Hansen 1876-1941 *ApCAB X, NatCAB 31*
Oviatt, Delmar Thomas 1911-1971 *WhAm 5*
Ovid 043BC-018?AD *McGEWB*
Oviedo, Juan Antonio 1670-1757 *ApCAB*
Oviedo Y Valdes, Gonzalez Hernando 1478-1557 *Drake*
Oviedo Y Valdez, Gonzalo Fernandez De 1478-1557 *ApCAB*
Ovington, Earle 1879-1936 *WhAm 1*
Ovington, Irene Helen 1836-1905 *WhAm 1*
Ovington, Mary White 1865-1951 *WhAm 3*
Owen, Abraham 1769-1811 *ApCAB, Drake*
Owen, Alfred 1829- *NatCAB 1, TwCBDA*
Owen, Allen Ferdinand 1816-1865 *BiAUS, BiDrAC, WhAm H*
Owen, Allison 1869-1951 *WhAm 3*
Owen, Anna Reese 1878- *WomWWA 14*
Owen, Arthur David Kemp 1904- *WhAm 5*
Owen, Arthur Kirk 1882-1960 *NatCAB 48*
Owen, Bill 1942- *IIBEAAW*
Owen, Carl Maynard 1879-1954 *NatCAB 40, WhAm 3*
Owen, Charles Archibald 1885-1951 *WhAm 3*
Owen, Charles Sumner 1869-1946 *WhAm 2*
Owen, Clifford H 1878- *WhAm 6*
Owen, D T 1878-1947 *WhAm 2*
Owen, Daniel 1732-1812 *NatCAB 7*
Owen, David Blair 1908-1960 *WhAm 4*
Owen, David Dale 1807-1860 *ApCAB, BiAUS, DcAmB, DcScB, Drake, NatCAB 8, NewYHSD, TwCBDA, WhAm H*
Owen, David Edward 1898-1968 *WhAm 4, WhAm 5*
Owen, Edward 1838- *WhAm 4*
Owen, Edward Thomas 1850-1931 *DcAmB, NatCAB 41*
Owen, Edwin Iorwerth 1825-1867 *TwCBDA*
Owen, Elizabeth Kenyon 1875- *WomWWA 14*
Owen, Ella Seaver 1852- *AmWom*
Owen, Emmett Marshall 1877-1939 *BiDrAC, WhAm 1*
Owen, Fred K 1865-1940 *WhAm 1*
Owen, George *NewYHSD*
Owen, George 1552-1613 *DcScB*
Owen, George, Jr. *NewYHSD*
Owen, George Hodges 1912-1974 *WhAm 6*
Owen, George Washington 1795-1837 *TwCBDA*
Owen, George Washington 1796-1837 *BiDrAC, Drake, WhAm H*
Owen, George Washington 1798-1839 *BiAUS*
Owen, Goronwy 1722-1780? *ApCAB*
Owen, Griffith *NewYHSD*
Owen, Griffith 1647?-1717 *ApCAB, DcAmB, Drake, WhAm H*
Owen, James 1784-1865 *ApCAB, BiAUS, BiDrAC, NatCAB 12, WhAm H*
Owen, James 1872-1949 *NatCAB 37, WhAm 3*
Owen, John *WhAm H*
Owen, John 1787-1841 *ApCAB, BiAUS, Drake, NatCAB 4, TwCBDA*

Owen, John 1805-1882 *ApCAB*
Owen, John Jason 1803-1869 *ApCAB, Drake, NatCAB 13, TwCBDA*
Owen, John Paul 1889-1954 *WhAm 3*
Owen, John S 1849-1939 *WhAm 1*
Owen, John Wilson 1871-1949 *WhAm 2*
Owen, Joseph 1814-1870 *ApCAB*
Owen, Joshua Thomas 1821-1887 *ApCAB, NatCAB 5, TwCBDA*
Owen, Kenneth Marvin 1899-1966 *WhAm 4*
Owen, L F 1871-1954 *WhAm 3*
Owen, Louis Franklin 1871-1954 *NatCAB 45*
Owen, Marie Bankhead 1869- *WomWWA 14*
Owen, Mary Alicia 1858-1935 *AmWom, NatCAB 13, WhAm 1, WomWWA 14*
Owen, Raymond Moses 1872-1943 *NatCAB 32*
Owen, Richard *NewYHSD*
Owen, Sir Richard 1804-1892 *AsBiEn, DcScB, McGEWB*
Owen, Richard 1810-1890 *ApCAB, NatCAB 14, TwCBDA*
Owen, Richard Blakelock 1889-1927 *NatCAB 22*
Owen, Robert Dale 1771-1858 *ApCAB, Drake, EncAAH, McGEWB, NatCAB 6, WhAm H*
Owen, Robert Dale 1800-1877 *ApCAB, BiDrAC, NatCAB 9, WhAmP*
Owen, Robert Dale 1801-1877 *AmBi, BiAUS, DcAmB, Drake, McGEWB, TwCBDA, WebAB, WhAm H*
Owen, Robert Latham 1856-1947 *ApCAB X, BiDrAC, DcAmB S4, NatCAB 14, NatCAB 37, REnAW, WhAm 2, WhAmP*
Owen, Russell 1889-1952 *WhAm 3*
Owen, Ruth Bryan 1885-1954 *BiDrAC, WhAmP*
Owen, Selwyn Nelson 1836- *NatCAB 4*
Owen, Sidney Marcus 1838- *NatCAB 14*
Owen, Stephen Walker 1837-1916 *WhAm 1*
Owen, Stewart Douglas 1898-1970 *WhAm 5*
Owen, Thomas Henry 1873-1938 *NatCAB 29, WhAm 1*
Owen, Thomas McAdory 1866-1920 *DcAmB S1, NatCAB 19, TwCBDA, WhAm 1*
Owen, Walter Cecil 1868-1934 *WhAm 1*
Owen, Walter Edwin 1907-1975 *WhAm 6*
Owen, Wesley M 1869-1917 *WhAm 1*
Owen, Wilfred Campbell 1894-1951 *NatCAB 40*
Owen, William Baxter 1843-1917 *WhAm 1*
Owen, William Baxter 1844-1917 *NatCAB 11*
Owen, William Bishop 1866-1928 *BiDAmEd, NatCAB 23, WhAm 1*
Owen, William Dale 1846-1906? *BiDrAC, TwCBDA*
Owen, William Florence 1844-1906 *DcAmB*
Owen, William Frazer 1856-1943 *WhAm 2*
Owen, William Otway 1854-1924 *WhAm 1*
Owen, William Russell 1879-1938 *WhAm 1*
Owens *NewYHSD*
Owens, Frederick William 1880-1961 *WhAm 4*
Owens, George, Jr. *NewYHSD*
Owens, George Washington 1852- *ApCAB X*
Owens, George Welshman 1786-1856 *BiAUS, BiDrAC, WhAm H*
Owens, Griffith *NewYHSD*
Owens, Grover Thomas 1887-1954 *WhAm 3*
Owens, Hamilton 1888-1967 *WhAm 4*
Owens, Heber Williams 1869-1925 *ApCAB X*
Owens, Helen Brewster 1881- *WomWWA 14*
Owens, James Bryan 1816-1889 *BiDConf*
Owens, James Cleveland *WebAB*
Owens, James Francis 1878-1942 *WhAm 2*
Owens, James W 1837-1900 *BiDrAC, TwCBDA*
Owens, Jesse 1913- *McGEWB, WebAB*
Owens, John E 1823-1886 *Drake, NatCAB 5*
Owens, John Edmond 1823-1886 *DcAmB, WhAm H*
Owens, John Edward 1824-1886 *ApCAB, TwCBDA*
Owens, John Edwin 1836-1922 *ApCAB X, NatCAB 24, WhAm 1*
Owens, John Whitefield 1884-1968 *WhAm 5*
Owens, Leo Edward 1889-1975 *WhAm 6*

Owens, Louis Joseph John 1882-1944 *NatCAB 33*
Owens, Madison Townsend 1852-1929 *WhAm 1*
Owens, Michael Joseph 1859-1923 *ApCAB X, DcAmB, NatCAB 13, NatCAB 28, WhAm 1*
Owens, Pauline Dabney 1877- *WhoColR*
Owens, Perry 1852-1919 *REnAW*
Owens, Ray L 1891- *WhAm 3*
Owens, Robert Bowie 1870-1940 *WhAm 1*
Owens, S Logan 1879-1951 *NatCAB 40*
Owens, Sara E 1865- *WomWWA 14*
Owens, Thomas Leonard 1897-1948 *BiDrAC, WhAm 2*
Owens, Walter D 1903-1952 *WhAm 3*
Owens, William 1840- *ApCAB Sup*
Owens, William Claiborne 1849-1925 *BiDrAC*
Owens-Adair, Bethenia Angelina 1840-1926 *NotAW*
Owings, Pauline James 1868- *WomWWA 14*
Owler, Martha Tracy *AmWom*
Owlett, Gilbert Mason 1892-1957 *WhAm 3*
Owre, Alfred 1870-1935 *AmBi, BiDAmEd, DcAmB S1, WhAm 1*
Owre, Erling 1877-1961 *NatCAB 49*
Owre, Oscar 1880-1950 *NatCAB 39*
Owsley, Alvin Mansfield 1888-1967 *NatCAB 54, WhAm 4*
Owsley, Bryan Young 1798-1849 *BiAUS, BiDrAC, WhAm H*
Owsley, Charles Frederick 1880- *WhAm 6*
Owsley, Charles Henry 1846-1935 *NatCAB 39*
Owsley, Frank Lawrence 1890-1956 *WhAm 3*
Owsley, William 1782-1862 *ApCAB, BiAUS, DcAmB, Drake, NatCAB 13, TwCBDA, WhAm H*
Owst, Wilberfoss George 1861-1928 *WhAm 1*
Oxenbridge, John 1609-1674 *ApCAB, Drake*
Oxenden, Ashton 1808- *ApCAB*
Oxendine, Alexander W 1759-1869 *Drake*
Oxenstierna, Count Axel Gustafsson 1593-1654 *McGEWB*
Oxley, James Macdonald 1855- *ApCAB*
Oxnam, Garfield Bromley 1891-1963 *WebAB, WhAm 4*
Oxnam, Robert Fisher 1915-1974 *WhAm 6*
Oxnam, William Clarence 1874-1963 *NatCAB 49*
Oxnard, Benjamin Alexander 1855-1924 *WhAm 1*
Oxnard, Henry Thomas 1860-1922 *WhAm 1*
Oxnard, Robert 1853-1930 *WhAm 1, WhAm 1C*
Oxnard, Thomas 1901-1965 *WhAm 4*
Oxner, George Dewey 1898-1962 *WhAm 4*
Oxtoby, Frederic Breading 1881-1941 *WhAm 1*
Oxtoby, James Veech 1872-1940 *NatCAB 30*
Oxtoby, Walter Ewing 1876-1934 *WhAm 1*
Oxtoby, William Henry 1871-1938 *WhAm 1*
Oyama, Iwao 1843-1916 *WhoMilH*
Oyen, Henry 1883-1921 *WhAm 1*
Oyen, Valborg Hansine 1907-1968 *WhAm 5*
Oyster, Earl Franklin 1883-1955 *NatCAB 47*
Oyster, James F 1851-1925 *WhAm 1*
Ozanam, Jacques 1640-1717? *DcScB*
Ozanne, Pierre 1737-1813 *NewYHSD*
Ozawa, Jisaburo 1896-1966 *WhWW-II*
Ozbirn, Mrs. E Lee d1974 *WhAm 6*
Ozenfant, Amedee-Jullen 1886-1966 *WhAm 4*
Ozersky, Aleksandr Dmitrievich 1813-1880 *DcScB*
Ozlin, Thomas William 1884-1944 *WhAm 2*
Ozmun, Edward Henry 1857- *WhAm 1*

P

Pa, Chin 1904- *McGEWB*
Paap, Hans 1894?-1966 *IlBEAAW*
Paarlberg, Don 1911- *EncAAH*
Paasikivi, Juho Kusti 1870-1956 *WhAm 3*
Pablos, Juan *ApCAB Sup*
Pabodie, Charles A *NewYHSD*
Pabodie, Edwin A *NewYHSD*
Pabodie, William Jewett 1812?-1870 *Drake*
Pabst, Charles Frederick 1887-1971 *WhAm 5*
Pabst, Fred 1869-1958 *WhAm 3*
Pabst, Frederick 1836-1904 *NatCAB 3*,
    WhAm 1
Paca, William 1740-1799 *AmBi, ApCAB,
    BiAUS, BiDrAC, DcAmB, Drake,
    NatCAB 9, TwCBDA, WhAm H,
    WhAmP*
Pacchioni, Antonio 1665-1726 *DcScB*
Pace, Charles Ashford 1869-1940 *NatCAB 41*
Pace, Charles Nelson 1877-1955 *WhAm 4*
Pace, Edward Aloysius 1861-1938 *BiDAmEd,
    DcAmB S2, NatCAB 40, WhAm 1*
Pace, Frank 1872- *WhAm 5*
Pace, Harry Herbert 1884- *WhoColR*
Pace, Homer St. Clair 1879-1942 *NatCAB 30,
    WhAm 2*
Pace, Jerome Grant 1867- *WhAm 1*
Pace, Julian Harrison 1878- *WhAm 1*
Pace, Leo L 1898-1963 *WhAm 4*
Pace, Lula *WomWWA 14*
Pace, Mary Anna 1880-1922 *WhAm 1,
    WomWWA 14*
Pace, Pearl Carter 1896-1970 *WhAm 5*
Pace, Stephen 1891-1970 *BiDrAC*
Pace, Thomas A 1901-1969 *WhAm 5*
Pacent, Louis Gerard 1893-1952 *WhAm 3*
Pacey, William Cyril Desmond 1917-1975
    WhAm 6
Pach, Walter 1883-1958 *WhAm 3*
Pacheco, Romnaldo 1831-1899 *NatCAB 4*
Pacheco, Romualdo 1831-1899 *BiAUS,
    BiDrAC, DcAmB, TwCBDA, WhAmP*
Pacheco Y Osorio, Rodrigo d1650? *ApCAB*
Pachelbel, Carl Theodorus 1690-1750 *WhAm H*
Pachelbel, Johann 1653-1706 *McGEWB*
Pacher, Michael 1435?-1498 *McGEWB*
Pachler, William Joseph 1904-1970 *WhAm 5*
Pachmann, Vladimir De 1848-1933 *WhAm 1*
Pachucki, Adolf Kasimer 1903-1975 *WhAm 6*
Pacini, Filippo 1812-1883 *DcScB*
Pacinotti, Antonio 1841-1912 *DcScB*
Pacioli, Luca 1445?-1517 *DcScB*
Pack, Charles Lathrop 1857-1937 *AmBi,
    DcAmB S2, EncAAH, NatCAB 28,
    WhAm 1*
Pack, Frederick James 1875-1938 *WhAm 1*
Pack, George Willis 1831- *WhAm 4*
Pack, Randolph Greene 1890-1956 *WhAm 3*
Pack, Robert Francis 1874-1961 *WhAm 4*
Pack, Robert Wallace 1885-1965 *WhAm 4*
Packard, Alpheus Spring 1798-1884 *AmBi,
    ApCAB, DcAmB, Drake, TwCBDA,
    WhAm H*
Packard, Alpheus Spring 1839-1905 *AmBi,
    ApCAB, BiDAmEd, DcAmB, DcScB,
    EncAAH, NatCAB 3, TwCBDA,
    WhAm 1*
Packard, Alton 1870-1929 *WhAm 1*
Packard, Ansel Alva 1894-1957 *NatCAB 47*
Packard, Arthur Joseph 1901-1974 *WhAm 6*
Packard, Arthur Worthington 1901-1953
    WhAm 3
Packard, Bertram E 1876-1945 *WhAm 2*
Packard, Burdett Aden 1847-1935 *WhAm 1*

Packard, Charles Stuart Wood 1860-1937
    WhAm 1
Packard, Elizabeth Parsons Ware 1816-1897
    NotAW
Packard, Francis Randolph 1870-1950
    NatCAB 39, WhAm 3
Packard, Frank Edward 1873-1961 *NatCAB 50*
Packard, Frank Edward 1880-1961 *WhAm 4*
Packard, Frank Lucius 1877-1942 *WhAm 2*
Packard, Frederick Adolphus 1794-1867
    ApCAB, DcAmB, Drake, WhAm H
Packard, George 1868-1949 *WhAm 2*
Packard, George Arthur 1869- *WhAm 5*
Packard, George Byron 1852-1927 *WhAm 1*
Packard, George Randolph 1872-1936 *WhAm 1*
Packard, Hezekiah 1761-1849 *ApCAB,
    TwCBDA*
Packard, Horace 1855-1936 *WhAm 1*
Packard, James Ward 1863-1928 *DcAmB,
    NatCAB 20, WhAm 1*
Packard, Jasper 1832-1899 *ApCAB, BiAUS,
    BiDrAC, TwCBDA, WhAm 1*
Packard, John Cooper 1892-1956 *NatCAB 43*
Packard, John Hooker 1832-1907 *ApCAB,
    DcAmB, NatCAB 6, WhAm 1*
Packard, John Quackenbos 1822-1908
    NatCAB 16
Packard, Joseph 1812-1902 *ApCAB,
    ApCAB Sup, DcAmB, TwCBDA,
    WhAm 1*
Packard, Joseph 1842-1923 *WhAm 1*
Packard, Laurence Bradford 1887-1955
    WhAm 3
Packard, Lawrence Ralph 1877-1957
    NatCAB 48
Packard, Lewis Richard 1836-1884 *ApCAB,
    NatCAB 4, WhAm H*
Packard, Luther William 1873-1950
    NatCAB 40
Packard, Mary Secord *WomWWA 14*
Packard, Ralph Gooding 1840- *WhAm 4*
Packard, Rawson 1813?- *NewYHSD*
Packard, Richard Alexander 1884-1945
    NatCAB 38
Packard, Samuel Ware 1847-1937 *NatCAB 10,
    NatCAB 27*
Packard, Silas Sadler 1826-1898 *ApCAB,
    BiDAmEd, DcAmB, NatCAB 3,
    WhAm H*
Packard, Sophia B 1824-1891 *BiDAmEd,
    NatCAB 2, NotAW*
Packard, Walter Eugene 1884-1966 *NatCAB 53,
    WhAm 4*
Packard, Warren 1892-1929 *NatCAB 22*
Packard, William Alfred 1830-1909 *TwCBDA,
    WhAm 1*
Packard, William Doud 1861-1923 *NatCAB 20*
Packard, Winthrop 1862-1943 *WhAm 2*
Packer, Asa 1805-1879 *AmBi, BiAUS,
    BiDrAC, DcAmB, NatCAB 7, TwCBDA,
    WhAm H, WhAmP*
Packer, Asa 1806-1879 *ApCAB*
Packer, Edith Crozier 1878- *WomWWA 14*
Packer, Elizabeth Ella 1871- *WomWWA 14*
Packer, Francis Herman 1873-1957 *WhAm 3*
Packer, Frank 1906-1974 *WhAm 6*
Packer, Fred Little 1886-1956 *NatCAB 46,
    WhAm 3*
Packer, Gibson David 1859-1929 *NatCAB 22*
Packer, Herbert Leslie 1925-1972 *WhAm 5*
Packer, Horace Billings 1851-1940 *BiDrAC,
    TwCBDA, WhAm 3*
Packer, James Cameron 1863-1919 *NatCAB 18*
Packer, John Black 1824-1891 *BiAUS,*

*BiDrAC, NatCAB 7, TwCBDA,
    WhAm H*
Packer, William Fisher 1807-1870 *ApCAB,
    BiAUS, DcAmB, Drake, NatCAB 2,
    TwCBDA, WhAm H*
Packman, James Joseph 1907-1969 *WhAm 5*
Packwood, Robert William 1932- *BiDrAC*
Packwood, William Henderson 1832-1917
    NatCAB 8
Pacsu, Eugene 1891-1972 *NatCAB 56*
Paddleford, Clementine Haskin 1900-1967
    WhAm 4
Paddock, Algernon Sidney 1830-1897 *ApCAB,
    BiAUS, BiDrAC, DcAmB, NatCAB 2,
    TwCBDA, WhAm H, WhAmP*
Paddock, Alva Adams 1887-1961 *NatCAB 50*
Paddock, Benjamin Henry 1828-1891 *ApCAB,
    DcAmB, NatCAB 6, TwCBDA,
    WhAm H*
Paddock, Buckley B 1844-1922 *WhAm 1*
Paddock, Caroline Bolles 1839- *WomWWA 14*
Paddock, Charles William 1900-1943
    NatCAB 32, WhAm 2
Paddock, George Arthur 1885-1964 *BiDrAC*
Paddock, George Arthur 1885-1965 *WhAm 4*
Paddock, George Hussey 1852-1934
    NatCAB 28
Paddock, George Laban 1832-1910 *NatCAB 15*
Paddock, Hiram Lester 1860-1948 *NatCAB 36,
    WhAm 2*
Paddock, John Adams 1825-1894 *ApCAB,
    DcAmB, NatCAB 3, TwCBDA,
    WhAm H*
Paddock, Lucius Carver 1859-1940 *WhAm 1*
Paddock, Miner Hamlin 1846- *WhAm 4*
Paddock, R B 1891- *WhAm 3*
Paddock, Robert Lewis 1869-1939 *NatCAB 14,
    NatCAB 29, WhAm 1*
Paddock, Stuart Ranson 1881-1968 *NatCAB 57*
Paddock, Wendell 1866- *WhAm 3*
Paddock, Willard Dryden 1873-1956 *WhAm 3,
    WhAm 5*
Padelford, Frank William 1872-1944 *WhAm 2*
Padelford, Frederick Morgan 1875-1942
    NatCAB 33, WhAm 2
Padelford, Seth 1807-1878 *BiAUS, NatCAB 9,
    TwCBDA*
Padelford, Silas Catching *WhAm 5*
Paden, William Mitchel 1854- *WhAm 4*
Paderewski, Ignace Jan 1860-1941 *ApCAB X,
    McGEWB, WhAm 1*
Padgham, Dora Adele 1892-1976 *WhAm 6*
Padgett, Earl Calvin 1893-1946 *NatCAB 37,
    WhAm 2*
Padgett, Everett Ervin 1878-1951 *NatCAB 39*
Padgett, Lemuel Phillips 1855-1922 *BiDrAC,
    NatCAB 23, WhAm 1, WhAmP*
Padgett, Lemuel Phillips, Jr. 1897-1957
    WhAm 4
Padgham, Elizabeth 1874- *WomWWA 14*
Padilha, Francisco d1627 *ApCAB*
Padilla, Diego Francisco 1754-1829 *ApCAB*
Padilla, Ezequiel 1890-1971 *WhAm 5*
Padilla, Juan De 1500?-1539 *ApCAB*
Padilla, Juan De 1500?-1544? *DcAmB,
    WhAm H*
Padilla, Juan Jose d1750? *ApCAB*
Padilla Y Estrada, Jose Antonio De 1696-1760
    ApCAB
Padmore, George 1902?-1959 *McGEWB*
Padoa, Alessandro 1868-1937 *DcScB*
Paduani, Louis *NewYHSD*
Padway, Joseph A 1891-1947 *WhAm 2*
Paeff, Bashka 1893- *BiCAW*

Paepcke, Walter Paul 1896-1960 *WhAm 3A, WhAm 4*
Paetow, Louis John 1880-1928 *NatCAB 21, WhAm 1*
Paez, Jose Antonio 1787-1873 *Drake*
Paez, Jose Antonio 1790-1873 *ApCAB, McGEWB*
Paff, J Willard 1877-1955 *NatCAB 47*
Paffard, Frederic Chauncey 1876-1962 *NatCAB 48*
Pagan, Bolivar 1897-1961 *BiDrAC, WhAmP*
Pagan, Bolivar 1899-1961 *WhAm 4*
Pagan, Oliver Elwood 1858-1932 *WhAm 1*
Paganini, Christophani *NewYHSD*
Paganini, Niccolo 1782-1840 *McGEWB*
Pagano, Giuseppe 1872-1959 *DcScB, DcScB Sup*
Paganucci, Anthony 1893-1954 *NatCAB 40*
Page, Alanson Sumner, II 1887-1961 *NatCAB 50*
Page, Alby *NewYHSD*
Page, Alfred Rider 1859-1931 *NatCAB 25, WhAm 1*
Page, Arthur Clinton 1888-1953 *WhAm 3*
Page, Arthur Wilson 1883-1960 *WhAm 4*
Page, Benjamin 1792-1858 *ApCAB Sup, Drake*
Page, Benjamin 1840-1929 *NatCAB 29*
Page, Benjamin Edwin 1877-1926 *NatCAB 32*
Page, Bertrand A 1873-1941 *WhAm 1*
Page, Birdie Sinclair 1871- *WomWWA 14*
Page, Calvin 1845-1919 *WhAm 1*
Page, Carroll Smalley 1843-1925 *BiDrAC, NatCAB 1, NatCAB 8, TwCBDA, WhAm 1, WhAmP*
Page, Carter 1758-1825 *ApCAB*
Page, Charles *NewYHSD, WhAm 1*
Page, Charles 1829-1906 *WhAm 1*
Page, Charles 1861-1926 *NatCAB 28, WhAm 1*
Page, Charles Edward 1840- *NatCAB 18*
Page, Charles Grafton 1812-1868 *ApCAB, DcAmB, Drake, NatCAB 5, WhAm H*
Page, Charles Harrison 1843-1912 *BiDrAC*
Page, Charles Randolph 1878- *WhAm 6*
Page, Clarence Winslow 1879-1950 *NatCAB 42*
Page, Curtis Hidden 1870-1946 *WhAm 2*
Page, David Cook 1801-1878 *ApCAB Sup*
Page, David Perkins 1810-1848 *ApCAB, BiDAmEd, DcAmB, WhAm H*
Page, David Perkins 1816-1848 *Drake*
Page, DeWitt 1869-1940 *NatCAB 31*
Page, Earl Dexter 1893-1964 *WhAm 4*
Page, Edward Day 1856-1919 *WhAm 1*
Page, Edward Sydenham 1868-1917 *NatCAB 27*
Page, Elizabeth Fry *WhAm 5, WomWWA 14*
Page, Ellen Frances 1842-1913 *WomWWA 14, WomWWA 14a*
Page, Elwin Lawrence 1876- *WhAm 5*
Page, Emily Rebecca 1834-1862 *ApCAB*
Page, Frank C Bauman 1870-1938 *NatCAB 35*
Page, Frank Copeland 1887-1950 *WhAm 3*
Page, Frederick Harlan 1860- *WhAm 5*
Page, Gay *WomWWA 14*
Page, George Bispham *WhAm 2*
Page, George Franklin 1844-1939 *NatCAB 29*
Page, George T 1859-1941 *WhAm 1*
Page, Grace Rand 1870- *WomWWA 14*
Page, H *NewYHSD*
Page, H C *NewYHSD*
Page, Henry 1841-1913 *BiDrAC, WhAm 1*
Page, Herman 1866-1942 *NatCAB 33, WhAm 2*
Page, Horace Francis 1833-1890 *BiAUS, BiDrAC, TwCBDA, WhAm H, WhAmP*
Page, Howard Wurts 1862-1932 *NatCAB 25*
Page, Hugh Nelson 1788-1871 *ApCAB, TwCBDA*
Page, Inman Edward 1853-1935 *BiDAmEd, WhoColR*
Page, J Seaver 1844- *ApCAB X*
Page, James 1795-1875 *ApCAB*
Page, James Morris 1864-1936 *WhAm 1, WhAm 4*
Page, James Rathwell 1884-1962 *WhAm 4*
Page, John 1627-1692 *ApCAB*
Page, John 1743-1808 *AmBi, BiAUS, DcAmB,*

Drake
Page, John 1744-1808 *ApCAB, BiDrAC, NatCAB 3, TwCBDA, WhAm H, WhAmP*
Page, John 1787-1865 *ApCAB, BiAUS, BiDrAC, Drake, NatCAB 11, TwCBDA, WhAm H, WhAmP*
Page, John Boardman 1826-1885 *BiAUS, NatCAB 8, TwCBDA*
Page, John Chatfield 1887-1955 *WhAm 3*
Page, John Henry 1842-1916 *NatCAB 16, WhAm 1*
Page, John Lincoln 1878- *WhoColR*
Page, John Randolph 1876-1960 *WhAm 4*
Page, Kirby 1890-1957 *NatCAB 47, WhAm 3*
Page, LaFayette 1863-1929 *NatCAB 22*
Page, Leigh 1884-1952 *DcAmB S5, NatCAB 42, WhAm 3*
Page, Lewis Coues 1869-1956 *WhAm 3*
Page, Logan Waller 1870-1918 *WhAm 1*
Page, Mann 1691-1730 *ApCAB, DcAmB, WhAm H*
Page, Mann 1749-1781 *ApCAB, BiAUS, BiDrAC, TwCBDA, WhAm H, WhAmP*
Page, Marie Danforth 1869-1940 *NatCAB 29, WhAm 1, WomWWA 14*
Page, Matthew 1659-1703 *ApCAB*
Page, Milton Edwin 1869-1948 *NatCAB 38*
Page, Nathaniel Clifford 1866- *WhAm 4*
Page, Oran Thaddeus 1908-1954 *DcAmB S5*
Page, Ralph Walter 1881-1963 *WhAm 2, WhAm 4*
Page, Richard Channing Moore 1841-1898 *ApCAB, TwCBDA*
Page, Richard Gregory 1887-1951 *WhAm 3*
Page, Richard Lucian 1807-1901 *BiDConf, DcAmB, NatCAB 8, TwCBDA, WebAMB, WhAm 1*
Page, Richard Marshall 1888-1961 *NatCAB 49*
Page, Robert d1840 *BiAUS*
Page, Robert 1764-1840 *ApCAB*
Page, Robert 1765-1840 *BiDrAC, WhAm H*
Page, Robert G 1901-1970 *WhAm 5*
Page, Robert Lee 1878-1954 *NatCAB 41*
Page, Robert M 1919-1968 *WhAm 5*
Page, Robert Newton 1859-1933 *BiDrAC, WhAm 1, WhAmP*
Page, Robert Powel, Jr. 1879-1949 *WhAm 2*
Page, Roger McKeene 1876-1942 *WhAm 2*
Page, Russel Smith 1877-1941 *NatCAB 31*
Page, S P *NewYHSD*
Page, Samuel 1823-1852 *NewYHSD*
Page, Samuel Davis 1840- *ApCAB, NatCAB 15*
Page, Samuel Davis 1840-1921 *WhAm 1*
Page, Samuel Davis 1840-1922 *NatCAB 26*
Page, Sarah Nichols *NewYHSD*
Page, Sherman 1779-1853 *BiAUS, BiDrAC, WhAm H*
Page, Sophy Ellen 1879- *WomWWA 14*
Page, Thomas Jefferson 1808-1899 *AmBi, ApCAB, DcAmB, NatCAB 10, TwCBDA, WebAMB, WhAm H*
Page, Thomas Jefferson 1815?-1899 *Drake*
Page, Thomas Nelson 1853-1922 *AmBi, ApCAB, ApCAB X, DcAmB, McGEWB, NatCAB 1, NatCAB 19, TwCBDA, WhAm 1*
Page, Thomas Walker 1866-1937 *DcAmB S2, WhAm 1*
Page, Walter Gilman 1862-1934 *WhAm 1*
Page, Walter Hines 1855-1918 *AmBi, ApCAB X, DcAmB, EncAAH, EncAB, McGEWB, NatCAB 3, NatCAB 19, TwCBDA, WebAB, WhAm 1*
Page, Walter Oliver 1882-1960 *NatCAB 51*
Page, William 1811-1885 *AmBi, ApCAB, BnEnAmA, DcAmB, Drake, NatCAB 11, NewYHSD, TwCBDA, WhAm H*
Page, William Byrd 1817-1877 *ApCAB*
Page, William Herbert 1868-1952 *WhAm 3*
Page, William Hussey 1827-1888 *ApCAB Sup*
Page, William Hussey 1861- *ApCAB X, NatCAB 17*
Page, William Nelson 1854-1932 *WhAm 1*
Page, William Tyler 1868-1942 *WhAm 2*
Pagenkopf, Alfred Albert 1887-1958 *NatCAB 47*

Pagenstecher, Albrecht 1839-1926 *NatCAB 13, NatCAB 28*
Pagenstecher, Albrecht, III 1904-1946 *NatCAB 45*
Pagenstecher, Albrecht, Jr. 1873-1964 *NatCAB 52*
Pages, Pierre Marie F, Viscount De 1748-1793 *ApCAB*
Paget, Sir James 1814-1899 *BiHiMed*
Paget, Lowell 1898-1967 *WhAm 4*
Pagett, Mrs. *NewYHSD*
Paggatt, L *NewYHSD*
Pagnol, Marcel Paul 1895-1974 *WhAm 6*
Pahlow, Edwin William 1878-1942 *WhAm 2*
Pahlow, Gertrude Curtis Brown d1937 *WhAm 1*
Paige, Abbie L *WomWWA 14*
Paige, Allan Wallace 1855- *NatCAB 7*
Paige, Alonzo Christopher 1797-1868 *ApCAB, Drake*
Paige, Calvin DeWitt 1848-1930 *BiDrAC, WhAm 1*
Paige, Clifford E 1884-1958 *WhAm 3*
Paige, David Raymond 1844-1901 *BiDrAC*
Paige, DelRomig 1901-1962 *NatCAB 49, WhAm 4*
Paige, Elbridge Gerry 1816?-1859 *Drake*
Paige, Hildegard Brooks 1875-1920 *WhAm 1*
Paige, Hildegarde Brooks 1875-1920 *WomWWA 14*
Paige, J F *NewYHSD*
Paige, James 1863-1940 *NatCAB 33*
Paige, Leroy Robert 1906- *WebAB*
Paige, Lucius Robinson 1802-1896 *ApCAB, Drake, NatCAB 9*
Paige, Raymond North 1900-1965 *WhAm 4*
Paige, Robert Myron 1908-1965 *WhAm 4*
Paige, Sidney 1880- *WhAm 6*
Pain, A *NewYHSD*
Pain, Charles Esmond, Jr. 1896-1966 *NatCAB 53*
Pain, Jacob *NewYHSD*
Pain, Philip *WhAm H*
Paine *NewYHSD*
Paine, Albert Bigelow 1861-1937 *AmBi, DcAmB S2, NatCAB 13, NatCAB 28, TwCBDA, WhAm 1*
Paine, Albert Ware 1812-1907 *WhAm 1*
Paine, Bayard Henry 1872-1955 *NatCAB 42, WhAm 3*
Paine, Bryon 1827-1871 *WhAm H*
Paine, Byron 1827-1871 *ApCAB, BiAUS, DcAmB, NatCAB 4*
Paine, Charles 1799-1853 *ApCAB, BiAUS, DcAmB, Drake, TwCBDA, WhAm H*
Paine, Charles 1799-1855 *NatCAB 8*
Paine, Charles 1830-1906 *NatCAB 12, WhAm 1*
Paine, Charles Jackson 1833-1916 *ApCAB, DcAmB, NatCAB 1, TwCBDA, WhAm 1*
Paine, Charles Leslie 1914-1963 *WhAm 4*
Paine, Clara Audrea 1875- *WhAm 5*
Paine, Eleazar A 1815-1882 *ApCAB*
Paine, Eleazer A 1815-1882 *TwCBDA*
Paine, Elijah 1757-1842 *AmBi, ApCAB, BiAUS, BiDrAC, DcAmB, Drake, NatCAB 8, TwCBDA, WhAm H*
Paine, Elijah 1796-1853 *AmBi, ApCAB, BiAUS, Drake*
Paine, Ellery Burton 1875- *WhAm 5*
Paine, Emory Madison 1901-1963 *NatCAB 50*
Paine, Ephraim 1730-1785 *ApCAB, BiAUS, BiDrAC, TwCBDA, WhAm H*
Paine, Everett 1855-1925 *NatCAB 24*
Paine, Francis Brinley Hebard 1869-1917 *WhAm 1*
Paine, Francis Ward 1888-1940 *NatCAB 30, WhAm 1*
Paine, Frank Cabot 1890-1952 *NatCAB 41*
Paine, George Eustis 1893-1953 *WhAm 3*
Paine, George H 1884-1949 *WhAm 3*
Paine, George Milton 1833-1917 *NatCAB 18*
Paine, George Porter 1909-1974 *WhAm 6*
Paine, Gregory Lansing 1877-1950 *WhAm 2*
Paine, Halbert E 1826-1905 *BiAUS, Drake*
Paine, Halbert Eleazar 1826-1905 *ApCAB*
Paine, Halbert Eleazer 1826-1905 *BiDrAC,*

DcAmB, NatCAB 10, TwCBDA,
WhAm 1
Paine, Harlan Lloyd 1884-1971 *WhAm 5*
Paine, Harriet Eliza 1845-1910 *TwCBDA,*
WhAm 1
Paine, Henry Gallup 1859-1929 *WhAm 1*
Paine, Henry Warren 1810-1893 *DcAmB,*
NatCAB 11, WhAm H
Paine, Henry William 1810- *ApCAB*
Paine, Horace Marshfield 1827-1903 *ApCAB,*
WhAm 1
Paine, Howard Simmons 1856- *WhAm 3*
Paine, Hugh E 1905-1973 *WhAm 5*
Paine, James Lawrence 1865-1943 *NatCAB 34,*
WhAm 2
Paine, John Adams 1887-1966 *NatCAB 52*
Paine, John Alsop 1840-1912 *AmBi, ApCAB,*
DcAmB, NatCAB 13, TwCBDA,
WhAm 1
Paine, John Gregg 1889-1947 *WhAm 2*
Paine, John Howard 1883-1964 *NatCAB 52*
Paine, John Knowles 1839- *ApCAB,*
NatCAB 7, TwCBDA
Paine, John Knowles 1839-1905 *McGEWB*
Paine, John Knowles 1839-1906 *AmBi,*
BiDAmEd, DcAmB, WhAm 1
Paine, Karl 1875- *WhAm 5*
Paine, Levi Leonard 1832-1902 *TwCBDA*
Paine, Lucy Theodora *WomWWA 14*
Paine, Margaret Humphreys *WomWWA 14*
Paine, Martyn 1794-1877 *ApCAB, DcAmB,*
Drake, NatCAB 11, WhAm H
Paine, Nathan 1869-1947 *NatCAB 35*
Paine, Nathaniel 1832-1917 *WhAm 1*
Paine, Nathaniel Emmons 1853-1948 *WhAm 2*
Paine, Paul Mayo 1869-1955 *NatCAB 42,*
WhAm 3
Paine, Ralph Delahaye 1871-1925 *DcAmB,*
NatCAB 25, WhAm 1
Paine, Rene Evans 1870-1935 *NatCAB 40*
Paine, Robert 1799-1882 *ApCAB, DcAmB,*
Drake, NatCAB 10, TwCBDA, WhAm H
Paine, Robert Edward 1898-1951 *NatCAB 40*
Paine, Robert Findlay 1856-1940 *WhAm 1*
Paine, Robert Treat 1731-1814 *AmBi, ApCAB,*
BiAUS, BiDrAC, DcAmB, Drake,
NatCAB 5, TwCBDA, WebAB,
WhAm H, WhAmP
Paine, Robert Treat 1773-1811 *ApCAB,*
DcAmB, Drake, NatCAB 4, WebAB,
WhAm H
Paine, Robert Treat 1812-1872 *BiDrAC,*
WhAm H
Paine, Robert Treat 1835-1910 *AmBi,*
ApCAB Sup, ApCAB X, DcAmB,
NatCAB 13, NatCAB 26, TwCBDA,
WhAm 1
Paine, Robert Treat 1861-1943 *ApCAB X,*
NatCAB 32, WhAm 2
Paine, Robert Treat 1900-1965 *WhAm 4*
Paine, Roger W 1887-1964 *WhAm 4*
Paine, Roland D 1900-1972 *WhAm 5*
Paine, Rowlett 1879- *WhAm 6*
Paine, Sidney Small 1887-1972 *NatCAB 57*
Paine, Stuart Douglas Lansing 1910-1961
NatCAB 49
Paine, Susan 1792-1862 *NewYHSD*
Paine, Susannah 1792-1862 *NewYHSD*
Paine, T O 1825?- *NewYHSD*
Paine, Thomas d1859 *Drake*
Paine, Thomas 1737-1809 *AmBi, ApCAB,*
DcAmB, DcAmReB, Drake, EncAB,
McGEWB, NatCAB 5, TwCBDA,
WebAB, WhAm H, WhAmP
Paine, Thomas Harden 1836-1903 *NatCAB 8*
Paine, Timothy Otis 1824- *ApCAB*
Paine, W *NewYHSD*
Paine, William 1750-1833 *ApCAB, Drake*
Paine, William 1821- *ApCAB*
Paine, William Alfred 1855-1929 *ApCAB X,*
NatCAB 24, WhAm 1
Paine, William Cushing 1834-1889 *ApCAB X*
Paine, William Henry 1828-1890 *NatCAB 21*
Paine, William Wiseham 1817-1882 *BiDrAC,*
WhAm H
Paine, Willis Seaver 1848-1927 *WhAm 1*
Painleve, Paul 1863-1933 *DcScB*
Painter, Albert Elza 1860-1942 *NatCAB 36*

Painter, Carl Wesley 1892-1971 *WhAm 5*
Painter, Charles Fairbank 1869-1947
NatCAB 38, NatCAB 47, WhAm 2
Painter, Eleanor 1891-1947 *NatCAB 44*
Painter, Franklin Verzelius Newton 1852-1931
BiDAmEd, NatCAB 10, TwCBDA,
WhAm 1
Painter, Gamaliel 1743-1819 *ApCAB, BiAUS,*
DcAmB, Drake, NatCAB 12, WhAm H
Painter, George Alexander Stephen 1864-
WhAm 4
Painter, Henry McMahon 1863-1934 *WhAm 1*
Painter, Robert Cornell 1868-1944 *NatCAB 34*
Painter, Russell Floyd 1911-1971 *WhAm 5*
Painter, Sidney 1902-1960 *WhAm 3*
Painter, Theophilus Shickel 1889-1969 *DcScB,*
NatCAB 55, WhAm 5
Painter, William 1838-1906 *DcAmB,*
NatCAB 31, WhAm HA, WhAm 4
Pair, James David 1873- *WhoColR*
Paisley, James Alexander 1866-1932
NatCAB 41
Paist, Theresa Wilbur 1880- *WhAm 6*
Pajeau, Charles Hamilton 1875-1952
NatCAB 46
Pajot, Louis E *NewYHSD*
Pake, Edward Howe 1888-1962 *NatCAB 49*
Pakenham, Sir Edward Michael 1778-1815
AmBi, ApCAB, Drake
Palache, Charles 1869-1954 *WhAm 3*
Palacio, Diego Garcia De 1530?-1580? *ApCAB*
Palacios, Alfredo L 1881- *WhAm 6*
Palacky, Frantisek 1798-1876 *McGEWB*
Palade, George Emil 1912- *AsBiEn*
Palafox Y Melzi, Jose De 1780-1847 *WhoMilH*
Palafox Y Mendoza, Juan 1600-1659 *ApCAB*
Palamar, Michael 1915-1970 *WhAm 5*
Palamas, Kostes 1859-1943 *McGEWB*
Paldi, Ange *NewYHSD*
Palen, Frederick Pomeroy 1872-1933
NatCAB 16, WhAm 1
Palen, Gilbert Ezekiel 1832- *NatCAB 3*
Palen, Joseph G d1875 *BiAUS*
Palen, Rufus 1807-1844 *BiAUS, BiDrAC,*
WhAm H
Palen, Rufus James 1843-1916 *WhAm 1*
Palen-Klar, Adolphe J, VonDer 1870-
ApCAB X
Palencia, Isabel De 1881- *WhAm 6*
Palenske, Reinhold H 1884-1954? *IlBEAAW*
Palestrina, Giovanni Pierluigi Da 1525?-1594
McGEWB
Paley, Jay 1885-1960 *NatCAB 52*
Paley, John 1871-1907 *DcAmB*
Paley, Robert L *IlBEAAW*
Paley, Samuel 1875-1963 *WhAm 4*
Paley, William 1743-1805 *DcScB, McGEWB*
Palfray, Warwick 1787-1838 *Drake*
Palfrey, Francis Winthrop 1831-1889 *AmBi,*
ApCAB
Palfrey, John Carver 1833-1906 *ApCAB,*
DcAmB, NatCAB 17
Palfrey, John Gorham 1795-1881 *BiAUS*
Palfrey, John Gorham 1796-1881 *AmBi,*
ApCAB, BiDrAC, DcAmB, Drake,
NatCAB 7, TwCBDA, WhAm H
Palfrey, John Gorham 1875-1945 *NatCAB 35,*
WhAm 2
Palfrey, Sara Hammond 1823- *ApCAB,*
TwCBDA, WhAm 4
Palfrey, Sarah Hammond 1823- *NatCAB 7*
Palfrey, Warwick 1787-1838 *ApCAB*
Palfrey, William 1741-1780 *ApCAB*
Palikao, Cousin-Montauban, Comte De
1796-1878 *WhoMilH*
Palisa, Johann 1848-1925 *DcScB*
Palisot DeBeauvois, Ambrose Marie F J
1752-1820 *ApCAB*
Palissard, Louis *NewYHSD*
Palissy, Bernard 1510?-1590? *DcScB*
Palladin, Vladimir Ivanovich 1859-1922 *DcScB*
Palladino, Lawrence Benedict 1837-1927
DcAmB, REnAW
Palladio, Andrea 1508-1580 *McGEWB*
Pallas, Pyotr Simon 1741-1811 *DcScB*
Pallen, Conde Benoist 1858-1929 *DcAmB,*
NatCAB 26, WhAm 1
Pallen, Montrose Anderson 1836-1890 *ApCAB,*

NatCAB 5
Pallenlief, Andrew *NewYHSD*
Pallette, Edward Choate 1904-1973 *WhAm 6*
Pallette, Edward Marshall 1874-1944
ApCAB X, NatCAB 33, WhAm 2
Palliser, Charles 1853- *WhAm 4*
Palliser, John 1817- *ApCAB*
Palliser, Melvin G 1873-1940 *WhAm 1*
Pallotti, Francis Antonio 1886-1946
NatCAB 37, WhAm 2
Palm, Franklin Charles 1890-1973 *NatCAB 57,*
WhAm 6
Palma, Ricardo 1833-1919 *McGEWB*
Palma, Tomas Estrada 1835-1908 *ApCAB Sup,*
WhAm 1
Palma Y Romay, Ramon 1812-1860 *ApCAB*
Palma Y Velasquez, Rafael 1874-1939 *WhAm 2*
Palmaro, Marcel A d1969 *WhAm 5*
Palmatary, James T *NewYHSD*
Palmer, A Emerson d1925 *WhAm 1C*
Palmer, Mrs. A Lynde *WomWWA 14*
Palmer, Mrs. A M *WomWWA 14*
Palmer, Aaron Joseph 1904-1971 *NatCAB 57*
Palmer, Abraham John 1847-1922 *WhAm 1*
Palmer, Adaline Osburn 1817-1906 *NewYHSD*
Palmer, Adelaide *WomWWA 14*
Palmer, Agnes Lizzie 1874- *WhAm 5*
Palmer, Albert DeForest 1869-1940 *NatCAB 41,*
WhAm 1
Palmer, Albert Gallatin 1813- *ApCAB*
Palmer, Albert Kenny Craven 1887-1942
WhAm 2
Palmer, Albert Marshman 1838-1905 *AmBi,*
ApCAB, DcAmB, NatCAB 1, WhAm 1
Palmer, Albert Robert 1880-1947 *WhAm 2*
Palmer, Albert Wentworth 1879-1954
NatCAB 43, WhAm 3
Palmer, Alden Claude 1887-1972 *WhAm 6*
Palmer, Alexander Mitchell 1872-1936
ApCAB X, BiDrAC, BiDrUSE,
DcAmB S2, EncAB, McGEWB,
NatCAB 27, WebAB, WhAm HA,
WhAm 1, WhAm 4A, WhAmP
Palmer, Alfred Lee 1835-1914 *NatCAB 17*
Palmer, Alice Elvira Freeman 1855-1902 *AmBi,*
AmWom, BiDAmEd, DcAmB, NatCAB 7,
NotAW, TwCBDA, WebAB, WhAm 1
Palmer, Alonzo Benjamin 1815-1887 *ApCAB,*
DcAmB, WhAm H
Palmer, Andrew Henry 1886-1942 *WhAm 2*
Palmer, Anna Alexander 1845- *WomWWA 14*
Palmer, Anna Campbell 1854-1928 *AmWom,*
NatCAB 22, TwCBDA, WhAm 1,
WomWWA 14
Palmer, Anthony 1675?-1749 *AmBi, ApCAB,*
NatCAB 13
Palmer, Archie Emerson 1853-1925 *WhAm 1*
Palmer, Arnold 1929- *WebAB*
Palmer, Arthur 1889-1954 *WhAm 3*
Palmer, Arthur C *NewYHSD*
Palmer, Arthur Hubbell 1859-1918 *WhAm 1*
Palmer, Arthur William 1861-1904 *WhAm 1*
Palmer, Aulick 1843- *WhAm 4*
Palmer, Bartlett Joshua 1881-1961 *NatCAB 47,*
WhAm 4
Palmer, Bell Elliott 1873- *WhAm 5*
Palmer, Ben Whipple 1889-1946 *NatCAB 50*
Palmer, Benjamin C *NewYHSD*
Palmer, Benjamin Morgan 1781-1847 *ApCAB,*
Drake
Palmer, Benjamin Morgan 1818-1902 *ApCAB,*
BiDConf, DcAmB, DcAmReB,
NatCAB 11, TwCBDA, WhAm 1
Palmer, Beriah 1740-1812 *BiAUS, BiDrAC,*
WhAm H
Palmer, Bertha Honore 1849-1918 *AmWom,*
ApCAB Sup, ApCAB X, DcAmB,
NotAW, TwCBDA, WebAB, WhAm 1,
WomWWA 14
Palmer, Bertha Rachel 1880-1959 *WhAm 3*
Palmer, Bessie Draper 1880- *WomWWA 14*
Palmer, Blanche Lillian 1869- *WomWWA 14*
Palmer, Bradley Webster 1866-1946 *WhAm 2*
Palmer, Bruce Bartlett 1908-1973 *WhAm 6*
Palmer, C H *NewYHSD*
Palmer, C K *NewYHSD*
Palmer, C William 1886-1965 *WhAm 4*

Palmer, Carleton Humphreys 1891-1971
NatCAB 55, WhAm 5
Palmer, Carroll Edwards 1903-1972
NatCAB 56, WhAm 5
Palmer, Ch B R *NewYHSD*
Palmer, Charles Conger 1892-1963 *NatCAB 50*
Palmer, Charles Forrest 1892-1973 *WhAm 6*
Palmer, Charles M 1856-1949 *WhAm 2*
Palmer, Charles Ray 1834-1914 *WhAm 1*
Palmer, Charles Rees 1870-1932 *NatCAB 25*
Palmer, Charles Richard 1881-1947
NatCAB 34
Palmer, Charles Skeele 1858-1939 *NatCAB 45,*
WhAm 1
Palmer, Chase 1856-1927 *NatCAB 21,*
WhAm 1
Palmer, Chauncey Davis 1839-1917 *NatCAB 24,*
WhAm 1
Palmer, Chesley Robert 1881-1968 *NatCAB 56,*
WhAm 5
Palmer, Claude Irwin 1871-1931 *WhAm 1*
Palmer, Clyde Eber 1876-1957 *WhAm 3*
Palmer, Cornelius Solomon 1844-1932 *WhAm 1*
Palmer, Courtlandt 1800-1874 *ApCAB*
Palmer, Courtlandt 1843-1888 *ApCAB*
Palmer, Cyrus Maffet 1887-1959 *BiDrAC*
Palmer, Daniel David 1845-1913 *AmBi,*
DcAmB, NatCAB 18, WebAB,
WhAm HA, WhAm 4
Palmer, David 1815-1894 *NatCAB 18*
Palmer, David J 1938- *WhAm 5*
Palmer, Dean 1889-1942 *WhAm 2*
Palmer, E Laurence 1888-1970 *NatCAB 56,*
WhAm 6
Palmer, Edgar 1880-1943 *NatCAB 32,*
WhAm 2
Palmer, Edmund Janes 1856-1917 *NatCAB 18*
Palmer, Edna Louise *WomWWA 14*
Palmer, Edward 1802-1886 *ApCAB*
Palmer, Edward 1831-1911 *DcScB*
Palmer, Edward A 1825-1862 *NatCAB 8*
Palmer, Edward Herendeen 1854-1931
NatCAB 41
Palmer, Edward L, Jr. 1877-1952 *WhAm 3*
Palmer, Edward Rush 1871-1942 *NatCAB 35*
Palmer, Edward S *NewYHSD*
Palmer, Edwin R 1895-1963 *WhAm 4*
Palmer, Elbridge Woodman 1886-1953
WhAm 3
Palmer, Eleanor Perry 1864- *WomWWA 14*
Palmer, Elihu 1764-1806 *ApCAB, DcAmB,*
DcAmReB, Drake, WhAm H
Palmer, Elizabeth Paine 1863- *WomWWA 14*
Palmer, Erastus Dow 1817-1904 *AmBi,*
ApCAB, BnEnAmA, DcAmB, Drake,
NatCAB 5, NewYHSD, TwCBDA,
WhAm 1
Palmer, Everett Walter 1906-1971 *WhAm 5*
Palmer, Fanny 1812?-1876 *NewYHSD*
Palmer, Fanny Purdy 1839- *AmWom,*
WhAm 4
Palmer, Frances Flora Bond 1812-1876
IlBEAAW, NotAW, WhAm H
Palmer, Francesca DiMaria *WomWWA 14*
Palmer, Francis Asbury 1812-1902 *TwCBDA*
Palmer, Francis Eber 1863- *WhAm 5*
Palmer, Francis Leseure 1863- *WhAm 5*
Palmer, Francis Wayland 1827-1907 *BiAUS,*
BiDrAC
Palmer, Frank Herbert 1853-1936 *WhAm 1*
Palmer, Frank Nelson 1859- *WhAm 3*
Palmer, Frank Wayland 1827-1907 *ApCAB,*
TwCBDA, WhAm 1
Palmer, Fred Chester 1910-1970 *WhAm 5*
Palmer, Frederic 1848-1932 *WhAm 1*
Palmer, Frederic, Jr. 1878-1967 *WhAm 4*
Palmer, Frederick 1873-1958 *ApCAB X,*
NatCAB 46, WhAm 3
Palmer, George Herbert 1842-1933 *AmBi,*
ApCAB X, BiDAmEd, DcAmB,
NatCAB 6, TwCBDA, WebAB, WhAm 1
Palmer, George Louis 1901-1956 *WhAm 3*
Palmer, George Smith 1855-1934 *NatCAB 29*
Palmer, George Thomas 1875-1943 *NatCAB 32*
Palmer, George Washington 1835-1887 *ApCAB*
Palmer, George Washington 1864- *WhAm 4*
Palmer, George William 1818-1916 *BiAUS,*
BiDrAC

Palmer, Gordon Davis 1896-1956 *WhAm 3*
Palmer, Hannah Borden 1843- *AmWom*
Palmer, Harold Gilbert 1897-1958 *WhAm 3*
Palmer, Harriet Warner 1857- *WomWWA 14*
Palmer, Harry Price 1877-1919 *NatCAB 18*
Palmer, Henrietta Lee 1834- *ApCAB,*
WhAm 1
Palmer, Henry E 1841-1911 *WhAm 1*
Palmer, Henry L 1819-1909 *WhAm 1*
Palmer, Henry Robinson 1867- *WhAm 4*
Palmer, Henry Wilber 1839-1913 *BiDrAC,*
WhAm 1
Palmer, Henry Wilbur 1839-1913 *DcAmB,*
NatCAB 17
Palmer, Horatio Richmond 1834-1907 *ApCAB,*
BiDAmEd, DcAmB, NatCAB 7,
WhAm 1
Palmer, Howard 1883-1944 *WhAm 2*
Palmer, Innis Newton 1824-1900 *ApCAB,*
DcAmB, NatCAB 12, TwCBDA,
WhAm H
Palmer, Innis Newton 1825?-1900 *Drake*
Palmer, Irving Allston 1866-1936 *WhAm 1*
Palmer, J *NewYHSD*
Palmer, J Culbert 1896-1972 *NatCAB 56*
Palmer, James 1865-1943 *NatCAB 32*
Palmer, James Croxall 1811-1883 *ApCAB,*
DcAmB, NatCAB 8, TwCBDA,
WhAm H
Palmer, James Shedden 1810-1867 *ApCAB,*
DcAmB, Drake, NatCAB 4, TwCBDA,
WebAMB, WhAm H
Palmer, Jane *NewYHSD*
Palmer, Joel 1810-1881 *DcAmB, WhAm H*
Palmer, John *ApCAB*
Palmer, John 1785-1840 *BiAUS, BiDrAC,*
WhAm H
Palmer, John 1842-1905 *NatCAB 8*
Palmer, John M 1817-1900 *BiAUS*
Palmer, John Mayo 1848-1903 *ApCAB X*
Palmer, John McAuley 1817-1900 *AmBi,*
ApCAB X, BiDrAC, DcAmB,
NatCAB 11, TwCBDA, WhAm 1,
WhAmP
Palmer, John McAuley 1870-1955 *DcAmB S5,*
NatCAB 44, WhAm 3
Palmer, John McCauley 1817-1900 *ApCAB,*
Drake
Palmer, John William 1825-1906 *Drake*
Palmer, John William 1866-1958 *BiDrAC*
Palmer, John William 1886-1958 *WhAm 3*
Palmer, John Williamson 1825-1906 *AmBi,*
ApCAB, DcAmB, NatCAB 8, TwCBDA,
WhAm 1
Palmer, Joseph d1788 *BiAUS, Drake*
Palmer, Joseph 1716-1788 *DcAmB, WhAm H*
Palmer, Joseph 1718-1788 *NatCAB 4*
Palmer, Joseph 1796-1871 *ApCAB, Drake*
Palmer, Julia Ann *NewYHSD*
Palmer, Julius Auboineau 1840- *WhAm 1*
Palmer, Leigh Carlyle 1873-1955 *NatCAB 46,*
WhAm 3
Palmer, Lelia Belinda 1854- *WomWWA 14*
Palmer, Leroy Sheldon 1887-1944 *NatCAB 42,*
WhAm 2
Palmer, Leslie Richard 1877-1930 *ApCAB X,*
NatCAB 17, WhAm 1
Palmer, Lizzie Pitts Merrill 1838-1916 *NotAW*
Palmer, Loren 1881-1930 *WhAm 1*
Palmer, Lowell Melvin 1845-1915 *ApCAB X*
Palmer, Lucia A *WomWWA 14*
Palmer, Lucian Horatio 1855- *WhoColR*
Palmer, Lynde *WhAm 1*
Palmer, Margaretta *WomWWA 14*
Palmer, Martin Franklin 1905-1965 *WhAm 4*
Palmer, Minnie 1865- *ApCAB*
Palmer, Mitchell 1872-1936 *AmBi*
Palmer, Nathaniel Brown 1799-1877 *AmBi,*
DcAmB, McGEWB, NatCAB 25,
TwCBDA, WhAm H
Palmer, Pauline d1938 *BiCAW, WhAm 1,*
WomWWA 14
Palmer, Philip Mason 1880-1951 *WhAm 3*
Palmer, Phoebe Worrall 1807-1874 *ApCAB,*
DcAmReB, NotAW
Palmer, Potter 1826-1902 *ApCAB Sup,*
DcAmB, NatCAB 12, TwCBDA, WebAB,
WhAm 1

Palmer, Mrs. Potter 1849-1918 *DcAmB,*
NotAW, WhAm 1
Palmer, Potter 1875-1943 *WhAm 2*
Palmer, R D *NewYHSD*
Palmer, Randolph *NewYHSD*
Palmer, Ray 1808-1887 *AmBi, ApCAB,*
DcAmB, Drake, NatCAB 8, TwCBDA,
WhAm H
Palmer, Ray 1878-1947 *ApCAB X,*
NatCAB 38, WhAm 2
Palmer, Richard Stuart 1899-1972 *NatCAB 57*
Palmer, Robert 1887-1957 *WhAm 3*
Palmer, Robert Clinton 1875-1927 *NatCAB 24*
Palmer, Robert Dilworth 1870-1922 *NatCAB 6*
Palmer, Robert M 1820-1862 *BiAUS,*
NatCAB 13
Palmer, Rose Amelia *WomWWA 14*
Palmer, Samuel Sterling 1861-1930 *WhAm 1*
Palmer, Sarah Ellen *WomWWA 14*
Palmer, Seymour *NewYHSD*
Palmer, Silas H 1874-1963 *WhAm 4*
Palmer, Solon 1823-1903 *NatCAB 14*
Palmer, Sophia French 1853-1920 *NotAW*
Palmer, Stanley Gustavus 1887-1975 *WhAm 6*
Palmer, Stephen Squires 1853-1913 *NatCAB 21,*
WhAm 1
Palmer, Stuart 1905-1968 *WhAm 4*
Palmer, Sylvanus *NewYHSD*
Palmer, Theodore Sherman 1868-1955
NatCAB 44, WhAm 3
Palmer, Theresa *NewYHSD*
Palmer, Thomas 1859- *NatCAB 6*
Palmer, Thomas Waverly 1860-1926
NatCAB 20, WhAm 1
Palmer, Thomas Waverly 1891-1968 *WhAm 5*
Palmer, Thomas Witherell 1830-1913 *ApCAB,*
BiDrAC, DcAmB, NatCAB 11, TwCBDA,
WhAm 1
Palmer, Truman Fayette 1851-1922 *NatCAB 20*
Palmer, Truman Garrett 1858-1925 *NatCAB 20,*
WhAm 1
Palmer, Virginia Lincoln *WomWWA 14*
Palmer, Walter C 1804-1883 *NatCAB 5*
Palmer, Walter Launt 1854-1932 *AmBi,*
ApCAB, DcAmB, NatCAB 7, TwCBDA,
WhAm 1
Palmer, Walter Walker 1882-1950 *DcAmB S4,*
WhAm 3
Palmer, Warren Sherman 1858- *WhAm 4*
Palmer, William Adams d1860 *BiAUS, Drake*
Palmer, William Adams 1781-1860 *BiDrAC,*
DcAmB, NatCAB 8, TwCBDA,
WhAm H, WhAmP
Palmer, William Adams 1791-1860 *ApCAB*
Palmer, William Beach 1854- *WhAm 4*
Palmer, William Fleet 1862-1942 *NatCAB 31*
Palmer, William Franklin 1859-1909
NatCAB 16
Palmer, William Gay 1877-1942 *NatCAB 33*
Palmer, William Hailes 1882-1954 *NatCAB 43*
Palmer, William Henry 1828-1878 *ApCAB*
Palmer, William Henry 1830?-1878 *DcAmB,*
WhAm H
Palmer, William Irving 1869-1929 *ApCAB X*
Palmer, William Jackson 1836-1909 *AmBi,*
DcAmB, NatCAB 12, NatCAB 23,
REnAW, WhAm 1
Palmer, William Pendleton 1861-1927
ApCAB X, WhAm 1
Palmer, William Pitt 1805-1884 *ApCAB,*
Drake
Palmer, William Spencer 1906-1972 *WhAm 5*
Palmer, William Thomas 1874-1927
NatCAB 23
Palmer, Willis Lucellius 1854- *NatCAB 5*
Palmer, Williston Birkhimer 1899-1973
WhAm 6
Palmer, Zoe Wyndham *WomWWA 14*
Palmerlee, Thomas Richardson 1908-1965
NatCAB 51
Palmerston, Viscount *WhAm H*
Palmerston, Henry John Temple, Viscount
1784-1865 *McGEWB*
Palmie, Anna Helene 1863- *WomWWA 14*
Palmie, Marguerite Thiel *WomWWA 14*
Palmieri, Luigi 1807-1896 *AsBiEn*
Palmisano, Vincent Luke 1882-1953 *BiDrAC*
Palmore, Hovey Duncan 1885-1961 *NatCAB 48*

Palmore, William Beverly 1844-1914 *DcAmB, WhAm 1*
Palmquist, Elim Arthur Eugene 1873- *WhAm 5*
Palms, Charles Louis 1871-1925 *NatCAB 18, NatCAB 22*
Palms, Francis 1884-1943 *NatCAB 33*
Palomino, Juan Alonso d1553 *ApCAB*
Palou, Francisco 1722?-1789? *DcAmB, WhAm H*
Paltenghi, A *NewYHSD*
Paltsits, Victor Hugo 1867-1952 *DcAmLiB, NatCAB 17, TwCBDA, WhAm 3*
Palumbo, Leonard 1921-1974 *WhAm 6*
Pam, Hugo 1870-1930 *NatCAB 25*
Pam, Max 1865-1925 *NatCAB 14, WhAm 1*
Pambour, Francois Marie Guyonneau De 1795- *DcScB*
Pammel, Louis Hermann 1862-1931 *DcAmB, NatCAB 10, WhAm 1, WhAm 1C*
Pan, Ku 032-092 *McGEWB*
Panabaker, Frank S 1895?- *IlBEAAW*
Panaretoff, Stephen 1853- *WhAm 4*
Panassie, Hughes Louis Marle Henri 1912-1974 *WhAm 6*
Panat, Charles Louis Etienne 1762-1834 *ApCAB*
Panbourne, Oliver *WhAm 1*
Pancoast, Henry Khunrath 1875-1939 *DcAmB S2, NatCAB 35, WhAm 1*
Pancoast, Henry Spackman 1858-1928 *TwCBDA, WhAm 1*
Pancoast, Joseph 1805-1882 *AmBi, ApCAB, BiHiMed, DcAmB, Drake, NatCAB 10, TwCBDA, WhAm H*
Pancoast, Mary Soper 1872- *WomWWA 14*
Pancoast, Russell Thorn 1899-1972 *WhAm 6*
Pancoast, Seth 1823-1889 *ApCAB, DcAmB, WhAm H*
Pancoast, Thomas Jessup 1865-1941 *WhAm 1*
Pancoast, William Henry 1835-1897 *AmBi, ApCAB, NatCAB 10, TwCBDA*
Pancost, E Ellsworth 1895-1954 *WhAm 3*
Pander, Christian Heinrich 1794-1865 *DcScB*
Pandit, Vijaya Lakshmi 1900- *McGEWB*
Pandolfi, Frank Louis 1901-1975 *WhAm 6*
Pane-Gasser, John 1897-1964 *WhAm 4*
Panero, Guy Bompard 1892-1961 *NatCAB 49*
Panet, Charles Eugene 1830- *ApCAB*
Paneth, F A 1887-1958 *WhAm 3*
Paneth, Friedrich Adolf 1887-1958 *DcScB*
Pangborn, Earl Leroy 1897-1964 *WhAm 4*
Pangborn, Frederic Werden 1855- *WhAm 4*
Pangborn, Georgia Wood 1872- *WhAm 5, WomWWA 14*
Pangborn, Joseph Gladding 1844-1914 *NatCAB 16*
Pangborn, Thomas Wesley 1880-1967 *WhAm 4*
Panico, Giovanni 1895-1962 *WhAm 4*
Pankhurst, Emmeline 1858-1928 *McGEWB*
Pannekoek, Antonie 1873-1960 *DcScB*
Pannell, Faye 1912-1969 *WhAm 5*
Pannell, Henry Clifton 1897-1946 *WhAm 2*
Pannill, Charles Jackson 1879-1955 *WhAm 3*
Pannill, David Harry 1880-1940 *NatCAB 35*
Pannill, Gordon 1889-1952 *NatCAB 41*
Pannill, William Letcher 1880-1940 *NatCAB 35*
Panofsky, Erwin 1892-1968 *BiDAmEd, WebAB, WhAm 4A*
Pansy *DcAmB S1, NotAW, WhAm 1, WomWWA 14*
Pantin, Santiago Iglesias *BiDrAC, WhAmP*
Panton, Henry *NewYHSD*
Panton, William 1742?-1801 *DcAmB, WhAm H*
Pantsios, Athan Anastason 1912-1974 *WhAm 6*
Panum, Peter Ludvig 1820-1885 *BiHiMed*
Panunzio, Constantine Maria 1884-1964 *WhAm 4*
Panyushkin, Alexander S 1905-1974 *WhAm 6*
Paoli, J *NewYHSD*
Papagos, Alexander 1883-1955 *WhAm 3, WhWW-II*
Papanek, Ernst 1900-1973 *WhAm 6*
Papanicolaou, George Nicholas 1883-1962 *DcScB, NatCAB 50, WhAm 4*
Pape, Eric 1870-1938 *ApCAB X, NatCAB 38, TwCBDA, WhAm 1*
Pape, Henrietta Louise 1873- *WomWWA 14*

Pape, William J 1873-1961 *WhAm 4*
Paper, Joseph 1896-1962 *NatCAB 50*
Papesh, Alexander Anthony 1928-1971 *WhAm 6*
Papez, James Wenceslas 1883-1958 *NatCAB 48, WhAm 4*
Papi, Gennaro 1886-1941 *WhAm 1*
Papin, Denis 1647-1712? *AsBiEn, DcScB*
Papineau, Louis Joseph 1786-1871 *McGEWB*
Papineau, Louis Joseph 1789-1871 *ApCAB, Drake*
Pappenheim, Eugenie 1853- *AmWom*
Pappenheim, Gottfried Heinrich, Graf Zu 1594-1632 *WhoMilH*
Pappenheimer, Alwin M 1878-1955 *WhAm 3*
Papprill, Henry *NewYHSD*
Pappus Of Alexandria 260?- *AsBiEn, DcScB*
Paquet, Anselme Homere 1830- *ApCAB*
Paquet, Anthony C 1814-1882 *NewYHSD, WhAm H*
Paquette, Charles Alfred 1872- *WhAm 5*
Paquin, Albert Joseph, Jr. 1921-1967 *WhAm 4*
Paquin, J Ubalde 1878-1963 *NatCAB 51*
Paquin, Lawrence G d1967 *WhAm 4*
Paquin, Paul 1860-1916 *NatCAB 6, WhAm 1*
Paquin, Samuel Savil 1868-1943 *WhAm 2*
Paracelsus, Philippus Aureolus 1493-1541 *AsBiEn, BiHiMed, McGEWB*
Paracelsus, Theophrastus P A B Von H 1493?-1541 *DcScB*
Paradies, Isaac Jacob 1886-1967 *NatCAB 54*
Paradis, Edouard Antoine 1850-1924 *NatCAB 19*
Paradis, Marjorie 1886-1970 *NatCAB 57*
Paradise, Frank Ilsley 1859-1926 *WhAm 1*
Paradise, John 1783-1833 *NewYHSD*
Paradise, John 1783-1834 *ApCAB*
Paradise, John Wesley 1809-1862 *ApCAB, NewYHSD*
Paradise, Philip Herschel 1905- *IlBEAAW*
Paraguassu *ApCAB*
Paramananda, Swami d1940 *WhAm 1*
Paramesvara 1380?-1460? *DcScB*
Paramino, John Francis 1888-1956 *NatCAB 42*
Parana, Honorio Hermeto Carneiro Leao 1801-1856 *ApCAB*
Parangua, Francisco Villela Barbosa 1769-1846 *ApCAB*
Parce, Inez Lorena Taggart *WomWWA 14*
Parcel, John Ira 1878- *WhAm 6*
Parcells, Charles Abram 1888-1948 *NatCAB 36*
Parde, Phineas *NewYHSD*
Pardee, Ario 1810-1892 *ApCAB, DcAmB, NatCAB 11, WhAm H*
Pardee, Ariovistus 1810-1892 *TwCBDA*
Pardee, C Marvin 1894-1947 *NatCAB 38*
Pardee, Don Albert 1837-1919 *DcAmB, NatCAB 18, TwCBDA, WhAm 1*
Pardee, Dwight Whitfield 1822-1893 *NatCAB 15*
Pardee, George Cooper 1857-1941 *NatCAB 13, NatCAB 30, WhAm 1*
Pardee, Harold Ensign Bennett 1886-1972 *WhAm 5*
Pardee, Israel Platt 1852-1934 *NatCAB 26, WhAm 1*
Pardee, James Thomas 1867-1944 *NatCAB 47, WhAm 2*
Pardee, Joseph Thomas 1871-1960 *NatCAB 53*
Pardies, Ignace Gaston 1636-1673 *DcScB*
Pardo, Ambroise *NewYHSD*
Pardo, Felipe 1860- *WhAm 4*
Pardo, Manuel 1834-1878 *ApCAB*
Pardoe, John *NewYHSD*
Pardoe, William Dolton 1883-1955 *NatCAB 45*
Pardow, William O'Brien 1847- *NatCAB 4*
Pardow, William O'Brien 1847-1908 *WhAm 1*
Pardow, William O'Brien 1847-1909 *DcAmB*
Pardridge, William DeWeese 1916-1975 *WhAm 6*
Pardue, Lit J 1870-1944 *NatCAB 34*
Pardue, Louis A 1900-1963 *WhAm 4*
Pare, Ambroise 1510?-1590 *AsBiEn, BiHiMed, DcScB, McGEWB*
Pare, Francis Michael 1902-1948 *NatCAB 36*
Paredes, Ignacio 1703-1770? *ApCAB*
Paredes, Jose Gregorio 1779-1839 *ApCAB*
Paredes, Mariano d1849 *Drake*

Paredes, Quintin 1884- *BiDrAC*
Paredes Y Arrillaga, Mariano 1797-1849 *ApCAB*
Pareja, Antonio 1760?-1813 *ApCAB*
Pareja, Francisco d1628 *ApCAB, Drake*
Pareja, Jose 1812?-1865 *ApCAB*
Pareja, Juan De 1608-1670 *ApCAB Sup*
Parenago, Pavel Petrovich 1906-1960 *DcScB*
Parent, Alphonse Marie 1906-1970 *WhAm 5*
Parent, Antoine 1666-1716 *DcScB*
Parent, Etienne 1801-1874 *ApCAB, Drake*
Parent, Pierre *ApCAB*
Parent, Simon Napoleon 1855- *ApCAB Sup*
Parente, Pascal Prosper 1890-1971 *WhAm 5*
Parentz, Ernest *NewYHSD*
Parepa-Rosa, Euphrosyne 1836-1874 *ApCAB*
Paret, Anna Parmly *WomWWA 14*
Paret, J Parmly 1870- *WhAm 5*
Paret, Thomas Dunkin 1837- *ApCAB, WhAm H*
Paret, William 1826-1911 *ApCAB, NatCAB 6, TwCBDA, WhAm 1*
Pareto, Vilfredo 1848-1923 *McGEWB*
Paretti, Andrew 1891-1955 *NatCAB 43*
Pargellis, Stanley 1898-1968 *DcAmLiB, WhAm 4*
Parham, Edwin Fuller 1900-1953 *NatCAB 41*
Parham, Frederick William 1856-1927 *NatCAB 10, WhAm 1*
Parham, James A 1881- *WhAm 6*
Paris, Auguste Jean, Jr. 1874-1955 *WhAm 3*
Paris, Charles Wesley 1916-1972 *WhAm 6*
Paris, Frances Johnston 1862- *WomWWA 14*
Paris, Harold Persico 1925- *BnEnAmA*
Paris, John W 1860- *ApCAB X*
Paris, W Francklyn 1871-1954 *WhAm 3*
Paris, Walter 1842-1906 *DcAmB, IlBEAAW, NatCAB 7*
Paris, William Edward 1893-1955 *WhAm 3*
Parisen, Mister *NewYHSD*
Parisen, J *NewYHSD*
Parisen, Otto 1723-1811 *NewYHSD*
Parisen, Philip d1822 *NewYHSD*
Parisen, William D 1800-1832 *NewYHSD*
Parish *NewYHSD*
Parish, Charles Louis 1830?-1902 *IlBEAAW*
Parish, Charles Louis *see also* Parrish, Charles Louis
Parish, Edward Codman 1873-1962 *NatCAB 48*
Parish, Edward Jenkins 1874-1955 *NatCAB 46*
Parish, Elijah 1762-1825 *ApCAB, DcAmB, Drake, NatCAB 4, WhAm H*
Parish, John Carl 1881-1939 *WhAm 1*
Parish, Walter Alvis 1887-1959 *WhAm 3*
Parish, William Jackson 1907-1964 *WhAm 4*
Parish, Sir Woodbine 1796-1882 *ApCAB*
Parisien *NewYHSD*
Parjeaux *NewYHSD*
Park, A *NewYHSD*
Park, Ambrose Berry 1852-1915 *NatCAB 17*
Park, Asa d1827 *NewYHSD*
Park, Benjamin 1777-1835 *BiAUS*
Park, Calvin 1774-1847 *ApCAB*
Park, Charles Abraham 1882-1966 *NatCAB 52*
Park, Charles Caldwell 1860-1931 *WhAm 1*
Park, Charles Edwards 1873-1962 *WhAm 4*
Park, Charles Francis 1869-1944 *WhAm 2*
Park, Chung Hee 1917- *McGEWB*
Park, Clara Cahill *WomWWA 14*
Park, David 1911-1960 *BnEnAmA*
Park, David Edgar 1849- *NatCAB 18*
Park, Edith Beam *WomWWA 14*
Park, Edward Amasa 1808-1900 *WhAm 1*
Park, Edward Cahill 1895-1967 *NatCAB 53, WhAm 4*
Park, Edwards Albert 1877-1969 *WhAm 5*
Park, Edwards Amasa 1808-1900 *ApCAB, DcAmB, Drake, NatCAB 9, TwCBDA*
Park, Frank 1864-1925 *BiDrAC, WhAm 4, WhAmP*
Park, Franklin Atwood 1868-1938 *NatCAB 28, WhAm 1*
Park, George 1871-1951 *NatCAB 38*
Park, Grace Burtt 1876- *WomWWA 14*
Park, Guy Brasfield 1872- *WhAm 2*
Park, Isabelle Springer 1895-1975 *WhAm 6*
Park, J A 1893-1952 *WhAm 3*
Park, J Edgar 1879-1956 *NatCAB 46,*

WhAm 3

Park, James 1820-1883 *ApCAB, DcAmB, WhAm H*
Park, James 1892-1970 *NatCAB 57*
Park, John 1775-1852 *ApCAB, Drake*
Park, John Alsey 1885-1956 *WhAm 3*
Park, John Duane 1819-1896 *NatCAB 12*
Park, John Rocky 1833-1900 *BiDAmEd, NatCAB 22*
Park, Joseph 1705-1777 *NatCAB 8*
Park, Julian 1888-1965 *WhAm 4*
Park, Sir Keith 1892-1975 *WhWW-II*
Park, L W *NewYHSD*
Park, Lawrence 1873- *WhAm 1*
Park, Linton 1826- *NewYHSD, WhAm H*
Park, Lottie Crego *WomWWA 14*
Park, Marion Edwards 1875-1960 *WhAm 4, WomWWA 14*
Park, Maud Wood 1871-1955 *DcAmB S5, WhAm 3*
Park, Maybelle M *WomWWA 14*
Park, Milton 1846-1914 *TwCBDA, WhAm 1*
Park, Orlando 1901-1969 *NatCAB 55*
Park, Orville Augustus 1872-1943 *NatCAB 37, WhAm 2*
Park, Paul Archibald 1884-1954 *NatCAB 46*
Park, Richard Henry 1832-1890? *NewYHSD*
Park, Robert Emory 1868-1942 *WhAm 2*
Park, Robert Ezra 1864-1944 *DcAmB S3, NatCAB 37, WebAB, WhAm 2*
Park, Roswell 1807-1869 *ApCAB, DcAmB, Drake, NatCAB 8, TwCBDA, WhAm H*
Park, Roswell 1852-1914 *AmBi, ApCAB X, DcAmB, NatCAB 8, WhAm 1*
Park, Royal Wheeler 1897-1941 *WhAm 1*
Park, S *NewYHSD*
Park, Sam 1857-1937 *ApCAB X, NatCAB 27, WhAm 1*
Park, Samuel Culver 1869-1920 *WhAm 1*
Park, Trenor William 1823-1882 *ApCAB, DcAmB, NatCAB 13, TwCBDA, WhAm H*
Park, William *NewYHSD*
Park, William d1961 *WhAm 4*
Park, William Gray 1848-1909 *NatCAB 27*
Park, William Hallock 1863-1939 *AmBi, DcAmB S2, McGEWB, WhAm 1*
Park, William Lee 1859- *WhAm 4*
Parke, Benjamin 1777-1835 *ApCAB, BiDrAC, DcAmB, Drake, NatCAB 16, TwCBDA, WhAm H*
Parke, Benjamin 1801- *Drake*
Parke, Francis Neal 1871-1955 *WhAm 3*
Parke, Harry Wiswall 1891-1947 *NatCAB 35*
Parke, Henry Charles 1892-1968 *NatCAB 55*
Parke, Henry Hall 1876-1957 *NatCAB 46*
Parke, Henry Walter 1901-1970 *WhAm 5*
Parke, Hervey Coke 1827-1899 *NatCAB 24*
Parke, Hervey Coke 1873-1951 *NatCAB 40*
Parke, Jessie Burns 1879-1964 *NatCAB 50*
Parke, John 1750?- *Drake*
Parke, John 1754-1789 *ApCAB, DcAmB, NatCAB 13, WhAm H*
Parke, John Grubb 1827-1900 *AmBi, ApCAB, DcAmB, Drake, NatCAB 12, TwCBDA, WhAm 1*
Parke, John Shepard 1896-1954 *WhAm 3*
Parke, Joseph 1705-1777 *ApCAB, Drake*
Parke, Mary *NewYHSD*
Parke, N Grier 1884-1961 *NatCAB 49*
Parke, Samuel 1853-1940 *NatCAB 29*
Parke, Thomas 1749-1835 *ApCAB*
Parke, Thomas 1901-1965 *NatCAB 51*
Parke, Thomas Albert 1849-1895 *ApCAB X*
Parke, William More 1878-1962 *NatCAB 48, WhAm 4*
Parker, Mister 1822?- *NewYHSD*
Parker, A *NewYHSD*
Parker, A Warner 1872-1939 *WhAm 1*
Parker, Abraham X 1831-1909 *BiDrAC, TwCBDA*
Parker, Addison Bennett 1869-1944 *WhAm 2*
Parker, Adella *WomWWA 14*
Parker, Alan Phares 1901-1970 *NatCAB 57*
Parker, Albert George, Jr. 1892-1958 *NatCAB 44, WhAm 3*
Parker, Alexander Wilson 1898-1972 *WhAm 5*
Parker, Alexis DuPont 1859-1932 *NatCAB 23,*

WhAm 1

Parker, Alice 1864- *AmWom*
Parker, Alice Bennett *WomWWA 14*
Parker, Alton Brooks 1851-1926 *ApCAB Sup, NatCAB 10*
Parker, Alton Brooks 1852-1926 *AmBi, ApCAB X, DcAmB, NatCAB 27, TwCBDA, WhAm 1, WhAmP*
Parker, Alvin Pierson 1850-1924 *DcAmB*
Parker, Amasa Junius 1807-1890 *ApCAB, BiAUS, BiDrAC, DcAmB, Drake, NatCAB 2, TwCBDA, WhAm H*
Parker, Amasa Junius 1843-1938 *NatCAB 2, TwCBDA, WhAm 2*
Parker, Amory 1918-1967 *WhAm 4*
Parker, Andrew 1805-1864 *BiAUS, BiDrAC, WhAm H*
Parker, Arthur Caswell 1881-1955 *DcAmB S5, WhAm 3*
Parker, Augusta Talcott 1877- *WomWWA 14*
Parker, Ben Hutchinson 1902-1969 *NatCAB 55, WhAm 5*
Parker, Benjamin 1759-1845 *NatCAB 5*
Parker, Benjamin Franklin 1839-1912 *WhAm 1*
Parker, Bonnie *REnAW*
Parker, Bowdoin Strong 1841- *NatCAB 15*
Parker, C R *NewYHSD*
Parker, Carleton Hubbell 1878-1918 *DcAmB, NatCAB 19*
Parker, Caroline Miller 1874- *WomWWA 14*
Parker, Charles 1809- *NatCAB 1*
Parker, Charles A 1909-1959 *WhAm 3*
Parker, Charles Barnsdall 1853- *WhAm 4*
Parker, Charles Christopher 1920-1955 *McGEWB, WhAm HA, WhAm 4*
Parker, Charles David 1853- *NatCAB 16*
Parker, Charles Edward d1909 *WhAm 1*
Parker, Charles Edward 1872-1933 *WhAm 1*
Parker, Charles H 1795?-1819 *NewYHSD*
Parker, Charles Morton 1868-1934 *WhAm 1*
Parker, Charles Wolcott 1862-1948 *NatCAB 46, WhAm 2*
Parker, Charlie 1920-1955 *DcAmB S5, WebAB*
Parker, Chauncey David 1873- *WhAm 5*
Parker, Chauncey Goodrich 1864-1943 *NatCAB 35, WhAm 2*
Parker, Chauncey Goodrich, Jr. 1897-1953 *WhAm 3*
Parker, Cola Godden 1890-1962 *WhAm 4*
Parker, Cortlandt 1818-1907 *ApCAB, DcAmB, NatCAB 12, NatCAB 36, TwCBDA, WhAm 1*
Parker, Cortlandt 1884-1960 *NatCAB 50, WhAm 3*
Parker, Cynthia Ann 1827?-1864? *NotAW*
Parker, Daingerfield 1832-1925 *WhAm 1*
Parker, Daniel 1781-1844 *DcAmReB*
Parker, Daniel 1782-1846 *ApCAB, Drake*
Parker, Daniel Francis 1893-1967 *WhAm 4*
Parker, DeWitt Henry 1885-1949 *WhAm 2*
Parker, Dexter Wright 1849- *NatCAB 18*
Parker, Donald 1874-1949 *NatCAB 39*
Parker, Dorothy Rothschild 1893-1967 *McGEWB, WebAB, WhAm 4*
Parker, Edgar 1840- *Drake, NewYHSD*
Parker, Edith Putnam 1886-1961 *WhAm 4*
Parker, Edmund Southard d1921 *WhAm 1*
Parker, Edward Burns 1895-1958 *NatCAB 47, WhAm 3*
Parker, Edward Cary 1881-1939 *WhAm 1*
Parker, Edward Clifton 1874-1961 *NatCAB 50*
Parker, Edward Frost 1867-1938 *WhAm 1*
Parker, Edward Griffin 1825-1868 *ApCAB, Drake*
Parker, Edward J 1869-1961 *WhAm 4*
Parker, Edward Leslie 1881-1956 *NatCAB 42*
Parker, Edward Lutwyche 1785-1850 *ApCAB, Drake*
Parker, Edward Mason 1860-1941 *NatCAB 30*
Parker, Edward Melville 1855-1925 *NatCAB 25, WhAm 1*
Parker, Edward Pickering 1912-1974 *WhAm 6*
Parker, Edward Sanders, Jr. 1872-1933 *WhAm 1*
Parker, Edward Wheeler 1860- *NatCAB 14, WhAm 4*
Parker, Edwin Augustus 1872-1929 *NatCAB 39*

Parker, Edwin Brewington 1868-1929 *ApCAB X, DcAmB, NatCAB 21, WhAm 1*
Parker, Edwin Pond 1836-1920 *DcAmB, NatCAB 25, WhAm 1*
Parker, Edwin Wallace 1833-1901 *DcAmB, NatCAB 5, WhAm H*
Parker, Eila Moore Johnson 1900-1973 *WhAm 6*
Parker, Eli S 1828-1895 *BiAUS*
Parker, Elizabeth Chandler *WomWWA 14*
Parker, Elizabeth Kittredge 1881- *WomWWA 14*
Parker, Elizabeth Middleton Bryan 1881- *WomWWA 14*
Parker, Ely Samuel 1828-1895 *ApCAB, DcAmB, NatCAB 5, TwCBDA, WebAMB, WhAm H*
Parker, Emma Harriet 1863- *WomWWA 14*
Parker, Emmett Newton 1859-1939 *WhAm 1*
Parker, Evan James 1894-1964 *WhAm 4*
Parker, Fitzgerald Sale 1863- *WhAm 1*
Parker, Fletcher Douglas 1888-1963 *WhAm 4*
Parker, Forrest Hoffman 1837-1918 *NatCAB 38*
Parker, Foxhall Alexander 1821-1879 *AmBi, ApCAB, DcAmB, Drake, NatCAB 5, TwCBDA, WebAMB, WhAm H*
Parker, Frances 1875- *WhAm 5, WomWWA 14*
Parker, Frances T 1871- *WomWWA 14*
Parker, Francis Hubert 1850-1927 *WhAm 1*
Parker, Francis Lejau 1873- *WhAm 5*
Parker, Francis Warner 1858-1922 *WhAm 1*
Parker, Francis Wayland 1837-1902 *AmBi, ApCAB, BiDAmEd, DcAmB, TwCBDA, WebAB, WhAm 1*
Parker, Frank 1872-1947 *NatCAB 35, WhAm 2*
Parker, Frank Wilson 1860-1932 *WhAm 1*
Parker, Franklin Eddy 1867- *WhAm 1*
Parker, Franklin Eddy, Jr. 1895-1963 *NatCAB 50, WhAm 4*
Parker, Franklin Nutting 1867- *WhAm 5*
Parker, Frederic, Jr. 1890-1969 *WhAm 5*
Parker, Frederic Charles Wesby 1872-1945 *WhAm 2*
Parker, Frederick Livingston 1874-1951 *NatCAB 39*
Parker, Gabe Edward 1878- *WhAm 6*
Parker, George d1868 *NewYHSD*
Parker, George Albert 1856-1939 *WhAm 1*
Parker, George Amos 1853-1926 *WhAm 1*
Parker, George Bertrand 1886-1949 *NatCAB 39, WhAm 2*
Parker, George Frederick 1847-1928 *NatCAB 24, WhAm 1*
Parker, George Hoffman 1863-1919 *NatCAB 18*
Parker, George Howard 1864-1955 *DcAmB S5, WhAm 3*
Parker, George Leroy *REnAW*
Parker, George Proctor 1885- *WhAm 1*
Parker, George Swinnerton 1866-1952 *NatCAB 40, WhAm 3*
Parker, George Washington 1836-1913 *NatCAB 6, NatCAB 12*
Parker, Gertrude Waterhouse 1858- *WomWWA 14*
Parker, Gilbert LaFayette 1832-1915 *NatCAB 16*
Parker, Glenn Lane d1946 *WhAm 2*
Parker, Grady P 1903-1972 *WhAm 5*
Parker, H Wayne 1904-1967 *WhAm 5*
Parker, Harry Lee 1894-1959 *NatCAB 48, WhAm 3*
Parker, Harry McDoel 1859-1921 *NatCAB 25*
Parker, Hattie Rowland *WomWWA 14*
Parker, Helen Almena *AmWom*
Parker, Helen Eliza Fitch 1827-1874 *ApCAB, TwCBDA*
Parker, Henry *NatCAB 1*
Parker, Henry 1690?-1777 *ApCAB*
Parker, Henry 1690-1778? *TwCBDA*
Parker, Henry Griffith 1866-1953 *NatCAB 46, WhAm 3*
Parker, Henry Hodges 1834-1927 *NatCAB 22*
Parker, Henry Pickering 1875-1925 *NatCAB 21*

Parker, Henry Taylor 1867-1934 *DcAmB S1, WhAm 1*
Parker, Henry Webster 1822- *Drake, TwCBDA*
Parker, Henry Webster 1824- *ApCAB*
Parker, Henry William 1860- *NatCAB 15*
Parker, Herbert 1856-1939 *AmBi, NatCAB 29, WhAm 1*
Parker, Herschel Clifford 1867- *NatCAB 14, WhAm 4*
Parker, Hilon Adelbert 1841-1911 *WhAm 1*
Parker, Homer Cling 1885-1946 *BiDrAC, WhAm 2*
Parker, Horatio Gilbert 1859- *ApCAB Sup*
Parker, Horatio Newton 1871-1946 *WhAm 2*
Parker, Horatio William 1863-1919 *AmBi, ApCAB X, BiDAmEd, DcAmB, McGEWB, NatCAB 11, NatCAB 35, TwCBDA, WhAm 1*
Parker, Hosea Washington 1833-1922 *BiAUS, BiDrAC, TwCBDA, WhAm 1*
Parker, Hugh E 1887-1956 *WhAm 3*
Parker, Sir Hyde 1739-1807 *ApCAB, Drake, WhoMilH*
Parker, Isaac 1768-1830 *ApCAB, BiAUS, BiDrAC, DcAmB, Drake, NatCAB 2, TwCBDA, WhAm H*
Parker, Isaac Charles 1838-1896 *BiAUS, BiDrAC, DcAmB, REnAW, TwCBDA, WhAm H*
Parker, J Brooks Bloodgood 1889-1951 *NatCAB 45*
Parker, J Heber 1881-1956 *NatCAB 46, WhAm 3*
Parker, J Roy 1895-1957 *WhAm 3*
Parker, James 1714?-1770 *DcAmB, WhAm H*
Parker, James 1768-1837 *BiAUS, BiDrAC, WhAm H*
Parker, James 1776-1868 *ApCAB, BiAUS, BiDrAC, DcAmB, Drake, TwCBDA, WhAm H, WhAmP*
Parker, James 1854-1934 *NatCAB 25, WhAm 1*
Parker, James Cutler Dunn 1828-1916 *DcAmB, NatCAB 5, TwCBDA, WhAm 1*
Parker, James Cutter Dunn 1828-1916 *ApCAB*
Parker, James Edmund 1896-1946 *WhAm 2*
Parker, James Henry 1843-1915 *NatCAB 3, NatCAB 16, WhAm 1*
Parker, James I 1857- *WhAm 4*
Parker, James K 1880?-1963 *IIBEAAW*
Parker, James Phillips 1874-1948 *NatCAB 42*
Parker, James Southworth 1867-1933 *BiDrAC, WhAm 1, WhAmP*
Parker, James Wentworth 1886-1957 *NatCAB 44, WhAm 3*
Parker, Jameson 1909-1972 *WhAm 5*
Parker, Jane Marsh 1836-1913 *DcAmB, NatCAB 10, TwCBDA, WhAm 4*
Parker, Jo A 1869- *WhAm 5*
Parker, Joel 1795-1875 *AmBi, ApCAB, BiAUS, DcAmB, Drake, NatCAB 12, TwCBDA, WhAm H*
Parker, Joel 1799-1873 *ApCAB, DcAmB, Drake, NatCAB 7, TwCBDA, WhAm H*
Parker, Joel 1816-1888 *AmBi, ApCAB, BiAUS, DcAmB, NatCAB 5, TwCBDA, WhAm H*
Parker, John 1729-1775 *DcAmB, NatCAB 1, WebAB, WebAMB, WhAm H*
Parker, John 1749-1822 *ApCAB, TwCBDA*
Parker, John 1759-1832 *BiAUS, BiDrAC, WhAm H*
Parker, John 1875-1952 *WhAm 3*
Parker, John, Jr. *NewYHSD*
Parker, John Adams 1827- *WhAm 4*
Parker, John Adams 1827-1900 *TwCBDA*
Parker, John Adams 1829- *ApCAB*
Parker, John Adams, Jr. 1827?-1905? *NewYHSD*
Parker, John Bernard 1870-1951 *WhAm 3*
Parker, John Castiereagh, Jr. 1879-1953 *NatCAB 41, WhAm 6*
Parker, John Cortlandt 1818-1907 *DcAmB*
Parker, John D 1831- *WhAm 4*
Parker, John Emilius 1879-1951 *NatCAB 39*

Parker, John Gowans 1883-1953 *WhAm 3*
Parker, John Henry 1866-1942 *WhAm 2*
Parker, John Johnston 1885-1958 *NatCAB 47, WhAm 3*
Parker, John Mason 1805-1873 *BiAUS, BiDrAC, TwCBDA, WhAm H*
Parker, John Milliken 1863-1939 *DcAmB S2, NatCAB 29, WhAm 1, WhAmP*
Parker, John Walter 1879- *WhoColR*
Parker, Joseph *NewYHSD*
Parker, Joseph 1810-1887 *NatCAB 7*
Parker, Joseph Benson 1841-1915 *NatCAB 17, WhAm 1*
Parker, Josiah 1751-1810 *BiAUS, BiDrAC, DcAmB, TwCBDA, WhAm H, WhAmP*
Parker, Julia Evelina Smith *WhAm H*
Parker, Julius Frederick 1910-1966 *WhAm 4*
Parker, Junius 1867-1944 *NatCAB 33, WhAm 2*
Parker, Kenneth Colburn 1892-1961 *NatCAB 49, WhAm 4*
Parker, L Maud *WomWWA 14*
Parker, Laigh C 1902-1959 *WhAm 3*
Parker, Lawton S 1868-1954 *WhAm 3*
Parker, Leonard Fletcher 1825- *TwCBDA, WhAm 1*
Parker, Leonard Moody 1789-1854 *ApCAB*
Parker, Lewis Wardlwa 1865- *WhAm 4*
Parker, Life, Jr. 1822- *NewYHSD*
Parker, Linus 1829-1885 *ApCAB, TwCBDA*
Parker, Linus Marcellus 1884-1947 *NatCAB 42*
Parker, Lottie Blair d1937 *NatCAB 10, WhAm 1, WomWWA 14*
Parker, Louise Merritt 1868- *WomWWA 14*
Parker, Lovell Hallet 1882-1961 *WhAm 4*
Parker, M S *NewYHSD*
Parker, Marion W 1907-1966 *WhAm 4*
Parker, Matthew *NewYHSD*
Parker, Maude d1959 *WhAm 3*
Parker, Maurice 1916-1974 *WhAm 6*
Parker, Millard Mayhew 1849-1928 *NatCAB 27, WhAm 4*
Parker, Morris Ketchum 1878-1925 *NatCAB 26*
Parker, Moses Greeley 1842-1917 *WhAm 1*
Parker, Myron Melvin 1843-1929 *NatCAB 40, WhAm 4*
Parker, Nahum 1760-1839 *ApCAB, BiAUS, BiDrAC, NatCAB 5, TwCBDA, WhAm H*
Parker, Nathan 1782-1833 *Drake*
Parker, Nathaniel 1802- *NewYHSD*
Parker, Permelia Jane Marsh 1836- *ApCAB*
Parker, Peter *BiAUS*
Parker, Sir Peter 1721-1811 *ApCAB*
Parker, Sir Peter 1723-1811 *Drake*
Parker, Sir Peter 1786-1814 *ApCAB*
Parker, Peter 1804-1888 *ApCAB, DcAmB, NatCAB 10, TwCBDA, WhAm H*
Parker, Philip Stanley 1867-1939 *NatCAB 42*
Parker, Quanah 1840?- *ApCAB Sup*
Parker, Quanah 1845?-1911 *DcAmB, DcAmReB, WebAB*
Parker, Ralph Robinson 1888-1949 *WhAm 2*
Parker, Ralzemond Allen 1843- *NatCAB 15*
Parker, Raymond 1922- *BnEnAmA*
Parker, Rea 1880-1948 *NatCAB 37*
Parker, Richard d1780 *Drake*
Parker, Richard 1810-1893 *BiAUS, BiDrAC, WhAm H, WhAmP*
Parker, Richard E 1777-1840 *BiAUS, Drake*
Parker, Richard Elliot 1783-1840 *DcAmB, WhAm H*
Parker, Richard Elliott 1783-1840 *ApCAB, BiDrAC, NatCAB 11, TwCBDA*
Parker, Richard Green 1798-1869 *ApCAB, BiDAmEd, DcAmB, Drake, WhAm H*
Parker, Richard Wayne 1848-1923 *BiDrAC, NatCAB 36, TwCBDA, WhAm 1, WhAmP*
Parker, Robert 1906-1955 *WhAm 3*
Parker, Robert Hunt 1892-1969 *WhAm 5*
Parker, Robert Meade 1864- *ApCAB X, NatCAB 15*
Parker, Robert Randolph 1880-1942 *NatCAB 42*
Parker, Robert Shumate 1884-1941 *WhAm 2*
Parker, Rolla Jabish 1857-1921 *NatCAB 19*

Parker, Ross Isaac 1890-1973 *WhAm 6*
Parker, Ruth Louise *WomWWA 14*
Parker, Samuel 1744-1804 *ApCAB, Drake, NatCAB 6, TwCBDA*
Parker, Samuel 1779-1866 *ApCAB, DcAmB, Drake, NatCAB 7, TwCBDA, WhAm H*
Parker, Samuel Chester 1880-1924 *DcAmB, WhAm 1*
Parker, Samuel Parker 1805-1880 *TwCBDA*
Parker, Samuel Wilson 1805-1859 *BiAUS, BiDrAC, WhAm H*
Parker, Severn Eyre 1787-1836 *BiAUS, BiDrAC, WhAm H*
Parker, Sophy Gordon 1849- *WomWWA 14*
Parker, Stanley Vincent 1885-1968 *NatCAB 54, WhAm 5*
Parker, Susan Duroe 1859- *WomWWA 14*
Parker, Theodore 1810-1860 *AmBi, ApCAB, DcAmB, DcAmReB, Drake, EncAB, McGEWB, NatCAB 2, TwCBDA, WebAB, WhAm H*
Parker, Theodore Bissell 1889-1944 *DcAmB S3, WhAm 2*
Parker, Thomas *BiAUS*
Parker, Thomas 1595-1677 *ApCAB, DcAmB, Drake, NatCAB 12, WhAm H*
Parker, Thomas 1753-1820 *ApCAB, Drake*
Parker, Thomas Cleveland 1904-1967 *WhAm 4*
Parker, Thomas H 1801- *NewYHSD*
Parker, Torrance 1872-1945 *WhAm 2*
Parker, Valeria Hopkins 1879-1959 *WhAm 3A, WomWWA 14*
Parker, W S *NewYHSD*
Parker, Walter Huntington 1884-1968 *WhAm 5*
Parker, Walter Robert 1865-1955 *WhAm 3*
Parker, Walter Scott 1849-1933 *NatCAB 35*
Parker, Walter Winfield 1889-1957 *NatCAB 46, WhAm 3*
Parker, Watson 1924- *EncAAH*
Parker, Wesby Reed 1903-1967 *WhAm 4*
Parker, Willard 1800-1884 *AmBi, ApCAB, BiHiMed, DcAmB, NatCAB 9, TwCBDA, WhAm H*
Parker, Willard 1857- *WhAm 4*
Parker, Willard Justin 1887-1960 *NatCAB 45*
Parker, William Allen 1866-1934 *NatCAB 26*
Parker, William Belmont 1871-1934 *WhAm 1*
Parker, William Edward 1876-1942 *WhAm 2*
Parker, William Gordon 1875- *WhAm 5*
Parker, William Harwar 1826-1896 *ApCAB, DcAmB, TwCBDA, WebAMB, WhAm H*
Parker, William Henry 1847-1908 *BiDrAC, WhAm 1*
Parker, William Henry 1873-1956 *NatCAB 45*
Parker, William Henry 1902-1966 *WhAm 5*
Parker, William McCready 1870-1943 *NatCAB 32, WhAm 2*
Parker, William Riley 1906-1968 *NatCAB 54, WhAm 5*
Parker, William Stanley 1877- *WhAm 5*
Parker, Winthrop 1857-1937 *NatCAB 27*
Parker, Woodruff John 1880-1930 *NatCAB 22*
Parkerson, Jesse Jones 1884-1959 *WhAm 4*
Parkes, Alexander 1813-1890 *AsBiEn*
Parkes, Charles Herbert 1872- *WhAm 4*
Parkes, Sir Henry 1815-1896 *McGEWB*
Parkes, Henry Bamford 1904-1972 *WhAm 5*
Parkes, W *NewYHSD*
Parkes, William Ross 1869- *WhAm 5*
Parkhill, Charles Breckinridge 1859-1933 *NatCAB 9, WhAm 1*
Parkhill, James William 1855- *WhAm 4*
Parkhurst, Charles 1845-1921 *DcAmB, WhAm 1*
Parkhurst, Charles Henry 1842-1933 *AmBi, ApCAB, ApCAB X, DcAmB, DcAmReB, NatCAB 4, TwCBDA, WhAm 1*
Parkhurst, Christopher Francis 1854-1925 *NatCAB 24, WhAm 1*
Parkhurst, Daniel S *NewYHSD*
Parkhurst, Emelie Tracy Y Swett 1863-1892 *AmWom*
Parkhurst, Frederic Augustus 1877- *WhAm 5*
Parkhurst, Frederic Hale 1864-1921 *WhAm 1*
Parkhurst, Frederick Hale 1864-1921 *NatCAB 26*
Parkhurst, Helen 1887-1973 *BiDAmEd*
Parkhurst, Helen 1892-1973 *WhAm 6*

Parkhurst, Helen Huss 1887-1959 *WhAm 3*
Parkhurst, Howard Elmore 1848-1916 *TwCBDA, WhAm 1*
Parkhurst, John Adelbert 1861-1925 *DcAmB, DcScB, NatCAB 20, WhAm 1*
Parkhurst, John Foster 1843-1906 *WhAm 1*
Parkhurst, John Gibson 1824-1906 *NatCAB 7, WhAm 1*
Parkhurst, Lewis 1856-1949 *WhAm 2*
Parkhurst, Ralph Richards 1872-1955 *NatCAB 43*
Parkindon, Thomas Ignatius 1881-1959 *WhAm 3*
Parkington, E *WomWWA 14*
Parkins, Almon Ernest 1879-1940 *BiDAmEd, NatCAB 38, WhAm 1*
Parkins, Sir J *NewYHSD*
Parkinson, Amy *WomWWA 14*
Parkinson, Burney Lynch 1887-1972 *WhAm 5*
Parkinson, Daniel Baldwin 1845-1923 *NatCAB 10, TwCBDA, WhAm 1*
Parkinson, Donald Berthold 1895-1945 *NatCAB 35*
Parkinson, Donald Berthold 1895-1946 *WhAm 2*
Parkinson, James 1755-1824 *BiHiMed, DcScB*
Parkinson, John 1861-1935 *NatCAB 26*
Parkinson, John Barber 1834-1927 *NatCAB 13, WhAm 1*
Parkinson, Richard *NewYHSD*
Parkinson, Richard 1748-1815 *ApCAB, Drake*
Parkinson, Robert Henry 1849-1927 *WhAm 1*
Parkinson, Sydney 1745?-1771 *DcScB*
Parkinson, Thomas Ignatius 1881-1959 *NatCAB 47*
Parkinson, William 1774-1848 *ApCAB, Drake*
Parkinson, William Jensen 1899- *IIBEAAW*
Parkinson, William Lynn 1902-1959 *NatCAB 48, WhAm 4*
Parkinson, William Nimon 1886-1971 *NatCAB 57, WhAm 5*
Parkisen *NewYHSD*
Parkman, Ebenezer 1703-1782 *Drake*
Parkman, Ebenezer 1703-1789 *ApCAB*
Parkman, Francis 1788-1852 *ApCAB, Drake, TwCBDA*
Parkman, Francis 1823-1893 *AmBi, ApCAB, DcAmB, Drake, EncAAH, EncAB, McGEWB, NatCAB 1, REnAW, TwCBDA, WebAB, WhAm H*
Parkman, George 1791-1849 *ApCAB*
Parkman, Henry 1850-1924 *ApCAB X, NatCAB 20, WhAm 1*
Parkman, Henry 1894-1958 *WhAm 3*
Parks, Addison Karrick 1875-1943 *WhAm 2*
Parks, Albert Henry 1890-1954 *NatCAB 43*
Parks, Alonzo *NewYHSD*
Parks, Asa *NewYHSD*
Parks, Charles Darling 1869-1929 *NatCAB 22*
Parks, Charles Wellman 1863-1930 *NatCAB 22, WhAm 1*
Parks, Clifford C 1860-1937 *WhAm 1*
Parks, E Taylor 1898-1966 *WhAm 4*
Parks, Edd Winfield 1906-1968 *NatCAB 54, WhAm 5*
Parks, Edward Lamay 1851-1930 *WhAm 1*
Parks, Elton 1882-1943 *NatCAB 38*
Parks, Ethel R d1963 *WhAm 4*
Parks, Floyd Lavinius 1896-1959 *WhAm 3*
Parks, Frances P 1856- *WomWWA 14*
Parks, Frank Thomas 1890-1959 *WhAm 4*
Parks, Fred Willard 1872-1941 *NatCAB 31*
Parks, Frederick *NewYHSD*
Parks, George Winant 1856-1929 *ApCAB X, NatCAB 31*
Parks, Gorham 1793-1877 *BiAUS*
Parks, Gorham 1794-1877 *BiDrAC, WhAm H*
Parks, Grace Runyan 1868- *WomWWA 14*
Parks, Henry Blanton *WhoColR*
Parks, Henry Martin 1872-1945 *WhAm 3*
Parks, J *NewYHSD*
Parks, James Lewis 1848-1912 *WhAm 1*
Parks, James Lewis 1886-1934 *WhAm 1*
Parks, John Louis 1908-1972 *WhAm 5*
Parks, John Shields 1870- *WhAm 5*
Parks, Leighton 1852-1938 *TwCBDA, WhAm 1*
Parks, Margaret *WomWWA 14*

Parks, Marvin McTyeire 1872-1926 *NatCAB 24, WhAm 1*
Parks, Mary Leitch 1857- *WomWWA 14*
Parks, Richard *NewYHSD*
Parks, Robert Lee McAllister 1902- *WhAm 3*
Parks, Rufus 1837-1913 *WhAm 1*
Parks, Samuel Augustus 1822-1877 *NewYHSD*
Parks, Samuel C *BiAUS*
Parks, Samuel Conant 1859-1944 *WhAm 2*
Parks, Tilman Bacon 1872-1950 *BiDrAC, WhAm 3, WhAmP*
Parks, Wilbur George 1904-1975 *WhAm 6*
Parks, William d1750 *NatCAB 20*
Parks, William 1696?-1750 *AmBi*
Parks, William 1698?-1750 *DcAmB, WhAm H*
Parks, Wythe Marchant 1856-1938 *NatCAB 28, WhAm 1*
Parkyns, George Isham 1749?-1820? *NewYHSD, WhAm H*
Parlange, Charles 1851-1907 *TwCBDA, WhAm 1*
Parlette, Ralph 1870-1930 *WhAm 1*
Parley, Peter 1793-1860 *AmBi, DcAmB, WebAB, WhAm H*
Parlin, Albert Norton 1848-1927 *NatCAB 21*
Parlin, Frank Edson 1860-1939 *WhAm 1*
Parlin, H T 1879-1951 *WhAm 3*
Parlin, William Henry 1847-1920 *WhAm 1*
Parloa, Maria 1843-1909 *NotAW, WhAm 1*
Parlow, Mary Kathleen 1890- *WomWWA 14*
Parma, Alessandro Farnese, Duque Di 1545-1592 *WhoMilH*
Parmele, Harris Barnum 1901-1965 *WhAm 4*
Parmele, Mary Platt 1843-1911 *WhAm 1*
Parmelee, Amy Olgen 1882- *WomWWA 14*
Parmelee, Charles N 1805?- *NewYHSD*
Parmelee, Cullen Warner 1874-1947 *NatCAB 41, WhAm 3*
Parmelee, Elmer Eugene 1839-1861 *NewYHSD*
Parmelee, Henry Francis 1875-1934 *WhAm 1*
Parmelee, Howard Coon 1874-1959 *NatCAB 45, WhAm 3*
Parmelee, Julius Hall 1883-1961 *NatCAB 49, WhAm 4*
Parmelee, Lewis Dwight 1896- *WhAm 3*
Parmelee, Theodore Nelson 1804-1874 *ApCAB*
Parmenides *McGEWB*
Parmenides 540?BC- *AsBiEn*
Parmenides Of Elea 515?BC-450?BC *DcScB*
Parmenter, Bertice Marvin 1867-1945 *WhAm 2*
Parmenter, Charles Sylvester 1860-1922 *WhAm 1*
Parmenter, Charles Winfield 1852- *WhAm 4*
Parmenter, Christine Whiting 1877-1953 *WhAm 3*
Parmenter, Derric Choate 1890-1958 *NatCAB 43*
Parmenter, Frederick James 1880-1962 *NatCAB 50, WhAm 6*
Parmenter, George Freeman 1877-1955 *WhAm 3*
Parmenter, Henry Earl 1861-1941 *NatCAB 30*
Parmenter, Roswell A 1821- *NatCAB 1, WhAm 4*
Parmenter, William 1789-1866 *BiAUS, BiDrAC, TwCBDA, WhAm H*
Parmentier, Andrew 1780-1830 *DcAmB S1, WhAm H*
Parmentier, Antoine-Augustin 1737-1813 *DcScB*
Parmentier, Auguste Henry 1752-1816? *ApCAB*
Parmentier, Jehan 1494-1530 *ApCAB*
Parmigianino 1503-1540 *McGEWB*
Parmley, Joseph William 1861-1940 *WhAm 1*
Parmley, Walter Camp 1862-1934 *WhAm 1*
Parmly, Charles Howard 1868-1917 *NatCAB 17*
Parmly, Eleazar 1797-1874 *DcAmB, NatCAB 28, WhAm H*
Parnall, Christopher 1880-1960 *WhAm 4*
Parnas, Jakub Karol 1884-1949 *DcScB*
Parnell, Charles Stewart 1846-1891 *McGEWB*
Parnell, Harvey 1880-1936 *NatCAB 26, WhAm 1*
Parpart, Arthur Kemble 1903-1965 *NatCAB 51, WhAm 4*
Parr, Charles McKew 1884-1976 *WhAm 6*
Parr, Harry L 1880-1964 *WhAm 4*

Parr, Henry A *NatCAB 12*
Parr, Jerome Henry 1909- *WhAm 3*
Parr, Joseph Greer 1881-1952 *WhAm 3*
Parr, Ral 1877-1939 *NatCAB 29*
Parr, Samuel Wilson 1857-1931 *AmBi, DcAmB, WhAm 1*
Parr, William David 1855-1918 *WhAm 1*
Parra, Antonio DeLa *ApCAB*
Parra, Francisco 1500?-1560 *ApCAB*
Parran, Thomas 1860-1955 *BiDrAC, WhAm 4*
Parran, Thomas 1892-1968 *WhAm 4*
Parreno, Jose Julian 1728-1785 *ApCAB*
Parrett, Arthur N 1896-1956 *WhAm 3*
Parrett, William Fletcher 1825-1895 *BiDrAC, WhAm H*
Parrington, Vernon Louis 1871-1929 *AmBi, DcAmB, EncAAH, McGEWB, NatCAB 25, REnAW, WebAB, WhAm 1*
Parriott, Foster Brooks 1878-1957 *NatCAB 49, WhAm 3*
Parriott, James Deforis 1880-1948 *WhAm 2*
Parris, Albion Keith 1788-1857 *ApCAB, BiAUS, BiDrAC, DcAmB, Drake, NatCAB 6, WhAm H, WhAmP*
Parris, Albion Keith 1798-1857 *TwCBDA*
Parris, Alexander 1780-1852 *BnEnAmA, DcAmB, WhAm H*
Parris, Samuel 1653-1719? *DcAmB, WhAm H*
Parris, Samuel 1653-1720 *AmBi, ApCAB, Drake, NatCAB 13*
Parris, Virgil Delphini 1807-1874 *BiAUS, BiDrAC, WhAm H, WhAmP*
Parrisen *NewYHSD*
Parrisen, J *NewYHSD*
Parrish, Alan Jay 1885-1968 *NatCAB 54*
Parrish, Albert Garrett 1850- *WhAm 3*
Parrish, Anne *NewYHSD*
Parrish, Anne 1760-1800 *DcAmB, WhAm H*
Parrish, Anne 1888-1957 *WhAm 3*
Parrish, Anne Lodge 1850?- *IIBEAAW*
Parrish, Carl 1904-1965 *WhAm 4*
Parrish, Celestia Susannah 1853-1918 *BiDAmEd, DcAmB, NotAW, TwCBDA, WhAm 1, WomWWA 14*
Parrish, Charles 1826-1896 *DcAmB, NatCAB 9, WhAm H*
Parrish, Charles Henry 1859- *WhoColR*
Parrish, Charles Louis 1830?-1902 *IIBEAAW, NewYHSD*
Parrish, Clara Weaver d1925 *WhAm 1, WomWWA 14*
Parrish, Dillwyn d1885 *NatCAB 5*
Parrish, Dillwyn 1894-1941 *NatCAB 38*
Parrish, Edith May Winch 1874- *WomWWA 14*
Parrish, Edward 1822-1872 *AmBi, ApCAB, BiDAmEd, DcAmB, Drake, NatCAB 5, TwCBDA, WhAm H*
Parrish, Edward James 1846-1920 *NatCAB 38*
Parrish, George 1872-1941 *NatCAB 30*
Parrish, George Randall 1858- *ApCAB X*
Parrish, Henry James 1859-1942 *NatCAB 32*
Parrish, Isaac 1804-1860 *BiAUS, BiDrAC, WhAm H*
Parrish, Isaac 1811-1852 *ApCAB, NatCAB 12, WhAm H*
Parrish, Jack McPherson 1893-1952 *NatCAB 45*
Parrish, James Ware 1862-1940 *NatCAB 30*
Parrish, Jean 1920?- *IIBEAAW*
Parrish, John 1729-1807 *ApCAB*
Parrish, John Bertrand 1877- *WhAm 5*
Parrish, John Wells 1865-1949 *NatCAB 37*
Parrish, Joseph 1779-1840 *ApCAB, DcAmB, Drake, NatCAB 12, TwCBDA, WhAm H*
Parrish, Joseph 1818-1891 *ApCAB, NatCAB 12, TwCBDA*
Parrish, Joseph Alfred Deans 1882-1951 *NatCAB 38*
Parrish, Karl Calvin 1877-1933 *WhAm 1*
Parrish, Lucian Walton 1878-1922 *BiDrAC, NatCAB 20, WhAm 1*
Parrish, Maxfield Frederick 1870-1966 *BnEnAmA, IIBEAAW, NatCAB 12, NatCAB 53, TwCBDA, WebAB, WhAm 4*
Parrish, Philip Hammon 1896- *WhAm 3*
Parrish, Randall 1858-1923 *WhAm 1*

Parrish, Robert Lewis 1876-1915 *WhAm 1*
Parrish, Samuel 1830-1889 *NatCAB 25*
Parrish, Samuel Longstreth 1849- *ApCAB X*
Parrish, Stephen 1846-1938 *AmBi, ApCAB, NatCAB 38, TwCBDA, WhAm 1*
Parrish, Thomas 1837-1899 *IIBEAAW*
Parrish, Thomas Clarkson 1846-1899 *NatCAB 24*
Parrish, William 1885- *WhoColR*
Parrisien *NewYHSD*
Parrot, Raymond Townley 1880-1962 *NatCAB 48*
Parrott, Alonzo Leslie 1891-1976 *WhAm 6*
Parrott, Claude Byron 1895-1963 *WhAm 4*
Parrott, Enoch G 1814-1879 *Drake*
Parrott, Enoch Greenleaf 1814-1879 *ApCAB, NatCAB 4, TwCBDA*
Parrott, Enoch Greenleafe 1815-1879 *DcAmB, WebAMB, WhAm H*
Parrott, James Marion 1874-1934 *WhAm 1*
Parrott, John Fabyan 1767-1836 *BiAUS, BiDrAC, WhAm H*
Parrott, John Francis 1768-1836 *ApCAB, NatCAB 11, TwCBDA*
Parrott, Marcus Junius 1828-1879 *BiAUS, BiDrAC, WhAm H*
Parrott, Percival John 1873-1953 *NatCAB 44*
Parrott, Percival John 1874-1953 *WhAm 3*
Parrott, Robert Parker 1804-1877 *AmBi, ApCAB, DcAmB, NatCAB 5, TwCBDA, WebAB, WebAMB, WhAm H*
Parrott, Roger Sheffield 1883-1950 *NatCAB 50*
Parrott, Thomas Marc 1866-1960 *WhAm 3*
Parrott, William Samuel 1844-1915 *IIBEAAW*
Parry, Angenette 1857-1939 *NatCAB 29*
Parry, Caleb 1735?-1776 *ApCAB*
Parry, Caleb Hillier 1755-1822 *BiHiMed*
Parry, Charles 1814-1861 *NatCAB 10*
Parry, Charles Christopher 1823-1890 *DcAmB, NatCAB 13, WhAm H*
Parry, Charles Thomas 1821-1887 *DcAmB, NatCAB 1, WhAm H*
Parry, David Maclean 1852-1915 *WhAm 1*
Parry, David McLean 1852-1915 *NatCAB 12*
Parry, Emma Louise *WhAm 3*
Parry, Frances Camp *WomWWA 14*
Parry, John Jay 1889-1954 *WhAm 3*
Parry, John Stubbs 1843-1876 *DcAmB, WhAm H*
Parry, Josephine Lincoln 1884- *WomWWA 14*
Parry, Sidney Loren 1902-1968 *WhAm 5*
Parry, Thomas 1795-1870 *ApCAB*
Parry, Will H 1864-1917 *NatCAB 18, WhAm 1*
Parry, Sir William Edward 1790-1855 *ApCAB, Drake*
Parry, William Jones 1865-1947 *NatCAB 35*
Parschall, Nathaniel 1804-1866 *ApCAB*
Parsell, Abraham 1792?- *NewYHSD*
Parsell, Charles Victor 1851-1920 *WhAm 1*
Parsell, John H *NewYHSD*
Parseval-Deschenes, Alexander Ferdinand 1790-1860 *ApCAB*
Parseval DesChenes, Marc-Antoine 1755-1836 *DcScB*
Parshall, DeWitt 1864-1956 *IIBEAAW, WhAm 3*
Parshall, Douglass Ewell 1899- *IIBEAAW*
Parshall, Howard Percival 1891-1968 *NatCAB 54*
Parshall, Ralph Leroy 1881-1959 *NatCAB 49*
Parshley, Howard Madison 1884-1953 *NatCAB 40, WhAm 3*
Parsly, Elmer Griffith 1886-1972 *NatCAB 56*
Parson, Hubert Templeton 1872-1940 *WhAm 1*
Parson, Samuel H *BiAUS*
Parson, Willard Sigsbee 1898-1957 *NatCAB 45*
Parsons *NewYHSD*
Parsons, Albert Richard 1848-1887 *DcAmB, WhAm H*
Parsons, Albert Ross 1847-1933 *DcAmB, NatCAB 2, TwCBDA, WhAm 1*
Parsons, Albert Stevens 1841-1922 *ApCAB X, WhAm 1*
Parsons, Alice Beal 1886-1962 *NatCAB 50, WhAm 4*
Parsons, Alice Knight 1855- *WhAm 4, WomWWA 14*

Parsons, Alice Tullis Lord 1878- *WomWWA 14*
Parsons, Andrew 1817-1855 *NatCAB 5, TwCBDA*
Parsons, Andrew Clarkson 1881- *WhAm 6*
Parsons, Anson Virgil 1799-1882 *ApCAB*
Parsons, Archibald Livingstone 1875-1953 *WhAm 3*
Parsons, Arthur Barrette 1887-1966 *WhAm 4*
Parsons, Arthur Hudson, Jr. 1910-1959 *WhAm 3*
Parsons, Azariah Worthington 1857-1931 *WhAm 1*
Parsons, Brackett 1896-1970 *NatCAB 56*
Parsons, C Leland 1919-1973 *WhAm 6*
Parsons, Charles 1821-1910 *AmBi, ApCAB, NewYHSD, TwCBDA, WhAm HA, WhAm 1, WhAm 4*
Parsons, Charles 1824- *NatCAB 12*
Parsons, Charles 1829-1904 *NatCAB 4, WhAm 1*
Parsons, Sir Charles Algernon 1854-1931 *AsBiEn, McGEWB*
Parsons, Charles B 1875-1967 *WhAm 4*
Parsons, Charles Baldwin 1835- *WhAm 1*
Parsons, Charles Carroll 1838-1878 *ApCAB, TwCBDA*
Parsons, Charles Francis 1872-1944 *WhAm 2*
Parsons, Charles H 1821-1910 *IIBEAAW*
Parsons, Charles Henry 1892-1963 *NatCAB 47*
Parsons, Charles Lathrop 1867-1954 *NatCAB 14, NatCAB 47, WhAm 3*
Parsons, Charles William 1823- *ApCAB*
Parsons, Clara Doolittle 1873- *WomWWA 14*
Parsons, Claude VanCleve 1895-1941 *BiDrAC, WhAm 1*
Parsons, Clelia Sara Howson *WomWWA 14*
Parsons, Daniel *NewYHSD*
Parsons, David *NewYHSD*
Parsons, David 1749-1823 *ApCAB*
Parsons, Donald Johnson 1909-1969 *NatCAB 54, WhAm 5*
Parsons, Eben 1896-1969 *NatCAB 55*
Parsons, Eben Burt 1835-1913 *WhAm 1*
Parsons, Edgerton 1875-1929 *NatCAB 45*
Parsons, Edith Barretto *WomWWA 14*
Parsons, Edmund Byrd 1864-1938 *WhAm 1*
Parsons, Edward Alexander 1878-1962 *WhAm 4*
Parsons, Edward Lambe 1868-1960 *NatCAB 51, WhAm 4*
Parsons, Edward Smith 1863-1943 *NatCAB 33, WhAm 2*
Parsons, Edward T 1842-1876 *BiAUS*
Parsons, Edward Young 1842-1876 *BiDrAC, WhAm H*
Parsons, Elsie Worthington Clews 1875-1941 *DcAmB S3, NotAW, REnAW, WebAB, WhAm 2*
Parsons, Emily Elizabeth 1824-1880 *NotAW*
Parsons, Emma Follin *WhAm 5*
Parsons, Enoch 1769-1846 *ApCAB, NatCAB 1*
Parsons, Ernest William 1873- *WhAm 5*
Parsons, Ernestine 1884-1967 *IIBEAAW*
Parsons, Eugene 1855-1933 *WhAm 1*
Parsons, Fannie Griscom 1850-1923 *BiCAW, WhAm 1*
Parsons, Florence Whitin *WomWWA 14*
Parsons, Floyd William 1880-1941 *NatCAB 30, WhAm 1*
Parsons, Frances Theodora 1861- *TwCBDA, WhAm 4*
Parsons, Francis 1871-1937 *WhAm 1*
Parsons, Frank 1854-1908 *BiDAmEd, DcAmB, McGEWB, NatCAB 11, TwCBDA, WhAm 1*
Parsons, Frank Alvah 1868-1930 *WhAm 1*
Parsons, Frank Alvah 1869-1930 *AmBi*
Parsons, Frank Nesmith 1854-1934 *NatCAB 13, NatCAB 27, WhAm 1, WhAm 1C*
Parsons, Frank T, Jr. 1906-1957 *NatCAB 47*
Parsons, Frederick Williams 1875-1957 *NatCAB 45, WhAm 3*
Parsons, Geoffrey 1879-1956 *NatCAB 46, WhAm 3*
Parsons, George Frederic 1840-1893 *NatCAB 8*
Parsons, George Whitwell 1850- *ApCAB X*

Parsons, Georgiana Hull 1840- *WomWWA 14*
Parsons, Harry DeBerkeley 1862-1935 *NatCAB 28, WhAm 1*
Parsons, Mrs. Henry *WhAm 1*
Parsons, Henry Betts 1855-1885 *ApCAB*
Parsons, Henry C 1840- *NatCAB 14*
Parsons, Henry Spaulding 1894-1965 *NatCAB 51*
Parsons, Herbert 1869-1925 *ApCAB X, BiDrAC, NatCAB 14, NatCAB 32, WhAm 1*
Parsons, J Lester d1957 *WhAm 3*
Parsons, J Russell 1896-1970 *WhAm 5*
Parsons, James Alpheus 1868-1945 *NatCAB 43*
Parsons, James Hepburn 1832-1876 *NatCAB 42*
Parsons, James Herbert 1831-1905 *NewYHSD*
Parsons, James Kelly 1877- *WhAm 5*
Parsons, James Russell, Jr. 1861-1905 *TwCBDA, WhAm 1*
Parsons, John 1820-1910 *ApCAB X, NatCAB 16*
Parsons, John B 1850- *WhAm 4*
Parsons, John Calvin 1897-1968 *NatCAB 54, WhAm 5*
Parsons, John Edward 1829-1915 *DcAmB, NatCAB 28, WhAm 1*
Parsons, John Frederick 1908-1969 *WhAm 5*
Parsons, John Purl 1889-1956 *NatCAB 46*
Parsons, Jonathan 1705-1776 *ApCAB, Drake*
Parsons, Joseph Greeley 1877-1950 *NatCAB 39*
Parsons, Joseph Lewis 1867-1943 *NatCAB 32*
Parsons, Kenyon 1860-1925 *NatCAB 20*
Parsons, Lawrence Buell 1897-1966 *NatCAB 53*
Parsons, Lester Shields 1886-1960 *WhAm 4*
Parsons, Levi 1822-1887 *ApCAB*
Parsons, Lewis Baldwin 1798-1855 *ApCAB*
Parsons, Lewis Baldwin 1818-1907 *ApCAB, DcAmB, WhAm 1*
Parsons, Lewis Eliphalet 1817-1895 *BiAUS, DcAmB, NatCAB 10, TwCBDA, WhAm H*
Parsons, Lewis Morgan 1898- *WhAm 5*
Parsons, Llewellyn Bradley 1897-1968 *NatCAB 54, WhAm 4A, WhAm 5*
Parsons, Louella O 1893-1972 *WebAB, WhAm 5*
Parsons, Mabel 1872- *WomWWA 14*
Parsons, Mae Frances 1872- *WomWWA 14*
Parsons, Marion Randall 1880- *WhAm 6*
Parsons, May Hall Childs *WomWWA 14*
Parsons, Monroe M 1819-1865 *Drake*
Parsons, Mosby Monroe 1819-1865 *ApCAB*
Parsons, Mosby Monroe 1822-1865 *TwCBDA*
Parsons, Mosby Munroe 1822-1865 *BiDConf*
Parsons, Orrin Sheldon 1866-1943 *IIBEAAW*
Parsons, Payn Bigelow 1872-1931 *WhAm 1, WhAm 1C*
Parsons, Philip Archibald 1879-1943 *WhAm 2*
Parsons, Ralph Monroe 1896-1974 *WhAm 6*
Parsons, Reginald Hascall 1873-1955 *NatCAB 46, WhAm 3*
Parsons, Richard 1847-1926 *WhAm 1*
Parsons, Richard C 1826-1899 *BiAUS*
Parsons, Richard Chappel 1826-1899 *BiDrAC*
Parsons, Richard Chappell 1826-1899 *NatCAB 6*
Parsons, Robert Stevens 1873-1928 *WhAm 1*
Parsons, Robert William 1877-1933 *NatCAB 35*
Parsons, Samuel 1844-1923 *NatCAB 13, NatCAB 26, TwCBDA, WhAm 1*
Parsons, Samuel Bowne 1819-1906 *DcAmB*
Parsons, Samuel Holden 1737-1789 *AmBi, ApCAB, BiAUS, DcAmB, Drake, NatCAB 1, TwCBDA, WebAMB, WhAm H*
Parsons, Starr 1869-1948 *WhAm 2*
Parsons, Talcott 1902- *EncAB, McGEWB, WebAB*
Parsons, Theophilus 1750-1813 *AmBi, ApCAB, BiAUS, DcAmB, Drake, NatCAB 5, TwCBDA, WebAB, WhAm H*
Parsons, Theophilus 1797-1882 *AmBi, ApCAB, DcAmB, Drake, NatCAB 5, TwCBDA, WebAB, WhAm H*
Parsons, Thomas Smith 1873-1923 *WhAm 1*

Parsons, Thomas William 1819-1892 *AmBi,
ApCAB, DcAmB, Drake, NatCAB 5,
WhAm H*
Parsons, Usher 1788-1868 *ApCAB, DcAmB,
Drake, NatCAB 8, WhAm H*
Parsons, Wallace Emery d1957 *WhAm 3*
Parsons, Walter Wood 1874- *ApCAB X*
Parsons, Wilfrid 1887-1958 *NatCAB 44,
WhAm 3*
Parsons, Willard H 1898-1969 *WhAm 5*
Parsons, William d1757 *ApCAB*
Parsons, William 1867-1942 *WhAm 2*
Parsons, William, Earl Of Rosse 1800-1867
DcScB
Parsons, William B 1856-1924 *NatCAB 26*
Parsons, William Barclay 1859-1932 *AmBi,
DcAmB, NatCAB 12, NatCAB 14,
TwCBDA, WhAm 1*
Parsons, William Barclay 1888-1973
NatCAB 57, WhAm 5
Parsons, William Edward 1872-1939 *WhAm 1*
Parsons, William Hinckley 1864-1948
NatCAB 38
Parsons, William Lewis 1884-1972 *WhAm 5*
Parsons, William Moody 1825-1923 *NatCAB 6*
Parsons, William Sterling 1901-1953 *WhAm 3*
Parsons, William Wood 1850-1925 *WhAm 1*
Parsons, Willis Edwards 1857- *WhAm 4*
Partch, Harry 1901-1974 *WhAm 6*
Partington, Mrs. *DcAmB*
Partington, Frederick Eugene d1924 *WhAm 1*
Partington, James Riddick 1886-1965 *DcScB*
Partipilo, Anthony Victor 1900-1966 *WhAm 5*
Partlow, Ira Judson 1876-1952 *WhAm 3*
Partlow, William Dempsey 1877- *WhAm 5*
Partner, Winnie Leroy 1891-1962 *WhAm 4*
Parton, Arthur 1842-1914 *AmBi, ApCAB,
DcAmB, NatCAB 13, TwCBDA,
WhAm 1*
Parton, Charles Higginson 1908-1966
NatCAB 53
Parton, Ernest 1845-1933 *AmBi, ApCAB,
TwCBDA, WhAm 1*
Parton, Ethel 1862- *WomWWA 14*
Parton, Henry Woodbridge 1858-1933 *ApCAB,
WhAm 1*
Parton, James 1822-1891 *AmBi, ApCAB,
DcAmB, Drake, NatCAB 1, TwCBDA,
WebAB, WhAm H*
Parton, Lemuel Frederick d1943 *WhAm 2*
Parton, Sara Payson Willis 1811-1872 *AmBi,
AmWom, ApCAB, DcAmB, Drake,
EncAB, NatCAB 1, NotAW, TwCBDA,
WebAB, WhAm H*
Partridge, Albert Gerry 1880-1952 *WhAm 3*
Partridge, Alden 1785-1854 *AmBi, ApCAB,
BiDAmEd, DcAmB, Drake, NatCAB 18,
TwCBDA, WebAMB, WhAm H*
Partridge, Bellamy 1877-1960 *NatCAB 47,
WhAm 4*
Partridge, Charles Patrick 1897-1966 *WhAm 4*
Partridge, Charles Sumner 1856-1916
NatCAB 18
Partridge, Donald Barrows 1891-1946 *BiDrAC,
WhAm 2*
Partridge, Earle Everard 1900- *WebAMB*
Partridge, Edward Lasell 1853-1930
ApCAB Sup, NatCAB 21, WhAm 1
Partridge, Everett Percy 1902-1969 *NatCAB 55,
WhAm 5*
Partridge, Frances Rosamond 1851-
WomWWA 14
Partridge, Frank Charles 1861-1943 *BiDrAC,
NatCAB 32, WhAm 2*
Partridge, Frederick William 1824-1899
TwCBDA
Partridge, George 1740-1828 *ApCAB, BiAUS,
BiDrAC, Drake, NatCAB 10, TwCBDA,
WhAm H*
Partridge, George Everett 1870-1953 *WhAm 3*
Partridge, James R d1884 *BiAUS*
Partridge, James R 1824-1884 *NatCAB 7*
Partridge, James Rudolph 1823?-1884 *DcAmB,
WhAm H*
Partridge, John Frederick 1891-1953
NatCAB 42
Partridge, John Slater 1870-1926 *WhAm 1*
Partridge, Joseph *NewYHSD*

Partridge, Mary Elizabeth 1832-
WomWWA 14
Partridge, Nehemiah *NewYHSD*
Partridge, Oliver 1712-1792 *ApCAB, Drake,
NatCAB 13*
Partridge, Richard 1681-1759 *DcAmB,
WhAm H*
Partridge, Robert Glenn 1903-1963 *NatCAB 51*
Partridge, Roland Edward 1901-1960
NatCAB 45
Partridge, Samuel 1790-1883 *BiAUS, BiDrAC*
Partridge, Sidney Catlin 1857-1930 *NatCAB 25,
TwCBDA, WhAm 1*
Partridge, Warren Graham 1854- *NatCAB 12*
Partridge, William Ordway 1861-1930 *AmBi,
ApCAB Sup, ApCAB X, BnEnAmA,
DcAmB, NatCAB 6, NatCAB 23,
TwCBDA, WhAm 1*
Parvin, Theodore Sutton 1817-1901 *ApCAB,
DcAmB, NatCAB 8, TwCBDA,
WhAm 1*
Parvin, Theophilus 1829-1898 *ApCAB,
DcAmB, NatCAB 4, WhAm H*
Paryzek, Harry Vincent 1892-1958 *NatCAB 43*
Pas, Ion 1895-1974 *WhAm 6*
Pascal, Blaise 1623-1662 *AsBiEn, DcScB,
McGEWB*
Pascal, Etienne 1588-1651 *DcScB*
Pascalis, Felix A Ouviere 1750?-1833 *Drake*
Pascalis-Ouviere, Felix 1750?-1840 *ApCAB*
Pascalis-Ouvriere, Felix 1750?-1833 *DcAmB,
WhAm H*
Pascall, Thomas M 1880- *WhAm 6*
Pasch, Moritz 1843-1930 *DcScB*
Paschal, Franklin Cressey 1890-1947 *WhAm 2*
Paschal, George Washington 1812-1878 *ApCAB,
DcAmB, TwCBDA, WhAm H*
Paschal, Thomas Moore 1845-1919 *BiDrAC*
Paschall, Clarence 1872-1951 *NatCAB 39*
Paschall, Edwin 1799-1869 *ApCAB*
Paschall, J E 1896-1974 *WhAm 6*
Paschall, John 1879-1953 *WhAm 3*
Paschall, Nathaniel 1802-1866 *Drake*
Paschen, Henry Daniel 1882-1959 *NatCAB 49*
Paschen, Louis Carl Heinrich Friedrich
1865-1947 *DcScB*
Paschkes, Otto 1885-1955 *NatCAB 43*
Pasco, James Denham 1883-1943 *NatCAB 36*
Pasco, Samuel 1834-1917 *ApCAB, BiDrAC,
DcAmB, NatCAB 1, TwCBDA,
WhAm 1, WhAmP*
Pashkovsky, Theophilus Nicholas 1874-1950
WhAm 3
Paskett, Winifred Llewellyn 1884-
WomWWA 14
Paskievich, Ivan Fedorovich 1782-1856
WhoMilH
Pasko, Wesley Washington 1840-1897
NatCAB 2, TwCBDA
Pasko, Wesly Washington 1840-1897 *WhAm H*
Pasma, Henry Kay *WhAm 2*
Pasmore, Henry Bickford 1858-1944 *WhAm 2*
Pasolini, Pier Paolo 1922-1975 *WhAm 6*
Pasquin, Anthony 1761-1818 *DcAmB,
WhAm H*
Pass, James 1856-1913 *NatCAB 39*
Pass, Joe 1887-1950 *NatCAB 38*
Pass, Richard Henry 1893-1964 *NatCAB 52*
Passaconaway 1580?-1669? *ApCAB, Drake*
Passannate, Charles 1887-1956 *WhAm 3*
Passano, Edward Boteler 1872-1946
NatCAB 36, WhAm 2
Passarelli, Luigi Alfonso 1895-1953 *WhAm 3*
Passavant, William Alfred 1821-1894 *AmBi,
ApCAB, DcAmB, WhAm H*
Passman, Otto Ernest 1900- *BiDrAC*
Passmore, Ellis Pusey 1869-1928 *WhAm 1*
Passmore, Joseph Clarkson 1818-1866 *ApCAB,
Drake*
Passmore, Lincoln Knight 1850-1935 *ApCAB X,
WhAm 1*
Passmore, Susie Came 1864- *WomWWA 14*
Pasternack, Josef Alexander 1880-1940
NatCAB 38
Pasternak, Boris Leonidovich 1890-1960
McGEWB
Pasternak, Boris Leonidovitch 1890-1960
WhAm 4

Pasteur, Herbert Neale 1892-1967 *NatCAB 53*
Pasteur, Louis 1822-1895 *AsBiEn, BiHiMed,
DcScB, McGEWB*
Pastor, Antonio 1837-1908 *DcAmB*
Pastor, Antonio 1840-1908 *NatCAB 16*
Pastor, Julio Rey *DcScB*
Pastor, Tony 1837-1908 *WebAB*
Pastore, John Orlando 1907- *BiDrAC*
Pastorius, Francis Daniel 1651-1719? *ApCAB,
BiDAmEd, DcAmB, NatCAB 11,
WhAm H*
Pastorius, Francis Daniel 1651-1720? *AmBi,
DcAmReB, WebAB*
Pasvolsky, Leo 1893-1953 *DcAmB S5,
WhAm 3*
Patai, Imre Franz 1894-1949 *NatCAB 37*
Patania, G F B *NewYHSD*
Patch, Alexander McCarrell 1889-1945
*DcAmB S3, NatCAB 38, WebAMB,
WhAm 2, WhWW-II, WhoMilH*
Patch, Edgar Leonard 1851-1924 *NatCAB 25*
Patch, Edith Marion 1876-1954 *NatCAB 18,
WhAm 3, WomWWA 14*
Patch, Frank Wallace 1862-1923 *WhAm 1*
Patch, Fred Roswell 1853-1938 *NatCAB 35*
Patch, Helen Elizabeth 1891-1959 *WhAm 3*
Patch, Howard Rollin 1889-1963 *NatCAB 50*
Patch, Kate Whiting 1870-1909 *WhAm 1*
Patch, Mary Greene 1871- *WomWWA 14*
Patch, Maurice Byron 1852-1913 *NatCAB 16*
Patch, Nathaniel Jordan Knight d1913
WhAm 1
Patch, Ralph Reginald 1882-1957 *WhAm 3*
Patch, Richard Harkness 1888-1954
NatCAB 46
Patch, Sam 1807?-1829 *DcAmB, WebAB,
WhAm H*
Patch, Samuel 1807?-1829 *ApCAB*
Patch, Samuel 1807?-1830 *NatCAB 5*
Patch, Samuel, Jr. *NewYHSD*
Patchen, Kenneth 1911-1972 *WhAm 5*
Patchin, Frank Glines 1861-1925 *NatCAB 22,
WhAm 1*
Patchin, Jared 1828-1892 *NatCAB 6*
Patchin, Philip Halsey 1884-1954 *WhAm 3*
Patchin, Robert Halsey 1881-1955 *NatCAB 45,
WhAm 3*
Pate, Charles Earnest 1880-1961 *NatCAB 50*
Pate, Maurice 1894-1965 *NatCAB 51,
WhAm 4*
Pate, Randolph McCall 1898-1961 *WebAMB,
WhAm 4*
Pate, Walter Romny 1877- *WhAm 5*
Pate, William *NewYHSD*
Patek, Stanislaw 1866- *WhAm 4*
Patel, Vallabhbhai 1875-1950 *McGEWB*
Patenaude, Esioff Leon 1875- *WhAm 5*
Patenotre, Eleanor Elverson 1870- *WhAm 5*
Pater, Walter Horatio 1839-1894 *McGEWB*
Paterno, Joseph 1881-1939 *NatCAB 29*
Paterson, Albert Barnett 1883-1952
NatCAB 41, WhAm 3
Paterson, Alexander Horn 1878-1941
NatCAB 30
Paterson, Andrew Barton 1864-1941 *McGEWB*
Paterson, Donald Gildersleeve 1892-1961
BiDAmEd, NatCAB 53, WhAm 4
Paterson, Isabel d1961 *WhAm 4*
Paterson, James Venn 1867-1947 *NatCAB 17,
WhAm 2*
Paterson, John 1707-1762 *NatCAB 3*
Paterson, John 1744-1808 *AmBi, ApCAB,
BiDrAC, DcAmB, NatCAB 3, TwCBDA,
WhAm H*
Paterson, John 1801-1883 *ApCAB*
Paterson, John *see also* Patterson, John
Paterson, Robert Gildersleeve 1882-1964
WhAm 4
Paterson, VanRensselaer 1850?-1902 *WhAm 1*
Paterson, William 1665-1719 *ApCAB*
Paterson, William 1745-1806 *AmBi, ApCAB,
BiAUS, BiDrAC, DcAmB, McGEWB,
NatCAB 1, TwCBDA, WebAB,
WhAm H, WhAmP*
Paterson, William *see also* Patterson, William
Paterson, William Bothwell 1875-1933
NatCAB 25
Paterson, William Burns 1849-1915 *BiDAmEd*

Paterson, William Tait 1884-1970 *WhAm 5*
Patigian, Haig 1876-1950 *NatCAB 18,*
 WhAm 3
Patillo, Henry 1726-1801 *ApCAB, DcAmB,*
 WhAm H
Patino, Albina Rodriguez 1872-1953
 NatCAB 40
Patino, Simon Iturri 1862-1947 *McGEWB,*
 NatCAB 40, WhAm 2
Patitz, J F Max 1866-1937 *NatCAB 27*
Patman, Wright 1893-1976 *BiDrAC, WhAm 6*
Patmos, Martin 1901-1971 *WhAm 6*
Paton, A R *NewYHSD*
Paton, Alan Stewart 1903- *McGEWB*
Paton, Alexander Sinclair 1854-1926 *ApCAB X*
Paton, James Morton 1863-1944 *WhAm 2*
Paton, Julia Bayles 1874- *WomWWA 14*
Paton, Lewis Bayles 1864-1932 *DcAmB,*
 WhAm 1
Paton, Stewart 1865-1942 *WhAm 2*
Paton, Thomas Bugard 1861-1933 *NatCAB 16,*
 WhAm 1
Paton, William Agnew 1848-1918 *WhAm 1*
Paton, William Kennell 1894-1959 *WhAm 3*
Patri, Angelo 1877-1965 *BiDAmEd, WhAm 4*
Patriarche, Valance St. Just 1875-
 WomWWA 14
Patrick, Saint d460? *McGEWB*
Patrick, David Lyall 1899-1969 *WhAm 5*
Patrick, Dora Smith 1869- *WomWWA 14*
Patrick, Edwin Dawless 1894-1945 *WhAm 2*
Patrick, Fannie Brown 1864- *WomWWA 14*
Patrick, Fred Albert 1857-1931 *NatCAB 44,*
 WhAm 1
Patrick, George Edward 1851-1916 *WhAm 1*
Patrick, George Neill 1880- *WhAm 6*
Patrick, George Thomas White 1857-1949
 TwCBDA, WhAm 2
Patrick, Hugh Talbot 1860-1939 *DcAmB S2,*
 NatCAB 30, WhAm 1
Patrick, John Hayward 1901- *WhAm 5*
Patrick, Joseph Cecil 1892-1965 *WhAm 4*
Patrick, Joseph Henry 1866-1946 *NatCAB 35*
Patrick, Luther 1891-1957 *WhAm 3*
Patrick, Luther 1894-1957 *BiDrAC*
Patrick, Lytle Neale 1883-1947 *NatCAB 34*
Patrick, Marsena Rudolph 1811-1888 *ApCAB,*
 DcAmB, Drake, TwCBDA, WhAm H
Patrick, Mary Mills 1850-1940 *DcAmB S2,*
 NotAW, TwCBDA, WhAm 1,
 WomWWA 14
Patrick, Mason Mathews 1863-1942 *DcAmB S3,*
 NatCAB 44, WebAMB, WhAm 1
Patrick, Ransom Rathbone 1906-1971 *WhAm 5*
Patrick, Rembert Wallace 1909-1967 *WhAm 6*
Patrick, Robert F 1903-1967 *WhAm 5*
Patrick, Robert Goodlett 1866-1920 *WhAm 1*
Patrick, Roy Leonard 1876-1953 *NatCAB 46,*
 WhAm 3
Patrick, Ted 1901-1964 *WhAm 4*
Patrick, William Reuben 1869-1962
 NatCAB 52
Patridge, Lelia Ellen *WomWWA 14*
Patrizi, Francesco 1529-1597 *DcScB*
Patry, Frederick Lorimer 1897-1968
 NatCAB 54
Patt, John Francis 1905-1972 *WhAm 5*
Pattangall, William Robinson 1865-1942
 WhAm 2
Pattee, Alida Frances *WomWWA 14*
Pattee, Ernest Noble 1864-1946 *WhAm 2*
Pattee, Fred Lewis 1853-1950 *BiDAmEd,*
 WhAm 3
Pattee, Fred Lewis 1863-1950 *NatCAB 39,*
 TwCBDA
Pattee, William Sullivan 1846-1911 *TwCBDA,*
 WhAm 1
Patten, Amos Williams 1848-1924 *WhAm 1*
Patten, Bradley Merrill 1889-1971 *WhAm 5*
Patten, Charles Edward 1865-1918 *NatCAB 38*
Patten, Charles Harreld 1909- *WhAm 5*
Patten, Cora Mel 1869- *WomWWA 14*
Patten, David 1888-1975 *WhAm 6*
Patten, Edith Sylvia 1869- *WomWWA 14*
Patten, Edward James 1905- *BiDrAC*
Patten, Emily A 1858- *WomWWA 14*
Patten, Frank Chauncy 1855-1934 *NatCAB 24*

Patten, George Washington 1808-1882 *ApCAB,*
 Drake, NatCAB 13
Patten, George Yager 1876-1951 *WhAm 3*
Patten, Gilbert 1866-1945 *DcAmB S3,*
 NatCAB 34, WebAB, WhAm 2
Patten, Harold Ambrose 1907-1969 *BiDrAC*
Patten, Helen Philbrook 1865- *WhAm 4*
Patten, Helen Philbrook 1868- *WomWWA 14*
Patten, Henry 1871-1955 *WhAm 3*
Patten, James A 1852-1928 *DcAmB, WhAm 1*
Patten, James Horace 1877-1940 *WhAm 1*
Patten, Jeanie Maury Coyle 1855-
 WomWWA 14
Patten, John 1746-1800 *BiDrAC, WhAm H,*
 WhAmP
Patten, John 1746-1801 *ApCAB, Drake,*
 TwCBDA
Patten, John *see also* Patton, John
Patten, John Alanson 1867-1916 *NatCAB 17,*
 WhAm 1
Patten, Mary Pohlman 1826- *WomWWA 14*
Patten, Ryder 1897-1957 *NatCAB 48*
Patten, Simon Nelson 1852-1922 *DcAmB,*
 McGEWB, NatCAB 11, TwCBDA,
 WhAm 1
Patten, Thomas Gedney 1861-1939 *BiDrAC,*
 WhAm 1
Patten, William 1763-1839 *ApCAB, Drake,*
 TwCBDA
Patten, William 1861-1932 *AmBi, DcAmB,*
 NatCAB 24, WhAm 1
Patten, William Hardman 1865-1936
 NatCAB 27
Patten, William Samuel 1800-1873 *ApCAB*
Patten, William Taylor 1875-1947 *NatCAB 37*
Patten, Zeboim Cartter 1840-1925 *NatCAB 21*
Patten, Zeboim Charles 1874-1948 *WhAm 2*
Patten, Zebulon S *NewYHSD*
Pattengill, Henry Romaine 1852-1918
 NatCAB 19
Patterson, A Truman 1882-1945 *NatCAB 35*
Patterson, Ada *WomWWA 14*
Patterson, Adam Edward 1876- *WhoColR*
Patterson, Adoniram Judson 1827-1909
 WhAm 1
Patterson, Alexander Evans 1887-1948
 WhAm 2
Patterson, Alice Higinbotham 1880-
 WomWWA 14
Patterson, Alice Maria 1869- *WomWWA 14*
Patterson, Alicia d1963 *WhAm 4*
Patterson, Alvah Worrell 1870-1938 *WhAm 1*
Patterson, Andrew 1843- *WhAm 4*
Patterson, Andrew Dickson 1854- *ApCAB Sup*
Patterson, Andrew Henry 1870-1928
 NatCAB 21, WhAm 1
Patterson, Anne Virginia Sharp *WomWWA 14*
Patterson, Antoinette DeCourcey 1866-1925
 WhAm 1
Patterson, Antoinette DeCoursey 1866-1925
 BiCAW, WomWWA 14
Patterson, Archibald Williams 1858- *WhAm 4*
Patterson, Arthur L 1902-1966 *WhAm 4*
Patterson, Ashby Metcalfe 1889-1971
 NatCAB 56
Patterson, Austin McDowell 1876-1956
 WhAm 3
Patterson, Burd Shippen 1857-1924 *WhAm 1*
Patterson, Caleb Perry 1880- *WhAm 6*
Patterson, Carl George 1877-1950 *NatCAB 53*
Patterson, Carl VanSchaick 1888-1965
 NatCAB 56
Patterson, Carlile Pollock 1816-1881 *ApCAB,*
 BiAUS, NatCAB 4
Patterson, Catherine Norris d1943 *WhAm 2*
Patterson, Charles Adams 1876-1922
 NatCAB 19
Patterson, Charles Brodie 1854-1917 *WhAm 1*
Patterson, Charles Ector 1877-1947 *NatCAB 35*
Patterson, Charles Edward 1842-1913 *WhAm 1*
Patterson, Charles Howard 1859- *WhAm 4*
Patterson, Charles Loeser 1855-1930
 NatCAB 50, WhAm 1
Patterson, Charles Lord 1905-1962 *WhAm 4*
Patterson, Charles Thompson 1862-1915
 NatCAB 16
Patterson, Charlotte Wise 1879-
 WomWWA 14

Patterson, Christopher Salmon 1823-
 ApCAB Sup
Patterson, Christopher Stuart 1842-1924
 ApCAB, NatCAB 20, WhAm 1
Patterson, Curtis John 1889-1960 *NatCAB 50*
Patterson, Daniel Cleveland 1882-1946
 NatCAB 35
Patterson, Daniel T 1786-1839 *Drake*
Patterson, Daniel Tod 1786-1839 *AmBi,*
 ApCAB
Patterson, Daniel Todd 1786-1839 *DcAmB,*
 TwCBDA, WebAMB, WhAm H
Patterson, David H, Jr. 1875- *WhAm 5*
Patterson, David Trotter 1818-1891 *BiDrAC,*
 WhAm H
Patterson, David Trotter 1819-1891 *ApCAB,*
 BiAUS, NatCAB 12, TwCBDA
Patterson, E R 1888-1970 *NatCAB 57*
Patterson, Edith Clarke *WomWWA 14*
Patterson, Edmund Booth 1864- *WhAm 4*
Patterson, Edward 1839-1910 *NatCAB 13,*
 WhAm 1
Patterson, Edward P *NewYHSD*
Patterson, Edward White 1895-1940 *BiDrAC,*
 WhAm 1
Patterson, Edwin Wilhite 1889-1965 *BiDAmEd,*
 NatCAB 51
Patterson, Edwin Wilhite 1899-1965 *WhAm 5*
Patterson, Eleanor Medill 1881-1948
 DcAmB S4, NotAW
Patterson, Eleanor Medill 1884-1948 *WebAB,*
 WhAm 2
Patterson, Elizabeth 1785-1879 *AmBi*
Patterson, Elizabeth Hutchinson 1871-
 WomWWA 14
Patterson, Ellis Ellwood 1897- *BiDrAC*
Patterson, Ernest Minor 1870-1969 *WhAm 5*
Patterson, Ernest Odell 1874- *WhAm 5*
Patterson, Everett M 1906-1962 *WhAm 4*
Patterson, Flora Wambaugh 1847-1928
 WhAm 1, WomWWA 14
Patterson, Francis Engle 1827-1862 *ApCAB,*
 TwCBDA
Patterson, Francis Ford, Jr. 1867-1935 *BiDrAC,*
 NatCAB 29, WhAm 1
Patterson, Frank Allen 1878-1944 *WhAm 2*
Patterson, Frank Miner 1873-1939 *WhAm 1*
Patterson, Fred D 1871- *WhoColR*
Patterson, Frederick Beck 1892-1971 *WhAm 5*
Patterson, Frederick William 1877-1965
 WhAm 4
Patterson, Garnet Levi 1905-1967 *NatCAB 54*
Patterson, Gaylard Hawkins 1866-1940
 WhAm 1
Patterson, George 1824- *ApCAB*
Patterson, George 1828-1901 *TwCBDA*
Patterson, George Francis 1874- *WhAm 5*
Patterson, George Herbert 1836- *TwCBDA*
Patterson, George Robert 1863-1906 *BiDrAC,*
 WhAm 1
Patterson, George Seth 1883-1951 *NatCAB 42*
Patterson, George Stuart 1868- *WhAm 4*
Patterson, George Washington 1799-1879
 BiDrAC, WhAm H
Patterson, George Washington 1864-1930
 NatCAB 35, WhAm 1
Patterson, Gerard Francis 1867-1944 *WhAm 2*
Patterson, Gertrude A 1877- *WhoColR*
Patterson, Gilbert Brown 1863-1922 *BiDrAC,*
 WhAm 4
Patterson, Giles Jared 1885-1963 *WhAm 4*
Patterson, Graham Creighton 1881-1969
 WhAm 5
Patterson, Grove Hiram 1881-1956 *WhAm 3*
Patterson, H *NewYHSD*
Patterson, Hannah Jane 1879-1937 *NotAW,*
 WhAm 6, WomWWA 14
Patterson, Harold C d1960 *WhAm 4*
Patterson, Harry Howard 1872-1945
 NatCAB 36
Patterson, Harry Jacob 1866-1948 *WhAm 2,*
 WhAm 3
Patterson, Henry Stuart 1874-1957 *NatCAB 44*
Patterson, Isaac Lee 1859-1929 *NatCAB 25,*
 WhAm 1
Patterson, James d1972 *WhAm 5*
Patterson, James Albert 1864-1923 *NatCAB 14,*
 WhAm 3

Patterson, James Colebrook 1839- *ApCAB Sup*
Patterson, James Kennedy 1833-1922 *BiDAmEd, DcAmB, NatCAB 11, TwCBDA, WhAm 1*
Patterson, James Lawson d1937 *WhAm 1*
Patterson, James O'Hanlon 1857-1911 *BiDrAC, WhAm 1*
Patterson, James S 1832-1916 *NewYHSD*
Patterson, James Thomas 1908- *BiDrAC*
Patterson, James Willis 1823-1893 *ApCAB, BiAUS, BiDAmEd, BiDrAC, DcAmB, NatCAB 11, TwCBDA, WhAm H*
Patterson, Jane Lippitt 1829- *WhAm 4*
Patterson, John *BiAUS*
Patterson, John 1744-1808 *Drake*
Patterson, John 1771-1848 *BiAUS, BiDrAC, WhAm H*
Patterson, John *see also* Paterson, John
Patterson, John Fulton 1856-1924 *WhAm 1*
Patterson, John Henry 1843-1920 *WhAm 1*
Patterson, John Henry 1844-1922 *AmBi, DcAmB, NatCAB 13, NatCAB 20, WebAB, WhAm 1*
Patterson, John James 1830-1912 *ApCAB, BiAUS, BiDrAC, NatCAB 12, TwCBDA*
Patterson, John Letcher 1861-1937 *WhAm 1, WhAm 1C*
Patterson, John Neville 1910-1970 *WhAm 5*
Patterson, John Thomas 1878-1960 *NatCAB 47, WhAm 4*
Patterson, Joseph *NewYHSD*
Patterson, Joseph 1783-1868 *NatCAB 5*
Patterson, Joseph 1808-1887 *ApCAB*
Patterson, Joseph Emmett 1838-1925 *NatCAB 38*
Patterson, Joseph McDowell 1865- *WhAm 1*
Patterson, Joseph Medill 1879-1946 *DcAmB S4, NatCAB 36, WhAm 2*
Patterson, Joseph T 1907-1969 *WhAm 5*
Patterson, Josiah 1837- *TwCBDA*
Patterson, Josiah 1837-1903 *NatCAB 8*
Patterson, Josiah 1837-1904 *BiDrAC, WhAmP*
Patterson, Juliet C *WomWWA 14*
Patterson, LaFayette Lee 1888- *BiDrAC*
Patterson, Lamar Gray 1865- *WhAm 4*
Patterson, Lemuel B 1869-1927 *WhAm 1*
Patterson, Lillian Beatrice 1900-1954 *WhAm 3*
Patterson, Mrs. Lindsay *WhAm 5*
Patterson, Lindsay 1858-1922 *NatCAB 20*
Patterson, Mrs. Lindsay Bramlette *WomWWA 14*
Patterson, Malcolm Rice 1861-1935 *BiDrAC, NatCAB 14, TwCBDA, WhAm 1, WhAmP*
Patterson, Margaret Jordan *WomWWA 14*
Patterson, Margaret Morehead 1874- *WomWWA 14*
Patterson, Margaret Norris *WomWWA 14*
Patterson, Marion Dean 1876-1950 *NatCAB 40, WhAm 2*
Patterson, Mary Frances *WomWWA 14*
Patterson, Mary King 1885-1975 *WhAm 6*
Patterson, Merib Rowley *WomWWA 14*
Patterson, Minnie Ward *AmWom*
Patterson, Morehead 1897-1962 *NatCAB 49, WhAm 4*
Patterson, Morris 1809-1878 *ApCAB, DcAmB, WhAm H*
Patterson, Mortimer Bliss 1875-1957 *NatCAB 47*
Patterson, Otto 1890-1967 *WhAm 5*
Patterson, Paul 1888-1954 *WhAm 3*
Patterson, Paul Chenery 1878-1952 *WhAm 3*
Patterson, Paul Linton 1900-1956 *NatCAB 43, WhAm 3*
Patterson, Proctor 1862-1947 *NatCAB 38*
Patterson, Ralph Morris 1904-1972 *WhAm 5*
Patterson, Raymond Albert 1856-1909 *NatCAB 25, WhAm 1*
Patterson, Reese Williams 1883-1940 *NatCAB 30*
Patterson, Richard Cunningham, Jr. d1966 *WhAm 4*
Patterson, Robert 1743-1824 *ApCAB, BiAUS, DcAmB, Drake, NatCAB 1, NatCAB 26, TwCBDA, WhAm H*
Patterson, Robert 1753-1827 *AmBi, ApCAB, Drake, NatCAB 10*

Patterson, Robert 1792-1881 *ApCAB, DcAmB, Drake, NatCAB 10, TwCBDA, WhAm H*
Patterson, Robert 1819- *ApCAB*
Patterson, Robert 1829- *ApCAB*
Patterson, Robert 1869-1931 *NatCAB 33*
Patterson, Robert Clendening 1883-1952 *NatCAB 42*
Patterson, Robert Covert 1887-1949 *NatCAB 37*
Patterson, Robert Dempster 1896-1972 *WhAm 6*
Patterson, Robert Foster 1905-1969 *WhAm 5*
Patterson, Robert Franklin 1836- *WhAm 1*
Patterson, Robert Giles 1891-1959 *NatCAB 48*
Patterson, Robert Irwin 1842-1916 *NatCAB 17*
Patterson, Robert Maskell 1787-1854 *ApCAB, BiAUS, Drake, NatCAB 1, NatCAB 26, TwCBDA*
Patterson, Robert Mayne 1832- *ApCAB, TwCBDA*
Patterson, Robert Mayne 1832-1911 *DcAmB*
Patterson, Robert Mayne 1832-1912 *WhAm 1*
Patterson, Robert Porter 1891-1952 *BiDrUSE, DcAmB S5, WhAm 3*
Patterson, Robert Urie 1877-1950 *NatCAB 46, WhAm 3*
Patterson, Robert Wilson 1814-1894 *TwCBDA*
Patterson, Robert Wilson 1850-1910 *NatCAB 12, TwCBDA, WhAm 1*
Patterson, Roscoe Conkling 1876-1954 *BiDrAC, WhAm 3*
Patterson, Ross Vernet 1877-1938 *WhAm 1, WhAm 1C*
Patterson, Roswell Henry 1860-1936 *NatCAB 33*
Patterson, Rufus Lenoir 1872-1943 *ApCAB X, DcAmB S3, NatCAB 16, WhAm 2*
Patterson, Russell Louis 1891-1950 *NatCAB 40*
Patterson, Samuel Finley 1867-1926 *NatCAB 22, WhAm 4*
Patterson, Samuel Sharpless 1855-1914 *NatCAB 17*
Patterson, Samuel White 1883-1975 *WhAm 6*
Patterson, Seely Benedict, Jr. 1885-1951 *NatCAB 42*
Patterson, Shirley Gale 1884-1938 *WhAm 1*
Patterson, Simon Truby 1885-1937 *NatCAB 32*
Patterson, Stuart Hayt 1871-1934 *NatCAB 41*
Patterson, Theresa Homet *WomWWA 14*
Patterson, Thomas 1764-1841 *BiAUS, BiDrAC, TwCBDA, WhAm H*
Patterson, Thomas 1856-1929 *NatCAB 34, WhAm 1*
Patterson, Thomas Edward 1867- *WhAm 4*
Patterson, Thomas H 1819- *Drake*
Patterson, Thomas H 1820-1888 *NatCAB 4*
Patterson, Thomas H 1820-1890 *ApCAB*
Patterson, Thomas Harman 1820-1889 *DcAmB, WhAm H*
Patterson, Thomas Harmon 1820-1889 *TwCBDA*
Patterson, Thomas J 1808?- *BiAUS, BiDrAC, WhAm H*
Patterson, Thomas MacDonald 1839-1916 *BiDrAC, DcAmB, WhAmP*
Patterson, Thomas MacDonald 1840-1916 *BiAUS, NatCAB 12, TwCBDA, WhAm 1*
Patterson, Ulysses S Grant 1867- *WhoColR*
Patterson, Virginia Sharpe 1841-1913 *AmWom, WhAm 1*
Patterson, Walter *BiAUS, BiDrAC, WhAm H*
Patterson, Walter Kennedy 1844-1932 *WhAm 1*
Patterson, William 1745-1806 *Drake*
Patterson, William 1752-1835 *DcAmB, NatCAB 18, WhAm H*
Patterson, William 1789-1838 *BiAUS, BiDrAC, WhAm H*
Patterson, William 1790-1868 *BiAUS, BiDrAC, WhAm H*
Patterson, William 1820?- *NewYHSD*
Patterson, William *see also* Paterson, William
Patterson, William Brown 1873- *WhAm 1*
Patterson, William Chamberlain 1813-1883 *NatCAB 13*
Patterson, William Francis 1898-1959 *WhAm 4*
Patterson, William Harvey 1918-1974 *WhAm 6*
Patterson, William Henry 1854- *NatCAB 15*

Patterson, William James 1880-1955 *NatCAB 43, WhAm 3*
Patterson, William Leslie 1879-1969 *WhAm 5*
Patterson, William Morehouse 1872-1942 *NatCAB 30*
Patterson, William Morrison 1880- *WhAm 6*
Patterson, William R 1868-1929 *WhAm 1*
Patterson, Wright A 1870-1954 *WhAm 3*
Patteson, S Louise 1853- *WhAm 4*
Patteson, Seargent Smith Prentiss 1856-1931 *WhAm 1*
Patteson, Susannah Louise 1853- *WomWWA 14*
Patti, Adelina 1843-1919 *AmWom, ApCAB, Drake, NatCAB 7, NotAW, TwCBDA, WhAm 1*
Patti, Carlo 1842-1873 *ApCAB*
Patti, Carlotta 1840-1889 *ApCAB, Drake*
Patti, P *NewYHSD*
Pattie, James Ohio 1804- *ApCAB*
Pattie, James Ohio 1804-1850? *DcAmB, WebAB, WhAm H*
Pattie, James Ohio 1804?-1851? *REnAW*
Pattie, Sylvester 1782-1828? *ApCAB, REnAW*
Pattillo, Henry 1726-1801 *NatCAB 7*
Pattillo, Nathan Allen 1867-1936 *WhAm 1*
Pattison, Alice M G 1860- *WomWWA 14*
Pattison, Everett Wilson 1839-1919 *WhAm 1*
Pattison, Frank Ambler 1866-1946 *NatCAB 34*
Pattison, Granville Sharp 1791-1851 *DcAmB, NatCAB 6, WhAm H*
Pattison, Granville Sharpe 1791-1851 *ApCAB, Drake, TwCBDA*
Pattison, Harold 1869- *WhAm 5*
Pattison, Harry Archibald 1877-1957 *NatCAB 46*
Pattison, Isaac Caldwell, Jr. 1908-1967 *WhAm 4*
Pattison, James 1724-1805 *ApCAB, Drake*
Pattison, James William 1844-1915 *DcAmB, WhAm 1*
Pattison, John 1859- *WhAm 4*
Pattison, John M 1847-1906 *BiDrAC, DcAmB, NatCAB 14, NatCAB 45, WhAm 1*
Pattison, John R 1860-1940 *WhAm 1*
Pattison, John Williams 1884-1957 *NatCAB 43*
Pattison, Martin 1841-1918 *NatCAB 18, WhAm 1*
Pattison, Mary Stranahan Hart 1869- *WomWWA 14*
Pattison, Robert Emory 1850-1904 *ApCAB, DcAmB, NatCAB 1, TwCBDA, WhAm 1*
Pattison, Robert Everett 1800-1874 *ApCAB, Drake, NatCAB 8, TwCBDA*
Pattison, Robert J 1838-1903 *NewYHSD*
Pattison, Salem Griswold 1859- *WhAm 4*
Pattison, Thomas 1822-1891 *ApCAB, DcAmB, NatCAB 4, TwCBDA, WhAm H*
Pattison, Thomas Harwood 1838-1904 *WhAm 1*
Pattison, William J 1870-1939 *WhAm 1*
Patton, Abby Hutchinson 1829-1892 *AmWom, NotAW*
Patton, Abigail Hutchinson 1829-1892 *WhAm H*
Patton, Abigail Jemima 1829-1892 *NatCAB 10*
Patton, Albert F 1883-1959 *WhAm 4*
Patton, Alfred Spencer 1825-1888 *ApCAB*
Patton, Bertha Estelle Meader 1880- *WomWWA 14*
Patton, Carl Safford 1866-1939 *WhAm 1*
Patton, Cassia 1861- *WomWWA 14*
Patton, Charles Emory 1859-1937 *BiDrAC, WhAm 4*
Patton, Clarke Campbell 1883-1942 *NatCAB 32*
Patton, Cornelius Howard 1860-1939 *NatCAB 30, WhAm 1, WhAm 1C*
Patton, David Henry 1837-1914 *BiDrAC*
Patton, David Hubert 1894-1968 *WhAm 5*
Patton, Earnest Dock 1885-1940 *NatCAB 30*
Patton, Francine Elizabeth 1846- *WomWWA 14*
Patton, Francis Landey 1843-1932 *AmBi, ApCAB, DcAmB, DcAmReB, NatCAB 5, TwCBDA, WhAm 1*
Patton, Frank Bennett 1865-1928 *NatCAB 22*
Patton, Fred 1888-1951 *WhAm 3*

Patton, G Farrar 1853-1934 *NatCAB 24,*
WhAm 1
Patton, George Smith, Jr. 1885-1945
DcAmB S3, EncAB, McGEWB,
NatCAB 37, WebAB, WebAMB,
WhAm 2, WhWW-II, WhoMilH
Patton, George William 1876-1955 *NatCAB 41*
Patton, Harriet A 1840- *WomWWA 14*
Patton, Harris Patterson 1893-1970 *NatCAB 57*
Patton, Haskell Riley 1894-1965 *WhAm 4*
Patton, Henry William 1856- *WhAm 1*
Patton, Horace Bushnell 1858-1929 *WhAm 1*
Patton, Isabella Mack 1878- *WomWWA 14*
Patton, J Allen 1866-1944 *NatCAB 33*
Patton, Jacob Harris 1812-1903 *ApCAB,*
TwCBDA, WhAm 1
Patton, James 1824- *ApCAB*
Patton, James Lee 1869-1935 *NatCAB 25*
Patton, James McDowell 1876-1930 *WhAm 1*
Patton, James Welch 1900-1973 *WhAm 6*
Patton, Jesse Rush 1891-1963 *NatCAB 51*
Patton, John 1745-1804 *ApCAB Sup*
Patton, John 1746-1801 *BiAUS*
Patton, John 1823-1897 *BiAUS, BiDrAC,*
WhAm H
Patton, John 1850-1907 *BiDrAC, NatCAB 12,*
TwCBDA, WhAm 1
Patton, John *see also* Patten, John
Patton, John Denniston 1829-1904 *BiDrAC*
Patton, John Mercer d1858 *BiAUS*
Patton, John Mercer 1796-1858 *ApCAB,*
TwCBDA
Patton, John Mercer 1797-1858 *BiDrAC,*
DcAmB, WhAm H
Patton, John Shelton 1857-1932 *WhAm 1*
Patton, John Woodbridge 1843-1921
NatCAB 21
Patton, Joseph McIntyre 1860-1930 *WhAm 1*
Patton, Katharine d1941 *WhAm 2*
Patton, Leroy Thompson 1880-1957 *WhAm 3*
Patton, Nannie Leary *WomWWA 14*
Patton, Nat 1883-1957 *WhAm 3*
Patton, Nat 1884-1957 *BiDrAC, WhAmP*
Patton, Normand Smith 1852-1915 *WhAm 1*
Patton, Odis Knight 1889-1967 *WhAm 5*
Patton, R M 1809-1885 *BiAUS*
Patton, Raymond Stanton 1882-1937
NatCAB 29, WhAm 1
Patton, Robert 1755-1814 *ApCAB*
Patton, Robert Bridges 1794-1839 *ApCAB*
Patton, Robert Howard 1860-1939 *WhAm 1*
Patton, Robert Miller 1809-1885 *NatCAB 10,*
TwCBDA
Patton, Robert Williams 1869-1944 *NatCAB 33,*
WhAm 2
Patton, Walter Melville 1863-1928 *WhAm 1*
Patton, Willard 1853-1924 *WhAm 1*
Patton, William 1798-1879 *ApCAB, DcAmB,*
NatCAB 10, TwCBDA, WhAm H
Patton, William 1824?- *NewYHSD*
Patton, William Augustus 1849-1927 *WhAm 1*
Patton, William Macfarland 1845-1905
WhAm 1
Patton, William Weston 1821-1889 *ApCAB,*
NatCAB 10, TwCBDA, WhAm H
Pattullo, George 1879- *REnAW, WhAm 6*
Patty, Willard Walter 1892-1962 *NatCAB 50,*
WhAm 4
Paty, Raymond Ross 1896-1957 *WhAm 3*
Pau, Paul Marie Cesar Gerald 1848-1932
WhoMilH
Pauger, Adrien De d1726 *DcAmB*
Paugher, Adrien De d1726 *WhAm H*
Pauk, Henry Ernst 1864-1940 *NatCAB 32*
Pauker, Ana d1960 *WhAm 4*
Paul I 1754-1801 *McGEWB*
Paul I 1901-1964 *WhAm 4*
Paul III 1468-1549 *McGEWB*
Paul IV 1476-1559 *McGEWB*
Paul VI 1897- *McGEWB*
Paul, Father 1863-1940 *DcAmB S2*
Paul Frederic-W, Duke Of Wurttemberg
1797-1860 *NewYHSD*
Paul Of Aegina *DcScB*
Paul Of Alexandria *DcScB*
Paul Of Venice 1370?-1429 *DcScB*
Paul, Prince Regent Of Yugoslavia 1893-1976
WhWW-II

Paul, Saint d067? *McGEWB*
Paul, A J Drexel 1884-1958 *WhAm 3*
Paul, Alice 1885- *BiCAW, WebAB,*
WomWWA 14
Paul, Amasa Copp 1857-1936 *NatCAB 16,*
WhAm 1
Paul, Arthur 1898-1976 *WhAm 6*
Paul, Augustus Chouteau 1842- *ApCAB*
Paul, Charles Edward 1876- *WhAm 5*
Paul, Charles Ferguson 1902- *WhAm 4*
Paul, Charles Howard 1875-1941 *WhAm 1*
Paul, Charles Thomas 1869-1940 *WhAm 1*
Paul, Eleanor Frances 1875- *WomWWA 14*
Paul, Elliot Harold 1891-1958 *WhAm 3*
Paul, Eugene 1830?- *NewYHSD*
Paul, Frederick William 1797-1860 *ApCAB*
Paul, Gabriel 1781-1845 *WhAm H*
Paul, Gabriel Rene 1813-1886 *ApCAB, Drake,*
NatCAB 12, TwCBDA
Paul, George Philip 1879- *WhAm 6*
Paul, Harry Gilbert 1874-1945 *NatCAB 41,*
WhAm 2
Paul, Henry C 1851-1933 *NatCAB 32*
Paul, Henry Martyn 1851-1931 *ApCAB,*
DcAmB, NatCAB 10, TwCBDA,
WhAm 1
Paul, Howard 1835- *ApCAB*
Paul, Isabelle Featherstone 1835?-1879 *ApCAB*
Paul, J Gilman D'Arcy 1887-1972 *WhAm 5*
Paul, J W S *NewYHSD*
Paul, James Washington 1868-1945 *NatCAB 33*
Paul, Jeremiah, Jr. d1820 *NewYHSD,*
WhAm H
Paul, John *DcAmB, NewYHSD, TwCBDA,*
WebAB, WhAm H
Paul, John 1839-1901 *BiDrAC, TwCBDA,*
WhAm 1
Paul, John 1883-1964 *BiDrAC, WhAm 4*
Paul, John Benjamin 1915-1974 *WhAm 6*
Paul, John Harland 1900-1971 *WhAm 6*
Paul, John Haywood 1877- *WhAm 5*
Paul, John Rodman 1852-1941 *NatCAB 41,*
WhAm 1
Paul, John Rodman 1893-1971 *NatCAB 55,*
WhAm 5
Paul, Jose Jesus 1825-1870 *ApCAB*
Paul, Joseph Edward 1917-1969 *WhAm 6*
Paul, Josephine Bay 1900-1962 *WhAm 4*
Paul, Joshua Hughes 1863-1939 *WhAm 1*
Paul, Mary Frances *WomWWA 14*
Paul, Maury Henry Biddle 1890-1942 *WhAm 2*
Paul, Nanette Baker 1866-1928 *BiCAW,*
WhAm 1, WomWWA 14
Paul, Randolph Evernghim 1890-1956
NatCAB 45, WhAm 3
Paul, Ray Sherman 1896-1957 *WhAm 3*
Paul, Rodman Wilson 1912- *REnAW*
Paul, Sarah Woodman 1859- *WhAm 4,*
WomWWA 14
Paul, Willard Augustus 1855-1926 *WhAm 1*
Paul, Willard Stewart 1894-1966 *NatCAB 52,*
WhAm 4
Paul, William Brown 1897-1962 *WhAm 4*
Paul, William Edward 1880- *WhAm 6*
Paul, William Glae 1893-1960 *WhAm 4*
Paulding, Charles Cook 1868-1938 *WhAm 1*
Paulding, Charles Pearson 1872-1905
NatCAB 17
Paulding, Hiram 1797-1878 *AmBi, ApCAB,*
DcAmB, Drake, NatCAB 4, TwCBDA,
WebAB, WebAMB, WhAm H
Paulding, James Kirke 1778-1860 *AmBi,*
BiAUS, BiDrUSE, DcAmB, NatCAB 7,
TwCBDA, WebAB, WhAm H
Paulding, James Kirke 1779-1860 *ApCAB,*
Drake
Paulding, John 1758-1818 *AmBi, ApCAB,*
Drake, NatCAB 13, TwCBDA
Paulding, Leonard 1826-1867 *ApCAB*
Paulding, Richard A *NewYHSD*
Paulding, William, Jr. 1769-1854 *ApCAB,*
BiAUS
Paulding, William, Jr. 1770-1854 *BiDrAC,*
WhAm H
Paulen, Ben Sanford 1869-1961 *NatCAB 45,*
WhAm 4, WhAm 5
Pauley, Elbert L 1877-1950 *NatCAB 41*
Pauley, Scott Samuel 1910-1970 *WhAm 5*

Paulhamus, W H d1925 *WhAm 1*
Pauli, Hertha 1909-1973 *WhAm 5*
Pauli, Simon *DcScB*
Pauli, Wolfgang Ernst 1900-1958 *AsBiEn,*
DcScB, McGEWB, WhAm 3
Paulin, Thomas *NewYHSD*
Pauling *NewYHSD*
Pauling, Linus Carl 1901- *AsBiEn, EncAB,*
McGEWB, WebAB
Paulisa *DcScB*
Paull, Lee Cunningham 1889-1958 *NatCAB 48,*
WhAm 4
Paulli, Simon 1603-1680 *DcScB*
Paullin, Charles Oscar d1944 *WhAm 2*
Paullin, George Washington 1864-1933
NatCAB 25
Paullin, James Edgar 1881-1951 *NatCAB 39,*
WhAm 3
Paullin, William 1812-1871 *ApCAB*
Paullu-Inca 1510?-1550? *ApCAB*
Paulsen, August 1871-1927 *NatCAB 37*
Paulsen, Howard C d1959 *WhAm 3*
Paulson, Daniel McKee 1895-1928 *NatCAB 23*
Paulson, Frederick Holroyd 1898-1959
WhAm 4
Paulson, Mary Wild 1872- *WomWWA 14*
Paulson, Richard Hulet 1906-1965 *WhAm 4*
Paulus, Francis Petrus 1862-1933 *NatCAB 17,*
WhAm 1
Paulus, Friedrich 1890-1957 *WhWW-II,*
WhoMilH
Pauly, August 1850-1914 *DcScB*
Pauly, Edward Stanley 1870-1948 *NatCAB 36*
Pauly, Karl Bone 1900-1963 *WhAm 4*
Paumgartner, Bernhard 1887-1971 *WhAm 5*
Paunack, August Oscar 1879-1954 *WhAm 3*
Pauncefote 1828- *ApCAB Sup*
Paur, Emil 1855- *WhAm 4*
Pausch, George 1740?-1796 *ApCAB*
Paust, Elnar Bernhardt 1907-1973 *WhAm 5*
Paustovsky, Konstantin Georgievich 1892-1968
WhAm 5
Pauw, Cornelius De 1739-1799 *Drake*
Paver, John Milton, III 1900-1972 *NatCAB 57*
Pavese, Cesare 1908-1950 *McGEWB*
Pavey, Frank Dunlap 1860-1946 *NatCAB 35*
Pavia, Virgil Carl 1912-1972 *NatCAB 56*
Pavie, Theodore Marie 1811- *ApCAB*
Pavlidis, Isaac Michael 1877-1959 *NatCAB 44*
Pavloska, Irene 1890-1962 *WhAm 4*
Pavloska, Aleksei Petrovich 1854-1929 *DcScB*
Pavlov, Dimitry *WhWW-II*
Pavlov, Ivan Petrovich 1849-1936 *AsBiEn,*
DcScB, McGEWB
Pavlov, Ivan Petrovitch 1849-1936 *BiHiMed*
Pavon Y Jimenez, Jose Antonio 1754-1840
DcScB Sup
Pavy, Octave Pierre 1844-1884 *ApCAB,*
DcAmB, NatCAB 7, WhAm H
Pawley, James, Sr. *NewYHSD*
Pawling, Levi 1773-1845 *BiAUS, BiDrAC,*
WhAm H
Pawlowski, Bogumil 1898-1971 *WhAm 6*
Pawlowski, Felix Wladyslaw 1876-1951
WhAm 3
Pawnee Bill *DcAmB S3, WhAm 1*
Pax, Walter Thomas 1903-1960 *WhAm 4*
Paxon, Edward M 1824- *ApCAB*
Paxon, Frederic John 1865-1939 *WhAm 1*
Paxson, Anna Richardson 1877-
WomWWA 14
Paxson, Edgar Samuel 1852-1919 *IIBEAAW,*
REnAW, WhAm 1
Paxson, Edward M 1824-1905 *NatCAB 5,*
TwCBDA, WhAm 1
Paxson, Frederic Logan 1877-1948 *NatCAB 39,*
WhAm 2
Paxson, Frederick Logan 1877-1948 *REnAW*
Paxson, Helen J 1883- *WomWWA 14*
Paxson, Henry Douglas 1945-1975 *WhAm 6*
Paxson, Samuel Edgar 1852-1919 *ApCAB X*
Paxson, W A 1850- *WhAm 4*
Paxton, Alexander Gallatin 1896-1974
WhAm 6
Paxton, Charles 1704-1788 *ApCAB, Drake*
Paxton, Columbus Sherman 1879-1950
NatCAB 41
Paxton, Edwin John 1877-1961 *NatCAB 50,*

WhAm 4, WhAm 5

Paxton, Elisha Franklin 1828-1863 *ApCAB, Drake, TwCBDA*

Paxton, Eliza *NewYHSD*

Paxton, J Hall 1899-1952 *WhAm 3*

Paxton, James Dunlop 1860-1949 *WhAm 3*

Paxton, James Whitehead 1821- *NatCAB 7*

Paxton, John Gallatin 1859-1928 *WhAm 1*

Paxton, John Randolph 1843-1923 *ApCAB, WhAm 1*

Paxton, John Richard 1906-1968 *WhAm 5*

Paxton, Joseph 1786-1861 *ApCAB*

Paxton, Joseph Francis 1864-1939 *WhAm 1, WhAm 1C*

Paxton, Joseph Rupert 1827-1867 *ApCAB, Drake*

Paxton, Kenneth T 1906-1971 *WhAm 5*

Paxton, Myra Reading Gulick *WomWWA 14*

Paxton, Philip *WhAm H*

Paxton, Thomas Barbour 1835-1922 *NatCAB 28, WhAm 1*

Paxton, Thomas Barbour, Jr. 1873-1930 *NatCAB 22*

Paxton, Thomas Rice 1847-1940 *NatCAB 34*

Paxton, William Francis, II 1907-1974 *WhAm 6*

Paxton, William McClung 1819-1916 *NatCAB 16*

Paxton, William McGregor 1869-1941 *WhAm 1*

Paxton, William Miller 1824-1904 *NatCAB 12, TwCBDA, WhAm 1*

Paxton, William Percy 1879-1953 *WhAm 3*

Payan, Elisco 1825- *ApCAB*

Payen, Anselme 1795-1871 *AsBiEn, DcScB*

Payen DeNoylan, Gilles-Augustin 1697-1751 *WhAm H*

Payer, Harry Franklin 1875-1952 *NatCAB 42*

Payer, Julius 1842- *ApCAB*

Payeras, Mariano 1739-1823 *WhAm H*

Paykull, Gustaf 1757-1826 *DcScB*

Paylor, I Irvin *WomWWA 14*

Payne, Adaline Maria Brown 1834- *WomWWA 14*

Payne, Alfred 1815?-1893 *NewYHSD*

Payne, Annie Amelia Allis *WomWWA 14*

Payne, Anthony Monck-Mason 1911-1970 *WhAm 5*

Payne, Arthur Coyle 1864-1952 *NatCAB 39*

Payne, Bruce Ryburn 1874-1937 *BiDAmEd, DcAmB S2, NatCAB 32, WhAm 1*

Payne, Byron Samuel 1876-1949 *WhAm 3*

Payne, Calvin Nathaniel 1844-1926 *NatCAB 24*

Payne, Charles *NewYHSD*

Payne, Charles Albert 1860- *WhAm 4*

Payne, Charles Edward 1879-1947 *WhAm 2*

Payne, Charles Henry 1830-1899 *ApCAB, NatCAB 4, TwCBDA, WhAm 1*

Payne, Charles Rockwell 1880-1926 *WhAm 1*

Payne, Cheals W 1846- *ApCAB X*

Payne, Christopher Harrison 1848-1925 *DcAmB, WhAm 4, WhoColR*

Payne, Christy 1874-1962 *WhAm 4*

Payne, Daniel Alexander 1811-1893 *AmBi, ApCAB, BiDAmEd, DcAmB, DcAmReB, NatCAB 4, TwCBDA, WhAm H*

Payne, David L 1836-1884 *NatCAB 19*

Payne, David Wells 1841-1921 *NatCAB 19*

Payne, Devall 1764-1830 *ApCAB*

Payne, Duval 1764-1830 *Drake*

Payne, E George 1877-1953 *WhAm 3*

Payne, Edgar Alwin 1882-1947 *IIBEAAW*

Payne, Edward Duggan 1836- *ApCAB*

Payne, Edward Townsend 1853-1922 *NatCAB 19*

Payne, Edward Waldron 1857- *WhAm 1*

Payne, Elisabeth Stancy d1944 *WhAm 2*

Payne, Elisha 1731-1807 *TwCBDA*

Payne, Elizabeth Rebecca Clark 1862- *WomWWA 14*

Payne, Eloisa R *NewYHSD*

Payne, Eugene Beauharnais 1835-1910 *WhAm 1*

Payne, F Ursula *WhAm 5*

Payne, Franklin Storey 1896-1970 *NatCAB 57, WhAm 5*

Payne, Frederick George 1904- *BiDrAC*

Payne, Frederick Huff 1876-1960 *WhAm 3*

Payne, Gavin Lodge 1869-1939 *NatCAB 30*

Payne, George Atlanta *WhoColR*

Payne, George Frederick 1853-1923 *NatCAB 20, WhAm 1*

Payne, George Henry 1876-1945 *NatCAB 34, WhAm 2*

Payne, George W 1888- *WhoColR*

Payne, George Witheridge 1843-1915 *NatCAB 42*

Payne, Guy 1877-1956 *NatCAB 47*

Payne, Henry *NewYHSD*

Payne, Henry B 1810-1896 *AmBi, ApCAB, BiAUS, BiDrAC, DcAmB, NatCAB 1, NatCAB 36, TwCBDA, WhAm H, WhAmP*

Payne, Henry Clay 1843-1904 *BiDrUSE, DcAmB, NatCAB 9, NatCAB 14, TwCBDA, WhAm 1*

Payne, James *NewYHSD*

Payne, Jason Elihu 1874-1941 *WhAm 2*

Payne, Jennie MacKay 1877- *WomWWA 14*

Payne, John 1815-1874 *ApCAB, NatCAB 5, TwCBDA*

Payne, John A 1900-1947 *WhAm 2*

Payne, John Barton 1855-1935 *AmBi, ApCAB X, BiDrUSE, DcAmB S1, NatCAB 10, WhAm 1*

Payne, John Bayly d1938 *WhAm 1*

Payne, John Carroll 1855-1936 *NatCAB 26, WhAm 4*

Payne, John H 1883-1961 *WhAm 4*

Payne, John Howard 1791-1852 *AmBi, DcAmB, McGEWB, NatCAB 2, TwCBDA, WebAB, WhAm H*

Payne, John Howard 1792-1852 *ApCAB, Drake*

Payne, John M *NewYHSD*

Payne, Kenneth Wilcox 1890-1962 *WhAm 4*

Payne, Leon Mather 1915-1972 *NatCAB 57, WhAm 5*

Payne, Leonidas Warren, Jr. 1873-1945 *WhAm 2*

Payne, Lewis Thornton Powell 1845-1865 *WhAm H*

Payne, Mary Earle 1856- *WomWWA 14*

Payne, Matthew Mountjoy *Drake*

Payne, Milton Jameson 1829- *NatCAB 9*

Payne, Montgomery Ashby 1906-1970 *WhAm 5*

Payne, Oliver Hazard 1839-1917 *DcAmB, NatCAB 35, WhAm 1*

Payne, Oliver Hiram 1901-1961 *WhAm 4*

Payne, Philip 1867- *WhAm 4*

Payne, Robert Lee 1857-1918 *WhAm 1*

Payne, Sereno Elisha 1843-1914 *AmBi, ApCAB Sup, BiDrAC, DcAmB, EncAAH, NatCAB 10, TwCBDA, WhAm 1, WhAmP*

Payne, W Harvey 1894-1969 *NatCAB 56*

Payne, Walter Seth 1837- *NatCAB 4*

Payne, Will 1865-1954 *TwCBDA, WhAm 3*

Payne, William Harold 1836-1907 *ApCAB, BiDAmEd, DcAmB, NatCAB 5, NatCAB 8, TwCBDA, WhAm 4*

Payne, William Henry Fitzhugh 1830-1904 *ApCAB Sup, BiDConf, TwCBDA, WhAm 1*

Payne, William Kenneth 1903-1963 *WhAm 4*

Payne, William Knapp 1874-1965 *WhAm 4*

Payne, William Morton 1858-1919 *DcAmB, NatCAB 11, TwCBDA, WhAm 1*

Payne, William Wallace 1837-1928 *ApCAB, WhAm 1*

Payne, William Winter 1805-1874 *TwCBDA*

Payne, William Winter 1807-1874 *BiDrAC, WhAm H*

Payne, Winfred Eustace 1892-1963 *NatCAB 52*

Payne, Winter W 1807- *BiAUS*

Paynter, John Henry 1838-1890 *NatCAB 44*

Paynter, Lemuel 1788-1863 *BiAUS, BiDrAC, WhAm H*

Paynter, Rowland Gardiner 1874-1944 *NatCAB 35*

Paynter, Samuel 1768-1845 *BiAUS, NatCAB 11, TwCBDA*

Paynter, Thomas Hanson 1851-1921 *BiDrAC, NatCAB 12, TwCBDA, WhAm 1, WhAmP*

Payot, Annie Eliza Evans 1847-1927 *NatCAB 21*

Payson, Charles Henry 1853-1933 *NatCAB 26*

Payson, Edward 1783-1827 *ApCAB, DcAmB, Drake, NatCAB 10, WhAm H*

Payson, Edward 1813-1890 *NatCAB 10*

Payson, Edward Saxton 1842- *WhAm 4*

Payson, Eliot Robertson 1846-1945 *WhAm 2*

Payson, Fanny Sturgis 1871- *WomWWA 14*

Payson, Franklin Conant 1856-1930 *WhAm 1*

Payson, George Shipman 1845-1923 *WhAm 1*

Payson, Herbert 1860-1940 *NatCAB 39*

Payson, Joan Whitney 1903-1975 *WhAm 6*

Payson, Laurence G 1894-1962 *WhAm 4*

Payson, Lewis Edwin 1840-1909 *BiDrAC, WhAmP*

Payson, Lieutenant Howard *WebAB*

Payson, Phillips 1736-1801 *ApCAB, Drake*

Payson, Seth 1758-1820 *ApCAB, DcAmB, Drake, WhAm H*

Payson, William Farquhar 1876-1939 *NatCAB 38, TwCBDA, WhAm 1*

Payton, Jacob Simpson 1884-1963 *WhAm 4*

Payton, Philip A, Jr. 1876- *WhoColR*

Paz, Ezequiel P 1871-1953 *WhAm 3*

Paz, Jose Maria 1789-1854 *ApCAB*

Paz Estenssoro, Victor 1907- *McGEWB*

Paz Soldan, Mariano Felipe 1821- *ApCAB*

Paz Soldan, Mateo 1814-1860 *ApCAB*

Pazmany, Peter 1570-1637 *McGEWB*

Peabody, Andrew Preston 1811-1893 *AmBi, ApCAB, DcAmB, Drake, NatCAB 3, TwCBDA, WhAm H*

Peabody, Anna Howe 1876- *WomWWA 14*

Peabody, Arthur 1858-1942 *WhAm 2*

Peabody, Augustus Stephen 1873-1934 *ApCAB X, WhAm 1*

Peabody, Cecil Hobart 1855-1934 *AmBi, DcAmB S1, NatCAB 24, WhAm 1*

Peabody, Charles 1867-1939 *WhAm 1*

Peabody, Charles Augustus 1814-1901 *ApCAB Sup, TwCBDA, WhAm 1*

Peabody, Charles Augustus 1849-1931 *WhAm 1*

Peabody, Dean, Jr. 1888-1951 *WhAm 3*

Peabody, Elizabeth Gertrude 1864- *WomWWA 14*

Peabody, Elizabeth Palmer 1804-1894 *AmBi, AmWom, ApCAB, BiDAmEd, DcAmB, Drake, McGEWB, NatCAB 12, NotAW, TwCBDA, WebAB, WhAm H*

Peabody, Endicott 1857-1944 *BiDAmEd, DcAmB S3, WhAm 2*

Peabody, Ephraim 1807-1856 *ApCAB, Drake*

Peabody, Ernest H 1869-1965 *WhAm 4*

Peabody, Everett 1830-1862 *NatCAB 4*

Peabody, Everett 1831-1862 *ApCAB*

Peabody, Francis 1854-1938 *WhAm 1*

Peabody, Francis Greenwood 1847-1936 *DcAmB S2, DcAmReB, TwCBDA, WhAm 1*

Peabody, Francis Howard 1831-1905 *NatCAB 28*

Peabody, Francis Stuyvesant 1859-1922 *NatCAB 18, WhAm 1*

Peabody, Francis Weld 1881-1927 *WhAm 1*

Peabody, Frank Everett 1856-1918 *NatCAB 26*

Peabody, Franklin Winchester 1826- *NewYHSD*

Peabody, Frederick Forrest 1859-1927 *NatCAB 36, WhAm 1*

Peabody, Frederick William 1862- *WhAm 1*

Peabody, George 1795-1869 *AmBi, ApCAB, DcAmB, Drake, EncAB, McGEWB, NatCAB 5, TwCBDA, WebAB, WhAm H*

Peabody, George Foster 1852-1938 *DcAmB S2, NatCAB 15, NatCAB 27, WhAm 1*

Peabody, George Harman *NatCAB 3, WhAm 5*

Peabody, George Livingston 1850-1914 *NatCAB 24, WhAm 1*

Peabody, Harry Ernest 1865-1940 *WhAm 2*

Peabody, Helen Sophia 1859- *WhAm 4*

Peabody, Henry Clay 1838-1911 *WhAm 1*

Peabody, Mrs. Henry Wayland 1861-1949 *WhAm 3*

Peabody, Mrs. James *NewYHSD*

Peabody, James Hamilton 1852-1917
NatCAB 1, WhAm 1
Peabody, James Terry White 1845-1916
NatCAB 16
Peabody, John Endicott 1853-1921 *ApCAB X*
Peabody, Joseph 1757-1844 *ApCAB, DcAmB,
NatCAB 5, WhAm H*
Peabody, Josephine Preston 1874-1922 *AmBi,
ApCAB X, BiCAW, DcAmB,
NatCAB 13, NatCAB 19, NotAW,
TwCBDA, WhAm 1, WomWWA 14*
Peabody, Kate Nichols Trask *NotAW*
Peabody, Lucy Evelyn 1865- *WhAm 4,
WomWWA 14*
Peabody, Lucy Whitehead McGill 1861-1949
DcAmB S4, NotAW, WomWWA 14
Peabody, M M *NewYHSD*
Peabody, Malcolm Endicott 1888-1974
WhAm 6
Peabody, Mary Jane *NewYHSD*
Peabody, Natalie Clews 1890- *WomWWA 14*
Peabody, Nathaniel 1741-1823 *AmBi, ApCAB,
BiDrAC, DcAmB, Drake, NatCAB 5,
TwCBDA, WhAmP*
Peabody, Nathaniel 1742-1823 *WhAm H*
Peabody, Nelson John 1883-1966 *NatCAB 52*
Peabody, Oliver William Bourn 1799-1848 *AmBi,
ApCAB, DcAmB, Drake, NatCAB 8,
WhAm H*
Peabody, Robert Swain 1845-1917 *BnEnAmA,
DcAmB, NatCAB 12, NatCAB 51,
WhAm 1*
Peabody, Ruth Eaton 1898-1967 *IIBEAAW*
Peabody, Selim Hobart 1829-1903 *BiDAmEd,
DcAmB, NatCAB 1, TwCBDA,
WhAm 1*
Peabody, Sophia Amelia 1811-1871 *NewYHSD*
Peabody, Stuyvesant 1888-1946 *NatCAB 41,
WhAm 2*
Peabody, William Bourn Oliver 1799-1847
*ApCAB, DcAmB, Drake, NatCAB 8,
WhAm H*
Peabody, William Rodman 1874-1941 *WhAm 1*
Peabody, William Wirt 1836- *NatCAB 12*
Peace *NewYHSD*
Peace, Bony Hampton 1873-1934 *WhAm 1*
Peace, Katherine Heyl *WomWWA 14*
Peace, Roger Craft 1899-1968 *BiDrAC,
WhAm 5*
Peace, Samuel Thomas 1879-1964 *NatCAB 51*
Peace, Willis Grandy 1875-1941 *NatCAB 39*
Peach, Robert English 1920-1971 *NatCAB 56,
WhAm 5*
Peach, Robert Westly 1863-1936 *NatCAB 29,
WhAm 1*
Peachey, Mrs. *NewYHSD*
Peacock *NewYHSD*
Peacock, Dred 1864-1934 *TwCBDA, WhAm 1*
Peacock, George 1791-1858 *DcScB*
Peacock, John *NewYHSD*
Peacock, Joseph Leishman 1873-1954 *WhAm 3*
Peacock, M A 1898-1950 *WhAm 3*
Peacock, Robert 1883-1956 *NatCAB 46*
Peacock, Thomas Bevill 1812-1882 *BiHiMed*
Peacock, Thomas Brower 1852-1919
ApCAB Sup
Peacock, Thomas Brower 1856-1919 *WhAm 1*
Peacock, Thomas Love 1785-1866 *McGEWB*
Peacock, Virginia Tatnall 1873- *WhAm 5,
WomWWA 14*
Peacock, Wesley, Sr. 1865-1941 *WhAm 1*
Peairs, Hervey B 1866-1940 *WhAm 1*
Peak, J Elmer 1888-1960 *WhAm 4*
Peak, John Lee 1839-1910 *NatCAB 13,
TwCBDA, WhAm 1*
Peak, Walter Clyde 1882-1967 *NatCAB 53*
Peake, Alonzo William 1890-1958 *WhAm 3*
Peake, Elmore Elliott 1871- *WhAm 5*
Peaks, Archibald Garfield 1880-1918 *WhAm 1*
Peaks, Mary Bradford 1880- *WomWWA 14*
Peale, Albert Charles 1849-1913 *WhAm 1*
Peale, Albert Charles 1849-1914 *NatCAB 21*
Peale, Anna Claypoole 1791-1878 *ApCAB,
BnEnAmA, DcAmB, NewYHSD, NotAW,
WhAm H*
Peale, Charles Clifford 1870-1955 *WhAm 3*
Peale, Charles Willson 1741-1827 *AmBi,
ApCAB, BnEnAmA, DcAmB, DcScB,*

*EncAB, IIBEAAW, McGEWB,
NewYHSD, TwCBDA, WebAB,
WhAm H*
Peale, Charles Wilson 1741-1827 *Drake,
NatCAB 6*
Peale, Emma Clara 1814- *NewYHSD*
Peale, Franklin 1795-1870 *NewYHSD,
WhAm H*
Peale, Miss J M *NewYHSD*
Peale, James 1749-1831 *ApCAB, BnEnAmA,
DcAmB, NewYHSD, TwCBDA,
WhAm H*
Peale, James, Jr. 1779-1876 *ApCAB*
Peale, James, Jr. 1789-1876 *NewYHSD*
Peale, Margaretta Angelica 1795-1882
NewYHSD, NotAW
Peale, Maria 1787-1866 *NewYHSD*
Peale, Mary Jane 1827-1902 *NewYHSD*
Peale, Mundy Ingalls 1906-1972 *WhAm 6*
Peale, Norman Vincent 1898- *WebAB*
Peale, Raphael 1774-1825 *DcAmB, Drake,
WhAm H*
Peale, Raphaelle 1774-1825 *ApCAB,
BnEnAmA, NewYHSD*
Peale, Rembrandt d1934 *WhAm 1*
Peale, Rembrandt 1778-1860 *AmBi, ApCAB,
BnEnAmA, DcAmB, DcScB, DcScB Sup,
Drake, McGEWB, NatCAB 5,
NewYHSD, TwCBDA, WhAm H*
Peale, Mrs. Rembrandt 1800?-1869 *NewYHSD*
Peale, Richard P 1903-1972 *WhAm 6*
Peale, Rosalba Carriera 1799-1874 *NewYHSD*
Peale, Rubens 1784-1864 *BnEnAmA*
Peale, Rubens 1784-1865 *NewYHSD*
Peale, Sarah Miriam 1800-1885 *ApCAB,
BnEnAmA, DcAmB, NewYHSD, NotAW,
WhAm H*
Peale, Titian Ramsay 1799-1885 *BnEnAmA,
DcAmB, DcScB, IIBEAAW, NewYHSD,
WhAm H*
Peale, Titian Ramsay 1800-1885 *NatCAB 21*
Peale, Titian Ramsey 1800-1885 *ApCAB*
Peale, Washington 1825-1868 *NewYHSD*
Pean DeSaint-Gilles, Leon 1832-1862 *DcScB*
Peano, Giuseppe 1858-1932 *AsBiEn, DcScB*
Pearce, Arthur Williams 1874- *NatCAB 14*
Pearce, Charles A 1906-1970 *WhAm 5*
Pearce, Charles Edward 1842-1902 *BiDrAC,
TwCBDA, WhAm 1*
Pearce, Charles Sidney 1808-1972 *WhAm 5*
Pearce, Charles Sprague 1851- *ApCAB,
NatCAB 11, TwCBDA*
Pearce, Charles Sprague 1851-1914 *AmBi,
DcAmB, WhAm 1*
Pearce, Charles Sprague 1851-1924 *ApCAB X*
Pearce, Charles Sumner 1877-1965 *NatCAB 51,
WhAm 4*
Pearce, Charles Tabb 1871-1953 *NatCAB 42*
Pearce, Clinton Ellicott 1891-1967 *WhAm 4*
Pearce, Cromwell 1772-1852 *ApCAB, Drake*
Pearce, Dutee Jerauld 1789-1849 *ApCAB,
BiDrAC, Drake, TwCBDA, WhAm H,
WhAmP*
Pearce, Dutte Jerauld 1789-1849 *BiAUS*
Pearce, Duttee Jerauld 1789-1849 *NatCAB 12*
Pearce, Edward 1833-1899 *NatCAB 8*
Pearce, Edward Douglas 1849-1923 *NatCAB 6*
Pearce, Elsie Simmons 1888- *WomWWA 14*
Pearce, Eugene Hamer 1843-1914 *WhAm 1*
Pearce, Eugene Lovick 1875-1963 *NatCAB 50*
Pearce, Eva F 1876- *WhAm 5*
Pearce, Hart L *NewYHSD*
Pearce, Haywood Jefferson 1871-1943 *WhAm 2*
Pearce, Helen Spang 1895- *IIBEAAW*
Pearce, James Alfred 1804-1862 *BiDrAC,
NatCAB 10, TwCBDA, WhAmP*
Pearce, James Alfred 1805-1862 *ApCAB,
BiAUS, DcAmB, Drake, WhAm H*
Pearce, James Alfred 1840- *WhAm 1*
Pearce, James Newton 1873-1936 *WhAm 1*
Pearce, James William 1924-1975 *WhAm 6*
Pearce, John Arthur 1871-1927 *NatCAB 22*
Pearce, John Elias 1876-1935 *WhAm 1*
Pearce, John Jackson *WhoColR*
Pearce, John Jamison 1826-1912 *BiAUS,
BiDrAC*
Pearce, John Musser 1908-1960 *WhAm 3*
Pearce, Liston Houston 1838-1924 *WhAm 1*
Pearce, Louise 1885-1959 *WhAm 3*

Pearce, Mary Bunting *WomWWA 14*
Pearce, Matthew Chalmers 1891-1966
NatCAB 53
Pearce, Maunsel Bennett 1902-1965
NatCAB 52
Pearce, McLeod Milligan 1874-1948
NatCAB 35, WhAm 2
Pearce, Mildred Tenney Brown *WomWWA 14*
Pearce, Myron La 1821-1914 *NatCAB 16*
Pearce, Nina Marie MacClure 1879-
WomWWA 14
Pearce, Richard 1837-1927 *DcAmB, WhAm 4*
Pearce, Richard Mills, Jr. 1874-1930 *BiDAmEd,
DcAmB, NatCAB 15, WhAm 1*
Pearce, Stephen Austen 1836-1900 *DcAmB,
WhAm H*
Pearce, Warren Frederick 1885-1964
NatCAB 51, WhAm 4
Pearce, Webster Houston 1876-1940 *WhAm 1*
Pearce, William *NewYHSD*
Pearce, William 1862-1947 *WhAm 2*
Pearce, William, Jr. *NewYHSD*
Pearce, William Cliff 1864- *WhAm 4*
Pearce, William Greene 1859-1952 *WhAm 3*
Pearce, William Herbert 1870-1951
NatCAB 40
Pearcy, Frank 1895-1974 *WhAm 6*
Peard, Frank Furnival 1868- *WhAm 4*
Peare, Robert Swaim 1901-1951 *NatCAB 46,
WhAm 3*
Pearl, Joseph 1885-1974 *WhAm 6*
Pearl, Mary Jeanette 1900-1966 *WhAm 5*
Pearl, Raymond 1879-1940 *DcAmB S2,
DcScB, NatCAB 15, WebAB, WhAm 1*
Pearl, Sarah Wood *NewYHSD*
Pearlstein, Philip 1924- *BnEnAmA*
Pearlstone, Hyman 1876-1966 *WhAm 4*
Pearmain, Alice Whittemore Upton 1863-
WhAm 4, WomWWA 14
Pearmain, Sumner Bass 1859- *WhAm 4*
Pearne, Wesley Ulysses 1851-1917 *WhAm 1*
Pearre, George Alexander 1860-1923 *BiDrAC,
TwCBDA, WhAm 1, WhAmP*
Pears, Sidney John 1900-1975 *WhAm 6*
Pears, Thomas Clinton 1849-1926 *NatCAB 22*
Pearsall, Benjamin Simon 1866-1935
NatCAB 42, WhAm 1
Pearsall, Charles H C 1887-1958 *WhAm 3*
Pearsall, Frederick Leonidas 1874-1945
NatCAB 36
Pearsall, James Welch 1839-1918 *WhAm 1*
Pearsall, Robert Ellis 1889-1963 *WhAm 4*
Pearse, Arthur Sperry 1877-1956 *NatCAB 47,
WhAm 3*
Pearse, Carroll Gardner 1858-1948 *NatCAB 42,
WhAm 4*
Pearse, John Barnard Swett 1842-1914 *ApCAB,
DcAmB, NatCAB 26, WhAm 4*
Pearse, Langdon 1877-1956 *NatCAB 43,
WhAm 3*
Pearse, Patrick Henry 1879-1916 *McGEWB*
Pearson, Albert Jackson 1846-1905 *BiDrAC*
Pearson, Alfred John 1869-1939 *ApCAB X,
NatCAB 36, WhAm 1*
Pearson, Alfred L 1838-1903 *ApCAB,
TwCBDA, WhAm 1*
Pearson, Andrew C 1873-1933 *WhAm 1*
Pearson, Arthur Emmons 1869-1934 *ApCAB X,
WhAm 1, WhAm 1C*
Pearson, Charles William 1846-1905 *WhAm 1*
Pearson, Chester Page 1873-1956 *NatCAB 43*
Pearson, Daniel Cecil 1881- *WhAm 6*
Pearson, Drew 1897-1969 *WebAB, WhAm 5*
Pearson, E Pennington 1886-1944 *NatCAB 37*
Pearson, Edmund Lester 1880-1937 *DcAmB S2,
DcAmLiB, NatCAB 28, WhAm 1*
Pearson, Edward Jones 1863-1928 *DcAmB,
NatCAB 23, WhAm 1*
Pearson, Edward Lowry 1880- *ApCAB X*
Pearson, Eliphalet 1752-1826 *ApCAB,
BiDAmEd, DcAmB, Drake, NatCAB 10,
TwCBDA, WhAm H*
Pearson, Elizabeth Ware Winsor
WomWWA 14
Pearson, Frank Bail 1853- *WhAm 4*
Pearson, Fred Stark 1861-1915 *DcAmB,
WhAm 1*

Pearson, Frederick 1842-1890 *NatCAB 26*
Pearson, Frederick Fanning Ayer 1888-1958 *NatCAB 45*
Pearson, Frederick Stark 1861-1915 *ApCAB X, NatCAB 18*
Pearson, George 1751-1828 *DcScB*
Pearson, George Frederick 1796-1867 *ApCAB, TwCBDA*
Pearson, George Frederick 1799-1867 *Drake*
Pearson, Gerald H J 1893-1969 *WhAm 5*
Pearson, Gustaf Adolph 1880-1949 *WhAm 2*
Pearson, Harry *NewYHSD*
Pearson, Harry A 1910-1973 *WhAm 6*
Pearson, Helen Sleeper *WomWWA 14*
Pearson, Henry 1864- *WhoColR*
Pearson, Henry Carr 1871- *WhAm 5*
Pearson, Henry Clemens 1858-1936 *NatCAB 27, WhAm 1*
Pearson, Henry Greenleaf 1870-1939 *WhAm 1*
Pearson, Herbert William 1850-1916 *NatCAB 18*
Pearson, Herron Carney 1890-1953 *BiDrAC, WhAm 3*
Pearson, Hesketh 1887-1964 *WhAm 4*
Pearson, James Blackwood 1920- *BiDrAC*
Pearson, James John 1858-1926 *WhAm 1*
Pearson, James Larkin 1879- *WhAm 6*
Pearson, Jay Frederick Wesley 1901-1965 *NatCAB 52, WhAm 4*
Pearson, Joel Gottfred 1891-1963 *NatCAB 51*
Pearson, John James 1800-1888 *ApCAB, BiDrAC, NatCAB 14, WhAm H*
Pearson, Jonathan 1813-1887 *ApCAB, TwCBDA*
Pearson, Joseph *NewYHSD*
Pearson, Joseph 1776-1834 *BiAUS, BiDrAC, TwCBDA, WhAm H, WhAmP*
Pearson, Joseph Reed 1880-1955 *NatCAB 46*
Pearson, Joseph Thurman, Jr. 1876-1951 *NatCAB 40, WhAm 3*
Pearson, Josephine Anderson 1870- *WhAm 5*
Pearson, Karl 1857-1936 *DcScB*
Pearson, Leon Morris 1899-1963 *WhAm 4*
Pearson, Leonard 1868-1909 *DcAmB, WhAm 1*
Pearson, Lester Bowles 1897-1972 *McGEWB, WhAm 5*
Pearson, Lola Clark 1871-1951 *WhAm 3, WomWWA 14*
Pearson, Lucy Wright 1864- *WomWWA 14*
Pearson, Matthew Edgar 1862-1948 *WhAm 3*
Pearson, Norman Holmes 1909-1975 *WhAm 6*
Pearson, Oscar William 1895-1957 *NatCAB 47, WhAm 3*
Pearson, Paul Martin 1871-1938 *NatCAB 37, WhAm 1*
Pearson, Peter Henry 1864-1940 *WhAm 1*
Pearson, Ralph M 1883- *WhAm 3*
Pearson, Raymond Allen 1873-1939 *DcAmB S2, NatCAB 15, WhAm 1*
Pearson, Richard Metcalf 1899-1957 *NatCAB 46, WhAm 3*
Pearson, Richard Mumford 1805-1878 *ApCAB, BiAUS*
Pearson, Richmond 1852-1923 *BiDrAC, NatCAB 14, TwCBDA, WhAm 1*
Pearson, Richmond Mumford 1805-1878 *BiDConf, DcAmB, NatCAB 11, TwCBDA, WhAm H*
Pearson, Robert d1891 *NewYHSD*
Pearson, Robert Caldwell 1807-1867 *NatCAB 36*
Pearson, Robert Logan 1882-1952 *WhAm 3*
Pearson, Samuel 1862- *WhAm 4*
Pearson, Thomas 1893-1963 *NatCAB 50, WhAm 4*
Pearson, Thomas Gilbert 1873-1943 *DcAmB S3, NatCAB 33, WhAm 2*
Pearson, Walter Washington 1862- *WhAm 4*
Pearson, William *NewYHSD*
Pearson, William 1854- *NatCAB 14*
Pearson, William Alexander 1879-1959 *WhAm 3*
Pearson, William Edward 1869- *ApCAB X*
Pearson, William Frederick 1880-1957 *NatCAB 48*
Pearson, William Gaston 1859- *WhoColR*
Pearson, William Henry 1832- *ApCAB X*

Pearson, William Lazarus 1849-1935 *WhAm 3*
Pearson, William Norman 1924-1968 *WhAm 5*
Pearson, William Simpson 1849-1919 *NatCAB 18*
Pearson, William Thomas 1884-1968 *NatCAB 54*
Pearson, William Wilson 1869-1944 *NatCAB 35*
Pearsons, Daniel Kimball 1820-1912 *AmBi, ApCAB, DcAmB, NatCAB 24, TwCBDA, WhAm 1*
Peary, Josephine Diebitsch 1863-1955 *DcAmB S5, WhAm 3, WomWWA 14*
Peary, Robert Edward 1856-1920 *ApCAB Sup*
Peary, Robert Edwin 1856-1920 *AmBi, AsBiEn, DcAmB, McGEWB, NatCAB 14, NatCAB 37, TwCBDA, WebAB, WebAMB, WhAm 1*
Pease, Abraham PerLee 1847- *ApCAB X*
Pease, Alan W d1955 *WhAm 3*
Pease, Albert Sheldon 1828-1914 *NatCAB 16*
Pease, Alfred Humphreys 1838-1882 *ApCAB, DcAmB, WhAm H*
Pease, Alonzo *NewYHSD*
Pease, Anson 1819-1896 *ApCAB X*
Pease, Arthur Stanley 1881-1964 *WhAm 4*
Pease, Benjamin F 1822- *NewYHSD*
Pease, C W *NewYHSD*
Pease, Calvin 1776-1839 *BiAUS, DcAmB, Drake, NatCAB 7, WhAm H*
Pease, Calvin 1813-1863 *ApCAB, Drake, NatCAB 2, TwCBDA*
Pease, Charles Edward 1836- *NatCAB 10*
Pease, Charles Giffin 1854-1941 *NatCAB 31, WhAm 1*
Pease, Charles Henry 1873-1933 *WhAm 1*
Pease, Edward Allen 1865-1940 *NatCAB 30*
Pease, Edward M *BiAUS*
Pease, Elisha Marshall 1812-1883 *DcAmB, NatCAB 9, TwCBDA, WhAm H, WhAmP*
Pease, Ernest Mondell 1859-1936 *AmBi, WhAm 1*
Pease, Eva May 1870- *WomWWA 14*
Pease, Francis Gladheim 1881-1938 *AmBi, WhAm 1*
Pease, Francis Gladhelm 1881-1938 *DcScB*
Pease, Fred Atwood 1873-1955 *NatCAB 44*
Pease, Frederick Henry 1839-1909 *WhAm 1*
Pease, Harry E *NewYHSD*
Pease, Henry *NewYHSD*
Pease, Henry Roberts 1835-1907 *ApCAB, BiAUS, BiDrAC, NatCAB 12, TwCBDA*
Pease, Herbert Hoyt 1881-1967 *NatCAB 53, WhAm 4*
Pease, Joseph Ives 1809-1883 *ApCAB, DcAmB, NewYHSD, WhAm H*
Pease, Kingsley Eugene 1875- *WhAm 5*
Pease, Laurette Eustis Potts *WomWWA 14*
Pease, Leonora Elizabeth *NatCAB 17*
Pease, Lucius Curtis 1869-1963 *IlBEAAW, WhAm 5*
Pease, Murray 1903-1964 *WhAm 4*
Pease, Nell Christmas McMullin 1883- *IlBEAAW*
Pease, Nelson Livingston 1831-1872 *NatCAB 20*
Pease, Phineas 1826- *ApCAB*
Pease, Ralph Clifford 1874-1964 *NatCAB 51*
Pease, Richard H 1813-1869 *NewYHSD*
Pease, Robert Norton 1895-1964 *NatCAB 50, WhAm 4*
Pease, Rollin 1879- *WhAm 6*
Pease, Rose Winchester 1842- *WomWWA 14*
Pease, Seth *BiAUS*
Pease, Theodore Calvin 1887-1948 *WhAm 2*
Pease, Zephaniah W 1861-1933 *WhAm 1*
Peaslee, Abbie Ann 1849- *WomWWA 14*
Peaslee, Amos Jenkins 1887-1969 *NatCAB 56, WhAm 5*
Peaslee, Charles Hazen 1804-1866 *BiAUS, BiDrAC, TwCBDA, WhAm H*
Peaslee, Edmund Randolph 1814-1878 *ApCAB, DcAmB, Drake, NatCAB 10, WhAm H*
Peaslee, Horace Whittier 1884-1959 *WhAm 3*
Peaslee, John Bradley 1842-1912 *NatCAB 14, TwCBDA, WhAm 1*
Peaslee, Robert James 1864-1936 *NatCAB 27,*

WhAm 1
Peasley, A M *NewYHSD*
Peat *NewYHSD*
Peat, Miss *NewYHSD*
Peat, Wilbur David 1898-1966 *NatCAB 53, WhAm 4*
Peate, John 1820-1903 *WhAm 1*
Peattie, Donald Culross 1898-1964 *WhAm 4*
Peattie, Elia Wilkinson 1862-1935 *AmWom, TwCBDA, WhAm 1, WomWWA 14*
Peattie, Louise Redfield 1900-1965 *WhAm 4*
Peattie, Robert 1857-1930 *WhAm 1*
Peattie, Roderick 1891-1955 *NatCAB 41, WhAm 3*
Peavey, Frank Hutchinson 1850-1901 *DcAmB, WhAm H*
Peavey, Frank Hutchison 1850-1901 *NatCAB 6*
Peavey, Hubert Haskell 1881-1937 *BiDrAC, WhAmP*
Peavey, Leroy Deering 1876-1937 *WhAm 1*
Peavy, Anderson Jasper 1866-1942 *NatCAB 32*
Peavy, George Wilcox 1869-1951 *NatCAB 41, WhAm 3*
Peavy, William Asa 1904-1961 *NatCAB 48*
Peay, Austin 1876-1927 *DcAmB, NatCAB 33, WhAm 1*
Pebbles, Francis Marion 1839-1928 *NatCAB 23*
Pebbles, Frank Marion 1839-1928 *NewYHSD*
Pech, James 1830- *ApCAB*
Pech, James 1839- *WhAm 4*
Pecham, John 1230?-1292 *DcScB*
Pechan, Albert Raymond 1902-1969 *NatCAB 55*
Pechin, Edmund Cash 1834-1928 *WhAm 1*
Peck, Adelbert Henry 1862- *NatCAB 14*
Peck, Alice Malana 1851- *WomWWA 14*
Peck, Alice Russell 1857- *WomWWA 14*
Peck, Allen Steele 1880-1951 *WhAm 3*
Peck, Andrew 1836-1917 *ApCAB X*
Peck, Annie Smith 1850-1935 *AmBi, AmWom, NatCAB 15, NotAW, WhAm 1, WomWWA 14*
Peck, Asahel 1803-1879 *NatCAB 8, TwCBDA*
Peck, Bayard Livingston 1869-1931 *NatCAB 23, WhAm 1*
Peck, Carson Christopher 1858-1915 *ApCAB X, NatCAB 25*
Peck, Cassius Reuben 1880-1963 *NatCAB 51, WhAm 6*
Peck, Cecil Clay 1880- *WhAm 6*
Peck, Charles H 1817- *NatCAB 9*
Peck, Charles Horton 1833-1917 *DcAmB, NatCAB 13, WhAm 3*
Peck, Charles Howard 1870-1927 *DcAmB, WhAm 1*
Peck, Clarence Ives 1841-1916 *NatCAB 17*
Peck, Clarissa Clark 1817-1884 *ApCAB Sup*
Peck, Darius Edward 1877-1944 *WhAm 2*
Peck, Ebenezer 1805-1881 *ApCAB, BiAUS*
Peck, Edith Weld *WomWWA 14*
Peck, Edson Sheldon 1862-1937 *NatCAB 27*
Peck, Edward Porter 1855-1937 *WhAm 1*
Peck, Edwin James 1806-1876 *ApCAB*
Peck, Elijah Wolsey 1799-1888 *NatCAB 8, TwCBDA*
Peck, Emelyn Foster 1878- *WomWWA 14*
Peck, Epaphroditus 1860-1938 *WhAm 1*
Peck, Erasmus Darwin 1808-1876 *BiAUS, BiDrAC, WhAm H*
Peck, Eugenia Caldwell 1860- *WomWWA 14*
Peck, Ferdinand Wythe 1848-1924 *ApCAB, NatCAB 3, TwCBDA, WhAm 1*
Peck, Frank 1864-1943 *NatCAB 34*
Peck, Frederick Burritt 1860-1925 *NatCAB 21, WhAm 1*
Peck, Frederick Stanhope 1868-1947 *ApCAB X, NatCAB 35, WhAm 2*
Peck, George 1797-1876 *ApCAB, DcAmB, Drake, TwCBDA, WhAm H*
Peck, George 1834-1913 *NatCAB 16*
Peck, George Bacheler 1843-1934 *NatCAB 6, WhAm 1*
Peck, George Clarke 1865-1927 *WhAm 1*
Peck, George Lyman 1858-1932 *NatCAB 23, WhAm 1*
Peck, George Melancthon 1843-1935 *NatCAB 31*
Peck, George Record 1843-1923 *DcAmB,*

Peet, Stephen 1795-1855 *ApCAB, Drake*
Peet, Stephen Denison 1830-1914 *ApCAB, TwCBDA*
Peet, Stephen Denison 1831-1914 *AmBi, DcAmB, WhAm 4*
Peet, W Creighton 1871-1937 *NatCAB 28*
Peet, William 1822-1895 *NatCAB 7*
Peet, William 1847-1934 *NatCAB 26, WhAm 1*
Peet, William Wheelock 1851- *WhAm 4*
Peetsch, Charles *NewYHSD*
Peffer, Harry Creighton 1873-1934 *WhAm 1*
Peffer, Henry Ira 1879-1952 *WhAm 3*
Peffer, Nathaniel 1890-1964 *WhAm 4*
Peffer, Susie Hayes 1879- *WomWWA 14*
Peffer, William Alfred 1831-1912 *AmBi, ApCAB Sup, BiDrAC, DcAmB, EncAAH, NatCAB 1, REnAW, TwCBDA, WhAm 1, WhAmP*
Pefferle, Leslie George 1895-1955 *NatCAB 43*
Pegler, Westbrook James 1894-1969 *WebAB, WhAm 5*
Pegram, George Braxton 1876-1958 *NatCAB 49, WhAm 3*
Pegram, George Herndon 1855-1937 *ApCAB X, NatCAB 9, NatCAB 28, WhAm 1*
Pegram, J Edward 1880-1951 *NatCAB 44*
Pegram, John 1773-1831 *BiAUS, BiDrAC, TwCBDA, WhAm H*
Pegram, John 1832-1865 *AmBi, ApCAB, BiDConf, Drake, NatCAB 5, TwCBDA, WebAMB*
Pegram, John Combe 1842-1909 *WhAm 1*
Pegram, Robert Baker 1811-1894 *ApCAB, TwCBDA*
Pegram, Robert Baker, III 1874- *WhAm 5*
Pegram, William Howell 1846- *NatCAB 3*
Pegram, William Johnson 1841-1865 *ApCAB, Drake, TwCBDA*
Pegues, Albert Shipp 1872-1960 *WhAm 4, WhAm 5*
Pegues, Albert Witherspoon 1859- *WhoColR*
Pegues, Boykin Witherspoon 1874- *WhAm 5*
Peguy, Charles Pierre 1873-1914 *McGEWB*
Pehrson, Ernest William 1880-1953 *WhAm 4*
Pei, I M 1917- *BnEnAmA*
Peik, Wesley Earnest 1886-1951 *WhAm 3*
Peint, Girault *NewYHSD*
Peirce *NewYHSD*
Peirce, Arthur Winslow 1860-1934 *WhAm 1*
Peirce, Benjamin 1778-1831 *ApCAB, Drake, NatCAB 10, TwCBDA, WhAm H*
Peirce, Benjamin 1809-1880 *AmBi, ApCAB, BiDAmEd, DcAmB, DcScB, Drake, EncAB, NatCAB 8, TwCBDA, WebAB, WhAm H*
Peirce, Benjamin Mills 1844-1870 *NatCAB 10, WhAm H*
Peirce, Benjamin Osgood 1854-1914 *AmBi, ApCAB, DcAmB, DcScB, NatCAB 20, TwCBDA, WhAm 1*
Peirce, Bertha *BiCAW*
Peirce, Bradford Kinney 1819-1889 *ApCAB, DcAmB, Drake, TwCBDA, WhAm H*
Peirce, Charles Henry 1814-1855 *ApCAB*
Peirce, Charles Santiago Sanders 1839-1914 *AmBi, ApCAB, BiDAmEd, DcAmB, DcScB, EncAB, McGEWB, NatCAB 8, TwCBDA, WebAB, WhAm 1*
Peirce, Clarence Andrew 1860-1960 *WhAm 4*
Peirce, Cyrus 1790-1860 *BiDAmEd, DcAmB, Drake, WhAm H*
Peirce, Cyrus Newlin 1829-1909 *WhAm 1*
Peirce, Ebenezer Weaver 1822- *ApCAB, Drake, NatCAB 11, NatCAB 13, TwCBDA*
Peirce, Eliza Metcalf *WomWWA 14*
Peirce, Frances Elizabeth 1857- *AmWom*
Peirce, Frederic Marshall 1910-1974 *WhAm 6*
Peirce, George 1883-1919 *NatCAB 24*
Peirce, George James 1868-1954 *NatCAB 41, WhAm 3*
Peirce, Gerry 1900- *IlBEAAW*
Peirce, Miss H T *NewYHSD*
Peirce, Harold 1856-1932 *WhAm 1*
Peirce, Harry H 1891-1954 *WhAm 3*
Peirce, Hattie Wasmuth 1870- *WomWWA 14*
Peirce, Hayford 1883-1946 *NatCAB 34*
Peirce, Henry Augustus 1808-1885 *BiAUS,*

DcAmB, WhAm H
Peirce, Herbert Benjamin 1887-1955 *NatCAB 44*
Peirce, Herbert Henry Davis 1849-1916 *NatCAB 27, WhAm 1*
Peirce, James Mills 1834-1906 *AmBi, ApCAB, BiDAmEd, DcAmB, NatCAB 10, TwCBDA, WhAm 1*
Peirce, John 1836-1897 *NatCAB 10*
Peirce, Joseph 1748-1812 *BiDrAC, WhAm H*
Peirce, Joshua H *IlBEAAW, NewYHSD*
Peirce, Katharine Upham *WomWWA 14*
Peirce, Leona May 1863- *WomWWA 14*
Peirce, Louise Fagan *WomWWA 14*
Peirce, Mary Robinson 1873- *WomWWA 14*
Peirce, Melusina Fay 1836- *TwCBDA, WhAm 4, WomWWA 14*
Peirce, Paul Skeels 1874-1951 *NatCAB 41, WhAm 3*
Peirce, Robert Bruce Fraser 1843-1898 *BiDrAC*
Peirce, Sara Estelle 1862- *WomWWA 14*
Peirce, Silas 1860-1922 *WhAm 1*
Peirce, Thomas 1786-1850 *ApCAB, Drake*
Peirce, Thomas May 1837-1896 *NatCAB 5, NatCAB 36*
Peirce, Thomas May, Jr. 1878- *WhAm 6*
Peirce, Thomas Mitchell 1864- *WhAm 4*
Peirce, Waldo 1884-1970 *NatCAB 55, WhAm 5*
Peirce, William 1590-1641 *ApCAB, DcAmB, Drake, WhAm H*
Peirce, William Foster 1868-1967 *NatCAB 8, TwCBDA, WhAm 4*
Peirce, William Henry 1865-1944 *NatCAB 34, WhAm 2*
Peirce, William J *NewYHSD*
Peirce, William Shannon 1815-1887 *ApCAB*
Peirce, William Sullivan 1864-1923 *NatCAB 19, WhAm 1*
Peiresc, Nicolas Claude Fabri De 1580-1637 *DcScB*
Peirse, Sir Richard 1892-1970 *WhWW-II*
Peirson, Alden 1873- *WhAm 1*
Peirson, Lydia Jane Wheeler 1802-1862 *ApCAB, Drake*
Peis *NewYHSD*
Peis, Lewis *NewYHSD*
Peiser, Solomon d1951 *WhAm 3*
Peissner, Elias 1826- *Drake*
Peixoto, Floriano 1839-1895 *McGEWB*
Peixoto, Ignacio Jose DeAlvarenga 1748-1792 *ApCAB*
Peixotto, Benjamin Franklin 1834-1890 *ApCAB, DcAmB, WhAm H*
Peixotto, Daniel Levy Maduro 1800-1843 *ApCAB*
Peixotto, Ernest Clifford 1869-1940 *IlBEAAW, NatCAB 14, NatCAB 30, WhAm 1*
Peixotto, Jessica Blanche 1864-1941 *NotAW, WhAm 1, WomWWA 14*
Peixotto, Sidney Salzado 1866-1925 *WhAm 1*
Pekelharing, Cornelis Adrianus 1848-1922 *DcScB*
Pekenino, Michele *NewYHSD*
Pelage, Magloire 1769-1840 *ApCAB*
Pelagius d430? *McGEWB*
Pelby, Mrs. *NewYHSD*
Pelby, Rosalie French 1793-1855 *Drake*
Pelby, Rosalie French 1793-1857 *ApCAB*
Pelby, William 1793-1850 *ApCAB*
Pelenyi, John 1885-1974 *WhAm 6*
Peletier, Jacques 1517-1582 *DcScB*
Pelham, Arleigh 1880-1957 *NatCAB 48*
Pelham, Charles 1835-1908 *BiAUS, BiDrAC*
Pelham, Henry 1748?-1806 *DcAmB*
Pelham, Henry 1749-1806 *BnEnAmA, NewYHSD, WhAm H*
Pelham, Herbert 1602-1673 *ApCAB, Drake*
Pelham, John 1838-1863 *DcAmB, WebAMB, WhAm H*
Pelham, John 1865-1917 *NatCAB 18, WhAm 1*
Pelham, Laura Dainty 1849- *WomWWA 14*
Pelham, Mary Singleton Copley 1710?-1789 *NotAW*
Pelham, Peter d1751 *ApCAB•*
Pelham, Peter 1695?-1751 *BnEnAmA, DcAmB, WhAm H*

Pelham, Peter 1697-1751 *NewYHSD*
Pelham, Robert A 1859-1943 *DcAmB S3*
Pelham, Thomas Walter 1861- *NatCAB 2*
Pelissier, Aimable Jean Jacques 1794-1864 *WhoMilH*
Pell, Anna Johnson 1883- *WomWWA 14*
Pell, Claiborne DeBorda 1918- *BiDrAC*
Pell, Edward Leigh 1861-1943 *WhAm 2*
Pell, Ella Ferris 1846-1922 *WhAm 1, WomWWA 14*
Pell, F Livingston 1873-1945 *NatCAB 47*
Pell, George Pierce 1870-1938 *WhAm 1*
Pell, Herbert Claiborne 1884-1961 *ApCAB X, BiDrAC, NatCAB 47, WhAm 4*
Pell, Howland Haggerty 1872-1949 *NatCAB 37*
Pell, James Albert 1899-1962 *WhAm 4*
Pell, John 1611-1685 *DcScB*
Pell, John L E 1876- *WhAm 5*
Pell, Philip 1753-1811 *BiDrAC, WhAm H*
Pell, Robert Conger 1835-1868 *Drake*
Pell, Robert L *NatCAB 5*
Pell, Robert Paine 1860-1941 *WhAm 1*
Pell, Samuel Osgood 1873- *NatCAB 14*
Pell, Stephen H P 1874-1950 *WhAm 3*
Pell, William Henry Dannat 1888-1962 *WhAm 4*
Pell, Williamson 1881-1949 *WhAm 2*
Pell, Williamson, Jr. 1911-1972 *NatCAB 56, WhAm 5*
Pellegrin, Francis *NewYHSD*
Pellegrini, Carlos 1846- *ApCAB Sup*
Pellepart, Pierre 1606-1667 *ApCAB*
Pelletier, Bertrand 1761-1797 *DcScB*
Pelletier, Charles Alphonse Pentaleon 1837- *ApCAB*
Pelletier, Louis Philippe 1857- *ApCAB Sup*
Pelletier, Pierre Joseph 1788-1842 *AsBiEn, DcScB*
Pelletier, William Joseph 1897-1947 *NatCAB 42*
Pellett, Frank Chapman 1879-1951 *WhAm 3*
Pellett, LeGrand Warren 1877-1945 *NatCAB 33*
Pellew, Charles Ernest 1863- *WhAm 5*
Pellew, Edward 1757-1833 *WhoMilH*
Pellew, George 1859-1892 *NatCAB 4, WhAm H*
Pellew, Henry Edward 1828-1923 *DcAmB, WhAm 1*
Pelley, John Jeremiah 1878-1946 *NatCAB 36, WhAm 2*
Pelley, William Dudley 1890-1965 *WhAm 4*
Pellicer, Anthony Dominic 1824-1880 *WhAm H*
Pellicer, Anthony Dominic 1825-1880 *ApCAB, NatCAB 13*
Pellicier, Anthony Domenec Ambrose 1824-1880 *TwCBDA*
Pelly, Thomas Minor 1902-1973 *BiDrAC, WhAm 6*
Pelotas, Patricio J C DaC, Viscount Of 1740?-1827 *ApCAB*
Peloubet, Francis Nathan 1831-1920 *ApCAB, DcAmB, TwCBDA, WhAm 1*
Pelouze, Louis Henry 1841-1878 *ApCAB*
Pelouze, Theophile-Jules 1807-1867 *DcScB*
Pelouze, William Nelson 1865-1943 *NatCAB 33, WhAm 2*
Pelstring, Herman Joseph 1882-1956 *NatCAB 46*
Peltason, Paul Evans 1898-1974 *WhAm 6*
Pelter, Fred Paul 1875-1928 *WhAm 1*
Peltier, Florence 1862- *WomWWA 14*
Peltier, George Leo 1888-1975 *WhAm 6*
Peltier, Jean Charles Athanase 1785-1845 *DcScB*
Pelton, Carl Homer 1879-1943 *NatCAB 36*
Pelton, Ernest Williams 1880-1947 *NatCAB 35*
Pelton, Guy Ray 1824-1890 *BiDrAC, WhAm H*
Pelton, Guy Ray 1825-1890 *BiAUS*
Pelton, Lester Allen 1829- *NatCAB 13*
Pelton, Oliver 1798-1882 *NewYHSD*
Pelton, Roger Trowbridge 1880- *WhAm 6*
Peltz, William Law Learned 1882-1961 *NatCAB 49*
Peluse, Samuel 1895-1963 *NatCAB 51*
Pelz, Paul Johann 1841-1918 *NatCAB 25*
Pelz, Paul Johannes 1841-1918 *DcAmB,*

WhAm 1
Pelzer, Arthur 1865-1951 *NatCAB 40*
Pelzer, Francis Joseph 1826-1916 *NatCAB 17*
Pelzer, Lewis 1879-1946 *REnAW*
Pelzer, Louis 1879-1946 *WhAm 2*
Pember, Phoebe Yates Levy 1823-1913 *NotAW*
Pemberton, Brock 1885-1950 *DcAmB S4,*
WhAm 2
Pemberton, Ebenezer 1671-1717 *ApCAB,*
Drake
Pemberton, Ebenezer 1704-1779 *ApCAB,*
Drake
Pemberton, Ebenezer 1747?-1835 *NatCAB 10*
Pemberton, Frank Arthur 1884-1952
NatCAB 39
Pemberton, Henry 1694-1771 *DcScB*
Pemberton, Henry 1826-1911 *WhAm 1*
Pemberton, Henry, Jr. 1855-1913 *NatCAB 15*
Pemberton, Israel 1685-1754 *ApCAB*
Pemberton, Israel 1715-1779 *ApCAB, DcAmB,*
Drake, NatCAB 5, WhAm H
Pemberton, James 1723-1808 *ApCAB*
Pemberton, James 1723-1809 *DcAmB,*
WhAm H
Pemberton, James 1724-1809 *Drake*
Pemberton, John 1727-1795 *ApCAB, DcAmB,*
Drake, WhAm H
Pemberton, John Clifford 1814-1881 *ApCAB,*
BiDConf, DcAmB, NatCAB 10,
TwCBDA, WebAMB, WhAm H,
WhoMilH
Pemberton, John Clifford 1818?-1881 *Drake*
Pemberton, John DeJarnette 1887-1967
WhAm 4
Pemberton, Leander Munsell 1845- *NatCAB 18*
Pemberton, Phineas 1650-1702 *ApCAB, Drake*
Pemberton, Ralph 1877-1949 *WhAm 2*
Pemberton, Thomas 1728-1807 *ApCAB, Drake*
Pemberton, Virginia Carroll 1856-
WomWWA 14
Pemberton, Walter Henry 1857-1928
NatCAB 21
Pemberton, William Young 1842-1922
NatCAB 12, WhAm 1
Pena, Tonita 1895-1949 *IlBEAAW*
Pena Y Pena, Manuel DeLa 1789-1850 *ApCAB*
Penabert, F *NewYHSD*
Penafiel, Alfonso *ApCAB*
Penalosa Briceno, Diego Dioniso De 1622?-1687?
DcAmB, WhAm H
Penalver Y Cardenas, Luis Ignatius 1749-1810
WhAm H
Penberthy, Grover Cleveland 1886-1959
WhAm 3
Pence, Arthur W 1898- *WhAm 3*
Pence, Edward Hart 1868-1936 *WhAm 1,*
WhAm 1C
Pence, John Wesley 1896-1959 *WhAm 3*
Pence, Lafayette 1857-1923 *BiDrAC,*
WhAm 1
Pence, Thomas Jones 1873-1916 *WhAm 1*
Pence, William David 1865-1946 *WhAm 2*
Penck, Albrecht 1858-1945 *DcScB*
Penck, Walther 1888-1923 *DcScB*
Pendell, William Delcamp 1914-1961
NatCAB 50
Pendelton, Charles Sutphin 1879-1948 *WhAm 2*
Pender, Harold 1879-1959 *NatCAB 48,*
WhAm 3
Pender, William Dorsey 1833-1863 *Drake*
Pender, William Dorsey 1834-1863 *AmBi,*
ApCAB, BiDConf, DcAmB, NatCAB 9,
TwCBDA, WebAMB, WhAm H
Penderecki, Krzysztof 1933- *McGEWB*
Pendergast *NewYHSD*
Pendergast, Ella Worth 1851- *WomWWA 14*
Pendergast, John Joseph 1906-1967 *WhAm 4*
Pendergast, Thomas Joseph 1872-1945
DcAmB S3
Pendergrast, Austin 1829-1874 *ApCAB*
Pendergrast, Garrett Jesse 1802-1862 *ApCAB,*
Drake, WebAMB
Pendexter, Hugh 1875-1940 *NatCAB 30,*
WhAm 1
Pendleton, Albert Huntington 1901-1972
WhAm 5
Pendleton, Charles Rittenhouse 1850-1913
WhAm 1

Pendleton, Edmund 1721-1803 *AmBi, ApCAB,*
BiAUS, BiDrAC, DcAmB, Drake,
McGEWB, NatCAB 10, TwCBDA,
WebAB, WhAm H, WhAmP
Pendleton, Edmund 1843-1910 *NatCAB 15*
Pendleton, Edmund 1845-1910 *WhAm 1*
Pendleton, Edmund Henry 1788-1862 *BiAUS,*
BiDrAC, WhAm H
Pendleton, Edmund Monroe 1815-1884 *ApCAB,*
DcAmB, WhAm H
Pendleton, Edward Waldo 1849- *NatCAB 5*
Pendleton, Edwin Conway 1847-1919
NatCAB 42, WhAm 1
Pendleton, Edwin Seymour 1877-1936
NatCAB 29
Pendleton, Ellen Fitz 1864-1936 *AmBi,*
BiDAmEd, DcAmB S2, NotAW,
WhAm 1, WomWWA 14
Pendleton, Elliott Hunt 1859-1926 *NatCAB 21,*
WhAm 1
Pendleton, Fields Seeley 1870-1923 *NatCAB 29*
Pendleton, Francis Key d1930 *WhAm 1*
Pendleton, Frederick Starr 1867- *ApCAB X*
Pendleton, George 1800-1875 *NatCAB 6*
Pendleton, George Cassety 1845-1913 *BiDrAC*
Pendleton, George Hunt 1825-1889 *AmBi,*
ApCAB, BiAUS, BiDrAC, DcAmB,
Drake, EncAAH, McGEWB, NatCAB 3,
TwCBDA, WhAm H, WhAmP
Pendleton, Henry 1750?-1789 *ApCAB, BiAUS,*
Drake
Pendleton, James Madison 1811-1891 *ApCAB,*
DcAmB, WhAm H
Pendleton, James Monroe 1822-1889 *BiAUS,*
BiDrAC, WhAm H
Pendleton, John B 1798-1866 *DcAmB,*
NewYHSD, WhAm H
Pendleton, John Overton 1851-1916 *BiDrAC,*
TwCBDA
Pendleton, John Strother 1802-1868 *BiAUS,*
BiDrAC, DcAmB, NatCAB 12, TwCBDA,
WhAm H
Pendleton, Joseph Henry 1860-1942
NatCAB 46, WebAMB, WhAm 1
Pendleton, Joseph Saxton 1873-1944
NatCAB 33
Pendleton, Leila Amos *WhoColR*
Pendleton, Louis 1861-1939 *NatCAB 10,*
TwCBDA, WhAm 1
Pendleton, Mary Fay 1863- *WomWWA 14*
Pendleton, Moses 1884-1950 *NatCAB 39,*
WhAm 3
Pendleton, Nathanael 1756-1821 *BiDrAC*
Pendleton, Nathanael Greene 1793-1861
BiDrAC, WhAmP
Pendleton, Nathanael Greene 1793-1891
WhAm H
Pendleton, Nathaniel d1821 *Drake*
Pendleton, Nathaniel 1746-1821 *NatCAB 3*
Pendleton, Nathaniel 1756-1821 *ApCAB,*
TwCBDA
Pendleton, Nathaniel Dandridge 1865-1936
WhAm 1
Pendleton, Nathaniel Greene 1793-1861 *ApCAB,*
BiAUS, TwCBDA
Pendleton, Nathaniel Greene 1793-1869
NatCAB 10
Pendleton, Nathaniel Willis 1898-1968
NatCAB 54
Pendleton, Robert L 1890-1957 *WhAm 3*
Pendleton, Robert Lewis 1865- *WhoColR*
Pendleton, Ruth Jane 1910-1973 *WhAm 6*
Pendleton, Thomas P 1885-1954 *WhAm 3*
Pendleton, W L Marcy 1865- *WhAm 4*
Pendleton, William *NewYHSD*
Pendleton, William Frederic 1845-1927
NatCAB 21
Pendleton, William Gibson 1880- *WhAm 6*
Pendleton, William Kimbrough 1817-1899
BiDAmEd, DcAmB, NatCAB 22,
TwCBDA, WhAm H
Pendleton, William Nelson 1809-1883 *ApCAB,*
BiDConf, DcAmB, Drake, NatCAB 10,
TwCBDA, WebAMB, WhAm H
Pendleton, William S 1795-1879 *NewYHSD,*
WhAm H
Pendock, Charles William 1890-1951
NatCAB 44

Pendray, Leatrice M 1905-1971 *WhAm 5*
Penelon, Henri 1827-1885 *IlBEAAW,*
NewYHSD
Penfield *NewYHSD*
Penfield, Adele Ernst 1875- *WomWWA 14*
Penfield, Anne Wightman *WomWWA 14*
Penfield, Clarence Miller 1882-1951 *WhAm 3*
Penfield, E Jean Nelson 1872- *WomWWA 14*
Penfield, Edward 1866-1925 *AmBi, BnEnAmA,*
DcAmB, IlBEAAW, TwCBDA, WhAm 1
Penfield, Frederic Courtland 1855-1922
ApCAB X, DcAmB, NatCAB 15,
TwCBDA, WhAm 1
Penfield, Georgia May *WomWWA 14*
Penfield, Jean Nelson 1872- *WhAm 6*
Penfield, Roderic Campbell 1864-1921 *WhAm 1*
Penfield, Samuel Lewis 1856-1906 *WhAm 1*
Penfield, Sarah Elizabeth Hoyt *WomWWA 14*
Penfield, Smith Newell 1837- *NatCAB 11,*
WhAm 4
Penfield, Thornton B 1867-1958 *WhAm 3*
Penfield, Walter Scott 1879-1931 *WhAm 1*
Penfield, Wilder Graves 1891- *McGEWB*
Penfield, William Lawrence 1846-1909 *AmBi,*
DcAmB, WhAm 1
Penfold, William *NewYHSD*
Pengelley, Arthur Lorne 1879-1922 *WhAm 1*
Penhale, Clayton Archbold 1883-1950 *WhAm 3*
Penhallegon, William Hitt 1849- *WhAm 4*
Penhallow, Benjamin H *NewYHSD*
Penhallow, David Pearce 1854-1910
NatCAB 20, WhAm 1
Penhallow, Dunlap Pearce 1880- *WhAm 6*
Penhallow, Samuel 1665-1726 *ApCAB,*
DcAmB, Drake, NatCAB 8, WhAm H
Penick, Albert Dorset 1908-1967 *NatCAB 55,*
WhAm 4
Penick, Charles Clifton 1843-1914 *ApCAB,*
DcAmB, NatCAB 11, TwCBDA,
WhAm 1
Penick, Daniel Allen 1869-1964 *NatCAB 52*
Penick, Edwin Anderson 1887-1959 *NatCAB 43,*
WhAm 3
Penick, Issac Newton 1859- *WhAm 5*
Penick, John Newton 1869-1967 *WhAm 4*
Penick, Sydnor Barksdale 1882-1953
NatCAB 43
Penieres, Jean Augustin De 1762-1820 *ApCAB*
Penington, Edward 1667-1701 *DcAmB,*
WhAm H
Penington, Edward 1667-1711 *ApCAB*
Penington, Edward 1726-1796 *ApCAB,*
DcAmB, TwCBDA
Penington, Edward *see also* Pennington, Edward
Penington, Henry 1807-1858 *ApCAB*
Penington, John 1768-1793 *ApCAB, Drake*
Penington, John 1799-1867 *ApCAB, Drake,*
TwCBDA
Penington, John Brown 1825-1902 *BiDrAC,*
WhAmP
Penington, Meta Roberts 1837-1885 *ApCAB*
Penland, George Harvey 1888-1958 *WhAm 4*
Penley, Albert Manchester 1847-1927
NatCAB 23
Penman, John Simpson 1864-1949 *WhAm 3*
Penmork *NewYHSD*
Penn, Albert Miller 1881-1962 *NatCAB 50*
Penn, Albert Miller 1885-1962 *WhAm 4*
Penn, Alexander Gordon 1799-1866 *BiAUS,*
BiDrAC, WhAm H
Penn, Arthur Ambrose 1875-1941 *NatCAB 31*
Penn, Arthur Ambrose 1880-1941 *WhAm 1*
Penn, Granville 1761-1844 *ApCAB*
Penn, Hannah Callowhill 1671-1726 *NotAW*
Penn, Hannah Callowhill 1671-1733 *ApCAB*
Penn, I Garland 1867-1930 *WhAm 1,*
WhoColR
Penn, Irving 1917- *BnEnAmA*
Penn, James Gilmore 1877-1942 *NatCAB 39*
Penn, James H 1880- *WhoColR*
Penn, John 1700-1746 *ApCAB*
Penn, John 1729-1795 *AmBi, ApCAB, BiAUS,*
DcAmB, Drake, NatCAB 2, TwCBDA,
WhAm H
Penn, John 1740-1788 *AmBi, DcAmB*
Penn, John 1741-1788 *ApCAB, BiDrAC,*
Drake, NatCAB 7, TwCBDA, WhAm H,
WhAmP

Pepper, Irvin St. Clair 1876-1913 *BiDrAC*
Pepper, Irvin St. Clare 1876-1913 *WhAm 1*
Pepper, John Alfred 1896-1925 *ApCAB X*
Pepper, John Robertson 1850-1931 *WhAm 1*
Pepper, Julia 1868- *WomWWA 14*
Pepper, Mary *NewYHSD*
Pepper, O H Perry 1884-1962 *WhAm 4*
Pepper, Stephen Coburn 1891-1972 *NatCAB 57,*
WhAm 5
Pepper, William 1810-1864 *ApCAB, DcAmB,*
WhAm H
Pepper, William 1843-1898 *AmBi, ApCAB,*
BiDAmEd, DcAmB, NatCAB 1,
TwCBDA, WebAB, WhAm H
Pepper, William 1874-1947 *DcAmB S4,*
WhAm 2
Pepper, William Mullin, Jr. 1903-1975 *WhAm 6*
Pepperday, Thomas M 1886-1956 *WhAm 3*
Pepperell, Sir William 1696-1759 *McGEWB*
Pepperman, W Leon 1876- *WhAm 5*
Pepperrell, Sir William 1696-1759 *AmBi,*
ApCAB, DcAmB, Drake, NatCAB 3,
TwCBDA, WebAB, WebAMB, WhAm H
Pepperrell, Sir William 1746-1816 *ApCAB*
Peppler, Charles William 1872- *WhAm 5*
Pepys, Samuel 1633-1703 *McGEWB*
Pequignot, Clarence Francis 1894-1966
NatCAB 51
Pequignot, Mary Boland 1852- *WhAm 4,*
WomWWA 14
Perabo, Ernst 1845-1920 *WhAm 1*
Perabo, Johann Ernst 1845-1920 *DcAmB,*
NatCAB 8
Perakos, Peter George 1885-1972 *NatCAB 57*
Peralli *NewYHSD*
Peralta, Gaston De 1520?-1580? *ApCAB*
Peralta, Manuel Maria De 1847- *ApCAB*
Peralta, Pedro De 1584?-1666 *DcAmB,*
WhAm H
Peralta, Pedro De 1585?-1666 *WebAB*
Peralta-Barnuevo, Pedro 1663-1743 *ApCAB*
Perard, Victor Semon 1870-1957 *WhAm 3*
Peratee, Sebastian *NewYHSD*
Perce, Elbert 1831-1869 *ApCAB, Drake*
Perce, Legrand Winfield 1836-1911 *BiAUS,*
BiDrAC
Percel, Madame De *NewYHSD*
Percell, John *NewYHSD*
Perceval, Don Louis 1908- *IIBEAAW*
Perceval, John 1680-1748 *ApCAB*
Perche, Napoleon Joseph 1805-1883 *ApCAB,*
DcAmB, NatCAB 5, TwCBDA,
WhAm H
Percheron, Etienne 1613-1675 *ApCAB*
Percival, Arthur Ernest 1887-1966 *WhWW-II,*
WhoMilH
Percival, Chester Smith 1822-1892 *NatCAB 2*
Percival, Edwin 1793- *NewYHSD*
Percival, Harold Waldwin 1868- *WhAm 4*
Percival, Henry 1810?- *NewYHSD*
Percival, Henry Robert 1854- *WhAm 1*
Percival, James Gates 1785-1856 *AmBi*
Percival, James Gates 1795-1856 *ApCAB,*
DcAmB, Drake, NatCAB 8, TwCBDA,
WhAm H
Percival, John 1779-1862 *ApCAB, DcAmB,*
Drake, NatCAB 11, NatCAB 20,
WebAMB, WhAm H
Percival, Olive May Graves 1868- *WhAm 4,*
WomWWA 14
Percival, Shirley 1884-1952 *NatCAB 39*
Percival, Thomas 1740-1804 *BiHiMed*
Percy, Atlee Lane 1880- *WhAm 6*
Percy, Charles Harting 1919- *BiDrAC*
Percy, Earl Hugh 1742-1817 *Drake*
Percy, Elizabeth Sutton 1879- *WomWWA 14*
Percy, Florence *NotAW*
Percy, Frederick Bosworth 1856-1928 *WhAm 1*
Percy, George 1580-1632 *AmBi, DcAmB,*
NatCAB 13, WhAm H
Percy, George 1586-1632 *ApCAB*
Percy, Hugh 1742-1817 *ApCAB*
Percy, Isabelle Clark 1882- *WomWWA 14*
Percy, James Fulton 1864-1946 *NatCAB 34,*
WhAm 2
Percy, John 1817-1889 *DcScB*
Percy, LeRoy 1860-1929 *BiDrAC, NatCAB 4,*
NatCAB 15

Percy, LeRoy 1861-1929 *WhAm 1*
Percy, Mary Cruttenden *WomWWA 14*
Percy, Nelson Mortimer 1875-1958 *ApCAB X,*
NatCAB 44, WhAm 3
Percy, Walker 1864-1917 *WhAm 1*
Percy, William 1744-1819 *ApCAB*
Percy, William Alexander 1885-1942
DcAmB S3, WhAm 1
Perdue, Eugene Hartley 1845- *WhAm 4*
Perdue, Rosa M 1870- *WomWWA 14*
Perea, Francisco 1830-1913 *BiDrAC, WhAmP*
Perea, Francisco 1831-1913 *BiAUS*
Perea, Pedro 1852-1906 *BiDrAC, REnAW,*
WhAm 1, WhAmP
Peregoy, Charles E *NewYHSD*
Peregrinus, Petrus 1240?- *AsBiEn, McGEWB*
Pereira, Antonio 1641-1702 *ApCAB*
Pereira, Benedictus 1535-1610 *DcScB*
Pereira, Duarte Pacheco 1460?-1533 *DcScB*
Pereira, Francisco DeLemos DeFaria 1735-1822
ApCAB
Pereira, Irene Rice 1907-1971 *BnEnAmA,*
WhAm 5
Pereira, Jose Clemente 1787-1854 *ApCAB*
Pereira, Jose Saturnino DaCosta 1773-1852
ApCAB
Pereira, Nuno Marques 1652-1718 *ApCAB*
Pereira DaSilva, Joao Manoel 1818- *ApCAB*
Pereire, Jacob Emile 1800-1875 *ApCAB*
Perelli, Achille 1822-1891 *NewYHSD,*
WhAm H
Perelli, Cesar *NewYHSD*
Perelman, Sidney Joseph 1904- *WebAB*
Peres, Israel Hyman 1867-1925 *NatCAB 20,*
WhAm 4
Peres, Joseph Jean Camille 1890-1962 *DcScB*
Peretz, Isaac Loeb 1851-1915 *McGEWB*
Perez, Andres Aznar 1831-1894 *ApCAB Sup*
Perez, Jose Joaquin 1801- *ApCAB, Drake*
Perez, Jose Joaquin 1845- *ApCAB*
Perez, Juan Pio 1798-1859 *ApCAB*
Perez, Pedro Ildefonso 1826-1869 *ApCAB*
Perez, Santiago 1830- *ApCAB*
Perez DeUrdininea, Jose Maria 1782-1865
ApCAB
Perez DeVargas, Bernardo 1500?- *DcScB*
Perez DeVillagra, Gaspar 1555-1620 *WhAm H*
Perez DeZambrana, Luisa 1837- *ApCAB*
Pergler, Charles 1882-1954 *WhAm 3*
Pergolesi, Giovanni Battista 1710-1736
McGEWB
Perham, G Sheldon 1893-1955 *NatCAB 45*
Perham, Josiah 1803-1868 *DcAmB, WhAm H*
Perham, Sidney 1817-1907 *TwCBDA*
Perham, Sidney 1819-1907 *ApCAB, BiAUS,*
BiDrAC, Drake, NatCAB 6, WhAm 1
Perham, William Sidney 1905-1968 *NatCAB 54*
Periam, Jonathan 1823-1911 *DcAmB*
Pericles 495?BC-429BC *McGEWB*
Perignon, Catherine D, Marquis De 1754-1818
WhoMilH
Perigord, Paul 1882-1959 *NatCAB 48,*
WhAm 3
Perilli, John William 1878-1926 *NatCAB 21*
Perillo, Gregory *IIBEAAW*
Perin, Charles Page 1861-1937 *DcAmB S2,*
WhAm 1
Perin, Florence Nightingale Hobart 1869-
WhAm 5, WomWWA 14
Perin, George Landor 1854-1921 *ApCAB X,*
WhAm 1
Perin, Oliver 1821-1880 *NatCAB 26*
Perinchief, Octavius 1829-1877 *ApCAB*
Perine, Edward TenBroeck 1870-1941 *WhAm 1*
Perine, George Edward 1837-1885 *NewYHSD*
Perine, T B *NewYHSD*
Perine, Tyler Cooke 1876- *WomWWA 14*
Pering, Cornelius 1806-1881 *NewYHSD*
Perini, Louis Robert, Jr. d1972 *WhAm 5*
Perinor, Mister *NewYHSD*
Perisho, Elwood Chappell d1935 *WhAm 1*
Perit, Pelatiah 1785-1864 *ApCAB, NatCAB 1*
Peritz, Ismar John 1863-1950 *WhAm 3*
Perkin, Richard Scott 1906-1969 *NatCAB 54,*
WhAm 5
Perkin, Sir William Henry 1838-1907 *AsBiEn,*
DcScB
Perkin, William Henry, Jr. 1860-1929 *DcScB*

Perkins, Miss *NewYHSD*
Perkins, Abraham 1768-1839 *NewYHSD*
Perkins, Agnes Frances 1875- *WhAm 5,*
WomWWA 14
Perkins, Albert Cornelius 1833-1896
NatCAB 10
Perkins, Albert Thompson 1865-1936 *WhAm 1*
Perkins, Alice Sullivan *WomWWA 14*
Perkins, Angie Villette Warren 1854-1921
NatCAB 19, WomWWA 14
Perkins, Angie Villette Warren 1858-1921
WhAm 1
Perkins, Bertram Lucius 1922-1972 *WhAm 5*
Perkins, Bishop 1787-1866 *BiAUS, BiDrAC,*
WhAm H
Perkins, Bishop W 1841-1894 *NatCAB 3*
Perkins, Bishop Walden 1841-1894 *BiDrAC,*
TwCBDA, WhAm H, WhAmP
Perkins, Bishop Walter 1841-1894 *ApCAB Sup*
Perkins, Carl Dewey 1912- *BiDrAC*
Perkins, Carroll Norman 1880-1954
NatCAB 45, WhAm 3
Perkins, Charles Albert 1858-1945 *NatCAB 36,*
WhAm 2
Perkins, Charles Allen 1832-1892 *ApCAB Sup*
Perkins, Charles Callahan 1823-1886 *AmBi,*
ApCAB, DcAmB, NatCAB 4, NewYHSD,
TwCBDA, WhAm H
Perkins, Charles Edwin 1871- *WhAm 5*
Perkins, Charles Elliott 1840-1907 *DcAmB,*
NatCAB 14, REnAW, WhAm 1
Perkins, Charles Elliott 1881-1943 *NatCAB 32,*
WhAm 2
Perkins, Charles Enoch 1832-1917 *WhAm 1*
Perkins, Charles G 1849- *NatCAB 4*
Perkins, Charles Harvey 1889-1963 *WhAm 4*
Perkins, Charles Henry 1830-1904 *NatCAB 2*
Perkins, Charles Plummer 1848-1913 *WhAm 1*
Perkins, Clarence 1878-1946 *WhAm 2*
Perkins, DeForest H 1873- *WhAm 1*
Perkins, Della Foote *WomWWA 14*
Perkins, Donald 1912-1973 *WhAm 6*
Perkins, Dwight Heald 1867-1941 *DcAmB S3,*
WhAm 1
Perkins, E Benson 1881-1964 *WhAm 4*
Perkins, E G *NewYHSD*
Perkins, Edgar Almon 1866-1956 *NatCAB 46*
Perkins, Edmund Taylor 1864-1921 *NatCAB 17,*
WhAm 1
Perkins, Edna Brush 1880-1930 *NatCAB 26,*
WomWWA 14
Perkins, Edward Ellsworth 1863-1952
NatCAB 39
Perkins, Edward Henry 1886-1936 *NatCAB 32*
Perkins, Edwin Carter 1875-1958 *NatCAB 48*
Perkins, Edwin Ruthven, Jr. 1879-1960
WhAm 3
Perkins, Eli 1839-1910 *DcAmB*
Perkins, Elias 1767-1845 *BiAUS, BiDrAC,*
WhAm H
Perkins, Elisha 1741-1799 *AmBi, ApCAB,*
DcAmB, Drake
Perkins, Elisha 1742-1799 *WhAm H*
Perkins, Elisha Henry 1850-1931 *WhAm 1*
Perkins, Elizabeth B 1861- *WomWWA 14*
Perkins, Elizabeth Peck 1735?-1807 *NotAW*
Perkins, Elizabeth Ward 1873- *WhAm 5*
Perkins, Emily Swan 1866-1941 *WhAm 1*
Perkins, Emma Maude *WomWWA 14*
Perkins, Florence Tobey 1873- *WomWWA 14*
Perkins, Frances 1880-1965 *WhAm 4*
Perkins, Frances 1882-1965 *BiDrUSE, EncAB,*
McGEWB, WebAB, WhAmP,
WomWWA 14
Perkins, Francis Davenport 1897-1970 *WhAm 5*
Perkins, Frank Sutherland 1879-1921
ApCAB X
Perkins, Frank Walley 1844-1922 *WhAm 1*
Perkins, Fred Bartlett 1897-1969 *NatCAB 56,*
WhAm 5
Perkins, Frederic Beecher 1828-1899 *ApCAB,*
DcAmB, TwCBDA, WhAm H
Perkins, Frederic Williams 1870-1943 *WhAm 2*
Perkins, Frederick 1857-1940 *WhAm 1*
Perkins, Frederick Beecher 1828-1899
DcAmLiB
Perkins, Frederick Orville 1879- *WhAm 6*

Perkins, Frederick Payne 1881-1950
NatCAB 39
Perkins, Frederick Powers 1904-1975 *WhAm 6*
Perkins, Frederick Stanton 1832-1899
NewYHSD
Perkins, George Clement 1832-1923 *TwCBDA*
Perkins, George Clement 1839-1923
ApCAB Sup, BiDrAC, DcAmB,
NatCAB 4, WhAm 1, WhAmP
Perkins, George Douglas 1840-1914 *BiDrAC,*
DcAmB, TwCBDA, WhAm 1, WhAmP
Perkins, George Hamilton 1835-1899
NatCAB 26
Perkins, George Hamilton 1836-1899 *ApCAB,*
DcAmB, NatCAB 13, TwCBDA,
WhAm H
Perkins, George Henry 1844-1933 *ApCAB,*
DcAmB, NatCAB 10, WhAm 1
Perkins, George Lathrop 1788-1888
ApCAB Sup
Perkins, George Napier 1841- *WhoColR*
Perkins, George Roberts 1812-1876 *ApCAB,*
Drake, TwCBDA
Perkins, George Walbridge 1862-1920 *DcAmB,*
EncAB, NatCAB 15, WebAB, WhAm 1
Perkins, George Walbridge 1895-1960
NatCAB 44, WhAm 3
Perkins, Granville 1830-1895 *ApCAB,*
IlBEAAW, NewYHSD
Perkins, Harold E 1900-1952 *WhAm 3*
Perkins, Harold Oliver 1904-1968 *NatCAB 57*
Perkins, Henry 1803- *NewYHSD*
Perkins, Henry Augustus 1873-1959
NatCAB 44, WhAm 3
Perkins, Henry Farnham 1877- *WhAm 5*
Perkins, Henry Jason 1859-1927 *NatCAB 22*
Perkins, Henry Southwick 1833- *ApCAB*
Perkins, Herbert Farrington 1864-1936
WhAm 1
Perkins, Horace, Jr. *NewYHSD*
Perkins, J J 1874-1960 *NatCAB 49*
Perkins, J R *NewYHSD*
Perkins, Jacob 1766-1849 *AmBi, ApCAB,*
DcAmB, Drake, NatCAB 10, NewYHSD,
WhAm H
Perkins, James Blenn 1881-1948 *NatCAB 36*
Perkins, James Breck 1847-1910 *AmBi,*
ApCAB, BiDrAC, DcAmB, NatCAB 13,
TwCBDA, WhAm 1, WhAmP
Perkins, James Handasyd 1810-1849 *ApCAB,*
DcAmB, Drake, WhAm H
Perkins, James Handasyd 1876-1940
DcAmB S2, NatCAB 34, WhAm 1
Perkins, James McDaniel 1863- *WhAm 4*
Perkins, Janet Russell 1853-1933 *WhAm 1,*
WomWWA 14
Perkins, Jared 1793-1854 *BiAUS, BiDrAC,*
WhAm H
Perkins, Jennie Saunders 1832- *TwCBDA*
Perkins, John, Jr. 1819-1885 *BiAUS, BiDConf,*
BiDrAC, WhAm H, WhAmP
Perkins, John Carroll 1862- *WhAm 3*
Perkins, John Marion 1877-1946 *NatCAB 42*
Perkins, John Russell 1868-1923 *NatCAB 32,*
WhAm 1
Perkins, John Winslow 1866-1922 *ApCAB X*
Perkins, Jonathan Cogswell 1809-1877 *ApCAB,*
Drake
Perkins, Joseph *NewYHSD*
Perkins, Joseph 1788-1842 *NewYHSD*
Perkins, Joseph 1819-1885 *ApCAB*
Perkins, Julius Edson 1845-1875 *ApCAB*
Perkins, Justin 1805-1869 *ApCAB, DcAmB,*
Drake, NatCAB 10, WhAm H
Perkins, Lee *NewYHSD*
Perkins, Lucy Ann d1975 *WhAm 6*
Perkins, Lucy Fitch 1865-1937 *AmBi,*
NatCAB 33, NotAW, WhAm 1,
WomWWA 14
Perkins, Marlin 1905- *WebAB*
Perkins, Mary Smyth *WomWWA 14*
Perkins, Maurice 1836-1901 *ApCAB,*
WhAm 1
Perkins, Maxwell Evarts 1884-1947 *DcAmB S4,*
NatCAB 37, WebAB, WhAm 2
Perkins, Mertie Aldrich 1879- *WomWWA 14*
Perkins, Milo Randolph 1900-1972 *WhAm 5*

Perkins, Miriam Nancy Shelton Rogers
WomWWA 14
Perkins, Nathan 1749-1838 *ApCAB, Drake*
Perkins, Nathaniel 1803-1847 *NewYHSD*
Perkins, Nathaniel James 1877- *WhAm 5*
Perkins, Orman Clarence 1892-1958
NatCAB 46
Perkins, Ralph 1886-1964 *WhAm 4*
Perkins, Ralph Sherburne 1884-1955
NatCAB 46
Perkins, Randolph 1871-1936 *BiDrAC,*
WhAm 1, WhAmP
Perkins, Rebecca Clarendon Talbot
WomWWA 14
Perkins, Reece Wilmer *WhAm 1*
Perkins, Richard Marlin *WebAB*
Perkins, Robert Patterson 1861-1924 *WhAm 1*
Perkins, Roger Griswold 1874-1936 *NatCAB 26,*
WhAm 1
Perkins, Roy Stanley 1890-1944 *NatCAB 34*
Perkins, Rufus Lord 1819-1909 *NatCAB 16*
Perkins, S Albert 1865-1955 *WhAm 3*
Perkins, S Lee *NewYHSD*
Perkins, Samuel 1767-1850 *ApCAB, Drake*
Perkins, Samuel Elliott 1811-1879 *ApCAB,*
DcAmB, Drake, TwCBDA, WhAm H
Perkins, Sarah Annie 1842- *WomWWA 14*
Perkins, Sarah Maria Clinton 1824- *AmWom*
Perkins, Sidney Albert 1865-1955 *NatCAB 46*
Perkins, Simon 1771-1844 *ApCAB,*
NatCAB 10
Perkins, Susan E H *WomWWA 14*
Perkins, Thomas Clark 1919-1969 *WhAm 5*
Perkins, Thomas Handasyd 1764-1854 *AmBi,*
ApCAB, DcAmB, Drake, NatCAB 5,
TwCBDA, WhAm H
Perkins, Thomas Jefferson 1873-1952 *WhAm 3*
Perkins, Thomas Leavitt 1839-1922 *NatCAB 19*
Perkins, Thomas Lee 1905-1973 *WhAm 6*
Perkins, Thomas Nelson 1870-1937 *DcAmB S2,*
WhAm 1
Perkins, Walter Eugene *WhAm 5*
Perkins, Walton 1847-1929 *WhAm 1*
Perkins, William Allan 1880-1960 *WhAm 4*
Perkins, William Harvey 1894-1967 *WhAm 4A*
Perkins, William Oscar 1831-1902 *ApCAB,*
NatCAB 9, WhAm 1
Perkins, William R 1877-1962 *WhAm 4*
Perkins, William Robertson 1875-1945
NatCAB 44, WhAm 2
Perkins, Worcester 1891-1952 *NatCAB 40*
Perky, Henry D 1843-1906 *NatCAB 13,*
NatCAB 24
Perky, Kirtland Irving 1867-1939 *BiDrAC,*
NatCAB 32, WhAm 1
Perl, A *NewYHSD*
Perlberg, Harry James 1889-1962 *NatCAB 49*
Perlea, Ionel 1900-1970 *WhAm 5*
Perley, Henry Fullerton 1831- *ApCAB*
Perley, Ira 1799-1874 *ApCAB, DcAmB,*
NatCAB 12, TwCBDA, WhAm H
Perley, Martin VanBuren 1835-1926
NatCAB 20
Perley, Mary Elizabeth 1863- *AmWom*
Perley, Sidney 1858-1928 *NatCAB 21,*
WhAm 1
Perlitz, Charles Albert, Jr. 1903-1964 *WhAm 4*
Perlman, David 1909-1972 *WhAm 6*
Perlman, Jacob 1898-1968 *WhAm 5*
Perlman, Louis Henry 1861- *ApCAB X,*
NatCAB 16
Perlman, Nathan David 1887-1952 *BiDrAC,*
WhAm 3
Perlman, Philip Benjamin 1890-1960
NatCAB 45, WhAm 4
Perlman, Selig 1888-1959 *WhAm 3*
Perlmann, Gertrude Erika 1912-1974 *WhAm 6*
Perlmuter, Meyer Hirsh 1876-1964 *NatCAB 50*
Perlmutter, Irving K 1915-1972 *WhAm 6*
Perlmutter, Oscar William 1920-1975 *WhAm 6*
Perlstein, Meyer Aaron 1902-1969 *WhAm 5*
Perlzweig, William Alexander 1891-1949
NatCAB 38, WhAm 2
Perman, Ronald James 1920-1972 *NatCAB 56*
Permar, Howard Henry 1889-1963 *NatCAB 48*
Permar, Robert 1895-1948 *WhAm 2*
Pernot, Emile Francis 1859-1927 *NatCAB 21*
Pero, Giuseppe d1963 *WhAm 4*

Pero, Lorenzo *NewYHSD*
Peron, Francois 1775-1810 *DcScB*
Peron, Juan Domingo 1895- *McGEWB*
Peron, Juan Domingo 1895-1974 *WhAm 6*
Peron, Juan Domingo 1895-1975 *WhWW-II*
Perot, Jean-Baptiste Gaspard G Alfred
1863-1925 *DcScB*
Perot, T Morris, Jr. 1872-1945 *WhAm 2*
Perot, Thomas Morris 1828-1902 *ApCAB,*
WhAm 1
Perotin *McGEWB*
Perovani, Joseph d1835 *NewYHSD*
Perrault, Claude 1613-1688 *DcScB, McGEWB*
Perrault, Pierre 1611-1680 *DcScB*
Perreault, Francis Joseph 1750-1844 *ApCAB*
Perrein, Jean 1749-1805 *Drake*
Perrein, Jean 1749-1805 *ApCAB*
Perret, Andrew *NewYHSD*
Perret, Auguste 1874-1954 *McGEWB,*
WhAm 3
Perret, Charles E *NewYHSD*
Perret, Frank Alvord 1867- *NatCAB 15,*
WhAm 4
Perret, Henry *NewYHSD*
Perret, Jacques 1595-1674 *ApCAB*
Perret, Paulin *NewYHSD*
Perrett, Antoinette Rehmann 1880-
WomWWA 14
Perretta, Louis 1904-1966 *NatCAB 52*
Perrie, Celsus Price 1874-1934 *NatCAB 28*
Perrier, Edmond 1844-1921 *DcScB*
Perrier, Georges 1872-1946 *DcScB*
Perrigo, James 1859- *WhAm 3*
Perrigo, Lynn 1904- *REnAW*
Perrill, Augustus Leonard 1807-1882 *BiAUS,*
BiDrAC, WhAm H
Perrin, Abner Monroe 1829-1864 *ApCAB*
Perrin, Beranger *NewYHSD*
Perrin, Bernadotte 1847-1920 *DcAmB,*
NatCAB 12, TwCBDA, WhAm 1
Perrin, Charles Courtney 1884-1968
NatCAB 56
Perrin, Dwight Stanley 1888-1952 *WhAm 3*
Perrin, Edward Burt 1838-1932 *NatCAB 36*
Perrin, Eloi Philibert 1674-1713 *ApCAB*
Perrin, Ethel 1871-1962 *BiDAmEd*
Perrin, Fleming Allen Clay 1884-1944 *WhAm 2*
Perrin, Frank L 1862- *WhAm 5*
Perrin, Halford Guy 1905-1974 *WhAm 6*
Perrin, Herbert Towle 1893-1962 *NatCAB 50,*
WhAm 4
Perrin, Jean Baptiste 1870-1942 *AsBiEn,*
DcScB
Perrin, John 1857-1931 *ApCAB X, WhAm 1*
Perrin, John William d1924 *WhAm 1*
Perrin, Lee James 1884-1946 *NatCAB 35,*
WhAm 2
Perrin, Marshall Livingston 1855-1935
WhAm 1
Perrin, Porter Gale 1896-1962 *BiDAmEd,*
NatCAB 50, WhAm 4
Perrin, Raymond St. James 1849-1915 *WhAm 1*
Perrin, Willard Taylor 1850-1929 *NatCAB 13,*
WhAm 1
Perrin DuLac, Francois Marie 1766-1824
ApCAB
Perrine, Charles Dillon 1867-1951 *DcAmB S5,*
DcScB, NatCAB 13, WhAm 4
Perrine, Enoch 1853-1920 *WhAm 1*
Perrine, Frederic Auten Combs 1862-1908
DcAmB, NatCAB 19, WhAm 1
Perrine, Grace Halbert 1868- *WomWWA 14*
Perrine, Henry 1797-1840 *DcAmB, WhAm H*
Perrine, Henry Pratt 1891-1954 *WhAm 3*
Perrine, Irving 1884-1955 *WhAm 4*
Perrine, Matthew LaRue 1777-1836 *ApCAB,*
Drake
Perrine, VanDearing 1869-1955 *NatCAB 45,*
WhAm 3
Perrinet, Charles Gaston 1791-1849 *ApCAB*
Perrins, Harlan Bassett 1894-1950 *NatCAB 39*
Perroncito, Edoardo 1847-1936 *DcScB*
Perronet, Jean-Rodolphe 1708-1794 *DcScB*
Perrot, Emile George 1872-1954 *NatCAB 43*
Perrot, Nicholas 1644- *Drake*
Perrot, Nicholas 1644-1718 *WhAm H*
Perrot, Nicolas 1644-1697? *ApCAB*
Perrot, Nicolas 1644-1717 *WebAB*

Perrot, Nicolas 1644-1718? *AmBi, DcAmB, REnAW*

Perrot, Pierre 1632-1681 *ApCAB*

Perrotet, Gustave Samuel 1793-1867 *ApCAB*

Perrotin, Henri Joseph Anastase 1845-1904 *DcScB*

Perry, Mrs. Aaron *WomWWA 14*

Perry, Aaron Fyfe 1815-1893 *BiDrAC, WhAm H*

Perry, Agnes *NotAW*

Perry, Albertus 1873-1940 *WhAm 1*

Perry, Alexander James 1828-1913 *ApCAB, WhAm 1*

Perry, Alfred Tyler 1854-1912 *NatCAB 25*

Perry, Alfred Tyler 1858-1912 *TwCBDA, WhAm 1*

Perry, Alice Maud 1858- *WomWWA 14*

Perry, Amos 1812-1899 *ApCAB, Drake, NatCAB 2*

Perry, Andre James 1909-1963 *WhAm 4*

Perry, Antoinette 1888-1946 *DcAmB S4, NatCAB 37, NotAW, WhAm 2*

Perry, Antonio 1871-1944 *NatCAB 11, WhAm 2*

Perry, Archibald Preston 1875-1961 *NatCAB 50*

Perry, Arthur 1857-1930 *ApCAB X, WhAm 1*

Perry, Arthur Cecil 1873-1961 *WhAm 4*

Perry, Arthur Franklin 1866-1941 *NatCAB 31, WhAm 2*

Perry, Arthur Latham 1830-1905 *ApCAB, DcAmB, Drake, NatCAB 10, WhAm 1*

Perry, Barbour *WhAm 4*

Perry, Ben Edwin 1892-1968 *WhAm 5*

Perry, Benjamin Franklin 1805-1886 *ApCAB, BiAUS, DcAmB, NatCAB 12, TwCBDA, WhAm H*

Perry, Bertrand James 1874-1960 *WhAm 4*

Perry, Bliss 1860-1954 *ApCAB Sup, DcAmB S5, NatCAB 10, NatCAB 46, TwCBDA, WhAm 3*

Perry, C H *NewYHSD*

Perry, Carlotta 1848- *AmWom*

Perry, Carroll 1869-1937 *WhAm 1*

Perry, Charles 1851-1929 *WhAm 1*

Perry, Charles Coffin 1857-1924 *NatCAB 39*

Perry, Charles Milton 1876-1942 *WhAm 2*

Perry, Christopher James 1859- *WhoColR*

Perry, Christopher Raymond 1760-1818 *Drake*

Perry, Christopher Raymond 1761-1818 *ApCAB, DcAmB, WhAm H*

Perry, Claibourne Gordon 1889-1957 *NatCAB 54*

Perry, Clara Greenleaf 1871- *WomWWA 14*

Perry, Clarence Arthur 1872-1944 *DcAmB S3, WhAm 2*

Perry, Clay Lamont 1920- *WhAm 5*

Perry, Cyrus Curley 1901-1955 *NatCAB 44*

Perry, David 1841-1908 *WhAm 1*

Perry, David Brainerd 1839-1912 *TwCBDA, WhAm 1*

Perry, Donald Putnam 1895-1957 *WhAm 4*

Perry, Edith Dean Weir 1875- *WomWWA 14*

Perry, Edward *NewYHSD*

Perry, Edward Aylesworth 1831-1889 *BiDConf, DcAmB, NatCAB 11, TwCBDA, WhAm H*

Perry, Edward Aylesworth 1833-1889 *ApCAB*

Perry, Edward Baxter 1855-1924 *DcAmB, WhAm 1*

Perry, Edward Delavan 1854-1938 *WhAm 1*

Perry, Eli 1799-1881 *ApCAB, BiDrAC, WhAm H*

Perry, Eli 1802-1881 *BiAUS*

Perry, Elliott 1884-1972 *NatCAB 57*

Perry, Emma Elizabeth 1879- *WomWWA 14*

Perry, Enoch 1863-1953 *NatCAB 43*

Perry, Enoch Wood 1830-1915 *TwCBDA*

Perry, Enoch Wood 1831-1915 *ApCAB, DcAmB, IIBEAAW, NewYHSD, WhAm 1*

Perry, Ernest Bert 1876-1962 *WhAm 4*

Perry, Ernest James 1873-1949 *WhAm 2*

Perry, Eugene Ashton 1864-1948 *NatCAB 34*

Perry, Everett Robbins 1876-1933 *WhAm 1*

Perry, Franklin *NewYHSD*

Perry, Fred Jerome 1872-1955 *NatCAB 45*

Perry, Gardner Browne 1882-1964 *NatCAB 50*

Perry, George Dorn 1887-1940 *WhAm 1*

Perry, George F *NewYHSD*

Perry, George Hough 1888-1945 *WhAm 2*

Perry, George Russell 1849- *NatCAB 10*

Perry, George Sessions 1910-1956 *WhAm 3*

Perry, Hector H 1876- *WhAm 5*

Perry, Henry Eldredge 1889-1950 *WhAm 2*

Perry, Horatio Justus 1824-1891 *ApCAB, NatCAB 10*

Perry, Hoyt Ogden 1893-1966 *WhAm 4*

Perry, Hunter 1887-1969 *NatCAB 54*

Perry, Ione 1839- *NewYHSD*

Perry, Isaac Newton 1846- *WhAm 4*

Perry, Isaac Newton 1847- *NatCAB 11*

Perry, James Clifford 1864-1936 *WhAm 1*

Perry, James DeWolf 1839-1927 *WhAm 1*

Perry, James DeWolf 1871-1947 *WhAm 2*

Perry, John 1897-1972 *WhAm 5*

Perry, John Edward 1870- *WhoColR*

Perry, John Franklin 1890-1946 *NatCAB 41*

Perry, John Holliday 1881-1952 *WhAm 3*

Perry, John Hoyt 1848-1928 *WhAm 1*

Perry, John Jasiel 1811- *BiAUS*

Perry, John Jasiel 1811-1897 *BiDrAC, WhAm H*

Perry, John Jasiel 1811-1899 *NatCAB 13*

Perry, John Lester 1881-1952 *WhAm 3*

Perry, John Morris d1951 *WhAm 3*

Perry, John Richard 1899-1955 *NatCAB 43, WhAm 3*

Perry, Joseph Franklin 1846- *WhAm 4*

Perry, Julia B 1860- *WomWWA 14*

Perry, Kenneth 1899-1964 *WhAm 4*

Perry, Lawrence d1954 *WhAm 3*

Perry, Lewis 1877-1970 *WhAm 5*

Perry, Lewis Ebenezer 1899-1963 *NatCAB 50, WhAm 4*

Perry, Lilla Cabot 1848-1933 *NatCAB 26, WhAm 1, WomWWA 14*

Perry, Louis Clausiel 1877-1926 *NatCAB 22, WhAm 1*

Perry, Lyman Spencer 1897-1975 *WhAm 6*

Perry, Lynn 1884-1969 *NatCAB 55*

Perry, Madison S 1814-1865 *BiAUS, NatCAB 11*

Perry, Marsden Jasiel 1850-1935 *WhAm 1*

Perry, Mathew Calbraith 1794-1858 *Drake*

Perry, Matthew Calbraith 1794-1858 *AmBi, ApCAB, BiAUS, DcAmB, EncAB, McGEWB, NatCAB 4, TwCBDA, WebAB, WebAMB, WhAm H, WhoMilH*

Perry, Matthew Calbraith 1821-1873 *ApCAB, TwCBDA*

Perry, Middleton Lee 1868- *WhAm 5*

Perry, Nehemiah 1816-1881 *BiAUS, BiDrAC, NatCAB 11, WhAm H*

Perry, Newel Lewis 1873-1961 *NatCAB 48*

Perry, Nora 1831-1896 *DcAmB, WhAm H*

Perry, Nora 1841-1896 *AmWom, ApCAB, NatCAB 15, TwCBDA*

Perry, Oliver Hazard 1785-1819 *AmBi, ApCAB, DcAmB, Drake, EncAB, McGEWB, NatCAB 4, REnAW, TwCBDA, WebAB, WebAMB, WhAm H, WhoMilH*

Perry, Oscar Butler 1876-1945 *WhAm 2*

Perry, R H *BiAUS*

Perry, R Ross 1846-1915 *WhAm 1*

Perry, Ralph Barton 1876-1957 *McGEWB, NatCAB 43, WhAm 3*

Perry, Richard Ross, Jr. 1871- *WhAm 5*

Perry, Richard Wilbert 1872-1957 *NatCAB 47*

Perry, Roland Hinton 1870-1941 *NatCAB 9, WhAm 1*

Perry, Roy Vincelle 1889-1959 *WhAm 4*

Perry, Rufus Lewis 1834-1895 *DcAmB, WhAm H*

Perry, Rufus Lewis 1872- *WhoColR*

Perry, Sarah Alexander 1768-1830 *ApCAB*

Perry, Stella George Stern 1877- *WhAm 3, WomWWA 14*

Perry, Stuart 1814-1890 *DcAmB, WhAm H*

Perry, Stuart Hoffman 1874-1957 *WhAm 3*

Perry, Thomas 1844-1918 *TwCBDA, WhAm 1*

Perry, Thomas Johns 1807-1871 *BiAUS, BiDrAC, WhAm H*

Perry, Thomas Sergeant 1845-1928 *ApCAB, DcAmB, NatCAB 21, TwCBDA,*

WhAm 1

Perry, Wallace 1883-1956 *NatCAB 45, WhAm 3*

Perry, Walter Scott 1855-1934 *DcAmB S1, WhAm 1*

Perry, William *BiAUS*

Perry, William 1788-1887 *ApCAB, DcAmB, NatCAB 11, WhAm H*

Perry, William Alfred 1835-1916 *ApCAB X*

Perry, William Edward Carver 1893-1961 *NatCAB 50*

Perry, William Flake 1823-1901 *BiDAmEd, DcAmB, NatCAB 8, TwCBDA, WhAm 1*

Perry, William Graves 1883-1975 *WhAm 6*

Perry, William Hayes 1832- *WhAm 4*

Perry, William Hayne 1837-1902 *ApCAB*

Perry, William Hayne 1839-1902 *BiDrAC, TwCBDA*

Perry, William L d1967 *WhAm 5*

Perry, William Stevens 1832-1898 *ApCAB, DcAmB, Drake, NatCAB 3, TwCBDA, WhAm H*

Perryman, Francis Spencer 1896-1959 *WhAm 4*

Perryman, Walter Lewis, Jr. 1923-1966 *WhAm 4*

Persac, Adrian *NewYHSD*

Perse, Saint-John 1887-1975 *McGEWB, WhAm 6*

Perseus *DcScB*

Pershing, Cyrus L 1825-1903 *WhAm 1*

Pershing, Howell Terry 1858-1935 *WhAm 1*

Pershing, James Hammond 1863-1948 *WhAm 2*

Pershing, John Joseph 1860-1948 *ApCAB X, DcAmB S4, EncAB, McGEWB, NatCAB 35, REnAW, WebAMB, WhAm 2, WhoMilH*

Persico, E Luigi 1791-1860 *NewYHSD, WhAm H*

Persico, Gennaro d1859? *NewYHSD*

Persico, Ignatius 1823-1895 *ApCAB, NatCAB 12, TwCBDA*

Persinger, Louis 1887-1966 *NatCAB 53*

Persinger, Louis 1887-1967 *WhAm 4*

Perskie, Joseph B 1885-1957 *WhAm 3*

Persky, Jack Albert 1894-1962 *NatCAB 54*

Persky, Samuel Alexander 1887-1964 *NatCAB 49*

Person, Edward Samuel 1872-1930 *NatCAB 44*

Person, Harlow Stafford 1875-1955 *NatCAB 45, WhAm 3*

Person, Hiram Grant 1866-1923 *WhAm 1*

Person, Hjalmer T 1903-1974 *WhAm 6*

Person, John Elmer 1889-1967 *WhAm 4*

Person, John L 1907-1969 *WhAm 5*

Person, Robert S 1857- *WhAm 4*

Person, Rollin Harlow 1850-1917 *NatCAB 17*

Person, Seymour Howe 1879-1957 *BiDrAC, NatCAB 46, WhAm 3*

Person, Thomas *BiAUS, Drake*

Person, Thomas 1733-1800 *DcAmB, WhAm H*

Person, Thomas 1740?-1799 *ApCAB*

Person, William 1793-1818 *Drake*

Personius, Ely Watson 1875-1944 *NatCAB 35*

Personne, Jacques 1816-1880 *DcScB*

Persons, Augustus Archilus 1866-1917 *WhAm 1*

Persons, Frederick Torrel 1869-1948 *WhAm 2*

Persons, Gordon 1902-1965 *WhAm 4*

Persons, Henry 1834-1910 *BiDrAC*

Persons, James White 1879-1964 *NatCAB 52*

Persons, John Cecil 1888-1974 *WhAm 6*

Persons, John Williams 1899-1972 *WhAm 5*

Persons, Remus Charles 1850-1924 *NatCAB 18*

Persons, Truman Streckfus *WebAB*

Persons, Warren Milton 1878-1937 *DcAmB S2, WhAm 1, WhAm 1C*

Persons, William Frank 1876-1955 *WhAm 3*

Persoon, Christiaan Hendrik 1761-1836 *DcScB*

Persoz, Jean-Francois 1805-1868 *DcScB*

Pertain, Charles Andree 1913-1974 *WhAm 6*

Perth, James Eric Drummond, Earl Of 1876-1951 *McGEWB*

Peruani, Joseph *NewYHSD*

Perugino 1450?-1523 *McGEWB*

Perul, Madame De *NewYHSD*

Perutz, Max Ferdinand 1914- *AsBiEn*

Peruzzi, Mario 1875-1955 *NatCAB 45*

Pesado, Jose Joaquin 1801-1861 *ApCAB*

Pescara, Fernando Francesco, Marchese Di 1490-1525 *WhoMilH*

Peschau, Ferdinand William Elias 1849- *ApCAB, WhAm 1*

Pescheret, Leon Rene 1892-1961 *IlBEAAW*

Peschges, John Hubert 1881- *WhAm 2*

Peschowsky, Michael Igor *WebAB*

Pescud, Peter Francisco 1850- *NatCAB 11*

Peska, Frank 1885-1962 *NatCAB 50*

Pesquera, Jose Lorenzo 1882-1950 *BiDrAC*

Pessao, Jose Elloy 1792-1841 *ApCAB*

Pessen, Edward 1920- *EncAAH*

Pessou, Louis *NewYHSD*

Pestalozzi, Johann Heinrich 1746-1827 *McGEWB*

Petain, Henri Philippe Omer 1856-1951 *McGEWB, WhWW-II, WhoMilH*

Peteet, Walton 1869- *WhAm 5*

Petegorsky, David W 1915-1956 *WhAm 3*

Petek, Poko d1972 *IlBEAAW*

Peter I 1672-1725 *McGEWB*

Peter I 1844-1921 *McGEWB*

Peter III 1239?-1285 *McGEWB*

Peter Abano *DcScB*

Peter Abelard *DcScB*

Peter Bonus *DcScB*

Peter Canisius, Saint 1521-1597 *McGEWB*

Peter Claver, Saint 1580-1654 *McGEWB*

Peter II, King Of Yugoslavia 1923-1970 *WhWW-II*

Peter Of Abano 1250-1315 *BiHiMed*

Peter Of Ailly *DcScB*

Peter Of Dacia *DcScB*

Peter Peregrinus *DcScB*

Peter Philomena Of Dacia *DcScB*

Peter, Saint d065? *McGEWB*

Peter The Great 1672-1725 *WhoMilH*

Peter, Alfred Meredith 1857- *WhAm 4*

Peter, Arthur 1873-1943 *NatCAB 32, WhAm 2*

Peter, Edward Compston 1862-1923 *NatCAB 37*

Peter, George 1779-1861 *BiAUS, BiDrAC, WhAm H*

Peter, Hugh 1598-1660 *DcAmB, WhAm H*

Peter, J Vinson 1898-1963 *NatCAB 51*

Peter, John Frederick 1746-1813 *DcAmB, WhAm H*

Peter, Luther Crouse 1869-1942 *WhAm 2*

Peter, Marc 1873-1966 *WhAm 4, WhAm 5*

Peter, Philip Adam 1832?- *WhAm 4*

Peter, Robert 1805-1894 *ApCAB, DcAmB, Drake, NatCAB 4, WhAm H*

Peter, Robert 1897-1951 *NatCAB 39*

Peter, Sarah Anne Worthington King 1800-1877 *AmBi, ApCAB, DcAmB, NotAW, TwCBDA, WhAm H*

Peter, William Frederick 1883-1956 *NatCAB 44, WhAm 3*

Peterdi, Gabor 1915- *BnEnAmA*

Peterkin, Daniel 1872-1941 *WhAm 1*

Peterkin, George William 1841-1916 *ApCAB, DcAmB, NatCAB 12, TwCBDA, WhAm 1*

Peterkin, John Boddington 1886-1969 *NatCAB 54*

Peterkin, Julia Mood 1880-1961 *WhAm 4*

Peterkin, William Gardner 1870-1941 *NatCAB 32, WhAm 2*

Peterman, Claude Lewis 1888-1971 *NatCAB 57*

Peterman, Mynie Gustav 1896-1971 *WhAm 5*

Petermann, Albert E 1877-1944 *WhAm 2*

Peters, Absalom 1793-1869 *ApCAB, DcAmB, Drake, WhAm H*

Peters, Albert Theodore 1868- *WhAm 4*

Peters, Alice E H 1845- *AmWom*

Peters, Amelia C 1843- *WomWWA 14*

Peters, Andrew d1822 *Drake*

Peters, Andrew James 1872-1938 *BiDrAC, NatCAB 40, WhAm 1, WhAmP*

Peters, Belvart January 1805- *NatCAB 12*

Peters, Bernard 1827- *NatCAB 1*

Peters, C *NewYHSD*

Peters, Carl 1856-1918 *McGEWB*

Peters, Carl F W 1844-1894 *DcScB*

Peters, Charles Clinton 1881-1973 *WhAm 6*

Peters, Charles Rollo 1862-1928? *IlBEAAW, WhAm 4*

Peters, Christian August Friedrich 1806-1880 *DcScB*

Peters, Christian Heinrich Friedrich 1813-1890 *DcScB*

Peters, Christian Henry Frederick 1813-1890 *AmBi, ApCAB, DcAmB, NatCAB 13, TwCBDA, WhAm H*

Peters, Cortez Wilson 1906-1964 *NatCAB 52*

Peters, Curtis Arnoux 1879-1933 *NatCAB 25, WebAB*

Peters, David Wilbur 1889-1951 *WhAm 3*

Peters, Don Preston 1877-1943 *NatCAB 35*

Peters, Edward Dyer 1849-1917 *ApCAB, DcAmB, WhAm 1*

Peters, Edwin Chandlee 1836-1917 *ApCAB X, NatCAB 16*

Peters, Eleanor Bradley *WomWWA 14*

Peters, Elizabeth 1640- *ApCAB*

Peters, Frances *BiCAW*

Peters, Frederick Romer 1874-1935 *NatCAB 35, WhAm 1*

Peters, Gabriella Brooke Farman *WomWWA 14*

Peters, George Absalom 1821-1894 *NatCAB 11*

Peters, George Boddie 1850- *WhAm 4*

Peters, George Henry 1854-1916 *WhAm 1*

Peters, George Nathaniel Henry 1825- *ApCAB*

Peters, George Silas 1846-1928 *NatCAB 21*

Peters, Grace Rarey *WomWWA 14*

Peters, Guy Melvin 1880-1948 *NatCAB 36*

Peters, H LeBaron 1882-1940 *NatCAB 30*

Peters, Harry Alfred 1879- *WhAm 6*

Peters, Heber Wallace 1892-1971 *WhAm 5*

Peters, Herbert Grayson 1895-1951 *NatCAB 41*

Peters, Howard H 1877-1963 *NatCAB 51*

Peters, Hugh 1599-1660 *ApCAB, Drake, NatCAB 8*

Peters, Hugh 1807-1831 *ApCAB, Drake*

Peters, J *NewYHSD*

Peters, J, Sr. *NewYHSD*

Peters, J A 1832-1901 *WhAm 1*

Peters, James 1909-1967 *WhAm 5*

Peters, James Arthur 1922-1972 *WhAm 5*

Peters, James Lee 1889-1952 *NatCAB 41, WhAm 3*

Peters, John 1889-1956 *NatCAB 42*

Peters, John Abram 1832-1901 *TwCBDA*

Peters, John Andrew 1822-1904 *BiAUS, BiDrAC, DcAmB, NatCAB 9, TwCBDA, WhAm 1, WhAmP*

Peters, John Andrew 1864-1953 *BiDrAC, WhAm 4, WhAmP*

Peters, John Charles 1819-1893 *AmBi, ApCAB, DcAmB, Drake, WhAm H*

Peters, John Dwight 1911- *WhAm 4*

Peters, John E *NewYHSD*

Peters, John Punnett 1852-1921 *ApCAB X, DcAmB, NatCAB 13, TwCBDA, WhAm 1*

Peters, John Punnett 1887-1955 *NatCAB 42, WhAm 3*

Peters, John Russell 1896-1968 *WhAm 5*

Peters, John Samuel 1772-1857 *TwCBDA*

Peters, John Samuel 1772-1858 *NatCAB 10*

Peters, John Samuel 1778-1858 *BiAUS*

Peters, John Thompson 1765-1834 *ApCAB, BiAUS, Drake*

Peters, Leonard Constance 1850-1928 *NatCAB 21*

Peters, LeRoy Samuel 1882-1941 *NatCAB 31, WhAm 2*

Peters, Leslie H 1916?- *IlBEAAW*

Peters, Lewis Edwin 1843- *WhAm 4*

Peters, Lulu Hunt d1930 *WhAm 1*

Peters, Madison Clinton 1859-1918 *DcAmB, NatCAB 2, WhAm 1*

Peters, Marian Phelps 1868- *WhAm 4*

Peters, Mason Summers 1844-1914 *BiDrAC*

Peters, Phillis Wheatley 1754?-1784 *DcAmB*

Peters, R Earl 1886-1952 *NatCAB 41, WhAm 3*

Peters, Ralph 1853-1923 *NatCAB 51, WhAm 1*

Peters, Ralph, Jr. 1908-1957 *WhAm 3*

Peters, Raymond Elmer 1903-1973 *WhAm 5*

Peters, Richard 1704-1776 *ApCAB, DcAmB, Drake, NatCAB 13, WhAm H*

Peters, Richard 1743-1828 *BiDrAC, TwCBDA,*

Peters, Richard 1744-1828 *AmBi, ApCAB, BiAUS, DcAmB, Drake, NatCAB 12*

Peters, Richard 1780-1848 *ApCAB, TwCBDA*

Peters, Richard 1810-1889 *DcAmB, NatCAB 3, WhAm H*

Peters, Russell Holt 1899-1975 *WhAm 6*

Peters, Miss S A *NewYHSD*

Peters, Samuel Andrew 1735-1826 *ApCAB, DcAmB, Drake, NatCAB 8, WhAm H*

Peters, Samuel Jarvis 1801-1855 *ApCAB*

Peters, Samuel Ritter 1842-1910 *BiDrAC, TwCBDA, WhAm 1, WhAmP*

Peters, Thomas Minott 1810-1888 *NatCAB 7*

Peters, Thomas Pollock 1868-1936 *WhAm 1*

Peters, Thomas Willing 1855-1917 *WhAm 1*

Peters, W T *NewYHSD*

Peters, Walter Harvest 1885-1949 *WhAm 3*

Peters, William *NewYHSD*

Peters, William Allison 1858-1929 *NatCAB 35*

Peters, William Allison, Jr. 1890-1948 *NatCAB 39*

Peters, William Cumming 1805-1866 *ApCAB, DcAmB, WhAm H*

Peters, William E 1829- *WhAm 4*

Peters, William Henry 1881-1936 *WhAm 1*

Peters, William John 1863-1942 *WhAm 2*

Peters, William Rogers 1849-1917 *NatCAB 22*

Peters, William Thompson, Jr. 1828- *NewYHSD*

Petersen, Andrew Nicholas 1870-1952 *BiDrAC, WhAm 5*

Petersen, Carl Edward 1897-1944 *WhAm 2*

Petersen, Charles 1906-1974 *WhAm 6*

Petersen, Elmore 1888-1959 *NatCAB 46*

Petersen, Gordon Cole 1914-1956 *NatCAB 46*

Petersen, Hans 1872-1924 *NatCAB 20*

Petersen, Harriet Lea Murray d1973 *WhAm 6*

Petersen, Hjalmar 1890-1968 *NatCAB 53, WhAm 5*

Petersen, Johan Erik Christian 1839-1874 *ApCAB*

Petersen, John Eric Christian 1839-1874 *Drake*

Petersen, Julius 1839-1910 *DcScB*

Petersen, Leroy A 1893-1974 *WhAm 6*

Petersen, Martin 1866-1956 *WhAm 3, WhAm 4*

Petersen, Peter 1935- *EncAAH*

Petersen, Ralph Clarence 1907-1956 *NatCAB 47*

Petersen, Robert Warren 1925-1973 *WhAm 6*

Petersen, Theodore Scarborough 1896-1966 *WhAm 4*

Petersen, William Earl 1892-1971 *WhAm 5*

Petersen, William Ferdinand 1887-1950 *NatCAB 39, WhAm 3*

Petersilea, Carlyle 1844- *ApCAB*

Peterson, A H M *NewYHSD*

Peterson, Albert Edmund 1906-1974 *WhAm 6*

Peterson, Alfred Emanuel 1873-1938 *WhAm 1*

Peterson, Alfred Walter 1900-1965 *WhAm 4*

Peterson, Anna Lockwood 1878- *WomWWA 14*

Peterson, Arthur 1851-1932 *ApCAB, WhAm 1*

Peterson, B Walker 1852-1925 *NatCAB 6*

Peterson, Bedford Forrest 1910-1972 *NatCAB 57*

Peterson, C *NewYHSD*

Peterson, Charles Jacobs 1819-1887 *ApCAB, DcAmB, Drake, NatCAB 28, TwCBDA, WhAm H*

Peterson, Charles Simeon 1873-1943 *WhAm 2*

Peterson, Donald Bolch 1911-1973 *WhAm 6*

Peterson, Duane Lansing 1890-1962 *NatCAB 49*

Peterson, Edward 1860-1925 *NatCAB 20*

Peterson, Elmer George 1882-1958 *WhAm 3*

Peterson, Elmer Theodore 1884-1969 *WhAm 5*

Peterson, Ervin Albert 1878-1947 *NatCAB 36*

Peterson, Frederick 1859-1938 *NatCAB 16, NatCAB 47, WhAm 1*

Peterson, Gordon Elmer 1913-1967 *NatCAB 54*

Peterson, H *NewYHSD*

Peterson, Hannah Mary Bouvier 1811-1870 *ApCAB*

Peterson, Harold Leslie 1922- *EncAAH*

Peterson, Harry Claude 1876-1941 *WhAm 1*

Peterson, Helen W 1915- *REnAW*

Peterson, Henry 1818-1891 *ApCAB*, *DcAmB*, *Drake*, *TwCBDA*, *WhAm H*
Peterson, Henry 1868-1957 *NatCAB 45*
Peterson, Henry John 1877-1957 *WhAm 3*
Peterson, Herbert 1870-1943 *WhAm 2*
Peterson, Hugh 1898-1961 *BiDrAC*, *WhAmP*
Peterson, J Marvin 1902-1954 *WhAm 3*
Peterson, J Whitney 1898-1959 *WhAm 3*
Peterson, James Aslak 1859-1928 *NatCAB 21*
Peterson, James Earl, Sr. 1891- *WhAm 2*
Peterson, James Hardin 1894- *BiDrAC*
Peterson, Jane *WomWWA 14*
Peterson, John Barney 1850-1944 *BiDrAC*
Peterson, John Barney 1851-1944 *WhAm 4*
Peterson, John Bertram 1871-1944 *WhAm 2*
Peterson, John LeRoy 1895-1969 *NatCAB 56*
Peterson, John Valdemar 1898-1968 *WhAm 5*
Peterson, Jonathan 1867-1929 *ApCAB X*
Peterson, Joseph 1878-1935 *NatCAB 42*, *WhAm 1*
Peterson, Karl Mikhailovich 1828-1881 *DcScB*
Peterson, Kate Oelzner *WomWWA 14*
Peterson, Lawrence Eugene 1897-1963 *WhAm 4*
Peterson, Lawrence John 1903-1957 *WhAm 3*
Peterson, Marie Dahle 1862- *WomWWA 14*
Peterson, Mary Alida Orswell *WomWWA 14*
Peterson, Maude Gridley 1871- *WomWWA 14*
Peterson, May 1889-1952 *WhAm 3*
Peterson, Mell Andrew 1908-1970 *WhAm 5*
Peterson, Merrill Daniel 1921- *EncAAH*
Peterson, Morris Blaine 1906- *BiDrAC*
Peterson, Niss C *NewYHSD*
Peterson, Olof August 1865-1933 *WhAm 1*
Peterson, Oscar Charles 1857- *NatCAB 17*
Peterson, Peter 1866-1940 *WhAm 1*
Peterson, Reuben 1862-1942 *ApCAB X*, *NatCAB 34*, *WhAm 1*
Peterson, Robert Evans 1812- *ApCAB*
Peterson, Robert Evans 1812-1894 *TwCBDA*
Peterson, Robert Evans 1815-1874 *NatCAB 8*, *WhAm H*
Peterson, Roger Tory 1908- *WebAB*
Peterson, Ruben Olof 1899-1958 *NatCAB 49*
Peterson, Sarah Webb 1820- *ApCAB*
Peterson, Theophilos Beasley 1821-1890 *TwCBDA*
Peterson, Theophilus Beasley 1821-1890 *ApCAB*
Peterson, Thomas Franklin 1902-1962 *NatCAB 53*
Peterson, Virgil Lee 1882-1956 *WhAm 3*
Peterson, Virgilia 1904-1966 *WhAm 4*
Peterson, Walter Fritiof 1929- *EncAAH*
Peterson, William H 1880-1960 *WhAm 4*
Petheram, Charles Creglow 1887-1963 *NatCAB 51*
Pethick, Harry H 1888-1966 *WhAm 4*
Pethick-Lawrence, Frederick William 1871-1961 *WhAm 4*
Peticolas, Arthur Edward 1820?- *NewYHSD*
Peticolas, Ben Catlin 1907-1960 *NatCAB 49*
Peticolas, Edward F 1793-1853? *IlBEAAW*, *NewYHSD*
Peticolas, Jane Pitfield Braddick 1791-1852 *NewYHSD*
Peticolas, Marion Goodwin 1844- *WomWWA 14*
Peticolas, Philippe Abraham 1760-1841 *NewYHSD*
Peticolas, Theodore V 1797- *NewYHSD*
Petigru, Caroline 1819- *ApCAB*, *NewYHSD*
Petigru, James Lewis 1789-1863 *AmBi*, *ApCAB*, *NatCAB 9*, *TwCBDA*
Petigru, James Louis 1789-1863 *DcAmB*, *Drake*, *WebAB*, *WhAm H*
Petion, Alexander 1770-1818 *ApCAB*
Petion, Anne Alexander Sabes 1770-1818 *Drake*
Petit, Alexis Therese 1791-1820 *AsBiEn*, *DcScB*
Petit, Louis Le *ApCAB*
Petit, Pierre 1594?-1677 *DcScB*
Peto, John Frederick 1854-1907 *BnEnAmA*, *McGEWB*
Peto, Sir Samuel Morton 1809- *ApCAB*, *Drake*
Petosiris, Pseudo- *DcScB*
Petrarch 1304-1374 *McGEWB*
Petrasch, Carl Schurz 1866-1927 *NatCAB 23*

Petrequin, Edouard Albert 1870-1949 *NatCAB 42*
Petretti, Mario John 1914-1960 *NatCAB 48*
Petri, Carl Johan 1856- *WhAm 4*
Petri, Frederick Richard 1824-1857 *IlBEAAW*
Petri, Richard 1824-1857 *NewYHSD*
Petrie, Cordia Greer *WomWWA 14*
Petrie, Flinders 1853-1942 *DcScB*
Petrie, Flora Rebekah *WomWWA 14*
Petrie, George 1793-1879 *BiAUS*, *BiDrAC*, *WhAm H*
Petrie, George 1866-1947 *BiDAmEd*, *WhAm 2*
Petrie, George Laurens 1840-1931 *WhAm 1*
Petrie, George Marshall 1868-1930 *NatCAB 38*
Petrie, James MacFarlin 1883-1922 *NatCAB 20*
Petrie, M Josephine *WomWWA 14*
Petrie, Sir William Matthew Flinders 1853-1942 *McGEWB*
Petriken, David 1788-1849 *BiAUS*
Petrikin, David 1788-1847 *BiDrAC*, *WhAm H*
Petrikin, William Lloyd 1871-1951 *NatCAB 54*, *WhAm 3*
Petroff, Strashimer Alburtus 1883-1948 *WhAm 2*
Petronella, Samuel James 1908-1953 *NatCAB 44*
Petronius Arbiter d066? *McGEWB*
Petrov, Ivan 1896-1950 *WhWW-II*
Petrov, Nikolay Pavlovich 1836-1920 *DcScB*
Petrov, Vasily Vladimirovich 1761-1834 *DcScB*
Petrovsky, Ivan Georgievich 1901-1973 *DcScB*
Petrunkevitch, Alexander 1875-1964 *WhAm 4*
Petrunkevitch, Wanda Hartshorn 1875- *WomWWA 14*
Petrus *DcScB*
Petrus Bonus *DcScB*
Petry, Edward Jacob 1880-1939 *WhAm 1*
Petry, Loren Clifford 1887-1970 *NatCAB 55*
Pett, John *NewYHSD*
Pettee, Charles Holmes 1853-1938 *WhAm 3*
Pettee, George Daniel 1864- *WhAm 4*
Pettee, James Horace 1851-1920 *WhAm 1*
Pettee, Julia 1872-1967 *DcAmLiB*, *WomWWA 14*
Pettee, Lemuel Gardner 1875- *WhAm 3*
Pettee, Otis 1795-1853 *ApCAB*
Pettee, William Henry 1838-1904 *ApCAB*, *WhAm 1*
Pettee, William Jay 1867-1928 *WhAm 1*
Pettees, John J d1864 *BiAUS*
Pettegrew, Jon Price 1937-1974 *WhAm 6*
Pettegrew, Marion Edgar 1908-1972 *WhAm 5*
Pettengill, Amos 1780-1830 *Drake*
Pettengill, George 1877-1959 *WhAm 3*
Pettengill, Heman Judson 1851-1931 *NatCAB 31*, *WhAm 1*, *WhAm 1C*
Pettengill, Samuel Barrett 1886-1974 *BiDrAC*, *WhAm 6*
Pettenkofer, Max Josef Von 1818-1901 *DcScB*
Pettenkofer, Max Joseph Von 1818-1901 *AsBiEn*
Petter, Rodolphe C 1865-1935 *WhAm 2*
Petter, Rodolphe C 1865-1947 *WhAm 2C*
Petterson, LeRoy David 1885-1970 *WhAm 5*
Petterson, Ness C *NewYHSD*
Pettersson, Hans 1888-1966 *DcScB*
Pettet, Isabella M 1848- *AmWom*
Pettet, Zellmer Roswell 1880-1962 *WhAm 4*
Pettey, Charles Calvin 1849- *ApCAB Sup*
Petteys, Alonzo 1887-1968 *WhAm 5*
Petti, Cherubino 1888-1966 *NatCAB 54*
Pettibone, Augustus Herman 1835-1918 *BiDrAC*, *TwCBDA*, *WhAm 1*
Pettibone, Daniel *NewYHSD*
Pettibone, Frank G 1861- *WhAm 4*
Pettibone, George A *WhAm 4*
Pettibone, Holman Dean 1889-1962 *NatCAB 48*, *WhAm 4*
Pettibone, Minnie Mathewson 1870- *WomWWA 14*
Pettibone, Rufus 1784-1825 *NatCAB 16*
Pettibone, Wilson Boyd 1858- *WhAm 4*
Petticord, Paul Parker 1907-1975 *WhAm 6*
Pettiford, William Reuben 1840?- *WhoColR*
Pettigrew, Belle L *WomWWA 14*
Pettigrew, Bertrand Linwood 1874-1947 *NatCAB 35*
Pettigrew, Charles d1807 *Drake*

Pettigrew, Charles 1743-1807 *DcAmB*, *NatCAB 7*
Pettigrew, Charles 1744-1807 *WhAm H*
Pettigrew, Charles 1748-1807 *ApCAB*, *TwCBDA*
Pettigrew, Ebenezer 1783-1848 *ApCAB*, *BiAUS*, *BiDrAC*, *WhAm H*
Pettigrew, George Atwood 1858-1938 *WhAm 1*
Pettigrew, James Johnston 1828-1862 *BiDConf*
Pettigrew, James Johnston 1828-1863 *AmBi*, *ApCAB*, *DcAmB*, *NatCAB 9*, *TwCBDA*, *WebAMB*
Pettigrew, James Johnston 1828-1866 *WhAm H*
Pettigrew, James Louis *WebAB*
Pettigrew, Richard Franklin 1848-1926 *ApCAB Sup*, *BiDrAC*, *DcAmB*, *EncAAH*, *NatCAB 2*, *REnAW*, *TwCBDA*, *WhAm 1*, *WhAmP*
Pettigrew, Thomas Joseph 1791-1865 *BiHiMed*
Pettijohn, Charles Clyde 1881-1948 *WhAm 2*
Pettijohn, Grace Smith 1876- *WomWWA 14*
Pettijohn, John J 1875-1923 *WhAm 1*
Pettijohn, Julia Ivans 1918-1975 *WhAm 6*
Pettingell, Frank Hervey 1868-1926 *ApCAB X*, *WhAm 1*
Pettingill, Amos 1780-1830 *ApCAB*
Pettingill, John Hancock 1815-1887 *ApCAB*, *TwCBDA*
Pettingill, William LeRoy 1866-1950 *WhAm 3*
Pettis *NewYHSD*
Pettis, Charles Emerson 1901-1972 *WhAm 5*
Pettis, Clifford Robert 1877-1927 *NatCAB 20*, *WhAm 1*
Pettis, Jerry Lyle 1916-1975 *BiDrAC*, *WhAm 6*
Pettis, S Newton 1828-1900 *BiAUS*, *NatCAB 11*
Pettis, Solomon Newton 1827-1900 *BiDrAC*
Pettis, Spencer Darwin 1802-1831 *BiAUS*, *BiDrAC*, *WhAm H*, *WhAmP*
Pettit, Charles 1736-1806 *ApCAB*, *BiAUS*, *BiDrAC*, *DcAmB*, *Drake*, *NatCAB 11*, *TwCBDA*, *WhAm H*
Pettit, Curtis Hussey 1833-1914 *NatCAB 37*
Pettit, Frederick Robinson 1884-1919 *NatCAB 17*
Pettit, George Albert Joseph 1858-1917 *NatCAB 14*, *TwCBDA*, *WhAm 1*
Pettit, Harvey P 1893-1966 *NatCAB 52*, *WhAm 4*
Pettit, Henry 1842-1921 *TwCBDA*, *WhAm 1*
Pettit, Henry Corbin 1863-1913 *NatCAB 15*
Pettit, Horace 1860-1914 *NatCAB 25*
Pettit, John 1807-1877 *ApCAB*, *BiAUS*, *BiDrAC*, *NatCAB 4*, *TwCBDA*, *WhAm H*, *WhAmP*
Pettit, John Upfold 1820-1881 *BiAUS*, *BiDrAC*, *TwCBDA*, *WhAm H*
Pettit, Katherine Rhoda 1868-1936 *BiDAmEd*, *NotAW*
Pettit, Mortlock Stratton 1887-1962 *NatCAB 48*
Pettit, Paul Bruce 1920-1972 *WhAm 6*
Pettit, Roswell Talmadge 1885-1953 *NatCAB 45*
Pettit, Silas Wright 1844-1908 *NatCAB 31*
Pettit, Thomas McKean 1797-1853 *ApCAB*, *BiAUS*, *DcAmB*, *Drake*, *NatCAB 12*, *WhAm H*
Pettitt, Byron Buck 1910-1969 *WhAm 5*
Pettrich, Ferdinand Friedrich August 1798-1872 *IlBEAAW*, *NewYHSD*
Pettrich, Frederick August Ferdinand 1798-1872 *NewYHSD*
Pettus, Edmund Winston 1821-1907 *ApCAB Sup*, *BiDConf*, *BiDrAC*, *DcAmB*, *NatCAB 12*, *TwCBDA*, *WhAm 1*, *WhAmP*
Pettus, Erle 1877-1960 *NatCAB 49*, *WhAm 4*
Pettus, Frances Stevenson 1872- *WomWWA 14*
Pettus, Isabella Mary *WomWWA 14*
Pettus, James Thomas 1874-1971 *NatCAB 57*, *WhAm 5*
Pettus, John Jones 1813-1864 *Drake*
Pettus, John Jones 1813-1867 *BiDConf*, *NatCAB 13*, *TwCBDA*
Pettus, John Wilson 1872- *WhoColR*
Pettus, Maia 1874-1956 *WomWWA 14*

Pettus, Maia 1875-1956 WhAm 3
Pettus, Martha Elvira WomWWA 14
Pettus, Sarah Lydia DeForest WomWWA 14
Pettus, William Bacon 1880-1959 WhAm 3
Pettus, William Jerdone 1862- WhAm 5
Petty, Alonzo McAllister 1860-1937 WhAm 1
Petty, Alonzo Ray 1887-1932 WhAm 1
Petty, C Wallace 1884-1932 WhAm 1
Petty, David Milton 1885-1960 NatCAB 47
Petty, James William 1904-1965 WhAm 4
Petty, Julia DeBernien Davis WomWWA 14
Petty, Mary WomWWA 14
Petty, Mary Louise 1878- WhoColR
Petty, Nelson Lane 1869-1945 NatCAB 34
Petty, Orlando Henderson 1874- WhAm 1
Petty, Orville Anderson 1874-1942 WhAm 2
Petty, VanAlvin 1889-1942 NatCAB 32
Petty, William 1623-1687 DcScB
Petty, William 1737-1805 WhAm H
Pettys, Anna C WhAm 6
Petzoldt, William A 1872-1960 WhAm 4
Peuerbach, Georg Von 1423-1461 DcScB
Peugnet, Ramsay 1870-1944 NatCAB 33
Peurbach, Georg Von 1423-1461 AsBiEn
Peurifoy, John E 1907-1955 WhAm 3
Pevsner, Antoine 1884-1962 WhAm 4
Pevsner, Antoine 1886-1962 McGEWB
Pew, Arthur E, Jr. 1898-1965 WhAm 4
Pew, Helen Jennings Thompson 1883-1963
  NatCAB 57
Pew, Howard 1882-1971 NatCAB 57
Pew, J Howard 1882-1971 WhAm 5
Pew, James NewYHSD
Pew, James Edgar 1870-1946 NatCAB 41,
  WhAm 2
Pew, John Brooks 1877-1960 WhAm 4
Pew, John G d1954 WhAm 3
Pew, Joseph Newton 1848-1912 NatCAB 21
Pew, Joseph Newton, Jr. 1886-1963 WhAm 4
Pew, Marlen Edwin 1878-1936 NatCAB 43,
  WhAm 1
Pew, Robert 1862-1925 NatCAB 47
Pexton, George Ellsworth 1863-1939 WhAm 1
Peyer, Johann Conrad 1653-1712 DcScB
Peynada, Francisco J 1867- WhAm 4
Peyraud, Frank Charles 1858-1948 WhAm 2
Peyri, Antonio 1765-1832? ApCAB
Peyser, Ethan Allen 1897-1958 NatCAB 46,
  WhAm 4
Peyser, Julius I d1953 WhAm 3
Peyser, Theodore Albert 1873-1937 BiDrAC,
  WhAm 1
Peyssonnel, Jean Andre 1694-1759 DcScB
Peyton, Bailie 1803-1878 BiAUS
Peyton, Bailie 1803-1878 ApCAB, BiDrAC,
  NatCAB 7, TwCBDA, WhAm H
Peyton, Bernard 1896-1975 WhAm 6
Peyton, Bernard Robertson 1886-1959 WhAm 3
Peyton, Bertha Menzler d1947 WhAm 2
Peyton, Charles Dewey 1898-1963 WhAm 4
Peyton, Ephraim Geoffrey 1802-1876 ApCAB,
  NatCAB 7, TwCBDA
Peyton, Ephraim Geoffrey 1876-1950 WhAm 3
Peyton, Garland 1892-1964 WhAm 5
Peyton, Harlan Ide 1894-1958 NatCAB 50,
  WhAm 4
Peyton, Isaac Newton 1842-1913 NatCAB 17
Peyton, Jesse Enlows 1815-1897 ApCAB Sup
Peyton, John Howe 1778-1847 ApCAB,
  NatCAB 4, TwCBDA
Peyton, John Howe 1864-1918 WhAm 1
Peyton, John Lewis 1824-1896 ApCAB,
  DcAmB, NatCAB 4, TwCBDA,
  WhAm H
Peyton, John Lewis 1825-1896 Drake
Peyton, Joseph Hopkins 1808-1845 BiDrAC,
  WhAm H
Peyton, Joseph Hopkins 1813-1845 BiAUS
Peyton, Lawrence Washington Howe 1872-1949
  NatCAB 38
Peyton, Randolph Victor 1863- WhoColR
Peyton, Robert Ludwell Yates 1822-1863
  BiDConf
Peyton, Robert Ludwell Yates 1825-1863
  NatCAB 5
Peyton, Samuel Oldham 1804-1870 BiAUS,
  BiDrAC, TwCBDA, WhAm H

Peyton, William Madison 1804-1868
  ApCAB Sup
Pezard, Albert 1875-1927 DcScB
Pezenas, Esprit 1692-1776 DcScB
Pezet, Federico Alfonso 1859- WhAm 4
Pezet, Juan Antonio 1806- ApCAB
Pezuela, Jacobo DeLa 1811-1882 ApCAB
Pezuela, Joaquin DeLa 1761-1830 ApCAB
Pezuela, Juan Manuel 1810- ApCAB
Pfaelzer, Monroe 1892-1960 NatCAB 51
Pfaff, Franz 1860-1926 WhAm 1
Pfaff, Johann Friedrich 1765-1825 DcScB
Pfaff, Norman Joseph 1895-1958 NatCAB 48
Pfaff, Orange Garrett 1857-1927 NatCAB 20,
  WhAm 1
Pfaff, William 1871-1940 WhAm 1
Pfaffenberger, Edith Myers 1869-
  WomWWA 14
Pfahler, George Edward 1874-1957 NatCAB 49,
  WhAm 3
Pfahler, William H 1844-1908 WhAm 1
Pfannmuller, Julius F W 1889-1961 NatCAB 50
Pfanstiehl, Carl 1887-1942 WhAm 2
Pfanstiehl, Carl 1888-1942 NatCAB 32
Pfarr, John S 1906-1968 NatCAB 56
Pfatteicher, Ernst Philip Henry 1874-1943
  NatCAB 33, WhAm 2
Pfau, Gustavus 1800?- NewYHSD
Pfeffer, Clarence Augustus 1884-1950
  NatCAB 39
Pfeffer, Delmont Kahler d1974 WhAm 6
Pfeffer, Edward Charles 1884-1954 WhAm 3
Pfeffer, F NewYHSD
Pfeffer, Wilhelm Friedrich Philipp 1845-1920
  AsBiEn, DcScB
Pfefferle, Benjamin Lefever 1882-1944
  NatCAB 34
Pfeifer, Carl 1834-1888 Drake
Pfeifer, Joseph Lawrence 1892-1974 BiDrAC,
  WhAm 6
Pfeifer, Otto John, Jr. 1905-1970 NatCAB 56
Pfeiffenberger, James Mather 1879-1963
  NatCAB 50, WhAm 4
Pfeiffenschneider, Justus 1861- WhAm 4
Pfeiffer NewYHSD
Pfeiffer, Annie Merner 1860-1946 WhAm 2
Pfeiffer, C Leonard 1896-1958 NatCAB 48
Pfeiffer, Carl 1834-1888 ApCAB
Pfeiffer, Carl 1838-1888 WhAm H
Pfeiffer, Charles Frederick 1852-1921
  NatCAB 47
Pfeiffer, Edward 1857- WhAm 4
Pfeiffer, Frederick 1872-1934 NatCAB 26
Pfeiffer, Jacob NewYHSD
Pfeiffer, Jacob 1861-1946 WhAm 2
Pfeiffer, Ludwig Georg 1805-1877 ApCAB
Pfeiffer, Oscar Joseph 1858- WhAm 4
Pfeiffer, Paul 1875-1951 DcScB
Pfeiffer, Robert Henry 1892-1958 NatCAB 43,
  WhAm 3
Pfeiffer, Timothy Newell 1886-1971 WhAm 5
Pfeiffer, Victor Wilbur 1913-1960 NatCAB 49
Pfeiffer, William Louis 1907- BiDrAC
Pfeil, John Simon 1889-1967 WhAm 5
Pfeil, Stephen 1854- WhAm 4
Pfeiler, William Karl 1897-1970 WhAm 5
Pfenninger, Jacob NewYHSD
Pfetsch, Carl P 1817-1898 NewYHSD
Pfingst, Adolph Otto 1869-1944 NatCAB 33,
  WhAm 2
Pfister, Alfred 1880-1964 NatCAB 51
Pfister, Jean Jacques 1878-1949 WhAm 2
Pfister, Joseph Clement 1867-1948 WhAm 2
Pfister, Lester 1897-1970 EncAAH
Pfisterer, Henry Albert 1908-1972 WhAm 5
Pflager, Harry Miller 1866-1951 WhAm 3
Pflager, Henry Barber 1903-1972 WhAm 5
Pfleiderer, Arthur Burdett 1898-1969
  NatCAB 56
Pflueger, John Seiberling 1898-1967 WhAm 4
Pfluger, Eduard Friedrich Wilhelm 1829-1910
  DcScB
Pfohl, John Kenneth 1874-1967 WhAm 4A
Pforzheimer, Carl Howard 1879-1957 WhAm 3
Pfost, Gracie Bowers 1906-1965, BiDrAC,
  WhAm 4, WhAmP
Pfotenhauer, Frederick 1859-1939 WhAm 1
Pfund, A Herman 1879-1948 WhAm 2

Pfund, August Herman 1879-1949 DcAmB S4,
  NatCAB 37
Phair, John J 1904-1970 WhAm 5
Phalen, Charles Stephen 1883-1947 NatCAB 45
Phalen, Harold Romaine 1889-1955 WhAm 3
Phalen, James Matthew 1872-1954 NatCAB 45,
  WhAm 3
Phalen, Paul Stephens 1881-1938 WhAm 1
Phaneuf, Joseph Stanislas 1888-1957
  NatCAB 46
Phaneuf, Louis Eusebe 1884-1953 WhAm 3
Pharis, Charles Sheldon 1898-1960 NatCAB 49
Pharr, Henry Eugene 1884-1960 NatCAB 52
Pharr, Henry Newton 1872- NatCAB 14
Pharr, Hurieosco Austill 1891- WhAm 5
Pharr, John Newton 1829-1903 NatCAB 14
Pheiffer, William Townsend 1898- BiDrAC
Phelan, Andrew J 1907-1973 WhAm 6
Phelan, Balfour 1894-1973 WhAm 6
Phelan, Charles T 1840- NewYHSD
Phelan, David Samuel 1841-1915 DcAmB
Phelan, Edward Joseph 1888-1967 WhAm 4A
Phelan, Florence B 1872- WomWWA 14
Phelan, Florence Lanahan 1880-
  WomWWA 14
Phelan, Hunt 1873-1942 NatCAB 33
Phelan, James 1821-1873 ApCAB, BiDConf,
  NatCAB 36, TwCBDA
Phelan, James 1821-1892 NatCAB 8
Phelan, James 1824-1892 DcAmB, WhAm H
Phelan, James 1856-1891 ApCAB, BiDrAC,
  DcAmB, NatCAB 36, TwCBDA,
  WhAm H
Phelan, James Duval 1861-1930 AmBi,
  BiDrAC, DcAmB, NatCAB 8, WhAm 1
Phelan, James J 1871-1934 WhAm 1
Phelan, James M 1914-1974 WhAm 6
Phelan, John 1879-1952 WhAm 3
Phelan, John Dennis 1809-1879 ApCAB,
  NatCAB 36
Phelan, John Joseph 1851-1936 NatCAB 31
Phelan, Michael 1816-1871 ApCAB
Phelan, Michael Francis 1875-1941 BiDrAC,
  NatCAB 31, WhAm 1
Phelan, Richard 1825-1904 ApCAB
Phelan, Richard 1828-1904 NatCAB 6,
  TwCBDA, WhAm 1
Phelan, Robert Early 1886-1948 NatCAB 36
Phelan, Sidney M, Jr. 1886-1950 WhAm 3
Phelan, Thomas Aloysius 1844-1914
  NatCAB 31
Phelan, Warren Waverly 1869-1935 WhAm 1
Phelan, William Rowe 1917-1972 WhAm 6
Phelon, Howard Burdette 1904-1972
  NatCAB 57
Phelps, Abel Mix 1851-1902 NatCAB 12
Phelps, Abner 1779-1873 ApCAB
Phelps, Albert Caruthers 1875-1912
  NatCAB 16
Phelps, Albert Charles 1873-1937 WhAm 1
Phelps, Almira Hart Lincoln 1793-1884 ApCAB,
  BiDAmEd, DcAmB, Drake, NatCAB 11,
  NotAW, TwCBDA, WhAm H
Phelps, Alvernon WomWWA 14
Phelps, Amos Augustus 1805-1847 ApCAB,
  NatCAB 2
Phelps, Andrew Henry 1888-1962 WhAm 4
Phelps, Anna Redfield 1852- WomWWA 14
Phelps, Anson Greene 1781-1853 AmBi,
  ApCAB, DcAmB, Drake, NatCAB 12,
  WhAm H
Phelps, Arthur Stevens 1863-1948 WhAm 2
Phelps, Ashton 1853-1919 WhAm 1
Phelps, Austin 1820-1890 AmBi, ApCAB,
  DcAmB, Drake, NatCAB 9, TwCBDA,
  WhAm H
Phelps, Benjamin Kinsman 1832-1880
  NatCAB 40
Phelps, Charles 1834-1913 NatCAB 46,
  WhAm 1
Phelps, Charles Edward 1833-1908 ApCAB,
  BiAUS, BiDrAC, DcAmB, NatCAB 29,
  TwCBDA, WhAm 1
Phelps, Charles Edward, Jr. 1871-1918
  WhAm 1
Phelps, Charles Edward Davis 1851- WhAm 4
Phelps, Charles Henry 1853-1933 NatCAB 8,
  WhAm 1

Phelps, Clarence Lucien 1881-1964 *WhAm 4*
Phelps, Darwin 1807-1879 *BiAUS, BiDrAC, WhAm H*
Phelps, David McCord, Jr. 1895-1956 *NatCAB 45*
Phelps, Delos Porter 1837-1914 *WhAm 1*
Phelps, Dudley 1861-1952 *NatCAB 40*
Phelps, Dudley Farleigh 1876-1932 *NatCAB 26*
Phelps, E *NewYHSD*
Phelps, Earl Francis 1875-1966 *NatCAB 51*
Phelps, Earle Bernard 1876-1953 *NatCAB 40, WhAm 3*
Phelps, Edmund Joseph 1845- *NatCAB 15*
Phelps, Edward Bunnell 1863-1915 *WhAm 1*
Phelps, Edward John 1822-1900 *AmBi, ApCAB, DcAmB, NatCAB 5, TwCBDA, WhAm 1*
Phelps, Edward Shethar 1858-1939 *WhAm 1*
Phelps, Elisha 1779-1847 *ApCAB, BiAUS, BiDrAC, NatCAB 11, TwCBDA, WhAm H*
Phelps, Eliza Bowen *WomWWA 14*
Phelps, Elizabeth 1815-1852 *Drake, NatCAB 9, TwCBDA*
Phelps, Elizabeth Steward 1815-1852 *WomWWA 14*
Phelps, Elizabeth Stuart 1815-1852 *AmBi, ApCAB, NotAW, TwCBDA*
Phelps, Elizabeth Stuart 1844-1911 *AmBi, ApCAB, DcAmB, NotAW*
Phelps, Erskine Mason 1839-1910 *NatCAB 14, WhAm 1*
Phelps, Esmond 1888-1950 *WhAm 3*
Phelps, Frank Wesley 1878-1949 *NatCAB 38*
Phelps, George Dwight 1803-1872 *ApCAB*
Phelps, George Harrison 1883-1945 *WhAm 2*
Phelps, George May 1820-1888 *ApCAB Sup, NatCAB 7*
Phelps, George Turner 1867-1920 *WhAm 1*
Phelps, Gertrude Lindall 1867- *WomWWA 14*
Phelps, Guy Fitch d1933 *WhAm 1*
Phelps, Guy Merritt 1887-1946 *WhAm 2*
Phelps, Guy Rowland 1802-1869 *ApCAB, DcAmB, WhAm H*
Phelps, Harry 1861- *WhAm 1*
Phelps, Helen Watson d1944 *WhAm 2, WomWWA 14*
Phelps, Henry Willis 1863-1944 *WhAm 2*
Phelps, Isaac King 1872- *WhAm 5*
Phelps, J Manley 1891-1971 *WhAm 5*
Phelps, James 1822-1900 *BiAUS, BiDrAC, TwCBDA, WhAm H*
Phelps, James Ivey 1875-1947 *WhAm 2*
Phelps, Jessie 1870- *WomWWA 14*
Phelps, John 1824-1886 *ApCAB*
Phelps, John Jay 1861-1948 *NatCAB 17, NatCAB 37, WhAm 2*
Phelps, John Noble 1912-1968 *WhAm 5*
Phelps, John Smith 1814-1886 *ApCAB, ApCAB X, BiAUS, BiDrAC, DcAmB, NatCAB 5, NatCAB 12, TwCBDA, WhAm H, WhAmP*
Phelps, John Wolcott 1813-1885 *AmBi, ApCAB, Drake, TwCBDA*
Phelps, Lancelot 1784-1866 *BiDrAC, WhAm H*
Phelps, Launcelot 1784-1866 *BiAUS*
Phelps, Lawrence 1852- *WhAm 4*
Phelps, Leland Daniel 1902-1972 *NatCAB 57*
Phelps, Luis James 1864-1939 *NatCAB 38*
Phelps, Marian *WhAm 4*
Phelps, Martha Austin *WomWWA 14*
Phelps, Mary *WomWWA 14*
Phelps, Mary Ward 1878- *WomWWA 14*
Phelps, Mason Elliott 1885-1945 *NatCAB 35*
Phelps, Minna Belle *WomWWA 14*
Phelps, Noah 1740-1809 *ApCAB*
Phelps, Noah Amherst 1788-1872 *ApCAB*
Phelps, O Draper 1881-1951 *NatCAB 41*
Phelps, Oliver 1749-1809 *AmBi, ApCAB, BiAUS, BiDrAC, DcAmB, Drake, NatCAB 7, WhAm H*
Phelps, Pauline *WomWWA 14*
Phelps, Philip 1826-1896 *TwCBDA*
Phelps, Royal 1809-1884 *ApCAB*
Phelps, Ruth Shepard 1876- *WhAm 5, WomWWA 14*
Phelps, Samuel Shethar 1793-1855 *ApCAB,*

BiAUS, BiDrAC, Drake, NatCAB 8, TwCBDA, WhAm H, WhAmP
Phelps, Seth Ledyard 1824-1885? *NatCAB 12*
Phelps, Sheffield 1864- *NatCAB 11*
Phelps, Shelton Joseph 1884-1948 *NatCAB 39, WhAm 2*
Phelps, Stanford Newton 1904-1961 *NatCAB 49*
Phelps, Stephen 1839-1930 *NatCAB 25, TwCBDA, WhAm 1*
Phelps, Stowe 1869-1952 *NatCAB 42*
Phelps, Sylvanus Dryden 1816- *ApCAB, Drake*
Phelps, Thomas Stowell 1822-1901 *ApCAB, DcAmB, NatCAB 4, TwCBDA, WhAm 1*
Phelps, Thomas Stowell, Jr. 1848-1915 *WhAm 1*
Phelps, Timothy Guy 1824-1899 *BiAUS, BiDrAC, WhAm H*
Phelps, Wilbur Moorehead 1877-1949 *NatCAB 38*
Phelps, William 1599-1672 *ApCAB*
Phelps, William Franklin 1822-1907 *ApCAB, BiDAmEd, DcAmB, NatCAB 12, WhAm 4*
Phelps, William Henry 1872-1939 *WhAm 1*
Phelps, William Henry 1874-1963 *NatCAB 51*
Phelps, William Lyon 1865-1943 *ApCAB X, BiDAmEd, DcAmB S3, NatCAB 32, WhAm 2*
Phelps, William Wallace 1826-1873 *BiAUS, BiDrAC, WhAm H*
Phelps, William Walter 1839-1894 *ApCAB, BiAUS, BiDrAC, DcAmB, NatCAB 7, TwCBDA, WhAm H, WhAmP*
Phelps, William Wines 1792-1872 *ApCAB*
Phelps, William Woodward 1869-1938 *NatCAB 30, WhAm 1*
Phelps-Rider, Alice d1973 *WhAm 6*
Phemister, Dallas Burton 1882-1951 *NatCAB 40, WhAm 3*
Phenix, George Perley 1864-1930 *NatCAB 26, WhAm 1, WhAm 1C*
Phibun Songkhram, Luang 1897-1964 *McGEWB*
Phidias *McGEWB*
Phifer, Fred Wood 1876-1935 *WhAm 1*
Philbin, Eugene Ambrose 1857-1920 *ApCAB X, NatCAB 12, WhAm 1*
Philbin, Mary 1905- *ApCAB X*
Philbin, Philip Joseph 1898-1972 *BiDrAC, WhAm 5*
Philbrick, Grace Elizabeth Mathews *WomWWA 14*
Philbrick, Helen Fitch 1880- *WomWWA 14*
Philbrick, Herbert Shaw 1875-1963 *WhAm 4*
Philbrick, Inez C 1866- *WomWWA 14*
Philbrick, John Alden 1899-1952 *NatCAB 41*
Philbrick, John Dudley 1818-1886 *AmBi, ApCAB, BiDAmEd, NatCAB 12*
Philbrick, Otis 1888-1973 *NatCAB 57*
Philbrick, Stacey *IIBEAAW*
Philbrook, Warren Coffin 1857-1933 *WhAm 1*
Phile, Philip d1793 *WhAm H*
Philenia *WhAm H*
Philes, George Philip 1828- *ApCAB, Drake*
Philinus Of Cos *DcScB*
Philip 1639?-1676 *AmBi, ApCAB, DcAmB, Drake, EncAB, McGEWB, NatCAB 10, TwCBDA, WebAB, WebAMB, WhAm H*
Philip *see also* King Philip
Philip II 382BC-336BC *McGEWB*
Philip II 1165-1223 *McGEWB*
Philip II 1527-1598 *McGEWB, WhoMilH*
Philip III 1578-1621 *McGEWB*
Philip IV 1268-1314 *McGEWB*
Philip IV 1605-1665 *McGEWB*
Philip V 1683-1746 *McGEWB*
Philip VI 1293-1350 *McGEWB*
Philip The Good 1396-1467 *McGEWB*
Philip, Albert 1887-1954 *NatCAB 41*
Philip, Alexander Philip Wilson 1770-1851 *BiHiMed*
Philip, Alexander Philips Wilson 1770-1851? *DcScB*
Philip, Andre 1902-1970 *WhAm 5*
Philip, Frederick William 1814-1841 *NewYHSD*
Philip, George 1880-1948 *NatCAB 36, WhAm 2*

Philip, Hoffman 1872-1951 *NatCAB 44, WhAm 3*
Philip, John Jay 1924-1974 *WhAm 6*
Philip, John Woodward 1840-1900 *ApCAB Sup, DcAmB, NatCAB 9, TwCBDA, WebAMB, WhAm 1*
Philip, Scotty 1857-1911 *REnAW*
Philip, William H *NewYHSD*
Philipp, Emanuel Lorenz 1861-1925 *DcAmB, NatCAB 19, WhAm 1*
Philipp, M Bernard 1848-1929 *NatCAB 26*
Philipp, Richard 1874-1959 *WhAm 3*
Philippe, Robert Rene 1906-1968 *WhAm 5*
Philippes DeKerhallet, Charles Marie 1809-1863 *ApCAB*
Philippi, E Martin d1946 *WhAm 2*
Philippoteaux, Paul Dominick 1846- *ApCAB, NewYHSD*
Philipps, Richard 1661-1751 *Drake*
Philips *NewYHSD*
Philips, Carlin 1871- *WhAm 5*
Philips, George Morris 1851-1920 *TwCBDA, WhAm 1*
Philips, Jesse Evans 1862- *WhAm 4*
Philips, John F 1834-1919 *WhAm 1*
Philips, John Fines 1834-1919 *TwCBDA*
Philips, John Finis 1834-1919 *BiAUS, BiDrAC, DcAmB, NatCAB 26*
Philips, Joseph *NatCAB 5*
Philips, Martin Wilson 1806-1889 *DcAmB, WhAm H*
Philips, Samuel 1823- *ApCAB*
Philips, Samuel F 1824-1903 *NatCAB 5*
Philips, William Commons 1857-1942 *NatCAB 31*
Philips, William Pyle 1882-1950 *NatCAB 39, WhAm 3*
Philipse, Frederick 1626-1702 *ApCAB, DcAmB, NatCAB 14, WhAm H*
Philipse, Frederick 1690-1751 *ApCAB*
Philipse, Frederick 1695-1751 *NatCAB 14*
Philipse, Frederick 1746-1785 *ApCAB, TwCBDA*
Philipse, Margaret Hardenbrook *NotAW*
Philipse, Mary 1730-1825 *NewYHSD*
Philipson, David 1862-1949 *DcAmB S4, DcAmReB, NatCAB 13, WhAm 2*
Phillene, Ferdinand J *NewYHSD*
Philleo, Calvin W 1822-1858 *Drake*
Philleo, Prudence Crandall 1803-1890 *BiDAmEd, TwCBDA*
Philler, George d1916 *WhAm 1*
Phillibrowne, Thomas *NewYHSD*
Phillip, Arthur 1738-1814 *McGEWB*
Phillip, Hardie d1973 *WhAm 6*
Philippe, Gerald Lloyd 1909-1968 *NatCAB 54, WhAm 5*
Phillippi, Joseph Martin 1869-1926 *WhAm 1*
Phillippi, Stanley Isaac 1900-1971 *WhAm 5*
Phillippo, James M *ApCAB*
Phillipps, Adelaide 1833-1882 *ApCAB, NotAW, TwCBDA*
Phillipps, H Godfrey 1879-1940 *NatCAB 30*
Phillips *NewYHSD*
Phillips, Mrs. *NewYHSD*
Phillips, Adelaide 1833-1882 *AmBi, Drake, NatCAB 6*
Phillips, Albanus 1871-1949 *NatCAB 38, WhAm 2*
Phillips, Albanus, Jr. 1902-1970 *WhAm 5*
Phillips, Albert William 1838- *ApCAB X*
Phillips, Alexander Hamilton 1866-1937 *WhAm 1*
Phillips, Alexander Lacy 1859- *WhAm 1*
Phillips, Alexander Roy 1880-1945 *NatCAB 35, WhAm 2*
Phillips, Alexander VanCleve 1868-1956 *WhAm 3*
Phillips, Alfred Edward 1863-1931 *WhAm 1*
Phillips, Alfred Noroton 1894-1970 *BiDrAC, WhAm 5*
Phillips, Ammi 1787?-1865 *NewYHSD*
Phillips, Ammi 1788-1865 *BnEnAmA*
Phillips, Andrew Wheeler 1844-1915 *WhAm 1*
Phillips, Arthur Edward 1867-1932 *NatCAB 23*
Phillips, Arthur L 1872-1937 *WhAm 1*
Phillips, Asa Emory 1869-1936 *WhAm 1*
Phillips, Barnet 1828-1905 *ApCAB, WhAm 1*

Phillips, Benjamin Dwight 1885-1968 *WhAm 5*
Phillips, Benjamin R *NewYHSD*
Phillips, Benjamin Troup 1840-1918
 NatCAB 19
Phillips, Bernard 1915-1974 *WhAm 6*
Phillips, Bert G 1868-1956 *REnAW*
Phillips, Bert Geer 1868-1956 *WhAm 5*
Phillips, Bert Greer 1868-1956 *IlBEAAW*
Phillips, Bradley Hatch 1870-1938 *NatCAB 32*
Phillips, Cabell Beverly Hatchett 1904-1975
 WhAm 6
Phillips, Carl Chrisler 1883-1956 *WhAm 3*
Phillips, Carl LeRoy 1894-1965 *NatCAB 51,*
 WhAm 4
Phillips, Catherine Coffin 1874-1942
 NatCAB 32, WhAm 2
Phillips, Charles *NewYHSD*
Phillips, Charles 1822-1889 *TwCBDA*
Phillips, Charles 1880-1933 *WhAm 1*
Phillips, Charles C *NewYHSD*
Phillips, Charles Clarence 1880-1945
 NatCAB 37
Phillips, Charles Eaton 1877-1945 *NatCAB 34*
Phillips, Charles Evert 1889- *WhoColR*
Phillips, Charles Gordon 1892-1970 *WhAm 5*
Phillips, Charles Henry 1858-1951 *WhAm 3,*
 WhoColR
Phillips, Charles Henry, Jr. 1882- *WhoColR*
Phillips, Charles L 1889-1965 *WhAm 4*
Phillips, Charles Leonard 1856- *WhAm 4*
Phillips, Charles Menamin 1884-1961
 NatCAB 48
Phillips, Chauncey Hatch 1837- *NatCAB 7,*
 WhAm 4
Phillips, Claire Dooner 1887- *IlBEAAW*
Phillips, Claude Anderson 1871-1960
 NatCAB 49
Phillips, Coles 1912-1959 *WhAm 3*
Phillips, Cyrus William 1870-1936 *NatCAB 28*
Phillips, Daniel Conrad 1834-1916 *ApCAB X*
Phillips, David Graham 1867-1911 *AmBi,*
 DcAmB, McGEWB, NatCAB 14,
 WhAm 1
Phillips, Dayton Edward 1910- *BiDrAC*
Phillips, Duane Seneca 1834-1917 *WhAm 1*
Phillips, Duncan 1886-1966 *NatCAB 52,*
 WhAm 4
Phillips, Edna M d1970 *WhAm 5*
Phillips, Edward Charles 1877-1952 *WhAm 3*
Phillips, Elizabeth Buford 1843-1925
 NatCAB 20
Phillips, Elliot Schuyler 1893-1966 *NatCAB 52,*
 WhAm 4
Phillips, Ellis Laurimore 1873-1959 *NatCAB 46,*
 WhAm 3
Phillips, Elsie LaGrange Cole 1879-
 WomWWA 14
Phillips, Ethel Calvert d1947 *WhAm 2*
Phillips, Everett Franklin 1878-1951
 NatCAB 48, WhAm 5
Phillips, Florence Hall *WomWWA 14*
Phillips, Francis Clifford 1850-1920 *DcAmB,*
 NatCAB 18, WhAm 1
Phillips, Frank 1873-1950 *DcAmB S4,*
 NatCAB 38, REnAW, WhAm 3
Phillips, Frank Lyman 1879-1963 *NatCAB 48*
Phillips, Frank McGinley 1874- *WhAm 5*
Phillips, Frank Reith 1876-1942 *NatCAB 31,*
 WhAm 2
Phillips, Fremont Orestes 1856-1936 *BiDrAC*
Phillips, G W Macpherson 1888-1955
 NatCAB 42
Phillips, George 1593-1644 *ApCAB, DcAmB,*
 Drake, WhAm H
Phillips, George Felter 1892-1971 *WhAm 5*
Phillips, George Searle 1816-1889 *ApCAB Sup*
Phillips, George W 1822?- *NewYHSD*
Phillips, George W F 1853- *WhoColR*
Phillips, George Wallace 1879- *WhAm 6*
Phillips, Glenn Randall 1894-1970 *WhAm 5*
Phillips, Gordon 1927- *IlBEAAW*
Phillips, Harmon 1903-1975 *WhAm 6*
Phillips, Harold Cooke 1892-1966 *WhAm 4*
Phillips, Harold Meyer 1874-1967 *NatCAB 54*
Phillips, Harriet Sophia 1849- *WomWWA 14*
Phillips, Harry Clinton 1880- *WhAm 4*
Phillips, Harry Hungerford Spooner, Jr.
 1901-1968 *NatCAB 54, WhAm 5*

Phillips, Harry Irving 1889-1965 *WhAm 4*
Phillips, Henry 1838-1895 *ApCAB, DcAmB,*
 TwCBDA, WhAm H
Phillips, Henry, Jr. *Drake*
Phillips, Henry A d1950 *WhAm 3*
Phillips, Henry Albert 1880-1951 *NatCAB 38,*
 WhAm 3
Phillips, Henry Bayard 1881- *WhAm 6*
Phillips, Henry Disbrow 1882-1955 *WhAm 3*
Phillips, Henry J *NewYHSD*
Phillips, Henry Lee 1889-1975 *WhAm 6*
Phillips, Henry Myer 1811-1884 *ApCAB,*
 BiAUS, BiDrAC, WhAm H
Phillips, Henry Wallace 1869-1930 *WhAm 1*
Phillips, Herbert Ostrander 1858-1936
 NatCAB 31
Phillips, Herbert Stanton 1871-1962
 NatCAB 52, WhAm 4
Phillips, Hiram Wendell 1850-1924 *ApCAB X*
Phillips, Irna 1901-1973 *WhAm 6*
Phillips, J Warne 1863-1939 *NatCAB 31*
Phillips, James 1792-1867 *ApCAB*
Phillips, James Andrew 1873-1949 *NatCAB 38,*
 WhAm 2
Phillips, James David 1868- *WhAm 5*
Phillips, James Frederick 1900-1973
 NatCAB 57, WhAm 5, WhAm 6
Phillips, James Laughlin 1884-1918 *NatCAB 20*
Phillips, James McIlvaine 1874-1945
 NatCAB 34
Phillips, James Templeman 1877- *WhoColR*
Phillips, Jasper Tappan 1884- *WhoColR*
Phillips, Jay Campbell 1873-1948 *NatCAB 13,*
 WhAm 2
Phillips, Jesse J 1837-1901 *NatCAB 12,*
 WhAm 1
Phillips, Jesse Snyder 1871-1954 *NatCAB 45,*
 WhAm 3
Phillips, John *BiAUS, BiDrAC, WhAm H*
Phillips, John d1726 *Drake*
Phillips, John 1719-1795 *AmBi, ApCAB,*
 BiDAmEd, DcAmB, Drake, NatCAB 10,
 TwCBDA, WhAm H
Phillips, John 1770-1823 *ApCAB, BiAUS,*
 Drake
Phillips, John 1800-1874 *DcScB*
Phillips, John 1822- *NewYHSD*
Phillips, John 1879-1929 *ApCAB X,*
 NatCAB 21, WhAm 1
Phillips, John 1887- *BiDrAC*
Phillips, John Bakewell 1854-1911 *WhAm 1*
Phillips, John Benjamin 1854-1921 *NatCAB 19*
Phillips, John Burton 1866-1923 *WhAm 1*
Phillips, John Charles 1838-1885 *NatCAB 47*
Phillips, John Charles 1876-1938 *NatCAB 29,*
 WhAm 1
Phillips, John Clayton 1870-1943 *NatCAB 33,*
 WhAm 2
Phillips, John Daniel 1870-1925 *NatCAB 6*
Phillips, John George 1888-1964 *WhAm 4*
Phillips, John Gibson 1897-1951 *NatCAB 40*
Phillips, John Herbert 1853-1921 *WhAm 1*
Phillips, John MacFarlane 1861-1953
 NatCAB 49
Phillips, John Marshall 1905-1953 *NatCAB 50,*
 WhAm 3
Phillips, John McFarlane 1861-1953 *WhAm 3*
Phillips, John Milton 1820-1889 *NatCAB 12*
Phillips, John Owen 1891-1961 *NatCAB 48*
Phillips, John Reed 1899-1964 *NatCAB 52*
Phillips, John Sanburn 1861-1949 *DcAmB S4,*
 NatCAB 38, WhAm 2
Phillips, John Spinning 1895-1975 *WhAm 6*
Phillips, Kathryn Sisson 1879-1970 *WhAm 5*
Phillips, L Vance 1858- *AmWom*
Phillips, Lee Allen 1871-1938 *ApCAB X,*
 NatCAB 28, WhAm 1
Phillips, Lee Eldas 1876-1944 *NatCAB 33,*
 WhAm 2
Phillips, Lena Madesin 1881-1955 *DcAmB S5,*
 WhAm 3
Phillips, Leon Chase 1890-1958 *NatCAB 56,*
 WhAm 3
Phillips, Leroy 1870- *WhAm 5*
Phillips, Levi Benjamin 1868-1945 *NatCAB 37,*
 WhAm 2
Phillips, Lewis Strong 1818-1886 *NatCAB 2*
Phillips, Llewellyn 1869-1923 *NatCAB 19,*

 WhAm 1
Phillips, Louis 1893-1959 *WhAm 3*
Phillips, Marie Tello 1874- *WhAm 5*
Phillips, Marvin Hurston 1907-1967
 NatCAB 53
Phillips, Mary Martha *WomWWA 14*
Phillips, Mary Walker 1923- *BnEnAmA*
Phillips, Maud Gillette 1860- *WomWWA 14*
Phillips, Maude Gillette 1860- *AmWom,*
 WhAm 4
Phillips, Merton Ogden 1900-1958 *WhAm 3*
Phillips, Mervyn Claire 1898-1957 *NatCAB 46*
Phillips, Michael James 1876- *WhAm 5*
Phillips, Milton Eves 1844-1909 *WhAm 1*
Phillips, Minnie Holman 1861- *WomWWA 14*
Phillips, Morris 1834-1904 *ApCAB,*
 NatCAB 9, TwCBDA, WhAm 1
Phillips, Nelson 1873-1939 *NatCAB 17,*
 NatCAB 29, WhAm 1
Phillips, Norman Ethelbert 1894-1961 *WhAm 4*
Phillips, Paul Chrisler 1883-1956 *NatCAB 44,*
 WhAm 3
Phillips, Percival 1877-1937 *WhAm 1*
Phillips, Percy Wilson 1892-1969 *WhAm 5*
Phillips, Philip 1807-1884 *BiAUS, BiDrAC,*
 NatCAB 11, WhAm H
Phillips, Philip 1834-1895 *AmBi, ApCAB,*
 DcAmB, Drake, NatCAB 7, WhAm H
Phillips, Philip Lee *WhAm 1*
Phillips, Phoebe Foxcraft d1818 *ApCAB*
Phillips, Ray Edmund 1889-1967 *WhAm 4*
Phillips, Richard Harvey 1866- *WhAm 4*
Phillips, Richard Jones 1861- *WhAm 1*
Phillips, Richard William 1845-1916
 NatCAB 17
Phillips, Robert 1890-1944 *WhAm 2*
Phillips, Roger Sherman 1922-1969 *WhAm 5*
Phillips, Rosalie 1876- *WomWWA 14*
Phillips, Rosina Olive 1872- *WomWWA 14*
Phillips, Rowley Wilhelm 1890-1974 *WhAm 6*
Phillips, S J *NewYHSD*
Phillips, Samuel 1690-1771 *ApCAB,*
 NatCAB 10
Phillips, Samuel 1750-1802 *TwCBDA*
Phillips, Samuel 1751-1802 *ApCAB*
Phillips, Samuel 1752-1802 *AmBi, DcAmB,*
 Drake, NatCAB 10, WhAm H
Phillips, Samuel Edgar 1891-1951 *WhAm 3*
Phillips, Stephen Clarendon 1801-1857 *ApCAB,*
 BiAUS, BiDrAC, Drake, NatCAB 11,
 TwCBDA, WhAm H
Phillips, T D 1891-1960 *WhAm 4*
Phillips, Theodore Evelyn Reece 1868-1942
 DcScB
Phillips, Thomas Ashley 1881-1957 *WhAm 3*
Phillips, Thomas Henry 1847-1924 *NatCAB 21*
Phillips, Thomas I 1887-1956 *WhAm 3*
Phillips, Thomas Raphael 1892-1965 *WhAm 4*
Phillips, Thomas Wharton 1835-1912
 ApCAB X, BiDrAC, DcAmB, WhAm 1
Phillips, Thomas Wharton, Jr. 1874-1956
 BiDrAC, WhAm 3
Phillips, Timothy Redfield 1879-1953 *WhAm 3*
Phillips, Sir Tom 1888-1941 *WhWW-II*
Phillips, Ulrich Bonnell 1877-1934 *AmBi,*
 DcAmB S1, EncAAH, NatCAB 44,
 WhAm 1
Phillips, Waite 1883-1964 *WhAm 4*
Phillips, Wallace Banta 1886-1952 *WhAm 3*
Phillips, Walter Joseph 1884-1963 *IlBEAAW*
Phillips, Walter Polk 1846-1920 *DcAmB,*
 NatCAB 19
Phillips, Walter Sargeant 1905-1975 *WhAm 6*
Phillips, Walter Shelley 1867-1940 *IlBEAAW*
Phillips, Watson Lyman 1850-1944 *WhAm 2*
Phillips, Watson Provost 1863-1926 *NatCAB 20*
Phillips, Wendell 1811-1884 *AmBi, ApCAB,*
 DcAmB, Drake, EncAB, McGEWB,
 NatCAB 2, TwCBDA, WebAB,
 WhAm H
Phillips, Wendell 1921-1975 *WhAm 6*
Phillips, Wendell Christopher 1857-1934
 NatCAB 25, WhAm 1
Phillips, Wiley Johnson 1846- *NatCAB 5*
Phillips, Willard 1784-1873 *ApCAB, DcAmB,*
 Drake, NatCAB 7, TwCBDA, WhAm H
Phillips, William 1731-1781 *ApCAB, Drake*
Phillips, William 1750-1827 *ApCAB, DcAmB,*

Drake, WhAm H
Phillips, William 1775-1828 *DcScB*
Phillips, William 1814?-1874 *WhAm H*
Phillips, William 1878-1968 *NatCAB 14,*
 WhAm 4A
Phillips, William Addison 1824-1893 *BiDrAC,*
 DcAmB, NatCAB 8, TwCBDA,
 WhAm H, WhAmP
Phillips, William Addison 1826-1893 *BiAUS*
Phillips, William Battle 1857-1918 *WhAm 1*
Phillips, William Eric 1893-1964 *WhAm 4*
Phillips, William F *BiAUS*
Phillips, William Fowke Ravenel 1863-1935
 TwCBDA, WhAm 1
Phillips, William Henry 1871-1945 *NatCAB 34*
Phillips, William Irving 1847- *WhAm 4*
Phillips, William Segar 1842-1919 *NatCAB 17*
Phillips, William Wirt 1796-1865 *ApCAB,*
 Drake
Phillips, Ze Barney Thorne 1875-1942
 NatCAB 34, WhAm 2
Phillipson, Irving Joseph 1882-1955 *NatCAB 44,*
 WhAm 3
Phillipson, Samuel 1865- *NatCAB 18*
Phillpotts, Eden 1862-1960 *WhAm 4*
Philo Judaeus 020?BC-045?AD *McGEWB*
Philo Of Byzantium *DcScB*
Philolaus 480?BC- *AsBiEn, DcScB*
Philon 300?BC- *AsBiEn*
Philoon, Mary A 1853- *WomWWA 14*
Philoponus *DcScB*
Philp, John W 1874-1948 *WhAm 2*
Philp, Mary Roberts 1881- *WomWWA 14*
Philp, William H *NewYHSD*
Philpott, Gordon 1894-1965 *WhAm 4*
Philpott, Harvey Cloyd, Sr. 1909-1961 *WhAm 4*
Philpott, Peter Willey 1865- *WhAm 4*
Philputt, Allan Bearden 1856-1925 *WhAm 1*
Philputt, James M 1860- *WhAm 1*
Philson, Robert 1759-1831 *BiAUS, BiDrAC,*
 WhAm H
Phin, John 1830-1913 *WhAm 1*
Phin, John 1832-1913 *ApCAB*
Phinizy, Bowdre 1871-1931 *WhAm 1*
Phinizy, Charles H 1835- *NatCAB 5*
Phinizy, Ferdinand 1819-1889 *DcAmB,*
 WhAm H
Phinizy, Hamilton 1864-1938 *WhAm 1*
Phinney, Deidamia *NewYHSD*
Phinney, Ethel Warner 1875- *WomWWA 14*
Phinney, Frank Ferguson 1870-1920 *ApCAB X*
Phinney, Horatio Augustus 1860-1938
 NatCAB 31
Phinney, Jessie Woodward 1855-
 WomWWA 14
Phippen, George 1916-1966 *IIBEAAW*
Phippen, John *NewYHSD*
Phippen, Walter Gray 1876-1967 *NatCAB 53*
Phipps, Don Holcomb 1906-1970 *WhAm 5*
Phipps, Frank Huntington 1843-1925 *WhAm 1*
Phipps, G W *NewYHSD*
Phipps, Henry 1755-1831 *Drake*
Phipps, Henry 1839-1930 *AmBi, ApCAB X,*
 DcAmB, NatCAB 43, WhAm 1
Phipps, John Shaffer 1874-1958 *WhAm 3*
Phipps, Joseph Allen 1865-1951 *NatCAB 47*
Phipps, Lawrence Cowle 1862-1958 *ApCAB X,*
 BiDrAC, WhAm 3, WhAmP
Phipps, Luther James 1898-1969 *NatCAB 55*
Phipps, Mary Elizabeth Williams 1851-
 WomWWA 14
Phipps, Michael Grace 1910-1973 *WhAm 5*
Phipps, Sir William 1651-1695 *AmBi*
Phipps, William C *NewYHSD*
Phipps, William Wallace 1842-1914
 NatCAB 17
Phips, Spencer 1685-1757 *ApCAB, Drake*
Phips, Sir William 1650?-1694? *DcAmB*
Phips, Sir William 1650?-1695 *McGEWB*
Phips, Sir William 1651-1695 *AmBi, ApCAB,*
 Drake, NatCAB 6, WebAB, WebAMB,
 WhAm H
Phister, Elijah Conner 1822-1887 *BiDrAC,*
 WhAm H
Phister, Montgomery 1852- *WhAm 4*
Phisterer, Frederick 1836-1909 *DcAmB,*
 NatCAB 17
Phlegar, Archer A 1846-1912 *WhAm 1*

Phoebus, William 1754-1831 *ApCAB*
Phoenix, Charles E 1871- *WhAm 5*
Phoenix, J Phillips 1788-1859 *BiAUS*
Phoenix, John 1823-1861 *AmBi, DcAmB*
Phoenix, Jonas Phillips 1788-1859 *BiDrAC,*
 TwCBDA, WhAm H
Phoenix, Lloyd 1841-1926 *ApCAB X,*
 WhAm 1
Phoenix, Stephen Whitney 1839-1881 *ApCAB,*
 TwCBDA
Pholien, Joseph 1884-1968 *WhAm 4A*
Photius 820?-891 *McGEWB*
Phraner, Wilson 1822- *WhAm 4*
Phyfe, Duncan 1768-1854 *AmBi, BnEnAmA,*
 DcAmB, McGEWB, NatCAB 19,
 WebAB, WhAm H
Phyfe, William Henry Pinkney 1855-1915
 NatCAB 15, NatCAB 24, WhAm 1
Physic, Phillip Syng 1768-1837 *Drake*
Physick, Philip Syng 1768-1837 *AmBi, ApCAB,*
 BiDAmEd, BiHiMed, DcAmB,
 NatCAB 6, WhAm H
Physick, Philip Syng 1769-1837 *TwCBDA*
Physick, W *NewYHSD*
Phythian, Robert Lees 1835-1917 *NatCAB 13,*
 WhAm 1
Piaat, Sarah Morgan Bryan 1836- *WhAm 4*
Piaf, Edith 1915-1963 *WhAm 4*
Piaget, Jean 1896- *McGEWB*
Piane, John Michaeles 1890-1968 *NatCAB 53*
Pianese, Giuseppe 1864-1933 *DcScB,*
 DcScB Sup
Piankhi *McGEWB*
Piar, Manuel Carlos 1782-1817 *ApCAB*
Piasecki, Peter F 1876- *WhAm 5*
Piastro, Mishel 1892-1970 *WhAm 5*
Piatt, Abram Sanders 1821- *ApCAB,*
 TwCBDA
Piatt, Cecil 1878-1949 *NatCAB 39*
Piatt, Donn 1819-1891 *ApCAB, DcAmB,*
 NatCAB 13, TwCBDA, WhAm H,
 WhAmP
Piatt, Jacob Wykoff 1801-1857 *ApCAB*
Piatt, John Hooper 1781-1822 *ApCAB*
Piatt, John James 1835-1917 *ApCAB, DcAmB,*
 Drake, NatCAB 8, TwCBDA, WhAm 1
Piatt, Louise Kirby 1826-1864 *ApCAB*
Piatt, Sarah Morgan Bryan 1836-1919 *AmWom,*
 ApCAB, DcAmB, NatCAB 8, NotAW,
 TwCBDA, WomWWA 14
Piatti, Anthony *NewYHSD*
Piatti, Patrizio 1825-1888 *ApCAB Sup,*
 NewYHSD
Piazza, Ferdinand 1902-1968 *WhAm 5*
Piazzi, Giuseppe 1746-1826 *AsBiEn, DcScB*
Piazzoni, Gottardo 1872- *WhAm 5*
Pibul Songgram, Luang 1897-1964 *WhAm 4*
Picard, Charles Emile 1856-1941 *DcScB*
Picard, Frank A 1889-1963 *WhAm 4*
Picard, George Henry 1850-1916 *ApCAB,*
 TwCBDA, WhAm 1
Picard, Jean 1620-1682 *AsBiEn, DcScB*
Picard, Peter *NewYHSD*
Picard, Peter M, Jr. *NewYHSD*
Picard, Ralph Alan 1898-1952 *WhAm 3*
Picasso, Pablo Ruiz 1881-1973 *McGEWB,*
 WhAm 5
Piccard, Auguste 1884-1962 *AsBiEn, DcScB,*
 McGEWB
Piccard, Jean Felix 1884-1963 *NatCAB 47,*
 WebAB, WhAm 4
Picchi, Frederick *NewYHSD*
Piccirilli, Attilio 1868-1945 *WhAm 2*
Piccirilli, Furio 1868-1949 *ApCAB X,*
 WhAm 3
Piccolomini, Arcangelo 1525-1586 *DcScB*
Piccolomini, Ottavio 1599-1656 *WhoMilH*
Pichardo Y Tapia, Esteban 1799-1879 *ApCAB*
Pichegru, Charles 1761-1804 *WhoMilH*
Pichel, Irving 1891-1954 *WhAm 3*
Picher, Oliver Sheppard 1875-1920 *NatCAB 20*
Pichon, Thomas d1781 *Drake*
Pick, Albert 1869-1955 *NatCAB 43, WhAm 3*
Pick, Bernard 1842-1917 *TwCBDA*
Pick, Bernhard 1842-1917 *ApCAB,*
 NatCAB 10, WhAm 1
Pick, Lewis Andrew 1890-1956 *NatCAB 46,*
 WhAm 3

Pickands, Henry Sparks 1875-1929 *ApCAB X*
Pickands, James 1839-1896 *ApCAB X*
Pickard, Andrew Ezra 1878- *WhAm 6*
Pickard, Florence Willingham 1862-1930
 NatCAB 27, WhAm 1
Pickard, Frederick William 1871-1952 *WhAm 3*
Pickard, Greenleaf Whittier 1877-1956
 NatCAB 45, WhAm 3
Pickard, John 1858-1937 *NatCAB 27,*
 WhAm 1
Pickard, John Coleman 1900-1970 *NatCAB 57*
Pickard, Josiah Little 1824-1914 *BiDAmEd,*
 NatCAB 12, TwCBDA, WhAm 1
Pickard, Samuel Nelson 1897-1973 *WhAm 5*
Pickard, Samuel Thomas 1828-1915 *DcAmB,*
 TwCBDA, WhAm 1
Pickard, Ward Wilson 1878-1943 *WhAm 2*
Pickard, William Lowndes 1861-1935
 NatCAB 27, WhAm 1
Pickel, Adele Jackson *WomWWA 14*
Pickel, Frank Welborn 1864-1922 *WhAm 1*
Pickel, Margaret Barnard 1897-1955 *WhAm 3*
Pickell, Frank Gerald 1885-1936 *WhAm 1*
Pickells, Charles William 1874- *WhAm 5*
Picken, A *NewYHSD*
Picken, Andrew Belfrage 1802-1849 *ApCAB*
Picken, Joanna Belfrage 1798-1849 *ApCAB*
Picken, Lillian Hoxie 1856- *AmWom*
Picken, Lillian Hoxie 1857- *WhAm 4*
Picken, William Henry 1895-1947 *NatCAB 36*
Pickens, Andrew 1732-1817 *TwCBDA*
Pickens, Andrew 1739-1817 *AmBi, ApCAB,*
 BiAUS, BiDrAC, DcAmB, Drake,
 NatCAB 1, WebAMB, WhAm H
Pickens, Andrew 1779-1838 *Drake,*
 NatCAB 12, TwCBDA
Pickens, Andrew Calhoun 1881-1944
 NatCAB 33, WhAm 2
Pickens, Andrew Lee 1890-1969 *NatCAB 55*
Pickens, Charles Henry 1856-1923 *NatCAB 20*
Pickens, Ezekiel 1794-1860 *ApCAB Sup*
Pickens, Francis W 1807-1869 *BiAUS, Drake*
Pickens, Francis Wilkinson 1805-1869 *AmBi,*
 ApCAB, BiDConf, BiDrAC, DcAmB,
 NatCAB 12, TwCBDA, WhAm H
Pickens, Israel 1780-1827 *ApCAB, BiAUS,*
 BiDrAC, DcAmB, Drake, NatCAB 10,
 TwCBDA, WhAm H, WhAmP
Pickens, James Madison 1872- *WhAm 5*
Pickens, Lucy Petway Holcombe 1832-1899
 NotAW
Pickens, Minnie G McAlpine 1880- *WhoColR*
Pickens, Samuel O 1846- *WhAm 4*
Pickens, William 1881-1954 *DcAmB S5,*
 WhAm 3, WhoColR
Pickens, William Augustus *WhAm 1*
Picker, James 1882-1963 *NatCAB 50*
Pickerell, George Henry 1858- *WhAm 4*
Pickering, Abner 1854- *WhAm 4*
Pickering, Charles 1805-1878 *AmBi, ApCAB,*
 DcAmB, Drake, NatCAB 13, TwCBDA,
 WhAm H
Pickering, Charles Whipple 1815-1888 *ApCAB,*
 Drake, TwCBDA
Pickering, Edward Charles 1846-1919 *AmBi,*
 ApCAB, ApCAB X, AsBiEn, BiDAmEd,
 DcAmB, DcScB, McGEWB, NatCAB 6,
 TwCBDA, WebAB, WhAm 1
Pickering, Ernest 1893-1974 *WhAm 6*
Pickering, Henry 1781-1831 *ApCAB*
Pickering, Henry 1781-1838 *Drake*
Pickering, John 1737-1805 *ApCAB, BiAUS,*
 Drake, NatCAB 3, TwCBDA, WhAm H
Pickering, John 1738?-1805 *DcAmB*
Pickering, John 1777-1846 *AmBi, ApCAB,*
 DcAmB, Drake, NatCAB 7, TwCBDA,
 WhAm H
Pickering, Loring 1812-1892 *NatCAB 25*
Pickering, Loring 1888-1959 *NatCAB 48,*
 WhAm 3
Pickering, Octavius 1791-1868 *ApCAB*
Pickering, Octavius 1792-1868 *Drake*
Pickering, Sarah Maria 1858- *WomWWA 14*
Pickering, Timothy 1745-1829 *AmBi, ApCAB,*
 BiAUS, BiDrAC, BiDrUSE, DcAmB,
 Drake, EncAB, McGEWB, NatCAB 1,
 TwCBDA, WebAB, WebAMB, WhAm H,
 WhAmP

Pickering, W J 1878-1954 *NatCAB 45*
Pickering, William *BiAUS*
Pickering, William Alfred 1870-1930 *WhAm 1*
Pickering, William Henry 1858-1938 *AmBi,*
ApCAB, ApCAB X, AsBiEn, DcScB,
NatCAB 33, TwCBDA, WebAB,
WhAm 1
Picket, Albert 1771-1850 *BiDAmEd, DcAmB,*
WhAm H
Pickett, Albert James 1810-1858 *ApCAB,*
DcAmB, Drake, EncAAH, NatCAB 9,
WhAm H
Pickett, Bethel Stewart 1882-1975 *WhAm 6*
Pickett, Byron M *Drake*
Pickett, Charles Edgar 1866-1930 *BiDrAC,*
WhAm 1
Pickett, Charles Henry 1875- *WhoColR*
Pickett, Clarence Evan 1884-1965 *WhAm 4*
Pickett, Fermen Layton 1881-1940 *WhAm 1*
Pickett, George Edward 1825-1875 *AmBi,*
ApCAB, BiDConf, DcAmB, Drake,
NatCAB 5, TwCBDA, WebAB,
WebAMB, WhAm H, WhoMilH
Pickett, Hugh Dale 1900-1957 *WhAm 3*
Pickett, James C 1793-1872 *ApCAB, BiAUS*
Pickett, James Chamberlain 1795-1872
NatCAB 13
Pickett, James Chamberlayne 1793-1872
DcAmB, TwCBDA, WhAm H
Pickett, John C *BiAUS*
Pickett, John Erasmus 1885-1952 *WhAm 3*
Pickett, John T 182-?-189-? *BiDConf*
Pickett, Joseph 1848-1919 *BnEnAmA*
Pickett, Josiah 1822- *NatCAB 12*
Pickett, LaSalle Corbell 1848-1931 *WhAm 1,*
WomWWA 14
Pickett, Lasell Carbell 1848- *AmWom*
Pickett, Mary *WomWWA 14*
Pickett, Thomas Augustus 1906- *BiDrAC*
Pickett, Thomas Edward 1841-1913 *WhAm 1*
Pickett, Warren Wheeler 1895-1952 *WhAm 3*
Pickett, William *REnAW*
Pickett, William Clendenin 1870-1907 *WhAm 1*
Pickett, William Hiram 1916-1963 *NatCAB 52*
Pickford, Mary 1893- *WebAB*
Pickhardt, William Paul 1881-1941 *WhAm 1*
Pickil, Alexander d1840? *NewYHSD*
Picking, Henry Forry 1840-1899 *AmBi,*
ApCAB Sup, TwCBDA, WhAm 1
Pickle, George Wesley 1845- *WhAm 4*
Pickle, James Jarrell 1913- *BiDrAC*
Pickler, Alice M A 1848- *WomWWA 14*
Pickler, John Alfred 1844-1910 *BiDrAC,*
TwCBDA, WhAmP
Picklesimer, Hayes 1899-1969 *WhAm 5*
Pickman, Benjamin, Jr. 1763-1843 *BiAUS,*
BiDrAC, WhAm H
Pickman, Dudley Leavitt 1850-1938
NatCAB 39
Picknell, William Lamb 1853-1897 *AmBi,*
BnEnAmA, DcAmB, WhAm H
Picknell, William Lamb 1854-1897 *ApCAB,*
NatCAB 10, TwCBDA
Pickop, George Brooks 1875-1941 *NatCAB 33*
Pickrel, William Gillespie 1888-1966 *WhAm 4*
Pickrell, Homer P 1885-1971 *WhAm 5*
Pickrell, Maude Ingram 1880- *WomWWA 14*
Pickthall, Marjorie Lowry Christie
WomWWA 14
Pico DellaMirandola, Conte Giovanni 1463-1494
McGEWB
Picoff, Ronald Chester 1935-1974 *WhAm 6*
Picot *NewYHSD*
Picot, Louis Julien 1853-1924 *WhAm 1*
Picotte, Susan LaFlesche 1865-1915 *NotAW*
Picquet, Francois 1708-1781 *ApCAB,*
WhAm H
Pictet, Marc-Auguste 1752-1825 *DcScB*
Pictet, Raoul-Pierre 1846-1929 *AsBiEn, DcScB*
Picton, David Means, Jr. 1888-1951
NatCAB 40
Picton, John Moore White 1804-1858 *ApCAB*
Picton, Sir Thomas 1785-1815 *WhoMilH*
Picton, Thomas 1822-1891 *ApCAB, DcAmB,*
NatCAB 13, WhAm H
Pidansat DeMairobert, Mathieu Francois
1727-1779 *ApCAB*

Pidcock, Brian Morris Henzell 1930-1971
WhAm 6
Pidcock, James Nelson 1836-1899 *BiDrAC*
Piddock, Charles Albert 1849-1907 *NatCAB 7,*
WhAm 1
Pidge, John Bartholomew Gough 1844-
NatCAB 3, WhAm 4
Pidgin, Charles Felton 1844-1923 *AmBi,*
DcAmB, NatCAB 13, WhAm 1
Pieck, Wilhelm 1876-1960 *WhAm 4*
Piek, Stefaan 1876-1939 *NatCAB 29*
Piel, Michael 1849-1915 *ApCAB X*
Pielsticker, Fred Alonzo 1876-1931 *NatCAB 23*
Pienovi *NewYHSD*
Pieper, Emil G 1872-1938 *WhAm 1*
Pieper, Ezra H 1902-1950 *WhAm 3*
Pieper, Franz August Otto 1852-1931 *ApCAB,*
DcAmB, TwCBDA, WhAm 1
Pieper, John Jacob 1886-1939 *WhAm 1*
Pieper, William Charles 1910-1961 *WhAm 4*
Pier, Arthur Stanwood 1874-1966 *NatCAB 53,*
WhAm 4
Pier, Caroline Hamilton 1870- *AmWom*
Pier, Garrett Chatfield 1875-1943 *WhAm 2*
Pier, Harriet Hamilton 1872- *AmWom*
Pier, Kate Hamilton 1845-1925 *AmWom,*
NatCAB 21
Pier, Kate Hamilton 1868- *AmWom*
Pier, William Lauren Cook 1888-1964
NatCAB 50, WhAm 4
Pierce *NewYHSD*
Pierce, Albert Russell 1869-1948 *NatCAB 42*
Pierce, Alfred Mann 1874- *WhAm 5*
Pierce, Andrew Granville 1864-1950
NatCAB 39
Pierce, Anna Eloise d1956 *WhAm 3*
Pierce, Arthur Henry 1867-1914 *WhAm 1*
Pierce, Arthur Sylvanus 1875-1963 *WhAm 4*
Pierce, Benjamin 1757-1839 *BiAUS, DcAmB,*
Drake, NatCAB 3, NatCAB 11,
TwCBDA, WhAm H, WhAmP
Pierce, Benjamin 1759-1839 *AmBi*
Pierce, Benjamin 1809- *BiAUS*
Pierce, Bessie Louise 1888-1974 *WhAm 6*
Pierce, Byron Root 1829-1924 *ApCAB,*
TwCBDA, WhAm 1
Pierce, Carleton Custer 1877- *WhAm 5*
Pierce, Carlton Brownell 1857-1928
NatCAB 29
Pierce, Caroline Low 1848- *WomWWA 14*
Pierce, Charles Campbell 1858-1921
NatCAB 19
Pierce, Charles Franklin 1844-1920 *WhAm 1*
Pierce, Charles Milton 1916-1974 *WhAm 6*
Pierce, Charles Sumner 1874-1949 *WhAm 3*
Pierce, Charles Wilson 1823-1907 *BiAUS,*
BiDrAC
Pierce, Claude Connor 1878-1944 *WhAm 2*
Pierce, Clay Arthur 1873- *WhAm 5*
Pierce, Clifford Davis 1898-1974 *WhAm 6*
Pierce, Cornelia Marvin 1873-1957 *DcAmLiB*
Pierce, Daniel Thompson 1875- *WhAm 5*
Pierce, Dante Melville 1880-1955 *WhAm 3*
Pierce, David *NewYHSD*
Pierce, Earle Vaydor 1869- *WhAm 5*
Pierce, Edward Allen d1974 *WhAm 6*
Pierce, Edward Allen 1855-1948 *NatCAB 38*
Pierce, Edward Elisha 1856-1939 *NatCAB 29*
Pierce, Edward J d1974 *WhAm 6*
Pierce, Edward Lillie 1829-1897 *ApCAB,*
DcAmB, NatCAB 4, TwCBDA,
WhAm H
Pierce, Edward Lillie 1866-1954 *WhAm 3*
Pierce, Edward Peter 1852-1938 *WhAm 1*
Pierce, Elias Davidson 1824-1897 *REnAW*
Pierce, Elizabeth Cumings 1850- *AmWom*
Pierce, Flora McDonald *WomWWA 14*
Pierce, Florence K 1884- *WomWWA 14*
Pierce, Francis Marshal 1847- *WhAm 4*
Pierce, Frank 1857-1924 *ApCAB X,*
NatCAB 20
Pierce, Frank 1864- *WhAm 4*
Pierce, Frank Grainger 1904-1958 *NatCAB 48*
Pierce, Frank Reynolds 1901- *WhAm 3*
Pierce, Frank W 1893-1964 *WhAm 4*
Pierce, Franklin 1804-1869 *AmBi, ApCAB,*
BiAUS, BiDrAC, BiDrUSE, DcAmB,
Drake, EncAAH, EncAB, McGEWB,

NatCAB 4, TwCBDA, WebAB,
WhAm H, WhAmP
Pierce, Frederick Clifton 1856- *ApCAB,*
TwCBDA
Pierce, Frederick Clifton 1858- *NatCAB 10*
Pierce, Frederick Clifton 1859- *WhAm 1*
Pierce, Frederick Ernest 1878-1963 *WhAm 4*
Pierce, Frederick Louis 1860-1935 *WhAm 1*
Pierce, George Edmond 1794-1871 *ApCAB,*
Drake, TwCBDA
Pierce, George Edmund 1794-1871 *NatCAB 7*
Pierce, George Edwin 1887-1951 *WhAm 3*
Pierce, George Foster 1811-1884 *ApCAB,*
BiDConf, DcAmB, Drake, NatCAB 1,
NatCAB 5, TwCBDA, WhAm H
Pierce, George Warren 1889-1965 *WhAm 4*
Pierce, George Washington 1872-1956 *DcScB,*
WhAm 3
Pierce, George William 1908-1975 *WhAm 6*
Pierce, Gilbert Ashville d1901 *ApCAB Sup,*
NatCAB 1, TwCBDA
Pierce, Gilbert Ashville 1839-1901 *BiDrAC,*
DcAmB, WhAmP
Pierce, Gilbert Ashville 1841-1901 *WhAm 1*
Pierce, Grace Adele d1923 *WhAm 1,*
WomWWA 14
Pierce, Harold Marshall 1896-1961 *NatCAB 48*
Pierce, Hartell *NewYHSD*
Pierce, Helen Frances 1861- *WomWWA 14*
Pierce, Heman Winthrop 1850- *NatCAB 12*
Pierce, Henry A 1808- *NatCAB 5*
Pierce, Henry Clay d1927 *WhAm 1*
Pierce, Henry Clay 1840?-1927 *NatCAB 12*
Pierce, Henry Clay 1849-1927 *ApCAB X*
Pierce, Henry Douglas 1848-1929 *NatCAB 22*
Pierce, Henry Hill 1875-1940 *WhAm 1*
Pierce, Henry Lillie 1825-1896 *ApCAB,*
BiAUS, BiDrAC, DcAmB, NatCAB 4,
TwCBDA, WhAm H
Pierce, Henry Miller 1831-1902 *TwCBDA*
Pierce, Henry Niles 1820-1899 *ApCAB,*
NatCAB 5, TwCBDA, WhAm 1
Pierce, Imogene S *WomWWA 14*
Pierce, Jack Reed 1918-1965 *NatCAB 51*
Pierce, James Buchanan 1891-1943 *NatCAB 36*
Pierce, James Oscar 1836- *TwCBDA*
Pierce, Jane Means Appleton 1806-1863
AmWom, ApCAB, NatCAB 4, NotAW,
TwCBDA
Pierce, Jason Noble 1880-1948 *WhAm 2*
Pierce, John d1788 *Drake*
Pierce, John 1773-1849 *ApCAB, Drake*
Pierce, John Davis 1797-1882 *ApCAB,*
BiDAmEd, DcAmB, WhAm H
Pierce, John Robinson 1910- *AsBiEn*
Pierce, Joseph *BiAUS*
Pierce, Joseph Hart 1855-1932 *WhAm 1*
Pierce, Joshua *NewYHSD*
Pierce, Josiah, Jr. 1861-1902 *NatCAB 5,*
WhAm 1
Pierce, Lawrence Blunt 1859-1919 *WhAm 1*
Pierce, Leonard A 1885-1960 *WhAm 4*
Pierce, Lorne 1890-1961 *WhAm 4*
Pierce, Lovick 1785-1879 *ApCAB, TwCBDA*
Pierce, Lucy France 1877- *WomWWA 14*
Pierce, Lyman L 1868-1940 *WhAm 1*
Pierce, Marion Barnwell 1883-1953 *NatCAB 44*
Pierce, Martha 1873- *IIBEAAW*
Pierce, Marvin 1893-1969 *WhAm 5*
Pierce, Mary Rosetta Fitch *WomWWA 14*
Pierce, Newton Barris 1856-1917 *WhAm 1*
Pierce, Nicholas *NewYHSD*
Pierce, Norval Harvey 1863-1946 *WhAm 2*
Pierce, Oliver Willard 1869- *WhAm 5*
Pierce, Oscar Hawkes 1840-1916 *NatCAB 16*
Pierce, Palmer Eddy 1865-1940 *WhAm 1*
Pierce, Ray Vaughn 1840-1914 *BiDrAC,*
WhAm 4
Pierce, Raymond Clark 1887-1961 *NatCAB 49*
Pierce, Rice Alexander 1848-1936 *BiDrAC,*
WhAmP
Pierce, Rice Alexander 1849-1936 *TwCBDA,*
WhAm 4
Pierce, Richard Donald 1915-1973 *WhAm 6*
Pierce, Robert Fletcher Young 1852- *WhAm 4*
Pierce, Robert Layne 1901-1968 *NatCAB 54,*
WhAm 4A
Pierce, Roger 1882-1959 *WhAm 4*

Pierce, Sarah 1767-1852 *BiDAmEd, NotAW*
Pierce, Shanghai 1834-1900 *REnAW*
Pierce, Shelly 1898-1956 *WhAm 3*
Pierce, Sylvester P 1814- *NatCAB 3*
Pierce, Thomas Lewis 1877-1955 *NatCAB 42*
Pierce, Thomas Murray 1877-1954 *NatCAB 45*
Pierce, Ulrica Dahlgren *WomWWA 14*
Pierce, Ulysses Grant Baker 1865-1943
NatCAB 31, WhAm 2
Pierce, V Mott 1865-1942 *NatCAB 31*
Pierce, W Conway 1895-1974 *WhAm 6*
Pierce, W J *NewYHSD*
Pierce, Wallace Edgar 1881-1940 *BiDrAC,
NatCAB 29*
Pierce, Wallace Lincoln 1853-1920 *ApCAB X,
WhAm 1*
Pierce, Walter Marcus 1861-1954 *BiDrAC,
WhAm 3, WhAmP*
Pierce, Walworth 1877-1965 *NatCAB 54,
WhAm 4*
Pierce, William, Jr. *NewYHSD*
Pierce, William J *NewYHSD*
Pierce, William Kasson 1851 *NatCAB 14*
Pierce, William Kasson 1859- *WhAm 4*
Pierce, William Leigh 1740?- *BiAUS, Drake*
Pierce, William Leigh 1740?-1789 *BiDrAC,
DcAmB, TwCBDA, WhAm H*
Pierce, William Leigh 1740?-1806? *ApCAB,
NatCAB 7*
Pierce, William Oscar 1835- *TwCBDA*
Pierce, Winslow Shelby 1857-1938 *NatCAB 28,
WhAm 1*
Pierce, Winslow Smith 1819-1888 *ApCAB Sup*
Piercy, Esther June 1905-1967 *DcAmLiB*
Piercy, Frederick 1830-1891 *IIBEAAW,
NewYHSD*
Pieri, Louis Arthur Raymond 1897-1967
WhAm 4
Pieri, Mario 1860-1913 *DcScB*
Pierie, George Gorgas, Jr. 1873-1955
NatCAB 48
Pierie, William *NewYHSD*
Pieriot, Lucille Georgette 1928-1975 *WhAm 6*
Piero Della Francesca 1415?-1492 *DcScB,
McGEWB*
Pierola, Nicolas 1839- *ApCAB*
Pierola, Nicolas De 1798-1857 *ApCAB*
Pieron, Henri 1881-1964 *WhAm 4*
Pierpoint, John 1805-1882 *NatCAB 4*
Pierpont, Francis Harrison 1814-1899 *AmBi,
BiAUS, DcAmB, NatCAB 5,
NatCAB 35, REnAW, TwCBDA,
WhAm H*
Pierpont, Henry Edwards *WhAm 5*
Pierpont, James d1938 *WhAm 1*
Pierpont, James 1659?-1714 *DcAmB,
TwCBDA*
Pierpont, James 1660-1714 *WhAm H*
Pierpont, James 1661-1714 *NatCAB 1*
Pierpont, James 1866- *NatCAB 16*
Pierpont, John 1785-1866 *ApCAB, BiDAmEd,
DcAmB, Drake, NatCAB 6, WhAm H*
Pierpont, John 1805-1882 *ApCAB, TwCBDA*
Pierre *DcScB*
Pierre, LePicard 1624-1679 *ApCAB*
Pierrepont, Edward 1860-1885 *ApCAB*
Pierrepont, Edwards 1817-1892 *AmBi, ApCAB,
BiAUS, BiDrUSE, DcAmB, Drake,
NatCAB 4, TwCBDA, WhAm H*
Pierrepont, Henry Evelyn 1808-1888 *ApCAB,
NatCAB 5, NatCAB 20*
Pierrepont, Henry Evelyn, Jr. 1845-1911
NatCAB 23
Pierrepont, Hezekiah Beers 1768-1838 *ApCAB*
Pierrepont, James 1659-1714 *ApCAB*
Pierrepont, John Jay 1849-1923 *NatCAB 20*
Pierrepont, R Stuyvesant 1882-1950
NatCAB 41
Pierrepont, Robert Low 1876-1944 *WhAm 2*
Pierrepont, William Constable 1803-1885
ApCAB
Pierrie, William *NewYHSD*
Pierron, Jean *ApCAB*
Piers, Constance Fairbanks 1866-
WomWWA 14
Piersel, Alba Chambers 1867-1934 *WhAm 1*
Piersol, Florence Lukens 1865- *WomWWA 14*
Piersol, George Arthur 1856-1924 *NatCAB 33,*

WhAm 1
Piersol, George Morris 1880-1966 *WhAm 4*
Pierson, Abraham 1608-1678 *ApCAB*
Pierson, Abraham 1609-1678 *DcAmB,
WhAm H*
Pierson, Abraham 1641-1707 *ApCAB, Drake,
NatCAB 1*
Pierson, Abraham 1645?-1707 *BiDAmEd,
DcAmB, TwCBDA, WhAm H*
Pierson, Arthur Tappan 1837-1911 *DcAmB,
DcAmReB, NatCAB 13, TwCBDA,
WhAm 1*
Pierson, Bowen Whiting 1858-1907 *NatCAB 36*
Pierson, Charles Ernest 1906-1967 *WhAm 4*
Pierson, Charles Wheeler 1864-1934
NatCAB 26, WhAm 1
Pierson, Coen Gallatin 1901-1972 *WhAm 5*
Pierson, David Lawrence 1865-1938
NatCAB 28
Pierson, Delavan Leonard 1867-1938 *WhAm 1*
Pierson, Edward Donahue 1872- *WhoColR*
Pierson, Emily 1881- *WomWWA 14*
Pierson, Fanny Eaton *WomWWA 14*
Pierson, Farrand Baker 1876-1928 *ApCAB X*
Pierson, George Wilson 1904- *REnAW*
Pierson, Grace Rappleye 1879- *WomWWA 14*
Pierson, Hamilton Wilcox 1817-1888 *ApCAB,
DcAmB, Drake, TwCBDA, WhAm H*
Pierson, Henry Rufus 1819-1890 *ApCAB Sup,
TwCBDA*
Pierson, Isaac 1770-1833 *BiAUS, BiDrAC,
Drake, WhAm H*
Pierson, Isaac 1843-1919 *WhAm 1*
Pierson, Israel Coriell 1843-1908 *NatCAB 25,
WhAm 1*
Pierson, J Fred 1839-1932 *WhAm 1*
Pierson, Jeremiah Halsey 1766-1855 *BiAUS,
BiDrAC, WhAm H*
Pierson, Job 1791-1860 *BiAUS, BiDrAC,
WhAm H*
Pierson, John Frederick 1839-1932 *NatCAB 47*
Pierson, Lewis Eugene 1870-1954 *NatCAB 15,
WhAm 3*
Pierson, Margaret 1858- *WomWWA 14*
Pierson, Paul R B *NewYHSD*
Pierson, Philip Hale 1886-1946 *NatCAB 34*
Pierson, Romaine 1868-1932 *WhAm 1,
WhAm 1C*
Pierson, Sarah *NewYHSD*
Pierson, Silas Gilbert 1866-1946 *WhAm 2*
Pierson, Thomas B 1800-1866 *BiAUS*
Pierson, Thomas Haines 1873-1942 *NatCAB 31*
Pierson, William 1830-1900 *NatCAB 5,
WhAm 1*
Pierson, William 1871-1935 *NatCAB 28,
WhAm 1*
Pierson, William Montgomery 1842-1904
NatCAB 8
Pierson, William Whatley 1890-1966
NatCAB 51
Pierz, Franz 1785-1880 *DcAmB, WhAm H*
Pieters, Adrian John 1866-1940 *WhAm 1*
Pieters, Aleida Johanna 1876-1936 *WhAm 1*
Pietrafesa, Joseph John 1885-1968 *NatCAB 56*
Pietro, Cartaino DiSciarrino 1886-1918
WhAm 1
Pietsch, Karl 1860-1930 *WhAm 1*
Pietsch, Theodore Wells 1868-1930 *WhAm 1*
Piette, Louis-Edouard-Stanislas 1827-1906
DcScB
Piety, Charles Eberle 1898-1965 *NatCAB 52*
Piez, Charles 1866-1933 *DcAmB S1,
NatCAB 24, WhAm 1*
Pifer, Drury Augustus 1905-1971 *WhAm 5*
Piffard, Henry Granger 1842-1910 *WhAm 1*
Pigafetta, Francesco Antonio 1491-1535 *ApCAB*
Pigal *NewYHSD*
Pigalle *NewYHSD*
Pigeon, Richard 1882-1970 *WhAm 5*
Pigford, Albert Winfrey 1883-1942 *NatCAB 34*
Pigford, Clarence E 1873-1945 *WhAm 2*
Piggot, Charles Snowden 1892-1973 *WhAm 6*
Piggot, Robert 1795-1887 *ApCAB, DcAmB,
NewYHSD, WhAm H*
Piggott, James 1739?-1799 *DcAmB, WhAm H*
Pigman, George Wood 1843-1920 *WhAm 1*
Pigot *NewYHSD*
Pigot, Sir Robert 1720-1796 *ApCAB, Drake*

Pigott, Edward 1753-1825 *DcScB*
Pigott, James M 1894-1969 *WhAm 5*
Pigott, James Protus 1852-1919 *BiDrAC*
Pigott, John Thomas 1885-1965 *WhAm 4*
Pigott, Nathaniel d1804 *DcScB*
Pigott, Paul 1900-1961 *WhAm 4*
Pigott, William 1860-1929 *NatCAB 23*
Pigott, William, Jr. 1895-1947 *NatCAB 36*
Pigott, William Trigg 1861-1944 *WhAm 2*
Pigou, Arthur Cecil 1877-1959 *McGEWB*
Piguet, Leon A 1894-1962 *WhAm 4*
Pihlblad, Ernst Frederick 1873-1943 *WhAm 2*
Pike, Albert 1809-1891 *AmBi, ApCAB,
DcAmB, Drake, NatCAB 1, REnAW,
TwCBDA, WebAB, WebAMB, WhAm H*
Pike, Austin Franklin 1819-1886 *ApCAB,
BiAUS, BiDrAC, NatCAB 10, TwCBDA,
WhAm H*
Pike, Charles Burrall 1871-1941 *WhAm 2*
Pike, Charles Joseph 1866-1931 *NatCAB 24*
Pike, Chester Lincoln 1867-1936 *NatCAB 37*
Pike, Clayton Warren 1866-1938 *WhAm 1*
Pike, Douglas Henry 1908-1974 *WhAm 6*
Pike, Eva Frances 1857- *WomWWA 14*
Pike, Frances West Atherton 1819- *ApCAB,
Drake*
Pike, Frank Henry 1876-1953 *NatCAB 42,
WhAm 3*
Pike, Frederick Augustus d1886 *BiAUS*
Pike, Frederick Augustus 1816-1886 *BiDrAC,
WhAm H*
Pike, Frederick Augustus 1817-1886 *ApCAB,
NatCAB 11, TwCBDA*
Pike, Gordon Brainerd 1865-1925 *NatCAB 24*
Pike, Granville Ross 1856- *WhAm 4*
Pike, H Harvey 1887-1973 *WhAm 6*
Pike, Harry Hale 1874- *WhAm 5*
Pike, James 1818-1895 *BiAUS, BiDrAC,
WhAm H*
Pike, James Albert 1913-1969 *DcAmReB,
NatCAB 56, WhAm 5*
Pike, James Shepherd 1811-1882 *ApCAB,
BiAUS, DcAmB, NatCAB 11, TwCBDA,
WhAm H*
Pike, Joseph *NewYHSD*
Pike, Joseph Brown 1866- *WhAm 4*
Pike, Maria Louisa d1892 *TwCBDA*
Pike, Mary H 1827-1908 *Drake*
Pike, Mary Hayden Green 1824-1908 *DcAmB,
NotAW*
Pike, Mary Hayden Green 1825-1908 *ApCAB*
Pike, Nicholas 1743-1819 *BiDAmEd, Drake*
Pike, Nicholas 1818-1905 *NatCAB 24*
Pike, Nicolas 1743-1819 *DcAmB, NatCAB 20,
WhAm H*
Pike, Otis Grey 1921- *BiDrAC*
Pike, Percy Mortimer 1882-1963 *NatCAB 50,
WhAm 4*
Pike, Robert 1616?-1708 *DcAmB, WhAm H*
Pike, Robert Dickson 1855-1955 *NatCAB 46*
Pike, Robert Gordon 1822-1898 *NatCAB 24*
Pike, Robert Gordon 1851-1917 *NatCAB 19,
WhAm 1*
Pike, S *NewYHSD*
Pike, Sumner Tucker 1891-1976 *WhAm 6*
Pike, William Allen 1858-1927 *NatCAB 21*
Pike, William John 1864-1923 *WhAm 1*
Pike, Zebulon Montgomery 1779-1813 *AmBi,
ApCAB, BiAUS, DcAmB, Drake,
EncAAH, McGEWB, NatCAB 2,
REnAW, TwCBDA, WebAB, WebAMB,
WhAm H*
Pilat, Carl Francis 1876- *NatCAB 15,
WhAm 5*
Pilat, Ignatz Anton 1820-1870 *ApCAB*
Pilat, Ignaz Anton 1820-1870 *DcAmB,
NatCAB 15, WhAm H*
Pilatre DeRozier, Jean Francois 1754-1785
DcScB
Pilbrow, Edward *NewYHSD*
Pilcher, Cobb 1904-1949 *NatCAB 38*
Pilcher, Elijah Homes 1810-1887 *ApCAB*
Pilcher, James Evelyn 1857-1911 *WhAm 1*
Pilcher, James Taft 1880-1947 *NatCAB 36,
WhAm 2*
Pilcher, John Leonard 1898- *BiDrAC,
WhAmP*
Pilcher, Joshua 1790-1843 *DcAmB, REnAW,*

WhAm H

Pilcher, Lewis Frederick d1941 *WhAm 1*
Pilcher, Lewis Stephen 1845-1934 *DcAmB S1,
NatCAB 32, WhAm 1*
Pilcher, Paul Monroe 1876-1917 *DcAmB*
Pile, William Anderson 1829-1889 *ApCAB,
BiAUS, BiDrAC, NatCAB 11, TwCBDA,
WhAm H*
Piles, Samuel Henry 1858-1940 *BiDrAC,
NatCAB 14, WhAm 1, WhAmP*
Pilgrim, Charles Winfield 1855-1934
NatCAB 25, WhAm 4
Pilgrim, James *NewYHSD*
Pilie, J *NewYHSD*
Pilkington, Adam 1810-1856 *NewYHSD*
Pilkington, James 1851-1929 *DcAmB*
Pilkington, James E *NewYHSD*
Pillars, Charles Adrian 1870-1937 *NatCAB 34,
WhAm 1*
Pillemer, Louis 1908-1957 *WhAm 3*
Pilliner, C A *NewYHSD*
Pilliner, Frederick J *NewYHSD*
Pilling, George Platt 1891-1943 *NatCAB 33*
Pilling, James Constantine 1846-1895 *AmBi,
ApCAB, ApCAB X, DcAmB,
NatCAB 15, TwCBDA, WhAm H*
Pilliod, Thomas Joseph 1887-1962 *NatCAB 49*
Pillion, John Raymond 1904- *BiDrAC,
WhAmP*
Pillmore, Joseph 1734?-1825 *Drake*
Pillner, George *NewYHSD*
Pillow, George *NewYHSD*
Pillow, Gideon Johnson 1806-1878 *AmBi,
ApCAB, DcAmB, Drake, NatCAB 9,
TwCBDA, WebAMB, WhAm H*
Pillsbury, Albert Enoch 1849-1930 *NatCAB 11,
WhAm 1*
Pillsbury, Alfred Fiske 1869-1950 *WhAm 3*
Pillsbury, Amos 1805-1873 *ApCAB*
Pillsbury, Amos *see also* Pilsbury, Amos
Pillsbury, Arthur Judson 1854-1937 *WhAm 1*
Pillsbury, Arthur Low 1869-1925 *NatCAB 20*
Pillsbury, Charles Alfred 1842-1899
*ApCAB Sup, DcAmB, EncAAH,
McGEWB, WebAB, WhAm H, WhAm 1*
Pillsbury, Charles Lucien 1872-1959
NatCAB 44
Pillsbury, Charles Stinson 1878-1939
NatCAB 30, WhAm 1
Pillsbury, Edwin S 1867-1955 *WhAm 4*
Pillsbury, Eleanor Bellows 1913-1971 *WhAm 5*
Pillsbury, Evans Searle 1843- *WhAm 4*
Pillsbury, George Alfred 1816-1898
ApCAB Sup, NatCAB 13
Pillsbury, George Bigelow 1876-1951
NatCAB 39, WhAm 5
Pillsbury, Harriette Brown 1871-1957 *WhAm 3*
Pillsbury, Harry Nelson 1872-1906 *AmBi,
DcAmB, NatCAB 13, WhAm 1*
Pillsbury, Henry Church 1881-1955 *NatCAB 48,
WhAm 3*
Pillsbury, Horace Davis 1873-1940 *NatCAB 31,
WhAm 1*
Pillsbury, John Elliott 1846-1919 *DcAmB,
NatCAB 20, WhAm 1*
Pillsbury, John Henry 1846-1910 *WhAm 1*
Pillsbury, John Sargent 1828-1901 *AmBi,
ApCAB Sup, DcAmB, NatCAB 10,
TwCBDA, WhAm 1, WhAmP*
Pillsbury, John Sargent 1878-1968 *NatCAB 54,
WhAm 5*
Pillsbury, Nelle Pendleton Winston 1878-
WomWWA 14
Pillsbury, Oliver 1817-1888 *ApCAB*
Pillsbury, Parker 1809-1898 *AmBi, ApCAB,
DcAmB, NatCAB 2, TwCBDA,
WhAm H*
Pillsbury, Rosecrans W 1863- *WhAm 1*
Pillsbury, Tom G 1915?- *IlBEAAW*
Pillsbury, Walter Bowers 1872-1960 *BiDAmEd,
NatCAB 15, NatCAB 44, WhAm 4,
WhAm 5*
Pillsbury, William Howard 1880-1953 *WhAm 3*
Pilmore, Joseph 1739-1825 *ApCAB, DcAmB,
WhAm H*
Pilon, Germain 1535?-1590 *McGEWB*
Pilsbry, Henry Augustus 1862-1957
NatCAB 47, WhAm 3

Pilsbury, Amos 1805-1873 *DcAmB, WhAm H*
Pilsbury, Amos *see also* Pillsbury, Amos
Pilsbury, Timothy 1789-1858 *BiAUS, BiDrAC,
WhAm H*
Pilsudski, Joseph 1867-1935 *McGEWB,
WhoMilH*
Pilsworth, Malcolm Nevil 1894-1965 *WhAm 4*
Pilzer, Maximilian 1890-1958 *WhAm 3*
Pim, Bedford Clapperton Trevelyan 1826-1886
ApCAB
Pim, Louis Tousard 1828-1888 *NatCAB 12*
Pim, W Paul 1885-1950 *WhAm 3*
Pimat, P Mignon *NewYHSD*
Pimentel, Manoel 1650-1719 *ApCAB*
Pimsleur, Solomon 1900-1962 *NatCAB 46*
Pina, Ramon 1819-1861 *ApCAB*
Pinanski, Abraham Edward 1887-1949
WhAm 2
Pinanski, Samuel 1893-1972 *WhAm 5*
Pinchback, Pinckney Benton Stewart 1837-1921
ApCAB, DcAmB, TwCBDA, WhAm 1
Pinchbeck, Raymond Bennett 1900-1957
WhAm 3
Pincheira, Jose Antonio 1801?-1850? *ApCAB*
Pincherle, Salvatore 1853-1936 *DcScB*
Pinchot, Amos Richards Eno 1873-1944
DcAmB S3, NatCAB 32, WhAm 2
Pinchot, Cornelia Bryce 1881-1960 *WhAm 4*
Pinchot, Gifford 1865-1946 *ApCAB X,
DcAmB S4, EncAAH, EncAB, McGEWB,
NatCAB 11, NatCAB 14, NatCAB 36,
REnAW, TwCBDA, WebAB, WhAm 2*
Pinchot, James Wallace 1831-1908 *ApCAB X,
WhAm 1*
Pinckard, Harold Recenus 1897-1972 *WhAm 5*
Pinckard, James Steptoe 1859-1926 *NatCAB 30*
Pinckard, William Henderson 1893-1957
NatCAB 52
Pinckney, Camilla Scott *WomWWA 14*
Pinckney, Charles 1757-1824 *AmBi, BiDrAC,
DcAmB, McGEWB, WebAB, WhAm H,
WhAmP*
Pinckney, Charles 1758-1824 *ApCAB, BiAUS,
Drake, NatCAB 12, TwCBDA*
Pinckney, Charles Cotesworth 1745-1825
McGEWB
Pinckney, Charles Cotesworth 1746-1825 *AmBi,
ApCAB, BiAUS, DcAmB, Drake,
NatCAB 2, TwCBDA, WebAB,
WhAm H, WhAmP*
Pinckney, Charles Cotesworth 1812- *ApCAB*
Pinckney, Charles Cotesworth 1812-1898
TwCBDA
Pinckney, Charles Cotesworth 1812-1899
WhAm 1
Pinckney, Eliza Lucas 1722?-1793 *AmBi*
Pinckney, Elizabeth Lucas 1722?-1793 *DcAmB,
NotAW, WhAm H*
Pinckney, Elizabeth Lucas 1723?-1793 *EncAB*
Pinckney, Francis Douglas 1900-1974 *WhAm 6*
Pinckney, Henry Laurens 1794-1863 *ApCAB,
BiAUS, BiDrAC, DcAmB, Drake,
NatCAB 11, WhAm H, WhAmP*
Pinckney, John Adams 1905-1972 *WhAm 5*
Pinckney, John McPherson 1845-1905 *BiDrAC*
Pinckney, Josephine Lyons Scott 1895-1957
WhAm 3
Pinckney, Merritt Willis 1859-1920 *NatCAB 19,
WhAm 1*
Pinckney, Thomas 1750-1828 *AmBi, ApCAB,
BiAUS, BiDrAC, DcAmB, Drake,
NatCAB 12, TwCBDA, WebAB,
WhAm H, WhAmP*
Pincus, Gregory Goodwin 1903-1967 *AsBiEn,
DcScB, WhAm 4*
Pindall, James 1783?-1825 *BiAUS, BiDrAC,
WhAm H*
Pindall, Xenophon Overton 1873-1935 *WhAm 1*
Pindar 522?BC-438BC *McGEWB*
Pindar, John Hothersall 1794-1868 *ApCAB*
Pindar, John Sigsbee 1835-1907 *BiDrAC*
Pindar, Susan 1820?- *ApCAB*
Pindell, Henry Means 1860-1924 *ApCAB X,
NatCAB 18, WhAm 1*
Pindell, Richard d1833 *NatCAB 18*
Pine, David Andrew 1891-1970 *WhAm 5*
Pine, Frank Woodworth 1869-1919 *WhAm 1*
Pine, James *NewYHSD*

Pine, James 1885-1953 *WhAm 3*
Pine, James K P 1841- *NatCAB 3*
Pine, John B 1857-1922 *WhAm 1*
Pine, Mabel Edna Durand 1874-
WomWWA 14
Pine, Robert Edge 1730?-1788 *ApCAB,
BnEnAmA, DcAmB, NewYHSD,
WhAm H*
Pine, Robert Edge 1742-1788 *Drake*
Pine, Theodore E 1828-1905 *NewYHSD*
Pine, William Bliss 1877-1942 *BiDrAC,
NatCAB 40, WhAmP*
Pineda, Juan De 1520?-1606 *ApCAB*
Pinel, Jacques 1640-1693 *ApCAB*
Pinel, Philippe 1745-1826 *AsBiEn, BiHiMed,
DcScB, McGEWB*
Pinelo, Antonio DeLeon 1589-1675? *ApCAB*
Piner, Robert T 1889-1958 *NatCAB 49*
Pinero, Jesus T 1897-1952 *BiDrAC, WhAm 3,
WhAmP*
Pinero Jimenez, Jesus Toribio 1897-1952
DcAmB S5
Piness, George 1891-1970 *WhAm 5*
Pineyro, Enrique 1839- *ApCAB*
Pingre, Alexandre-Gui 1711-1796 *DcScB*
Pingree, Edwin Daniel 1862-1933 *NatCAB 27*
Pingree, George Elmer 1876- *WhAm 6*
Pingree, Harriet Cummings Blake 1859-
WomWWA 14
Pingree, Hazen S 1840-1901 *ApCAB Sup,
NatCAB 7, WhAm 1*
Pingree, Hazen Smith 1840-1901 *TwCBDA*
Pingree, Hazen Stuart 1840-1901 *DcAmB,
EncAAH*
Pingree, James 1862-1924 *NatCAB 6*
Pingree, Samuel Everett 1832-1922 *ApCAB,
NatCAB 8, TwCBDA, WhAm 1*
Pingry, William Morrill 1806-1885 *ApCAB Sup*
Pinheiro, Don J 1870- *WhoColR*
Pinheiro, Sylvestre Ferreira, Marquis De
1769-1847 *ApCAB*
Pinillos, Claudio M De 1782-1853 *ApCAB*
Pink, Charlotte 1896-1973 *WhAm 6*
Pink, Louis Heaton 1882-1955 *WhAm 3*
Pinkard, Maceo 1897-1962 *NatCAB 48*
Pinkerton, Alfred S 1856-1922 *NatCAB 6*
Pinkerton, Allan 1819-1884 *AmBi, ApCAB,
DcAmB, EncAB, McGEWB, NatCAB 3,
TwCBDA, WebAB, WhAm H*
Pinkerton, E J *NewYHSD*
Pinkerton, Kathrene 1887-1967 *WhAm 4A*
Pinkerton, Lewis Letig 1812-1875 *DcAmB,
WhAm H*
Pinkerton, Lowell Call 1894-1959 *WhAm 3*
Pinkerton, Robert Allan, II 1904-1967
NatCAB 53
Pinkerton, Roy David 1885-1974 *WhAm 6*
Pinkerton, William Allan 1846-1923 *WhAm 1*
Pinkett, Harold Thomas 1914- *EncAAH*
Pinkham, Isabelle Foote 1872- *WomWWA 14*
Pinkham, Lucile Deen 1904-1960 *WhAm 4*
Pinkham, Lucius Eugene 1850-1922
NatCAB 17, WhAm 1
Pinkham, Lydia Estes 1819-1883 *AmBi,
DcAmB, NotAW, WebAB, WhAm H*
Pinkham, Spencer 1902-1969 *NatCAB 55*
Pinkham, Wenona Osborne 1882-1930
ApCAB X
Pinkham, William Cyprian 1844- *ApCAB*
Pinkley, Roy H 1877- *WhAm 6*
Pinkney, Charles 1797-1835 *NatCAB 13*
Pinkney, Edward Coate 1802-1828 *ApCAB,
Drake, NatCAB 6*
Pinkney, Edward Coote 1802-1828 *AmBi,
DcAmB, WhAm H*
Pinkney, Edward J *NewYHSD*
Pinkney, Frederick 1804-1873 *ApCAB,
NatCAB 6*
Pinkney, Ninian 1771-1825 *NatCAB 8*
Pinkney, Ninian 1776-1825 *ApCAB*
Pinkney, Ninian 1811-1877 *ApCAB, DcAmB,
WhAm H*
Pinkney, Samuel J *NewYHSD*
Pinkney, William 1764-1822 *AmBi, ApCAB,
BiAUS, BiDrAC, BiDrUSE, DcAmB,
Drake, NatCAB 5, TwCBDA, WebAB,
WhAm H, WhAmP*
Pinkney, William 1810-1883 *ApCAB,*

NatCAB 6, TwCBDA

Pinn, James Luther 1877- *WhoColR*
Pinnell, Emmett Louis 1915- *WhAm 5*
Pinnell, Leroy Kenneth d1972 *WhAm 5*
Pinneo, Dotha Stone d1924 *WhAm 1, WomWWA 14*
Pinner, Max 1851-1887 *WhAm H*
Pinner, Max 1891-1948 *NatCAB 37, WhAm 2*
Pinney, E Jay 1847- *WhAm 4*
Pinney, Eunice Griswold 1770-1849 *BnEnAmA, NewYHSD, NotAW*
Pinney, George Miller, Jr. 1856- *WhAm 4*
Pinney, Harry Bowman 1875- *WhAm 5*
Pinney, Nelson James 1906-1967 *NatCAB 57*
Pinney, Norman 1800-1862 *ApCAB, NatCAB 5*
Pinney, Norman 1804-1862 *BiDAmEd, DcAmB, WhAm H*
Pino, Jose 1866-1954 *DcAmB S5*
Pinoli, Signor A *NewYHSD*
Pinski, David 1872- *WhAm 5*
Pinson, William Washington 1854-1930 *WhAm 1*
Pinsonneault, Peter Adolphus 1815-1883 *ApCAB Sup*
Pint, Joseph *NewYHSD*
Pintard, John 1759-1844 *ApCAB, DcAmB, Drake, NatCAB 3, TwCBDA, WhAm H*
Pintard, Lewis 1732-1818 *ApCAB, DcAmB, WhAm H*
Pinten, Joseph Gabriel 1867-1945 *WhAm 2*
Pinter, Harold 1930- *McGEWB*
Pintner, Rudolf 1884-1942 *WhAm 2*
Pinto, Alva Sherman 1872-1944 *WhAm 2*
Pinto, Anibal 1824-1884 *ApCAB*
Pinto, Bento Teixeira d1610? *ApCAB*
Pinto, Francisco Antonio 1785?-1858 *ApCAB*
Pinto, Isaac 1720-1791 *DcAmB, McGEWB, WhAm H*
Pinto, Salvatore 1905-1966 *WhAm 4*
Pinza, Ezio 1892-1957 *NatCAB 46, WhAm 3*
Pinzon, Arias Martin 1465-1510 *ApCAB*
Pinzon, Francisco Martin 1462?-1500 *ApCAB*
Pinzon, Martin Alonso 1441-1493 *ApCAB*
Pinzon, Martin Alonzo 1441-1493 *Drake*
Pinzon, Vicente Yanez 1460?-1524? *ApCAB*
Pinzon, Vincenzio Yanez 1460?-1524? *Drake*
Piotrowska, Helena 1873- *WomWWA 14*
Piper, Alexander Ross 1865-1952 *WhAm 3*
Piper, Arthur 1845- *WhAm 4*
Piper, Charles Vancouver 1867-1926 *DcAmB, EncAAH, WhAm 1*
Piper, Edgar Bramwell 1865-1928 *WhAm 1*
Piper, Edwin Ford 1871-1939 *WhAm 1*
Piper, Elizabeth Bridge 1883- *WomWWA 14*
Piper, Fred LeRoy 1858-1940 *WhAm 4*
Piper, Henry 1840-1914 *NatCAB 16*
Piper, Horace L 1842- *WhAm 4*
Piper, James 1874-1965 *WhAm 4*
Piper, Jonathan 1885-1951 *NatCAB 42*
Piper, Leonore Evelina Simonds 1859-1950 *NotAW*
Piper, Lewis Allie 1897-1971 *NatCAB 57*
Piper, Margaret Rebecca 1879- *WhAm 6, WomWWA 14*
Piper, Ralph Crosby 1890-1963 *NatCAB 50*
Piper, Raymond F 1888-1962 *WhAm 4*
Piper, Richard Upton 1818- *ApCAB*
Piper, William 1774-1852 *BiAUS, BiDrAC, WhAm H*
Piper, William A 1825-1899 *BiAUS*
Piper, William Adam 1826-1899 *BiDrAC*
Piper, William Scott 1882-1937 *NatCAB 30*
Piper, William Thomas 1881-1970 *NatCAB 56, WhAm 5*
Pipes, Louis A 1910-1971 *WhAm 5*
Pipes, Martin Luther 1850-1932 *WhAm 1*
Pipkin, Charles Wooten 1899-1941 *WhAm 1*
Pipkin, Hermon Clyde 1886-1949 *NatCAB 40*
Pippenger, Wayne Grise 1906-1975 *WhAm 6*
Pippett, Roger 1895-1963 *WhAm 4*
Pippin, Horace 1888-1946 *DcAmB S4, McGEWB*
Pipping, Hugo Edvard 1895-1975 *WhAm 6*
Piquenard, Alfred H d1876 *WhAm H*
Pirandello, Luigi 1867-1936 *McGEWB*
Piranesi, Giovanni Battista 1720-1778 *McGEWB*

Pirani, Eugenio Di 1852- *WhAm 4*
Pirazzini, Agide 1875-1934 *WhAm 1, WhAm 1C*
Pirce, William Almy 1824-1891 *BiDrAC, NatCAB 11, WhAm H*
Pire, Dominique Georges 1910-1969 *WhAm 5*
Pirelli, Alberto 1882-1971 *WhAm 5*
Pirenne, Jean Henri Otto Lucien Marie 1862-1935 *McGEWB*
Pires, Francisco 1520?-1586 *ApCAB*
Pires, Tome 1470?-1540? *DcScB*
Piri Rais, Muhyi Al-Din 1470-1554 *DcScB*
Pirie, Emma Elizabeth d1951 *WhAm 3*
Pirie, Frederick W 1893-1956 *WhAm 3*
Pirie, Gordon Lennox 1880-1944 *NatCAB 33*
Pirie, John Taylor 1871-1940 *WhAm 1*
Pirie, John Thomas 1827- *NatCAB 7*
Pirie, Samuel Carson 1864-1938 *WhAm 1*
Pirkey, Everett Leighton 1915-1963 *WhAm 4*
Pirkey, Henry Warren, Jr. 1907-1972 *WhAm 6*
Pirkey, Russell Johnson 1883-1925 *NatCAB 21*
Pirkle, Lewis Henry 1873-1948 *NatCAB 38*
Pirnie, Alexander 1903- *BiDrAC*
Pirogoff, Nikolai Ivanovich 1810-1881 *BiHiMed*
Pirogov, Nikolay Ivanovich 1810-1881 *DcScB*
Pirquet, Clemens Freiherr Von 1874- *WhAm 5*
Pirroli *NewYHSD*
Pirrson, James W *NewYHSD*
Pirsch, Peter 1866-1954 *NatCAB 40*
Pirsson, James W 1833-1888 *WhAm H*
Pirsson, Louis Valentine 1860-1919 *BiDAmEd, DcAmB, NatCAB 10, NatCAB 28, WhAm 1*
Pirtle, Henry 1798-1880 *ApCAB, NatCAB 10*
Pirtle, James Speed 1840- *WhAm 1*
Pisanello 1395?-1455 *McGEWB*
Pisani, C *NewYHSD*
Pisani, F *NewYHSD*
Pisano *DcScB*
Pisar, Charles Juneau 1890-1955 *WhAm 3*
Piscator, Erwin 1893-1966 *WhAm 4*
Pise, Charles Constantine 1801-1866 *DcAmB, WhAm H*
Pise, Charles Constantine 1802-1866 *ApCAB, Drake, TwCBDA*
Pise, Lewis *NewYHSD*
Piser, Alfred Lionel 1909-1974 *WhAm 6*
Pishbourne *NewYHSD*
Pishtey, Joseph Josephson 1899-1972 *WhAm 5*
Piskaret, Simon 1602-1646 *ApCAB*
Piso, Willem 1611?-1678 *DcScB*
Pison, Willem 1596-1681 *ApCAB*
Pison, William 1596-1681 *Drake*
Pissarro, Camille 1830-1903 *McGEWB*
Pistole, Martha Harris 1865- *WomWWA 14*
Piston, Walter Hamor 1894- *McGEWB, WebAB*
Pitalesharo 1787?-1832? *REnAW*
Pitaval, John Baptist 1858-1928 *NatCAB 15, WhAm 1*
Pitblado, Euphemia Wilson *AmWom*
Pitcairn, Archibald 1652-1713 *DcScB*
Pitcairn, Harold Frederick 1897-1960 *WhAm 4*
Pitcairn, Hugh 1845-1911 *NatCAB 21*
Pitcairn, John d1775 *Drake*
Pitcairn, John 1722-1775 *AmBi, DcAmB, WhAm H*
Pitcairn, John 1740?-1775 *ApCAB*
Pitcairn, John 1841-1916 *DcAmB, NatCAB 16*
Pitcairn, Norman Bruce 1881-1948 *WhAm 2*
Pitcairn, Raymond 1885-1966 *WhAm 4*
Pitcairn, Robert 1836-1909 *NatCAB 11, WhAm 1*
Pitcher, Charles Sidney 1874- *WhAm 5*
Pitcher, Ethelwyn *WomWWA 14*
Pitcher, James Robertson 1845- *NatCAB 2*
Pitcher, Mary Merrill 1856- *WomWWA 14*
Pitcher, Molly 1744-1823 *NatCAB 9, TwCBDA*
Pitcher, Molly 1754-1832 *AmBi, DcAmB, NotAW, WebAB, WhAm H*
Pitcher, Nathaniel 1777-1836 *ApCAB, BiAUS, BiDrAC, NatCAB 3, TwCBDA, WhAm H*
Pitcher, Thomas Gamble 1824-1895 *ApCAB, Drake, NatCAB 13, TwCBDA*
Pitcher, William Leonard 1871-1954 *NatCAB 48*

Pitcher, Zina 1797-1872 *ApCAB, DcAmB, NatCAB 12, WhAm H*
Pitchford, John Henry 1857-1923 *NatCAB 20, WhAm 1*
Pitchlynn, Peter Perkins 1806-1881 *ApCAB, DcAmB, WhAm H*
Pitfield, Robert Lucas 1870- *WhAm 5*
Pitiscus, Bartholomeo 1561-1613 *DcScB*
Pitkin, Edith Winifred 1877- *WomWWA 14*
Pitkin, Francis Alexander 1899-1969 *WhAm 5*
Pitkin, Frederick Walker 1837-1886 *ApCAB, DcAmB, NatCAB 6, TwCBDA, WhAm H, WhAmP*
Pitkin, George 1709-1806 *ApCAB*
Pitkin, George Philo 1885-1943 *NatCAB 34*
Pitkin, John 1707-1790 *ApCAB*
Pitkin, John Robert Graham 1841-1901 *NatCAB 11*
Pitkin, Joseph 1696-1762 *ApCAB*
Pitkin, Robert James 1864-1957 *NatCAB 43*
Pitkin, Stephen Henderson 1860-1933 *NatCAB 35*
Pitkin, Timothy 1727-1812 *ApCAB*
Pitkin, Timothy 1765-1847 *BiAUS*
Pitkin, Timothy 1766-1847 *AmBi, ApCAB, BiDrAC, DcAmB, Drake, NatCAB 11, TwCBDA, WhAm H, WhAmP*
Pitkin, Walter Boughton 1878-1953 *DcAmB S5, WebAB, WhAm 3*
Pitkin, William 1635-1694 *ApCAB, DcAmB, WhAm H*
Pitkin, William 1664-1723 *ApCAB, BiAUS, Drake*
Pitkin, William 1694-1769 *ApCAB, BiAUS, DcAmB, Drake, NatCAB 10, TwCBDA, WhAm H*
Pitkin, William 1725-1789 *ApCAB, DcAmB, TwCBDA, WhAm H*
Pitkin, William Roger 1877-1938 *NatCAB 29*
Pitkin, William Taft 1867-1949 *NatCAB 38*
Pitkin, Wolcott H 1881-1954 *WhAm 3*
Pitman, Annie Maria 1874- *WomWWA 14*
Pitman, Benn 1822-1910 *AmBi, ApCAB, BiDAmEd, DcAmB, NatCAB 4, TwCBDA, WhAm 1*
Pitman, Charles Wesley d1871 *BiAUS, BiDrAC*
Pitman, Frank Wesley 1882-1949 *WhAm 2*
Pitman, J Asbury 1867-1952 *WhAm 3*
Pitman, James Fling 1890-1952 *NatCAB 43*
Pitman, James Hall 1896-1958 *WhAm 4*
Pitman, John 1784-1864 *BiAUS*
Pitman, John 1785-1863 *NatCAB 8*
Pitman, John 1842-1933 *WhAm 1*
Pitman, Marie J 1850- *ApCAB*
Pitman, Norman Hinsdale 1876-1925 *WhAm 1*
Pitman, Theodore B 1892-1956 *IIBEAAW*
Pitman, Thomas *NewYHSD*
Pitner, Thomas Jefferson 1842-1920 *WhAm 1*
Pitney, John Oliver Halsted 1860-1928 *WhAm 1*
Pitney, Mahlon 1858-1924 *ApCAB X, BiDrAC, DcAmB, NatCAB 15, WebAB, WhAm 1, WhAmP*
Pitney, Shelton 1893-1946 *WhAm 2*
Pitot, Henri 1695-1771 *DcScB*
Pitou, Augustus d1915 *WhAm 1*
Pitou, Louis Ange 1769-1828? *ApCAB*
Pitt, Miss *NewYHSD*
Pitt, Dale Leatham 1884-1955 *NatCAB 43*
Pitt, David Alexander 1877-1949 *WhAm 3*
Pitt, Joseph B *NewYHSD*
Pitt, Louis Wetherbee 1893-1959 *WhAm 3*
Pitt, Robert Healy 1853-1937 *WhAm 1*
Pitt, William 1708-1778 *McGEWB, WhAm H*
Pitt, William 1759-1806 *ApCAB, McGEWB*
Pitt, William Percival 1870-1950 *NatCAB 40*
Pitt-Rivers, Augustus Henry Lane Fox 1827-1900 *DcScB*
Pitta, Sebastiao DaRocha 1660-1738 *ApCAB*
Pittenger, Lemuel Arthur 1873-1955 *WhAm 3*
Pittenger, William 1840-1905 *ApCAB, NatCAB 11, TwCBDA, WhAm 1*
Pittenger, William Alvin 1885-1951 *BiDrAC, NatCAB 41, WhAm 3, WhAmP*
Pittfield, William *NewYHSD*
Pittis, Albert 1873-1927 *NatCAB 20*
Pittis, Henry *NewYHSD*

Pittis, Thomas 1807?- *New YHSD*
Pittman, Alfred d1961 *WhAm 4*
Pittman, Charles Wesley 1838-1871 *WhAm H*
Pittman, Ernest Wetmore 1889-1970 *WhAm 5*
Pittman, Hannah Daviess 1840- *WhAm 4,*
WomWWA 14
Pittman, Hobson 1899-1972 *WhAm 5*
Pittman, Key 1872-1940 *ApCAB X, BiDrAC,*
DcAmB S2, EncAAH, NatCAB 34,
REnAW, WhAm 1, WhAmP
Pittman, Marvin Summers 1882-1954 *BiDAmEd,*
WhAm 3
Pittman, Nathan Rowland 1856-1919 *WhAm 1*
Pittman, Owen Willis 1903-1954 *NatCAB 48*
Pittman, Thomas Merritt 1857-1932
NatCAB 37
Pittman, Vail Montgomery 1883-1964 *WhAm 4*
Pittman, William Buckner 1876-1936 *WhAm 1*
Pittner, F J *New YHSD*
Pittock, Henry Lewis 1835-1919 *NatCAB 16,*
WhAm 1
Pittock, Henry Lewis 1836-1919 *DcAmB*
Pitts, Alexander Davidson 1851-1928 *WhAm 1*
Pitts, Edmund Levi 1839- *ApCAB*
Pitts, Hiram Abial 1799-1860 *NatCAB 13*
Pitts, Hiram Avery 1800?-1860 *DcAmB,*
EncAAH, WhAm H
Pitts, James 1712-1776 *ApCAB*
Pitts, John 1668- *ApCAB*
Pitts, John 1738-1815 *ApCAB*
Pitts, John Abraham 1849- *NatCAB 8*
Pitts, Kate Isabel DuVal *WomWWA 14*
Pitts, Lendall 1737-1787 *ApCAB*
Pitts, Llewellyn William 1906-1967 *WhAm 4,*
WhAm 5
Pitts, Mary Helen McCrea Weaver 1898-1969
WhAm 5
Pitts, Noah Odas 1875-1963 *NatCAB 50*
Pitts, Robert Newton 1866-1940 *NatCAB 30*
Pitts, Thomas 1779-1836 *ApCAB*
Pittsinger, Eliza A 1837- *AmWom*
Pitzer, Alexander White 1834-1927 *ApCAB,*
TwCBDA, WhAm 1
Pitzman, Julius 1837-1923 *NatCAB 22*
Pitzner, Alwin Frederick 1897-1953
NatCAB 40
Pius II 1405-1464 *McGEWB*
Pius IV 1499-1565 *McGEWB*
Pius V 1504-1572 *McGEWB*
Pius VI 1717-1799 *McGEWB*
Pius VII 1740-1823 *McGEWB*
Pius IX 1792-1878 *McGEWB*
Pius X 1835-1914 *McGEWB*
Pius XI 1857-1939 *McGEWB*
Pius XII 1876-1958 *McGEWB, WhAm 3*
Piutti, Anna Adams 1858- *WomWWA 14*
Piver, Sara Elizabeth Early d1969 *WhAm 5*
Pixley, Albert John 1879-1954 *NatCAB 44*
Pixley, Frank 1867-1919 *NatCAB 20,*
WhAm 1
Pixley, Henry David 1892-1960 *WhAm 4*
Pizarro, Francisco 1471?-1541 *Drake*
Pizarro, Francisco 1474?-1541 *McGEWB,*
WhoMilH
Pizarro, Francisco 1475?-1541 *WhAm H*
Pizarro, Francisco 1476-1541 *ApCAB*
Pizarro, Gonzalo 1506-1548 *ApCAB*
Pizarro, Hernando 1474-1578 *ApCAB*
Pizarro, Jose Alfonso 1689-1762 *ApCAB*
Pizarro, Juan 1500?-1536 *ApCAB*
Pizi *WebAB*
Pizitz, Louis 1868-1959 *WhAm 3*
Pizzetti, Ildebrando 1880-1968 *WhAm 4A*
Pizzini, Andrew 1844-1913 *NatCAB 50*
Plaatje, Solomon Tshekisho 1878-1932
McGEWB
Place, Charles Edward Stewart 1894-1957
NatCAB 46
Place, Chester Allen 1862- *NatCAB 9*
Place, Ira Adelbert 1854-1928 *NatCAB 14,*
NatCAB 21, WhAm 1
Place, Perley Oakland 1873-1946 *WhAm 2*
Place, Roland Percy 1891-1967 *WhAm 4*
Place, Willard Fiske 1896-1961 *WhAm 4*
Plachy, Fred Joseph 1901-1972 *WhAm 5*
Placide, Alexander d1812 *WhAm H*
Placide, Henry 1799-1870 *ApCAB, DcAmB,*
Drake, NatCAB 8, WhAm H

Placide, Suzanne *NotAW*
Placide, Thomas 1808-1877 *ApCAB*
Plack, William L 1854-1944 *WhAm 2*
Plaehn, Erma Belle 1906-1974 *WhAm 6*
Plafker, Nathan Victor 1905- *WhAm 6*
Plagens, Joseph Casimir 1880-1943 *NatCAB 38,*
WhAm 2
Plaggemeyer, Harry Ward 1881-1953
NatCAB 44
Plain, Bartholomew *New YHSD*
Plaisted, Frederick William 1865-1943
WhAm 2
Plaisted, Harris Merrill 1828-1898 *ApCAB,*
ApCAB Sup, BiAUS, BiDrAC, DcAmB,
NatCAB 6, TwCBDA, WhAm H,
WhAmP
Plamenatz, John Petrov 1912-1975 *WhAm 6*
Plamondon, Alfred Daniel, Jr. 1899-1965
WhAm 4
Plamondon, Charles Ambrose 1856-1915
NatCAB 30
Plamondon, Charles Ambrose, Jr. 1889-1958
NatCAB 48
Plana, Giovanni 1781-1864 *DcScB*
Planck, Max Karl Ernst Ludwig 1858-1947
AsBiEn, DcScB, McGEWB, WhAm 4
Planje, Christian William 1905-1973 *WhAm 6*
Plank, Kenneth Robert 1907-1973 *WhAm 6*
Plank, William Bertolette 1886-1956 *WhAm 3*
Plankers, Arthur Gottfried 1889-1964
NatCAB 51
Plankinton, John 1820-1891 *NatCAB 1*
Plankinton, William 1844-1905 *NatCAB 16*
Plankinton, William Woods 1881- *NatCAB 16*
Plant, David 1783-1851 *BiAUS, BiDrAC,*
WhAm H
Plant, Henry Bradley 1819-1899 *DcAmB,*
NatCAB 11, NatCAB 18, REnAW,
WhAm 1
Plant, Henry Bradley 1895-1938 *NatCAB 18,*
NatCAB 27
Plant, John David 1888-1958 *NatCAB 47*
Plant, Louis Clark 1870-1966 *NatCAB 52*
Plant, Marion Borchers 1907-1968 *WhAm 5*
Plant, Morton Freeman 1852-1918 *NatCAB 18,*
WhAm 1
Plant, Oscar Henry 1875-1939 *NatCAB 29,*
WhAm 1
Plant, Philip Morgan 1901-1941 *NatCAB 31*
Plante, Gaston 1834-1889 *AsBiEn*
Planten, John Rutger 1835-1912 *NatCAB 16*
Plantou, Madame Anthony *New YHSD*
Plants, Tobias Avery 1811-1887 *BiAUS,*
BiDrAC, WhAm H
Plantz, Myra Goodwin 1856-1914 *BiCAW,*
WhAm 1, WomWWA 14
Plantz, Samuel 1859-1924 *ApCAB X,*
NatCAB 25, TwCBDA, WhAm 1
Planudes, Maximus 1255?-1305 *DcScB*
Plaschke, Paul Albert 1880-1954 *WhAm 4*
Plaskett, John Stanley 1865-1941 *DcScB*
Plassmann, Ernst 1823-1877 *ApCAB,*
New YHSD, WhAm H
Plassmann, Thomas 1879-1959 *WhAm 3*
Plaster, Jerry Glen 1935-1970 *WhAm 5*
Plastiras, Nicholas 1833-1953 *WhAm 3*
Plate, H Robinson 1877-1941 *NatCAB 30*
Plate, Ludwig Hermann 1862-1937 *DcScB*
Plate, Walter 1925-1972 *WhAm 5*
Plateau, Joseph Antoine Ferdinand 1801-1883
DcScB
Platen, C *New YHSD*
Plater, Felix *DcScB*
Plater, George d1792 *Drake*
Plater, George 1735-1792 *BiDrAC, DcAmB,*
NatCAB 9, TwCBDA, WhAm H,
WhAmP
Plater, George 1736-1792 *ApCAB, BiAUS*
Plater, Thomas 1769-1830 *BiAUS, BiDrAC,*
WhAm H, WhAmP
Plath, Sylvia 1932-1963 *WhAm 4*
Platner, John Winthrop 1865-1921 *NatCAB 19,*
WhAm 1
Platner, Samuel Ball 1863-1921 *DcAmB,*
NatCAB 12, TwCBDA, WhAm 1
Plato 427?BC-347?BC *AsBiEn*
Plato 427?BC-348?BC *DcScB*
Plato 428BC-347BC *McGEWB*

Plato Of Tivoli *DcScB*
Platou, Ralph Victor 1909-1968 *WhAm 5*
Platt, Mrs. *New YHSD*
Platt, Alethea Hill *WomWWA 14*
Platt, Alfred 1789-1872 *NatCAB 27*
Platt, Alice Wadsworth 1879- *WomWWA 14*
Platt, Casper 1892-1965 *NatCAB 51,*
WhAm 4
Platt, Charles 1744-1827 *NatCAB 2*
Platt, Charles 1869- *WhAm 1*
Platt, Charles Adams 1861-1933 *AmBi,*
ApCAB, BnEnAmA, DcAmB,
NatCAB 11, NatCAB 27, TwCBDA,
WhAm 1
Platt, Charles Alexander 1884-1965 *WhAm 4*
Platt, Clark Murray 1824-1900 *NatCAB 27*
Platt, Edmund 1865-1939 *BiDrAC, WhAm 1*
Platt, Eleanor d1974 *WhAm 6*
Platt, Elsie Hawley 1857- *WomWWA 14*
Platt, Frank Hinchman 1854-1926 *ApCAB X*
Platt, Frank Lafayette 1864-1927 *NatCAB 28*
Platt, Franklin 1844-1900 *ApCAB, NatCAB 5,*
WhAm 1
Platt, Frederick Gideon 1848-1932 *NatCAB 29*
Platt, Frederick Joseph 1871-1959 *WhAm 3*
Platt, George *New YHSD*
Platt, George W 1839-1899 *IIBEAAW,*
New YHSD
Platt, H *New YHSD*
Platt, Harvey P 1827- *WhAm 4*
Platt, Henry Clay 1840-1904 *NatCAB 5,*
WhAm 1
Platt, Henry Russell 1866-1931 *WhAm 1*
Platt, Howard V 1865- *WhAm 4*
Platt, Irving Gibbs 1860-1896 *NatCAB 27*
Platt, Isaac Hull 1853-1912 *NatCAB 15,*
WhAm 1
Platt, James C d1882 *New YHSD*
Platt, James Delaney 1838-1920 *NatCAB 19*
Platt, James Henry, Jr. 1837-1894 *BiAUS,*
BiDrAC, WhAm H
Platt, James Perry 1851-1913 *WhAm 1*
Platt, John 1864-1942 *WhAm 2*
Platt, John I 1839-1907 *NatCAB 25*
Platt, John O 1874-1947 *WhAm 2*
Platt, Jonas 1769-1834 *ApCAB, BiAUS,*
BiDrAC, Drake, NatCAB 11, TwCBDA,
WhAm H
Platt, Joseph Brereton 1895-1968 *NatCAB 54,*
WhAm 4A
Platt, Joseph Curtis 1816-1887 *NatCAB 8*
Platt, Julia Barlow *WomWWA 14*
Platt, Laura N 1865- *WomWWA 14*
Platt, Lewis Alfred 1854-1919 *NatCAB 27*
Platt, Livingston 1885-1968 *WhAm 5*
Platt, Orville Hitchcock 1827-1905 *AmBi,*
ApCAB, BiDrAC, DcAmB, NatCAB 2,
TwCBDA, WebAB, WhAm 1, WhAmP
Platt, Philo Tousey 1880-1928 *NatCAB 21*
Platt, Robert Swanton 1891-1964 *WhAm 4*
Platt, Rutherford 1894-1975 *WhAm 6*
Platt, Samuel 1874-1964 *NatCAB 53,*
WhAm 5
Platt, Sarah Sophia Chase *NotAW*
Platt, Thomas Collier 1833-1910 *AmBi,*
ApCAB, BiAUS, BiDrAC, DcAmB,
EncAB, McGEWB, NatCAB 11,
TwCBDA, WebAB, WhAm 1, WhAmP
Platt, Walter Brewster 1853-1922 *NatCAB 32*
Platt, Willard Harold 1854-1926 *ApCAB X*
Platt, William Henry 1821-1898 *ApCAB,*
TwCBDA
Platt, William Popham 1858-1926 *NatCAB 21,*
WhAm 1
Platt, William Smith 1822-1886 *NatCAB 27*
Platt, Zephaniah d1807 *BiAUS*
Platt, Zephaniah 1735-1807 *BiDrAC,*
WhAm H
Platt, Zephaniah 1740-1807 *ApCAB,*
TwCBDA
Platt, Zephaniah 1796-1871 *ApCAB,*
TwCBDA
Platten, John Wesley d1954 *WhAm 3*
Plattenberger *New YHSD*
Plattenburg, Jessie Thatcher 1861-
WomWWA 14
Platter, Felix 1536-1614 *BiHiMed, DcScB*
Plattner, Karl Friedrich 1800-1858 *DcScB*

Platzek, M Warley 1854-1932 *NatCAB 12,* *WhAm 1*
Platzman, Robert Leroy 1918-1973 *WhAm 6*
Plauche, Vance Gabriel 1897- *BiDrAC*
Plaut, Edward 1891-1972 *WhAm 5*
Plautus 254?BC-184?BC *McGEWB*
Player, John 1847- *NatCAB 11*
Player, William Oscar, Jr. 1906-1951 *WhAm 3*
Playfair, John 1748-1819 *DcScB*
Playfair, Lyon 1818-1898 *DcScB*
Playter, Harold 1877- *WhAm 5*
Plaza, Manuel 1772-1845? *ApCAB*
Plaza, Nicanor 1844- *ApCAB*
Plaza Lasso, Galo 1906- *McGEWB*
Pleadwell, Frank Lester 1872-1957 *WhAm 3*
Pleasant, Carl 1886-1930 *NatCAB 25*
Pleasant, Mary Ellen 1814?-1904 *NotAW*
Pleasant, Ruffin Golson 1871-1937 *WhAm 1*
Pleasanton, Alfred 1824-1897 *TwCBDA*
Pleasanton, Augustus James 1808-1894 *TwCBDA*
Pleasanton, Stephen d1855 *BiAUS*
Pleasants, Albert C *NewYHSD*
Pleasants, Henry, Jr. 1884-1963 *WhAm 4*
Pleasants, J Hall 1873-1957 *WhAm 3*
Pleasants, James 1769-1836 *BiAUS, BiDrAC,* *DcAmB, Drake, NatCAB 5, WhAm H,* *WhAmP*
Pleasants, James 1769-1839 *ApCAB,* *TwCBDA*
Pleasants, James Jay, Jr. 1907-1950 *WhAm 3*
Pleasants, John Hampden 1797-1846 *ApCAB,* *DcAmB, NatCAB 7, TwCBDA,* *WhAm H*
Pleasonton, Alfred 1824-1897 *AmBi, ApCAB,* *DcAmB, Drake, NatCAB 4, WebAMB,* *WhAm H*
Pleasonton, Augustus James 1808-1894 *ApCAB,* *NatCAB 10, WhAm H*
Plecker, D A *NewYHSD*
Plee, Auguste 1787-1825 *ApCAB*
Plehn, Carl Copping 1867-1945 *NatCAB 36,* *TwCBDA, WhAm 2*
Pleissner, Ogden Minton 1905- *IlBEAAW*
Plekhanov, Georgi Valentinovich 1856-1918 *McGEWB*
Plencic, Marcus Antonius 1705-1786 *DcScB*
Plenty Coups 1848-1932 *REnAW*
Plessis, Francis Xavier 1694- *ApCAB*
Plessis, Joseph Octave 1762-1825 *Drake*
Plessis, Joseph Octave 1763-1825 *ApCAB*
Plessis, Pacificus Du *ApCAB*
Plessner, Theodore d1946 *WhAm 2*
Plessys, Pacificus Du *ApCAB*
Pleville LePeley, Georges Rene 1726-1805 *ApCAB*
Plicator, Frank *NewYHSD*
Plimpton, Etta Ferry 1867- *WomWWA 14*
Plimpton, Florus Beardsley 1830-1886 *NatCAB 5*
Plimpton, George Ames 1927- *WebAB*
Plimpton, George Arthur 1837-1911 *NatCAB 16*
Plimpton, George Arthur 1855-1936 *DcAmB S2,* *NatCAB 9, NatCAB 27, WhAm 1*
Plimpton, George Lincoln 1865-1946 *NatCAB 35, WhAm 3*
Plimpton, Hannah R Cope 1841- *AmWom*
Plimpton, Helen Louise Sheppard 1878- *WomWWA 14*
Plimpton, Herbert Moseley 1859-1948 *NatCAB 55*
Plimpton, James Leonard 1828- *NatCAB 7*
Plimpton, Jenny Faulkner *WomWWA 14*
Plimpton, Russell Arthur 1891-1975 *WhAm 6*
Pliny 023?-079 *AsBiEn, DcScB, McGEWB*
Pliny The Younger 061?-113? *McGEWB*
Plocher, Jacob J d1820 *NewYHSD*
Plock, Richard Henry 1908-1959 *WhAm 3A*
Ploeser, Walter Christian 1907- *BiDrAC*
Plonk, Emma Laura 1890-1966 *WhAm 4*
Plonk, Joseph Calvin 1852-1939 *NatCAB 30*
Plot, Robert 1640-1696 *DcScB*
Plotinus 204?-270 *DcScB*
Plotinus 205-270 *McGEWB*
Plotkin, Oscar Hillel 1897-1950 *NatCAB 38*
Plotz, Harry 1890-1947 *DcAmB S4*

Plough, Kenneth Atchinson 1891-1947 *NatCAB 49*
Plowden, Eldridge Rodgers 1899-1975 *WhAm 6*
Plowhead, Ruth Gipson 1877- *WhAm 6*
Plowman, George Taylor 1869-1932 *DcAmB,* *NatCAB 23, WhAm 1*
Plowman, Idora M 1843- *AmWom*
Plowman, Thomas Scales 1843-1919 *BiDrAC*
Pluche, Noel-Antoine 1688-1761 *DcScB*
Plucker, Julius 1801-1868 *AsBiEn, DcScB*
Pluemer, Adolph 1851- *WhAm 4*
Plum, David Banks 1869-1948 *WhAm 2*
Plum, Harry Clarke 1871- *WhAm 1*
Plum, Harry Grant 1868-1956 *WhAm 3*
Plum, Margaret Budington *WomWWA 14*
Plum, Matthias 1865-1928 *NatCAB 21*
Plumb *NewYHSD*
Plumb, Albert Hale 1829-1907 *WhAm 1*
Plumb, Charles Sumner 1860-1939 *AmBi,* *NatCAB 38, TwCBDA, WhAm 1,* *WhAm 1C*
Plumb, David Smith 1852- *NatCAB 5*
Plumb, Edward Lee 1827- *ApCAB*
Plumb, Fayette Rumsey 1877-1966 *WhAm 4*
Plumb, Glenn Edward 1866-1922 *DcAmB,* *WhAm 1*
Plumb, Joseph 1791-1870 *ApCAB,* *NatCAB 12*
Plumb, Josiah Burr 1816-1888 *ApCAB*
Plumb, Mrs. L H 1841- *AmWom*
Plumb, Louis Jackson 1883-1942 *NatCAB 39*
Plumb, Preston B 1837-1891 *ApCAB, BiDrAC,* *DcAmB, NatCAB 2, TwCBDA,* *WhAm H, WhAmP*
Plumb, Ralph 1816-1903 *BiDrAC*
Plumbe, George Edward 1837-1912 *WhAm 1*
Plumbe, John 1809-1857 *DcAmB, WhAm H*
Plume, David Scott 1829-1907 *NatCAB 26*
Plume, Joseph William 1839-1918 *ApCAB Sup,* *TwCBDA*
Plume, Joseph Williams 1839-1918 *WhAm 1*
Plume, Stephen Kellogg 1881-1950 *WhAm 3*
Plumer, Arnold 1801-1869 *BiAUS, BiDrAC,* *WhAm H*
Plumer, George 1762-1843 *BiAUS, BiDrAC,* *WhAm H*
Plumer, Harrison Lorenzo 1814- *NewYHSD*
Plumer, Herbert Charles 1857-1932 *WhoMilH*
Plumer, Jacob P *NewYHSD*
Plumer, James Marshall 1899-1960 *NatCAB 49*
Plumer, William 1759-1850 *ApCAB, BiAUS,* *BiDrAC, DcAmB, Drake, NatCAB 11,* *TwCBDA, WhAm H, WhAmP*
Plumer, William 1789-1854 *ApCAB, BiDrAC,* *TwCBDA, WhAm H, WhAmP*
Plumer, William 1790-1854 *BiAUS*
Plumer, William Henry 1831-1915 *NatCAB 17*
Plumer, William Swan 1802-1880 *ApCAB,* *DcAmB, Drake, NatCAB 9, TwCBDA,* *WhAm H*
Plumier, Charles 1646-1704 *ApCAB, DcScB*
Plumley, Benjamin Rush 1816-1887 *ApCAB,* *Drake*
Plumley, Charles Albert 1875-1964 *BiDrAC,* *NatCAB 18, WhAm 4*
Plumley, Frank 1844-1924 *BiDrAC, DcAmB,* *NatCAB 26, WhAm 1*
Plumley, W Franklin 1877-1959 *NatCAB 47*
Plummer, Adrian *NewYHSD*
Plummer, Andrew 1698?-1756 *DcScB*
Plummer, Charles Griffin 1859-1936 *WhAm 1*
Plummer, Cora Elisabeth Burbank 1864- *WomWWA 14*
Plummer, Daniel Clarence 1896-1956 *WhAm 3*
Plummer, Edward *NewYHSD*
Plummer, Edward Clarence 1863-1932 *WhAm 1*
Plummer, Edward Clarence 1864-1932 *NatCAB 23*
Plummer, Edward Hinkley 1855-1927 *WhAm 1*
Plummer, Edwin *NewYHSD*
Plummer, Frank Everett 1858- *WhAm 4*
Plummer, Franklin E d1847 *BiDrAC,* *WhAm H*
Plummer, Franklin E d1852 *BiAUS*
Plummer, Frederick Byron 1885-1947 *NatCAB 35*
Plummer, Henry 1837?-1864 *DcAmB, REnAW,* *WhAm H*

Plummer, Henry Crozier 1875-1946 *DcScB*
Plummer, Henry Stanley 1874-1936 *DcAmB S2,* *NatCAB 29*
Plummer, Henry Vinton 1876- *WhoColR*
Plummer, James Kemp 1886- *WhAm 3*
Plummer, John Watrous 1924-1968 *WhAm 5*
Plummer, Jonathan 1761-1819 *DcAmB,* *WhAm H*
Plummer, Joseph B 1820-1862 *ApCAB, Drake*
Plummer, Joseph Henry 1876- *WhoColR*
Plummer, Mary Redfield *WomWWA 14*
Plummer, Mary Wright 1856-1916 *DcAmB,* *DcAmLiB, NatCAB 21, NotAW,* *TwCBDA, WhAm 1, WomWWA 14*
Plummer, R *NewYHSD*
Plummer, Ralph Walter 1874- *WhAm 5*
Plummer, Samuel Craig 1865-1952 *NatCAB 41,* *WhAm 5*
Plummer, Walter Percy 1883-1933 *WhAm 1*
Plummer, William *NewYHSD*
Plummer, William Alberto 1865-1925 *WhAm 1*
Plumptre, Adelaide Mary Wynne 1871- *WomWWA 14*
Plumsted, Clement 1680-1745 *ApCAB*
Plumsted, William 1708-1765 *ApCAB*
Plunkert, William Joseph 1900-1972 *WhAm 6*
Plunket, James Dace 1839- *TwCBDA*
Plunkett, Charles Peshall 1864-1931 *DcAmB,* *NatCAB 25, WhAm 1*
Plunkett, Charles Timothy 1855-1927 *NatCAB 23, WhAm 1*
Plunkett, Edward Milton 1886-1948 *WhAm 2*
Plunkett, Flavius Ogburn 1886-1946 *NatCAB 36*
Plunkett, Guy Downs 1894-1963 *NatCAB 50*
Plunkett, Harriette M 1826- *AmWom*
Plunkett, Theodore Robinson 1882-1946 *NatCAB 35*
Plunkett, William Brown 1850-1917 *WhAm 1*
Plutarch 046?-120? *McGEWB*
Plyler, Alva Washington 1867- *WhAm 5*
Plyler, John Laney 1894-1966 *WhAm 4*
Plyler, Marion Timothy 1867- *WhAm 5*
Plym, Francis John 1869-1940 *WhAm 1*
Plymire, Reginald Floyd 1909-1972 *WhAm 5*
Plympton, Almira George 1852- *WomWWA 14*
Plympton, Eben 1853-1915 *WhAm 1*
Plympton, George Washington 1827-1907 *AmBi,* *ApCAB, NatCAB 9, TwCBDA, WhAm 1*
Plympton, Gilbert Motier 1835- *NatCAB 11*
Plympton, Joseph 1787-1860 *ApCAB, Drake*
Po, Chu-I 772-846 *McGEWB*
Po-Chedley, Donald Stephen 1917-1969 *WhAm 5*
Poag, Thomas E d1974 *WhAm 6*
Poage, Josephine K 1867- *WomWWA 14*
Poage, Margaret Annie *WomWWA 14*
Poage, William Robert 1899- *BiDrAC,* *EncAAH*
Pobedonostsev, Konstantin Petrovich 1827-1907 *McGEWB*
Pocahontas 1594?-1617 *NatCAB 7*
Pocahontas 1595?-1616? *NotAW*
Pocahontas 1595?-1617 *AmBi, DcAmB,* *Drake, EncAAH, McGEWB, WebAB,* *WhAm H*
Pocahontas 1596?-1617 *EncAB*
Pocker, Victor 1902-1950 *NatCAB 39*
Pockman, Philetus Theodore 1853-1919 *WhAm 1*
Podell, Bertram L 1925- *BiDrAC*
Podell, David Louis 1884-1947 *NatCAB 36,* *WhAm 2*
Podesta, Joseph Sentenus 1877-1957 *NatCAB 46*
Podesta, Stephen *NewYHSD*
Poe, Adam 1804-1868 *Drake*
Poe, Clarence 1881-1964 *NatCAB 52,* *WhAm 4*
Poe, David Louis 1883-1961 *NatCAB 46*
Poe, Edgar Allan 1809-1849 *AmBi, ApCAB,* *DcAmB, EncAB, McGEWB, NatCAB 1,* *TwCBDA, WebAB, WhAm H*
Poe, Edgar Allan 1811-1849 *Drake*
Poe, Edgar Allan 1871-1961 *WhAm 4*
Poe, Elisabeth Ellicott 1886-1947 *WhAm 2*
Poe, Elizabeth Arnold Hopkins 1787?-1811 *NotAW, WhAm H*

Poe, Floyd 1877- *WhAm 5*
Poe, James W 1857- *WhoColR*
Poe, John Prentiss d1909 *WhAm 1*
Poe, John William 1850-1923 *NatCAB 6*, *WhAm 1*
Poe, Lavinia Marian 1890- *WhoColR*
Poe, Orlando M 1832-1895 *REnAW*
Poe, Orlando Metcalf 1832-1895 *NatCAB 6*, *TwCBDA*
Poe, Orlando Metcalfe 1832-1895 *ApCAB*, *DcAmB*, *NatCAB 5*, *WebAMB*, *WhAm H*
Poe, Pascal Eugene, Jr. 1904-1963 *WhAm 4*
Poe, Philip Livingston 1879-1970 *NatCAB 55*
Poebel, Arno 1881-1958 *WhAm 3*
Poehler, Henry 1833-1912 *BiDrAC*
Poehler, W A 1904-1971 *WhAm 5*
Poehlmann, Adolph H 1860- *ApCAB X*
Poehlmann, August Franklin 1869- *ApCAB X*
Poehlmann, John William 1867-1916 *ApCAB X*
Poels, Henry Andrew 1868- *WhAm 4*
Poensgen, Lillie Elizabeth Muller *WomWWA 14*
Poeppig, Eduard 1797-1868 *ApCAB*
Poetker, Albert Henry 1887-1960 *NatCAB 47*, *WhAm 4*
Poett, Henry Williams 1872-1938 *NatCAB 42*
Poey, Andres 1826- *ApCAB*
Poey, Felipe 1799- *ApCAB*
Poff, Richard Harding 1923- *BiDrAC*
Poffenbarger, George 1861-1941 *WhAm 4*
Poffenbarger, Livia Simpson 1862-1937 *WhAm 1*
Pogany, Willy 1882-1955 *NatCAB 44*, *WhAm 3*
Poggendorff, Johann Christian 1796-1877 *DcScB*
Poggiale, Antoine-Baudoin 1808-1879 *DcScB*
Pogson, Norman Robert 1829-1891 *AsBiEn*
Pogue, Henry 1829-1903 *NatCAB 13*, *NatCAB 32*
Pogue, Mabel Wood 1883- *WomWWA 14*
Pogue, Robert West 1872-1937 *NatCAB 28*
Pogue, Samuel 1832-1912 *NatCAB 24*
Pogzeba, Wolfgang 1936- *IlBEAAW*
Pohl, Edward *NewYHSD*
Pohl, Hugo David 1878-1960 *IlBEAAW*
Pohl, Johann Emanuel 1784-1834 *ApCAB*
Pohl, Joseph Louis 1901-1967 *NatCAB 55*
Pohl, Karl 1895-1947 *NatCAB 38*
Pohlers, Richard Camillo 1901-1959 *WhAm 3*
Pohlman, Augustus Grote 1879-1950 *WhAm 3*
Pohlmann, Julius 1848-1910 *WhAm 1*
Poillon, Howard Andrews 1879-1954 *WhAm 3*
Poillon, William Clark 1872- *WhAm 5*
Poincare, Jules Henri 1854-1912 *AsBiEn*, *DcScB*, *McGEWB*
Poincare, Raymond 1860-1934 *McGEWB*
Poincy, A *NewYHSD*
Poincy, Paul 1833-1909 *NewYHSD*
Poindexter, Claude Hendricks 1901-1974 *WhAm 6*
Poindexter, George 1779-1853 *AmBi*, *ApCAB*, *BiAUS*, *DcAmB*, *Drake*, *REnAW*, *TwCBDA*, *WhAm H*
Poindexter, George 1779-1855 *BiDrAC*, *NatCAB 13*, *WhAmP*
Poindexter, James Thomas 1832-1891 *NewYHSD*
Poindexter, Joseph Boyd 1869-1951 *WhAm 3*
Poindexter, Miles 1868-1946 *BiDrAC*, *DcAmB S4*, *NatCAB 15*, *WhAm 2*, *WhAmP*
Poinier, Lela M Peet *WomWWA 14*
Poinsett, Joel Roberts 1779-1851 *AmBi*, *ApCAB*, *BiAUS*, *BiDrAC*, *BiDrUSE*, *DcAmB*, *Drake*, *EncAB*, *NatCAB 6*, *TwCBDA*, *WebAB*, *WhAm H*, *WhAmP*
Poinsot, Louis 1777-1859 *DcScB*
Point, Father Nicholas 1799-1868 *NewYHSD*, *WhAm H*
Point, Father Nicolas 1799-1868 *IlBEAAW*
Point DuSable, Jean Baptiste d1800? *WhAm H*
Pointel, J B *NewYHSD*
Pointis, Jean B L Desjean, Baron De 1645-1707 *ApCAB*
Points, Arthur Jones 1904-1969 *WhAm 5*
Poirier, Charles Joseph 1886-1947 *NatCAB 36*

Poirier, Pascal 1852- *ApCAB*
Poiseuille, Jean Leonard Marie 1797-1869 *DcScB*
Poisson, Julien *NewYHSD*
Poisson, Modest Jules Adolphe 1849- *ApCAB*
Poisson, Simeon-Denis 1781-1840 *DcScB*, *DcScB Sup*
Poitevent, Eliza Jane *NotAW*
Poivre, Pierre 1719-1786 *DcScB*
Pokagon, Leopold 1775-1841 *REnAW*
Polacco, Giorgi 1875-1960 *WhAm 4*
Polachek, Victor Henry 1876-1940 *WhAm 1*
Polack, William Gustave 1890-1950 *WhAm 3*
Polak, John Osborn 1870-1931 *DcAmB*
Polak, John Osborn 1871-1931 *NatCAB 25*, *WhAm 1*
Polakov, Walter Nicholas 1879- *WhAm 6*
Polanco-Abreu, Santiago 1920- *BiDrAC*
Poland, John Carroll 1847-1927 *NatCAB 21*
Poland, John Scroggs 1836-1898 *AmBi*, *ApCAB*
Poland, Luke Potter 1815-1887 *ApCAB*, *BiAUS*, *BiDrAC*, *DcAmB*, *NatCAB 5*, *TwCBDA*, *WhAm H*, *WhAmP*
Poland, Mary L *WomWWA 14*
Poland, William Carey 1846-1929 *BiDAmEd*, *NatCAB 10*, *NatCAB 22*, *WhAm 1*
Polanyi, Karl 1886-1964 *McGEWB*, *WhAm 4*
Polasek, Albin 1879-1965 *WhAm 4*
Polayes, Silik Herman 1899-1962 *NatCAB 50*
Poldeman, William F *NewYHSD*
Poldervaart, Arie 1909-1969 *NatCAB 55*, *WhAm 5*
Poldervaart, Arie 1918-1964 *NatCAB 51*
Pole, Elizabeth 1588-1654 *NatCAB 4*, *WhAm H*
Pole, John William d1958 *WhAm 3*
Polelonema, Otis 1902- *IlBEAAW*
Poleman, Horace Irvin 1905-1965 *NatCAB 53*, *WhAm 4*
Poleni, Giovanni 1683-1761 *DcScB*
Poleri, David Samuel 1927-1967 *WhAm 4A*
Polette, Antoine 1807-1887 *ApCAB*
Polhamus, Jose Nelson 1871- *WhAm 5*
Polhem, Christopher 1661-1751 *AsBiEn*
Polhemus, Abraham 1812-1857 *ApCAB*
Polhemus, James H 1887-1965 *WhAm 4*
Polhemus, James Higbie 1884-1926 *NatCAB 20*
Poli, Giuseppe Saverio 1746-1825 *DcScB*
Poli, S Z 1858-1937 *NatCAB 27*
Polifeme, Charles 1863- *NatCAB 10*
Polignac, Camille A J M, Count De 1832- *ApCAB*
Poling, Daniel Alfred 1884-1968 *NatCAB 54*, *WhAm 5*
Poling, Daniel V 1865- *WhAm 4*
Poliniere, Pierre 1671-1734 *DcScB*
Politella, Joseph 1910-1975 *WhAm 6*
Politi, Leo 1908- *IlBEAAW*
Politzer, Adam 1835-1920 *BiHiMed*
Politzer, Jerome 1887-1959 *NatCAB 48*
Polivka, Jaroslav Joseph 1886-1960 *WhAm 3*
Poliziano, Angelo 1454-1494 *McGEWB*
Polk, Albert Fawcett 1869-1955 *BiDrAC*, *WhAm 5*
Polk, Charles 1787-1857 *BiAUS*
Polk, Charles 1788-1857 *NatCAB 11*, *TwCBDA*
Polk, Charles Peale 1767-1822 *BnEnAmA*, *NewYHSD*, *WhAm H*
Polk, Christine Stevens 1870- *WomWWA 14*
Polk, Forrest Raymond 1888-1965 *WhAm 4*
Polk, Frank 1909- *IlBEAAW*
Polk, Frank Lyon 1871-1943 *DcAmB S3*, *WhAm 2*
Polk, Harry Herndon 1875-1949 *NatCAB 39*
Polk, Henry Christopher 1851-1915 *NatCAB 17*
Polk, James Gould 1896-1959 *BiDrAC*, *WhAm 3*, *WhAmP*
Polk, James Knox 1795-1849 *AmBi*, *ApCAB*, *BiAUS*, *BiDrAC*, *BiDrUSE*, *DcAmB*, *Drake*, *EncAAH*, *EncAB*, *McGEWB*, *NatCAB 6*, *TwCBDA*, *WebAB*, *WhAm H*, *WhAmP*
Polk, Leonidas 1806-1864 *AmBi*, *ApCAB*, *BiDConf*, *DcAmB*, *DcAmReB*, *Drake*, *NatCAB 11*, *TwCBDA*, *WebAB*,

WebAMB, *WhAm H*, *WhoMilH*
Polk, Leonidas Lafayette 1837-1892 *DcAmB*, *EncAAH*, *McGEWB*, *WhAm H*
Polk, Lucius Eugene 1833- *ApCAB*
Polk, Lucius Eugene 1833-1892 *BiDConf*, *DcAmB*, *WhAm H*
Polk, Lucius Eugene 1833-1893 *TwCBDA*
Polk, Ralph Lane 1849-1923 *WhAm 1*
Polk, Rufus King 1866-1902 *BiDrAC*, *TwCBDA*, *WhAm 1*
Polk, Sarah Chambers 1887- *WomWWA 14*
Polk, Sarah Childress 1803-1891 *AmWom*, *ApCAB*, *NatCAB 6*, *NotAW*, *TwCBDA*, *WhAm H*
Polk, Thomas 1724?-1794 *NatCAB 11*
Polk, Thomas 1732?-1793 *ApCAB*, *TwCBDA*
Polk, Thomas 1732?-1794 *DcAmB*, *WhAm H*
Polk, Thomas Gilchrist 1790-1869 *ApCAB*
Polk, Trusten 1811-1876 *ApCAB*, *BiAUS*, *BiDrAC*, *DcAmB*, *Drake*, *NatCAB 12*, *TwCBDA*, *WhAm H*
Polk, William 1758-1834 *ApCAB*, *DcAmB*, *NatCAB 11*, *TwCBDA*, *WhAm H*
Polk, William Hawkins 1815-1862 *ApCAB*, *BiAUS*, *BiDrAC*, *NatCAB 11*, *TwCBDA*, *WhAm H*, *WhAmP*
Polk, William Mecklenburg 1844-1918 *ApCAB*, *DcAmB*, *NatCAB 2*, *NatCAB 26*, *TwCBDA*, *WhAm 1*
Polk, Willis Jefferson 1867-1924 *DcAmB*
Pollack, Abou David 1908-1971 *WhAm 6*
Pollack, Ervin Harold 1913-1972 *DcAmLiB*, *WhAm 5*
Pollack, Flora 1865- *WomWWA 14*
Pollack, Louis 1921-1970 *WhAm 5*
Pollack, Norman 1933- *EncAAH*
Pollaiuolo, Antonio 1432?-1498 *McGEWB*
Pollak, Egon 1879- *WhAm 6*
Pollak, Gustav 1849-1919 *DcAmB*, *WhAm 1*
Pollak, Robert 1903-1971 *WhAm 5*
Pollak, Virginia Morris 1898-1967 *WhAm 4*
Pollak, Walter Heilprin 1887-1940 *DcAmB S2*, *WhAm 1*
Pollan, Arthur Adair 1885-1958 *NatCAB 48*, *WhAm 3*
Pollard, Albert Frederick 1869-1948 *McGEWB*
Pollard, Arthur Gayton 1843-1930 *WhAm 1*
Pollard, C J *NewYHSD*
Pollard, Calvin 1797-1850 *NewYHSD*
Pollard, Cash Blair 1900-1959 *WhAm 3*
Pollard, Charles Louis 1872-1945 *WhAm 2*
Pollard, Clark Nickerson 1834-1920 *NatCAB 19*
Pollard, Claude 1874- *WhAm 5*
Pollard, Edward A d1851 *Drake*
Pollard, Edward Albert 1828-1872 *ApCAB*
Pollard, Edward Albert 1831-1872 *AmBi*
Pollard, Edward Alfred 1831-1872 *BiDConf*, *DcAmB*, *NatCAB 11*, *WhAm H*
Pollard, Edward Bagby 1864-1927 *WhAm 1*
Pollard, Ernest Mark 1869-1939 *BiDrAC*, *WhAm 5*
Pollard, Grace Putnam 1871- *WomWWA 14*
Pollard, Harold Stanley 1878-1953 *WhAm 3*
Pollard, Harry Strange 1900-1971 *WhAm 5*
Pollard, Henry *NewYHSD*
Pollard, Henry Douglas 1872-1942 *NatCAB 30*, *WhAm 2*
Pollard, Henry G *NewYHSD*
Pollard, Henry Moses 1836-1904 *BiDrAC*
Pollard, Henry Rives 1833-1868 *ApCAB*
Pollard, Isaac 1830-1916 *WhAm 1*
Pollard, John 1802-1885 *NewYHSD*
Pollard, John Cheetham 1926-1971 *NatCAB 57*
Pollard, John Garland 1871-1937 *NatCAB 31*, *WhAm 1*
Pollard, John William Hobbs 1872-1957 *NatCAB 47*, *WhAm 5*
Pollard, Joseph Percival 1869-1911 *DcAmB*
Pollard, Joseph Percival 1898-1960 *NatCAB 48*
Pollard, Josephine 1834-1892 *AmWom*
Pollard, Josephine 1840?-1892 *ApCAB*
Pollard, Josephine 1842?-1892 *TwCBDA*
Pollard, Leslie Lawrence 1886- *WhoColR*
Pollard, Luke *NewYHSD*
Pollard, Marie A N Granier-Dowell *ApCAB*
Pollard, Percival 1869-1911 *WhAm 1*
Pollard, Richard 1790-1851 *BiAUS*,

NatCAB 12
Pollard, Robert Nelson 1880- *WhAm 6*
Pollard, Warren Randolph 1898-1966
  NatCAB 53, WhAm 4
Pollard, William *NewYHSD*
Pollard, William B, Sr. 1896-1957 *WhAm 3*
Pollard, William Jefferson 1860-1913 *WhAm 1*
Pollard, Zilla Hopkins 1865- *WomWWA 14*
Pollender, Aloys 1800-1879 *DcScB*
Polley, Lenore Vance *WomWWA 14*
Polley, Samuel Cleland 1864- *WhAm 2*
Pollia, Joseph P 1894-1954 *WhAm 3*
Pollitt, Levin Irving 1866-1953 *NatCAB 42, WhAm 5*
Pollitz, Edward Alan 1900-1968 *NatCAB 52*
Pollitzer, Anita d1975 *WhAm 6*
Pollitzer, Sigmund 1859-1937 *BiHiMed, NatCAB 29, WhAm 1*
Pollman, William 1867-1930 *WhAm 1*
Pollock, Anna Marble 1876- *WomWWA 14*
Pollock, Benjamin Reathe 1865- *WhAm 4*
Pollock, Channing 1880-1946 *DcAmB S4, NatCAB 34, WhAm 2*
Pollock, Charles Andrew 1853- *WhAm 1*
Pollock, Clement Perry 1905-1973 *WhAm 6*
Pollock, Edwin Taylor 1870-1943 *WhAm 2*
Pollock, Henry Meeker 1877-1954 *NatCAB 42*
Pollock, Hester McLean *BiCAW*
Pollock, Horatio Milo 1868-1950 *WhAm 3*
Pollock, Howard Wallace 1920- *BiDrAC*
Pollock, Jackson 1912-1956 *BnEnAmA, EncAB, McGEWB, WebAB, WhAm HA, WhAm 4*
Pollock, James 1810-1890 *ApCAB, BiAUS, BiDrAC, DcAmB, Drake, NatCAB 2, TwCBDA, WhAm H, WhAmP*
Pollock, Jennie H 1843- *WomWWA 14*
Pollock, John C 1857-1937 *WhAm 1*
Pollock, Lewis John 1886-1966 *NatCAB 54, WhAm 4*
Pollock, Louise Plessner 1832-1901 *AmWom, BiDAmEd*
Pollock, Mary Regina *WomWWA 14*
Pollock, Oliver 1737-1823 *ApCAB, DcAmB, TwCBDA, WebAB, WhAm H*
Pollock, Pinckney Daniel 1859- *NatCAB 13, TwCBDA, WhAm 1*
Pollock, Raymond 1876-1951 *NatCAB 41*
Pollock, Simon Oscar 1868- *WhAm 4*
Pollock, Susan Plessner 1852- *WomWWA 14*
Pollock, Thomas *NewYHSD*
Pollock, Thomas Cithcart 1873-1948 *WhAm 2*
Pollock, Walter Briesler 1856-1928 *WhAm 1*
Pollock, Wayne 1902-1967 *WhAm 4A*
Pollock, William Pegues 1870-1922 *BiDrAC, NatCAB 19*
Polo, Marco 1254?-1324? *AsBiEn, McGEWB*
Polo Y Bernabe, Luis 1858- *ApCAB Sup*
Polock, Moses 1817-1903 *DcAmB*
Polsky, Bert Alfred 1881- *WhAm 6*
Polsley, Daniel Haymond 1803-1877 *BiAUS, BiDrAC, WhAm H*
Poltchaninoff, Nicholas John 1892-1950
  NatCAB 39
Polter *NewYHSD*
Polter, Samuel *NewYHSD*
Poltoratzky, Marianna A 1906-1968 *WhAm 5*
Polushkin, Eugene Paul 1880-1964 *NatCAB 49*
Polverel, Etienne 1742-1795 *ApCAB*
Polyak, Stephen 1889-1955 *WhAm 3*
Polybios 203?BC-120BC *McGEWB*
Polyblank, Ellen Albertina *NotAW*
Polykleitos *McGEWB*
Polyzoides, Adamantios Theophilus 1885-1969
  WhAm 5
Pomarede, Edwards *NewYHSD*
Pomarede, Leon 1807?-1892 *IIBEAAW, NewYHSD, WhAm H*
Pombal, Sebastiao Jose DeC, Marques De
  1699-1782 *McGEWB*
Pombo, Manuel De 1769-1829 *ApCAB*
Pomerat, Charles Marc 1905-1964 *WhAm 4*
Pomerene, Atlee 1863-1937 *AmBi, BiDrAC, DcAmB S2, NatCAB 16, NatCAB 28, WhAm 1*
Pomerene-Haney, Jennie *WomWWA 14*
Pomeroy, Allan 1906-1966 *WhAm 4*
Pomeroy, Benjamin 1704-1784 *ApCAB, Drake,*

TwCBDA
Pomeroy, Brenton Crane 1891-1941
  NatCAB 32
Pomeroy, Charles 1825-1891 *BiAUS, BiDrAC, WhAm H*
Pomeroy, Daniel Eleazer 1868-1965 *WhAm 4*
Pomeroy, Earl S 1915- *REnAW*
Pomeroy, Edward Stuart 1884-1954
  NatCAB 41
Pomeroy, Elizabeth Ella 1882-1966 *WhAm 4*
Pomeroy, Eltweed 1860- *WhAm 1*
Pomeroy, Genie Clark 1867- *AmWom*
Pomeroy, Horace Burton 1879-1957
  NatCAB 43
Pomeroy, Howard Edwin 1900-1975 *WhAm 6*
Pomeroy, James Edmund 1867-1922
  NatCAB 19
Pomeroy, John Larrabee 1883-1941 *NatCAB 30, WhAm 1*
Pomeroy, John Norton 1826?-1885 *Drake*
Pomeroy, John Norton 1828-1885 *AmBi, ApCAB, DcAmB, WhAm H*
Pomeroy, John Norton 1866-1924 *WhAm 1*
Pomeroy, Laura Skeel 1833-1911 *NewYHSD*
Pomeroy, Marcus Mills 1833-1896 *ApCAB, DcAmB, WhAm H*
Pomeroy, Mark Mills 1833-1896 *NatCAB 2, TwCBDA*
Pomeroy, Oren Day 1834-1902 *NatCAB 20*
Pomeroy, Ralph Brouwer 1876-1935 *WhAm 1*
Pomeroy, Samuel Clarke 1816-1891 *ApCAB, BiAUS, BiDrAC, DcAmB, NatCAB 12, TwCBDA, WhAm H*
Pomeroy, Seth 1706-1777 *AmBi, ApCAB, DcAmB, Drake, NatCAB 1, TwCBDA, WebAMB, WhAm H*
Pomeroy, Theodore Medad 1824-1905 *ApCAB, BiAUS, BiDrAC, NatCAB 12, TwCBDA, WhAm 1*
Pommayrac *NewYHSD*
Pompey 106BC-048BC *McGEWB*
Pompidou, Georges Jean Raymond 1911-1974
  WhAm 6
Pompilly, Grace Thome *WomWWA 14*
Pomponazzi, Pietro 1462-1525 *DcScB, McGEWB*
Pomponius Mela *DcScB*
Pomroy, Rebecca Rossignol 1817-1884 *ApCAB*
Ponce DeLeon, Juan 1460?-1521 *AmBi, ApCAB, DcAmB, Drake, McGEWB, NatCAB 11, REnAW, WebAB, WhAm H*
Poncelet, Jean Victor 1788-1867 *AsBiEn, DcScB*
Poncher, Henry George 1902-1955 *NatCAB 45, WhAm 3*
Ponchon, Anthony 1820?- *NewYHSD*
Poncia, Antonio 1793?- *NewYHSD*
Pond, Allen Bartlit 1858-1929 *DcAmB, NatCAB 21, WhAm 1*
Pond, Alonzo Smith 1905-1959 *WhAm 3*
Pond, Anson Phelps 1856- *WhAm 4*
Pond, Ashley 1827-1910 *NatCAB 32, WhAm 1*
Pond, Benjamin d1815 *BiAUS*
Pond, Benjamin 1768-1923 *BiDrAC*
Pond, Bremer Whidden 1884-1959 *NatCAB 45, WhAm 3*
Pond, C H *BiAUS*
Pond, Charles Bailey 1883-1958 *NatCAB 48*
Pond, Charles Fremont 1856-1929 *WhAm 1*
Pond, Chester Henry 1844-1912 *NatCAB 15*
Pond, Dana 1881-1962 *WhAm 4*
Pond, David F *NewYHSD*
Pond, Elihu Bartlit 1826-1898 *NatCAB 22*
Pond, Enoch 1791-1882 *ApCAB, DcAmB, Drake, TwCBDA, WhAm H*
Pond, Francis Jones 1871- *WhAm 5*
Pond, Frederick Eugene 1856-1925 *ApCAB, DcAmB, NatCAB 10, TwCBDA, WhAm 1*
Pond, George Edward 1837-1899 *ApCAB, DcAmB, NatCAB 10, TwCBDA, WhAm 1*
Pond, George Gilbert 1861-1920 *NatCAB 20, WhAm 1*
Pond, Gideon 1810-1878 *REnAW*
Pond, Irving Kane 1857-1939 *ApCAB X,*

DcAmB S2, NatCAB 18, WhAm 1
Pond, James B 1889-1961 *WhAm 4*
Pond, James Burton 1838-1903 *AmBi, DcAmB, NatCAB 1, TwCBDA, WhAm 1*
Pond, John Allan 1914-1973 *WhAm 5*
Pond, Nathan Patchen 1832-1921 *NatCAB 18*
Pond, Nella Brown 1858- *AmWom*
Pond, Peter 1740-1807 *AmBi, DcAmB, REnAW, WhAm H*
Pond, Philip 1866- *WhAm 2*
Pond, Robert Andrew 1892-1970 *NatCAB 55, WhAm 5*
Pond, Samuel William 1808-1891 *ApCAB, DcAmB, REnAW, TwCBDA, WhAm H*
Pond, Silvanus Billings 1792-1871 *WhAm H*
Pond, Theodore Hanford 1873-1933 *WhAm 1*
Pond, Theron Tilden 1800-1852 *NatCAB 8*
Pond, Wilf Pocklington d1936 *WhAm 1*
Pond, William Adams 1824-1885 *ApCAB*
Ponder, Amos Lee 1887-1959 *NatCAB 47*
Ponder, James 1819-1897 *BiAUS, NatCAB 11, TwCBDA*
Poniatowski, Prince Josef Anton 1763-1813
  WhoMilH
Ponnamperuma, Cyril 1923- *AsBiEn*
Pons, Francois Raymond Joseph De 1751-1812?
  ApCAB
Pons, Jean Louis 1761-1831 *AsBiEn, DcScB*
Pons, Lilly d1976 *WhAm 6*
Pont-Au-Sable, Jean Baptiste *WhAm H*
Pont Briand, Henri DuBriel De 1709-1760 *Drake*
Pontbriand, Henry Mary DuBreil De 1709-1760
  ApCAB
Ponte, Lorenzo Da 1749-1838 *Drake*
Pontedera, Giulio 1688-1757 *DcScB*
Pontelli, M L De *NewYHSD*
Ponteves-Gien, Henry Jean B, Viscount De
  1740-1790 *ApCAB*
Pontgibaud, Charles Albert DeMore 1758-1837
  ApCAB Sup
Pontgrave, Sieur De *ApCAB*
Pontiac 1720?-1769 *AmBi, ApCAB, DcAmB, Drake, EncAAH, EncAB, McGEWB, NatCAB 10, WebAB, WebAMB, WhAm H, WhoMilH*
Pontin, Marie Juliette Everett 1873-
  WomWWA 14
Pontius, Albert William 1879-1923 *WhAm 1*
Pontius, Miller Hall 1891-1960 *NatCAB 46*
Ponton, Mungo Melanchthon 1860- *WhoColR*
Pontormo 1494-1556 *McGEWB*
Pook, Samuel Hartt 1827-1901 *ApCAB, NatCAB 4, TwCBDA, WhAm 1*
Pook, Samuel Moore 1804-1878 *ApCAB*
Pool, David DeSola 1885-1970 *WhAm 5*
Pool, Earl 1891-1962 *NatCAB 50*
Pool, Eugene Hillhouse 1874-1949 *WhAm 2*
Pool, George Franklin 1910- *WhAm 6*
Pool, Joe Richard 1911-1968 *BiDrAC, WhAm 5*
Pool, John 1826-1884 *ApCAB, BiAUS, BiDrAC, DcAmB, NatCAB 12, TwCBDA, WhAm H, WhAmP*
Pool, Joseph 1835- *NatCAB 10*
Pool, Judith Graham 1919-1975 *WhAm 6*
Pool, Leonidas Moore 1871-1929 *WhAm 1*
Pool, Maria Louise 1841-1898 *ApCAB Sup, DcAmB, NatCAB 6, TwCBDA, WhAm H*
Pool, Marvin Bemis 1869-1950 *NatCAB 43*
Pool, Solomon 1832-1901 *NatCAB 13, TwCBDA*
Pool, Walter Freshwater 1850-1883 *BiDrAC, WhAm H, WhAmP*
Pool, William Pohlman 1869-1941 *NatCAB 33*
Poole, Abram 1882-1961 *WhAm 4*
Poole, Amos Ritchie 1893-1960 *NatCAB 48*
Poole, Cecil Percy 1865-1921 *WhAm 1*
Poole, Charles Augustus 1849- *WhAm 4*
Poole, Charles Hubbard 1840-1906 *WhAm 1*
Poole, Daniel 1797-1864 *NatCAB 7*
Poole, DeWitt Clinton 1885-1952 *WhAm 3*
Poole, Edward 1609-1664 *NatCAB 7*
Poole, Edward Valentine 1826-1887 *NatCAB 7*
Poole, Elijah *WebAB*
Poole, Ernest Cook 1880-1950 *ApCAB X, DcAmB S4, NatCAB 18, WhAm 2*
Poole, Eugene Alonzo 1841-1912 *WhAm 1*

Poole, Fanny Huntington Runnells 1863-1940 *WhAm 2, WomWWA 14*
Poole, Fenn E 1906-1952 *WhAm 3*
Poole, Fitch 1803-1873 *ApCAB, DcAmB, NatCAB 6, TwCBDA, WhAm H*
Poole, Frank Augustus 1871-1957 *NatCAB 52*
Poole, Franklin Osborne 1872-1943 *WhAm 2*
Poole, Frederic 1863-1936 *WhAm 1*
Poole, George Amos 1843-1918 *NatCAB 18*
Poole, Gerald Ogden 1905-1960 *NatCAB 48*
Poole, Herman 1849- *WhAm 4*
Poole, Hester Martha 1833- *NatCAB 11*
Poole, Hester Martha 1843?- *AmWom*
Poole, John 1875- *WhAm 5*
Poole, John Hudson 1878-1940 *NatCAB 42*
Poole, Lynn D 1910-1969 *WhAm 5*
Poole, Murray Edward 1857-1925 *NatCAB 7, TwCBDA, WhAm 1*
Poole, Reuben Brooks 1834-1895 *DcAmLiB*
Poole, Robert Franklin 1893-1958 *NatCAB 46, WhAm 3*
Poole, Robert Terrell 1872-1940 *NatCAB 30*
Poole, Rufus Gilbert 1902-1968 *WhAm 5*
Poole, Samuel, II 1713-1795? *NatCAB 7*
Poole, Samuel, III 1736-1830 *NatCAB 7*
Poole, Sidman Parmelee 1893-1955 *NatCAB 46, WhAm 3*
Poole, Theodore Lewis 1840-1900 *BiDrAC*
Poole, William Frederick 1821-1894 *AmBi, ApCAB, DcAmB, DcAmLiB, Drake, NatCAB 6, TwCBDA, WhAm H*
Poole, William Frederick 1868-1926 *NatCAB 22*
Poole, William H 1830?- *NewYHSD*
Pooler, Charles Alfred 1909-1972 *WhAm 5*
Pooley, A *NewYHSD*
Pooley, Charles A 1854-1932 *WhAm 1*
Pooley, Edward Murray 1898-1969 *WhAm 5*
Pooley, Guy Elwood 1891-1956 *NatCAB 52*
Pooley, James Henry 1839-1897 *ApCAB, NatCAB 10*
Pooley, Thomas Rickett 1841-1926 *NatCAB 21*
Pooley, Thomas Rickett 1843-1926 *NatCAB 1*
Pooley, Thomas Rickett 1846-1934 *NatCAB 25*
Poons, Larry 1937- *BnEnAmA*
Poor, Agnes Blake 1842-1922 *NatCAB 19, WhAm 1, WomWWA 14*
Poor, Artemas Brockway 1879-1943 *NatCAB 34*
Poor, Charles Henry 1808-1882 *ApCAB, DcAmB, Drake, NatCAB 7, TwCBDA, WhAm H*
Poor, Charles Lane 1866-1951 *DcScB, NatCAB 14, NatCAB 38, WhAm 3*
Poor, Charles Marshall 1872- *WhAm 5*
Poor, Clarence Henry 1860-1920 *NatCAB 18*
Poor, Cornelia Longstreet 1849- *WomWWA 14*
Poor, Daniel 1789-1855 *ApCAB, DcAmB, Drake, TwCBDA, WhAm H*
Poor, Daniel Warren 1818-1897 *ApCAB, TwCBDA*
Poor, Edward Eri 1861-1951 *NatCAB 47*
Poor, Edward Eri 1889-1957 *NatCAB 47*
Poor, Edward Erie 1837-1900 *NatCAB 14*
Poor, Enoch 1736-1780 *AmBi, ApCAB, DcAmB, Drake, NatCAB 1, TwCBDA, WebAMB, WhAm H*
Poor, Frank A 1880-1956 *WhAm 3*
Poor, Fred Arthur 1870-1953 *WhAm 3*
Poor, Henry Varnum 1812-1905 *DcAmB, EncAAB, WebAB*
Poor, Henry Varnum 1880-1931 *NatCAB 25*
Poor, Henry Varnum 1888-1970 *BnEnAmA, IlBEAAW, WhAm 5*
Poor, Henry Varnum 1914-1972 *NatCAB 57*
Poor, Henry William 1844-1915 *ApCAB X, NatCAB 16, WhAm 1*
Poor, James Harper 1862- *ApCAB X*
Poor, John 1752-1829 *BiDAmEd, DcAmB, WhAm H*
Poor, John Alfred 1808-1871 *ApCAB, DcAmB, Drake, WhAm H*
Poor, John Merrill 1871-1933 *NatCAB 25, WhAm 1*
Poor, Jonathan D *NewYHSD*
Poor, Mary Adelaide 1863- *WomWWA 14*
Poor, Ruel Whitcomb 1860-1941 *WhAm 1*
Poor, Russell Spurgeon 1899-1972 *WhAm 5*

Poor, Walter Everett 1885-1950 *WhAm 3*
Poor, Wharton 1888-1974 *WhAm 6*
Poor, William Bunker 1901-1973 *WhAm 6*
Poore, Benjamin Andrew 1863-1940 *WhAm 1*
Poore, Benjamin Perley 1820-1887 *AmBi, ApCAB, DcAmB, Drake, NatCAB 8, TwCBDA, WhAm H*
Poore, Charles Graydon 1902-1971 *WhAm 5*
Poore, Henry Rankin 1859-1940 *ApCAB Sup, IlBEAAW, NatCAB 5, TwCBDA, WhAm 1*
Poorman, Alfred Peter 1877-1952 *NatCAB 41, WhAm 3*
Poorman, Christian L 1825- *NatCAB 4*
Poos, Edgar Everett 1894-1967 *NatCAB 54*
Pop Chalee 1908- *IlBEAAW*
Pope d1690 *WebAB, WebAMB*
Pope d1692 *EncAAH*
Pope, Mrs. *NewYHSD*
Pope, Abby Linden *BiCAW*
Pope, Albert Augustus 1843-1909 *ApCAB, DcAmB, NatCAB 1, WebAB, WhAm 1*
Pope, Alexander 1688-1744 *McGEWB*
Pope, Alexander 1849-1924 *BnEnAmA, NatCAB 10, WhAm 1*
Pope, Alfred Atmore 1842-1913 *NatCAB 17, WhAm 1*
Pope, Allan Melvill 1879-1963 *NatCAB 53, WhAm 4*
Pope, Amy Elizabeth 1869- *WhAm 5*
Pope, Anna Isabella 1877- *WomWWA 14*
Pope, Arthur 1880- *WhAm 6*
Pope, Arthur Upham 1881-1969 *WhAm 5*
Pope, Bayard Foster 1887-1968 *WhAm 5*
Pope, Burrell Thomas 1813-1868 *BiAUS*
Pope, Carey Joseph 1858-1932 *WhAm 1*
Pope, Caroline Augusta 1846- *ApCAB*
Pope, Charles Alexander 1818-1870 *ApCAB, Drake, NatCAB 12*
Pope, Charles R 1832-1899 *NatCAB 8*
Pope, Clifford Hillhouse 1899-1974 *WhAm 6*
Pope, Cora Scott Pond 1856- *AmWom*
Pope, Curran 1866-1934 *WhAm 1*
Pope, E Marion 1909-1966 *NatCAB 53*
Pope, Edward Waldron 1845- *WhAm 4*
Pope, Elfrieda Hochbaum 1877- *WomWWA 14*
Pope, Emily Frances 1846- *ApCAB*
Pope, Eugene Madison 1859-1934 *NatCAB 25*
Pope, Francis Horton 1876-1971 *WhAm 5*
Pope, Franklin Leonard 1840-1895 *AmBi, ApCAB, DcAmB, NatCAB 7, TwCBDA, WhAm H*
Pope, Frederick 1877- *WhAm 5*
Pope, George 1844-1918 *NatCAB 18, WhAm 1*
Pope, George Andrew 1864-1942 *NatCAB 54*
Pope, Georgina Fane 1862- *WomWWA 14*
Pope, Gustavus Debrille 1873-1952 *WhAm 3*
Pope, Harold Linder 1879-1961 *NatCAB 53, WhAm 6*
Pope, Henry Francis 1867-1950 *NatCAB 39, WhAm 3*
Pope, Herbert 1870-1958 *WhAm 3*
Pope, James Colledge 1826-1885 *ApCAB*
Pope, James Pinckney 1884-1966 *BiDrAC*
Pope, James Worden 1846-1919 *WhAm 1*
Pope, John 1770-1845 *ApCAB, BiAUS, BiDrAC, Drake, NatCAB 10, TwCBDA, WhAm H, WhAmP*
Pope, John 1798-1876 *ApCAB, Drake, TwCBDA*
Pope, John 1820-1880 *NewYHSD, WhAm H*
Pope, John 1822-1892 *AmBi, ApCAB, DcAmB, REnAW, WebAMB, WhAm H, WhoMilH*
Pope, John 1823-1892 *Drake, NatCAB 4, TwCBDA*
Pope, John Dudley 1856- *WhAm 4*
Pope, John Henry 1824-1889 *ApCAB*
Pope, John Hunter 1845- *ApCAB*
Pope, John Russell 1874-1937 *AmBi, DcAmB S2, NatCAB 28, WhAm 1*
Pope, Joseph 1854- *ApCAB Sup*
Pope, Joseph Anthony 1908-1961 *NatCAB 50*
Pope, Joseph Daniel 1820-1908 *BiDConf*
Pope, Larry Jacob 1937-1975 *WhAm 6*
Pope, Liston 1909-1974 *WhAm 6*

Pope, Marion Manville 1859- *AmWom*
Pope, Menry 1881- *WhoColR*
Pope, Nathaniel 1784-1850 *ApCAB, BiAUS, BiDrAC, DcAmB, NatCAB 9, WhAm H*
Pope, O C 1842- *NatCAB 3*
Pope, Patrick Hamilton 1806-1841 *BiAUS, BiDrAC, WhAm H*
Pope, Percival Clarence 1841-1922 *WhAm 1*
Pope, Ralph Elton 1875-1959 *WhAm 3*
Pope, Ralph Wainwright 1844-1929 *NatCAB 27, WhAm 1*
Pope, Richard 1827- *ApCAB*
Pope, Roy L 1904-1973 *WhAm 6*
Pope, Sarah *NewYHSD*
Pope, Saxton Temple 1875-1926 *NatCAB 20*
Pope, Theodate *NatCAB 30*
Pope, Thomas *NewYHSD*
Pope, Thomas Benjamin d1891 *NewYHSD*
Pope, Thomas Eliot 1848-1928 *NatCAB 21*
Pope, Walter Lyndon 1889-1969 *WhAm 5*
Pope, Willard 1867-1949 *NatCAB 38*
Pope, Willard Smith 1832-1895 *NatCAB 20*
Pope, William Carroll 1847-1913 *NatCAB 36*
Pope, William Hayes 1870-1916 *NatCAB 26, WhAm 1*
Pope, Sir William Jackson 1870-1939 *AsBiEn, DcScB*
Pope, Young John 1841-1911 *NatCAB 13, WhAm 1*
Popejoy, Thomas Lafayette 1902-1975 *WhAm 6*
Popeney, Harry Virgil 1885-1958 *NatCAB 51*
Popenoe, Charles Broadwell 1887-1929 *NatCAB 22*
Popenot *NewYHSD*
Popham, Sir Francis *ApCAB*
Popham, George 1550?-1608 *AmBi, ApCAB, DcAmB, Drake, WhAm H*
Popham, Sir John 1531-1607 *ApCAB*
Popham, William 1752-1849 *NatCAB 4*
Popkin, John Snelling 1771-1852 *ApCAB, Drake*
Popma, Gerritt Jacob 1904-1967 *WhAm 4*
Popoff, Stephen 1885-1931 *WhAm 1*
Popov, Aleksandr Nikiforivich 1840?-1881 *DcScB*
Popov, Aleksandr Stepanovich 1859-1906 *DcScB*
Popov, Alexander Stepanovich 1859-1905 *AsBiEn*
Popov, Markian 1902- *WhWW-II*
Popov-Veniaminov, Joann 1797-1879 *WhAm H*
Popovic, Vladimir 1914-1972 *WhAm 5*
Poppel, John *NewYHSD*
Poppen, Anna Trebel 1874- *WomWWA 14*
Poppen, Emmanuel Frederick 1874-1961 *WhAm 4*
Poppen, Hero Tjarks 1867-1944 *NatCAB 33*
Poppenheim, Christopher Pritchard 1839-1901 *NatCAB 17*
Poppenheim, Louisa Bouknight 1868- *WomWWA 14*
Poppenheim, Mary Barnett 1866-1936 *WhAm 1, WomWWA 14*
Poppenhusen, Conrad Herman 1872-1949 *WhAm 2*
Popper, Sir Karl Raimund 1902- *McGEWB*
Popper, William 1874-1963 *WhAm 4*
Poppleton, Andrew Jackson 1830-1896 *ApCAB X*
Poppleton, E F 1834-1899 *BiAUS*
Poppleton, Earley Franklin 1834-1899 *BiDrAC*
Poppleton, William Sears 1866-1913 *NatCAB 16*
Poppo, Martin Joseph 1903-1963 *NatCAB 50*
Poray, Stan Pociecha 1888-1948 *IlBEAAW*
Porcallo DeFigueroa, Vasco 1494-1550 *ApCAB*
Porcher, Miss *NewYHSD*
Porcher, Francis Peyre 1824-1895 *TwCBDA*
Porcher, Francis Peyre 1825-1895 *ApCAB, BiDConf, DcAmB, Drake Sup, WhAm H*
Poret DeBlosseville, Benique Ernest 1799-1882 *ApCAB*
Poret DeBlosseville, Jules A Rene 1802-1834 *ApCAB*
Poretsky, Platon Sergeevich 1846-1907 *DcScB*
Pormort, Philemon 1595?-1656? *DcAmB, WhAm H*
Porras, Belisario 1856- *WhAm 4*
Porrez, Martin De 1579-1639 *ApCAB*

Porritt, Annie Gertrude 1861- *BiCAW,*
WomWWA 14
Porritt, Edward 1860-1921 *WhAm 1*
Porro, Francis Porro Y Peinado d1802? *ApCAB,*
NatCAB 7
Porro, Ignazio 1801-1875 *DcScB*
Porro, Thomas J 1891-1959 *WhAm 4*
Porskievies, Anthony Joseph 1883-1948
NatCAB 38
Port, Mary Alice *WomWWA 14*
Porta, Armando Joseph 1904-1967 *NatCAB 54*
Porta, Giacomo Della 1537?-1602 *McGEWB*
Porta, Giambattista Della 1535-1615 *DcScB,*
McGEWB
Porta, Luigi 1800-1875 *DcScB*
Portail, M Pontel Du *NewYHSD*
Portal, Antoine 1742-1832 *DcScB*
Portal, Sir Charles 1893-1971 *WhWW-II,*
WhoMilH
Portal, Wyndham Raymond 1885-1949
WhAm 2
Portales, Diego Jose Victor 1793-1837 *ApCAB*
Portales Plazazuelos, Diego Jose Victor
1793-1837 *McGEWB*
Porte Crayon *NewYHSD*
Portela, Epifanio 1855- *WhAm 4*
Porteous, James 1849-1922 *NatCAB 20*
Porteous, John 1850-1939 *NatCAB 39*
Porter, A W Noel 1885-1963 *WhAm 4*
Porter, Albert d1930 *WhAm 1*
Porter, Albert Gallatin 1824-1897 *ApCAB,*
BiAUS, BiDrAC, DcAmB, NatCAB 13,
TwCBDA, WhAm H, WhAmP
Porter, Alexander 1785-1844 *AmBi, DcAmB*
Porter, Alexander 1786-1844 *ApCAB, BiAUS,*
BiDrAC, Drake, NatCAB 13, TwCBDA,
WhAm H
Porter, Alexander James 1822-1888 *NatCAB 8,*
TwCBDA
Porter, Alice Downey 1856- *WomWWA 14*
Porter, Alice Hobbins 1854- *AmWom*
Porter, Andrew 1743-1813 *ApCAB, DcAmB,*
Drake, NatCAB 1, TwCBDA, WhAm H
Porter, Andrew 1819-1872 *Drake Sup*
Porter, Andrew 1820-1872 *ApCAB, TwCBDA*
Porter, Arthur Kingsley 1883-1933 *BiDAmEd,*
DcAmB S1, NatCAB 28, NatCAB 40,
WhAm 1
Porter, Arthur LeMoyne 1873- *WhAm 5*
Porter, Augustus S 1798-1872 *BiAUS*
Porter, Augustus Seymour 1798-1872 *BiDrAC,*
WhAm H
Porter, Augustus Steele 1798-1872 *ApCAB,*
NatCAB 11, TwCBDA
Porter, Benjamin Curtis d1908 *TwCBDA,*
WhAm 1
Porter, Benjamin Curtis 1843-1908 *ApCAB,*
NatCAB 26
Porter, Benjamin Curtis 1845-1908 *AmBi,*
DcAmB
Porter, Benjamin Fickling 1808- *ApCAB,*
Drake
Porter, Bruce 1865-1953 *NatCAB 51,*
WhAm 5
Porter, Charles A 1839- *NatCAB 3*
Porter, Charles Allen 1866-1931 *NatCAB 23,*
WhAm 1
Porter, Charles Burnham 1840-1909 *WhAm 1*
Porter, Charles Howell 1833-1897 *BiAUS,*
BiDrAC, WhAm H
Porter, Charles Orlando 1919- *BiDrAC*
Porter, Charles Scott 1897-1966 *WhAm 4*
Porter, Charles Talbot 1826-1910 *AmBi,*
NatCAB 20
Porter, Mrs. Charles Vernon *WomWWA 14*
Porter, Charles Vernon 1885-1962 *WhAm 4*
Porter, Charley Lyman 1889-1966 *WhAm 4*
Porter, Charlotte Endymion d1942
WomWWA 14
Porter, Charlotte Endymion 1857-1942 *NotAW*
Porter, Charlotte Endymion 1859-1942
TwCBDA
Porter, Charlotte Williams 1840- *WhAm 4,*
WomWWA 14
Porter, Clara Chamberlain *WomWWA 14*
Porter, Claude Rodman 1872-1946 *NatCAB 45,*
WhAm 2
Porter, Clyde Alden 1897-1955 *NatCAB 42*

Porter, Cole Albert 1891-1964 *McGEWB*
Porter, Cole Albert 1892-1964 *EncAB*
Porter, Cole Albert 1893-1964 *WebAB,*
WhAm 4
Porter, Cyrus Kinne 1828-1910 *NatCAB 2*
Porter, Dana 1901-1967 *WhAm 4*
Porter, David 1761-1851 *ApCAB, Drake*
Porter, David 1780-1843 *AmBi, ApCAB,*
BiAUS, DcAmB, Drake, NatCAB 2,
NewYHSD, TwCBDA, WebAB,
WebAMB, WhAm H
Porter, David Dixon 1813-1891 *AmBi, ApCAB,*
DcAmB, Drake, NatCAB 2, TwCBDA,
WebAB, WebAMB, WhAm H, WhoMilH
Porter, David Dixon 1878-1944 *WhAm 2*
Porter, David H 1804-1828 *ApCAB*
Porter, David Richard 1882-1973 *WhAm 6*
Porter, David Rittenhouse 1788-1867 *ApCAB,*
BiAUS, DcAmB, Drake, NatCAB 2,
TwCBDA, WhAm H
Porter, David Tinsley 1827-1898 *NatCAB 8*
Porter, Delia Lyman 1858-1933 *WhAm 1,*
WomWWA 14
Porter, Dwight 1855-1935 *WhAm 1*
Porter, Earle Sellers 1888-1951 *NatCAB 42,*
WhAm 3
Porter, Ebenezer 1772-1834 *ApCAB, DcAmB,*
Drake, NatCAB 10, TwCBDA, WhAm H
Porter, Edward Arthur Gribbon 1895-1974
WhAm 6
Porter, Edwin Stanton 1870-1941 *DcAmB S3,*
NatCAB 30
Porter, Elbert Stothoff 1820-1888 *NatCAB 9,*
TwCBDA
Porter, Eleanor Hodgman 1868-1920 *BiCAW,*
NatCAB 18, NotAW, WhAm 1
Porter, Eliphalet 1758-1833 *ApCAB, Drake,*
NatCAB 7, TwCBDA
Porter, Eliza Emily Chappell 1807-1888 *NotAW*
Porter, Ella Caruthers 1864- *WomWWA 14*
Porter, Ernest Warren 1873- *WhAm 5*
Porter, Eugene Hoffman 1856-1929 *WhAm 1*
Porter, F Addison 1859-1941 *WhAm 1*
Porter, Fairfield 1907-1975 *BnEnAmA,*
WhAm 6
Porter, Fitz-John 1822-1901 *AmBi, ApCAB,*
DcAmB, Drake, NatCAB 4, TwCBDA,
WebAMB, WhAm 1
Porter, Fitz John 1889-1946 *NatCAB 35*
Porter, Florence Collins 1853-1930 *AmWom,*
BiCAW, WhAm 1, WomWWA 14
Porter, Frank Chamberlin 1859-1946 *WhAm 2*
Porter, Frank M 1892-1962 *WhAm 4*
Porter, Frank Monroe 1857-1936 *WhAm 1*
Porter, Fred Thomas 1904-1971 *NatCAB 57,*
WhAm 5
Porter, Gene Stratton d1924 *WomWWA 14*
Porter, Gene Stratton 1863-1924 *DcAmB S1,*
EncAAH, NotAW, WebAB
Porter, Gene Stratton 1868-1924 *AmBi,*
NatCAB 15, WhAm 1
Porter, George 1920- *AsBiEn*
Porter, George B 1790-1834 *BiAUS, Drake*
Porter, George Bryan 1791-1834 *ApCAB,*
NatCAB 5, TwCBDA
Porter, George Edwin 1878-1954 *NatCAB 43*
Porter, George French 1881-1927 *WhAm 1*
Porter, George W 1806?-1856 *ApCAB, Drake*
Porter, Georgia Pulsifer *WomWWA 14*
Porter, Georgia Whidden *WomWWA 14*
Porter, Gilbert Edwin 1863-1942 *NatCAB 31,*
WhAm 2
Porter, Gilchrist 1817-1894 *BiAUS, BiDrAC,*
WhAm H
Porter, Harold Everett 1887-1936 *WhAm 1*
Porter, Helen Talbot 1872- *WomWWA 14*
Porter, Henry Alanson 1886-1968 *WhAm 5*
Porter, Henry Alford 1871-1946 *WhAm 2*
Porter, Henry Dwight 1845-1916 *WhAm 1*
Porter, Henry H 1835-1910 *WhAm 1*
Porter, Henry Hobart 1865-1947 *ApCAB X,*
WhAm 2
Porter, Henry Kirke 1840-1921 *BiDrAC,*
NatCAB 13, NatCAB 29, WhAm 1
Porter, Henry Miller 1838-1937 *NatCAB 28,*
WhAm 1
Porter, Henry Moses 1872- *WhoColR*
Porter, Henry Ogden 1823-1872 *ApCAB*

Porter, Henry Phillip 1879- *WhoColR*
Porter, Henry Ware *WhoColR*
Porter, Holbrook Fitz-John 1858-1933 *DcAmB,*
WhAm 1
Porter, Horace 1837-1921 *AmBi, ApCAB,*
ApCAB X, DcAmB, NatCAB 4,
NatCAB 28, TwCBDA, WhAm 1
Porter, Horace 1863-1940 *NatCAB 31*
Porter, Hubert Elmer Volney 1861-
NatCAB 16
Porter, Hugh 1897-1960 *WhAm 4*
Porter, Hugh Omega 1898-1966 *WhAm 4*
Porter, Irvin Lourie 1881- *WhAm 6*
Porter, J D Forest *BiAUS*
Porter, J DeForest *BiAUS Sup*
Porter, J Elmer 1865-1961 *NatCAB 49*
Porter, J Sherman 1872- *WhAm 5*
Porter, J T *NewYHSD*
Porter, James d1859 *Drake*
Porter, James 1787-1839 *BiAUS, BiDrAC,*
WhAm H
Porter, James 1808-1888 *ApCAB*
Porter, James A d1970 *WhAm 5*
Porter, James Davis 1828-1912 *ApCAB,*
BiAUS, DcAmB, NatCAB 7, TwCBDA,
WhAm 1
Porter, James Dunlop 1909-1969 *WhAm 5*
Porter, James Henry 1829- *NatCAB 2*
Porter, James Hyde 1873-1949 *NatCAB 38,*
WhAm 2
Porter, James Madison 1793-1862 *ApCAB,*
BiAUS, BiDrUSE, DcAmB, Drake,
NatCAB 6, WhAm H
Porter, James Madison, III 1864- *WhAm 4*
Porter, James Pertice 1873-1956 *WhAm 3*
Porter, James Temple 1873-1931 *WhAm 1*
Porter, James W 1887-1959 *WhAm 3*
Porter, Jermain Gildersleeve 1852-1933 *DcAmB,*
NatCAB 13, WhAm 1
Porter, Joe Frank 1880-1951 *WhAm 3*
Porter, John *BiAUS, BiDrAC, NewYHSD,*
WhAm H
Porter, John Addison 1822-1866 *ApCAB,*
DcAmB, Drake, TwCBDA, WhAm H
Porter, John Addison 1856-1900 *ApCAB,*
NatCAB 9, NatCAB 28, TwCBDA,
WhAm 1
Porter, John Clinton 1872-1959 *WhAm 3*
Porter, John Edward 1857- *WhoColR*
Porter, John Henry 1876-1922 *WhAm 1*
Porter, John J *NewYHSD*
Porter, John Jermain 1880-1956 *NatCAB 46,*
WhAm 6
Porter, John Kilham 1819-1892 *ApCAB Sup,*
NatCAB 3, TwCBDA
Porter, John Lincoln 1864-1938 *NatCAB 29,*
WhAm 1
Porter, John Luke 1813-1893 *DcAmB,*
WebAMB, WhAm H
Porter, John Lupher 1868-1937 *NatCAB 28,*
WhAm 1
Porter, John S *NewYHSD*
Porter, John William 1863-1937 *WhAm 1*
Porter, Joseph Franklin 1863-1942 *WhAm 2*
Porter, Joseph Yates 1847-1927 *WhAm 1*
Porter, Josephine Perry 1874- *WomWWA 14*
Porter, Joshua 1730-1825 *ApCAB, TwCBDA*
Porter, Josiah 1830-1894 *NatCAB 5*
Porter, Kate Leland Lincoln *WomWWA 14*
Porter, Katherine 1872- *WomWWA 14*
Porter, Katherine Anne 1890- *McGEWB,*
WebAB
Porter, Kenneth Wiggins 1905- *REnAW*
Porter, Kirk Harold 1891-1972 *WhAm 5*
Porter, Lester Gilbert 1903-1970 *NatCAB 55,*
WhAm 5
Porter, Linn Boyd 1851-1916 *WhAm 1*
Porter, Louis Hopkins 1874-1946 *NatCAB 35,*
WhAm 2
Porter, Lucius Chapin 1880-1958 *NatCAB 47,*
WhAm 3
Porter, Lydia Ann Emerson 1816- *ApCAB*
Porter, M *NewYHSD*
Porter, Margaret Cochran Dewar 1872-
WomWWA 14
Porter, Marion Otis 1875- *WomWWA 14*
Porter, Melissa Patterson 1873- *WomWWA 14*
Porter, Miles Fuller 1856-1933 *NatCAB 32,*

WhAm 1
Porter, Miles Fuller, Jr. 1887-1952 NatCAB 41
Porter, Milton Brockett 1869-1960 NatCAB 49
Porter, Minor Gibson 1865-1947 NatCAB 38
Porter, Moses 1755-1822 ApCAB, Drake
Porter, Newton Hazelton 1877-1945 WhAm 2
Porter, Noah 1781-1866 ApCAB
Porter, Noah 1811-1892 AmBi, ApCAB,
   BiDAmEd, DcAmB, Drake, NatCAB 1,
   TwCBDA, WhAm H
Porter, Oliver Saffold 1836-1914 NatCAB 33
Porter, Otho Dandrith 1864- WhoColR
Porter, Paul Aldermandt 1904-1975 WhAm 6
Porter, Peter Augustus 1827-1864 ApCAB
Porter, Peter Augustus 1853-1925 BiDrAC
Porter, Peter B 1773-1844 BiAUS
Porter, Peter Buel 1773-1844 ApCAB, Drake,
   NatCAB 5, TwCBDA
Porter, Peter Buell 1773-1844 AmBi, BiDrAC,
   BiDrUSE, DcAmB, WhAm H
Porter, Phil 1887-1965 WhAm 4
Porter, Pleasant 1840-1907 NatCAB 19
Porter, Quincy 1897-1966 WhAm 4
Porter, Robert Henry 1876-1952 NatCAB 48
Porter, Robert Langley 1870-1965 WhAm 4
Porter, Robert Percival 1852-1917 DcAmB,
   WhAm 1
Porter, Robert Percival 1854-1917 NatCAB 12
Porter, Roland Guyer 1894-1953 NatCAB 40,
   WhAm 3
Porter, Rose 1845-1906 AmWom, NatCAB 10,
   WhAm 1
Porter, Royal A 1877- WhAm 5
Porter, Rufus 1792-1884 ApCAB, BnEnAmA,
   DcAmB, NatCAB 7, NewYHSD,
   TwCBDA, WhAm H
Porter, Russell Williams 1871-1949 DcAmB S4,
   WhAm 2
Porter, Ruth Wadsworth Furness
   WomWWA 14
Porter, Samuel 1760-1825 ApCAB
Porter, Samuel 1810-1901 ApCAB, DcAmB,
   NatCAB 25, WhAm 1
Porter, Samuel Doak 1896-1966 NatCAB 52
Porter, Sarah 1813-1900 ApCAB, BiDAmEd,
   DcAmB, NatCAB 10, NotAW, TwCBDA,
   WhAm H
Porter, Seton 1882-1953 WhAm 3
Porter, Silas Wright 1857-1937 WhAm 1
Porter, Stephen Geyer 1869-1930 BiDrAC,
   DcAmB, WhAm 1, WhAmP
Porter, Stephen Twombly 1816-1850
   NewYHSD
Porter, Susan Creighton WomWWA 14
Porter, Sydney 1867-1910 WhAm 1
Porter, Theodoric 1849-1920 NatCAB 25,
   WhAm 1
Porter, Theodoric Henry 1817-1846 ApCAB
Porter, Therese Study WomWWA 14
Porter, Thomas 1734-1833 ApCAB, BiAUS,
   Drake
Porter, Thomas Conrad 1822-1901 ApCAB,
   DcAmB, NatCAB 11, TwCBDA,
   WhAm 1
Porter, Thomas Edward 1896-1956 NatCAB 45
Porter, Timothy H d1840? BiAUS, BiDrAC,
   WhAm H
Porter, Valentine Mott 1870-1915 WhAm 1
Porter, W Evelyn NatCAB 5
Porter, Washington 1843-1922 ApCAB X
Porter, Washington, II 1893- ApCAB X
Porter, Washington Tullis 1850-1933
   NatCAB 24, WhAm 1
Porter, Whitney Clair 1897-1970 WhAm 5
Porter, William Arnold 1906-1976 WhAm 6
Porter, William Augustus 1821-1886 ApCAB,
   BiAUS, Drake
Porter, William Curren 1910-1965 WhAm 4
Porter, William David 1809-1864 AmBi,
   ApCAB, NatCAB 2, TwCBDA
Porter, William David 1810-1864 Drake
Porter, William David 1850-1930 WhAm 1
Porter, William Dodge 1831-1912 NatCAB 18
Porter, William E NewYHSD
Porter, William Gove 1858-1927 WhAm 1
Porter, William Hamilton 1890-1937
   NatCAB 32
Porter, William Henry 1853-1933 WhAm 1

Porter, William Henry 1861-1926 WhAm 1
Porter, William Impey 1919-1965 NatCAB 51
Porter, William Luther 1918-1975 WhAm 6
Porter, William N 1886-1973 WhAm 5
Porter, William Sidney 1862-1910 ApCAB X
Porter, William Stratton 1887-1964
   NatCAB 50
Porter, William Surber 1867-1948 NatCAB 37
Porter, William Sydney 1862-1910 AmBi,
   DcAmB, NatCAB 15, WebAB
Porter, William Townsend 1862-1949
   DcAmB S4, NatCAB 15, WhAm 2
Porter, William Trotter 1806-1858 Drake
Porter, William Trotter 1809-1858 ApCAB,
   DcAmB, TwCBDA, WhAm H
Porter, William Wagener 1856-1928 WhAm 1
Porter, William Wallace 1864- WhAm 5
Porterfield, Allen Wilson 1878-1952 WhAm 3
Porterfield, Austin Roy 1876-1961 NatCAB 50
Porterfield, Charles 1750-1780 ApCAB, Drake,
   TwCBDA
Porterfield, Frank William 1860-1937
   NatCAB 28
Porterfield, Lewis Broughton 1879-1942
   WhAm 2
Porterfield, Robert 1752-1843 ApCAB, Drake,
   TwCBDA
Porterfield, Robert Huffard 1905-1971
   NatCAB 57, WhAm 5
Porterfield, William Hempstead 1872-1927
   NatCAB 21
Porterie, Gaston Louis 1885-1953 NatCAB 42,
   WhAm 3
Portevin, Albert Marcel Germain Rene
   1880-1962 DcScB, WhAm 4
Portier, Michael 1795-1859 DcAmB, Drake,
   NatCAB 7, TwCBDA, WhAm H
Portier, Michel 1795-1859 ApCAB
Portier, Paul 1866-1962 DcScB
Portillo, Jacinto De 1490?-1566 ApCAB
Portinari, Candido 1903-1962 McGEWB,
   WhAm 4
Portlock, Nathaniel 1748?-1817 ApCAB,
   NewYHSD
Portman, Eric 1908-1969 WhAm 5
Portmann, Ursus Victor 1887-1966 WhAm 4
Portner, Edward 1835?- NewYHSD
Portner, Robert 1837- NatCAB 10
Portner, William 1888-1948 NatCAB 36
Portnoff, Alexander 1887-1949 WhAm 2
Portocarrero Laso DeLaVega, Melchor De
   1636-1705 ApCAB
Portola, Gaspar De 1723?-1784? AmBi,
   DcAmB, McGEWB, WebAB, WhAm H
Portor, Laura Spencer d1957 WhAm 3
Portuondo, Bernardo 1840- ApCAB
Pory, John 1570?-1635? ApCAB, NatCAB 8
Pory, John 1572-1635 DcAmB, WhAm H
Posadas, Gervasio Antonio 1757-1832 ApCAB
Posegate, Mabel d1957 WhAm 3
Poseidonius 135?BC-050?BC AsBiEn
Poseidonius see also Posidonius
Posepny, Franz 1836-1895 DcScB
Posey, Alexander Lawrence 1873-1908 DcAmB,
   NatCAB 19, REnAW
Posey, Benjamin Lane 1827-1888 ApCAB Sup
Posey, Carnot 1818-1863 ApCAB, Drake
Posey, Chester Alfred 1896-1971 WhAm 5
Posey, Francis Blackburn 1848-1915 BiDrAC
Posey, Leroy R 1880- WhAm 6
Posey, Thomas 1750-1818 ApCAB, BiAUS,
   BiDrAC, DcAmB, Drake, NatCAB 13,
   TwCBDA, WhAm H
Posey, Walter Brownlow 1922- EncAAH
Posey, William Campbell 1866-1934 WhAm 1
Posidonius 135?BC-051?BC DcScB
Posidonius see also Poseidonius
Posner, Abraham 1865-1935 NatCAB 27
Posner, Edwin Forest 1890-1969 NatCAB 55,
   WhAm 5
Posner, Harry 1879-1962 NatCAB 46
Posner, Harry 1889-1962 WhAm 4
Posner, Jacob David 1889-1923 NatCAB 20
Posner, Louis Samuel WhAm 5
Posner, Stanley I 1909-1965 WhAm 4
Posse, Nils 1862-1895 BiDAmEd
Posse, Baroness Rose WhAm 5,
   WomWWA 14

Possel, Rene De 1905-1974 WhAm 6
Posselt, Emanuel Anthony 1858- NatCAB 10
Posselwhite, George W 1822?- NewYHSD
Post, Abner 1844-1934 NatCAB 29
Post, Alfred Charles 1806-1886 AmBi, ApCAB,
   NatCAB 9, TwCBDA
Post, Alice Thacher 1853-1947 WhAm 2,
   WomWWA 14
Post, Amalia Barney Simons 1836- AmWom
Post, Augustus 1873-1952 DcAmB S5
Post, Caroline Lathrop 1824- AmWom
Post, Chandler Rathfon 1881-1959 WhAm 3
Post, Charles Addison 1886-1973 WhAm 6
Post, Charles Cyrel 1846- TwCBDA
Post, Charles Henderson 1856-1925
   NatCAB 24
Post, Charles Johnson 1873-1956 WhAm 3
Post, Charles William 1854-1914 DcAmB,
   NatCAB 14, NatCAB 25, WebAB,
   WhAm 1
Post, Chester Leroy 1880-1950 WhAm 3
Post, Christian Frederick 1710?-1785 ApCAB,
   DcAmB, NatCAB 25, WebAB, WhAm H
Post, Edward C NewYHSD
Post, Edwin 1851-1932 WhAm 1
Post, Elwyn Donald 1899-1961 WhAm 4
Post, Emil Leon 1897-1954 DcScB
Post, Emily Price d1960 WhAm 4
Post, Emily Price 1872-1960 NatCAB 44
Post, Emily Price 1873-1960 WebAB
Post, Frank Truman 1862-1941 WhAm 1
Post, Franklin Grotus 1880-1962 NatCAB 54
Post, Fred Burton 1894-1966 NatCAB 53
Post, George Adam 1854-1925 WhAm 1
Post, George Adams 1854-1925 BiDrAC,
   DcAmB, NatCAB 25
Post, George Brown 1837-1913 NatCAB 13
Post, George Browne 1837-1913 AmBi,
   DcAmB, NatCAB 15, WhAm 1
Post, George Browne 1890-1952 NatCAB 44
Post, George Edward 1838-1909 DcAmB,
   NatCAB 13, TwCBDA, WhAm 1
Post, Herbert Wilson 1886-1960 WhAm 4
Post, Hoyt Garrod 1884-1958 WhAm 3
Post, Isaac 1798-1872 ApCAB, DcAmB,
   WhAm H
Post, James Douglass 1863-1921 BiDrAC,
   WhAm 1
Post, James Howell 1859-1938 ApCAB X,
   NatCAB 14, WhAm 1
Post, James Otis 1873-1951 NatCAB 42,
   WhAm 3
Post, Janet Greig 1871- WomWWA 14
Post, Joseph 1803-1888 ApCAB
Post, Joseph Walter 1869-1969 NatCAB 54
Post, Josephine Fowler 1870-1946 WhAm 2
Post, Jotham, Jr. 1771-1817 BiAUS, BiDrAC,
   WhAm H
Post, Kenneth 1904-1955 NatCAB 42,
   WhAm 3
Post, Lawrence T 1887-1959 WhAm 3
Post, Lawrence Tyler 1887-1958 NatCAB 53
Post, Levi Arnold 1889-1971 WhAm 5
Post, Louis Freeland 1849-1928 DcAmB,
   NatCAB 18, TwCBDA, WhAm 1
Post, Marjorie Merriweather 1887-1973
   WhAm 6
Post, Martin Hayward 1851-1914 NatCAB 15,
   NatCAB 19, WhAm 1
Post, Mary Elizabeth 1840- WomWWA 14
Post, Mary Ellen WomWWA 14
Post, Mary Tanner 1868- WomWWA 14
Post, Melville Davisson 1871-1930 DcAmB,
   WhAm 1
Post, Minturn 1808-1869 ApCAB, Drake
Post, Morton Everel 1840-1933 BiDrAC,
   WhAmP
Post, Philip Sidney 1833-1895 ApCAB,
   BiDrAC, NatCAB 4, TwCBDA,
   WhAm H, WhAmP
Post, Philip Sidney 1869-1920 NatCAB 19
Post, Regis Henri 1870-1944 WhAm 2
Post, Roswell Olcott 1850- WhAm 4
Post, Sarah E 1853- AmWom
Post, Truman Marcellus 1810-1886 ApCAB,
   DcAmB, WhAm H
Post, Waldron Kintzing 1868-1955 WhAm 3
Post, Wilbur E 1877-1963 WhAm 4

Post, Wiley 1898-1935 *AmBi, WebAB*
Post, Wiley 1899-1935 *DcAmB S1*
Post, Wiley 1900-1935 *WhAm 1*
Post, William Merritt 1856-1935 *WhAm 1*
Post, William Stone 1866-1940 *WhAm 1*
Post, Wright 1766-1828 *ApCAB, DcAmB, Drake, NatCAB 9, TwCBDA, WhAm H*
Poste, Jennie May *WomWWA 14*
Postell, Benjamin 1760-1801 *ApCAB, Drake*
Postl, Carl 1793-1864 *DcAmB*
Postl, Karl Anton *WhAm H*
Postle, James Martin 1861-1951 *NatCAB 40*
Postle, Wilbur Everett 1860- *WhAm 1*
Postlethwaite, Robert Hodgshon 1862- *WhAm 4*
Postlethwaite, William Wallace 1870- *WhAm 5*
Postley, Brooke *NatCAB 3*
Postley, Clarence Ashley 1849-1908 *NatCAB 3, NatCAB 16*
Postley, Sterling 1877-1928 *NatCAB 16, NatCAB 39*
Postnikov, Fedor Alexis 1872- *WhAm 5*
Poston, Charles D 1825-1902 *BiAUS*
Poston, Charles Debrill 1825-1902 *DcAmB*
Poston, Charles Debrille 1825-1902 *BiDrAC, REnAW, WhAmP*
Poston, Charles Pebrille 1825-1902 *WhAm H*
Poston, Elias McClellan 1862-1931 *WhAm 1*
Poston, Ephriam 1865- *WhoColR*
Poston, Lawrence Sanford, Jr. 1902-1974 *WhAm 6*
Poston, Mollie 1872- *WhoColR*
Potain, Pierre-Carl-Edouard 1825-1901 *BiHiMed*
Potamian, Brother 1847-1917 *DcAmB*
Potanin, Grigory Nikolaevich 1835-1920 *DcScB*
Potanou 1525?-1570? *ApCAB*
Pote, William, Jr. 1718-1755? *ApCAB Sup*
Poteat, Edwin McNeill 1861-1937 *WhAm 1*
Poteat, Edwin McNeill 1892-1955 *WhAm 3*
Poteat, Edwin McNiel 1861-1937 *NatCAB 14*
Poteat, Hubert McNeil 1886-1958 *WhAm 3*
Poteat, James Douglass 1903-1950 *WhAm 2*
Poteat, William Louis 1856-1938 *BiDAmEd, NatCAB 28, WhAm 1*
Potemkin, Grigori Aleksandrovich 1739-1791 *McGEWB*
Potemkin, Prince Grigori Alexandrovich 1731-1791 *WhoMilH*
Pothier, Aram J 1854-1928 *NatCAB 15, WhAm 1*
Potocki, Jerzy 1889-1961 *WhAm 4*
Potratz, Herbert August 1902-1975 *WhAm 6*
Pott, Francis Lister Hawks 1864-1947 *WhAm 2*
Pott, Francis Lister Hawks 1864-1949 *DcAmB S4*
Pott, Johann Heinrich 1692-1777 *DcScB*
Pott, John d1642? *DcAmB, NatCAB 13, WhAm H*
Pott, Percivall 1714-1788 *BiHiMed*
Pott, William Sumner Appleton 1892-1967 *WhAm 4A*
Pottenger, Francis Marion 1869-1961 *ApCAB X, NatCAB 13, NatCAB 16, WhAm 4*
Potter, A 1825- *BiAUS*
Potter, Albert Edwin 1873-1949 *NatCAB 38*
Potter, Albert Franklin 1859- *WhAm 4*
Potter, Albert Knight 1864- *WhAm 4*
Potter, Alfred Claghorn 1867-1940 *WhAm 1*
Potter, Alfred Knight 1880-1936 *WhAm 1*
Potter, Allen 1818-1885 *BiDrAC, WhAm H*
Potter, Alonzo 1800-1865 *AmBi, ApCAB, BiDAmEd, DcAmB, Drake, NatCAB 3, TwCBDA, WhAm H*
Potter, Anna Louise Arnold 1867- *WomWWA 14*
Potter, Austin 1873-1944 *NatCAB 33*
Potter, Barrett 1857-1926 *NatCAB 28*
Potter, Burton Willis 1843- *WhAm 4*
Potter, Carlton Frasier 1883-1962 *NatCAB 48*
Potter, Chandler Eastman 1807-1868 *ApCAB, Drake, NatCAB 7*
Potter, Charles 1908-1970 *NatCAB 56, WhAm 5*
Potter, Charles Edward 1916- *BiDrAC*
Potter, Charles Francis 1885-1962 *NatCAB 52, WhAm 4*

Potter, Charles Lewis 1864-1928 *WhAm 1*
Potter, Charles Nelson 1852-1927 *NatCAB 3, NatCAB 35, TwCBDA, WhAm 1*
Potter, Chester Delos 1862-1921 *NatCAB 19*
Potter, Chester Magee 1899-1956 *WhAm 3*
Potter, Clarkson 1880- *WhAm 6*
Potter, Clarkson Nott 1825-1882 *AmBi, ApCAB, BiAUS, BiDrAC, NatCAB 3, TwCBDA, WhAm H, WhAmP*
Potter, Cora Urquhart d1936 *AmWom, WhAm 1, WomWWA 14*
Potter, Crowell *NewYHSD*
Potter, David 1874- *WhAm 5*
Potter, David Morris 1910-1971 *EncAB, WhAm 5*
Potter, Delbert Maxwell *WhAm 5*
Potter, Dexter Burton 1840-1917 *NatCAB 17*
Potter, Edward Clark 1800-1826 *NewYHSD*
Potter, Edward Clark 1857-1923 *AmBi, DcAmB, NatCAB 26, WhAm 1*
Potter, Edward Eells 1833-1902 *ApCAB, TwCBDA*
Potter, Edward Eels 1833-1902 *WhAm 1*
Potter, Edward Elmer 1823-1889 *ApCAB, TwCBDA*
Potter, Edward Tuckerman 1831- *ApCAB, NewYHSD*
Potter, Edwin Augustus 1842-1936 *WhAm 1*
Potter, Eliphalet Nott 1836-1901 *AmBi, ApCAB, DcAmB, NatCAB 7, TwCBDA, WhAm 1*
Potter, Eliphalet Nott 1878- *NatCAB 14*
Potter, Elisha Reynolds 1764-1835 *ApCAB, BiAUS, BiDrAC, Drake, NatCAB 2, TwCBDA, WhAm H, WhAmP*
Potter, Elisha Reynolds 1811-1882 *ApCAB, BiAUS, BiDAmEd, BiDrAC, DcAmB, Drake, TwCBDA, WhAm H, WhAmP*
Potter, Ellen Culver 1871-1958 *WhAm 3, WomWWA 14*
Potter, Emery Davis 1804-1896 *BiAUS, BiDrAC, WhAm H*
Potter, Ezra Barker 1848-1921 *NatCAB 19*
Potter, Florence Hollister Dangerfield 1868- *BiCAW, WomWWA 14*
Potter, Frances Boardman Squire 1867-1914 *BiCAW, NatCAB 15*
Potter, Francis Drake 1876-1941 *NatCAB 30*
Potter, Francis Marmaduke 1888-1952 *NatCAB 43*
Potter, Frank B 1891-1970 *WhAm 5*
Potter, Frank Maxson 1873-1950 *WhAm 2A*
Potter, George Milton 1875- *WhAm 5*
Potter, George Reuben 1895-1954 *NatCAB 42*
Potter, George W 1899-1959 *WhAm 3*
Potter, Mrs. Gurdon *WomWWA 14*
Potter, Harrison Corbet 1864-1927 *NatCAB 20*
Potter, Harry S 1869- *WhAm 5*
Potter, Hazard Arnold 1810-1869 *ApCAB*
Potter, Hazard Arnold 1811-1869 *Drake*
Potter, Helen Margaret 1887- *WomWWA 14*
Potter, Henry *NewYHSD*
Potter, Henry 1765-1857 *ApCAB, BiAUS, NatCAB 11, TwCBDA*
Potter, Henry Codman 1834-1908 *ApCAB X, NatCAB 14, TwCBDA, WhAm 1*
Potter, Henry Codman 1835-1908 *AmBi, ApCAB, DcAmB, NatCAB 1, WebAB*
Potter, Henry Noel 1869- *WhAm 5*
Potter, Henry Richardson 1877-1946 *NatCAB 34*
Potter, Henry Sayre 1798-1884 *NatCAB 12*
Potter, Henry Staples 1848- *WhAm 1*
Potter, Hollis Elmer 1880-1964 *NatCAB 53*
Potter, Homer Dexter 1878-1924 *WhAm 1*
Potter, Horatio 1802-1887 *AmBi, ApCAB, DcAmB, Drake, NatCAB 1, TwCBDA, WhAm H*
Potter, Irving White 1868-1956 *NatCAB 43*
Potter, Isabella Abbe *NatCAB 14, WomWWA 14*
Potter, Isaiah 1746-1817 *Drake*
Potter, Israel Ralph 1744-1826? *ApCAB, NatCAB 14*
Potter, James 1729-1789 *ApCAB, DcAmB, TwCBDA, WhAm H*
Potter, Mrs. James Brown *WhAm 1*
Potter, Janet Gregor 1854- *WomWWA 14*

Potter, Jennie O'Neill 1867- *AmWom*
Potter, Jerome Whitfield 1851-1923 *NatCAB 21*
Potter, John Fox 1817-1899 *ApCAB, BiAUS, BiDrAC, NatCAB 8, TwCBDA, WhAm H*
Potter, John Milton 1906-1947 *WhAm 2*
Potter, John S 1809-1869 *ApCAB, NatCAB 5*
Potter, John Wesley 1864- *WhAm 4*
Potter, Joseph Adams 1816-1888 *ApCAB Sup*
Potter, Joseph Hayden 1822-1892 *TwCBDA*
Potter, Joseph Hayden 1823-1892 *NatCAB 4*
Potter, Joseph Haydn 1822-1892 *ApCAB*
Potter, Julian Whitfield 1889-1926 *NatCAB 21*
Potter, Justin 1898-1961 *NatCAB 50, WhAm 4*
Potter, Louis McClellan 1873-1912 *DcAmB, NatCAB 26, WhAm 1*
Potter, Lucy I Johnson 1859- *WomWWA 14*
Potter, Mabel L 1873- *WomWWA 14*
Potter, Margaret Horton 1881-1911 *TwCBDA, WhAm 1*
Potter, Marion Craig 1863- *WomWWA 14*
Potter, Marion E 1869-1953 *WhAm 3, WomWWA 14*
Potter, Mark Winslow 1866-1942 *NatCAB 31, WhAm 2*
Potter, Mary Knight d1915 *WhAm 1, WomWWA 14*
Potter, Mary Pratt 1864- *WomWWA 14*
Potter, Mary Ross 1871- *WhAm 5*
Potter, Mary Sargent 1878- *WomWWA 14*
Potter, Nathaniel 1770-1843 *ApCAB, DcAmB, NatCAB 5, WhAm H*
Potter, Nathaniel Bowditch 1869-1919 *ApCAB X, NatCAB 19, NatCAB 26, WhAm 5*
Potter, Orlando Brunson 1823-1894 *BiDrAC, NatCAB 1, TwCBDA, WhAm H*
Potter, Orrin W 1836-1907 *WhAm 1*
Potter, Paul Meredith 1853-1921 *DcAmB, WhAm 1*
Potter, Platt 1800-1891 *ApCAB, DcAmB, NatCAB 10, TwCBDA, WhAm H*
Potter, Robert 1800?- *BiAUS*
Potter, Robert 1800?-1841 *BiDrAC*
Potter, Robert 1800?-1842 *DcAmB, NatCAB 25, WhAm H*
Potter, Robert 1864-1930 *NatCAB 22*
Potter, Robert Brown 1829-1887 *AmBi, ApCAB, DcAmB, Drake, NatCAB 4, TwCBDA, WhAm H*
Potter, Rockwell Harmon 1874-1967 *WhAm 4*
Potter, Roderick 1879-1959 *WhAm 4*
Potter, Russell Sherwood 1897-1966 *NatCAB 51*
Potter, Ruth Nellis 1880- *WomWWA 14*
Potter, Samuel *NewYHSD*
Potter, Samuel John d1804 *BiAUS*
Potter, Samuel John 1739-1804 *ApCAB, NatCAB 13*
Potter, Samuel John 1751?-1804 *TwCBDA*
Potter, Samuel John 1753-1804 *BiDrAC, WhAm H*
Potter, Samuel Otway Lewis 1846- *WhAm 4*
Potter, Stephen 1900-1969 *WhAm 5*
Potter, Thomas Albert 1883-1949 *WhAm 2*
Potter, Thomas J 1840-1888 *ApCAB*
Potter, Thomas Paine *WhAm 5*
Potter, Thompson Eldridge 1849-1916 *NatCAB 13, NatCAB 19*
Potter, W C *NewYHSD*
Potter, Wilfrid Carne 1861-1947 *NatCAB 35, WhAm 2*
Potter, William 1852-1926 *NatCAB 13, NatCAB 27, TwCBDA, WhAm 1*
Potter, William Appleton 1842-1909 *BnEnAmA*
Potter, William Bancroft 1863-1934 *DcAmB S1, WhAm 1*
Potter, William Bleecker 1846-1914 *ApCAB, NatCAB 13, WhAm 1*
Potter, William Bleeker 1846-1914 *TwCBDA*
Potter, William Chapman 1874-1957 *ApCAB X, WhAm 3*
Potter, William Frederick 1855-1905 *NatCAB 26*
Potter, William Henry 1856-1928 *ApCAB X, WhAm 1*

Potter, William J 1883-1964 *IlBEAAW,*
WhAm 4
Potter, William James 1829-1893 *DcAmB,*
WhAm H
Potter, William James 1830-1893 *NatCAB 13,*
TwCBDA
Potter, William Parker 1850-1917 *WhAm 1*
Potter, William Plumer 1857-1918 *NatCAB 11,*
WhAm 1
Potter, William W 1869-1940 *NatCAB 39,*
WhAm 5
Potter, William Warren 1838-1911 *WhAm 1*
Potter, William Wilson 1792-1839 *BiAUS,*
BiDrAC, WhAm H
Potter, Winfield Tuthill 1889-1949 *NatCAB 38*
Potterton, Thomas Edward 1868-1933 *WhAm 1*
Potthast, Edward Henry 1857-1927 *IlBEAAW,*
NatCAB 22, WhAm 1
Pottier, Auguste 1823-1896 *NatCAB 6*
Pottle, Emory Bemsley 1815-1891 *BiAUS,*
BiDrAC, WhAm H
Pottle, Juliet Wilbor Tompkins 1871-
WomWWA 14
Potts, Alexander Douglas 1898-1957
NatCAB 47
Potts, Alfred Fremont 1856-1927 *NatCAB 20,*
WhAm 1
Potts, Allen 1866-1930 *NatCAB 25*
Potts, Anna M Longshore 1829- *AmWom*
Potts, Benjamin Franklin 1836-1887
ApCAB Sup, DcAmB, NatCAB 11,
WhAm H
Potts, Charles Edwin 1873-1956 *NatCAB 44,*
WhAm 3
Potts, Charles Sower 1864-1930 *ApCAB X,*
DcAmB, NatCAB 26, WhAm 1
Potts, Charles Wesley 1877-1927 *NatCAB 20*
Potts, David, Jr. 1794-1863 *BiAUS, BiDrAC,*
TwCBDA, WhAm H
Potts, David Matthew 1906- *BiDrAC*
Potts, Francis Lanier 1860-1910 *NatCAB 26*
Potts, Frederic Augustus 1836-1888
NatCAB 32
Potts, George 1801-1864 *Drake*
Potts, George 1802-1864 *ApCAB*
Potts, Harrison Isaac 1870-1955 *NatCAB 46*
Potts, Heston Nelson 1900-1968 *TwCBDA*
Potts, Horace Miles 1875-1961 *NatCAB 49*
Potts, James Henry 1848-1942 *ApCAB,*
NatCAB 10, WhAm 2
Potts, James Henry 1855-1926 *WhAm 1*
Potts, John *NatCAB 13*
Potts, John 1838- *ApCAB*
Potts, Jonathan 1745-1781 *ApCAB, DcAmB,*
NatCAB 12, TwCBDA, WhAm H
Potts, Jonathan 1747-1781 *Drake*
Potts, Joseph D 1829-1893 *NatCAB 5*
Potts, Louis Moses 1877- *WhAm 1*
Potts, Richard 1753-1808 *ApCAB, BiAUS,*
BiDrAC, DcAmB, Drake, NatCAB 11,
TwCBDA, WhAm H
Potts, Robert 1835-1913 *WhAm 1*
Potts, Robert Joseph 1877-1962 *WhAm 4*
Potts, Roy C 1881- *WhAm 6*
Potts, Stacy Gardner 1799-1865 *ApCAB*
Potts, Stacy Gardner 1800-1865 *Drake*
Potts, Templin Morris 1855-1927 *NatCAB 22,*
WhAm 1
Potts, William 1838-1908 *TwCBDA, WhAm 1*
Potts, William McCleery 1856-1943
NatCAB 35
Potts, William Stephens 1802-1852 *ApCAB,*
Drake, NewYHSD
Potts, William Stevens 1802-1852 *TwCBDA*
Potts, Willis John 1895-1968 *WhAm 5*
Potts, Wylodine Gabbert 1898- *WhAm 5*
Potwin, Clara Brewster 1862- *WomWWA 14*
Potzger, John Ernest 1886-1955 *NatCAB 43,*
WhAm 3
Pou, Edward William 1863-1934 *BiDrAC,*
DcAmB S1, NatCAB 26, TwCBDA,
WhAm 1, WhAmP
Pou, James Hinton 1861-1935 *NatCAB 26,*
WhAm 1
Pouch, Alfred Johnson 1844-1899 *NatCAB 23*
Pouch, William Henry 1875-1959 *WhAm 3*
Poucher, Florence Lucinda Holbrook
WomWWA 14

Poucher, J Wilson 1859-1948 *NatCAB 36*
Poucher, Morris Richard 1859-1936
NatCAB 33
Pouchet, Felix-Archimede 1800-1872 *DcScB*
Pouchot, M 1712-1769 *ApCAB, Drake*
Pouillet, Claude-Servais-Mathias 1790-1868
DcScB
Pouilly, Jacques Nicholas Bussiere De
WhAm H
Pouilly, Joseph De *WhAm H*
Poujade, Joseph 1852- *NatCAB 6*
Poulenc, Francis 1899-1963 *McGEWB,*
WhAm 4
Poulos, Raleigh Anest 1922-1975 *WhAm 6*
Poulsen, Valdemar 1869-1942 *AsBiEn*
Poulson, C Norris 1895- *BiDrAC*
Poulson, Edna Snell 1843- *WomWWA 14*
Poulson, Niels 1843-1911 *DcAmB,*
NatCAB 14
Poulson, Zachariah 1761-1844 *ApCAB,*
DcAmB, Drake, NatCAB 10, WhAm H
Poulsson, Anne Emilie 1853-1939 *TwCBDA,*
WhAm 1, WomWWA 14
Poulsson, Emilie 1853-1939 *NatCAB 10*
Poulton, William Edward 1910-1958
NatCAB 43
Pound, Sir Alfred Dudley Pickman Rogers
1877-1943 *WhoMilH*
Pound, Arthur 1884-1966 *WhAm 4*
Pound, Cuthbert Winfred 1864-1935
DcAmB S1, NatCAB 25, WhAm 1
Pound, Sir Dudley 1877-1943 *WhWW-II*
Pound, Earl Clifford 1876-1945 *WhAm 2*
Pound, Ezra Loomis 1885-1972 *EncAB,*
McGEWB, WebAB, WhAm 5
Pound, G C 1891-1968 *WhAm 5*
Pound, Jere M 1864-1935 *WhAm 1, WhAm 4*
Pound, Louise 1872-1958 *BiDAmEd,*
NatCAB 46, WhAm 3, WomWWA 14
Pound, Roscoe 1870-1964 *BiDAmEd,*
McGEWB, WebAB, WhAm 4
Pound, Stephen Bosworth 1833-1911
NatCAB 29
Pound, Thaddeus Coleman 1833-1914 *BiDrAC*
Pound, Thomas 1650?-1703 *DcAmB,*
WhAm H
Poundmaker 1826-1886 *ApCAB*
Poupard, James *NewYHSD*
Pourfour DuPetit, Francois 1664-1741 *DcScB*
Pourtales, Louis Francois De d1880 *WhAm H*
Pourtales, Louis Francois De 1823-1880 *AmBi,*
DcAmB, DcScB
Pourtales, Louis Francois De 1824-1880 *ApCAB,*
TwCBDA
Pousette-Dart, Nathaniel 1886-1965 *WhAm 4*
Pousette-Dart, Richard 1916- *BnEnAmA*
Poussin, Guillaume Tell Lavallee 1795?-1850?
ApCAB
Poussin, Nicolas 1594-1665 *McGEWB*
Poussin, William Tell *Drake*
Poutrincourt, Jean DeBiencourt 1557-1615
ApCAB
Poveda, Francisco 1796-1881 *ApCAB*
Powalky, Karl Rudolph 1817-1881 *DcScB*
Powderly, Terence Vincent 1849-1924 *AmBi,*
ApCAB Sup, ApCAB X, DcAmB,
EncAB, McGEWB, NatCAB 8,
TwCBDA, WebAB, WhAm 1, WhAmP
Powdermaker, Hortense 1900-1970 *NatCAB 55,*
WhAm 5
Powe, Thomas Erasmus 1872-1941 *WhAm 2*
Powel, Elizabeth Willing *ApCAB*
Powel, Harford 1887-1956 *WhAm 3*
Powel, Harney Twiggs 1847-1923 *NatCAB 6*
Powel, John Hare 1786-1856 *ApCAB, DcAmB,*
NatCAB 10, WhAm H
Powel, John Hare *see also* Powell, John Hare
Powel, Samuel 1739-1793 *ApCAB,*
NatCAB 11
Powel, Samuel 1776-1841 *BiAUS*
Powel, Samuel 1884-1945 *NatCAB 35*
Powel, Samuel *see also* Powell, Samuel
Powell *DcAmB, WebAB, WhAm H*
Powell, Aaron Macy 1832-1899 *ApCAB,*
NatCAB 5, TwCBDA
Powell, Adam Clayton 1865-1953 *DcAmB S5,*
WhoColR
Powell, Adam Clayton, Jr. 1908-1972 *BiDrAC,*

EncAB, WebAB, WhAm 5, WhAmP
Powell, Alden L 1902-1950 *WhAm 3*
Powell, Alfred H 1781-1831 *BiAUS, BiDrAC,*
WhAm H
Powell, Alma Webster 1874-1930 *DcAmB,*
WomWWA 14
Powell, Anthony 1905- *McGEWB*
Powell, Arthur Gray 1873-1951 *NatCAB 47,*
WhAm 3
Powell, Arthur James Emery 1864-1956
IlBEAAW, WhAm 3
Powell, Asa L 1912- *IlBEAAW*
Powell, Baden 1796-1860 *DcScB*
Powell, Benjamin Harrison 1881-1960
NatCAB 48, WhAm 4
Powell, Caroline Amelia d1935 *WhAm 2,*
WhAm 5, WomWWA 14
Powell, Carroll A 1892-1948 *WhAm 2*
Powell, Cecil Frank 1903-1969 *AsBiEn, DcScB,*
WhAm 5
Powell, Charles Francis 1843-1907 *WhAm 1*
Powell, Charles L 1861-1929 *WhAm 1*
Powell, Charles Stuart 1749-1811 *Drake,*
WhAm H
Powell, Charles Underhill 1876-1956
NatCAB 48, WhAm 3
Powell, Charlotte Agnes *BiCAW*
Powell, Cuthbert 1775-1849 *BiAUS, BiDrAC,*
WhAm H
Powell, David 1831- *WhAm 1*
Powell, David Alva 1883-1948 *NatCAB 39*
Powell, Dawn d1965 *WhAm 4*
Powell, Desmond Stevens 1899-1964 *WhAm 4*
Powell, Dick 1904-1963 *WhAm 4*
Powell, Doane 1881-1951 *WhAm 3*
Powell, Donald Adams 1900-1972 *WhAm 5*
Powell, E Alexander 1879-1957 *NatCAB 46,*
WhAm 3
Powell, E Harrison 1888-1966 *WhAm 4*
Powell, E Henry 1909-1961 *NatCAB 49*
Powell, Earl 1924-1966 *WhAm 4*
Powell, Edward 1850-1941 *NatCAB 35*
Powell, Edward Alexander 1838-1925 *WhAm 1*
Powell, Edward Henry 1909-1961 *WhAm 4*
Powell, Edward Lindsay 1860-1933 *WhAm 1*
Powell, Edward Payson 1833-1915 *DcAmB,*
NatCAB 16, TwCBDA, WhAm 1
Powell, Edward Thomson 1874- *WhAm 5*
Powell, Elmer Ellsworth 1861-1947 *NatCAB 41,*
WhAm 2
Powell, Elmer Nathaniel 1869-1946 *NatCAB 36,*
WhAm 2
Powell, Emma Webster *WomWWA 14*
Powell, Ernest Willard 1875-1928 *NatCAB 21*
Powell, Francis Edward 1863-1938 *NatCAB 31*
Powell, Frank Henry 1883-1949 *NatCAB 38*
Powell, Fred Wilbur 1881-1943 *WhAm 2*
Powell, Frederick 1859- *WhAm 4*
Powell, G Thomas 1874-1963 *NatCAB 51,*
WhAm 4, WhAm 5
Powell, George 1823- *Drake*
Powell, George Harold 1872-1922 *AmBi,*
ApCAB X, DcAmB, NatCAB 20,
WhAm 1
Powell, George Kelsey 1845-1910 *NatCAB 41*
Powell, George May 1835-1905 *WhAm 1*
Powell, George Townsend 1843-1927
NatCAB 21
Powell, Gertrude Wilson 1874- *WomWWA 14*
Powell, H M T *IlBEAAW, NewYHSD*
Powell, Hannah Belle Clark *WomWWA 14*
Powell, Henry Watson 1733-1814 *ApCAB,*
Drake
Powell, Howell Aubrey 1846- *NatCAB 12*
Powell, Hugh John 1877-1955 *NatCAB 42*
Powell, Hunter Holmes 1843- *WhAm 1*
Powell, J T *NewYHSD*
Powell, J W 1834-1902 *BiAUS Sup*
Powell, James Alexander 1888-1948
NatCAB 40
Powell, James Robert 1814-1883 *NatCAB 18*
Powell, Jessie Elizabeth 1866- *WomWWA 14*
Powell, John 1882-1963 *WhAm 4*
Powell, John Benjamin 1886-1947 *DcAmB S4,*
WhAm 2
Powell, John H 1869-1935 *WhAm 1,*
WhAm 1C
Powell, John Hare 1786-1856 *Drake*

Powell, John Hare *see also* Powel, John Hare
Powell, John Lee 1859- *WhAm 4*
Powell, John Stephen 1857-1921 *NatCAB 19*
Powell, John Wesley 1834-1902 *AmBi, ApCAB, DcAmB, DcScB, EncAAH, EncAB, McGEWB, NatCAB 3, REnAW, TwCBDA, WebAB, WhAm H*
Powell, Joseph 1828-1904 *BiDrAC*
Powell, Joseph 1848-1904 *BiAUS*
Powell, Joseph Cyrus 1854-1904 *NatCAB 13*
Powell, Joseph Wright 1877-1954 *NatCAB 41, WhAm 3*
Powell, Joseph Yancey 1888-1965 *WhAm 4*
Powell, Junius L 1891-1966 *WhAm 4*
Powell, Junius Levert 1843-1925 *NatCAB 20*
Powell, Lawrence Clark 1906- *BiDAmEd*
Powell, Lazarus Whitehead 1812-1867 *ApCAB, BiAUS, BiDrAC, DcAmB, Drake, NatCAB 13, TwCBDA, WhAm H, WhAmP*
Powell, Legh Richmond, Jr. 1884-1969 *NatCAB 55*
Powell, Leslie Charles 1894-1954 *NatCAB 45*
Powell, Lester Davis 1891-1961 *NatCAB 50*
Powell, Leven 1737-1810 *NatCAB 8, NatCAB 19*
Powell, Levin 1737-1810 *BiDrAC, WhAm H*
Powell, Levin 1738-1810 *ApCAB, BiAUS, Drake*
Powell, Levin M 1800?-1885 *Drake*
Powell, Levin Minn 1803-1885 *NatCAB 1, TwCBDA*
Powell, Levin Myne 1800-1885 *ApCAB*
Powell, Lewis Franklin, Jr. 1907- *WebAB*
Powell, Lonie Gertrude Hamacher 1867- *WomWWA 14*
Powell, Louis W 1866-1913 *NatCAB 17*
Powell, Louise Mathilde 1871-1943 *NotAW*
Powell, Lucien Whiting 1846-1930 *DcAmB, IIBEAAW, NatCAB 23, WhAm 1*
Powell, Lula E 1879-1953 *WhAm 3*
Powell, Lyman Pierson 1866-1946 *NatCAB 15, NatCAB 34, WhAm 2*
Powell, Lyman Theodore, Jr. 1902-1974 *WhAm 6*
Powell, Maud 1867-1920 *AmWom*
Powell, Maud 1868-1920 *AmBi, DcAmB, NatCAB 13, NotAW, WhAm 1, WomWWA 14*
Powell, Nancy Morell 1880- *WomWWA 14*
Powell, Nathan 1869- *WhAm 5*
Powell, Noble Cilley 1891-1968 *NatCAB 54, WhAm 5*
Powell, Paul d1970 *WhAm 5*
Powell, Paul Mahlon 1881-1944 *NatCAB 33*
Powell, Paulus 1809-1874 *BiAUS, BiDrAC, WhAm H, WhAmP*
Powell, Paulus Prince 1892-1963 *WhAm 4*
Powell, Rachel Hopper 1864- *WhAm 4*
Powell, Ralph Lorin 1917-1975 *WhAm 6*
Powell, Ray E 1887-1973 *WhAm 6*
Powell, Richard 1767-1834 *BiHiMed*
Powell, Richard Holmes 1875-1947 *WhAm 2*
Powell, Richard Sterling 1876- *WhAm 5*
Powell, Robert 1851-1930 *WhAm 1*
Powell, Samuel *NewYHSD*
Powell, Samuel 1776-1841 *BiDrAC, WhAm H*
Powell, Samuel *see also* Powel, Samuel
Powell, Sarah Harrison *WomWWA 14*
Powell, Snelling 1758-1821 *DcAmB, Drake, WhAm H*
Powell, Talcott Williams 1900-1937 *WhAm 1*
Powell, Theophilus Orgain 1837-1907 *NatCAB 2*
Powell, Thomas 1809-1887 *ApCAB, DcAmB, WhAm H*
Powell, Thomas 1837-1916 *WhAm 1*
Powell, Thomas Carr d1945 *WhAm 2*
Powell, Thomas Edward 1842- *WhAm 4*
Powell, Thomas Reed 1880-1955 *DcAmB S5, WhAm 3*
Powell, W Byrd 1799-1866 *Drake*
Powell, Walker 1828- *ApCAB*
Powell, Warren Thomson 1884-1946 *WhAm 3*
Powell, Weldon 1903-1965 *WhAm 4*
Powell, William Bramwell 1836-1904 *BiDAmEd, DcAmB, NatCAB 13, WhAm 1*
Powell, William Byrd 1799-1866 *DcAmB,*

WhAm H
Powell, William Byrd 1799-1867 *ApCAB*
Powell, William Dan 1873-1943 *NatCAB 35, WhAm 2*
Powell, William David 1854- *WhAm 1*
Powell, William Dinsmoor 1756-1834 *Drake*
Powell, William Frank 1845-1920 *WhoColR*
Powell, William Frank 1848-1920 *NatCAB 12, WhAm 1*
Powell, William Hamilton 1856- *WhAm 4*
Powell, William Henry 1823-1879 *ApCAB, BiAUS, DcAmB, NatCAB 19, NewYHSD, TwCBDA, WhAm H*
Powell, William Henry 1825-1904 *ApCAB, TwCBDA, WhAm 1*
Powell, William M 1862- *WhAm 4*
Powell, William Mennig 1893-1951 *NatCAB 40*
Powell, Wilson Marcy 1834-1915 *NatCAB 17*
Powell, Wilson Marcy 1872-1935 *WhAm 1*
Powell, Wilson Marcy 1903-1974 *NatCAB 57, WhAm 6*
Powelson, Abram James 1893-1974 *WhAm 6*
Powelson, Wilfrid VanNest 1872- *WhAm 5*
Power, Charles Gavan 1888-1968 *WhAm 5*
Power, Curtis Garland 1902-1966 *NatCAB 53*
Power, Effie Louise 1873-1969 *DcAmLiB*
Power, Ethel B 1881- *WhAm 6*
Power, Frank W 1886- *WhAm 3*
Power, Frederick Belding 1853-1927 *ApCAB, DcAmB, DcScB, NatCAB 28, WhAm 1*
Power, Frederick Dunglison 1851-1911 *DcAmB, WhAm 1*
Power, Frederick Tyrone 1869-1931 *DcAmB*
Power, Frederick Tyrone *see also* Power, Tyrone
Power, Henry 1623-1668 *DcScB*
Power, Howard Anderson 1893-1957 *WhAm 3*
Power, James Edward 1876- *WhAm 5*
Power, John *NewYHSD*
Power, John 1792-1849 *DcAmB, WhAm H*
Power, John Joseph, Jr. 1911-1968 *WhAm 5*
Power, John Logan 1834-1901 *BiDConf*
Power, Lawrence Geoffrey 1841- *ApCAB*
Power, Michael 1804-1848 *ApCAB*
Power, Thomas Charles 1839-1923 *ApCAB Sup, ApCAB X, BiDrAC, NatCAB 1, NatCAB 19, TwCBDA, WhAm 1, WhAmP*
Power, Thomas S 1905-1970 *WhAm 6*
Power, Tyrone 1797-1841 *ApCAB, Drake, NatCAB 13*
Power, Tyrone 1869-1931 *AmBi, DcAmB*
Power, Tyrone 1914-1958 *WhAm 3*
Powers, A G *NewYHSD*
Powers, Albert Henry 1862-1930 *NatCAB 42*
Powers, Asahel L 1813- *NewYHSD*
Powers, Augustin Jay 1873-1956 *NatCAB 42*
Powers, Caleb 1869-1932 *AmBi, BiDrAC, WhAm 1, WhAmP*
Powers, Carol Hoyt 1868-1940 *WhAm 1, WomWWA 14*
Powers, Charles Andrew 1858-1922 *NatCAB 20, WhAm 1*
Powers, Daniel William 1818-1897 *DcAmB, NatCAB 10, WhAm H*
Powers, David Lane 1896-1968 *BiDrAC*
Powers, Delmar Thomas 1865-1948 *WhAm 2*
Powers, Donald Howard 1901-1968 *NatCAB 54*
Powers, Edward 1830- *ApCAB*
Powers, Edwin Booth 1880-1949 *NatCAB 38, WhAm 2*
Powers, Eliza Howard 1802-1887 *ApCAB*
Powers, Emma Hardy 1863- *WomWWA 14*
Powers, Eugene Paul 1913-1968 *WhAm 5*
Powers, Franklin Brown 1887-1960 *WhAm 4*
Powers, Fred Perry 1849-1927 *NatCAB 21*
Powers, Fred William 1888-1951 *NatCAB 42*
Powers, Frederick Alton 1855-1923 *NatCAB 25, WhAm 1*
Powers, George Herman 1840-1913 *NatCAB 15*
Powers, George McClellan 1861-1938 *NatCAB 17, WhAm 1*
Powers, Gershom 1789-1831 *BiAUS, BiDrAC, WhAm H*
Powers, Grant 1784-1841 *ApCAB, Drake*
Powers, Grover Francis 1887-1968 *WhAm 5*
Powers, Harry Huntington 1859- *WhAm 4*
Powers, Harry Joseph 1859-1941 *WhAm 1, WhAm 2*

Powers, Hiram 1805-1873 *AmBi, ApCAB, BiAUS, BnEnAmA, DcAmB, Drake, EncAB, IIBEAAW, McGEWB, NatCAB 3, NewYHSD, TwCBDA, WebAB, WhAm H*
Powers, Horace Henry 1835-1913 *BiDrAC, NatCAB 17, TwCBDA, WhAm 1, WhAmP*
Powers, Horatio Nelson 1826-1890 *ApCAB, NatCAB 10, WhAm H*
Powers, Hugh Winfield 1860-1938 *WhAm 1*
Powers, J *NewYHSD*
Powers, James Knox 1851-1913 *BiDAmEd, NatCAB 12, NatCAB 15, TwCBDA, WhAm 1*
Powers, James T *NewYHSD*
Powers, James T 1862- *WhAm 4*
Powers, Jerome 1892-1957 *NatCAB 48*
Powers, John Craig 1869-1955 *WhAm 3*
Powers, Joseph Harrell 1910-1967 *WhAm 5*
Powers, Joseph Neely 1869-1939 *NatCAB 33, WhAm 1*
Powers, Joshua Dever 1844-1923 *NatCAB 25*
Powers, LeGrand 1851-1933 *WhAm 4*
Powers, Leland Todd 1857-1920 *WhAm 1*
Powers, Leon Walter 1888-1959 *WhAm 3*
Powers, Leonard Stewart 1919-1972 *WhAm 6*
Powers, Levi Moore 1864-1920 *WhAm 1*
Powers, Llewellyn 1836-1908 *BiDrAC, NatCAB 13, TwCBDA, WhAmP*
Powers, Llewellyn 1838-1908 *WhAm 1*
Powers, Luther Milton 1853- *WhAm 1*
Powers, Oliver *NewYHSD*
Powers, Orlando Woodworth 1851-1914 *TwCBDA, WhAm 1*
Powers, Pliny H 1895-1966 *WhAm 4*
Powers, Preston 1843- *ApCAB, TwCBDA*
Powers, Ralph Averill 1893-1971 *NatCAB 56, WhAm 5*
Powers, Ridgely Ceylon 1836-1912 *BiAUS, NatCAB 13, WhAm 1*
Powers, Ridgley Ceylon 1836-1912 *TwCBDA*
Powers, Robert A *NewYHSD*
Powers, Robert Davis, Jr. 1908-1971 *WhAm 5*
Powers, S *NewYHSD*
Powers, Samuel Leland 1847-1929 *NatCAB 24*
Powers, Samuel Leland 1848-1929 *BiDrAC, NatCAB 11, TwCBDA, WhAm 1*
Powers, Samuel Ralph 1887-1970 *NatCAB 57, WhAm 5*
Powers, Sidney 1890-1932 *NatCAB 25, WhAm 1, WhAm 1C*
Powers, Sue McFall 1878- *WhAm 6*
Powers, Thomas E 1870-1939 *AmBi*
Powers, Thomas Jefferson 1875- *WhAm 5*
Powers, Tom 1890-1955 *WhAm 3*
Powers, William Dudley 1849- *WhAm 4*
Powers, William Herman 1900-1964 *NatCAB 51*
Powers, William L 1863-1927 *WhAm 1*
Powers, William Penn 1842-1928 *NatCAB 20*
Powers, William T 1911-1974 *WhAm 6*
Powhatan 1550?-1618 *AmBi, ApCAB, DcAmB, Drake, McGEWB, NatCAB 10, REnAW, WebAB, WhAm H*
Powley, N R 1885-1956 *WhAm 3*
Powlison, Charles Ford 1865-1942 *WhAm 2*
Pownal, Thomas *NatCAB 12*
Pownal, Mrs. d1796 *WhAm H*
Pownall, Charles Alan 1887-1975 *WhAm 6*
Pownall, Thomas 1720-1805 *ApCAB, NatCAB 7*
Pownall, Thomas 1722-1805 *AmBi, DcAmB, Drake, NewYHSD, WhAm H*
Powning, H Glenn, Jr. 1899-1968 *NatCAB 55*
Powys, John Cowper 1872-1963 *WhAm 4*
Powys, Llewelyn 1884-1939 *WhAm 2*
Poyas, Catharine Gendron 1813-1882 *ApCAB*
Poydras, Julian d1824 *BiAUS*
Poydras, Julien d1824 *ApCAB, Drake*
Poydras, Julien DeLalande 1746-1824 *DcAmB*
Poydras, Julien DeLallande 1740-1824 *BiDrAC*
Poydras, Julien DeLallande 1746-1824 *WhAm H*
Poydras DeLalande, Julien 1746-1824 *TwCBDA*
Poynter, Charles William McCorkle 1875-1950 *NatCAB 39, WhAm 3*
Poynter, Clara E 1876- *WomWWA 14*

Poynter, Clara Martin 1846-1937 *WhAm 1*
Poynter, Henrietta Malkiel 1901-1968
NatCAB 53, WhAm 4A
Poynter, Juliet Jameson 1881-1974 *WhAm 6*
Poynter, Mary Augusta Mason *WomWWA 14*
Poynter, Paul 1875-1950 *WhAm 3*
Poynter, William Amos 1848-1909 *NatCAB 12,
TwCBDA, WhAm 1*
Poynting, John Henry 1852-1914 *DcScB*
Poynton, John Albert d1934 *WhAm 1*
Poyntz, James M 1838-1904 *WhAm 1*
Poyntz, Juliet Stuart 1886- *WomWWA 14*
Poznanski, Gustavus 1804-1879 *DcAmB,
WhAm H*
Pracht, Charles Frederick 1880-1950 *BiDrAC,
WhAm 6*
Prado, Juan De 1716-1770? *ApCAB*
Prado, Mariano Ignacio 1826- *ApCAB*
Prado Ugarteche, Manuel 1889-1967 *McGEWB,
WhAm 4*
Prados, Madame *NewYHSD*
Pradt, Louis Augustus 1851- *WhAm 4*
Praeger, Arnold 1887-1972 *NatCAB 57*
Praeger, Herman Albert 1884-1961 *NatCAB 49*
Praeger, Otto d1948 *WhAm 2*
Praetorius, Michael 1571?-1621 *McGEWB*
Prager, Anna Goslin 1869- *WomWWA 14*
Prahl, Augustus John 1901-1970 *WhAm 5*
Prall, Anning Smith 1869-1937 *NatCAB 38*
Prall, Anning Smith 1870-1937 *BiDrAC,
WhAm 1, WhAmP*
Prall, Charles Edward 1891-1964 *WhAm 4*
Prall, David Wight 1886-1940 *DcAmB S2,
WhAm 1*
Prall, John Howard 1855-1918 *NatCAB 6*
Prall, Robert M *NewYHSD*
Prall, William 1853-1933 *NatCAB 7,
WhAm 1*
Prandtauer, Jakob 1660-1726 *McGEWB*
Prandtl, Ludwig 1875-1953 *DcScB*
Prang, Louis 1824-1909 *DcAmB, NatCAB 11,
NewYHSD, TwCBDA, WhAm 1*
Prang, Mary Amelia Dana Hicks 1836-1927
*BiDAmEd, DcAmB, NatCAB 27, NotAW,
TwCBDA, WhAm 1, WomWWA 14*
Pranishnikopf, Ivan P d1910? *IIBEAAW*
Prankard, Harry Irving, II 1902-1964 *WhAm 4*
Prasad, Rajendra 1884-1963 *McGEWB,
WhAm 4*
Prat, Agustin Arturo 1848-1879 *ApCAB*
Prather, Homer Lee 1873-1921 *NatCAB 22*
Prather, Perry Franklin 1894-1967 *WhAm 4A*
Prather, Thomas J 1866- *WhAm 4*
Pratt, Agnes Edwards Rothery d1954 *WhAm 3*
Pratt, Alice Edwards 1860- *WomWWA 14*
Pratt, Alvaro 1876- *ApCAB X*
Pratt, Anna Beach 1867-1932 *NotAW,
WomWWA 14*
Pratt, Arthur 1842- *NatCAB 1*
Pratt, Arthur Peabody 1872- *WhAm 5*
Pratt, Auguste Goubert 1881-1970 *NatCAB 54,
WhAm 5*
Pratt, Beatrice M *WomWWA 14*
Pratt, Bela Lyon 1867-1917 *AmBi, ApCAB X,
DcAmB, NatCAB 14, WhAm 1*
Pratt, Benjamin 1710-1763 *ApCAB, Drake,
NatCAB 7*
Pratt, Calvin Edward 1828-1896 *ApCAB,
TwCBDA*
Pratt, Caroline 1867-1954 *BiDAmEd*
Pratt, Charles 1830-1891 *AmBi, ApCAB,
ApCAB X, DcAmB, NatCAB 9,
NatCAB 26, TwCBDA, WhAm H*
Pratt, Charles 1892-1956 *NatCAB 45,
WhAm 3*
Pratt, Charles Augustus 1862-1951 *NatCAB 39*
Pratt, Charles Clarence 1854-1916 *BiDrAC,
NatCAB 17, WhAm 3*
Pratt, Charles Dudley 1900-1970 *WhAm 5*
Pratt, Charles H *NewYHSD*
Pratt, Charles Henry 1881-1950 *WhAm 3*
Pratt, Charles Millard 1855-1935 *NatCAB 28,
TwCBDA, WhAm 1*
Pratt, Charles Stebbings 1901-1970 *WhAm 5*
Pratt, Charles Stuart 1854- *WhAm 4*
Pratt, Chester Mayo 1878-1944 *NatCAB 33*
Pratt, Clifford 1893-1954 *NatCAB 49*
Pratt, Dallas Bache 1849-1929 *NatCAB 29*

Pratt, Daniel 1799-1873 *AmBi, BiDConf,
DcAmB, WhAm H*
Pratt, Daniel 1806- *BiAUS*
Pratt, Daniel 1809-1887 *ApCAB, DcAmB,
WhAm H*
Pratt, Daniel 1866- *WhAm 2*
Pratt, Daniel Darwin 1813-1877 *ApCAB,
BiAUS, BiDrAC, NatCAB 11, TwCBDA,
WhAm H*
Pratt, Daniel Johnson 1827-1884 *ApCAB*
Pratt, Don Forrester 1892-1944 *WhAm 2*
Pratt, Donald Roy 1910-1970 *NatCAB 56*
Pratt, Dwight Mallory 1852-1922 *WhAm 1*
Pratt, Edward Barton 1853- *WhAm 4*
Pratt, Edwin Hartley 1849-1930 *NatCAB 11,
WhAm 1*
Pratt, Eliot Deming 1903-1969 *NatCAB 55*
Pratt, Eliza Anna Farman 1837-1907 *DcAmB*
Pratt, Eliza Jane 1902- *BiDrAC*
Pratt, Ella Farman 1837-1907 *WhAm 1*
Pratt, Elsie Seelye 1873- *WomWWA 14*
Pratt, Enoch 1781-1860 *ApCAB, Drake*
Pratt, Enoch 1808-1896 *AmBi, ApCAB,
DcAmB, NatCAB 2, TwCBDA,
WhAm H*
Pratt, Fletcher 1897-1956 *NatCAB 46,
WhAm 3*
Pratt, Florence Gibb d1935 *WhAm 1*
Pratt, Francis Ashbury 1827-1902 *DcAmB*
Pratt, Francis Cole 1867-1930 *NatCAB 27*
Pratt, Frank Randall 1876-1954 *WhAm 3*
Pratt, Frederic Bayley 1865-1945 *NatCAB 34,
WhAm 2*
Pratt, Frederic Richardson 1908-1966
NatCAB 52
Pratt, Frederick Haven 1873-1958 *DcScB,
NatCAB 46, WhAm 3*
Pratt, Frederick Sanford 1872-1968 *WhAm 5*
Pratt, Frederick Sumner 1845-1924 *NatCAB 32*
Pratt, George Collins 1882-1968 *WhAm 5*
Pratt, George Dupont 1869-1935 *ApCAB X,
NatCAB 29, WhAm 1*
Pratt, George Dwight 1864- *WhAm 4*
Pratt, George Kenneth 1891-1957 *NatCAB 44,
WhAm 3*
Pratt, George Watson 1830-1861 *ApCAB*
Pratt, Grace Tyler *WomWWA 14*
Pratt, Hannah T 1854- *AmWom*
Pratt, Harcourt Joseph 1866-1934 *BiDrAC,
NatCAB 25, WhAm 4*
Pratt, Harold Henry 1877-1950 *NatCAB 41*
Pratt, Harold Irving 1877-1939 *NatCAB 29,
WhAm 1*
Pratt, Harold Irving 1904-1975 *WhAm 6*
Pratt, Harry Edward 1901-1956 *NatCAB 46,
WhAm 3*
Pratt, Harry Emerson 1884-1957 *WhAm 3*
Pratt, Harry Hayt 1864-1932 *BiDrAC,
WhAm 1*
Pratt, Harry Noyes 1879-1944 *NatCAB 41,
WhAm 2*
Pratt, Harry Rogers 1884-1956 *WhAm 3*
Pratt, Helen Sherman 1869-1923 *NatCAB 6*
Pratt, Henry Cheever 1803-1880 *IIBEAAW,
NewYHSD, WhAm H*
Pratt, Henry Conger 1882-1966 *WhAm 4*
Pratt, Henry Otis 1838-1931 *BiAUS, BiDrAC*
Pratt, Henry Sherring 1859-1946 *WhAm 2*
Pratt, Herbert Lee 1871-1945 *NatCAB 33,
WhAm 2*
Pratt, Howard Lewis 1850-1914 *NatCAB 16*
Pratt, J *NewYHSD*
Pratt, James Alfred 1873- *WhAm 5*
Pratt, James Bissett 1875-1944 *DcAmB S3,
NatCAB 32, WhAm 2*
Pratt, James Timothy 1802-1887 *BiDrAC,
WhAm H*
Pratt, James Timothy 1805-1887 *BiAUS*
Pratt, John 1753-1824 *NatCAB 12*
Pratt, John 1800-1882 *NatCAB 1, TwCBDA*
Pratt, John 1831-1900? *DcAmB, NatCAB 3*
Pratt, John Francis 1848- *WhAm 4*
Pratt, John Henry 1809-1871 *DcScB*
Pratt, John L d1975 *WhAm 6*
Pratt, John Lowell 1906-1968 *WhAm 5*
Pratt, John Sherring 1875-1959 *NatCAB 48*
Pratt, John Stanford Mullin 1881-1960
NatCAB 47

Pratt, John Teele 1873-1927 *NatCAB 21,
WhAm 1*
Pratt, John Teele, Jr. 1903-1969 *NatCAB 54*
Pratt, Joseph Hersey 1872-1942 *WhAm 2*
Pratt, Joseph Hyde 1870-1942 *WhAm 2*
Pratt, Joseph Marmaduke 1891-1946 *BiDrAC,
WhAm 2*
Pratt, Julia Stebbings 1871- *WomWWA 14*
Pratt, Julius Howard 1821- *NatCAB 1*
Pratt, LeGage 1852-1911 *BiDrAC*
Pratt, LeGage 1853-1911 *WhAm 1*
Pratt, Lewellyn 1832-1913 *NatCAB 16,
WhAm 1*
Pratt, Lorus 1855-1923? *IIBEAAW*
Pratt, Louisa Kirby d1864 *Drake*
Pratt, Lucy 1874- *WhAm 5*
Pratt, Mabel Dodge 1873- *WomWWA 14*
Pratt, Mary G Landon 1857- *WomWWA 14*
Pratt, Matthew 1734-1805 *ApCAB, BnEnAmA,
DcAmB, Drake, NatCAB 14, NewYHSD,
WhAm H*
Pratt, Minnie Gertrude Mills 1875-
WomWWA 14
Pratt, Nellie Pearse DeWolfe 1868-
WomWWA 14
Pratt, O C *BiAUS*
Pratt, Oliver Garrett 1882-1963 *NatCAB 48*
Pratt, Orson 1811-1881 *AmBi, ApCAB,
BiDAmEd, DcAmB S1, NatCAB 7,
NatCAB 16, REnAW, TwCBDA,
WhAm H*
Pratt, Orville Charles, Jr. 1882-1944
NatCAB 38
Pratt, Orville Clyde 1873- *WhAm 3*
Pratt, Parley Parker 1807-1857 *AmBi, ApCAB,
DcAmB, DcAmReB, NatCAB 7,
NatCAB 16, TwCBDA, WhAm H*
Pratt, Pascal Paoli 1819-1905 *NatCAB 8,
NatCAB 26, WhAm 1*
Pratt, Peter d1730 *ApCAB*
Pratt, Phinehas 1590-1680 *ApCAB, Drake*
Pratt, Ralph 1872-1924 *ApCAB X*
Pratt, Ransom 1857-1932 *NatCAB 23*
Pratt, Richard Henry 1840-1924 *BiDAmEd,
DcAmB, NatCAB 13, REnAW,
WebAMB, WhAm 1*
Pratt, Richardson 1894-1959 *WhAm 3*
Pratt, Robert M 1811-1880 *ApCAB,
NewYHSD, TwCBDA*
Pratt, Ruth Sears Baker 1877-1965 *BiDrAC,
NatCAB 51, WhAm 4*
Pratt, Samuel Wheeler 1838-1910 *ApCAB,
NatCAB 4, TwCBDA, WhAm 1*
Pratt, Sedgwick 1845-1920 *WhAm 1*
Pratt, Seely Fournier 1893-1949 *NatCAB 43*
Pratt, Sereno Stansbury 1858-1915 *DcAmB,
WhAm 1*
Pratt, Sherman 1900-1964 *NatCAB 50*
Pratt, Silas Gamaliel 1846-1916 *AmBi,
ApCAB X, DcAmB, NatCAB 10,
WhAm 1*
Pratt, Steve 1917-1973 *WhAm 6*
Pratt, Stewart Camden 1885-1951 *WhAm 3*
Pratt, Thomas G 1805-1869 *BiAUS, Drake*
Pratt, Thomas George 1804-1869 *ApCAB,
BiDrAC, DcAmB, NatCAB 9, TwCBDA,
WhAm H, WhAmP*
Pratt, Thomas William *WhoColR A*
Pratt, Thomas Willis 1812-1875 *DcAmB,
NatCAB 22, WhAm H*
Pratt, Waldo Selden 1857-1939 *DcAmB S2,
NatCAB 16, TwCBDA, WhAm 1*
Pratt, Wallace 1831-1907 *NatCAB 4,
WhAm 1*
Pratt, Walter Merriam 1880-1973 *WhAm 6*
Pratt, William Hall Brace 1842-1916
NatCAB 34
Pratt, William Henry *WebAB*
Pratt, William Maynard 1867-1946 *NatCAB 41*
Pratt, William Veazie 1869-1957 *NatCAB 46,
WebAMB, WhAm 3*
Pratt, Zadock 1790-1871 *ApCAB, BiAUS,
BiDrAC, DcAmB, Drake, NatCAB 9,
TwCBDA, WhAm H*
Pratte, Bernard 1771-1836 *DcAmB, WhAm H*
Pratviel, Louis *NewYHSD*
Pratz, LePage Du d1775 *Drake*
Praxagoras 350?BC- *AsBiEn*

Praxagoras Of Cos 340?BC- *DcScB*
Praxiteles *McGEWB*
Pray, Charles Nelson 1868-1963 *BiDrAC, WhAm 4*
Pray, Frances Abbie Laraway *WomWWA 14*
Pray, Isaac Clark 1813-1869 *AmBi, ApCAB, DcAmB, Drake, NatCAB 13, TwCBDA, WhAm H*
Pray, James Sturgis 1871-1929 *NatCAB 27, WhAm 1*
Pray, Job d1789 *Drake*
Pray, Lewis Glover 1793-1882 *ApCAB*
Pray, Malvina *NotAW*
Pray, Publius Rutilius Rufus 1795-1840 *ApCAB*
Pray, Theron Brown 1849- *WhAm 4*
Preber, Christian *DcAmB*
Preble, Alice Hosmer 1865- *WomWWA 14*
Preble, Edward 1761-1807 *AmBi, ApCAB, DcAmB, Drake, NatCAB 8, TwCBDA, WebAMB, WhAm H*
Preble, Edward A 1871-1957 *WhAm 3*
Preble, Edwin Burnham 1854-1920 *NatCAB 19*
Preble, Fred Myron 1855-1928 *WhAm 1*
Preble, George Henry 1816-1885 *AmBi, ApCAB, DcAmB, Drake, NatCAB 8, TwCBDA, WhAm H*
Preble, Harriet 1795-1854 *ApCAB*
Preble, Jedediah 1707-1784 *ApCAB, Drake*
Preble, Robert Bruce 1866-1948 *WhAm 2*
Preble, William Pitt 1783-1857 *ApCAB, BiAUS, DcAmB, Drake, NatCAB 13, TwCBDA, WhAm H*
Preble, William Pitt, Jr. 1854- *WhAm 4*
Precour, Madame Peter *NewYHSD*
Predlove *NewYHSD*
Preetorius, Edward Louis 1866-1915 *NatCAB 16*
Preetorius, Emil 1827-1905 *DcAmB, WhAm 1*
Prefontaine, Aymery 1720-1767 *ApCAB*
Pregeant, Victor Eugene, III 1922-1972 *WhAm 5*
Pregl, Fritz 1869-1930 *AsBiEn, DcScB, McGEWB*
Prehn, Arthur William 1884-1951 *NatCAB 41*
Prejean, Louis Agerin 1877-1949 *NatCAB 42*
Prell, Charles Martin 1887-1960 *NatCAB 49*
Prellwitz, Edith Mitchill 1865-1944 *WhAm 2, WomWWA 14*
Prellwitz, Henry 1865-1940 *WhAm 1*
Prem, F Herbert 1891-1974 *NatCAB 57*
Premchand 1880-1936 *McGEWB*
Preminger, Marion Mill 1913-1972 *NatCAB 57*
Preminger, Otto Ludwig 1906- *WebAB*
Prence, Thomas 1600-1673 *AmBi*
Prence, Thomas 1601-1673 *ApCAB*
Prendergast, Albert Collins 1853-1922 *NatCAB 19, WhAm 1*
Prendergast, Charles d1948 *WhAm 2*
Prendergast, Edmond Francis 1843-1918 *ApCAB Sup, NatCAB 15, WhAm 1*
Prendergast, Edmund Francis 1843-1918 *TwCBDA*
Prendergast, James M 1851-1920 *WhAm 1*
Prendergast, James William 1875-1938 *NatCAB 30*
Prendergast, John *IlBEAAW, NewYHSD*
Prendergast, Joseph 1866- *NatCAB 18*
Prendergast, Marcia Kettelle 1888- *WomWWA 14*
Prendergast, Maurice Brazil 1859-1924 *BnEnAmA, McGEWB*
Prendergast, Maurice Brazil 1861-1923 *WhAm 1*
Prendergast, Maurice Brazil 1861-1924 *DcAmB, NatCAB 30*
Prendergast, William A 1867-1954 *WhAm 3*
Prentice, Bernon Sheldon 1882-1948 *WhAm 2*
Prentice, Bessie E 1872- *WhoColR*
Prentice, Donald Bishop 1889-1971 *NatCAB 57*
Prentice, E Parmalee 1863-1955 *WhAm 3*
Prentice, George Denison 1802-1870 *ApCAB, Drake, NatCAB 3, TwCBDA*
Prentice, George Dennison 1802-1870 *AmBi, DcAmB, WhAm H*
Prentice, George Gordon 1865-1941 *NatCAB 31, WhAm 1*
Prentice, George W *NewYHSD*
Prentice, James M 1868- *WhoColR*

Prentice, James Stuart 1889-1972 *WhAm 5*
Prentice, John Hill 1874-1925 *NatCAB 14, NatCAB 31*
Prentice, Leon Hamline 1847- *NatCAB 16*
Prentice, Samuel Oscar 1850-1924 *DcAmB, NatCAB 16, WhAm 1*
Prentice, Sartell 1867-1937 *NatCAB 42, WhAm 1*
Prentice, William Kelly 1871-1964 *NatCAB 50, WhAm 4*
Prentice, William Packer 1834-1915 *WhAm 1*
Prentis, Henning Webb, Jr. 1884-1959 *WhAm 3*
Prentis, Robert Riddick 1855-1931 *NatCAB 18, NatCAB 24, WhAm 1*
Prentiss, Addison *NewYHSD*
Prentiss, Albert Nelson 1836-1896 *NatCAB 4, TwCBDA*
Prentiss, Anna McCauley *WomWWA 14*
Prentiss, Benjamin Mayberry 1819-1901 *AmBi, ApCAB, DcAmB, Drake, WebAMB*
Prentiss, Benjamin Maybury 1819-1901 *NatCAB 5, TwCBDA, WhAm 1*
Prentiss, Charles 1774-1820 *ApCAB, Drake, TwCBDA*
Prentiss, Daniel Webster 1843-1899 *NatCAB 3, WhAm 1*
Prentiss, Elizabeth Payson 1818-1878 *ApCAB, DcAmB, NatCAB 7, NotAW, TwCBDA, WhAm H*
Prentiss, Francis Fleury 1858-1937 *NatCAB 31, WhAm 1, WhAm 1C*
Prentiss, George Aldrich 1809-1868 *ApCAB, Drake*
Prentiss, George Lewis 1816-1903 *ApCAB, DcAmB, NatCAB 7, TwCBDA, WhAm 1*
Prentiss, Henry 1846- *ApCAB X*
Prentiss, Henry 1848- *NatCAB 14*
Prentiss, Henry James 1867-1931 *WhAm 1*
Prentiss, Janet *WomWWA 14*
Prentiss, John Holmes 1784-1861 *ApCAB, BiAUS, BiDrAC, NatCAB 11, WhAm H*
Prentiss, John Holmes 1785-1861 *Drake*
Prentiss, John William 1898-1953 *NatCAB 42*
Prentiss, John Wing 1875-1938 *NatCAB 28, WhAm 1*
Prentiss, Nathaniel Smith *NewYHSD*
Prentiss, Robert Jerome 1909-1972 *NatCAB 57*
Prentiss, Roger Gaylord, Jr. 1904-1961 *NatCAB 52*
Prentiss, Samuel 1759-1818 *ApCAB, Drake*
Prentiss, Samuel 1782-1857 *ApCAB, BiAUS, BiDrAC, DcAmB, Drake, NatCAB 8, TwCBDA, WhAm H*
Prentiss, Samuel Loomis 1862-1942 *NatCAB 38*
Prentiss, Sarah J 1823-1877 *NewYHSD*
Prentiss, Seargent Smith 1808-1850 *AmBi, DcAmB, NatCAB 7, WhAm H*
Prentiss, Sergeant Smith 1808-1850 *ApCAB, BiAUS, BiDrAC, Drake, TwCBDA*
Prentiss, Theodore 1815-1906 *ApCAB*
Prentiss, Theodore 1818-1906 *WhAm 3*
Prentiss, Thomas 1747-1814 *Drake*
Prentke, Herbert Emanuel 1896-1963 *NatCAB 50*
Prerau, Sydney 1900-1968 *NatCAB 53*
Presbrey, Eugene Wiley 1853-1931 *DcAmB, WhAm 1*
Presbrey, Frank 1855-1936 *WhAm 1*
Presbrey, Oliver Stetson 1849-1921 *NatCAB 19*
Presby, Charlotte Sulley *WhAm 5*
Prescott, Albert Benjamin 1832-1905 *AmBi, ApCAB, DcAmB, NatCAB 13, TwCBDA, WhAm 1*
Prescott, Annie 1860- *WomWWA 14*
Prescott, Anson Ward 1873- *WhAm 5*
Prescott, Arthur Taylor 1863- *WhAm 5*
Prescott, Augusta *WomWWA 14*
Prescott, Benjamin 1687-1777 *ApCAB, Drake*
Prescott, Benjamin Franklin 1833-1895 *NatCAB 11, TwCBDA*
Prescott, Charles Frederick 1859-1919 *NatCAB 18*
Prescott, Charles Henry 1857-1923 *NatCAB 20, WhAm 1*
Prescott, Cyrus Dan 1836-1902 *BiDrAC*
Prescott, Daniel Alfred 1898-1970 *NatCAB 56,*

WhAm 5
Prescott, DeWitt Clinton 1841-1918 *NatCAB 17*
Prescott, Dorothy *WhAm 1*
Prescott, Edward Purcell 1904-1973 *WhAm 5*
Prescott, Frank Clarke 1859-1934 *WhAm 1*
Prescott, Frederick Clarke 1871-1957 *NatCAB 45, WhAm 3*
Prescott, George Bartlett 1830-1894 *AmBi, ApCAB, DcAmB, NatCAB 5, TwCBDA, WhAm H*
Prescott, Gustavus Linnemann 1867-1946 *NatCAB 48*
Prescott, Harriet Beardslee 1866- *WomWWA 14*
Prescott, Harry Lockwood 1873-1948 *NatCAB 37*
Prescott, Henry Washington 1874-1943 *WhAm 2*
Prescott, John S d1949 *WhAm 3*
Prescott, Katharine T *WomWWA 14*
Prescott, Mary Newmarch 1849-1888 *ApCAB, NatCAB 8, WhAm H*
Prescott, Oliver 1731-1804 *ApCAB, DcAmB, Drake, WhAm H*
Prescott, Oliver 1762-1827 *ApCAB*
Prescott, Oliver 1868-1938 *NatCAB 34, WhAm 1*
Prescott, Plumer 1833-1881 *NewYHSD*
Prescott, Richard 1725-1788 *ApCAB, Drake*
Prescott, Robert 1725-1816 *ApCAB, Drake*
Prescott, Samuel 1751-1777? *DcAmB, WebAB, WebAMB, WhAm H*
Prescott, Samuel Cate 1872-1962 *NatCAB 50, WhAm 4*
Prescott, Stedman 1896-1968 *WhAm 5*
Prescott, William 1726-1795 *AmBi, ApCAB, DcAmB, Drake, NatCAB 1, TwCBDA, WebAB, WebAMB, WhAm H*
Prescott, William 1762-1844 *ApCAB, Drake*
Prescott, William 1788-1875 *ApCAB*
Prescott, William Henry 1840-1908 *NatCAB 24*
Prescott, William Hickling 1796-1859 *AmBi, ApCAB, DcAmB, Drake, EncAAH, McGEWB, NatCAB 6, TwCBDA, WebAB, WhAm H*
Prescott, William Ray 1892-1965 *WhAm 4*
Prescott, William Warren 1855-1944 *NatCAB 32*
Prescott, Winward 1886-1932 *NatCAB 25*
Presl, Karel Boriwoj 1794-1852 *DcScB*
Presley, Elvis Aron 1935- *EncAB, WebAB*
Press, Otto 1880- *WhAm 6*
Press, Samuel David 1875- *WhAm 5*
Presser, Theodore 1848-1925 *DcAmB, NatCAB 20, WhAm 1*
Pressey, Henry Albert 1873- *WhAm 5*
Pressey, Sidney Leavitt 1888- *BiDAmEd*
Pressly, Charles Payson 1860-1945 *NatCAB 33*
Pressly, Frank Young 1853- *WhAm 4*
Pressly, John Taylor 1795-1870 *NatCAB 7*
Pressly, Mason Wylie 1859- *WhAm 4*
Pressman, Joel J 1901-1968 *WhAm 4A*
Presstman, Stephen Wilson 1794-1843 *ApCAB*
Prest, Edward Jabez 1870-1941 *NatCAB 35*
Prest, William Morton 1862- *WhAm 5*
Prestes, Luiz Carlos 1898- *McGEWB*
Preston, Adelaide B 1871- *WhAm 5*
Preston, Andrew Woodbury 1846-1924 *NatCAB 14, NatCAB 26, WhAm 1*
Preston, Ann 1813-1872 *AmBi, AmWom, ApCAB, DcAmB, NatCAB 10, NotAW, TwCBDA, WhAm H*
Preston, Anna Louise 1862- *WomWWA 14*
Preston, Annie A 1840- *WomWWA 14*
Preston, Arthur Murray 1913-1968 *WhAm 5*
Preston, Austin Roe 1894-1956 *WhAm 3*
Preston, Byron Webster 1858-1939 *WhAm 1*
Preston, Cecil Anthony 1852-1922 *WhAm 1*
Preston, Charles Finney 1829-1877 *ApCAB*
Preston, Charles Miller 1874-1947 *WhAm 2*
Preston, David 1826-1887 *ApCAB*
Preston, Douglas A 1858-1929 *WhAm 1*
Preston, Edward Stouter 1884-1947 *NatCAB 36*
Preston, Elwyn Greeley 1866-1951 *WhAm 3*
Preston, Erasmus Darwin 1851-1906 *WhAm 1*

Preston, Frances Folsom Cleveland 1864-1947 *NotAW, WhAm 2, WomWWA 14*
Preston, Francis 1765-1835 *ApCAB, BiAUS, NatCAB 11, TwCBDA*
Preston, Francis 1765-1836 *BiDrAC, WhAm H*
Preston, George H 1890-1972 *WhAm 5*
Preston, George Junkin 1858-1908 *WhAm 1*
Preston, Guy Henry 1864-1952 *WhAm 3*
Preston, H Raymond 1874-1944 *NatCAB 34*
Preston, Harold 1858-1938 *WhAm 1*
Preston, Harriet Waters 1836-1911 *AmBi, DcAmB*
Preston, Harriet Waters 1843-1911 *ApCAB, NatCAB 8, TwCBDA, WhAm 1*
Preston, Herbert R 1861-1937 *WhAm 1*
Preston, Howard Hall 1885-1952 *WhAm 3*
Preston, Howard Payne 1884-1968 *NatCAB 54, WhAm 4A*
Preston, Howard Willis 1859-1936 *WhAm 1*
Preston, Isaac Trimble 1793-1852 *ApCAB, BiAUS, Drake*
Preston, Jacob Alexander 1796-1868 *BiAUS, BiDrAC, WhAm H*
Preston, James Harry 1860-1938 *WhAm 1*
Preston, James Patton 1774-1843 *ApCAB, NatCAB 5, TwCBDA*
Preston, James Patton 1775-1843 *BiAUS, Drake*
Preston, John Fisher 1872- *WhAm 5*
Preston, John J Davis 1892-1953 *NatCAB 42*
Preston, John Smith 1809-1881 *AmBi, ApCAB, BiDConf, DcAmB, Drake, NatCAB 11, TwCBDA, WhAm H*
Preston, John Thomas Lewis 1811-1890 *NatCAB 28, TwCBDA*
Preston, John White 1877-1958 *NatCAB 53, WhAm 5*
Preston, John Williams 1908-1966 *NatCAB 53*
Preston, Jonas 1764-1836 *ApCAB, DcAmB, WhAm H*
Preston, Jonathan 1801-1888 *WhAm H*
Preston, Josephine Corliss 1873-1958 *BiDAmEd, WhAm 3*
Preston, Julius Hervey 1858-1921 *NatCAB 35*
Preston, Keith 1884-1927 *NatCAB 21, WhAm 1*
Preston, Malcolm Greenhough 1905-1971 *WhAm 5*
Preston, Margaret Junkin 1820-1897 *AmBi, DcAmB, NotAW, TwCBDA, WhAm H*
Preston, Margaret Junkin 1825?-1897 *AmWom, ApCAB, NatCAB 7*
Preston, Marie Maples 1878- *WomWWA 14*
Preston, May Wilson 1873-1949 *NotAW, WomWWA 14*
Preston, Ord 1874-1949 *WhAm 3*
Preston, Paul *WhAm H*
Preston, Porter Johnstone 1870-1950 *NatCAB 39*
Preston, Prince Hulon, Jr. 1908-1961 *BiDrAC, WhAm 4, WhAmP*
Preston, Robert J d1967 *WhAm 5*
Preston, Robert Louis 1904-1974 *WhAm 6*
Preston, Roger 1900-1954 *WhAm 3*
Preston, Samuel 1665-1743 *ApCAB*
Preston, Thomas Jex, Jr. 1862- *WhAm 4*
Preston, Thomas L 1897-1957 *WhAm 3*
Preston, Thomas Lewis 1812- *ApCAB, NatCAB 11*
Preston, Thomas Ross 1868-1953 *WhAm 3*
Preston, Thomas Ross 1869-1953 *NatCAB 46*
Preston, Thomas Scott 1824-1891 *ApCAB, DcAmB, Drake, NatCAB 2, TwCBDA, WhAm H*
Preston, Walter 1819-1867 *BiDConf*
Preston, Walter Creigh 1895-1950 *NatCAB 40*
Preston, Willard 1785-1853 *NatCAB 2*
Preston, Willard 1785-1856 *Drake, TwCBDA*
Preston, William 1729-1781 *NatCAB 11*
Preston, William 1729-1783 *ApCAB*
Preston, William 1806-1887 *ApCAB*
Preston, William 1816- *BiAUS*
Preston, William 1816-1862 *Drake*
Preston, William 1816-1887 *BiDConf, BiDrAC, DcAmB, NatCAB 9, TwCBDA, WhAm H*
Preston, William Ballard 1805-1862 *AmBi,*

ApCAB, BiAUS, BiDConf, BiDrAC, BiDrUSE, DcAmB, Drake, NatCAB 4, TwCBDA, WhAm H
Preston, William Bowker 1887-1960 *NatCAB 49*
Preston, William Campbell 1794-1860 *ApCAB, BiAUS, BiDrAC, DcAmB, Drake, NatCAB 11, TwCBDA, WhAm H*
Prestridge, John Newton 1853-1913 *WhAm 1*
Prestwich, Joseph 1812-1896 *DcScB*
Prestwich, Thomas Wendell 1884-1953 *NatCAB 42*
Pretlove, David *NewYHSD*
Pretorius, Andries 1798-1853 *McGEWB*
Prettyman, Anna Yardley 1873- *WomWWA 14*
Prettyman, Cornelius William 1872-1946 *NatCAB 38, NatCAB 47, WhAm 2*
Prettyman, E Barrett 1891-1971 *WhAm 5*
Prettyman, Forrest Johnston 1860-1945 *WhAm 2*
Prettyman, Virgil 1874- *WhAm 5*
Preus, Christian Keyser 1852-1921 *DcAmB*
Preus, Jacob Aall Ottesen 1883-1961 *WhAm 4*
Preus, Ove J H 1880-1951 *WhAm 3*
Preuss, Arthur 1871-1934 *WhAm 1*
Preuss, Charles 1803-1854 *IIBEAAW, NewYHSD, REnAW*
Preuss, Lawrence 1905-1956 *WhAm 3*
Preusser, Christian 1826- *NatCAB 3*
Prevalaye, Pierre Dimas, Marquis De 1745-1816 *ApCAB*
Previtali, Giuseppe 1879-1969 *NatCAB 55*
Prevost, Abbe 1697-1763 *McGEWB*
Prevost, Augustine 1725?-1786 *ApCAB, Drake*
Prevost, Charles Mallet 1818-1887 *ApCAB, TwCBDA*
Prevost, Clifford Alfred 1898-1976 *WhAm 6*
Prevost, Eugene-Prosper 1809-1872 *WhAm H*
Prevost, Francois Marie 1764?-1842 *DcAmB, WhAm H*
Prevost, Sir George 1767-1816 *ApCAB, Drake*
Prevost, Henry Clay 1860-1927 *NatCAB 23*
Prevost, Isaac-Benedict 1755-1819 *DcScB*
Prevost, Jean-Louis 1790-1850 *DcScB*
Prevost, John B *BiAUS*
Prevost, Louis-Constant 1787-1856 *DcScB*
Prevost, Pierre 1751-1839 *AsBiEn, DcScB*
Prevost, Victor 1820- *NewYHSD*
Prevost, William S *NewYHSD*
Prevost-Paradol, Lucien Anatole 1829-1870 *ApCAB*
Prewitt, Ethan C 1903-1971 *WhAm 6*
Preyer, Allan Talmage 1891-1965 *WhAm 4*
Preyer, Carl Adolph 1863-1947 *WhAm 2*
Preyer, Lunsford Richardson 1919- *BiDrAC*
Preyer, Thierry William 1841-1897 *DcScB*
Preyer, William Yost 1888-1970 *NatCAB 56, WhAm 5*
Priber, Christian Gottlieb d1743? *REnAW*
Priber, Christian Gottlieb d1745? *DcAmB, WhAm H*
Priborsky, Benjamin Harrison 1891-1954 *NatCAB 43*
Pribram, Ernest August 1879-1940 *WhAm 1*
Price, Abel Fitzwater 1847-1919 *WhAm 1*
Price, Ada Aikman 1871- *WomWWA 14*
Price, Andrew 1854-1909 *BiDrAC, TwCBDA*
Price, Andrew 1890-1955 *NatCAB 44, WhAm 3*
Price, Bertram John 1878-1944 *WhAm 2*
Price, Bruce 1845-1903 *ApCAB, DcAmB, NatCAB 13, WhAm 1*
Price, Burr 1888-1952 *WhAm 3*
Price, Butler Delaplaine 1845-1919 *WhAm 1*
Price, Carl Fowler 1881-1948 *WhAm 2*
Price, Charles Browne 1869-1939 *WhAm 1*
Price, Charles Melvin 1905- *BiDrAC*
Price, Charles Richard 1885- *WhoColR*
Price, Charles S 1852- *WhAm 4*
Price, Charles Wilson 1857-1934 *WhAm 1, WhAm 1C*
Price, Chester B 1885-1962 *WhAm 4*
Price, Christopher Herbert 1908-1974 *WhAm 6*
Price, Clayton S 1874-1950 *IIBEAAW, REnAW*
Price, Clifton 1867-1942 *NatCAB 31*
Price, David 1790-1854 *WhoMilH*
Price, David Edward 1826-1883 *ApCAB*

Price, David James 1884-1951 *WhAm 3*
Price, Edmund Taber 1895-1968 *NatCAB 55*
Price, Edwin R 1889-1962 *WhAm 4*
Price, Eldridge Cowman 1854- *WhAm 1*
Price, Eli Kirk 1797-1884 *ApCAB, DcAmB, Drake, NatCAB 10, WhAm H*
Price, Eli Kirk 1860-1933 *DcAmB S1*
Price, Elida Ann 1859- *WhoColR*
Price, Ellen H Evans *WomWWA 14*
Price, Emma Paul 1878- *WomWWA 14*
Price, Emory Hilliard 1899- *BiDrAC*
Price, Enoch Jones 1864-1945 *WhAm 2*
Price, Ethel Vermilye Gale *WomWWA 14*
Price, Evan John 1840- *ApCAB Sup*
Price, Francis 1890-1965 *WhAm 4*
Price, Frank 1852-1927 *WhAm 1*
Price, Frank J 1860-1939 *WhAm 1*
Price, Frank Wilson 1895-1974 *WhAm 6*
Price, Franklin Haines 1882-1958 *WhAm 3*
Price, George 1826- *NewYHSD*
Price, George Clinton 1860- *WhAm 4*
Price, George Edmund 1848-1938 *WhAm 1*
Price, George Hunter 1858-1927 *WhAm 1*
Price, George McCready 1870-1963 *WhAm 4*
Price, George Merriman 1865-1956 *WhAm 3*
Price, George Moses 1864-1942 *DcAmB S3, WhAm 2*
Price, George Washington Fergus 1830-1899 *NatCAB 2, TwCBDA*
Price, Granville 1906-1974 *WhAm 6*
Price, Hannibal 1875- *WhAm 5*
Price, Harriet Kilson 1868- *WhoColR*
Price, Harrison Jackson 1868-1945 *NatCAB 33, WhAm 2*
Price, Harvey Lee 1874-1951 *WhAm 3*
Price, Henry Ferris 1884-1955 *WhAm 4*
Price, Henry Vernon 1910-1973 *WhAm 6*
Price, Hickman 1886-1939 *NatCAB 29, WhAm 1*
Price, Hiram 1814-1901 *ApCAB, BiAUS, BiDrAC, DcAmB, TwCBDA, WhAm 1, WhAmP*
Price, Hobert 1899-1965 *WhAm 4*
Price, Homer Charles 1875-1943 *WhAm 3*
Price, Howard Campbell 1872-1950 *WhAm 3*
Price, Hugh Hiram 1859-1904 *BiDrAC*
Price, Ira Maurice 1856-1939 *NatCAB 4, NatCAB 30, WhAm 1*
Price, J St. Clair 1888-1975 *WhAm 6*
Price, Jacob Embury 1853-1935 *WhAm 1*
Price, James Frame 1853-1922 *NatCAB 32*
Price, James Houston 1861- *WhAm 4*
Price, James Hubert 1878-1943 *NatCAB 34, WhAm 2*
Price, James Latimer 1840-1912 *NatCAB 20, WhAm 1*
Price, James Woods 1877-1951 *WhAm 3*
Price, Janice M *WomWWA 14*
Price, Jesse Dashiell 1863-1939 *BiDrAC, WhAm 1*
Price, John *NewYHSD*
Price, John 1661- *ApCAB*
Price, John Charles 1854- *ApCAB Sup*
Price, John D 1892-1957 *WhAm 3*
Price, John Ewing 1857-1928 *NatCAB 33*
Price, John G 1871-1930 *WhAm 1*
Price, John Garland 1868-1957 *NatCAB 43*
Price, John Roy 1900-1975 *WhAm 6*
Price, Joseph 1853-1911 *DcAmB*
Price, Joseph 1876-1950 *NatCAB 38*
Price, Joseph Lindon 1911-1968 *WhAm 5*
Price, Joseph Morris 1870-1949 *NatCAB 37*
Price, Julian 1867-1946 *NatCAB 34, WhAm 2*
Price, Julius Mendes 1857-1924 *IIBEAAW*
Price, Kenneth 1935- *BnEnAmA*
Price, Lee 1917-1962 *WhAm 4*
Price, Leontyne 1927- *WebAB*
Price, Lucien 1883-1964 *WhAm 4*
Price, Lucy Catharine *WomWWA 14*
Price, Margaret 1912-1968 *WhAm 5*
Price, Margaret Wright 1910-1973 *WhAm 5*
Price, Marshall Langton 1878-1915 *WhAm 1*
Price, Miles Oscar 1890-1968 *DcAmLiB, NatCAB 55, WhAm 5*
Price, Milo B 1867-1940 *NatCAB 30, WhAm 1*
Price, Miriam Sutro 1871- *WomWWA 14*

Price, Mona B 1877- *WomWWA 14*
Price, Norman Mills 1877-1951 *IlBEAAW*
Price, Ore Lee 1877- *WhAm 5*
Price, Orlo Josiah 1870-1943 *NatCAB 37, WhAm 2*
Price, Oscar Jay 1845-1929 *WhAm 1*
Price, Overton Westfeldt 1873-1914 *WhAm 1*
Price, P Frank 1864-1954 *WhAm 3*
Price, R Holleman 1900-1963 *WhAm 4*
Price, Raymond B 1872- *WhAm 5*
Price, Richard 1723-1791 *ApCAB, Drake, McGEWB*
Price, Richard Nye 1830- *WhAm 1*
Price, Richard Rees 1875- *WhAm 5*
Price, Robert *NewYHSD*
Price, Robert Beverly 1832- *WhAm 4*
Price, Robert Dale 1927- *BiDrAC*
Price, Robert Henderson 1864- *WhAm 4*
Price, Robert Martin 1867-1940 *WhAm 1*
Price, Rodman M 1816-1894 *BiAUS, Drake*
Price, Rodman McCamley 1816-1894 *ApCAB, BiDrAC, DcAmB, TwCBDA, WhAm H, WhAmP*
Price, Rodman McCauley 1816-1894 *NatCAB 5*
Price, Roger 1696?-1762 *ApCAB*
Price, Sadie F d1903 *WhAm 1*
Price, Samuel 1805-1884 *ApCAB, BiDrAC, NatCAB 5, TwCBDA, WhAm H*
Price, Samuel D 1869-1932 *WhAm 1*
Price, Samuel Woodson 1828-1918 *NewYHSD, WhAm HA, WhAm 4*
Price, Silas Eber 1860-1934 *WhAm 1*
Price, Simeon Taylor 1849-1912 *NatCAB 34*
Price, Stephen 1782-1840 *DcAmB, WhAm H*
Price, Sterling 1809-1867 *AmBi, ApCAB, BiAUS, BiDConf, BiDrAC, DcAmB, Drake, NatCAB 12, REnAW, TwCBDA, WebAMB, WhAm H*
Price, Theodore Hazeltine 1861-1935 *DcAmB S1, NatCAB 14, WhAm 1*
Price, Theophilus Townsend 1828- *ApCAB*
Price, Thomas 1874-1933 *NatCAB 25*
Price, Thomas Frederick 1860-1919 *DcAmB*
Price, Thomas Lawson 1809-1870 *ApCAB, BiAUS, BiDrAC, DcAmB, TwCBDA, WhAm H, WhAmP*
Price, Thomas Randolph 1839-1903 *AmBi, DcAmB, NatCAB 12, WhAm 1*
Price, V Hugh 1916-1962 *NatCAB 50*
Price, Viola Millron 1901-1975 *WhAm 6*
Price, Walter Edwin 1867-1952 *NatCAB 41*
Price, Walter L 1895-1962 *WhAm 4*
Price, Walter Winston 1866-1943 *WhAm 2*
Price, Warren Elbridge 1864- *WhAm 4*
Price, Warwick James 1870- *WhAm 1*
Price, Weston Andrew Valleau 1870-1948 *NatCAB 40*
Price, William Cecil 1818-1907 *BiAUS, DcAmB, WhAm HA, WhAm 4*
Price, William Edmund 1883-1951 *NatCAB 40*
Price, William Francis 1909-1973 *WhAm 6*
Price, William Gray, Jr. 1869- *WhAm 5*
Price, William Henry 1855- *WhAm 4*
Price, William Hundley, Jr. 1926-1972 *WhAm 5*
Price, William James Monroe 1867- *WhoColR*
Price, William Jennings 1873-1952 *NatCAB 41, WhAm 3*
Price, William Pierce 1835-1908 *BiAUS, BiDrAC, NatCAB 7, WhAm 1*
Price, William Raleigh 1875-1936 *WhAm 1*
Price, William Sylvester 1901-1974 *WhAm 6*
Price, William Thompson 1824-1886 *BiDrAC, WhAm H*
Price, William Thompson 1846-1920 *DcAmB, WhAm 1*
Price, William Wightman 1871- *WhAm 5*
Prichard, Alice H 1869- *WomWWA 14*
Prichard, Augustus Bedlow 1854- *WhAm 4*
Prichard, Frank Perley 1853-1918 *NatCAB 28, WhAm 1*
Prichard, Harold Adye 1882-1944 *NatCAB 33, WhAm 2*
Prichard, James Cowles 1786-1848 *DcScB*
Prichard, Lev H 1883-1949 *WhAm 2*
Prichard, Lucius Warner 1864-1949 *NatCAB 38*

Prichard, Lucy Elizabeth 1876- *WomWWA 14*
Prichard, Sarah Johnson 1830-1909 *TwCBDA, WhAm 1*
Prichard, Theodore Jan 1902-1974 *WhAm 6*
Prichard, Vernon E 1892-1949 *WhAm 2*
Prickett, Alva Leroy 1890-1973 *WhAm 6*
Prickett, Henry E *BiAUS*
Prickett, Joe Milroy 1887-1952 *WhAm 3*
Prickett, William 1894-1964 *WhAm 4*
Prickitt, William Augustus 1839-1929 *WhAm 1*
Priddy, Bessie Leach 1871- *WomWWA 14*
Priddy, Lawrence 1874-1944 *WhAm 2*
Pride, Cecil Benjamin 1893-1962 *NatCAB 50*
Pride, Frederick W R 1904-1972 *WhAm 5*
Pride, H Hammond 1891-1973 *WhAm 6*
Pride, Maynard Prince 1914-1973 *NatCAB 57, WhAm 6*
Pride, William Thomas 1881-1952 *NatCAB 40*
Prideaux, John 1718-1759 *ApCAB, Drake*
Pridemore, Auburn Lorenzo 1837-1900 *BiDrAC*
Pridgen, William d1845 *Drake*
Pridgeon, Charles Hamilton 1863-1932 *WhAm 1*
Pridham, Henry *NewYHSD*
Pridi, Phanomyong 1901- *McGEWB*
Pridmore, John Edmund Oldaker 1867-1940 *WhAm 1*
Prien, Gunther 1908-1941 *WhWW-II*
Priest, Alan 1898-1969 *WhAm 5*
Priest, Alice Lucinda 1866- *WomWWA 14*
Priest, Charles Albert 1876-1961 *NatCAB 49*
Priest, Edward Dwight 1861-1931 *DcAmB*
Priest, Francis I *NewYHSD*
Priest, George Madison 1873-1947 *WhAm 2*
Priest, Henry Samuel 1853-1930 *NatCAB 6, WhAm 1*
Priest, Ira Allen 1856- *TwCBDA, WhAm 4*
Priest, Irwin G 1886-1932 *WhAm 1*
Priest, Ivy Baker 1905-1975 *WhAm 6*
Priest, James Percy 1900-1956 *BiDrAC, NatCAB 46, WhAm 3, WhAmP*
Priest, Joseph *NewYHSD*
Priest, Joseph Kilbourne 1890-1948 *NatCAB 37*
Priest, Josiah 1790?-1850? *ApCAB, Drake*
Priest, Mary Charlotte *WomWWA 14*
Priest, Walter Scott 1860-1929 *WhAm 1*
Priest, Wells Blodgett 1888- *WhAm 3*
Priest, William *NewYHSD*
Priestley, George Colin 1862-1938 *WhAm 1*
Priestley, Herbert Ingram 1875-1944 *NatCAB 34, WhAm 2*
Priestley, James d1821 *BiDAmEd, DcAmB, NatCAB 8, WhAm H*
Priestley, John Gillies 1879-1941 *DcScB*
Priestley, Joseph 1733-1804 *AmBi, ApCAB, AsBiEn, BiHiMed, DcAmB, DcAmReB, DcScB, Drake, McGEWB, NatCAB 6, TwCBDA, WhAm H*
Priestly, James d1821 *TwCBDA*
Prieto, Joaquin 1786-1854 *ApCAB*
Prillerman, Byrd 1859- *WhoColR*
Prim, Payne Page 1822-1899 *NatCAB 13*
Prim Y Prats, Juan 1814-1870 *WhoMilH*
Priman, Jacob 1892-1971 *NatCAB 57*
Primaticcio, Francesco 1504-1570 *McGEWB*
Prime, Benjamin Young 1733-1791 *ApCAB, Drake, NatCAB 6*
Prime, Benjamin Youngs 1733-1791 *DcAmB, TwCBDA, WhAm H*
Prime, Ebenezer 1700-1779 *ApCAB, NatCAB 7, TwCBDA*
Prime, Ebenezer Scudder 1847-1912 *WhAm 1*
Prime, Edward Dorr Griffin 1814-1891 *AmBi, ApCAB, DcAmB, NatCAB 7, TwCBDA, WhAm H*
Prime, Frederick 1846-1915 *ApCAB, NatCAB 4, WhAm 1*
Prime, Frederick Edward 1829-1900 *ApCAB, WhAm 1*
Prime, H F *NewYHSD*
Prime, Nathaniel Scudder 1785-1856 *ApCAB, Drake, NatCAB 7, TwCBDA, WhAm H*
Prime, Ralph Earl 1840-1920 *WhAm 1*
Prime, Rufus 1805-1885 *ApCAB*
Prime, Samuel Irenaeus 1812-1885 *AmBi, ApCAB, DcAmB, Drake, NatCAB 7, TwCBDA, WhAm H*

Prime, Samuel Thornton Kemeys 1834-1907 *WhAm 1*
Prime, Wendell 1837- *NatCAB 7*
Prime, William Albert 1863-1936 *NatCAB 29*
Prime, William Cowper 1825-1905 *AmBi, ApCAB, DcAmB, Drake, NatCAB 13, TwCBDA, WhAm 1*
Prime-Stevenson, Edward Irenaeus *WhAm 4*
Primer, Sylvester 1842-1913 *WhAm 1*
Primo DeRivera, J, Marques D'Estella 1870-1930 *WhoMilH*
Primo DeRivera, Jose 1903-1936 *WhoMilH*
Primo DeRivera Y Orbaneja, Miguel 1870-1930 *McGEWB*
Primrose, John 1873-1955 *WhAm 3*
Prims, James Edwin 1931-1969 *WhAm 5*
Primus, Nelson A 1843- *NewYHSD*
Prince, Alexander Louis 1884-1938 *NatCAB 28*
Prince, Arthur Warren 1879-1951 *WhAm 3*
Prince, Benjamin F 1840-1933 *WhAm 1*
Prince, Charles Henry 1837-1912 *BiAUS, BiDrAC*
Prince, Charles Lemuel 1914-1965 *NatCAB 52*
Prince, Edmond Mortimer 1876-1943 *NatCAB 32*
Prince, Edward Ernest 1858- *ApCAB Sup*
Prince, Eugene Mitchell 1897-1965 *WhAm 4*
Prince, Frank Moody 1854-1941 *WhAm 1*
Prince, Frederick Henry 1633- *NatCAB 10*
Prince, Frederick Henry 1859-1953 *DcAmB S5, NatCAB 45, WhAm 3*
Prince, Frederick Octavius 1818-1899 *NatCAB 10*
Prince, George Harrison 1861-1933 *WhAm 1*
Prince, George Washington 1854-1939 *BiDrAC, TwCBDA, WhAm 1, WhAmP*
Prince, George Washington 1878- *WhoColR*
Prince, Helen Choate 1857- *TwCBDA, WhAm 4*
Prince, Henry 1811-1892 *ApCAB, Drake, TwCBDA*
Prince, Henry Axtell 1861-1930 *NatCAB 22*
Prince, Jean Charles 1804-1860 *ApCAB*
Prince, John 1751-1836 *ApCAB, Drake, NatCAB 7*
Prince, John Charles d1860 *Drake*
Prince, John Dyneley 1868-1945 *NatCAB 43, TwCBDA, WhAm 2*
Prince, John Tilden 1844-1916 *WhAm 1*
Prince, John W 1892-1962 *WhAm 4*
Prince, L Bradford 1840-1922 *ApCAB X, NatCAB 1, WhAm 1*
Prince, LeBaron Bradford 1840-1922 *ApCAB, DcAmB, NatCAB 20, TwCBDA, WhAmP*
Prince, Lemuel Benton 1892-1961 *NatCAB 50*
Prince, Leon Cushing 1875-1937 *NatCAB 27, WhAm 1*
Prince, Leon Nathaniel 1906-1970 *WhAm 5*
Prince, Lucinda W *WomWWA 14*
Prince, Luke, Jr. *NewYHSD*
Prince, Mary Catharine Burckle Beardsley *WomWWA 14*
Prince, Mildred Mallon 1897-1961 *NatCAB 47*
Prince, Morris Watson 1843-1932 *NatCAB 26*
Prince, Morton Henry 1854-1929 *AmBi, ApCAB X, DcAmB, NatCAB 25, WhAm 1*
Prince, Nathan 1698-1748 *ApCAB, Drake*
Prince, Nathan Dyer 1878-1942 *WhAm 2*
Prince, Norman 1887-1915 *ApCAB X*
Prince, Oliver Hillhouse d1837 *BiAUS, Drake*
Prince, Oliver Hillhouse 1782-1837 *TwCBDA*
Prince, Oliver Hillhouse 1787?-1837 *ApCAB, BiDrAC, NatCAB 11, WhAm H*
Prince, Sydney Rhodes 1876-1948 *NatCAB 38, WhAm 2*
Prince, Thomas 1600-1673 *AmBi, NatCAB 7*
Prince, Thomas 1601-1673 *Drake*
Prince, Thomas 1687-1758 *AmBi, ApCAB, DcAmB, Drake, NatCAB 7, TwCBDA, WhAm H*
Prince, Thomas 1722-1748 *ApCAB, Drake*
Prince, Walter Franklin 1863-1934 *NatCAB 24, WhAm 1*
Prince, William 1725?-1802 *DcAmB, WhAm H*
Prince, William 1766-1842 *ApCAB, DcAmB,*

Prony, Gaspard-Francois-Clair-M Riche De 1755-1839 *DcScB*
Proper, Datus DeWitt 1844- *WhAm 4*
Proper, Datus Edwin 1896-1965 *WhAm 4*
Proper, Ida Sedgwick *WomWWA 14*
Propert, Frank Cantrell 1884-1955 *NatCAB 47*
Prophet, The *DcAmB*, *WebAB*
Propp, Morris 1884-1933 *NatCAB 24*
Propper DeCallejon, Don Eduardo 1896-1972 *WhAm 5*
Propst, Walter William 1885-1940 *NatCAB 30*
Proschowski, Frantz James Edward 1868- *WhAm 4*
Proseus, Edna Louise 1877- *WomWWA 14*
Proskauer, Joseph M 1877-1971 *WhAm 5*
Prosper *NewYHSD*
Prosper, Henri *NewYHSD*
Pross, Edward Lawrence 1908-1957 *NatCAB 46*
Prosser, Anna Weed 1846- *AmWom*
Prosser, Charles Allen 1871-1952 *BiDAmEd*, *NatCAB 42*, *WhAm 5*
Prosser, Charles Smith 1860-1916 *DcAmB*, *NatCAB 12*, *TwCBDA*, *WhAm 1*
Prosser, Gabriel 1775?-1800 *McGEWB*
Prosser, Herman Alfred 1875-1958 *NatCAB 47*
Prosser, Paul Pittman 1880-1936 *WhAm 1*
Prosser, Seward 1871-1942 *NatCAB 31*, *WhAm 2*
Prosser, William Farrand 1834-1911 *BiAUS*, *BiDrAC*
Prosswimmer, Paul E 1902-1973 *WhAm 6*
Protagoras 484?BC-414?BC *McGEWB*
Protas, Maurice 1899-1970 *NatCAB 54*
Prothero, James Harrison 1862-1929 *WhAm 1*
Protheroe, Daniel 1866-1934 *NatCAB 6*, *WhAm 1*
Protin, Victor *NewYHSD*
Protitch, Dragoslav 1902-1974 *WhAm 6*
Prottengeier, Conrad Gottfried 1872-1949 *WhAm 2*
Proud, Robert 1728-1813 *AmBi*, *ApCAB*, *BiDAmEd*, *DcAmB*, *Drake*, *WhAm H*
Proudfit, Alexander Moncrief 1770-1843 *ApCAB*, *Drake*
Proudfit, Andrew Ellis 1857-1919 *NatCAB 18*
Proudfit, David Law 1842-1897 *ApCAB*, *NatCAB 8*, *WhAm H*
Proudfit, John Williams 1803-1870 *ApCAB*
Proudfoot, Louis Alexander 1869-1927 *NatCAB 20*
Proudhon, Pierre Joseph 1809-1864 *McGEWB*
Proudman, William 1826- *NewYHSD*
Proust, Joseph Louis 1754-1826 *AsBiEn*, *DcScB*
Proust, Marcel 1871-1922 *McGEWB*
Prout, Frank J 1883-1967 *WhAm 4*
Prout, G R 1899-1953 *WhAm 3*
Prout, Henry Goslee *WhAm 5*
Prout, V A *NewYHSD*
Prout, William 1785-1850 *AsBiEn*, *BiHiMed*, *DcScB*
Prout, William Christopher 1886-1927 *ApCAB X*, *NatCAB 21*, *WhAm 1*
Proutt, Frederick George 1870-1934 *NatCAB 33*
Prouty, Charles Azro 1853-1921 *DcAmB*, *WhAm 1*
Prouty, Charles Newton 1842-1916 *ApCAB X*
Prouty, Charles Tyler 1909-1974 *WhAm 6*
Prouty, George Herbert 1862-1918 *NatCAB 14*, *WhAm 1*
Prouty, John Goodell 1865-1923 *NatCAB 20*
Prouty, Lewis Isaac 1872-1951 *NatCAB 38*
Prouty, Olive Higgins 1882-1974 *NatCAB 57*, *WhAm 6*
Prouty, Solomon Francis 1854-1927 *BiDrAC*, *WhAm 4*
Prouty, William Frederick 1879-1949 *NatCAB 38*, *WhAm 6*
Prouty, Winston Lewis 1906-1971 *BiDrAC*, *WhAm 5*
Provancher, Leon 1820- *ApCAB*
Provence, Herbert Winston 1873- *WhAm 5*
Provence, Samuel Moore 1844- *WhAm 4*
Provencher, Jean Norbert 1787-1853 *ApCAB*
Provine, John William 1866-1949 *WhAm 2*
Provine, Loring Harvey 1880- *WhAm 6*

Provine, Robert Calhoun 1902-1966 *WhAm 4*
Provinse, John H 1897-1965 *WhAm 4*
Provoost, Mary Spratt *NotAW*
Provoost, Samuel 1742-1815 *AmBi*, *ApCAB*, *DcAmB*, *DcAmReB*, *Drake*, *NatCAB 1*, *TwCBDA*
Provoost, Samuel 1743-1815 *WhAm H*
Provost, Andrew J 1834-1925 *NatCAB 21*
Provost, Etienne 1782?-1850 *DcAmB*, *REnAW*, *WhAm H*
Provost, Pierre Eusebe 1909-1967 *NatCAB 56*
Provost, Ray 1902-1961 *NatCAB 50*
Provosty, Michel 1889-1958 *NatCAB 44*
Provosty, Oliver Otis 1852-1924 *NatCAB 20*
Provosty, Olivier Otis 1852-1924 *DcAmB*, *WhAm 1*
Prowazek, Stanislaus VonLanov 1875-1915 *DcScB*
Prowell, George R 1849-1928 *WhAm 1*
Prowers, John Wesley 1838-1884 *REnAW*
Prowse, Robert *IIBEAAW*
Prowse, Robert John 1906-1969 *WhAm 5*
Proxmire, William 1915- *BiDrAC*
Prucha, Francis Paul 1921- *REnAW*
Prudden, Lillian E 1852- *WomWWA 14*
Prudden, Paul Peter 1881-1949 *NatCAB 37*
Prudden, Russell Field 1893-1969 *WhAm 5*
Prudden, Theophil Mitchell 1849-1924 *AmBi*, *DcAmB*, *DcScB*, *NatCAB 9*, *TwCBDA*, *WhAm 1*
Pruden, Daniel R *NewYHSD*
Pruden, Oscar L d1902 *WhAm 1*
Prud'homme, John Francis Eugene 1800-1892 *ApCAB*, *DcAmB*, *NewYHSD*, *TwCBDA*, *WhAm H*
Prud'hon, Pierre Paul 1758-1823 *McGEWB*
Prugh, Byron Edgar Peart 1859-1941 *NatCAB 31*, *WhAm 1*
Pruit, Lee Tinkle 1898-1954 *NatCAB 41*
Pruit, Willie Franklin 1865- *AmWom*
Pruitt, A Kelly 1924- *IIBEAAW*
Pruitt, John Dowman 1886-1964 *NatCAB 51*
Pruitt, John Henry 1896-1918 *NatCAB 19*
Pruitt, Raymond S 1887-1957 *WhAm 3*
Pruner, Joseph Alderson 1861-1945 *NatCAB 33*
Pruner Bey, Franz Ignace 1808-1882 *DcScB*
Prunty, Merle Charles 1888-1972 *WhAm 5*
Prurnacke, Charles *NewYHSD*
Prussing, Eugene Ernst 1855- *WhAm 1*
Prutton, Carl Frederick 1898-1970 *NatCAB 55*, *WhAm 5*
Prutzman, C Darrell 1904-1971 *NatCAB 57*
Prutzman, Paul Wyckoff 1876-1953 *NatCAB 41*
Pruyn, Charles Lansing 1852-1906 *NatCAB 26*
Pruyn, H Sewall 1904-1968 *WhAm 5*
Pruyn, Isaac 1816- *NatCAB 7*
Pruyn, John VanSchaick Lansing 1811-1877 *ApCAB*, *BiAUS*, *BiDrAC*, *DcAmB*, *NatCAB 3*, *TwCBDA*, *WhAm H*
Pruyn, Robert Clarence 1847-1934 *NatCAB 26*, *WhAm 4*
Pruyn, Robert Hewson 1815-1882 *ApCAB*, *BiAUS*, *DcAmB*, *NatCAB 13*, *TwCBDA*, *WhAm H*
Pruyn, Samuel 1820-1908 *NatCAB 26*
Pryanishnikov, Dmitry Nikolaevich 1865-1948 *DcScB*
Pryber, Christian *DcAmB*
Pryor, Alice Knight 1879- *WomWWA 14*
Pryor, Arthur W 1870-1942 *DcAmB S3*, *NatCAB 40*, *WhAm 2*
Pryor, David Hampton 1934- *BiDrAC*
Pryor, Edward Bailey 1854- *WhAm 1*
Pryor, Frederick Lincoln 1875-1961 *NatCAB 49*
Pryor, George *NewYHSD*
Pryor, Helen Brenton 1897-1972 *NatCAB 57*
Pryor, Ike T 1852-1937 *WhAm 1*
Pryor, Isaac Thomas 1852-1937 *NatCAB 28*
Pryor, James Chambers 1871-1947 *NatCAB 35*, *WhAm 2*
Pryor, John Henry 1859-1923 *NatCAB 20*
Pryor, Louisa Isabelle 1884- *WomWWA 14*
Pryor, Luke 1820-1900 *ApCAB Sup*, *BiDrAC*, *NatCAB 12*, *TwCBDA*
Pryor, Nathaniel 1775?-1831 *DcAmB*, *WhAm H*

Pryor, Ralph H 1898-1969 *WhAm 5*
Pryor, Roger 1901-1974 *WhAm 6*
Pryor, Roger Atkinson 1828-1919 *AmBi*, *ApCAB*, *ApCAB X*, *BiAUS*, *BiDConf*, *BiDrAC*, *DcAmB*, *NatCAB 9*, *TwCBDA*, *WhAm 1*
Pryor, Samuel Frazier 1865-1934 *NatCAB 27*, *WhAm 1*
Pryor, Sara Agnes Rice 1830-1912 *NotAW*, *WhAm 1*
Pryor, Stewart Wylie 1864-1918 *NatCAB 18*
Pryor, Thomas Brady 1869-1952 *WhAm 3*
Pryor, William Rice d1904 *WhAm 1*
Pryor, William S 1821- *NatCAB 12*
Przhevalsky, Nikolai Mikhailovich 1839-1888 *McGEWB*
Przhevalsky, Nikolay Mikhaylovich 1839-1888 *DcScB*
Psellus, Michael 1018-1078 *DcScB*
Ptacek, Charles William 1905-1968 *NatCAB 55*
Ptolemy 075?- *AsBiEn*
Ptolemy 100?-170? *DcScB*, *McGEWB*
Ptolemy II 308BC-246BC *McGEWB*
Ptolemy I Soter 367?BC-283BC *McGEWB*
Publicker, Harry d1951 *WhAm 3*
Puccini, Giacomo 1858-1924 *McGEWB*
Puchner, Irving A 1899-1968 *WhAm 5*
Pucinski, Roman Conrad 1919- *BiDrAC*
Puckett, B Earl 1897-1976 *WhAm 6*
Puckett, Charles Alexander 1889-1970 *WhAm 5*
Puckett, Erastus Paul 1882-1959 *WhAm 3*
Puckett, Newbell Niles 1897-1967 *WhAm 4*
Puckett, William Olin 1906-1972 *WhAm 5*
Puckette, Charles McDonald 1887-1957 *WhAm 3*
Puckhaber, Edward Frederick Jacob 1895-1953 *NatCAB 42*
Puckner, William August 1864-1932 *WhAm 1*
Puddefoot, William George 1842-1925 *NatCAB 12*, *WhAm 1*
Pudor, H *NewYHSD*
Puelicher, Albert Siefert 1897-1963 *NatCAB 52*, *WhAm 4*
Puelicher, John Huegin 1869-1935 *WhAm 1*
Puente, Giuseppe Del 1841-1900 *WhAm H*
Puente, Juan Eligio 1720?-1780? *ApCAB*
Puerbach, Georg Von 1423-1461 *DcScB Sup*
Puerta, Cristobal Martinez 1580-1623 *ApCAB*
Puestow, Charles Bernard 1902-1973 *NatCAB 57*
Puette, Ross 1887-1971 *NatCAB 56*
Pueyrredon, Juan Martin De 1775?-1840? *ApCAB*
Pufendorf, Baron Samuel Von 1632-1694 *McGEWB*
Puffer, Charles Chenery 1841-1915 *NatCAB 17*
Puffer, Harold Reuben 1897-1960 *NatCAB 48*
Puffer, J Adams 1872-1958 *WhAm 3*
Puffer, Kate Fairbanks *WomWWA 14*
Puffer, Louis Blackmer 1886-1951 *NatCAB 40*
Puffer, Reuben 1756-1829 *ApCAB*
Pugachev, Emelyan Ivanovich 1742-1775 *McGEWB*
Puget, Peter Richings 1797-1871 *DcAmB*, *WhAm H*
Pugh, Arthur Benton 1854-1916 *WhAm 1*
Pugh, Charles Edmund 1841-1913 *NatCAB 16*, *WhAm 1*
Pugh, Eliza Lofton 1841- *ApCAB*
Pugh, Ellis 1656-1718 *ApCAB*, *DcAmB*, *Drake*, *WhAm H*
Pugh, Esther *AmWom*
Pugh, Evan 1828-1864 *ApCAB*, *BiDAmEd*, *DcAmB*, *NatCAB 11*, *TwCBDA*, *WhAm H*
Pugh, George Bernard 1872-1933 *WhAm 1*
Pugh, George Ellis 1822-1876 *ApCAB*, *BiAUS*, *BiDrAC*, *DcAmB*, *Drake*, *NatCAB 4*, *TwCBDA*, *WhAm H*
Pugh, Griffith Thompson 1874- *WhAm 5*
Pugh, James Lawrence 1820-1907 *ApCAB*, *BiAUS*, *BiDConf*, *BiDrAC*, *NatCAB 1*, *TwCBDA*, *WhAm 1*, *WhAmP*
Pugh, John 1761-1842 *BiAUS*, *BiDrAC*, *WhAm H*
Pugh, John Howard 1827-1905 *BiDrAC*
Pugh, John Jones 1864-1946 *WhAm 2*

Pugh, Leonard Eugene 1875-1931 *NatCAB 22*
Pugh, Philip Sidney 1892-1958 *NatCAB 44*
Pugh, Robert Chalfant 1857-1935 *WhAm 1*
Pugh, Samuel Johnson 1850-1922 *BiDrAC,*
WhAm 4
Pugh, Sarah 1800-1884 *NotAW*
Pugh, William Barrow 1889-1950 *WhAm 3*
Pugh, William Leonard 1874- *WhAm 5*
Pugh, William Samuel 1871-1954 *WhAm 3*
Pugin, Augustus Welby Northmore 1812-1852
McGEWB
Pugmire, Ernest Ivison 1888-1953 *WhAm 3*
Pugni, Louis *NewYHSD*
Pugsley, Charles William 1878-1940 *WhAm 1*
Pugsley, Chester DeWitt 1887-1973 *ApCAB X,*
WhAm 6
Pugsley, Clara Elizabeth Holbrook 1855-
WomWWA 14
Pugsley, Cornelius Amory 1850-1936 *ApCAB X,*
BiDrAC, NatCAB 26, WhAm 1
Pugsley, Emma Catherine Gregory d1928
NatCAB 22
Pugsley, Isaac Platt 1843-1915 *NatCAB 16*
Pugsley, Jacob Joseph 1838-1920 *BiDrAC*
Puiseux, Victor 1820-1883 *DcScB*
Pujo, Arsene Paulin 1861-1939 *BiDrAC,*
DcAmB S2, WhAm 1, WhAmP
Pujo, Arsene Paulin 1861-1940 *AmBi*
Pulaski, Casimir 1747?-1779 *McGEWB*
Pulaski, Casimir 1748-1779 *AmBi, DcAmB,*
Drake, NatCAB 1, TwCBDA, WhAm H
Pulaski, Edwin Joseph 1910-1970 *NatCAB 55*
Pulaski, Kazimierz 1747-1779 *WebAB,*
WebAMB
Pulaski, Kazimierz 1748-1779 *ApCAB*
Pulci, Luigi 1432-1484 *McGEWB*
Puleston, Sir John Henry 1830- *ApCAB Sup*
Puleston, William Dilworth 1881- *WhAm 6*
Pulford, John 1837-1896 *ApCAB Sup*
Pulfrich, Carl 1858-1927 *DcScB*
Pulido, Augusto F 1873- *WhAm 5*
Pulitzer, Albert 1851-1909 *WhAm 1*
Pulitzer, Joseph 1847-1911 *AmBi, ApCAB,*
ApCAB X, BiDrAC, DcAmB, EncAB,
McGEWB, NatCAB 1, WebAB,
WhAm 1
Pulitzer, Joseph, Jr. 1885-1955 *DcAmB S5,*
WhAm 3
Pulitzer, Ralph 1879-1939 *DcAmB S2,*
NatCAB 37, WhAm 1
Pulitzer, Walter 1878-1926 *WhAm 1*
Pullen, Daniel Dee 1885-1923 *NatCAB 17*
Pullen, Elisabeth Cavazza *NatCAB 8,*
WhAm 5, WomWWA 14
Pullen, Eugene Henry 1832-1899 *NatCAB 4*
Pullen, Herbert Armitage 1874-1935 *WhAm 1*
Pullen, Roscoe LeRoy 1915-1960 *NatCAB 50,*
WhAm 3
Pullen, Stanley Thomas 1843-1910 *NatCAB 17*
Pullen, Sue Vesta 1861- *AmWom*
Pullen, William Russell 1919-1974 *WhAm 6*
Puller, Edwin Seward 1868- *WhAm 2*
Puller, Lewis Burwell 1898-1971 *NatCAB 57,*
WebAMB
Pulley, Frederick 1875- *WhAm 5*
Pulliam, David Lloyd 1852-1931 *NatCAB 27*
Pulliam, Eugene Collins 1889-1975 *WhAm 6*
Pulliam, Roscoe 1896-1944 *NatCAB 51,*
WhAm 2
Pulliam, William Ellis 1871-1949 *WhAm 3*
Pulling, Arthur Clement 1887-1963 *WhAm 4*
Pullman, George Mortimer 1831-1897 *AmBi,*
ApCAB, DcAmB, EncAB, McGEWB,
NatCAB 11, REnAW, TwCBDA,
WebAB, WhAm H
Pullman, James Minton 1836-1903 *ApCAB,*
WhAm 1
Pullman, John 1912-1971 *WhAm 5*
Pullman, John Stephenson 1871-1943
NatCAB 33, WhAm 2
Pully, Bernard Shaw 1910-1972 *WhAm 5*
Puls, Arthur John 1857- *NatCAB 16*
Pulse, Earl Burton 1908-1959 *NatCAB 47*
Pulsifer, Adelaide Pennell *BiCAW*
Pulsifer, Augustus Moses 1834-1910
NatCAB 39
Pulsifer, David 1802-1894 *ApCAB, TwCBDA*

Pulsifer, Harold Trowbridge 1886-1948
NatCAB 36, WhAm 2
Pulsifer, Harry Bridgman 1879-1947 *WhAm 2*
Pulsifer, Julia 1878- *WomWWA 14*
Pulsifer, Lawson Valentine 1881- *WhAm 6*
Pulsifer, Nathan Trowbridge 1851-1931
WhAm 1, WhAm 1C
Pulsifer, William E 1852-1931 *WhAm 1,*
WhAm 1C
Pulte, Joseah Hippolyt 1811-1884 *Drake*
Pulte, Joseph Hippolyt 1811-1884 *ApCAB,*
DcAmB, WhAm H
Pultz, Leon M 1904-1970 *WhAm 5*
Pulver, Arthur Wadworth 1859-1904 *WhAm 1*
Pulvermacher, Joseph 1886-1962 *NatCAB 47,*
WhAm 4
Pumacahua, Mateo 1760?-1815 *ApCAB*
Pummill, James 1828- *Drake*
Pumpelly, Harmon 1795-1882 *NatCAB 8*
Pumpelly, Josiah Collins 1839-1920 *WhAm 1*
Pumpelly, Mary Hollenback Welles 1803-1879
ApCAB
Pumpelly, Rafael 1837-1923 *REnAW*
Pumpelly, Raphael 1837-1923 *AmBi, ApCAB,*
DcAmB, DcScB, NatCAB 6, TwCBDA,
WebAB, WhAm 1
Punchard, George 1806-1880 *ApCAB*
Punderford, John Keeler 1870-1936 *WhAm 1*
Punderson, E M *NewYHSD*
Punderson, Lemuel S *NewYHSD*
Punnett, Reginald Crundall 1875-1967 *DcScB*
Puntenny, Minnie Ethel *WomWWA 14*
Pupin, Michael Idvorsky 1858-1935 *AmBi,*
ApCAB X, AsBiEn, DcAmB S1, DcScB,
McGEWB, NatCAB 13, NatCAB 26,
WebAB, WhAm 1
Puppel, I Darin 1909-1973 *WhAm 6*
Purce, Charles Lee 1856-1905 *WhAm 1*
Purcell, Charles Henry 1883-1951 *NatCAB 41,*
WhAm 3
Purcell, Edward B *NewYHSD*
Purcell, Edward B, Jr. *NewYHSD*
Purcell, Edward Mills 1912- *AsBiEn, WebAB*
Purcell, Francis Andrew 1872- *WhAm 5*
Purcell, Ganson 1905-1967 *WhAm 4A*
Purcell, George William 1888-1952 *WhAm 3*
Purcell, Graham Boynton, Jr. 1919- *BiDrAC*
Purcell, Henry *NewYHSD*
Purcell, Henry 1659-1695 *McGEWB*
Purcell, Henry 1848-1931 *WhAm 1*
Purcell, John Baptist 1800-1883 *ApCAB,*
DcAmB, DcAmReB, Drake, NatCAB 5,
TwCBDA, WhAm H
Purcell, Martha Grassham 1867-
WomWWA 14
Purcell, Richard J 1887-1950 *WhAm 3*
Purcell, Rosanna *NewYHSD*
Purcell, Theodore Vincent 1866-1957 *WhAm 3*
Purcell, Thomas Williamson 1881-1940
NatCAB 30
Purcell, William 1830-1905 *NatCAB 1,*
WhAm 1
Purcell, William Edward 1856-1928 *BiDrAC,*
WhAm 1
Purcell, William Gray 1880-1964 *BnEnAmA*
Purcell, William Henry 1864-1944 *NatCAB 35*
Purcell, William Henry 1866-1944 *WhAm 2*
Purcell And Elmslie *BnEnAmA*
Purchas, Samuel 1577-1628 *ApCAB, Drake*
Purdin, William A *NewYHSD*
Purdon, Alexander d1970 *WhAm 5*
Purdon, Charles DeLaCherois 1850- *WhAm 4*
Purdon, John 1784-1835 *ApCAB, Drake*
Purdon, Josephine Wilson 1874- *WomWWA 14*
Purdue, Albert Homer 1861-1917 *WhAm 1*
Purdue, Ida Pace 1869- *WomWWA 14*
Purdue, John 1801-1876 *ApCAB Sup*
Purdue, John 1802-1876 *DcAmB, WhAm H*
Purdum, Smith White 1876-1945 *WhAm 2*
Purdy, Albert J 1835?-1909 *NewYHSD*
Purdy, Charles 1850-1928 *ApCAB X*
Purdy, Corydon Tyler 1859-1944 *DcAmB S3,*
NatCAB 12, WhAm 2
Purdy, Edward Amos 1877-1945 *NatCAB 34*
Purdy, Edward Amos 1879-1945 *WhAm 2*
Purdy, George Flint 1905-1969 *DcAmLiB,*
WhAm 5
Purdy, Ken William 1913-1972 *WhAm 5*

Purdy, Lawson 1863-1959 *NatCAB 43,*
WhAm 3
Purdy, Milton Dwight 1866-1937 *AmBi,*
WhAm 1
Purdy, Ray Foote 1898-1965 *NatCAB 52*
Purdy, Richard Augustus 1863-1925 *WhAm 1*
Purdy, Richard Townsend 1906-1972 *WhAm 5*
Purdy, Ross Coffin 1875-1949 *WhAm 3*
Purdy, Smith Meade 1796-1870 *BiAUS,*
BiDrAC, WhAm H
Purdy, Thomas C 1846- *WhAm 4*
Purdy, Victor William 1885-1958 *WhAm 4*
Purdy, Warren Grafton 1843-1910 *WhAm 1*
Purdy, William Henry 1874-1925 *NatCAB 23*
Purin, Charles Maltador 1872- *WhAm 5*
Purington, Beulah Frances 1883-
WomWWA 14
Purington, Florence 1862-1950 *WhAm 3*
Purington, George Colby 1848-1909 *WhAm 1*
Purington, Louise C 1844- *WomWWA 14*
Purinton, Alice May 1877- *WomWWA 14*
Purinton, Daniel Boardman 1850-1933
NatCAB 1, NatCAB 28, TwCBDA,
WhAm 1
Purinton, Edward Earle 1878-1945 *WhAm 3*
Purinton, George Dana 1856-1897 *NatCAB 8,*
TwCBDA
Purinton, Herbert Ronelle 1867-1934 *WhAm 1*
Purkinje, Jan Evangelista 1787-1869 *AsBiEn*
Purkiss, Albert C 1907-1967 *WhAm 5*
Purks, Paul Edwin 1898-1953 *NatCAB 45*
Purkyne, Jan Evangelista 1787-1869 *DcScB*
Purkyne, Johannes Evangelista 1787-1869
BiHiMed
Purman, William James 1840-1928 *ApCAB,*
BiAUS, BiDrAC
Purmort, Charles Hiram 1847- *WhAm 4*
Purmort, LaDoyt Gilman 1895-1966
NatCAB 53, WhAm 4
Purnell, Benjamin 1861-1927 *DcAmB S1,*
WhAm HA, WhAm 4
Purnell, Fillmore Rider 1868- *WhoColR*
Purnell, Frank 1886-1953 *WhAm 3*
Purnell, Fred Sampson 1882-1939 *BiDrAC,*
WhAm 1, WhAmP
Purnell, Maurice Eugene 1906-1972
NatCAB 57, WhAm 6
Purnell, Oscar M 1858- *WhAm 4*
Purnell, Thomas Richard 1846-1908 *TwCBDA*
Purnell, Thomas Richard 1847-1908 *WhAm 1*
Purnell, William C 1903-1971 *WhAm 5*
Purnell, William Henry 1826-1902 *DcAmB,*
WhAm H
Purnell, William Reynolds 1886-1955
NatCAB 46, WhAm 3
Purple, Albert Elijah 1843-1924 *NatCAB 20*
Purple, Edwin Ruthven 1831-1879 *ApCAB*
Purple, Mayo Smith 1860-1942 *NatCAB 31*
Purple, Norman Higgins 1808-1863 *ApCAB,*
Drake
Purple, Samuel Smith 1822-1900 *ApCAB,*
DcAmB, Drake, NatCAB 6, WhAm 1
Purrington, Caleb P *NewYHSD*
Purrington, Henry J 1825- *NewYHSD*
Purrington, J *NewYHSD*
Purrington, William Archer 1852-1926
WhAm 1
Purry, Jean Pierre 1675-1736 *DcAmB,*
WhAm H
Purse, Thomas 1802-1872 *NatCAB 2*
Pursell, Anna Ford 1860- *WomWWA 14*
Pursell, Henry D *NewYHSD*
Pursh, Frederic 1774-1820 *Drake*
Pursh, Frederick 1774-1820 *AmBi, ApCAB,*
DcAmB, DcScB, WhAm H
Purtell, William Arthur 1897- *BiDrAC*
Purucker, Gottfried De 1874-1942 *WhAm 2*
Purves, Austin Montgomery 1854-1915
ApCAB X
Purves, Clifford Burrough 1902-1965 *WhAm 4*
Purves, Dale Benson 1901-1966 *WhAm 4*
Purves, Edmund Randolph 1897-1964 *WhAm 4*
Purves, George Tybout 1852-1901 *TwCBDA,*
WhAm 1
Purviance, David 1766-1847 *DcAmB,*
WhAm H
Purviance, Hugh Young 1799- *Drake*
Purviance, Hugh Young 1799-1882 *TwCBDA*

Purviance, Hugh Young 1799-1883 *ApCAB,*
NatCAB 11
Purviance, Samuel Anderson 1809-1882 *BiAUS,*
BiDrAC, WhAm H
Purviance, Samuel Dinsmore 1774-1806? *BiAUS,*
BiDrAC, WhAm H
Purvin, Jennie Franklin 1873- *WomWWA 14*
Purvis, Charles B 1842- *WhAm 4*
Purvis, James William 1914-1955 *NatCAB 52*
Purvis, Joseph Dixon 1882-1939 *NatCAB 29*
Purvis, Robert 1810-1898 *ApCAB, McGEWB,*
NatCAB 1, TwCBDA
Purvis, William Edmond 1865-1940 *WhAm 1*
Puryear, Bennet 1826-1914 *DcAmB, TwCBDA*
Puryear, Bennett 1826-1914 *NatCAB 11*
Puryear, Charles 1860- *WhAm 3*
Puryear, Richard Clauselle 1801-1867 *BiAUS,*
BiDConf, BiDrAC, WhAm H
Puryear, Vernon John 1901-1970 *WhAm 6*
Pusey, Brown 1869-1953 *WhAm 3*
Pusey, Caleb 1650-1726 *NatCAB 10*
Pusey, Caleb 1650?-1727 *ApCAB, DcAmB,*
WhAm H
Pusey, Edward Bouverie 1800-1882 *McGEWB*
Pusey, Edwin Davis 1870- *WhAm 5*
Pusey, Lea 1820-1896 *NatCAB 34*
Pusey, William Allen 1865-1940 *DcAmB S2,*
NatCAB 34, WhAm 1
Pusey, William Henry Mills 1826-1900 *BiDrAC*
Pushkin, Aleksandr Sergeevich 1799-1837
McGEWB
Pushman, Hovsep d1966 *WhAm 4*
Pushmataha 1764?-1824 *REnAW*
Pushmataha 1765?-1824 *DcAmB, NatCAB 8*
Pushmatahaw 1765?-1824 *ApCAB, WhAm H*
Puterbaugh, Jay G 1876-1965 *WhAm 4*
Puterbaugh, Leslie D 1858-1918 *WhAm 1*
Puterbaugh, Margaret May Lohr 1873-
WomWWA 14
Puthuff, Hanson Duvall 1875-1972 *IIBEAAW,*
WhAm 5
Putman, Donald 1927- *IIBEAAW*
Putman, Floyd Fosket 1880-1958 *NatCAB 47*
Putman, Russell Lorain 1895-1973 *WhAm 6*
Putnam, Albert William 1877-1955 *WhAm 3*
Putnam, Albigence Waldo 1799-1869 *ApCAB,*
Drake, TwCBDA
Putnam, Alfred Porter 1827-1906 *NatCAB 9,*
TwCBDA, WhAm 1
Putnam, Alice Harvey Whiting 1841-1919
BiDAmEd, NotAW
Putnam, Amelia Earhart 1898-1937 *AmBi*
Putnam, Arthur 1873-1930 *AmBi, DcAmB,*
IIBEAAW, NatCAB 21, WhAm 1
Putnam, Arthur Smith 1862-1920 *NatCAB 19*
Putnam, Bertha Haven 1872-1960 *NatCAB 43,*
WomWWA 14
Putnam, Bessie Lucina 1859- *WomWWA 14*
Putnam, Borden Roger 1895-1973 *WhAm 6*
Putnam, Brenda 1890-1975 *BiCAW, WhAm 6,*
WomWWA 14
Putnam, Carolyn Elizabeth 1857-
WomWWA 14
Putnam, Charles Pickering 1844-1914 *DcAmB,*
NatCAB 16
Putnam, Clara Belle Rood 1861-
WomWWA 14
Putnam, Clarence Irwin 1879- *WhAm 6*
Putnam, Claude Adams 1890-1966 *WhAm 4*
Putnam, David A 1816?-1840 *NewYHSD*
Putnam, Dora Park 1859- *WomWWA 14*
Putnam, Eben 1868-1933 *DcAmB, NatCAB 14,*
NatCAB 23, TwCBDA, WhAm 1
Putnam, Eben Fiske Appleton 1891-1953
NatCAB 41, WhAm 3
Putnam, Edmund 1800?- *NewYHSD*
Putnam, Edward Kirby 1868-1939 *WhAm 1*
Putnam, Edwin 1840-1925 *WhAm 1*
Putnam, Elizabeth 1862- *BiCAW,*
WomWWA 14
Putnam, Emily James Smith 1865-1944 *NotAW,*
TwCBDA, WhAm 2, WomWWA 14
Putnam, Francis J 1903-1967 *WhAm 4*
Putnam, Frederic Ward 1839-1915 *AmBi,*
ApCAB X, DcAmB, DcScB, NatCAB 23,
TwCBDA, WhAm 1
Putnam, Frederick Ward 1839-1915 *ApCAB,*
NatCAB 3

Putnam, George 1872-1961 *WhAm 4*
Putnam, George 1889-1960 *WhAm 3*
Putnam, George Ellsworth 1887-1939 *WhAm 1*
Putnam, George Haven 1844-1930 *AmBi,*
ApCAB, ApCAB X, DcAmB, NatCAB 2,
TwCBDA, WhAm 1
Putnam, George Herbert 1861-1955 *DcAmLiB*
Putnam, George Jacob 1866- *WhAm 4*
Putnam, George Lansing 1844- *NatCAB 11*
Putnam, George Martin 1864-1951 *WhAm 3*
Putnam, George Palmer 1814-1872 *AmBi,*
ApCAB, DcAmB, Drake, NatCAB 2,
TwCBDA, WhAm H
Putnam, George Palmer 1887-1950 *WhAm 2*
Putnam, George Rockwell 1865-1953
NatCAB 42, WhAm 3
Putnam, George W 1812?- *NewYHSD*
Putnam, Gideon 1763-1812 *DcAmB, WhAm H*
Putnam, Gideon 1764-1812 *ApCAB*
Putnam, Haldimand Sumner 1835-1863 *ApCAB*
Putnam, Harold 1889-1956 *NatCAB 45*
Putnam, Harrington 1851-1937 *WhAm 1*
Putnam, Harvey 1793-1855 *BiAUS, BiDrAC,*
TwCBDA, WhAm H
Putnam, Helen Cordelia 1857-1951 *DcAmB S5,*
WhAm 3, WomWWA 14
Putnam, Henry 1778-1822 *ApCAB*
Putnam, Henry St. Clair 1861-1924 *WhAm 1*
Putnam, Herbert 1861-1955 *ApCAB Sup,*
DcAmB S5, NatCAB 9, NatCAB 44,
TwCBDA, WebAB, WhAm 3
Putnam, Israel 1718-1790 *AmBi, ApCAB,*
DcAmB, Drake, McGEWB, NatCAB 1,
TwCBDA, WebAB, WebAMB, WhAm H
Putnam, Israel 1878-1918 *ApCAB X,*
NatCAB 21
Putnam, James 1725-1789 *ApCAB*
Putnam, James Jackson 1846-1918 *BiHiMed,*
DcAmB, NatCAB 18, WhAm 1
Putnam, James Osborne 1818-1903 *ApCAB,*
DcAmB, NatCAB 10, TwCBDA,
WhAm 1
Putnam, James William 1865-1940 *NatCAB 41,*
WhAm 1
Putnam, James Wright 1860-1938 *NatCAB 28,*
WhAm 1
Putnam, John Beaman 1893-1951 *NatCAB 40*
Putnam, John Bishop 1848-1915 *WhAm 1*
Putnam, John Phelps 1817-1882 *ApCAB*
Putnam, John Pickering 1847-1917 *WhAm 1*
Putnam, John Risley 1876-1949 *WhAm 2*
Putnam, Katherine Hunt 1792-1869 *ApCAB*
Putnam, Kathrine Scobey *WomWWA 14*
Putnam, Lucy Chase 1859- *WomWWA 14*
Putnam, Mark Edson 1886-1960 *NatCAB 49,*
WhAm 4
Putnam, Mary 1842-1906 *AmBi*
Putnam, Mary B 1872- *WomWWA 14*
Putnam, Mary Nicoll Woodward 1834-1923
BiCAW, WomWWA 14
Putnam, Mary Perkins *WomWWA 14*
Putnam, Mary Traill Spence Lowell 1810-1898
ApCAB, Drake, NatCAB 12, TwCBDA
Putnam, Nina Wilcox 1888-1962 *NatCAB 46,*
WhAm 4, WomWWA 14
Putnam, Osgood 1860-1919 *NatCAB 29*
Putnam, Phil Hezekiah Isaac 1908-1966
NatCAB 54
Putnam, Ralph 1876-1923 *ApCAB X*
Putnam, Rex 1890-1967 *BiDAmEd*
Putnam, Robert Bruce 1891-1960 *NatCAB 49*
Putnam, Roger Lowell 1893-1972 *NatCAB 57*
Putnam, Rufus 1738-1824 *AmBi, ApCAB,*
BiAUS, DcAmB, Drake, NatCAB 1,
TwCBDA, WebAB, WebAMB, WhAm H
Putnam, Russell Benjamin 1878-1959 *WhAm 3*
Putnam, Ruth d1931 *WhAm 1*
Putnam, Ruth 1856-1931 *DcAmB*
Putnam, Ruth 1858-1931 *BiCAW,*
WomWWA 14
Putnam, Sallie A Brock 1845?- *ApCAB,*
TwCBDA
Putnam, Salmon W 1815-1872 *NatCAB 11*
Putnam, Samuel 1768-1853 *ApCAB, BiAUS,*
Drake, TwCBDA
Putnam, Samuel Porter 1838-1896 *ApCAB Sup*
Putnam, Sarah A Brock *AmWom*
Putnam, Sarah A Brock 1840?- *NatCAB 10*

Putnam, Stephen Greeley 1852- *WhAm 4*
Putnam, Thomas Milton 1875-1942 *WhAm 2*
Putnam, Warren Edward 1857-1927 *WhAm 1,*
WhAm 2
Putnam, William Allen 1847-1936 *NatCAB 28*
Putnam, William Hutchinson 1878-1958
WhAm 3
Putnam, William LeBaron 1835-1918 *ApCAB,*
DcAmB, TwCBDA, WhAm 1
Putnam, William LeBarron 1835-1918
NatCAB 19
Putnam, William Lowell 1840-1861 *ApCAB*
Putnam, William Lowell 1861-1924 *ApCAB X,*
NatCAB 34, WhAm 1
Putnam, William Pitt 1870-1961 *NatCAB 48*
Putnam, William Rowell 1876-1957 *WhAm 3*
Putney, Albert Hutchinson 1872-1928 *WhAm 1*
Putney, Elmore Martin 1895-1951 *NatCAB 42,*
WhAm 3
Putney, William Wallace 1893-1969
NatCAB 55
Putnik, Radomir 1847-1917 *WhoMilH*
Putts, B Swayne 1882-1952 *NatCAB 41*
Puvis DeChavannes, Pierre 1824-1898 *McGEWB*
Puys, Zachary Du *ApCAB*
Puysegur, Antoine Hyacinthe 1752-1809
ApCAB
Puzinas, Paul Peter 1907- *WhAm 5*
Pye, David Walter 1870-1951 *NatCAB 14,*
NatCAB 42
Pye, Watts Orson 1878-1926 *DcAmB*
Pye, William Satterlee 1880- *WhAm 6*
Pyeatt, John Samuel 1874-1946 *WhAm 2*
Pyke, W E 1896-1959 *WhAm 4*
Pyle, Adam, Jr. 1888-1960 *NatCAB 50*
Pyle, Annie Sanborn 1859- *WomWWA 14*
Pyle, Charles C 1882?-1939 *WebAB*
Pyle, Dan 1875-1964 *NatCAB 52*
Pyle, Ellen *WomWWA 14*
Pyle, Ernest Taylor 1900-1945 *DcAmB S3,*
WebAB, WebAMB, WhAm 2, WhWW-II
Pyle, Ernie 1900-1945 *NatCAB 33*
Pyle, Gladys 1890- *BiDrAC*
Pyle, Hannah Cadbury 1872- *WomWWA 14*
Pyle, Helen Mary 1908-1970 *WhAm 5*
Pyle, Howard 1853-1911 *AmBi, ApCAB,*
DcAmB, IIBEAAW, NatCAB 9,
NatCAB 29, TwCBDA, WebAB,
WhAm 1
Pyle, John Sherman 1865-1951 *NatCAB 40,*
WhAm 4
Pyle, Joseph Gilpin 1853-1930 *WhAm 1*
Pyle, Katharine d1938 *WhAm 1,*
WomWWA 14
Pyle, Margery *WomWWA 14*
Pyle, Robert 1877-1951 *DcAmB S5, WhAm 3*
Pyle, Walter Lytle 1871-1921 *DcAmB,*
NatCAB 19, WhAm 1
Pyle, William H 1875-1946 *WhAm 2*
Pyles, John Wylie 1901-1951 *NatCAB 39*
Pyles, Nellie E 1869- *WomWWA 14*
Pym, John 1584-1643 *McGEWB*
Pynchon, Charles 1719-1783 *ApCAB*
Pynchon, Edwin 1856-1914 *NatCAB 20*
Pynchon, John 1621-1703 *ApCAB, TwCBDA*
Pynchon, John 1626?-1702? *DcAmB*
Pynchon, John 1626?-1703 *AmBi, WhAm H*
Pynchon, Joseph 1737-1794 *ApCAB*
Pynchon, Thomas Ruggles 1760-1796 *ApCAB*
Pynchon, Thomas Ruggles 1823-1904 *ApCAB,*
DcAmB, NatCAB 3, TwCBDA,
WhAm 1
Pynchon, William 1590-1662 *AmBi, ApCAB,*
DcAmB, Drake, NatCAB 7, TwCBDA,
WhAm H
Pynchon, William 1723-1789 *ApCAB*
Pyne, Frederick Glover 1879-1962 *WhAm 4*
Pyne, George Rovillo 1853-1911 *WhAm 1*
Pyne, H Rivington 1892-1952 *NatCAB 42*
Pyne, Moses Taylor 1855-1921 *ApCAB X,*
NatCAB 19, TwCBDA, WhAm 1
Pyne, Percy Rivington 1857-1929 *NatCAB 22*
Pyne, Percy Rivington, II 1882-1950 *WhAm 1,*
WhAm 3
Pyne, R L *NewYHSD*
Pyne, R S *NewYHSD*
Pyott, Wilford Henry 1890-1957 *NatCAB 48*
Pyre, George John 1912-1967 *WhAm 5*

Pyre, James Francis Augustin 1871-1934
  WhAm 1
Pyrke, Berne Ashley 1875-1953 *WhAm 4*
Pyrlaeus, John Christopher 1713-1779 *ApCAB*
Pyrlaus, John Christopher 1713-1779
  NatCAB 6
Pyron, Walter Braxton 1882-1951 *NatCAB 40,*
  WhAm 3
Pyrtle, E Ruth *WhAm 5*
Pythagoras 575?BC-495?BC *McGEWB*
Pythagoras 582?BC-497?BC *AsBiEn*
Pythagoras Of Samos 560?BC-480?BC *DcScB*
Pytheas Of Massalia 300?BC- *AsBiEn, DcScB*
Pyun, Yung-Tai 1892-1969 *WhAm 5*

Q

Qabajaqi, Al- *DcScB*
Qabisi, Abu Al-Saqr Abd Al-Aziz Ibn, Al- *DcScB*
Qadi Zada Al-Rumi 1364?-1436? *DcScB*
Qalasadi, Abu L-Hasan Ali Ibn M, Al- 1412-1486 *DcScB*
Qarashi, Al- *DcScB*
Qassim, Abdul Karim d1963 *WhAm 4*
Qazwini, Zakariya Ibn Muhammad, Al- 1203?-1283 *DcScB*
Quackenbos, George Payn 1826-1881 *ApCAB, BiDAmEd, NatCAB 13, TwCBDA*
Quackenbos, George Payne 1826-1881 *Drake*
Quackenbos, John Duncan 1848-1926 *ApCAB, BiDAmEd, NatCAB 6, TwCBDA, WhAm 1*
Quackenboss, Alexander 1866-1933 *NatCAB 28, WhAm 4*
Quackenbush, John Adam 1828-1908 *BiDrAC*
Quackenbush, John Adams 1828-1908 *TwCBDA*
Quackenbush, Larry 1916-1967 *WhAm 4*
Quackenbush, Stephen Platt 1823-1890 *ApCAB, DcAmB, NatCAB 4, TwCBDA, WhAm H*
Quade, Maurice Northrop 1900-1966 *NatCAB 52, WhAm 4*
Quade, Omar H 1886-1965 *WhAm 4*
Quaid, John Erskell 1884-1948 *NatCAB 37*
Quaife, Milo Milton 1880-1959 *REnAW, WhAm 3*
Quail, Frank Adgate 1865- *WhAm 5*
Quaile, George Emerson 1867-1934 *WhAm 1*
Quain, Edwin Alphonsus 1906-1975 *WhAm 6*
Quain, Eric P 1870-1962 *NatCAB 51, WhAm 5*
Quain, Frances Dunn *WomWWA 14*
Quaintance, Altus Lacy 1870- *WhAm 5*
Qualtrough, Edward Francis 1850-1913 *WhAm 1*
Quam, James Philip 1880-1956 *NatCAB 43*
Quanah 1845?-1911 *AmBi, DcAmB, WebAB, WebAMB, WhAm HA, WhAm 4*
Quanah Parker 1845?-1911 *REnAW*
Quantrell, Ernest E 1881-1962 *WhAm 4*
Quantrill, William Clarke 1837-1865 *DcAmB, WebAB, WebAMB, WhAm H*
Quarles, Benjamin 1904- *EncAAH*
Quarles, Charles 1846-1908 *NatCAB 16, WhAm 1*
Quarles, Charles Bullen 1884-1968 *WhAm 5*
Quarles, Donald A 1894-1959 *WhAm 3*
Quarles, Edwin Latham 1880-1932 *WhAm 1*
Quarles, James d1950 *WhAm 3*
Quarles, James Addison 1837-1907 *WhAm 1*
Quarles, James Minor 1823-1901 *BiAUS, BiDrAC*
Quarles, James Thomas 1877- *WhAm 5*
Quarles, Joseph Very 1843-1911 *ApCAB Sup, BiDrAC, NatCAB 13, TwCBDA, WhAm 1*
Quarles, Joseph Very, III 1874-1946 *NatCAB 35, WhAm 2*
Quarles, Julian Minor 1848-1929 *BiDrAC*
Quarles, Louis 1883-1972 *WhAm 5*
Quarles, Ralph Petty 1855-1921 *NatCAB 13, TwCBDA, WhAm 1*
Quarles, Robert Thomas 1850-1914 *NatCAB 17*
Quarles, Tunstall 1770?-1855 *BiAUS, BiDrAC, WhAm H*
Quarles, William Charles 1870-1939 *NatCAB 29, WhAm 1*
Quarre, Ferdinand *NewYHSD*
Quarre, Frederick *NewYHSD*
Quarter, William 1806-1848 *ApCAB, DcAmB,*

NatCAB 9, TwCBDA, WhAm H
Quartley, Arthur 1839-1886 *ApCAB, DcAmB, NatCAB 11, NewYHSD, TwCBDA, WhAm H*
Quartley, Frederick William 1808-1874 *ApCAB, NewYHSD*
Quasdanovich, Sigismond Mathias 1742-1796 *ApCAB*
Quasimodo, Salvatore 1901-1968 *McGEWB, WhAm 5*
Quatrefages DeBreau, Jean-Louis-A De 1810-1892 *DcScB*
Quattrocchi, Edmondo 1889-1966 *WhAm 4*
Quaw, John C *NewYHSD*
Quay, Arthur Hayes 1895-1951 *WhAm 3*
Quay, Matthew Stanley 1833-1904 *AmBi, ApCAB, BiDrAC, DcAmB, McGEWB, NatCAB 1, TwCBDA, WebAB, WhAm 1, WhAmP*
Quayle, Henry Joseph 1876- *WhAm 5*
Quayle, John Francis 1866-1930 *WhAm 1*
Quayle, John Francis 1868-1930 *BiDrAC*
Quayle, John Harrison 1874-1944 *NatCAB 35*
Quayle, John Harrison 1874-1945 *WhAm 2*
Quayle, Oliver A, Jr. 1894-1956 *WhAm 3*
Quayle, Osborne R 1898-1954 *WhAm 3*
Quayle, William Alfred 1860-1925 *DcAmB, NatCAB 6, TwCBDA, WhAm 1*
Quealy, Patrick J 1857-1930 *WhAm 1*
Quealy, Susan Jane 1870-1956 *WhAm 3*
Queby, John *NewYHSD*
Queck-Berner, Clarie Lyon *WomWWA 14*
Queckenstedt, Hans 1876-1918 *BiHiMed*
Queen, Ellery *WebAB*
Queen, Emmet 1854- *NatCAB 12*
Queen, James 1824-1877? *NewYHSD*
Queen, Walter W 1824-1893 *ApCAB, DcAmB, NatCAB 4, TwCBDA, WhAm H*
Queeny, Edgar Monsanto 1897-1968 *WhAm 5*
Queeny, John Francis 1859-1933 *NatCAB 24, WhAm 1*
Queipo, Manuel Abad 1760?-1820? *ApCAB*
Queipo, Vicente Vasquez 1804- *ApCAB*
Queiros, Pedro Fernandes De 1560-1614 *ApCAB*
Quelch, John 1665?-1704 *DcAmB, WhAm H*
Quenstedt, Friedrich 1809-1889 *DcScB*
Quentin, Charles Henry 1621-1683 *ApCAB*
Querard, Louis Francois 1706-1749 *ApCAB*
Querbes, Andrew 1864-1939 *WhAm 1*
Quercetanus, Josephus *DcScB*
Quercia, Jacopo Della 1374?-1438 *McGEWB*
Quereau, Edmund Chase 1868- *WhAm 4*
Quertin, George Albert 1869- *NatCAB 16*
Query, Walter Graham 1877- *WhAm 5*
Quesada, Elwood Richard 1904- *WebAMB*
Quesada, Gonzalo De 1868- *ApCAB Sup*
Quesada, Gonzalo Jimenez De 1495-1597 *ApCAB*
Quesada, Manuel 1833-1886 *Drake Sup*
Quesada, Manuel Castro 1877- *WhAm 5*
Quesada, Manuel De 1830?-1886 *ApCAB*
Quesada, Vicente Gaspar 1830- *ApCAB*
Quesenbury, William 1822-1888 *NewYHSD*
Quesnay, Alexandre-Marie 1755-1820 *DcAmB, NewYHSD, WhAm H*
Quesnel, Dieudonne-Gabriel Louis 1749-1801 *ApCAB*
Quesnel, Joseph 1749-1809 *ApCAB*
Quesnel, Joseph 1750-1809 *Drake*
Questa, Edward J 1898-1962 *WhAm 4*
Quetelet, Lambert Adolphe Jacques 1796-1874 *AsBiEn, DcScB, McGEWB*
Quetzalcohuatl *ApCAB*

Quevedo Y Villegas, Francisco Gomez De 1580-1645 *McGEWB*
Quezon, Manuel Luis 1878-1944 *BiDrAC, DcAmB S3, McGEWB, WhAmP, WhWW-II*
Quezon Y Molina, Manuel Luis 1878-1944 *WhAm 2*
Quff, Amin Al-Dawlah Abu Al-F, Ibn Al- 1233-1286 *DcScB*
Quhi, Abu Sahl Wayjan Ibn Rustam, Al- *DcScB*
Quiat, Ira L 1891-1967 *WhAm 5*
Quick, Charles William 1822- *ApCAB*
Quick, George W 1861- *WhAm 4*
Quick, H B *NewYHSD*
Quick, Herbert 1861-1925 *NatCAB 25, WhAm 1*
Quick, Isaac *NewYHSD*
Quick, Israel *NewYHSD*
Quick, John Herbert 1861-1925 *AmBi, DcAmB, EncAAH, REnAW*
Quick, Walter 1861- *WhAm 4*
Quick, William *NewYHSD*
Quickenborne, Charles Van 1788-1857 *ApCAB*
Quickert, Marvin H 1929-1974 *WhAm 6*
Quidor, George W 1817?- *NewYHSD*
Quidor, John 1801-1881 *AmBi, BnEnAmA, DcAmB, NewYHSD, WhAm H*
Quie, Albert Harold 1923- *BiDrAC*
Quier, Edwin Addams 1869-1939 *NatCAB 47*
Quigan, Frank Joseph 1890-1952 *NatCAB 39*
Quigg, Eugene Kramer 1896-1950 *NatCAB 39*
Quigg, James F 1900-1960 *WhAm 4*
Quigg, Lemuel Ely 1863-1919 *ApCAB X, BiDrAC, DcAmB, NatCAB 18, WhAm 4*
Quigg, Murray Townsend 1891-1956 *NatCAB 43*
Quiggle, Edmund Blanchard 1886-1935 *WhAm 1*
Quigley, Edward B 1895- *IIBEAAW*
Quigley, Harold Scott 1889-1968 *NatCAB 55*
Quigley, Harry Nelson 1866-1936 *WhAm 1*
Quigley, Isaac Moore 1856- *NatCAB 12*
Quigley, Jack Clement 1930-1975 *WhAm 6*
Quigley, James Cloyd 1887-1960 *WhAm 4*
Quigley, James Edward 1854-1915 *DcAmB, NatCAB 12, TwCBDA, WhAm 1*
Quigley, James Edward 1855-1915 *ApCAB Sup*
Quigley, James Knight 1880-1964 *NatCAB 51*
Quigley, James Michael 1918- *BiDrAC*
Quigley, John Paul 1896-1967 *NatCAB 53, WhAm 4A*
Quigley, Margery Closey 1886-1968 *DcAmLiB*
Quigley, Martin Joseph 1890-1964 *WhAm 4*
Quigley, Samuel 1873-1946 *WhAm 3*
Quigley, Thomas M 1889-1974 *WhAm 6*
Quigley, William Middleton 1890-1957 *WhAm 3*
Quilici, George L d1969 *WhAm 5*
Quill, Michael J 1905-1966 *WhAm 4*
Quillen, Isaac James 1909-1967 *BiDAmEd, WhAm 4*
Quillen, James Henry 1916- *BiDrAC*
Quillen, Robert 1887-1948 *WhAm 2*
Quiller-Couch, Arthur Thomas 1863-1944 *WhAm 2*
Quilliam, J *NewYHSD*
Quillian, Paul Whitfield 1895- *WhAm 2*
Quillian, William Fletcher 1880-1960 *NatCAB 50*
Quimby, A Judson 1875-1958 *NatCAB 43*
Quimby, Althea Coffin 1858- *WomWWA 14*
Quimby, Brooks 1897-1968 *WhAm 5*
Quimby, Charles Elihu 1853-1921 *WhAm 1*
Quimby, Harriet 1884-1912 *WhAm 1,*

Wom WWA 14
Quimby, Neal Frederic 1907-1961 WhAm 4
Quimby, Phineas Parkhurst 1802-1866 AmBi,
    DcAmB, NatCAB 11, WhAm H
Quimby, Silas Everard 1837- NatCAB 14
Quin, Charles Kennon 1877- WhAm 5
Quin, Clinton Simon 1883-1956 NatCAB 44,
    WhAm 3
Quin, Huston 1876-1938 NatCAB 28,
    WhAm 1
Quin, Percy Edwards 1872-1932 BiDrAC,
    WhAm 1, WhAmP
Quinan, John Russell 1822-1890 DcAmB,
    WhAm H
Quinby, Edward McConahay 1851-1909
    NatCAB 17
Quinby, Florence Cole Wom WWA 14
Quinby, Frank Haviland 1868- WhAm 1
Quinby, George Washington 1810-1884 ApCAB,
    Drake
Quinby, H Anna 1871- Wom WWA 14
Quinby, Henry Brewer 1846-1924 NatCAB 14,
    WhAm 1
Quinby, Henry Cole 1872-1922 NatCAB 25
Quinby, Isaac Ferdinand 1820?-1891 Drake
Quinby, Isaac Ferdinand 1821-1891 ApCAB,
    DcAmB, TwCBDA, WhAm H
Quinby, Lillian Baker Wom WWA 14
Quinby, Watson Fell 1825- TwCBDA
Quinby, William Carter 1877- WhAm 5
Quinby, William Emory 1835-1908 ApCAB Sup,
    NatCAB 1, TwCBDA, WhAm 1
Quincey, Josiah 1744-1775 WhAm H
Quincke, Georg Hermann 1834-1924 DcScB
Quincke, Heinrich Irenaeus 1842-1922 BiHiMed
Quincy, Abraham Howard 1767-1840 ApCAB
Quincy, Charles Frederick 1856-1927
    NatCAB 23, WhAm 1, WhAm 1C
Quincy, Edmund 1602-1635 ApCAB
Quincy, Edmund 1627-1698 ApCAB
Quincy, Edmund 1681-1738 ApCAB, Drake,
    NatCAB 13
Quincy, Edmund 1703-1788 ApCAB
Quincy, Edmund 1808-1877 AmBi, ApCAB,
    DcAmB, Drake, NatCAB 6, WhAm H
Quincy, Eliza Susan 1773-1850 ApCAB
Quincy, Eliza Susan 1798-1884 ApCAB
Quincy, Henry Parker 1838-1899 NatCAB 15
Quincy, John 1689-1767 ApCAB, Drake
Quincy, Josiah 1709-1784 ApCAB, NatCAB 6
Quincy, Josiah 1744-1775 AmBi, ApCAB,
    DcAmB, Drake, NatCAB 1, TwCBDA,
    WhAmP
Quincy, Josiah 1772-1864 AmBi, ApCAB,
    BiAUS, BiDAmEd, BiDrAC, DcAmB,
    Drake, NatCAB 6, TwCBDA, WebAB,
    WhAm H, WhAmP
Quincy, Josiah 1793-1875 ApCAB
Quincy, Josiah 1802-1882 ApCAB, Drake,
    NatCAB 6
Quincy, Josiah 1859-1919 ApCAB Sup,
    NatCAB 19, TwCBDA, WhAm 1
Quincy, Josiah Hatch 1860-1930 NatCAB 24
Quincy, Josiah Phillips 1829-1910 ApCAB,
    DcAmB, NatCAB 7, WhAm 1
Quincy, Josiah Phillips 1830-1910 Drake
Quincy, Mary Adams BiCAW, Wom WWA 14
Quincy, Samuel 1735-1789 ApCAB
Quincy, Samuel Miller 1833- ApCAB, Drake
Quine, Willard VanOrman 1908- McGEWB,
    WebAB
Quine, William Edward 1847-1922 DcAmB S1,
    WhAm 1
Quiner, Joanna 1801-1873 New YHSD
Quinlan, Francis Joseph 1852-1936 NatCAB 27
Quinlan, George Austin 1880- WhAm 6
Quinlan, John 1826-1883 ApCAB, NatCAB 13,
    TwCBDA, WhAm H
Quinlan, Joseph Albert 1889-1959 NatCAB 49,
    WhAm 3
Quinlivan, Ray James 1894-1961 WhAm 4
Quinn, Arthur Hobson 1875-1960 WhAm 4
Quinn, Bernard G 1879- WhAm 6
Quinn, Charles Henry 1876- WhAm 5
Quinn, Daniel Hellenist 1861-1918 NatCAB 18,
    WhAm 1
Quinn, Daniel Joseph 1864-1940 WhAm 1
Quinn, Edmond Thomas 1868-1929 AmBi,

DcAmB, NatCAB 26, WhAm 1
Quinn, Edward James 1897-1975 WhAm 6
Quinn, Isabel Lowe Wom WWA 14
Quinn, James Baird 1843-1915 WhAm 1
Quinn, James Cochrane 1845- ApCAB
Quinn, James H 1857-1930 WhAm 1
Quinn, James Leland 1875-1960 BiDrAC,
    WhAm 5
Quinn, James Mark 1892-1955 NatCAB 45
Quinn, John 1839-1903 BiDrAC
Quinn, John 1870-1924 NatCAB 18, WhAm 1
Quinn, John Francis 1888-1971 WhAm 5
Quinn, John Joseph 1892-1947 NatCAB 35,
    WhAm 2
Quinn, Karl Vincent 1902-1962 NatCAB 49
Quinn, Michael Joseph Francis 1851-
    ApCAB Sup
Quinn, Murtha Patrick 1858-1940 NatCAB 31
Quinn, Patrick Henry 1869-1956 NatCAB 44,
    WhAm 3
Quinn, Peter Anthony 1904- BiDrAC
Quinn, Ralph Hughes 1893-1940 WhAm 1
Quinn, Robert Emmett 1894-1975 WhAm 6
Quinn, Terence John 1836-1878 BiDrAC,
    WhAm H
Quinn, Theodore Kinget 1893-1961 WhAm 4
Quinn, Thomas Charles 1864- WhAm 4
Quinn, Thomas Vincent 1903- BiDrAC
Quinn, Vernon 1881- WhAm 6
Quinn, William 1820-1887 TwCBDA
Quinn, William 1821-1887 ApCAB
Quinn, William Joseph 1879-1960 NatCAB 45
Quint, Alonzo Hall 1828-1896 ApCAB, Drake,
    TwCBDA
Quint, Louis H New YHSD
Quint, Wilder Dwight 1863-1936 WhAm 1
Quintana, Agustin 1660?-1734 ApCAB
Quintana, Ben 1923-1944 IIBEAAW
Quintana, Joe A IIBEAAW
Quintana Roo, Andres 1787-1851 ApCAB
Quintard, Charles Todd 1824-1898 ApCAB,
    BiDConf, DcAmB, Drake, NatCAB 5,
    TwCBDA, WhAm H
Quintard, Edward 1867-1936 WhAm 1
Quintard, George William 1822-1913 ApCAB X,
    DcAmB, NatCAB 2, WhAm 1
Quintero, J Marshall 1871-1960 NatCAB 49
Quintero, Juan BiDConf
Quintero, Lamar Charles 1863-1921 WhAm 1
Quintilian 035?-099? McGEWB
Quintin, D S New YHSD
Quinton New YHSD
Quinton, Amelia Stone 1833-1926 AmWom,
    NotAW, TwCBDA
Quinton, Cornelia Bentley Sage d1936 WhAm 1
Quinton, Harold 1899-1969 WhAm 5
Quinton, John Henry 1850-1939 WhAm 1
Quinton, William 1838-1916 WhAm 1
Quintrell, Mary Corinne 1839- Wom WWA 14
Quirino, Elpidio 1890-1956 McGEWB,
    WhAm 3
Quirk, Francis Joseph 1907- WhAm 6
Quirk, George Russell 1881-1962 NatCAB 48
Quirk, James Robert 1884-1932 WhAm 1
Quirk, James Thomas 1911-1969 WhAm 5
Quirk, John F 1859- WhAm 4
Quirk, Lillian DeFrank Park 1849-
    Wom WWA 14
Quirk, Raphael Joseph 1901-1949 NatCAB 37
Quirke, Terence Thomas 1886-1947 WhAm 2,
    WhAm 2C
Quiroga, Jose 1707-1804 Drake
Quiroga, Juan Facundo 1788?-1835 McGEWB
Quiroga, Juan Facundo 1790-1835 ApCAB
Quiroga, Vasco De 1470-1565 ApCAB
Quiros, Agustin De 1566-1622 ApCAB
Quirot New YHSD
Quirt, Howard Arthur 1891-1968 NatCAB 57
Quirt, Walter W 1902- IIBEAAW
Quisenberry, Anderson Chenault 1850-1921
    NatCAB 19, WhAm 1
Quisenberry, Hiter Nelson 1865- WhAm 4
Quisenberry, Russell A 1893-1966 WhAm 4
Quisenberry, T Edwin 1891-1964 NatCAB 52
Quisling, Vidkun 1887-1945 WhWW-II
Quitman, Frederick Henry 1760-1832 ApCAB,
    NatCAB 11, TwCBDA
Quitman, John Anthony 1798-1858 AmBi,

DcAmB, REnAW, WebAMB, WhAm H
Quitman, John Anthony 1799-1858 ApCAB,
    BiAUS, BiDrAC, Drake, NatCAB 13,
    TwCBDA
Quoniam DeSchompre, Guy Emile M Joseph
    1905-1958 WhAm 3
Quoy, Jean-Rene-Constant 1790-1869 DcScB
Qurra, Ibn DcScB
Qusta Ibn Luqa Al-Balabakki DcScB
Qutayba, Abu Muhammad Abdallah Ibn, Ibn
    828-889? DcScB
Qutb Al-Din Al-Shirazi 1236-1311 DcScB
Quynn, Allen George 1894-1971 WhAm 5

R

Raab, Ferdinand *NewYHSD*
Raab, Francis 1813?- *NewYHSD*
Raab, Harold Sherman 1915-1961 *NatCAB 45*
Raab, Henry 1837-1901 *TwCBDA*
Raab, Julius 1891-1964 *WhAm 4*
Raab, Merrill Emanuel 1891-1965 *NatCAB 51*
Raab, Wilhelm 1895-1970 *WhAm 5*
Raabe, Arthur Edward 1898-1965 *WhAm 4*
Raasch, Richard Frederic 1921-1971 *WhAm 6*
Rabaud, Charles Hector 1711-1764 *ApCAB*
Rabaut, Louis Charles 1886-1961 *BiDrAC,*
WhAm 4, WhAmP
Rabb, Albert Livingston 1893-1939 *NatCAB 30*
Rabb, Kate Milner 1866-1937 *WhAm 1,*
WomWWA 14
Rabbeth, James, Jr. 1824-1858? *NewYHSD*
Rabbino, Bernhard 1860-1933 *NatCAB 24*
Rabe, Robert Emanuel 1925-1974 *WhAm 6*
Rabe, Rudolph Frederick 1841- *NatCAB 5*
Rabearivelo, Jean Joseph 1901-1937 *McGEWB*
Rabel, Ernst 1874- *WhAm 5*
Rabelais, Francois 1494?-1553? *DcScB,*
McGEWB
Raben, John Gerard 1905-1961 *NatCAB 50*
Rabenort, William Louis 1870-1938 *WhAm 1*
Raber, Benedict Frederick 1882-1949
NatCAB 38
Raber, Oran Lee 1893-1940 *NatCAB 31,*
WhAm 1
Rabi, Isidor Isaac 1898- *AsBiEn, McGEWB,*
WebAB
Rabillon, Leonce 1814-1886 *NewYHSD*
Rabin, Benjamin J 1896-1969 *BiDrAC*
Rabin, Michael 1936-1972 *WhAm 5*
Rabineau, Francis *NewYHSD*
Rabinoff, Max 1877-1966 *WhAm 4*
Rabinoff, Sophie 1889-1957 *NatCAB 43*
Rabinovitz, Joseph 1878-1967 *WhAm 4A*
Rabinowitch, Eugene 1901-1971 *WhAm 6*
Rabinowitz, Aaron 1884-1973 *NatCAB 57*
Rabinowitz, Jerome *WebAB*
Rabinowitz, Louis Max 1887-1957 *NatCAB 49*
Rabinowitz, Sidney Hellman 1890-1961
NatCAB 49
Rabl, Carl 1853-1917 *DcScB*
Raboch, Wenzel Albert 1854-1942 *WhAm 2,*
WhAm 4
Raborg, Benjamin 1871-1918 *IIBEAAW*
Rabourdin, Henry Etienne 1711-1764 *ApCAB*
Rabun, William 1771-1819 *ApCAB,*
NatCAB 1, TwCBDA
Raburn, William 1771-1819 *BiAUS, Drake*
Rabuski, Theodore *NewYHSD*
Rabut, Paul 1914- *IIBEAAW*
Raby, James Joseph 1874-1934 *DcAmB,*
WhAm 1
Racca, Vittorio 1876-1957 *WhAm 4*
Race, John Abner 1914- *BiDrAC*
Race, John H 1862-1954 *TwCBDA, WhAm 3*
Race, U Grant 1864-1952 *NatCAB 40*
Race, Walter Loomis 1864-1953 *NatCAB 42*
Rachford, Benjamin Knox 1857-1929 *DcAmB,*
NatCAB 42, WhAm 1
Rachmaninoff, Sergei 1873-1943 *WhAm 2*
Rachmaninoff, Sergei Vasilyevich 1873-1943
DcAmB S3
Rachmaninov, Sergei Vasilievich 1873-1943
McGEWB
Rachmiel, Jean 1871- *WhAm 5*
Racine, Albert 1907- *IIBEAAW*
Racine, Antoine 1822- *ApCAB*
Racine, Jean Baptiste 1639-1699 *McGEWB*
Rackemann, Francis Minot 1887-1973 *WhAm 5*

Rackham, Horace Hatcher 1858-1933
NatCAB 24
Rackley, Frank Bailey 1916-1973 *WhAm 6*
Rackley, John Ralph 1907-1969 *WhAm 5*
Rada, Juan De d1542 *ApCAB*
Radbill, Samuel 1894-1956 *WhAm 3*
Radbourne, William H 1838-1914 *NewYHSD*
Radcliff, Jacob 1764-1841 *NatCAB 13*
Radcliff, Jacob 1764-1844 *DcAmB, WhAm H,*
WhAmP
Radcliffe, Amos Henry 1870-1950 *BiDrAC,*
WhAm 3
Radcliffe, Charles 1777?-1807 *NewYHSD*
Radcliffe, George Lovick 1877-1974 *BiDrAC,*
WhAm 6
Radcliffe, Harry Southwell 1894-1968
WhAm 4A
Radcliffe, Jessie Walker *WomWWA 14*
Radcliffe, John 1650-1714 *BiHiMed*
Radcliffe, John Anderson 1881-1944
NatCAB 34
Radcliffe, Margaret Porter 1863-
WomWWA 14
Radcliffe, McCluney 1854-1936 *NatCAB 27*
Radcliffe, T B *NewYHSD*
Radcliffe, Thomas 1794-1841 *ApCAB*
Radcliffe, Wallace 1842-1930 *NatCAB 22,*
WhAm 1
Radden, Thomas M *NewYHSD*
Raddi, Giuseppe 1770-1829 *ApCAB*
Radebaugh, Randolph Foster 1846-1927
NatCAB 21
Radek, Karl Bernardovich 1885-1939 *McGEWB*
Radeke, Eliza Greene Metcalf 1854-
WomWWA 14
Rademacher, Hans 1892-1969 *DcScB,*
WhAm 5
Rademacher, Joseph 1840-1900 *ApCAB,*
NatCAB 12, TwCBDA, WhAm 1
Rader, Frank 1848-1897 *NatCAB 8*
Rader, Paul 1879-1938 *NatCAB 28, WhAm 1*
Rader, Perry Scott 1859- *WhAm 4*
Rader, Robert Fort 1901-1965 *WhAm 4*
Rader, William 1862-1930 *WhAm 1*
Radetzky VonRadetz, Joseph Wenzel, Graf
1766-1858 *WhoMilH*
Radford, Arthur William 1896-1973 *WebAMB,*
WhAm 6
Radford, Benjamin Johnson 1838-1933
WhAm 1
Radford, Cyrus Sugg 1868-1951 *NatCAB 41,*
WhAm 3
Radford, George Stanley 1881- *WhAm 6*
Radford, Grace Anna Bennett 1870-
WomWWA 14
Radford, James Matthew 1861-1933
NatCAB 47
Radford, Robert Somerville 1869-1936 *WhAm 1*
Radford, William d1890 *Drake*
Radford, William 1808-1890 *ApCAB,*
NatCAB 4, TwCBDA
Radford, William 1809-1890 *AmBi, DcAmB,*
WebAMB, WhAm H
Radford, William 1814-1870 *BiAUS, BiDrAC,*
WhAm H
Radford, William A 1865- *WhAm 4*
Radford, William H 1909-1966 *WhAm 4*
Radhakrishnam, Sarvepalli 1888-1975 *WhAm 6*
Radhakrishnan, Sarvepalli 1888-1975 *McGEWB*
Radiguet, Maximilien Rene 1816- *ApCAB*
Radin, Edward David 1909-1966 *WhAm 4*
Radin, Max 1880-1950 *DcAmB S4,*
NatCAB 39, WhAm 3
Radin, Paul 1883-1959 *McGEWB, WebAB,*

WhAm 3
Radinsky, Ellis 1904-1955 *WhAm 3*
Radisson, Pierre Esprit 1636?-1710? *AmBi,*
ApCAB Sup, DcAmB, McGEWB,
WebAB, WhAm H
Radl, Emanuel 1873-1942 *DcScB*
Radliff, William Clarence 1889-1963
NatCAB 50
Radner, William 1908-1951 *NatCAB 41,*
WhAm 3
Radnitz, Gerty *WebAB*
Rado, Sandor 1890-1972 *WhAm 5*
Rado, Tibor 1895-1965 *DcScB, WhAm 4*
Radolfi, Alexander Rado *WhWW-II*
Radon, Johann 1887-1956 *DcScB*
Rados, Andrew 1888-1949 *NatCAB 38*
Radosavljevich, Paul Rankov 1879-1958
WhAm 3
Radwan, Edmund Patrick 1911-1959 *BiDrAC,*
WhAm 4
Radzat, Gilbert Francke 1939-1974 *WhAm 6*
Rae, Bruce 1892-1962 *NatCAB 47, WhAm 4*
Rae, Charles Whiteside 1847-1908 *NatCAB 15,*
WhAm 1
Rae, John 1796-1872 *DcAmB, WhAm H*
Rae, John 1813- *ApCAB, Drake*
Rae, John 1882-1963 *IIBEAAW, WhAm 4*
Rae, John Broadfoot 1867-1941 *NatCAB 42*
Rae, Luzerne 1811-1854 *ApCAB*
Rae, William McLane 1913-1965 *WhAm 4*
Raeder, Erich 1876-1960 *WhWW-II,*
WhoMilH
Raegener, Louis Christian 1856-1928 *WhAm 4*
Raegner, Louis Christian 1856-1928 *ApCAB X*
Raemaekers, Louis 1869- *WhAm 3*
Raemer, Clifford M 1903-1967 *WhAm 5*
Raen, Isaac *NewYHSD*
Raff, Emma Scott *WomWWA 14*
Raff, George Wertz 1825-1888 *ApCAB, Drake*
Raff, Richard Davis 1898-1963 *WhAm 4*
Raffeiner, John Stephen 1785-1861 *DcAmB,*
WhAm H
Raffeneau-Delile, Alyre 1778-1850 *ApCAB*
Rafferty, James A d1951 *WhAm 3*
Rafferty, Peter Philip 1874-1924 *NatCAB 6*
Rafferty, William *NatCAB 1*
Rafferty, William Carroll 1859-1941 *WhAm 1*
Raffety, William Edward 1876-1937 *WhAm 1*
Raffles, Sir Thomas Stamford Bingley 1781-1826
DcScB, McGEWB
Raffman, Halsey Lester 1911-1973 *WhAm 6*
Rafinesque, Constantine Samuel 1773-1840
NatCAB 8
Rafinesque, Constantine Samuel 1783-1840
AmBi, DcAmB, DcScB, EncAAH, EncAB,
WebAB, WhAm H
Rafinesque, Constantine Samuel 1783-1842
TwCBDA
Rafinesque, Constantine Samuel 1784-1842
ApCAB
Rafinesque, Constantine Smaltz 1784-1842
Drake
Rafn, Carl Christian 1795-1864 *Drake*
Rafn, Karl Christian 1795-1864 *ApCAB*
Rafsky, Henry Aaron 1890-1954 *NatCAB 41*
Rafter, George W 1851-1907 *DcAmB,*
NatCAB 12
Raftery, John Henry 1866- *WhAm 4*
Raftery, Oliver Tenry 1853-1919 *WhAm 1*
Ragan, Emily Lee 1839- *WomWWA 14*
Ragan, Frank Xavier 1897-1972 *WhAm 5*
Ragan, Willis Eugene 1852- *NatCAB 2*
Ragen, Joseph Edward 1896-1971 *NatCAB 56,*
WhAm 5

Raggio, Dante Alaghiere 1873-1945
  NatCAB 38
Raghavananda Sarman *DcScB*
Ragins, Alex Benjamin 1908-1960 *NatCAB 50*
Ragir, Benjamin A 1913-1958 *WhAm 3*
Raglan, Fitzroy James Henry Somerset
  1788-1855 *WhoMilH*
Ragland, Fountain Gage 1856- *WhoColR*
Ragland, Fountain Washington *WhoColR A*
Ragland, George 1876-1957 *WhAm 3*
Ragland, Samuel Evan 1874-1949 *WhAm 3*
Ragland, William T 1866- *WhAm 5*
Rago, Henry Anthony 1915-1969 *WhAm 5*
Ragon, Heartsill 1885-1940 *BiDrAC, WhAm 1,*
  WhAmP
Ragozin, Zenaide Alexeievna 1835?- *ApCAB,*
  WhAm 5
Ragsdale, Bartow Davis 1861- *WhAm 2*
Ragsdale, Edward Tillottson 1897-1971
  NatCAB 57, WhAm 5
Ragsdale, James W 1848- *WhAm 4*
Ragsdale, James Willard 1872-1919 *BiDrAC,*
  WhAm 1
Ragsdale, Lulah 1866- *AmWom*
Ragsdale, Tallulah 1866- *WhAm 3*
Ragsdale, VanHubert 1892- *WhAm 3*
Ragsdale, Virginia *WomWWA 14*
Ragueneau, Paul 1605-1680 *ApCAB*
Raguet, Condy 1784-1842 *ApCAB, BiAUS,*
  DcAmB, Drake, WhAm H
Ragusa, Signor *NewYHSD*
Rahi, Michel 1912-1973 *WhAm 6*
Rahman, Abdul d1960 *WhAm 4*
Rahman, Tunku Abdul 1903-1960 *WhAm 3*
Rahmn, Elza Lothner 1872- *WhAm 5*
Rahn, John 1862-1921 *NatCAB 19*
Rahn, Otto 1881-1957 *NatCAB 49, WhAm 3*
Rahner, Karl 1904- *McGEWB*
Raht, August Wilhelm 1843-1916 *DcAmB*
Rahv, Philip d1973 *WhAm 6*
Rai, Lala Lajpat 1865-1928 *McGEWB*
Raible, John Robert 1869-1948 *NatCAB 36,*
  WhAm 2
Raiford, Lemuel Charles 1872-1944 *WhAm 2*
Raiford, Theo Sidney 1903-1966 *NatCAB 54*
Raiguel, George Earle 1880- *WhAm 6*
Rail-Splitter, The *EncAAH*
Railey, Fleming G 1884-1961 *WhAm 4*
Railey, Howard Hannabal 1867- *WhoColR*
Railey, Thomas Tarlton 1885-1956 *WhAm 3*
Railsback, Thomas Fisher 1932- *BiDrAC*
Raimond, C E *WomWWA 14*
Raimondi, Antonio 1825-1890 *ApCAB Sup*
Raimondi, Luigi 1912-1975 *WhAm 6*
Rain, Isaac *NewYHSD*
Raine, James Watt 1869-1949 *WhAm 2*
Raine, Wendell Phillips 1881-1952 *NatCAB 39*
Raine, William MacLeod 1871-1954 *WhAm 3*
Rainer, John C 1900?- *REnAW*
Rainer, Joseph 1845- *NatCAB 9, WhAm 4*
Raines, George Neely 1908-1959 *WhAm 3*
Raines, John 1840-1909 *AmBi, ApCAB Sup,*
  BiDrAC, DcAmB, TwCBDA, WhAm 1
Raines, John Marlin 1907-1971 *WhAm 5*
Rainey, Anson 1848-1922 *NatCAB 23,*
  WhAm 1
Rainey, Ellenora McBride *WomWWA 14*
Rainey, Gertrude Malissa Nix Pridgett
  1886-1939 *DcAmB S2, NotAW*
Rainey, Henry Thomas 1860-1934 *AmBi,*
  BiDrAC, DcAmB S1, EncAAH,
  NatCAB 24, WebAB, WhAm 1, WhAmP
Rainey, John William 1880-1923 *BiDrAC,*
  WhAm 1
Rainey, Joseph Hayne 1832-1887 *ApCAB,*
  BiAUS, BiDrAC, DcAmB, NatCAB 11,
  TwCBDA, WhAm H, WhAmP
Rainey, Lilius Bratton 1876-1959 *BiDrAC,*
  WhAm 5
Rainey, Ma 1886-1939 *WhAm HA, WhAm 4*
Rainey, Paul James 1877-1923 *NatCAB 19*
Rainey, Warren Robert 1887-1941 *NatCAB 35*
Rains, Albert M 1902- *BiDrAC, WhAmP*
Rains, Claude 1889-1967 *WhAm 4*
Rains, Gabriel James d1881 *Drake*
Rains, Gabriel James 1803-1881 *ApCAB,*
  DcAmB, NatCAB 4, TwCBDA,
  WebAMB, WhAm H

Rains, Gabriel James 1804-1881 *BiDConf*
Rains, George Washington 1817-1898 *ApCAB,*
  BiDConf, DcAmB, NatCAB 4, TwCBDA, WhAm H
Rains, James Edward 1833-1862 *ApCAB,*
  Drake, TwCBDA
Rains, John 1750?-1821 *ApCAB*
Rains, Leon 1870-1954 *WhAm 3*
Rainsborow, William d1648 *Drake*
Rainsford, Miss *NewYHSD*
Rainsford, Kerr 1882-1947 *NatCAB 38*
Rainsford, William Stephen 1850-1933 *AmBi,*
  ApCAB, DcAmB S1, NatCAB 1,
  NatCAB 42, TwCBDA, WhAm 1
Rainwater, Charles Cicero 1838-1902
  NatCAB 25
Rainwater, Clarence Elmer 1884-1925
  NatCAB 21
Rainwater, Clarence Elmer 1884-1934 *WhAm 1*
Rairden, Bradstreet Stinson 1858-1944 *WhAm 2*
Raisa, Rosa 1893-1963 *WhAm 4*
Raisz, Erwin Josephus 1893-1968 *NatCAB 56*
Raitt, Effie Isabel 1878-1945 *WhAm 2*
Raizen, Charles Sanford 1892-1967 *WhAm 4*
Rajagopalachari, Chakravarti 1879-1972
  McGEWB
Rajagopalacharya, Chakravarti 1879-1972
  WhAm 5
Rajaraja I *McGEWB*
Rak, Mary Kidder 1879-1958 *WhAm 3*
Rake, Geoffrey William 1904-1958 *WhAm 3*
Rake, John Frederick 1878- *WhAm 6*
Rakeman, Carl 1878- *WhAm 6*
Raker, John Edward 1863-1926 *BiDrAC,*
  NatCAB 20, WhAm 1, WhAmP
Rakoczy, George, I 1593-1648 *WhoMilH*
Rakotomalala, Louis 1901-1968 *WhAm 5*
Rale, Sebastien 1654?-1724 *DcAmB,*
  WhAm H
Rale, Sebastien 1657?-1724 *AmBi*
Rale, Sebastien 1658-1724 *Drake*
Ralegh, Sir Walter 1552-1618 *ApCAB,*
  NatCAB 7
Raleigh, Henry Patrick 1880- *WhAm 6*
Raleigh, Sir Walter 1552?-1618 *Drake,*
  EncAAH, McGEWB, WhAm H
Raley, John Wesley 1902-1968 *WhAm 5*
Rall d1776 *Drake*
Rall, Charles Rudolph 1855- *ApCAB X*
Rall, Edward Everett 1876- *WhAm 5*
Rall, Harris Franklin 1870-1964 *WhAm 4*
Rall, Johann Gottlieb 1720?-1776 *ApCAB*
Ralli, Elaine Pandia 1894-1968 *WhAm 5*
Ralls, Arthur Williams 1881- *WhAm 6*
Ralls, John Perkins 1822-1904 *BiDConf*
Ralls, John Wallace 1916-1962 *NatCAB 50*
Ralph, James 1695?-1762 *AmBi, ApCAB,*
  DcAmB, Drake, NatCAB 8, WhAm H
Ralph, John A *NewYHSD*
Ralph, Julian 1853-1903 *AmBi, ApCAB Sup,*
  DcAmB, NatCAB 1, TwCBDA
Ralph, Lester 1876-1927 *TwCBDA, WhAm 2*
Ralph, Richard Folsom 1869-1949 *NatCAB 38*
Ralph, Stuart Harrison 1893-1956 *WhAm 3*
Ralph, W *NewYHSD*
Ralston, Alexander 1771-1827 *NatCAB 12*
Ralston, Anderson Wheeler 1899-1948 *WhAm 2*
Ralston, Burrell Otto 1887-1970 *WhAm 5*
Ralston, Byron Brown 1890-1971 *WhAm 5*
Ralston, Fanny Marion *WomWWA 14*
Ralston, George Washington 1819-1843
  NewYHSD
Ralston, Harriet Newell 1828- *AmWom*
Ralston, Jackson Harvey 1857-1945 *NatCAB 37,*
  WhAm 2
Ralston, James Grier 1815-1880 *TwCBDA*
Ralston, James Kenneth 1896- *IlBEAAW*
Ralston, James Layton 1881-1948 *WhAm 3*
Ralston, John Chester 1867-1928 *WhAm 1*
Ralston, Oliver Caldwell 1887-1965 *NatCAB 52,*
  WhAm 4
Ralston, Robert *NewYHSD*
Ralston, Robert 1761-1836 *ApCAB*
Ralston, Samuel 1756-1851 *ApCAB, Drake*
Ralston, Mrs. Samuel M 1861-1954 *WhAm 3*
Ralston, Samuel Moffett 1857-1925 *ApCAB X,*
  BiDrAC, DcAmB, NatCAB 15, WhAm 1
Ralston, Sara Burns Rankin *WomWWA 14*
Ralston, Thomas Neely 1806- *ApCAB*

Ralston, William Chapman 1826-1875 *ApCAB,*
  DcAmB, NatCAB 7, NatCAB 24,
  REnAW, WhAm H
Ralston, William Chapman 1863- *WhAm 5*
Ralston, William Spencer 1870-1940
  NatCAB 30
Rama Khamhaeng 1239?-1299? *McGEWB*
Ramadier, Paul 1888-1961 *WhAm 4*
Ramage, Adam d1850 *Drake*
Ramage, Carroll Johnson 1874-1937 *WhAm 1*
Ramage, Eleanor Dinsmore 1883-
  WomWWA 14
Ramage, James Savage 1868-1956 *WhAm 3*
Ramage, John 1748?-1802 *BnEnAmA, DcAmB,*
  NewYHSD, WhAm H
Ramage, Samuel Young 1853-1940 *NatCAB 30*
Ramaker, Albert John 1860-1946 *WhAm 2*
Ramakrishna, Sri 1833-1886 *McGEWB*
Ramaley, Francis 1870-1942 *WhAm 2*
Raman, Sir Chandrasekhar Venkata 1888-1970
  McGEWB
Raman, Sir Chandrasekhara Venkata 1888-1970
  AsBiEn, DcScB, WhAm 6
Ramani, Radhakrishna 1901-1970 *WhAm 5*
Ramanujan, Srinivasa Aaiyangar 1887-1920
  DcScB
Ramanujan Aiyangar, Srinivasa 1887-1920
  McGEWB
Ramazzini, Bernardini 1633-1714 *BiHiMed*
Rambaud, George Gibier 1875- *WhAm 5*
Rambaut, Mary Lucinda Bonney 1816-1900
  AmWom, ApCAB Sup, BiDAmEd,
  DcAmB, NatCAB 6, NotAW, TwCBDA,
  WhAm 1
Rambaut, Thomas 1819-1890 *ApCAB Sup,*
  TwCBDA
Rambeau, Morjorie 1889-1970 *WhAm 5*
Rambo, Ormond 1859-1935 *NatCAB 30*
Rameau, Jean Philippe 1683-1764 *McGEWB*
Ramee, Joseph Jacques 1764-1842 *BnEnAmA,*
  DcAmB, NewYHSD, WhAm H
Ramee, Stanislas Henri DeLa 1747-1803
  ApCAB
Ramer, John Edward 1868-1926 *NatCAB 28*
Rames, Jean Baptiste 1832-1894 *DcScB*
Ramet, Nicolas 1673-1735 *ApCAB*
Ramey, Frank Marion 1881-1942 *BiDrAC,*
  WhAm 3
Ramey, Homer Alonzo 1891-1960 *BiDrAC,*
  WhAm 3A
Ramey, Roger Maxwell 1905-1963 *NatCAB 51*
Ramey, W Albert 1899-1968 *NatCAB 55*
Ramirez, Alejandro 1777-1821 *ApCAB*
Ramirez, Francisco 1823-1869 *ApCAB, Drake*
Ramirez, Ignacio 1818-1879 *ApCAB*
Ramirez, Pedro Pablo 1884-1962 *WhAm 4*
Ramirez DeQuinones, Pedro d1570? *ApCAB*
Ramm, Charles Adolph d1951 *WhAm 4*
Rammacher, John Joseph 1880-1938
  NatCAB 29
Rammelkamp, Charles Henry 1874-1932
  NatCAB 22, WhAm 1
Rammelsberg, Karl Friedrich 1813-1899 *DcScB*
Rammer, August J 1885-1960 *WhAm 4*
Ramon *IlBEAAW*
Ramon, Gaston 1886-1963 *DcScB*
Ramon Y Cajal, Santiago 1852-1934 *AsBiEn,*
  BiHiMed, DcScB
Ramond DeCarbonnieres, Louis F E 1755-1827
  DcScB
Ramos Arizpe, Miguel 1775-1843 *ApCAB*
Ramsauer, Carl Wilhelm 1879-1955 *DcScB*
Ramsay, Alexander 1754?-1824 *DcAmB,*
  WhAm H
Ramsay, Alexander *see also* Ramsey, Alexander
Ramsay, Andrew Crombie 1814-1891 *DcScB*
Ramsay, Arch Gibson 1882-1956 *NatCAB 42*
Ramsay, Sir Bertram Home 1883-1945
  WhWW-II, WhoMilH
Ramsay, Charles Cornell 1857-1942
  NatCAB 37
Ramsay, Claude Clinton 1865-1930 *ApCAB X,*
  NatCAB 25
Ramsay, David *NewYHSD*
Ramsay, David 1749-1815 *AmBi, ApCAB,*
  BiAUS, BiDrAC, BiHiMed, DcAmB,
  Drake, McGEWB, TwCBDA, WhAm H
Ramsay, David *see also* Ramsey, David

Ramsay, David Marshall 1857- *WhAm 3*
Ramsay, David Marshall *see also* Ramsey, David
Marshall
Ramsay, Erskine 1864-1953 *DcAmB S5,*
NatCAB 41, WhAm 3
Ramsay, Francis Munroe 1835-1914 *ApCAB,*
DcAmB, NatCAB 4, NatCAB 15,
TwCBDA, WhAm 1
Ramsay, Franklin Pierce 1856-1926 *NatCAB 22*
Ramsay, George Douglas 1802-1882 *ApCAB,*
DcAmB, Drake, TwCBDA, WhAm H
Ramsay, James Graham 1823-1903 *BiDConf*
Ramsay, Jean Barnett 1868- *WomWWA 14*
Ramsay, Jennie C Blodget *WomWWA 14*
Ramsay, John Breckinridge 1846-1921
NatCAB 25
Ramsay, Kerr Craige 1911-1951 *NatCAB 45*
Ramsay, Martha Laurens 1759-1811 *ApCAB,*
NotAW
Ramsay, Nathaniel d1817 *BiAUS, Drake*
Ramsay, Nathaniel 1741-1817 *BiDrAC,*
DcAmB, NatCAB 26, TwCBDA,
WhAm H
Ramsay, Nathaniel 1751-1817 *ApCAB*
Ramsay, Robert 1780-1849 *BiAUS*
Ramsay, Robert 1840-1899 *NatCAB 31*
Ramsay, Robert *see also* Ramsey, Robert
Ramsay, Robert Ewart 1876-1949 *NatCAB 38*
Ramsay, Robert Lee 1880- *WhAm 6*
Ramsay, Robert Lincoln 1877-1956 *BiDrAC,*
WhAm 3, WhAmP
Ramsay, Thomas Henry 1869-1940 *WhAm 1*
Ramsay, Thomas Kennedy 1826-1886 *ApCAB*
Ramsay, Sir William 1852-1916 *AsBiEn,*
DcScB, McGEWB
Ramsay, William Gouverneur 1866-1916
NatCAB 27
Ramsaye, Terry 1885-1954 *WhAm 3*
Ramsburg, C J 1877-1954 *WhAm 3*
Ramsdell, Bailey Edwin 1890-1963 *NatCAB 51*
Ramsdell, Charles William 1877-1942 *WhAm 2*
Ramsdell, Edwin George 1886-1960 *NatCAB 45,*
WhAm 3A
Ramsdell, Frank Ellsworth 1862- *NatCAB 13*
Ramsdell, George Allen 1834-1900 *NatCAB 11,*
NatCAB 37, TwCBDA
Ramsdell, Harry Thomas 1856-1934
NatCAB 35
Ramsdell, Julia Alice Carter *WomWWA 14*
Ramsdell, Lewis Stephen 1895-1975 *WhAm 6*
Ramsdell, Marshall Albert 1887-1954
NatCAB 43
Ramsdell, Robert Leroy 1882-1953 *NatCAB 43*
Ramsdell, Washington Irving 1900-1965
WhAm 4
Ramsden, Jesse 1735-1800 *DcScB*
Ramsen, Halsey Edmund 1885-1957 *WhAm 3*
Ramser, Charles Ernest 1885-1962 *WhAm 4*
Ramses II *McGEWB*
Ramseur, Stephen Dodson 1837-1864 *ApCAB,*
BiDConf, DcAmB, Drake, NatCAB 4,
TwCBDA, WebAMB, WhAm H
Ramseur, Walter Gassaway 1894-1968
NatCAB 52
Ramsey, Alexander 1754?-1824 *ApCAB, Drake*
Ramsey, Alexander 1815-1903 *ApCAB, BiAUS,*
BiDrAC, BiDrUSE, DcAmB, Drake,
NatCAB 10, REnAW, TwCBDA,
WhAm 1, WhAmP
Ramsey, Alexander *see also* Ramsay, Alexander
Ramsey, Alfred 1860- *WhAm 4*
Ramsey, Charles Cyrus 1862-1917 *NatCAB 18*
Ramsey, D Hiden 1891-1966 *WhAm 4*
Ramsey, David 1749-1815 *NatCAB 7*
Ramsey, David *see also* Ramsay, David
Ramsey, David Marshall 1857- *NatCAB 11*
Ramsey, David Marshall *see also* Ramsay, David
Marshall
Ramsey, DeWitt Clinton 1888-1961 *NatCAB 46,*
WhAm 4
Ramsey, Donald James 1903-1968 *NatCAB 54*
Ramsey, Frank Plumpton 1903-1930 *DcScB,*
McGEWB
Ramsey, George 1878-1950 *WhAm 2*
Ramsey, George Junkin 1857-1928 *WhAm 1*
Ramsey, George Samuel 1874-1941 *NatCAB 34,*
WhAm 2
Ramsey, Grace Keys 1875- *WomWWA 14*

Ramsey, Horace Marion 1880-1942 *WhAm 2*
Ramsey, James B 1892-1965 *WhAm 4*
Ramsey, James Basil 1893-1969 *WhAm 5*
Ramsey, James Gattys McGregor 1796-1884
ApCAB
Ramsey, James Gettys McGrady 1797-1884
TwCBDA
Ramsey, James Gettys McGready 1797-1884
DcAmB, WhAm H
Ramsey, John Patterson 1864- *WhAm 4*
Ramsey, John Rathbone 1862-1933 *BiDrAC,*
WhAm 1
Ramsey, Joseph, Jr. 1850-1916 *NatCAB 7,*
NatCAB 12, WhAm 1
Ramsey, Leonidas William 1891-1947 *WhAm 2*
Ramsey, Leonidas Willing 1891-1947
NatCAB 36
Ramsey, Lewis A 1873-1941 *IIBEAAW*
Ramsey, Lulu A *AmWom*
Ramsey, Marathon Montrose 1867- *WhAm 4*
Ramsey, Mary Grant Burrows 1869-
WomWWA 14
Ramsey, Norman Foster 1882-1963 *WhAm 4*
Ramsey, Rachel *NewYHSD*
Ramsey, Robert 1780-1849 *BiDrAC,*
WhAm H
Ramsey, Robert 1863-1927 *NatCAB 25*
Ramsey, Robert *see also* Ramsay, Robert
Ramsey, Rolla Roy 1872-1955 *NatCAB 42,*
WhAm 3
Ramsey, Samuel A 1856- *NatCAB 3*
Ramsey, William 1779-1831 *BiAUS, BiDrAC,*
WhAm H
Ramsey, William F 1855-1922 *WhAm 1*
Ramsey, William Sterrett 1810-1840 *BiAUS,*
BiDrAC, WhAm H
Ramsey, Willis Hinksman 1861-1936 *WhAm 1*
Ramseyer, Christian William 1875-1943
BiDrAC, NatCAB 32, WhAm 2, WhAmP
Ramseyer, John Alvin 1908-1968 *WhAm 5*
Ramsower, Harry C 1880- *WhAm 6*
Ramspeck, Robert C Word 1890-1972 *BiDrAC,*
WhAm 5
Ramstad, Niles Oliver 1875-1952 *NatCAB 41,*
WhAm 5
Ramus, Carl 1872- *WhAm 5*
Ramus, Peter 1515-1572 *DcScB*
Ramus, Petrus 1515-1572 *McGEWB*
Rance, Sir Hubert Elvin 1898-1974 *WhAm 6*
Ranchin, Francois 1560-1641 *BiHiMed*
Ranck, Clayton Haverstick 1876- *WhAm 5*
Ranck, Edward Carty 1879- *WhAm 6*
Ranck, George Washington 1841-1900 *WhAm 1*
Ranck, George Washington 1841-1901
TwCBDA
Ranck, Henry Haverstick 1868-1948 *WhAm 2*
Ranck, Joseph Alvin 1866-1951 *NatCAB 39*
Ranck, Paul Sensenich 1889-1955 *NatCAB 46*
Ranck, Samuel H 1866-1952 *WhAm 3*
Ranck, Than Vanneman 1874-1947 *WhAm 2*
Rancon, Victor *NewYHSD*
Rand, Addison Crittenden 1841-1900 *DcAmB,*
NatCAB 11, WhAm H
Rand, Arthur Henry, Jr. 1915-1972 *WhAm 5*
Rand, Asa 1783-1871 *ApCAB, Drake*
Rand, Avery Lewis 1851-1918 *NatCAB 39*
Rand, Ayn 1905- *WebAB*
Rand, Benjamin 1856-1934 *DcAmB S1,*
WhAm 1
Rand, Benjamin Howard 1792-1862 *ApCAB*
Rand, Benjamin Howard 1827-1883 *ApCAB,*
Drake
Rand, Caroline Amanda Sherfey 1828-1905
NotAW
Rand, Charles Frederic 1856-1927 *ApCAB X,*
NatCAB 21, WhAm 1
Rand, Christopher 1912-1968 *WhAm 5*
Rand, Claire Forbes 1873- *WomWWA 14*
Rand, Clayton Thomas 1891-1971 *WhAm 5*
Rand, Edgar Eugene 1905-1955 *NatCAB 45,*
WhAm 3
Rand, Edward Augustus 1837-1903 *NatCAB 13,*
WhAm 1
Rand, Edward Kennard 1871-1945 *DcAmB S3,*
WhAm 2
Rand, Edward Lothrop 1859-1924 *WhAm 1*
Rand, Edward Sprague 1782-1863 *ApCAB,*
DcAmB, WhAm H

Rand, Edward Sprague 1834-1897 *ApCAB,*
Drake, TwCBDA
Rand, Ellen Gertrude Emmet 1875-1941 *NotAW*
Rand, Ellen Gertrude Emmet 1876-1941
NatCAB 40, WhAm 2
Rand, F *NewYHSD*
Rand, Frank Chambless 1876-1949 *NatCAB 39,*
WhAm 2
Rand, Frank Prentice 1889-1971 *WhAm 5*
Rand, Frederick Henry 1846-1933 *WhAm 2*
Rand, George Franklin 1891-1942 *WhAm 2*
Rand, Gertrude 1886-1970 *WhAm 5*
Rand, Henry Hale 1909-1962 *WhAm 4*
Rand, Herbert Wilbur 1872-1960 *WhAm 4*
Rand, Isaac 1743-1822 *ApCAB, Drake*
Rand, James Henry 1859-1944 *DcAmB S3*
Rand, James Henry 1886-1968 *NatCAB 54,*
WhAm 5
Rand, Jasper Raymond 1837-1900 *NatCAB 11,*
NatCAB 30
Rand, Jasper Raymond 1874-1909 *NatCAB 14,*
NatCAB 30
Rand, John Clark 1842-1911 *NatCAB 28*
Rand, John Goffe 1801-1873 *NewYHSD,*
WhAm H
Rand, John Langdon 1861-1942 *WhAm 2*
Rand, John Prentice 1857- *WhAm 1*
Rand, Lyman Fiske 1848-1928 *NatCAB 33*
Rand, Margaret Arnold 1868- *WomWWA 14*
Rand, Marion Howard 1824-1849 *ApCAB*
Rand, Mary Frances Abbott 1840- *WhAm 4*
Rand, Sally 1904- *WebAB*
Rand, Silas Tertius 1810- *ApCAB*
Rand, Stephen 1844-1915 *NatCAB 16,*
WhAm 1
Rand, Theodore Dehon 1836-1903 *ApCAB,*
WhAm 1
Rand, Theodore Harding 1835- *ApCAB,*
ApCAB Sup
Rand, William, Jr. 1866-1931 *WhAm 1*
Rand, William Blanchard 1913-1975 *WhAm 6*
Rand, William Wilberforce 1816-1909 *ApCAB,*
WhAm 1
Randal, Florence Hamilton *WomWWA 14*
Randall, Adelia Miner 1872- *WomWWA 14*
Randall, Adin 1829-1868 *ApCAB X*
Randall, Albert Borland 1879-1945 *NatCAB 36,*
WhAm 2
Randall, Alexander 1803-1881 *BiAUS,*
BiDrAC, WhAm H
Randall, Alexander 1883-1951 *WhAm 3*
Randall, Alexander Williams 1819-1872 *AmBi,*
ApCAB, BiAUS, BiDrUSE, DcAmB,
Drake, NatCAB 2, TwCBDA, WhAm H
Randall, Archibald 1797-1846 *BiAUS, Drake,*
NatCAB 4
Randall, Benjamin 1749-1808 *DcAmB,*
NatCAB 4, WhAm H
Randall, Benjamin 1789-1857 *BiAUS*
Randall, Benjamin 1789-1859 *BiDrAC,*
WhAm H
Randall, Blanchard 1856-1942 *WhAm 2*
Randall, Burton Alexander 1858-1932
ApCAB X, DcAmB, NatCAB 25,
WhAm 1
Randall, Charles Hiram 1865-1951 *BiDrAC,*
WhAm 4
Randall, Charles Percy 1866-1928 *NatCAB 22*
Randall, Charles Sturtevant 1824-1904 *BiDrAC*
Randall, Clarence Belden 1891-1967 *WhAm 4*
Randall, Clifford Ellsworth 1876-1934 *BiDrAC*
Randall, Clyde Nathaniel 1906-1970 *WhAm 5*
Randall, Daniel Richard 1864-1936 *WhAm 1*
Randall, David Anton 1905-1975 *WhAm 6*
Randall, David Austin 1813-1884 *ApCAB,*
NatCAB 10, WhAm H
Randall, Edward 1860-1944 *NatCAB 35,*
WhAm 2
Randall, Edward Caleb 1860-1935 *WhAm 1*
Randall, Edwin Jarvis 1869-1964 *WhAm 4*
Randall, Edwin M 1822-1895 *NatCAB 12*
Randall, Edwin Mortimer, Jr. 1862-1939
NatCAB 14, WhAm 1
Randall, Emilius Oviatt 1850-1919 *NatCAB 10,*
TwCBDA, WhAm 1
Randall, Emma Pearson 1874- *WomWWA 14*
Randall, Eugene Wilson 1859-1940 *WhAm 1*
Randall, Evelyn 1860- *WomWWA 14*

Randall, Frank Alfred 1883-1950 *WhAm 3*
Randall, Frank Hall 1877-1958 *WhAm 4*
Randall, Frank Lange 1856-1921 *WhAm 1*
Randall, George *NewYHSD*
Randall, George Archibald 1887-1941 *WhAm 1*
Randall, George Maxwell 1810-1873 *ApCAB,
NatCAB 8, TwCBDA*
Randall, George Morton 1841-1918 *TwCBDA,
WhAm 1*
Randall, George William 1912-1975 *WhAm 6*
Randall, Henry Leroy 1891-1947 *NatCAB 42*
Randall, Henry Stephens 1811-1876 *ApCAB,
DcAmB, Drake, WhAm H*
Randall, James Garfield 1881-1953 *DcAmB S5,
NatCAB 39, WhAm 3*
Randall, James Ryder 1839-1908 *AmBi,
ApCAB, ApCAB X, DcAmB, NatCAB 8,
TwCBDA, WhAm 1*
Randall, John Arthur 1881- *WhAm 6*
Randall, John Edgar 1861-1955 *NatCAB 43*
Randall, John Hammond 1899-1959
NatCAB 48, WhAm 4
Randall, John Herman 1871-1946 *WhAm 2*
Randall, John Witt 1813- *ApCAB, Drake*
Randall, Lawrence Merill 1895-1969
NatCAB 55
Randall, Lawrence Merrill 1895-1969 *WhAm 5*
Randall, Lillian Craig 1858- *WomWWA 14*
Randall, Merle 1888-1950 *NatCAB 39,
WhAm 2*
Randall, Minnie Josephine Smith 1867-1955
NatCAB 42
Randall, Otis Everett 1860-1946 *WhAm 2*
Randall, Paul King, Jr. 1928-1971 *WhAm 5*
Randall, R C d1951 *WhAm 3*
Randall, Robert Henry 1890-1966 *NatCAB 52,
WhAm 4*
Randall, Robert Richard 1740?-1801 *ApCAB,
TwCBDA*
Randall, Robert Richard 1750?-1801 *DcAmB,
NatCAB 11, WhAm H*
Randall, Ruth Painter 1892-1971 *WhAm 5*
Randall, Samuel 1778-1864 *DcAmB,
WhAm H*
Randall, Samuel Bond 1860-1904 *WhAm 1*
Randall, Samuel Haskell 1836- *NatCAB 11*
Randall, Samuel Jackson 1828-1890 *AmBi,
ApCAB, BiAUS, BiDrAC, DcAmB,
EncAB, NatCAB 3, TwCBDA, WebAB,
WhAm H, WhAmP*
Randall, Samuel Sidwell 1809-1881 *ApCAB,
BiDAmEd, DcAmB, NatCAB 10,
NatCAB 18, WhAm H*
Randall, T *BiAUS*
Randall, William Bradley 1857- *ApCAB X*
Randall, William Harrison 1812-1881 *BiAUS,
BiDrAC, WhAm H*
Randall, William Joseph 1909- *BiDrAC*
Randall, William Trafton 1860- *WhAm 4*
Randall, Wyatt William 1867-1930 *DcAmB,
WhAm 1, WhAm 1C*
Randau, Clem J 1895-1954 *WhAm 3*
Randegger, Giuseppe Aldo 1874- *WhAm 5*
Randel, Elias, Jr. *NewYHSD*
Randell, Abraham R *NewYHSD*
Randell, Choice Boswell 1857-1945 *BiDrAC,
WhAm 4, WhAmP*
Randell, Elias, Jr. *NewYHSD*
Randle, Clint Wilson 1910-1964 *NatCAB 51,
WhAm 4*
Randle, Edwin Buster 1856-1944 *NatCAB 35*
Randle, Thurman 1890-1957 *WhAm 3*
Randles, Andrew J 1877- *WhAm 5*
Randolph, A Philip 1889- *McGEWB*
Randolph, Alfred Magill 1836-1918 *ApCAB,
DcAmB, NatCAB 7, TwCBDA,
WhAm 1*
Randolph, Anson Davies Fitz 1820-1896
ApCAB Sup, NatCAB 8
Randolph, Asa Philip 1889- *EncAB, WebAB*
Randolph, Benjamin 1737?-1791 *BnEnAmA*
Randolph, Bessie Carter 1885-1966 *NatCAB 52,
WhAm 4*
Randolph, Beverley 1754-1797 *NatCAB 5,
WhAm H*
Randolph, Beverley 1755-1797 *ApCAB*
Randolph, Beverly d1797 *BiAUS, Drake*
Randolph, Beverly 1754-1797 *TwCBDA*

Randolph, Carman Fitz 1856- *WhAm 1*
Randolph, Edgar Eugene 1878- *WhAm 6*
Randolph, Edmund 1753-1813 *BiAUS, DcAmB,
Drake, EncAB, McGEWB, NatCAB 1,
TwCBDA*
Randolph, Edmund 1819-1861 *DcAmB,
WhAm H*
Randolph, Edmund 1820-1861 *ApCAB,
NatCAB 1*
Randolph, Edmund Jenings 1753-1813 *AmBi*
Randolph, Edmund Jennings 1753-1813 *ApCAB,
BiDrAC, BiDrUSE, WebAB, WhAm H,
WhAmP*
Randolph, Edward *Drake*
Randolph, Edward 1620?-1694 *ApCAB*
Randolph, Edward 1632?-1703 *AmBi, DcAmB,
WhAm H*
Randolph, Edward 1640?-1700? *NatCAB 8*
Randolph, Edward Hughes 1858-1934 *WhAm 1*
Randolph, Edward Washburn *NewYHSD*
Randolph, Epes 1856-1921 *DcAmB, WhAm 1*
Randolph, Francis Fitz 1889-1973 *WhAm 6*
Randolph, George F 1856-1926 *WhAm 1*
Randolph, George Wythe 1802?-1867 *Drake*
Randolph, George Wythe 1815-1867 *WhAm H*
Randolph, George Wythe 1818-1867 *AmBi,
BiDConf, DcAmB, NatCAB 10*
Randolph, George Wythe 1818-1878 *ApCAB,
TwCBDA*
Randolph, Grace Fitz *WomWWA 14*
Randolph, Harold 1861-1927 *WhAm 1*
Randolph, Harriet *WomWWA 14*
Randolph, Harrison 1871-1954 *NatCAB 47,
TwCBDA, WhAm 3*
Randolph, Harry Ward 1864-1933 *NatCAB 24*
Randolph, Henry Fitz 1856-1892 *ApCAB Sup*
Randolph, Hollins Nicholas 1872-1938 *WhAm 1*
Randolph, Innes 1837-1887 *NatCAB 19,
NewYHSD*
Randolph, Isham 1687-1742 *ApCAB*
Randolph, Isham 1848-1920 *ApCAB X,
DcAmB, NatCAB 19, WhAm 1*
Randolph, Jacob 1796-1836 *ApCAB*
Randolph, Jacob 1796-1848 *DcAmB, Drake,
NatCAB 10, WhAm H*
Randolph, James Fitz 1791-1871 *ApCAB,
BiAUS, NatCAB 3, TwCBDA*
Randolph, James Fitz 1791-1872 *BiDrAC,
WhAm H*
Randolph, James Henry 1825-1900 *BiDrAC*
Randolph, James Thompson 1817-1874
NewYHSD
Randolph, Jennings 1902- *BiDrAC*
Randolph, Sir John 1693?-1736? *DcAmB*
Randolph, Sir John 1693-1737 *AmBi, ApCAB,
NatCAB 8, WhAm H*
Randolph, John 1727?-1784 *ApCAB, DcAmB,
WhAm H*
Randolph, John 1773-1833 *AmBi, ApCAB,
BiAUS, BiDrAC, DcAmB, Drake,
EncAAH, EncAB, McGEWB, NatCAB 5,
TwCBDA, WebAB, WhAm H, WhAmP*
Randolph, John Cooper Fitz 1846-1911
WhAm 1
Randolph, John Wiloughby 1896-1960
NatCAB 49
Randolph, Joseph Fitz *NewYHSD*
Randolph, Joseph Fitz 1803-1873 *BiAUS,
BiDrAC, TwCBDA, WhAm H*
Randolph, Joseph Fitz 1843-1932 *WhAm 1,
WhAm 1C*
Randolph, Lee F 1880- *WhAm 6*
Randolph, Lewis VanSyckle Fitz 1838-1921
NatCAB 7, NatCAB 26, WhAm 1
Randolph, Lingan Strother 1859-1922
NatCAB 19, WhAm 1
Randolph, Martha Jefferson 1772-1836
NatCAB 3, NatCAB 5, NotAW
Randolph, Mary Randolph 1762-1828 *NotAW*
Randolph, Nathaniel Archer 1858-1887 *ApCAB*
Randolph, Peter *BiAUS*
Randolph, Peyton d1775 *BiAUS*
Randolph, Peyton 1721-1775 *AmBi, ApCAB,
BiDrAC, BiDrUSE, DcAmB, NatCAB 2,
TwCBDA, WhAm H*
Randolph, Peyton 1723-1775 *Drake*
Randolph, Peyton 1779-1828 *ApCAB*
Randolph, Richard 1691-1748 *ApCAB*

Randolph, Robert Isham 1883-1951 *WhAm 3*
Randolph, Robert Lee 1860-1919 *WhAm 1*
Randolph, Sarah Nicholas 1839-1892 *ApCAB,
DcAmB, TwCBDA, WhAm H*
Randolph, Susan Strong 1867- *WomWWA 14*
Randolph, Theodore Fitz 1826-1883 *BiAUS,
BiDrAC, DcAmB, WhAm H, WhAmP*
Randolph, Theodore Frelinghuysen 1816-1883
ApCAB, NatCAB 5, TwCBDA
Randolph, Thomas Jefferson 1792-1875 *AmBi,
ApCAB, DcAmB, NatCAB 5, TwCBDA,
WhAm H*
Randolph, Thomas Jefferson 1868-1926
NatCAB 20
Randolph, Thomas Mann 1741-1793 *ApCAB*
Randolph, Thomas Mann 1768-1828 *ApCAB,
BiAUS, BiDrAC, DcAmB, Drake,
NatCAB 5, TwCBDA, WhAm H,
WhAmP*
Randolph, Tom 1854-1918 *WhAm 1*
Randolph, Virginia Estelle 1875- *WhoColR*
Randolph, Wallace F 1841-1910 *WhAm 1*
Randolph, Warren 1826-1899 *NatCAB 2*
Randolph, Wassell 1880-1970 *NatCAB 55*
Randolph, William 1650-1711 *ApCAB*
Randolph, William 1651?-1711 *AmBi, DcAmB,
WhAm H*
Randolph, William 1681- *ApCAB*
Randolph, William Mann 1870-1944 *WhAm 2*
Randolph, William Mortimer 1837- *NatCAB 7*
Randolph, Woodruff 1892-1966 *WhAm 4*
Rane, Frank William 1868-1933 *WhAm 1*
Raneri, Ray 1908-1960 *NatCAB 47*
Raney, George Pettus 1845-1911 *DcAmB,
NatCAB 12, TwCBDA, WhAm 1*
Raney, John Henry 1849-1928 *BiDrAC*
Raney, McKendree Llewellyn 1877-1964
DcAmLiB, WhAm 5
Raney, Murray 1885-1966 *NatCAB 51*
Raney, Richard Beverly 1860-1909 *WhAm 1*
Raney, William Eugene 1916-1964 *WhAm 4*
Ranganatha *DcScB*
Rangel, Ignacio d1549 *ApCAB*
Rangeler, William Francis 1869-1949 *WhAm 2*
Ranger, Henry Ward 1858-1916 *AmBi,
BnEnAmA, DcAmB, NatCAB 15,
WhAm 1*
Ranger, Richard H 1889-1962 *WhAm 4*
Ranger, Walter Eugene 1855-1941 *WhAm 1*
Ranjit Singh 1780-1839 *McGEWB*
Rank, Joseph Arthur 1888-1972 *WhAm 5*
Rank, Otto 1884-1939 *McGEWB, WhAm 4*
Ranke, Leopold Von 1795-1886 *McGEWB*
Ranken, David, Jr. 1835- *NatCAB 12*
Ranken, Ellen Mary Halliday 1854-
WomWWA 14
Ranken, John Francis 1875-1933 *NatCAB 37*
Ranken-Jordan, Mary A L *WomWWA 14*
Ranker, Emery Romaine 1896-1957
NatCAB 45
Rankin, B Kirk 1874-1936 *WhAm 1*
Rankin, Carroll Watson 1864-1945 *WhAm 3*
Rankin, Christopher 1788-1826 *BiAUS,
BiDrAC, WhAm H*
Rankin, David 1825-1910 *WhAm 1*
Rankin, David Nevin 1834- *ApCAB*
Rankin, Edward Watkinson 1850-1932
NatCAB 48
Rankin, Egbert Guernsey 1856- *NatCAB 2,
WhAm 4*
Rankin, Ellen Houser 1852- *NatCAB 8*
Rankin, Emmet Woollen d1954 *WhAm 3*
Rankin, Fred Wharton 1886-1954 *WhAm 3*
Rankin, George Clark 1849-1915 *WhAm 1*
Rankin, Henry Bascom 1837-1927 *WhAm 1*
Rankin, Isaac Ogden 1852-1936 *WhAm 1*
Rankin, James Doig 1855-1949 *NatCAB 39,
WhAm 2*
Rankin, James Walter 1870-1951 *NatCAB 39*
Rankin, James Warren 1859- *WhoColR*
Rankin, Jean Sherwood 1856- *WomWWA 14*
Rankin, Jeanette 1880-1973 *REnAW*
Rankin, Jeannette 1880-1973 *BiDrAC, EncAB,
WebAB, WhAm 5, WhAmP*
Rankin, Jeremiah Eames 1828-1904 *ApCAB,
DcAmB, NatCAB 5, TwCBDA,
WhAm 1*
Rankin, John 1793-1886 *ApCAB, NatCAB 2,*

WhAm H
Rankin, John Chambers 1816-1900 *ApCAB, NatCAB 11, WhAm 1*
Rankin, John Elliott 1882-1960 *BiDrAC, WhAm 4, WhAmP*
Rankin, John Hall 1868-1952 *WhAm 3*
Rankin, John Mercer 1873-1947 *WhAm 2*
Rankin, John Watkins 1919-1972 *WhAm 5*
Rankin, Joseph 1833-1886 *BiDrAC, WhAm H*
Rankin, Martha Clark *WomWWA 14*
Rankin, McKee 1844-1914 *DcAmB*
Rankin, Milledge Theron 1894-1953 *WhAm 3*
Rankin, Pressley Robinson 1885-1958 *NatCAB 47*
Rankin, Rebecca Browning 1887-1965 *WhAm 4*
Rankin, Stacy Barcroft 1855-1919 *NatCAB 19*
Rankin, Thomas 1738?-1810 *ApCAB*
Rankin, Thomas Ernest 1872-1953 *WhAm 3*
Rankin, Walter Mead 1857-1947 *WhAm 2*
Rankin, Watson Smith 1879-1970 *NatCAB 56, WhAm 6*
Rankin, Wellington Duncan 1884-1966 *NatCAB 53, WhAm 4*
Rankin, William Bradshaw 1825-1903 *NatCAB 7, WhAm 1*
Rankin, William Brodshaw 1825-1903 *TwCBDA*
Rankin, William Durham 1876-1943 *WhAm 2*
Rankin, William Finley 1861-1918 *NatCAB 17*
Rankin, William Hector 1878- *ApCAB X*
Rankin, William Ivy 1895-1970 *NatCAB 56*
Rankin, William Thomasson 1854- *WhAm 4*
Rankin, William Walter 1882-1961 *NatCAB 49*
Rankine, Alexander Oliver 1881-1956 *DcScB*
Rankine, DeLancey 1867-1934 *NatCAB 25*
Rankine, James 1827-1896 *NatCAB 12, TwCBDA*
Rankine, William Birch 1858-1905 *DcAmB, NatCAB 13*
Rankine, William John Macquorn 1820-1872 *AsBiEn, DcScB*
Ranney, Ambrose Arnold 1821-1899 *ApCAB, BiDrAC, TwCBDA, WhAm 1*
Ranney, Ambrose Loomis 1848-1905 *DcAmB, WhAm 1*
Ranney, Frederick Eli 1853-1922 *NatCAB 36*
Ranney, George Alfred 1874-1947 *WhAm 2*
Ranney, Henry Clay 1829-1913 *NatCAB 3, WhAm 1*
Ranney, Henry Joseph 1800?-1865 *NatCAB 17, WhAm H*
Ranney, John L 1815-1866 *Drake*
Ranney, Leo 1884-1950 *NatCAB 40, WhAm 3*
Ranney, LeRoy Wilson 1888-1953 *NatCAB 48*
Ranney, Rufus Percival 1813-1891 *ApCAB, DcAmB, Drake, NatCAB 13, WhAm H*
Ranney, Walter Roy 1879-1930 *NatCAB 22*
Ranney, William Tylee 1813-1857 *ApCAB, BnEnAmA, DcAmB, IlBEAAW, NewYHSD, WhAm H*
Ranney, Winthrop Rodgers 1900-1951 *WhAm 3*
Ranno, Frederick Sebastian 1910-1965 *NatCAB 52, WhAm 4*
Ranous, Dora Knowlton 1859-1916 *NatCAB 17, WhAm 1, WomWWA 14*
Ranow, George R 1893-1954 *WhAm 3*
Ransdell, Daniel Moore 1842-1912 *WhAm 1*
Ransdell, Joseph Eugene 1858-1954 *ApCAB X, BiDrAC, NatCAB 15, TwCBDA, WhAm 3, WhAmP*
Ranseen, Mattis C 1845-1920 *WhAm 1*
Ransford, Charles Orrin 1868- *WhAm 5*
Ransford, Nettie 1838- *AmWom*
Ransier, Alonzo Jacob 1834-1882 *BiAUS, BiDrAC, WhAm H, WhAmP*
Ransier, Alonzo Jacob 1836-1882 *ApCAB*
Ransley, Harry Clay 1863-1941 *BiDrAC, WhAm 1, WhAmP*
Ransohoff, J Louis 1880-1958 *NatCAB 47*
Ransohoff, Joseph 1853-1921 *ApCAB X, DcAmB, NatCAB 19, WhAm 1*
Ransom, Alexander *NewYHSD*
Ransom, Alice Ruth Carter 1865- *WomWWA 14*
Ransom, Ann Baldwin 1871- *WomWWA 14*
Ransom, Brayton Howard 1879-1925 *WhAm 1*
Ransom, Caroline L Ormes 1838-1910 *NewYHSD, WhAm HA, WhAm 4*
Ransom, Eliza Taylor *BiCAW*

Ransom, Elmer 1892-1942 *WhAm 3*
Ransom, Epaphroditus 1797-1859 *BiAUS, NatCAB 1, TwCBDA*
Ransom, Frank Leslie 1865-1947 *WhAm 2*
Ransom, Freeman Bailey 1884- *WhoColR*
Ransom, George Brinkerhoff 1851-1924 *WhAm 1*
Ransom, George Marcellus 1820-1889 *ApCAB, TwCBDA*
Ransom, John Crowe 1888-1974 *McGEWB, WebAB, WhAm 6*
Ransom, Louis Liscolm 1831-1927? *NewYHSD*
Ransom, Marion 1866- *WomWWA 14*
Ransom, Marion 1867- *WhAm 4*
Ransom, Mathew W 1826-1904 *BiAUS*
Ransom, Matt Whitaker 1826-1904 *AmBi, ApCAB, BiDConf, BiDrAC, DcAmB, TwCBDA, WhAmP*
Ransom, Matthew Whitaker 1826-1904 *NatCAB 10, WhAm 1*
Ransom, Paul Carlton 1863-1907 *NatCAB 16*
Ransom, Rastus Seneca 1839-1914 *ApCAB Sup, NatCAB 12, WhAm 1*
Ransom, Reverdy Cassius 1861- *WhoColR*
Ransom, Robert 1828-1893 *AmBi, TwCBDA*
Ransom, Robert 1830?- *ApCAB*
Ransom, Robert, Jr. 1828-1892 *BiDConf*
Ransom, Ronald 1882-1947 *WhAm 2*
Ransom, Thomas Edward Greenfield 1834-1864 *AmBi, ApCAB, DcAmB, Drake, NatCAB 4, TwCBDA, WebAMB, WhAm H*
Ransom, Thomas Eugene Greenfield 1834-1864 *NatCAB 16*
Ransom, Truman Bishop 1802-1847 *ApCAB, Drake, NatCAB 5, NatCAB 18, TwCBDA*
Ransom, William Lynn 1883-1949 *NatCAB 40, WhAm 3*
Ransom-Kehler, Mrs. Keith *WomWWA 14*
Ransome, Amy Cordoba Rock 1872- *WomWWA 14*
Ransome, Frederick Leslie 1868-1935 *AmBi, DcAmB S1, NatCAB 26, WhAm 1*
Ranson, Arthur Jones 1873- *WhAm 5*
Ranson, Stephen Walter 1880-1942 *DcAmB S3, WhAm 2*
Ransonnier, Jean Jacques 1600-1640 *ApCAB*
Rantoul, Augustus Neal 1865- *WhAm 4*
Rantoul, Neal 1870-1956 *NatCAB 46, WhAm 3*
Rantoul, Robert 1778-1848 *NatCAB 11*
Rantoul, Robert 1778-1858 *ApCAB, DcAmB, TwCBDA, WhAm H*
Rantoul, Robert, Jr. 1805-1852 *AmBi, ApCAB, BiAUS, BiDrAC, DcAmB, Drake, NatCAB 11, TwCBDA, WhAm H*
Rantoul, Robert Samuel 1832-1922 *ApCAB, NatCAB 11, NatCAB 41, TwCBDA, WhAm 1*
Rantoul, William Gibbons 1867-1949 *WhAm 2*
Rantz, Lowell Addison 1912-1964 *WhAm 4*
Ranum, Arthur 1870-1934 *WhAm 1, WhAm 1C*
Ranvier, Louis-Antoine 1835-1922 *DcScB*
Ranyard, Arthur Cowper 1845-1894 *DcScB*
Rao, K Kirshna 1924-1970 *WhAm 5*
Raoul, Gaston C 1874-1960 *WhAm 4*
Raoul, Louis *NewYHSD*
Raoul, William Greene 1843- *NatCAB 1*
Raoult, Francois Marie 1830-1901 *AsBiEn, DcScB*
Raousset-Boulbon, Gaston Raoul 1817-1854 *ApCAB Sup*
Rapacki, Adam 1909-1970 *WhAm 5*
Rapacz, Max Peter 1892-1964 *NatCAB 50*
Rapaelje, Sarah De 1625-1700? *ApCAB*
Rapallo, Charles Anthony 1823-1887 *ApCAB*
Rapallo, Charles Antonio 1823-1887 *NatCAB 12, TwCBDA*
Rapaport, David 1911-1960 *NatCAB 50*
Rapee, Erno 1891-1945 *WhAm 2*
Rapee, Leon Andre 1903- *WhAm 5*
Raper, B W *NewYHSD*
Raper, Charles Lee 1870-1957 *NatCAB 47, WhAm 3, WhAm 4*
Raper, James Arthur 1887-1948 *NatCAB 36*
Raper, John Robert 1911-1974 *WhAm 6*

Raphael 1483-1520 *McGEWB*
Raphael, Father *WhoColR*
Raphall, Morris Jacob 1798-1868 *ApCAB, DcAmB, Drake, TwCBDA, WhAm H*
Rapier, James T 1840-1883 *BiAUS*
Rapier, James Thomas 1837-1883 *BiDrAC, WhAm H, WhAmP*
Rapier, Thomas Gwynn *WhAm 5*
Rapp, George 1757-1847 *AmBi, DcAmB, DcAmReB, EncAAH, McGEWB, WhAm H*
Rapp, George 1770-1847 *ApCAB, Drake, NatCAB 4*
Rapp, Jean 1772-1788 *WhoMilH*
Rapp, Wilhelm 1827-1907 *DcAmB, WhAm 1*
Rapp, William Jourdan 1895-1942 *WhAm 2*
Rappaport, Max Edward 1908-1965 *NatCAB 51, WhAm 4*
Rappaport, Percy 1895-1971 *NatCAB 56, WhAm 5*
Rappard, William Emmanuel 1883-1958 *WhAm 3*
Rappe, Louis Amadeus 1801-1877 *ApCAB, TwCBDA, WhAm H*
Rappe, Louis Amedeus 1801-1877 *NatCAB 5*
Rappe, Mary *NewYHSD*
Rappleye, Elbert 1867-1923 *NatCAB 6*
Rappold, Marie 1880-1957 *WhAm 3*
Rappold-Berger, Marie Winterrath 1878- *NatCAB 15*
Rappolo, Joseph Leon 1902-1943 *WhAm 4*
Rapport, David 1891-1970 *WhAm 5*
Rapport, David M 1886-1953 *NatCAB 41*
Rapuano, Michael 1904-1975 *WhAm 6*
Raquet, Condy 1784-1842 *NatCAB 11*
Rarey, John S 1828-1866 *ApCAB, Drake*
Rarey, John Solomon 1827-1866 *DcAmB, WhAm H*
Rarick, Clarence Edmund 1879-1941 *WhAm 2*
Rarick, John Richard 1924- *BiDrAC*
Rariden, James 1795-1856 *BiAUS, BiDrAC, WhAm H*
Rarig, Frank M R 1880-1963 *WhAm 4*
Rasbach, Oscar 1888-1975 *WhAm 6*
Rasberry, John Lee 1900-1957 *NatCAB 43*
Rasch, Albertina 1896-1967 *WhAm 4A*
Rasch, Carl 1866-1961 *NatCAB 48*
Raschen, Henry 1854?-1937? *IlBEAAW*
Raschen, John Frederick Louis 1875-1958 *NatCAB 47, WhAm 3*
Raschig, Frank Elmer 1887-1960 *WhAm 3*
Rasco, Richmond Austin 1871-1931 *WhAm 1*
Rascoe, Burton 1892-1957 *WhAm 3*
Rasely, Hiram Newton 1887-1955 *WhAm 3*
Rash, Frank Dillman 1878- *WhAm 6*
Rashevsky, Nicolas 1899-1972 *WhAm 6*
Rashi 1040-1105 *McGEWB*
Rashid Ali, El-Gaylani *WhWW-II*
Rasines, Antonio P 1848-1917 *NatCAB 17*
Raskob, John Jakob 1879-1950 *DcAmB S4, NatCAB 38, WhAm 3*
Rasle, Sebastien d1724 *DcAmB*
Rasle, Sebastien 1657?-1724 *AmBi*
Rasle, Sebastien 1658-1724 *ApCAB*
Rasmus, Henry 1859- *NatCAB 7*
Rasmusen, Bertil Mathias 1862- *WhAm 4*
Rasmusen, Edward A 1882-1949 *WhAm 2*
Rasmussen, Albert Terrill 1911-1969 *WhAm 5*
Rasmussen, Andrew Theodore 1883-1955 *NatCAB 45*
Rasmussen, Earl 1915-1964 *NatCAB 51*
Rasmussen, Frederik 1876-1932 *WhAm 1*
Rasmussen, George 1872-1936 *NatCAB 27*
Rasmussen, Harry Elwood 1893-1968 *NatCAB 54*
Rasmussen, James Peter 1853-1948 *NatCAB 37*
Rasmussen, Knud Johan Victor 1879-1933 *McGEWB*
Rasmussen, Marius Peter 1893-1970 *WhAm 5*
Rasmussen, Nils *NewYHSD*
Rasmussen, Otto Mills 1913-1958 *WhAm 3*
Rasmussen, Wayne David 1915- *EncAAH*
Rasor, Samuel Eugene 1873-1950 *WhAm 3*
Raspail, Francois-Vincent 1794-1878 *DcScB*
Raspe, Rudolf Erich 1737-1794 *DcScB*
Rasputin, Grigori Efimovich 1872-1916 *McGEWB*
Rassau, J H *NewYHSD*

Rassieur, Leo 1844-1929 *NatCAB 4*, *WhAm 1*
Rassieur, Louis 1876-1953 *NatCAB 45*
Rassweiler, Henry Haeseler 1842-1928
    NatCAB 21
Rastetter, William Charles 1874-1940
    NatCAB 35
Raszenski, Alexandre *NewYHSD*
Raszewski, Alexandre *NewYHSD*
Ratchford, Michael D 1860- *WhAm 4*
Ratcliff, Dillwyn Fritschel 1898-1961
    NatCAB 49
Ratcliff, Hubert McRae 1890-1956 *NatCAB 45*
Ratcliff, John Moses 1892-1953 *WhAm 3*
Ratcliffe, John d1609? *NatCAB 13*,
    WhAm H
Ratcliffe, William Cummins 1839-1920
    NatCAB 8
Ratcliffe, William Lea 1862-1916 *NatCAB 40*
Rateau, Auguste Camille Edmond 1863-1930
    DcScB
Ratellier, Francis *NewYHSD*
Rath, Howard Harbin 1898-1971 *NatCAB 56*,
    WhAm 5
Rath, John Washington 1872-1951 *NatCAB 41*
Rath, Ruben A 1892-1956 *WhAm 3*
Rath, W John 1872-1951 *WhAm 3*
Rathbone, Albert 1868-1943 *WhAm 2*
Rathbone, Alfred Day, IV 1897-1949 *WhAm 2*
Rathbone, Estes George 1848- *NatCAB 7*
Rathbone, Henry Bailey 1871-1945 *WhAm 2*
Rathbone, Henry Reed 1837- *ApCAB*
Rathbone, Henry Riggs 1870-1928 *BiDrAC*,
    WhAm 1
Rathbone, Jared Lawrence 1844-1907 *ApCAB*,
    WhAm 1
Rathbone, John Finley 1819- *WhAm 1*
Rathbone, John Finley 1821- *ApCAB*
Rathbone, Josephine Adams 1864-1941
    DcAmLiB, *NotAW*, *WhAm 1*
Rathbone, Justus Henry 1839-1889 *DcAmB*,
    WhAm H
Rathbone, Justus Henry 1839-1890 *NatCAB 2*
Rathbone, Philip St. John Basil d1967 *WhAm 4*
Rathborne, J Cornelius 1909-1954 *WhAm 3*
Rathborne, St. George Henry 1854-1938
    WhAm 1
Rathbun, Charles Addison 1867-1927
    NatCAB 21
Rathbun, D R *NewYHSD*
Rathbun, Edward Harris 1866-1948 *NatCAB 38*,
    WhAm 2
Rathbun, Elmer Jeremiah 1870-1952 *WhAm 3*
Rathbun, George Arthur 1868- *ApCAB X*
Rathbun, George Oscar 1803-1870 *BiAUS*,
    BiDrAC, *WhAm H*
Rathbun, H H 1891-1948 *WhAm 2*
Rathbun, Harriet M 1840- *AmWom*
Rathbun, John Campbell 1915-1972 *WhAm 6*
Rathbun, John Charles 1882-1958 *NatCAB 49*,
    WhAm 3
Rathbun, Mary Jane 1860-1943 *NotAW*,
    WhAm 4, *WomWWA 14*
Rathbun, Richard 1852-1918 *DcAmB*,
    NatCAB 13, *TwCBDA*, *WhAm 1*
Rathbun, Valentine 1723- *Drake*
Rathel, Otis Alfonso 1890- *WhoColR*
Rathenau, Walther 1867-1922 *McGEWB*
Rather, Howard C 1895-1950 *WhAm 3*
Rather, John Thomas, Jr. 1896-1968 *WhAm 5*
Rathje, Frank C 1882-1967 *WhAm 4*
Rathke, Martin Heinrich 1793-1860 *DcScB*
Rathmann, Carl Gustav 1853-1930 *WhAm 1*
Rathmann, Walter Lincoln 1880-1954 *WhAm 3*
Rathom, John Revelstoke 1868-1923 *ApCAB X*,
    NatCAB 20, *WhAm 1*
Rathvon, Nathaniel Peter 1891-1972 *WhAm 5*
Rathvon, William Roedel 1854-1939 *WhAm 1*
Ratliff, Alexander L 1881-1944 *WhAm 2*
Ratner, Bret 1893-1957 *WhAm 3*
Ratoff, Gregory 1897-1960 *WhAm 4*
Ratshesky, Abraham C 1864-1943 *NatCAB 33*,
    WhAm 2
Rattelman, William Adam 1893-1956 *WhAm 3*
Rattenbury, Bertha 1894- *WomWWA 14*
Rattermann, Heinrich Armin 1832-1923 *DcAmB*
Rattigan, Charles F 1865- *WhAm 4*
Rattner, Abraham 1895- *BnEnAmA*
Rattner, Herbert 1900-1962 *NatCAB 53*,

WhAm 4
Rattray, William Jordan 1835-1883 *ApCAB*
Ratzel, Friedrich 1844-1904 *DcScB*, *McGEWB*
Ratzlaff, Carl Johann 1895-1951 *WhAm 3*
Rau, Albert George 1868-1942 *WhAm 2*
Rau, Sir Benegal Rama 1889-1953 *WhAm 3*
Rau, Charles 1826-1887 *ApCAB*, *DcAmB*,
    NatCAB 2, *TwCBDA*, *WhAm H*
Rau, Jacob 1821?- *NewYHSD*
Rau, Roscoe Russel 1896-1965 *WhAm 4*
Raub, Albert Newton 1840-1904 *BiDAmEd*,
    NatCAB 38, *TwCBDA*
Raub, Edward B 1871-1955 *WhAm 3*
Raub, Edwin Stanley 1920-1966 *NatCAB 53*
Raub, Kenneth Charles 1910-1962 *WhAm 4*
Raub, William Longstreth 1867- *WhAm 4*
Rauch, Frederick Augustus 1806-1841
    BiDAmEd, *DcAmB*, *Drake*, *WhAm H*
Rauch, Friedrich August 1806-1841 *ApCAB*,
    NatCAB 11, *TwCBDA*
Rauch, Friedrich Augustus 1806-1841
    DcAmReB
Rauch, George Washington 1876-1940 *BiDrAC*,
    NatCAB 31, *WhAm 5*, *WhAmP*
Rauch, Harry Lee 1890- *WhAm 3*
Rauch, John Henry 1828-1894 *ApCAB*,
    DcAmB, *NatCAB 12*, *TwCBDA*,
    WhAm H
Rauch, Rudolph Stewart 1892-1971 *WhAm 5*
Rauch, William *NewYHSD*
Raudenbush, David Webb 1906-1969 *WhAm 5*
Raudenbush, George King 1899-1956 *WhAm 3*
Raue, Charles Godlove 1820-1896 *ApCAB*,
    NatCAB 3
Raue, Charles Gottlieb 1820-1896 *DcAmB*,
    WhAm H
Rauers, John Jacob 1877-1943 *NatCAB 36*
Rauh, Bertha Floersheim 1865- *WhAm 5*
Rauh, Enoch 1857-1919 *ApCAB X*
Rauh, Flora Mayer 1870- *WomWWA 14*
Rauh, Henry 1852-1922 *NatCAB 19*
Rauh, Joseph Louis 1875-1943 *NatCAB 34*
Rauh, Leopold 1850-1915 *NatCAB 49*
Rauh, Samuel Elias 1853-1935 *NatCAB 26*
Raul, Minnie Louise d1955 *WhAm 3*
Raulin, Jules 1836-1896 *DcScB*
Raulston, John Tate 1868-1956 *NatCAB 44*
Rault, Joseph Matthew 1893-1965 *WhAm 4*
Raum, Green Berry 1829-1909 *ApCAB*, *BiAUS*,
    BiDrAC, *DcAmB*, *Drake*, *NatCAB 13*,
    TwCBDA, *WhAm 1*
Raumer, Friedrich Ludwig Georg Von 1781-1873
    ApCAB
Rausch, Emil Henry 1874-1938 *WhAm 1*
Rauschenbach, Charles William 1889-1951
    NatCAB 44
Rauschenberg, Robert 1925- *BnEnAmA*,
    EncAB, *McGEWB*, *WebAB*
Rauschenbusch, Augustus 1816- *ApCAB*,
    WhAm 1
Rauschenbusch, Walter 1861-1918 *DcAmB*,
    DcAmReB, *EncAB*, *McGEWB*,
    NatCAB 19, *WebAB*, *WhAm 1*
Rauschner, Henry *NewYHSD*
Rauschner, John Christian 1760- *NewYHSD*
Rauskolb, Fred Willis 1868-1922 *NatCAB 19*
Rautenstrauch, Walter 1880-1951 *DcAmB S5*,
    WhAm 3
Rauwolf, Leonhard 1535-1596 *DcScB*
Ravalli, Anthony 1812-1884 *NatCAB 3*,
    REnAW
Ravalli, Antonio 1811-1884 *DcAmB*, *WhAm H*
Ravdin, Isidor Schwaner 1894-1972 *WhAm 5*
Ravdin, Robert Glenn 1923-1972 *WhAm 6*
Ravel, Gabriel 1810- *ApCAB*
Ravel, Maurice Joseph 1875-1937 *McGEWB*
Ravel, Vincent Marvin 1914-1969 *WhAm 5*
Ravel Family *ApCAB*
Ravelli, Father *NewYHSD*
Raven *EncAAH*
Raven, Anton Adolph 1833-1919 *ApCAB X*,
    NatCAB 14, *NatCAB 23*
Raven, Anton Adolph 1895-1955 *WhAm 3*
Raven, John Howard 1870-1949 *NatCAB 39*,
    WhAm 2
Ravenal, Mazyck Porcher 1861-1946
    NatCAB 38
Ravenel, Beatrice Witte 1870-1956 *WhAm 3*

Ravenel, Edmund 1797-1871 *DcAmB*,
    WhAm H
Ravenel, Florence Leftwich *WomWWA 14*
Ravenel, Gaillard FitzSimons 1886-1956
    NatCAB 53
Ravenel, Harriott Harry 1832-1912 *WhAm 4*
Ravenel, Harriott Horry Rutledge 1832-1912
    DcAmB, *WomWWA 14*
Ravenel, Henry William 1814-1887 *AmBi*,
    ApCAB, *DcAmB*, *NatCAB 10*, *TwCBDA*,
    WhAm H
Ravenel, Marguerite *WomWWA 14*
Ravenel, Mazyck Porcher 1861-1946 *DcAmB S4*,
    WhAm 2
Ravenel, St. Julien 1819-1882 *ApCAB*, *DcAmB*,
    NatCAB 10, *TwCBDA*, *WhAm H*
Ravenel, William DeChastignier 1859-
    WhAm 4
Ravenhill, Alice 1859- *WomWWA 14*
Ravenscroft, Edward Hawks 1871-1951
    NatCAB 37, *WhAm 3*
Ravenscroft, Elizabeth Fish *WomWWA 14*
Ravenscroft, John Stark 1772-1830 *ApCAB*,
    DcAmB, *Drake*, *NatCAB 6*, *TwCBDA*,
    WhAm H
Raveson, Sherman Harold 1907-1974 *WhAm 6*
Ravitch, Saul 1902-1952 *NatCAB 39*
Ravlin, Grace 1885-1956 *IIBEAAW*, *WhAm 3*
Ravndal, G Bie 1865-1950 *NatCAB 38*,
    WhAm 2A
Ravogli, Augustus 1851- *NatCAB 12*,
    WhAm 4
Ravoux, Augustin 1815-1906 *DcAmB*
Raw, Jacob *NewYHSD*
Rawdon, Francis 1754-1826 *Drake*
Rawdon, Freeman 1801?-1859 *NewYHSD*
Rawdon, Henry M *NewYHSD*
Rawdon, Ralph *NewYHSD*
Rawdon-Hastings, Francis 1754-1826 *AmBi*,
    ApCAB, *NewYHSD*
Rawhouser, Minnie Oglevee 1882-
    WomWWA 14
Rawidowicz, Simon 1897-1957 *NatCAB 50*,
    WhAm 3
Rawl, Bernard Hazelius 1876-1924 *WhAm 1*
Rawle, Francis 1660?-1727 *ApCAB*,
    NatCAB 6
Rawle, Francis 1662?-1726? *DcAmB*,
    WhAm H
Rawle, Francis 1846-1930 *ApCAB*, *DcAmB*,
    NatCAB 17, *TwCBDA*, *WhAm 1*
Rawle, Henry 1833- *ApCAB*
Rawle, James 1842-1912 *NatCAB 18*,
    WhAm 1
Rawle, William 1759-1836 *AmBi*, *ApCAB*,
    DcAmB, *Drake*, *NatCAB 7*, *TwCBDA*
Rawle, William 1759-1856 *WhAm H*
Rawle, William 1788-1858 *ApCAB*,
    NatCAB 10, *TwCBDA*
Rawle, William Brooke *TwCBDA*
Rawle, William Brooke-Rawle 1843- *ApCAB*
Rawle, William Henry 1823-1889 *AmBi*,
    ApCAB, *DcAmB*, *NatCAB 10*, *TwCBDA*,
    WhAm H
Rawleigh, William Thomas 1870- *WhAm 5*
Rawles, Jacob Beekman 1839-1919 *WhAm 1*
Rawles, Thomas Howard 1897-1962
    NatCAB 53
Rawles, William A 1863-1936 *TwCBDA*,
    WhAm 1
Rawley, Joseph Pearson 1886-1937 *WhAm 1*
Rawlings, Eugene Hubbard 1865-1939 *WhAm 1*
Rawlings, Henry *NewYHSD*
Rawlings, Marjorie Kinnan 1896-1953
    DcAmB S5, *WhAm 3*
Rawlings, Moses d1809 *Drake*
Rawlings, Moses 1740?-1808 *ApCAB*
Rawlings, Norborne L 1894-1972 *WhAm 5*
Rawlings, Stuart Lamar 1875-1940 *NatCAB 30*
Rawlins, Cora Monnier 1864- *WomWWA 14*
Rawlins, George Herndon 1901-1963 *WhAm 4*
Rawlins, John Aaron 1831-1869 *AmBi*, *ApCAB*,
    BiAUS, *BiDrUSE*, *DcAmB*, *Drake*,
    NatCAB 4, *TwCBDA*, *WhAm H*
Rawlins, Joseph Lafayette 1850-1926
    ApCAB Sup, *BiDrAC*, *NatCAB 11*,
    TwCBDA, *WhAmP*
Rawlins, Joseph Lafayette 1850-1927 *WhAm 1*

Rawlins, William Thomas 1877-1928
NatCAB 40, WhAm 1
Rawlinson, Frank Joseph 1871-1937 *DcAmB S2,
WhAm 1*
Rawlinson, Sir Henry Creswicke 1810-1895
AsBiEn
Rawlinson, Henry Seymour 1864-1925
WhoMilH
Rawll, Herbert Frederic 1881-1947 *ApCAB X,
NatCAB 35*
Rawls, Julian Lamar 1881-1948 *NatCAB 35*
Rawls, Morgan 1829-1906 *BiDrAC*
Rawls, Walter Cecil 1895-1964 *NatCAB 51*
Rawls, William Lee 1883-1946 *NatCAB 44*
Rawn, A M 1888-1968 *NatCAB 55*
Rawn, Arnold Edward 1906-1973 *WhAm 6*
Rawn, Ira Griffith 1855-1910 *WhAm 1*
Rawschnor *NewYHSD*
Rawson, Albert Leighton 1828-1902 *TwCBDA,
WhAm 1*
Rawson, Albert Leighton 1829-1902 *ApCAB,
NewYHSD*
Rawson, Carl Wendell 1884-1970 *WhAm 5*
Rawson, Charles Augustus 1867-1936 *BiDrAC,
NatCAB 27, WhAm 1*
Rawson, E M *NewYHSD*
Rawson, Edward 1615-1693 *ApCAB, Drake,
NatCAB 13*
Rawson, Edward Kirk 1846- *WhAm 4*
Rawson, Edward Lincoln 1864-1948
NatCAB 37
Rawson, Edward Stephen 1868-1935
NatCAB 27
Rawson, Eleanor *NewYHSD*
Rawson, Frederick Holbrook 1872-1937
NatCAB 43, WhAm 1
Rawson, Grindall 1659-1715 *ApCAB*
Rawson, Rebecca 1656- *ApCAB*
Rawstorne, Edward *NewYHSD*
Rawstorne, Edwin *NewYHSD*
Ray, Albert Hoyt 1865-1925 *NatCAB 23*
Ray, Anna Chapin 1865-1945 *TwCBDA,
WhAm 2, WomWWA 14*
Ray, Anna Elizabeth *WomWWA 14*
Ray, Arthur Benning 1889-1951 *WhAm 3*
Ray, Charles Andrew 1864- *WhAm 1*
Ray, Charles Bennett 1807-1886 *DcAmB,
WhAm H*
Ray, Charles Henry 1821-1870 *NatCAB 7,
NatCAB 29, WhAm H*
Ray, Charles Wayne 1872-1928 *WhAm 1*
Ray, Charlotte E 1850-1911 *NotAW*
Ray, Cornelius 1755-1827 *NatCAB 1*
Ray, David Heydorn 1878-1960 *WhAm 4*
Ray, E Lansing 1884-1955 *WhAm 3*
Ray, Edgar Knapp 1844-1906 *NatCAB 16*
Ray, Edward Chittenden 1849- *WhAm 4*
Ray, Franklin Arnold 1862-1938 *WhAm 1*
Ray, Frederick Augustus, Jr. 1871- *WhAm 5*
Ray, G J 1876-1962 *WhAm 4*
Ray, George Washington 1844-1925 *BiDrAC,
NatCAB 2, TwCBDA, WhAm 1,
WhAmP*
Ray, Guy W 1897-1950 *WhAm 3*
Ray, Harvey Cincinnatus 1889- *WhoColR*
Ray, Herbert James 1893-1970 *WhAm 5*
Ray, Hugh Edwin 1866-1940 *NatCAB 36*
Ray, Isaac 1807-1881 *ApCAB, DcAmB,
Drake, WhAm H*
Ray, James Brown 1794-1848 *ApCAB, BiAUS,
NatCAB 13, TwCBDA*
Ray, James Morrison 1860-1918 *NatCAB 24*
Ray, Jefferson Davis 1860-1951 *WhAm 3*
Ray, John 1627-1705 *DcScB, McGEWB*
Ray, John 1628-1705 *AsBiEn*
Ray, John 1816-1888 *ApCAB*
Ray, John Arthur 1879- *WhAm 6*
Ray, John David 1904-1969 *NatCAB 55*
Ray, John Edwin 1852-1918 *WhAm 1*
Ray, John Henry 1886-1975 *BiDrAC,
WhAm 6, WhAmP*
Ray, Joseph 1807-1855 *Drake*
Ray, Joseph 1807-1865 *BiDAmEd, NatCAB 1,
WhAm H*
Ray, Joseph Johnson *IIBEAAW*
Ray, Joseph R, Sr. 1887- *WhAm 4*
Ray, Joseph Warren 1849-1928 *BiDrAC*
Ray, Louise Crenshaw 1890-1956 *WhAm 3*

Ray, Man 1890- *BnEnAmA, McGEWB,
WebAB*
Ray, Marie Beynon d1969 *WhAm 5*
Ray, Milton Smith 1881-1946 *NatCAB 34,
WhAm 2*
Ray, Ossian 1835-1892 *BiDrAC, WhAm H*
Ray, P Henry 1842-1911 *WhAm 1*
Ray, P Orman 1875- *WhAm 5*
Ray, Philip Alexander 1911-1970 *WhAm 5*
Ray, Prafulla Chandra 1861-1944 *DcScB*
Ray, Rachel Beasley 1849- *AmWom*
Ray, Randolph 1886-1963 *WhAm 4*
Ray, Reginald Piffard 1880-1960 *NatCAB 48*
Ray, Robert Darwin 1817-1891 *NatCAB 13*
Ray, Robert Donald 1924- *IIBEAAW*
Ray, Robert Jackson 1883-1936 *NatCAB 27*
Ray, Russel 1878-1950 *NatCAB 40*
Ray, S J 1891-1970 *WhAm 5*
Ray, Satyajit 1921- *McGEWB*
Ray, Simon 1635-1737 *NatCAB 8*
Ray, Sybil Duncan 1860- *WomWWA 14*
Ray, T Bronson 1868-1934 *WhAm 1*
Ray, T Bronson 1883-1936 *WhAm 1*
Ray, Thomas William 1883-1958 *NatCAB 48*
Ray, William 1771-1827 *Drake, NatCAB 1*
Ray, William Henry 1812-1881 *BiAUS,
BiDrAC, WhAm H*
Ray, William Wallace 1880- *WhAm 6*
Raybold, Walter James 1864-1938 *WhAm 1*
Rayburn, Robert Henry 1866-1944 *NatCAB 36*
Rayburn, Sam Taliaferro 1882-1961 *BiDrAC,
WhAm 4, WhAmP*
Rayburn, Samuel Taliaferro 1882-1961 *EncAAH,
EncAB, McGEWB, WebAB*
Raycorft, Joseph Edward 1867-1955 *WhAm 3*
Rayer, Pierre-Francois 1793-1867 *BiHiMed*
Rayet, Georges Antoine Pons 1839-1906 *DcScB*
Rayfiel, Leo Frederick 1888- *BiDrAC*
Rayleigh *DcScB*
Rayleigh, John William Strutt, Baron 1842-1919
AsBiEn, McGEWB
Raymer, Albert Reesor 1862-1931 *WhAm 1*
Raymond Of Marseilles *DcScB*
Raymond, Alexander Gillespie 1909-1956
WhAm 3
Raymond, Anan 1890-1975 *WhAm 6*
Raymond, Andrew VanVranken 1854-1918
NatCAB 7, TwCBDA, WhAm 1
Raymond, Anna Almy 1888-1935 *WhAm 1*
Raymond, Annie Louise Cary 1842- *AmWom*
Raymond, Benjamin 1774-1824 *TwCBDA*
Raymond, Benjamin Wright 1801-1883 *ApCAB,
DcAmB, NatCAB 12, TwCBDA,
WhAm H*
Raymond, Bradford Paul 1846-1916 *NatCAB 9,
TwCBDA, WhAm 1*
Raymond, C Rexford 1872-1958 *WhAm 3*
Raymond, Carrie Isabelle Rice 1857- *AmWom*
Raymond, Charles Beebe 1866-1945
NatCAB 36, WhAm 2
Raymond, Charles Henry 1834- *NatCAB 13*
Raymond, Mrs. Charles M *WomWWA 14*
Raymond, Charles Walker 1842-1913 *DcAmB,
WhAm 1*
Raymond, Clifford Samuel 1875-1950 *WhAm 3*
Raymond, Daniel 1780?-1849? *NatCAB 13*
Raymond, Daniel 1786-1849? *DcAmB,
WhAm 1*
Raymond, Donat 1880-1963 *WhAm 4*
Raymond, Dora Neill 1888-1961 *WhAm 4*
Raymond, Edith Eaton 1853- *WomWWA 14*
Raymond, Edward Brackett 1869-1922
NatCAB 22
Raymond, Emma Marcy 1856- *AmWom*
Raymond, Ernest 1888-1974 *WhAm 6*
Raymond, Evelyn Hunt 1843-1910 *TwCBDA,
WhAm 1, WomWWA 14*
Raymond, Frances Effinger 1863-
WomWWA 14
Raymond, Fred Morton 1876-1946 *WhAm 2*
Raymond, Frederick Wingate 1874- *WhAm 5*
Raymond, George H *NewYHSD*
Raymond, George Lansing 1839-1929 *ApCAB,
ApCAB X, BiDAmEd, DcAmB,
NatCAB 8, TwCBDA, WhAm 1*
Raymond, Harry Howard 1864-1935
DcAmB S1, WhAm 1
Raymond, Henry Ingle 1857- *WhAm 4*

Raymond, Henry Jarvis 1820-1869 *AmBi,
ApCAB, BiAUS, BiDrAC, DcAmB,
Drake, NatCAB 8, TwCBDA, WebAB,
WhAm H, WhAmP*
Raymond, Henry Warren 1847-1925 *NatCAB 6,
TwCBDA, WhAm 1*
Raymond, Howard Monre 1872-1943 *WhAm 2*
Raymond, Howard Monroe 1872-1943
ApCAB X
Raymond, Irving Edward 1875-1962
NatCAB 57
Raymond, James 1796-1858 *ApCAB*
Raymond, James Irving 1843-1905 *NatCAB 14*
Raymond, Jerome Hall 1869-1928 *NatCAB 25,
TwCBDA, WhAm 1*
Raymond, John Baldwin 1844-1886 *BiDrAC,
WhAm H*
Raymond, John Howard 1814-1878 *ApCAB,
BiDAmEd, DcAmB, NatCAB 5,
TwCBDA, WhAm H*
Raymond, John Marshall 1852-1920 *ApCAB X*
Raymond, John T 1836-1887 *AmBi, ApCAB,
DcAmB, TwCBDA, WhAm H*
Raymond, Jonathan Stone 1894-1963 *WhAm 4*
Raymond, Joseph Howard 1845-1915 *WhAm 1*
Raymond, Josephine Hunt *WhAm 5,
WomWWA 14*
Raymond, Katharine Platt *WomWWA 14*
Raymond, Lee Roy 1887-1953 *NatCAB 42*
Raymond, Mabel K *WomWWA 14*
Raymond, Mary Elizabeth 1867- *WhAm 3,
WomWWA 14*
Raymond, Maud Mary Wotring 1867- *WhAm 4,
WomWWA 14*
Raymond, Miner 1811-1897 *ApCAB, DcAmB,
WhAm H*
Raymond, Neil Charles 1896-1965 *NatCAB 54*
Raymond, Nell Charles 1895-1965 *WhAm 4*
Raymond, Percy Edward 1879-1952 *DcScB,
WhAm 6*
Raymond, Robert Fulton 1858- *WhAm 1*
Raymond, Robert Raikes 1819-1888 *ApCAB*
Raymond, Rossiter Worthington 1840-1918
*ApCAB, BiAUS Sup, DcAmB, NatCAB 8,
TwCBDA, WhAm 1*
Raymond, Thomas Lynch 1875-1928 *WhAm 1*
Raymond, Wayte 1886-1956 *NatCAB 42*
Raymond, Wilbur Samuel 1852-1914
NatCAB 17
Raymond, William Galt 1859-1926 *NatCAB 17,
WhAm 1*
Raymond, William Lee 1877-1942 *WhAm 2*
Raynal, Guillaume Thomas Francois 1713-1793
ApCAB
Raynal, William Thomas Francis 1714-1796
Drake
Raynaud, Maurice 1834-1881 *BiHiMed*
Rayner, Emily C 1847- *AmWom*
Rayner, Emma d1926 *WhAm 1,
WomWWA 14*
Rayner, Ernest Adolphus 1878- *WhAm 6*
Rayner, Isidor 1850-1912 *BiDrAC, DcAmB,
NatCAB 13, TwCBDA, WhAm 1,
WhAmP*
Rayner, Kenneth 1808-1884 *ApCAB, BiAUS,
BiDrAC, TwCBDA, WhAm H*
Rayner, Kenneth 1810?-1884 *DcAmB*
Rayner, Robert J *NewYHSD*
Rayner, Thomas W *NewYHSD*
Raynolds, Frederic A 1874- *NatCAB 1*
Raynolds, Herbert F 1874- *WhAm 5*
Raynolds, John Madison 1878- *WhAm 6*
Raynolds, Joshua Saxton 1845-1932
NatCAB 18, WhAm 1, WhAm 1C
Raynolds, Robert Frederick 1902-1965
NatCAB 51, WhAm 4
Raynolds, William Franklin 1820- *ApCAB*
Raynor, Hayden 1906-1963 *WhAm 4*
Raynor, Mortimer Williams 1879-1935
NatCAB 27
Rayon, Ignacio Lopez 1773-1827 *ApCAB*
Rayon, Ramon 1775-1839 *ApCAB*
Raysor, Charles Luke 1882- *WhoColR*
Raysor, Thomas Middleton 1895-1974 *WhAm 6*
Rayton, Wilbur Brambley 1884-1946
NatCAB 35
Rayton, Willis MacNair 1909-1957 *NatCAB 46*
Razafkeriefo, Paul Andrea 1895- *WhoColR*

Razi, Al- 865?-925 *McGEWB*
Razi, Abu Bakr Muhammad Ibn Z, Al-854?-925? *DcScB*
Razmadze, Andrei Mikhailovich 1889-1929 *DcScB*
Razmara, Ali 1901-1951 *WhAm 3*
Razran, Gregory 1901-1973 *WhAm 6*
Re Qua, Alice Haven 1865- *WomWWA 14*
Rea, Carolyn Morse 1877- *WomWWA 14*
Rea, Daniel, Jr. 1743- *NewYHSD*
Rea, David 1831-1901 *BiAUS Sup, BiDrAC*
Rea, Edith Oliver *ApCAB X, BiCAW*
Rea, Gardner 1892-1966 *WhAm 4*
Rea, George Bronson 1869-1936 *WhAm 1*
Rea, Mrs. Henry R 1865- *WhAm 5*
Rea, Henry Robinson 1863-1919 *ApCAB X, NatCAB 23*
Rea, John 1755-1829 *ApCAB, BiAUS, BiDrAC, Drake, TwCBDA, WhAm H*
Rea, John Andrew d1941 *WhAm 1*
Rea, John Dougan 1880-1933 *WhAm 1*
Rea, John Patterson 1840-1900 *ApCAB, NatCAB 6, WhAm 1*
Rea, Mary Kathleen Coyle *WomWWA 14*
Rea, Paul Marshall 1878-1948 *WhAm 2*
Rea, Robert 1877- *WhAm 5*
Rea, Robert Chenoweth 1889-1957 *NatCAB 47*
Rea, Robert Laughlin 1827-1899 *NatCAB 14*
Rea, Samuel 1855-1929 *AmBi, ApCAB X, DcAmB, NatCAB 15, WhAm 1*
Rea, Stanley Leroy 1912-1967 *NatCAB 54*
Reach, Alfred James 1840-1928 *DcAmB*
Read *NewYHSD*
Read, Abigail Dickinson Dreer *WomWWA 14*
Read, Abner 1821-1863 *ApCAB, NatCAB 7*
Read, Albert Cushing 1887-1967 *NatCAB 53, WebAMB, WhAm 4A*
Read, Almon Heath 1790-1844 *BiAUS, BiDrAC, WhAm H*
Read, Benjamin Stalker 1876-1935 *WhAm 1*
Read, Cecil Byron 1901-1972 *WhAm 5*
Read, Charles 1713?-1774 *DcAmB*
Read, Charles 1715-1774 *WhAm H*
Read, Charles 1715-1780? *ApCAB, NatCAB 12*
Read, Charles Barnum 1858-1912 *NatCAB 31*
Read, Charles Francis 1876-1946 *WhAm 2*
Read, Charles O 1846-1926 *WhAm 1*
Read, Charles William 1840-1890 *DcAmB, WebAMB, WhAm H*
Read, Clark Phares 1921-1973 *WhAm 6*
Read, Conyers 1881-1959 *NatCAB 48, WhAm 3*
Read, Daniel 1757-1836 *DcAmB, Drake, NatCAB 7, WhAm H*
Read, Daniel 1757-1841 *ApCAB*
Read, Daniel 1805-1878 *ApCAB, BiDAmEd, DcAmB, NatCAB 8, TwCBDA, WhAm H*
Read, Daniel 1825- *NatCAB 5*
Read, Donald F *NewYHSD*
Read, Edward Griffin 1844-1933 *NatCAB 24*
Read, Edward Parker 1868- *WhoColR*
Read, Effie Alberta *WomWWA 14*
Read, Elizabeth C Bunnell 1834- *AmWom*
Read, Elmer Joseph 1862- *NatCAB 4*
Read, Flora Alice 1862- *WomWWA 14*
Read, Florence Matilda 1885-1973 *WhAm 6*
Read, George *NewYHSD*
Read, George 1733-1798 *AmBi, ApCAB, BiAUS, BiDrAC, DcAmB, Drake, NatCAB 3, TwCBDA, WebAB, WhAm H, WhAmP*
Read, George Campbell d1862 *Drake*
Read, George Campbell 1787?-1862 *ApCAB, DcAmB, TwCBDA, WebAMB, WhAm H*
Read, George Campbell 1788?-1862 *NatCAB 6*
Read, George Isaac 1886- *WhoColR*
Read, George Windle 1860-1934 *DcAmB S1, WebAMB, WhAm 1*
Read, George Windle, Jr. 1900-1974 *WhAm 6*
Read, Gerald Howard 1913- *BiDAmEd*
Read, Granville Moorman 1894-1962 *NatCAB 50, WhAm 4*
Read, Harlan Eugene 1880-1963 *WhAm 4*
Read, Harmon Pumpelly 1860- *NatCAB 4*
Read, Harold D 1902-1945 *WhAm 2*
Read, Helen Appleton 1887-1974 *WhAm 6*

Read, Helen Leah 1864- *WomWWA 14*
Read, Henrietta Fanning *Drake*
Read, Henry E 1824-1869 *BiDConf*
Read, Herbert 1893-1968 *WhAm 5*
Read, Herbert Harold 1889-1970 *WhAm 6*
Read, Hollis 1802-1887 *ApCAB, TwCBDA*
Read, Horace Emerson 1898-1975 *WhAm 6*
Read, Isaac 1746-1778 *ApCAB*
Read, J *BiAUS*
Read, Jacob d1816 *BiAUS*
Read, Jacob 1751-1816 *BiDrAC*
Read, Jacob 1752-1816 *ApCAB, DcAmB, Drake, NatCAB 2, TwCBDA, WhAm H*
Read, James 1716-1793 *ApCAB*
Read, James 1743-1822 *ApCAB*
Read, James Alexander *NewYHSD*
Read, James B 1803?- *NewYHSD*
Read, Jane Maria 1853- *AmWom*
Read, John *NewYHSD*
Read, John d1749 *Drake*
Read, John 1673-1749 *ApCAB*
Read, John 1679?-1749 *DcAmB*
Read, John 1680-1750 *WhAm H*
Read, John 1688-1756 *ApCAB, NatCAB 6*
Read, John 1769-1854 *ApCAB, DcAmB, WhAm H*
Read, John Elliot 1845- *WhAm 4*
Read, John Joseph 1842-1910 *TwCBDA, WhAm 1*
Read, John Meredith 1797-1874 *ApCAB, BiAUS, DcAmB, Drake, NatCAB 4, TwCBDA, WhAm H*
Read, John Meredith 1837-1896 *AmBi, ApCAB, BiAUS, DcAmB, NatCAB 2, TwCBDA, WhAm H*
Read, John Royall 1881- *WhAm 6*
Read, Katharine Bell *WomWWA 14*
Read, Lazarus H *BiAUS*
Read, Louis Wilson 1828- *ApCAB Sup*
Read, Luella Jane 1878- *WomWWA 14*
Read, Mary Lillian 1878- *WhAm 6, WomWWA 14*
Read, Maurice Gallison 1905-1966 *NatCAB 53, WhAm 4*
Read, Melbourne Stuart 1869-1927 *WhAm 1*
Read, Nathan 1759-1849 *AmBi, ApCAB, BiDrAC, DcAmB, Drake, NatCAB 4, WhAm H*
Read, Nathan 1760-1849 *BiAUS*
Read, Nicholas 1841?- *NewYHSD*
Read, Oliver Middleton 1889-1972 *WhAm 5*
Read, Opie 1852-1939 *NatCAB 1, TwCBDA, WhAm 1*
Read, Opie Percival 1852-1939 *AmBi, ApCAB Sup, WebAB*
Read, Opie Pope 1852-1939 *DcAmB S2, EncAAH*
Read, Ruth Sears 1862- *WomWWA 14*
Read, Samuel Roberson 1860-1942 *NatCAB 33*
Read, Theodore 1836-1865 *ApCAB*
Read, Thomas 1740-1788 *ApCAB, DcAmB, TwCBDA, WhAm H*
Read, Thomas 1745-1817 *ApCAB*
Read, Thomas 1746-1823 *ApCAB*
Read, Thomas 1881-1962 *NatCAB 50, WhAm 4*
Read, Thomas Albert 1913-1966 *NatCAB 51, WhAm 4*
Read, Thomas B d1829 *BiAUS*
Read, Thomas Buchanan 1822-1872 *AmBi, ApCAB, DcAmB, Drake, IIBEAAW, NatCAB 6, NewYHSD, TwCBDA, WhAm H*
Read, Thomas Thornton 1880-1947 *NatCAB 38, WhAm 2*
Read, Waldemer Pickett 1897-1975 *WhAm 6*
Read, William 1607-1679 *NewYHSD*
Read, William Augustus 1858-1916 *ApCAB X, WhAm 1*
Read, William B 1820-1880 *BiAUS*
Read, William Brown 1817-1880 *BiDrAC, WhAm H*
Read, William Franklin 1833-1916 *NatCAB 18*
Read, William Lewis 1851-1915 *WhAm 1*
Read, William Thackara 1878-1954 *WhAm 3*
Reade, Edwin Godwin 1812-1894 *BiAUS, BiDConf, BiDrAC, DcAmB, NatCAB 11, WhAm H*

Reade, Herbert Wight 1867-1921 *NatCAB 29*
Reade, John 1837- *ApCAB*
Reade, John Moore 1876-1937 *WhAm 1*
Reade, Philip 1844- *WhAm 1*
Reader, Francis Smith 1842- *WhAm 4*
Reader, Frank Eugene 1868-1947 *NatCAB 36*
Reader, Frank Smith 1842- *NatCAB 7*
Reader, George W 1820?- *NewYHSD*
Reader, Samuel J *NewYHSD*
Reading, Earl Of 1860- *WhAm 4*
Reading, Arthur Henry 1863- *NatCAB 16*
Reading, John Roberts 1826-1886 *BiAUS, BiDrAC, WhAm H*
Reading, Pearson B 1816-1868 *NatCAB 15*
Reading, Richard William 1882-1952 *WhAm 3*
Reading, Rufus D Isaacs, Marquess Of 1860-1935 *McGEWB*
Reading, William *NewYHSD*
Readio, Wilfred Allen 1895-1961 *WhAm 4*
Ready *NewYHSD*
Ready, Charles 1802-1878 *BiAUS, BiDrAC, TwCBDA, WhAm H*
Ready, Frank A 1884-1961 *WhAm 4*
Ready, Joseph Louis 1895-1955 *NatCAB 43, WhAm 3*
Ready, Lester Seward 1888-1947 *WhAm 2*
Ready, Michael Joseph 1893-1957 *WhAm 3*
Ready, Samuel 1789-1871 *ApCAB*
Reagan, Frank Joseph 1883-1955 *NatCAB 44, WhAm 3*
Reagan, John Henninger 1818-1905 *AmBi, ApCAB, BiAUS, BiDConf, BiDrAC, DcAmB, Drake, NatCAB 1, REnAW, TwCBDA, WhAm 1, WhAmP*
Reagan, Lewis M 1904-1961 *WhAm 4*
Reagan, Ronald Wilson 1911- *EncAB*
Realf, Richard 1834-1878 *ApCAB, DcAmB, NatCAB 8, WhAm H*
Reals, Willis Howard 1892-1967 *NatCAB 53, WhAm 4A, WhAm 5*
Ream, Carducis Plantagenet 1838-1917 *NatCAB 17*
Ream, Carducius Plantagenet 1836?-1917 *NewYHSD*
Ream, Norman Bruce 1844-1915 *DcAmB, NatCAB 9, NatCAB 16, WhAm 1*
Ream, Robert Clarke 1882-1957 *NatCAB 47*
Ream, Vinnie 1847-1914 *NotAW*
Ream, Vinnie 1850- *NatCAB 1*
Reames, Alfred Evan 1870-1943 *BiDrAC, WhAm 2*
Reams, Frazier 1897-1971 *WhAm 5*
Reams, Henry Frazier 1897-1971 *BiDrAC*
Reamy, Thaddeus Asbury 1829-1909 *ApCAB, NatCAB 12, WhAm 1*
Reaney, George Humes 1887-1947 *WhAm 2*
Reaney, Joseph Hamblin 1864-1947 *NatCAB 34*
Reaney, Thomas A 1916- *IIBEAAW*
Rear, George William 1873-1942 *NatCAB 31*
Rearick, Allan Chamberlain 1874-1940 *WhAm 1*
Rease, William H 1818?- *NewYHSD*
Reaser, Matthew Howell 1863- *WhAm 4*
Reaser, Wilbur Aaron 1860- *WhAm 4*
Reason, Henry J *NewYHSD*
Reason, Patrick Henry 1817- *NewYHSD*
Reason, Philip H *NewYHSD*
Reasoner, Mathew Aaron 1875-1947 *NatCAB 34*
Reath, Benjamin Brannon 1862-1919 *NatCAB 23*
Reath, Theodore Wood 1866- *WhAm 4*
Reath, Thomas 1890-1975 *WhAm 6*
Reaugh, Charles Franklin 1860-1945 *IIBEAAW*
Reaumur, Rene Antoine Ferchault De 1683-1757 *AsBiEn, DcScB*
Reaves, J Ullman 1885-1959 *NatCAB 49*
Reaves, Samuel Watson 1875-1950 *WhAm 3*
Reavis, Charles Frank 1870-1932 *BiDrAC, WhAm 1, WhAmP*
Reavis, Isaac *BiAUS*
Reavis, James Addison 1843-1914 *REnAW*
Reavis, James Bradley 1848-1912 *NatCAB 5, TwCBDA*
Reavis, James Bradly 1848-1912 *WhAm 1*
Reavis, James Overton 1872- *WhAm 5*
Reavis, Logan Uriah 1831-1889 *ApCAB,*

TwCBDA

Reavis, William Claude 1881-1955 *BiDAmEd,*
WhAm 3

Reavley, Lester S 1894-1965 *WhAm 4*

Rebasz, Enrith Trabue Pattison 1860-
WomWWA 14

Rebasz, Eurith Trabue Pattison 1860- *WhAm 4*

Rebec, George 1868-1944 *WhAm 2*

Rebeck, Henry Milton 1913-1964 *NatCAB 54*

Reber, Anna Marie Walton 1882-
WomWWA 14

Reber, Grote 1911- *AsBiEn*

Reber, James Lenhardt 1838-1917 *ApCAB X*

Reber, John 1858-1931 *BiDrAC, WhAm 3*

Reber, John U 1893-1955 *WhAm 3*

Reber, Louis Ehrhart 1858-1948 *NatCAB 37,*
WhAm 2

Reber, Samuel 1864-1933 *NatCAB 24,*
WhAm 1

Reber, Samuel 1903-1971 *WhAm 5*

Rebert, Charles Muthart 1882-1951
NatCAB 41

Rebert, Clara Mickley 1857- *WomWWA 14*

Rebert, G Nevin 1889-1948 *WhAm 2*

Rebeske, Edward Carl 1863-1940 *NatCAB 36*

Rebety, Victor *NewYHSD*

Rebichon, Emile *NewYHSD*

Rebichon, Theodorus *NewYHSD*

Rebisso, Louis T 1837-1899 *NewYHSD*

Rebole, Henry *NewYHSD*

Rebori, Andrew Nicholas 1886-1966 *WhAm 4*

Reboucas, Manoel Mauricio 1792-1866 *ApCAB*

Rebrassier, Russell Edmund 1890-1964
NatCAB 51

Rebscher, J M 1887-1961 *WhAm 4*

Rebuck, Charles Stough 1873-1928 *NatCAB 29*

Recabarren DeMarin, Luisa 1777-1839 *ApCAB*

Reccord, Augustus Phineas 1870-1946 *WhAm 2*

Recht, Albert William 1898-1962 *NatCAB 48*

Recht, Charles 1887-1965 *WhAm 4*

Reck, B Harry 1888-1960 *NatCAB 48*

Reck, Franklin Mering 1896-1965 *WhAm 4*

Reck, Hans 1886-1937 *DcScB*

Reckford, Louis Joseph 1866-1928 *ApCAB X*

Reckling, William Joseph 1904-1966 *WhAm 4*

Reckly, Mary D *WomWWA 14*

Reckmeyer, Luella d1962 *WhAm 4*

Recknagel, Arthur Bernard 1883-1962
NatCAB 47, WhAm 4

Reckord, Milton A 1879-1975 *WhAm 6*

Reclus, Elie Armand Ebenhezer 1843- *ApCAB*

Reclus, Elisee 1830-1905 *DcScB*

Reclus, Jean Jacques Elisee 1830-1905 *ApCAB*

Recoley, Julius *NewYHSD*

Record, George Lawrence 1859-1933 *AmBi*

Record, James Lucius 1857-1944 *NatCAB 34,*
WhAm 2

Record, James Robert 1885-1973 *WhAm 6*

Record, Samuel James 1881-1945 *DcAmB S3,*
NatCAB 33, WhAm 2

Recorde, Robert 1510?-1558 *DcScB,*
McGEWB

Records, Edward 1887-1960 *WhAm 4*

Records, Ralph LaFayette 1883-1965 *WhAm 4*

Recto, Claro M 1890-1960 *McGEWB*

Rector, Edward 1863-1925 *NatCAB 24,*
WhAm 1

Rector, Elbridge Lee 1847-1929 *WhAm 1*

Rector, Frank 1851-1933 *WhAm 1*

Rector, Henry Massey 1816-1899 *BiAUS,*
BiDConf, DcAmB, NatCAB 10, REnAW,
TwCBDA, WhAm H

Rector, John Benjamin 1837-1898 *TwCBDA,*
WhAm 4

Rector, Lizzie E 1866-1955 *WhAm 3,*
WomWWA 14

Rector, Thomas Marion 1894-1950 *NatCAB 41,*
WhAm 3

Rector, Walter Whiting 1887-1953 *WhAm 3*

Red, Samuel Clark 1861-1940 *NatCAB 32*

Red, William Stuart, Jr. 1898-1960 *NatCAB 47*

Red Bird 1788?-1828 *REnAW*

Red Cloud 1822-1909 *AmBi, DcAmB,*
McGEWB, REnAW, WebAB, WebAMB,
WhAm HA, WhAm 4

Red Eagle 1765-1824 *DcAmB*

Red Eagle 1780?-1824 *AmBi, WebAMB,*
WhAm H

Red-Jacket 1750?-1830 *NatCAB 13*

Red Jacket 1751-1830 *ApCAB, Drake*

Red Jacket 1756?-1830 *REnAW, WebAB*

Red Jacket 1758?-1830 *AmBi, DcAmB,*
WhAm H

Red Wing 1750?-1825? *DcAmB, WhAm H*

Redd, F Marion 1876-1956 *NatCAB 45*

Reddall, Frederic 1856- *WhAm 4*

Reddall, Henry Frederick 1852- *ApCAB*

Redden, Laura Catherine *TwCBDA*

Redden, Monroe Minor 1901- *BiDrAC*

Redden, William Rufus 1881-1952 *NatCAB 41*

Reddick, Donald 1883-1955 *WhAm 3*

Reddick, Harry Ernest 1892-1957 *NatCAB 52*

Redding *NewYHSD*

Redding, Mister *NewYHSD*

Redding, Benjamin Barnard 1824-1882 *ApCAB*

Redding, Charles Joseph Vincent 1879-1946
NatCAB 34

Redding, Charles Summerfield 1883-1959
WhAm 3

Redding, George Hyde 1892-1956 *NatCAB 44*

Redding, Isabella Remshart *WomWWA 14*

Redding, John MacLean 1908-1965 *WhAm 4*

Rediger, Joseph Deighn 1858-1932 *NatCAB 23*

Redding, Joseph Deighn 1859-1932 *WhAm 1,*
WhAm 1C

Redding, Leo L 1867-1936 *WhAm 1*

Redding, Otis 1942-1967 *WhAm 4A*

Redding, Robert Jordan 1836-1914 *WhAm 1*

Redding, William *NewYHSD*

Reddish, George Fults 1894-1962 *WhAm 4*

Reddix, Jacob L 1897-1973 *WhAm 6*

Reddon, Laura C *Drake*

Rede, Wyllys 1859- *NatCAB 2, WhAm 4*

Redeke, Ernest William 1906-1962 *WhAm 4*

Redelheim, Abraham Aaron 1897-1965
NatCAB 50

Reder, Bernard 1897-1966 *WhAm 4*

Redfearn, Daniel Huntley 1884-1963 *WhAm 4*

Redfearn, David Townley 1915-1969
NatCAB 55

Redfern, Donald Verne 1915-1965 *WhAm 4*

Redfern, Merrill F 1901-1952 *WhAm 3*

Redfern, Peter 1821-1912 *BiHiMed*

Redfield, Amasa Angell 1837-1902 *ApCAB,*
DcAmB, NatCAB 26, WhAm 1

Redfield, Anna Maria Treadwell 1800-1888
NatCAB 2, TwCBDA

Redfield, Casper Lavater 1853-1943 *WhAm 2*

Redfield, Edward Willis 1869-1965 *WhAm 4*

Redfield, Henry Stephen 1851-1926 *NatCAB 20,*
WhAm 1

Redfield, Isaac Fletcher 1804-1876 *ApCAB,*
BiAUS, DcAmB, Drake, NatCAB 7,
TwCBDA, WhAm H

Redfield, John Howard 1815- *ApCAB*

Redfield, John Vermilye 1878-1956 *NatCAB 47*

Redfield, Justus Starr 1810-1888 *ApCAB,*
DcAmB, NatCAB 7, WhAm H

Redfield, Lewis Hamilton 1792-1882 *NatCAB 2*

Redfield, Robert 1870-1921 *ApCAB X*

Redfield, Robert 1897-1958 *McGEWB,*
NatCAB 44, WebAB, WhAm 3

Redfield, William C 1789-1857 *AmBi, ApCAB,*
DcAmB, DcScB, Drake, NatCAB 7,
TwCBDA, WhAm H

Redfield, William Cox 1858-1932 *AmBi,*
BiDrAC, BiDrUSE, DcAmB, WhAm 1,
WhAmP

Redfield, William D *NewYHSD*

Redfield, William Goodrich 1870-1941
NatCAB 31

Redhead, Edwin Richard 1851-1924 *NatCAB 6,*
WhAm 1

Redhefer, Raymond Lindley 1880-1972
NatCAB 56

Redi, Francesco 1626-1697 *AsBiEn*

Redi, Francesco 1626-1698? *DcScB*

Redick, John Irwin 1828- *NatCAB 11*

Rediger, Michel Jon 1939-1969 *WhAm 5*

Redin, William H *NewYHSD*

Reding, John Randall 1805-1892 *BiAUS,*
BiDrAC, WhAm H

Reding, W *NewYHSD*

Redington, Paul Goodwin 1878-1942 *WhAm 1,*
WhAm 2

Redington, Ruth Holley Cabeen 1888-
WomWWA 14

Redlin, Rolland W 1920- *BiDrAC*

Redman, Ben Ray 1896-1961 *WhAm 4*

Redman, Harry Newton 1869- *WhAm 5*

Redman, John 1722-1808 *ApCAB, BiHiMed,*
DcAmB, Drake, WhAm H

Redman, Joseph Reasor 1891-1968 *WhAm 5*

Redman, Lawrence Vincent 1880-1946
NatCAB 38, WhAm 2

Redman, Theodore Miller 1900-1962
NatCAB 49

Redman, William H 1833?- *NewYHSD*

Redmayne, Robert 1826?- *NewYHSD*

Redmond, Daniel George 1896-1955 *WhAm 3*

Redmond, Daniel Walter 1876-1934 *WhAm 1*

Redmond, Granville 1871-1935 *WhAm 1*

Redmond, John Harris 1912-1974 *WhAm 6*

Redmond, Kenneth H 1895-1975 *WhAm 6*

Redmond, Maurice Snowden 1889-1952
NatCAB 49

Redon, Odilon 1840-1916 *McGEWB*

Redoute, Pierre-Joseph 1759-1840 *DcScB*

Redpath, James 1833-1891 *AmBi, ApCAB,*
DcAmB, Drake Sup, NatCAB 13,
TwCBDA, WhAm H

Redstone, Edward H 1882-1950 *WhAm 3*

Redtenbacher, Ferdinand Jakob 1809-1863
DcScB

Redway, Jacques Wardlaw 1849-1942 *ApCAB,*
BiDAmEd, NatCAB 4, NatCAB 31,
WhAm 2

Redway, Jaques Wardlaw 1849-1942 *TwCBDA*

Redway, Laurance David 1890-1960
NatCAB 45

Redwine, Martha Bush *WomWWA 14*

Redwood, Abraham d1788 *Drake*

Redwood, Abraham 1709-1788 *ApCAB,*
DcAmB, WhAm H

Redwood, Abraham 1710-1788 *TwCBDA*

Redwood, Allen C 1844-1922 *IIBEAAW*

Redwood, Mary Buchanan Coale 1861-
WomWWA 14

Redwood, William Morris 1872-1955
NatCAB 45

Reeb, James Joseph 1927-1965 *WhAm 4*

Reece, Brazilla Carroll 1889-1961 *BiDrAC,*
NatCAB 49, WhAm 4, WhAmP

Reece, Mrs. Carroll 1898-1970 *WhAm 5*

Reece, Ernest James 1881- *WhAm 6*

Reece, Louise Goff 1898-1970 *BiDrAC*

Reece, Richard H 1879-1954 *WhAm 3*

Reech, Ferdinand 1805-1884 *DcScB*

Reed *NewYHSD*

Reed, A F 1894-1963 *WhAm 4*

Reed, Abner 1771-1866 *NewYHSD*

Reed, Albert Alison 1866-1947 *NatCAB 36*

Reed, Albert Augustus 1868-1951 *NatCAB 38,*
WhAm 5

Reed, Albert Granberry 1870-1932 *WhAm 1*

Reed, Alfred 1839-1918 *WhAm 1*

Reed, Alfred Zantzinger 1875-1949 *WhAm 2*

Reed, Allen Visscher 1838-1917 *WhAm 1*

Reed, Amy Louise 1872-1949 *WhAm 2,*
WomWWA 14

Reed, Andrew 1788-1862 *ApCAB*

Reed, Anna Yeomans 1871- *WhAm 5*

Reed, Anna Yeomans 1873- *WomWWA 14*

Reed, Annie Martha *WomWWA 14*

Reed, Benjamin E 1844- *NatCAB 2*

Reed, Boardman 1842-1917 *WhAm 1*

Reed, C Lawson 1888-1923 *NatCAB 21*

Reed, Caleb 1797-1854 *ApCAB, Drake*

Reed, Caroline Gallup 1821- *ApCAB Sup,*
WomWWA 14

Reed, Caroline Keating *AmWom*

Reed, Carroll Roscoe 1884-1959 *WhAm 3*

Reed, Cass Arthur 1884-1949 *NatCAB 49,*
WhAm 3

Reed, Charles Alfred Lee 1856-1928
NatCAB 12, NatCAB 24, WhAm 1

Reed, Charles Bert 1866-1940 *NatCAB 31,*
WhAm 1

Reed, Charles Dana 1875-1945 *WhAm 2*

Reed, Charles John 1858- *WhAm 4*

Reed, Charles Manning 1803-1871 *BiAUS,*
BiDrAC, WhAm H

Reed, Charles Shadrach 1862- *NatCAB 17*

Reed, Charles Wesley 1867-1949 *NatCAB 40*
Reed, Chauncey William 1890-1956 *BiDrAC,*
WhAm 3, WhAmP
Reed, Chester Allyn 1860- *WhAm 4*
Reed, Clare Osborne 1868- *WhAm 5,*
WomWWA 14
Reed, Clinton 1892-1954 *NatCAB 50*
Reed, Clyde Martin 1871-1949 *BiDrAC,*
NatCAB 47, WhAm 2, WhAmP
Reed, Daniel Alden 1875-1959 *BiDrAC,*
NatCAB 51, WhAm 3, WhAmP
Reed, David 1790-1870 *ApCAB, DcAmB,*
Drake, NatCAB 12, WhAm H
Reed, David Aiken 1880-1953 *BiDrAC,*
DcAmB S5, NatCAB 52, WhAm 3
Reed, David Allen 1850-1932 *BiDAmEd*
Reed, Doel 1894- *IIBEAAW*
Reed, Donald Ross 1906-1971 *WhAm 5*
Reed, E Glenn 1890-1958 *NatCAB 47*
Reed, E Howard 1878-1943 *NatCAB 33*
Reed, Earl Frederick 1894-1963 *NatCAB 52,*
WhAm 4
Reed, Earl Howell 1863-1931 *AmBi, DcAmB,*
WhAm 1
Reed, Earl Howell 1884-1968 *WhAm 4A*
Reed, Earl Meusel 1895- *IIBEAAW*
Reed, Edna Gertrude Young 1875-
WomWWA 14
Reed, Edward Bliss 1872-1940 *WhAm 1*
Reed, Edward Cambridge 1793-1883 *BiAUS,*
BiDrAC, WhAm H
Reed, Edwin 1835-1908 *WhAm 1*
Reed, Edwin Clarence 1877- *WhAm 5*
Reed, Edwin O 1824?- *NewYHSD*
Reed, Elizabeth Armstrong 1842-1915 *DcAmB,*
NatCAB 1, NatCAB 15, NotAW,
TwCBDA, WhAm 1, WomWWA 14
Reed, Elmer Ellsworth 1862-1926 *WhAm 1*
Reed, Emma Louise Fetzer 1866-
WomWWA 14
Reed, Erastus R *NewYHSD*
Reed, Esther DeBerdt 1746-1780 *ApCAB,*
NotAW
Reed, Eugene Elliott 1866-1940 *BiDrAC*
Reed, Fannie Blauvelt 1875- *WomWWA 14*
Reed, Fishe P *NewYHSD*
Reed, Florence 1883-1967 *WhAm 4A*
Reed, Florence Campbell 1860- *AmWom*
Reed, Forrest Francis 1897-1975 *WhAm 6*
Reed, Francis Cables 1903-1974 *WhAm 6*
Reed, Frank Fremont 1857-1926 *WhAm 1*
Reed, Frank Hynes 1890-1957 *NatCAB 46,*
WhAm 3
Reed, Frank Lefevre 1871- *WhAm 5*
Reed, Frank Otis 1876-1928 *WhAm 2*
Reed, Frank Walker 1881- *WhAm 6*
Reed, Franklin Hancock 1880-1931 *WhAm 1*
Reed, George Edward 1846-1930 *NatCAB 6,*
TwCBDA, WhAm 1
Reed, George Henry 1905-1975 *WhAm 6*
Reed, George Letchworth 1900-1970 *WhAm 5*
Reed, George Matthew 1878- *WhAm 6*
Reed, George William 1878-1957 *WhAm 3*
Reed, Grace Holt 1874- *WomWWA 14*
Reed, Guy Euclid 1890-1959 *WhAm 3*
Reed, Harlow John 1918-1971 *WhAm 5*
Reed, Harrison 1813- *NatCAB 11*
Reed, Harry Bertram 1872-1939 *WhAm 1*
Reed, Harry E 1892-1961 *WhAm 4*
Reed, Harry Gibson 1855- *WhoColR*
Reed, Harry James 1887-1960 *NatCAB 49,*
WhAm 4
Reed, Harry Lathrop 1867-1964 *NatCAB 52,*
WhAm 4
Reed, Helen Leah *WhAm 5, WomWWA 14*
Reed, Henry *BnEnAmA*
Reed, Henry 1846- *ApCAB*
Reed, Henry Albert 1844-1930 *WhAm 1*
Reed, Henry Clay 1899-1972 *WhAm 5*
Reed, Henry Gooding 1810- *NatCAB 10*
Reed, Henry Hope 1808-1854 *ApCAB, DcAmB,*
Drake, NatCAB 2, TwCBDA, WhAm H
Reed, Henry Morrison 1880-1947 *NatCAB 38,*
WhAm 2
Reed, Henry Thomas 1846-1924 *WhAm 1*
Reed, Herbert 1876- *WhAm 5*
Reed, Hollis 1802- *Drake*
Reed, Horace 1870- *WhAm 5*

Reed, Horace 1876-1953 *NatCAB 45*
Reed, Horatio Blake 1837-1888 *ApCAB*
Reed, Howard Sprague 1876-1950 *NatCAB 40,*
WhAm 3
Reed, Hugh 1850- *ApCAB*
Reed, Hugh Daniel 1875-1937 *WhAm 1*
Reed, Isaac d1778 *Drake*
Reed, Isaac 1809-1887 *BiDrAC, WhAm H*
Reed, Isaac 1810-1887 *BiAUS*
Reed, Ivy Kellerman 1877- *WhAm 5,*
WomWWA 14
Reed, Izah B *NewYHSD*
Reed, J Henry 1868- *WhoColR*
Reed, James 1722-1807 *DcAmB*
Reed, James 1724-1807 *ApCAB, Drake,*
NatCAB 1, WhAm H
Reed, James 1834-1921 *DcAmB, NatCAB 14,*
TwCBDA, WhAm 4
Reed, James 1881-1941 *NatCAB 30*
Reed, James Alexander 1861-1944 *ApCAB X,*
BiDrAC, DcAmB S3, NatCAB 15,
NatCAB 34, WhAm 2, WhAmP
Reed, James Byron 1881-1935 *BiDrAC,*
WhAm 1
Reed, James Calvin 1869-1949 *WhAm 3*
Reed, James Hay 1853-1927 *DcAmB,*
WhAm 1
Reed, James Oliver 1861-1925 *NatCAB 21*
Reed, John *NewYHSD*
Reed, John 1673?-1749 *NatCAB 19*
Reed, John 1751-1831 *ApCAB, BiAUS,*
BiDrAC, Drake, NatCAB 2, TwCBDA,
WhAm H, WhAmP
Reed, John 1757-1845 *DcAmB, WhAm H*
Reed, John 1760-1848? *ApCAB*
Reed, John 1777-1845 *ApCAB*
Reed, John 1781-1860 *ApCAB, BiAUS,*
BiDrAC, Drake, NatCAB 2, TwCBDA,
WhAm H, WhAmP
Reed, John 1786-1850 *ApCAB*
Reed, John 1789-1850 *NatCAB 16*
Reed, John Alton 1898-1962 *WhAm 4*
Reed, John B *NewYHSD*
Reed, John C 1902-1952 *NatCAB 44,*
WhAm 3
Reed, John Calvin 1836-1910 *WhAm 1*
Reed, John Hamilton *WhoColR*
Reed, John Oren 1856-1916 *WhAm 1*
Reed, John S *NewYHSD*
Reed, John Silas 1887-1920 *DcAmB, EncAB,*
McGEWB, NatCAB 19, WebAB,
WhAm 1, WhAm 4A
Reed, Joseph 1741-1785 *AmBi, ApCAB,*
BiAUS, BiDrAC, DcAmB, Drake,
NatCAB 1, NatCAB 2, TwCBDA,
WhAm H, WhAmP
Reed, Joseph 1772-1846 *ApCAB*
Reed, Joseph Abram 1847-1919 *NatCAB 18*
Reed, Joseph Rea 1835-1925 *BiDrAC,*
NatCAB 12, NatCAB 21, WhAm 1
Reed, Joseph Verner 1902-1973 *WhAm 6*
Reed, Kenneth White 1889-1958 *NatCAB 46*
Reed, Leo Augustine 1901-1963 *NatCAB 50*
Reed, Lowell Jacob 1886-1966 *WhAm 4*
Reed, Luman 1781-1836 *DcAmB*
Reed, Luman 1787-1836 *WhAm H*
Reed, Luther Dotterer 1873-1972 *WhAm 5*
Reed, Lydia MacMillan *WomWWA 14*
Reed, Lyman Aaron 1860-1927 *NatCAB 22*
Reed, M W 1895-1975 *WhAm 6*
Reed, Marjorie 1915- *IIBEAAW*
Reed, Martin Monroe 1912-1963 *NatCAB 52,*
WhAm 4
Reed, Mary 1854-1943 *DcAmB S3, NotAW*
Reed, Mary Dean 1875- *WhAm 5*
Reed, Mary Williams 1872- *WhAm 5*
Reed, Milton 1848-1932 *WhAm 1*
Reed, Myron Winslow 1836-1899 *NatCAB 18*
Reed, Myrtle 1874-1911 *DcAmB, NotAW,*
TwCBDA
Reed, Nathan Parker 1874-1941 *NatCAB 30*
Reed, P *NewYHSD*
Reed, Perley Isaac 1887-1973 *WhAm 5*
Reed, Peter Fishe 1817-1887 *NewYHSD*
Reed, Philip 1760-1829 *ApCAB, BiAUS,*
BiDrAC, Drake, NatCAB 7, TwCBDA,
WhAm H
Reed, Philip Loring 1883-1964 *WhAm 4*

Reed, Phillip Allen 1934-1972 *WhAm 6*
Reed, Ralph John 1883-1939 *NatCAB 29,*
WhAm 1
Reed, Ralph Thomas 1890-1968 *NatCAB 53,*
WhAm 4A
Reed, Rebecca Theresa 1813?- *ApCAB*
Reed, Richard Clark 1851-1925 *DcAmB,*
WhAm 1
Reed, Richard Cumming Stockton 1825-
NatCAB 12
Reed, Richard Forman 1861-1926 *WhAm 1*
Reed, Robert Bowman 1881-1944 *NatCAB 34,*
WhAm 2
Reed, Robert Cameron 1860-1928 *WhAm 1*
Reed, Robert Lafayette 1905-1965 *NatCAB 51*
Reed, Robert Rentoul 1807-1864 *BiAUS,*
BiDrAC, WhAm H
Reed, Robert Rentoul 1876-1945 *ApCAB X,*
NatCAB 34, WhAm 2
Reed, Rodman Smith, Jr. 1904-1961 *WhAm 4*
Reed, Roland 1852-1901 *NatCAB 13,*
WhAm 1
Reed, Rosa Aurelia Nichols 1870-
WomWWA 14
Reed, Sampson 1800-1880 *ApCAB, DcAmB,*
Drake, WhAm H
Reed, Samuel *NewYHSD*
Reed, Samuel Clarke 1877-1943 *NatCAB 33*
Reed, Samuel Macon 1879- *WhAm 6*
Reed, Sarah A 1838-1934 *WhAm 1*
Reed, Seth 1744-1797 *NatCAB 13*
Reed, Simeon Gannett 1830-1895 *DcAmB,*
REnAW, WhAm H
Reed, Stanley Forman 1884- *WebAB*
Reed, Mrs. Stanley Forman 1887-
WomWWA 14
Reed, Stuart Felix 1866-1935 *BiDrAC,*
WhAm 1, WhAmP
Reed, Stuart Royden 1884-1960 *NatCAB 48,*
WhAm 4
Reed, Sylvanus Albert 1854-1935 *AmBi,*
WhAm 1
Reed, Theodore Byington 1888-1958
NatCAB 43
Reed, Thomas Brackett 1839-1902 *AmBi,*
ApCAB, BiDrAC, DcAmB, EncAB,
McGEWB, NatCAB 2, TwCBDA,
WebAB, WhAm 1, WhAmP
Reed, Thomas Buck d1829 *ApCAB, TwCBDA*
Reed, Thomas Buck 1780?-1829 *NatCAB 4*
Reed, Thomas Buck 1787-1829 *BiDrAC,*
WhAm H
Reed, Thomas Harrison 1881-1971 *WhAm 5*
Reed, Thomas Milburne 1857-1928 *WhAm 1*
Reed, Verner Zevola 1863-1919 *NatCAB 19,*
WhAm 1
Reed, Victor Joseph 1905-1971 *WhAm 5*
Reed, W B 1836- *NatCAB 1*
Reed, Walter 1851-1902 *AmBi, AsBiEn,*
BiHiMed, DcAmB, DcScB, EncAB,
McGEWB, NatCAB 13, NatCAB 33,
WebAB, WhAm H
Reed, Walter Lawrence 1877-1956 *WhAm 3*
Reed, Warren Augustus 1871-1927 *WhAm 1*
Reed, Washington 1891-1951 *WhAm 3*
Reed, Wayne Otis 1911-1974 *WhAm 6*
Reed, Willard 1870-1944 *WhAm 2*
Reed, William d1837 *BiAUS, Drake*
Reed, William 1776-1837 *BiDrAC,*
NatCAB 11, WhAm H
Reed, William 1777-1837 *ApCAB*
Reed, William Bradford 1806-1876 *AmBi,*
ApCAB, BiAUS, BiAUS Sup, DcAmB,
Drake, NatCAB 7, TwCBDA, WhAm H
Reed, William Hale 1874-1950 *NatCAB 40,*
WhAm 3
Reed, William M 1892-1956 *WhAm 3*
Reed, William Randolph 1868-1936 *NatCAB 27*
Reed, William Reynolds 1915-1971 *WhAm 5*
Reed, William Shields 1778-1853 *TwCBDA*
Reed, William Shields *see also* Reid, William
Shields
Reed, William Thomas, Jr. 1903-1966 *WhAm 4*
Reed And Barton *BnEnAmA*
Reeder, Alexander *NewYHSD*
Reeder, Andrew Horatio 1807-1864 *AmBi,*
ApCAB, DcAmB, NatCAB 8, TwCBDA,
WhAm H

Reeder, Andrew Horatio 1808?-1864 *Drake*
Reeder, Benjamin F 1834?- *NewYHSD*
Reeder, Charles 1817-1900 *ApCAB,*
NatCAB 11
Reeder, Charles L 1864- *WhAm 4*
Reeder, Charles Leonard 1876- *WhAm 5*
Reeder, Edwin Hewett 1892-1957 *WhAm 3*
Reeder, Edwin Thorley 1908-1963 *WhAm 4*
Reeder, Frank 1845-1912 *NatCAB 4,*
WhAm 1
Reeder, Glezen Asbury, Jr. *WhAm 5*
Reeder, Grace Amelia 1888-1960 *WhAm 4*
Reeder, J H *NewYHSD*
Reeder, Ward Glen 1891-1962 *WhAm 4*
Reeder, William Augustus 1849-1929 *BiDrAC,*
TwCBDA, WhAm 4, WhAmP
Reeder, William Herron 1848-1911 *WhAm 1*
Reedy, Daniel M 1854-1927 *NatCAB 22*
Reedy, Fred Owen 1891-1958 *NatCAB 47*
Reedy, J Martin 1889-1955 *WhAm 3*
Reedy, Leonard Howard 1899-1956 *IIBEAAW*
Reedy, Rose Stroman 1904-1969 *WhAm 5*
Reedy, William Marion 1862-1920 *DcAmB,*
NatCAB 19, WhAm 1
Reel, Estelle 1866- *WomWWA 14*
Reeman, Edmund Henry 1881-1950 *WhAm 3*
Reemelin, Oscar Ben 1881- *WhAm 6*
Reen, Charles 1827?- *NewYHSD*
Reep, Samuel Austen 1912-1970 *WhAm 5*
Rees, Albert William 1877- *WhAm 5*
Rees, Alfred Cornelius 1876-1941 *WhAm 1*
Rees, Byron Johnson 1877-1920 *WhAm 1*
Rees, Charles Mayrant 1862-1932 *NatCAB 16*
Rees, Corwin Pottenger 1848-1924 *WhAm 1*
Rees, Edward Herbert 1886-1969 *BiDrAC,*
WhAm 5
Rees, Edwin Henry 1922-1974 *WhAm 6*
Rees, Ernest 1876-1951 *NatCAB 41*
Rees, George E 1845- *WhAm 4*
Rees, James 1802- *Drake*
Rees, James 1821-1889 *DcAmB, NatCAB 23,*
WhAm H
Rees, John Krom 1851-1907 *ApCAB, DcAmB,*
NatCAB 11, TwCBDA, WhAm 1
Rees, Kelley 1878-1954 *NatCAB 40*
Rees, Mrs. Lewis *NewYHSD*
Rees, Maurice H 1880-1945 *WhAm 2*
Rees, Robert Irwin 1871-1936 *NatCAB 27,*
WhAm 1
Rees, Rollin Raymond 1865-1935 *BiDrAC,*
WhAm 4
Rees, Ruby Almeda *WomWWA 14*
Rees, Thomas 1850-1933 *WhAm 1*
Rees, Thomas Henry 1863-1942 *WhAm 2*
Rees, Thomas Mankell 1925- *BiDrAC*
Rees, William Henry 1882-1952 *NatCAB 41,*
WhAm 3
Reese, Abram 1829-1908 *DcAmB*
Reese, Albert Moore 1872-1965 *WhAm 4*
Reese, Benjamin Harrison 1888-1974 *WhAm 6*
Reese, Charles H 1895-1968 *WhAm 5*
Reese, Charles Lee 1862-1940 *DcAmB S2,*
NatCAB 30, WhAm 1
Reese, Chauncey B 1837-1870 *ApCAB*
Reese, Clarence 1896-1972 *NatCAB 57*
Reese, Curtis Williford 1887-1961 *WhAm 4*
Reese, Dale F 1883-1957 *WhAm 3*
Reese, David Addison 1794-1871 *BiAUS,*
BiDrAC, WhAm H
Reese, David Meredith 1800-1861 *ApCAB,*
Drake
Reese, Frederick Focke 1854-1936 *NatCAB 14,*
WhAm 1
Reese, George Lee 1872- *WhAm 5*
Reese, Gilbert A 1885-1943 *WhAm 2*
Reese, Herbert Meredith 1873-1954 *WhAm 3*
Reese, Isaac 1821-1908 *DcAmB*
Reese, J Allen 1905-1964 *WhAm 4*
Reese, Jacob 1825-1907 *DcAmB*
Reese, James Mitchell 1858-1922 *NatCAB 6*
Reese, John D 1907-1973 *WhAm 6*
Reese, John Davies 1893-1958 *NatCAB 47*
Reese, John James 1818-1892 *ApCAB, DcAmB,*
NatCAB 6, WhAm H
Reese, Joseph Hammond 1896-1968 *WhAm 5*
Reese, Leal Wiley 1894-1954 *NatCAB 44*
Reese, Levi H 1806-1851 *ApCAB*
Reese, Lizette Woodworth 1856-1935 *AmWom,*

DcAmB S1, NatCAB 1, NotAW,
WhAm 1, WhAm 2
Reese, Lowell Otus 1866-1948 *WhAm 3*
Reese, Manoah Bostic 1839-1917 *NatCAB 8,*
WhAm 1
Reese, Mary Bynon 1832- *AmWom*
Reese, Millard 1880-1955 *WhAm 3*
Reese, Owen 1896-1970 *NatCAB 55*
Reese, Robert Grigg 1866-1926 *NatCAB 20*
Reese, Scott Charles 1903-1966 *WhAm 5*
Reese, Seaborn 1846-1907 *BiDrAC*
Reese, T T 1867-1957 *WhAm 3*
Reese, Theodore Irving 1873-1931 *WhAm 1*
Reese, Thomas 1742-1794 *ApCAB*
Reese, Thomas 1742-1796 *Drake*
Reese, Warren Stone 1841-1897 *NatCAB 10*
Reese, Webster Paul 1879- *WhAm 6*
Reese, Wilbur Ford 1917-1971 *NatCAB 57,*
WhAm 5
Reese, William Brown 1793-1859 *TwCBDA*
Reese, William Brown 1793-1860 *ApCAB*
Reese, William M 1847- *NatCAB 1*
Reese, William Smythe 1850- *TwCBDA*
Reeser, Edwin B 1873- *WhAm 5*
Reeside, John Bernard, Jr. 1889-1958 *WhAm 3*
Reesman, Budd Aaron 1907-1968 *WhAm 5*
Reeve, Arthur Benjamin 1880-1936 *NatCAB 26,*
WhAm 1, WhAm 6
Reeve, Charles Asa 1875-1949 *NatCAB 39*
Reeve, Charles McCormick 1847- *TwCBDA,*
WhAm 4
Reeve, Felix Alexander 1836-1920 *WhAm 1*
Reeve, Isaac VanDuzen 1813- *ApCAB, Drake*
Reeve, James Knapp 1856-1933 *WhAm 1*
Reeve, John Charles 1826-1920 *NatCAB 20*
Reeve, Katharine Roosevelt 1887-
WomWWA 14
Reeve, Margaretta Willis 1871- *WomWWA 14*
Reeve, Sidney Armor 1866-1941 *WhAm 1*
Reeve, Tapping 1744-1823 *ApCAB, BiDAmEd,*
DcAmB, Drake, McGEWB, NatCAB 6,
TwCBDA, WebAB, WhAm H
Reeve, William David 1883-1961 *BiDAmEd,*
WhAm 4
Reeve, William Foster, III 1892-1972 *WhAm 5*
Reeverts, Emma 1898-1973 *WhAm 6*
Reeves, Albert Lee, Jr. 1906- *BiDrAC*
Reeves, Alec Harley 1902-1971 *WhAm 5*
Reeves, Alfred Gandy 1859-1927 *WhAm 1*
Reeves, Archie R 1898- *WhAm 5*
Reeves, Arthur Middleton 1856-1891 *DcAmB,*
WhAm H
Reeves, Beauford Houston 1892-1955
NatCAB 44
Reeves, Charles Francis 1854- *WhAm 4*
Reeves, Daniel F d1971 *WhAm 5*
Reeves, Elizabeth Hoffman 1862-
WomWWA 14
Reeves, Francis Brewster 1836-1922 *ApCAB X,*
NatCAB 21, WhAm 1, WhAm 1C
Reeves, Frank Daniel 1916-1973 *WhAm 5*
Reeves, George Curtis 1905-1969 *WhAm 5*
Reeves, Henry Augustus 1832-1916 *BiDrAC*
Reeves, Henry Augustus 1833-1916 *BiAUS*
Reeves, Herbert James 1884-1964 *WhAm 4*
Reeves, Ira Louis 1872-1939 *NatCAB 18,*
WhAm 1
Reeves, Isaac Stockton Keith 1850-1917
WhAm 1
Reeves, J Franklin 1886-1946 *NatCAB 35*
Reeves, James Aloysius Wallace 1892-1947
WhAm 2
Reeves, James Haynes 1870- *WhAm 5*
Reeves, Jeremiah Bascom 1884-1946 *WhAm 2*
Reeves, Jeremiah E 1845-1920 *NatCAB 18*
Reeves, Jesse Siddall 1872-1942 *WhAm 2*
Reeves, John 1752-1829 *ApCAB*
Reeves, John Dudley, Jr. 1924-1964 *WhAm 4*
Reeves, John Richard Thomas, Jr. 1877-
WhAm 5
Reeves, John Ruel 1906-1959 *WhAm 3*
Reeves, John Toy 1863-1926 *NatCAB 20*
Reeves, John Walter, Jr. 1888-1967 *WhAm 4*
Reeves, Joseph Mason 1872-1948 *DcAmB S4,*
WebAMB, WhAm 2
Reeves, Marian Calhoun Legare 1854-1898
ApCAB, NatCAB 4
Reeves, Micajah Rufus 1877-1942 *NatCAB 31*

Reeves, Ollie Clarence 1891-1965 *NatCAB 51*
Reeves, Owen Thornton 1829- *WhAm 4*
Reeves, Paul Beatty 1889-1971 *NatCAB 56*
Reeves, Perry Willard 1878-1946 *WhAm 2*
Reeves, Reuben A 1821- *NatCAB 1*
Reeves, Robert James 1898-1968 *WhAm 4A*
Reeves, Russell Henry 1905-1974 *WhAm 6*
Reeves, Ruth 1892-1966 *WhAm 4*
Reeves, Samuel J 1818-1878 *NatCAB 13*
Reeves, Thomas Rosser 1876-1951 *WhAm 3*
Reeves, W H *NewYHSD*
Reeves, Walter 1848-1909 *BiDrAC, TwCBDA,*
WhAm 1
Reeves, Walter Perkins 1884-1957 *WhAm 3*
Reeves, William Harvey 1895-1970 *WhAm 6*
Reeves, William Peters 1865-1945 *WhAm 2*
Reeves, Winona Evans 1871- *WhAm 5,*
WomWWA 14
Refregier, Anton 1905- *BnEnAmA*
Regal, Mary Lucinda 1863- *WomWWA 14*
Regalbuto, Samuel Biagio 1898-1958
NatCAB 46
Regamey, Felix Elie 1844-1907 *IIBEAAW*
Regan, Agnes Gertrude 1869-1943 *DcAmB S3,*
NotAW
Regan, Ben 1910-1970 *WhAm 5*
Regan, Frank Stewart 1862-1944 *WhAm 2*
Regan, Frank W d1967 *WhAm 4*
Regan, James Joseph 1905-1974 *WhAm 6*
Regan, James L 1850- *WhAm 1*
Regan, John E 1883-1946 *NatCAB 33*
Regan, Kenneth Mills 1893-1959 *BiDrAC,*
NatCAB 50
Regan, Louis John 1892-1955 *WhAm 3*
Regar, Robert Smith 1882-1955 *WhAm 3*
Regener, Erich Rudolph Alexander 1881-1955
DcScB
Regensburger, Richard William 1899-1957
WhAm 3
Regenstein, Meyer 1869-1946 *NatCAB 35*
Reger, David Bright 1882-1958 *WhAm 3*
Reges, George Henry 1887-1964 *NatCAB 50*
Regiomontanus, Johannes 1436-1476 *AsBiEn,*
DcScB, McGEWB
Register, Edward Chauncey 1860-1920
NatCAB 18, WhAm 1
Register, Francis Henry 1859-1929 *WhAm 1*
Register, George Scott 1901-1972 *WhAm 5*
Register, Henry Bartol d1956 *WhAm 3*
Regnault, Henri Victor 1810-1878 *AsBiEn,*
DcScB
Regnier, Eugene Arthur 1893-1956 *NatCAB 46*
Rehan, Ada 1857-1916 *NotAW*
Rehan, Ada 1859-1916 *AmWom, ApCAB*
Rehan, Ada 1860-1916 *AmBi, DcAmB,*
NatCAB 1, TwCBDA, WebAB, WhAm 1,
WomWWA 14
Rehberger, George Edward 1880- *WhAm 6*
Rehder, Alfred 1863-1949 *WhAm 2*
Reherd, Herbert Ware 1869-1952 *WhAm 3*
Rehm, Theodore A 1901-1974 *WhAm 6*
Rehn, Frank Knox Morton 1848-1914 *AmBi,*
ApCAB, DcAmB, NatCAB 9, TwCBDA,
WhAm 1
Rehn, Isaac *NewYHSD*
Rehn, John *NewYHSD*
Rehn, Michael *NewYHSD*
Rehnquist, William Hubbs 1924- *WebAB*
Rehse, George Washington 1868- *WhAm 4*
Reiber, Aaron Eli 1863-1947 *NatCAB 36*
Reich, Ferdinand 1799-1882 *AsBiEn*
Reich, Jacques 1852-1923 *ApCAB Sup,*
WhAm 1
Reich, Johann Mathias 1768-1833 *NewYHSD,*
WhAm H
Reich, John 1768-1833 *NewYHSD*
Reich, Max Isaac 1867-1945 *WhAm 2*
Reich, Paul Derr 1884-1956 *NatCAB 42*
Reichard, George Nicholas 1834-1884
NatCAB 5
Reichard, Gladys Amanda 1893-1955 *WhAm 3*
Reichard, John Davis 1889-1961 *WhAm 4*
Reichard, Robert Albert 1875-1953 *NatCAB 44*
Reichelt, Ferdinand *NewYHSD*
Reichardt, John *NewYHSD*
Reichardt, Konstantin 1904-1976 *WhAm 6*
Reichart, James Hyter 1885-1950 *NatCAB 38*
Reiche, F *NewYHSD*

Reiche, J F *NewYHSD*
Reichel, Charles Gotthold 1751-1825 *ApCAB,
DcAmB, NatCAB 4, TwCBDA,
WhAm H*
Reichel, Frank Hartranft 1897-1964 *WhAm 4*
Reichel, George Valentine 1863-1914
NatCAB 17
Reichel, Levin Theodore 1812-1878 *ApCAB,
NatCAB 7, TwCBDA*
Reichel, William Cornelius 1824-1876 *ApCAB,
DcAmB, NatCAB 5, NewYHSD,
TwCBDA, WhAm H*
Reichelderfer, Luther 1874-1945 *WhAm 2*
Reichenau, Walter Von 1884-1942 *WhoMilH*
Reichenau, Walther Von 1884-1942 *WhWW-II*
Reichenbach, Georg Friedrich Von 1771-1826
DcScB
Reichenbach, Hans 1891-1953 *DcAmB S5,
DcScB*
Reichenbach, Herman Rudolph 1898-1958
NatCAB 46
Reichenbach, Karl Ludwig 1788-1869 *DcScB*
Reichert, Edward Tyson 1855-1931 *NatCAB 23,
WhAm 1, WhAm 1C*
Reichert, Frederick Leet 1894-1969 *NatCAB 55*
Reichert, Irving Frederick 1895-1968
WhAm 4A
Reichert, Karl Bogislaus 1811-1883 *DcScB*
Reichert, Rudolph Edward 1887-1965 *WhAm 4*
Reichert, Mother Thomas 1868- *WhAm 5*
Reichhelm, Edward Paul 1843- *NatCAB 14*
Reichman, Hyrum Reid 1907-1967 *NatCAB 54*
Reichmann, Alexander Frederick 1868-1948
NatCAB 42
Reichmann, Carl 1859- *WhAm 4*
Reichmann, Donald August 1919-1971 *WhAm 5*
Reichstein, Tadeus 1897- *McGEWB*
Reichstein, Tadeusz 1897- *AsBiEn*
Reick, William Charles 1864-1924 *DcAmB,
WhAm 1*
Reid *NewYHSD*
Reid, Albert Turner 1873-1955 *WhAm 3*
Reid, Alberta Bancroft 1873- *WhAm 5,
WomWWA 14*
Reid, Alexander Hamilton 1864-1938
NatCAB 29
Reid, Cecil Latta 1882-1955 *NatCAB 45*
Reid, Charles Chester 1868-1922 *BiDrAC,
WhAm 4, WhAmP*
Reid, Charles Dwight 1886-1964 *NatCAB 50*
Reid, Charles Hamilton 1891-1954 *NatCAB 43*
Reid, Charles Martin 1882- *WhoColR*
Reid, Charles Simpson 1897-1947 *NatCAB 37,
WhAm 2*
Reid, Charles Wesley 1843- *WhAm 4*
Reid, Charlotte Thompson 1913- *BiDrAC*
Reid, Christian *DcAmB, NotAW*
Reid, Daniel Gray 1858-1925 *NatCAB 19,
WhAm 1*
Reid, David Boswell 1805-1863 *ApCAB,
DcAmB, Drake, WhAm H*
Reid, David Settle 1813-1891 *ApCAB, BiAUS,
BiDrAC, DcAmB, Drake, NatCAB 4,
TwCBDA, WhAm H, WhAmP*
Reid, Delafayette 1915-1970 *WhAm 5*
Reid, Duncan Earl 1905-1973 *WhAm 6*
Reid, E C 1900-1958 *WhAm 3*
Reid, E Emmet 1872-1973 *WhAm 6*
Reid, Edward Snover 1871-1925 *NatCAB 32*
Reid, Elisabeth Mills 1858-1931 *NatCAB 22,
NotAW*
Reid, Eliza Anna 1842- *WomWWA 14*
Reid, Elliott Gray 1900-1968 *WhAm 5*
Reid, Ernest Alexander 1888-1965 *NatCAB 52*
Reid, Ernest Welcome 1891-1966 *WhAm 4*
Reid, Ernest Welcome 1897-1966 *NatCAB 51*
Reid, Eva Charlotte *WomWWA 14*
Reid, Fergus 1862-1941 *NatCAB 35,
WhAm 2*
Reid, Frank R 1879-1945 *BiDrAC, WhAm 2,
WhAmP*
Reid, Frank R 1910-1962 *NatCAB 48*
Reid, Frederick Horman 1880-1943 *WhAm 2*
Reid, George 1733-1815 *ApCAB, Drake*
Reid, George Croghan 1840-1914 *WhAm 1*
Reid, George T 1871-1927 *WhAm 1*
Reid, Gilbert 1857-1927 *DcAmB, WhAm 1*
Reid, Harry Fielding 1859-1944 *DcScB,*

NatCAB 33, WhAm 2
Reid, Harry Maurrelle 1853- *NatCAB 7*
Reid, Helen Dwight 1901-1965 *NatCAB 51,
WhAm 4*
Reid, Helen Rogers 1882-1970 *BiCAW,
NatCAB 56, WhAm 5, WomWWA 14*
Reid, Henry John Edward 1895-1968 *WhAm 5*
Reid, Hugh Thompson 1811-1874 *ApCAB*
Reid, Hugo 1810-1852 *REnAW*
Reid, Ira DeAugustine 1901-1968 *BiDAmEd,
WhAm 5*
Reid, J J *NewYHSD*
Reid, James *NatCAB 6*
Reid, James L 1844-1910 *AmBi, DcAmB,
EncAAH, WhAm HA, WhAm 4*
Reid, James Randolph 1718- *WhAm H*
Reid, James Randolph 1750-1789 *BiDrAC*
Reid, James Wesley 1849-1902 *BiDrAC*
Reid, James William 1851-1943 *NatCAB 32*
Reid, Jessie 1861- *WomWWA 14*
Reid, John *NewYHSD*
Reid, John 1722-1807 *ApCAB, Drake*
Reid, John 1832?- *NewYHSD*
Reid, John 1840-1916 *NatCAB 22*
Reid, John 1875-1948 *NatCAB 36*
Reid, John, Jr. 1879- *WhAm 6*
Reid, John Joseph 1887-1953 *NatCAB 41*
Reid, John Morrison 1820-1896 *ApCAB,
DcAmB, NatCAB 13, TwCBDA,
WhAm H*
Reid, John Simpson 1856- *WhAm 4*
Reid, John William 1821-1881 *BiAUS,
BiDrAC, WhAm H*
Reid, Julia 1846- *WomWWA 14*
Reid, Kenneth 1893-1960 *NatCAB 50,
WhAm 4*
Reid, Kenneth Alexander 1895-1956 *WhAm 3*
Reid, Leonard Corrigan 1887-1953 *NatCAB 42*
Reid, Loudon Corsan 1893-1969 *WhAm 5*
Reid, Mary Elizabeth *WomWWA 14*
Reid, Mary Hiester *WomWWA 14*
Reid, Mary Thompson 1871- *WomWWA 14*
Reid, Mayne 1818-1883 *ApCAB, DcAmB,
Drake*
Reid, Mont Rogers 1889-1943 *DcAmB S3,
NatCAB 34, WhAm 2*
Reid, O L 1875- *WhAm 5*
Reid, Ogden Mills 1882-1947 *DcAmB S4,
NatCAB 33, WebAB, WhAm 2*
Reid, Ogden Rogers 1925- *BiDrAC*
Reid, Orleanis 1875- *WhoColR*
Reid, Philip Joseph 1865-1930 *WhAm 1*
Reid, Richard 1896-1961 *WhAm 4*
Reid, Robert 1862-1929 *AmBi, BnEnAmA,
DcAmB, IIBEAAW, WhAm 1*
Reid, Robert 1863-1929 *NatCAB 6*
Reid, Robert Haley 1906-1972 *WhAm 5*
Reid, Robert Raymond 1789-1841 *ApCAB,
BiDrAC, Drake, NatCAB 11, REnAW,
TwCBDA, WhAm H*
Reid, Robert Raymond 1789-1844 *BiAUS*
Reid, Sam Chester 1818-1897 *ApCAB,
TwCBDA*
Reid, Samuel Chester 1783-1861 *AmBi,
ApCAB, DcAmB, Drake, NatCAB 8,
TwCBDA, WebAMB, WhAm H*
Reid, Silas Hinkle 1870- *WhAm 3*
Reid, Sydney 1857- *WhAm 4*
Reid, T Roy 1889-1969 *WhAm 5*
Reid, Thomas 1710-1796 *McGEWB*
Reid, Thomas Mayne 1818-1883 *DcAmB,
WhAm H*
Reid, Thorburn 1864-1933 *WhAm 3*
Reid, Walter Williamson 1881-1960 *WhAm 3*
Reid, Mrs. Whitelaw *NotAW*
Reid, Whitelaw 1837-1912 *AmBi, ApCAB,
ApCAB X, DcAmB, Drake, EncAB,
NatCAB 3, NatCAB 22, TwCBDA,
WebAB, WhAm 1*
Reid, Will J 1889-1956 *WhAm 3*
Reid, Willard Placide 1862-1925 *NatCAB 20*
Reid, Sir William 1791-1858 *ApCAB*
Reid, William 1816- *ApCAB*
Reid, William 1886-1965 *WhAm 4*
Reid, William Alfred 1871-1954 *NatCAB 42,
WhAm 5*
Reid, William Clifford 1868-1941 *NatCAB 31,
WhAm 2*

Reid, William Duncan 1885-1949 *WhAm 2*
Reid, William James 1834-1902 *ApCAB,
NatCAB 6, WhAm 1*
Reid, William James, Jr. 1871-1943 *WhAm 2*
Reid, William Max 1839-1911 *WhAm 1*
Reid, William R d1950 *WhAm 3*
Reid, William Shields 1778-1853 *DcAmB,
NatCAB 2, WhAm H*
Reid, William Shields *see also* Reed, William
Shields
Reid, William Thomas 1842- *NatCAB 2*
Reid, William Thomas 1843- *TwCBDA,
WhAm 4*
Reid, William Wallace 1891-1923 *ApCAB X*
Reid, William Wharry 1799-1866 *DcAmB*
Reidemeister, Kurt Werner Friedrich 1893-1971
DcScB
Reider, Edith Shope *WomWWA 14*
Reider, Frank R 1879-1957 *NatCAB 47*
Reidy, Ben Thomas 1895-1963 *NatCAB 51*
Reidy, Daniel Joseph 1884-1967 *WhAm 4*
Reidy, E T 1903-1975 *WhAm 6*
Reidy, Peter Joseph 1900-1971 *NatCAB 56,
WhAm 5*
Reiersen, Johan Reinert 1810-1864 *DcAmB*
Reiersen, Johan Reinhart 1810-1864 *WhAm H*
Reif, Edward Clarence 1888-1961 *NatCAB 49,
WhAm 4*
Reif, Ernest Carl 1908-1956 *NatCAB 46*
Reif, Herbert R 1898-1971 *WhAm 5*
Reifel, Benjamin 1906- *BiDrAC, REnAW*
Reifenstein, Edward Conrad 1880- *WhAm 6*
Reifenstein, Edward Conrad, Jr. 1908-1975
WhAm 6
Reiff, Cecil K 1888-1952 *WhAm 3*
Reiff, Evan Allard 1907-1962 *WhAm 4*
Reiffel, Charles 1862-1942 *IIBEAAW,
WhAm 2*
Reifsnider, Anna Cyrene Ellis 1850-1932
NatCAB 23
Reifsnider, Calvin Kryder 1847-1924
NatCAB 26
Reifsnider, Charles Shriver 1875-1958 *WhAm 3*
Reifsnider, Lawrence Fairfax 1887-1956
NatCAB 42, WhAm 3
Reifsnyder, Howard 1869-1929 *NatCAB 25*
Reigart, Henry *NewYHSD*
Reigart, John Franklin 1863-1946 *NatCAB 34*
Reiger, John Franklin 1943- *EncAAH*
Reiger, Siegfried Heinrich 1920-1970 *WhAm 5*
Reighard, Jacob Ellsworth 1861-1942
NatCAB 16, WhAm 5
Reighley, Lyster Cooper 1891-1956 *NatCAB 49*
Reignolds, Catherine Mary 1836-1911 *NotAW*
Reignolds, Catherine May 1837-1911 *BiCAW*
Reihl, Charles Wesley 1867-1948 *NatCAB 37*
Reik, Henry Ottridge 1868-1938 *WhAm 1*
Reik, Theodor 1888-1969 *WhAm 5*
Reil, Johann Christian 1759-1813 *DcScB*
Reiland, Karl 1871- *WhAm 5*
Reiley, Henry Baker 1875-1962 *NatCAB 48*
Reiley, Isaac Henry 1843- *NatCAB 1*
Reiley, John Arndt 1816-1878 *ApCAB Sup*
Reiley, Katharine Campbell 1873-
WomWWA 14
Reiley, Mary Trimble 1858-1878 *ApCAB Sup*
Reilley, Florence Jones 1875- *WomWWA 14*
Reilley, Mrs. J Eugene 1861-1941 *WhAm 1*
Reilley, Laura Holmes 1861-1941
WomWWA 14
Reilly, Charles Gilbert 1888-1918 *ApCAB X*
Reilly, Edgar Austin 1900-1952 *NatCAB 39*
Reilly, Edward Joseph 1905-1953 *NatCAB 44*
Reilly, Frank Joseph 1906-1967 *WhAm 4*
Reilly, Frank Kennicott 1863-1932 *WhAm 1*
Reilly, Henry Joseph 1881-1963 *WhAm 4*
Reilly, James Aloysius 1904-1953 *WhAm 3*
Reilly, James Bernard 1845-1924 *BiAUS,
BiDrAC, TwCBDA*
Reilly, James W 1842?- *ApCAB*
Reilly, James William 1828- *TwCBDA*
Reilly, James William 1839-1910 *WhAm 1*
Reilly, John 1836-1904 *BiAUS, BiDrAC*
Reilly, John Chrysostom 1845-1907 *ApCAB X*
Reilly, John David 1868-1971 *WhAm 5*
Reilly, John Liguori 1853-1945 *WhAm 2*
Reilly, Joseph F 1906-1974 *WhAm 6*
Reilly, Joseph John 1881-1951 *WhAm 3*

Reilly, Marion 1879-1928 *DcAmB*,
NatCAB 26
Reilly, Maurice Thomas 1900-1962 *NatCAB 47*,
WhAm 4
Reilly, Michael Kieran 1869-1944 *BiDrAC*,
NatCAB 34, *WhAmP*
Reilly, Michael Kiernan 1869-1944 *WhAm 2*
Reilly, Peter C 1869-1952 *WhAm 3*
Reilly, Thomas Daniel 1927-1974 *WhAm 6*
Reilly, Thomas Lawrence 1858-1924 *BiDrAC*,
WhAm 4
Reilly, Thomas Peter 1884-1965 *NatCAB 54*
Reilly, Walter Benedict 1888-1961 *NatCAB 49*,
WhAm 4
Reilly, William John 1899-1970 *WhAm 5*
Reilly, William Robison 1884-1957 *NatCAB 50*
Reilly, Wilson 1811-1885 *BiAUS*, *BiDrAC*,
WhAm H
Reily, E Mont d1954 *WhAm 3*
Reily, George W 1870-1954 *WhAm 3*
Reily, James 1811-1863 *TwCBDA*
Reily, John 1752-1810 *ApCAB*
Reily, Joseph *NewYHSD*
Reily, Luther 1794-1854 *BiAUS*, *BiDrAC*,
WhAm H
Reily, William McClellan 1837- *ApCAB*
Reim, Hugo 1883-1953 *NatCAB 44*
Reimann, Stanley Philip 1891-1968 *NatCAB 54*,
WhAm 4A
Reimensnyder, Junius Benjamin 1841- *ApCAB*
Reimer, Marie *WhAm 5*, *WomWWA 14*
Reimer, Rudolph 1875-1948 *NatCAB 36*
Reimers, Frederick W 1877-1958 *WhAm 3*
Reimert, William Daniel 1902-1969 *NatCAB 55*
Reimert, William Daniel 1902-1971 *WhAm 5*
Reimold, Orlando Schairer 1873-1962 *WhAm 4*
Rein, Charles Robert 1904-1957 *NatCAB 46*
Reina Maldonado, Pedro d1661 *ApCAB*
Reinagle, Alexander 1756-1809 *DcAmB*, *Drake*,
WhAm H
Reinagle, Hugh 1788?-1834 *NewYHSD*
Reinagle, Hugh 1790?-1834 *ApCAB*
Reinagle, T *NewYHSD*
Reinberger, Joseph A *NewYHSD*
Reindahl, Knute 1858- *WhAm 1*
Reinecke, Edwin 1924- *BiDrAC*
Reineke, George Ferdinand 1871-1957
NatCAB 46
Reiner, Fritz 1888-1963 *WhAm 4*
Reiner, Harry Chauncey 1869-1940 *NatCAB 34*
Reiner, Joseph 1881-1934 *WhAm 1*
Reinertsen, Emma May Alexander 1853-
AmWom
Reines, Frederick 1918- *AsBiEn*
Reinhard, Adolph Earl 1895-1968 *WhAm 5*
Reinhard, L Andrew 1891-1964 *WhAm 4*
Reinhardt, Ad 1913-1967 *BnEnAmA*,
WhAm 4
Reinhardt, Aurelia Isabel Henry 1877-1948
BiDAmEd, *DcAmB S4*, *NotAW*, *WhAm 2*,
WomWWA 14
Reinhardt, Berna Lapham 1885- *WomWWA 14*
Reinhardt, Charles William 1858- *WhAm 4*
Reinhardt, Django 1910-1953 *WhAm 4A*
Reinhardt, Emil Fred 1888-1969 *WhAm 5*
Reinhardt, Emma d1973 *WhAm 6*
Reinhardt, G Frederick 1911-1971 *WhAm 5*
Reinhardt, George Frederick 1869-1914
NatCAB 15, *WhAm 1*
Reinhardt, Guenther 1904-1968 *WhAm 5*
Reinhardt, Gustav Adolph 1881- *WhAm 6*
Reinhardt, James Melvin 1894-1974 *WhAm 6*
Reinhardt, Max 1873-1943 *WhAm 2*
Reinhardt, Paul 1888-1945 *NatCAB 33*
Reinhardt, Ralph Homer 1907-1968 *WhAm 5*
Reinhart, Albert Grantley 1854-1926
NatCAB 20
Reinhart, Benjamin Franklin 1829-1885 *ApCAB*,
DcAmB, *IIBEAAW*, *NatCAB 11*,
NewYHSD, *TwCBDA*, *WhAm H*
Reinhart, Charles Stanley 1844-1896 *AmBi*,
ApCAB, *DcAmB*, *NatCAB 7*, *TwCBDA*,
WhAm H
Reinhart, Earl F 1898-1949 *WhAm 3*
Reinhart, Joseph W 1851-1911 *NatCAB 6*,
WhAm 1
Reinhaus, Stanley Marx 1889-1956 *WhAm 3*

Reinheimer, Bartel Hilen 1889-1949
NatCAB 40, *WhAm 2*
Reinheimer, Howard Emanuel 1899-1970
NatCAB 54
Reinhold, Caspar *NewYHSD*
Reinhold, Eli Spayd 1847-1928 *WhAm 1*
Reinhold, Erasmus 1511-1553 *AsBiEn*, *DcScB*
Reinhold, James P 1905-1961 *WhAm 4*
Reinhold, Rudolph *NewYHSD*
Reinholdt, Julius William 1869- *WhAm 1*
Reinholdt, Julius William 1890-1958 *WhAm 4*
Reinicke, Frederick George 1888-1969 *WhAm 5*
Reinke, Amadeus Abraham 1822-1889 *ApCAB*,
NatCAB 7, *NewYHSD*, *TwCBDA*
Reinke, Edwin Eustace 1887-1945 *WhAm 2*
Reinke, Jonathan 1860-1928 *NatCAB 22*
Reinke, Samuel 1790?- *NewYHSD*
Reinke, Samuel 1791-1875 *ApCAB*,
NatCAB 7, *TwCBDA*
Reinking, Otto August 1890-1962 *NatCAB 46*,
WhAm 4
Reinsch, Paul Samuel 1869-1923 *DcAmB*,
NatCAB 19
Reinsch, Paul Samuel 1870-1923 *WhAm 1*
Re'is *DcScB*
Reis, Arthur M 1883-1947 *WhAm 2*
Reis, Francisco Sotero Dos 1800-1871 *ApCAB*
Reis, Robert 1850-1918 *ApCAB X*
Reiser, Armand Edouard 1924-1968 *WhAm 5*
Reiser, Oliver Leslie 1895-1974 *WhAm 6*
Reisinger, Blanche Genevieve 1877-
WomWWA 14
Reisinger, Curt H 1891-1964 *WhAm 4*
Reisinger, Harold Carusi 1876-1945 *WhAm 2*
Reisinger, Hugo 1856-1914 *DcAmB*,
NatCAB 14, *NatCAB 16*, *WhAm 1*
Reisinger, Robert Louis 1889-1947 *NatCAB 39*
Reisman, Morton 1907-1967 *WhAm 5*
Reisner, Christian Fichthorne 1872-1940
NatCAB 37, *WhAm 1*
Reisner, Edward Hartman 1885-1958
NatCAB 47, *WhAm 3*
Reisner, George Andrew 1867-1942 *ApCAB X*,
DcAmB S3, *WhAm 2*
Reisner, Martin A *NewYHSD*
Reiss, Elias 1869-1958 *NatCAB 44*
Reiss, Fritz Winold 1888?-1953 *IIBEAAW*
Reiss, Jacob Lawrence 1873-1955 *NatCAB 43*,
WhAm 3
Reiss, Julian Jacob 1899-1959 *NatCAB 50*
Reiss, William Anthony 1884-1959 *NatCAB 48*
Reissner, Albert 1883-1970 *WhAm 5*
Reissner, Martin A *NewYHSD*
Reist, Henry Gerber 1862-1942 *NatCAB 31*,
WhAm 2
Reiter, Bernard L d1968 *WhAm 5*
Reiter, George Cook d1930 *WhAm 1*
Reiter, Hans 1881-1969 *BiHiMed*
Reith, Francis C 1914-1960 *WhAm 4*
Reitinger, T Philip 1895-1957 *NatCAB 46*
Reitler, Joseph 1883-1948 *NatCAB 36*
Reitman, Joseph *NewYHSD*
Reitz, John Augustus 1815-1891 *NatCAB 34*
Reitz, Walter R 1885-1957 *WhAm 3*
Reitze, Chester Nelson 1883-1956 *NatCAB 45*
Reitzel, Albert Emmet d1960 *WhAm 4*
Reitzel, Marques E 1896-1963 *WhAm 4*
Reitzel, Robert 1849-1898 *DcAmB*, *WhAm H*
Reizenstein, Elmer *WebAB*
Relf, Henry Clark 1898-1959 *NatCAB 47*
Relf, Richard 1892-1956 *NatCAB 47*
Relf, Samuel 1776-1823 *ApCAB*
Relfe, James Hugh 1791-1863 *BiAUS*, *BiDrAC*,
WhAm H
Relin, Bernard 1914-1974 *WhAm 6*
Reller, Charles J 1904-1961 *WhAm 4*
Rellstab, John 1858-1930 *DcAmB*, *NatCAB 8*,
WhAm H
Relyea, Charles M 1863- *WhAm 4*
Relyea, Eleanor Wood 1872- *WomWWA 14*
Relyea, Richard Jacqmein, II 1909-1970
NatCAB 56
Remak, Gustavus, Jr. 1861-1944 *NatCAB 33*,
WhAm 2
Remak, Robert 1815-1865 *AsBiEn*, *BiHiMed*,
DcScB
Remann, Frederick 1847-1895 *BiDrAC*,
WhAm H

Remarque, Erich Maria 1898-1970 *McGEWB*,
WhAm 5
Rembaugh, Bertha 1876-1950 *WhAm 3*,
WomWWA 14
Rembert, Arthur Gaillard 1860- *WhAm 4*
Rembert, George William Francis 1879-
WhAm 6
Rembrandt Harmensz VanRijn 1606-1669
McGEWB
Remecke, Adolphe *NewYHSD*
Remeneye, Edward *NewYHSD*
Remensnyder, Junius Benjamin 1843-1927
NatCAB 10, *WhAm 1*
Remenyi, Joseph 1892-1956 *WhAm 3*
Remer, Charles Frederick 1889-1972 *WhAm 5*
Remer, Helen *WhAm 1*
Remesal, Antonio De 1570-1639 *ApCAB*
Remey, Charles Mason 1874- *WhAm 6*
Remey, George Collier 1841-1928 *ApCAB Sup*,
DcAmB, *NatCAB 10*, *TwCBDA*,
WebAMB, *WhAm 1*
Remick, Christian 1726- *NewYHSD*
Remick, Christine L 1882- *WomWWA 14*
Remick, Eliot Wickham 1876-1953 *NatCAB 40*
Remick, Grace May *WhAm 5*
Remick, J Gould 1897-1962 *WhAm 4*
Remick, James Waldron 1860-1943 *WhAm 2*
Remick, Jerome Homer 1868-1931 *NatCAB 22*
Remington, Carl 1880-1919 *ApCAB X*
Remington, Eliphalet 1793-1861 *AmBi*,
DcAmB, *NatCAB 9*, *TwCBDA*, *WebAB*,
WhAm H
Remington, Elizabeth 1825-1917 *NewYHSD*
Remington, Elizabeth Thompson 1883-
WomWWA 14
Remington, Franklin 1865-1955 *NatCAB 16*,
WhAm 3
Remington, Frederic 1831- *NatCAB 7*
Remington, Frederic 1861-1909 *AmBi*,
ApCAB X, *DcAmB*, *EncAAH*, *EncAB*,
IIBEAAW, *McGEWB*, *NatCAB 22*,
REnAW, *WebAB*, *WhAm 1*
Remington, Frederick 1861-1909 *BnEnAmA*,
TwCBDA
Remington, Harold 1865-1937 *NatCAB 29*,
WhAm 1
Remington, Harvey Foote 1863- *WhAm 2*
Remington, Joseph Price 1847-1918 *ApCAB*,
DcAmB, *NatCAB 5*, *NatCAB 33*,
WhAm 1
Remington, Mary E 1859- *WomWWA 14*
Remington, Philo 1816-1889 *AmBi*, *ApCAB*,
DcAmB, *NatCAB 9*, *WebAB*, *WhAm H*
Remington, Preston 1897-1958 *WhAm 3*
Remington, S J *IIBEAAW*
Remington, Stephen 1803-1869 *ApCAB*
Remington, William Procter 1879-1963
NatCAB 50, *WhAm 4*
Remington, William Walter 1917-1954
DcAmB S5
Remley, Mary Ellen Warren 1868-
WomWWA 14
Remley, Milton 1844-1929 *NatCAB 16*,
WhAm 1
Remmel, Arthur Kizer 1886-1941 *NatCAB 32*,
WhAm 1
Remmel, Ellen Cates 1888-1961 *WhAm 4*
Remmel, Harmon Liveright 1852-1927
NatCAB 8, *WhAm 1*
Remmel, Valentine 1853- *WhAm 4*
Remmey, Charles H *NewYHSD*
Remon, Cantera Alejandro 1912-1973 *WhAm 6*
Remon Cantera, Jose Antonio 1908-1955
WhAm 3
Remond, Charles Lennox 1810-1873 *McGEWB*
Remond, Charles Lenox 1810-1873 *DcAmB*,
NatCAB 2, *WhAm H*
Remond, Sarah Parker 1826-1887? *NotAW*
Remondino, Peter Charles 1846-1926
NatCAB 14, *NatCAB 42*, *WhAm 1*
Remouit, L *NewYHSD*
Remsburg, John Eleazer 1848-1919 *ApCAB Sup*,
WhAm 1
Remsen, Charles 1856-1921 *NatCAB 41*
Remsen, Daniel Smith 1853-1935 *WhAm 1*
Remsen, Ira 1846-1927 *AmBi*, *ApCAB*,
BiDAmEd, *DcAmB*, *DcScB*, *NatCAB 9*,
NatCAB 37, *TwCBDA*, *WebAB*,

WhAm 1

Remsen, Richard 1821-1914 *NatCAB 16*
Remster, Charles 1862-1937 *WhAm 1*
Remus, Peter *NewYHSD*
Remy, Alfred 1870-1937 *NatCAB 44,
WhAm 1*
Remy, Arthur Frank Joseph 1871-1954
NatCAB 44
Remy, Charles Frederick 1860- *WhAm 5*
Remy, Egbertina 1880-1956 *NatCAB 44*
Remy, Henri 1811-1867 *DcAmB, WhAm H*
Remy, Jules 1826- *ApCAB*
Remy, Paul Edouard 1711-1784 *ApCAB*
Remy, William Henderson 1892-1968
NatCAB 54
Renahan, John Alfred 1865-1923 *NatCAB 21*
Renan, Ernest 1823-1892 *McGEWB*
Renard, Alphonse Francois 1842-1903 *DcScB*
Renard, Gustave Henri 1673-1741 *ApCAB*
Renaud *NewYHSD*
Renaud, Etlenne Bernardeau 1880- *WhAm 6*
Renaud, George Louis 1870-1949 *NatCAB 37*
Renaud, Pierre Francois 1641-1703 *ApCAB*
Renaud, Ralph Edward 1881-1948 *WhAm 2*
Renauld, Cesar Auguste 1701-1734 *ApCAB*
Renault, Antoine *NewYHSD*
Renault, Bernard 1836-1904 *DcScB*
Renault, John Francis *NewYHSD*
Renault, Philip Francois d1744? *ApCAB*
Renaut, Joseph-Louis 1844-1917 *DcScB*
Rencher, Abraham 1798-1883 *BiAUS, BiDrAC,
NatCAB 12, TwCBDA, WhAm H,
WhAmP*
Rend, Joseph Paul 1870-1935 *NatCAB 26*
Rend, William Patrick 1840-1915 *WhAm 1*
Rendall, Isabella Pratt 1857- *WomWWA 14*
Rendall, John Ballard 1847-1924 *WhAm 1*
Rendall, Raymond Eaton 1892-1949
NatCAB 38
Render, Mayme Ellen 1871- *WomWWA 14*
Rendleman, John Samuel 1927-1976 *WhAm 6*
Rendu, Henri 1844-1902 *BiHiMed*
Renevier, Eugene 1831-1906 *DcScB*
Renfrew, Carrie *AmWom*
Renfro, Harold Bell 1915-1972 *WhAm 6*
Renfrow, William Cary 1845-1922 *TwCBDA,
WhAm 1*
Rengino, Luis 1520?-1580? *ApCAB*
Reni, Guido 1575-1642 *McGEWB*
Renick, Felix 1770-1848 *DcAmB, WhAm H*
Renier, Joseph Emile d1966 *WhAm 4*
Reniers, Peter *NewYHSD*
Renison, Robert John 1875-1957 *WhAm 3*
Renker, Henry Gilbert 1881-1947 *NatCAB 36*
Renkert, Oliver William 1878-1937 *NatCAB 32*
Rennay, Leon 1878- *WhAm 6*
Renne, Roland Roger 1905- *REnAW*
Rennebohm, Oscar 1889-1968 *WhAm 5*
Rennell, James 1742-1830 *DcScB*
Rennelson, Clara H 1845- *WhAm 4,
WomWWA 14*
Rennenkampf, Paul Karlovich Von 1853-1918
WhoMilH
Renner, Frederic G 1897- *REnAW*
Renner, George Thomas, Jr. 1900-1955
BiDAmEd, NatCAB 45, WhAm 3
Renner, Karl 1870-1950 *McGEWB, WhAm 3*
Renner, Otto 1883-1960 *WhAm 4*
Rennert, Hugo Albert 1858-1927 *NatCAB 22,
WhAm 1*
Rennie, Joseph 1860-1943 *WhAm 2*
Rennie, Sylvester Wilding 1903-1971 *WhAm 5*
Rennie, Thomas Alexander Cumming 1904-1956
NatCAB 49, WhAm 3
Reno, Claude Trexler 1882-1961 *WhAm 4*
Reno, Conrad 1859-1933 *TwCBDA, WhAm 1*
Reno, Doris Smith 1907-1973 *WhAm 5*
Reno, Guy Benjamin 1892-1972 *WhAm 5*
Reno, Itti Kinney 1862- *AmWom, WhAm 4,
WomWWA 14*
Reno, Jesse Lee 1823-1862 *AmBi, ApCAB,
DcAmB, Drake, NatCAB 4, TwCBDA,
WebAMB, WhAm H*
Reno, Jesse Wilford 1861-1947 *NatCAB 38,
WhAm 4*
Reno, Marcus Albert d1889 *REnAW*
Reno, Marcus Albert 1834-1889 *NatCAB 4,
WebAMB*

Reno, Marcus Albert 1835-1889 *ApCAB*
Reno, Milo 1866-1936 *DcAmB S2, EncAAH*
Renoir, Alexander *NewYHSD*
Renoir, Pierre Auguste 1841-1919 *McGEWB*
Renouf, Mae Page 1875- *WomWWA 14*
Renouf Edward 1846- *WhAm 1*
Renouvin, Pierre Eugene Georges 1893-1974
WhAm 6
Renshaw, Alfred 1891-1953 *NatCAB 40*
Renshaw, Alfred Howard 1861-1939 *ApCAB X,
WhAm 1*
Renshaw, Henry 1845-1928 *NatCAB 21*
Renshaw, James 1784-1846 *Drake*
Renshaw, Raemer Rex 1880-1938 *WhAm 1*
Renshaw, Richard T 1821- *Drake*
Renshaw, William Bainbridge 1815?-1863 *Drake*
Renshaw, William Bainbridge 1816-1863
ApCAB, NatCAB 12
Rentfro, Robert Byron 1874-1953 *NatCAB 41*
Rentner, Maurice 1889-1958 *NatCAB 57*
Renton, David Malcolm 1878-1947 *NatCAB 41*
Renton, Herbert Stanley 1854-1939 *NatCAB 29*
Rentschler, Calvin Balthaser 1897-1973
WhAm 6
Rentschler, Frederic Brant 1877-1956
NatCAB 45
Rentschler, Frederick Brant 1887-1956
WhAm 3
Rentschler, George Adam 1892-1972
NatCAB 57, WhAm 5
Rentschler, Gordon Sohn 1885-1948
NatCAB 38, WhAm 2
Rentschler, Harvey Clayton 1881-1949
WhAm 2
Renwick, Edward Anderson 1860- *NatCAB 18*
Renwick, Edward Sabine 1823-1912 *ApCAB,
DcAmB, NatCAB 11, TwCBDA,
WhAm 1*
Renwick, Henry Brevoort 1817-1895 *ApCAB,
DcAmB, NatCAB 11, TwCBDA,
WhAm H*
Renwick, James 1790-1862 *NatCAB 11*
Renwick, James 1790-1863 *ApCAB, TwCBDA*
Renwick, James 1792-1863 *DcAmB, Drake,
NewYHSD, WhAm H*
Renwick, James 1818-1895 *AmBi, ApCAB,
BnEnAmA, DcAmB, McGEWB,
NatCAB 11, TwCBDA, WebAB,
WhAm H*
Renwick, Jean 1773-1850 *ApCAB Sup*
Renwick, Pamela Helen Goodwin 1845-
WomWWA 14
Renwick, Ward James 1873-1961 *NatCAB 47*
Renwick, William Whetten 1864-1933 *WhAm 1*
Renyx, Guy Worden 1868-1956 *WhAm 3*
Renz, Carl Julius 1839-1921 *NatCAB 19*
Reoch, Robert 1840-1918 *NatCAB 36*
Repass, Joseph Wharton 1861-1919 *WhAm 1*
Repass, William Carlyle 1896-1945 *WhAm 2*
Replogle, Jacob Leonard 1876-1948 *NatCAB 16,
WhAm 2*
Reppert, Charles Miller 1880-1939 *NatCAB 30*
Repplier, Agnes 1855-1950 *ApCAB Sup,
DcAmB S4, NotAW, WhAm 3*
Repplier, Agnes 1858-1950 *WomWWA 14*
Repplier, Agnes 1859-1950 *NatCAB 9,
TwCBDA*
Reppy, Alison 1893-1958 *WhAm 3*
Reppy, Roy Valentine 1878-1943 *WhAm 2*
Repsold, Adolf 1806-1871 *DcScB*
Repsold, Johann Adolf 1838-1919 *DcScB*
Repsold, Johann Georg 1770-1830 *DcScB*
Requa, Earl Francis 1904-1970 *WhAm 5*
Requa, Isaac Lawrence 1828-1905 *NatCAB 6*
Requa, Mark Lawrence 1865-1937 *DcAmB S2,
NatCAB 27*
Requa, Mark Lawrence 1866-1937 *WhAm 1*
Requesens, Luis DeZuniga Y 1528-1576
WhoMilH
Requier, Augustus Julian 1825-1887 *ApCAB,
DcAmB, Drake, WhAm H*
Resa, Alexander John 1887-1964 *BiDrAC*
Rese, Frederick 1791-1871 *DcAmB,
NatCAB 13, WhAm H*
Resnick, Joseph Yale 1924-1969 *BiDrAC,
WhAm 5*
Resnick, Milton 1917- *BnEnAmA*
Resor, Stanley Burnet 1879-1962 *NatCAB 53,*

WhAm 4
Respighi, Lorenzo 1824-1889 *DcScB*
Respighi, Ottorino 1879-1936 *McGEWB*
Resseguie, Frederic John 1874-1956 *NatCAB 50*
Resser, Charles Elmer 1889-1943 *NatCAB 32*
Ressler, Edwin DeVore 1869-1926 *WhAm 1*
Restarick, Henry Bond 1854-1933 *DcAmB S1,
NatCAB 13, TwCBDA, WhAm 1*
Restein, Edmund B 1837-1891 *NewYHSD*
Restein, Edmund P 1837-1891 *NewYHSD*
Restein, Ludwig 1838?- *NewYHSD*
Restell, Madame *NotAW*
Reston, James Barrett 1909- *WebAB*
Restrepo, Jose Manuel 1780-1860? *ApCAB*
Rethers, Harry Frederick 1870-1941
NatCAB 30, WhAm 1
Reti-Forbes, Jean 1911-1972 *WhAm 6*
Retief, Pieter 1780-1838 *McGEWB*
Rettger, Leo Frederick 1874-1954 *NatCAB 42,
WhAm 5*
Rettig, H Earl 1903-1969 *WhAm 5*
Rettig, John 1860?-1932 *IIBEAAW*
Retzius, Anders Adolf 1796-1860 *AsBiEn,
BiHiMed, DcScB*
Retzius, Magnus Gustaf 1842-1919 *BiHiMed,
DcScB*
Retzsch, Frederick August Moritz 1779-1857
NewYHSD
Reu, Johann Michael 1869-1943 *WhAm 2*
Reuben, Odell Richardson 1918-1970 *WhAm 5*
Reuben, Robert Ervin 1918-1964 *WhAm 4*
Reuchlin, Johann 1455-1522 *McGEWB*
Reul, Matilda E 1857- *WomWWA 14*
Reuleaux, Franz 1829-1905 *DcScB*
Reuling, George 1839-1915 *ApCAB, DcAmB,
NatCAB 34, WhAm 1*
Reuss, August Emanuel 1811-1873 *DcScB*
Reuss, Franz Ambrosius 1761-1830 *DcScB*
Reuss, Henry Schoellkopf 1912- *BiDrAC*
Reussner, Robert *NewYHSD*
Reusswig, William 1902- *IIBEAAW*
Reuter, Dominic 1856-1933 *DcAmB*
Reuter, Edward Byron 1880-1946 *NatCAB 36*
Reuter, Edward Byron 1882-1946 *WhAm 2*
Reuter, Irving Jacob 1885-1972 *WhAm 5*
Reuter, Rudolph Ernst d1973 *WhAm 5*
Reuterdahl, Arvid 1876-1933 *WhAm 1*
Reuterdahl, Henry 1871-1925 *AmBi,
ApCAB X, DcAmB, WhAm 1*
Reuther, Walter Philip 1907-1970 *EncAB,
McGEWB, WebAB, WhAm 5*
Reutlinger, Harry F d1962 *WhAm 4*
Revel, Bernard 1885-1940 *BiDAmEd,
DcAmB S2, WhAm 1*
Reveley, Ellen G 1840- *WomWWA 14*
Reveley, Ida Louise 1870- *WomWWA 14*
Revell, Alexander Hamilton 1858-1931
NatCAB 1, WhAm 1
Revell, Fleming H, Jr. 1882- *WhAm 5*
Revell, Fleming Hewitt 1849-1931 *DcAmB,
NatCAB 26, WhAm 1*
Revelle, Thomas P 1868-1937 *WhAm 1*
Revels, Hiram R 1822-1901 *ApCAB, BiAUS,
NatCAB 11, TwCBDA*
Revels, Hiram Rhoades 1822-1901 *BiDAmEd,
DcAmB, McGEWB, WebAB, WhAm H*
Revels, Hiram Rhodes 1827-1901 *BiDrAC,
WhAmP*
Revercomb, William Chapman 1895- *BiDrAC*
Revercomb, William McMath 1880-1957
NatCAB 46
Revere, C H *NewYHSD*
Revere, Clinton T 1873-1949 *WhAm 2*
Revere, Edward H R 1867-1957 *WhAm 3*
Revere, Edward Hutchinson Robbins 1827-1862
ApCAB, NatCAB 4
Revere, Joseph Warren 1812-1880 *ApCAB,
DcAmB, IIBEAAW, NatCAB 4,
NewYHSD, TwCBDA, WebAMB,
WhAm H*
Revere, Paul 1735-1818 *AmBi, ApCAB,
BnEnAmA, DcAmB, Drake, EncAB,
McGEWB, NatCAB 1, NewYHSD,
TwCBDA, WebAB, WebAMB, WhAm H*
Revere, Paul, Jr. 1760-1813 *NatCAB 21*
Revere, Paul Joseph 1832-1863 *ApCAB,
NatCAB 7, TwCBDA*
Reverend, J *NewYHSD*

Reverend, T *NewYHSD*
Reverman, Theodore Henry 1877-1941 *WhAm 1*
Reviere *NewYHSD*
Revill, Milton Kirtley 1900-1955 *NatCAB 45,*
  WhAm 3
Revillagigedo, Juan Pacheco, Conde De
  1740-1799 *McGEWB*
Reville, Albert 1826- *ApCAB*
Revoil, Benedict Henry 1816- *ApCAB*
Revson, Charles Haskell 1906-1975 *WhAm 6*
Rew, Charles D 1856-1897 *TwCBDA*
Rew, Henry Cunningham 1839- *NatCAB 10*
Rew, Irwin 1868-1958 *WhAm 3*
Rex, Charles D 1856-1897 *TwCBDA*
Rex, Charles Henry 1903-1973 *WhAm 6*
Rex, George 1817-1879 *NatCAB 12*
Rex, Walter Edwin 1847-1916 *NatCAB 21*
Rexdale, Robert 1859-1929 *WhAm 1*
Rexford, Eben Eugene 1848-1916 *ApCAB,*
  NatCAB 10, TwCBDA, WhAm 1
Rexford, Frank A 1876-1941 *WhAm 1*
Rey, Abel 1873-1940 *DcScB*
Rey, Anthony 1807-1846 *ApCAB*
Rey, Anthony 1807-1847 *WhAm H*
Rey, Jacques Joseph 1820- *NewYHSD*
Rey, Jean 1582?-1645? *DcScB*
Rey Pastor, Julio 1888-1962 *DcScB*
Reybold, Eugene 1884-1961 *WhAm 4*
Reyburn, John Edgar 1845-1914 *BiDrAC,*
  NatCAB 5, WhAm 1, WhAmP
Reyburn, Laurens H 1897-1962 *WhAm 4*
Reyburn, Robert 1833-1909 *WhAm 1*
Reyburn, Samuel Wallace 1872-1962 *ApCAB X,*
  WhAm 4
Reyburn, William Stuart 1882-1946 *BiDrAC,*
  WhAmP
Reye, Theodor 1838-1919 *DcScB*
Reyerson, Lloyd Hilton 1893-1969 *NatCAB 55,*
  WhAm 5
Reyes, Alfonso 1889-1959 *McGEWB,*
  WhAm 3
Reyes, Rafael 1850-1920 *McGEWB*
Reymert, Martin Luther 1883-1953 *NatCAB 42,*
  WhAm 3
Reymond, Emil DuBois 1818-1896 *BiHiMed*
Reyna, Francisco DeLa 1520?- *DcScB*
Reynal, Eugene 1902-1968 *WhAm 5*
Reynal, Louis 1905-1960 *WhAm 4*
Reynal, Louis Samuel 1868-1943 *NatCAB 35*
Reynard, Charles Arthur 1915-1959
  NatCAB 48
Reynard, Grant 1887-1968 *WhAm 5*
Reynaud, Paul 1878-1966 *WhAm 4,*
  WhWW-II
Reynders, John V W d1944 *WhAm 2*
Reyneau, Charles Rene 1656-1728 *DcScB*
Reynes, Mrs. Joseph 1805- *NewYHSD*
Reyniers, James A 1908-1967 *WhAm 4A*
Reynolds, Alexander Welch 1817-1876 *ApCAB,*
  DcAmB, TwCBDA, WhAm H
Reynolds, Alfred 1853-1936 *NatCAB 27,*
  WhAm 1
Reynolds, Allen Holbrook 1869-1941 *WhAm 1*
Reynolds, Amelia Stead *WomWWA 14*
Reynolds, Amesbury L 1847- *WhAm 4*
Reynolds, Arthur 1868-1943 *NatCAB 33,*
  WhAm 2
Reynolds, Arthur Rowley 1854-1935
  NatCAB 29
Reynolds, Benjamin 1849-1913 *NatCAB 25*
Reynolds, Bruce Dodson 1894-1957 *NatCAB 46,*
  WhAm 5
Reynolds, C Hal 1890-1958 *NatCAB 48*
Reynolds, Carl Vernon 1872- *WhAm 5*
Reynolds, Carroll Foster 1910-1975 *WhAm 6*
Reynolds, Catherine 1782?-1864 *NewYHSD*
Reynolds, Charles Alexander 1842?-1876
  DcAmB, WhAm H
Reynolds, Charles Bingham 1854-1940 *WhAm 1*
Reynolds, Charles Lee 1874- *WhAm 5*
Reynolds, Charles Ransom 1877- *WhAm 5*
Reynolds, Charles Vaughn 1891-1940
  NatCAB 30
Reynolds, Chester A 1887-1958 *WhAm 3*
Reynolds, Clarence 1880- *WhAm 6*
Reynolds, Clarence James 1853-1919
  NatCAB 18
Reynolds, Clarence Kelly 1890-1963
  NatCAB 48

Reynolds, Conger 1891-1971 *WhAm 5*
Reynolds, Cuyler 1866- *WhAm 4*
Reynolds, Daniel Harris 1832-1902 *ApCAB,*
  TwCBDA
Reynolds, Dudley Sharpe 1842-1915 *WhAm 1*
Reynolds, Edward 1866-1929 *NatCAB 22*
Reynolds, Edwin 1831-1909 *DcAmB,*
  NatCAB 2, WhAm 1
Reynolds, Edwin Ruthvin 1816-1908 *BiDrAC*
Reynolds, Edwin Stanton 1869-1935
  NatCAB 31
Reynolds, Elmer Lewis 1890-1964 *WhAm 4*
Reynolds, Elmer Robert 1846-1907 *ApCAB,*
  TwCBDA, WhAm 1
Reynolds, Emanuel *NewYHSD*
Reynolds, Ernest Shaw 1884-1961 *WhAm 4*
Reynolds, Frank Bernard 1874- *WhAm 1*
Reynolds, Frank James 1890-1958 *WhAm 3*
Reynolds, Frank William 1901-1971 *WhAm 5*
Reynolds, Frederic Philip 1877-1952
  NatCAB 41
Reynolds, Frederick Jesse 1857-1931 *WhAm 1*
Reynolds, George Delachaumette 1841-1921
  NatCAB 7, WhAm 1
Reynolds, George Greenwood 1821-1913
  NatCAB 9, WhAm 1
Reynolds, George McClelland 1865-1940
  DcAmB S2, WhAm 1
Reynolds, George William 1868-1944 *WhAm 2*
Reynolds, Gideon 1813-1896 *BiAUS, BiDrAC,*
  WhAm H
Reynolds, Grace Morrison 1880- *WhAm 3*
Reynolds, H Walter 1901-1972 *WhAm 6*
Reynolds, Harry Badger 1874-1958 *NatCAB 50*
Reynolds, Harry St. Clair 1880-1956
  NatCAB 44
Reynolds, Harry Vollmer 1896-1951
  NatCAB 39
Reynolds, Henry James 1852-1949 *NatCAB 38,*
  WhAm 2
Reynolds, Henry Vose 1861-1922 *NatCAB 19*
Reynolds, Herbert Byron 1888-1968 *WhAm 5*
Reynolds, Horatio McLeod 1857-1929
  NatCAB 25
Reynolds, Hugh Elba 1900-1968 *NatCAB 54*
Reynolds, Igantius Aloysius 1798-1855
  WhAm H
Reynolds, Ignatius Aloysius 1798-1855 *ApCAB,*
  Drake, NatCAB 12, TwCBDA
Reynolds, Irving Carey 1893-1968 *NatCAB 54*
Reynolds, Isham E 1879-1949 *WhAm 2A*
Reynolds, Jackson Eli 1873- *WhAm 5*
Reynolds, James B 1779-1851 *BiAUS, BiDrAC,*
  WhAm H
Reynolds, James Banks 1833-1882 *NatCAB 14*
Reynolds, James Bronson 1861-1924
  NatCAB 10, WhAm 1
Reynolds, James Burton 1870-1948 *WhAm 2*
Reynolds, James E 1926- *IIBEAAW*
Reynolds, James Richard 1870- *WhoColR*
Reynolds, John *NewYHSD*
Reynolds, John 1700?-1776 *ApCAB, Drake,*
  NatCAB 1
Reynolds, John 1713-1788 *DcAmB, WhAm H*
Reynolds, John 1788-1865 *DcAmB,*
  NatCAB 11, TwCBDA
Reynolds, John 1789-1865 *ApCAB, BiAUS,*
  BiDrAC, Drake, WhAm H
Reynolds, John 1883-1966 *NatCAB 51*
Reynolds, John Cromwell 1810-1849 *NatCAB 3*
Reynolds, John Douglas 1869- *WhoColR*
Reynolds, John Edwin 1863- *WhAm 1*
Reynolds, John Fulton 1820-1863 *AmBi,*
  ApCAB, DcAmB, Drake, NatCAB 4,
  TwCBDA, WebAMB, WhAm H
Reynolds, John Gililford 1859- *WhAm 4*
Reynolds, John Hazard 1819-1875 *BiAUS,*
  BiDrAC, WhAm H
Reynolds, John Henry 1900-1968 *WhAm 5*
Reynolds, John Hughes 1846- *WhAm 1*
Reynolds, John Lacey, Jr. 1910-1963 *WhAm 4*
Reynolds, John Merriman 1848-1933 *BiDrAC,*
  WhAm 1
Reynolds, John N *Drake*
Reynolds, John P 1825?- *NatCAB 12*
Reynolds, John Parker 1820-1912 *ApCAB,*
  TwCBDA, WhAm 1
Reynolds, John Whitcome 1875-1958 *WhAm 3*

Reynolds, John Wilkins 1875-1942 *NatCAB 38*
Reynolds, Joseph *Drake*
Reynolds, Joseph 1785-1864 *BiAUS, BiDrAC,*
  WhAm H
Reynolds, Joseph B 1871-1937 *WhAm 1*
Reynolds, Joseph Jones 1822-1899 *AmBi,*
  ApCAB, DcAmB, Drake, NatCAB 9,
  TwCBDA, WhAm H, WhAm 1
Reynolds, Joseph Smith 1839-1911 *ApCAB,*
  WhAm 1
Reynolds, Sir Joshua 1723-1792 *McGEWB*
Reynolds, Joshua W *NewYHSD*
Reynolds, Kate Beatty *WomWWA 14*
Reynolds, Lawrence 1889-1961 *WhAm 4*
Reynolds, Milton 1892-1976 *WhAm 6*
Reynolds, Morley Punshon 1868-1935
  NatCAB 33
Reynolds, Mortimer Fabricius 1814-1892
  NatCAB 8
Reynolds, Myra 1853-1936 *NotAW, WhAm 1,*
  WomWWA 14
Reynolds, Myron Herbert 1865-1929 *WhAm 1*
Reynolds, Nellie Austin *WomWWA 14*
Reynolds, Oliver Charlick 1884-1970 *WhAm 6*
Reynolds, Osborne 1842-1912 *DcScB*
Reynolds, Paul Revere 1864-1944 *WhAm 2*
Reynolds, Powell Benton 1841-1914 *WhAm 1*
Reynolds, Quentin 1902-1965 *WhAm 4*
Reynolds, R Foster 1887-1955 *NatCAB 42*
Reynolds, Ralph Arthur 1893-1956 *NatCAB 46*
Reynolds, Richard 1827-1918 *NewYHSD*
Reynolds, Richard Joshua 1850-1918
  NatCAB 18
Reynolds, Richard Joshua 1906-1964
  NatCAB 53, WhAm 4
Reynolds, Richard Samuel 1881-1955
  DcAmB S5, WhAm 3
Reynolds, Robert F 1818?- *NewYHSD*
Reynolds, Robert John 1838-1909 *NatCAB 11,*
  TwCBDA, WhAm 1
Reynolds, Robert M 1826- *BiAUS,*
  NatCAB 12
Reynolds, Robert Rice 1884-1963 *BiDrAC,*
  NatCAB 50, WhAm 4
Reynolds, Royal 1881- *WhAm 6*
Reynolds, Sadie Davis *WomWWA 14*
Reynolds, Samuel Godfrey 1801-1881 *DcAmB,*
  WhAm H
Reynolds, Samuel Guilford 1868- *WhAm 4*
Reynolds, Samuel Williams 1890- *BiDrAC*
Reynolds, Thomas *NewYHSD*
Reynolds, Thomas 1796-1844 *BiAUS, Drake,*
  NatCAB 12, TwCBDA
Reynolds, Thomas C 1821-1887 *BiDConf*
Reynolds, Thomas Harvey 1866-1943 *WhAm 2*
Reynolds, Victor George Fassett 1905-1973
  NatCAB 57, WhAm 6
Reynolds, Virginia 1866-1903 *WhAm 1*
Reynolds, Walter Ford 1880-1942 *WhAm 2*
Reynolds, Wellington George 1880-1941
  NatCAB 31
Reynolds, Wellington Jarard 1866- *WhAm 4*
Reynolds, Wiley Richard 1879-1948
  NatCAB 37, WhAm 2
Reynolds, William 1815-1879 *ApCAB, DcAmB,*
  NatCAB 2, TwCBDA, WhAm H
Reynolds, William David 1846- *NatCAB 17*
Reynolds, William Henry 1868-1931
  NatCAB 25
Reynolds, William Howard 1922-1972 *WhAm 5*
Reynolds, William Morton 1812-1876 *ApCAB,*
  Drake, TwCBDA
Reynolds, William Neal 1863-1951 *DcAmB S5,*
  WhAm 3
Reynoso, Alvaro 1820?- *ApCAB*
Reza Shah Pahlavi 1878-1944 *McGEWB*
Rezanov, Nikolai Petrovich 1764-1807 *AmBi,*
  DcAmB, WhAm H
Reze, Frederic 1791-1871 *TwCBDA*
Reze, Frederick 1797-1871 *ApCAB*
Reznikoff, Charles 1894-1976 *WhAm 6*
Reznor, Jesse T 1870-1919 *NatCAB 22*
Rhaesa, William A 1909-1970 *WhAm 5*
Rhawn, William Henry 1832-1898 *NatCAB 12*
Rhazes *DcScB*
Rhazes 850?-932 *BiHiMed*
Rhazes 860?-930? *AsBiEn*
Rhea, Clarance Ward 1890-1956 *NatCAB 46*

Rhea, David M 1863-1924 *NatCAB 6*
Rhea, Hiawatha W 1870- *WhoColR*
Rhea, Hortense d1899 *WhAm 1*
Rhea, John 1753-1832 *BiAUS, BiDrAC, DcAmB, TwCBDA, WhAm H, WhAmP*
Rhea, John Stockdale 1855-1924 *BiDrAC, TwCBDA, WhAm 4, WhAmP*
Rhea, William Edward 1889-1946 *WhAm 2*
Rhea, William Francis 1858-1931 *BiDrAC*
Rhea, William Francis 1859-1931 *TwCBDA, WhAm 4*
Rhead, Frederick Hurten 1880-1942 *NatCAB 41*
Rhead, Louis John 1857-1926 *WhAm 1*
Rheaume, Louis 1873-1955 *WhAm 3*
Rhee, Syngman 1875-1965 *McGEWB, WhAm 4*
Rheem, Richard Scoffield 1903-1971 *WhAm 5*
Rhees, Benjamin Rush 1860- *TwCBDA*
Rhees, Harriet Chapin Seelye *WomWWA 14*
Rhees, John Morgan 1760-1804 *WhAm H*
Rhees, Morgan John 1760-1804 *ApCAB, DcAmB S1, Drake*
Rhees, N *IlBEAAW*
Rhees, Rush 1860-1939 *DcAmB S2, NatCAB 12, NatCAB 29, WhAm 1*
Rhees, William Jones 1830-1907 *ApCAB, DcAmB, NatCAB 12, TwCBDA, WhAm 1*
Rhein, Meyer Louis 1860-1928 *NatCAB 38*
Rheinhardt, Rudolph H *WhAm 1*
Rheinstrom, Henry 1884-1960 *WhAm 4*
Rheita, Anton Maria Schyrlaeus De 1597-1660 *DcScB*
Rheticus 1514-1576 *AsBiEn*
Rheticus, George Joachim 1514-1574 *DcScB*
Rhett, A Burnet 1877-1946 *WhAm 2*
Rhett, Robert Barnwell 1800-1876 *AmBi, ApCAB, BiAUS, BiDConf, BiDrAC, DcAmB, Drake, McGEWB, NatCAB 4, TwCBDA, WebAB, WhAm H, WhAmP*
Rhett, Robert Barnwell 1854-1901 *NatCAB 12*
Rhett, Robert Goodwyn 1862-1939 *NatCAB 11, WhAm 1*
Rhett, Thomas Grimke 1824?-1878 *NatCAB 4*
Rhett, Thomas Grimke 1825?-1878 *ApCAB*
Rhetts, Charles Edward 1910-1971 *WhAm 5*
Rhind, Alexander Colden 1821-1897 *ApCAB, DcAmB, Drake, NatCAB 4, TwCBDA, WebAMB, WhAm H*
Rhind, C *NewYHSD*
Rhind, Charles d1847? *DcAmB, WhAm H*
Rhind, John Massey 1858-1936 *WhAm 1*
Rhind, John Massey 1860?-1936 *AmBi, IlBEAAW*
Rhine, Abraham Benedict 1877-1941 *WhAm 1*
Rhine, Alice Hyneman 1840- *ApCAB*
Rhine, Joseph Banks 1895- *AsBiEn, WebAB*
Rhinedesbacher *NewYHSD*
Rhinehart, Barton Arthur 1895-1964 *NatCAB 51*
Rhinehart, Darmon Artelle 1887-1954 *NatCAB 43*
Rhinelander, Philip Mercer 1869-1939 *WhAm 1*
Rhinelander, T J Oakley 1853-1946 *WhAm 4*
Rhinelander, T J Oakley 1858-1946 *NatCAB 37*
Rhinelander, W H *NewYHSD*
Rhinelander, William 1825-1908 *NatCAB 37*
Rhinelander, William Christopher 1790-1878 *NatCAB 37*
Rhinock, Joseph Lafayette 1863-1926 *BiDrAC, WhAm 1*
Rhoad, Albert Oliver 1902-1962 *WhAm 4*
Rhoades, Clifford Thomas 1901-1951 *NatCAB 39*
Rhoades, Cornelia Harsen 1863-1940 *WhAm 1, WomWWA 14*
Rhoades, Edward Henry, Jr. 1872-1949 *WhAm 3*
Rhoades, Electa E 1848- *WomWWA 14*
Rhoades, Isabella Carter 1849- *WomWWA 14*
Rhoades, John Harsen 1838-1906 *NatCAB 22, WhAm 1*
Rhoades, John Harsen 1869-1943 *NatCAB 30*
Rhoades, John Harson 1869-1943 *WhAm 2*
Rhoades, Lewis Addison 1860-1910 *WhAm 1*
Rhoades, Lyman 1881-1960 *WhAm 4*
Rhoades, Mabel Carter 1875- *WhAm 5,*

WomWWA 14
Rhoades, Mary Prentice 1848- *WomWWA 14*
Rhoades, Nelson Osgood 1869-1928 *WhAm 1*
Rhoades, Ralph Omer 1895-1961 *NatCAB 52, WhAm 4*
Rhoades, Robert Channing 1903-1971 *NatCAB 56*
Rhoades, Verne 1881-1969 *NatCAB 55*
Rhoades, William Caldwell Plunkett 1845-1923 *WhAm 1*
Rhoades, William H *NewYHSD*
Rhoads, Charles James 1872-1954 *WhAm 3*
Rhoads, Cornelius Packard 1898-1959 *WhAm 3*
Rhoads, Edwin Mathias 1889-1938 *NatCAB 37*
Rhoads, J Snowdon 1867-1936 *NatCAB 28*
Rhoads, James Evans 1828-1895 *DcAmB, NatCAB 13, TwCBDA, WhAm H*
Rhoads, Joseph J 1890-1951 *WhAm 3*
Rhoads, Lewis Thomas 1875-1938 *NatCAB 29*
Rhoads, McHenry 1858-1943 *WhAm 2*
Rhoads, Samuel 1711-1784 *ApCAB, BiDrAC, NatCAB 13, TwCBDA, WhAm H*
Rhoads, Samuel *see also* Rhodes, Samuel
Rhoads, Samuel Nicholson 1862- *WhAm 5*
Rhoads, Thomas Jefferson Boyer 1837-1919 *NatCAB 18*
Rhoads, Thomas Leidy 1870-1940 *NatCAB 37*
Rhoads, Webster Strunk 1858-1941 *NatCAB 31*
Rhoads, William *NewYHSD*
Rhode, Chris Simeon 1890-1969 *NatCAB 55*
Rhode, Clarence J 1913-1958 *WhAm 3*
Rhode, Homer Jonas 1877-1949 *NatCAB 38*
Rhode, Paul Peter 1871-1945 *WhAm 2*
Rhodehamel, Harry E 1876-1969 *NatCAB 56*
Rhodes, Albert 1840- *ApCAB*
Rhodes, Albert James 1864-1921 *NatCAB 19*
Rhodes, Anne 1860- *WomWWA 14*
Rhodes, Augustus Loring 1821- *NatCAB 12*
Rhodes, Bradford 1845-1924 *WhAm 1*
Rhodes, Bradford 1848-1924 *NatCAB 10*
Rhodes, Cecil John 1853-1902 *McGEWB*
Rhodes, Charles Dudley 1865-1948 *WhAm 3*
Rhodes, Daniel 1911- *BnEnAmA*
Rhodes, Donald Gene 1931-1974 *WhAm 6*
Rhodes, E Washington 1895-1970 *NatCAB 56*
Rhodes, Edward Everett 1868-1959 *WhAm 3*
Rhodes, Elisha Hunt 1842- *WhAm H*
Rhodes, Eugene Manlove 1869-1934 *AmBi, DcAmB S1, EncAAH, NatCAB 45, REnAW*
Rhodes, Eugene Manlove 1869-1935 *WhAm 1*
Rhodes, Foster Twichell 1906-1967 *NatCAB 54, WhAm 5*
Rhodes, Frederic Harrison 1878-1942 *WhAm 2*
Rhodes, Frederick Leland 1870-1933 *WhAm 1*
Rhodes, George F *NewYHSD*
Rhodes, George Milton 1898- *BiDrAC, WhAmP*
Rhodes, George Pearson 1871-1940 *WhAm 1*
Rhodes, Harrison 1871-1929 *WhAm 1*
Rhodes, Henry Abraham 1863-1954 *WhAm 3*
Rhodes, James Ford 1848-1927 *AmBi, DcAmB, EncAAH, McGEWB, NatCAB 7, TwCBDA, WebAB, WhAm 1*
Rhodes, James Mauran 1848-1925 *NatCAB 28*
Rhodes, Jeremiah 1862-1938 *WhAm 1*
Rhodes, John Bower 1899-1966 *WhAm 4*
Rhodes, John Franklin 1889-1944 *WhAm 2*
Rhodes, John Jacob 1916- *BiDrAC*
Rhodes, Laura Andrews 1854- *AmWom*
Rhodes, Leland Smiley 1889-1958 *NatCAB 47*
Rhodes, Marion Edward 1868-1928 *WhAm 4*
Rhodes, Marion Edwards 1868-1928 *BiDrAC*
Rhodes, Mary 1782?-1853 *NotAW*
Rhodes, Mary Smiley 1862- *WomWWA 14*
Rhodes, Mosheim 1837- *ApCAB, WhAm 4*
Rhodes, Robert 1840-1863 *NatCAB 8*
Rhodes, Robert Clinton 1887-1948 *WhAm 2*
Rhodes, Robert E 1826-1864 *Drake*
Rhodes, Rufus Napoleon 1856-1910 *WhAm 1*
Rhodes, Samuel 1711-1784 *BiAUS*
Rhodes, Samuel *see also* Rhoads, Samuel
Rhodes, Stephen Holbrook 1825-1908 *NatCAB 11*
Rhodes, Stephen Holbrook 1825-1909 *WhAm 1*
Rhodes, Willard E 1912-1968 *WhAm 5*
Rhodes, William Castle 1869-1914 *NatCAB 16*
Rhodes, William H *NewYHSD*

Rhodes, William Henry 1822-1852 *NatCAB 7*
Rhodin, Carl Jonas 1877-1932 *NatCAB 24*
Rhone, Daniel Nelson 1873- *WhoColR*
Rhone, Rosamond Dodson 1855- *WhAm 4, WomWWA 14*
Rhudy, William Porter 1899-1960 *NatCAB 49*
Rhyne, Brice Wilson 1917-1972 *WhAm 5*
Rhys, Noel Andrew 1899-1973 *WhAm 6*
Riach, May Turner 1886-1946 *NatCAB 34*
Rial, John *NewYHSD*
Riale, Franklin Neiman 1859-1935 *WhAm 1*
Riall, Sir Phineas 1769?-1851 *ApCAB, Drake*
Riano Y Gayangos, Don Juan 1865-1939 *WhAm 1*
Ribak, Louis Leon 1903?- *IlBEAAW*
Ribar, Ivan 1884-1968 *WhAm 5*
Ribas, Andres Perez De 1576-1655 *ApCAB*
Ribas, Jose Felix 1775-1815 *ApCAB*
Ribaucour, Albert 1845-1893 *DcScB*
Ribault, Jean 1520?-1565 *AmBi, Drake, REnAW*
Ribaut, Jean 1520?-1565 *AmBi, ApCAB, DcAmB, WhAm H*
Ribbentrop, Joachim Von 1893-1946 *WhWW-II*
Ribble, Frederick D G 1898-1971 *WhAm 5*
Ribby, Eugene Giles 1899-1948 *NatCAB 37*
Ribeiro Santos, Carlos 1813-1882 *DcScB*
Ribera, Jusepe De 1591-1652 *McGEWB*
Ribgy, Edmund 1901-1964 *WhAm 4*
Ribicoff, Abraham Alexander 1910- *BiDrAC, BiDrUSE*
Ribner, Irving 1921-1972 *WhAm 5*
Riboni, Giacinto *NewYHSD*
Ricarby, George *NewYHSD*
Ricard, Jerome Sixtus 1850-1930 *NatCAB 23, WhAm 1*
Ricardo, David 1772-1823 *McGEWB*
Ricardo, Harry Ralph 1885-1974 *WhAm 6*
Ricardo, Mrs. R J *NewYHSD*
Ricaud, James Barroll 1808-1866 *ApCAB, BiAUS, BiDrAC, TwCBDA, WhAm H*
Ricaurte, Antonio 1792-1814 *ApCAB*
Riccati, Jacopo Francesco 1676-1754 *DcScB*
Riccati, Vincenzo 1707-1775 *DcScB*
Ricci, Matteo 1552-1610 *DcScB, McGEWB*
Ricci, Michelangelo 1619-1682 *DcScB*
Ricci, Ostilio 1540-1603 *DcScB*
Ricci, Ulysses Anthony 1888-1960 *WhAm 4*
Ricci-Curbastro, Gregorio 1853-1925 *DcScB*
Riccioli, Giambattista 1598-1671 *DcScB*
Riccioli, Giovanni Battista 1598-1671 *AsBiEn*
Riccius, Hermann Porter 1883-1965 *WhAm 4*
Ricciuto, Harry Adrian 1921-1974 *WhAm 6*
Ricco, Annibale 1844-1919 *DcScB*
Rice, Abigail Ruth Burton 1895-1968 *WhAm 5*
Rice, Agnes Downey 1889- *WomWWA 14*
Rice, Albert E 1847-1921 *WhAm 1*
Rice, Albert White 1883-1965 *WhAm 4*
Rice, Alexander Hamilton 1818-1895 *ApCAB, BiAUS, BiDrAC, DcAmB, Drake, NatCAB 1, TwCBDA, WhAm H, WhAmP*
Rice, Alexander Hamilton 1875-1956 *WhAm 3*
Rice, Alice Caldwell Hegan 1870-1942 *DcAmB S3, NatCAB 14, NotAW, WhAm 1, WomWWA 14*
Rice, Alice May Bates 1868- *AmWom*
Rice, Allen Thorndike 1851-1889 *AmBi*
Rice, Allen Thorndike 1853-1889 *ApCAB, NatCAB 3*
Rice, Alonzo Leora 1867- *WhAm 4*
Rice, Americus Vespucius 1835-1904 *ApCAB, BiAUS, BiDrAC, NatCAB 4*
Rice, Arthur Edmund 1880-1941 *NatCAB 30*
Rice, Arthur Henry 1900-1975 *WhAm 6*
Rice, Arthur Hitchcock 1854-1927 *NatCAB 22*
Rice, Arthur Hyde 1878-1955 *NatCAB 47*
Rice, Arthur Louis 1870-1946 *WhAm 2*
Rice, Arthur Wallace 1869-1938 *NatCAB 29, WhAm 1*
Rice, Ben H, Jr. 1889-1964 *WhAm 4*
Riee, Benjamin Franklin 1828-1905 *ApCAB, BiAUS, BiDrAC, NatCAB 12*
Rice, Benjamin Franklin 1875-1924 *WhAm 1*
Rice, Benjamin Holt 1782-1856 *ApCAB*
Rice, Cale Young 1872-1943 *NatCAB 34, WhAm 2*
Rice, Calvin L *NewYHSD*

Rice, Calvin Winsor 1868-1934 *DcAmB S1,*
NatCAB 25, *WhAm 1*
Rice, Charles 1841-1901 *DcAmB,* *WhAm H*
Rice, Charles A 1873- *WhAm 5*
Rice, Charles Ainsworth 1896-1959 *NatCAB 43*
Rice, Charles Allen Thorndike 1851-1889
DcAmB, *TwCBDA,* *WhAm H*
Rice, Charles Atwood 1876- *WhAm 6*
Rice, Charles DeLos 1859-1939 *NatCAB 35*
Rice, Charles Edmund 1846-1919 *WhAm 1*
Rice, Charles Francis 1851-1927 *WhAm 1*
Rice, Charles Frank 1868-1928 *NatCAB 23*
Rice, Charles M 1882-1950 *WhAm 3*
Rice, Chester Williams 1888-1951 *NatCAB 40*
Rice, Clarence Thornton 1881-1967 *NatCAB 53*
Rice, Claton Silas 1883-1972 *WhAm 5*
Rice, Craig 1908-1957 *WhAm 3*
Rice, Dan 1823-1900 *AmBi,* *DcAmB,* *WebAB,*
WhAm H
Rice, Daniel 1822- *ApCAB*
Rice, Daniel 1823- *NatCAB 3*
Rice, David 1733-1816 *ApCAB,* *DcAmB,*
DcAmReB, *Drake,* *TwCBDA,* *WhAm H*
Rice, Devereux Dunlap 1898-1948 *NatCAB 41,*
WhAm 2
Rice, E A *NewYHSD*
Rice, Edith Florence *WomWWA 14*
Rice, Edmund 1819-1889 *BiDrAC,* *DcAmB,*
NatCAB 3, *WhAm H,* *WhAmP*
Rice, Edmund 1842-1906 *ApCAB Sup,*
WhAm 1
Rice, Edward Irving 1868- *WhAm 1*
Rice, Edward Loranus 1871-1960 *WhAm 3*
Rice, Edward Thomson 1886-1957 *NatCAB 46*
Rice, Edward Young 1820-1883 *BiAUS,*
BiDrAC, *WhAm H*
Rice, Edwin Wilbur 1831-1929 *ApCAB,*
DcAmB, *NatCAB 3,* *TwCBDA,*
WhAm 1
Rice, Edwin Wilbur 1862-1935 *DcAmB S1,*
NatCAB 26, *WhAm 1*
Rice, Elbridge Washburn 1870-1941
NatCAB 31
Rice, Eleanor Elkins 1861-1937 *NatCAB 29*
Rice, Elliott Warren 1835-1887 *ApCAB,*
NatCAB 5, *TwCBDA*
Rice, Elmer Leopold 1892-1967 *McGEWB,*
WebAB, *WhAm 4*
Rice, Elwood Ernest 1879-1958 *NatCAB 47*
Rice, Emery *NewYHSD*
Rice, Emory Clark 1897-1970 *NatCAB 56*
Rice, Ernest 1872-1950 *NatCAB 39,* *WhAm 3*
Rice, Ernest Gary 1909-1960 *NatCAB 47*
Rice, Ethel 1877- *NatCAB 18*
Rice, Eugene 1891-1967 *WhAm 4A*
Rice, F Willis 1848-1931 *WhAm 1*
Rice, Fenelon Bird 1841-1901 *BiDAmEd,*
DcAmB, *WhAm H*
Rice, Florence Frances 1855- *WomWWA 14*
Rice, Frank James 1869-1917 *WhAm 1*
Rice, Frank Sumner 1850-1898 *NatCAB 6*
Rice, Franklin Pierce 1852-1919 *WhAm 1*
Rice, Fred Ball 1866-1933 *NatCAB 32*
Rice, Frederick Adolph 1888-1959 *WhAm 3*
Rice, George Brackett 1859- *WhAm 2*
Rice, George Edward 1822-1861 *ApCAB,*
Drake
Rice, George Samuel 1866-1950 *DcAmB S4,*
NatCAB 38, *WhAm 2*
Rice, George Staples 1849-1920 *NatCAB 12,*
WhAm 1
Rice, Grantland 1880-1954 *DcAmB S5,*
NatCAB 41, *WebAB,* *WhAm 3*
Rice, Greek Lent 1886-1950 *NatCAB 39,*
WhAm 3
Rice, Hamilton 1875-1956 *NatCAB 45*
Rice, Harmon Howard 1870- *WhAm 5*
Rice, Harry Lee 1862-1951 *WhAm 3*
Rice, Harvey 1800-1891 *ApCAB,* *Drake,*
NatCAB 13, *TwCBDA*
Rice, Heber Holbrook 1882- *WhAm 3*
Rice, Henry 1835-1914 *WhAm 1*
Rice, Henry H 1816- *BiAUS*
Rice, Henry Izard Bacon 1881- *WhAm 6*
Rice, Henry Mower 1816-1894 *ApCAB,*
DcAmB, *NatCAB 12,* *TwCBDA*
Rice, Henry Mower 1817-1894 *BiDrAC,*
NatCAB 21, *WhAm H,* *WhAmP*

Rice, Herbert Ambrose 1866-1929 *WhAm 1*
Rice, Herbert Howard 1870-1938 *NatCAB 29,*
WhAm 1
Rice, Herbert Leigh 1876-1932 *WhAm 1*
Rice, Herbert Wayland 1869-1941 *WhAm 1*
Rice, Hermon Read 1886-1956 *NatCAB 45*
Rice, Howard Crosby 1878-1965 *WhAm 4*
Rice, Mrs. Isaac L 1860- *NatCAB 14*
Rice, Mrs. Isaac L *see also* Rice, Julia Barnett
Rice, Isaac Leopold 1850-1915 *ApCAB,*
ApCAB X, *DcAmB,* *NatCAB 11,*
WhAm 1
Rice, Jack Horton 1911-1967 *WhAm 4*
Rice, James Clay 1829-1864 *ApCAB,* *Drake,*
NatCAB 5, *TwCBDA*
Rice, James Edward 1865-1953 *BiDAmEd,*
NatCAB 45, *WhAm 5*
Rice, James H 1843- *NatCAB 1*
Rice, James Henry, Jr. 1868-1935 *WhAm 1*
Rice, James R 1824- *NewYHSD*
Rice, Jeannie Durant 1862-1919 *NatCAB 18*
Rice, Jeannie Durant 1863-1919 *WomWWA 14*
Rice, Jerome Bonaparte 1841- *NatCAB 5*
Rice, John 1866- *WhAm 5*
Rice, John Andrew 1862-1930 *WhAm 1,*
WhAm 1C
Rice, John Andrew 1888-1968 *BiDAmEd,*
WhAm 5
Rice, John Birchard 1832-1893 *BiDrAC,*
WhAm H
Rice, John Blake 1809-1874 *BiAUS,* *BiDrAC,*
WhAm H
Rice, John Campbell 1864-1937 *WhAm 1*
Rice, John E *NewYHSD*
Rice, John H 1816- *BiAUS*
Rice, John Hodgen 1870-1940 *WhAm 1*
Rice, John Holt 1777-1831 *ApCAB,* *DcAmB,*
DcAmReB, *Drake,* *NatCAB 2,* *TwCBDA,*
WhAm H
Rice, John Holt 1818-1878 *NatCAB 2*
Rice, John Hovey 1816-1911 *BiDrAC,*
TwCBDA, *WhAm 1*
Rice, John Joseph 1871- *NatCAB 16*
Rice, John Lovell 1840-1923 *NatCAB 33*
Rice, John McConnell 1831-1895 *BiAUS,*
BiAUS Sup, *BiDrAC,* *WhAm H*
Rice, John Pierrepont 1879-1941 *WhAm 2*
Rice, John V, Jr. 1871- *NatCAB 15*
Rice, John Winter 1891-1971 *NatCAB 56,*
WhAm 5
Rice, Jonas Shearn 1855-1931 *ApCAB X,*
WhAm 1
Rice, Jonathan 1843- *NatCAB 12*
Rice, Joseph J 1871-1938 *WhAm 1*
Rice, Joseph Lee, Jr. 1902-1974 *WhAm 6*
Rice, Joseph Mayer 1857-1934 *BiDAmEd,*
NatCAB 12, *WhAm 1*
Rice, Joseph R *NewYHSD*
Rice, Julia Barnett 1860- *ApCAB X,* *BiCAW*
Rice, Julia Barnett *see also* Rice, Mrs. Isaac
Leopold
Rice, Julia Hyneman Barnett 1860-
WomWWA 14
Rice, Juliet Powell 1849- *WomWWA 14*
Rice, Katharine McDowell *WomWWA 14*
Rice, Kingsley Loring 1898-1960 *WhAm 4*
Rice, Laban Lacy 1870- *WhAm 5*
Rice, Leon Leftwich 1885-1966 *NatCAB 55*
Rice, Lewis Albert 1861-1941 *NatCAB 30*
Rice, Lewis Frederick 1839-1909 *WhAm 1*
Rice, Lloyd Preston 1889-1958 *WhAm 3*
Rice, Luther 1783-1836 *ApCAB,* *DcAmB,*
DcAmReB, *Drake,* *NatCAB 3,* *TwCBDA,*
WhAm H
Rice, M Wilfred 1909-1968 *WhAm 5*
Rice, Maurice Smythe 1912-1962 *WhAm 4*
Rice, Merton Stacher 1872-1943 *WhAm 2*
Rice, N L 1807-1877 *Drake*
Rice, Nathan Lewis 1807-1877 *ApCAB,*
DcAmB, *NatCAB 3,* *TwCBDA,*
WhAm H
Rice, Paran Flint 1859- *ApCAB X*
Rice, Paul Harper 1893-1958 *NatCAB 43,*
WhAm 3
Rice, Paul North 1888-1967 *DcAmLiB,*
WhAm 4
Rice, Philip Blair 1904-1956 *WhAm 3*
Rice, Ralph Herbert 1873-1956 *NatCAB 44*

Rice, Richard Ashley 1878-1955 *NatCAB 43,*
WhAm 3
Rice, Richard Austin 1846-1925 *WhAm 1*
Rice, Richard Henry 1863-1922 *ApCAB X,*
DcAmB, *NatCAB 30,* *WhAm 1*
Rice, Robert *NewYHSD*
Rice, Robert 1874- *WhAm 5*
Rice, Rosella 1827- *ApCAB,* *NatCAB 5*
Rice, Samuel Allen 1828-1864 *ApCAB,* *Drake,*
NatCAB 5, *TwCBDA*
Rice, Samuel Davies 1877-1931 *NatCAB 43*
Rice, Samuel Farrow 1816-1890 *NatCAB 4,*
TwCBDA
Rice, Septimus P 1825?- *NatCAB 3*
Rice, Stephen Ewing 1905-1958 *WhAm 3*
Rice, Stuart Arthur 1889-1969 *WhAm 5*
Rice, Theron Hall 1867-1922 *WhAm 1*
Rice, Theron Moses 1829-1895 *BiDrAC,*
WhAm H
Rice, Thomas 1768-1854 *BiAUS,* *BiDrAC,*
WhAm H
Rice, Thomas Dartmouth 1808-1860 *AmBi,*
ApCAB, *DcAmB,* *Drake,* *EncAAH,*
NatCAB 11, *WebAB,* *WhAm H*
Rice, Thomas Stevens 1878-1942 *WhAm 2*
Rice, Thurman Brooks 1888-1952 *BiDAmEd,*
NatCAB 41, *WhAm 3*
Rice, Victor Moreau 1818-1869 *ApCAB,*
BiDAmEd, *DcAmB,* *NatCAB 14,*
WhAm H
Rice, Vietts Lysander 1844- *NatCAB 1*
Rice, W Merton 1878-1957 *NatCAB 45*
Rice, W W *NewYHSD*
Rice, Wallace 1859-1939 *NatCAB 13,*
TwCBDA, *WhAm 1*
Rice, Walter Percival 1855-1941 *NatCAB 30*
Rice, Willard Martin 1817-1904 *NatCAB 3,*
WhAm 1
Rice, William *NewYHSD*
Rice, William 1821-1897 *NatCAB 6*
Rice, William 1867-1932 *WhAm 1*
Rice, William Ball 1840-1909 *ApCAB X,*
NatCAB 32, *WhAm 1*
Rice, William Gorham 1856- *ApCAB Sup,*
WhAm 4
Rice, William Hyde 1846-1924 *NatCAB 40*
Rice, William Marsh 1816-1900 *DcAmB,*
NatCAB 29, *WhAm H*
Rice, William Morton Jackson 1854-1922
WhAm 1
Rice, William North 1845-1928 *ApCAB,*
BiDAmEd, *DcAmB,* *NatCAB 12,*
TwCBDA, *WhAm 1*
Rice, William Seltzer 1873- *IIBEAAW*
Rice, William Seward 1865-1937 *NatCAB 28*
Rice, William Stafford 1889-1956 *NatCAB 45*
Rice, William Whitney 1826-1896 *BiDrAC,*
TwCBDA, *WhAm H,* *WhAmP*
Rice-Keller, Inez *WomWWA 14*
Rich, A H *NewYHSD*
Rich, Adelbert Petty 1860-1933 *NatCAB 28,*
WhAm 1
Rich, Aileen Nutten 1874- *WomWWA 14*
Rich, Arnold Rice 1893-1968 *WhAm 5*
Rich, Benjamin Leroy 1878- *WhAm 6*
Rich, Burdett Alberto 1854-1925 *WhAm 1*
Rich, Carl W 1898-1972 *BiDrAC,* *WhAm 5*
Rich, Charles 1771-1824 *BiAUS,* *BiDrAC,*
TwCBDA, *WhAm H,* *WhAmP*
Rich, Charles 1865-1953 *NatCAB 41*
Rich, Charles Alonzo 1855-1943 *ApCAB,*
WhAm 2
Rich, Charles Coulson 1809-1883 *REnAW*
Rich, Charles Howard 1860-1948 *NatCAB 36*
Rich, Earl Arthur 1921-1967 *NatCAB 53*
Rich, Edgar Judson 1864-1948 *WhAm 2*
Rich, Ednah Anne 1871- *WhAm 5*
Rich, Edson Prosper 1858- *WhAm 4*
Rich, Edward Antoine 1876-1933 *NatCAB 24*
Rich, Edward P 1879-1937 *WhAm 1*
Rich, Edwin Gile 1879- *WhAm 6*
Rich, Ellen Moore 1843- *WomWWA 14*
Rich, Elmer 1882-1967 *NatCAB 53,* *WhAm 4*
Rich, Eugene Conklin Clark 1903-1957
NatCAB 48
Rich, Giles Willard 1875-1949 *WhAm 2*
Rich, Harvey J *NewYHSD*
Rich, Helen Hinsdale 1827- *AmWom*

Rich, Hiram 1832- *NatCAB 9*
Rich, Isaac 1801-1872 *ApCAB, DcAmB, NatCAB 11, TwCBDA, WhAm H*
Rich, J Harry 1888-1966 *NatCAB 52*
Rich, Jacob 1832-1913 *NatCAB 15*
Rich, John A 1855- *WhAm 4*
Rich, John Frederick 1902-1973 *WhAm 6*
Rich, John Harrison 1856-1924 *NatCAB 26, WhAm 1*
Rich, John Lyon 1884-1956 *WhAm 3*
Rich, John Tyler 1841-1926 *BiDrAC, NatCAB 5, NatCAB 29, TwCBDA, WhAm 1*
Rich, Joseph Carlos 1859-1927 *NatCAB 24*
Rich, Josephine Arnold 1874- *WomWWA 14*
Rich, Julia Ashley 1862- *WomWWA 14*
Rich, Laura Tuttle 1873- *WomWWA 14*
Rich, Mary Perry *WomWWA 14*
Rich, Michael Bond 1855-1930 *NatCAB 38*
Rich, Obadiah 1777-1850 *ApCAB*
Rich, Obadiah 1783-1850 *DcAmB, Drake, WhAm H*
Rich, Obadiah 1809-1888 *BnEnAmA*
Rich, Raymond Thomas 1899-1959 *WhAm 3*
Rich, Richard H 1901-1975 *WhAm 6*
Rich, Sir Robert 1587-1658 *WhAm H*
Rich, Robert Fleming 1883-1968 *BiDrAC, NatCAB 56, WhAm 5*
Rich, Ronald Emil 1907-1959 *WhAm 3*
Rich, S Grover 1885-1963 *NatCAB 50*
Rich, S Heath 1856-1947 *WhAm 2*
Rich, Thaddeus 1885-1969 *WhAm 5*
Rich, Theodore Scott 1867-1944 *NatCAB 34*
Rich, Walter John 1869-1925 *NatCAB 23*
Rich, William Fleming 1862-1943 *NatCAB 40*
Rich, William Thayer 1862-1942 *NatCAB 32*
Rich, Williston C 1882-1952 *WhAm 3*
Richard I 1157-1199 *McGEWB*
Richard II 1367-1400 *McGEWB*
Richard III 1452-1485 *McGEWB, WhoMilH*
Richard Of Wallingford 1292?-1336 *DcScB*
Richard Swineshead *DcScB*
Richard, Charles 1854-1940 *WhAm 1*
Richard, Ernst J 1859-1914 *WhAm 1*
Richard, Gabriel 1764-1832 *BiAUS, Drake, NatCAB 20*
Richard, Gabriel 1767-1832 *ApCAB, BiDrAC, DcAmB, WhAm H*
Richard, Harold Charles 1884-1958 *WhAm 3*
Richard, Irwin 1881- *WhAm 6*
Richard, James William 1843-1909 *DcAmB, WhAm 1*
Richard, John H 1807?- *NewYHSD, WhAm H*
Richard, Jules Antoine 1862-1956 *DcScB*
Richard, Louis Francois 1757-1806 *ApCAB*
Richard, Louis Paul Emile 1795-1849 *DcScB*
Richard, Matthias 1758-1830 *WhAm H*
Richard, Stephen *NewYHSD*
Richards, Albert Norton 1822- *ApCAB*
Richards, Alfred Ernest 1874-1946 *NatCAB 35, WhAm 2*
Richards, Alfred Newton 1876-1966 *WhAm 4*
Richards, Alice Haliburton 1860-1936 *WhAm 1*
Richards, Augustus Loring 1879-1951 *NatCAB 40*
Richards, Benjamin *NewYHSD*
Richards, Benjamin Wood 1797-1851 *ApCAB, NatCAB 10*
Richards, Bernard Gerson 1877- *WhAm 5*
Richards, Byron Ulysses 1866-1939 *NatCAB 32*
Richards, Calvin Adams 1828-1892 *NatCAB 8*
Richards, Charles Brinckerhoff 1833-1919 *DcAmB, NatCAB 25, WhAm 1*
Richards, Charles Gorman 1872- *WhAm 5*
Richards, Charles Herbert 1839-1925 *ApCAB, DcAmB, WhAm 1*
Richards, Charles Howard 1868-1949 *NatCAB 40*
Richards, Charles Lenmore 1877-1953 *BiDrAC, WhAm 5, WhAmP*
Richards, Charles Malone 1871- *WhAm 5*
Richards, Charles Russ 1871-1941 *NatCAB 32, WhAm 1*
Richards, Charles Russell 1865-1936 *BiDAmEd, WhAm 1*
Richards, Charles Walter 1877- *WhAm 1*

Richards, Charles Weeborn 1869-1961 *NatCAB 49*
Richards, Cornelia Holroyd 1822-1892 *ApCAB, TwCBDA*
Richards, Cornelia Wells Walter *NotAW*
Richards, Cyril Fuller 1894-1954 *WhAm 3*
Richards, Cyrus Smith 1808-1885 *ApCAB*
Richards, David 1828-1897 *NewYHSD*
Richards, David 1829-1897 *ApCAB Sup, NatCAB 40*
Richards, DeForest 1846-1903 *NatCAB 11, TwCBDA, WhAm 1*
Richards, Dickinson Woodruff 1895-1973 *WebAB, WhAm 5*
Richards, Donald 1919-1953 *WhAm 3*
Richards, Eben 1866-1942 *NatCAB 31, WhAm 2*
Richards, Edgar 1858- *NatCAB 11, WhAm 4*
Richards, Edward A d1956 *WhAm 3*
Richards, Edward Augustus 1855-1930 *NatCAB 33*
Richards, Edward F 1903-1965 *WhAm 4*
Richards, Edward Osgood 1857-1928 *NatCAB 31*
Richards, Ellen Henrietta Swallow 1842-1911 *AmBi, AmWom, ApCAB, BiDAmEd, DcAmB, NatCAB 7, NotAW, TwCBDA, WhAm 1*
Richards, Emerson Lewis 1884-1963 *WhAm 4*
Richards, Emily S Tanner 1850-1929 *WhAm 1, WomWWA 14*
Richards, Emma Louise *WomWWA 14*
Richards, Erwin Hart 1851-1928 *WhAm 1*
Richards, Eugene Lamb 1838-1912 *WhAm 1*
Richards, Eugene Scott 1904-1965 *WhAm 4*
Richards, Florence D *WomWWA 14*
Richards, Francis Henry 1850- *NatCAB 7*
Richards, Francis John 1901-1965 *DcScB*
Richards, Franklin Batchelder 1862-1940 *NatCAB 30*
Richards, Franklin Dewey 1821-1899 *NatCAB 7, NatCAB 16*
Richards, Franklin Snyder 1849- *NatCAB 18*
Richards, Frederick DeBourg 1822-1903 *IlBEAAW, NewYHSD*
Richards, Frederick Thompson 1864-1921 *WhAm 1*
Richards, George d1814 *ApCAB, Drake Sup*
Richards, George 1833-1900 *NatCAB 10, WhAm 1*
Richards, George 1849-1930 *WhAm 1*
Richards, George 1872-1948 *WhAm 2*
Richards, George Arthur 1889-1951 *NatCAB 42*
Richards, George Franklin 1861-1950 *WhAm 3*
Richards, George Gill 1883-1950 *NatCAB 39, WhAm 3*
Richards, George Handyside 1901-1958 *WhAm 3*
Richards, George Herbert 1863-1919 *NatCAB 19*
Richards, George Huntington 1882-1969 *WhAm 5*
Richards, George Lyman 1863-1933 *NatCAB 24*
Richards, George Warren 1869-1955 *NatCAB 46, WhAm 3*
Richards, Harriet Roosevelt *WomWWA 14*
Richards, Harry Sanger 1868-1929 *WhAm 1*
Richards, Helen Dorothy Whiton *ApCAB*
Richards, Henry 1848-1949 *NatCAB 38*
Richards, Henry Melchior Muhlenberg 1848-1935 *WhAm 1*
Richards, Herbert Maule 1871-1928 *WhAm 1*
Richards, Herbert Montague 1904-1970 *WhAm 5*
Richards, Ira 1879-1961 *NatCAB 47*
Richards, Irving Trefethen 1896-1967 *NatCAB 53, WhAm 4*
Richards, Ivor Armstrong 1893- *McGEWB, WebAB*
Richards, J R *NewYHSD*
Richards, Jacob 1773-1816 *BiAUS, BiDrAC, WhAm H*
Richards, James 1766-1843 *Drake*
Richards, James 1767-1843 *ApCAB, NatCAB 4*

Richards, James Alexander Dudley 1845-1911 *BiDrAC*
Richards, James Austin 1878- *WhAm 6*
Richards, James L 1858-1955 *WhAm 3*
Richards, James Prioleau 1894- *BiDrAC*
Richards, Janet Elizabeth Hosmer d1948 *WhAm 2, WomWWA 14*
Richards, Jean Marie 1872- *WhAm 5*
Richards, John *BiAUS*
Richards, John d1694 *Drake*
Richards, John 1753-1822 *BiDrAC, WhAm H*
Richards, John 1765-1850 *BiDrAC, WhAm H*
Richards, John 1797-1859 *Drake*
Richards, John 1831-1889 *NewYHSD*
Richards, John Evan 1856-1932 *NatCAB 23, WhAm 1*
Richards, John Francisco 1834-1922 *NatCAB 20*
Richards, John Gardiner 1864-1941 *NatCAB 45, WhAm 1*
Richards, John H *NewYHSD*
Richards, John H 1807?- *NewYHSD*
Richards, John Kelvey 1856-1909 *DcAmB, NatCAB 13, NatCAB 29, WhAm 1*
Richards, John P Moore 1847- *ApCAB X*
Richards, John Thomas 1851-1942 *WhAm 2*
Richards, John William 1803-1854 *ApCAB*
Richards, Jonas DeForest 1809-1872 *TwCBDA*
Richards, Joseph Ernest 1881- *NatCAB 16*
Richards, Joseph H *WhAm 5*
Richards, Joseph Havens Cowles 1851-1923 *TwCBDA, WhAm 1*
Richards, Joseph Thomas 1845- *NatCAB 14*
Richards, Joseph William 1864-1921 *DcAmB, NatCAB 13, WhAm 1*
Richards, Laura Elizabeth Howe 1850-1943 *DcAmB S3, NatCAB 15, NatCAB 39, NotAW, TwCBDA, WebAB, WhAm 2, WomWWA 14*
Richards, Lee Greene 1878-1950 *IlBEAAW*
Richards, Lela Horn 1870- *WhAm 5*
Richards, Lewis Loomis 1881-1940 *WhAm 1*
Richards, Linda Judson 1841-1930 *BiDAmEd, NotAW*
Richards, Louise d1966 *WhAm 5*
Richards, Louise Parks 1852- *WomWWA 14*
Richards, Maria Tolman 1821- *ApCAB*
Richards, Mark 1760-1844 *BiAUS, BiDrAC, WhAm H*
Richards, Mark Allred 1883-1942 *NatCAB 33*
Richards, Mary Anne Mitchell 1936-1975 *WhAm 6*
Richards, Matthias 1757-1830 *BiAUS*
Richards, Matthias 1758-1830 *BiDrAC*
Richards, Matthias Henry 1841-1898 *ApCAB, TwCBDA*
Richards, N *NewYHSD*
Richards, Nancy Dryden *WomWWA 14*
Richards, Nathan Charles 1864-1943 *WhAm 2*
Richards, Paul Snelgrove 1892-1958 *NatCAB 47*
Richards, Paul Stanley 1870- *WhAm 5*
Richards, Paul William 1874-1956 *WhAm 3*
Richards, Perry Douglas 1880-1947 *NatCAB 36*
Richards, Preston 1905-1957 *WhAm 3*
Richards, Ralph H 1892-1967 *WhAm 5*
Richards, Ralph Strother 1881- *WhAm 2*
Richards, Ralph Webster 1879- *WhAm 6*
Richards, Ray 1894-1950 *WhAm 3*
Richards, Rezin Howard 1901-1963 *WhAm 4*
Richards, Robert Hallowell 1844-1945 *ApCAB, DcAmB S3, NatCAB 12, TwCBDA, WhAm 2*
Richards, Robert Haven 1873-1951 *WhAm 3*
Richards, Robert Kenneth 1913-1969 *NatCAB 54*
Richards, Robert Watt 1900-1963 *WhAm 4*
Richards, Roger G 1925- *WhAm 5*
Richards, Rosalind 1874- *WhAm 5*
Richards, Samuel 1853-1893 *NatCAB 6*
Richards, Samuel H d1957 *WhAm 3*
Richards, Seth Mason 1850-1910 *NatCAB 21*
Richards, Stephen L 1879-1959 *NatCAB 49, WhAm 3*
Richards, Stewart Watson 1903-1975 *WhAm 6*
Richards, T Addison 1820-1900 *NatCAB 8, WhAm 1*
Richards, Theodore 1867-1948 *NatCAB 40*

Richards, Theodore William 1868-1928 *AmBi, ApCAB Sup, AsBiEn, DcAmB, DcScB, McGEWB, NatCAB 12, WebAB, WhAm 1*
Richards, Thomas Addison 1820-1900 *AmBi, ApCAB, DcAmB, NewYHSD, TwCBDA*
Richards, Thomas Cole 1866-1936 *WhAm 1*
Richards, Thomas W *NewYHSD*
Richards, Mrs. Waldo d1927 *WhAm 1*
Richards, Walter Alan 1891-1961 *NatCAB 49*
Richards, Willard 1804-1854 *NatCAB 16*
Richards, William 1792-1847 *ApCAB, Drake, NatCAB 4*
Richards, William 1793-1847 *BiDAmEd, DcAmB, WhAm H*
Richards, William Alford 1849-1912 *NatCAB 11, TwCBDA, WhAm 1*
Richards, Sir William Buell 1815-1889 *ApCAB*
Richards, William Carey 1817-1892 *Drake*
Richards, William Carey 1818-1892 *ApCAB, TwCBDA*
Richards, William Henry 1856- *WhAm 4, WhoColR*
Richards, William Joseph 1863- *WhAm 4*
Richards, William Phillips 1855-1925 *NatCAB 20*
Richards, William Rogers 1853-1910 *WhAm 1*
Richards, William Trost 1833-1905 *AmBi, ApCAB, BnEnAmA, DcAmB, NatCAB 12, NewYHSD, TwCBDA, WhAm 1*
Richards, Zalmon 1811-1899 *BiDAmEd, DcAmB, NatCAB 13, WhAm H*
Richardson, Abby Sage 1837-1900 *NatCAB 5, TwCBDA, WhAm 1*
Richardson, Albert Deane 1833-1869 *ApCAB, DcAmB, Drake, NatCAB 8, TwCBDA, WhAm H*
Richardson, Alexander Henderson 1872- *WhAm 5*
Richardson, Alice Miller *WomWWA 14*
Richardson, Allan Harvey 1872-1955 *NatCAB 42*
Richardson, Andrew 1799-1876 *NewYHSD*
Richardson, Anna Euretta 1883-1931 *DcAmB, WhAm 1*
Richardson, Anna Steese 1865-1949 *WhAm 2*
Richardson, Arthur St. George 1863- *WhoColR*
Richardson, Basil 1866-1937 *WhAm 1*
Richardson, Beale Howard 1843- *NatCAB 4*
Richardson, Benjamin 1835-1926 *NewYHSD*
Richardson, Benjamin Ward 1828-1896 *BiHiMed, DcScB*
Richardson, Carrie Lavinia *WomWWA 14*
Richardson, Charles 1841-1922 *WhAm 1*
Richardson, Charles Francis 1851-1913 *ApCAB, BiDAmEd, DcAmB, NatCAB 9, TwCBDA, WhAm 1*
Richardson, Charles Freemont 1862-1939 *WhAm 1*
Richardson, Charles Fremont 1862-1939 *NatCAB 30*
Richardson, Charles Henry 1862-1935 *NatCAB 26, WhAm 1*
Richardson, Charles Tiffany 1880- *WhAm 6*
Richardson, Charles Williamson 1861-1929 *DcAmB, NatCAB 22, WhAm 1*
Richardson, Clarence H 1890-1955 *WhAm 3*
Richardson, Clifford 1856-1932 *AmBi, NatCAB 33, WhAm 1, WhAm 1C*
Richardson, Clifford Harry 1888-1958 *NatCAB 44*
Richardson, David Arthur 1875-1953 *NatCAB 47*
Richardson, David Crockett 1845- *WhAm 4*
Richardson, David Nelson 1832- *ApCAB X*
Richardson, David Plunket 1833-1904 *BiDrAC*
Richardson, Donald Delos 1900-1957 *NatCAB 46*
Richardson, Donovan MacNeely 1894-1967 *WhAm 4A*
Richardson, Dorothy d1955 *WhAm 3*
Richardson, Dorothy 1878- *WomWWA 14*
Richardson, Dwight Sumner 1850-1930 *NatCAB 28*
Richardson, Edmund 1818-1886 *ApCAB, DcAmB, WhAm H*
Richardson, Edmund F 1862- *NatCAB 12*

Richardson, Edward 1789-1876 *ApCAB*
Richardson, Edward Adams 1859-1919 *NatCAB 18*
Richardson, Edward Elliott 1873-1950 *WhAm 3*
Richardson, Edward Henderson 1877-1971 *NatCAB 56, WhAm 5*
Richardson, Edward Peirson 1881-1944 *WhAm 2*
Richardson, Edwin Sanders 1875-1950 *WhAm 3*
Richardson, Elisabeth Mathews 1872- *WomWWA 14*
Richardson, Ellen A 1845-1911 *WhAm 1*
Richardson, Elliot Lee 1920- *BiDrUSE*
Richardson, Elliott Verne 1868-1929 *WhAm 1*
Richardson, Elmo 1930- *EncAAH*
Richardson, Elsie Greenwood Pillsbury 1877- *WomWWA 14*
Richardson, Emma Adelia Rice *WomWWA 14*
Richardson, Ernest Cushing 1860-1939 *ApCAB Sup, DcAmLiB, NatCAB 13, TwCBDA, WhAm 1*
Richardson, Ernest Gladstone 1874-1947 *WhAm 2*
Richardson, Florence Amidon 1868- *WomWWA 14*
Richardson, Florence Wyman 1855- *WomWWA 14*
Richardson, Francis 1681-1729 *BnEnAmA*
Richardson, Francis 1705?-1782 *BnEnAmA*
Richardson, Francis Asbury 1838-1926 *WhAm 1*
Richardson, Francis Harrie 1898-1975 *WhAm 6*
Richardson, Francis Henry 1855- *NatCAB 13*
Richardson, Francis Henry 1859-1934 *WhAm 1*
Richardson, Frank Chase 1859-1918 *WhAm 1*
Richardson, Frank Howard 1882- *WhAm 6*
Richardson, Frederick *NewYHSD*
Richardson, Frederick 1862-1937 *WhAm 1*
Richardson, Frederick Albert 1873- *WhAm 5*
Richardson, Frederick Dawson 1884-1954 *NatCAB 48*
Richardson, Friend William 1869-1943 *NatCAB 53, WhAm 2*
Richardson, G Reid 1879-1937 *NatCAB 27*
Richardson, George *NewYHSD*
Richardson, George Adams 1887-1958 *NatCAB 47, WhAm 3*
Richardson, George Burr 1872-1949 *NatCAB 38, WhAm 5*
Richardson, George Francis 1829-1912 *NatCAB 15*
Richardson, George Frederick 1850-1923 *BiDrAC*
Richardson, George Lynde 1867-1935 *WhAm 1*
Richardson, George Parker 1850-1919 *NatCAB 18*
Richardson, George Tilton d1938 *WhAm 1*
Richardson, Granville Alfred 1860- *ApCAB X*
Richardson, Guy A 1882-1960 *WhAm 4*
Richardson, H George 1901-1971 *WhAm 5*
Richardson, Harriet *WomWWA 14*
Richardson, Harry Alden 1853-1928 *BiDrAC, NatCAB 14, WhAm 1, WhAmP*
Richardson, Henry *NewYHSD*
Richardson, Henry Brown 1837-1909 *WhAm 1*
Richardson, Henry Handel 1870-1946 *McGEWB*
Richardson, Henry Hobson 1836-1886 *BnEnAmA*
Richardson, Henry Hobson 1838-1886 *AmBi, ApCAB, DcAmB, DcAmLiB, EncAB, McGEWB, NatCAB 6, TwCBDA, WebAB, WhAm H*
Richardson, Henry Smith 1885-1972 *NatCAB 57, WhAm 5*
Richardson, Hester Dorsey 1862-1923 *AmWom, WhAm 1, WomWWA 14*
Richardson, Hilary Goode 1874- *WhAm 5*
Richardson, Holden Chester 1878- *WhAm 6*
Richardson, Howard Gray 1885-1944 *NatCAB 34*
Richardson, Hugh 1869- *WhAm 5*
Richardson, Ira 1871-1958 *WhAm 3*
Richardson, Israel Bush 1815-1862 *ApCAB, DcAmB, NatCAB 12, TwCBDA, WhAm H*
Richardson, Israel Bush 1819-1862 *Drake*
Richardson, J F *NewYHSD*

Richardson, James 1817-1863 *ApCAB*
Richardson, James B 1770-1836 *BiAUS*
Richardson, James Bailey 1832-1911 *WhAm 1*
Richardson, James Burchell 1770-1836 *TwCBDA*
Richardson, James Burchill 1770-1836 *NatCAB 12*
Richardson, James Daniel 1843-1914 *BiDrAC, DcAmB, NatCAB 17, TwCBDA, WhAm 1, WhAmP*
Richardson, James Daniel 1875-1950 *NatCAB 37*
Richardson, James H *NewYHSD*
Richardson, James Hugh 1894-1963 *WhAm 4*
Richardson, James Julius 1868-1933 *WhAm 1*
Richardson, James McDowell 1884-1971 *NatCAB 55*
Richardson, James Montgomery 1858-1925 *BiDrAC, WhAm 4*
Richardson, James Otto 1878-1974 *WhAm 6*
Richardson, James Parmelee 1878-1947 *WhAm 2*
Richardson, Jennie May *WomWWA 14*
Richardson, John *Drake*
Richardson, Sir John 1787-1865 *ApCAB, Drake*
Richardson, John 1797-1863? *ApCAB*
Richardson, John Breckinridge, Jr. 1876-1958 *NatCAB 47*
Richardson, John Fram 1808-1868 *ApCAB*
Richardson, John Manly 1831-1898 *TwCBDA*
Richardson, John Moore 1880-1941 *NatCAB 32*
Richardson, John Peter 1801-1864 *ApCAB, BiAUS, BiDrAC, Drake, NatCAB 12, TwCBDA, WhAm H*
Richardson, John Peter 1831-1899 *ApCAB Sup, NatCAB 12*
Richardson, John S 1908-1969 *WhAm 5*
Richardson, John Smythe 1777-1850 *ApCAB, BiAUS, NatCAB 12, TwCBDA*
Richardson, John Smythe 1828-1894 *ApCAB, BiDrAC, TwCBDA, WhAm H*
Richardson, Jonathan James 1839- *ApCAB X*
Richardson, Joseph 1711-1784 *BnEnAmA, DcAmB, WhAm H*
Richardson, Joseph 1778-1871 *ApCAB, BiAUS, BiDrAC, TwCBDA, WhAm H*
Richardson, Joseph, Jr. 1752-1831 *BnEnAmA*
Richardson, Josiah Crosby 1842-1918 *NatCAB 18*
Richardson, Julius Caesar 1851-1910 *NatCAB 17*
Richardson, Katharine Berry d1933 *WhAm 1*
Richardson, L C *NewYHSD*
Richardson, Leon Burr 1878-1951 *BiDAmEd, NatCAB 39*
Richardson, Leon Josiah 1868-1966 *WhAm 4*
Richardson, Lunsford 1854-1919 *NatCAB 37*
Richardson, Lunsford 1891-1953 *WhAm 3*
Richardson, M S 1895-1971 *WhAm 5*
Richardson, Marcella Percy *WomWWA 14*
Richardson, Margaret Foster 1881- *WomWWA 14*
Richardson, Marion Solomon 1895-1971 *NatCAB 57*
Richardson, Mark E 1905-1972 *WhAm 5*
Richardson, Mark Wyman 1867- *ApCAB X, WhAm 4*
Richardson, Mary Lilias *WomWWA 14*
Richardson, Mary Meylert *WomWWA 14*
Richardson, Mary Neal 1859- *WomWWA 14*
Richardson, Mary Raymond 1851- *WomWWA 14*
Richardson, Maurice Howe 1851-1912 *DcAmB, NatCAB 13, NatCAB 18, WhAm 1*
Richardson, Nathaniel 1754-1827 *BnEnAmA*
Richardson, Nathaniel Smith 1810-1883 *ApCAB, Drake*
Richardson, Norman Egbert 1878-1945 *WhAm 2*
Richardson, Norval 1877-1940 *WhAm 1*
Richardson, Oliver Huntington 1866-1936 *WhAm 1*
Richardson, Orlando Brown 1842-1921 *ApCAB X*
Richardson, Sir Owen Willans 1879-1959 *AsBiEn, DcScB, WhAm 3*
Richardson, Philip d1948 *WhAm 2*

Richardson, Richard *NewYHSD*
Richardson, Richard 1704-1780 *ApCAB*,
TwCBDA
Richardson, Richard 1704-1781 *Drake*
Richardson, Robert 1806-1876 *DcAmB*,
WhAm H
Richardson, Robert Charlwood, Jr. 1882-1954
WhAm 3
Richardson, Robert Kimball 1876-1952
WhAm 3
Richardson, Robert Newton 1841- *WhAm 3*
Richardson, Robert Price 1896-1967 *WhAm 5*
Richardson, Robert William 1851- *WhAm 4*
Richardson, Rodney Hall 1860-1936
NatCAB 36
Richardson, Roland George Dwight 1878-1949
WhAm 2
Richardson, Roy Mundy Davidson 1895-1968
NatCAB 54, *WhAm 5*
Richardson, Rufus Byam 1845-1914 *DcAmB*,
WhAm 1
Richardson, Rupert Norval 1891- *EncAAH*,
REnAW
Richardson, Russell 1881- *WhAm 6*
Richardson, S *NewYHSD*
Richardson, Mrs. Samuel *NewYHSD*
Richardson, Samuel 1689-1761 *McGEWB*
Richardson, Sarah Felt Bryant *WomWWA 14*
Richardson, Sarah Lyman Dickinson
WomWWA 14
Richardson, Seth Whitley 1880-1953 *WhAm 3*
Richardson, Sid Williams 1891-1959 *WhAm 3*,
WhAm 4
Richardson, Solon Osmond, III 1887-1956
NatCAB 48
Richardson, T M *NewYHSD*
Richardson, Thomas Franklin 1855-1915
NatCAB 19
Richardson, Thomas Meriwether 1848-1915
NatCAB 43
Richardson, Tobias Gibson 1827-1892 *DcAmB*,
WhAm H
Richardson, Warfield Creath 1823-1914
WhAm 1
Richardson, Wilds Preston 1861-1929 *DcAmB*,
WebAMB, *WhAm 1*
Richardson, Willard 1802-1875 *DcAmB*,
WhAm H
Richardson, Willard Durant 1857-1938
NatCAB 28
Richardson, Willard Samuel 1866-1952
WhAm 3
Richardson, William 1743-1786 *TwCBDA*
Richardson, William 1839-1914 *BiDrAC*,
WhAmP
Richardson, William 1845-1914 *TwCBDA*,
WhAm 1
Richardson, William Adams 1821-1896 *AmBi*,
ApCAB, *BiAUS*, *BiDrUSE*, *DcAmB*,
NatCAB 4, *TwCBDA*, *WhAm H*
Richardson, William Alexander 1811-1875
ApCAB, *BiAUS*, *BiDrAC*, *Drake*,
WhAm H, *WhAmP*
Richardson, William Cummings 1854-1935
WhAm 1
Richardson, William D 1876-1936 *WhAm 1*
Richardson, William Eddy 1861-1923 *WhAm 1*
Richardson, William Edwin 1900-1971 *WhAm 5*
Richardson, William Emanuel 1886-1948
BiDrAC, *WhAm 2*
Richardson, William Franklin 1852-1925
WhAm 1
Richardson, William Henry 1906-1960
NatCAB 48
Richardson, William Howard 1869- *WhoColR*
Richardson, William King 1859-1951
NatCAB 39, *WhAm 5*
Richardson, William Lambert 1842-1932
DcAmB, *NatCAB 25*, *WhAm 1*
Richardson, William Lloyd 1901-1973
NatCAB 56, *WhAm 5*
Richardson, William Merchant 1774-1838
ApCAB, *BiAUS*, *BiDrAC*, *DcAmB*, *Drake*,
NatCAB 4, *TwCBDA*, *WhAm H*,
WhAmP
Richardson, William Ormiston 1879-1925
ApCAB X

Richardson, William Payson 1864-1945
NatCAB 35
Richardson, William Reuben 1866- *WhoColR*
Richardson, William Samuel 1893-1962
WhAm 4
Richardson, William Symmes 1873-1931
WhAm 1
Richardson, William Waddle 1877-1945
NatCAB 34
Richardson, William Wightman 1866-1912
NatCAB 18
Richardson, Wilson Gaines 1825-1886 *TwCBDA*
Richardt, Ferdinand Joachim 1819-1895
IlBEAAW, *NewYHSD*
Richart, Duncan Grant 1887-1950 *WhAm 3*
Richart, Frank Erwin 1892-1951 *WhAm 3*
Richberg, Donald Randall 1881-1960
NatCAB 49, *WhAm 4*
Riche, Charles Swift 1864-1936 *WhAm 1*
Riche, George Inman 1833- *ApCAB*
Riche, Jean Baptiste 1780?-1847 *ApCAB*,
Drake
Riche DeProny, Gaspard-Francois-C-M *DcScB*
Richel, George William 1905-1970 *WhAm 5*
Richel, Nicolas Antoine 1745-1799 *ApCAB*
Richelieu, Cardinal Armand Jean DuP De
1585-1642 *McGEWB*
Richepanse, Antoine 1770-1803 *ApCAB*
Richer, Jean 1630-1696 *AsBiEn*, *DcScB*
Richer DeBelleval, Pierre *DcScB*
Richery, Joseph De 1757-1799 *ApCAB*
Riches *NewYHSD*
Richeson, Frank St. Clair 1889-1954
NatCAB 46
Richeson, John Jacob 1874-1964 *WhAm 4*,
WhAm 5
Richeson, Vern Noah 1889-1951 *NatCAB 39*
Richet, Charles Robert 1850-1935 *AsBiEn*,
DcScB, *McGEWB*
Richet, Jules Cesar 1697-1776 *ApCAB*
Richey, Albert Sutton 1874-1936 *WhAm 1*
Richey, Anna Gertrude 1873- *WomWWA 14*
Richey, Frank O 1878-1964 *NatCAB 52*
Richey, Frederick David 1884-1955 *WhAm 3*
Richey, Lawrence 1885-1959 *WhAm 3*
Richey, Matthew 1803-1883 *ApCAB*
Richey, Matthew Henry 1828- *ApCAB*
Richey, S Hunter 1882-1949 *NatCAB 37*
Richey, Thomas B 1887-1949 *WhAm 2*
Richhart, William Shirley 1881-1941
NatCAB 32
Richier, Germaine 1904-1959 *McGEWB*
Richings, Caroline Mary 1827-1884 *ApCAB*,
Drake, *NatCAB 9*
Richings, Peter 1797-1871 *ApCAB*, *Drake*,
NatCAB 7
Richings, Peter 1798-1871 *DcAmB*, *WhAm H*
Richison, Earl 1889-1962 *NatCAB 52*
Richling, Don Jose 1874- *WhAm 5*
Richman, Arthur 1886-1944 *WhAm 2*
Richman, Frank Nelson 1881-1956 *NatCAB 54*,
WhAm 4
Richman, Irving Berdine 1861-1938 *TwCBDA*,
WhAm 1
Richman, Julia 1855-1912 *BiDAmEd*, *NotAW*
Richman, Nathan G 1868-1941 *NatCAB 31*
Richmann, Georg Wilhelm 1711-1753 *DcScB*
Richmond, Adam 1889-1959 *WhAm 3*
Richmond, Agnes M *WomWWA 14*
Richmond, Altha Louisa 1850- *WomWWA 14*
Richmond, Charles Alexander 1862-1940
NatCAB 30, *WhAm 1*
Richmond, Charles Alexander 1863-1940
NatCAB 14
Richmond, Charles Blair 1893-1968 *WhAm 5*
Richmond, Charles Gordon Lennox 1764-1820
ApCAB, *Drake*
Richmond, Charles Herbert 1840-1904
NatCAB 17
Richmond, Charles Wallace 1868-1932 *DcAmB*,
NatCAB 23, *WhAm 1*
Richmond, Dean 1804-1866 *ApCAB*, *DcAmB*,
Drake, *WhAm H*, *WhAmP*
Richmond, Edward Gould 1851-1903
NatCAB 19
Richmond, Euphemia Johnson 1825- *AmWom*,
NatCAB 4, *WhAm 1*, *WomWWA 14*

Richmond, Frederic Courtis 1862-1940
WhAm 1
Richmond, George Chalmers 1870- *WhAm 5*
Richmond, George Ernest 1880-1925
NatCAB 24
Richmond, Gerald Hunt 1877-1930 *NatCAB 32*
Richmond, Grace Smith 1866-1959 *WhAm 3*,
WomWWA 14
Richmond, Harold Anthony 1871-1948
NatCAB 38
Richmond, Harold Bours 1892-1970 *WhAm 5*
Richmond, Hiram H 1810-1885 *BiAUS*
Richmond, Hiram Lawton 1810-1885 *BiDrAC*,
WhAm H
Richmond, James Buchanan 1842-1910 *BiDrAC*
Richmond, James Cook 1808-1866 *ApCAB*,
Drake
Richmond, James Howell 1884-1945 *WhAm 2*
Richmond, Jeannette Davis Nightingale 1879-
WomWWA 14
Richmond, Jewett Melvin 1831-1899
NatCAB 21
Richmond, John Lambert 1785-1855 *DcAmB*,
WhAm H
Richmond, John Wilkes 1775-1857 *DcAmB*,
WhAm H
Richmond, Jonathan 1774-1853 *BiAUS*,
BiDrAC, *WhAm H*
Richmond, Kenneth Calvin 1894-1969 *WhAm 5*
Richmond, Leonard *IlBEAAW*
Richmond, Lewis 1824-1894 *NatCAB 12*
Richmond, Lizzie R 1850- *AmWom*
Richmond, Mary Ellen 1861-1928 *DcAmB*,
NatCAB 21, *NotAW*, *WhAm 1*,
WomWWA 14
Richmond, Sarah Abigail Adams 1821-1866
ApCAB
Richmond, William 1797-1858 *ApCAB*
Richmond, William Henry 1821- *NatCAB 9*
Richter, Albert B 1845-1898 *IlBEAAW*
Richter, Arthur William 1883-1952 *NatCAB 39*
Richter, Conrad Michael 1890-1968 *McGEWB*,
REnAW, *WhAm 5*
Richter, Emil Heinrich 1869- *WhAm 5*
Richter, Gisela Marie Augusta 1882-1972
WhAm 5
Richter, Henry Joseph 1838-1916 *ApCAB*,
NatCAB 12, *TwCBDA*, *WhAm 1*
Richter, Hieronymus Theodor 1824-1898?
AsBiEn
Richter, Jeremias Benjamin 1762-1807 *DcScB*
Richter, Johann Paul Friedrich 1763-1825
McGEWB
Richter, John Frederick 1897-1954 *NatCAB 41*,
WhAm 3
Richter, Julius 1876-1974 *WhAm 6*
Richter, Otto Clarence 1899-1962 *NatCAB 49*
Richter, Paul Ernest 1896-1949 *NatCAB 38*,
WhAm 2
Richter, Richard *NewYHSD*
Richter, Richard Biddle 1901-1971 *WhAm 5*
Richter, Theodore John 1882-1950 *NatCAB 40*
Richthofen, Ferdinand Von 1833-1905 *DcScB*
Richthofen, Lothar Von 1894-1922 *WhoMilH*
Richthofen, Manfred Freiherr Von 1892-1918
WhoMilH
Richtmyer, Floyd Karker 1881-1939 *DcAmB S2*,
DcScB, *WhAm 1*
Ricimer, Flavius d472 *McGEWB*
Rickard, Arthur Purdy 1884-1960 *NatCAB 49*
Rickard, Brent Neville 1885-1951 *WhAm 3*
Rickard, Edgar 1874-1951 *NatCAB 42*,
WhAm 5
Rickard, George Lewis 1871-1929 *DcAmB*,
WebAB, *WhAm HA*, *WhAm 4*
Rickard, Richard Darke 1856-1946 *WhAm 2*
Rickard, Thomas Arthur 1864- *WhAm 5*
Rickards, George Collins 1860-1933 *WhAm 1*
Rickards, James S 1883-1949 *WhAm 2*
Rickards, John Ezra 1848- *NatCAB 11*,
TwCBDA
Rickel, Henry William 1833-1910 *NatCAB 24*
Rickenbacker, Edward Vernon 1890-1973
ApCAB X, *WebAB*, *WebAMB*, *WhAm 5*
Rickenbacker, Edward Veron 1890-1973
WhoMilH
Ricker, Alvan Bolster 1850-1933 *NatCAB 24*

Ricker, George Alfred Joy 1863-1933 *NatCAB 12, WhAm 1*
Ricker, Hiram 1809-1893 *NatCAB 2*
Ricker, Hiram Weston 1857-1930 *NatCAB 24*
Ricker, Marilla Marks Young 1840-1920 *NatCAB 17, NotAW, WhAm 1, WomWWA 14*
Ricker, Marrilla M 1840-1920 *AmWom*
Ricker, Mary Stowell 1871- *WomWWA 14*
Ricker, N Clifford 1843-1924 *WhAm 1*
Ricker, Nathan Clifford 1843-1924 *BiDAmEd*
Ricker, Robert Edwin 1828-1894 *NatCAB 6*
Rickerby, Arthur Burroughs 1921-1972 *WhAm 5*
Rickerson, Maude Williams 1869- *WomWWA 14*
Rickert, Edith 1871-1938 *NotAW, WhAm 1*
Rickert, Frederick William 1878-1950 *NatCAB 39*
Rickert, J *NewYHSD*
Rickert, Martha Edith 1871-1938 *DcAmB S2, WomWWA 14*
Rickert, Thomas A 1876-1941 *WhAm 1*
Ricket, Thomas *NewYHSD*
Ricketson, Daniel 1813-1898 *DcAmB, WhAm H*
Ricketson, Walton 1839-1923 *NewYHSD, WhAm 1*
Ricketts, Claude Bertram 1877-1951 *NatCAB 39*
Ricketts, Claude Vernon 1906-1964 *NatCAB 52, WhAm 4*
Ricketts, Edwin Burnley 1883-1956 *NatCAB 46*
Ricketts, Edwin Darlington 1867-1937 *BiDrAC, WhAmP*
Ricketts, Howard Taylor 1871-1910 *AsBiEn, DcAmB S1, DcScB, NatCAB 34*
Ricketts, James Brewerton 1817-1887 *AmBi, ApCAB, DcAmB, Drake, NatCAB 4, TwCBDA, WhAm H*
Ricketts, Louis Davidson 1859-1940 *NatCAB 33, WhAm 1*
Ricketts, Palmer Chamberlaine 1856-1934 *DcAmB S1, NatCAB 26, WhAm 1*
Ricketts, Pierre DePeyster d1918 *WhAm 1*
Ricketts, Robert Bruce 1839- *NatCAB 5*
Rickey, Branch Wesley 1881-1965 *EncAB, WebAB, WhAm 4*
Rickey, George 1907- *BnEnAmA*
Rickey, James Walter 1871-1943 *WhAm 2*
Rickey, Minna Blair *WomWWA 14*
Rickey, Walter Josiah 1871-1935 *NatCAB 31*
Rickly, Samuel Strasser 1819- *NatCAB 11*
Rickmers, Edna Allen *WomWWA 14*
Rickner, Louis *NewYHSD*
Rickoff, Andrew Jackson 1824-1899 *ApCAB, BiDAmEd, NatCAB 4*
Rickover, Hyman George 1900- *AsBiEn, WebAB, WebAMB*
Ricks, Augustus J 1843-1906 *WhAm 1*
Ricks, David Absalom 1877-1954 *NatCAB 45*
Ricks, Edgar Ethelred 1877- *WhoColR*
Ricks, James Benjamin 1852-1906 *NatCAB 17, WhAm 1*
Ricks, Jesse Jay 1879-1944 *WhAm 2*
Ricks, William Benjamin 1866-1963 *WhAm 4*
Ricksecker, Peter 1791-1873 *NatCAB 5*
Ricord, Alexander 1798-1876 *ApCAB*
Ricord, Elizabeth 1788-1865 *ApCAB, Drake*
Ricord, Frederick William 1819-1897 *ApCAB, DcAmB, NatCAB 8, TwCBDA, WhAm H*
Ricord, Jean Baptiste 1777-1837 *ApCAB*
Ricord, Philippe 1800-1889 *ApCAB, BiHiMed, DcAmB, WhAm H*
Ridabock, Raymond Budd 1904-1970 *WhAm 5*
Riddell, Agnes Rutherford *WomWWA 14*
Riddell, Guy Crosby 1882-1959 *WhAm 4*
Riddell, Herman Ellis 1890-1966 *WhAm 4*
Riddell, John L 1807- *Drake*
Riddell, John Leonard 1807-1865 *DcAmB, NatCAB 21, WhAm H*
Riddell, John Leonard 1807-1867 *ApCAB*
Riddell, John Tate 1885-1945 *NatCAB 35*
Riddell, Robert Gerald 1908-1951 *WhAm 3*
Riddell, William Hugh 1897-1958 *WhAm 3*
Riddell, William Renwick 1852-1945 *WhAm 2*
Ridder, Bernard Herman 1883-1975 *WhAm 6*

Ridder, Herman 1851-1915 *DcAmB, NatCAB 22, WhAm 1*
Ridder, Herman Henry 1908-1969 *WhAm 5*
Ridder, Joseph E 1886-1966 *WhAm 4*
Ridder, Victor Frank 1886-1963 *WhAm 4*
Riddick, Carl Wood 1872-1960 *BiDrAC, WhAm 5*
Riddick, Diamond Matthew 1873- *WhoColR*
Riddick, James Edward 1849-1907 *WhAm 1*
Riddick, Thomas Kader 1851- *WhAm 4*
Riddick, Wallace Carl 1864-1942 *WhAm 2*
Riddick, Walter Garrett 1883-1953 *WhAm 3*
Riddle, Adeline *WomWWA 14*
Riddle, Albert Gallatin 1816-1902 *AmBi, ApCAB, BiAUS, BiDrAC, DcAmB, NatCAB 2, TwCBDA, WhAm 1, WhAmP*
Riddle, David Hunter 1805-1888 *NatCAB 24, TwCBDA*
Riddle, Edith Gillette Ward *WomWWA 14*
Riddle, Finis Ewing 1870-1953 *NatCAB 43*
Riddle, George Peabody 1851-1910 *DcAmB, NatCAB 13, TwCBDA, WhAm 1*
Riddle, George Peabody 1853-1910 *ApCAB*
Riddle, George Read 1817-1867 *BiAUS, BiDrAC, NatCAB 4, TwCBDA, WhAm H, WhAmP*
Riddle, George Reade 1817-1867 *ApCAB, Drake*
Riddle, H T 1834-1879 *BiAUS*
Riddle, H Warner 1880-1962 *NatCAB 50*
Riddle, Harry Carson 1869- *NatCAB 18*
Riddle, Harry Earle 1894-1962 *NatCAB 48*
Riddle, Harry Marvin 1855-1937 *NatCAB 38*
Riddle, Haywood Yancey 1834-1879 *BiDrAC, WhAm H*
Riddle, James Henry 1916-1966 *NatCAB 54*
Riddle, James Marion, Jr. 1913-1970 *WhAm 5*
Riddle, John Wallace 1864-1941 *NatCAB 14, NatCAB 30, WhAm 2*
Riddle, Joseph 1753-1836 *BiAUS*
Riddle, Julia *WomWWA 14*
Riddle, Lawrence Edward 1876-1951 *NatCAB 39*
Riddle, Lincoln Ware 1880-1921 *WhAm 1*
Riddle, Mary Althea *WomWWA 14*
Riddle, Matthew Brown 1836-1916 *ApCAB, DcAmB, NatCAB 13, TwCBDA, WhAm 1*
Riddle, Oscar 1877-1968 *WhAm 5*
Riddle, Samuel Doyle 1861-1951 *DcAmB S5*
Riddle, Theodate Pope d1946 *BiCAW, WhAm 2*
Riddle, William 1860- *WhAm 4*
Riddle, William R *NewYHSD*
Riddleberger, Harrison Holt 1844-1890 *ApCAB, BiDrAC, NatCAB 13, TwCBDA, WhAm H*
Riddles, Leonard 1910- *IIBEAAW*
Rideal, Charles Frederick 1858- *WhAm 4*
Rideal, Eric Keightley 1890-1974 *WhAm 6*
Rideing, William Henry 1853- *ApCAB, TwCBDA*
Rideing, William Henry 1853-1918 *AmBi, DcAmB*
Rideing, William Henry 1853-1919 *WhAm 1*
Ridenour, Gerald Marcellus 1901-1972 *NatCAB 57*
Ridenour, Louis N, Jr. 1911-1959 *WhAm 3*
Rideout, Frances Reed 1887- *WomWWA 14*
Rideout, Helen B *WomWWA 14*
Rideout, Henry Milner 1877-1927 *DcAmB, NatCAB 14, WhAm 1*
Rider, Alexander *NewYHSD*
Rider, Arthur Fremont 1885-1962 *DcAmLiB*
Rider, Arthur William 1863- *WhAm 4*
Rider, Charles R 1895-1961 *WhAm 4*
Rider, Dwight George 1897-1966 *NatCAB 53*
Rider, Fremont 1885-1962 *NatCAB 50, WhAm 4*
Rider, George Thomas 1829- *ApCAB, Drake*
Rider, Ira Edgar 1868-1906 *BiDrAC, WhAm 4*
Rider-Kelsey, Corinne 1877-1947 *NotAW*
Ridgaway, Henry Bascom 1830-1895 *ApCAB, DcAmB, NatCAB 9, TwCBDA*
Ridgaway, Henry Baseom 1830-1895 *WhAm H*
Ridge, Albert Alphonso 1898-1967 *WhAm 4*
Ridge, Isaac M 1825- *NatCAB 12*

Ridge, John 1801?-1839 *ApCAB, NatCAB 8*
Ridge, John R d1867 *ApCAB*
Ridge, Lola 1873-1941 *NotAW*
Ridge, Major 1771?-1839 *AmBi, ApCAB, DcAmB, WhAm H*
Ridge, Martin 1923- *EncAAH*
Ridgeley, Charles Goodwin 1784-1848 *ApCAB, TwCBDA*
Ridgeley, Henry Moore 1778-1847 *BiAUS*
Ridgeley, Henry Moore 1779-1847 *WhAm H*
Ridgely, Benjamin H 1861-1908 *WhAm 1*
Ridgely, Charles 1738-1785 *ApCAB, Drake*
Ridgely, Charles Carnan d1829 *Drake*
Ridgely, Charles Carnan 1760-1829 *TwCBDA*
Ridgely, Charles Carnan 1762-1829 *ApCAB, NatCAB 9*
Ridgely, Charles Goodwin 1784-1848 *DcAmB, Drake, WhAm H*
Ridgely, Daniel B 1813-1868 *Drake*
Ridgely, Daniel Boone 1813-1868 *ApCAB, TwCBDA*
Ridgely, Daniel Bowly 1813-1868 *DcAmB, WhAm H*
Ridgely, Edwin Reed 1844-1927 *BiDrAC*
Ridgely, Elizabeth Frazier 1868- *WomWWA 14*
Ridgely, Henry 1869-1940 *WhAm 1*
Ridgely, Henry Moore 1778-1847 *ApCAB, NatCAB 4, TwCBDA*
Ridgely, Henry Moore 1779-1847 *BiDrAC, WhAmP*
Ridgely, Hilliard Samuel 1874- *WhAm 5*
Ridgely, Irwin Oliver 1892-1965 *NatCAB 51*
Ridgely, James Lot 1807-1881 *ApCAB*
Ridgely, Kate Deering *WomWWA 14*
Ridgely, Nicholas 1762-1830 *ApCAB, DcAmB, NatCAB 4, TwCBDA, WhAm H*
Ridgely, Richard 1755-1824 *BiAUS, BiDrAC, WhAm H*
Ridgely, William Barret 1858-1920 *NatCAB 27, WhAm 1*
Ridges, Robert Paul 1903-1972 *WhAm 5*
Ridgeway, George L 1901-1968 *WhAm 5*
Ridgeway, Robert d1869 *BiAUS*
Ridgley, Douglas Clay 1868-1952 *WhAm 3*
Ridgway, Amos Caryl 1860- *WhAm 4*
Ridgway, Arthur Osbourne 1870-1953 *WhAm 3*
Ridgway, Erman Jesse 1867-1943 *WhAm 2*
Ridgway, Gail Hamilton 1884- *WomWWA 14*
Ridgway, Grant 1868- *WhAm 5*
Ridgway, Henry Bascom 1830-1895 *ApCAB Sup*
Ridgway, Howard Eugene 1905-1974 *WhAm 6*
Ridgway, John J 1843- *NatCAB 1*
Ridgway, Joseph 1783-1861 *BiAUS, BiDrAC, WhAm H*
Ridgway, Mathew Bunker 1895- *WebAB*
Ridgway, Matthew Bunker 1895- *McGEWB, WebAMB, WhWW-II*
Ridgway, Robert 1823-1870 *BiDrAC, WhAm H*
Ridgway, Robert 1850-1929 *AmBi, ApCAB, DcAmB, DcScB, NatCAB 8, TwCBDA, WhAm 1*
Ridgway, Robert 1862-1938 *DcAmB S2, NatCAB 39, WhAm 1*
Ridgway, Thomas 1861- *WhAm 4*
Ridgway, W *NewYHSD*
Ridgway, William Hance 1856-1945 *WhAm 2*
Ridings, Eugene Ware 1899-1969 *WhAm 5*
Ridings, Percy 1879-1960 *NatCAB 49*
Ridley, Clarence Self 1883-1969 *WhAm 5*
Ridley, Essex *NewYHSD*
Ridley, Mary Kent 1864- *WomWWA 14*
Ridlon, John 1852-1936 *NatCAB 17, WhAm 1*
Ridlon, Joseph Randall 1882-1973 *WhAm 6*
Ridpath, John Clark 1840-1900 *AmBi, ApCAB, BiDAmEd, DcAmB, NatCAB 6, TwCBDA*
Ridpath, John Clark 1841-1900 *WhAm 1*
Ridpath, Robert Ferguson 1876-1950 *WhAm 3*
Ridpath, William Marion 1845-1914 *NatCAB 30*
Ridsdale, Percival Sheldon 1872-1953 *WhAm 3*
Ridwan, Abu'l-Hasan Ali Ibn Ali, Ibn 998-1069? *DcScB*
Riebel, Frank A 1903-1972 *WhAm 5*

Riebenack, Max 1844- *NatCAB 14*
Rieber, Charles Henry 1866-1948 *WhAm 2*
Rieber, Torkild 1882-1968 *WhAm 5*
Riechmann, Donald August 1919-1971 *WhAm 6*
Riecke, Eduard 1845-1915 *DcScB*
Riecken, William Emil 1892-1958 *WhAm 3*
Ried, William Wharry 1799-1866 *WhAm H*
Riedel, Edward Gustave 1892-1969 *NatCAB 55*
Riedel, Karl Heinrich 1879-1946 *WhAm 2*
Riedesel, Frederica Charlotte Louisa 1746-1808
  ApCAB, Drake
Riedesel, Baron Friedrich Adolph 1738-1800
  ApCAB, Drake
Riefler, Winfield William 1897-1974 *WhAm 6*
Riefstahl, Rudolf M 1880- *WhAm 6*
Riegel, Benjamin D d1941 *WhAm 1*
Riegel, Byron 1906-1975 *WhAm 6*
Riegel, Catherine Thirza 1911-1974 *WhAm 6*
Riegel, John Leidy 1819-1893 *NatCAB 26*
Riegel, Robert Edgar 1897- *EncAAH, REnAW*
Rieger, Johann Georg Joseph Anton 1811-1869
  DcAmB, WhAm H
Rieger, William Henry 1862- *WhAm 4*
Riegger, Wallingford 1885-1961 *WhAm 4*
Riegle, Charles Milton 1869-1949 *NatCAB 37*
Riegle, Donald Wayne, Jr. 1938- *BiDrAC*
Riehl, Emil A 1837-1925 *NatCAB 20*
Riehl, Gustav 1855-1943 *BiHiMed*
Riehle, Theodore Martin 1891-1949 *WhAm 2*
Riehlman, Roy Walter 1899- *BiDrAC,
  WhAmP*
Riekarts, Frederick *NewYHSD*
Rieke, Marcus Clarence 1909-1962 *WhAm 4*
Riel, John Michael 1861-1937 *NatCAB 28*
Riel, Louis 1844-1885 *ApCAB, McGEWB,
  REnAW, WhAm H*
Riely, John William 1839-1900 *WhAm 1*
Rieman, Charles Ellet 1870-1954 *NatCAB 45,
  WhAm 5*
Rieman, Charles Stanley 1877-1957 *NatCAB 45*
Rieman, Taylor Goodwin 1872- *WomWWA 14*
Riemann, Georg Friedrich Bernard 1826-1866
  McGEWB
Riemann, Georg Friedrich Bernhard 1826-1866
  AsBiEn, DcScB
Riemenschneider, Albert 1878-1950 *NatCAB 43,
  WhAm 3*
Riemenschneider, Karl 1844-1925 *NatCAB 20*
Riemenschneider, Tilman 1468-1531 *McGEWB*
Riemer, Guido Carl Leo 1873-1953 *NatCAB 44,
  WhAm 3*
Rienhoff, William 1858-1937 *NatCAB 27*
Rienzi, Cola Di 1313?-1354 *McGEWB*
Riepe, Carl Christoph 1885-1969 *WhAm 5*
Riepp, Mother Benedicta 1825-1862 *NotAW*
Ries, Adam 1492-1559 *DcScB*
Ries, Elias Elkan 1862-1928 *WhAm 1*
Ries, Heinrich 1871-1951 *WhAm 3*
Ries, Iwan 1872-1949 *NatCAB 38*
Riesenberg, Felix 1879-1939 *NatCAB 29,
  WhAm 1*
Riesenberg, Sidney H 1885- *IIBEAAW*
Riesenfeld, Hugo 1879-1939 *NatCAB 38,
  NatCAB 47*
Riesenfeld, Hugo 1885-1939 *WhAm 1*
Riesenfeld, Victor S 1887-1964 *NatCAB 50*
Rieser, Leonard Moos 1893-1959 *WhAm 3*
Riesman, David 1867-1940 *WhAm 1*
Riesman, David 1909- *BiDAmEd, EncAB,
  WebAB*
Riesman, Eleanor Fleisher 1882-
  WomWWA 14
Riesman, John Penrose 1912-1972 *NatCAB 56,
  WhAm 6*
Riesz, Frigyes 1880-1956 *DcScB*
Riethmuller, Richard Henri 1881- *WhAm 2*
Rietmuller, James 1915-1942 *WhAm 5*
Rietveld, Gerrit Thomas 1888-1964 *McGEWB*
Rietz, Henry Lewis 1875-1943 *WhAm 2*
Rieve, Emil 1892-1975 *WhAm 6*
Rife, John Maynard 1917-1969 *WhAm 5*
Rife, John Winebrenner 1846-1908 *BiDrAC*
Riff, David Morris 1891-1966 *NatCAB 53*
Riffinburg, William *NewYHSD*
Rifkin, Bernard 1878-1955 *NatCAB 43*
Rigali, G *NewYHSD*
Rigaud, Baron Antoine 1758-1820 *ApCAB*
Rigaud, Benoit Joseph Andre 1761-1811 *ApCAB*

Rigby, Cecil 1891-1949 *NatCAB 38*
Rigby, William Cattron 1871-1945 *NatCAB 35,
  WhAm 2*
Rigby, William Otto 1872-1943 *WhAm 3*
Rigby, William Titus 1841-1929 *ApCAB X,
  WhAm 1, WhAm 1C*
Rigdon, Charles Loammi 1876- *WhAm 5*
Rigdon, Jonathan 1858-1933 *WhAm 1*
Rigdon, Sidney 1793-1876 *AmBi, ApCAB,
  DcAmB, DcAmReB, NatCAB 7,
  NatCAB 16, WhAm H*
Riger, Robert 1924- *IIBEAAW*
Rigg, Earl William 1905-1949 *NatCAB 38*
Rigg, Ephraim 1892-1960 *NatCAB 49,
  WhAm 4*
Rigg, George Burton 1872- *WhAm 6*
Rigg, James Albert 1881-1959 *NatCAB 49*
Rigg, John Adam 1854- *ApCAB X*
Rigg, Walker Adam 1874-1960 *ApCAB X*
Rigg, Walter Adam 1874-1960 *NatCAB 47*
Rigge, William Francis 1857-1927 *DcAmB,
  WhAm 1*
Riggin, Fred Leroy 1885-1971 *NatCAB 57*
Riggins, H McLeod 1900-1973 *WhAm 5*
Riggins, Ivan Webster 1874-1945 *NatCAB 34*
Riggins, Richard William 1896-1967
  NatCAB 53
Riggins, Russell Myers 1894-1961 *WhAm 4*
Riggio, Vincent 1877-1960 *NatCAB 49,
  WhAm 4*
Riggs, Albert Rose 1875-1971 *NatCAB 57*
Riggs, Alexander Brown 1842-1919 *WhAm 1*
Riggs, Alfred Longley 1837-1916 *WhAm 1*
Riggs, Anna Rankin *AmWom*
Riggs, Arthur Stanley 1879- *WhAm 6*
Riggs, Austen Fox 1876-1940 *NatCAB 30,
  WhAm 1*
Riggs, Charles Edward 1869-1963 *NatCAB 50,
  WhAm 4*
Riggs, Charlotte Symington *WomWWA 14*
Riggs, Edward 1844-1913 *WhAm 1*
Riggs, Edward Gridley 1856-1924 *WhAm 1*
Riggs, Elias 1810-1901 *AmBi, ApCAB,
  DcAmB, NatCAB 3, TwCBDA,
  WhAm 1*
Riggs, Elisha Francis 1851-1910 *NatCAB 15*
Riggs, Ernest Wilson 1881-1952 *WhAm 3*
Riggs, Francis Behn 1881- *WhAm 6*
Riggs, George Washington 1813-1881 *ApCAB,
  DcAmB, NatCAB 28, WhAm H*
Riggs, Harold Walter 1894-1954 *NatCAB 43*
Riggs, Henry Earle 1865-1949 *WhAm 2*
Riggs, Henry Harrison 1875-1943 *WhAm 3*
Riggs, James Forsyth 1852-1918 *WhAm 1*
Riggs, James Gilbert 1861-1936 *WhAm 1*
Riggs, James Milton 1839-1933 *BiDrAC,
  WhAm 1*
Riggs, James Stevenson 1853-1936 *NatCAB 26,
  WhAm 4*
Riggs, Jetur Rose 1809-1869 *BiAUS, BiDrAC,
  WhAm H*
Riggs, John Davis Seaton 1851- *TwCBDA,
  WhAm 1*
Riggs, John Mankey 1810-1885 *DcAmB,
  WhAm H*
Riggs, Joseph A 1899-1973 *WhAm 6*
Riggs, Kate Douglas 1857- *ApCAB Sup*
Riggs, Kate Douglas Wiggin *BiDAmEd,
  WhAm 1, WomWWA 14*
Riggs, Kate Douglas Wiggin 1859- *TwCBDA*
Riggs, Lewis 1789-1870 *BiAUS, BiDrAC,
  WhAm H*
Riggs, Louis Warner 1862- *WhAm 4*
Riggs, Lynn 1899-1954 *NatCAB 45, REnAW*
Riggs, Norman Colman 1870-1943 *WhAm 2*
Riggs, Robert 1896-1970 *WhAm 5*
Riggs, Robert Baird 1855-1929 *WhAm 1*
Riggs, Samuel Agnew 1835-1920 *NatCAB 11,
  NatCAB 29*
Riggs, Stephen Return 1812-1883 *AmBi,
  ApCAB, DcAmB, DcAmReB, NatCAB 3,
  TwCBDA, WhAm H*
Riggs, Theodore Foster 1874- *WhAm 5*
Riggs, Theodore Scott 1907-1970 *NatCAB 56,
  WhAm 5*
Riggs, Thomas 1873-1945 *NatCAB 33,
  WhAm 2*
Riggs, Walter Merritt 1873-1924 *NatCAB 19,*

WhAm 1
Riggs, William Henry 1837-1924 *ApCAB X,
  DcAmB*
Righi, Augusto 1850-1920 *AsBiEn, DcScB*
Righter, Chester Newell 1824-1856 *ApCAB*
Righter, Eva Cornelia Foster *WomWWA 14*
Righter, Thomas McNair 1847-1918
  NatCAB 17
Rightmire, George Washington 1868-1952
  NatCAB 39, WhAm 3
Rightor, Henry 1870-1922 *WhAm 1*
Riglander, Jacob Wolff 1840-1929 *ApCAB X*
Riglander, Moses Montefiore 1878-1932
  NatCAB 24
Rigling, Alfred 1868-1940 *NatCAB 30*
Rignall, Raymond H 1904-1960 *WhAm 4*
Rigney, Hugh McPheeters 1873-1950 *BiDrAC,
  WhAm 3*
Rigsbee, Albert Vinson 1925-1969 *WhAm 5*
Rigsbee, Alice Davidson 1874- *WomWWA 14*
Rihani, Ameen 1876-1940 *WhAm 1*
Rihbany, Abraham Mitrie 1869-1944 *WhAm 2,
  WhAm 3*
Rihl, Walter Alday 1903-1960 *NatCAB 48*
Riis, Erling d1965 *WhAm 4*
Riis, Jacob August 1849-1914 *AmBi, DcAmB,
  EncAB, McGEWB, NatCAB 13,
  TwCBDA, WebAB, WhAm 1*
Riis, Mary Phillips 1877- *WomWWA 14*
Riis, Roger William 1894-1953 *WhAm 3*
Riisager, Knudage 1897-1974 *WhAm 6*
Riker, Albert Burdsall 1852-1929 *NatCAB 23,
  WhAm 1*
Riker, Andrew Lawrence 1868-1930 *AmBi,
  NatCAB 15, NatCAB 22, WhAm 1*
Riker, Carleton Berrian 1890-1952 *NatCAB 39*
Riker, Carroll Livingston 1854-1931 *WhAm 1*
Riker, Chandler White 1855-1919 *NatCAB 18*
Riker, Clarence Bayley 1863-1947 *NatCAB 39*
Riker, Franklin Wing 1876-1958 *WhAm 3*
Riker, Irving 1896-1970 *WhAm 5*
Riker, James 1822-1889 *ApCAB, TwCBDA*
Riker, John Jackson 1858- *NatCAB 8*
Riker, John Lafayette d1862 *ApCAB*
Riker, John Lawrence 1830-1909 *NatCAB 8,
  WhAm 1*
Riker, Martina Grubbs 1867- *WomWWA 14*
Riker, Richard 1773-1842 *ApCAB, NatCAB 3*
Riker, Samuel 1743-1823 *BiAUS, BiDrAC,
  WhAm H*
Riker, Samuel 1832-1911 *NatCAB 8*
Riker, Samuel 1868-1936 *NatCAB 33*
Riker, Thad Weed 1880-1952 *WhAm 3*
Rilea, Thomas Edward 1895-1959 *WhAm 3*
Riley, Alice Cushing Donaldson 1867-1955
  NatCAB 44
Riley, Benjamin Franklin 1849-1925 *DcAmB,
  NatCAB 9, TwCBDA, WhAm 1*
Riley, Bennet 1786-1852 *Drake*
Riley, Bennet 1787-1853 *DcAmB, WebAMB,
  WhAm H*
Riley, Bennett 1787-1853 *ApCAB, NatCAB 4,
  TwCBDA*
Riley, Bert Clair 1891-1962 *WhAm 4*
Riley, Bryan M 1874- *WhAm 1*
Riley, Cassius Marcellus 1844- *WhAm 2*
Riley, Charles Edwin 1909-1965 *NatCAB 53*
Riley, Charles Valentine 1843-1895 *AmBi,
  ApCAB, DcAmB, NatCAB 9, TwCBDA,
  WhAm H*
Riley, Corinne Boyd 1893- *BiDrAC*
Riley, Donald 1890-1946 *NatCAB 35*
Riley, Earl 1890-1965 *WhAm 4*
Riley, Edward 1894-1962 *WhAm 4*
Riley, Edward Barnes 1883-1965 *NatCAB 51*
Riley, Elizabeth Angela 1870?-1921 *NatCAB 6,
  WomWWA 14*
Riley, Evelyn C *WomWWA 14*
Riley, Franklin Lafayette 1868-1929
  NatCAB 24, TwCBDA, WhAm 1
Riley, Franklin Wilbert 1868- *WhoColR*
Riley, George Washington 1866-1954
  NatCAB 40, WhAm 3
Riley, Gertrude E A 1872- *ApCAB X*
Riley, Harrison Barnett 1862-1944 *NatCAB 32*
Riley, Hattie E Fossette 1847- *WomWWA 14*
Riley, Henry Alsop 1887-1966 *NatCAB 53,
  WhAm 5*

Riley, Henry Chauncey 1835- *ApCAB*
Riley, Henry Hiram 1813-1888 *ApCAB*
Riley, Henry Ware 1902-1959 *WhAm 3*
Riley, Herbert Douglas 1904-1973 *WhAm 5*
Riley, Isaac Woodbridge 1869-1933 *DcAmB*
Riley, James 1775-1840 *Drake*
Riley, James 1777-1840 *ApCAB*
Riley, James 1848- *WhAm 4*
Riley, James Breinig 1894-1958 *WhAm 3*
Riley, James Whitcomb 1849-1916 *AmBi,*
   ApCAB X, DcAmB, EncAAH, McGEWB,
   WebAB
Riley, James Whitcomb 1852?-1916 *ApCAB*
Riley, James Whitcomb 1853-1916 *NatCAB 6,*
   TwCBDA, WhAm 1
Riley, Jeremiah H *NewYHSD*
Riley, Joe Shelby 1865- *ApCAB X*
Riley, John *NewYHSD*
Riley, John Alexander 1888-1955 *WhAm 3*
Riley, John B 1852-1919 *WhAm 1*
Riley, John Campbell 1828-1879 *ApCAB*
Riley, John Gilmore 1857- *WhoColR*
Riley, John Jacob 1895-1962 *BiDrAC,*
   WhAm 4, WhAmP
Riley, John Stewart 1899-1965 *WhAm 4*
Riley, Kenneth Pauling 1919- *IIBEAAW*
Riley, Leonard William 1872-1945 *NatCAB 34,*
   WhAm 2
Riley, Lewis Adams 1847-1925 *ApCAB X,*
   NatCAB 31, WhAm 1
Riley, Mary G 1883-1939 *IIBEAAW*
Riley, Melville Fuller 1872-1938 *WhAm 1*
Riley, Phil Madison 1882-1926 *WhAm 1*
Riley, Philip Henry 1898-1950 *WhAm 3*
Riley, Robert Sanford 1874-1926 *ApCAB X,*
   NatCAB 20
Riley, Thomas Harrison, Jr. 1880-1945
   NatCAB 35
Riley, Thomas James 1870-1931 *WhAm 1*
Riley, Thomas Joseph 1908-1970 *WhAm 5*
Riley, Walter James 1875-1973 *WhAm 6*
Riley, William Albert 1876-1963 *NatCAB 51*
Riley, William Bell 1861-1947 *DcAmB S4,*
   WhAm 2
Riley, William F 1884-1956 *WhAm 3*
Riley, William G 1897-1953 *WhAm 3*
Riley, William Henry 1859-1941 *NatCAB 32*
Riley, William Henry 1900-1942 *NatCAB 32*
Riley, Woodbridge 1869-1933 *WhAm 1*
Rilke, Rainer Maria 1875-1926 *McGEWB,*
   WhAm 4A
Rima, Tommaso 1775-1843 *DcScB*
Rimbaud, Jean Nicolas Arthur 1854-1891
   McGEWB
Rimer, Edward Sherrard 1877-1955 *NatCAB 42*
Rimington, Critchell 1907-1976 *WhAm 6*
Rimini, Giacomo d1952 *WhAm 3*
Rimmer, Caroline Hunt 1851- *WhAm 4*
Rimmer, Harry 1890-1952 *NatCAB 41,*
   WhAm 3
Rimmer, John Wilfred 1889-1956 *WhAm 4*
Rimmer, William 1816-1879 *AmBi, ApCAB,*
   BnEnAmA, DcAmB, McGEWB,
   NatCAB 4, NewYHSD, WebAB,
   WhAm H
Rimmer, William 1821- *Drake*
Rimprecht, Johann Baptist 1801-1877
   NewYHSD
Rimprecht, John 1801-1877 *NewYHSD*
Rimsky-Korsakov, Nikolai Andreevich 1844-1908
   McGEWB
Rinaker, John Irving 1830-1915 *BiDrAC*
Rinaker, Samuel Mayo 1887-1964 *WhAm 4*
Rinaldini, Benito 1695-1760? *ApCAB*
Rinaldo, Philip Sidney 1877-1931 *NatCAB 24*
Rinck, A D *NewYHSD*
Rincon, Antoine Del d1641 *Drake*
Rincon, Antonio Del 1541-1601 *ApCAB*
Rind, Clementina 1740?-1774 *NotAW*
Rindge, Frederick Hastings 1857-1905
   ApCAB X, DcAmB, NatCAB 9,
   NatCAB 16
Rindge, Samuel Knight 1888- *ApCAB X*
Rindisbacher, Peter 1806-1834 *IIBEAAW,*
   NewYHSD, REnAW, WhAm H
Rindlaub, John Henry 1865-1950 *NatCAB 38*
Rindlaub, Martin Phillip, Jr. 1874-1928
   NatCAB 22

Rine, John Alfred 1878-1944 *NatCAB 35*
Rinehart, George Franklin 1864- *NatCAB 16,*
   WhAm 4
Rinehart, Henry R 1890-1966 *WhAm 4*
Rinehart, Hollis 1871-1943 *NatCAB 40*
Rinehart, James Fleece 1901-1955 *NatCAB 44,*
   WhAm 3
Rinehart, Jay Don 1891-1964 *NatCAB 50*
Rinehart, Mary Roberts 1876-1958 *ApCAB X,*
   WebAB, WhAm 3, WomWWA 14
Rinehart, Roy James 1880-1957 *WhAm 3*
Rinehart, Stanley Marshall 1867-1932
   NatCAB 25
Rinehart, Stanley Marshall, Jr. 1897-1969
   WhAm 5
Rinehart, William Henry 1825-1874 *AmBi,*
   ApCAB, BnEnAmA, DcAmB, NatCAB 2,
   NewYHSD, TwCBDA, WhAm H
Rinek, John Oswald 1890-1962 *NatCAB 48*
Riner, John Alden 1850-1923 *WhAm 1*
Riner, William A 1878-1955 *WhAm 3*
Rines, George Edwin 1858-1951 *WhAm 3*
Riney, Earl Alvin 1885-1955 *WhAm 3*
Ring, Arthur Hallam 1874-1935 *NatCAB 32*
Ring, Blanche 1877-1961 *WhAm 4*
Ring, Charles Augustus 1845-1903 *NatCAB 25*
Ring, Clark Lombard 1862-1933 *NatCAB 31*
Ring, David *NewYHSD*
Ring, Floyd Orval 1921-1970 *WhAm 6*
Ring, G Oram 1861-1933 *NatCAB 24*
Ring, Richard Warner 1901-1958 *WhAm 3*
Ring, Welding 1846-1929 *ApCAB X,*
   NatCAB 21, WhAm 1
Ringer, Paul Henry 1881-1952 *WhAm 3*
Ringer, Sydney 1835-1910 *BiHiMed, DcScB*
Ringer, Thomas Tazzell 1884- *WhoColR*
Ringgold, Cadwalader 1802-1867 *ApCAB,*
   DcAmB, Drake, NewYHSD, TwCBDA,
   WebAMB, WhAm H
Ringgold, George Hay 1814-1864 *ApCAB,*
   Drake
Ringgold, Samuel 1770-1829 *ApCAB, BiAUS,*
   BiDrAC, TwCBDA, WhAm H, WhAmP
Ringgold, Samuel 1800-1846 *ApCAB,*
   NatCAB 7
Ringgold, William 1723- *NatCAB 3*
Ringius, Carl Sigfrid 1879-1950 *NatCAB 39*
Ringland, Adam Weir *WhAm 5*
Ringland, Joseph Ford 1901-1957 *WhAm 3*
Ringle, Arthur Levi 1901-1963 *WhAm 4*
Ringle, John 1884-1942 *NatCAB 31*
Ringle, William Edgar 1872-1924 *NatCAB 20*
Ringleb, Friedrich Otto 1900-1966 *NatCAB 53*
Ringler, Frederick Anton 1852-1929 *NatCAB 3,*
   NatCAB 37
Ringley, James Patrick 1895-1965 *WhAm 4*
Ringling, Charles 1863-1926 *DcAmB, WebAB,*
   WhAm HA, WhAm 4
Ringling, Henry E 1906-1955 *NatCAB 46,*
   WhAm 3
Ringling, John Nicholas 1866-1936 *NatCAB 40,*
   WhAm 1
Ringling, Robert Edward 1897-1950
   NatCAB 38, WhAm 2
Ringo, Daniel 1800?-1873 *NatCAB 13*
Ringo, Helen d1952 *WhAm 3*
Ringo, Hugh Fay 1884-1945 *WhAm 2*
Ringo, John 1844?-1882 *REnAW*
Ringold, James 1879- *WhAm 6*
Ringold, Thomas *BiAUS*
Rings, Daniel d1873 *BiAUS*
Rings, Edythe Patterson 1877- *WomWWA 14*
Ringstad, Edward Olson 1871- *WhAm 5*
Ringwalt, Ralph Curtis 1874-1946 *NatCAB 36,*
   WhAm 5
Ringwood, John Francis 1863-1930 *NatCAB 22*
Rink, Heinrik Johannes 1819- *ApCAB Sup*
Rink, John J *NewYHSD*
Rink, Joseph Aloysius 1858-1923 *NatCAB 36*
Rinkel, Herbert John 1896-1963 *NatCAB 51*
Rinkenbach, William Henry 1894-1965
   WhAm 4
Rinkoff, Barbara Jean 1923-1975 *WhAm 6*
Rinman, Sven 1720-1792 *DcScB*
Rinn, Daniel Frederick 1863-1950 *NatCAB 47*
Rinsland, Henry Daniel 1889-1971 *WhAm 5*
Rinzler, Seymour Harold 1914-1970
   NatCAB 54

Rio, Andres Manuel Del 1764-1849 *DcScB*
Rio, Antonio Del 1745-1789? *ApCAB*
Rio, Diego Del 1580?-1644 *ApCAB*
Rio Branco, Jose DaS Paranhos, Barao Do
   1845-1912 *McGEWB*
Rio DeLaLoza, Leopoldo 1807-1873 *ApCAB*
Rio-Hortega, Pio Del 1882-1945 *DcScB*
Riolan, Jean, Jr. 1580-1657 *DcScB*
Rion, Hanna 1875-1924 *WhAm 1*
Rion, James Henry 1828-1886 *NatCAB 4*
Rions, Francois C H D'Albert, Count De
   1728-1802 *ApCAB*
Riopel, Edmund Eusebius 1846-1916
   NatCAB 50
Riordan, Daniel Joseph 1870-1923 *BiDrAC,*
   WhAm 1, WhAmP
Riordan, Laurence Michael 1890-1965
   NatCAB 51
Riordan, Leo 1903-1975 *WhAm 6*
Riordan, Michael Robert 1927-1969
   NatCAB 54
Riordan, Patrick William 1841-1914 *ApCAB,*
   DcAmB, NatCAB 12, NatCAB 15,
   TwCBDA, WhAm 1
Riordan, Roger 1848-1904 *WhAm 1*
Riordan, Timothy Allen 1858- *WhAm 4*
Riordan, William O 1890-1950 *WhAm 3*
Riordon, Raymond 1877-1940 *WhAm 1*
Rios *NewYHSD*
Rios, Juan Antonio 1888-1946 *WhAm 2*
Riotte, Charles N *BiAUS*
Ripley, Aiden Lassell 1896-1969 *NatCAB 55*
Ripley, Alden Lassell 1896-1969 *WhAm 5*
Ripley, Alfred Lawrence 1858-1943 *WhAm 2*
Ripley, Charles Trescott 1886-1949 *WhAm 2*
Ripley, Chauncey B 1835-1893 *NatCAB 2*
Ripley, Christopher Gore 1822-1881
   NatCAB 12, TwCBDA
Ripley, Clements 1892-1954 *WhAm 3*
Ripley, Daniel Campbell 1850-1912 *NatCAB 23*
Ripley, Edith Helen Wheeler *WomWWA 14*
Ripley, Edward Hastings 1839-1915 *ApCAB X,*
   DcAmB, NatCAB 16
Ripley, Edward Lafayette 1876-1944 *WhAm 3*
Ripley, Edward Payson 1845-1920 *DcAmB,*
   NatCAB 18, REnAW, WhAm 1
Ripley, Eleazar Wheelock 1782-1839 *ApCAB,*
   BiAUS, BiDrAC, DcAmB, NatCAB 3,
   TwCBDA, WebAMB, WhAm H
Ripley, Eleazer Wheelock 1782-1839 *AmBi,*
   Drake
Ripley, Eva Gowing 1870- *WomWWA 14*
Ripley, Ezra 1751-1841 *ApCAB, DcAmB,*
   Drake, NatCAB 7, WhAm H
Ripley, Frederic Herbert 1854- *WhAm 4*
Ripley, George 1802-1880 *AmBi, ApCAB,*
   DcAmB, DcAmReB, Drake, EncAB,
   McGEWB, NatCAB 3, TwCBDA,
   WebAB, WhAm H
Ripley, Giles Emmett 1874-1943 *WhAm 2*
Ripley, Henry Jones 1798-1875 *ApCAB, Drake,*
   NatCAB 3
Ripley, Hubert G d1942 *WhAm 2*
Ripley, James Wheelock 1786-1835 *BiAUS,*
   BiDrAC, WhAm H
Ripley, James Wolfe 1794-1870 *AmBi, ApCAB,*
   DcAmB, Drake, NatCAB 3, TwCBDA,
   WhAm H
Ripley, Joseph 1854-1940 *WhAm 1*
Ripley, Joseph Pierce 1889-1974 *WhAm 6*
Ripley, Katharine Ball 1899-1955 *WhAm 3*
Ripley, Lauren William 1864- *WhAm 4*
Ripley, Lucy Fairfield Perkins d1949 *WhAm 2*
Ripley, Martha George Rogers 1843-1912
   AmWom, NotAW
Ripley, Mary A 1831- *AmWom*
Ripley, Mary Churchill 1831- *WhAm 4*
Ripley, Robert Harris 1876-1931 *NatCAB 23,*
   WhAm 1
Ripley, Robert LeRoy 1893-1949 *DcAmB S4,*
   NatCAB 41, WebAB, WhAm 2
Ripley, Roswell Sabin 1823?-1863 *Drake*
Ripley, Roswell Sabine 1823-1887 *ApCAB,*
   BiDConf, DcAmB, NatCAB 3, TwCBDA,
   WhAm H
Ripley, Sarah Alden Bradford 1793-1867
   NotAW
Ripley, Sophia Willard Dana 1803-1861 *NotAW*

Ripley, Theron Monroe 1868-1936 *NatCAB 27*
Ripley, Thomas C *BiAUS, BiDrAC, WhAm H*
Ripley, Thomas Emerson 1865-1956 *NatCAB 46, WhAm 4*
Ripley, Wilber Franklin 1878- *WhAm 6*
Ripley, William Zebina 1867-1941 *ApCAB X, DcAmB S3, NatCAB 32, WhAm 1*
Rippel, Julius S 1868-1950 *WhAm 3*
Ripperger, Helmut Lothar 1897-1974 *WhAm 6*
Rippey, Edwin Floyd 1885-1960 *WhAm 4*
Rippey, Harian Watson 1874-1946 *WhAm 2*
Rippin, Jane Deeter 1882-1953 *WhAm 3*
Ripple, Ezra Hoyt 1842- *NatCAB 4*
Ripple, Michael Joseph 1875-1938 *WhAm 1*
Ripton, Benjamin Henry 1858-1936 *NatCAB 27, WhAm 1*
Ris, Bernard 1862- *ApCAB X*
Risch, Otto Carl 1893-1956 *NatCAB 42*
Risdon, Fulton 1880- *WhAm 6*
Risdon, Richard P *NewYHSD*
Riseman, Joseph Ephraim Frank 1903-1974 *WhAm 6*
Riser, Luther Allen 1877-1960 *NatCAB 49*
Riser, William Henry, Jr. 1911-1961 *WhAm 4*
Rishell, Charles Wesley 1850-1908 *WhAm 1*
Rishell, James Dyson 1858- *WhAm 4*
Rishell, Robert 1925?- *IIBEAAW*
Rising, Henry 1869-1939 *WhAm 1*
Rising, Johan Claesson 1600?-1672 *ApCAB*
Rising, Johan Classon 1617-1672 *DcAmB, WhAm H*
Rising, Willard Bradley 1839-1910 *ApCAB, NatCAB 12, NatCAB 25, WhAm 1*
Risitine, Frederick Pearce 1871-1959 *WhAm 4*
Risk, Charles Francis 1897-1943 *BiDrAC, WhAm 2*
Risley, Edward Hammond 1877-1963 *NatCAB 52*
Risley, Edward Henry 1881-1943 *NatCAB 32*
Risley, Edwin H 1842- *WhAm 4*
Risley, Elijah 1787-1870 *BiAUS, BiDrAC, WhAm H*
Risley, H S *NewYHSD*
Risley, John Ewing 1840- *NatCAB 12*
Risley, John Ewing 1843- *TwCBDA*
Risley, Louise Robinson 1870- *WomWWA 14*
Risley, Paul L 1906-1971 *WhAm 5*
Risley, Richard Voorhees 1874-1904 *TwCBDA, WhAm 1*
Risley, Samuel Doty 1845-1920 *ApCAB, NatCAB 7, WhAm 1*
Risley, Theodore Granville 1864- *WhAm 4*
Risner, Friedrich d1580? *DcScB*
Risner, Henry Clay 1860-1948 *ApCAB X*
Risner, Henry Clay 1869-1948 *WhAm 2*
Risom, Jens 1916- *BnEnAmA*
Rissberger, Harold P d1972 *WhAm 6*
Risse, Louis Aloys 1850- *NatCAB 4*
Risser, Frederic Emanuel 1900-1971 *NatCAB 57*
Risser, Hubert Elias 1914-1974 *WhAm 6*
Risser, James Vaulx 1910-1973 *NatCAB 57*
Risser, Louis Henry 1880-1949 *NatCAB 39*
Rissman, Henry Louis 1880-1946 *NatCAB 35*
Risso, Charles *NewYHSD*
Ristad, Ditlef G 1863-1938 *WhAm 1*
Risteen, Allan Douglas 1866-1932 *NatCAB 24*
Rister, Carl Coke 1889-1955 *DcAmB S5, REnAW, WhAm 3*
Ristine, Frank Humphrey 1884-1958 *NatCAB 47, WhAm 3*
Ristine, George W 1846-1918 *WhAm 1*
Ristori, Adelaide 1822- *ApCAB*
Ristoro D'Arezzo 1210?-1282? *DcScB*
Ritch, John Warren 1822- *ApCAB, WhAm 4*
Ritchey, Charles James 1885-1959 *WhAm 4*
Ritchey, Della 1873- *WomWWA 14*
Ritchey, George Willis 1864-1945 *DcAmB S3, DcScB, WhAm 4*
Ritchey, Thomas 1801-1863 *BiAUS, BiDrAC, WhAm H*
Ritchie, Adele d1930 *WhAm 1*
Ritchie, Albert Cabell 1876-1936 *AmBi, DcAmB S2, NatCAB 29, WhAm 1, WhAmP*
Ritchie, Alexander Hay 1822-1895 *AmBi, ApCAB, DcAmB, NewYHSD, TwCBDA,*

WhAm H
Ritchie, Andrew, Jr. 1782-1862 *NewYHSD*
Ritchie, Andrew Jackson 1868-1948 *WhAm 2*
Ritchie, Anna Cora Mowatt 1819-1870 *AmBi, AmWom, DcAmB, Drake, NatCAB 3, NotAW*
Ritchie, Arthur 1849-1921 *WhAm 1*
Ritchie, Beulah Boyd 1864- *WomWWA 14*
Ritchie, Byron Foster 1853-1928 *BiDrAC*
Ritchie, David 1812-1867 *BiAUS, BiDrAC, TwCBDA, WhAm H*
Ritchie, David 1836-1874 *ApCAB*
Ritchie, Eliza 1856- *WomWWA 14*
Ritchie, James Monroe 1829-1918 *BiDrAC*
Ritchie, John 1831-1887 *BiAUS, BiDrAC, WhAm H*
Ritchie, John 1853-1939 *WhAm 1*
Ritchie, John A d1950 *WhAm 2*
Ritchie, John M *NewYHSD*
Ritchie, John William 1808- *ApCAB*
Ritchie, John Woodside 1871-1943 *WhAm 2*
Ritchie, Morris 1861-1952 *NatCAB 40*
Ritchie, Neil 1897- *WhWW-II*
Ritchie, Nelvia E Webb d1948 *WhAm 2*
Ritchie, Robert 1798-1870 *ApCAB, TwCBDA*
Ritchie, Robert 1800-1870 *Drake*
Ritchie, Robert Estes 1892-1965 *NatCAB 52*
Ritchie, Robert Welles 1879-1942 *NatCAB 32, WhAm 2*
Ritchie, Ryerson 1856- *WhAm 4*
Ritchie, Sarah Lourie 1862- *WomWWA 14*
Ritchie, Thomas 1778-1854 *AmBi, ApCAB, BiAUS, DcAmB, Drake, NatCAB 7, WhAm H*
Ritchie, William 1886-1956 *WhAm 3*
Ritchie, Sir William Johnston 1813- *ApCAB*
Ritenour, Joseph Paul 1879-1952 *NatCAB 40*
Riter, Benjamin Franklin 1859-1925 *NatCAB 6*
Riter, Frank Miller 1855-1935 *WhAm 1*
Riter, Franklin 1886-1966 *NatCAB 53, WhAm 4*
Riter, Henry Gilbert, III 1892-1958 *NatCAB 46, WhAm 3*
Riter, William Delamater 1874-1927 *NatCAB 20, WhAm 1*
Ritman, Louis 1892-1963 *WhAm 4*
Ritmiller, LeRoy Frederick 1915-1971 *NatCAB 57*
Ritner, Joseph 1779-1869 *BiAUS, Drake*
Ritner, Joseph 1780-1869 *ApCAB, DcAmB, NatCAB 2, TwCBDA, WhAm H*
Ritschel, Wilhelm 1864-1949 *WhAm 3*
Ritschel, William 1864-1949 *IIBEAAW*
Ritschl, Albrecht Benjamin 1822-1889 *McGEWB*
Ritt, Joseph Fels 1893-1951 *DcScB, WhAm 3*
Rittenberg, David 1906-1970 *WhAm 5*
Rittenberg, Henry H 1879-1969 *WhAm 5*
Rittenberg, Louis 1892-1962 *WhAm 4*
Rittenhouse, Anne *WomWWA 14*
Rittenhouse, Charles Augustus, III 1903-1965 *NatCAB 50*
Rittenhouse, Daniel Franklin 1882-1943 *WhAm 2*
Rittenhouse, David 1732-1796 *AmBi, ApCAB, BiAUS, DcAmB, DcScB, Drake, EncAB, McGEWB, NatCAB 1, TwCBDA, WebAB, WhAm H*
Rittenhouse, Elmer Ellsworth 1861-1920 *WhAm 1*
Rittenhouse, Frank Austin 1885-1950 *NatCAB 40*
Rittenhouse, George Brown 1878-1925 *NatCAB 23, WhAm 1*
Rittenhouse, Jessie Bell 1869-1948 *NotAW*
Rittenhouse, Jessie Belle 1869-1948 *DcAmB S4, WhAm 2, WomWWA 14*
Rittenhouse, Laura Jacinta 1841- *AmWom*
Rittenhouse, Moses Franklin 1846-1915 *ApCAB X, NatCAB 17, WhAm 1*
Rittenhouse, William 1644-1708 *ApCAB, DcAmB, WhAm H*
Ritter, Abraham 1792-1860 *ApCAB, Drake*
Ritter, Burwell C 1810-1880 *BiAUS*
Ritter, Burwell Clark 1810-1880 *BiDrAC*
Ritter, Burwell Clarke 1810-1880 *WhAm H*
Ritter, C Lloyd 1865-1945 *NatCAB 35*
Ritter, Claude Dowd 1880-1948 *WhAm 3*

Ritter, Edward Frederick 1869-1933 *WhAm 1*
Ritter, Eli Foster 1838-1913 *NatCAB 30*
Ritter, Elizabeth Emma 1875- *WomWWA 14*
Ritter, Fanny Raymond 1830-1890 *ApCAB, TwCBDA*
Ritter, Francis Oliver 1858-1938 *NatCAB 28*
Ritter, Frank 1845-1915 *NatCAB 43*
Ritter, Frederic Louis 1828-1892 *TwCBDA*
Ritter, Frederic Louis 1834- *ApCAB*
Ritter, Frederic Louis 1834-1891 *AmBi, BiDAmEd, DcAmB, NatCAB 7, WhAm H*
Ritter, Halsted Lockwood 1868-1951 *NatCAB 43, WhAm 3*
Ritter, Harry Wilbur 1888- *ApCAB X*
Ritter, Henry 1816-1853 *ApCAB*
Ritter, Howard L 1916-1967 *WhAm 5*
Ritter, Johann Wilhelm 1776-1810 *AsBiEn, DcScB*
Ritter, John 1779-1851 *BiAUS, BiDrAC, WhAm H*
Ritter, Joseph Elmer d1967 *WhAm 4*
Ritter, Karl 1779-1859 *McGEWB*
Ritter, Louis E 1864-1934 *WhAm 1*
Ritter, Paul 1865-1921 *WhAm 1*
Ritter, Philip 1867-1953 *NatCAB 50*
Ritter, Richard Wallace 1890-1945 *NatCAB 36*
Ritter, Tex Maurice Woodward 1907-1974 *EncAAH*
Ritter, Thelma 1905-1969 *WhAm 5*
Ritter, Verus Taggart 1883-1942 *WhAm 2*
Ritter, William Emerson 1856-1944 *DcAmB S3, NatCAB 16, WhAm 2*
Ritter, William Ernest 1873-1950 *NatCAB 39*
Ritter, William Leonard 1898-1971 *WhAm 5*
Ritter, William McClellan 1864-1952 *NatCAB 41*
Rittersporn, Bernard Andrew 1897-1974 *WhAm 6*
Rittman, Walter Frank 1883-1954 *NatCAB 44, WhAm 3*
Rittmaster, Alexander, III 1916-1969 *WhAm 5*
Ritvo, Max 1896-1962 *NatCAB 53*
Ritz, Harold Arthur 1873-1948 *NatCAB 36, WhAm 2*
Ritz, Walter 1878-1909 *DcScB*
Ritzema, Johannes 1710-1795 *ApCAB, NatCAB 12*
Ritzman, Allen Zachariah 1885-1953 *NatCAB 42*
Ritzman, Ernest George 1875-1955 *WhAm 3*
Riva Aguero, Jose 1783-1858 *ApCAB*
Riva Palacio, Mariano 1803-1880 *ApCAB*
Riva-Rocci, Scipione 1863-1937 *DcScB*
Rivadavia, Bernardino 1780-1845 *ApCAB, McGEWB*
Rivas, Angel DeSaavedra, Duque De 1791-1865 *McGEWB*
Rivas, Damaso De 1874- *WhAm 5*
Rive, Leon 1809?- *NewYHSD*
Rive-King, Julie 1854-1937 *NotAW*
Rive-King, Julie 1859-1937 *WomWWA 14*
Rivenburg, Romeyn Henry 1874-1961 *NatCAB 49, WhAm 4*
Rivera, Antonio De d1560? *ApCAB*
Rivera, Diego 1886-1957 *McGEWB, WhAm 3*
Rivera, Fructuoso 1788?-1854 *McGEWB*
Rivera, Jose Eustacio 1888-1928 *McGEWB*
Rivera, Jose Fructuoso 1790-1854 *ApCAB, Drake*
Rivera, Jose Garibi 1889-1972 *WhAm 5*
Rivera, Luis Munoz 1859-1916 *BiDrAC, DcAmB, WhAm 1, WhAmP*
Rivera Carballo, Julio Adalberto 1921-1973 *WhAm 6*
Rivero, Mariano Eduardo De 1799-1857 *ApCAB*
Rivers, Eurith Dickinson 1895-1967 *WhAm 4*
Rivers, G L Buist 1896-1963 *NatCAB 51, WhAm 4*
Rivers, James *NewYHSD*
Rivers, L Mendel 1905-1970 *WhAm 5*
Rivers, Larry 1923- *BnEnAmA*
Rivers, Lidie Avirett *WomWWA 14*
Rivers, Lucius Mendel 1905-1970 *BiDrAC, NatCAB 56, WhAmP*
Rivers, Moultrie Rutledge 1868-1940 *WhAm 1*
Rivers, Pearl *NotAW*
Rivers, Ralph Julian 1903- *BiDrAC*

Rivers, Richard Henderson 1814-1894 *ApCAB,*
TwCBDA
Rivers, Thomas 1819-1863 *BiAUS, BiDrAC,*
WhAm H
Rivers, Thomas Milton 1888-1962 *WhAm 4*
Rivers, William Cannon 1866-1943 *WhAm 2*
Rivers, William James 1822-1909 *ApCAB,*
DcAmB, Drake
Rivers, William Walter 1863- *WhAm 4*
Rives, Alexander 1806-1885 *NatCAB 19*
Rives, Alfred Landon 1830-1903 *ApCAB,*
BiDConf, NatCAB 20, WhAm 1
Rives, Amelie Louise 1863-1945 *ApCAB,*
NotAW, TwCBDA, WomWWA 14
Rives, Edwin Earle 1898-1953 *WhAm 3*
Rives, F Bayard 1890-1969 *NatCAB 53*
Rives, Francis Everod 1792-1861 *BiAUS,*
BiDrAC, WhAm H
Rives, Fred A 1910-1963 *NatCAB 51*
Rives, George Lockhart 1849-1917 *DcAmB,*
NatCAB 22, WhAm 1
Rives, George Lockhart 1849-1918 *ApCAB X*
Rives, John Cook 1795-1864 *ApCAB, DcAmB,*
NatCAB 3, WhAm H
Rives, John Cook 1796?-1864 *BiAUS, Drake*
Rives, Judith Page Walker 1802-1882 *ApCAB*
Rives, Thomas 1806- *BiAUS, NatCAB 13*
Rives, Tom Christopher 1892-1975 *WhAm 6*
Rives, William Cabell 1792-1868 *BiDConf,*
BiDrAC, WhAm H, WhAmP
Rives, William Cabell 1793-1868 *AmBi,*
ApCAB, BiAUS, DcAmB, Drake,
NatCAB 6, TwCBDA
Rives, Zeno John 1874-1939 *BiDrAC,*
WhAm 5
Rives-Wheeler, Hallie Ermine 1878- *WhAm 1*
Rives-Wheeler, Hallie Erminie 1878-
WomWWA 14
Rivett, Albert Cherbury David 1885-1961 *DcScB*
Riviere, Edward 1804?- *NewYHSD*
Riviere, Peter *NewYHSD*
Riviere DePrecourt, Emile-Valere 1835-1922
DcScB
Rivington, James 1724-1802 *ApCAB, DcAmB,*
Drake, NatCAB 3, WhAm H
Rivinus, Augustus Quirinus *DcScB*
Rivinus, Francis Markoe 1882-1951 *NatCAB 40,*
WhAm 3
Rivitz, Hiram S d1951 *WhAm 3*
Rivkin, William Robert 1919-1967 *WhAm 4*
Rivlin, Harry N 1904- *BiDAmEd*
Rix, Carl Barnett 1878-1963 *WhAm 4*
Rix, Charles Northrup 1843-1927 *WhAm 1*
Rix, Frank Reader 1853-1919 *WhAm 1*
Rix, Harriet Hale 1863- *WomWWA 14*
Rix, Julian Walbridge 1850-1903 *DcAmB,*
IIBEAAW
Rixey, George Foreman 1888-1974 *WhAm 6*
Rixey, John Franklin 1854-1907 *BiDrAC,*
TwCBDA, WhAm 1, WhAmP
Rixey, Presley Marion 1852-1928 *NatCAB 21,*
WhAm 1
Rixford, Elizabeth M Leach 1866-1956
WhAm 3
Rixford, Emmet 1865-1938 *NatCAB 35,*
WhAm 1
Rixford, Gulian Pickering 1838-1930
NatCAB 35
Rixinger, Francis *NewYHSD*
Rizal, Jose 1861-1896 *McGEWB*
Rizer, Henry Clay 1891- *WhAm 4*
Rizley, Ross 1892-1969 *BiDrAC*
Roach, Abby Meguire 1876- *WhAm 5,*
WomWWA 14
Roach, Alden G 1901-1956 *WhAm 3*
Roach, Aurelia 1865- *AmWom*
Roach, David James 1887-1953 *WhAm 3*
Roach, Dee 1875-1950 *NatCAB 41*
Roach, Howard Laverne 1898-1968 *NatCAB 54*
Roach, Isaac 1786-1848 *ApCAB*
Roach, John 1813-1887 *AmBi, DcAmB,*
TwCBDA, WhAm H
Roach, John 1815-1887 *ApCAB, NatCAB 3*
Roach, John Baker 1839-1908 *NatCAB 15*
Roach, John Millard 1851-1924 *WhAm 1*
Roach, Philip Francis 1881- *WhAm 6*
Roach, Sidney Crain 1876-1934 *BiDrAC,*
WhAm 5

Roach, Thomas Watson 1847-1927 *WhAm 1*
Roach, William Allen 1874-1920 *NatCAB 18*
Roach, William Nathaniel 1840-1902
ApCAB Sup, BiDrAC, NatCAB 5,
TwCBDA, WhAmP
Roach, William Robert 1862-1937 *NatCAB 28*
Roadhouse, Chester Linwood 1881-1969
WhAm 5
Roadman, Earl Alan 1885-1967 *NatCAB 54*
Roads, Charles 1855- *WhAm 4*
Roads, William Michael 1860-1919 *NatCAB 22*
Roadstrum, Victor N 1872-1967 *WhAm 4*
Roan, Augustus Morrow 1898-1959 *NatCAB 57*
Roane, Archibald *BiAUS*
Roane, Archibald 1755-1818 *TwCBDA*
Roane, Archibald 1759?-1819 *DcAmB,*
WhAm H
Roane, Archibald 1760-1817 *NatCAB 7*
Roane, John d1869 *BiAUS*
Roane, John J *BiAUS*
Roane, John Jones 1794-1869 *BiDrAC,*
WhAm H, WhAmP
Roane, John Selden 1817-1857 *Drake*
Roane, John Selden 1817-1867 *ApCAB, BiAUS,*
DcAmB, NatCAB 10, WhAm H
Roane, John Selden 1817-1869 *TwCBDA*
Roane, John T d1838 *BiAUS*
Roane, John T 1754-1838 *TwCBDA*
Roane, John T 1766-1838 *BiDrAC, WhAm H,*
WhAmP
Roane, Spencer 1762-1822 *ApCAB, BiAUS,*
DcAmB, Drake, WhAm H
Roane, William H 1788-1845 *BiAUS*
Roane, William Harrison 1788-1845 *ApCAB,*
NatCAB 4, TwCBDA
Roane, William Henry 1787-1845 *BiDrAC,*
WhAm H
Roantree, Robert Peter 1895-1950 *NatCAB 38*
Roark, Charles Wickliffe 1887-1929 *BiDrAC*
Roark, Edward Lee 1898-1953 *NatCAB 42*
Roark, Mary Creegan *WomWWA 14*
Roark, Raymond Jefferson 1890-1966
NatCAB 53
Roark, Ruric Nevel 1859-1909 *BiDAmEd,*
DcAmB, WhAm 1
Robb, Anna Bennett *WomWWA 14*
Robb, Charles Henry 1867-1939 *WhAm 1*
Robb, Charles W 1822-1894 *NatCAB 7*
Robb, Clair E 1905-1965 *WhAm 4*
Robb, E Donald 1880-1942 *WhAm 2*
Robb, Edward 1857-1934 *BiDrAC, TwCBDA,*
WhAm 4, WhAmP
Robb, Elise DeLaFontaine d1969 *WhAm 5*
Robb, Emilie D Taylor 1845- *WomWWA 14*
Robb, Eugene Spivey 1910-1969 *NatCAB 55,*
WhAm 5
Robb, Hunter 1863-1940 *WhAm 1*
Robb, Isabel Adams Hampton 1860-1910
BiDAmEd, NotAW
Robb, James 1814-1881 *ApCAB, DcAmB,*
WhAm H
Robb, James Burch 1817-1876 *ApCAB*
Robb, James Hampden 1846- *ApCAB,*
WhAm 1
Robb, James Milton 1884-1964 *NatCAB 52*
Robb, John Scott 1839- *NatCAB 5*
Robb, Max d1975 *WhAm 6*
Robb, Richard Alexander 1909-1971
NatCAB 57, WhAm 5
Robb, Russell 1864-1927 *NatCAB 37,*
WhAm 1
Robb, Russell 1900-1957 *WhAm 3*
Robb, Samuel A 1851-1928 *BnEnAmA*
Robb, Seymour 1901-1961 *WhAm 4*
Robb, Thomas Bruce 1885-1966 *WhAm 4*
Robb, Walter Eagleson 1865-1941 *NatCAB 32*
Robb, Walter Johnson 1880- *WhAm 6*
Robb, William Lispenard 1861-1933 *DcAmB S1,*
WhAm 1
Robb, Willis Oscar 1858-1933 *WhAm 1*
Robbe-Grillet, Alain 1922- *McGEWB*
Robbia, Luca Della 1399?-1482 *McGEWB*
Robbie, Alexander Cumming 1866- *WhAm 4*
Robbie, Reuben *BiAUS*
Robbins, Alexander Henry 1875-1922 *WhAm 1*
Robbins, Alfred Augustus 1837-1919 *ApCAB X*
Robbins, Alice Emily *WomWWA 14*
Robbins, Ammi Ruhamah 1740-1813 *ApCAB,*

Drake, NatCAB 1
Robbins, Arthur Graham 1862-1947
NatCAB 39, WhAm 4
Robbins, Asher 1757-1845 *BiAUS, BiDrAC,*
TwCBDA, WhAm H, WhAmP
Robbins, Ashur 1757-1845 *ApCAB, Drake,*
NatCAB 1
Robbins, Benjamin H 1904-1960 *WhAm 4*
Robbins, Burnett W 1876-1952 *WhAm 3*
Robbins, Chandler 1738-1799 *ApCAB,*
NatCAB 2
Robbins, Chandler 1810-1882 *ApCAB, DcAmB,*
Drake, NatCAB 2, WhAm H
Robbins, Chandler 1834-1928 *ApCAB X*
Robbins, Charles Burton 1877-1943 *WhAm 2*
Robbins, Charles Columbus 1872-1940
NatCAB 36
Robbins, Charles D *IIBEAAW*
Robbins, Charles F 1886-1957 *WhAm 3*
Robbins, Charles Leonidas 1876-1938 *WhAm 1*
Robbins, Charles Pern 1872-1959 *NatCAB 47*
Robbins, Edmund Yard 1867-1942 *WhAm 2*
Robbins, Edward Denmore 1853-1932
NatCAB 34, WhAm 1
Robbins, Edward Everett 1860-1919 *BiDrAC,*
NatCAB 7, NatCAB 16
Robbins, Edward Everett 1861-1919 *WhAm 1*
Robbins, Edward Fuller 1863-1920 *ApCAB X*
Robbins, Edward Hutchinson 1758-1829
ApCAB Sup
Robbins, Edward Rutledge 1870- *WhAm 5*
Robbins, Edwin Clyde 1883-1947 *WhAm 2*
Robbins, Eliza 1786-1853 *ApCAB Sup*
Robbins, Ellen 1828-1905 *NewYHSD*
Robbins, Francis LeBaron 1830-1920 *ApCAB,*
NatCAB 26, WhAm 1
Robbins, Francis LeBaron 1855-1911
NatCAB 14, WhAm 1
Robbins, Franklin G 1876- *WhAm 5*
Robbins, Frederick Chapman 1916- *AsBiEn,*
WebAB
Robbins, Frederick Wright 1857- *WhAm 4*
Robbins, Gaston Ahi 1858-1902 *BiDrAC,*
TwCBDA, WhAm 5
Robbins, George Ridgway 1850- *WhAm 4*
Robbins, George Robbins 1808-1875 *BiDrAC,*
WhAm H
Robbins, George Robbins 1812-1875 *BiAUS*
Robbins, Harry Clark 1890-1960 *WhAm 4*
Robbins, Harry Pelham 1874-1946 *WhAm 2*
Robbins, Harry Wolcott 1883-1954 *WhAm 3*
Robbins, Hayes 1873-1941 *WhAm 1*
Robbins, Henry Alfred 1839- *NatCAB 5*
Robbins, Henry Spencer 1853-1932 *WhAm 1*
Robbins, Herbert Daniel 1862-1947 *NatCAB 36*
Robbins, Horace Wolcott 1842-1904 *ApCAB,*
NatCAB 13, NewYHSD, TwCBDA,
WhAm 1
Robbins, Howard Chandler 1876-1952
NatCAB 40, WhAm 3
Robbins, Irvin 1839-1911 *WhAm 1*
Robbins, Jane Elizabeth 1860-1946 *NotAW*
Robbins, Jerome 1918- *WebAB*
Robbins, Jim 1916-1966 *WhAm 4*
Robbins, John 1808-1880 *BiAUS, BiAUS Sup,*
BiDrAC, WhAm H
Robbins, John Jacob 1894-1959 *NatCAB 45*
Robbins, John Louis 1886-1944 *NatCAB 33*
Robbins, John Williams 1856-1938 *WhAm 1*
Robbins, John Young 1884-1942 *NatCAB 31*
Robbins, Joseph Chandler 1874-1962 *WhAm 4,*
WhAm 5
Robbins, Laurence Ballard 1887-1965 *WhAm 4*
Robbins, Leonard H 1877-1947 *WhAm 2*
Robbins, Louise Barnum 1844- *WomWWA 14*
Robbins, Luke *NewYHSD*
Robbins, Marvin S 1813- *NewYHSD*
Robbins, Mary Caroline 1841-1912 *WhAm 1,*
WomWWA 14
Robbins, Merton Covey 1875-1937 *NatCAB 37,*
WhAm 1
Robbins, Milton Herbert 1903-1971 *WhAm 5*
Robbins, Milton Holley, Jr. 1871- *WhAm 5*
Robbins, Olive E 1869- *WomWWA 14*
Robbins, Omer Ellsworth 1890-1973 *WhAm 6*
Robbins, Rainard Benton 1886-1951
NatCAB 40

Robbins, Reginald Chauncey 1871-1955
  WhAm 3
Robbins, Rensselaer David Chanceford
  1811-1882 *ApCAB*
Robbins, Richard Whitfield 1892-1971 *WhAm 5*
Robbins, Royal 1788-1861 *ApCAB, Drake,*
  NatCAB 2
Robbins, Royal 1865-1928 *NatCAB 34,*
  WhAm 1
Robbins, Samuel Dowse 1887-1968 *NatCAB 54,*
  WhAm 5
Robbins, Thomas 1777-1856 *ApCAB, DcAmB,*
  Drake, NatCAB 2, WhAm H
Robbins, Thomas Hinckley, Jr. 1900-1972
  NatCAB 57, WhAm 5
Robbins, Walter 1875-1956 *WhAm 3*
Robbins, Warren Delano 1885-1935 *NatCAB 28,*
  WhAm 1
Robbins, Wilford Lash 1859-1927 *WhAm 1*
Robbins, Wilfred William 1884-1952 *WhAm 3*
Robbins, William McKendree 1828-1905 *BiAUS,*
  BiDrAC
Robe, Charles Franklin 1841-1910 *WhAm 1*
Rober, Ernest 1867-1947 *NatCAB 40*
Roberdeau, Daniel 1727-1795 *ApCAB, BiAUS,*
  BiDrAC, DcAmB, Drake, NatCAB 2,
  TwCBDA, WhAm H
Roberdeau, Isaac 1763-1829 *ApCAB, DcAmB,*
  Drake, NatCAB 2, WhAm H
Roberds, William Greene 1884-1963 *WhAm 4*
Roberson, Frank Remont 1871-1916 *WhAm 1*
Roberson, Virgil Odell, Jr. 1908-1973 *WhAm 6*
Roberson, Wescott 1875-1938 *NatCAB 36*
Robert I 1274-1329 *McGEWB*
Robert II 1316-1390 *McGEWB*
Robert III 1337?-1406 *McGEWB*
Robert Guiscard, Count Of Apulia 1016-1085
  McGEWB
Robert Of Lincoln *DcScB*
Robert, Alexander *NewYHSD*
Robert, Ann Maria 1802-1888 *ApCAB*
Robert, Christopher Rhinelander 1802-1878
  AmBi, ApCAB, DcAmB, NatCAB 10,
  TwCBDA, WhAm H
Robert, Daniel Rutgers 1885-1944 *NatCAB 34*
Robert, Dent Hayes 1863-1917 *NatCAB 17*
Robert, Henry Martyn 1837-1923 *AmBi,*
  ApCAB, DcAmB S1, NatCAB 10,
  NatCAB 27, TwCBDA, WebAB,
  WebAMB, WhAm 1
Robert, James Marshall 1885-1964 *NatCAB 51,*
  WhAm 4
Robert, Joseph Thomas 1807-1884 *ApCAB,*
  TwCBDA
Robert, Joseph Thomas 1835- *WhAm 4*
Robert, Sarah Emily Corbin 1886-1972
  WhAm 5
Robert, William Pierre 1873-1963 *WhAm 4*
Roberts, Ada Palmer 1852- *AmWom*
Roberts, Adam *NewYHSD*
Roberts, Albert Houston 1868-1946 *NatCAB 40,*
  WhAm 2
Roberts, Alexander Crippen 1878- *WhAm 6*
Roberts, Allen *NewYHSD*
Roberts, Anna Monsch 1870- *WomWWA 14*
Roberts, Anna Smith 1827-1858 *ApCAB,*
  Drake
Roberts, Anne Mason d1971 *WhAm 5*
Roberts, Anthony Ellmaker 1803-1885 *BiAUS,*
  BiDrAC, WhAm H
Roberts, Arthur Boardman 1884-1965
  NatCAB 51
Roberts, Arthur Jeremiah 1867-1927
  NatCAB 21, WhAm 1
Roberts, Benjamin Franklin 1880-1949
  WhAm 3
Roberts, Benjamin H 1897-1955 *WhAm 3*
Roberts, Benjamin Kearney 1846-1921
  WhAm 1
Roberts, Benjamin Stone 1810-1875 *AmBi,*
  DcAmB, TwCBDA, WhAm H
Roberts, Benjamin Stone 1811-1875 *ApCAB,*
  Drake, NatCAB 5
Roberts, Benjamin Titus 1823-1893 *AmBi,*
  DcAmB, WhAm H
Roberts, Benson Howard 1853-1930 *WhAm 1*
Roberts, Bishop d1739 *NewYHSD*
Roberts, Brigham Henry 1857-1933 *AmBi,*

  BiDrAC, DcAmB, REnAW, WhAm 1
Roberts, Carl Glennis 1886- *WhoColR*
Roberts, Chalmes 1870- *WhAm 5*
Roberts, Charles Asaph 1879-1964 *WhAm 4*
Roberts, Charles B 1842-1899 *BiAUS*
Roberts, Charles Bayle 1842-1899 *NatCAB 3*
Roberts, Charles Boyle 1842-1899 *BiDrAC*
Roberts, Charles Burleson 1892-1953 *WhAm 3*
Roberts, Charles DuVal 1873-1966 *WhAm 4*
Roberts, Charles George Douglas 1860-1943
  ApCAB, ApCAB Sup, NatCAB 11,
  WhAm 3
Roberts, Charles H 1821- *NatCAB 2*
Roberts, Charles Humphrey 1847- *WhAm 4*
Roberts, Charles Wesley 1883-1947 *WhAm 2*
Roberts, Charlotte Fitch 1859-1917 *NatCAB 19,*
  WhAm 1, WomWWA 14
Roberts, Clarence 1890-1942 *WhAm 2*
Roberts, Clarence Joseph 1873-1931
  NatCAB 18, NatCAB 27, WhAm 1
Roberts, Clifford 1896-1959 *WhAm 3*
Roberts, Coleman Williams 1891-1969
  NatCAB 56
Roberts, Colette Jacqueline 1910-1971 *WhAm 5*
Roberts, Columbus 1870-1950 *NatCAB 39*
Roberts, Cyrus Swan 1841-1917 *WhAm 1*
Roberts, David Evan 1854- *NatCAB 16*
Roberts, David Renshaw 1911- *WhAm 6*
Roberts, Delmar 1901-1963 *WhAm 4*
Roberts, Donald F 1902-1965 *WhAm 4*
Roberts, Dorothea Klumpke 1861-1942
  NatCAB 31
Roberts, Douglas James 1892-1957 *NatCAB 47*
Roberts, Dwight Conklin 1898- *WhAm 6*
Roberts, Edmund 1784-1836 *ApCAB, BiAUS,*
  DcAmB, TwCBDA, WhAm H
Roberts, Edward Alexander 1893-1965
  WhAm 4
Roberts, Edward David 1864-1920 *NatCAB 19*
Roberts, Edward Dodson 1877- *WhAm 5*
Roberts, Edward Howell 1895-1954 *WhAm 3*
Roberts, Edwin Ewing 1870-1933 *BiDrAC,*
  WhAm 1, WhAmP
Roberts, Eillis Henry 1827-1918 *BiAUS*
Roberts, Elizabeth Hill Bissell *WomWWA 14*
Roberts, Elizabeth Madox 1881-1941
  DcAmB S3, NotAW
Roberts, Elizabeth Madox 1886-1941 *WebAB,*
  WhAm 1
Roberts, Elizabeth Wentworth 1871-1927
  DcAmB
Roberts, Ellis Henry 1827-1918 *AmBi, ApCAB,*
  BiDrAC, DcAmB, NatCAB 11, TwCBDA,
  WhAm 1, WhAmP
Roberts, Ellsworth A 1896-1960 *WhAm 4*
Roberts, Elmer 1863-1937 *WhAm 1*
Roberts, Elzey 1892-1962 *WhAm 4*
Roberts, Emma Sellew *WomWWA 14*
Roberts, Ernest Porter 1869- *WhAm 5*
Roberts, Ernest William 1858-1924 *BiDrAC,*
  TwCBDA, WhAm 1, WhAmP
Roberts, Florence 1871-1927 *WhAm 1,*
  WomWWA 14
Roberts, Frank Calvin, Jr. 1894-1966 *WhAm 4*
Roberts, Frank Harold Hanna 1897-1966
  WhAm 4
Roberts, Frank Hubert 1916-1972 *WhAm 5*
Roberts, Frank Hunt Hurd 1869-1937
  NatCAB 28, WhAm 1
Roberts, Frank Needham 1897-1975 *WhAm 6*
Roberts, Fred Henry 1856-1920 *ApCAB X*
Roberts, Frederick Madison 1879- *WhoColR*
Roberts, Frederick Sleigh 1832-1913 *WhoMilH*
Roberts, Frederick Sleigh 1832-1914 *McGEWB*
Roberts, Frederick Walton 1876-1955
  NatCAB 47
Roberts, Frederick William 1913-1972
  NatCAB 57
Roberts, George 1884-1968 *WhAm 5*
Roberts, George Brooke 1833-1897 *ApCAB Sup,*
  DcAmB, NatCAB 13, WhAm H
Roberts, George Edward Theodore 1877-
  WhAm 5
Roberts, George Evan 1857-1948 *NatCAB 12,*
  WhAm 2
Roberts, George Litch 1836-1929 *ApCAB Sup,*
  WhAm 1
Roberts, George Lucas 1860-1941 *WhAm 1*

Roberts, George Newman 1874-1940 *WhAm 1*
Roberts, George Washington 1833-1862 *ApCAB,*
  Drake, NatCAB 11
Roberts, George Watson 1866-1931 *NatCAB 23*
Roberts, George Whiting 1903-1964
  NatCAB 50
Roberts, Glenn 1927-1964 *WebAB*
Roberts, H K *NewYHSD*
Roberts, Harlan Page 1854-1925 *WhAm 1*
Roberts, Harold DeWitt 1887-1956 *WhAm 3*
Roberts, Harris Lee 1858-1918 *WhAm 1*
Roberts, Harvey Morehouse 1886-1949
  NatCAB 37
Roberts, Helen Troth Chambers 1869-
  WomWWA 14
Roberts, Henry 1830-1917 *NatCAB 17*
Roberts, Henry 1853-1929 *NatCAB 13,*
  NatCAB 47, WhAm 1
Roberts, Henry Clemens 1918-1964 *NatCAB 54*
Roberts, Henry Lithgow 1916-1972 *WhAm 5*
Roberts, Henry Stoutte 1913-1974 *WhAm 6*
Roberts, Herbert Ray 1913- *BiDrAC*
Roberts, Herbert Rufus 1865-1950 *WhAm 3*
Roberts, Howard 1843-1900 *AmBi, ApCAB,*
  DcAmB, TwCBDA, WhAm 1
Roberts, I H *NewYHSD*
Roberts, Ina Brevoort 1874- *WhAm 5,*
  WomWWA 14
Roberts, Isaac 1829-1904 *DcScB*
Roberts, Isaac Phillips 1833-1928 *NatCAB 4,*
  WhAm 1
Roberts, Isaac Warner 1881- *WhAm 6*
Roberts, Issachar Jacob 1802-1871 *DcAmB,*
  WhAm H
Roberts, J H *NewYHSD*
Roberts, Jack 1920- *IIBEAAW*
Roberts, James Arthur 1847-1922 *NatCAB 5,*
  WhAm 1
Roberts, James Booth 1818- *ApCAB*
Roberts, James Cole 1863- *WhAm 1*
Roberts, James Henry 1876- *WhoColR*
Roberts, James Hudson 1851- *WhAm 4*
Roberts, James Waid 1858-1937 *NatCAB 28*
Roberts, Job 1756-1851 *DcAmB, WhAm H*
Roberts, Job 1757-1851 *ApCAB*
Roberts, John 1768-1803 *NewYHSD*
Roberts, John Bingham 1852-1924 *NatCAB 13,*
  WhAm 1
Roberts, John Emerson 1853- *WhAm 4*
Roberts, John Lake 1902-1961 *NatCAB 50*
Roberts, John Louis 1901-1970 *NatCAB 56*
Roberts, John S 1892-1953 *WhAm 3*
Roberts, John Stacey 1876-1938 *NatCAB 27*
Roberts, John Thomas 1852-1924 *NatCAB 21*
Roberts, John Wright 1815-1875 *ApCAB,*
  NatCAB 5
Roberts, Jonathan 1771-1854 *ApCAB, BiAUS,*
  BiDrAC, DcAmB, NatCAB 4, TwCBDA,
  WhAm H, WhAmP
Roberts, Jonathan Manning 1821-1888 *ApCAB*
Roberts, Jonathan William 1821- *NatCAB 9,*
  WhAm 4
Roberts, Joseph 1814- *ApCAB*
Roberts, Joseph Harry Newton 1892-1959
  WhAm 3
Roberts, Joseph Hayward 1887-1954
  NatCAB 49
Roberts, Joseph Jenkins 1809-1876 *ApCAB,*
  DcAmB, WhAm H
Roberts, Joseph Thomas 1909-1975 *WhAm 6*
Roberts, Kate Louise d1941 *WhAm 2*
Roberts, Katharine Eggleston 1895-1968
  WhAm 4A
Roberts, Kathleen Elizabeth d1975 *WhAm 6*
Roberts, Kenneth 1885-1957 *NatCAB 48,*
  WhAm 3
Roberts, Kenneth Allison 1912- *BiDrAC,*
  WhAmP
Roberts, Kingsley 1893-1947 *WhAm 2*
Roberts, Lloyd Sherwood 1900-1968 *WhAm 5*
Roberts, Lydia Jane d1965 *WhAm 4*
Roberts, Madison Hines 1895-1961 *NatCAB 49,*
  WhAm 4
Roberts, Malcolm Ferguson 1894-1971
  WhAm 5
Roberts, Maria M *WomWWA 14*
Roberts, Marshall Owen 1814-1880 *ApCAB,*

DcAmB, NatCAB 3, WhAm H
Roberts, Marvin S *NewYHSD*
Roberts, Mary d1761 *NewYHSD*
Roberts, Mary Fanton 1871-1956 *WhAm 3, WomWWA 14*
Roberts, Mary M 1877-1959 *WhAm 3*
Roberts, Milnor 1877- *WhAm 6*
Roberts, Milton Josiah 1851-1893 *NatCAB 44*
Roberts, Morton 1927-1964 *WhAm 4*
Roberts, N Suttle 1894-1956 *NatCAB 48*
Roberts, Nathan B *NewYHSD*
Roberts, Nathan Selleck 1843- *NatCAB 2*
Roberts, Nathan Smith 1776-1852 *DcAmB, WhAm H*
Roberts, Nicholas 1878-1945 *NatCAB 34*
Roberts, Nicholas Franklin 1849- *WhoColR*
Roberts, Norman James 1860-1940 *NatCAB 32*
Roberts, Octavia 1875- *WomWWA 14*
Roberts, Odin 1867-1934 *WhAm 1*
Roberts, Oral 1918- *WebAB*
Roberts, Oran Milo 1815-1898 *AmBi, ApCAB, BiDAmEd, BiDConf, DcAmB, NatCAB 9, REnAW, TwCBDA, WhAm H*
Roberts, Owen Josephus 1875-1955 *DcAmB S5, WebAB, WhAm 3*
Roberts, Percival, Jr. 1857-1943 *WhAm 2*
Roberts, Peter 1859-1932 *WhAm 1*
Roberts, Phill Tandy, Jr. 1898-1960 *NatCAB 47, WhAm 4*
Roberts, Richard Brook 1758-1788 *NatCAB 2*
Roberts, Robert 1821?- *NewYHSD*
Roberts, Robert 1848-1939 *WhAm 1*
Roberts, Robert 1872-1940 *NatCAB 36*
Roberts, Robert Ellis 1809-1888 *ApCAB*
Roberts, Robert Jeffries 1849-1920 *BiDAmEd*
Roberts, Robert Richford 1776-1843 *Drake*
Roberts, Robert Richford 1778-1843 *ApCAB, DcAmB, NatCAB 9, TwCBDA, WhAm H*
Roberts, Robert Whyte 1784-1865 *BiAUS, BiDrAC, WhAm H*
Roberts, Roy 1906-1975 *WhAm 6*
Roberts, Roy Allison 1887-1967 *WhAm 4*
Roberts, Sam Earl 1887-1966 *NatCAB 53*
Roberts, Samuel 1763-1830 *ApCAB*
Roberts, Samuel Blakeslee 1894-1970 *NatCAB 57*
Roberts, Samuel Jennings 1897-1971 *WhAm 5*
Roberts, Samuel Judson 1858-1913 *NatCAB 17, WhAm 1*
Roberts, Sara Weeks *BiCAW, WomWWA 14*
Roberts, Seldon L 1871-1930 *WhAm 1*
Roberts, Shelby Saufley 1874-1936 *WhAm 1*
Roberts, Solomon White 1811-1882 *ApCAB, DcAmB, NatCAB 27, WhAm H*
Roberts, Stanley Burroughs 1855-1933 *WhAm 1*
Roberts, Steele Foster 1850-1913 *NatCAB 15*
Roberts, Stephen B 1902-1970 *WhAm 5*
Roberts, Steward Ralph 1878-1941 *WhAm 1*
Roberts, T Scott 1878-1956 *WhAm 3*
Roberts, Tarlton Taylor 1874- *WhAm 5*
Roberts, Theodore 1861-1928 *DcAmB, WhAm 1*
Roberts, Theodore Newlin 1861- *ApCAB X*
Roberts, Thomas 1885-1959 *NatCAB 48*
Roberts, Thomas Humphrey 1891-1967 *NatCAB 54*
Roberts, Thomas Paschall 1843- *ApCAB, TwCBDA, WhAm 4*
Roberts, Thomas Reaser 1923-1968 *WhAm 5*
Roberts, Thomas Sadler 1858-1946 *WhAm 2*
Roberts, Trevor V 1894-1961 *WhAm 4*
Roberts, Vasco Harold 1874-1910 *WhAm 1*
Roberts, W *NewYHSD*
Roberts, W Frank 1879-1957 *WhAm 3*
Roberts, W Lewis 1877-1960 *NatCAB 49*
Roberts, Walter 1870-1958 *NatCAB 44*
Roberts, Walter Adolphe 1886-1962 *WhAm 4*
Roberts, Walter Nelson 1898-1966 *WhAm 4*
Roberts, Warren Russell 1863-1944 *NatCAB 41, WhAm 2*
Roberts, Wes 1903-1975 *WhAm 6*
Roberts, Wightman Durand 1873-1927 *WhAm 1*
Roberts, Willa Mae 1887-1961 *WhAm 4*
Roberts, William *Drake*
Roberts, William 1809-1887 *ApCAB, TwCBDA*

Roberts, William 1811?- *NewYHSD*
Roberts, William 1829?- *NewYHSD*
Roberts, William 1879-1952 *NatCAB 39*
Roberts, William Allerton 1900-1968 *WhAm 5*
Roberts, William Alva 1897-1955 *WhAm 3*
Roberts, William Burchard 1875-1957 *NatCAB 44*
Roberts, William Charles 1832-1903 *ApCAB, DcAmB, NatCAB 2, TwCBDA, WhAm 1*
Roberts, William Henry 1844-1920 *ApCAB Sup, DcAmB, TwCBDA, WhAm 1*
Roberts, William J *NewYHSD*
Roberts, William Milnor 1810-1881 *AmBi, ApCAB, DcAmB, NatCAB 13, NatCAB 29, WhAm H*
Roberts, William Milnor 1810-1882 *TwCBDA*
Roberts, William Randall 1830-1897 *BiAUS, BiDrAC, DcAmB, NatCAB 8, TwCBDA, WhAm H, WhAmP*
Roberts-Austen, William Chandler 1843-1902 *DcScB*
Robertson, A James 1867- *WhAm 5*
Robertson, A Willis 1887-1971 *BiDrAC, WhAm 5, WhAmP*
Robertson, Abram Heaton 1850-1924 *WhAm 1*
Robertson, Agnes Kelly 1833-1916 *NotAW*
Robertson, Alexander *NewYHSD*
Robertson, Alexander d1841 *Drake*
Robertson, Alexander 1768-1841 *ApCAB*
Robertson, Alexander 1772-1841 *NewYHSD*
Robertson, Alexander George Morison 1867-1947 *NatCAB 37, WhAm 2*
Robertson, Alexander Martin 1867-1933 *NatCAB 25*
Robertson, Alexander Mitchell 1855-1934 *WhAm 1*
Robertson, Alfred Worcester 1889-1958 *NatCAB 43*
Robertson, Alice d1922 *WhAm 1*
Robertson, Alice Mary 1854-1931 *AmBi, BiDrAC, DcAmB, NotAW, WhAm 1, WhAmP*
Robertson, Andrew Wells 1880-1965 *WhAm 4*
Robertson, Ann Eliza Worcester 1826-1905 *NotAW*
Robertson, Anthony Lispenard 1808-1868 *ApCAB, BiAUS, Drake*
Robertson, Mrs. Archibald *NewYHSD*
Robertson, Archibald 1745?-1813 *NewYHSD*
Robertson, Archibald 1765-1835 *ApCAB, DcAmB, NewYHSD, WhAm H*
Robertson, Archibald Thomas 1863-1934 *NatCAB 25, WhAm 1*
Robertson, Argyll 1837-1909 *BiHiMed*
Robertson, Ashley Herman 1867-1930 *AmBi, DcAmB, NatCAB 24, WhAm 1*
Robertson, Ben 1903-1943 *NatCAB 32, WhAm 2*
Robertson, Benjamin Franklin 1873-1943 *NatCAB 32*
Robertson, Beverly Holcombe 1827-1910 *TwCBDA, WhAm 1*
Robertson, Carl Trowbridge 1876-1935 *WhAm 1*
Robertson, Cary 1902-1975 *WhAm 6*
Robertson, Charles 1858- *WhAm 4*
Robertson, Charles Barr 1868-1919 *WhAm 1*
Robertson, Charles Franklin 1835-1886 *ApCAB, NatCAB 6, TwCBDA*
Robertson, Charles M 1877-1961 *WhAm 4*
Robertson, Charles Raymond 1889-1951 *BiDrAC, WhAm 3, WhAmP*
Robertson, Charlotte Reeves 1751-1843 *ApCAB, NatCAB 2*
Robertson, David Allan 1880-1961 *WhAm 4*
Robertson, David Brown 1876-1961 *WhAm 4*
Robertson, David Ritchie 1911-1961 *WhAm 4*
Robertson, Sir Dennis Holme 1890-1963 *McGEWB, WhAm 4*
Robertson, Donald 1860-1926 *WhAm 1*
Robertson, Edward P 1860-1941 *WhAm 1*
Robertson, Edward Vivian 1881-1963 *BiDrAC, WhAm 4*
Robertson, Edward White 1823-1887 *ApCAB, BiDrAC, NatCAB 2, TwCBDA, WhAm H, WhAmP*

Robertson, Edwin Wales 1863-1928 *WhAm 1*
Robertson, Ella Broadus 1872-1945 *WhAm 2*
Robertson, Eugene Philip 1841-1917 *NatCAB 17*
Robertson, Felix Davis 1871-1941 *NatCAB 41*
Robertson, Felix Huston 1839-1928 *WhAm 1*
Robertson, Frank Harmon 1895-1938 *NatCAB 29*
Robertson, Frank Wade 1868-1938 *NatCAB 29*
Robertson, Fred 1871- *WhAm 5*
Robertson, Frederick Young 1858-1938 *NatCAB 29*
Robertson, George 1790-1871 *Drake*
Robertson, George 1790-1874 *AmBi, ApCAB, BiAUS, BiDrAC, DcAmB, NatCAB 1, TwCBDA, WhAm H*
Robertson, George 1852-1914 *WhAm 1*
Robertson, George 1878-1960 *WhAm 4*
Robertson, George Hepburn 1884-1955 *NatCAB 41*
Robertson, George J *NewYHSD*
Robertson, George Lawrence 1902-1956 *WhAm 3*
Robertson, Georgia Trowbridge 1852- *AmWom*
Robertson, Grace Barrett *WomWWA 14*
Robertson, Graziella Ridgway 1852- *BiCAW*
Robertson, Harold Eugene 1878-1946 *NatCAB 38, WhAm 2*
Robertson, Harold Hansard 1878-1950 *WhAm 3*
Robertson, Harrison 1856-1939 *NatCAB 29, TwCBDA, WhAm 1*
Robertson, Harrison Marshall 1892-1958 *NatCAB 43, WhAm 3*
Robertson, Heaton Ridgway 1882-1953 *NatCAB 42*
Robertson, Holcombe McGavock 1874- *WhAm 5*
Robertson, Howard Percy 1903-1961 *NatCAB 50, WhAm 4*
Robertson, Ina Law 1867-1916 *NatCAB 17*
Robertson, J Breathitt 1892-1952 *WhAm 3*
Robertson, James 1710?-1788 *ApCAB, Drake*
Robertson, James 1740- *DcAmB*
Robertson, James 1740-1812? *WhAm H*
Robertson, James 1742-1814 *AmBi, ApCAB, DcAmB, Drake, EncAAH, NatCAB 2, REnAW, TwCBDA, WhAm H*
Robertson, James Alexander 1873-1939 *DcAmB S2, WhAm 1*
Robertson, James Brooks Ayres 1871-1938 *NatCAB 51, WhAm 1*
Robertson, James G 1878- *WhAm 6*
Robertson, James Rood 1864-1932 *NatCAB 23, WhAm 1*
Robertson, Jarratt Padgett 1898-1959 *NatCAB 49*
Robertson, Jerome Bonaparte 1815-1891 *BiDConf, DcAmB, WhAm H*
Robertson, John *NewYHSD*
Robertson, John 1787-1873 *ApCAB, BiAUS, BiDrAC, DcAmB, NatCAB 2, TwCBDA, WhAm H, WhAmP*
Robertson, John Alexander 1867-1922 *NatCAB 35*
Robertson, John Brunt 1917-1965 *WhAm 4*
Robertson, John Dill 1871-1931 *WhAm 1*
Robertson, John Ewart 1820-1879 *NewYHSD*
Robertson, John Parish 1793?-1843 *ApCAB*
Robertson, John Ross 1841- *ApCAB*
Robertson, John Roy *NewYHSD*
Robertson, John Stevenston 1866-1937 *WhAm 1*
Robertson, Joseph Andrew 1849-1939 *ApCAB X, WhAm 1*
Robertson, Joseph Gibb 1820- *ApCAB*
Robertson, Lawrence Vernon 1906-1971 *WhAm 5*
Robertson, Leroy Jasper 1896-1971 *NatCAB 56, WhAm 5*
Robertson, Louis Alexander 1856- *WhAm 4*
Robertson, Lucy Henderson 1850- *WhAm 4, WomWWA 14*
Robertson, Lucy Love Crissey 1873- *WomWWA 14*
Robertson, Lyle Lynn 1905-1972 *NatCAB 57*
Robertson, Maria Louisa *WomWWA 14*
Robertson, Marion Clinton 1885-1953 *WhAm 3*
Robertson, Miles Edgar 1889-1972 *NatCAB 57,*

Robinson, Charles Mulford 1869-1917 *DcAmB, NatCAB 21, WhAm 1*
Robinson, Charles Seymour 1829-1899 *AmBi, ApCAB, DcAmB, NatCAB 9, TwCBDA, WhAm H*
Robinson, Charles Snelling 1864- *WhAm 4*
Robinson, Christopher 1760-1798 *ApCAB*
Robinson, Christopher 1806-1889 *BiAUS, BiDrAC, DcAmB, NatCAB 12, WhAm H*
Robinson, Christopher Blackett 1837- *ApCAB*
Robinson, Clara Schouten 1868- *WomWWA 14*
Robinson, Clarence C 1879- *WhAm 6*
Robinson, Clark Shove 1888-1947 *NatCAB 35*
Robinson, Claude Everett 1900-1961 *NatCAB 46, WhAm 4*
Robinson, Clement Franklin 1882-1964 *WhAm 4*
Robinson, Clinton Frederick 1902-1962 *WhAm 4*
Robinson, Coleman Townsend 1838-1872 *NatCAB 21*
Robinson, Conway 1805-1884 *ApCAB, DcAmB, Drake, NatCAB 1, TwCBDA, WhAm H*
Robinson, Corinne Roosevelt 1861-1933 *BiCAW, WhAm 1*
Robinson, Cornelius 1805-1867 *BiDConf*
Robinson, Cyrus 1870-1930 *WhAm 1*
Robinson, Daisy Maude Orleman 1868-1942 *NatCAB 32*
Robinson, Daisy Michaud Orleman 1868-1942 *WomWWA 14*
Robinson, David 1754-1843 *ApCAB, NatCAB 1*
Robinson, David Hunter 1911-1973 *WhAm 6*
Robinson, David Moore 1880-1958 *ApCAB X, WhAm 3*
Robinson, DeLorme Wilson 1854-1910 *WhAm 1*
Robinson, Doane 1856-1946 *WhAm 3*
Robinson, Donald Allister 1881- *WhAm 6*
Robinson, Donald Edward 1901-1959 *NatCAB 48*
Robinson, Douglas d1918 *WhAm 1*
Robinson, Dwight Nelson 1886-1941 *WhAm 2*
Robinson, Dwight Parker 1869-1955 *WhAm 3*
Robinson, Edgar Eugene 1887- *REnAW*
Robinson, Edith 1858- *WhAm 4, WomWWA 14*
Robinson, Edward 1794-1863 *AmBi, ApCAB, DcAmB, Drake, NatCAB 2, TwCBDA, WhAm H*
Robinson, Edward 1796-1857 *BiAUS, BiDrAC, WhAm H*
Robinson, Mrs. Edward 1797-1869 *NatCAB 2*
Robinson, Edward 1858-1931 *AmBi, DcAmB, NatCAB 23, TwCBDA, WhAm 1*
Robinson, Edward Arlington 1869-1935 *EncAB, NatCAB 15*
Robinson, Edward G 1893-1973 *WhAm 5*
Robinson, Edward Henry 1862-1916 *NatCAB 17*
Robinson, Edward Levi 1864-1943 *WhAm 2*
Robinson, Edward Mott 1800-1865 *AmBi, DcAmB, NatCAB 25, WhAm H*
Robinson, Edward Stevens 1893-1937 *DcAmB S2, NatCAB 28, WhAm 1*
Robinson, Edward VanDyke 1867-1915 *DcAmB, WhAm 1*
Robinson, Edwin Arlington 1869-1935 *AmBi, DcAmB S1, McGEWB, NatCAB 33, WebAB, WhAm 1*
Robinson, Edwin Marshall 1888-1963 *NatCAB 48*
Robinson, Edwin Meade 1878-1946 *WhAm 2*
Robinson, Elizabeth Bash Sloan 1882- *WomWWA 14*
Robinson, Erdis 1872-1953 *WhAm 3*
Robinson, Ernest Franklin 1872- *WhAm 2*
Robinson, Esther Tontant DeBeauregard *WomWWA 14*
Robinson, Ethel Brown Blackwell 1870-1947 *NatCAB 36, WomWWA 14*
Robinson, Ezekial Gilman 1815-1894 *WhAm H*
Robinson, Ezekiel Gilman 1815-1894 *ApCAB, BiDAmEd, DcAmB, Drake, NatCAB 1, NatCAB 8, TwCBDA*
Robinson, F DeLancey 1872-1938 *NatCAB 29*

Robinson, Fannie Ruth 1847- *AmWom, WhAm 5*
Robinson, Fayette d1859 *ApCAB, Drake*
Robinson, Florence Evey 1881- *WomWWA 14*
Robinson, Florence Richardson d1936 *WhAm 1*
Robinson, Florence Vincent 1864-1937 *WomWWA 14*
Robinson, Florence Vincent 1874-1937 *WhAm 1*
Robinson, Frank *NewYHSD*
Robinson, Frank M 1845- *ApCAB X*
Robinson, Frank Neall 1874-1915 *NatCAB 18*
Robinson, Frank Torrey 1845-1898 *TwCBDA*
Robinson, Frank Upham 1841-1927 *NatCAB 22, WhAm 1*
Robinson, Frank Wisner 1874-1948 *NatCAB 41, WhAm 2*
Robinson, Franklin Clement 1852-1910 *NatCAB 14, WhAm 1*
Robinson, Fred Carlton 1902-1966 *NatCAB 55*
Robinson, Fred J 1870- *WhAm 5*
Robinson, Fred Norris 1871-1966 *WhAm 4*
Robinson, Frederic Hugo 1890-1923 *NatCAB 35*
Robinson, Frederick Austin 1860-1913 *NatCAB 16*
Robinson, Frederick Bertrand 1883-1941 *BiDAmEd, WhAm 1*
Robinson, Frederick Byron 1855-1910 *DcAmB*
Robinson, Sir Frederick Phillipse 1763-1852 *ApCAB, Drake*
Robinson, G Canby 1878-1960 *NatCAB 46, WhAm 4*
Robinson, George Dexter 1834-1896 *ApCAB, BiDrAC, NatCAB 1, TwCBDA, WhAm H, WhAmP*
Robinson, George Foreman 1844-1917 *NatCAB 41*
Robinson, George Henry 1865- *ApCAB X*
Robinson, George Joseph 1870-1940 *NatCAB 29*
Robinson, George Livingstone 1864-1958 *NatCAB 43, WhAm 3*
Robinson, George Thomas 1868-1944 *WhAm 2*
Robinson, George William 1866-1947 *WhAm 2*
Robinson, George Wilse 1871-1958 *WhAm 3*
Robinson, Gerard B 1898-1959 *WhAm 3*
Robinson, Gerold Tanquary 1892-1971 *WhAm 5*
Robinson, Gifford Simeon 1843-1936 *NatCAB 12, WhAm 1*
Robinson, Gustavus Hill 1881-1972 *WhAm 5*
Robinson, Hamilton W 1814-1879 *NatCAB 10*
Robinson, Harold Clinton 1892-1965 *NatCAB 51*
Robinson, Harold McAfee 1881-1939 *WhAm 1*
Robinson, Harriet Jane Hanson 1825-1911 *AmWom, ApCAB, DcAmB, NatCAB 3, NotAW, TwCBDA, WhAm H*
Robinson, Harrison Sidney 1877-1947 *WhAm 2*
Robinson, Harry Charles 1869- *WhAm 2*
Robinson, Harry Perry 1859-1930 *WhAm 1*
Robinson, Helen Ring d1923 *WhAm 1, WomWWA 14*
Robinson, Henry Cornelius 1832-1900 *DcAmB, WhAm H*
Robinson, Henry Douglas 1859-1913 *NatCAB 30*
Robinson, Henry Douglas 1860-1913 *WhAm 1*
Robinson, Henry Mauris 1868-1937 *NatCAB 30, WhAm 1*
Robinson, Henry Morton 1898-1961 *WhAm 4*
Robinson, Henry Pynchon 1840-1913 *NatCAB 16*
Robinson, Henry R *NewYHSD*
Robinson, Henry Seymour 1868-1926 *NatCAB 29, WhAm 1*
Robinson, Hope Dunlap 1883- *WomWWA 14*
Robinson, Horatio Nelson 1806-1867 *ApCAB, Drake, NatCAB 2, TwCBDA*
Robinson, Howard Lee 1887-1963 *WhAm 5*
Robinson, Howard West 1896-1971 *WhAm 5*
Robinson, Hubbell 1905-1974 *WhAm 6*
Robinson, Ira Ellsworth 1869-1951 *NatCAB 40, WhAm 3*
Robinson, J C *NewYHSD*
Robinson, J F *BiAUS*
Robinson, Jack Roosevelt 1919-1972 *EncAB, McGEWB, WebAB, WhAm 5*

Robinson, James Carroll 1822-1886 *BiAUS, TwCBDA*
Robinson, James Carroll 1823-1886 *BiDrAC, WhAm H, WhAmP*
Robinson, James Dixon 1871-1948 *WhAm 2*
Robinson, James Dixon, Jr. 1905-1967 *NatCAB 54, WhAm 4*
Robinson, James E 1868-1932 *WhAm 1*
Robinson, James Fisher 1800-1892 *NatCAB 13*
Robinson, James Harvey 1863-1936 *AmBi, BiDAmEd, DcAmB S2, McGEWB, TwCBDA, WebAB, WhAm 1*
Robinson, James Hathaway 1892-1963 *WhAm 4*
Robinson, James Lawrence Prever 1880-1947 *NatCAB 48*
Robinson, James Lee 1872-1931 *WhAm 1*
Robinson, James Lukin *ApCAB*
Robinson, James McClellan 1861-1942 *BiDrAC, TwCBDA, WhAm 4, WhAmP*
Robinson, James Milton 1919-1974 *WhAm 6*
Robinson, James Sidney 1827-1892 *ApCAB, BiDrAC, TwCBDA, WhAm H*
Robinson, James Sidney 1828-1892 *Drake*
Robinson, James Wallace 1826-1898 *BiAUS, BiDrAC*
Robinson, James William 1878-1964 *BiDrAC, WhAmP*
Robinson, Jane Marie Bancroft 1847-1932 *AmWom, BiCAW, NotAW, WhAm 1, WomWWA 14*
Robinson, Jesse Mathews 1889-1949 *WhAm 3*
Robinson, John *NewYHSD*
Robinson, John d1829 *NewYHSD*
Robinson, John 1575?-1625 *ApCAB, Drake, NatCAB 2, WhAm H*
Robinson, John 1683-1749 *NatCAB 13*
Robinson, John 1704-1766 *DcAmB, WhAm H*
Robinson, John 1761-1828 *ApCAB*
Robinson, John 1768-1843 *ApCAB, NatCAB 2*
Robinson, John 1806-1888 *NatCAB 3*
Robinson, John 1832?- *NewYHSD*
Robinson, John 1846-1925 *WhAm 1*
Robinson, Sir John Beverley 1791-1863 *Drake, McGEWB*
Robinson, John Beverley 1853-1923 *NatCAB 19, WhAm 1*
Robinson, Sir John Beverly 1791-1863 *ApCAB*
Robinson, John Beverly 1820- *ApCAB*
Robinson, John Buchanan 1846-1933 *BiDrAC*
Robinson, John Bunyan 1834- *TwCBDA*
Robinson, John Cleveland 1817-1897 *AmBi, ApCAB, DcAmB, Drake, NatCAB 4, TwCBDA, WebAMB, WhAm H*
Robinson, John Edward 1849-1922 *WhAm 1*
Robinson, John Eustace 1876- *WhoColR*
Robinson, John Franklin 1843-1921 *NatCAB 27*
Robinson, John Gilbert 1872-1935 *NatCAB 27*
Robinson, John Hiram 1826-1900 *NatCAB 14*
Robinson, John Kelly 1842-1908 *NatCAB 11, NatCAB 24*
Robinson, John Larne 1813-1860 *BiAUS, BiDrAC, WhAm H*
Robinson, John M 1793-1843 *ApCAB, BiAUS, NatCAB 13*
Robinson, John M 1908-1963 *WhAm 4*
Robinson, John Marshall 1851-1910 *WhAm 1*
Robinson, John McCracken 1794-1843 *BiDrAC, WhAm H*
Robinson, John McCraken 1794-1843 *TwCBDA*
Robinson, John Mitchell 1827-1896 *DcAmB, NatCAB 7, WhAm H*
Robinson, John Mitchell 1828-1896 *TwCBDA*
Robinson, John Moseley 1887-1963 *NatCAB 51*
Robinson, John Norris 1831-1878 *NatCAB 15*
Robinson, John Q 1898-1973 *WhAm 6*
Robinson, John Seaton 1856-1903 *BiDrAC, WhAm 3*
Robinson, John Sherman 1880-1951 *WhAm 3*
Robinson, John Staniford 1804-1860 *ApCAB, BiAUS, Drake, NatCAB 8, TwCBDA*
Robinson, John Trumbull 1871-1937 *WhAm 1*
Robinson, John W 1866-1947 *WhAm 2*
Robinson, John William 1875-1966 *NatCAB 52*
Robinson, Jonah Leroy 1856- *NatCAB 13*
Robinson, Jonathan 1756-1819 *ApCAB, BiAUS, BiDrAC, Drake, NatCAB 2, TwCBDA, WhAm H, WhAmP*
Robinson, Joseph 1874-1943 *WhAm 2*

Robinson, Joseph E 1873- *WhAm 3*
Robinson, Joseph Gibson 1909-1963 *WhAm 4*
Robinson, Joseph Patterson *WhoColR*
Robinson, Joseph Taylor 1872-1937 *AmBi, ApCAB X, BiDrAC, DcAmB S2, NatCAB 36, WhAm 1, WhAmP*
Robinson, Julia Almira d1942 *WhAm 2*
Robinson, Karl Frederic 1904-1967 *WhAm 4*
Robinson, Lee I 1884-1966 *NatCAB 52*
Robinson, Leland Rex 1893-1966 *WhAm 4*
Robinson, Lelia Walker 1885- *WhoColR*
Robinson, Lennox 1886-1958 *WhAm 3*
Robinson, Leonard George 1875- *WhAm 2*
Robinson, Leonidas Dunlap 1867-1941 *BiDrAC, WhAm 4*
Robinson, Leora Bettison 1840- *AmWom*
Robinson, Lewis Taylor 1868-1931 *AmBi*
Robinson, Lewis Wood 1840-1903 *TwCBDA, WhAm 1*
Robinson, Louis Newton 1880-1952 *WhAm 3*
Robinson, Lucien Moore 1858-1932 *WhAm 1, WhAm 1C*
Robinson, Lucius 1810-1891 *ApCAB, NatCAB 3, TwCBDA*
Robinson, Lucius Franklin 1863-1941 *WhAm 1*
Robinson, Lucius W d1941 *WhAm 1*
Robinson, Lucius Waterman 1855-1935 *NatCAB 26, WhAm 1*
Robinson, Luther Emerson 1867-1945 *WhAm 3*
Robinson, Lydia Gillingham 1875- *WhAm 5, WomWWA 14*
Robinson, Mabel Louise 1874-1962 *NatCAB 47, WhAm 4*
Robinson, Mark Prever 1852-1915 *NatCAB 36*
Robinson, Mary Barber 1854- *WomWWA 14*
Robinson, Mary Dummett Nauman *WhAm 5*
Robinson, Mary H 1875- *WomWWA 14*
Robinson, Mary Levering 1875- *WomWWA 14*
Robinson, Mary Nauman *WomWWA 14*
Robinson, Mary Yandes 1864- *WhAm 4*
Robinson, Matthew 1713-1800 *ApCAB, Drake*
Robinson, Maurice Henry d1946 *WhAm 2*
Robinson, Merritt M 1810?-1850 *ApCAB, Drake*
Robinson, Millard Lyman 1880-1947 *WhAm 2*
Robinson, Milton Stapp 1832-1892 *BiAUS, BiDrAC, WhAm H*
Robinson, Moncure 1802-1891 *DcAmB, NatCAB 8, WhAm H*
Robinson, Morris 1759-1815 *ApCAB*
Robinson, Moses d1813 *BiAUS*
Robinson, Moses 1740-1813 *NatCAB 8*
Robinson, Moses 1741-1813 *ApCAB, BiDrAC, Drake, TwCBDA, WhAmP*
Robinson, Moses 1742-1813 *DcAmB, WhAm H*
Robinson, Myron Potter 1871-1932 *NatCAB 23*
Robinson, Myron Wilber 1881- *WhAm 6*
Robinson, Nelson Lemuel 1857-1944 *NatCAB 35*
Robinson, Noel 1892-1944 *WhAm 2*
Robinson, Oliver Pearce 1853-1917 *NatCAB 17*
Robinson, Orin Pomeroy, Jr. 1891-1956 *WhAm 3*
Robinson, Orville 1801-1882 *BiAUS, BiDrAC, WhAm H*
Robinson, Otis Hall 1835-1912 *DcAmLiB*
Robinson, Pat 1891-1964 *WhAm 4*
Robinson, Paul Gervais 1834-1913 *NatCAB 16, WhAm 4*
Robinson, Pauline *NewYHSD*
Robinson, R R 1885-1948 *WhAm 2*
Robinson, Rachel *WomWWA 14*
Robinson, Ray 1920- *WebAB*
Robinson, Remus Grant 1904-1970 *WhAm 5*
Robinson, Reuel 1858-1927 *NatCAB 38*
Robinson, Richard Hallett Meredith 1875-1951 *NatCAB 41, WhAm 3*
Robinson, Richard Lee 1872-1939 *WhAm 1*
Robinson, Sir Robert 1886-1975 *AsBiEn, WhAm 6*
Robinson, Robert Francis 1893-1957 *NatCAB 45*
Robinson, Robert Gibson 1886-1958 *NatCAB 47*
Robinson, Robert Pomeroy 1884-1953 *NatCAB 43*
Robinson, Robert Pyle 1869-1939 *NatCAB 29,*

WhAm 1
Robinson, Rodney Potter 1890-1950 *WhAm 3*
Robinson, Roswell Raymond 1835-1923 *NatCAB 31*
Robinson, Rowland Evans 1833-1900 *DcAmB, WhAm 1*
Robinson, Samuel 1707-1767 *ApCAB, NatCAB 1*
Robinson, Samuel 1738-1813 *ApCAB*
Robinson, Samuel 1877-1947 *WhAm 2*
Robinson, Samuel Murray 1882-1972 *WhAm 5*
Robinson, Sanford 1873-1942 *WhAm 2*
Robinson, Sara Tappann Doolittle 1827- *TwCBDA, WhAm 4*
Robinson, Sarah Tappan Doolittle 1827- *ApCAB*
Robinson, Sidney W 1903-1974 *WhAm 6*
Robinson, Silas Arnold 1840-1927 *NatCAB 20, WhAm 1*
Robinson, Snowden *NewYHSD*
Robinson, Solon 1803-1880 *ApCAB, DcAmB, Drake, EncAAH, NatCAB 3, TwCBDA, WhAm H*
Robinson, Solon 1895-1964 *WhAm 4*
Robinson, Stephen Bernard 1880-1964 *WhAm 4*
Robinson, Stewart MacMaster 1893-1965 *WhAm 4*
Robinson, Stillman Williams 1838-1910 *ApCAB, BiDAmEd, DcAmB, NatCAB 10, NatCAB 35, TwCBDA, WhAm 1*
Robinson, Stuart d1881 *Drake*
Robinson, Stuart 1814-1881 *ApCAB, DcAmB, TwCBDA, WhAm H*
Robinson, Stuart 1816-1881 *NatCAB 1*
Robinson, Sumers Corson 1831-1903 *NatCAB 6*
Robinson, Theodore 1852-1896 *BnEnAmA, DcAmB, McGEWB, WhAm H*
Robinson, Theodore Douglas 1883-1934 *NatCAB 25, WhAm 1*
Robinson, Theodore Winthrop 1862-1948 *WhAm 2*
Robinson, Therese Albertina L VonJakob 1797-1869 *ApCAB*
Robinson, Therese Albertine L VonJakob 1797-1869 *Drake*
Robinson, Therese Albertine L VonJakob 1797-1870 *DcAmB, WhAm H*
Robinson, Thomas *NewYHSD*
Robinson, Thomas 1834-1888 *NewYHSD*
Robinson, Thomas 1835-1888 *NatCAB 5*
Robinson, Thomas, Jr. 1800-1843 *BiAUS, BiDrAC, WhAm H*
Robinson, Thomas John Bright 1868-1958 *BiDrAC, WhAm 3, WhAmP*
Robinson, Thomas Linton 1880-1940 *WhAm 1*
Robinson, Thomas Pendleton 1878-1954 *NatCAB 41*
Robinson, Thomas Raymond 1892-1957 *NatCAB 47*
Robinson, Thomas William 1900-1971 *NatCAB 56*
Robinson, Tracy 1833- *WhAm 4*
Robinson, V Gilpin 1851-1942 *NatCAB 37*
Robinson, Victor 1886-1947 *NatCAB 35, WhAm 2*
Robinson, Virginia Pollard 1883- *WomWWA 14*
Robinson, Wallace Freeman 1830-1920 *ApCAB X*
Robinson, Walter Augustin 1854- *NatCAB 3*
Robinson, Waltour Moss 1850-1933 *NatCAB 13, NatCAB 25, WhAm 4*
Robinson, Wilfred Henry 1882-1948 *WhAm 3*
Robinson, Wilfreid 1871- *WhAm 5*
Robinson, William *NewYHSD*
Robinson, William 1785-1868 *WhAm H*
Robinson, William 1840-1921 *DcAmB, WhAm HA, WhAm 4*
Robinson, William Alexander 1843-1917 *WhAm 1*
Robinson, William Alexander 1884-1950 *WhAm 3*
Robinson, William Arthur 1881-1951 *NatCAB 39*
Robinson, William Callyhan 1834-1911 *DcAmB, NatCAB 3, TwCBDA, WhAm 1*
Robinson, William Christopher 1867-1962 *WhAm 4*

Robinson, William Courtland 1865-1938 *WhAm 1*
Robinson, William Davis 1775?- *NatCAB 18*
Robinson, William Dean 1898-1957 *WhAm 3*
Robinson, William Duffield 1856-1931 *WhAm 1*
Robinson, William Edward 1900-1969 *NatCAB 54, WhAm 5*
Robinson, William Erigena 1814-1892 *AmBi, ApCAB, BiAUS, BiDrAC, DcAmB, NatCAB 3, TwCBDA, WhAm H*
Robinson, William H 1909-1973 *WhAm 5*
Robinson, William Henry 1766-1836 *ApCAB*
Robinson, William Henry 1848-1910 *WhAm 3*
Robinson, William Henry 1867-1938 *NatCAB 34, WhAm 1*
Robinson, William Henry 1897-1955 *WhAm 3*
Robinson, William Josephus 1867-1936 *NatCAB 35*
Robinson, William Josephus 1869-1936 *WhAm 1*
Robinson, William M 1878-1961 *WhAm 4*
Robinson, William Morrison, Jr. 1891-1965 *WhAm 4*
Robinson, William Oswald 1846-1927 *NatCAB 21*
Robinson, William Proudfit 1862-1929 *NatCAB 23*
Robinson, William Samuel 1874-1954 *NatCAB 43*
Robinson, William Smith 1861-1945 *NatCAB 33, WhAm 2*
Robinson, William Stevens 1818-1876 *ApCAB, DcAmB, Drake Sup, NatCAB 3, TwCBDA, WhAm H*
Robinson, William Theodore 1877-1953 *WhAm 3*
Robinson, William Wallace, Jr. 1846-1917 *WhAm 1*
Robinson, Winifred Josephine 1867- *WomWWA 14*
Robinson, Wirt 1864-1929 *WhAm 1*
Robiquet, Pierre-Jean 1780-1840 *DcScB*
Robison, David Fullerton 1816-1859 *BiAUS, BiDrAC, WhAm H*
Robison, Frank DeHass 1852-1908 *NatCAB 18*
Robison, Henry Barton 1866-1953 *WhAm 3*
Robison, Henry John 1894- *WhAm 6*
Robison, Howard Winfield 1915- *BiDrAC*
Robison, Jeannie Floyd-Jones 1853- *WomWWA 14*
Robison, John 1739-1805 *DcScB*
Robison, John Keeler 1870-1938 *NatCAB 29*
Robison, Lyman Miner 1837- *NatCAB 1*
Robison, Samuel Shelburn 1867-1952 *NatCAB 41, WhAm 3*
Robison, William 1851-1928 *ApCAB X*
Robison, William Ferretti 1871-1944 *WhAm 2*
Robitaille, Louis 1836- *ApCAB*
Robitaille, Theodore 1834- *ApCAB*
Robitschek, Fritz Otto 1907-1962 *NatCAB 52*
Robledo, Jorje d1546 *ApCAB*
Roblee, William Wallace 1872-1944 *NatCAB 37*
Robles Pezuela, Manuel 1810-1862 *ApCAB*
Robnett, David Barton 1890-1947 *NatCAB 44*
Robnett, Dudley Anderson 1895-1948 *NatCAB 36*
Robnett, Ronald Herbert 1905-1954 *WhAm 3*
Robot, Isidore 1837-1887 *ApCAB Sup, DcAmB, WhAm H*
Robsion, John Marshall 1873-1948 *BiDrAC, WhAmP*
Robsion, John Marshall 1878-1948 *WhAm 2*
Robsion, John Marshall, Jr. 1904- *BiDrAC, WhAmP*
Robsjohn-Gibbings, Terence Harold 1905- *BnEnAmA*
Robson, Eleanor Elsie *WomWWA 14*
Robson, Elizabeth 1842- *WomWWA 14*
Robson, Frank E 1859-1948 *WhAm 2*
Robson, James A 1851-1916 *WhAm 1*
Robson, Mrs. John J 1885- *WomWWA 14*
Robson, Martin Cecil 1908-1971 *WhAm 5*
Robson, May 1858-1942 *DcAmB S3, NotAW, WhAm 2*
Robson, May Waldron 1868-1925 *WhAm 1, WomWWA 14*
Robson, Stuart 1836-1903 *AmBi, DcAmB,*

NatCAB 2, TwCBDA, WhAm 1
Robus, Hugo 1885-1964 *BnEnAmA, WhAm 4*
Roby, Harlow Stanley 1872-1954 *NatCAB 43*
Roby, Ida Hall 1857- *AmWom*
Roby, Joseph 1871-1954 *NatCAB 40*
Roby, Lelia P 1848- *AmWom*
Roby, Maude Gordon *WomWWA 14*
Roby, Samuel Sidney Breese 1866-1931
NatCAB 40
Robyn, Alfred George 1860-1935 *NatCAB 7, WhAm 1*
Robyn, Charles *NewYHSD*
Robyn, Edward 1820-1862 *NewYHSD, WhAm H*
Roca, Julio Argentino 1843-1914 *ApCAB Sup, McGEWB*
Rocafuerte, Vicente 1783-1847 *ApCAB*
Rocap, James E 1881- *WhAm 6*
Rocha, Justiniano Jose Da 1812-1863 *ApCAB*
Rochambeau, Comte De 1725-1807 *WebAB, WebAMB, WhAm H*
Rochambeau, D M J DeV, Viscount De
1750-1813 *ApCAB, WhoMilH*
Rochambeau, Jean B D DeVimeur, Count De
1725-1807 *AmBi, ApCAB, DcAmB, Drake, McGEWB, NatCAB 1, TwCBDA, WhoMilH*
Roche, Alexandre DeLa 1594-1667 *ApCAB*
Roche, Ambrose Francis 1854-1935 *WhAm 1*
Roche, Arthur Somers 1883-1935 *DcAmB S1, NatCAB 38, WhAm 1*
Roche, David *NewYHSD*
Roche, Edouard Albert 1820-1883 *DcScB*
Roche, Frederick W 1914-1971 *WhAm 5*
Roche, James Jeffrey 1847-1908 *ApCAB, DcAmB, NatCAB 8, TwCBDA, WhAm 1*
Roche, John A 1844-1904 *NatCAB 3, NatCAB 33, WhAm 1*
Roche, John Francis 1874-1950 *NatCAB 43*
Roche, John Joseph 1899-1967 *WhAm 4*
Roche, John Pierre 1889-1960 *WhAm 3*
Roche, Joseph T 1865- *WhAm 4*
Roche, Kevin 1922- *BnEnAmA*
Roche, Martin d1927 *WhAm 1*
Roche, Michael Joseph 1878-1964 *WhAm 4*
Roche, Theodore Joseph 1876-1958 *NatCAB 51*
Roche, Troilus DeM, Marquis DeLa 1549-1606
ApCAB
Roche, Walter 1895-1962 *NatCAB 51*
Roche, William James 1853- *WhAm 1*
Rochefort, Cesar De 1630-1691 *ApCAB*
Rochefoucauld-L D'E, F A F, Duke DeLa
1747-1827 *ApCAB*
Rochefoucauld Liancourt, F A, Duke DeLa
1747-1829 *Drake*
Rochejacquelein, Henri DuV, Comte De
1772-1794 *WhoMilH*
Rochejacquelein, Louis De 1777-1815 *WhoMilH*
Rocheleau, Walter Claver 1881-1952
NatCAB 41
Rochester, Anna 1880- *WomWWA 14*
Rochester, Edward Sudler 1885-1946 *WhAm 2*
Rochester, Nathaniel 1752-1831 *ApCAB, DcAmB, NatCAB 9, TwCBDA, WhAm H*
Rochester, Thomas Fortescue 1823-1887
ApCAB, NatCAB 25
Rochester, William Beatty 1789-1838 *BiAUS, BiDrAC, WhAm H*
Rochester, William Beatty 1826-1909 *ApCAB, TwCBDA, WhAm 1*
Rochford, Richard Augustine 1889-1953
NatCAB 42
Rochlen, Ava Michael 1891-1969 *WhAm 5*
Rochon, Julius *NewYHSD*
Rock, George Frederick 1907-1959 *NatCAB 53, WhAm 3*
Rock, George Henry 1868-1946 *NatCAB 36, WhAm 2*
Rock, John 1836-1904 *DcAmB*
Rock, John Swett 1825-1866 *EncAB*
Rock, William Elijah 1861- *WhoColR*
Rockefeller, Abby Greene Aldrich 1874-1948
DcAmB S4, NatCAB 46, NotAW
Rockefeller, Franklin 1845-1917 *NatCAB 21*
Rockefeller, John Davidson 1839-1937 *TwCBDA*
Rockefeller, John Davison 1839-1937 *AmBi,*

ApCAB Sup, DcAmB S2, EncAB, McGEWB, NatCAB 11, NatCAB 29, WebAB, WhAm 1
Rockefeller, John Davison, Jr. 1874-1960
McGEWB, NatCAB 44, WhAm 4
Rockefeller, Laura Celestia Spelman 1839-
BiCAW
Rockefeller, Lewis Kirby 1875-1948 *BiDrAC, NatCAB 41*
Rockefeller, Lewis Kirby 1877-1948 *WhAm 5*
Rockefeller, Nelson Aldrich 1908- *EncAB, WebAB*
Rockefeller, Percy Avery 1878-1934 *WhAm 1*
Rockefeller, William 1841-1922 *AmBi, ApCAB Sup, DcAmB, NatCAB 11, WhAm 1*
Rockefeller, William Goodsell 1870-1922
WhAm 1
Rockefeller, Winthrop 1912-1973 *WhAm 5, WhAm 6*
Rockenbach, Samuel Dickerson 1869- *WhAm 3*
Rocker, Nicholas *NewYHSD*
Rockett, James Francis 1884-1948 *WhAm 2*
Rockey, Abraham B 1799- *NewYHSD*
Rockey, Alpha Eugene 1857-1927 *NatCAB 21, WhAm 1*
Rockey, Howard 1886-1934 *WhAm 1*
Rockey, Keller E 1888-1970 *WhAm 5*
Rockhill, Clayton 1861-1918 *ApCAB X, NatCAB 28*
Rockhill, William 1793-1865 *BiAUS, BiDrAC, WhAm H*
Rockhill, William Woodville 1853-1914 *EncAB*
Rockhill, William Woodville 1854-1914 *AmBi, DcAmB, NatCAB 8, WebAB, WhAm 1*
Rockingham, Charles Watson Wentworth
1730-1782 *ApCAB, Drake, McGEWB, WhAm H*
Rockne, Knute Kenneth 1888-1931 *AmBi, DcAmB, McGEWB, NatCAB 25, WebAB, WhAm 1*
Rockwell, Albert 1877-1951 *NatCAB 39*
Rockwell, Alfred Perkins 1834-1903 *WhAm 1*
Rockwell, Alfred Perkins 1834-1923
NatCAB 21
Rockwell, Alphonso David 1840-1933 *ApCAB, DcAmB, WhAm 1*
Rockwell, Anna Gaylord 1857- *WomWWA 14*
Rockwell, Augustus *NewYHSD*
Rockwell, Charles 1806-1882 *ApCAB*
Rockwell, Charles Bristed 1848-1929
NatCAB 36
Rockwell, Charles H 1852-1907 *WhAm 1*
Rockwell, Charles Henry 1840-1908 *WhAm 1*
Rockwell, Charles W *BiAUS*
Rockwell, Cleveland 1837-1907 *IlBEAAW*
Rockwell, David Ladd 1877- *WhAm 5*
Rockwell, Edward Henry 1869-1943
NatCAB 32, WhAm 2
Rockwell, Fenton 1839-1913 *NatCAB 33*
Rockwell, Fletcher Webster 1877- *WhAm 5*
Rockwell, Francis Williams 1844-1929 *BiDrAC, TwCBDA, WhAmP*
Rockwell, Franklin Hard 1844-1911
NatCAB 39
Rockwell, Herbert George 1872-1927
NatCAB 21
Rockwell, Homer 1902-1971 *WhAm 5*
Rockwell, Horace 1811-1877 *NewYHSD*
Rockwell, Hosea Hunt 1840-1918 *BiDrAC*
Rockwell, J Edson 1816-1882 *Drake*
Rockwell, James Otis 1807-1831 *Drake*
Rockwell, James Otis 1808-1831 *ApCAB*
Rockwell, James Wade 1890-1962 *NatCAB 51*
Rockwell, Joel Edson 1816-1882 *ApCAB, NatCAB 9*
Rockwell, John A 1804-1861 *BiAUS*
Rockwell, John Arnold 1803-1861 *ApCAB, BiDrAC, Drake, WhAm H*
Rockwell, Joseph Henry 1862-1927 *NatCAB 28, WhAm 1*
Rockwell, Julius 1805-1888 *ApCAB, BiAUS, BiDrAC, Drake, NatCAB 11, TwCBDA, WhAm H, WhAmP*
Rockwell, Julius Ensign 1860-1926 *WhAm 1*
Rockwell, Kiffin Yates 1892-1916 *DcAmB, WebAMB, WhAm HA, WhAm 4*
Rockwell, Leo Lawrence 1888-1967 *NatCAB 54*

Rockwell, Mary Fairchild 1862- *WomWWA 14*
Rockwell, Maryelda 1909-1970 *WhAm 5*
Rockwell, Norman Percevel 1894- *IlBEAAW, WebAB*
Rockwell, Robert Fay 1886-1950 *BiDrAC, WhAm 3, WhAmP*
Rockwell, Samuel 1847- *WhAm 4*
Rockwell, Walter F 1899-1973 *WhAm 6*
Rockwell, William Hayden 1867-1930 *WhAm 1*
Rockwell, William Walker 1874-1958 *WhAm 3*
Rockwood, Charles Greene, Jr. 1843-1913
ApCAB, NatCAB 7, NatCAB 16, TwCBDA, WhAm 1
Rockwood, Ebenezer Arthur 1839- *NatCAB 3*
Rockwood, Elbert William 1860-1935 *WhAm 1*
Rockwood, Frank Ernest 1852-1935 *WhAm 1*
Rockwood, George Gardner 1832-1911
ApCAB Sup, NatCAB 13, WhAm 1
Rockwood, George Ichabod 1868-1959
NatCAB 50, WhAm 5
Rockwood, George Otis 1872-1935 *NatCAB 48*
Rockwood, Laura Clarke *WomWWA 14*
Rockwood, Robert Everett 1887-1958 *WhAm 3*
Rockwood, William Moore 1874-1945
NatCAB 34
Rodale, Jerome Irving 1898-1971 *WhAm 5*
Rodd, Thomas 1849-1929 *NatCAB 12, NatCAB 36, WhAm 4*
Rodda, F C 1880-1963 *WhAm 4*
Rodda, Frederick Constans 1880-1963
NatCAB 50
Rodden, H *NewYHSD*
Roddenbery, Seaborn Anderson 1870-1913
BiDrAC, WhAm 1
Roddewig, Clair M 1903-1975 *WhAm 6*
Roddewig, Paulo 1857-1938 *NatCAB 44*
Roddey, Philip Dale 1818-1897 *ApCAB*
Roddey, Philip Dale 1820-1897 *DcAmB, TwCBDA, WhAm H*
Roddey, Philip Dale 1826-1897 *BiDConf*
Roddey, William Joseph 1861- *WhAm 4*
Roddis, Hamilton 1875-1960 *NatCAB 50, WhAm 3*
Roddy, Gilbert Morgan 1910-1972 *WhAm 5*
Roddy, Harry Justin 1856-1943 *NatCAB 47, WhAm 1, WhAm 2*
Roddy, James E 1905-1965 *WhAm 4*
Roddy, William Franklin 1871-1940 *WhAm 1*
Rode, Alfred 1895-1969 *WhAm 5*
Rode, Paul Peter 1873- *NatCAB 15*
Rode, Ralph Becker 1893-1953 *WhAm 3*
Rodebush, Worth Huff 1887-1959 *NatCAB 50, WhAm 4*
Rodefer, Charles Mayger 1881-1965 *WhAm 4*
Rodeheaver, Homer Alvan 1880-1955
NatCAB 45, WhAm 3
Rodell, Marie Freid d1975 *WhAm 6*
Roden, Carl Bismarck 1870-1956 *NatCAB 47, WhAm 3*
Roden, Carl Bismarck 1871-1956 *DcAmLiB*
Roden, Elizabeth Bowman 1883-
WomWWA 14
Roden, Henry Wisdom 1895-1963 *NatCAB 50, WhAm 4*
Rodenbaugh, Henry Nathan 1879-1966
WhAm 4
Rodenbeck, Adolph Julius d1960 *WhAm 3A*
Rodenberg, William August 1865-1937 *BiDrAC, NatCAB 28, WhAm 1, WhAmP*
Rodenbough, Theophilus Francis 1828-1912
AmBi
Rodenbough, Theophilus Francis 1838-1912
ApCAB, DcAmB, NatCAB 10, TwCBDA, WhAm 1
Roder, Martin 1851-1895 *WhAm H*
Rodes, John Barret 1870-1970 *NatCAB 57*
Rodes, Robert Emmett 1826-1864 *NatCAB 5*
Rodes, Robert Emmett 1829-1864 *ApCAB, BiDConf, DcAmB, TwCBDA, WebAMB, WhAm H*
Rodewald, Fred C *IlBEAAW*
Rodey, Bernard Shandon 1856-1927 *BiDrAC, WhAm 1, WhAmP*
Rodey, Pearce Coddington 1889-1958
NatCAB 54, WhAm 3
Rodger, James George 1852- *TwCBDA, WhAm 4*
Rodgers *NewYHSD*

Rodgers, Arthur 1848-1902 *NatCAB 8*
Rodgers, Bert 1893-1951 *NatCAB 40*
Rodgers, C R P 1818-1892 *Drake*
Rodgers, Christopher Raymond Perry 1818-1892
ApCAB
Rodgers, Christopher Raymond Perry 1819-1892
*AmBi, DcAmB, NatCAB 4, TwCBDA,
WebAMB, WhAm H*
Rodgers, Cleveland 1885-1956 *WhAm 3*
Rodgers, Cowan 1878-1936 *WhAm 1*
Rodgers, David John 1912-1968 *WhAm 5*
Rodgers, Elizabeth Flynn 1847-1939 *NotAW*
Rodgers, Frederick 1842-1917 *TwCBDA,
WhAm 1*
Rodgers, George Washington 1787-1832 *AmBi,
ApCAB, DcAmB, Drake, NatCAB 4,
TwCBDA, WebAMB, WhAm H*
Rodgers, George Washington 1822-1863 *AmBi,
ApCAB, DcAmB, NatCAB 4, TwCBDA,
WebAMB, WhAm H*
Rodgers, Helen Z M 1876- *WomWWA 14*
Rodgers, Henry Darling 1879-1957 *NatCAB 47,
WhAm 6*
Rodgers, Hickman Price 1859-1922 *NatCAB 19*
Rodgers, James Linn 1861-1930 *WhAm 1*
Rodgers, James Webb 1822-1896 *TwCBDA*
Rodgers, James Webb *see also* Rogers, James
Webb
Rodgers, John 1727-1811 *ApCAB, DcAmB,
Drake, NatCAB 5, TwCBDA, WhAm H*
Rodgers, John 1771-1838 *ApCAB, Drake,
NatCAB 5, TwCBDA*
Rodgers, John 1773-1838 *AmBi, DcAmB,
WebAB, WebAMB, WhAm H*
Rodgers, John 1811-1882 *Drake*
Rodgers, John 1812-1882 *AmBi, ApCAB,
DcAmB, NatCAB 5, NatCAB 25,
TwCBDA, WebAB, WebAMB, WhAm H*
Rodgers, John 1881-1926 *DcAmB, NatCAB 20,
WebAMB, WhAm 1*
Rodgers, John Augustus 1848-1933 *NatCAB 27,
WhAm 1*
Rodgers, John Gilmour 1861-1923 *NatCAB 24*
Rodgers, John Gilmour 1863-1923 *WhAm 1*
Rodgers, John Isaac 1839-1931 *WhAm 1*
Rodgers, Joshua *NewYHSD*
Rodgers, Philip R d1965 *WhAm 4*
Rodgers, Raymond 1899-1968 *WhAm 5*
Rodgers, Raymond Perry 1849-1925
NatCAB 26, WhAm 1
Rodgers, Richard Charles 1902- *EncAB,
McGEWB, WebAB*
Rodgers, Robert Lewis 1875-1960 *BiDrAC,
WhAm 4*
Rodgers, Robert Perry 1895-1934 *NatCAB 27*
Rodgers, Ted Vincent, Sr. 1888-1960
NatCAB 49, WhAm 4
Rodgers, Thomas Slidell 1858-1931 *NatCAB 25,
WhAm 1*
Rodgers, William 1903-1972 *WhAm 5*
Rodgers, William Baker 1865- *NatCAB 11*
Rodgers, William Blackstock 1845-1914
WhAm 1
Rodgers, William Cunningham 1856-1921
WhAm 1
Rodgers, William Ledyard 1860-1944
NatCAB 33, WhAm 2
Rodgers, William S S 1886-1965 *WhAm 4*
Rodgers, William Thomas 1861-1931 *WhAm 1*
Rodholm, Ansgar Kolhede 1906-1951
NatCAB 40
Rodick, David Owen 1893-1946 *NatCAB 36*
Rodick, Serenus Burleigh 1897-1948
NatCAB 36
Rodin, Auguste 1840-1917 *McGEWB*
Rodino, Peter Wallace, Jr. 1909- *BiDrAC*
Rodkey, Robert Gordon 1885-1956 *WhAm 3*
Rodman, Clarence James 1891-1972 *WhAm 5*
Rodman, Henrietta 1877- *WomWWA 14*
Rodman, Hugh 1859-1940 *WebAMB,
WhAm 1*
Rodman, Isaac Peace 1822-1862 *ApCAB,
DcAmB, Drake, NatCAB 4, WhAm H*
Rodman, Isaac Peace 1822-1863 *TwCBDA*
Rodman, Isaac Pierce 1822-1862 *NatCAB 4*
Rodman, Jennie Williams 1863- *WomWWA 14*
Rodman, John Croom 1870-1941 *WhAm 1*
Rodman, John Stewart 1883-1958 *WhAm 3*

Rodman, T Clifford 1895-1966 *WhAm 4*
Rodman, Thomas J 1821-1871 *Drake Sup*
Rodman, Thomas Jackson 1815-1871 *DcAmB,
WebAMB, WhAm H*
Rodman, Thomas Jefferson 1815-1871 *AmBi,
ApCAB, TwCBDA*
Rodman, Thomas Jefferson 1818-1871
NatCAB 4
Rodman, Walter Sheldon 1883-1946 *WhAm 2*
Rodman, Warren Anson 1895- *WhAm 4*
Rodman, William 1757-1824 *BiAUS, BiDrAC,
WhAm H*
Rodman, William Blount 1817-1893 *NatCAB 7*
Rodman, William Blount 1889- *WhAm 2*
Rodman, William Louis 1858-1916 *NatCAB 27,
WhAm 1*
Rodney, Caesar 1728-1784 *AmBi, ApCAB,
BiDrAC, DcAmB, NatCAB 5, TwCBDA,
WhAm H, WhAmP*
Rodney, Caesar 1730?-1783 *BiAUS, Drake*
Rodney, Caesar Augustus 1772-1824 *ApCAB,
BiAUS, BiDrAC, BiDrUSE, DcAmB,
NatCAB 3, TwCBDA, WhAm H,
WhAmP*
Rodney, Caleb 1767-1840 *BiAUS, TwCBDA*
Rodney, Daniel 1764-1846 *ApCAB, BiAUS,
BiDrAC, Drake, NatCAB 11, TwCBDA,
WhAm H, WhAmP*
Rodney, George Brydges d1883 *BiAUS*
Rodney, Baron George Brydges 1718-1792
ApCAB, McGEWB, WhoMilH
Rodney, George Brydges 1800-1883 *NatCAB 13*
Rodney, George Brydges 1803-1883 *BiDrAC,
WhAm H, WhAmP*
Rodney, George Brydges 1842-1927 *WhAm 1*
Rodney, John Leonard 1869-1922 *NatCAB 20*
Rodney, Keith Reeves 1875-1956 *NatCAB 47*
Rodney, Richard Seymour 1882-1963 *WhAm 4*
Rodney, Thomas 1744-1811 *ApCAB, BiAUS,
BiDrAC, DcAmB, NatCAB 1, TwCBDA,
WhAm H, WhAmP*
Rodney, William 1652-1708 *NatCAB 5*
Rodo, Jose Enrique 1872-1917 *McGEWB*
Rodrigues, Joao *DcScB*
Rodriguez, Cayetano Jose 1761-1823 *ApCAB*
Rodriguez, Diego 1597-1668 *ApCAB*
Rodriguez, Jose Ignacio 1831-1907 *WhAm 1*
Rodriguez, Manuel 1786-1818 *ApCAB*
Rodriguez, Manuel DelSocorro 1758-1818
ApCAB
Rodriguez, Manuel Domingo 1780-1840 *ApCAB*
Rodriguez-Serra, Manuel 1871- *WhAm 5*
Rodriquez, Abelardo 1889-1967 *WhAm 4*
Rodway *NewYHSD*
Rodzinski, Artur 1892-1958 *NatCAB 47,
WhAm 3*
Roe, Arthur 1878-1942 *WhAm 2*
Roe, Azel Stevens 1798-1886 *ApCAB, Drake,
NatCAB 4, WhAm H*
Roe, Charles Francis 1848-1922 *ApCAB Sup,
NatCAB 7, TwCBDA, WhAm 1*
Roe, Clarence Sage 1889-1962 *NatCAB 50*
Roe, Clifford Griffith 1875-1934 *WhAm 1*
Roe, Dudley George 1881-1970 *BiDrAC,
WhAm 6*
Roe, Edward Drake, Jr. 1859-1929 *WhAm 1*
Roe, Edward Payson 1838-1888 *AmBi, ApCAB,
DcAmB, NatCAB 7, TwCBDA,
WhAm H*
Roe, Edwin Powell 1867-1940 *NatCAB 30*
Roe, Elizabeth Emmons *WomWWA 14*
Roe, Francis Asbury 1823-1901 *AmBi, ApCAB,
DcAmB, NatCAB 12, TwCBDA,
WhAm 1*
Roe, Frederick William 1874- *WhAm 5*
Roe, George 1861- *WhAm 4*
Roe, George Henry 1852-1894 *NatCAB 38*
Roe, George Mortimer 1848- *NatCAB 12*
Roe, Gilbert Ernstein 1865-1929 *DcAmB,
NatCAB 22, WhAm 1*
Roe, Gwyneth King *WomWWA 14*
Roe, Henry 1829- *ApCAB*
Roe, Herman 1886-1961 *NatCAB 52,
WhAm 4*
Roe, James A 1896-1967 *BiDrAC, WhAm 4*
Roe, John Ernest 1906-1956 *NatCAB 47*
Roe, John Orlando 1849-1915 *WhAm 1*
Roe, Joseph Hyram 1892-1967 *WhAm 5*

Roe, Joseph Wickham 1871-1960 *NatCAB 57,
WhAm 4*
Roe, Nicholas *NewYHSD*
Roe, Nora Ardella 1856- *WhAm 4*
Roe, Robert A 1924- *BiDrAC*
Roe, Vingie Eve 1879-1958 *WhAm 3*
Roe, William Clarke 1859-1925 *NatCAB 21*
Roe, William Edgar 1857-1934 *WhAm 1*
Roeber, Edward Charles 1913-1969 *WhAm 6*
Roeber, Eugene Franz 1867-1917 *NatCAB 17,
WhAm 1*
Roebling, Charles Gustavus 1849-1918
NatCAB 39
Roebling, Donald 1909-1959 *NatCAB 44*
Roebling, Ferdinand William 1842-1917
NatCAB 35, WhAm 1
Roebling, Ferdinand William, Jr. 1878-1936
NatCAB 31, WhAm 1
Roebling, John Augustus 1806-1869 *AmBi,
ApCAB, DcAmB, Drake, EncAB,
McGEWB, NatCAB 4, TwCBDA,
WebAB, WhAm H*
Roebling, Washington Augustus 1837-1926
*AmBi, ApCAB, DcAmB, McGEWB,
NatCAB 4, NatCAB 26, TwCBDA,
WebAB, WhAm 1*
Roebuck, Arthur Wentworth 1878- *WhAm 6*
Roebuck, John 1718-1794 *DcScB*
Roebuck, John Arthur 1802-1879 *ApCAB*
Roebuck, John Ransom 1876-1965 *WhAm 4,
WhAm 5*
Roedder, Edwin Carl Lothar Clemens 1873-1945
WhAm 2
Roeder, Adolph 1857- *WhAm 4*
Roeder, Bernard Franklin 1911-1971 *WhAm 5*
Roeder, Effie Ebey 1869- *WomWWA 14*
Roeder, Elmer 1884-1959 *NatCAB 47*
Roeder, Elsa 1883- *WomWWA 14*
Roeder, Fred Vincent 1904-1967 *WhAm 5*
Roeder, Geraldine Morgan 1868- *WhAm 4,
WomWWA 14*
Roediger, Henry Lederer 1882-1963
NatCAB 51
Roeding, George Christian 1868-1928 *DcAmB,
NatCAB 40, NatCAB 47*
Roehm, Alfred Isaac 1880-1949 *WhAm 2*
Roehner, Wilhelm *NewYHSD*
Roehr, Julius Edward 1859-1930 *WhAm 1*
Roehrig, Frederic Louis Otto 1819-1908
WhAm 1
Roehrig, Mary Gavina Hungerford 1862-
WomWWA 14
Roelker, Bernard 1816-1888 *ApCAB*
Roelker, Charles Rafael d1910 *WhAm 1*
Roelker, Millicent Turle 1882- *WomWWA 14*
Roelker, William Greene 1886-1953 *WhAm 3*
Roelofs, Howard Dykema 1893-1974 *WhAm 6*
Roelse, Harold Vincent 1894-1960 *NatCAB 48*
Roemer *DcScB*
Roemer, Erwin William 1890-1960 *NatCAB 48*
Roemer, Ferdinand 1818-1891 *DcScB,
WhAm H*
Roemer, Friedrich Adolph 1809-1869 *DcScB*
Roemer, Henry A d1969 *WhAm 5*
Roemer, Jean 1815- *ApCAB*
Roemer, John Lincoln 1865-1940 *NatCAB 38,
WhAm 1*
Roemer, Joseph 1884-1955 *BiDAmEd,
WhAm 3*
Roemer, Karl Ferdinand 1818-1891 *DcAmB*
Roemer, Olaus 1644-1710 *AsBiEn*
Roemershauser, Alvin E 1907-1968 *WhAm 5*
Roemler, Charles Oscar 1873-1950 *NatCAB 39*
Roen, John 1887-1970 *NatCAB 55*
Roenigk, Marion Chase 1880- *WomWWA 14*
Roenne, Torben Henning 1919-1973 *WhAm 6*
Roentgen, Wilhelm 1845-1923 *DcScB*
Roentgen, Wilhelm Conrad 1845-1923
McGEWB
Roentgen, Wilhelm Konrad 1845-1923 *AsBiEn*
Roepnack, Howard 1904-1963 *NatCAB 50*
Roerich, Nicholas Konstantin 1874-1947
IIBEAAW, WhAm 2
Roesch, Charles Edward 1886-1936 *WhAm 1*
Roesch, Karl Alexander 1903-1969 *WhAm 5*
Roesch, Walter Alfred 1917-1962 *WhAm 4*
Roeschlaub, Robert Sawers 1843- *NatCAB 12*

Roesel VonRosenhof, August Johann 1705-1759 *DcScB*

Roesen, Severin 1848-1871 *BnEnAmA, NewYHSD*

Roeser, Charles Franklin 1887-1949 *NatCAB 40*

Roeser, William Frederick 1901-1964 *NatCAB 51*

Roess, Martin John 1880-1952 *NatCAB 41*

Roessel, Maximilian Louis 1872-1958 *NatCAB 46*

Roessing, Jennie Bradley 1881- *WomWWA 14*

Roessler, John Edward 1859-1941 *NatCAB 42, WhAm 4*

Roessner, Elmer 1900-1972 *WhAm 5*

Roeth, Burton Albert 1907-1966 *NatCAB 52*

Roethke, Rudolph Walter 1884-1949 *NatCAB 45*

Roethke, Theodore 1908-1963 *McGEWB, WebAB, WhAm 4*

Roethke, William A C 1907- *WhAm 4*

Roethlisberger, Fritz Jules 1898-1974 *WhAm 6*

Roetken, Alfred Allen 1902-1970 *NatCAB 55*

Roetter, Paulus 1806-1894 *IIBEAAW, NewYHSD, WhAm H*

Roettinger, Philip 1852-1935 *NatCAB 27*

Roever, William 1830-1898 *NatCAB 16*

Roever, William Henry 1874-1951 *WhAm 3*

Roey, Cardinal Joseph Van 1874-1961 *WhWW-II*

Roff, Allen Archiland 1881-1948 *NatCAB 37*

Rogan, Fred Leon 1880- *WhAm 3*

Rogan, James S 1888-1954 *WhAm 3*

Rogan, Ralph Frederic 1875-1955 *WhAm 3*

Roge, Mrs. Adolphe *WomWWA 14*

Roge, Charlotte Fiske Bates 1838- *AmWom*

Roger II 1095-1154 *McGEWB*

Roger Of Hereford *DcScB*

Roger, Henri-Louis 1809-1891 *BiHiMed*

Roger, Juan 1540?-1618 *ApCAB*

Rogers *NewYHSD*

Rogers, Albert Clark 1850-1923 *NatCAB 19*

Rogers, Albert Edward 1884-1945 *NatCAB 34*

Rogers, Alexander Hamilton 1868-1942 *NatCAB 37*

Rogers, Alfred Moore 1897-1964 *WhAm 4*

Rogers, Alfred Thomas 1873-1948 *WhAm 2*

Rogers, Allan Buttrick 1931-1962 *WhAm 4*

Rogers, Allen 1876-1938 *WhAm 1*

Rogers, Allen Hastings 1871-1938 *WhAm 1*

Rogers, Amsiah 1884- *WhoColR*

Rogers, Andrew Jackson 1828-1900 *BiAUS, BiDrAC, NatCAB 7*

Rogers, Anne Day *WomWWA 14*

Rogers, Anthony Astley Cooper 1821-1899 *BiAUS, BiDrAC*

Rogers, Arthur 1864-1938 *WhAm 1*

Rogers, Arthur 1885-1947 *NatCAB 36*

Rogers, Arthur Amzi 1881- *WhAm 6*

Rogers, Arthur Curtis 1856-1917 *NatCAB 17, WhAm 1*

Rogers, Arthur Kenyon 1868-1936 *WhAm 1, WhAm 1C*

Rogers, Arthur Leon 1883-1962 *NatCAB 51*

Rogers, Arthur Small 1869-1964 *WhAm 4*

Rogers, Austin Flint 1877-1957 *WhAm 3*

Rogers, Austin Leonard 1855-1937 *WhAm 1*

Rogers, B Talbot 1865-1934 *NatCAB 38, WhAm 1*

Rogers, Bernard 1893-1968 *NatCAB 55, WhAm 5*

Rogers, Bernard William 1921- *WebAMB*

Rogers, Bruce 1870-1957 *WebAB, WhAm 3*

Rogers, Burton R 1879- *WhAm 6*

Rogers, Byron Giles 1900- *BiDrAC*

Rogers, Carl Ransom 1902- *BiDAmEd*

Rogers, Cassius Clay 1869-1944 *NatCAB 32*

Rogers, Celeste Elizabeth *WomWWA 14*

Rogers, Cephas Brainerd 1836-1919 *WhAm 1*

Rogers, Charles *NewYHSD*

Rogers, Charles 1800-1874 *BiAUS, BiDrAC, WhAm H*

Rogers, Charles A 1840?- *IIBEAAW, NewYHSD*

Rogers, Charles Butler 1865-1937 *WhAm 1*

Rogers, Charles Buxton 1852- *NatCAB 5*

Rogers, Charles Cassius 1847- *NatCAB 11*

Rogers, Charles Custis 1856-1917 *WhAm 1*

Rogers, Charles Darius 1866- *WhAm 1*

Rogers, Charles Edwin 1874-1942 *WhAm 2*

Rogers, Charles Gardner 1875-1950 *WhAm 3*

Rogers, Charles Pingrey 1865-1943 *NatCAB 33*

Rogers, Charlotte Boardman 1878- *WhAm 6, WomWWA 14*

Rogers, Clara Kathleen Barnett 1844-1931 *DcAmB, WhAm 1, WomWWA 14*

Rogers, Clinton 1832-1924 *NatCAB 28*

Rogers, Crawford Stanley 1885-1956 *NatCAB 45*

Rogers, D *NewYHSD*

Rogers, Daisy Fiske d1954 *WhAm 3*

Rogers, Daniel *BiAUS*

Rogers, David *NewYHSD*

Rogers, David Banks 1868-1954 *NatCAB 44, WhAm 4*

Rogers, David Barss 1899-1967 *WhAm 4*

Rogers, David Camp 1878-1959 *WhAm 4*

Rogers, Donald Aquilla 1901-1969 *WhAm 5*

Rogers, Donald G 1892-1958 *WhAm 3*

Rogers, Dwight Laing 1886-1954 *BiDrAC, WhAm 3, WhAmP*

Rogers, E Albert 1874-1942 *NatCAB 31*

Rogers, Earl Bertram 1874-1953 *NatCAB 40*

Rogers, Ebenezer Platt 1817-1881 *ApCAB*

Rogers, Edith Nourse 1881-1960 *BiDrAC, NatCAB 44, WhAm 4, WhAmP*

Rogers, Edmund James Armstrong 1852-1922 *WhAm 1*

Rogers, Edward *NewYHSD*

Rogers, Edward 1787-1857 *BiAUS, BiDrAC, WhAm H*

Rogers, Edward Sidney 1875-1949 *WhAm 2*

Rogers, Edward Standiford 1826-1899 *WhAm H*

Rogers, Edward Staniford 1826-1899 *DcAmB*

Rogers, Effie Louise Hoffman 1855- *AmWom*

Rogers, Elizabeth Ann 1829-1921 *BiDAmEd, NotAW*

Rogers, Elizabeth Anna Rowley 1856- *WomWWA 14*

Rogers, Elizabeth Selden White 1868- *WomWWA 14*

Rogers, Elliot 1872-1948 *NatCAB 38*

Rogers, Emma Ferdon Winner *AmWom, WomWWA 14*

Rogers, Ernest Albert 1866- *WhAm 5*

Rogers, Ernest Andrew 1881-1957 *WhAm 3*

Rogers, Ernest Elias 1866-1945 *NatCAB 34, WhAm 2*

Rogers, Eustace Barron 1855-1929 *NatCAB 21, WhAm 1*

Rogers, Ezekiel 1590-1660 *ApCAB*

Rogers, Fairman 1833-1900 *AmBi, ApCAB, NatCAB 11, TwCBDA, WhAm 1*

Rogers, Florence Gertrude Dyer 1875- *WomWWA 14*

Rogers, Floyd Leslie 1895-1954 *NatCAB 43*

Rogers, Floyd Sterling, Jr. 1906-1966 *WhAm 4*

Rogers, Fordyce Huntington 1840-1914 *NatCAB 16*

Rogers, Francis 1870-1951 *NatCAB 43, WhAm 3*

Rogers, Francis Medad 1838-1916 *NatCAB 17*

Rogers, Frank Henkels 1884-1951 *NatCAB 41*

Rogers, Franklin Whiting 1854- *ApCAB*

Rogers, Frazier 1893-1959 *WhAm 3*

Rogers, Fred A 1869-1949 *WhAm 3*

Rogers, Fred S 1871-1949 *WhAm 2*

Rogers, Fred William 1849-1940 *NatCAB 42*

Rogers, Frederick Morris 1872- *WhAm 5*

Rogers, Frederick Titsworth 1859- *WhAm 4*

Rogers, Frederick Tuttle 1859-1932 *NatCAB 33*

Rogers, Frederick William 1859-1937 *NatCAB 33*

Rogers, George Adelmer 1852-1935 *NatCAB 26*

Rogers, George Alfred 1876-1936 *WhAm 1*

Rogers, George Bartlett 1909-1967 *WhAm 4*

Rogers, George Benjamin 1868-1936 *NatCAB 27*

Rogers, George Blake 1864- *WhAm 4*

Rogers, George Clarke 1838- *ApCAB*

Rogers, George Frederick 1887-1948 *BiDrAC, WhAm 2*

Rogers, George H *NewYHSD*

Rogers, George McIntosh 1879-1949 *WhAm 3*

Rogers, George Thomas 1875-1959 *NatCAB 44*

Rogers, George Vernor 1876-1961 *WhAm 4*

Rogers, Goodloe Harold 1891-1969 *NatCAB 55*

Rogers, Gordon B 1901-1967 *WhAm 4*

Rogers, Grace Dean McLeod *WomWWA 14*

Rogers, Grace Jeannette Haynes 1854- *WomWWA 14*

Rogers, Grace Rainey 1867-1943 *NotAW*

Rogers, H G *BiAUS*

Rogers, Harriet Burbank 1834-1919 *BiDAmEd, DcAmB, NotAW, WhAm HA, WhAm 4*

Rogers, Harry Clayton 1877- *WhAm 5*

Rogers, Harry H 1877-1957 *WhAm 3*

Rogers, Harry Lovejoy 1867-1925 *NatCAB 24, WhAm 1*

Rogers, Harry Stanley 1890-1957 *NatCAB 43, WhAm 3*

Rogers, Helen Worthington 1869- *WomWWA 14*

Rogers, Henry Darwin 1808-1866 *AmBi, ApCAB, DcAmB, DcScB, NatCAB 1, NatCAB 7, TwCBDA, WhAm H*

Rogers, Henry Darwin 1809-1866 *Drake*

Rogers, Henry H d1909 *WhAm 1*

Rogers, Henry Huddleston 1840-1909 *NatCAB 22*

Rogers, Henry Huddleston, II 1879-1935 *NatCAB 47, WhAm 1*

Rogers, Henry Huttleston 1839-1909 *NatCAB 19*

Rogers, Henry Huttleston 1840-1909 *AmBi, DcAmB*

Rogers, Henry J 1811-1879 *ApCAB, DcAmB, Drake, NatCAB 4, WhAm H*

Rogers, Henry Munroe 1839-1937 *WhAm 1*

Rogers, Henry Treat 1846- *WhAm 1*

Rogers, Henry W *NewYHSD*

Rogers, Henry Wade 1853-1926 *AmBi, ApCAB X, BiDAmEd, DcAmB, NatCAB 13, NatCAB 26, TwCBDA, WhAm 1*

Rogers, Henry Whittingham 1824-1855 *NewYHSD*

Rogers, Herbert Wesley 1890-1964 *WhAm 4*

Rogers, Hopewell Lindenberger 1876-1948 *WhAm 2*

Rogers, Horatio 1836-1904 *ApCAB, NatCAB 10, TwCBDA, WhAm 1*

Rogers, Howard Jason 1861-1927 *WhAm 1*

Rogers, Howard Joseph 1894-1957 *NatCAB 42, WhAm 3*

Rogers, Hubert E d1958 *WhAm 3*

Rogers, Isaiah 1800-1869 *BnEnAmA, DcAmB, WhAm H*

Rogers, J Speed 1891-1955 *WhAm 3*

Rogers, Jacob 1829-1914 *NatCAB 18*

Rogers, Jacob C d1900 *ApCAB X*

Rogers, James 1795-1873 *BiAUS, BiDrAC, WhAm H*

Rogers, James 1826- *ApCAB*

Rogers, James Blythe 1802-1852 *ApCAB, DcAmB, NatCAB 8, WhAm H*

Rogers, James Blythe 1803-1852 *Drake, TwCBDA*

Rogers, James Frederick 1870-1965 *WhAm 4*

Rogers, James Gamble 1867-1947 *DcAmB S4, WhAm 2*

Rogers, James Grafton 1883-1971 *WhAm 5*

Rogers, James Harris 1850-1929 *ApCAB, NatCAB 21, WhAm 1*

Rogers, James Harris 1856-1929 *DcAmB*

Rogers, James Harvey 1886-1939 *AmBi, DcAmB S2, NatCAB 31, WhAm 1*

Rogers, James Hotchkiss 1857-1940 *NatCAB 35, WhAm 1*

Rogers, James Murchison 1868-1958 *NatCAB 44*

Rogers, James Sterling 1871- *WhAm 5*

Rogers, James Tracy 1864- *WhAm 4*

Rogers, James Webb 1822-1896 *ApCAB*

Rogers, James Webb *see also* Rodgers, James Webb

Rogers, Jason 1868-1932 *WhAm 1*

Rogers, Jesse Armstead 1913-1962 *NatCAB 53*

Rogers, John 1631-1684 *ApCAB, Drake, NatCAB 6, TwCBDA*

Rogers, John 1648-1721 *ApCAB, DcAmB, WebAB, WhAm H*

Rogers, John 1723-1789 *ApCAB, BiAUS,*

BiDrAC, Drake, WhAm H
Rogers, John 1808?-1888? NewYHSD
Rogers, John 1813-1879 BiAUS, BiDrAC, WhAm H
Rogers, John 1827-1902 NatCAB 6
Rogers, John 1829-1904 AmBi, ApCAB, BnEnAmA, DcAmB, Drake, McGEWB, NatCAB 8, NewYHSD, TwCBDA, WebAB, WhAm 1
Rogers, John 1866-1939 WhAm 1
Rogers, John 1899-1967 NatCAB 53
Rogers, John Almanza Rowley 1828-1906 DcAmB, TwCBDA
Rogers, John Edward 1884-1950 WhAm 2
Rogers, John Henry 1845-1911 BiDrAC, TwCBDA, WhAm 1
Rogers, John I 1904-1963 WhAm 4
Rogers, John Ignatius 1843-1910 DcAmB
Rogers, John Ignatius 1844-1910 NatCAB 14
Rogers, John Jacob 1881-1925 BiDrAC, WhAm 1, WhAmP
Rogers, John Lenzie 1889-1967 NatCAB 53
Rogers, John Milton 1874-1926 NatCAB 21
Rogers, John Rankin 1838-1901 DcAmB, NatCAB 12, REnAW, TwCBDA, WhAm 1
Rogers, John Raphael 1856-1934 DcAmB, WhAm 1
Rogers, John Shillito 1876-1935 NatCAB 42
Rogers, John William 1894-1965 WhAm 4
Rogers, Jonathan Clark 1885-1967 NatCAB 54
Rogers, Joseph Egerton 1880-1951 WhAm 3
Rogers, Joseph Morgan 1861-1922 WhAm 1
Rogers, Julia Ellen 1866- WhAm 4, WomWWA 14
Rogers, Laussat Richter 1866-1957 NatCAB 48
Rogers, Lawrence Harrison 1883-1959 NatCAB 50
Rogers, Lebbeus Harding 1847- WhAm 4
Rogers, Leslie Charles 1896-1961 NatCAB 51
Rogers, Lester Burton 1875- WhAm 5
Rogers, Lester Cushing 1893-1972 NatCAB 57, WhAm 5
Rogers, Lina Lavanche 1870- WomWWA 14
Rogers, Lore Alford 1875- WhAm 5
Rogers, Louis William 1859- WhAm 4
Rogers, Malcolm Joseph 1905-1972 WhAm 5
Rogers, Marvin Carson 1904-1968 WhAm 5
Rogers, Mary Cecilia 1820?-1841 ApCAB
Rogers, Mary Cochrane 1869- WhAm 5
Rogers, Mary Fletcher AmWom
Rogers, Mary Josephine 1882-1955 DcAmB S5
Rogers, Mary Phelps Christie WomWWA 14
Rogers, Max d1932 WhAm 1
Rogers, May 1852- WhAm 4
Rogers, McLain 1874-1960 WhAm 3
Rogers, Michael G 1805?-1832 NewYHSD
Rogers, Molton Cropper 1786-1863 NatCAB 16
Rogers, Moses 1779-1821 DcAmB, WhAm H
Rogers, Moses 1779-1822 NatCAB 4
Rogers, Moses 1780-1822 ApCAB Sup, TwCBDA
Rogers, Nathaniel 1598-1655 ApCAB, Drake
Rogers, Nathaniel 1788-1844 ApCAB, NewYHSD
Rogers, Nathaniel Peabody 1794-1846 ApCAB, Drake, NatCAB 2
Rogers, Olive Henrietta Warner 1867- WomWWA 14
Rogers, Oscar Harrison 1857-1941 NatCAB 30, WhAm 1
Rogers, Paul Grant 1921- BiDrAC
Rogers, Philip Fletcher 1870-1928 WhAm 1
Rogers, Platt 1884-1956 NatCAB 48
Rogers, Pleas Blair 1895-1974 WhAm 6
Rogers, Ralph NewYHSD
Rogers, Randolph 1825-1892 AmBi, ApCAB, BiAUS, BnEnAmA, DcAmB, Drake, IlBEAAW, NatCAB 8, NewYHSD, TwCBDA, WhAm H
Rogers, Robert NewYHSD
Rogers, Robert 1727-1800? ApCAB, NatCAB 7
Rogers, Robert 1730?-1800? Drake
Rogers, Robert 1731-1795 AmBi, DcAmB, EncAAH, McGEWB, WebAB, WebAMB, WhAm H, WhoMilH

Rogers, Robert Cameron 1862-1912 NatCAB 15, WhAm 1
Rogers, Robert Emmons 1888-1941 WhAm 1
Rogers, Robert Empie 1813-1884 ApCAB, DcAmB, NatCAB 7, TwCBDA, WhAm H
Rogers, Robert Empie 1814-1884 Drake
Rogers, Robert Samuel 1900-1968 NatCAB 53, WhAm 5
Rogers, Robert William 1864-1930 DcAmB, NatCAB 23, TwCBDA, WhAm 1
Rogers, Sampson, Jr. d1972 WhAm 5
Rogers, Samuel H 1907-1968 WhAm 5
Rogers, Samuel Lyle 1859- WhAm 4
Rogers, Samuel St. George 1832-1880 BiDConf
Rogers, Sarah NewYHSD
Rogers, Scott Moncrief 1871-1953 NatCAB 42
Rogers, Sherman Skinner 1830-1900 NatCAB 8, WhAm 1
Rogers, Sion Hart 1825-1874 BiAUS, BiDrAC, WhAm H
Rogers, Stephen 1826-1878 DcAmB, WhAm H
Rogers, Theodora Isabella Wormley 1876- WomWWA 14
Rogers, Theodore 1831- NatCAB 11
Rogers, Thomas 1792-1856 DcAmB, NatCAB 19, WhAm H
Rogers, Thomas Arthur 1887-1944 NatCAB 33
Rogers, Thomas Jones 1781-1832 ApCAB, BiAUS, BiDrAC, Drake, TwCBDA, WhAm H
Rogers, Thomas Wesley 1900-1973 WhAm 6
Rogers, Tyler Stewart 1895-1967 WhAm 4
Rogers, Vance 1908-1962 WhAm 4
Rogers, Waldo Henry 1908-1964 WhAm 4
Rogers, Walter Alexander 1868-1944 NatCAB 34, WhAm 2
Rogers, Walter Black 1883-1945 NatCAB 34
Rogers, Walter Edward 1908- BiDrAC, WhAmP
Rogers, Walter Stowell 1877-1965 WhAm 4
Rogers, Warren Lincoln 1877-1938 WhAm 1
Rogers, Weaver Henry 1876-1936 WhAm 1
Rogers, Will 1879-1935 AmBi, DcAmB S1, NatCAB 33, REnAW, WebAB, WhAm 1
Rogers, Will 1898- BiDrAC
Rogers, Will see also Rogers, William Penn Adair
Rogers, Will Vann, Jr. 1911- BiDrAC
Rogers, Willard Benjamin 1888-1964 WhAm 4
Rogers, William 1751-1824 ApCAB, Drake, NatCAB 8, TwCBDA
Rogers, William Allen 1854-1931 AmBi, DcAmB, IlBEAAW, NatCAB 24, REnAW, WhAm 1
Rogers, William Arthur 1851-1946 NatCAB 35, WhAm 2
Rogers, William Augustus 1832-1898 AmBi, ApCAB, DcAmB, TwCBDA, WhAm H
Rogers, William Banks 1857-1937 NatCAB 27, WhAm 1
Rogers, William Barton 1804-1882 AmBi, ApCAB, BiDAmEd, DcAmB, DcScB, NatCAB 7, TwCBDA, WhAm H
Rogers, William Barton 1805-1882 Drake
Rogers, William Boddie 1856- WhAm 1
Rogers, William Charles 1890-1970 NatCAB 56
Rogers, William Crowninshield 1823-1888 DcAmB, WhAm H
Rogers, William F 1870-1952 WhAm 4
Rogers, William Findlay 1820-1899 BiDrAC
Rogers, William Harlow 1884-1967 WhAm 4
Rogers, William King 1863-1921 WhAm 1
Rogers, William Loveland 1911-1968 WhAm 5
Rogers, William McMillan 1890-1951 NatCAB 52
Rogers, William Nathaniel 1892-1945 BiDrAC, NatCAB 39, WhAm 2
Rogers, William Oscar 1825- TwCBDA, WhAm 4
Rogers, William Penn Adair 1879-1935 EncAAH, EncAB
Rogers, William Penn Adair see also Rogers, Will
Rogers, William Pennock 1842-1916 WhAm 1
Rogers, William Perry 1857-1921 NatCAB 20, WhAm 1
Rogers, William Pierce 1913- BiDrUSE
Rogers, Winfield Scott 1853-1931 NatCAB 24
Rogers, Woodes 1665?-1732 ApCAB, Drake

Rogers, Wynne 1845?- NatCAB 11
Rogers, Wynne Grey 1874- WhAm 2
Rogers-Moore, Alice Medora WomWWA 14
Rogerson, Charles Edward 1855-1932 WhAm 1
Roget, Peter Mark 1779-1869 BiHiMed
Rogge, Albert Paul 1865-1946 NatCAB 35
Roggewen, Jacob 1669-1733 ApCAB Sup
Rogliano, Francis Teobaldo 1915-1973 WhAm 6
Rogosin, I 1887-1971 WhAm 5
Rohan, James Michael 1867-1947 NatCAB 36
Rohault, Jacques 1620-1675 DcScB
Rohbach, James Alexander 1864-1930 WhAm 1
Rohde, Gilbert 1894-1944 BnEnAmA, NatCAB 33
Rohde, Lewin Jorgen 1786-1857 ApCAB
Rohde, Max Spencer 1884-1973 WhAm 6
Rohde, Ruth Bryan Owen 1885-1954 DcAmB S5, WhAm 3
Rohde, William F NewYHSD
Rohe, Alice WomWWA 14
Rohe, Charles Henry 1846- WhAm 1
Rohe, George Henry 1851-1899 DcAmB, NatCAB 7, WhAm 1
Roheim, Geza 1891-1953 DcAmB S5
Rohland, Cora Dolbee 1856- WomWWA 14
Rohland, Paul 1884-1953 IlBEAAW
Rohlfing, Charles Carroll 1902-1954 WhAm 3
Rohlfs, Anna Katharine Green 1846-1935 AmBi, AmWom, DcAmB S1, NatCAB 9, NotAW, TwCBDA, WhAm 1
Rohlfs, Mrs. Charles WomWWA 14
Rohlfs, Charles 1853-1936 NatCAB 9, WhAm 1
Rohlman, Henry P 1876-1957 WhAm 3
Rohm, Robert 1934- BnEnAmA
Rohn, Karl 1855-1920 DcScB
Rohn, Oscar 1870-1923 NatCAB 20, WhAm 1
Rohner, Mister NewYHSD
Rohnstock, J Henry 1879-1956 WhAm 3
Rohr, Elizabeth 1908-1958 WhAm 3
Rohr, Frederick Hilmer 1896-1965 WhAm 4
Rohrbach, John Francis Deems 1889-1968 WhAm 5
Rohrbach, John J 1896-1953 WhAm 3
Rohrbough, Edward Gay 1874-1956 BiDrAC, WhAm 3
Rohrbough, Ralph Virgil 1901-1961 WhAm 4
Rohrer, Albert Lawrence 1856-1951 NatCAB 42, WhAm 3
Rohrer, George Redsecker 1853-1935 NatCAB 37
Rohrer, Karl 1848-1913 WhAm 1
Rohrer, Perry Lawrence 1898-1970 NatCAB 55
Rohrlich, Chester 1900-1974 WhAm 6
Rohwer, Henry 1847-1916 WhAm 1
Rohwer, Sievert Allen 1888-1951 NatCAB 39
Roig, Antonio A 1888-1956 WhAm 3
Roig, Harold Joseph 1885-1972 WhAm 5
Roisman, Joseph 1900-1974 WhAm 6
Rojankovsky, Feodor S 1891-1970 WhAm 5
Rojas, Gabriel De d1548 ApCAB
Rojas, Juan Ramon 1784-1824 ApCAB
Rojas, P Ezequiel 1844-1914 WhAm 1
Rojas Pinilla, Gustavo 1900-1975 McGEWB, WhAm 6
Rojtman, Marc Bori 1917-1967 NatCAB 54, WhAm 4
Rokitansky, Carl Von 1804-1878 BiHiMed
Rokossovski, Konstantin Konstantinovich 1896-1968 WhoMilH
Rokossovsky, Konstantin 1896-1968 WhWW-II
Roland, John NewYHSD
Roland, Oliver 1850-1910 NatCAB 16
Roland, Ruth ApCAB X
Rolander, Daniel 1720-1774 ApCAB
Rolando, Luigi 1773-1831 DcScB
Rolapp, Henry Hermann 1860-1936 NatCAB 17, WhAm 1
Roler, Edward Oscar Fitzalan 1835- WhAm 4
Rolette, Jean Joseph 1781-1842 DcAmB, WhAm H
Rolf, Emma NewYHSD
Rolfe, Alfred Grosvenor 1860-1942 WhAm 2
Rolfe, Charles Wesley 1850-1934 WhAm 1
Rolfe, Daniel Thomas 1868-1968 WhAm 5
Rolfe, Emma NewYHSD
Rolfe, George William 1864-1942 WhAm 2
Rolfe, Henry Winchester 1858- WhAm 4

Rolfe, Ida Brown 1852- *WomWWA 14*
Rolfe, John *NewYHSD*
Rolfe, John 1585-1622 *AmBi, ApCAB Sup, DcAmB, EncAAH, EncAB, McGEWB, WhAm H*
Rolfe, John A 1799-1862 *NewYHSD*
Rolfe, John Carew 1859-1943 *NatCAB 32, WhAm 2*
Rolfe, John Furman 1880-1937 *WhAm 1*
Rolfe, Stanley Herbert 1887-1949 *WhAm 2*
Rolfe, William James 1827-1910 *AmBi, ApCAB, DcAmB, NatCAB 4, TwCBDA, WhAm 1*
Rolfinck, Guerner 1599-1673 *DcScB*
Rolfing, R C 1891-1974 *WhAm 6*
Rolfs, Fred Maas 1875- *WhAm 5*
Rolfs, Peter Henry 1865-1944 *WhAm 2*
Rolker, Charles M 1852-1927 *ApCAB X*
Roll, Albert Thomas 1881-1956 *NatCAB 42*
Rolland, Romain 1866-1944 *McGEWB*
Rolland, Romaine 1866-1944 *WhAm 2*
Rolle, Albert *NewYHSD*
Rolle, Dennis 1730?-1797 *ApCAB, Drake*
Rolle, Michel 1652-1719 *DcScB*
Rolle Of Hampole, Richard 1290?-1349 *McGEWB*
Rollefson, Gerhard Krohn 1900-1955 *WhAm 3*
Roller, Charles S, Jr. 1879-1963 *WhAm 4*
Roller, Robert Douglas, Jr. 1879-1935 *NatCAB 26, WhAm 1*
Roller, Thomas J 1878-1946 *WhAm 3*
Roller, William Wallace 1841- *NatCAB 6*
Rollert, Edward Dumas 1912-1969 *WhAm 5*
Rolleston, George 1829-1881 *DcScB*
Rollet, Joseph-Pierre-Martin 1824-1894 *DcScB*
Rollin, Ambroise Lucien 1692-1749 *ApCAB*
Rollinat, Andre 1741-1793 *ApCAB*
Rollings, George 1856-1912 *NatCAB 16*
Rollins, Albert Sidney 1877-1952 *NatCAB 41*
Rollins, Alice Marland Wellington 1847-1897 *AmWom, ApCAB, DcAmB, NatCAB 8, TwCBDA, WhAm H*
Rollins, Andrew Peachey 1884-1966 *NatCAB 53*
Rollins, Ben 1878-1962 *NatCAB 50*
Rollins, Carl Purington 1880-1960 *WhAm 4*
Rollins, Charles Cogswell 1832-1914 *NatCAB 19*
Rollins, Charles E, Jr. d1957 *WhAm 3*
Rollins, Charles Leonard 1856- *WhAm 4*
Rollins, Clara Sherwood 1874- *WhAm 5*
Rollins, Daniel Ashton 1879-1952 *NatCAB 42*
Rollins, Daniel G 1842- *ApCAB*
Rollins, Edward A *BiAUS*
Rollins, Edward Henry 1824-1889 *ApCAB, BiAUS, BiDrAC, DcAmB, TwCBDA, WhAm H, WhAmP*
Rollins, Edward Henry 1825-1889 *NatCAB 7*
Rollins, Edward Warren 1850-1929 *ApCAB X, WhAm 1*
Rollins, Ellen Chapman 1831-1881 *ApCAB*
Rollins, Francis Willard 1893-1966 *NatCAB 52*
Rollins, Frank West 1860-1915 *DcAmB, NatCAB 11, TwCBDA, WhAm 1*
Rollins, George Sherman 1864-1916 *WhAm 1*
Rollins, Hyder Edward 1889-1958 *WhAm 3*
Rollins, James Sidney 1812-1888 *ApCAB, BiAUS, BiDrAC, DcAmB, NatCAB 8, TwCBDA, WhAm H*
Rollins, James Wingate 1858-1935 *WhAm 1*
Rollins, John Fox 1893-1961 *WhAm 4*
Rollins, Mary Harris *WomWWA 14*
Rollins, Montgomery 1867-1918 *WhAm 1*
Rollins, Philip Ashton 1869-1950 *REnAW*
Rollins, Richard Russell 1906-1964 *NatCAB 50*
Rollins, Thornton 1840-1935 *WhAm 1*
Rollins, Wallace Eugene 1870-1959 *WhAm 3*
Rollins, Walter Huntington 1869-1939 *NatCAB 29, WhAm 1*
Rollins, Warren Eliphalet 1861-1962 *IIBEAAW*
Rollins, Weld Allen 1874-1952 *NatCAB 41*
Rollinson, Charles 1793?-1833 *NewYHSD*
Rollinson, S O *NewYHSD*
Rollinson, William 1760-1840? *NatCAB 7*
Rollinson, William 1762-1842 *DcAmB, NewYHSD, WhAm H*
Rollo 860?-932? *McGEWB*
Rollston, Adelaide Day *AmWom*

Roloff, Louis *NewYHSD*
Rolph, George Morrison 1873-1932 *NatCAB 35*
Rolph, James 1869-1934 *DcAmB S1, NatCAB 25, WhAm 1*
Rolph, John 1792-1870 *ApCAB*
Rolph, John A 1799-1862 *Drake, NewYHSD*
Rolph, John Gladwyn 1889-1958 *WhAm 3*
Rolph, Samuel Wyman 1889-1962 *WhAm 4*
Rolph, Thomas 1820?-1883 *ApCAB*
Rolph, Thomas 1885-1956 *BiDrAC*
Rolphe, John 1786-1870 *Drake*
Rolshoven, Julius 1858-1930 *DcAmB, IIBEAAW, NatCAB 26, WhAm 1*
Rolt-Wheeler, Francis William 1876-1960 *WhAm 4*
Rolvaag, Ole Edvart 1876-1931 *AmBi, DcAmB, EncAAH, McGEWB, WebAB, WhAm 1*
Rolvagg, Ole Edvart 1876-1931 *REnAW*
Rolz-Bennett, Jose 1918-1972 *WhAm 5*
Rom, Jack 1912-1965 *NatCAB 51*
Roma, Caro 1866-1937 *WhAm 1, WomWWA 14*
Romains, Jules 1885-1972 *WhAm 5*
Roman, Andre Bienvenu 1795-1866 *BiAUS, DcAmB, Drake, NatCAB 10, WhAm H*
Roman, Andrew Bienvenu 1795-1866 *TwCBDA*
Roman, Andrew Bienvenue 1785-1866 *ApCAB*
Roman, Charles Victor 1864- *WhoColR*
Roman, Frederick William d1948 *WhAm 2*
Roman, J Dixon 1809-1867 *BiAUS*
Roman, James Dixon 1809-1867 *BiDrAC, WhAm H*
Roman, Victor M Reyes Y 1872-1950 *WhAm 3*
Roman Nose d1868 *REnAW*
Romanes, George John 1848-1894 *DcScB*
Romanoff, Michael 1892?-1971 *WebAB*
Romanowitz, Harry Alex 1901-1971 *WhAm 5*
Romans, Bernard 1720?-1784 *ApCAB, BnEnAmA, DcAmB, Drake, NatCAB 7, NewYHSD, WhAm H*
Romans, John Francis 1904-1974 *WhAm 6*
Romare, Paul 1828- *NatCAB 5*
Romay, Tomas 1769-1849 *ApCAB*
Romayne, Nicholas 1756-1817 *DcAmB, Drake, WhAm H*
Rombauer, Roderick Emile 1833-1924 *NatCAB 25, WhAm 4*
Romberg, Moritz Heinrich 1795-1873 *BiHiMed*
Romberg, Sigmund 1887-1951 *DcAmB S5, WebAB, WhAm 3*
Rombro, Jacob 1858-1922 *DcAmB*
Rome, Charles A 1896-1959 *WhAm 3*
Rome DeL'Isle, Jean-Baptiste Louis 1736-1790 *DcScB*
Romegar *NewYHSD*
Romeike, Henry 1855-1903 *DcAmB, NatCAB 3, WhAm 1*
Romein, Peter DeH *NewYHSD*
Romeis, Jacob 1835-1904 *BiDrAC*
Romer *DcScB*
Romer, Alfred Sherwood 1894-1973 *WhAm 6*
Romer, Arthur C 1897-1962 *WhAm 4*
Romer, Eugeniusz Mikolaj 1871-1954 *DcScB*
Romer, Frank 1895-1947 *NatCAB 34*
Romer, Ole Christensen 1644-1710 *DcScB*
Romera-Navarro, Miguel 1888-1954 *WhAm 4*
Romero, Felix 1831- *ApCAB Sup*
Romero, Matias 1837- *ApCAB*
Romero, Trinidad 1835-1918 *BiDrAC, WhAmP*
Romey, William Henry 1878-1950 *NatCAB 39*
Romeyn, James 1797-1859 *ApCAB, TwCBDA*
Romeyn, James VanCampen 1765-1840 *ApCAB*
Romeyn, Jeremiah 1768-1818 *ApCAB*
Romeyn, John Brodhead 1777-1825 *ApCAB, TwCBDA*
Romeyn, John Brodhead 1778-1825 *Drake*
Romeyn, Nicholas 1756-1817 *ApCAB*
Romeyn, Theodore Bayard 1827-1885 *ApCAB, TwCBDA*
Romeyn, Theodoric Dirck 1744-1804 *ApCAB, Drake, TwCBDA*
Romfh, Edward Coleman 1880-1952 *NatCAB 39, WhAm 6*
Romig, Edgar Franklin 1890-1963 *WhAm 4*
Romig, John Samuel 1869-1930 *WhAm 1*
Rominger, Carl Ludwig 1820-1907 *WhAm 1*
Romjue, Milton Andrew 1874-1968 *BiDrAC*

Rommel, Erwin 1891-1944 *McGEWB, WhWW-II, WhoMilH*
Rommel, George McCullough 1876-1945 *WhAm 2*
Romnes, H I 1907-1973 *WhAm 6*
Romney, George 1734-1802 *McGEWB*
Romney, George Wilcken 1907- *BiDrUSE*
Romney, Miles 1806-1877 *NewYHSD*
Romoda, Joseph J 1907-1966 *WhAm 4*
Romualdez, Miguel 1881- *WhAm 6*
Romualdez, Norberto 1875- *WhAm 5*
Romulo, Carlos Pena 1899- *McGEWB*
Romulo, Carlos Pena 1901- *BiDrAC*
Ronalds, George L *NewYHSD*
Ronaldson, Douglass S 1835?- *NewYHSD*
Ronaldson, James 1780?-1841 *NatCAB 12*
Ronan, Daniel John 1914-1969 *BiDrAC, WhAm 5*
Ronan, James Joseph 1884-1959 *WhAm 4*
Ronayne, Maurice 1828-1903 *ApCAB, WhAm 1*
Roncalio, Teno 1916- *BiDrAC*
Ronckendorff, William 1812-1891 *ApCAB, Drake, NatCAB 4, TwCBDA*
Ronde, Lambertus De *ApCAB*
Rondeau, Jose 1773-1834 *ApCAB*
Rondel, Frederic 1826-1892 *TwCBDA*
Rondel, Frederick 1826-1892 *NewYHSD*
Rondelet, Guillaume 1507-1566 *DcScB*
Rondon, Candido Mariano DaSilva 1865-1958 *McGEWB*
Rondthaler, Edward 1817-1855 *ApCAB*
Rondthaler, Edward 1842-1931 *DcAmB, NatCAB 5, WhAm 1*
Rondthaler, Howard Edward 1871-1956 *WhAm 3*
Rongy, Abraham Jacob 1878-1949 *WhAm 2*
Ronne, Torben 1919-1973 *WhAm 6*
Ronnebeck, Arnold 1885-1947 *WhAm 2*
Ronneberg, Earl Fridthjov 1905-1972 *WhAm 5*
Ronon, Gerald 1890-1960 *WhAm 4*
Ronsard, Pierre De 1524-1585 *McGEWB*
Ronsheim, Anna Paebst 1860- *WomWWA 14*
Rontgen, Wilhelm Conrad Von 1845-1923 *BiHiMed, DcScB*
Rood, A Edward 1899-1961 *WhAm 4*
Rood, Dorothy B A 1890-1965 *WhAm 4*
Rood, Henry Martyn 1853-1914 *NatCAB 16*
Rood, James Theron 1876-1934 *WhAm 1*
Rood, John 1902-1974 *WhAm 6*
Rood, Katharine A 1861- *WomWWA 14*
Rood, Ogden Nicholas 1831-1902 *AmBi, ApCAB, DcAmB, DcScB, NatCAB 13, TwCBDA, WhAm 1*
Rood, Paul William 1899-1956 *WhAm 3*
Rood, Roland 1863-1927 *NatCAB 21*
Rood, Stephen *NewYHSD*
Rook, Charles Alexander 1861-1946 *WhAm 2*
Rook, Edward Francis 1870-1960 *IIBEAAW, WhAm 4*
Rook, Gustav S 1915-1970 *WhAm 5*
Rooke, Lawrence 1622-1662 *DcScB*
Rooker, Frederick Zadok 1861-1907 *TwCBDA, WhAm 1*
Rooker, Samuel Saffel 1800?-1875? *NewYHSD*
Rooks, John J 1877-1933 *NatCAB 24*
Rooks, Lowell W 1893-1973 *WhAm 6*
Roome, Kenneth Andrew 1901-1967 *WhAm 5*
Roome, W Harris 1861-1934 *NatCAB 39*
Roomen, Adriaan Van 1561-1615 *DcScB*
Roon, Albrecht Theodor Emil Von 1803-1879 *WhoMilH*
Rooney, Edward Stanton 1905-1970 *NatCAB 57*
Rooney, Frederick Bernard 1925- *BiDrAC*
Rooney, Henry Michael 1878-1954 *NatCAB 43*
Rooney, John James 1903-1975 *BiDrAC, WhAm 6*
Rooney, John Jerome 1866-1934 *ApCAB Sup, TwCBDA, WhAm 1*
Rooney, Marie Collins d1949 *WhAm 2*
Rooney, Mary Frances 1877- *WomWWA 14*
Roop, Hervin Ulysses 1868-1955 *TwCBDA*
Roop, Hervin Ulysses 1868-1955 *WhAm 3*
Roop, James Clawson 1888-1972 *WhAm 5*
Roorbach, George Byron 1878-1934 *WhAm 1*
Roorbach, Orville Augustus 1803-1861 *ApCAB, DcAmLiB, Drake*

Roos, Charles Frederick 1901-1958 *WhAm 3*
Roos, Delmar Gerle 1887-1960 *NatCAB 44,*
WhAm 3
Roos, Edwin G 1894-1971 *WhAm 5*
Roos, Frank John, Jr. 1903-1967 *WhAm 4*
Roos, George Anthony 1885-1953 *NatCAB 49*
Roos, John Frederick Fitzgerald *NewYHSD*
Roos, Leonard Henrik 1787-1827 *NewYHSD*
Roos, Robert Achille 1883-1951 *NatCAB 41,*
WhAm 3
Roos, Walter L 1890-1972 *WhAm 5*
Roosa, Daniel Bennett St. John 1838-1908 *AmBi,*
ApCAB, DcAmB, NatCAB 9, TwCBDA,
WhAm 1
Roosevelt, Alice Hathaway Lee 1861-1884
NotAW
Roosevelt, Anna Eleanor 1884-1962 *EncAB,*
McGEWB, WhAm 4, WhAmP
Roosevelt, Blanche 1856-1898 *ApCAB Sup*
Roosevelt, Cornelius VanSchaick 1794-1871
NatCAB 8
Roosevelt, Cornelius VanSchaik 1794-1871
ApCAB
Roosevelt, Edith Kermit Carow 1861-1948
NatCAB 14, NotAW, TwCBDA,
WhAm 2, WhAm 2C, WomWWA 14
Roosevelt, Eleanor 1884-1962 *NatCAB 57,*
WebAB, WhWW-II
Roosevelt, Franklin Delano 1882-1945
ApCAB X, BiDrAC, BiDrUSE,
DcAmB S3, EncAAH, EncAB, McGEWB,
NatCAB 37, WebAB, WhAm HA,
WhAm 2, WhAm 2C, WhAm 4A,
WhAmP, WhWW-II
Roosevelt, Franklin Delano, Jr. 1914- *BiDrAC*
Roosevelt, George Emlen 1887-1963
NatCAB 51, WhAm 4
Roosevelt, George Washington 1844-1907
WhAm 1
Roosevelt, Henry Latrobe 1879-1936
NatCAB 32, WhAm 1
Roosevelt, Hilborne Lewis 1849-1886 *ApCAB,*
DcAmB, NatCAB 26, WhAm H
Roosevelt, J West 1858-1896 *NatCAB 24*
Roosevelt, James 1828-1900 *ApCAB X,*
NatCAB 24
Roosevelt, James 1907- *BiDrAC*
Roosevelt, James Henry 1800-1863 *ApCAB,*
NatCAB 12, TwCBDA
Roosevelt, James I 1795-1875 *BiDrAC,*
TwCBDA, WhAm H
Roosevelt, James I 1796-1875 *BiAUS*
Roosevelt, James John 1795-1875 *ApCAB*
Roosevelt, James Roosevelt 1854-1927
NatCAB 26
Roosevelt, John Ellis 1853-1939 *NatCAB 29*
Roosevelt, Kermit 1889-1943 *DcAmB S3,*
NatCAB 33, WhAm 2
Roosevelt, Nicholas 1767-1854 *NatCAB 12,*
TwCBDA
Roosevelt, Nicholas I 1767-1854 *DcAmB*
Roosevelt, Nicholas I 1767-1854 *ApCAB,*
REnAW, WhAm H
Roosevelt, Philip J 1892-1941 *WhAm 2*
Roosevelt, Robert Barnwell 1829-1906 *AmBi,*
ApCAB, BiAUS, BiDrAC, DcAmB,
Drake, NatCAB 3, TwCBDA, WhAm 1
Roosevelt, Samuel Montgomery 1858-1920
NatCAB 12
Roosevelt, Samuel Montgomery 1864-1920
WhAm 1
Roosevelt, Mrs. Theodore d1960 *WhAm 4*
Roosevelt, Theodore 1831-1878 *ApCAB*
Roosevelt, Theodore 1858-1919 *AmBi, ApCAB,*
ApCAB Sup, BiDrAC, BiDrUSE,
DcAmB, EncAAH, EncAB, McGEWB,
NatCAB 9, NatCAB 11, NatCAB 14,
REnAW, TwCBDA, WebAB, WebAMB,
WhAm HA, WhAm 1, WhAm 4A,
WhAmP
Roosevelt, Theodore, Jr. 1887-1944 *DcAmB S3,*
NatCAB 48, WebAMB, WhAm 2
Roosevelt, W Emlen 1857-1930 *WhAm 1*
Root, Alice Nairn *WomWWA 14*
Root, Amos Ives 1839-1923 *AmBi, DcAmB,*
NatCAB 25, WhAm 1
Root, Anna Conant Brenson 1865-
WomWWA 14

Root, Arthur Lewis 1859-1921 *NatCAB 6*
Root, Azariah Smith 1862-1927 *DcAmLiB,*
NatCAB 22, WhAm 1
Root, Benjamin Trexler 1881-1956 *NatCAB 46*
Root, Chapman Jay 1864-1945 *NatCAB 34*
Root, Chapman Jay 1867-1945 *WhAm 2*
Root, Charles Stevens 1874-1930 *NatCAB 23*
Root, David 1790-1873 *ApCAB*
Root, E Tallmadge 1865-1948 *WhAm 2*
Root, Edward Clary 1877- *WhAm 5*
Root, Edward King 1854-1937 *NatCAB 27*
Root, Edwin Alvin 1860- *WhAm 4*
Root, Edwin Park 1861-1938 *WhAm 1*
Root, Eleazer 1802-1887 *TwCBDA*
Root, Elihu 1845- *ApCAB, ApCAB Sup,*
ApCAB X, NatCAB 7, NatCAB 14,
TwCBDA
Root, Elihu 1845-1937 *AmBi, BiDrAC,*
DcAmB S2, EncAB, McGEWB,
NatCAB 26, WebAB, WebAMB,
WhAm 1, WhAmP, WhoMilH
Root, Elihu 1845-1939 *BiDrUSE*
Root, Elihu, Jr. 1881-1967 *NatCAB 53,*
WhAm 4
Root, Elisha King 1808-1865 *DcAmB,*
NatCAB 18, WhAm H
Root, Elmira *NewYHSD*
Root, Erastus 1772-1846 *BiAUS*
Root, Erastus 1773-1846 *ApCAB, BiDrAC,*
DcAmB, Drake, TwCBDA, WhAm H,
WhAmP
Root, Ernest Rob 1862- *WhAm 5*
Root, Frank Albert 1837-1926 *DcAmB,*
WhAm 1
Root, Frank Douglas 1851- *WhAm 4*
Root, Frank Kimball 1856- *NatCAB 17*
Root, Frederic Woodman 1846-1916 *ApCAB,*
DcAmB, NatCAB 9, WhAm 1
Root, Frederick Stanley 1853-1906 *WhAm 1*
Root, George Frederick 1820-1895 *AmBi,*
ApCAB, BiDAmEd, DcAmB, Drake,
EncAB, NatCAB 9, TwCBDA, WhAm H
Root, George Frederick 1871-1932 *NatCAB 25*
Root, Helen E *WomWWA 14*
Root, Howard Frank 1890-1967 *WhAm 4*
Root, Jesse 1736-1822 *ApCAB, BiDrAC,*
DcAmB, NatCAB 4, WhAmP
Root, Jesse 1737-1822 *BiAUS, Drake,*
TwCBDA, WhAm H
Root, Jesse L 1860-1947 *WhAm 3*
Root, John Gilbert 1835-1910 *NatCAB 6*
Root, John Wellborn 1850-1891 *DcAmB,*
EncAB, NatCAB 8, WebAB, WhAm H
Root, John Wellborn 1887-1963 *WhAm 4*
Root, Joseph Cullen 1844-1913 *NatCAB 15,*
WhAm 1
Root, Joseph Edward 1854-1933 *NatCAB 29,*
WhAm 1
Root, Joseph M 1817-1879 *BiAUS*
Root, Joseph Moseley 1807-1879 *TwCBDA*
Root, Joseph Mosley 1807-1879 *BiDrAC,*
WhAm H
Root, Joseph Pomeroy 1826-1885 *BiAUS,*
DcAmB, NatCAB 13, WhAm H
Root, Josiah Goodrich 1801-1883 *NatCAB 2*
Root, Louis Carroll 1868-1939 *WhAm 1*
Root, Lyman C 1840- *WhAm 1*
Root, Mary Pauline 1859- *WhAm 4,*
WomWWA 14
Root, Milo Adelbert 1863-1917 *WhAm 1*
Root, Oren 1838-1907 *TwCBDA, WhAm 1*
Root, Oren 1873-1948 *WhAm 2*
Root, Reuben Marion 1854-1924 *NatCAB 6*
Root, Robert Cromwell 1858- *WhAm 4*
Root, Robert Kilburn 1877-1950 *WhAm 3*
Root, Russell C *NewYHSD*
Root, Stella Quinby 1872- *WomWWA 14*
Root, Walter Harold 1888-1954 *WhAm 3*
Root, Walter Stanton 1902-1972 *WhAm 5*
Root, William Campbell 1903-1969 *WhAm 5*
Root, William Ruffle 1900-1932 *NatCAB 35*
Root, William T 1882-1945 *WhAm 2*
Root, William Webster 1867-1932 *WhAm 1*
Root, Winfred Trexler 1879-1947 *NatCAB 37,*
WhAm 2
Rooth, Ivar 1888-1972 *WhAm 5*
Roots, Benajah Guernsey 1811-1888 *NatCAB 5*
Roots, Emily Margaret *WomWWA 14*

Roots, Logan Herbert 1841- *NatCAB 13*
Roots, Logan Herbert 1870-1945 *WhAm 2*
Roots, Logan Holt 1841-1893 *BiAUS, BiDrAC,*
NatCAB 5, WhAm H
Roots, Philander Keep 1838- *NatCAB 5*
Roozeboom, Hendrik Willem Bakhuis 1854-1907
AsBiEn, DcScB
Roper, Alvin Whitehead 1883-1930 *WhAm 1*
Roper, Daniel Calhoun 1867-1943 *BiDrUSE,*
DcAmB S3, NatCAB 31, WhAm 2
Roper, Denney Warren 1869-1949 *WhAm 3*
Roper, Edward 1857-1891 *IIBEAAW*
Roper, John Caswell 1873-1958 *WhAm 3*
Roper, John Lonsdale 1835-1921 *NatCAB 20*
Roper, John Wesley 1898-1963 *WhAm 4*
Roper, Lewis Murphree 1870-1938 *WhAm 1*
Roper, Robert Poore 1915-1965 *NatCAB 52,*
WhAm 4
Roper, William Bryham 1870-1964 *NatCAB 50*
Roper, William Hamilton 1904-1960
NatCAB 46
Roper, William Winston 1880-1933 *WhAm 1*
Ropers, Harold 1904-1966 *WhAm 5*
Ropes, Charles Joseph Hardy 1851-1915
WhAm 1
Ropes, George *NewYHSD*
Ropes, George 1788-1819 *NewYHSD*
Ropes, Hannah Anderson 1808-1863
ApCAB Sup
Ropes, James Hardy 1866-1933 *DcAmB,*
NatCAB 25, WhAm 1
Ropes, Jessie Naudine Alexander 1872-
WomWWA 14
Ropes, John Codman 1836-1899 *AmBi,*
ApCAB, DcAmB, NatCAB 11, TwCBDA,
WhAm 1
Ropes, Joseph 1770-1850 *DcAmB, WhAm H*
Ropes, Joseph 1812-1885 *NewYHSD*
Ropes, Sarah F Chapman *WomWWA 14*
Ropes, William Ladd 1825-1912 *WhAm 1*
Roquen, August *NewYHSD*
Roraback, Alberto T 1849-1923 *WhAm 1*
Roraback, Charles Pierson 1901-1964
NatCAB 50
Roraback, J Henry 1870-1937 *NatCAB 27,*
WhAm 1
Rorabaugh, Guy Oscar 1911-1970 *WhAm 5*
Rorer, David 1806-1884 *DcAmB, WhAm H*
Rorer, Gerald Francis 1908-1976 *WhAm 6*
Rorer, Herbert Crawley 1906-1962 *NatCAB 49*
Rorer, James Birch 1876- *WhAm 5*
Rorer, Sarah Tyson 1849-1937 *TwCBDA,*
WhAm 1
Rorer, Sarah Tyson Hester 1849-1937
NatCAB 16
Rorer, Sarah Tyson Heston 1849-1937
BiDAmEd, NotAW
Rorer, Virgil Eugene 1867-1944 *WhAm 2*
Rorick, Horton Clifford 1866-1946 *NatCAB 33*
Rorick, John C 1834- *WhAm 4*
Rorimer, James J 1905-1966 *NatCAB 52,*
WhAm 4
Rorimer, Louis 1872-1939 *WhAm 1*
Rorison, Arda Bates *WomWWA 14*
Rorke, Margaret Hayden 1883-1969
NatCAB 54
Rorschach, Hermann 1884-1922 *AsBiEn*
Rorty, James 1890-1973 *WhAm 6*
Rorty, Malcolm Churchill 1875-1936
NatCAB 27, WhAm 1
Rosa, Charles Arthur 1862-1921 *NatCAB 19*
Rosa, Daniele 1857-1944 *DcScB*
Rosa, Edward Bennett 1861-1921 *DcAmB,*
NatCAB 13, NatCAB 26, WhAm 1
Rosa, Elinor Baldwin 1872- *WomWWA 14*
Rosa, Salvator 1615-1673 *McGEWB*
Rosa Of Lima, Santa 1586-1617 *ApCAB*
Rosamond, William Irby 1912-1973 *WhAm 6*
Rosanes, Jakob 1842-1922 *DcScB*
Rosanoff, Martin Andre 1874-1951 *WhAm 3*
Rosario *REnAW*
Rosas, Juan Manuel Ortiz De 1793-1877
ApCAB, Drake, McGEWB
Rosati, James 1912- *BnEnAmA*
Rosati, Joseph 1789-1843 *ApCAB, DcAmB,*
NatCAB 13, TwCBDA, WhAm H
Rosbaud, Hans 1895-1962 *WhAm 4*
Rosbrugh, John 1714-1777 *ApCAB*

Rosburg, August Henry 1883-1953 *NatCAB 42*
Rosch, Joseph 1879- *WhAm 6*
Roscio, Juan German 1769-1821 *ApCAB*
Roscoe, Henry Enfield 1833-1915 *DcScB*
Rose, Abram John 1854-1929 *ApCAB X*
Rose, Albert Chatellier 1887-1966 *WhAm 4*
Rose, Aquila 1695?-1723 *ApCAB, DcAmB, Drake, NatCAB 8, WhAm H*
Rose, Arnold M 1918-1968 *WhAm 4*
Rose, Arthur Herbert 1883-1961 *NatCAB 49*
Rose, Benjamin 1828- *NatCAB 12*
Rose, Benjamin Morris 1898-1969 *WhAm 5*
Rose, Bessie Belle Williams 1878- *WomWWA 14*
Rose, Billy 1899-1966 *WhAm 4*
Rose, Carl Graham, Sr. 1892-1963 *NatCAB 48*
Rose, Carlton Raymond 1873- *WhAm 5*
Rose, Charles Bedell 1879-1962 *WhAm 4*
Rose, Chauncey 1794-1877 *ApCAB, DcAmB, TwCBDA, WhAm H*
Rose, D Kenneth 1902-1963 *WhAm 4*
Rose, Dana d1968 *WhAm 5*
Rose, David S 1856- *WhAm 4*
Rose, Don 1881-1965 *NatCAB 53, WhAm 6*
Rose, Donald Frank 1890-1964 *WhAm 4*
Rose, Dwight Chappell 1897-1969 *WhAm 5*
Rose, E H 1897-1968 *WhAm 5*
Rose, Edward *DcAmB*
Rose, Edward d1833? *REnAW*
Rose, Edward d1834 *WhAm H*
Rose, Edward Everley 1862-1939 *WhAm 1*
Rose, Elihu *NewYHSD*
Rose, Ellen Alida 1843- *AmWom*
Rose, Elmer Jay 1893-1965 *NatCAB 51*
Rose, Ernestine 1880-1961 *DcAmLiB*
Rose, Ernestine Louise Lasmond Potowsky 1810-1892 *ApCAB*
Rose, Ernestine Louise Siismondi P 1810-1892 *DcAmB, NotAW, WhAm H*
Rose, Flora 1874-1959 *WhAm 3, WomWWA 14*
Rose, Floyd 1875-1950 *WhAm 3*
Rose, Forrest Hobart 1899-1969 *WhAm 5*
Rose, Frank Bramwell 1836-1910 *WhAm 1*
Rose, Frank Watson 1917-1969 *WhAm 5*
Rose, Frederick Dodds 1882-1945 *NatCAB 35*
Rose, Frederick Holland 1866-1946 *NatCAB 47*
Rose, George B 1860-1942 *NatCAB 32*
Rose, George B 1860-1943 *WhAm 2*
Rose, George Basil 1860- *NatCAB 7*
Rose, George DeForest 1879-1950 *NatCAB 39*
Rose, George Maclean 1829- *ApCAB*
Rose, George P *NewYHSD*
Rose, George Phelps 1864-1947 *NatCAB 51*
Rose, Gustav 1798-1873 *DcScB*
Rose, Guy 1867-1925 *IIBEAAW, WhAm 1*
Rose, Heinrich 1795-1864 *DcScB*
Rose, Heloise Durant *WhAm 5*
Rose, Henry Howard 1856- *WhAm 4*
Rose, Henry Martin 1858- *WhAm 1*
Rose, Henry Nelson 1875-1955 *NatCAB 41*
Rose, Henry Reuben 1866-1950 *WhAm 3*
Rose, Herschel Hampton 1877-1945 *WhAm 2*
Rose, Howard Smith 1887-1971 *NatCAB 57*
Rose, Hugh Edward 1869-1945 *WhAm 2*
Rose, Hugh Henry 1801-1885 *WhoMilH*
Rose, Iver 1899-1972 *NatCAB 57*
Rose, John *NewYHSD*
Rose, Sir John 1820- *ApCAB*
Rose, John Andrew 1908-1962 *NatCAB 50*
Rose, John Carter 1861-1927 *DcAmB, NatCAB 28, WhAm 1*
Rose, John Kerr 1905-1974 *WhAm 6*
Rose, John Marshall 1856-1923 *BiDrAC, WhAm 1*
Rose, Joseph Nelson 1862-1928 *AmBi, DcAmB, NatCAB 27, WhAm 1*
Rose, Josiah Tryon 1869-1951 *WhAm 3*
Rose, Kurt Eugene 1909-1972 *WhAm 6*
Rose, Landon Cabell 1872-1931 *WhAm 1, WhAm 1C*
Rose, Laura *WomWWA 14*
Rose, Leo Stanton 1871-1946 *WhAm 2*
Rose, Lisle Abbott 1904-1955 *NatCAB 45, WhAm 3*
Rose, Mabel Austin Harris *WomWWA 14*
Rose, Mabel Estey 1877- *WomWWA 14*
Rose, Marcus A 1888-1964 *WhAm 4*

Rose, Martha Emily Parmelee 1834-1923 *AmWom, NatCAB 11, WhAm 1, WomWWA 14*
Rose, Mary Davies Schwartz 1874-1941 *BiDAmEd*
Rose, Mary Davies Swartz 1874-1941 *DcAmB S3, NotAW, WhAm 1*
Rose, Mary Dunning 1872- *WomWWA 14*
Rose, Maurice 1899-1945 *WhAm 2*
Rose, Morris Erich 1911-1967 *NatCAB 54*
Rose, Paul Howard 1881-1955 *NatCAB 45*
Rose, Philip Sheridan 1872-1962 *WhAm 4*
Rose, Ray Clarke 1870- *WhAm 5*
Rose, Robert Evstafieff 1879-1946 *NatCAB 39*
Rose, Robert Forest 1868- *WhAm 4*
Rose, Robert Given 1865-1942 *NatCAB 32*
Rose, Robert Hugh 1876- *WhAm 5*
Rose, Robert Lawson 1804-1877 *BiAUS, BiDrAC, WhAm H*
Rose, Robert Selden 1774-1835 *BiAUS, BiDrAC, WhAm H*
Rose, Robert Selden 1887-1964 *NatCAB 50*
Rose, Rufus Edwards 1847-1931 *ApCAB X, WhAm 1*
Rose, S Brandt 1901-1971 *WhAm 5*
Rose, Mrs. S E F 1862- *WomWWA 14*
Rose, Thomas Ellwood 1830-1907 *ApCAB, WhAm 1*
Rose, Thomas Elwood 1830-1907 *NatCAB 4*
Rose, U M 1834-1913 *NatCAB 7, WhAm 1*
Rose, Uriah Milton 1834-1913 *DcAmB*
Rose, Wallace Dickinson 1887-1928 *WhAm 1*
Rose, Walter Malins 1872-1908 *DcAmB, NatCAB 17, NatCAB 19, WhAm 1*
Rose, Walter Washington 1887-1958 *NatCAB 47*
Rose, Wickliffe 1862-1931 *DcAmB S1, NatCAB 31, WhAm 1*
Rose, William Brandon 1862-1946 *WhAm 2*
Rose, William Clayton 1890-1973 *WhAm 6*
Rose, William Cumming 1887- *AsBiEn*
Rose, William Ganson 1878-1957 *WhAm 3*
Rose, William Gray 1829-1899 *NatCAB 11*
Rose, William Hazael 1852- *WhAm 4*
Rosebault, Charles Jerome 1864-1944 *WhAm 2*
Roseboro, Viola *WomWWA 14*
Rosebrugh, Abner Mulholland 1835- *ApCAB*
Rosebush, Judson George 1878-1948 *WhAm 2*
Rosecrans, Egbert 1891-1948 *WhAm 2*
Rosecrans, Sylvester Horton 1827-1878 *ApCAB, DcAmB, NatCAB 9, TwCBDA, WhAm H*
Rosecrans, William Starke 1818-1898 *WhoMilH*
Rosecrans, William Starke 1819-1898 *AmBi, ApCAB, BiAUS, BiDrAC, DcAmB, Drake, NatCAB 4, TwCBDA, WebAB, WebAMB, WhAm H*
Rosecrans, William Starke 1889-1965 *WhAm 5*
Rosekrans, John Newton d1966 *WhAm 4*
Rosekrans, Sarah H Didriksen 1901-1970 *WhAm 6*
Roseland, Harry 1866-1950 *NatCAB 11, WhAm 3*
Roselius, Christian 1803-1873 *ApCAB, DcAmB, WhAm H*
Roseman, Alvin 1910-1974 *WhAm 6*
Rosemond, Fred Leslie 1861-1948 *NatCAB 35*
Rosen, Baron d1921 *WhAm 2*
Rosen, Abraham Nathaniel 1895-1967 *NatCAB 53*
Rosen, Charles 1872-1957 *NatCAB 47*
Rosen, Charles 1878-1950 *WhAm 3*
Rosen, Charles F 1910-1970 *WhAm 5*
Rosen, Joseph A 1878-1949 *DcAmB S4*
Rosen, Julius Jack 1919-1969 *WhAm 5*
Rosen, Louis Leucht 1900-1954 *NatCAB 44*
Rosen, Lucie Bigelow Dodge 1889-1968 *NatCAB 54*
Rosen, Max 1900-1956 *WhAm 3*
Rosen, Peter 1850-1906 *WhAm 3*
Rosen, Raymond 1893-1952 *NatCAB 45*
Rosen, Samuel 1898-1969 *WhAm 5*
Rosen, Theodore 1895-1940 *NatCAB 30*
Rosen, Victor Hugo 1911-1973 *WhAm 5*
Rosen, Walter Tower 1875-1951 *NatCAB 38*
Rosenau, Frederick J d1974 *WhAm 6*
Rosenau, Milton Joseph 1869-1946 *DcAmB S4, NatCAB 42, WhAm 2*

Rosenau, Myra B Frank 1877- *WomWWA 14*
Rosenbach, Abraham Simon Wolf 1876-1952 *DcAmB S5, WhAm 3*
Rosenbach, Joseph Bernhardt 1897-1951 *WhAm 3*
Rosenbach, Philip Hyman 1863-1953 *DcAmB S5*
Rosenbaum, David 1910-1974 *WhAm 6*
Rosenbaum, David Howell, Jr. 1908- *IlBEAAW*
Rosenbaum, Edward Philip 1916-1963 *WhAm 4*
Rosenbaum, Joseph 1838-1919 *NatCAB 17*
Rosenbaum, Lewis Newman 1881-1956 *WhAm 3*
Rosenbaum, Otho Bane 1871- *WhAm 5*
Rosenbaum, Samuel Rawlins 1888-1972 *WhAm 5*
Rosenbaum, Solomon Guedalia 1868-1937 *WhAm 1*
Rosenberg, Abraham Hayyim 1838-1925 *DcAmB*
Rosenberg, Alfred 1893-1946 *WhWW-II*
Rosenberg, Arthur 1889-1943 *WhAm 2*
Rosenberg, Charles G *NewYHSD*
Rosenberg, Edwin 1890-1969 *NatCAB 54*
Rosenberg, Ethel 1915-1953 *DcAmB S5, WebAB*
Rosenberg, Hans Oswald 1879-1940 *DcScB*
Rosenberg, Henry 1824-1893 *DcAmB, NatCAB 9, WhAm H*
Rosenberg, Henry A 1898-1955 *WhAm 3*
Rosenberg, Heyman 1874-1952 *NatCAB 48*
Rosenberg, Horace Louis 1891-1955 *NatCAB 45*
Rosenberg, Israel 1875-1956 *NatCAB 42, WhAm 3*
Rosenberg, James N 1874-1970 *WhAm 5*
Rosenberg, Julius 1918-1953 *DcAmB S5, WebAB*
Rosenberg, Maurice D 1866-1944 *NatCAB 33*
Rosenberg, Maurice David 1909-1950 *NatCAB 38*
Rosenberg, Philip 1913-1966 *NatCAB 53*
Rosenberg, S L Millard 1869-1934 *WhAm 1*
Rosenberg, Samuel 1896-1972 *WhAm 5*
Rosenberg, William Allen 1893-1955 *NatCAB 45*
Rosenberger, Absalom 1849- *WhAm 4*
Rosenberger, Carl 1872-1957 *WhAm 3*
Rosenberger, Gerald E d1967 *WhAm 4*
Rosenberger, Harry Emerson 1885-1963 *NatCAB 51*
Rosenberger, Johann Karl Ferdinand 1845-1899 *DcScB*
Rosenberger, Otto August 1800-1890 *DcScB*
Rosenberry, Alvan Avery 1883-1947 *NatCAB 35*
Rosenberry, Lois Carter Kimball Mathews 1873- *WhAm 5*
Rosenberry, Marvin Bristol 1868-1958 *WhAm 3*
Rosenberry, Morris Claude 1889-1957 *WhAm 3*
Rosenblatt, Josef 1882-1933 *NatCAB 28*
Rosenblatt, Joseph 1882-1933 *DcAmB*
Rosenblatt, Mandell 1891-1966 *NatCAB 53*
Rosenblatt, Morris S 1891-1965 *NatCAB 52*
Rosenblatt, Sol A 1900-1968 *WhAm 5*
Rosenbloom, Benjamin Louis 1880-1965 *BiDrAC, WhAm 6*
Rosenblueth, Arturo Stearns 1900-1970 *DcScB, WhAm 5*
Rosenblum, David Hyman 1898-1959 *NatCAB 47*
Rosenblum, Frank 1888-1973 *WhAm 5*
Rosenblum, Herman 1887- *WhAm 5*
Rosenblum, Jacob Joseph 1897-1971 *WhAm 5*
Rosenblum, William Franklin 1892-1968 *NatCAB 53, WhAm 4A*
Rosenbusch, Harry 1836-1914 *DcScB*
Rosencrantz, Albert Carl 1842-1920 *NatCAB 38*
Rosendale, Simon Wolf 1842-1937 *NatCAB 27*
Rosendale, Simon Wolfe 1842-1937 *WhAm 1*
Rosenfeld, James Wendel 1884-1961 *NatCAB 48*
Rosenfeld, Maurice 1867-1939 *WhAm 1, WhAm 1C*
Rosenfeld, Morris 1862-1923 *AmBi, DcAmB*
Rosenfeld, Mortimer Centinnial 1876-1943 *NatCAB 33*
Rosenfeld, Paul Leopold 1890-1946 *DcAmB S4,*

WhAm 2

Rosenfeld, Sydney 1855-1931 *WhAm 1*
Rosenfield, John 1900-1966 *WhAm 4*
Rosenfield, William Maxwell 1892-1957
NatCAB 48
Rosengarten, Adolph George 1870-1946
WhAm 2
Rosengarten, Frederic 1877-1955 *WhAm 3*
Rosengarten, George 1887-1953 *NatCAB 41*
Rosengarten, George David 1869-1936
NatCAB 35, WhAm 1
Rosengarten, Joseph George 1835- *ApCAB,*
WhAm 4
Rosengrant, E Judson 1863- *WhAm 4*
Rosenhain, Johann Georg 1816-1887 *DcScB*
Rosenhain, Walter 1875-1834 *DcScB*
Rosenheim, Alfred Faist 1859-1943 *WhAm 2*
Rosenheim, Arthur 1865-1942 *DcScB*
Rosenheimer, Ward Irving 1893-1967
NatCAB 53
Rosenhirsch, Leo Leonard 1901-1952
NatCAB 39
Rosenhof, August Johann Roesel Von *DcScB*
Rosenholtz, Joseph Leon 1863- *WhAm 4*
Rosenkampff, Arthur H 1884-1952 *WhAm 3*
Rosenkrans, Addison Priest 1875-1952
NatCAB 39
Rosenkrans, Carl Benjamin 1886-1945
NatCAB 35
Rosenkrans, Lillian Margaret 1871-
WomWWA 14
Rosenman, Samuel Irving 1896-1973 *WhAm 5*
Rosenmiller, Joseph Lewis 1897-1962
NatCAB 47, WhAm 4
Rosenquest, Eugene Haskins 1869-1936
NatCAB 35
Rosenquist, James 1933- *BnEnAmA*
Rosenschein, Charles Saul 1889-1957
NatCAB 45
Rosenshine, Albert Adolph 1882-1950
NatCAB 53
Rosensohn, Etta Lasker 1885-1966 *WhAm 4*
Rosenson, Alexander Moses 1900-1969
WhAm 5
Rosenstadt, Bernard Sidney 1896-1970
NatCAB 55
Rosenstein, A Louis 1910-1973 *NatCAB 57*
Rosenstein, David 1895-1963 *WhAm 4*
Rosenstengel, W E 1896-1958 *WhAm 3*
Rosenstern, Iwan 1882-1973 *WhAm 6*
Rosenstiel, Lewis S 1891-1976 *WhAm 6*
Rosenstock, Arthur 1903-1975 *WhAm 6*
Rosenstock-Huessy, Eugen 1888-1973 *WhAm 5*
Rosenthal, Adolph Henry 1906-1962
NatCAB 47
Rosenthal, Albert 1863-1939 *ApCAB,*
WhAm 1
Rosenthal, Benjamin 1875-1950 *NatCAB 37*
Rosenthal, Benjamin 1881-1950 *WhAm 3*
Rosenthal, Benjamin Stanley 1923- *BiDrAC*
Rosenthal, David S 1900-1954 *WhAm 3*
Rosenthal, Doris 1895?-1971 *IlBEAAW,*
WhAm 5
Rosenthal, Harry 1886-1973 *NatCAB 57*
Rosenthal, Henry Samuel 1864-1945
NatCAB 34
Rosenthal, Herman 1843-1917 *DcAmB,*
NatCAB 11, WhAm 1
Rosenthal, Ida Cohen 1886-1973 *NatCAB 57,*
WhAm 5
Rosenthal, Jean 1912-1969 *WhAm 5*
Rosenthal, Leonard 1874-1955 *NatCAB 44*
Rosenthal, Lessing 1868-1949 *WhAm 2*
Rosenthal, Lewis 1856- *ApCAB*
Rosenthal, Louis N *NewYHSD*
Rosenthal, Louis S 1890-1943 *WhAm 2*
Rosenthal, Max 1833-1918 *ApCAB, DcAmB,*
NatCAB 20, NewYHSD, TwCBDA,
WhAm 1
Rosenthal, Max 1865-1936 *NatCAB 27*
Rosenthal, Moritz 1866-1934 *WhAm 1*
Rosenthal, Morris *NewYHSD*
Rosenthal, Morris Sigmund 1897-1958
NatCAB 43, WhAm 3
Rosenthal, Sam 1891-1973 *WhAm 6*
Rosenthal, Samuel 1906-1965 *NatCAB 51*
Rosenthal, Samuel H 1878-1926 *NatCAB 23*
Rosenthal, Sarah G d1970 *WhAm 5*

Rosenthal, Simon *NewYHSD*
Rosenthal, Toby Edward 1848-1917 *AmBi,*
ApCAB, DcAmB, NatCAB 13, WhAm 1
Rosenthal, William 1881-1958 *NatCAB 48*
Rosenthall, Louis Samuel Philip 1890-1943
NatCAB 31
Rosenwald, Julius 1862-1932 *AmBi, DcAmB,*
EncAAH, EncAB, McGEWB,
NatCAB 26, WebAB, WhAm 1
Rosenzweig, Franz 1886-1929 *McGEWB*
Roser, Henry Harvoleau 1863- *WhAm 4*
Rosett, Joshua 1875-1940 *NatCAB 30*
Rosett, Leo J 1892-1952 *NatCAB 39*
Rosewald, Julie 1850- *AmWom*
Rosewater, Andrew 1848-1909 *WhAm 1*
Rosewater, Charles Colman 1874-1946
WhAm 2
Rosewater, Edward 1841-1906 *DcAmB,*
NatCAB 13, REnAW, WhAm 1
Rosewater, Stanley Meinrath 1885-1951
WhAm 3
Rosewater, Victor 1871-1940 *DcAmB S2,*
NatCAB 13, WhAm 1
Rosewater, William Marcus 1870-1935
NatCAB 27
Rosienkiewicz, Martin *NewYHSD*
Rosier, James 1575?-1635? *ApCAB, Drake*
Rosier, Joseph 1870-1951 *BiDrAC,*
NatCAB 40, WhAm 3
Rosin, Harry 1897-1973 *WhAm 6*
Rosing, Leonard August 1861-1909 *WhAm 1*
Rosing, Vladimir 1890-1963 *WhAm 4*
Rosling, George 1900-1973 *WhAm 5*
Rosmini-Serbati, Antonio 1797-1855 *McGEWB*
Rosner, David 1898-1959 *NatCAB 48*
Ross, Miss *NewYHSD*
Ross, Mister *NewYHSD*
Ross, Mrs. *NewYHSD*
Ross, Abel Hastings 1831-1893 *DcAmB,*
NatCAB 30, WhAm H
Ross, Adeline Rebecca 1876- *WomWWA 14*
Ross, Albert *WhAm 1*
Ross, Albert 1846-1926 *NatCAB 20, WhAm 1*
Ross, Albert Randolph 1869- *WhAm 3*
Ross, Alexander 1742-1827 *ApCAB, Drake*
Ross, Alexander 1783-1856 *AmBi, ApCAB,*
DcAmB, REnAW, WhAm H
Ross, Alexander Coffman 1812-1883 *ApCAB,*
DcAmB, NatCAB 20, WhAm H
Ross, Alexander Milton 1832- *ApCAB*
Ross, Alfred Joseph 1906-1971 *WhAm 5*
Ross, Allan Charles 1871- *WhAm 5*
Ross, Annie 1882- *WomWWA 14*
Ross, Araminta 1821?-1913 *AmBi, DcAmB*
Ross, Arthur Amasa 1791-1864 *NatCAB 8*
Ross, Arthur Leonidas 1895-1963 *WhAm 4*
Ross, Arthur M 1916-1970 *WhAm 5*
Ross, Austin C 1893-1960 *WhAm 3*
Ross, Barnaby *WebAB*
Ross, Bennett Battle 1864-1930 *NatCAB 25,*
NatCAB 26, WhAm 1
Ross, Bernard Rogan *WhAm H*
Ross, Betsy 1752-1836 *AmBi, ApCAB Sup,*
DcAmB, NatCAB 12, NotAW, WebAB,
WhAm H
Ross, Carmon 1884-1946 *WhAm 2*
Ross, Charles *NewYHSD*
Ross, Charles Adam 1882-1956 *NatCAB 43*
Ross, Charles Benjamin 1876-1946 *NatCAB 36,*
REnAW, WhAm 2
Ross, Charles Edward 1874-1954 *NatCAB 44*
Ross, Charles Griffith 1885-1950 *DcAmB S4,*
NatCAB 42, WhAm 3
Ross, Charles Wilson 1881-1946 *NatCAB 36*
Ross, Clarence Frisbee 1870-1942 *WhAm 2*
Ross, Clarence Samuel 1880- *WhAm 6*
Ross, Clay Campbell 1892-1947 *WhAm 2*
Ross, Clinton 1861-1920 *TwCBDA, WhAm 1*
Ross, Connor Daniel 1884-1955 *NatCAB 43*
Ross, Custer Enoch 1883-1946 *NatCAB 35*
Ross, David d1800 *BiAUS*
Ross, David 1750?-1800 *ApCAB*
Ross, David 1755-1800 *BiDrAC, WhAm H*
Ross, David 1865-1931 *NatCAB 24*
Ross, David 1891-1975 *WhAm 6*
Ross, David Alexander 1819-1897 *ApCAB Sup*
Ross, David E 1871-1943 *WhAm 2*
Ross, David Francis 1925-1975 *WhAm 6*

Ross, Denman Waldo 1853-1935 *DcAmB S1,*
WhAm 1
Ross, Donald 1890-1963 *WhAm 4*
Ross, Donald Garrett 1861-1939 *NatCAB 36*
Ross, Donald James 1872-1948 *NatCAB 39*
Ross, Earle Dudley 1885-1973 *EncAAH,*
NatCAB 57, WhAm 5
Ross, Edmund Gibson 1826-1907 *ApCAB,*
BiAUS, BiDrAC, DcAmB, NatCAB 13,
TwCBDA, WhAm HA, WhAm 4,
WhAmP
Ross, Edward Alsworth 1866- *NatCAB 18,*
TwCBDA, WhAm 5
Ross, Edward Alsworth 1866-1951 *DcAmB S5,*
McGEWB
Ross, Edward Alsworth 1866-1961 *EncAB*
Ross, Edward C 1801-1851 *Drake*
Ross, Elijah Walker 1872-1956 *NatCAB 49*
Ross, Emory 1887-1973 *NatCAB 57,*
WhAm 5
Ross, Erskine Mayo 1845-1928 *ApCAB X,*
DcAmB, WhAm 1, WhAm 1C
Ross, Ethel Darroch 1879- *WomWWA 14*
Ross, F Clair 1895-1956 *NatCAB 47*
Ross, Felix Brunot 1884-1962 *NatCAB 51*
Ross, Frank Alexander 1880-1943 *NatCAB 50*
Ross, Frank Alexander 1888-1968 *NatCAB 55,*
WhAm 5
Ross, Frank Elmore 1874-1960 *DcScB*
Ross, Frank Elmore 1874-1966 *WhAm 4*
Ross, Frank James 1913-1963 *WhAm 4*
Ross, Frank Mackenzie 1891-1971 *WhAm 5*
Ross, Frank Pierce 1869-1947 *NatCAB 34*
Ross, Frederick Augustus 1796-1883 *ApCAB*
Ross, Frederick Jeffery 1879-1957 *WhAm 3*
Ross, G A Johnston 1865-1937 *WhAm 1*
Ross, George 1730-1776 *NatCAB 10*
Ross, George 1730-1779 *AmBi, ApCAB,*
BiAUS, BiDrAC, DcAmB, Drake,
TwCBDA, WhAm H, WhAmP
Ross, George Gallious 1879- *WhoColR*
Ross, George Gates 1814-1856 *NewYHSD*
Ross, George Gould 1894-1961 *NatCAB 49*
Ross, George Hews 1854-1929 *NatCAB 21,*
WhAm 1
Ross, George William 1841- *ApCAB*
Ross, Gertrude *BiCAW*
Ross, Harold Ellis 1881- *WhAm 6*
Ross, Harold Wallace 1892-1951 *DcAmB S5,*
WebAB, WhAm 3
Ross, Harry Beach 1870-1955 *NatCAB 52*
Ross, Harry Seymour 1868-1948 *WhAm 2*
Ross, Henry Davis 1861-1945 *NatCAB 17,*
WhAm 2
Ross, Henry Howard 1790-1862 *ApCAB,*
BiAUS, BiDrAC, WhAm H
Ross, Homer Lachlin 1867- *WhAm 4*
Ross, Hubert Washington 1874- *WhoColR*
Ross, Isaac Nelson 1856- *WhoColR A*
Ross, Jack Ferrill 1791-1837 *TwCBDA*
Ross, James *Drake, NatCAB 5*
Ross, James 1761?-1847 *BiAUS*
Ross, James 1762-1847 *ApCAB, BiDrAC,*
DcAmB, Drake, NatCAB 5, TwCBDA,
WhAm H
Ross, James 1811- *ApCAB*
Ross, James 1835-1871 *ApCAB*
Ross, James Adrian 1883-1961 *NatCAB 48*
Ross, James Alexander 1867- *WhoColR*
Ross, James Archbald 1886-1970 *NatCAB 56*
Ross, Sir James Clark 1800-1862 *DcScB,*
McGEWB
Ross, Sir James Clarke 1800-1862 *ApCAB*
Ross, James Delmage 1871-1939 *AmBi,*
WhAm 1
Ross, James Delmage McKenzie 1872-1939
DcAmB S2
Ross, James Hubert 1875-1962 *NatCAB 48*
Ross, James Lycurgus 1901-1965 *WhAm 4*
Ross, John 1714-1776 *ApCAB*
Ross, John 1726-1800 *ApCAB, NatCAB 5*
Ross, John 1770-1834 *BiAUS, BiDrAC,*
NatCAB 16, TwCBDA, WhAm H
Ross, Sir John 1777-1856 *ApCAB, Drake*
Ross, John 1790-1866 *AmBi, ApCAB,*
DcAmB, Drake, McGEWB, NatCAB 11,
REnAW, WebAB, WhAm H
Ross, John 1818-1871 *ApCAB*

Ross, Sir John 1829- *ApCAB*
Ross, John Alexander, Jr. 1878- *WhAm 6*
Ross, John Dawson 1853-1939 *WhAm 1*
Ross, John Elliot 1884-1946 *NatCAB 34, WhAm 2*
Ross, John Frederick 1883-1962 *NatCAB 49*
Ross, John Jacob 1871-1935 *WhAm 3*
Ross, John Jones 1832- *ApCAB*
Ross, John Mason 1874-1944 *WhAm 2*
Ross, John O 1885-1966 *WhAm 4*
Ross, John Ogg 1884-1966 *NatCAB 56*
Ross, John Quincy 1873-1922 *NatCAB 6*
Ross, John Walker 1868-1937 *WhAm 1*
Ross, John Walton 1843-1920 *NatCAB 19*
Ross, John Wesley 1841-1902 *NatCAB 11, WhAm 1*
Ross, John William d1925 *WhAm 1*
Ross, John William 1852- *WhAm 4*
Ross, John William 1896-1965 *WhAm 4*
Ross, Jonathan 1826-1905 *ApCAB Sup, BiDrAC, NatCAB 7, TwCBDA, WhAm 1*
Ross, Joseph 1855-1925 *ApCAB X*
Ross, Joseph 1914-1966 *NatCAB 52, WhAm 4*
Ross, Julian Lenhart 1903-1972 *WhAm 5*
Ross, Lawrence Sullivan 1838-1898 *ApCAB, BiDConf, DcAmB, NatCAB 9, TwCBDA, WhAm H*
Ross, Leonard Fulton 1823- *ApCAB*
Ross, Leonard Fulton 1823-1901 *TwCBDA*
Ross, Leonard Fulton 1823-1902 *WhAm 1*
Ross, Leroy Williams 1883-1921 *WhAm 1*
Ross, Lester J 1890-1953 *WhAm 3*
Ross, Letitia Roano Dowdell d1952 *WhAm 3*
Ross, Lewis H 1901-1969 *NatCAB 54*
Ross, Lewis P 1843-1916 *WhAm 1*
Ross, Lewis Tenney 1896-1958 *NatCAB 48, WhAm 3*
Ross, Lewis Williams 1897-1969 *NatCAB 57*
Ross, Lewis Winans 1812-1895 *BiAUS, BiDrAC, TwCBDA, WhAm H*
Ross, Linn Carnahan 1880-1949 *NatCAB 41*
Ross, Louis 1859- *NatCAB 18*
Ross, Louis Warren 1893-1966 *NatCAB 51*
Ross, Louise 1846- *WomWWA 14*
Ross, Luther Sherman 1864- *WhAm 4*
Ross, Miss M *NewYHSD*
Ross, Mabel Landers 1874- *WomWWA 14*
Ross, Malcolm 1895-1965 *WhAm 4*
Ross, Martin 1762-1827 *DcAmB, WhAm H*
Ross, Michael 1898-1963 *WhAm 4*
Ross, Milan 1861- *NatCAB 8*
Ross, Lady Mildred *WomWWA 14*
Ross, Miles 1827-1903 *BiDrAC*
Ross, Miles 1828-1903 *BiAUS*
Ross, Nellie Tayloe 1880?- *WebAB, WhAmP*
Ross, Ogden 1893-1968 *WhAm 5*
Ross, Ora Thompson *WomWWA 14*
Ross, Patrick Hore Warriner 1858-1928 *NatCAB 16, WhAm 1*
Ross, Perley Ason 1883-1938 *WhAm 1*
Ross, Peter V 1870-1947 *WhAm 2*
Ross, Philip James 1875-1952 *WhAm 3*
Ross, Robert *NewYHSD*
Ross, Robert d1814 *Drake*
Ross, Robert 1766-1814 *AmBi, WhoMilH*
Ross, Robert 1770?-1814 *ApCAB*
Ross, Robert Edwin 1871-1941 *WhAm 1*
Ross, Robert Tripp 1903- *BiDrAC*
Ross, Sir Ronald 1857-1932 *AsBiEn, BiHiMed, DcScB*
Ross, Samuel Herman 1906-1959 *NatCAB 47*
Ross, Samuel Louis 1892-1970 *WhAm 5*
Ross, Sarah Gridley 1880-1962 *WhAm 4, WomWWA 14*
Ross, Sobieski 1828-1877 *BiAUS, BiDrAC, WhAm H*
Ross, Stoyte O 1906-1973 *WhAm 6*
Ross, Thomas 1806-1865 *BiAUS, BiDrAC, WhAm H*
Ross, Thomas Joseph 1893-1975 *WhAm 6*
Ross, Thomas R 1789-1869 *BiAUS*
Ross, Thomas Randolph 1788-1869 *BiDrAC, WhAm H, WhAmP*
Ross, Thorvald Salicath 1887-1965 *NatCAB 52*
Ross, Virginia Evelyn 1857- *AmWom*
Ross, Walter Daniel 1858-1922 *NatCAB 19*

Ross, Walter Lint 1865-1939 *NatCAB 35, WhAm 1*
Ross, Walter Willard 1866- *NatCAB 17*
Ross, Wilbert Davidson 1870-1944 *WhAm 2*
Ross, William Alanson 1878-1947 *NatCAB 34*
Ross, William Bradford 1873-1924 *NatCAB 20, WhAm 1*
Ross, William Edson 1879-1959 *NatCAB 47*
Ross, William Henry Harrison 1814- *BiAUS*
Ross, William Henry Harrison 1814-1887 *TwCBDA*
Ross, William Henry Harrison 1814-1890 *NatCAB 11*
Ross, William Horace 1875-1947 *WhAm 2*
Ross, William Hugh 1862-1955 *NatCAB 44*
Ross, William Lytle 1859-1939 *NatCAB 37*
Ross, William McAlister 1850-1934 *NatCAB 42*
Ross, William McAllister 1850-1934 *WhAm 1*
Ross, William Octavius 1853-1920 *NatCAB 18*
Ross, William Potter 1820-1891 *NatCAB 19*
Ross, Worth Gwynn 1854-1916 *WhAm 1*
Rossbach, Edgar Hilary 1903-1952 *WhAm 3*
Rossbach, Edward 1914- *BnEnAmA*
Rossby, Carl-Gustaf Arvid 1898-1957 *DcScB, WebAB, WhAm 3*
Rossdale, Albert Berger 1878-1968 *BiDrAC, WhAm 6*
Rosse, Christ *NewYHSD*
Rosse, Herman 1887-1965 *NatCAB 51*
Rosse, Leon *NewYHSD*
Rosse, William Parsons, Earl Of 1800-1867 *AsBiEn, DcScB*
Rosseau, Percival Leonard 1859-1937 *NatCAB 28, WhAm 1*
Rossel, Elisabeth Paul Edouard 1765-1829 *ApCAB*
Rosseler, Rudolf Lucy 1897-1958 *WhWW-II*
Rossell, John Settles 1856-1934 *WhAm 1*
Rossell, William 1761-1840 *BiAUS*
Rossell, William Trent 1849-1919 *WhAm 1*
Rosselle, William Quay 1869- *WhAm 5*
Rossen, Ralph 1909-1974 *WhAm 6*
Rossen, Robert 1908-1966 *WhAm 4*
Rosser, John Elijah 1881- *WhAm 5*
Rosser, Leonidas 1815- *ApCAB*
Rosser, Luther E B 1870- *WhoColR*
Rosser, Luther Zeigler 1859-1923 *WhAm 1*
Rosser, Thomas Lafayette 1836-1910 *AmBi, ApCAB, BiDConf, DcAmB, NatCAB 3, TwCBDA, WhAm 1*
Rosser, William James 1892-1962 *NatCAB 49*
Rosset, Joseph *NewYHSD*
Rosseter, John Henry 1869- *WhAm 5*
Rossette, John Baptiste d1797 *NewYHSD*
Rossetter, George W d1959 *WhAm 3*
Rossetti, Christina Georgina 1830-1894 *McGEWB*
Rossetti, Dante Gabriel 1828-1882 *McGEWB*
Rossetti, Francesco 1833-1885 *DcScB*
Rossetti, John Baptiste d1797 *NewYHSD*
Rossetti, Victor H 1877-1960 *WhAm 4*
Rossey, Chris C 1889-1946 *WhAm 2*
Rossey, Christopher Columbus 1889-1946 *NatCAB 34*
Rossi, Angelo Joseph 1878-1948 *NatCAB 37, WhAm 2*
Rossi, Bruno Benedetto 1905- *AsBiEn*
Rossi, Jean *NewYHSD*
Rossi, Louis Mansfield 1877-1944 *WhAm 2*
Rossi, Luigi 1598?-1653 *McGEWB*
Rossi, Luis Banchero 1930-1972 *WhAm 5*
Rossi, Paul A 1929- *IIBEAAW*
Rossi, Tobias *NewYHSD*
Rossin, Clara Lewisohn 1880-1927 *ApCAB X*
Rossin, Edgar Lewis 1901-1948 *NatCAB 36*
Rossini, Gioacchino 1792-1868 *McGEWB*
Rossiter, Clinton 1917-1970 *WhAm 5*
Rossiter, Dudley Lounsbery 1895-1970 *NatCAB 55*
Rossiter, Edward VanWyck 1844-1910 *WhAm 1*
Rossiter, Ehrick Kensett 1854-1941 *WhAm 2*
Rossiter, Fred J 1895-1964 *WhAm 4*
Rossiter, Frederick McGee 1870- *WhAm 5*
Rossiter, Joseph Pynchon 1789-1826 *NewYHSD*
Rossiter, Margaret 1944- *EncAAH*

Rossiter, Perceval Sherer 1874-1957 *NatCAB 48, WhAm 5*
Rossiter, Stealy Bales 1842-1914 *WhAm 1*
Rossiter, Thomas P 1818-1871 *Drake*
Rossiter, Thomas Prichard 1817-1871 *ApCAB, TwCBDA*
Rossiter, Thomas Prichard 1818-1871 *AmBi, DcAmB, NatCAB 4, NewYHSD, WhAm H*
Rossiter, Thomas Pritchard 1818-1871 *IIBEAAW*
Rossiter, William Sidney 1861-1929 *DcAmB, NatCAB 23, WhAm 1*
Rosskopf, Myron Frederick 1907-1973 *BiDAmEd*
Rosslin, Eucharius d1526 *BiHiMed*
Rosslyn, John *WhAm 4*
Rossman, George 1885-1967 *WhAm 4*
Rossman, Joseph 1899-1972 *WhAm 5*
Rossman, Lillie Baker 1860- *WomWWA 14*
Rossman, Samuel S 1896-1971 *WhAm 5*
Rosso, Il 1495-1540 *McGEWB*
Rosso, Augusto 1885-1964 *WhAm 4*
Rosson, L R 1910-1963 *NatCAB 56*
Rost, Christian *NewYHSD*
Rost, Pierre A 1797-1868 *BiAUS, Drake*
Rost, Pierre Adolph 1797-1868 *ApCAB*
Rost, Pierre Adolphe 1797-1868 *NatCAB 11*
Rostaing, A *NewYHSD*
Rostaing, Just Antoine H M, Marquis De 1740-1825 *Drake*
Rostaing, Just Antoine H M, Marquis De 1740-1826 *ApCAB*
Rostan, L *NewYHSD*
Rostan, Leon Louis 1790-1866 *DcScB*
Rostenkowski, Daniel David 1928- *BiDrAC*
Roster, D *NewYHSD*
Rostock, Frank Witte 1882-1960 *NatCAB 48, WhAm 4*
Rostovtzeff, Michael Ivanovich 1870-1952 *McGEWB, NatCAB 39, WhAm 3*
Rostovtzeff, Michael Ivanovitch 1870-1952 *DcAmB S5*
Rostow, Walt Whitman 1916- *EncAB*
Roszak, Theodore 1907- *BnEnAmA*
Roszel, Brantz Mayer 1869-1938 *WhAm 1*
Rotan, Kate Sturm McCall 1851- *WomWWA 14*
Rotch, Abbott Lawrence 1861-1912 *AmBi, DcAmB, NatCAB 15, TwCBDA, WhAm 1*
Rotch, Arthur 1850-1894 *ApCAB, DcAmB, NatCAB 11, WhAm H*
Rotch, Charity Rodman 1766-1824 *ApCAB*
Rotch, Thomas Morgan 1849-1914 *DcAmB, NatCAB 19, WhAm 1*
Rotch, William 1734-1828 *DcAmB, WhAm H*
Rotch, William 1844-1925 *ApCAB X, NatCAB 15, WhAm 1*
Rotchford, Hugh Babb 1905-1969 *WhAm 5*
Rote, Mary Krueger 1858- *WomWWA 14*
Roth, Almon Edward 1886-1964 *NatCAB 51*
Roth, Ben 1909-1960 *WhAm 3*
Roth, Charles Robert 1873-1954 *NatCAB 45*
Roth, Daniel K 1872-1968 *NatCAB 54*
Roth, Feri 1899- *WhAm 5*
Roth, Filibert 1858-1925 *NatCAB 21, WhAm 1*
Roth, Frederick George Richard 1872-1944 *NatCAB 37, WhAm 2*
Roth, George Byron 1879- *WhAm 6*
Roth, George J *NewYHSD*
Roth, Helen Bernheim *WomWWA 14*
Roth, Henry 1872-1949 *NatCAB 38*
Roth, Henry Warren 1838-1918 *WhAm 1*
Roth, John 1726-1791 *ApCAB, NatCAB 5*
Roth, John Ernest 1868-1954 *WhAm 4*
Roth, Justus Ludwig Adolph 1818-1892 *DcScB*
Roth, Lester 1881-1952 *NatCAB 42*
Roth, Lester Bertram 1899-1945 *NatCAB 36*
Roth, Paul Hoerlein 1880-1967 *NatCAB 53, WhAm 4*
Roth, Philip Milton 1933- *WebAB*
Roth, Stephen John 1908-1974 *WhAm 6*
Roth, Theophilus Buechle 1853- *TwCBDA*
Roth, William Henry 1874-1949 *NatCAB 37*
Roth, William Philip 1881-1963 *NatCAB 55, WhAm 4*

Roth, William Victor, Jr. 1921- *BiDrAC*
Rothafel, Samuel Lionel 1881-1936 *DcAmB S2,*
WhAm HA, WhAm 4
Rothas, Jacob *NewYHSD*
Rothberg, Maurice 1907-1972 *WhAm 6*
Rothberg, Sidney 1914-1970 *WhAm 5*
Rothchild, Herbert Lionel 1881-1935
NatCAB 27
Rothe, Emil 1826-1895 *NatCAB 28*
Rothe, Guillermo 1879- *WhAm 6*
Rothenberg, Joel Elmer 1912-1958 *NatCAB 43*
Rothenberg, Milton 1916-1973 *WhAm 5*
Rothenberg, Morris 1884-1950 *WhAm 3*
Rothenberg, Theresa 1888- *WomWWA 14*
Rothenburger, William Frederic 1874- *WhAm 5*
Rothermel, Amos Cornelius 1864-1946 *WhAm 2*
Rothermel, John Goodhart 1847-1928 *WhAm 1*
Rothermel, John Hoover 1856-1922 *BiDrAC,*
WhAm 1
Rothermel, Peter Frederick 1812-1895
NatCAB 4
Rothermel, Peter Frederick 1817-1895 *AmBi,*
ApCAB, DcAmB, Drake, NewYHSD,
TwCBDA, WhAm H
Rothermel, Peter Frederick 1850-1929
NatCAB 4, NatCAB 24
Rothgeb, Wade Hampton 1881-1928 *ApCAB X*
Rothier, Leon 1874- *WhAm 5*
Rothko, Mark 1903-1970 *BnEnAmA, EncAB,*
McGEWB, WebAB, WhAm 5
Rothkovich, Marcus *WebAB*
Rothman, Stephen 1894-1963 *WhAm 4*
Rothmann, Christoph d1608? *DcScB*
Rothrock, Addison May 1903-1971 *NatCAB 56*
Rothrock, Addison May 1908-1971 *WhAm 5*
Rothrock, David Andrew 1864- *WhAm 4*
Rothrock, Edward Streicher 1896-1964
WhAm 4
Rothrock, James Harvey 1829-1899 *NatCAB 12*
Rothrock, Joseph Trimble 1839-1922 *ApCAB,*
DcAmB, NatCAB 19, TwCBDA,
WhAm 1
Rothrock, Mary Utopia 1890-1976 *DcAmLiB*
Rothschild, Alonzo 1862-1915 *WhAm 1*
Rothschild, Karl 1897-1969 *WhAm 5*
Rothschild, Louis F 1869-1957 *WhAm 3*
Rothschild, Marcus Adolphus 1887-1936
NatCAB 29, WhAm 1
Rothschild, Maurice d1949 *WhAm 2*
Rothschild, Maurice Leopold 1864-1941
NatCAB 30
Rothschild, V Henry 1834-1911 *NatCAB 26*
Rothschild, Walter Nathan 1892-1960
NatCAB 44, WhAm 4
Rothstein, Irma d1971 *WhAm 5*
Rothstein, Morton 1926- *EncAAH*
Rothwell, Annie 1837- *AmWom*
Rothwell, Bernard Joseph 1859-1948
NatCAB 38, WhAm 2
Rothwell, Gideon Frank 1836-1894 *BiDrAC,*
WhAm H
Rothwell, J *NewYHSD*
Rothwell, Richard Pennefather 1836-1901
DcAmB, WhAm 1
Rothwell, Richard Pennefather 1837-1901
NatCAB 10
Rothwell, Will A 1863- *WhAm 1*
Rothwell, William Herbert 1876-1933
NatCAB 43
Rotmistrov, Pavel 1901- *WhWW-II*
Rotnem, Ralph Arthur 1903-1973 *WhAm 5*
Rotours, Jean Julien Angot, Baron Des
1773-1844 *ApCAB*
Rott, Reuben Paul 1907-1968 *NatCAB 54*
Rottenburg, Baron De d1832 *Drake*
Rottermund, Baron De 1813-1858 *ApCAB*
Rottger, Curtis Hoopes 1864- *WhAm 4*
Rottler, Clarence Theodore 1889-1958
NatCAB 48
Rottman, Ad *NewYHSD*
Rottman, Henry Maxwell 1902-1958
NatCAB 48
Rottmayr, Johann Michael 1654-1730
McGEWB
Rotunda, Dominic Peter 1895-1960 *NatCAB 48*
Rotzell, Willett Enos 1871-1913 *NatCAB 12,*
WhAm 1
Rouanez, P P *NewYHSD*

Rouard, John *NewYHSD*
Rouarie, Armand Taffin, Marquis DeLa
1756-1793 *ApCAB, TwCBDA*
Rouault, Georges 1871-1958 *McGEWB,*
WhAm 3
Roucolle, Adrienne 1875- *WhAm 5*
Roudebush, Alfred Holt 1873-1946 *WhAm 2*
Roudebush, Allen Cowen 1884-1960
NatCAB 48
Roudebush, Francis Wilshira 1899-1975
WhAm 6
Roudebush, George Shotwell 1828- *TwCBDA*
Roudebush, Richard Lowell 1918- *BiDrAC*
Rouelle, Guillaume-Francois 1703-1770 *DcScB*
Rouelle, Hilaire-Marin 1718-1779 *DcScB*
Rouelle, Jean 1751?- *DcScB*
Rouget, Charles Marie Benjamin 1824-1904
BiHiMed, DcScB
Rougut, Michael *NewYHSD*
Rouiller, Charles 1922-1973 *WhAm 6*
Rouillier, Karl Frantsovich 1814-1858 *DcScB*
Rouland, Orlando 1871-1945 *IIBEAAW,*
WhAm 2
Roulard, Charles 1751-1787 *ApCAB*
Roulery, Reuben *NewYHSD*
Roulhac, Thomas Ruffin 1846- *WhAm 4*
Roullston, Marjorie Hillis 1890-1971 *WhAm 5*
Roulstone, George 1767-1804 *DcAmB,*
WhAm H
Roulstone, William Bradford 1883-1953
NatCAB 45
Roumfort, Augustus Louis 1796-1878 *ApCAB*
Round, Louis David 1866-1938 *NatCAB 28*
Round, William Marshall Fitts 1845-1906
ApCAB, DcAmB, TwCBDA, WhAm 1
Rounding, William *NewYHSD*
Rounds, Arthur Charles 1862-1928 *WhAm 1*
Rounds, Dora Madeleine 1873- *WomWWA 14*
Rounds, Leslie Raymond 1886-1965 *WhAm 4*
Rounds, Ralph Stowell 1864-1948 *WhAm 2*
Rounds, Sterling Parker 1828-1887 *ApCAB*
Rounseville, Robert Field 1919-1974 *WhAm 6*
Rountree, Carl 1893-1962 *NatCAB 54*
Rountree, George 1855-1942 *WhAm 2*
Rountree, Walter Scott 1873-1940 *NatCAB 30*
Roupel, George *NewYHSD*
Rouquette, Adrien Emmanuel 1813-1887
ApCAB, DcAmB, Drake, TwCBDA,
WhAm H
Rouquette, Francois Dominique 1810-1890
ApCAB, DcAmB, WhAm H
Rourke, Anthony J J 1904- *WhAm 6*
Rourke, Constance Mayfield 1885-1941
DcAmB S3, NatCAB 32, NotAW,
WhAm 1
Rourke, Frank W 1892-1964 *WhAm 4*
Rous, Francis Peyton 1879-1970 *AsBiEn,*
McGEWB
Rous, John d1760 *ApCAB, Drake*
Rous, Peyton 1879-1970 *NatCAB 55, WebAB,*
WhAm 5
Rouse, Adelaide Louise d1912 *WhAm 1*
Rouse, Arthur Blythe 1874-1956 *BiDrAC,*
WhAm 5, WhAmP
Rouse, G *NewYHSD*
Rouse, Henry Clark 1853-1906 *NatCAB 6,*
WhAm 1
Rouse, John Delos 1838- *WhAm 4*
Rouse, John Gould 1884-1961 *WhAm 4*
Rouse, Louis Austin 1915-1975 *WhAm 6*
Roush, Dwight Irvin 1875-1954 *NatCAB 48*
Roush, Franklin Winbert 1877-1951
NatCAB 42
Roush, Gar A 1883-1955 *NatCAB 48,*
WhAm 3
Roush, John Edward 1920- *BiDrAC*
Roush, Oliver Eugene d1970 *WhAm 5*
Rousmaniere, Edmund Swett 1858-1926
ApCAB X, WhAm 1
Rouss, Charles Broadway 1836-1902 *NatCAB 8,*
WhAm 1
Rousse, Thomas Andrew 1901-1961 *NatCAB 55,*
WhAm 4
Rousseau, Charles M 1848-1918 *NatCAB 19*
Rousseau, Edme *NewYHSD*
Rousseau, Harry Harwood 1870-1930 *DcAmB,*
NatCAB 26, WhAm 1
Rousseau, Henri 1844-1910 *McGEWB*

Rousseau, Henry Harwood 1909-1972
NatCAB 57
Rousseau, Jean Jacques 1712-1778 *McGEWB*
Rousseau, Lovell Harrison 1818-1869 *AmBi,*
ApCAB, BiAUS, BiDrAC, DcAmB,
Drake, NatCAB 4, TwCBDA, WhAm H
Rousseau, Richard Hilaire 1815-1872 *BiAUS,*
NatCAB 12
Rousseau, Theodore 1812-1867 *McGEWB,*
NewYHSD
Rousseau, Theodore 1912-1973 *WhAm 6*
Roussel, Albert 1869-1937 *McGEWB*
Roussel, Gabriel Edmond 1717-1781 *ApCAB*
Rousselot, John Harbin 1927- *BiDrAC*
Rousselot, Louis M 1902-1974 *WhAm 6*
Rousselot DeSurgy, Jacques Philibert 1737-1791
ApCAB
Rousseve, Ferdinand Lucien 1904-1965
NatCAB 52, WhAm 4
Routh, Edward John 1831-1907 *DcScB*
Routh, Eugene Coke 1874- *WhAm 5*
Routh, James 1879- *WhAm 6*
Routh, Sir Randolph J 1787-1858 *ApCAB*
Routhier, Adolphe Basile 1839- *ApCAB Sup*
Routley, Thomas Clarence 1889-1963 *WhAm 4*
Routt, Eliza Franklin 1842- *AmWom*
Routt, John Long 1826-1907 *NatCAB 1,*
NatCAB 6, TwCBDA, WhAm 1
Routzahn, Evart Grant 1869-1939 *WhAm 1*
Routzohn, Harry Nelson 1881-1953 *BiDrAC,*
WhAm 3
Roux, Alexander 1813-1886 *BnEnAmA*
Roux, Edwin Timanus 1876-1946 *NatCAB 36*
Roux, Francis *NewYHSD*
Roux, Pierre Paul Emile 1853-1933 *DcScB*
Roux, Wilhelm 1850-1924 *DcScB*
Roux DeRochelle, Jean Baptiste Gaspard
1762-1849 *ApCAB*
Rouxel, Gustave Augustin 1840-1908 *TwCBDA,*
WhAm 1
Rovelstad, A M 1881- *WhAm 6*
Rovensky, Joseph Charles 1886-1952 *WhAm 3*
Rovenstine, E A 1895-1960 *WhAm 4*
Rover, Henry *NewYHSD*
Rover, Leo Aloysius 1888-1960 *WhAm 4*
Rovereto, Gaetano 1870-1952 *DcScB*
Roversi, Louis 1859-1927 *WhAm 1*
Row, Edgar Charles 1896-1973 *WhAm 6*
Row, Robert Keable 1858-1932 *NatCAB 17,*
WhAm 1
Row, William Hamilton 1907-1961 *WhAm 4*
Rowan, Andrew Summers 1857-1943
NatCAB 31, WebAMB, WhAm 2
Rowan, Andrew Summers 1859-1943
ApCAB Sup
Rowan, Charles A 1874-1940 *WhAm 1*
Rowan, Charles Joseph 1874-1948 *WhAm 2*
Rowan, Hugh Williamson 1894-1973 *WhAm 6*
Rowan, John d1855 *BiAUS*
Rowan, John 1771-1843 *TwCBDA*
Rowan, John 1773-1843 *BiDrAC, DcAmB,*
Drake, NatCAB 6, WhAm H
Rowan, John 1773-1853 *ApCAB, BiAUS*
Rowan, Joseph 1870-1930 *BiDrAC, WhAm 1*
Rowan, Richard Wilmer 1894-1964 *WhAm 4*
Rowan, Stephen Clegg 1808-1890 *AmBi,*
ApCAB, DcAmB, Drake, NatCAB 2,
TwCBDA, WebAMB, WhAm H
Rowan, Thomas Leslie 1908-1972 *WhAm 5*
Rowan, Sir William 1789-1879 *ApCAB*
Rowan, William A 1882-1961 *BiDrAC,*
WhAm 4
Rowand, William *NewYHSD*
Rowbottom, Harry Emerson 1884-1934 *BiDrAC,*
WhAm 1
Rowcliff, Gilbert 1881-1963 *WhAm 4*
Rowe, Albert Holmes 1889-1970 *WhAm 5*
Rowe, Alice Ethel 1884- *WomWWA 14*
Rowe, Allan Winter 1879-1934 *DcScB,*
WhAm 1
Rowe, Anna Forrest 1857-1920 *NatCAB 20*
Rowe, Arthur Taylor 1883-1935 *NatCAB 27*
Rowe, Benjamin Ackley 1884-1937 *WhAm 1*
Rowe, Bert Bessac 1862-1959 *NatCAB 36*
Rowe, Casper Hartman 1860-1928 *NatCAB 32*
Rowe, Clarence Herbert 1878-1930 *IIBEAAW*
Rowe, Clifford Paul 1905-1968 *WhAm 5*
Rowe, E R *NewYHSD*

Rowe, Edmund 1892- *BiDrAC*
Rowe, Ellis Lewis 1858-1942 *NatCAB 31*
Rowe, Eugene Charles 1870-1946 *NatCAB 41*
Rowe, Frank Elmer 1885-1968 *NatCAB 55*
Rowe, Fred Nelcy 1883-1965 *NatCAB 53*
Rowe, Frederick William 1863-1946 *BiDrAC,
WhAm 2*
Rowe, Gilbert Hume 1904-1971 *NatCAB 57*
Rowe, Gilbert Theodore 1875-1965 *WhAm 4*
Rowe, Guy 1894-1969 *WhAm 5*
Rowe, Hartley 1882-1966 *WhAm 4*
Rowe, Henrietta Gould 1835-1910 *WhAm 1*
Rowe, Henry Clarke 1851- *NatCAB 8,
WhAm 4*
Rowe, Henry Kalloch 1869-1941 *WhAm 1*
Rowe, Jesse Perry 1871- *WhAm 5*
Rowe, John Jay 1885-1965 *NatCAB 51*
Rowe, John Leroy 1914-1975 *WhAm 6*
Rowe, Joseph Eugene 1883-1939 *WhAm 1*
Rowe, L Earle 1882-1937 *NatCAB 28,
WhAm 1*
Rowe, L K *NewYHSD*
Rowe, Leo Stanton 1871-1946 *DcAmB S4,
NatCAB 12, NatCAB 18, TwCBDA*
Rowe, Peter 1807-1876 *BiAUS, BiDrAC,
WhAm H*
Rowe, Peter Trimble 1856-1942 *TwCBDA,
WhAm 2*
Rowe, Robert G 1895- *WhAm 5*
Rowe, Stuart Henry 1869- *WhAm 5*
Rowe, Theodore Spurling 1902-1973 *WhAm 6*
Rowe, Wallace Hurtte 1861-1919 *ApCAB X,
NatCAB 18*
Rowe, Walter Ellsworth 1875-1952 *WhAm 3*
Rowe, William Henry 1858-1919 *NatCAB 18*
Rowe, William Stanhope 1857-1941 *WhAm 1*
Rowe, William Vincent 1861-1930 *NatCAB 22*
Rowell, Chester Harvey 1867-1948 *DcAmB S4,
WhAm 2*
Rowell, Franklin Pierce 1850-1927 *NatCAB 21*
Rowell, George Presbury 1838-1908 *DcAmB,
NatCAB 2, WhAm 1*
Rowell, George Smith 1846- *WhAm 4*
Rowell, Henrietta Kingdon *WomWWA 14*
Rowell, Henry Thompson 1904-1974 *WhAm 6*
Rowell, Hugh Grant 1892-1963 *WhAm 4*
Rowell, James G 1883-1956 *WhAm 3*
Rowell, John W 1835-1924 *NatCAB 5,
WhAm 1*
Rowell, Jonathan Harvey 1833-1908 *BiDrAC,
WhAm 1*
Rowell, Joseph Cummings 1853-1938 *WhAm 1*
Rowell, Mary Coyne *WomWWA 14*
Rowell, Ross Erastus 1884-1947 *WhAm 2*
Rowell, Samuel 1815- *NewYHSD*
Rowell, Teresina Peck 1872- *WomWWA 14*
Rowell, Wilbur Everett 1862-1946 *NatCAB 40,
WhAm 2*
Rowell, Wilfrid Asa 1877-1956 *NatCAB 48,
WhAm 3*
Rowerdink, William Henry 1859-1923
NatCAB 19
Rowland, Adoniram Judson 1840-1917 *WhAm 1*
Rowland, Alfred 1844-1898 *BiDrAC*
Rowland, Arthur John 1867-1934 *WhAm 1*
Rowland, Benjamin, Jr. 1904-1972 *WhAm 5*
Rowland, Charles Hedding 1860-1921 *BiDrAC,
WhAm 4*
Rowland, Charles Leonard 1852-1926 *WhAm 1*
Rowland, Clarence H d1969 *WhAm 5*
Rowland, David *BiAUS*
Rowland, Dunbar 1864-1937 *ApCAB X,
WhAm 1*
Rowland, Earle 1894-1951 *NatCAB 45*
Rowland, Eron Opha *WomWWA 14*
Rowland, Harry Tatem 1899-1955 *NatCAB 42,
WhAm 3*
Rowland, Helen *WomWWA 14*
Rowland, Henry *NewYHSD*
Rowland, Henry Augustus 1804-1859 *ApCAB,
Drake*
Rowland, Henry Augustus 1848-1901 *AmBi,
ApCAB, AsBiEn, DcAmB, DcScB,
EncAB, McGEWB, NatCAB 11,
TwCBDA, WebAB, WhAm 1*
Rowland, Henry Cottrell 1874-1933 *DcAmB,
WhAm 1*
Rowland, Henry James 1843-1909 *NatCAB 16*

Rowland, Hiram Arthur 1881-1958 *NatCAB 45*
Rowland, Howard Johnson 1862-1926
NatCAB 21
Rowland, James Marshall Hanna 1867-1954
WhAm 3
Rowland, James S *NewYHSD*
Rowland, Jasper Morgan 1879-1932
NatCAB 24
Rowland, Joseph Medley 1880-1938 *WhAm 1*
Rowland, Kate Mason d1916 *TwCBDA,
WhAm 1, WomWWA 14*
Rowland, Robert Meredith 1872-1961
NatCAB 50
Rowland, Roger Whittaker 1895-1974 *WhAm 6*
Rowland, Russell Sturgis 1874-1938
NatCAB 29
Rowland, Thomas Fitch 1831-1907 *DcAmB,
NatCAB 12*
Rowland, Vernon Cecil 1883-1963 *WhAm 4*
Rowland, William 1828- *NatCAB 5*
Rowland, William Denton 1879-1949
NatCAB 37
Rowland, William Samuel 1881-1936
NatCAB 28, WhAm 1
Rowlands, John *WebAB*
Rowlands, William 1807-1866 *DcAmB,
NatCAB 26, WhAm H*
Rowlandson, Mary White 1635?-1678 *ApCAB,
DcAmB, Drake, NatCAB 8, NotAW,
WhAm H*
Rowlee, Willard Winfield 1861-1923 *WhAm 1*
Rowlett, Robert 1888-1937 *WhAm 1*
Rowley, Alfred Merriman 1875-1942
NatCAB 31
Rowley, Claude Arthur 1882-1945 *NatCAB 34*
Rowley, Edith 1877- *WomWWA 14*
Rowley, Francis Harold 1854-1952 *NatCAB 43,
WhAm 3*
Rowley, Frank Ellis 1869-1913 *NatCAB 16*
Rowley, Frank S 1896-1952 *WhAm 3*
Rowley, George 1892-1962 *WhAm 4*
Rowley, John 1866-1928 *WhAm 1*
Rowley, Mabel A *WomWWA 14*
Rowley, Reuben *NewYHSD*
Rowley, Thomas Algeo 1808- *ApCAB*
Rowley, William C 1863- *WhAm 4*
Rowley, William Reuben 1824-1886 *ApCAB*
Rowning, John 1701?-1771 *DcScB*
Rowntree, Harold 1865-1943 *NatCAB 35*
Rowntree, Jennie 1890-1974 *WhAm 6*
Rowntree, Leonard George 1883-1959
NatCAB 44
Rowse, J B *NewYHSD*
Rowse, Samuel *NewYHSD*
Rowse, Samuel Worcester 1822-1901 *ApCAB,
DcAmB, NatCAB 30, NewYHSD,
WhAm H*
Rowson, Charlotte 1779?-1855 *ApCAB*
Rowson, Susanna Haswell 1762-1824 *AmBi,
ApCAB, DcAmB, Drake, NatCAB 9,
NotAW, WebAB, WhAm H*
Roxas, Manuel 1892-1948 *McGEWB,
WhAm 2*
Roxborough, Alexander *NewYHSD*
Roxborough, William 1829?- *NewYHSD*
Roxy 1881-1936 *DcAmB*
Roy, Alphonse 1897-1967 *BiDrAC*
Roy, Arthur J 1869-1948 *WhAm 2*
Roy, Charles Dunbar 1866-1937 *NatCAB 34*
Roy, Francis Albert 1907-1970 *WhAm 5*
Roy, Herbert Francis 1876-1939 *NatCAB 30*
Roy, James Evans d1974 *WhAm 6*
Roy, Joseph Edmond 1858- *ApCAB Sup*
Roy, Lillian Elizabeth 1868-1932 *WhAm 1*
Roy, P A 1889-1949 *WhAm 2*
Roy, Philip Seddon 1861- *WhAm 4*
Roy, Ram Mohun 1772-1833 *McGEWB*
Roy, Reuben Finnell 1854- *WhAm 4*
Roy, Sharat Kumar 1897-1962 *NatCAB 50,
WhAm 4*
Roy, Victor Leander, Sr. 1871- *WhAm 5*
Royal, Forrest Betton 1893-1945 *NatCAB 34,
WhAm 2*
Royal, George 1853-1931 *WhAm 1*
Royal, Joseph 1837- *ApCAB*
Royal, Paul Ambrose 1891-1956 *NatCAB 48*
Royal, Ralph *WhAm 1*
Royall, Anne Newport 1769-1854 *AmBi,*

ApCAB, DcAmB, Drake, EncAB,
NotAW, WebAB, WhAm H
Royall, Isaac 1720?-1781 *ApCAB, Drake*
Royall, John Mabery 1874- *WhoColR*
Royall, Kenneth Claiborne 1894-1971 *BiDrUSE,
NatCAB 57, WhAm 5*
Royall, Nina Almirall 1878- *WomWWA 14*
Royall, Page Aylett *WomWWA 14*
Royall, Ralph 1881-1954 *WhAm 3*
Royall, Tucker 1877- *WhAm 1*
Royall, William 1823-1893 *NatCAB 25*
Royall, William Bailey 1844-1928 *WhAm 1*
Royall, William Bedford 1825- *ApCAB*
Royall, William L 1844-1911 *NatCAB 18*
Royalty, Paul 1899-1960 *WhAm 4*
Roybal, Edward Ross 1916- *BiDrAC*
Royce, Alexander Burgess 1894-1968 *WhAm 4*
Royce, Asa Marshfield 1876-1963 *WhAm 4*
Royce, Clayton Elbert 1886-1947 *NatCAB 45*
Royce, Donald 1900-1969 *WhAm 5*
Royce, Frederick Page 1868-1933 *WhAm 1*
Royce, George Monroe 1850- *WhAm 1*
Royce, Homer Elihu 1819-1891 *BiAUS,
BiDrAC, NatCAB 4, TwCBDA,
WhAm H*
Royce, Homer Elihu 1820-1891 *ApCAB*
Royce, J B *NatCAB 4*
Royce, Josiah 1855-1916 *AmBi, ApCAB,
DcAmB, DcAmReB, EncAB, McGEWB,
NatCAB 11, NatCAB 25, REnAW,
TwCBDA, WebAB, WhAm 1*
Royce, Luman Herbert 1868-1935 *WhAm 1*
Royce, Robert Russel 1902- *WhAm 5*
Royce, Sarah Eleanor Bayliss 1819-1891
NotAW, WhAm H
Royce, Sarah Grace *WomWWA 14*
Royce, Stephen 1787-1868 *ApCAB, BiAUS,
Drake, NatCAB 8, TwCBDA*
Roye, Edward James 1815-1872 *ApCAB,
DcAmB, WhAm H*
Roye, T B *NatCAB 4*
Royer, Arnold Lennel 1912-1971 *WhAm 5*
Royer, J E E 1885-1957 *WhAm 3*
Royer, J Elliott 1881-1961 *NatCAB 53*
Royer, R Stuart 1884-1951 *NatCAB 39*
Royer, Edwin Milton 1862-1942 *WhAm 2*
Royle, Vernon 1846- *NatCAB 12*
Roys, Cyrus Dustan 1836-1915 *ApCAB X,
NatCAB 17*
Roys, Mabel Milham *WomWWA 14*
Royse, Lemuel Willard 1847-1946 *BiDrAC*
Royse, Samuel Durham 1878-1945 *NatCAB 34,
WhAm 2*
Royster, Frank Sheppard 1849-1928
NatCAB 39
Royster, Hubert Ashley 1871- *WhAm 5*
Royster, James Finch 1880-1930 *DcAmB,
NatCAB 27, WhAm 1*
Royster, Lawrence Thomas 1874- *WhAm 5*
Royster, Salibelle 1895-1975 *WhAm 6*
Royster, Stephen Sampson 1867-1948
NatCAB 38
Royster, Thomas Sampson 1890-1939
NatCAB 36
Royston, Grandison Delaney 1809-1889
BiDConf
Rozan, Josef Samuel 1904-1965 *NatCAB 52*
Rozar, Allen Robert 1898-1949 *NatCAB 39*
Roze, Pierre Gustave 1812-1882 *ApCAB*
Rozhdestvenski, Zinovy Petrovich 1848-1909
WhoMilH
Rozhdestvensky, Dmitry Sergeevich 1876-1940
DcScB
Rozier, J Ad 1817-1896 *NatCAB 10*
Rozmarek, Charles 1897-1973 *WhAm 6*
Ruan, Carrie Frazer *WomWWA 14*
Ruark, Robert Chester 1915-1965 *WhAm 4*
Rubattel, Rodolphe 1896-1961 *WhAm 4*
Rubel, A C 1895-1967 *WhAm 4*
Ruben, Barney d1959 *WhAm 3*
Ruben, Jose 1888-1969 *NatCAB 55*
Rubendall, Clarence 1883-1950 *WhAm 3*
Rubens, Harry 1850-1920 *WhAm 1*
Rubens, Heinrich 1865-1922 *DcScB*
Rubens, Horatio Seymour 1869-1941 *WhAm 1*
Rubens, Peter Paul 1577-1640 *McGEWB*
Rubenstein, Emil 1880-1952 *NatCAB 39*
Rubey, Thomas Lewis 1862-1928 *BiDrAC,*

WhAm 1, WhAmP

Rubey, William Walden 1898-1974 *WhAm 6*
Rubin, Bernard Daniel 1893-1948 *NatCAB 35*
Rubin, I Louis 1900-1959 *NatCAB 47*
Rubin, J Robert 1882-1958 *WhAm 3*
Rubin, Reuven 1893-1974 *WhAm 6*
Rubin, William 1871-1928 *NatCAB 22*
Rubin, William Benjamin 1873- *ApCAB X,*
WhAm 5
Rubin DeLaBorbolla, Daniel Fernando 1907-
WhAm 5
Rubina, Signor *NewYHSD*
Rubinkam, Nathaniel Irwin 1851-1919 *WhAm 1*
Rubinovitz, George 1914-1971 *WhAm 5*
Rubinow, Isaac Max 1875-1936 *DcAmB S2,*
WhAm 1
Rubinowicz, Wojciech 1889-1974 *WhAm 6*
Rubinstein, Arthur 1889- *WebAB*
Rubinstein, Beryl 1898-1952 *NatCAB 39,*
WhAm 3
Rubinstein, Helena 1870-1965 *NatCAB 50,*
WhAm 4
Rubio, Antonio 1888-1955 *WhAm 3*
Rubio, David 1884-1962 *WhAm 4*
Ruble, Joseph Shirk 1877-1935 *NatCAB 28*
Ruble, Zulema Alice 1861- *WomWWA 14*
Rublee, George 1868-1957 *WhAm 3*
Rublee, Horace 1829-1896 *ApCAB Sup,*
BiAUS, DcAmB, NatCAB 1, WhAm H
Rublee, William Alvah 1861-1910 *WhAm 1*
Rubler, Louis *NewYHSD*
Rubner, Max 1854-1932 *AsBiEn, BiHiMed,*
DcScB
Rubsamen, Walter Howard 1911-1973 *WhAm 6*
Ruby, Edward Ernest 1874- *WhAm 5*
Ruby, Emery Haskett, Jr. 1909-1965
NatCAB 52
Ruby, Harry 1895-1974 *WhAm 6*
Ruby, John Wesley 1902-1972 *NatCAB 57*
Ruby, Lionel 1899-1972 *WhAm 5*
Ruby, Robert 1921- *EncAAH*
Ruch, Giles Murrel 1892-1943 *WhAm 2*
Ruchstuhl, Frederick Wellington 1858-
ApCAB X
Ruckdeschel, Charles *NewYHSD*
Ruckdeschel, J Charles *NewYHSD*
Rucker *NewYHSD*
Rucker, Allen Willis 1897-1964 *WhAm 4*
Rucker, Atterson Walden 1847-1924 *BiDrAC,*
WhAmP
Rucker, Atterson Walden 1847-1927 *WhAm 2*
Rucker, Casper Bell 1886-1948 *WhAm 2*
Rucker, Daniel Henry 1812-1910 *ApCAB,*
Drake, TwCBDA, WhAm 1
Rucker, Edmund Winchester 1835-1924
NatCAB 20
Rucker, Edwin Timothy 1853-1918 *NatCAB 29*
Rucker, Elbert Marion 1866-1926 *WhAm 1*
Rucker, Howard Lewis 1852- *NatCAB 6*
Rucker, James Bernard 1879-1961 *NatCAB 50*
Rucker, Louis H 1842-1906 *WhAm 1*
Rucker, Marvin Pierce 1881-1953 *NatCAB 42,*
WhAm 4
Rucker, Tinsley White 1848-1926 *BiDrAC*
Rucker, William Colby 1875-1930 *NatCAB 32,*
WhAm 1
Rucker, William Waller 1855-1936 *BiDrAC,*
TwCBDA, WhAm 1, WhAmP
Ruckle, Thomas 1776-1853 *NewYHSD*
Ruckle, Thomas Coke 1811-1891 *NewYHSD*
Ruckman, John Wilson 1858-1921 *WhAm 1*
Ruckmick, Christian Alban 1886-1961 *WhAm 4*
Ruckstuhl, Frederic Wellington 1853-1942
TwCBDA
Ruckstull, F Wellington 1853-1942 *WhAm 2*
Ruckstull, Frederic Wellington 1853-1942
BnEnAmA, NatCAB 32
Ruckstull, Frederick Wellington 1853-1942
DcAmB S3
Rudbeck, Olof 1630-1702 *AsBiEn, DcScB*
Rudd, Anson 1819- *NatCAB 1*
Rudd, George Arthur 1852-1933 *NatCAB 25*
Rudd, Herbert Finley 1877-1948 *NatCAB 37*
Rudd, John Churchill 1779-1848 *ApCAB,*
Drake
Rudd, Judson Archer 1902-1970 *WhAm 5*
Rudd, Nathaniel *NewYHSD*
Rudd, Stephen Andrew 1874-1936 *BiDrAC,*

Rudd, Thomas Brown 1898-1955 *NatCAB 43,*
WhAm 3
Rudd, William Platt 1851-1929 *NatCAB 12,*
WhAm 1
Ruddell, Clementine Tucker 1875-
WomWWA 14
Rudder, James Earl 1910-1970 *WhAm 5*
Ruddiman, Edsel Alexander 1864-1954
NatCAB 45, WhAm 3, WhAm 5
Ruddock, Albert Billings 1886- *ApCAB X*
Ruddock, John Carroll 1891-1964 *WhAm 4*
Ruddock, Malcolm Irving 1912-1961 *WhAm 4*
Ruddy, Edward Michael 1899-1969 *WhAm 5*
Ruddy, Ella Giles *WomWWA 14*
Ruddy, Howard Shaw 1856-1922 *WhAm 1*
Rude, Ellen Sergeant 1838- *AmWom*
Rude, Joe Christopher 1905-1974 *WhAm 6*
Rudenberg, Reinhold 1883-1961 *DcScB,*
NatCAB 47, WhAm 4
Rudenko, William Bernard 1905-1966 *WhAm 4*
Ruder, William Ernst 1886-1963 *WhAm 4*
Ruderman, James d1966 *WhAm 6*
Rudersdorff, Hermine 1822-1882 *WhAm H*
Rudge, William Edwin 1876-1931 *DcAmB,*
WhAm 1
Rudick, Harry J 1899-1964 *WhAm 4*
Rudiger, August E 1818?- *NewYHSD*
Rudin, John 1876-1959 *NatCAB 43*
Rudinger, Ellen Eckstein 1915-1971 *WhAm 5*
Rudio, Ferdinand 1856-1929 *DcScB*
Rudisill, Carl Augustus 1884-1949 *NatCAB 55*
Rudisill, James Jefferson 1900-1958 *NatCAB 48*
Rudkin, Frank H 1864-1931 *NatCAB 18,*
WhAm 1
Rudkin, Margaret Fogarty 1897-1967 *WhAm 4*
Rudo, Stephen Istvan 1897-1960 *NatCAB 45*
Rudolf I 1218?-1291 *McGEWB*
Rudolff, Christoff *DcScB*
Rudolph, Alexander Joseph 1850?-1917
DcAmLiB
Rudolph, Charles 1868- *WhAm 4*
Rudolph, Cuna Hugo 1860-1932 *WhAm 1*
Rudolph, Cuno Hugo 1860-1932 *NatCAB 25*
Rudolph, Ernest *NewYHSD*
Rudolph, Herbert Blaine 1894-1957 *WhAm 3*
Rudolph, Herman Louis 1909-1975 *WhAm 6*
Rudolph, Irving 1897-1964 *WhAm 4*
Rudolph, Jacob H 1886-1960 *WhAm 3*
Rudolph, Louis N 1886-1949 *NatCAB 37*
Rudolph, Michael 1754?-1794? *ApCAB, Drake*
Rudolph, Michael 1754-1795 *NatCAB 12*
Rudolph, Paul 1918- *BnEnAmA*
Rudolph, Pauline Dohn *WomWWA 14*
Rudolph, Robert Livingston 1865-1930 *WhAm 1*
Rudolphi, Karl Asmund 1771-1832 *DcScB*
Rudorf, Cornelis Van 1769-1813 *ApCAB*
Rudy, James Augustus 1851-1919 *NatCAB 18*
Rue, Lars 1893-1965 *WhAm 4*
Rue, Levi Lingo 1860-1931 *NatCAB 18,*
WhAm 1
Rue, Milton 1899-1968 *WhAm 5*
Rue, Ralph H 1902-1966 *WhAm 4*
Rueb, Rolland Richmond 1918-1960
NatCAB 50
Ruebush, Ephraim 1833-1924 *NatCAB 20*
Ruebush, James Hott 1865-1948 *WhAm 3*
Rueckert, Frederick 1855-1941 *NatCAB 30*
Ruedemann, Albert Darwin 1897-1971 *WhAm 6*
Ruedemann, Rudolf 1864-1956 *DcScB,*
WhAm 3
Ruediger, Gustav F 1876-1935 *WhAm 1*
Ruediger, William Carl 1874-1947 *WhAm 2*
Ruef, Abraham 1864-1936 *DcAmB S2,*
McGEWB, REnAW
Ruehe, Harrison August 1888-1953 *WhAm 3*
Ruehl, Victor Eugene 1881-1942 *NatCAB 32*
Ruekberg, Nathan 1890-1949 *NatCAB 38*
Ruel, Jean 1474-1537 *DcScB*
Rueling, George 1839-1915 *NatCAB 27*
Ruen, Charles *NewYHSD*
Ruetenik, Herman Julius 1826- *WhAm 4*
Ruf, Frank Aloysius 1856-1923 *NatCAB 6*
Ruff, Charles Frederick 1818-1885 *ApCAB*
Ruff, G Elson 1904-1972 *WhAm 5*
Ruff, Robert Hamric 1887-1942 *WhAm 2*
Ruffennach, Cyril Francis 1903-1966
NatCAB 51

Ruffer, Marc Armand 1859-1917 *DcScB*
Ruffin, Armand Gustave 1731-1789 *ApCAB*
Ruffin, Edmund 1794-1865 *AmBi, ApCAB,*
DcAmB, Drake, EncAAH, EncAB,
McGEWB, NatCAB 5, WebAB,
WebAMB, WhAm H, WhAmP
Ruffin, Edmund Sumter 1861-1949 *NatCAB 41*
Ruffin, George Lewis 1834-1886 *ApCAB*
Ruffin, James Edward 1893- *BiDrAC*
Ruffin, Josephine St. Pierre 1842-1924 *NotAW,*
WomWWA 14
Ruffin, Margaret Ellen Henry *WhAm 5,*
WomWWA 14
Ruffin, Sterling 1866-1949 *WhAm 2*
Ruffin, Thomas 1787-1870 *AmBi, ApCAB,*
BiDConf, DcAmB, NatCAB 6, TwCBDA,
WhAm H
Ruffin, Thomas 1820-1863 *BiAUS, BiDConf,*
BiDrAC, WhAm H, WhAmP
Ruffin, Thomas 1824-1889 *NatCAB 7*
Ruffini, Angelo 1864-1929 *DcScB*
Ruffini, Elise Erna d1970 *WhAm 5*
Ruffini, Paolo 1765-1822 *DcScB*
Ruffner, Charles Shumway 1880-1939
NatCAB 31, WhAm 1
Ruffner, David 1767-1837 *NatCAB 11*
Ruffner, Ernest Howard 1845- *WhAm 4*
Ruffner, Henry d1861 *Drake*
Ruffner, Henry 1789-1861 *ApCAB, NatCAB 3,*
TwCBDA
Ruffner, Henry 1790-1861 *BiDAmEd, DcAmB,*
WhAm H
Ruffner, William Henry 1824-1908 *BiDAmEd,*
DcAmB, NatCAB 12, WhAm 1
Ruffo, Giordano *DcScB*
Rufinus *DcScB*
Rufus Of Ephesus *BiHiMed, DcScB*
Rufus, Will Carl 1876-1946 *WhAm 2*
Rufz DeLavison, Etienne 1806- *ApCAB*
Rugen, Myrtle Louise 1904-1971 *WhAm 6*
Rugendas, Johann Moritz 1802-1858 *ApCAB*
Ruger, Thomas Howard 1833-1907 *ApCAB,*
DcAmB, Drake, NatCAB 1, TwCBDA,
WhAm 1
Ruger, Washington *NewYHSD*
Ruger, William Crawford 1824-1892 *ApCAB,*
NatCAB 5, TwCBDA
Rugg, Arthur Prentice 1862-1938 *DcAmB S2,*
NatCAB 17, NatCAB 33, WhAm 1
Rugg, Charles Belcher 1890-1962 *NatCAB 50,*
WhAm 4
Rugg, Ellen Marshall *WomWWA 14*
Rugg, Frederic Waldo 1855-1932 *WhAm 1*
Rugg, Harold Ordway 1886-1960 *BiDAmEd,*
WebAB, WhAm 4
Rugg, Henry Warren 1833-1910 *WhAm 1*
Rugg, Herbert Dean 1891-1960 *WhAm 4*
Rugg, Robert Billings 1886-1946 *WhAm 2*
Rugg, Walter Sylvester 1866-1940 *NatCAB 30*
Ruggles, Alice Morrill 1879- *WomWWA 14*
Ruggles, Arthur Hiler 1881-1961 *WhAm 4*
Ruggles, Benjamin d1837 *BiAUS*
Ruggles, Benjamin 1783-1857 *ApCAB,*
BiDrAC, Drake, NatCAB 13, TwCBDA,
WhAm H, WhAmP
Ruggles, Carl 1876-1971 *WhAm 5*
Ruggles, Charles 1892-1970 *WhAm 5*
Ruggles, Charles Herman 1789-1865 *ApCAB,*
BiDrAC, NatCAB 11, TwCBDA,
WhAm H
Ruggles, Charles Herman 1790?-1865 *BiAUS*
Ruggles, Clyde Orval 1878-1958 *NatCAB 46,*
WhAm 3
Ruggles, Colden L'Hommedieu 1869-1933
WhAm 1
Ruggles, Daniel 1810-1897 *ApCAB, Drake,*
TwCBDA
Ruggles, E, Jr. *NewYHSD*
Ruggles, E Wood 1861-1942 *WhAm 2*
Ruggles, Edward 1817-1867 *Drake, NewYHSD*
Ruggles, Edwin Pakenham 1873-1940
NatCAB 29
Ruggles, George David 1833-1904 *ApCAB,*
NatCAB 12, TwCBDA, WhAm 1
Ruggles, Henry Joseph 1813-1906 *WhAm 1*
Ruggles, Horace Fowle 1869-1944 *NatCAB 33*
Ruggles, John d1874 *BiAUS*
Ruggles, John 1789-1874 *BiDrAC,*

NatCAB 12, TwCBDA, WhAm H,
WhAmP
Ruggles, John 1790-1874 *ApCAB*
Ruggles, Mary *NewYHSD*
Ruggles, May Sleeper 1861- *WomWWA 14*
Ruggles, Nathaniel 1761-1819 *BiAUS, BiDrAC,*
TwCBDA, WhAm H
Ruggles, Oliver W d1923 *WhAm 1*
Ruggles, Samuel Bulkley 1800-1881 *ApCAB,*
DcAmB, Drake, NatCAB 13, TwCBDA,
WhAm H
Ruggles, Theo Alice 1871- *AmWom*
Ruggles, Timothy 1711-1795 *AmBi, ApCAB,*
BiAUS, DcAmB, Drake, NatCAB 2,
TwCBDA, WhAm H
Ruggles, William 1797-1877 *ApCAB*
Ruggles, William Benjamin 1827- *ApCAB Sup*
Ruggles, William Burroughs 1853- *WhAm 4*
Rugh, Charles Edward 1867-1938 *NatCAB 28,*
WhAm 4
Ruhe, Percy Bott 1881-1962 *WhAm 4*
Ruhemann, Helmut 1891-1973 *WhAm 6*
Ruhf, Charles Theodore 1893-1960 *NatCAB 48*
Ruhl, Arthur Brown 1876-1935 *DcAmB S1,*
WhAm 5
Ruhl, Christian H 1853- *WhAm 4*
Ruhl, E Blair 1892-1950 *NatCAB 39*
Ruhl, James Brough 1864- *WhAm 3*
Ruhl, Julia Slocum Walker 1861-
WomWWA 14
Ruhl, Robert Waldo 1880-1967 *WhAm 4*
Ruhland, George Clemens 1878-1958
NatCAB 43
Ruhland, John *NewYHSD*
Ruhlender, Henry 1867- *WhAm 4*
Ruhmkorff, Heinrich Daniel 1803-1877 *DcScB*
Ruhoff, John Richard 1908-1973 *WhAm 6*
Ruhrah, John 1872-1935 *DcAmB S1,*
WhAm 1
Ruini, Carlo 1530?-1598 *DcScB*
Ruisdael, Jacob Van 1628?-1682 *McGEWB*
Ruiz, Cortines Adolfo 1891-1973 *WhAm 6*
Ruiz, Hipolito 1754-1816 *DcScB*
Ruiz, Jose Martinez 1873-1967 *McGEWB,*
WhAm 4
Ruiz, Juan 1283?-1350? *McGEWB*
Ruiz Guinazo, Enrique 1884-1967 *WhAm 4*
Ruland, Lloyd Stanton 1889-1953 *WhAm 3*
Ruland, Martin 1569-1611 *DcScB*
Rule, Arthur Richards 1876-1950 *NatCAB 41,*
WhAm 3
Rule, James Noble 1876-1938 *WhAm 1*
Rule, Rebecca 1856- *WomWWA 14*
Rule, William 1839-1928 *WhAm 1*
Rulein, Ulrich 1465?-1523 *DcScB*
Rulison, Nelson Somerville 1842-1897 *ApCAB,*
TwCBDA
Rulison, Nelson Somerville 1843-1897
NatCAB 1
Rullman, Walter Ames 1885-1962 *NatCAB 50*
Rulon, Phillip Justin 1900-1968 *WhAm 5*
Rumbaugh, Lynn Hamilton 1904-1964
NatCAB 51
Rumble, Douglas 1880- *WhAm 6*
Rumble, Mrs. Stephen *NewYHSD*
Rumbold, Caroline Thomas 1877-
WomWWA 14
Rumbold, Frank Meeker 1862- *WhAm 4*
Rumbold, Thomas Frazier 1830-1901 *WhAm 1*
Rumely, Edward A 1882-1964 *WhAm 4*
Rumely, V P 1889-1964 *WhAm 4*
Rumely, William Nicholas 1858-1936 *WhAm 3*
Rumford *DcScB*
Rumford, Count 1753-1814 *EncAB,*
NewYHSD, TwCBDA, WhAm H
Rumford, Benjamin Thompson, Count 1753-1814
AmBi, ApCAB, AsBiEn, DcAmB, Drake,
McGEWB, NatCAB 5, WebAB
Rumford, Countess Sarah 1774-1852 *ApCAB*
Rumi, Al- *DcScB*
Rumi, Jalai Ed-Din 1207-1273 *McGEWB*
Ruminagui d1534 *ApCAB*
Ruml, Beardsley 1894-1960 *EncAB,*
NatCAB 44, WhAm 3A
Rummel, Delbert 1875-1937 *NatCAB 30*
Rummel, Joseph F 1876-1964 *WhAm 4*
Rummler, Susan Harding 1874- *WomWWA 14*

Rummler, William Richard 1865-1948
NatCAB 37
Rumney, John Gaine 1850-1941 *NatCAB 31*
Rumovsky, Stepan Yakovlevich 1734-1812
DcScB
Rumpf, Arthur Newell 1908-1968 *WhAm 5*
Rumple, J N W 1841-1903 *WhAm 1*
Rumple, Jethro 1827- *ApCAB, TwCBDA*
Rumple, John Nicholas William 1841-1903
BiDrAC
Rumpler, Maude Lucas 1874- *WomWWA 14*
Rumpler, William *NewYHSD*
Rumsey, Benjamin d1808 *BiAUS*
Rumsey, Benjamin 1730?-1808 *ApCAB,*
NatCAB 7, TwCBDA
Rumsey, Benjamin 1734-1808 *BiDrAC,*
WhAm H
Rumsey, Charles Cary 1879-1922 *DcAmB,*
NatCAB 25, WhAm 1
Rumsey, David 1810-1883 *BiAUS, BiDrAC,*
NatCAB 11, WhAm H
Rumsey, Dexter Phelps 1893-1966 *WhAm 4*
Rumsey, Edward 1796-1868 *BiAUS, BiDrAC,*
WhAm H
Rumsey, Elida Barker *NotAW*
Rumsey, Eugene Aertsen 1867-1944
NatCAB 35
Rumsey, Hiram *NewYHSD*
Rumsey, Israel Parsons 1836- *WhAm 4*
Rumsey, James 1743-1792 *AmBi, ApCAB,*
DcAmB, Drake, NatCAB 5, TwCBDA,
WebAB, WhAm H
Rumsey, Julian Sidney 1823-1886 *ApCAB*
Rumsey, Mary Harriman 1881-1934 *DcAmB S1,*
NatCAB 25, NotAW, WhAm 1
Rumsey, William 1841-1903 *DcAmB,*
NatCAB 11, WhAm 1
Rumsfeld, Donald Henry 1932- *BiDrAC*
Runcie, Constance Faunt LeRoy 1836-1911
AmWom, DcAmB, NatCAB 7, WhAm 1
Rundall, Charles Owen 1885-1953 *NatCAB 42,*
WhAm 3
Rundell, Annie Stevens *WomWWA 14*
Rundell, Oliver Samuel 1881-1957 *WhAm 3*
Rundle, George Mortimer 1855- *WhAm 4*
Rundle, Samuel H 1832-1922 *NatCAB 19*
Rundles, Walter Zell 1895-1964 *NatCAB 51*
Rundlet, Mabel Tower 1877- *WomWWA 14*
Rundquist, George E 1896-1969 *WhAm 5*
Rundstedt, Gerd Von 1875-1953 *WhWW-II*
Rundstedt, Karl Rudolf Gerd Von 1875-1953
McGEWB, WhoMilH
Rundt, Charles Godfrey 1713-1764 *ApCAB*
Runge, Carl David Tolme 1856-1927 *DcScB*
Runge, Edith Amelie 1916-1971 *WhAm 5*
Runge, Friedlieb Ferdinand 1794-1867 *DcScB*
Runge, John *NewYHSD*
Rungius, Carl Clemens Moritz 1869-1959
IlBEAAW, NatCAB 45, WhAm 3
Runk, John 1791-1872 *BiAUS, BiDrAC,*
WhAm H
Runkle, Benjamin Piatt 1837-1916 *TwCBDA,*
WhAm 1
Runkle, Bertha 1879- *BiCAW, TwCBDA,*
WomWWA 14
Runkle, Delmer 1856-1936 *WhAm 1*
Runkle, Erwin William 1869-1941 *WhAm 1*
Runkle, Harry Godley 1858- *WhAm 4*
Runkle, Harry Maize 1889-1962 *NatCAB 46,*
WhAm 4
Runkle, John Daniel 1822-1902 *ApCAB,*
BiDAmEd, DcAmB, Drake, NatCAB 6,
TwCBDA, WhAm 1
Runkle, Lucia Gilbert 1837-1923 *BiCAW*
Runkle, Lucia Isabella 1844- *ApCAB,*
WhAm 4, WomWWA 14
Runkles, Cornelius A 1832-1888 *ApCAB*
Runnells, Clive 1877-1935 *WhAm 1*
Runnells, John Edmunds 1876-1964 *NatCAB 50*
Runnells, John Sumner 1844-1929 *WhAm 1*
Runnels, Hardin R d1873 *NatCAB 9,*
TwCBDA
Runnels, Harrison R *BiAUS*
Runnels, Hiram G 1790?-1857 *BiAUS,*
NatCAB 13
Runnels, Orange Scotch 1847-1929 *NatCAB 14*
Runnels, Orange Scott 1847-1929 *WhAm 1*
Runnels, Richard Stitt 1923-1974 *WhAm 6*

Runner, Harvey Evan 1897-1961 *WhAm 4*
Running, Theodore Rudolph 1866- *WhAm 5*
Runyan, Elmer Gardner 1862- *WhAm 4*
Runyan, William B 1877-1953 *WhAm 3*
Runyon, Damon 1880-1946 *DcAmB S4,*
NatCAB 39
Runyon, Damon 1884-1946 *WebAB, WhAm 2*
Runyon, John William 1887-1967 *WhAm 4*
Runyon, Laura Louisa 1862- *WomWWA 14*
Runyon, Mefford 1861-1928 *ApCAB X*
Runyon, Peter P 1787-1871 *BiAUS*
Runyon, Theodore 1822-1896 *ApCAB Sup,*
NatCAB 7, TwCBDA
Runyon, W Parker 1861-1928 *WhAm 1*
Runyon, William Nelson 1871-1931 *WhAm 1*
Ruoff, Henry Woldmar 1865-1935 *WhAm 1*
Ruopp, Harold Washington 1899-1961 *WhAm 4*
Ruotolo, Onorio 1888-1966 *WhAm 4*
Rupe, Dallas Gordon 1902-1970 *WhAm 5*
Rupe, William Stephen 1886-1959 *NatCAB 46*
Rupel, I Walker 1900-1971 *WhAm 5*
Rupert Of The Rhine, Prince 1619-1682
WhoMilH
Rupert, Frank 1865-1922 *NatCAB 36*
Rupertus, William Henry 1889-1945
NatCAB 36, WhAm 2
Rupley, Arthur Ringwalt 1868-1920 *BiDrAC,*
WhAm 4
Rupley, Joseph William 1902-1968 *WhAm 5*
Rupp, Charles, Jr. 1908-1970 *NatCAB 55,*
WhAm 5
Rupp, Christian *NewYHSD*
Rupp, Frederic Carl 1877-1932 *NatCAB 29*
Rupp, George Herbert 1889-1954 *NatCAB 44*
Rupp, Isaac Daniel 1803-1878 *Drake*
Rupp, Israel Daniel 1803-1878 *ApCAB,*
DcAmB, TwCBDA, WhAm H
Rupp, Lawrence Henry 1881-1936 *WhAm 1*
Rupp, Norman Nienstedt 1882-1942
NatCAB 33
Rupp, Otto Burton 1877-1962 *WhAm 4*
Rupp, Werner Andrew 1880-1963 *NatCAB 53,*
WhAm 4
Rupp, William 1839-1904 *DcAmB, WhAm 1*
Ruppe, Philip Edward 1926- *BiDrAC*
Ruppel, Louis 1903-1958 *WhAm 3*
Ruppenthal, Jacob Christian 1869-1964
WhAm 4
Ruppert, George E d1948 *WhAm 2*
Ruppert, Jacob 1842-1915 *NatCAB 3,*
NatCAB 29
Ruppert, Jacob, Jr. 1867-1939 *BiDrAC,*
DcAmB S2, NatCAB 11, NatCAB 29,
TwCBDA, WhAm 1, WhAmP
Ruppert, Max King 1899-1962 *WhAm 4*
Rupprecht, Prince Of Bavaria 1869-1955
WhoMilH
Rupprecht, Frederick Kelsey 1872-1954
WhAm 3
Ruprecht, Jenny Terrill 1840- *AmWom*
Rurik d873? *McGEWB*
Rusbatch, Samuel *NewYHSD*
Rusby, Henry Hurd 1855-1940 *BiDAmEd,*
DcAmB S2, TwCBDA, WhAm 1
Ruscelli, Girolamo d1565? *DcScB Sup*
Ruschenberger, William S W 1807- *ApCAB,*
Drake
Ruschenberger, William S W 1807-1895
TwCBDA
Ruschenberger, William S W 1807-1905
NatCAB 13
Rush, Miss *NewYHSD*
Rush, Benjamin 1741-1813 *TwCBDA*
Rush, Benjamin 1745-1813 *AmBi, ApCAB,*
BiAUS, BiDAmEd, BiDrAC, BiHiMed,
DcAmB, Drake, EncAB, McGEWB,
WebAB, WhAmP
Rush, Benjamin 1746-1813 *DcScB, NatCAB 3,*
WhAm H
Rush, Benjamin 1811-1877 *ApCAB,*
NatCAB 3
Rush, Benjamin 1869-1948 *WhAm 2*
Rush, Charles Andrew 1862- *WhAm 4*
Rush, Charles Everett 1885-1958 *DcAmLiB,*
NatCAB 46
Rush, Christopher 1777-1873 *ApCAB,*
TwCBDA
Rush, Franklin Smithwick 1865-1933 *WhAm 1*

Rush, Gertrude E Durden 1880- *WhoColR*
Rush, Guy Mansfield 1882-1962 *WhAm 4*
Rush, Ira *NewYHSD*
Rush, J *NewYHSD*
Rush, Mrs. Jacob *NewYHSD*
Rush, Jacob 1746-1820 *ApCAB, Drake, NatCAB 5, TwCBDA, WhAm H*
Rush, James 1786-1869 *ApCAB, DcAmB, Drake, NatCAB 6, TwCBDA, WhAm H*
Rush, James Buchanan 1861- *WhoColR*
Rush, John 1782-1853 *NewYHSD*
Rush, John Andrew 1865-1943 *WhAm 2*
Rush, Judson Randolph 1865- *ApCAB X*
Rush, Madelon Reine Francis *WhAm 6*
Rush, Olive 1873-1966 *IlBEAAW, WhAm 4, WomWWA 14*
Rush, Rachel Lionne Adsit 1885-
WomWWA 14
Rush, Richard 1780-1859 *AmBi, ApCAB, BiAUS, BiDrUSE, DcAmB, Drake, NatCAB 5, TwCBDA, WebAB, WhAm H*
Rush, Sylvester R 1860-1932 *WhAm 1*
Rush, Thomas E 1867-1927 *WhAm 1*
Rush, Wilbur Miller 1911-1969 *NatCAB 55*
Rush, William 1756-1833 *AmBi, ApCAB, BnEnAmA, DcAmB, McGEWB, NatCAB 8, NewYHSD, TwCBDA, WebAB, WhAm H*
Rushd, Abu'l-Walid Muhammad Ibn, Ibn 1126-1198 *DcScB*
Rushing, James Andrew 1903-1972 *WhAm 5*
Rushmore, David Barker 1873-1940 *ApCAB X, WhAm 1*
Rushmore, Edward 1845- *WhAm 4*
Rushmore, Jane P 1864- *WomWWA 14*
Rushmore, John Dikeman 1845- *WhAm 4*
Rushmore, Stephen 1875-1960 *NatCAB 50, WhAm 5*
Rushton, Herbert J 1878-1947 *WhAm 2*
Rushton, Joseph Augustine 1874-1956
NatCAB 45
Rushton, Joseph Howard 1849-1922
NatCAB 19
Rushton, Ray 1868-1940 *WhAm 1*
Rushton, Richard Holt 1851-1910 *WhAm 1*
Rusk, David Dean 1909- *BiDrUSE, EncAB*
Rusk, Evelyn Carroll 1900-1964 *NatCAB 51*
Rusk, Harry Welles 1852-1926 *BiDrAC, TwCBDA, WhAmP*
Rusk, Henry Perly 1884-1954 *WhAm 3*
Rusk, J Wayne, Jr. 1905-1968 *NatCAB 54*
Rusk, Jeremiah M 1830-1893 *BiAUS*
Rusk, Jeremiah McClain 1830-1893 *DcAmB*
Rusk, Jeremiah McLain *NatCAB 12*
Rusk, Jeremiah McLain 1830-1893 *AmBi, ApCAB, BiDrAC, BiDrUSE, EncAAH, NatCAB 1, TwCBDA, WhAm H, WhAmP*
Rusk, John 1849-1910 *WhAm 1*
Rusk, Ralph Leslie 1888-1962 *WhAm 4*
Rusk, Thomas Jefferson d1856 *BiAUS*
Rusk, Thomas Jefferson 1802-1856 *ApCAB, Drake*
Rusk, Thomas Jefferson 1803-1857 *AmBi, BiDrAC, DcAmB, NatCAB 3, TwCBDA, WhAm H, WhAmP*
Rusk, William Dougherty 1850- *NatCAB 13*
Ruska, Ernst August Friedrich 1906- *AsBiEn*
Ruskin, Jerrold Harold 1912-1968 *WhAm 5*
Ruskin, John 1819-1900 *BnEnAmA, McGEWB*
Ruskin, Simon Lyon 1897-1958 *NatCAB 44*
Ruslander, Phoebe Jane 1868- *WomWWA 14*
Rusling, Emily Wood *WomWWA 14*
Rusling, James Fowler 1834-1918 *NatCAB 8, NatCAB 35, WhAm 1*
Rusling, James Wood 1874-1947 *NatCAB 35*
Russ, Horace P 1820-1862 *Drake*
Russ, Horace P 1821-1863 *ApCAB*
Russ, Hugh McMaster 1900-1971 *WhAm 5*
Russ, Imanuel Christian Charles 1795-1857
NatCAB 7
Russ, John *NewYHSD*
Russ, John 1767-1832 *BiAUS*
Russ, John 1767-1833 *BiDrAC, WhAm H*
Russ, John Denison 1801-1881 *ApCAB, TwCBDA, WhAm H*
Russ, John Dennison 1801-1881 *AmBi, DcAmB*

Russ, John Megginson 1891-1969 *NatCAB 56, WhAm 5*
Russ, John T 1904-1954 *WhAm 3*
Russel, Albert Lacy 1902-1952 *NatCAB 41*
Russel, Edgar 1862-1925 *NatCAB 20, WhAm 1*
Russel, Florence Kimball 1873- *WomWWA 14*
Russel, George Howard 1847-1915 *ApCAB X, NatCAB 35, WhAm 1*
Russel, George Howard *see also* Russell, George Howard
Russel, Henry 1852-1920 *WhAm 1*
Russel, Walter S 1855-1935 *WhAm 1*
Russell, Ada Dwyer *WomWWA 14*
Russell, Addison Peale 1826- *NatCAB 6, TwCBDA, WhAm 1*
Russell, Albert Cuyp 1838-1917 *NewYHSD*
Russell, Albert Hyatt 1904-1960 *WhAm 4*
Russell, Albert Jonathan 1831-1896 *BiDAmEd*
Russell, Alexander 1880-1953 *WhAm 3*
Russell, Lord Alexander George 1821- *ApCAB*
Russell, Alexander Jamieson 1807- *ApCAB*
Russell, Alexander Wilson 1824-1908 *WhAm 1*
Russell, Alfred 1830- *WhAm 1*
Russell, Alfred Pierpont, Jr. 1881- *WhoColR*
Russell, Alys Whitall Pearsall Smith
WomWWA 14
Russell, Annie d1936 *WomWWA 14*
Russell, Annie 1864-1936 *AmBi, DcAmB S2, NatCAB 13, NotAW*
Russell, Annie 1869-1936 *WhAm 1*
Russell, Archibald 1811-1871 *ApCAB*
Russell, Archibald Douglas 1853-1919
NatCAB 41
Russell, Arthur Joseph 1861- *WhAm 4*
Russell, Arthur Perkins 1871-1946 *WhAm 2*
Russell, Benjamin 1761-1845 *AmBi, ApCAB, DcAmB, Drake, TwCBDA, WhAm H*
Russell, Benjamin 1804-1870? *WhAm H*
Russell, Benjamin 1804-1885 *NewYHSD*
Russell, Benjamin 1876-1941 *NatCAB 31*
Russell, Benjamin Edward 1845-1909 *BiDrAC, WhAmP*
Russell, Bertrand Arthur William, Earl 1872-1970 *AsBiEn, DcScB, McGEWB, WhAm 5*
Russell, Bruce Alexander 1903-1963 *WhAm 4*
Russell, Chambers 1713-1767 *ApCAB*
Russell, Charles 1893-1957 *WhAm 3*
Russell, Charles Addison 1852-1902 *BiDrAC, TwCBDA, WhAm 1, WhAmP*
Russell, Charles Augustus 1886-1962
NatCAB 48, WhAm 4
Russell, Charles Edward 1860-1941 *DcAmB S3, McGEWB, WhAm 1*
Russell, Charles Hazen 1845-1912 *NatCAB 25*
Russell, Charles Hinton 1903- *BiDrAC*
Russell, Charles Howland 1851-1921 *ApCAB X, NatCAB 26, WhAm 1*
Russell, Charles Marion 1864-1926 *BnEnAmA, IlBEAAW, McGEWB, REnAW*
Russell, Charles Marion 1865-1926 *WhAm 1*
Russell, Charles Partridge 1883-1953 *WhAm 4*
Russell, Charles Taze 1852-1916 *AmBi, ApCAB X, DcAmB, DcAmReB, McGEWB, NatCAB 12, WebAB, WhAm 1*
Russell, Charles Theodore 1815-1896
NatCAB 11
Russell, Charles Tier 1877-1958 *WhAm 3*
Russell, Charles Wells 1818-1867 *BiDConf*
Russell, Charles Wells 1856-1927 *DcAmB, NatCAB 15, WhAm 1*
Russell, Claude Charles 1873-1934 *NatCAB 25*
Russell, Clinton Warden 1891-1943 *WhAm 2*
Russell, Daniel 1873-1947 *WhAm 2*
Russell, Daniel Lindsay 1845-1908 *BiDrAC, NatCAB 13, TwCBDA, WhAm 1*
Russell, David *NewYHSD*
Russell, David Abel 1780-1861 *ApCAB, BiAUS, BiDrAC, TwCBDA, WhAm H*
Russell, David Allan 1820-1864 *ApCAB*
Russell, David Allen 1820-1864 *AmBi, DcAmB, Drake, NatCAB 4, TwCBDA, WhAm H*
Russell, Donald Stuart 1906- *BiDrAC*
Russell, Doris Aurelia 1902-1962 *WhAm 4*
Russell, Earle Leander 1890-1947 *NatCAB 35*
Russell, Edmund A 1866- *WhAm 4*

Russell, Edward Hamilton 1899-1965
NatCAB 51
Russell, Edward Hutson 1869- *WhAm 5*
Russell, Edward John 1872-1965 *DcScB, DcScB Sup*
Russell, Edward Lafayette 1845-1911
NatCAB 8, WhAm 1
Russell, Edward Percy 1896-1967 *NatCAB 53*
Russell, Edward Perry 1857-1940 *NatCAB 30*
Russell, Edward Wesley 1869-1923 *NatCAB 35*
Russell, Elbert 1871- *WhAm 3*
Russell, Elias Harlow 1836- *WhAm 4*
Russell, Elizabeth Augusta S 1832- *AmWom*
Russell, Emerson Colby 1890-1928 *NatCAB 21*
Russell, Ernest John 1870-1956 *NatCAB 42, WhAm 3*
Russell, Ethel Clinton 1879- *WomWWA 14*
Russell, Faris R 1883-1969 *WhAm 5*
Russell, Florence Ely 1869- *WomWWA 14*
Russell, Francis Thayer 1828-1910 *ApCAB, WhAm 3*
Russell, Francis Wayland 1865- *WhAm 5*
Russell, Frank 1868-1903 *NatCAB 12, WhAm 1*
Russell, Frank Berryman 1890-1958
NatCAB 46
Russell, Frank F 1904-1969 *WhAm 5*
Russell, Frank Greenleaf 1883- *WhoColR*
Russell, Frank Marion 1895-1972 *WhAm 5*
Russell, Frederick Fuller 1870-1960 *WhAm 4*
Russell, George 1837-1924 *WhAm 1*
Russell, George Edmond 1877-1953 *WhAm 3*
Russell, George Harvey 1866- *WhAm 1*
Russell, George Howard 1847-1915 *NatCAB 12*
Russell, George Howard *see also* Russel, George Howard
Russell, George Jeffrey 1878-1948 *NatCAB 36*
Russell, George Louis, Jr. 1896-1947 *WhAm 2*
Russell, Gordon James 1859-1919 *BiDrAC, WhAm 1, WhAmP*
Russell, Grace Lillibridge 1872- *WomWWA 14*
Russell, Green Pinckney 1863- *WhoColR*
Russell, H *NewYHSD*
Russell, H Earle 1889-1971 *WhAm 5*
Russell, Harry Luman 1866-1954 *BiDAmEd, NatCAB 16, NatCAB 43, WhAm 3*
Russell, Harry Newton 1862-1936 *WhAm 1*
Russell, Harvey Clarence 1883- *WhoColR*
Russell, Helen Gertrude 1901-1968 *WhAm 5*
Russell, Helen Victoria Crocker 1896-1966
NatCAB 53, WhAm 4
Russell, Henry 1810?- *ApCAB*
Russell, Henry 1815- *NatCAB 5*
Russell, Henry 1874-1936 *WhAm 2*
Russell, Henry Benajah 1859-1945 *TwCBDA, WhAm 2*
Russell, Henry Chamberlaine 1836-1907 *DcScB, DcScB Sup*
Russell, Henry Dozier 1889-1972 *WhAm 5*
Russell, Henry Moore 1851-1915 *WhAm 1*
Russell, Henry Norris 1877-1957 *ApCAB X, AsBiEn, DcScB, WebAB, WhAm 3*
Russell, Herbert Edwin 1860-1927 *WhAm 1*
Russell, Herman 1878-1956 *WhAm 3*
Russell, Horace 1843-1913 *NatCAB 27, WhAm 1*
Russell, Horace 1889-1973 *WhAm 6*
Russell, Horace Marvin 1846- *NatCAB 14*
Russell, Howard Hyde 1855-1946 *NatCAB 13, WhAm 2*
Russell, Howard Willis 1901-1965 *NatCAB 51*
Russell, Hub Searles 1885-1963 *REnAW*
Russell, Irwin 1853-1879 *DcAmB, NatCAB 4, WhAm H*
Russell, Isaac Franklin 1857-1931 *TwCBDA, WhAm 1*
Russell, Israel Cook 1852-1906 *AmBi, ApCAB, DcAmB, NatCAB 10, TwCBDA, WhAm 1*
Russell, J J d1953 *WhAm 3*
Russell, J Stuart 1892-1960 *WhAm 4*
Russell, James 1640-1709 *ApCAB*
Russell, James Earl 1864-1945 *BiDAmEd, DcAmB S3, TwCBDA, WhAm 2*
Russell, James McPherson 1786-1870 *BiAUS, BiDrAC, WhAm H*
Russell, James Solomon 1857-1935 *AmBi, DcAmB S1, WhAm 1*

Russell, James Townsend 1861-1929
NatCAB 21
Russell, Jane Anne 1911-1967 *WhAm 4*
Russell, Jeremiah 1786-1867 *BiAUS, BiDrAC,
WhAm H*
Russell, John 1772-1842 *BiAUS, BiDrAC,
WhAm H*
Russell, John, Earl 1792-1878 *McGEWB*
Russell, John 1885-1956 *WhAm 3*
Russell, John Andrew 1865- *WhAm 1*
Russell, John Edward 1848-1917 *WhAm 1*
Russell, John Edwards 1834-1903 *BiDrAC,
TwCBDA*
Russell, John Henry 1827-1897 *ApCAB,
DcAmB, NatCAB 5, TwCBDA,
WhAm H*
Russell, John Henry 1872-1947 *NatCAB 39,
WebAMB, WhAm 2*
Russell, John Newton 1864-1941 *NatCAB 30*
Russell, Jonathan 1771-1832 *ApCAB, BiAUS,
BiDrAC, DcAmB, Drake, NatCAB 8,
TwCBDA, WhAm H*
Russell, Joseph *BiAUS, BiDrAC, WhAm H*
Russell, Joseph 1702-1815 *NatCAB 13*
Russell, Joseph 1719-1804 *DcAmB, WhAm H*
Russell, Joseph Ballister 1852-1929 *NatCAB 24,
WhAm 1*
Russell, Joseph Henry 1855- *WhAm 1*
Russell, Joseph Holt 1891-1964 *WhAm 4*
Russell, Joseph James 1854-1922 *BiDrAC,
WhAmP*
Russell, Joseph Shoemaker 1795- *NewYHSD*
Russell, Joshua Edward 1866-1953 *WhAm 3*
Russell, Joshua Edward 1867-1953 *BiDrAC*
Russell, Kenneth Sherman 1907-1974 *WhAm 6*
Russell, L Case 1876- *WhAm 5*
Russell, Lee Maurice 1875-1943 *NatCAB 33,
WhAm 2*
Russell, Leslie W 1840-1903 *BiDrAC*
Russell, Lillian 1861- *NatCAB 4,
WomWWA 14*
Russell, Lillian 1861-1921 *WhAm 1*
Russell, Lillian 1861-1922 *AmBi, DcAmB,
NotAW, WebAB*
Russell, Lillian 1862- *AmWom*
Russell, Lillian Hillyard *WomWWA 14*
Russell, Linus Eli 1848-1917 *NatCAB 16*
Russell, Louis Arthur 1854-1925 *WhAm 1*
Russell, Lydia Smith *NewYHSD*
Russell, Manley Holland 1908-1969 *WhAm 5*
Russell, Margaret Clarke *WomWWA 14*
Russell, Martin James 1845-1900 *NatCAB 10,
WhAm 1*
Russell, Mother Mary Baptist 1829-1898
DcAmB, NotAW, WhAm H
Russell, Melodia Chapman 1863-
WomWWA 14
Russell, Melvin Gray, Jr. 1922-1974 *WhAm 6*
Russell, Morgan 1886-1953 *BnEnAmA*
Russell, Mrs. Moses B 1810?- *NewYHSD*
Russell, Moses B 1810?-1884 *NewYHSD*
Russell, Nelson Gorham 1872-1956 *NatCAB 48*
Russell, Nelson Vance 1895-1951 *WhAm 3*
Russell, Noadiah 1659-1713 *ApCAB*
Russell, Norman Felt Shelton 1880-1954
NatCAB 42, WhAm 3
Russell, Olive Stewart 1885- *WomWWA 14*
Russell, Osborne 1814-1865? *DcAmB,
WhAm H*
Russell, Osborne 1814-1892 *REnAW*
Russell, Pastor *WhAm 1*
Russell, Paul Snowden 1893-1950 *WhAm 2*
Russell, Peter 1755?-1825? *ApCAB*
Russell, Philip Winfred 1877-1941 *NatCAB 32*
Russell, Richard 1612-1674 *ApCAB*
Russell, Richard 1612-1676 *Drake*
Russell, Richard Brevard 1861-1938
NatCAB 37, WhAm 1

Russell, Richard Brevard 1897-1971 *EncAB,
NatCAB 56, WhAm 5, WhAmP*
Russell, Richard Joel 1895-1971 *WhAm 5*
Russell, Richard Manning 1891- *BiDrAC*
Russell, Robert 1925-1965 *WhAm 4*
Russell, Robert Lee 1900-1955 *WhAm 3*
Russell, Robert McWatty 1858-1921
NatCAB 19, WhAm 1
Russell, Robert Watrous 1906-1962 *WhAm 4*

Russell, Sam Morris 1889- *BiDrAC*
Russell, Samuel, Jr. 1873-1935 *NatCAB 34,
WhAm 5*
Russell, Samuel Lyon 1816-1891 *BiAUS,
BiDrAC, WhAm H*
Russell, Scott 1895-1950 *WhAm 3*
Russell, Sol Smith 1848-1902 *AmBi, DcAmB,
NatCAB 10, WhAm 1*
Russell, Stanley Addison 1889-1958 *WhAm 3*
Russell, Stephen S C 1836?- *NewYHSD*
Russell, Talcott Huntington 1847-1917
NatCAB 25, WhAm 1
Russell, Thomas 1758-1801 *NatCAB 8*
Russell, Thomas 1825-1887 *BiAUS,
NatCAB 13*
Russell, Thomas Halbert 1880-1933 *NatCAB 24,
WhAm 1*
Russell, Thomas Henry 1880-1928 *ApCAB X*
Russell, Thomas Herbert 1862- *WhAm 4*
Russell, Thomas Wright 1880- *WhAm 6*
Russell, W C *NewYHSD*
Russell, Walter Bowman 1871-1963 *DcAmReB,
WhAm 4*
Russell, Walter C 1892-1954 *WhAm 3*
Russell, Walter Earle 1869-1948 *WhAm 2*
Russell, Willard Lorane 1898-1974 *WhAm 6*
Russell, William 1690-1761 *ApCAB*
Russell, William 1758-1825 *ApCAB, Drake*
Russell, William 1763-1842 *Drake*
Russell, William 1782-1845 *BiAUS, BiDrAC,
TwCBDA, WhAm H, WhAmP*
Russell, William 1798-1873 *ApCAB,
BiDAmEd, DcAmB, Drake, WhAm H*
Russell, William Augustus 1831-1899 *BiDrAC,
TwCBDA*
Russell, William Delano 1851-1937 *NatCAB 37*
Russell, William Edmonston 1872-1956
NatCAB 47
Russell, William Eustis 1857-1896 *AmBi,
ApCAB Sup, DcAmB, NatCAB 1,
TwCBDA*
Russell, William Eustus 1857-1896 *WhAm H*
Russell, William Felton 1934- *WebAB*
Russell, William Fiero 1812-1896 *BiAUS,
BiDrAC, WhAm H*
Russell, William Fletcher 1890-1956 *BiDAmEd,
WhAm 3*
Russell, William Henry 1802-1873 *DcAmB,
WhAm H*
Russell, William Hepburn 1812-1870
NatCAB 20
Russell, William Hepburn 1812-1872 *DcAmB,
REnAW, WhAm H*
Russell, William Hepburn 1857-1911
NatCAB 15, WhAm 1
Russell, William Logie 1863-1951 *NatCAB 39,
WhAm 3, WhAm 5*
Russell, William Loughlin 1918-1962 *WhAm 4*
Russell, William T 1863-1927 *WhAm 1*
Russell, William Worthington 1859-
NatCAB 15, WhAm 4
Russin, Robert I 1914- *IIBEAAW*
Russo, Joseph Daniel 1893-1957 *NatCAB 48*
Russum, B C 1892-1956 *WhAm 3*
Russum, Carl 1892-1956 *NatCAB 42*
Russum, Sarah Elizabeth 1877- *WhAm 5*
Russwurm, John Brown 1799-1851 *DcAmB,
McGEWB, WebAB, WhAm H*
Rust, Adlai H 1892-1974 *WhAm 6*
Rust, Albert 1818-1870 *BiAUS, BiDConf,
BiDrAC, WhAm H*
Rust, Charles Herbert 1869-1953 *WhAm 3*
Rust, Edgar Carter 1882-1963 *NatCAB 50*
Rust, George Henry 1839-1908 *NatCAB 16*
Rust, Harry Lee, Jr. 1893-1967 *NatCAB 54*
Rust, Henry Bedinger 1872-1936 *NatCAB 46,
WhAm 1*
Rust, John Daniel 1892-1954 *DcAmB S5,
NatCAB 42, WhAm 3*
Rust, John Franklin 1835-1899 *NatCAB 32*
Rust, John Franklin 1882-1938 *NatCAB 29*
Rust, Josephine V 1839- *WomWWA 14*
Rust, Mack Donald 1900-1966 *WhAm 4*
Rust, Marshall 1857-1916 *NatCAB 16*
Rust, Nathaniel Johnson 1833- *NatCAB 3*
Rust, Richard Frederick 1872-1928 *NatCAB 23*
Rust, Richard Sutton 1815-1906 *DcAmB,
NatCAB 4*

Rust, Walter L 1892-1958 *WhAm 3*
Rustad, Elmer Lewis 1908-1975 *WhAm 6*
Ruste, Martha Oline 1872- *WomWWA 14*
Rustgard, John 1863-1950 *NatCAB 39,
WhAm 2*
Rustin, Bayard 1910- *EncAB*
Rustin, Charles Bradley 1836-1900 *NatCAB 18*
Rustin, Henry 1865- *WhAm 4*
Ruston, John Edward 1872-1932 *WhAm 1*
Ruston, William Otis 1852-1922 *WhAm 1*
Rusznyak, Istvan 1889-1974 *WhAm 6*
Rutan, Charles Hercules 1851-1914 *WhAm 1*
Rutan, Harold Duane 1898-1956 *WhAm 3*
Rutan, Thomas Benton 1837-1903 *NatCAB 6*
Ruter, Martin 1785-1838 *ApCAB, DcAmB,
Drake, TwCBDA*
Rutford, Skuli 1897-1968 *NatCAB 55*
Rutgers, Henry 1745-1830 *AmBi, ApCAB,
DcAmB, Drake, NatCAB 3, TwCBDA,
WhAm H*
Ruth, Carl Douglas 1884-1936 *WhAm 1*
Ruth, Earl Baker 1916- *BiDrAC*
Ruth, George Herman 1894-1948 *WhAm 2*
Ruth, George Herman 1895-1948 *DcAmB S4,
EncAB, McGEWB, WebAB*
Ruth, Henry Swartley 1899-1956 *NatCAB 46,
WhAm 3*
Ruth, John A 1918-1972 *WhAm 5*
Ruth, John P 1895-1971 *WhAm 5*
Rutherfoord, John 1792-1865 *NatCAB 5*
Rutherfoord, John 1792-1866 *ApCAB,
TwCBDA*
Rutherfoord, John Coles 1825-1866 *ApCAB*
Rutherfoord, Thomas 1766-1852 *ApCAB*
Rutherfoord, Thomas 1879-1952 *NatCAB 41*
Rutherfoord, Thomas Meldrum 1848-1914
NatCAB 16
Rutherford, Albert Greig 1879-1941 *BiDrAC,
WhAm 1*
Rutherford, Alexander H 1876-1955 *WhAm 3*
Rutherford, Alexander W 1826-1851 *NewYHSD*
Rutherford, Allan 1839- *BiAUS, BiAUS Sup*
Rutherford, Annie O *WomWWA 14*
Rutherford, Arthur Robert 1868-1944
NatCAB 33
Rutherford, Charles Henry 1872-1955
NatCAB 44
Rutherford, Charles Henry, Jr. 1906-1973
WhAm 6
Rutherford, Clarendon 1854-1933 *WhAm 1*
Rutherford, Daniel 1749-1819 *AsBiEn, DcScB*
Rutherford, Ernest, Baron Of Nelson 1871-1937
AsBiEn, DcScB, McGEWB
Rutherford, Forest 1871-1938 *NatCAB 27*
Rutherford, Friend Smith 1820-1864 *ApCAB*
Rutherford, George H 1899-1966 *WhAm 4*
Rutherford, Griffith 1731?-1794? *Drake*
Rutherford, Griffith 1731?-1800? *ApCAB,
TwCBDA, WebAMB*
Rutherford, Harry Kenneth 1883-1964
NatCAB 50
Rutherford, J C *NewYHSD*
Rutherford, J T 1921- *BiDrAC*
Rutherford, Jane Meade *WomWWA 14*
Rutherford, John *BiAUS, NewYHSD*
Rutherford, John 1760-1840 *BiAUS*
Rutherford, John 1869-1947 *NatCAB 35*
Rutherford, John 1895-1965 *WhAm 4*
Rutherford, John *see also* Rutherfurd, John
Rutherford, Joseph Franklin 1869-1942
ApCAB X, DcAmB S3, DcAmReB
Rutherford, Margaret 1892-1972 *WhAm 5*
Rutherford, Mildred Lewis 1851-1928 *NotAW,
TwCBDA, WhAm 1, WomWWA 14*
Rutherford, Mildred Lewis 1852-1928 *AmWom,
NatCAB 10*
Rutherford, Minnie Ursula Oliver 1868- *NotAW,
WomWWA 14*
Rutherford, Paul 1913-1964 *NatCAB 51*
Rutherford, Robert 1728-1803 *BiAUS, BiDrAC,
WhAm H*
Rutherford, Samuel 1870-1932 *BiDrAC,
WhAm 1*
Rutherford, Samuel Morton 1859-1922
WhAm 1
Rutherford, Seymour Suffel 1885-1972
NatCAB 57

Rutherford, William Oliver 1874-1935
NatCAB 26
Rutherford, Williams 1818-1896 *NatCAB 9,*
TwCBDA
Rutherfurd, John 1760-1840 *ApCAB, BiDrAC,*
NatCAB 2, TwCBDA, WhAm H,
WhAmP
Rutherfurd, John *see also* Rutherford, John
Rutherfurd, Lewis Morris 1816-1892 *AmBi,*
ApCAB, DcAmB, DcScB, NatCAB 6,
TwCBDA, WhAm H
Ruthrauff, Florence May Barlow 1865-
WomWWA 14
Ruthrauff, John Mosheim 1846-1902 *TwCBDA,*
WhAm 1
Ruthven, Alexander G 1882-1971 *WhAm 5*
Ruthven, Edwin C *NewYHSD*
Rutimeyer, Karl Ludwig 1825-1895 *DcScB*
Rutkins, Harry Bernard 1903-1962 *NatCAB 47*
Rutland, James Richard 1879-1948 *WhAm 2*
Rutledge, Ann Mays 1813-1835 *NotAW,*
WhAm H
Rutledge, Archibald 1883-1973 *WhAm 6*
Rutledge, Benjamin Huger 1861- *WhAm 4*
Rutledge, Carl P 1894-1952 *WhAm 3*
Rutledge, Edward 1749-1800 *AmBi, ApCAB,*
BiAUS, BiDrAC, DcAmB, Drake,
NatCAB 12, TwCBDA, WhAm H,
WhAmP
Rutledge, Edward 1797-1832 *ApCAB, Drake*
Rutledge, Edward 1797-1836 *TwCBDA*
Rutledge, Francis Huger 1799-1866 *ApCAB,*
Drake, NatCAB 13, TwCBDA
Rutledge, George Perry 1869-1947 *WhAm 2*
Rutledge, Hugh d1811 *Drake*
Rutledge, Hugh 1740?-1811 *NatCAB 5,*
NatCAB 13
Rutledge, Hugh 1741?-1811 *ApCAB*
Rutledge, John 1739-1800 *AmBi, ApCAB,*
BiAUS, BiDrAC, DcAmB, Drake,
McGEWB, NatCAB 1, TwCBDA,
WebAB, WhAm H, WhAmP
Rutledge, John, Jr. 1766-1819 *ApCAB,*
BiDrAC, TwCBDA, WhAm H, WhAmP
Rutledge, Thomas G 1917-1963 *WhAm 4*
Rutledge, Wiley Blount 1894-1949 *DcAmB S4,*
NatCAB 38, WebAB, WhAm 2
Rutman, Darrett 1929- *EncAAH*
Rutt, Christian Louis 1859-1936 *WhAm 1*
Ruttenber, Edward Manning 1824-1907 *ApCAB*
Ruttenber, Edward Manning 1825-1907
WhAm 1
Rutter, Frank Roy 1874-1926 *WhAm 1*
Rutter, George *NewYHSD*
Rutter, Henley Chapman 1849-1910 *WhAm 1*
Rutter, J Wood 1883-1957 *NatCAB 47*
Rutter, James H 1836-1885 *NatCAB 1*
Rutter, Josiah Baldwin 1892-1951 *WhAm 3*
Rutter, Robert Lewis 1867-1948 *ApCAB X,*
NatCAB 37, WhAm 4
Rutter, Thomas 1824-1895 *NatCAB 7*
Rutz, Anthony Alexander 1874-1928 *ApCAB X*
Rutzler, John Enoch, Jr. 1903-1960 *NatCAB 47*
Ruud, Edwin 1854-1932 *NatCAB 24*
Ruud, Martin Bronn 1885-1941 *WhAm 1*
Ruutz-Rees, C 1865-1954 *WomWWA 14*
Ruutz-Rees, Caroline 1865-1954 *BiCAW,*
WhAm 3
Ruutz-Rees, Janet Emily Meugens 1842-1924
BiCAW, NatCAB 20, WomWWA 14
Ruwe, Edgar Clement 1891-1957 *NatCAB 42*
Ruxton, George Frederick Augustus 1820-1848
ApCAB, Drake
Ruxton, William Vernon Chickering 1891-1959
NatCAB 43
Ruyl, Beatrice Baxter 1879- *WhAm 6,*
WomWWA 14
Ruyle, John Bryan 1896-1952 *WhAm 3*
Ruysbroeck, Jan Van 1293-1381 *McGEWB*
Ruysch, Frederik 1638-1731 *BiHiMed, DcScB*
Ruyter, Michiel Adriaanzoon De 1607-1676
WhoMilH
Ruz, Joaquin 1772-1850 *ApCAB*
Ruzicka, Charles 1896-1952 *WhAm 3*
Ruzicka, Leopold 1887- *AsBiEn*
Ruzicka, Rudolph Frank 1883-1966 *NatCAB 52*
Ryall, D B 1798-1864 *BiAUS*
Ryall, Daniel Bailey 1798-1864 *BiDrAC,*

WhAm H
Ryals, Thomas Edward 1863-1943 *WhAm 2*
Ryan, Abraham Hall 1837-1903 *NatCAB 5*
Ryan, Abram Joseph 1838-1886 *DcAmB,*
WhAm H
Ryan, Abram Joseph 1839-1886 *ApCAB,*
NatCAB 5, TwCBDA
Ryan, Andrew Warren 1902-1960 *NatCAB 51*
Ryan, Archie Lowell 1881- *WhAm 6*
Ryan, Arthur 1884-1972 *WhAm 5*
Ryan, Arthur Clayton 1879-1927 *DcAmB*
Ryan, Bertha Parker 1870- *WomWWA 14*
Ryan, C D 1895-1947 *WhAm 2*
Ryan, Clendenin J 1905-1957 *WhAm 3*
Ryan, Coletta 1876- *WomWWA 14*
Ryan, Cornelius Edward 1896-1972 *WhAm 5*
Ryan, Cornelius John 1920-1974 *WhAm 6*
Ryan, Daniel Alphonsus 1873-1933 *NatCAB 24*
Ryan, Daniel Joseph 1855-1923 *NatCAB 19,*
WhAm 1
Ryan, Dennis d1786 *WhAm H*
Ryan, Edward Francis 1878-1956 *WhAm 3*
Ryan, Edward George 1810-1880 *ApCAB,*
DcAmB, NatCAB 12, TwCBDA,
WhAm H
Ryan, Edward William 1884-1923 *WhAm 1*
Ryan, Elmer James 1907-1958 *BiDrAC,*
WhAm 3, WhAmP
Ryan, Emmons Blackburn 1832-1919
NatCAB 19
Ryan, Evelyn Althea Murphy 1869-1951
WhAm 3
Ryan, Francis Joseph 1916-1963 *WhAm 4*
Ryan, Frank Xavier 1872-1916 *NatCAB 17*
Ryan, Franklin Winton d1957 *WhAm 3*
Ryan, Frederick Behrens 1883-1955 *WhAm 3*
Ryan, George Joseph 1872-1949 *WhAm 2*
Ryan, George Parker 1842-1877 *ApCAB*
Ryan, Harold Martin 1911- *BiDrAC*
Ryan, Harris Joseph 1866-1924 *WhAm 1*
Ryan, Harris Joseph 1866-1934 *DcAmB S1,*
NatCAB 28
Ryan, Henry 1775-1832 *ApCAB Sup*
Ryan, Ida Annah *WomWWA 14*
Ryan, James 1848-1923 *ApCAB, NatCAB 12,*
TwCBDA, WhAm 1, WhAm 3
Ryan, James Augustine 1867-1956 *WhAm 3*
Ryan, James Hugh 1886-1947 *NatCAB 35*
Ryan, James Hugh 1886-1948 *WhAm 2*
Ryan, James L *NewYHSD*
Ryan, James Wilfrid 1858-1907 *BiDrAC,*
WhAm 4
Ryan, John *NewYHSD*
Ryan, John 1810-1861 *NatCAB 4, TwCBDA*
Ryan, John Augustine 1869-1945 *DcAmB S3,*
DcAmReB, EncAB, NatCAB 39,
WhAm 2
Ryan, John D 1864-1933 *WhAm 1*
Ryan, John Dale 1915- *WebAMB*
Ryan, John Denis 1864-1933 *AmBi,*
NatCAB 23
Ryan, John Dennis 1864-1933 *DcAmB,*
REnAW
Ryan, John Harold 1885-1961 *WhAm 4*
Ryan, John J, Jr. 1901-1963 *WhAm 4*
Ryan, John Thomas 1884-1941 *NatCAB 30*
Ryan, John William 1919-1970 *WhAm 5*
Ryan, Joseph Bernard 1891-1964 *NatCAB 51*
Ryan, Lewis Cook 1891-1961 *WhAm 4*
Ryan, Marah Ellis 1860-1934 *AmWom,*
WhAm 4, WomWWA 14
Ryan, Marah Ellis 1866-1934 *WhAm 1*
Ryan, Martin Francis 1874-1935 *WhAm 1*
Ryan, Matthew Joseph 1864-1927 *NatCAB 22*
Ryan, Maurice Orton 1899-1962 *NatCAB 50*
Ryan, Michael 1845- *NatCAB 12*
Ryan, Michael J 1862-1943 *WhAm 2*
Ryan, Michael Sylvester 1875-1931 *WhAm 1*
Ryan, O'Neill 1860-1939 *NatCAB 36,*
WhAm 1
Ryan, Patrick John 1831-1911 *ApCAB,*
DcAmB, NatCAB 6, TwCBDA,
WhAm 1
Ryan, Patrick John 1908- *WhAm 4*
Ryan, Patrick L 1876- *WhAm 5*
Ryan, Raymond Richard 1884-1934 *WhAm 1*
Ryan, Robert 1913-1973 *WhAm 5*
Ryan, Stanley Martin 1898-1957 *WhAm 3*

Ryan, Stephen Vincent 1825-1896 *ApCAB,*
DcAmB, NatCAB 12, TwCBDA,
WhAm H
Ryan, Thomas 1827-1903 *NatCAB 10,*
TwCBDA
Ryan, Thomas 1837-1914 *BiDrAC,*
NatCAB 12, TwCBDA, WhAm 1,
WhAmP
Ryan, Thomas Curran 1841-1911 *WhAm 1*
Ryan, Thomas Fortune 1851-1928 *DcAmB,*
EncAB, WebAB, WhAm 1
Ryan, Thomas Francis 1872- *NatCAB 16*
Ryan, Thomas Jefferson 1890-1968 *BiDrAC*
Ryan, Timothy Alphonsus 1889-1945
NatCAB 34
Ryan, Timothy Edward 1859-1911 *WhAm 1*
Ryan, Tom 1922- *IIBEAAW*
Ryan, Vincent J 1884-1951 *WhAm 3*
Ryan, Walter D'Arcy 1870-1934 *DcAmB,*
NatCAB 26
Ryan, Will Carson, Jr. 1885-1968 *BiDAmEd,*
WhAm 5
Ryan, William 1840-1925 *BiDrAC*
Ryan, William 1851-1920 *WhAm 1*
Ryan, William Albert Charles 1843-1873
ApCAB
Ryan, William Andrew 1900-1953 *NatCAB 43*
Ryan, William Fitts 1922-1972 *BiDrAC,*
WhAm 5
Ryan, William Henry 1860-1939 *BiDrAC,*
TwCBDA, WhAm 1, WhAmP
Ryan, William King 1827-1895 *ApCAB X*
Ryan, William Patrick 1895- *WhAm 1*
Ryan, William Redmond *ApCAB, NewYHSD*
Ryan, William Thomas 1839- *ApCAB*
Ryan, William Thomas 1882-1939 *WhAm 1*
Rybalko, Pavel 1894-1948 *WhWW-II*
Rybeck, William Howard 1894-1973
NatCAB 57
Ryberg, Eric William 1884-1951 *NatCAB 41*
Ryberg, William Enoch 1892-1950 *NatCAB 41*
Rybner, Cornelius Martin 1855-1929
NatCAB 25
Rybner, Martin Cornelius 1853-1929 *DcAmB,*
WhAm 1
Ryburn, Frank M 1884-1964 *WhAm 4*
Ryckman, Charles Silcott 1898-1966 *WhAm 4*
Ryckmans, Pierre 1891-1959 *WhAm 3*
Rydberg, Johannes Robert 1854-1919 *DcScB*
Rydberg, Per Axel 1860-1931 *AmBi, DcAmB,*
NatCAB 26, WhAm 1
Ryden, George Herbert 1884-1941 *WhAm 1*
Ryder, Albert Pinkham 1847-1917 *AmBi,*
ApCAB, DcAmB, EncAB,
IIBEAAW, McGEWB, WebAB, WhAm 1
Ryder, Albert Pynkham 1847-1917 *NatCAB 10*
Ryder, Arthur Hilton 1875-1944 *WhAm 2*
Ryder, Arthur William 1877-1938 *WhAm 1*
Ryder, Charles Jackson 1848-1917 *NatCAB 12,*
WhAm 1
Ryder, Charles Wolcott 1892-1960 *WhAm 4*
Ryder, Chauncey Foster 1868-1949 *WhAm 2*
Ryder, Edgar Lee 1860-1936 *NatCAB 30*
Ryder, Frederick Milliachip 1862-1939
WhAm 1
Ryder, George Hope 1872-1946 *WhAm 2*
Ryder, Harry Osborne 1880- *WhAm 1*
Ryder, J F *NewYHSD*
Ryder, James 1800-1860 *ApCAB, Drake,*
TwCBDA
Ryder, Jeannette Ford 1866- *WomWWA 14*
Ryder, John Adam 1852-1895 *NatCAB 16*
Ryder, Oscar Baxter 1885-1972 *WhAm 5*
Ryder, Platt Powell 1821-1896 *ApCAB,*
NatCAB 11, NewYHSD, TwCBDA
Ryder, Robert Oliver 1875-1936 *WhAm 1*
Ryder, Thomas Philander 1836-1887 *WhAm H*
Ryder, William Henry 1822-1888 *ApCAB*
Ryder, William Henry 1842-1918 *NatCAB 10,*
WhAm 1
Ryder, Worth Allen 1884-1960 *NatCAB 50*
Ryding, Herbert Charles 1863-1946 *NatCAB 52*
Rydstrom, Arthur Gordon 1905-1976 *WhAm 6*
Rydz-Smigly, Edward 1886-1943 *WhWW-II*
Ryer, Fletcher Ferris 1862-1911 *NatCAB 17*
Ryerson, Adolphus Egerton 1803-1882 *ApCAB,*
Drake, McGEWB
Ryerson, Arthur 1851-1912 *NatCAB 30*

Ryerson, Caroline Hutchinson 1859-
 WomWWA 14
Ryerson, Edward Larned 1854-1928
 NatCAB 21, WhAm 1
Ryerson, Edward Larned 1886-1971 *WhAm 5*
Ryerson, Edwin Warner 1872-1961 *NatCAB 45,*
 WhAm 4
Ryerson, John 1800-1878 *ApCAB*
Ryerson, Joseph Turner 1880-1947 *WhAm 2*
Ryerson, Luther L *NewYHSD*
Ryerson, Martin 1815-1875 *BiAUS*
Ryerson, Martin 1818-1887 *ApCAB*
Ryerson, Martin Antoine 1856-1932 *DcAmB,*
 WhAm 1
Ryerson, William Newton 1874- *WhAm 5*
Rygel, John 1888-1955 *WhAm 3*
Rygg, Andrew Nilsen 1868-1951 *WhAm 3*
Rygh, George Taylor 1860- *WhAm 4*
Ryken, Theodore James 1797-1871 *WhAm H*
Rykens, Paul 1888-1965 *WhAm 4*
Ryker, Edward *NewYHSD*
Rykert, Annie M *WomWWA 14*
Rylance, Joseph Hine 1826-1907 *ApCAB,*
 WhAm 1
Ryland, Cally *WomWWA 14*
Ryland, Charles Hill 1836- *TwCBDA*
Ryland, Edward 1880- *WhAm 6*
Ryland, Isaac Palmer 1861-1940 *NatCAB 40*
Ryland, James Fleet 1875-1951 *NatCAB 40*
Ryland, John Peter 1911-1973 *WhAm 6*
Ryland, Joseph R 1863-1928 *WhAm 1*
Ryland, Mark *NewYHSD*
Ryland, Robert 1805-1899 *ApCAB, DcAmB,*
 NatCAB 11, TwCBDA, WhAm H
Ryland, Robert Knickerbocker 1894-1964
 NatCAB 51
Ryland, Robert Knight 1873-1951 *NatCAB 40,*
 WhAm 3
Ryland, William Semple 1836-1906 *NatCAB 27,*
 TwCBDA, WhAm 1
Ryle, Gilbert 1900- *McGEWB*
Ryle, John 1817-1887 *ApCAB*
Ryle, John Francis 1882-1958 *NatCAB 43*
Ryle, Thomas J 1894-1954 *NatCAB 43*
Ryle, William Thornicroft 1858-1898
 ApCAB Sup
Rylee, William Jackson 1905-1961 *WhAm 4*
Ryman, James H T 1855-1926 *WhAm 1*
Rymer, S Bradford 1879-1959 *NatCAB 52*
Rynd, Francis 1801-1861 *BiHiMed*
Rynders, Isaiah *NatCAB 3*
Rynearson, Edward 1867-1932 *WhAm 1*
Rynning, Ole 1809-1838 *DcAmB, WhAm H*
Ryon, Elijah William 1883-1922 *NatCAB 6*
Ryon, Harrison 1892-1970 *WhAm 5*
Ryon, John Lesley 1894-1961 *NatCAB 49*
Ryon, John Walker 1825-1901 *BiDrAC*
Ryon, Walter Gohring 1874-1925 *ApCAB X*
Ryons, Joseph Leslie 1902-1961 *WhAm 4*
Ryors, Alfred 1812-1858 *NatCAB 4,*
 TwCBDA
Rys, C F W 1877-1946 *WhAm 2*
Rys, Carl Frederick Wilhelm 1877-1946
 NatCAB 40
Ryter, Joseph Francis 1914- *BiDrAC*
Ryttenberg, Isabelle Levy 1849- *WomWWA 14*
Ryus, Celeste Nellis 1877- *WhAm 5*

S

Sa, Estacio De 1530?-1567 *ApCAB*
Sa, Mem De 1504-1572 *McGEWB*
Sa, Salvador Correa De 1594-1688 *ApCAB*
Sa, Simao Pereira De 1701-1769? *ApCAB*
Saadia Ben Joseph Al-Fayumi 882-942
  McGEWB
Saal, Irving Randolph 1879- *WhAm 6*
Saalfield, Ada Louise 1865- *WhAm 5*
Saalfield, Adah Louise Sutton 1865-
  WomWWA 14
Saalfield, Albert George 1886-1959 *WhAm 3*
Saalfield, Robert Sutton 1894-1963 *NatCAB 50*
Saar, Louis Victor Franz 1868-1937
  NatCAB 37, WhAm 1
Saarinen, Aline Bernstein 1914-1972 *WhAm 5*
Saarinen, Eero 1910-1961 *BnEnAmA,*
  McGEWB, WebAB, WhAm 4
Saarinen, Eliel 1873-1950 *BnEnAmA,*
  McGEWB, WebAB, WhAm 3
Saarinen, Gottlieb Eliel 1873-1950 *DcAmB S4*
Saavedra, Cornelio 1760-1829 *ApCAB*
Saavedra, Hernando Arias De 1556-1625?
  ApCAB
Saavedra, Juan De d1554 *ApCAB*
Saavedra Guzman, Antonio 1550?-1620 *ApCAB*
Saavedra Lamas, Carlos 1878-1959 *McGEWB*
Sabacher, George William, Jr. 1919-1973
  WhAm 5
Sabath, Adolph Joachim 1866-1952 *BiDrAC,*
  DcAmB S5, WhAm 3, WhAmP
Sabatier, Armand 1834-1910 *DcScB*
Sabatier, Paul 1854-1941 *AsBiEn, DcScB,*
  McGEWB
Sabatini, Rafael 1875-1950 *WhAm 2*
Sabato, Ernesto 1911- *McGEWB*
Sabbatai Zevi 1626-1676 *McGEWB*
Sabean, Bernard Stowe 1881-1957 *NatCAB 46*
Saben, Mowry 1870-1950 *WhAm 3*
Sabichi, Frank 1842-1900 *NatCAB 43*
Sabin, Albert Bruce 1906- *AsBiEn, WebAB*
Sabin, Alvah 1793-1885 *BiAUS, BiDrAC,*
  WhAm H, WhAmP
Sabin, Alvah Horton 1851-1940 *NatCAB 41,*
  WhAm 1
Sabin, Charles Hamilton 1868-1933 *ApCAB X,*
  DcAmB, NatCAB 16, WhAm 1
Sabin, Dwight May 1843-1902 *BiDrAC,*
  NatCAB 2, TwCBDA, WhAmP
Sabin, Dwight May 1844-1902 *ApCAB*
Sabin, Dwight May 1845-1902 *WhAm 1*
Sabin, Edwin Legrand 1870- *WhAm 5*
Sabin, Elbridge Hosmer 1865-1934 *WhAm 1*
Sabin, Elijah Robinson 1776-1818 *ApCAB,*
  NatCAB 6
Sabin, Ella Clara 1850-1949 *AmWom*
Sabin, Ellen Clara 1850-1949 *BiDAmEd,*
  NotAW, WhAm 2, WomWWA 14
Sabin, Florence Rena 1871-1953 *BiDAmEd,*
  BiHiMed, DcAmB S5, DcScB,
  NatCAB 40, WhAm 3, WomWWA 14
Sabin, Frances Ellis 1870-1943 *WhAm 2*
Sabin, Georgia Minerva Judd *WomWWA 14*
Sabin, Henry 1829-1918 *WhAm 1*
Sabin, John I 1847-1902 *NatCAB 21*
Sabin, Joseph 1821-1881 *AmBi, ApCAB,*
  DcAmB, DcAmLiB, Drake, NatCAB 6,
  WhAm H
Sabin, Lorenzo 1803-1877 *ApCAB*
Sabin, Louis Carlton 1867-1950 *NatCAB 45,*
  WhAm 3
Sabin, Wallace Arthur 1869- *WhAm 1*
Sabine, Sir Edward 1788-1883 *ApCAB, DcScB*
Sabine, George Holland 1880-1961 *WhAm 4*
Sabine, George Krans, Jr. 1889-1919 *ApCAB X*

Sabine, James 1774-1845 *TwCBDA*
Sabine, Jane Downes Kelly *WomWWA 14*
Sabine, Lorenzo 1803-1877 *BiAUS, BiDrAC,*
  DcAmB, Drake, NatCAB 5, TwCBDA,
  WhAm H
Sabine, Paul Earls 1879-1958 *DcScB*
Sabine, Wallace Clement Ware 1868-1919
  AsBiEn, DcAmB, DcScB, NatCAB 15,
  NatCAB 27, WhAm 1, WhAm 2
Sabine, William Tufnell 1838-1913 *NatCAB 15,*
  WhAm 1
Sabo, Betty 1928- *IIBEAAW*
Sabouraud, Raymond 1864-1938 *BiHiMed*
Sacagawea d1812? *AmBi*
Sacagawea 1787?-1812? *DcAmB, WebAB,*
  WhAm H
Sacagawea 1790?-1812? *REnAW*
Sacajawea *AmBi*
Sacajawea 1786?-1812? *NotAW*
Sacajawea 1788?-1824? *NatCAB 13*
Saccheri, Girolamo 1667-1733 *DcScB*
Sacco, Luigi 1769-1836 *DcScB*
Sacco, Nicola 1891-1927 *AmBi, DcAmB,*
  McGEWB, WebAB, WhAm 4
Sacco And Vanzetti *McGEWB*
Sachar, Abram Leon 1899- *BiDAmEd*
Sacheverell, John *NewYHSD*
Sachs, Alexander 1893-1973 *WhAm 6*
Sachs, Bernard *NewYHSD*
Sachs, Bernard 1858-1943 *WhAm 2*
Sachs, Bernard 1858-1944 *DcAmB S3,*
  NatCAB 34, WhAm 2C
Sachs, Carl 1893-1962 *NatCAB 49*
Sachs, Curt 1881-1959 *WebAB, WhAm 3*
Sachs, Ernest 1879-1958 *NatCAB 48,*
  WhAm 3
Sachs, Frederick *NewYHSD*
Sachs, George 1896-1960 *NatCAB 49*
Sachs, Hanns 1881-1947 *DcAmB S4*
Sachs, Hans 1494-1576 *McGEWB*
Sachs, Howard Joseph 1891-1969 *WhAm 5*
Sachs, James Henry 1907-1971 *NatCAB 57,*
  WhAm 5
Sachs, Joseph 1870-1946 *NatCAB 35,*
  WhAm 2
Sachs, Julius 1849-1934 *BiDAmEd, DcAmB,*
  NatCAB 13, WhAm 1
Sachs, Julius Von 1832-1897 *AsBiEn, DcScB*
Sachs, Lambert *NewYHSD*
Sachs, Morris Bernard 1896-1957 *NatCAB 48,*
  WhAm 3
Sachs, Nathan Irwin 1891-1928 *ApCAB X*
Sachs, Nelly 1891-1970 *McGEWB, WhAm 5*
Sachs, Paul Joseph 1878-1965 *WhAm 4*
Sachs, Samuel 1851-1935 *NatCAB 35*
Sachs, Teviah 1902-1959 *WhAm 3*
Sachs, Theodore Bernard 1868-1916 *DcAmB*
Sachse, August *NewYHSD*
Sachse, Edward 1804-1873 *NewYHSD*
Sachse, Helena V 1875- *WhAm 5*
Sachse, John Henry David *NewYHSD*
Sachse, Julius Friedrich 1842-1919 *DcAmB,*
  NatCAB 25, WhAm 1
Sachse, Richard 1881- *WhAm 3*
Sachse, Theodore 1815?- *NewYHSD*
Sachse, William *NewYHSD*
Sachsse, Dorothea Kotzschmar *WomWWA 14*
Sack, Alexander Naoum 1890-1955 *WhAm 3*
Sack, Henri S 1903-1972 *WhAm 5*
Sack, Leo R 1889-1956 *NatCAB 42, WhAm 3*
Sacket, Delos Bennet 1822-1885 *ApCAB,*
  Drake, TwCBDA
Sackett, Arthur Johnson 1884-1975 *WhAm 6*
Sackett, Augustine 1841-1914 *NatCAB 16*

Sackett, Carl Leroy 1876- *WhAm 5*
Sackett, Clara Elizabeth *WomWWA 14*
Sackett, Earl L 1897-1970 *WhAm 5*
Sackett, Esther *NewYHSD*
Sackett, Frederic Moseley 1840-1913
  NatCAB 17
Sackett, Frederic Moseley 1868-1941
  NatCAB 37, WhAm 1
Sackett, Frederic Mosely 1868-1941 *BiDrAC,*
  WhAmP
Sackett, Henry Woodward 1853-1929 *DcAmB,*
  NatCAB 7, WhAm 1
Sackett, Margaret Ferguson 1882-
  WomWWA 14
Sackett, Robert Lemuel 1867-1946 *WhAm 2*
Sackett, Samuel Jefferson 1882-1967 *WhAm 4*
Sackett, Sheldon F 1902-1968 *WhAm 5*
Sackett, Walter George 1880- *WhAm 6*
Sackett, William A 1811-1895 *BiAUS*
Sackett, William August 1811-1895 *WhAm H*
Sackett, William Augustus 1811-1895 *BiDrAC*
Sackett, William Augustus 1812-1895 *ApCAB*
Sackett, William Edgar 1848-1926 *WhAm 1*
Sacks, Emanuel 1902-1958 *NatCAB 43*
Sacks, Emanuel 1904-1958 *WhAm 3*
Sacks, Leon 1902- *BiDrAC*
Sacks, William 1874-1937 *NatCAB 27*
Sackville, Lord *WhAm H*
Sackville-West, Lionel 1827-1908 *WhAm HA,*
  WhAm 4
Sackville-West, Victoria 1892-1962 *WhAm 4*
Saco, Jose Antonio 1797-1879 *ApCAB*
Sacrobosco, Johannes De d1256? *DcScB*
Sadacca, Henri 1894-1969 *WhAm 5*
Sadafi, Al- *DcScB*
Sadd, Henry S *NewYHSD*
Sadd, Walter Allen 1863- *WhAm 5*
Sade, Donatien A Francois, Comte De 1740-1814
  McGEWB
Sadi, Shaikh Muslih-Al-Din 1184?-1291
  McGEWB
Sadlak, Antoni Nicholas 1908-1969 *BiDrAC,*
  WhAm 5
Sadleir, Michael 1888- *WhAm 3*
Sadler, E J 1879-1947 *WhAm 2*
Sadler, Frank Howard 1880- *WhAm 6*
Sadler, Herbert Charles 1872-1948 *WhAm 2*
Sadler, Hilda Ridley 1881- *WomWWA 14*
Sadler, Lena Kellogg 1875-1939 *WhAm 1*
Sadler, Lewis Lamont 1843- *NatCAB 14*
Sadler, McGruder Ellis 1896-1966 *NatCAB 53,*
  WhAm 4
Sadler, Raymond Farrell, II 1920-1965
  NatCAB 51
Sadler, Reinhold 1848-1906 *NatCAB 11,*
  TwCBDA, WhAm 1
Sadler, Rufus 1816?- *NewYHSD*
Sadler, Rupert 1816?- *NewYHSD*
Sadler, Sylvester Baker 1876-1931 *WhAm 1*
Sadler, Thomas William 1831-1896 *BiDrAC,*
  WhAm H
Sadler, Walter Clifford 1891-1959 *NatCAB 47*
Sadler, Wilbur Fisk 1840-1916 *WhAm 1*
Sadler, William Paul 1895-1961 *NatCAB 49*
Sadler, William Samuel 1875-1969 *NatCAB 54*
Sadlier, Anna Theresa 1854- *ApCAB,*
  WomWWA 14
Sadlier, Denis 1817-1885 *DcAmB, WhAm H*
Sadlier, Mary Anne Madden 1820-1903 *ApCAB,*
  DcAmB, Drake, NotAW
Sadow, Leonard Bernard 1914- *WhAm 6*
Sadowski, George Gregory 1903-1961 *BiDrAC,*
  WhAm 4, WhAmP
Sadtler, Benjamin 1823-1901 *ApCAB,*

781

NatCAB 5, TwCBDA
Sadtler, Delia Cromwell Banks *WomWWA 14*
Sadtler, Helena V Sachse 1875- *WomWWA 14*
Sadtler, John Philip Benjamin 1823-1901
DcAmB
Sadtler, John Phillip Benjamin 1823-1901
WhAm H
Sadtler, Philip Bridges 1884-1964 *NatCAB 49*
Sadtler, Samuel Philip 1847-1923 *AmBi,*
ApCAB, DcAmB, NatCAB 5, TwCBDA,
WhAm 1
Sadwin, Sherwood Herbert 1921-1964
NatCAB 51
Saenderl, Simon 1800-1879 *DcAmB, WhAm H*
Saenger, Oscar 1868-1929 *NatCAB 14,*
WhAm 1
Saenz, Manuel *NewYHSD*
Saenz, Pena Luis 1824- *ApCAB Sup*
Saerchinger, Cesar 1884-1971 *WhAm 5*
Safanie, Murray D 1899-1968 *WhAm 4*
Safay, Fred A 1898-1952 *WhAm 3*
Saffin, William *WhAm HA, WhAm 4*
Saffold, Reuben 1788-1847 *ApCAB, BiAUS,*
Drake, NatCAB 4, TwCBDA
Saffold, William Berney 1867-1941 *NatCAB 37,*
WhAm 2
Safford, Agnes Mabel d1932 *WhAm 1*
Safford, Anne Williston 1869- *WomWWA 14*
Safford, Anson Peacely-Killen 1830-1891
BiDAmEd
Safford, Gertrude Sunderland 1873-
WomWWA 14
Safford, Harry Robinson 1875-1943
NatCAB 32, WhAm 2
Safford, James Merrill 1822-1907 *ApCAB,*
DcAmB, NatCAB 8, TwCBDA,
WhAm 1
Safford, Mary Augusta 1851- *NatCAB 14,*
WhAm 4, WomWWA 14
Safford, Mary Jane 1834-1891 *AmWom,*
NotAW
Safford, Mary Joanna *WomWWA 14*
Safford, Truman Henry 1836-1901 *AmBi,*
ApCAB, DcAmB, Drake, NatCAB 13,
TwCBDA, WhAm 1
Safford, William Edwin 1859-1926 *DcAmB,*
NatCAB 20, WhAm 1
Safford, William Harrison 1821- *ApCAB,*
Drake
Sagan, Carl 1934- *AsBiEn*
Sagard-Theodat, Gabriel *ApCAB*
Sagaz, Angel 1913-1975 *WhAm 6*
Sage, Adoniram Judson 1836- *NatCAB 13*
Sage, Agnes Carolyn 1854- *WhAm 4,*
WomWWA 14
Sage, Balthazar-Georges 1740-1824 *DcScB*
Sage, Bernard Janin 1821-1902 *DcAmB,*
WhAm H
Sage, Charles Gurdon 1895-1967 *WhAm 4*
Sage, Charles H 1891-1972 *WhAm 6*
Sage, Cornelia Bentley *WomWWA 14*
Sage, Dean 1841-1902 *NatCAB 32*
Sage, Dean 1875-1943 *NatCAB 32, WhAm 2*
Sage, Eben Charles 1855-1927 *NatCAB 21,*
WhAm 1
Sage, Ebenezer 1755-1834 *BiAUS, BiDrAC,*
WhAm H
Sage, Evan Taylor 1881-1936 *WhAm 1*
Sage, Florence Eleanor 1858- *AmWom*
Sage, Gardner Avery 1813-1882 *ApCAB*
Sage, Henry Manning 1868-1933 *NatCAB 25*
Sage, Henry Williams 1814-1897 *AmBi,*
ApCAB, DcAmB, NatCAB 4, TwCBDA,
WhAm H
Sage, Henry Williams 1872-1938 *NatCAB 32*
Sage, John Charles 1866-1919 *NatCAB 25,*
WhAm 1
Sage, John Davis 1877-1928 *WhAm 1*
Sage, John Hall 1847-1925 *NatCAB 20,*
NatCAB 21, WhAm 1
Sage, Josephine Bentley *WomWWA 14*
Sage, Kay 1898-1963 *WhAm 4*
Sage, Letitia *NewYHSD*
Sage, Margaret Olivia Slocum 1828-1918 *AmBi,*
DcAmB, NatCAB 16, NotAW, WebAB,
WomWWA 14
Sage, Russell 1816-1906 *AmBi, ApCAB,*
BiAUS, BiDrAC, DcAmB, NatCAB 10,

TwCBDA, WebAB, WhAm 1
Sage, Mrs. Russell 1828-1918 *NotAW,*
WhAm 1
Sage, William 1864- *TwCBDA, WhAm 4*
Sage, William Evans 1859-1913 *NatCAB 16*
Sage, William Hampden 1859-1922 *WhAm 1*
Sage, William Henry 1844-1924 *NatCAB 32*
Sage, William Henry 1852-1942 *NatCAB 38*
Sagean, Mathieu 1655?-1710? *ApCAB*
Sagebeer, Joseph Evans 1861-1940 *WhAm 1*
Sageman, Hattie Vera Bacon *WomWWA 14*
Sagendorph, George 1879- *ApCAB X*
Sagendorph, Kent 1902-1958 *WhAm 3*
Sagendorph, Robb Hansell 1900-1970
NatCAB 55, WhAm 5
Sager, Abram 1810-1877 *ApCAB*
Sager, Clarence Lane 1891-1955 *NatCAB 41*
Sager, Edward Anton 1872-1943 *WhAm 2*
Sager, Frederick Whitney 1869-1919
NatCAB 17
Sager, George Josiah 1840-1914 *NatCAB 26*
Sager, Hiram Norton 1859-1924 *NatCAB 20*
Sager, Joseph *NewYHSD*
Sager, Washington Budd 1881-1950
NatCAB 39
Sagnac, Georges M M 1869-1928 *DcScB*
Sagner, Stanley 1907-1964 *NatCAB 52*
Sagoyewatha *WebAB*
Sagoyewatha 1750?-1830 *NatCAB 13*
Sagoyewatha 1758?-1830 *AmBi*
Sagra, Ramon DeLa 1798-1871 *ApCAB*
Sague, James Edward 1862-1930 *NatCAB 26,*
WhAm 4
Saha, Meghnad 1893-1956 *WhAm 4*
Saha, Meghnad 1894-1956 *DcScB*
Sahagun, Bernardino De d1590 *ApCAB, Drake*
Sahler, Charles Oliver 1854-1917 *WhAm 1*
Sahler, Daniel DuBois 1829-1882 *ApCAB X,*
NatCAB 16
Sahler, Helen Gertrude 1877-1950 *BiCAW,*
NatCAB 39, WhAm 3
Sahlgren, G F Joran 1884-1971 *WhAm 5*
Sahlin, Henry 1893-1956 *NatCAB 42*
Saicho 767-822 *McGEWB*
Said, Maraghai Mohammad d1973 *WhAm 6*
Said, Seyyid 1790-1856 *McGEWB*
Saidla, Leo Erval Alexandre 1889-1961
WhAm 4
Saigh, Ibn Al- *DcScB*
Saigo, Takamori 1827-1877 *McGEWB*
Sailer, Joseph 1867-1928 *WhAm 1*
Sailer, William Augustus 1861-1937
NatCAB 28
Sailly, Peter 1754-1826 *BiAUS, BiDrAC,*
WhAm H
Sainsbury, William Charles 1882-1956 *WhAm 3*
Saint, Harry Young 1873- *WhAm 6*
Saint, Lawrence 1885-1961 *WhAm 4*
Saint, Percy 1870- *WhAm 5*
St. Alary, E *NewYHSD*
St. Ange, Louis DeBellerive 1698?-1774
WhAm H
St. Ange DeBellerive, Louis 1698?-1774 *DcAmB*
Saint Armand, Dreux *NewYHSD*
Saint-Arnaud, Armand Jacques Leroy De
1801-1854 *WhoMilH*
Saint-Aulaire, Felix A DeB, Marquis De 1801-
NewYHSD
Saint-Aulaire, Felix Achille 1801- *WhAm H*
Saint Castin, Jean V DeL'A, Baron De 1650-1712
ApCAB
St. Clair, Arthur 1734-1818 *ApCAB, BiAUS,*
BiDrAC, BiDrUSE, Drake, NatCAB 1,
TwCBDA
St. Clair, Arthur 1736-1818 *AmBi, DcAmB,*
McGEWB, REnAW, WebAB, WebAMB
St. Clair, Arthur 1737-1818 *WhAm H*
St. Clair, Byron Wagner 1892-1946 *NatCAB 36*
St. Clair, George Arthur 1848-1926 *NatCAB 41*
St. Clair, Harry Hull 1879-1953 *NatCAB 40*
St. Clair, Leonard Pressley 1870-1960 *WhAm 4*
St. Clair, Margaret Ann 1868- *WomWWA 14*
St. Clair, William Henry 1877-1943 *NatCAB 33*
St. Clair-Moss, Luella W 1865- *WhAm 4*
St. Come, John Francis Buisson De 1658?-1707
ApCAB
Saint-Cosme, Jean Francois Buisson De
1658?-1707 *WhAm H*

St. Cyr, John Alexander 1890-1966 *WhAm 4*
St. Cyr, John Mary Irenus 1804-1883 *ApCAB*
St. Denis, Louis Juchereau De 1676-1744
DcAmB, WhAm H
Saint-Denis, Michel Jacques 1897-1971
WhAm 5
St. Denis, Ruth 1877-1968 *WebAB*
St. Denis, Ruth 1878?-1968 *McGEWB*
St. Denis, Ruth 1879-1968 *WhAm 5*
Saint-Exupery, Antoine De 1900-1944
McGEWB
St. Gaudens, Annetta Johnson 1869-
WomWWA 14
Saint-Gaudens, Augustus 1848-1907 *AmBi,*
ApCAB, ApCAB X, BnEnAmA, DcAmB,
EncAB, McGEWB, NatCAB 1,
NatCAB 8, TwCBDA, WebAB, WhAm 1
Saint-Gaudens, Homer Schiff 1880-1958
NatCAB 48, WhAm 3
Saint Gaudens, Louis 1854-1913 *ApCAB,*
WhAm 1
St. George, Katharine Price Collier 1896-
BiDrAC, WhAmP
St. George, Sir Thomas Bligh 1765?-1837
ApCAB
St. George, William Sterne 1852- *WhAm 4*
St. Germain, Fernand Joseph 1928- *BiDrAC*
Saint Ges *NewYHSD*
Saint Hilaire, A F C Prouvencal De 1799-1853
ApCAB, DcScB
St. Husson, Sieur De *WhAm H*
St. John *NewYHSD*
St. John, Benjamin Pennington 1898-1968
NatCAB 54
St. John, Charles 1818-1891 *BiAUS, BiDrAC,*
WhAm H
St. John, Charles Edward 1857-1935 *DcAmB S1,*
DcScB, NatCAB 26, WhAm 1
St. John, Charles Elliott 1856-1916 *TwCBDA,*
WhAm 1
St. John, Charles Griffin 1873- *WhAm 5*
St. John, Charles J 1862- *WhAm 4*
St. John, Cynthia Morgan 1852-1919 *AmWom,*
WhAm 1, WomWWA 14
St. John, Daniel Bennett 1808-1890 *BiAUS,*
BiDrAC, WhAm H
St. John, Edward Porter 1866- *WhAm 4*
St. John, Emma Celestia Brownell
WomWWA 14
St. John, Everitte 1844-1908 *WhAm 1*
St. John, Fordyce Barker 1884-1973 *WhAm 6*
St. John, Francis Regis 1908-1971 *DcAmLiB,*
WhAm 5
St. John, Gamaliel Cyrus 1848-1933
NatCAB 24
St. John, George Clair 1877-1966 *NatCAB 53,*
WhAm 4
St. John, Guy Bascom 1878- *WhAm 6*
St. John, Harry Mark 1888-1965 *NatCAB 52*
St. John, Henry 1783-1869 *BiAUS, BiDrAC,*
WhAm H
St. John, Howell W 1834- *NatCAB 12,*
NatCAB 13
St. John, Isaac Munroe 1827-1880 *ApCAB,*
BiDConf, DcAmB, TwCBDA, WhAm H
St. John, J Hector *WebAB, WhAm H*
St. John, John Pierce 1833-1916 *AmBi, ApCAB,*
DcAmB, NatCAB 8, TwCBDA,
WhAm 1
St. John, John Price 1833-1916 *WhAm HA,*
WhAm 4
St. John, Martha Everett *WomWWA 14*
St. John, Robert Lester 1884-1939 *NatCAB 29*
St. John, Samuel Benedict 1845-1909 *WhAm 1*
St. John, Susan Hely 1833-1913 *NewYHSD*
St. John, Theodore Raymond 1880-1958
WhAm 3
St. John, Thomas Raymond 1911-1970
WhAm 5
St. John, William Pope 1849-1897 *NatCAB 2*
Saint-Just, Louis Antoine Leon De 1767-1794
McGEWB
St. Just, Luc Letelliere De 1820-1881 *ApCAB*
St. Laurent, Louis Stephen 1882-1973 *McGEWB,*
WhAm 5
St. Lausson, Simon Francois Daumont d1674
WhAm H
St. Leger, Barry 1737-1789 *AmBi, ApCAB,*

Drake, *WhAm H*

St. Lewis, Roy 1891-1969 *WhAm 5*

St. Luc, LaCorne De 1712-1784 *ApCAB*

St. Lusson, Simon F Daumont, Sieur De d1674
ApCAB, DcAmB

St. Martin, Alexis 1804-1887 *AmBi*

St. Martin, Louis 1820-1893 *BiAUS, BiDrAC,*
WhAm H

Saint Maur, Kate Vandenhoff 1869-
WomWWA 14

Saint-Memin, Charles B Julien Fevret De
1770-1844 *NatCAB 18*

Saint-Memin, Charles B Julien Fevret De
1770-1852 *ApCAB, DcAmB, IlBEAAW,*
NewYHSD, WhAm H

Saint-Mery, Moreau De 1750-1819 *AmBi,*
DcAmB

St. Onge, William Leon 1914-1970 *BiDrAC,*
WhAm 5

St. Ours, Charles Louis Roch 1753-1834 *ApCAB*

St. Ours, Francis Xavier 1714?-1759 *ApCAB*

St. Ours, Jean Baptiste De 1668-1747 *ApCAB*

Saint-Palais, Jacques Maurice Landes De
1811-1875 *WhAm H*

St. Palais, James M DeL D'Aussac De 1811-1877
ApCAB, NatCAB 12, TwCBDA

Saint-Pierre, Charles I Castel, Abbe De
1658-1743 *McGEWB*

Saint Pierre, Legardeur Jacques De 1698-1755
ApCAB

St. Real, Joseph Remi Vallieres De 1787-1847
ApCAB

Saint Remy, Madame De *NewYHSD*

Saint-Saens, Charles Camille 1835-1921
McGEWB

Saint-Simon, Claude Anne, Duke De 1740-1819
ApCAB Sup

Saint Simon, Claude Anne, Marquis De
1743-1819 *Drake*

Saint-Simon, Claude DeRouvroy, Comte De
1760-1825 *McGEWB*

Saint Simon, Claude Henri, Count De 1760-1825
ApCAB

Saint-Simon, Louis DeRouvroy, Duc De
1675-1755 *McGEWB*

St. Sure, Adolphus Frederic 1869-1949
WhAm 2

Saint Vallier, Jean Baptist DeL C De 1653-1727
ApCAB, Drake

Saint-Venant, Adhemar Jean Claude B De
1797-1886 *DcScB*

St. Victor, Hugh Of *DcScB*

Saint Victor, Jacques B M, Count De 1770-1858
ApCAB

Saint Vincent, Gregorius 1584-1667 *DcScB*

St. Vincent, John Jervis 1735-1823 *WhoMilH*

St. Vrain, Ceran DeHault DeLassus De
1802-1870 *DcAmB, REnAW, WebAB,*
WhAm H

Sainte-Beuve, Charles Augustin 1804-1869
McGEWB

Sainte-Claire Deville, Charles 1814-1876
ApCAB

Sainte-Claire Deville, Henri Etienne 1818-1881
AsBiEn

Sainte-Claire Deville, Henri Etienne 1818-1883
ApCAB

Sainte-Croix, Gaetan X G DePascalis 1708-1762
ApCAB

Sainte-Croix, Louis M P E DeRenouard De 1809-
ApCAB

Sainte-Mesme, Marquis De *DcScB*

Saintin, Jules Emile 1829-1894 *ApCAB,*
IlBEAAW, NewYHSD

Saionji, Kimmochi 1849-1940 *McGEWB*

Sait, Edward McChesney 1881-1943
NatCAB 33, WhAm 2

Saito, Hirosi 1886-1939 *WhAm 1*

Saito, Yoshitsugu *WhWW-II*

Sajous, Charles Eucharist DeMedicis 1852-1929
NatCAB 9

Sajous, Charles Euchariste 1852-1929 *ApCAB*

Sajous, Charles Euchariste De'Medici 1852-1929
WhAm 1

Sajous, Charles Euchariste DeMedicis 1852-1929
DcAmB

Sakel, Manfred Joshua 1900-1957 *WhAm 3*

Sakharov, Vladimir Vladimirovich 1902-1969
DcScB

Sakolski, Aaron Morton 1880-1955 *NatCAB 46,*
WhAm 3

Saks, Horace Andrew 1882-1925 *NatCAB 20*

Saks, Ira 1893-1966 *NatCAB 51*

Saks, Stanislaw 1897-1942 *DcScB*

Sala, Angelo 1576-1637 *DcScB*

Sala, Antoine 1897-1973 *WhAm 6*

Sala, George Augustus Henry 1828- *ApCAB*

Sala, J Roland 1907-1963 *NatCAB 49*

Salaberry, Charles M D'Irumberry De 1778-1829
ApCAB

Salaberry, Charles Michel, D'Iramberry
1778-1829 *Drake*

Saladin 1138-1193 *McGEWB*

Salant, Aaron Bennett 1878-1967 *NatCAB 54*

Salant, William 1870- *WhAm 5*

Salant, William Aaron 1916-1966 *NatCAB 52*

Salas, Mariano 1797-1867 *ApCAB*

Salas, Rafael Sabastian 1862-1921 *NatCAB 6*

Salaverry, Felipe Santiago De 1806-1836
ApCAB

Salazar, Antonio 1889-1972 *WhWW-II*

Salazar, Antonio DeOliveira 1889-1970
McGEWB

Salazar, Diego De d1521 *ApCAB*

Salazar, Francisco *NewYHSD*

Salazar, Jose De *NewYHSD*

Salazar, Jose Maria 1785-1828 *ApCAB*

Salazar, Ontonio DeOliveira 1880-1970
WhAm 5

Salazar, Ruben 1928-1970 *WhAm 5*

Salazar Argumedo, Carlos 1863- *WhAm 5*

Salazar DeEspinosa, Juan De d1566? *ApCAB*

Salb, John Paul 1855-1925 *NatCAB 44*

Salcedo, Francisco 1550?- *ApCAB*

Saldanha, Joao Carlos Oliveira, Duke De
1791-1876 *ApCAB*

Sale, Charles Partlow 1885-1936 *WhAm 1*

Sale, George 1856- *WhAm 1*

Sale, John Burress 1818-1876 *BiDConf*

Sale, John Wesley 1840-1913 *NatCAB 16*

Sale, Samuel 1854-1937 *WhAm 1*

Salem, Hermann R 1892-1966 *WhAm 4*

Salerno, George Fred 1909-1970 *WhAm 5*

Salerno, Vito Lorenzo 1915-1971 *WhAm 5*

Sales, Francis 1771-1854 *ApCAB, NatCAB 5*

Sales, Grover Grauman 1887-1967 *NatCAB 53*

Sales, Mrs. Harry Nathan *WomWWA 14*

Sales, Murray W 1865-1951 *WhAm 3*

Sales Laterriere, Mark Pascal 1792- *ApCAB*

Sales Laterriere, Peter De 1789-1834 *ApCAB*

Salesky, Bernard Leonard 1903-1963 *WhAm 4*

Saliba, Michel Moses 1875-1944 *NatCAB 33*

Saliers, Earl Adolphus 1884-1952 *WhAm 3*

Salinas, Pedro 1891-1951 *WhAm 3*

Salinas, Porfirio 1910- *IlBEAAW*

Salinas Y Cordoba, Buenaventura De d1653
ApCAB

Salinger, Benjamin I 1861-1931 *WhAm 1*

Salinger, Harry 1883-1951 *WhAm 3*

Salinger, Jerome David 1919- *EncAB, WebAB*

Salinger, Pierre Emil George 1925- *BiDrAC*

Salisbury, Albert 1843-1911 *BiDAmEd,*
DcAmB, NatCAB 11, WhAm 1

Salisbury, Bert Eugene 1870-1946 *NatCAB 35*

Salisbury, C B *NewYHSD*

Salisbury, Cornelius 1882-1970 *IlBEAAW*

Salisbury, Edward Elbridge 1814-1901 *ApCAB,*
DcAmB, NatCAB 11, TwCBDA,
WhAm H

Salisbury, Evelyn 1823- *ApCAB*

Salisbury, George Robert 1855- *WhAm 4*

Salisbury, Gertrude Franklin 1858-
WomWWA 14

Salisbury, James Henry 1823-1905 *ApCAB,*
DcAmB, NatCAB 8, WhAm 1

Salisbury, Lucius Albert 1882-1970 *NatCAB 55,*
NatCAB 56

Salisbury, Morse 1898-1962 *WhAm 4*

Salisbury, Paul 1903?-1973 *IlBEAAW*

Salisbury, Robert Cecil, Marquess Of 1830-1903
McGEWB

Salisbury, Rollin Daniel 1858-1922 *DcAmB,*
DcScB, WhAm 1

Salisbury, Rollin Daniel 1859-1922 *NatCAB 11*

Salisbury, Ronnie *WomWWA 14*

Salisbury, Rosine Howard 1887-1975 *IlBEAAW*

Salisbury, Stanton W 1891-1966 *WhAm 4*

Salisbury, Stephen 1835- *NatCAB 7*

Salisbury, Stuart McFarland 1885- *WhAm 3*

Salisbury, Sylvester d1680? *ApCAB*

Salisbury, Winifred 1880- *WomWWA 14*

Salit, Norman 1896-1960 *WhAm 4*

Salk, Jonas Edward 1914- *AsBiEn, McGEWB,*
WebAB

Salkeld, Howard Bernard 1880-1966
NatCAB 53

Salkey, J Sydney 1888-1954 *NatCAB 48*

Sallee, Webster Irby 1882-1938 *NatCAB 27*

Salley, Alexander Samuel, Jr. 1871- *TwCBDA,*
WhAm 4

Salley, Nathaniel Moss 1876- *WhAm 5*

Salley, William Henry 1867- *WhoColR*

Sallmon, William Henry 1866-1938 *TwCBDA,*
WhAm 1

Sallness, Fritchof Theodore 1900-1966
NatCAB 51

Sallo, Denys De 1626-1669 *DcScB*

Sallust 086BC-035?BC *McGEWB*

Salm-Salm, Prince 1828-1870 *WhAm H*

Salm-Salm, Princess 1840-1912 *WhAm HA,*
WhAm 4

Salm Salm, Agnes 1842-1881? *ApCAB*

Salm-Salm, Princess Agnes E Leclercq Joy
1840-1912 *DcAmB, TwCBDA*

Salm Salm, Agnes Joy, Princess Zu 1840-1912
ApCAB X

Salm Salm, Prince Felix 1828-1870 *ApCAB*

Salm Salm, Felix, Prince Zu 1828-1870
ApCAB X

Salm-Salm, Prince Felix J N M 1828-1870
NatCAB 11

Salmaggi, Alfredo 1886-1975 *WhAm 6*

Salmanowitz, Jules Moses 1887-1968
NatCAB 54

Salmans, Levi Brimner 1855- *WhAm 4*

Salmon, Alvah Glover 1868- *WhAm 4*

Salmon, Daniel Elmer 1850-1914 *DcAmB,*
EncAAH, WhAm 1

Salmon, David Alden 1879- *WhAm 6*

Salmon, Edwin Ashley 1902-1965 *WhAm 4*

Salmon, George 1819-1904 *DcScB*

Salmon, J *NewYHSD*

Salmon, Joshua S 1846-1902 *BiDrAC,*
WhAm 1

Salmon, Lucy Maynard 1853-1927 *DcAmB,*
NotAW, WhAm 1, WomWWA 14

Salmon, Robert 1775?-1842? *NewYHSD*

Salmon, Robert 1775?-1844? *BnEnAmA*

Salmon, Thomas William 1876-1927 *DcAmB,*
NatCAB 21, WhAm 1

Salmon, Udall Julius 1904-1963 *NatCAB 50,*
WhAm 4

Salmon, William Charles 1868-1925 *BiDrAC,*
WhAm 1

Salmon, Wilmer Wesley 1866-1936 *NatCAB 25,*
WhAm 1

Salnave, Silvain 1832-1870 *Drake*

Salnave, Sylvain 1832-1870 *ApCAB*

Salomon, Edward 1828- *TwCBDA*

Salomon, Edward 1830- *NatCAB 12*

Salomon, Erich 1886-1944 *WhAm 4*

Salomon, Fred Z d1961 *WhAm 4*

Salomon, Frederick 1826-1897 *ApCAB, Drake,*
TwCBDA

Salomon, Haym 1740?-1785 *AmBi, ApCAB,*
DcAmB, NatCAB 11, WebAB, WhAm H,
WhAmP

Salomon, Hayne 1740?-1785 *Drake*

Salomon, Henry 1879-1943 *NatCAB 32*

Salomon, Henry, Jr. 1917-1958 *NatCAB 46*

Salomon, Herbert 1883-1951 *WhAm 3*

Salomon, Louis Etienne Felicite 1820-1888
ApCAB Sup

Salomon, William 1823?- *NewYHSD*

Salomonsen, Carl Julius 1847-1924 *DcScB*

Saloutos, Theodore 1910- *EncAAH*

Salpeter, Harry 1895-1967 *WhAm 5*

Salpeter, High 1911-1969 *WhAm 5*

Salpointe, Jean Baptist 1825-1898 *ApCAB,*
NatCAB 12, TwCBDA

Salpointe, Jean Baptiste 1825-1898 *REnAW*

Salpointe, John Baptist 1825-1898 *WhAm H*

Salsburg, Zevi Walter 1928-1970 *WhAm 5*

Salsbury, Joseph Edward 1887-1967
  NatCAB 53
Salsbury, Lant King 1867-1938 *WhAm 1*
Salsbury, Nathan 1846-1902 *NatCAB 8*
Salsgiver, Paul L 1907-1954 *WhAm 3*
Salsich, LeRoy 1879-1957 *WhAm 3*
Salt, Albert Lincoln 1865-1945 *NatCAB 34,
  WhAm 2*
Salten, Felix 1869-1945 *WhAm 2*
Salter, Ann Elizabeth *NewYHSD*
Salter, John Cleveland 1873-1950 *NatCAB 42*
Salter, John Thomas 1898-1973 *WhAm 6*
Salter, Leslie Earnest 1895-1964 *WhAm 4*
Salter, Lewis Spencer 1891-1965 *WhAm 4*
Salter, Mary Turner 1856-1938 *WhAm 1,
  WomWWA 14*
Salter, Moses Buckingham 1841- *NatCAB 4,
  TwCBDA, WhAm 4*
Salter, Richard 1723-1787 *Drake, NatCAB 11*
Salter, Richard 1723-1789 *ApCAB*
Salter, Richard Gene 1926- *WhAm 5*
Salter, Robert Mundhenk 1892-1955
  NatCAB 45, WhAm 3
Salter, Sumner 1856-1944 *WhAm 2*
Salter, Wilbur Mitchell 1881-1964 *NatCAB 51*
Salter, William 1821-1910 *DcAmB,
  NatCAB 13, WhAm 1*
Salter, William Dayton 1794-1869 *ApCAB,
  Drake, TwCBDA*
Salter, William Mackintire 1853-1931 *DcAmB,
  NatCAB 24, WhAm 1*
Salter, William Thomas 1901-1952 *WhAm 3*
Salterlee, Samuel K 1818- *NatCAB 3*
Saltonstall, Dudley 1738-1796 *ApCAB,
  DcAmB, Drake, NatCAB 7, TwCBDA,
  WebAMB, WhAm H*
Saltonstall, Gurdon 1666-1724 *AmBi, ApCAB,
  DcAmB, Drake, NatCAB 1, TwCBDA,
  WhAm H*
Saltonstall, Gurdon 1708-1785 *ApCAB, Drake*
Saltonstall, Leverett 1754-1782 *ApCAB*
Saltonstall, Leverett 1781-1845 *BiAUS*
Saltonstall, Leverett 1783-1845 *ApCAB,
  BiDrAC, Drake, TwCBDA, WhAm H*
Saltonstall, Leverett 1825- *ApCAB*
Saltonstall, Leverett 1892- *BiDrAC, WhAmP*
Saltonstall, Nathaniel 1639-1707 *ApCAB,
  NatCAB 5*
Saltonstall, Nathaniel 1746-1815 *ApCAB*
Saltonstall, Nathaniel 1903-1971 *WhAm 5*
Saltonstall, Sir Richard 1586-1658? *AmBi,
  ApCAB, Drake*
Saltonstall, Richard 1610-1694 *ApCAB,
  DcAmB, WhAm H*
Saltonstall, Richard 1703-1756 *ApCAB,
  BiAUS, Drake*
Saltonstall, Richard 1732-1785 *ApCAB*
Saltonstall, William Wanton 1793-1862 *ApCAB*
Saltus, Edgar Evertson 1855-1921 *DcAmB,
  NatCAB 19*
Saltus, Edgar Evertson 1858-1921 *AmBi,
  ApCAB, NatCAB 7, TwCBDA, WhAm 1*
Saltus, Evelyn Noyes 1871- *WomWWA 14*
Saltus, Francis Saltus 1850-1889 *NatCAB 6*
Saltus, Rollin Sanford 1869-1934 *NatCAB 29*
Saltzgaber, Gaylord Miller 1846-1930
  NatCAB 28, WhAm 1
Saltzman, Charles McKinley 1871-1942
  NatCAB 33, WhAm 2
Saltzman, Joel 1915-1967 *WhAm 4*
Saltzmann, John C *NewYHSD*
Salvage, Sir Samuel Agar 1876-1946
  NatCAB 35, WhAm 2
Salvant, Robert Milton 1889-1958 *WhAm 3*
Salvatierra, Juan Maria De 1648-1717 *ApCAB,
  WhAm H*
Salvatore, Victor 1884-1965 *WhAm 4*
Salvatorelli, Luigi 1886-1974 *WhAm 6*
Salvemini, Gaetano 1873-1957 *McGEWB,
  WhAm 3*
Salvert, Perier Du 1690?- *ApCAB*
Salvert, Perrier Du 1690?- *Drake*
Salviani, Ippolito 1514-1572 *DcScB*
Salvignac, Jean *NewYHSD*
Salvini, Tommaso 1830- *ApCAB*
Salway, William *NatCAB 16*
Salzedo, Carlos 1885-1961 *NatCAB 45,
  WhAm 4*

Salzer, Benjamin Franklin 1867-1915
  NatCAB 16
Salzman, Carl Conrad 1901-1964 *NatCAB 50*
Salzman, Joseph 1819-1874 *ApCAB,
  WhAm H*
Sam, Tiresias Agustin Simon 1834-
  ApCAB Sup
Samalman, Alexander 1904-1956 *WhAm 3*
Samans, Walter 1882-1968 *NatCAB 54*
Samaras, Lucas 1936- *BnEnAmA*
Samaroff, Olga 1882-1948 *BiDAmEd,
  DcAmB S4, NotAW, WhAm 2*
Samarqandi, Najib Al-Din Abu Hamid, Al-
  d1222 *DcScB*
Samarqandi, Shams Al-Din Muhammad, Al-
  DcScB
Samawal, Ibn Yahya Al-Maghribi, Al- d1180?
  DcScB
Samberg, Harry Hyman 1904-1972 *NatCAB 57*
Sames, Albert Morris 1873-1958 *WhAm 3*
Samfield, Max 1844-1915 *WhAm 1*
Samford, Frank Park 1893-1973 *WhAm 6*
Samford, John A 1905-1968 *WhAm 5*
Samford, Thomas Drake 1868-1947 *WhAm 2*
Samford, William Hodges 1866-1940
  NatCAB 31, WhAm 1
Samford, William James 1844-1901 *BiDrAC,
  NatCAB 19, TwCBDA*
Saminsky, Lazare 1882-1959 *NatCAB 44,
  WhAm 3*
Sammann, Detlef 1857- *NatCAB 10*
Sammarco, G Mario 1873- *WhAm 5*
Sammartino, Peter 1904- *BiDAmEd*
Sammet, G Victor 1880-1958 *WhAm 3*
Sammis, Arthur Maxwell 1911-1970 *WhAm 5*
Sammis, Donald Stuart 1889-1968 *NatCAB 57*
Sammis, Frances Hobbs Drake *WomWWA 14*
Sammis, Russel Fleet 1876-1957 *NatCAB 46*
Sammond, Frederic 1895-1966 *WhAm 4*
Sammond, Herbert Stavely 1871-1963 *WhAm 4,
  WhAm 5*
Sammons, F Elmer 1888-1959 *WhAm 3*
Sammons, Hume Leon 1871-1942 *NatCAB 35*
Sammons, Thomas 1762-1838 *BiAUS, BiDrAC,
  WhAm H*
Sammons, Thomas 1863-1935 *WhAm 1*
Sammons, Wheeler 1889-1956 *WhAm 3*
Sammons, William Henry 1861-1944 *WhAm 2*
Samoset 1590?-1653? *ApCAB, WebAB*
Samouri, Claude *NewYHSD*
Samoylov, Aleksandr Filippovich 1867-1930
  DcScB
Sampey, John Richard 1863-1946 *NatCAB 36,
  WhAm 2*
Sampey, John Richard, Jr. 1896-1967 *WhAm 5*
Sample, John Glen 1891-1971 *WhAm 5*
Sample, John Thomas 1883-1968 *NatCAB 54*
Sample, Paul Lindsay 1897-1953 *WhAm 3*
Sample, Paul Starrett 1896-1974 *IIBEAAW,
  WhAm 6*
Sample, Robert Fleming 1829-1905 *ApCAB,
  TwCBDA, WhAm 1*
Sample, Samuel Caldwell 1796-1855 *BiAUS,
  BiDrAC, WhAm H*
Sample, Samuel Williamson 1855- *WhAm 4*
Sample, William Devore 1929-1971 *WhAm 6*
Sample, William Dodge 1898-1946 *WhAm 2*
Sample, William Roderick 1866- *WhAm 4*
Sampsell, Marshall Emmett 1874- *WhAm 5*
Sampsell, Marshall Grosscup 1904-1973
  WhAm 6
Sampson, Alden 1853-1925 *WhAm 1*
Sampson, Archibald J 1839-1921 *NatCAB 3,
  TwCBDA, WhAm 1*
Sampson, Arthur William 1884-1967
  NatCAB 53
Sampson, Charles Bradford 1868-1940
  NatCAB 32
Sampson, Clark Hamilton 1850-1904
  NatCAB 12, NatCAB 16
Sampson, Deborah 1760-1827 *AmBi, ApCAB,
  Drake, NatCAB 8, NotAW, WebAMB*
Sampson, Emma Speed 1868-1947 *NatCAB 37,
  WhAm 2*
Sampson, Ezekiel Silas 1831-1892 *BiAUS,
  BiDrAC, WhAm H*
Sampson, Ezra 1749-1823 *ApCAB, Drake*
Sampson, Flemon Davis 1873-1967 *WhAm 4*

Sampson, Francis Asbury 1842-1918 *WhAm 1*
Sampson, Francis Smith 1814-1854 *ApCAB,
  Drake*
Sampson, George Arthur 1881-1966
  NatCAB 52
Sampson, Henry Ellis 1879-1944 *WhAm 2*
Sampson, Henry Thomas 1907-1967 *WhAm 4*
Sampson, Homer Lazelle 1880-1945
  NatCAB 34
Sampson, John *NewYHSD*
Sampson, John Albertson 1873-1946 *WhAm 2*
Sampson, John Patterson 1837- *ApCAB,
  NatCAB 4, WhoColR*
Sampson, John Patterson 1839- *TwCBDA*
Sampson, John Pattrson 1837- *WhAm 4*
Sampson, Martin Wright 1866-1930 *DcAmB,
  NatCAB 28, WhAm 1*
Sampson, Oscar Hallet 1829-1904 *ApCAB X*
Sampson, Ralph Allen 1866-1939 *DcScB*
Sampson, Thornton Rogers 1852-1915 *TwCBDA,
  WhAm 1*
Sampson, William 1763-1836 *Drake*
Sampson, William 1764-1836 *ApCAB, DcAmB,
  WhAm H*
Sampson, William 1818-1866 *NatCAB 12*
Sampson, William 1859-1922 *NatCAB 20*
Sampson, William Emmett 1886-1959
  NatCAB 47
Sampson, William Harkness 1808-1892
  TwCBDA
Sampson, William James, Jr. 1896-1969
  WhAm 5
Sampson, William Thomas 1840-1902 *AmBi,
  ApCAB, ApCAB Sup, ApCAB X,
  DcAmB, NatCAB 9, TwCBDA,
  WebAMB, WhAm 1*
Sampson, Zabdiel 1781-1828 *BiAUS, BiDrAC,
  WhAm H*
Sampter, Jessie Ethel 1883-1938 *NotAW*
Sams, Earl Corder 1884-1950 *NatCAB 39,
  WhAm 3*
Sams, Howard Waldemar 1897-1974 *WhAm 6*
Sams, James Hagood, Jr. 1903-1970 *WhAm 5*
Sams, Oliver Newton 1862-1932 *WhAm 1*
Sams, Robert Shields 1905-1969 *WhAm 5*
Samson, George Clement 1848-1922 *WhAm 1*
Samson, George Whitefield 1819-1896 *ApCAB,
  Drake, NatCAB 3, WhAm H*
Samson, George Whitfield 1819-1896 *TwCBDA*
Samson, Simeon 1736-1789 *ApCAB Sup*
Samson, William Holland 1860-1917 *WhAm 1*
Samsonov, Alexander Vasilievich 1859-1914
  WhoMilH
Samudragupta *McGEWB*
Samuel 1056?BC-1004BC *McGEWB*
Samuel, Bernard 1880-1954 *WhAm 3*
Samuel, Bunford 1857-1949 *WhAm 2*
Samuel, E Roger 1889-1967 *NatCAB 54*
Samuel, Edmund William 1857-1930 *BiDrAC,
  WhAm 1*
Samuel, Elizabeth Ida *WomWWA 14*
Samuel, Green B 1794-1859 *BiAUS*
Samuel, Henry Paul 1886-1938 *WhAm 1*
Samuel, Herbert 1870-1963 *WhAm 4*
Samuel, Mary Alexander *WomWWA 14*
Samuel, Maurice 1895-1972 *WhAm 5*
Samuel, Ralph E 1892-1967 *WhAm 4*
Samuel, Webster Marshall 1834-1905
  NatCAB 8
Samuel, William M G 1815-1902 *IIBEAAW*
Samuels, Adelaide Florence 1845- *ApCAB*
Samuels, Arthur Hiram 1888-1938 *WhAm 1*
Samuels, Benjamin 1878-1961 *WhAm 4*
Samuels, Bernard 1876-1959 *NatCAB 49*
Samuels, Clifford Elroy 1919-1973 *NatCAB 57*
Samuels, Edward Augustus 1836-1908 *ApCAB,
  DcAmB, TwCBDA, WhAm 1*
Samuels, Green Berry 1806-1859 *BiDrAC,
  WhAm H*
Samuels, Maurice Victor 1873-1945 *WhAm 2*
Samuels, Morton 1870-1941 *NatCAB 38*
Samuels, Samuel 1823-1908 *DcAmB, WhAm 1*
Samuels, Samuel 1825-1908 *ApCAB,
  NatCAB 1*
Samuels, Saul Simon 1895-1961 *NatCAB 48*
Samuels, Susan Blagge Caldwell 1848- *ApCAB*
Samuels, W G M *NewYHSD*
Samuelson, Agnes d1963 *WhAm 4*

Samuelson, Paul Anthony 1915- *EncAB, McGEWB, WebAB*
Samy, Mahmoud 1881-1936 *WhAm 1*
Samyn *NewYHSD*
San Buenaventura, Gabriel De *ApCAB*
San Carlos, Jose Miguel, Duke De 1771-1828 *ApCAB*
San Martin, Jose De 1778-1850 *ApCAB, Drake, WhoMilH*
San Martin, Tomas De 1482-1554 *ApCAB*
San Roman, Miguel De 1802-1863 *ApCAB, Drake*
San Souci, Emery John 1857-1936 *WhAm 1*
Sanarelli, Giuseppe 1864-1940 *DcScB*
Sanborn, Alvan Francis 1866- *WhAm 4*
Sanborn, Andrew Eliason 1857-1918 *NatCAB 23*
Sanborn, Arthur Loomis 1850-1920 *WhAm 1*
Sanborn, Benjamin H 1851-1926 *WhAm 1*
Sanborn, Charles Henry 1821- *WhAm 3*
Sanborn, Charles Henry 1822- *ApCAB*
Sanborn, Clarence Herbert 1868-1927 *NatCAB 21*
Sanborn, Edwin David 1808-1885 *ApCAB, DcAmB, NatCAB 9, TwCBDA, WhAm H*
Sanborn, Elwin Roswell d1947 *WhAm 2*
Sanborn, Franklin Benjamin 1831-1917 *AmBi, ApCAB, DcAmB, NatCAB 8, TwCBDA, WhAm 1*
Sanborn, Frederic Rockwell 1899-1973 *WhAm 6*
Sanborn, Gertrude Stillman 1876- *WomWWA 14*
Sanborn, Helen Josephine 1857-1917 *WhAm 1, WomWWA 14*
Sanborn, Henry Nichols 1879-1926 *WhAm 1*
Sanborn, Herbert Charles 1873-1967 *WhAm 4*
Sanborn, John Albert 1901-1966 *WhAm 4*
Sanborn, John Bell 1876-1933 *WhAm 1*
Sanborn, John Benjamin 1826-1904 *AmBi, ApCAB, NatCAB 5, TwCBDA, WhAm 1*
Sanborn, John Benjamin 1883-1964 *NatCAB 51*
Sanborn, John Carfield 1885-1968 *BiDrAC, WhAm 5*
Sanborn, John Pitts d1941 *WhAm 1*
Sanborn, John Sewell 1819-1877 *ApCAB*
Sanborn, Joseph Brown 1855-1934 *WhAm 1*
Sanborn, Kate *AmWom*
Sanborn, Katharine Abbott 1839-1917 *ApCAB, NatCAB 9*
Sanborn, Katherine Abbott 1839-1917 *DcAmB, TwCBDA, WhAm 1, WomWWA 14*
Sanborn, Louise Kirkland 1866- *WomWWA 14*
Sanborn, Mary Farley 1853-1941 *WhAm 3, WomWWA 14*
Sanborn, Susan Dana 1861- *WomWWA 14*
Sanborn, Walter Henry 1845-1928 *ApCAB X, DcAmB, NatCAB 12, NatCAB 47, TwCBDA, WhAm 1*
Sanborn, William Edward 1876-1949 *NatCAB 38*
Sanborne, Henry Kendall 1860- *WhAm 4*
Sancan, J *NewYHSD*
Sanches, Affonso 1430?-1486? *ApCAB*
Sanchez, Allan Juan 1908-1970 *WhAm 5*
Sanchez, Francisco 1550?-1623 *DcScB*
Sanchez, George Isidore 1906-1972 *BiDAmEd*
Sanchez, Jose Bernardo 1778-1833 *WhAm H*
Sanchez, Labrador Jose 1717-1799 *ApCAB*
Sanchez, Nellie VanDeGrift 1856-1935 *WhAm 1*
Sanchez DeAguilar, Pedro 1555-1640? *ApCAB*
Sanchez-Latour, Francisco 1876-1927 *WhAm 1*
Sanchez Rey, Matteo *ApCAB Sup*
Sanchez Y Tapia, Lino *IlBEAAW*
Sanctorio 1561-1636 *DcScB, McGEWB*
Sanctorius, Sanctorius 1561-1636 *AsBiEn*
Sand, George 1804-1876 *McGEWB*
Sand, Inge 1928-1974 *WhAm 6*
Sand, John F *NewYHSD*
Sandage, Allan Rex 1926- *AsBiEn*
Sandager, Harry 1887-1955 *BiDrAC*
Sandall, Charles Edward 1876- *WhAm 5*
Sandall, Mary Lucy *WomWWA 14*
Sandberg, Karl Ferdinand Marius 1855-1949 *NatCAB 38*
Sandborn, Manly Jay 1869-1926 *NatCAB 20*

Sandburg, Carl August 1878-1967 *ApCAB X, EncAAH, EncAB, McGEWB, WebAB, WhAm 4*
Sandefer, Jefferson Davis 1868-1940 *WhAm 1*
Sandelands, James 1636-1692 *ApCAB Sup*
Sandell, Perry James 1911-1968 *WhAm 4*
Sandeman, Robert 1718-1771 *ApCAB, DcAmB, Drake, NatCAB 13, TwCBDA, WhAm H*
Sander, A H 1892- *IlBEAAW*
Sander, Enno 1822- *NatCAB 13*
Sander, John Ferdinand 1898-1969 *WhAm 5*
Sander, Ludwig 1906-1975 *WhAm 6*
Sanders *NewYHSD*
Sanders, Alvin Howard 1860- *WhAm 4*
Sanders, Andrew *NewYHSD*
Sanders, Archie Dovell 1857-1941 *BiDrAC, WhAm 1, WhAmP*
Sanders, Audley Owenton 1878-1962 *NatCAB 52*
Sanders, Billington McCarter 1789-1852 *NatCAB 6*
Sanders, Billington McCarter 1789-1854 *DcAmB, WhAm H*
Sanders, Charles Finley 1869-1959 *WhAm 3*
Sanders, Charles Walton 1805-1889 *BiDAmEd, DcAmB, NatCAB 2, WhAm H*
Sanders, Clarence Elmer 1885-1949 *NatCAB 37*
Sanders, Daniel Clarke 1768-1850 *ApCAB, DcAmB, Drake, NatCAB 2, TwCBDA, WhAm H*
Sanders, Daniel Jackson 1847-1907 *BiDAmEd, DcAmB, NatCAB 2, WhAm H*
Sanders, Elizabeth Elkins 1762-1851 *ApCAB, DcAmB, Drake, NotAW, WhAm H*
Sanders, Ellen Jones 1870- *WomWWA 14*
Sanders, Euclid 1853- *WhAm 4*
Sanders, Everett 1882-1950 *BiDrAC, NatCAB 41, WhAm 3, WhAmP*
Sanders, F *NewYHSD*
Sanders, Frank Knight 1861-1933 *DcAmB, NatCAB 25, TwCBDA, WhAm 1*
Sanders, Frederic William 1864- *TwCBDA, WhAm 4*
Sanders, Frederick Morton 1876-1944 *NatCAB 33*
Sanders, George 1906-1972 *WhAm 5*
Sanders, George Nicholas 1812-1873 *DcAmB, WhAm H*
Sanders, Harold Frederick 1906-1959 *WhAm 3*
Sanders, Hedwig 1869- *WomWWA 14*
Sanders, Helen Fitzgerald 1883- *WomWWA 14*
Sanders, Henry Arthur 1868-1956 *WhAm 3*
Sanders, Henry James 1828-1905 *NatCAB 17*
Sanders, Henry Martin 1849-1921 *WhAm 1*
Sanders, Henry Nevill 1869- *WhAm 5*
Sanders, James Glossbrenner 1880-1957 *NatCAB 44*
Sanders, James Harvey 1832-1899 *DcAmB, WhAm H*
Sanders, Jared Young 1869-1944 *BiDrAC, NatCAB 14, NatCAB 41, WhAm 4, WhAmP*
Sanders, Jared Young, Jr. 1892-1944 *WhAm 2*
Sanders, Jared Young, Jr. 1892-1960 *BiDrAC, NatCAB 49, WhAm 4, WhAmP*
Sanders, John 1810-1858 *ApCAB*
Sanders, John Adams 1866- *WhAm 4*
Sanders, John Caldwell Calhoun 1840-1864 *TwCBDA*
Sanders, John Chapin 1825- *NatCAB 12*
Sanders, John Oliver 1881- *WhAm 6*
Sanders, Joseph M 1866-1927 *WhAm 1*
Sanders, Lee Stanley 1913-1970 *WhAm 5*
Sanders, Loren Addison 1874- *NatCAB 16*
Sanders, Louis Peck d1940 *WhAm 1*
Sanders, Minerva Amanda Lewis 1837-1912 *DcAmLiB*
Sanders, Morgan Gurley 1878-1956 *BiDrAC, WhAm 3, WhAmP*
Sanders, Newell 1850-1939 *BiDrAC, WhAm 1, WhAmP*
Sanders, Robert David 1898-1954 *NatCAB 43, WhAm 3*
Sanders, Robert L 1906-1975 *WhAm 6*
Sanders, Samuel D 1880-1961 *WhAm 4*
Sanders, Sue A Pike 1842- *AmWom*
Sanders, Thomas 1839-1911 *DcAmB*
Sanders, Thomas Henry 1885- *WhAm 3*

Sanders, Thomas Jefferson 1855-1946 *TwCBDA, WhAm 2*
Sanders, W Burton 1893-1961 *NatCAB 49, WhAm 4*
Sanders, W C *NewYHSD*
Sanders, Walter Benjamin 1906-1972 *WhAm 5*
Sanders, Wilbur Fisk 1834-1905 *ApCAB Sup, DcAmB, NatCAB 1, REnAW, WhAm 1*
Sanders, Wilbur Fiske 1834-1905 *BiDrAC, TwCBDA, WhAmP*
Sanders, William Brownell 1854-1929 *WhAm 1*
Sanders, William King 1905-1973 *WhAm 6*
Sanders, William Price 1833-1863 *ApCAB, Drake, NatCAB 5*
Sanderson *NewYHSD*
Sanderson, Charles Rupert 1887-1956 *WhAm 3*
Sanderson, Charles Wesley 1838-1905 *NewYHSD*
Sanderson, Dwight 1878-1944 *NatCAB 34, WhAm 2*
Sanderson, Edward 1829-1889 *NatCAB 1*
Sanderson, Edward Frederick 1874- *WhAm 5*
Sanderson, Edwin Nash 1862-1932 *WhAm 1*
Sanderson, Eugene Claremont 1859- *WhAm 4*
Sanderson, Ezra Dwight 1878-1944 *DcScB S3, DcScB*
Sanderson, George *NewYHSD*
Sanderson, George 1810-1886 *NatCAB 10, WhAm H*
Sanderson, George 1847-1924 *NatCAB 19*
Sanderson, George Andrew 1850-1925 *WhAm 1*
Sanderson, George Augustus 1863- *WhAm 1*
Sanderson, Henry 1808-1880 *NewYHSD, WhAm H*
Sanderson, Henry 1868-1934 *WhAm 1*
Sanderson, Henry Stephen 1878- *WhAm 6*
Sanderson, Ivan Terence 1911-1973 *NatCAB 57*
Sanderson, John 1783-1844 *ApCAB, DcAmB, Drake, NatCAB 6, WhAm H*
Sanderson, John 1891-1958 *WhAm 3*
Sanderson, John Pease 1816-1871 *BiDConf*
Sanderson, John Philip 1818-1864 *ApCAB, NatCAB 6*
Sanderson, John S B *DcScB*
Sanderson, Joseph 1823- *ApCAB, NatCAB 5, TwCBDA, WhAm 4*
Sanderson, Julia 1887-1975 *WhAm 6*
Sanderson, Lewis R 1891-1964 *WhAm 4*
Sanderson, Lucien 1857-1933 *NatCAB 25*
Sanderson, Musie Woollen 1852- *WomWWA 14*
Sanderson, Paul Thomas 1888-1944 *NatCAB 34*
Sanderson, Sir Percy 1842- *WhAm 4*
Sanderson, Richard Philip Charles 1858-1942 *NatCAB 31*
Sanderson, Robert 1608-1693 *BnEnAmA, DcAmB, WhAm H*
Sanderson, Robert Louis 1851- *WhAm 4*
Sanderson, Roy Voter 1892-1962 *NatCAB 50*
Sanderson, Samuel Gilbert 1895-1969 *WhAm 5*
Sanderson, Sewall Allyn 1873-1942 *NatCAB 37*
Sanderson, Sibyl Swift 1865-1903 *DcAmB, NotAW, WhAm 1*
Sanderson, Silas W 1824-1886 *NatCAB 12*
Sanderson, Susan Ferguson *WomWWA 14*
Sanderson, Sybil 1865-1903 *AmWom*
Sanderson, Thomas Harvey 1879-1964 *NatCAB 51*
Sanderson, Walter W d1973 *WhAm 5*
Sanderson, William 1905- *IlBEAAW*
Sandes, Margaret Isabelle 1849- *AmWom*
Sandford, Edward 1809-1854 *ApCAB, Drake*
Sandford, James T *BiDrAC, WhAm H*
Sandford, John d1857 *BiAUS*
Sandford, Jonah *BiAUS*
Sandford, Lewis H 1806?-1852 *BiAUS, Drake*
Sandford, Lewis Halsey 1807-1852 *ApCAB*
Sandford, Thomas 1762-1808 *BiAUS, BiDrAC, WhAm H*
Sandham, Henry 1842-1910 *DcAmB, NatCAB 6*
Sandham, J Henry 1842-1912 *IlBEAAW*
Sandholzer, Leslie Adrian 1903-1941 *NatCAB 37*
Sandidge, John Milton 1817-1890 *BiAUS, BiDrAC, WhAm H*
Sandifer, Joseph Randolph 1878-1956 *WhAm 3*
Sandiford, Ralph 1693?-1733 *ApCAB*

Sandison, George Henry 1850- *WhAm 4*
Sandler, Jacob Koppel 1856-1931 *DcAmB*
Sandlin, John Nicholas 1872-1957 *BiDrAC,*
  WhAm 5, WhAmP
Sandlin, Marlin Elijah 1909-1974 *WhAm 6*
Sandman, Charles William, Jr. 1921- *BiDrAC*
Sandmeyer, Jacques *NewYHSD*
Sandor, Mathias 1857-1920 *IIBEAAW,*
  WhAm 1
Sandor, Pal 1901-1972 *WhAm 5*
Sandoval, Alfonso De d1652 *ApCAB*
Sandoval, Gonzalo De 1496?-1528 *ApCAB*
Sandoval, Hilary Joseph, Jr. 1930-1973
  WhAm 6
Sandoval Silva Y Mendoza, Gaspar De 1640?-
  ApCAB
Sandoz, Mari Susette 1907-1966 *EncAAH,*
  REnAW, WhAm 4
Sandrok, Edward George 1913-1967 *WhAm 5*
Sands, Master *NewYHSD*
Sands, Alexander H, Jr. 1891-1960 *WhAm 4*
Sands, Alexander Hamilton 1828-1887 *ApCAB,*
  Drake
Sands, Alfred R *NewYHSD*
Sands, Benjamin Aymar 1853-1917 *ApCAB X,*
  NatCAB 24, WhAm 1
Sands, Benjamin Franklin 1811-1883 *ApCAB,*
  NatCAB 4, TwCBDA, WebAMB
Sands, Benjamin Franklin 1812-1883 *BiAUS,*
  DcAmB, Drake, WhAm H
Sands, Comfort 1740?-1834 *NatCAB 1*
Sands, Comfort 1748-1834 *DcAmB, WhAm H*
Sands, David 1745-1818 *ApCAB, DcAmB,*
  Drake, WhAm H
Sands, Diana Patricia 1934-1973 *WhAm 6*
Sands, Edward Emmet 1877-1923 *NatCAB 20*
Sands, Frank 1863-1951 *WhAm 3*
Sands, George Lincoln 1845- *WhAm 1*
Sands, Georgiana *WomWWA 14*
Sands, Henry Berton 1830-1888 *AmBi, ApCAB,*
  NatCAB 9
Sands, Herbert Stead 1874-1944 *WhAm 2*
Sands, James Hoban 1845-1911 *NatCAB 20,*
  TwCBDA, WhAm 1
Sands, John *NewYHSD*
Sands, Joshua 1757-1835 *BiDrAC, WhAm H*
Sands, Joshua 1758-1835 *BiAUS*
Sands, Joshua Ratoon 1795-1883 *ApCAB,*
  DcAmB, Drake, NatCAB 4, TwCBDA,
  WhAm H
Sands, Lawrence Eyster 1859-1928 *NatCAB 41,*
  WhAm 1
Sands, Louis 1826-1905 *NatCAB 34*
Sands, Louis Clinton 1858-1922 *NatCAB 22*
Sands, Louis Joseph 1860- *NatCAB 7*
Sands, Merrill Burr 1884-1951 *WhAm 3*
Sands, Nina DeLong 1877- *WomWWA 14*
Sands, Oliver Jackson 1870-1964 *WhAm 4*
Sands, Richard *NewYHSD*
Sands, Robert Charles 1799-1832 *AmBi,*
  ApCAB, DcAmB, Drake, NatCAB 8,
  TwCBDA, WhAm H
Sands, Robert Marcena 1876-1937 *NatCAB 31*
Sands, Stafford Lofthouse 1913-1972 *WhAm 6*
Sands, Thomas Edmund 1869- *WhAm 5*
Sands, William Franklin 1874-1946 *NatCAB 14,*
  NatCAB 41, WhAm 2
Sandstead, Harold Russell 1904-1955
  NatCAB 46
Sandsten, Emil Peter 1868- *WhAm 4*
Sandstrom, Emil 1886-1962 *WhAm 4*
Sandstrom, Ivar 1852-1889 *BiHiMed*
Sandt, George Washington 1854-1931 *WhAm 1,*
  WhAm 1C
Sandusky, William H 1813-1846 *IIBEAAW*
Sandweiss, David Jacob 1898-1962 *WhAm 4*
Sandy, Percy Tsisete 1918- *IIBEAAW*
Sandy, William Charles 1876-1957 *NatCAB 47,*
  WhAm 5
Sandy, William Charles 1915-1972 *WhAm 6*
Sandys, Edwin *NewYHSD*
Sandys, Sir Edwin 1561-1629 *ApCAB,*
  McGEWB
Sandys, Edwyn William 1860- *WhAm 1*
Sandys, George 1577?-1643? *DcAmB*
Sandys, George 1577-1644 *ApCAB*
Sandys, George 1578-1644 *AmBi, WhAm H*
Sandzen, Sven Birger 1871-1954 *IIBEAAW,*

  WhAm 3
Saner, John Crawford 1874-1948 *WhAm 2*
Saner, Robert Edward Lee 1871-1938
  ApCAB X, NatCAB 35, WhAm 1
Sanford *NewYHSD*
Sanford, Albert Hart 1866-1956 *NatCAB 46,*
  WhAm 3
Sanford, Alfred Fanton 1875-1946 *WhAm 2*
Sanford, Alice Boardman Poinier
  WomWWA 14
Sanford, Alice Emily Harris 1874-
  WomWWA 14
Sanford, Allan Douglas 1869-1950 *WhAm 2*
Sanford, Anna M 1867- *WomWWA 14*
Sanford, Annie Tomlinson 1870-
  WomWWA 14
Sanford, Arthur Hawley 1882-1959 *NatCAB 47,*
  WhAm 3
Sanford, Carlton Elisha 1847-1915 *NatCAB 17*
Sanford, Caroline Hamlin 1854- *WomWWA 14*
Sanford, Charles Edwin 1830-1914 *NatCAB 31*
Sanford, Charles F 1854- *WhAm 4*
Sanford, Charles Glover 1856-1930 *NatCAB 26*
Sanford, Charles W 1796-1878 *ApCAB*
Sanford, Chester Milton 1872-1944 *WhAm 2*
Sanford, Conley Hall 1893-1953 *WhAm 3*
Sanford, Daniel Sammis 1859-1936 *WhAm 1*
Sanford, David 1737-1810 *ApCAB*
Sanford, David C 1800-1864 *BiAUS*
Sanford, Edmund Clark 1859-1924 *DcAmB,*
  NatCAB 12, WhAm 1
Sanford, Edward 1805-1876 *ApCAB, Drake,*
  TwCBDA
Sanford, Edward Field, Jr. 1886-1951 *WhAm 3*
Sanford, Edward J 1826- *BiAUS*
Sanford, Edward Terry 1865-1930 *AmBi,*
  ApCAB X, DcAmB, NatCAB 21,
  TwCBDA, WebAB, WhAm 1
Sanford, Elias Benjamin 1843-1932 *DcAmB,*
  DcAmReB, NatCAB 24, WhAm 1
Sanford, Ezekiel 1796-1822 *ApCAB, Drake*
Sanford, Fernando 1854-1948 *WhAm 2*
Sanford, Fillmore Hargrave 1914-1967
  WhAm 4
Sanford, Francis Baird 1871-1949 *NatCAB 38,*
  WhAm 2
Sanford, Frank Goodwin 1874- *WhAm 5*
Sanford, Frank Seymour 1872-1956 *NatCAB 43*
Sanford, G P *NewYHSD*
Sanford, George Bliss 1842-1908 *WhAm 1*
Sanford, George T *NewYHSD*
Sanford, Giles 1783-1866 *WhAm H*
Sanford, Graham 1876-1942 *WhAm 2*
Sanford, Harold Williams 1890-1950 *WhAm 3*
Sanford, Harriet Sophia *WomWWA 14*
Sanford, Harry Charles 1869-1928 *ApCAB X,*
  NatCAB 21
Sanford, Henry Lindsay 1873-1938 *WhAm 1*
Sanford, Henry Shelton 1823-1891 *ApCAB,*
  BiAUS, DcAmB, NatCAB 7, TwCBDA,
  WhAm H
Sanford, Hugh Wheeler 1879-1961 *NatCAB 52,*
  WhAm 4
Sanford, Isaac *NewYHSD*
Sanford, J *NewYHSD*
Sanford, James Clark 1859-1926 *WhAm 1*
Sanford, James T *BiAUS*
Sanford, John 1600?- *NatCAB 10*
Sanford, John 1803-1857 *BiDrAC, WhAm H*
Sanford, John 1851-1939 *BiDrAC, NatCAB 1,*
  NatCAB 40, WhAm 1
Sanford, John B 1869- *WhAm 5*
Sanford, John Edgar 1879-1965 *WhAm 4*
Sanford, John W A 1798-1870 *BiDrAC,*
  WhAm H
Sanford, Jonah 1789-1867 *BiAUS*
Sanford, Jonah 1790-1867 *BiDrAC, WhAm H*
Sanford, Joseph 1797-1831 *ApCAB, Drake*
Sanford, Joseph Perry 1816-1901 *TwCBDA*
Sanford, Joseph William 1889-1952 *WhAm 3*
Sanford, Leonard Cutler 1868-1950 *NatCAB 42*
Sanford, Lockwood 1817?- *NewYHSD*
Sanford, Louis Childs 1867-1948 *WhAm 2*
Sanford, M M *NewYHSD*
Sanford, Maria L 1836-1920 *WhAm 1*
Sanford, Maria Louisa 1836-1920 *NatCAB 20*
Sanford, Maria Louise 1836-1920 *BiDAmEd,*
  NotAW, WomWWA 14

Sanford, Maude Tiel 1868- *WomWWA 14*
Sanford, Myron Reed d1939 *WhAm 1*
Sanford, Nathan 1777-1838 *ApCAB, BiDrAC,*
  DcAmB, NatCAB 3, TwCBDA,
  WhAm H, WhAmP
Sanford, Nathan 1779-1838 *BiAUS, Drake*
Sanford, Orin Grover 1877-1948 *WhAm 2*
Sanford, Peleg 1639-1701 *NatCAB 10*
Sanford, Robert Nevitt 1909- *BiDAmEd*
Sanford, Rollin Brewster 1874-1957 *BiDrAC,*
  WhAm 5
Sanford, Roscoe Frank 1883-1958 *WhAm 3*
Sanford, Steadman Vincent 1871-1945
  NatCAB 35, WhAm 2
Sanford, Stephen 1826-1913 *BiAUS, BiDrAC,*
  NatCAB 40
Sanford, Thaddeus 1791-1867 *ApCAB*
Sanford, Thomas Ryland 1878- *WhAm 6*
Sanfuentes, Salvador 1817-1860 *ApCAB*
Sang, Philip David 1902-1975 *WhAm 6*
Sangallo *McGEWB*
Sanger, Alexander 1847-1925 *WhAm 1*
Sanger, Anthony *NewYHSD*
Sanger, Charles Robert 1860-1912 *DcAmB,*
  NatCAB 28, WhAm 1
Sanger, Frank Dyer 1864-1935 *NatCAB 33*
Sanger, Frederick 1918- *AsBiEn, McGEWB*
Sanger, George Partridge 1819-1890 *ApCAB,*
  DcAmB, NatCAB 11, WhAm H
Sanger, Henry Hubbell 1866-1956 *NatCAB 45,*
  WhAm 3
Sanger, Henry L *NewYHSD*
Sanger, John Bernard 1891-1955 *NatCAB 42*
Sanger, John Pomeroy 1900-1951 *WhAm 3*
Sanger, Joseph Prentice 1840-1926 *NatCAB 27,*
  TwCBDA, WhAm 1
Sanger, Margaret Higgins d1966 *WhAm 4*
Sanger, Margaret Higgins 1879-1966
  NatCAB 52
Sanger, Margaret Higgins 1883-1966 *EncAB,*
  WebAB
Sanger, Margaret Higgins 1884-1966 *McGEWB*
Sanger, Paul Weldon 1906-1968 *WhAm 5*
Sanger, Ralph 1786-1860 *Drake*
Sanger, Ralph G 1905-1968 *WhAm 4A*
Sanger, Wendolin *NewYHSD*
Sanger, William Cary 1853-1921 *ApCAB X,*
  NatCAB 20, WhAm 1
Sanger, William Thomas 1885-1975 *WhAm 6*
Sanger, William Wallace 1819-1872
  ApCAB Sup
Sanger, Winnie Monroney 1874- *WhAm 5*
Sanger, Zedekiah 1748-1820 *Drake*
Sangren, Paul Vivian 1897-1967 *NatCAB 53*
Sangren, Paul Vivian 1898-1967 *WhAm 4*
Sangster *NewYHSD*
Sangster, Charles 1822- *ApCAB, Drake*
Sangster, John Herbert 1831- *ApCAB*
Sangster, Margaret Elizabeth Munson 1838-1912
  AmBi, AmWom, ApCAB, DcAmB,
  NatCAB 6, NotAW, TwCBDA,
  WhAm 1
Sangteller *NewYHSD*
Sanial, Lucien 1836- *WhAm 4*
Sanio, Karl Gustav 1832-1891 *DcScB*
Sankey, Ira Allan 1874-1915 *WhAm 1*
Sankey, Ira David 1840-1908 *AmBi, ApCAB,*
  DcAmB, DcAmReB, NatCAB 7,
  TwCBDA, WhAm 1
SanMartin, Jose De 1778-1850 *McGEWB*
Sanmicheli, Michele 1484?-1559 *McGEWB*
Sanner, Sydney 1873- *WhAm 5*
Sanno, James Madison Johnston 1840-1907
  WhAm 1
Sansay, Madame *NewYHSD*
Sansbury, Marvin Orville 1891-1962 *WhAm 4*
Sansom, Sir George 1883-1965 *WhAm 4*
Sansom, Joseph *NewYHSD*
Sansom, Marion 1852-1932 *WhAm 1*
Sansom, Odette 1912- *WhWW-II*
Sansom, Thomas Haughton 1891-1955
  NatCAB 43
Sanson, Thomas Haughton 1891-1955
  NatCAB 42
SanSouci, Emery John 1857-1936 *NatCAB 30*
Sansoucy, A Eugene 1880-1950 *NatCAB 40*
Sansovino, Jacopo 1486-1570 *McGEWB*
Sansum, William David 1880-1948 *WhAm 2*

Santa Ana, Antonio Lopez De 1794-1876
McGEWB
Santa Ana, Antonio Lopez De 1798-1876 *Drake*
Santa Anna, Antonio Lopez De 1794-1876
WhoMilH
Santa Anna, Antonio Lopez De 1795?-1876
ApCAB, WhAm H
Santa Cruz, Alvaro DeBazan, Marques De
1526-1588 *WhoMilH*
Santa Cruz, Andres 1792-1865 *ApCAB*
Santa Cruz, Andres 1800?- *Drake*
Santa Cruz, Andres De 1792-1865 *McGEWB*
Santa Cruz, Maria DeLasMercedes 1789-1852
ApCAB
Santa Cruz, Raimundo 1620?-1662 *ApCAB*
Santa Maria, Domingo 1825- *ApCAB*
Santacilia, Pedro 1829- *ApCAB*
Santamaria, Bartholomew Augustine 1915-
McGEWB
Santana, Pedro 1801-1864 *ApCAB, Drake,
McGEWB*
Santander, Francisco DePaula 1792-1840
ApCAB, Drake, McGEWB
Santangelo, Alfred Edward 1912- *BiDrAC,
WhAmP*
Santayana, George 1863-1952 *DcAmB S5,
EncAB, McGEWB, TwCBDA, WebAB,
WhAm 3*
Sante, Christopher Alfred 1919-1972 *WhAm 5*
Sante, Hans Heinrich 1908-1971 *WhAm 5*
Sante, LeRoy 1890-1964 *NatCAB 51,
WhAm 4*
Santee, Ellis Monroe 1862-1931 *WhAm 1*
Santee, Harris Ellett 1864-1936 *NatCAB 27,
WhAm 1*
Santee, Ross 1888-1965 *REnAW*
Santee, Ross 1889-1965 *IlBEAAW*
Santella *NewYHSD*
Santello *NewYHSD*
Santelman, Elmar William 1905-1973 *WhAm 6*
Santelmann, William Henry 1863-1932
WhAm 2
Santorini, Giovanni Domenico 1681-1737 *DcScB*
Santorio, Santorio 1561-1636 *BiHiMed, DcScB*
Santos, Eduardo 1888-1974 *WhAm 6*
Santos, Epifanio DeLos 1871-1928 *WhAm 1*
Santos-Dumont, Alberto 1873-1932 *McGEWB*
Sanville, Florence Lucas 1876- *WomWWA 14*
Saphore, Edwin Warren d1944 *WhAm 2*
Sapir, Edward 1884-1939 *DcAmB S2,
McGEWB, NatCAB 33, REnAW,
WebAB, WhAm 1*
Sapiro, Aaron 1884-1959 *EncAAH, WhAm 3*
Saporta, Louis Charles Joseph Gaston De
1823-1896 *DcScB*
Sapp, Arthur Henry 1883-1946 *WhAm 2*
Sapp, Frederick Arthur 1877-1955 *NatCAB 45*
Sapp, Ruth Bent 1877-1951 *NatCAB 47*
Sapp, William Fletcher 1824-1890 *BiDrAC,
WhAm H*
Sapp, William Frederick 1856-1917 *NatCAB 30,
WhAm 1*
Sapp, William Robinson 1804-1875 *BiAUS,
BiDrAC, WhAm H*
Sappho 625?BC-570BC *McGEWB*
Sappington, Clarence Olds 1889-1949
NatCAB 39, WhAm 2
Sappington, G Ridgely 1883-1948 *NatCAB 37*
Sappington, John 1776-1856 *DcAmB, REnAW,
WhAm H*
Sappington, John Harvard 1924-1944
NatCAB 39
Sappington, Samuel Watkins 1874-1951
WhAm 3
Sapru, Sir Tej Bahadur 1875-1949 *McGEWB*
Sar, Samuel Leib 1893-1962 *WhAm 4*
Saraceni, Gene *WebAB*
Saraiva, Matheus d1761 *ApCAB*
Saravia, Francisco 1530?-1630 *ApCAB*
Saravia, Melchor Bravo De d1579? *ApCAB*
Sarazen, Gene 1901- *WebAB*
Sarazin, Mrs. L *NewYHSD*
Sarbacher, George William, Jr. 1919-1973
BiDrAC
Sarber, Adelaide Stringfield 1871-
WomWWA 14
Sarchet, Corbin Marquand 1871- *WhAm 5*
Sard, Grange 1843- *WhAm 1*

Sard, Russell Ellis 1882-1948 *NatCAB 38*
Sardeau, Helene 1899-1969 *NatCAB 55,
WhAm 5*
Sardeson, Frederick William 1866-1958
WhAm 3
Sarett, Lew 1888-1954 *WhAm 3*
Sarg, Tony 1880-1942 *DcAmB S3,
NatCAB 33*
Sarg, Tony 1882-1942 *WhAm 2*
Sargeant, Edmund Eugene 1860-1930
ApCAB X
Sargeant, Frank Wadleigh 1860- *WhAm 5*
Sargeant, Gaston 1880- *WhAm 6*
Sargeant, Nathaniel Peaslee 1731-1791 *ApCAB,
BiAUS, Drake, NatCAB 4, TwCBDA*
Sargeant, William Gaston 1881-1918
NatCAB 17
Sargeant, William H 1868-1935 *WhAm 1*
Sargent, Aaron Augustus 1827-1887 *ApCAB,
BiAUS, BiDrAC, DcAmB, Drake Sup,
NatCAB 13, TwCBDA, WhAm H,
WhAmP*
Sargent, Amor Hartley 1876-1968 *NatCAB 54,
WhAm 5*
Sargent, Archer Downing 1906-1971 *WhAm 5*
Sargent, Charles Rankin 1884-1940 *NatCAB 32*
Sargent, Charles Sprague 1841-1927 *AmBi,
ApCAB, ApCAB X, DcAmB, EncAAH,
NatCAB 13, NatCAB 26, TwCBDA,
WhAm 1*
Sargent, Charles Wesley 1894-1963 *WhAm 4*
Sargent, Christiana Keadie Swan 1777-1867
NewYHSD
Sargent, Christopher Gilbert 1872- *WhAm 5*
Sargent, Dudley Allen 1849-1924 *ApCAB X,
BiDAmEd, DcAmB, NatCAB 7,
WhAm 1*
Sargent, Edward 1877- *WhAm 5*
Sargent, Edwin William 1848- *ApCAB X,
NatCAB 16*
Sargent, Epes 1812-1880 *Drake*
Sargent, Epes 1813-1880 *AmBi, ApCAB,
BiDAmEd, DcAmB, NatCAB 7,
TwCBDA, WhAm H*
Sargent, Fitzwilliam 1820-1889 *ApCAB,
DcAmB, WhAm H*
Sargent, Fitzwilliam 1892-1955 *WhAm 3*
Sargent, Frank Pierce 1854-1908 *DcAmB,
WhAm 1*
Sargent, Franklin Haven 1856-1923 *NatCAB 6,
WhAm 1*
Sargent, Fred Wesley 1876-1940 *WhAm 1*
Sargent, Frederick 1859-1919 *DcAmB,
NatCAB 22, WhAm 1*
Sargent, Frederick LeRoy 1863-1928 *TwCBDA,
WhAm 1*
Sargent, George Frederick 1841-1901
NatCAB 11
Sargent, George Henry 1828- *NatCAB 11*
Sargent, George Henry 1867-1931 *DcAmB,
WhAm 1*
Sargent, Harriet E 1854- *WomWWA 14*
Sargent, Helen Sanborn 1870- *WomWWA 14*
Sargent, Henry 1770-1845 *AmBi, ApCAB,
BnEnAmA, DcAmB, Drake, NatCAB 5,
NewYHSD, WhAm H*
Sargent, Henry Barry 1905-1967 *WhAm 4*
Sargent, Henry Bradford 1851-1927 *WhAm 1*
Sargent, Henry Winthrop 1810-1882 *ApCAB,
DcAmB, TwCBDA, WhAm H*
Sargent, Herbert Howland 1858-1921
NatCAB 19, TwCBDA, WhAm 1
Sargent, Horace Binney 1821- *ApCAB*
Sargent, Mrs. I T *NewYHSD*
Sargent, James 1824-1910 *ApCAB, DcAmB,
NatCAB 3, WhAm 1*
Sargent, James Clyde 1892-1954 *WhAm 3*
Sargent, John Davis 1871-1945 *NatCAB 35*
Sargent, John Garibaldi 1860-1939 *ApCAB X,
BiDrUSE, NatCAB 32, WhAm 1*
Sargent, John Harris 1814-1893 *NatCAB 16*
Sargent, John Osborne 1810-1891 *Drake*
Sargent, John Osborne 1811-1891 *ApCAB,
DcAmB, NatCAB 9, WhAm H*
Sargent, John Singer 1856-1925 *AmBi, ApCAB,
ApCAB X, BnEnAmA, DcAmB, EncAB,
McGEWB, NatCAB 11, TwCBDA,
WebAB, WhAm 1*

Sargent, Jonathan Everett 1816-1890
NatCAB 12, TwCBDA
Sargent, Joseph Bradford 1822-1907
NatCAB 28
Sargent, Ledyard Worthington 1882- *WhAm 1*
Sargent, Lucius Manlius 1786-1867 *ApCAB,
DcAmB, Drake, NatCAB 4, TwCBDA,
WhAm H*
Sargent, Lucius Manlius, Jr. 1826-1864 *ApCAB,
Drake*
Sargent, Mary Forward Kooser 1875-1963
NatCAB 50
Sargent, May Pardridge *WomWWA 14*
Sargent, Nathan 1794-1875 *ApCAB, BiAUS,
DcAmB, NatCAB 13, WhAm H*
Sargent, Nathan 1849-1907 *WhAm 1*
Sargent, Nathan Burnham 1839-1924
NatCAB 6
Sargent, Noel Gharrett 1894- *WhAm 5*
Sargent, Paul Dudley 1745-1828 *ApCAB,
Drake, TwCBDA*
Sargent, Paul Dudley 1873- *WhAm 5*
Sargent, Porter E 1872-1951 *WhAm 3,
WhAm 5*
Sargent, Walter 1868-1927 *BiDAmEd,
WhAm 1*
Sargent, William Cooper 1849-1922 *NatCAB 6*
Sargent, William Dunlap 1845-1911
NatCAB 25
Sargent, William Durham 1863-1940 *WhAm 1*
Sargent, William Edward 1856- *WhAm 4*
Sargent, William Isaac 1882-1961 *NatCAB 50*
Sargent, Winthrop 1753-1820 *AmBi, ApCAB,
BiAUS, DcAmB, Drake, NatCAB 13,
TwCBDA, WhAm H*
Sargent, Winthrop 1753-1823 *REnAW*
Sargent, Winthrop 1825-1870 *AmBi, ApCAB,
DcAmB, Drake, NatCAB 7, TwCBDA,
WhAm H*
Sargent, Winthrop 1853-1932 *NatCAB 25*
Sargon II *McGEWB*
Sargon Of Agade *McGEWB*
Sarit Thanarat 1908-1963 *McGEWB*
Sarkisian, Dickran Manouk 1875-1947
NatCAB 37
Sarles, Elmore Yocum 1859-1929 *ApCAB X,
NatCAB 13, WhAm 1*
Sarmiento, Domingo Faustino 1811-1888
ApCAB, Drake, McGEWB
Sarmiento DeSotomayor, Garcia 1590?-1655
ApCAB
Sarmiento Gamboa, Pedro De 1530?-1590?
ApCAB
Sarmiento Valladares, Jose 1650?-1717 *ApCAB*
Sarnoff, David 1891-1971 *EncAB, McGEWB,
NatCAB 56, WebAB, WhAm 5*
Sarony, Hector *NewYHSD*
Sarony, Napoleon 1821-1896 *NewYHSD,
WhAm H*
Saroyan, William 1908- *McGEWB, WebAB*
Sarper, Selim 1899-1968 *WhAm 5*
Sarpi, Paolo 1552-1623 *DcScB, McGEWB*
Sarpy, Peter A 1805-1865 *DcAmB, WhAm H*
Sarrail, Maurice Paul Emmanuel 1856-1929
WhoMilH
Sarrasin, Michel 1659-1734 *ApCAB*
Sars, Michael 1805-1869 *DcScB*
Sartain, Emily 1841-1927 *AmBi, AmWom,
ApCAB, BiDAmEd, DcAmB,
NatCAB 13, NotAW, TwCBDA,
WhAm 1, WomWWA 14*
Sartain, Harriet *WomWWA 14*
Sartain, Henry 1833-1895? *NewYHSD*
Sartain, John 1808-1897 *AmBi, ApCAB,
DcAmB, Drake, NatCAB 6, NewYHSD,
TwCBDA, WhAm H*
Sartain, Paul Judd 1861-1944 *WhAm 2*
Sartain, Samuel 1830-1906 *ApCAB, DcAmB,
NewYHSD, TwCBDA, WhAm 1*
Sartain, William 1843-1924 *AmBi, ApCAB,
DcAmB, NatCAB 13, TwCBDA,
WhAm 1*
Sarther, John M 1889-1957 *WhAm 3*
Sarton, George Alfred Leon 1884-1956 *DcScB,
McGEWB, NatCAB 45, WebAB,
WhAm 3*
Sartori, Giovanni *NewYHSD*
Sartori, Joseph Francis 1858-1946 *NatCAB 52,*

WhAm 2

Sartori, Lewis Constant 1812-1899 *ApCAB, TwCBDA*
Sartori, Louis Constant 1812-1899 *WhAm 1*
Sartorius, August Matern 1888-1926 *NatCAB 20*
Sartorius, Irving A 1893-1959 *WhAm 3*
Sartre, Jean Paul 1905- *McGEWB*
Sartwell, Edwin Wesley 1879-1950 *NatCAB 41*
Sartwell, Henry Parker 1792-1867 *ApCAB, DcAmB, Drake, WhAm H*
Sartz, Richard Sophus Nielsen 1852-1920 *WhAm 1*
Sarvis, Guy Walter 1879- *WhAm 6*
Sarychev, Gavriil Andreevich 1763-1831 *DcScB*
Sase *NewYHSD*
Saslavsky, Alexander 1876-1924 *DcAmB, WhAm 1*
Sasnett, William Jacob 1820-1865 *ApCAB, Drake*
Sasoonan d1747 *ApCAB*
Sass, George Herbert 1845-1908 *WhAm 1*
Sass, Herbert Ravenel 1884-1958 *WhAm 3*
Sassacus 1560?-1637 *ApCAB, DcAmB, WhAm H*
Sasscer, Lansdale Ghiselin 1893-1964 *BiDrAC, WhAm 4*
Sasser, James Archibald 1897-1953 *NatCAB 41*
Sassetta 1400?-1450 *McGEWB*
Sassman, G C *NewYHSD*
Sassman, John C *NewYHSD*
Sassoon, Siegfried Loraine 1886-1967 *McGEWB, WhAm 4*
Sastroamidjojo, Ali 1903-1975 *WhAm 6*
Satananda *DcScB*
Satanta 1830?-1878 *EncAAH, REnAW*
Satchell, James *NewYHSD*
Satenstein, Edward d1968 *WhAm 5*
Satenstein, Sidney 1900-1961 *WhAm 4*
Sater, John Elbert 1854-1937 *WhAm 1*
Saterlee, Gerald Britton 1893-1957 *WhAm 3*
Sathre, Jacob Cornelius 1867-1922 *WhAm 1*
Sathre, Peter O 1878- *WhAm 6*
Satie, Erik 1866-1925 *McGEWB*
Sato, Eisaku 1901-1975 *McGEWB, WhAm 6*
Sato, Nobuhiro 1769-1850 *DcScB*
Sato, Nobukage 1674-1732 *DcScB*
Sato, Nobusue 1724-1784 *DcScB*
Satolli, Francesco 1839-1910 *DcAmReB*
Satolli, Francis 1831- *ApCAB Sup*
Satter, Gustav 1832-1879 *WhAm H*
Satter, Mark J 1916-1965 *WhAm 5*
Satterfield, Charles Nathan 1879-1944 *NatCAB 37*
Satterfield, Dave Edward, Jr. 1894-1946 *BiDrAC, NatCAB 38, WhAm 2, WhAmP*
Satterfield, David Edward, III 1920- *BiDrAC*
Satterfield, John 1839- *NatCAB 5*
Satterfield, John Martin 1876-1932 *NatCAB 25*
Satterfield, John Vines, Jr. 1902-1966 *WhAm 5*
Satterfield, M H 1904-1949 *WhAm 3*
Satterfield, Robert Samuel 1873-1945 *NatCAB 36, WhAm 2*
Satterlee, Churchill 1867-1904 *NatCAB 16*
Satterlee, Eugene 1847-1910 *WhAm 1*
Satterlee, Francis LeRoy 1847- *NatCAB 7*
Satterlee, George Reese 1873-1928 *ApCAB X, WhAm 1*
Satterlee, Henry Yates 1843-1908 *AmBi, ApCAB, DcAmB, NatCAB 10, TwCBDA, WhAm 1*
Satterlee, Herbert Livingston 1863-1947 *NatCAB 39, WhAm 2*
Satterlee, Hugh 1880-1963 *WhAm 4*
Satterlee, Richard Sherwood 1798-1880 *ApCAB, DcAmB, WhAm H*
Satterlee, Richard Smith 1798-1880 *NatCAB 11*
Satterlee, Walter 1844-1908 *ApCAB, NatCAB 13, TwCBDA, WhAm 1*
Satterthwait, John Jackson 1854-1941 *NatCAB 46*
Satterthwaite, Laura Henderson 1861- *WomWWA 14*
Satterthwaite, Livingston 1909-1959 *WhAm 3*
Satterthwaite, Thomas Edward 1843-1934 *NatCAB 12, WhAm 1*
Satterwhite, James King 1880- *WhoColR*

Sattgast, Charles Richard 1899-1964 *NatCAB 51, WhAm 4*
Sattler, Eric Ericson 1859-1926 *WhAm 1*
Sattler, George Albert 1887-1958 *NatCAB 49*
Sattler, Hubert 1817-1904 *NewYHSD*
Sattler, Robert 1855-1939 *NatCAB 30, WhAm 1*
Sattler, William Martin 1910-1969 *WhAm 5*
Sattley, Ida Belle Newkirk *WomWWA 14*
Sauckel, Fritz 1894-1946 *WhWW-II*
Saud III 1880-1953 *WhAm 3*
Sauer, Carl Ortwin 1889-1975 *McGEWB, WhAm 6*
Sauer, Emil 1881-1949 *WhAm 4*
Sauer, LeRoy Dagobert 1894-1959 *WhAm 3*
Sauer, Mack 1896-1960 *NatCAB 47*
Sauer, Paul Kurt 1890-1957 *NatCAB 46*
Sauer, William Emil 1875- *WhAm 3*
Sauerbrei, Harold 1916-1975 *WhAm 6*
Sauerbruch, Ferdinand 1875-1951 *BiHiMed*
Sauereisen, Christian Fred 1884-1965 *NatCAB 52*
Sauerhering, Edward 1864-1924 *BiDrAC*
Sauerwein, Allan 1875- *WhAm 5*
Sauerwein, Charles D 1839-1918 *NewYHSD*
Sauerwein, Frank Peters 1871-1910 *IIBEAAW*
Sauerwine, Calvin Elias 1880-1962 *NatCAB 50*
Sauganash 1780?-1841 *AmBi, ApCAB, DcAmB*
Saugrain DeVigni, Antoine Francois 1763-1820? *DcAmB, WhAm H*
Saul *McGEWB*
Saul, Charles Dudley 1880-1947 *WhAm 2*
Saul, Chief Terry 1921- *IIBEAAW*
Saul, Ezra Victor 1925-1970 *NatCAB 57*
Saul, Maurice Bower 1883-1974 *WhAm 6*
Saul, Walter Biddle 1881-1966 *NatCAB 52, WhAm 4*
Saulnier, Henry E *NewYHSD*
Saulsbury, Eli 1817-1893 *ApCAB, BiAUS, BiDrAC, DcAmB, NatCAB 11, TwCBDA, WhAm H, WhAmP*
Saulsbury, Gore 1815-1881 *WhAmP*
Saulsbury, Gove 1815-1881 *BiAUS, DcAmB, NatCAB 11, TwCBDA, WhAm H*
Saulsbury, Willard 1820-1892 *ApCAB, BiAUS, BiDrAC, DcAmB, NatCAB 11, TwCBDA, WhAm H, WhAmP*
Saulsbury, Willard 1861-1927 *BiDrAC, DcAmB, NatCAB 15, WhAm 1, WhAmP*
Saund, Dalip Singh 1899-1973 *BiDrAC, WhAm 5, WhAmP*
Saunders *NewYHSD*
Saunders, Alvin 1817-1899 *ApCAB, BiAUS, BiDrAC, DcAmB, NatCAB 13, TwCBDA, WhAm H, WhAmP*
Saunders, Arthur Percy 1869-1953 *WhAm 3*
Saunders, Mrs. Bacon *WomWWA 14*
Saunders, Bacon 1855-1925 *NatCAB 28*
Saunders, Benjamin H 1894-1973 *WhAm 6*
Saunders, Carl Maxon 1890-1974 *WhAm 6*
Saunders, Carleton Earl 1878-1949 *NatCAB 39*
Saunders, Sir Charles 1705?-1775 *ApCAB*
Saunders, Sir Charles Edward 1867-1937 *McGEWB*
Saunders, Charles Francis 1859-1941 *WhAm 1*
Saunders, Charles Gurley 1847-1918 *NatCAB 18, WhAm 1*
Saunders, Charles W 1902-1964 *WhAm 5*
Saunders, Clarence 1881-1953 *ApCAB X, DcAmB S5*
Saunders, Daniel 1796-1872 *NatCAB 11*
Saunders, Daniel 1822-1917 *NatCAB 17*
Saunders, Dealton 1869- *WhAm 5*
Saunders, Dudley Dunn 1835- *WhAm 1*
Saunders, Edward Watts 1854-1927 *NatCAB 21*
Saunders, Edward Watts 1860-1921 *BiDrAC, WhAm 1, WhAmP*
Saunders, Ephraim Dod 1808-1872 *ApCAB*
Saunders, Eugene Davis 1853-1914 *WhAm 1*
Saunders, Eugene Davis 1898-1969 *NatCAB 56, WhAm 5*
Saunders, Frederic 1807-1902 *Drake*
Saunders, Frederick 1807-1902 *ApCAB, DcAmB, NatCAB 2, TwCBDA, WhAm 1*
Saunders, Frederick A 1875-1963 *WhAm 4*

Saunders, George Lethbridge 1807-1863 *NewYHSD*
Saunders, Grace Elder *WomWWA 14*
Saunders, Harold Eugene 1890-1961 *WhAm 4*
Saunders, Harold William 1909-1974 *WhAm 6*
Saunders, Henry Dmochowski 1810-1863 *NewYHSD, WhAm H*
Saunders, Irvine 1914-1958 *NatCAB 49*
Saunders, Jessie Cassidy 1861- *WomWWA 14*
Saunders, John 1754-1834 *ApCAB, Drake*
Saunders, John Monk 1897-1940 *WhAm 1*
Saunders, John Richard 1869-1934 *NatCAB 39, WhAm 1*
Saunders, John Turner 1898-1953 *NatCAB 43*
Saunders, Joseph H 1876-1945 *WhAm 2*
Saunders, Joseph Taylor 1885-1942 *WhAm 2*
Saunders, Kenneth James 1883-1937 *WhAm 1*
Saunders, Lawrence 1890-1968 *NatCAB 54, WhAm 5*
Saunders, Louise Sheffield Brownell 1870- *WomWWA 14*
Saunders, Lowell Waller 1901-1954 *WhAm 3*
Saunders, Margaret Marshall 1861- *WomWWA 14*
Saunders, Marshall 1861-1947 *WhAm 2*
Saunders, Mary A 1849- *AmWom*
Saunders, Merrell Kerby 1909-1973 *WhAm 6*
Saunders, Michael Graham 1920-1975 *WhAm 6*
Saunders, Paul Hill 1870-1947 *WhAm 2*
Saunders, Paul Rome 1916-1974 *WhAm 6*
Saunders, Prince 1775?-1839 *DcAmB, Drake, WhAm H*
Saunders, Prince 1775?-1840 *ApCAB*
Saunders, Richard *WebAB*
Saunders, Richard Loesch 1892-1963 *NatCAB 50, WhAm 4*
Saunders, Richard West 1874- *ApCAB X*
Saunders, Ripley Dunlap 1856-1915 *WhAm 1*
Saunders, Robert 1805-1868 *NatCAB 3*
Saunders, Robert Chancellor 1864-1922 *WhAm 1*
Saunders, Romulus Mitchell 1791-1867 *ApCAB, BiAUS, BiDrAC, DcAmB, Drake, NatCAB 13, TwCBDA, WhAm H, WhAmP*
Saunders, Roy Farra 1879-1957 *NatCAB 47*
Saunders, Samuel James 1862- *WhAm 3*
Saunders, Sophia *NewYHSD*
Saunders, Thomas Brady 1882-1968 *NatCAB 55*
Saunders, W C *NewYHSD*
Saunders, W V 1898-1974 *WhAm 6*
Saunders, Walter Hyde 1870-1935 *NatCAB 26*
Saunders, Walter Mills 1866- *WhAm 4*
Saunders, William 1822-1900 *AmBi, DcAmB, EncAAH, NatCAB 10, WhAm H*
Saunders, William Laurence 1835-1891 *DcAmB, NatCAB 5, WhAm H*
Saunders, William Lawrence 1856-1931 *ApCAB X, DcAmB, NatCAB 14, NatCAB 26, WhAm 1*
Saunders, William Louis 1858-1946 *NatCAB 36*
Saunderson, Henry Hallam 1871-1957 *WhAm 3*
Saur, Christopher 1693-1758 *AmBi, DcAmB*
Saur, Christopher 1721-1784 *AmBi*
Saurel, Paul 1871-1934 *WhAm 1*
Sauret, Emile 1852- *WhAm 4*
Saurin, Joseph 1659-1737 *DcScB*
Saussure, Horace Benedict De 1740-1799 *DcScB*
Saussure, Nicolas-Theodore De 1767-1845 *DcScB*
Sauters, William Davis 1869-1917 *NatCAB 17*
Sauthoff, Harry 1879-1966 *BiDrAC, WhAm 6*
Sauvageau, Camille-Francois 1861-1936 *DcScB*
Sauve, Paul 1907-1959 *WhAm 3*
Sauveur, Albert 1863-1939 *DcAmB S2, DcScB, NatCAB 29, WhAm 1*
Sauveur, Baudoin 1779-1832 *ApCAB*
Sauveur, Joseph 1653-1716 *DcScB*
Savage, A J *NewYHSD*
Savage, Albert Russell 1847-1917 *NatCAB 20, WhAm 1*
Savage, Alexander Duncan 1848- *WhAm 4*
Savage, Alfred Orville 1911-1968 *WhAm 5*
Savage, Annie Douglas 1896-1971 *IIBEAAW*
Savage, Arthur Harold 1872-1933 *NatCAB 38*
Savage, Arthur William 1857-1938 *WhAm 1*
Savage, Boutelle 1910-1970 *NatCAB 56*

Savage, Charles Albert 1866- *WhAm 4*
Savage, Charles C 1820- *Drake*
Savage, Charles Raymon 1906- *BiDrAC*
Savage, Charles Winfred 1869- *WhAm 5*
Savage, Courtenay 1890-1946 *WhAm 2*
Savage, Edward 1761-1817 *AmBi, ApCAB, BnEnAmA, DcAmB, Drake, NewYHSD, WhAm H*
Savage, Edward Hartwell 1812- *ApCAB*
Savage, Elmer Seth 1884-1943 *NatCAB 34, WhAm 2*
Savage, Eudora Helen 1870- *WomWWA 14*
Savage, Eugene Francis 1883- *BnEnAmA*
Savage, Ezra Perin 1842-1920 *NatCAB 12, TwCBDA, WhAm 4*
Savage, Ezra Perrin 1842-1920 *NatCAB 30*
Savage, Francis Martin 1855-1934 *NatCAB 28, WhAm 1*
Savage, George Martin 1849-1938 *TwCBDA, WhAm 1*
Savage, George Slocum Folger 1817- *WhAm 4*
Savage, Giles Christopher 1854-1930 *AmBi, WhAm 1, WhAm 1C*
Savage, Harlow Dow 1880-1942 *WhAm 1*
Savage, Henry Wilson 1859-1927 *DcAmB, WhAm 1*
Savage, Hiram Newton 1861-1934 *WhAm 1, WhAm 1C*
Savage, Howard Paul 1884-1944 *NatCAB 33*
Savage, James 1784-1873 *AmBi, ApCAB, DcAmB, Drake, NatCAB 9, TwCBDA, WhAm H*
Savage, James Edwin 1903-1972 *WhAm 5*
Savage, John 1779-1863 *ApCAB, BiAUS, BiDrAC, Drake, TwCBDA, WhAm H*
Savage, John 1828-1888 *ApCAB, DcAmB, Drake, NatCAB 11, TwCBDA, WhAm H*
Savage, John A d1864 *Drake*
Savage, John Houston 1815-1904 *ApCAB, ApCAB Sup, BiAUS, BiDrAC, Drake, TwCBDA, WhAm 1*
Savage, John Lucian 1879-1967 *WhAm 4*
Savage, John Marbacher 1864- *WhAm 4*
Savage, John Simpson 1841-1884 *BiAUS, BiDrAC, WhAm H*
Savage, Joseph d1814 *Drake*
Savage, Leonard Jimmie 1917-1971 *WhAm 5*
Savage, Marion Alexander 1885-1946 *WhAm 2*
Savage, Marion Alexander 1885-1947 *NatCAB 36*
Savage, Maxwell 1876-1948 *WhAm 2*
Savage, Michael Joseph 1872-1940 *McGEWB*
Savage, Millard Bridgman 1896-1958 *NatCAB 48*
Savage, Minnie Stebbins 1850- *AmWom*
Savage, Minot Judson 1841-1918 *AmBi, ApCAB, DcAmB, NatCAB 1, TwCBDA, WhAm 1*
Savage, Philip Henry 1868-1899 *DcAmB, NatCAB 10, WhAm 1*
Savage, Richard Henry 1846-1903 *ApCAB Sup, TwCBDA, WhAm 1*
Savage, Samuel Phillips d1797 *Drake*
Savage, Seth Cameron 1869-1946 *NatCAB 36*
Savage, Theodore Fiske 1885-1957 *WhAm 3*
Savage, Thomas Edmund 1866- *WhAm 4*
Savage, Thomas Staughton 1804-1880 *DcAmB, NatCAB 26, WhAm H*
Savage, Toy Dixon 1878-1941 *WhAm 2*
Savage, Watson Lewis 1859-1931 *AmBi, WhAm 1*
Savant, Domenico Pietro 1886-1968 *NatCAB 54*
Savart, Felix 1791-1841 *DcScB*
Savasorda *DcScB*
Saver, John S *NewYHSD*
Savery, Thomas 1650?-1715 *AsBiEn*
Savery, William 1721-1787 *DcAmB, WhAm H*
Savery, William 1721-1788 *BnEnAmA*
Savery, William 1750-1804 *DcAmB, WhAm H*
Savery, William 1875-1945 *WhAm 2*
Savidge, Emily Louise 1860- *WomWWA 14*
Savidge, Eugene Coleman 1863-1924 *NatCAB 31, WhAm 1*
Savidge, Frank Raymond 1866-1928 *WhAm 1*
Savigny, Friedrich Karl Von 1779-1861 *McGEWB*
Savigny, Marie-Jules-Cesar Lelorgne De 1777-1851 *DcScB*

Saville, Bruce Wilder 1893-1939 *WhAm 1*
Saville, Caleb Mills 1865-1960 *NatCAB 47, WhAm 5*
Saville, Marshall Howard 1867-1935 *AmBi, DcAmB S1, NatCAB 28, WhAm 1*
Saville, Richard Littlehale 1819-1897 *NatCAB 22*
Saville, Thorndike 1892-1969 *WhAm 5*
Saville, Wilson Gordon 1897-1954 *NatCAB 42*
Savino, Patrick Ronald 1917-1974 *WhAm 6*
Savitt, Sam *IIBEAAW*
Savonarola, Girolamo 1452-1498 *McGEWB*
Savord, Catherine Ruth 1894-1966 *DcAmLiB*
Savord, Ruth 1894-1966 *WhAm 4*
Savorgnan, Alessandro 1908-1973 *WhAm 5*
Savory, George Washington 1856- *WhAm 4*
Savory, Thomas C *NewYHSD*
Savoy, Prew 1899-1956 *NatCAB 49*
Savoy, William Joseph 1908-1970 *NatCAB 55*
Sawada, Kyoichi 1936-1970 *WhAm 5*
Sawbridge, Edward 1861-1953 *NatCAB 43*
Sawders, James Caleb 1894-1960 *WhAm 4*
Sawdon, Will Miller 1873-1952 *NatCAB 40*
Sawhill, Donald Vere 1891-1955 *NatCAB 49*
Sawin, Edward D *NewYHSD*
Sawin, J W *NewYHSD*
Sawin, Theophilus Parsons 1841-1906 *WhAm 1*
Sawin, Wealthy O *NewYHSD*
Sawkins, James G *NewYHSD*
Sawtelle, Charles Greene 1834-1913 *ApCAB, NatCAB 28, TwCBDA, WhAm 1*
Sawtelle, Cullen 1805-1887 *BiAUS, BiDrAC, WhAm H*
Sawtelle, George 1892-1967 *NatCAB 54, WhAm 4*
Sawtelle, Henry Allen 1832-1885 *ApCAB*
Sawtelle, Julia Hedden Worthington 1890- *WomWWA 14*
Sawtelle, Lelia Robinson 1850-1891 *NatCAB 3*
Sawtelle, William Henry 1868-1934 *WhAm 1*
Sawtelle, William Luther 1871-1926 *WhAm 1*
Sawvel, Franklin B 1850- *WhAm 4*
Sawyer, A R *NewYHSD*
Sawyer, Alan Kenneth 1904-1973 *WhAm 6*
Sawyer, Alfred Isaac 1828-1891 *NatCAB 5*
Sawyer, Andrew Jackson 1844-1924 *NatCAB 20*
Sawyer, Anna Laura Margaret *WomWWA 14*
Sawyer, Ansley Wilcox 1885-1955 *NatCAB 45*
Sawyer, Antonia 1863- *NatCAB 16*
Sawyer, Belinda A *NewYHSD*
Sawyer, Bonner Dupree 1902-1972 *WhAm 5*
Sawyer, C Adrian, Jr. 1881-1952 *WhAm 3*
Sawyer, Carl Walker 1881-1966 *WhAm 4*
Sawyer, Caroline M 1812-1894 *Drake*
Sawyer, Caroline Mehetabel 1812-1894 *ApCAB*
Sawyer, Caroline Mehitabel 1812-1894 *TwCBDA*
Sawyer, Caroline Mehitable Fisher 1812-1894 *NotAW*
Sawyer, Charles 1887- *BiDrUSE*
Sawyer, Charles Baldwin 1894-1964 *NatCAB 53, WhAm 4*
Sawyer, Charles Elbridge 1874-1959 *NatCAB 45*
Sawyer, Charles Elmer 1860-1924 *NatCAB 21, WhAm 1*
Sawyer, Charles Francis 1869-1938 *NatCAB 37*
Sawyer, Charles Henry 1840-1908 *NatCAB 11, TwCBDA, WhAm 1*
Sawyer, Charles Pike 1854-1935 *WhAm 1*
Sawyer, Charles Winthrop 1868- *WhAm 4*
Sawyer, Donald Hubbard 1879-1941 *NatCAB 31, WhAm 1*
Sawyer, Edgar Philetus 1842- *NatCAB 8, NatCAB 16*
Sawyer, Edward 1828- *NatCAB 12*
Sawyer, Edward 1836-1916 *NatCAB 17*
Sawyer, Edward Duren 1863-1926 *ApCAB X*
Sawyer, Edward Warren 1876-1932 *IIBEAAW*
Sawyer, Edwin Forrest 1849- *NatCAB 8*
Sawyer, Frederic William 1810-1875? *Drake*
Sawyer, Frederick Adolphus 1822-1891 *ApCAB, BiAUS, BiDrAC, NatCAB 3, TwCBDA, WhAm H*
Sawyer, Frederick William 1810-1875? *ApCAB*
Sawyer, George Frederick 1875-1941 *WhAm 1*
Sawyer, Georgia Pope 1873- *WomWWA 14*

Sawyer, Grace Ethel 1877- *WomWWA 14*
Sawyer, Harold Everett 1889-1969 *WhAm 5*
Sawyer, Harold Merriam 1882-1951 *NatCAB 40*
Sawyer, Henry Buckland 1871-1950 *NatCAB 38, WhAm 5*
Sawyer, Hiram Arthur 1875-1946 *NatCAB 35, WhAm 2*
Sawyer, Horace Bucklin 1797-1860 *ApCAB, Drake, TwCBDA*
Sawyer, J Estcourt 1846-1914 *WhAm 1*
Sawyer, Jacob Henry 1896-1961 *NatCAB 51*
Sawyer, James Emery Cochran 1842- *NatCAB 4*
Sawyer, James George 1911-1963 *NatCAB 53*
Sawyer, James J 1813-1888 *NewYHSD*
Sawyer, John 1755-1858 *Drake*
Sawyer, John Gilbert 1825-1898 *BiDrAC*
Sawyer, John Pascal 1862-1945 *NatCAB 35, WhAm 2*
Sawyer, John Talbott 1843- *NatCAB 11, WhAm 4*
Sawyer, Joseph Dillaway 1849-1933 *WhAm 1*
Sawyer, Joseph Henry 1842- *WhAm 4*
Sawyer, Leicester Ambrose 1807-1898 *ApCAB, DcAmB, Drake, TwCBDA, WhAm H*
Sawyer, Lemuel 1777-1852 *ApCAB, BiAUS, BiDrAC, DcAmB, TwCBDA, WhAm H, WhAmP*
Sawyer, Lewis Ernest 1867-1923 *BiDrAC*
Sawyer, Lorenzo 1820-1891 *ApCAB, BiAUS, DcAmB, NatCAB 13, TwCBDA, WhAm H*
Sawyer, Lucy Sargent 1840- *AmWom, NatCAB 5*
Sawyer, Luke Eugene 1887-1969 *NatCAB 55*
Sawyer, Mary Alma 1854- *WhAm 4, WomWWA 14*
Sawyer, Mary Pepperell *WomWWA 14*
Sawyer, Mildred Conway *WomWWA 14*
Sawyer, Moses Havens 1827-1909 *NatCAB 2*
Sawyer, Paul Backus 1879-1946 *WhAm 2*
Sawyer, Philetus 1816-1900 *ApCAB, ApCAB X, BiAUS, BiDrAC, DcAmB, NatCAB 1, TwCBDA, WhAm 1, WhAmP*
Sawyer, Philip 1868-1949 *WhAm 2*
Sawyer, Philip Ayer 1877-1949 *IIBEAAW*
Sawyer, Prince Edwin 1874-1954 *WhAm 3*
Sawyer, Raymond Terry 1879-1938 *NatCAB 43*
Sawyer, Raymond Terry, Jr. 1912-1962 *NatCAB 51*
Sawyer, Rollin Augustus 1830-1915 *WhAm 1*
Sawyer, Ruth 1880-1970 *WhAm 5*
Sawyer, S T 1800-1865 *BiAUS*
Sawyer, Samuel Locke 1813-1890 *BiDrAC, WhAm H*
Sawyer, Samuel Nelson 1858-1939 *NatCAB 31, WhAm 1*
Sawyer, Samuel Tredwell 1800-1865 *BiDrAC, WhAm H*
Sawyer, Samuel Woodson 1878-1949 *WhAm 3*
Sawyer, Sylvanus 1822-1895 *ApCAB, DcAmB, NatCAB 4, TwCBDA, WhAm H*
Sawyer, Thomas H *NewYHSD*
Sawyer, Thomas Jefferson 1804-1899 *ApCAB, DcAmB, Drake, TwCBDA, WhAm 1*
Sawyer, Walter Howard 1867-1923 *DcAmB, NatCAB 26*
Sawyer, Walter Hulme 1861-1931 *WhAm 1*
Sawyer, Walter Leon 1862-1915 *WhAm 1*
Sawyer, Wells Moses 1863-1960 *NatCAB 48, WhAm 5*
Sawyer, Wesley Caleb 1839- *WhAm 4*
Sawyer, Wilbur Augustus 1879-1951 *DcAmB S5, NatCAB 52, WhAm 3*
Sawyer, Willard Gilbert 1900-1960 *NatCAB 49*
Sawyer, William 1803-1877 *BiAUS, BiDrAC, WhAm H*
Sawyer, William Henry 1867-1947 *NatCAB 35*
Sawyer, William L 1905-1966 *WhAm 4*
Sawyers, Francis Lazelle 1895-1956 *NatCAB 46*
Sawyers, Mott Randolph 1870- *WhAm 6*
Sax, George David 1904-1974 *WhAm 6*
Sax, Karl 1892-1973 *WhAm 6*
Saxbe, William Bart 1916- *BiDrAC*
Saxe, G A DeSantos 1876-1911 *WhAm 1*

Saxe, Hermann Maurice, Comte De 1696-1750
 McGEWB, WhoMilH
Saxe, James Alfred 1863-1948 *NatCAB 37*
Saxe, John Godfrey 1816-1887 *AmBi, ApCAB,
 DcAmB, Drake, NatCAB 1, TwCBDA,
 WhAm H*
Saxe, John Godfrey 1877-1953 *WhAm 3*
Saxe, Martin 1874-1967 *WhAm 4*
Saxe, Sigmond 1861-1944 *NatCAB 32*
Saxe, Thomas Edward, II 1903-1975 *WhAm 6*
Saxe-Weimar, Karl Bernhard, Duke Of
 1792-1862 *Drake*
Saxe-Weimar-Eisenach, Carl B, Duke Of
 1792-1862 *ApCAB*
Saxman, Marcus Wilson, Jr. 1895-1968
 NatCAB 55, WhAm 5
Saxon, Cora Long *WomWWA 14*
Saxon, Elizabeth Lyle 1832-1915 *AmWom,
 NatCAB 16*
Saxon, Henry Elbert 1904-1968 *NatCAB 55*
Saxon, Lyle 1891-1946 *WhAm 3*
Saxon, Olin Glenn 1892-1962 *WhAm 4*
Saxon, William 1857- *ApCAB X*
Saxton, Charles T 1846-1903 *NatCAB 4,
 WhAm 1*
Saxton, Eugene Francis 1884-1943 *DcAmB S3*
Saxton, Francis Marion 1864- *WhAm 1*
Saxton, John G 1860- *WhAm 4*
Saxton, Joseph 1799-1873 *AmBi, ApCAB,
 DcAmB, DcScB, NatCAB 9, TwCBDA,
 WhAm H*
Saxton, Luther Calvin 1806-1866 *ApCAB*
Saxton, Lynn Mateer 1874-1941 *NatCAB 31*
Saxton, Rufus 1824-1908 *ApCAB, Drake,
 NatCAB 4, TwCBDA, WhAm 1*
Say, Benjamin d1813 *BiAUS*
Say, Benjamin 1755-1813 *DcAmB, WhAm H*
Say, Benjamin 1756-1813 *ApCAB, BiDrAC,
 TwCBDA*
Say, Jean Baptiste 1767-1832 *McGEWB*
Say, Lucy Way Sistare 1801-1886 *NewYHSD,
 WhAm H*
Say, Thomas 1709-1796 *ApCAB*
Say, Thomas 1787-1834 *AmBi, ApCAB,
 DcAmB, DcScB, Drake, NatCAB 6,
 TwCBDA, WebAB, WhAm H*
Sayen, Clarence Nicholas 1919-1965 *WhAm 4*
Sayers, Albert Jefferson 1870-1931 *NatCAB 24*
Sayers, Dorothy Leigh 1893-1957 *WhAm 3*
Sayers, Joseph Draper 1841-1929 *BiDrAC,
 NatCAB 9, TwCBDA, WhAm 1,
 WhAmP*
Sayers, Orline Walton *WomWWA 14*
Sayers, Reagan 1914-1969 *WhAm 5*
Sayers, Royd Ray 1885-1965 *NatCAB 51*
Sayle, Robert G 1860-1940 *NatCAB 30*
Sayler, Henry 1856-1939 *NatCAB 29*
Sayler, Henry Benton 1836-1900 *BiAUS,
 BiDrAC*
Sayler, James Knox Polk 1839- *WhAm 4*
Sayler, John William 1908- *WhAm 6*
Sayler, Milton 1831-1892 *ApCAB, BiAUS,
 BiDrAC, WhAm H*
Sayler, Oliver Martin 1887-1958 *WhAm 3*
Sayler, Samuel M 1856- *WhAm 4*
Sayles, Frederic Clark 1835-1903 *NatCAB 10,
 NatCAB 26*
Sayles, Henry 1852- *WhAm 4*
Sayles, John 1825-1897 *ApCAB, DcAmB,
 TwCBDA, WhAm H*
Sayles, John Manville 1877-1956 *WhAm 3*
Sayles, Mary Buell 1878- *WomWWA 14*
Sayles, Robert Wilcox 1878-1942 *NatCAB 32,
 WhAm 2*
Saylor, Harry Truax 1893-1973 *WhAm 6*
Saylor, Henry Hodgman 1880-1967 *NatCAB 53,
 WhAm 4*
Saylor, John Galen 1902- *BiDAmEd*
Saylor, John Henry 1904-1966 *WhAm 4*
Saylor, John Phillips 1908-1973 *BiDrAC,
 WhAm 6*
Saylor, Parry Dorland 1878-1942 *NatCAB 31*
Sayour, Elias 1906-1961 *NatCAB 46*
Sayre, A Nelson 1901-1967 *NatCAB 52,
 WhAm 5*
Sayre, Anthony Dickinson 1858-1931 *WhAm 1*
Sayre, Caryl Henry 1889-1963 *NatCAB 50,
 WhAm 4*

Sayre, Daniel Clemens 1903-1957 *WhAm 3*
Sayre, David Austen 1793-1870 *ApCAB*
Sayre, Farrand 1861-1952 *WhAm 3*
Sayre, Francis Bowes 1885-1972 *McGEWB,
 WhAm 5*
Sayre, Harrison Monell 1894-1974 *WhAm 6*
Sayre, Herbert Armistead 1866-1916 *WhAm 1*
Sayre, Ira Terry 1858- *NatCAB 17*
Sayre, Lewis Albert 1820-1900 *AmBi, ApCAB,
 DcAmB, NatCAB 2, TwCBDA,
 WhAm 1*
Sayre, Louise M 1858- *WomWWA 14*
Sayre, Lucius Elmer 1847-1925 *NatCAB 22,
 WhAm 1*
Sayre, Monell 1875-1936 *WhAm 1*
Sayre, Morris 1885-1953 *NatCAB 42,
 WhAm 3*
Sayre, Paul 1894-1959 *WhAm 3*
Sayre, Phoebe Ann *TwCBDA*
Sayre, Reginald Hall 1859-1929 *DcAmB,
 NatCAB 21, WhAm 1*
Sayre, Robert Harold 1885-1960 *NatCAB 50,
 WhAm 1*
Sayre, Robert Heysham 1824-1907 *DcAmB,
 NatCAB 5, WhAm 1*
Sayre, Stephen 1734-1818 *ApCAB, Drake*
Sayre, Stephen 1736-1818 *DcAmB, TwCBDA,
 WhAm H*
Sayre, Theodore Burt 1874-1954 *WhAm 3*
Sayre, Wallace Stanley 1905-1972 *WhAm 5*
Sayre, William Lynison 1840- *NatCAB 5*
Sayres, Edward Smith 1797-1877 *NatCAB 15*
Sayres, Edward Smith 1799-1877 *ApCAB*
Sayres, Edward Stalker 1850- *NatCAB 15*
Sayres, Philip Cooke 1904-1963 *WhAm 4*
Sayres, William Seaman 1851-1916 *WhAm 1*
Sayward, Mary Edith 1870- *WomWWA 14*
Sayward, S Janet 1855- *WhAm 4*
Sayward, William Henry 1845- *WhAm 4*
Sayward, William James 1875-1945 *WhAm 2*
Sbarboro, Alfred Enrico 1875- *WhAm 5*
Sbarboro, Chevalier Andrea 1839-1923
 WhAm 1
Sbarretti, Donatus 1856-1939 *WhAm 3*
Scacki, Francisco *NewYHSD*
Scadding, Charles 1861-1914 *NatCAB 20,
 WhAm 1*
Scadding, Henry 1813- *ApCAB, Drake*
Scaeva *WhAm H*
Scafarello, Peter Joseph 1899-1972 *NatCAB 57*
Scaife, Alan Magee 1900-1958 *WhAm 3*
Scaife, Lauriston Livingston 1907-1970
 WhAm 5
Scaife, Roger Livingston 1875-1951 *WhAm 3*
Scaife, Walter Bell 1858- *WhAm 4*
Scaife, William Lucien 1853-1924 *NatCAB 20*
Scala, Francis M 1819?-1903 *WhAm 2*
Scala, Norman Philip 1894-1953 *WhAm 3*
Scales, A H 1868-1952 *WhAm 3*
Scales, Alfred Moore 1827-1892 *ApCAB,
 BiAUS, BiDrAC, NatCAB 4, TwCBDA,
 WhAm H, WhAmP*
Scales, Alfred Moore 1870-1940 *WhAm 2*
Scales, James 1907-1966 *WhAm 4*
Scales, Joseph E 1891-1959 *WhAm 4*
Scaliger, Joseph Justus 1540-1609 *AsBiEn*
Scaliger, Julius Caesar 1484-1558 *DcScB*
Scallan, Thomas 1770?-1830 *ApCAB*
Scallon, William 1855-1951 *NatCAB 47*
Scamman, John Fairfield 1786-1858 *BiDrAC,
 WhAm H*
Scammell, Alexander 1746-1781 *ApCAB*
Scammell, Alexander 1747-1781 *DcAmB,
 Drake, NatCAB 2, TwCBDA, WhAm H*
Scammell, Scott 1876-1954 *NatCAB 47*
Scammon, Charles Mellville 1825- *ApCAB*
Scammon, Charles Tenfant 1840-1876
 NatCAB 7
Scammon, Eliakim Parker 1816-1894 *ApCAB,
 NatCAB 7, TwCBDA*
Scammon, John F 1786-1858 *BiAUS*
Scammon, Jonathan Young 1812-1890 *ApCAB,
 DcAmB, NatCAB 7, TwCBDA,
 WhAm H*
Scandberger, August *NewYHSD*
Scandrett, Henry Alexander 1876-1957
 NatCAB 44, WhAm 3
Scandrett, Richard B, Jr. 1891-1969 *WhAm 5*

Scanlan, John Jerome 1909-1970 *WhAm 5*
Scanlan, Joseph D 1876-1939 *WhAm 1*
Scanlan, Lawrence 1843-1915 *ApCAB,
 DcAmB, NatCAB 12, TwCBDA,
 WhAm 1*
Scanland, John Milton 1874-1939 *NatCAB 29*
Scanlon, Charles 1869-1927 *NatCAB 20,
 WhAm 1*
Scanlon, Cornelius Thomas 1906-1959
 NatCAB 51
Scanlon, David Howard 1875-1950 *WhAm 3*
Scanlon, Edward J 1893-1967 *WhAm 4*
Scanlon, Michael Joseph 1861-1930 *NatCAB 22*
Scanlon, Thomas Edward 1896-1955 *BiDrAC,
 WhAm 3*
Scannel, Richard 1845-1916 *WhAm 1*
Scannell, David D 1874- *WhAm 5*
Scannell, Edward John 1876-1950 *NatCAB 38*
Scannell, Raymond Christopher 1906-1962
 NatCAB 50
Scannell, Richard 1844- *ApCAB, NatCAB 13*
Scannell, Richard 1845- *TwCBDA*
Scarborough, Byron 1912-1968 *WhAm 5*
Scarborough, Dallas 1882-1957 *NatCAB 43*
Scarborough, Daniel Culpepper 1852- *WhAm 4*
Scarborough, Dorothy 1878-1935 *BiCAW,
 DcAmB S1, WhAm 1*
Scarborough, George Moore 1875- *WhAm 5*
Scarborough, Harold Ellicott 1897-1935
 WhAm 1
Scarborough, Henry 1889-1962 *NatCAB 50*
Scarborough, J Elliott 1906-1966 *NatCAB 52*
Scarborough, James Blaine 1885-1974 *WhAm 6*
Scarborough, John *NewYHSD*
Scarborough, John 1831-1914 *ApCAB,
 NatCAB 3, TwCBDA, WhAm 1*
Scarborough, Lee Rutland 1870-1945
 DcAmB S3, WhAm 2
Scarborough, Robert Bethea 1861-1927 *BiDrAC,
 TwCBDA, WhAm 3*
Scarborough, Warren 1901-1962 *WhAm 4*
Scarborough, William Harrison 1812-1871
 NewYHSD, WhAm H
Scarborough, William Sanders 1852-1926
 BiDAmEd
Scarborough, William Sanders 1854-1926
 WhAm 1, WhoColR
Scarborough, William Saunders 1852-1926
 ApCAB, DcAmB, NatCAB 12
Scarborough, Y Wilcox 1895-1956 *NatCAB 46*
Scarbrough, William 1776-1838 *DcAmB,
 NatCAB 2, WhAm H*
Scarff, Paul Brown 1871-1940 *WhAm 1*
Scarlatti, Domenico 1685-1757 *McGEWB*
Scarlatti, Pietro Alessandro Gaspare 1660-1725
 McGEWB
Scarlett, Frank M 1891-1971 *WhAm 5*
Scarlett, Samuel 1775?- *NewYHSD*
Scarlett, William 1883-1973 *WhAm 5*
Scarpa, Antonio 1752-1832 *BiHiMed, DcScB*
Scarpello, Gaetano 1903-1974 *WhAm 6*
Scarr, James Henry 1867-1936 *WhAm 1*
Scarritt, Nathan 1821-1890 *NatCAB 19*
Scarritt, Nathan Spencer 1898-1965 *WhAm 4*
Scarritt, William Russell 1846-1931
 NatCAB 23
Scarritt, Winthrop Eugene 1857-1911
 NatCAB 28, WhAm 1
Scarseth, George Dewey 1898-1962 *NatCAB 49,
 WhAm 4*
Scarth, William Bain 1837- *ApCAB*
Scasserra, Benedict Benjamin 1905-1968
 NatCAB 54
Scatchard, George 1892-1973 *WhAm 6*
Scates, Douglas Edgar 1898-1967 *BiDAmEd,
 WhAm 5*
Scates, Walter Bennett 1808-1887 *ApCAB,
 NatCAB 12*
Scattergood, Alfred Garrett 1878-1954
 NatCAB 46, WhAm 3
Scattergood, David *NewYHSD*
Scattergood, Ezra Frederick 1871-1947
 NatCAB 36, WhAm 2
Scattergood, Thomas 1748-1814 *DcAmB,
 WhAm H*
Scattergood, Thomas 1754-1814 *ApCAB*
Scattergood, Thomas 1841-1907 *NatCAB 32*

Scavullo, Angelo Carmelo 1888-1965
NatCAB 52
Scervini, Frank Angelo 1907-1962 *NatCAB 46*
Schaaf, Anton 1869- *WhAm 5*
Schaaf, Clarence W 1892-1958 *WhAm 3*
Schaaf, Edward Oswald 1869-1939 *WhAm 1*
Schaaf, Ferdinand Richard 1878- *WhAm 6*
Schaaf, Royal Albert 1892-1964 *WhAm 4*
Schaal, Earl Volk 1892-1967 *NatCAB 54*
Schaap, Michael 1874-1957 *WhAm 3*
Schaare, Harry J 1922- *IIBEAAW*
Schabarum, Bruno Rudolph 1903-1952
NatCAB 39
Schaber, Charles Frederick 1873-1954
NatCAB 45
Schaberg, Herman Henry 1848- *NatCAB 6*
Schachner, Nathan 1895-1955 *NatCAB 43,*
WhAm 3
Schacht, Hjalmar Horace Greeley 1877-1970
McGEWB, WhWW-II
Schaddelee, Richard 1873-1966 *WhAm 4*
Schade, George Herman 1907-1961 *NatCAB 52*
Schade, Louis 1829-1903 *NatCAB 21*
Schadeberg, Henry Carl 1913- *BiDrAC*
Schadle, Jacob Evans 1849-1908 *DcAmB,*
NatCAB 9, NatCAB 12
Schaeberle, John Martin 1853-1924 *DcAmB,*
DcScB, NatCAB 26, TwCBDA, WhAm 1
Schaefer, Abraham Maurice 1900-1965
NatCAB 51
Schaefer, Albert A 1884- *WhAm 2*
Schaefer, Anthony *NewYHSD*
Schaefer, Bertha d1971 *WhAm 5*
Schaefer, Edgar Frederick 1896-1954
NatCAB 44, WhAm 3
Schaefer, Edwin Martin 1887-1950 *BiDrAC,*
WhAmP
Schaefer, Frederic 1877-1955 *WhAm 3*
Schaefer, George Gustave 1857-1927 *ApCAB X*
Schaefer, Gertrude Rose Keegan 1886-1944
NatCAB 34
Schaefer, Harold LeRoy 1893-1952 *NatCAB 44*
Schaefer, Herbert William 1885-1947
NatCAB 36
Schaefer, Hugo H 1891-1967 *WhAm 4*
Schaefer, J Louis 1867-1927 *NatCAB 25*
Schaefer, Jack Warner 1907- *REnAW*
Schaefer, Mathilde 1909- *IIBEAAW*
Schaefer, Milner Baily 1912-1970 *WhAm 5*
Schaefer, Otto Edward 1874-1939 *NatCAB 32*
Schaefer, Paul Herman 1879-1937 *NatCAB 42*
Schaefer, Rudolph Jay 1863-1923 *NatCAB 30*
Schaefer, Vincent Joseph 1906- *AsBiEn*
Schaeffer *NewYHSD*
Schaeffer, Albert Charles 1907-1957 *WhAm 3*
Schaeffer, Charles Ashmead 1843-1898
NatCAB 26, TwCBDA
Schaeffer, Charles Edmund 1867- *WhAm 5*
Schaeffer, Charles Frederick 1807-1879 *ApCAB,*
DcAmB, Drake, WhAm H
Schaeffer, Charles William 1813-1896 *ApCAB,*
DcAmB, Drake, NatCAB 7, WhAm H
Schaeffer, David Frederick 1787-1837 *ApCAB,*
DcAmB, Drake, WhAm H
Schaeffer, Frederick Christian 1792-1831
DcAmB, Drake, WhAm H
Schaeffer, Frederick Christian 1792-1832
ApCAB
Schaeffer, Frederick Christopher 1890-1945
NatCAB 40
Schaeffer, Frederick David 1760-1836 *ApCAB,*
DcAmB, WhAm H
Schaeffer, George W 1917-1959 *WhAm 3*
Schaeffer, Harry Brent 1891-1975 *WhAm 6*
Schaeffer, Henry 1881- *WhAm 6*
Schaeffer, J Nevin 1882-1942 *NatCAB 41*
Schaeffer, J Parsons 1878-1970 *NatCAB 55,*
WhAm 6
Schaeffer, John Ahlum 1886-1941 *NatCAB 30,*
WhAm 1
Schaeffer, John Simon *NewYHSD*
Schaeffer, Nathan Christ 1849-1919 *BiDAmEd,*
DcAmB, NatCAB 14, NatCAB 22,
TwCBDA, WhAm 1
Schaeffer, Ralph William 1890-1949
NatCAB 38
Schaeffer, Robert E 1929-1972 *WhAm 5*
Schaeffer, Robert L 1881-1965 *WhAm 5*

Schaeffer, Samuel Andrew 1879-1950
NatCAB 39
Schaeffer, William Butler 1865-1951
NatCAB 40
Schaeffer, William Christ 1851-1921
NatCAB 20, WhAm 1
Schaerf, Adolf 1890-1965 *WhAm 4*
Schaerff, Charles *NewYHSD*
Schaerff, J W *NewYHSD*
Schafer *DcScB*
Schafer, Frederick Ferdinand 1841- *IIBEAAW*
Schafer, John Charles 1893-1962 *BiDrAC*
Schafer, Joseph 1867-1941 *REnAW, WhAm 1*
Schafer, Mac Henry 1906-1916 *WhAm 3*
Schafer, Samuel M 1840-1918 *NatCAB 17*
Schaff, Charles Ellsworth 1856-1945
NatCAB 35, WhAm 2
Schaff, David Schley 1852- *NatCAB 13,*
WhAm 1
Schaff, Frederic Alan 1884-1950 *WhAm 2*
Schaff, Merle Saunders 1899-1971 *NatCAB 57*
Schaff, Morris 1840-1929 *WhAm 1*
Schaff, Philip 1819-1893 *AmBi, ApCAB,*
DcAmB, DcAmReB, Drake, McGEWB,
NatCAB 3, TwCBDA, WebAB,
WhAm H
Schaff, Philip Haynes 1886-1961 *NatCAB 49*
Schaff, William Frank d1957 *WhAm 3*
Schaffer, Aaron 1894-1957 *WhAm 3*
Schaffer, Charles 1838-1903 *WhAm 1*
Schaffer, David Nicholas 1880-1938
NatCAB 28
Schaffer, Louis Hutzler 1930-1973 *WhAm 6*
Schaffer, Margaret Eliza 1869- *AmWom*
Schaffer, Margaret Ellen 1870- *WomWWA 14*
Schaffer, Mary Townsend Sharples 1861-
WhAm 4
Schaffer, Otto George 1886-1970 *WhAm 5*
Schaffer, William I 1867- *WhAm 5*
Schaffner, Ernestine *AmWom*
Schaffner, John Henry 1866-1939 *WhAm 1*
Schaffner, Louis 1827-1914 *NatCAB 16*
Schaffner, Margaret Anna *WomWWA 14*
Schaffner, Robert C 1876-1946 *WhAm 2*
Schafhirt, William Gurley 1865-1952
NatCAB 40
Schaiberger, Elmer George 1901-1959
NatCAB 48
Schaible, Philip John 1899-1971 *NatCAB 57*
Schain, Josephine 1886- *WomWWA 14*
Schairer, John Frank 1904-1970 *WhAm 5*
Schairer, Otto Sorg 1879- *WhAm 6*
Schaldach, William Joseph 1896- *IIBEAAW*
Schall, John Hubley 1871-1947 *WhAm 2*
Schall, Nina Dennis 1880-1961 *NatCAB 49*
Schall, Thomas David 1877-1935 *DcAmB S1,*
WhAm 1
Schall, Thomas David 1878-1935 *BiDrAC,*
WhAmP
Schaller, Albert 1856-1934 *NatCAB 26,*
WhAm 1, WhAm 1C
Schaller, George J 1873-1964 *WhAm 4*
Schaller, Waldemar Theodore 1882-1967
WhAm 4
Schamberg, Jay Frank 1870-1934 *DcAmB,*
NatCAB 30, WhAm 1
Schamberg, Morton Livingston 1882-1918
BnEnAmA
Schanck, John 1740-1823 *Drake*
Schanck, John Stillwell 1817-1898 *ApCAB,*
TwCBDA
Schanck, Thomas Ely 1860-1945 *NatCAB 34*
Schandein, Emil 1840-1888 *NatCAB 3*
Schanen, William Frank, Jr. 1913-1971
NatCAB 57
Schanfarber, Edwin J 1886-1944 *NatCAB 34*
Schanfarber, Tobias 1862-1942 *WhAm 2*
Schank, John 1740-1823 *ApCAB*
Schantz, Adam, Jr. 1867-1921 *NatCAB 20*
Schaper, William August 1869- *WhAm 5*
Schapiro, J Salwyn 1879-1973 *WhAm 6*
Schapsmeier, Edward Lewis 1927- *EncAAH*
Schapsmeier, Frederick Herman 1927- *EncAAH*
Schardt, Hans 1858-1931 *DcScB*
Scharf, John Thomas 1843-1898 *AmBi,*
ApCAB, DcAmB, NatCAB 7, TwCBDA,
WhAm H
Scharff, Maurice Roos 1888-1967 *NatCAB 53,*

WhAm 5
Scharl, Josef 1896-1954 *WhAm 3*
Scharnagel, Isabel Mona 1906-1953 *WhAm 3*
Scharnhorst, Gerhard Johann David Von
1755-1813 *McGEWB, WhoMilH*
Scharps, Andrew 1905-1971 *WhAm 5*
Scharps, Benjamin 1864-1943 *NatCAB 33*
Scharrer, Ernst Albert 1905-1965 *NatCAB 52*
Schartow, Frank Ernst 1882-1949 *NatCAB 43*
Schattenburg, O Lee 1894-1943 *NatCAB 40*
Schattschneider, Elmer Eric 1892-1971
WhAm 5
Schatz, Carl F 1906-1970 *WhAm 5*
Schatz, Nathan Arthur 1893-1956 *WhAm 3*
Schatz, William Jackson 1876-1964 *NatCAB 51*
Schatzlein, Charles *IIBEAAW*
Schaub, Carl Francis 1802-1944 *NatCAB 33*
Schaub, Edward Leroy 1881-1953 *NatCAB 42,*
WhAm 5
Schaub, Frederick 1855-1937 *WhAm 1*
Schaub, Howard Churchill 1863-1947 *WhAm 2*
Schaub, Ira Obed 1880-1971 *WhAm 5*
Schaub, Mother Jerome 1856-1942 *WhAm 2*
Schaub, Robert C 1904-1958 *WhAm 3*
Schaudinn, Fritz Richard 1871-1906 *AsBiEn,*
BiHiMed, DcScB
Schaufelberger, John William d1916
NatCAB 17
Schauffler, Adolph Frederick 1845-1919
NatCAB 18, WhAm 1
Schauffler, Adolphus Frederick 1845-1919
ApCAB Sup
Schauffler, Edward William 1839-1916
WhAm 1
Schauffler, Goodrich Capen 1896-1966
WhAm 4
Schauffler, Henry Albert 1837-1905 *DcAmB*
Schauffler, Henry Park 1870-1930 *WhAm 1*
Schauffler, Rachel Capen 1876- *WhAm 5,*
WomWWA 14
Schauffler, Robert Haven 1879-1964 *WhAm 4*
Schauffler, Robert McEwen 1871-1958
NatCAB 48
Schauffler, William Gottlieb 1798-1883 *ApCAB,*
DcAmB, NatCAB 18, TwCBDA,
WhAm H
Schauffler, William Gray 1863-1933 *WhAm 1*
Schaufus, Charles Patrick 1922-1974 *WhAm 6*
Schautz, Walter Louis 1900-1963 *NatCAB 48*
Schayer, Milton M 1876-1935 *WhAm 1*
Schealer, Samuel Raymond 1887-1964 *WhAm 4*
Schebera, Ernst Hans 1888-1949 *NatCAB 37*
Schebosh, John Joseph 1721-1788 *ApCAB,*
NatCAB 5
Schechter, Solomon 1847-1915 *DcAmReB,*
WebAB, WhAm 1
Schechter, Solomon 1849-1915 *McGEWB,*
NatCAB 13
Schechter, Solomon 1850-1915 *AmBi, DcAmB*
Schedler, Carl Robert 1904-1965 *WhAm 4*
Schedler, Dean L 1914-1970 *WhAm 5*
Schedler, Joseph *NewYHSD*
Scheel, Fritz 1852-1907 *DcAmB*
Scheel, Sophie Bade 1859- *WomWWA 14*
Scheele, Carl Wilhelm 1732-1786 *BiHiMed*
Scheele, Carl Wilhelm 1742-1786 *DcScB*
Scheele, Karl Wilhelm 1742-1786 *AsBiEn,*
McGEWB
Scheeline, Julia Schoenfeld 1878- *WhAm 6*
Scheer, Edward Waldemar 1875-1949 *WhAm 2*
Scheer, George Adam 1848-1925 *NatCAB 20*
Scheer, Reinhard Karl Friedrich 1863-1929
WhoMilH
Scheerer, William 1855-1944 *NatCAB 33*
Scheetz, Francis Harley 1894-1968 *NatCAB 54,*
WhAm 5
Scheff, Fritzi 1878-1954 *NatCAB 40*
Scheff, Fritzi 1880-1954 *WomWWA 14*
Scheff, Fritzi 1882-1954 *WhAm 3*
Scheffauer, Frederick Carl 1878-1969
NatCAB 57
Scheffauer, Herman George 1878-1927
WhAm 1
Scheffers, Georg 1866-1945 *DcScB*
Scheffey, Lewis Cass 1893-1969 *NatCAB 55,*
WhAm 5
Scheffler, Richard Lee 1893-1967 *NatCAB 53*
Schegk, Jakob 1511-1587 *DcScB*

Scheiber, Harry A 1935- *REnAW*
Scheiberling, Edward Nicholas 1888-1967
WhAm 4, WhAm 5
Scheible, Charles Frederick 1869-1935 *WhAm 1*
Scheible, William F *NewYHSD*
Scheide, Lester Beach 1897-1953 *NatCAB 42*
Scheidenhelm, Frederick William 1884-1959
NatCAB 43, WhAm 4
Scheifer, H *NewYHSD*
Scheiman, William Henry 1873-1949
NatCAB 38
Schein, Ernest 1899-1967 *WhAm 5*
Schein, Marcel 1902-1960 *WhAm 3*
Schein, Samuel Bernard 1883-1952 *NatCAB 41*
Scheiner, Christoph 1573-1650 *DcScB*
Scheiner, Christoph 1575-1650 *AsBiEn*
Scheiner, Julius 1858-1913 *DcScB*
Scheirich, Henry J, Jr. 1902-1968 *NatCAB 54*
Scheldrup, Nicolay Hilmar 1873-1968 *WhAm 5*
Schele DeVere, Maximilian 1820-1898 *DcAmB,*
WhAm H
Schell, Augustus 1812-1884 *ApCAB, DcAmB,*
NatCAB 3, WhAm H
Schell, Edwin Allison 1859-1937 *WhAm 1*
Schell, Francis H 1834-1909 *IIBEAAW,*
NewYHSD
Schell, Frank Cresson 1857-1942 *WhAm 2*
Schell, Frederick A 1838?- *NewYHSD*
Schell, Herbert Hannan 1892-1973 *WhAm 6*
Schell, John J *NewYHSD*
Schell, Ralph Garfield 1892-1958 *WhAm 3*
Schell, Richard 1810-1879 *BiAUS, BiDrAC,*
WhAm H
Schell, Samuel Duvall 1896-1975 *WhAm 6*
Schell, Walker 1857-1915 *NatCAB 16*
Schell, William Elias 1861-1935 *TwCBDA,*
WhAm 1
Schell, William Peter 1878- *WhAm 6*
Schellberg, William Henry 1881- *WhAm 6*
Schellenbach, Lorena Egbert 1873-
WomWWA 14
Schellenberg, Walther 1911- *WhWW-II*
Schellenen, C *NewYHSD*
Schelling, Ernest Henry 1876-1939 *AmBi,*
DcAmB S2, NatCAB 32, WhAm 1
Schelling, Felix Emanuel 1858-1945 *BiDAmEd,*
DcAmB S3, WhAm 2
Schelling, Felix Emmanuel 1858-1945 *TwCBDA*
Schelling, Frederick Wilhelm Joseph Von
1775-1854 *DcScB*
Schelling, Friedrich Wilhelm Joseph Von
1775-1854 *McGEWB*
Schelm, George William 1890-1950 *NatCAB 39*
Schem, Alexander Jacob 1826-1881 *ApCAB,*
DcAmB, TwCBDA, WhAm H
Scheman, Louis 1907-1972 *WhAm 6*
Schemm, Ferdinand Ripley 1899-1955
NatCAB 51
Schemmel, Robert Charles 1867-1953
NatCAB 42
Schenandoa 1706?-1816 *DcAmB*
Schenberg, Joseph 1881-1946 *NatCAB 35*
Schenck, Abraham Henry 1775-1831 *BiDrAC,*
WhAm H
Schenck, Abraham Henry 1777-1831 *BiAUS*
Schenck, Albert Frederick 1877-1931
NatCAB 25
Schenck, Benjamin Robinson 1872-1920
NatCAB 32, WhAm 1
Schenck, Charles Lott 1870-1959 *NatCAB 48*
Schenck, Charles Meigs 1850-1933 *WhAm 1*
Schenck, Daniel Dow 1875-1918 *NatCAB 35*
Schenck, David 1835-1902 *NatCAB 8,*
TwCBDA
Schenck, Edgar Craig 1909-1959 *WhAm 3*
Schenck, Edwin Saxton 1867- *WhAm 4*
Schenck, Eunice Morgan 1884-1955 *WhAm 3*
Schenck, Ferdinand Schureman 1790-1860
BiAUS, BiDrAC, WhAm H
Schenck, Ferdinand Schureman 1845-1925
DcAmB, WhAm 1
Schenck, Frederick Brett 1851-1913
NatCAB 15
Schenck, Hassil Eli 1893-1971 *WhAm 5*
Schenck, Henry A 1856-1922 *NatCAB 24*
Schenck, Hollister V 1888-1960 *WhAm 4*
Schenck, Hubert Gregory 1897-1960 *WhAm 4*

Schenck, Isaac VanWart 1844-1913
NatCAB 24
Schenck, James Findlay 1807-1882 *ApCAB,*
DcAmB, Drake, NatCAB 5, TwCBDA,
WhAm H
Schenck, James R *NewYHSD*
Schenck, John H *NewYHSD*
Schenck, Joseph M d1961 *WhAm 4*
Schenck, Leopold 1843-1886 *NatCAB 4*
Schenck, Lewis Richardson 1880-1923
NatCAB 35
Schenck, Martin Adrian 1882-1956 *NatCAB 42,*
WhAm 3
Schenck, Michael 1876-1948 *WhAm 2*
Schenck, Nicholas d1969 *WhAm 5*
Schenck, Noah Hunt 1825- *Drake*
Schenck, Noah Hunt 1825-1885 *ApCAB,*
TwCBDA
Schenck, Noah Hunt 1825-1895 *NatCAB 9*
Schenck, Paul Fornshell 1899-1968 *BiDrAC,*
WhAm 5, WhAmP
Schenck, Paul Wadsworth 1874- *WhAm 5*
Schenck, Peter Lawrence 1843- *WhAm 4*
Schenck, Robert Cumming 1809-1890 *AmBi,*
ApCAB, BiAUS, BiDrAC, DcAmB,
Drake, NatCAB 3, TwCBDA, WhAm H,
WhAmP
Schenck, Robert Cumming 1905-1967
NatCAB 54, WhAm 4
Schenck, Schuyler Charles 1842-1913
NatCAB 16
Schenck, William Edward 1819-1904 *ApCAB,*
Drake, TwCBDA, WhAm 1
Schenk, Francis Joseph 1901-1969 *WhAm 5*
Schenk, Henry L 1898-1973 *WhAm 5*
Schenk, John Otto 1861-1942 *NatCAB 32*
Schenk, Rachel Katherine 1899-1973 *DcAmLiB*
Schenuit, Alfons William 1864- *WhAm 4*
Schenuit, Frank George 1894-1948 *NatCAB 36*
Schepflin, William Frederick 1886-1957
NatCAB 47
Schepp, Leopold 1841-1926 *NatCAB 20*
Scheppegrell, William 1860- *NatCAB 11,*
WhAm 1
Scher, Phillip George 1880- *WhAm 6*
Scherbak, Boris 1923-1965 *WhAm 4*
Scherbonnier, Henry *NewYHSD*
Scherchen, Hermann 1891-1966 *WhAm 5*
Scherck, Gordon 1903-1967 *WhAm 5*
Scherer, Gordon Harry 1906- *BiDrAC,*
WhAmP
Scherer, James Augustin Brown 1870-1944
NatCAB 32, WhAm 2
Scherer, John Hamilton 1899-1967 *NatCAB 53*
Scherer, John Jacob, Jr. 1881-1956 *WhAm 3*
Scherer, Melanchthon Gideon Groseclose
1861-1932 *NatCAB 28, WhAm 1*
Scherer, Paul Ehrman 1892-1969 *WhAm 5*
Scherer, Robert Pauli 1906-1960 *NatCAB 48,*
WhAm 4
Scherer, Tilden 1876- *WhAm 5*
Scherer, Walter Henry 1880-1951 *NatCAB 45,*
WhAm 3
Schereschewsky, John Forby 1909-1969
WhAm 5
Schereschewsky, Joseph Williams 1873-1940
WhAm 1
Schereschewsky, Samuel Isaac Joseph 1831-1906
ApCAB, DcAmB, NatCAB 13, TwCBDA,
WhAm 1
Scherger, George Lawrence 1874-1941 *WhAm 1*
Scherle, William Joseph 1923- *BiDrAC*
Scherman, Harry 1887-1969 *WhAm 5*
Schermerhorn, Abraham Maus 1791-1855
BiAUS, BiDrAC, WhAm H
Schermerhorn, Agnes Anne 1869-
WomWWA 14
Schermerhorn, Arthur Frederic 1860- *WhAm 4*
Schermerhorn, Frederick Augustus 1844-1919
WhAm 1
Schermerhorn, James 1865-1941 *WhAm 2*
Schermerhorn, Julian Hiram 1876-1953
NatCAB 40
Schermerhorn, Martin Kellogg 1841-1923
NatCAB 20, WhAm 4
Schermerhorn, Richard, Jr. 1877-1962
NatCAB 49, WhAm 5
Schermerhorn, Simon Jacob 1827-1901 *BiDrAC*

Schermerhorn, William David 1871-1942
WhAm 2
Schermerhorn, William Erwin 1852-1930
NatCAB 22
Scheron, William *NewYHSD*
Scherr, Harry 1881-1963 *WhAm 4*
Scherr, Harry, Jr. 1915-1972 *WhAm 5*
Schertz, Helen Pitkin 1877- *WhAm 5,*
WomWWA 14
Schertzinger, Victor 1888-1941 *NatCAB 32*
Scherzer, Albert H 1865-1916 *WhAm 1*
Scherzer, Karl Von 1821- *ApCAB*
Schetky, Caroline 1790-1852 *NewYHSD*
Schetky, John Christian 1778-1874 *NewYHSD*
Scheuch, Frederick Charles 1871-1954
NatCAB 44, WhAm 5
Scheuchzer, Johann Jakob 1672-1733 *DcScB*
Scheuer, James Haas 1920- *BiDrAC*
Scheuerle, Joe 1873-1948 *IIBEAAW*
Scheuermann, Hugo E 1887-1957 *WhAm 3*
Scheuermann, Joseph *NewYHSD*
Scheurer, Peter Arthur 1885-1944 *NatCAB 37*
Scheve, Edward Benjamin 1865-1924 *DcAmB,*
WhAm 1
Schevill, Ferdinand 1868-1954 *NatCAB 47,*
WhAm 3
Schevill, Rudolph 1874-1946 *BiDAmEd,*
DcAmB S4, NatCAB 35, WhAm 2
Schevill, William V 1864- *WhAm 4*
Scheyer, Bell Krolik 1875- *WomWWA 14*
Schiaparelli, Elsa d1973 *WhAm 6*
Schiaparelli, Giovanni Virginio 1835-1910
AsBiEn, DcScB
Schick, Bela 1877-1967 *NatCAB 53, WebAB,*
WhAm 4
Schick, Herman John 1878-1949 *WhAm 2*
Schick, Jacob 1877-1937 *NatCAB 30*
Schick, John Michael 1848-1913 *WhAm 1*
Schick, Lawrence 1897-1967 *WhAm 4*
Schick-Gutierrez, Rene 1903-1966 *WhAm 4*
Schickard, Wilhelm 1592-1635 *DcScB*
Schickhaus, Edward 1898-1969 *WhAm 5*
Schickillemy d1748 *DcAmB*
Schiedt, Richard Conrad Francis 1859-
WhAm 5
Schiefelbein, Harry Theodore 1897-1960
NatCAB 47
Schiefer, Henry *NewYHSD*
Schieffelen, Ed 1850?-1897 *WhAm 4*
Schieffelin, Bradhurst 1824- *ApCAB,*
WhAm 1
Schieffelin, Samuel Bradhurst 1811-1900
ApCAB, NatCAB 4, WhAm 1
Schieffelin, William Jay 1866-1955 *ApCAB X,*
NatCAB 44, WhAm 3
Schieffer *NewYHSD*
Schieffer, Herman *NewYHSD*
Schieffer, Paul *NewYHSD*
Schiele, Arthur Roland 1886-1939 *NatCAB 29*
Schierberg, George Bernard 1892-1967
WhAm 5
Schieren, Charles A 1842-1915 *NatCAB 3*
Schieren, Charles Adolf 1842-1915 *NatCAB 26*
Schieren, Charles Adolph 1842-1915 *DcAmB,*
WhAm 1
Schieren, Charles Albert, Jr. 1869-1932
NatCAB 14, NatCAB 23
Schieren, George Arthur 1904-1951 *NatCAB 40*
Schiff, Hugo Josef 1834-1915 *DcScB*
Schiff, Jacob Henry 1847-1920 *AmBi, DcAmB,*
EncAB, McGEWB, NatCAB 13,
WhAm 1
Schiff, Leo F 1885-1957 *WhAm 3*
Schiff, Leonard Isaac 1915-1971 *WhAm 5*
Schiff, Mary Burch *WomWWA 14*
Schiff, Moritz 1823-1896 *BiHiMed, DcScB*
Schiff, Mortimer L 1877-1931 *WhAm 1*
Schiff, Robert William 1886-1971 *WhAm 5*
Schiff, Sydney Kaufman 1900-1973 *WhAm 6*
Schiffeler, Curt Conrad 1892-1969 *WhAm 5*
Schiffer, Herbert Michael 1890-1952 *WhAm 3*
Schiffler, Andrew Charles 1889-1970 *BiDrAC*
Schiffner, Carl Edmund 1891-1953 *WhAm 3*
Schifreen, Clement Solomon 1901-1967
NatCAB 53
Schilcock, Charles *NewYHSD*
Schilder, Paul Ferdinand 1886-1940 *WhAm 1*
Schildhauer, Edward 1872-1953 *NatCAB 42*

Schildkraut, Joseph 1896-1964 *WhAm 4*
Schildkraut, Rudolf 1862-1930 *AmBi*
Schiller, Avery Reubens 1890-1974 *WhAm 6*
Schiller, Gottfried *NewYHSD*
Schiller, Johann Christoph Friedrich Von 1759-1805 *McGEWB*
Schiller, Margaret Crosby *WomWWA 14*
Schiller, Max d1952 *WhAm 3*
Schiller, Walter 1887-1960 *NatCAB 48*
Schiller, William Bacon 1859-1935 *NatCAB 35, WhAm 1*
Schilling, Etta Acuff *WomWWA 14*
Schilling, George A 1850- *WhAm 4*
Schilling, Gustav 1803-1881 *WhAm H*
Schilling, Hugo Karl 1861-1931 *DcAmB, NatCAB 23, WhAm 1*
Schilling, Joseph T 1893-1957 *WhAm 3*
Schilling, William Frank 1872- *WhAm 5*
Schillinger, Arnold Arthur 1912-1965 *WhAm 4*
Schillinger, Joseph 1895-1943 *DcAmB S3*
Schimmel, Louis William 1860-1933 *NatCAB 26*
Schimmel, Wilhelm 1817-1890 *BnEnAmA*
Schimmel, William Berry 1906- *IlBEAAW*
Schimmelfennig, Alexander 1824-1865 *Drake*
Schimmelin, Alexander Oliver 1645?-1707 *ApCAB*
Schimmelpfennig, Alexander 1824-1865 *ApCAB, TwCBDA*
Schimonsky, Stanislas *IlBEAAW, NewYHSD*
Schimper, Andreas Franz Wilhelm 1856-1901 *DcScB*
Schimper, Karl Friedrich 1803-1867 *DcScB*
Schimper, Wilhelm Philipp 1808-1880 *DcScB*
Schimpf, Henry William 1868- *WhAm 4*
Schimpf, Willis Henry 1911-1959 *NatCAB 50*
Schimpff, Charles Henry 1897-1975 *WhAm 6*
Schinasi, Solomon 1861- *NatCAB 10*
Schindel, John Randolph 1875-1941 *NatCAB 32, WhAm 1*
Schindel, Samuel John Bayard 1871-1921 *NatCAB 19, WhAm 1*
Schindler, Jacob John 1868-1922 *WhAm 1*
Schindler, John Albert 1903-1957 *NatCAB 46*
Schindler, Kurt 1882-1935 *DcAmB S1, WhAm 1*
Schindler, Raymond Campbell d1959 *WhAm 3*
Schindler, Rudolf 1888-1968 *WhAm 5*
Schindler, Rudolph Michael 1887-1953 *BnEnAmA, DcAmB S5*
Schindler, Solomon 1842-1915 *DcAmB, McGEWB, NatCAB 7, WhAm 1*
Schine, J Myer 1892-1971 *WhAm 5*
Schinkel, Karl Friedrich 1781-1841 *McGEWB*
Schinner, Augustin Francis 1863-1937 *WhAm 1*
Schinner, Augustine Francis 1863-1937 *NatCAB 15*
Schinoski, Wallace Charles 1913-1971 *NatCAB 56*
Schinotti, C A *NewYHSD*
Schinotti, E *NewYHSD*
Schinz, Albert 1870-1943 *DcAmB S3, WhAm 2*
Schinz, Walter 1874-1957 *NatCAB 47*
Schiotz, Aksel 1906-1975 *WhAm 6*
Schipa, Tito 1890-1965 *WhAm 4*
Schipfer, Lloyd Albert 1883-1955 *NatCAB 46*
Schipper, Gerrit 1775-1830? *NewYHSD*
Schirach, Baldur Von 1907-1974 *WhWW-II*
Schirer, George 1885-1970 *WhAm 5*
Schirm, Charles Reginald 1864-1918 *BiDrAC, WhAm 4*
Schirmer, Alice Phelps Goodwin *WomWWA 14*
Schirmer, Frank Anton 1863-1942 *NatCAB 32*
Schirmer, Gustav 1829-1893 *DcAmB, WebAB, WhAm H*
Schirmer, Gustave 1890-1965 *WhAm 4*
Schirmer, Rudolph Edward 1859-1919 *DcAmB*
Schirokauer, Arno C 1899-1954 *WhAm 3*
Schirra, Walter Marty, Jr. 1923- *WebAMB*
Schisler, Darwin Gale 1933- *BiDrAC*
Schiwetz, Edward M 1898- *IlBEAAW*
Schjelderup, Harald Krabbe 1895- *WhAm 6*
Schjellerup, Hans Carl F Christian 1827-1887 *DcScB*
Schlacht, Harry H 1893-1961 *NatCAB 47*
Schlacks, Charles Henry 1865-1941 *WhAm 1*
Schladermundt, Herman T 1863-1937 *WhAm 1*

Schladermundt, Peter 1907-1975 *WhAm 6*
Schladitz, E 1862-1910 *WhAm 1*
Schlaefer, Edward George 1895-1963 *WhAm 4*
Schlafli, Ludwig 1814-1895 *DcScB*
Schlager *NewYHSD*
Schlagintweit, Robert Von 1833-1885 *ApCAB*
Schlaikjer, Erich Maren 1905-1972 *WhAm 5, WhAm 6*
Schlaikjer, Oscar Asmus 1901-1966 *NatCAB 52*
Schlake, William E 1863-1940 *WhAm 1*
Schlanger, Ben 1904-1971 *WhAm 5*
Schlanser, Adam Edward 1880-1964 *NatCAB 50*
Schlapp, Max Gustav 1869-1928 *NatCAB 15, WhAm 1*
Schlarman, Joseph H 1879-1951 *NatCAB 38, NatCAB 47, WhAm 3*
Schlatter, Michael 1716-1790 *ApCAB, DcAmB, DcAmReB, Drake, WhAm H*
Schlebecker, John 1923- *EncAAH*
Schlee, Stanley Curren 1910-1972 *NatCAB 57, WhAm 6*
Schleeter, Howard Behling 1903- *IlBEAAW*
Schlegel, Charles 1865-1967 *NatCAB 54*
Schlegel, Fridolin *NewYHSD*
Schlegel, Friedrich Von 1772-1829 *McGEWB*
Schlegel, H Franklin 1867-1941 *WhAm 1*
Schlegel, Herman Theodore 1870-1940 *NatCAB 31*
Schlegel, Mathilde *WomWWA 14*
Schleich, Charles F *NewYHSD*
Schleicher, Gustave 1823-1879 *BiAUS, BiDrAC, NatCAB 11, TwCBDA, WhAm H*
Schleicher, Lou Lane *WomWWA 14*
Schleiden, Jacob Mathias 1804-1881 *DcScB*
Schleiden, Matthias Jakob 1804-1881 *AsBiEn*
Schleiermacher, Friedrich Ernst Daniel 1768-1834 *McGEWB*
Schleif, William 1868- *WhAm 4*
Schlein, Maurice Irving 1902-1949 *NatCAB 37*
Schlenz, Harry Edward 1905-1969 *WhAm 5*
Schlereth, C Q 1884-1950 *WhAm 3*
Schlesinger, Armin Ardery 1883-1962 *WhAm 4*
Schlesinger, Arthur Meier 1888-1965 *McGEWB, WebAB, WhAm 4*
Schlesinger, Arthur Meier, Jr. 1917- *EncAAH, EncAB, WebAB*
Schlesinger, Benjamin 1876-1932 *DcAmB, WhAm HA, WhAm 4*
Schlesinger, Bruno Walter *WebAB*
Schlesinger, Edward Ralph 1911-1974 *WhAm 6*
Schlesinger, Elmer 1880-1928 *NatCAB 24*
Schlesinger, Elmer 1880-1929 *WhAm 1*
Schlesinger, Frank 1871-1943 *DcAmB S3, DcScB, NatCAB 14, NatCAB 32, WhAm 2*
Schlesinger, Hermann Irving 1882-1960 *BiDAmEd, WhAm 4*
Schlesinger, Lee Cahn 1912-1954 *NatCAB 44*
Schlesinger, Louis 1865-1942 *WhAm 1, WhAm 2*
Schlesinger, Monroe Jacob 1892-1955 *NatCAB 43*
Schlesinger, Sara Rosenfeld *WomWWA 14*
Schlesselman, J Theodore 1877-1948 *NatCAB 37*
Schlesser, George Ernest 1907-1973 *NatCAB 57, WhAm 6*
Schleussner, Philip Otto 1878-1931 *NatCAB 25*
Schley, Evander Baker 1883-1953 *WhAm 3*
Schley, George 1795-1846 *NewYHSD*
Schley, Grant Barney 1845-1917 *NatCAB 1, WhAm 1*
Schley, Grant Barney 1880-1936 *NatCAB 34*
Schley, James Montfort 1852-1924 *NatCAB 26*
Schley, Julian Larcombe 1880-1965 *WhAm 4*
Schley, Kenneth Baker 1881-1944 *WhAm 2*
Schley, Reeve 1881-1960 *NatCAB 45, WhAm 4*
Schley, William 1786-1858 *ApCAB, BiAUS, BiDrAC, Drake, NatCAB 1, TwCBDA, WhAm H*
Schley, Winfield Scott 1839- *ApCAB, ApCAB Sup, NatCAB 4, NatCAB 9, TwCBDA*
Schley, Winfield Scott 1839-1909 *AmBi, DcAmB, WebAMB*

Schley, Winfield Scott 1839-1911 *ApCAB X, WhAm 1*
Schleyer, O L d1954 *WhAm 3*
Schlichter, Charles Henry 1874-1948 *NatCAB 37*
Schlick, Florilla S 1869- *WomWWA 14*
Schlick, Friedrich Albert Moritz 1882-1936 *McGEWB*
Schlick, John Joseph 1920-1964 *NatCAB 51*
Schlick, Moritz 1882-1936 *DcScB*
Schlieder, Frederick 1873- *WhAm 5*
Schlieffen, Alfred, Graf Von 1833-1913 *WhoMilH*
Schliemann, Heinrich 1822-1890 *AmBi, DcScB, McGEWB, WhAm H*
Schling, Max 1874-1943 *WhAm 2*
Schling, Max, Jr. 1914-1971 *WhAm 5*
Schlink, Theodore Aloysius 1890-1971 *NatCAB 57*
Schlivek, Kaufman 1881-1955 *NatCAB 44*
Schloerb, Rolland Walter 1893-1958 *WhAm 3*
Schlosberg, Harold 1904-1964 *WhAm 4*
Schloss, Henry William 1855- *NatCAB 14*
Schloss, Oscar Menderson 1882-1952 *WhAm 3*
Schlossberg, Joseph 1875-1971 *WhAm 5*
Schlotheim, Ernst Friedrich, Baron Von 1765-1832 *DcScB*
Schlotman, Joseph Bernard 1882-1951 *NatCAB 42*
Schlotterbeck, Eda Clark *WomWWA 14*
Schlotterbeck, Julius Otto 1865-1917 *WhAm 1*
Schlotterer, Ray C 1898-1966 *WhAm 4*
Schlotthauer, Carl Frank 1893-1959 *NatCAB 48*
Schlottman, Richard Henry 1888-1955 *WhAm 3*
Schluederberg, Carl George 1880-1938 *NatCAB 29*
Schlueter, Edward Benjamin 1880-1952 *WhAm 3*
Schlueter, Newell William 1902-1961 *NatCAB 50*
Schlueter, Robert Ernst 1872-1955 *WhAm 3*
Schlumberger, Charles 1825-1905 *DcScB*
Schlundt, Herman 1869-1937 *NatCAB 41, WhAm 1, WhAm 1C*
Schluraff, Helen Margaret 1884- *WomWWA 14*
Schluter, Andreas 1660?-1714 *McGEWB*
Schlutz, Frederic William 1880-1944 *NatCAB 33, WhAm 2*
Schmaling, Hannah Nichols 1863- *WomWWA 14*
Schmauk, Theodore Emanuel 1860-1920 *DcAmB, NatCAB 19, WhAm 1*
Schmedeman, Albert George 1864-1946 *NatCAB 33, WhAm 2*
Schmedtgen, William Herman 1862- *WhAm 4*
Schmeisser, Harry Christian 1885- *WhAm 5*
Schmeisser, William Christian 1880-1941 *NatCAB 46*
Schmelkes, Franz Charles 1899-1942 *NatCAB 32*
Schmeltzer, John Emile 1882-1943 *NatCAB 34*
Schmerling, Philippe-Charles 1791-1836 *DcScB*
Schmertz, Robert J 1928-1975 *WhAm 6*
Schmick, Franklin Bush 1904-1973 *WhAm 6*
Schmick, William Frederick 1883-1963 *WhAm 4*
Schmid, Edwin Alexander 1890-1955 *NatCAB 45*
Schmid, Henry Ernest 1834-1926 *NatCAB 21*
Schmid, Joseph John 1875-1957 *NatCAB 49*
Schmid, William Ernest 1890-1960 *NatCAB 49*
Schmidel, Casimir Christoph 1718-1792 *DcScB*
Schmidel, Ulrich 1511?-1570? *ApCAB*
Schmidhauser, John Richard 1922- *BiDrAC*
Schmidlapp, Carl Jacob 1888-1960 *NatCAB 48, WhAm 4*
Schmidlapp, Jacob Godfrey 1849-1919 *ApCAB X, NatCAB 19, WhAm 1*
Schmidlin, Theodor 1917-1974 *WhAm 6*
Schmidt *NewYHSD*
Schmidt, Adolph D, Jr. 1912-1964 *WhAm 4*
Schmidt, Albert H 1883-1957 *IlBEAAW*
Schmidt, Alfred Francis William 1873-1966 *NatCAB 54, WhAm 5*
Schmidt, Alwin E 1900- *IlBEAAW*

Schmidt, Anna Seaton *WomWWA 14*
Schmidt, Arthur Alexander 1901-1969 *WhAm 5*
Schmidt, Arthur Paul 1846-1921 *DcAmB*
Schmidt, August *NewYHSD*
Schmidt, Austin G 1883-1960 *WhAm 4*
Schmidt, Bernhard Voldemar 1879-1935 *DcScB*
Schmidt, Bernhard Voldemar 1879-1955 *AsBiEn*
Schmidt, Carl August Von 1840-1929 *DcScB*
Schmidt, Carl Bernard 1872- *NatCAB 16*
Schmidt, Carl Louis August 1885-1946
 DcAmB S4, NatCAB 34, WhAm 2
Schmidt, Charles Gottlieb 1851-1930
 NatCAB 22
Schmidt, Edward Charles 1874-1942
 NatCAB 32, WhAm 2
Schmidt, Edward Julius 1865-1945 *NatCAB 37*
Schmidt, Edward William 1866- *WhAm 4*
Schmidt, Elmer Frederick Edward 1889-1959
 WhAm 3
Schmidt, Emil G 1900-1958 *WhAm 3*
Schmidt, Erhard 1876-1959 *DcScB*
Schmidt, Erich Friedrich 1897-1964
 NatCAB 51, WhAm 4
Schmidt, Ernest R 1895-1971 *WhAm 5*
Schmidt, Ernst Johannes 1877-1933 *DcScB*
Schmidt, Erwin Rudolph 1890-1961 *WhAm 4*
Schmidt, Francis Albert 1885-1944 *WhAm 2*
Schmidt, Frank Henry 1900- *WhAm 5*
Schmidt, Frank Wilhelm 1899-1969 *NatCAB 55*
Schmidt, Frederick *NewYHSD*
Schmidt, Frederick 1826?- *NewYHSD*
Schmidt, Frederick Augustus 1837-1928 *ApCAB,*
 TwCBDA, WhAm 4
Schmidt, Frederick William 1862-1917
 NatCAB 16
Schmidt, Friedrich August 1837-1928 *DcAmB*
Schmidt, Friedrich Georg Gottlob 1868-1945
 WhAm 2
Schmidt, George August 1885-1961 *NatCAB 50,*
 WhAm 4
Schmidt, George Kaspar 1869-1939 *NatCAB 29*
Schmidt, George Small 1861-1935 *WhAm 1*
Schmidt, Gerhard Carl Nathaniel 1865-1949
 DcScB
Schmidt, Gustavus 1795-1877 *ApCAB Sup*
Schmidt, Hans 1865-1930 *NatCAB 50*
Schmidt, Harry 1886-1968 *WhAm 4*
Schmidt, Henry Immanuel 1806- *ApCAB*
Schmidt, Herbert William 1904-1966 *WhAm 4*
Schmidt, Hubert Glasgow 1905- *EncAAH*
Schmidt, Johann Friedrich Julius 1825-1884
 DcScB
Schmidt, John Charles 1859-1923 *NatCAB 38*
Schmidt, Joseph Martin 1846-1931 *WhAm 1*
Schmidt, Karl P 1890-1957 *WhAm 3*
Schmidt, Louis Bernard 1879- *WhAm 6*
Schmidt, Louis David 1896-1968 *NatCAB 55*
Schmidt, Louis Ernst 1869-1957 *WhAm 3*
Schmidt, Maarten 1929- *AsBiEn*
Schmidt, Mabel Pearson 1875- *WomWWA 14*
Schmidt, Minna 1866- *BiCAW*
Schmidt, Nathaniel 1862-1939 *DcAmB S2,*
 WhAm 1
Schmidt, Orvis Adrian 1912-1967 *WhAm 5*
Schmidt, Otto Leopold 1863-1935 *ApCAB X,*
 NatCAB 29, WhAm 1
Schmidt, Paul Gerhard 1876-1957 *WhAm 3*
Schmidt, Peter 1822-1867 *NewYHSD*
Schmidt, Peter Paul 1912-1969 *WhAm 5*
Schmidt, Petrus Johannes 1896-1952 *WhAm 3*
Schmidt, Richard Ernst 1865-1959 *NatCAB 47,*
 WhAm 3
Schmidt, Ruth Hanchett 1875- *WomWWA 14*
Schmidt, Solomon 1806?- *NewYHSD*
Schmidt, Traugott 1830-1897 *NatCAB 46*
Schmidt, Violet Jayne 1867- *WomWWA 14*
Schmidt, Walter A 1895-1975 *WhAm 6*
Schmidt, Walter August 1883-1962 *NatCAB 50,*
 WhAm 4
Schmidt, Walter Seton 1885-1957 *WhAm 3*
Schmidt, William 1855-1931 *WhAm 1*
Schmidt, William, Jr. d1955 *WhAm 3*
Schmidt, William Richard 1889-1966 *WhAm 4*
Schmidt-Isserstedt, Hans Paul Ernst 1900-1973
 WhAm 6
Schmidtke, Edwin Calvin 1899-1952
 NatCAB 42
Schmiedeberg, Oswald 1838-1921 *BiHiMed*

Schmiedel *DcScB*
Schmitt, Aaron Franklin 1870-1949 *NatCAB 39*
Schmitt, Anton 1860-1926 *NatCAB 20*
Schmitt, Arthur J 1893-1971 *WhAm 5*
Schmitt, Bernadotte Everly 1886-1969
 NatCAB 55
Schmitt, Cooper Davis 1859-1910 *WhAm 3*
Schmitt, Eugene August 1879-1958 *NatCAB 43*
Schmitt, Fred 1870-1945 *NatCAB 35*
Schmitt, Gladys 1909-1972 *WhAm 5*
Schmitt, Julius *NewYHSD*
Schmitt, Oscar Charles 1894-1953 *NatCAB 42,*
 WhAm 3
Schmitt, Roland G 1890-1964 *WhAm 4*
Schmitt, Rupert P 1890- *WhAm 3*
Schmitz, Carl Ludwig 1900-1967 *WhAm 4*
Schmitz, Dietrich 1890-1970 *WhAm 5*
Schmitz, Henry 1892-1965 *WhAm 4*
Schmitz, Herbert Eugene 1901-1960
 NatCAB 48, WhAm 3A
Schmitz, Herbert Walter 1894-1960
 NatCAB 46
Schmitz, John George 1930- *BiDrAC*
Schmitz, Joseph William 1905-1966 *WhAm 4*
Schmitz, Leonard Stockwell 1908-1974
 WhAm 6
Schmitz, M S *NewYHSD*
Schmitz, Woodrow Adolph 1912-1973 *WhAm 6*
Schmoller, Gustav Friedrich Von 1838-1917
 McGEWB
Schmolze, Karl Heinrich 1823-1861 *NewYHSD*
Schmon, Arthur Albert 1895-1964 *WhAm 4*
Schmuck, Elmer Nicholas 1882-1936
 NatCAB 31, WhAm 1
Schmucker, Beale Melanchthon 1827-1888
 ApCAB, DcAmB, NatCAB 7, WhAm H
Schmucker, John George 1771-1854 *ApCAB,*
 DcAmB, NatCAB 5, WhAm H
Schmucker, Katherine Elizabeth 1861-
 WomWWA 14
Schmucker, Samuel Christian 1860- *WhAm 5*
Schmucker, Samuel D 1844-1911 *WhAm 1*
Schmucker, Samuel Mosheim 1823-1863 *AmBi,*
 ApCAB, Drake, NatCAB 5, TwCBDA
Schmucker, Samuel Simon 1799-1873 *ApCAB,*
 DcAmB, DcAmReB, Drake, NatCAB 5,
 TwCBDA, WebAB, WhAm H
Schmus, Elmer Ezra 1892-1959 *WhAm 3*
Schmutz, Charles Austin 1900-1974 *WhAm 6*
Schnabel, Artur 1882-1951 *DcAmB S5,*
 WhAm 3
Schnabel, Charles J 1867- *WhAm 1*
Schnabel, Edward *NewYHSD*
Schnabel, Katie Childress 1874- *WomWWA 14*
Schnabel, Truman Gross 1886-1971 *WhAm 5*
Schnackenberg, Elmer Jacob 1889-1968
 WhAm 5
Schnader, William A 1886-1968 *WhAm 5*
Schnakenberg, Henry 1892-1970 *NatCAB 55,*
 WhAm 5
Schnarr, D *NewYHSD*
Schnauffer, Carl Heinrich 1823-1854 *DcAmB,*
 WhAm H
Schnauffer, William 1903-1950 *NatCAB 39*
Schnebly, John Thomas 1910-1974 *WhAm 6*
Schneck, Benjamin Shroder 1806-1874 *ApCAB*
Schneckenburger, Walter William 1882-1951
 NatCAB 48
Schnecker, Peter August 1850-1903 *WhAm 1*
Schneder, David Bowman 1857-1938 *WhAm 1*
Schnee, Verne H 1898-1957 *WhAm 3*
Schneebeli, G Adolph 1853-1923 *WhAm 3,*
 WhAm 4
Schneebeli, Gustav Adolphus 1853-1923 *BiDrAC*
Schneebeli, Herman Theodore 1907- *BiDrAC*
Schneideman, Theodore Benjamin 1861-1931
 NatCAB 24
Schneider, Adolph Benedict 1866-1946
 WhAm 2
Schneider, Albert 1862-1928 *TwCBDA*
Schneider, Albert 1863-1928 *DcAmB,*
 NatCAB 13, WhAm 1
Schneider, Albert Edward Rupert 1874-1954
 NatCAB 42
Schneider, Albert Francis 1853-1932
 NatCAB 24
Schneider, Alma Kittredge 1901-1975 *WhAm 6*
Schneider, B Aubrey 1912-1960 *NatCAB 51*

Schneider, Benjamin 1807-1877 *DcAmB,*
 WhAm H
Schneider, Benjamin Bernard 1891-1957
 NatCAB 47
Schneider, Carl E 1903-1966 *WhAm 4*
Schneider, Charles B 1821?- *NewYHSD*
Schneider, Charles Conrad 1843-1916
 NatCAB 11, NatCAB 18, WhAm 1
Schneider, Clement Joseph 1927-1972 *WhAm 5*
Schneider, Edward Alexander 1901-1972
 WhAm 5
Schneider, Edward Christian 1874-1954
 WhAm 3
Schneider, Erich 1900-1970 *WhAm 5*
Schneider, Frederick William 1862-1941
 WhAm 2
Schneider, Friedrich Anton 1831-1890 *DcScB*
Schneider, George 1823-1905 *ApCAB, DcAmB,*
 NatCAB 10
Schneider, George 1897-1971 *WhAm 5*
Schneider, George John 1877-1939 *BiDrAC,*
 WhAm 1, WhAmP
Schneider, Hans 1863-1926 *NatCAB 20*
Schneider, Harvey C 1895-1962 *NatCAB 50*
Schneider, Herman 1872-1939 *BiDAmEd,*
 DcAmB S2, NatCAB 37, WhAm 1
Schneider, Ila Roberts 1873- *WomWWA 14*
Schneider, J Walter 1905-1944 *NatCAB 33*
Schneider, Joseph 1845-1927 *NatCAB 2,*
 WhAm 1
Schneider, Nathaniel Churchill 1839-1895
 NatCAB 17
Schneider, Oscar Albert 1898-1961 *WhAm 4*
Schneider, Otto Henry 1865-1950 *NatCAB 39*
Schneider, Ralph Edward 1909-1964 *WhAm 4*
Schneider, Samuel Hiram 1886-1939 *WhAm 1,*
 WhAm 1C
Schneider, Stanley Frederick 1929-1975
 WhAm 6
Schneider, Theodore 1703-1764 *DcAmB,*
 WhAm H
Schneider, Vincent Augustine 1900-1963
 NatCAB 49
Schneider, Walter Arthur 1899-1956 *WhAm 3*
Schneider, William B 1898-1964 *WhAm 4*
Schneider, Wilmar Rufus 1913-1974 *WhAm 6*
Schneiderhahn, Edward Vincent Paul 1874-1948
 NatCAB 37
Schneiderhohn, Hans 1887-1962 *DcScB*
Schneiders, Alexander A 1909-1968 *WhAm 5*
Schneidewind, Richard 1900-1970 *WhAm 5*
Schneierson, Samuel Simon 1901-1974
 NatCAB 57
Schneirla, Theodore Christian 1902-1968
 WhAm 5
Schnell, Henry Ferdinand 1878-1956
 NatCAB 45
Schneller, Frederic Andrew 1906-1960
 NatCAB 48, WhAm 4
Schneller, George Otto 1843-1895 *DcAmB,*
 NatCAB 8, WhAm H
Schner, Charles, Jr. 1911-1963 *NatCAB 51*
Schnering, Otto Young 1891-1953 *NatCAB 41,*
 WhAm 3
Schnerr, Leander 1836-1920 *DcAmB*
Schniewind, Ewald Heinrich 1887- *ApCAB X*
Schnitzer, Cordelia M 1850- *WomWWA 14*
Schnitzius, Henry Joseph 1897-1957
 NatCAB 43
Schnitzler, Arthur 1862-1931 *McGEWB*
Schnitzler, John William 1882- *WhAm 1*
Schnur, George Henry, Jr. 1861-1939 *WhAm 1*
Schnurpel, Hans Karl 1896-1973 *WhAm 6*
Schnurr, Martin K 1898-1965 *WhAm 4*
Schnute, William Jacob 1914-1972 *WhAm 6*
Schobeck, Arthur Ellwyn 1893-1962 *WhAm 4*
Schoch, Eugene Paul 1871- *WhAm 5*
Schock, Clarence 1865-1955 *NatCAB 45*
Schocken, Theodore 1914-1975 *WhAm 6*
Schodde, George Henry 1854-1917 *ApCAB,*
 DcAmB, NatCAB 26, WhAm 1
Schoder, Ernest William 1879-1968 *NatCAB 5,*
 WhAm 5
Schoelcher, Victor 1804- *ApCAB*
Schoellkopf, Alfred Hugo 1893-1942
 NatCAB 43, WhAm 2
Schoellkopf, Arthur 1856-1913 *NatCAB 17*

Schoellkopf, Carl Phillip Hugo 1862-1928
  NatCAB 23
Schoellkopf, J Fred, IV 1910-1969 *WhAm 5*
Schoellkopf, Jacob Frederick 1819-1899
  NatCAB 31
Schoellkopf, Jacob Frederick 1858-1942
  NatCAB 31, WhAm 2
Schoellkopf, Paul Arthur 1884-1947 *WhAm 2*
Schoemaker, Daniel Martin 1867-1951
  WhAm 3
Schoemaker, Helen Taylor 1865-
  WomWWA 14
Schoen, Charles Thomas 1844-1917 *NatCAB 25,*
  WhAm 4
Schoen, Edward, Jr. 1911-1974 *WhAm 6*
Schoen, Frank Joseph 1884-1955 *NatCAB 43*
Schoen, John Edmund 1898-1967 *NatCAB 53,*
  WhAm 5
Schoenberg, Arnold 1874-1951 *DcAmB S5,*
  EncAB, McGEWB, WebAB, WhAm 3
Schoenberg, Hyman 1886-1952 *NatCAB 41*
Schoenberger, George Christian 1875-1928
  NatCAB 26
Schoene, William Jay 1879- *WhAm 6*
Schoeneck, Edward 1875- *WhAm 5*
Schoeneck, Henry William 1884-1956
  NatCAB 45
Schoenefeld, Henry 1857- *NatCAB 11,*
  WhAm 4
Schoenemann, Oscar Paul 1899-1974 *WhAm 6*
Schoenen, Percy Leopold 1891-1953
  NatCAB 40
Schoener, Jacob B 1805-1846? *NewYHSD*
Schoenfeld, H F Arthur 1889-1952 *WhAm 3*
Schoenfeld, Hermann 1861-1926 *WhAm 1*
Schoenfeld, William Alfred 1888-1959
  NatCAB 46, WhAm 3
Schoenflies, Arthur Moritz 1853-1928 *DcScB*
Schoenheimer, Rudolf 1898-1941 *AsBiEn,*
  DcAmB S3
Schoenhof, Jacob 1839-1903 *DcAmB*
Schoenleber, Gretchen Bertha 1890-1953
  NatCAB 45
Schoenleber, Otto J 1858- *NatCAB 16*
Schoenrich, Herbert 1883-1957 *NatCAB 48*
Schoenstein, Paul 1902-1974 *WhAm 6*
Schoepf, Albin Francisco 1822-1886 *ApCAB*
Schoepf, W Kesley 1864-1927 *WhAm 1*
Schoepfle, Chester Seitz 1892-1957 *NatCAB 46,*
  WhAm 3
Schoeppel, Andrew Frank 1894-1962 *BiDrAC,*
  WhAm 4
Schoepperle, Victor 1890-1962 *WhAm 4*
Schoetz, Max 1884-1927 *WhAm 1*
Schoff, Charles Henry 1871-1957 *NatCAB 47*
Schoff, Frederick 1848-1922 *NatCAB 19*
Schoff, George Calix 1867-1914 *NatCAB 16*
Schoff, Hannah Kent d1940 *WhAm 1,*
  WomWWA 14
Schoff, Hannah Kent 1850?-1940 *NatCAB 18*
Schoff, Hannah Kent 1853-1940 *NotAW*
Schoff, Stephen Alonzo 1818-1904 *ApCAB,*
  DcAmB, NewYHSD, TwCBDA,
  WhAm 1
Schoff, Wilfred Harvey 1874-1932 *WhAm 1*
Schoffman, Leonard 1916-1972 *NatCAB 56*
Schofield, Albert George 1912-1970 *WhAm 5*
Schofield, Charles Edwin 1894-1951 *WhAm 3*
Schofield, Frank Herman 1869-1942 *WhAm 2*
Schofield, Frank Lee 1849-1925 *WhAm 1*
Schofield, Frank Michel 1873-1947 *NatCAB 37*
Schofield, Harvey A 1877-1941 *WhAm 1*
Schofield, Henry 1866-1918 *DcAmB, WhAm 1*
Schofield, John McAllister 1831-1906 *AmBi,*
  ApCAB, BiAUS, BiDrUSE, DcAmB,
  Drake, NatCAB 4, TwCBDA, WebAB,
  WebAMB, WhAm 1
Schofield, Martha 1839-1916 *NotAW*
Schofield, Mary Lyon Cheney 1868-1943
  NatCAB 36, WhAm 2
Schofield, William 1857-1912 *NatCAB 15,*
  WhAm 1
Schofield, William Henry 1870-1920 *DcAmB,*
  WhAm 1
Scholder, Charles Orin 1869-1934 *NatCAB 25*
Scholder, Fritz 1937- *IIBEAAW*
Scholem, Gershom 1897- *McGEWB*
Scholer, Henry Charles 1891-1957 *NatCAB 43*

Scholer, Walter 1890-1972 *WhAm 5*
Scholes, Charles Marcel 1903-1972 *WhAm 6*
Scholes, Samuel Ray 1884-1974 *WhAm 6*
Scholfield, John 1834-1893 *NatCAB 13,*
  TwCBDA
Scholfield, William Rufus 1883-1970
  NatCAB 56
Scholl, David Henry 1893-1966 *NatCAB 53*
Scholl, Frank John 1884-1967 *NatCAB 54*
Scholl, Guilford Darby 1879-1950 *NatCAB 38*
Scholl, Gustave *NewYHSD*
Scholl, Hans 1917-1943 *WhWW-II*
Scholl, John William 1869-1952 *WhAm 3*
Scholl, Sophie 1920-1943 *WhWW-II*
Scholl, William John 1862-1932 *NatCAB 28*
Scholl, William M 1882-1968 *WhAm 5*
Scholle, Hardinge 1896-1969 *WhAm 5*
Scholler, Adolph 1884-1939 *NatCAB 29*
Scholler, Henry Herbert 1888-1936 *NatCAB 30*
Scholte, Hendrick Peter 1805-1868 *WhAm H*
Scholte, Hendrik Peter 1805-1868 *DcAmB*
Scholtz, Henry George 1866-1936 *NatCAB 31*
Scholtz, Joseph D 1890-1972 *WhAm 5*
Scholz, Emil Maurice 1881-1948 *WhAm 2*
Scholz, Karl William Henry 1886-1962
  WhAm 4
Scholz, Richard Frederick 1880-1924 *WhAm 1*
Scholze, George Ernest 1874-1947 *NatCAB 38*
Schomberg, Friedrich, Graf Von 1615-1690
  WhoMilH
Schomburg, Arthur Alfonso 1874-1938
  DcAmLiB, WhoColR
Schomburgk, Robert Herman 1804-1865
  ApCAB
Schomer, Nahum Meir 1849-1905 *DcAmB*
Schommer, John J 1884-1960 *WhAm 4*
Schomp, Albert Linden 1880-1957 *NatCAB 50,*
  WhAm 3
Schonbein, Christian Friedrich 1799-1868
  AsBiEn, DcScB
Schonberg, Arnold 1874-1951 *WebAB*
Schonberg, Charles L *NewYHSD*
Schonberg, David L *NewYHSD*
Schonberg, James *NewYHSD*
Schonberger, E D 1875- *WhAm 5*
Schonborn, Anton d1871 *IIBEAAW*
Schondelmeier, Charles Theodore 1844-1927
  NatCAB 21
Schoney, Theodosia Secor Fowler 1871-
  WomWWA 14
Schonfarber, Gordon 1894-1951 *NatCAB 40*
Schonfeld, Eduard 1828-1891 *DcScB*
Schonfeld, William Albrecht 1906-1970
  NatCAB 55, WhAm 5
Schongauer, Martin 1435?-1491 *McGEWB*
Schonhardt, Henri 1877-1953 *WhAm 3*
Schonherr, Carl Johan 1772-1848 *DcScB*
Schonitzer, Rudolph Ignatius 1889-1968
  NatCAB 55
Schonland, Basil Ferdinand Jamieson 1896-1972
  DcScB
Schonlein, Johann Lucas 1793-1864 *BiHiMed,*
  DcScB
Schoofs, Orlando Peter 1894-1950 *NatCAB 41*
Schoolcraft, Arthur Allen 1897-1959 *WhAm 4*
Schoolcraft, Henry Rowe 1793-1864 *AmBi,*
  ApCAB, BiAUS, DcAmB, DcScB, Drake,
  EncAAH, EncAB, IIBEAAW, McGEWB,
  NatCAB 5, NewYHSD, REnAW,
  TwCBDA, WebAB, WhAm H
Schoolcraft, John Lawrence 1804-1860 *BiAUS,*
  BiDrAC, WhAm H
Schoolcraft, Lawrence 1760-1840 *ApCAB*
Schoolcraft, Mary Howard *ApCAB*
Schooler, Lewis 1848- *WhAm 4*
Schooley, Arthur 1868-1952 *NatCAB 40*
Schooley, Harry Barnum 1869-1953
  NatCAB 42
Schoolfield, Benjamin Lucky 1888-1958
  NatCAB 47
Schoolfield, Mary Louisa 1839- *WomWWA 14*
Schoolhouse, Charles 1832-1913 *NatCAB 15*
Schoolhouse, Lewis 1862- *NatCAB 15*
Schoonhoven, Helen Butterfield 1869-1958
  WhAm 3
Schoonhoven, Helen Butterfield 1870-1958
  WomWWA 14

Schoonhoven, John James 1864-1936
  NatCAB 26, WhAm 1, WhAm 1C
Schoonmaker, Augustus 1828- *ApCAB*
Schoonmaker, Cornelius Corneliusen 1745-1796
  ApCAB, BiAUS, BiDrAC, TwCBDA,
  WhAm H
Schoonmaker, Cornelius Marius 1839-1889
  TwCBDA
Schoonmaker, Edwin Davies 1873-1940
  NatCAB 37, WhAm 1
Schoonmaker, Frederic Palen 1870-1945
  WhAm 2
Schoonmaker, John Harp 1868-1951
  NatCAB 40
Schoonmaker, Marius 1811-1894 *ApCAB,*
  BiAUS, BiDrAC, TwCBDA
Schoonmaker, Martinus 1737-1824 *ApCAB*
Schoonmaker, Nancy M 1873-1965 *WhAm 4*
Schoonover, Anna Bonnell Day 1871-
  WomWWA 14
Schoonover, Draper Talman 1872-1956
  NatCAB 42, WhAm 3
Schoonover, Frank Earle 1877-1972 *IIBEAAW,*
  WhAm 5
Schoonover, Warren 1838-1919 *NatCAB 6*
Schooten, Frans Van 1615?-1660 *DcScB*
Schooten, Sarah Schilling 1894-1974 *WhAm 6*
Schopenhauer, Arthur 1788-1860 *McGEWB*
Schopf, Johann David 1752-1800 *DcAmB,*
  WhAm H
Schopfer, William-Henri 1900-1962 *DcScB*
Schopflin, Jack 1907-1963 *WhAm 4*
Schoregge, Charles William 1889-1961
  NatCAB 51
Schorer, William Carl 1878-1967 *NatCAB 54*
Schorer, William Conrad 1906-1969
  NatCAB 55
Schorger, Arlie William 1884-1972 *WhAm 5*
Schorlemmer, Carl 1834-1892 *DcScB*
Schorling, Raleigh 1887-1950 *BiDAmEd,*
  NatCAB 38, WhAm 3
Schorner, Ferdinand 1892- *WhoMilH*
Schorner, Friedrich 1892- *WhWW-II*
Schorr, Friedrich 1888-1953 *NatCAB 41*
Schorsch, Alexander Peter 1882-1957 *WhAm 3*
Schortemeier, Frederick Edward 1889-1965
  WhAm 4
Schott, Arthur 1813?-1875 *IIBEAAW,*
  NewYHSD
Schott, Charles Anthony 1826-1901 *ApCAB,*
  DcAmB, DcScB, TwCBDA, WhAm 1
Schott, Charles Mandeville, Jr. 1846-1919
  NatCAB 18
Schott, Gaspar 1608-1666 *DcScB*
Schott, Henry 1873-1926 *WhAm 1*
Schott, Lawrence Frederick 1907-1963
  WhAm 4
Schott, Max 1876-1955 *NatCAB 47, WhAm 3*
Schott, Otto Friedrich 1851-1935 *DcScB*
Schotten, Julius John 1858- *NatCAB 12*
Schottky, Friedrich Hermann 1851-1935 *DcScB*
Schouler, James 1839-1920 *AmBi, ApCAB,*
  DcAmB, NatCAB 11, TwCBDA,
  WhAm 1
Schouler, John 1846-1917 *TwCBDA, WhAm 1*
Schouler, William 1814-1872 *ApCAB, DcAmB,*
  Drake, WhAm H
Schour, Isaac 1900-1964 *WhAm 4*
Schoute, Pieter Hendrik 1846-1923 *DcScB*
Schouten, Jan Arnoldus 1883-1971 *DcScB*
Schouten, Willem Cornelis 1567-1625 *ApCAB*
Schouten, William Cornelius 1580?-1625
  McGEWB
Schouw, Joakim Frederik 1789-1852 *DcScB*
Schoyen, A Robert 1917-1967 *NatCAB 53*
Schoyer, Alfred McGill 1859- *WhAm 4*
Schoyer, Raphael *NewYHSD*
Schoyer, Samuel Chadwick 1840-1890
  NatCAB 31
Schrade, Leo Franz 1903-1964 *WhAm 5*
Schrader *NewYHSD*
Schrader, Charles E 1890-1969 *WhAm 5*
Schrader, Frank Charles 1860-1944 *WhAm 2*
Schrader, Franz 1891-1962 *WhAm 4*
Schrader, Fred L 1891-1963 *WhAm 4*
Schrader, Frederick Franklin 1857-1943
  WhAm 2
Schrader, George H *WhAm 5*

Schrader, Robert Estes 1915-1974 *WhAm 6*
Schrader, Theodore *NewYHSD*
Schradieck, Henry 1846-1918 *DcAmB, NatCAB 20, WhAm 4*
Schrafft, George Frederick 1870-1928 *NatCAB 26*
Schrag, Karl 1912- *BnEnAmA*
Schrage, Annie Thayer 1863- *WomWWA 14*
Schrage, Arthur Anthony 1880-1951 *NatCAB 42*
Schrager, Victor Lupu 1878-1944 *NatCAB 33*
Schrakamp, Josepha *WhAm 5*
Schram, Jack Aron 1908-1961 *WhAm 4*
Schramm, E Frank 1883-1967 *WhAm 4*
Schramm, Louis 1902-1957 *NatCAB 46*
Schrank, Raymond Edward 1912-1973 *WhAm 6*
Schratchley, Francis Arthur 1858- *WhAm 4*
Schrech, Horst 1885- *IIBEAAW*
Schreckengast, Isaac Butler 1864-1935 *NatCAB 26, WhAm 1*
Schrecker, Paul 1889-1963 *WhAm 4*
Schreiber, Carl Frederick 1886-1960 *NatCAB 47, WhAm 3*
Schreiber, Collingwood 1831- *ApCAB*
Schreiber, Georges 1904- *IIBEAAW*
Schreiber, Manuel 1907-1974 *WhAm 6*
Schreiber, Martin 1876-1941 *NatCAB 31*
Schreiber, Walter 1884-1958 *WhAm 3*
Schreibers, Karl Franz Anton Von 1775-1852 *DcScB*
Schreiner, Bernard Francis 1886-1951 *NatCAB 39*
Schreiner, Charles 1838-1927 *REnAW*
Schreiner, Emma Tolbert 1856- *WomWWA 14*
Schreiner, George Abel 1875- *WhAm 5*
Schreiner, Myrta Scott 1866- *WomWWA 14*
Schreiner, Oswalk 1875- *WhAm 5*
Schreiner, Mrs. T *NewYHSD*
Schrembs, Joseph 1866-1945 *DcAmB S3, NatCAB 15, WhAm 2*
Schrenk, Hermann Von d1953 *WhAm 3*
Schreyvogel, Charles 1861-1912 *IIBEAAW, NatCAB 13, REnAW, WhAm 1*
Schriber, Louis 1878-1950 *WhAm 3*
Schricker, Henry Frederick 1883-1966 *WhAm 4*
Schrider, Peter Paul 1903-1966 *NatCAB 51*
Schrieck, Sister Louise VanDer 1813-1886 *DcAmB, WhAm H*
Schrieffer, John Robert 1931- *WebAB*
Schriever, William 1894-1958 *WhAm 3*
Schriver, Edmund 1812-1899 *ApCAB, DcAmB, Drake, TwCBDA, WhAm H*
Schrock, Robert D 1884-1960 *NatCAB 51*
Schroder, Friedrich Wilhelm Karl Ernst 1841-1902 *DcScB*
Schroder, William Henry 1914-1970 *NatCAB 56, WhAm 5*
Schrodinger, Erwin 1887-1961 *AsBiEn, DcScB, McGEWB, WhAm 4*
Schroeder, Albert William 1917-1966 *WhAm 4*
Schroeder, Alwin 1855- *WhAm 4*
Schroeder, Bernard Anthony 1900-1957 *NatCAB 48, WhAm 3*
Schroeder, C *NewYHSD*
Schroeder, Carl A 1903-1965 *WhAm 4*
Schroeder, David R *NewYHSD*
Schroeder, Ernest Charles 1865- *WhAm 1*
Schroeder, Francis *BiAUS, NatCAB 4*
Schroeder, Frederick Antony 1833-1899 *NatCAB 2, WhAm 1*
Schroeder, George William 1914-1971 *WhAm 6*
Schroeder, Henry Alfred 1906-1975 *WhAm 6*
Schroeder, Henry Franklin 1870-1955 *NatCAB 46*
Schroeder, John *NewYHSD*
Schroeder, John Charles 1897-1954 *WhAm 3*
Schroeder, John Frederick 1800-1857 *ApCAB, DcAmB, Drake, NatCAB 11, WhAm H*
Schroeder, Joseph Edwin 1905-1967 *WhAm 5*
Schroeder, Louis Clausen 1881-1938 *NatCAB 28*
Schroeder, May Catherine 1872- *WomWWA 14*
Schroeder, Paul Henry 1897-1968 *NatCAB 54*
Schroeder, Paul Louis 1894-1966 *WhAm 4*
Schroeder, Reginald 1855- *WhAm 4*

Schroeder, Rudolph William 1886-1952 *DcAmB S5, WhAm 3*
Schroeder, Seaton 1849-1922 *DcAmB, NatCAB 28, TwCBDA, WhAm 1*
Schroeder, Walter 1878-1967 *WhAm 4*
Schroeder, Werner William 1892-1960 *WhAm 4*
Schroeder, William Edward 1867-1926 *WhAm 1*
Schroeder VanDerKolk, Jacobus L C 1797-1862 *DcScB*
Schroers, John 1858- *NatCAB 12*
Schroeter, Heinrich Eduard 1829-1892 *DcScB*
Schroff, Joseph 1887-1967 *NatCAB 54, WhAm 4*
Schropp, Rutledge Clifton 1922-1973 *WhAm 6*
Schroter, Johann Hieronymus 1745-1816 *DcScB*
Schrotter, Anton Von 1802-1875 *DcScB*
Schrunk, Terry Doyle 1913-1975 *WhAm 6*
Schrup, Charles Joseph 1886-1949 *NatCAB 38, WhAm 2C*
Schubart, William Howard 1892-1953 *NatCAB 41*
Schubert, Franz Peter 1797-1828 *McGEWB*
Schubert, George Peter 1883-1964 *NatCAB 50*
Schubert, Hermann Casar Hannibal 1848-1911 *DcScB*
Schubring, Edward John Bernhard 1878-1959 *NatCAB 48*
Schuchard, Carl 1827-1883 *IIBEAAW, NewYHSD*
Schuchardt, Rudolph Frederick 1875-1932 *NatCAB 25, WhAm 1*
Schuchardt, William Herbert 1874-1958 *WhAm 3*
Schuchert, Charles 1858-1942 *DcAmB S3, DcScB, NatCAB 15, WhAm 2*
Schuck, Arthur Aloys 1895-1963 *WhAm 4*
Schuck, Arthur Frederick 1896-1971 *WhAm 5*
Schuckman, George *NewYHSD*
Schuckman, William *NewYHSD*
Schuelein, Hermann 1884- *WhAm 5*
Schuell, Hildred Magdalene 1906-1970 *NatCAB 55*
Schuerman, William Henry 1859-1932 *WhAm 1*
Schuessele, Christian 1826-1879 *DcAmB*
Schuette, Conrad Herman Louis 1843-1926 *ApCAB, WhAm 1*
Schuette, Curt Nicolaus 1895-1975 *WhAm 6*
Schuette, Walter Erwin 1867-1955 *WhAm 3*
Schuette, William Herman 1912-1959 *WhAm 4*
Schuetz, Leonard William 1887-1944 *BiDrAC, WhAm 2, WhAmP*
Schuh, Henry Frederick 1890-1965 *WhAm 4*
Schuhmann, George William 1865-1931 *WhAm 1*
Schuirmann, Roscoe Ernest 1890-1971 *WhAm 5*
Schule, James Raymond 1920-1970 *WhAm 5*
Schuler, Anthony Joseph 1869-1944 *NatCAB 15, WhAm 2*
Schuler, Donald Vern 1927-1974 *WhAm 6*
Schuler, Hans 1874-1951 *NatCAB 39, WhAm 3*
Schuler, Loring Ashley 1886-1968 *WhAm 5*
Schulgen, George Francis 1900-1955 *WhAm 3*
Schulhoff, Henry Bernard 1904-1968 *WhAm 5*
Schull, Herman Walter 1875- *WhAm 5*
Schuller, Gunther 1925- *McGEWB, WebAB*
Schuller, John D *NewYHSD*
Schullinger, Rudolph Nicholas 1896-1969 *NatCAB 56, WhAm 5*
Schulmaier, A Talmage 1893- *WhAm 3*
Schulman, Abraham S 1899-1954 *NatCAB 42*
Schulman, Jack Henry 1904-1967 *WhAm 4*
Schulman, Samuel 1864-1955 *NatCAB 42, WhAm 3*
Schulte, David Albert 1873-1949 *NatCAB 39, WhAm 2*
Schulte, Hermann VonWechlinger 1876-1932 *NatCAB 23, WhAm 1*
Schulte, John H 1923-1972 *WhAm 6*
Schulte, John Walter 1914-1968 *NatCAB 54*
Schulte, Walter Biersach 1888-1957 *NatCAB 49*
Schulte, William Henry 1889-1957 *WhAm 3*
Schulte, William Theodore 1890-1966 *BiDrAC*
Schultes, Johann 1595-1645 *BiHiMed*
Schultheis, Christian *NewYHSD*
Schultheiss, Carl Max 1885-1961 *WhAm 4*

Schultz *NewYHSD*
Schultz, Alfred Paul 1878- *WhAm 6*
Schultz, Alfred Reginald 1876-1943 *NatCAB 41, WhAm 2*
Schultz, Carl Emil 1909-1966 *NatCAB 51*
Schultz, Charles 1893-1948 *NatCAB 37*
Schultz, Charles Monroe 1922- *WebAB*
Schultz, Clifford Griffith 1890-1958 *NatCAB 43, WhAm 3*
Schultz, Clinton M 1851- *WhAm 4*
Schultz, Dutch *DcAmB S1, WebAB*
Schultz, Edward Garfield 1878-1961 *NatCAB 48*
Schultz, Edward Waters 1919-1972 *WhAm 5*
Schultz, Ernst William 1877-1938 *WhAm 1*
Schultz, Frederick *NewYHSD*
Schultz, George F 1869- *WhAm 5*
Schultz, Hart Merriam *IIBEAAW*
Schultz, Henry 1893-1938 *DcAmB S2, WhAm HA, WhAm 4*
Schultz, Jackson Smith 1815-1891 *NatCAB 12, TwCBDA*
Schultz, James Willard 1859-1947 *WhAm 2*
Schultz, John Christian 1840- *ApCAB*
Schultz, John Richie 1884-1947 *NatCAB 36, WhAm 2*
Schultz, Louis 1867- *WhAm 5*
Schultz, Marion Louise McLean 1880- *WomWWA 14*
Schultz, Oscar Theodore 1877-1947 *NatCAB 16, NatCAB 39*
Schultz, Roy Henry 1918-1970 *NatCAB 57*
Schultz, William *NewYHSD*
Schultz, William Eben 1887-1964 *WhAm 4*
Schultz, William Henry 1873-1955 *NatCAB 42*
Schultz, William Lightfoot 1876-1950 *NatCAB 37*
Schultze, Arthur 1860- *WhAm 4*
Schultze, Augustus 1840-1918 *DcAmB, NatCAB 8, WhAm 1*
Schultze, Carl Emil 1866-1939 *WhAm 1*
Schultze, Leonard 1877-1951 *WhAm 3*
Schultze, Max Johann Sigismund 1825-1874 *AsBiEn, DcScB*
Schulz, Armand 1876-1956 *NatCAB 47*
Schulz, Carl Gustav 1867- *ApCAB X, WhAm 4*
Schulz, Edward Hugh 1873-1951 *NatCAB 38, WhAm 3*
Schulz, Eugene George 1901-1960 *NatCAB 49*
Schulz, Leo 1865-1944 *WhAm 2*
Schulz, William Frederick 1872-1956 *NatCAB 45*
Schulze, Franz Ferdinand 1815-1873 *DcScB*
Schulze, Margaret 1894-1943 *NatCAB 34*
Schulze, Paul 1864-1948 *WhAm 2*
Schulze, Paul, Jr. 1895-1959 *NatCAB 48, WhAm 3*
Schulze, Theodore A 1860-1922 *NatCAB 6*
Schulze, Victor Ewald 1904-1970 *NatCAB 55*
Schumacher, Anton Herbert 1908-1968 *WhAm 5*
Schumacher, Ferdinand 1822-1908 *NatCAB 2, WhAm 1*
Schumacher, Frederick William 1863-1957 *NatCAB 52*
Schumacher, Heinrich Christian 1780-1850 *DcScB*
Schumacher, Henry Cyril 1893-1971 *WhAm 5*
Schumacher, James Madison 1843- *NatCAB 5*
Schumacher, Matthew Aloysius 1879-1966 *WhAm 4*
Schumacher, Thomas Milton 1862-1948 *WhAm 2*
Schumaker, Frank 1876-1924 *ApCAB X*
Schumaker, John Godfrey 1826-1905 *BiAUS, BiDrAC, TwCBDA*
Schuman, Robert 1886-1963 *McGEWB, WhAm 4*
Schuman, William Howard 1910- *EncAB, WebAB*
Schumann, Edward Armin 1879-1970 *WhAm 5*
Schumann, John Joseph, Jr. 1889-1964 *WhAm 4*
Schumann, Paul R 1876- *IIBEAAW*
Schumann, Robert Alexander 1810-1856 *McGEWB*
Schumann, Victor 1841-1913 *DcScB*
Schumann-Heink, Ernestine 1861-1936 *AmBi,*

DcAmB S2, NatCAB 14, NotAW, WebAB, WhAm 1, WomWWA 14
Schumm, Herman Charles 1889-1955 *WhAm 3*
Schumo, Elmer Mansfield 1883-1958 *NatCAB 45*
Schumpert, Thomas Edgar 1866- *NatCAB 11*
Schumpeter, Joseph Alois 1883-1950 *DcAmB S4, EncAB, McGEWB, WebAB, WhAm 2*
Schunck, Henry Edward 1820-1903 *DcScB*
Schuneman, Martin Gerretsen 1764-1827 *BiAUS, BiDrAC, WhAm H*
Schunk, Arthur John 1876- *WhAm 5*
Schupp, Otto d1941 *WhAm 4*
Schupp, Robert William 1890-1946 *WhAm 2*
Schur, Issai 1875-1941 *DcScB*
Schureman, Alfred *NewYHSD*
Schureman, Alphonso B *NewYHSD*
Schureman, James d1824 *BiAUS, Drake*
Schureman, James 1756-1824 *BiDrAC, TwCBDA, WhAm H, WhAmP*
Schureman, James 1757-1824 *ApCAB, NatCAB 2*
Schureman, John d1818 *Drake*
Schuricht, Carl 1880-1967 *WhAm 4*
Schurman, George Wellington d1931 *WhAm 1*
Schurman, Jacob Gould 1854-1942 *ApCAB, DcAmB S3, NatCAB 4, NatCAB 40, TwCBDA, WebAB, WhAm 2*
Schurman, Jacob Gould, III 1916- *WhAm 6*
Schurmeier, Theodore Leopold 1852- *NatCAB 7*
Schurz, Carl 1829-1906 *AmBi, ApCAB, BiAUS, BiDrAC, BiDrUSE, DcAmB, Drake, EncAAH, EncAB, McGEWB, NatCAB 3, REnAW, TwCBDA, WebAB, WhAm 1, WhAmP*
Schurz, Carl Lincoln 1871-1924 *WhAm 1*
Schurz, Margarethe Meyer 1833-1876 *BiDAmEd, NotAW*
Schurz, William Lytle 1886-1962 *WhAm 4*
Schuschnigg, Kurt Von 1897- *McGEWB*
Schussele, Christian 1824?-1879 *ApCAB, NewYHSD, TwCBDA*
Schussele, Christian 1826-1879 *DcAmB, WhAm H*
Schuster, Arnauld *NewYHSD*
Schuster, Arthur 1851-1934 *DcScB*
Schuster, George Lee 1891-1966 *WhAm 4*
Schuster, Lena Aldrich 1875- *WomWWA 14*
Schuster, Lester James 1896-1960 *NatCAB 49*
Schuster, Sigismund 1807- *NewYHSD*
Schutt, Harold Smith 1884-1963 *NatCAB 47, WhAm 4*
Schutt, Mary H M 1870- *WomWWA 14*
Schutt, Warren Ellis 1883-1955 *NatCAB 43*
Schutte, Louis Henry 1874-1957 *WhAm 3*
Schuttler, Peter 1812-1865 *DcAmB, WhAm H*
Schutz, Heinrich 1585-1672 *McGEWB*
Schutz, J *NewYHSD*
Schutz, William Jack 1906-1970 *NatCAB 55*
Schutze, Martin 1866-1950 *WhAm 3*
Schutzer, Paul George 1930-1967 *WhAm 5*
Schutzman, Julius 1915-1962 *NatCAB 48, WhAm 4*
Schuyler, Aaron 1828-1913 *ApCAB, TwCBDA, WhAm 1*
Schuyler, Anthony 1816- *ApCAB*
Schuyler, Catherine VanRensselaer 1734-1803 *ApCAB, NotAW*
Schuyler, Daniel J 1873-1952 *WhAm 3*
Schuyler, Elizabeth Scammell 1882- *WomWWA 14*
Schuyler, Eugene 1840-1890 *AmBi, ApCAB, DcAmB, NatCAB 8, TwCBDA, WhAm H*
Schuyler, George Lee 1811-1890 *ApCAB, NatCAB 1*
Schuyler, George Washington 1810-1888 *ApCAB, DcAmB, NatCAB 26, WhAm H*
Schuyler, Georgina 1841-1923 *BiCAW*
Schuyler, Hamilton 1862-1933 *NatCAB 24, WhAm 1*
Schuyler, James Dix 1848-1912 *DcAmB, NatCAB 18, WhAm 1*
Schuyler, Johannes 1668-1747 *ApCAB Sup*
Schuyler, Karl Cortlandt 1877-1933 *BiDrAC, NatCAB 25, WhAm 1*
Schuyler, Leonora Rogers *WomWWA 14*

Schuyler, Livingston Rowe 1868-1931 *WhAm 1*
Schuyler, Louis Sandford 1852-1878 *ApCAB*
Schuyler, Louisa Lee 1837-1926 *BiCAW, DcAmB, NatCAB 20, NotAW*
Schuyler, Margarita 1701-1782 *ApCAB Sup, DcAmB*
Schuyler, Margurita 1701-1782 *WhAm H*
Schuyler, Montgomery 1814-1896 *ApCAB, NatCAB 7, TwCBDA*
Schuyler, Montgomery 1843-1914 *AmBi, ApCAB, DcAmB, NatCAB 15, TwCBDA, WhAm 1*
Schuyler, Montgomery 1877-1955 *NatCAB 44, WhAm 3*
Schuyler, Peter 1657-1724 *ApCAB, DcAmB, Drake, TwCBDA, WhAm H*
Schuyler, Peter 1710-1762 *ApCAB, Drake, TwCBDA*
Schuyler, Philip Jeremiah 1768-1835 *BiAUS, BiDrAC, WhAm H*
Schuyler, Philip John 1733-1804 *AmBi, ApCAB, BiAUS, BiDrAC, DcAmB, Drake, McGEWB, NatCAB 1, TwCBDA, WebAB, WebAMB, WhAm H*
Schuyler, Philippa Duke d1967 *WhAm 4*
Schuyler, Remington 1877- *IIBEAAW*
Schuyler, Sidney Schieffelin 1864- *NatCAB 14*
Schuyler, Walter Scribner 1850-1932 *WhAm 1*
Schuyler, William 1855-1914 *WhAm 1*
Schwab, Charles Michael 1862-1939 *AmBi, ApCAB X, DcAmB S2, EncAB, McGEWB, NatCAB 14, WebAB, WhAm 1*
Schwab, Francis Xavier 1874-1946 *WhAm 2*
Schwab, Gustav Henry 1851-1912 *NatCAB 11, WhAm 1*
Schwab, Harvey A 1887-1956 *WhAm 3*
Schwab, John Christopher 1865-1916 *DcAmB, NatCAB 26, TwCBDA, WhAm 1*
Schwab, John George 1865-1943 *WhAm 2*
Schwab, Martin Constan 1880-1947 *WhAm 2*
Schwab, Paul Josiah 1894-1966 *WhAm 4*
Schwab, Robert Sidney 1903-1972 *NatCAB 57, WhAm 5*
Schwab, Roy Valentine 1902-1968 *WhAm 5*
Schwab, Sidney Isaac 1871-1947 *WhAm 2*
Schwabacher, Albert E 1888-1964 *WhAm 4*
Schwabacher, James Herbert 1881-1958 *NatCAB 47, WhAm 3*
Schwabe, George Blaine 1886-1952 *BiDrAC, NatCAB 41, WhAm 3, WhAmP*
Schwabe, H August 1843-1916 *WhAm 1*
Schwabe, Heinrich Samuel 1789-1875 *AsBiEn*
Schwabe, Max 1905- *BiDrAC*
Schwabe, Samuel Heinrich 1789-1875 *DcScB*
Schwacke, John Henry 1879-1942 *WhAm 2*
Schwager, Solomon 1890-1948 *NatCAB 37*
Schwain, Frank Robert 1913-1967 *WhAm 4*
Schwalm, Earl George 1907-1964 *WhAm 4*
Schwalm, Vernon Franklin 1887-1972 *NatCAB 56, WhAm 5*
Schwamb, Herbert Hadley 1897-1960 *NatCAB 46, WhAm 4*
Schwamb, Peter 1858- *WhAm 4*
Schwamm, Harvey 1904-1958 *WhAm 3*
Schwan, Phi *NewYHSD*
Schwan, Theodore 1839-1926 *ApCAB Sup, TwCBDA*
Schwan, Theodore 1841-1926 *WhAm 1*
Schwann, Theodor Ambrose Hubert 1810-1882 *AsBiEn, BiHiMed, DcScB, McGEWB*
Schwardt, Herbert Henry 1903-1962 *WhAm 4*
Schwarg, Genevieve Ives Allen 1861- *WomWWA 14*
Schwarts, John 1793-1860 *BiAUS*
Schwartz, A Charles 1895-1967 *WhAm 4*
Schwartz, Andrew Thomas 1867-1942 *NatCAB 18, WhAm 2*
Schwartz, B Davis 1902-1969 *WhAm 5*
Schwartz, Bertha 1901-1961 *NatCAB 51*
Schwartz, C *NewYHSD*
Schwartz, Carl Konrad 1885-1955 *NatCAB 44*
Schwartz, Charles d1969 *WhAm 5*
Schwartz, Christian *NewYHSD*
Schwartz, Delmore 1913-1966 *WhAm 4*
Schwartz, Frederick *NewYHSD*
Schwartz, Hans Jorgen 1876- *WhAm 3*
Schwartz, Harry Adolph 1880-1954 *NatCAB 43*

Schwartz, Harry Wolfe 1899-1950 *NatCAB 39*
Schwartz, Harwood Muzzy 1881-1945 *WhAm 2*
Schwartz, Henry Herman 1869-1955 *BiDrAC, WhAmP*
Schwartz, Herbert J 1887-1955 *WhAm 3*
Schwartz, Herbert Woodworth 1857-1921 *NatCAB 19*
Schwartz, Isaac Hillson 1912-1970 *WhAm 5*
Schwartz, Jack William 1905-1968 *WhAm 5*
Schwartz, Jacob, Jr. 1846- *ApCAB, DcAmLiB*
Schwartz, James Ernest 1843-1900 *NatCAB 17*
Schwartz, John 1793-1860 *BiDrAC, WhAm H*
Schwartz, Julia Augusta 1873- *WhAm 5, WomWWA 14*
Schwartz, Karl 1863-1924 *WhAm 1*
Schwartz, Lew 1907-1971 *WhAm 5*
Schwartz, Lewis Harry 1880-1961 *NatCAB 48*
Schwartz, Louis 1883-1963 *WhAm 4*
Schwartz, Maurice 1882-1954 *NatCAB 42*
Schwartz, Maurice 1890-1964 *WhAm 4*
Schwartz, Milton Henry 1905-1970 *WhAm 5*
Schwartz, R Plato 1892-1965 *NatCAB 51*
Schwartz, Robert S 1921-1964 *NatCAB 50*
Schwartz, Samuel D 1890-1968 *WhAm 5*
Schwartz, Walter Marshall, Sr. 1877- *WhAm 5*
Schwartz, William Daniel 1870-1952 *NatCAB 41*
Schwartz, William Leonard 1888-1955 *NatCAB 43*
Schwartz, William Spencer 1904-1971 *WhAm 5*
Schwartze, Johan Georg 1814?-1874 *NewYHSD*
Schwarz, Arthur 1868-1939 *NatCAB 31*
Schwarz, Berthold Theodore Dominic 1899-1969 *WhAm 5*
Schwarz, Charles Edward 1874-1938 *NatCAB 42*
Schwarz, Edward R 1899-1961 *WhAm 4*
Schwarz, Eugene Amandus 1844-1928 *DcAmB, NatCAB 29*
Schwarz, Frank Henry 1894-1951 *WhAm 3*
Schwarz, Frederick August Otto 1836- *NatCAB 11*
Schwarz, Frederick August Otto 1902-1974 *WhAm 6*
Schwarz, George Frederick 1868-1931 *NatCAB 22, WhAm 1*
Schwarz, Guenter 1913-1974 *WhAm 6*
Schwarz, H Stanley 1890-1955 *NatCAB 43*
Schwarz, Helen Geneva 1899-1960 *WhAm 4*
Schwarz, Henry Frederick 1866-1925 *NatCAB 30*
Schwarz, Henry Frederick 1906-1971 *WhAm 5*
Schwarz, Herman 1876-1945 *NatCAB 33*
Schwarz, Hermann Amandus 1843-1921 *DcScB*
Schwarz, Melbert 1898-1957 *NatCAB 47*
Schwarz, Otto Henry 1888-1950 *WhAm 3*
Schwarz, Paul Edgar 1891-1950 *NatCAB 39*
Schwarz, Ralph Jacob 1880-1943 *NatCAB 32*
Schwarz, William Tefft 1888-1967 *WhAm 4*
Schwarzburger, Carl 1850- *WhAm 4*
Schwarze, William Nathaniel 1875-1948 *WhAm 2*
Schwarzenbach, Ernest Blackbrook 1898-1968 *WhAm 5*
Schwarzenbach, Robert 1839-1904 *ApCAB X*
Schwarzenbach, Robert J F 1875- *ApCAB X*
Schwarzenberg, Friedrich Karl 1800-1870 *WhoMilH*
Schwarzenberg, Karl Philip, Furst Zu 1771-1820 *WhoMilH*
Schwarzkopf, Albert Beauregard 1861-1945 *NatCAB 34*
Schwarzmann, Herman J 1843-1891 *WhAm H*
Schwarzschild, Karl 1873-1916 *DcScB*
Schwarzschild, William Harry 1879-1952 *WhAm 3*
Schwatka, Frederick 1849-1892 *AmBi, ApCAB, DcAmB, NatCAB 3, TwCBDA, WhAm H*
Schwatt, Isaac Joachim 1867-1934 *WhAm 1*
Schwebach, James 1847-1921 *ApCAB Sup, NatCAB 12, TwCBDA, WhAm 1*
Schwebel, Lewis *NewYHSD*
Schwebel, Lewis, Jr. *NewYHSD*
Schwedtman, F Charles 1867-1952 *WhAm 3*
Schweet, Richard S 1918-1967 *NatCAB 53*
Schwegler, Raymond Alfred 1874-1952 *WhAm 3*

Schweickhard, Dean Merrill 1892- *BiDAmEd*
Schweig, Joel 1893-1973 *NatCAB 56*
Schweigardt, Frederick William 1885-1948 *WhAm 2*
Schweigger, Johann Salomo Christoph 1779-1857 *AsBiEn, DcScB*
Schweikart, Ferdinand Karl 1780-1859 *DcScB*
Schweiker, Richard Schultz 1926- *BiDrAC*
Schweikert, Harry Christian 1877-1937 *WhAm 1*
Schweinfurth, Charles Frederick 1856-1919 *WhAm 1*
Schweinfurth, Julius Adolph 1858-1931 *ApCAB X, WhAm 1*
Schweinhaut, Henry Albert 1902-1970 *WhAm 5*
Schweinitz, Edmund Alexander De 1825-1887 *AmBi, ApCAB, DcAmB, Drake, WhAm H*
Schweinitz, Edmund Alexander Von 1825-1887 *TwCBDA*
Schweinitz, Emil Adolphus De 1816-1879 *ApCAB, TwCBDA*
Schweinitz, Emil Alexander De 1855- *ApCAB Sup*
Schweinitz, Emil Alexander De 1866-1904 *AmBi, DcAmB, TwCBDA, WhAm 1*
Schweinitz, George Edmund De 1858-1938 *DcAmB S2, WhAm 1*
Schweinitz, Lewis David Von 1780-1834 *AmBi, ApCAB, DcAmB, Drake, NatCAB 8, TwCBDA*
Schweiter, Henry 1844-1925 *NatCAB 20*
Schweiter, Leo Henry 1917-1972 *WhAm 5*
Schweitzer, Albert 1875-1964 *WhAm 4*
Schweitzer, Albert 1875-1965 *McGEWB*
Schweitzer, Edmund Oscar 1875-1949 *NatCAB 45*
Schweitzer, Paul 1840-1911 *WhAm 1*
Schweizer, Albert Charles 1900-1949 *WhAm 3*
Schweizer, J Otto 1863-1955 *WhAm 5*
Schweizer, Jacob Otto 1863-1955 *NatCAB 41*
Schwellenbach, Edgar Ward 1887-1957 *WhAm 3*
Schwellenbach, Lewis Baxter 1894-1948 *BiDrAC, BiDrUSE, DcAmB S4, NatCAB 39, WhAm 2, WhAmP*
Schwenckfeld, Kaspar Von 1489?-1561 *McGEWB*
Schwendener, Simon 1829-1919 *DcScB*
Schwengel, Frank Rudolph 1885-1974 *WhAm 6*
Schwengel, Frederick Delbert 1907- *BiDrAC*
Schwentker, Francis Frederic 1904-1954 *WhAm 3*
Schwep, C Frank 1872-1946 *NatCAB 35*
Schweppe, Charles Hodgdon 1880-1941 *NatCAB 31, WhAm 1*
Schweppe, Laura Shedd 1880-1937 *NatCAB 50*
Schweppe, Richard Jewett 1876-1940 *NatCAB 33*
Schwerin, Rennie Pierre 1858-1936 *NatCAB 26*
Schwerin, Richard DeCantillon 1899-1941 *NatCAB 31*
Schwert, Pius Louis 1892-1941 *BiDrAC, NatCAB 30, WhAm 1*
Schwertner, August John 1870-1939 *WhAm 1*
Schwertner, Augustus John 1870-1939 *NatCAB 33*
Schwidetzky, Oscar O R 1874-1963 *WhAm 4*
Schwiering, Conrad 1916- *IIBEAAW*
Schwietert, Arthur Henry 1896-1966 *WhAm 4*
Schwimmer, Rosika 1877-1948 *DcAmB S4, NotAW*
Schwinbeck, Joseph Carl 1863-1936 *NatCAB 30*
Schwind, Etta Mae Powell 1878- *WomWWA 14*
Schwind, Joseph Louis 1902-1948 *NatCAB 38*
Schwindt, Robert *NewYHSD*
Schwing, Edward Beynroth 1870-1950 *NatCAB 43*
Schwingel, Vincent John 1903-1967 *WhAm 5*
Schwinger, Julian Seymore 1918- *WebAB*
Schwinger, Julian Seymour 1918- *AsBiEn*
Schwinn, Frederick Sievers 1889-1968 *WhAm 5*
Schwinn, Sidoine Jordan 1905-1963 *WhAm 4*
Schwitalla, Alphonse Mary 1882-1965 *WhAm 4*
Schwitter, Fridolin *NewYHSD*
Schwitter, George *NewYHSD*
Schwitter, Joseph *NewYHSD*

Schwob, Jacques 1883-1949 *NatCAB 42*
Schwob, Simon 1886-1954 *NatCAB 42*
Schwode, Andrea *NewYHSD*
Schwyzer, Arnold 1864-1944 *NatCAB 34, WhAm 2*
Schwyzer, Gustav 1867-1951 *NatCAB 40*
Sciaraffa, Gerard James 1915-1963 *NatCAB 50*
Scibetta, Samuel Louis 1893-1953 *NatCAB 41*
Scidmore, Eliza Ruhamah 1856-1928 *BiCAW, DcAmB, TwCBDA, WhAm 1*
Scidmore, Eliza Ruhamah 1866-1928 *WomWWA 14*
Scidmore, George Hawthorne 1854-1922 *WhAm 1*
Scilla, Agostino 1629-1700 *DcScB*
Scipio Africanus Major, Publius C 236BC-183?BC *McGEWB*
Scipio Africanus Minor, Publius C A 185?BC-129BC *McGEWB*
Scipio, Lynn A 1876- *WhAm 5*
Scism, Don 1893-1954 *WhAm 3*
Sclater, John Robert Paterson 1876-1949 *WhAm 3*
Sclater, Philip Lutley 1829-1913 *DcScB*
Scobie, Ronald 1893-1969 *WhWW-II*
Scoblick, James Paul 1909- *BiDrAC*
Scofield, Carl Schurz 1875-1966 *WhAm 4*
Scofield, Cora Louisa 1870- *WomWWA 14*
Scofield, Cyrus Ingerson 1843-1921 *DcAmReB, WhAm 1*
Scofield, Edson Mason 1867-1939 *NatCAB 29*
Scofield, Edward 1842-1925 *NatCAB 12, TwCBDA, WhAm 1*
Scofield, Elizabeth Clark 1845-1914 *ApCAB X*
Scofield, Glenni William 1817-1891 *ApCAB, BiAUS, BiDrAC, NatCAB 11, TwCBDA, WhAm H, WhAmP*
Scofield, John Adams 1892-1956 *NatCAB 42*
Scofield, Levi Tucker 1842-1917 *ApCAB X, NatCAB 12*
Scofield, Louis A 1895- *WhAm 4*
Scofield, M Adda *WomWWA 14*
Scofield, Nettie McDougall 1881- *WomWWA 14*
Scofield, Perry Lee 1890-1975 *WhAm 6*
Scofield, Walter Keeler 1839-1910 *WhAm 1*
Scofield, William Bacon 1864-1930 *WhAm 1*
Scoggin, Margaret Clara 1905-1968 *DcAmLiB*
Scoggins, Charles Elbert 1888-1955 *WhAm 3*
Scoles, John *NewYHSD*
Scollard, Clinton 1860-1932 *AmBi, ApCAB X, DcAmB, NatCAB 23, TwCBDA, WhAm 1*
Scollard, Clinton 1861-1932 *ApCAB*
Scollay, Catherine d1863 *NewYHSD*
Scolponeti, Joseph Aloysius 1893-1959 *NatCAB 57*
Sconce, Harvey James 1875-1943 *WhAm 2*
Scoon, Robert 1886- *WhAm 5*
Scoones, Sir Geoffrey 1893-1975 *WhWW-II*
Scopes, John T d1970 *WhAm 5*
Scorah, Ralph Louis 1901-1969 *NatCAB 55*
Score, John Nelson Russell 1896-1949 *NatCAB 47, WhAm 2*
Scoresby, William 1790-1857 *ApCAB*
Scorpio, Angelo 1896-1951 *NatCAB 42*
Scot, DcScB, NewYHSD
Scot, Robert *NewYHSD*
Scotson-Clark, George Frederick 1872-1927 *NatCAB 21, WhAm 1*
Scott, A Lincoln 1899-1953 *NatCAB 41*
Scott, Abraham M *BiAUS*
Scott, Abram M d1833 *NatCAB 13, TwCBDA*
Scott, Albert Lyon 1878-1946 *WhAm 2*
Scott, Albert Woodburn, Jr. 1869- *WhAm 5*
Scott, Alberta Garber 1869- *WomWWA 14*
Scott, Alexander Armstrong 1887-1965 *WhAm 4*
Scott, Alfred Bowne 1846-1908 *NatCAB 31*
Scott, Alfred James, Jr. 1881-1940 *WhAm 1*
Scott, Alfred Malley 1883-1954 *NatCAB 43*
Scott, Alfred Witherspoon 1896-1974 *WhAm 6*
Scott, Andrew *BiAUS*
Scott, Andrew 1757-1839 *ApCAB*
Scott, Angelo Cyrus 1857-1949 *NatCAB 37, WhAm 2*
Scott, Anna B 1856- *WomWWA 14*

Scott, Anna Grace 1880- *WomWWA 14*
Scott, Arthur Carroll 1865-1940 *NatCAB 34, WhAm 1*
Scott, Arthur Curtis 1873- *WhAm 5*
Scott, Arthur Hoyt 1875-1927 *NatCAB 40*
Scott, Austin 1848-1922 *DcAmB, NatCAB 3, TwCBDA, WhAm 1*
Scott, Bertha Drake 1866- *WomWWA 14*
Scott, Bertha Lane *WomWWA 14*
Scott, Betty 1874- *WomWWA 14*
Scott, Bruce 1874-1939 *NatCAB 28, WhAm 1*
Scott, Buford 1895-1973 *WhAm 6*
Scott, Byron Nicholson 1903- *BiDrAC*
Scott, Campbell 1869-1960 *NatCAB 49*
Scott, Carlyle MacRoberts 1873-1945 *WhAm 2*
Scott, Carrie Emma 1874-1943 *WhAm 2*
Scott, Charles 1733-1813 *ApCAB, NatCAB 13, TwCBDA*
Scott, Charles 1733-1820 *BiAUS, Drake*
Scott, Charles 1739?-1813 *AmBi, DcAmB, WebAMB, WhAm H*
Scott, Charles 1811-1861 *ApCAB, TwCBDA*
Scott, Charles 1847-1916 *NatCAB 17, WhAm 1*
Scott, Charles Felton 1864-1944 *NatCAB 13, WhAm 2*
Scott, Charles Frederick 1860-1938 *BiDrAC, TwCBDA, WhAm 1, WhAmP*
Scott, Charles Hepburn 1886-1962 *IIBEAAW*
Scott, Charles Herrington 1870- *WhAm 5*
Scott, Charles Lewis 1827-1899 *BiAUS, BiDrAC, NatCAB 12*
Scott, Charles Lewis 1883-1954 *NatCAB 44, WhAm 3*
Scott, Charles Payson Gurley 1853- *WhAm 4*
Scott, Charles Ulysses 1870-1966 *NatCAB 53*
Scott, Charlotte Angas 1858-1931 *NotAW, WhAm 1, WomWWA 14*
Scott, Clyde F 1881- *WhAm 6*
Scott, Colin Alexander 1861-1925 *DcAmB, NatCAB 26, WhAm 1*
Scott, Cornelia Porter Leland 1844- *WomWWA 14*
Scott, Cyril Meir 1879- *WhAm 6*
Scott, D R 1887-1954 *WhAm 3*
Scott, David *BiDrAC, WhAm H*
Scott, David Cook 1884-1951 *NatCAB 40*
Scott, David James 1828-1912 *NatCAB 29*
Scott, Donald 1879-1967 *WhAm 4*
Scott, Donald Corwin 1878-1945 *NatCAB 39*
Scott, Donnell Everett 1887-1955 *WhAm 3*
Scott, Dred 1795-1858 *AmBi, DcAmB, EncAB, McGEWB, WhAm H*
Scott, Dred 1810?-1857? *ApCAB, NatCAB 2*
Scott, Dukinfield Henry 1854-1934 *DcScB*
Scott, Duncan Jackson 1880- *WhoColR*
Scott, E Harrison 1883-1955 *NatCAB 44*
Scott, Earl Francis 1874-1940 *WhAm 1*
Scott, Eben Greenough 1836- *WhAm 4*
Scott, Eda Vernaz 1870- *WomWWA 14*
Scott, Edward *NewYHSD*
Scott, Edward E 1866- *WhoColR*
Scott, Edwin William 1902-1974 *WhAm 6*
Scott, Ellen C 1862-1936 *WhAm 1*
Scott, Elmer 1866-1954 *WhAm 3*
Scott, Elmer Ellsworth 1863-1943 *NatCAB 36*
Scott, Elmer Eugene 1879-1945 *NatCAB 34*
Scott, Elmon 1853- *TwCBDA, WhAm 4*
Scott, Elmon 1863- *NatCAB 12*
Scott, Emily Maria Spafard 1832- *AmWom, NatCAB 11, WhAm 4, WomWWA 14*
Scott, Emma Look 1858- *WomWWA 14*
Scott, Emmett Jay 1873-1957 *EncAB, NatCAB 43, WhAm 3, WhoColR*
Scott, Ernest 1875-1934 *WhAm 1*
Scott, Ernest 1903-1973 *NatCAB 57, WhAm 6*
Scott, Ernest Darius 1872- *WhAm 5*
Scott, Ernest Findlay 1868-1954 *WhAm 3*
Scott, Eugene Crampton 1889-1972 *WhAm 5*
Scott, Fanny Elizabeth 1876- *WomWWA 14*
Scott, Fitzhugh 1881-1957 *WhAm 3*
Scott, Florence Bucklin 1860- *WomWWA 14*
Scott, Frances Gage 1849- *WomWWA 14*
Scott, Francis Eugene 1848-1917 *NatCAB 17*
Scott, Francis Markoe 1848-1922 *WhAm 1*
Scott, Frank Augustus 1873-1949 *WhAm 2*

Scott, Frank Douglas 1878-1951 *BiDrAC, WhAmP*
Scott, Frank Hall 1848-1912 *WhAm 1*
Scott, Frank Hamline 1857-1931 *WhAm 1*
Scott, Frank Jesup 1828- *NatCAB 13, WhAm 4*
Scott, Franklin William 1877-1950 *WhAm 2*
Scott, Fred Newton 1860- *NatCAB 14*
Scott, Fred Newton 1860-1930 *WhAm 1*
Scott, Fred Newton 1860-1931 *AmBi, DcAmB*
Scott, Frederic William 1862-1939 *NatCAB 30, WhAm 1*
Scott, Frederick Andrew 1866- *WhAm 4*
Scott, Frederick George 1861- *ApCAB Sup*
Scott, Frederick Hossack 1879-1958 *WhAm 3*
Scott, Garfield 1881-1955 *WhAm 3*
Scott, George 1849-1938 *NatCAB 28, WhAm 4*
Scott, George Alexander 1887-1957 *NatCAB 44*
Scott, George Christian 1873-1947 *NatCAB 35*
Scott, George Cromwell 1864-1948 *BiDrAC, WhAm 2*
Scott, George Eaton 1871-1939 *WhAm 1*
Scott, George Gilmore 1873- *WhAm 5*
Scott, George Montgomery 1835-1915 *NatCAB 18*
Scott, George Winfield 1875-1944 *WhAm 2*
Scott, Gordon Hatler 1901-1970 *WhAm 5*
Scott, Gustavus 1753- *BiAUS*
Scott, Gustavus 1753-1800 *BiDrAC, DcAmB, WhAm H*
Scott, Gustavus 1753-1801 *ApCAB, NatCAB 2, TwCBDA*
Scott, Gustavus Hall 1812-1882 *ApCAB, Drake, NatCAB 3, TwCBDA*
Scott, Guy Charles 1863-1909 *WhAm 1*
Scott, Hamilton Gray 1883-1943 *WhAm 2*
Scott, Hardie 1907- *BiDrAC*
Scott, Harold Bartlett 1884-1938 *NatCAB 30*
Scott, Harold Wilson 1896- *WhAm 5*
Scott, Harold Winfield 1898?- *IIBEAAW*
Scott, Harriet Maria d1906 *WhAm 1*
Scott, Harvey David 1818-1891 *BiDrAC, WhAm H*
Scott, Harvey David 1818-1892 *BiAUS*
Scott, Harvey Whitefield 1838-1910 *ApCAB X, DcAmB, NatCAB 1, NatCAB 16, WhAm 1*
Scott, Helen 1851- *WomWWA 14*
Scott, Henri 1876-1942 *WhAm 2*
Scott, Henry Clarkson 1859-1911 *NatCAB 16*
Scott, Henry Clay 1930-1974 *WhAm 6*
Scott, Henry D 1893-1947 *WhAm 2*
Scott, Henry Edwards 1859-1944 *WhAm 2*
Scott, Henry Lee 1814-1886 *ApCAB, Drake*
Scott, Henry Pepper 1859-1933 *NatCAB 30*
Scott, Henry Tiffany 1846-1927 *WhAm 1*
Scott, Henry Wilson 1866-1935 *WhAm 2*
Scott, Herbert 1872- *WhAm 5*
Scott, Hermon Hosmer 1909-1975 *WhAm 6*
Scott, Hugh Briar 1891-1960 *WhAm 4*
Scott, Hugh Doggett, Jr. 1900- *BiDrAC*
Scott, Hugh Lenox 1853-1934 *AmBi, DcAmB S1, NatCAB 14, NatCAB 26, WebAMB, WhAm 1*
Scott, Hugh McDonald 1848-1909 *WhAm 1*
Scott, Ida Gray 1860- *WomWWA 14*
Scott, Irving Murray 1837-1903 *ApCAB, DcAmB, NatCAB 6, TwCBDA, WhAm 1*
Scott, Isaac Franklin 1868- *WhoColR*
Scott, Isaac MacBurney 1866-1942 *WhAm 2*
Scott, Isaiah Benjamin 1854-1931 *NatCAB 14, WhAm 1, WhoColR*
Scott, J G d1974 *WhAm 6*
Scott, Jack Garrett 1895-1956 *WhAm 3*
Scott, James *BiAUS*
Scott, James 1806-1857 *ApCAB*
Scott, James B *NewYHSD*
Scott, James Brown 1866-1943 *DcAmB S3, WebAB, WhAm 2*
Scott, James Edward 1874- *WhAm 5*
Scott, James Francis 1856-1929 *NatCAB 22*
Scott, James Frederick 1873-1952 *NatCAB 42*
Scott, James Hutchison 1868- *WhAm 4*
Scott, James Powell 1909- *IIBEAAW*
Scott, James Ralph 1888-1968 *NatCAB 54*
Scott, James Robert 1886-1956 *NatCAB 44*

Scott, James Wilmot 1849-1895 *ApCAB X, DcAmB, NatCAB 2, WhAm H*
Scott, Jeanette 1864-1937 *WomWWA 14*
Scott, Jeannette 1864-1937 *WhAm 1*
Scott, Jessie 1912- *IIBEAAW*
Scott, Job 1751-1793 *DcAmB, Drake, NatCAB 11, WhAm H*
Scott, John *BiAUS*
Scott, John d1850 *BiAUS, Drake*
Scott, John 1630?-1696 *DcAmB, WhAm H*
Scott, John 1634?-1696 *AmBi*
Scott, John 1781-1850 *NatCAB 19*
Scott, John 1782-1861 *BiAUS, TwCBDA*
Scott, John 1784-1850 *BiDrAC, WhAm H*
Scott, John 1785-1861 *BiDrAC, WhAm H, WhAmP*
Scott, John 1820-1907 *ApCAB, ApCAB Sup, NatCAB 8, TwCBDA*
Scott, John 1821-1889 *NatCAB 34*
Scott, John 1824- *BiAUS, NatCAB 12, TwCBDA*
Scott, John 1824-1889 *ApCAB*
Scott, John 1824-1896 *BiDrAC, NatCAB 24, TwCBDA, WhAm H*
Scott, John 1824-1903 *WhAm 1*
Scott, John 1907- *IIBEAAW*
Scott, John Adams 1867-1947 *DcAmB S4, NatCAB 35, WhAm 2*
Scott, John Addison 1852-1950 *WhAm 3*
Scott, John Andrew 1892-1950 *NatCAB 39*
Scott, John Calvin 1877-1952 *NatCAB 40*
Scott, John Eugene 1851-1913 *NatCAB 30*
Scott, John Frederick 1841-1895 *NatCAB 17*
Scott, John Guier 1819-1892 *BiAUS, BiDrAC, WhAm H*
Scott, John Hart 1847- *TwCBDA, WhAm 4*
Scott, John Jay 1860- *WhoColR*
Scott, John Loughran 1846- *WhAm 4*
Scott, John Lynn 1899-1949 *NatCAB 39*
Scott, John M 1824-1898 *NatCAB 12, TwCBDA*
Scott, John Marcy 1902-1968 *WhAm 5*
Scott, John McCorkle 1866-1945 *NatCAB 37*
Scott, John Morin 1730-1784 *AmBi, ApCAB, BiAUS, BiDrAC, DcAmB, Drake, NatCAB 2, TwCBDA, WhAm H, WhAmP*
Scott, John Morin 1789-1858 *ApCAB*
Scott, John Prindle 1877-1932 *DcAmB, WhAm 1*
Scott, John Randolph 1805-1856 *NatCAB 13, WhAm H*
Scott, John Reed 1869- *NatCAB 14, WhAm 5*
Scott, John Roger Kirkpatrick 1873-1945 *BiDrAC, WhAm 2*
Scott, John Rudolph 1809-1856 *ApCAB*
Scott, John Scanlin 1871-1919 *NatCAB 18*
Scott, John White Allen 1815-1907 *NewYHSD*
Scott, John William 1870-1932 *WhAm 1*
Scott, John Witherspoon 1800-1892 *ApCAB Sup, NatCAB 1, TwCBDA*
Scott, John Work 1807-1879 *BiDAmEd, NatCAB 20, TwCBDA*
Scott, John Zachary Holladay 1843- *NatCAB 9*
Scott, Jonathan French 1882-1942 *WhAm 2*
Scott, Joseph 1867-1958 *NatCAB 16, WhAm 3*
Scott, Joseph T *NewYHSD*
Scott, Josiah 1803-1879 *NatCAB 12*
Scott, Julia Green 1839-1923 *NatCAB 20, WhAm 1, WomWWA 14*
Scott, Julia H 1809-1842 *Drake*
Scott, Julian 1846-1901 *ApCAB, IIBEAAW, TwCBDA, WhAm 1*
Scott, Leroy 1875-1929 *DcAmB, NatCAB 26, WhAm 1*
Scott, Leslie Grant 1886- *WomWWA 14*
Scott, Leslie M 1878- *WhAm 6*
Scott, Levi 1802-1882 *ApCAB, TwCBDA*
Scott, Lilian S *WomWWA 14*
Scott, Llewellyn Davis 1871-1939 *WhAm 1*
Scott, Lloyd Nudd 1875-1966 *NatCAB 52*
Scott, Lockburn Bertie 1862-1951 *NatCAB 40*
Scott, Lon Allen 1888-1931 *BiDrAC, WhAm 1*
Scott, Louis Allen 1895-1975 *WhAm 6*
Scott, Lucy Jameson 1843-1920 *WhAm 1, WomWWA 14*

Scott, Margaret T *WomWWA 14*
Scott, Margaretta Morris 1878- *WomWWA 14*
Scott, Martin 1788-1847 *ApCAB, Drake*
Scott, Martin J 1865-1954 *WhAm 3*
Scott, Mary 1851- *AmWom*
Scott, Mary 1860- *WomWWA 14*
Scott, Mary Augusta 1851-1918 *WhAm 1, WomWWA 14*
Scott, Mary Kennard *WomWWA 14*
Scott, Mary McKay 1851- *WomWWA 14*
Scott, Mary Sophia 1838- *AmWom*
Scott, Mary Stuart 1870- *WomWWA 14*
Scott, Miriam Finn 1881-1944 *WomWWA 14*
Scott, Miriam Finn 1882-1944 *BiDAmEd, NatCAB 36, WhAm 2*
Scott, Nancy Elnora 1879- *WomWWA 14*
Scott, Nathan Bay 1841-1924 *NatCAB 19, WhAm 1*
Scott, Nathan Bay 1842-1924 *BiDrAC, NatCAB 13, TwCBDA, WhAmP*
Scott, Nicholas *WhWW-II*
Scott, Norman 1889-1942 *WhAm 3*
Scott, Norman 1928-1968 *WhAm 5*
Scott, Orange 1800-1847 *ApCAB, DcAmB, DcAmReB, NatCAB 2, TwCBDA, WhAm H*
Scott, Oreon Earle 1871-1956 *WhAm 3*
Scott, Owen 1848-1928 *BiDrAC*
Scott, Palmer 1897-1970 *NatCAB 55*
Scott, Paul Ryrie 1895-1967 *WhAm 4*
Scott, Paul Whitten 1869-1950 *WhAm 3*
Scott, Philip B 1912-1961 *WhAm 4*
Scott, Philip Drennen 1855- *WhAm 4*
Scott, R D 1878- *WhAm 6*
Scott, Ralph James 1905- *BiDrAC, WhAmP*
Scott, Richard 1605-1681? *NatCAB 11*
Scott, Richard 1607-1681? *ApCAB, Drake*
Scott, Richard Hamilton 1858-1917 *NatCAB 20, WhAm 1*
Scott, Richard Hugh 1869-1944 *WhAm 2*
Scott, Richard John Ernst 1863-1932 *NatCAB 25, WhAm 1*
Scott, Richard William 1825- *ApCAB*
Scott, Robert 1860- *WhAm 4*
Scott, Robert Eden 1808-1862 *ApCAB Sup, BiDConf, NatCAB 19*
Scott, Robert Falcon 1868-1912 *AsBiEn, McGEWB*
Scott, Robert Gillam 1907-1957 *NatCAB 45*
Scott, Robert Gray 1894-1947 *NatCAB 38*
Scott, Robert Kingston 1826-1900 *AmBi, ApCAB, BiAUS, DcAmB, Drake, NatCAB 12, TwCBDA, WhAm 1*
Scott, Robert Lee, Jr. 1908- *WebAMB*
Scott, Robert Lindsay 1873-1953 *WhAm 3*
Scott, Robert Nicholson 1838-1887 *ApCAB, NatCAB 2, WhAm H*
Scott, Roger Burdette 1913-1968 *WhAm 5*
Scott, Roy Vernon 1927- *EncAAH*
Scott, Roy Wesley 1888-1957 *WhAm 3*
Scott, Rufus Leonard 1835- *NatCAB 1*
Scott, Russell Burton 1902-1967 *NatCAB 54, WhAm 5*
Scott, Ruth Spencer 1879- *WomWWA 14*
Scott, S Spencer 1892-1971 *WhAm 5*
Scott, Samuel Bryan 1878-1941 *NatCAB 30*
Scott, Samuel Parsons 1846-1929 *DcAmB, WhAm 1*
Scott, Sutton Selwyn 1829-1907 *TwCBDA, WhAm 1*
Scott, Thomas 1739-1796 *BiAUS, BiDrAC, WhAm H*
Scott, Thomas 1772-1856 *BiAUS, Drake, NatCAB 5*
Scott, Thomas 1841- *ApCAB*
Scott, Thomas Alexander d1881 *BiAUS*
Scott, Thomas Alexander 1823-1881 *AmBi, DcAmB, EncAB, REnAW, WhAm H*
Scott, Thomas Alexander 1824-1881 *ApCAB, NatCAB 13, TwCBDA*
Scott, Thomas Blythe 1863-1928 *ApCAB X*
Scott, Thomas Fielding 1805-1867 *Drake*
Scott, Thomas Fielding 1807-1867 *ApCAB, DcAmB, NatCAB 5, TwCBDA, WhAm H*
Scott, Thomas Morton 1824-1911 *WhAm 1*
Scott, Thomas S *NewYHSD*
Scott, Tom 1913-1961 *WhAm 4*

Scott, Tully 1857-1924 *NatCAB 23*, *WhAm 1*
Scott, W Roger 1897-1960 *NatCAB 50*
Scott, Sir Walter 1771-1832 *McGEWB*
Scott, Walter 1796-1861 *ApCAB*, *DcAmB*, *DcAmReB*, *NatCAB 2*, *WhAm H*
Scott, Walter 1861-1935 *ApCAB X*, *WhAm 1*
Scott, Walter Canfield 1869-1951 *WhAm 3*
Scott, Walter Dill 1869-1955 *BiDAmEd*, *DcAmB S5*, *NatCAB 42*, *WhAm 3*
Scott, Walter E, Jr. 1895-1959 *WhAm 3*
Scott, Walter Edward 1870?-1954 *DcAmB S5*
Scott, Walter Edward 1872-1954 *WebAB*
Scott, Walter Quincy 1841- *NatCAB 7*, *NatCAB 10*
Scott, Wendell G 1905-1972 *WhAm 5*
Scott, Wilfred Welday 1876-1932 *WhAm 1*
Scott, Will 1877-1937 *WhAm 1*
Scott, Willard 1850- *WhAm 4*
Scott, William 1804-1862 *DcAmB*, *NatCAB 12*, *WhAm H*
Scott, William 1850-1906 *NatCAB 24*, *WhAm 1*
Scott, William Alexander 1870- *WhoColR*
Scott, William Amasa 1862-1944 *TwCBDA*, *WhAm 2*
Scott, William Anderson 1813-1885 *ApCAB*, *DcAmB*, *NatCAB 2*, *TwCBDA*, *WhAm H*
Scott, William Anderson 1833-1885 *Drake*
Scott, William Berryman 1858-1947 *DcAmB S4*, *DcScB*, *NatCAB 13*, *NatCAB 36*, *WhAm 2*
Scott, William Cowper 1817-1854 *ApCAB*
Scott, William Earl Dodge 1852-1910 *NatCAB 13*, *WhAm 1*
Scott, William Edouard 1884-1964 *NatCAB 50*, *WhAm 4*
Scott, William Edward 1884-1964 *WhoColR*
Scott, William Forse 1844- *WhAm 4*
Scott, William Henry 1840-1937 *NatCAB 7*, *NatCAB 29*, *TwCBDA*
Scott, William Henry 1846-1920 *WhAm 1*
Scott, William Kerr 1896-1958 *BiDrAC*, *NatCAB 44*, *WhAm 3*, *WhAmP*
Scott, William Lawrence 1828-1891 *ApCAB Sup*, *BiDrAC*, *DcAmB*, *WhAm H*
Scott, William Lloyd 1915- *BiDrAC*
Scott, William Robertson 1860-1926 *NatCAB 24*, *WhAm 1*
Scott, William Sherley 1856-1941 *WhAm 1*
Scott, William Wilson 1902-1961 *WhAm 4*
Scott, Willis Howard 1896-1960 *WhAm 4*
Scott, Winfield 1786-1866 *AmBi*, *ApCAB*, *BiAUS*, *DcAmB*, *Drake*, *EncAB*, *McGEWB*, *NatCAB 3*, *REnAW*, *TwCBDA*, *WebAB*, *WebAMB*, *WhAm H*, *WhoMilH*
Scott, Winfield 1849-1911 *ApCAB X*
Scott, Winfield Germain 1854-1919 *NatCAB 19*
Scott, Winfield Townley 1910-1968 *WhAm 5*
Scott, Zar Delevan 1848-1931 *NatCAB 27*
Scott-Hunter, George 1874- *WhAm 5*
Scotten, Robert McGregor 1891- *WhAm 5*
Scotten, Samuel Chatman 1851-1920 *WhAm 1*
Scotti, Antonio 1868-1936 *WhAm 1*
Scottow, Joshua 1615-1698 *ApCAB Sup*, *Drake*
Scotus *DcScB*
Scoullek, James Brown 1820-1899 *ApCAB*
Scouller, James Brown 1820-1899 *WhAm 1*
Scouller, John Crawford 1858-1925 *WhAm 1*
Scovel, Henry Sydney 1858-1918 *NatCAB 17*
Scovel, Henry Sylvester 1869-1905 *DcAmB*
Scovel, John Combs 1845-1923 *NatCAB 20*
Scovel, Sylvester 1796-1849 *NatCAB 2*
Scovel, Sylvester 1869-1905 *DcAmB*, *WhAm 1*
Scovel, Sylvester Fithian 1835-1910 *TwCBDA*, *WhAm 1*
Scovell, Josiah Thomas 1841-1915 *NatCAB 16*
Scovell, Melville Amasa 1855-1912 *DcAmB*, *EncAAH*, *NatCAB 15*, *WhAm 1*
Scovern, John 1845-1923 *NatCAB 20*
Scovil, Samuel 1857-1950 *NatCAB 39*, *WhAm 3*
Scovill, Guy Norman 1874-1950 *NatCAB 41*
Scovill, Hiram Thompson 1885-1962 *NatCAB 50*
Scoville, Annie Beecher *WhAm 5*

Scoville, Harold Ralph 1910-1974 *WhAm 6*
Scoville, Helen M *WomWWA 14*
Scoville, Jonathan 1830-1891 *BiDrAC*, *WhAm H*
Scoville, Joseph Alfred 1811-1864 *ApCAB*
Scoville, Joseph Alfred 1815-1864 *DcAmB*, *NatCAB 5*, *WhAm H*
Scoville, Robert 1876-1934 *WhAm 1*
Scoville, Samuel, Jr. 1872-1950 *WhAm 3*
Scoville, Susie Ray Greene *WomWWA 14*
Scoville, Wilbur Lincoln 1865-1942 *NatCAB 40*, *WhAm 4*
Scranton, Benjamin Hand 1856-1936 *NatCAB 30*
Scranton, Cassius A 1885-1970 *WhAm 5*
Scranton, George W 1811-1861 *BiAUS*, *Drake*
Scranton, George Whitefield 1811-1861 *ApCAB*, *WhAm H*
Scranton, George Whitfield 1811-1861 *AmBi*, *BiDrAC*, *DcAmB*, *NatCAB 9*, *WhAmP*
Scranton, Joel 1798- *NatCAB 11*
Scranton, Joseph Augustine 1838-1908 *BiDrAC*, *WhAmP*
Scranton, Joseph Hand 1813-1872 *ApCAB*, *NatCAB 10*
Scranton, Lida 1868- *AmWom*
Scranton, Marion Margery Warren 1884-1960 *WhAm 4*
Scranton, William Dowd 1875-1950 *NatCAB 40*
Scranton, William Walker 1844-1916 *NatCAB 25*
Scranton, William Warren 1917- *BiDrAC*
Scranton, Worthington 1876-1955 *WhAm 3*
Screven, James d1778 *Drake*
Screven, James 1738-1778 *TwCBDA*
Screven, James 1744?-1778 *ApCAB*
Screven, James Proctor 1799-1859 *NatCAB 3*
Screven, John 1827-1900 *NatCAB 2*
Screven, William 1629-1713 *ApCAB*
Screws, William Preston 1875- *WhAm 5*
Screws, William Wallace 1839-1913 *DcAmB*, *WhAm 1*
Scriabin, Alexander Nikolayevich 1871-1915 *McGEWB*
Scriber, William Edward 1859-1915 *NatCAB 17*
Scribner, Arthur Hawley 1859-1932 *NatCAB 36*, *WhAm 1*
Scribner, Charles 1821-1871 *AmBi*, *ApCAB*, *DcAmB*, *NatCAB 6*, *TwCBDA*, *WhAm H*
Scribner, Charles 1854-1930 *AmBi*, *DcAmB*, *WhAm 1*
Scribner, Charles 1890-1952 *DcAmB S5*, *NatCAB 45*, *WhAm 3*
Scribner, Charles Ezra 1858-1926 *NatCAB 13*, *NatCAB 41*, *WhAm 1*
Scribner, Ernest Varian 1855-1918 *NatCAB 35*
Scribner, Frank Jay 1888-1966 *WhAm 4*
Scribner, Frank Kimball 1867-1935 *WhAm 1*
Scribner, Frank Lamson 1851-1938 *AmBi*
Scribner, George Kline 1891-1962 *WhAm 4*
Scribner, Gilbert Hilton 1831-1910 *WhAm 1*
Scribner, Gilbert Hilton 1890-1966 *WhAm 4*, *WhAm 5*
Scribner, Harvey 1850-1913 *WhAm 1*
Scribner, Helen Culbertson Annan *WomWWA 14*
Scribner, Josephine Eleanor Pittman 1869- *WomWWA 14*
Scribner, Lucy Skidmore 1853-1931 *NatCAB 23*, *WhAm 1*
Scriggs, William L *BiAUS*
Scripps, Edward Wyllis 1854-1926 *AmBi*, *DcAmB*, *EncAB*, *McGEWB*, *NatCAB 28*, *WebAB*, *WhAm 1*
Scripps, Ellen Browning 1836-1932 *DcAmB*, *NatCAB 28*, *NotAW*, *WebAB*
Scripps, Helen Knappen 1865- *WomWWA 14*
Scripps, James Edmund 1835-1906 *ApCAB X*, *DcAmB*, *NatCAB 15*, *NatCAB 28*, *WebAB*, *WhAm 1*
Scripps, James George 1886-1921 *NatCAB 22*
Scripps, John Locke 1818-1866 *NatCAB 7*, *WhAm H*
Scripps, Robert Paine 1895-1938 *AmBi*, *DcAmB S2*, *WhAm 1*, *WhAm 1C*

Scripps, William Armiger 1838-1914 *NatCAB 36*
Scripps, William Edmund 1882-1952 *DcAmB S5*, *WhAm 3*
Scripps, William John 1905-1965 *NatCAB 52*
Scripture, Edward Wheeler 1864- *NatCAB 10*, *WhAm 4*
Scripture, May Kirk 1864- *WomWWA 14*
Scripture, William Ellis 1843-1933 *WhAm 1*
Scriven, George Percival 1854-1940 *NatCAB 8*, *WhAm 1*
Scriver, Delia M 1855- *WomWWA 14*
Scriver, Robert Macfie 1914- *IIBEAAW*
Scrivner, Errett Power 1898- *BiDrAC*
Scrivner, Richard Hosea 1880-1948 *NatCAB 36*
Scroggs, Joseph Whitefield 1852- *WhAm 4*
Scroggs, William Oscar 1879-1957 *WhAm 3*
Scroggy, Thomas Edmund 1843-1915 *BiDrAC*
Scrope, George Julius Poulett 1797-1876 *DcScB*
Scruggs, Anderson M 1897-1955 *WhAm 3*
Scruggs, Loyd 1875- *WhAm 5*
Scruggs, Mary Isabell Dial *WomWWA 14*
Scruggs, Richard Mitchell 1822- *NatCAB 7*, *NatCAB 12*
Scruggs, William Lindsay 1834-1912 *NatCAB 2*
Scruggs, William Lindsay 1836-1912 *DcAmB*, *TwCBDA*, *WhAm 1*
Scruggs, William Marvin 1889-1951 *WhAm 3*
Scrugham, James Graves 1880-1945 *BiDrAC*, *NatCAB 36*, *REnAW*, *WhAm 2*, *WhAmP*
Scrugham, William W 1819-1867 *BiAUS*
Scrugham, William Warburton 1860-1944 *WhAm 2*
Scrutchin, Charles W 1866- *WhoColR*
Scrymser, James Alexander 1839-1918 *DcAmB*, *NatCAB 18*, *WhAm 1*
Scudder, Mrs. A M *NewYHSD*
Scudder, Charles Locke 1860-1949 *WhAm 2*
Scudder, David Coit 1835-1862 *ApCAB*
Scudder, Doremus 1858-1942 *WhAm 2*
Scudder, Edward Wallace 1882-1953 *WhAm 3*
Scudder, Frank Dyckman 1888-1942 *NatCAB 32*
Scudder, Henry Blatchford 1844-1917 *NatCAB 18*
Scudder, Henry Joel 1825-1886 *ApCAB*, *BiAUS*, *BiDrAC*, *WhAm H*
Scudder, Henry Martyn 1822-1895 *AmBi*, *ApCAB*, *TwCBDA*
Scudder, Horace Elisha 1838-1902 *AmBi*, *ApCAB*, *DcAmB*, *Drake*, *NatCAB 1*, *TwCBDA*, *WhAm 1*
Scudder, Hubert Baxter 1888-1968 *BiDrAC*, *WhAm 5*
Scudder, Isaac W 1818-1881 *BiAUS*
Scudder, Isaac Williamson 1816-1881 *BiDrAC*, *WhAm H*
Scudder, James Long 1836-1881 *NewYHSD*
Scudder, Janet 1869-1940 *NotAW*
Scudder, Janet 1873-1940 *WhAm 1*, *WomWWA 14*
Scudder, Janet 1874-1940 *BiCAW*, *NatCAB 14*, *NatCAB 15*
Scudder, Jared Waterbury 1830- *ApCAB*
Scudder, John 1793-1855 *ApCAB*, *DcAmB*, *Drake*, *NatCAB 2*, *TwCBDA*, *WhAm H*
Scudder, John A d1810 *BiAUS*
Scudder, John Anderson 1759-1836 *BiDrAC*, *WhAm H*
Scudder, John Milton 1829-1894 *DcAmB*, *NatCAB 28*, *WhAm H*
Scudder, Marvyn 1875-1935 *NatCAB 27*
Scudder, Moses Lewis 1843-1917 *WhAm 1*
Scudder, Myron Tracy 1860-1935 *WhAm 1*
Scudder, Nathaniel 1733-1781 *ApCAB*, *BiAUS*, *BiDrAC*, *DcAmB*, *Drake*, *NatCAB 4*, *TwCBDA*, *WhAm H*, *WhAmP*
Scudder, Raymond Barnes 1850-1917 *NatCAB 18*
Scudder, Samuel Hubbard 1837-1911 *AmBi*, *ApCAB*, *DcAmB*, *DcScB*, *NatCAB 3*, *NatCAB 24*, *TwCBDA*, *WhAm 1*
Scudder, Silas Doremus 1833-1877 *ApCAB*
Scudder, Theodore Townsend 1889-1953 *NatCAB 41*
Scudder, Townsend 1865-1960 *BiDrAC*, *NatCAB 44*, *WhAm 3*

Scudder, Treadwell *BiAUS*
Scudder, Tredwell 1778-1834 *BiDrAC,*
WhAm H
Scudder, Vida Dutton 1861-1954 *ApCAB,*
DcAmB S5, NatCAB 4, TwCBDA,
WhAm 3, WomWWA 14
Scudder, Wallace McIlvaine 1853-1931
NatCAB 25, WhAm 1
Scudder, Zeno 1807-1857 *BiAUS, BiDrAC,*
WhAm H
Scull, Edward 1818-1900 *BiDrAC*
Scull, Florence Prall *WomWWA 14*
Scull, John 1765-1828 *DcAmB, WhAm H*
Scull, Nicholas 1687-1762 *NatCAB 9*
Scull, Nicholas 1700?- *ApCAB*
Scullen, Anthony James 1889-1970 *WhAm 5*
Scullin, James Henry 1876-1953 *McGEWB*
Scullin, John 1836-1920 *DcAmB, NatCAB 12*
Scullin, Stella Wade 1884- *WomWWA 14*
Scully, Arthur Murtland 1882-1948 *NatCAB 37*
Scully, C Alison 1887-1954 *WhAm 3*
Scully, Cornelius Decatur 1878- *WhAm 6*
Scully, Hugh Day 1883-1968 *WhAm 5*
Scully, James Wall 1838-1918 *NatCAB 17,*
WhAm 1
Scully, John 1846-1917 *NatCAB 2*
Scully, John Sullivan 1844-1914 *ApCAB X,*
NatCAB 16
Scully, Thomas Joseph 1868-1921 *BiDrAC,*
WhAm 1, WhAmP
Scully, William 1821-1906 *EncAAH*
Scully, William A 1894-1969 *WhAm 5*
Scully, William Augustine d1936 *WhAm 1C*
Scully, William Augustine 1881-1936
NatCAB 27
Scully, William Augustine 1886-1936 *WhAm 1*
Scupham, George William 1889-1969 *WhAm 5*
Scupin, Carl Albert 1901-1972 *WhAm 5*
Scurry, Richardson 1811-1862 *BiAUS,*
BiDrAC, WhAm H
Seaberg, Stanley Stephen 1929- *EncAAH*
Seaberry, Virgil Theodore 1892-1960 *WhAm 4*
Seaborg, Glenn Theodore 1912- *AsBiEn,*
WebAB
Seabra, Vicente Coelho De 1766-1804 *ApCAB*
Seabring, Andrew T *NewYHSD*
Seabrook, Ava Gould 1870- *WomWWA 14*
Seabrook, Benjamin Whitemarsh 1795-1856
TwCBDA
Seabrook, Charles Franklin 1881-1964
NatCAB 53, WhAm 4
Seabrook, Harry Hartshorne 1859-1930
NatCAB 24
Seabrook, Whitemarsh Benjamin d1855 *Drake*
Seabrook, Whitemarsh Benjamin 1792-1855
NatCAB 12
Seabrook, Whitemarsh Benjamin 1795-1855
BiAUS
Seabrook, William Buehler 1886-1945 *WhAm 2*
Seabrooke, Thomas Q 1860-1913 *WhAm 1*
Seabury, Catharine Regina *WomWWA 14*
Seabury, Charles Ward 1876-1966 *WhAm 4*
Seabury, David 1885-1960 *NatCAB 49,*
WhAm 3, WhAm 4
Seabury, Dwight 1863-1931 *NatCAB 27*
Seabury, Francis William 1868-1946 *WhAm 2*
Seabury, George John 1844-1909 *DcAmB*
Seabury, George Tilley 1880-1945 *WhAm 2*
Seabury, Humphrey Woodman 1817-1891
ApCAB X
Seabury, John Cozzens 1848-1935 *NatCAB 34*
Seabury, Samuel 1706-1764 *ApCAB*
Seabury, Samuel 1729-1796 *AmBi, ApCAB,*
DcAmB, DcAmReB, Drake, EncAB,
McGEWB, NatCAB 3, TwCBDA,
WebAB, WhAm H
Seabury, Samuel 1801-1872 *ApCAB, DcAmB,*
Drake, TwCBDA, WhAm H
Seabury, Samuel 1873-1958 *WhAm 3*
Seabury, William Jones 1837-1916 *ApCAB,*
TwCBDA, WhAm 1
Seabury, William Marston 1878-1949 *WhAm 2*
Seachrest, Effie M *WhAm 3*
Seacord, Frederick Howard 1875-1949
NatCAB 38
Seacrest, Frederick Snively 1894-1971 *WhAm 5*
Seacrest, Joseph Claggett 1864-1942
NatCAB 37, WhAm 2

Seager *NewYHSD*
Seager, Miss *NewYHSD*
Seager, Allan 1906-1968 *WhAm 5*
Seager, Charles Allen 1872-1948 *WhAm 2*
Seager, Edward 1809?-1886 *NewYHSD*
Seager, Henry Rogers 1870-1930 *AmBi,*
DcAmB, NatCAB 22, WhAm 1
Seager, Lawrence H 1860-1937 *WhAm 1*
Seager, Sarah *NewYHSD*
Seager, William S *NewYHSD*
Seagle, Nathan Adolphus 1868-1957
NatCAB 43
Seagle, Oscar 1877-1945 *WhAm 2*
Seago, Erwin 1902-1968 *WhAm 5*
Seagrave, Frank Evans 1860-1934 *WhAm 1*
Seagrave, Gordon Stiffer 1897-1965 *WhAm 4*
Seagrave, Gordon Stifler 1897-1965 *WebAMB*
Seagrave, Louis H 1892-1966 *WhAm 4*
Seagrave, Walter Howard 1881-1949
NatCAB 37
Seagrove, Gordon Kay 1890-1963 *WhAm 4*
Seal, John Frederick 1894-1964 *WhAm 4*
Seal, Roderick *BiAUS*
Seale, Ellis Chase 1878-1960 *NatCAB 49*
Sealey, Alfred 1815?-1868? *NewYHSD*
Sealey, James Harris 1892-1925 *NatCAB 22*
Sealock, William Elmer 1877-1935 *WhAm 1*
Seals, Carl H 1882-1955 *WhAm 3*
Seals, John H *WhAm 5*
Seals, John Henry d1906 *NatCAB 2*
Sealsfield, Charles 1793-1864 *ApCAB, DcAmB,*
NatCAB 2, WhAm H
Sealsfield, Charles 1797-1864 *Drake*
Sealy, Frank L 1858-1938 *WhAm 1*
Sealy, George 1835-1901 *NatCAB 9,*
NatCAB 35
Sealy, George 1880-1944 *NatCAB 35*
Sealy, John 1822-1884 *NatCAB 11*
Seaman, A Owen 1878- *WhAm 6*
Seaman, Arthur Edmund 1858-1937 *WhAm 1*
Seaman, Augusta Huiell 1879-1950 *WhAm 3*
Seaman, Charles *NewYHSD*
Seaman, Cleora Augusta 1814-1869
NatCAB 23
Seaman, Elizabeth Cochrane 1865?-1922
NotAW
Seaman, Elizabeth Cochrane 1867-1922 *DcAmB,*
WebAB, WhAm HA, WhAm 4
Seaman, Emery *NewYHSD*
Seaman, Eugene Cecil 1881-1950 *WhAm 3*
Seaman, Ezra Champion 1805-1880 *ApCAB*
Seaman, George Milton 1876-1936 *NatCAB 28,*
WhAm 1
Seaman, Gilbert Edmund 1869-1941 *WhAm 1*
Seaman, Harold Hibbard 1879-1966
NatCAB 51
Seaman, Harry Joseph 1898-1966 *NatCAB 52*
Seaman, Henry *NewYHSD*
Seaman, Henry Bowman 1861-1940 *WhAm 1*
Seaman, Henry John 1805-1861 *BiAUS,*
BiDrAC, WhAm H
Seaman, Irving 1881- *WhAm 6*
Seaman, John Thompson 1898-1955 *WhAm 3*
Seaman, Joseph Husband 1865-1948
NatCAB 37
Seaman, Laura Rice 1876- *WomWWA 14*
Seaman, Louis Livingston 1851-1932 *ApCAB X,*
NatCAB 5, WhAm 1
Seaman, Margaret Laurie 1869- *WomWWA 14*
Seaman, Valentine 1770-1817 *ApCAB, Drake*
Seaman, William Grant 1866- *WhAm 4*
Seaman, William Henry 1837-1910 *NatCAB 14,*
WhAm 1
Seaman, William Henry 1842-1915 *NatCAB 20,*
WhAm 1
Seamans, Byron George 1862-1927 *NatCAB 23*
Seamans, Clarence Walker 1854-1915
ApCAB X, NatCAB 26, WhAm 1
Seamans, Frank 1876-1955 *NatCAB 45*
Searby, Edmund Wilson 1896-1944 *WhAm 2*
Searby, William Martin 1835-1909 *NatCAB 20*
Search, Preston Willis 1853-1932 *WhAm 1*
Search, Theodore Corson 1841- *NatCAB 12,*
WhAm 1
Searcy, Chesley Hunter 1881-1935 *WhAm 1*
Searcy, Mrs. Earle Benjamin d1968 *WhAm 5*
Searcy, Hubert Floyd 1908-1971 *WhAm 5*
Searcy, James Thomas 1839- *WhAm 4*

Searer, Jay Charles 1914-1967 *WhAm 5*
Seares, Frederick Hanley 1873-1964 *DcScB,*
WhAm 6
Searight, James Allison 1836-1915 *NatCAB 16*
Searing, Anne Eliza Pidgeon 1857-
WomWWA 14
Searing, Ernest 1877-1961 *NatCAB 52*
Searing, Florence E 1868- *AmWom*
Searing, Hudson Roy 1895-1957 *WhAm 3*
Searing, John A 1814- *BiAUS*
Searing, John Alexander 1805-1876 *BiDrAC,*
WhAm H
Searing, Laura Catharine Redden 1840-1923
TwCBDA
Searing, Laura Catherine Redden 1840-1923
AmWom, ApCAB, DcAmB, NatCAB 9,
WhAm 4, WomWWA 14
Searl, Kelly Stephen 1862-1942 *NatCAB 31*
Searle, Alonzo T 1857- *WhAm 4*
Searle, Arthur 1837-1920 *ApCAB, DcAmB,*
NatCAB 18, NatCAB 19, TwCBDA,
WhAm 1
Searle, Augustus Leach 1863-1955 *WhAm 3*
Searle, Charles James 1865-1933 *WhAm 1*
Searle, Charles Putnam 1854-1917 *WhAm 1*
Searle, Cyril *NewYHSD*
Searle, Dominic Francis 1859-1943 *NatCAB 47*
Searle, Edith MacDonald 1886- *WomWWA 14*
Searle, Franklin Elijah 1853-1916 *NatCAB 17*
Searle, George 1751?-1796 *NewYHSD*
Searle, George James 1860-1954 *NatCAB 45*
Searle, George Mary 1839-1918 *ApCAB,*
TwCBDA, WhAm 1
Searle, George W 1826- *Drake*
Searle, Harriet Richardson *WhAm 5*
Searle, Helen Marshall 1880- *WomWWA 14*
Searle, Helen R *NewYHSD*
Searle, James 1730?-1797 *ApCAB, BiAUS,*
BiDrAC, Drake, NatCAB 4, TwCBDA
Searle, James 1733-1797 *DcAmB, WhAm H*
Searle, John *NewYHSD*
Searle, John Preston 1854-1922 *DcAmB,*
WhAm 1
Searle, Robert Wyckoff 1894-1967 *NatCAB 53,*
WhAm 4, WhAm 5
Searle, William Beecher 1862-1913 *NatCAB 17*
Searles, Colbert 1873- *WhAm 5*
Searles, Helen McGaffey 1856- *WomWWA 14*
Searles, John Ennis d1908 *WhAm 1*
Searles, John William 1870-1933 *WhAm 1*
Searles, William Henry 1837-1921 *WhAm 1*
Searls, Carroll 1894-1970 *WhAm 5*
Searls, David Thomas 1905-1972 *NatCAB 57,*
WhAm 5
Searls, Niles 1825- *NatCAB 13*
Searls, Robert McMurray 1886-1953
NatCAB 42
Sears *EncAAH*
Sears, Anna Wentworth *WomWWA 14*
Sears, Barnas 1802-1880 *ApCAB, BiDAmEd,*
DcAmB, Drake, NatCAB 1, NatCAB 8,
TwCBDA, WhAm H
Sears, Charles Brown 1870-1950 *NatCAB 39,*
WhAm 3
Sears, Charles Edwin 1878-1956 *NatCAB 43*
Sears, Charles Hatch 1870-1943 *WhAm 2*
Sears, Chauncey Howe 1853-1925 *NatCAB 21*
Sears, Clara Endicott 1863-1960 *BiCAW,*
NatCAB 47
Sears, Clinton Brooks 1844-1912 *WhAm 1*
Sears, Ed *NewYHSD*
Sears, Edmund Hamilton 1810-1876 *ApCAB,*
DcAmB, Drake, NatCAB 8, TwCBDA,
WhAm H
Sears, Edmund Hamilton 1852-1942
NatCAB 31, WhAm 2
Sears, Edward I 1819-1876 *ApCAB*
Sears, Francis Philip 1869- *WhAm 5*
Sears, Francis W 1898-1975 *WhAm 6*
Sears, Frank Irving 1872-1956 *WhAm 3*
Sears, Franklin Warren 1863- *NatCAB 7*
Sears, Fred Coleman 1866-1949 *WhAm 3*
Sears, Frederic William 1859-1934 *WhAm 1*
Sears, Frederick W 1858-1934 *WhAm 1,*
WhAm 1C
Sears, George Gray 1859-1940 *NatCAB 30,*
WhAm 1
Sears, George Wallace 1878- *WhAm 6*

Sears, Harriet Robinson Harrington
WomWWA 14
Sears, Harry Johnson 1885-1962 *NatCAB 49*
Sears, Herbert Mason 1867-1942 *WhAm 2*
Sears, Hess Thatcher 1912-1973 *WhAm 5*
Sears, Isaac 1729-1786 *ApCAB, Drake,
NatCAB 1, TwCBDA*
Sears, Isaac 1730-1786 *DcAmB, WebAB,
WhAm H*
Sears, James Hamilton 1855-1915 *WhAm 1*
Sears, Jesse Brundage 1876- *WhAm 5*
Sears, John Sylvester 1867-1958 *NatCAB 44*
Sears, John VanDerZee 1835-1926 *NatCAB 21,
WhAm 4*
Sears, Joseph Hamblen 1865-1946 *NatCAB 13,
WhAm 2*
Sears, Julia Seton *WomWWA 14*
Sears, Julian D 1891-1970 *WhAm 5*
Sears, Kenneth Craddock 1890-1961 *WhAm 4*
Sears, Laurence 1896-1958 *WhAm 3*
Sears, Lester Merriam 1888-1967 *WhAm 4*
Sears, Lorenzo 1838-1916 *TwCBDA, WhAm 1*
Sears, Louise A Boesche *WomWWA 14*
Sears, Lulu Jean Ledgerwood 1883-
WomWWA 14
Sears, Millicent Lura 1881- *WomWWA 14*
Sears, Minnie Earl 1873-1933 *DcAmLiB*
Sears, Nathan Pratt 1886-1946 *WhAm 2*
Sears, Nathaniel Clinton 1854-1934
NatCAB 16, WhAm 1
Sears, Philip Mason 1899-1973 *WhAm 6*
Sears, Philip Shelton 1867-1953 *IIBEAAW,
WhAm 3*
Sears, Richard 1867-1943 *NatCAB 32*
Sears, Richard Dudley 1861-1943 *DcAmB S3*
Sears, Richard Warren 1863-1914 *AmBi,
ApCAB X, DcAmB, EncAAH, WebAB,
WhAm 1*
Sears, Robert 1810- *ApCAB, Drake*
Sears, Robert 1810-1891 *TwCBDA*
Sears, Robert 1810-1892 *DcAmB, NatCAB 7,
WhAm H*
Sears, Russell Adams 1869-1932 *WhAm 1*
Sears, Samuel Powers 1895-1964 *WhAm 4*
Sears, Sarah Choate 1858-1935 *WhAm 1,
WomWWA 14*
Sears, Taber 1870-1950 *WhAm 3*
Sears, Thad Perce 1892-1965 *NatCAB 53*
Sears, Walter Herbert 1847-1911 *WhAm 1*
Sears, Walter James 1869-1929 *WhAm 1*
Sears, Willard Thomas 1837-1920 *WhAm 1*
Sears, William Barnas 1832- *NatCAB 14*
Sears, William Henry 1858-1933 *WhAm 1*
Sears, William Joseph 1874-1944 *BiDrAC,
WhAm 2, WhAmP*
Sears, William Richards 1869-1925 *NatCAB 22*
Sears, Willis Gratz 1860-1949 *BiDrAC,
WhAm 5, WhAmP*
Sears, Zelda 1873-1935 *WhAm 1*
Searson, James William 1873-1927 *WhAm 1*
Seashore, August Theodore 1871-1934 *WhAm 1*
Seashore, Carl Emil 1866-1949 *BiDAmEd,
DcAmB S4, WhAm 2*
Seashore, Harold Gustav 1906-1965
NatCAB 52
Seashore, Robert Holmes 1902-1951
NatCAB 41, WhAm 3
Seastone, Charles Victor 1872-1940 *WhAm 1*
Seastone, Charles Victor 1908-1974 *WhAm 6*
Seath, Ethel 1879- *WomWWA 14*
Seaton, Charles Williams 1831-1885
NatCAB 12
Seaton, Frederick Andrew 1909-1974 *BiDrAC,
BiDrUSE, EncAAH, WhAm 6*
Seaton, John Lawrence 1873-1961 *WhAm 4,
WhAm 5*
Seaton, Kendall Gordon 1893-1948 *NatCAB 37*
Seaton, Roy Andrew 1884-1970 *WhAm 5*
Seaton, William Biggs 1855-1927 *NatCAB 45*
Seaton, William Winston 1785-1864 *TwCBDA*
Seaton, William Winston 1785-1866 *ApCAB,
BiAUS, DcAmB, Drake, NatCAB 2*
Seaton, William Winston 1785-1885 *WhAm H*
Seattle 1780?-1866 *ApCAB Sup*
Seattle 1786?-1866 *DcAmB, WhAm H*
Seaver, Ebenezer 1763-1844 *BiAUS, BiDrAC,
TwCBDA, WhAm H, WhAmP*
Seaver, Edwin Pliny 1838-1917 *WhAm 1*

Seaver, Frank Roger 1883-1964 *NatCAB 52,
WhAm 4A*
Seaver, Fred Jay 1877-1970 *WhAm 5*
Seaver, Henry Latimer 1878-1975 *WhAm 6*
Seaver, Homer Carlton 1889-1941 *NatCAB 31*
Seaver, Kenneth 1877- *WhAm 5*
Seaver, Mary Patterson *WomWWA 14*
Seaverns, Clara I 1866- *WomWWA 14*
Seaverns, Joel Herbert 1860- *WhAm 4*
Seavey, Clyde Leroy 1874-1943 *WhAm 2*
Seavey, Julian Ruggles 1857-1940 *IIBEAAW*
Seavey, Thomas *NewYHSD*
Seavey, Warren Abner 1880-1966 *NatCAB 53,
WhAm 4*
Seavey, William L *NewYHSD*
Seawell, Aaron Ashley Flowers 1864-1950
WhAm 3
Seawell, Emmet 1862-1939 *WhAm 1*
Seawell, Henry 1772-1835 *NatCAB 7*
Seawell, Herbert Floyd 1869- *WhAm 5*
Seawell, Molly Elliot 1860-1916 *AmWom,
ApCAB Sup, DcAmB, NatCAB 7,
TwCBDA, WomWWA 14*
Seawell, Molly Elliott 1860-1916 *WhAm 1*
Seawell, Washington 1802-1888 *ApCAB,
Drake*
Seay, Abraham Jefferson 1832-1915 *TwCBDA,
WhAm 1*
Seay, Edward Tucker 1868-1941 *NatCAB 41,
WhAm 2*
Seay, Frank 1881-1920 *WhAm 1*
Seay, George James 1862-1952 *NatCAB 10,
WhAm 3*
Seay, Harry Lauderdale 1872-1957 *WhAm 3*
Seay, Thomas 1846-1896 *NatCAB 10,
TwCBDA*
Seay, William A 1831- *NatCAB 7*
Seay, William Albert 1920-1969 *WhAm 5*
Sebald, Hobarth *NewYHSD*
Sebald, Hugo *NewYHSD*
Sebald, Weber William 1888-1967 *NatCAB 52,
WhAm 4*
Sebast, Frederick Martin 1892-1955 *WhAm 3*
Sebastian, Benjamin 1745?-1834 *DcAmB,
WhAm H*
Sebastian, Jerome D d1960 *WhAm 4*
Sebastian, John 1849-1914 *WhAm 1*
Sebastian, S Powell 1879- *WhoColR*
Sebastian, William King d1865 *BiAUS*
Sebastian, William King 1812-1865 *BiDrAC,
WhAm H, WhAmP*
Sebastian, William King 1814-1865 *ApCAB,
NatCAB 4, TwCBDA*
Sebbelov, Gerda 1885- *WomWWA 14*
Sebben, Edward Wilbert 1855-1926 *NatCAB 22*
Sebelius, Keith George 1916- *BiDrAC*
Sebelius, Sven Johan 1874- *WhAm 3*
Sebenius, John Uno 1862-1932 *NatCAB 27,
WhAm 1*
Seber, William Franklin 1884-1935 *NatCAB 26*
Sebree, Edmund B 1898-1966 *WhAm 4*
Sebree, J Emmett 1878-1952 *NatCAB 39*
Sebree, Uriel 1848-1922 *WhAm 1*
Sebrell, John Ney 1871-1947 *NatCAB 35*
Sebring, Emma Goodeve *WomWWA 14*
Sebring, Harold Leon 1898-1968 *WhAm 5*
Sebring, Harriet McPherson 1862-
WomWWA 14
Sebron, Hyppolite Victor Valentin 1801-1897
NewYHSD
Secchi, Pietro Angelo 1818-1878 *AsBiEn,
DcScB*
Seccomb, John 1708-1792 *DcAmB, WhAm H*
Seccomb, John 1708-1793 *ApCAB, Drake,
NatCAB 7*
Seccomb, Joseph 1706-1760 *ApCAB*
Seccombe, James 1893-1970 *BiDrAC*
Sechenov, Ivan Mikhaylovich 1829-1905 *DcScB*
Secher, Samuel 1771-1839 *WhAm H*
Seckel, Joshua C *NewYHSD*
Seckendorff, Max Gebhard 1852-1911 *WhAm 1*
Seckler-Hudson, Catheryn 1902-1963 *WhAm 4*
Secondari, John Hermes 1919-1975 *WhAm 6*
Secor, Charles Edgar 1881-1958 *NatCAB 48*
Secor, David Pell 1824-1909 *NewYHSD*
Secor, John Alstyne 1847- *WhAm 4*
Secord, Arthur Wellesley 1891-1957 *WhAm 3*
Secord, Eugene William 1903-1968 *NatCAB 54*

Secord, Frederick 1884-1964 *NatCAB 51,
WhAm 4*
Secoy, Harry Raymond 1890-1960 *NatCAB 49*
Secrest, Robert Thompson 1904- *BiDrAC*
Secrist, Horace 1881-1943 *WhAm 2*
Secunda, Sholom 1894-1974 *WhAm 6*
Seddon, James Alexander 1815-1880 *AmBi,
ApCAB, BiAUS, BiDConf, BiDrAC,
DcAmB, Drake, NatCAB 6, TwCBDA,
WhAm H, WhAmP*
Seddon, Richard John 1845-1906 *McGEWB*
Seddon, William Little 1862-1937 *WhAm 1*
Sedella, Antoine 1748-1829 *DcAmB*
Sedeno, Antonio d1538 *ApCAB*
Seder, Arthur Raymond 1889-1969 *WhAm 5*
Sederholm, Johannes Jakob 1863-1934 *DcScB*
Sedges, John *WebAB*
Sedgewick, Robert 1848- *ApCAB Sup*
Sedgley, Reginald Francis 1876-1938
NatCAB 32
Sedgwick, Adam 1785-1873 *AsBiEn, DcScB,
McGEWB*
Sedgwick, Allan E 1881-1941 *WhAm 2*
Sedgwick, Anne Douglas 1873-1935 *AmBi,
DcAmB S1, NotAW, WhAm 1,
WomWWA 14*
Sedgwick, Arthur George 1844-1915 *ApCAB,
DcAmB, NatCAB 27, WhAm 1*
Sedgwick, C B 1815-1883 *BiAUS*
Sedgwick, Catharine Maria 1789-1867 *AmBi,
DcAmB, Drake, NatCAB 1, NotAW,
TwCBDA, WhAm H*
Sedgwick, Catherine Maria 1789-1867 *AmWom,
ApCAB*
Sedgwick, Charles Baldwin 1815-1883 *BiDrAC,
WhAm H*
Sedgwick, Elizabeth Dwight *ApCAB*
Sedgwick, Ellery 1872-1960 *WhAm 4*
Sedgwick, Francis Minturn 1904-1967
IIBEAAW, NatCAB 54, WhAm 5
Sedgwick, Henry Dwight 1785-1831 *ApCAB,
Drake, NatCAB 2, TwCBDA, WhAm H*
Sedgwick, Henry Dwight 1824-1903 *TwCBDA,
WhAm 1*
Sedgwick, Henry Dwight 1861-1957
NatCAB 47, WhAm 3
Sedgwick, John 1813-1864 *AmBi, ApCAB,
DcAmB, Drake, NatCAB 4, TwCBDA,
WebAMB, WhAm H*
Sedgwick, John 1829- *ApCAB*
Sedgwick, Julius Parker 1876-1923 *NatCAB 27,
WhAm 1*
Sedgwick, Mary Aspinwall Bend 1878-
WomWWA 14
Sedgwick, Paul J 1896-1973 *WhAm 6*
Sedgwick, Robert d1656 *Drake*
Sedgwick, Robert 1590?-1656 *ApCAB,
NatCAB 2*
Sedgwick, Robert 1613?-1656 *AmBi, DcAmB,
WhAm H*
Sedgwick, Samuel Hopkins 1848-1919
NatCAB 14, WhAm 1
Sedgwick, Susan Anne Livingston Ridley
1788-1867 *TwCBDA*
Sedgwick, Susan Anne Livingston Ridley
1789?-1867 *ApCAB, NewYHSD*
Sedgwick, Theodore 1746-1813 *AmBi, ApCAB,
BiAUS, BiDrAC, DcAmB, Drake,
NatCAB 2, TwCBDA, WebAB,
WhAm H, WhAmP*
Sedgwick, Theodore 1780-1839 *ApCAB,
DcAmB, Drake, NatCAB 2, TwCBDA,
WhAm H*
Sedgwick, Theodore 1811-1859 *ApCAB,
DcAmB, Drake, NatCAB 2, TwCBDA,
WhAm H*
Sedgwick, William Thompson 1855-1921
*BiHiMed, DcAmB, NatCAB 13, TwCBDA,
WhAm 1*
Sedita, Frank Albert 1907-1975 *WhAm 6*
Sedlander, Norman Robert 1920-1974 *WhAm 6*
Sedlar, Sasa 1913-1975 *WhAm 6*
Sedley, Henry 1831-1899 *WhAm 1*
Sedley, Henry 1835- *ApCAB*
Sedley, William Henry 1806-1872 *ApCAB,
DcAmB, NatCAB 13*
Sedov, Georgy Yakovlevich 1877-1914 *DcScB*
See, Elliot M, Jr. 1927-1966 *WhAm 4*

See, Harold Philip 1907-1972 *WhAm 5*

See, Horace 1835-1909 *DcAmB, NatCAB 2, WhAm 1*

See, Salvator *NewYHSD*

See, Thomas Jefferson Jackson 1866-1962 *ApCAB X, DcScB, NatCAB 13, TwCBDA, WhAm 4*

Seebeck, Thomas 1770-1831 *DcScB*

Seebeck, Thomas Johann 1770-1831 *AsBiEn*

Seebirt, Eli Fowler 1878-1955 *NatCAB 47, WhAm 3*

Seebold, Herman DeBachelle 1875-1950 *NatCAB 42*

Seeburg, Justus Percival 1871- *ApCAB X*

Seeck, George Conrad 1898-1973 *NatCAB 57*

Seeckt, Hans Von 1866-1936 *WhoMilH*

Seed, Miles Ainscough 1843-1913 *ApCAB X, DcAmB*

Seeds, Jacob Jordan 1858-1945 *NatCAB 35*

Seeds, Russel M 1864- *WhAm 4*

Seegal, David 1899-1972 *NatCAB 57, WhAm 5*

Seeger, Alan 1888-1916 *AmBi, DcAmB, NatCAB 20, WebAMB, WhAm 4*

Seeger, Charles Louis 1886-1943 *WhAm 2*

Seeger, Edwin W 1892-1955 *WhAm 3*

Seeger, Eugene 1853- *WhAm 4*

Seeger, John August 1854-1938 *NatCAB 46*

Seeger, Pete 1919- *EncAAH, WebAB*

Seeger, Stanley Joseph 1889-1952 *NatCAB 39, WhAm 5*

Seeger, Walter Gustave 1886-1969 *NatCAB 55, WhAm 5*

Seegers, John Conrad 1867-1936 *WhAm 1*

Seegmiller, Wilhelmina 1866-1913 *WhAm 1*

Seelbach, Louis 1890-1971 *WhAm 5*

Seele, Keith C 1898-1971 *WhAm 6*

Seeler, Albert Otto 1915-1976 *WhAm 6*

Seeler, Edgar Viguers 1867-1929 *NatCAB 41, WhAm 1*

Seeley, Dana Elisha 1868-1957 *NatCAB 46*

Seeley, Elias P 1791-1846 *NatCAB 5, WhAm H*

Seeley, Frank Barrows 1872-1951 *WhAm 3*

Seeley, Halstead Harley 1876-1952 *NatCAB 41*

Seeley, John Edward 1810-1875 *BiAUS, BiDrAC, WhAm H*

Seeley, Lauren Earl 1898-1968 *NatCAB 55*

Seeley, Levi 1847-1928 *BiDAmEd, WhAm 1*

Seeley, Morton Claude 1885-1957 *NatCAB 48*

Seeley, W Parker 1892-1953 *NatCAB 42*

Seeley, Walter James 1894-1974 *WhAm 6*

Seeley, Ward Francis 1888-1960 *NatCAB 50*

Seelig, Gabriel 1874-1953 *NatCAB 40*

Seelig, M G 1874- *WhAm 5*

Seeliger, Hugo Von 1849-1924 *DcScB*

Seelman, Ernest Paris 1876-1970 *NatCAB 57*

Seelos, Francis X 1819-1867 *WhAm H*

Seelve, Laurens Hickok 1889-1960 *WhAm 4*

Seely, Bertha Warner 1883- *WomWWA 14*

Seely, Clark Chester 1886-1920 *NatCAB 18*

Seely, Elias P *BiAUS*

Seely, Florence Corinne 1865- *WomWWA 14*

Seely, Fred B 1884-1968 *NatCAB 54*

Seely, Fred Loring 1871-1942 *NatCAB 32, WhAm 2*

Seely, Henry B 1838-1901 *TwCBDA*

Seely, Henry Martyn 1828-1917 *TwCBDA, WhAm 1*

Seely, Herman Gastrell 1891-1958 *WhAm 3*

Seely, Linus 1848-1923 *NatCAB 19*

Seely, Walter Hoff 1873-1936 *WhAm 1*

Seely-Brown, Horace, Jr. 1908- *BiDrAC*

Seelye, Anne Ide Barrows *WomWWA 14*

Seelye, Elizabeth Eggleston 1858-1923 *AmWom, WhAm 3, WomWWA 14*

Seelye, Elwyn Eggleston 1884-1959 *NatCAB 46*

Seelye, Julius Hawley 1824-1895 *AmBi, ApCAB, BiAUS, BiDAmEd, BiDrAC, DcAmB, NatCAB 5, NatCAB 6, TwCBDA, WhAm H, WhAmP*

Seelye, Laurens Clark 1837-1924 *ApCAB, TwCBDA*

Seelye, Laurens Hickok 1889-1960 *NatCAB 45*

Seelye, Laurenus Clark 1837-1924 *AmBi, BiDAmEd, DcAmB, NatCAB 7, NatCAB 38, WhAm 1*

Seelye, Theodore Edward 1887-1963 *WhAm 4*

Seelye, Walter Clark 1873-1961 *NatCAB 51*

Seelye, Wilber Morgan 1899-1964 *NatCAB 51*

Seelye, William James 1857-1931 *NatCAB 22*

Seem, Ralph Berger 1880-1941 *WhAm 1*

Seeman, Berthold 1825-1871 *ApCAB*

Seep, Joseph 1838-1928 *NatCAB 52*

Seerie, David Duff 1862-1917 *NatCAB 32*

Seering, Harold Albert 1902-1956 *NatCAB 44*

Seerley, Frank Newell 1859- *WhAm 4*

Seerley, Homer Horatio 1848-1932 *BiDAmEd, WhAm 1*

Seerley, John Joseph 1852-1931 *BiDrAC*

Seery, Irving Peter 1890-1966 *NatCAB 53*

Sees, John Vincent 1875-1946 *NatCAB 35, WhAm 2*

Seested, August Frederick 1864-1928 *WhAm 1*

Seever, William John 1860- *WhAm 2*

Seevers, Charles Hamilton 1907-1965 *WhAm 4*

Seevers, William Henry 1822-1895 *DcAmB, NatCAB 12, WhAm H*

Seferiades, George 1900-1971 *WhAm 5*

Seferis, George 1900-1971 *McGEWB*

Seffel, E A, Jr. *IIBEAAW*

Sefrit, Frank Ira 1867-1950 *WhAm 3*

Sefstrom, Nils Gabriel 1787-1845 *AsBiEn*

Sefton, John 1805-1868 *ApCAB, Drake*

Segal, George 1924- *BnEnAmA, WebAB*

Segal, Paul Moses 1899-1968 *WhAm 5*

Segar, Elzie Crisler 1895-1938 *WebAB*

Segar, Joseph Eggleston 1804- *BiAUS*

Segar, Joseph Eggleston 1804-1880 *BiDrAC, WhAm H*

Segar, Joseph Eggleston 1804-1885 *ApCAB*

Segar, William S 1823-1887 *NewYHSD*

Segel, David 1894-1972 *WhAm 5*

Seger, Charles Bronson 1867-1940 *WhAm 1*

Seger, George Nicholas 1866-1940 *BiDrAC, WhAm 1, WhAmP*

Seger, George Nicholas 1868-1940 *NatCAB 45*

Seger, Gerhart Henry 1896-1967 *WhAm 4*

Seger, Sarah Hardenberg 1851- *WomWWA 14*

Seghers, Charles Jean 1839-1886 *DcAmB, WhAm H*

Seghers, Charles John 1839-1886 *ApCAB, NatCAB 13, TwCBDA*

Segner, Janos-Andras 1704-1777 *DcScB*

Segni, Antonio 1891-1972 *WhAm 5*

Segre, Corrado 1863-1924 *DcScB*

Segre, Emilio Gino 1905- *AsBiEn, WebAB*

Seguin Aine 1786-1875 *DcScB*

Seguin, Ann Childe 1809- *ApCAB*

Seguin, Armand 1767-1835 *DcScB*

Seguin, Mrs. Arthur Edward Shelden *Drake*

Seguin, Arthur Edward Shelden 1809-1852 *Drake*

Seguin, Arthur Edward Sheldon 1809-1852 *ApCAB*

Seguin, Edouard 1812-1880 *AmBi, ApCAB, DcAmB, NatCAB 15, TwCBDA, WhAm H*

Seguin, Edward Constant 1843-1898 *AmBi, DcAmB, TwCBDA, WhAm H*

Seguin, Marc 1786-1875 *DcScB*

Segur, Louis Philippe, Count De 1753-1830 *ApCAB*

Segur, Louis-Philippe, Count De 1753-1832 *Drake*

Segur, Rosa L 1833- *AmWom*

Segura, Juan Bautista d1571 *ApCAB*

Segurola, Sebastian De 1740-1789 *ApCAB*

Seibel, Frederick Otto 1886-1969 *WhAm 5*

Seibel, George 1872-1958 *WhAm 3*

Seibels, Edwin Granville 1866-1954 *WhAm 3*

Seibels, George Goldthwaite 1872- *WhAm 5*

Seibels, J J 1816-1865 *BiAUS*

Seibels, John Jacob 1816-1865 *NatCAB 12*

Seibels, Temple 1874-1960 *NatCAB 51*

Seiberling, Albert Franklin 1866-1948 *NatCAB 47*

Seiberling, Charles Willard 1861-1946 *ApCAB X, WhAm 2*

Seiberling, Francis 1870-1945 *BiDrAC, WhAm 2*

Seiberling, Frank Augustus 1859-1955 *ApCAB X, DcAmB S5, WhAm 3*

Seiberling, Gertrude F *WomWWA 14*

Seiberling, James Henry 1835-1916 *NatCAB 47*

Seiberling, John Frederick 1834-1903 *ApCAB X*

Seibert *NewYHSD*

Seibert, Edward *NewYHSD*

Seibert, Gertrude Woodcock 1864- *WomWWA 14*

Seibert, Henry *NewYHSD*

Seibert, Jacob *NewYHSD*

Seibert, James Walter 1915-1963 *WhAm 4*

Seibert, John F 1868-1939 *WhAm 1*

Seibert, Robert T 1861-1917 *ApCAB X*

Seibert, Walter R 1908-1965 *WhAm 4*

Seibert, William Adam 1859-1919 *WhAm 1*

Seibold, Louis 1863-1945 *DcAmB S3, WhAm 2*

Seibold, Myron James 1908-1970 *WhAm 5*

Seidel, Charles Frederick *NewYHSD*

Seidel, Emil 1864-1947 *WhAm 2*

Seidel, Frederick *NewYHSD*

Seidel, George Lukas Emil 1864-1947 *DcAmB S4*

Seidel, Harry George 1890-1943 *NatCAB 32*

Seidel, Harry George 1922-1973 *WhAm 6*

Seidel, John George 1902-1973 *WhAm 6*

Seidel, Nathaniel 1718-1782 *ApCAB, NatCAB 2*

Seidel, Philipp Ludwig Von 1821-1896 *DcScB*

Seidel, Toscha 1899-1962 *WhAm 4*

Seidemann, Henry Peter 1883-1954 *WhAm 3*

Seidenbusch, Rupert 1830-1895 *NatCAB 12*

Seidenbush, Rupert 1830-1895 *ApCAB, TwCBDA, WhAm H*

Seidensticker, Oswald 1825-1894 *DcAmB, WhAm H*

Seiders, George Melville 1844-1915 *WhAm 1*

Seidl, Anton 1850-1898 *ApCAB Sup, ApCAB X, DcAmB, NatCAB 8, TwCBDA, WhAm H*

Seidl, Frank J, Sr. 1880- *WhAm 6*

Seidlitz, Walter George 1899-1974 *WhAm 6*

Seidman, Frank Edward 1891-1972 *NatCAB 56*

Seidner, Howard Mayo 1921-1968 *WhAm 5*

Seids, James Vane 1894-1941 *NatCAB 31*

Seids, John William 1871-1965 *NatCAB 51*

Seif, William Henry 1859-1921 *NatCAB 5, WhAm 1*

Seifart, Fritz 1894-1964 *NatCAB 50*

Seifer, Arthur Fred 1911-1973 *NatCAB 57*

Seifert, F *NewYHSD*

Seifert, Henry 1824-1911 *NewYHSD*

Seifert, Mathias Joseph 1866-1947 *NatCAB 16, WhAm 2*

Seifert, William Alexander 1876-1956 *NatCAB 49*

Seifferth, Anton 1712-1785 *NatCAB 2*

Seifriz, William 1888-1955 *WhAm 3*

Seigle, John Sanders 1914-1973 *WhAm 5*

Seignobosc, Francoise 1897-1961 *WhAm 4*

Seil, Gilbert Edward 1888-1946 *NatCAB 37*

Seil, Harvey Ambrose 1882-1951 *NatCAB 38, NatCAB 44*

Seile, Simeon B *NewYHSD*

Seiler, Alice Faye 1881- *WomWWA 14*

Seiler, Carl 1849-1905 *DcAmB, NatCAB 28*

Seiler, Frederick *NewYHSD*

Seime, Reuben Ingmar 1907-1969 *WhAm 6*

Seinsheimer, J Fellman 1881-1951 *WhAm 3*

Seip, Theodore Lorenzo 1842-1903 *ApCAB, DcAmB, NatCAB 5, TwCBDA, WhAm 1*

Seipp, Philip Walter 1877- *NatCAB 17*

Seiss, Joseph Augustus 1823-1904 *ApCAB, DcAmB, Drake, NatCAB 7, TwCBDA, WhAm 1*

Seiter, Edward Alvin 1867-1941 *NatCAB 34*

Seitz, Albert Blazier 1898-1962 *WhAm 4*

Seitz, Charles Edward 1890-1972 *WhAm 5*

Seitz, Charles Lewis 1878-1957 *NatCAB 49*

Seitz, Don Carlos 1862-1935 *AmBi, DcAmB S1, WhAm 1*

Seitz, Earl William 1865-1942 *NatCAB 30*

Seitz, Frank Noah 1909-1969 *WhAm 5*

Seitz, George Albert 1897-1947 *WhAm 2*

Seitz, Ira James 1868-1971 *WhAm 5*

Seitz, John *NewYHSD*

Seitz, Louis Arthur 1861-1928 *NatCAB 21*

Seitz, Mildred E 1862- *WomWWA 14*

Seitz, Roland Forrest 1867-1946 *NatCAB 45*

Seitz, William Chapin 1914-1974 *WhAm 6*

Seiver, George Otto 1898-1964 *WhAm 4*

Seixas, Gershom Mendes 1745-1816 *NatCAB 4*
Seixas, Gershom Mendes 1746-1816 *DcAmB,*
WhAm H
Sejo 1417-1468 *McGEWB*
Sejong 1397-1450 *McGEWB*
Sejour, Victor 1817-1874 *DcAmB, WhAm H*
Sekera, Zdenek 1905-1973 *WhAm 5*
Sekers, Nicholas Thomas 1910-1972 *WhAm 5*
Seki, Takakazu 1642?-1708 *DcScB*
Sekimachi, Kay 1926- *BnEnAmA*
Sel, B *NewYHSD*
Sel, John B d1832 *NewYHSD*
Selby, Augustine Dawson 1859-1924 *WhAm 1*
Selby, Charles Baxter 1872-1933 *WhAm 1*
Selby, Clarence Davey 1878- *WhAm 6*
Selby, F *NewYHSD*
Selby, Francis Marion 1856-1946 *NatCAB 45*
Selby, George Dyar 1846-1927 *NatCAB 31*
Selby, Howard Williams 1891-1953 *NatCAB 47,*
WhAm 3
Selby, Mark Webster 1876- *WhAm 5*
Selby, Thomas Jefferson 1840-1917 *BiDrAC,*
WhAm 4
Selby, William 1739?-1798 *DcAmB, WhAm H*
Selby, William Gifford 1884-1956 *NatCAB 45*
Selden, Armistead Inge, Jr. 1921- *BiDrAC*
Selden, Charles A 1870- *WhAm 5*
Selden, Dudley d1855 *BiAUS, BiDrAC,*
WhAm H
Selden, Edwin VanDeusen 1858- *NatCAB 16*
Selden, Elizabeth Rodman *WomWWA 14*
Selden, George Baldwin 1846-1922 *DcAmB,*
NatCAB 20, WebAB, WhAm 4
Selden, Henry Rogers 1805-1885 *ApCAB,*
NatCAB 4, TwCBDA
Selden, John Harris 1848- *NatCAB 1*
Selden, Joseph *BiAUS*
Selden, Joseph Luther 1884-1959 *NatCAB 47*
Selden, Lynde 1891-1972 *WhAm 5*
Selden, Samuel Lee 1800-1876 *ApCAB,*
NatCAB 4, TwCBDA
Selden, William *BiAUS*
Selden, William 1808-1887 *NatCAB 10*
Seldes, Gilbert Vivian 1893-1970 *WebAB,*
WhAm 5
Seldom, Benjamin Franklin 1884- *WhoColR*
Seldomridge, Harry Hunter 1864-1927 *BiDrAC,*
WhAm 4
Selecman, Charles Claude 1874-1958
NatCAB 43, WhAm 3
Selekman, Benjamin Morris 1893-1962
NatCAB 47, WhAm 4
Seleucus 190?BC- *AsBiEn*
Seleucus I, Nikator 358?BC-281BC *McGEWB*
Seley, Jason 1919- *BnEnAmA*
Self, James Cuthbert 1876-1955 *NatCAB 45,*
WhAm 3
Self, William King 1918-1975 *WhAm 6*
Selfredge, Thomas Oliver 1804-1902 *Drake*
Selfridge, Brice 1890-1962 *NatCAB 50*
Selfridge, Harry Gordon 1857?-1947 *WebAB,*
WhAm 2
Selfridge, Thomas Oliver 1804-1902 *ApCAB,*
NatCAB 7, TwCBDA, WhAm 1
Selfridge, Thomas Oliver 1836-1924 *AmBi,*
DcAmB, TwCBDA, WebAMB, WhAm 1
Selfridge, Thomas Oliver 1837-1924 *ApCAB,*
NatCAB 7
Selig, Lester North 1893-1968 *WhAm 5*
Selig, William Nicholas 1864-1948 *DcAmB S4,*
WhAm 2
Seliger, Robert V 1900-1953 *WhAm 3*
Seligman, Albert Joseph 1859-1935 *NatCAB 32,*
WhAm 1
Seligman, Arthur 1871-1933 *DcAmB,*
NatCAB 26
Seligman, Arthur 1873-1933 *WhAm 1*
Seligman, Ben Baruch 1912-1970 *NatCAB 56*
Seligman, Ben Baruch 1912-1972 *WhAm 5*
Seligman, DeWitt James 1853-1933 *NatCAB 1,*
NatCAB 23
Seligman, Edwin Robert Anderson 1861-1939
AmBi, ApCAB Sup, ApCAB X,
DcAmB S2, McGEWB, NatCAB 10,
TwCBDA, WebAB, WhAm 1
Seligman, George Washington 1858-1929
NatCAB 30
Seligman, Henry 1857-1933 *NatCAB 14,*

WhAm 1
Seligman, Isaac Newton 1855-1917 *DcAmB*
Seligman, Isaac Newton 1856-1917 *ApCAB X,*
NatCAB 3, WhAm 1
Seligman, James 1823-1916 *ApCAB X*
Seligman, Jefferson 1858-1937 *WhAm 1*
Seligman, Jesse 1821-1894 *TwCBDA*
Seligman, Jesse 1825-1894 *NatCAB 4*
Seligman, Jesse 1827-1894 *DcAmB, WhAm H*
Seligman, Joseph 1819-1880 *DcAmB,*
NatCAB 3, WebAB, WhAm H
Seligman, Joseph Lionel 1887-1944 *NatCAB 36*
Seligman, Selig Jacob 1918-1969 *WhAm 5*
Seligmann, Kurt 1900-1962 *WhAm 4*
Selijns, Henricus 1636-1701 *DcAmB,*
WhAm H
Selikovitsch, Goetzel 1863-1926 *DcAmB*
Selim I 1470?-1520 *McGEWB, WhoMilH*
Selim III 1761-1808 *McGEWB*
Selinger, Emily Harris McGary 1854- *AmWom,*
WomWWA 14
Selinger, Jean Paul 1850-1909 *WhAm 1*
Selke, George Albert 1888-1970 *WhAm 5*
Selke, W Erich 1885-1966 *WhAm 5*
Selkirk, Alexander 1676-1723 *ApCAB, Drake*
Selkirk, Edward 1809- *ApCAB*
Selkirk, Thomas 1774-1820 *Drake*
Selkirk, Thomas Douglas, Earl Of 1771-1820
ApCAB, McGEWB
Sell, Edward Herman Miller 1832-1920
NatCAB 3, WhAm 1
Sell, G William 1871-1941 *NatCAB 30*
Sell, Henry Blackman 1889-1974 *WhAm 6*
Sell, Henry Thorne 1854-1928 *WhAm 1*
Sell, John Steel 1857-1922 *NatCAB 6*
Sell, Lewis L 1890-1958 *WhAm 3*
Sellar, Robert F 1884-1951 *WhAm 3*
Sellards, Elias Howard 1875- *WhAm 5*
Sellars, Roy Wood 1880-1973 *WhAm 6*
Selleck, Nathaniel Benedict 1898-1959
NatCAB 49
Selleck, Virgil Dural 1877-1945 *NatCAB 35*
Selleck, Willard Chamberlain 1856-1941
WhAm 2
Selleck, William Alson 1857-1949 *NatCAB 38,*
WhAm 2
Selleck, William Edwin 1841-1917 *NatCAB 18*
Sellen, Arthur Godfrey 1893-1963 *WhAm 4*
Sellers, Charles Grier 1923- *EncAAH*
Sellers, Charles Victor 1865-1941 *NatCAB 31*
Sellers, Coleman 1827-1907 *AmBi, ApCAB,*
DcAmB, NatCAB 11, TwCBDA,
WhAm 1
Sellers, Coleman, III 1893-1957 *NatCAB 45*
Sellers, Coleman, Jr. 1852-1922 *NatCAB 45*
Sellers, Coleman, Jr. 1852-1923 *WhAm 1*
Sellers, David Foote 1874-1949 *NatCAB 36,*
WhAm 2
Sellers, Edwin Jaquett 1865- *WhAm 4*
Sellers, Frank Harrold 1864-1938 *NatCAB 29*
Sellers, Franklin Peter 1847-1927 *NatCAB 21*
Sellers, George Escol 1808-1899 *NewYHSD*
Sellers, Horace Wells 1857-1933 *NatCAB 26,*
WhAm 1
Sellers, Isaiah 1802?-1864 *DcAmB, REnAW,*
WhAm H
Sellers, James Clark 1891-1973 *WhAm 6*
Sellers, James Freeman 1862-1936 *NatCAB 48,*
WhAm 1
Sellers, John, Jr. 1826- *NatCAB 12*
Sellers, Kathryn 1870-1939 *ApCAB X,*
WhAm 1
Sellers, Mary Morley 1870- *WomWWA 14*
Sellers, Matthew Bacon 1869-1932 *DcAmB,*
NatCAB 15, WhAm 1
Sellers, Robert Daniel 1901-1965 *NatCAB 52,*
WhAm 4
Sellers, Robert Henry 1857- *WhAm 4*
Sellers, Sandford 1854-1938 *WhAm 1*
Sellers, Walton Preston 1901-1969 *WhAm 6*
Sellers, William 1824-1905 *ApCAB, DcAmB,*
NatCAB 7, TwCBDA, WhAm 1
Sellers, William Ferris 1856-1933 *NatCAB 43*
Sellery, George Clarke 1872-1962 *WhAm 4*
Sellew, George Tucker 1866- *WhAm 4*
Sellew, Walter Ashbel 1844-1929 *WhAm 1*
Selling, Bernard Benjamin 1873-1918
NatCAB 45

Selling, Lowell Sinn 1902-1955 *NatCAB 45*
Sellman, Albert Hall 1894-1967 *NatCAB 53*
Sellman, William Nelson 1885-1965 *WhAm 4*
Sells, C H *IlBEAAW*
Sells, Cato *WhAm 5*
Sells, Elijah 1814-1897 *BiAUS, NatCAB 13*
Sells, Elijah Watt 1858-1924 *NatCAB 13,*
WhAm 1
Sells, Lewis 1841-1907 *NatCAB 16*
Sells, Sam Riley 1871-1935 *BiDrAC, WhAmP*
Sellstedt, Lars Gustaf 1819-1911 *ApCAB,*
DcAmB, NatCAB 8, NewYHSD,
TwCBDA, WhAm 1
Selman, John Henry 1839-1896 *REnAW*
Selmer, Ernst Westerlund 1890-1971 *WhAm 5*
Selover, Lola Hord 1859- *WomWWA 14*
Sels, Helen Adelaide VanLoben 1882-
WomWWA 14
Selser, James Clyde, Jr. 1912-1956 *WhAm 3*
Seltzer, Charles Alden 1875-1942 *WhAm 1*
Seltzer, Maurice Bishop 1897-1963 *NatCAB 50*
Seltzer, Olaf Carl 1877?-1957 *IlBEAAW,*
REnAW
Seltzer, Theodore 1870-1957 *WhAm 3*
Selvage, Watson 1873- *WhAm 5*
Selvidge, Robert Washington 1872-1941
BiDAmEd, WhAm 2
Selvig, Conrad George 1877-1953 *BiDrAC,*
NatCAB 42, WhAm 3, WhAmP
Selwin *NewYHSD*
Selwyn, Alfred Richard Cecil 1824-1902 *ApCAB,*
DcScB
Selwyn, Edgar 1875-1944 *NatCAB 38,*
WhAm 2
Selye, Lewis 1803-1883 *BiDrAC, WhAm H*
Selye, Lewis 1808-1883 *BiAUS*
Selyns, Henricus 1636-1701 *ApCAB, DcAmB,*
NatCAB 12
Selz, Lawrence Hochstadter 1904-1962
WhAm 4
Selznick, David Oliver 1902-1965 *NatCAB 54,*
WebAB, WhAm 4
Selznick, Lewis Joseph 1872-1933 *NatCAB 41*
Seman, Philip Louis 1881-1957 *NatCAB 48,*
WhAm 3
Semans, Edwin Walker 1901-1971 *WhAm 5*
Semans, Harry Merrick 1867- *WhAm 5*
Sembach, J 1881- *WhAm 6*
Sembower, Alta Brunt 1878- *WhAm 6,*
WomWWA 14
Sembower, Charles Jacob 1871- *WhAm 5*
Sembrich, Marcella 1858-1935 *DcAmB S1,*
NatCAB 25, NotAW, WhAm 1
Semelroth, William James 1858- *WhAm 4*
Semenov, Nikolai Nikolaevich 1896- *McGEWB*
Semenov, Nikolay Nikolaevich 1896- *AsBiEn*
Semler, George Herbert 1891-1954 *WhAm 3*
Semmann, Liborius 1873- *WhAm 5*
Semmelweis, Ignaz Philipp 1818-1865 *DcScB,*
McGEWB
Semmelweis, Ignaz Phillip 1818-1865 *BiHiMed*
Semmelweiss, Ignaz Philipp 1818-1865 *AsBiEn*
Semmes, Alexander Aldebaran 1825-1885
ApCAB, NatCAB 5, TwCBDA
Semmes, Alexander Jenkins 1828-1898 *ApCAB,*
DcAmB, WhAm H
Semmes, Benedict Joseph 1789-1863 *BiAUS,*
BiDrAC, WhAm H
Semmes, John Edward 1851-1925 *NatCAB 31*
Semmes, John Edward 1881-1967 *NatCAB 54,*
WhAm 4A
Semmes, Raphael 1809-1877 *AmBi, ApCAB,*
BiDConf, DcAmB, McGEWB, NatCAB 4,
TwCBDA, WebAB, WebAMB, WhAm H
Semmes, Raphael 1810-1877 *Drake*
Semmes, Thomas Jenkins 1824-1899 *BiDConf,*
DcAmB, NatCAB 10, WhAm H
Semnacher, William M 1839- *WhAm 4*
Semon, Richard Wolfgang 1859-1918 *DcScB*
Semper, Carl Gottfried 1832-1893 *DcScB*
Semple, Ellen Churchill 1863-1932 *AmBi,*
DcAmB, NatCAB 35, NotAW, WhAm 1,
WomWWA 14
Semple, Eugene 1840-1908 *NatCAB 19*
Semple, Helen Merrick *WomWWA 14*
Semple, Henry Churchill 1822-1894
NatCAB 17
Semple, Henry Churchill 1853-1925 *WhAm 1*

Semple, James 1798-1866 *ApCAB*, *BiDrAC*,
NatCAB 4, *TwCBDA*, *WhAm H*
Semple, James 1799-1866 *Drake*
Semple, James 1800-1867 *BiAUS*
Semple, John Bonner 1869-1947 *NatCAB 37*
Semple, Robert 1766?-1816 *ApCAB*, *Drake*
Semple, Robert Baylor 1769-1831 *ApCAB*,
Drake, *NatCAB 12*, *TwCBDA*
Semple, William Tunstall 1881-1962 *WhAm 4*
Semrad, Charles A 1885-1965 *NatCAB 52*
Semsch, Otto Francis 1872- *WhAm 5*
Semyonov-Tyan-Shansky, Petr Petrovich
1827-1914 *DcScB*
Sen, Ram Camul 1783-1844 *McGEWB*
Senac, Jean-Baptiste 1693?-1770 *DcScB*
Senan, Jose Francisco DePaula 1760-1823
WhAm H
Senanayake, Don Stephen 1884-1952 *WhAm 3*
Senanayake, Dudley Shelton 1911-1973
WhAm 5
Senarmont, Henri Hureau De 1808-1862 *DcScB*
Sence, Leonard *NewYHSD*
Sencenbaugh, Charles Wilber d1950 *WhAm 3*
Sendivogius, Michael 1566-1636 *DcScB*
Sendorf, Reinhardt *NewYHSD*
Senear, Francis Eugene 1889-1958 *NatCAB 47*,
WhAm 3
Senebier, Jean 1742-1809 *DcScB*
Seneca, Lucius Annaeus 004?BC-065AD *DcScB*,
McGEWB
Senecal, Louis Adelard 1829-1887 *ApCAB*
Senecal, Raymond Ernest 1892-1943
NatCAB 36
Seneff, Edward H 1867-1932 *WhAm 1*
Sener, J Frederick 1833-1920 *NatCAB 21*
Sener, James B 1837-1903 *BiAUS*
Sener, James Beverley 1837-1903 *BiDrAC*,
WhAm H
Sener, James Beverly 1837-1903 *ApCAB*
Senesh, Hannah 1921-1944 *WhWW-II*
Seney, George Ebbert 1832-1905 *BiDrAC*,
TwCBDA, *WhAmP*
Seney, George Ingraham 1826-1893 *ApCAB*,
DcAmB, *TwCBDA*, *WhAm H*
Seney, Henry William 1900-1965 *NatCAB 51*,
WhAm 4
Seney, Joshua *BiAUS*
Seney, Joshua 1750-1799 *ApCAB*
Seney, Joshua 1756-1798 *BiDrAC*, *TwCBDA*,
WhAm H, *WhAmP*
Senfl, Ludwig 1486?-1543? *McGEWB*
Senft, Craig T 1915-1975 *WhAm 6*
Senger, William 1874-1955 *NatCAB 44*
Senghor, Leopold Sedar 1906- *McGEWB*
Sengier, Edgar d1963 *WhAm 4*
Sengle, Robert Louis 1894-1942 *NatCAB 31*
Sengstack, John F 1893-1970 *WhAm 5*
Sengteller, Alexander 1813?- *NewYHSD*
Senior, C F *NewYHSD*
Senior, Clair Marcil 1901-1965 *WhAm 4*
Senior, Clarence 1903-1974 *WhAm 6*
Senior, Harold Dickinson 1870-1938 *WhAm 1*
Senior, John Lawson 1879-1946 *NatCAB 34*,
WhAm 2
Senior, Joseph Howe 1870- *WhAm 5*
Senior, Samuel Palmer 1874-1962 *WhAm 4*
Senn, Nicholas 1844-1908 *AmBi*, *ApCAB Sup*,
ApCAB X, *DcAmB*, *NatCAB 6*,
WhAm 1
Senn, Thomas J 1871-1947 *WhAm 2*
Senn, William Nicholas 1876-1947 *NatCAB 34*
Sennacherib *McGEWB*
Senner, George Frederick, Jr. 1921- *BiDrAC*
Senner, Joseph Henry 1846-1908 *WhAm 1*
Sennert, Daniel 1572-1637 *DcScB*
Sennet, George Burritt 1840-1900 *WhAm H*
Sennett, George Burritt 1840-1900 *DcAmB*,
NatCAB 24
Sennett, John T *NewYHSD*
Sennett, Mack 1884-1960 *McGEWB*, *WebAB*,
WhAm HA, *WhAm 4*
Sennett, Mack 1890-1960 *ApCAB X*
Senning, John Peter 1884-1954 *WhAm 3*
Senour, Charles 1892-1972 *WhAm 6*
Sensenbrenner, Frank Jacob 1864-1952
WhAm 3
Sensenbrenner, John Stlip 1886-1973 *WhAm 6*
Senseney, George Eyster 1874-1943 *NatCAB 33*,

WhAm 2
Sensenich, Roscoe Lloyd 1882-1963 *NatCAB 50*,
WhAm 4
Sensenig, David Martin 1840-1907 *WhAm 1*
Sensing, Thurman 1900-1971 *NatCAB 56*
Sentell, George Washington 1863- *WhAm 3*
Sentelle, Mark Edgar 1874-1949 *WhAm 3*
Senter, DeWitt Clinton 1834- *BiAUS*,
NatCAB 7
Senter, Erasmus Gilbert 1865-1942 *NatCAB 34*
Senter, Isaac 1755-1799 *ApCAB*, *Drake*
Senter, J Herbert 1842- *ApCAB X*
Senter, John Henry 1848-1916 *WhAm 1*
Senter, Leon B 1889-1965 *WhAm 4*
Senter, Ralph Townsend 1876-1948 *WhAm 2*
Senter, William T 1802-1849 *BiAUS*
Senter, William Tandy 1801-1848 *BiDrAC*,
WhAm H
Sentner, David d1975 *WhAm 6*
Sentner, Richard Faulkner 1902-1971 *WhAm 5*
Seppelt, Ian Howe 1909-1973 *WhAm 6*
Septenville, C E Langlois, Baron De 1835-
ApCAB
Sequoya 1770?-1843 *EncAAH*, *WebAB*
Sequoyah 1770?-1843 *AmBi*, *DcAmB*,
McGEWB, *REnAW*, *WhAm H*
Sera, J *NewYHSD*
Serafin, Tullio 1878-1968 *WhAm 4A*
Serakoff, Leonard 1921-1967 *WhAm 5*
Sercey, Pierre Cesar C G, Marquis De 1753-1836
ApCAB
Serena, Elmer Porter 1905-1964 *NatCAB 51*
Serenbetz, George Benjamin 1874-1951
NatCAB 41
Serenus *DcScB*
Seress, Raoul d1968 *WhAm 4A*
Sergeant, Elizabeth Shepley 1881-1965
WhAm 4
Sergeant, Erastus 1742-1814 *ApCAB*, *Drake*,
NatCAB 2
Sergeant, Henry Clark 1834-1907 *DcAmB*,
NatCAB 15
Sergeant, John 1710-1749 *ApCAB*, *DcAmB*,
Drake, *NatCAB 1*, *WhAm H*
Sergeant, John 1747-1824 *ApCAB*, *NatCAB 1*
Sergeant, John 1779-1852 *ApCAB*, *BiAUS*,
BiDrAC, *DcAmB*, *Drake*, *NatCAB 2*,
TwCBDA, *WhAm H*, *WhAmP*
Sergeant, Jonathan Dickinson 1746-1793
ApCAB, *BiAUS*, *BiDrAC*, *DcAmB*, *Drake*,
NatCAB 2, *TwCBDA*, *WhAm H*,
WhAmP
Sergeant, Thomas 1782-1860 *ApCAB*, *BiAUS*,
DcAmB, *Drake*, *NatCAB 2*, *TwCBDA*,
WhAm H
Sergel, Charles Hubbard 1861-1926 *WhAm 1*
Sergent, Edmond 1876-1969 *DcScB*
Serles, Earl Roy 1890-1957 *NatCAB 44*,
WhAm 3
Serles, Frank Rose 1877-1963 *NatCAB 50*
Serlin, Oscar 1901-1971 *WhAm 5*
Serling, Rod 1924-1975 *WhAm 6*
Serna, Jose DeLa 1770-1832 *ApCAB*
Serotta, Elliott Cecil 1912-1971 *WhAm 6*
Serov, Ivan 1905- *WhWW-II*
Serpell, Goldsborough McDowell 1837-1912
NatCAB 29
Serpell, Susan Watkins d1912 *WhAm 1*,
WomWWA 14
Serra, Angel 1640?-1700? *ApCAB*
Serra, Junipero 1713-1784 *ApCAB Sup*,
DcAmB, *DcAmReB*, *EncAB*, *McGEWB*,
REnAW, *WebAB*, *WhAm H*
Serra, Richard 1939- *BnEnAmA*
Serra Junipero, Miguel Jose 1713-1784 *AmBi*
Serrano, Emelia Benic *AmWom*
Serrano Y Dominguez, Francisco 1810-1885
ApCAB
Serrell, Edward Wellman 1826-1906 *ApCAB*,
DcAmB, *TwCBDA*, *WebAMB*
Serrell, Edward Wellmann 1826-1906 *WhAm 1*
Serrell, Henry R *NewYHSD*
Serres, Antoine Etienne Reynaud Augustin
1786-1868 *DcScB*
Serres, Olivier De 1539-1619 *DcScB*
Serres DeMesples, Marcel Pierre T De 1780-1862
DcScB
Serret, Joseph Alfred 1819-1885 *DcScB*

Serries, Mavis McGrew 1925-1975 *WhAm 6*
Serrill, William Jones 1862-1952 *WhAm 3*
Sertoli, Enrico 1842-1910 *DcScB*
Serturner, Friedrich Wilhelm Adam F 1783-1841
DcScB
Serullas, Georges-Simon 1774-1832 *DcScB*
Serurier, Jean Mathieu Phibilert 1742-1819
WhoMilH
Serven, Abram Ralph 1862-1942 *NatCAB 32*,
WhAm 2
Servetus, Michael 1509-1553 *BiHiMed*
Servetus, Michael 1511?-1553 *AsBiEn*, *DcScB*,
McGEWB
Service, Francis G *BiAUS*
Service, Robert William 1874-1958 *WhAm 3*
Servien, Claude 1493-1549 *ApCAB*
Serviss, Frederick LeVerne 1895-1954 *WhAm 3*
Serviss, Garrett Putman 1851-1929 *ApCAB X*,
TwCBDA, *WhAm 1*
Serviss, Garrett Putnam 1851-1929 *NatCAB 11*
Servois, Francois-Joseph 1767-1847 *DcScB*
Servoss, Henry Laidlaw 1877-1951 *NatCAB 39*
Servoss, Thomas Lowery 1786-1866 *ApCAB*,
DcAmB, *WhAm H*
Serz, John 1810?- *NewYHSD*
Seskis, I J d1951 *WhAm 3*
Sesse Y Lacasta, Martin De 1751?-1808 *DcScB*
Sesshu, Toyo 1420-1506 *McGEWB*
Sessinghaus, Gustavus 1838-1887 *BiDrAC*,
WhAm H
Session, Walter L *BiAUS*
Sessions, Charles H 1868-1942 *WhAm 2*
Sessions, Clarence Nathaniel 1890-1963
NatCAB 51
Sessions, Clarence William 1859-1931 *WhAm 1*
Sessions, Darius d1809 *Drake*
Sessions, Henry Howard 1847-1915 *ApCAB X*,
DcAmB
Sessions, Kate Olivia 1857-1940 *NotAW*
Sessions, Kenosha 1862- *WhAm 2*
Sessions, Roger Huntington 1896- *McGEWB*,
WebAB
Sessions, Walter Loomis 1820-1896 *BiDrAC*,
WhAm H
Sessions, Walter Loomis 1824-1896 *TwCBDA*
Sessions, William Edwin 1857-1920 *ApCAB X*,
NatCAB 18, *WhAm 1*
Sessums, Davis 1858-1929 *NatCAB 11*,
TwCBDA, *WhAm 1*
Sestini, Benedict 1816-1890 *DcAmB*,
WhAm H
Setchell, William Albert 1864-1943 *DcAmB S3*,
DcScB, *NatCAB 32*, *WhAm 2*
Seth, James 1860-1924 *DcAmB*
Seth, Julien Orem 1883-1963 *WhAm 4*
Sethness, Helga Midling 1865- *BiCAW*,
WomWWA 14
Seton, Eliza Ann 1774-1821 *Drake*
Seton, Elizabeth Ann Bayley 1774-1821 *AmBi*,
ApCAB, *BiDAmEd*, *DcAmB*, *DcAmReB*,
McGEWB, *NatCAB 2*, *NotAW*,
TwCBDA, *WebAB*, *WhAm H*
Seton, Ernest Thompson 1860-1946 *ApCAB X*,
DcAmB S4, *IIBEAAW*, *NatCAB 36*,
WhAm 2
Seton, Grace Gallatin Thompson 1872-1959
BiCAW, *NatCAB 47*, *WhAm 3*,
WomWWA 14
Seton, Julia 1862- *NatCAB 16*, *WhAm 4*
Seton, Robert 1839-1927 *ApCAB*, *DcAmB*,
NatCAB 1, *TwCBDA*, *WhAm 1*
Seton, Samuel Waddington 1789-1869 *ApCAB*
Seton, William 1835-1905 *ApCAB*, *DcAmB*,
TwCBDA
Seton-Thompson, Ernest Evan 1860-1946
NatCAB 9
Setterfield, Hugh E 1900-1953 *WhAm 3*
Settergren, Bror Knute 1871-1949 *NatCAB 40*
Setti, Giulio 1869-1938 *WhAm 2*
Settle, Evan Evans 1848-1899 *BiDrAC*,
WhAm 1
Settle, George Thomas 1863-1930 *NatCAB 22*
Settle, George Thomas 1865-1930 *WhAm 1*
Settle, Josiah Thomas 1850- *WhoColR*
Settle, Thomas *BiAUS*
Settle, Thomas d1857 *BiAUS*
Settle, Thomas 1789-1857 *BiDrAC*, *TwCBDA*,
WhAm H

Settle, Thomas 1791-1857 *ApCAB*
Settle, Thomas 1831-1888 *ApCAB, DcAmB, NatCAB 12, TwCBDA, WhAm H*
Settle, Thomas 1865-1919 *BiDrAC, NatCAB 18, TwCBDA*
Settle, Warner Ellmore 1850-1929 *WhAm 4*
Settle, Warner Elmore 1850-1929 *NatCAB 23*
Setty *NewYHSD*
Setze, Julius Adolphus 1871-1955 *WhAm 3*
Setzer, Richard Woodrow 1918-1969 *WhAm 5*
Setzler, Frank Maryl 1902-1975 *WhAm 6*
Seubert, Edward George 1876-1949 *WhAm 2*
Seurat, Georges Pierre 1859-1891 *McGEWB*
Seuseman, Gottlob 1742-1808 *ApCAB, NatCAB 2*
Seuseman, Joachim 1710?-1772 *ApCAB, NatCAB 2*
Seuss, Doctor *WebAB*
Seuter, DeWitt Clinton 1834-1898 *TwCBDA*
Sever, Anne Elizabeth Parsons 1810-1879 *ApCAB*
Sever, George Francis 1866- *WhAm 4*
Severance, Allen Dudley 1865-1929 *NatCAB 21*
Severance, Benjamin J *NewYHSD*
Severance, Carolina Maria Seymour 1820-1914 *NotAW*
Severance, Caroline Maria Seymour 1820-1914 *AmBi, AmWom, DcAmB, NatCAB 8, WhAm 1*
Severance, Cordenio Arnold 1862-1925 *ApCAB X, NatCAB 19, WhAm 1*
Severance, Emily A 1840- *WomWWA 14*
Severance, Frank Hayward 1856-1931 *DcAmB, NatCAB 26, WhAm 1*
Severance, Henry Ormal 1867-1942 *WhAm 2*
Severance, John Long 1863-1936 *WhAm 1*
Severance, Juliet H 1833- *AmWom*
Severance, Lena Lilian *WomWWA 14*
Severance, Louis Henry 1838-1913 *DcAmB, NatCAB 15*
Severance, Luther 1797-1855 *ApCAB, BiAUS, BiDrAC, Drake, NatCAB 13, TwCBDA, WhAm H, WhAmP*
Severance, Mark Sibley 1846-1931 *NatCAB 25, WhAm 4*
Severance, Mary Frances 1863- *BiCAW*
Severance, Mary Francis 1863- *WomWWA 14*
Severance, Sarah M 1835- *WomWWA 14*
Severance, Solon Long 1834-1915 *NatCAB 22*
Severens, Henry Franklin 1835-1923 *NatCAB 19, TwCBDA, WhAm 4*
Severgin, Vasily Mikhaylovich 1765-1826 *DcScB*
Severi, Francesco 1879-1961 *DcScB*
Severin, Charles 1808?- *NewYHSD*
Severin, Christian 1562-1647 *DcScB*
Severini, Gino 1883-1966 *McGEWB*
Severino, Marco Aurelio 1580-1656 *DcScB*
Severinus, Petrus 1542?-1602 *DcScB*
Severn, Edmund 1862-1942 *WhAm 3*
Severns, William Harrison 1888-1956 *NatCAB 43*
Severs, John Ward 1890-1966 *WhAm 4*
Seversky, Alexander P De 1894-1974 *WhAm 6*
Severson, Harold Clifford 1910-1972 *WhAm 6*
Severson, Harry Ashton 1877-1957 *NatCAB 43*
Severson, Lewis Everett 1896-1960 *WhAm 4*
Severson, Lloyd John 1914-1965 *NatCAB 51*
Severtsov, Aleksey Nikolaevich 1866-1936 *DcScB*
Severus, Lucius Septimius 146-211 *McGEWB*
Severy, Melvin Linwood 1863- *WhAm 4*
Severy, Wendell Linwood 1918-1968 *NatCAB 54*
Severyn, Charles 1808?- *NewYHSD*
Sevey, Robert 1898-1951 *WhAm 3*
Sevier, Ambrose H 1802-1848 *BiAUS, Drake*
Sevier, Ambrose Hundley 1801-1848 *ApCAB, BiDrAC, DcAmB, NatCAB 2, REnAW, TwCBDA, WhAm H, WhAmP*
Sevier, Charles Edwin 1889-1952 *NatCAB 41, WhAm 3*
Sevier, Clara Driscoll 1881- *NotAW, WhAm 6, WomWWA 14*
Sevier, Henry Hulme 1878-1940 *NatCAB 30, WhAm 1, WhAm 2*
Sevier, John 1744-1815 *BiAUS*
Sevier, John 1745-1815 *AmBi, ApCAB, BiDrAC, DcAmB, Drake, EncAAH,*

McGEWB, NatCAB 3, REnAW, TwCBDA, WebAB, WebAMB, WhAm H, WhAmP
Sevier, John Alston 1889-1962 *NatCAB 47*
Sevier, Joseph Ramsey 1877- *WhAm 5*
Sevier, Landers 1866-1942 *WhAm 3*
Sevier, Randolph 1897-1966 *WhAm 4*
Sevigny, Albert 1880-1961 *WhAm 4*
Sevilla, Jose 1820?-1888 *ApCAB*
Sevitzky, Fabien 1893-1967 *WhAm 4*
Sewall, Arthur 1835-1900 *ApCAB Sup, DcAmB, NatCAB 10, TwCBDA, WhAm 1*
Sewall, Arthur Eugene 1882-1956 *NatCAB 45*
Sewall, Arthur Wollaston 1860-1939 *WhAm 1*
Sewall, Charles S 1779-1848 *BiDrAC, WhAm H*
Sewall, David 1735-1825 *ApCAB, Drake, TwCBDA*
Sewall, Edmund Devereux d1923 *WhAm 1*
Sewall, Frank 1837-1915 *DcAmB, TwCBDA, WhAm 1*
Sewall, Hannah Robie 1861- *WomWWA 14*
Sewall, Harold Marsh 1860-1924 *ApCAB Sup, DcAmB, NatCAB 12, NatCAB 21, TwCBDA, WhAm 1*
Sewall, Harriet Winslow 1819-1888 *NatCAB 10*
Sewall, Harriet Winslow 1819-1889 *WhAm H*
Sewall, Helen Sidney Ditmars 1881- *WomWWA 14*
Sewall, Henry 1855-1936 *AmBi, ApCAB X, NatCAB 26, WhAm 1*
Sewall, James Wingate 1884-1946 *NatCAB 35, WhAm 2*
Sewall, John Smith 1830-1911 *ApCAB, WhAm 1*
Sewall, Jonathan 1728-1796 *AmBi, ApCAB, DcAmB, Drake, NatCAB 2, WhAm H*
Sewall, Jonathan Mitchell 1745-1808 *Drake*
Sewall, Jonathan Mitchell 1748-1808 *ApCAB, DcAmB, NatCAB 2, WhAm H*
Sewall, Joseph 1688-1769 *ApCAB, Drake, NatCAB 2, TwCBDA*
Sewall, Joseph Addison 1830-1917 *DcAmB, NatCAB 6*
Sewall, Jotham 1760-1850 *ApCAB, NatCAB 2*
Sewall, Jotham Bradbury 1825- *NatCAB 12*
Sewall, Lee Goodrich 1907-1971 *WhAm 5*
Sewall, Lucy Ellen 1837-1890 *NotAW*
Sewall, May Eliza Wright Thompson 1844-1920 *AmWom, BiDAmEd, DcAmB, NatCAB 19, NotAW, TwCBDA, WhAm 1, WomWWA 14*
Sewall, Rufus King 1814-1903 *ApCAB, Drake, WhAm 1*
Sewall, Samuel 1652-1730 *AmBi, ApCAB, DcAmB, Drake, EncAB, McGEWB, NatCAB 5, TwCBDA, WebAB, WhAm H*
Sewall, Samuel 1724-1815 *ApCAB, Drake*
Sewall, Samuel 1757-1814 *ApCAB, BiAUS, BiDrAC, Drake, NatCAB 6, TwCBDA, WhAm H*
Sewall, Samuel 1785-1868 *ApCAB, Drake*
Sewall, Samuel Edmund 1799-1888 *NatCAB 10, TwCBDA*
Sewall, Samuel Swanton 1858-1935 *NatCAB 32*
Sewall, Stephen 1704-1760 *ApCAB, Drake, NatCAB 8*
Sewall, Stephen 1734-1804 *ApCAB, DcAmB, Drake, NatCAB 6, TwCBDA, WhAm H*
Sewall, Sydney 1912-1974 *WhAm 6*
Sewall, Thomas 1786-1845 *ApCAB*
Sewall, William Bartlett 1782-1869 *Drake*
Sewall, William Dunning 1861-1930 *NatCAB 21*
Seward, Albert Charles 1863-1941 *DcScB*
Seward, Allin Carey, Jr. 1909-1971 *WhAm 5*
Seward, Augustus Henry 1826-1876 *ApCAB*
Seward, Clarence Armstrong 1828-1897 *AmBi, ApCAB, NatCAB 9*
Seward, Coy Avon 1884-1939 *IIBEAAW, NatCAB 29, WhAm 1*
Seward, Frederick A *BiAUS*
Seward, Frederick William 1830-1915 *AmBi, ApCAB, DcAmB, NatCAB 11, WhAm 1*
Seward, George Frederick 1840-1910 *AmBi,*

ApCAB, BiAUS, DcAmB, NatCAB 7, TwCBDA, WhAm 1
Seward, George Winn 1906-1975 *WhAm 6*
Seward, Herbert Lee 1885-1966 *WhAm 4*
Seward, James 1832?- *NewYHSD*
Seward, James Lindsay 1813-1886 *BiAUS, BiDrAC, WhAm H*
Seward, Janet Watson 1839-1913 *WomWWA 14, WomWWA 14a*
Seward, John Perry 1868-1933 *NatCAB 24, WhAm 1*
Seward, Mary Coggeshall 1839- *WomWWA 14*
Seward, Percival Halvor 1871-1936 *NatCAB 27*
Seward, Samuel Swayze 1838- *WhAm 1*
Seward, Samuel Swayze, Jr. 1876-1932 *NatCAB 23, WhAm 1*
Seward, Sara Cornelia 1833-1891 *TwCBDA*
Seward, Theodore Frelinghausen 1835-1902 *TwCBDA*
Seward, Theodore Frelinghuysen 1835-1902 *ApCAB, DcAmB, NatCAB 11, WhAm 1*
Seward, William 1837-1905 *WhAm 1*
Seward, William Henry 1801-1872 *AmBi, ApCAB, BiAUS, BiDrAC, BiDrUSE, DcAmB, Drake, EncAAH, EncAB, McGEWB, NatCAB 2, TwCBDA, WebAB, WhAm H, WhAmP*
Seward, William Henry 1839-1920 *ApCAB, NatCAB 6, TwCBDA, WhAm 1*
Seward, William Henry 1864-1951 *NatCAB 44*
Sewell, Albert Henry 1847-1924 *WhAm 1*
Sewell, Amanda Brewster d1926 *WhAm 1, WomWWA 14*
Sewell, Amos 1901- *IIBEAAW*
Sewell, Anne B 1837- *WomWWA 14*
Sewell, Dan Roy 1904-1973 *WhAm 6*
Sewell, David 1735-1825 *BiAUS, NatCAB 11*
Sewell, Edmund Willoughby 1800- *ApCAB*
Sewell, H *NewYHSD*
Sewell, Harriet *NewYHSD*
Sewell, James *BiAUS*
Sewell, Jesse Parker 1876- *WhAm 5*
Sewell, John Stephen 1869-1940 *WhAm 1*
Sewell, Jonathan 1766-1839 *ApCAB, Drake*
Sewell, Lydia Amanda 1859- *NatCAB 13*
Sewell, Oscar Marion 1866-1936 *WhAm 1*
Sewell, Robert VanVorst 1860-1924 *WhAm 1*
Sewell, Warren Pelmer 1888- *WhAm 6*
Sewell, William Grant 1829-1862 *ApCAB, Drake*
Sewell, William Joyce 1835-1901 *ApCAB, BiDrAC, DcAmB, NatCAB 12, TwCBDA, WhAm 1, WhAmP*
Sexson, John Amherst 1881- *WhAm 6*
Sexton, Anne Harvey 1928-1974 *WhAm 6*
Sexton, Charles Willard 1854-1920 *NatCAB 26*
Sexton, Edward Bailey 1852-1932 *NatCAB 25*
Sexton, Franklin Barlow 1828-1900 *BiDConf*
Sexton, George Samuel 1867-1937 *WhAm 1*
Sexton, Harold Eustace 1888-1972 *WhAm 5*
Sexton, James Andrew 1844-1899 *ApCAB Sup, NatCAB 12*
Sexton, James Seymour 1854-1928 *NatCAB 21*
Sexton, John Chase 1859-1936 *WhAm 1*
Sexton, John Joseph 1911-1966 *NatCAB 51*
Sexton, John Moody 1909-1967 *WhAm 5*
Sexton, Lawrence Eugene 1859-1919 *WhAm 1*
Sexton, Leonidas 1827-1880 *BiDrAC, WhAm H*
Sexton, Lewis Albert 1876-1936 *WhAm 1*
Sexton, Martin Luther 1857-1922 *NatCAB 19*
Sexton, Pliny Titus 1840-1924 *NatCAB 20, WhAm 1*
Sexton, Samuel 1833-1896 *ApCAB Sup*
Sexton, Samuel H *NewYHSD*
Sexton, Sherman John 1892-1956 *NatCAB 45, WhAm 3*
Sexton, Thomas Lawrence 1839- *WhAm 4*
Sexton, Thomas Scott 1913-1973 *WhAm 5*
Sexton, Walton Roswell 1876-1943 *WhAm 2*
Sexton, William *NewYHSD*
Sexton, William Henry 1875-1963 *WhAm 4*
Sexton, William Thomas 1890-1955 *WhAm 3*
Sextus Empiricus *DcScB*
Seybert, Adam 1773-1825 *ApCAB, BiAUS, BiDrAC, DcAmB, Drake, NatCAB 4, TwCBDA, WhAm H*
Seybert, Henry 1801-1883 *DcAmB, WhAm H*

Seybert, John 1791-1860 *DcAmB, WhAm H*
Seybold, Henry *NewYHSD*
Seybolt, Robert Francis 1888-1951 *BiDAmEd, NatCAB 39, WhAm 3*
Seydlitz, Friedrich W, Freiherr Von 1721-1783 *WhoMilH*
Seyfert, Carl Keenan 1911-1960 *WhAm 4*
Seyfert, Samuel Ritter 1855-1939 *NatCAB 29*
Seyffarth, Gustavus 1796-1885 *ApCAB, DcAmB, WhAm H*
Seyffert, Anton 1712-1785 *ApCAB, NatCAB 2*
Seyffert, Leopold 1887-1956 *NatCAB 45, WhAm 3*
Seymore, Truman 1824-1891 *WhAm H*
Seymour, Alexander Duncan, Jr. 1884-1957 *NatCAB 47, WhAm 3*
Seymour, Arthur Bliss 1859-1933 *NatCAB 44, WhAm 1*
Seymour, Augustus Sherrill 1836-1897 *TwCBDA*
Seymour, Augustus Theodore 1873-1926 *WhAm 1*
Seymour, Augustus Theodore 1907- *WhAm 4*
Seymour, Burge Miles 1894-1967 *WhAm 4*
Seymour, Charles 1885-1963 *WhAm 4*
Seymour, Charles B 1829-1869 *ApCAB*
Seymour, Charles Milne 1882-1958 *WhAm 3*
Seymour, Charles Robert 1870-1952 *NatCAB 42*
Seymour, David L 1802-1867 *BiAUS*
Seymour, David Lowrey 1803-1867 *BiDrAC, WhAm H*
Seymour, Edward Woodruff 1832-1892 *ApCAB, BiDrAC, NatCAB 10, WhAm H, WhAmP*
Seymour, Elizabeth Day *WomWWA 14*
Seymour, Evelyn May 1857-1921 *DcAmLiB*
Seymour, Flora Warren Smith d1948 *BiCAW, WhAm 2*
Seymour, Francis Barnard 1856-1939 *NatCAB 29*
Seymour, Frederick 1856- *WhAm 1*
Seymour, Frederick Henri 1850-1913 *NatCAB 15*
Seymour, George Dudley 1859-1945 *WhAm 2*
Seymour, George Dudley 1859-1946 *NatCAB 38*
Seymour, George Franklin 1829-1906 *ApCAB, DcAmB, NatCAB 10, TwCBDA, WhAm 1*
Seymour, George Steele 1878-1945 *WhAm 2*
Seymour, Gideon Deming 1901-1954 *NatCAB 43, WhAm 3*
Seymour, Harold J 1894-1968 *WhAm 5*
Seymour, Harriet Ayer 1867-1944 *NatCAB 33*
Seymour, Harry Campbell 1861-1921 *NatCAB 18*
Seymour, Henry 1780-1837 *ApCAB*
Seymour, Henry William 1834-1906 *BiDrAC*
Seymour, Horatio 1778-1857 *ApCAB, BiAUS, BiDrAC, Drake, NatCAB 8, TwCBDA, WhAm H, WhAmP*
Seymour, Horatio 1810-1886 *AmBi, ApCAB, DcAmB, McGEWB, NatCAB 3, TwCBDA, WebAB, WhAm H*
Seymour, Horatio 1811-1886 *BiAUS, Drake*
Seymour, Horatio Winslow 1854-1920 *DcAmB, NatCAB 10, NatCAB 27, WhAm 1*
Seymour, Isaac 1798-1863 *NatCAB 23*
Seymour, J O *NewYHSD*
Seymour, James Alward 1864-1943 *WhAm 2*
Seymour, John *BnEnAmA*
Seymour, John d1709 *NatCAB 7*
Seymour, John B *NewYHSD*
Seymour, John F *NewYHSD*
Seymour, John Sammis 1848-1931 *NatCAB 12, WhAm 1*
Seymour, Joseph H *NewYHSD*
Seymour, Luda Wells *WomWWA 14*
Seymour, Mary Foot 1846-1893 *AmWom, NotAW*
Seymour, Mary Harrison 1835- *ApCAB, NatCAB 4, TwCBDA, WhAm 3*
Seymour, May *WomWWA 14*
Seymour, Morris Woodruff 1842-1920 *WhAm 1*
Seymour, Moses 1742-1826 *ApCAB*
Seymour, Nan Gilbert 1875- *WomWWA 14*

Seymour, Origen Storrs 1804-1881 *ApCAB, BiAUS, BiDrAC, NatCAB 10, TwCBDA, WhAm H, WhAmP*
Seymour, Origen Storrs 1872-1940 *NatCAB 32*
Seymour, Ralph Fletcher 1876-1966 *WhAm 4*
Seymour, Robert Gillin 1841-1912 *WhAm 1*
Seymour, Mrs. Robert Morris *WomWWA 14*
Seymour, Samuel 1775?- *IlBEAAW, NewYHSD, WhAm H*
Seymour, Storrs Ozias 1836- *WhAm 3*
Seymour, Thomas 1771-1848 *BnEnAmA*
Seymour, Thomas Day 1848-1907 *AmBi, DcAmB, NatCAB 12, TwCBDA, WhAm 1*
Seymour, Thomas H 1808-1868 *BiAUS*
Seymour, Thomas Hart 1807-1868 *AmBi, BiDrAC, DcAmB, NatCAB 10, WhAm H, WhAmP*
Seymour, Thomas Hart 1808-1868 *ApCAB, Drake*
Seymour, Thomas Henry 1808-1868 *TwCBDA*
Seymour, Truman 1824-1891 *AmBi, ApCAB, DcAmB, Drake, TwCBDA*
Seymour, William 1780?-1848 *BiAUS, BiDrAC, WhAm H*
Seymour, William 1855-1933 *DcAmB, WhAm 1*
Seymour, Lord William Frederick Ernest 1838- *ApCAB Sup*
Seymour, William J *DcAmReB*
Seymour, William Pierce 1825-1893 *NatCAB 4*
Seymour, William Wolcott 1861-1929 *WhAm 1*
Seymour, William Wotkyns 1853-1904 *WhAm 1*
Seyppel, Ferdinand *NewYHSD*
Seyrig, Henri Arnold 1895-1973 *WhAm 6*
Seys, John *BiAUS*
Seyss-Inquart, Artur Von 1892-1946 *WhWW-II*
Sezawa, Katsutada 1895-1944 *DcScB*
Sforza, Ludovico 1452-1508 *McGEWB*
Shaad, George Carl 1878-1936 *WhAm 1*
Shabaka *McGEWB*
Shabonee 1775?-1859 *AmBi, DcAmB, WhAm H*
Shack, Ferdinand 1856- *WhAm 4*
Shackelford, Edward Madison 1863-1943 *WhAm 2*
Shackelford, Elizabeth Putnam *WomWWA 14*
Shackelford, Francis 1909-1973 *WhAm 6*
Shackelford, George Scott 1897-1965 *NatCAB 52*
Shackelford, James H 1873- *WhoColR*
Shackelford, James M 1827-1909 *ApCAB, TwCBDA, WhAm 1*
Shackelford, Jesse Martin 1869-1941 *NatCAB 31*
Shackelford, Joel Walker 1851-1916 *NatCAB 17*
Shackelford, John Williams 1844-1883 *BiDrAC, WhAm H*
Shackelford, Virginia Randolph 1859- *WomWWA 14*
Shackelford, Virginius Randolph 1885-1949 *WhAm 2*
Shackelford, Walter Lawson 1896-1964 *NatCAB 51*
Shackford, John Walter 1878- *WhAm 6*
Shackford, Martha Hale 1875- *WhAm 5, WomWWA 14*
Shackleford, Dorsey William 1853-1936 *BiDrAC, WhAm 4, WhAmP*
Shackleford, Lena Wooten 1862- *WomWWA 14*
Shackleford, Orren Lyne 1881-1949 *NatCAB 38*
Shackleford, Robert Wooten 1890- *WhAm 4*
Shackleford, Thomas G *NatCAB 5*
Shackleford, Thomas Mitchell 1859-1927 *NatCAB 10, WhAm 1*
Shackleford, Thomas Mitchell, Jr. 1884-1973 *WhAm 5*
Shackleford, W S *NewYHSD*
Shackleton, Sir Ernest Henry 1874-1922 *McGEWB*
Shackleton, James Maxwell 1896-1968 *NatCAB 54*
Shackleton, Robert 1860-1923 *NatCAB 19, WhAm 1*

Shackleton, William 1883-1958 *NatCAB 47*
Shadbolt, Jack Leonard 1909- *IlBEAAW*
Shadburn, Morris Luther 1897-1970 *NatCAB 56*
Shadd, Mary Ann *NotAW*
Shadid, Michael Abraham 1881-1966 *WhAm 4*
Shadwick, William *BiAUS*
Shaeffer, Arthur Merrill 1893-1960 *NatCAB 48*
Shafer, Alexander Armstead 1907-1967 *NatCAB 53*
Shafer, Burr 1899-1965 *NatCAB 51*
Shafer, Don Cameron 1881- *WhAm 6*
Shafer, Frederick Charles 1886-1966 *NatCAB 53*
Shafer, George F 1888-1948 *WhAm 2*
Shafer, George H 1879- *WhAm 4*
Shafer, Harvey Gillette 1869-1933 *NatCAB 25*
Shafer, Helen Almira 1839-1894 *AmWom, ApCAB, BiDAmEd, DcAmB, NatCAB 7, TwCBDA, WhAm H*
Shafer, Jacob K 1823-1876 *BiAUS, BiDrAC, WhAm H, WhAmP*
Shafer, John Douglas 1848-1926 *ApCAB X, NatCAB 20, WhAm 1*
Shafer, Julius Edward 1878-1952 *NatCAB 42*
Shafer, Morris Luther 1903-1968 *WhAm 5*
Shafer, Paul Werntz 1893-1954 *BiDrAC, WhAm 3, WhAmP*
Shafer, Robert 1889-1956 *WhAm 3*
Shafer, Samuel C *NewYHSD*
Shafer, Sara Andrew d1913 *WhAm 1, WomWWA 14*
Shafer, Stewart Sherman 1864-1955 *NatCAB 47*
Shaffer *NewYHSD*
Shaffer, Bertram 1906-1974 *WhAm 6*
Shaffer, Charles Norman 1895-1962 *NatCAB 49, WhAm 4*
Shaffer, Cornelius Thadeus 1847-1919 *WhAm 1, WhoColR*
Shaffer, Edward H 1898-1944 *WhAm 2*
Shaffer, Elmer Ellsworth Dale 1917-1974 *WhAm 6*
Shaffer, Floyd Elmer 1889-1963 *WhAm 4*
Shaffer, Harold Stanley 1860-1970 *NatCAB 53*
Shaffer, Henry *NewYHSD*
Shaffer, Irene Yates 1870- *WomWWA 14*
Shaffer, James Newton 1811-1901 *ApCAB X*
Shaffer, John *NewYHSD*
Shaffer, John Charles 1853-1943 *WhAm 2, WhAm 5*
Shaffer, Joseph Crockett 1880-1958 *BiDrAC, NatCAB 43*
Shaffer, Joseph Crockett 1889-1958 *WhAm 3*
Shaffer, Katharine Boggs 1854- *WomWWA 14*
Shaffer, Kent 1885-1925 *NatCAB 21*
Shaffer, Lewis d1973 *WhAm 5*
Shaffer, Newton Melman 1846-1928 *ApCAB X, NatCAB 3, WhAm 1*
Shaffer, Philip Anderson 1881-1960 *WhAm 4*
Shaffer, Ray Osborn 1904-1964 *WhAm 4*
Shaffer, Roy Lee 1881- *WhAm 6*
Shaffer, William Frederick 1903-1962 *WhAm 4*
Shaffner, Henry Fries 1867-1941 *NatCAB 35, WhAm 1*
Shaffner, Taliaferro Preston 1818-1881 *ApCAB, NatCAB 10, WhAm H*
Shafroth, John Franklin 1854-1922 *BiDrAC, DcAmB, NatCAB 14, REnAW, TwCBDA, WhAm 1, WhAmP*
Shafroth, John Franklin 1887-1967 *WhAm 4*
Shafteberg, Lewis *NewYHSD*
Shafter, James McMillan 1816- *ApCAB*
Shafter, Oscar C d1873 *BiAUS*
Shafter, Oscar Lovell 1812-1873 *ApCAB, NatCAB 15*
Shafter, William Rufus 1835-1906 *AmBi, ApCAB Sup, DcAmB, NatCAB 9, TwCBDA, WebAB, WebAMB, WhAm 1*
Shaftesbury, Anthony A Cooper, Earl Of 1621-1683 *McGEWB*
Shaftesbury, Anthony A Cooper, Earl Of 1671-1713 *McGEWB*
Shaftesbury, Anthony A Cooper, Earl Of 1801-1885 *McGEWB*
Shaftesbury, Archie D 1893-1967 *WhAm 4*
Shah Jahan 1592-1666 *McGEWB*
Shahan, Thomas Joseph 1857-1932 *BiDAmEd,*

DcAmB, *NatCAB 5*, *WhAm 1*
Shahn, Ben 1898-1969 *BnEnAmA*, *EncAB*, *McGEWB*, *WhAm 5*
Shahn, Benjamin 1898-1969 *WebAB*
Shahpur II 310-379 *McGEWB*
Shaiken, Joseph 1905-1974 *WhAm 6*
Shaikewitz, Nahum Meir 1849-1905 *DcAmB*
Shainmark, Eliezer L 1900-1976 *WhAm 6*
Shainwald, Ralph Louis 1851- *NatCAB 16*
Shainwald, Richard Herman 1894-1955 *WhAm 3*
Shainwald, Richard S 1862-1954 *WhAm 3*
Shainwald, Ruth Hart *BiCAW*
Shaka 1787?-1828 *McGEWB*
Shakallamy d1748 *DcAmB*
Shakerley, Jeremy 1626-1655? *DcScB*
Shakespeare, Edward Oram 1846- *ApCAB*
Shakespeare, Monroe 1898-1945 *NatCAB 36*
Shakespeare, William 1564-1616 *McGEWB*
Shakespeare, William, Jr. d1950 *WhAm 3*
Shaler, Alexander 1827-1911 *ApCAB*, *Drake*, *NatCAB 4*, *TwCBDA*, *WhAm 1*
Shaler, Charles 1843-1915 *WhAm 1*
Shaler, Clarence Addison 1860-1941 *NatCAB 54*, *WhAm 2*
Shaler, Millard King 1880-1942 *NatCAB 32*
Shaler, Nathaniel Southgate 1841-1906 *ApCAB*, *BiDAmEd*, *DcAmB*, *DcScB*, *NatCAB 9*, *TwCBDA*, *WhAm 1*
Shaler, William d1833 *BiAUS*, *Drake*
Shaler, William 1773?-1833 *DcAmB*, *WhAm H*
Shaler, William 1778-1833 *ApCAB*, *NatCAB 4*
Shall, Frank Hiram 1875-1949 *NatCAB 39*
Shallberg, Gustavus Adolphus 1876-1959 *WhAm 3*
Shallcross, Cecil Fleetwood 1872-1947 *NatCAB 34*, *WhAm 2*
Shallcross, Thomas 1875-1960 *NatCAB 48*
Shallenberger, Ashton Cokayne 1862-1938 *BiDrAC*, *WhAm 1*, *WhAmP*
Shallenberger, Bella Glass 1869- *WomWWA 14*
Shallenberger, James Marion 1860-1944 *NatCAB 33*
Shallenberger, Martin C 1886-1951 *WhAm 3*
Shallenberger, William Shadrach 1839-1914 *TwCBDA*, *WhAm 1*
Shallenberger, William Shadrack 1839-1914 *BiDrAC*, *WhAmP*
Shallna, Anthony Oswald 1894-1971 *NatCAB 57*
Shallus, Francis 1774-1821 *NewYHSD*
Shalter, Irwin Maurer 1880- *WhAm 6*
Shambaugh, Benjamin Franklin 1871-1940 *REnAW*, *WhAm 1*
Shambaugh, Bertha M H 1871- *WhAm 5*, *WomWWA 14*
Shambaugh, George Elmer 1869-1947 *NatCAB 40*, *WhAm 5*
Shambora, William E 1900-1975 *WhAm 6*
Shamburger, Carl Shuford 1903-1967 *WhAm 5*
Shamel, Archibald Dixon 1878-1956 *NatCAB 46*, *WhAm 6*
Shammai *McGEWB*
Shamroy, Leon 1901-1974 *WhAm 6*
Shanafelt, Thomas M 1840- *WhAm 4*
Shanahan, David Edward 1862-1936 *WhAm 1*
Shanahan, Edmund Thomas 1868-1929 *WhAm 1*
Shanahan, Foss 1910-1964 *WhAm 4*
Shanahan, Jeremiah Francis 1834-1886 *ApCAB*, *NatCAB 13*, *TwCBDA*
Shanahan, John Daniel 1864- *WhAm 4*
Shanahan, John Walter 1846-1916 *NatCAB 21*, *WhAm 1*
Shanahan, T J 1902-1963 *WhAm 4*
Shananan, Jeremiah Francis 1834-1886 *WhAm H*
Shand, Robert Gordon 1896-1966 *WhAm 4*
Shand, S James 1882-1957 *WhAm 3*
Shand, William Munro 1881-1941 *NatCAB 36*
Shands, Aurelius Rives 1860-1941 *NatCAB 31*, *WhAm 1*
Shands, Bessie Nugent 1885- *WomWWA 14*
Shands, Courtney 1905-1968 *WhAm 5*
Shands, Garvin Dugas 1844-1917 *WhAm 1*

Shands, Ruebush George 1903-1967 *NatCAB 52*
Shane, George 1906-1969 *WhAm 5*
Shane, Joseph Brooks 1903-1974 *WhAm 6*
Shaner, Albert Lou Allen 1865-1945 *NatCAB 36*
Shang, Yang 390?BC-338BC *McGEWB*
Shank, Corwin Sheridan 1866-1947 *WhAm 2*
Shank, David d1831 *ApCAB*, *Drake*
Shank, Donald J 1910-1967 *WhAm 4*
Shank, John Jay 1898-1949 *NatCAB 38*
Shank, Samuel Herbert 1871- *WhAm 5*
Shankara 788?-820 *McGEWB*
Shankland, Edward Clapp 1854-1924 *NatCAB 13*, *WhAm 1*
Shankland, Sherwood Dodge 1874-1947 *WhAm 2*
Shankland, William H 1804- *BiAUS*
Shankle, Olin Estes 1880-1929 *NatCAB 24*
Shanklin, Arnold 1866- *NatCAB 14*, *WhAm 4*
Shanklin, George Bryan 1888-1961 *NatCAB 49*
Shanklin, George Sea 1807-1883 *BiAUS*, *BiDrAC*, *WhAm H*
Shanklin, John Gilbert d1903 *WhAm 1*
Shanklin, R Maurice 1868-1944 *NatCAB 34*
Shanklin, William Arnold 1862-1924 *WhAm 1*
Shanklin, William Arnold 1864-1924 *NatCAB 14*
Shanks *NewYHSD*
Shanks, David Carey 1861-1940 *WhAm 1*
Shanks, Henry Thomas 1896-1959 *WhAm 3*
Shanks, John P C 1826-1901 *BiAUS*
Shanks, John Peter Cleaver 1826-1901 *BiDrAC*, *WhAmP*
Shanks, John Peter Clever 1826-1901 *TwCBDA*
Shanks, Lewis Piaget 1878-1935 *WhAm 1*
Shanks, Maria Gore 1875- *WomWWA 14*
Shanks, Royal E 1912-1962 *WhAm 4*
Shanks, William 1812-1882 *DcScB*
Shanks, William Franklin Gore 1837-1905 *ApCAB*, *NatCAB 3*, *TwCBDA*, *WhAm 1*
Shanley, George Patrick 1879- *WhAm 6*
Shanley, James Andrew 1896-1965 *BiDrAC*, *WhAm 4*
Shanley, John 1852-1909 *ApCAB Sup*, *TwCBDA*, *WhAm 1*
Shanley, John Francis 1855-1911 *NatCAB 21*
Shanley, William Carleton Bayley 1871-1922 *NatCAB 32*
Shanly, Charles Dawson 1811-1875 *ApCAB*, *NatCAB 8*
Shanly, Walter 1819-1938 *ApCAB*, *Drake*
Shannahan, John Newton 1872-1938 *WhAm 1*
Shannon, Alice Avery 1869- *WomWWA 14*
Shannon, Claude Elwood 1916- *AsBiEn*, *McGEWB*
Shannon, Edgar Finley 1874-1938 *WhAm 1*
Shannon, Effie 1867-1954 *WhAm 3*, *WomWWA 14*
Shannon, Ellen Elizabeth Poppleton *WomWWA 14*
Shannon, Fred Albert 1893-1963 *EncAAH*, *WhAm 4*
Shannon, Frederick Franklin 1877- *NatCAB 10*, *WhAm 5*
Shannon, Freeland Blake 1877-1956 *NatCAB 45*
Shannon, George 1787-1836 *BiAUS*
Shannon, George Pope 1892-1964 *WhAm 4*
Shannon, Henry Edward 1867-1943 *NatCAB 47*
Shannon, Hugh Samuel 1872-1932 *NatCAB 24*
Shannon, James 1799-1859 *NatCAB 8*
Shannon, James Jebusa 1862- *NatCAB 14*, *WhAm 4*
Shannon, Joseph Bernard 1867-1943 *BiDrAC*, *NatCAB 32*, *WhAm 2*, *WhAmP*
Shannon, Lester Norman 1893-1960 *NatCAB 50*
Shannon, Mary Eulalie Fee 1824-1855 *Drake*
Shannon, Michael Francis 1887-1953 *NatCAB 42*
Shannon, Nellie 1863-1924 *WhAm 1*
Shannon, Peter C *BiAUS*
Shannon, Richard Cutts 1839-1920 *BiDrAC*, *NatCAB 12*, *TwCBDA*, *WhAm 1*
Shannon, Robert Thomas 1860-1931 *WhAm 1*
Shannon, Spencer Sweet 1893-1964 *WhAm 4*

Shannon, Thomas 1786-1843 *BiAUS*, *BiDrAC*, *WhAm H*, *WhAmP*
Shannon, Thomas Bowles 1827-1897 *BiAUS*, *BiDrAC*, *WhAm H*
Shannon, Thomas Vincent 1874-1959 *WhAm 3*
Shannon, W *NewYHSD*
Shannon, William 1861-1923 *NatCAB 23*
Shannon, William Duncan 1880- *WhoColR*
Shannon, Wilson 1802-1877 *AmBi*, *ApCAB*, *BiAUS*, *BiDrAC*, *DcAmB*, *Drake*, *NatCAB 8*, *TwCBDA*, *WhAm H*, *WhAmP*
Shannon, Wilson 1803-1877 *NatCAB 3*
Shanton, George Reynolds 1868-1930 *NatCAB 25*
Shantz, Harold 1894-1967 *NatCAB 53*
Shantz, Homer LeRoy 1876-1958 *WhAm 3*
Shapiro, Arthur 1910-1969 *NatCAB 54*, *WhAm 6*
Shapiro, Chaim 1886-1966 *NatCAB 54*
Shapiro, Harry 1887-1967 *WhAm 4A*
Shapiro, Harry Herschel 1892-1958 *NatCAB 47*
Shapiro, Joseph M 1888-1968 *WhAm 4A*, *WhAm 5*
Shapiro, Karl Jay 1913- *WebAB*
Shapiro, Morse Joseph 1893-1968 *NatCAB 54*
Shapiro, Shepard 1896-1966 *NatCAB 52*
Shapiro, William Mordecai 1890-1960 *NatCAB 48*
Shapleigh, Alfred Lee 1862-1945 *NatCAB 12*, *WhAm 2*
Shapleigh, Amelia 1868- *WomWWA 14*
Shapleigh, Augustus Frederick 1810- *NatCAB 5*
Shapleigh, Bertram Lincoln 1871-1940 *NatCAB 29*, *WhAm 1*
Shapleigh, Frank Henry 1842-1906 *ApCAB*, *IIBEAAW*, *NatCAB 8*, *WhAm 1*
Shapleigh, John Blasdel 1857- *NatCAB 16*
Shapleigh, Richard Waldron 1859-1933 *NatCAB 35*
Shapleigh, Waldron 1848-1901 *WhAm 1*
Shapley, Alan 1903-1973 *WhAm 5*
Shapley, Harlow 1885- *AsBiEn*, *McGEWB*
Shapley, Harlow 1885-1971 *EncAB*
Shapley, Harlow 1885-1972 *DcScB*, *WebAB*, *WhAm 5*
Shapley, Rufus Edmonds 1840-1906 *ApCAB*, *NatCAB 2*, *WhAm 4*
Shaporin, Yuri 1887-1966 *WhAm 4*
Shaposhnikov, Boris Mikhailovich 1882-1945 *WhWW-II*, *WhoMilH*
Sharber, Kate Trimble 1883- *WomWWA 14*
Sharer, William E *IIBEAAW*
Sharett, Moshe 1894-1965 *WhAm 4*
Sharfman, Isaiah Leo 1886-1969 *NatCAB 53*
Sharif Al-Idrisi, Al- *DcScB*
Sharkey, Emma Augusta 1858- *AmWom*
Sharkey, Joseph Edward 1877- *WhAm 5*
Sharkey, Thomas Clifford 1932-1973 *WhAm 6*
Sharkey, William Lewis d1873 *BiAUS*
Sharkey, William Lewis 1793-1873 *REnAW*
Sharkey, William Lewis 1797-1873 *ApCAB*, *NatCAB 12*, *NatCAB 13*, *TwCBDA*
Sharkey, William Lewis 1798-1873 *AmBi*, *DcAmB*, *WhAm H*
Sharman, Jackson Roger 1895-1957 *WhAm 3*
Sharon, Emmet Michael 1847- *NatCAB 16*
Sharon, Isaac Paul 1879-1957 *NatCAB 47*
Sharon, William 1821-1885 *ApCAB*, *BiAUS*, *BiDrAC*, *NatCAB 5*, *TwCBDA*, *WhAm H*, *WhAmP*
Sharon, William Evan 1852-1926 *NatCAB 21*
Sharonov, Vsevolod Vasilievich 1901-1964 *DcScB*
Sharood, Charles K 1849- *NatCAB 6*
Sharp, Mister *NewYHSD*
Sharp, Abbie Gardner *WomWWA 14*
Sharp, Alexander 1885-1975 *WhAm 6*
Sharp, Benjamin 1858-1915 *WhAm 1*
Sharp, Bertha Staples Pitman 1865- *WomWWA 14*
Sharp, Carl J 1893-1968 *WhAm 5*
Sharp, Clarence Bryan 1896-1974 *WhAm 6*
Sharp, Clayton Halsey 1869-1942 *NatCAB 31*, *WhAm 3*
Sharp, Dallas Lore 1870-1929 *AmBi*, *DcAmB*, *WhAm 1*

Sharp, Daniel 1783-1853 *ApCAB, DcAmB, Drake, NatCAB 12, TwCBDA, WhAm H*
Sharp, Eckley Grant 1866-1941 *WhAm 4*
Sharp, Edgar Allan 1876-1948 *BiDrAC, WhAm 2*
Sharp, Edward Raymond 1894-1961 *WhAm 4*
Sharp, Edwin Rees 1858- *WhAm 1*
Sharp, Edwin V *NewYHSD*
Sharp, Eliza Mary 1829- *NewYHSD*
Sharp, Estelle Avery 1858- *WomWWA 14*
Sharp, Frank Chapman 1866-1943 *NatCAB 33, WhAm 2*
Sharp, George Clough 1897-1972 *WhAm 5*
Sharp, George Gillies 1874-1960 *NatCAB 46, WhAm 4*
Sharp, George Henry 1834- *NewYHSD*
Sharp, George Matthews d1911 *WhAm 1*
Sharp, George W 1859-1919 *NatCAB 19*
Sharp, George Winters 1882-1953 *WhAm 3*
Sharp, Grace Hastings *WomWWA 14*
Sharp, Hallie Clough *WomWWA 14*
Sharp, Henry Staats 1902-1969 *WhAm 5*
Sharp, Hugh Rodney 1880- *WhAm 6*
Sharp, Hunter 1861-1923 *WhAm 1*
Sharp, Jacob 1817-1888 *ApCAB*
Sharp, Jacob 1835-1892 *TwCBDA*
Sharp, James *NewYHSD*
Sharp, James Clement 1818-1897 *NewYHSD*
Sharp, James H d1974 *WhAm 6*
Sharp, John 1820-1891 *DcAmB, WhAm H*
Sharp, Mrs. John C d1912 *WhAm 1*
Sharp, John Fletcher 1865-1927 *WhAm 1*
Sharp, John H 1874- *WhAm 5*
Sharp, Joseph C 1898-1946 *WhAm 2*
Sharp, Joseph Henry 1859-1953 *ApCAB X, IIBEAAW, NatCAB 11, NatCAB 18, REnAW, TwCBDA*
Sharp, Joseph Lessil 1914-1971 *WhAm 5*
Sharp, Katharine Lucinda 1865-1914 *BiDAmEd, DcAmB, DcAmLiB, NotAW, WhAm 1, WomWWA 14*
Sharp, Katherine Lucinda 1865-1914 *TwCBDA*
Sharp, Lester Whyland 1887-1961 *NatCAB 53*
Sharp, Louis Hovey 1875-1946 *IIBEAAW*
Sharp, Marlay Albert 1889-1959 *WhAm 3*
Sharp, Mary S 1876- *WomWWA 14*
Sharp, Paul Frederick 1918- *EncAAH*
Sharp, Philip Thomas 1831- *NewYHSD*
Sharp, Richard 1813-1895 *ApCAB X*
Sharp, Robert 1851-1931 *WhAm 1*
Sharp, Robert 1852-1931 *NatCAB 24*
Sharp, Robert Sherman 1869-1932 *WhAm 1*
Sharp, Solomon P d1835 *BiAUS*
Sharp, Solomon P 1780-1825 *BiDrAC, WhAm H, WhAmP*
Sharp, Thomas Enoch 1890-1957 *WhAm 3*
Sharp, Waldo Z 1870-1933 *WhAm 1*
Sharp, Walter Bedford 1897-1964 *WhAm 4*
Sharp, Walter Benona 1870-1912 *NatCAB 39*
Sharp, William 1802?- *NewYHSD, WhAm H*
Sharp, William 1900-1961 *NatCAB 46*
Sharp, William Barnard 1889-1961 *NatCAB 51*
Sharp, William Comely 1822-1897 *NewYHSD*
Sharp, William F 1885-1947 *WhAm 2*
Sharp, William Graves 1859-1922 *AmBi, ApCAB X, BiDrAC, DcAmB, NatCAB 19, WhAm 1, WhAmP*
Sharp, William Wilson 1891-1955 *WhAm 4*
Sharpe, Alfred Clarence 1850-1922 *WhAm 1*
Sharpe, Charles Tilley 1875-1950 *NatCAB 38*
Sharpe, Charles W d1876? *NewYHSD*
Sharpe, Cornelius N d1828 *NewYHSD*
Sharpe, Francis Robert 1870-1948 *WhAm 2*
Sharpe, George Bertram 1877-1923 *NatCAB 6*
Sharpe, George Henry 1828-1900 *ApCAB, TwCBDA*
Sharpe, Henry Augustus 1848-1919 *NatCAB 18, WhAm 1*
Sharpe, Henry Dexter 1872-1954 *WhAm 3*
Sharpe, Henry Granville 1858-1947 *NatCAB 36, WhAm 2*
Sharpe, Horatio 1718-1790 *DcAmB, NatCAB 7, WhAm H*
Sharpe, Jacob 1835-1892 *ApCAB Sup*
Sharpe, John C 1853-1942 *WhAm 2*
Sharpe, John Semple 1878-1946 *NatCAB 35*
Sharpe, Joseph Audley 1907-1952 *NatCAB 39*
Sharpe, Julia Graydon *WomWWA 14*

Sharpe, Leo Nelson 1885-1939 *NatCAB 29*
Sharpe, Merrell Quentin 1883-1962 *WhAm 4*
Sharpe, Merrell Quentin 1888-1962 *NatCAB 47*
Sharpe, Nelson 1858-1935 *NatCAB 26, WhAm 1*
Sharpe, Peter *BiAUS, BiDrAC, WhAm H*
Sharpe, Philip Burdette 1903-1961 *WhAm 4*
Sharpe, Richard 1813-1895 *NatCAB 9*
Sharpe, William 1742-1818 *ApCAB, BiAUS, BiDrAC, Drake, NatCAB 8, TwCBDA, WhAm H*
Sharpey, William 1802-1880 *DcScB*
Sharpey-Schafer, Sir Edward Albert 1850-1935 *AsBiEn, BiHiMed, DcScB*
Sharples, Ellen Wallace 1769-1849 *NewYHSD*
Sharples, Felix Thomas 1786?-1824? *NewYHSD*
Sharples, James 1751?-1811 *DcAmB, NewYHSD, TwCBDA, WhAm H*
Sharples, James, Jr. 1788?-1839 *NewYHSD*
Sharples, Philip M 1857-1944 *NatCAB 47, WhAm 4*
Sharples, Rolinda 1793?-1838 *NewYHSD*
Sharples, Stephen Paschall 1842-1923 *WhAm 1*
Sharpless, Frederic Cope 1880-1971 *WhAm 5*
Sharpless, Frederick F 1866-1951 *WhAm 3*
Sharpless, Isaac 1848-1920 *DcAmB, NatCAB 21, TwCBDA, WhAm 1*
Sharpless, James 1751?-1811 *ApCAB*
Sharpnack, Lew George 1905-1968 *NatCAB 54*
Sharps, Christian 1811-1874 *ApCAB, NatCAB 5*
Sharretts, Thaddeus Stevens 1850- *NatCAB 14*
Sharrock, Robert 1630-1684 *DcScB*
Sharron, John *NewYHSD*
Sharswood, George 1810-1883 *ApCAB, BiAUS, DcAmB, Drake, NatCAB 2, TwCBDA, WhAm H*
Sharswood, William 1836- *ApCAB, Drake*
Shartel, Cassius McLean 1860-1943 *BiDrAC*
Sharts, Joseph William 1875- *WhAm 5*
Shastid, Thomas Hall 1866-1947 *WhAm 2*
Shastri, Lal Bahadur 1904-1966 *WhAm 4*
Shaterian, William Shadrack 1884-1964 *NatCAB 50*
Shatir, Ala Al-Din Abul-Hasan, Ibn Al-1305?-1375? *DcScB*
Shatltuck, Harriette Lucy Robinson 1850- *WhAm 4*
Shatswell, James Arthur 1863-1947 *NatCAB 36*
Shattuc, William Bunn 1841-1911 *BiDrAC, TwCBDA, WhAm 1*
Shattuck, Aaron Draper 1832-1928 *ApCAB, DcAmB, Drake, NewYHSD, TwCBDA, WhAm 1*
Shattuck, Arthur 1881- *NatCAB 17, WhAm 3*
Shattuck, Charles Houston 1867-1931 *WhAm 1*
Shattuck, Corinna 1848- *TwCBDA*
Shattuck, Edward Stevens 1901-1965 *WhAm 4*
Shattuck, Edwin Chase 1870-1961 *NatCAB 49*
Shattuck, Edwin Paul 1873-1964 *WhAm 4*
Shattuck, Frank 1878- *WhAm 6*
Shattuck, Frank Garrett 1860- *ApCAB X*
Shattuck, Frederick Cheever 1847-1929 *DcAmB, NatCAB 12, WhAm 1*
Shattuck, George Brune 1844-1923 *DcAmB, WhAm 1*
Shattuck, George Burbank 1869-1934 *WhAm 1*
Shattuck, George Cheever 1879-1972 *WhAm 5*
Shattuck, George Cheyne 1783-1854 *ApCAB, DcAmB, Drake, NatCAB 12, TwCBDA, WhAm H*
Shattuck, George Cheyne 1813-1893 *DcAmB, TwCBDA, WhAm H*
Shattuck, George Lysander 1868-1955 *NatCAB 45*
Shattuck, H Morgan d1967 *WhAm 4A*
Shattuck, Harriette Robinson 1850- *AmWom, TwCBDA, WomWWA 14*
Shattuck, Helen Barnes 1878- *WomWWA 14*
Shattuck, Henry Lee 1879-1971 *NatCAB 57, WhAm 5*
Shattuck, Howard Francis 1887-1972 *WhAm 5*
Shattuck, J L *NewYHSD*
Shattuck, John Garrett 1884-1964 *WhAm 4*
Shattuck, Joseph Cummings 1835-1921 *BiDAmEd*

Shattuck, Lemuel 1793-1859 *ApCAB, BiHiMed, DcAmB, Drake, WhAm H*
Shattuck, Lemuel C 1866-1938 *WhAm 1*
Shattuck, Lillian *WomWWA 14*
Shattuck, Lydia White 1822-1889 *AmWom, NotAW*
Shattuck, Mayo Adams 1898-1952 *WhAm 3*
Shattuck, Orville Frank d1948 *NatCAB 38*
Shattuck, Samuel Walker 1841-1915 *NatCAB 18, WhAm 1*
Shattuck, Samuel Winthrop 1866-1915 *NatCAB 16*
Shattuck, William 1864-1946 *WhAm 3*
Shattuck, William Pitt 1860-1926 *NatCAB 21*
Shatunovsky, Samuil Osipovich 1859-1929 *DcScB*
Shatzer, Charles Gallatin 1877-1959 *NatCAB 48, WhAm 3*
Shaubena 1775?-1859 *AmBi, ApCAB, DcAmB*
Shauck, John Allen 1841-1918 *DcAmB, NatCAB 12, WhAm 1*
Shaughnessy, Clark Daniel 1892-1970 *WhAm 5*
Shaughnessy, Edward Henry 1882-1922 *NatCAB 19*
Shaughnessy, Gerald 1887-1950 *WhAm 3*
Shaughnessy, Sir Thomas George 1853-1923 *WhAm 1*
Shaver, A G *NewYHSD*
Shaver, Charles William 1890-1961 *WhAm 4*
Shaver, Clarence L 1876-1963 *NatCAB 51*
Shaver, Clement Lawrence 1867-1954 *WhAm 3*
Shaver, Dorothy 1897-1959 *NatCAB 56, WhAm 3*
Shaver, Emilie H 1869- *WomWWA 14*
Shaver, George Frederick 1855- *ApCAB, NatCAB 4, WhAm 4*
Shaver, Jesse Milton 1888-1961 *WhAm 4*
Shaver, Leonidas *BiAUS*
Shaver, Robert Ezekiel 1905-1973 *WhAm 6*
Shaver, Samuel M 1816?-1878 *NewYHSD*
Shaver, V Payson *NewYHSD*
Shaw *NewYHSD*
Shaw, A Vere 1887-1970 *NatCAB 56*
Shaw, Aaron 1811-1887 *BiAUS, BiDrAC, WhAm H*
Shaw, Adele Marie *WomWWA 14*
Shaw, Agnes Morton *WomWWA 14*
Shaw, Albert 1857-1947 *ApCAB, DcAmB S4, NatCAB 9, NatCAB 34, TwCBDA, WhAm 2*
Shaw, Albert Duane 1841-1901 *ApCAB, ApCAB Sup, BiDrAC, NatCAB 7, WhAm 1*
Shaw, Albert Sidney Johnston 1880- *WhAm 6*
Shaw, Anna Howard 1847-1919 *AmBi, AmWom, ApCAB X, DcAmB, McGEWB, NatCAB 14, NotAW, WhAm 1, WhAmP, WomWWA 14*
Shaw, Annie Cornelia 1852- *AmWom, ApCAB*
Shaw, Arch Wilkinson 1876-1962 *WhAm 4*
Shaw, Arthur Douglas 1902-1958 *NatCAB 49*
Shaw, Arvin Benjamin, Jr. 1889-1953 *NatCAB 40*
Shaw, Avery Albert 1870-1949 *NatCAB 35, WhAm 2*
Shaw, Caroline Budd Gallaudet 1848- *WomWWA 14*
Shaw, Charles 1782-1828 *ApCAB, Drake*
Shaw, Charles Bunsen 1894-1962 *DcAmLiB, NatCAB 46, WhAm 4*
Shaw, Charles Dannelly 1834-1909 *NatCAB 14*
Shaw, Charles Frederick 1881-1939 *WhAm 1*
Shaw, Charles Gray 1871-1949 *WhAm 2*
Shaw, Charles Green 1892-1974 *WhAm 6*
Shaw, Clara Hathorne *WomWWA 14*
Shaw, Clarence Reginald 1889-1950 *WhAm 3*
Shaw, Cornelia Dean 1845- *AmWom*
Shaw, Daniel Alexander 1866-1930 *NatCAB 44*
Shaw, David Alexander 1870-1933 *NatCAB 25*
Shaw, Dexter Nichols 1900-1973 *WhAm 6*
Shaw, Earl 1913-1965 *WhAm 4*
Shaw, Edgar Dwight 1871-1931 *AmBi, WhAm 1*
Shaw, Edgar William 1887-1939 *NatCAB 30*
Shaw, Edward Lyman 1875-1943 *NatCAB 32*
Shaw, Edward Richard 1850-1903 *DcAmB*
Shaw, Edward Richard 1855-1903 *WhAm 1*

Shaw, Edwin Adams 1876-1951 *WhAm 3*
Shaw, Edwin Coupland 1863-1941 *WhAm 2*
Shaw, Elijah 1793-1851 *DcAmB, WhAm H*
Shaw, Elizabeth Garman 1858- *WomWWA 14*
Shaw, Ellen Eddy *WomWWA 14*
Shaw, Elton Raymond 1886-1955 *NatCAB 48*
Shaw, Elwyn Riley 1888-1950 *WhAm 3*
Shaw, Emma 1846- *AmWom*
Shaw, Esmond 1902-1972 *WhAm 5*
Shaw, Eugene 1920-1974 *WhAm 6*
Shaw, Eugene Wesley 1881-1935 *WhAm 1*
Shaw, Flora Madlena Matheson *WomWWA 14*
Shaw, Florence DeGraff 1865- *WomWWA 14*
Shaw, Florence Sylvia Berlowitz d1963
  WhAm 4
Shaw, Frances Wills 1872-1937 *WhAm 1*
Shaw, Francis George 1809-1882 *ApCAB,
  NatCAB 8*
Shaw, Franck Gilliam 1891-1961 *NatCAB 51*
Shaw, Frank Harold 1872-1950 *NatCAB 40*
Shaw, Frank L 1877-1958 *WhAm 3*
Shaw, Frank Sargent 1862-1936 *NatCAB 35*
Shaw, Frank Thomas 1841-1923 *BiDrAC*
Shaw, Frederic Lonsdale 1880- *WhAm 6*
Shaw, Frederick Benjamin 1869- *WhAm 5*
Shaw, Frederick William 1882-1945
  NatCAB 36, WhAm 2
Shaw, Gardiner Howland 1893-1965 *WhAm 4*
Shaw, George Bernard 1856-1950 *McGEWB,
  WhAm 3*
Shaw, George Bernard 1905-1975 *WhAm 6*
Shaw, George Bullen 1854-1894 *BiDrAC,
  WhAm H*
Shaw, George Clayton 1863- *WhoColR*
Shaw, George Elmer 1861-1938 *WhAm 1*
Shaw, George Hamlin 1890-1956 *NatCAB 44,
  WhAm 3*
Shaw, Guy Loren 1881-1950 *BiDrAC,
  WhAm 6*
Shaw, Harriett McCreary Jackson 1865-1933
  WhAm 1, WomWWA 14
Shaw, Harry Judson 1873-1946 *NatCAB 35*
Shaw, Hartley 1874-1958 *NatCAB 46*
Shaw, Henry 1788-1857 *BiAUS, BiDrAC,
  WhAm H, WhAmP*
Shaw, Henry 1800-1889 *ApCAB, DcAmB,
  NatCAB 9, TwCBDA, WhAm H*
Shaw, Henry G 1879- *WhAm 6*
Shaw, Henry Larned Keith 1873-1941
  NatCAB 37, WhAm 1
Shaw, Henry Marchmore 1819-1864 *BiAUS,
  BiDrAC, WhAm H*
Shaw, Henry Wheeler 1818-1885 *AmBi,
  ApCAB, DcAmB, Drake, EncAAH,
  NatCAB 6, TwCBDA, WebAB,
  WhAm H*
Shaw, Hobart Doane 1879-1960 *WhAm 4*
Shaw, Howard Burton 1869-1943 *WhAm 2*
Shaw, Howard Elwin 1867-1924 *NatCAB 22*
Shaw, Howard VanDoren 1869-1926 *DcAmB,
  NatCAB 20, WhAm 1*
Shaw, Irving Roland 1887-1954 *NatCAB 43*
Shaw, J *NewYHSD*
Shaw, James *NewYHSD*
Shaw, James Boylan 1808- *ApCAB*
Shaw, James Byrnie 1866-1948 *WhAm 2*
Shaw, James Edward 1914-1974 *WhAm 6*
Shaw, Jesse Washington 1913-1964 *NatCAB 51*
Shaw, John 1773-1823 *ApCAB, DcAmB,
  Drake, NatCAB 8, TwCBDA, WebAMB,
  WhAm H*
Shaw, John 1778-1809 *ApCAB, DcAmB,
  Drake, NatCAB 8, WhAm H*
Shaw, John Balcom 1860- *WhAm 4*
Shaw, John Gilbert 1859-1932 *BiDrAC*
Shaw, John Jacob 1907-1974 *WhAm 6*
Shaw, John Knox 1876-1943 *NatCAB 32*
Shaw, John Maxwell 1851-1924 *NatCAB 31*
Shaw, John Stewart 1885-1952 *NatCAB 40,
  WhAm 3*
Shaw, John William 1863-1934 *NatCAB 15,
  WhAm 1*
Shaw, John William 1910-1968 *WhAm 4A*
Shaw, Joseph *NewYHSD*
Shaw, Joseph Alden 1836-1915 *WhAm 1*
Shaw, Joseph Henry 1872-1922 *NatCAB 6*
Shaw, Joshua 1776?-1860 *IlBEAAW*
Shaw, Joshua 1777?-1860 *BnEnAmA,*

NewYHSD, WhAm H
Shaw, Julia Williamson 1869- *WomWWA 14*
Shaw, Lacy 1886-1951 *NatCAB 40*
Shaw, Lemuel 1781-1861 *AmBi, ApCAB,
  DcAmB, Drake, EncAB, McGEWB,
  NatCAB 5, TwCBDA, WebAB,
  WhAm H*
Shaw, Leo Nelson 1893-1965 *WhAm 4*
Shaw, Leon Irwin 1885-1962 *NatCAB 51*
Shaw, Leslie Mortier 1848-1932 *AmBi,
  BiDrUSE, DcAmB, NatCAB 11,
  NatCAB 23, TwCBDA, WhAm 1*
Shaw, Leslie Mortimer 1848-1932 *ApCAB Sup,
  NatCAB 14*
Shaw, Lloyd 1890-1958 *NatCAB 48, WhAm 3*
Shaw, Louis Agassiz 1886-1940 *NatCAB 33*
Shaw, Lucien 1845-1933 *WhAm 1*
Shaw, Martha Cornelia 1878- *WomWWA 14*
Shaw, Mary d1929 *WomWWA 14*
Shaw, Mary 1854-1929 *DcAmB, NotAW*
Shaw, Mary 1860-1929 *WhAm 1*
Shaw, Mary Edna 1881- *WomWWA 14*
Shaw, Mary Stephens *WomWWA 14*
Shaw, Nathaniel 1735-1782 *DcAmB,
  WhAm H*
Shaw, Nellie DeBertrand 1874- *WomWWA 14*
Shaw, Oliver 1776-1849 *ApCAB*
Shaw, Oliver 1779-1848 *DcAmB, Drake,
  WhAm H*
Shaw, Oliver Abbott 1870-1945 *WhAm 2*
Shaw, Patrick 1913-1975 *WhAm 6*
Shaw, Paul Albert 1905-1970 *NatCAB 55*
Shaw, Paul Norval 1880-1957 *NatCAB 48*
Shaw, Paul Thornton 1877-1945 *NatCAB 35*
Shaw, Pauline Agassiz 1841-1917 *BiCAW,
  DcAmB, NatCAB 27, NotAW*
Shaw, Peter 1694-1764 *DcScB*
Shaw, Phillip 1909-1970 *NatCAB 55*
Shaw, Phillips Bassett 1895-1947 *NatCAB 37,
  WhAm 2*
Shaw, Quincy Adams 1825-1908 *NatCAB 27*
Shaw, Quincy Adams 1869-1960 *NatCAB 53,
  WhAm 4, WhAm 5*
Shaw, Ralph Martin 1869-1947 *NatCAB 17,
  WhAm 2*
Shaw, Ralph Robert 1907-1972 *DcAmLiB,
  WhAm 5*
Shaw, Ransford W 1856-1945 *NatCAB 36*
Shaw, Reuben T 1884-1949 *WhAm 3*
Shaw, Richard 1887-1958 *WhAm 3*
Shaw, Richard Norman 1831-1912 *McGEWB*
Shaw, Robert 1907-1972 *NatCAB 57,
  WhAm 5, WhAm 6*
Shaw, Robert Alfred 1865-1948 *WhAm 2*
Shaw, Robert Anderson 1870-1941 *WhAm 1*
Shaw, Robert Gould 1776-1853 *ApCAB, Drake*
Shaw, Robert Gould 1837-1863 *AmBi, ApCAB,
  Drake, EncAB, NatCAB 8, TwCBDA,
  WebAMB, WhAm H*
Shaw, Robert Gould 1850-1931 *NatCAB 30*
Shaw, Robert Kendall 1871- *WhAm 5*
Shaw, Robert Lawson 1916- *WebAB*
Shaw, Robert Sidey 1871-1953 *NatCAB 39,
  WhAm 3*
Shaw, Roger 1903-1959 *NatCAB 48,
  WhAm 3*
Shaw, Roy Wilbur 1880-1947 *NatCAB 37*
Shaw, Samuel 1754-1794 *ApCAB, DcAmB,
  Drake, NatCAB 5, WhAm H*
Shaw, Samuel 1768-1827 *BiAUS, BiDrAC,
  WhAm H, WhAmP*
Shaw, Samuel Gormley 1854- *WhAm 4*
Shaw, Silas Frederick 1877- *WhAm 6*
Shaw, Stephen William 1817-1900 *IlBEAAW,
  NewYHSD*
Shaw, Sterling Price 1872-1934 *WhAm 1*
Shaw, Sydney Dale 1879-1946 *IlBEAAW,
  WhAm 6*
Shaw, Thomas 1838-1901 *DcAmB,
  NatCAB 15, WhAm H*
Shaw, Thomas 1843- *WhAm 4*
Shaw, Thomas 1883-1958 *NatCAB 49*
Shaw, Thomas Mott 1878-1965 *NatCAB 51,
  WhAm 4*
Shaw, Thompson Darrah 1801-1874 *ApCAB*
Shaw, Tristam 1787-1843 *BiAUS*
Shaw, Tristram 1786-1843 *BiDrAC, WhAm H*
Shaw, Walter Adam 1866-1951 *WhAm 3*

Shaw, Walter Carlyle 1881-1962 *NatCAB 49,
  WhAm 6*
Shaw, Walter Keith 1868-1933 *WhAm 1*
Shaw, Wilbur 1902-1954 *DcAmB S5*
Shaw, William 1860-1941 *NatCAB 31*
Shaw, William Bristol 1863-1943 *WhAm 2*
Shaw, William Conner 1846- *NatCAB 6*
Shaw, William Edward 1869-1947 *NatCAB 36,
  WhAm 2*
Shaw, William Frederick 1910-1972 *WhAm 5*
Shaw, William James d1939 *WhAm 3*
Shaw, William Miller 1882-1930 *NatCAB 32*
Shaw, William Napier 1854-1945 *DcScB*
Shaw, William Smith 1778-1826 *ApCAB,
  DcAmB, WhAm H*
Shaw, William Tuckerman 1822-1909
  NatCAB 17
Shaw, Wilson Alexander 1846-1928 *NatCAB 12,
  NatCAB 24*
Shawan, Jacob Albright 1850- *NatCAB 14*
Shawan, Robert Foster 1885-1949 *NatCAB 39*
Shawcross, Sir Hartley 1902- *WhWW-II*
Shawhan, Narcissa Tayloe Maupin *WhAm 5*
Shawkey, Morris Purdy 1868-1941 *NatCAB 35,
  WhAm 1*
Shawn, Edwin M 1891-1972 *WhAm 5*
Shawn, Ted 1891-1972 *WebAB*
Shawnee Prophet *AmBi*
Shay, Frank 1888-1954 *WhAm 3*
Shayler, Ernest Vincent 1867-1947 *WhAm 2*
Shayn, Grigory Abramovich 1892-1956 *DcScB*
Shayne, Alexander 1881-1957 *NatCAB 48*
Shayne, Christopher Columbus 1844-
  NatCAB 7
Shayne, Margaret A Sloan *WomWWA 14*
Shays, Daniel 1747-1825 *AmBi, ApCAB,
  DcAmB, Drake, EncAAH, EncAB,
  McGEWB, NatCAB 2, TwCBDA,
  WebAB, WebAMB, WhAm H*
Shays, William P *NewYHSD*
Shazar, Zalman 1889-1974 *WhAm 6*
Shea, Andrew Bernard 1903-1972 *WhAm 5*
Shea, C Bernard 1835-1900 *NatCAB 21*
Shea, Charles Austin 1883-1942 *NatCAB 33*
Shea, Daniel William 1859-1930 *WhAm 1*
Shea, Edmund Burke 1892-1969 *WhAm 5*
Shea, Edward Lane 1892-1963 *NatCAB 52,
  WhAm 4*
Shea, George 1826- *ApCAB*
Shea, James R 1891-1952 *WhAm 3*
Shea, John *NewYHSD*
Shea, John Augustus 1802-1845 *ApCAB,
  Drake*
Shea, John Dawson Gilmary 1824-1892 *AmBi,
  ApCAB, DcAmB, Drake, EncAAH,
  NatCAB 6, TwCBDA, WhAm H*
Shea, John J 1898-1963 *WhAm 4*
Shea, John Joseph 1906-1974 *WhAm 6*
Shea, John Joseph 1922-1968 *WhAm 5*
Shea, Joseph 1829-1881 *NatCAB 2*
Shea, Joseph Bernard 1863-1930 *NatCAB 21,
  WhAm 1*
Shea, Joseph Hooker 1863-1928 *NatCAB 22,
  WhAm 1*
Shea, Lewis Anthony 1899-1971 *WhAm 5*
Shea, Sidney Morgan 1899-1967 *NatCAB 53*
Shea, Thomas Daniel 1894-1963 *NatCAB 50*
Shea, William Joseph 1900-1965 *NatCAB 51,
  WhAm 4*
Sheafe, James 1755-1829 *ApCAB, BiAUS,
  BiDrAC, NatCAB 2, TwCBDA,
  WhAm H*
Sheafer, Arthur Whitcomb 1856-1943 *WhAm 2*
Sheafer, Peter Wenrick 1819- *ApCAB*
Sheaff, Howard Martin 1889-1966 *NatCAB 51*
Sheaffe, Sir Roger Hale 1763-1851 *ApCAB,
  Drake*
Sheaffer, Craig Royer 1897-1961 *WhAm 4*
Sheaffer, Daniel Miller 1885-1960 *WhAm 4*
Sheaffer, M Clyde 1891-1966 *NatCAB 54*
Sheaffer, Walter A 1867-1946 *WhAm 2*
Sheakley, James 1829-1917 *BiDrAC, WhAmP*
Sheakley, James 1830-1917 *BiAUS,
  NatCAB 12*
Shean, Albert 1868-1949 *DcAmB S4*
Shean, Charles M d1925 *WhAm 1*
Shear, Cornelius Lott 1865-1956 *NatCAB 48,
  WhAm 4*

Shear, John Knox 1917-1958 *WhAm 3*
Shear, Theodore Leslie 1880-1945 *DcAmB S3,*
NatCAB 42, WhAm 2
Sheard, Titus 1841-1904 *WhAm 1*
Sheard, Virginia *WomWWA 14*
Sheardown, Annie Fillmore 1859- *AmWom*
Shearer *NewYHSD*
Shearer, Andrew 1850-1934 *WhAm 1*
Shearer, Augustus Hunt 1878-1941 *WhAm 1*
Shearer, Christopher H 1840-1926 *NewYHSD*
Shearer, Frances Burritt *WomWWA 14*
Shearer, George Lewis 1835-1919 *TwCBDA,*
WhAm 1
Shearer, Henry 1868- *WhAm 4*
Shearer, Howard Jacob 1885-1960 *NatCAB 49*
Shearer, J Harry 1868- *WhAm 4*
Shearer, John Bowie 1891-1963 *NatCAB 51*
Shearer, John Bunyan 1832-1919 *TwCBDA,*
WhAm 1
Shearer, John Louis 1857- *WhAm 4*
Shearer, John Sanford 1865-1922 *WhAm 1*
Shearer, Mary Butler 1871- *WomWWA 14*
Shearer, Maurice Edwin 1879- *WhAm 6*
Shearer, Thomas Laidlaw 1859-1946
NatCAB 35
Shearer, Tom Ellas 1906-1965 *WhAm 4,*
WhAm 5
Shearer, William Lete 1880-1971 *NatCAB 56*
Shearin, Hubert Gibson 1878-1919 *WhAm 1*
Shearin, Ruth Marguerite *WomWWA 14*
Shearman, Alfred Neal 1873-1934 *NatCAB 25*
Shearman, Frank Edward 1857-1942
NatCAB 41
Shearman, James A *NewYHSD*
Shearman, Margaret Hilles 1873-
WomWWA 14
Shearman, Sylvester G 1802-1868 *BiAUS*
Shearman, Thomas Gaskell 1834-1900 *AmBi,*
ApCAB, DcAmB, NatCAB 2, TwCBDA,
WhAm 1
Shearman, Thomas Gaskell 1868-1944
NatCAB 34
Shearn, Clarence John 1869-1953 *NatCAB 44,*
WhAm 3
Shears, Jessie E Hunter *WomWWA 14*
Shearson, Edward 1864-1950 *NatCAB 38*
Sheats, Charles Christopher 1839-1904 *BiAUS,*
BiDrAC
Sheats, William Nicholas 1851-1922 *BiDAmEd,*
WhAm 1
Sheatsley, Clarence Valentine 1873-1943
WhAm 2
Sheatsley, Jacob 1859- *WhAm 4*
Shebl, Joseph J 1913- *IIBEAAW*
Sheblessy, John Francis 1873-1938 *NatCAB 29*
Shebosch, John Joseph 1721-1788 *NatCAB 2*
Shecker, Herman *NewYHSD*
Shecut, John Linnaeus Edward Whitridge
1770-1836 *ApCAB, DcAmB, WhAm H*
Shedd, Agnes Jeffrey 1875- *WomWWA 14*
Shedd, Alice M 1870- *WomWWA 14*
Shedd, Clarence Prouty 1887-1973 *WhAm 6*
Shedd, Edward Avery 1851-1922 *ApCAB X*
Shedd, Fred Fuller 1871-1937 *DcAmB S2,*
WhAm 1
Shedd, Frederick 1861-1947 *NatCAB 35*
Shedd, George Clifford 1877-1937 *WhAm 1*
Shedd, Jeannette Bell *WomWWA 14*
Shedd, Joel Herbert 1834-1915 *ApCAB,*
DcAmB, NatCAB 13, WhAm 1
Shedd, John Cutler 1868-1933 *WhAm 1*
Shedd, John Graves 1850-1926 *DcAmB,*
NatCAB 17, WhAm 1
Shedd, Julia Ann Clark 1834- *ApCAB*
Shedd, Kendrick Philander 1866-1953
NatCAB 43
Shedd, Solon 1860-1941 *WhAm 2*
Shedd, Thomas Clark 1890-1959 *NatCAB 47,*
WhAm 3
Shedd, William Alfred 1868- *WhAm 4*
Shedd, William Ambrose 1865-1918 *DcAmB*
Shedd, William Greenough Thayer 1820-1894
AmBi, ApCAB, BiDAmEd, DcAmB,
Drake, NatCAB 7, TwCBDA, WhAm H
Shedden, Lucian Love 1849-1912 *WhAm 1*
Shedden, Robert Fitch 1867-1930 *NatCAB 22*
Shedlock, Marie L 1854-1935 *DcAmLiB*
Shedwick, John *NewYHSD*

Sheean, James B 1863-1941 *WhAm 3*
Sheean, James Vincent 1899-1975 *WhAm 6*
Sheedy, Dennis 1846-1923 *DcAmB, WhAm 1*
Sheedy, Herman James 1898-1967 *NatCAB 54*
Sheedy, Joseph Edward 1881-1955 *WhAm 3*
Sheedy, Morgan John 1896-1955 *NatCAB 45*
Sheedy, Morgan Madden 1853-1939 *NatCAB 6,*
WhAm 1
Sheedy, Winthrop Lawrence 1891-1965
NatCAB 52
Sheehan, Blanche Cecilia Bellamy 1868-
WomWWA 14
Sheehan, Daniel Michael 1902-1967 *WhAm 4A*
Sheehan, Donal 1907-1964 *WhAm 4*
Sheehan, Donald Henry 1917-1974 *WhAm 6*
Sheehan, J Eastman 1855-1951 *ApCAB X,*
WhAm 3
Sheehan, John Charles 1848-1916 *NatCAB 9,*
WhAm 1
Sheehan, John Vincent 1855-1916 *NatCAB 16*
Sheehan, Joseph Raymond 1888-1940 *WhAm 1,*
WhAm 1C
Sheehan, Perley Poore 1875- *WhAm 5*
Sheehan, Robert Francis, Jr. 1879-1947
NatCAB 35, WhAm 2
Sheehan, Robert John 1900-1962 *WhAm 4*
Sheehan, Robert Wade 1903-1971 *WhAm 5*
Sheehan, Timothy J 1835- *WhAm 4*
Sheehan, Timothy Patrick 1909- *BiDrAC*
Sheehan, Walter Brendan 1891-1964
NatCAB 51
Sheehan, William Francis 1859-1917 *ApCAB X,*
NatCAB 4, NatCAB 18, WhAm 1
Sheehan, William Mark 1887-1965 *WhAm 4*
Sheehan, Winfield R 1883-1945 *WhAm 2*
Sheehy, George Alexander 1866- *WhoColR*
Sheehy, Joe Warren 1910-1967 *WhAm 4*
Sheehy, Maurice S 1898-1972 *WhAm 5*
Sheeleigh, Matthias 1821- *ApCAB*
Sheeler, Charles 1883-1965 *BnEnAmA, EncAB,*
McGEWB, WebAB, WhAm 4
Sheely, William Clarence 1902- *WhAm 5*
Sheen, Daniel Robinson 1852- *WhAm 4*
Sheen, Fulton John 1895- *WebAB*
Sheen, M Roy 1884-1947 *NatCAB 37*
Sheep, William L 1881- *WhAm 6*
Sheerin, Charles Wilford 1897-1948 *WhAm 2*
Sheerin, James 1865-1933 *WhAm 1*
Sheerin, John Joseph 1893-1952 *NatCAB 41*
Sheets, Earl Wooddell 1886-1964 *NatCAB 52*
Sheets, Emily Churchill Thompson 1875-
WomWWA 14
Sheets, Frank Thomas 1890-1951 *WhAm 3*
Sheets, Frederick Hill 1859-1928 *NatCAB 21*
Sheets, Harold Frank 1883-1969 *NatCAB 57,*
WhAm 5
Sheets, Henry Eugene 1865-1956 *NatCAB 46*
Sheets, John *NewYHSD*
Sheets, Millard Owen 1907- *IIBEAAW,*
WhAm 4
Sheets, Nan Jane 1885- *IIBEAAW*
Sheffer, Daniel 1783-1880 *BiAUS, BiDrAC,*
WhAm H
Sheffer, Henry Maurice 1883-1964 *WhAm 4*
Sheffey, Daniel 1770-1830 *ApCAB, BiAUS,*
BiDrAC, NatCAB 4, TwCBDA,
WhAm H
Sheffey, Edward Fleming 1865-1933 *WhAm 1*
Sheffield, Ada Eliot 1869- *WomWWA 14*
Sheffield, Alfred Dwight 1871-1961 *WhAm 4*
Sheffield, Clarence Gleason 1885-1946
NatCAB 35
Sheffield, Devello Zelotes 1841-1913 *DcAmB,*
WhAm 1
Sheffield, Flora E Matteson 1861-
WomWWA 14
Sheffield, Frederick 1902-1971 *WhAm 5*
Sheffield, Isaac 1798-1845 *BnEnAmA,*
NewYHSD
Sheffield, J S 1902-1963 *WhAm 4*
Sheffield, James Rockwell 1864-1938 *ApCAB X,*
NatCAB 31, WhAm 1
Sheffield, Joseph Earl 1793-1882 *DcAmB,*
NatCAB 11, TwCBDA, WhAm H
Sheffield, Joseph Earle 1793-1882 *AmBi,*
ApCAB
Sheffield, Rena Cary *WomWWA 14*

Sheffield, Washington Kyle 1886-1969
NatCAB 57
Sheffield, William Henry 1874-1949
NatCAB 37
Sheffield, William Paine 1819-1907 *ApCAB,*
NatCAB 12, TwCBDA, WhAm 1
Sheffield, William Paine 1820-1907 *BiAUS,*
BiDrAC
Sheffield, William Paine 1857-1919 *BiDrAC,*
WhAm 1
Shegogue, Alfred M *NewYHSD*
Shegogue, James Hamilton 1806-1872
NewYHSD
Shegogue, James Henry 1810?-1879 *ApCAB*
Sheil, Bernard J d1969 *WhAm 5*
Sheil, George Knox 1825-1893 *BiAUS*
Shein, Harvey M 1933-1974 *WhAm 6*
Sheinin, John J 1900-1972 *WhAm 5*
Shelabarger, Samuel 1817- *BiAUS*
Shelburne, Lord *WhAm H*
Shelburne, James Madison 1867-1951
NatCAB 38, WhAm 3
Shelburne, Samuel Pinkney 1888-1956
NatCAB 50
Shelby, David Davie 1847-1914 *NatCAB 20,*
NatCAB 21, TwCBDA, WhAm 1
Shelby, Evan 1719-1794 *DcAmB, WebAMB,*
WhAm H
Shelby, Evan 1720-1794 *ApCAB, NatCAB 2*
Shelby, Gertrude Singleton Mathews 1881-1936
WhAm 1
Shelby, Isaac 1750-1826 *AmBi, ApCAB,*
BiAUS, DcAmB, Drake, NatCAB 3,
NatCAB 13, REnAW, TwCBDA,
WebAB, WebAMB, WhAm H
Shelby, John 1786-1859 *NatCAB 2*
Shelby, John Todd 1851-1920 *NatCAB 19,*
WhAm 1
Shelby, Joseph Orville 1830-1897 *BiDConf,*
DcAmB, WebAMB, WhAm H
Shelby, Joseph Orville 1831-1897 *ApCAB Sup,*
NatCAB 6, TwCBDA
Shelby, Peter Paul 1845-1916 *ApCAB X*
Shelby, Philemon Richard 1861-1925
NatCAB 20
Shelby, Robert Evart 1906-1955 *NatCAB 45,*
WhAm 3
Shelby, Thomas Hall 1881- *WhAm 6*
Shelby, William Read 1842-1930 *NatCAB 12,*
NatCAB 17, WhAm 1
Shelden, Carlos Douglas 1840-1904 *BiDrAC,*
WhAm 1, WhAmP
Shelden, Miriam Aldridge 1912-1975 *WhAm 6*
Sheldon, Addison Erwin 1861-1943 *WhAm 2*
Sheldon, Alexander 1766-1836 *ApCAB*
Sheldon, Arthur Frederick 1868-1935
NatCAB 27, WhAm 1
Sheldon, Benjamin Lillibridge 1877-1937
NatCAB 28
Sheldon, Benjamin Robbins 1812-1897
NatCAB 13
Sheldon, Caroline M 1860-1929 *WhAm 1,*
WomWWA 14
Sheldon, Charles 1867-1928 *WhAm 1*
Sheldon, Charles Albert 1898-1966 *NatCAB 51*
Sheldon, Charles Henry 1840-1898 *NatCAB 13,*
TwCBDA
Sheldon, Charles Mills 1866-1928 *WhAm 1*
Sheldon, Charles Monroe 1857-1946 *DcAmB S4,*
DcAmReB, NatCAB 34, TwCBDA,
WhAm 2
Sheldon, Charles Stuart 1842-1929 *NatCAB 25,*
WhAm 1
Sheldon, David Newton 1807-1889 *ApCAB,*
Drake, NatCAB 8, TwCBDA, WhAm H
Sheldon, Dean Ernst 1904-1964 *NatCAB 51*
Sheldon, Dean Howell 1908-1965 *NatCAB 53*
Sheldon, Edith Dudley 1877- *WomWWA 14*
Sheldon, Edward Austin 1823-1897 *AmBi,*
ApCAB, BiDAmEd, DcAmB, NatCAB 7,
WhAm H
Sheldon, Edward Brewster 1886-1946
NatCAB 34, WhAm 2
Sheldon, Edward Schock 1874-1958 *NatCAB 48*
Sheldon, Edward Stevens 1851-1925 *DcAmB,*
NatCAB 6, TwCBDA, WhAm 1
Sheldon, Edward Wright 1858-1934
NatCAB 29, WhAm 1

Sheldon, Emily Evans 1881- *WomWWA 14*
Sheldon, Frederick Beaumont 1856-1927
 WhAm 1
Sheldon, G L 1909-1970 *WhAm 5*
Sheldon, George 1818-1916 *NatCAB 17*
Sheldon, George Lawson 1870-1960 *NatCAB 56,*
 WhAm 3A
Sheldon, George Preston 1847-1909 *WhAm 1*
Sheldon, George Rumsey 1857-1919
 NatCAB 14, WhAm 1
Sheldon, George William 1843-1914 *ApCAB,*
 WhAm 1
Sheldon, Grace Carew 1855- *TwCBDA,*
 WhAm 5, WomWWA 14
Sheldon, Harold Horton 1893-1964 *WhAm 4*
Sheldon, Harry Ellsworth 1862-1937
 NatCAB 28
Sheldon, Helen Mary *WomWWA 14*
Sheldon, Henry Clay 1845-1928 *ApCAB,*
 TwCBDA, WhAm 1
Sheldon, Henry Davidson 1874-1948
 NatCAB 38, WhAm 2
Sheldon, Henry King 1826-1902 *NatCAB 22*
Sheldon, Henry Newton 1843-1926 *DcAmB,*
 NatCAB 20, WhAm 1
Sheldon, James 1817-1887 *TwCBDA*
Sheldon, Jennie Maria Arms *WomWWA 14*
Sheldon, John Lewis 1865-1947 *WhAm 3*
Sheldon, John McFarland 1905-1967
 NatCAB 52, WhAm 4
Sheldon, Joseph 1828-1911 *WhAm 1*
Sheldon, Joshua *NewYHSD*
Sheldon, Lionel Allen 1828-1917 *BiDrAC*
Sheldon, Lionel Allen 1829-1917 *ApCAB,*
 BiAUS
Sheldon, Lionel Allen 1831-1917 *TwCBDA,*
 WhAm 1
Sheldon, Lucy 1788-1889 *NewYHSD*
Sheldon, Mary Downing 1850-1898 *ApCAB,*
 DcAmB, NotAW
Sheldon, Mary French 1846- *AmWom*
Sheldon, Maurice Gerald 1894-1964
 NatCAB 51
Sheldon, Nettie Mae 1878- *WomWWA 14*
Sheldon, Pearl Gertrude 1885- *WomWWA 14*
Sheldon, Percy Ellsworth 1881-1945
 NatCAB 40
Sheldon, Porter 1831-1908 *BiAUS, BiDrAC*
Sheldon, Ralph Crowley 1862-1937 *NatCAB 45*
Sheldon, Ralph Edward 1883-1918 *WhAm 1*
Sheldon, Rowland Caldwell 1876-1936 *WhAm 1*
Sheldon, Roy Horton 1894-1970 *WhAm 5*
Sheldon, Samuel 1862-1920 *NatCAB 14,*
 WhAm 1
Sheldon, Smith 1811-1884 *ApCAB*
Sheldon, Theodore 1853-1905 *NatCAB 15*
Sheldon, Walter Lorenzo 1858-1907 *DcAmB,*
 TwCBDA, WhAm 1
Sheldon, William Adams 1872-1952
 NatCAB 41
Sheldon, William Evarts 1832-1900 *BiDAmEd,*
 DcAmB, NatCAB 5, WhAm H
Sheldon, William Henry 1840-1912 *NewYHSD*
Sheldon, Wilmon Henry 1875- *WhAm 5*
Sheldon, Winthrop Dudley 1839- *WhAm 4*
Sheldon-Williams, Inglis 1870-1940 *IIBEAAW*
Shelekhov, Grigorii Ivanovich 1747-1795
 DcAmB, WhAm H
Sheley, Basil LeRoy 1918-1961 *WhAm 4*
Shelford, Victor E 1877-1968 *WhAm 5*
Shell, George Washington 1831-1899 *BiDrAC*
Shellabarger, Adam 1846-1915 *NatCAB 17*
Shellabarger, Samuel 1817-1896 *ApCAB,*
 BiDrAC, Drake, NatCAB 2, TwCBDA,
 WhAm H
Shellabarger, Samuel 1888-1954 *DcAmB S5,*
 NatCAB 40, NatCAB 47, WhAm 3
Shelley, Charles Miller 1833-1907 *BiDConf,*
 BiDrAC, TwCBDA
Shelley, George Elgin 1873-1955 *WhAm 4*
Shelley, Guy Morrell 1924-1975 *WhAm 6*
Shelley, Harry Rowe 1858-1947 *TwCBDA,*
 WhAm 2
Shelley, Henry Charles *WhAm 5*
Shelley, Henry V 1890-1959 *WhAm 3*
Shelley, John Francis 1905-1974 *BiDrAC,*
 WhAm 6
Shelley, Mary Jane 1832- *AmWom*

Shelley, Oliver Hazard Perry 1875-1943
 WhAm 2
Shelley, Percy Bysshe 1792-1822 *McGEWB*
Shelley, Tully 1892-1966 *WhAm 4*
Shelley, Wayne Leo 1898-1957 *NatCAB 49*
Shelley, William Francis 1908-1968 *NatCAB 54*
Shelmire, Horace Weeks 1886-1965 *WhAm 4*
Shelmire, Lucy Cope 1854- *WomWWA 14*
Shelton, Albert Leroy 1875-1922 *DcAmB*
Shelton, Charles Eldred 1859-1940 *TwCBDA,*
 WhAm 1
Shelton, Don Odell 1867-1941 *WhAm 1*
Shelton, Dwight J 1886-1943 *NatCAB 39*
Shelton, E Kost 1888-1955 *WhAm 3*
Shelton, Edward Mason 1846-1928 *DcAmB*
Shelton, Frederic William 1814-1881 *Drake*
Shelton, Frederick Hart 1866-1924 *NatCAB 24*
Shelton, Frederick William 1814-1881 *ApCAB,*
 NatCAB 9
Shelton, Frederick William 1815-1881 *DcAmB,*
 WhAm H
Shelton, George Gregory 1853-1925
 NatCAB 30
Shelton, Hugh Todd 1891-1965 *NatCAB 51*
Shelton, James N 1872- *WhoColR*
Shelton, Jane DeForest *WhAm 5,*
 WomWWA 14
Shelton, Louise 1867-1934 *WhAm 1*
Shelton, Mary Howe 1860- *WomWWA 14*
Shelton, Orman Leroy 1895-1959 *WhAm 3*
Shelton, Rosalie Tomlinson 1861-
 WomWWA 14
Shelton, Samuel Azariah 1858-1948 *BiDrAC,*
 WhAm 4
Shelton, Thomas Garland 1885-1940
 NatCAB 32
Shelton, Thomas Wall 1870-1931 *WhAm 1*
Shelton, Whitford Huston 1885-1963 *WhAm 4*
Shelton, Willard Ellington 1905-1970 *WhAm 5*
Shelton, William 1798-1883 *ApCAB*
Shelton, William 1824- *TwCBDA*
Shelton, William Arthur 1875- *WhAm 5*
Shelton, William Hazen 1901-1955 *NatCAB 42*
Shelton, William Henry 1840- *TwCBDA,*
 WhAm 4
Shemeley, William Glovier 1887-1958
 NatCAB 46
Shemin, David 1911- *AsBiEn*
Shen, Kua 1031-1095 *DcScB*
Shenehon, Francis Clinton 1861-1939 *WhAm 1*
Sheneman, Hester Mary Dickerson d1969
 WhAm 5
Shenk, Hirmna Herr 1872-1954 *WhAm 3*
Shenk, John Wesley 1875-1959 *WhAm 3*
Shenker, William Scheinbaum 1909-1959
 NatCAB 47
Shenton, Herbert Newhard 1884- *WhAm 1*
Shepard, Alan Bartlett, Jr. 1923- *WebAMB*
Shepard, Andrew N 1862-1934 *WhAm 1,*
 WhAm 1C
Shepard, Annie Bartlett *WomWWA 14*
Shepard, Arthur St. John 1859-1930
 NatCAB 25
Shepard, Benjamin Arthur 1879-1945
 NatCAB 34
Shepard, Bertram David 1907-1966 *WhAm 4*
Shepard, Charles Biddle 1807-1843 *BiAUS,*
 BiDrAC, WhAm H
Shepard, Charles Edward 1848-1928 *WhAm 1*
Shepard, Charles Henry 1825-1910 *WhAm 1*
Shepard, Charles Sidney 1856-1934 *NatCAB 24,*
 WhAm 1
Shepard, Charles Upham 1804-1886 *ApCAB,*
 DcAmB, Drake, NatCAB 5, WhAm H
Shepard, Charles Upham 1842- *ApCAB*
Shepard, Clarence Erasmus 1869-1949
 NatCAB 40
Shepard, Daniel M *NewYHSD*
Shepard, David Chauncey 1828- *ApCAB X*
Shepard, Donald D'Arcy 1894-1966 *NatCAB 51*
Shepard, Earl Dorman 1870- *WhAm 5*
Shepard, Edward Martin 1854-1934
 NatCAB 12, WhAm 1
Shepard, Edward Morse 1850-1911 *DcAmB,*
 NatCAB 17, WhAm 1
Shepard, Edwin Malcolm 1843-1904 *TwCBDA,*
 WhAm 1

Shepard, Elizabeth DeAngelis 1830-1922
 NatCAB 22
Shepard, Ellie Josephine 1854- *WomWWA 14*
Shepard, Elliott Fitch 1833-1893 *AmBi,*
 ApCAB, ApCAB X, NatCAB 1
Shepard, Finley Johnson 1867-1942 *NatCAB 41,*
 WhAm 2
Shepard, Francis Henry 1874-1957 *NatCAB 48*
Shepard, Frank Edward 1865- *WhAm 4*
Shepard, Frank Russell 1868-1952 *WhAm 3*
Shepard, Fred Douglas 1855-1915 *DcAmB,*
 WhAm 1
Shepard, Frederick Job 1850-1934 *WhAm 1*
Shepard, George 1801-1868 *NatCAB 10*
Shepard, George Wanzor 1878-1958 *WhAm 3*
Shepard, Guy Conwell 1873-1938 *WhAm 1*
Shepard, Harriett Elma 1853-1946 *WhAm 2,*
 WomWWA 14
Shepard, Harvey Newton 1848-1936 *WhAm 1*
Shepard, Helen Miller Gould 1868-1938 *AmBi,*
 WhAm 1, WomWWA 14
Shepard, Horace B 1885-1944 *WhAm 2*
Shepard, Irving 1843-1916 *ApCAB*
Shepard, Irwin 1843-1916 *WhAm 1*
Shepard, Isaac Fitzgerald 1816-1889 *ApCAB,*
 TwCBDA
Shepard, James Edward 1875-1947 *BiDAmEd,*
 DcAmB S4, NatCAB 33, WhAm 2,
 WhoColR
Shepard, James Henry 1850-1918 *DcAmB,*
 NatCAB 17, WhAm 1
Shepard, Jean Edward, Jr. 1917-1971
 NatCAB 56
Shepard, Jesse 1848-1927 *AmBi*
Shepard, John, Jr. 1857-1948 *WhAm 2*
Shepard, John Frederick 1881-1965 *WhAm 4*
Shepard, John Leslie 1870-1931 *NatCAB 30*
Shepard, Lawrence Freeman 1887-1952
 NatCAB 47
Shepard, Lorenzo B 1821-1857 *NatCAB 3*
Shepard, Lulu Loveland *WomWWA 14*
Shepard, Luther Dimmick d1911 *WhAm 1*
Shepard, Marguerite 1879- *WomWWA 14*
Shepard, Marguerite Dunbar 1908-1957
 NatCAB 47
Shepard, Odell 1884-1967 *WhAm 4*
Shepard, Oscar Fred, II 1887-1971 *NatCAB 55*
Shepard, Oscar Frederick 1873-1950
 NatCAB 43
Shepard, Pattie Gilliam 1874- *WhoColR*
Shepard, Roger Bulkley 1885-1972 *NatCAB 57*
Shepard, Samuel 1739-1815 *ApCAB*
Shepard, Samuel 1772-1846 *Drake*
Shepard, Seth 1847-1917 *DcAmB, NatCAB 10,*
 WhAm 1
Shepard, Sidney 1814-1893 *NatCAB 22*
Shepard, Stuart Gore 1874-1936 *WhAm 1*
Shepard, Theodore F 1844- *WhAm 4*
Shepard, Thomas 1605-1649 *AmBi, ApCAB,*
 DcAmB, Drake, NatCAB 7, WhAm H
Shepard, Thomas 1635-1677 *ApCAB*
Shepard, Walter James 1876-1936 *NatCAB 44,*
 WhAm 1
Shepard, William 1737-1817 *ApCAB, BiDrAC,*
 DcAmB, Drake, NatCAB 2, WebAMB,
 WhAm H
Shepard, William see also Shepherd, William
Shepard, William Biddle 1799-1852 *BiAUS,*
 BiDrAC, WhAm H
Shepard, William Orville 1862-1931
 NatCAB 24, WhAm 1
Shepard, William Pierce 1870-1948 *WhAm 2*
Shepard, Woolsey Adams 1880-1960 *WhAm 4*
Shepardson, Charles Noah 1896-1975 *WhAm 6*
Shepardson, Francis Wayland 1862-1937
 WhAm 1
Shepardson, Frank Lucius 1861-1952 *WhAm 3*
Shepardson, George Defrees 1864-1926
 NatCAB 21, WhAm 1
Shepardson, John 1729- *NatCAB 8*
Shepardson, Ruth Pearson Chandler 1897-1949
 WhAm 2
Shepardson, Whitney Hart 1890-1966 *WhAm 4*
Sheperd, James Edward 1847-1910 *WhAm 1*
Shepheart, Frederick *NewYHSD*
Shepherd, Alexander Robey 1835-1902 *BiAUS,*
 DcAmB, NatCAB 13, TwCBDA,
 WhAm 1

Shepherd, Arthur 1880-1958 *NatCAB 47,*
  WhAm 4
Shepherd, Charles Reginald 1885-1964
  WhAm 4
Shepherd, Clifford John 1879-1939 *WhAm 1*
Shepherd, Ernest Stanley 1879-1949 *WhAm 2*
Shepherd, Fitch *NewYHSD*
Shepherd, Fred N 1878- *WhAm 6*
Shepherd, G S *NewYHSD*
Shepherd, George M 1823?- *NewYHSD*
Shepherd, Grace M *WhAm 5, WomWWA 14*
Shepherd, Harold 1897-1971 *WhAm 5*
Shepherd, Henry Bush 1906-1967 *NatCAB 54*
Shepherd, Henry Elliot 1844-1929 *ApCAB Sup,*
  NatCAB 33, WhAm 1
Shepherd, Henry Elliott 1844-1929 *TwCBDA*
Shepherd, J Clinton 1888- *IIBEAAW*
Shepherd, James Edward 1846-1910
  NatCAB 12, NatCAB 36
Shepherd, James Leftwich, Jr. 1893-1964
  NatCAB 52, WhAm 4
Shepherd, Jesse Lake 1867-1952 *NatCAB 41*
Shepherd, Judson O'Donald, III 1900-1957
  NatCAB 46
Shepherd, Lemuel Cornick, Jr. 1896- *WebAMB*
Shepherd, Mozelle Miller d1971 *WhAm 6*
Shepherd, N C *NewYHSD*
Shepherd, Nathaniel Graham 1835-1869
  ApCAB, Drake, NatCAB 8
Shepherd, Oliver Lathrop 1815- *ApCAB,*
  Drake
Shepherd, Patricia Drake d1972 *WhAm 5*
Shepherd, Pearce 1901-1969 *WhAm 5*
Shepherd, Russell E 1860-1944 *WhAm 2*
Shepherd, S Brown 1876-1946 *NatCAB 36*
Shepherd, Temperance Elizabeth Caulk 1874-
  WomWWA 14
Shepherd, Theodosia Burr 1845-1906 *WhAm 1*
Shepherd, Thomas Munroe 1856-1923
  NatCAB 6
Shepherd, Thomas S *NewYHSD*
Shepherd, William 1737-1817 *BiAUS,*
  TwCBDA
Shepherd, William *see also* Shepard, William
Shepherd, William Almon 1876-1963
  NatCAB 52
Shepherd, William Chauncey 1874-1966
  WhAm 4
Shepherd, William Chauncy 1874-1966
  NatCAB 55
Shepherd, William Gunn 1878-1933 *WhAm 1*
Shepherd, William Robert 1871-1934
  DcAmB S1, WhAm 1
Shepler, Joseph McGuire 1869-1951 *WhAm 3*
Shepler, Matthias 1790-1863 *BiDrAC,*
  WhAm H
Shepley, Ethan A H 1896-1975 *WhAm 6*
Shepley, Ether 1789-1877 *ApCAB, BiAUS,*
  BiDrAC, DcAmB, Drake, NatCAB 2,
  TwCBDA, WhAm H
Shepley, George Forster 1819-1878 *AmBi,*
  ApCAB
Shepley, George Foster 1819-1878 *BiAUS,*
  DcAmB, Drake, NatCAB 10, TwCBDA,
  WhAm H
Shepley, George Foster 1860-1903 *NatCAB 22,*
  WhAm 1
Shepley, George Leander 1854- *WhAm 1*
Shepley, Henry Richardson 1887-1962
  NatCAB 49, WhAm 4
Shepley, John 1787-1857 *ApCAB, NatCAB 2*
Shepley, John Rutledge 1817-1884 *NatCAB 26*
Sheplor, Matthias *BiAUS*
Shepp, Daniel B 1863-1940 *NatCAB 31*
Sheppard, Edward *NewYHSD*
Sheppard, Edwin W *NewYHSD*
Sheppard, Furman 1823- *ApCAB*
Sheppard, George 1819- *NatCAB 13*
Sheppard, Harper Donelson 1868-1951
  NatCAB 41
Sheppard, Harry Richard 1885-1969 *BiDrAC,*
  WhAm 5, WhAmP
Sheppard, Isaac A 1827- *NatCAB 2*
Sheppard, J Palmer 1875-1935 *NatCAB 26*
Sheppard, J Warren 1880-1943 *NatCAB 39*
Sheppard, Jack Murff 1917-1973 *WhAm 6*
Sheppard, James Carroll 1898-1964 *NatCAB 50,*
  WhAm 4

Sheppard, James J 1868-1914 *WhAm 1*
Sheppard, John Calhoun 1850-1931 *NatCAB 12,*
  WhAm 1
Sheppard, John Hannibal 1789-1873 *ApCAB,*
  Drake
Sheppard, John Levi 1852-1902 *BiDrAC,*
  WhAmP
Sheppard, John Levi 1854-1902 *TwCBDA,*
  WhAm 1
Sheppard, John Morris 1875-1941 *DcAmB S3*
Sheppard, John Rutherford 1873-1945 *WhAm 2*
Sheppard, John Shoemaker 1871-1948
  NatCAB 53, WhAm 2
Sheppard, Lawrence Baker 1897-1968
  NatCAB 54, WhAm 5
Sheppard, Lucius Elmer 1863-1934 *WhAm 1*
Sheppard, Morris 1875-1941 *ApCAB X,*
  BiDrAC, NatCAB 15, NatCAB 34,
  WhAm 2, WhAmP
Sheppard, Moses 1771-1857 *ApCAB*
Sheppard, Nathan 1834-1888 *ApCAB*
Sheppard, Richard H *NewYHSD*
Sheppard, Robert Clay 1914-1964 *NatCAB 50*
Sheppard, Robert Dickinson 1846- *NatCAB 13,*
  WhAm 4
Sheppard, Samuel Edward 1882-1948
  DcAmB S4, NatCAB 52, WhAm 2
Sheppard, Thomas Trovillo 1892-1948
  NatCAB 36
Sheppard, Walter Wade 1856-1935 *WhAm 1*
Sheppard, Warren 1858-1937 *WhAm 1*
Sheppard, Warren Wood 1855-1937
  NatCAB 13
Sheppard, William Bostwick 1860-1934
  WhAm 1
Sheppard, William Henry 1865- *WhAm 4,*
  WhoColR
Sheppard, William Ludlow 1833-1912
  NewYHSD
Sheppard, William Ludwell 1833-1912
  IIBEAAW, NatCAB 19
Shepperd, Augustine Henry 1792-1864 *BiDrAC,*
  WhAm H, WhAmP
Shepperd, Augustus H 1792-1864 *BiAUS*
Shepperd, John Henry 1869-1939 *WhAm 1*
Shepperson, Archibald Bolling 1897-1962
  WhAm 4
Sheppey, Marshall 1869-1945 *WhAm 2*
Sheps, Mindel Cherniack 1913-1973 *WhAm 6*
Shera, Jesse Hauk 1903- *BiDAmEd*
Shera, John Fletcher 1865- *NatCAB 9*
Sherard, William 1659-1728 *DcScB*
Sheraton, James Paterson 1841- *ApCAB*
Sheraton, Thomas 1751-1806 *McGEWB*
Sherbakoff, Constantine Dmitriev 1878-1965
  WhAm 4
Sherberg, Ralph Omer 1905-1972 *NatCAB 56*
Sherbon, Florence Brown 1869-1944 *WhAm 2*
Sherbrooke, Sir John Coape 1760?-1830 *ApCAB,*
  Drake
Sherbune, John Samuel 1757-1830 *TwCBDA*
Sherburne, Andrew 1765-1831 *ApCAB, Drake*
Sherburne, Elmer David 1868-1929 *ApCAB X*
Sherburne, Ernest C 1878-1952 *WhAm 3*
Sherburne, Harold Hewitt 1912-1975 *WhAm 6*
Sherburne, Henry d1824 *Drake, NatCAB 9*
Sherburne, Henry 1674-1757 *NatCAB 13*
Sherburne, John Henry 1794-1850? *ApCAB,*
  Drake
Sherburne, John Henry 1877-1959 *WhAm 4*
Sherburne, John Samuel 1757-1830 *ApCAB,*
  BiAUS, BiDrAC, Drake, WhAm H,
  WhAmP
Sherburne, Mary Patterson Harris 1878-
  WomWWA 14
Sherburne, Moses *BiAUS*
Sherby, Daniel 1908-1954 *WhAm 3*
Shere, Lewis 1895-1971 *NatCAB 55,*
  WhAm 5
Sheredine, Upton 1740-1800 *BiAUS, BiDrAC,*
  WhAm H
Sherer, Albert W 1883-1973 *WhAm 6*
Sherer, Dunham B 1877-1965 *WhAm 4*
Sherer, John *NewYHSD*
Sherer, Rex W 1876- *WhAm 5*
Sherer, Samuel Luckett 1866-1928 *NatCAB 21*
Sherer, William 1837- *NatCAB 9, WhAm 4*
Sheridan, Ann 1915-1967 *WhAm 4*

Sheridan, Edward Francis 1907-1974 *WhAm 6*
Sheridan, Edwin Everitt 1887-1961 *NatCAB 51*
Sheridan, Emma V *AmWom*
Sheridan, George Augustus 1840-1896 *BiDrAC,*
  WhAm H
Sheridan, George Augustus 1842-1896
  NatCAB 3
Sheridan, Harold James 1885-1961 *WhAm 4*
Sheridan, John Edward 1902- *BiDrAC*
Sheridan, John Lawrence 1893-1964 *WhAm 4*
Sheridan, Lawrence Vinnedge 1887-1972
  WhAm 5
Sheridan, Leo J 1897-1975 *WhAm 6*
Sheridan, Michael Stephen 1869-1958
  NatCAB 49
Sheridan, Michael Vincent 1840-1918
  ApCAB Sup, TwCBDA, WhAm 1
Sheridan, Philip Edward Anthony 1884-1965
  NatCAB 51
Sheridan, Philip Henry 1831-1888 *AmBi,*
  ApCAB, DcAmB, Drake, EncAAH,
  EncAB, McGEWB, NatCAB 4, REnAW,
  TwCBDA, WebAB, WebAMB, WhAm H,
  WhoMilH
Sheridan, Richard Brinsley 1751-1816
  McGEWB
Sheridan, Sarah MacDonald 1876- *WhAm 5,*
  WomWWA 14
Sheridan, Thomas Francis 1859- *WhAm 4*
Sheridan, Thomas Harold 1886-1952 *WhAm 3*
Sheridan, Wilbur Fletcher 1863-1920 *WhAm 1*
Sheridan, William E 1839-1887 *NatCAB 2*
Sheridan, William Patrick 1861-1934
  NatCAB 25
Sheriff, Andrew Rothwell 1872- *NatCAB 17*
Sheriff, Robert Cedric 1896-1975 *WhAm 6*
Sherill, George Raymond 1892-1963 *WhAm 4*
Sherk, Florence Nightingale *WomWWA 14*
Sherk, Kenneth Wayne 1907-1972 *WhAm 5*
Sherley, Joseph Swagar 1871-1941 *BiDrAC,*
  WhAmP
Sherley, Swagar 1871-1941 *NatCAB 31,*
  WhAm 1
Sherlock *NewYHSD*
Sherlock, Charles Reginald 1857- *WhAm 4*
Sherlock, Chelsia C 1895-1938 *WhAm 1*
Sherlock, Robert Aloysius 1870-1930
  NatCAB 25
Sherman, A Josephine *WomWWA 14*
Sherman, Alfred Leavenworth 1870-1938
  NatCAB 28
Sherman, Allan 1924-1973 *WhAm 6*
Sherman, Althea Rosina 1853-1943 *WhAm 2*
Sherman, Andrew Magoun 1844-1921 *WhAm 1*
Sherman, Arthur Outram 1864-1949
  NatCAB 44
Sherman, Bertram Evart 1877-1913 *NatCAB 16*
Sherman, Buren Robinson 1836-1904 *ApCAB,*
  NatCAB 11, TwCBDA, WhAm 1
Sherman, Byron 1824-1899 *NatCAB 16*
Sherman, Carl 1890-1956 *NatCAB 45,*
  WhAm 3
Sherman, Carl Benjamin 1915-1974 *WhAm 6*
Sherman, Caroline Kempton 1842-
  WomWWA 14
Sherman, Charles Colebrook 1860-1927
  WhAm 1
Sherman, Charles Day 1843-1927 *NatCAB 39*
Sherman, Charles Lawrence 1905-1968
  WhAm 5
Sherman, Charles Lawton 1894-1954 *WhAm 3*
Sherman, Charles Lewis 1876-1969 *NatCAB 55*
Sherman, Charles Phineas 1874-1962
  NatCAB 50, WhAm 6
Sherman, Charles Pomeroy 1847-1944 *WhAm 2*
Sherman, Charles R 1788-1829 *BiAUS, Drake*
Sherman, Charles T *BiAUS*
Sherman, Christopher Elias 1869-1940
  NatCAB 29, WhAm 1
Sherman, Clarence Edgar 1887-1974 *DcAmLiB*
Sherman, Clifford Gould 1887-1964 *WhAm 4*
Sherman, Clifton Lucien 1866-1946 *WhAm 2*
Sherman, DeWitt Halsey 1864-1940
  NatCAB 41
Sherman, Edgar Jay 1902-1973 *WhAm 6*
Sherman, Edgar Leslie 1873-1946 *NatCAB 38*
Sherman, Edward Augustine 1871-1940
  WhAm 1

Sherman, Edwin Allen 1829-1914 *NewYHSD*
Sherman, Eleanor Boyle Ewing 1824-1888
  AmWom
Sherman, Elijah Bernis 1832-1910 *NatCAB 3,*
  WhAm 1
Sherman, Ellen Amelia 1849- *WomWWA 14*
Sherman, Ellen Burns 1867-1956 *NatCAB 46,*
  WhAm 3, WomWWA 14
Sherman, Forrest Percival 1896-1951
  DcAmB S5, WebAMB, WhAm 3
Sherman, Frank A 1887- *WhAm 4*
Sherman, Frank Asbury 1841-1915 *NatCAB 9,*
  WhAm 1
Sherman, Frank Dempster 1860-1916 *DcAmB,*
  NatCAB 7, TwCBDA, WhAm 1
Sherman, Frank Maynard 1879-1960
  NatCAB 44
Sherman, Franklin 1877-1947 *WhAm 2*
Sherman, Frederick Carl 1888-1957 *NatCAB 46,*
  WhAm 3, WhWW-II
Sherman, George E 1810?- *NewYHSD*
Sherman, Georgiana H *WhoColR*
Sherman, Gordon Edward 1854-1925 *WhAm 1*
Sherman, H M, Jr. 1906-1966 *WhAm 4*
Sherman, Harry Bartine 1865-1932 *NatCAB 24*
Sherman, Harry Mitchell 1854-1921
  NatCAB 21, WhAm 1
Sherman, Helen 1879- *WomWWA 14*
Sherman, Henry 1808-1879 *ApCAB, BiAUS,*
  TwCBDA
Sherman, Henry Clapp 1875-1955 *AsBiEn,*
  DcAmB S5, NatCAB 45, WhAm 3
Sherman, Henry John 1869-1952 *NatCAB 42*
Sherman, Henry Stoddard 1879-1956
  NatCAB 45, WhAm 3
Sherman, Homer Henkel 1870-1948 *WhAm 2*
Sherman, Hoyt 1827-1904 *WhAm 1*
Sherman, J W 1808-1881 *BiAUS*
Sherman, J W *see also* Sherman, Judson W
Sherman, James Morgan 1890-1956
  NatCAB 47, WhAm 3
Sherman, James Schoolcraft 1855-1912 *AmBi,*
  ApCAB X, BiDrAC, BiDrUSE, DcAmB,
  NatCAB 14, WebAB, WhAm 1, WhAmP
Sherman, John 1613-1685 *ApCAB, DcAmB,*
  Drake, NatCAB 7, WhAm H
Sherman, John 1772-1828 *ApCAB, Drake*
Sherman, John 1823-1900 *AmBi, ApCAB,*
  BiAUS, BiDrAC, BiDrUSE, DcAmB,
  Drake, EncAAH, EncAB, McGEWB,
  NatCAB 3, TwCBDA, WebAB, WhAm 1,
  WhAmP
Sherman, John Ames 1852- *NatCAB 13*
Sherman, John Dickinson 1859-1926 *WhAm 1*
Sherman, John Francis 1888-1934 *WhAm 1*
Sherman, John H *NewYHSD*
Sherman, John James 1913-1973 *WhAm 6*
Sherman, John K 1898-1969 *WhAm 5*
Sherman, Judson W 1808-1881 *BiDrAC,*
  WhAm H
Sherman, Judson W *see also* Sherman, J W
Sherman, Juliet Durand 1868- *WomWWA 14*
Sherman, Lawrence William, Jr. 1928-1969
  WhAm 5
Sherman, Lawrence Yates 1858-1939 *BiDrAC,*
  NatCAB 15, WhAm 1
Sherman, Lenore Walton 1920- *IlBEAAW*
Sherman, Leora Chase *WomWWA 14*
Sherman, Lewis Frank 1917-1974 *WhAm 6*
Sherman, Loren Albert 1844-1914 *NatCAB 16*
Sherman, Louis Ralph 1886-1953 *WhAm 3*
Sherman, Lucius Adelno 1847-1933 *NatCAB 8,*
  NatCAB 24, WhAm 1
Sherman, Lucy McFarland 1838-1878
  NewYHSD
Sherman, Margaret Stewart *AmWom*
Sherman, Marrietta R 1862- *AmWom*
Sherman, Mary Belle King 1862-1935 *NotAW,*
  WhAm 1
Sherman, Mary Isabella 1852- *WomWWA 14*
Sherman, Maurice Sinclair 1873-1947 *WhAm 2*
Sherman, Merritt Masters 1854-1937 *WhAm 1*
Sherman, Mildred P 1898-1961 *WhAm 4*
Sherman, Moses Hazeltine 1853-1932
  ApCAB X, WhAm 1
Sherman, Mrs. P A *NewYHSD*
Sherman, Philemon Tecumseh 1867- *WhAm 4*
Sherman, Philip Darrell 1881-1957 *NatCAB 46*

Sherman, Philip Francis 1898-1973 *WhAm 6*
Sherman, Ray Eugene 1885-1947 *WhAm 2*
Sherman, Robert Minot 1773-1844 *BiAUS*
Sherman, Roger 1721-1793 *AmBi, ApCAB,*
  BiAUS, BiDrAC, DcAmB, Drake,
  EncAB, McGEWB, NatCAB 2,
  TwCBDA, WebAB, WhAm H, WhAmP
Sherman, Roger 1872-1957 *WhAm 3*
Sherman, Roger Minot 1773-1844 *ApCAB,*
  Drake
Sherman, Roger Minot 1773-1844 *NatCAB 11*
Sherman, Roger Minott 1773-1844 *NatCAB 11*
Sherman, Ruth Bartlett Mears *WomWWA 14*
Sherman, Sidney 1805-1873 *NatCAB 2*
Sherman, Socrates Norton 1801-1873 *BiAUS,*
  BiDrAC, WhAm H
Sherman, Stephen Fish 1874-1936 *NatCAB 27*
Sherman, Stuart Pratt 1881-1926 *AmBi,*
  DcAmB, NatCAB 21
Sherman, Stuart Pratt 1881-1927 *WhAm 1*
Sherman, Thomas B 1891-1968 *WhAm 5*
Sherman, Thomas Ewing 1856- *WhAm 4*
Sherman, Thomas Townsend 1853-1931
  WhAm 1
Sherman, Thomas West 1813-1879 *ApCAB,*
  DcAmB, Drake, NatCAB 8, TwCBDA,
  WebAMB, WhAm H
Sherman, Wells Alvord 1868-1939 *WhAm 1*
Sherman, William Arthur 1878-1950 *WhAm 3*
Sherman, William Bowen 1907-1971 *WhAm 5*
Sherman, William Carrington 1888-1927
  NatCAB 21
Sherman, William O'Neill 1880-1954
  NatCAB 43, WhAm 3
Sherman, William Tecumseh 1820-1891 *AmBi,*
  ApCAB, BiAUS, BiDrUSE, DcAmB,
  Drake, EncAB, McGEWB, NatCAB 4,
  REnAW, TwCBDA, WebAB, WebAMB,
  WhAm H, WhoMilH
Sherman, William Watts 1842-1912
  NatCAB 30
Sherman, William Winslow 1833-1908 *WhAm 1*
Shero, Lucius Rogers 1891-1968 *WhAm 5*
Shero, William Francis 1863-1943 *WhAm 2*
Sherpick, Eugene Arthur 1895-1964 *WhAm 4*
Sherrard, Charles Cornell 1857- *WhAm 4*
Sherrard, Glenwood John 1895-1958 *WhAm 3*
Sherrard, Thomas Herrick 1874-1941 *WhAm 1*
Sherred, Jacob 1756-1821 *ApCAB Sup*
Sherrerd, William D 1816-1869 *WhAm H*
Sherriff, Andrew Rothwell 1872-1935
  NatCAB 18, WhAm 1
Sherrill, Alvan Foote 1842- *WhAm 4*
Sherrill, Charles Hitchcock 1867-1936 *AmBi,*
  NatCAB 14, NatCAB 37, WhAm 1
Sherrill, Clarence Osborne 1876-1959
  NatCAB 49, WhAm 5
Sherrill, Edwin Stanton 1854- *WhAm 4*
Sherrill, Eliakim 1813-1863 *BiAUS, BiDrAC,*
  NatCAB 13, WhAm H
Sherrill, Flake Anderson 1899-1963 *NatCAB 52*
Sherrill, Frank Ceburn 1871-1942 *NatCAB 35*
Sherrill, Gibbs Wynkoop 1908-1957 *WhAm 3*
Sherrill, J Garland 1868-1949 *NatCAB 38*
Sherrill, James Winn 1890-1955 *NatCAB 43,*
  WhAm 3
Sherrill, John Bascom 1864-1934 *WhAm 1*
Sherrill, Lewis Joseph 1892-1957 *WhAm 3*
Sherrill, Miles Osborne 1841-1919 *WhAm 1*
Sherrill, Miles Standish 1877-1965 *WhAm 4*
Sherrill, R E 1899-1953 *WhAm 3*
Sherrill, Ruth Erwin 1900-1952 *WhAm 4*
Sherrill, Samuel Wells 1869- *WhAm 5*
Sherrill, Stephen H 1893-1956 *WhAm 3*
Sherrill, William Lander 1860- *WhAm 5*
Sherrington, Sir Charles Scott 1857-1952
  AsBiEn, BiHiMed, DcScB, McGEWB
Sherrod, Charles Chester 1882-1967
  NatCAB 53
Sherrod, Daniel Webster 1867- *WhoColR*
Sherrod, William Crawford 1835-1919 *BiAUS,*
  BiDrAC
Sherry, George Gregory 1929-1964 *WhAm 4*
Sherry, Louis 1856-1926 *DcAmB*
Sherts, J Hervey 1892-1969 *NatCAB 55*
Sherwell, G Butler 1904-1963 *WhAm 4*
Sherwell, Guillermo Antonio 1878-1926
  WhAm 1
Sherwin, Belle 1868-1955 *WhAm 3*

Sherwin, Carl Paxson 1885-1974 *WhAm 6*
Sherwin, Donald George 1894-1942 *NatCAB 31*
Sherwin, Henry Alden 1842-1916 *NatCAB 21,*
  WhAm 1
Sherwin, Isabel Fiske 1845- *WomWWA 14*
Sherwin, John Collins 1851-1919 *NatCAB 30*
Sherwin, John Collins 1852-1919 *WhAm 1*
Sherwin, John Crocker 1838-1904 *BiDrAC*
Sherwin, John H 1834- *NewYHSD*
Sherwin, Proctor Fenn 1891-1958 *WhAm 3*
Sherwin, Ralph Sidney 1876-1957 *WhAm 3*
Sherwin, Thomas *NewYHSD*
Sherwin, Thomas 1799-1869 *ApCAB, DcAmB,*
  Drake, NatCAB 11, WhAm H
Sherwin, Thomas 1799-1899 *BiDAmEd*
Sherwin, Thomas 1839-1914 *ApCAB X,*
  NatCAB 17, WhAm 1
Sherwood, A *NewYHSD*
Sherwood, Adiel 1791-1879 *ApCAB, DcAmB,*
  NatCAB 6, TwCBDA, WhAm H
Sherwood, Andrew 1848-1933 *WhAm 1*
Sherwood, Arnold Cooper 1892-1970 *WhAm 5*
Sherwood, Austin O *ApCAB X*
Sherwood, Carl G 1855-1938 *NatCAB 44,*
  WhAm 1
Sherwood, Carlton Montgomery 1895-1970
  WhAm 5
Sherwood, Emily Lee 1839- *WhAm 4*
Sherwood, Emily Lee 1843- *AmWom*
Sherwood, George Edward 1872-1957
  NatCAB 47
Sherwood, George Herbert 1876-1937
  NatCAB 28, WhAm 1
Sherwood, Grace Mabel 1884- *WomWWA 14*
Sherwood, Granville Hudson 1878-1923
  NatCAB 20, WhAm 1
Sherwood, Harold Homer 1891-1964
  NatCAB 51
Sherwood, Henry *NewYHSD*
Sherwood, Henry 1813-1896 *BiDrAC,*
  WhAm H
Sherwood, Henry 1817-1896 *BiAUS*
Sherwood, Henry J *NewYHSD*
Sherwood, Herbert Francis 1872-1930 *WhAm 1,*
  WhAm 1C
Sherwood, Isaac R 1835-1925 *BiAUS, BiDrAC,*
  DcAmB, NatCAB 2, TwCBDA,
  WhAm 1, WhAmP
Sherwood, J P *NewYHSD*
Sherwood, James Manning 1814-1890 *ApCAB,*
  TwCBDA
Sherwood, Jean 1848- *WomWWA 14*
Sherwood, Mrs. John *NotAW*
Sherwood, John D 1818- *ApCAB*
Sherwood, Jonathan William 1864-1944
  NatCAB 33
Sherwood, Josephine *WomWWA 14*
Sherwood, Kate Brownlee 1841-1914 *AmWom*
Sherwood, Katharine Margaret Brownlee
  1841-1914 *DcAmB, NotAW, TwCBDA,*
  WhAm 1
Sherwood, Katherine Margaret Brownlee
  1841-1914 *NatCAB 2, WomWWA 14*
Sherwood, Margaret Pollock 1864-1955
  WhAm 3, WomWWA 14
Sherwood, Mary 1856-1935 *NotAW,*
  WomWWA 14
Sherwood, Mary C 1839- *WomWWA 14*
Sherwood, Mary Elizabeth Wilson 1826-1903
  DcAmB, NotAW
Sherwood, Mary Elizabeth Wilson 1830-1903
  AmWom, ApCAB, NatCAB 5, TwCBDA,
  WhAm 1
Sherwood, Noble Pierce 1882-1961 *WhAm 4*
Sherwood, Paul James 1866-1929 *NatCAB 22*
Sherwood, Robert Emmet 1896-1955
  DcAmB S5, McGEWB, WebAB,
  WhAm 3
Sherwood, Rosina Emmet 1854-1948 *AmWom,*
  NatCAB 17, WhAm 3, WomWWA 14
Sherwood, Samuel 1779-1862 *BiAUS, BiDrAC,*
  WhAm H
Sherwood, Samuel Burr 1767-1833 *BiAUS,*
  BiDrAC, WhAm H
Sherwood, Sidney 1860-1901 *WhAm 1*
Sherwood, Thomas Adiel 1834-1918 *DcAmB,*
  NatCAB 7, TwCBDA, WhAm 4
Sherwood, Thomas Kilgore 1903-1976 *WhAm 6*

Sherwood, Thomas Russell 1827- *NatCAB 12*
Sherwood, Walker Fanton 1859-1947
 NatCAB 43
Sherwood, William 1875-1951 *WhAm 3*
Sherwood, William Carman 1871-1936
 NatCAB 27
Sherwood, William Davies 1883-1959
 NatCAB 48
Sherwood, William Hall 1854-1911 *AmBi,*
 ApCAB, DcAmB, NatCAB 9, TwCBDA,
 WhAm 1
Sherwood-Dunn, Berkeley *WhAm 5*
Sherzer, Allen Firman 1890-1962 *NatCAB 49*
Sherzer, Jane B *WomWWA 14*
Sherzer, William Hittell 1860-1932 *WhAm 1*
Shettel, Raymond 1913-1967 *NatCAB 53*
Shetter, Stella Cross 1880-1936 *WhAm 1*
Sheue *NewYHSD*
Shevelson, S Harris 1916-1959 *WhAm 3*
Shevlin, Edwin Charles 1867-1927 *NatCAB 26*
Shevlin, Edwin Leonard 1898-1950 *NatCAB 38*
Shevlin, Thomas Henry 1852-1912 *ApCAB X*
Shevlin, Thomas Leonard 1883-1915 *ApCAB X,*
 NatCAB 18
Shew, Joel 1816-1855 *ApCAB, Drake*
Shewan, Edwin Arthur 1877-1945 *NatCAB 33*
Shewan, James 1848-1914 *NatCAB 17,*
 NatCAB 26
Shewhart, Walter Andrew 1891-1967 *WhAm 4*
Shewmake, John Troup 1826-1898 *BiDConf*
Shewmake, Oscar Lane 1882-1963 *WhAm 4*
Shewman, Eben B 1876-1959 *WhAm 3*
Sheys, William P *NewYHSD*
Shiber, Etta 1878-1948 *WhAm 2*
Shibley, Alice Smith Patterson 1862- *WhAm 4*
Shibukawa, Harumi 1639-1715 *DcScB*
Shick, William Franklin 1864-1928 *NatCAB 21*
Shick Calamys d1748 *DcAmB*
Shidehara, Baron Kijuro 1872- *WhAm 5*
Shideler, James Henry 1914- *EncAAH*
Shideler, W H 1886-1958 *WhAm 3*
Shidy, Leland Perry 1851-1935 *WhAm 1*
Shiek, Harriet L 1873- *WomWWA 14*
Shiel, George Knox 1825-1893 *BiDrAC,*
 WhAm H, WhAmP
Shield, Lansing P d1960 *WhAm 3, WhAm 4*
Shields *NewYHSD*
Shields, A C d1943 *WhAm 2*
Shields, Albert Stepney Latchworth 1850-1916
 NatCAB 18
Shields, Albert William 1885-1956 *NatCAB 47*
Shields, Benjamin Glover 1808- *BiAUS,*
 BiDrAC, NatCAB 13, WhAm H
Shields, Charles *NewYHSD*
Shields, Charles R 1861-1939 *WhAm 1*
Shields, Charles Woodruff 1825-1904 *ApCAB,*
 DcAmB, Drake, NatCAB 13, TwCBDA,
 WhAm 1
Shields, Charlotte Elliott 1880- *WomWWA 14*
Shields, Clarence Vance 1883-1943 *NatCAB 46*
Shields, E Southard 1883-1950 *NatCAB 40*
Shields, Ebenezer J 1778-1846 *BiAUS, BiDrAC,*
 WhAm H
Shields, Edmund Claude 1871-1947 *WhAm 2*
Shields, Edwin John 1912-1973 *WhAm 6*
Shields, Edwin Willis 1866-1920 *NatCAB 43*
Shields, Emily L 1883-1964 *WhAm 4*
Shields, G O 1846-1925 *WhAm 1*
Shields, George Howell 1842-1924 *DcAmB,*
 WhAm 1
Shields, George Oliver 1846-1925 *DcAmB*
Shields, George Robert 1879-1947 *WhAm 2*
Shields, James 1762-1831 *BiAUS, BiDrAC,*
 WhAm H
Shields, James 1806-1879 *AmBi, DcAmB,*
 WebAMB
Shields, James 1810-1879 *ApCAB, BiAUS,*
 BiDrAC, Drake, NatCAB 8, TwCBDA,
 WhAm H, WhAmP
Shields, James Percy 1889-1953 *NatCAB 43*
Shields, John Franklin 1869-1947 *WhAm 2*
Shields, John Knight 1855-1934 *NatCAB 26*
Shields, John Knight 1858-1934 *AmBi,*
 BiDrAC, DcAmB S1, WhAm 1, WhAmP
Shields, Litton Edward 1852-1933 *NatCAB 24*
Shields, Lytton James 1887-1936 *NatCAB 35*
Shields, Mary 1820-1880 *ApCAB, NatCAB 3*
Shields, Patrick Henry 1773-1848 *ApCAB,*
 TwCBDA

Shields, Paul Vincent 1889-1962 *WhAm 4*
Shields, Roy Franklin 1888-1966 *NatCAB 56,*
 WhAm 4
Shields, Thomas Edward 1862-1921 *BiDAmEd,*
 DcAmB, WhAm 1
Shields, Thomas H *NewYHSD*
Shields, Thomas Todhunter 1873-1955 *WhAm 3*
Shields, William *NewYHSD*
Shields, William Bayard *BiAUS*
Shields, William S 1853-1933 *WhAm 1*
Shiels, Albert 1865-1940 *WhAm 1*
Shiels, George Franklin 1863-1943 *WhAm 2*
Shiels, James 1902-1968 *WhAm 5*
Shiels, William *NewYHSD*
Shientag, Bernard Lloyd 1887- *WhAm 3*
Shier, Calrton S 1875-1957 *WhAm 3*
Shifferstine, Edgar Efraim 1876-1948
 NatCAB 39
Shifflet, Glynne Williams 1907-1971
 NatCAB 57
Shigemitsu, Mamoru 1881-1957 *WhWW-II*
Shigemitsu, Mamoru 1887-1957 *WhAm 3*
Shigg, William *NewYHSD*
Shih, Ko-Fa d1644 *McGEWB*
Shih, Le 274-333 *McGEWB*
Shikellamy d1748 *DcAmB, WhAm H*
Shillaber, Benjamin Penhallow 1814-1890 *AmBi,*
 ApCAB, DcAmB, Drake, NatCAB 6,
 TwCBDA, WhAm H
Shillady, John R 1875- *WhAm 5*
Shilling, Alexander d1937 *WhAm 1*
Shillinglaw, David Lee 1889-1976 *WhAm 6*
Shiloah, Reuven 1909-1959 *WhAm 3*
Shilov, Nikolay Aleksandrovich 1872-1930
 DcScB
Shimeall, Richard Cunningham 1803-1874
 ApCAB
Shimek, Bohumil 1861- *WhAm 1*
Shimer, Florence Henry 1879- *WomWWA 14*
Shimer, Hervey Woodburn 1872-1965 *WhAm 4*
Shimer, Porter William 1857-1938 *NatCAB 29,*
 WhAm 1
Shimer, William Robert 1883-1946 *NatCAB 35*
Shimmon, John Gill 1884-1945 *NatCAB 35*
Shimonsky *NewYHSD*
Shimp, Herbert Gilby 1887-1943 *NatCAB 31,*
 WhAm 2
Shindler, A Zeno 1813?- *NewYHSD*
Shindler, Mary Stanley Bunce Palmer 1810-
 ApCAB, Drake
Shine, Francis Eppes 1871-1922 *WhAm 1*
Shine, James Henry 1846-1920 *NatCAB 37*
Shingask *ApCAB*
Shingle, John Delroy 1883-1962 *NatCAB 56*
Shingle, Robert Witt 1876-1935 *NatCAB 38*
Shingler, Don Gilmore 1896-1963 *NatCAB 50,*
 WhAm 4
Shinkle, A Clifford 1877-1944 *NatCAB 34*
Shinkle, Edward Marsh 1878-1966 *WhAm 4*
Shinkman, Paul Alfred 1897-1975 *WhAm 6*
Shinn, Anne O'Hagan *WomWWA 14*
Shinn, Asa 1781-1853 *ApCAB, DcAmB,*
 WhAm H
Shinn, Charles Howard 1852-1924 *NatCAB 10,*
 TwCBDA, WhAm 1
Shinn, Charles Moses 1847-1931 *NatCAB 22*
Shinn, Everett 1876-1953 *BnEnAmA,*
 DcAmB S5, WhAm 3
Shinn, Everett 1876-1955 *NatCAB 44*
Shinn, Florence Scovel d1940 *WhAm 1,*
 WomWWA 14
Shinn, George Wolfe 1839-1910 *ApCAB,*
 NatCAB 5, TwCBDA, WhAm 1
Shinn, Henry Arthur 1890-1948 *WhAm 2*
Shinn, James Thornton 1834-1907 *NatCAB 25*
Shinn, John Calvin 1918-1973 *WhAm 6*
Shinn, Josiah Hazen 1849-1917 *BiDAmEd*
Shinn, Milicent Washburn 1858-1940 *NotAW,*
 WhAm 1, WomWWA 14
Shinn, Richard Randolph 1889-1950
 NatCAB 39
Shinn, William Norton 1782-1871 *BiAUS,*
 BiDrAC, WhAm H
Shinn, William Powell 1834-1892 *ApCAB Sup,*
 NatCAB 11
Shinran 1173-1262 *McGEWB*
Shipherd, H Robinson 1878- *WhAm 6*

Shipherd, John Jay 1802-1844 *DcAmB,*
 NatCAB 2, WhAm H
Shipherd, Zebulon Rudd 1768-1841 *BiAUS,*
 BiDrAC, WhAm H
Shiple, George J 1891-1958 *WhAm 3*
Shipley, Antoinette Cary 1871- *WomWWA 14*
Shipley, Caleb Wright 1861-1940 *NatCAB 31*
Shipley, Charles Raymond 1883-1961 *WhAm 4*
Shipley, Edward Ellis 1861- *WhAm 4*
Shipley, Frederick William 1871-1945
 NatCAB 17, WhAm 2
Shipley, George 1867-1944 *WhAm 2*
Shipley, George Edward 1927- *BiDrAC*
Shipley, Grant Batchelder 1880-1962
 NatCAB 48
Shipley, Henry H 1830?- *NewYHSD*
Shipley, Katharine Morris 1867-1929
 NatCAB 23
Shipley, Maynard 1872-1934 *WhAm 1*
Shipley, Richard Larkin 1879-1947 *WhAm 2*
Shipley, Samuel R 1828-1908 *WhAm 1*
Shipley, Walter Cleveland 1903-1966
 NatCAB 54
Shipley, Walter Penn 1860-1942 *WhAm 2*
Shipley, William *NewYHSD*
Shipley, William 1693- *NatCAB 12*
Shipley, William Stewart 1879-1951
 NatCAB 39, WhAm 3
Shipman, Andrew Jackson 1857-1915 *DcAmB,*
 NatCAB 15
Shipman, Arthur Leffingwell 1864-1937
 WhAm 1
Shipman, Benjamin Jonson 1853- *WhAm 4*
Shipman, Carolyn *WomWWA 14*
Shipman, George Elias 1820- *ApCAB*
Shipman, Herbert 1869-1930 *NatCAB 18,*
 WhAm 1
Shipman, Jacob Shaw 1832-1905 *NatCAB 18*
Shipman, James Shelby 1898-1969 *NatCAB 54*
Shipman, Louis Evan 1869-1933 *NatCAB 45,*
 WhAm 1
Shipman, Nathaniel 1828-1906 *BiAUS,*
 NatCAB 19, TwCBDA, WhAm 1
Shipman, Paul Roberts 1827-1917 *ApCAB X*
Shipman, Samuel d1937 *WhAm 1*
Shipman, William Davis 1818-1898
 ApCAB Sup, NatCAB 11, TwCBDA
Shipman, William Rollin 1836-1908 *WhAm 1*
Shipp, Albert Micajah 1819-1887 *ApCAB,*
 DcAmB, NatCAB 9, TwCBDA,
 WhAm H
Shipp, Barnard 1813- *TwCBDA, WhAm 4*
Shipp, Bernard 1813- *ApCAB*
Shipp, Cameron 1903-1961 *WhAm 4*
Shipp, D Harvey 1908-1966 *NatCAB 52*
Shipp, Frederic B 1868-1932 *WhAm 1*
Shipp, Jesse Allison 1864- *NatCAB 14*
Shipp, Leland Parmater 1904-1969 *NatCAB 55*
Shipp, Margaret Busbee 1871- *WomWWA 14*
Shipp, Scott 1839-1917 *DcAmB, NatCAB 25,*
 TwCBDA, WebAMB, WhAm 1
Shipp, Thomas Roerty d1952 *WhAm 3*
Shippee, Lester Burrell 1879-1944 *WhAm 2*
Shippee, Wanton Allen 1847-1922 *NatCAB 25*
Shippen, Edward 1639-1712 *ApCAB, DcAmB,*
 NatCAB 10, NatCAB 18, WhAm H
Shippen, Edward 1703-1781 *ApCAB,*
 TwCBDA
Shippen, Edward 1728?-1806 *DcAmB,*
 McGEWB
Shippen, Edward 1729-1806 *ApCAB, BiAUS,*
 Drake, NatCAB 10, TwCBDA, WhAm H
Shippen, Edward 1821- *ApCAB*
Shippen, Edward 1826-1911 *ApCAB,*
 NatCAB 10, WhAm 1
Shippen, Eugene Rodman 1865-1959 *WhAm 3*
Shippen, Georgiana Truman *WomWWA 14*
Shippen, Joseph 1679-1741 *ApCAB*
Shippen, Joseph 1732-1810 *ApCAB*
Shippen, Joseph 1839-1923 *WhAm 1*
Shippen, Margaret 1760-1804 *AmBi*
Shippen, Rush Rhees 1828- *WhAm 1*
Shippen, William 1712-1801 *ApCAB, BiDrAC,*
 Drake, NatCAB 10, TwCBDA, WhAm H
Shippen, William, Jr. d1808 *BiAUS*
Shippen, William, Jr. 1735-1808 *Drake*
Shippen, William, Jr. 1736-1808 *ApCAB,*
 BiDAmEd, BiHiMed, DcAmB,

NatCAB 10, TwCBDA, WhAm H
Shipper *NewYHSD*
Shipper, Nicholas L *NewYHSD*
Shippey, Lee 1884-1969 *WhAm 5*
Shippin, William 1745?-1777 *ApCAB*
Ships, Nicholas *NewYHSD*
Shipsey, Edward 1890-1954 *WhAm 3*
Shipstead, Henrik 1881-1960 *ApCAB X,
BiDrAC, WhAm 4, WhAmP*
Shipton, A W 1893-1964 *WhAm 4*
Shipton, Audus Walton 1893-1964 *NatCAB 51*
Shipton, Clifford Kenyon 1902-1973 *DcAmLiB*
Shipton, Clifford Kenyon 1902-1974 *WhAm 6*
Shipton, James Ancil 1867-1926 *WhAm 1*
Shir, Martin M 1897-1974 *WhAm 6*
Shira, John William 1886-1963 *NatCAB 50*
Shirakatsi, Anania 620?-685? *DcScB*
Shiras, Alexander Eakin 1812-1875 *ApCAB*
Shiras, George, III 1859-1942 *BiDrAC,
WhAm 2*
Shiras, George, Jr. 1832-1924 *ApCAB Sup,
DcAmB, NatCAB 2, TwCBDA, WebAB,
WhAm 1*
Shiras, Oliver Perry 1833-1916 *DcAmB,
TwCBDA, WhAm 1*
Shirazi, Al- *DcScB*
Shire, Moses 1857-1913 *NatCAB 45*
Shirer, John Wesley 1899-1974 *WhAm 6*
Shirer, William Lawrence 1904- *WebAB*
Shires, Henry Herbert 1886-1961 *NatCAB 48*
Shirk, A Urban 1890-1956 *NatCAB 43*
Shirk, Ida Morrison Murphy 1860-
WomWWA 14
Shirk, James W d1873 *NatCAB 5*
Shirk, Joseph Henry 1881-1953 *NatCAB 44*
Shirlaw, Walter 1838-1909 *AmBi, ApCAB,
BnEnAmA, DcAmB, IlBEAAW,
NatCAB 11, NewYHSD, TwCBDA,
WhAm 1*
Shirley, Dame *NotAW*
Shirley, Archie Turner 1863- *WhoColR*
Shirley, Cassius Clay 1859- *WhAm 4*
Shirley, John Milton 1831-1887 *ApCAB*
Shirley, Paul 1820-1876 *ApCAB*
Shirley, Robert Kirby 1899-1956 *WhAm 3*
Shirley, William 1693-1771 *ApCAB, Drake,
NatCAB 7*
Shirley, William 1694-1771 *AmBi, DcAmB,
WebAB, WhAm H*
Shirley, William Wayne 1900-1973 *DcAmLiB*
Shirvington, J *NewYHSD*
Shivaji 1627-1680 *McGEWB*
Shive, Benjamin Milam 1862-1925 *NatCAB 21*
Shive, John W 1877- *WhAm 5*
Shive, Raymond O 1883-1962 *NatCAB 49*
Shively, Benjamin Franklin 1857-1916 *BiDrAC,
NatCAB 14, WhAm 1, WhAmP*
Shively, Carlton Adamson 1890-1952 *WhAm 3*
Shively, Robert Rex 1888-1956 *NatCAB 48*
Shiverick, Asa 1816-1894 *NatCAB 35*
Shiverick, Asa 1877-1937 *NatCAB 27,
WhAm 1*
Shivers, Charles Hendry DeTurck 1887-1969
NatCAB 56
Shivers, R Kevin 1902-1962 *WhAm 4*
Shizuki, Tadao 1760-1806 *DcScB*
Shlenker, Irvin Morris 1905-1971 *WhAm 5*
Shlionsky, Herman 1903-1966 *NatCAB 53*
Shmalhauzen, Ivan Ivanovich 1884-1963 *DcScB*
Shmishkiss, Joseph 1882-1956 *NatCAB 44*
Shnirelman, Lev Genrikhovich 1905-1938 *DcScB*
Shnydore, Ignatius *NewYHSD*
Shoaf, Lilian Noyes 1871- *WomWWA 14*
Shoaff, Carrie M 1849- *AmWom*
Shoaff, Fred B 1877- *WhAm 4*
Shoals, George 1903-1960 *WhAm 4*
Shober, Charles *NewYHSD*
Shober, Francis Edwin 1831-1896 *BiAUS,
BiDrAC, WhAm H*
Shober, Francis Emanuel 1860-1919 *BiDrAC,
WhAm 4*
Shober, Gottlieb 1756-1838 *ApCAB*
Shober, John Bedford 1859-1912 *NatCAB 24*
Shober, John Bedford 1893-1959 *WhAm 4*
Shobert, Alonzo *NewYHSD*
Shobonier 1775?-1859 *AmBi, DcAmB*
Shock, Thomas Macy 1892-1962 *WhAm 4*
Shock, William Henry 1821-1905 *ApCAB,*

NatCAB 6, WhAm 4
Shockleidge, R *NewYHSD*
Shockley, Frank William 1884-1954 *WhAm 3*
Shockley, M Augustus Wroten 1874- *WhAm 5*
Shockley, William Bradford 1910- *AsBiEn,
EncAB, WebAB*
Shoe, Grace Ellen *WomWWA 14*
Shoemaker, Andrew *NewYHSD*
Shoemaker, Charles Chalmers 1860-1937
WhAm 2
Shoemaker, Charles Frederick 1841- *WhAm 1*
Shoemaker, Daniel Naylor 1869- *WhAm 5*
Shoemaker, Ella O *WomWWA 14*
Shoemaker, Francis Henry 1889-1958 *BiDrAC*
Shoemaker, Franklin 1826-1878 *NatCAB 28*
Shoemaker, George Washington 1861- *ApCAB*
Shoemaker, Gottlieb *NewYHSD*
Shoemaker, Harlan 1875-1943 *NatCAB 32,
WhAm 2*
Shoemaker, Harry J 1855-1918 *NatCAB 17*
Shoemaker, Henry Francis 1845-1918
NatCAB 8, WhAm 1
Shoemaker, Henry Wharton 1882-1958
WhAm 3
Shoemaker, J Ferris 1838-1915 *NatCAB 17*
Shoemaker, J Warren 1898-1964 *NatCAB 50*
Shoemaker, John Veitch 1852-1910 *NatCAB 13*
Shoemaker, John Vietch 1852-1910 *WhAm 1*
Shoemaker, Joseph Addison 1872- *WhAm 5*
Shoemaker, Lazarus Denison 1819-1893 *BiAUS,
BiDrAC, WhAm H*
Shoemaker, Lewis Foulke 1867-1931
NatCAB 23
Shoemaker, Louis Pierce 1856- *NatCAB 5*
Shoemaker, Mary Craig 1862- *WomWWA 14*
Shoemaker, Michael Myers 1853-1924
TwCBDA, WhAm 1
Shoemaker, Rachel Hinkle 1838-1915 *AmWom,
WhAm 1, WomWWA 14*
Shoemaker, Raymond L d1963 *WhAm 4*
Shoemaker, Richard Heston 1907-1970
DcAmLiB, WhAm 5
Shoemaker, Robert 1817-1896 *NatCAB 5,
WhAm H*
Shoemaker, Robert 1858-1926 *NatCAB 20*
Shoemaker, Samuel Moor 1821-1884
NatCAB 11
Shoemaker, Samuel Moor 1893-1963 *WhAm 4*
Shoemaker, Thomas Howard 1851-1936
NatCAB 28
Shoemaker, Waite Almon 1860-1916 *WhAm 1*
Shoemaker, William Lee 1931- *WebAB*
Shoemaker, William Lukens 1822- *ApCAB*
Shoemaker, William Rawle 1863-1938 *WhAm 1*
Shoenberg, Sydney Melville 1881- *WhAm 6*
Shoffner, John 1892-1944 *NatCAB 37*
Shoffstall, Arthur Scott 1876- *WhAm 3*
Shofner, Orman Eugene 1938- *WhAm 6*
Shohat, James Alexander 1886-1944
NatCAB 33, WhAm 2
Shohl, Alfred Theodore 1889-1946 *NatCAB 35*
Shohl, Walter Max 1885-1970 *WhAm 5*
Shokalsky, Yuly Mikhaylovich 1856-1940
DcScB
Sholem Aleichem 1859-1916 *McGEWB*
Sholes, Charles Clark 1816-1867 *ApCAB*
Sholes, Christopher Latham 1819-1890 *AmBi,
ApCAB, DcAmB, NatCAB 3, WebAB,
WhAm H*
Sholes, Justin Grant 1871-1952 *NatCAB 42*
Sholl, Anna McClure *WomWWA 14*
Sholley, Sidney Llewellyn 1896-1963
NatCAB 52, WhAm 4
Sholokhov, Mikhail Aleksandrovich 1905-
McGEWB
Sholtz, David 1891-1953 *WhAm 3*
Shomo, E H 1907-1972 *WhAm 5*
Shonk, George Washington 1850-1900 *BiDrAC*
Shonle, Horace Abbott 1892-1947 *NatCAB 36*
Shonnard, Christy Fox d1975 *WhAm 6*
Shonnard, Eugenie Frederica 1886- *IlBEAAW*
Shonts, Theodore Perry 1856-1919 *DcAmB,
WhAm 1*
Shontz, Vernon Lloyd 1889-1954 *WhAm 3*
Shook, Alfred Montgomery 1845-1923 *DcAmB,
WhAm 1*
Shook, Charles Francis 1894-1966 *WhAm 4*
Shook, Edgar 1894-1970 *WhAm 5*

Shook, Glenn Alfred 1882-1954 *WhAm 3*
Shoong, Joe 1879-1961 *NatCAB 51*
Shoonmaker, Marius 1811-1894 *WhAm H*
Shoop, Clarence Adelbert 1907-1968 *WhAm 4A*
Shoop, Duke 1905-1957 *WhAm 3*
Shoop, John Daniel 1857-1918 *WhAm 1*
Shope, Irvin Shorty 1900- *IlBEAAW*
Shope, Richard Edwin 1901-1966 *WhAm 4*
Shope, Simeon P 1837-1920 *NatCAB 12,
WhAm 1*
Shopen, Earl Reginald 1902-1965 *NatCAB 51*
Shor, Franc Marion Luther 1914-1974 *WhAm 6*
Shor, George Gershon 1884-1967 *WhAm 5*
Shorb, James DeBarth 1842-1896 *NatCAB 40*
Shore, Clarence Albert 1873-1933 *WhAm 1*
Shore, Maurice J 1901-1961 *WhAm 4*
Shores, Louis 1904- *BiDAmEd*
Shores, Robert James 1881- *WhAm 6*
Shorey, Clyde Everett 1882-1965 *NatCAB 51,
WhAm 4*
Shorey, Edwin Roy 1884-1964 *NatCAB 50*
Shorey, Marian Lydia 1874- *WomWWA 14*
Shorey, Paul 1857-1934 *AmBi, DcAmB,
NatCAB 11, WhAm 1*
Shoriki, Matsutaro 1885-1969 *WhAm 5*
Shorr, Ephraim 1897-1956 *NatCAB 45*
Short, Albert 1866- *WhAm 5*
Short, Carlton Byrce 1888-1946 *NatCAB 35*
Short, Charles 1821-1886 *ApCAB, DcAmB,
Drake, NatCAB 7, TwCBDA, WhAm H*
Short, Charles Wilkins 1794-1863 *ApCAB,
DcAmB, NatCAB 4, TwCBDA,
WhAm H*
Short, Dewey Jackson 1898- *BiDrAC, WhAmP*
Short, Don Levingston 1903- *BiDrAC*
Short, Francis Burgette 1868-1936 *WhAm 1*
Short, Frank Hamilton 1862-1920 *NatCAB 19,
WhAm 1*
Short, Frank Rice 1876-1949 *NatCAB 38*
Short, James 1710-1768 *DcScB*
Short, Jeffrey Robson 1880-1955 *NatCAB 47*
Short, John Thomas 1850-1883 *TwCBDA*
Short, Joseph Hudson, Jr. 1904-1952
DcAmB S5, WhAm 3, WhAm 4
Short, Josephine Helena *WhAm 1,
WomWWA 14*
Short, Livingston Lyman d1963 *WhAm 4*
Short, Luke L 1854-1893 *REnAW*
Short, Omar Jackson 1867-1906 *NatCAB 8*
Short, Sidney Howe 1858-1902 *DcAmB,
NatCAB 13, WhAm 1*
Short, Wallace Mertin 1866- *WhAm 5*
Short, Walter Campbell 1880-1949 *DcAmB S4,
NatCAB 40, WebAMB, WhAm 2*
Short, William 1759-1849 *AmBi, ApCAB,
BiAUS, DcAmB, Drake, NatCAB 4,
TwCBDA, WhAm H*
Short, William Harrison 1868-1935 *NatCAB 26,
WhAm 1*
Short, Zuber Nathaniel 1873- *WhAm 5*
Shortall, John George 1838-1908 *ApCAB,
NatCAB 6, WhAm 1*
Shortall, Thomas Francis 1896-1964 *WhAm 4*
Shortell, Joseph Henry 1891-1951 *NatCAB 39*
Shorter, Eli Sims 1823-1879 *BiAUS, BiDrAC,
WhAm H*
Shorter, James Alexander 1817- *ApCAB*
Shorter, James Hargraves 1842-1920
NatCAB 19
Shorter, John Gill 1818-1872 *ApCAB, BiAUS,
BiDConf, DcAmB, NatCAB 10,
TwCBDA, WhAm H*
Shortle, Abraham Given 1871-1922 *WhAm 1*
Shortlidge, Evan G 1844-1913 *NatCAB 18*
Shortlidge, Jonathan Chauncey 1872-1941
WhAm 1
Shortridge, Charles M 1857- *WhAm 4*
Shortridge, Edward C D 1830- *NatCAB 13*
Shortridge, Eli C D 1819-1898 *REnAW*
Shortridge, Elwill Samuel 1869-1947
NatCAB 37
Shortridge, N Parker d1915 *WhAm 1*
Shortridge, Samuel Morgan 1861-1952
*ApCAB X, BiDrAC, NatCAB 45,
WhAm 3, WhAmP*
Shortridge, Wilson Peter 1880- *WhAm 6*
Shorts, Bruce Carman 1878-1945 *WhAm 2*
Shorts, Robert Perry 1879-1975 *WhAm 6*

Shortt, Elizabeth Smith 1859- *WomWWA 14*
Shortt, Elster Clayton 1907-1961 *WhAm 4*
Shortz, Edwin, Jr. 1876-1953 *NatCAB 42*
Shostakovich, Dmitri Dmitrievich 1906-1975 *McGEWB, WhAm 6*
Shotoku, Taishi 573-621 *McGEWB*
Shott, Allen Thurman 1887-1970 *NatCAB 56*
Shott, Hugh Ike 1866-1953 *BiDrAC, WhAm 3, WhAmP*
Shott, Hugh Ike 1868-1953 *NatCAB 46*
Shott, James Howard 1895-1957 *NatCAB 46*
Shotwell, Abel V 1883-1958 *WhAm 3*
Shotwell, H C *NewYHSD*
Shotwell, James Thomson 1874-1965 *WhAm 4*
Shotwell, Martha Beebe 1855- *WomWWA 14*
Shoudy, Loyal Ambrose 1880-1950 *WhAm 3*
Shoudy, William Allen 1878- *WhAm 6*
Shoulders, Harrison H 1886-1963 *NatCAB 51, WhAm 4*
Shoulders, James *REnAW*
Shoup, Arthur Glendinning 1880-1942 *WhAm 2*
Shoup, David Monroe 1904- *WebAMB*
Shoup, Earl Leon 1886-1953 *WhAm 3*
Shoup, Eldon Campbell 1897-1954 *WhAm 3*
Shoup, Francis Asbury 1834-1896 *ApCAB, BiDConf, DcAmB, TwCBDA, WhAm H*
Shoup, George Laird 1836-1904 *ApCAB Sup, BiDrAC, DcAmB, NatCAB 1, NatCAB 12, REnAW, TwCBDA, WhAm 1, WhAmP*
Shoup, Guy V 1872- *WhAm 5*
Shoup, Mary Eloise Howard 1872- *WomWWA 14*
Shoup, Merrill Edgar 1899-1964 *WhAm 4*
Shoup, Oliver Henry 1869-1940 *NatCAB 30, WhAm 1*
Shoup, Paul 1874-1946 *NatCAB 35, WhAm 2*
Shourds, George Washington *NewYHSD*
Shourds, John *NewYHSD*
Shouse, James D 1903-1965 *WhAm 4*
Shouse, Jouett 1879-1968 *BiDrAC, WhAm 6*
Shove, Benjamin 1829-1906 *NatCAB 21*
Shove, Eugene Percy 1855-1939 *WhAm 1*
Shover, John 1927- *EncAAH*
Show, Arley Barthlow 1856-1920 *WhAm 1*
Showalter, Anthony Johnson 1858-1924 *WhAm 1*
Showalter, Arthur Jennings Bryan 1898-1961 *NatCAB 48*
Showalter, Howard Westwood 1881-1963 *NatCAB 50*
Showalter, Jackson Whipps 1860-1935 *WhAm 1*
Showalter, Joseph Baltzell 1851-1932 *BiDrAC, TwCBDA, WhAm 4*
Showalter, Noah David 1869-1937 *BiDAmEd, WhAm 1*
Showalter, William Joseph 1878-1935 *WhAm 1*
Shower, George Theodore 1841-1923 *WhAm 1*
Shower, Jacob 1803-1879 *BiAUS, BiDrAC, WhAm H*
Showerman, Grant 1870-1935 *DcAmB S1, NatCAB 27, WhAm 1*
Showers, J Balmer 1879-1962 *NatCAB 50, WhAm 4*
Showman, Harry Munson 1889-1943 *WhAm 2*
Shrader, Alfred *NewYHSD*
Shrader, E Roscoe 1878-1960 *NatCAB 48*
Shrader, Edwin Roscoe 1879-1960 *IIBEAAW*
Shrady, George Frederick 1837-1907 *DcAmB, NatCAB 7, TwCBDA, WhAm 1*
Shrady, Henry Merwin 1871-1922 *AmBi, DcAmB, IIBEAAW, NatCAB 13, NatCAB 30, TwCBDA, WhAm 1*
Shrady, John 1830- *NatCAB 4*
Shramek, Joseph Marius 1879-1961 *NatCAB 50*
Shrank, William *NewYHSD*
Shreeve, John 1823?- *NewYHSD*
Shreeves, John 1823?- *NewYHSD*
Shreve, Ann Lux Buchanan *WomWWA 14*
Shreve, Charles Everett 1905-1972 *WhAm 5*
Shreve, Earl Owen 1881- *WhAm 6*
Shreve, Eugene Sheldon 1895-1949 *NatCAB 37*
Shreve, Forrest 1878-1950 *NatCAB 40, WhAm 3*
Shreve, Henry Miller 1785-1851 *AmBi, DcAmB, Drake, McGEWB, REnAW, WebAB, WhAm H*
Shreve, Henry Miller 1785-1854 *ApCAB,*

Shreve, Milton William 1858-1939 *BiDrAC, WhAm 1, WhAmP*
Shreve, Ralph Febrey 1882-1955 *NatCAB 44*
Shreve, Richmond Harold 1877-1946 *NatCAB 38, WhAm 2*
Shreve, Ruth Bentley 1881- *WomWWA 14*
Shreve, Samuel Henry 1829-1884 *ApCAB*
Shreve, Thomas Hopkins 1808-1853 *ApCAB, DcAmB, Drake, WhAm H*
Shreve, Wickliffe Winston 1903-1964 *WhAm 4*
Shrimpton, Elizabeth Latimer 1875- *WomWWA 14*
Shriner, Charles Anthony 1853- *WhAm 3*
Shriner, Herb 1918-1970 *WhAm 5*
Shriver, Alfred 1894-1963 *WhAm 4*
Shriver, Alfred Jenkins 1867-1939 *WhAm 1*
Shriver, Garner E 1912- *BiDrAC*
Shriver, George McLean 1868-1942 *WhAm 2*
Shriver, John Shultz 1857-1915 *WhAm 1*
Shriver, Samuel Henry 1903-1969 *NatCAB 56*
Shriver, T Herbert 1846-1917 *NatCAB 17*
Shriver, William Payne 1872-1957 *WhAm 3*
Shroder, William Jacob 1876-1952 *WhAm 3*
Shropshire, Courtney William 1877-1965 *WhAm 4*
Shroyer, Curtis Clinton 1894-1973 *WhAm 6*
Shroyer, John Ulysses 1882-1960 *NatCAB 54*
Shrum, George Dixon 1896-1959 *NatCAB 49, WhAm 4*
Shryock, Burnett Henry, Sr. 1904-1971 *WhAm 5*
Shryock, Gideon 1802-1880 *BnEnAmA, WhAm H*
Shryock, Henry William 1861-1935 *WhAm 1*
Shryock, Joseph Grundy 1880-1956 *NatCAB 47, WhAm 3*
Shryock, Richard Harrison 1893-1972 *NatCAB 56, WhAm 5*
Shtokman, Vladimir Borisovich 1909-1968 *DcScB*
Shuart, William Herbert 1852-1944 *NatCAB 35*
Shubert, Jacob J 1880-1963 *EncAB, WhAm 4*
Shubert, John 1908-1962 *NatCAB 52*
Shubert, Lee 1873?-1953 *DcAmB S5*
Shubert, Lee 1875-1953 *WebAB*
Shubert, Lee 1883-1953 *WhAm 3*
Shubert, Levi 1875?-1953 *EncAB*
Shubert, Samuel 1876?-1905 *EncAB*
Shubow, Joseph Shalom 1899-1969 *NatCAB 55*
Shubrick, Edward Rutledge 1794-1844 *ApCAB, Drake, TwCBDA*
Shubrick, Irvine 1797-1849 *Drake*
Shubrick, Irvine 1798-1845 *WhAm 4*
Shubrick, Irvine 1798-1849 *ApCAB, TwCBDA*
Shubrick, John Taylor 1788-1815 *Drake*
Shubrick, John Templar 1788-1815 *ApCAB*
Shubrick, John Templer 1788-1815 *DcAmB, NatCAB 8, TwCBDA, WebAMB, WhAm H*
Shubrick, Thomas 1755-1810 *Drake*
Shubrick, Thomas Branford 1825-1847 *ApCAB*
Shubrick, William Branford 1790-1874 *AmBi, ApCAB, DcAmB, Drake, NatCAB 2, TwCBDA, WebAMB, WhAm H*
Shuck, Henrietta Hall 1817-1844 *ApCAB*
Shuck, Jehu Lewis 1812-1863 *ApCAB, DcAmB, WhAm H*
Shuey, Edwin Longstreet 1857-1924 *ApCAB X, DcAmB, NatCAB 11, WhAm 1*
Shuey, Lillian Hinman 1853- *WhAm 4*
Shuey, Sarah Isabel 1850- *WomWWA 14*
Shuey, Theodore Frelinghuysen 1845-1933 *NatCAB 25*
Shuey, William John 1827-1920 *ApCAB X, DcAmB, NatCAB 6, WhAm 1*
Shufeldt, Robert Wilson 1822-1895 *ApCAB, DcAmB, NatCAB 4, TwCBDA, WebAMB, WhAm H*
Shufeldt, Robert Wilson 1850-1934 *AmBi, NatCAB 6, WhAm 1*
Shuff, John A d1970 *WhAm 5*
Shuford, A Alex, Jr. 1905-1971 *WhAm 5*
Shuford, Abel Alexander 1841-1912 *NatCAB 36*
Shuford, Adrian Lafayette 1884-1957 *NatCAB 47*
Shuford, Alonzo Craig 1858-1933 *BiDrAC,*

WhAm 4, WhAmP
Shuford, Forrest Herman 1897-1954 *WhAm 3*
Shuford, George Adams 1895-1962 *BiDrAC, WhAm 4*
Shuford, William Burder 1907-1967 *NatCAB 53*
Shugerman, Abe Louis 1918-1960 *WhAm 4*
Shugg, Richard *NewYHSD*
Shuja Ibn Aslam, Al-Misri *DcScB*
Shukers, Carroll Franklin 1905-1970 *NatCAB 56*
Shulenberger, Ephraim Adams 1860-1918 *NatCAB 17*
Shuler, Carl Frederick 1875-1957 *NatCAB 47*
Shuler, Ellis W 1881-1954 *WhAm 3*
Shuler, Nettie Rogers 1862-1939 *NotAW, WomWWA 14*
Shuler, Robert Pierce 1880- *WhAm 6*
Shulkin, Anatol 1901-1961 *NatCAB 48*
Shull, Aaron Franklin 1881-1961 *DcScB, WhAm 4*
Shull, Charles Albert 1879- *WhAm 6*
Shull, Charles Graves 1878-1950 *WhAm 3*
Shull, Deloss Carlton 1858-1938 *NatCAB 15, WhAm 1*
Shull, Deloss P 1887-1964 *WhAm 4*
Shull, Frank Leslie 1869-1960 *NatCAB 50, WhAm 5*
Shull, George Harrison 1874-1940 *EncAAH*
Shull, George Harrison 1874-1954 *DcAmB S5, WhAm 3*
Shull, J Marion 1872-1948 *WhAm 2*
Shull, J Rush 1886-1964 *NatCAB 51*
Shull, James Wilson 1855-1937 *NatCAB 29*
Shull, Joseph Horace 1848-1944 *BiDrAC, WhAm 2*
Shull, Josiah 1855-1927 *NatCAB 21*
Shullenberger, William Arthur 1881- *WhAm 6*
Shulman, Charles Emanuel 1900-1968 *NatCAB 57, WhAm 5*
Shulman, Harry 1903-1955 *NatCAB 41, WhAm 4*
Shulters, Hoyt Volney 1868-1932 *WhAm 1*
Shultz, Charles *NewYHSD*
Shultz, Emanuel 1819-1912 *BiDrAC*
Shultz, George Pratt 1920- *BiDrUSE*
Shultz, Henry Augustus 1800-1885 *NatCAB 2*
Shultz, Henry Augustus 1806-1885 *ApCAB, NatCAB 13*
Shultz, John Ernest 1914-1973 *NatCAB 56*
Shultz, John Fair 1884-1954 *NatCAB 42*
Shultz, Theodore 1770-1850 *ApCAB, NatCAB 2*
Shultz, William John 1902-1970 *WhAm 5*
Shulz, Adolph Robert 1869-1963 *WhAm 4*
Shulze, John Andrew 1775-1852 *BiAUS, DcAmB, Drake, NatCAB 2, TwCBDA, WhAm H*
Shulze, Maurice 1878-1945 *NatCAB 35*
Shumaker, E Ellsworth 1862- *WhAm 4*
Shumaker, Edward Earl 1882- *ApCAB X*
Shumaker, Edward Seitz 1867-1929 *NatCAB 21, WhAm 1*
Shumaker, Ross Webster 1895-1964 *NatCAB 51, WhAm 4*
Shuman, Abraham 1838-1918 *WhAm 1*
Shuman, Davis 1912-1966 *WhAm 4*
Shuman, Edwin Llewellyn 1863-1941 *NatCAB 15, NatCAB 32, WhAm 1*
Shuman, Frank 1862-1918 *NatCAB 19*
Shuman, John Franklin 1884-1961 *WhAm 4*
Shuman, John William 1885-1956 *NatCAB 46*
Shuman, Milton G 1866- *NatCAB 7*
Shuman, Royal Lewis 1879-1957 *NatCAB 46*
Shumard, Benjamin Franklin 1820-1869 *NatCAB 8*
Shumate, Roger V 1900-1954 *WhAm 3*
Shumate, Wade Hampton 1879- *WhAm 6*
Shumberger, John Calvin 1873-1958 *WhAm 4*
Shumberger, John Calvin, Jr. 1904-1970 *NatCAB 57*
Shumway, Adelina Ritter 1875- *WhAm 6*
Shumway, Daniel Bussier 1868-1940 *WhAm 1*
Shumway, Edgar Solomon 1856-1928 *WhAm 1*
Shumway, Edward D 1885-1963 *WhAm 4*
Shumway, Florence Snow 1859- *WomWWA 14*
Shumway, Henry Colton 1807-1884 *NewYHSD*
Shumway, Henry Cotton 1807-1884 *ApCAB,*

TwCBDA
Shumway, Mary Ida 1856- *WomWWA 14*
Shumway, Sherman N 1895-1954 *WhAm 3*
Shumway, Waldo 1891-1956 *WhAm 3*
Shumway, Walter Bradley 1852-1934 *WhAm 1*
Shun, Chih 1638-1661 *WhoMilH*
Shunk, Caroline Saxe Merrill *WomWWA 14*
Shunk, Francis Rawn 1788-1848 *ApCAB,*
BiAUS, DcAmB, Drake, NatCAB 2,
TwCBDA, WhAm H
Shunk, Joseph Lorain 1844-1936 *WhAm 1*
Shunk, William Alexander 1857-1921 *WhAm 1*
Shunk, William Findlay 1830-1907 *WhAm 1*
Shupe, Henry Fox 1860-1926 *WhAm 1*
Shuping, Clarence Leroy 1886-1971 *NatCAB 56,*
WhAm 5
Shurcliff, Arthur Asahel 1870-1957 *WhAm 3*
Shurly, Burt Russell 1871-1950 *NatCAB 39,*
WhAm 5
Shurly, Ernest Lorenzo 1845-1913 *NatCAB 21*
Shurter, Edwin DuBois 1863-1946 *NatCAB 34,*
WhAm 2
Shurter, Robert Lafevre 1907-1974 *WhAm 6*
Shurtleff, Charles Allerton 1857-1941 *WhAm 1*
Shurtleff, Ernest Warburton 1862-1917 *ApCAB,*
WhAm 1
Shurtleff, Eugene d1957 *WhAm 3*
Shurtleff, Flavel 1879- *WhAm 6*
Shurtleff, Fred 1867- *NatCAB 13*
Shurtleff, George Augustus 1819- *NatCAB 7*
Shurtleff, Glen Kassimer 1860-1909 *WhAm 1*
Shurtleff, Margaret Homer Nichols 1879-
BiCAW
Shurtleff, Nathaniel Bradstreet 1810-1874
ApCAB, DcAmB, Drake, TwCBDA,
WhAm H
Shurtleff, Robert 1760-1827 *AmBi*
Shurtleff, Roswell Morse 1838-1915 *AmBi,*
ApCAB, DcAmB, IIBEAAW,
NatCAB 10, NewYHSD, TwCBDA,
WhAm 1
Shurtleff, Stephen Currier 1838-1898
NatCAB 18
Shurtliff, Lewis Warren 1835- *NatCAB 7*
Shuster *NewYHSD*
Shuster, Arnauld *NewYHSD*
Shuster, George Nauman 1894-1977 *BiDAmEd*
Shuster, Sigismund 1807- *NewYHSD*
Shuster, William Howard 1893-1969 *IIBEAAW*
Shuster, William Morgan 1877-1960
NatCAB 15, NatCAB 47, WhAm 4
Shute, A Lincoln 1865-1947 *WhAm 2*
Shute, Daniel 1722-1802 *Drake*
Shute, Daniel Kerfoot 1858-1935 *WhAm 1*
Shute, Emmett R 1889-1965 *WhAm 4*
Shute, Furman Robbins 1873-1947 *NatCAB 35*
Shute, Hattie Josephine *WomWWA 14*
Shute, Henry Augustus 1856-1943 *WhAm 2*
Shute, Henry Damon 1871- *ApCAB X*
Shute, Miriam Helen 1879- *WomWWA 14*
Shute, Nevil 1899-1960 *WhAm 3, WhAm 4*
Shute, Mrs. R W *NewYHSD*
Shute, Samuel 1653-1742 *ApCAB, Drake*
Shute, Samuel 1653-1743 *NatCAB 7*
Shute, Samuel 1662-1742 *DcAmB, WhAm H*
Shute, Samuel Moore 1823-1902 *ApCAB,*
WhAm 1
Shutter, Marion Daniel 1853-1939 *NatCAB 31,*
WhAm 1
Shuttleworth, V Craven 1900-1965 *NatCAB 51,*
WhAm 4
Shutts, Frank Barker 1870-1947 *WhAm 2*
Shvernik, Nikola 1888-1970 *WhAm 5*
Shy, George Milton 1919-1967 *WhAm 4A*
Siamese Twins 1811-1874 *DcAmB*
Sias, Ernest J d1955 *WhAm 3*
Sibal, Abner Woodruff 1921- *BiDrAC*
Sibberson, Ernest Christian 1885-1956
NatCAB 46
Sibelius, Jean Julius Christian 1865-1957
McGEWB, WhAm 3
Sibell, Muriel Vincent *IIBEAAW*
Siberell, Lloyd E 1905-1968 *WhAm 5*
Sibert, William Luther 1860-1935 *AmBi,*
DcAmB S1, NatCAB 17, NatCAB 35,
WebAMB, WhAm 1
Sibiel, Alexander 1709-1791 *ApCAB*
Sibler, Charles Jgnatz 1896-1959 *NatCAB 43*

Sibley, Bolling 1873-1949 *WhAm 2*
Sibley, Clyde Lawson 1899-1968 *WhAm 5*
Sibley, Edwin Henry 1857- *WhAm 4*
Sibley, Frank J 1847- *WhAm 4*
Sibley, Frederic Merrill 1883-1945 *NatCAB 34*
Sibley, Frederick Hubbard 1872-1941 *BiDAmEd,*
NatCAB 36, WhAm 1
Sibley, Frederick W 1852-1918 *WhAm 1*
Sibley, George Champlain 1782-1863 *ApCAB,*
DcAmB, Drake, NatCAB 2, WhAm H
Sibley, George H 1898-1974 *WhAm 6*
Sibley, Harper 1885-1959 *NatCAB 49,*
WhAm 3
Sibley, Henry Hastings 1811-1891 *AmBi,*
ApCAB, BiAUS, BiDrAC, DcAmB,
Drake, NatCAB 10, REnAW, TwCBDA,
WebAMB, WhAm H, WhAmP
Sibley, Henry Hopkins 1815?-1886 *Drake*
Sibley, Henry Hopkins 1816-1886 *ApCAB,*
NatCAB 2, TwCBDA, WebAMB
Sibley, Hiram 1807-1888 *AmBi, ApCAB,*
DcAmB, NatCAB 4, TwCBDA, WebAB,
WhAm H
Sibley, Hiram Luther 1836-1920 *WhAm 1*
Sibley, Jane Eliza 1838- *NatCAB 1*
Sibley, Jennie E *AmWom*
Sibley, John 1757-1837 *DcAmB, WhAm H*
Sibley, John Langdon 1804-1885 *ApCAB,*
DcAmB, DcAmLiB, Drake, NatCAB 11,
TwCBDA, WhAm H
Sibley, Jonas 1762-1834 *BiAUS, BiDrAC,*
WhAm H
Sibley, Joseph Crocker 1850-1926 *BiDrAC,*
DcAmB, NatCAB 27, TwCBDA,
WhAm 1, WhAmP
Sibley, Josiah 1877- *WhAm 5*
Sibley, Louise F M Lyndon *WomWWA 14*
Sibley, Mark Hopkins 1796-1852 *ApCAB,*
BiAUS, BiDrAC, WhAm H
Sibley, Mary 1861- *WomWWA 14*
Sibley, Mary Easton 1800-1878 *NotAW*
Sibley, Preston B 1840-1914 *NatCAB 16*
Sibley, Robert 1881-1958 *WhAm 3*
Sibley, Rufus Adams 1841- *NatCAB 18,*
WhAm 4
Sibley, Samuel Hale 1873-1958 *NatCAB 53,*
WhAm 3
Sibley, Solomon 1769-1846 *ApCAB, BiAUS,*
BiDrAC, Drake, NatCAB 2, WhAm H,
WhAmP
Sibley, William Crapen 1832-1902 *NatCAB 2*
Sibley, William Giddings 1860-1935 *WhAm 1*
Sibley, Willis Emory 1857-1950 *NatCAB 44*
Sibolt *NewYHSD*
Sicalamous d1748 *DcAmB*
Sicard, Montgomery 1836-1900 *ApCAB Sup,*
DcAmB, NatCAB 10, TwCBDA,
WhAm 1
Siceloff, L Parker 1880- *WhAm 6*
Siciliano, Angelo *WebAB*
Sicilianos, Demetrios Constantine 1880-
WhAm 6
Sick, Emil George 1894-1964 *WhAm 4*
Sickel, Horatio Gates 1817-1890 *ApCAB,*
NatCAB 5
Sickel, William George 1868-1929 *WhAm 1*
Sickels, David Banks 1837-1918 *NatCAB 10,*
WhAm 1
Sickels, Frederick Ellsworth 1819-1895 *DcAmB,*
WhAm H
Sickels, Ivin 1853-1943 *WhAm 2*
Sickels, John Edmund 1857- *NatCAB 5*
Sickels, John Stewart 1888-1957 *NatCAB 46*
Sickenberger, Jesse Urban 1878-1962
NatCAB 50
Sickert, Walter Richard 1860-1942 *McGEWB*
Sickles, Carlton Ralph 1921- *BiDrAC*
Sickles, Daniel Edgar 1819-1914 *DcAmB*
Sickles, Daniel Edgar 1821-1914 *BiAUS,*
Drake
Sickles, Daniel Edgar 1823-1914 *ApCAB,*
NatCAB 3
Sickles, Daniel Edgar 1825-1914 *AmBi,*
BiDrAC, NatCAB 12, TwCBDA, WebAB,
WebAMB, WhAm 1, WhAmP
Sickles, Nicholas 1801-1845 *BiAUS, BiDrAC,*
WhAm H
Sickles, Noel Douglas 1910?- *IIBEAAW*

Sicotte, Louis V 1812- *ApCAB*
Sidarouss, Pasha 1873- *WhAm 3*
Sidbury, James Buren 1886-1967 *WhAm 4*
Siddall, Hugh Wagstaff 1885-1948 *WhAm 2*
Siddall, John MacAlpine 1874-1923
NatCAB 19, WhAm 1
Siddons, Frederick Lincoln 1864-1931
NatCAB 23, WhAm 1
Siddons, Mary Frances Scott d1896 *AmWom*
Sidell, William Henry 1810-1873 *ApCAB,*
DcAmB, WhAm H
Siders, Walter Raleigh 1870-1940 *WhAm 1*
Sidgreaves, Sir Arthur F 1882-1946 *WhAm 3*
Sidgwick, Henry 1838-1900 *McGEWB*
Sidgwick, Nevil Vincent 1873-1952 *AsBiEn,*
DcScB
Sidi Muhammed d1791? *WhAm H*
Sidis, Boris 1867-1923 *DcAmB, NatCAB 24,*
WhAm 1
Sidley, Robert William 1905-1961 *NatCAB 49*
Sidley, William Pratt 1868-1958 *NatCAB 49,*
WhAm 3
Sidlo, Thomas L 1888-1955 *WhAm 3*
Sidney, Margaret 1844-1924 *DcAmB, NotAW,*
WhAm 1
Sidney, Sir Philip 1554-1586 *McGEWB*
Sido, George Henry 1887-1955 *WhAm 3*
Sidore, Saul O 1907-1964 *NatCAB 53*
Sidwell, Frances Haldeman *WomWWA 14*
Sidwell, Thomas Watson 1859-1936 *WhAm 1*
Siebecker, Robert George 1854-1922
NatCAB 19, WhAm 1
Siebel, Ewald Herbert 1875-1932 *NatCAB 45*
Siebel, John Ewald 1845-1919 *WhAm 1*
Siebenthal, Claude Ellsworth 1869-1930
WhAm 1
Sieber, Al 1844-1907 *DcAmB S1, REnAW,*
WebAMB
Sieber, George Washington 1854- *ApCAB X*
Siebert *NewYHSD*
Siebert, Albert Franklin 1878-1960 *NatCAB 48*
Siebert, Annie Ware Sabine *WomWWA 14*
Siebert, Selmar 1808- *NewYHSD*
Siebert, Wilbur Henry 1866-1961 *NatCAB 13,*
NatCAB 49, WhAm 4
Siebold, Carl Theodor Ernst Von 1804-1885
DcScB
Siebold, Karl Theodor Ernst Von 1804-1885
AsBiEn
Sieck, Louis John 1884-1952 *WhAm 3*
Siedenburg, Frederic 1872-1939 *WhAm 1*
Siedentopf, Henry Friedrich Wilhelm 1872-1940
DcScB
Sieder, Otto Ferdinand 1881-1969 *NatCAB 55,*
WhAm 5
Siedlecki, Michal 1873-1940 *DcScB*
Siefert, Henry Otto Rudolf 1841- *WhAm 4*
Sieff, Israel Moses 1889-1972 *WhAm 5*
Siefkin, C Gordon 1908-1960 *WhAm 4*
Siefkin, Forest DeWitt 1891-1964 *WhAm 4*
Siefkin, George 1895-1954 *NatCAB 43,*
WhAm 4
Sieg, Lee Paul 1879-1963 *WhAm 4*
Siegbahn, Karl Manne Georg 1886- *AsBiEn*
Siegel, Alfred J 1871-1926 *NatCAB 22*
Siegel, David Porter 1895-1958 *WhAm 3*
Siegel, David Tevel 1896-1957 *WhAm 3*
Siegel, Irwin 1924-1970 *WhAm 5*
Siegel, Isaac 1880-1947 *BiDrAC, WhAm 2,*
WhAmP
Siegel, Keeve Milton 1923-1975 *WhAm 6*
Siegel, Lester 1893-1971 *WhAm 5*
Siegel, Roy Richard 1896-1964 *WhAm 4*
Siegel, William Ely 1909-1973 *WhAm 6*
Siegfried, Clarence Simon 1881-1957
NatCAB 47
Siegler *NewYHSD*
Siegler, Samuel Lewis 1894-1953 *NatCAB 40*
Siegman, Sidney Bertram 1883-1951
NatCAB 38
Siegmund, Joseph Valentine 1893-1965
NatCAB 52
Siegnars, Charles *NewYHSD*
Siegrist, Mary d1953 *WhAm 3*
Sielaff, Gustav Julius 1878-1956 *WhAm 3*
Siemens, Charles William 1823-1883 *DcScB*
Siemens, Ernst Werner Von 1816-1892 *DcScB*
Siemens, Sir William 1823-1883 *AsBiEn*

Sieminski, Alfred Dennis 1911- *BiDrAC*
Siemon, Daniel William 1898-1959 *WhAm 4*
Siemonn, George 1874-1952 *WhAm 3*
Siems, Allan Gleason 1888-1943 *NatCAB 33, WhAm 2*
Siems, Peter 1842-1917 *NatCAB 26*
Siemsen, Walter Johannes 1901-1959 *NatCAB 48*
Sieni, Cyril *WhAm H*
Sienkiewicz, Henryk 1846-1916 *McGEWB*
Sieroty, Adolph 1876-1937 *NatCAB 36*
Sierpinski, Waclaw 1882-1969 *DcScB*
Sierra, Justo 1848-1912 *McGEWB*
Siersema, Reynold Clinton 1900-1967 *NatCAB 54*
Sies, Raymond William 1878-1922 *WhAm 1*
Sietz, Lewis *NewYHSD*
Sievers, Fred John 1880-1952 *WhAm 3*
Sievers, Frederick William 1872-1966 *WhAm 4*
Sievert, Leo Ellsworth 1898-1962 *WhAm 4*
Siewers, William Albert 1873-1923 *NatCAB 34*
Sieyes, Emmanuel Jospeh, Comte 1748-1836 *McGEWB*
Sifferlen, Isabel Rees 1873- *WomWWA 14*
Sifton, Clifford 1861- *ApCAB Sup*
Sifton, Harry Austin 1867-1935 *WhAm 1*
Sifton, Victor 1897-1961 *WhAm 4*
Sigall, Joseph De 1892-1953 *WhAm 3*
Sigaud DeLafond, Joseph-Aignan 1730-1810 *DcScB*
Sigel, Albert 1827-1884 *ApCAB*
Sigel, Emil *NewYHSD*
Sigel, Franz 1824-1902 *AmBi, ApCAB, DcAmB, Drake, NatCAB 4, TwCBDA, WebAMB, WhAm 1*
Sigel, Franz 1872-1922 *WhAm 1*
Siger Of Brabant 1240?-1284? *DcScB*
Sigerfoos, Charles Peter 1865-1944 *WhAm 2*
Sigerist, Henry Ernest 1891-1957 *NatCAB 46, WhAm 4*
Sigismund 1368-1437 *McGEWB*
Sigismund III, Vasa 1566-1632 *WhoMilH*
Sigler, Thomas Amon 1879-1957 *WhAm 3*
Sigman, Jules Israel 1904- *WhAm 6*
Sigman, Morris 1881-1931 *DcAmB*
Sigmon, Jesse Caleb 1885-1967 *NatCAB 54*
Sigmund, Frederick Lester 1866- *TwCBDA, WhAm 4*
Sigmund, Jay G 1885-1937 *WhAm 1*
Signay, Joseph 1778-1850 *ApCAB, Drake*
Signer, Merton I 1900-1956 *WhAm 3*
Signorelli, Luca 1445?-1523 *McGEWB*
Sigogne, Mande d1850? *ApCAB*
Sigorgne, Pierre 1719-1809 *DcScB*
Sigourney, Lydia Howard Huntley 1791-1865 *AmBi, AmWom, ApCAB, DcAmB, Drake, NatCAB 1, NotAW, TwCBDA, WebAB, WhAm H*
Sigsbee, Charles Dwight 1845-1923 *AmBi, ApCAB Sup, ApCAB X, DcAmB, NatCAB 9, TwCBDA, WebAB, WebAMB, WhAm 1*
Siguenza Y Gongora, Carlos De 1645-1700 *ApCAB, DcScB*
Sihanouk, Prince Norodom 1922- *McGEWB*
Sihler, Ernest Gottlieb 1853-1942 *WhAm 1*
Sijzi, Abu Said Ahmad Ibn Muhammad, Al-945?-1020? *DcScB*
Sikelianos, Eva Palmer 1874- *WomWWA 14*
Sikes, Clarence S 1869- *WhAm 5*
Sikes, Enoch Walter 1868-1941 *NatCAB 34, WhAm 1*
Sikes, George Cushing 1868-1928 *WhAm 1*
Sikes, Madeleine Wallin *WomWWA 14*
Sikes, Robert Lee Fulton 1906- *BiDrAC*
Sikes, William Wirt 1836-1883 *ApCAB, DcAmB, TwCBDA, WhAm H*
Sikorski, Wladyslaw 1881-1943 *WhWW-II*
Sikorsky, Igor Ivan 1889-1972 *McGEWB, WebAB, WhAm 5*
Silber, Frederick David 1873-1935 *NatCAB 30*
Silber, Isadore Bert 1895-1964 *NatCAB 51*
Silber, William Beinhauer 1826- *NatCAB 5*
Silberberg, Martin 1895-1966 *NatCAB 52*
Silberberg, Mendel B 1886-1965 *WhAm 4*
Silberman, Alfred M 1890-1948 *WhAm 2*
Silberman, M J d1959 *WhAm 4*
Silbersack, Walter Frank 1902-1960 *WhAm 4*

Silberstein, Ludwik 1872-1948 *WhAm 2*
Silbert, Samuel 1894-1959 *NatCAB 45*
Silcox, Ferdinand Augustus 1882-1939 *DcAmB S2, NatCAB 29, WhAm 1*
Silcox, John B 1847- *WhAm 4*
Siler, Eugene 1900- *BiDrAC, WhAmP*
Siler, Joseph Franklin 1875-1960 *NatCAB 57*
Siler, Vinton Earnest 1909-1971 *NatCAB 56, WhAm 5*
Silin, Charles Intervale 1897-1974 *WhAm 6*
Silk, William Wallace 1875-1952 *NatCAB 39*
Silkett, Albert Frank 1904-1969 *WhAm 5*
Silkman, James Bailey 1819-1888 *ApCAB*
Silknitter, G F 1879-1954 *WhAm 3*
Silkworth, William Duncan 1873-1951 *NatCAB 39*
Sill, Anna Peck 1816-1889 *BiDAmEd, DcAmB, NotAW, WhAm H*
Sill, Ebenezer Enoch 1822- *NewYHSD*
Sill, Edward Roland 1841-1887 *TwCBDA*
Sill, Edward Rowland 1841-1887 *AmBi, ApCAB, BiDAmEd, DcAmB, NatCAB 7, WhAm H*
Sill, Frederick Herbert 1874-1952 *NatCAB 41, WhAm 3*
Sill, John Mahelm Berry 1831-1901 *NatCAB 10, TwCBDA, WhAm 1*
Sill, John Mahelon Berry 1831-1901 *ApCAB*
Sill, Joseph 1801-1854 *NewYHSD*
Sill, Joshua Woodrow 1831-1862 *ApCAB, Drake, NatCAB 5, TwCBDA*
Sill, Louise Morgan d1961 *WhAm 4, WomWWA 14*
Sill, Thomas Hale 1783-1856 *BiAUS, BiDrAC, WhAm H*
Sillanpaa, Frans Emil 1888-1964 *WhAm 4*
Sillcocks, Henry 1876-1957 *NatCAB 45*
Sille, Nicasius De 1600?- *ApCAB*
Sillen, Lars Gunnar 1916-1970 *WhAm 5*
Siller, Hilda 1861- *AmWom*
Sillery, Noel Brulart De 1577-1640 *ApCAB*
Silletti, Frank Candid 1895- *ApCAB X*
Silliman, Augustus Ely 1807-1884 *ApCAB, NatCAB 6, TwCBDA, WhAm H*
Silliman, Benjamin 1779-1864 *AmBi, ApCAB, AsBiEn, BiDAmEd, DcAmB, DcScB, Drake, EncAB, McGEWB, NatCAB 2, TwCBDA, WebAB, WhAm H*
Silliman, Benjamin, Jr. 1816-1885 *AmBi, ApCAB, BiDAmEd, DcAmB, DcScB, Drake, NatCAB 2, TwCBDA, WebAB, WhAm H*
Silliman, Benjamin Douglas 1805-1901 *ApCAB, NatCAB 6, TwCBDA*
Silliman, Blanche Goodman 1865- *WomWWA 14*
Silliman, Charles Augustus 1830-1906 *WhAm 1*
Silliman, Gold Selleck 1730?-1790 *Drake*
Silliman, Gold Selleck 1732-1790 *ApCAB, TwCBDA, WebAMB*
Silliman, Gold Selleck 1777-1868 *ApCAB*
Silliman, Harry Inness 1876- *WhAm 5*
Silliman, Justus Mitchell 1842-1896 *ApCAB, NatCAB 11, TwCBDA*
Silliman, Reuben Daniel 1871-1961 *WhAm 4*
Silloway, Thomas William 1828-1910 *ApCAB, TwCBDA, WhAm 1*
Sills, Kenneth Charles Morton 1879-1954 *NatCAB 44, WhAm 3*
Sills, Milton 1882-1930 *DcAmB, WhAm 1*
Silone, Ignazio 1900- *McGEWB*
Siloti, Alexander Ilyitch 1863-1945 *DcAmB S3*
Silsbee, Arthur Boardman 1854-1924 *WhAm 1*
Silsbee, Joshua S 1815-1855 *ApCAB, Drake*
Silsbee, Martha 1858- *WomWWA 14*
Silsbee, Nathaniel 1773-1850 *ApCAB, BiAUS, BiDrAC, DcAmB, Drake, NatCAB 12, TwCBDA, WhAm H, WhAmP*
Silsbury, George M *NewYHSD*
Silsby, Samuel Schoppee 1898-1956 *NatCAB 45*
Silsby, Wilson 1883-1952 *WhAm 3*
Silva, Francis Augustus 1835-1886 *ApCAB, NewYHSD*
Silva, Jose Laurencio 1792-1873 *ApCAB*
Silva, William Posey 1859-1948 *WhAm 2*
Silveira, Joseph N *NewYHSD*
Silver, Abba Hillel 1893-1963 *McGEWB,*

NatCAB 50, WhAm 4*
Silver, Arthur Elmer 1879-1975 *WhAm 6*
Silver, Ernest Leroy 1876-1949 *NatCAB 37, WhAm 3*
Silver, Francis Aloysius 1895- *WhAm 6*
Silver, Gray 1870-1935 *NatCAB 27*
Silver, Gray 1871-1935 *DcAmB S1, WhAm 1*
Silver, H Percy d1934 *WhAm 1*
Silver, Jesse Forrest 1872- *WhAm 5*
Silver, Maurice A 1893-1960 *NatCAB 46*
Silver, Maxwell 1891-1966 *WhAm 4*
Silver, Thomas 1813-1888 *ApCAB, DcAmB, NatCAB 6, WhAm H*
Silver, William 1870-1934 *NatCAB 27*
Silvera, Frank Alvin 1914-1970 *WhAm 5*
Silvercruys, Baron 1893-1975 *WhAm 6*
Silvercruys, Suzanne d1973 *WhAm 6*
Silverman, Alexander 1881-1962 *NatCAB 16, WhAm 4*
Silverman, Archibald 1880-1966 *WhAm 4*
Silverman, David 1909-1959 *WhAm 3*
Silverman, Irving 1912-1973 *WhAm 5*
Silverman, Joseph 1860-1930 *AmBi, ApCAB X, DcAmB, NatCAB 26, WhAm 1*
Silverman, Leslie 1914-1966 *NatCAB 52, WhAm 4*
Silverman, Morris 1894-1972 *WhAm 5*
Silverman, Roland E 1911-1974 *WhAm 6*
Silverman, Sime 1872-1933 *NatCAB 24*
Silverman, Sime 1873-1933 *DcAmB, WebAB, WhAm HA, WhAm 4*
Silvers, Earl Reed 1891-1948 *WhAm 2*
Silvers, Louis 1889-1954 *DcAmB S5*
Silverson, Harry 1910-1963 *NatCAB 53*
Silverson, William 1852-1924 *NatCAB 20*
Silverstein, Joseph Lee 1898-1950 *NatCAB 46*
Silverstein, Max 1878-1955 *NatCAB 43*
Silverthorn, William Henry 1850-1910 *NatCAB 18*
Silverthorne, George Morrill 1877-1953 *NatCAB 44*
Silvester, Lindsay McDonald 1889-1963 *WhAm 4*
Silvester, Peter d1845 *BiAUS*
Silvester, Peter 1734-1808 *BiDrAC, WhAm H*
Silvester, Peter Henry 1807-1882 *BiAUS, BiDrAC, WhAm H*
Silvester, Richard William 1857- *WhAm 4*
Silvestri, George 1911-1967 *NatCAB 53*
Silveus, William Arents 1875- *WhAm 5*
Silvia, Frank Machado 1882-1948 *NatCAB 39*
Silvis, Richard Shippen 1907-1960 *NatCAB 49*
Silvius, George Harold 1908- *BiDAmEd*
Silzer, George Sebastian 1870-1940 *NatCAB 34, WhAm 1*
Sim, F L 1834-1894 *NatCAB 2*
Sim, John Robert 1849-1925 *WhAm 1*
Simcock, John 1630?-1703 *Drake, NatCAB 16*
Simcoe, John Graves 1752-1806 *AmBi, ApCAB, Drake*
Simenon, Georges 1903- *McGEWB*
Simer, Parke Harvey 1897-1972 *NatCAB 56*
Simeral, Charles Delmar 1875-1947 *NatCAB 37*
Simes, Lewis Mallalieu 1889-1974 *WhAm 6*
Simes, Mary Jane 1807-1872 *NewYHSD*
Simic, Stanoje 1893-1970 *WhAm 5*
Simitiere *NewYHSD*
Simitiere, Pierre Eugene Du d1784 *ApCAB*
Simitiere, Pierre Eugene Du d1788 *Drake*
Simkhovitch, Mary Melinda Kingsbury 1867-1951 *DcAmB S5, WhAm 3, WomWWA 14*
Simkhovitch, Vladimir Gregorievitch 1874-1959 *WhAm 3*
Simkins, Arthur 1750?-1826 *ApCAB*
Simkins, Eldred 1779-1831 *BiDrAC, WhAm H*
Simkins, Eldred 1779-1832 *ApCAB, BiAUS, NatCAB 11, TwCBDA*
Simkins, Henry Walter 1868-1925 *WhAm 1*
Simkins, William Stewart 1842-1929 *WhAm 1*
Simler, George Brenner 1921-1972 *WhAm 5*
Simley, Irvin T 1887-1967 *WhAm 5*
Simmang, John Schelnick 1906-1969 *NatCAB 56*
Simmel, Georg 1858-1918 *McGEWB*
Simmill, Elvin Raymond 1906-1971 *WhAm 5*

Simmonds, Albert Carleton, Jr. 1902-1963
  NatCAB 50, *WhAm 4*
Simmonds, Frank William 1876-1971 *WhAm 5*
Simmonds, Robert 1892-1952 *NatCAB 39*
Simmone *NewYHSD*
Simmons, Aaron Trabue 1876-1963 *NatCAB 50*
Simmons, Abraham *NewYHSD*
Simmons, Allen Thurman 1888-1965
  NatCAB 51
Simmons, Caesar Felton 1866- *WhoColR*
Simmons, Charles Ezra 1840-1918 *NatCAB 29*
Simmons, Daniel Augustus 1873- *WhAm 5*
Simmons, David Andrew 1897-1951 *WhAm 3*
Simmons, Dayton Cooper 1877- *WhAm 5*
Simmons, Donald MacLaren 1889-1961
  NatCAB 45
Simmons, Dwight Lane 1898-1970 *WhAm 5*
Simmons, Edward Alfred 1875-1931
  NatCAB 24, *WhAm 1*
Simmons, Edward Campbell 1839-1920
  NatCAB 26, *WhAm 1*
Simmons, Edward Emerson 1852-1931 *AmBi*,
  DcAmB, *NatCAB 13*, *WhAm 1*
Simmons, Edward Helfenstein 1870-1937
  NatCAB 30
Simmons, Edward Henry Harriman 1876-1955
  WhAm 3
Simmons, Edward Peynado 1893-1951
  NatCAB 40
Simmons, Elizabeth Margret 1891-1947
  WhAm 2
Simmons, Emma Brown 1861- *WomWWA 14*
Simmons, Ernest J 1903-1972 *WhAm 5*
Simmons, Fay Alton 1878-1929 *ApCAB X*,
  NatCAB 22
Simmons, Franklin 1839-1913 *AmBi*,
  BnEnAmA, *DcAmB*, *NatCAB 11*,
  NewYHSD, *TwCBDA*, *WhAm 1*
Simmons, Franklin 1842-1913 *ApCAB*
Simmons, Furnifold McLendel 1854-1940
  ApCAB X, *BiDrAC*, *DcAmB S2*,
  NatCAB 12, *NatCAB 35*, *TwCBDA*,
  WhAmP
Simmons, Furnifold McLendell 1854-1940
  WhAm 1
Simmons, George Abel 1791-1857 *BiAUS*,
  BiDrAC, *WhAm H*
Simmons, George E 1898-1972 *WhAm 5*
Simmons, George Finlay 1895-1955 *WhAm 3*
Simmons, George Frederick 1814-1855 *ApCAB*,
  Drake, *NatCAB 7*, *TwCBDA*
Simmons, George Henry 1852-1937 *DcAmB S2*,
  WhAm 1
Simmons, George Welch 1878-1930 *WhAm 1*
Simmons, Grant G, Sr. 1893-1974 *WhAm 6*
Simmons, Gustavus Lincoln 1832- *NatCAB 7*
Simmons, Hannah Coralynn 1877-
  WomWWA 14
Simmons, Henry Clay 1845-1899 *TwCBDA*,
  WhAm 1
Simmons, Henry Martyn 1841- *WhAm 1*
Simmons, Hezzleton Erastus 1885-1954
  NatCAB 43
Simmons, J P 1891-1961 *WhAm 4*
Simmons, James 1821- *ApCAB*
Simmons, James Fowler 1795-1864 *ApCAB*,
  BiAUS, *BiDrAC*, *Drake*, *NatCAB 9*,
  TwCBDA, *WhAm H*
Simmons, James Henry 1867- *WhAm 5*
Simmons, James Samuel 1861-1935 *BiDrAC*
Simmons, James Stevens 1890-1954 *DcAmB S5*,
  NatCAB 49, *WhAm 3*
Simmons, James William 1885-1969 *WhAm 5*
Simmons, James Wright *ApCAB*
Simmons, John 1796-1870 *Drake*
Simmons, John Anderson 1892-1962
  NatCAB 50
Simmons, John F 1892-1968 *WhAm 4A*
Simmons, John James 1862-1948 *NatCAB 37*
Simmons, John Paul 1880-1946 *NatCAB 35*
Simmons, Joseph Edward 1841-1910 *ApCAB*,
  NatCAB 2, *WhAm 1*
Simmons, Leo 1860-1930 *NatCAB 22*
Simmons, Leo Charles 1900-1959 *WhAm 3*
Simmons, Lessie Southgate 1863-1914 *WhAm 1*,
  WomWWA 14
Simmons, Lucretia VanTuyl *WomWWA 14*
Simmonds, Medora Aiken *WomWWA 14*

Simmons, Robert Cantrell 1894-1967 *WhAm 4*
Simmons, Robert Glenmore 1891-1969 *BiDrAC*,
  NatCAB 57
Simmons, Roscoe Conkling Murray 1878-1951
  DcAmB S5
Simmons, S *NewYHSD*
Simmons, Thomas *BiAUS Sup*
Simmons, Thomas Jackson 1864-1942 *WhAm 2*
Simmons, Thomas Jefferson 1837-1905 *DcAmB*,
  NatCAB 2, *TwCBDA*, *WhAm H*,
  WhAm 3
Simmons, Virgil M 1893-1958 *WhAm 3*
Simmons, Wallace Delafield 1867- *WhAm 4*
Simmons, Walter Mayes 1903-1968 *NatCAB 54*
Simmons, Warren Seabury 1867-1944 *WhAm 2*
Simmons, Will 1884- *WhAm 2*
Simmons, William Hayne 1785?- *ApCAB*
Simmons, William Johnson 1849- *ApCAB*
Simmons, William Joseph 1880-1945
  DcAmB S3
Simmons, William Marvin 1885-1940 *WhAm 1*
Simmons, Zalmon Gilbert 1828-1910
  NatCAB 15
Simms, Albert Gallatin 1882-1964 *BiDrAC*,
  WhAm 4, *WhAmP*
Simms, Beverley Singleton 1910-1972
  NatCAB 57
Simms, Charles Harries 1868-1941 *NatCAB 36*
Simms, Daisy Florence 1873-1923 *NotAW*
Simms, Edward Francis 1870-1938 *NatCAB 33*
Simms, Ephraim Fitch 1803-1886 *NatCAB 12*
Simms, Jeptha Root 1807-1883 *ApCAB*, *Drake*,
  NatCAB 7, *TwCBDA*, *WhAm H*
Simms, John Field 1885-1954 *WhAm 3*
Simms, Joseph 1833-1920 *ApCAB*, *NatCAB 7*,
  WhAm 1
Simms, Lewis Wesley 1885-1957 *WhAm 3*
Simms, P Marion 1869-1946 *WhAm 2*
Simms, Ruth Hanna McCormick 1880-1944
  DcAmB S3, *NatCAB 34*, *NotAW*,
  WhAm 2
Simms, S Champan 1863-1937 *WhAm 1*
Simms, William David 1860- *WhoColR*
Simms, William E 1822-1898 *BiAUS*
Simms, William Elliot 1822-1898 *WhAm H*
Simms, William Elliott 1822-1898 *BiDConf*,
  DcAmB
Simms, William Emmett 1822-1898 *BiDrAC*
Simms, William Gilmore 1806-1870 *AmBi*,
  ApCAB, *DcAmB*, *Drake*, *McGEWB*,
  NatCAB 6, *TwCBDA*, *WebAB*,
  WhAm H
Simms, William Philip 1881-1957 *NatCAB 47*,
  WhAm 3
Simon Bredon *DcScB*
Simon De Phares 1450?-1499? *DcScB*
Simon, Abram 1872-1938 *NatCAB 28*,
  WhAm 1
Simon, Andre Louis 1877-1970 *WhAm 5*
Simon, August *NewYHSD*
Simon, Augustus D *NewYHSD*
Simon, Benedict 1824?- *NewYHSD*
Simon, Charles Edmund 1866-1927 *WhAm 1*
Simon, Clarence Joseph 1911-1974 *WhAm 6*
Simon, Clarence Turkle 1897-1967 *WhAm 5*
Simon, D Bernard 1906-1953 *NatCAB 41*
Simon, Dennis 1830?- *NewYHSD*
Simon, Dionis 1830?- *NewYHSD*
Simon, Edward Paul 1878-1949 *WhAm 2*
Simon, Etienne 1747-1809 *ApCAB*
Simon, Sir Francis 1893-1956 *WhAm 3*
Simon, Franklin 1865-1934 *WhAm 1*
Simon, Franz Eugen 1893-1956 *DcScB*
Simon, Frederick M 1886-1957 *WhAm 4*
Simon, George Dewey 1898-1944 *NatCAB 35*
Simon, Grant Miles 1887-1967 *WhAm 5*
Simon, Henry William 1901-1970 *WhAm 5*
Simon, Herbert James 1905-1968 *NatCAB 56*
Simon, Herman 1850- *NatCAB 14*
Simon, Mrs. Hiram Esli 1860- *WomWWA 14*
Simon, Sir John 1816-1904 *BiHiMed*
Simon, Joseph 1851-1935 *ApCAB Sup*,
  BiDrAC, *NatCAB 13*, *TwCBDA*,
  WhAm 1, *WhAmP*
Simon, Jules Francois 1814-1896 *McGEWB*
Simon, Julian Edwin 1901-1965 *WhAm 4*
Simon, Leon Charles 1876-1953 *WhAm 3*
Simon, Louis A d1958 *WhAm 3*

Simon, Naif Louis 1914-1968 *NatCAB 55*,
  WhAm 5
Simon, Nathan David 1864-1927 *NatCAB 20*
Simon, Neil 1927- *WebAB*
Simon, Pedro Antonio 1560?-1630? *ApCAB*
Simon, Richard Leo 1899-1960 *NatCAB 44*,
  WhAm 4
Simon, Robert 1852-1901 *NatCAB 14*
Simon, Sam Seymour 1888-1964 *NatCAB 50*
Simon, Webster Godman 1892-1974 *WhAm 6*
Simon, William 1844-1916 *NatCAB 17*,
  WhAm 1
Simon, Yves Rene 1903-1961 *NatCAB 50*,
  WhAm 4
Simond, Alfred 1740-1801 *ApCAB*
Simond, Louis 1767-1831 *NewYHSD*,
  WhAm H
Simond, Maynard Ewing 1888-1963 *WhAm 4*
Simonds, Alvan Tracy 1876-1941 *NatCAB 31*,
  WhAm 1
Simonds, Daniel 1847-1913 *ApCAB X*
Simonds, Frank Herbert 1878-1936 *AmBi*,
  DcAmB S2, *WhAm 1*
Simonds, Frederic William 1853-1941 *TwCBDA*,
  WhAm 1
Simonds, George Sherwin 1874-1938 *WhAm 1*
Simonds, George W *NewYHSD*
Simonds, Gifford Kingsbury 1880-1941
  NatCAB 33, *WhAm 1*
Simonds, Godfrey Baldwin 1904-1952 *WhAm 3*
Simonds, Guy 1903-1974 *WhWW-II*
Simonds, James Persons 1878-1964 *WhAm 4*
Simonds, Martha Rumsey 1857- *WomWWA 14*
Simonds, Ossian Cole 1855-1931 *NatCAB 22*,
  WhAm 1
Simonds, William 1822-1859 *ApCAB*, *Drake*,
  NatCAB 5, *WhAm H*
Simonds, William Adams 1887-1963 *WhAm 4*
Simonds, William Edgar 1841-1903 *TwCBDA*,
  WhAm 1
Simonds, William Edgar 1842-1903 *BiDrAC*,
  NatCAB 1
Simonds, William Edward 1860-1947 *ApCAB X*,
  WhAm 2
Simone, G F Edgardo 1890-1948 *WhAm 2*
Simoni, Antonio *NewYHSD*
Simonin, D *NewYHSD*
Simonin, Isaac Moore 1856-1926 *NatCAB 27*
Simonin, Louis Laurent 1830- *ApCAB*
Simonne, T *NewYHSD*
Simonov, Konstantin Mikhailovich 1915-
  McGEWB
Simons, Misses *NewYHSD*
Simons, Algie Martin 1870-1950 *DcAmB S4*,
  WhAm 3
Simons, Amory Coffin 1869- *WhAm 5*
Simons, Charles *NewYHSD*
Simons, Charles Caspar 1876-1964 *WhAm 4*
Simons, Emogene Sanford 1880-
  WomWWA 14
Simons, Francis X *NewYHSD*
Simons, George 1834-1917 *IIBEAAW*,
  NewYHSD
Simons, George Albert 1874-1952 *WhAm 3*
Simons, Grace Churchyard 1866-
  WomWWA 14
Simons, Hans 1893-1972 *NatCAB 56*,
  WhAm 5
Simons, Helen Savage 1873- *WomWWA 14*
Simons, Henry Calvert 1899-1946 *DcAmB S4*
Simons, Howard Perry 1907-1972 *WhAm 5*
Simons, Irving 1884-1951 *NatCAB 39*
Simons, James 1839-1919 *NatCAB 18*,
  WhAm 1
Simons, Jessie Vanderbilt *WomWWA 14*
Simons, John P *NewYHSD*
Simons, Joseph *NewYHSD*
Simons, Kenneth W 1898-1948 *WhAm 2*
Simons, Manley Hale 1879- *WhAm 6*
Simons, Manning 1846-1911 *NatCAB 16*
Simons, May Wood d1948 *WhAm 2*,
  WomWWA 14
Simons, Michael Laird 1843-1880 *ApCAB*
Simons, Milton E *NewYHSD*
Simons, Minot 1868-1941 *WhAm 1*
Simons, Robert Edward 1865- *WhoColR*
Simons, Samuel 1792-1847 *BiAUS*, *BiDrAC*,
  WhAm H

Simons, Sarah Emma 1867- *WhAm 4,*
WomWWA 14
Simons, Seymour Broudy 1896-1949
NatCAB 39
Simons, Thomas Young 1828-1878 *ApCAB,*
NatCAB 11
Simons, Wilford Collins 1871-1952 *WhAm 3*
Simonson, Gustave 1864- *WhAm 4*
Simonson, Henry James, Jr. 1894-1967
WhAm 4A
Simonson, John Smith 1796-1881 *ApCAB,*
Drake
Simonson, Lee 1888-1967 *WebAB, WhAm 4*
Simonson, William A 1865-1937 *WhAm 1*
Simonton, Charles Bryson 1838-1911 *BiDrAC,*
NatCAB 8
Simonton, Charles Henry 1829-1904 *DcAmB,*
NatCAB 12, TwCBDA, WhAm 1
Simonton, Ida Vera d1931 *WhAm 1,*
WomWWA 14
Simonton, James William 1823-1882 *ApCAB,*
DcAmB, WhAm H
Simonton, John Wiggins 1826-1903 *WhAm 1*
Simonton, William 1788-1846 *BiAUS, BiDrAC,*
WhAm H
Simovic, Dusan 1882- *WhWW-II*
Simpers, Robert Nichols 1851- *NatCAB 7*
Simpich, Frederick 1878-1950 *WhAm 2*
Simpkins, George W 1909-1966 *WhAm 4*
Simpkins, John 1862-1898 *BiDrAC,*
NatCAB 7
Simpkins, Nathaniel Stone 1861-1919
NatCAB 18
Simpkins, Nathaniel Stone, Jr. 1885-1918
NatCAB 30
Simplicius 500?-533? *DcScB*
Simps, James C *NewYHSD*
Simpson, Aemilius d1831 *ApCAB*
Simpson, Albert Benjamin 1843-1919 *DcAmB*
Simpson, Albert Benjamin 1844-1919 *WhAm 1*
Simpson, Alex, Jr. 1855-1935 *WhAm 1*
Simpson, Alexander 1811- *ApCAB*
Simpson, Alfred Dexter 1891-1955 *WhAm 3*
Simpson, Belle Buckingham *WomWWA 14*
Simpson, Burton Thorne 1873-1946 *NatCAB 35*
Simpson, Charles Jay 1878-1952 *NatCAB 50*
Simpson, Charles Torrey 1846-1932 *DcAmB S1,*
NatCAB 23, WhAm 1
Simpson, Charles William 1879- *WhAm 6*
Simpson, Clarence L 1896-1969 *WhAm 5*
Simpson, Clarence Oliver 1879- *WhAm 6*
Simpson, Corelli C W 1837- *AmWom*
Simpson, Cuthbert Aikman 1892-1969 *WhAm 5*
Simpson, David Ferguson 1860-1925
NatCAB 20, WhAm 1
Simpson, Earnest Clyde 1872-1946 *NatCAB 34*
Simpson, Edmund Shaw 1784-1848 *ApCAB,*
DcAmB, Drake, WhAm H
Simpson, Edna Huestis 1882- *WomWWA 14*
Simpson, Edna Oakes 1891- *BiDrAC*
Simpson, Edward 1824-1888 *AmBi, ApCAB,*
DcAmB, NatCAB 11, TwCBDA,
WhAm H
Simpson, Edward 1860-1930 *NatCAB 41,*
WhAm 1
Simpson, Elsie Carson 1872- *WomWWA 14*
Simpson, Floyd Robert 1906-1974 *WhAm 6*
Simpson, Frances 1863- *WhAm 4,*
WomWWA 14
Simpson, Frances May 1875- *WomWWA 14*
Simpson, Frank Edward 1869-1948 *WhAm 2*
Simpson, Frank Farrow 1868-1948 *NatCAB 37,*
WhAm 1
Simpson, Frank Leslie 1875- *WhAm 5*
Simpson, Friench 1848-1923 *WhAm 1*
Simpson, Sir George 1796?-1860 *ApCAB,*
Drake
Simpson, George Barton 1881-1954 *NatCAB 41*
Simpson, George Gaylord 1902- *WebAB*
Simpson, George Semmes 1818-1885 *ApCAB*
Simpson, Grace Sybrandt *WomWWA 14*
Simpson, H Lee 1878-1948 *NatCAB 36*
Simpson, Harold Taylor 1892-1966 *NatCAB 51*
Simpson, Harold Vernon 1897-1962 *NatCAB 51*
Simpson, Hartley 1900-1967 *WhAm 5*
Simpson, Helen Augusta 1868- *WomWWA 14*
Simpson, Henry 1790-1868 *ApCAB, Drake*
Simpson, Herbert Downs 1876-1962 *WhAm 4*

Simpson, Herman 1873- *WhAm 5*
Simpson, Howard Edwin 1874-1938 *WhAm 1*
Simpson, Howard Woodworth 1892-1963
NatCAB 52
Simpson, I *NewYHSD*
Simpson, J J *NewYHSD*
Simpson, James 1796-1876 *NatCAB 12*
Simpson, James 1874-1939 *NatCAB 46,*
WhAm 1
Simpson, James, Jr. 1905-1960 *BiDrAC,*
WhAm 3
Simpson, James Alexander 1775-1848
NewYHSD
Simpson, James Alexander 1805?- *NewYHSD*
Simpson, James Alexander 1890-1973 *WhAm 6*
Simpson, James C *NewYHSD*
Simpson, James Clarke 1864-1948 *WhAm 2*
Simpson, James Hervey 1812?-1883 *Drake*
Simpson, James Hervey 1813-1883 *ApCAB,*
DcAmB, WebAMB, WhAm H
Simpson, James Inglis 1885-1958 *WhAm 3*
Simpson, Sir James Young 1811-1870 *AsBiEn,*
BiHiMed
Simpson, Jean Emerson 1900-1962 *NatCAB 49*
Simpson, Jeremiah 1842-1905 *BiDrAC,*
WebAB, WhAmP
Simpson, Jerry 1842-1905 *DcAmB, EncAAH,*
EncAB, NatCAB 1, REnAW, TwCBDA,
WhAm 1
Simpson, Jesse L 1884-1973 *WhAm 6*
Simpson, John *NewYHSD*
Simpson, John 1812-1885 *ApCAB*
Simpson, John 1840-1914 *WhAm 1*
Simpson, John Andrew 1871-1934 *DcAmB,*
WhAm 1
Simpson, John Childs 1889-1962 *WhAm 4*
Simpson, John Dixon 1858- *WhAm 4*
Simpson, John Frederick 1928-1973 *WhAm 6*
Simpson, John G *NewYHSD*
Simpson, John Nathan 1869-1947 *WhAm 2*
Simpson, John R 1907-1969 *WhAm 5*
Simpson, John Reid 1879-1965 *NatCAB 52*
Simpson, John Roy 1876-1956 *NatCAB 44,*
WhAm 3
Simpson, John William 1889-1973 *WhAm 6*
Simpson, John Woodruff 1850-1920 *ApCAB X,*
NatCAB 25, WhAm 1
Simpson, Joseph *NewYHSD*
Simpson, Joseph 1794?- *NewYHSD*
Simpson, Joseph Warren 1872- *WhAm 2*
Simpson, Josephine Sarles 1862- *BiCAW,*
WhAm 4, WomWWA 14
Simpson, Josiah *BiAUS*
Simpson, Josiah 1815-1874 *ApCAB*
Simpson, Kathrine Woodford *WomWWA 14*
Simpson, Kemper 1893-1970 *WhAm 5*
Simpson, Kenneth Farrand 1895-1941 *BiDrAC,*
WhAm 1
Simpson, Kenneth Miller 1882-1957 *WhAm 3*
Simpson, Kirke Larue 1881-1972 *WhAm 5*
Simpson, Leslie Butler 1885-1961 *NatCAB 50*
Simpson, Lizzie M *WomWWA 14*
Simpson, Lola Jean 1880- *WhAm 6*
Simpson, Louis 1877-1949 *NatCAB 37*
Simpson, Marcus DeLafayette 1824-1909
ApCAB, TwCBDA, WhAm 1
Simpson, Mathew 1810-1884 *Drake*
Simpson, Matthew 1811-1884 *AmBi, ApCAB,*
DcAmB, DcAmReB, NatCAB 7,
TwCBDA, WebAB, WhAm H
Simpson, Michael 1740-1813 *ApCAB, Drake*
Simpson, Michael Hodge 1809-1884 *DcAmB,*
NatCAB 10, WhAm H
Simpson, Milward Lee 1897- *BiDrAC*
Simpson, Oramel Hinckley 1870-1932
NatCAB 25
Simpson, Orville 1861-1944 *NatCAB 34*
Simpson, Richard Franklin 1798-1882 *BiAUS,*
BiDrAC, WhAm H
Simpson, Richard Lee 1873-1947 *NatCAB 36,*
WhAm 5
Simpson, Richard Murray 1900-1960 *BiDrAC,*
WhAm 3, WhAm 4, WhAmP
Simpson, Robert 1886-1934 *WhAm 1*
Simpson, Robert Edward 1869- *WhAm 5*
Simpson, Robert Tennent 1837- *WhAm 1*
Simpson, Roy E 1893- *BiDAmEd*
Simpson, Samuel 1814-1894 *NatCAB 10*

Simpson, Samuel 1868-1955 *WhAm 3*
Simpson, Sidney Elmer 1894-1958 *BiDrAC,*
WhAm 3, WhAmP
Simpson, Sidney Post 1898-1949 *WhAm 2*
Simpson, Sloan 1876- *WhAm 5*
Simpson, Solomon L *NewYHSD*
Simpson, Stanley Gibson 1900-1961
NatCAB 48
Simpson, Stephen 1789-1854 *ApCAB, DcAmB,*
Drake, NatCAB 5, WhAm H
Simpson, Sumner 1874-1953 *WhAm 3*
Simpson, Sutherland 1863-1926 *WhAm 1*
Simpson, Thomas 1710-1761 *DcScB*
Simpson, Thomas 1808-1840 *ApCAB*
Simpson, Thomas Henry 1859-1923 *NatCAB 20*
Simpson, Thomas McNider, Jr. 1882-1965
WhAm 4
Simpson, Virgil Earl 1875-1943 *WhAm 2*
Simpson, W Arthur 1887-1971 *NatCAB 56*
Simpson, Wallace 1880- *IIBEAAW*
Simpson, Wallis Warfield *WebAB*
Simpson, William 1823-1899 *IIBEAAW*
Simpson, William 1839-1905 *NatCAB 24*
Simpson, William Augustus 1854- *WhAm 4*
Simpson, William B 1876-1948 *WhAm 2*
Simpson, William David 1875-1950 *NatCAB 40*
Simpson, William Dunlap 1823-1890 *BiDConf,*
DcAmB, NatCAB 12, TwCBDA,
WhAm H
Simpson, William Edgar 1856-1919 *NatCAB 17*
Simpson, William Gibson 1896-1956
NatCAB 45
Simpson, William H d1872 *NewYHSD*
Simpson, William Hood 1888- *WebAMB*
Simpson, William James 1877-1932 *WhAm 1*
Simpson, William Kelly 1855-1914 *DcAmB,*
WhAm 1
Simpson, William R 1826?- *NewYHSD*
Simpson, William Robert 1922-1975 *WhAm 6*
Simpson, William Thomas 1855-1915
NatCAB 26
Simpson, Willie Perry 1872- *WomWWA 14*
Simrall, Horatio F 1818- *NatCAB 5*
Simrall, James 1781-1823 *NatCAB 38*
Simrall, John Graham 1840-1905 *NatCAB 38*
Simrall, Josephine Price 1869-1949 *WhAm 2,*
WomWWA 14
Simrell, William LeGrand 1863-1933 *WhAm 1*
Sims, Miss *NewYHSD*
Sims, Alexander D 1803-1848 *BiAUS*
Sims, Alexander Dromgoole 1803-1848 *ApCAB,*
BiDrAC, WhAm H
Sims, Alexander Drumgoole 1803-1848
NatCAB 12
Sims, Alfred Varley 1864-1944 *NatCAB 33*
Sims, Alva Ray 1909-1964 *WhAm 4*
Sims, Cecil 1893-1968 *WhAm 5*
Sims, Cecil LaVell 1902-1963 *NatCAB 51*
Sims, Charles Abercrombie 1866-1942 *WhAm 2*
Sims, Charles N 1835-1908 *ApCAB, DcAmB,*
NatCAB 13, TwCBDA, WhAm HA,
WhAm 4
Sims, Clifford Stanley 1839-1896 *ApCAB,*
Drake, TwCBDA
Sims, Clifford Stanley 1868-1935 *WhAm 1*
Sims, Dillon Odell 1889-1957 *NatCAB 47*
Sims, Edward Dromgoole 1805-1845 *ApCAB,*
Drake
Sims, Edward Drumgoole 1805-1845 *NatCAB 7*
Sims, Edwin W 1870-1948 *WhAm 2*
Sims, Felix Rice 1863- *WhoColR*
Sims, Frederick William 1828-1875 *BiDConf*
Sims, Frederick Wilmer 1862-1925 *NatCAB 19,*
WhAm 1
Sims, George Henry 1871- *WhoColR*
Sims, George Pence 1901-1969 *NatCAB 56*
Sims, Harry Marion 1851- *ApCAB, WhAm 4*
Sims, Henry Augustus 1832-1875 *ApCAB*
Sims, Henry Upson 1873-1961 *NatCAB 46,*
WhAm 4
Sims, Hollie Turner 1884- *WhoColR*
Sims, Hugo Sheridan, Jr. 1921- *BiDrAC*
Sims, James Marion 1813-1883 *AmBi, ApCAB,*
BiHiMed, DcAmB, NatCAB 2, TwCBDA,
WebAB, WhAm H
Sims, James Peacock 1849-1882 *ApCAB*
Sims, John Francis 1862-1926 *NatCAB 20,*
WhAm 1

Sims, Leonard Henly 1807-1886 *BiAUS,*
BiDrAC, WhAm H
Sims, Marian McCamy 1899-1961 *WhAm 4*
Sims, Newell LeRoy 1878-1965 *WhAm 4*
Sims, Otis Astor 1874- *WhoColR*
Sims, Ray 1888-1961 *NatCAB 49*
Sims, Richard Maury 1874-1935 *WhAm 1*
Sims, Samuel *NewYHSD*
Sims, Thetus Willrette 1852-1939 *BiDrAC,*
NatCAB 35, TwCBDA, WhAmP
Sims, Thetus Wilrette 1852-1939 *WhAm 1*
Sims, Walter Arthur 1880- *WhAm 6*
Sims, William Henry 1837-1920 *NatCAB 6*
Sims, William Sowden 1858-1936 *AmBi,*
ApCAB X, DcAmB S2, EncAB,
McGEWB, NatCAB 27, WebAB,
WebAMB, WhAm 1
Sims, Winfield Scott 1844-1918 *AmBi, ApCAB,*
DcAmB, TwCBDA, WhAm 1
Simson, R *NewYHSD*
Simson, Robert 1687-1768 *DcScB*
Simson, Sampson 1780-1857 *ApCAB*
Sina, Abu Ali Al-Husayn, Ibn 980-1037
DcScB Sup
Sina, Abu Ali Al-Hussein Ibn A, Ibn 980-1037
DcScB
Sinan, Kodja Mimar 1489-1578 *McGEWB*
Sinan Ibn Thabit Ibn Qurra, Abu Said 880?-943
DcScB
Sinatra, Frank 1915- *WebAB*
Sinatra, Frank Albert 1917- *EncAB*
Sincerbeaux, Frank H 1874-1969 *WhAm 5*
Sinclair, Aileen Cleveland Higgins 1882-
WomWWA 14
Sinclair, Alexander Doull 1828- *WhAm 4*
Sinclair, Alexander Grant 1842-1915 *WhAm 1*
Sinclair, Angus 1841-1919 *WhAm 1*
Sinclair, Arthur 1780?-1831 *Drake*
Sinclair, Carrie Bell 1839- *ApCAB*
Sinclair, Catherine *NotAW*
Sinclair, Charles *BiAUS*
Sinclair, Daniel Alison 1871-1947 *NatCAB 38*
Sinclair, Dohrman James 1860-1915
NatCAB 16
Sinclair, Earle Westwood 1874-1944 *WhAm 2*
Sinclair, Harold Augustus 1907-1966 *WhAm 4*
Sinclair, Harry Ford 1876-1956 *WebAB,*
WhAm 3
Sinclair, Henry Harbinson 1858-1914
NatCAB 15
Sinclair, Herbert 1875-1931 *NatCAB 35*
Sinclair, James Herbert 1871-1943 *BiDrAC,*
EncAAH, WhAm 2, WhAmP
Sinclair, John 1836-1916 *NatCAB 16*
Sinclair, John Elbridge 1838-1915 *WhAm 1*
Sinclair, John Franklin 1885-1950 *WhAm 3*
Sinclair, John Stephens 1897-1972 *WhAm 5*
Sinclair, L *NewYHSD*
Sinclair, Lee Wiley 1836-1916 *WhAm 1*
Sinclair, Peter *NewYHSD*
Sinclair, Peter 1825- *ApCAB*
Sinclair, Peter Thomas 1906-1970 *WhAm 5*
Sinclair, Robert Soutter 1872-1937 *WhAm 1*
Sinclair, Thomas, Jr. 1832?- *NewYHSD*
Sinclair, Thomas S 1805?-1881 *NewYHSD*
Sinclair, Upton Beale 1878-1968 *McGEWB*
Sinclair, Upton Beall 1878-1968 *ApCAB X,*
EncAAH, EncAB, NatCAB 14, WebAB
Sinclair, William 1827?- *NewYHSD*
Sinclair, William 1835-1905 *TwCBDA,*
WhAm 1
Sinclair, William Albert 1858- *WhAm 4*
Sinclair, William Richardson 1884-1965
NatCAB 52, WhAm 4
Sindeband, Maurice Leonard 1887-1971
WhAm 5
Sindelar, Paul Joseph 1929-1974 *WhAm 6*
Sindell, Theodore Thurston 1905-1957
NatCAB 47
Sinek, William J 1881-1964 *WhAm 4*
Sinek, William Jackson 1877-1964 *NatCAB 51*
Sinex, Thomas Henry 1824- *NatCAB 5*
Singer, Berthold 1860- *WhAm 5*
Singer, Edgar Arthur, Jr. 1873-1954 *WhAm 3*
Singer, Frederic 1847-1923 *WhAm 1*
Singer, Frederick George 1897-1971 *WhAm 5*
Singer, Harold Douglas 1875-1940 *WhAm 1*
Singer, Harold Ralph 1891-1942 *WhAm 2*

Singer, Henry B 1873- *WhAm 6*
Singer, Isaac Bashevis 1904- *McGEWB,*
WebAB
Singer, Isaac Merrit 1811-1875 *DcAmB,*
WebAB, WhAm H
Singer, Isaac Merritt 1811-1875 *AmBi, ApCAB,*
NatCAB 5, TwCBDA
Singer, Isaac Merritt 1812-1875 *NatCAB 30*
Singer, Isidor 1859-1939 *NatCAB 14*
Singer, Isidore 1859-1939 *WhAm 1*
Singer, Israel Joshua 1893-1944 *DcAmB S3,*
WhAm 2
Singer, John *NewYHSD*
Singer, Otto 1833-1894 *AmBi, NatCAB 7,*
WhAm H
Singer, Russell E 1897-1975 *WhAm 6*
Singer, Willard Edison 1904-1972 *WhAm 5*
Singer, William H, Jr. 1868-1943 *WhAm 2*
Singer, William Henry 1835-1909 *NatCAB 23*
Singerly, William Miskey 1832-1898 *ApCAB,*
DcAmB, NatCAB 1, WhAm H
Singh, Raja Sir Maharaj 1878- *WhAm 6*
Singher, Heron Orlando 1914-1973 *NatCAB 57*
Singiser, Theodore Frelinghuysen 1845-1907
BiDrAC
Single, J F *NewYHSD*
Singletary, B Henry 1890-1964 *WhAm 4*
Singleton, Mister *NewYHSD*
Singleton, Albert Olin 1882-1947 *WhAm 2*
Singleton, Asa Leon 1876-1943 *WhAm 2*
Singleton, Esther 1865-1930 *AmBi, DcAmB,*
TwCBDA, WhAm 1, WomWWA 14
Singleton, George 1892-1945 *NatCAB 34*
Singleton, J Milton 1893-1961 *NatCAB 50*
Singleton, James Washington 1811-1892
BiDrAC, DcAmB, WhAm H
Singleton, Marvin Edward 1872-1938
NatCAB 43, WhAm 1
Singleton, Micajah Thomas 1892-1959
NatCAB 47
Singleton, Ortho Robards 1814-1889 *BiDConf*
Singleton, Otho Robards 1814-1889 *BiAUS,*
BiDrAC, TwCBDA, WhAm H, WhAmP
Singleton, Richard 1851-1921 *NatCAB 31*
Singleton, Richard Henry 1865- *WhoColR*
Singleton, Thomas Day d1833 *BiAUS,*
BiDrAC, WhAm H
Singleton, William Daniel 1908-1969 *WhAm 5*
Singley, Albert Henry 1905-1974 *WhAm 6*
Singley, B Lloyd 1864- *WhAm 4*
Singmaster, Elsie 1879-1958 *WhAm 3,*
WomWWA 14
Singmaster, James Arthur 1878-1962 *WhAm 4*
Singmaster, John Alden 1852-1926 *WhAm 1*
Sink, Charles Albert 1879-1972 *WhAm 5*
Sink, Emory Walter 1887-1965 *NatCAB 51*
Sink, H Hoyle 1888-1968 *NatCAB 54*
Sink, Robert Frederick 1905-1965 *WhAm 4*
Sinkler, Charles 1874-1952 *NatCAB 48*
Sinkler, John P B 1875-1959 *WhAm 3*
Sinkler, Wharton 1845-1910 *WhAm 1*
Sinn, Joseph Albert 1854- *NatCAB 10*
Sinnett, Francis *NewYHSD*
Sinnett, John Albert 1863-1919 *NatCAB 18*
Sinnickson, Clement Hall 1834-1919 *BiAUS,*
BiDrAC
Sinnickson, Thomas d1817 *ApCAB,*
NatCAB 2
Sinnickson, Thomas 1744-1817 *BiDrAC,*
WhAm H
Sinnickson, Thomas 1745-1817 *BiAUS, Drake*
Sinnickson, Thomas 1786-1873 *BiAUS,*
BiDrAC, WhAm H
Sinnott, Alfred Arthur 1877-1954 *WhAm 3*
Sinnott, Annie E Rogers 1842- *WomWWA 14*
Sinnott, Arthur Joseph 1886-1944 *NatCAB 34,*
WhAm 2
Sinnott, Edmund Ware 1888-1968 *BiDAmEd,*
WhAm 4A
Sinnott, Elizabeth 1878- *WomWWA 14*
Sinnott, James Butterfield 1842-1917
NatCAB 17
Sinnott, Michael *WebAB*
Sinnott, Nicholas John 1870-1929 *BiDrAC,*
WhAm 1, WhAmP
Sinsel, Rupert Alston 1904-1972 *WhAm 5*
Sinte-Galeshka *WebAB*
Sinton, David 1808-1900 *NatCAB 13*

Sintzenich, Eugene *NewYHSD*
Sinz, Walter Alexander 1881-1966 *WhAm 4*
Siodmak, Robert d1973 *WhAm 5*
Sions, Harry 1906-1974 *WhAm 6*
Sioussat, St. George Leakin 1878-1960
NatCAB 45, WhAm 4
Sipe, William Allen 1844-1935 *BiDrAC*
Siple, Paul Allman 1908-1968 *WhAm 5*
Sippel, Bettie Manroe *WhAm 5*
Sippi, Grace Hamilton 1880- *WomWWA 14*
Sipple, Chester Ellsworth 1894-1967 *WhAm 4*
Sipple, Leslie B 1880- *WhAm 6*
Sippy, Bertram Welton 1866-1924 *WhAm 1*
Sippy, John Johnson 1879-1949 *WhAm 3*
Siqueiros, David Alfaro 1896-1972 *McGEWB,*
WhAm 6
Siqueland, Tryggve Albert 1888-1937 *WhAm 1*
Sire, Joseph A 1795-1854 *REnAW*
Sires, Ronald Vernon 1901-1970 *WhAm 5*
Siringo, Charles A 1855-1928 *DcAmB,*
REnAW
Sirois, Edward Devlin 1898-1968 *NatCAB 55,*
WhAm 4A
Siroky, Villem 1902-1971 *WhAm 5*
Sirota, William 1900-1961 *NatCAB 47*
Sirovich, William Irving 1882-1939 *BiDrAC,*
WhAm 1, WhAmP
Sirrine, Joseph Emory 1872- *WhAm 5*
Sisam, Charles Herschel 1879-1964 *NatCAB 51,*
WhAm 6
Sisavang Vong 1885-1959 *WhAm 3*
Sisco, Frank Thayer 1889-1965 *WhAm 4*
Sisco, Gordon A 1891-1953 *WhAm 3*
Siscoe, Frank Gotch 1913-1971 *WhAm 5*
Sise, Lincoln Fleetford 1874-1942 *WhAm 2*
Sise, Paul F 1879-1951 *WhAm 3*
Sisk, Albert Wesley 1860-1936 *NatCAB 35*
Sisk, Bernice Frederic 1910- *BiDrAC*
Siskind, Aaron 1903- *BnEnAmA*
Sisley, Lyman A d1927 *WhAm 1*
Sismondi, Jean Charles L Simonde De 1773-1842
McGEWB
Sisson, A Elverton 1851- *NatCAB 16*
Sisson, Charles Newton 1892-1947 *WhAm 2*
Sisson, Charles Peck 1890-1947 *NatCAB 36,*
WhAm 2
Sisson, Edgar Grant 1875-1948 *WhAm 2*
Sisson, Edward Octavius 1869-1949 *BiDAmEd,*
WhAm 3
Sisson, Francis Hinckley 1871-1933 *NatCAB 24,*
WhAm 1
Sisson, Fred James 1879-1949 *WhAm 2*
Sisson, Frederick James 1879-1949 *BiDrAC*
Sisson, Jean 1892- *WhAm 5*
Sisson, Rufus Lasher 1860-1936 *NatCAB 27*
Sisson, Septimus 1865- *WhAm 1*
Sisson, Thomas Upton 1869-1923 *BiDrAC,*
WhAm 1, WhAmP
Sistiaga, Sebastian 1690?-1756 *ApCAB*
Sisto, Louis Stanley 1899-1972 *WhAm 5*
Sites, Frank Crawford 1864-1935 *BiDrAC,*
WhAm 4
Sitgreaves, Charles 1803-1878 *BiAUS, BiDrAC,*
TwCBDA, WhAm H
Sitgreaves, John d1801 *BiAUS*
Sitgreaves, John d1802 *Drake*
Sitgreaves, John 1740?-1802 *ApCAB,*
NatCAB 20, TwCBDA
Sitgreaves, John 1757-1802 *BiDrAC,*
WhAm H
Sitgreaves, Lorenzo 1811?-1888 *ApCAB,*
BiAUS
Sitgreaves, Samuel 1764-1824 *ApCAB, BiAUS*
Sitgreaves, Samuel 1764-1827 *BiDrAC,*
NatCAB 2, TwCBDA, WhAm H
Sitgreaves, W K *NewYHSD*
Sithole, Ndabaningi 1920- *McGEWB*
Sitjar, Buenaventura 1739-1808 *ApCAB,*
WhAm H
Sitter, Willem De 1872-1934 *AsBiEn, DcScB*
Sitterley, James Eugene 1877-1945 *NatCAB 34*
Sitterly, Charles Fremont 1861-1945 *WhAm 2*
Sittig, Isabel W 1863- *WomWWA 14*
Sittig, Lena Wilson 1855- *NatCAB 12*
Sitting Bull 1831?-1890 *REnAW, WebAB,*
WebAMB
Sitting Bull 1834?-1890 *AmBi, DcAmB,*
EncAAH, EncAB, McGEWB, WhAm H,

WhoMilH
Sitting Bull 1837?-1890 *ApCAB, NatCAB 13*
Sittler, Edward Lewis, Jr. 1908- *BiDrAC*
Sitton, Charles Edward 1848-1890 *NatCAB 17*
Sitwell, Edith 1887-1964 *McGEWB, WhAm 4*
Sitwell, Osbert d1969 *WhAm 5*
Sivaji 1627-1680 *WhoMilH*
Sivertsen, Peter M 1891-1962 *NatCAB 51*
Sivertson, Martin 1887-1960 *NatCAB 48*
Siviter, Anna Pierpont 1859-1932 *TwCBDA, WhAm 1, WomWWA 14*
Siviter, William Henry 1858-1939 *WhAm 1*
Sivolella, Nicholas William 1905-1968 *NatCAB 54*
Sivraj, J A *NewYHSD*
Sivright, Cal 1886-1945 *NatCAB 34, WhAm 2*
Sivyer, Frederick Lincoln 1879-1949 *NatCAB 48*
Sixt VonArmin, Friedrich 1851-1936 *WhoMilH*
Sixt VonArmin, Hans-Heinrich 1890-1952 *WhoMilH*
Sixtus V 1520-1590 *McGEWB*
Sizer, Lawrence Bradford 1902-1972 *WhAm 5*
Sizer, Nelson 1812-1897 *DcAmB, NatCAB 3, WhAm H*
Sizer, Theodore 1892-1967 *WhAm 4*
Sizoo, Joseph Richard 1885-1966 *WhAm 4*
Sjolander, John Peter 1851- *NatCAB 13, WhAm 4*
Sjoqvist, Erik 1903-1975 *WhAm 6*
Skae, Edward Askin 1909-1967 *NatCAB 53*
Skaggs, William Henry 1861-1947 *WhAm 2*
Skalovsky, Samuel 1904-1961 *NatCAB 50*
Skaniadariio 1735?-1815 *DcAmB, WhAm H*
Skapski, Adam Stanislas 1902-1968 *WhAm 5*
Skariatina, Irina d1962 *WhAm 4*
Skarstedt, Ernst Teofil 1857-1929 *WhAm 2*
Skaug, Arne 1906-1974 *WhAm 6*
Skaug, Julius 1881- *WhAm 6*
Skead, James 1817-1884 *ApCAB*
Skeel, Adelaide *WhAm 5*
Skeel, Arthur Julius 1874-1942 *NatCAB 32*
Skeel, Emily E F *WomWWA 14*
Skeel, Ernst Laughlin 1881-1952 *NatCAB 41*
Skeel, Franklin Deuel 1851-1923 *WhAm 1*
Skeel, Roland Edward 1869-1925 *WhAm 1*
Skeele, Anna Katherine 1896-1963 *IIBEAAW*
Skeele, Walter Fisher 1865-1935 *WhAm 1*
Skeels, Homer Griffith 1916-1954 *NatCAB 44*
Skeels, Homer Lucius 1875-1947 *NatCAB 46*
Skeels, Irving Thomas 1896-1954 *NatCAB 43*
Skeels, Wines Harris 1876- *WhAm 5*
Skeen, John A 1903- *WhAm 3*
Skeer, Jacob 1893-1953 *NatCAB 41*
Skeetop, Frederick Elmer 1889-1926 *ApCAB X*
Skelley, William Charles 1896-1950 *WhAm 3*
Skelly, James Thomas 1877-1936 *NatCAB 27*
Skelly, William Grove 1878-1957 *WhAm 3*
Skelton, Charles 1806-1879 *BiAUS, BiDrAC, WhAm H*
Skelton, Henneriette 1842-1900 *AmWom*
Skelton, Henrietta 1842-1900 *WhAm 1*
Skelton, John 1460?-1529 *McGEWB*
Skelton, Leslie James 1848-1929 *IIBEAAW, WhAm 1*
Skelton, William B 1871-1964 *WhAm 4*
Skenando 1706-1816 *ApCAB, NatCAB 9*
Skenandoa 1706?-1816 *DcAmB, WhAm H*
Skene, Alexander Johnston Chalmers 1837-1900 *ApCAB, DcAmB, NatCAB 5, WhAm 1*
Skene, Andrew Motz d1849 *ApCAB*
Skene, Andrew Philip 1753-1826 *ApCAB*
Skene, Philip d1810 *Drake*
Skene, Philip 1720?-1810 *NatCAB 18*
Skene, Philip 1725-1810 *ApCAB*
Skene, Philip Orkney 1790?-1837 *ApCAB*
Skerpan, Alfred Andrew 1914-1967 *WhAm 5*
Skerrett, Joseph Salathiel 1833-1896 *TwCBDA*
Skerrett, Joseph Salathiel 1833-1897 *ApCAB Sup*
Skerrett, Mark Nicholas 1869-1952 *NatCAB 41*
Skevington, Samuel John 1871-1944 *NatCAB 41, WhAm 2*
Skewes, James Henry 1888-1958 *WhAm 3*
Skiddy, William 1795-1870 *NatCAB 7*
Skiddy, William Wheelwright 1845- *NatCAB 7*

Skidmore, Anna Theodora 1872- *WomWWA 14*
Skidmore, Charles H 1875- *WhAm 5*
Skidmore, Hubert Standish 1911-1946 *WhAm 2*
Skidmore, Lemuel 1891-1964 *WhAm 4*
Skidmore, Louis 1897-1962 *NatCAB 50, WhAm 4, WhAm 5*
Skiff, Frank Vernon 1869-1933 *NatCAB 23*
Skiff, Frederick James Volney 1851-1921 *NatCAB 12, WhAm 1*
Skifter, Hector Randolph 1901-1964 *NatCAB 52, WhAm 4*
Skiles, Jonah William Durward 1903-1966 *WhAm 4*
Skiles, William Vernon 1879-1947 *NatCAB 36, WhAm 2*
Skiles, William Woodburn 1849-1904 *BiDrAC, WhAm 1*
Skillern, Ross Hall 1875-1930 *DcAmB, WhAm 1*
Skillin, John 1746-1800 *NewYHSD, WhAm H*
Skillin, Samuel d1816 *NewYHSD*
Skillin, Simeon *NewYHSD*
Skillin, Simeon 1716-1778 *BnEnAmA, NewYHSD, WhAm H*
Skillin, Simeon, III 1766-1830 *NewYHSD*
Skillin, Simeon, Jr. 1756?-1806 *NewYHSD, WhAm H*
Skilling, David Miller 1868- *WhAm 5*
Skilling, William Thompson 1866- *WhAm 5*
Skillman, Frank Sherman 1907-1963 *NatCAB 50*
Skillman, Thomas Julien 1876-1939 *NatCAB 28, WhAm 1*
Skilton, Alice Thomas *WomWWA 14*
Skilton, Charles Sanford 1868-1941 *NatCAB 34, WhAm 1*
Skilton, DeWitt Clinton 1839-1913 *WhAm 1*
Skilton, John Davis 1867-1951 *WhAm 3*
Skilton, Julius Augustus 1833- *ApCAB*
Skinker, Alexander Rives 1883-1918 *NatCAB 28*
Skinker, Thomas Keith 1845-1924 *NatCAB 35*
Skinner, Aaron Nichols 1845- *TwCBDA*
Skinner, Aaron Nichols 1845-1918 *DcAmB, NatCAB 20*
Skinner, Aaron Nichols 1845-1919 *WhAm 1*
Skinner, Alanson Buck 1886-1925 *DcAmB*
Skinner, Alburn Edward 1872- *WhAm 5*
Skinner, Allan David 1874-1942 *NatCAB 33*
Skinner, Avery Warner 1870-1937 *NatCAB 27, WhAm 1*
Skinner, Belle 1866-1928 *BiCAW, NatCAB 23, WhAm 1*
Skinner, Beverly Oden 1875- *WhAm 5*
Skinner, Burrhus Frederic 1904- *BiDAmEd, EncAB, McGEWB, WebAB*
Skinner, Charles Drake 1874-1950 *WhAm 3*
Skinner, Charles Edward 1865-1950 *NatCAB 38, WhAm 3*
Skinner, Charles Edward 1897-1958 *WhAm 3*
Skinner, Charles H 1889-1974 *WhAm 6*
Skinner, Charles Montgomery 1852-1907 *TwCBDA, WhAm 1*
Skinner, Charles Rufus 1844-1928 *AmBi, ApCAB, BiDAmEd, BiDrAC, DcAmB, NatCAB 10, TwCBDA, WhAm 1*
Skinner, Charles W d1860 *Drake*
Skinner, Charles Wilbur 1864- *WhAm 2*
Skinner, Charlotte B 1879- *IIBEAAW*
Skinner, Clarence Aurelius 1871- *WhAm 5*
Skinner, Clarence Edward 1868- *WhAm 4*
Skinner, Clarence Russell 1881-1949 *WhAm 2*
Skinner, Constance Lindsay d1939 *WhAm 1*
Skinner, Constance Lindsay 1877-1939 *NotAW*
Skinner, Constance Lindsay 1879?-1939 *AmBi*
Skinner, Cortlandt 1728-1799 *ApCAB, Drake*
Skinner, David A 1877- *WhAm 5*
Skinner, David Edward 1867-1933 *NatCAB 27*
Skinner, David Salmon 1844- *NatCAB 3*
Skinner, David William 1902-1974 *WhAm 6*
Skinner, Edward Holman 1881-1953 *NatCAB 39, WhAm 3*
Skinner, Eleanor Louise d1951 *WhAm 3*
Skinner, Emory Fisk 1833-1913 *NatCAB 17*
Skinner, Ernest Brown 1863-1935 *WhAm 1*
Skinner, Ernest M 1866- *WhAm 5*
Skinner, Eugene William 1896-1966 *WhAm 4*

Skinner, Ezekiel 1777-1855 *ApCAB*
Skinner, Frank Woodward 1858- *WhAm 4*
Skinner, Frederick Gustavus 1814- *ApCAB*
Skinner, Frederick Henry 1886-1944 *NatCAB 37*
Skinner, George Alfred 1870-1949 *NatCAB 43*
Skinner, George Ure 1805-1867 *ApCAB*
Skinner, Halcyon 1824-1900 *DcAmB, NatCAB 5, WhAm H*
Skinner, Harold Stanfield 1907-1967 *WhAm 4*
Skinner, Harry 1855-1929 *BiDrAC, DcAmB, EncAAH, WhAm 4, WhAmP*
Skinner, Helen Bowen 1872- *WomWWA 14*
Skinner, Henrietta Channing Dana 1857-1928 *TwCBDA, WhAm 1, WomWWA 14*
Skinner, Henry 1861-1926 *NatCAB 21, WhAm 1*
Skinner, Howard K d1971 *WhAm 5*
Skinner, Hubert Marshall 1855-1916 *WhAm 1*
Skinner, James 1835-1924 *NatCAB 30*
Skinner, James Atcheson 1826- *ApCAB*
Skinner, James M, Jr. 1914-1974 *WhAm 6*
Skinner, James Mortimer 1889-1953 *NatCAB 45, WhAm 3*
Skinner, James W 1855- *WhAm 4*
Skinner, James Washburn 1838-1912 *NatCAB 16*
Skinner, John 1750?-1827 *ApCAB, Drake*
Skinner, John Harrison 1874-1942 *WhAm 2*
Skinner, John Herbert 1864-1958 *NatCAB 47*
Skinner, John R M *NewYHSD*
Skinner, John Stuart 1788-1851 *ApCAB, BiAUS, DcAmB, Drake, EncAAH, NatCAB 2, WhAm H*
Skinner, Joseph Allen 1862-1946 *NatCAB 34, WhAm 2*
Skinner, Laura *WomWWA 14*
Skinner, Laurence Hervey 1897- *WhAm 2*
Skinner, LeGrand 1845-1922 *NatCAB 19*
Skinner, Lewis Bailey 1874- *WhAm 5*
Skinner, Lilian Marchant *WomWWA 14*
Skinner, Mark 1813-1887 *ApCAB*
Skinner, Onias C 1817-1877 *NatCAB 5*
Skinner, Otis 1858-1942 *DcAmB S3, NatCAB 11, NatCAB 32, WebAB, WhAm 1*
Skinner, Otis Ainsworth 1807-1861 *ApCAB, Drake, TwCBDA*
Skinner, Paul Butler 1885-1969 *WhAm 5*
Skinner, Philip Kearney d1826 *Drake*
Skinner, Philip Kearney d1826 *ApCAB*
Skinner, R Dana 1893-1941 *NatCAB 47*
Skinner, Richard 1778-1833 *ApCAB, BiAUS, BiDrAC, Drake, TwCBDA, WhAm H, WhAmP*
Skinner, Richard 1778-1853 *NatCAB 8*
Skinner, Robert P 1866-1960 *WhAm 4*
Skinner, St. John B L *BiAUS*
Skinner, Stella 1857-1922 *WhAm 1*
Skinner, Thomas Clagett 1869-1934 *WhAm 1*
Skinner, Thomas Gregory 1842-1907 *BiDrAC, WhAmP*
Skinner, Thomas Harvey 1791-1871 *ApCAB, DcAmB, Drake, NatCAB 7, TwCBDA, WhAm H*
Skinner, Thomas Harvey 1820-1892 *TwCBDA*
Skinner, Thomson Joseph 1752-1809 *BiAUS, BiDrAC, WhAm H*
Skinner, William *NewYHSD*
Skinner, William 1824-1902 *DcAmB, NatCAB 23, WhAm H*
Skinner, William 1857-1947 *NatCAB 37, WhAm 2*
Skinner, William Converse 1855- *ApCAB X*
Skinner, William Converse 1888-1962 *WhAm 4*
Skinner, William Woolford 1874- *WhAm 5*
Skipper, Glenn Blount 1887- *WhAm 1*
Skipworth *NewYHSD*
Skirving, John *IIBEAAW, NewYHSD*
Skobolev, Mikhail Dimitrievich 1843-1882 *WhoMilH*
Skoda, Josef 1805-1881 *DcScB*
Skoda, Joseph 1805-1881 *BiHiMed*
Skog, Charles Arthur 1887-1965 *WhAm 4*
Skogh, Harriet Mathilda 1861- *WhAm 6*
Skogmo, Philip Waldo 1896-1949 *WhAm 3*
Skolem, Albert Thoralf 1887-1963 *DcScB*
Skoog, Andrew Leonard 1877- *WhAm 5*

Skoog, Bertil O 1914-1975 *WhAm 6*
Skoog, Karl Frederick 1878-1936 *WhAm 1*
Skorneck, Alan Bernard 1917-1974 *WhAm 6*
Skorzeny, Otto 1908- *WhWW-II*
Skottsberg, Carl Johan F 1880-1963 *WhAm 4*
Skouras, George P d1964 *WhAm 4*
Skouras, Spyros Panagiotes 1893-1971 *WebAB, WhAm 5*
Skraup, Zdenko Hans 1850-1910 *DcScB*
Skryabin, Konstantin Ivanovich 1878-1972 *DcScB*
Skubitz, Joe 1906- *BiDrAC*
Skuce, Walter Charles 1904-1973 *WhAm 6*
Skulnik, Menasha 1894-1970 *WhAm 5*
Skyberg, Herman Fridtjof 1896-1968 *NatCAB 54*
Slabaugh, Harold Watson 1896-1970 *WhAm 5*
Slack, Abraham 1811?- *NewYHSD*
Slack, Abram 1811?- *NewYHSD*
Slack, Allen Burnham 1810-1888 *NatCAB 17*
Slack, Charles Morse 1901-1970 *NatCAB 56*
Slack, Charles Morse 1901-1971 *WhAm 5*
Slack, Charles William 1858-1945 *WhAm 2*
Slack, Elijah 1784-1866 *ApCAB, Drake, TwCBDA*
Slack, James Richard 1818-1881 *ApCAB*
Slack, John Mark, Jr. 1915- *BiDrAC*
Slack, John Taylor 1857-1939 *NatCAB 35*
Slack, L Ert 1874- *WhAm 5*
Slack, Leighton P 1867-1938 *WhAm 1*
Slack, Munsey 1877-1939 *WhAm 1*
Slack, Robert M 1842?- *NewYHSD*
Slack, William J *NewYHSD*
Slade, Albert Arthur 1876- *WhAm 5*
Slade, Annie Malcom 1878- *WomWWA 14*
Slade, Arthur Joseph 1893-1971 *WhAm 5*
Slade, Benjamin 1873-1951 *NatCAB 41*
Slade, Caleb Arnold 1882-1961 *WhAm 4*
Slade, Caroline McCormick d1952 *WhAm 3*
Slade, Charles d1834 *BiAUS, BiDrAC, WhAm H*
Slade, Charles Blount 1874-1942 *WhAm 2*
Slade, Charlotte Keach Boone 1874- *WomWWA 14*
Slade, Daniel Denison 1823- *ApCAB*
Slade, Emma Maleen Hardy 1847- *WhAm 4, WomWWA 14*
Slade, George Theron 1871-1941 *WhAm 1*
Slade, James Jeremiah 1831-1917 *NatCAB 17*
Slade, John C 1880-1963 *WhAm 4*
Slade, Joseph Alfred 1824?-1864 *DcAmB, WhAm H*
Slade, S V *NewYHSD*
Slade, William 1786-1859 *ApCAB, BiAUS, BiDrAC, DcAmB, Drake, NatCAB 8, TwCBDA, WhAm H, WhAmP*
Slade, William Adams 1874-1950 *WhAm 3*
Sladen, Fred Winchester 1867-1945 *NatCAB 34, WhAm 2*
Slafter, Alonzo 1801-1864 *NewYHSD*
Slafter, Edmund Farwell 1816-1906 *ApCAB, DcAmB, TwCBDA, WhAm 1*
Slaght, William Ernest Andrew 1875-1932 *WhAm 1*
Slagle, Anna Riemann 1868- *WomWWA 14*
Slagle, Christian W 1821-1882 *NatCAB 21*
Slagle, Dean 1889-1961 *WhAm 4*
Slagle, Eleanor Clarke 1871-1942 *NotAW*
Slagle, Robert Lincoln 1865-1920 *WhAm 1*
Slagle, Robert Lincoln 1865-1929 *BiDAmEd, NatCAB 25*
Slanetz, Charles Arthur 1899-1964 *NatCAB 56*
Slaney, John *NewYHSD*
Slarrow, Malcolm G 1891-1958 *WhAm 3*
Slate, Frederick 1852-1930 *WhAm 1*
Slate, William L 1884-1974 *WhAm 6*
Slaten, Arthur Wakefield 1880-1944 *WhAm 2*
Slater *NewYHSD*
Slater, A James 1902-1967 *WhAm 4*
Slater, Alpheus Brayton 1832- *NatCAB 9*
Slater, Caroline I A 1869- *WomWWA 14*
Slater, Denniston Lyon 1927-1971 *WhAm 5*
Slater, Elsie Pomeroy McElroy *WomWWA 14*
Slater, Fred C 1864- *WhAm 4*
Slater, George 1841-1889 *NatCAB 2*
Slater, George Basset 1804-1843 *NatCAB 24*
Slater, George Washington, Jr. 1872- *WhoColR*
Slater, Harry George 1908-1970 *WhAm 5*

Slater, Henry Byron 1850-1931 *NatCAB 24*
Slater, Horatio Nelson 1808-1888 *NatCAB 24*
Slater, Horatio Nelson, II 1835-1899 *NatCAB 24*
Slater, Hughes DeCourcy 1874- *WhAm 5*
Slater, James Harvey 1826-1899 *ApCAB Sup, BiAUS, BiDrAC, NatCAB 4, TwCBDA, WhAmP*
Slater, Jennie E *WomWWA 14*
Slater, John 1776-1843 *NatCAB 8*
Slater, John 1860-1948 *NatCAB 39*
Slater, John Fox 1815-1884 *AmBi, ApCAB, DcAmB, NatCAB 12, TwCBDA, WhAm H*
Slater, Mary White 1870- *WomWWA 14*
Slater, Paul Raymond 1903-1967 *NatCAB 54*
Slater, S M *NewYHSD*
Slater, Samuel 1768-1835 *AmBi, ApCAB, DcAmB, Drake, EncAB, McGEWB, NatCAB 4, NatCAB 24, TwCBDA, WebAB, WhAm H*
Slater, William Albert 1857-1919 *NatCAB 18, WhAm 4*
Slater, William Kershaw 1893-1970 *WhAm 5*
Slater, Woodson Taylor 1858- *WhAm 4*
Slaton, John Marshall 1866-1955 *NatCAB 52, WhAm 3*
Slattery *NewYHSD*
Slattery, Charles Lewis 1867-1930 *DcAmB, NatCAB 21, WhAm 1*
Slattery, Harry 1887-1949 *WhAm 2*
Slattery, James Michael 1878-1948 *BiDrAC, WhAm 2*
Slattery, John Joseph 1866-1926 *NatCAB 20*
Slattery, John Lawrence 1878- *WhAm 6*
Slattery, John Theodore d1938 *WhAm 1, WhAm 1C*
Slattery, Margaret d1947 *WhAm 2*
Slattery, Michael *NewYHSD*
Slatton, Charles Stewart 1895-1951 *WhAm 3*
Slaught, Herbert Ellsworth 1861-1937 *NatCAB 28, WhAm 1*
Slaughter, Albert Lloyd 1889-1952 *NatCAB 42*
Slaughter, Christopher C 1837-1919 *NatCAB 32, WhAm 1*
Slaughter, Danely Philip 1911-1970 *NatCAB 55, WhAm 5*
Slaughter, Donald 1905-1952 *WhAm 3*
Slaughter, Elizabeth Vanuxem Kennedy 1876-1960 *NatCAB 44*
Slaughter, Fenton Mercer 1826-1897 *NatCAB 41*
Slaughter, Gabriel 1767?-1820 *ApCAB*
Slaughter, Gabriel 1767?-1830 *BiAUS, Drake, NatCAB 13, TwCBDA*
Slaughter, Gertrude Elizabeth Taylor 1870- *WomWWA 14*
Slaughter, Harvey Leroy 1900-1961 *WhAm 4*
Slaughter, Henry Proctor 1871- *WhoColR*
Slaughter, Howard S 1890- *WhoColR*
Slaughter, James Edwin 1827-1901 *BiDConf*
Slaughter, John Horton 1841-1922 *NatCAB 23, REnAW*
Slaughter, John William 1884-1949 *NatCAB 43*
Slaughter, John Willis 1878-1964 *WhAm 4*
Slaughter, Leslie A 1892- *WhoColR*
Slaughter, Moses Stephen 1860-1923 *WhAm 1*
Slaughter, Philip 1808-1890 *ApCAB, DcAmB, TwCBDA, WhAm H*
Slaughter, Robert K *NewYHSD*
Slaughter, Roger Caldwell 1905- *BiDrAC*
Slaughter, Seth Warren 1893-1970 *WhAm 5*
Slaughter, William Bank 1798-1879 *ApCAB*
Slaughter, William Herbert 1875-1952 *NatCAB 41*
Slaughter, Mrs. Winston Henry *WomWWA 14*
Slaughton, Mrs. *NewYHSD*
Slaven, Henry Bartholomew 1853-1904 *NatCAB 3, NatCAB 16, WhAm 1*
Slavens, Luther Clay 1836-1923 *NatCAB 6*
Slavens, Thomas Horace 1863-1954 *WhAm 3*
Slavin, Matthew 1853-1915 *NatCAB 17*
Slavin, Robert Joseph 1907-1961 *WhAm 4*
Slawson, Chester Baker 1898-1964 *WhAm 4*
Slawter, John David 1886-1957 *NatCAB 46*
Slayden, James Luther 1853-1924 *BiDrAC, NatCAB 19, TwCBDA, WhAm 1, WhAmP*

Slaymaker, Amos 1755-1837 *BiAUS, BiDrAC, WhAm H*
Slaymaker, Philip K 1877-1954 *WhAm 3*
Slaymaker, Samuel Redsecker 1867-1940 *NatCAB 32*
Slayter, Games 1896-1964 *NatCAB 50, WhAm 4*
Slayter, Donald Kent 1924- *WebAMB*
Slayton, Mary Rose 1938-1973 *WhAm 6*
Slechta, Andrew 1870-1939 *NatCAB 30, WhAm 1*
Sledd, Benjamin 1864-1940 *WhAm 1*
Sledge, Edward Simmons 1887-1954 *NatCAB 45*
Sledge, William Henry 1855- *NatCAB 5*
Sledge, William Whitfield 1898-1964 *NatCAB 51, WhAm 4*
Slee, Daniel Grover 1892-1960 *NatCAB 45*
Slee, J Noah H 1861- *ApCAB X*
Slee, John B 1875-1947 *WhAm 2*
Sleeper, Albert Edson 1862-1934 *NatCAB 24, WhAm 1*
Sleeper, Charles Frederick *NewYHSD*
Sleeper, Harold Reeve 1893-1960 *NatCAB 48, WhAm 4*
Sleeper, Henry Dike 1865-1948 *WhAm 2*
Sleeper, Herbert Sumner 1865-1922 *NatCAB 6*
Sleeper, Jacob 1802-1889 *DcAmB, NatCAB 11, WhAm H*
Sleeper, John *NewYHSD*
Sleeper, John Sherburne 1794-1878 *ApCAB, Drake, NatCAB 13*
Sleesman, Maie Close 1855- *WomWWA 14*
Sleeter, Richard L 1916-1972 *WhAm 6*
Sleicher, John Albert 1848-1921 *NatCAB 13, WhAm 1*
Sleight, Charles Lee 1856- *WhAm 4*
Sleight, Mary Breck *TwCBDA, WomWWA 14*
Slemmer, Adam Jacoby 1828-1868 *AmBi, ApCAB, Drake, NatCAB 4, TwCBDA, WebAMB*
Slemons, Clyde Calderwood 1874-1953 *NatCAB 45, WhAm 5*
Slemons, J Morris 1876-1948 *WhAm 2*
Slemons, W F 1830-1918 *BiAUS*
Slemons, William Ferguson 1830-1918 *BiDrAC, WhAmP*
Slemp, Campbell 1839-1907 *BiDrAC, WhAm 1, WhAmP*
Slemp, Campbell Bascom 1870-1943 *BiDrAC, DcAmB S3, WhAm 2, WhAmP*
Slenker, Elmina Drake 1827- *ApCAB, NatCAB 7, WhAm 1*
Slenker, Elmira Drake 1827- *NatCAB 5*
Slentz, Samuel D 1877-1955 *WhAm 3*
Slep, Daniel Neff 1872-1953 *NatCAB 45*
Slep, Harry 1836-1922 *NatCAB 39*
Slepian, Joseph 1891-1969 *WhAm 5*
Slessor, Sir John 1897- *WhWW-II*
Sleyster, Rock 1879-1942 *NatCAB 33, WhAm 2*
Slezak, Leo 1875-1946 *WhAm 2*
Slicer, Henry 1801-1874 *ApCAB*
Slicer, Thomas Roberts 1847-1916 *ApCAB Sup, DcAmB, NatCAB 14, WhAm 1*
Slicer, Thomas Rogers 1847-1916 *TwCBDA*
Slichter, Allen McKinnon 1898-1974 *WhAm 6*
Slichter, Charles Sumner 1864-1946 *TwCBDA, WhAm 2*
Slichter, Sumner Huber 1892-1959 *WhAm 3*
Slichter, Walter Irvine 1873-1958 *NatCAB 47, WhAm 5*
Slick, Thomas Baker 1883-1930 *NatCAB 29*
Slick, Thomas Baker 1916-1962 *WhAm 4*
Slick, Thomas Whitten 1869-1959 *WhAm 3*
Slidell, John 1793-1871 *AmBi, ApCAB, BiAUS, BiDConf, BiDrAC, DcAmB, Drake, EncAB, McGEWB, NatCAB 2, REnAW, TwCBDA, WebAB, WhAm H*
Slidell, Thomas 1805?-1860 *NatCAB 7*
Slifer, Hiram Joseph 1857-1919 *WhAm 1*
Sligh, Charles Robert 1850-1927 *ApCAB X, NatCAB 16, NatCAB 46*
Sligh, Edith Clark 1869- *WomWWA 14*
Sligh, Thomas Standifer 1890-1927 *NatCAB 21*
Slim, Mongi 1908-1969 *WhAm 5*
Slim, Sir William Joseph 1891-1970 *WhAm 5,*

WhWW-II, WhoMilH

Slingerland, John I 1804-1861 *BiAUS, BiDrAC, WhAm H*

Slingerland, Mark Vernon 1864-1909 *NatCAB 13, WhAm 1*

Slingland, George Kuett 1895-1974 *WhAm 6*

Slinglandt, Jacob 1813?- *NewYHSD*

Slingluff, Frank 1886-1947 *NatCAB 38*

Slingluff, Jesse 1870-1957 *WhAm 3*

Slingluff, William Herman 1865-1930 *NatCAB 24*

Slinkard, William Lycurgus 1864-1950 *NatCAB 38*

Slinker, Clay Dean 1864-1943 *WhAm 2*

Slipher, Earl C 1883-1964 *DcScB*

Slipher, Vesto Melvin 1875-1969 *AsBiEn, DcScB, WebAB, WhAm 5*

Sliter, Arthur Beekman 1868-1950 *NatCAB 39*

Sloan, A Scott 1820-1895 *BiAUS*

Sloan, Alfred Pritchard, Jr. 1875-1966 *ApCAB X, McGEWB, WhAm 4*

Sloan, Andrew 1845-1883 *BiAUS, BiDrAC, WhAm H*

Sloan, Andrew Scott 1820-1895 *BiDrAC, WhAm H*

Sloan, Anna M 1876- *WomWWA 14*

Sloan, Benjamin 1836- *NatCAB 13, WhAm 4*

Sloan, Boyd 1895-1970 *NatCAB 56*

Sloan, Charles Henry 1863-1946 *BiDrAC, WhAm 2*

Sloan, Duncan Lindley 1874- *WhAm 5*

Sloan, Earl Sawyer 1848-1923 *ApCAB X, NatCAB 20*

Sloan, Edgar J 1870-1942 *WhAm 2*

Sloan, Edwin Plummer 1876-1935 *NatCAB 26*

Sloan, Edwin Plummer 1878-1935 *WhAm 1*

Sloan, Fergus Martin 1903-1963 *WhAm 4*

Sloan, Frances Blake 1873- *WomWWA 14*

Sloan, Frank Theodore 1869-1940 *NatCAB 35*

Sloan, George Arthur 1893-1955 *DcAmB S5, NatCAB 44, WhAm 3*

Sloan, George Beale 1831-1904 *WhAm 1*

Sloan, Gordon McGregor 1898-1959 *WhAm 4*

Sloan, Harold Paul 1881-1961 *WhAm 4*

Sloan, Hubert John 1903-1974 *WhAm 6*

Sloan, Ithamar Conkey 1822-1898 *BiAUS, BiDrAC*

Sloan, James d1811 *BiAUS, BiDrAC, WhAm H*

Sloan, James Forman 1874-1933 *AmBi, DcAmB, WhAm HA, WhAm 4*

Sloan, James Wallace 1870-1938 *NatCAB 28*

Sloan, John Alexander 1839-1886 *NatCAB 7*

Sloan, John Benson 1877-1957 *NatCAB 49*

Sloan, John Francis 1874-1947 *NatCAB 34*

Sloan, John French 1871-1951 *BnEnAmA, DcAmB S5, EncAB, IIBEAAW, McGEWB, NatCAB 40, WebAB, WhAm 3*

Sloan, John James 1868-1927 *NatCAB 21*

Sloan, Junius R 1827-1900 *NewYHSD*

Sloan, Laurence Henry 1889-1949 *WhAm 2*

Sloan, LeRoy Hendrick 1892-1961 *WhAm 4*

Sloan, Marianna d1954 *WhAm 4, WomWWA 14*

Sloan, Mary Herron 1915-1974 *WhAm 6*

Sloan, Matthew Scott 1881-1945 *DcAmB S3, NatCAB 34, WhAm 2*

Sloan, R Beverley 1883-1950 *NatCAB 40*

Sloan, Richard Elihu 1857-1933 *DcAmB, NatCAB 26, WhAm 1*

Sloan, Robert James 1902-1964 *WhAm 4*

Sloan, Samuel 1815-1884 *ApCAB, BnEnAmA, Drake, NewYHSD*

Sloan, Samuel 1817-1907 *ApCAB, DcAmB, TwCBDA, WhAm 1*

Sloan, Samuel 1864-1939 *WhAm 1*

Sloan, Thomas Wylie 1868-1949 *WhAm 3*

Sloan, Tod 1874-1933 *DcAmB*

Sloan, William Franklin 1879-1958 *WhAm 3*

Sloan, William Wesley 1892-1956 *NatCAB 48*

Sloane, A B *NewYHSD*

Sloane, Alfred Baldwin 1872-1924 *WhAm 1*

Sloane, Alfred Baldwin 1872-1925 *NatCAB 31*

Sloane, Charles Swift 1859-1923 *WhAm 1*

Sloane, Eric 1910- *IIBEAAW*

Sloane, George 1888-1946 *NatCAB 52*

Sloane, Sir Hans 1660-1753 *ApCAB, BiHiMed,*

DcScB

Sloane, Henry Thompson 1845-1937 *NatCAB 37*

Sloane, James Renwick 1881-1955 *NatCAB 45*

Sloane, James Renwick Wilson 1823-1886 *ApCAB, TwCBDA*

Sloane, John 1779-1856 *ApCAB, BiAUS, BiDrAC, TwCBDA, WhAm H*

Sloane, John 1834-1905 *NatCAB 37, WhAm 1*

Sloane, John 1883-1971 *NatCAB 56*

Sloane, John Eyre 1886-1970 *NatCAB 56*

Sloane, Jonathan 1785-1854 *BiAUS, BiDrAC, WhAm H*

Sloane, Joseph Curtis 1873- *WhAm 5*

Sloane, Rush Richard 1828- *ApCAB, WhAm 5*

Sloane, Thomas Morrison 1854- *WhAm 1*

Sloane, Thomas O'Conor 1851-1940 *ApCAB, WhAm 1*

Sloane, William 1873-1922 *NatCAB 30, WhAm 1*

Sloane, William 1906-1974 *WhAm 6*

Sloane, William A 1854-1930 *WhAm 1*

Sloane, William Douglas 1844-1915 *NatCAB 30*

Sloane, William Milligan 1850-1928 *AmBi, ApCAB, BiDAmEd, DcAmB, NatCAB 9, NatCAB 21, TwCBDA, WhAm 1*

Sloane, William Woodard 1885-1954 *NatCAB 41*

Sloat, John Drake 1780-1867 *ApCAB, Drake, NatCAB 2, NatCAB 6, TwCBDA*

Sloat, John Drake 1781-1867 *AmBi, DcAmB, WebAB, WebAMB, WhAm H*

Slobin, Hermon Lester 1883-1951 *WhAm 3*

Slobodkin, Louis 1903-1975 *WhAm 6*

Slocomb, Edwin Pliny 1823-1865 *NewYHSD*

Slocomb, Florence White Seaver 1867- *WomWWA 14*

Sloctemeyer, Hugo Ferdinand 1884-1937 *WhAm 1*

Slocum, Arthur Gaylord 1847-1924 *NatCAB 13, TwCBDA, WhAm 1*

Slocum, Cella Boucher 1856- *WomWWA 14*

Slocum, Charles Elihu 1841-1915 *NatCAB 7, NatCAB 16, WhAm 1*

Slocum, Chester Andrews 1885-1959 *NatCAB 47*

Slocum, Clarence Alfred 1904-1957 *WhAm 3*

Slocum, Clarence Rice 1868-1912 *WhAm 4*

Slocum, Estelle Woodruff 1870- *WomWWA 14*

Slocum, Frances 1773-1847 *DcAmB, NatCAB 10, NotAW*

Slocum, Frances 1773-1851 *ApCAB*

Slocum, Francis 1773-1847 *WhAm H*

Slocum, Frederick 1873-1944 *WhAm 2*

Slocum, George 1865-1933 *NatCAB 24*

Slocum, George Warren 1881-1961 *WhAm 4*

Slocum, Grace Leila *WomWWA 14*

Slocum, Henry W 1827-1894 *BiAUS*

Slocum, Henry Wadsworth 1827-1894 *Drake*

Slocum, Henry Warner 1827-1894 *AmBi, ApCAB, BiDrAC, DcAmB, NatCAB 4, NatCAB 24, TwCBDA, WebAMB, WhAm H*

Slocum, Herbert Jermain 1855-1928 *NatCAB 24, WhAm 1*

Slocum, Jane Mariah 1842- *AmWom, WomWWA 14*

Slocum, Jesse d1820 *BiAUS*

Slocum, John S 1824- *NatCAB 8*

Slocum, Joseph 1800-1890 *NatCAB 5, WhAm H*

Slocum, Joseph Warren 1833- *NatCAB 5*

Slocum, Joshua 1844-1910? *DcAmB, WhAm HA, WhAm 4*

Slocum, Lorimer B 1898-1957 *WhAm 3*

Slocum, M Harvey 1887-1961 *NatCAB 51*

Slocum, Richard William 1901-1957 *WhAm 3*

Slocum, Samuel 1792-1861 *DcAmB, NatCAB 7, WhAm H*

Slocum, Stephen Elmer 1875- *WhAm 5*

Slocum, Thomas Williams 1867-1937 *NatCAB 29, WhAm 1*

Slocum, William Frederick 1851-1934 *NatCAB 13, TwCBDA, WhAm 1*

Slocumb, Ezekiel 1750?-1840 *ApCAB*

Slocumb, Jesse 1780-1820 *ApCAB, BiDrAC, WhAm H*

Sloman, Ernest Gaynor 1895-1952 *WhAm 3*

Slonaker, James Rollin 1866-1954 *NatCAB 42*

Slonecker, J G 1851- *WhAm 4*

Sloneker, Howard L 1890-1963 *WhAm 4*

Sloop, Jacob H *NewYHSD*

Sloper, Andrew Jackson 1849-1933 *WhAm 1*

Sloper, Leslie Akers 1883-1949 *WhAm 2*

Sloss, James Withers 1820-1890 *DcAmB, WhAm H*

Sloss, Joseph 1865-1939 *NatCAB 29*

Sloss, Joseph Humphrey 1826-1911 *BiAUS, BiDrAC*

Sloss, Louis 1823-1902 *DcAmB, NatCAB 26, WhAm H*

Sloss, Marcus Cauffman 1869-1958 *WhAm 4*

Slosson, Annie Trumbull 1838-1926 *WhAm 1, WomWWA 14*

Slosson, Edwin Emery 1865-1929 *AmBi, DcAmB, NatCAB 32, WhAm 1*

Slosson, Leonard B 1875-1946 *WhAm 2*

Slosson, May Genevieve Preston 1858-1943 *NatCAB 35, WomWWA 14*

Slotkin, Samuel 1885-1965 *WhAm 4*

Slott, Mollie 1893-1967 *WhAm 4*

Slottman, George Vincent 1903-1958 *NatCAB 44, WhAm 3*

Slough, John P 1829-1867 *ApCAB, BiAUS, Drake*

Slover, Samuel LeRoy 1873-1959 *NatCAB 49, WhAm 4*

Slowe, Lucy Diggs 1885-1937 *NotAW*

Sluder, Jefferson Davis 1915-1969 *NatCAB 55*

Sluse, Rene-Francois De 1622-1685 *DcScB*

Sluss, Homer Oscar 1871-1929 *WhAm 1*

Sluss, John William 1867-1961 *WhAm 4*

Slusser, Charles Edward 1897-1963 *NatCAB 51, WhAm 4*

Sluter, Claus 1350?-1406? *McGEWB*

Sluter, George Ludewig 1837-1909 *ApCAB, TwCBDA, WhAm 1*

Slutsky, Evgeny Evgenievich 1880-1948 *DcScB*

Slutz, Frank D 1882-1956 *WhAm 3*

Sly, John Fairfield 1893-1965 *NatCAB 52, WhAm 4*

Sly, William James 1867-1940 *WhAm 1*

Slye, Maud 1879-1954 *WhAm 3*

Slyke, Donald Dexter Van *DcScB*

Smadel, Joseph Edwin 1907-1963 *WhAm 4*

Smaill, Edith Margaret *WomWWA 14*

Small, Albion Woodbury 1854-1926 *AmBi, BiDAmEd, DcAmB, McGEWB, NatCAB 8, NatCAB 25, TwCBDA, WhAm 1*

Small, Alex 1895-1965 *WhAm 4*

Small, Alvan Edmond 1811-1886 *DcAmB, WhAm H*

Small, Alvin Edmond 1811-1866 *ApCAB*

Small, Alvin Edmond 1811-1886 *NatCAB 3*

Small, Andrew Buchanan 1863- *WhAm 4*

Small, Benjamin Francis 1919-1973 *WhAm 5*

Small, Beulah *WomWWA 14*

Small, Charles C 1876- *WhAm 5*

Small, Elden 1876- *WhAm 1*

Small, Ernest Gregor 1888-1944 *NatCAB 34, WhAm 2*

Small, Francis Aloysius 1916-1974 *WhAm 6*

Small, Frank, Jr. 1896-1973 *BiDrAC, WhAm 6*

Small, Frederick Michael 1878-1947 *NatCAB 36*

Small, Frederick Percival 1874-1958 *WhAm 3*

Small, Frederick Rieth 1898-1955 *NatCAB 47*

Small, George G *NewYHSD*

Small, Harold Patten 1888-1942 *NatCAB 31*

Small, Harold Patten 1888-1943 *WhAm 2*

Small, Henry Beaumont 1831- *ApCAB*

Small, John 1726-1796 *ApCAB, Drake*

Small, John Bryan 1845- *TwCBDA*

Small, John Clay 1873- *WhAm 5*

Small, John D 1893-1963 *WhAm 4*

Small, John Humphrey 1858-1946 *BiDrAC, TwCBDA, WhAm 2, WhAmP*

Small, John Kunkel 1869-1938 *WhAm 1*

Small, Len 1862-1936 *WhAm 1*

Small, Leslie Charles 1886-1957 *NatCAB 44*

Small, Lisle Francis 1895-1969 *NatCAB 55*

Small, Lyndon Frederick 1897-1957
NatCAB 44
Small, Michael Peter 1831- *ApCAB*
Small, Philip Lindsley 1890-1963 *WhAm 4*
Small, Robert Scott 1891-1931 *WhAm 1*
Small, Sam 1851-1931 *WhAm 1*
Small, Sergine Anne 1949-1974 *WhAm 6*
Small, Sidney Aylmer 1876- *WhAm 5*
Small, Sydney French 1893- *WhAm 6*
Small, Thomas Frederick 1880- *WhoColR*
Small, Vivian Blanche 1875-1946 *WhAm 2,*
WomWWA 14
Small, W A 1894-1975 *WhAm 6*
Small, Willard Stanton 1870-1943 *WhAm 2*
Small, William Bradbury 1817-1878 *BiAUS,*
BiDrAC, WhAm H
Small, William Fraser McPherson 1844-1929
NatCAB 34
Smallcomb, Glen Oliver 1895-1961 *NatCAB 48*
Smallens, Alexander 1889-1972 *WhAm 5*
Smalley, Bradley Barlow 1835-1909 *WhAm 1*
Smalley, David A 1809- *BiAUS*
Smalley, Eugene Virgil 1841-1899 *ApCAB,*
DcAmB, WhAm H, WhAm 1
Smalley, Frank 1846-1931 *NatCAB 15,*
WhAm 1
Smalley, Frank Mather 1877-1957 *WhAm 3*
Smalley, Frank Newell 1874-1921 *NatCAB 19*
Smalley, George Oakley 1885-1956 *NatCAB 50*
Smalley, George Washburn 1833-1916 *AmBi,*
ApCAB, DcAmB, NatCAB 3, TwCBDA,
WhAm 1
Smalley, Harrison Standish 1878-1912 *WhAm 1*
Smalley, John 1734-1820 *ApCAB, Drake*
Smalley, Katherine 1865?- *IIBEAAW*
Smalley, William Cameron 1880- *WhAm 6*
Smalley, William Winsor 1850-1916
NatCAB 17
Smalls, Robert 1839-1915 *ApCAB, BiAUS,*
BiDrAC, DcAmB, NatCAB 12, TwCBDA,
WebAB, WebAMB, WhAm HA,
WhAm 4, WhAmP
Smalls, Robert 1839-1916 *McGEWB*
Smallsreed, George A, Sr. 1898-1964 *WhAm 4*
Smallwood, Charles 1812-1873 *ApCAB*
Smallwood, Della Graeme *WhAm 5,*
WomWWA 14
Smallwood, Eleanor Stanley 1876-
WomWWA 14
Smallwood, Robert Bartly 1893-1974 *WhAm 6*
Smallwood, Walter Charles 1890-1955
NatCAB 46
Smallwood, William *NewYHSD*
Smallwood, William 1732-1792 *AmBi, ApCAB,*
DcAmB, Drake, NatCAB 1, NatCAB 9,
TwCBDA, WebAMB, WhAm H
Smallwood, William Hillary 1841-1919
NatCAB 19
Smallwood, William Martin 1873-1949
NatCAB 42, WhAm 2
Smarius, Cornelius Francis 1823-1870 *ApCAB*
Smarius, S J 1823-1870 *Drake*
Smart, Allen Rich 1867-1940 *NatCAB 33*
Smart, Charles 1841-1905 *WhAm 1*
Smart, Charles Allen 1904-1967 *NatCAB 56,*
WhAm 4
Smart, David Archibald 1892-1952 *DcAmB S5,*
NatCAB 43, WhAm 3
Smart, E Hodgson 1873-1942 *WhAm 2,*
WhAm 2C
Smart, Elizabeth Allen *WhAm 4*
Smart, Ephraim Knight 1813-1872 *BiAUS,*
BiDrAC, WhAm H
Smart, Frank Leroy 1862-1936 *WhAm 1*
Smart, George Thomas 1863-1928 *WhAm 1*
Smart, Isabella Thompson *WomWWA 14*
Smart, Jackson Wyman 1898-1971 *NatCAB 55,*
WhAm 5
Smart, James Dede 1882-1950 *NatCAB 41,*
WhAm 3
Smart, James Henry 1841-1900 *BiDAmEd,*
DcAmB, NatCAB 6, WhAm 1
Smart, James Stevenson 1842-1903 *BiAUS,*
BiDrAC
Smart, John *NewYHSD*
Smart, John Stuart, Jr. 1913-1969 *NatCAB 57,*
WhAm 5
Smart, Leroy d1936 *WhAm 1C*

Smart, Reginald Hughes 1903-1968 *NatCAB 55*
Smart, Richard Addison 1872- *WhAm 5*
Smart, Thomas 1853-1921 *NatCAB 20*
Smart, Walter Kay 1878- *WhAm 6*
Smathers, George Armistead 1913- *BiDrAC*
Smathers, William Howell 1891-1955 *BiDrAC,*
WhAm 3
Smay, Joseph Edgar 1898-1974 *WhAm 6*
Smead, Isaac David 1849- *NatCAB 3*
Smead, Wesley 1800-1871 *ApCAB*
Smeallie, John Morris 1886-1947 *NatCAB 42,*
WhAm 2
Smeaton, John 1724-1792 *DcScB, McGEWB*
Smedberg, Carl Gustav 1869-1933 *NatCAB 27*
Smedes, Susan Dabney 1840- *AmWom,*
ApCAB
Smedley, Agnes 1892?-1950 *NotAW*
Smedley, Agnes 1894-1950 *DcAmB S4,*
WhAm 3
Smedley, Graham Best 1879-1954 *NatCAB 41,*
WhAm 3
Smedley, Isaac G 1855- *NatCAB 3*
Smedley, M Harvey 1902-1968 *WhAm 5*
Smedley, Samuel Lightfoot 1832- *NatCAB 3*
Smedley, William Thomas 1858-1920 *DcAmB,*
IIBEAAW, NatCAB 10, TwCBDA,
WhAm 1
Smeeth, Edwin Elliott 1862-1925 *NatCAB 40*
Smeeth, Jennie Harwood 1869- *WomWWA 14*
Smekal, Adolf Gustav Stephan 1895-1959
DcScB
Smellie, Robert *IIBEAAW*
Smellie, William 1697-1763 *BiHiMed*
Smelo, Leon Samuel 1911-1975 *WhAm 6*
Smelt, Dennis 1750?- *BiAUS, BiDrAC,*
WhAm H
Smeltz, George Washington 1884-1967
WhAm 4
Smeltzer, Clarence Harry 1900- *WhAm 5*
Smeltzer, Hugh Walter 1879-1961 *NatCAB 48*
Smeltzer, Josiah Pearce 1819-1887 *TwCBDA*
Smelzer, Baxter Timothy 1852- *WhAm 4*
Smemo, Johannes 1898-1973 *WhAm 6*
Smertenko, Clara Millerd 1873- *WhAm 5*
Smet, Peter John De 1801-1873 *Drake,*
NatCAB 2
Smet, Father Pierre-Jean De 1801-1873
NewYHSD, WhAm H
Smetana, Bedrich 1824-1884 *McGEWB*
Smetters, Samuel Tupper 1871- *ApCAB X*
Smibert, John 1684?-1752? *Drake*
Smibert, John 1688-1751 *AmBi, BnEnAmA,*
DcAmB, McGEWB, NewYHSD, WebAB,
WhAm H
Smibert, Nathaniel 1735-1756 *NewYHSD*
Smick, Helen Godwin *WomWWA 14*
Smick, Kimber Cleaver 1853-1925 *NatCAB 6*
Smiedel, Ulrich *Drake*
Smigel, Erwin O 1917-1973 *WhAm 6*
Smiles, Clyde Jeffrey 1885-1958 *NatCAB 48*
Smiley, Albert Keith 1827-1912 *ApCAB Sup*
Smiley, Albert Keith 1828-1912 *DcAmB,*
NatCAB 15, TwCBDA, WhAm 1
Smiley, Charles Newton 1873-1943 *WhAm 2*
Smiley, Charles Wesley 1846-1926 *NatCAB 2,*
WhAm 1
Smiley, Daniel 1855-1930 *ApCAB X,*
WhAm 1
Smiley, David Elmer 1879-1960 *WhAm 4*
Smiley, Dean Franklin 1894-1969 *WhAm 5*
Smiley, Elmer Ellsworth 1862-1911 *TwCBDA,*
WhAm 1
Smiley, Francis Edward 1858- *WhAm 4*
Smiley, John Stanley 1885-1945 *WhAm 2*
Smiley, Lillian Fletcher 1861- *WomWWA 14*
Smiley, Lyda May 1906-1962 *WhAm 4*
Smiley, Sarah Frances 1830- *WhAm 4*
Smiley, Thomas 1861-1940 *NatCAB 31*
Smiley, William Brownlee 1856-1931 *WhAm 1*
Smiley, William Henry 1854-1934 *WhAm 1*
Smiley, William Henry 1854-1934 *WhAm 2*
Smilie, John d1813 *BiAUS*
Smilie, John 1741-1812 *ApCAB, BiDrAC,*
Drake, NatCAB 2, WhAm H, WhAmP
Smilie, John 1742-1813 *TwCBDA*
Smillie, Alice Marjorie Adamson 1882-
WomWWA 14
Smillie, Charles Francis 1848- *NatCAB 14*

Smillie, George D 1840-1921 *Drake*
Smillie, George Frederick Cumming 1854-1924
WhAm 1
Smillie, George Henry 1840-1921 *ApCAB,*
DcAmB, IIBEAAW, NatCAB 8,
NewYHSD, TwCBDA, WhAm 1
Smillie, Helen Sheldon Jacobs 1854-1926
WhAm 1, WomWWA 14
Smillie, Irene Rose *WomWWA 14*
Smillie, James 1807-1885 *ApCAB, DcAmB,*
NatCAB 2, NewYHSD, TwCBDA,
WhAm H
Smillie, James David 1833-1909 *AmBi, ApCAB,*
DcAmB, IIBEAAW, NatCAB 10,
NewYHSD, TwCBDA, WhAm 1
Smillie, Nellie Sheldon Jacobs 1854-1926
ApCAB, TwCBDA
Smillie, Thomas W 1843- *WhAm 4*
Smillie, William Cumming 1813-1908 *ApCAB,*
NatCAB 2, NewYHSD
Smillie, William Main 1835-1888 *ApCAB,*
NatCAB 2
Smillie, Wilson George 1886-1971 *WhAm 5*
Smirke, *NewYHSD*
Smiser, James A 1862- *WhAm 1*
Smissman, Edward Ervin 1925-1974 *WhAm 6*
Smith 1747?-1834? *NewYHSD*
Smith, Messrs. *NewYHSD*
Smith, Mister *NewYHSD*
Smith, Miss A *NewYHSD*
Smith, A C *NewYHSD*
Smith, A Edward 1902-1962 *NatCAB 49*
Smith, A Frank 1889-1962 *WhAm 4*
Smith, Abbie Nora 1856- *WomWWA 14*
Smith, Abby Hadassah 1797-1878 *DcAmB,*
NotAW, WhAm H, WhAmP
Smith, Abel I 1843-1916 *NatCAB 27*
Smith, Abiel Leonard 1857-1946 *WhAm 2*
Smith, Abiel Leonard, Jr. 1891-1928 *ApCAB X*
Smith, Abner 1843- *NatCAB 10*
Smith, Abraham E 1848-1915 *WhAm 1*
Smith, Abraham Herr 1815-1894 *BiDrAC,*
WhAm H
Smith, Abram Alexander 1847-1915 *WhAm 1*
Smith, Acheson 1878-1933 *NatCAB 24*
Smith, Adam 1723-1790 *McGEWB*
Smith, Addison Gillespie 1851-1933 *NatCAB 32*
Smith, Addison R 1872-1946 *WhAm 2*
Smith, Addison Taylor 1862-1956 *BiDrAC,*
WhAm 3, WhAmP
Smith, Adelaide 1870- *WomWWA 14*
Smith, Adeline Avery 1862- *WomWWA 14*
Smith, Adolphus 1828?- *NewYHSD*
Smith, Adrian W 1860-1892 *WhAm H*
Smith, Alan 1887-1953 *NatCAB 41*
Smith, Alan Penneman 1840- *ApCAB,*
NatCAB 3
Smith, Alaric M 1859-1943 *NatCAB 35*
Smith, Albert 1793-1867 *BiAUS, BiDrAC,*
WhAm H
Smith, Albert 1805-1870 *BiAUS, BiDrAC,*
NewYHSD, WhAm H
Smith, Albert C 1894-1974 *WhAm 6*
Smith, Albert Charles 1906-1972 *WhAm 5*
Smith, Albert Delmont 1886-1962 *NatCAB 50*
Smith, Albert Edward 1874-1958 *WhAm 4*
Smith, Albert Edwin 1860-1941 *WhAm 1*
Smith, Albert Herman 1867-1950 *NatCAB 39*
Smith, Albert Holmes 1835-1885 *DcAmB,*
NatCAB 12, NatCAB 25, WhAm H
Smith, Sir Albert James 1824- *ApCAB*
Smith, Albert William 1856-1942 *NatCAB 35,*
WhAm 2
Smith, Albert William 1862-1927 *NatCAB 24,*
WhAm 1
Smith, Albridge Clinton 1881-1951 *WhAm 3*
Smith, Alcock C *BiAUS*
Smith, Alexander 1865-1922 *DcAmB,*
NatCAB 20, WhAm 1
Smith, Alexander Coke 1849-1906 *NatCAB 13,*
TwCBDA, WhAm 1
Smith, Alexander Hamilton 1833-1922
NatCAB 19
Smith, Alexander Rogers 1861- *WhAm 4*
Smith, Alexander Wyly 1861-1925 *WhAm 1*
Smith, Alexander Wyly, Jr. 1886-1964
NatCAB 54
Smith, Alfred Aloysius 1854?-1927 *IIBEAAW*

Smith, Alfred Baker 1825- *ApCAB*
Smith, Alfred Emanuel 1873-1944 *ApCAB X, DcAmB S3, EncAAH, EncAB, NatCAB 32, WebAB, WhAm 2, WhAmP*
Smith, Alfred Emmanuel 1873-1944 *McGEWB*
Smith, Alfred Ferdinand 1877-1953 *NatCAB 40*
Smith, Alfred Franklin 1869- *WhAm 5*
Smith, Alfred George 1875-1928 *ApCAB X*
Smith, Alfred H 1893-1961 *WhAm 4*
Smith, Alfred Holland 1863-1924 *DcAmB, NatCAB 20, WhAm 1*
Smith, Alfred Oscar 1888-1930 *NatCAB 22*
Smith, Alfred Theodore 1874-1939 *WhAm 1*
Smith, Alice Josephine Bristol *WomWWA 14*
Smith, Alice Ravenel Huger 1876- *WhAm 5*
Smith, Allan 1883-1963 *NatCAB 51*
Smith, Allard 1876-1933 *NatCAB 24, WhAm 1*
Smith, Allen 1849-1927 *WhAm 1*
Smith, Allen, Jr. 1810-1890 *NewYHSD*
Smith, Allen John 1863-1926 *NatCAB 20, WhAm 1*
Smith, Allen S 1906-1966 *WhAm 4*
Smith, Alonzo Covert 1887-1943 *NatCAB 35*
Smith, Alonzo DeGrate 1890-1970 *NatCAB 56*
Smith, Alphonse J 1883-1935 *WhAm 1*
Smith, Alson Jesse 1908-1965 *WhAm 5*
Smith, Alva J 1840-1906 *WhAm 1*
Smith, Alvin Augustine 1884-1943 *WhAm 2*
Smith, Amanda Berry 1837-1915 *NotAW, WhoColR*
Smith, Amor, Jr. 1840- *NatCAB 10*
Smith, Andrew Heermance 1837-1910 *NatCAB 5, WhAm 1*
Smith, Andrew Jackson 1814?-1897 *Drake*
Smith, Andrew Jackson 1815-1897 *AmBi, ApCAB, DcAmB, NatCAB 11, TwCBDA, WebAMB, WhAm H*
Smith, Andrew Thomas 1862-1928 *WhAm 1*
Smith, Angus 1822-1898 *NatCAB 11*
Smith, Anna Harris *WomWWA 14*
Smith, Anna Tolman d1917 *WhAm 1, WomWWA 14*
Smith, Annie Dawson 1868- *WomWWA 14*
Smith, Annie E *WomWWA 14*
Smith, Annie Morrill 1856- *WhAm 4, WomWWA 14*
Smith, Annie Shaw *WomWWA 14*
Smith, Archibald Carey 1837-1911 *NewYHSD*
Smith, Archibald Cary 1837-1911 *ApCAB, DcAmB, NatCAB 1, TwCBDA, WhAm 1*
Smith, Arta Morris 1856- *WomWWA 14*
Smith, Arthur 1785-1853 *BiAUS, BiDrAC, WhAm H*
Smith, Arthur 1884-1947 *NatCAB 42*
Smith, Arthur A 1875- *WhAm 5*
Smith, Arthur Albert 1907-1965 *NatCAB 52*
Smith, Arthur Alexander 1888-1962 *NatCAB 49*
Smith, Arthur Bessey 1875-1959 *NatCAB 47*
Smith, Arthur Cosslett 1852-1926 *WhAm 1*
Smith, Arthur Crittenden 1863-1923 *NatCAB 20*
Smith, Arthur Donaldson 1864-1939 *AmBi, WhAm 1*
Smith, Arthur Donaldson 1866-1939 *NatCAB 13*
Smith, Arthur George 1868-1916 *WhAm 1*
Smith, Arthur George 1889-1951 *NatCAB 41*
Smith, Arthur Henderson 1845-1932 *AmBi, DcAmB, WhAm 1*
Smith, Arthur L J 1860-1946 *WhAm 2*
Smith, Arthur Laws 1880-1959 *NatCAB 48*
Smith, Arthur Leland 1863-1928 *ApCAB X, NatCAB 23*
Smith, Arthur Maxson 1873-1962 *NatCAB 50*
Smith, Arthur Mumford 1903-1968 *WhAm 5*
Smith, Arthur Raphael 1879-1952 *NatCAB 45*
Smith, Arthur St. Clair 1873-1942 *NatCAB 42, WhAm 2*
Smith, Asa Dodge 1804-1877 *ApCAB, DcAmB, Drake, NatCAB 9, TwCBDA, WhAm H*
Smith, Asenath Maria 1833-1916 *NatCAB 6*
Smith, Ashbel 1805-1886 *ApCAB, DcAmB, NatCAB 10, WhAm H*
Smith, Augustine 1770-1840 *AmBi*

Smith, Augustine Coleman 1864-1928 *ApCAB X*
Smith, Augustus Wardlaw 1862-1934 *NatCAB 32, WhAm 1*
Smith, Augustus William 1802-1866 *ApCAB, Drake, NatCAB 9, TwCBDA*
Smith, Aurine Williams 1863- *WomWWA 14*
Smith, Avis E 1851- *WomWWA 14*
Smith, Azariah 1817-1851 *ApCAB, DcAmB, Drake, WhAm H*
Smith, B Holly 1858-1920 *NatCAB 8, WhAm 1*
Smith, Ballard *BiAUS, BiDrAC*
Smith, Barbara Stella 1888- *WomWWA 14*
Smith, Barry Congar 1877-1952 *WhAm 3*
Smith, Barton 1852-1935 *WhAm 1*
Smith, Benjamin 1750-1829 *ApCAB, BiAUS, NatCAB 4, TwCBDA*
Smith, Benjamin A, II 1916- *BiDrAC*
Smith, Benjamin Bosworth 1794-1884 *ApCAB, Drake, NatCAB 3, TwCBDA*
Smith, Benjamin Eli 1857-1913 *DcAmB, TwCBDA, WhAm 1*
Smith, Benjamin Franklin 1830-1927 *NatCAB 21, NewYHSD*
Smith, Benjamin M 1900-1949 *WhAm 3*
Smith, Benjamin Mosby 1811-1893 *ApCAB, DcAmB, WhAm H*
Smith, Bernard 1776-1835 *BiAUS, BiDrAC, WhAm H*
Smith, Bernard B 1902-1970 *NatCAB 54*
Smith, Bertha Helena 1892- *WomWWA 14*
Smith, Bessie 1894-1937 *DcAmB S2, NotAW, WhAm HA, WhAm 4*
Smith, Bessie 1898?-1937 *WebAB*
Smith, Betty 1896-1972 *WhAm 5*
Smith, Beverly Waugh, Jr. 1898-1972 *WhAm 5*
Smith, Blaine Spray d1955 *WhAm 3*
Smith, Bloomfield *NewYHSD*
Smith, Boardman H 1826- *BiAUS*
Smith, Bolton 1861-1935 *WhAm 1*
Smith, Boyd Milford 1887-1973 *WhAm 6*
Smith, Bradford 1909-1964 *WhAm 4*
Smith, Brainard Gardner 1846-1930 *NatCAB 22*
Smith, Bridges 1848-1930 *WhAm 1*
Smith, Brown Sylvester 1863- *WhoColR*
Smith, Bruce 1892-1955 *DcAmB S5, NatCAB 44, WhAm 3*
Smith, Bruce Donald 1885-1952 *NatCAB 39, WhAm 3*
Smith, Bryce Byram 1877-1962 *NatCAB 49*
Smith, Bryce Byram 1878-1962 *WhAm 4*
Smith, Buckingham 1810-1871 *ApCAB, DcAmB, Drake, WhAm H*
Smith, Bunnie Othanel 1903- *BiDAmEd*
Smith, Burnett 1877-1958 *NatCAB 47*
Smith, Burton 1864-1944 *NatCAB 14, WhAm 2*
Smith, Byron Caldwell 1849-1877 *DcAmB, WhAm H*
Smith, Byron Laflin 1853-1914 *WhAm 1*
Smith, C Elmer 1863-1936 *NatCAB 32*
Smith, C Fred 1867-1936 *NatCAB 28*
Smith, C H Erskine 1934-1973 *WhAm 6*
Smith, C Kenneth 1898-1964 *NatCAB 51*
Smith, C Kirby 1894-1963 *NatCAB 52*
Smith, C Morton 1867-1938 *NatCAB 28*
Smith, Caleb 1723-1762 *Drake*
Smith, Caleb Blood 1808-1864 *ApCAB, BiAUS, BiDrAC, BiDrUSE, DcAmB, Drake, NatCAB 2, TwCBDA, WhAm H*
Smith, Cameron C 1861-1932 *NatCAB 35, WhAm 1*
Smith, Carl T 1906-1966 *WhAm 4*
Smith, Carlos Green 1813-1892 *NatCAB 12, TwCBDA*
Smith, Caroline Lackland 1885- *WomWWA 14*
Smith, Carrie Josephine 1860- *WomWWA 14*
Smith, Carroll 1878-1945 *NatCAB 36*
Smith, Carroll Earll 1832- *NatCAB 4, WhAm 4*
Smith, Carson Willard 1881-1945 *NatCAB 35*
Smith, Catharine C 1879- *WomWWA 14*
Smith, Catherine N *NewYHSD*
Smith, Cecil A 1910- *IIBEAAW*
Smith, Cecil H 1860- *WhAm 4*
Smith, Cecil Michener 1906-1956 *WhAm 3*

Smith, Charles *NewYHSD*
Smith, Charles 1765-1836 *ApCAB*
Smith, Charles 1768-1808 *ApCAB, Drake*
Smith, Charles 1770-1836 *Drake*
Smith, Charles 1855-1945 *NatCAB 35*
Smith, Charles A 1861-1916 *NatCAB 19*
Smith, Charles Adam 1809-1879 *ApCAB*
Smith, Charles Alfonso 1864-1924 *BiDAmEd*
Smith, Charles Alphonso 1864-1924 *DcAmB, WhAm 1*
Smith, Charles Axel 1852-1925 *ApCAB X, NatCAB 17, WhAm 1*
Smith, Charles Bennett 1870-1939 *BiDrAC, WhAm 1*
Smith, Charles Blood 1850- *WhAm 1*
Smith, Charles Brooks 1844-1899 *BiDrAC*
Smith, Charles C *NewYHSD*
Smith, Charles Card 1827-1918 *WhAm 1*
Smith, Charles Carman 1866-1951 *WhAm 3*
Smith, Charles Copeland 1878- *WhAm 6*
Smith, Charles Dennison 1855-1925 *NatCAB 21, WhAm 1*
Smith, Charles Edward 1904-1967 *WhAm 4*
Smith, Charles Edward 1904-1970 *WhAm 5*
Smith, Charles Edward 1905-1959 *NatCAB 47*
Smith, Charles Emory 1842-1908 *AmBi, ApCAB, BiDrUSE, DcAmB, NatCAB 1, NatCAB 11, TwCBDA, WhAm 1*
Smith, Charles Ernest d1939 *WhAm 1*
Smith, Charles Ferguson 1805?-1862 *Drake*
Smith, Charles Ferguson 1807-1862 *AmBi, ApCAB, DcAmB, NatCAB 11, TwCBDA, WebAMB, WhAm H*
Smith, Charles Forster 1852-1931 *DcAmB, NatCAB 12, TwCBDA, WhAm 1*
Smith, Charles G 1891-1967 *WhAm 4A*
Smith, Charles George Percy 1917-1972 *WhAm 6*
Smith, Charles Grover 1888-1969 *WhAm 5*
Smith, Charles H *NewYHSD*
Smith, Charles H d1903 *Drake Sup*
Smith, Charles Hadden 1872-1941 *NatCAB 39*
Smith, Charles Harold 1860-1931 *NatCAB 23*
Smith, Charles Henry 1826-1903 *AmBi, ApCAB, BiDConf, DcAmB, EncAAH, NatCAB 3, WebAB, WhAm 1*
Smith, Charles Henry 1827-1902 *ApCAB, DcAmB, NatCAB 8, WhAm 1*
Smith, Charles Henry 1827-1903 *TwCBDA*
Smith, Charles Henry 1828-1903 *TwCBDA*
Smith, Charles Henry 1833- *NatCAB 5*
Smith, Charles Henry 1842-1933 *WhAm 1*
Smith, Charles Howard 1884-1950 *WhAm 3*
Smith, Charles J 1854- *WhAm 4*
Smith, Charles Jacob 1882-1967 *WhAm 4*
Smith, Charles Johnson 1864-1945 *NatCAB 39*
Smith, Charles L 1812?- *IIBEAAW, NewYHSD*
Smith, Charles Lavens 1885-1955 *NatCAB 45, WhAm 3*
Smith, Charles Lee 1865-1951 *NatCAB 14, WhAm 3*
Smith, Charles Lysle 1895-1972 *WhAm 5*
Smith, Charles Manley 1868-1937 *NatCAB 30, WhAm 1*
Smith, Charles Perley 1878-1948 *WhAm 2*
Smith, Charles Perrin 1819-1883 *ApCAB, DcAmB, WhAm H*
Smith, Charles Plimpton 1847-1937 *NatCAB 29*
Smith, Charles Robinson 1855-1930 *NatCAB 30*
Smith, Charles Shaler 1836-1886 *ApCAB, DcAmB, NatCAB 3, WhAm H*
Smith, Charles Sidney 1843-1922 *WhAm 1*
Smith, Charles Spencer 1852-1923 *WhAm 1, WhoColR*
Smith, Charles Sprague 1853-1910 *AmBi, DcAmB, WhAm 1*
Smith, Charles Stephenson 1877-1964 *WhAm 4*
Smith, Charles Stewart 1832-1909 *NatCAB 1, NatCAB 24, WhAm 1*
Smith, Charles Sumner *WhoColR*
Smith, Charles Sumner 1857-1927 *WhAm 1*
Smith, Charles Theodore 1865-1939 *WhAm 1*
Smith, Charles W *NewYHSD*
Smith, Charles W 1822?- *NewYHSD*
Smith, Charles W 1846-1921 *NatCAB 28*
Smith, Charles Wenham 1851-1920 *WhAm 1*

Smith, Charles Wesley 1877-1956 *DcAmLiB*
Smith, Charles Whitefoord 1856-1923
NatCAB 20
Smith, Charles William 1840-1914 *NatCAB 13,*
WhAm 1
Smith, Charles William 1896-1976 *WhAm 6*
Smith, Charles William Thomas 1847-
WhoColR
Smith, Charlotte Louise 1853- *AmWom*
Smith, Chauncey 1819-1895 *DcAmB*
Smith, Chauncey Wayland 1885- *WhAm 1*
Smith, Chauncy 1819-1895 *WhAm H*
Smith, Chester Alexander 1881-1962
NatCAB 50
Smith, Chester C 1888-1947 *WhAm 2*
Smith, Chester F 1890-1964 *WhAm 4*
Smith, Christopher Columbus 1861-1939
NatCAB 47
Smith, Clara Alzina Hapgood Higgins
WomWWA 14
Smith, Clara Eastman *WomWWA 14*
Smith, Clarence Beaman 1870- *WhAm 5*
Smith, Clarence Edwin 1885-1959 *WhAm 4*
Smith, Clarence Henry 1875-1947 *NatCAB 36*
Smith, Clarence James 1874-1940 *WhAm 1*
Smith, Claribel *WomWWA 14*
Smith, Clay 1876-1930 *WhAm 1*
Smith, Clayton Moran 1884-1967 *NatCAB 53*
Smith, Clement Lawrence 1844-1909 *ApCAB,*
NatCAB 7, TwCBDA, WhAm 1
Smith, Clifford Lewis 1867-1936 *NatCAB 27*
Smith, Clifford P 1869-1945 *WhAm 2*
Smith, Clinton DeWitt 1854-1916 *NatCAB 17,*
WhAm 1
Smith, Clustor Quentin 1890-1966 *WhAm 4*
Smith, Clyde Harold 1876-1940 *BiDrAC,*
WhAm 1
Smith, Collie Jackson *WomWWA 14*
Smith, Constance Elizabeth 1922-1970
NatCAB 56
Smith, Cotesworth P d1863 *NatCAB 5*
Smith, Cotton Mather 1731-1806 *ApCAB,*
Drake
Smith, Courtland 1884-1970 *WhAm 5*
Smith, Courtney Craig 1916-1969 *WhAm 5*
Smith, Mrs. Creagh *NewYHSD*
Smith, Curtis Pendleton 1860-1919 *NatCAB 18*
Smith, Cyril James 1909-1974 *WhAm 6*
Smith, Cyrus Rowlett 1899- *BiDrUSE*
Smith, D Lesesne 1877-1947 *NatCAB 36*
Smith, D R *NewYHSD*
Smith, Dan 1865-1934 *IIBEAAW, REnAW*
Smith, Dan Morgan 1873-1947 *WhAm 2*
Smith, Daniel *NewYHSD*
Smith, Daniel d1818 *BiAUS, Drake*
Smith, Daniel 1740?-1818 *ApCAB, NatCAB 2,*
TwCBDA
Smith, Daniel 1748-1818 *BiDrAC, DcAmB,*
WhAm H
Smith, Daniel 1789-1822 *Drake*
Smith, Daniel 1806-1852 *ApCAB*
Smith, Daniel Appleton White 1840-1921
WhAm 1
Smith, Daniel B 1792-1883 *ApCAB, BiDAmEd,*
DcAmB, NatCAB 5, WhAm H
Smith, Daniel Fletcher, Jr. 1910-1971 *WhAm 5*
Smith, Daniel Luther Bertrand 1874-1950
NatCAB 39
Smith, Daniel T *NewYHSD*
Smith, Daniel W *NewYHSD*
Smith, David *NewYHSD*
Smith, David d1841 *NewYHSD*
Smith, David 1906-1965 *BnEnAmA, EncAB,*
McGEWB, WebAB, WhAm 4
Smith, David Eugene 1860-1944 *BiDAmEd,*
DcAmB S3, TwCBDA, WhAm 2
Smith, David H 1844-1904 *NewYHSD,*
WhAm H
Smith, David Highbaugh 1854-1928 *BiDrAC,*
TwCBDA, WhAm 4, WhAmP
Smith, David M 1809-1881 *ApCAB*
Smith, David Morton 1854-1931 *WhAm 1*
Smith, David Nevin 1909-1964 *WhAm 4*
Smith, David Parker 1889-1958 *NatCAB 47*
Smith, David Stanley 1877-1949 *NatCAB 38,*
WhAm 2
Smith, David Thomas 1840- *WhAm 1*
Smith, David V *NewYHSD*

Smith, David V 1921- *WhAm 6*
Smith, Sir David William 1764-1837 *ApCAB*
Smith, Dean Tyler 1860-1933 *NatCAB 25,*
WhAm 1
Smith, DeCost 1864-1939 *IIBEAAW*
Smith, Delavan 1861-1922 *NatCAB 19,*
WhAm 1
Smith, Delazon 1816-1860 *ApCAB, BiAUS,*
BiDrAC, NatCAB 11, TwCBDA,
WhAm H
Smith, Delbert O 1876-1964 *NatCAB 51*
Smith, Delos Hamilton 1884-1963 *WhAm 4*
Smith, Delos Owen 1905-1973 *WhAm 6*
Smith, Dena 1899- *WhAm 5*
Smith, Dietrich Conrad 1840-1914 *BiDrAC*
Smith, Dilman M K 1902- *WhAm 5*
Smith, Donald 1861-1921 *NatCAB 20*
Smith, Sir Donald Alexander 1820-1914
McGEWB
Smith, Sir Donald Alexander 1821-1914 *ApCAB*
Smith, Donald Baker 1894-1972 *NatCAB 56*
Smith, Donald Borden 1896-1959 *WhAm 3*
Smith, Donald Jenckes 1892-1964 *WhAm 4*
Smith, Dora Valentine 1893- *BiDAmEd*
Smith, Dorland 1875-1945 *NatCAB 34*
Smith, Dorman Henry 1892-1956 *WhAm 3*
Smith, Douglas Forrest 1893-1973 *WhAm 5*
Smith, Douglas York 1905-1965 *NatCAB 51*
Smith, Mrs. Draper *WomWWA 14*
Smith, Dudley Crofford 1892-1950 *WhAm 3*
Smith, Dwight Timothy 1868-1936 *NatCAB 27*
Smith, E C E d1950 *WhAm 3*
Smith, E Gerard 1903-1954 *NatCAB 47*
Smith, E Howard 1895-1970 *WhAm 5*
Smith, E Hugh 1883-1967 *NatCAB 54*
Smith, E Kearney 1895-1950 *NatCAB 39*
Smith, E Norman d1957 *WhAm 3*
Smith, E Otis 1871-1934 *WhAm 1*
Smith, E P *NewYHSD*
Smith, Earl Baldwin 1888-1956 *NatCAB 48,*
WhAm 3
Smith, Earl Baxter 1896-1975 *WhAm 6*
Smith, Earl Clemons 1886-1961 *NatCAB 52*
Smith, Earl Edward 1904-1963 *WhAm 4*
Smith, Earle Clement 1891-1960 *NatCAB 49,*
WhAm 4
Smith, Ed Sinclair 1897-1960 *WhAm 4*
Smith, Edgar 1857-1938 *WhAm 1*
Smith, Edgar Bronson 1853-1937 *WhAm 1*
Smith, Edgar Fahs 1854-1928 *AmBi, DcAmB,*
DcScB, NatCAB 13, NatCAB 21
Smith, Edgar Fahs 1856-1928 *NatCAB 15,*
WhAm 1
Smith, Edgar Lawrence 1882-1971 *NatCAB 55*
Smith, Edgar Moncena 1845-1924 *TwCBDA*
Smith, Edgar Moncena 1846-1924 *WhAm 3*
Smith, Edgar Wadsworth 1894-1960 *WhAm 4*
Smith, Edmund Kirby 1824-1893 *AmBi,*
ApCAB, BiDConf, DcAmB, NatCAB 8,
TwCBDA, WhAm H
Smith, Edmund Kirby 1825?-1893 *Drake*
Smith, Edmund Kirby 1871-1929 *WhAm 1*
Smith, Edmund Munroe 1854-1926
ApCAB Sup, DcAmB, TwCBDA,
WhAm 4
Smith, Edmund Reuel 1829-1911 *NewYHSD*
Smith, Edna Kenderdine 1879- *WomWWA 14*
Smith, Edna Leah 1889- *WomWWA 14*
Smith, Edward *NewYHSD*
Smith, Edward 1818?-1874 *DcScB*
Smith, Edward Brinton 1861-1918 *NatCAB 17,*
WhAm 1
Smith, Edward Curtis 1854-1935 *NatCAB 13,*
NatCAB 26, TwCBDA, WhAm 1
Smith, Edward Darrell d1819 *Drake*
Smith, Edward Delafield 1826-1878 *ApCAB,*
Drake, NatCAB 11, WhAm H
Smith, Edward Devereux 1876- *WhAm 5*
Smith, Edward Everett 1856-1917 *NatCAB 16*
Smith, Edward Everett 1861- *WhAm 5*
Smith, Edward G 1886-1956 *WhAm 3*
Smith, Edward Grandison 1868- *WhAm 2*
Smith, Edward Hanson 1889-1961 *WhAm 4*
Smith, Edward Henry 1809-1885 *BiAUS,*
BiDrAC, WhAm H
Smith, Edward Iungerich 1855-1912
NatCAB 16
Smith, Edward Laurence 1875-1923 *WhAm 1*

Smith, Edward Laurence 1877-1923 *WhAm 1*
Smith, Edward Lincoln 1865-1940 *WhAm 1*
Smith, Edward Needham 1902-1951
NatCAB 40
Smith, Edward North 1868-1943 *WhAm 2*
Smith, Edward Page 1871-1955 *NatCAB 43*
Smith, Edward Parmelee 1827-1876 *ApCAB,*
BiAUS
Smith, Edward Parson 1860-1930 *WhAm 1*
Smith, Edward St. Clair 1879- *WhAm 6*
Smith, Edward Staples Cousens 1894-1971
NatCAB 57
Smith, Edward Warren 1915-1974 *WhAm 6*
Smith, Edward Wier 1854-1930 *NatCAB 23*
Smith, Edward William Peter 1885-1942
NatCAB 32
Smith, Edward Willis 1872- *WhAm 5*
Smith, Edwin 1851-1912 *TwCBDA, WhAm 1*
Smith, Edwin Augustus 1843-1919 *NatCAB 30*
Smith, Edwin B *NewYHSD*
Smith, Edwin B 1835?- *BiAUS*
Smith, Edwin Bert 1880- *WhAm 6*
Smith, Edwin Bradbury 1832- *WhAm 4*
Smith, Edwin Burritt 1854-1906 *WhAm 1*
Smith, Edwin E 1862-1934 *WhAm 1*
Smith, Edwin Sumter 1861-1926 *WhAm 1*
Smith, Edwin Whittier 1857-1937 *WhAm 1*
Smith, Egbert Watson 1862-1944 *WhAm 2*
Smith, Elbert Benjamin 1920- *EncAAH*
Smith, Elbert Luther, Jr. 1926-1974 *WhAm 6*
Smith, Elbert Sidney 1847-1934 *WhAm 1*
Smith, Eleanor 1858-1942 *BiDAmEd,*
NatCAB 35, WomWWA 14
Smith, Eli 1801-1857 *AmBi, ApCAB, DcAmB,*
Drake, NatCAB 8, TwCBDA, WhAm H
Smith, Elias 1769-1846 *ApCAB, DcAmB,*
Drake, WhAm H
Smith, Elias A Cappelen 1873-1949 *WhAm 2*
Smith, Elihu Hubbard 1771-1796 *NatCAB 9*
Smith, Elihu Hubbard 1771-1798 *ApCAB,*
DcAmB, Drake, WhAm H
Smith, Elisabeth Howell 1854- *WhAm 4,*
WomWWA 14
Smith, Elise Bennett 1872- *WomWWA 14*
Smith, Eliza Roxey Snow 1804-1887 *DcAmB,*
NotAW
Smith, Elizabeth Anne O'Linn 1876-
WomWWA 14
Smith, Elizabeth Hight 1877- *WomWWA 14*
Smith, Elizabeth J *AmWom*
Smith, Elizabeth Laban 1856- *WomWWA 14*
Smith, Elizabeth Oakes Prince 1806-1893 *AmBi,*
AmWom, ApCAB, DcAmB, Drake,
NatCAB 9, NotAW, TwCBDA,
WhAm H
Smith, Elizur Goodrich 1822- *Drake*
Smith, Ella May Dunning 1860- *WomWWA 14*
Smith, Ellen M Cyr d1920 *WhAm 1,*
WomWWA 14
Smith, Elliott 1875-1943 *WhAm 2*
Smith, Ellison DuRant 1864-1944 *ApCAB X,*
DcAmB S3, WhAm 2
Smith, Ellison DuRant 1866-1944 *BiDrAC,*
NatCAB 14, NatCAB 38, WhAmP
Smith, Ellison Griffith 1854-1935 *WhAm 1*
Smith, Elmer Boyd 1860-1943 *IIBEAAW,*
WhAm 5
Smith, Elmer Dennison 1854-1939 *WhAm 2*
Smith, Elmer William 1868-1950 *WhAm 3*
Smith, Elmo 1909-1968 *WhAm 5*
Smith, Elsworth Fayssoux 1825-1896
NatCAB 27
Smith, Elva Sophronia 1871-1965 *DcAmLiB,*
WhAm 5
Smith, Emeline Sherman 1823- *Drake*
Smith, Emily James *NotAW*
Smith, Emily L Goodrich 1830- *AmWom*
Smith, Emma Adelia Flint *WomWWA 14*
Smith, Emma Hale 1804-1879 *NotAW*
Smith, Emma Pow 1848- *AmWom*
Smith, Emory Byington 1886- *WhoColR*
Smith, Ephraim Kirby 1807-1847 *ApCAB*
Smith, Erasmus Darwin 1806-1883 *ApCAB,*
DcAmB, WhAm H
Smith, Erasmus Deshine 1814-1882 *WhAm H*
Smith, Erasmus Peshine 1814-1882 *ApCAB,*
NatCAB 13
Smith, Erastus d1838 *NatCAB 2*

Smith, Erastus Gilbert 1855-1937 *WhAm 1*
Smith, Erminnie Adelle Platt 1836-1886 *NotAW*
Smith, Erminnie Adelle Platt 1836-1886 *AmBi,*
ApCAB, DcAmB, NatCAB 13, TwCBDA,
WhAm H
Smith, Ernest Ashton 1868-1926 *NatCAB 24,*
WhAm 1
Smith, Ernest Charles 1864- *WhAm 4*
Smith, Ernest Ellsworth 1867-1930 *WhAm 1,*
WhAm 1C
Smith, Ernest Gray 1873-1945 *NatCAB 33,*
WhAm 2
Smith, Ernest Martin 1887-1970 *NatCAB 55*
Smith, Ernest Ollington 1880- *WhoColR*
Smith, Erwin E 1888-1947 *IlBEAAW*
Smith, Erwin Fletcher 1902-1974 *WhAm 6*
Smith, Erwin Frank 1854-1927 *EncAAH*
Smith, Erwin Frink 1854-1927 *DcAmB, DcScB,*
NatCAB 20, WhAm 1
Smith, Erwin Jesse 1866-1925 *WhAm 1*
Smith, Estelle Turrell 1854- *AmWom*
Smith, Ethan 1762-1849 *ApCAB, Drake*
Smith, Ethan Henry 1864-1937 *WhAm 1,*
WhAm 2
Smith, Ethelbert Walton 1885-1958 *WhAm 3*
Smith, Ethelynde 1888- *WomWWA 14*
Smith, Eugene 1839-1928 *NatCAB 26*
Smith, Eugene 1860-1912 *WhAm 1*
Smith, Eugene Allen 1841-1927 *ApCAB,*
DcAmB, NatCAB 6, TwCBDA,
WhAm 1
Smith, Eugene Hanes 1853-1925 *WhAm 1*
Smith, Eugenie Marie Raye *WomWWA 14*
Smith, Eva Augusta Ford Cline *WomWWA 14*
Smith, Eva Jane *WomWWA 14*
Smith, Eva Munson 1843- *AmWom,*
WomWWA 14
Smith, Everett 1862-1933 *NatCAB 40,*
WhAm 4
Smith, Everett Russell 1846-1917 *NatCAB 19*
Smith, Everett William 1897-1961 *WhAm 4*
Smith, Ezekiel Ezra 1852-1933 *ApCAB,*
WhAm 3, WhoColR
Smith, F Berkeley 1868- *WhAm 4*
Smith, F Janney 1888-1966 *NatCAB 53,*
WhAm 5
Smith, Fannie Douglass 1865- *AmWom*
Smith, Ferdinand Conrad 1892-1958 *WhAm 3*
Smith, Ferris 1883-1957 *WhAm 3*
Smith, Fitz-Henry, Jr. 1873- *WhAm 5*
Smith, Floyd Frank 1895-1956 *NatCAB 44*
Smith, Ford Arthur 1883-1946 *NatCAB 36*
Smith, Forrest 1886-1962 *NatCAB 51,*
WhAm 4
Smith, Forrest Allan 1897-1971 *NatCAB 57*
Smith, Frances Gist *WomWWA 14*
Smith, Frances Gordon Burton 1870-
WomWWA 14
Smith, Frances Grace *WomWWA 14*
Smith, Frances M Owston *AmWom*
Smith, Frances Stanton 1871-1931 *NatCAB 27,*
WhAm 5, WomWWA 14
Smith, Frances Wheeler 1850- *WomWWA 14*
Smith, Francis 1720?-1791 *ApCAB, Drake*
Smith, Francis Alward 1898-1962 *WhAm 4*
Smith, Francis Asbury 1837-1915 *WhAm 1*
Smith, Francis Drexel 1874-1956 *IlBEAAW,*
NatCAB 49
Smith, Francis Edward 1878- *WhAm 6*
Smith, Francis Edwin 1877- *WhAm 5*
Smith, Francis Gurney 1818-1878 *ApCAB,*
NatCAB 10
Smith, Francis Henney 1812-1890 *ApCAB,*
BiDAmEd, DcAmB, Drake, NatCAB 26,
TwCBDA, WhAm H
Smith, Francis Henry 1829-1928 *WhAm 1*
Smith, Francis Hopkinson 1838-1915 *AmBi,*
ApCAB, ApCAB X, DcAmB, NatCAB 5,
NewYHSD, TwCBDA, WhAm 1
Smith, Francis Marion 1846-1931 *DcAmB,*
NatCAB 28, WebAB, WhAm 1
Smith, Francis O J 1806-1876 *BiAUS*
Smith, Francis Ormand Jonathan 1806-1876
BiDrAC, WhAm H
Smith, Francis Osmond Jon 1806-1876 *ApCAB*
Smith, Francis Raphael 1911- *BiDrAC*
Smith, Francis Shubael 1819-1887 *NatCAB 21*
Smith, Frank 1822- *ApCAB*

Smith, Frank 1857-1942 *NatCAB 31,*
WhAm 1
Smith, Frank 1884-1954 *NatCAB 43*
Smith, Frank Austin 1866-1948 *WhAm 2*
Smith, Frank Biddle 1859-1909 *NatCAB 19*
Smith, Frank Bulkeley 1864-1918 *WhAm 1*
Smith, Frank C 1892-1971 *WhAm 5*
Smith, Frank Carol 1904-1962 *NatCAB 52*
Smith, Frank Channing, Jr. 1877-1952
NatCAB 40, WhAm 3
Smith, Frank Earling 1877- *ApCAB X*
Smith, Frank Ellis 1918- *BiDrAC*
Smith, Frank Gerard 1878- *WhAm 6*
Smith, Frank Graham 1910-1965 *NatCAB 52*
Smith, Frank Grigsby 1872-1950 *WhAm 3*
Smith, Frank Hill 1842- *ApCAB*
Smith, Frank Hill 1879-1963 *NatCAB 53*
Smith, Frank Kirk 1905-1957 *NatCAB 50*
Smith, Frank Leslie 1867-1950 *BiDrAC,*
DcAmB S4, WhAm 3
Smith, Frank Macpherson 1894-1951
NatCAB 39
Smith, Frank Marshall 1866-1937 *NatCAB 40,*
WhAm 1
Smith, Frank Owens 1859-1924 *BiDrAC,*
WhAm 1
Smith, Frank Sullivan 1851-1920 *WhAm 1*
Smith, Frank Webster 1854-1943 *WhAm 2*
Smith, Frank Whitney 1867-1946 *WhAm 2*
Smith, Franklin G 1867-1968 *WhAm 5*
Smith, Franklin Gatewood *WhoColR A*
Smith, Franklin Guest 1840-1912 *WhAm 1*
Smith, Franklin Orion 1867-1941 *WhAm 1*
Smith, Franklin Pratt 1864- *NatCAB 17*
Smith, Fred Andrew 1907-1972 *WhAm 5*
Smith, Fred Bruce 1897-1968 *NatCAB 54*
Smith, Fred Burton 1865-1936 *DcAmB S2,*
WhAm 1
Smith, Fred Emory 1894-1963 *WhAm 4*
Smith, Fred Lester 1887-1962 *NatCAB 53*
Smith, Fred Louis 1862-1941 *NatCAB 30*
Smith, Fred M 1888-1946 *WhAm 2*
Smith, Fred Merwin 1862-1928 *NatCAB 21*
Smith, Frederic Augustus d1852 *NewYHSD*
Smith, Frederic William 1880- *WhAm 6*
Smith, Frederick *NewYHSD*
Smith, Frederick 1773-1830 *BiAUS,*
NatCAB 16
Smith, Frederick 1807?- *NewYHSD*
Smith, Frederick Appleton 1849-1922 *WhAm 1*
Smith, Frederick Arthur 1875- *WhAm 5*
Smith, Frederick Augustus 1844-1919
ApCAB X, NatCAB 12, NatCAB 19,
WhAm 1
Smith, Frederick B *NewYHSD*
Smith, Frederick Cleveland 1884-1956 *BiDrAC,*
NatCAB 44, WhAm 3, WhAmP
Smith, Frederick Glazier 1867-1948
NatCAB 36
Smith, Frederick H 1869- *WhAm 1*
Smith, Frederick Madison 1874-1946
NatCAB 37, WhAm 2
Smith, Frederick Miller 1870- *WhAm 5*
Smith, Fredrika Shumway 1877-1968
NatCAB 55
Smith, Freling H 1844-1926 *ApCAB X*
Smith, G Edwin 1870-1961 *NatCAB 48*
Smith, G G *NewYHSD*
Smith, G Morris 1891-1962 *NatCAB 46*
Smith, Gean 1851-1928 *IlBEAAW*
Smith, Geddes 1890-1953 *NatCAB 44*
Smith, Gena *WomWWA 14*
Smith, Genie M 1852- *AmWom*
Smith, George *BiAUS, BiDrAC, NewYHSD,*
WhAm H
Smith, George d1902 *TwCBDA*
Smith, George 1804-1882 *ApCAB*
Smith, George 1806-1899 *AmBi, DcAmB*
Smith, George 1808-1899 *ApCAB, NatCAB 7*
Smith, George Albert 1817-1875 *NatCAB 16*
Smith, George Albert 1858-1942 *WhAm 1*
Smith, George Albert 1870-1951 *DcAmB S5,*
NatCAB 39, WhAm 3
Smith, George Albert, Jr. 1905-1969
NatCAB 55, WhAm 5
Smith, George Bancroft 1857- •*ApCAB X*
Smith, George C 1886-1973 *WhAm 6*
Smith, George Carson 1855-1916 *NatCAB 13,*

WhAm 1
Smith, George D *WhoColR*
Smith, George D 1889-1965 *WhAm 4*
Smith, George Edson Philip 1873- *WhAm 5*
Smith, George Everett 1859-1921 *NatCAB 19*
Smith, George F *NewYHSD*
Smith, George Ferguson 1868-1942 *NatCAB 32*
Smith, George Frederick 1865-1952 *NatCAB 49*
Smith, George Frederick 1897-1974 *WhAm 6*
Smith, George Gilbert 1883-1963 *WhAm 4*
Smith, George Girdler 1795-1878 *NewYHSD*
Smith, George H 1843- *NatCAB 5*
Smith, George Handy 1836- *NatCAB 3*
Smith, George Harris 1873-1947 *WhAm 2*
Smith, George Hathorn 1885-1952 *NatCAB 41,*
WhAm 3
Smith, George Henry 1847-1937 *WhAm 1*
Smith, George Henry 1873-1931 *DcAmB*
Smith, George Hunter 1861-1939 *WhAm 3*
Smith, George Jay 1866- *WhAm 4*
Smith, George Joseph 1859-1913 *BiDrAC,*
WhAm 4
Smith, George L d1959 *WhAm 3*
Smith, George L 1840-1884 *BiAUS*
Smith, George Luke 1837-1884 *BiDrAC,*
WhAm H
Smith, George M d1962 *WhAm 4*
Smith, George M 1847-1920 *WhAm 1*
Smith, George McPhail 1878-1943 *NatCAB 35*
Smith, George Milton 1879-1951 *WhAm 3*
Smith, George Otis 1871-1944 *DcAmB S3,*
NatCAB 14, NatCAB 35, WhAm 2
Smith, George P F 1896-1962 *WhAm 4*
Smith, George Rodney 1850- *WhAm 4*
Smith, George Ross 1864-1952 *BiDrAC,*
WhAm 4
Smith, George Sumner 1863-1926 *NatCAB 24*
Smith, George Theodore 1855-1940 *WhAm 1*
Smith, George Valentine 1883-1943 *NatCAB 34*
Smith, George Wallace 1894-1959 *WhAm 3*
Smith, George Walter Vincent 1832-1923
WhAm 1
Smith, George Washington 1800-1876 *ApCAB,*
Drake
Smith, George Washington 1837-1898
ApCAB Sup
Smith, George Washington 1846-1907 *BiDrAC,*
TwCBDA, WhAm 1, WhAmP
Smith, George Watson 1862- *ApCAB X*
Smith, George Weissinger 1864- *WhAm 1*
Smith, George Willard 1884-1968 *NatCAB 54*
Smith, George William 1762-1811 *BiAUS,*
Drake, NatCAB 5, TwCBDA
Smith, George William 1862-1900 *NatCAB 13*
Smith, George Williamson 1836-1925 *ApCAB,*
NatCAB 3, TwCBDA, WhAm 1
Smith, Georgine Northrop Wetherill 1873-1955
NatCAB 48
Smith, Gerald Birney 1868-1929 *DcAmB,*
WhAm 1
Smith, Gerald Hewitt 1912-1955 *NatCAB 45,*
WhAm 3
Smith, Gerald Leigh 1908-1970 *NatCAB 55*
Smith, Gerrit 1797-1874 *AmBi, ApCAB,*
BiAUS, BiDrAC, DcAmB, Drake,
McGEWB, NatCAB 2, TwCBDA,
WebAB, WhAm H
Smith, Gerrit 1838-1915 *NatCAB 15*
Smith, Gerrit 1859-1962 *TwCBDA, WhAm 1*
Smith, Gerritt 1859-1912 *NatCAB 14*
Smith, Gertrude *WomWWA 14*
Smith, Gertrude d1917 *WhAm 1*
Smith, Gertrude E Dietrich 1880-
WomWWA 14
Smith, Gertrude Robinson 1881-1963
NatCAB 48
Smith, Gilbert Morgan 1885-1959 *NatCAB 47,*
WhAm 3
Smith, Giles Alexander 1829-1876 *ApCAB,*
DcAmB, Drake, TwCBDA, WhAm H
Smith, Gladys Ffoulke 1881- *WomWWA 14*
Smith, Gladys Mary *WebAB*
Smith, Glen Edward 1888-1957 *NatCAB 43*
Smith, Goldwin 1823-1910 *ApCAB, Drake,*
WhAm 1
Smith, Gomer Griffith 1896-1953 *BiDrAC,*
NatCAB 41
Smith, Gordon Arthur 1886-1944 *WhAm 2*

Smith, Gordon Laidlaw 1893-1967 *NatCAB 54*
Smith, Grace Coburn 1871- *WomWWA 14*
Smith, Graeme McGregor 1875-
WomWWA 14
Smith, Grafton Adrian 1925-1970 *WhAm 5*
Smith, Grafton Elliot *DcScB*
Smith, Grant 1864-1923 *NatCAB 20*
Smith, Green Clay 1826-1895 *BiDrAC,*
WhAm H
Smith, Green Clay 1830-1895 *BiAUS, Drake*
Smith, Green Clay 1832-1895 *AmBi, ApCAB,*
NatCAB 11, TwCBDA
Smith, Gregory L 1853-1929 *NatCAB 7,*
WhAm 1
Smith, Gretchen Hart 1902-1974 *WhAm 6*
Smith, Griffin 1885-1955 *NatCAB 43,*
WhAm 3
Smith, Gustavus Woodson 1820?-1896 *Drake*
Smith, Gustavus Woodson 1822-1896 *ApCAB,*
BiDConf, DcAmB, NatCAB 7, TwCBDA,
WebAMB, WhAm H
Smith, Guy Chester 1890-1973 *WhAm 6*
Smith, Guy Lincoln 1898-1968 *WhAm 5*
Smith, H A Hammond 1860-1927 *NatCAB 29*
Smith, H Alexander 1880-1966 *WhAm 4*
Smith, H Alexander, Jr. 1909-1964 *NatCAB 49*
Smith, H Alexander *see also* Smith, Howard
Alexander
Smith, H Allen 1906-1976 *WhAm 6*
Smith, H Allen 1909-1976 *BiDrAC*
Smith, H Burns 1874-1958 *NatCAB 44*
Smith, H DeWitt 1888-1962 *NatCAB 49*
Smith, H Gordon 1891-1975 *WhAm 6*
Smith, Hal Horace 1873-1944 *WhAm 2*
Smith, Hal Horace, Jr. 1903-1973 *WhAm 5*
Smith, Hamilton 1840-1900 *DcAmB,*
WhAm H
Smith, Hamilton Lamphere 1818-1903
NatCAB 12, TwCBDA, WhAm 1
Smith, Hamilton Lanphere 1819-1903 *ApCAB*
Smith, Hannah 1849- *WomWWA 14*
Smith, Hannah Whitall 1832-1911 *DcAmB,*
NotAW
Smith, Hariette Knight 1855- *WhAm 4*
Smith, Harlan Ingersoll 1872-1940 *TwCBDA,*
WhAm 1
Smith, Harmon 1872-1934 *NatCAB 26,*
WhAm 1
Smith, Harold Babbitt 1869-1932 *BiDAmEd,*
DcAmB, WhAm 1
Smith, Harold Dewey 1898-1947 *DcAmB S4,*
NatCAB 35, WhAm 2
Smith, Harold Elno 1882-1932 *NatCAB 25*
Smith, Harold Leonard 1896-1971 *WhAm 5*
Smith, Harold Stephen 1893-1970 *WhAm 5*
Smith, Harold Travis 1887- *WhAm 3*
Smith, Harold Vincent 1889-1962 *NatCAB 50,*
WhAm 4
Smith, Harold Wellington 1878-1952 *WhAm 3*
Smith, Harriet Louise Goetsch 1872-
WomWWA 14
Smith, Harriet Lummis d1947 *WhAm 2,*
WomWWA 14
Smith, Harrison 1888-1971 *WhAm 5*
Smith, Harry Alexander 1866-1929 *WhAm 1*
Smith, Harry Alexander 1869-1928 *WhAm 1*
Smith, Harry Bache 1860-1936 *DcAmB S2,*
TwCBDA, WhAm 1
Smith, Harry C 1863- *WhoColR*
Smith, Harry DeForest 1869- *WhAm 5*
Smith, Harry Eaton 1869-1931 *WhAm 1*
Smith, Harry James 1880-1918 *DcAmB,*
NatCAB 18, WhAm 1
Smith, Harry Lester 1876-1951 *WhAm 3*
Smith, Harry Pearse 1885-1953 *WhAm 3*
Smith, Harry Scott 1883-1957 *NatCAB 46*
Smith, Harry Worcester 1865-1945 *WhAm 2*
Smith, Haviland 1905- *WhAm 5*
Smith, Hay Watson 1868-1940 *WhAm 1*
Smith, Helen Evertson 1839- *WhAm 4,*
WomWWA 14
Smith, Helen Fairchild 1836- *WomWWA 14*
Smith, Helen Florene 1877- *WomWWA 14*
Smith, Helen Morton 1859- *AmWom*
Smith, Henry *BiAUS, NewYHSD*
Smith, Henry 1784-1851 *NatCAB 9*
Smith, Sir Henry 1812-1868 *ApCAB*
Smith, Henry 1820-1874 *ApCAB*

Smith, Henry 1838-1916 *BiDrAC*
Smith, Henry Augustine 1874-1952 *NatCAB 18,*
NatCAB 42, WhAm 3
Smith, Henry Augustus 1850-1934 *NatCAB 25*
Smith, Henry Augustus Middleton 1853-1924
DcAmB, WhAm 1
Smith, Henry Bloomfield, Jr. 1885-1972
NatCAB 57
Smith, Henry Boynton 1815- *Drake*
Smith, Henry Boynton 1815-1876 *ApCAB*
Smith, Henry Boynton 1815-1877 *AmBi,*
DcAmB, NatCAB 5, TwCBDA,
WhAm H
Smith, Henry Bradford 1882-1938 *WhAm 1*
Smith, Henry Cassorte 1856-1911 *BiDrAC*
Smith, Henry Cassorte 1859-1911 *WhAm 1*
Smith, Henry Chawner 1886-1961 *NatCAB 52*
Smith, Henry Cooper 1862- *WhAm 4*
Smith, Henry Erskine *WhAm 5*
Smith, Henry Few *NewYHSD*
Smith, Henry Gerrish 1870-1959 *WhAm 3*
Smith, Henry Hollingsworth 1815-1890 *AmBi,*
ApCAB
Smith, Henry Hollingsworth 1818-1890 *Drake*
Smith, Henry John Stanley 1826-1883 *DcScB*
Smith, Henry Justin 1875-1936 *DcAmB S2,*
WhAm 1
Smith, Henry Kay 1875-1943 *NatCAB 32*
Smith, Henry Leavitt 1848-1918 *NatCAB 25,*
WhAm 1
Smith, Henry Lee 1868-1957 *NatCAB 46*
Smith, Henry Lee, Jr. 1913-1972 *NatCAB 56,*
WhAm 5
Smith, Henry Lester 1876-1963 *BiDAmEd,*
WhAm 4
Smith, Henry Louis 1859-1951 *BiDAmEd,*
DcAmB S5, NatCAB 15, NatCAB 40,
TwCBDA, WhAm 3
Smith, Henry M, Jr. 1859-1936 *WhAm 1*
Smith, Henry Michelet 1886-1957 *WhAm 3*
Smith, Henry Monmouth 1868-1950 *WhAm 3*
Smith, Henry Nash 1906- *REnAW*
Smith, Henry P, III 1911- *BiDrAC*
Smith, Henry Perkins 1871-1939 *NatCAB 29*
Smith, Henry Preserved 1847-1927 *DcAmB,*
DcAmReB, NatCAB 23, WhAm 1
Smith, Henry Rittenhouse Wolf 1876-1949
NatCAB 38
Smith, Henry S *NewYHSD*
Smith, Henry Tomlinson 1866-1930 *WhAm 1*
Smith, Henry Tomlinson 1867-1930 *NatCAB 22*
Smith, Henry W *NewYHSD*
Smith, Herbert A 1866-1944 *WhAm 2*
Smith, Herbert Atwood 1878-1959 *WhAm 3*
Smith, Herbert Booth 1883-1967 *NatCAB 53,*
WhAm 4
Smith, Herbert Dwight 1894-1959 *NatCAB 48*
Smith, Herbert Edward 1886-1968 *NatCAB 54*
Smith, Herbert Edward 1889-1968 *WhAm 5*
Smith, Herbert Eugene 1857-1933 *NatCAB 24,*
WhAm 1
Smith, Herbert Huntington 1851-1919 *WhAm 1*
Smith, Herbert Knox 1869-1931 *NatCAB 42,*
WhAm 1
Smith, Herbert McKelden 1876-1960
NatCAB 48
Smith, Herbert Wilson 1888-1970 *WhAm 5*
Smith, Herman Henry 1876-1957 *NatCAB 46*
Smith, Herman Lyle 1892-1950 *WhAm 3*
Smith, Herr A 1815- *BiAUS*
Smith, Hezekiah 1737-1805 *ApCAB, DcAmB,*
WhAm H
Smith, Hezekiah Bradley 1816-1887 *ApCAB,*
BiDrAC, WhAm H
Smith, Hezekiah Wright 1828- *ApCAB,*
NewYHSD
Smith, Hilda Josephine 1880- *WomWWA 14*
Smith, Hiram 1817-1890 *DcAmB, WhAm H*
Smith, Hiram Moore 1884-1946 *WhAm 2*
Smith, Hiram Ypsilanti 1843-1894 *BiDrAC,*
WhAm H
Smith, Hoke 1855-1931 *AmBi, ApCAB Sup,*
ApCAB X, BiDrAC, BiDrUSE, DcAmB,
EncAAH, NatCAB 1, TwCBDA, WebAB,
WhAm 1, WhAmP
Smith, Holland McTyeire 1882-1967 *WebAMB,*
WhAm 4, WhWW-II
Smith, Holmes 1863-1937 *WhAm 1*

Smith, Homer 1867-1934 *WhAm 1*
Smith, Homer A A 1875-1940 *WhAm 1*
Smith, Homer William 1895-1962 *DcScB,*
NatCAB 52, WhAm 4
Smith, Horace 1808-1893 *DcAmB,*
NatCAB 10, WhAm H
Smith, Horace Boardman 1826-1888 *BiDrAC,*
WhAm H
Smith, Horace Herbert 1868- *WhAm 4*
Smith, Horace Strong 1826-1899 *NatCAB 13*
Smith, Horace Wemyss 1825- *ApCAB, Drake*
Smith, Horatio Elwin 1886-1946 *DcAmB S4,*
WhAm 2
Smith, Hosea Hildreth 1820- *TwCBDA*
Smith, Hoval Arnold 1876-1953 *NatCAB 40*
Smith, Howard Alexander 1880-1966 *BiDrAC*
Smith, Howard Alexander *see also* Smith, H
Alexander
Smith, Howard Anthony 1888-1963 *WhAm 4*
Smith, Howard Caswell 1871-1965 *NatCAB 51,*
WhAm 4
Smith, Howard Cloid 1896-1966 *NatCAB 54*
Smith, Howard Dwight 1886-1958 *WhAm 3*
Smith, Howard Lee 1898-1952 *NatCAB 42*
Smith, Howard Leland 1894-1974 *WhAm 6*
Smith, Howard Leslie 1861- *WhAm 4*
Smith, Howard Remus 1872- *NatCAB 17,*
WhAm 5
Smith, Howard Wayne 1870-1951 *NatCAB 48,*
WhAm 3
Smith, Howard Worth 1883- *BiDrAC,*
WhAmP
Smith, Hubert Winston 1907-1971 *WhAm 5*
Smith, Hugh Allison 1873- *WhAm 5*
Smith, Hugh Carnes 1873-1946 *WhAm 2*
Smith, Hugh F, Jr. 1892-1946 *WhAm 2*
Smith, Hugh McCormick 1865-1941
NatCAB 33, WhAm 1
Smith, Huntington 1857- *WhAm 4*
Smith, Hurlbut William 1865-1951 *WhAm 3*
Smith, Huron H 1883-1933 *WhAm 1*
Smith, Hyrum 1800-1844 *NatCAB 16*
Smith, I B *NewYHSD*
Smith, Ian Douglas 1919- *McGEWB*
Smith, Ida B Wise 1871-1952 *WhAm 3,*
WomWWA 14
Smith, Ida Kendrick *WomWWA 14*
Smith, Ida Spooner *WomWWA 14*
Smith, Ignatius 1889-1957 *WhAm 3*
Smith, Ira B 1852- *NatCAB 12*
Smith, Irving Gardner 1899-1965 *WhAm 4*
Smith, Isaac d1807 *BiAUS, Drake*
Smith, Isaac 1736-1807 *ApCAB*
Smith, Isaac 1740-1807 *BiDrAC, WhAm H*
Smith, Isaac 1761-1834 *BiAUS, BiDrAC,*
WhAm H
Smith, Isaac Butler 1867-1941 *NatCAB 33,*
WhAm 2
Smith, Isaac Townsend 1813- *ApCAB,*
WhAm 4
Smith, Isabel Elizabeth 1845-1938 *AmWom,*
WhAm 1, WomWWA 14
Smith, Isabella Gwynn 1867- *WhoColR*
Smith, Isaiah Perley 1836- *WhAm 4*
Smith, Israel 1759-1810 *ApCAB, BiAUS,*
BiDrAC, DcAmB, Drake, NatCAB 8,
TwCBDA, WhAm H, WhAmP
Smith, Israel A 1876-1958 *WhAm 3*
Smith, Ivy May 1874- *WomWWA 14*
Smith, Mrs. J *NewYHSD*
Smith, J Allen 1850-1920 *NatCAB 19*
Smith, J Brodie 1861-1947 *NatCAB 17,*
NatCAB 34
Smith, J Burritt 1852-1914 *WhAm 1*
Smith, J Emil 1880-1969 *NatCAB 55,*
WhAm 5
Smith, J Miller 1862-1934 *NatCAB 26*
Smith, J Neil 1895-1971 *WhAm 5*
Smith, J Paul 1890-1955 *NatCAB 43,*
WhAm 3
Smith, J Waldo 1861-1933 *NatCAB 15,*
NatCAB 24
Smith, Jack Wilkinson 1873-1949 *IIBEAAW*
Smith, Jacob, Jr. *NewYHSD*
Smith, Jacob Getlar 1898-1958 *WhAm 3*
Smith, Jacob Hurd 1840-1918 *WhAm 1*
Smith, James *NewYHSD*
Smith, James 1713-1806 *BiAUS, BiDrAC,*

WhAmP
Smith, James 1719?-1806 *AmBi, DcAmB, NatCAB 2, WhAm H*
Smith, James 1720?-1806 *ApCAB, Drake, TwCBDA*
Smith, James 1737-1812 *ApCAB, Drake*
Smith, James 1737-1813 *WhAm H*
Smith, James 1737?-1814? *AmBi, DcAmB*
Smith, James 1808- *ApCAB*
Smith, James, Jr. 1851- *ApCAB Sup, NatCAB 12, TwCBDA*
Smith, James, Jr. 1851-1926 *WhAm 1*
Smith, James, Jr. 1851-1927 *BiDrAC, DcAmB*
Smith, James Allen 1860-1924 *DcAmB*
Smith, James Allen 1860-1926 *WhAm 1*
Smith, James Allwood 1865-1920 *WhAm 1*
Smith, James Argyle 1831-1901 *BiDConf, WhAm 4*
Smith, James Baker 1836- *NatCAB 1*
Smith, James Beattie 1901-1956 *NatCAB 43*
Smith, James Cosslett 1857-1917 *NatCAB 17*
Smith, James D 1872-1955 *WhAm 3*
Smith, James Dickinson 1829-1909 *NatCAB 15*
Smith, James Dickinson 1832-1909 *WhAm 1*
Smith, James E *New YHSD*
Smith, James Edward 1759-1828 *DcScB*
Smith, James Ellwood 1851-1936 *WhAm 1*
Smith, James Elwood 1851-1936 *NatCAB 12*
Smith, James Francis 1859-1928 *AmBi, DcAmB, TwCBDA, WhAm 1*
Smith, James Frank 1868-1920 *WhAm 1*
Smith, James Franklin 1882- *WhoColR*
Smith, James Gerald 1897-1946 *WhAm 2*
Smith, James Henderson 1882-1953 *NatCAB 42*
Smith, James Henry Oliver 1857-1935 *WhAm 1*
Smith, James Irwin 1827- *WhAm 4*
Smith, James Kellum 1893-1961 *NatCAB 48, WhAm 4*
Smith, James Leonard 1864- *WhoColR*
Smith, James Lewis 1827-1897 *NatCAB 2*
Smith, James McCune 1813-1865 *DcAmB, WhAm H*
Smith, James McLain 1838-1905 *WhAm 1*
Smith, James Milton 1823-1890 *ApCAB, BiAUS, BiDConf, NatCAB 1, TwCBDA*
Smith, James P 1803?-1888 *New YHSD*
Smith, James Perrin 1864-1931 *DcAmB, WhAm 1*
Smith, James Porter 1882-1940 *WhAm 1*
Smith, James Power 1837- *WhAm 4*
Smith, James Sheppard 1871-1931 *WhAm 1*
Smith, James Strudwick 1790-1859 *BiAUS, BiDrAC, WhAm H*
Smith, James Thomas 1866-1928 *NatCAB 24*
Smith, James Vernon 1926- *BiDrAC*
Smith, James W 1893-1955 *WhAm 3*
Smith, James Walter 1868-1948 *WhAm 2*
Smith, James Willison 1879-1942 *WhAm 2*
Smith, James Youngs 1809-1876 *ApCAB, BiAUS, DcAmB, Drake, NatCAB 9, TwCBDA, WhAm H*
Smith, Jane Luella Dowd 1847- *NatCAB 2, TwCBDA, WhAm 4, WomWWA 14*
Smith, Jane Luella Dowd *see also* Smith, Luella Dowd
Smith, Jane Norman 1874-1953 *WhAm 3*
Smith, Jane Noyes 1848- *WomWWA 14*
Smith, Jay Briasted Roe 1869-1953 *NatCAB 42*
Smith, Jeanie Oliver Davidson d1925 *AmWom, WhAm 1, WomWWA 14*
Smith, Jedediah Kilburn 1770-1828 *BiAUS, BiDrAC, WhAm H*
Smith, Jedediah Strong 1798-1831 *AmBi, DcAmB, WhAm H*
Smith, Jedediah Strong 1799-1831 *EncAAH, McGEWB, REnAW, WebAB*
Smith, Jennie Cora Morse *WomWWA 14*
Smith, Jennie Merrylees 1861- *WomWWA 14*
Smith, Jeremiah 1759-1842 *ApCAB, BiDrAC, DcAmB, Drake, NatCAB 2, NatCAB 11, TwCBDA, WhAm H, WhAmP*
Smith, Jeremiah 1759-1843 *BiAUS*
Smith, Jeremiah 1837-1921 *DcAmB, WhAm 1*
Smith, Jeremiah, Jr. 1870-1935 *AmBi, DcAmB S1, WhAm 1*
Smith, Jerome Carruth 1874-1936 *NatCAB 30*
Smith, Jerome Howard 1861?-1941 *IlBEAAW*

Smith, Jerome Howard 1861-1942 *REnAW*
Smith, Jerome VanCrowninshield 1800-1879 *ApCAB, Drake*
Smith, Jesse C 1808-1888 *ApCAB*
Smith, Jesse Merrick 1848-1927 *NatCAB 22, WhAm 1*
Smith, Jessie Earnestine Shirley 1866-1918 *NatCAB 18*
Smith, Jessie Willcox 1863-1935 *AmBi, NatCAB 26, NotAW, WhAm 1, WomWWA 14*
Smith, Jim Clifford 1894-1947 *WhAm 2*
Smith, Job Lewis 1827-1897 *ApCAB, DcAmB, WhAm H*
Smith, Joe Frazer 1897-1957 *WhAm 3*
Smith, Joe L 1880-1962 *WhAm 4*
Smith, Joel Perry 1912-1975 *WhAm 6*
Smith, Joel West 1837-1924 *DcAmB, WhAm 1*
Smith, John *New YHSD*
Smith, John d1631 *Drake, TwCBDA*
Smith, John d1664 *NatCAB 10*
Smith, John d1815 *Drake*
Smith, John 1579?-1631 *AmBi, DcAmB, EncAAH, EncAB, NatCAB 13, WhAm H*
Smith, John 1579-1632 *ApCAB*
Smith, John 1580?-1631 *McGEWB, WebAB, WebAMB*
Smith, John 1722-1771 *ApCAB, NatCAB 13*
Smith, John 1735-1816 *ApCAB, BiAUS, BiDrAC, NatCAB 6, TwCBDA*
Smith, John 1735?-1824? *DcAmB, WhAm H*
Smith, John 1750-1836 *BiAUS, BiDrAC, WhAm H, WhAmP*
Smith, John 1752-1809 *ApCAB, BiDAmEd, Drake, NatCAB 9, WhAm H*
Smith, John 1752-1816 *ApCAB, BiAUS, BiDrAC, NatCAB 11, TwCBDA, WhAm H, WhAmP*
Smith, John 1784-1868 *NatCAB 17*
Smith, John 1789-1858 *ApCAB, BiAUS, BiDrAC, TwCBDA, WhAm H*
Smith, John, Jr. *New YHSD*
Smith, John A *New YHSD*
Smith, John Adam 1864-1941 *NatCAB 31*
Smith, John Addison Baxter 1845-1918 *WhAm 1*
Smith, John Ambler 1847-1892 *BiAUS, BiDrAC, WhAm H*
Smith, John Armstrong 1814-1892 *BiAUS, BiDrAC, WhAm H*
Smith, John Augustine 1782-1865 *ApCAB, ApCAB Sup, DcAmB, Drake, NatCAB 3, TwCBDA, WhAm H*
Smith, John B *BiAUS, New YHSD*
Smith, John Bernhard 1858-1912 *DcAmB*
Smith, John Bernhardt 1858-1912 *NatCAB 13, NatCAB 15, TwCBDA, WhAm 1*
Smith, John Beyea 1815- *NatCAB 5*
Smith, John Blair 1756-1799 *ApCAB, DcAmB, Drake, NatCAB 2, TwCBDA, WhAm H*
Smith, John Butler 1838-1914 *NatCAB 11, TwCBDA, WhAm 1*
Smith, Mrs. John Calvin *New YHSD*
Smith, John Calvin *New YHSD*
Smith, John Charles 1907-1965 *WhAm 4*
Smith, John Corson 1832-1910 *WhAm 1*
Smith, John Cotton 1765-1845 *ApCAB, BiAUS, BiDrAC, DcAmB, Drake, NatCAB 10, TwCBDA, WhAm H, WhAmP*
Smith, John Cotton 1810-1879 *ApCAB*
Smith, John Cotton 1826-1882 *ApCAB, DcAmB, NatCAB 8, WhAm H*
Smith, John Day 1845-1933 *WhAm 1*
Smith, John Elijah 1871- *WhAm 5*
Smith, John Eliphalet 1878-1963 *NatCAB 52*
Smith, John Eugene 1816-1897 *ApCAB, DcAmB, Drake, NatCAB 12, TwCBDA, WhAm H*
Smith, John F *New YHSD*
Smith, John Ferdinand D *Drake*
Smith, John Frederick 1860-1952 *NatCAB 40, WhAm 3*
Smith, John Gregory 1818-1891 *ApCAB, BiAUS, DcAmB, Drake, NatCAB 8, TwCBDA, WhAm H*
Smith, John H 1882- *ApCAB X*
Smith, John Hammond 1867-1932 *NatCAB 23,*

WhAm 1, WhAm 1C
Smith, John Henry 1848-1911 *NatCAB 16*
Smith, John Henry, Jr. 1894-1950 *WhAm 3*
Smith, John Hyatt 1824-1886 *ApCAB, BiDrAC, WhAm H*
Smith, John Jay 1798-1881 *ApCAB, DcAmB, Drake, WhAm H*
Smith, John Joseph 1896-1968 *WhAm 5*
Smith, John Joseph 1904- *BiDrAC*
Smith, John L *New YHSD*
Smith, John Lawrence 1818-1883 *AmBi, ApCAB, DcAmB, NatCAB 6, TwCBDA, WhAm H*
Smith, John Lawrence 1889-1950 *NatCAB 44, WhAm 3*
Smith, John Lewis 1877-1950 *WhAm 3*
Smith, John Lockhart *New YHSD*
Smith, John M C 1853-1923 *BiDrAC, WhAm 1, WhAmP*
Smith, John Merlin Powis 1866-1932 *DcAmB, NatCAB 42, WhAm 1*
Smith, John P 1883-1948 *WhAm 2*
Smith, John Powell 1846-1918 *NatCAB 18*
Smith, John Quincy 1824-1901 *BiAUS, BiDrAC*
Smith, John Rowson 1810-1864 *DcAmB, IlBEAAW, New YHSD, WhAm H*
Smith, John Rubens 1775-1849 *BiDAmEd, DcAmB, New YHSD, WhAm H*
Smith, John Sabine 1843- *NatCAB 3*
Smith, John Sloan 1907-1969 *NatCAB 57, WhAm 5*
Smith, John Spear 1790?-1866 *ApCAB, NatCAB 12*
Smith, John Speed 1792-1854 *ApCAB, BiAUS, BiDrAC, Drake, WhAm H*
Smith, John T *BiAUS, BiDrAC, WhAm H*
Smith, John Talbot 1855-1923 *ApCAB, WhAm 1*
Smith, John Thomas 1879-1947 *NatCAB 35, WhAm 2*
Smith, John Walter 1845-1925 *BiDrAC, NatCAB 13, TwCBDA, WhAm 1, WhAmP*
Smith, John Walter 1900-1972 *WhAm 5*
Smith, John Warren 1863-1940 *WhAm 1*
Smith, John Wesley 1859-1927 *NatCAB 20*
Smith, John Wesley 1863-1931 *WhAm 1*
Smith, Jonas Waldo 1861-1933 *AmBi, DcAmB, WhAm 1*
Smith, Jonathan 1842-1930 *NatCAB 22*
Smith, Jonathan Bayard d1812 *BiAUS*
Smith, Jonathan Bayard 1741-1812 *Drake, NatCAB 4*
Smith, Jonathan Bayard 1742-1812 *ApCAB, BiDrAC, DcAmB, TwCBDA, WhAm H*
Smith, Jonathan Ritchie 1852-1936 *WhAm 1*
Smith, Joseph 1790-1877 *ApCAB, DcAmB, Drake, NatCAB 4, TwCBDA, WhAm H*
Smith, Joseph 1796-1868 *ApCAB, Drake*
Smith, Joseph 1805-1844 *AmBi, ApCAB, DcAmB, DcAmReB, Drake, EncAAH, EncAB, McGEWB, NatCAB 7, NatCAB 16, WebAB, WhAm H*
Smith, Joseph 1832-1914 *ApCAB, DcAmB, WhAm 1*
Smith, Joseph 1853-1929 *WhAm 1*
Smith, Joseph, Jr. 1805-1844 *REnAW, TwCBDA*
Smith, Joseph Adams 1837-1907 *WhAm 1*
Smith, Joseph B d1862 *NatCAB 6*
Smith, Joseph B 1798-1876 *New YHSD*
Smith, Joseph Brodie 1861-1947 *WhAm 2*
Smith, Joseph Earl 1888-1970 *WhAm 5*
Smith, Joseph Fielding 1838-1918 *DcAmB, NatCAB 7, NatCAB 16, REnAW, WhAm 1*
Smith, Joseph Fielding 1876-1972 *WhAm 5*
Smith, Joseph Fielding 1899-1964 *WhAm 4*
Smith, Joseph Francis 1865-1942 *WhAm 2*
Smith, Joseph Lee 1776-1846 *ApCAB, BiAUS*
Smith, Joseph Lee Kirby 1836-1862 *ApCAB, TwCBDA*
Smith, Joseph Lindon 1863-1950 *NatCAB 39, WhAm 3*
Smith, Joseph Luther 1880-1962 *BiDrAC*
Smith, Joseph Mather 1789-1866 *ApCAB, Drake, NatCAB 6, WhAm H*

Smith, Joseph Newton 1887-1951 *WhAm 3*
Smith, Joseph P 1897-1964 *WhAm 4*
Smith, Joseph Richard 1850-1920 *NatCAB 43*
Smith, Joseph Richards 1873-1954 *NatCAB 47*
Smith, Joseph Rowe 1802-1868 *ApCAB, Drake*
Smith, Joseph Rowe 1831-1911 *WhAm 1*
Smith, Joseph Russell 1874- *WhAm 6*
Smith, Joseph Showalter 1824-1884 *BiAUS,*
   BiDrAC, WhAm H
Smith, Joseph Thomas 1883-1951 *NatCAB 38*
Smith, Joseph Thomas 1895-1965 *WhAm 4*
Smith, Josephine Tatnall 1854- *WomWWA 14*
Smith, Josephine Wernicke d1953 *WhAm 3*
Smith, Joshua Hett 1736-1818 *ApCAB, Drake*
Smith, Joshua Toulmin 1816-1869 *ApCAB*
Smith, Josiah 1704-1781 *ApCAB, Drake*
Smith, Josiah 1738-1803 *BiDrAC, WhAm H*
Smith, Josiah 1745-1803 *BiAUS*
Smith, Josiah Renick 1851-1914 *WhAm 1*
Smith, Josiah Torrey 1815- *ApCAB*
Smith, Judson 1837-1906 *ApCAB, DcAmB,*
   NatCAB 14, TwCBDA, WhAm 1
Smith, Jules Andre 1880- *WhAm 6*
Smith, Julia 1792-1886 *WhAmP*
Smith, Julia E 1792-1892 *NatCAB 7*
Smith, Julia Evalina 1792-1886 *ApCAB*
Smith, Julia Evelina 1792- *NotAW*
Smith, Julia Evelina 1792-1886 *DcAmB,*
   WhAm H
Smith, Julia Holmes 1839-1930 *AmWom,*
   NatCAB 22, WhAm 1, WhAm 1C,
   WomWWA 14
Smith, Julius Clarence 1889-1968 *WhAm 5*
Smith, Julius Paul 1842-1904 *NatCAB 25*
Smith, June C 1876-1947 *WhAm 2*
Smith, Junius 1780-1853 *ApCAB, DcAmB,*
   Drake, NatCAB 19, WhAm H
Smith, Justin Almerin 1819- *ApCAB*
Smith, Justin Harvey 1857-1930 *AmBi,*
   DcAmB, WhAm 1
Smith, K Wesley 1892-1961 *WhAm 4*
Smith, Kate 1909- *WebAB*
Smith, Kate Douglas *NotAW*
Smith, Katharine Ware *WomWWA 14*
Smith, Kenneth Gladstone 1892-1945 *WhAm 2*
Smith, Kirby 1824-1893 *AmBi*
Smith, Kirby Flower 1862-1918 *WhAm 1*
Smith, Langdon 1858-1908 *WhAm 1*
Smith, Lanta Wilson *WomWWA 14*
Smith, Laura Rountree 1876-1924 *WhAm 1,*
   WomWWA 14
Smith, Lawrence 1893-1966 *WhAm 4*
Smith, Lawrence Henry 1892-1958 *BiDrAC,*
   WhAm 3, WhAmP
Smith, Lawrence Meredith Clemson 1902-1975
   WhAm 6
Smith, Lawrence Weld 1895-1974 *WhAm 6*
Smith, Lee Herbert 1856- *NatCAB 17*
Smith, Lee Stewart 1844- *NatCAB 17*
Smith, Lee Thompson d1963 *WhAm 4*
Smith, Lemon Lawrence 1881-1954 *NatCAB 44*
Smith, Lemuel Augustus, Sr. 1878-1950
   WhAm 3
Smith, Lemuel Fish 1873-1951 *NatCAB 40*
Smith, Lemuel Franklin 1890-1956 *NatCAB 45,*
   WhAm 3
Smith, Leo R 1905-1963 *WhAm 4*
Smith, Leon E 1894-1961 *WhAm 4*
Smith, Leon Edgar 1884-1975 *WhAm 6*
Smith, Leon Perdue 1869-1937 *WhAm 1*
Smith, Leon Perdue 1899-1964 *WhAm 4*
Smith, Leon Rutherford 1875-1918 *NatCAB 18*
Smith, Leona Jones 1912-1969 *WhAm 5*
Smith, Leonard Bacon 1873-1957 *WhAm 3,*
   WhAm 4
Smith, Leonard Minuse 1894- *WhAm 2*
Smith, Leonidas D'Entrecasteaux 1866-1932
   WhAm 1
Smith, LeRoy Artemas 1843-1926 *NatCAB 21*
Smith, LeRoy Henry 1897-1954 *NatCAB 44*
Smith, Leslie Raymond 1873-1932 *NatCAB 24*
Smith, Levi 1844-1917 *NatCAB 17*
Smith, Levi Pease 1885-1970 *NatCAB 56,*
   WhAm 5
Smith, Lewis Elden 1906-1964 *WhAm 4*
Smith, Lewis Martin 1894-1958 *WhAm 3*
Smith, Lewis Wilbur 1876-1952 *WhAm 3*
Smith, Lewis Worthington 1866-1947 *WhAm 2*

Smith, Lillian 1897-1966 *WhAm 4*
Smith, Lillian Church 1865- *WomWWA 14*
Smith, Lillian Scoresby *WomWWA 14*
Smith, Lillian W *IIBEAAW*
Smith, Livingston 1879- *WhAm 6*
Smith, Livingston Waddell 1876-1956 *WhAm 3*
Smith, Lizzie Williams 1853- *WomWWA 14*
Smith, Lloyd Dewitt 1873- *WhAm 5*
Smith, Lloyd Gaston 1891-1958 *WhAm 3*
Smith, Lloyd Logan Pearsall 1865-1946
   DcAmB S4
Smith, Lloyd Pearsall 1822-1886 *AmBi,*
   ApCAB, DcAmB, DcAmLiB, WhAm H
Smith, Lloyd Raymond 1883-1944 *NatCAB 33,*
   WhAm 2
Smith, Lloyd Waddell 1870- *WhAm 5*
Smith, Lloyd Weir 1886-1950 *WhAm 3*
Smith, Lochlan *NewYHSD*
Smith, Logan Pearsall 1865-1946 *WhAm 2*
Smith, Lois Ellen *WomWWA 14*
Smith, Lon A 1869-1947 *NatCAB 36*
Smith, Lothrop 1906-1949 *WhAm 3*
Smith, Lottie Millard 1871- *WomWWA 14*
Smith, Louie Henrie 1872- *WhAm 5*
Smith, Louie Myers *WomWWA 14*
Smith, Louise Allen *WomWWA 14*
Smith, Louise Kirkhuff *WomWWA 14*
Smith, Louise Porter 1848- *WomWWA 14*
Smith, Lowell Herbert 1892-1945 *NatCAB 37,*
   WhAm 2
Smith, Lucius 1883- *WhoColR*
Smith, Lucius Edwin 1822- *ApCAB*
Smith, Lucy Hahn Cunningham 1871-
   WomWWA 14
Smith, Lucy Harth 1888-1955 *DcAmB S5*
Smith, Luella Dowd 1847- *AmWom, ApCAB*
Smith, Luella Dowd *see also* Smith, Jane Luella
   Dowd
Smith, Lura Eugenie Brown *WomWWA 14*
Smith, Lura Eugenie Brown 1854- *WhAm 4*
Smith, Lura Eugenie Brown 1864- *AmWom*
Smith, Lurenda Beverly 1844- *WomWWA 14*
Smith, Luther Ely 1873-1951 *NatCAB 41,*
   WhAm 3
Smith, Luther M 1826-1879 *NatCAB 1,*
   TwCBDA
Smith, Luther Pinkney 1861-1926 *NatCAB 20*
Smith, Luther Wesley 1897-1971 *NatCAB 56,*
   WhAm 5
Smith, Lybrand Palmer 1891-1948 *WhAm 2*
Smith, Lyman Atwater 1884-1950 *NatCAB 39*
Smith, Lyman Cornelius 1850-1910 *NatCAB 14,*
   NatCAB 35, TwCBDA, WhAm 1
Smith, Lyndon Ambrose 1854-1918 *WhAm 1*
Smith, Lyndon Arnold 1795-1865 *Drake*
Smith, Lynwood Herbert 1893-1955
   NatCAB 45, WhAm 3
Smith, Mabell Shippie Clarke 1864-1942
   WhAm 2, WomWWA 14
Smith, Madison Roswell 1850-1919 *BiDrAC,*
   NatCAB 19, WhAm 4
Smith, Mahlon Ellwood 1884-1966 *WhAm 4*
Smith, Mrs. Mai Davis *WomWWA 14*
Smith, Marcus 1829-1874 *ApCAB, DcAmB,*
   Drake, NatCAB 26, WhAm H
Smith, Marcus Aurelius 1851-1924 *BiDrAC,*
   NatCAB 26, WhAmP
Smith, Marcus Aurelius 1852-1924 *NatCAB 15,*
   WhAm 1
Smith, Margaret Bayard 1778-1844 *ApCAB,*
   DcAmB, Drake, NotAW, WhAm H
Smith, Margaret Cary 1881- *WomWWA 14*
Smith, Margaret Chase 1897- *BiDrAC*
Smith, Margaret Keiver *WomWWA 14*
Smith, Margaret Nichols 1875- *WomWWA 14*
Smith, Margaret Vowell 1839- *WhAm 4,*
   WomWWA 14
Smith, Marion 1884-1947 *WhAm 2*
Smith, Marion Couthouy d1931 *WhAm 1,*
   WomWWA 14
Smith, Marion Gertrude d1951 *WhAm 3*
Smith, Marion Parris 1879- *WomWWA 14*
Smith, Marjorie C 1903-1972 *WhAm 5*
Smith, Mark *WhAm H*
Smith, Mark A 1886- *WhAm 2*
Smith, Marshall Alexander 1869-1937
   NatCAB 27
Smith, Martha Jane 1867- *WomWWA 14*

Smith, Martha Pearson 1836- *AmWom*
Smith, Martha Rose Kapantaes 1927-1970
   WhAm 5
Smith, Martin Fernard 1891-1954 *BiDrAC,*
   WhAm 3, WhAmP
Smith, Martin Luther 1819-1866 *ApCAB,*
   BiDConf, DcAmB, Drake, NatCAB 5,
   TwCBDA, WhAm H
Smith, Marvin Boren 1877-1952 *NatCAB 41,*
   WhAm 3
Smith, Mary 1842-1878 *NewYHSD*
Smith, Mary A *NewYHSD*
Smith, Mary Alice *WomWWA 14*
Smith, Mary Almira 1850- *WomWWA 14*
Smith, Mary Bartlett *WomWWA 14*
Smith, Mary Belle 1862- *AmWom*
Smith, Mary Cynthia 1882- *WhAm 6*
Smith, Mary Eleanor Diehl *WomWWA 14*
Smith, Mary Elizabeth 1880-1915 *WhAm 1*
Smith, Mary Emma Colby *WomWWA 14*
Smith, Mary Emmons 1864- *WomWWA 14*
Smith, Mary Frances Dibble *WomWWA 14*
Smith, Mary Frazer *WomWWA 14*
Smith, Mary Louise Riley 1842- *ApCAB,*
   WomWWA 14
Smith, Mary Louise Riley 1852- *AmWom*
Smith, Mary Priscilla Wilson *NewYHSD*
Smith, Mary Prudence Wells 1840-1930 *ApCAB,*
   TwCBDA, WhAm 1, WomWWA 14
Smith, Mary Stewart 1834- *AmWom*
Smith, Mary Virginia Agate *WomWWA 14*
Smith, Mason 1902-1966 *WhAm 4*
Smith, Mathew Charles 1868-1941 *NatCAB 30*
Smith, Matt Ryan 1866-1930 *NatCAB 24*
Smith, Matthew d1958 *WhAm 3*
Smith, Matthew F 1882-1926 *WhAm 1*
Smith, Matthew Hale 1816-1879 *ApCAB,*
   Drake, NatCAB 2, TwCBDA, WhAm H
Smith, Matthew John Wilfred 1891-1960
   WhAm 4
Smith, Max 1874- *WhAm 5*
Smith, May Riley 1842-1927 *WhAm 1*
Smith, McGregor 1899-1972 *WhAm 5*
Smith, Melancthon d1958 *BiAUS*
Smith, Melancthon 1724-1798 *NatCAB 3*
Smith, Melancthon 1744-1798 *BiDrAC*
Smith, Melancthon 1809-1893 *Drake*
Smith, Melancton 1724-1798 *ApCAB,*
   TwCBDA
Smith, Melancton 1744-1798 *DcAmB,*
   WhAm H
Smith, Melancton 1780-1818 *ApCAB*
Smith, Melancton 1810-1893 *AmBi, ApCAB,*
   DcAmB, NatCAB 5, TwCBDA,
   WebAMB
Smith, Melvin Montgomery 1906-1974
   WhAm 6
Smith, Meriwether 1730-1790 *ApCAB,*
   BiDrAC, TwCBDA, WhAm H
Smith, Meriwether 1730-1794 *DcAmB*
Smith, Merle Negley 1872- *WhAm 5*
Smith, Merriman 1913-1970 *NatCAB 56,*
   WhAm 5
Smith, Merriwether *BiAUS, Drake*
Smith, Mildred Catharine d1973 *WhAm 6*
Smith, Milo Augustus 1844-1922 *NatCAB 37*
Smith, Milo Pettibone 1835-1926 *NatCAB 20*
Smith, Milton Hannibal 1836-1921 *DcAmB,*
   WhAm 1
Smith, Milton Truman 1901-1958 *WhAm 3*
Smith, Minna Caroline d1929 *WhAm 1,*
   WomWWA 14
Smith, Minnehaha Lovell McKinlay
   WomWWA 14
Smith, Minnie Louise 1863-1927 *NatCAB 21*
Smith, Monroe William 1901-1973 *WhAm 6*
Smith, Mordon 1881- *WhAm 6*
Smith, Morgan 1868-1935 *NatCAB 27*
Smith, Morgan Lewis 1821-1874 *AmBi,*
   DcAmB, WebAMB, WhAm H
Smith, Morgan Lewis 1822-1874 *ApCAB,*
   TwCBDA
Smith, Moses 1901-1964 *WhAm 4*
Smith, Munroe 1854- *NatCAB 11, WhAm 1*
Smith, Muriel 1881- *WomWWA 14*
Smith, Murray 1891-1955 *WhAm 3*
Smith, Myron Bement 1897-1970 *NatCAB 55*
Smith, Myrtle Holm 1875-1951 *WhAm 3*

Smith, Nathan 1762-1828 *ApCAB, NatCAB 3*
Smith, Nathan 1762-1829 *AmBi, BiDAmEd, BiHiMed, DcAmB, Drake, TwCBDA, WebAB, WhAm H*
Smith, Nathan 1769-1835 *ApCAB, NatCAB 5*
Smith, Nathan 1770-1835 *BiDrAC, DcAmB, Drake, TwCBDA, WhAm H, WhAmP*
Smith, Nathan 1770-1836 *BiAUS*
Smith, Nathan Ryno 1797-1877 *AmBi, ApCAB, DcAmB, NatCAB 3, WhAm H*
Smith, Nathaniel 1762-1822 *ApCAB, BiAUS, BiDrAC, DcAmB, Drake, NatCAB 2, TwCBDA, WhAm H, WhAmP*
Smith, Nathaniel Waite 1873- *WhAm 5*
Smith, Neal Edward 1920- *BiDrAC*
Smith, Nelson 1828-1916 *NatCAB 6*
Smith, Newman 1889-1964 *WhAm 4*
Smith, Nicholas 1836-1911 *WhAm 1*
Smith, Nicholas 1836-1919 *NatCAB 40*
Smith, Nicholas 1837- *NatCAB 1*
Smith, Nicholas T 1829-1907 *NatCAB 18*
Smith, Nicol Hamilton 1899-1970 *WhAm 5*
Smith, Nila Banton 1890-1976 *BiDAmEd*
Smith, Nixola Greeley *NotAW*
Smith, Nora Archibald *NotAW, TwCBDA, WomWWA 14*
Smith, Nora Archibald 1859-1934 *NatCAB 26, WhAm 1*
Smith, Norman Kemp 1872- *WhAm 5*
Smith, Norman Murray 1883-1968 *NatCAB 54, WhAm 5*
Smith, Oberlin 1840-1926 *NatCAB 12, WhAm 1*
Smith, O'Brien 1756?-1811 *BiDrAC, WhAm H*
Smith, Olive White 1846- *AmWom*
Smith, Oliver 1766-1845 *ApCAB, DcAmB, Drake, TwCBDA, WhAm H*
Smith, Oliver Cotton 1859-1915 *NatCAB 19*
Smith, Oliver Hampton 1794-1849 *BiAUS*
Smith, Oliver Hampton 1794-1859 *ApCAB, BiDrAC, DcAmB, Drake, NatCAB 5, TwCBDA, WhAm H*
Smith, Oliver Prince 1893- *WebAMB*
Smith, Oney Percy 1902-1950 *NatCAB 39*
Smith, Onnie Warren 1872-1941 *WhAm 1*
Smith, Oramandal 1842-1915 *WhAm 3*
Smith, Orlando Jay 1842-1908 *NatCAB 24, WhAm 1*
Smith, Orma Jacob 1879-1948 *WhAm 2*
Smith, Ormond Gerald 1860-1933 *DcAmB S1, NatCAB 25, WhAm 1*
Smith, Orrin Harold 1884-1973 *WhAm 6*
Smith, Orrin Leroy 1870-1929 *NatCAB 31*
Smith, Orsino Cecil 1887-1958 *NatCAB 47*
Smith, Orson 1841-1923 *ApCAB X, NatCAB 20, WhAm 1*
Smith, Orvil Weaver 1880-1955 *NatCAB 44*
Smith, Osborn L 1819-1878 *NatCAB 1*
Smith, Oscar Franklin 1884-1941 *NatCAB 35*
Smith, Oscar Frommel 1891-1950 *NatCAB 41*
Smith, Otis 1800-1865 *NatCAB 26*
Smith, Otis David 1831-1905 *NatCAB 26, WhAm 1*
Smith, Otterbein Oscar 1858-1934 *WhAm 1*
Smith, Owen Lun West 1851- *NatCAB 14, WhAm 4*
Smith, P C *NewYHSD*
Smith, Parke Gillespie 1890-1969 *NatCAB 56*
Smith, Parker 1902-1949 *NatCAB 40*
Smith, Paul Appollis 1825-1912 *NatCAB 18*
Smith, Paul Edward 1908-1968 *WhAm 5*
Smith, Paul Francis 1902-1964 *WhAm 4*
Smith, Paul Glen 1930-1971 *WhAm 6*
Smith, Paul Jordan 1885-1971 *WhAm 5*
Smith, Paul Kauvar 1893- *IlBEAAW*
Smith, Paul Kenneth 1908-1960 *WhAm 4*
Smith, Payson 1873-1963 *BiDAmEd, WhAm 4*
Smith, Pearl Long 1871- *WomWWA 14*
Smith, Percey Franklyn 1867-1956 *WhAm 3*
Smith, Percy Roy 1894-1964 *NatCAB 50*
Smith, Percy William 1900-1967 *NatCAB 54, WhAm 4A*
Smith, Perry 1783-1852 *ApCAB, BiAUS, BiDrAC, NatCAB 5, TwCBDA, WhAm H*
Smith, Perry Coke 1899-1973 *WhAm 6*
Smith, Perry Dunlap 1888-1967 *NatCAB 53,*

Smith, *WhAm 4*
Smith, Persifer Frazer 1798-1858 *NatCAB 7*
Smith, Persifer Frazer 1798-1858 *AmBi, ApCAB, DcAmB, Drake, TwCBDA, WebAMB, WhAm H*
Smith, Persifor Frazer 1808-1882 *ApCAB, Drake*
Smith, Peter 1768-1837 *ApCAB, DcAmB, WhAm H*
Smith, Peter P 1877-1960 *WhAm 3*
Smith, Philip Edward 1884-1970 *DcScB, WhAm 5*
Smith, Philip Sidney 1877-1949 *NatCAB 36, WhAm 3*
Smith, Phillips Waller 1906- *WhAm 4*
Smith, Pierre Reublin 1898-1961 *NatCAB 49*
Smith, Preserved 1880-1941 *DcAmB S3, WhAm 1*
Smith, Preston 1823-1863 *ApCAB, Drake, TwCBDA*
Smith, Preston Carter 1857-1897 *NatCAB 17*
Smith, Quintius Cincinnatus 1842- *WhAm 4*
Smith, R Blackwell, Jr. 1915-1971 *WhAm 5*
Smith, R Gordon 1887-1952 *NatCAB 41*
Smith, R K *NewYHSD*
Smith, R P *NewYHSD*
Smith, Racy Hawkins 1898-1952 *NatCAB 39*
Smith, Rae *NewYHSD*
Smith, Ralph Chester 1892-1963 *WhAm 4*
Smith, Ralph Eliot 1874- *WhAm 5*
Smith, Ralph Green 1906-1969 *NatCAB 55*
Smith, Ralph M 1883-1951 *WhAm 3*
Smith, Ralph Tyler 1915-1972 *BiDrAC, WhAm 5*
Smith, Ralph Winfield 1871- *WhAm 5*
Smith, Randle Jasper 1908-1962 *WhAm 4*
Smith, Ray L 1886-1954 *WhAm 3*
Smith, Raymond Abner 1875- *WhAm 5*
Smith, Raymond Ralston 1876-1965 *NatCAB 51*
Smith, Raymond Underwood 1875-1958 *NatCAB 49, WhAm 3*
Smith, Rea 1876-1935 *NatCAB 31*
Smith, Red *WebAB*
Smith, Reed 1881-1943 *WhAm 2*
Smith, Reginald Heber 1889-1966 *WhAm 4*
Smith, Reuben Robert 1900-1969 *WhAm 5*
Smith, Rex 1898-1959 *NatCAB 48*
Smith, Rex 1900-1959 *WhAm 3*
Smith, Richard 1735-1803 *ApCAB, BiAUS, BiDrAC, DcAmB, TwCBDA, WhAm H*
Smith, Richard 1823- *ApCAB*
Smith, Richard Hewlett 1859-1945 *WhAm 2*
Smith, Richard Paul 1889-1964 *NatCAB 54, WhAm 4*
Smith, Richard Penn 1799-1854 *ApCAB, DcAmB, Drake, WhAm H*
Smith, Richard Penn 1837-1887 *ApCAB*
Smith, Richard R 1885-1957 *WhAm 3*
Smith, Richard Root 1869-1940 *NatCAB 29, WhAm 1*
Smith, Richard Somers 1813-1877 *ApCAB, DcAmB, Drake, NatCAB 7, NewYHSD, WhAm H*
Smith, Mrs. Richmond *WomWWA 14*
Smith, Richmond Mayo 1854-1901 *AmBi*
Smith, Robert *NewYHSD*
Smith, Robert 1689-1768 *DcScB*
Smith, Robert 1722?-1777 *BnEnAmA, DcAmB, WhAm H*
Smith, Robert 1723-1793 *ApCAB, Drake*
Smith, Robert 1732-1801 *ApCAB, DcAmB, Drake, NatCAB 12, TwCBDA, WhAm H*
Smith, Robert 1757-1842 *AmBi, ApCAB, BiAUS, BiDrUSE, DcAmB, Drake, NatCAB 3, TwCBDA, WhAm H*
Smith, Robert 1802-1867 *BiAUS, BiDrAC, WhAm H, WhAmP*
Smith, Robert 1904-1955 *NatCAB 44*
Smith, Robert Alexander C 1857-1933 *DcAmB, WhAm 1*
Smith, Robert Angus 1817-1884 *DcScB*
Smith, Robert Armstrong 1827- *WhAm 4*
Smith, Robert Aura 1899-1959 *WhAm 3*
Smith, Robert B *NewYHSD*
Smith, Robert Barnwell 1800-1876 *AmBi, BiDrAC, DcAmB, WebAB*
Smith, Robert Brandon 1891- *WhAm 2*

Smith, Robert Burns 1854-1908 *NatCAB 11, TwCBDA, WhAm 1*
Smith, Robert Chester 1904-1962 *WhAm 4*
Smith, Robert Edwin 1866-1941 *WhAm 3*
Smith, Robert Edwin 1920-1974 *WhAm 6*
Smith, Robert Fitch 1894-1964 *WhAm 4*
Smith, Robert Floyd 1861- *WhoColR*
Smith, Robert Frederick 1806-1893 *ApCAB Sup*
Smith, Robert H 1888-1960 *WhAm 4*
Smith, Robert Hardy 1813-1878 *DcAmB, NatCAB 8, WhAm H*
Smith, Robert Hardy 1814-1878 *BiDConf*
Smith, Robert Hays 1877- *WhAm 5*
Smith, Robert Henry 1845-1917 *NatCAB 17*
Smith, Robert John 1859-1942 *NatCAB 32*
Smith, Robert Keating 1865-1931 *WhAm 1*
Smith, Robert Lansing 1890-1962 *NatCAB 48*
Smith, Robert Lee 1893-1961 *WhAm 4*
Smith, Robert Louis 1874-1953 *NatCAB 42*
Smith, Robert Metcalf 1886-1952 *WhAm 3*
Smith, Robert P 1863- *WhAm 4*
Smith, Robert Palmer 1895-1961 *NatCAB 49*
Smith, Robert Paterson 1903-1971 *WhAm 5*
Smith, Robert Seneca 1880-1939 *WhAm 1*
Smith, Robert Shufeldt 1861- *WhAm 4*
Smith, Robert Sidney 1877-1935 *DcAmB S1, WhAm HA, WhAm 4*
Smith, Robert Sidney 1904-1969 *WhAm 5*
Smith, Robert Tecumseh 1900-1958 *NatCAB 46*
Smith, Robert Waverley 1865-1930 *WhAm 1*
Smith, Robert William 1916-1975 *WhAm 6*
Smith, Robinson 1876- *WhAm 5*
Smith, Rodney 1829-1915 *NatCAB 17, WhAm 1*
Smith, Rodney 1860-1947 *DcAmReB*
Smith, Roland Cotton 1860-1934 *TwCBDA, WhAm 1*
Smith, Roland Kidder 1870-1937 *WhAm 1*
Smith, Roswell 1797- *Drake*
Smith, Roswell 1829-1892 *ApCAB, DcAmB, NatCAB 1, TwCBDA, WhAm H*
Smith, Roswell T *NewYHSD*
Smith, Roy Campbell 1858-1940 *WhAm 1*
Smith, Roy Harmon 1879-1963 *NatCAB 53, WhAm 4*
Smith, Roy Kenneth 1885-1957 *NatCAB 44*
Smith, Roy Lemon 1887-1963 *NatCAB 51*
Smith, Roy Leon 1879-1932 *WhAm 1*
Smith, Ruby Green *WomWWA 14*
Smith, Ruel Perley 1869-1937 *WhAm 1*
Smith, Rufus Biggs 1854-1923 *NatCAB 23*
Smith, Rufus D 1884-1953 *WhAm 3*
Smith, Russell 1812-1896 *ApCAB, DcAmB, NewYHSD, WhAm H*
Smith, Ruth Ann Cook 1869- *WhAm 5*
Smith, S Archibald 1870-1954 *WhAm 3*
Smith, S Fahs 1864-1942 *NatCAB 31*
Smith, S Jennie d1904 *WhAm 1*
Smith, S L 1875- *WhAm 5*
Smith, S Morgan 1839-1903 *NatCAB 35*
Smith, S Stephenson 1897-1961 *NatCAB 50*
Smith, Sadie Adams 1845- *WhAm 4*
Smith, Samray 1914-1968 *WhAm 5*
Smith, Samuel *BiAUS, BiDrAC, WhAm H*
Smith, Samuel 1720-1776 *ApCAB, Drake*
Smith, Samuel 1752-1839 *ApCAB, BiAUS, BiDrAC, DcAmB, Drake, NatCAB 1, TwCBDA, WhAm H, WhAmP*
Smith, Samuel 1765-1842 *BiDrAC, WhAm H, WhAmP*
Smith, Samuel 1767-1842 *BiAUS*
Smith, Samuel 1786?- *NewYHSD*
Smith, Samuel 1852- *WhAm 4*
Smith, Samuel, Jr. d1812 *NewYHSD*
Smith, Samuel A 1795-1861 *BiAUS, BiDrAC, WhAm H*
Smith, Samuel Axley 1822- *BiAUS*
Smith, Samuel Axley 1822-1863 *BiDrAC, WhAm H*
Smith, Samuel Axley 1822-1864 *TwCBDA*
Smith, Samuel B 1871-1937 *NatCAB 29*
Smith, Samuel Calvin 1881-1939 *NatCAB 35, WhAm 1*
Smith, Samuel Edwin 1861-1928 *NatCAB 30, WhAm 1*
Smith, Samuel Emerson 1788-1860 *ApCAB,*

BiAUS, Drake, NatCAB 6, TwCBDA

Smith, Samuel Francis 1808-1895 *AmBi, ApCAB, DcAmB, Drake, NatCAB 6, TwCBDA, WebAB, WhAm H*

Smith, Samuel George 1852-1915 *ApCAB X, NatCAB 6, WhAm 1*

Smith, Samuel Harrison 1772-1845 *ApCAB, DcAmB, Drake, NatCAB 20, WhAm H*

Smith, Samuel Jonathan 1867-1914 *NatCAB 16*

Smith, Samuel Joseph 1771-1835 *ApCAB, Drake*

Smith, Samuel Lewis 1867-1932 *NatCAB 24*

Smith, Samuel Miller 1865-1956 *NatCAB 45*

Smith, Samuel P *NewYHSD*

Smith, Samuel Stanhope 1750-1819 *ApCAB, BiDAmEd, DcAmB, Drake, NatCAB 2, TwCBDA, WhAm H*

Smith, Samuel Stephenson 1897-1961 *WhAm 4*

Smith, Samuel W 1800- *ApCAB*

Smith, Samuel William 1852-1931 *BiDrAC, NatCAB 28, TwCBDA, WhAm 1, WhAmP*

Smith, Sanford Willard 1869-1929 *NatCAB 22*

Smith, Sarah Effie 1863- *WomWWA 14*

Smith, Sarah Katharine *WomWWA 14*

Smith, Sarah Lanman 1802-1836 *ApCAB, Drake*

Smith, Sarah Louisa Hickman 1811-1832 *ApCAB*

Smith, Sarah Louisa P 1811-1832 *Drake*

Smith, Seba 1792-1868 *AmBi, ApCAB, DcAmB, Drake, NatCAB 8, TwCBDA, WebAB, WhAm H*

Smith, Selden Cornelius 1874-1939 *NatCAB 29*

Smith, Seth MacCuen 1863-1929 *WhAm 1*

Smith, Seymour Wemyss 1896-1932 *WhAm 1, WhAm 1C*

Smith, Sherman Everett 1909-1973 *WhAm 6*

Smith, Sherrill 1881-1951 *WhAm 3*

Smith, Shirley Wheeler 1875-1959 *NatCAB 49, WhAm 3*

Smith, Sidney 1823- *ApCAB*

Smith, Sidney 1877-1935 *WhAm 1*

Smith, Sidney 1883-1958 *WhAm 4*

Smith, Sidney Earle 1897-1959 *WhAm 3*

Smith, Sidney Irving 1843-1926 *ApCAB, DcScB, WhAm 1*

Smith, Sidney Mason 1842-1902 *WhAm 1*

Smith, Sidney Paul 1904- *IIBEAAW*

Smith, Sion Bass 1865-1954 *WhAm 3*

Smith, Sol 1801-1869 *NatCAB 26*

Smith, Soloman Franklin 1808-1869 *WhAm H*

Smith, Solomon Albert 1877-1963 *NatCAB 51, WhAm 4*

Smith, Solomon Franklin 1801-1869 *ApCAB, DcAmB, Drake, NatCAB 2*

Smith, Sophia 1796-1870 *ApCAB, DcAmB, NatCAB 7, NotAW, TwCBDA, WhAm H*

Smith, Spencer Henry 1829-1917 *ApCAB X, NatCAB 17*

Smith, Stanton Kinnie 1904-1967 *NatCAB 53*

Smith, Starbuck 1872-1955 *NatCAB 46*

Smith, Stephen 1823-1922 *ApCAB, DcAmB, NatCAB 2, WhAm 1*

Smith, Stephen 1880-1947 *NatCAB 40*

Smith, Stevenson 1883-1950 *WhAm 3*

Smith, Stiles Curtiss 1831-1907 *NatCAB 24*

Smith, Stuart Gross 1900-1958 *NatCAB 47*

Smith, Stuart Robertson 1867-1937 *WhAm 1*

Smith, Susan Mason 1765-1845 *ApCAB*

Smith, Susan T d1965 *WhAm 4*

Smith, Sydney 1869-1948 *NatCAB 36, WhAm 2A*

Smith, Sylvester Clark 1858-1913 *BiDrAC, WhAm 1, WhAmP*

Smith, T Guilford 1839-1912 *WhAm 1*

Smith, T Guilford *see also* Smith, Thomas Guilford

Smith, T J *NewYHSD*

Smith, T M *NewYHSD*

Smith, Temple Doswell 1846-1926 *NatCAB 20*

Smith, Theobald 1859-1934 *AmBi, BiHiMed, DcAmB S1, DcScB, EncAB, NatCAB 35, WebAB, WhAm 1*

Smith, Theobold 1859-1934 *EncAAH*

Smith, Theodate Louise 1859-1914 *DcAmB*

Smith, Theodate Louise 1860-1914 *WomWWA 14*

Smith, Theodore Clarke 1870-1960 *WhAm 4*

Smith, Theodore Parker 1860- *WhoColR*

Smith, Theophilus Washington 1784-1846 *ApCAB*

Smith, Theresa Herriott Voss *WomWWA 14*

Smith, Thomas *BnEnAmA, NewYHSD*

Smith, Thomas d1846 *BiAUS, BiDrAC, WhAm H*

Smith, Thomas 1702-1795 *ApCAB, Drake*

Smith, Thomas 1745-1809 *ApCAB, BiAUS, BiDrAC, Drake, TwCBDA, WhAm H*

Smith, Thomas 1799-1876 *BiAUS, BiDrAC, WhAm H*

Smith, Thomas 1808-1885 *BiDAmEd*

Smith, Thomas 1835- *NatCAB 5, WhAm 4*

Smith, Thomas 1836- *WhAm 4*

Smith, Thomas A *NewYHSD*

Smith, Thomas Adams 1781-1844 *DcAmB S1, WhAm H*

Smith, Thomas Alexander 1850-1932 *BiDrAC*

Smith, Thomas Arthur 1896-1965 *WhAm 4*

Smith, Thomas Berry 1850-1933 *WhAm 1, WhAm 1C*

Smith, Thomas Church Haskell 1819-1897 *ApCAB, TwCBDA*

Smith, Thomas Francis 1865-1923 *BiDrAC, WhAm 1*

Smith, Thomas Franklin 1833-1916 *WhAm 1*

Smith, Thomas Guilford 1839-1912 *NatCAB 4*

Smith, Thomas Guilford *see also* Smith, T Guilford

Smith, Thomas H *NewYHSD*

Smith, Thomas Henry 1841-1931 *NatCAB 25*

Smith, Thomas James 1830?-1870 *REnAW*

Smith, Thomas Jefferson d1857 *Drake*

Smith, Thomas Jefferson 1836- *ApCAB X*

Smith, Thomas Jefferson 1877- *WhAm 5*

Smith, Thomas Kilby 1820-1887 *ApCAB, NatCAB 8, TwCBDA, WhAm H*

Smith, Thomas Kilby 1871-1944 *NatCAB 35*

Smith, Thomas L d1871 *BiAUS*

Smith, Thomas L 1805- *Drake*

Smith, Thomas Lochlan 1835-1884 *ApCAB, NewYHSD*

Smith, Thomas Marshall 1880-1947 *NatCAB 37*

Smith, Thomas Mather 1796-1864 *NatCAB 7*

Smith, Thomas Mather 1797-1864 *ApCAB, Drake, TwCBDA*

Smith, Thomas Newill 1909- *WhAm 5*

Smith, Thomas Octavius 1859-1925 *WhAm 1*

Smith, Thomas R 1880-1942 *WhAm 2*

Smith, Thomas Vernor 1890-1964 *BiDrAC, WhAm 4*

Smith, Thomas White 1906-1971 *NatCAB 57*

Smith, Thomas William 1865- *WhAm 5*

Smith, Thurber Montgomery 1893-1950 *WhAm 3*

Smith, Tony 1912- *BnEnAmA*

Smith, Truman 1791-1884 *ApCAB, BiAUS, BiDrAC, DcAmB, Drake, NatCAB 12, TwCBDA, WhAm H, WhAmP*

Smith, Tryphena Goldsbury 1801-1836 *NewYHSD*

Smith, Ulysses Simpson 1869-1946 *WhAm 2*

Smith, Uriah 1832-1903 *DcAmB, WhAm 1*

Smith, Valentine William 1868-1941 *NatCAB 31*

Smith, Vernon Corbett 1892-1963 *NatCAB 50*

Smith, Vincent E d1972 *WhAm 5*

Smith, Vincent Weaver 1892-1964 *WhAm 4*

Smith, Vine Harold 1874-1957 *NatCAB 45, WhAm 5*

Smith, Virginia Thrall 1836-1903 *NotAW*

Smith, Vivian Thomas 1886-1953 *WhAm 3*

Smith, Vivus Wood 1804-1881 *NatCAB 5*

Smith, Von *NewYHSD*

Smith, W *NewYHSD*

Smith, W A 1870-1958 *WhAm 3*

Smith, W Eugene 1919- *BnEnAmA*

Smith, W Herbert 1901-1964 *NatCAB 51*

Smith, W Heyward 1898-1964 *NatCAB 52*

Smith, W J 1823-1913 *BiAUS*

Smith, W J *see also* Smith, William Jay

Smith, Wade Cothran 1869- *WhAm 5*

Smith, Walker *WebAB*

Smith, Walt Allen 1910-1971 *WhAm 5*

Smith, Walter Bedell 1895-1961 *WebAB, WebAMB, WhAm 4*

Smith, Walter Byron 1878-1945 *NatCAB 34, WhAm 2*

Smith, Walter Driscoll 1875-1955 *WhAm 3*

Smith, Walter George 1854-1924 *ApCAB X, NatCAB 18, NatCAB 21, WhAm 1*

Smith, Walter H *BiAUS*

Smith, Walter H B 1901-1959 *WhAm 4*

Smith, Walter Inglewood 1862-1922 *BiDrAC, DcAmB, WhAm 1, WhAmP*

Smith, Walter Lloyd 1856-1928 *WhAm 1*

Smith, Walter McMynn 1869-1938 *WhAm 1*

Smith, Walter Robinson 1875-1937 *WhAm 1*

Smith, Walter Tenney 1870-1940 *WhAm 1, WhAm 2*

Smith, Walter Wellesley 1905- *WebAB*

Smith, Walter Winfred 1877-1949 *WhAm 2*

Smith, Warren DuPre 1880-1950 *NatCAB 41, WhAm 3*

Smith, Warren Greene 1849-1910 *NatCAB 17*

Smith, Warren Horton 1896-1965 *NatCAB 52*

Smith, Warren Lounsbury 1914-1972 *NatCAB 56, WhAm 5*

Smith, Warren Robert 1888-1957 *WhAm 3*

Smith, Wayne Carleton 1901-1964 *WhAm 4*

Smith, Wendell 1914-1972 *WhAm 5*

Smith, Wesley 1805-1888 *ApCAB Sup*

Smith, Weston 1901- *WhAm 6*

Smith, Wilbert Lewis 1852-1937 *NatCAB 33, WhAm 1*

Smith, Wilbur Cleveland 1884-1952 *WhAm 3*

Smith, Wilbur Fisk 1856-1940 *WhAm 1*

Smith, Wilbur Richard Carroll 1872-1941 *NatCAB 30*

Smith, Willard Adelbert 1849-1923 *WhAm 1*

Smith, Willard Mallalien 1888-1959 *NatCAB 48*

Smith, William *BiAUS, BiDrAC, NewYHSD, WhAm H*

Smith, William d1814 *BiAUS, Drake*

Smith, William 1655-1705 *NatCAB 12*

Smith, William 1697-1769 *ApCAB, DcAmB, NatCAB 11, WhAm H*

Smith, William 1726-1803 *Drake*

Smith, William 1727-1803 *ApCAB, BiDAmEd, DcAmB, DcAmReB, McGEWB, NatCAB 1, TwCBDA, WebAB, WhAm H*

Smith, William 1728-1793 *ApCAB, BiAUS, DcAmB, Drake, EncAB, NatCAB 11, WhAm H*

Smith, William 1728-1814 *BiDrAC, WhAm H*

Smith, William 1730-1814 *ApCAB, TwCBDA*

Smith, William 1751-1837 *BiDrAC*

Smith, William 1753-1821 *Drake*

Smith, William 1754?-1821 *ApCAB, DcAmB, WhAm H*

Smith, William 1762-1840 *ApCAB, BiAUS, BiDrAC, DcAmB, Drake, NatCAB 2, TwCBDA, WhAm H, WhAmP*

Smith, William 1769-1839 *AsBiEn, DcScB*

Smith, William 1769-1847 *ApCAB*

Smith, William 1770-1857 *NatCAB 4*

Smith, William 1796-1887 *ApCAB, NatCAB 5, TwCBDA*

Smith, William 1797-1887 *BiAUS, BiDConf, BiDrAC, DcAmB, Drake, WhAm H, WhAmP*

Smith, William 1803-1873 *ApCAB, Drake, TwCBDA*

Smith, William 1811?- *NewYHSD*

Smith, William 1818-1912 *NatCAB 15*

Smith, William 1831-1912 *NatCAB 4, WhAm 1*

Smith, William Abbott 1867-1917 *NatCAB 30*

Smith, William Alden 1859-1932 *BiDrAC, NatCAB 14, NatCAB 16, NatCAB 26, TwCBDA, WhAm 1, WhAmP*

Smith, William Alexander 1820-1911 *NatCAB 2, WhAm 1*

Smith, William Alexander 1828-1888 *BiAUS, BiDrAC, WhAm H*

Smith, William Alexander 1843-1934 *NatCAB 26*

Smith, William Alexander 1853-1922 *NatCAB 6*

Smith, William Alexander 1882- *WhoColR*

Smith, William Alexander 1896-1956
NatCAB 45

Smith, William Andrew 1802-1870 *ApCAB,
DcAmB, TwCBDA, WhAm H*

Smith, William Anton 1880- *WhAm 6*

Smith, William Arthur 1918- *IIBEAAW*

Smith, William Austin 1872-1922 *WhAm 1*

Smith, William Bailey 1873-1926 *NatCAB 20*

Smith, William Benjamin 1850-1934 *NatCAB 9,
NatCAB 35, WhAm 1*

Smith, William Binns 1885-1952 *NatCAB 41*

Smith, William C *NewYHSD*

Smith, William Carlton 1874-1930 *NatCAB 22*

Smith, William Carpenter 1865-1913
NatCAB 16

Smith, William Clarke 1857-1942 *WhAm 1,
WhAm 2*

Smith, William Cunningham 1871-1943
WhAm 2

Smith, William D 1800?- *NewYHSD*

Smith, William Dee 1882-1948 *NatCAB 36*

Smith, William E *NewYHSD*

Smith, William E 1824-1883 *ApCAB,
NatCAB 12, TwCBDA*

Smith, William E 1829-1890 *BiAUS, TwCBDA*

Smith, William Eason 1868-1948 *WhAm 2*

Smith, William Edward 1873-1946 *WhAm 2*

Smith, William Edward 1874-1946 *NatCAB 37*

Smith, William Ephraim 1829-1890 *BiDConf,
BiDrAC, WhAm H*

Smith, William Ernest 1852-1888 *ApCAB*

Smith, William Ernest 1892-1969 *NatCAB 55*

Smith, William Farrar 1824-1903 *AmBi,
ApCAB, DcAmB, Drake, NatCAB 7,
TwCBDA, WebAMB, WhAm 1*

Smith, William Francis 1904-1968 *WhAm 4A*

Smith, William Good *NewYHSD*

Smith, William Griswold 1869-1943 *WhAm 2*

Smith, William H H 1814- *NatCAB 4*

Smith, William Haimes 1847-1929 *NatCAB 22*

Smith, William Hall 1866- *WhAm 4*

Smith, William Harrison 1848- *NatCAB 1,
WhAm 4*

Smith, William Hawley 1845-1922 *WhAm 1*

Smith, William Henry 1806-1872 *DcAmB,
WhAm H*

Smith, William Henry 1833-1896 *AmBi,
ApCAB, DcAmB, NatCAB 19, TwCBDA,
WhAm H*

Smith, William Henry 1859-1933 *WhAm 1*

Smith, William Henry 1873-1938 *NatCAB 28*

Smith, William Henry 1873-1954 *WhAm 4*

Smith, William Hinckle 1861-1943 *NatCAB 31,
WhAm 2*

Smith, William Hopton 1882-1945 *WhAm 2*

Smith, William Hugh 1826-1899 *BiAUS,
NatCAB 10, TwCBDA*

Smith, William Jay 1823-1913 *BiDrAC*

Smith, William Jay *see also* Smith, W J

Smith, William Jones 1855-1954 *NatCAB 50*

Smith, William Jones 1881-1958 *WhAm 3*

Smith, William Loughton 1758-1812 *ApCAB,
BiAUS, BiDrAC, DcAmB, Drake,
NatCAB 12, TwCBDA, WhAm H*

Smith, William M 1862- *WhoColR*

Smith, William Mason 1851-1936 *NatCAB 51*

Smith, William Mason 1874-1964 *WhAm 4*

Smith, William McKennan 1868-1948
NatCAB 37

Smith, William Moore 1759-1821 *ApCAB,
Drake*

Smith, William N 1864-1931 *NatCAB 22*

Smith, William Nathan Harrell 1812-1889
*ApCAB, BiAUS, BiDConf, BiDrAC,
DcAmB, NatCAB 13, TwCBDA,
WhAm H*

Smith, William O *NewYHSD*

Smith, William Oliver 1894-1960 *WhAm 4*

Smith, William Orlando 1859-1932 *BiDrAC,
WhAm 4*

Smith, William Owen 1848-1929 *NatCAB 40,
WhAm 1, WhAm 2*

Smith, William Palmer 1852- *ApCAB X*

Smith, William Pitt *NatCAB 3*

Smith, William R *NewYHSD*

Smith, William Redwood 1851-1935
NatCAB 28

Smith, William Robert 1863-1924 *BiDrAC,
WhAm 1, WhAmP*

Smith, William Roy 1876- *WhAm 5*

Smith, William Rudolph 1787-1868 *ApCAB,
Drake*

Smith, William Russell d1896 *BiAUS, Drake*

Smith, William Russell 1813-1896 *ApCAB*

Smith, William Russell 1815-1896 *BiDConf,
BiDrAC, DcAmB, NatCAB 12, TwCBDA,
WhAm H, WhAmP*

Smith, William Ruthven 1868-1941 *WhAm 1*

Smith, William S 1821- *NewYHSD*

Smith, William Skeldon Adamson 1860-1953
WhAm 3

Smith, William Sooy 1830-1916 *ApCAB,
DcAmB, NatCAB 4, TwCBDA,
WhAm 1*

Smith, William Stephens 1755-1816 *ApCAB,
BiAUS, BiDrAC, DcAmB, Drake,
NatCAB 4, WebAMB, WhAm H*

Smith, William Stevenson 1907-1969 *WhAm 5*

Smith, William Strother 1857-1927 *WhAm 1*

Smith, William Sydney 1764-1840 *WhoMilH*

Smith, William Thayer 1839-1909 *NatCAB 9,
NatCAB 25, WhAm 1*

Smith, William Thomas 1884- *WhAm 2*

Smith, William Thompson Russell 1812-1896?
IIBEAAW, NewYHSD

Smith, William Walker 1874-1932 *WhAm 1*

Smith, William Wallace, II 1888-1955
NatCAB 17, NatCAB 44, WhAm 3

Smith, William Walter 1868-1942 *WhAm 2*

Smith, William Walter 1883-1959 *NatCAB 50*

Smith, William Ward 1888-1966 *NatCAB 53,
WhAm 4*

Smith, William Waugh 1845-1912 *AmBi,
ApCAB, DcAmB, TwCBDA, WhAm 1*

Smith, William Wickham 1859-1912
NatCAB 16

Smith, William Wilberforce 1858-1943
WhAm 2

Smith, Willis 1887-1953 *BiDrAC, WhAm 3*

Smith, Willis, Jr. 1921-1971 *WhAm 5*

Smith, Wilmot M 1852-1906 *WhAm 1*

Smith, Wilmot Mott 1887-1961 *NatCAB 50*

Smith, Wilson 1897-1965 *DcScB*

Smith, Wilson George 1855-1929 *NatCAB 11,
TwCBDA, WhAm 1*

Smith, Wilson Levering 1878-1931 *NatCAB 23*

Smith, Winchell 1871-1933 *DcAmB,
NatCAB 24, WhAm 1*

Smith, Winford Henry 1877-1961 *WhAm 4*

Smith, Wint 1892- *BiDrAC*

Smith, Winthrop Hiram 1893-1961 *WhAm 4*

Smith, Woodruff 1895-1960 *NatCAB 47*

Smith, Worthington 1795-1856 *ApCAB, Drake,
NatCAB 2, TwCBDA, WhAm H*

Smith, Worthington Curtis 1819-1894 *TwCBDA*

Smith, Worthington Curtis 1823-1894 *BiAUS,
BiDrAC, WhAm H*

Smith, Xanthus Russell 1839-1929 *ApCAB,
DcAmB, IIBEAAW, NatCAB 21,
NewYHSD*

Smith, Young Berryman 1889-1960 *WhAm 4*

Smith, Zachariah Frederick 1827-1911 *ApCAB,
BiDAmEd, WhAm 1*

Smith, Zemro Augustus 1837- *WhAm 1*

Smith, Zilpha Drew 1852-1926 *NotAW,
WhAm 1, WomWWA 14*

Smith Irisarri, Antonio 1832-1877 *ApCAB*

Smith-Petersen, Marius Nygaard 1886-1953
NatCAB 42, WhAm 3

Smithe, Ferdinand Ludwig 1869-1938
NatCAB 30

Smithee, James Newton 1842-1905 *NatCAB 7,
WhAm 1*

Smithells, Arthur 1860-1939 *DcScB*

Smither, Henry Carpenter 1873-1930 *WhAm 1*

Smither, James d1797 *BnEnAmA, NewYHSD*

Smither, James, Jr. *NewYHSD*

Smither, James Madison 1908-1964 *NatCAB 50*

Smitherman, Andrew Jackson 1883- *WhoColR*

Smithers, Bertha *WomWWA 14*

Smithers, Christopher Dunkin 1865-1952
NatCAB 39

Smithers, Ernest Leonard 1867-1940 *WhAm 1*

Smithers, Kate Eloise Brett 1857-
WomWWA 14

Smithers, Mabel Brinkley 1880- *WomWWA 14*

Smithers, Nathaniel B 1818-1896 *BiAUS*

Smithers, Nathaniel Barratt 1818-1896 *BiDrAC*

Smithers, Nathaniel Barrett 1818-1896
WhAm H

Smithers, William West 1864-1947 *WhAm 2*

Smithey, Louis Philippe 1890-1966 *WhAm 4*

Smithey, Royall Bascom 1851-1925 *WhAm 1*

Smithey, William Royall 1881-1967 *WhAm 5*

Smithies, Frank 1880-1937 *WhAm 1*

Smithman, John Bernhardt 1844-1932
NatCAB 25

Smithson, James 1754?-1829 *ApCAB,
NatCAB 3*

Smithson, James 1765-1829 *EncAAH,
TwCBDA, WhAm H*

Smithson, James Lewis Macie 1765-1829 *Drake*

Smithson, James Louis Macie 1765-1829 *DcScB*

Smithson, Mary Isabel *WomWWA 14*

Smithson, Noble 1841- *WhAm 1*

Smithson, Robert 1938- *BnEnAmA*

Smithson, William Walpole 1874-1931 *WhAm 1*

Smithwick, John Harris 1872-1948 *BiDrAC,
WhAm 3*

Smithy, Horace Gilbert 1880-1971 *NatCAB 57*

Smithy, Horace Gilbert 1914-1948 *NatCAB 38*

Smits, Andreas 1870-1948 *DcScB*

Smitz, M *NewYHSD*

Smock, Ada Mima 1877- *WomWWA 14*

Smock, Augustus Hobart 1870-1926
NatCAB 20

Smock, Harry Berdan 1912-1972 *WhAm 6*

Smock, John Conover 1842-1926 *ApCAB,
NatCAB 11, TwCBDA, WhAm 1*

Smock, Ledru Pierson 1857-1933 *NatCAB 25*

Smock, P Monroe 1874- *WhAm 5*

Smock, Wendell Merritt 1901-1964 *WhAm 4*

Smohalla 1815?-1907 *AmBi, DcAmB,
WebAB, WhAm HA, WhAm 4*

Smoke, Kenneth Ludwig 1903-1970 *NatCAB 55*

Smoky, Lois 1907- *IIBEAAW*

Smoley, Constantine Kenneth 1869-1952
WhAm 3

Smollett, Tobias George 1721-1771 *BiHiMed,
McGEWB*

Smolnikar, Andreas Bernardus *NatCAB 12*

Smolnikar, Marian 1872-1917 *DcScB*

Smoot, Charles Head 1878-1933 *NatCAB 24,
WhAm 1*

Smoot, Lewis Egerton 1876-1962 *NatCAB 50*

Smoot, Reed 1862-1941 *ApCAB X, BiDrAC,
DcAmB S3, NatCAB 13, NatCAB 35,
REnAW, TwCBDA, WhAm 1, WhAmP*

Smoot, Thomas Arthur 1871-1937 *WhAm 1*

Smucker, Samuel Mosheim 1823-1863
NatCAB 5

Smucker, Willard Earl 1891-1970 *NatCAB 56*

Smull, Jacob Barstow 1874-1962 *ApCAB X,
WhAm 4*

Smull, Thomas Jefferson, Jr. 1875-1962
WhAm 4

Smulski, John Franklin 1867-1928 *ApCAB X,
NatCAB 21, WhAm 1*

Smutny, Rudolf 1897-1974 *WhAm 6*

Smuts, Jan Christiaan 1870-1950 *WhAm 3,
WhWW-II*

Smuts, Jan Christian 1870-1950 *McGEWB*

Smutz, Laura Katharine 1883- *WomWWA 14*

Smybert, John 1684?-1751 *ApCAB,
NatCAB 5*

Smybert, John 1688-1751 *AmBi*

Smybert, Nathaniel 1734-1756 *ApCAB*

Smykal, Richard 1900-1958 *WhAm 3*

Smylie, Charles Albert 1858-1902 *NatCAB 5*

Smyly, Arthur Leopold 1884-1951 *NatCAB 40*

Smyser, Martin Luther 1851-1908 *BiDrAC,
WhAm 1*

Smyser, William Emory 1866-1935 *WhAm 1*

Smyth, Albert Henry 1863-1907 *DcAmB,
TwCBDA, WhAm 1*

Smyth, Alexander 1765-1830 *ApCAB, BiAUS,
BiDrAC, DcAmB, Drake, WebAMB,
WhAm H*

Smyth, Andrew Woods 1833- *ApCAB*

Smyth, Calvin Mason, Jr. 1895-1967 *WhAm 4*

Smyth, Charles Henry, Jr. 1866-1937 *WhAm 1*

Smyth, Charles Piazzi 1819-1900 *DcScB*

Smyth, Clement 1810-1865 *ApCAB, Drake,*

NatCAB 12

Smyth, Clement Biddle 1827-1901 *NatCAB 29*
Smyth, Clifford 1866- *WhAm 4*
Smyth, Constantine Joseph 1859-1924
NatCAB 19, WhAm 1
Smyth, David McConnell 1833- *NatCAB 7*
Smyth, David Wilson 1880-1949 *NatCAB 37*
Smyth, Egbert Coffin 1829-1904 *AmBi,*
ApCAB, DcAmB, NatCAB 10, TwCBDA,
WhAm 1
Smyth, Ellison Adger 1847-1942 *NatCAB 32,*
WhAm 2
Smyth, Ellison Adger 1863-1941 *WhAm 1*
Smyth, Eugene Leslie 1857-1932 *IIBEAAW*
Smyth, Francis Scott 1895-1972 *WhAm 5*
Smyth, Frederick *NatCAB 12*
Smyth, Frederick 1819-1899 *BiAUS,*
NatCAB 11, TwCBDA
Smyth, George Washington 1803-1866 *BiAUS,*
BiDrAC, WhAm H
Smyth, Henry Field 1875-1954 *WhAm 3*
Smyth, Henry Lloyd 1862-1944 *NatCAB 34,*
WhAm 2
Smyth, Herbert Crommelin 1870-1944
NatCAB 33, WhAm 2
Smyth, Herbert Weir 1857-1937 *AmBi,*
DcAmB S2, NatCAB 13, NatCAB 28,
WhAm 1
Smyth, Hugh Patrick 1855-1927 *NatCAB 21*
Smyth, James Adger 1838-1920 *WhAm 1*
Smyth, John 1869-1935 *NatCAB 26*
Smyth, John Ferdinand D *ApCAB*
Smyth, John Henry 1844-1908 *DcAmB,*
NatCAB 12
Smyth, Julian Kennedy 1856-1921 *DcAmB,*
WhAm 1
Smyth, Margarita Pumpelly 1873- *WhAm 5,*
WomWWA 14
Smyth, Newman 1843-1925 *AmBi, DcAmB,*
NatCAB 26, TwCBDA, WhAm 1
Smyth, P Somers 1877-1929 *NatCAB 26*
Smyth, S Gordon 1859-1930 *WhAm 3*
Smyth, Samuel Phillips Newman 1843- *ApCAB,*
NatCAB 13
Smyth, Thomas 1808-1873 *ApCAB, DcAmB,*
Drake, NatCAB 2, WhAm H
Smyth, Thomas A d1865 *ApCAB, Drake,*
NatCAB 2
Smyth, Thomas Lawrence 1890-1962
NatCAB 50
Smyth, Timothy Clement 1810-1865 *WhAm H*
Smyth, William d1877 *NewYHSD*
Smyth, William 1797-1868 *ApCAB, BiDAmEd,*
DcAmB, Drake, NatCAB 10, TwCBDA,
WhAm H
Smyth, William 1824-1870 *BiAUS, BiDrAC,*
WhAm H
Smyth, William Ellsworth 1861-1922 *WhAm 1*
Smyth, William Henry 1855-1940 *NatCAB 18,*
WhAm 1
Smyth, Wilma Louise 1915-1969 *WhAm 5*
Smyth, Winfield Scott 1872-1940 *WhAm 1*
Smythe, Arnold Miller 1893-1971 *NatCAB 56*
Smythe, Arthur Livermore 1881-1939
NatCAB 29
Smythe, Augustine Thomas 1842-1962
NatCAB 10, WhAm 1
Smythe, Augustine Thomas 1885-1962
NatCAB 50
Smythe, Clement 1810-1865 *TwCBDA*
Smythe, George Franklin 1852-1934 *WhAm 1*
Smythe, George Winfred 1899-1969 *WhAm 5*
Smythe, Henry Maxwell 1844- *NatCAB 13*
Smythe, J Henry, Jr. 1883-1956 *WhAm 3*
Smythe, Sir James Carmichael 1775?-1838
ApCAB
Smythe, Marion Augustus 1884-1951
NatCAB 39
Smythe, Robert L *NewYHSD*
Smythe, Sidney Thomas 1862-1923 *WhAm 1*
Smythe, William Ellsworth 1861-1922
NatCAB 17, REnAW, TwCBDA
Snader, E Roland, Jr. 1895-1948 *NatCAB 36*
Snader, Edward Roland 1855- *NatCAB 3*
Snaer, Jonathan *NewYHSD*
Snaith, William Theodore 1908-1974 *WhAm 6*
Snape, John 1870-1941 *WhAm 2*
Snapp, Carl Foster 1888-1945 *NatCAB 35*

Snapp, H 1822-1895 *BiAUS*
Snapp, Henry 1822-1895 *BiDrAC, WhAm H*
Snapp, Howard Malcolm 1855-1938 *BiDrAC,*
WhAm 4
Snare, Frederick 1862-1946 *WhAm 3*
Snarr, Frederic Earle 1909-1959 *WhAm 4*
Snarr, Otto Welton 1886-1966 *WhAm 4*
Snavely, Guy Everett 1881-1974 *BiDAmEd,*
WhAm 6
Snavely, Hershel Robert 1882-1955 *NatCAB 48*
Snavely, John Robert 1913-1964 *WhAm 4*
Snead, Louise Hammond Willis *WomWWA 14*
Snead, Samuel Jackson 1912- *WebAB*
Snead, Thomas Burton 1878-1942 *NatCAB 41*
Snead, Thomas Lowndes 1828- *ApCAB*
Snead, Thomas Lowndes 1828-1890 *BiDConf,*
DcAmB, WhAm H
Snead, Thomas Lowndes 1828-1891 *NatCAB 1*
Sneath, E Hershey 1857-1935 *NatCAB 26,*
WhAm 1
Sneath, Laura Stephenson *WomWWA 14*
Sneath, Mrs. Samuel B *WhAm 5*
Sneath, Samuel Baugher 1828-1915 *NatCAB 17*
Sneath, William Henry 1878-1962 *NatCAB 48*
Snedden, David Samuel 1868-1951 *BiDAmEd,*
WhAm 5
Sneddon, James Prentice 1863-1921 *ApCAB X,*
NatCAB 22
Snedecor, George W 1881- *WhAm 6*
Snedecor, James George 1855-1916 *WhAm 1*
Snedeker, Caroline Dale 1871-1956 *WhAm 3,*
WomWWA 14
Snedeker, Charles Dippolt 1861-1935 *WhAm 1*
Snedeker, Charles Henry 1856-1926
NatCAB 20
Sneed, Albert Lee 1884-1967 *WhAm 4A*
Sneed, Frank William 1862- *NatCAB 9*
Sneed, Frank Woolford 1862-1923 *NatCAB 23,*
WhAm 1
Sneed, John Louis Taylor 1820-1901 *ApCAB,*
TwCBDA, WhAm 1
Sneed, William Henry 1812-1869 *BiAUS,*
BiDrAC, WhAm H
Sneed, William Lent 1881-1941 *WhAm 2*
Snegireff, Leonid Sergius 1908-1963
NatCAB 51
Snel, Willebrord 1580-1626 *DcScB*
Snelham, John Sydney 1884-1964 *NatCAB 50,*
WhAm 4
Snell, Albert Conrad 1871-1954 *NatCAB 46*
Snell, Albert M 1896-1960 *WhAm 3*
Snell, Bertrand Hollis 1870-1958 *BiDrAC,*
NatCAB 43, WhAm 3, WhAmP
Snell, Earl 1895-1947 *WhAm 2*
Snell, Ebenzer Strong 1801-1874 *NatCAB 5*
Snell, George 1820-1893 *WhAm H*
Snell, Henry Bayley 1858-1943 *WhAm 2*
Snell, J Henry 1890-1961 *NatCAB 48*
Snell, John Leslie 1923-1972 *WhAm 5*
Snell, Merwin-Marie 1863- *TwCBDA*
Snell, Nellie C *WomWWA 14*
Snell, Novia Z 1860-1927 *NatCAB 28*
Snell, P *NewYHSD*
Snell, Ralph Meeker 1876-1934 *NatCAB 27*
Snell, Roy Judson 1878- *WhAm 6*
Snell, Thomas 1774-1862 *ApCAB, Drake*
Snell, Willebrord VanRoijen 1591-1626 *AsBiEn*
Snell, William R *NewYHSD*
Snelling, Charles Mercer 1862-1939
NatCAB 34, WhAm 1
Snelling, Henry Hornor 1882-1969 *NatCAB 55*
Snelling, Henry Hunt 1817-1897 *ApCAB,*
DcAmB, WhAm H
Snelling, Josiah 1782-1828 *DcAmB, Drake,*
NatCAB 2, TwCBDA, WebAMB,
WhAm H
Snelling, Josiah 1782-1829 *ApCAB*
Snelling, Rodman Paul 1861-1935 *WhAm 1*
Snelling, Walter Otheman 1880-1965 *WhAm 4*
Snelling, William Joseph 1804-1848 *ApCAB,*
DcAmB, Drake, NatCAB 2, WhAm H
Snelson, Kenneth 1927- *BnEnAmA*
Snelson, Robert Edward Lee 1893-1957
NatCAB 45
Snetcher, Paul Revere 1895-1965 *NatCAB 52*
Snethen, Nicholas 1769-1845 *ApCAB, DcAmB,*
Drake, NatCAB 2, WhAm H
Sneve, Haldor 1865-1924 *WhAm 1*

Snevily, Henry Mansfield 1886-1954 *WhAm 3*
Snider, Clyde Frank 1904-1971 *WhAm 5*
Snider, Denton Jaques 1841-1925 *ApCAB,*
DcAmB, TwCBDA, WhAm 1
Snider, George *NewYHSD*
Snider, Joseph Lyons 1894-1955 *WhAm 3*
Snider, Luther Crocker 1882-1947 *WhAm 2*
Snider, Samuel Prather 1845-1928 *BiDrAC,*
WhAm 4
Snidow, Gordon 1936- *IIBEAAW*
Sniff, Littleton Moore 1849-1922 *NatCAB 19,*
WhAm 1
Sniffen, Culver Channing 1844-1930
NatCAB 22, WhAm 1
Sniffen, D Austin 1873-1950 *NatCAB 38*
Snively, John Harrison 1842-1922 *NatCAB 19*
Snively, Mary Agnes *WomWWA 14*
Snively, Samuel Frisby 1859- *WhAm 4*
Snively, William Andrew 1833-1901 *WhAm 1*
Snoberger, Rantz E 1893-1965 *WhAm 4*
Snoddy, Cary Alexander 1875-1956 *NatCAB 47*
Snoddy, Elmer Ellsworth 1863-1936 *WhAm 1*
Snoddy, Leland Bradley 1898-1950 *WhAm 3*
Snodgrass, Charles Edward 1866-1936 *BiDrAC,*
WhAm 4
Snodgrass, David E 1894-1963 *WhAm 4*
Snodgrass, David LaFayette 1851-1917
NatCAB 12, WhAm 1
Snodgrass, George Merrill 1879-1939 *WhAm 1*
Snodgrass, Henry Clay 1848-1931 *BiDrAC*
Snodgrass, John Fryall 1804-1854 *BiAUS,*
BiDrAC, WhAm H
Snodgrass, John Harold d1943 *WhAm 2*
Snodgrass, Robert 1836- *WhAm 1*
Snodgrass, Robert Evans 1875-1962
NatCAB 49, WhAm 5
Snodgrass, Robert Richard 1902- *WhAm 5*
Snodgrass, Samuel Robert 1906-1975 *WhAm 6*
Snodgrass, William Davis 1796-1886 *ApCAB*
Snook, Homer Clyde 1878-1942 *NatCAB 35,*
WhAm 2
Snook, John Stout 1862-1952 *BiDrAC,*
WhAm 5
Snook, John Wilson 1876- *WhAm 5*
Snorri Sturluson 1179-1241 *McGEWB*
Snover, Horace Greeley 1847-1924 *BiDrAC*
Snow, Agnes Kune *WomWWA 14*
Snow, Albert Sydney 1845-1932 *WhAm 1*
Snow, Alpheus Henry 1859-1920 *WhAm 1*
Snow, Alva Edson 1860- *WhAm 4*
Snow, Benjamin Warner 1860- *WhAm 1*
Snow, Bruce 1894-1958 *NatCAB 46*
Snow, Caleb Hopkins 1796-1835 *ApCAB,*
Drake
Snow, Carmel 1890-1961 *WhAm 4*
Snow, Charles Armstrong 1862-1920 *WhAm 1*
Snow, Charles Ernest 1910-1967 *WhAm 4A*
Snow, Charles Henry 1863-1957 *NatCAB 48,*
WhAm 3
Snow, Charles Percy 1905-1972 *McGEWB*
Snow, Charles Wesley 1835-1918 *NatCAB 18*
Snow, Chauncey Depew 1889-1964 *WhAm 4*
Snow, David William 1851-1924 *NatCAB 20*
Snow, Donald Francis 1877-1958 *BiDrAC,*
WhAm 1
Snow, Edgar Parks 1905-1972 *WhAm 5*
Snow, Edward Neil 1916-1966 *NatCAB 52*
Snow, Edwin Miller 1820-1888 *NatCAB 13*
Snow, Elbert Clay 1855- *WhAm 4*
Snow, Elbridge Gerry 1841-1925 *ApCAB X,*
NatCAB 2, NatCAB 25, WhAm 1
Snow, Elinor Kimball Bruce 1871-
WomWWA 14
Snow, Eliza Roxey 1804-1887 *DcAmB, NotAW,*
REnAW, WhAm H
Snow, Ellen *BiCAW*
Snow, Ellen Frances Jewell 1862-
WomWWA 14
Snow, Ernest Albert 1875-1928 *WhAm 1*
Snow, Erva Goodwin *WomWWA 14*
Snow, F Herbert 1865-1942 *NatCAB 33*
Snow, Floyd Demarcus 1898-1964 *NatCAB 50*
Snow, Francis 1876- *WhAm 5*
Snow, Francis Huntington 1840-1908 *AmBi,*
DcAmB, NatCAB 9, TwCBDA,
WhAm 1
Snow, Franklin Augustus 1856-1942
NatCAB 31, WhAm 2

Snow, Frederic 1864-1935 *WhAm 1*
Snow, Harold Robert 1895-1957 *NatCAB 46*
Snow, Henry Sanger 1856- *WhAm 4*
Snow, Herman Wilber 1836-1914 *BiDrAC*
Snow, J Parker 1848-1934 *WhAm 3*
Snow, Jenny Emily *New YHSD*
Snow, Jesse Baker 1868-1947 *NatCAB 34*
Snow, Jessie Baker 1868-1947 *DcAmB S4*
Snow, John 1813-1858 *BiHiMed, DcScB*
Snow, John Albert 1871-1926 *NatCAB 22*
Snow, John Ben 1883- *WhAm 5*
Snow, Julia Warner 1863- *WomWWA 14*
Snow, Lawrence Crosby 1886-1943 *NatCAB 41*
Snow, Leslie Perkins 1862-1934 *NatCAB 29, WhAm 1*
Snow, Leslie Whitmore 1890-1958 *NatCAB 46*
Snow, Leslie Whitmore 1890-1959 *WhAm 3*
Snow, Levi Tracy 1860-1949 *NatCAB 41*
Snow, Lorenzo 1814-1901 *AmBi, ApCAB Sup, DcAmB, NatCAB 7, NatCAB 16, WhAm 1*
Snow, Lorenzo 1819-1901 *TwCBDA*
Snow, Louis Franklin 1862-1934 *WhAm 1*
Snow, Marshall Solomon 1842-1916 *ApCAB, NatCAB 11, TwCBDA, WhAm 1*
Snow, Mary S 1857- *WomWWA 14*
Snow, Neil Worthington 1880-1914 *NatCAB 19*
Snow, Sydney Bruce 1878-1944 *WhAm 2*
Snow, Walter Bradlee 1860- *WhAm 4*
Snow, Warren Howland 1886-1963 *WhAm 4*
Snow, Willard Groesbeck 1913-1957 *NatCAB 48*
Snow, William Benham 1895-1974 *WhAm 6*
Snow, William Brackett 1897-1972 *NatCAB 56*
Snow, William Dunham 1832-1910 *ApCAB, WhAm 1*
Snow, William Freeman 1874-1950 *DcAmB S4, NatCAB 39, WhAm 3*
Snow, William Josiah 1868-1946 *WhAm 2*
Snow, William Parker 1817- *ApCAB*
Snow, William W 1812-1886 *BiAUS, BiDrAC, WhAm H*
Snow, Zerubbabel *BiAUS*
Snow, Zerubbabel Levi 1854-1922 *NatCAB 19*
Snowden, Albert Alexander 1876-1927 *NatCAB 22*
Snowden, Archibald Loudon 1837-1912 *ApCAB, NatCAB 12, TwCBDA, WhAm 1*
Snowden, George Grant 1865-1919 *NatCAB 24*
Snowden, James Henry 1852-1936 *WhAm 1*
Snowden, James Ross 1809-1878 *DcAmB, TwCBDA, WhAm H*
Snowden, James Ross 1810-1878 *ApCAB, BiAUS, Drake, NatCAB 13*
Snowden, Madeline Gaston *WomWWA 14*
Snowden, R Brinkley 1869- *WhAm 5*
Snowden, Robert Bogardus 1836-1909 *NatCAB 32, WhAm 1*
Snowden, Roy Ross 1885-1968 *NatCAB 54*
Snowden, Thomas 1857-1930 *DcAmB, WhAm 1*
Snowden, Yates 1858-1933 *WhAm 1*
Snuggs, Henry Lawrence 1904-1970 *NatCAB 57*
Snure, John *WhAm 1*
Snyder, A Cecil 1907-1959 *WhAm 3*
Snyder, Adam Wilson 1799-1842 *BiDrAC, WhAm H*
Snyder, Adam Wilson 1801-1842 *BiAUS*
Snyder, Addison Hogan 1879- *WhAm 6*
Snyder, Alban Goshorn 1877- *WhAm 5*
Snyder, Albert Whitcomb 1842-1914 *WhAm 1*
Snyder, Alice D 1887-1943 *NotAW*
Snyder, Arthur 1899-1964 *WhAm 4*
Snyder, Baird, III d1946 *WhAm 2*
Snyder, Carl 1869-1946 *WhAm 2*
Snyder, Carl J 1896-1956 *WhAm 3*
Snyder, Charles B J 1860- *WhAm 4*
Snyder, Charles Edward 1877-1950 *NatCAB 46, WhAm 3*
Snyder, Charles McCoy 1859- *WhAm 4*
Snyder, Charles Philip 1847-1915 *BiDrAC, WhAmP*
Snyder, Charles Philip 1879-1964 *WhAm 4*
Snyder, Charles William 1870- *WhoColR*
Snyder, Christopher 1755?-1770 *ApCAB*

Snyder, Clarence Hubert 1897-1967 *NatCAB 53*
Snyder, Donald Kenneth 1889-1950 *NatCAB 40*
Snyder, Edgar Callender 1860-1940 *WhAm 1*
Snyder, Edmund Bowman 1831-1895 *ApCAB X, NatCAB 11*
Snyder, Edward 1835- *WhAm 1*
Snyder, Edwin Reagan 1872-1925 *DcAmB*
Snyder, Eldredge 1901-1967 *WhAm 4*
Snyder, Emma Morrill 1876- *WomWWA 14*
Snyder, Erwin Paul 1891-1975 *WhAm 6*
Snyder, Eva Smith 1862- *WomWWA 14*
Snyder, Franklyn Bliss 1884-1958 *BiDAmEd, WhAm 3*
Snyder, Fred Beal 1859-1951 *WhAm 3*
Snyder, Frederic Sylvester 1868- *WhAm 5*
Snyder, George *New YHSD*
Snyder, George 1820?- *New YHSD*
Snyder, George Gordon 1908-1969 *WhAm 6*
Snyder, George Walter King 1907-1969 *NatCAB 56*
Snyder, Grace Lesta 1863- *WomWWA 14*
Snyder, Harry 1867-1927 *NatCAB 21, WhAm 1*
Snyder, Henry 1858-1923 *WhAm 1*
Snyder, Henry George 1879-1950 *WhAm 3*
Snyder, Henry M *New YHSD*
Snyder, Henry Nelson 1865-1949 *NatCAB 37, WhAm 2*
Snyder, Henry Steinman 1869-1941 *NatCAB 31, WhAm 1*
Snyder, Henry W *New YHSD*
Snyder, Homer Peter 1863-1937 *BiDrAC, NatCAB 28, WhAm 1*
Snyder, Howard McC 1881-1970 *WhAm 5*
Snyder, J Luther 1873-1957 *NatCAB 43*
Snyder, J Ralph 1885-1960 *WhAm 3*
Snyder, Jefferson 1848-1926 *WhAm 1*
Snyder, John 1793-1850 *BiAUS, BiDrAC, WhAm H*
Snyder, John Buell 1877-1946 *BiDrAC, NatCAB 35, WhAmP*
Snyder, John Buell 1879-1946 *WhAm 2*
Snyder, John Francis 1830-1921 *DcAmB*
Snyder, John I, Jr. 1909-1965 *WhAm 4*
Snyder, John Ludwig 1746-1860 *Drake*
Snyder, John Otterbein 1867- *WhAm 5*
Snyder, John Taylor 1893-1956 *WhAm 3*
Snyder, John Wesley 1869-1950 *NatCAB 43*
Snyder, John Wesley 1895- *BiDrUSE*
Snyder, Jonathan LeMoyne 1859-1919 *NatCAB 24, WhAm 1*
Snyder, Kate Anor Cosad 1877- *WomWWA 14*
Snyder, Leroy Edwin 1879-1944 *WhAm 2*
Snyder, Marion Gene 1928- *BiDrAC*
Snyder, Mary J Dunlap *WomWWA 14*
Snyder, Melvin Claude 1898- *BiDrAC*
Snyder, Meredith Pinxton 1859-1937 *WhAm 1*
Snyder, Monroe B 1848-1932 *WhAm 1, WhAm 1C*
Snyder, Morton Ives 1884-1964 *NatCAB 51*
Snyder, Murray 1911-1969 *WhAm 5*
Snyder, Nicholas R 1860- *WhAm 4*
Snyder, Oliver P 1833-1882 *BiAUS, BiDrAC, WhAm H, WhAmP*
Snyder, Oscar John 1866-1947 *WhAm 2*
Snyder, Peter Frederick 1889-1963 *NatCAB 48*
Snyder, Philip *New YHSD*
Snyder, Reginald Clare 1873-1941 *WhAm 1*
Snyder, Robert *New YHSD*
Snyder, Robert McClure 1852- *NatCAB 13*
Snyder, Robert McClure 1876-1937 *WhAm 1*
Snyder, Sibyl Thurston 1876- *WomWWA 14*
Snyder, Simon 1759-1819 *ApCAB, BiAUS, DcAmB, Drake, NatCAB 2, TwCBDA, WhAm H*
Snyder, Simon 1839-1912 *ApCAB Sup, TwCBDA, WhAm 1*
Snyder, Ted 1881-1965 *NatCAB 52*
Snyder, Thomas C 1843- *NatCAB 12*
Snyder, Thomas Elliott 1885-1970 *NatCAB 56*
Snyder, Thomas Iaegar 1879-1955 *NatCAB 42*
Snyder, Valentine P d1934 *WhAm 1*
Snyder, Virgil 1869-1950 *NatCAB 38, WhAm 2*
Snyder, W L *IIBEAAW*
Snyder, William Edward 1877-1949 *WhAm 3*
Snyder, William Henry 1829-1910 *New YHSD*

Snyder, William John 1863-1946 *NatCAB 35*
Snyder, William Lamartine 1848- *WhAm 4*
Snyder, William P, Jr. 1888-1967 *WhAm 4*
Snyder, William Penn 1861-1921 *ApCAB X, NatCAB 49*
Snyder, Wilson Isaac 1856- *NatCAB 18*
Snyder, Zachariah Xenophon 1850-1915 *WhAm 1*
Soane, Sir John 1753-1837 *McGEWB*
Soans, Cyril Arthur 1884-1973 *NatCAB 57, WhAm 6*
Soaper, William Henderson 1876-1947 *NatCAB 47*
Soares, Theodore Gerald 1869-1952 *BiDAmEd, NatCAB 42, WhAm 5*
Sobel, Bernard d1964 *WhAm 4*
Sobel, Isador 1858-1939 *NatCAB 16, NatCAB 30*
Sobeloff, Simon E 1894-1973 *WhAm 6*
Sober, Herbert Alexander 1918-1974 *WhAm 6*
Sobieske, Thaddeus *New YHSD*
Sobieski, Eugene Thaddeus Standalus John 1842- *ApCAB Sup*
Sobieski, John 1842- *WhAm 4*
Sobiloff, Hyman Jordan 1912-1970 *WhAm 5*
Sobin, Irving Maxwell 1894-1973 *NatCAB 57*
Sobol, Louis 1896-1948 *WhAm 2*
Sobolev, Arkady A 1903-1964 *WhAm 4*
Sobolewski, J Friedrich Eduard 1808-1872 *DcAmB*
Sobolewski, J Friedrich Edvard 1808-1872 *WhAm H*
Sobrero, Ascanio 1812-1888 *AsBiEn*
Sockman, Ralph Washington 1889-1970 *ApCAB X, DcAmReB, NatCAB 55, WhAm 5*
Socolofsky, Homer Edward 1922- *EncAAH*
Socrates 469BC-399BC *McGEWB*
Socrates 470?BC-399BC *AsBiEn*
Soddy, Frederick 1877-1956 *AsBiEn, DcScB, McGEWB, WhAm 3*
Soden, Arthur Henry 1843-1925 *ApCAB X*
Soden, Francis Henry 1857-1914 *NatCAB 16*
Soderblom, Nathan 1866-1931 *McGEWB*
Sodero, Cesare 1886-1947 *NatCAB 38*
Sodt, William George 1893-1955 *WhAm 3*
Soemmerring, Samuel Thomas 1755-1830 *DcScB*
Soergel, E W d1949 *WhAm 3*
Soffel, Joseph August 1902-1974 *WhAm 6*
Sogge, Tillman M 1903-1958 *WhAm 3*
Soglow, Otto 1900-1973 *WhAm 6*
Sohier, William Davies 1858-1938 *NatCAB 14, NatCAB 29*
Sohn, Edward Adam 1868-1942 *NatCAB 38*
Sohn, Joseph 1862-1935 *ApCAB X*
Sohn, Joseph 1867-1935 *WhAm 1*
Sohn, Leo Bailey 1892-1962 *NatCAB 50*
Sohncke, Leonhard 1842-1897 *DcScB*
Sohon, Frederick Wyatt 1894-1972 *WhAm 5*
Sohon, Gustavus 1825-1903 *IIBEAAW, New YHSD*
Sohon, Harry 1904-1961 *NatCAB 48*
Soiland, Albert 1873-1946 *NatCAB 40, WhAm 2*
Soissons, Charles DeBourbon, Count De 1565-1612 *ApCAB*
Sojourner Truth 1775?-1883 *AmBi, ApCAB*
Sokel, George Joseph 1892-1958 *NatCAB 47*
Sokhotsky, Yulian-Karl Vasilievich 1842-1927 *DcScB*
Sokol, J Kenneth 1911-1972 *NatCAB 57*
Sokoloff, Nikolai 1886-1965 *NatCAB 52, WhAm 4*
Sokoloff, Ruth H Ottaway 1886-1955 *WhAm 3*
Sokolov, Dmitry Ivanovich 1788-1852 *DcScB*
Sokolovsky, Vasili Danilovich 1897-1968 *WhoMilH*
Sokolovsky, Vasiliy 1897-1968 *WhWW-II*
Sokolow, Alexander Theodore 1891-1934 *WhAm 1, WhAm 1C*
Sokolsky, George Ephraim 1893-1962 *NatCAB 49, WhAm 4*
Sol, Ch'ong 680?-750 *McGEWB*
Solana, Alonso De 1530?-1600 *ApCAB*
Solander, Daniel Carl 1733-1782 *DcScB*
Solano, Juan 1504?-1580 *ApCAB*
Solar, Mercedes Marin De 1804-1866 *ApCAB*
Solari, Marie Magdelene 1849- *BiCAW*

Solari, Mary M 1849- *AmWom*
Solberg, Charles Orrin 1869-1944 *WhAm 2*
Solberg, Marshall 1887-1949 *NatCAB 37*
Solberg, Thorvald 1852-1949 *DcAmLiB,*
WhAm 2
Solberg, Thorvald Arthur 1894-1964
NatCAB 52
Solbert, Oscar Nathaniel d1958 *WhAm 3*
Solchaga, Miguel 1674-1718 *ApCAB*
Soldan, Frank Louis 1842-1908 *BiDAmEd,*
DcAmB, NatCAB 12
Soldani, Ambrogio 1736-1808 *DcScB*
Soldner, Johann Georg Von 1776-1833 *DcScB*
Soldner, Paul 1921- *BnEnAmA*
Soldwedel, Frederic 1886- *IlBEAAW*
Soleil, Jean-Baptiste-Francois 1798-1878 *DcScB*
Soler, Juan Jose 1880- *WhAm 6*
Soleri, Paolo 1919- *BnEnAmA*
Solether, Pliny Louis 1887-1952 *WhAm 3*
Soley, James Russell 1850-1911 *AmBi, ApCAB,*
DcAmB, NatCAB 11, NatCAB 16,
TwCBDA, WhAm 1
Soley, Mayo Hallton 1907-1949 *WhAm 3*
Solf Y Muro, Alfredo 1878- *WhAm 5*
Solger, Reinhold Ernst Friedrich Karl 1817-1866
DcAmB, Drake, WhAm H
Solheim, Arthur Oliver 1921-1968 *WhAm 5*
Soliday, David Shriver 1895-1969 *WhAm 5*
Soliday, Joseph Henry d1947 *WhAm 2*
Solinsky, Francis Joseph 1857-1932 *NatCAB 34*
Solis, Antonio De 1610-1686 *Drake*
Solis, Isaac Nathan 1857- *WhAm 4*
Solis, Jeanne Cady *WomWWA 14*
Solis, Juan Diaz De 1470?-1516 *McGEWB*
Solis-Cohen, Jacob DaSilva 1838-1927 *DcAmB,*
NatCAB 10
Solis-Cohen, Myer 1877-1960 *NatCAB 47*
Solis-Cohen, Solomon 1857-1948 *ApCAB X,*
WhAm 2
Solis Y Rivadeneyra, Antonio De 1610-1686
ApCAB
Sollas, William Johnson 1849-1936 *DcScB*
Sollenberger, John Burtner 1897-1967
NatCAB 54
Sollenberger, Richard Talbot 1907-1975
WhAm 6
Sollers, Augustus Rhodes 1814-1862 *BiAUS,*
BiDrAC, WhAm H
Solley, Fred Palmer 1866-1950 *NatCAB 45*
Solley, John Beach 1872-1947 *NatCAB 33*
Sollitt, Sumner Shannon 1902-1964 *NatCAB 50,*
WhAm 4
Sollmann, Torald Hermann 1874-1965 *WhAm 4*
Sollott, Ralph Preston 1908-1953 *WhAm 3*
Solly, Samuel Edwin 1845-1906 *WhAm 1*
Solly, William Franklin 1858-1927 *NatCAB 21*
Solomon *McGEWB*
Solomon, Barbara Stauffacher 1932- *BnEnAmA*
Solomon, Charles 1889-1963 *NatCAB 49*
Solomon, Edward *BiAUS*
Solomon, Edward Davis 1875-1957 *WhAm 4*
Solomon, Frank 1888-1954 *NatCAB 44*
Solomon, Gabriel Roberts 1880-1956
NatCAB 45
Solomon, Hannah Greenebaum 1858-1942
NatCAB 36, NotAW, WomWWA 14
Solomon, J *NewYHSD*
Solomon, Louis H 1892-1964 *WhAm 4*
Solomon, Sidney L 1902-1975 *WhAm 6*
Solomons, Adolphus Simeon 1826-1910 *DcAmB*
Solon *McGEWB*
Solon, C *NewYHSD*
Solon, Faustin Johnson 1894-1964 *WhAm 4*
Solon, Harry 1873- *WhAm 5*
Solon, Leon Victor 1886- *WhAm 5*
Solorzano Y Pereira, Juan De 1575-1654
ApCAB
Soloviev, Vladimir Sergeevich 1853-1900
McGEWB
Solow, Herbert 1903-1964 *WhAm 4*
Soltes, Mordecai 1893-1957 *WhAm 3*
Solvay, Ernest 1838-1922 *AsBiEn, DcScB*
Solzhenitsyn, Alexander Isayevich 1918-
McGEWB
Sombart, Werner 1863-1941 *McGEWB*
Somer, Frank Alois 1895-1957 *NatCAB 47*
Somerall, James Bentley 1917-1975 *WhAm 6*

Somerby, Frederic Thomas 1814-1870?
NewYHSD
Somerby, Frederic Thomas 1814-1871 *ApCAB*
Somerby, Horatio Gates 1805-1872 *ApCAB,*
NewYHSD
Somerby, Lorenzo 1816-1883 *NewYHSD*
Somerndike, John Mason 1877-1939 *WhAm 1*
Somers, Andrew Lawrence 1895-1949 *BiDrAC,*
WhAm 2, WhAmP
Somers, Arthur Sylvester 1866-1932
NatCAB 24
Somers, Daniel McLean 1841-1912 *NatCAB 16*
Somers, Frederic Maxwell 1850-1894
NatCAB 22
Somers, Frederick Maxwell 1850-1894
NatCAB 1
Somers, James Alpheus 1869-1939 *NatCAB 29*
Somers, Joseph L 1844-1914 *NatCAB 18*
Somers, Joseph Patrick 1919-1974 *WhAm 6*
Somers, Orlando Allen 1843-1921 *NatCAB 19,*
WhAm 1
Somers, Peter J 1850-1924 *BiDrAC,*
NatCAB 2
Somers, Richard 1778-1804 *ApCAB, DcAmB,*
Drake, NatCAB 8, TwCBDA, WebAMB
Somers, Richard H 1881- *WhAm 6*
Somerset, Edward Seymour, Duke Of 1506-1552
McGEWB
Somervell, Alexander 1820-1854 *NatCAB 5*
Somervell, Brehon Burke 1892-1955 *DcAmB S5,*
WebAMB, WhAm 3, WhWW-II
Somerville, Alexander 1811-1885 *ApCAB*
Somerville, C C 1859- *WhoColR*
Somerville, Ethel Blackmore 1883-
WomWWA 14
Somerville, Frederick Howland 1872- *WhAm 5*
Somerville, Harry Philip 1889-1960 *WhAm 4*
Somerville, Henderson Middleton 1837-1915
NatCAB 7, NatCAB 18, TwCBDA,
WhAm 1
Somerville, James Alexander 1867-1939
WhAm 1
Somerville, Sir James Fownes 1882-1949
WhAm 2, WhWW-II, WhoMilH
Somerville, M *NewYHSD*
Somerville, Mary Fairfax Greig 1780-1872
DcScB
Somerville, Ormond 1868-1928 *WhAm 1*
Somerville, Pearl Cliffe 1877-1954 *WhAm 3*
Somerville, Randolph 1891-1958 *WhAm 3*
Somerville, Thomas Hugh 1850- *WhAm 4*
Somerville, William Clark 1790-1826
NatCAB 11, WhAm H
Somerville, William Clarke 1790-1826 *ApCAB*
Somes, Daniel Eton 1815-1888 *BiAUS,*
BiDrAC, WhAm H
Somigli, Carlo Maria 1863- *NatCAB 17*
Somma, Gerard Jerry 1892-1960 *NatCAB 44*
Sommer, Alvin Henry 1900-1966 *WhAm 4*
Sommer, Charles G 1864-1925 *WhAm 1*
Sommer, Daniel Philip 1892-1963 *WhAm 4*
Sommer, Ernst August 1870-1936 *WhAm 1*
Sommer, Frank Henry 1872-1957 *NatCAB 48,*
WhAm 3
Sommer, Frederick 1905- *BnEnAmA*
Sommer, Henry Getz d1952 *WhAm 3*
Sommer, Hugo Henry 1896-1953 *NatCAB 42*
Sommer, Luther Allen 1878-1946 *WhAm 2*
Sommer, Martin S 1869- *WhAm 5*
Sommer, Otto *IlBEAAW*
Sommer, Peter W 1869-1924 *WhAm 1*
Sommer, Reuben E 1899-1961 *WhAm 4*
Sommer, William H 1882-1950 *WhAm 3*
Sommerfeld, Arnold Johannes Wilhelm
1868-1951 *AsBiEn, DcScB*
Sommerhof, Roy Andrew 1903-1961
NatCAB 47
Sommerich, Otto Charles 1877-1968 *WhAm 4A*
Sommering *DcScB*
Sommers, Charles G 1791-1868 *Drake*
Sommers, Charles George 1793-1868 *ApCAB,*
NatCAB 13
Sommers, Charles Leissring 1870- *WhAm 5*
Sommers, Henry Cantine 1861- *WhAm 4*
Sommers, Katharine Higgins 1878-
WomWWA 14
Sommers, Martin 1900-1963 *WhAm 4*
Sommers, May A C *WomWWA 14*

Sommers, Paul Bergen 1885-1958 *WhAm 3*
Sommerville, Charles William 1867-1938
WhAm 1
Sommerville, Duncan McLaren Young 1879-1934
DcScB
Sommerville, Maxwell 1829-1904 *NatCAB 12,*
TwCBDA, WhAm 1
Sommerville, Robert Leonard 1906-1968
NatCAB 54
Sommerville, Walter Byers 1854-1924
NatCAB 20, WhAm 1
Somov, Osip Ivanovich 1815-1876 *DcScB*
Somoza, Anastasio 1896-1956 *McGEWB,*
WhAm 3
Somoza, Luis 1922-1967 *WhAm 4*
Somsen, Henry Northrop 1875-1955
NatCAB 42
Son Of Many Beads 1866?-1954 *DcAmB S5*
Sondern, Frederic Ewald 1867- *WhAm 5*
Sondley, F A 1857- *WhAm 3*
Sones, Warren Wesley David 1888-1958
NatCAB 45, WhAm 3
Sonfield, Robert Leon 1893-1972 *WhAm 5*
Soniat, Leonce Martin 1841-1922 *WhAm 1*
Sonin, Nikolay Yakovlevich 1849-1915 *DcScB*
Sonjo 1552-1608 *McGEWB*
Sonnabend, Abraham M 1896-1964 *WhAm 4*
Sonnakolb, Franklin Schuyler 1864- *WhAm 4*
Sonne, Fred Theodore 1899-1965 *WhAm 4*
Sonne, Hans Christian 1891-1971 *NatCAB 57*
Sonneborn, Siegmund Bachrach 1872-1940
NatCAB 30
Sonneck, Oscar George Theodore 1873-1928
DcAmB, DcAmLiB, EncAAH,
NatCAB 25, WhAm 1
Sonnedecker, Thomas Harry 1857- *WhAm 4*
Sonnenberg, Henry L 1915-1955 *WhAm 3*
Sonnenschein, Hugo 1883-1956 *WhAm 3*
Sonnerat, Pierre 1748-1814 *DcScB*
Sonnett, John Francis 1912-1969 *WhAm 5*
Sonneysyn, H O 1900-1969 *WhAm 5*
Sonnichsen, Albert 1878-1931 *DcAmB,*
WhAm 1
Sonnichsen, Charles Leland 1901- *REnAW*
Sonnichsen, Yngvar 1873?-1940 *IlBEAAW*
Sonnichsen, Yngvar 1875-1940 *WhAm 1*
Sonnier, Keith 1941- *BnEnAmA*
Sonnini DeManoncourt, Charles N S 1751-1812
ApCAB
Sonntag, Alfred E 1903-1965 *NatCAB 52*
Sonntag, George 1786-1841 *ApCAB, Drake*
Sonntag, Marcus S 1859-1936 *WhAm 1*
Sonntag, William Louis 1822-1900 *ApCAB,*
NewYHSD, WhAm 1
Sonrel, Antoine *NewYHSD*
Sonsteby, John J 1879-1941 *WhAm 1*
Sontag, Henriette 1805-1854 *ApCAB*
Sontag, Raymond James 1897-1972 *WhAm 5*
Sontheimer, Goley Donald 1909-1970
NatCAB 54
Sonthonax, Leger Felicite 1763-1813 *ApCAB*
Soong, T V 1891-1971 *WhAm 5*
Sooy, William Frank 1880-1947 *NatCAB 38*
Sooysmith, Charles 1856-1916 *DcAmB,*
WhAm 1
Soper, Alexander Coburn 1846-1930 *WhAm 1*
Soper, Arthur William 1838-1901 *NatCAB 12*
Soper, Augustus 1852- *NatCAB 11*
Soper, Edmund Davison 1876-1961 *NatCAB 50,*
WhAm 4
Soper, Erastus Burrows 1841-1917 *WhAm 1*
Soper, George Albert 1870-1948 *WhAm 2*
Soper, George Edmond 1857-1927 *NatCAB 21*
Soper, Henry Marlin 1850-1911 *NatCAB 11,*
WhAm 1
Soper, Horace Wendell 1867- *WhAm 5*
Soper, John Harris 1846-1944 *NatCAB 48,*
WhAm 1
Soper, Mabel Browning *WomWWA 14*
Soper, Morris Ames 1873-1963 *WhAm 4*
Soper, Pliny Leland 1861-1913 *NatCAB 26,*
WhAm 4
Soper, Richard F 1810?-1862? *NewYHSD*
Soper, Willard Burr 1882-1939 *NatCAB 29*
Sophian, Lawrence Henry 1903-1959 *WhAm 3*
Sophocles 496BC-406BC *McGEWB*
Sophocles, Evangelinus Apostolides 1800?-1883
NatCAB 5

Sophocles, Evangelinus Apostolides 1805?-1883
  BiDAmEd, DcAmB, WhAm H
Sophocles, Evangelinus Apostolides 1807-1883
  ApCAB
Sophoulis, Themistocles d1949 *WhAm 3*
Sopkin, Alvin Abraham 1901-1967 *NatCAB 54*
Soranus Of Ephesus *DcScB*
Sorby, Henry Clifton 1826-1908 *DcScB*
Sordoni, Andrew John, Jr. 1916-1967 *WhAm 5*
Sordoni, Andrew John, Sr. 1887-1963 *WhAm 4*
Sorel, Albert 1842-1906 *McGEWB*
Sorel, Georges 1847-1922 *McGEWB*
Soren, John Johnston d1889 *NewYHSD*
Soreng, Edgar Martin 1884-1958 *NatCAB 47*
Sorensen, Carl Walter 1900-1961 *NatCAB 52*
Sorensen, Charles E 1881-1968 *WhAm 5*
Sorensen, John Hjelmhof 1923-1969 *WhAm 5*
Sorensen, Royal Wasson 1882-1965 *WhAm 4*
Sorensen, Soren Peter Lauritz 1868-1939
  AsBiEn, DcScB
Sorenson, Elias 1825-1911 *REnAW*
Sorenson, Roy 1900-1966 *WhAm 5*
Sorg, Paul John 1840-1902 *ApCAB X,*
  BiDrAC, NatCAB 18, WhAm 1
Sorg, Theodore 1888-1955 *WhAm 3*
Sorge, Friedrich Adolph 1828-1906 *DcAmB*
Sorge, Richard 1895-1944 *WhWW-II*
Sorgel, William Richard 1884-1958 *NatCAB 48*
Soriano, Andres 1898-1964 *WhAm 4*
Sorin, Edward Frederick 1814-1893 *ApCAB,*
  BiDAmEd, DcAmB, TwCBDA, WebAB,
  WhAm H
Sorin, Sarah Inslee Herring 1861-1914
  NatCAB 36
Sorlie, Arthur Gustav 1874-1928 *NatCAB 33,*
  WhAm 1
Sorokin, Pitirim Alexandrovitch 1889-1968
  McGEWB, WebAB, WhAm 4A
Sorrel, Gilbert Moxley 1838-1901 *BiDConf*
Sorrell, Lewis Carlyle 1889-1962 *NatCAB 49,*
  WhAm 4
Sorrells, John Harvey 1896-1948 *WhAm 2*
Sorsby, William Brooks 1858- *NatCAB 13,*
  WhAm 4
Sortwell, Alvin Foye 1854-1910 *NatCAB 34*
Sorver, Edwin RafSnyder 1897-1967
  NatCAB 53
Sosigenes 090?BC- *AsBiEn, DcScB*
Sosin, Jack Marvin 1928- *EncAAH*
Soske, Joshua Lawrence 1903-1966 *NatCAB 53*
Soskin, William 1899-1952 *WhAm 3*
Sosman, Merrill C 1890-1959 *WhAm 3*
Sosman, Robert Browning 1881-1967 *WhAm 5*
Sosnowski, John Bartholomew 1883-1968
  BiDrAC
Sotatsu, Tawaraya 1570?-1643? *McGEWB*
Sothell, Seth d1694 *NatCAB 12*
Sotheran, Alice Hyneman 1840- *WhAm 4*
Sotheran, Charles 1847-1902 *ApCAB,*
  WhAm 1
Sothern, Edward Askew 1826-1881 *AmBi,*
  DcAmB, NatCAB 5, TwCBDA,
  WhAm H
Sothern, Edward Askew 1830-1881 *ApCAB,*
  Drake
Sothern, Edward Hugh 1859-1933 *AmBi,*
  ApCAB X, DcAmB, NatCAB 5,
  TwCBDA, WebAB, WhAm 1
Sothern, Edward Lytton 1856-1887 *NatCAB 5*
Sothoron, James T 1842- *NatCAB 7*
Soto, Bernardo 1853- *ApCAB*
Soto, Domingo De 1494?-1560 *DcScB*
Soto, Hernando De 1500?-1542 *AmBi, DcAmB*
Soto, Marco Aurelio 1846- *ApCAB*
Sotomayor, Cristobal De d1511 *ApCAB*
Sotomayor, Pedro De 1554-1631 *ApCAB*
Sotta *NewYHSD*
Sotter, George William 1879-1953 *WhAm 3*
Sotzin, Heber Allen 1893-1960 *WhAm 3*
Soubin, Pierre 1625-1676 *ApCAB*
Soubise, Charles DeRohan, Prince De 1715-1787
  WhoMilH
Soublette, Carlos 1790-1870 *ApCAB, Drake*
Souby, A Max 1880-1922 *WhAm 1*
Soucek, Apollo 1897-1955 *NatCAB 42,*
  WhAm 3
Souchon, Edmond 1841-1924 *DcAmB,*
  NatCAB 9, WhAm 1

Souder, Casper 1819-1868 *ApCAB*
Souder, Charles Granville 1881-1967
  NatCAB 54
Souder, Edwin Mills 1872-1947 *WhAm 2*
Souder, George B *NewYHSD*
Souder, Harrison 1870-1938 *NatCAB 28*
Souders, John Cloyd 1872-1955 *NatCAB 44*
Souer, Louis Joseph 1844- *NatCAB 9*
Souers, Loren Edmunds 1882-1961 *NatCAB 49,*
  WhAm 4
Souers, Sidney William 1892-1973 *WhAm 5*
Souers, Warren Earl 1916-1975 *WhAm 6*
Soufert *NewYHSD*
Soufflot, Jacques Germain 1713-1780 *McGEWB*
Soulaibe, Louis Ferdinand 1587-1656 *ApCAB*
Soulages, Pierre 1919- *McGEWB*
Soulard, Andrew Livingston 1841- *NatCAB 3*
Soulavie, Jean-Louis Giraud 1752-1813 *DcScB*
Soule, Andrew MacNairn 1872-1934 *WhAm 1*
Soule, Asa Titus 1824-1890 *WhAm H*
Soule, Carolina Augusta White 1824-1903
  TwCBDA
Soule, Caroline Augusta White 1824-1903
  ApCAB, Drake, NotAW
Soule, Caroline Gray 1855- *WhAm 4*
Soule, Charles, Jr. *NewYHSD*
Soule, Charles, Sr. 1809-1869 *NewYHSD*
Soule, Charles Carroll 1842-1913 *WhAm 1*
Soule, Clara *NewYHSD*
Soule, Edward Lee 1882-1971 *WhAm 5*
Soule, Elizabeth Helena *WomWWA 14*
Soule, Elizabeth Sterling 1884-1972 *WhAm 5*
Soule, Frank 1871-1957 *NatCAB 46*
Soule, George 1834-1926 *ApCAB, ApCAB X,*
  BiDAmEd, DcAmB, NatCAB 1,
  WhAm 1
Soule, George Carroll 1885-1957 *NatCAB 47*
Soule, Gideon Lane 1796-1879 *NatCAB 10*
Soule, Henri Remy 1903-1966 *WhAm 4*
Soule, Joshua 1781-1867 *ApCAB, DcAmB,*
  Drake, NatCAB 5, TwCBDA, WhAm H
Soule, Malcolm Herman 1896-1951 *WhAm 3*
Soule, Nathan *BiAUS, BiDrAC, WhAm H*
Soule, Octavia *NewYHSD*
Soule, Pierre d1870 *BiAUS*
Soule, Pierre 1801-1870 *BiDConf, BiDrAC,*
  DcAmB, Drake, McGEWB, WebAB,
  WhAm H, WhAmP
Soule, Pierre 1802-1870 *AmBi, ApCAB,*
  NatCAB 3, TwCBDA
Soule, Richard 1812-1877 *ApCAB, NatCAB 2*
Soule, Robert Homer 1900-1952 *NatCAB 40,*
  WhAm 3
Soule, Winsor 1883-1954 *NatCAB 43,*
  WhAm 3
Soules, Mary E 1910-1971 *WhAm 6*
Souleyet, Louis-Francois-Auguste 1811-1852
  DcScB
Soulouque, Faustin 1789-1867 *Drake*
Soulouque, Faustin Elie 1785-1867 *ApCAB*
Soult, Nicolas Jean DeDieu 1769-1851
  WhoMilH
Soupe, Marie Joseph 1738-1794 *ApCAB*
Sourdis, Evarista 1908-1970 *WhAm 5*
Sourian, Zareh Missak 1904-1967 *NatCAB 53*
Sousa, Carlos Martins Pereira 1884-1965
  WhAm 4
Sousa, John Philip 1854-1932 *AmBi,*
  ApCAB Sup, ApCAB X, DcAmB,
  EncAB, McGEWB, NatCAB 9,
  NatCAB 33, WebAB, WebAMB,
  WhAm 1
Sousa, John Philip 1856-1932 *TwCBDA*
Sousa, Martim Afonso De 1500?-1564
  McGEWB
Sousa, Martim Afonso De *see also* Souza, Martim
  Affonso De
Souser, Kenneth 1905-1970 *WhAm 5*
Soutar, Richard Gray 1888-1964 *NatCAB 51*
Souter, Dale 1887-1964 *NatCAB 51*
South, Charles Lacy 1892-1965 *BiDrAC*
South, F Floyd 1892-1955 *NatCAB 47*
South, James 1785-1867 *DcScB*
South, Jerry C 1867-1930 *WhAm 1*
South, John Glover 1873-1940 *NatCAB 29,*
  WhAm 1
South, Lillian H 1880- *WhAm 6*
Southack, Cyprian 1662-1745 *DcAmB,*

WhAm H
Southall, James Cocke 1828-1897 *DcAmB,*
  NatCAB 19, WhAm H
Southall, James H 1841-1901 *NatCAB 8*
Southall, James Powell Cocke 1871-1962
  NatCAB 50, WhAm 4
Southall, Robert Goode 1852-1924 *BiDrAC,*
  WhAm 4
Southam, H S d1954 *WhAm 3*
Southam, J D 1909-1954 *WhAm 3*
Southampton, Henry Wriothesley, Earl Of
  1573-1624 *ApCAB*
Southard, E Francis 1868-1939 *NatCAB 30*
Southard, Elmer Ernest 1876-1920 *AmBi,*
  DcAmB, NatCAB 19, WhAm 1
Southard, Frank Elwyn 1890-1963 *NatCAB 50*
Southard, George Franklin 1852-1930 *WhAm 1*
Southard, George Henry 1841-1913 *NatCAB 30*
Southard, Harry Green 1878-1959 *WhAm 4*
Southard, Henry 1747-1842 *BiDrAC,*
  WhAm H, WhAmP
Southard, Henry 1749-1842 *ApCAB, BiAUS,*
  NatCAB 1, TwCBDA
Southard, Isaac 1783-1850 *BiAUS, BiDrAC,*
  WhAm H, WhAmP
Southard, James Harding 1851-1918 *WhAm 1*
Southard, James Harding 1851-1919 *BiDrAC,*
  WhAmP
Southard, Louis Carver 1854-1922 *NatCAB 16,*
  WhAm 1
Southard, Lucien H 1827-1881 *DcAmB,*
  WhAm H
Southard, Lydia 1875- *WomWWA 14*
Southard, Milton Isaiah 1836-1905 *BiAUS,*
  BiDrAC, NatCAB 3, TwCBDA
Southard, Samuel Lewis 1787-1842 *ApCAB,*
  BiAUS, BiDrAC, BiDrUSE, DcAmB,
  Drake, NatCAB 6, TwCBDA, WhAm H,
  WhAmP
Southard, Samuel Lewis 1819-1859 *Drake*
Souther, George Hawley 1864-1949 *NatCAB 39*
Souther, Henry 1865- *WhAm 1*
Southerd, Lucien H 1827-1881 *WhAm H*
Southerland, Clarence Andrew 1889-1973
  WhAm 6
Southerland, J Julien 1884-1950 *WhAm 3*
Southerland, Susan George 1862-
  WomWWA 14
Southerland, William Henry Hudson 1852-1933
  WhAm 1
Southern, Allen Carriger 1878-1967 *WhAm 4*
Southern, Julia Marlowe *DcAmB S4*
Southern, William Neil, Jr. 1864-1956 *WhAm 3*
Southgate, George Thompson 1886-1946
  WhAm 2
Southgate, Horatio 1812-1894 *ApCAB,*
  DcAmB S1, Drake, NatCAB 13,
  TwCBDA, WhAm H
Southgate, James Haywood 1859- *ApCAB Sup,*
  TwCBDA
Southgate, James Haywood 1859-1915
  NatCAB 17
Southgate, James Haywood 1859-1917 *WhAm 1*
Southgate, John Frederick 1831-1858
  NewYHSD
Southgate, Louise 1857- *WomWWA 14*
Southgate, Richard 1893-1946 *WhAm 2*
Southgate, Thomas Somerville 1868-1928
  NatCAB 21, WhAm 1
Southgate, William 1782-1811 *NewYHSD*
Southgate, William Wright 1800-1849 *BiAUS,*
  BiDrAC, WhAm H
Southmayd, Charles Ferdinand 1824-1911
  DcAmB, NatCAB 15
Southward, George 1803-1876 *NewYHSD*
Southwick, Albert Plympton 1855- *WhAm 4*
Southwick, Elsie Whitmore 1881-
  WomWWA 14
Southwick, George Newell 1863-1912 *BiDrAC,*
  TwCBDA, WhAm 1, WhAmP
Southwick, George Rinaldo 1859-1930
  NatCAB 23, WhAm 1
Southwick, Henry Lawrence 1863-1932
  WhAm 1
Southwick, John Claflin 1835-1896 *NatCAB 16*
Southwick, John Leonard 1858-1932
  NatCAB 31, WhAm 1
Southwick, Soloman 1773-1839 *WhAm H*

Southwick, Solomon 1773-1839 *ApCAB*,
DcAmB, *NatCAB 4*
Southwick, Solomon 1774?-1839 *Drake*
Southworth, Albert Sands 1811-1894 *BnEnAmA*,
NatCAB 28
Southworth, Alice Berry 1863- *WomWWA 14*
Southworth, Constant 1614-1685 *ApCAB*
Southworth, Edward Franklin 1872-1946
NatCAB 34
Southworth, Emma Dorothy Eliza Nevitte
1818-1899 *Drake*
Southworth, Emma Dorothy Eliza Nevitte
1819-1899 *AmBi, AmWom, ApCAB,
DcAmB, NatCAB 1, NotAW, TwCBDA,
WebAB, WhAm 1*
Southworth, Franklin Chester 1863-1944
NatCAB 45, WhAm 2
Southworth, George Champlin Shepard 1842-
WhAm 4
Southworth, George Clark 1890-1972 *WhAm 5*
Southworth, Gertrude VanDuyn *WomWWA 14*
Southworth, Inez M Southworth 1880-
WomWWA 14
Southworth, James Larry 1913-1970
NatCAB 56
Southworth, John Willard 1919-1962
NatCAB 48
Southworth, Melvin Deane 1883-1967 *WhAm 4*
Southworth, Nathaniel 1806-1858 *ApCAB,
Drake, NewYHSD*
Southworth, Thomas Shepard 1861-1940
NatCAB 36, WhAm 1
Soutine, Chaim 1894-1943 *McGEWB*
Soutman, Cornelius 1686-1751 *ApCAB*
Soutter, Charles Broughton 1845-1917
NatCAB 17
Soutter, Robert 1870-1933 *NatCAB 24*
Souvanna Phouma, Prince 1901- *McGEWB*
Souvestre, Henry Victurnien 1729-1782 *ApCAB*
Souza, Martim Affonso De d1550? *ApCAB*
Souza, Martim Affonso De *see also* Sousa,
Martim Afonso De
Souza, Pero Lopes 1500?-1539 *ApCAB*
Souza, Thome De d1560? *ApCAB*
Sovak, Francis Washington 1885-1939
NatCAB 29
Sowards, Joseph 1840?-1863? *ApCAB*
Sowden, William Henry 1840-1907 *BiDrAC*
Sowder, Charles Robert 1870-1942 *NatCAB 31*
Sowdon, Arthur John Clark 1835-1911
NatCAB 10, WhAm 1
Sowell, Ashley B 1893-1945 *WhAm 2*
Sowell, Ellis Mast 1902-1956 *NatCAB 45,
WhAm 3*
Sowell, Ingram Cecil 1889-1947 *WhAm 2*
Sowell, Paul Dibrell 1904-1971 *WhAm 5*
Sower, Charles Gilbert, Sr. 1821-1902 *ApCAB,
WhAm 1*
Sower, Christopher 1693-1758 *AmBi, ApCAB,
DcAmB, Drake, WhAm H*
Sower, Christopher 1721-1784 *AmBi, ApCAB,
DcAmB, Drake, NatCAB 13, WhAm H*
Sower, Christopher 1754-1799 *ApCAB,
DcAmB, WhAm H*
Sowerby, James 1757-1822 *DcScB*
Sowerby, Leo 1895-1968 *WhAm 5*
Sowers, Daniel Henry 1867-1927 *NatCAB 23*
Sowers, Don Conger 1883-1942 *WhAm 2*
Sowers, Joseph Cullen 1909-1972 *WhAm 5*
Sowles, Lewis William 1884-1956 *NatCAB 43*
Sowles, Melvin Henry 1882-1951 *NatCAB 39*
Soyer, Isaac 1907- *BnEnAmA*
Soyer, Moses 1899-1974 *BnEnAmA, WhAm 6*
Soyer, Raphael 1899- *BnEnAmA*
Soyinka, Wole 1935- *McGEWB*
Spaak, Paul Henri 1899-1972 *McGEWB,
WhAm 5, WhWW-II*
Spaatz, Carl 1891-1974 *WebAB, WebAMB,
WhAm 6, WhWW-II, WhoMilH*
Spachner, John Victor 1898-1974 *WhAm 6*
Spackman, Cyril Saunders 1887-1963 *WhAm 4*
Spackman, G Donald 1895-1957 *NatCAB 48*
Spackman, Harold Burton 1899-1957 *WhAm 3*
Spackman, James Guie 1889-1959 *NatCAB 47*
Spaeth, Adolph 1839-1910 *ApCAB, DcAmB,
TwCBDA, WhAm 1*
Spaeth, Bernard Anton 1885-1958 *WhAm 3*
Spaeth, John Duncan 1868-1954 *DcAmB S5,*

WhAm 3
Spaeth, Otto Lucien 1897-1966 *WhAm 4*
Spaeth, Reynold Albrecht 1886-1925 *WhAm 1*
Spaeth, Sigmund 1885-1965 *WhAm 4*
Spafard, Mrs. Edwin *NewYHSD*
Spafford, Edward Elwell 1878-1941 *NatCAB 36,
WhAm 2*
Spafford, Elizabeth H *NewYHSD*
Spafford, Emily Hazard Dakin 1866-
WomWWA 14
Spafford, Frederick Angier 1855-1922 *WhAm 1*
Spafford, George Catlin 1864-1943 *NatCAB 32,
WhAm 2*
Spafford, Jessie I *WomWWA 14*
Spahn, Ronald Arthur 1907-1969 *NatCAB 55*
Spahn, Warren Edward 1921- *WebAB*
Spahr, Boyd Lee 1880-1970 *NatCAB 55,
WhAm 5*
Spahr, Charles Barzillai 1860-1904 *DcAmB,
TwCBDA, WhAm 1*
Spahr, George W 1839- *WhAm 1*
Spahr, Herman Louis 1875-1953 *WhAm 3*
Spahr, Jean Gurney Fine *WomWWA 14*
Spahr, Walter Earl 1891-1970 *NatCAB 56,
WhAm 5*
Spaid, Arthur Rusmiselle Miller 1866-
WhAm 4
Spaid, William Wesley 1903-1972 *WhAm 5*
Spaid, William Winfield 1880-1938 *WhAm 1*
Spaide, Rolland Lee 1884-1945 *NatCAB 34*
Spaight, Richard Dobbs 1758-1802 *ApCAB,
BiAUS, BiDrAC, DcAmB, Drake,
NatCAB 4, TwCBDA, WhAm H,
WhAmP*
Spaight, Richard Dobbs 1796-1850 *ApCAB,
BiAUS, BiDrAC, Drake, TwCBDA,
WhAm H, WhAmP*
Spain, Charles Lyle 1869-1950 *NatCAB 38,
WhAm 2A*
Spain, Charles R 1913-1965 *WhAm 4*
Spain, Gail Elliott 1898-1963 *WhAm 4*
Spain, Will Cook 1891-1956 *WhAm 3*
Spainhour, Mrs. *NewYHSD*
Spalckhaver, William 1837-1919 *NatCAB 17*
Spalding, Albert 1888-1953 *DcAmB S5,
NatCAB 42, WebAB, WhAm 3*
Spalding, Albert Goodwill 1850-1915 *DcAmB,
NatCAB 3, WebAB, WhAm 1*
Spalding, Alfred Baker 1874- *WhAm 5*
Spalding, Alice Huntington 1875- *WhAm 5*
Spalding, Benedict Joseph 1810-1868 *Drake*
Spalding, Benedict Joseph 1812-1868 *ApCAB,
NatCAB 5*
Spalding, Burleigh Folsom 1853-1934 *BiDrAC,
NatCAB 18, WhAm 1, WhAmP*
Spalding, Catherine 1793-1858 *AmBi, ApCAB,
BiDAmEd, DcAmB, NotAW, WhAm H*
Spalding, Charles Hubbard 1837- *WhAm 4*
Spalding, Effie Almira Southworth 1860-
WomWWA 14
Spalding, Eliza Hart d1843? *WhAm H*
Spalding, Eliza Hart 1807-1851 *NewYHSD,
NotAW*
Spalding, Elizabeth 1870?-1954 *IIBEAAW*
Spalding, Elizabeth Hill 1854- *WhAm 4,
WomWWA 14*
Spalding, Franklin Spencer 1865-1914 *DcAmB,
NatCAB 15, WhAm 1*
Spalding, Frederick Putnam 1857-1923
WhAm 1
Spalding, George 1836- *ApCAB Sup*
Spalding, George 1836-1915 *BiDrAC*
Spalding, George 1837- *WhAm 4*
Spalding, George Burley 1835- *ApCAB,
NatCAB 3*
Spalding, George Burley 1835-1914 *WhAm 1*
Spalding, George R 1877- *WhAm 5*
Spalding, Harriet Mabel 1862- *AmWom*
Spalding, Henry Harmon 1803?-1843 *WhAm H*
Spalding, Henry Harmon 1803-1874 *REnAW*
Spalding, Henry Harmon 1804-1874 *ApCAB,
NatCAB 2*
Spalding, Hughes 1886-1969 *WhAm 5*
Spalding, J Walter 1856-1931 *WhAm 1*
Spalding, Jack Johnson 1856-1938 *WhAm 1*
Spalding, James Alfred 1846-1938 *WhAm 1*
Spalding, James Field 1839-1921 *NatCAB 34,
WhAm 1*

Spalding, James Reed 1821-1872 *ApCAB,
NatCAB 5*
Spalding, James Walter 1856-1931 *NatCAB 3*
Spalding, Jesse 1833-1904 *WhAm 1*
Spalding, John Franklin 1828-1902 *ApCAB,
NatCAB 3, TwCBDA, WhAm 1*
Spalding, John Lancaster 1840-1916 *ApCAB,
BiDAmEd, DcAmB, DcAmReB,
NatCAB 10, TwCBDA, WhAm 1*
Spalding, Katherine Moody 1859-
WomWWA 14
Spalding, Keith 1877-1961 *WhAm 4,
WhAm 5*
Spalding, Lyman 1775-1821 *AmBi, ApCAB,
DcAmB, Drake, NatCAB 2, WhAm H*
Spalding, Martin John 1810-1872 *ApCAB,
DcAmB, DcAmReB, Drake, NatCAB 1,
TwCBDA, WhAm H*
Spalding, Otis Burgess 1875-1940 *NatCAB 31*
Spalding, Phebe Estelle 1859-1937 *WhAm 1,
WomWWA 14*
Spalding, Philip Leffingwell 1871-1938
NatCAB 30, WhAm 1
Spalding, Rufus Paine 1797-1886 *BiAUS*
Spalding, Rufus Paine 1798-1886 *ApCAB,
BiDrAC, Drake, NatCAB 5, TwCBDA,
WhAm H*
Spalding, Simon 1742-1814 *ApCAB*
Spalding, Solomon 1761-1816 *Drake*
Spalding, Solomon *see also* Spaulding, Solomon
Spalding, Susan Marr *AmWom*
Spalding, Thomas d1851 *BiAUS*
Spalding, Thomas 1774-1851 *BiDrAC, DcAmB*
Spalding, Thomas 1776-1851 *WhAm H*
Spalding, Volney Morgan 1849-1918 *DcAmB,
NatCAB 10, TwCBDA, WhAm 1*
Spalding, Walter Raymond 1865-1962 *WhAm 4*
Spalding, William Andrew 1852-1941
NatCAB 8, NatCAB 31, WhAm 1
Spallanzani, Lazzaro 1729-1799 *AsBiEn,
BiHiMed, DcScB, McGEWB*
Spamer, Richard 1856-1938 *WhAm 1*
Spampinato, Clemente 1912- *IIBEAAW*
Spang, Joseph Peter, Jr. 1893-1969 *NatCAB 56,
WhAm 5*
Spang, O S *NewYHSD*
Spangenberg, Augustus Gottlieb 1704-1792
*AmBi, ApCAB, DcAmB, DcAmReB,
Drake, NatCAB 1, WhAm H*
Spangenberg, Ferdinand T 1820?- *NewYHSD*
Spangler, Clair Grove 1902-1960 *NatCAB 46*
Spangler, David 1796-1856 *BiAUS, BiDrAC,
WhAm H*
Spangler, Harrison Earl 1879-1965 *WhAm 4*
Spangler, Henry Thomas 1853-1934
NatCAB 33, WhAm 4
Spangler, Henry Wilson 1858-1912 *DcAmB,
WhAm 1*
Spangler, Jacob 1767-1843 *BiDrAC, WhAm H*
Spangler, Jacob 1768-1843 *BiAUS*
Spangler, James Williams 1874-1957
NatCAB 47, WhAm 5
Spangler, John Mayne 1889-1954 *NatCAB 44*
Spangler, Lena Margaret Norton 1859-
WomWWA 14
Spangler, Timon John 1869-1926 *WhAm 1*
Spanier, Francis Joseph 1906-1967 *WhAm 4*
Spann, Otis 1930-1970 *WhAm 5*
Sparber, Jean Leah Weinstein 1923-1972
WhAm 6
Spargo, John 1876-1966 *NatCAB 52,
WhAm 4*
Spargo, John Webster 1896-1956 *NatCAB 43,
WhAm 3*
Spargur, John Mitchell 1879-1956 *NatCAB 44*
Sparhawk, Frances Campbell *WomWWA 14*
Sparhawk, Frances Campbell 1847- *AmWom,
NatCAB 10, WhAm 4*
Sparhawk, Frances Campbell 1858?- *ApCAB*
Sparhawk, John, Jr. 1857-1918 *NatCAB 18*
Sparkes, Boyden 1890-1954 *WhAm 3*
Sparkes, Fannie J *WomWWA 14*
Sparkman, James Truslow 1842- *ApCAB*
Sparkman, John Jackson 1899- *BiDrAC*
Sparkman, Stephen Milancthon 1849-1929
BiDrAC, NatCAB 6, WhAm 4, WhAmP
Sparks, Arthur Watson 1870?-1919 *IIBEAAW,
WhAm 1*

Sparks, Charles Isaac 1872-1937 *BiDrAC,*
WhAm 1
Sparks, Chauncey 1884-1968 *WhAm 5*
Sparks, Edward *NewYHSD*
Sparks, Edwin Erle 1859-1924 *NatCAB 20*
Sparks, Edwin Erle 1860-1924 *DcAmB,*
WhAm 1
Sparks, Frank Hugh 1891-1964 *NatCAB 54,*
WhAm 4
Sparks, Frank Melville 1877-1950 *WhAm 3*
Sparks, George McIntosh 1888-1958
NatCAB 52, WhAm 3
Sparks, Jared 1789-1866 *AmBi, ApCAB,*
BiDAmEd, DcAmB, Drake, EncAB,
McGEWB, NatCAB 5, TwCBDA,
WebAB, WhAm H
Sparks, John 1843-1908 *NatCAB 26,*
WhAm 1
Sparks, Joseph 1865- *WhAm 4*
Sparks, N R 1900-1972 *WhAm 5*
Sparks, Sir T Ashley 1877-1963 *WhAm 4*
Sparks, Thomas Ayres 1881-1954 *WhAm 3*
Sparks, Thomas J 1868-1946 *WhAm 2*
Sparks, Will 1862-1937 *IIBEAAW, WhAm 1*
Sparks, Will Morris 1872-1950 *NatCAB 40,*
WhAm 2
Sparks, William Andrew Jackson 1828-1904
BiAUS, BiDrAC, DcAmB, TwCBDA,
WhAmP
Sparks, William F *IIBEAAW*
Sparks, William Harris 1800-1882 *TwCBDA*
Sparks, William Henry 1800-1882 *ApCAB,*
NatCAB 5, WhAm H
Sparling, Edna McKenzie 1865- *WomWWA 14*
Sparling, Maurice Clinton 1898-1965
NatCAB 51
Sparling, Samuel Edwin 1866- *WhAm 4*
Sparre, Fin 1879-1944 *NatCAB 33*
Sparrow, Carroll Mason 1880-1941 *WhAm 1*
Sparrow, Edward 1810-1882 *BiDConf*
Sparrow, Edward Wheeler 1846-1913
ApCAB X, NatCAB 49
Sparrow, Patrick J 1802-1867 *NatCAB 2*
Sparrow, Ray F 1898-1961 *WhAm 4*
Sparrow, Stanwood Willston 1888-1952
NatCAB 44, WhAm 3
Sparrow, Thomas 1746?- *BnEnAmA,*
NewYHSD
Sparrow, William 1801-1874 *ApCAB, DcAmB,*
NatCAB 5, WhAm H
Sparrow, William S 1875- *WhoColR*
Sparrow, William Warburton Knox 1870-1939
WhAm 1
Sparrow, William Warburton Knox 1879-1939
NatCAB 29
Spartacus d071BC *McGEWB*
Spates, John *NewYHSD*
Spatta, George 1893- *WhAm 5*
Spaulding, Alice Howard 1878- *WomWWA 14*
Spaulding, Charles Clinton 1874-1952
DcAmB S5, NatCAB 42, WhoColR
Spaulding, Charles Kent 1865-1938 *NatCAB 27*
Spaulding, Charles Walter, Jr. 1889-1970
NatCAB 56
Spaulding, Edward 1824- *ApCAB*
Spaulding, Edward Gleason 1873-1940
DcAmB S2, NatCAB 31, WhAm 1
Spaulding, Elbridge Gerry 1809-1897 *ApCAB,*
BiAUS, BiDrAC, DcAmB, NatCAB 6,
TwCBDA, WhAm H
Spaulding, Elsie Myers *WomWWA 14*
Spaulding, Eugene Ristine 1889-1966 *WhAm 5*
Spaulding, Forrest Brisbin 1892-1965 *WhAm 4*
Spaulding, Francesca DiMaria *WomWWA 14*
Spaulding, Francis Trow 1896-1950 *WhAm 3*
Spaulding, Frank Ellsworth 1866-1960
BiDAmEd, WhAm 4
Spaulding, Frederic Henry 1892-1974 *WhAm 6*
Spaulding, George Lawson 1864-1921 *WhAm 1*
Spaulding, Grace *IIBEAAW*
Spaulding, Helim G 1869-1943 *WhAm 2*
Spaulding, Henry Foster 1816-1893 *NatCAB 5*
Spaulding, Henry George 1837-1920
NatCAB 18, WhAm 4
Spaulding, Huntley Norvel 1869-1955
ApCAB X
Spaulding, Huntley Nowell 1869-1955 *WhAm 3*
Spaulding, John Cecil 1879-1954 *WhAm 3*

Spaulding, John Pearson 1923-1974 *WhAm 6*
Spaulding, Leila Clement 1878- *WomWWA 14*
Spaulding, Levi 1791-1873 *ApCAB, DcAmB,*
WhAm H
Spaulding, Major Franklin 1900-1964 *WhAm 4*
Spaulding, Mary Elizabeth Trow
WomWWA 14
Spaulding, Nathan Weston 1829- *ApCAB,*
NatCAB 13, WhAm 1
Spaulding, Oliver Lyman 1833-1922 *BiDrAC,*
DcAmB, NatCAB 20, TwCBDA,
WhAm 1
Spaulding, Oliver Lyman 1875-1947
NatCAB 35, WhAm 2
Spaulding, Ralph Edgar 1884-1950 *NatCAB 38*
Spaulding, Rolland Harty 1873-1942
NatCAB 18, WhAm 2
Spaulding, Solomon 1761-1816 *ApCAB*
Spaulding, Solomon *see also* Spalding, Solomon
Spaulding, Sumner 1892-1952 *WhAm 3*
Spaulding, William 1881-1954 *NatCAB 43*
Spaulding, William Stuart 1865-1937 *WhAm 1*
Spayd, Milferd Aaron 1900-1965 *WhAm 5*
Speakman, Esther *NewYHSD*
Speakman, Frank L 1874- *WhAm 5*
Speakman, G Dixon 1903-1956 *NatCAB 50,*
WhAm 3
Speakman, Harold 1888-1928 *WhAm 1*
Speakman, Willard Allen 1864-1936
NatCAB 38
Speakman, William Cyrus 1868-1930
NatCAB 22
Speaks, John 1896-1965 *NatCAB 51*
Speaks, John Charles 1859-1945 *BiDrAC,*
NatCAB 34, WhAm 2
Speaks, Oley 1874-1948 *DcAmB S4*
Speaks, Oley 1876-1948 *NatCAB 41,*
WhAm 2
Spear, Albert Moore 1852-1929 *NatCAB 21,*
WhAm 1
Spear, Arthur Prince 1879-1959 *WhAm 4*
Spear, Catherine Swan Brown 1814- *AmWom*
Spear, Charles 1801-1863 *ApCAB, DcAmB,*
Drake, WhAm H
Spear, Ellis 1834-1917 *ApCAB, NatCAB 13,*
WhAm 1
Spear, Ellwood Barker 1875- *WhAm 5*
Spear, Frank Bennett 1872-1949 *NatCAB 44*
Spear, James Milton 1843-1921 *NatCAB 28*
Spear, John William 1856-1943 *NatCAB 40*
Spear, John William 1859-1943 *WhAm 2*
Spear, Joseph *NewYHSD*
Spear, Lawrence York 1870-1950 *NatCAB 38,*
WhAm 3
Spear, Lewis Benson 1868-1959 *WhAm 3*
Spear, Nathaniel 1867-1947 *WhAm 2*
Spear, Rachel Cooper 1879- *WomWWA 14*
Spear, Ray 1878- *WhAm 6*
Spear, Samuel P 1815-1875 *ApCAB*
Spear, Samuel Thayer 1812-1891 *ApCAB,*
NatCAB 3, WhAm H
Spear, Thomas Truman 1803-1882? *NewYHSD*
Spear, Walter Evans 1874-1940 *NatCAB 30*
Spear, William F *NewYHSD*
Spear, William Thomas 1833-1913 *NatCAB 18*
Spear, William Thomas 1834-1913 *DcAmB,*
NatCAB 12, WhAm 1
Speare, Charles Frederic 1874-1961 *WhAm 4*
Speare, Dorothy 1897-1951 *NatCAB 40,*
WhAm 3
Speare, Edward Ray 1872-1960 *WhAm 4*
Speare, Frank Palmer 1869- *WhAm 5*
Speare, Morris Edmund d1974 *WhAm 6*
Speare, Sceva 1868-1964 *NatCAB 51*
Speare, William Martin 1908-1968 *WhAm 5*
Spearing, J Zach 1864-1942 *WhAm 2*
Spearing, James Zacharie 1864-1942 *BiDrAC*
Spearing, Joseph Hall 1853- *WhAm 4*
Spearing, Thomas P *NewYHSD*
Spearl, George 1882-1948 *WhAm 2*
Spearman, Frank Hamilton 1859-1937 *AmBi,*
NatCAB 28, WhAm 1
Spears, John Randolph 1850-1936 *NatCAB 9,*
WhAm 1
Spears, Lawrence Napoleon 1880- *WhAm 6*
Spears, Raymond Smiley 1876-1950 *WhAm 4*
Spears, Samuel Tilden 1877-1936 *WhAm 1*
Spears, William Oscar 1885-1966 *NatCAB 54,*

WhAm 4
Spease, Edward 1883-1957 *NatCAB 46,*
WhAm 3
Specht, Frederick William 1890-1973 *WhAm 6*
Speck, Frank Gouldsmith 1881-1950
DcAmB S4, WhAm 2A
Speck, William Alfred 1864-1928 *NatCAB 29*
Specthrie, Samuel Waldo 1908-1973 *WhAm 6*
Spector, Benjamin 1893-1976 *WhAm 6*
Spectorsky, Auguste C 1910-1972 *WhAm 5*
Spedding, Frank Harold 1902- *AsBiEn*
Spee, Maximilian Graf Von 1861-1914
WhoMilH
Speece, Conrad 1776-1836 *ApCAB, Drake*
Speed, Bessie Frances *WomWWA 14*
Speed, Carleton Donaldson, Jr. 1903-1970
NatCAB 55
Speed, Horace 1852- *WhAm 4*
Speed, James 1812-1887 *AmBi, ApCAB,*
BiAUS, BiDrUSE, DcAmB, Drake,
NatCAB 2, TwCBDA, WhAm H
Speed, James Breckinridge 1844-1912
NatCAB 39, WhAm 1
Speed, John Gilmer 1852-1909 *ApCAB*
Speed, John Gilmer 1853-1909 *NatCAB 10,*
TwCBDA, WhAm 1
Speed, Joshua Fry 1814-1882 *ApCAB*
Speed, Keats 1879-1952 *WhAm 3*
Speed, Kellogg 1879-1955 *NatCAB 45,*
WhAm 3
Speed, Thomas 1768-1842 *BiAUS, BiDrAC,*
WhAm H
Speed, Thomas 1841- *WhAm 4*
Speed, U Grant 1935?- *IIBEAAW*
Speed, Virginia Perrin 1881- *WhAm 5*
Speed, William Shallcross 1873-1955
NatCAB 50, WhAm 3
Speer, Albert 1905- *WhWW-II*
Speer, Alfred Alten 1858-1935 *WhAm 1*
Speer, Emma Bailey 1872-1961 *NatCAB 52,*
WhAm 4
Speer, Emory 1848-1918 *BiDrAC, DcAmB,*
NatCAB 6, TwCBDA, WhAm 1
Speer, J Ramsey 1870-1941 *WhAm 2*
Speer, James Henry 1867-1952 *WhAm 3*
Speer, John 1817- *NatCAB 7*
Speer, Peter Moore 1862-1933 *BiDrAC,*
NatCAB 24, WhAm 1
Speer, Robert Elliott 1867-1947 *DcAmB S4,*
DcAmReB, NatCAB 36, TwCBDA,
WhAm 2
Speer, Robert Kenneth 1898-1959 *WhAm 3*
Speer, Robert Milton 1838-1890 *BiAUS,*
BiDrAC, WhAm H
Speer, Robert Walter 1855-1918 *NatCAB 18,*
WhAm 1
Speer, Theodora Armstrong *WomWWA 14*
Speer, Thomas Jefferson 1837-1872 *BiDrAC,*
WhAm H
Speer, William 1822-1904 *ApCAB, DcAmB,*
TwCBDA, WhAm 1
Speer, William H 1868-1959 *WhAm 3*
Speer, William McMurtrie 1865-1923 *WhAm 1*
Speers, Chester Henry 1860- *WhAm 4*
Speers, James M 1862-1941 *WhAm 1*
Speers, John Boyd 1830-1895 *NatCAB 12*
Speers, Theodore Cuyler 1899-1964 *NatCAB 53,*
WhAm 4
Speers, Wallace Carter 1896-1963 *NatCAB 51*
Speers, William Ewing 1889-1960 *NatCAB 48,*
WhAm 4
Speicher, Eugene Edward 1883-1962 *BnEnAmA,*
WhAm 4
Speidel, Edward 1859-1948 *WhAm 2*
Speidel, Frederick George 1889-1944
NatCAB 39
Speidel, Hans 1897- *WhWW-II*
Speidel, John George 1855- *NatCAB 17*
Speidel, Merritt Charles 1879-1960 *WhAm 3*
Speidel, Thomas D 1908-1957 *WhAm 3*
Speiden, Clement Coote 1866-1926 *ApCAB X,*
NatCAB 27
Speight, Jesse 1795-1847 *ApCAB, BiAUS,*
BiDrAC, NatCAB 11, TwCBDA,
WhAm H, WhAmP
Speir, Louis Dean 1869-1967 *NatCAB 53*
Speir, Samuel Fleet 1838-1895 *ApCAB,*
DcAmB, NatCAB 4, WhAm H

Speirs, Richard Joseph 1903-1967 *NatCAB 54*
Speiser, Ephraim Avigdor 1902-1965 *WhAm 4*
Speiser, Mortimer Dudley 1899-1967
 NatCAB 52
Speke, John Hanning 1827-1864 *McGEWB*
Spekke, Arnolds 1887-1972 *WhAm 5*
Spelfogel, Morris Richard 1907-1969 *WhAm 5*
Spellacy, Edmund Frank 1906-1968 *WhAm 5*
Spellacy, Thomas Joseph 1880-1957 *WhAm 3*
Spellman, Cardinal Francis Joseph 1889-1967
 DcAmReB, EncAB, McGEWB, WebAB,
 WhAm 4
Spellmeyer, Henry 1847-1910 *NatCAB 13,*
 WhAm 1
Spelman, Deborah Rose d1822 *BiCAW*
Spelman, Henry 1600?-1622 *ApCAB, Drake*
Spelman, John Dillon 1889-1929 *NatCAB 22*
Spelman, Lucy Henry 1810-1897 *BiCAW*
Spelsberg, Walter William 1900-1966
 NatCAB 53
Spemann, Hans 1869-1941 *AsBiEn, DcScB,*
 McGEWB
Spence, Brent 1874-1967 *BiDrAC, WhAm 4A,*
 WhAmP
Spence, Carroll 1818-1896 *BiAUS,*
 NatCAB 12
Spence, Cary Fletcher 1869-1943 *NatCAB 33*
Spence, Clara Beebe 1862-1923 *NatCAB 20,*
 WhAm 1
Spence, David 1881-1957 *NatCAB 46*
Spence, Fannie 1864- *WomWWA 14*
Spence, Frederick 1872-1943 *WhAm 2*
Spence, Homer Roberts 1891-1973 *NatCAB 57,*
 WhAm 6
Spence, John 1766-1829 *ApCAB*
Spence, John Fletcher 1828-1912 *NatCAB 1,*
 TwCBDA, WhAm 1
Spence, John Lee 1863- *WhAm 4*
Spence, John Selby 1788-1840 *ApCAB, BiAUS,*
 BiDrAC, NatCAB 7, TwCBDA,
 WhAm H, WhAmP
Spence, John Selby 1909-1973 *WhAm 5*
Spence, Kenneth Monroe 1886-1957 *WhAm 3*
Spence, Kenneth Wartinbee 1907-1967
 WhAm 4
Spence, Matthew Johnstone 1907-1966
 NatCAB 53
Spence, Robert Trail 1785?-1826 *Drake*
Spence, Robert Traill 1785?-1826 *TwCBDA*
Spence, Robert Traill 1785?-1827 *ApCAB*
Spence, Thomas A 1810-1877 *BiAUS*
Spence, Thomas Adam 1810-1877 *ApCAB*
Spence, Thomas Ara 1810-1877 *BiDrAC,*
 WhAm H, WhAmP
Spence, Thomas Humphreys 1867-1937
 NatCAB 27
Spence, Walter 1867- *WhAm 4*
Spence, William Grant 1885-1954 *NatCAB 42*
Spence, William H 1875-1935 *WhAm 1*
Spence, William Kenneth 1898-1967 *WhAm 4*
Spencer, Abner Peck *ApCAB*
Spencer, Alfred, Jr. 1851-1934 *NatCAB 26,*
 WhAm 1
Spencer, Almon Edwin 1867- *WhAm 4*
Spencer, Ambrose 1765-1848 *ApCAB, BiAUS,*
 BiDrAC, DcAmB, Drake, NatCAB 3,
 TwCBDA, WhAm H, WhAmP
Spencer, Anna Carpenter Garlin 1851-1931
 AmBi, DcAmB, NotAW, WhAm 1,
 WhAmP, WomWWA 14
Spencer, Arthur Coe 1871- *WhAm 5*
Spencer, Asa 1747-1828 *ApCAB, NatCAB 3*
Spencer, Asa 1805?- *NewYHSD*
Spencer, Asa, Jr. *NewYHSD*
Spencer, Aubrey George 1785-1872 *ApCAB*
Spencer, Bella Zilfa 1840?-1867 *ApCAB,*
 Drake
Spencer, Benjamin R *NewYHSD*
Spencer, Bertrand Edwin 1884-1941
 NatCAB 30
Spencer, Bunyan 1854-1932 *WhAm 1*
Spencer, Byron 1893-1964 *WhAm 4*
Spencer, C Luther 1887-1960 *NatCAB 48,*
 WhAm 4
Spencer, Caroline Elizabeth 1861-1928
 NatCAB 21
Spencer, Charles Achilles 1813-1881
 NatCAB 13

Spencer, Charles Eldridge, Jr. 1882-1953
 WhAm 3
Spencer, Charles Winthrop 1868-1928
 NatCAB 21
Spencer, Christopher Miner 1833-1922 *DcAmB,*
 NatCAB 13, NatCAB 22
Spencer, Clarence Garfield 1881-1964
 NatCAB 51
Spencer, Claudius Buchanan 1856-1934
 WhAm 1
Spencer, Clayton C 1894-1972 *WhAm 6*
Spencer, Cornelia Ann Phillips 1825-1908
 ApCAB, DcAmB, NotAW, TwCBDA
Spencer, Corwin H 1851-1906 *NatCAB 12,*
 WhAm 1
Spencer, Dumaresq 1895-1918 *NatCAB 21*
Spencer, Earl Elwen 1889-1937 *NatCAB 27*
Spencer, Earl Winfield 1852- *NatCAB 17*
Spencer, Edgar A 1847-1911 *WhAm 1*
Spencer, Edward Buckham Taylor 1863-1945
 NatCAB 34, WhAm 2
Spencer, Elihu 1721-1784 *ApCAB, DcAmB,*
 Drake, NatCAB 5, WhAm H
Spencer, Elijah 1775-1852 *BiAUS, BiDrAC,*
 WhAm H
Spencer, Elizabeth C 1878- *WomWWA 14*
Spencer, Elizabeth Dwight 1841-
 WomWWA 14
Spencer, Ema 1862- *WomWWA 14*
Spencer, Emily Meredith Read *WomWWA 14*
Spencer, Evelene Armstrong 1867- *WhAm 4*
Spencer, F Erle 1891-1955 *NatCAB 42*
Spencer, Fannie M 1860?- *NatCAB 11*
Spencer, Francis Elias 1834- *ApCAB*
Spencer, Francis Marion 1842-1930 *WhAm 1*
Spencer, Frank E 1884-1952 *WhAm 3*
Spencer, Frank Robert 1879-1957 *WhAm 3*
Spencer, Frederick Asher 1885-1952
 NatCAB 40
Spencer, Frederick Collins 1863-1935
 NatCAB 27
Spencer, Frederick R 1806-1875 *ApCAB,*
 NatCAB 5, NewYHSD
Spencer, G P *NewYHSD*
Spencer, George Albert 1914-1973 *WhAm 5*
Spencer, George Eliphaz 1835-1893 *BiAUS*
Spencer, George Eliphaz 1836-1893 *ApCAB,*
 BiDrAC, NatCAB 13, TwCBDA,
 WhAm H
Spencer, George Hazelton 1866-1936 *WhAm 1*
Spencer, George Lloyd 1893- *BiDrAC*
Spencer, George Moreland 1871-1938
 NatCAB 30
Spencer, Gertrude Armstrong 1874-
 WomWWA 14
Spencer, Gertrude Longworth 1881-
 WomWWA 14
Spencer, Grace Ione *WomWWA 14*
Spencer, Guilford Lawson 1858-1925 *WhAm 1*
Spencer, Guy Raymond 1878- *WhAm 6*
Spencer, Harley Orton 1916-1974 *WhAm 6*
Spencer, Hazelton 1893-1944 *WhAm 2*
Spencer, Henry Benning 1872-1956 *NatCAB 45*
Spencer, Henry James 1884-1944 *NatCAB 33*
Spencer, Henry Russell 1879-1970 *WhAm 5*
Spencer, Herbert 1820-1903 *AsBiEn, DcScB,*
 McGEWB, WhAm H
Spencer, Herbert 1879-1969 *NatCAB 56*
Spencer, Herbert Lincoln 1894-1960
 NatCAB 51, WhAm 3
Spencer, Herbert Ransom 1856- *NatCAB 16*
Spencer, Herbert Reynolds 1894-1968
 NatCAB 56
Spencer, Herbert Ruthven 1849-1900
 NatCAB 13
Spencer, Hiram Ladd 1829- *NatCAB 7*
Spencer, Horatio Nelson 1842-1915 *NatCAB 5,*
 WhAm 1
Spencer, Howard Bonnell 1870- *WhAm 6*
Spencer, Ichabod Smith 1798-1854 *ApCAB,*
 Drake, NatCAB 5, WhAm H
Spencer, Ira Hobart 1873-1928 *NatCAB 21*
Spencer, Irene Keyes 1892-1971 *WhAm 6*
Spencer, J Brookes 1888-1959 *WhAm 3*
Spencer, J C *NewYHSD*
Spencer, J W 1851-1921 *WhAm 1*
Spencer, James Bradley 1781-1848 *ApCAB,*
 BiAUS, BiDrAC, WhAm H

Spencer, James Clark 1826-1901 *ApCAB,*
 WhAm 1
Spencer, James Clark 1827-1901 *NatCAB 1*
Spencer, James Grafton 1844-1926 *BiDrAC*
Spencer, James Harland 1908-1970 *WhAm 5*
Spencer, James Morton 1854- *WhAm 4*
Spencer, Jesse Ames 1816-1898 *ApCAB,*
 DcAmB, Drake, TwCBDA, WhAm H
Spencer, Job B 1829- *NewYHSD*
Spencer, John 1885-1957 *WhAm 3*
Spencer, John C 1787-1855 *BiAUS*
Spencer, John Canfield 1788-1855 *AmBi,*
 ApCAB, BiDrAC, BiDrUSE, DcAmB,
 Drake, NatCAB 6, TwCBDA, WhAm H,
 WhAmP
Spencer, John Mitchell 1883-1954 *WhAm 3*
Spencer, John R 1854- *WhAm 4*
Spencer, John Thompson 1846-1924
 NatCAB 45
Spencer, John Wesley 1864-1939 *WhAm 1*
Spencer, Joseph 1714-1789 *ApCAB, BiAUS,*
 BiDrAC, DcAmB, Drake, NatCAB 1,
 WebAMB, WhAm H
Spencer, Joseph B *NewYHSD*
Spencer, Joseph William 1850- *ApCAB*
Spencer, Joseph William Winthrop 1851-
 NatCAB 14
Spencer, Josephine *AmWom*
Spencer, Joshua Austin 1790-1857 *ApCAB Sup*
Spencer, Kenneth 1888-1946 *NatCAB 35,*
 WhAm 2
Spencer, Kenneth Aldred 1902-1960
 NatCAB 49, WhAm 3
Spencer, Lee Bowen 1914-1970 *WhAm 5*
Spencer, Leonard James 1870-1959 *DcScB*
Spencer, Lilian Graham 1855- *WomWWA 14*
Spencer, Lilian White d1953 *WhAm 3*
Spencer, Lilly Martin 1822-1902 *NotAW*
Spencer, Lily Martin 1822-1902 *NewYHSD*
Spencer, Lorillard 1827-1888 *ApCAB X*
Spencer, Lorillard 1859-1912 *NatCAB 16*
Spencer, Lorillard 1860-1912 *ApCAB X,*
 WhAm 1
Spencer, Lorillard 1883-1939 *NatCAB 28,*
 WhAm 1
Spencer, Lyle Manly 1911-1968 *WhAm 5*
Spencer, Lyman Potter 1840-1915 *NatCAB 18,*
 NewYHSD
Spencer, M Lyle 1881-1969 *WhAm 5*
Spencer, Margaret Smith Henry 1850-
 WomWWA 14
Spencer, Mary 1835-1923 *NewYHSD*
Spencer, Mary Acheson 1863- *WomWWA 14*
Spencer, Mary Cass *WomWWA 14*
Spencer, Mary R *WomWWA 14*
Spencer, Nelson Stanley 1856-1934 *NatCAB 33*
Spencer, Nelson Strong 1857-1949 *NatCAB 37*
Spencer, Nicholas d1689 *NatCAB 13*
Spencer, Niles 1893-1952 *BnEnAmA,*
 WhAm 3
Spencer, Oliver Martin 1849-1924 *WhAm 1*
Spencer, Omar Corwin 1881-1964 *NatCAB 50,*
 WhAm 6
Spencer, Paul 1866-1927 *NatCAB 26,*
 WhAm 1
Spencer, Paul Bertram 1881-1932 *NatCAB 23*
Spencer, Percy Craig 1893-1969 *WhAm 5*
Spencer, Percy Lebaron 1894-1970 *WhAm 5*
Spencer, Pitman Clemens 1793-1860 *DcAmB,*
 WhAm H
Spencer, Pitman Curtius 1790-1861 *ApCAB*
Spencer, Platt R 1801-1864 *Drake*
Spencer, Platt Rogers 1800-1864 *AmBi,*
 ApCAB, BiDAmEd, DcAmB, NatCAB 8,
 TwCBDA, WhAm H
Spencer, Richard 1796-1868 *BiAUS, BiDrAC,*
 WhAm H
Spencer, Richard 1902-1962 *WhAm 4*
Spencer, Richard Pratt 1820-1910 *NatCAB 28*
Spencer, Robert 1879-1931 *AmBi, DcAmB,*
 WhAm 1
Spencer, Robert Closson 1829-1916 *NatCAB 8*
Spencer, Robert Closson, Jr. 1864-1953
 NatCAB 42, WhAm 3
Spencer, Robert Lyle 1887-1945 *WhAm 2*
Spencer, Robert Nelson 1877- *WhAm 5*
Spencer, Samuel 1847-1906 *ApCAB X,*
 DcAmB, NatCAB 12, NatCAB 14,

WhAm 1

Spencer, Samuel Riley 1874-1953 *WhAm 3*
Spencer, Sara Andrews 1837-1909 *AmBi,
ApCAB, WhAm 1*
Spencer, Sarah Elizabeth 1887- *WhoColR*
Spencer, Selden Palmer 1862-1925 *ApCAB X,
BiDrAC, NatCAB 20, WhAm 1,
WhAmP*
Spencer, Selina *NewYHSD*
Spencer, Shelby Cruthirds 1886-1967
NatCAB 53
Spencer, Theodore 1800-1870 *ApCAB,
NatCAB 5*
Spencer, Theodore 1902-1949 *NatCAB 35,
WhAm 2*
Spencer, Thomas 1793-1857 *ApCAB, Drake,
NatCAB 5, WhAm H*
Spencer, Vernon 1875-1949 *WhAm 2*
Spencer, W H *NewYHSD*
Spencer, Walker Brainerd 1868-1941
NatCAB 44, WhAm 1
Spencer, Walter Tuttle 1869-1928 *ApCAB X*
Spencer, William *NewYHSD*
Spencer, William d1640 *NatCAB 5*
Spencer, William Ambrose 1793-1854 *ApCAB,
Drake, NatCAB 5*
Spencer, William Brainerd 1835-1882 *BiDrAC*
Spencer, William Brinerd 1835-1882 *WhAm H*
Spencer, William Gear 1886-1960 *NatCAB 47*
Spencer, William Homer 1888-1966 *WhAm 4*
Spencer, William L 1879-1960 *WhAm 4*
Spencer, William Loring *ApCAB, WhAm 5*
Spencer, William Vaughan 1899-1940
NatCAB 46, WhAm 1
Spencer, Willing 1877-1952 *NatCAB 45,
WhAm 5*
Spencer Jones, Harold 1890-1960 *DcScB*
Spencer-Nairn, Sir Robert 1880-1960 *WhAm 4*
Spener, Philipp Jakob 1635-1705 *McGEWB*
Spengel, August John 1856-1917 *NatCAB 18*
Spengler, John Arthur 1868-1949 *NatCAB 38*
Spengler, Oswald 1880-1936 *McGEWB*
Spens, Conrad E 1875-1931 *WhAm 1*
Spens, Nathaniel 1838-1916 *IlBEAAW*
Spenser, Edmund 1552?-1599 *McGEWB*
Spenser, Willard 1852-1933 *NatCAB 29*
Spenzer, John George 1864-1932 *WhAm 1,
WhAm 1C*
Speranski, Count Mikhail Mikhailovich
1772-1839 *McGEWB*
Speranza, Gino 1872-1927 *WhAm 1*
Sperber, Jacob d1963 *WhAm 4*
Sperling, Melitta 1899-1973 *WhAm 6*
Spero, Sterling D 1896-1976 *WhAm 6*
Speroni, John L *NewYHSD*
Sperr, Frederick William 1856-1929
NatCAB 21, WhAm 1
Sperrle, Hugo 1885-1953 *WhWW-II*
Sperry, Albert Francis 1900-1962 *NatCAB 52*
Sperry, Charles Stillman 1847-1911 *NatCAB 14,
NatCAB 21, WebAMB, WhAm 1*
Sperry, Earl Evelyn 1875-1939 *NatCAB 29,
WhAm 4*
Sperry, Elmer Ambrose 1860-1930 *AmBi,
ApCAB X, AsBiEn, DcAmB, DcScB,
EncAB, NatCAB 15, NatCAB 23,
WebAB, WhAm 1*
Sperry, Eugene Edward 1876-1945 *NatCAB 34*
Sperry, Frederick Edward 1886-1946
NatCAB 36
Sperry, John Alexander 1896-1964 *NatCAB 51*
Sperry, Leavenworth Porter 1883-1958
NatCAB 43, WhAm 3
Sperry, Leonard Boyd 1879-1959 *NatCAB 47*
Sperry, Lewis 1848-1922 *BiDrAC, NatCAB 7,
WhAm 4*
Sperry, Lyman Beecher 1841-1923 *WhAm 1*
Sperry, Marcy Leavenworth 1877-1949
NatCAB 38, WhAm 2
Sperry, Mark Leavenworth 1842-1926
NatCAB 44
Sperry, Nehemiah Day 1827-1911 *BiDrAC,
DcAmB, TwCBDA, WhAm 1, WhAmP*
Sperry, Paul 1879- *WhAm 6*
Sperry, Theodore S 1822- *NewYHSD*
Sperry, Thomas Alexander 1864-1913
NatCAB 15

Sperry, Watson Robertson 1842-1926
NatCAB 1, WhAm 1
Sperry, Willard Gardner 1847- *WhAm 4*
Sperry, Willard Learoyd 1882-1954 *DcAmB S5,
WhAm 3*
Speusippus 408?BC-339BC *DcScB*
Spewack, Samuel 1899-1971 *WhAm 5*
Speyer, Ellin L Prince 1850-1921 *ApCAB X,
NatCAB 25*
Speyer, Ellin Leslie Prince Lowery 1849-1921
NotAW
Speyer, James Joseph 1861-1941 *DcAmB S3,
NatCAB 36, WhAm 1*
Speyer, Leonora 1872-1956 *WhAm 3*
Speyers, Arthur Bayard 1846-1918 *WhAm 1*
Sphujidhvaja *DcScB*
Spicer, Anne Higginson d1935 *WhAm 1*
Spicer, Clarence Winfred 1875-1939 *WhAm 1*
Spicer, Clinton Elbert 1869- *WhAm 5*
Spicer, Edward Holland 1906- *REnAW*
Spicer, Eleanor W d1974 *WhAm 6*
Spicer, Frank William 1878-1950 *NatCAB 38*
Spicer, Henry Russell 1909-1968 *WhAm 5*
Spicer, Mabel Alberta *WomWWA 14*
Spicer, Morgan Vardry 1894-1958 *NatCAB 46*
Spicer, Robert Barclay 1869- *WhAm 5*
Spicer, William Ambrose 1865- *WhAm 5*
Spicer, William Francis 1820-1878 *ApCAB,
TwCBDA*
Spicer-Simson, Margaret 1874- *WhAm 5,
WomWWA 14*
Spicer-Simson, Theodore 1871-1959 *WhAm 3*
Spickelmier, Ernest 1895-1953 *NatCAB 41*
Spicker, Max 1858-1912 *DcAmB*
Spiegel, Adriaan VanDen 1578-1625 *DcScB*
Spiegel, Charles Albert 1861-1926 *NatCAB 20*
Spiegel, Edwin John 1894-1967 *WhAm 4*
Spiegel, Frederick Siegfried 1858-1925
WhAm 1
Spiegel, Frederick William 1898-1975 *WhAm 6*
Spiegel, Modie Joseph d1943 *WhAm 2*
Spiegel, Rollin William 1885-1950 *NatCAB 39*
Spiegelberg, Isaac Newton 1859-1927
ApCAB X, NatCAB 31
Spiegelberg, Willi 1844-1929 *ApCAB X*
Spiegelberg, William Isaac 1863-1932
NatCAB 25
Spiegelius *DcScB*
Spiegle, Charles 1831?- *NewYHSD*
Spieker, Edward Henry 1859-1918 *WhAm 1*
Spieker, George Frederick 1844-1913 *ApCAB,
WhAm 1*
Spielbergen, Georg Van 1557-1621 *ApCAB*
Spieler, George *NewYHSD*
Spieler, William F *NewYHSD*
Spielmacher, John LeRoy 1895-1949
NatCAB 37
Spielman, Marvin Andrew 1906-1957
NatCAB 46
Spielvogel, Siegfried Werner 1892-1959
NatCAB 50
Spier, George William 1854-1924 *NatCAB 20*
Spier, Leslie 1893-1961 *WhAm 4*
Spiering, Theodore Bernays 1871-1925 *DcAmB,
NatCAB 20, WhAm 1*
Spiers, H Waldo 1885-1942 *NatCAB 31*
Spies, Albert 1862-1910 *WhAm 1*
Spies, August Vincent Theodore 1855-1887
ApCAB, WhAm H
Spies, Tom Douglas 1902-1960 *NatCAB 43,
WhAm 3*
Spiess, Carlos Augustus 1899-1964 *WhAm 4*
Spiess, Joseph Charles 1884-1964 *NatCAB 51*
Spieth, Lawrence Caleb 1883-1963 *WhAm 4*
Spight, Thomas 1841-1924 *BiDrAC, WhAmP*
Spigner, W H 1866- *WhoColR*
Spike, Robert Warren 1923-1966 *WhAm 4*
Spillane, Edward 1859- *WhAm 4*
Spillane, Frank Morrison *WebAB*
Spillane, Mickey 1918- *WebAB*
Spillane, Richard 1864-1936 *WhAm 2*
Spiller, Harold Alfred 1895-1965 *WhAm 4*
Spiller, Robert Kent 1878-1949 *NatCAB 38*
Spiller, William Gibson 1863-1940 *NatCAB 29,
WhAm 1*
Spillers, Charles Lee 1901-1962 *WhAm 4*
Spillman, Ora Seldon 1881-1941 *WhAm 1*
Spillman, William Jasper 1863-1931 *DcAmB,*

EncAAH, WhAm 1
Spilman, Bernard Washington 1871-1950
NatCAB 40, WhAm 5
Spilman, Edward Guthrie 1855-1930 *WhAm 1*
Spilman, Lewis Hopkins 1860-1938 *WhAm 1*
Spilman, Robert Scott 1876-1958 *WhAm 3*
Spilman, Robert Scott, Jr. 1908-1969 *WhAm 5*
Spilsbury, Edmund Gybbon 1845-1920 *DcAmB,
WhAm 1*
Spilsbury, Edmund Gybbon 1847-1920
NatCAB 13
Spinden, Herbert Joseph 1879-1967 *WhAm 4*
Spindle, Richard Buckner, Jr. 1886-1954
NatCAB 43
Spindler, Garold Ralph 1902-1961 *WhAm 4*
Spindler, John *NewYHSD*
Spingarn, Arthur B 1878-1971 *WhAm 5*
Spingarn, Joel Elias 1875-1939 *AmBi,
DcAmB S2, EncAB, NatCAB 17,
WebAB, WhAm 1*
Spingold, Nathan Breiter 1886-1958 *WhAm 3*
Spining, George Lawrence 1840-1923 *WhAm 1*
Spink, Cyrus 1793-1859 *BiDrAC, WhAm H*
Spink, Edgar George 1867-1927 *NatCAB 40*
Spink, J G Taylor 1888-1962 *WhAm 4*
Spink, Leland Kenneth 1899-1957 *NatCAB 47*
Spink, Mary Angela 1863-1939 *NatCAB 40,
WhAm 1, WhAm 2, WomWWA 14*
Spink, S L 1831-1881 *BiAUS*
Spink, Solomon Lewis 1831-1881 *BiDrAC,
WhAm H, WhAmP*
Spink, Urbana 1879-1952 *NatCAB 40*
Spinka, Matthew 1890-1972 *WhAm 5*
Spinks, Lewis 1879-1946 *WhAm 2*
Spinner, Francis Elias 1802-1890 *ApCAB,
BiAUS, BiDrAC, DcAmB, Drake,
NatCAB 12, TwCBDA, WhAm H*
Spinney, George Wilbur 1889-1948 *WhAm 2*
Spinney, Louis Bevier 1869-1951 *NatCAB 40,
WhAm 3*
Spinning, Alfred A *NewYHSD*
Spinning, C S *NewYHSD*
Spinning, James M 1892-1973 *WhAm 6*
Spinola, Ambrogio DeFilippo 1569-1630
WhoMilH
Spinola, Francis Barretto 1821-1891 *ApCAB,
BiDrAC, NatCAB 4, TwCBDA,
WhAm H*
Spinoza, Baruch 1632-1677 *McGEWB*
Spire, Georg Von 1496?-1540 *ApCAB*
Spires, Joseph H 1853-1913 *NatCAB 16*
Spiro, Charles 1850-1933 *NatCAB 3,
WhAm 1*
Spiro, Solon 1863-1929 *ApCAB X,
NatCAB 17, WhAm 4*
Spittall, John 1811?- *NewYHSD*
Spitz, Armand Neustadter 1904-1971
NatCAB 56, WhAm 5
Spitz, Leo 1888-1956 *NatCAB 43, WhAm 3*
Spitz, Sophie 1910-1956 *NatCAB 46*
Spitzer, Aaron Bovee 1823-1892 *NatCAB 11*
Spitzer, Adelbert Lorenzo 1852- *NatCAB 11*
Spitzer, Carl Bovee 1877-1962 *NatCAB 51*
Spitzer, Ceilan Milo 1849-1919 *NatCAB 11,
WhAm 1*
Spitzer, Garrett 1817-1891 *NatCAB 11*
Spitzer, Lyman, Jr. 1914- *AsBiEn*
Spitzer, Max 1883-1949 *NatCAB 38*
Spitzer, Nellie Tefft 1874- *WomWWA 14*
Spitzer, Nicholas 1783-1868 *NatCAB 11*
Spitzer, Sidney 1875-1933 *NatCAB 18,
NatCAB 46*
Spitzka, Edward Anthony 1876-1922 *AmBi,
DcAmB, NatCAB 19, WhAm 1*
Spitzka, Edward Charles 1852-1914 *AmBi,
ApCAB, DcAmB, NatCAB 19, WhAm 1*
Spivack, Robert Gerald 1915-1970 *WhAm 5*
Spivak, Charles David 1861-1927 *DcAmB,
WhAm 1*
Spivey, Ludd Myrl 1886-1962 *WhAm 4*
Spivey, Thomas Sawyer 1856-1938 *WhAm 1*
Spix, Johann Baptist Von 1781-1826 *DcScB*
Splane, William Williams 1859-1926
NatCAB 32
Splawn, Andrew Jackson 1845-1917
NatCAB 17
Splint, Sarah Field 1883-1959 *WhAm 3,
WomWWA 14*

Spring, Laurence Ellsworth 1898-1963 *WhAm 4*
Spring, LaVerne Ward 1876-1932 *WhAm 1*
Spring, Leverett Wilson 1840-1917 *DcAmB,*
  TwCBDA, WhAm 1
Spring, Marshall 1742-1818 *Drake*
Spring, Robert 1813-1876 *ApCAB*
Spring, Samuel 1746-1819 *AmBi, ApCAB,*
  DcAmB, Drake, NatCAB 5
Spring, Samuel 1747-1819 *WhAm H*
Spring, Samuel 1888- *WhAm 6*
Spring, Samuel Newton 1875-1952 *WhAm 3*
Spring, Walthere Victor 1848-1911 *DcScB*
Spring, William Arthur 1866-1940 *NatCAB 30*
Spring-Rice, Sir Cecil Arthur 1859-1918
  WhAm 1
Springer, Alfred 1854-1946 *WhAm 2*
Springer, Carlie McClure *WomWWA 14*
Springer, Charles 1857-1932 *DcAmB S1,*
  WhAm 1
Springer, Durand William 1866- *WhAm 4*
Springer, Edward Thomas 1885-1964 *WhAm 4*
Springer, Francis Edwin 1872-1940 *WhAm 1*
Springer, Frank 1848-1927 *DcAmB,*
  NatCAB 20, WhAm 1
Springer, Franklin Wesley 1870-1933 *WhAm 1*
Springer, George Peter 1919-1972 *WhAm 5*
Springer, Gertrude Lynch 1869- *WomWWA 14*
Springer, John Franklin 1866-1943 *WhAm 2*
Springer, John McKendree 1873- *WhAm 5*
Springer, John Wallace 1859- *WhAm 4*
Springer, Marguerite Warren 1872- *ApCAB X*
Springer, Raymond Smiley 1882-1947 *BiDrAC,*
  NatCAB 36, WhAm 2, WhAmP
Springer, Rebecca Ruter 1832-1904 *AmWom,*
  ApCAB, TwCBDA, WhAm 1
Springer, Reuben Runyan 1800-1884 *ApCAB,*
  DcAmB, WhAm H
Springer, Russell Severance 1880-1953
  NatCAB 47
Springer, Thomas Grant 1873- *WhAm 5*
Springer, Warren 1844-1912 *ApCAB X*
Springer, Willard, Jr. 1886-1956 *NatCAB 44*
Springer, William Lee 1909- *BiDrAC*
Springer, William McKendree 1836-1903
  ApCAB, BiAUS, BiDrAC, DcAmB,
  NatCAB 11, TwCBDA, WhAm 1,
  WhAmP
Springfield, John Frank 1862-1955 *NatCAB 44*
Springford, Herbert Henry 1878-1942
  NatCAB 31
Springhorn, Carl 1887-1971 *WhAm 5*
Springmeyer, George 1881-1955 *WhAm 6*
Springmeyer, George Adolphus 1883-1955
  NatCAB 44
Springmeyer, Henry Edward 1901-1968
  NatCAB 54
Springs, Andrew Wilton 1869- *WhoColR*
Springs, Birdie E McLain 1886- *WhoColR*
Springs, Eli Baxter 1852-1933 *NatCAB 24*
Springs, Elliot White 1896-1959 *WebAB,*
  WebAMB
Springs, Elliott White 1896-1959 *NatCAB 48,*
  WhAm 3
Springs, Holmes Buck 1879-1951 *WhAm 3*
Springs, Lena Jones *ApCAB X, BiCAW*
Springs, Mrs. Leroy d1942 *WhAm 2*
Springs, Leroy 1861-1931 *WhAm 1*
Springweiler, Erwin Frederick 1896-1968
  WhAm 5
Sproat, Ebenezer 1752-1805 *ApCAB, Drake*
Sprogell, Harry E 1911-1972 *WhAm 6*
Sprong, Severn D 1873-1946 *WhAm 2*
Spross, Charles Gilbert 1874-1961 *WhAm 4,*
  WhAm 5
Sprott, Jarl Sigurd 1881-1949 *NatCAB 37,*
  WhAm 2
Sproul, Elliott Wilford 1856-1935 *BiDrAC,*
  NatCAB 25, WhAm 1
Sproul, John *NewYHSD*
Sproul, Joseph Plummer 1884-1938 *NatCAB 28*
Sproul, Robert Gordon 1891-1975 *BiDAmEd,*
  WhAm 6
Sproul, William Cameron 1870-1928 *DcAmB,*
  NatCAB 21, WhAm 1
Sproul, William Henry 1867-1932 *BiDrAC,*
  WhAm 1, WhAmP
Sproule, Andrew 1831-1912 *NatCAB 17*
Sproule, Charles H 1853-1904 *WhAm 1*

Sproule, Ralph Piggins 1894-1969 *NatCAB 54*
Sproule, William 1858-1935 *DcAmB S1,*
  WhAm 1
Sproull, Thomas 1803-1892 *ApCAB, DcAmB,*
  NatCAB 7, WhAm H
Sproull, William Oliver 1848-1911 *WhAm 1*
Sprour, John *NewYHSD*
Sprouse, Claude Willard 1888-1952 *WhAm 3*
Sprout, Will Carleton 1886- *WhAm 4*
Sprowl, Charles Orr 1877-1955 *NatCAB 42*
Sprowl, James Allen 1906-1963 *NatCAB 50,*
  WhAm 4
Sprowls, Joseph Barnett, Jr. 1912-1971
  WhAm 5
Spruance, Benton M 1904-1967 *WhAm 4A*
Spruance, Frank Palin 1887-1972 *NatCAB 57*
Spruance, Presley 1785-1863 *ApCAB, BiAUS,*
  BiDrAC, NatCAB 4, TwCBDA,
  WhAm H
Spruance, Raymond 1886-1969 *WhWW-II*
Spruance, Raymond Ames 1886-1969
  NatCAB 55, WebAB, WebAMB,
  WhAm 5
Spruance, Raymond Arnes 1886-1969 *WhoMilH*
Spruance, Russell 1890-1960 *NatCAB 49*
Spruance, William Corbit 1831-1913
  NatCAB 33
Spruance, William Corbit 1873-1935 *WhAm 1*
Spruce, Everett Franklin 1908- *IlBEAAW*
Spruce, Richard 1817-1893 *DcScB*
Sprung, Adolf Friedrich Wichard 1848-1909
  DcScB
Sprunger, Elmer 1915?- *IlBEAAW*
Sprunt, Alexander 1852-1937 *WhAm 1*
Sprunt, Alexander, Jr. 1898-1973 *WhAm 5*
Sprunt, James 1846-1924 *DcAmB*
Sprunt, James 1847-1924 *NatCAB 20*
Spruor, John *NewYHSD*
Spry, William d1772 *ApCAB*
Spry, William 1864-1929 *NatCAB 15,*
  WhAm 1
Spurck, Richard Francis 1896-1952 *NatCAB 42*
Spurgeon, William Albertus 1852-1940
  NatCAB 32
Spurgeon, William Porter 1867-1920 *WhAm 1*
Spurgin, William Fletcher 1838-1904 *WhAm 1*
Spurling, Oliver Cromwell 1874- *NatCAB 18*
Spurlock, Isabella Smiley Davis 1843- *AmWom*
Spurney, Anton Benjamin 1879-1950
  NatCAB 39
Spurr, Arthur Clinton 1889-1971 *NatCAB 57*
Spurr, Elizabeth Albright 1870-1934
  NatCAB 27
Spurr, Josiah Edward 1870-1950 *DcAmB S4,*
  WhAm 2A, WhAm 3
Spurr, William Alfred 1905-1975 *WhAm 6*
Spurzheim, Johann Christoph 1776-1832 *DcScB*
Spurzheim, Johann Kaspar 1776-1832 *WhAm H*
Spurzheim, John Gaspard 1776-1832 *Drake*
Spykman, Nicholas John 1893-1943 *WhAm 2*
Squanto d1622 *AmBi, DcAmB, WebAB,*
  WhAm H
Squibb, Edward Hamilton 1853-1929
  NatCAB 32
Squibb, Edward Robinson 1819-1900 *DcAmB,*
  NatCAB 19, WebAB, WhAm H
Squier, Carl B 1893-1967 *WhAm 4A*
Squier, Ephraim George 1821-1888 *AmBi,*
  ApCAB, BiAUS, DcAmB, Drake,
  NatCAB 4, TwCBDA, WhAm H
Squier, Frank 1840- *NatCAB 3*
Squier, George Owen 1865-1934 *AmBi,*
  DcAmB, NatCAB 24, WhAm 1
Squier, Herbert Northrup 1880-1963
  NatCAB 50
Squier, J Bentley 1873-1948 *NatCAB 35,*
  WhAm 2
Squier, Lee Welling 1859- *WhAm 4*
Squier, Miles Powell 1792-1866 *ApCAB,*
  NatCAB 8, WhAm H
Squier, Rosie Gardner 1876- *WomWWA 14*
Squiers, Arnon Lyon 1869-1921 *WhAm 1*
Squiers, Herbert Goldsmith 1859-1911 *DcAmB,*
  NatCAB 14, WhAm 1
Squire, Amos Osborne 1876-1949 *WhAm 2*
Squire, Andrew 1850-1934 *ApCAB X,*
  NatCAB 9, WhAm 1
Squire, Carrie Ranson 1869- *WomWWA 14*

Squire, Edward Jacob 1886-1967 *WhAm 4A*
Squire, Feargus O'Conner Bowden 1850-1932
  NatCAB 24
Squire, Frances 1867-1914 *WhAm 1*
Squire, Francis Hagar 1902-1956 *WhAm 3*
Squire, John Peter 1819-1893 *NatCAB 2*
Squire, Mary E 1859- *BiCAW*
Squire, Watson Carbosso 1838-1926 *TwCBDA*
Squire, Watson Carvosso 1838-1926
  ApCAB Sup, BiDrAC, DcAmB,
  NatCAB 3, NatCAB 27, WhAm 1,
  WhAmP
Squire-Potter, Frances 1867- *WomWWA 14*
Squires, Alden Wood 1906-1971 *NatCAB 56*
Squires, C Clyde 1883-1970 *IlBEAAW*
Squires, Charles William 1877-1948 *WhAm 2*
Squires, David Denton 1906-1973 *WhAm 6*
Squires, George Forbes 1894-1956 *WhAm 3*
Squires, Grant 1863-1928 *NatCAB 26*
Squires, Henry 1850-1928 *IlBEAAW*
Squires, James Duane 1904- *BiDAmEd*
Squires, Lawrence 1887-1928 *IlBEAAW*
Squires, Lindley Sturges 1890-1949 *NatCAB 38*
Squires, Mark 1878-1938 *NatCAB 38*
Squires, Mary Smyth *BiCAW, WomWWA 14*
Squires, Ralph Anthony 1906-1962 *WhAm 4*
Squires, S A *NewYHSD*
Squires, Vernon Purinton 1866-1930 *WhAm 1*
Squires, Walter Albion 1874- *WhAm 5*
Squires, William Henry Tappey 1875-1948
  WhAm 2
Sridhara *DcScB*
Sripati *DcScB*
Ssu-Ma, Ch'ien 145BC-090?BC *McGEWB*
Ssu-Ma, Hsiang-Ju 179?BC-117BC *McGEWB*
Ssu-Ma, Kuang 1019-1086 *McGEWB*
Staack, John George 1878- *WhAm 6*
Staaf, Oscar 1880-1958 *WhAm 3*
Staake, William Heaton 1846-1924 *WhAm 1*
Stabler, Herman 1879-1942 *WhAm 2*
Stabler, Howard Douglas 1887-1963 *WhAm 4*
Stabler, James Pleasants 1839- *WhAm 4*
Stabler, John Gates 1871-1940 *NatCAB 34,*
  WhAm 1
Stabler, Jordan Herbert 1885-1938 *WhAm 1*
Stabler, Laird Joseph 1865-1939 *WhAm 1*
Stableton, John Kay 1858-1939 *WhAm 4*
Stace, Arthur William 1875-1950 *WhAm 2*
Stace, Walter Terence 1886-1967 *NatCAB 55,*
  WhAm 5
Stacey, Alfred Edwin 1846-1940 *WhAm 1*
Stacey, Alfred Edwin, Jr. 1885-1975 *WhAm 6*
Stacey, Anna Lee d1943 *WhAm 2*
Stacey, John Franklin 1859-1941 *WhAm 1*
Stacey, John Markell 1918-1973 *WhAm 6*
Stack, Edmund John 1874-1957 *BiDrAC,*
  WhAm 5
Stack, Edward 1755?- *NatCAB 11*
Stack, Frederic William 1871- *WhAm 5*
Stack, James Aloysius 1887-1951 *NatCAB 37*
Stack, John 1906-1972 *WhAm 5*
Stack, Joseph Michael 1895-1952 *WhAm 3*
Stack, Joseph W 1893-1954 *WhAm 3*
Stack, Michael Joseph 1888-1960 *BiDrAC*
Stack, Morton Myer 1901-1967 *NatCAB 54*
Stackel, Paul Gustav 1862-1919 *DcScB*
Stacker, Antoine *NewYHSD*
Stackhouse, Daniel Morrell 1866-1943
  NatCAB 34
Stackhouse, Eli Thomas 1824-1892 *BiDrAC,*
  WhAm H
Stackhouse, Perry James 1875-1944
  NatCAB 33, WhAm 2
Stackhouse, Powell 1840-1927 *NatCAB 22*
Stackhouse, Thomas Bascom 1857-1939
  NatCAB 48
Stackhouse, Wesley Thomas 1865- *WhAm 4*
Stackpole, Albert Hummel 1897-1971 *WhAm 5*
Stackpole, Edward J 1894-1967 *WhAm 4A*
Stackpole, Edward James 1861-1936
  NatCAB 27, WhAm 1
Stackpole, Everett Schermerhorn 1850-
  WhAm 1
Stackpole, Harrison Clinton 1875-1945
  NatCAB 43
Stackpole, James Hall 1902-1964 *WhAm 4*
Stackpole, Joseph Lewis 1838-1904 *ApCAB X*
Stackpole, Patrick M *NewYHSD*

Stackpole, Pierpont L 1875-1936 *WhAm 1*
Stacy, James 1830- *ApCAB*
Stacy, Merrill E d1966 *WhAm 4*
Stacy, Thomas Ford 1891-1962 *NatCAB 49*
Stacy, Thomas Hobbs 1850-1927 *WhAm 1*
Stacy, Walter Parker 1884-1951 *DcAmB S5,*
NatCAB 40, WhAm 3
Stad, Ben 1885-1946 *NatCAB 35*
Stadden, Corry Montague 1870-1916 *WhAm 1*
Stadelman, William Francis 1869-1928
WhAm 1
Staden, Hans 1520-1565? *ApCAB*
Stadie, William Christopher 1886-1959
WhAm 3
Stadler, Charles A 1848- *WhAm 4*
Stadler, Lewis John 1896-1954 *NatCAB 45,*
WhAm 3
Stadler, William Lewis 1897-1972 *WhAm 5*
Stadtfeld *NewYHSD*
Stadtfeld, Joseph 1861-1943 *WhAm 2*
Staebler, Neil Oliver 1905- *BiDrAC*
Stael *NewYHSD*
Stael, Germaine De 1766-1817 *McGEWB*
Stael, Nicolas De 1914-1955 *McGEWB*
Staff, Samuel George 1900-1965 *NatCAB 51*
Stafford, Aaron 1787-1886 *NatCAB 5*
Stafford, Charles Lewis 1844-1930 *WhAm 1*
Stafford, Clarence Eugene 1906-1974 *WhAm 6*
Stafford, Cora Elder 1897-1964 *WhAm 4*
Stafford, Dale Bernard 1908-1973 *WhAm 6*
Stafford, Denis Joseph 1860- *NatCAB 12*
Stafford, Geoffrey Wardle 1898-1958 *WhAm 3*
Stafford, George Thomas 1894-1968
NatCAB 54
Stafford, Harold Earle 1895-1945 *NatCAB 34*
Stafford, John Aloysius 1857- *WhAm 4*
Stafford, John M *NewYHSD*
Stafford, John Richard 1874- *WhAm 5*
Stafford, Leroy Augustus 1869-1923
NatCAB 19
Stafford, Maria Brewster Brooks 1809-
AmWom
Stafford, Maude Humes 1884- *WomWWA 14*
Stafford, Maurice L 1885-1957 *WhAm 3*
Stafford, Ogburn Fletcher 1903-1969
NatCAB 55
Stafford, Orin Fletcher 1873-1941 *WhAm 1*
Stafford, Robert Theodore 1913- *BiDrAC*
Stafford, Thomas Polhill 1866-1942 *WhAm 2*
Stafford, Wendell Phillips 1861- *WhAm 5*
Stafford, William Bascom 1901-1964 *WhAm 4*
Stafford, William Henry 1869-1957 *BiDrAC,*
WhAmP
Stafseth, H J 1890-1968 *WhAm 5*
Stage, Charles Willard 1868-1946 *NatCAB 35*
Stage, Charles Willard 1868-1947 *WhAm 2*
Stage, Miriam Gertrude Kerruish 1870-1929
NatCAB 21, WomWWA 14
Stager, Anson 1825-1885 *ApCAB, DcAmB,*
NatCAB 4, WhAm H
Stager, Emil *NewYHSD*
Stager, John Mickle 1881-1963 *NatCAB 50*
Stagg, Amos Alonzo 1862-1965 *NatCAB 11,*
NatCAB 18, WebAB, WhAm 4
Stagg, Charles d1735 *WhAm H*
Stagg, Charles Tracey 1878-1939 *WhAm 1*
Stagg, James Paul 1862-1927 *NatCAB 21*
Stagg, John Weldon 1864-1915 *WhAm 1*
Stagg, Stella Robertson 1875- *WomWWA 14*
Staggers, Harley Orrin 1907- *BiDrAC*
Stagi, Pietro *NewYHSD*
Stahel, Julius 1825-1912 *ApCAB, DcAmB,*
Drake, NatCAB 4, TwCBDA, WhAm 1
Stahl, Bernice Margaret 1886- *WomWWA 14*
Stahl, Georg Ernst 1659?-1734 *DcScB*
Stahl, Georg Ernst 1660-1734 *AsBiEn,*
McGEWB
Stahl, George Ernst 1660-1734 *BiHiMed*
Stahl, John Meloy 1860-1944 *WhAm 2*
Stahl, Karl Friedrich 1855-1946 *NatCAB 35,*
WhAm 2
Stahl, William Harris 1908-1969 *NatCAB 54,*
WhAm 5
Stahlberg, Frederik 1877-1937 *NatCAB 27*
Stahle, James Alonzo 1829-1912 *BiDrAC*
Stahley, Joseph 1900?- *IIBEAAW*
Stahlman, E B, Jr. 1898-1974 *WhAm 6*
Stahlman, Edward Bushrod 1843-1930 *DcAmB,*

Stahlman, Edward Bushrod 1844-1930
NatCAB 8
Stahlnecker, William Griggs 1849-1902 *BiDrAC*
Stahlschmidt, Arthur Edward 1863- *WhAm 4*
Stahly, Edward Harry 1896-1961 *NatCAB 50*
Stahr, Henry Irvin 1880-1962 *NatCAB 50,*
WhAm 4
Stahr, John Summers 1841-1915 *DcAmB,*
NatCAB 12, TwCBDA, WhAm 1
Stahr, Paul 1883- *IIBEAAW*
Staiger, Monsieur *NewYHSD*
Staigg, Richard M 1820?-1881 *Drake*
Staigg, Richard Morell 1817-1881 *NewYHSD*
Staigg, Richard Morrell 1817-1881 *ApCAB,*
TwCBDA
Stainback, Ingram Macklin 1883-1961 *WhAm 4*
Stainback, Willard Edward 1906-1965
NatCAB 51
Stair, Charles Augustus 1879- *WhAm 6*
Stair, Edward Douglas 1859-1951 *NatCAB 39,*
WhAm 5
Stair, J William 1884-1963 *NatCAB 48*
Staiti, Henry Thomas 1876-1933 *NatCAB 32*
Stakely, Charles A 1903-1965 *WhAm 5*
Stakely, Charles Averett d1937 *WhAm 1*
Stalbaum, Lynn Ellsworth 1920- *BiDrAC*
Stalberg, Jonah 1894-1955 *WhAm 3*
Stalder, Jackson R 1915-1968 *WhAm 5*
Stalder, Walter 1881-1949 *WhAm 2*
Staley, A Rollin 1907-1968 *WhAm 5*
Staley, Allen Conkling 1885-1960 *NatCAB 49,*
WhAm 4
Staley, Augustus Eugene 1867-1940
NatCAB 33, WhAm 1
Staley, Augustus Eugene, Jr. 1903-1975
WhAm 6
Staley, Cady 1840-1928 *DcAmB, NatCAB 11,*
WhAm 4
Staley, Ellis Judd 1877-1943 *NatCAB 41*
Staley, John Richard 1901-1964 *WhAm 4*
Staley, John Wilson 1871-1928 *NatCAB 23,*
WhAm 1
Staley, R C 1888-1963 *WhAm 4*
Stalfort, John Alfred 1887-1954 *NatCAB 51*
Stalin, Joseph Vissarionovich 1879-1953
McGEWB, WhAm 3, WhAm 4,
WhWW-II
Stalions, B R 1905-1955 *NatCAB 42*
Stalker, Arthur William 1860-1930 *WhAm 1*
Stalker, E *NewYHSD*
Stalker, Gale Hamilton 1889- *BiDrAC*
Stalker, John Nellis 1881- *WhAm 6*
Stall, Albert H 1900- *WhAm 6*
Stall, Sylvanus 1847-1915 *ApCAB, WhAm 1*
Stallard, Carton Sherman 1905-1975 *WhAm 6*
Stallcup, John Calhoun 1841-1915 *NatCAB 16*
Stallings, Jesse Francis 1856-1928 *BiDrAC,*
WhAm 4
Stallings, Laurence 1894-1968 *NatCAB 55,*
WhAm 4A
Stallmann, Esther Laverne 1903-1969 *DcAmLiB*
Stallo, Edmund Kittredge 1864-1947
NatCAB 35
Stallo, Johann Bernhard 1823-1900 *DcAmB,*
DcScB
Stallo, John Bernard 1823-1900 *NatCAB 11*
Stallo, John Bernhard 1823-1900 *ApCAB,*
TwCBDA, WhAm 1
Stallworth, James Adams 1822-1861 *BiAUS,*
BiDrAC, WhAm H
Stallworth, Nicholas Eugene 1874-1941
WhAm 1
Stalnaker, Frank Douglas 1860-1932
NatCAB 23
Stalnaker, Frank Douglas 1862-1932 *WhAm 1*
Stalnaker, Luther Winfield 1892-1954 *WhAm 3*
Stam, Colin Ferguson 1896-1966 *NatCAB 52,*
WhAm 4
Stam, Jacob 1899- *WhAm 5*
Stambaugh, Armstrong Alexander 1885-1961
WhAm 4
Stambaugh, Henry H 1858-1919 *NatCAB 20*
Stambaugh, John 1862-1927 *WhAm 1*
Stambul, Joseph 1892-1959 *NatCAB 44*
Stamm, Earle Williams 1894-1963 *NatCAB 50,*
WhAm 4
Stamm, Edward P 1892-1964 *WhAm 4*

Stamm, Frederick Keller 1883-1961 *NatCAB 47*
Stamm, Frederick Keller 1886-1961 *WhAm 4*
Stamm, John Samuel 1878-1956 *NatCAB 43,*
WhAm 3
Stamm, Martin 1847-1918 *NatCAB 21*
Stamm, Vincil R 1901-1968 *WhAm 5*
Stamos, Theodoros 1922- *BnEnAmA*
Stamp, Adele H 1893-1974 *WhAm 6*
Stamper, Dave 1883-1963 *NatCAB 52*
Stampioen, Jan Jansz 1610-1689? *DcScB*
Stampp, Kenneth 1912- *EncAAH*
Stamps, Thomas Dodson 1893-1964 *WhAm 4*
Stanard, Edwin Obed 1832-1914 *BiDrAC,*
NatCAB 5, NatCAB 26, WhAm 1
Stanard, Mary Mann Page Newton 1865-1929
DcAmB, WhAm 1, WomWWA 14
Stanard, Robert d1846 *BiAUS, Drake*
Stanard, William Glover 1858-1933 *DcAmB,*
WhAm 1
Stanberry, Henry 1803-1881 *Drake*
Stanberry, William 1788-1873 *BiAUS*
Stanbery, Henry 1803-1881 *ApCAB, BiAUS,*
BiDrUSE, DcAmB, NatCAB 2,
TwCBDA, WhAm H
Stanbery, William 1788-1873 *BiDrAC,*
WhAm H
Stanbro, William Woodrow 1913-1972 *WhAm 6*
Stanbury, Walter Albert 1884-1954 *WhAm 3*
Stanchfield, John Barry 1855-1921 *ApCAB X,*
DcAmB, NatCAB 14, WhAm 1
Stancliff, Evert Lee 1887-1956 *WhAm 3*
Stancliff, J W 1814- *NewYHSD*
Stanclift, Henry Clay 1864-1948 *WhAm 2*
Standard, Edwin Obed 1832-1914 *BiAUS*
Standeford, Elisha D 1831- *BiAUS*
Standen, George William 1867-1942
NatCAB 31
Standen, William Thomas 1852- *WhAm 4*
Stander, Henricus Johannes 1894-1948
WhAm 2
Standerin, Ann Lee 1736-1784 *AmBi*
Standeven, Herbert Leslie 1878-1942 *WhAm 2*
Standeven, James Wylie 1916-1972 *WhAm 5,*
WhAm 6
Standifer, James d1836 *BiAUS*
Standifer, James d1837 *BiDrAC, WhAm H,*
WhAmP
Standifer, Sarah Blanche *WomWWA 14*
Standiford, Elisha David 1831-1887 *BiDrAC,*
WhAm H
Standish, Burt L *DcAmB S3, WebAB*
Standish, Clara May 1882- *WomWWA 14*
Standish, Frederick Dana 1852- *NatCAB 16*
Standish, H P *NewYHSD*
Standish, Henry *NewYHSD*
Standish, John VanNess 1825-1919 *NatCAB 18,*
TwCBDA, WhAm 1
Standish, Miles 1583?-1656 *EncAAH*
Standish, Miles 1584?-1656 *AmBi, Drake,*
NatCAB 5, WebAB, WebAMB
Standish, Miles 1858-1932 *NatCAB 23*
Standish, Miles 1887-1949 *NatCAB 38*
Standish, Myles 1584?-1656 *AmBi, ApCAB,*
DcAmB, McGEWB, TwCBDA,
WhAm H
Standish, Myles 1847-1915 *ApCAB X*
Standish, Myles 1851-1928 *NatCAB 23,*
WhAm 1
Standish, Myles 1898-1957 *NatCAB 47*
Standish, Philander 1835-1918 *EncAAH*
Standish, S H 1883-1953 *WhAm 3*
Standish, William Colburn 1879- *NatCAB 18*
Standley, William Harrison 1872-1963
WebAMB, WhAm 4
Standt, Ruth Wells *WomWWA 14*
Stanfield, Agnes *NotAW*
Stanfield, F W *NewYHSD*
Stanfield, J Fisher 1901-1958 *WhAm 3*
Stanfield, Richard Semei 1877-1934
NatCAB 26
Stanfield, Robert Nelson 1877-1945 *BiDrAC,*
WhAm 2, WhAmP
Stanfield, Theodore 1874- *WhAm 5*
Stanfill, William Abner 1892- *BiDrAC*
Stanford, Alan Griffith 1894-1961 *NatCAB 48*
Stanford, Albert Clinton 1895-1952 *WhAm 3*
Stanford, Arthur Willis 1859-1921 *NatCAB 19*

Stanford, Edward Valentine 1897-1966
WhAm 4
Stanford, Mrs. Henry *WomWWA 14*
Stanford, Homer Reed 1865- *WhAm 3*
Stanford, Jane Lathrop 1825-1905 *NatCAB 24,*
WhAm 1
Stanford, Jane Lathrop 1828-1905 *AmWom,*
NotAW, TwCBDA
Stanford, John 1754-1834 *ApCAB Sup,*
DcAmB, Drake, WhAm H
Stanford, John Anderson 1875-1951
NatCAB 40
Stanford, Leland 1824-1893 *AmBi, ApCAB,*
BiAUS, BiDrAC, DcAmB, Drake,
EncAB, McGEWB, NatCAB 2, REnAW,
TwCBDA, WebAB, WhAm H, WhAmP
Stanford, Rawghlie Clement 1879-1963
NatCAB 52, WhAm 4
Stanford, Richard 1767-1816 *BiAUS, BiDrAC,*
TwCBDA, WhAm H, WhAmP
Stanford, Thomas Welton 1832-1918 *NatCAB 2*
Stanford, Wesley Matthias 1846- *NatCAB 13,*
TwCBDA, WhAm 4
Stang, William 1854-1907 *DcAmB,*
NatCAB 15
Stange, Charles Henry 1880-1936 *WhAm 1*
Stangeland, Charles Emil 1881- *WhAm 6*
Stangeland, Katharina Marie 1877- *WhAm 5*
Stangl, Franz *WhWW-II*
Stangland, Benjamin F 1848- *WhAm 4*
Stanhope, Leon Eugene 1873-1956 *NatCAB 43*
Staniar, Ethel Ball 1885- *WomWWA 14*
Staniford, Thomas 1789-1855 *Drake*
Stanislaus, I V Stanley 1870- *WhAm 5*
Stanislavsky, Constantin 1863-1938 *McGEWB*
Stankiewicz, Richard 1922- *BnEnAmA*
Stanlaws, Penrhyn 1877-1957 *WhAm 3*
Stanley, Abram R 1816- *NewYHSD*
Stanley, Albert Augustus 1851-1932 *AmBi,*
BiDAmEd, DcAmB, WhAm 1
Stanley, Alfred Thomas 1868-1965 *NatCAB 52*
Stanley, Alice Dana Knox 1877- *WomWWA 14*
Stanley, Ann Lee 1736-1784 *AmBi*
Stanley, Anthony Dumond 1810-1853 *ApCAB,*
Drake
Stanley, Augustus Owsley 1867-1958 *ApCAB X,*
BiDrAC, NatCAB 45, WhAm 3,
WhAmP
Stanley, Carleton Wellesley 1886-1971
WhAm 5
Stanley, Caroline Abbot 1849-1919 *WhAm 1,*
WomWWA 14
Stanley, Cassius Miller 1878-1964 *WhAm 4*
Stanley, Charles Harvey 1843-1913 *NatCAB 16*
Stanley, Charles St. George *IIBEAAW*
Stanley, Clarance 1897-1972 *WhAm 5*
Stanley, Court Roger 1884-1970 *NatCAB 56*
Stanley, David S 1828-1902 *Drake*
Stanley, David Sloan 1828-1902 *ApCAB,*
NatCAB 4
Stanley, David Sloane 1828-1902 *AmBi,*
DcAmB, TwCBDA, WhAm 1
Stanley, Edmund 1847-1928 *WhAm 3*
Stanley, Edmund Allport 1888-1956
NatCAB 43
Stanley, Edward d1833 *Drake*
Stanley, Edward 1808-1872 *BiAUS, TwCBDA*
Stanley, Edward North 1858-1948 *NatCAB 47*
Stanley, Edwin James 1848-1919 *WhAm 1*
Stanley, Edwin M 1909-1971 *WhAm 5*
Stanley, Emma E 1853- *WomWWA 14*
Stanley, Emory Day 1881-1968 *WhAm 4A*
Stanley, Fabius 1815-1882 *Drake*
Stanley, Fabius *see also* Stanly, Fabius
Stanley, Francis Edgar 1849-1918 *DcAmB,*
NatCAB 18, WebAB, WhAm HA,
WhAmP
Stanley, Frank Arthur 1874-1960 *WhAm 4*
Stanley, Fred Grant 1885-1962 *NatCAB 48*
Stanley, Frederic Bartlett 1874-1943 *WhAm 2*
Stanley, Lord Frederick Arthur 1841- *ApCAB*
Stanley, Frederick Jonte 1848- *WhAm 4*
Stanley, Freelan O 1849-1940 *WebAB,*
WhAm 1
Stanley, George James 1877-1960 *NatCAB 48,*
WhAm 4
Stanley, Harold 1885-1963 *WhAm 4*
Stanley, Harvey *NewYHSD*

Stanley, Helen 1889-1966 *WhAm 4*
Stanley, Sir Henry Morton 1840-1904 *ApCAB*
Stanley, Sir Henry Morton 1841-1904 *AmBi,*
DcAmB, McGEWB, NatCAB 4, WebAB,
WhAm 1
Stanley, Hiram Alonzo 1859- *NatCAB 13,*
WhAm 4
Stanley, Hugh Wright 1874-1955 *WhAm 3*
Stanley, J M 1814-1872 *Drake*
Stanley, James G 1881-1947 *WhAm 2*
Stanley, James M 1814-1872 *NatCAB 6*
Stanley, John d1834 *BiAUS*
Stanley, John Joseph 1863-1926 *ApCAB X,*
WhAm 1
Stanley, John Mix 1814-1872 *BnEnAmA,*
DcAmB, IIBEAAW, NewYHSD, REnAW,
WhAm H
Stanley, Louise 1883-1954 *WhAm 3,*
WomWWA 14
Stanley, Maurice 1887-1966 *WhAm 4*
Stanley, Osso Willis 1887-1963 *WhAm 4*
Stanley, Philip B 1883-1963 *WhAm 4*
Stanley, Robert Crooks 1876-1951 *DcAmB S5,*
NatCAB 55, WhAm 3
Stanley, Thomas Bahnson 1890-1970 *BiDrAC,*
WhAm 5
Stanley, W E 1848-1910 *WhAm 1*
Stanley, Walter Lawrence 1871-1943 *WhAm 2*
Stanley, Wendell Meredith 1904-1971 *AsBiEn,*
McGEWB, NatCAB 57, WebAB,
WhAm 5
Stanley, William 1858-1916 *DcAmB,*
NatCAB 24, WhAm 1
Stanley, William 1891-1946 *NatCAB 35,*
WhAm 2
Stanley, William Edward 1848-1910
NatCAB 13
Stanley, William Eugene 1844-1910
NatCAB 30
Stanley, William Eugene 1891-1953 *WhAm 3*
Stanley, William Henry 1880-1959 *WhAm 4*
Stanley, Winifred Claire 1909- *BiDrAC*
Stanley Brothers *WebAB*
Stanley-Brown, Joseph 1858-1941 *NatCAB 33,*
WhAm 1, WhAm 2
Stanly, Edward 1810-1872 *BiDrAC, DcAmB,*
WhAm H, WhAmP
Stanly, Edward 1811?-1872 *ApCAB*
Stanly, Fabius 1815-1882 *ApCAB, NatCAB 4,*
TwCBDA
Stanly, Fabius *see also* Stanley, Fabius
Stanly, John 1774-1834 *BiDrAC, WhAm H,*
WhAmP
Stanly, John Wright 1742?-1789 *NatCAB 10*
Stannard, Albert Clinton 1881- *WhAm 6*
Stannard, E Tappan d1949 *WhAm 3*
Stannard, George Jennison 1820-1886 *TwCBDA*
Stannard, George Jerrison 1820-1886 *ApCAB,*
NatCAB 12
Stannard, Julia Ione 1869- *WomWWA 14*
Stannard, Margaret J 1861- *WhAm 4,*
WomWWA 14
Stannius, Hermann Friedrich 1808-1883 *DcScB*
Stans, Maurice Hubert 1908- *BiDrUSE*
Stansbury, Arthur J 1781-1845? *ApCAB,*
NewYHSD
Stansbury, Ele 1861- *WhAm 4*
Stansbury, Ellis Meredith *WomWWA 14*
Stansbury, Howard 1806-1863 *AmBi, ApCAB,*
BiAUS, DcAmB, Drake, WebAMB,
WhAm H
Stansbury, Joseph 1742-1809 *DcAmB*
Stansbury, Joseph 1750-1809 *ApCAB,*
NatCAB 8, WhAm H
Stansbury, Karl E 1879-1965 *WhAm 4*
Stansbury, Paul William 1897-1964 *WhAm 4*
Stansbury, Philip 1802?-1870? *ApCAB*
Stansbury, Tobias E 1756-1849 *Drake*
Stansel, Valentine 1621-1705 *ApCAB*
Stansell, Robert Basil 1875- *WhAm 5*
Stansfield, F W *NewYHSD*
Stansfield, John Heber 1878-1953 *IIBEAAW*
Stanson, George Curtin 1885- *IIBEAAW*
Stanton, A Glenn 1895-1969 *WhAm 5*
Stanton, Benjamin 1809-1872 *BiAUS, BiDrAC,*
WhAm H
Stanton, Benjamin Irving 1853-1898
NatCAB 16

Stanton, Charles *NewYHSD*
Stanton, Charles Spelman 1868-1947 *WhAm 2*
Stanton, Daniel 1708-1770 *ApCAB, Drake*
Stanton, Edgar Williams 1850-1920
NatCAB 19
Stanton, Edith N 1882- *WomWWA 14*
Stanton, Edward Cornelius 1888-1960
NatCAB 48
Stanton, Edwin Forward 1901-1968 *NatCAB 56*
Stanton, Edwin Lamson 1842-1877 *NatCAB 20*
Stanton, Edwin McMasters 1814-1869 *AmBi,*
ApCAB, BiAUS, BiDrUSE, DcAmB,
Drake, EncAB, McGEWB, NatCAB 2,
WebAB, WhAm H
Stanton, Edwin McMasters 1815-1869
TwCBDA
Stanton, Elizabeth Cady 1815-1902 *AmBi,*
AmWom, ApCAB, BiCAW, DcAmB,
DcAmReB, EncAB, McGEWB,
NatCAB 3, NotAW, TwCBDA, WebAB,
WhAm 1, WhAmP
Stanton, Elizabeth Cady 1816-1902 *Drake*
Stanton, Forrest Quillian 1886-1953
NatCAB 41
Stanton, Frank Lebby 1857-1927 *DcAmB,*
NatCAB 11, WhAm 1
Stanton, Frank M 1890-1963 *WhAm 4*
Stanton, Frank McMillan *WhAm 3*
Stanton, Frederic Perry 1814-1894 *ApCAB,*
TwCBDA
Stanton, Frederick Perry 1814-1894 *BiAUS,*
BiDrAC, DcAmB, NatCAB 8, WhAm H,
WhAmP
Stanton, Frederick Skiff 1857-1915 *ApCAB X*
Stanton, Harry Leavenworth 1875- *WhAm 5*
Stanton, Henry 1796?-1856 *ApCAB, Drake*
Stanton, Henry Brewster 1805-1887 *AmBi,*
ApCAB, ApCAB X, DcAmB, NatCAB 2,
TwCBDA, WhAm H
Stanton, Henry Francis 1894-1953 *WhAm 3*
Stanton, Henry Thompson 1834- *ApCAB*
Stanton, Henry Thompson 1886-1954 *WhAm 3*
Stanton, Horace Coffin 1849-1925 *WhAm 1*
Stanton, James Norman 1879-1962 *NatCAB 50*
Stanton, John 1830-1906 *NatCAB 4,*
NatCAB 14, WhAm 1
Stanton, John Gilman 1848-1927 *WhAm 1*
Stanton, John William 1924- *BiDrAC*
Stanton, Jonathan Young 1834-1918 *WhAm 1*
Stanton, Joseph, Jr. 1739-1807 *ApCAB, BiAUS,*
BiDrAC, NatCAB 5, TwCBDA,
WhAm H, WhAmP
Stanton, Lucy M 1875-1931 *WhAm 1,*
WomWWA 14
Stanton, Nathaniel Brown 1893-1946
NatCAB 40
Stanton, Oscar Fitzalan 1834-1924 *ApCAB,*
TwCBDA, WhAm 1
Stanton, Philip Ackley 1868- *WhAm 4*
Stanton, Phineas, Jr. 1817-1867 *NewYHSD*
Stanton, Richard Henry 1812-1891 *ApCAB,*
BiAUS, BiDrAC, DcAmB, Drake,
NatCAB 10, TwCBDA, WhAm H
Stanton, Robert 1889-1974 *WhAm 6*
Stanton, Robert Brewster 1846-1922
NatCAB 26, WhAm 1
Stanton, Robert Livingston 1810-1885 *ApCAB,*
NatCAB 26, TwCBDA
Stanton, Samuel Cecil 1856-1949 *NatCAB 39*
Stanton, Stephen Berrien 1864- *WhAm 5*
Stanton, Stiles Trumbull 1849-1888 *ApCAB*
Stanton, Thaddeus Harlan 1835-1900 *WhAm 1*
Stanton, Thaddeus Harlan 1835-1908
NatCAB 16
Stanton, Theodore 1851-1925 *ApCAB,*
NatCAB 11, WhAm 1
Stanton, Thomas 1615?-1678 *ApCAB Sup*
Stanton, Thomas Elwood 1881- *WhAm 6*
Stanton, Thomas Ernest 1865-1931 *DcScB*
Stanton, Timothy William 1860-1953
NatCAB 40, WhAm 3
Stanton, William 1843-1927 *WhAm 1*
Stanton, William Henry 1843-1900 *BiDrAC*
Stanton, William Henry 1874- *WhoColR*
Stanton, William Mortimer 1890-1957
NatCAB 46
Stanton, Zed Silloway 1848-1921 *NatCAB 19*
Stanwick, John 1740-1798 *WhAm H*

Stanwix, John 1690?-1765 *ApCAB, Drake*
Stanwood, A *NewYHSD*
Stanwood, Cornelia McKinne 1875-
 WomWWA 14
Stanwood, Daniel Caldwell 1869-1951
 NatCAB 41
Stanwood, Edward 1841-1923 *ApCAB Sup,*
 DcAmB, NatCAB 9, TwCBDA,
 WhAm 1
Stanwood, Isaac Augustus 1839- *NatCAB 14*
Stanwood, Louise Brockway 1858-
 WomWWA 14
Stapel, Henry Frederick 1858-1918 *NatCAB 17*
Stapf, Lowell Harvey 1899-1953 *NatCAB 42*
Staples, Abram Penn 1858-1913 *WhAm 1*
Staples, Abram Penn 1885-1951 *WhAm 3*
Staples, Alva Sherwood 1873-1958 *NatCAB 47*
Staples, Arthur Gray 1861-1940 *WhAm 1*
Staples, Bernice Dunning 1882- *WomWWA 14*
Staples, Carlton Albert 1827-1904 *NatCAB 8*
Staples, Charles Henry 1885-1950 *WhAm 3*
Staples, Charles Jason 1856- *WhAm 4*
Staples, Charles Job 1873-1949 *NatCAB 40*
Staples, Helen M 1845- *WomWWA 14*
Staples, Henry Franklin 1870-1938 *WhAm 1*
Staples, John Jacob d1806 *ApCAB*
Staples, John Norman 1881-1947 *WhAm 2*
Staples, Owen George 1838- *NatCAB 11*
Staples, Percy A 1883-1956 *WhAm 3*
Staples, Philip Clayton 1882-1949 *WhAm 2*
Staples, Seth Stitt 1868- *WhAm 4*
Staples, Thomas S 1879-1957 *WhAm 3*
Staples, Waller Redd 1826-1897 *ApCAB,*
 BiDConf, DcAmB, TwCBDA, WhAm H
Staples, William Edward 1863-1930
 NatCAB 22
Staples, William Read 1798-1868 *ApCAB,*
 BiAUS, DcAmB, Drake, NatCAB 8,
 TwCBDA, WhAm H
Stapleton, Ammon 1850-1916 *WhAm 1*
Stapleton, Benjamin F 1869-1950 *WhAm 3*
Stapleton, Charles W 1851-1935 *NatCAB 26*
Stapleton, Luke D 1869-1923 *WhAm 1*
Stapleton, Luke Daniel 1895-1948 *NatCAB 38*
Stapleton, Patience 1861-1893 *NatCAB 8*
Stapleton, William 1847- *WhAm 4*
Stapp, John Paul 1910- *WebAMB*
Starbird, Alfred 1875-1956 *WhAm 3*
Starbird, Mary Ann *NewYHSD*
Starbuck, A A 1878- *WomWWA 14*
Starbuck, Alexander 1841-1925 *NatCAB 20*
Starbuck, Calvin Washburn 1822-1870 *ApCAB*
Starbuck, Edwin Diller 1866-1947 *DcAmB S4,*
 WhAm 1
Starbuck, Kathryn Helene 1887-1965
 NatCAB 53, WhAm 4
Starbuck, Mary Coffyn 1644?-1717 *NotAW*
Starbuck, Raymond Donald 1878-1965
 WhAm 4
Starbuck, William David Lent 1886-1954
 NatCAB 41
Starck, Taylor 1889-1974 *WhAm 6*
Starcke, Viggo 1895-1974 *WhAm 6*
Stare, Fredrick Arthur 1877-1966 *NatCAB 53*
Starek, Fred 1873- *WhAm 5*
Staren, John Edgar 1902-1966 *WhAm 4*
Stariha, John N 1845-1915 *NatCAB 15,*
 WhAm 1
Starin, John Henry 1825-1909 *BiDrAC,*
 DcAmB, NatCAB 2, WhAm 1
Starin, John Henry 1827-1909 *ApCAB*
Stark, Abe 1893-1972 *NatCAB 57*
Stark, Abe 1894-1972 *WhAm 5*
Stark, Albert Philander 1863- *WhAm 4*
Stark, Andrew 1790-1849 *ApCAB*
Stark, Benjamin 1820- *ApCAB, BiAUS,*
 NatCAB 4
Stark, Benjamin 1820-1878 *TwCBDA*
Stark, Benjamin 1820-1898 *BiDrAC*
Stark, Caleb 1804-1864 *ApCAB, Drake*
Stark, Charles Gager 1835- *NatCAB 4*
Stark, Clarence Oscar 1898-1967 *WhAm 5*
Stark, Clay Hamilton 1894-1953 *NatCAB 43*
Stark, Dudley Scott 1894-1971 *WhAm 5*
Stark, Edward Josef 1858-1918 *DcAmB*
Stark, Edwin Jackson 1898-1964 *WhAm 4*
Stark, Edwin M d1967 *WhAm 4*
Stark, Eugene Miller 1886-1961 *NatCAB 49*

Stark, Francis Raymond 1877- *WhAm 5*
Stark, G Harold 1894-1973 *WhAm 6*
Stark, George W 1884-1966 *WhAm 4*
Stark, Harold 1898-1953 *NatCAB 46*
Stark, Harold Raynsford 1880-1972 *WebAMB,*
 WhAm 5, WhWW-II
Stark, Harry Rodgers 1864- *WhAm 4*
Stark, Henry Ignatius d1946 *WhAm 2*
Stark, Henry Jacob Lutcher 1887-1965 *REnAW,*
 WhAm 4
Stark, Johannes 1874-1957 *AsBiEn, DcScB*
Stark, John 1728-1822 *AmBi, ApCAB,*
 DcAmB, Drake, NatCAB 1, TwCBDA,
 WebAB, WebAMB, WhAm H, WhoMilH
Stark, John Francis 1851-1920 *NatCAB 18*
Stark, Joshua 1828- *NatCAB 2*
Stark, Lloyd Crow 1886-1972 *NatCAB 57,*
 WhAm 5
Stark, Louis 1888-1954 *DcAmB S5*
Stark, Louis 1889-1954 *WhAm 3*
Stark, Mary *WomWWA 14*
Stark, Orton K 1898-1968 *WhAm 5*
Stark, Otto 1859-1926 *NatCAB 20, WhAm 1*
Stark, Paul Clarence 1891-1974 *WhAm 6*
Stark, Sidney 1893-1960 *NatCAB 48*
Stark, Washington 1834-1914 *NatCAB 16*
Stark, William 1724-1776? *ApCAB,*
 NatCAB 5
Stark, William 1820?-1873 *ApCAB*
Stark, William 1825?-1873 *NatCAB 5*
Stark, William Everett 1873- *WhAm 6*
Stark, William Ledyard 1853-1922 *BiDrAC,*
 WhAm 4, WhAmP
Starkenborgh, J N, Baron Tjarda Van 1822-1895
 NewYHSD
Starkenborgh, William T Van *NewYHSD*
Starkey *NewYHSD*
Starkey, Frank Thomas 1892-1968 *BiDrAC*
Starkey, George 1628-1665 *DcScB*
Starkey, George R 1823- *NatCAB 3*
Starkey, Harold Bellamy 1896-1973 *WhAm 6*
Starkey, James *NewYHSD*
Starkey, Jennie O 1863- *AmWom*
Starkey, Jo-Anita 1895- *IlBEAAW*
Starkey, Newton B 1843-1919 *NatCAB 18*
Starkey, Thomas Alfred 1819-1903 *TwCBDA,*
 WhAm 1
Starkey, Thomas Alfred 1824-1903 *ApCAB,*
 NatCAB 3
Starkloff, Max C 1859- *WhAm 5*
Starks, Edwin Chapin 1867-1932 *DcAmB S1,*
 NatCAB 24
Starks, James Rockelle 1873- *WhoColR*
Starks, Samuel W 1865?-1908 *DcAmLiB*
Starks, William Henry Lord 1826- *WhAm 4*
Starkweather, Amelia Minerva *AmWom,*
 WomWWA 14
Starkweather, Chauncey Clark 1851- *WhAm 1*
Starkweather, David Austin 1802-1876 *BiAUS,*
 BiDrAC, NatCAB 8, WhAm H
Starkweather, George Anson 1794-1879 *BiAUS,*
 BiDrAC, WhAm H
Starkweather, Henry Howard 1826-1876
 ApCAB, BiAUS, BiDrAC, NatCAB 11,
 WhAm H
Starkweather, Miss J M *NewYHSD*
Starkweather, John Converse 1830-1890 *ApCAB,*
 NatCAB 12, TwCBDA
Starkweather, John K 1891-1972 *WhAm 5*
Starkweather, Louis Pomeroy 1898-1958
 WhAm 3
Starkweather, Louise Jennie *WomWWA 14*
Starkweather, William Edward Bloomfield
 1879-1969 *WhAm 5*
Starling, Ernest Henry 1866-1927 *AsBiEn,*
 BiHiMed, DcScB
Starling, Lyne 1784-1848 *ApCAB Sup,*
 NatCAB 12
Starling, William 1839-1900 *NatCAB 26,*
 WhAm 1
Starnes, George Talmage 1895-1955 *WhAm 3*
Starnes, Henry 1816- *ApCAB*
Starnes, Joe 1895-1962 *BiDrAC, WhAm 4*
Starr *NewYHSD*
Starr, Alfred Adolphus 1820- *ApCAB*
Starr, Belle 1848-1889 *NotAW, REnAW,*
 WhAm H
Starr, Clara Eilene 1878- *WomWWA 14*

Starr, Cornelius V 1892-1968 *WhAm 5*
Starr, Eliza Allan 1824-1901 *ApCAB*
Starr, Eliza Allen 1824-1901 *DcAmB,*
 NatCAB 13, NewYHSD, NotAW,
 TwCBDA, WhAm 1
Starr, Eliza Ellen 1824-1901 *AmWom*
Starr, Ellen Gates 1859-1940 *AmBi, DcAmReB,*
 NotAW
Starr, Emma Blanche Tillinghast 1850-
 WomWWA 14
Starr, Floyd Tallmadge 1904-1971 *NatCAB 57*
Starr, Frances 1886-1973 *WhAm 6,*
 WomWWA 14
Starr, Frederick 1858-1933 *AmBi, DcAmB,*
 NatCAB 13, TwCBDA, WhAm 1
Starr, Frederick Ratchford 1821- *ApCAB*
Starr, George William 1862-1940 *NatCAB 30*
Starr, H Danforth 1905-1974 *WhAm 6*
Starr, Helen Knowlton 1880- *WhAm 6*
Starr, Henry Frank 1894-1969 *WhAm 5*
Starr, Ida May Hill 1859- *WhAm 4*
Starr, John Farson 1818-1904 *BiAUS, BiDrAC*
Starr, John Markham 1846-1921 *NatCAB 22*
Starr, Lee Anna *WhAm 5*
Starr, Louis 1849-1925 *DcAmB, WhAm 1*
Starr, Louis Edward 1897-1967 *WhAm 4*
Starr, Merritt 1856-1931 *DcAmB, WhAm 1*
Starr, Moses Allen 1854-1932 *AmBi, DcAmB,*
 NatCAB 16, WhAm 1
Starr, N B *NewYHSD*
Starr, Nathan 1860- *WhAm 3*
Starr, Oliver 1883-1961 *WhAm 4*
Starr, Paul Hart 1908-1972 *WhAm 6*
Starr, Raymond Wesley 1888-1968 *NatCAB 54,*
 WhAm 5
Starr, Samuel H 1810-1891 *NatCAB 4*
Starr, Thomas Harper 1858-1944 *NatCAB 34*
Starr, William *NewYHSD*
Starr, William Flavius 1897-1966 *NatCAB 53*
Starr, William G 1840- *TwCBDA, WhAm 4*
Starret, Thomas Cyrus 1855-1927 *NatCAB 38*
Starrett, Emma L *WomWWA 14*
Starrett, Goldwin 1874-1918 *NatCAB 24*
Starrett, Helen Ekin 1840-1920 *TwCBDA,*
 WhAm 1, WomWWA 14
Starrett, Henry Prince 1885-1933 *WhAm 1*
Starrett, Laroy S 1836-1922 *DcAmB,*
 NatCAB 18
Starrett, Lewis Frederick 1844- *WhAm 1*
Starrett, Milton Gerry 1861-1942 *WhAm 2*
Starrett, Paul 1866-1957 *WhAm 3*
Starrett, Ralph 1868-1930 *NatCAB 24*
Starrett, Theodore 1865-1917 *NatCAB 15,*
 NatCAB 24, WhAm 1
Starrett, Vincent 1886-1974 *WhAm 6*
Starrett, William Aiken 1877-1932 *DcAmB,*
 NatCAB 24, WhAm 1
Starrett, William Aikin 1877-1932 *ApCAB X*
Starring, Anna Mullett Farrar 1861-
 WomWWA 14
Starring, Frederick A 1834-1904 *WhAm 1*
Starring, Helen Swing 1862- *WomWWA 14*
Starring, Mason Brayman 1859-1934 *WhAm 1*
Starrs, William 1807-1873 *ApCAB*
Start, Charles Monroe 1839-1919 *NatCAB 13,*
 TwCBDA, WhAm 1
Start, Cora Angeline 1867- *WomWWA 14*
Start, Edwin Augustus 1863-1923 *WhAm 1*
Start, Henry R 1845- *WhAm 1*
Startsman, Daniel Harry 1885-1959
 NatCAB 49
Startzman, Clyde Kress 1890-1958 *NatCAB 48*
Starup, Edward *NewYHSD*
Stas, Jean Servais 1813-1891 *AsBiEn, DcScB*
Stason, E Blythe 1891-1972 *WhAm 5*
Stassen, Harold Edward 1907- *WebAB*
Stastny, Olga Frances 1878-1952 *WhAm 3*
Staszic, Stanislaw Wawrzyniec 1755-1826
 DcScB Sup
State, Charles 1854- *WhAm 4*
Statfeld, Moritz *NewYHSD*
Stathas, Pericles Peter 1898-1973 *WhAm 5*
Stathers, Birk Smith 1884-1945 *NatCAB 35,*
 WhAm 2
Stathers, Silas Cliffert 1871-1955 *NatCAB 46*
Statler, Alice Seidler 1882-1969 *WhAm 5*
Statler, Ellsworth Milton 1863-1928 *DcAmB,*
 WebAB, WhAm 1

Staton, Adolphus 1879-1964 *WhAm 4*
Staton, Harry 1879-1959 *WhAm 3*
Staton, Sally Baker 1875- *WomWWA 14*
Statter, Arthur Frederick 1870- *WhAm 5*
Stattler, George *NewYHSD*
Statton, Arthur Biggs 1870-1937 *WhAm 1*
Staub, Albert William 1880-1953 *WhAm 3*
Staub, Francis Reinhard 1893-1965 *NatCAB 51*
Staub, Gordon James 1919-1958 *WhAm 3*
Staub, Walter Adolph 1881-1945 *WhAm 2*
Stauber, Leslie Alfred 1907-1973 *WhAm 5*
Stauble, Wilbur Carl 1899-1972 *WhAm 5*
Stauch, Alfred 1836?- *NewYHSD*
Stauch, Edward 1830?- *NewYHSD*
Staude, Edwin Gustave 1876- *NatCAB 16*
Staudinger, Hermann 1881-1965 *AsBiEn,*
DcScB, WhAm 4
Staudt, Karl Georg Christian Von 1798-1867
DcScB
Stauffacher, Charles Henry 1879-1956 *WhAm 3*
Stauffacher, Edward L 1901-1966 *WhAm 4*
Stauffen, Ernest, Jr. 1883-1950 *NatCAB 40,*
WhAm 3
Stauffenberg, Claus Von 1907-1944 *WhWW-II*
Stauffer, B Grant 1877-1950 *NatCAB 39*
Stauffer, Charles Albert 1880-1970 *WhAm 5*
Stauffer, Clinton Raymond 1875-1960 *WhAm 4*
Stauffer, David McNeely 1845-1913 *DcAmB,*
NatCAB 9, WhAm 1
Stauffer, Donald Alfred 1902-1952 *NatCAB 42,*
WhAm 3
Stauffer, Grant 1888-1949 *NatCAB 38,*
WhAm 2
Stauffer, Herbert Milton 1914-1970
NatCAB 57, WhAm 5
Stauffer, Jacob 1808-1880 *NewYHSD*
Stauffer, Ralph Daniel 1898-1956 *NatCAB 45*
Stauffer, Simon Walter 1888- *BiDrAC*
Stauffer, Vernon 1875-1925 *WhAm 1*
Staufft, Hannah Ophelia 1868- *WomWWA 14*
Staughton *NewYHSD*
Staughton, William 1770-1829 *ApCAB,*
DcAmB, Drake, NatCAB 3, TwCBDA,
WhAm H
Staunton *NewYHSD*
Staunton, Frederick Marshall 1866-1926
NatCAB 38
Staunton, Schuyler *WebAB*
Staunton, Sidney Augustus 1850-1939
NatCAB 28, WhAm 1
Staunton, William 1803-1889 *ApCAB,*
NatCAB 5, TwCBDA, WhAm H
Staunton, William Field 1860-1947 *ApCAB X,*
NatCAB 40, WhAm 2
Stavely, Albert Livingston 1863-1939
NatCAB 29
Staves, William Hickman 1904-1962
NatCAB 48
Stayton, Edward M 1874-1954 *WhAm 3*
Stayton, John William 1830-1894 *DcAmB,*
NatCAB 4, WhAm H
Stayton, Joseph Markham 1864-1923 *WhAm 1*
Stayton, Robert Weldon 1886-1963 *WhAm 4*
Stayton, William H 1861-1942 *WhAm 2*
Steacie, Edgar William Richard 1900-1962
DcScB, WhAm 4
Stead, John 1885-1949 *NatCAB 37*
Stead, John Edward 1851-1923 *DcScB*
Stead, Robert 1856-1943 *NatCAB 9,*
WhAm 2
Stead, William Henry 1899-1959 *WhAm 3*
Steadman, Alva Edgar 1894-1964 *WhAm 4*
Steadman, Chester Chandler 1892-1973
WhAm 6
Steadman, J H *BiAUS*
Steadman, John Marcellus, Jr. 1889-1945
NatCAB 35, WhAm 2
Steadwell, B Samuel 1871-1947 *WhAm 2*
Steadwell, Clara Oswald 1875- *WomWWA 14*
Steag, Jacob *NewYHSD*
Steagall, Henry Bascom 1873-1943 *BiDrAC,*
DcAmB S3, WhAm 2, WhAmP
Stealey, Orlando O 1842-1928 *WhAm 1*
Stealey, Sydnor Lorenzo 1897-1969 *WhAm 5*
Stealy, Clair Lazarus 1890-1956 *NatCAB 52*
Stearley, Ralph Francis 1898-1973 *NatCAB 57,*
WhAm 5
Stearly, Wilson Reiff 1869-1941 *NatCAB 34,*

WhAm 1
Stearne, Allen Michener 1882-1956 *NatCAB 46,*
WhAm 3
Stearnes, Reaumur Coleman 1866-1945
WhAm 2
Stearns, Abel 1798-1871 *DcAmB, WhAm H*
Stearns, Albert Warren 1885-1959 *WhAm 3*
Stearns, Alfred Ernest 1871-1949 *NatCAB 13,*
WhAm 2
Stearns, Anna E 1862- *WomWWA 14*
Stearns, Arthur French 1864- *WhAm 4*
Stearns, Asahel 1774-1839 *ApCAB, BiAUS,*
BiDrAC, DcAmB, Drake, WhAm H
Stearns, Betsey Ann 1830- *AmWom*
Stearns, Carl Leo 1892-1972 *WhAm 5*
Stearns, Charles 1752-1826 *Drake*
Stearns, Charles 1753-1826 *ApCAB*
Stearns, Charles Andrews 1858-1927
NatCAB 22
Stearns, Charles Cummings 1850-1924
WhAm 1
Stearns, Charles Falconer 1866-1946
NatCAB 40, WhAm 2
Stearns, Charles Woodward 1818-1887 *ApCAB*
Stearns, Eben Sperry 1819-1887 *BiDAmEd,*
DcAmB, NatCAB 8, WhAm H
Stearns, Eben Sperry 1821-1887 *ApCAB,*
TwCBDA
Stearns, Edith Shaffer d1958 *WhAm 3*
Stearns, Edward Carl 1856- *NatCAB 11*
Stearns, Edward Josiah 1810- *ApCAB*
Stearns, Ezra Scollay 1838-1915 *NatCAB 2*
Stearns, Foster Waterman 1881-1956 *BiDrAC,*
WhAm 3
Stearns, Frank Ballou 1878-1955 *DcAmB S5,*
NatCAB 45
Stearns, Frank Preston 1846-1917 *NatCAB 8,*
WhAm 1
Stearns, Frank Waterman 1856-1939
DcAmB S2, WhAm 1
Stearns, Frederic Baldwin 1874-1959
NatCAB 48
Stearns, Frederic Pike 1851-1919 *DcAmB,*
NatCAB 14, WhAm 1
Stearns, Frederic William 1867-1936
NatCAB 40
Stearns, Frederick Sweet 1881- *WhAm 6*
Stearns, Frederick William 1867-1936 *WhAm 1*
Stearns, George Luther 1809-1867 *ApCAB,*
DcAmB, Drake, NatCAB 8, WhAm H
Stearns, Gustav 1874-1951 *WhAm 3*
Stearns, Harold Edmund 1891-1943 *DcAmB S3,*
WhAm 2
Stearns, Helen Elizabeth Sweet *WomWWA 14*
Stearns, Henry Putnam 1828-1905 *DcAmB,*
NatCAB 22, WhAm 1
Stearns, Irving Ariel 1845-1920 *DcAmB,*
NatCAB 11
Stearns, James Pierce 1840-1922 *NatCAB 34*
Stearns, John 1770-1848 *ApCAB, Drake,*
NatCAB 6
Stearns, John Barker 1894-1973 *WhAm 6*
Stearns, John Glazier 1795-1874 *ApCAB*
Stearns, John Newton 1829-1895 *ApCAB,*
DcAmB, NatCAB 6, TwCBDA,
WhAm H
Stearns, John William 1839- *TwCBDA,*
WhAm 4
Stearns, John William 1840- *ApCAB*
Stearns, Jonathan French 1808- *ApCAB*
Stearns, Joseph Barker 1831- *ApCAB Sup*
Stearns, Joyce Clennam 1893-1948 *NatCAB 37,*
WhAm 2
Stearns, Junius Brutus 1810-1885 *ApCAB,*
IlBEAAW, NewYHSD, WhAm H
Stearns, Justus Smith 1845-1933 *NatCAB 36*
Stearns, Lewis French 1847-1892 *DcAmReB*
Stearns, Lutie Eugenia 1866-1943 *BiCAW,*
DcAmLiB, NotAW, WhAm 5,
WomWWA 14
Stearns, Marcellus Lovejoy 1829-1891
NatCAB 11
Stearns, Marcellus Lovejoy 1839-1891 *TwCBDA*
Stearns, Marshall Winslow 1908-1966 *WhAm 4*
Stearns, Mary Ann H *WhAm H*
Stearns, Neele Edward 1907-1962 *WhAm 4*
Stearns, Nellie George 1855- *AmWom,*
WomWWA 14

Stearns, Oakman Sprague 1817- *ApCAB*
Stearns, Oliver 1807-1885 *DcAmB, NatCAB 9,*
TwCBDA, WhAm H
Stearns, Onslow 1810-1878 *NatCAB 3,*
NatCAB 11, TwCBDA
Stearns, Osborne Putnam 1888-1963 *WhAm 4*
Stearns, Ozora Pierson 1831-1896 *ApCAB,*
BiDrAC, NatCAB 10, TwCBDA,
WhAm H
Stearns, Robert Edwards Carter 1827-1909
DcAmB, WhAm 1
Stearns, Robert Lyon 1872-1939 *NatCAB 31*
Stearns, Samuel 1747-1809 *Drake*
Stearns, Samuel 1747-1819 *ApCAB*
Stearns, Samuel Horatio 1801-1837 *ApCAB,*
Drake
Stearns, Sarah Burger 1836- *AmWom,*
ApCAB, NatCAB 10, TwCBDA,
WhAm 1
Stearns, Shubal 1706-1771 *DcAmB, DcAmReB,*
WhAm H
Stearns, Spencer 1891-1957 *NatCAB 47*
Stearns, Theodore 1880-1935 *WhAm 1*
Stearns, Wallace Nelson 1866-1934 *WhAm 1*
Stearns, Wilbur Watkins 1890-1946
NatCAB 35
Stearns, William *NewYHSD*
Stearns, William Augustus 1805-1876 *ApCAB,*
DcAmB, Drake, NatCAB 5, TwCBDA,
WhAm H
Stearns, William French 1834-1874 *ApCAB*
Stearns, William Guilford 1865-1937 *WhAm 1*
Stearns, William Marion 1856-1939 *WhAm 1*
Stebbing, Thomas Roscoe Rede 1835-1926
DcScB
Stebbins, Arthur D d1950 *WhAm 2, WhAm 3*
Stebbins, Byron H 1876-1967 *WhAm 4*
Stebbins, Carlos *NewYHSD*
Stebbins, Catharine A F 1823- *AmWom*
Stebbins, Edith Endicott 1876- *WomWWA 14*
Stebbins, Edwin Allen 1879-1954 *NatCAB 41,*
WhAm 3
Stebbins, Emma 1815-1882 *ApCAB,*
NatCAB 8, NewYHSD, NotAW,
TwCBDA, WhAm H
Stebbins, Ethel 1873- *WomWWA 14*
Stebbins, Eunice 1872- *WomWWA 14*
Stebbins, Frances Russell Palmer 1850-
WomWWA 14
Stebbins, G Waring 1869- *WhAm 5*
Stebbins, George Coles 1846-1945 *NatCAB 35,*
WhAm 2
Stebbins, George Edwin 1882-1947 *NatCAB 37*
Stebbins, Henry Constant 1865-1921
NatCAB 19
Stebbins, Henry Endicott 1905-1973 *WhAm 6*
Stebbins, Henry George 1811-1881 *BiDrAC,*
WhAm H
Stebbins, Henry George 1812-1881 *BiAUS*
Stebbins, Henry Hamlin 1839- *WhAm 3*
Stebbins, Henry Hamlin, Jr. 1881-1952
NatCAB 41
Stebbins, Homer Adolph 1884-1962 *WhAm 4*
Stebbins, Horatio 1821-1902 *DcAmB,*
NatCAB 24, WhAm H
Stebbins, Horatio Ward 1878-1933 *NatCAB 24*
Stebbins, J Cooper 1874-1947 *NatCAB 35*
Stebbins, Joel 1878- *WhAm 6*
Stebbins, John W 1819- *WhAm 4*
Stebbins, Kathleen B 1905-1962 *WhAm 4*
Stebbins, Lewis Abryam 1863- *ApCAB X*
Stebbins, Lucy Ward 1880- *WhAm 6*
Stebbins, Mary Elizabeth 1818- *NatCAB 13*
Stebbins, Rufus Phineas 1810-1885 *ApCAB Sup,*
DcAmB, NatCAB 12, WhAm H
Stebler, William John 1902-1960 *WhAm 4*
Stec, Michael John 1899-1959 *NatCAB 48*
Stecher, Frederich Wilhelm George 1866-1916
NatCAB 25
Stecher, Henry William 1856-1935 *WhAm 1,*
WhAm 1C
Stecher, Karl 1891-1965 *NatCAB 51*
Stecher, Robert Morgan 1896-1972 *WhAm 5*
Stechow, Wolfgang 1896-1974 *WhAm 6*
Stechschulte, Victor Cyril 1893-1955 *WhAm 3*
Steciuk, Basil W 1910-1975 *WhAm 6*
Steck, Charles Calvin 1884- *WhAm 5*
Steck, Daniel Frederic 1881-1950 *BiDrAC,*

NatCAB 40, WhAm 3
Steck, George 1829-1897 *DcAmB, WhAm H*
Steckbeck, Walter 1880-1956 *NatCAB 47*
Steckel, Abram Peters 1879-1954 *WhAm 3*
Steckel, Louis Joseph Rene 1844- *ApCAB*
Stecker, Margaret Loomis 1885-
  WomWWA 14
Stecker, Mary Bates *WomWWA 14*
Stecker, Robert Donald 1901-1959 *WhAm 4*
Steckler, Alfred 1856- *WhAm 4*
Steckler, Samuel Price 1886-1963 *NatCAB 53*
Steddom, Rice Price 1864- *WhAm 5*
Stedingk, Curt Bogislaus L C, Count Von
  1746-1836 *ApCAB, Drake*
Stedman, Alexander 1703-1794 *NatCAB 17*
Stedman, Arthur Wallace 1855- *NatCAB 14*
Stedman, Charles 1745?-1812 *ApCAB, Drake*
Stedman, Charles Manly 1841-1930 *BiDrAC,
  WhAm 1, WhAmP*
Stedman, Edmund Clarence 1833-1908 *AmBi,
  ApCAB, ApCAB X, DcAmB, Drake,
  NatCAB 3, TwCBDA, WhAm 1*
Stedman, Frank Haywood 1859-1939
  NatCAB 31
Stedman, George Woolverton 1864-1954
  WhAm 3
Stedman, Giles Chester 1897-1961 *WhAm 4*
Stedman, Griffin Alexander 1838-1864 *ApCAB,
  Drake, NatCAB 5*
Stedman, Henry Rust 1849-1926 *WhAm 1*
Stedman, John Gabriel 1745-1797 *ApCAB,
  Drake*
Stedman, John Moore 1864-1949 *NatCAB 41,
  WhAm 2*
Stedman, John Weiss 1880-1952 *WhAm 3*
Stedman, Louise Adella 1907- *WhAm 5*
Stedman, Marshall Willis 1859-1935
  NatCAB 26
Stedman, Nathan Alexander 1854-1927
  NatCAB 38
Stedman, Thomas Lathrop 1853-1938 *WhAm 1*
Stedman, William 1765-1831 *BiAUS, BiDrAC,
  TwCBDA, WhAm H*
Steed, J Lyman 1880-1941 *WhAm 2*
Steed, Robert Dennis 1880-1944 *WhAm 2*
Steed, Thomas Jefferson 1904- *BiDrAC*
Steedly, Benjamin Broadus 1874-1932 *WhAm 1*
Steedman, Carrie Howard 1874-
  WomWWA 14
Steedman, Charles 1811- *ApCAB, Drake*
Steedman, Charles 1811-1889 *NatCAB 4*
Steedman, Charles 1811-1890 *AmBi, DcAmB,
  TwCBDA, WhAm H*
Steedman, Edwin Harrison 1873-1961 *WhAm 4*
Steedman, George Fox 1871-1940 *NatCAB 30*
Steedman, James Barrett 1818-1883 *ApCAB,
  Drake, NatCAB 4, TwCBDA*
Steedman, James Blair 1817-1883 *AmBi,
  DcAmB, WhAm H*
Steedman, Virginia Chase *WomWWA 14*
Steel, Alfred B *NewYHSD*
Steel, Alfred G B 1886-1949 *WhAm 2*
Steel, David 1893-1970 *WhAm 6*
Steel, George Alexander 1846- *WhAm 1*
Steel, George Drexel 1896- *ApCAB X*
Steel, Henry Miller 1840-1911 *NatCAB 28*
Steel, James W 1799-1879 *NewYHSD*
Steel, John 1825?- *NewYHSD*
Steel, Rowe Summerville 1899-1970 *WhAm 5*
Steel, Westbrook 1889- *WhAm 5*
Steel, William 1809-1881 *ApCAB*
Steele, Mister *NewYHSD*
Steele, Mrs. A *NewYHSD*
Steele, Aaron John 1835-1917 *NatCAB 20*
Steele, Albert Wilbur 1862-1925 *WhAm 1*
Steele, Alfred N 1901-1959 *WhAm 3*
Steele, Alice Bradbury *WomWWA 14*
Steele, Alice Garland 1880- *WhAm 6*
Steele, Annie Follansbee 1850- *WomWWA 14*
Steele, Ashbel 1796- *Drake*
Steele, Benjamin Hinman 1837-1873
  NatCAB 20
Steele, Charles 1857-1939 *NatCAB 14,
  WhAm 1*
Steele, Daniel *NewYHSD*
Steele, Mrs. Daniel *NewYHSD*
Steele, Daniel 1824-1914 *DcAmB, NatCAB 12,
  TwCBDA, WhAm 1*

Steele, Daniel Atkinson King 1852-1931
  NatCAB 22, WhAm 1
Steele, David 1827-1906 *TwCBDA, WhAm 1*
Steele, David McConnell 1873-1945 *WhAm 2*
Steele, Edgar Clarence 1856- *WhAm 4*
Steele, Esther Baker 1835-1911 *AmWom,
  WhAm 1*
Steele, Francis Joseph 1908-1965 *NatCAB 50*
Steele, Frank B 1864- *WhAm 5*
Steele, Frederic 1821-1868 *Drake*
Steele, Frederic Dorr 1873-1944 *WhAm 2*
Steele, Frederick 1819-1868 *ApCAB, DcAmB,
  NatCAB 4, TwCBDA, WebAMB,
  WhAm H*
Steele, Frederick Morgan 1851- *NatCAB 14*
Steele, George Louis 1891-1953 *NatCAB 42*
Steele, George McKendree 1823-1902 *TwCBDA*
Steele, George W 1798-1842 *WhAm H*
Steele, George Washington 1839-1922 *BiDrAC,
  NatCAB 1, TwCBDA, WhAm 1,
  WhAmP*
Steele, Gilbert Victor 1887-1950 *NatCAB 39*
Steele, Harry Lee 1874-1938 *WhAm 1*
Steele, Heath McClung 1884-1956 *WhAm 3*
Steele, Henry Joseph 1860-1933 *BiDrAC,
  WhAm 1*
Steele, Henry Maynadier 1865-1909
  NatCAB 14, WhAm 1
Steele, Hiram Roswell 1842-1929 *WhAm 1,
  WhAm 1C*
Steele, Isaac Nevett 1809-1891 *NatCAB 12,
  NatCAB 14, NatCAB 29*
Steele, James 1765-1845 *ApCAB*
Steele, James Dallas 1864-1928 *WhAm 1,
  WhAm 1C*
Steele, James King 1875-1937 *NatCAB 33,
  WhAm 1*
Steele, Joel Dorman 1836-1886 *AmBi, ApCAB,
  BiDAmEd, DcAmB, NatCAB 3,
  WhAm H*
Steele, John 1755?-1805? *ApCAB, Drake*
Steele, John 1758-1827 *ApCAB, Drake,
  NatCAB 5*
Steele, John 1764-1815 *ApCAB, BiAUS,
  BiDrAC, DcAmB, Drake, TwCBDA,
  WhAm H*
Steele, John 1870-1947 *WhAm 2*
Steele, John Benedict 1814-1866 *BiAUS,
  BiDrAC, WhAm H*
Steele, John Dutton 1905- *WhAm 5*
Steele, John Hardy 1789-1865 *NatCAB 11,
  TwCBDA*
Steele, John Hardy 1792-1865 *BiAUS, Drake*
Steele, John Murray 1900-1969 *WhAm 5*
Steele, John Nelson 1853-1933 *NatCAB 14,
  WhAm 1*
Steele, John Nevett 1796-1853 *BiAUS,
  BiDrAC, WhAm H*
Steele, Joseph M 1865- *WhAm 5*
Steele, Katharyn Albani 1871- *WomWWA 14*
Steele, Leda Crawford *WomWWA 14*
Steele, Leon Charles 1889-1945 *WhAm 2*
Steele, Leslie Jasper 1868-1929 *BiDrAC,
  WhAm 1*
Steele, Mark Boyden 1877-1948 *NatCAB 36*
Steele, Sir Richard 1672-1729 *McGEWB*
Steele, Robert Benson *NewYHSD*
Steele, Robert Denham 1901-1972 *WhAm 5*
Steele, Robert Hampton 1938- *BiDrAC*
Steele, Robert McCurdy 1882-1962 *NatCAB 52*
Steele, Robert W 1820-1901 *NatCAB 11*
Steele, Robert Wilbur 1857-1910 *NatCAB 20,
  WhAm 1*
Steele, Robert Wilbur 1891-1969 *NatCAB 56,
  WhAm 5*
Steele, Rowena Granice 1824- *AmWom*
Steele, Rufus Milas 1877-1935 *AmBi,
  NatCAB 26, WhAm 1*
Steele, Sandra 1938- *IlBEAAW*
Steele, Sanford Henry 1847-1920 *NatCAB 21*
Steele, Sidney John 1877- *WhAm 5*
Steele, Theodore Clement 1847-1926 *WhAm 1*
Steele, Thomas Jefferson 1853-1920 *BiDrAC,
  NatCAB 19, WhAm 1*
Steele, Thomas M 1878-1944 *WhAm 2*
Steele, Thomas Sedgwick 1845-1903 *NatCAB 8,
  WhAm 1*
Steele, Walter David 1870-1954 *NatCAB 44*

Steele, Walter Leak 1823-1891 *BiDrAC,
  WhAm H*
Steele, Walter Simeon 1890-1960 *WhAm 3*
Steele, Walter Wallace 1865-1924 *NatCAB 23*
Steele, Wilbur Daniel 1886-1970 *WhAm 5*
Steele, Wilbur Fletcher 1851- *WhAm 4*
Steele, William 1819-1885 *ApCAB, NatCAB 4*
Steele, William Edward 1886-1958 *NatCAB 44*
Steele, William Gaston 1820-1892 *BiAUS,
  BiDrAC, WhAm H*
Steele, William Hamilton 1844-1919
  NatCAB 18
Steele, William LaBarthe 1875-1949 *WhAm 2*
Steele, William Porter 1817-1864 *NewYHSD*
Steele, William Randolph 1842-1901 *BiAUS,
  BiDrAC, WhAmP*
Steelhammer, Arvid Morris 1887-1961
  NatCAB 49
Steell, Graham 1851-1942 *BiHiMed*
Steell, Willis d1941 *WhAm 1, WhAm 2*
Steelman, Fannie Lawrence 1867-
  WomWWA 14
Steels, John 1825?- *NewYHSD*
Steen, Alexander E d1862 *Drake*
Steen, Fred E 1879- *WhAm 6*
Steen, Harold Karl 1935- *EncAAH*
Steen, Marguerite 1894-1975 *WhAm 6*
Steenberg, Richard Wilbur 1906-1963 *WhAm 4*
Steenbock, Harry 1886-1967 *NatCAB 54,
  WhAm 4A*
Steendam, Jacob 1616-1672 *ApCAB, DcAmB,
  WhAm H*
Steene, William 1883-1965 *NatCAB 52*
Steene, William 1893-1965 *WhAm 4*
Steenerson, Halvor 1852-1926 *BiDrAC,
  WhAm 1, WhAmP*
Steenrod, Lewis 1810-1862 *BiAUS, BiDrAC,
  WhAm H*
Steenrod, Norman Earl 1910-1971 *WhAm 5*
Steenstra, Peter Henry 1833-1911 *ApCAB,
  WhAm 1*
Steenstrup, Christian 1873-1955 *NatCAB 42*
Steenstrup, Japetus Smith 1813-1897 *DcScB*
Steenwyck, Cornelis d1684 *DcAmB, WhAm H*
Steep, Thomas 1880-1944 *WhAm 2*
Steeper, John *NewYHSD*
Steeps, Henry John 1883-1955 *NatCAB 45*
Steere, Arnold 1792-1832 *NewYHSD*
Steere, Joseph Beal 1842-1940 *WhAm 1*
Steere, Joseph Hall 1852-1936 *WhAm 1*
Steere, Kenneth David 1884-1963 *WhAm 4*
Steere, Lloyd Randol 1880-1961 *NatCAB 50,
  WhAm 4*
Steers, Alfred Ernst 1860-1948 *NatCAB 35*
Steers, Arnold 1792-1832 *NewYHSD*
Steers, Edna Louise 1883- *WomWWA 14*
Steers, George 1820-1856 *DcAmB, NatCAB 4,
  WhAm H*
Steers, George 1821-1856 *Drake*
Steers, Henry 1832-1903 *NatCAB 6,
  NatCAB 25*
Steers, J Rich 1868-1936 *NatCAB 51*
Steers, J Rich 1898-1964 *NatCAB 51*
Steers, Newton Ivan 1876-1944 *NatCAB 33*
Steers, William Edward 1906-1976 *WhAm 6*
Stees, Washington Moore 1826-1890 *NatCAB 6*
Steese, James Gordon 1882-1958 *NatCAB 50,
  WhAm 3*
Steese, Jay Ceylon 1869-1962 *NatCAB 49*
Stefan, Josef 1835-1893 *AsBiEn, DcScB*
Stefan, Karl 1884-1951 *BiDrAC, WhAm 3,
  WhAmP*
Stefan, Ross 1934- *IlBEAAW*
Stefanini, Francois Ange Antoine 1909-1948
  WhAm 2
Stefansson, Vilhjalmur 1879-1962 *ApCAB X,
  McGEWB, WebAB, WhAm 4*
Steffan, Edward *NewYHSD*
Steffan, Eugene *NewYHSD*
Steffan, Roger 1893-1955 *WhAm 3*
Steffen, Randy 1915?- *IlBEAAW*
Steffens, Cornelius M 1866-1933 *WhAm 1*
Steffens, Joseph Lincoln 1866-1936 *EncAB*
Steffens, Lincoln 1866-1936 *AmBi, DcAmB S2,
  McGEWB, NatCAB 14, REnAW,
  WebAB, WhAm 4*
Steffens, Theodore Henry 1883-1956 *WhAm 3*
Steffensen, Vern R 1905-1965 *NatCAB 51*

Steffensen, Vernal R 1905-1965 *WhAm 4*
Steffey, Otto 1898-1958 *NatCAB 44*
Steffian, Edwin Theodore 1899-1974 *WhAm 6*
Steffke, Wesley Alvin 1906-1968 *NatCAB 54*
Stegagnini, Louis *NewYHSD*
Stegeman, Gebhard 1890-1949 *WhAm 2*
Steger, Christian Talbot 1893-1951 *WhAm 3*
Steger, John Valentine 1854-1916 *NatCAB 16*
Steger, Julius d1959 *WhAm 3*
Steger, Peyton 1883- *WhAm 1*
Steggerda, Morris 1900-1950 *NatCAB 38*
Stegnani, Louis *NewYHSD*
Stegner, Charles Bryant 1892-1963 *NatCAB 50*
Stegner, Wallace 1909- *REnAW*
Stehle, Aurelius Aloysius 1877-1930 *DcAmB,*
  WhAm 1
Stehle, Richard Brehm 1898-1967 *NatCAB 53*
Steichen, Edouard Jean 1879-1973 *EncAB*
Steichen, Edward Jean 1879-1973 *BnEnAmA,*
  McGEWB, WebAB, WhAm 5
Steider, Doris 1924- *IlBEAAW*
Steidtmann, Waldo E 1896-1955 *WhAm 3*
Steiger, Albert 1860-1938 *NatCAB 30*
Steiger, Emil Herman 1871-1929 *NatCAB 16,*
  NatCAB 37
Steiger, Ernst 1832-1917 *ApCAB, WhAm 1*
Steiger, George 1869-1944 *WhAm 2*
Steiger, Sam 1929- *BiDrAC*
Steiger, William Albert 1938- *BiDrAC*
Steigers, William Corbet 1845-1923 *WhAm 1*
Steigers, William Corbet 1847-1923
  NatCAB 12
Steiguer, Louis Rudolph De *WhAm 2*
Steil, William Nicholas 1876- *WhAm 5*
Stein *NewYHSD*
Stein, A *NewYHSD*
Stein, Albert Harvey 1917-1972 *WhAm 5*
Stein, Beatrice Borg 1881-1958 *NatCAB 47*
Stein, Blanche Harnish 1868- *WomWWA 14*
Stein, Charles *NewYHSD*
Stein, Conrad 1701-1762 *ApCAB*
Stein, David 1887-1959 *NatCAB 47*
Stein, Earl Roscoe 1886-1957 *NatCAB 48*
Stein, Edward Thomas 1899- *WhAm 4*
Stein, Evaleen 1863-1923 *AmWom, DcAmB,*
  WhAm 1, WomWWA 14
Stein, Frank Louis 1878- *ApCAB X*
Stein, Fred M 1874-1950 *NatCAB 39*
Stein, Fred W, Sr. 1905-1970 *WhAm 5*
Stein, Frederick William 1905-1970 *NatCAB 56*
Stein, Gertrude 1874-1946 *DcAmB S4, EncAB,*
  McGEWB, NatCAB 38, NotAW,
  WebAB, WhAm 2
Stein, Hannah 1920-1973 *WhAm 6*
Stein, Harold 1902-1966 *NatCAB 53,*
  WhAm 4
Stein, Baron Heinrich F Karl 1757-1831
  McGEWB
Stein, Henry Frederick Andrew 1867-1948
  NatCAB 40
Stein, I Melville 1894-1965 *WhAm 4*
Stein, Jacob *NewYHSD*
Stein, James Rauch 1868- *WhAm 5*
Stein, Johan Willem Jakob Antoon 1871-1951
  DcScB
Stein, John Bethune 1869-1947 *NatCAB 34*
Stein, John Philip 1836-1909 *WhAm 1*
Stein, Leo Daniel 1872-1947 *DcAmB S4*
Stein, Louis P 1893-1952 *WhAm 3*
Stein, Maurice 1919-1972 *NatCAB 57*
Stein, Otto Jacob 1867-1938 *NatCAB 29*
Stein, Philip 1898-1955 *NatCAB 41*
Stein, Robert 1857-1917 *WhAm 1*
Stein, William Howard 1911- *WebAB*
Stein, William Philip 1873-1953 *NatCAB 43*
Steinbach, Everett Mark 1905-1968 *WhAm 5*
Steinbach, Milton 1902-1970 *WhAm 5*
Steinbeck, John Ernst 1902-1968 *EncAAH,*
  EncAB, McGEWB, REnAW, WebAB,
  WhAm 5
Steinbel, Roger Nelson 1810- *ApCAB*
Steinberg, Milton 1903-1950 *WhAm 3*
Steinberg, Samuel Sidney 1891-1968 *WhAm 4A*
Steinberg, Saul 1914- *WebAB*
Steinberger, Franklin Jennings 1900-1973
  WhAm 6
Steinbiss, Herman William 1853- *NatCAB 12*
Steinbock, Max 1917-1975 *WhAm 6*

Steinbrecher, Paul 1879-1937 *NatCAB 27*
Steinbright, Harold Dixon 1898-1954
  NatCAB 43
Steinbrink, Meier 1880-1967 *WhAm 4A*
Steinbrugge, Edward Donald 1917-1975
  WhAm 6
Steindel, Bruno 1869- *WhAm 5*
Steindler, Arthur 1878-1959 *WhAm 3*
Steindorff, Georg 1861-1951 *WhAm 3*
Steinecke, Henry F *NewYHSD*
Steinegger, Henry 1831?- *IlBEAAW,*
  NewYHSD
Steinem, Pauline *WhAm 4, WomWWA 14*
Steinen, William 1887-1965 *WhAm 4*
Steiner, Bernard Christian 1867-1926 *DcAmB,*
  DcAmLiB, NatCAB 18, NatCAB 26,
  TwCBDA, WhAm 1
Steiner, Bernard Sigfried 1905-1974 *WhAm 6*
Steiner, Burghard 1857-1923 *NatCAB 6*
Steiner, Celestin John 1898-1971 *WhAm 5*
Steiner, Edward Alfred 1866-1956 *NatCAB 48,*
  WhAm 3
Steiner, Emma R *AmWom*
Steiner, Jakob 1796-1863 *DcScB*
Steiner, Jesse Frederick 1880- *WhAm 6*
Steiner, Leo K 1870-1944 *WhAm 2*
Steiner, Lewis Henry 1827-1892 *ApCAB,*
  DcAmB, NatCAB 11, TwCBDA,
  WhAm H
Steiner, Louis John 1902-1963 *NatCAB 49*
Steiner, Max 1888-1971 *WhAm 5*
Steiner, Ralph 1899- *BnEnAmA*
Steiner, Robert Eugene 1862-1955 *WhAm 3*
Steiner, Sam Simon 1865-1955 *NatCAB 46*
Steiner, Walter Ralph 1870-1942 *WhAm 2*
Steiner, William Howard 1894-1966
  NatCAB 51, WhAm 4
Steiner, Williams Kossuth 1874-1945 *WhAm 2*
Steinert, Alan 1901-1969 *WhAm 5*
Steinert, Morris 1831-1912 *DcAmB*
Steinert, William Joseph 1880- *WhAm 6*
Steinetz, Bernard G d1966 *WhAm 4*
Steinfeld, Albert 1854-1935 *WhAm 1*
Steinfeld, Martha L 1880- *WomWWA 14*
Steingruber-Wildgans, Ilona *WhAm 5*
Steinhagen, E Harvey 1903-1970 *NatCAB 56*
Steinhardt, Laurence Adolph 1892-1950
  DcAmB S4, NatCAB 40, WhAm 2
Steinhart, Frank 1864-1938 *WhAm 1*
Steinhart, Jesse H 1881-1966 *WhAm 4*
Steinhauer, Henry Bird 1804-1885 *ApCAB*
Steinhaus, Arthur H 1897-1970 *BiDAmEd,*
  WhAm 5
Steinhaus, Edward A 1914-1969 *WhAm 5*
Steinhefer, Juan 1650?-1716 *ApCAB*
Steinheil, Karl August 1801-1870 *DcScB*
Steinheimer, Anna Scott *WomWWA 14*
Steinhorst, Henry 1892-1956 *NatCAB 46*
Steininger, Fred H 1915-1973 *WhAm 5*
Steinitz, Ernst 1871-1928 *DcScB*
Steinitz, William 1836-1900 *ApCAB, DcAmB,*
  WebAB, WhAm 1
Steinitz, William 1837-1900 *NatCAB 10*
Steinkamp, George Riegler 1916-1966
  NatCAB 54
Steinke, Bettina 1913- *IlBEAAW*
Steinkraus, Herman W 1890-1974 *WhAm 6*
Steinle, Roland Joseph 1896-1966 *WhAm 4,*
  WhAm 5
Steinman, Andrew Jackson 1836-1917
  NatCAB 6, WhAm 1
Steinman, David Barnard 1886-1960 *WebAB,*
  WhAm 4
Steinman, James Hale 1886-1962 *WhAm 4*
Steinmayer, Reinhard August 1892-1968
  NatCAB 55
Steinmetz, Charles Proteus 1865-1923 *AmBi,*
  AsBiEn, DcAmB, DcScB, EncAB,
  McGEWB, NatCAB 13, NatCAB 23,
  WebAB, WhAm 1
Steinmetz, Friedrich Von 1796-1877 *WhoMilH*
Steinmetz, Joseph Allison 1870-1928 *WhAm 1*
Steinmetz, Maurice 1904-1969 *WhAm 5*
Steinmeyer, Ferdinand 1720-1786 *DcAmB*
Steinreich, Kenneth Pease 1899-1965 *WhAm 4*
Steinsapir, Saul P 1904-1973 *WhAm 5*
Steinway, Albert 1840-1877 *ApCAB*
Steinway, C F Theodore 1825-1889 *NatCAB 2*

Steinway, Charles Herman 1857-1919
  NatCAB 18, WhAm 1
Steinway, Christian Friedrich Theodore
  1825-1889 *DcAmB, WhAm H*
Steinway, Frederick Theodore 1860- *ApCAB X,*
  NatCAB 18
Steinway, Henry Engelhard 1797-1871 *AmBi,*
  ApCAB, DcAmB, NatCAB 2, WhAm H
Steinway, Henry Englehard 1797-1871 *WebAB*
Steinway, Theodore E 1883-1957 *WhAm 3*
Steinway, William 1835-1896 *ApCAB X,*
  DcAmB, EncAB, WhAm H
Steinway, William 1836-1896 *ApCAB Sup,*
  NatCAB 2
Steinway, William Richard 1881-1960 *WhAm 4*
Steinweg, Heinrich Engelhard *WebAB*
Steinweg, William Louis 1852- *WhAm 4*
Steinwehr, Adolph W Friedrich, Baron Von
  1822-1877 *ApCAB, Drake, TwCBDA*
Steivel, Gustav *NewYHSD*
Steiwer, Frederick 1883-1939 *BiDrAC,*
  NatCAB 29, WhAm 1, WhAmP
Stejneger, Leonhard Hess 1851-1943
  DcAmB S3, DcScB, NatCAB 14,
  TwCBDA, WhAm 2
Steklov, Vladimir Andreevich 1864-1926 *DcScB*
Stella, Antonio 1868-1927 *NatCAB 20,*
  WhAm 1
Stella, Frank Philip 1936- *BnEnAmA, EncAB,*
  McGEWB, WebAB
Stella, Joseph 1877-1946 *BnEnAmA,*
  DcAmB S4, IlBEAAW, McGEWB,
  NatCAB 36
Stella, Joseph 1880-1946 *WhAm 2*
Stelle, Charles Clarkson 1910-1964 *WhAm 4*
Stelle, John 1891-1962 *WhAm 4*
Stelle, Lucy Page *WomWWA 14*
Steller, Georg Wilhelm 1709-1746 *DcScB*
Stellhorn, Frederick William 1841-1919
  NatCAB 24, WhAm 1
Stelluti, Francesco 1577-1652 *DcScB*
Stellwagen, Charles K 1818?- *NewYHSD*
Stellwagen, Edward James 1854-1932 *WhAm 1*
Stellwagen, Henry S d1866 *Drake*
Stellwagen, Seiforde Michael 1890-1946
  WhAm 2
Stellwagen, Thomas Cook 1841-1918
  NatCAB 28
Stelter, Benjamin F 1882-1958 *WhAm 3*
Stelwagon, Henry Weightman 1853-1919
  NatCAB 19, WhAm 1
Stelzle, Charles 1869-1941 *DcAmB S3,*
  DcAmReB, WhAm 1
Stem, Allen Hartzell 1856-1931 *NatCAB 23*
Stembel, Roger Nelson 1810-1900 *Drake,*
  NatCAB 5, TwCBDA, WhAm 1
Stembler, Harry Abraham 1882-1964
  NatCAB 50
Stemler, Otto Adolph 1872-1953 *WhAm 3*
Stemmler, Theodore Washington 1885-1974
  WhAm 6
Stempel, Guido Hermann 1868-1955 *WhAm 3*
Stempf, Victor Herman 1893-1946 *WhAm 2*
Stemple, Dayton Reuben 1900-1964
  NatCAB 51
Stemple, Frank 1894-1964 *NatCAB 50,*
  WhAm 4
Stenberg, Thornton Rice 1895-1963 *NatCAB 50*
Stendhal 1783-1842 *McGEWB*
Stengel, Alfred 1868-1939 *DcAmB S2,*
  WhAm 1
Stengel, Arthur Wise 1895-1964 *NatCAB 51*
Stengel, Casey 1890-1975 *WhAm 6*
Stengel, Charles Dillon 1891- *WebAB*
Stengel, Erwin 1902-1973 *WhAm 6*
Stengel, Frederick William 1874- *WhAm 5*
Stenger, William Shearer 1832?-1918 *BiAUS*
Stenger, William Shearer 1840-1918 *BiDrAC*
Stengle, Charles Irwin 1869-1953 *BiDrAC,*
  WhAm 3
Stennis, John Cornelius 1901- *BiDrAC*
Steno, Nicolaus 1638-1686 *AsBiEn, DcScB,*
  McGEWB
Stensen, Niels 1638-1686 *BiHiMed, DcScB*
Stensland, Paul O 1847- *NatCAB 9*
Stenson, Charles Ernest 1887-1954 *NatCAB 41*
Stentz, John Clyde 1880- *WhAm 6*
Stenzel, Lula Vinette 1872- *WhAm 5,*

WomWWA 14

Stepanov, Vyacheslav Vassilievich 1889-1950 *DcScB*

Stepelton, Norman Allen 1912-1970 *WhAm 5*

Stephan, Arthur Theodore 1913-1973 *WhAm 6*

Stephan, Edouard Jean Marie 1837-1923 *DcScB*

Stephan, Frank Lawrence 1886-1953 *WhAm 3*

Stephan, Frederick Franklin 1903-1971 *WhAm 5*

Stephan, George 1862-1944 *WhAm 2*

Stephan, Martin 1777-1846 *DcAmReB*

Stephan, Walter George 1877-1957 *NatCAB 47*

Stephanus Of Alexandria *DcScB*

Stephanus, Carolus *DcScB*

Stephen 1096?-1154 *McGEWB*

Stephen Harding, Saint d1134 *McGEWB*

Stephen Of Antioch *DcScB*

Stephen, Adam 1730?-1791 *ApCAB, Drake, TwCBDA, WebAMB*

Stephen, Elizabeth Willisson 1856- *AmWom*

Stephen, Sir George 1829- *ApCAB*

Stephen, George 1876-1955 *WhAm 3*

Stephen, James 1759-1832 *ApCAB*

Stephen, John d1844 *BiAUS*

Stephen, Laura Rose 1866- *WomWWA 14*

Stephen, Sir Leslie 1832-1904 *McGEWB*

Stephens *NewYHSD*

Stephens, A E S 1900-1973 *WhAm 6*

Stephens, Abednego 1812-1841 *ApCAB*

Stephens, Abraham P 1796-1859 *BiAUS, BiDrAC, WhAm H*

Stephens, Agnes Lavinia 1856- *WomWWA 14*

Stephens, Albert Lee, Sr. 1874-1965 *WhAm 4*

Stephens, Alexander Hamilton 1812-1883 *AmBi, ApCAB, BiAUS, BiDConf, BiDrAC, DcAmB, Drake, EncAAH, EncAB, McGEWB, NatCAB 3, TwCBDA, WebAB, WhAm H, WhAmP*

Stephens, Alice Barber 1858-1932 *DcAmB, NatCAB 13, NatCAB 23, NotAW, TwCBDA, WhAm 1, WomWWA 14*

Stephens, Ambrose Everett Burnside 1862-1927 *BiDrAC, WhAm 1*

Stephens, Ann Sophia 1810-1886 *NotAW*

Stephens, Ann Sophia 1813-1886 *ApCAB, DcAmB, Drake, NatCAB 10, TwCBDA, WhAm H*

Stephens, Benjamin Hughl 1869- *WhAm 5*

Stephens, Charles Asbury 1844-1931 *DcAmB*

Stephens, Charles Asbury 1845-1931 *NatCAB 13, TwCBDA*

Stephens, Charles Asbury 1847-1931 *AmBi, NatCAB 23, WhAm 1*

Stephens, Charles H 1855?-1931 *IIBEAAW*

Stephens, Charles Randall 1862-1921 *ApCAB X*

Stephens, Charlotte E 1854- *WhoColR*

Stephens, Claude P 1890-1959 *WhAm 4*

Stephens, Clyde Harrison 1890-1965 *WhAm 4*

Stephens, Dan Voorhees 1868-1939 *BiDrAC, WhAm 1, WhAmP*

Stephens, Dan Vorhees 1868-1939 *NatCAB 29*

Stephens, Daniel 1778-1850 *ApCAB, NatCAB 5*

Stephens, Daniel Mallory 1893-1961 *NatCAB 48, WhAm 4*

Stephens, David Stubert 1847-1921 *WhAm 1*

Stephens, Edwin Lewis 1872-1938 *WhAm 1*

Stephens, Edwin William 1849-1931 *DcAmB, WhAm 1*

Stephens, Ernest James 1889-1941 *NatCAB 31*

Stephens, Ernest Lenwood, Jr. 1894-1955 *NatCAB 45*

Stephens, Ferris J 1893-1969 *NatCAB 57, WhAm 5*

Stephens, Frances Ramsay *WomWWA 14*

Stephens, Frank 1859-1935 *WhAm 1*

Stephens, Frank Fletcher 1878- *WhAm 6*

Stephens, George 1873-1946 *WhAm 2*

Stephens, George Asbury 1873-1952 *WhAm 3*

Stephens, George Ware 1878-1940 *WhAm 1*

Stephens, George Washington 1819-1902 *NatCAB 32*

Stephens, Guy Frederic 1888-1965 *WhAm 4*

Stephens, Harley Clifford 1900-1971 *WhAm 5*

Stephens, Harold Montelle 1886-1955 *NatCAB 42, WhAm 3*

Stephens, Harriet Marion 1823-1858 *ApCAB, Drake*

Stephens, Harry T d1948 *WhAm 2*

Stephens, Henry Louis 1824-1882 *ApCAB, IIBEAAW, NatCAB 5, NewYHSD*

Stephens, Henry Morse 1857-1919 *DcAmB, NatCAB 13, WhAm 1*

Stephens, Herbert Taylor 1864-1929 *NatCAB 22, WhAm 1*

Stephens, Howard V 1887-1952 *WhAm 3*

Stephens, Hubert Durrett 1875-1946 *ApCAB X, BiDrAC, WhAm 2, WhAmP*

Stephens, James 1882-1950 *McGEWB, WhAm 3*

Stephens, James C 1894-1969 *WhAm 5*

Stephens, John Edmondson 1874-1919 *NatCAB 6*

Stephens, John Hall 1847-1924 *BiDrAC, TwCBDA, WhAm 4, WhAmP*

Stephens, John Harris 1913-1965 *NatCAB 52*

Stephens, John Leonard 1852-1934 *NatCAB 17, WhAm 1*

Stephens, John Lloyd 1805-1852 *AmBi, ApCAB, BiAUS, DcAmB, Drake, NatCAB 5, TwCBDA, WhAm H*

Stephens, John Vant 1857-1946 *NatCAB 34, WhAm 2*

Stephens, Kate 1853-1938 *BiCAW, NotAW, WhAm 1, WomWWA 14*

Stephens, Lawrence Vest 1858-1923 *TwCBDA, WhAm 1*

Stephens, Leroy 1841- *WhAm 4*

Stephens, Linton 1823-1872 *ApCAB, BiDConf, DcAmB, WhAm H*

Stephens, Lon V 1858- *NatCAB 12*

Stephens, Louis L 1875-1960 *WhAm 4*

Stephens, Luther *NewYHSD*

Stephens, Marietta Louise 1850- *WomWWA 14*

Stephens, Marion Ream 1877- *WomWWA 14*

Stephens, Martin Bates 1862-1923 *NatCAB 20, WhAm 1*

Stephens, Minnie *WomWWA 14*

Stephens, Nanna J Wilson 1860- *WomWWA 14*

Stephens, Oren Melson 1914-1969 *WhAm 5*

Stephens, Percy Rector 1876-1942 *WhAm 2*

Stephens, Philander 1788-1842 *BiAUS, BiDrAC, WhAm H*

Stephens, Philip B 1900-1972 *WhAm 5*

Stephens, Powell 1874-1954 *NatCAB 43*

Stephens, Redmond Davis 1874-1931 *WhAm 1*

Stephens, Robert Allan 1878-1942 *WhAm 2*

Stephens, Robert Grier, Jr. 1913- *BiDrAC*

Stephens, Robert Neilson 1867-1906 *TwCBDA, WhAm 1*

Stephens, Roswell Powell 1874-1954 *WhAm 3*

Stephens, Russell Stout 1893-1965 *WhAm 4*

Stephens, Theodore Pierson 1896-1963 *WhAm 4*

Stephens, Thomas *ApCAB, NewYHSD*

Stephens, Thomas Henry 1863-1932 *NatCAB 28*

Stephens, Uriah Smith 1821-1882 *AmBi, DcAmB, EncAB, McGEWB, NatCAB 1, WebAB, WhAm H*

Stephens, Victor Emmanuel 1887-1966 *NatCAB 53*

Stephens, W Barclay 1869- *WhAm 5*

Stephens, Ward 1869-1940 *NatCAB 36*

Stephens, Ward 1879-1940 *WhAm 1*

Stephens, Wiley Webster 1867-1954 *NatCAB 41*

Stephens, William *BiAUS, NewYHSD*

Stephens, William 1671-1753 *AmBi, ApCAB, Drake, NatCAB 1*

Stephens, William Dennison 1859-1944 *BiDrAC, NatCAB 33, WhAm 2, WhAmP*

Stephenson *NewYHSD*

Stephenson, Benjamin d1822 *BiAUS, BiDrAC, WhAm H*

Stephenson, Benjamin Franklin 1823-1871 *DcAmB, NatCAB 14, WebAMB, WhAm H*

Stephenson, Carl 1886-1954 *DcAmB S5, WhAm 3*

Stephenson, Charles S 1887-1965 *NatCAB 51, WhAm 4*

Stephenson, Edward Morris 1853-1926 *WhAm 1*

Stephenson, Elmer 1877-1959 *NatCAB 47*

Stephenson, Franklin Bache 1848- *WhAm 4*

Stephenson, George 1781-1848 *AsBiEn, McGEWB*

Stephenson, George Malcolm 1883-1958 *WhAm 3*

Stephenson, Gilbert Thomas 1884-1972 *WhAm 5*

Stephenson, Henry Thew 1870- *WhAm 5*

Stephenson, Isaac 1829-1918 *BiDrAC, DcAmB, NatCAB 14, WhAm 1, WhAmP*

Stephenson, James 1764-1833 *BiAUS, BiDrAC, TwCBDA, WhAm H*

Stephenson, James 1898-1941 *WhAm 2*

Stephenson, James Pomeroy 1845-1937 *WhAm 3*

Stephenson, James S 1780-1831 *BiAUS*

Stephenson, James S *see also* Stevenson, James S

Stephenson, John 1809-1893 *ApCAB Sup, DcAmB, NatCAB 7, TwCBDA, WhAm H*

Stephenson, John Gould 1828-1883 *BiAUS, DcAmLiB*

Stephenson, Joseph Maxwell 1892- *WhAm 2*

Stephenson, Junius Winfield 1885-1930 *ApCAB X*

Stephenson, Luther 1830- *NatCAB 7*

Stephenson, Margaret Elizabeth Coulter 1881- *WomWWA 14*

Stephenson, Mathew 1776?-1834? *ApCAB*

Stephenson, Nathaniel Wright 1867-1935 *DcAmB S1, WhAm 1*

Stephenson, Orlistus Bell 1867- *WhAm 4*

Stephenson, Peter 1823-1860? *NatCAB 8, NewYHSD*

Stephenson, Robert 1803-1859 *McGEWB*

Stephenson, Rome Charles 1865-1934 *WhAm 1*

Stephenson, S Town 1910-1964 *WhAm 4*

Stephenson, Sam 1868-1942 *WhAm 2*

Stephenson, Samuel Merritt 1831-1907 *BiDrAC, WhAmP*

Stephenson, Sarah 1876- *WomWWA 14*

Stephenson, Stuart Augustus 1878-1938 *NatCAB 28*

Stephenson, Thomas *NewYHSD*

Stephenson, Wendell Holmes 1899-1970 *WhAm 5*

Stephenson, William 1856- *WhAm 4*

Stephenson, William B, Jr. 1880-1955 *WhAm 3*

Stephenson, William Benjamin 1915-1964 *WhAm 4*

Stephenson, William Lawrence 1880-1963 *WhAm 4*

Stephenson, William Prettyman 1868- *WhAm 5*

Stephenson, William Worth 1857-1914 *WhAm 1*

Stepling, Joseph 1716-1778 *DcScB*

Stepp, Morris Daniel 1872-1944 *NatCAB 33*

Steppat, Leo 1910-1965 *WhAm 4*

Steptoe, Edward Jenner 1816-1865 *BiAUS, Drake*

Steptoe, Philip Pendleton 1877-1944 *WhAm 2*

Sterett, Andrew 1760?-1807 *ApCAB*

Sterett, Andrew 1778-1807 *DcAmB, WebAMB, WhAm H*

Sterett, Isaac Sears 1801-1863 *ApCAB*

Sterett, Samuel 1758-1833 *BiDrAC, WhAm H*

Sterigere, John Benton 1793-1852 *BiAUS, BiDrAC, WhAm H*

Sterki, Victor 1846-1933 *DcAmB, WhAm 1*

Sterley, William F 1859- *WhAm 4*

Sterling *NewYHSD*

Sterling, Ada *WomWWA 14*

Sterling, Adaline Wheelock *WomWWA 14*

Sterling, Alexander Frederick 1817-1885 *NatCAB 16*

Sterling, Ansel 1782-1853 *BiAUS, BiDrAC, WhAm H*

Sterling, Antoinette *AmWom*

Sterling, Bruce Foster 1870-1945 *BiDrAC, WhAm 5*

Sterling, Clarence Irving, Jr. 1905-1963 *NatCAB 49*

Sterling, Donald Justus 1887-1954 *WhAm 3*

Sterling, Edward Canfield 1834-1911 *WhAm 1*

Sterling, Ernest Albert 1878- *WhAm 6*

Sterling, Frederick Augustine 1876-1957 *WhAm 3*

Sterling, George 1869-1926 *DcAmB, WhAm 1*

Sterling, George Mathleson 1910-1967 *WhAm 5*
Sterling, Graham Lee 1904-1972 *WhAm 5*
Sterling, Guy 1860- *WhAm 1*
Sterling, James 1701?-1763 *DcAmB, WhAm H*
Sterling, John Allen 1857-1918 *BiDrAC, WhAm 1, WhAmP*
Sterling, John C 1888-1964 *WhAm 4*
Sterling, John Ewart Wallace 1906- *BiDAmEd*
Sterling, John Whalen 1816-1885 *DcAmB, WhAm H*
Sterling, John William 1844-1918 *DcAmB, NatCAB 10, NatCAB 19, WhAm 1*
Sterling, Mary E *NewYHSD*
Sterling, Micah 1781-1844 *BiAUS*
Sterling, Micah 1784-1844 *BiDrAC, WhAm H*
Sterling, Richard 1812-1883 *ApCAB*
Sterling, Ross Shaw 1875-1949 *DcAmB S4, NatCAB 38, WhAm 2*
Sterling, Sara Hawks *WomWWA 14*
Sterling, Theodore 1827-1912 *NatCAB 7, WhAm 1*
Sterling, Thomas 1851-1930 *ApCAB X, BiDrAC, NatCAB 15, WhAm 1, WhAm 1C, WhAmP*
Sterling, W T 1906-1951 *WhAm 3*
Stern, Adolph 1878- *WhAm 6*
Stern, Alfred Whital 1881-1960 *WhAm 4*
Stern, Bernhard Joseph 1894-1956 *WhAm 3*
Stern, Bill 1907-1971 *WhAm 5*
Stern, Carl 1902-1971 *NatCAB 56*
Stern, Catherine 1894-1973 *NatCAB 57*
Stern, Charles Frank 1880- *WhAm 6*
Stern, Charles Mann 1876-1961 *NatCAB 49*
Stern, David Becker 1880-1960 *WhAm 4*
Stern, Edgar Bloom 1886-1959 *NatCAB 47, WhAm 4*
Stern, Edith Mendel 1901-1975 *WhAm 6*
Stern, Elizabeth Gertrude Levin 1889-1954 *NatCAB 39, WhAm 3*
Stern, Erich Cramer 1879-1969 *NatCAB 54*
Stern, Felix 1877-1949 *NatCAB 42*
Stern, Frances 1873-1947 *NotAW*
Stern, Frederick David 1897-1960 *NatCAB 45*
Stern, Gerson *NewYHSD*
Stern, Gladys Bertha 1890-1973 *WhAm 6*
Stern, Gustav 1904-1969 *NatCAB 53*
Stern, Henry Root 1882-1959 *WhAm 3*
Stern, Horace 1878-1969 *WhAm 5*
Stern, Isaac 1920- *WebAB*
Stern, Isaac Farber 1871-1949 *WhAm 3*
Stern, Jo Lane 1848-1932 *WhAm 1*
Stern, Joseph Smith 1891-1971 *NatCAB 57, WhAm 5*
Stern, Joseph William 1870-1934 *DcAmB, WhAm HA, WhAm 4*
Stern, Julius 1878-1960 *NatCAB 45*
Stern, Julius David 1886-1971 *WhAm 5*
Stern, Kurt Guenter 1904-1956 *WhAm 3*
Stern, Lawrence Fish 1888-1967 *WhAm 4*
Stern, Leo 1895-1973 *WhAm 6*
Stern, Leopold 1848-1928 *ApCAB X*
Stern, Louis 1847-1922 *WhAm 1*
Stern, Louis 1904-1972 *WhAm 5*
Stern, Maurice 1855-1919 *NatCAB 18*
Stern, Nathan 1878-1945 *WhAm 2*
Stern, Oscar David 1888-1973 *WhAm 6*
Stern, Otto 1888-1969 *AsBiEn, DcScB, McGEWB, WebAB*
Stern, Percival 1880-1970 *NatCAB 57*
Stern, Samuel Rika 1855-1937 *NatCAB 27*
Stern, Siegfried 1896-1952 *NatCAB 39*
Stern, Sigmund 1878-1955 *WhAm 3*
Stern, Simon Adler 1838-1904 *WhAm 1*
Stern, William Bernhard 1912- *WhAm 5*
Stern, William Wolf 1887-1965 *NatCAB 51*
Sternau, Herbert 1899-1972 *NatCAB 56*
Sternberg, Charles Hazellus 1850-1943 *WhAm 2*
Sternberg, Constantin I, Edler Von 1852-1924 *DcAmB*
Sternberg, Erich 1901-1965 *NatCAB 54*
Sternberg, George Miller 1838-1915 *AmBi, ApCAB, ApCAB X, BiHiMed, DcAmB, NatCAB 4, TwCBDA, WebAB, WhAm 1*
Sternberg, Kaspar Maria Von 1761-1838 *DcScB*
Sternberg, Louis 1886-1963 *NatCAB 50*
Sternberg, Pavel Karlovich 1865-1920 *DcScB*

Sternberg, Walter 1905-1966 *NatCAB 53, WhAm 4*
Sternberger, Bertha Strauss 1877- *WomWWA 14*
Sternberger, Estelle Miller d1971 *WhAm 5*
Sternbergh, J Hervey 1890-1949 *NatCAB 37*
Sternbergh, James Hervey 1834-1913 *NatCAB 10, NatCAB 31*
Sternbergh, Katharine Eleanor Cornell 1890-1950 *NatCAB 39*
Sternburg, Herman VonSpeck- 1852-1908 *WhAm 1*
Sterne, Albert Eugene 1866-1931 *WhAm 1*
Sterne, Eugene Herman 1872-1955 *NatCAB 44*
Sterne, Laurence 1713-1768 *McGEWB*
Sterne, Maurice 1877-1957 *NatCAB 42, WhAm 3*
Sterne, Maurice 1878?-1957 *BnEnAmA, IlBEAAW*
Sterne, Niel Paul 1883-1939 *WhAm 1*
Sterne, Simon 1839-1901 *AmBi, ApCAB, DcAmB, WhAm 1*
Sterne, Stuart 1845-1905 *DcAmB*
Sterne, Theodore Eugene 1907-1970 *WhAm 5*
Sterner, Albert Edward 1863-1946 *NatCAB 11, TwCBDA, WhAm 2*
Sterner, Marie 1877- *BiCAW*
Sternhagen, John Meier 1888-1954 *WhAm 3*
Sternhell, Charles Max 1915-1971 *WhAm 5*
Sterrett, Andrew d1807 *Drake*
Sterrett, Frances Roberta d1947 *WhAm 2*
Sterrett, H Willard 1894-1951 *NatCAB 43*
Sterrett, Henry Hatch Dent 1880- *WhAm 6*
Sterrett, James Macbride 1847-1923 *DcAmB*
Sterrett, James Macbridge 1847-1923 *WhAm 1*
Sterrett, James Patterson 1822- *NatCAB 13*
Sterrett, James Ralston 1853-1939 *WhAm 1*
Sterrett, John Robert Sitlington 1851-1914 *AmBi, DcAmB, TwCBDA, WhAm 1*
Sterrett, Joseph Edmund 1870-1934 *NatCAB 26*
Sterrett, Robert John 1877-1943 *NatCAB 36*
Sterrett, Samuel d1833 *BiAUS*
Sterrs, Willis Edward 1868- *WhoColR*
Sterry, Frederic 1866-1933 *NatCAB 37*
Sterry, Thomas N *NewYHSD*
Stetcher, Karl 1831?-1924 *NewYHSD*
Stetefeldt, Carl August 1838-1896 *ApCAB, DcAmB, WhAm H*
Stetson, Augusta Emma Simmons 1842-1928 *ApCAB X, DcAmB, DcAmReB, NatCAB 18, NotAW, WhAm 1, WomWWA 14*
Stetson, Caleb Rochford 1871-1932 *WhAm 1*
Stetson, Charles 1801-1863 *BiAUS, BiDrAC, WhAm H*
Stetson, Charles Augustus 1810-1888 *ApCAB, DcAmB, WhAm H*
Stetson, Charles Walter 1858-1911 *DcAmB, NatCAB 9, WhAm 1*
Stetson, Charles Wyllys 1869-1958 *NatCAB 46*
Stetson, Charlotte Perkins 1860-1935 *NotAW, TwCBDA*
Stetson, Eugene William 1881-1959 *NatCAB 44, WhAm 3*
Stetson, Francis Lynde 1846-1920 *ApCAB X, DcAmB, NatCAB 14, WhAm 1*
Stetson, George Albert 1889-1959 *NatCAB 47*
Stetson, George Warren 1876-1942 *NatCAB 36*
Stetson, Harlan True 1885-1964 *WhAm 4*
Stetson, Henry Crosby 1900-1955 *DcAmB S5, WhAm 3*
Stetson, Herbert Lee 1847-1935 *NatCAB 37, WhAm 4*
Stetson, Herbet Lee 1848-1935 *TwCBDA*
Stetson, Isaiah Kidder 1858-1940 *WhAm 1*
Stetson, John Batterson 1830-1906 *AmBi, DcAmB, NatCAB 11, TwCBDA, WebAB, WhAm 1*
Stetson, John Batterson, Jr. 1884-1952 *NatCAB 42*
Stetson, Katharine Beecher 1885- *WomWWA 14*
Stetson, Lemuel 1804- *BiAUS*
Stetson, Lemuel 1804-1868 *BiDrAC, WhAm H*
Stetson, Lemuel 1804-1886 *ApCAB X*
Stetson, Paul Clifford 1884-1937 *WhAm 1*

Stetson, Raymond Herbert 1872-1950 *WhAm 3*
Stetson, Thomas Drew 1827-1916 *NatCAB 2, WhAm 4*
Stetson, William Wallace 1849-1910 *BiDAmEd, DcAmB, NatCAB 17, WhAm 1*
Stetson, Willis Kimball 1848-1942 *TwCBDA*
Stetson, Willis Kimball 1858-1942 *WhAm 1*
Stetten, DeWitt 1881-1951 *WhAm 3*
Stettheimer, Florine 1871-1944 *NotAW*
Stettinius, Edward R, Jr. 1900-1949 *McGEWB, WhAm 2, WhWW-II*
Stettinius, Edward Reilley, Jr. 1900-1949 *BiDrUSE*
Stettinius, Edward Reilly, Jr. 1900-1949 *DcAmB S4, EncAB, NatCAB 38*
Stettinius, Edward Riley 1865-1925 *DcAmB, WhAm 1*
Stettinius, Samuel Enredy 1768-1815 *NewYHSD*
Stettinius, William Carrington 1895-1937 *NatCAB 28*
Stettner, Ludwig Wilhelmin 1887-1964 *WhAm 4*
Steuart, George Hume 1828-1903 *ApCAB Sup, BiDConf, TwCBDA, WhAm 1*
Steuart, James Aloysius 1828-1903 *ApCAB, WhAm 1*
Steuart, Leonard Pinkney 1879-1966 *NatCAB 52*
Steuart, Richard Sprigg 1797-1876 *ApCAB*
Steuben, Baron Von d1864 *Drake*
Steuben, Baron Von 1730-1794 *WebAB, WebAMB*
Steuben, Frederick W Augustus, Baron Von 1730-1794 *AmBi, Drake, McGEWB, NatCAB 1*
Steuben, Frederick William A H F Von 1730-1794 *ApCAB*
Steuben, Friedrich W A, Freiherr Von 1730-1794 *WhoMilH*
Steuben, Friedrich W L G Augustin Von 1730-1794 *DcAmB, WhAm H*
Steuben, Friedrich Wilhelm A H F Von 1730-1794 *TwCBDA*
Steuer, August 1902-1969 *NatCAB 54*
Steuer, Max David 1869-1940 *NatCAB 54*
Steuer, Max David 1870-1940 *DcAmB S2, WhAm HA, WhAm 4*
Steuermann, Edward 1892-1964 *WhAm 4*
Steunenberg, Frank 1861-1905 *REnAW*
Steunenburg, Frank 1861-1905 *NatCAB 12*
Stevenot, Fred Gabriel 1877- *WhAm 5*
Stevens *NewYHSD*
Stevens, Aaron Fletcher 1819-1887 *ApCAB, BiAUS, BiDrAC, Drake, WhAm H*
Stevens, Abbot 1888-1958 *NatCAB 47*
Stevens, Abel 1815-1897 *AmBi, ApCAB, DcAmB, Drake, NatCAB 8, TwCBDA, WhAm H*
Stevens, Adeline Chapman *WomWWA 14*
Stevens, Adie Allan 1845- *WhAm 3*
Stevens, Albert Clark 1854-1919 *WhAm 1*
Stevens, Albert William 1886-1949 *NatCAB 37*
Stevens, Alden 1907-1968 *WhAm 5*
Stevens, Alexander H Hogden 1789-1869 *TwCBDA*
Stevens, Alexander Henry 1834-1916 *NatCAB 31*
Stevens, Alexander Hodgden 1789-1869 *NatCAB 9*
Stevens, Alexander Hodgdon 1789-1869 *ApCAB, DcAmB, Drake, WhAm H*
Stevens, Alexander Raymond 1876-1968 *WhAm 5*
Stevens, Alice Bartlett *WomWWA 14*
Stevens, Alviso Burdett 1853-1940 *NatCAB 18, WhAm 1*
Stevens, Alzina Parsons 1849-1900 *AmWom, NotAW*
Stevens, Ambrose *NewYHSD*
Stevens, Amelia *NewYHSD*
Stevens, Andrew Frazier, Jr. 1868- *WhoColR*
Stevens, Anna C Mann 1889-1969 *WhAm 5*
Stevens, Anne Evans Shipman 1859-1939 *NatCAB 17, NatCAB 32*
Stevens, Arthur Albert 1865-1944 *NatCAB 34, WhAm 4*
Stevens, Ashton 1872-1951 *DcAmB S5,*

Stewart, Alexander Turney 1802-1876
  ApCAB X
Stewart, Alexander Turney 1803-1876 *AmBi,*
  ApCAB, BiAUS, DcAmB, Drake, EncAB,
  McGEWB, NatCAB 7, TwCBDA,
  WebAB, WhAm H
Stewart, Alfred William 1884-1957 *NatCAB 43*
Stewart, Allison Vance 1856-1919 *WhAm 1*
Stewart, Alpheus Lloyd 1890-1948 *WhAm 2*
Stewart, Alphonso Chase 1848-1916 *WhAm 1*
Stewart, Alvan 1790-1849 *AmBi, ApCAB,*
  DcAmB, NatCAB 2, WhAm H
Stewart, Andrew 1791-1872 *BiDrAC, DcAmB,*
  WhAm H, WhAmP
Stewart, Andrew 1792-1872 *BiAUS, TwCBDA*
Stewart, Andrew 1867-1942 *NatCAB 30*
Stewart, Andrew, Jr. 1836-1903 *BiDrAC,*
  WhAmP
Stewart, Andrew Perry 1848- *NatCAB 7*
Stewart, Archibald *ApCAB, BiAUS*
Stewart, Arthur Thomas 1892- *BiDrAC*
Stewart, Austin 1793?-1860? *ApCAB*
Stewart, Austin 1799-1865 *NatCAB 14*
Stewart, Balfour 1828-1887 *AsBiEn, DcScB*
Stewart, Ben A 1889-1967 *NatCAB 54*
Stewart, Caroline Taylor *WomWWA 14*
Stewart, Cecil Parker 1881-1945 *WhAm 2*
Stewart, Charles *NewYHSD*
Stewart, Charles 1729-1800 *ApCAB, BiDrAC,*
  Drake, WhAm H
Stewart, Charles 1778-1869 *AmBi, ApCAB,*
  DcAmB, Drake, NatCAB 8, TwCBDA,
  WebAMB, WhAm H
Stewart, Charles 1826-1895 *WhAm H*
Stewart, Charles 1836-1895 *BiDrAC,*
  TwCBDA
Stewart, Charles 1869- *WhoColR*
Stewart, Charles Allan 1907-1973 *WhAm 5*
Stewart, Charles D 1868- *WhAm 5*
Stewart, Charles James 1775-1837 *ApCAB,*
  Drake
Stewart, Charles Leslie 1890-1974 *WhAm 6*
Stewart, Charles Samuel 1795-1870 *ApCAB,*
  Drake
Stewart, Charles Seaforth 1823-1904 *ApCAB,*
  WhAm 1
Stewart, Charles West 1859-1929 *WhAm 1*
Stewart, Colin C 1873-1944 *WhAm 2*
Stewart, Cora L 1867- *WomWWA 14*
Stewart, Cora Wilson 1875-1958 *BiDAmEd,*
  WomWWA 14
Stewart, David 1800-1858 *ApCAB, BiAUS,*
  BiDrAC, NatCAB 4, WhAm H
Stewart, David 1856- *WhAm 4*
Stewart, David Denison 1858- *WhAm 1*
Stewart, David Wallace 1887- *BiDrAC*
Stewart, DeLisle 1870-1941 *WhAm 1*
Stewart, Donald Barton 1885-1949 *NatCAB 37*
Stewart, Donald Farquharson 1882- *WhAm 2*
Stewart, Donald Mitchell 1913-1965
  NatCAB 51
Stewart, Douglas 1873-1926 *WhAm 1*
Stewart, Douglas Hunt 1860-1933 *WhAm 1*
Stewart, Dugald 1753-1828 *McGEWB*
Stewart, Duncan 1905-1969 *WhAm 5*
Stewart, Duncan James 1899-1963 *NatCAB 52*
Stewart, Edwin 1837-1933 *ApCAB Sup,*
  DcAmB, TwCBDA, WhAm 1
Stewart, Electra Maria Sheldon 1817- *ApCAB*
Stewart, Eliza Daniel 1816-1908 *AmWom,*
  DcAmB, NatCAB 7, NotAW, WhAm 1
Stewart, Eliza H B 1856- *WomWWA 14*
Stewart, Ella Seass 1871- *WhAm 5,*
  WomWWA 14
Stewart, Ethelbert 1857-1936 *NatCAB 27,*
  WhAm 1
Stewart, Ferdinand Augustus 1862- *WhoColR*
Stewart, Ferdinand Campbell 1815- *ApCAB*
Stewart, Ford 1909-1971 *WhAm 5*
Stewart, Forrest Ewart 1879- *WhoColR*
Stewart, Francis Robert 1874- *WhAm 5*
Stewart, Francis Torrens 1877-1920 *WhAm 1*
Stewart, Frank Corwin 1853-1920 *NatCAB 19*
Stewart, Frank Mann 1894-1961 *WhAm 4*
Stewart, Frank R 1910-1964 *WhAm 4*
Stewart, Fred 1906-1970 *WhAm 5*
Stewart, Fred Carlton 1868-1946 *WhAm 2*
Stewart, Frederick William 1894- *WhAm 5*

Stewart, George 1848- *ApCAB*
Stewart, George 1888-1957 *WhAm 3*
Stewart, George 1892-1972 *WhAm 5*
Stewart, George Adolph 1885-1955 *NatCAB 45*
Stewart, George Black 1854-1932 *TwCBDA,*
  WhAm 1
Stewart, George Craig 1879-1940 *NatCAB 33,*
  WhAm 1
Stewart, George David 1862-1933 *NatCAB 23,*
  WhAm 1
Stewart, George Harlan 1858-1914 *NatCAB 20,*
  WhAm 1
Stewart, George James 1895-1957 *WhAm 3*
Stewart, George Neil 1860-1930 *DcAmB,*
  DcScB, NatCAB 23, WhAm 1
Stewart, George Pheldon 1874- *WhoColR*
Stewart, George Scott, Jr. 1888-1949
  NatCAB 37
Stewart, George Taylor 1855-1940 *WhAm 1*
Stewart, George Walter 1876-1956 *WhAm 3*
Stewart, George Washington 1859- *WhoColR*
Stewart, Georgiana 1870- *WomWWA 14*
Stewart, Gideon Tabor 1824-1909 *ApCAB,*
  WhAm 1
Stewart, Gilbert Henry 1878-1957 *WhAm 3*
Stewart, Grace Bliss 1885-1969 *WhAm 5*
Stewart, Graeme 1853-1905 *WhAm 1*
Stewart, H Lockett 1897-1958 *NatCAB 44*
Stewart, Hal Wilson 1896-1964 *NatCAB 51*
Stewart, Harlon L 1861- *WhAm 4*
Stewart, Harold Edison 1903-1975 *WhAm 6*
Stewart, Harold Morgan 1897-1966 *NatCAB 53*
Stewart, Harry Eaton 1887-1948 *NatCAB 36*
Stewart, Hugh Parlane 1856-1914 *NatCAB 16*
Stewart, Humphrey John 1854-1932 *DcAmB,*
  WhAm 1
Stewart, Irvine Emerson 1893-1965 *NatCAB 54*
Stewart, Isabel Maitland 1878-1963 *BiDAmEd,*
  WhAm 4
Stewart, Ivey Withers 1888-1966 *WhAm 4*
Stewart, J Adger 1877-1954 *NatCAB 45*
Stewart, J D d1943 *WhAm 2*
Stewart, Jacob Henry 1829-1884 *ApCAB,*
  BiDrAC, WhAm H
Stewart, James 1775-1821 *BiDrAC, WhAm H*
Stewart, James 1775-1822 *BiAUS*
Stewart, James 1799-1864 *ApCAB*
Stewart, James 1845-1923 *NatCAB 22*
Stewart, James 1898-1957 *WhAm 3*
Stewart, James Augustus 1808-1879 *BiAUS,*
  BiDrAC, WhAm H
Stewart, James Christian 1865-1942 *WhAm 2*
Stewart, James Fleming 1851-1904 *BiDrAC,*
  NatCAB 5, WhAm 1
Stewart, James Garfield 1880-1959 *NatCAB 45*
Stewart, James Garfield 1881-1959 *WhAm 3*
Stewart, James Kennedy 1901-1960 *NatCAB 47*
Stewart, Jane Agnes d1944 *WhAm 2,*
  WomWWA 14
Stewart, Jennie E Douglas 1854-
  WomWWA 14
Stewart, John *Drake*
Stewart, John d1820 *BiAUS, BiDrAC,*
  WhAm H
Stewart, John 1773-1858 *ApCAB*
Stewart, John 1795-1860 *BiAUS, BiDrAC,*
  WhAm H
Stewart, John 1839- *WhAm 1*
Stewart, John A *NewYHSD*
Stewart, John Aikman 1822-1926 *DcAmB,*
  WhAm 1
Stewart, John Alexander 1900-1968 *WhAm 5*
Stewart, John Appleton 1865-1928 *WhAm 1*
Stewart, John David 1833-1894 *BiDrAC,*
  WhAm H
Stewart, John Faulkner 1877-1962 *NatCAB 50*
Stewart, John George 1890-1970 *BiDrAC,*
  NatCAB 55
Stewart, John Hamilton 1917- *WhAm 6*
Stewart, John Hetsler 1903-1971 *NatCAB 57*
Stewart, John Knox 1853-1919 *BiDrAC,*
  WhAm 4
Stewart, John Lammey 1867-1927 *WhAm 1*
Stewart, John Leighton 1876-1940 *NatCAB 34,*
  WhAm 1
Stewart, John Leslie 1911-1971 *WhAm 5*
Stewart, John Minor 1856-1940 *WhAm 1*
Stewart, John Quincy 1894-1972 *WhAm 5*

Stewart, John T 1833-1901 *NatCAB 16*
Stewart, John Truesdale 1868-1928 *WhAm 1*
Stewart, John Wolcott 1825-1915 *BiAUS,*
  BiDrAC, NatCAB 8, TwCBDA,
  WhAm 1, WhAmP
Stewart, Joseph 1859-1929 *NatCAB 22,*
  WhAm 1
Stewart, Joseph Spencer 1863-1934 *BiDAmEd,*
  WhAm 1
Stewart, Joseph William Alexander 1852-1947
  WhAm 2
Stewart, Judd 1867- *WhAm 4*
Stewart, Julius L 1855- *WhAm 4*
Stewart, LeConte 1891- *IIBEAAW*
Stewart, Lever Flegal 1887-1930 *NatCAB 22*
Stewart, Lillian Kimball 1860- *WomWWA 14*
Stewart, Lispenard 1855-1927 *WhAm 1*
Stewart, Logan Henry 1879- *WhoColR*
Stewart, Lowry Alexander 1893-1954
  NatCAB 43
Stewart, Maco 1871-1938 *NatCAB 38*
Stewart, Malcolm Chilson 1913-1970 *WhAm 5*
Stewart, Malcolm Montrose 1877-1937
  WhAm 1
Stewart, Margarita Abraham 1853-
  WomWWA 14
Stewart, Maria W Miller 1803-1879 *NotAW*
Stewart, Marshall Bowyer 1880- *WhAm 6*
Stewart, Mary *WomWWA 14*
Stewart, Matthew 1717-1785 *DcScB*
Stewart, McLeod 1847- *ApCAB*
Stewart, Merch Bradt 1875-1934 *NatCAB 26,*
  WhAm 1
Stewart, Morris Albion 1902-1961 *WhAm 4*
Stewart, Nathaniel Bacon 1871-1931 *WhAm 1*
Stewart, Norman Hamilton 1885-1970
  NatCAB 55
Stewart, Oline Johnson *WhAm 5*
Stewart, Oliver J *NewYHSD*
Stewart, Oliver Wayne 1867-1937 *WhAm 1*
Stewart, Oscar Milton 1869-1944 *WhAm 2*
Stewart, Paul 1892-1950 *BiDrAC, WhAm 3,*
  WhAmP
Stewart, Paul Morton 1888-1957 *NatCAB 47,*
  WhAm 3
Stewart, Paul Perry 1876-1941 *NatCAB 31*
Stewart, Paul Rich 1887-1974 *WhAm 6*
Stewart, Paul William 1899-1955 *WhAm 3*
Stewart, Percy Hamilton 1867-1951 *BiDrAC,*
  NatCAB 40, WhAm 3
Stewart, Philip 1760-1830 *Drake*
Stewart, Philip *see also* Stuart, Philip
Stewart, Philip Battell 1865- *WhAm 5*
Stewart, Philo Penfield 1798-1868 *DcAmB,*
  NatCAB 2, WhAm H
Stewart, Potter 1915- *WebAB*
Stewart, Pythias *NewYHSD*
Stewart, Randall 1896-1964 *WhAm 4*
Stewart, Redmond Conyngham 1873-1936
  NatCAB 27
Stewart, Rex William 1907-1967 *WhAm 4A*
Stewart, Richard Franklin 1862-1939
  NatCAB 36
Stewart, Richard Siegfried 1912-1957 *WhAm 3*
Stewart, Roach Sidney 1881-1948 *NatCAB 38*
Stewart, Robert 1839-1915 *DcAmB, WhAm 1*
Stewart, Robert Ernest 1885-1966 *NatCAB 52*
Stewart, Robert Giffen 1892-1948 *WhAm 3*
Stewart, Robert Laird 1840- *WhAm 4*
Stewart, Robert M 1805- *BiAUS*
Stewart, Robert M 1815-1871 *Drake*
Stewart, Robert Marcellus 1815-1871 *DcAmB,*
  NatCAB 12, WhAm H
Stewart, Robert Mercellus 1815-1871 *ApCAB,*
  TwCBDA
Stewart, Robert Wright 1866-1947 *WhAm 2*
Stewart, Robina Lamont *WomWWA 14*
Stewart, Rolland Maclaren 1878- *WhAm 6*
Stewart, Rosalie 1890- *BiCAW*
Stewart, Ross 1897-1975 *WhAm 6*
Stewart, Rowe 1876-1940 *NatCAB 30,*
  WhAm 1
Stewart, Russ 1909-1974 *WhAm 6*
Stewart, Russell C 1859-1942 *WhAm 1,*
  WhAm 2
Stewart, Ruth Lincoln Phelan 1884-
  WomWWA 14
Stewart, S *NewYHSD*

Stewart, Samuel Vernon 1872-1939 *NatCAB 15,*
NatCAB 30, WhAm 1
Stewart, Samuel White 1867-1955 *NatCAB 49*
Stewart, Sarah A 1839- *WomWWA 14*
Stewart, Sarah E 1858- *WomWWA 14*
Stewart, Seymour 1867-1927 *NatCAB 23*
Stewart, Thomas Dale 1890-1958 *NatCAB 47*
Stewart, Thomas Elliott 1824-1904 *BiAUS,*
BiDrAC
Stewart, Thomas James 1856- *NatCAB 5*
Stewart, Thomas Jamison 1848-1917
NatCAB 12, WhAm 1
Stewart, Thomas McCants 1854- *ApCAB,*
WhAm 4
Stewart, Thomas Milton 1866-1945 *WhAm 2*
Stewart, Tom 1892-1972 *WhAm 5*
Stewart, Virgil Adam 1809- *ApCAB*
Stewart, W Denning 1888-1965 *NatCAB 52*
Stewart, Walter 1756?-1796 *ApCAB, Drake*
Stewart, Walter Allan 1889-1970 *NatCAB 55,*
WhAm 5
Stewart, Walter Leslie 1888-1974 *WhAm 6*
Stewart, Walter W 1885-1958 *WhAm 3*
Stewart, Wilbur Filson 1885-1967 *WhAm 4*
Stewart, William 1802-1856 *ApCAB*
Stewart, William 1810-1876 *BiDrAC,*
WhAm H
Stewart, William 1811-1876 *BiAUS*
Stewart, William Alexander 1825-1892
NatCAB 2
Stewart, William Alvah 1903-1953 *WhAm 3*
Stewart, William Blair 1867-1933 *NatCAB 25*
Stewart, Sir William Drummond *WhAm H*
Stewart, William Finney Bay 1849- *WhAm 4*
Stewart, William H *NewYHSD*
Stewart, William Henry 1831-1913 *WhAm 1*
Stewart, William Holmes 1868-1954
NatCAB 40
Stewart, William Kilborne 1875-1944 *WhAm 2*
Stewart, William Lyman 1868-1930 *WhAm 1*
Stewart, William Lyman, Jr. 1897-1963
NatCAB 50, WhAm 4
Stewart, William Mitton 1859-1913 *BiDAmEd,*
NatCAB 20
Stewart, William Morris 1827-1909 *ApCAB,*
BiDrAC, DcAmB, NatCAB 1, REnAW,
TwCBDA, WebAB, WhAm 1, WhAmP
Stewart, William Moylan 1890-1962
NatCAB 52
Stewart, William Rhinelander 1852-1929
DcAmB, NatCAB 22, WhAm 1
Stewart, William Richard 1864- *WhoColR*
Stewart, William Shaw 1838-1903 *WhAm 1*
Stewel, Gustav *NewYHSD*
Steyerman, Sidney Victor 1892-1966
NatCAB 52
Steyne, Alan Nathaniel 1898-1946 *WhAm 2*
Stibbs, John Henry 1909-1975 *WhAm 6*
Stibitz, George 1856-1944 *WhAm 2*
Stich, Adolph Carl 1846-1915 *NatCAB 16*
Stickel, Fred George, Jr. 1887-1969 *NatCAB 54*
Stickel, William Chrysostom 1863-1926
ApCAB X
Stickle, Fred Ellsworth 1915-1964 *NatCAB 51*
Stickle, John Wesley 1876- *WhAm 5*
Stickler, Joseph William 1854- *NatCAB 7*
Stickles, Arndt Mathis 1872- *WhAm 5*
Stickley, Ezra Eugenius 1839-1915 *WhAm 3*
Stickley, Gustav 1858- *NatCAB 14, WhAm 4*
Stickley, Mary Louise *WomWWA 14*
Stickney, Albert 1839-1908 *WhAm 1*
Stickney, Alpheus Beede 1840-1916 *DcAmB,*
NatCAB 19, WhAm 1
Stickney, Amos 1843-1924 *WhAm 1*
Stickney, Austin 1831-1896 *NatCAB 15*
Stickney, Benjamin Rollin 1871-1946
NatCAB 33
Stickney, Edward Swan 1824-1880 *NatCAB 9*
Stickney, Herman Osman 1867-1936 *WhAm 1*
Stickney, John 1742-1826 *ApCAB*
Stickney, Joseph L 1848-1907 *WhAm 1*
Stickney, Julia Noyes 1830- *WhAm 4*
Stickney, Louis R 1879- *WhAm 6*
Stickney, Mehitabel *NewYHSD*
Stickney, Samuel Crosby 1865- *WhAm 4*
Stickney, William Brunswick Curry 1845-1930
NatCAB 26

Stickney, William Wallace 1853-1932
NatCAB 25, TwCBDA, WhAm 1
Stickroth, Harry I 1890-1922 *NatCAB 6*
Stidger, William Leroy 1885-1949 *WhAm 2*
Stidley, Leonard Albert 1898-1958 *NatCAB 47,*
WhAm 3
Stidolph *NewYHSD*
Stidun, James *NewYHSD*
Stiebel, Augustus *NewYHSD*
Stiebel, Frances *WomWWA 14*
Stieff, Gideon Numsen 1893-1970 *NatCAB 57*
Stieffel, Hermann 1826-1882 *IIBEAAW,*
NewYHSD, WhAm H
Stieg, Max 1889-1969 *WhAm 5*
Stiegel, Henrick Wilhelm Von 1730-1783
NatCAB 11
Stiegel, Henry William 1729-1785 *AmBi,*
BnEnAmA, DcAmB, McGEWB, WebAB,
WhAm H
Stiegler, Richard 1909-1967 *NatCAB 53*
Stieglitz, Alfred 1864-1946 *BnEnAmA,*
DcAmB S4, EncAB, McGEWB, WebAB,
WhAm 2
Stieglitz, Julius Oscar 1867-1937 *DcAmB S2,*
NatCAB 15, NatCAB 27, WhAm 1
Stieglitz, Leopold 1867-1956 *NatCAB 45*
Stieltjes, Thomas Jan 1856-1894 *DcScB*
Stieren, Edward 1873-1946 *NatCAB 35*
Stifel, Edward William 1869-1947 *NatCAB 36*
Stifel, Michael 1487?-1567 *DcScB*
Stifft, M *NewYHSD*
Stifler, Cloyd Burnley 1876- *WomWWA 14*
Stifler, James Madison 1839-1902 *WhAm 1*
Stifler, James Madison 1875-1949 *WhAm 2*
Stifler, William Warren 1883-1954 *NatCAB 44*
Stiger, Cornelia Harter 1877- *WomWWA 14*
Stigler, William Grady 1891-1952 *BiDrAC,*
DcAmB S5, WhAm 3, WhAmP
Stignani, Ebe d1974 *WhAm 6*
Stiha, Vladin 1910?- *IIBEAAW*
Stiles, Charles Wardell 1867-1941 *DcAmB S3,*
DcScB, TwCBDA, WhAm 1
Stiles, Edward H 1836- *NatCAB 4, WhAm 4*
Stiles, Eliza Huestis 1879- *WomWWA 14*
Stiles, Ezra 1727-1795 *AmBi, ApCAB,*
BiDAmEd, DcAmB, DcAmReB, Drake,
NatCAB 1, TwCBDA, WebAB,
WhAm H
Stiles, Fred Bailey 1887-1970 *WhAm 5*
Stiles, George K 1873- *WhAm 5*
Stiles, George P *BiAUS*
Stiles, George Whitfield 1877-1970 *NatCAB 57*
Stiles, Henry Reed 1832-1909 *ApCAB,*
DcAmB, Drake, NatCAB 13, TwCBDA
Stiles, Hinson 1893-1970 *WhAm 5*
Stiles, Israel Newton 1833- *ApCAB*
Stiles, James Esmond 1889-1960 *WhAm 4*
Stiles, James F, Jr. 1892-1965 *WhAm 4*
Stiles, Jeremiah 1771-1826 *NewYHSD*
Stiles, John Dodson 1822-1896 *BiDrAC,*
WhAm H
Stiles, John Dodson 1823-1896 *BiAUS,*
TwCBDA
Stiles, Joseph Clay 1795-1875 *ApCAB*
Stiles, Karl Amos 1895-1968 *NatCAB 54*
Stiles, Meredith Newcomb 1880-1937 *WhAm 1*
Stiles, Norman Charles 1834- *NatCAB 10*
Stiles, Percy Goldthwait 1875-1936 *WhAm 1*
Stiles, Samuel 1796-1861 *NewYHSD*
Stiles, Theodore Lamme 1848-1925 *WhAm 1*
Stiles, William Curtis 1851-1911 *WhAm 1*
Stiles, William Henry 1808-1865 *ApCAB,*
BiAUS, BiDrAC, Drake, NatCAB 12,
WhAm H
Stiles, William M *NewYHSD*
Stilicho, Flavius d408 *McGEWB*
Still, Alfred 1869- *WhAm 5*
Still, Andrew Taylor 1828-1917 *AmBi, DcAmB,*
NatCAB 14, NatCAB 26, WebAB,
WhAm 1
Still, Ardella Dockery 1880- *WomWWA 14*
Still, Clyfford 1904-1967 *BnEnAmA, WhAm 4*
Still, George Anderson 1882-1922 *NatCAB 22*
Still, George Frederick 1868-1941 *BiHiMed*
Still, Summerfield Saunders 1851-1931
NatCAB 22
Still, William 1821-1902 *ApCAB, DcAmB,*
McGEWB, NatCAB 2, WhAm 1

Still, William Grant 1895- *McGEWB, WebAB*
Stille, Alfred 1813-1900 *AmBi, ApCAB,*
BiHiMed, DcAmB, Drake, NatCAB 9,
TwCBDA, WhAm 1
Stille, Charles Janeway 1819-1899 *ApCAB,*
BiDAmEd, DcAmB, Drake, NatCAB 1,
TwCBDA, WhAm 1
Stille, Mary Ingram 1844- *WomWWA 14*
Stille, Mary Ingram 1854- *AmWom*
Stille, Moreton 1822-1855 *ApCAB, Drake*
Stille, Wilhelm Hans 1876-1966 *DcScB*
Stillings, Charles Arthur 1871-1917 *WhAm 1*
Stillings, Ephraim Bailey 1846-1917 *WhAm 1*
Stillman, Albert Leeds 1883-1959 *NatCAB 50*
Stillman, Charles Clark 1877-1952 *WhAm 3*
Stillman, Emma Pomplitz 1858- *WomWWA 14*
Stillman, Ernest Goodrich 1884-1949
NatCAB 40
Stillman, George K 1821?- *NewYHSD*
Stillman, George Schley 1912-1964 *NatCAB 52*
Stillman, James 1850-1918 *DcAmB,*
NatCAB 15, WhAm 1
Stillman, James Alexander 1873-1944
NatCAB 32, WhAm 2
Stillman, John Maxson 1852-1923 *NatCAB 20,*
WhAm 1
Stillman, Joseph Frederick 1848-1932
NatCAB 26
Stillman, Mary Wight *WomWWA 14*
Stillman, Paul Roscoe 1871-1945 *WhAm 2*
Stillman, Samuel 1737-1807 *DcAmB, Drake,*
WhAm H
Stillman, Samuel 1738-1807 *AmBi, ApCAB*
Stillman, Stanley 1861-1934 *NatCAB 18,*
WhAm 1
Stillman, Thomas Bliss 1806-1866 *ApCAB*
Stillman, Thomas Bliss 1852-1915 *DcAmB,*
WhAm 1
Stillman, Thomas Bliss 1852-1916 *NatCAB 16*
Stillman, Thomas Edgar 1837-1906 *DcAmB,*
NatCAB 15
Stillman, Walter Negley 1883-1956 *NatCAB 44,*
WhAm 3
Stillman, William James 1828-1901 *AmBi,*
ApCAB, DcAmB, NatCAB 10,
NewYHSD, WhAm 1
Stillman, William Olin 1856-1924 *NatCAB 1,*
WhAm 1
Stillson, Hamilton 1857-1948 *NatCAB 37*
Stillwagon, G B *NewYHSD*
Stillwell, Ephraim Posey 1887-1965 *NatCAB 52*
Stillwell, Homer Allison 1860-1918 *NatCAB 17,*
WhAm 1
Stillwell, Leander 1843- *WhAm 4*
Stillwell, Lewis Buckley 1863-1941 *NatCAB 14,*
WhAm 1
Stillwell, Thomas Neel 1830-1874 *BiDrAC,*
WhAm H
Stillwell, William Burney 1851-1927 *WhAm 1*
Stilphen, Charles Augustus 1877-1956
NatCAB 47
Stilson, Edward 1867-1933 *NatCAB 25*
Stilson, Mary E 1854- *WomWWA 14*
Stilson, Oscar Reeves 1876- *WhAm 5*
Stilwell, Abner J 1889-1962 *WhAm 4*
Stilwell, Arthur Edward 1859-1928 *NatCAB 14,*
WhAm 1
Stilwell, Clifford Scott 1890-1941 *NatCAB 31*
Stilwell, Edmund William 1880-1957 *WhAm 3*
Stilwell, Eugene Jay 1849-1933 *NatCAB 31*
Stilwell, Giles Heath 1854-1936 *NatCAB 27*
Stilwell, Herbert Fenton 1856-1935 *NatCAB 26,*
WhAm 1
Stilwell, John 1886-1963 *NatCAB 50*
Stilwell, Joseph Warren 1883-1946 *DcAmB S4,*
EncAB, McGEWB, NatCAB 33, WebAB,
WebAMB, WhAm 2, WhWW-II,
WhoMilH
Stilwell, Laura Jean Libbey 1862-
WomWWA 14
Stilwell, Silas Moore 1800-1881 *ApCAB,*
DcAmB, NatCAB 11, WhAm H
Stilwell, Simpson Everett 1849-1903 *DcAmB*
Stilwell, Thomas L 1830-1874 *BiAUS*
Stilwell, Thomas N 1830-1874 *NatCAB 13*
Stilwell, Wilber Moore 1908-1974 *WhAm 6*
Stimets, Charles Calvin 1850- *WhAm 4*
Stimpson, George William 1896-1952 *WhAm 3*

Stimpson, Helen Josephine 1872-
    WomWWA 14
Stimpson, Herbert Baird 1869- *WhAm 5*
Stimpson, William 1832-1872 *ApCAB, DcAmB,
    DcScB, NatCAB 7, WhAm H*
Stimpson, William G 1865-1940 *WhAm 1*
Stimson, Alexander Lovett 1816-1906 *ApCAB,
    DcAmB*
Stimson, Alice Bartlett 1854- *WomWWA 14*
Stimson, Arthur Marston 1876- *WhAm 5*
Stimson, Charles Douglas 1857-1929
    NatCAB 28, WhAm 1
Stimson, Charles Willard 1879-1952
    NatCAB 52
Stimson, Daniel MacMartin 1844-1922
    WhAm 1
Stimson, Earl 1873-1936 *NatCAB 29*
Stimson, Fred Spencer 1868-1921 *NatCAB 19*
Stimson, Frederic Jessup 1855-1943 *NatCAB 44*
Stimson, Frederic Jesup 1855-1943 *ApCAB,
    DcAmB S3, NatCAB 10, TwCBDA,
    WhAm 2*
Stimson, Harriet Overton 1862-1936
    NatCAB 28
Stimson, Henry 1867-1950 *WhWW-II*
Stimson, Henry Albert 1842-1936 *NatCAB 13,
    TwCBDA, WhAm 1*
Stimson, Henry Lewis 1867-1950 *BiDrUSE,
    DcAmB S4, McGEWB, NatCAB 37,
    WebAB, WhAm 3*
Stimson, Henry Louis 1867-1950 *EncAB*
Stimson, John Ward 1850-1930 *ApCAB,
    BiDAmEd, WhAm 1, WhAm 1C*
Stimson, Julia Catherine 1881-1948 *DcAmB S4,
    NotAW, WebAMB, WhAm 2,
    WomWWA 14*
Stimson, Lewis Atterbury 1844-1917 *AmBi,
    ApCAB X, DcAmB, WhAm 1*
Stimson, Maie Elizabeth French 1888-
    WomWWA 14
Stimson, Marshall 1876-1951 *NatCAB 41*
Stimson, Mary Estella Courtright Davis 1862-
    WomWWA 14
Stimson, Philip Moen 1888-1971 *NatCAB 57,
    WhAm 5*
Stimson, Rufus Whittaker 1868-1947 *BiDAmEd,
    WhAm 4*
Stimson, Thomas Douglas 1884-1931
    NatCAB 23, WhAm 1
Stinchfield, Augustus White 1842-1917
    NatCAB 38
Stinchfield, Frederick Harold 1881-1950
    NatCAB 38, WhAm 2
Stinchfield, Roger Adams 1904-1970 *WhAm 5*
Stine, Charles Milton Altland 1882-1954
    *DcAmB S5, DcScB, NatCAB 47,
    WhAm 3*
Stine, George Haeberle 1897-1952 *NatCAB 41*
Stine, H Stanley 1901-1966 *NatCAB 53*
Stine, John William, Jr. 1903-1959 *WhAm 3*
Stine, Milton Henry 1853-1940 *WhAm 1*
Stine, Oscar Clemen 1884-1974 *WhAm 6*
Stine, Victor Francis 1893-1958 *NatCAB 47*
Stine, Wilbur Morris 1863-1934 *WhAm 1*
Stineman, Jacob C 1842-1913 *NatCAB 16*
Stiner, Louis *NewYHSD*
Stines, Norman Caswell 1881-1955 *NatCAB 44*
Stiness, John Henry 1840-1913 *DcAmB,
    NatCAB 12, TwCBDA, WhAm 1*
Stiness, Walter Russell 1854-1924 *BiDrAC,
    WhAm 4*
Stinson, Anna Carroll *WomWWA 14*
Stinson, John Turner 1865- *WhAm 5*
Stinson, K William 1930- *BiDrAC*
Stinson, Paul Raymond 1884-1956 *NatCAB 47*
Stinson, Robert V, Jr. 1892-1957 *NatCAB 45*
Stinson, Walter Samuel 1901-1959 *NatCAB 49*
Stinson, William H *NewYHSD*
Stires, Ernest Milmore 1866-1951 *WhAm 3*
Stires, Manning 1876-1962 *NatCAB 51*
Stirk, Samuel *BiDrAC*
Stirlen, Eugene Dare 1900-1967 *WhAm 4*
Stirling *NewYHSD*
Stirling, Lord *Drake, WebAMB*
Stirling, Allan 1844-1927 *NatCAB 21*
Stirling, Arthur Churchill 1912-1965
    NatCAB 51
Stirling, David 1915- *WhWW-II*

Stirling, Emma Maitland 1839- *AmWom*
Stirling, J Bowman 1870- *WhAm 5*
Stirling, James 1692-1770 *DcScB*
Stirling, John William 1910-1975 *WhAm 6*
Stirling, Matthew Williams 1896-1975 *WhAm 6*
Stirling, Sir Thomas d1808 *ApCAB, Drake*
Stirling, Lord William 1726-1783 *AmBi,
    DcAmB*
Stirling, William Arthur *NewYHSD*
Stirling, William Robert 1851-1918 *NatCAB 17*
Stirling, Yates 1843-1929 *NatCAB 38,
    TwCBDA, WhAm 1*
Stirling, Yates, Jr. 1872-1948 *NatCAB 49,
    WhAm 2*
Stirman, Wilbur Fitzalan 1856-1928
    NatCAB 22
Stirner, Max 1806-1856 *McGEWB*
Stirton, Ruben Arthur 1901-1966 *WhAm 4*
Stites, Fletcher Wilbur d1933 *WhAm 1*
Stites, Henry J 1816-1891 *NatCAB 12*
Stites, John 1850-1938 *WhAm 1*
Stites, John Randolph 1836- *NewYHSD*
Stites, Raymond Somers 1899-1974 *WhAm 6*
Stith, Robert Marcus 1874-1943 *NatCAB 35*
Stith, William 1689-1755 *ApCAB, Drake,
    TwCBDA*
Stith, William 1707-1755 *AmBi, DcAmB,
    NatCAB 3, WhAm H*
Stith, Wilmer Curtis 1858- *WhAm 4*
Stitt, Edward Rhodes 1867-1948 *DcAmB S4,
    NatCAB 39, WhAm 2*
Stitt, Edward Walmsley 1862-1927 *WhAm 1*
Stitt, Edward Walmsley 1893-1971 *NatCAB 56*
Stitt, Hobart 1880- *IlBEAAW*
Stitt, Howard Leigh 1885-1958 *NatCAB 43*
Stitt, William Britton 1898-1969 *WhAm 5*
Stiven, Frederic Benjamin 1882-1947 *WhAm 2*
Stivers, Edwin Jacob 1835- *WhAm 4*
Stivers, Frank Adams 1868-1946 *NatCAB 33*
Stivers, John Lawrence 1883-1958 *NatCAB 46*
Stivers, Kazia Armington 1840- *WhAm 4*
Stivers, Moses Dunning 1828-1895 *BiDrAC,
    WhAm H*
Stix, Charles Aaron 1861- *NatCAB 12*
Stix, Erma Kingsbacher 1884- *WomWWA 14*
Stix, Ernest William 1878-1955 *WhAm 3*
Stix, Sylvan L 1871- *WhAm 5*
Stoaks, Charles E 1900- *WhAm 4*
Stobaeus, John Baptist 1844-1918 *NatCAB 6*
Stobbs, George Russell 1877-1966 *BiDrAC,
    WhAm 4*
Stobie, Charles S 1845-1931 *IlBEAAW*
Stobo, Robert 1727-1770? *ApCAB, Drake*
Stobo, Robert 1727-1772? *DcAmB, WhAm H*
Stock, Alfred 1876-1946 *AsBiEn, DcScB*
Stock, Alvin Meredith 1896-1959 *NatCAB 48*
Stock, Chester 1892-1950 *DcScB, WhAm 3*
Stock, Frederick August 1872-1942 *DcAmB S3,
    WhAm 2*
Stock, Harry T 1891-1958 *WhAm 3*
Stock, Joseph Whiting 1815-1855 *BnEnAmA,
    NewYHSD, WhAm H*
Stock, Leo Francis 1878- *WhAm 6*
Stockard, Charles Rupert 1879-1939 *AmBi,
    ApCAB X, DcAmB S2, NatCAB 30,
    WhAm 1*
Stockard, Henry Jerome 1858-1914 *WhAm 1*
Stockard, Lester Napier 1893-1960 *NatCAB 47*
Stockard, Virginia Alice Cottey 1848-1940
    WhAm 1
Stockbarger, Donald C 1895-1952 *WhAm 3*
Stockberger, Warner W 1872-1944 *NatCAB 35,
    WhAm 2*
Stockbridge, Francis Brown 1826-1894 *ApCAB,
    BiDrAC, NatCAB 1, TwCBDA,
    WhAm H*
Stockbridge, Frank Parker 1870-1940 *WhAm 1*
Stockbridge, George Henry 1870-1957
    NatCAB 46
Stockbridge, Henry 1856-1924 *BiDrAC,
    DcAmB, WhAm 1*
Stockbridge, Henry Smith 1822-1895 *AmBi,
    ApCAB, DcAmB, WhAm H*
Stockbridge, Horace Edward 1857-1930 *DcAmB,
    EncAAH, NatCAB 14, WhAm 1*
Stockbridge, Levi 1820-1904 *ApCAB, DcAmB,
    EncAAH, NatCAB 5*
Stockdale, Allen Arthur 1875- *WhAm 5*

Stockdale, Grant 1915-1963 *WhAm 4*
Stockdale, John M 1822-1897 *NatCAB 17*
Stockdale, Paris Buell 1896-1962 *NatCAB 52,
    WhAm 4*
Stockdale, Shields Craig 1872-1961 *NatCAB 49*
Stockdale, Thomas Ringland 1828-1899 *BiDrAC,
    DcAmB, TwCBDA, WhAm H*
Stockder, Archibald Herbert 1889-1967
    WhAm 4
Stocker, Corinne 1871- *AmWom*
Stocker, Frank Anthony 1812?- *NewYHSD*
Stocker, Harry Emilius 1876-1929 *WhAm 1*
Stockham, Alice Bunker 1833-1912 *AmWom,
    WhAm 1, WomWWA 14*
Stockham, Charles 1820- *NatCAB 3*
Stockham, Edward Villeroy 1863- *WhAm 1*
Stockham, William Henry 1861-1923
    NatCAB 19, WhAm 1
Stockhardt, Karl Georg 1842-1913 *DcAmB*
Stockhausen, Karlheinz 1928- *McGEWB*
Stockhausen, William Edward 1912-1974
    WhAm 6
Stocking, Charles Francis 1873- *WhAm 5*
Stocking, Charles Hendrickson 1842-1926
    NatCAB 30
Stocking, Charles Howard 1882-1958 *WhAm 3*
Stocking, George Ward 1892-1975 *WhAm 6*
Stocking, Harriet Bliss 1871- *WomWWA 14*
Stocking, Jay Thomas 1870-1936 *WhAm 1*
Stocking, William Alonzo, Jr. 1872-1926
    WhAm 1
Stockley, Charles Clark 1819-1901 *NatCAB 11,
    TwCBDA*
Stockman, Dora Hall 1872- *WomWWA 14*
Stockman, Lowell 1901-1962 *BiDrAC,
    WhAm 4*
Stockslager, Charles Oscar 1847- *NatCAB 14,
    WhAm 4*
Stockslager, Strother Madison 1842-1930
    BiDrAC
Stockstrom, Louis d1945 *WhAm 2*
Stockton, Alfred Augustus 1842- *ApCAB*
Stockton, Charles G 1853-1931 *DcAmB,
    WhAm 1*
Stockton, Charles Herbert 1845- *NatCAB 13,
    TwCBDA*
Stockton, Charles Herbert 1845-1923 *WhAm 1*
Stockton, Charles Herbert 1845-1924 *DcAmB,
    NatCAB 25*
Stockton, Charles Stacy 1836-1912 *NatCAB 15*
Stockton, Edward A, Jr. 1886-1948 *WhAm 2*
Stockton, Ernest 1888-1954 *WhAm 3*
Stockton, Francis Richard 1834-1902 *AmBi,
    ApCAB, ApCAB X, NatCAB 1,
    NewYHSD, TwCBDA, WhAm 1*
Stockton, Frank Richard 1834-1902 *DcAmB,
    WebAB*
Stockton, Fred Everett 1877-1938 *WhAm 1*
Stockton, Frederick Eugene 1883-1949
    NatCAB 38
Stockton, George 1854-1917 *WhAm 1*
Stockton, Harry Mitchell 1854-1928 *ApCAB X*
Stockton, Howard 1842-1932 *NatCAB 26,
    WhAm 1*
Stockton, J Roy 1892-1972 *WhAm 5*
Stockton, Jack Potter 1891-1953 *NatCAB 41*
Stockton, Jessie D A 1866- *WomWWA 14*
Stockton, John Drean 1836-1877 *ApCAB,
    NewYHSD, TwCBDA*
Stockton, John Potter 1825-1900 *BiAUS*
Stockton, John Potter 1826-1900 *ApCAB,
    BiDrAC, DcAmB, Drake Sup,
    NatCAB 13, TwCBDA, WhAm H,
    WhAmP*
Stockton, Joseph 1833-1907 *WhAm 1*
Stockton, Joseph Denniston 1907-1960 *WhAm 4*
Stockton, Kenneth E 1893-1950 *WhAm 3*
Stockton, Louise 1838-1914 *NatCAB 8,
    TwCBDA, WhAm 5*
Stockton, Mary Alice 1867- *WomWWA 14*
Stockton, N Allen 1859-1934 *NatCAB 29*
Stockton, Philip 1874-1940 *NatCAB 29,
    WhAm 1*
Stockton, Richard 1730-1781 *AmBi, ApCAB,
    BiAUS, BiDrAC, DcAmB, Drake,
    NatCAB 12, TwCBDA, WhAm H,
    WhAmP*
Stockton, Richard 1764-1828 *ApCAB, BiAUS,*

Stokes, S Emlen 1894-1972 *NatCAB 57*
Stokes, Thomas 1882-1952 *NatCAB 50*
Stokes, Thomas 1906-1975 *WhAm 6*
Stokes, Thomas Lunsford, Jr. 1898-1958 *WhAm 3*
Stokes, William 1804-1878 *BiHiMed*
Stokes, William Brickly 1814-1897 *ApCAB Sup, BiAUS, DcAmB, TwCBDA, WhAm H*
Stokes, William E 1878- *WhAm 6*
Stokes, William Earl Dodge 1852-1926 *DcAmB*
Stokes, William Herman 1894-1957 *NatCAB 43, WhAm 3*
Stokes, William John Blackman 1857-1935 *NatCAB 27*
Stokes, William Royal 1870-1930 *NatCAB 21*
Stokowski, Leopold 1882- *WebAB*
Stokowski, Olga Samaroff 1882-1948 *BiDAmEd, NatCAB 36, NotAW*
Stoland, Ole Olufson 1881-1959 *WhAm 3*
Stolberg, Benjamin 1891-1951 *DcAmB S5, WhAm 3*
Stolbrand, Carlos John Meuller 1821- *ApCAB*
Stolee, Michael J 1871-1946 *WhAm 2*
Stoletov, Aleksandr Grigorievich 1839-1896 *DcScB*
Stoll, Charles Augustus 1872-1939 *WhAm 1*
Stoll, Donald Earl 1917-1970 *NatCAB 56*
Stoll, Harry 1905-1962 *WhAm 4*
Stoll, Philip Henry 1874-1958 *BiDrAC, WhAm 3*
Stoll, Richard Charles 1876-1949 *WhAm 2*
Stolle, Antonie 1850- *WomWWA 14*
Stoller, James Hough 1857- *WhAm 4*
Stoller, Morton Joseph 1917-1963 *WhAm 4*
Stolper, Gustav 1888-1947 *WhAm 2*
Stoltz, Charles Edward 1920-1971 *WhAm 5*
Stoltz, Robert Bear 1890-1948 *WhAm 2*
Stolypin, Piotr Arkadevich 1862-1911 *McGEWB*
Stolz, Benjamin 1867-1937 *WhAm 1*
Stolz, Harry Phillip 1899-1964 *NatCAB 51*
Stolz, Joseph 1861-1941 *WhAm 1*
Stolz, Karl Ruf 1884-1943 *WhAm 2*
Stolz, Leon 1893-1968 *WhAm 5*
Stolz, Otto 1842-1905 *DcScB*
Stolzenbach, J Roland 1892-1961 *NatCAB 50*
Stomberg, Andrew Adin 1871-1943 *WhAm 2*
Stone, Abraham 1890-1959 *WhAm 3*
Stone, Albert Jmes 1873-1950 *WhAm 3*
Stone, Alexander W d1854 *BiAUS*
Stone, Alfred 1834-1908 *NatCAB 11, WhAm 1*
Stone, Alfred Holt 1870-1955 *WhAm 3*
Stone, Alfred Parish 1813-1865 *BiAUS, BiDrAC, WhAm H*
Stone, Allison 1873-1940 *WhAm 1*
Stone, Amasa 1818-1883 *AmBi, ApCAB, DcAmB, NatCAB 11, WhAm H*
Stone, Andrew J 1840-1926 *NatCAB 21*
Stone, Andrew Jackson 1859- *WhAm 4*
Stone, Andrew Leete 1815- *ApCAB, Drake*
Stone, Arthur Fairbanks 1863-1944 *WhAm 2*
Stone, Arthur John 1847-1938 *WhAm 1*
Stone, Arthur Kingsbury 1861-1952 *NatCAB 43*
Stone, Arthur Parker 1870-1961 *NatCAB 50*
Stone, Barton Warren d1844 *REnAW*
Stone, Barton Warren 1772-1844 *ApCAB, DcAmB, DcAmReB, WebAB, WhAm H*
Stone, Barton Warren 1774-1844 *AmBi*
Stone, Benjamin, Jr. *NewYHSD*
Stone, Benjamin Bellows Grant 1829-1906 *NewYHSD*
Stone, Caleb 1898- *WhAm 4*
Stone, Calvin Perry 1892-1954 *NatCAB 52, WhAm 3*
Stone, Carlos Huntington 1857-1934 *WhAm 1*
Stone, Carlos Melville 1846-1908 *NatCAB 15*
Stone, Celia M 1876- *WomWWA 14*
Stone, Charles Arthur 1893-1944 *NatCAB 33, WhAm 2*
Stone, Charles Augustus 1867-1941 *DcAmB S3, WhAm 1*
Stone, Charles Edwin 1887-1956 *WhAm 3*
Stone, Charles Francis 1843-1910 *WhAm 1*
Stone, Charles Frederic 1883-1970 *WhAm 5*
Stone, Charles Holmes 1890-1965 *WhAm 4*
Stone, Charles Newhall 1884-1954 *WhAm 3*
Stone, Charles Pomeroy 1824-1887 *AmBi,*

ApCAB, DcAmB, NatCAB 11, TwCBDA, WebAMB, WhAm H
Stone, Charles Pomeroy 1826-1887 *Drake*
Stone, Charles Warren 1843-1912 *BiDrAC, TwCBDA, WhAm 1*
Stone, Charles Waterman 1874-1938 *NatCAB 29, WhAm 1*
Stone, Charles Wellington 1853-1927 *ApCAB X, NatCAB 20, WhAm 1*
Stone, Claude Ulysses 1879-1957 *NatCAB 44*
Stone, Claudius Ulysses 1879-1957 *BiDrAC, WhAm 3*
Stone, Cliff Winfield 1874- *WhAm 5*
Stone, Clifford Hannibal 1888-1952 *NatCAB 40*
Stone, Clyde Ernest 1876-1948 *NatCAB 51, WhAm 2*
Stone, Collins 1812-1870 *ApCAB*
Stone, David 1770-1818 *ApCAB, BiAUS, BiDrAC, DcAmB, Drake, NatCAB 4, TwCBDA, WhAm H, WhAmP*
Stone, David Lamme 1876- *WhAm 5*
Stone, David Marvin 1817-1895 *ApCAB, DcAmB, NatCAB 1, TwCBDA, WhAm H*
Stone, David Mavine 1817-1895 *Drake*
Stone, Donald Lane 1886-1968 *NatCAB 55*
Stone, Eben Francis 1822-1895 *BiDrAC, TwCBDA, WhAm H*
Stone, Ebenezer Whittier 1801-1880 *NatCAB 4, WhAm H*
Stone, Ebenezer Whitton 1801-1880 *ApCAB*
Stone, Edmund *NewYHSD*
Stone, Edward Carleton 1878-1964 *NatCAB 52*
Stone, Edward Durell 1902- *BnEnAmA, WebAB*
Stone, Edwin Martin 1805-1883 *ApCAB, Drake*
Stone, Elihu David 1888-1952 *NatCAB 41*
Stone, Elizabeth 1811-1872 *NewYHSD*
Stone, Ellen A *WomWWA 14*
Stone, Ellen Maria 1846-1927 *AmBi, DcAmB, WhAm 1, WomWWA 14*
Stone, Emanuel Olson 1860- *WhAm 4*
Stone, Emerson Law 1895-1953 *WhAm 3*
Stone, Frank Burrill 1860- *NatCAB 17*
Stone, Frank Folsom 1886-1952 *NatCAB 41*
Stone, Fred 1835?- *NewYHSD*
Stone, Fred Andrew 1873-1959 *WhAm 3*
Stone, Fred Denton 1875-1956 *WhAm 3*
Stone, Frederick 1820-1899 *ApCAB, BiAUS, BiDrAC, NatCAB 3, TwCBDA, WhAm 1, WhAmP*
Stone, Frederick Dawson 1841-1897 *ApCAB Sup, NatCAB 9, TwCBDA*
Stone, Frederick E 1871- *WhAm 5*
Stone, G Edmund 1903-1961 *NatCAB 48*
Stone, Galen Luther 1862-1926 *ApCAB X, NatCAB 33*
Stone, George 1811?- *NewYHSD*
Stone, George Cameron 1859-1935 *NatCAB 33*
Stone, George Edward 1860-1941 *WhAm 1*
Stone, George Frederick 1836-1912 *NatCAB 15, WhAm 1*
Stone, George Hapgood 1841-1917 *WhAm 1*
Stone, George Nelson 1840-1901 *NatCAB 13*
Stone, George Washington 1811-1894 *DcAmB, NatCAB 4, TwCBDA, WhAm H*
Stone, George Whitefield 1840-1923 *WhAm 1*
Stone, H Charles 1873- *WhAm 5*
Stone, H Chase d1966 *WhAm 5*
Stone, Hannah Mayer 1893-1941 *NatCAB 30*
Stone, Harlan Fiske 1872-1946 *ApCAB X, BiDrUSE, DcAmB S4, EncAB, McGEWB, NatCAB 34, WebAB, WhAm 2*
Stone, Harold 1878-1958 *WhAm 3*
Stone, Harriet 1869- *WomWWA 14*
Stone, Harry Benjamin 1879-1966 *NatCAB 54*
Stone, Harry Everette 1883-1959 *WhAm 4*
Stone, Harry R 1896-1965 *WhAm 4*
Stone, Henry *NewYHSD*
Stone, Henry Lane 1842-1922 *NatCAB 19, WhAm 1*
Stone, Henry Lewis 1885-1969 *NatCAB 54*
Stone, Herbert Lawrence 1871-1955 *WhAm 3*
Stone, Herbert Stuart 1871- *WhAm 5*
Stone, Horace Greeley 1852-1923 *WhAm 1*

Stone, Horace M 1890-1944 *WhAm 2*
Stone, Horatio 1808-1875 *BnEnAmA, DcAmB, NewYHSD, WhAm H*
Stone, Horatio 1810?-1875 *BiAUS*
Stone, Horatio Odell 1811-1877 *NatCAB 3*
Stone, Hugh Lamar 1885-1967 *WhAm 4*
Stone, Imogen *WomWWA 14*
Stone, Isaac Frank 1867- *NatCAB 14*
Stone, Isaac Scott 1851-1935 *NatCAB 38, WhAm 4*
Stone, Isabelle 1870- *WhAm 5, WomWWA 14*
Stone, Isabelle 1884- *WomWWA 14*
Stone, Isidor Feinstein 1907- *WebAB*
Stone, Ivan McKinley 1899-1971 *WhAm 5*
Stone, J Austin 1847-1969 *NatCAB 55*
Stone, J McWilliams 1896-1970 *WhAm 5*
Stone, James *BiAUS*
Stone, James Andrus Blinn d1888 *TwCBDA*
Stone, James Clifton 1878- *WhAm 6*
Stone, James H 1847- *NatCAB 1*
Stone, James Kent 1840-1921 *ApCAB, DcAmB, NatCAB 7, TwCBDA*
Stone, James Lauriston 1873- *WhAm 5*
Stone, James Samuel 1852-1928 *ApCAB, NatCAB 5, WhAm 1*
Stone, James W 1813-1854 *BiAUS, BiDrAC, WhAm H*
Stone, Jane Dransfield 1875- *WomWWA 14*
Stone, Jennie Woodbury 1857- *WomWWA 14*
Stone, John Augustus 1800-1834 *DcAmB, WhAm H*
Stone, John Augustus 1801-1834 *ApCAB, Drake, NatCAB 8*
Stone, John Bestor 1842-1925 *NatCAB 20*
Stone, John Charles 1867-1940 *BiDAmEd, NatCAB 31, WhAm 1*
Stone, John Francis 1860-1900 *WhAm 1*
Stone, John Hamilton 1872-1930 *NatCAB 22*
Stone, John Haskins 1745-1804 *BiAUS, Drake*
Stone, John Holden 1881-1935 *NatCAB 25, WhAm 1*
Stone, John Hoskins 1745-1804 *ApCAB, NatCAB 9, TwCBDA*
Stone, John Marshall 1830-1900 *DcAmB, NatCAB 1, NatCAB 13, TwCBDA, WhAm 1*
Stone, John Osgood 1813-1876 *ApCAB, ApCAB X*
Stone, John Paul 1902-1966 *WhAm 5*
Stone, John Pittman 1890-1969 *WhAm 5*
Stone, John Seely 1795-1882 *ApCAB, DcAmB, Drake, TwCBDA, WhAm H*
Stone, John Stone 1869-1943 *ApCAB X, DcAmB S3, NatCAB 14, NatCAB 34, WhAm 2*
Stone, John Theodore 1859-1920 *NatCAB 19, WhAm 1*
Stone, John Timothy 1868- *ApCAB X*
Stone, John Wesley 1838-1922 *BiDrAC, DcAmB, NatCAB 22, WhAm 1*
Stone, John Wesley 1908-1955 *NatCAB 44*
Stone, Joseph Cecil 1870-1948 *WhAm 2*
Stone, Joseph Champlin 1829-1902 *BiDrAC*
Stone, Joseph E 1874-1952 *WhAm 3*
Stone, Joseph Mason 1820-1887 *NatCAB 17*
Stone, Judson F 1873-1958 *WhAm 3*
Stone, Julius Frederick 1855-1947 *WhAm 2*
Stone, Kenneth Franklin 1904-1952 *NatCAB 48, WhAm 3*
Stone, Kimbrough 1875-1958 *WhAm 3*
Stone, L A 1900-1967 *WhAm 4*
Stone, L Joseph 1912-1975 *WhAm 6*
Stone, Lauson 1883-1948 *WhAm 2*
Stone, Lee Alexander 1879- *WhAm 6*
Stone, Lewis 1879-1953 *WhAm 3*
Stone, Livingston 1835-1912 *WhAm 1*
Stone, Lucinda Hinsdale 1814-1900 *AmWom, BiDAmEd, NatCAB 13, NotAW*
Stone, Lucy 1818-1893 *AmBi, AmWom, ApCAB, DcAmB, Drake, McGEWB, NatCAB 2, NatCAB 29, NotAW, TwCBDA, WebAB, WhAm H, WhAmP*
Stone, Malcolm Bowditch 1881-1965 *NatCAB 55, WhAm 4*
Stone, Margaret *NewYHSD*
Stone, Margaret Manson Barbour 1841- *WhAm 4*

Stone, Marilla Lee 1868- *WomWWA 14*
Stone, Martha Elvira 1816- *AmWom*
Stone, Martha M 1858- *WomWWA 14*
Stone, Mason Sereno 1857- *WhAm 4*
Stone, Melville Elijah 1848-1929 *AmBi,*
ApCAB, ApCAB X, DcAmB, EncAB,
NatCAB 1, NatCAB 21, WebAB,
WhAm 1
Stone, Michael Jenifer 1747-1812 *BiDrAC,*
NatCAB 11, WhAm H, WhAmP
Stone, Michael Jenifer 1750?-1812 *ApCAB,*
BiAUS
Stone, N *NewYHSD*
Stone, N I 1873-1966 *WhAm 4*
Stone, Nat 1866-1931 *WhAm 1*
Stone, Ormond 1847-1933 *AmBi, ApCAB,*
DcAmB S1, NatCAB 6, WhAm 1
Stone, Patrick Thomas 1889-1963 *WhAm 4*
Stone, Philip Carlton 1911-1968 *WhAm 5*
Stone, Raleigh Webster 1889-1969 *WhAm 5*
Stone, Ralph 1868-1957 *WhAm 3*
Stone, Ralph Walter 1876-1964 *WhAm 4*
Stone, Richard French 1844-1913 *DcAmB,*
NatCAB 30
Stone, Robert 1866-1957 *NatCAB 46*
Stone, Robert Elwin 1891-1971 *WhAm 5*
Stone, Robert Franklin 1895-1968 *WhAm 5*
Stone, Robert Glenn 1881-1945 *NatCAB 38*
Stone, Robert Spencer 1895-1966 *NatCAB 53,*
WhAm 5
Stone, Royal Augustus 1875-1942 *WhAm 2*
Stone, Rufus Barrett 1847-1929 *WhAm 1*
Stone, Samuel 1602-1663 *ApCAB, DcAmB,*
Drake, NatCAB 7, WhAm H
Stone, Samuel M 1869-1959 *WhAm 3*
Stone, Theodore 1895-1962 *NatCAB 49*
Stone, Theodore Thaddeus 1897-1952 *WhAm 3*
Stone, Thomas 1743-1787 *AmBi, ApCAB,*
BiAUS, BiDrAC, DcAmB, Drake,
NatCAB 8, TwCBDA, WhAm H,
WhAmP
Stone, Thomas Treadwell 1801-1875? *ApCAB,*
NatCAB 2, WhAm H
Stone, Tillie McGill 1874- *WomWWA 14*
Stone, Ulysses Stevens 1878-1962 *BiDrAC,*
WhAm 6
Stone, Walker 1904-1973 *WhAm 5*
Stone, Walter King 1875-1949 *WhAm 3*
Stone, Walter Moreland 1884-1955 *NatCAB 44*
Stone, Walter Robinson 1872-1937 *NatCAB 28,*
WhAm 1, WhAm 1C
Stone, Warren 1808-1872 *ApCAB, DcAmB,*
NatCAB 5, WhAm H
Stone, Warren 1843-1883 *ApCAB*
Stone, Warren Sanford 1860-1925 *DcAmB,*
NatCAB 22, WhAm 1
Stone, Wilbur Fisk 1833-1920 *DcAmB,*
NatCAB 19, WhAm 1
Stone, Willard 1916- *IIBEAAW, REnAW*
Stone, Willard John 1877-1943 *NatCAB 36,*
WhAm 2
Stone, William 1603?-1660? *DcAmB*
Stone, William 1603?-1695? *ApCAB*
Stone, William 1605-1660? *NatCAB 7,*
WhAm H
Stone, William 1764-1840 *TwCBDA*
Stone, William 1791-1853 *BiAUS, BiDrAC,*
WhAm H
Stone, William Addison 1862-1924 *NatCAB 20*
Stone, William Alexis 1846-1920 *ApCAB Sup,*
BiDrAC, NatCAB 13, NatCAB 24,
WhAm HA, WhAm 1, WhAm 4
Stone, William Henry 1828-1901 *BiAUS,*
BiDrAC
Stone, William J 1798-1865 *NewYHSD*
Stone, William Joel 1848-1918 *ApCAB Sup,*
BiDrAC, DcAmB, NatCAB 12, TwCBDA,
WhAm 1, WhAmP
Stone, William Johnson 1841-1923 *BiDrAC,*
TwCBDA, WhAmP
Stone, William Leete 1792-1844 *AmBi,*
ApCAB, DcAmB, Drake, EncAAH,
NatCAB 7, TwCBDA, WhAm H
Stone, William Leete 1835-1908 *AmBi,*
ApCAB, DcAmB, NatCAB 11, TwCBDA,
WhAm 1
Stone, William Milo 1827-1893 *BiAUS,*
NatCAB 11, TwCBDA

Stone, William Murray 1779-1838 *ApCAB,*
Drake, NatCAB 6, TwCBDA
Stone, William Oliver 1830-1875 *ApCAB,*
DcAmB, NewYHSD, WhAm H
Stone, William S 1910-1968 *WhAm 5*
Stone, William Stephen 1867-1946 *NatCAB 35*
Stone, Wilson S 1907-1968 *WhAm 5*
Stone, Winthrop Ellsworth 1862-1921
NatCAB 21, TwCBDA, WhAm 1
Stone, Witmer 1866-1939 *DcAmB S2,*
TwCBDA, WhAm 1
Stonebarger, Herbert Hayes 1879-1960
NatCAB 50
Stonecipher, John Franklin 1852-1919
NatCAB 18
Stonehouse, Ned Bernard 1902-1962 *WhAm 4*
Stoneman, Abigail *NotAW*
Stoneman, Bertha 1866-1943 *NotAW,*
WomWWA 14
Stoneman, Frank B 1857-1941 *WhAm 1*
Stoneman, George 1822-1894 *AmBi, ApCAB,*
DcAmB, Drake, NatCAB 4, TwCBDA,
WebAMB, WhAm H
Stoner, Dayton 1883-1944 *WhAm 2*
Stoner, Frank E 1894-1965 *WhAm 4*
Stoner, Frank Rahm, Jr. 1903-1971 *NatCAB 57*
Stoner, George Hiram 1917-1971 *WhAm 5*
Stoner, Marcus Woodward 1878-1954
NatCAB 44
Stoner, William David 1893-1966 *WhAm 4*
Stoner, William Wirt 1875-1954 *NatCAB 47*
Stoner, Winifred Sackville d1931 *BiCAW,*
WhAm 1
Stoneroad, Rebecca 1865- *WomWWA 14*
Stoney, George Franklin 1886-1959 *NatCAB 49*
Stoney, George Johnstone 1826-1911 *AsBiEn,*
DcScB
Stong, Philip Duffield 1899-1957 *NatCAB 43,*
WhAm 3
Stonier, Harold 1890-1957 *NatCAB 43,*
WhAm 3
Stonorov, Oskar 1905-1970 *WhAm 5*
Stoody, Winston Flavius 1892-1967 *NatCAB 54*
Stookey, Byron Polk 1887-1966 *NatCAB 52,*
WhAm 4
Stookey, Lyman Brumbaugh 1878-1940
WhAm 1
Stookey, Stephen Wharton 1859-1951
NatCAB 47, WhAm 3
Stooksbury, William Lafayette 1866- *WhAm 4*
Stoops, Harry Eugene 1863-1922 *NatCAB 19*
Stoops, Herbert Morton 1887?-1948 *IIBEAAW*
Stoops, John Dashiell 1873-1973 *WhAm 6*
Stoothoff, Everett O 1905-1973 *WhAm 5*
Stoper, Frank *NewYHSD*
Stopford, Sir Montagu 1892-1971 *WhWW-II*
Stopford, William 1847-1928 *NatCAB 21*
Stopka, Andrzej Wieslaw 1904-1973 *WhAm 6*
Stoppel, Arthur Edward 1897-1957 *NatCAB 44*
Storckman, Clem Franklin 1899-1970 *WhAm 5*
Storelli, Felix Marie Ferdinand 1778-1854
IIBEAAW
Storer, Bellamy 1796-1875 *BiDrAC,*
NatCAB 11, WhAm H, WhAmP
Storer, Bellamy 1798?-1875 *ApCAB, BiAUS*
Storer, Bellamy 1844-1922 *ApCAB Sup*
Storer, Bellamy 1847-1922 *BiDrAC, DcAmB,*
NatCAB 11, TwCBDA, WhAm 1,
WhAmP
Storer, Catherine *NewYHSD*
Storer, Clement 1760-1830 *ApCAB, BiAUS,*
BiDrAC, NatCAB 7, TwCBDA,
WhAm H
Storer, David Humphreys 1804-1891 *ApCAB,*
DcAmB, Drake, NatCAB 11, TwCBDA,
WhAm H
Storer, Elizabeth Drinker *WomWWA 14*
Storer, Francis Humphreys 1832-1914 *ApCAB,*
DcAmB, Drake, EncAAH, NatCAB 11,
TwCBDA, WhAm 1
Storer, George Butler 1866-1920 *NatCAB 19*
Storer, George Butler 1899-1975 *WhAm 6*
Storer, George Washington 1789-1864 *ApCAB,*
Drake, TwCBDA
Storer, Grace Ayrault *WomWWA 14*
Storer, Horatio Robinson 1830-1922 *ApCAB,*
ApCAB X, DcAmB, Drake, NatCAB 10,
NatCAB 11, TwCBDA, WhAm 1

Storer, John Humphreys 1859-1935 *ApCAB X,*
NatCAB 14, WhAm 1
Storer, Katharine DeLamater 1870-
WomWWA 14
Storer, Malcolm 1862-1935 *NatCAB 41*
Storer, Maria Longworth Nichols 1849-1932
NatCAB 11, NotAW, WhAm 1,
WomWWA 14
Storer, Norman Wilson 1868-1947 *WhAm 3*
Storer, Robert Treat Paine 1893-1962 *WhAm 4*
Storey, Carroll Lawrence 1877-1924
NatCAB 20
Storey, Douglass Doty 1888-1953 *NatCAB 43*
Storey, James Walker 1896-1956 *NatCAB 47*
Storey, Moorfield 1845-1929 *AmBi, DcAmB,*
EncAB, NatCAB 12, TwCBDA,
WhAm 1, WhAmP
Storey, Robert Gerald, Jr. 1921-1962 *WhAm 4*
Storey, Thomas Andrew 1875-1943 *WhAm 2*
Storey, Walter Rendell 1881-1953 *WhAm 3*
Storey, Wilbur Fisk 1819-1884 *ApCAB,*
DcAmB, WhAm H
Storey, Willard Monroe 1875-1949 *NatCAB 37*
Storey, William Benson 1857-1940 *ApCAB X,*
WhAm 1
Storing, James Alvin 1905-1967 *NatCAB 53,*
WhAm 4
Stork, Charles Augustus 1838-1883 *ApCAB*
Stork, Charles Augustus Gottlieb 1764-1831
ApCAB
Stork, Charles Wharton 1881-1971 *NatCAB 56,*
WhAm 6
Stork, Fred William 1881-1956 *NatCAB 44*
Stork, Theophilus 1814-1874 *ApCAB*
Storke, Arthur Ditchfield 1894-1949
NatCAB 38, WhAm 2
Storke, Frederic Eliot 1855-1926 *NatCAB 22*
Storke, Helen Landon *WomWWA 14*
Storke, Sophia Dickerman *WomWWA 14*
Storke, Thomas More 1876-1971 *BiDrAC,*
WhAm 5
Storm, Ashley Van 1861-1943 *NatCAB 32*
Storm, Frederic 1844-1935 *BiDrAC*
Storm, G F *NewYHSD*
Storm, George 1830-1913 *NewYHSD*
Storm, Hans Otto 1895-1942 *WhAm 2*
Storm, Jack 1927-1975 *WhAm 6*
Storm, John 1910-1959 *NatCAB 47*
Storm, John Brutzman 1838-1901 *BiAUS,*
BiDrAC
Storm, John M 1899-1951 *WhAm 3*
Storm, Katherine L *WomWWA 14*
Storm, Mildred Raum 1911- *WhAm 5*
Storm, Theodor 1817-1888 *McGEWB*
Stormer, Fredrik Carl Mulertz 1874-1957
DcScB
Storms, Albert Boynton 1860-1933 *NatCAB 13,*
WhAm 1
Storms, Christian S *NewYHSD*
Storms, Jane McManus *NotAW*
Storms, John *NewYHSD*
Stormzand, Martin James 1879- *WhAm 6*
Storrow, Charles 1841-1927 *NatCAB 21*
Storrow, Charles Storer 1809-1904 *DcAmB,*
NatCAB 21
Storrow, James Jackson 1837-1897 *DcAmB,*
WhAm H
Storrow, James Jackson 1864-1926 *NatCAB 33,*
WhAm 1
Storrs, Augustus 1819-1892 *NatCAB 42*
Storrs, Caryl B 1870-1920 *WhAm 1*
Storrs, Charles Backus 1794-1833 *ApCAB,*
Drake, NatCAB 2, TwCBDA
Storrs, Emery Alexander 1835-1885 *ApCAB*
Storrs, Frank Vance 1873-1939 *NatCAB 29*
Storrs, George Draper 1866-1940 *NatCAB 35*
Storrs, Harry Asahel 1861- *WhAm 5*
Storrs, Henry Martyn 1827-1894 *NatCAB 9*
Storrs, Henry Randolph 1787-1837 *ApCAB,*
BiAUS, BiDrAC, Drake, NatCAB 11,
TwCBDA, WhAm H, WhAmP
Storrs, John 1885-1956 *BnEnAmA, WhAm 4*
Storrs, John Tyler 1889-1964 *NatCAB 51*
Storrs, Leonard Kip 1842-1923 *WhAm 3*
Storrs, Lewis Austin 1866-1945 *NatCAB 37,*
WhAm 2
Storrs, Lucius Seymour 1869-1945 *WhAm 5*
Storrs, Richard Salter 1787-1873 *ApCAB,*

DcAmB, Drake, WhAm H
Storrs, Richard Salter 1821-1900 *ApCAB,*
DcAmB, Drake, NatCAB 8, TwCBDA,
WhAm 1
Storrs, Robert Williamson, III 1912- *WhAm 5*
Storrs, William Lucius 1795-1861 *ApCAB,*
BiAUS, BiDrAC, Drake, NatCAB 7,
TwCBDA, WhAm H, WhAmP
Story *NewYHSD*
Story, Daisy Allen *WomWWA 14*
Story, Douglas 1872- *WhAm 5*
Story, Emma Eames 1867- *ApCAB Sup,*
TwCBDA
Story, Francis Quarles 1845- *WhAm 4*
Story, George Henry 1835- *ApCAB,*
ApCAB Sup, TwCBDA
Story, George Henry 1835-1922 *WhAm 1*
Story, George Henry 1835-1923 *NewYHSD*
Story, Isaac 1774-1803 *DcAmB, Drake,*
NatCAB 13, WhAm H
Story, John Patten 1841-1915 *WhAm 1*
Story, Joseph 1779-1845 *AmBi, ApCAB,*
BiAUS, BiDAmEd, BiDrAC, DcAmB,
Drake, EncAB, McGEWB, NatCAB 2,
TwCBDA, WebAB, WhAm H, WhAmP
Story, Julian 1857-1919 *DcAmB, NatCAB 19,*
TwCBDA, WhAm 1
Story, Nelson, Jr. 1874-1932 *WhAm 1*
Story, Russell McCulloch 1883-1942
NatCAB 37, WhAm 2
Story, Thomas C *NewYHSD*
Story, Walter P 1883- *WhAm 3*
Story, Walter Scott 1879-1955 *WhAm 3*
Story, William *BiAUS*
Story, Mrs. William Cumming 1855?-1932
NatCAB 16
Story, Mrs. William Cumming 1857-1932
NatCAB 26
Story, William Edward 1850-1930 *DcAmB,*
NatCAB 24, WhAm 1
Story, William Wetmore 1819-1895 *AmBi,*
ApCAB, BnEnAmA, DcAmB, Drake,
NatCAB 5, NewYHSD, TwCBDA,
WhAm H
Storz, Todd 1924-1964 *WhAm 4*
Stose, George Willis 1869-1960 *WhAm 4*
Stoskopf, Michael 1845-1919 *NatCAB 18*
Stoskopf, William Brewster 1878- *WhAm 6*
Stoss, Veit 1445?-1533 *McGEWB*
Stossel, Anatoli Mikhailovich 1848-1915
WhoMilH
Stote, Theodore *NewYHSD*
Stotesbury, Edward Townsend 1849-1938
DcAmB S2, WhAm 1
Stotesbury, Louis William 1870-1948
NatCAB 40, WhAm 2
Stothard, James *NewYHSD*
Stothard, R *NewYHSD*
Stotsenburg, Evan Brown 1865-1937 *WhAm 1*
Stott, Henry Gordon 1866-1917 *DcAmB,*
NatCAB 14, WhAm 1
Stott, John H *NewYHSD*
Stott, Louis Lathrop 1906-1964 *NatCAB 51*
Stott, Mary Perry 1842- *AmWom*
Stott, Roscoe Gilmore 1880-1957 *WhAm 3*
Stott, William *NewYHSD*
Stott, William Taylor 1836- *NatCAB 9,*
TwCBDA
Stotts, William *NewYHSD*
Stotz, Charles Frederick 1872-1948 *NatCAB 36*
Stotz, Edward, Jr. 1896-1964 *NatCAB 51,*
WhAm 4
Stoudenmire, Dallas 1845-1882 *REnAW*
Stoudt, John Baer 1878-1944 *WhAm 2*
Stoudt, Morris Eugene 1895-1953 *NatCAB 41*
Stouffer, Gordon A 1905-1956 *WhAm 3*
Stouffer, Samuel Andrew 1900-1960 *McGEWB,*
WhAm 4
Stouffer, Vernon Bigelow 1901-1974 *WhAm 6*
Stougaard, Holger 1892-1949 *NatCAB 37*
Stough, Charles Francis 1873-1953 *NatCAB 41*
Stough, Henry Wellington 1870-1939 *WhAm 1*
Stoughton, Mrs. *NewYHSD*
Stoughton, Bradley 1873-1959 *NatCAB 14,*
NatCAB 47, WhAm 3
Stoughton, Charles Bradley 1841-1898
NatCAB 14
Stoughton, Charles William d1945 *WhAm 2*

Stoughton, Clarence Charles 1895-1975
WhAm 6
Stoughton, Edwin Henry 1838-1868 *ApCAB*
Stoughton, Edwin Wallace 1818-1882 *ApCAB,*
DcAmB, NatCAB 3, WhAm H
Stoughton, Israel d1645 *ApCAB, Drake*
Stoughton, William 1631-1701 *AmBi, DcAmB,*
Drake, WhAm H
Stoughton, William 1632-1701 *ApCAB,*
NatCAB 7
Stoughton, William Lewis 1827-1888 *ApCAB,*
BiAUS, BiDrAC, Drake, NatCAB 11,
TwCBDA, WhAm H
Stout, Aaron James 1872-1947 *WhAm 4*
Stout, Arlow Burdette 1876-1957 *WhAm 3*
Stout, Arthur Purdy 1885-1967 *WhAm 4A*
Stout, Arthur Wendel 1889-1969 *NatCAB 56*
Stout, Benjamin Middleton 1889-1956
NatCAB 43
Stout, Byron Gray 1829-1896 *BiDrAC,*
WhAm H
Stout, Charles Banks 1882-1965 *WhAm 5*
Stout, Charles F C 1869-1952 *ApCAB X*
Stout, Charles Frederick Cloua 1869-1952
WhAm 5
Stout, Charles Frederick Clous 1869-1952
NatCAB 46
Stout, Charles Herman 1864-1928 *ApCAB X,*
NatCAB 32
Stout, Elmer William 1876-1962 *NatCAB 50,*
WhAm 4
Stout, Frank Wallace 1875-1955 *NatCAB 42*
Stout, Franklin *NewYHSD*
Stout, George Abeel 1876- *WhAm 5*
Stout, George Clymer 1862-1932 *ApCAB X,*
WhAm 1
Stout, George H 1807-1852 *NewYHSD*
Stout, Gilbert Leonidas 1898-1963 *NatCAB 51*
Stout, H Elton 1900-1961 *NatCAB 50*
Stout, Henry Elbert 1873- *WhAm 5*
Stout, Henry Rice 1843-1914 *WhAm 1*
Stout, Hiram Miller 1905-1972 *WhAm 5*
Stout, Howard A 1874-1959 *WhAm 3*
Stout, Irving Wright 1903-1972 *WhAm 6*
Stout, Jacob *BiAUS*
Stout, James *NewYHSD*
Stout, James Coffin 1869-1930 *WhAm 1*
Stout, James DeForest 1783-1868 *NewYHSD*
Stout, James Huff 1848-1910 *NatCAB 34,*
WhAm 1
Stout, James Varick 1809-1860 *NewYHSD*
Stout, John Benjamin 1805-1877 *NewYHSD*
Stout, John Elbert 1867-1942 *WhAm 2*
Stout, John William 1909-1965 *NatCAB 53*
Stout, Joseph Duerson 1886-1944 *WhAm 2*
Stout, Lansing 1828-1870 *BiAUS*
Stout, Lansing 1828-1871 *BiDrAC, WhAm H*
Stout, Lawrence Edward 1898-1966 *WhAm 5*
Stout, Oscar VanPelt 1865-1935 *NatCAB 26,*
WhAm 1
Stout, Ralph Emerson 1866-1926 *WhAm 1*
Stout, Rex Todhunter 1886-1975 *WhAm 6*
Stout, Rufus Sea 1868- *WhoColR*
Stout, Selatie Edgar 1871-1969 *WhAm 5*
Stout, Tom 1879-1965 *BiDrAC, WhAm 4*
Stout, W Frank 1867- *NatCAB 16*
Stout, Wesley Winans 1890-1971 *WhAm 5*
Stout, William *NewYHSD*
Stout, William Bushnell 1880-1956 *WhAm 3*
Stout, William Cill 1820- *NewYHSD*
Stoutenburgh, Mrs. *NewYHSD*
Stovall, L 1887- *WhoColR*
Stovall, Pleasant Alexander 1857-1935 *AmBi,*
DcAmB S1, NatCAB 26, WhAm 1
Stovall, Wallace Fisher 1869-1950 *NatCAB 12,*
WhAm 3
Stovall, William Robert 1905-1963 *NatCAB 52,*
WhAm 4
Stove, Serine Eisteinsen 1879- *WomWWA 14*
Stover, Charles Clark 1877-1948 *NatCAB 37*
Stover, Elias Steever 1836-1927 *NatCAB 25*
Stover, George Henry 1871-1915 *WhAm 1*
Stover, Georgia Hulse McLeod *WomWWA 14*
Stover, Holly 1883-1963 *NatCAB 50*
Stover, James Harney 1849- *NatCAB 12*
Stover, John Ford 1912- *EncAAH*
Stover, John Hubler 1833-1889 *BiAUS,*
BiDrAC, WhAm H

Stover, Jordan Homer, III 1911-1974 *WhAm 6*
Stover, Joseph Woodman 1837- *NatCAB 14*
Stover, Lora Agan 1881- *WomWWA 14*
Stover, Martin Luther 1845-1921 *NatCAB 12,*
WhAm 1
Stover, Russell 1888-1954 *NatCAB 43*
Stover, William Miller 1867- *WhAm 4*
Stow, Alexander Wolcott 1804-1854
NatCAB 12
Stow, Baron 1801-1869 *ApCAB, DcAmB,*
Drake, WhAm H
Stow, Charles Messer 1880-1952 *WhAm 3*
Stow, Frederic Henry 1814-1872 *NatCAB 5*
Stow, Frederick Enos 1870-1940 *NatCAB 32*
Stow, Hobart Hamilton 1837- *NatCAB 12*
Stow, John *NewYHSD*
Stow, Marcellus H 1902-1957 *WhAm 3*
Stow, Micollius Noel 1915- *WhAm 4*
Stow, Silas 1773-1827 *BiAUS, BiDrAC,*
WhAm H
Stowe, Ancel Roy Monroe 1882-1952
NatCAB 39
Stowe, Annie Bigelow 1879- *WomWWA 14*
Stowe, Ansel Roy Monroe 1882-1952 *WhAm 4*
Stowe, Calvin Ellis 1802-1886 *AmBi, ApCAB,*
BiDAmEd, DcAmB, Drake, NatCAB 10,
TwCBDA, WhAm H
Stowe, Charles Edward 1850- *WhAm 4*
Stowe, Emily Howard Jennings 1831- *AmWom*
Stowe, Franklin Day Locke 1879-1964
NatCAB 51
Stowe, Frederick Arthur 1870-1938 *WhAm 1*
Stowe, Harriet Elizabeth Beecher 1811-1896
AmBi, DcAmB, DcAmReB, EncAAH,
EncAB, McGEWB, NatCAB 1, NotAW,
TwCBDA, WebAB, WhAm H, WhAmP
Stowe, Harriet Elizabeth Beecher 1812-1896
AmWom, ApCAB, Drake
Stowe, Harvey Julius 1907-1971 *NatCAB 56*
Stowe, Lyman Beecher 1880-1963 *NatCAB 48,*
WhAm 4
Stowe, Robert Lee 1866-1963 *NatCAB 49,*
WhAm 4
Stowell, Calvin Llewellyn 1845-1920 *NatCAB 8*
Stowell, Calvin Llewellyn 1854-1920 *WhAm 1*
Stowell, Charles Frederick 1853-1933 *WhAm 1*
Stowell, Charles Henry 1850-1932 *ApCAB,*
WhAm 1
Stowell, E Channing 1866-1941 *NatCAB 32*
Stowell, Ellery Cory 1875-1958 *NatCAB 47,*
WhAm 3
Stowell, Frederick M 1870-1932 *WhAm 1*
Stowell, Henry 1834-1918 *NatCAB 17*
Stowell, Jay Samuel 1883-1966 *WhAm 4*
Stowell, Kenneth Kingsley 1894-1969 *WhAm 5*
Stowell, Leon Carl 1891-1976 *WhAm 6*
Stowell, Louisa Maria Reed 1850- *ApCAB*
Stowell, Louise Maria Reed 1850- *AmWom,*
WhAm 4, WomWWA 14
Stowell, Mary A *WomWWA 14*
Stowell, Nathan Wilson 1851- *ApCAB X*
Stowell, Thomas Blanchard 1846-1927
BiDAmEd, NatCAB 21, WhAm 1
Stowell, William Henry Harrison 1840-1922
BiAUS, BiDrAC, WhAm 1
Stower, John G *BiAUS, BiDrAC, WhAm H*
Stowers, Walter Haslip 1859- *WhoColR*
Strabel, Thelma d1959 *WhAm 3*
Strabo 063?BC-019AD *AsBiEn*
Strabo 063?BC-025?AD *DcScB*
Strabo 064?BC-023?AD *McGEWB*
Straccia, Frank Alexander 1916-1975 *WhAm 6*
Strachan, Donald Cheyne 1892-1957
NatCAB 46
Strachan, Grace Charlotte *WomWWA 14*
Strachan, John 1778-1867 *ApCAB, Drake,*
McGEWB
Strachan, Joseph 1859-1926 *NatCAB 21*
Strachan, Kenneth 1902-1956 *NatCAB 45*
Strachan, Paul Ambrose 1894-1972 *WhAm 5*
Strachan, Sir Richard John, Baronet 1760-1828
WhoMilH
Strachan, Thomas Curr, Jr. 1901-1957 *WhAm 4*
Strachauer, Arthur Clarence 1883-1957
WhAm 4
Strachauer, Arthur Clarence 1884-1957
NatCAB 47

Strachauer, Gertrude Louise Hale 1880-
  WomWWA 14
Strachey, John 1671-1743 *DcScB*
Strachey, John 1901-1963 *WhAm 4*
Strachey, Lionel 1864- *WhAm 4*
Strachey, William *AmBi, ApCAB, DcAmB,
  Drake, NatCAB 8, WhAm H*
Strackbein, John 1914-1963 *NatCAB 50*
Strader, Bernard Earl 1892-1949 *WhAm 2*
Strader, Jacob 1795-1860 *Drake*
Strader, Otto *BiAUS*
Strader, P W 1818-1881 *BiAUS*
Strader, Peter Wilson 1818-1881 *BiDrAC,
  WhAm H*
Stradley, Bland Lloyd 1889-1957 *NatCAB 46,
  WhAm 3*
Stradley, Leighton Paxton 1880-1956 *WhAm 3*
Stradling, George Flowers 1867-1932
  NatCAB 24, WhAm 4
Straehley, Clifford John 1896-1965 *NatCAB 52*
Straehley, Erwin, Sr. 1868-1947 *WhAm 2*
Strafer, Harriette R 1873- *WhAm 5*
Strafford, Thomas Wentworth, Earl Of
  1593-1641 *McGEWB*
Stragnell, Gregory 1888-1963 *WhAm 5*
Strahalm, Franz S 1879-1935 *IIBEAAW*
Strahan, Charles *NewYHSD*
Strahan, Charles Morton 1864-1947 *WhAm 2*
Strahan, Hazel Blair 1898-1963 *WhAm 4*
Strahan, Kay Cleaver 1888-1941 *WhAm 1*
Strahan, R S 1835- *NatCAB 13*
Strahlmann, Louis 1892-1952 *NatCAB 41*
Strahm, Victor H 1895-1957 *WhAm 3*
Strahorn, Robert Edmond 1852-1944 *REnAW*
Strahorn, Robert Edmund 1852-1944
  NatCAB 6, WhAm 2
Straidy *NewYHSD*
Straight, Herbert Randall 1874-1963 *WhAm 4*
Straight, Mrs. Johnson W 1844- *WomWWA 14*
Straight, Willard Dickerman 1880-1918
  ApCAB X, DcAmB, WhAm 1
Strain, Isaac G 1821-1857 *AmBi, ApCAB,
  DcAmB, Drake, WhAm H*
Strain, John Dougal 1879-1947 *NatCAB 39*
Strait, Horace Burton 1835-1894 *BiAUS,
  BiDrAC, WhAmP*
Strait, Thomas Jefferson 1846-1924 *BiDrAC,
  TwCBDA, WhAm 4*
Straiton, John 1830- *NatCAB 3*
Strake, George William 1894-1969 *NatCAB 57,
  WhAm 5*
Strakosch, Maurice 1825-1887 *ApCAB,
  WhAm H*
Strakosch, Max 1835- *ApCAB*
Stralem, Donald S 1903-1976 *WhAm 6*
Stranahan, Clara Harrison *AmWom*
Stranahan, Edgar Howard 1875-1944 *WhAm 2*
Stranahan, Frank Duane 1876-1965 *NatCAB 54*
Stranahan, J S T 1808-1898 *BiAUS*
Stranahan, James Adamson, Jr. 1910-1964
  NatCAB 50
Stranahan, James Samuel Thomas 1808-1898
  *ApCAB, BiDrAC, DcAmB, NatCAB 3,
  WhAm H*
Stranahan, Nevada Northrop 1861- *WhAm 4*
Stranahan, Robert Allen 1886-1962 *NatCAB 52,
  WhAm 4*
Strand, John Andrew 1910-1970 *NatCAB 57*
Strand, Paul 1890- *BnEnAmA, WebAB*
Strand, William 1911-1974 *WhAm 6*
Strandberg, George Robert 1888-1960
  NatCAB 47
Strandjord, Nels Magne 1920-1968 *WhAm 5*
Strang, Elmore Steele 1889-1964 *WhAm 4*
Strang, James Jesse 1813-1856 *DcAmB,
  REnAW, WebAB, WhAm H*
Strang, James Jesse 1820?-1856 *NatCAB 8*
Strang, Lewis Clinton 1869-1935 *TwCBDA,
  WhAm 1*
Strang, Ray C 1893-1957 *IIBEAAW*
Strang, Robert Hallock Wright 1881- *WhAm 6*
Strang, Ruth May 1895-1971 *BiDAmEd*
Strang, S Bartow 1882-1954 *NatCAB 46,
  WhAm 3*
Strang, William Frederick 1883-1960
  NatCAB 48
Strange, John 1789-1832 *NatCAB 22*
Strange, John 1852-1923 *NatCAB 16,*

WhAm 1
Strange, Joseph W *NewYHSD*
Strange, Mary Margaret 1854- *WomWWA 14*
Strange, Michael 1890-1950 *DcAmB S4,
  NatCAB 39, NotAW, WhAm 3*
Strange, Orman Morton 1901-1965 *NatCAB 53*
Strange, Robert 1796-1854 *AmBi, ApCAB,
  BiAUS, BiDrAC, Drake, NatCAB 7,
  TwCBDA, WhAm H*
Strange, Robert 1857-1914 *NatCAB 16,
  WhAm 1*
Strange, Robert 1888-1949 *WhAm 3*
Strange, Thomas B 1831- *ApCAB*
Stransky, Franklin J 1878-1960 *WhAm 4*
Stransky, Josef 1874-1936 *WhAm 1*
Strasburger, Christopher *NewYHSD*
Strasburger, Eduard Adolf 1844-1912 *AsBiEn,
  DcScB*
Strasburger, Milton 1876-1955 *WhAm 3*
Strasenburgh, Robert John 1864-1928
  NatCAB 26
Strassburger, Ralph Beaver 1883-1959
  ApCAB X, WhAm 4
Strasser *NewYHSD*
Strasser, Frederick *NewYHSD*
Strassman, Fritz 1902- *AsBiEn*
Strassmann, George Samuel 1890-1972
  WhAm 6
Stratemeyer, Edward 1862-1930 *ApCAB X,
  DcAmB, NatCAB 16, NatCAB 32,
  TwCBDA, WebAB, WhAm 1*
Stratemeyer, George E 1890-1969 *WhAm 5*
Strater, Charles Godfrey 1856-1937
  NatCAB 32
Strater, William Edward 1866-1908
  NatCAB 43
Strath, William 1906-1975 *WhAm 6*
Strathalmond, Lord 1888-1970 *WhAm 5*
Strathcona, Baroness Isabella Sophia
  WomWWA 14
Strathearn, Harold 1890-1950 *WhAm 3*
Strathearn, Robert P 1875?- *IIBEAAW*
Strathearn, Sophia 1865- *WomWWA 14*
Strato Of Lampsacus 340?BC-270?BC *AsBiEn,
  DcScB*
Straton, John Roach 1875-1929 *DcAmB,
  NatCAB 29, WhAm 1*
Stratte, Joseph J 1847-1954 *NatCAB 43*
Stratton, Albert Lorenzo 1882-1920 *ApCAB X*
Stratton, Anna Booth 1859- *WomWWA 14*
Stratton, Anna Reese *WomWWA 14*
Stratton, Charles Carroll 1833- *ApCAB*
Stratton, Charles Creighton 1796-1859 *BiAUS,
  BiDrAC, Drake, NatCAB 5, TwCBDA,
  WhAm H*
Stratton, Charles Sherwood 1838-1883 *AmBi,
  ApCAB, DcAmB, Drake, NatCAB 10,
  WhAm H*
Stratton, Clarence 1880-1950 *WhAm 3*
Stratton, Clif 1886-1970 *WhAm 5*
Stratton, Clif, Jr. 1918-1967 *WhAm 4A*
Stratton, Don B 1899-1958 *WhAm 3*
Stratton, Dorothy Constance 1899- *WebAMB*
Stratton, Frederick Alexander 1880-1954
  NatCAB 45
Stratton, Frederick Eugene 1847-1928 *WhAm 1*
Stratton, Frederick John Marrion 1881-1960
  DcScB
Stratton, Frederick Smith 1859-1915 *WhAm 1*
Stratton, George Malcolm 1865-1957
  NatCAB 13, WhAm 3
Stratton, Harold M 1878-1962 *WhAm 4*
Stratton, Henry Dwight 1824-1867 *ApCAB*
Stratton, John 1769-1804 *BiAUS, BiDrAC,
  WhAm H*
Stratton, John Leake Newbold 1817-1899
  BiAUS, BiDrAC
Stratton, Lloyd 1895-1961 *WhAm 4*
Stratton, Margaret Elizabeth 1844- *WhAm 4,
  WomWWA 14*
Stratton, Melville Norcross 1884-1968 *WhAm 5*
Stratton, Mercy Lavinia Warren Bump
  1841-1919 *ApCAB, NotAW*
Stratton, Nathan Taylor 1813-1887 *BiAUS,
  BiDrAC, WhAm H*
Stratton, Philip Bryan 1897-1968 *NatCAB 55*
Stratton, Samuel Sommerville 1898-1969
  WhAm 5

Stratton, Samuel Studdiford 1916- *BiDrAC*
Stratton, Samuel Wesley 1861-1931 *AmBi,
  DcAmB, NatCAB 13, WebAB, WhAm 1*
Stratton, William Buck 1865-1938 *NatCAB 29,
  WhAm 1, WhAm 1C*
Stratton, William D d1892 *NewYHSD*
Stratton, William F *NewYHSD*
Stratton, William Grant 1914- *BiDrAC*
Stratton-Porter, Gene 1863-1924 *DcAmB,
  NotAW, WebAB, WomWWA 14*
Straub, Christian Markle 1804- *BiAUS,
  BiDrAC, WhAm H*
Straub, Lorenz George 1901-1963 *NatCAB 52,
  WhAm 4*
Straub, Maria 1838- *AmWom*
Straub, Oscar Itin 1865-1922 *WhAm 1*
Straub, Walter F 1897-1964 *WhAm 4*
Straube, Oscar 1899-1958 *NatCAB 49*
Strauch, John Balthasar 1869-1945 *NatCAB 35,
  WhAm 2*
Strauch, Peter D 1836- *NatCAB 2*
Strauchen, Edmund Rudolph Meade 1910-1963
  NatCAB 50
Straughn, James Henry 1877- *WhAm 5*
Straughn, William Ringgold 1882-1936
  WhAm 1
Straumanis, Martin Edward 1898-1973
  WhAm 6
Straup, Daniel Newton 1862-1945 *NatCAB 33,
  WhAm 2*
Straus, Aaron 1864-1958 *WhAm 3*
Straus, Adolph D 1839-1925 *WhAm 1*
Straus, David C 1882-1954 *NatCAB 43*
Straus, Henry Lobe 1896-1949 *NatCAB 42*
Straus, Herbert Nathan 1881-1933 *NatCAB 24,
  WhAm 1*
Straus, Hugh Grant 1890-1961 *NatCAB 50*
Straus, Isidor 1845-1912 *AmBi, ApCAB X,
  BiDrAC, DcAmB, McGEWB,
  NatCAB 10, WebAB, WhAm 1*
Straus, Jesse Isidor 1872-1936 *AmBi,
  DcAmB S2, NatCAB 27, WhAm 1*
Straus, Lazarus 1809-1898 *NatCAB 23*
Straus, Lina Gutherz 1854-1930 *NatCAB 22*
Straus, M Franklin 1871-1954 *NatCAB 47*
Straus, Martin Louis, II 1896-1958 *NatCAB 48*
Straus, Martin Louis, II 1897-1958 *WhAm 3*
Straus, Michael Wolf 1897-1970 *NatCAB 55,
  WhAm 5*
Straus, Nathan 1848-1931 *AmBi, ApCAB X,
  DcAmB, NatCAB 10, NatCAB 22,
  WebAB, WhAm 1*
Straus, Nathan 1889-1961 *NatCAB 45,
  WhAm 4*
Straus, Oscar 1870-1954 *WhAm 3*
Straus, Oscar Solomon 1850- *ApCAB,
  ApCAB Sup, NatCAB 10, NatCAB 14,
  TwCBDA*
Straus, Oscar Solomon 1850-1926 *AmBi,
  DcAmB, NatCAB 40, WebAB, WhAm 1*
Straus, Oscar Solomon 1850-1931 *BiDrUSE*
Straus, Percy Selden 1876-1944 *DcAmB S3,
  NatCAB 40, WhAm 2*
Straus, Robert E 1903-1973 *WhAm 6*
Straus, Roger Williams 1891-1957 *NatCAB 45,
  WhAm 3*
Straus, Samuel J Tilden 1876- *WhAm 5*
Straus, Simon William 1866-1930 *AmBi,
  ApCAB X, DcAmB, WhAm 1*
Strauss, A J *WomWWA 14*
Strauss, Abraham 1887-1946 *NatCAB 42*
Strauss, Albert 1864-1929 *NatCAB 22,
  WhAm 1*
Strauss, Charles 1854-1934 *NatCAB 27,
  WhAm 1*
Strauss, David Friedrich 1808-1874 *McGEWB*
Strauss, Ferdinand 1852-1922 *NatCAB 19*
Strauss, Harold 1907-1975 *WhAm 6*
Strauss, Henry Harrison 1882-1958 *WhAm 3*
Strauss, Herbert Donald 1909-1973 *WhAm 5*
Strauss, Israel 1873-1955 *NatCAB 43*
Strauss, Johann, Jr. 1825-1899 *McGEWB*
Strauss, Joseph 1861-1948 *NatCAB 37,
  WhAm 2*
Strauss, Joseph Baermann 1870-1938 *AmBi,
  DcAmB S2, NatCAB 27, WhAm 1*
Strauss, Juliet Virginia 1863-1918 *NatCAB 2,
  WhAm 3*

Strauss, Leo 1899-1973 *WhAm 6*
Strauss, Leopold 1844-1914 *NatCAB 16*
Strauss, Levi 1829?-1902 *WebAB*
Strauss, Lewis Lichtenstein 1896-1974 *BiDrUSE,
WhAm 6*
Strauss, Maurice Benjamin 1904-1974 *WhAm 6*
Strauss, Maurice J 1893-1958 *WhAm 3*
Strauss, Morris *NewYHSD*
Strauss, Moses *NewYHSD*
Strauss, Moses 1872-1938 *WhAm 1*
Strauss, Raphael *NewYHSD*
Strauss, Richard 1864-1949 *McGEWB,
WhAm 2*
Strauss, William 1851-1902 *NatCAB 30*
Straussenberg, Artur Freiherr Arz Von
1857-1935 *WhoMilH*
Strausser, Clayton Edward 1892-1956
NatCAB 45
Strauther, D H *NewYHSD*
Stravinsky, Igor Fedorovich 1882-1971 *EncAB,
McGEWB, WebAB, WhAm 5*
Straw, Ezekiel Albert 1819-1882 *NatCAB 11*
Straw, William Parker 1878-1953 *WhAm 3*
Strawbridge, Frederic H 1866- *WhAm 5*
Strawbridge, George 1844-1914 *NatCAB 15*
Strawbridge, James Dale 1824-1890 *BiAUS,
BiDrAC, WhAm H*
Strawbridge, Robert d1781 *ApCAB, DcAmB,
WhAm H*
Strawbridge, Ruth Gawthorpe Knowles 1880-
WhAm 6
Strawbridge, William Correy 1848-1908
NatCAB 3, WhAm 1
Strawn, Eugene William 1907-1971 *NatCAB 56*
Strawn, Jacob 1800-1865 *DcAmB, WhAm H*
Strawn, Julia Clark 1868-1942 *NatCAB 31,
WhAm 2*
Strawn, Lester Herbert 1855- *WhAm 4*
Strawn, Silas Hardy 1866-1946 *DcAmB S4,
NatCAB 34, WhAm 2*
Strawn, Silas Hardy 1866-1949 *ApCAB X*
Strawn, Taylor 1889-1938 *NatCAB 31*
Strayer, Arthur Clare 1891-1962 *NatCAB 49*
Strayer, Edward Ray 1897-1951 *NatCAB 38*
Strayer, George Drayton 1876-1962 *BiDAmEd,
WhAm 4*
Strayer, Louis William 1869-1922 *WhAm 1*
Strayer, Paul 1885- *IIBEAAW*
Strayer, Paul Johnston 1912-1961 *WhAm 4*
Strayer, Paul Moore 1871-1929 *NatCAB 21,
WhAm 4*
Straznicky, Edward R 1820-1876 *ApCAB*
Stream, John Joseph 1870-1943 *NatCAB 33*
Streamer, A Camp 1885-1950 *WhAm 3*
Streamer, Charles Walker 1892-1939
NatCAB 42
Streamer, Volney d1915 *WhAm 1*
Strean, Maria Judson d1949 *WhAm 2,
WomWWA 14*
Streat, Hearn W d1946 *WhAm 2*
Streb, Charles Alexis 1888-1962 *WhAm 4*
Strebel, Ralph Frederick 1894-1959 *WhAm 3*
Streblow, Albert George 1894-1962 *NatCAB 54,
WhAm 4*
Strecker, Edward 1867-1938 *NatCAB 28*
Strecker, Edward Adam 1886-1959 *NatCAB 48*
Strecker, Edward Adam 1887-1959 *WhAm 3*
Strecker, Herman 1836-1901 *NatCAB 10,
NewYHSD, WhAm 1*
Strecker, John Kern 1875-1933 *WhAm 1*
Streckfus, Joseph Leo 1887-1960 *NatCAB 48*
Streeper, Gertrude Mitchell *WomWWA 14*
Streepey, George William 1908-1965 *WhAm 4*
Streeruwitz, William H Ritter Von 1833-
WhAm 4
Street, Alfred Billings 1811-1881 *ApCAB,
DcAmB, Drake, NatCAB 11, TwCBDA,
WhAm H*
Street, Augustus Russell 1791-1866 *ApCAB,
DcAmB, Drake, WhAm H*
Street, Austin 1824?- *NewYHSD*
Street, Claude Everett 1868-1945 *NatCAB 37*
Street, Claude Lorrain 1834- *NewYHSD*
Street, Frank 1893-1944 *IIBEAAW*
Street, Franklin *NewYHSD*
Street, Ida Maria 1856- *WhAm 4,
WomWWA 14*
Street, J Fletcher 1880-1944 *WhAm 2*

Street, Jacob Richard 1860-1920 *WhAm 1*
Street, James Howell 1903-1954 *NatCAB 42,
WhAm 3*
Street, John Northcott 1898-1964 *WhAm 4*
Street, Joseph Montfort 1782-1840 *DcAmB,
NatCAB 13, WhAm H*
Street, Julian 1879-1947 *NatCAB 34,
WhAm 2*
Street, Margaret Berry 1891-1967 *NatCAB 54*
Street, Oliver Day 1866-1944 *WhAm 2*
Street, Randall S 1780-1841 *BiAUS, BiDrAC,
WhAm H*
Street, Reuben C 1826- *NewYHSD*
Street, Robert 1796-1865 *NewYHSD,
WhAm H*
Street, Robert Gould 1843- *WhAm 1*
Street, Rubens 1826- *NewYHSD*
Street, Thaddeus 1863-1920 *NatCAB 19*
Street, Theophilus 1829?- *NewYHSD*
Street, Thomas Atkins 1872-1936 *WhAm 1*
Street, Thomas Grinter 1892-1946 *NatCAB 35*
Street, Webster 1846-1909 *WhAm 1*
Street, Whiting 1790-1878 *ApCAB*
Streete, Thomas 1622-1689 *DcScB*
Streeter, Carroll Perry 1898-1975 *WhAm 6*
Streeter, Edward Clark 1874-1947 *NatCAB 37,
WhAm 6*
Streeter, Edward W 1846-1919 *ApCAB X*
Streeter, F B *BiAUS*
Streeter, Frank Sherwin 1853-1922 *NatCAB 16,
WhAm 1*
Streeter, George Linius 1873-1948 *DcAmB S4,
DcScB, NatCAB 37, WhAm 2*
Streeter, George Wellington d1921 *WhAm 4*
Streeter, John Williams 1841-1905 *WhAm 1*
Streeter, Leander R *NewYHSD*
Streeter, Lilian Carpenter 1854- *NatCAB 17,
WomWWA 14*
Streeter, Robert Leroy 1880-1932 *NatCAB 30*
Streeter, Ruth Cheney 1895- *WebAMB*
Streeter, Stella Georgiana 1874- *WomWWA 14*
Streeter, Thomas Winthrop 1883-1965
NatCAB 51, REnAW, WhAm 4
Streeton, Sir Arthur Ernest 1867-1943
McGEWB
Streeton, Nora Clench *WomWWA 14*
Streett, David 1855-1915 *NatCAB 2,
WhAm 1*
Streett, St. Clair 1893-1970 *WhAm 5*
Streicher, Julius 1885-1946 *WhWW-II*
Streight, Abdel D 1829-1892 *TwCBDA*
Streightoff, Frank Hatch 1886-1935
NatCAB 28, WhAm 1
Streisand, Barbra 1942- *WebAB*
Streit, Carl Frederick 1875-1960 *NatCAB 49*
Streit, Paul Henry 1891-1976 *WhAm 6*
Streit, Samuel Frederick 1870-1933 *NatCAB 31,
WhAm 6*
Strench, Donald Davis 1921-1974 *WhAm 6*
Streng, J Truman 1896-1953 *WhAm 3*
Streng, Jesse F 1880-1973 *WhAm 6*
Stresemann, Gustav 1878-1929 *McGEWB*
Stretch, David Albert 1908-1972 *WhAm 5*
Stretch, Olive Minerva 1901-1971 *WhAm 6*
Streun, John Arnold 1882-1956 *NatCAB 45*
Stribling, Cornelius Kinchiloe 1796-1880
*ApCAB, Drake, NatCAB 4, TwCBDA,
WebAMB*
Stribling, Thomas Sigismund 1881-1965
EncAAH, WhAm 4
Stribling, William Austell 1873-1928
NatCAB 22
Stricker, Frederick David 1875-1959
NatCAB 45, WhAm 5
Stricker, John d1825 *Drake*
Stricker, Paul Frederick 1893-1963 *WhAm 4*
Strickland, Arthur Barsalou 1879-1952
NatCAB 40
Strickland, Charles Hobart 1859- *WhAm 4*
Strickland, David Joseph 1883-1956
NatCAB 44
Strickland, Francis Lorette 1871-1959 *WhAm 3*
Strickland, Frederic Hastings 1856-1939
WhAm 1
Strickland, Frederick Guy 1869- *WhAm 5*
Strickland, George 1797-1851 *NewYHSD*
Strickland, George Wilson 1875- *WhoColR*
Strickland, Hardy 1818-1884 *BiDConf*

Strickland, Horace Gilmore 1905-1962
NatCAB 49
Strickland, John Frank 1860-1921 *NatCAB 43*
Strickland, John Thomas 1915-1958
NatCAB 48
Strickland, Lily d1958 *WhAm 3*
Strickland, Martha 1853- *AmWom*
Strickland, O F *BiAUS*
Strickland, Peter 1837- *NatCAB 9*
Strickland, Randolph 1823-1880 *BiAUS,
BiDrAC, WhAm H*
Strickland, Robert Marion 1895-1946 *WhAm 2*
Strickland, Samuel 1809-1867 *ApCAB, Drake*
Strickland, Silas A d1970 *WhAm 5*
Strickland, Teresa Hammond *WomWWA 14*
Strickland, William 1787?-1854 *AmBi,
ApCAB, DcAmB, Drake, NatCAB 20,
WhAm H*
Strickland, William 1788-1854 *BnEnAmA,
NewYHSD*
Strickland, William Peter 1809-1884 *ApCAB,
Drake*
Strickler, Cyrus Warren, Sr. 1873-1953
NatCAB 54, WhAm 5
Strickler, Earl T 1908-1974 *WhAm 6*
Strickler, Givens Brown 1840-1913 *NatCAB 2,
WhAm 1, WhAm 1C*
Strickler, Harrison Kennedy 1888-1965
NatCAB 51
Strickler, John 1902-1961 *WhAm 4*
Strickler, Thomas Johnson 1883-1958 *WhAm 3*
Strickler, Woodrow Mann 1912-1975 *WhAm 6*
Stride, Joseph Burton 1894-1956 *WhAm 3*
Strieby, William 1852-1920 *WhAm 1*
Strietmann, A P 1873-1960 *WhAm 4*
Stright, Hayden Leroy 1898-1975 *WhAm 6*
Strijdom, Johannes Gerhardus 1893-1958
WhAm 3
Strike, C J 1895- *WhAm 2*
Strindberg, August 1849-1912 *McGEWB*
Strine, Howard Francis 1879-1962 *NatCAB 48*
Stringer, Arthur 1874-1950 *NatCAB 15,
WhAm 3*
Stringer, George Alfred 1845-1923 *NatCAB 13,
WhAm 1*
Stringer, Henry Delphos 1907-1974 *WhAm 6*
Stringer, Lawrence Beaumont 1866-1942
BiDrAC, WhAm 2
Stringer, Samuel 1734-1817 *ApCAB, Drake*
Stringfellow, Benjamin Franklin 1840-1913
WebAMB
Stringfellow, Douglas R 1922-1966 *BiDrAC*
Stringfellow, Franklin 1840-1913 *DcAmB*
Stringfellow, Henry Martyn 1839-1912
WhAm 1
Stringfield, Lamar 1897-1959 *WhAm 3*
Stringham, Edwin John 1890-1974 *WhAm 6*
Stringham, Irving 1847-1909 *WhAm 1*
Stringham, James S 1775-1817 *ApCAB, Drake*
Stringham, Silas Horton 1797-1876 *DcAmB,
WebAMB, WhAm H*
Stringham, Silas Horton 1798-1876 *ApCAB,
Drake, NatCAB 2, TwCBDA*
Stringham, Warde Barlow 1898-1968 *WhAm 5*
Stringham, Washington Irving 1847-1909
DcAmB
Stripling, Joseph Newton 1850- *NatCAB 5*
Stritch, Samuel Alphonsus 1887-1958 *WhAm 3*
Strobel, Charles Louis 1852-1936 *DcAmB S2,
WhAm 1*
Strobel, Edward Henry 1855-1908 *DcAmB,
NatCAB 12, TwCBDA, WhAm 1*
Strobel, Louisa Catherine 1803-1883 *NewYHSD*
Strobel, Max *IIBEAAW, NewYHSD*
Strobel, Oscar A 1891-1967 *IIBEAAW*
Strobel, Walter Emil 1877-1950 *NatCAB 39*
Strobel, William Daniel 1808-1884 *ApCAB*
Strobridge, Hines *NewYHSD*
Strobridge, Idah Meacham 1855-1932 *WhAm 1,
WomWWA 14*
Strobridge, James Harvey 1827-1921
NatCAB 19
Strock, Daniel 1851-1927 *WhAm 1*
Strodach, Paul Zeller 1876-1947 *WhAm 2*
Strode, Aubrey Ellis 1873-1946 *NatCAB 34*
Strode, George King 1886-1958 *WhAm 3*
Strode, Henry Aubrey 1844-1898 *NatCAB 35*
Strode, Jesse Burr 1845-1924 *BiDrAC*

Stroebe, Lilian L 1875- *WomWWA 14*
Stroeck, Charles Henry 1871-1937 *NatCAB 34*
Stroessner, Alfredo 1912- *McGEWB*
Stroh, Donald Armpriester 1892-1953
  NatCAB 44, WhAm 3
Stroh, George 1861-1916 *NatCAB 18*
Stroh, John Roscoe 1891-1935 *NatCAB 27*
Stroheim, Erich Von 1885-1957 *WebAB*
Strohl, Everett Lee 1906-1973 *WhAm 6*
Strohm, Adam Julius 1870-1951 *DcAmLiB,*
  NatCAB 40, WhAm 5
Strohm, Gertrude 1843- *AmWom, WhAm 4*
Strohm, John 1793-1884 *BiAUS, BiDrAC,*
  WhAm H
Strohmeyer, Friedrich 1776-1835 *AsBiEn*
Strohmeyer, George Dewey 1898-1965
  NatCAB 50
Strohschein, Don Frederick 1904-1959
  NatCAB 48
Strom, Carl Walther 1899-1969 *WhAm 5*
Stromberg, Alfred 1861-1913 *NatCAB 15*
Stromberg, Gustaf Benjamin 1882-1962 *DcScB,*
  WhAm 4
Stromberg, Hunt 1894-1968 *WhAm 5*
Stromgren, Svante Elis 1870-1947 *DcScB*
Stromme, Peer Olsen 1856-1921 *DcAmB,*
  NatCAB 19, WhAm 1
Stromquist, Victor Harold 1893-1959
  NatCAB 45
Strong, Adele M Smith *WomWWA 14*
Strong, Alan Hartwell 1856-1925 *NatCAB 34*
Strong, Angelia Longfellow 1865-
  WomWWA 14
Strong, Ann Gilchrist 1875- *WomWWA 14*
Strong, Anna Louise 1885-1970 *WhAm 5,*
  WomWWA 14
Strong, Augustus Hopkins 1836-1921 *ApCAB,*
  DcAmB, DcAmReB, NatCAB 12,
  TwCBDA, WhAm 1
Strong, Austin 1881-1952 *WhAm 3*
Strong, Benjamin 1872-1928 *DcAmB, EncAB,*
  NatCAB 33, WhAm 1
Strong, Beulah 1866- *WomWWA 14*
Strong, Caleb 1745-1819 *AmBi, ApCAB,*
  BiAUS, BiDrAC, DcAmB, Drake,
  NatCAB 1, TwCBDA, WhAm H,
  WhAmP
Strong, Charles Arthur 1882-1947 *NatCAB 38*
Strong, Charles Augustus 1862-1940
  DcAmB S2, NatCAB 31, WhAm 1
Strong, Charles Hall 1850-1915 *WhAm 1*
Strong, Charles Hamot 1853-1936 *NatCAB 27*
Strong, Charles Henry 1871-1960 *WhAm 4*
Strong, Charles Howard 1865-1949 *WhAm 2*
Strong, Charles Lyman 1826-1883 *DcAmB,*
  NatCAB 17, WhAm H
Strong, Charles Stanley 1906-1962 *WhAm 4*
Strong, Clinton Aaron 1874-1938 *NatCAB 29*
Strong, Edgar Eugene 1841- *NatCAB 16*
Strong, Edward Kellogg, Jr. 1884-1963
  BiDAmEd, NatCAB 51, WhAm 4
Strong, Edward Newton 1827-1895 *ApCAB X*
Strong, Edward Theodore 1877-1955
  NatCAB 42
Strong, Edward Trask 1840-1909 *TwCBDA,*
  WhAm 1
Strong, Edwin Atson 1834- *WhAm 4*
Strong, Elnathan Ellsworth 1832-1914 *WhAm 1*
Strong, Elsie 1874- *WomWWA 14*
Strong, Ernest Melvin 1881-1961 *NatCAB 48*
Strong, Frank 1859-1934 *BiDAmEd,*
  NatCAB 13, TwCBDA, WhAm 1
Strong, Frank Raleigh 1870-1950 *NatCAB 39*
Strong, Frederick Finch 1872- *WhAm 5*
Strong, Frederick Smith 1855-1935 *WhAm 1*
Strong, George Alexander 1859- *WhAm 4*
Strong, George Crockett 1832-1863 *ApCAB,*
  Drake, NatCAB 5, TwCBDA, WhAm H
Strong, George Frederic 1897- *WhAm 3*
Strong, George H *NewYHSD*
Strong, George Temple 1820-1875 *NatCAB 3*
Strong, George Templeton 1820-1875 *ApCAB*
Strong, George Veazey 1880-1946 *NatCAB 33,*
  WhAm 2
Strong, Harriet Williams Russell 1844-
  NatCAB 17
Strong, Harriet Williams Russell 1844-1926
  DcAmB

Strong, Harriet Williams Russell 1844-1929
  NotAW
Strong, Harry Allen 1888- *WhAm 3*
Strong, Harry Eugene 1893-1967 *WhAm 4A*
Strong, Hattie Maria 1864-1950 *WhAm 3*
Strong, Hattie Marie 1864- *NatCAB 24*
Strong, Henry 1829-1911 *NatCAB 41*
Strong, Henry Alvah 1838-1919 *NatCAB 20,*
  NatCAB 24, WhAm 1
Strong, Howard *NewYHSD*
Strong, Isobel *WomWWA 14*
Strong, Jacob Hill 1885-1960 *NatCAB 47*
Strong, James 1783-1847 *BiAUS, BiDrAC,*
  TwCBDA, WhAm H
Strong, James 1822-1894 *ApCAB, DcAmB,*
  Drake, NatCAB 13, TwCBDA, WhAm H
Strong, James Edward 1864-1929 *NatCAB 22*
Strong, James George 1870-1938 *BiDrAC,*
  WhAm 1, WhAmP
Strong, James Hooker 1814-1882 *ApCAB,*
  DcAmB, Drake, NatCAB 11, TwCBDA,
  WebAMB, WhAm H
Strong, James Woodward 1833-1913 *BiDAmEd,*
  DcAmB, NatCAB 24, TwCBDA,
  WhAm 1
Strong, Jedediah 1738-1802 *ApCAB, BiAUS,*
  BiDrAC, TwCBDA, WhAm H
Strong, John 1738-1816 *ApCAB*
Strong, John Henry 1866- *WhAm 4*
Strong, John Wesley *WhoColR A*
Strong, Joseph 1753-1834 *ApCAB*
Strong, Joseph D 1852-1900 *IIBEAAW*
Strong, Josiah 1847-1916 *ApCAB, DcAmB,*
  DcAmReB, EncAB, NatCAB 9, WebAB,
  WhAm 1
Strong, Julia Worthington *WomWWA 14*
Strong, Julius Levi 1828-1872 *BiAUS, BiDrAC,*
  WhAm H
Strong, L Corrin 1892-1966 *NatCAB 52,*
  WhAm 4
Strong, Latham Cornell 1845-1879 *ApCAB*
Strong, Lee Abram 1886-1941 *NatCAB 33,*
  WhAm 1
Strong, Luther Martin 1838-1903 *BiDrAC*
Strong, Marie Livingston 1878- *WomWWA 14*
Strong, Marshall Mason 1813-1864 *ApCAB*
Strong, Mary *WomWWA 14*
Strong, Mary Elizabeth *WomWWA 14*
Strong, Moses McCure 1810-1894 *ApCAB Sup,*
  DcAmB, WhAm H
Strong, Nathan 1748-1816 *ApCAB, Drake*
Strong, Nathan Leroy 1859-1939 *BiDrAC,*
  WhAm 1, WhAmP
Strong, Nehemiah 1730-1807 *ApCAB, Drake*
Strong, O Gregory 1881-1955 *NatCAB 43*
Strong, Oliver Smith 1806-1874 *ApCAB*
Strong, Oliver Smith 1864-1951 *NatCAB 39*
Strong, Ormand Butler 1878-1954 *WhAm 3*
Strong, Paschal Neilson 1793-1825 *ApCAB,*
  NatCAB 12
Strong, Reuben Myron 1872-1964 *WhAm 4*
Strong, Richard Pearson 1872-1948 *ApCAB X,*
  DcAmB S4, WhAm 2
Strong, Robert Alexander 1884-1955 *WhAm 3*
Strong, Samuel 1762-1832 *ApCAB*
Strong, Samuel Henry 1825- *ApCAB*
Strong, Samuel M 1906-1959 *WhAm 3*
Strong, Selah 1737-1815 *ApCAB*
Strong, Selah Brewster 1792-1872 *ApCAB,*
  BiAUS, BiDrAC, NatCAB 11, WhAm H
Strong, Selah Brewster 1873-1945 *NatCAB 47,*
  WhAm 4
Strong, Simeon 1736-1805 *ApCAB, BiAUS,*
  Drake
Strong, Solomon 1780-1850 *BiAUS, BiDrAC,*
  WhAm H
Strong, Stephen 1791-1866 *BiAUS, BiDrAC,*
  WhAm H
Strong, Sterling Price 1862-1936 *BiDrAC,*
  WhAm 4
Strong, Susan DeLancey VanRensselaer 1851-
  WomWWA 14
Strong, Sydney Dix 1860-1938 *WhAm 1*
Strong, Sylvester Emory 1837-1913 *WhAm 1*
Strong, Theodore 1790-1869 *AmBi, ApCAB,*
  DcAmB, Drake, NatCAB 9, TwCBDA,
  WhAm H
Strong, Theodore 1863-1928 *NatCAB 47*

Strong, Theron George 1846-1924 *WhAm 1*
Strong, Theron Rudd 1802-1873 *ApCAB,*
  BiAUS, BiDrAC, WhAm H, WhAmP
Strong, Thomas Morris 1797-1861 *ApCAB*
Strong, Thomas Nelson 1853- *WhAm 4*
Strong, Thomas Shepard 1834-1909
  NatCAB 25
Strong, Thomas W *NewYHSD*
Strong, Titus 1787-1855 *ApCAB, Drake*
Strong, Walter *NewYHSD*
Strong, Walter Ansel 1883-1931 *DcAmB,*
  NatCAB 24, WhAm 1
Strong, Wayne F 1907-1957 *WhAm 3*
Strong, Wendell Melville 1871-1942 *WhAm 2*
Strong, William *BiAUS*
Strong, William 1763-1840 *BiAUS, BiDrAC,*
  TwCBDA, WhAm H
Strong, William 1808-1895 *ApCAB, BiAUS,*
  BiDrAC, DcAmB, Drake Sup, NatCAB 1,
  NatCAB 21, TwCBDA, WebAB,
  WhAm H, WhAmP
Strong, William Barstow 1837-1914 *DcAmB,*
  WhAm 1
Strong, William Duncan 1899-1962 *NatCAB 49,*
  WhAm 4
Strong, William Ellsworth 1860-1934 *WhAm 1*
Strong, William Emerson 1840- *ApCAB*
Strong, William Kerley 1805-1868 *ApCAB*
Strong, William Lafayette 1827-1900
  ApCAB Sup, DcAmB, WhAm 1
Strong, William Thaddeus 1854-1919
  NatCAB 17
Strong, William Walker 1883-1955 *WhAm 3*
Strongman, John Henry 1855-1933 *NatCAB 26*
Stroobant, L *NewYHSD*
Stroock, James E 1891-1965 *WhAm 4*
Stroock, Joseph 1869- *ApCAB X*
Stroock, Solomon Marcuse 1873-1941
  NatCAB 30, WhAm 1
Strosacker, Charles John 1882-1963
  NatCAB 52, WhAm 4
Strosser *NewYHSD*
Strother, Dan J F 1872- *WhAm 5*
Strother, David Hunter 1816-1888 *AmBi,*
  ApCAB, DcAmB, NewYHSD, TwCBDA,
  WhAm H
Strother, David Hunter 1816-1898 *NatCAB 9*
Strother, Emily Viele 1868- *WomWWA 14*
Strother, French 1883-1933 *WhAm 1*
Strother, George French 1783-1840 *BiAUS,*
  BiDrAC, WhAm H, WhAmP
Strother, James French 1811-1860 *BiAUS,*
  BiDrAC, WhAm H
Strother, James French 1868-1930 *BiDrAC,*
  WhAmP
Strother, James French 1870-1930 *WhAm 1*
Strother, James H 1896-1966 *WhAm 4*
Strother, Philip Williams 1839-1922
  NatCAB 19
Strotz, Charles Nicolas 1868-1928 *NatCAB 28*
Stroud, Benjamin Kendrick 1881-1950
  NatCAB 39
Stroud, C Malone 1903-1950 *NatCAB 42*
Stroud, Ethan Beden 1893-1949 *NatCAB 39*
Stroud, George McDowell 1795-1875 *ApCAB,*
  BiAUS, Drake
Stroud, Morris Wistar 1860-1941 *WhAm 1*
Stroud, Robert 1890-1963 *WebAB*
Stroud, Thomas *NewYHSD*
Stroud, William Daniel 1891-1959 *WhAm 3*
Stroup, Thomas Andrew 1885-1943 *WhAm 2*
Strouse, D J 1879- *WhAm 6*
Strouse, Myer 1825-1878 *BiAUS, BiDrAC,*
  WhAm H
Strouse, Raphael *NewYHSD*
Strout, Charles Henry 1857- *WhAm 4*
Strout, Edwin Albert 1871-1952 *WhAm 3*
Strout, Harold Frederick 1883-1945
  NatCAB 33
Strout, Sarah Willard 1858- *WomWWA 14*
Strout, Sewall Cushing 1827-1914 *NatCAB 5,*
  WhAm 1
Strover, Carl Bernhard Wittekind 1865-1941
  WhAm 1
Strowbridge, Joseph Allen 1870-1942
  NatCAB 44
Strowd, Wallace Headen 1889-1946
  NatCAB 34

Strowd, William Franklin 1832-1911 *BiDrAC, WhAmP*
Strozier, Fred Lewis 1908-1969 *WhAm 5*
Strozier, Harry Stone 1889-1949 *NatCAB 38*
Strozier, Robert Manning 1906-1960 *NatCAB 50, WhAm 3A*
Struass, Nathan 1868-1933 *WhAm 1*
Strub, Paul 1917-1972 *WhAm 5*
Strubberg, Friedrich Armand 1806-1889 *DcAmB, WhAm H*
Strube, Gustav 1867- *WhAm 5*
Struble, Arthur Dewey 1894- *WebAMB*
Struble, George R 1836- *WhAm 4*
Struble, Isaac S 1843-1913 *BiDrAC*
Struble, Mildred 1894-1949 *WhAm 2*
Struble, Stanley 1865-1955 *NatCAB 46*
Struck, Ferdinand Theodore 1886-1943 *BiDAmEd, WhAm 2*
Strudwick, Edmund 1854-1928 *NatCAB 28, WhAm 1*
Strudwick, Edmund Charles Fox 1802-1879 *DcAmB, WhAm H*
Strudwick, William E d1812 *BiAUS*
Strudwick, William Francis d1812 *BiDrAC, WhAm H*
Struensee, Karl 1595?-1650? *ApCAB*
Strum, Louie Willard 1890-1954 *WhAm 3*
Strunk, Harry Decosta 1892-1960 *NatCAB 49*
Strunk, William 1869-1946 *WhAm 2*
Strunsky, Simeon 1879-1948 *DcAmB S4, NatCAB 37, WhAm 2*
Struss, Jozef 1510-1568 *DcScB*
Struther, Jan 1901-1953 *WhAm 3*
Struthers, G H 1914-1966 *WhAm 4*
Struthers, Joseph 1865-1923 *WhAm 1*
Struthers, Robert 1879-1951 *WhAm 4*
Strutt, John William, Baron Rayleigh 1842-1919 *DcScB*
Strutt, Robert John, Baron Rayleigh 1875-1947 *DcScB*
Struve, Amalie d1862 *ApCAB*
Struve, Friedrich Georg Wilhelm Von 1793-1864 *AsBiEn, DcScB, McGEWB*
Struve, Georg Otto Hermann 1886-1933 *DcScB*
Struve, Gustav Von 1805-1870 *ApCAB, DcAmB, WhAm H*
Struve, Gustav Wilhelm Ludwig 1858-1920 *DcScB*
Struve, Henry G 1836- *ApCAB X, NatCAB 11*
Struve, Karl Hermann 1854-1920 *DcScB*
Struve, Otto 1897-1963 *AsBiEn, DcScB, WebAB, WhAm 4*
Struve, Otto Wilhelm 1819-1905 *DcScB*
Struye, Paul 1896-1974 *WhAm 6*
Strycker, Jacobus Gerritsen 1619-1687 *NewYHSD*
Strydonck DeBurkel, Victor Van 1876-1953 *WhWW-II*
Stryke, Anna Clegg 1884- *WomWWA 14*
Stryker, James 1792-1864 *ApCAB, Drake*
Stryker, John 1740-1776 *ApCAB*
Stryker, John Dana 1856-1935 *NatCAB 26*
Stryker, Josiah 1880- *WhAm 6*
Stryker, Lloyd Paul 1885-1955 *DcAmB S5, NatCAB 42, WhAm 3*
Stryker, Melancthon Woolsey 1851-1929 *ApCAB Sup, BiDAmEd, DcAmB, NatCAB 7, NatCAB 26, TwCBDA, WhAm 1*
Stryker, Samuel Stanhope 1842-1929 *WhAm 1*
Stryker, William Scudder 1838-1900 *ApCAB, NatCAB 3, TwCBDA, WhAm 1*
Strype, Frederick C *NewYHSD*
Stuart, Albert F 1824- *NewYHSD*
Stuart, Albert Rhett 1906-1973 *WhAm 5*
Stuart, Alexander *BiAUS, NewYHSD*
Stuart, Alexander 1673-1742 *DcScB*
Stuart, Alexander 1810-1879 *ApCAB, NatCAB 10*
Stuart, Mrs. Alexander Hamilton *WomWWA 14*
Stuart, Alexander Hugh Holmes 1807-1891 *ApCAB, BiAUS, BiDrAC, BiDrUSE, DcAmB, Drake, NatCAB 6, TwCBDA, WhAm H*
Stuart, Alexander Tait 1848-1924 *NatCAB 17, WhAm 1*

Stuart, Allison Ellsworth 1886-1950 *NatCAB 45*
Stuart, Ambrose Pascal Sevilon 1820-1899 *ApCAB, WhAm 1*
Stuart, Andrew 1785-1840 *ApCAB*
Stuart, Sir Andrew 1812-1894 *ApCAB Sup*
Stuart, Andrew 1823-1872 *BiAUS, BiDrAC, WhAm H*
Stuart, Archibald 1757-1832 *DcAmB, WhAm H*
Stuart, Archibald 1795-1855 *BiAUS, BiDrAC, WhAm H*
Stuart, Carl Kirk 1890-1963 *WhAm 4*
Stuart, Carles A 1893-1962 *WhAm 4*
Stuart, Charles 1783?-1865 *ApCAB, DcAmB, WhAm H*
Stuart, Charles Arthur 1893-1962 *NatCAB 52*
Stuart, Charles Beebe 1814-1881 *ApCAB, DcAmB, Drake, WhAm H*
Stuart, Charles Duff 1854- *WhAm 4*
Stuart, Prince Charles Edward 1720-1788 *McGEWB, WhoMilH*
Stuart, Charles Edward 1810-1887 *ApCAB, BiAUS, BiDrAC, NatCAB 11, TwCBDA, WhAm H*
Stuart, Charles Edward 1881-1943 *WhAm 2*
Stuart, Charles Gilbert 1787?-1813 *NewYHSD*
Stuart, Charles Jenckes Barnes 1891-1964 *WhAm 4*
Stuart, Charles Macaulay 1853-1932 *DcAmB, NatCAB 23, WhAm 1*
Stuart, Charles T 1883-1958 *WhAm 3*
Stuart, Charles W T 1888-1951 *WhAm 3*
Stuart, Daniel Delehanty Vincent 1847-1932 *WhAm 1*
Stuart, David 1816-1868 *ApCAB, BiAUS, BiDrAC, TwCBDA, WhAm H*
Stuart, Della Tovrea 1888-1969 *WhAm 5*
Stuart, Donald Clive 1881-1943 *WhAm 3*
Stuart, Duane Reed 1873-1941 *WhAm 1*
Stuart, Edward 1888-1953 *WhAm 3*
Stuart, Edwin Roy 1874-1920 *WhAm 1*
Stuart, Edwin Sydney 1853-1937 *NatCAB 14, WhAm 1*
Stuart, Elbridge Amos 1856-1944 *DcAmB S3, NatCAB 32, WhAm 2*
Stuart, Elbridge Hadley 1887-1972 *WhAm 5*
Stuart, Eleanor *WhAm 1*
Stuart, Francis Hart 1846-1910 *WhAm 1*
Stuart, Francis Joseph 1878- *WhAm 6*
Stuart, Francis Lee 1866-1935 *DcAmB S1, NatCAB 27, WhAm 1*
Stuart, Frederick D 1816?- *IlBEAAW, NewYHSD*
Stuart, Frederick G *NewYHSD*
Stuart, Frederick T 1837-1913 *NewYHSD*
Stuart, George 1834?- *ApCAB*
Stuart, George 1843-1943 *WhAm 2*
Stuart, George Hay 1816-1890 *ApCAB, DcAmReB*
Stuart, George Okill 1776-1862 *ApCAB*
Stuart, George Rutledge 1857-1926 *WhAm 1*
Stuart, Gilbert Charles 1754-1828 *Drake*
Stuart, Gilbert Charles 1755-1828 *AmBi, ApCAB, BnEnAmA, DcAmB, EncAB, IlBEAAW, McGEWB, NatCAB 5, NewYHSD, TwCBDA, WebAB, WhAm H*
Stuart, Granville 1834-1918 *DcAmB, NatCAB 12, REnAW*
Stuart, H Worthington 1881-1931 *NatCAB 27*
Stuart, Hamilton 1813- *ApCAB*
Stuart, Harold Leonard 1881-1966 *WhAm 4*
Stuart, Harry Allen 1882- *WhAm 3*
Stuart, Helen Campbell *NotAW*
Stuart, Henry Carter 1855-1933 *NatCAB 15, NatCAB 33, WhAm 1*
Stuart, Henry Longan 1874-1928 *NatCAB 21*
Stuart, Henry Robson 1836-1903 *AmBi, DcAmB*
Stuart, Henry Waldgrave 1870-1951 *NatCAB 41, WhAm 5*
Stuart, Herbert William Z 1861-1921 *NatCAB 37*
Stuart, Holloway Ithamer 1865-1950 *WhAm 3*
Stuart, Ian 1902-1969 *WhAm 5*
Stuart, Isaac William 1809-1861 *ApCAB, DcAmB, Drake, WhAm H*

Stuart, James 1776-1849 *ApCAB*
Stuart, James 1780-1853 *ApCAB*
Stuart, James Arthur 1880-1975 *WhAm 6*
Stuart, James Austin 1899-1967 *WhAm 4*
Stuart, James E B 1832-1864 *Drake*
Stuart, James Edward 1842-1931 *WhAm 1*
Stuart, James Edwin 1897-1968 *WhAm 5*
Stuart, James Everett 1852-1941 *IlBEAAW, WhAm 1*
Stuart, James Ewell Brown 1833-1864 *AmBi, ApCAB, BiDConf, DcAmB, EncAB, McGEWB, NatCAB 4, TwCBDA, WebAB, WebAMB, WhAm H, WhoMilH*
Stuart, James Lyall 1872-1961 *WhAm 4*
Stuart, James Reeve 1834-1915 *NewYHSD, WhAm HA, WhAm 4*
Stuart, James Victor 1893-1962 *NatCAB 49*
Stuart, Jane 1810?-1888 *ApCAB*
Stuart, Jane 1812-1888 *NewYHSD*
Stuart, Jeb 1833-1864 *AmBi*
Stuart, Jessie Bonstelle *NotAW*
Stuart, John 1700?-1779 *ApCAB, DcAmB, WhAm H*
Stuart, John 1718-1784 *REnAW*
Stuart, John 1740-1811 *ApCAB, Drake*
Stuart, Sir John 1761-1815 *ApCAB, Drake*
Stuart, John 1877-1969 *WhAm 5*
Stuart, John Todd 1807-1885 *ApCAB, BiAUS, BiDrAC, DcAmB, NatCAB 3, TwCBDA, WhAm H*
Stuart, Josie Wanous 1870- *WomWWA 14*
Stuart, Mary Allan *WomWWA 14*
Stuart, Mary McCrea 1810-1891 *ApCAB Sup, NatCAB 7*
Stuart, Milo H 1871-1933 *WhAm 1*
Stuart, Montgomery Alexander 1881- *WhAm 6*
Stuart, Moses 1780-1852 *ApCAB, DcAmB, DcAmReB, Drake, NatCAB 6, TwCBDA, WhAm H*
Stuart, Oliver J *NewYHSD*
Stuart, Philip 1760-1830 *ApCAB, BiAUS, BiDrAC, WhAm H, WhAmP*
Stuart, Philip *see also* Stewart, Philip
Stuart, Pythias *NewYHSD*
Stuart, Robert 1785-1848 *AmBi, ApCAB, DcAmB, NatCAB 13, WhAm H*
Stuart, Robert C 1883-1964 *WhAm 4*
Stuart, Robert Douglas 1886-1975 *WhAm 6*
Stuart, Robert Leighton 1806-1882 *ApCAB, DcAmB, NatCAB 10, TwCBDA, WhAm H*
Stuart, Robert Terry 1880-1957 *WhAm 3*
Stuart, Robert Young 1883-1933 *NatCAB 25, WhAm 1*
Stuart, Ruth McEnery d1917 *TwCBDA, WhAm 1, WomWWA 14*
Stuart, Ruth McEnery 1849-1917 *AmBi, DcAmB, NotAW*
Stuart, Ruth McEnery 1860-1917 *NatCAB 4*
Stuart, Theresa Crystal 1885-1965 *WhAm 4*
Stuart, William 1821-1886 *ApCAB*
Stuart, William Francis 1905-1967 *NatCAB 53*
Stuart, William Hervey 1874- *WhAm 5*
Stuart, William Plato 1879-1960 *WhAm 4*
Stub, Hans Gerhard 1849-1931 *DcAmB, WhAm 1*
Stub, Jacob Aall Ottesen 1877- *WhAm 2*
Stubbers, Joseph 1857-1940 *NatCAB 30*
Stubbert, J Edward 1859- *WhAm 4*
Stubbins, Allan Linder 1907-1963 *WhAm 4*
Stubblefield, Frances Ogden d1959 *WhAm 3*
Stubblefield, Frank Albert 1907- *BiDrAC*
Stubblefield, William Higgason 1894-1963 *WhAm 4*
Stubbs, Henry Elbert 1881-1937 *BiDrAC, WhAm 1*
Stubbs, John Christian Spayd 1847- *NatCAB 6, WhAm 4*
Stubbs, John Osmon 1898-1972 *NatCAB 57, WhAm 5*
Stubbs, Joseph Edward 1850-1914 *BiDAmEd, NatCAB 16, TwCBDA, WhAm 1*
Stubbs, Mattie Wilma 1878-1940 *WhAm 3*
Stubbs, Merrill 1905-1972 *WhAm 5*
Stubbs, Ralph Sprengle 1882-1948 *ApCAB X, WhAm 2*
Stubbs, Truett Tristian 1907-1968 *WhAm 5*
Stubbs, Walter Roscoe 1858-1929 *DcAmB S1,*

Suckley, George 1830-1869 *ApCAB*
Suckley, Thomas Holy 1809-1888 *ApCAB*
Suckling, Sir John 1609-1642 *McGEWB*
Suckow, Ruth Ann Vivian 1892-1960 *EncAAH*,
  NatCAB 47, *WhAm 3*
Sucre, Antonia Jose De 1795-1830 *WhoMilH*
Sucre, Antonio Jose De 1793-1830 *Drake*
Sucre, Antonio Jose De 1795-1830 *ApCAB*,
  McGEWB
Sucre, Etienne Henry 1703-1745 *ApCAB*
Suczek, Robert 1883-1955 *NatCAB 44*
Suddards, William 1805- *ApCAB*
Sudden, Robert Cowperthwaite 1861-1932
  NatCAB 24
Sudds, William F 1843- *ApCAB*
Sudduth, Solon Bluch 1908-1963 *NatCAB 52*
Sudduth, William Xavier 1853-1915 *WhAm 1*
Sudermann, Hermann 1857-1928 *McGEWB*
Suderow, George Erich 1913-1961 *NatCAB 47*
Sudhoff, Karl Friedrich Jakob 1853-1938 *DcScB*
Sudjarwo, Tjondronegoro 1914-1972 *WhAm 5*
Sudler, Arthur Emory 1905-1968 *WhAm 5*
Sudler, Carroll Hopkins 1869-1958 *NatCAB 17*,
  NatCAB 45
Sudler, Mervin Tubman 1875- *WhAm 5*
Sudler, Susan Culbreth 1871- *WomWWA 14*
Sudler, Wright Spry 1879-1951 *NatCAB 41*
Sudlow, Elizabeth Williams 1878-1958 *WhAm 3*
Sudworth, George Bishop 1864-1927
  NatCAB 14, *WhAm 1*
Suess, Eduard 1831-1914 *DcScB*
Suetonius Tranquillus, Gaius 070?-135?
  McGEWB
Suffern, Arthur Elliott 1878- *WhAm 6*
Suffren, Charles Carroll 1854-1917 *NatCAB 18*,
  WhAm 1
Suffren, Martha Wentworth *WomWWA 14*
Suffren DeSaint-Tropez, Pierre Andre De
  1729-1788 *WhoMilH*
Sufi, Abu'i-Husayn Abd Al-Rahman, Al-
  903-986 *DcScB*
Sugar, David Israel 1894-1966 *NatCAB 52*
Sugarman, George 1912- *BnEnAmA*
Sugden, Walter S 1880-1938 *WhAm 1*
Sugg, Redding Stancil 1893-1958 *WhAm 3*
Suggs, Daniel Cato *WhoColR*
Sughrue, Timothy George 1889-1963 *WhAm 4*
Sugiyama, Hajime 1880-1945 *WhWW-II*
Suglian, Vinko Vladimir 1901-1964 *NatCAB 51*
Sugrue, Ralph Arthur 1880-1963 *NatCAB 50*
Sugrue, Thomas 1907-1953 *WhAm 3*
Suhr, Charles Louis 1877-1970 *WhAm 5*
Suhr, Otto Ernst Heinrich Hermann 1894-1957
  WhAm 3
Suhr, Robert Carl 1911-1974 *WhAm 6*
Suhrie, Ambrose Leo 1874-1956 *BiDAmEd*,
  WhAm 3
Sui, Wen-Ti 541-604 *McGEWB*
Suiko, Empress 554-628 *McGEWB*
Sukarno 1901-1970 *McGEWB*, *WhAm 5*
Sukarno, Achmed 1901-1970 *WhWW-II*
Suker, George Francis 1869-1933 *NatCAB 25*,
  WhAm 1
Suleiman I 1495-1566 *McGEWB*, *WhoMilH*
Sulerud, Allen Christen 1903-1974 *WhAm 6*
Sulla, Lucius Cornelius 138BC-078BC
  McGEWB
Sullavan, Margaret 1909-1960 *NatCAB 44*
Sullavan, Margaret 1911-1960 *WhAm 3*
Sullens, Frederick 1877-1957 *WhAm 3*
Sullivan, Albert Walter 1854-1938 *NatCAB 28*
Sullivan, Alexander 1847- *ApCAB Sup*,
  WhAm 4
Sullivan, Algernon Sydney 1826-1887 *ApCAB*,
  NatCAB 10, *NatCAB 24*
Sullivan, Amelia Lucy Owen *WomWWA 14*
Sullivan, Anne Mansfield 1866-1936 *AmBi*,
  NotAW, *WebAB*
Sullivan, Arthur George 1885-1941 *WhAm 2*
Sullivan, Arthur George 1885-1954 *WhAm 3*
Sullivan, Sir Arthur Seymour 1842-1900
  McGEWB
Sullivan, Charles 1794-1867 *NewYHSD*
Sullivan, Christopher Daniel 1870-1942 *BiDrAC*,
  WhAm 1, *WhAmP*
Sullivan, Corliss Esmonde 1876-1939
  NatCAB 30, *WhAm 1*
Sullivan, Daniel 1843-1931 *NatCAB 25*

Sullivan, Daniel Clifford 1908-1964 *WhAm 4*
Sullivan, David 1904-1976 *WhAm 6*
Sullivan, Dennis 1837- *NatCAB 12*
Sullivan, Dennis Francis 1898-1968 *WhAm 5*
Sullivan, Donal Mark 1910-1971 *WhAm 5*
Sullivan, Edward 1835?- *ApCAB*
Sullivan, Edward Dean 1888-1938 *WhAm 1*
Sullivan, Edward Joseph 1905-1962 *NatCAB 52*
Sullivan, Edward Vincent 1902-1974 *WebAB*,
  WhAm 6
Sullivan, Elizabeth Higgins 1874- *WhAm 5*
Sullivan, Elizabeth Higgins 1875-
  WomWWA 14
Sullivan, Eugene Cornelius 1872-1962 *WhAm 4*
Sullivan, Florence David 1883-1954 *WhAm 3*
Sullivan, Florence Leo 1902-1966 *NatCAB 51*
Sullivan, Francis John 1854-1930 *WhAm 1*
Sullivan, Francis Loftus 1903-1956 *WhAm 3*
Sullivan, Francis Paul 1885-1958 *WhAm 3*
Sullivan, Francis William 1894-1967 *WhAm 4*
Sullivan, Frank 1892-1976 *WhAm 6*
Sullivan, Gael Edward 1904-1956 *NatCAB 45*,
  WhAm 3
Sullivan, George 1771-1838 *ApCAB*, *BiDrAC*,
  DcAmB, *WhAm H*, *WhAmP*
Sullivan, George 1772-1838 *BiAUS*,
  NatCAB 11
Sullivan, George F 1886-1944 *WhAm 2*
Sullivan, George Hammond 1859-1956 *WhAm 3*
Sullivan, Harry Stack 1892-1949 *DcAmB S4*,
  EncAB, *McGEWB*, *WebAB*, *WhAm HA*,
  WhAm 4
Sullivan, Henry J 1905-1959 *WhAm 4*
Sullivan, Isaac Newton 1848-1938 *NatCAB 13*,
  WhAm 1
Sullivan, James 1744-1808 *AmBi*, *ApCAB*,
  BiAUS, *BiDrAC*, *DcAmB*, *Drake*,
  NatCAB 1, *TwCBDA*, *WhAm H*,
  WhAmP
Sullivan, James 1873-1931 *NatCAB 24*,
  WhAm 1
Sullivan, James Edward 1860-1914 *DcAmB*,
  WebAB, *WhAm 1*
Sullivan, James Edward 1861-1914 *NatCAB 15*
Sullivan, James Francis 1846-1930 *NatCAB 24*,
  WhAm 1
Sullivan, James Mark 1873-1920 *WhAm 1*
Sullivan, James Mark 1873-1933 *NatCAB 29*
Sullivan, James William 1848-1938 *DcAmB S2*,
  WhAm 4
Sullivan, Jeremiah 1794-1870 *ApCAB*
Sullivan, Jeremiah C 1830- *ApCAB*
Sullivan, Jeremiah Francis 1851-1928
  NatCAB 20, *WhAm 1*
Sullivan, Jeremiah Francis, Jr. 1891-1969
  WhAm 5
Sullivan, Jeremiah J 1845-1922 *WhAm 4*
Sullivan, Jeremiah Jay 1844-1922 *NatCAB 19*
Sullivan, Jeremiah John 1837-1928 *NatCAB 52*
Sullivan, Jerry B 1859-1948 *WhAm 2*
Sullivan, John *NewYHSD*
Sullivan, John 1740-1795 *AmBi*, *ApCAB*,
  BiAUS, *BiDrAC*, *DcAmB*, *Drake*,
  NatCAB 1, *TwCBDA*, *WebAB*,
  WebAMB, *WhAm H*, *WhAmP*,
  WhoMilH
Sullivan, John Andrew 1868-1927 *BiDrAC*,
  WhAm 4
Sullivan, John Augustine 1842-1902 *NatCAB 12*
Sullivan, John Berchmans 1897-1951 *BiDrAC*,
  WhAm 3
Sullivan, John Florence *WebAB*
Sullivan, John Francis 1896-1962 *NatCAB 50*
Sullivan, John Francis 1900-1954 *WhAm 3*
Sullivan, John James 1860-1930 *NatCAB 22*
Sullivan, John James 1877-1958 *NatCAB 46*,
  WhAm 3
Sullivan, John Joseph 1855-1926 *NatCAB 27*
Sullivan, John Langdon 1777-1865 *ApCAB*,
  Drake
Sullivan, John Lawrence 1858-1918 *AmBi*,
  DcAmB, *McGEWB*, *WebAB*, *WhAm HA*,
  WhAm 4
Sullivan, John Lawrence 1891-1949 *WhAm 3*
Sullivan, John Turner Sargent 1813-1838
  ApCAB
Sullivan, Laurence Fred 1885-1949 *NatCAB 40*
Sullivan, Lawrence 1898-1968 *WhAm 4A*

Sullivan, Leo Dennis 1901-1969 *WhAm 5*
Sullivan, Leonor Kretzer 1903- *BiDrAC*
Sullivan, Louis Henri 1856-1924 *AmBi*,
  BnEnAmA, *DcAmB*, *EncAB*, *McGEWB*,
  WebAB
Sullivan, Louis Henry 1856-1924 *WhAm 1*
Sullivan, Louis Robert 1892-1925 *DcAmB*,
  NatCAB 20
Sullivan, Lynde 1865-1939 *NatCAB 29*
Sullivan, Margaret Frances d1903 *ApCAB Sup*,
  WhAm 1
Sullivan, Margaret M 1890-1959 *WhAm 4*
Sullivan, Marie M B *WomWWA 14*
Sullivan, Mark 1874-1952 *DcAmB S5*,
  NatCAB 42, *WhAm 3*
Sullivan, Mark A 1878- *NatCAB 16*
Sullivan, Mary Josephine Quinn 1877-1939
  NotAW
Sullivan, Mary Mildred Hammond 1838-1933
  NatCAB 31
Sullivan, Matthew Ignatius 1857-1937
  NatCAB 28
Sullivan, Maurice J 1884-1962 *WhAm 4*
Sullivan, Maurice John 1881-1961 *NatCAB 48*,
  WhAm 4
Sullivan, Maurice Joseph 1884-1953 *BiDrAC*
Sullivan, May Lilian 1858- *WomWWA 14*
Sullivan, Michael 1838- *ApCAB*
Sullivan, Michael Crowley 1865-1928 *WhAm 1*
Sullivan, Michael Henry 1877-1959 *NatCAB 49*
Sullivan, Michael Xavier 1875-1963 *WhAm 4*
Sullivan, Oscar Matthias 1881-1955 *WhAm 3*
Sullivan, Owen d1756 *NewYHSD*
Sullivan, Owen J 1878-1957 *WhAm 3*
Sullivan, Patrick Francis 1856-1927 *NatCAB 15*,
  WhAm 1
Sullivan, Patrick J 1894-1967 *BnEnAmA*
Sullivan, Patrick Joseph 1865-1935 *BiDrAC*,
  NatCAB 43, *WhAm 1*, *WhAmP*
Sullivan, Patrick Joseph 1877-1946 *BiDrAC*,
  WhAm 5
Sullivan, Patrick U 1877-1946 *WhAm 2*
Sullivan, Paul E 1900-1958 *WhAm 3*
Sullivan, Peter John 1821-1883 *ApCAB*,
  BiAUS, *NatCAB 5*, *WhAm H*
Sullivan, Philip Leo 1889-1960 *WhAm 4*
Sullivan, Raymond F 1897-1969 *WhAm 5*
Sullivan, Roger Charles 1861-1920 *NatCAB 27*,
  WhAm 1
Sullivan, Roger G 1854-1918 *ApCAB X*
Sullivan, Russell 1881- *WhAm 6*
Sullivan, Thomas Allen 1869-1925 *NatCAB 28*
Sullivan, Thomas Crook 1833-1908 *WhAm 1*
Sullivan, Thomas Russell 1799-1862 *ApCAB*
Sullivan, Thomas Russell 1849-1916
  NatCAB 10, *NatCAB 16*, *WhAm 1*
Sullivan, Timothy Daniel 1862-1913 *BiDrAC*,
  DcAmB, *WebAB*, *WhAm 4*
Sullivan, Walter Bernard 1885-1921
  NatCAB 19
Sullivan, Walter Connor 1902-1952 *NatCAB 39*
Sullivan, Ward William 1883-1959 *NatCAB 50*
Sullivan, Will VanAmberg 1857- *TwCBDA*
Sullivan, William 1774-1839 *ApCAB*, *DcAmB*,
  Drake, *WhAm H*
Sullivan, William 1848- *NatCAB 10*
Sullivan, William Cleary 1880-1935 *WhAm 1*
Sullivan, William Edward 1897-1950
  NatCAB 39
Sullivan, William Henry 1864-1929 *DcAmB*
Sullivan, William Henry 1891-1959 *NatCAB 47*
Sullivan, William Laurence 1872-1935 *WhAm 1*
Sullivan, William Lawrence 1903-1967 *WhAm 4*
Sullivan, William VanAmberg 1857-
  NatCAB 12, *WhAm 4*
Sullivan, William VanAmberg 1857-1918
  BiDrAC
Sullivan, William VanAmberg 1857-1919
  NatCAB 45
Sullivant, Joseph 1809-1882 *NatCAB 30*
Sullivant, Michael Lucas 1807-1879 *ApCAB*
Sullivant, William Starling 1803-1873 *AmBi*,
  ApCAB, *DcAmB*, *NatCAB 8*, *TwCBDA*,
  WhAm H
Sulloway, Alvah Woodbury 1838-1928 *WhAm 1*
Sulloway, Cyrus Adam 1839-1917 *TwCBDA*
Sulloway, Cyrus Adams 1839-1917 *BiDrAC*,
  WhAm 1, *WhAmP*

Sully, Alfred 1820-1879 *Drake, IlBEAAW, NewYHSD, REnAW*

Sully, Alfred 1821-1879 *ApCAB, NatCAB 12, TwCBDA, WebAMB, WhAm H*

Sully, Alfred 1841-1909 *NatCAB 3, WhAm 1*

Sully, Blanche 1814-1898 *NewYHSD*

Sully, Daniel 1855-1910 *NatCAB 12, WhAm 1*

Sully, Daniel John 1861-1930 *DcAmB, WhAm 1*

Sully, Ellen Oldmixon 1816-1896 *NewYHSD*

Sully, Jane Cooper *NewYHSD*

Sully, John Murchison 1868-1933 *NatCAB 26, WhAm 1*

Sully, Lawrence 1769-1804 *NewYHSD*

Sully, Robert Matthew 1803-1855 *NewYHSD*

Sully, Rosalie Kemble 1818-1847 *NewYHSD*

Sully, Thomas 1783-1872 *AmBi, ApCAB, BnEnAmA, DcAmB, Drake, EncAB, NatCAB 5, NewYHSD, TwCBDA, WebAB, WhAm H*

Sully, Thomas 1855-1939 *NatCAB 9, NatCAB 29*

Sully, Thomas Wilcocks 1811-1847 *NewYHSD*

Sully, Wilberforce 1856- *NatCAB 14*

Sultan, Daniel Isom 1885-1947 *NatCAB 37, WebAMB, WhAm 2, WhWW-II*

Sulte, Benjamin 1841- *ApCAB*

Sulver, Gray 1871-1935 *EncAAH*

Sulzbacher, Louis 1842-1915 *WhAm 1*

Sulzberger, Arthur Hays 1891-1968 *WebAB, WhAm 5*

Sulzberger, Carl Fulton 1909-1964 *NatCAB 52*

Sulzberger, Cyrus Lindauer 1858-1932 *DcAmB, WhAm 1*

Sulzberger, Mayer 1843-1923 *DcAmB, NatCAB 15, WhAm 1*

Sulzburger, Ferdinand 1842-1915 *ApCAB X*

Sulzer, Albert Frederick 1878-1944 *WhAm 2*

Sulzer, Charles August 1879-1919 *BiDrAC, WhAm 1, WhAmP*

Sulzer, Hans A 1876-1959 *WhAm 3*

Sulzer, William 1863-1941 *ApCAB X, BiDrAC, DcAmB S3, NatCAB 3, TwCBDA, WhAm 1, WhAmP*

Sumichrast, Frederick Caesar De 1845- *WhAm 4*

Summa, Hugo 1859- *NatCAB 14*

Summerall, Charles Pelot 1867-1955 *DcAmB S5, WebAMB, WhAm 3*

Summerbell, Carlyle 1873-1935 *WhAm 1*

Summerbell, Martyn 1847-1939 *WhAm 1*

Summerbell, Robert Kerr 1904-1962 *WhAm 4*

Summerfield, Arthur Ellsworth 1899-1972 *BiDrUSE, WhAm 5*

Summerfield, Charles *WhAm H*

Summerfield, John 1798-1825 *ApCAB, Drake*

Summerfield, Lester D 1888-1966 *WhAm 4*

Summerfield, Solon E 1877-1947 *ApCAB X, WhAm 4*

Summerford, Dealva Clinton 1906-1969 *WhAm 5*

Summerhayes, Martha 1846-1911 *REnAW*

Summerlin, George Thomas 1872-1947 *NatCAB 43, WhAm 2*

Summers, Alex 1856-1933 *WhAm 1*

Summers, Andrew Rowan 1912-1968 *WhAm 5*

Summers, Augustus Neander 1856- *WhAm 4*

Summers, Caleb Edson 1881-1963 *NatCAB 50*

Summers, Cleon Aubrey 1881- *WhAm 6*

Summers, Elizabeth Montgomery *WomWWA 14*

Summers, Ella Florence 1864- *WomWWA 14*

Summers, Festus Paul 1895-1971 *WhAm 5*

Summers, George W d1868 *BiAUS*

Summers, George Washington 1805?-1868 *NatCAB 13*

Summers, George William 1804-1868 *BiDrAC, DcAmB, WhAm H*

Summers, Henry Elijah 1863- *WhAm 4*

Summers, Iverson Brooks 1864-1926 *NatCAB 20*

Summers, James Colling 1854-1929 *WhAm 1*

Summers, John Edward 1822- *WhAm 1*

Summers, John Edward 1858-1935 *NatCAB 17, NatCAB 28, WhAm 1*

Summers, John Hoagland 1896-1943 *NatCAB 32*

Summers, John William 1870-1937 *BiDrAC, NatCAB 28, WhAm 1, WhAmP*

Summers, Leland Laflin 1871-1927 *NatCAB 20, WhAm 1*

Summers, Lewis Preston 1868-1943 *WhAm 3*

Summers, Lionel Morgan 1905-1975 *WhAm 6*

Summers, Maddin 1877-1918 *WhAm 1*

Summers, Thomas Jefferson 1876-1952 *NatCAB 39*

Summers, Thomas Osmond 1812-1882 *ApCAB, DcAmB, Drake, TwCBDA, WhAm H*

Summers, Walter G 1889-1938 *WhAm 1*

Summers, Walter Lee 1888-1963 *WhAm 4*

Summers, William Henry 1897-1951 *WhAm 3*

Summers, William Thomas 1867-1938 *NatCAB 29*

Summerville, Amelia Shaw d1934 *WhAm 1, WomWWA 14*

Summerville, Stephen 1814?- *NewYHSD*

Summey, George 1853-1954 *NatCAB 48, TwCBDA, WhAm 3*

Summy, Clayton Frick 1852-1932 *NatCAB 18, NatCAB 24*

Sumner, Caroline Louise 1867- *WhAm 5, WomWWA 14*

Sumner, Charles 1811-1874 *AmBi, ApCAB, BiAUS, BiDrAC, DcAmB, Drake, EncAAH, EncAB, McGEWB, NatCAB 3, TwCBDA, WebAB, WhAm H, WhAmP*

Sumner, Charles Allen 1835-1903 *ApCAB, BiDrAC, WhAm 1*

Sumner, Charles Burt 1837- *WhAm 4*

Sumner, Charles Ralsey 1852-1928 *WhAm 1*

Sumner, Cid Ricketts 1890-1970 *WhAm 5*

Sumner, Clarence 1885-1952 *WhAm 3*

Sumner, Daniel Hadley 1837-1903 *BiDrAC*

Sumner, Edward Alleyne 1874-1948 *WhAm 2*

Sumner, Edward Arthur 1856-1913 *NatCAB 5, NatCAB 16*

Sumner, Edwin Vose d1863 *ApCAB*

Sumner, Edwin Vose 1796-1863 *Drake*

Sumner, Edwin Vose 1797-1863 *AmBi, ApCAB, DcAmB, NatCAB 4, REnAW, TwCBDA, WebAMB, WhAm H*

Sumner, Edwin Vose 1835-1912 *TwCBDA, WhAm 1*

Sumner, Francis Bertody 1874-1945 *DcAmB S3, DcScB, NatCAB 34, WhAm 2*

Sumner, Frederick Azel 1864-1933 *NatCAB 26, WhAm 1*

Sumner, G Lynn 1885-1952 *WhAm 3*

Sumner, George 1793-1855 *ApCAB, Drake*

Sumner, George 1817-1863 *ApCAB, Drake*

Sumner, George Watson 1841-1924 *NatCAB 10, TwCBDA, WhAm 1*

Sumner, Graham 1876-1946 *NatCAB 36*

Sumner, Guilford Herman 1857- *WhAm 1*

Sumner, Helen Laura 1876- *NotAW, WomWWA 14*

Sumner, Increase 1746-1799 *AmBi, ApCAB, BiAUS, DcAmB, Drake, NatCAB 1, TwCBDA, WhAm H*

Sumner, James Batcheller 1887-1955 *AsBiEn, DcAmB S5, DcScB, NatCAB 46, WebAB, WhAm 3*

Sumner, Jessie 1898- *BiDrAC*

Sumner, Jethro *Drake*

Sumner, Jethro 1730?-1790? *ApCAB, NatCAB 1*

Sumner, Jethro 1733?-1785 *DcAmB, TwCBDA, WebAMB, WhAm H*

Sumner, John 1735-1787 *ApCAB*

Sumner, John D 1904-1953 *WhAm 3*

Sumner, John Osborne 1863-1938 *WhAm 1*

Sumner, John Saxton 1876-1971 *NatCAB 56, WhAm 5*

Sumner, Joshua 1761-1831? *ApCAB*

Sumner, Osbourne Thomas 1862-1921 *NatCAB 22*

Sumner, Samuel Storrow 1842-1937 *TwCBDA, WhAm 1*

Sumner, Walter Taylor 1873-1935 *DcAmB S1, NatCAB 27, WhAm 1*

Sumner, William 1780-1838 *ApCAB*

Sumner, William Graham 1840-1910 *AmBi, ApCAB, BiDAmEd, DcAmB, EncAB, McGEWB, NatCAB 11, NatCAB 25, WebAB, WhAm 1*

Sumner, William H *NewYHSD*

Sumner, William Hyslop 1780-1861 *ApCAB, Drake, TwCBDA*

Sumners, Chester Lamar 1896-1959 *NatCAB 51, WhAm 4*

Sumners, Hatton William 1875-1962 *BiDrAC, WhAm 4, WhAmP*

Sumpter, William David 1872- *WhAm 5*

Sumter, Thomas 1734-1832 *AmBi, ApCAB, BiAUS, BiDrAC, DcAmB, Drake, NatCAB 1, TwCBDA, WebAB, WebAMB, WhAm H, WhAmP, WhoMilH*

Sumter, Thomas DeLage 1809-1874 *BiAUS, BiDrAC, WhAm H, WhAmP*

Sun, Gus 1868-1959 *NatCAB 49*

Sun, Yat-Sen 1866-1925 *McGEWB*

Sundance Kid *REnAW*

Sunday, William Ashley 1862-1935 *DcAmB S1, DcAmReB, EncAAH, McGEWB, WebAB*

Sunday, William Ashley 1863-1935 *AmBi, WhAm 1*

Sundback, Gideon 1880-1954 *NatCAB 47, WhAm 3*

Sundberg, Carl Andrew Lawrence 1898-1962 *WhAm 4*

Sundelius, Marie d1958 *WhAm 3*

Sunderland, Allan Boulter 1901-1956 *NatCAB 46*

Sunderland, Byron 1819- *NatCAB 10*

Sunderland, Edson Read 1874-1959 *WhAm 3*

Sunderland, Edwin Sherwood Stowell 1887-1964 *WhAm 4*

Sunderland, Eliza Jane Read 1839-1910 *AmWom, BiDAmEd, DcAmB, NatCAB 10, WhAm 1*

Sunderland, Jabez Thomas 1842-1936 *WhAm 1*

Sunderland, LaRoy 1804-1885 *DcAmB, Drake*

Sunderland, LeRoy 1802-1885 *ApCAB, NatCAB 5*

Sunderland, LeRoy 1804-1885 *WhAm H*

Sunderland, Lester Thomas 1867-1955 *NatCAB 46*

Sunderland, Thomas 1821-1886 *ApCAB*

Sunderland, Wilfred Wilt 1873-1948 *NatCAB 36, WhAm 2*

Sunderlin, Charles Algernon 1883-1951 *WhAm 3*

Sundfor, Zalia Harbaugh 1905- *WhAm 5*

Sundh, August 1864-1940 *NatCAB 29*

Sundheim, Anders M 1861-1945 *WhAm 2*

Sundheim, Trig *WhAm 6*

Sundiata Keita 1210?-1260? *McGEWB*

Sundman, Karl Frithiof 1873-1949 *DcScB*

Sundstrom, Frank Leander 1901- *BiDrAC*

Sundstrom, Jacob Otto 1846-1926 *NatCAB 23*

Sundstrom, Swan Reuben 1897-1956 *WhAm 3*

Sundt, Edwin Einar 1892- *WhAm 1*

Sundt, John Samuel 1900-1965 *NatCAB 51*

Sundwall, John 1880-1950 *NatCAB 39, WhAm 3*

Sung, T'ai-Tsu 927-976 *McGEWB*

Sunne, Dagny G 1881- *WomWWA 14*

Sunny, Bernard Edward 1856-1943 *NatCAB 42, WhAm 2*

Sunstrom, Mark A 1897-1960 *NatCAB 49, WhAm 4*

Suozzo, John 1921-1973 *WhAm 6*

Super, Charles William 1842-1939 *NatCAB 4, TwCBDA, WhAm 1*

Super, Ovando Byron 1848- *WhAm 4*

Suplee, Andrew Callender 1829?- *NewYHSD*

Suplee, Henry Harrison 1856- *WhAm 4*

Suplee, Thomas Danly 1846- *ApCAB*

Suppes, John Frederick 1884-1959 *NatCAB 43*

Supplee, William Wright 1832-1915 *NatCAB 34*

Suraci, Anthony Versace 1889-1965 *NatCAB 57*

Suramarit, Norodom d1960 *WhAm 3*

Sure, Barnett 1892-1960 *WhAm 4*

Surette, Thomas Whitney 1861-1941 *WhAm 1*

Surface, Frank Macy 1882-1965 *NatCAB 54, WhAm 4*

Surface, Harvey Adam 1867- *WhAm 4*

Suria, Tomas *NewYHSD*

Suringar, Willem Frederik Reinier 1832-1898 *DcScB*

Surkamp, Arthur 1893-1971 *WhAm 5*
Surles, Alexander D 1886-1947 *WhAm 2*
Surmann, John Fred 1889- *WhAm 5*
Surran, Edna M Walsh 1895-1974 *WhAm 6*
Surrat, Mary Eugenia Jenkins 1817-1865
  WhAm H
Surratt, John H 1844- *WhAm H*
Surratt, Mary Eugenia Jenkins 1817-1865
  NatCAB 4, WebAB
Surratt, Mary Eugenia Jenkins 1820?-1865
  NotAW
Surriage, Agnes *NotAW*
Surtlett, Margaret Homer Nichols 1879-
  WomWWA 14
Survilliers, Comtesse De *NewYHSD*
Susann, Jacqueline d1974 *WhAm 6*
Susini, Isabella d1862 *Drake*
Sussman, Otto 1879-1947 *NatCAB 33,
  WhAm 2*
Sutcliff, Robert d1811 *Drake*
Sutcliffe, Alice Crary *WomWWA 14*
Sutcliffe, Emerson Grant 1890-1967
  NatCAB 54
Sutcliffe, Thomas *ApCAB*
Suter, Charles Russell 1842-1920 *WhAm 1*
Suter, Francis Leon 1877-1967 *NatCAB 54,
  WhAm 5*
Suter, Heinrich 1848-1922 *DcScB*
Suter, Herbert Wallace, Jr. 1909-1960 *WhAm 4*
Suter, John Wallace 1859-1942 *WhAm 2*
Sutherland, Abby Ann 1871- *WhAm 6*
Sutherland, Alexander 1833- *ApCAB*
Sutherland, Allan 1871- *WhAm 5*
Sutherland, Annie d1943 *WhAm 2*
Sutherland, Arthur Eugene 1902-1973
  NatCAB 57, WhAm 5
Sutherland, Charles 1829-1895 *TwCBDA*
Sutherland, Charles 1830-1895 *NatCAB 4*
Sutherland, Charles Goldie 1877-1951
  NatCAB 40
Sutherland, Dan A 1869-1955 *WhAm 3*
Sutherland, Daniel Alexander 1869-1955
  BiDrAC, WhAmP
Sutherland, Daniel DeLloyd 1858-1927
  NatCAB 22
Sutherland, Dwight Lane 1900-1969
  NatCAB 55
Sutherland, Earl Wilbur, Jr. 1915-1974 *WebAB,
  WhAm 6*
Sutherland, Edna *WomWWA 14*
Sutherland, Edward Alexander 1865-1955
  NatCAB 46, WhAm 3
Sutherland, Edwin Hardin 1883-1950
  DcAmB S4, NatCAB 42, WhAm 3
Sutherland, Evelyn Greenleaf d1908 *WhAm 1*
Sutherland, George 1848-1943 *WhAm 2*
Sutherland, George 1862-1942 *ApCAB X,
  BiDrAC, DcAmB S3, NatCAB 13,
  NatCAB 31, WebAB, WhAm 2, WhAmP*
Sutherland, Gordon Alexander 1906-1957
  WhAm 3
Sutherland, Graham 1903- *McGEWB*
Sutherland, Howard 1865-1950 *BiDrAC,
  NatCAB 45, WhAm 2, WhAm 2C*
Sutherland, Howard Vigne 1868- *WhAm 4*
Sutherland, Jabez Gridley 1825-1902 *BiAUS,
  BiDrAC, NatCAB 11*
Sutherland, Joel B d1861 *BiAUS*
Sutherland, Joel B 1791-1861 *ApCAB, Drake,
  NatCAB 3, TwCBDA*
Sutherland, Joel Barlow 1792-1861 *BiDrAC,
  DcAmB, WhAm H*
Sutherland, John Bain 1889-1948 *WhAm 2*
Sutherland, John Preston 1854-1941 *WhAm 1*
Sutherland, Joseph Hooker 1898- *WhAm 5*
Sutherland, Josiah 1804-1887 *BiAUS, BiDrAC,
  WhAm H*
Sutherland, Lucinda Mae 1877- *WomWWA 14*
Sutherland, Richard K 1893-1966 *WhAm 4*
Sutherland, Robert Edward Lee 1878- *WhAm 6*
Sutherland, Roderick Dhu 1862-1915 *BiDrAC,
  WhAm 3, WhAmP*
Sutherland, Rosamond Lee *WomWWA 14*
Sutherland, Thomas Henry 1898-1972 *WhAm 6*
Sutherland, William 1859-1911 *DcScB*
Sutherland, William Andrew 1849-1908
  NatCAB 12, WhAm 1
Sutherland, William James 1865-1915 *WhAm 1*

Sutley, Margaret Hutchinson 1893-1947
  NatCAB 35
Sutliff, Helen Binninger 1867- *WomWWA 14*
Sutliff, Milo Joseph 1899-1964 *WhAm 4*
Sutliff, Phebe Temperance 1859- *TwCBDA,
  WhAm 4, WomWWA 14*
Sutliff, Vincent E 1900-1969 *WhAm 5*
Sutliffe, Albert 1830?- *ApCAB, Drake*
Sutlipp, Henry *NewYHSD*
Sutphen, Duncan Dunbar 1862-1953 *WhAm 3*
Sutphen, Henry Randolph 1875-1950
  NatCAB 16, NatCAB 46, WhAm 3
Sutphen, John Thomas 1849-1907 *NatCAB 6*
Sutphen, Martha Magill Watson 1864-
  WomWWA 14
Sutphen, Paul Frederick 1856-1929 *NatCAB 24*
Sutphen, William Gilbert VanTassel 1861-1945
  WhAm 2
Sutphin, Dudley Vanness 1875-1926
  NatCAB 23
Sutphin, Stuart Bruen 1881-1951 *NatCAB 40*
Sutphin, William Halstead 1887- *BiDrAC*
Sutro, Adolph Heinrich Joseph 1830-1898 *AmBi,
  ApCAB, DcAmB, NatCAB 13,
  NatCAB 21, REnAW, TwCBDA,
  WebAB, WhAm H*
Sutro, Alfred 1869-1945 *WhAm 2*
Sutro, Florence Clinton 1865-1906 *WhAm 1*
Sutro, Ludwig 1839-1920 *NatCAB 6*
Sutro, Oscar 1874-1935 *NatCAB 28,
  WhAm 1*
Sutro, Otto 1833-1896 *NatCAB 34*
Sutro, Otto 1833-1897 *NatCAB 2*
Sutro, Paul Emil 1866-1947 *NatCAB 35*
Sutro, Richard 1863-1930 *WhAm 1*
Sutro, Theodore 1845-1927 *NatCAB 3,
  WhAm 1*
Sutro, Mrs. Theodore 1865- *NatCAB 5*
Sutro, Victor 1876-1954 *NatCAB 41*
Sutter, Harry Blair 1891-1957 *WhAm 3*
Sutter, Henry Sylvester 1897-1950 *NatCAB 37*
Sutter, John Augustus 1803-1880 *AmBi,
  ApCAB, DcAmB, EncAAH, McGEWB,
  NatCAB 4, REnAW, WebAB, WhAm H*
Suttle, Andrew Dillard 1890-1964 *WhAm 4*
Sutton, Charles Edward 1914-1974 *WhAm 6*
Sutton, Charles R 1900-1963 *WhAm 5*
Sutton, Charles Wood 1877- *NatCAB 18,
  WhAm 5*
Sutton, Claude William 1883-1945 *WhAm 3*
Sutton, Dallas Gilchrist 1883-1970 *WhAm 5*
Sutton, David Nelson 1895-1974 *WhAm 6*
Sutton, Don C 1886-1968 *WhAm 4A*
Sutton, Donn 1905-1960 *WhAm 4*
Sutton, Frank 1859- *WhAm 4*
Sutton, Frank Spencer 1923-1974 *WhAm 6*
Sutton, Frederick Albert 1894-1950 *NatCAB 41*
Sutton, Frederick I 1886-1973 *WhAm 5*
Sutton, Harris Raymond 1888-1958 *NatCAB 48*
Sutton, James Patrick 1915- *BiDrAC*
Sutton, John Anderson 1853-1921 *NatCAB 27*
Sutton, John Brannen 1891-1944 *WhAm 2*
Sutton, Mrs. John Quarles *WomWWA 14*
Sutton, Joseph Lee 1924-1972 *WhAm 5*
Sutton, Joseph Wilson 1881- *WhAm 6*
Sutton, Lee Edwards, Jr. 1891-1964 *WhAm 4*
Sutton, Louis Valvelle 1889-1970 *WhAm 5*
Sutton, Loyd Hall 1885-1949 *WhAm 2*
Sutton, Mary Wooster Munson 1866- *WhAm 5,
  WomWWA 14*
Sutton, Ransome 1869-1934 *WhAm 1*
Sutton, Rhoades Stansbury 1841-1906
  NatCAB 12, WhAm 1
Sutton, Richard Lightburn 1878-1952
  NatCAB 40, WhAm 3
Sutton, Robert Lee 1863-1950 *NatCAB 39*
Sutton, Vida Ravenscroft 1880- *WomWWA 14*
Sutton, W *NewYHSD*
Sutton, W Henry 1863-1913 *WhAm 1*
Sutton, Walter Stanborough 1877-1916 *DcScB*
Sutton, Wilbur Ervin 1878-1949 *WhAm 2*
Sutton, William 1854- *WhAm 4*
Sutton, William James 1908-1972 *NatCAB 57*
Sutton, William Seneca 1860-1928 *BiDAmEd,
  DcAmB, NatCAB 21, WhAm 4*
Sutton, Willis Anderson 1879-1960 *NatCAB 48*
Suvorov, Aleksandr Vasilievich 1730-1800
  McGEWB

Suvorov, Alexander Vasilievich 1729-1800
  WhoMilH
Suydam, Charles Crooke 1836- *WhAm 4*
Suydam, Edward Howard 1885-1940 *IIBEAAW*
Suydam, Henry *NewYHSD*
Suydam, Henry 1891-1955 *WhAm 3*
Suydam, James Augustus 1819-1865 *ApCAB,
  Drake, NewYHSD*
Suydam, John Howard 1832-1909 *ApCAB,
  WhAm 1*
Suydam, John R 1858-1928 *ApCAB X*
Suydam, Richard Schoonmaker 1872-1954
  ApCAB X, NatCAB 48
Suydam, Vernon Andrew 1872-1955 *WhAm 3*
Suyker, Hector 1889-1973 *WhAm 5*
Suzor, Louis T 1834-1866 *ApCAB*
Suzuki, Daisetsu Teitaro 1870-1966 *WhAm 4*
Suzuki, Daisetz Teitaro 1870-1966 *DcAmReB*
Suzuki, Kantaro 1867-1948 *WhWW-II*
Suzzallo, Henry 1875-1933 *AmBi, BiDAmEd,
  DcAmB, NatCAB 24, WhAm 1*
Svanholm, Set 1904-1964 *WhAm 4*
Svedberg, The 1884-1971 *DcScB*
Svedberg, Theodor H E 1884-1971 *AsBiEn,
  WhAm 5*
Svedelius, Nils Eberhard 1873-1960 *DcScB,
  WhAm 4*
Svendsen, Henry Peter 1865-1910 *NatCAB 23*
Svendsen, Kester 1912-1968 *WhAm 5*
Sverdrup, Georg 1848-1907 *DcAmB, WhAm 1*
Sverdrup, George 1879-1937 *WhAm 1*
Sverdrup, Harald Ulrik 1888-1957 *DcScB,
  WhAm 3*
Sverdrup, Leif John 1898-1976 *WhAm 6*
Svevo, Italo 1861-1928 *McGEWB*
Svien, Hendrik Julius 1911-1972 *WhAm 6*
Svinin, Pavel Petrovitch 1787?-1839 *NewYHSD,
  WhAm H*
Svoboda, Ralph Edward 1901-1969 *WhAm 5*
Swab, Robert Dubs 1884-1960 *NatCAB 49*
Swabey, Marie Collins 1890-1966 *WhAm 4*
Swacker, Frank M 1879-1953 *WhAm 3*
Swackhamer, Chester Ray 1886-1957
  NatCAB 47
Swados, Harvey 1920-1972 *WhAm 5*
Swafford, Martina *AmWom*
Swaim, Curran 1826-1897 *NewYHSD*
Swaim, David Gaskill 1834- *ApCAB*
Swaim, H Nathan 1890-1957 *WhAm 3*
Swaim, Joseph Skinner 1851-1918 *WhAm 1*
Swaim, Loring Tiffany 1882-1964 *NatCAB 50*
Swaim, Verne Frank 1886-1954 *NatCAB 46*
Swain *NewYHSD*
Swain, Adeline Morrison 1820- *AmWom*
Swain, Benjamin Wilson 1866- *WhoColR*
Swain, Burton Franklin 1865-1933 *NatCAB 25*
Swain, Miss C *NewYHSD*
Swain, Charles Luther 1866-1933 *NatCAB 26*
Swain, Chester Odiorne 1877-1937 *NatCAB 33*
Swain, Clara A 1834-1910 *DcAmB, NotAW*
Swain, David Lowery 1801-1868 *NatCAB 4*
Swain, David Lowry 1801-1868 *ApCAB,
  BiAUS, BiDAmEd, BiDConf, DcAmB,
  Drake, NatCAB 13, TwCBDA, WhAm H*
Swain, Frances Morgan 1866- *WomWWA 14*
Swain, George Fillmore 1857-1931 *DcAmB S1,
  NatCAB 12, WhAm 1*
Swain, Harriet *NewYHSD*
Swain, Henry Huntington 1863-1941 *WhAm 1*
Swain, Henry Lawrence 1864-1940 *NatCAB 29,
  WhAm 1*
Swain, Howard Townsend 1868-1936
  NatCAB 27
Swain, James Barrett 1820-1895 *ApCAB,
  DcAmB, Drake, NatCAB 6, WhAm H*
Swain, James Ramsay 1872- *WhAm 5*
Swain, Joseph 1857-1927 *BiDAmEd,
  NatCAB 6, TwCBDA, WhAm 1*
Swain, Joseph Ward 1891-1971 *WhAm 5*
Swain, Philip William 1889-1958 *WhAm 3*
Swain, Rachel 1835- *WomWWA 14*
Swain, Richard LaRue 1860-1940 *NatCAB 30*
Swain, Robert Bunker 1822-1872 *NatCAB 12*
Swain, Robert Eckles 1875-1961 *NatCAB 57,
  WhAm 4*
Swain, Roland T *NewYHSD*
Swain, William 1803-1847 *NatCAB 19,
  NewYHSD*

Swaine, Robert Taylor 1886-1949 *WhAm 2*
Swainson, Otis William 1887-1969 *NatCAB 55*
Swainson, William 1789-1855 *ApCAB, DcScB, WhAm H*
Swales, Bradshaw Hall 1874-1928 *NatCAB 23*
Swallow, Alan 1915-1966 *WhAm 4*
Swallow, Ellen Henrietta *NotAW*
Swallow, George Clinton 1817-1899 *DcAmB*
Swallow, George Clinton 1817-1900 *WhAm 1*
Swallow, Silas Comfort 1839-1930 *DcAmB, NatCAB 24, WhAm 1*
Swalm, Albert Winfield 1845-1922 *NatCAB 20, WhAm 1*
Swalwell, Joseph Arthur 1873- *WhAm 5*
Swammerdam, Jan 1637-1680 *AsBiEn, BiHiMed, DcScB, McGEWB*
Swan, Alexander Hamilton 1831-1905 *REnAW*
Swan, Anna Georgina 1843- *WomWWA 14*
Swan, Caleb d1809 *ApCAB, Drake*
Swan, Clifford Melville 1877- *WhAm 3*
Swan, Edward Davis 1830-1915 *NatCAB 18*
Swan, Frank 1833-1915 *ApCAB X*
Swan, Frank Herbert 1873-1954 *NatCAB 43, WhAm 3*
Swan, Frederick William 1868-1955 *NatCAB 46*
Swan, Gustaf Nilsson 1856-1938 *WhAm 1*
Swan, Henry 1883-1971 *NatCAB 57*
Swan, Mrs. Henry Edson *WomWWA 14*
Swan, Henry Harrison 1840-1916 *NatCAB 21, WhAm 1*
Swan, James 1754-1830 *DcAmB, WhAm H*
Swan, James 1754-1831 *ApCAB, Drake*
Swan, James Edward 1920-1972 *WhAm 6*
Swan, James Hayes 1873-1958 *NatCAB 48*
Swan, John 1760-1793 *BiAUS, BiDrAC, WhAm H*
Swan, John Harold 1903-1957 *NatCAB 46*
Swan, John Mumford 1870-1949 *WhAm 3*
Swan, John Nesbit 1862-1937 *WhAm 1*
Swan, Joseph Edwards Corson 1897-1960 *WhAm 4*
Swan, Joseph Rockwell 1802-1884 *ApCAB, DcAmB, Drake, NatCAB 3, WhAm H*
Swan, Joseph Rockwell 1878-1948 *WhAm 2*
Swan, Joseph Rockwell 1878-1965 *WhAm 4*
Swan, Sir Joseph Wilson 1828-1914 *AsBiEn*
Swan, Lowell Benjamin 1910-1969 *WhAm 5*
Swan, Nathalie Henderson 1881- *WhAm 6*
Swan, Paul d1972 *WhAm 5*
Swan, Reuben Samuel 1850-1914 *NatCAB 17*
Swan, Richard Carl 1913-1962 *NatCAB 50*
Swan, Samuel 1771-1844 *BiAUS, BiDrAC, WhAm H, WhAmP*
Swan, Thomas Walter 1877- *WhAm 5*
Swan, Timothy 1758-1842 *ApCAB, DcAmB, Drake, WhAm H*
Swan, Verne Sturges 1891-1969 *WhAm 5*
Swan, William Batchelder 1825-1916 *NatCAB 17*
Swan, William Draper 1809-1864 *ApCAB, Drake*
Swan, William Graham 1821-1869 *BiDConf*
Swanberg, Harold 1891-1970 *WhAm 5*
Swander, John I 1833- *WhAm 4*
Swanebeck, Clarence W 1896-1970 *WhAm 5*
Swaney, Walter Glen 1891-1961 *NatCAB 46*
Swaney, William Bentley 1858-1946 *WhAm 2*
Swanish, Peter Theodore 1895-1971 *WhAm 5*
Swank, Fletcher B 1875-1950 *BiDrAC, WhAm 5, WhAmP*
Swank, James Moore 1832-1914 *ApCAB, DcAmB, NatCAB 20, WhAm 1*
Swanlund, Lester Herman 1908-1971 *WhAm 5*
Swann, Arthur Warton 1880-1914 *NatCAB 16*
Swann, Edward 1862-1945 *BiDrAC, WhAm 4*
Swann, Evans Samuel 1883-1960 *NatCAB 48*
Swann, Marguerite Gray 1878- *WomWWA 14*
Swann, Ralph Clay 1912-1967 *NatCAB 54, WhAm 4*
Swann, Thomas d1883 *BiAUS, Drake Sup*
Swann, Thomas 1805-1883 *ApCAB, TwCBDA*
Swann, Thomas 1806?-1883 *DcAmB, NatCAB 9*
Swann, Thomas 1809-1883 *BiDrAC, WhAm H, WhAmP*
Swann, Thomas Laurens 1841-1922 *NatCAB 29*
Swann, Thomas Wallace *WhoColR A*

Swann, William Francis Gray 1884-1962 *DcScB, NatCAB 53, WhAm 4*
Swansen, Sam T 1868-1958 *NatCAB 47*
Swansen, Sam T 1868-1959 *WhAm 3*
Swanson, Albert E 1896-1965 *WhAm 5*
Swanson, Albert Gustav 1906-1971 *WhAm 5*
Swanson, Carl Anton 1879-1949 *NatCAB 40*
Swanson, Charles Edward 1879-1970 *BiDrAC, WhAm 5*
Swanson, Clarence Emanuel 1898-1970 *WhAm 5*
Swanson, Claude Augustus 1862-1939 *AmBi, ApCAB X, BiDrAC, BiDrUSE, DcAmB S2, EncAAH, NatCAB 14, NatCAB 32, WhAm 1, WhAmP*
Swanson, Edgar Walfred 1899-1968 *NatCAB 54, WhAm 5*
Swanson, Gilbert Carl 1906-1968 *NatCAB 56*
Swanson, Jack N 1927- *IIBEAAW*
Swanson, John A 1874- *WhAm 2*
Swanson, Paul Gustaf 1895-1958 *WhAm 3*
Swanson, W Clarke 1908-1961 *NatCAB 49, WhAm 4*
Swanstrom, Otto 1874-1945 *NatCAB 42*
Swantee, Paul Frederick 1900-1970 *WhAm 5*
Swanton, Gerald F 1904-1955 *WhAm 3*
Swanton, John Reed 1873-1958 *WhAm 3*
Swanton, Lucy Ross *WomWWA 14*
Swanton, William T 1893-1970 *WhAm 5*
Swanwick, John 1740-1798 *BiAUS, BiDrAC*
Swart, James 1866-1927 *NatCAB 22*
Swart, John Alvah 1899-1962 *NatCAB 49*
Swart, Joseph 1899-1966 *WhAm 4*
Swart, Peter 1752-1829 *BiAUS, BiDrAC, WhAm H*
Swart, Robert Emerson 1901-1947 *WhAm 2*
Swart, Rose Chambers 1847- *WomWWA 14*
Swart, Walter Goodwin 1868-1946 *NatCAB 35, WhAm 2*
Swarthout, Donald Malcolm 1884-1962 *NatCAB 46, WhAm 4*
Swarthout, Elvin 1864-1935 *WhAm 1*
Swarthout, Gladys 1904-1969 *WhAm 5*
Swarthout, M French 1844- *AmWom*
Swarthout, Max VanLewen 1880- *WhAm 6*
Swartley, William Blaine 1884-1955 *NatCAB 43*
Swarts, Frederic Jean Edmond 1866-1940 *DcScB*
Swarts, Gardner Taber 1857-1925 *NatCAB 20, WhAm 1*
Swarts, Ralph Easterday 1891-1958 *NatCAB 45*
Swartsberg, Jerome F d1966 *WhAm 4*
Swartsel, Samuel Carey 1867-1958 *NatCAB 48*
Swartwood, Howard Albright 1890-1965 *WhAm 4*
Swartwout, Egerton 1870-1943 *WhAm 2*
Swartwout, Henry 1809-1892 *NatCAB 7*
Swartwout, Mary Cooke 1876- *WhAm 5*
Swartwout, Richard Henry 1874-1938 *NatCAB 44, WhAm 1*
Swartwout, Robert 1778-1833 *NatCAB 7*
Swartwout, Robert 1778-1838 *ApCAB*
Swartwout, Robert 1778-1848 *Drake*
Swartwout, Samuel 1783-1856 *ApCAB, DcAmB, WhAm H*
Swartwout, Samuel 1804-1867 *ApCAB*
Swartz, Charles Benjamin 1890-1951 *WhAm 3*
Swartz, Charles Kephart 1861-1949 *NatCAB 41, WhAm 2*
Swartz, Edward George 1866-1944 *NatCAB 17, NatCAB 40*
Swartz, Edward James 1848-1910 *WhAm 1*
Swartz, Harry R 1854- *ApCAB X*
Swartz, Harry Raymond 1874-1945 *WhAm 2*
Swartz, Herman Frank 1871- *WhAm 5*
Swartz, Jacob Hyams 1896-1971 *WhAm 6*
Swartz, Joel 1827- *ApCAB, WhAm 4*
Swartz, John Hancock 1835-1919 *NatCAB 19*
Swartz, Joshua William 1867-1959 *BiDrAC, WhAm 4*
Swartz, Katherine H 1862-1968 *WhAm 4A*
Swartz, Mark Truman 1875-1932 *NatCAB 38*
Swartz, Maud O'Farrell 1879-1937 *NotAW*
Swartz, Mifflin Wyatt 1874- *WhAm 5*
Swartz, Olaus 1760-1817 *ApCAB*
Swartz, Olof 1760-1818 *DcScB*

Swartz, Osman Ellis 1880-1971 *WhAm 5*
Swartz, Peter Charles 1882-1938 *NatCAB 29*
Swartz, Peter Winford 1880- *WhAm 6*
Swartz, Philip Allen 1889-1962 *WhAm 4*
Swartz, Samuel Jackson 1859-1905 *WhAm 1*
Swartz, Willis George 1902-1965 *WhAm 4*
Swartzbaugh, William Lamson 1923- *WhAm 4*
Swartzel, Karl Dale 1869-1941 *NatCAB 31*
Swasey, Albert Loring 1876-1956 *WhAm 3*
Swasey, Ambrose 1846-1937 *AmBi, DcAmB S2, NatCAB 11, NatCAB 27, WhAm 1*
Swasey, John Philip 1839-1928 *BiDrAC*
Swasey, William F *NewYHSD*
Swatane d1748 *ApCAB*
Swatland, Donald Clinton 1895-1962 *WhAm 4*
Swavely, Eli 1876- *WhAm 5*
Swayne, Alfred Harris 1870-1937 *WhAm 1*
Swayne, Charles 1842-1907 *TwCBDA, WhAm 1*
Swayne, Francis Bond 1850-1928 *ApCAB X*
Swayne, John Wager 1835- *Drake*
Swayne, Noah Haynes 1804-1884 *ApCAB, BiAUS, DcAmB, Drake, NatCAB 4, TwCBDA, WebAB, WhAm H*
Swayne, Samuel Edward 1859-1933 *NatCAB 27*
Swayne, Wager 1834-1902 *ApCAB, DcAmB, NatCAB 4, TwCBDA, WhAm 1*
Swayne, William Marshall 1828-1918 *NewYHSD*
Swayze, Francis Joseph 1861-1932 *NatCAB 23, WhAm 1*
Swayze, George Banghart Henry 1833- *WhAm 1*
Swearingen, Belle Comin 1871- *WomWWA 14*
Swearingen, Embry L 1863-1931 *WhAm 1, WhAm 1C*
Swearingen, Henry 1792?-1841 *BiAUS, BiDrAC, WhAm H*
Swearingen, Henry Chapman 1869-1932 *WhAm 1*
Swearingen, John Eldred 1875- *WhAm 5*
Swearingen, Joseph M 1854- *ApCAB X*
Swearingen, Lloyd Edward 1897-1972 *WhAm 5*
Swearingen, Mack Buckley 1902-1969 *WhAm 5*
Swearingen, Thomas V d1822 *BiAUS*
Swearingen, VanCicero 1873- *WhAm 5*
Swearingen, Victor Clarence 1899-1968 *WhAm 5*
Swearingen, William Van 1887- *ApCAB X*
Sweat, Lorenzo DeMedici 1818-1898 *BiAUS, BiDrAC*
Sweat, Margaret Jane Mussey 1823- *ApCAB, Drake*
Sweatman, Arthur 1834- *ApCAB*
Sweatt, William R *WhAm 1*
Swedenborg, Emanuel 1688-1772 *BiHiMed, DcScB, McGEWB*
Sweedler, Nathan 1885-1960 *NatCAB 45*
Sweedlun, Verne Sebastian 1901- *EncAAH*
Sweelinck, Jan Pieterszoon 1562-1621 *McGEWB*
Sweeney, Alvin Randolph 1881-1954 *NatCAB 42, WhAm 3*
Sweeney, Bo 1863-1917 *WhAm 1*
Sweeney, Charles Thomas 1869-1956 *NatCAB 50*
Sweeney, Dan 1880-1958 *IIBEAAW*
Sweeney, Dennis *NewYHSD*
Sweeney, Edward C 1906-1967 *WhAm 4*
Sweeney, Ella Louise 1872- *WomWWA 14*
Sweeney, George Clinton 1895-1966 *WhAm 5*
Sweeney, James G 1877- *WhAm 5*
Sweeney, James J 1898-1968 *WhAm 5*
Sweeney, James P 1894-1962 *WhAm 4*
Sweeney, John Joseph 1889-1952 *NatCAB 41*
Sweeney, John William 1869- *WhAm 5*
Sweeney, Loretta Crissman 1868- *WomWWA 14*
Sweeney, Martin Leonard 1885-1960 *BiDrAC, WhAm 4, WhAmP*
Sweeney, Mary Agnes 1883- *WomWWA 14*
Sweeney, Mildred I McNeal 1871- *WhAm 5*
Sweeney, Orland Russell 1882-1958 *WhAm 3*
Sweeney, Robert E 1924- *BiDrAC*
Sweeney, Robert Emmet 1882-1969 *NatCAB 55*
Sweeney, Sarah Clokey 1835- *WomWWA 14*
Sweeney, Thomas Bell, Sr. 1874-1957 *WhAm 3*

Sweeney, Thomas T *New YHSD*
Sweeney, Thomas William 1820-1892 *TwCBDA, WhAm H*
Sweeney, Thomas William 1899-1966 *NatCAB 51*
Sweeney, W N 1832-1895 *BiAUS*
Sweeney, Walter Campbell 1876-1963 *NatCAB 52*
Sweeney, Walter Campbell 1876-1965 *WhAm 4*
Sweeney, Walter Campbell 1909-1965 *NatCAB 53*
Sweeney, William Allison 1851- *WhoColR*
Sweeney, William Northcut 1832-1895 *BiDrAC, WhAm H*
Sweeney, William R 1911-1974 *WhAm 6*
Sweeney, Zachary Taylor 1849-1926 *NatCAB 20, WhAm 1*
Sweenie, Denis J 1834-1903 *WhAm 1*
Sweeny, Charles Amos 1908-1968 *WhAm 5*
Sweeny, E Arthur 1882-1947 *NatCAB 40*
Sweeny, George 1796-1877 *BiAUS, BiDrAC, WhAm H*
Sweeny, John 1821- *ApCAB*
Sweeny, Madeline G 1890- *WomWWA 14*
Sweeny, Mildred I McNeal 1871- *WomWWA 14*
Sweeny, Peter Barr 1825-1911 *DcAmB, WhAm HA, WhAm 4*
Sweeny, Robert O 1831-1902 *New YHSD*
Sweeny, Sarah Catherine 1876- *WomWWA 14*
Sweeny, Thomas William 1818-1892 *Drake*
Sweeny, Thomas William 1820-1892 *ApCAB, DcAmB, NatCAB 11*
Sweeny, William Montgomery 1871- *WhAm 5*
Sweet, Ada Celeste 1853-1928 *AmWom, WhAm 3, WhAm 4, WomWWA 14*
Sweet, Alexander Edwin 1841-1901 *ApCAB, NatCAB 6, WhAm 1*
Sweet, Alfred Henry 1890-1950 *WhAm 3*
Sweet, Anna Giffin 1863- *WomWWA 14*
Sweet, Arthur Jacob 1895-1953 *NatCAB 45*
Sweet, Benjamin Jeffrey 1832-1874 *AmBi, ApCAB*
Sweet, Burton Erwin 1867-1957 *BiDrAC, NatCAB 49*
Sweet, Carroll Fuller 1877- *WhAm 3*
Sweet, Charles 1811- *Drake*
Sweet, Charles Frederick 1869-1953 *NatCAB 42*
Sweet, Clinton Wesley 1841-1917 *NatCAB 20*
Sweet, Cyrus Bardeen 1861-1943 *NatCAB 32*
Sweet, Cyrus Bardeen 1900-1963 *WhAm 4*
Sweet, Edward Andrew 1837-1915 *NatCAB 17*
Sweet, Edwin Forrest 1847-1935 *BiDrAC, WhAm 1, WhAm 1C*
Sweet, Ellingham Tracy 1853- *WhAm 2*
Sweet, Elnathan 1837-1903 *ApCAB, WhAm 1*
Sweet, Frank Edwin 1861-1922 *NatCAB 19*
Sweet, Frank Herbert 1856-1930 *WhAm 1*
Sweet, Frederic E 1900-1973 *WhAm 6*
Sweet, Frederick A 1873-1936 *NatCAB 27*
Sweet, Frederick Benoni 1870-1941 *NatCAB 30*
Sweet, George Sullivan 1854- *WhAm 4*
Sweet, Harold Edward 1877- *WhAm 5*
Sweet, Homer DeLois 1826- *ApCAB*
Sweet, John Edson 1832-1916 *ApCAB, DcAmB, NatCAB 13, WhAm 1*
Sweet, John Henry Throop, Jr. 1884-1950 *WhAm 3*
Sweet, John Hyde 1880-1964 *BiDrAC, WhAm 4*
Sweet, Joseph Lyman 1852-1932 *NatCAB 24*
Sweet, Joshua Edwin 1876-1957 *WhAm 3*
Sweet, Louis Dennison 1863- *WhAm 1*
Sweet, Louis Matthews 1869-1950 *WhAm 3*
Sweet, Marguerite *WomWWA 14*
Sweet, Marion Atwood 1899-1970 *WhAm 5*
Sweet, Owen Jay 1845-1928 *WhAm 1*
Sweet, Paul Bailey 1881-1951 *NatCAB 43*
Sweet, Ralph William 1892-1961 *NatCAB 50*
Sweet, Robert Lockwood 1902-1958 *NatCAB 44*
Sweet, Silas A *New YHSD*
Sweet, Simeon *New YHSD*
Sweet, Thaddeus C 1872-1928 *BiDrAC, NatCAB 21, WhAm 1*
Sweet, Timothy Bailey 1841-1918 *WhAm 1*
Sweet, W Glenn 1875-1944 *NatCAB 34*

Sweet, William d1840 *New YHSD*
Sweet, William Ellery 1869-1942 *NatCAB 32, WhAm 2*
Sweet, William Luther 1868- *WhAm 4*
Sweet, William Merrick 1860-1926 *WhAm 1*
Sweet, William Warren 1881-1958 *WhAm 3*
Sweet, William Warren 1881-1959 *DcAmReB*
Sweet, Willis 1856-1925 *BiDrAC, WhAmP*
Sweet, Winifred *NotAW*
Sweetland, Cornelius Sowle 1845-1923 *WhAm 1*
Sweetland, Ernest John 1880-1950 *NatCAB 40*
Sweetland, Leon Hiram 1880- *WhAm 6*
Sweetland, Monroe Marsh 1860-1944 *NatCAB 34*
Sweetland, William Howard 1856-1932 *WhAm 1*
Sweets, David Matthis 1868-1932 *WhAm 1*
Sweets, Henry Hayes 1872-1952 *WhAm 3*
Sweetser, Arthur 1888-1968 *WhAm 4A*
Sweetser, Charles 1808-1864 *BiAUS, BiDrAC, WhAm H*
Sweetser, Charles Humphreys 1841-1871 *ApCAB, Drake*
Sweetser, Delight 1873-1903 *WhAm 1*
Sweetser, Edwin Chapin 1847-1929 *WhAm 1*
Sweetser, Henry Edward 1837-1870 *ApCAB*
Sweetser, John Anderson 1889-1944 *WhAm 2*
Sweetser, Kate Dickenson d1939 *WomWWA 14*
Sweetser, Kate Dickinson d1939 *WhAm 1*
Sweetser, Moses Foster 1848- *ApCAB*
Sweetser, William 1797-1875 *ApCAB*
Sweezey, Nelson *New YHSD*
Sweigard, Joseph Leonard 1871-1957 *NatCAB 50*
Sweinhart, Henry Lee 1878-1949 *NatCAB 38*
Sweitzer, Caesar 1911-1970 *WhAm 5*
Sweitzer, J Mearl 1900-1975 *WhAm 6*
Swem, Earl Gregg 1870-1965 *DcAmLiB*
Swem, Lee Allan 1899-1954 *WhAm 3*
Sweney, John Robson 1837-1899 *ApCAB, NatCAB 4*
Sweney, Joseph Henry 1845-1918 *BiDrAC, WhAm 1*
Swengel, Uriah Frantz 1846-1921 *WhAm 1*
Swenk, Myron Harmon 1883-1941 *WhAm 1*
Swenson, Amanda Carlson *AmWom*
Swenson, Annie Dinsdale *WomWWA 14*
Swenson, David Ferdinand 1876-1940 *DcAmB S2, NatCAB 29, WhAm 1*
Swenson, Eric Appleton 1884-1921 *NatCAB 23*
Swenson, Eric P d1945 *WhAm 2*
Swenson, Laurits Selmer 1865-1947 *WhAm 2*
Swenson, Laurits Solmer 1865-1947 *NatCAB 12*
Swenson, Lowell Harvey 1912-1963 *WhAm 4*
Swenson, Merrill G 1892-1960 *WhAm 4*
Swenson, O Frederick 1880-1957 *NatCAB 43*
Swenson, Stanley Prescott 1908-1974 *WhAm 6*
Swenson, Svante Magnus 1816-1896 *NatCAB 12*
Swenson, Swen Albin 1860-1927 *NatCAB 23*
Swensson, Carl Aaron 1857-1904 *ApCAB, DcAmB, NatCAB 21, WhAm 1*
Swensson, Emil C P 1858- *NatCAB 14*
Swensson, Otto Jordan 1885-1957 *NatCAB 43*
Swepston, John Elmer 1894-1961 *NatCAB 49, WhAm 4*
Swerdfeger, Elbert Byron 1876-1937 *WhAm 1*
Sweringen, Grace Fleming Van *WomWWA 14*
Swertfager, Walter Milton 1900-1961 *WhAm 4*
Swetland, Roger Williams 1861-1934 *NatCAB 14, WhAm 1*
Swett, Albert Louis 1850-1924 *NatCAB 20*
Swett, Arthur Hollister 1866-1953 *NatCAB 42*
Swett, Caroline Patton *WomWWA 14*
Swett, Cyrus A *New YHSD*
Swett, Frank Tracy 1869- *WhAm 5*
Swett, John 1830-1913 *BiDAmEd, DcAmB, NatCAB 10, WhAm 1*
Swett, John Appleton 1808-1854 *ApCAB, Drake*
Swett, Josiah 1814-1890 *ApCAB, NatCAB 18*
Swett, Leonard 1825-1889 *ApCAB, TwCBDA*
Swett, Louis William 1880-1930 *WhAm 1*
Swett, Mary Nye 1870- *WomWWA 14*
Swett, Moses *New YHSD*
Swett, Raymond Fuller 1885-1961 *NatCAB 48*

Swett, Samuel 1782-1866 *ApCAB, Drake, NatCAB 13*
Swett, Sophia Miriam d1912 *WhAm 1*
Swett, Susan Hartley d1907 *WhAm 1*
Swett, William 1825-1884 *ApCAB*
Swezey, Andrew Jackson 1869-1924 *NatCAB 20*
Swezey, Goodwin Deloss 1851-1934 *WhAm 1*
Swezey, Otto Herman 1869-1959 *NatCAB 50*
Swick, J Howard 1879-1952 *WhAm 6*
Swick, Jesse Howard 1879-1952 *BiDrAC*
Swierenga, Robert Peter 1935- *EncAAH*
Swieten, Gerard Van 1700-1772 *DcScB*
Swift, Albert George 1879-1959 *NatCAB 48*
Swift, Alden Brackett 1885-1936 *NatCAB 29*
Swift, Alice Mayhew *BiCAW*
Swift, Ann Waterman *New YHSD*
Swift, Archie Dean 1877-1961 *WhAm 4*
Swift, Benjamin 1780-1847 *NatCAB 3, TwCBDA*
Swift, Benjamin 1781-1847 *ApCAB, BiAUS, BiDrAC, WhAm H*
Swift, Carl Brown 1888-1930 *WhAm 1*
Swift, Charles Edward 1846-1925 *NatCAB 38*
Swift, Charles Henry 1872-1948 *WhAm 2*
Swift, Charles Henry 1885-1959 *NatCAB 52*
Swift, Claire Coburn 1876- *WomWWA 14*
Swift, Clarence Franklin 1861-1918 *WhAm 1*
Swift, Clarence Franklin 1861-1919 *NatCAB 17*
Swift, Clifford Jewett 1882-1955 *NatCAB 42*
Swift, Douglas 1882-1946 *WhAm 2*
Swift, Eben 1854-1938 *NatCAB 18, WhAm 1*
Swift, Ebenezer 1819-1885 *ApCAB, NatCAB 5*
Swift, Edgar James 1860-1932 *WhAm 1*
Swift, Edith Hale 1878- *BiCAW*
Swift, Edward Foster d1932 *WhAm 1*
Swift, Edward Wellington 1865- *WhAm 4*
Swift, Elijah Kent 1878-1959 *WhAm 3*
Swift, Elisha Pope 1792-1865 *ApCAB*
Swift, Ernest Fremont 1897-1968 *NatCAB 56, WhAm 5*
Swift, Ernest Gardner 1861-1926 *NatCAB 20*
Swift, Ernest John 1883-1941 *WhAm 1*
Swift, Eugene Clinton 1919-1973 *NatCAB 57, WhAm 6*
Swift, Fletcher Harper 1876-1947 *WhAm 2*
Swift, Frances Laura 1837- *AmWom*
Swift, George B 1845- *WhAm 4*
Swift, George Montague 1856-1925 *NatCAB 33*
Swift, George Robinson 1887- *BiDrAC*
Swift, George Wilkins 1882-1938 *NatCAB 28, WhAm 1*
Swift, Gustavus Franklin 1839-1903 *AmBi, ApCAB X, DcAmB, EncAAH, EncAB, NatCAB 14, WebAB, WhAm 1*
Swift, Gustavus Franklin 1881-1943 *WhAm 2*
Swift, Harold Higgins 1885-1962 *NatCAB 50, WhAm 4*
Swift, Harry Ladrew 1871-1955 *WhAm 3*
Swift, Heman 1733-1814 *Drake*
Swift, Henry Walton 1849- *NatCAB 16*
Swift, Herman Holst 1880-1954 *NatCAB 49*
Swift, Homer Fordyce 1881-1953 *NatCAB 40, WhAm 3*
Swift, Innis Palmer 1882-1953 *WhAm 3*
Swift, Ivan 1873-1945 *WhAm 2*
Swift, James Carroll 1869-1938 *WhAm 1*
Swift, James Marcus 1873-1946 *ApCAB X, WhAm 2*
Swift, Jireh, Jr. d1941 *WhAm 2*
Swift, John 1790-1873 *ApCAB*
Swift, John Edward 1879- *WhAm 6*
Swift, John Franklin 1829-1891 *DcAmB, NatCAB 13, NatCAB 18, TwCBDA, WhAm H*
Swift, John Trumbull 1861- *WhAm 4*
Swift, John White 1750-1819 *ApCAB*
Swift, Jonathan 1667-1745 *McGEWB*
Swift, Jonathan Williams 1808-1877 *ApCAB*
Swift, Joseph Gardiner 1783-1865 *NatCAB 10*
Swift, Joseph Gardner 1783-1865 *AmBi, ApCAB, DcAmB, Drake, TwCBDA, WhAm H*
Swift, Josiah Otis 1871-1948 *WhAm 2*
Swift, Lewis 1820-1913 *AmBi, ApCAB, DcAmB, NatCAB 4, TwCBDA, WhAm 1*

Swift, Lewis Burrie 1885-1967 *NatCAB 54*
Swift, Lindsay 1856-1921 *WhAm 1*
Swift, Linton Bishop 1888-1946 *DcAmB S4*
Swift, Louis Franklin 1861-1937 *DcAmB S2*,
  WhAm 1
Swift, Louise Russell Smith 1866-
  WomWWA 14
Swift, Lucian, Jr. 1848-1926 *NatCAB 6*,
  WhAm 3
Swift, Lucius Burrie 1844-1929 *DcAmB*
Swift, Marie Fitzgerald *WomWWA 14*
Swift, Nathan Butler 1911-1953 *WhAm 3*
Swift, Oscar William 1869-1940 *BiDrAC*,
  WhAm 1
Swift, Polemus Hamilton 1853-1935 *WhAm 1*
Swift, Raymond W 1895-1975 *WhAm 6*
Swift, Robert 1799-1872 *ApCAB*
Swift, Samuel 1782-1875 *ApCAB*, *Drake*
Swift, Samuel 1873-1914 *WhAm 1*
Swift, Willard Everett 1879-1947 *WhAm 2*
Swift, William 1848-1919 *NatCAB 26*,
  WhAm 1
Swift, William Everett 1871-1953 *NatCAB 40*
Swift, William Henry 1800-1879 *ApCAB*,
  DcAmB, *WhAm H*
Swift, Zephaniah 1759-1823 *AmBi*, *ApCAB*,
  BiAUS, *BiDrAC*, *DcAmB*, *Drake*,
  NatCAB 3, *TwCBDA*, *WhAm H*
Swigart, Charles H 1864- *WhAm 4*
Swigart, Clyde Arthur 1888-1973 *WhAm 6*
Swigart, Edmund Kearsley 1867-1934 *WhAm 1*
Swigart, Lavern Lake 1918-1970 *WhAm 6*
Swiger, Arlen Goff 1887-1960 *NatCAB 48*
Swiger, Wilbur Moore 1890-1939 *WhAm 1*
Swigert, Charles Frederick 1862-1935
  NatCAB 37
Swigert, William Gorrill 1898-1952 *NatCAB 41*
Swiggart, William Harris 1888-1966 *WhAm 4*
Swiggett, Douglas Worthington 1882-1950
  WhAm 2, *WhAm 3*
Swiggett, Glen Levin 1867-1961 *NatCAB 47*,
  WhAm 4
Swiler, Martha A *WomWWA 14*
Swim, Chester Lawrence 1894- *WhAm 5*
Swim, Dudley 1905-1972 *WhAm 5*
Swimmer, Jack 1900-1958 *NatCAB 45*
Swinburne, Algernon Charles 1837-1909
  McGEWB
Swinburne, John 1820-1889 *ApCAB*, *BiDrAC*,
  NatCAB 7, *WhAm H*
Swinburne, Louis Judson 1855-1887 *ApCAB*
Swinburne, Ralph Erskine 1853-1897 *NatCAB 2*
Swinburne, William Thomas 1847-1928
  WhAm 1
Swindall, Charles 1876-1939 *BiDrAC*,
  NatCAB 30, *WhAm 1*
Swinden, Jan Hendrik Van 1746-1823 *DcScB*
Swinderen, Jonkheer Reneke DeMarees Van
  1860- *WhAm 4*
Swindle, Robert Norris 1883-1957 *NatCAB 46*
Swindler, Mary Hamilton 1884-1967
  NatCAB 54, *WhAm 4*
Swineford, Alfred P 1836- *NatCAB 12*
Swinehart, Gerry 1903-1966 *WhAm 4*
Swinehart, James Allen 1856-1933 *NatCAB 32*
Swinerton, Alfred B 1883-1963 *WhAm 4*
Swineshead, Richard *DcScB*
Swiney, Daniel 1826- *WhAm 4*
Swiney, Florence VanPatten 1860-
  WomWWA 14
Swinford, Mac 1899-1975 *WhAm 6*
Swing, Albert Temple 1849-1925 *WhAm 1*
Swing, David 1830-1894 *ApCAB*, *DcAmB*,
  DcAmReB, *NatCAB 3*, *TwCBDA*,
  WhAm H
Swing, David Carrick 1864-1945 *IlBEAAW*,
  NatCAB 34
Swing, Frank Ulmer 1873-1948 *NatCAB 38*
Swing, Philip B *BiAUS*
Swing, Philip David 1884-1963 *BiDrAC*,
  NatCAB 49, *WhAm 4*
Swing, Raymond 1887-1968 *WhAm 5*
Swingle, D B d1944 *WhAm 2*
Swingle, Frank Bell 1874- *WhAm 5*
Swingle, Walter Tennyson 1871-1952
  NatCAB 54, *WhAm 3*
Swingle, William Alfred 1903-1967 *NatCAB 53*
Swingle, William S 1891-1973 *WhAm 6*

Swingler, William S 1901-1971 *WhAm 5*
Swinnerton, James Guilford 1875-1974
  IlBEAAW, *WhAm 6*
Swinney, E Earle 1884-1955 *NatCAB 44*
Swinney, Edward Fletcher 1857-1946
  NatCAB 13, *WhAm 2*
Swinney, Raymond Wooldridge 1892-1962
  NatCAB 49
Swint, John J 1879-1962 *WhAm 4*
Swint, Roger Cook 1875-1945 *NatCAB 38*
Swint, Samuel Hubert 1896-1962 *NatCAB 49*,
  WhAm 4
Swinton, Alfred 1826-1920 *NewYHSD*
Swinton, Frederick *NewYHSD*
Swinton, John 1829-1901 *DcAmB*, *TwCBDA*,
  WhAm 1
Swinton, John 1830-1901 *ApCAB*, *NatCAB 8*
Swinton, William 1833-1892 *AmBi*, *ApCAB*,
  BiDAmEd, *DcAmB*, *Drake*, *NatCAB 11*,
  TwCBDA, *WhAm H*
Swirbul, Leon A 1898-1960 *WhAm 4*
Swire, O L *NewYHSD*
Swiren, Max 1904-1969 *WhAm 5*
Swisher, Benjamin Franklin 1878-1959
  WhAm 3
Swisher, Charles Clinton d1940 *WhAm 1*
Swisher, Paul Leroy 1898-1958 *NatCAB 47*
Swisshelm, Jane Grey Cannon 1815-1884
  ApCAB, *DcAmB*, *NatCAB 2*, *NotAW*,
  REnAW, *WhAm H*
Swisshelm, Jane Grey Cannon 1816-1884 *Drake*
Switz, Theodore MacLean 1901-1971 *WhAm 5*
Switzer, George Washington 1854-1940
  WhAm 1
Switzer, Lucy Robbins Messer 1844- *AmWom*
Switzer, Mary Elizabeth 1900-1971 *NatCAB 56*,
  WhAm 5
Switzer, Maurice 1870-1929 *WhAm 1*
Switzer, Robert Mauck 1863-1952 *BiDrAC*,
  WhAm 4
Switzer, Roland Woodhill 1866-1918
  NatCAB 18
Switzer, Rufus 1855-1947 *NatCAB 36*
Switzler, Royall Hill 1878-1945 *NatCAB 38*
Switzler, William Franklin 1819-1906 *BiAUS*,
  DcAmB
Swoope, Jacob d1832 *BiAUS*, *BiDrAC*,
  WhAm H
Swoope, William Irvin 1862-1930 *BiDrAC*,
  WhAm 1
Swope, Ammon 1886-1963 *WhAm 4*
Swope, Belle McKinney Hays 1867-
  WomWWA 14
Swope, Charles Siegel 1899-1959 *WhAm 3*
Swope, Gerard 1872-1957 *NatCAB 45*,
  WebAB, *WhAm 3*
Swope, Guy Jacob 1892-1969 *BiDrAC*,
  WhAm 5
Swope, Herbert Bayard 1882-1958 *NatCAB 45*,
  WebAB, *WhAm 3*
Swope, John Augustus 1827-1910 *BiDrAC*
Swope, King 1893-1961 *BiDrAC*, *NatCAB 48*,
  WhAm 4
Swope, Logan Oliver 1847-1900 *ApCAB X*
Swope, Lorenzo Watson 1862-1939 *NatCAB 49*
Swope, Samuel Franklin 1809-1865 *BiDrAC*,
  WhAm H
Sword, James Brade 1839-1915 *ApCAB*,
  NewYHSD, *WhAm 1*
Sword, William Oscar 1896-1969 *NatCAB 55*
Swords, Henry Cotheal 1854-1924 *WhAm 1*
Swords, Robert Smith 1816-1881 *ApCAB*
Swords, Thomas 1806-1886 *ApCAB*,
  NatCAB 4
Swords, Thomas 1809?-1886 *Drake*
Swormstedt, Lyman Beecher 1853-1943
  NatCAB 32
Swormstedt, Mabel Godfrey 1869-
  WomWWA 14
Swrope, Samuel F *BiAUS*
Swyney, John *NewYHSD*
Sydenham, Charles E P Thompson, Baron
  1799-1841 *Drake*
Sydenham, Charles E P Thomson, Baron
  1799-1841 *ApCAB*, *McGEWB*
Sydenham, Thomas 1624-1689 *BiHiMed*,
  DcScB, *McGEWB*
Sydenstricker, Edgar 1881-1936 *DcAmB S2*,

NatCAB 27, *WhAm 1*
Sydenstricker, Lucy Alma Willis
  WomWWA 14
Sydenstricker, Pearl *WebAB*
Sydenstricker, Virgil Preston 1889-1964
  WhAm 4
Sydness, Joseph Truman 1912-1970 *WhAm 5*
Sydnor, Charles Sackett 1898-1954 *DcAmB S5*,
  WhAm 3
Sydnor, Eugene Beauharnais 1869-1949
  NatCAB 37
Sydnor, Giles Granville 1864-1941 *WhAm 2*
Syed Ahmed Khan 1817-1898 *McGEWB*
Sykes, Bernard Greenleaf 1869-1943
  NatCAB 32
Sykes, Charles Henry 1882-1942 *WhAm 2*
Sykes, David Allen 1858-1942 *NatCAB 34*
Sykes, Edward 1874- *WhAm 5*
Sykes, Edward Turner 1838- *WhAm 4*
Sykes, Eugene Octave 1876-1945 *NatCAB 34*,
  WhAm 2
Sykes, Frederick Henry 1863-1917 *NatCAB 26*,
  WhAm 1
Sykes, George d1880 *BiAUS*
Sykes, George 1802-1880 *BiDrAC*, *WhAm H*
Sykes, George 1822-1880 *AmBi*, *ApCAB*,
  DcAmB, *NatCAB 4*, *TwCBDA*,
  WhAm H
Sykes, George 1823?- *Drake*
Sykes, George 1840-1903 *NatCAB 34*
Sykes, Howard Calvin 1893-1966 *WhAm 4*
Sykes, James 1725-1792 *BiAUS*, *BiDrAC*,
  WhAm H
Sykes, James 1761-1822 *ApCAB*, *Drake*
Sykes, Jerome H d1903 *WhAm 1*
Sykes, John 1773-1858 *NewYHSD*
Sykes, Lawrence Granger 1887-1955
  NatCAB 46
Sykes, Lyman R *NewYHSD*
Sykes, Mabel 1868-1938 *WhAm 1*
Sykes, Martin Luther 1826- *NatCAB 3*
Sykes, M'Cready 1869-1952 *WhAm 3*
Sykes, Richard Eddy 1861-1942 *WhAm 2*
Sykes, Wilfred 1883-1964 *WhAm 4*
Syle, Louis DuPont 1857-1903 *WhAm 1*
Sylow, Peter Ludvig Mejdell 1832-1918 *DcScB*
Sylva, Marguerita d1957 *WhAm 3*
Sylvester II *DcScB*
Sylvester, Albert Lenthall 1903-1973 *WhAm 6*
Sylvester, Allie Lewis 1864-1961 *NatCAB 15*,
  WhAm 4
Sylvester, Charles Bradford 1865-1941
  NatCAB 32
Sylvester, Emma 1874- *WhAm 5*
Sylvester, Evander Wallace 1899-1960
  NatCAB 50, *WhAm 4*
Sylvester, Frederick Oakes 1869-1915 *DcAmB*,
  WhAm 1
Sylvester, Herbert Milton 1849- *ApCAB*,
  WhAm 4
Sylvester, James Joseph 1814-1897 *AmBi*,
  ApCAB, *DcAmB*, *DcScB*, *WhAm H*
Sylvester, Nathaniel Bartlett 1825- *ApCAB*
Sylvester, Richard H 1830- *NatCAB 3*
Sylvester, Robert 1907-1975 *WhAm 6*
Sylvie, Edouard 1670-1739 *ApCAB*
Sylvis, William H 1828-1869 *DcAmB*,
  McGEWB, *WebAB*, *WhAm H*
Sylvis, William Martin 1882-1947 *NatCAB 40*
Sylvius, Franciscus Dele Boe 1614-1672 *AsBiEn*,
  DcScB
Sylvius, Jacobus 1478-1555 *BiHiMed*, *DcScB*
Syme, Bernard Chapman 1888-1945
  NatCAB 34
Syme, Conrad Hunt 1868-1943 *WhAm 2*
Syme, James 1799-1870 *BiHiMed*
Syme, John P 1904-1970 *WhAm 5*
Syme, John William 1811-1865 *TwCBDA*
Symes, George Gifford 1840-1893 *BiDrAC*,
  WhAm H, *WhAmP*
Symes, J Foster 1878-1951 *WhAm 3*
Symes, John d1888 *NewYHSD*
Symington, Andrew James 1825- *ApCAB*
Symington, Donald 1881-1944 *NatCAB 33*,
  WhAm 2
Symington, James Mansfield 1894-1961
  NatCAB 50
Symington, James Wadsworth 1927- *BiDrAC*

Symington, Stuart 1901- *BiDrAC*
Symington, William Wallace 1873-1935
  NatCAB 26
Symmer, Robert 1707?-1763 *DcScB*
Symmers, Douglas 1879-1952 *WhAm 3*
Symmes, Edwin Joseph 1883-1935 *WhAm 1*
Symmes, Frank Jameson 1847-1916 *NatCAB 17,*
  WhAm 1
Symmes, Fred William 1879-1957 *NatCAB 46*
Symmes, John Cleves 1742-1814 *ApCAB,*
  BiAUS, BiDrAC, DcAmB, Drake,
  NatCAB 11, TwCBDA, WhAm H
Symmes, John Cleves 1780-1829 *ApCAB,*
  NatCAB 11
Symmes, Leslie Webb 1879- *WhAm 6*
Symmes, Peyton Short 1793-1861 *ApCAB,*
  NewYHSD
Symmes, Thomas 1678-1725 *ApCAB, Drake*
Symmes, Whitman 1873-1952 *NatCAB 44*
Symmes, William Bittle 1851-1928 *ApCAB X*
Symmes, Zechariah 1599-1671 *ApCAB*
Symmonds, Charles Jacobs 1866-1941 *WhAm 1*
Symon *NewYHSD*
Symonds, Brandreth 1863-1924 *WhAm 1*
Symonds, Frederick Martin 1846-1926 *WhAm 1*
Symonds, Gardiner 1903-1971 *NatCAB 57,*
  WhAm 5
Symonds, Joseph White 1840-1918 *NatCAB 15,*
  WhAm 1
Symonds, Nathaniel Millberry 1906-1968
  WhAm 5
Symonds, Percival Mallon 1893-1960 *BiDAmEd,*
  NatCAB 46, WhAm 4
Symonds, Thomas William 1849- *ApCAB Sup*
Symonds, Walter Stout 1891-1957 *WhAm 3*
Symonds, William Law 1833-1862 *ApCAB,*
  Drake
Symons, Arthur Henley 1872-1956 *NatCAB 47*
Symons, George Gardner 1863?-1930 *IIBEAAW*
Symons, George Gardner 1865-1930 *AmBi,*
  DcAmB, WhAm 1
Symons, Noel S 1897-1965 *WhAm 4*
Symons, Thomas Baddeley 1880-1970 *WhAm 5*
Symons, Thomas William 1849-1920 *DcAmB,*
  NatCAB 19, WhAm 1
Syms, Benjamin 1591?-1642? *DcAmB,*
  WhAm H
Syms, John George 1826- *NatCAB 7*
Synan, James William 1870-1926 *NatCAB 22*
Synesius Of Cyrene 370?-414? *DcScB*
Syng, Philip 1703-1789 *DcAmB, WhAm H*
Syng, Phillip 1703-1789 *BnEnAmA*
Synge, Edmund John Millington 1871-1909
  McGEWB
Synge, Millington Henry 1820?- *ApCAB*
Synge, Richard Laurence Millington 1914-
  AsBiEn
Synnestvedt, Arthur 1894-1965 *NatCAB 51*
Synnestvedt, Paul 1870- *NatCAB 17*
Synnott, Joseph J 1863-1899 *WhAm 1*
Synnott, Thomas Whitney 1845-1941 *WhAm 1*
Sypher, J Hale 1837-1905 *BiAUS*
Sypher, Jacob Hale 1837-1905 *BiDrAC*
Sypher, Jay Hale 1837-1905 *ApCAB Sup,*
  TwCBDA
Sypher, Josiah Rhinehart 1832- *ApCAB,*
  WhAm 4
Sypherd, Wilbur Owen 1877- *WhAm 5*
Syverton, Jerome T 1907-1961 *WhAm 4*
Syvertsen, Rolf Christian 1896-1960 *WhAm 4*
Syvret, Clara Maud *WomWWA 14*
Szabad, Emeric 1822- *ApCAB*
Szabo, Violette 1918-1945 *WhWW-II*
Szanto, Louis 1888-1952 *NatCAB 41*
Szasz, Otto 1884-1952 *NatCAB 41*
Sze, Sao-Ke Alfred 1877-1958 *WhAm 3*
Szebelledy, Laszlo 1901-1944 *DcScB*
Szechenyi, Countess L 1886- *WomWWA 14*
Szekely, Ernest 1888-1956 *NatCAB 46,*
  WhAm 3
Szell, George 1897-1970 *WebAB*
Szenes-Dugo, Andre 1895-1957 *NatCAB 43*
Szent-Gyorgyi, Albert Von 1893- *AsBiEn,*
  McGEWB, WebAB
Szepesi, Eugene Stevan 1880-1966 *NatCAB 53*
Szigeti, Joseph 1892-1973 *WhAm 5*
Szilard, Leo 1898-1964 *AsBiEn, DcScB,*
  McGEWB, WebAB, WhAm 4

Szily, Pal 1878-1945 *DcScB*
Szinnyey, Stephen Ivor 1863-1919 *WhAm 1*
Szkolny, John *ApCAB*
Szlupas, John 1861- *WhAm 4*
Szold, Benjamin 1829-1902 *DcAmB,*
  NatCAB 13
Szold, Henrietta 1860-1945 *DcAmB S3,*
  DcAmReB, McGEWB, NotAW,
  WhAm 2, WomWWA 14
Szumowska, Antoinette 1872-1938 *WhAm 1*
Szyk, Arthur 1894-1951 *DcAmB S5, WhAm 3*
Szymanowski, Karol 1882-1937 *McGEWB*

Taaffe, Martha Coffin 1868- WomWWA 14
Taba, Hilda 1902-1967 BiDAmEd,
  NatCAB 54
Tabaret, Joseph Henry 1828-1886 ApCAB
Tabari, Abul-Hasan Ahmad Ibn M, Al- DcScB
Tabari, Abul-Hasan Ali Ibn S Rabbam, Al-
  808?-861? DcScB
Tabari, Muhammad Ibn Jarir, Al- 839-923
  McGEWB
Tabb, John Banister 1845-1909 AmBi, DcAmB,
  NatCAB 13, TwCBDA, WhAm 1
Tabb, John Bannister 1845-1909 ApCAB X
Tabb, T Garnett 1875-1952 NatCAB 41
Tabell, Edmund Weber 1904-1965 WhAm 4
Taber NewYHSD
Taber, Albert Winnie 1892-1958 NatCAB 49
Taber, Clarence Wilbur 1870-1968 NatCAB 53
Taber, David Fairman 1891-1958 NatCAB 48,
  WhAm 3
Taber, Edward Smith 1826-1899 NatCAB 29
Taber, Erroll James Livingstone 1877-1947
  WhAm 2
Taber, Ethel Arnold Bell WomWWA 14
Taber, Frederic Crawford 1859-1930
  NatCAB 22
Taber, George Hathaway 1859-1940
  NatCAB 30
Taber, George Hathaway, Jr. 1890-1954
  WhAm 3
Taber, Harry Persons 1865- WhAm 4
Taber, Henry 1860-1936 WhAm 1
Taber, John 1880-1965 BiDrAC, WhAm 4,
  WhAmP
Taber, John Russell 1844-1922 NatCAB 26
Taber, Julia Marlowe 1870- TwCBDA
Taber, Louis John 1878-1960 NatCAB 49,
  WhAm 4
Taber, Marion Russell WomWWA 14
Taber, Mary Jane Howland 1834- WhAm 4,
  WomWWA 14
Taber, Norman Stephen 1891-1952 WhAm 3
Taber, Ralph Graham 1866- WhAm 4
Taber, Stephen 1821-1886 BiAUS, BiDrAC,
  WhAm H
Taber, Thomas, II 1785-1862 BiAUS, BiDrAC,
  WhAm H
Taber, W IIBEAAW
Taber, William Ira 1865-1931 WhAm 1
Tabert, Alfred T A BiAUS
Taboada, Antonio 1815- ApCAB
Tabor, Carl Henry 1893-1953 WhAm 3
Tabor, Edward A 1857- WhAm 4
Tabor, Horace Austin Warner 1830-1899 AmBi,
  ApCAB, BiDrAC, DcAmB, McGEWB,
  NatCAB 11, REnAW, TwCBDA,
  WhAm H, WhAmP
Tabor, Jeremiah Wilson 1839-1920 NatCAB 18
Tabor, John 1667- DcScB
Tabor, Mabel Rogers 1866- WomWWA 14
Tabor, Stephen J W 1815- BiAUS
Taboroff, Leonard Herbert 1914-1956
  NatCAB 49
Tabors, Robert Gustav 1914-1962 NatCAB 49,
  WhAm 4
Tac, Sixtus Le 1649-1699 ApCAB
Tacchini, Pietro 1838-1905 DcScB
Taccola, Mariano DiJacomo 1381-1458? DcScB
Tache, Alexander Antonine 1823- ApCAB
Tache, Sir Etienne Paschal 1795-1865 ApCAB,
  Drake
Tache, Joseph Charles 1820- ApCAB
Tachenius, Otto DcScB
Tacitus 056?-125? McGEWB
Tack, Augustus Vincent 1870-1949 NatCAB 39,

WhAm 2
Tackett, Boyd 1911- BiDrAC
Tackett, John Robert 1868- WhAm 4
Tackett, William Clarence 1897-1958 WhAm 3
Tacon, General d1855 Drake
Tacon, Miguel 1777-1855 ApCAB
Tacquet, Andreas 1612-1660 DcScB
Tadd, J Liberty 1854-1917 WhAm 1
Taeuber, Irene Barnes 1906-1974 WhAm 6
Taeusch, Carl Frederick 1889-1962 WhAm 4
Taewon'gun, Hungson 1820-1898 McGEWB
Tafaga, Joseph IIBEAAW
Tafawa Balewa, Sir Abubakar 1912-1966
  McGEWB
Tafel, Gustav 1830-1908 WhAm 1
Tafel, Johann Friedrich Leonhard 1800-
  ApCAB
Tafel, Rudolph Leonhard 1831- ApCAB
Taff, Joseph Alexander 1862- WhAm 2
Taffe, John 1827-1884 BiAUS, BiDrAC,
  WhAm H
Taffinder, Sherwoode Ayerst 1884-1965
  WhAm 4
Taft, Alphonso d1891 BiAUS Sup
Taft, Alphonso 1810-1891 ApCAB, BiDrUSE,
  DcAmB, TwCBDA, WhAm H
Taft, Alphonso 1814-1891 BiDrAC
Taft, Anna Sinton 1852-1931 NatCAB 23
Taft, Chamberlin 1891-1947 NatCAB 36
Taft, Charles Phelps 1843-1929 BiDrAC,
  DcAmB, NatCAB 1, NatCAB 23,
  TwCBDA, WhAm 1, WhAmP
Taft, Daniel Henry 1850-1915 NatCAB 17
Taft, David Gibson 1915-1962 WhAm 4
Taft, Edgar Sidney 1853-1930 NatCAB 21
Taft, Elihu Barber 1847- WhAm 4
Taft, Frances E Schlosser WomWWA 14
Taft, Frederick Harris 1857- ApCAB X
Taft, Frederick Lovett 1870-1913 NatCAB 17
Taft, George Wheaton 1865-1939 WhAm 1
Taft, Grace Ellis WomWWA 14
Taft, Harry Deward 1886-1956 WhAm 3
Taft, Harry Lee 1873-1953 NatCAB 41
Taft, Helen Herron 1861-1943 NatCAB 14,
  NotAW, WomWWA 14
Taft, Henry Waters 1859-1945 DcAmB S3,
  NatCAB 34, WhAm 2
Taft, Horace Dutton 1861-1943 BiDAmEd,
  NatCAB 35, WhAm 2
Taft, Hulbert 1877-1959 NatCAB 43,
  WhAm 3
Taft, John Holsten 1862-1941 NatCAB 31
Taft, Kendall B 1899-1972 WhAm 5
Taft, Kingsley Arter 1903-1970 BiDrAC,
  WhAm 5
Taft, Levi Rawson 1859- WhAm 4
Taft, Lorado Zadoc 1860-1936 AmBi, ApCAB,
  ApCAB Sup, ApCAB X, BnEnAmA,
  DcAmB S2, IIBEAAW, McGEWB,
  NatCAB 8, TwCBDA, WebAB, WhAm 1,
  WhAm 4A
Taft, Mary Hall WomWWA 14
Taft, Oren Byron 1846- NatCAB 16
Taft, Oren Edwin 1868-1958 NatCAB 47
Taft, Robert 1894-1955 WhAm 3
Taft, Robert, Jr. 1917- BiDrAC
Taft, Robert Alphonso 1889-1953 BiDrAC,
  DcAmB S5, EncAAH, EncAB,
  NatCAB 47, WebAB, WhAm 3, WhAmP
Taft, Robert Burbidge 1899-1951 WhAm 3
Taft, Robert Edward 1891-1960 NatCAB 47
Taft, Robert Wendell 1868-1934 WhAm 1
Taft, Royal Chapin 1823-1912 NatCAB 9,
  TwCBDA, WhAm 1

Taft, Russell Smith 1835-1902 NatCAB 4,
  TwCBDA, WhAm 1
Taft, Stephen Harris 1825-1918 ApCAB X
Taft, Waterman Allen 1849-1918 NatCAB 18
Taft, William Henry 1857-1930 NatCAB 11
Taft, William Howard 1857-1930 AmBi,
  ApCAB Sup, ApCAB X, BiDrAC,
  BiDrUSE, DcAmB, EncAAH, EncAB,
  McGEWB, NatCAB 14, NatCAB 23,
  TwCBDA, WebAB, WhAm 1, WhAmP
Tag, Casimir 1847-1913 WhAm 1
Tagg, Francis Thomas 1845-1923 WhAm 1
Taggard, Genevieve 1894-1948 DcAmB S4,
  NotAW, WhAm 2
Taggart, Arthur Fay 1884-1959 WhAm 3
Taggart, Byron Brown 1874-1941 NatCAB 30
Taggart, Charles Manson 1821-1853 Drake
Taggart, Cynthia 1802-1849 Drake
Taggart, David Alexander 1898-1970 WhAm 5
Taggart, David Arthur 1858-1922 NatCAB 19,
  WhAm 1
Taggart, Edward Thomas 1868-1925
  NatCAB 25
Taggart, Elmore Findlay 1858- WhAm 4
Taggart, Eugene Francis 1916-1951 WhAm 3
Taggart, Fenwick Gordon 1875-1962
  NatCAB 49
Taggart, Frank Fulton 1873-1945 WhAm 2
Taggart, James William 1859-1910 ApCAB X
Taggart, Jay Paul 1886-1949 NatCAB 39
Taggart, John G NewYHSD
Taggart, John Henry 1821-1892 NatCAB 5
Taggart, Joseph 1832-1915 NatCAB 38
Taggart, Joseph 1867-1938 BiDrAC,
  NatCAB 41, WhAm 4, WhAmP
Taggart, Marion Ames WhAm 5,
  WomWWA 14
Taggart, Moses 1843-1914 NatCAB 16
Taggart, Ralph Enos 1887-1951 WhAm 3
Taggart, Rush 1849-1922 WhAm 1
Taggart, Rush 1891-1965 NatCAB 54
Taggart, Samuel 1754-1825 ApCAB, BiAUS,
  BiDrAC, Drake, NatCAB 3, TwCBDA,
  WhAm H, WhAmP
Taggart, Thomas 1856-1929 BiDrAC, DcAmB,
  NatCAB 22, WhAm 1, WhAmP
Taggart, Thomas Douglas 1886-1949
  NatCAB 38, WhAm 2
Taggart, Walter Thomas 1872-1937 WhAm 1
Taggart, Walter Thomas 1872-1938
  NatCAB 29
Taggart, William Marcus 1852-1896 NatCAB 5
Taggart, William Rush 1849- NatCAB 14
Tagliabue, Giuseppe 1812-1873 WhAm H
Tagliabue, Giuseppe 1812-1878 ApCAB,
  DcAmB
Tagliacozzi, Gaspare 1545-1599 BiHiMed
Tagore, Rabindranath 1861-1941 McGEWB
Tague, John Robert 1859-1916 NatCAB 17
Tague, Peter Francis 1871-1941 BiDrAC,
  WhAm 1
Tah-Gah-Jute 1725?-1780 AmBi, WebAB
Taharqa McGEWB
Tahoma, Quincy 1921-1956 IIBEAAW
Tailer, William d1732 Drake
Tailfer, Patrick ApCAB
Tailor NewYHSD
Tailor, Stephen NewYHSD
Taine, Hippolyte Adolphe 1828-1893 McGEWB
Tainter, Charles Sumner 1854-1940 NatCAB 29,
  WhAm 1
Taintor, Henry Fox 1833- NatCAB 1
Taintor, Henry Fox 1833-1908 NatCAB 24

Taintor, Henry Fox 1833-1909 *WhAm 1*
Taintor, Jesse Fox 1851-1935 *WhAm 1*
Tait, Agnes 1897- *IIBEAAW*
Tait, Andrew Love 1901-1967 *NatCAB 54*
Tait, Arthur Fitzwilliam 1819-1905 *ApCAB,*
BnEnAmA, DcAmB, IIBEAAW,
NewYHSD, TwCBDA, WhAm 1
Tait, Charles d1835 *BiAUS*
Tait, Charles 1768-1835 *ApCAB, BiDrAC,*
DcAmB, NatCAB 4, TwCBDA,
WhAm H, WhAmP
Tait, Charles 1769-1835 *Drake*
Tait, Edgar Wendell 1886- *ApCAB X*
Tait, Edwin Edgar 1851- *ApCAB X*
Tait, Edwin Forbes 1894-1958 *NatCAB 48*
Tait, Frank Morrison 1874-1962 *WhAm 4*
Tait, George 1893-1952 *WhAm 3*
Tait, John Robinson 1834-1909 *ApCAB,*
ApCAB X, Drake, NatCAB 13,
NewYHSD, TwCBDA, WhAm 1
Tait, Julia Coman 1882- *WomWWA 14*
Tait, Peter Guthrie 1831-1901 *DcScB*
Tait, Robert Lawson 1854-1899 *BiHiMed*
Taite, Augustus *NewYHSD*
Taitt, Francis Marion 1862-1943 *WhAm 2*
Takach, Basil d1948 *WhAm 2*
Takaezu, Toshiko 1922- *BnEnAmA*
Takahashi, Korekiyo 1854-1936 *McGEWB*
Takahira, Kogoro 1854- *WhAm 4*
Takamine, Eben Takashi 1889-1953
NatCAB 48
Takamine, Jokichi 1854-1922 *AsBiEn, DcAmB,*
NatCAB 40, WhAm 1
Talamantes, Melchor 1750?-1809 *ApCAB*
Talavera Y Garces, Mariano 1777-1861 *ApCAB*
Talbert, Henry Payne 1884- *WhoColR*
Talbert, Horace 1859- *WhoColR*
Talbert, Joseph Truitt 1866-1920 *WhAm 1*
Talbert, Mary Burnett 1865- *WhoColR*
Talbert, Samuel Stubbs 1917-1972 *WhAm 5*
Talbert, William Herbert Hilton 1866-
WhoColR
Talbert, William Jasper 1846-1931 *BiDrAC,*
WhAm 4
Talbot, Ada Brown 1873- *WomWWA 14*
Talbot, Adolphus Robert 1859-1944 *WhAm 2*
Talbot, Alfred William 1884-1949 *NatCAB 37*
Talbot, Anna Charlotte Hedges 1868-
NatCAB 30
Talbot, Arthur Newell 1857-1942 *DcAmB S3,*
NatCAB 33, WhAm 2
Talbot, Edith Armstrong 1872- *WhAm 5*
Talbot, Ellen Bliss 1867-1968 *NatCAB 54,*
WhAm 4A, WomWWA 14
Talbot, Emily Fairbanks 1834-1900 *DcAmB*
Talbot, Emma L *WomWWA 14*
Talbot, Ethelbert 1848-1928 *ApCAB, DcAmB,*
NatCAB 8, TwCBDA, WhAm 1
Talbot, Eugene Solomon 1847-1924 *NatCAB 13,*
WhAm 1
Talbot, Fannie Sprague 1873- *WomWWA 14*
Talbot, Francis Xavier 1889-1953 *DcAmB S5,*
WhAm 3
Talbot, Frank 1864-1921 *NatCAB 6,*
NatCAB 19
Talbot, George Buheit 1896-1952 *NatCAB 40*
Talbot, George Frederick 1859-1938
NatCAB 40, NatCAB 47, WhAm 3
Talbot, George Newell 1849-1928 *ApCAB X*
Talbot, Guy Webster 1873- *WhAm 5*
Talbot, Henry Paul 1864-1927 *DcAmB,*
WhAm 1
Talbot, Howard 1865-1928 *WhAm 1*
Talbot, Isham 1773-1837 *ApCAB, BiAUS,*
BiDrAC, NatCAB 4, NatCAB 14,
TwCBDA, WhAm H
Talbot, Israel Tisdale 1829-1899 *DcAmB,*
NatCAB 11, WhAm 1
Talbot, James Martin 1883-1956 *NatCAB 42*
Talbot, Jesse 1806-1879 *NewYHSD*
Talbot, Joel Francis 1850-1944 *NatCAB 33*
Talbot, John 1645-1727 *ApCAB, DcAmB,*
DcAmReB, NatCAB 3, WhAm H
Talbot, John Edward 1879-1952 *NatCAB 41*
Talbot, John Gunnel 1844-1870 *ApCAB*
Talbot, John William 1863-1937 *WhAm 1*
Talbot, Joseph Cruikshank 1816-1883 *ApCAB,*
NatCAB 3, TwCBDA

Talbot, Joseph Edward 1901-1966 *BiDrAC*
Talbot, Katharine Streeper 1868-
WomWWA 14
Talbot, M W 1889-1972 *WhAm 5*
Talbot, Marion 1858-1948 *BiDAmEd,*
NatCAB 36, NotAW, WhAm 2,
WomWWA 14
Talbot, Marshall *NewYHSD*
Talbot, Mary White 1869-1952 *WhAm 3,*
WomWWA 14
Talbot, Mathew 1767-1827 *BiAUS, Drake*
Talbot, Matthew 1767-1827 *NatCAB 1*
Talbot, Mignon 1869- *WomWWA 14*
Talbot, Richard James 1874-1941 *NatCAB 31*
Talbot, Samson 1828-1873 *NatCAB 1,*
TwCBDA
Talbot, Silas d1813 *BiAUS*
Talbot, Silas 1750-1813 *Drake*
Talbot, Silas 1751-1813 *AmBi, ApCAB,*
BiDrAC, DcAmB, NatCAB 3, TwCBDA,
WebAMB, WhAm H
Talbot, Thomas 1818-1886 *ApCAB,*
NatCAB 1, TwCBDA
Talbot, Thomas H *BiAUS*
Talbot, Walter LeMar 1870-1943 *WhAm 2*
Talbot, William Hayden 1858-1930 *NatCAB 29*
Talbot, William Henry Fox 1800-1877 *AsBiEn,*
DcScB
Talbot, Winifred Luella Winter 1894-1970
WhAm 5
Talbot, Winthrop Tisdale 1866-1938
NatCAB 30
Talbott, Albert Gallatin 1808-1887 *BiAUS,*
BiDrAC, WhAm H
Talbott, E Guy 1883-1945 *WhAm 2*
Talbott, Harold E 1888-1957 *WhAm 3,*
WhAm 4
Talbott, Harry Elstner 1860-1921 *NatCAB 19*
Talbott, Henry James 1847-1921 *WhAm 1*
Talbott, Joshua Frederick Cockey 1843-1918
BiDrAC, WhAm 1, WhAmP
Talbott, Katharine Houk 1864-1935
NatCAB 27
Talbott, Kent Langhorne *WomWWA 14*
Talbott, Nelson S 1892-1952 *WhAm 3*
Talburt, Harold M 1895-1966 *WhAm 4*
Talcott, Allen Butler 1867-1908 *ApCAB X*
Talcott, Andrew 1797-1883 *ApCAB, DcAmB,*
NatCAB 13, WhAm H
Talcott, Burt Lacklen 1920- *BiDrAC*
Talcott, Charles Andrew 1857-1920 *BiDrAC,*
WhAm 1
Talcott, Edward N Kirk 1840-1901 *WhAm 1*
Talcott, Eliza 1836-1911 *DcAmB, NotAW*
Talcott, Fanny C Jones 1840- *WomWWA 14*
Talcott, George 1786-1862 *ApCAB*
Talcott, George Henry 1811-1854 *ApCAB*
Talcott, Harry R 1861- *NatCAB 7*
Talcott, Horace Gardner 1847-1917
NatCAB 17
Talcott, James 1835-1916 *ApCAB X,*
NatCAB 23
Talcott, James Frederick 1866-1944
NatCAB 32, WhAm 2
Talcott, John 1600?-1660 *ApCAB*
Talcott, John 1630?-1688 *ApCAB, Drake*
Talcott, John Butler 1824-1906 *ApCAB X,*
NatCAB 12
Talcott, Joseph 1669-1741 *ApCAB, DcAmB,*
NatCAB 10, TwCBDA, WhAm H
Talcott, Lucy 1899-1970 *NatCAB 54*
Talcott, Mancel 1817-1878 *ApCAB*
Talcott, Mary H 1820?-1888 *ApCAB*
Talcott, Samuel 1634-1691 *ApCAB*
Talcott, Sarah Whiting 1852- *WomWWA 14*
Talcott, Sebastian Visscher 1812- *ApCAB*
Talcott, Wait 1866-1943 *NatCAB 34*
Talcott, William *NewYHSD*
Talcott, William Ellsworth 1862-1947
NatCAB 35
Talcott, William Hubbard 1809-1868
NatCAB 9
Talen, W A *NewYHSD*
Talfourd, William Daniels 1823-1915
NatCAB 17
Taliaferro, Benjamin d1821 *BiAUS*
Taliaferro, Benjamin 1750-1821 *ApCAB,*
BiDrAC, WhAm H

Taliaferro, Benjamin 1751?-1821 *Drake*
Taliaferro, Harry Monroe 1882-1968 *WhAm 5*
Taliaferro, Henry Beckwith 1904-1958
WhAm 4
Taliaferro, Henry Burghardt 1890-1948
NatCAB 37
Taliaferro, James Govan 1798-1876 *NatCAB 1*
Taliaferro, James Piper 1847-1934 *ApCAB Sup,*
BiDrAC, NatCAB 10, TwCBDA,
WhAm 2, WhAmP
Taliaferro, John 1768-1852 *BiDrAC,*
WhAm H, WhAmP
Taliaferro, John 1768-1853 *ApCAB, BiAUS,*
TwCBDA
Taliaferro, Lawrence 1794-1871 *DcAmB,*
REnAW, WhAm H
Taliaferro, Nicholas Lloyd 1890-1961 *WhAm 4*
Taliaferro, Richard 1705-1779 *BnEnAmA*
Taliaferro, Sinclair 1853- *NatCAB 8*
Taliaferro, Thomas Hardy 1871-1941
NatCAB 37, WhAm 1
Taliaferro, Thomas Seddon 1864-1940
NatCAB 30
Taliaferro, Thomas Seddon, Jr. 1866-1940
WhAm 1
Taliaferro, William Booth 1822-1898 *ApCAB,*
BiDConf, DcAmB, NatCAB 5, TwCBDA,
WebAMB, WhAm H
Taliaferro, William Hay 1895-1973 *WhAm 6*
Tall, Lida Lee 1873-1942 *BiDAmEd, WhAm 2,*
WomWWA 14
Tall Bull 1815?-1869 *REnAW*
Tallant, Alice Weld 1875- *WomWWA 14*
Tallant, Hugh 1869-1952 *NatCAB 41,*
WhAm 3
Tallant, Jerome Landers 1894-1950 *NatCAB 46*
Tallant, Richard H 1853-1934 *IIBEAAW*
Tallchief, Maria 1925- *WebAB*
Talle, Henry Oscar 1892-1969 *BiDrAC,*
WhAm 5
Tallerday, Howard G d1946 *WhAm 2*
Talley, Bascom Destrehan, Jr. 1916-1971
WhAm 5
Talley, Dyer Findley 1865-1947 *WhAm 2*
Talley, James Columbus 1855-1921 *NatCAB 20*
Talley, James Ely 1864-1941 *NatCAB 38*
Talley, Lynn Porter 1881-1942 *NatCAB 32,*
WhAm 2
Talley, Thomas Washington *WhoColR*
Talleyrand, Charles Maurice De 1754-1838
McGEWB
Talleyrand-Perigord, Charles Maurice De
1754-1838 *WhAm H*
Talliafero, Richard d1755 *WhAm H*
Tallichet, Jules Henri 1877-1937 *WhAm 1*
Tallis, Thomas 1505?-1585 *McGEWB*
Tallmadge, Benjamin 1754-1835 *AmBi,*
ApCAB, BiAUS, BiDrAC, DcAmB,
Drake, NatCAB 1, TwCBDA, WhAm H,
WhAmP
Tallmadge, Frederick Augustus 1792-1869
ApCAB, BiAUS, BiDrAC, Drake,
NatCAB 3, WhAm H, WhAmP
Tallmadge, Grier 1826-1862 *ApCAB*
Tallmadge, Guy Kasten 1901-1966 *NatCAB 53,*
WhAm 4
Tallmadge, James, Jr. 1778-1853 *AmBi,*
ApCAB, BiDrAC, DcAmB, Drake,
NatCAB 3, WhAm H
Tallmadge, James, Jr. 1788-1853 *BiAUS*
Tallmadge, Mathias B *BiAUS*
Tallmadge, Nathaniel Pitcher 1795-1864
ApCAB, BiAUS, BiDrAC, Drake,
NatCAB 3, NatCAB 12, WhAm H,
WhAmP
Tallmadge, Thomas Eddy 1876-1940 *WhAm 1*
Tallmage, Nathaniel Pitcher 1795-1864
TwCBDA
Tallman, Boyd J 1858- *NatCAB 18*
Tallman, Clay 1874-1949 *NatCAB 38,*
WhAm 5
Tallman, Frank Gifford 1860-1938 *NatCAB 33*
Tallman, George Kemp 1874-1950 *NatCAB 39*
Tallman, Peleg 1764-1840 *ApCAB, BiDrAC,*
NatCAB 3, WhAm H
Tallman, Peleg 1764-1841 *BiAUS, Drake*
Tallman, Percy Lewis 1881-1960 *NatCAB 48*
Tallman, William Henry 1832-1902 *NatCAB 39*

Tallman, William Morrison 1808-1878
   NatCAB 39
Tally, Robert Emmet 1877-1936 *NatCAB 28,*
   WhAm 1
Tally, William F 1912-1964 *WhAm 4*
Talmadge, Constance 1900-1973 *WhAm 6*
Talmadge, Eugene 1884-1946 *DcAmB S4,*
   NatCAB 38, WhAm 2
Talmadge, Herman Eugene 1913- *BiDrAC,*
   EncAAH
Talmadge, Matthias Burnet 1774-1819 *ApCAB*
Talmadge, Norma 1897-1957 *NatCAB 48,*
   WhAm 3
Talmadge, Thomas DeWitt 1832-1902 *WhAm 1*
Talmage, Algernon M 1871-1939 *IlBEAAW*
Talmage, Charles Horace 1855-1925 *NatCAB 6*
Talmage, James Edward 1862-1933 *BiDAmEd,*
   DcAmB, NatCAB 16, WhAm 1
Talmage, John Frelinghuysen 1833-1881
   NatCAB 9
Talmage, John VanNest 1819-1892 *ApCAB,*
   DcAmB, WhAm H
Talmage, Samuel Kennedy 1798-1865 *ApCAB,*
   Drake, TwCBDA
Talmage, T DeWitt 1832-1902 *Drake*
Talmage, Thomas DeWitt 1832-1902 *AmBi,*
   ApCAB, DcAmB, DcAmReB, NatCAB 4,
   TwCBDA
Talman, Charles Fitzhugh 1874-1936 *WhAm 1*
Talman, E Lee 1905-1964 *WhAm 4*
Talon 1675?- *ApCAB*
Talon, Edouard 1759-1819 *ApCAB*
Talon, Jean 1626-1694 *McGEWB*
Talon, Jean-Baptiste 1625-1691 *ApCAB*
Talon, Pierre 1676-1700? *ApCAB, WhAm H*
Talton, Augustus 1854- *ApCAB*
Talvj 1797-1870 *DcAmB*
Tamarkin, Jacob David 1888-1945 *DcAmB S3,*
   WhAm 2
Tamaron, Pedro d1768 *DcAmB, WhAm H*
Tamburelli, Ercole 1899-1970 *NatCAB 55*
Tamerlane 1336-1405 *McGEWB*
Tamiris, Helen 1905-1966 *WhAm 4*
Tamiroff, Akim d1972 *WhAm 5*
Tamm, Igor 1895-1971 *WhAm 6*
Tamm, Igor Evgenievich 1895-1971 *DcScB*
Tamm, Igor Y 1895-1971 *WhAm 5*
Tamm, Igor Yevgenyevich 1895-1971 *AsBiEn*
Tammann, Gustav Heinrich Johann Apollon
   1861-1938 *DcScB*
Tammany *AmBi, ApCAB, DcAmB,*
   WhAm H
Tammen, Agnes Reid d1942 *WhAm 2*
Tammen, Harry Heye 1856-1924 *DcAmB S1,*
   NatCAB 20, WebAB, WhAm HA,
   WhAm 4
Tams, J Frederic 1847-1928 *ApCAB X*
Tanaka, Kotaro 1890-1974 *WhAm 6*
Tanaka, Raizo *WhWW-II*
Tanberg, Arthur Percival 1885-1963
   NatCAB 51
Tandowsky, Ralph Myron 1900-1968
   NatCAB 55
Taney, Mary Florence *WomWWA 14*
Taney, Roger Brooke 1777-1864 *AmBi,*
   ApCAB, BiAUS, BiDrUSE, DcAmB,
   Drake, EncAB, McGEWB, NatCAB 1,
   TwCBDA, WebAB, WhAm H
Tanfilev, Gavriil Ivanovich 1857-1928 *DcScB*
Tang, K Y 1900-1960 *WhAm 4*
T'ang, T'ai-Tsung 600-649 *McGEWB*
Tange, Kenzo 1913- *McGEWB*
Tangeman, Cornelius Hoagland 1877-1928
   NatCAB 32
Tangeman, Robert Stone 1910-1964
   NatCAB 51, WhAm 4
Tangeman, Walter W 1891-1966 *WhAm 4*
Tangley, Edwin Savory 1899-1973 *WhAm 6*
Tanguay, Ciprian 1819- *ApCAB*
Tanguay, Eva 1878-1947 *DcAmB S4, NotAW*
Tanguay, J Edgar 1876-1958 *NatCAB 46*
Tanguy, Yves 1900-1955 *BnEnAmA,*
   McGEWB, WhAm 3
Tani, Masayuki 1889-1962 *WhAm 4*
Tanizaki, Junichiro 1886-1965 *McGEWB,*
   WhAm 4
Tannahill, Mary Harvey *WomWWA 14*

Tannahill, Samuel O 1868-1935 *WhAm 1*
Tannatt, Thomas Redding 1833-1913
   NatCAB 17
Tanneberger, David 1728-1804 *DcAmB,*
   WhAm H
Tannehill, Adamson 1750-1820 *BiDrAC,*
   WhAm H
Tannehill, Adamson 1752-1817 *ApCAB*
Tannehill, Helen Train 1871- *WomWWA 14*
Tannehill, Wilkins 1787-1858 *ApCAB, Drake*
Tannen *NewYHSD*
Tannenbaum, Samuel Aaron 1874-1948
   NatCAB 36, WhAm 2
Tanner, A H 1833-1882 *BiAUS*
Tanner, Adolphus Hitchcock 1833-1882 *BiDrAC,*
   WhAm H
Tanner, Albert Hawes 1855-1932 *NatCAB 23*
Tanner, Allen Barnett 1898-1956 *NatCAB 44*
Tanner, Amy Eliza 1870- *WomWWA 14*
Tanner, Benjamin 1775-1848 *ApCAB, DcAmB,*
   NewYHSD, WhAm H
Tanner, Benjamin Tucker 1835-1923 *ApCAB,*
   DcAmB, DcAmReB, NatCAB 3,
   TwCBDA, WhAm 1, WhoColR
Tanner, Edward Allen 1837-1892 *NatCAB 28,*
   TwCBDA
Tanner, Edwin Platt 1874-1936 *WhAm 1*
Tanner, Eugene Simpson 1907-1970 *WhAm 5*
Tanner, Fred Wilbur 1888-1957 *WhAm 3*
Tanner, Frederick Chauncey 1878-1963
   WhAm 4
Tanner, George Clinton 1834- *WhAm 4*
Tanner, George Gordon 1854-1914 *NatCAB 23*
Tanner, Harold Brooks 1887-1968 *NatCAB 54,*
   WhAm 5
Tanner, Henry Ossawa 1859-1937 *AmBi,*
   ApCAB X, BnEnAmA, DcAmB S2,
   EncAB, McGEWB, NatCAB 3, WebAB,
   WhAm 1, WhoColR
Tanner, Henry S 1830?- *ApCAB*
Tanner, Henry Schenck 1786-1858 *ApCAB,*
   DcAmB, Drake, NewYHSD, WhAm H
Tanner, Jacob 1865- *WhAm 5*
Tanner, James 1844-1927 *ApCAB Sup,*
   DcAmB, NatCAB 1, WebAMB,
   WhAm 1
Tanner, Jesse *NewYHSD*
Tanner, Jessie Eagleson Oglevee *WomWWA 14*
Tanner, John 1780?-1846? *REnAW*
Tanner, John 1780?-1847 *ApCAB, Drake*
Tanner, John Henry 1861-1940 *NatCAB 29,*
   WhAm 1
Tanner, John Riley 1844-1901 *ApCAB Sup,*
   NatCAB 11, WhAm 1
Tanner, Kenneth Spencer 1890-1963 *WhAm 4*
Tanner, Kneland Clark 1898-1968 *NatCAB 54*
Tanner, Lillian Marsh 1863- *WomWWA 14*
Tanner, Rollin Harvelle 1874- *WhAm 5*
Tanner, Sheldon C 1900-1966 *WhAm 4*
Tanner, Willard Brooks 1858- *WhAm 4*
Tanner, William Vaughn 1881-1953 *WhAm 3*
Tanner, Zera Luther 1835-1906 *NatCAB 8,*
   WhAm 1
Tannery, Jules 1848-1910 *DcScB*
Tannery, Paul 1843-1904 *DcScB*
Tannrath, John Joseph 1864-1929 *WhAm 1*
Tanquary, Maurice Cole 1881-1944 *NatCAB 34*
Tansey, George Judd 1865- *NatCAB 12*
Tansey, Patrick Henry 1894-1976 *WhAm 6*
Tansil, John Bell 1881-1952 *WhAm 3*
Tansill, Charles Callan 1890-1964 *NatCAB 53,*
   WhAm 4
Tansley, John Oscroft 1844- *NatCAB 3*
Tanssen, T *NewYHSD*
Tantia Topi 1819-1859 *WhoMilH*
Tanturier *NewYHSD*
Tanzer, Laurence Arnold 1874-1963 *WhAm 4*
T'ao, Ch'ien 365-427 *McGEWB*
Tao-An 312-385 *McGEWB*
Tao-Hsuan 596-667 *McGEWB*
Tapia, Andres De 1480?-1540? *ApCAB Sup*
Tapin, Richard 1515?-1590 *ApCAB*
Tapke, Robert Joseph 1906-1962 *NatCAB 50*
Tapley, Jesse Fellowes 1824- *NatCAB 13*
Tapley, Walter Moore, Jr. 1898-1971 *WhAm 5*
Taplin, Frank Elijah 1875-1938 *NatCAB 28,*
   WhAm 1

Taplin, Mortimer Mason 1868-1913
   NatCAB 16
Taplinger, Richard Jacques 1911-1973 *WhAm 5*
Tapp, Ernest Marvin 1904-1971 *WhAm 6*
Tapp, Jesse W 1900-1967 *WhAm 4*
Tapp, Sidney C 1870- *WhAm 5*
Tappan, Arthur 1786-1865 *AmBi, ApCAB,*
   DcAmB, DcAmReB, Drake, McGEWB,
   NatCAB 2, TwCBDA, WebAB,
   WhAm H
Tappan, Benjamin 1773-1857 *ApCAB, BiAUS,*
   BiDrAC, DcAmB, Drake, NatCAB 5,
   TwCBDA, WhAm H
Tappan, Benjamin 1788-1863 *ApCAB*
Tappan, Benjamin 1856-1919 *ApCAB Sup,*
   NatCAB 18, WhAm 1
Tappan, Caroline Sturgis *NotAW*
Tappan, David 1752-1803 *ApCAB, Drake,*
   TwCBDA
Tappan, David Stanton 1845-1922 *NatCAB 21,*
   TwCBDA, WhAm 1
Tappan, Ebenezer 1815-1854 *NewYHSD*
Tappan, Eli Todd 1824-1888 *ApCAB Sup,*
   BiDAmEd, DcAmB, NatCAB 7,
   TwCBDA, WhAm H
Tappan, Eva March 1854-1930 *BiDAmEd,*
   DcAmB, NatCAB 22, NotAW, TwCBDA,
   WhAm 1, WomWWA 14
Tappan, Frank Girard 1882-1962 *WhAm 4*
Tappan, George Hooper 1833-1865 *NewYHSD*
Tappan, Henry Philip 1805-1881 *ApCAB,*
   BiDAmEd, DcAmB, NatCAB 1,
   TwCBDA, WhAm H
Tappan, Henry Philip 1806?-1881 *Drake*
Tappan, James Camp 1825-1906 *BiDConf*
Tappan, James Camp 1826-1906 *TwCBDA*
Tappan, John 1781-1871 *ApCAB, NatCAB 2*
Tappan, Lewis 1788-1873 *AmBi, ApCAB,*
   DcAmB, DcAmReB, McGEWB,
   NatCAB 2, TwCBDA, WebAB,
   WhAm H
Tappan, Lucy 1857- *WomWWA 14*
Tappan, Mason Weare 1817-1886 *ApCAB,*
   BiAUS, BiDrAC, WhAm H
Tappan, Paul Wilbur 1911-1964 *NatCAB 51,*
   WhAm 4
Tappan, Russell Golding 1896-1956 *NatCAB 45*
Tappan, William Bingham 1794-1849 *ApCAB,*
   Drake, NatCAB 5, WhAm H
Tappan, William Henry 1821-1907 *IlBEAAW,*
   NewYHSD
Tappen, Frederick Dobbs 1829-1902 *DcAmB,*
   NatCAB 12, WhAm 1
Tapper, Bertha Feiring 1859-1915 *DcAmB,*
   WhAm 1, WomWWA 14
Tapper, Thomas 1864-1958 *BiDAmEd,*
   TwCBDA, WhAm 3
Tappert, Theodore Gerhardt 1904-1973
   WhAm 6
Tappin, John Lindsley 1906-1964 *WhAm 4*
Tapscott, Ralph Henry 1885-1967 *WhAm 4*
Taqi Khan Amir-E Kabir, Mirza 1806?-1852
   McGEWB
Taquino, George James 1884-1953 *NatCAB 44,*
   WhAm 3
Taracouzio, Timothy Andrew 1897-1958
   WhAm 3
Taran, Leo Maurice 1902-1959 *NatCAB 45*
Tarasi, Rocco Francis 1903-1954 *NatCAB 42*
Taraval, Sigismond 1700- *ApCAB*
Tarbell, Arthur Wilson 1872-1946 *WhAm 2*
Tarbell, David Perry 1912-1957 *NatCAB 46*
Tarbell, Edmund Charles 1862-1938 *AmBi,*
   BnEnAmA, DcAmB S2, NatCAB 13,
   WhAm 1
Tarbell, Edmund N 1831?- *NewYHSD*
Tarbell, Frank Bigelow 1853-1920 *DcAmB,*
   WhAm 1
Tarbell, Gage E 1856-1936 *WhAm 1*
Tarbell, Horace Sumner 1838-1904 *NatCAB 28,*
   WhAm 1
Tarbell, Ida Minerva 1857-1944 *ApCAB X,*
   DcAmB S3, EncAB, McGEWB,
   NatCAB 14, NotAW, WebAB, WhAm 2,
   WomWWA 14
Tarbell, John Adams 1810-1864 *ApCAB*
Tarbell, John Adams 1811-1864 *Drake*
Tarbell, Joseph 1780?-1815 *ApCAB, DcAmB,*

Taylor, Alfred Simpson 1868-1942 *NatCAB 34,*
  WhAm 2
Taylor, Alice Maud 1879- *WomWWA 14*
Taylor, Alrutheus Ambush 1893-1954 *WhAm 3*
Taylor, Alva Edwards 1859-1941 *WhAm 1*
Taylor, Amos Elias 1893-1972 *WhAm 5*
Taylor, Amos Leavitt 1877-1965 *WhAm 4*
Taylor, Anna Heyward 1879-1956 *NatCAB 42*
Taylor, Anna May *WomWWA 14*
Taylor, Anna Rowena Goldsmith d1921 *BiCAW*
Taylor, Anne M Puffer 1888- *WomWWA 14*
Taylor, Annie Childs 1875- *WomWWA 14*
Taylor, Anson W H 1897-1948 *NatCAB 36*
Taylor, Anthony 1837-1894 *NatCAB 16*
Taylor, Archer 1890-1973 *WhAm 6*
Taylor, Archibald Alexander Edward 1834-1903
  ApCAB, DcAmB
Taylor, Archibald Boggs 1892-1962 *NatCAB 49*
Taylor, Archibald Wellington 1877-1953
  NatCAB 42, WhAm 3
Taylor, Arthur Herbert 1852-1922 *BiDrAC*
Taylor, Arthur Nelson 1867-1949 *NatCAB 38,*
  WhAm 4
Taylor, Asher *BiAUS*
Taylor, Asher Clayton 1842-1922 *WhAm 1*
Taylor, Aubrey E 1899-1947 *WhAm 2*
Taylor, Baker *NewYHSD*
Taylor, Barnard Cook 1850-1937 *WhAm 1*
Taylor, Barton S 1820- *NatCAB 5*
Taylor, Bayard 1825-1878 *AmBi, ApCAB,*
  DcAmB, Drake, IlBEAAW, NatCAB 3,
  NewYHSD, REnAW, TwCBDA, WebAB,
  WhAm H
Taylor, Benjamin Cook 1801-1881 *ApCAB,*
  Drake
Taylor, Benjamin Franklin 1819-1887 *ApCAB,*
  DcAmB, NatCAB 11, TwCBDA,
  WhAm H
Taylor, Benjamin Franklin 1822-1887 *Drake*
Taylor, Benjamin Irving 1877-1946 *BiDrAC,*
  WhAm 2
Taylor, Bert Leston 1866-1921 *DcAmB,*
  NatCAB 24, WebAB, WhAm 1
Taylor, Blair Dabney 1848-1930 *NatCAB 22*
Taylor, Brook 1685-1731 *DcScB, McGEWB*
Taylor, Burton Leo 1926-1974 *WhAm 6*
Taylor, Bushrod Bust 1832-1883 *ApCAB*
Taylor, C Bryson 1880- *WomWWA 14*
Taylor, Caleb Newbold 1813-1887 *BiDrAC,*
  WhAm H
Taylor, Caleb Newbold 1819-1887 *BiAUS*
Taylor, Carl 1871-1942 *NatCAB 32*
Taylor, Carson Lee 1889-1965 *WhAm 4*
Taylor, Charles 1819- *ApCAB*
Taylor, Charles Alonzo 1864-1942 *DcAmB S3*
Taylor, Charles Elisha 1842- *TwCBDA*
Taylor, Charles Elisha 1842-1915 *NatCAB 24*
Taylor, Charles Elisha 1842-1916 *WhAm 1*
Taylor, Charles Fayette 1827-1899 *AmBi,*
  ApCAB, DcAmB, NatCAB 9, WhAm H,
  WhAm 1
Taylor, Charles Fremont 1856-1919 *WhAm 1*
Taylor, Charles Gillies, Jr. 1883-1953 *WhAm 3*
Taylor, Charles Henry 1846-1921 *DcAmB,*
  NatCAB 2, NatCAB 35, WhAm 1
Taylor, Charles Henry 1863-1950 *NatCAB 39*
Taylor, Charles Henry 1867-1941 *WhAm 1*
Taylor, Charles Henry James 1857-1898
  NatCAB 5
Taylor, Charles Jay 1855-1929 *WhAm 1*
Taylor, Charles Keen 1879- *WhAm 6*
Taylor, Charles Lewis 1857-1922 *WhAm 1*
Taylor, Charles Lincoln 1875-1944 *NatCAB 54*
Taylor, Charles N 1869-1927 *NatCAB 21*
Taylor, Charles N 1869-1930 *ApCAB X*
Taylor, Charles Ralph 1877- *WhAm 5*
Taylor, Charles Ryall *NewYHSD*
Taylor, Charles Vincent 1885-1946 *DcScB*
Taylor, Charles Vincent 1895-1946 *WhAm 2*
Taylor, Charles William 1874-1943 *WhAm 2*
Taylor, Charlotte DeBernier Scarbrough
  1806-1861 *DcAmB, NatCAB 2, WhAm H*
Taylor, Chester Higbee 1887-1955 *NatCAB 42*
Taylor, Chester William 1883-1931 *BiDrAC,*
  WhAmP
Taylor, Christopher 1620?-1686 *ApCAB,*
  Drake
Taylor, Clara Sears 1878- *WomWWA 14*

Taylor, Claude Ambrose 1902-1966 *WhAm 4*
Taylor, Creed 1766-1836 *DcAmB, WhAm H*
Taylor, Daniel Albert 1895-1973 *WhAm 6*
Taylor, Daniel Richardson 1838- *ApCAB X*
Taylor, David Watson 1864-1940 *DcAmB S2,*
  NatCAB 15, NatCAB 30, WebAB,
  WebAMB, WhAm 1
Taylor, Dean Park 1902- *BiDrAC*
Taylor, Deems 1885-1966 *ApCAB X, WebAB,*
  WhAm 4
Taylor, Donald Stephen 1898-1970 *WhAm 5*
Taylor, Donald Wayne 1919-1975 *WhAm 6*
Taylor, E Alexis 1867- *WhAm 4*
Taylor, E Leland *WhAm 2*
Taylor, Earl Burt 1889-1946 *NatCAB 35,*
  WhAm 2
Taylor, Edmund Bernard 1877- *WhoColR*
Taylor, Edward 1642?-1729 *ApCAB,*
  McGEWB
Taylor, Edward 1645?-1729 *AmBi, DcAmB S1,*
  WebAB, WhAm H
Taylor, Edward Ballinger 1850-1922 *WhAm 1*
Taylor, Edward Livingston 1839-1910 *WhAm 1*
Taylor, Edward Livingston, Jr. 1869-1938
  BiDrAC
Taylor, Edward R 1908-1972 *WhAm 5*
Taylor, Edward Randolph 1844-1917 *WhAm 1*
Taylor, Edward Robeson 1838-1923 *TwCBDA,*
  WhAm 1
Taylor, Edward Thomas 1858-1941 *BiDrAC,*
  WhAm 1, WhAmP
Taylor, Edward Thompson 1793-1871 *AmBi,*
  ApCAB, DcAmB, NatCAB 13, WebAB,
  WhAm H
Taylor, Edward Thompson 1794-1871 *Drake*
Taylor, Edward Wyllys 1866-1932 *NatCAB 25*
Taylor, Edwin 1844-1926 *WhAm 3*
Taylor, Edwin Cassius 1874-1935 *NatCAB 28*
Taylor, Edwy Lycurgus 1879-1943 *NatCAB 33,*
  WhAm 2
Taylor, Edyth Elizabeth 1872- *WomWWA 14*
Taylor, Elbert Ozial 1843-1920 *NatCAB 20*
Taylor, Elfleda Whiting *WomWWA 14*
Taylor, Elisha Ephraim Leech 1815-1874
  ApCAB
Taylor, Eliza Ann *NewYHSD*
Taylor, Elizabeth 1826- *ApCAB*
Taylor, Elizabeth 1932- *WebAB*
Taylor, Elizabeth Roseman *WomWWA 14*
Taylor, Emerson Gifford 1874- *WhAm 5*
Taylor, Emily Drayton 1860- *WhAm 5,*
  WomWWA 14
Taylor, Emma Louisa Miller 1877-
  WomWWA 14
Taylor, Esther W 1826- *AmWom*
Taylor, Eugene Hartwell 1853-1924
  NatCAB 20, WhAm 4
Taylor, Ezra Booth 1823-1912 *BiDrAC,*
  TwCBDA, WhAm 1, WhAmP
Taylor, F Carroll 1884-1949 *WhAm 3*
Taylor, F W Howard 1891-1943 *WhAm 2*
Taylor, Fielding Lewis 1868-1942 *NatCAB 31*
Taylor, Fitch Waterman 1803-1865 *ApCAB,*
  Drake
Taylor, Fletcher Brandon 1892-1964
  NatCAB 52
Taylor, Florence Terwilliger 1885-
  WomWWA 14
Taylor, Floyd 1902-1951 *NatCAB 40,*
  WhAm 3
Taylor, Frances Brown 1861- *WomWWA 14*
Taylor, Frances Long *WomWWA 14*
Taylor, Francis Henry 1903-1957 *NatCAB 49,*
  WhAm 3
Taylor, Francis Matthew Sill 1851-1915
  WhAm 1
Taylor, Francis Winthrop 1878-1927
  NatCAB 22
Taylor, Frank 1842-1920 *WhAm 1*
Taylor, Frank 1844-1920 *NatCAB 19*
Taylor, Frank 1844-1922 *NatCAB 18*
Taylor, Frank Bursley 1860-1938 *DcAmB S2,*
  DcScB, WhAm 4
Taylor, Frank Eugene 1846-1913 *NatCAB 16*
Taylor, Frank Flagg 1875-1959 *WhAm 3*
Taylor, Frank Hendrickson 1855-1934
  NatCAB 26
Taylor, Frank J 1884-1958 *NatCAB 46*

Taylor, Frank J 1894-1972 *WhAm 5*
Taylor, Frank L 1900-1962 *WhAm 4*
Taylor, Frank Mansfield 1850-1930 *ApCAB X,*
  WhAm 1
Taylor, Frank Walter 1874-1921 *DcAmB,*
  WhAm 1
Taylor, Fred Manville 1855-1932 *DcAmB,*
  NatCAB 25, WhAm 1
Taylor, Frederic William 1860-1944 *WhAm 2*
Taylor, Frederick Clark 1866-1928 *NatCAB 30*
Taylor, Frederick Eugene 1867-1932 *WhAm 1*
Taylor, Frederick R 1887-1955 *WhAm 3*
Taylor, Frederick William 1853-1903
  NatCAB 13, TwCBDA, WhAm 1
Taylor, Frederick Winslow 1856-1915 *AmBi,*
  AsBiEn, DcAmB, DcScB, EncAB,
  NatCAB 14, NatCAB 23, WebAB,
  WhAm 1
Taylor, Geoffrey Ingram 1886-1975 *WhAm 6*
Taylor, George 1716-1781 *AmBi, ApCAB,*
  BiAUS, BiDrAC, DcAmB, Drake,
  NatCAB 5, TwCBDA, WhAm H,
  WhAmP
Taylor, George 1820-1894 *BiAUS, BiDrAC,*
  Drake, WhAm H
Taylor, George, Jr. 1879-1964 *WhAm 4*
Taylor, George Boardman 1832-1907 *ApCAB,*
  DcAmB, NatCAB 11, WhAm 1
Taylor, George Braxton 1860-1942 *WhAm 2*
Taylor, George Chadbourne 1868-1923
  ApCAB X, NatCAB 19
Taylor, George Chadbourne 1904-1962
  WhAm 4
Taylor, George Danforth 1888-1959
  NatCAB 48
Taylor, George H 1821-1896 *ApCAB,*
  NatCAB 5
Taylor, George Herbert 1853-1914 *NatCAB 6*
Taylor, George Hooper 1847-1922 *NatCAB 23*
Taylor, George K *BiAUS*
Taylor, George Lansing 1835- *ApCAB*
Taylor, George Mosser 1897-1959 *NatCAB 49,*
  WhAm 4
Taylor, George Ross 1898-1949 *NatCAB 37*
Taylor, George Sylvester 1822- *NatCAB 3*
Taylor, George Washington 1840-1925
  NatCAB 21
Taylor, George Washington 1849-1932 *BiDrAC,*
  TwCBDA, WhAm 4, WhAmP
Taylor, George William 1808-1862 *ApCAB,*
  Drake
Taylor, George William 1901- *WhAm 5*
Taylor, George Wood 1868-1921 *NatCAB 19*
Taylor, Glen Hearst 1904- *BiDrAC*
Taylor, Gordon Barclay 1905-1955 *NatCAB 48*
Taylor, Graham 1851-1938 *DcAmB S2,*
  NatCAB 29, WhAm 1
Taylor, Graham Romeyn 1880-1942
  NatCAB 31, WhAm 2
Taylor, Gus Floyd 1861-1952 *NatCAB 40*
Taylor, H M *NewYHSD*
Taylor, H Marshall 1881-1955 *NatCAB 43*
Taylor, Hannah E 1835- *AmWom*
Taylor, Hannis 1851-1922 *ApCAB Sup,*
  DcAmB, NatCAB 8, TwCBDA,
  WhAm 1
Taylor, Harden Franklin 1890-1966 *WhAm 4*
Taylor, Harold Alexander 1914- *BiDAmEd*
Taylor, Harold Claire 1905-1970 *NatCAB 55*
Taylor, Harris 1864-1952 *NatCAB 40,*
  WhAm 3
Taylor, Harry 1862-1930 *DcAmB, NatCAB 23,*
  WhAm 1
Taylor, Harry G 1880-1938 *WhAm 1*
Taylor, Harry Gordon 1891-1970 *WhAm 5*
Taylor, Harry Henry 1867-1952 *NatCAB 42*
Taylor, Harry Leonard 1866-1955 *NatCAB 47,*
  WhAm 3
Taylor, Harvey Birchard 1882-1959 *WhAm 3*
Taylor, Helen A *WomWWA 14*
Taylor, Henry, Jr. 1854-1945 *NatCAB 34*
Taylor, Henry A Coit 1841-1921 *ApCAB X,*
  WhAm 1
Taylor, Henry Carl 1873-1969 *EncAAH*
Taylor, Henry Charles 1873- *WhAm 6*
Taylor, Henry Clay 1845-1904 *ApCAB Sup*
Taylor, Henry Clay 1844-1917 *NatCAB 17*
Taylor, Henry Clay 1845-1904 *NatCAB 9,*

WhAm 1

Taylor, Henry Fitch 1853-1925 *WhAm 1*

Taylor, Henry Genet 1837-1916 *NatCAB 5, WhAm 1*

Taylor, Henry Kirby 1858-1934 *WhAm 1*

Taylor, Henry Lewis 1855- *WhAm 4*

Taylor, Henry Ling 1857-1923 *NatCAB 24, WhAm 1*

Taylor, Henry Longstreet 1857-1932 *WhAm 1*

Taylor, Henry Noble 1865-1932 *NatCAB 43*

Taylor, Henry Osborn 1856-1941 *DcAmB S3, NatCAB 35, WhAm 1*

Taylor, Henry Richmond 1869-1925 *ApCAB X*

Taylor, Herbert Addison 1876-1948 *WhAm 2*

Taylor, Herbert Worthington 1869-1931 *BiDrAC, WhAm 1*

Taylor, Hillsman 1884-1965 *WhAm 4*

Taylor, Hollinshead Nathan 1879-1931 *NatCAB 27*

Taylor, Holman 1874-1947 *NatCAB 37*

Taylor, Horace Adolphus 1837- *ApCAB Sup, WhAm 4*

Taylor, Howard 1865-1920 *WhAm 1*

Taylor, Howard Canning 1868-1949 *NatCAB 37, WhAm 2*

Taylor, Howard Emerson 1869-1934 *WhAm 1*

Taylor, Howard Floyd 1913-1962 *WhAm 4*

Taylor, Howard Rice 1892-1954 *WhAm 3*

Taylor, Hugh Stott 1890-1974 *WhAm 6*

Taylor, Irving Kurtz 1865-1939 *NatCAB 34*

Taylor, Isaac Ebenezer 1812-1889 *AmBi, ApCAB, NatCAB 9*

Taylor, Isaac Hamilton 1840-1936 *BiDrAC*

Taylor, Isaac Montrose 1857-1921 *WhAm 1*

Taylor, Isaac Stockton 1850-1917 *WhAm 1*

Taylor, Isaac Stockton 1851-1917 *NatCAB 12*

Taylor, J Edwin 1905-1964 *NatCAB 52*

Taylor, J Gurney 1872-1956 *NatCAB 48, WhAm 3*

Taylor, J Will 1880-1939 *NatCAB 42, WhAm 1*

Taylor, J Will *see also* Taylor, James Willis

Taylor, Jacob d1736? *ApCAB, Drake*

Taylor, Jacob d1745? *NatCAB 10*

Taylor, Jacob B 1898-1962 *WhAm 4*

Taylor, James *NewYHSD*

Taylor, James 1769-1848 *ApCAB, Drake*

Taylor, James 1869-1925 *ApCAB X*

Taylor, James Alfred 1878-1956 *BiDrAC, WhAm 3*

Taylor, James Anderson 1876- *WhAm 1*

Taylor, James Barnett 1804-1871 *ApCAB, DcAmB, WhAm H*

Taylor, James Bayard 1825-1878 *AmBi, DcAmB, WebAB*

Taylor, James Blackstone 1871-1956 *NatCAB 48*

Taylor, James Blackstone, Jr. 1897-1942 *NatCAB 48*

Taylor, James Brainerd 1801-1829 *ApCAB*

Taylor, James Earl 1839-1901 *IIBEAAW, NewYHSD, WhAm H*

Taylor, James H 1893-1972 *WhAm 5*

Taylor, James Henry 1871-1957 *NatCAB 43, WhAm 3*

Taylor, James Henry 1908-1968 *WhAm 5*

Taylor, James Knox 1857- *ApCAB Sup, WhAm 4*

Taylor, James L 1831?- *NewYHSD*

Taylor, James Lockerman 1847- *NatCAB 13*

Taylor, James Loockerman 1847- *ApCAB Sup, WhAm 4*

Taylor, James Milburn 1873- *WhAm 5*

Taylor, James Monroe 1848-1916 *ApCAB, DcAmB, NatCAB 5, TwCBDA, WhAm 1*

Taylor, James Morford 1843-1930 *WhAm 1*

Taylor, James Sherwood 1904-1975 *WhAm 6*

Taylor, James W 1833-1905 *WhAm 1*

Taylor, James Wickes 1819-1893 *ApCAB, DcAmB, TwCBDA, WhAm H*

Taylor, James Willis 1880-1939 *BiDrAC, WhAmP*

Taylor, James Willis *see also* Taylor, J Will

Taylor, Jane Fayrer 1869- *WomWWA 14*

Taylor, Jaquelin Plummer 1861-1950 *NatCAB 39*

Taylor, Jesse 1864-1916 *NatCAB 17*

Taylor, Jesse Reade 1880- *WhAm 6*

Taylor, John *BiDrAC, WhAm H*

Taylor, John d1824 *BiAUS, Drake*

Taylor, John 1745?-1806 *NewYHSD*

Taylor, John 1750-1824 *ApCAB, NatCAB 9, TwCBDA*

Taylor, John 1752-1833 *ApCAB, NatCAB 9*

Taylor, John 1752-1835 *DcAmB, Drake, WhAm H*

Taylor, John 1753-1824 *AmBi, DcAmB, EncAAH, EncAB, McGEWB, WebAB, WhAm H*

Taylor, John 1754-1824 *BiDrAC*

Taylor, John 1770-1832 *ApCAB, BiAUS, BiDrAC, Drake, NatCAB 12, TwCBDA, WhAm H, WhAmP*

Taylor, John 1808-1887 *AmBi, ApCAB, DcAmB, NatCAB 7, NatCAB 16, REnAW, WhAm H*

Taylor, John 1840- *NatCAB 2*

Taylor, John 1857-1914 *NatCAB 18*

Taylor, John Bellamy 1875-1963 *WhAm 4*

Taylor, John Blyth 1904-1968 *WhAm 5*

Taylor, John Chestnut 1893-1961 *NatCAB 48*

Taylor, John Clarence 1890- *BiDrAC*

Taylor, John Glanville 1823-1851 *ApCAB*

Taylor, John James 1808-1892 *BiAUS, BiDrAC, WhAm H*

Taylor, John Kepler 1892-1952 *NatCAB 48*

Taylor, John Lampkin 1805-1870 *BiAUS, BiDrAC, TwCBDA, WhAm H, WhAmP*

Taylor, John Lord 1811-1884 *NatCAB 26*

Taylor, John Louis 1769-1829 *AmBi, ApCAB, BiAUS, DcAmB, Drake, NatCAB 9, TwCBDA*

Taylor, John Madison 1855-1931 *NatCAB 18, WhAm 1*

Taylor, John May 1838-1911 *BiDrAC, NatCAB 3*

Taylor, John McLean 1828-1875 *ApCAB*

Taylor, John McNay 1905-1973 *WhAm 6*

Taylor, John Metcalf 1845-1918 *ApCAB X, WhAm 1*

Taylor, John Neilson 1805-1878 *ApCAB, Drake*

Taylor, John Orville 1807-1890 *ApCAB, BiDAmEd*

Taylor, John Phelps 1841-1915 *WhAm 1*

Taylor, John Robert 1876-1925 *ApCAB X*

Taylor, John Rodgers Meigs 1865-1949 *NatCAB 40*

Taylor, John Talford 1888-1958 *NatCAB 49*

Taylor, John Thomas 1885-1965 *WhAm 4*

Taylor, John W 1784-1854 *AmBi, ApCAB, BiAUS, BiDrAC, DcAmB, Drake, NatCAB 11, TwCBDA, WebAB, WhAm H, WhAmP*

Taylor, John Yeatman 1829-1911 *WhAm 1*

Taylor, Jonathan 1796-1848 *BiAUS, BiDrAC, WhAm H*

Taylor, Jonathan Kirkbride 1838-1916 *NatCAB 17*

Taylor, Joseph Danner 1830-1899 *BiDrAC, NatCAB 30, TwCBDA, WhAmP*

Taylor, Joseph Deems *WebAB*

Taylor, Joseph Fillmore 1889-1956 *WhAm 3*

Taylor, Joseph Hancock 1836-1885 *ApCAB*

Taylor, Joseph Jackson 1869-1943 *WhAm 2*

Taylor, Joseph Judson 1855- *WhAm 1*

Taylor, Joseph Pannel 1796-1864 *ApCAB*

Taylor, Joseph Penuel 1796-1864 *Drake*

Taylor, Joseph Richard 1858-1955 *WhAm 3*

Taylor, Joseph Robert 1873- *WhAm 5*

Taylor, Joseph Russell 1868-1933 *WhAm 1*

Taylor, Joseph Schimmel 1856-1932 *BiDAmEd, WhAm 1*

Taylor, Joseph Ward 1854-1932 *NatCAB 31*

Taylor, Joseph Wright 1810-1880 *DcAmB, WhAm H*

Taylor, Jude *NewYHSD*

Taylor, Julian Daniel 1846-1932 *WhAm 1*

Taylor, Junius LaFayette 1871- *WhoColR*

Taylor, Katharine Haviland d1941 *WhAm 1*

Taylor, Kenneth Ford 1903-1970 *NatCAB 57*

Taylor, Knox 1873-1922 *NatCAB 19*

Taylor, Lachlan 1815-1881 *ApCAB*

Taylor, Laurette 1884-1946 *DcAmB S4, NotAW*

Taylor, Laurette 1887-1946 *WhAm 2*

Taylor, Lawrence Augustus 1887-1928 *NatCAB 22*

Taylor, Lea Demarest 1883-1975 *WhAm 6*

Taylor, Lee Jackson 1886-1952 *NatCAB 41*

Taylor, Leland Russell 1912-1967 *WhAm 4A*

Taylor, Lester 1884-1950 *NatCAB 40*

Taylor, Lewis Harvie 1875-1940 *WhAm 1*

Taylor, Lillian E *WhAm 5*

Taylor, Lily Ross 1886-1969 *WhAm 5*

Taylor, Lloyd 1865-1944 *NatCAB 33*

Taylor, Lloyd E 1888-1957 *NatCAB 46*

Taylor, Lloyd William 1893-1948 *NatCAB 44, WhAm 2*

Taylor, Lodusky Jusrusha 1856-1923 *NatCAB 21, WhAm 4*

Taylor, Louis Sherman 1872-1965 *WhAm 4*

Taylor, Louise Clinton *WomWWA 14*

Taylor, Lucy Beaman Hobbs 1833-1910 *NotAW*

Taylor, Lydia Foulke 1884- *WomWWA 14*

Taylor, Mamie Love St. John *WomWWA 14*

Taylor, Margaret Mackall Smith d1852 *NatCAB 4*

Taylor, Margaret Mackall Smith 1788-1852 *NotAW*

Taylor, Margaret Mackall Smith 1790?-1852 *AmWom, ApCAB, TwCBDA*

Taylor, Marian J Winthrop 1838- *WomWWA 14*

Taylor, Marian Young 1908-1973 *NatCAB 57, WhAm 6*

Taylor, Marie Hansen 1829- *ApCAB, WhAm 4, WomWWA 14*

Taylor, Marion Sayle 1889-1942 *WhAm 1*

Taylor, Maris 1847- *WhAm 4*

Taylor, Marshall William 1846-1887 *ApCAB, DcAmB, WhAm H*

Taylor, Martha Smith 1829- *AmWom*

Taylor, Mary Cecilia 1827-1866 *ApCAB*

Taylor, Mary Elise Calhoon 1876- *WomWWA 14*

Taylor, Mary Frances Wigfall 1852- *WomWWA 14*

Taylor, Mary Imlay 1878-1938 *WhAm 1, WomWWA 14*

Taylor, Mary Isabella Morrison 1864- *WomWWA 14*

Taylor, Maurice 1895-1955 *WhAm 3*

Taylor, Maurice Craig 1894-1959 *NatCAB 49*

Taylor, Maxwell Davenport 1901- *WebAMB*

Taylor, Merris 1851- *WhAm 4*

Taylor, Mervyn Ross 1877-1953 *NatCAB 39*

Taylor, Miles 1805-1873 *BiAUS, BiDrAC, WhAm H*

Taylor, Mills James 1879-1974 *WhAm 6*

Taylor, Montgomery Meigs 1869-1952 *NatCAB 40, WhAm 3*

Taylor, Moses 1806-1882 *ApCAB, DcAmB, NatCAB 7, WhAm H*

Taylor, Moses 1871-1928 *ApCAB X, NatCAB 22, WhAm 1*

Taylor, Myron Charles 1874-1958 *NatCAB 44*

Taylor, Myron Charles 1874-1959 *WhAm 3*

Taylor, N H *NewYHSD*

Taylor, Nathan Alfred 1846-1915 *NatCAB 29*

Taylor, Nathaniel Green 1819-1887 *BiAUS, BiDrAC, WhAm H, WhAmP*

Taylor, Nathaniel Hapgood 1854-1926 *NatCAB 21*

Taylor, Nathaniel William 1786-1858 *ApCAB, DcAmB, DcAmReB, Drake, NatCAB 7, WhAm H*

Taylor, Nellie Grace *ApCAB X*

Taylor, Nelson 1821-1894 *ApCAB, BiAUS, BiDrAC, WhAm H*

Taylor, Nelson 1854-1912 *WhAm 1*

Taylor, Neumon 1876-1954 *NatCAB 44*

Taylor, Norman 1883-1967 *WhAm 5*

Taylor, Oliver Alden 1801-1851 *ApCAB, Drake*

Taylor, Oliver Guy 1883-1950 *WhAm 3*

Taylor, Oliver Swaine 1784-1885 *ApCAB*

Taylor, Ora Autumn 1878-1961 *WhAm 4*

Taylor, Orville d1969 *WhAm 5*

Taylor, Oury Wilburn 1885-1958 *WhAm 3*

Taylor, Paul Bennett 1905-1966 *WhAm 4*

Taylor, Peter *NewYHSD*

Taylor, Q C 1893-1965 *NatCAB 51*

Taylor, Ralph Wesley 1887-1973 *WhAm 6*

Taylor, Ransom Clarke 1829-1910 *NatCAB 34*
Taylor, Raynor 1747?-1825 *DcAmB, WhAm H*
Taylor, Reese Hale 1900-1962 *NatCAB 53, WhAm 4*
Taylor, Richard 1744-1826 *TwCBDA*
Taylor, Richard 1744-1827? *ApCAB Sup*
Taylor, Richard 1747-1825 *Drake*
Taylor, Richard 1826-1879 *AmBi, ApCAB, BiDConf, DcAmB, Drake, NatCAB 4, TwCBDA, WebAMB, WhAm H, WhoMilH*
Taylor, Richard 1902-1970 *WhAm 5*
Taylor, Richard Cowling 1789-1851 *ApCAB, DcAmB, Drake, NatCAB 9, WhAm H*
Taylor, Richard V 1859-1939 *WhAm 1*
Taylor, Robert 1763-1845 *BiAUS, BiDrAC, WhAm H*
Taylor, Robert Barnard 1774-1834 *Drake*
Taylor, Robert Barraud 1774-1834 *ApCAB*
Taylor, Robert Coleman 1863-1942 *NatCAB 31*
Taylor, Robert E Lee 1882-1952 *NatCAB 41*
Taylor, Robert Fenwick 1849- *NatCAB 12, WhAm 4*
Taylor, Robert Howard 1860-1936 *WhAm 1*
Taylor, Robert Jenks 1854-1939 *NatCAB 33*
Taylor, Robert John 1874- *WhAm 5*
Taylor, Robert Lee 1871- *WhAm 5*
Taylor, Robert Longley 1861-1923 *WhAm 1*
Taylor, Robert Love 1850-1912 *ApCAB Sup, BiDrAC, DcAmB, NatCAB 8, TwCBDA, WhAm 1, WhAmP*
Taylor, Robert Rochon 1899-1957 *NatCAB 43*
Taylor, Robert Stewart 1838-1918 *NatCAB 17, WhAm 1*
Taylor, Robert Tunstall 1867-1929 *DcAmB, NatCAB 29, WhAm 1*
Taylor, Robert William 1842- *ApCAB, WhAm 4*
Taylor, Roland Leslie 1868-1943 *NatCAB 32*
Taylor, Rolla S 1874- *IIBEAAW*
Taylor, Roy Arthur 1910- *BiDrAC*
Taylor, Royal 1800-1892 *ApCAB X*
Taylor, Rufus 1811- *ApCAB*
Taylor, S Earl 1873- *WhAm 5*
Taylor, S Gregory 1888-1948 *NatCAB 42*
Taylor, S N 1858- *WhAm 5*
Taylor, Samuel Alfred 1863-1950 *ApCAB X, NatCAB 46, WhAm 3*
Taylor, Samuel Harvey 1807-1871 *ApCAB, BiDAmEd, DcAmB, Drake, NatCAB 10, TwCBDA, WhAm H*
Taylor, Samuel Mac 1856-1916 *WhAm 1*
Taylor, Samuel Mitchell 1852-1921 *BiDrAC, WhAm 1, WhAmP*
Taylor, Samuel Priestly 1779-1874 *ApCAB*
Taylor, Sarah Ellen 1883- *WomWWA 14*
Taylor, Sarah Katherine Paine 1847- *AmWom, WomWWA 14*
Taylor, Sherman T 1872-1926 *NatCAB 23*
Taylor, Stephen William 1791-1856 *ApCAB, Drake, NatCAB 5, TwCBDA*
Taylor, Stevenson 1848-1926 *DcAmB, NatCAB 23*
Taylor, Stewart Munn 1884-1960 *NatCAB 48*
Taylor, Susie King 1848-1912 *McGEWB*
Taylor, T *NewYHSD*
Taylor, Thelma Marjorie Vogt d1971 *WhAm 6*
Taylor, Thomas *NewYHSD*
Taylor, Thomas 1820- *TwCBDA*
Taylor, Thomas 1860-1942 *WhAm 2*
Taylor, Thomas Hendricks 1885-1961 *WhAm 4*
Taylor, Thomas House 1799-1867 *ApCAB, Drake*
Taylor, Thomas Ivan 1909-1973 *WhAm 6*
Taylor, Thomas Nicholls 1868-1950 *WhAm 3*
Taylor, Thomas Ulvan 1858- *TwCBDA, WhAm 4*
Taylor, Vernon F 1888-1972 *WhAm 5*
Taylor, Victor V 1893-1944 *WhAm 2*
Taylor, Vincent Albert 1845-1922 *BiDrAC*
Taylor, Vincent George 1877-1959 *WhAm 3*
Taylor, Virgil Corydon 1817- *ApCAB, Drake*
Taylor, W Bayard 1896-1975 *WhAm 6*
Taylor, W H *NewYHSD*
Taylor, W Walter 1868- *WhoColR*
Taylor, Waller d1826 *Drake*
Taylor, Waller 1785?-1826 *TwCBDA*

Taylor, Waller 1786?-1826 *ApCAB, BiDrAC, NatCAB 4, WhAm H*
Taylor, Walter d1826 *BiAUS*
Taylor, Walter Andrews 1899-1963 *WhAm 4*
Taylor, Walter Fauntleroy 1870-1926 *ApCAB X, NatCAB 20*
Taylor, Walter Herron 1838-1916 *ApCAB, NatCAB 7, NatCAB 41, WhAm 1*
Taylor, Walter Herron 1887-1957 *NatCAB 43*
Taylor, Walter R 1813?- *NewYHSD*
Taylor, Walter S 1813?- *NewYHSD*
Taylor, Warner 1880-1958 *WhAm 3*
Taylor, Warren Howard 1846-1914 *NatCAB 17*
Taylor, Wayne Chatfield 1893-1967 *WhAm 4A*
Taylor, Will Samuel 1882-1968 *WhAm 5*
Taylor, William *BiAUS, NewYHSD*
Taylor, William 1764-1841 *NewYHSD*
Taylor, William 1788-1846 *BiAUS, BiDrAC*
Taylor, William 1791-1865 *BiDrAC, WhAm H*
Taylor, William 1793-1865 *BiAUS*
Taylor, William 1821-1902 *ApCAB, DcAmB, NatCAB 10, TwCBDA, WebAB, WhAm 1*
Taylor, William Albert 1881-1947 *WhAm 2*
Taylor, William Alexander 1837-1912 *WhAm 1*
Taylor, William Alton 1863-1949 *NatCAB 38, WhAm 2*
Taylor, William B *BiAUS*
Taylor, William Bower 1821- *ApCAB*
Taylor, William Chittenden 1886-1958 *NatCAB 49, WhAm 3*
Taylor, William Dana 1859-1911 *WhAm 1*
Taylor, William David, Jr. 1902-1975 *WhAm 6*
Taylor, William Dean 1849-1930 *NatCAB 21*
Taylor, William George Langworthy 1859-1941 *WhAm 1*
Taylor, William Henry 1835-1917 *NatCAB 18*
Taylor, William Henry 1836- *NatCAB 5*
Taylor, William Henry 1859-1928 *ApCAB X, NatCAB 15, WhAm 1*
Taylor, William Henry 1863-1926 *WhAm 1*
Taylor, William Henry 1877-1944 *NatCAB 33*
Taylor, William Hill 1869-1950 *NatCAB 41*
Taylor, William Howard 1882-1967 *NatCAB 54*
Taylor, William James 1867-1949 *WhAm 2*
Taylor, William James Romeyn 1823- *ApCAB*
Taylor, William Johnson 1861-1936 *WhAm 1*
Taylor, William Ladd 1854-1926 *DcAmB, IIBEAAW, NatCAB 12, TwCBDA, WhAm 1*
Taylor, William Lamborn 1853-1940 *NatCAB 31*
Taylor, William Lycurgus 1874-1957 *NatCAB 47*
Taylor, William Mackergo 1829-1895 *ApCAB, DcAmB, NatCAB 2, TwCBDA, WhAm H*
Taylor, William Marcus 1869-1947 *NatCAB 38*
Taylor, William Mode 1865-1947 *WhAm 2*
Taylor, William Osgood 1871-1955 *WhAm 3*
Taylor, William Penn *BiDrAC, WhAm H*
Taylor, William Rivers 1856-1941 *WhAm 1*
Taylor, William R *BiAUS Sup*
Taylor, William Robert 1818- *NatCAB 12, TwCBDA*
Taylor, William Robert 1820- *BiAUS*
Taylor, William Rogers 1811- *Drake*
Taylor, William Rogers 1811-1884 *WhAm H*
Taylor, William Rogers 1811-1889 *ApCAB, DcAmB, NatCAB 4, TwCBDA*
Taylor, William Septimus 1885-1949 *BiDAmEd, NatCAB 39, WhAm 2*
Taylor, William Sylvester 1853-1928 *TwCBDA, WhAm 1*
Taylor, William Vigneron 1780-1858 *DcAmB, NatCAB 4, TwCBDA, WhAm H*
Taylor, William Vigneron 1781-1858 *ApCAB, Drake*
Taylor, William Watts 1847-1913 *NatCAB 13, WhAm 1*
Taylor, Willis Ratcliffe 1897-1945 *WhAm 2*
Taylor, Zachary 1784-1850 *AmBi, ApCAB, BiAUS, BiDrAC, BiDrUSE, DcAmB, Drake, EncAAH, EncAB, McGEWB, NatCAB 4, REnAW, TwCBDA, WebAB, WebAMB, WhAm H, WhAmP,*

Taylor, Zachary 1849-1921 *BiDrAC*
Tazewell, Henry 1753-1799 *ApCAB, BiAUS, BiDrAC, DcAmB, Drake, NatCAB 2, TwCBDA, WhAm H, WhAmP*
Tazewell, Littleton W 1774-1860 *BiAUS*
Tazewell, Littleton Walker 1774-1860 *Drake*
Tazewell, Littleton Waller 1774-1860 *AmBi, ApCAB, BiDrAC, DcAmB, NatCAB 5, TwCBDA, WhAm H, WhAmP*
Tchaikovsky, Peter Ilyich 1840-1893 *McGEWB*
Tchelitchew, Pavel 1898-1957 *BnEnAmA*
Teach, Edward d1718 *WhAm H*
Teachenor, Frank Randall 1888-1953 *WhAm 3*
Tead, Edward Sampson 1852-1919 *WhAm 1*
Tead, Ordway 1891-1973 *WhAm 6*
Teagarden, Florence M 1887-1975 *WhAm 6*
Teagarden, Jack Weldon Leo 1905-1964 *WhAm 4*
Teagle, John 1848-1908 *NatCAB 32*
Teagle, Walter Clark 1878-1962 *NatCAB 53, WhAm 4*
Teague, Charles Collins 1873-1950 *NatCAB 39, WhAm 3*
Teague, Charles McKevett 1909-1974 *BiDrAC, WhAm 6*
Teague, Donald 1897- *IIBEAAW*
Teague, Eldred Burder 1820-1902 *NatCAB 19*
Teague, Olin Earl 1910- *BiDrAC*
Teague, Walter Dorwin 1883-1960 *NatCAB 50, WhAm 4*
Teague, William Thomas 1878-1958 *NatCAB 43*
Teal, Joseph Nathan 1858-1929 *WhAm 1*
Teall, Edward Hall 1885-1937 *NatCAB 28*
Teall, Edward Nelson 1880-1947 *WhAm 2*
Teall, Francis Augustus 1822-1894 *ApCAB, DcAmB, WhAm H*
Teall, Francis Horace 1850- *WhAm 4*
Teall, Gardner 1876-1956 *WhAm 3*
Teall, Jethro Justinian Harris 1849-1924 *DcScB*
Teall, William W 1818-1899 *NatCAB 6*
Teare, Daniel Wilson 1901-1968 *NatCAB 54*
Tearse, Harold Horton 1894-1972 *WhAm 5*
Teasdale, John Warren 1838-1921 *NatCAB 19*
Teasdale, Kenneth 1895-1970 *WhAm 5*
Teasdale, Sara 1884-1933 *AmBi, ApCAB X, DcAmB, NatCAB 39, NotAW, WebAB, WhAm 1, WomWWA 14*
Teasdale, William Bernard 1856-1907 *WhAm 1*
Teasdel, Mary 1863-1937 *IIBEAAW*
Tebbetts, Charles Edwin 1855- *WhAm 4*
Tebow, Louis Elliott 1910-1958 *NatCAB 48*
Techotlalatzin d1409 *ApCAB*
Tecto, Juan De 1468-1526 *ApCAB*
Tecum-Uman d1524 *ApCAB*
Tecumseh 1768?-1813 *AmBi, ApCAB, DcAmB, EncAAH, EncAB, McGEWB, NatCAB 11, REnAW, WebAB, WebAMB, WhAm H, WhoMilH*
Tecumseh 1770?-1813 *Drake*
Tedcastle, Arthur White 1855-1938 *NatCAB 30*
Tedder, Arthur William 1890-1967 *WhAm 4, WhWW-II, WhoMilH*
Tedesche, Leon Greenfield 1878-1956 *NatCAB 46, WhAm 3*
Tedford, William Hamill 1844-1917 *NatCAB 17*
Tedrow, Harry Beecher 1875-1921 *NatCAB 19, WhAm 1*
Tedyuskung 1700?-1763 *DcAmB, WhAm H*
Tee-Van, John 1897-1967 *WhAm 4A*
Teed, Ralph Herman 1898-1958 *NatCAB 49, WhAm 3*
Teedyuscung 1700?-1763 *ApCAB*
Teefy, Robert Baldwin 1859-1937 *NatCAB 27*
Teel, E 1830?- *NewYHSD*
Teel, Forrest 1904-1958 *WhAm 3*
Teel, Lewis Woods 1883- *IIBEAAW*
Teel, Warren Floyd 1868-1932 *WhAm 1*
Teele, Kenneth Robertson 1895-1968 *NatCAB 54*
Teele, Ray Palmer 1868-1927 *AmBi, NatCAB 20, WhAm 1*
Teele, Ray Palmer 1903-1974 *WhAm 6*
Teele, Stanley Ferdinand 1906-1967 *WhAm 4*
Teeple, John Edgar 1874-1931 *DcAmB S1, NatCAB 27, WhAm 1, WhAm 1C*

Teer, Nello Leguy 1888-1963 *NatCAB 50*

Teese, Frederick Halstead 1823-1894 *BiAUS, BiDrAC, WhAm H*

Teesing, H P H 1907-1973 *WhAm 6*

Teeter, Albert A 1888-1953 *WhAm 3*

Teeter, John Henry 1900-1966 *WhAm 4*

Teeters, Bert Alonzo 1897-1963 *WhAm 4*

Teeters, Negley King 1896-1971 *WhAm 5*

Teeters, Wilber John 1866- *WhAm 5*

Teetor, Charles Newton 1870-1937 *NatCAB 28*

Teetor, John Hamilton 1860-1939 *NatCAB 29*

Teetor, Lothair 1897-1962 *NatCAB 50, WhAm 4*

Teets, Harley O 1906-1957 *WhAm 3*

Teets, Herbert Mortimer 1872-1942 *NatCAB 31*

Teevan, John Charles 1880-1948 *WhAm 2*

Tefft, Benjamin Franklin 1813-1885 *ApCAB, Drake, NatCAB 12, NatCAB 13, WhAm H*

Tefft, Israel Keech 1794-1862 *ApCAB Sup*

Tefft, Lyman Beecher 1833-1926 *NatCAB 20, WhAm 1*

Tefft, Thomas Alexander 1826-1859 *ApCAB, Drake, WhAm H*

Tefft, William Wolcott 1882-1932 *NatCAB 23, WhAm 1*

Tegakouita, Catharine 1656-1680 *ApCAB*

Teganakoa, Stephen d1690 *ApCAB*

Teganissorens d1711? *ApCAB*

Tegarden, J B Hollis 1893-1954 *WhAm 3*

Teggart, Frederick John 1870-1946 *DcAmB S4, WhAm 2*

Tegtmeyer, William Hahne d1974 *WhAm 6*

Tehon, Leo Roy 1895-1954 *WhAm 3*

Teich, Max Louis 1873- *WhAm 5*

Teichert, Minerva Kohlhepp 1889- *IIBEAAW*

Teichmann, Ludwik Karol 1823-1895 *DcScB*

Teichmann, William C 1859- *WhAm 4*

Teigan, Henry George 1881-1941 *BiDrAC, WhAm 1, WhAmP*

Teilhard DeChardin, Pierre 1881-1955 *DcScB, McGEWB, WhAm HA, WhAm 4*

Teisseire, Armand *NewYHSD*

Teisserenc DeBort, Leon Philippe 1855-1913 *AsBiEn*

Tejada, M S De *NewYHSD*

Tejeda, Juan De *ApCAB*

Tekakwitha, Catherine 1656?-1680 *DcAmReB, NotAW*

Tekakwitha, Kateri 1656-1680 *WebAB*

Telemann, Georg Philipp 1681-1767 *McGEWB*

Telemaque *WebAB*

Telesio, Bernardino 1509-1588 *DcScB, McGEWB*

Telfair, Edward 1735-1807 *ApCAB, BiAUS, BiDrAC, DcAmB, Drake, NatCAB 1, TwCBDA, WhAm H, WhAmP*

Telfair, Thomas 1780-1818 *BiAUS, BiDrAC, WhAm H, WhAmP*

Telfer, John R *NewYHSD*

Telfer, Robert *NewYHSD*

Telford, Emma Paddock 1851- *WomWWA 14*

Telford, Mary Jewett 1839- *AmWom*

Telford, Robert Lee 1863-1934 *WhAm 1*

Teller, Edward 1908- *AsBiEn, EncAB, WebAB*

Teller, Henry Moore 1830-1914 *AmBi, ApCAB, BiDrAC, BiDrUSE, DcAmB, EncAAH, EncAB, NatCAB 4, NatCAB 15, REnAW, TwCBDA, WhAm 1, WhAmP*

Teller, Hugh Harlow 1896-1973 *WhAm 5*

Teller, Isaac 1798-1868 *BiAUS*

Teller, Isaac 1799-1868 *BiDrAC, WhAm H*

Teller, James Harvey 1850-1937 *WhAm 1*

Teller, John DuBois 1845-1922 *WhAm 1*

Teller, Ludwig 1911-1965 *BiDrAC, WhAm 4*

Teller, Philip Shepheard 1861-1930 *WhAm 1*

Teller, Steadman 1903-1955 *WhAm 4*

Tellier, Remigius Joseph 1796-1866 *ApCAB, Drake, NatCAB 2*

Tellkampf, Johann Ludwig 1808-1876 *ApCAB*

Tello, Juan Antonio De 1566-1654 *ApCAB Sup*

Tello, Julio C 1880-1947 *WhAm 2*

Tello, Manly 1842-1905 *NatCAB 21*

Tello DePortugal, Jose DeEspinosa 1763-1815 *ApCAB*

Telva, Marion 1897-1962 *WhAm 4*

Tembleque, Francisco *ApCAB*

Temkin, Samuel 1897-1963 *WhAm 4*

Temmey, Leo Albert 1894-1975 *WhAm 6*

Tempest, Marie Susan 1866-1942 *WhAm 2*

Tempka, Tadeusz 1885-1974 *WhAm 6*

Temple, Alice 1866-1946 *BiDAmEd*

Temple, Daniel 1789-1851 *ApCAB*

Temple, Daniel 1790-1851 *Drake*

Temple, Edward Arthur 1867-1924 *NatCAB 21, WhAm 1*

Temple, Edward Lowe 1844-1928 *NatCAB 7, TwCBDA, WhAm 1*

Temple, Harold Francis 1903-1961 *NatCAB 45, WhAm 4*

Temple, Henry John 1784-1865 *WhAm H*

Temple, Henry Willson 1864-1955 *BiDrAC, WhAm 3, WhAmP*

Temple, Jackson 1827-1902 *ApCAB, WhAm 1*

Temple, Sir John 1731-1798 *Drake*

Temple, Laura *WomWWA 14*

Temple, Mary Boyce *WhAm 5, WomWWA 14*

Temple, Oliver Perry 1820-1907 *ApCAB Sup, DcAmB, TwCBDA, WhAm 1*

Temple, Seth Justin 1867-1949 *NatCAB 38, WhAm 2*

Temple, Shirley 1928- *WebAB*

Temple, Walter Paul 1869- *WhAm 5*

Temple, William 1814-1863 *BiDrAC, TwCBDA, WhAm H*

Temple, William 1815-1863 *BiAUS, Drake*

Temple, William Chase 1862-1917 *NatCAB 18, WhAm 1*

Temple, William Greenville 1824-1894 *TwCBDA*

Temple, William Grenville 1824-1894 *ApCAB, DcAmB, NatCAB 4, WhAm H*

Templeton, Alec 1910-1963 *WhAm 4*

Templeton, Charles Augustus 1871-1955 *NatCAB 43, WhAm 3*

Templeton, Charlotte 1877- *WhAm 5*

Templeton, David Allison 1901-1959 *NatCAB 47*

Templeton, Fay 1865-1939 *NotAW, WhAm 1*

Templeton, Howard 1861-1937 *WhAm 1*

Templeton, James Scott 1871-1962 *NatCAB 50*

Templeton, Ralph Gordon 1916-1966 *NatCAB 54*

Templeton, Richard Harkness 1877- *WhAm 5*

Templeton, Samuel Moore 1853-1935 *WhAm 3*

Templeton, Stuart John 1889-1958 *NatCAB 43, WhAm 3*

Templeton, Thomas Weir 1867-1935 *BiDrAC, WhAm 3*

Templeton, William Craig 1863- *WhAm 4*

Templin, Lucinda DeLeftwich *WhAm 5*

Templin, Olin 1861-1943 *WhAm 2*

Templin, Richard Laurence 1893-1965 *WhAm 4*

TenBroeck, Abraham 1734-1810 *ApCAB, DcAmB, Drake, WhAm H*

TenBroeck, Albertina 1760-1840 *NewYHSD*

Tenbroeck, Carl 1885-1966 *WhAm 4*

TenBroeck, Drew 1888-1955 *NatCAB 41*

TenBroeck, Richard 1812-1892 *DcAmB, WhAm H*

TenBroek, Jacobus 1911-1968 *WhAm 5*

Tenbulzen, Lester Dale 1917-1973 *WhAm 6*

Tench, Thomas *NatCAB 9*

Tene-Ang Pote d1875 *WhAm H*

Tene-Angpote d1875 *DcAmB*

TenEick, Abraham S 1787-1844 *Drake*

Tener, Hampden Evans 1865-1948 *NatCAB 36*

Tener, John Kinley 1863-1946 *BiDrAC, WhAm 2, WhAmP*

Tenerowicz, Rudolph Gabriel 1890-1963 *BiDrAC*

Tenesy, George Stephan 1887-1948 *NatCAB 38*

TenEyck, Abraham S 1785-1844 *ApCAB*

TenEyck, Andrew 1888-1964 *NatCAB 50, WhAm 4*

TenEyck, Anthony 1810-1867 *BiAUS, NatCAB 12*

TenEyck, Egbert 1779-1844 *BiAUS, BiDrAC, WhAm H*

TenEyck, Henry James 1856-1887 *ApCAB*

TenEyck, Jay 1864-1943 *NatCAB 33*

TenEyck, John Conover 1814-1879 *ApCAB, BiAUS, BiDrAC, NatCAB 2, TwCBDA, WhAm H*

TenEyck, Maria Lovina 1846- *WomWWA 14*

TenEyck, Mills 1883-1957 *NatCAB 45*

TenEyck, Peter Gansevoort 1873-1944 *BiDrAC, NatCAB 18, WhAm 2*

TenEyck, Richard *NewYHSD*

TenEyck, Richard, Jr. *NewYHSD*

TenEyck, William Hoffman 1818-1908 *WhAm 1*

Tenggren, Gustaf Adolf 1896-1970 *WhAm 6*

TenHoor, Perry John 1892-1968 *NatCAB 54*

Tennant, John Hunter 1869-1933 *WhAm 1*

Tennant, Maurice Emerson 1883-1951 *NatCAB 39*

Tennant, Smithson 1761-1815 *AsBiEn, DcScB*

Tennant, W Brydon 1870-1940 *NatCAB 34*

Tennent, David Hilt 1873-1941 *DcScB, NatCAB 36, WhAm 1*

Tennent, Gilbert 1702-1764 *AmBi*

Tennent, Gilbert 1703-1764 *ApCAB, DcAmB, DcAmReB, Drake, McGEWB, NatCAB 8 TwCBDA, WebAB, WhAm H*

Tennent, John 1700?-1760? *DcAmB, WhAm H*

Tennent, John 1706-1732 *ApCAB*

Tennent, John 1707-1732 *NatCAB 8*

Tennent, W *NewYHSD*

Tennent, William 1673-1745 *AmBi*

Tennent, William 1673-1746 *ApCAB, BiDAmEd, DcAmB, DcAmReB, NatCAB 5, TwCBDA, WebAB, WhAm H*

Tennent, William 1705-1777 *ApCAB, DcAmB, Drake, NatCAB 8, WhAm H*

Tenney, Abby Amy Gove *ApCAB*

Tenney, Adna 1810-1900 *NewYHSD*

Tenney, Albert Ball 1873-1948 *WhAm 2*

Tenney, Alice Parker *WomWWA 14*

Tenney, Asa Wentworth 1833-1897 *ApCAB Sup, NatCAB 2*

Tenney, Charles Daniel 1857-1930 *DcAmB, WhAm 1*

Tenney, Charles H d1951 *WhAm 3*

Tenney, Charles Henry 1842-1919 *NatCAB 17*

Tenney, Charles Irving 1864-1945 *NatCAB 49, WhAm 2*

Tenney, Charles Rockwell 1854-1928 *NatCAB 43*

Tenney, Charles Wesley 1873- *WhAm 5*

Tenney, Daniel Kent 1834-1915 *NatCAB 16*

Tenney, Edward Davies 1859-1934 *NatCAB 36, WhAm 1, WhAm 1C*

Tenney, Edward Payson 1835-1916 *DcAmB, NatCAB 7, TwCBDA, WhAm 1*

Tenney, Frank Minard 1870-1957 *WhAm 3*

Tenney, Gena Branscombe *WomWWA 14*

Tenney, George Amos 1864-1947 *NatCAB 40*

Tenney, George Lee d1950 *WhAm 3*

Tenney, Grace Marten Kelley 1874- *WomWWA 14*

Tenney, Harral Straat 1883-1949 *NatCAB 38*

Tenney, Helen Mason 1860- *WomWWA 14*

Tenney, Henry Favill 1890-1971 *WhAm 5*

Tenney, Henry Martyn 1841-1932 *WhAm 1*

Tenney, Horace Kent 1859-1932 *WhAm 1*

Tenney, John S 1789-1869 *Drake*

Tenney, John Searle 1793-1869 *NatCAB 10*

Tenney, M B *NewYHSD*

Tenney, Minna Eliot *WomWWA 14*

Tenney, Otis Seth 1822-1916 *NatCAB 17*

Tenney, Samuel 1748-1816 *ApCAB, BiAUS, BiDrAC, Drake, NatCAB 5, WhAm H*

Tenney, Sanborn 1827-1877 *ApCAB*

Tenney, Sarah Brownson 1839-1876 *ApCAB, WhAm H*

Tenney, Tabitha Gilman 1762-1837 *ApCAB, DcAmB, NotAW, WhAm H*

Tenney, Ulysses Dow 1826-1908 *NewYHSD, WhAm 1*

Tenney, William Jewett 1811-1883 *DcAmB, Drake, WhAm H*

Tenney, William Jewett 1814-1883 *ApCAB, TwCBDA*

Tenney, William Lawrence 1862-1917 *WhAm 1*

Tenny, Charles Buckley 1871-1936 *WhAm 1*

Tenny, Lloyd Stanley 1876- *WhAm 5*

Tennyson, Baron Alfred 1809-1892 *McGEWB*

Tenoch *ApCAB*

WhAm H

Tenopyr, Joseph 1885-1961 *NatCAB 49*
TenRhyne, Willem 1647-1700 *DcScB*
Tenskwatawa *WebAB*
Tenskwatawa 1768-1813 *WhAm H*
Tenskwatawa 1768?-1834? *AmBi, DcAmB*
Tenskwatawa 1771?-1837 *DcAmReB*
Tenskwatawa 1778?-1837? *REnAW*
Tenzer, Herbert 1905- *BiDrAC*
Tepancaltzin d1103 *ApCAB*
Tepley, Marie L 1874- *WomWWA 14*
Tepoel, Louis John 1877- *WhAm 5*
Ter Borch, Gerard 1617-1681 *McGEWB*
Ter Poorten, Hein 1887-1948 *WhWW-II*
Terao, Takeo 1905-1974 *WhAm 6*
Terauchi, Hisaichi 1879-1945 *WhWW-II*
Terauchi, Count Seiki 1879-1946 *WhoMilH*
Terbell, Joseph Bodine 1863-1931 *NatCAB 37,*
 WhAm 1
Terence 195BC-159BC *McGEWB*
Teresa, Mother 1766?-1846 *AmBi, DcAmB,*
 WhAm H
Terhune, Albert Payson 1868- *NatCAB 10*
Terhune, Albert Payson 1872-1942 *DcAmB S3,*
 NatCAB 34, TwCBDA, WebAB,
 WhAm 2
Terhune, Anice Morris Stockton d1964 *BiCAW,*
 WhAm 4, WomWWA 14
Terhune, Edward Payson 1825?-1907 *ApCAB*
Terhune, Edward Payson 1830-1907 *WhAm 1*
Terhune, Everit Bogert 1876-1956 *WhAm 3*
Terhune, John Henry 1846-1909 *NatCAB 31*
Terhune, Mary Virginia Hawes d1922 *Drake,*
 WhAm 1
Terhune, Mary Virginia Hawes 1830-1922 *AmBi,*
 ApCAB, DcAmB, NotAW
Terhune, Mary Virginia Hawes 1831-1922
 AmWom, NatCAB 2, TwCBDA,
 WomWWA 14
Terhune, William Lewis 1850-1936 *WhAm 1*
Teriggi, A F *NewYHSD*
Teriggi, A M *NewYHSD*
Teriggi, F M *NewYHSD*
Terman, Lewis Madison 1877-1956 *BiDAmEd,*
 WebAB, WhAm 3
Termier, Pierre 1859-1930 *DcScB*
Termohlen, William Dewey 1898-1970 *WhAm 5*
Tern, C H *NewYHSD*
Ternant, Jean Baptiste 1750-1816 *ApCAB*
Ternant, Jean De 1750-1816 *Drake*
Ternaux, Henry 1807-1864 *ApCAB*
Ternaux Compans, Henri d1864 *Drake*
Ternay, Charles Lewis D'Arsac De 1722-1780
 Drake
Ternay, Charles Louis D'Arsae 1722-1780
 ApCAB
Ternes, William Peter 1877-1926 *NatCAB 22*
Terra, Gabriel 1873-1942 *McGEWB*
Terral, Samuel Heidelberg 1835-1903 *WhAm 1*
Terral, Thomas Jefferson 1884-1946
 NatCAB 40
Terral, Tom J 1884-1946 *WhAm 2*
Terrazas, Francisco De 1520?-1575 *ApCAB*
Terrell, Alexander Bismarck 1885- *WhoColR*
Terrell, Alexander Watkins 1827-1912 *WhAm 1*
Terrell, Alexander Watkins 1829-1912
 NatCAB 5
Terrell, Alton Truman 1872-1938 *NatCAB 28*
Terrell, Mrs. Ben *WomWWA 14*
Terrell, Charles Everett 1880- *WhAm 6*
Terrell, Edgar Allen 1894-1973 *NatCAB 57*
Terrell, Edwin Holland 1841-1910 *ApCAB Sup*
Terrell, Edwin Holland 1848-1910 *DcAmB,*
 NatCAB 1, TwCBDA, WhAm 1
Terrell, Frederick 1856-1940 *WhAm 1*
Terrell, George Butler 1862-1947 *BiDrAC,*
 WhAm 2
Terrell, Glanville 1859-1936 *NatCAB 27,*
 WhAm 1
Terrell, Glenn 1878-1964 *NatCAB 52*
Terrell, Henry Walker 1871-1921 *NatCAB 19*
Terrell, Isaiah Milligan 1859- *WhoColR*
Terrell, J O 1856-1923 *WhAm 1*
Terrell, James C 1806-1835 *BiDrAC,*
 WhAm H
Terrell, Joseph Meriwether 1861-1912 *BiDrAC,*
 NatCAB 12, TwCBDA, WhAm 1
Terrell, Marcelite Landry 1866- *WhoColR*
Terrell, Marjorie Smith 1891-1973 *WhAm 6*

Terrell, Mary Eliza Church 1863-1954
 DcAmB S5, NatCAB 52, WhAm 3
Terrell, Richard *NewYHSD*
Terrell, Mrs. Robert Allen 1877-
 WomWWA 14
Terrell, Robert Heberton 1857-1925
 NatCAB 47
Terrell, Robert Herberton 1857-1925 *WhoColR*
Terrell, Roy *WhAm 5*
Terrell, Scurry Latimer 1869- *WhAm 5*
Terrell, Wendell Phillips 1884- *WhoColR*
Terrell, William 1778-1855 *ApCAB, BiDrAC,*
 Drake, NatCAB 3, WhAm H
Terrell, William Dandridge 1871- *WhAm 5*
Terrell, William H 1876- *WhoColR*
Terres, John B 1847-1920 *WhAm 1*
Terrett, Colville Penrose 1852-1913 *NatCAB 16*
Terrett, William Rogers 1849-1902 *WhAm 1*
Terriberry, George Hitchings 1875-1948
 NatCAB 37, WhAm 2
Terriberry, Joseph Frederick 1857-1932
 NatCAB 34
Terriberry, William S 1871-1948 *WhAm 2,*
 WhAm 5
Terrien, Pierre-Esdras 1876- *WhAm 5*
Terriggi, A F *NewYHSD*
Terriggi, A M *NewYHSD*
Terriggi, F M *NewYHSD*
Terrill, Bertha Mary 1870- *WomWWA 14*
Terrill, Dean 1904-1972 *WhAm 5*
Terrill, James Barbour 1838-1864 *ApCAB*
Terrill, Mortimer Clark 1888-1944 *WhAm 2*
Terrill, William d1855 *BiAUS*
Terrill, William Rufus 1832-1862 *Drake*
Terrill, William Rufus 1834-1862 *ApCAB,*
 NatCAB 9
Terry, Adolphine Fletcher 1882-
 WomWWA 14
Terry, Adrian Russell 1808-1864 *ApCAB*
Terry, Albert Todd 1869-1947 *NatCAB 36*
Terry, Alfred Howe 1827-1890 *AmBi, ApCAB,*
 DcAmB, Drake, NatCAB 4, REnAW,
 TwCBDA, WebAB, WebAMB, WhAm H
Terry, Benjamin Stites 1857-1931 *NatCAB 9,*
 WhAm 1
Terry, Benjamin Taylor 1876-1955 *NatCAB 46*
Terry, Charles Appleton 1858-1939 *ApCAB X,*
 WhAm 1
Terry, Charles Guilford 1896-1962 *NatCAB 46,*
 WhAm 4
Terry, Charles Laymen, Jr. 1900-1970 *WhAm 5*
Terry, Charles Thaddeus 1867-1923
 NatCAB 12, NatCAB 38, WhAm 1
Terry, Clarissa *NewYHSD*
Terry, Clifford Edward 1885- *WhoColR*
Terry, David Dickson 1881-1963 *BiDrAC,*
 WhAm 4, WhAmP
Terry, David Smith 1823-1889 *DcAmB,*
 NatCAB 12, WhAm H
Terry, Edward Clinton 1850-1908 *NatCAB 17*
Terry, Eli 1772-1852 *ApCAB, DcAmB,*
 NatCAB 6, WebAB, WhAm H
Terry, Eliphalet 1826-1896 *NewYHSD*
Terry, Ellen 1848-1928 *WhAm 1*
Terry, Flora Lincoln 1865- *WomWWA 14*
Terry, Franklin Silas 1862-1926 *NatCAB 20*
Terry, George S d1911 *WhAm 1*
Terry, Henry Dwight 1812-1869 *ApCAB,*
 TwCBDA
Terry, Henry Taylor 1847- *WhAm 4*
Terry, Howard Leslie 1877- *WhAm 5*
Terry, John Orville 1796-1869 *ApCAB,*
 NatCAB 13, WhAm H
Terry, John Taylor 1822-1913 *NatCAB 3,*
 WhAm 1
Terry, John Taylor 1857-1942 *WhAm 2*
Terry, John Wharton 1860-1936 *NatCAB 27,*
 WhAm 1
Terry, John Young 1858- *WhAm 4*
Terry, Luther 1813-1869 *ApCAB, NewYHSD*
Terry, Marie Cady *WomWWA 14*
Terry, Marshall Orlando 1848-1933 *DcAmB,*
 NatCAB 16, NatCAB 27, WhAm 1
Terry, Milton Spenser 1840-1914 *ApCAB,*
 DcAmB, WhAm 1
Terry, Nathaniel 1768-1844 *BiAUS, BiDrAC,*
 WhAm H
Terry, Nathaniel Matson 1844-1938 *WhAm 1*

Terry, Oliver Perkins 1882-1933 *NatCAB 25*
Terry, Paul Washington 1887-1959 *WhAm 4*
Terry, Philip Roy 1880-1958 *NatCAB 46*
Terry, Randall B 1883-1955 *WhAm 3*
Terry, Robert James 1871-1966 *WhAm 4*
Terry, Robert Wood 1892-1949 *NatCAB 47*
Terry, Roderick 1849-1933 *NatCAB 10,*
 WhAm 1
Terry, Rose *NotAW*
Terry, Roy Albert 1887-1956 *NatCAB 47*
Terry, Samuel Walker 1894-1964 *NatCAB 54*
Terry, Seth 1780-1865 *BiAUS*
Terry, Seth Sprague 1862-1932 *NatCAB 26*
Terry, Silas Wright 1822-1911 *TwCBDA*
Terry, Silas Wright 1842-1911 *NatCAB 16,*
 WhAm 1
Terry, T Philip 1864- *WhAm 4*
Terry, Theodore Brainard 1843-1916 *WhAm 1*
Terry, Thomas Alexander 1885-1963 *WhAm 4*
Terry, Vashti Boardman 1839- *WomWWA 14*
Terry, W Eliphalet 1826-1896 *IIBEAAW*
Terry, Wallace Irving 1868- *WhAm 5*
Terry, Watt *WhoColR*
Terry, Will Albert 1864- *WhAm 4*
Terry, William 1824-1888 *ApCAB, BiAUS,*
 BiDConf, BiDrAC, WhAm H
Terry, William D *NewYHSD*
Terry, William Leake 1850-1917 *BiDrAC,*
 TwCBDA, WhAm 4, WhAmP
Terry, William Mershon, II 1920-1973
 NatCAB 57
Terry, William Michael 1916-1969 *WhAm 6*
Terry, William R d1865 *Drake*
Terry, William Richard 1827-1897 *ApCAB,*
 TwCBDA
Terryll, Richard *NewYHSD*
Terteling, Joseph Wesley 1895-1954
 NatCAB 47
Tertis, Lionel 1876-1975 *WhAm 6*
Tertre, John Baptist d1687 *Drake*
Tertullian 160?-220? *McGEWB*
Terwilliger, Charles VanOrden 1894-1962
 WhAm 4
Terwilliger, Lorenzo 1847-1905 *NatCAB 8*
Terzaghi, Karl 1883-1963 *WebAB, WhAm 4*
Teschemacher, Frank 1906-1932 *WhAm HA,*
 WhAm 4
Teschemacher, J E 1790-1853 *Drake*
Teschemacher, James Englebert 1790-1853
 ApCAB
Teschmaker, F *NewYHSD*
Teske, Edmund 1911- *BnEnAmA*
Teskey, Adeline Margaret *WomWWA 14*
Tesla, Nikola 1856-1943 *AsBiEn, DcAmB S3,*
 DcScB, McGEWB, WebAB, WhAm 2
Tesla, Nikola 1857-1943 *ApCAB Sup,*
 ApCAB X, NatCAB 6, TwCBDA
Tessier, Jules 1852- *ApCAB*
Tessier, Ulric Joseph 1817- *ApCAB*
Tessin, Germain *NewYHSD*
Tessitore, Nicola Joseph 1906-1967 *NatCAB 54*
Test, Charles Edward 1856-1910 *NatCAB 30*
Test, John 1771-1849 *BiAUS, BiDrAC,*
 WhAm H
Teste, Lucien Auguste 1765-1817 *ApCAB*
Testut, Charles 1818?-1892 *DcAmB,*
 WhAm H
Testut, Jean Leo 1849-1925 *DcScB*
Testwuide, Konrad Cullen 1879-1959
 NatCAB 48
Teszler, Andrew 1931-1971 *NatCAB 57*
Tete, Auguste J 1882-1944 *WhAm 2*
Teter, Eber 1846- *WhAm 4*
Teter, Lucius 1873-1950 *WhAm 3*
Tetinchoua *ApCAB*
Tetlepanquetzal d1525 *ApCAB*
Tetley, Edmund 1842- *ApCAB X*
Tetley, Frank Arthur 1866-1942 *NatCAB 33*
Tetley, William Birchall *NewYHSD*
Tetlow, John 1843-1911 *WhAm 1*
Tetlow, Percy 1875-1960 *NatCAB 50,*
 WhAm 5
Tetrazzini, Luisa 1874-1940 *WhAm 1*
Tetrick, W Guy 1883-1956 *NatCAB 45,*
 WhAm 3
Tetu, Louis David Henri 1849- *ApCAB*
Tetzotzomoc d1427 *ApCAB*
Teubner, George W *NewYHSD*

Teufert, Mabel Luella Kuhnley 1881-
WomWWA 14
Teuil, Val NewYHSD
Teulon, Edward A 1826?- NewYHSD
Teulon, Matthew H NewYHSD
Teusler, Rudolf Bolling 1876-1934 DcAmB,
WhAm 1
Tevis, Lloyd 1824-1899 DcAmB, NatCAB 8,
WebAB, WhAm H
Tew, David NewYHSD
Tew, James Dinsmore 1882-1964 WhAm 4
Tew, Susan Dinsmore WomWWA 14
Tewell, Harold Strong 1892-1972 WhAm 5
Tewes, Donald Edgar 1916- BiDrAC
Tewfik Pasha 1852-1892 McGEWB
Tewksbury, Donald George 1894-1958
BiDAmEd, NatCAB 43, WhAm 3
Tewksbury, Edith Malcolm 1878-
WomWWA 14
Tewksbury, Elwood Gardner 1865-1945
WhAm 2
Tewksbury, H Josiah Royal 1886-1937 WhAm 1
Tewksbury, William Davis 1885-1956 WhAm 3
Tewodros II 1820-1868 McGEWB
Tewson, W Orton 1877-1947 WhAm 2
Textor, G C 1900-1968 WhAm 5
Textor, Gordon Edmund 1902-1955 WhAm 3
Textor, Oscar 1860-1937 NatCAB 32
Thabit Ibn Qurra, Al-Sabi Al-Harrani 836-901
DcScB
Thach, Charles Coleman 1860-1921 BiDAmEd,
NatCAB 26, WhAm 1
Thach, James Harmon, Jr. 1900-1962 WhAm 4
Thach, Robert Gordon 1891-1955 NatCAB 44
Thachara, Alexander Montgomery 1848-1937
WhAm 1
Thacher, Archibald Gourlay 1876-1952
WhAm 3
Thacher, Arthur 1857-1934 WhAm 1
Thacher, Edwin 1839-1920 DcAmB,
NatCAB 7, WhAm 1
Thacher, Ethel Davies 1876- WomWWA 14
Thacher, George 1754-1824 ApCAB, BiAUS,
BiDrAC, DcAmB, Drake, NatCAB 2,
TwCBDA, WhAm H, WhAmP
Thacher, Henry Clarke 1881-1956 NatCAB 43
Thacher, J M 1836- BiAUS
Thacher, James 1754-1844 ApCAB, BiHiMed,
DcAmB, Drake, NatCAB 7, WhAm H
Thacher, James Kingsley 1847-1891
NatCAB 35
Thacher, John Boyd 1847-1909 DcAmB,
NatCAB 2, WhAm 1
Thacher, John Boyd 1882-1957 WhAm 4
Thacher, John Marshall 1836- ApCAB,
NatCAB 3
Thacher, John Seymour 1856-1922 WhAm 1
Thacher, Louis Bartlett 1867-1952 NatCAB 43
Thacher, Oxenbridge 1720-1765 ApCAB,
Drake, NatCAB 5
Thacher, Peter 1651-1727 ApCAB, DcAmB,
Drake, NatCAB 6, WhAm H
Thacher, Peter 1677-1738 ApCAB
Thacher, Peter 1716-1785 Drake
Thacher, Peter 1752-1802 ApCAB, DcAmB,
Drake, NatCAB 7, WhAm H
Thacher, Peter Oxenbridge 1776-1843 Drake
Thacher, Samuel 1776-1872 BiAUS
Thacher, Samuel see also Thatcher, Samuel
Thacher, Samuel Cooper 1785-1818 ApCAB,
DcAmB, Drake, NatCAB 5, WhAm H
Thacher, Sherman Day 1861-1931 WhAm 1
Thacher, Thomas 1620-1678 ApCAB, Drake
Thacher, Thomas 1756-1812 ApCAB,
NatCAB 5
Thacher, Thomas 1850-1919 ApCAB X,
NatCAB 14, NatCAB 24, WhAm 1
Thacher, Thomas Anthony 1815-1886 DcAmB,
NatCAB 11, WhAm H
Thacher, Thomas Antony 1815-1886 ApCAB
Thacher, Thomas Chander 1858-1945 WhAm 3
Thacher, Thomas Chandler 1858-1945 BiDrAC
Thacher, Thomas Day 1881-1950 DcAmB S4,
NatCAB 40, WhAm 3
Thacher, Thomas Oxenbridge 1884-1941
NatCAB 31
Thackara, Alexander Montgomery 1848-1937
NatCAB 27

Thackara, James 1767-1848 NewYHSD
Thackara, William 1791-1839 NewYHSD
Thacker, Carl Gale 1907-1975 WhAm 6
Thacker, J Ernest 1869-1945 WhAm 2
Thacker, May Dixon 1876- WomWWA 14
Thackeray, William Makepeace 1811-1863
McGEWB
Thackray, George Edward 1856-1944
NatCAB 35
Thackrey, Lyman Augustus 1897-1955
NatCAB 44, WhAm 3
Thackston, John Andy 1876- WhAm 5
Thaddaeus Florentinus DcScB
Thaden, John Frederick 1894-1968 NatCAB 54
Thaeler, Arthur David 1871-1932 NatCAB 23,
WhAm 1
Thaete, Edward H 1876- WhAm 5
Thalberg, Irving Grant 1899-1936 DcAmB S2,
NatCAB 27, WebAB, WhAm HA,
WhAm 4
Thales 624?BC-545?BC McGEWB
Thales 624BC-546BC AsBiEn
Thales 625?BC-547?BC DcScB
Thalheimer, Alvin 1894- WhAm 4
Thallon, Ida Carleton WomWWA 14
Thames, Mrs. E D 1875- WomWWA 14
Thames, Travis Butler 1856-1914 WhAm 1
Than, Karoly 1834-1908 DcScB
Thanarat, Marshal Sarit 1900-1963 WhAm 4
Thanet, Octave AmBi, ApCAB Sup,
DcAmB S1, NotAW, TwCBDA,
WhAm 1
Thannhauser, Siegfried Josef 1885-1962
NatCAB 51, WhAm 4
Thant, U 1909-1974 McGEWB, WhAm 6
Tharaldsen, Conrad Engerud 1884-1944
NatCAB 32, WhAm 2
Tharin, Robert Seymour Symmes 1830- ApCAB,
WhAm 4
Tharp, Benjamin C 1885-1964 WhAm 4
Tharp, Mabel Frances Robinson 1899-1973
WhAm 6
Tharp, William 1803-1865 NatCAB 11,
TwCBDA
Thatch, Edward WhAm H
Thatcher, Albert Garrett 1846-1928
NatCAB 38
Thatcher, Anna Susannah WomWWA 14
Thatcher, Benjamin Bussey 1809-1840 ApCAB,
DcAmB, Drake, NatCAB 13, WhAm H
Thatcher, Catharine Hall WomWWA 14
Thatcher, Edith Whiting 1877- WomWWA 14
Thatcher, George 1754-1824 DcAmB
Thatcher, George Bayard 1882-1946
NatCAB 37
Thatcher, George W 1833?- NewYHSD
Thatcher, George Wilson 1913-1971 WhAm 5
Thatcher, Henry Calvin 1842-1884 NatCAB 12
Thatcher, Henry Knox 1806-1880 ApCAB,
DcAmB, Drake, NatCAB 5, WebAMB,
WhAm H
Thatcher, Joseph Addison 1838-1918 WhAm 1
Thatcher, Joseph Adison 1838-1918 NatCAB 9
Thatcher, Mahlon D 1842-1965 WhAm 4
Thatcher, Mahlon Daniel 1839-1916 DcAmB,
NatCAB 18, WhAm 1
Thatcher, Maurice Hudson 1870-1973 BiDrAC,
WhAm 5, WhAmP
Thatcher, Moses 1842-1909 NatCAB 7,
WhAm 1
Thatcher, Oliver Joseph 1857- NatCAB 18,
WhAm 4
Thatcher, Roscoe Wilfred 1872-1933 DcAmB,
WhAm 1
Thatcher, Roy Davis 1879-1955 NatCAB 48
Thatcher, Samuel 1776-1872 BiDrAC,
WhAm H
Thatcher, Samuel see also Thacher, Samuel
Thatcher, Solon Otis 1830-1895 ApCAB Sup
Thatcher, W Ross 1917-1971 WhAm 5
Thauer, Ernest Moritz 1903-1972 NatCAB 57
Thaw, A Blair 1860-1937 NatCAB 28
Thaw, Benjamin 1859-1933 NatCAB 38
Thaw, Benjamin, Jr. 1888-1937 NatCAB 38
Thaw, Evelyn Nesbit 1884-1967 WhAm 4
Thaw, Harry Kendall 1871-1947 DcAmB S4
Thaw, Mary Copley d1929 WhAm 1,
WomWWA 14

Thaw, William 1818-1889 DcAmB,
NatCAB 17, WhAm H
Thaw, William 1893- ApCAB X
Thaxter, Adam Wallace 1832-1864 ApCAB,
Drake
Thaxter, Celia Laighton 1835-1894 AmBi,
AmWom, DcAmB, NotAW, WhAm H
Thaxter, Celia Laighton 1836-1894 ApCAB,
TwCBDA
Thaxter, Laighton Celia 1835-1894 NatCAB 1
Thaxter, Roland 1858-1932 AmBi, DcAmB,
DcScB, NatCAB 30, WhAm 1,
WhAm 1C
Thaxter, Sidney St. Felix 1883-1958 WhAm 4
Thayendanegea WebAB, WhAm H
Thayer, Abbott Henderson 1849-1921 AmBi,
BnEnAmA, DcAmB, WhAm H
Thayer, Abbott Henderson 1849-1921 ApCAB,
NatCAB 6
Thayer, Addison Sanford 1858-1923 WhAm 1
Thayer, Alexander Wheelock 1817-1897 AmBi,
ApCAB, DcAmB, NatCAB 8, WhAm H
Thayer, Amos Madden 1841-1905 DcAmB,
NatCAB 10, TwCBDA, WhAm 1
Thayer, Andrew Jackson 1818-1873 BiDrAC,
WhAm H
Thayer, Bayard 1862-1916 ApCAB X,
NatCAB 30
Thayer, Benjamin Bowditch 1862-1933
NatCAB 15, WhAm 1
Thayer, Benjamin W NewYHSD
Thayer, Bertha Cook 1877- WomWWA 14
Thayer, Charles Paine 1843- WhAm 1
Thayer, Charles Wheeler 1910-1969
NatCAB 56, WhAm 5
Thayer, Edward Claflin 1864-1949 NatCAB 38
Thayer, Edwin Force 1903-1975 WhAm 6
Thayer, Edwin Pope 1864- WhAm 3
Thayer, Eli 1819-1899 AmBi, ApCAB, BiAUS,
BiDrAC, DcAmB, McGEWB,
NatCAB 11, TwCBDA, WhAm H,
WhAmP
Thayer, Elihu 1747-1812 ApCAB, Drake
Thayer, Elizabeth Brooks Chatfield
WomWWA 14
Thayer, Emma Homan 1842-1908 AmWom,
IIBEAAW, TwCBDA, WhAm 1
Thayer, Emma Redington Lee 1874- WhAm 5
Thayer, Ernest Lawrence 1863-1940
NatCAB 33, WhAm 2
Thayer, Eugene 1838- ApCAB
Thayer, Eugene 1866- WhAm 4
Thayer, Eugene VanRensselaer 1881-1937
WhAm 1
Thayer, Ezra Ripley 1866-1915 DcAmB,
NatCAB 16, WhAm 1
Thayer, Floyd Kinyon 1896-1965 NatCAB 51,
WhAm 4
Thayer, Frank 1890-1965 NatCAB 52,
WhAm 4
Thayer, Frederick 1843-1924 NatCAB 20
Thayer, Frederick Morris 1896-1956 WhAm 3
Thayer, George Augustine 1839-1925 WhAm 1
Thayer, George Chapman, Jr. d1973 WhAm 6
Thayer, Gideon French 1793-1864 ApCAB Sup,
BiDAmEd, DcAmB, NatCAB 7,
WhAm H
Thayer, Harry Bates 1858-1936 NatCAB 15,
NatCAB 33, WhAm 1
Thayer, Harry Irving 1869-1926 ApCAB X,
BiDrAC, WhAm 1
Thayer, Helen Rand 1863- WhAm 4,
WomWWA 14
Thayer, Horace 1811- NewYHSD
Thayer, James Bradley 1831-1902 ApCAB Sup,
DcAmB, NatCAB 9, TwCBDA,
WhAm 1
Thayer, James Stansbury 1894-1950
NatCAB 38
Thayer, John 1755?-1815 ApCAB
Thayer, John 1758-1815 DcAmB, WhAm H
Thayer, John Adams 1861-1936 WhAm 1
Thayer, John Alden 1857-1917 BiDrAC,
WhAm 1, WhAmP
Thayer, John Borland 1862-1912 WhAm 1
Thayer, John Eliot 1862-1933 NatCAB 33,
WhAm 1
Thayer, John M 1847-1924 WhAm 1

Thoman, Leroy Delano 1851-1909 *ApCAB Sup,* *NatCAB 12, WhAm 1*
Thomas A Kempis 1380?-1471 *McGEWB*
Thomas Aquinas, Saint 1224?-1274 *McGEWB*
Thomas Of Cantimpre 1186?-1276? *DcScB*
Thomas, A E 1872-1947 *WhAm 2*
Thomas, Abel Charles 1807-1880 *ApCAB*
Thomas, Al *NewYHSD*
Thomas, Albert 1898-1966 *BiDrAC, WhAm 4,* *WhAmP*
Thomas, Albert D 1841-1925 *WhAm 1*
Thomas, Albert Harry 1870-1952 *WhAm 3*
Thomas, Albert Sidney 1873- *WhAm 5*
Thomas, Alfred Eugene 1877-1956 *NatCAB 43*
Thomas, Allen 1830-1907 *DcAmB, NatCAB 8*
Thomas, Allen Clapp 1846-1920 *NatCAB 19,* *WhAm 1*
Thomas, Allen Curry 1874-1952 *NatCAB 40*
Thomas, Amos Russell 1826-1895 *ApCAB,* *DcAmB, NatCAB 3, WhAm H*
Thomas, Andrew J 1875-1965 *WhAm 4*
Thomas, Arnon Daniels 1898-1966 *WhAm 4*
Thomas, Arthur Lloyd 1851-1924 *ApCAB Sup,* *NatCAB 1, NatCAB 45, TwCBDA,* *WhAm 1*
Thomas, Augustus 1857-1934 *AmBi, DcAmB,* *WhAm 1*
Thomas, Augustus 1859-1934 *NatCAB 14,* *TwCBDA*
Thomas, Augustus Orloff 1863-1935 *BiDAmEd,* *WhAm 1*
Thomas, Austin 1843-1922 *NatCAB 6*
Thomas, Beaumont 1910-1972 *WhAm 6*
Thomas, Benjamin Franklin 1813-1878 *ApCAB,* *BiDrAC, Drake, NatCAB 5, WhAm H*
Thomas, Benjamin Franklin 1850-1911 *WhAm 1*
Thomas, Benjamin Franklin 1853-1923 *NatCAB 20*
Thomas, Benjamin Platt 1902-1956 *NatCAB 47,* *WhAm 3*
Thomas, Benjamin S 1813- *BiAUS*
Thomas, Bernard P 1918- *IIBEAAW*
Thomas, Bryan M 1836-1905 *WhAm 1*
Thomas, Calvin 1854-1919 *BiDAmEd, DcAmB,* *NatCAB 16, NatCAB 29, TwCBDA,* *WhAm 1*
Thomas, Carl Clapp 1872-1938 *WhAm 1*
Thomas, Carrie M *WomWWA 14*
Thomas, Cecil Benton 1894-1956 *WhAm 3*
Thomas, Cecil Vincent 1892-1947 *NatCAB 36,* *WhAm 2*
Thomas, Charles *NewYHSD*
Thomas, Charles 1800?-1878 *ApCAB, Drake*
Thomas, Charles Doty 1861-1930 *NatCAB 26*
Thomas, Charles H *NewYHSD*
Thomas, Charles Holt 1850-1920 *NatCAB 19*
Thomas, Charles Lee 1881- *WhoColR*
Thomas, Charles Mitchell 1846-1908 *WhAm 1*
Thomas, Charles Monroe 1849-1916 *NatCAB 3,* *WhAm 1*
Thomas, Charles Preston 1864-1927 *WhAm 1*
Thomas, Charles Randolph 1827-1891 *BiAUS,* *BiDrAC, WhAm H, WhAmP*
Thomas, Charles Randolph 1861-1931 *BiDrAC,* *TwCBDA, WhAmP*
Thomas, Charles Randolph, Jr. 1888-1931 *WhAm 2*
Thomas, Charles Roberts 1891-1968 *NatCAB 54*
Thomas, Charles Samuel 1868-1945 *NatCAB 34*
Thomas, Charles Spalding 1849-1934 *AmBi,* *BiDrAC, DcAmB, NatCAB 13, TwCBDA,* *WhAm 1, WhAmP*
Thomas, Charles Swain 1868-1943 *WhAm 2*
Thomas, Chauncey 1850-1919 *WhAm 1*
Thomas, Christian Friedrich Theodore 1835-1905 *AmBi, DcAmB, WebAB*
Thomas, Christopher Yancy 1818-1879 *BiAUS,* *BiDrAC, WhAm H*
Thomas, Clarence Proctor 1889-1967 *NatCAB 54*
Thomas, Cleveland Anthoine 1912-1967 *WhAm 4, WhAm 5*
Thomas, Clifford Charles 1901-1958 *NatCAB 46*
Thomas, Clifford Ward 1902-1959 *NatCAB 47*

Thomas, Clinton Geraldys 1882-1950 *NatCAB 38*
Thomas, Columbus Eugene 1869- *WhAm 5*
Thomas, Cornelia Frances *WhAm H*
Thomas, Cullen Fleming 1868-1938 *WhAm 1*
Thomas, Cyrus 1825-1910 *AmBi, ApCAB,* *DcAmB, NatCAB 13, TwCBDA,* *WhAm 1*
Thomas, D B *BiAUS*
Thomas, Daniel W *NewYHSD*
Thomas, Darwin W 1894-1954 *WhAm 3*
Thomas, David 1762-1831 *BiAUS, BiDrAC,* *DcAmB, WhAm H, WhAmP*
Thomas, David 1776-1859 *ApCAB, Drake*
Thomas, David 1794-1882 *ApCAB, DcAmB,* *NatCAB 3, WhAm H*
Thomas, David Owen 1852-1925 *NatCAB 20*
Thomas, David W 1841- *NatCAB 2*
Thomas, David Wesley 1886-1958 *NatCAB 48*
Thomas, David Winton 1901-1972 *WhAm 5*
Thomas, David Yancey 1872-1943 *WhAm 2*
Thomas, Delphine Femanier 1890-1963 *WhAm 4*
Thomas, Douglas 1879-1933 *WhAm 1*
Thomas, Douglas Hamilton 1847-1919 *NatCAB 1, WhAm 1*
Thomas, Douglas Hamilton, Jr. 1872-1915 *WhAm 1*
Thomas, Dylan Marlais 1914-1953 *McGEWB,* *WhAm HA, WhAm 4*
Thomas, E A 1838-1890 *WhAm H*
Thomas, Earl Charles 1891-1948 *NatCAB 37*
Thomas, Earl Denison 1847-1921 *WhAm 1*
Thomas, Earl Tilman 1906-1970 *NatCAB 56*
Thomas, Eben Briggs d1919 *WhAm 1*
Thomas, Ebenezer Smith 1775-1845 *Drake,* *NatCAB 5, WhAm H*
Thomas, Ebenezer Smith 1780-1844 *ApCAB*
Thomas, Edith Matilda 1854-1925 *AmBi,* *AmWom, ApCAB, ApCAB X, DcAmB,* *NatCAB 9, NotAW, TwCBDA,* *WhAm 1, WomWWA 14*
Thomas, Edith Prince *WomWWA 14*
Thomas, Edward A *BiAUS*
Thomas, Edward Beers 1848- *WhAm 4*
Thomas, Edward Harper 1811-1869 *ApCAB*
Thomas, Edward Lloyd 1825-1898 *BiDConf*
Thomas, Edward Moseley 1879-1951 *WhAm 3*
Thomas, Edward Russell 1875-1926 *NatCAB 20*
Thomas, Edward Trudeau 1901-1973 *WhAm 6*
Thomas, Edwin Rittenhouse 1870-1944 *NatCAB 34*
Thomas, Edwin Ross 1850-1936 *NatCAB 28*
Thomas, Edwin Stark 1872-1952 *NatCAB 38,* *WhAm 5*
Thomas, Elbert Duncan 1883-1953 *BiDrAC,* *DcAmB S5, NatCAB 41, WhAm 3,* *WhAmP*
Thomas, Elisabeth Finley d1955 *WhAm 3*
Thomas, Elise Oliver Minton 1880- *WhoColR*
Thomas, Elisha Smith 1834-1895 *ApCAB,* *NatCAB 12, TwCBDA*
Thomas, Elizabeth M 1857- *WomWWA 14*
Thomas, Elizabeth M Utley 1880- *WomWWA 14*
Thomas, Ellen L 1853- *WomWWA 14*
Thomas, Elmer 1876-1965 *WhAm 4*
Thomas, Elwyn 1894-1971 *WhAm 5*
Thomas, Emma Mattoon 1857- *WomWWA 14*
Thomas, Esther Bradley *WomWWA 14*
Thomas, Esther Willits 1874- *WomWWA 14*
Thomas, Eugene Stuart 1900-1970 *WhAm 5*
Thomas, Eva Jane Swain 1853- *WomWWA 14*
Thomas, Evan 1853-1947 *NatCAB 36*
Thomas, Fanny Edgar *AmWom*
Thomas, Fay Mathew 1890-1974 *WhAm 6*
Thomas, Flavel Shurtleff 1852-1922 *WhAm 1*
Thomas, Francis 1799-1876 *ApCAB, BiAUS,* *BiDrAC, DcAmB, Drake, NatCAB 9,* *TwCBDA, WhAm H, WhAmP*
Thomas, Francis D 1896- *WhAm 3*
Thomas, Frank Andrew 1897-1955 *NatCAB 45*
Thomas, Frank Emmett 1895-1969 *WhAm 5*
Thomas, Frank H 1899-1952 *WhAm 3*
Thomas, Frank Morehead 1868-1921 *WhAm 1*
Thomas, Frank Waters 1878-1970 *BiDAmEd,* *WhAm 6*

Thomas, Franklin 1885-1952 *NatCAB 42*
Thomas, Franklin 1885-1953 *WhAm 3*
Thomas, Freddie Levy 1918-1974 *WhAm 6*
Thomas, Frederic Chichester 1858- *ApCAB X*
Thomas, Frederick Bradley 1921- *WhAm 5*
Thomas, Frederick Lionel 1892-1969 *WhAm 5*
Thomas, Frederick William 1806-1866 *DcAmB,* *WhAm H*
Thomas, Frederick William 1808-1866 *Drake*
Thomas, Frederick William 1811-1866 *ApCAB*
Thomas, Gabriel *ApCAB, Drake*
Thomas, George *NewYHSD*
Thomas, Sir George d1775 *Drake*
Thomas, Sir George 1695?-1774 *DcAmB,* *WhAm H*
Thomas, Sir George 1705?-1775 *ApCAB,* *NatCAB 2*
Thomas, George 1815?- *NewYHSD*
Thomas, George 1866-1951 *NatCAB 41*
Thomas, George Carroll 1881-1957 *NatCAB 47*
Thomas, George Clifford 1839-1909 *DcAmB,* *NatCAB 15, NatCAB 36*
Thomas, George Clifford, Jr. 1873-1932 *NatCAB 36*
Thomas, George H 1824-1868 *NewYHSD*
Thomas, George Henry 1816-1870 *AmBi,* *ApCAB, DcAmB, Drake, EncAB,* *McGEWB, NatCAB 4, TwCBDA,* *WebAB, WebAMB, WhAm H, WhoMilH*
Thomas, George Henry 1876-1966 *WhAm 4*
Thomas, George Herbert 1872-1935 *WhAm 1*
Thomas, George Jefferson 1878- *WhoColR*
Thomas, George Morgan 1828-1914 *BiDrAC,* *WhAm 4*
Thomas, George Washington, Jr. 1875- *WhoColR*
Thomas, Gerald Burison 1927-1972 *WhAm 5*
Thomas, Glen Herbert 1889-1962 *WhAm 4*
Thomas, Griffith 1820-1878 *WhAm H*
Thomas, Gus 1863-1951 *WhAm 3*
Thomas, Guy Alfred 1875-1946 *NatCAB 35*
Thomas, Guy Alfred 1879-1946 *WhAm 2*
Thomas, Harold Rudolph 1907-1974 *WhAm 6*
Thomas, Harry Randolph 1878-1965 *NatCAB 53*
Thomas, Henry *NewYHSD*
Thomas, Henry Atwell 1834-1904 *NewYHSD*
Thomas, Henry Bascom 1875-1958 *WhAm 3*
Thomas, Henry Franklin 1843-1912 *BiDrAC*
Thomas, Henry Goddard 1837-1897 *ApCAB,* *NatCAB 12, TwCBDA*
Thomas, Henry M 1861-1925 *NatCAB 20,* *WhAm 1*
Thomas, Henry Malcolm, Jr. 1891-1966 *NatCAB 51, WhAm 4*
Thomas, Henry Theodore 1844-1929 *NatCAB 22*
Thomas, Henry Wilton 1861- *WhAm 4*
Thomas, Herbert Alfred 1879-1956 *NatCAB 48*
Thomas, Herbert Henry 1875-1954 *NatCAB 44*
Thomas, Hiram Washington 1832-1909 *NatCAB 9, WhAm 1*
Thomas, Horace Davis 1905-1967 *WhAm 4*
Thomas, Horace Tucker 1874-1947 *NatCAB 38*
Thomas, Howard Dudley 1870- *WhAm 5*
Thomas, Hugh Hamshaw 1885-1962 *DcScB*
Thomas, Hugh Owens 1834-1891 *BiHiMed*
Thomas, I L *WhoColR A*
Thomas, Isaac 1735-1819 *ApCAB*
Thomas, Isaac 1784-1859 *BiAUS, BiDrAC,* *WhAm H*
Thomas, Isaac Biddle 1872-1920 *NatCAB 22*
Thomas, Isabella Ross 1856- *WomWWA 14*
Thomas, Isaiah 1749-1831 *AmBi, ApCAB,* *ApCAB X, DcAmB, Drake, NatCAB 6,* *NewYHSD, TwCBDA, WebAB*
Thomas, Isaiah 1750-1831 *WhAm H*
Thomas, J J *NewYHSD*
Thomas, J R 1830-1896 *Drake*
Thomas, J R *see also* Thomas, John Rogers
Thomas, Jackson Mash 1903-1963 *WhAm 4*
Thomas, James 1785-1845 *ApCAB, BiAUS,* *Drake, NatCAB 9, TwCBDA*
Thomas, James 1843- *WhAm 4*
Thomas, James Adrian, Jr. 1870-1918 *NatCAB 17*
Thomas, James Augustus 1862-1940 *WhAm 1*
Thomas, James Bishop 1871-1946 *WhAm 3*

Thomas, James C 1863- *WhoColR*
Thomas, James Houston 1808-1876 *BiAUS, BiDConf, BiDrAC, WhAm H*
Thomas, James John 1867- *WhAm 5*
Thomas, James Murphy 1877-1956 *NatCAB 47*
Thomas, James R 1812- *NatCAB 1*
Thomas, James Rufus 1863-1925 *NatCAB 20*
Thomas, James Shelby 1879- *WhAm 6*
Thomas, Jane *ApCAB*
Thomas, Jesse Burgess d1850 *BiAUS*
Thomas, Jesse Burgess 1777-1850 *NatCAB 11*
Thomas, Jesse Burgess 1777-1853 *ApCAB, BiDrAC, DcAmB, TwCBDA, WhAm H*
Thomas, Jesse Burgess 1806-1850 *TwCBDA*
Thomas, Jesse Burgess 1832-1915 *ApCAB, DcAmB, NatCAB 17, TwCBDA, WhAm 1*
Thomas, Jessie Beattie *WhAm 1*
Thomas, John *NewYHSD*
Thomas, John 1724-1776 *AmBi, DcAmB, WebAMB, WhAm H*
Thomas, John 1725-1776 *ApCAB, Drake, NatCAB 1, TwCBDA*
Thomas, John 1805-1871 *ApCAB, NatCAB 4*
Thomas, John 1829- *NatCAB 3*
Thomas, John 1874-1945 *BiDrAC, NatCAB 40, WhAmP*
Thomas, John Addison 1811-1858 *ApCAB, BiAUS*
Thomas, John Charles 1889-1960 *NatCAB 45, WhAm 4*
Thomas, John Chew 1764-1836 *BiAUS, BiDrAC, WhAm H*
Thomas, John Hampden 1848-1904 *WhAm 1*
Thomas, John Henry 1869-1931 *NatCAB 27*
Thomas, John Ira 1882-1940 *NatCAB 30*
Thomas, John J 1813- *BiDConf*
Thomas, John Jacobs 1810-1895 *AmBi, ApCAB, DcAmB, Drake, EncAAH, WhAm H*
Thomas, John Jenks 1861-1935 *WhAm 1*
Thomas, John Lewis, Jr. 1835-1893 *BiAUS, BiDrAC, WhAm H*
Thomas, John Lloyd 1857-1925 *WhAm 1*
Thomas, John Martin 1869-1952 *NatCAB 14, WhAm 3*
Thomas, John Michael 1875-1951 *NatCAB 44*
Thomas, John Montague 1874-1951 *WhAm 3*
Thomas, John Parnell 1895-1970 *BiDrAC, WhAm 5*
Thomas, John Peyre, Jr. 1857-1946 *WhAm 2*
Thomas, John Robert 1846-1914 *BiDrAC, TwCBDA, WhAm 1, WhAmP*
Thomas, John Rochester 1848-1901 *ApCAB Sup, NatCAB 9, WhAm 1*
Thomas, John Rogers 1829-1896 *NatCAB 8*
Thomas, John Rogers 1830-1896 *ApCAB*
Thomas, John Rogers *see also* Thomas, J R
Thomas, John S Ladd 1875-1959 *WhAm 3*
Thomas, John W 1874-1945 *WhAm 2*
Thomas, John Webster 1880-1951 *ApCAB X, NatCAB 43, WhAm 3*
Thomas, John William Elmer 1876-1965 *BiDrAC, EncAAH, WhAmP*
Thomas, John Wilson 1830-1906 *DcAmB*
Thomas, John Wilson, Jr. 1856-1913 *WhAm 1*
Thomas, Joseph 1811-1891 *AmBi, ApCAB, DcAmB, Drake, NatCAB 11, WhAm H*
Thomas, Joseph Brown 1879-1955 *WhAm 3*
Thomas, Joseph Dio 1843-1902 *NatCAB 6*
Thomas, Joseph F *NewYHSD*
Thomas, Joseph Loren 1873- *WhAm 5*
Thomas, Joseph Peter 1893-1948 *WhAm 2*
Thomas, Julius Albert 1896-1973 *NatCAB 57*
Thomas, Julius Graham 1886-1960 *NatCAB 48*
Thomas, Kirby d1931 *WhAm 1*
Thomas, Lee Emmett 1866- *WhAm 4*
Thomas, Leon Evan 1877-1958 *NatCAB 46*
Thomas, Leonard Moorhead 1878-1937 *NatCAB 36*
Thomas, Lera Millard 1900- *BiDrAC*
Thomas, Lester Chalmers 1900-1963 *NatCAB 50*
Thomas, Lewis F 1886-1950 *WhAm 3*
Thomas, Lewis Foulke 1815-1868 *ApCAB*
Thomas, Lewis Victor 1914-1965 *WhAm 4*
Thomas, Lillian Beynon 1874- *WomWWA 14*
Thomas, Lorenzo 1804-1875 *AmBi, ApCAB,*

BiAUS, DcAmB, Drake, NatCAB 11, TwCBDA, WebAMB, WhAm H
Thomas, Lot 1843-1905 *BiDrAC, WhAm 1*
Thomas, Lowell Jackson 1892- *WebAB*
Thomas, Lucien Irving 1876-1942 *WhAm 2*
Thomas, Lucy Stackhouse 1880- *WomWWA 14*
Thomas, Ludlow 1824-1849 *ApCAB X*
Thomas, M Carey 1857-1935 *NatCAB 13, WhAm 1*
Thomas, M Louise d1947 *WhAm 2*
Thomas, M Louise Palmer 1822- *NatCAB 13*
Thomas, M Louise Palmer 1830- *ApCAB*
Thomas, Majorie Helen 1885- *IIBEAAW*
Thomas, Marian Putnam MacQuinn 1877- *WomWWA 14*
Thomas, Marie *NewYHSD*
Thomas, Marshall 1867-1952 *NatCAB 40*
Thomas, Martha Carey 1857-1935 *AmBi, BiDAmEd, DcAmB S1, McGEWB, NotAW, TwCBDA, WebAB, WomWWA 14*
Thomas, Martha McCannon 1823- *ApCAB*
Thomas, Martin Henry 1865-1935 *WhAm 1*
Thomas, Mary Ann 1841- *AmWom*
Thomas, Mary Etta 1873- *WhoColR*
Thomas, Mary Frame Myers 1816-1888 *NotAW, TwCBDA*
Thomas, Mary Pettus 1857- *WomWWA 14*
Thomas, Mary VonErden 1825- *ApCAB*
Thomas, Mason Blanchard 1866-1912 *WhAm 1*
Thomas, Matt Grainger 1884-1952 *NatCAB 42*
Thomas, Maurice J 1902-1967 *WhAm 4A*
Thomas, Michael *NewYHSD*
Thomas, Morgan Hunsicker 1876-1961 *NatCAB 50*
Thomas, Nancy J Helm 1840- *WomWWA 14*
Thomas, Nathaniel Seymour 1867-1937 *NatCAB 31, WhAm 1*
Thomas, Norman Matoon 1884-1968 *DcAmReB*
Thomas, Norman Mattoon 1884-1968 *EncAB, McGEWB, NatCAB 55, WebAB, WhAm 5*
Thomas, Ormsby Brunson 1832-1904 *BiDrAC*
Thomas, P C 1906-1968 *WhAm 5*
Thomas, Paul Henwood 1926-1972 *WhAm 6*
Thomas, Paul Kirk Middlebrook 1875-1962 *WhAm 4*
Thomas, Percy Champion 1874-1951 *NatCAB 43, WhAm 5*
Thomas, Percy H 1872-1957 *WhAm 3*
Thomas, Philemon d1847 *BiAUS*
Thomas, Philemon 1763-1847 *BiDrAC, WhAm H*
Thomas, Philemon 1764-1847 *ApCAB, Drake, NatCAB 13*
Thomas, Philip Evan 1776-1861 *ApCAB, DcAmB, NatCAB 18, WhAm H*
Thomas, Philip Francis 1810-1890 *AmBi, ApCAB, BiAUS, BiDrUSE, DcAmB, Drake, NatCAB 5, TwCBDA, WhAm H, WhAmP*
Thomas, Phillip Francis 1810-1890 *BiDrAC*
Thomas, Phillips 1883-1958 *NatCAB 49*
Thomas, Ralph Llewellyn 1887-1965 *NatCAB 51, WhAm 4*
Thomas, Ralph W 1840-1920 *WhAm 1*
Thomas, Reuen 1840-1907 *NatCAB 13, WhAm 1*
Thomas, Richard 1744-1832 *BiAUS, BiDrAC, WhAm H*
Thomas, Richard Curd Pope 1872-1939 *WhAm 1*
Thomas, Richard Henry 1854-1904 *DcAmB, WhAm 1*
Thomas, Richard Simms 1866-1923 *NatCAB 22*
Thomas, Robert Bailey 1766-1846 *DcAmB, EncAAH, WhAm H*
Thomas, Robert Baily 1766-1846 *AmBi, ApCAB, Drake*
Thomas, Robert David 1909-1973 *WhAm 6*
Thomas, Robert Ellis 1920-1972 *WhAm 5*
Thomas, Robert Harper 1834- *ApCAB*
Thomas, Robert Horatio, Jr. 1861-1916 *NatCAB 17*
Thomas, Robert Mck, Jr. d1973 *WhAm 6*
Thomas, Robert P 1821-1864 *NatCAB 5*
Thomas, Robert Young, Jr. 1855-1925 *BiDrAC,*

WhAm 1, WhAmP
Thomas, Rolla L 1857-1932 *WhAm 1*
Thomas, Rolland Jay 1900-1967 *NatCAB 53, WhAm 4*
Thomas, Rose Fay 1852- *WomWWA 14*
Thomas, Roy Zachariah 1897- *WhAm 6*
Thomas, Royal David 1882-1960 *NatCAB 47*
Thomas, Samuel 1827- *NatCAB 3*
Thomas, Samuel 1840-1903 *NatCAB 25, WhAm 1*
Thomas, Samuel 1927- *WhAm 3*
Thomas, Samuel Bell 1871- *ApCAB X*
Thomas, Samuel Hinds 1852-1930 *NatCAB 25*
Thomas, Samuel Morgan 1903-1973 *WhAm 5*
Thomas, Sarah Grace Seely 1870- *WomWWA 14*
Thomas, Seth 1785-1859 *AmBi, ApCAB X, DcAmB, NatCAB 3, WebAB, WhAm H*
Thomas, Seth 1816-1888 *ApCAB, ApCAB X, NatCAB 3*
Thomas, Seth Edward 1841-1910 *ApCAB X, NatCAB 26*
Thomas, Seth Edward, Jr. 1876-1932 *NatCAB 53, WhAm 1*
Thomas, Sidney Gilchrist 1850-1885 *DcScB*
Thomas, Sophia N *WomWWA 14*
Thomas, Stanley Judson 1889-1960 *NatCAB 47, WhAm 4*
Thomas, Stanley Powers Rowland 1879- *WhAm 6*
Thomas, Stephen 1809- *ApCAB*
Thomas, Stephen Seymour 1868-1956 *IIBEAAW, WhAm 3*
Thomas, T Rowland 1874-1923 *NatCAB 20, WhAm 1*
Thomas, Thaddeus Peter 1867- *WhAm 4*
Thomas, Theodore 1835-1905 *AmBi, ApCAB, DcAmB, McGEWB, NatCAB 2, TwCBDA, WebAB, WhAm 1*
Thomas, Theodore Gaillard 1831-1903 *AmBi, ApCAB, DcAmB, Drake, NatCAB 3, NatCAB 26, WhAm 1*
Thomas, Thomas 1755-1824 *ApCAB, Drake*
Thomas, Thomas Ebenezer 1812-1875 *NatCAB 2, TwCBDA*
Thomas, Thomas M 1867- *WhoColR*
Thomas, Victor Philip 1863- *WhoColR*
Thomas, W Ray 1887-1957 *NatCAB 48*
Thomas, Walter Horstmann 1876-1948 *WhAm 2*
Thomas, Warren H 1837- *WhAm 4*
Thomas, Washington Butcher 1857-1929 *NatCAB 27, WhAm 1*
Thomas, Widgery 1901-1972 *NatCAB 57*
Thomas, Wilbur Kelsey 1882-1953 *WhAm 3*
Thomas, William 1853-1936 *WhAm 1, WhAm 1C*
Thomas, William Aubrey 1866-1951 *BiDrAC, WhAm 3, WhAmP*
Thomas, William David 1880-1936 *BiDrAC, NatCAB 27, WhAm 1*
Thomas, William Davy 1844- *WhAm 4*
Thomas, William Grasett 1822-1910 *NatCAB 25*
Thomas, William Henry Griffith 1861-1924 *NatCAB 39, WhAm 1*
Thomas, William Hill 1895-1962 *NatCAB 51*
Thomas, William Holcombe 1867-1945 *NatCAB 37, WhAm 2*
Thomas, William Isaac 1863-1947 *DcAmB S4, McGEWB, NatCAB 44, WhAm 2*
Thomas, William Matthews Merrick 1878-1951 *NatCAB 40*
Thomas, William Nathaniel 1892-1971 *WhAm 5*
Thomas, William Preston 1887-1962 *WhAm 4*
Thomas, William S 1858- *WhAm 4*
Thomas, William Silas 1826- *NatCAB 10*
Thomas, William Strobel 1868-1947 *NatCAB 38*
Thomas, William Sturgis 1871-1941 *WhAm 1*
Thomas, William Widgery 1839-1927 *ApCAB, DcAmB, NatCAB 2, TwCBDA, WhAm 1*
Thomas, Zoe Carey *WomWWA 14*
Thomasius, Christian 1655-1728 *McGEWB*
Thomason, George 1872-1947 *NatCAB 35*
Thomason, Harry Denny 1858- *NatCAB 7*

Thomason, Hugh French 1826- *BiDConf*
Thomason, John William, Jr. 1893-1944
  IlBEAAW, NatCAB 33, WhAm 2
Thomason, Robert Ewing 1879-1973 *BiDrAC,*
  WhAm 6
Thomason, Samuel Emory 1883-1944 *WhAm 2*
Thomasson, William Poindexter 1797-1882
  BiAUS, BiDrAC, WhAm H
Thomaz, Alvaro *DcScB*
Thomen, August Stephen Astor 1892-1943
  NatCAB 32, WhAm 2
Thomen, Otto John 1873-1952 *NatCAB 41*
Thomes, William Henry 1824-1895 *ApCAB,*
  DcAmB, WhAm H
Thompkins, Leonard Joseph 1934-1974
  WhAm 6
Thompson *NewYHSD*
Thompson, Miss A C *NewYHSD*
Thompson, Abraham G d1851 *Drake*
Thompson, Adaline Emerson 1859- *AmWom*
Thompson, Adele E 1849- *WomWWA 14*
Thompson, Albert 1853- *ApCAB*
Thompson, Albert Clifton 1842-1910 *BiDrAC,*
  TwCBDA, WhAm 1
Thompson, Albert F 1888-1965 *WhAm 4*
Thompson, Albert Riley 1879-1947 *NatCAB 36*
Thompson, Alexander Marshall 1872-1958
  WhAm 3
Thompson, Alexander Ramsay 1792-1837 *Drake*
Thompson, Alexander Ramsay 1794-1837
  ApCAB
Thompson, Alexander Ramsay 1822- *ApCAB*
Thompson, Alexis Wellington 1850-1923
  NatCAB 25
Thompson, Alfred Augustus 1852-1920
  NatCAB 18
Thompson, Alfred Charles 1898-1963 *WhAm 4*
Thompson, Alfred Clark 1867-1937 *WhAm 1*
Thompson, Alfred Wordsworth 1840-1896
  ApCAB, DcAmB, NewYHSD, WhAm H
Thompson, Allison John 1865-1939 *NatCAB 30*
Thompson, Almerin D *NewYHSD*
Thompson, Almon Harris 1839-1906 *WhAm 1*
Thompson, Amos Burt 1871-1965 *WhAm 4*
Thompson, Andrew Anderson 1880-1938
  NatCAB 32
Thompson, Lady Annie E *WomWWA 14*
Thompson, Arad 1786-1843 *NewYHSD*
Thompson, Arthur Scott 1876-1949 *WhAm 3*
Thompson, Arthur Webster 1875-1930
  ApCAB X, DcAmB, NatCAB 22,
  WhAm 1
Thompson, Augustus Charles 1812-1901 *ApCAB,*
  Drake, WhAm 1
Thompson, Basil 1892-1924 *WhAm 1*
Thompson, Beach 1864-1914 *NatCAB 27*
Thompson, Beach 1865-1914 *WhAm 1*
Thompson, Benjamin 1753-1814 *AmBi,*
  DcAmB, DcScB, Drake, EncAB,
  NewYHSD, TwCBDA, WebAB,
  WhAm H
Thompson, Benjamin 1798-1852 *BiAUS,*
  BiDrAC, WhAm H
Thompson, Benjamin F 1842-1884 *REnAW*
Thompson, C Bertrand 1882-1969 *WhAm 5*
Thompson, C Seymour 1879-1954 *WhAm 3*
Thompson, Calvin Miles 1866-1944 *WhAm 2*
Thompson, Carl Dean 1870-1949 *WhAm 2*
Thompson, Carmi Alderman 1870-1942
  NatCAB 37, WhAm 2
Thompson, Cecil Vincent Raymond 1906-1951
  WhAm 3
Thompson, Celeste DeLaureal 1839-
  WomWWA 14
Thompson, Cephas 1775-1856 *ApCAB,*
  NewYHSD
Thompson, Cephas Giovanni 1809-1888 *ApCAB,*
  BnEnAmA, DcAmB, Drake, NewYHSD,
  WhAm H
Thompson, Charles A *NewYHSD*
Thompson, Charles C B 1786-1832 *ApCAB,*
  Drake
Thompson, Charles Edwin 1870-1933 *WhAm 1*
Thompson, Charles Francis 1864-1937
  NatCAB 27
Thompson, Charles Fullington 1882-1954
  WhAm 3
Thompson, Charles H 1870- *WhAm 5*

Thompson, Charles Impey 1899-1958 *WhAm 3*
Thompson, Charles James 1862-1932 *BiDrAC,*
  WhAm 1, WhAmP
Thompson, Charles Lemeul 1839-1924
  DcAmReB
Thompson, Charles Lemuel 1839-1924 *ApCAB,*
  NatCAB 10, WhAm 1
Thompson, Charles Manfred 1877-1963
  WhAm 4
Thompson, Charles Miner 1864-1941 *WhAm 2*
Thompson, Charles Nebeker 1861-1949
  NatCAB 37, WhAm 3
Thompson, Charles Oliver 1836-1885 *ApCAB,*
  BiDAmEd, DcAmB, TwCBDA, WhAm H
Thompson, Charles Perkins 1827-1894 *BiAUS,*
  BiDrAC, WhAm H
Thompson, Charles Thaddeus d1925 *WhAm 1*
Thompson, Charles W *NewYHSD*
Thompson, Charles William 1851- *WhAm 1*
Thompson, Charles Willis 1871-1946 *WhAm 2*
Thompson, Charles Winston 1860-1904 *BiDrAC,*
  WhAm 1
Thompson, Charles Woody 1902-1962 *WhAm 4*
Thompson, Chester Charles 1893-1971 *BiDrAC,*
  WhAm 5
Thompson, Clara 1893-1958 *WhAm 3*
Thompson, Clarence Elmer 1888-1946
  NatCAB 35, WhAm 2
Thompson, Clark Wallace 1896- *BiDrAC,*
  WhAmP
Thompson, Clary 1912-1961 *WhAm 4*
Thompson, Clem Oren 1888- *WhAm 3*
Thompson, Clifford Griffeth 1882-1965
  WhAm 4
Thompson, Cyrus 1855-1930 *WhAm 1*
Thompson, D George d1870? *NewYHSD*
Thompson, Daniel Greenleaf 1850-1897 *AmBi,*
  ApCAB Sup, NatCAB 8
Thompson, Daniel Pierce 1795-1868 *AmBi,*
  ApCAB, DcAmB, Drake, NatCAB 6,
  TwCBDA, WhAm H
Thompson, Daniel Varney 1867-1932 *WhAm 1*
Thompson, D'Arcy Wentworth 1860-1948
  DcScB
Thompson, David 1770-1857 *AmBi, ApCAB,*
  DcAmB, McGEWB, REnAW, WebAB,
  WhAm H
Thompson, David 1798-1871 *NatCAB 18*
Thompson, David 1836- *ApCAB*
Thompson, David Alphaeus 1872-1935 *WhAm 1*
Thompson, David Decamp 1852-1908
  NatCAB 13, WhAm 1
Thompson, David Eugene 1854-1942
  NatCAB 14, WhAm 2
Thompson, David Newton 1859- *WhAm 4*
Thompson, David P 1834-1901 *DcAmB,*
  NatCAB 7, TwCBDA, WhAm 1
Thompson, David Pearson 1880-1930
  NatCAB 25
Thompson, Denman 1833-1911 *AmBi, DcAmB,*
  NatCAB 8, WhAm 1
Thompson, Dolly S *NewYHSD*
Thompson, Dorothy 1894-1961 *EncAB,*
  WebAB, WhAm 4
Thompson, Dwinel French 1846-1919 *WhAm 1*
Thompson, E E 1898-1968 *WhAm 5*
Thompson, Earl Avery 1891-1967 *NatCAB 53*
Thompson, Eben Francis 1859-1939 *NatCAB 31,*
  WhAm 1
Thompson, Edgar Camden 1880-1953
  NatCAB 44
Thompson, Edward 1843-1923 *NatCAB 19*
Thompson, Edward Archibald 1884-1959
  WhAm 3
Thompson, Edward Herbert 1856-1935
  DcAmB S1
Thompson, Edward Herbert 1860-1935
  WhAm 1
Thompson, Edward Murdock 1856-1941
  NatCAB 30
Thompson, Edward R 1808?-1879 *ApCAB*
Thompson, Edwin 1809-1888 *ApCAB,*
  NatCAB 2
Thompson, Effie Freeman *WomWWA 14*
Thompson, Egbert 1820-1881 *ApCAB,*
  TwCBDA
Thompson, Egbert 1822-1881 *DcAmB, Drake,*
  WhAm H

Thompson, Elbert-Nevius Sebring 1877-1948
  WhAm 2
Thompson, Eliza J 1813- *AmWom*
Thompson, Eliza Jane Trimble 1816-1905
  NotAW, WhAm 3
Thompson, Elizabeth 1821-1899 *ApCAB,*
  NatCAB 5, TwCBDA
Thompson, Elizabeth DeBow 1881-
  WomWWA 14
Thompson, Elizabeth Jane 1858-
  WomWWA 14
Thompson, Elizabeth McArthur d1956
  WhAm 3
Thompson, Elizabeth Rowell 1821-1899
  AmWom, NotAW
Thompson, Elizabeth W Ballard *WomWWA 14*
Thompson, Elizabeth Worts 1883-
  WomWWA 14
Thompson, Eloise Bibb 1878- *WhoColR*
Thompson, Ernest 1867-1945 *WhAm 2*
Thompson, Ernest Evan Seton 1860-
  ApCAB Sup
Thompson, Ernest Othmer 1892-1966 *WhAm 4*
Thompson, Ernest Seton *WhAm 2*
Thompson, Erwin W 1859- *WhAm 4*
Thompson, Estelle Clark 1862- *WomWWA 14*
Thompson, Eva Griffith 1842- *AmWom*
Thompson, Eva M Long 1862- *WomWWA 14*
Thompson, Fayette Lathrop 1862-1912
  WhAm 1
Thompson, Floyd Eugene 1887-1960
  NatCAB 53, WhAm 4
Thompson, Fountain Land 1854-1942 *BiDrAC,*
  NatCAB 31
Thompson, Francis 1838-1905 *NewYHSD*
Thompson, Francis Edward 1864-1939
  NatCAB 29
Thompson, Frank, Jr. 1918- *BiDrAC*
Thompson, Frank Abner 1880-1958 *WhAm 3*
Thompson, Frank Charles 1858-1940
  NatCAB 30
Thompson, Frank Dallas 1907-1969 *NatCAB 57*
Thompson, Frank Dutton 1876-1940 *WhAm 1*
Thompson, Frank Edward 1875-1943
  NatCAB 40, NatCAB 47, WhAm 2
Thompson, Frank Forrester 1870-1927 *WhAm 1*
Thompson, Frank Harrison 1859-1929
  ApCAB X
Thompson, Frank Marian 1860-1926
  NatCAB 20, WhAm 1
Thompson, Frank Victor 1874-1921 *WhAm 1*
Thompson, Fred Lawrence 1872- *WhAm 5*
Thompson, Count Frederic Diodati 1850-1906
  WhAm 1
Thompson, Frederic Lincoln 1869-1935
  WhAm 1
Thompson, Frederic Williams 1872-1919
  NatCAB 19
Thompson, Frederick Diodati 1847-1906
  NatCAB 18
Thompson, Frederick F 1836-1899 *NatCAB 6*
Thompson, Frederick Gregg 1898-1968
  WhAm 5
Thompson, Frederick Henry 1844-1939
  WhAm 1
Thompson, Frederick Ingate 1875-1952
  WhAm 3
Thompson, Frederick Oliver 1883-1953
  NatCAB 44
Thompson, George 1804-1878 *ApCAB*
Thompson, George 1840-1917 *NatCAB 3,*
  WhAm 1
Thompson, George 1857-1925 *WhAm 1*
Thompson, George B 1862-1930 *WhAm 1*
Thompson, George David 1899-1965
  NatCAB 52, WhAm 4
Thompson, George Farnsworth 1875-1959
  NatCAB 49
Thompson, George Hocken 1876-1953
  NatCAB 44
Thompson, George Jarvis 1886-1957
  NatCAB 45, WhAm 4
Thompson, George Kramer 1859- *NatCAB 6*
Thompson, George Smith 1840-1913
  NatCAB 15
Thompson, George Victor 1918-1968 *WhAm 5*
Thompson, George W 1806-1888 *BiAUS,*
  Drake

Thompson, George Wallace 1850-1921 *WhAm 1*
Thompson, George Washington 1806-1888
ApCAB
Thompson, George Western 1806-1888 *BiDrAC,*
WhAm H
Thompson, George Williston 1888-1969
WhAm 5
Thompson, Gertrude Falligant 1885-
WomWWA 14
Thompson, Gilbert 1839-1909 *WhAm 1*
Thompson, Gordon Grahame 1881-1957
NatCAB 44
Thompson, Gustave Whyte 1865-1942
NatCAB 17, WhAm 2
Thompson, Guy A 1875-1958 *WhAm 3*
Thompson, Hal Charles 1897-1964 *WhAm 4*
Thompson, Harold Alvin 1883-1948 *NatCAB 38*
Thompson, Harriet Pomeroy 1860-
WomWWA 14
Thompson, Harry Arthur 1867-1936 *WhAm 1*
Thompson, Harry Cecil 1897-1960 *NatCAB 49*
Thompson, Harry Ives 1840-1906 *NewYHSD*
Thompson, Harry LeRoy 1890-1953 *WhAm 3*
Thompson, Heber Samuel 1840-1911 *WhAm 1*
Thompson, Hedge 1780-1828 *BiAUS, BiDrAC,*
WhAm H
Thompson, Helen Dunbar *WomWWA 14*
Thompson, Helen Elizabeth 1857-1936
WhAm 1, WomWWA 14
Thompson, Helen Mulford d1974 *WhAm 6*
Thompson, Henry *NewYHSD*
Thompson, Henry 1849-1931 *NatCAB 24*
Thompson, Henry Adams 1837-1920 *TwCBDA,*
WhAm 1
Thompson, Henry Burling 1857-1935 *ApCAB X,*
NatCAB 26, WhAm 1
Thompson, Henry Dallas 1864-1927 *WhAm 1*
Thompson, Henry Lawrence 1871-1939
NatCAB 31
Thompson, Henry Mayo 1861-1947 *NatCAB 38*
Thompson, Henry Smith 1873-1944 *NatCAB 34*
Thompson, Hettie Linsley 1857- *WomWWA 14*
Thompson, Holland 1873-1940 *WhAm 1*
Thompson, Hollis Ring 1898-1944 *WhAm 2*
Thompson, Hugh Lindsay 1863-1949 *WhAm 2*
Thompson, Hugh Miller 1830-1902 *ApCAB,*
DcAmB, NatCAB 9, TwCBDA,
WhAm 1
Thompson, Hugh Smith 1836-1904 *ApCAB Sup,*
BiDAmEd, DcAmB, NatCAB 12,
NatCAB 24, TwCBDA, WhAm 1
Thompson, Huston 1875-1966 *NatCAB 52,*
WhAm 4
Thompson, Ira Fay 1877-1953 *NatCAB 43*
Thompson, Ira Francis 1885-1937 *WhAm 1*
Thompson, J David 1873-1932 *NatCAB 23*
Thompson, J Eric S 1898-1975 *WhAm 6*
Thompson, J Lewis 1875-1938 *NatCAB 34*
Thompson, J Pierce 1887-1947 *NatCAB 38*
Thompson, Jacob 1810-1885 *AmBi, ApCAB,*
BiAUS, BiDConf, BiDrAC, BiDrUSE,
DcAmB, Drake, NatCAB 5, REnAW,
TwCBDA, WhAm H, WhAmP
Thompson, James *BiAUS, NewYHSD*
Thompson, James 1806-1874 *ApCAB, BiAUS,*
BiDrAC, NatCAB 4, TwCBDA,
WhAm H
Thompson, James 1828-1880 *NatCAB 29*
Thompson, James Edwin 1863-1927 *WhAm 1*
Thompson, James F 1900-1956 *WhAm 3*
Thompson, James Goodhart 1911-1974
WhAm 6
Thompson, James Kidd 1874- *WhAm 5*
Thompson, James Livingston 1832- *WhAm 4*
Thompson, James Maurice 1844-1901 *DcAmB*
Thompson, James Ralph 1897-1968 *NatCAB 54,*
WhAm 5
Thompson, James Robert 1865-1922
NatCAB 20
Thompson, James Stratton 1899-1951 *WhAm 3*
Thompson, James Voorhees 1878-1952 *WhAm 3*
Thompson, James Walter 1847-1928 *ApCAB X,*
NatCAB 15, NatCAB 21, WebAB
Thompson, James Westfall 1869-1941 *WhAm 1*
Thompson, James Wilfred 1847-1927
NatCAB 21
Thompson, Jared D *NewYHSD*
Thompson, Jean M 1865- *WomWWA 14*

Thompson, Jean M 1867- *WhAm 5*
Thompson, Jeremiah 1784-1835 *DcAmB,*
WhAm H
Thompson, Jerome B 1814-1886 *ApCAB,*
BnEnAmA, DcAmB, IIBEAAW,
NewYHSD, WhAm H
Thompson, Joel 1760-1843 *BiAUS, BiDrAC,*
WhAm H
Thompson, John *NewYHSD*
Thompson, John d1789 *Drake*
Thompson, John d1944 *WhAm 2*
Thompson, John 1749-1823 *BiAUS, BiDrAC,*
WhAm H
Thompson, John 1776-1799 *DcAmB*
Thompson, John 1777-1799 *ApCAB*
Thompson, John 1777-1852 *TwCBDA*
Thompson, John 1800-1891 *NatCAB 6*
Thompson, John 1802-1891 *DcAmB,*
WhAm H
Thompson, John 1809-1890 *BiAUS, BiDrAC,*
WhAm H
Thompson, John 1873-1958 *WhAm 3*
Thompson, John *see also* Thomson, John
Thompson, John Allen 1878-1938 *NatCAB 31*
Thompson, John Bert 1878- *WhAm 6*
Thompson, John Bodine 1830-1907 *DcAmB*
Thompson, John Burton 1810-1874 *ApCAB,*
BiAUS, BiDrAC, NatCAB 12, TwCBDA,
WhAm H, WhAmP
Thompson, John C *NewYHSD*
Thompson, John Cameron 1872-1934 *WhAm 1*
Thompson, John E W 1855- *NatCAB 13*
Thompson, John Fairfield 1881-1968 *WhAm 5*
Thompson, John Fawdrey, Jr. 1919-1972
WhAm 5
Thompson, John Forbes 1920-1965 *NatCAB 52*
Thompson, John Gilbert 1862-1940 *WhAm 2*
Thompson, John Graves 1906-1962 *NatCAB 51,*
WhAm 4
Thompson, John Kerwin 1892-1975 *WhAm 6*
Thompson, John Lay 1869- *WhoColR*
Thompson, John Leverett 1835-1888 *ApCAB*
Thompson, John Maurice 1911-1958
NatCAB 47
Thompson, John McCandless 1829-1903
BiDrAC
Thompson, John Milton 1842-1922 *WhAm 1*
Thompson, John Q 1862-1913 *WhAm 1*
Thompson, John R 1865-1927 *NatCAB 21,*
WhAm 1
Thompson, John Reuben 1823-1873 *AmBi,*
ApCAB, BiDConf, DcAmB, Drake,
NatCAB 6, NatCAB 11, TwCBDA,
WhAm H
Thompson, John Rhey 1852-1904 *NatCAB 22*
Thompson, Sir John Sparrow David 1844-
ApCAB
Thompson, John Taliaferro 1860-1940
ApCAB X, NatCAB 16, NatCAB 29,
WebAMB, WhAm 1
Thompson, John Vaughan 1779-1847 *DcScB*
Thompson, John Wesley 1843- *NatCAB 2*
Thompson, John Winter 1867-1951 *WhAm 3*
Thompson, Jonathan 1773-1846 *ApCAB,*
NatCAB 18
Thompson, Joseph Addison 1860-1957 *WhAm 3*
Thompson, Joseph Bryan 1871-1918 *WhAm 1*
Thompson, Joseph Bryan 1871-1919 *BiDrAC*
Thompson, Joseph Hamilton 1900-1968
NatCAB 54, WhAm 5
Thompson, Joseph Henry 1871-1928
NatCAB 21
Thompson, Joseph Osgood 1863-1953 *WhAm 3*
Thompson, Joseph Parrish 1819-1879 *AmBi,*
ApCAB, DcAmB, Drake, NatCAB 10,
TwCBDA, WhAm H
Thompson, Joseph Peter 1818-1894 *ApCAB,*
TwCBDA
Thompson, Joseph Sexton 1878-1970
NatCAB 56, WhAm 5
Thompson, Joseph Whitaker 1861-1946
WhAm 2
Thompson, Josiah VanKirk 1854-1933 *DcAmB,*
NatCAB 14, WhAm 1
Thompson, Julia Prat 1862- *WomWWA 14*
Thompson, Kenworthy James 1881-1933
NatCAB 29

Thompson, Laforrest Holman 1848-1900
WhAm 1
Thompson, LaMarcus Adna 1848-1919
ApCAB X, NatCAB 19
Thompson, Landreth Worthington 1862-
NatCAB 3
Thompson, Launt 1833-1894 *AmBi, ApCAB,*
BnEnAmA, DcAmB, Drake, NatCAB 8,
NewYHSD, TwCBDA, WhAm H
Thompson, Laura Shafer 1876- *WomWWA 14*
Thompson, Lawrance Roger 1906-1973
WhAm 5
Thompson, Leonard Newton 1888-1967
NatCAB 54
Thompson, Leslie Prince 1880-1963 *WhAm 4*
Thompson, Leslie Stuart 1901-1959 *NatCAB 49*
Thompson, Leverett 1869-1921 *NatCAB 36*
Thompson, Lewis d1972 *WhAm 5*
Thompson, Lewis Eugene 1894-1968 *WhAm 5*
Thompson, Lewis O 1839-1887 *ApCAB,*
TwCBDA
Thompson, Lewis Ryers 1883-1954 *WhAm 3*
Thompson, Lily Wilkinson 1867-
WomWWA 14
Thompson, Lindsay Levant 1888-1956
NatCAB 44
Thompson, Llewellyn E, Jr. 1904-1972 *WhAm 5*
Thompson, Lucas P d1866 *BiAUS*
Thompson, Lucie Malone *WomWWA 14*
Thompson, M Gladys d1975 *WhAm 6*
Thompson, Malvina Cynthia 1893-1953
DcAmB S5
Thompson, Marcellus Hagans 1883-1939
ApCAB X, NatCAB 29
Thompson, Margaret Rice *WomWWA 14*
Thompson, Marietta 1803- *NewYHSD*
Thompson, Mark 1739-1803 *BiAUS*
Thompson, Mark *see also* Thomson, Mark
Thompson, Marshall Putnam 1869- *WhAm 5*
Thompson, Martin E 1786?-1877 *DcAmB,*
NewYHSD, WhAm H
Thompson, Marvin Russell 1905-1969
NatCAB 55
Thompson, Mary Dartt 1842- *WomWWA 14*
Thompson, Mary Harris 1829-1895 *BiCAW,*
NatCAB 13, NotAW
Thompson, Mary Sophia 1859- *AmWom*
Thompson, Mary Thaw 1856- *WomWWA 14*
Thompson, Maurice 1844-1901 *ApCAB,*
DcAmB, NatCAB 11, TwCBDA,
WhAm 1
Thompson, Maurice Wycliffe 1878-1954
WhAm 3
Thompson, Melville Withington 1871-1936
WhAm 1
Thompson, Merle Dow 1879-1970 *WhAm 5*
Thompson, Merriwether Jeff 1826-1876 *ApCAB,*
TwCBDA
Thompson, Mills 1875-1944 *WhAm 2*
Thompson, Milo Milton 1894-1945 *WhAm 2*
Thompson, Milton 1876-1931 *NatCAB 22*
Thompson, Milton John 1904-1971 *WhAm 5*
Thompson, Mortimer Neal 1831-1875 *AmBi*
Thompson, Myra 1860- *WomWWA 14*
Thompson, Neill Archie 1872-1922 *NatCAB 19*
Thompson, Noah D 1874- *WhoColR*
Thompson, Oscar Lee 1887-1945 *DcAmB S3,*
WhAm 2
Thompson, Oswald 1809-1866 *BiAUS*
Thompson, Owen Pierce 1852- *WhAm 4*
Thompson, Paul d1942 *WhAm 2*
Thompson, Paul Jennings 1890-1964 *WhAm 4*
Thompson, Percy Wallace 1858- *WhAm 4*
Thompson, Philip 1789-1836 *BiAUS, BiDrAC,*
WhAm H
Thompson, Philip Burton, Jr. 1845-1909 *BiDrAC*
Thompson, Philip Jacobs 1872-1952 *NatCAB 41*
Thompson, Philip Rootes 1766-1837 *BiAUS,*
BiDrAC, WhAm H
Thompson, Ralph Leroy 1873- *WhAm 5*
Thompson, Ralph Seymour 1847- *WhAm 4*
Thompson, Reuben Cyril Hill 1878-1951
NatCAB 48, WhAm 3
Thompson, Richard Edward 1848-1914
NatCAB 16
Thompson, Richard W 1865- *WhoColR*
Thompson, Richard Wigginton 1809-1900 *AmBi,*
ApCAB, BiAUS, BiDrAC, BiDrUSE,

DcAmB, NatCAB 3, TwCBDA,
WhAm 1
Thompson, Robert Andrew 1869-1941 *WhAm 1*
Thompson, Robert Augustine 1805-1876 *BiAUS,*
BiDrAC, WhAm H
Thompson, Robert Bruce 1906-1970 *WhAm 5*
Thompson, Robert Clark 1883-1929
NatCAB 23
Thompson, Robert Ellis 1844-1924 *AmBi,*
ApCAB, BiDAmEd, DcAmB,
NatCAB 10, TwCBDA, WhAm 1
Thompson, Robert Elmo 1895-1966 *WhAm 4*
Thompson, Robert Foster *WhAm 5*
Thompson, Robert Harvey 1847-1935 *WhAm 1*
Thompson, Robert Hezekiah Beattie 1884-1942
NatCAB 34
Thompson, Robert John 1865-1931 *WhAm 1*
Thompson, Robert LeRoy 1873-1937 *WhAm 3*
Thompson, Robert Long 1908-1958 *WhAm 4*
Thompson, Robert Means 1849-1930
DcAmB S1, NatCAB 3, NatCAB 15,
NatCAB 34, WhAm 1
Thompson, Robert S d1969 *WhAm 5*
Thompson, Roby Calvin 1898-1960 *WhAm 4*
Thompson, Ronald Burdick 1907-1975 *WhAm 6*
Thompson, Roy Leland 1891-1955 *WhAm 3*
Thompson, Rupert Campbell, Jr. 1905-1970
WhAm 5
Thompson, Russell Irvin 1898-1957 *NatCAB 43,*
WhAm 3
Thompson, Ruth 1887-1970 *BiDrAC*
Thompson, Sam Evans 1871-1956 *NatCAB 45,*
WhAm 5
Thompson, Sam H 1863-1956 *WhAm 3*
Thompson, Samuel 1783-1846 *ApCAB X*
Thompson, Samuel Hunter 1876-1952 *WhAm 3*
Thompson, Samuel Huston 1842- *WhAm 4*
Thompson, Samuel Rankin 1833-1896
BiDAmEd, DcAmB, NatCAB 7,
WhAm H
Thompson, Samuel Wesley 1825- *NatCAB 7*
Thompson, Sanford Eleazer 1867-1949 *WhAm 2*
Thompson, Seymour Dwight 1842-1904 *DcAmB,*
NatCAB 19
Thompson, Silvanus Phillips 1851-1916 *DcScB*
Thompson, Slason 1849-1935 *DcAmB S1,*
WhAm 1
Thompson, Smith 1767-1843 *BiAUS, Drake*
Thompson, Smith 1768-1843 *AmBi, ApCAB,*
BiDrUSE, DcAmB, NatCAB 6,
TwCBDA, WebAB, WhAm H
Thompson, Standish Fletcher 1925- *BiDrAC*
Thompson, Stith 1885-1976 *WhAm 6*
Thompson, Theo Ashton 1916-1965 *BiDrAC,*
WhAmP
Thompson, Theodore Strong 1842-1915
WhAm 1
Thompson, Theos Jardin 1918-1970 *WhAm 5*
Thompson, Thomas 1775?-1852 *NewYHSD*
Thompson, Thomas 1798-1869 *ApCAB*
Thompson, Thomas Barney 1876-1967
WhAm 4A
Thompson, Thomas Clarkson 1860-1938
WhAm 1
Thompson, Thomas Edward 1864- *WhAm 2*
Thompson, Thomas Gordon 1888-1961
WhAm 4
Thompson, Thomas Larkin 1838-1898 *BiDrAC,*
DcAmB, NatCAB 8, WhAm H
Thompson, Thomas Payne 1860-1924 *WhAm 1*
Thompson, Thomas W 1766-1820 *BiAUS,*
NatCAB 3, NatCAB 11
Thompson, Thomas Weston 1766-1821 *ApCAB,*
BiDrAC, TwCBDA, WhAm H
Thompson, Thor Arthur 1891-1957 *WhAm 3*
Thompson, Uldrick 1849-1942 *NatCAB 32*
Thompson, Vance 1863-1925 *NatCAB 20,*
TwCBDA, WhAm 1
Thompson, Vernon Percy 1898-1961
NatCAB 53
Thompson, Vinton Floyd 1898-1963 *NatCAB 50*
Thompson, W Stuart 1890-1968 *WhAm 5*
Thompson, Waddy 1769-1845 *TwCBDA*
Thompson, Waddy 1798-1868 *ApCAB, BiAUS,*
BiDrAC, DcAmB, Drake, NatCAB 3,
TwCBDA, WhAm H
Thompson, Waddy 1867-1939 *WhAm 1*

Thompson, Wade Vanzel 1895-1952
NatCAB 40
Thompson, Wallace 1883-1936 *WhAm 1,*
WhAm 1C
Thompson, Wallace 1896-1952 *NatCAB 46*
Thompson, Warren 1888-1962 *NatCAB 50*
Thompson, Wiley 1781-1835 *BiAUS,*
DcAmB, WhAm H, WhAmP
Thompson, Will Henry 1848- *NatCAB 11*
Thompson, Will L 1847-1909 *WhAm 1*
Thompson, Will Lamartine 1847-1909 *AmBi,*
DcAmB
Thompson, Will Lambertine 1847-1909
NatCAB 21
Thompson, Will Scroggs 1904-1959 *WhAm 4*
Thompson, Willard Chandler 1890-1954
WhAm 3
Thompson, Willard Owen 1899-1954 *WhAm 3*
Thompson, William *NewYHSD*
Thompson, William d1781 *Drake*
Thompson, William 1725?-1781 *ApCAB,*
NatCAB 1, TwCBDA
Thompson, William 1736-1781 *DcAmB,*
WebAMB, WhAm H
Thompson, William 1806-1889 *TwCBDA*
Thompson, William 1813-1897 *ApCAB Sup,*
BiAUS, BiDrAC, WhAm H
Thompson, William 1821-1865 *TwCBDA*
Thompson, William Barlum 1860- *WhAm 4*
Thompson, William Benbow 1890-1965
NatCAB 51
Thompson, William Bess 1865-1928 *WhAm 1*
Thompson, William Blaine, Jr. 1917-1970
WhAm 5
Thompson, William Boyce 1869-1930 *AmBi,*
ApCAB X, DcAmB, NatCAB 15,
NatCAB 22, WhAm 1
Thompson, William Dwight 1867-1943
NatCAB 34
Thompson, William Francis 1888-1965
NatCAB 52, WhAm 4
Thompson, William George 1830-1911 *BiDrAC*
Thompson, William Gilman 1856-1927 *DcAmB,*
WhAm 1
Thompson, William Goodrich 1864-1935
WhAm 1
Thompson, William H 1845?- *NatCAB 12*
Thompson, William Hale 1867-1944 *DcAmB S3*
Thompson, William Hale 1868-1944
NatCAB 44
Thompson, William Hale 1869-1944 *WhAm 2*
Thompson, William Henry 1853-1937 *BiDrAC,*
NatCAB 30, WhAm 1
Thompson, William Herbert 1878-1945
NatCAB 35, WhAm 2
Thompson, William Howard 1871-1928 *BiDrAC,*
NatCAB 15, WhAm 1
Thompson, William John 1771-1845 *NewYHSD*
Thompson, William Joseph 1864-1944 *WhAm 2*
Thompson, William Leland 1871-1957 *WhAm 3*
Thompson, William M *NewYHSD*
Thompson, William McLean 1904-1966
WhAm 4
Thompson, William N 1881- *WhAm 6*
Thompson, William Naylor 1842- *NatCAB 5*
Thompson, William Ormonde d1942 *WhAm 2*
Thompson, William Orvil 1870-1956
NatCAB 42
Thompson, William Oxley 1855-1933 *ApCAB X,*
BiDAmEd, DcAmB, NatCAB 12,
NatCAB 24, TwCBDA, WhAm 1
Thompson, William Reed 1845-1906
NatCAB 29
Thompson, William Rootes 1855-1947
NatCAB 39
Thompson, William Taliaferro 1886-1964
NatCAB 52, WhAm 4
Thompson, William Tappan 1812-1882 *AmBi,*
ApCAB, DcAmB, NatCAB 9, TwCBDA,
WhAm H
Thompson, William Thomas 1861-1951
WhAm 3
Thompson, William Townsend 1860- *WhAm 1*
Thompson, William W 1870- *WhAm 5*
Thompson, Wordsworth 1840-1896 *AmBi,*
NatCAB 7, NatCAB 8, TwCBDA
Thompson, Zadoc 1796-1856 *ApCAB*
Thompson, Zadoc 1796-1860 *NatCAB 6*

Thompson, Zadock 1796-1856 *DcAmB, Drake,*
WhAm H
Thoms, Adah B Samuels 1863?-1943 *NotAW*
Thoms, Craig Sharpe 1860-1945 *WhAm 2*
Thoms, Effie Walker 1866- *WomWWA 14*
Thoms, Herbert 1885-1972 *WhAm 5*
Thoms, William Edward 1870-1939 *WhAm 2*
Thoms, William M 1852- *WhAm 4*
Thomsen, Christian Jurgensen 1788-1865
AsBiEn, DcScB
Thomsen, Hans Peter Jorgen Julius 1826-1909
AsBiEn, DcScB
Thomsen, Hugo Adelberto 1850-1918
ApCAB X
Thomsen, Mark Lawrence 1872-1934 *WhAm 1*
Thomsen, Rasmus 1875-1948 *WhAm 2*
Thomson *NewYHSD*
Thomson, Alexander 1788-1848 *ApCAB,*
ApCAB X, BiAUS, BiDrAC,
NatCAB 12, WhAm H
Thomson, Alexander 1879-1939 *NatCAB 45,*
WhAm 1
Thomson, Alexander 1899-1949 *NatCAB 39*
Thomson, Archibald Wilson 1871-1928
NatCAB 23
Thomson, Arthur Conover 1871-1946
NatCAB 33, WhAm 2
Thomson, Benjamin 1640-1714 *NatCAB 9*
Thomson, Campbell *NewYHSD*
Thomson, Charles 1729-1824 *AmBi, ApCAB,*
BiAUS, DcAmB, Drake, NatCAB 2,
TwCBDA, WhAm H
Thomson, Charles Alexander 1893-1961
WhAm 4
Thomson, Charles Goff 1883-1937 *WhAm 1*
Thomson, Charles Marsh 1877-1943 *BiDrAC,*
WhAm 2
Thomson, Charles West 1798-1879 *ApCAB,*
Drake
Thomson, Sir Charles Wyville 1830-1882
AsBiEn, DcScB
Thomson, Chester Glasgow 1833-1911
NatCAB 27
Thomson, David 1893-1953 *NatCAB 45*
Thomson, David Sidney 1895-1958 *WhAm 3*
Thomson, Douglas Gillespie 1885-1936
NatCAB 27
Thomson, Douglas Hotchkiss 1885-1926
NatCAB 31
Thomson, Earl Henry 1902-1970 *NatCAB 55*
Thomson, Edgar Steiner 1871-1931 *NatCAB 22,*
WhAm 1, WhAm 1C
Thomson, Edward 1810-1870 *ApCAB, DcAmB,*
Drake, NatCAB 4, WhAm H
Thomson, Edward 1848- *WhAm 1*
Thomson, Edward Herrmann 1887-1967
NatCAB 53, WhAm 4
Thomson, Edward William 1849-1924 *DcAmB,*
WhAm 4
Thomson, Edwin Keith 1919-1960 *BiDrAC,*
WhAmP
Thomson, Elihu 1853-1937 *AmBi, ApCAB,*
DcAmB S2, DcScB, NatCAB 10,
NatCAB 27, TwCBDA, WebAB,
WhAm 1
Thomson, F DuPont 1869-1959 *NatCAB 49*
Thomson, Frances Howell Marston
WomWWA 14
Thomson, Francis Andrew 1879-1951
NatCAB 40, WhAm 3
Thomson, Frank 1841-1899 *ApCAB, DcAmB,*
NatCAB 13, TwCBDA, WhAm H
Thomson, Frank Graham 1874-1941
NatCAB 32
Thomson, Frederick Bordine 1809-1847 *ApCAB*
Thomson, Sir George Paget 1892-1975 *AsBiEn,*
McGEWB, WhAm 6
Thomson, Sir Godfrey Hilton 1881-1955
WhAm 3
Thomson, Henry Czar Merwin 1863-1926
NatCAB 29, WhAm 1
Thomson, Herbert Gordon 1870-1928
NatCAB 25
Thomson, J Faison 1888-1960 *NatCAB 49*
Thomson, J Oscar 1885-1956 *NatCAB 46*
Thomson, James *NewYHSD*
Thomson, James 1700-1748 *McGEWB*
Thomson, James Bates 1803-1883 *BiDAmEd*

Thomson, James Bates 1808-1883 *ApCAB*
Thomson, James Ellus M 1889-1962
NatCAB 48, WhAm 4
Thomson, James Lewis 1877-1966 *WhAm 4*
Thomson, James McIlhany 1878-1959 *WhAm 3*
Thomson, James P *NewYHSD*
Thomson, James Sutherland 1892-1972
WhAm 5
Thomson, James William 1836-1914 *WhAm 1*
Thomson, James William 1863-1938 *WhAm 1*
Thomson, Jane E 1885- *WomWWA 14*
Thomson, John *NewYHSD*
Thomson, John d1916 *WhAm 1*
Thomson, John 1776-1799 *DcAmB, WhAm H*
Thomson, John 1777-1852 *BiAUS*
Thomson, John 1780-1852 *BiDrAC, WhAm H,*
WhAmP
Thomson, John 1853-1926 *DcAmB*
Thomson, John *see also* Thompson, John
Thomson, John Cameron 1890-1966 *WhAm 4A*
Thomson, John Edgar 1808-1874 *ApCAB,*
DcAmB, EncAB, NatCAB 13, TwCBDA,
WhAm H
Thomson, John Renshaw 1800-1862 *ApCAB,*
BiAUS, BiDrAC, NatCAB 12, TwCBDA,
WhAm H
Thomson, Sir Joseph John 1856-1940 *AsBiEn,*
DcScB, McGEWB
Thomson, Keith 1919-1960 *WhAm 4*
Thomson, Lemon 1822- *NatCAB 4*
Thomson, Logan Gamble 1884-1946
NatCAB 49, WhAm 2
Thomson, Louisa A *WomWWA 14*
Thomson, Mabel Whitney 1877- *WomWWA 14*
Thomson, Malcolm d1961 *NatCAB 49*
Thomson, Mark 1739-1803 *BiDrAC, WhAm H,*
WhAmP
Thomson, Mark *see also* Thompson, Mark
Thomson, Mortimer Neal 1831-1875 *AmBi,*
DcAmB, WhAm H
Thomson, Mortimer Neal 1832-1875 *ApCAB,*
TwCBDA
Thomson, O R Howard 1873-1943 *NatCAB 32,*
WhAm 2
Thomson, Paul Swainston 1861-1932
NatCAB 23
Thomson, Peter Gibson 1851-1931 *WhAm 1*
Thomson, Philip Livingston 1879-1969 *WhAm 5*
Thomson, Procter 1919-1975 *WhAm 6*
Thomson, Reginald Heber 1856-1949 *WhAm 3*
Thomson, Robert Lyle 1855- *NatCAB 11*
Thomson, Robert William 1822-1873 *AsBiEn*
Thomson, Roy B 1881-1955 *WhAm 3*
Thomson, Samuel 1769-1843 *ApCAB, DcAmB,*
Drake, NatCAB 6, WhAm H
Thomson, Samuel Harrison 1813-1882 *ApCAB,*
NatCAB 10, WhAm H
Thomson, Samuel Harrison 1895-1975 *WhAm 6*
Thomson, Sarah *NewYHSD*
Thomson, T Kennard 1864-1952 *NatCAB 14,*
WhAm 4
Thomson, Thaddeus Austin 1853-1927
NatCAB 37, WhAm 1
Thomson, Thomas 1773-1852 *DcScB*
Thomson, Tom 1877-1917 *IIBEAAW,*
McGEWB
Thomson, Vernon Wallace 1905- *BiDrAC*
Thomson, Virgil Garnett 1896- *EncAAH,*
EncAB, McGEWB, WebAB
Thomson, W H Seward 1856- *WhAm 1*
Thomson, Walter Smith 1873-1947 *NatCAB 36*
Thomson, William 1726?-1796 *NatCAB 9*
Thomson, William 1727-1796 *ApCAB, DcAmB,*
Drake, WhAm H
Thomson, Sir William 1824-1907 *DcScB*
Thomson, William 1833-1907 *ApCAB,*
WhAm 1
Thomson, Sir William *see also* Kelvin, William
Thomson, Baron
Thomson, William Archibald, Jr. 1905-1974
WhAm 6
Thomson, William H d1946 *WhAm 2*
Thomson, William Hanna 1833-1918
NatCAB 23, WhAm 1
Thomson, William Judah 1841-1909 *WhAm 1*
Thomson, William McClure 1806-1894 *ApCAB,*
DcAmB, Drake, NatCAB 11, WhAm H
Thomson, William Nobel 1904-1975 *WhAm 6*

Thomte, Karl Adams 1909-1965 *NatCAB 51*
Thorame, Jean Pierre *NewYHSD*
Thorborg, Kerstin 1906-1970 *WhAm 5*
Thorburn, Grant 1773-1863 *ApCAB, DcAmB,*
Drake, NatCAB 7, TwCBDA, WhAm H
Thorburn, James 1830- *ApCAB*
Thorburn, John 1830- *ApCAB*
Thorburn, Thomas Rankin 1888-1962 *WhAm 4*
Thoreau, Henry David 1817-1862 *AmBi,*
ApCAB, DcAmB, Drake, EncAAH,
EncAB, McGEWB, NatCAB 2, REnAW,
TwCBDA, WebAB, WhAm H
Thoreau, Sophia 1819-1876 *NewYHSD*
Thorek, Max 1880-1960 *NatCAB 48,*
WhAm 3
Thorez, Maurice 1900-1964 *WhAm 4*
Thorfinn 980?-1016? *ApCAB, WhAm H*
Thorfinn, Karlsefni 980?-1016? *WebAB*
Thorgrimson, Oliver Bernard 1874-1960
NatCAB 53
Thorgrimson, Oliver Bernhard 1874-1960
WhAm 5
Thorington, James 1816-1887 *BiAUS, BiDrAC*
Thorington, James 1858-1944 *WhAm 2*
Thorington, William Sewell 1847-1915
NatCAB 38, WhAm 1
Thorkelson, Halsten Joseph 1875- *WhAm 5*
Thorkelson, Jacob 1876-1945 *BiDrAC,*
WhAm 5
Thorley, Charles 1854-1923 *NatCAB 19*
Thorn, Frank Manly 1836- *ApCAB,*
NatCAB 13, WhAm 4
Thorn, Henry Clare 1887-1962 *NatCAB 49*
Thorn, J C 1835-1898 *NewYHSD*
Thorn, James 1882- *WhAm 3*
Thorn, Linton *NewYHSD*
Thorn, Samuel Springate 1831-1916
NatCAB 17
Thornal, Benjamin Campbell 1908-1970
WhAm 5
Thornber, John James 1872- *WhAm 5*
Thornberry, William Homer 1909- *BiDrAC,*
WhAmP
Thornborough, Sir Edward 1758-1834 *ApCAB,*
Drake
Thornburg, Charles Lewis 1859-1944
NatCAB 38, WhAm 2
Thornburg, Delmar Leon 1881- *WhAm 6*
Thornburg, Zenas Charles 1872-1925 *WhAm 1*
Thornburgh, George 1847-1923 *WhAm 1*
Thornburgh, Jacob Montgomery 1837-1890
BiAUS, BiDrAC, WhAm H
Thornburgh, Thomas T 1843?-1879 *ApCAB*
Thorndike, Alden Augustus 1862-1925
NatCAB 33
Thorndike, Ashley Horace 1871-1933 *AmBi,*
DcAmB, NatCAB 51, WhAm 1
Thorndike, Augustus 1863-1940 *NatCAB 30,*
WhAm 4
Thorndike, Augustus Larkin 1861-1922
ApCAB X
Thorndike, Edward Lee 1874-1949 *ApCAB X,*
BiDAmEd, DcAmB S4, EncAB,
McGEWB, NatCAB 15, NatCAB 51,
WebAB, WhAm 2
Thorndike, George Quincy 1825?- *Drake*
Thorndike, George Quincy 1825?-1886 *ApCAB*
Thorndike, George Quincy 1825?-1887?
NewYHSD
Thorndike, Israel 1755-1832 *DcAmB,*
WhAm H
Thorndike, Israel 1757-1832 *ApCAB, Drake*
Thorndike, John James 1829?- *NewYHSD*
Thorndike, John Larkin 1844-1920 *NatCAB 20*
Thorndike, Lynn 1882-1965 *NatCAB 51,*
WhAm 4
Thorndike, Paul 1863-1939 *WhAm 1*
Thorndike, Townsend William 1872-1929
WhAm 1
Thorndike, Willis Hale 1872- *WhAm 5*
Thorne, Charles Embree 1846-1936 *WhAm 1*
Thorne, Charles Hallett 1868-1948 *WhAm 2*
Thorne, Charles Robert 1814-1893 *DcAmB,*
NatCAB 10, WhAm H
Thorne, Charles Robert 1840-1883 *ApCAB,*
DcAmB, WhAm H
Thorne, Chester 1863-1927 *NatCAB 21,*
WhAm 1

Thorne, Clifford 1878-1923 *ApCAB X,*
NatCAB 17, WhAm 1
Thorne, Edwin 1861-1935 *WhAm 1*
Thorne, Elisabeth Gertrude *WomWWA 14*
Thorne, Elisabeth Griffin 1873- *WhAm 5*
Thorne, Francis Burritt 1892-1950 *NatCAB 39*
Thorne, Frederick Wisner 1871-1960 *WhAm 4*
Thorne, Gertrude L Kemmerer *BiCAW*
Thorne, Henry Vane *NewYHSD*
Thorne, James Reynolds 1909-1970 *WhAm 5*
Thorne, John *NewYHSD*
Thorne, John Calvin 1873-1941 *NatCAB 30*
Thorne, Jonathan 1801- *NatCAB 3*
Thorne, Landon Ketcham 1888-1964
NatCAB 51, WhAm 4
Thorne, Lansing Stephen 1849-1917
NatCAB 17, WhAm 4
Thorne, Linton *NewYHSD*
Thorne, Oakleigh 1866-1948 *WhAm 2*
Thorne, Philip M 1885- *WhoColR*
Thorne, Ren Atherton 1901-1969 *NatCAB 55*
Thorne, Robert Julius 1875-1955 *WhAm 3*
Thorne, Samuel 1835-1915 *NatCAB 35,*
WhAm 1
Thorne, Samuel 1874-1963 *NatCAB 51*
Thorne, Samuel Brinckerhoff 1873-1930
NatCAB 22
Thorne, Thomas Jackson 1894-1947
NatCAB 36
Thorne, Victor Corse 1871-1948 *NatCAB 48*
Thorne, William 1863-1956 *NatCAB 48,*
WhAm 3
Thorne, William Henry 1839- *WhAm 4*
Thorne, William VanSchoonhoven 1865-1920
WhAm 1
Thorner, Max 1859-1899 *NatCAB 13*
Thornhill, Arthur Horace 1895-1970
NatCAB 57, WhAm 5
Thornley, Albert Edward 1886-1965
NatCAB 51
Thornley, Albert Joseph 1862-1943 *NatCAB 32*
Thornley, Fant Hill 1909-1970 *WhAm 5*
Thornley, May Rowland 1851- *WomWWA 14*
Thornley, William Henry 1869-1926
NatCAB 21
Thornquest, William Laten 1890-1956
NatCAB 45
Thornthwaite, Charles Warren 1899-1963
WhAm 4
Thornton, Albert Edward 1853-1907
NatCAB 16
Thornton, Anthony 1748-1828 *ApCAB*
Thornton, Anthony 1814-1904 *BiAUS, BiDrAC*
Thornton, Charles S 1851- *NatCAB 10*
Thornton, Charles Stead 1910-1974 *WhAm 6*
Thornton, Dan 1911-1976 *WhAm 6*
Thornton, E Quin 1866-1945 *WhAm 2*
Thornton, Edmund Braxtan 1856-1929
NatCAB 21
Thornton, Sir Edward 1817- *ApCAB*
Thornton, Edwin William 1863-1940 *WhAm 3*
Thornton, Eliza B 1795-1854 *ApCAB*
Thornton, Eric Laurence 1878- *WhAm 6*
Thornton, George Douglass 1874-1958
NatCAB 45
Thornton, Gustavus Brown 1835-1914 *ApCAB,*
TwCBDA, WhAm H
Thornton, Hamilton 1901-1972 *WhAm 5*
Thornton, Harrison John 1894-1952 *WhAm 3*
Thornton, Harrison Robertson 1858-1893
NatCAB 30
Thornton, Henry Clarke 1851-1930 *NatCAB 31*
Thornton, Sir Henry Worth 1871-1933 *AmBi,*
WhAm 1
Thornton, James B 1801-1838 *BiAUS, Drake,*
NatCAB 13
Thornton, James Bankhead 1806-1867 *ApCAB*
Thornton, James Bankhead Taylor 1856-1918
NatCAB 18
Thornton, James Brown 1861- *WhAm 1*
Thornton, James Goodlett 1891-1958
NatCAB 48
Thornton, James Shepard 1826-1875 *ApCAB,*
TwCBDA
Thornton, James Shepard 1827-1875 *NatCAB 4*
Thornton, Jesse Earl 1886-1965 *NatCAB 52*
Thornton, Jessy Quinn 1810-1888 *ApCAB Sup,*
DcAmB, WhAm H

Thornton, John Caldwell Calhoun 1834-1887
  NatCAB 41
Thornton, John Randolph 1846-1917 *BiDrAC,*
  NatCAB 18, WhAm 1
Thornton, John Thruston 1875-1955
  NatCAB 43
Thornton, John Wingate 1818-1878 *AmBi,*
  ApCAB, DcAmB, Drake, NatCAB 10,
  TwCBDA, WhAm H
Thornton, Lawson 1884-1957 *NatCAB 46*
Thornton, Leila Cameron Austell 1861-1931
  WhAm 1
Thornton, Mary Frances Deraismes
  WomWWA 14
Thornton, Matthew 1714?-1803 *AmBi, ApCAB,*
  BiAUS, BiDrAC, DcAmB, Drake,
  NatCAB 11, TwCBDA, WhAm H,
  WhAmP
Thornton, Mildred Valley 1900?- *IIBEAAW*
Thornton, Neda Sargent 1860- *WomWWA 14*
Thornton, Patrick M 1884-1959 *WhAm 3*
Thornton, Robert Lee 1880-1964 *WhAm 4*
Thornton, Sarah Andrews *WomWWA 14*
Thornton, Seth Barton 1814-1847 *ApCAB,*
  NatCAB 4
Thornton, T Eugene d1967 *WhAm 4*
Thornton, Thomas C 1794-1860 *ApCAB*
Thornton, Walter Edwin 1878-1960 *WhAm 4*
Thornton, Walter Francis 1866- *WhAm 4*
Thornton, William d1827 *ApCAB, BiAUS,*
  NatCAB 13
Thornton, William 1759-1828 *AmBi,*
  BnEnAmA, DcAmB, NewYHSD, WebAB,
  WhAm H
Thornton, William 1761-1828 *BiHiMed*
Thornton, Sir William 1775?-1840 *ApCAB,*
  Drake
Thornton, William A 1803-1866 *ApCAB*
Thornton, William Doniphan 1870-1953
  NatCAB 41, WhAm 3
Thornton, William Mynn 1851-1935
  NatCAB 30, WhAm 1
Thornton, William Mynn, Jr. 1883-1953
  NatCAB 42
Thornton, William Taylor 1843-1916 *TwCBDA,*
  WhAm 1
Thornton, William Tobin 1899-1954
  NatCAB 43
Thornton, William Wheeler 1851-1932
  WhAm 1
Thornton, Willis Wesley 1871-1929 *NatCAB 21*
Thornwell, James Henley 1811-1862 *Drake*
Thornwell, James Henley 1812-1862 *ApCAB,*
  BiDConf, DcAmB, DcAmReB,
  NatCAB 11, TwCBDA, WhAm H
Thoron, Benjamin Warder 1897-1975 *WhAm 6*
Thoroughman, James Chanslor 1904-1972
  WhAm 6
Thorp, Charles Monroe 1863-1942 *NatCAB 32,*
  WhAm 2
Thorp, Clark Elwin 1914-1968 *WhAm 5*
Thorp, Francis Newton 1857- *NatCAB 10*
Thorp, Frank 1842-1924 *WhAm 1*
Thorp, Frank Hall 1864- *WhAm 4*
Thorp, George Gowen 1868- *WhAm 4*
Thorp, Harry Walter 1865- *WhAm 4*
Thorp, John 1784-1848 *DcAmB, WhAm H*
Thorp, Mandana Coleman 1843- *AmWom*
Thorp, Orville 1875-1928 *NatCAB 23*
Thorp, Robert Taylor 1850-1938 *BiDrAC*
Thorp, Vivian Stanley 1876- *WomWWA 14*
Thorp, Willard Brown 1868-1952 *WhAm 3*
Thorp, William *BiAUS*
Thorp, Zephaniah *NewYHSD*
Thorpe, Burton Lee 1871- *WhAm 5*
Thorpe, Clarence DeWitt 1887-1959
  NatCAB 46
Thorpe, Drew Maxwell 1898-1965 *NatCAB 53,*
  WhAm 4
Thorpe, Ervin Llewellyn 1856-1919 *WhAm 1*
Thorpe, Everett Clark 1907- *IIBEAAW*
Thorpe, Francis Newton 1857-1926 *TwCBDA,*
  WhAm 1
Thorpe, George Cyrus 1875-1936 *WhAm 1*
Thorpe, George H *NewYHSD*
Thorpe, James Francis 1888-1953 *DcAmB S5,*
  WebAB, WhAm HA, WhAm 4
Thorpe, Jim 1888-1953 *EncAB*

Thorpe, Jocelyn Field 1872-1940 *DcScB*
Thorpe, Laura Eleanor 1856- *WomWWA 14*
Thorpe, Merle 1879-1955 *WhAm 3*
Thorpe, Rose Alnora Hartwick 1850-1939
  AmWom, ApCAB, DcAmB S2,
  NatCAB 10, NotAW, TwCBDA,
  WhAm 1, WomWWA 14
Thorpe, Roy Henry 1874-1951 *BiDrAC*
Thorpe, Spence Roane 1842-1905 *WhAm 4*
Thorpe, Spencer Roane 1842-1905 *NatCAB 16*
Thorpe, T W *NewYHSD*
Thorpe, Thomas Bangs 1815-1878 *ApCAB,*
  DcAmB, Drake, EncAAH, NatCAB 6,
  NewYHSD, REnAW, TwCBDA, WebAB,
  WhAm H
Thorpe, Thomas Edward 1845-1925 *DcScB*
Thors, Olafur 1892-1965 *WhAm 4*
Thors, Thor 1903-1965 *WhAm 4*
Thorsen, David S 1916-1968 *WhAm 5*
Thorson, Arthur Thomas 1901-1952
  NatCAB 42
Thorson, Gunnar Axel Wright 1906-1971
  WhAm 5
Thorson, Nelson Thor 1881-1951 *WhAm 3*
Thorson, Thomas 1848-1915 *WhAm 1*
Thorson, Truman C 1895-1966 *WhAm 4*
Thorton, Sir Henry Worth 1871-1933 *DcAmB*
Thorvald, Ericsson d1004 *ApCAB*
Thorvaldson, Gunnar S 1901-1969 *WhAm 5*
Thorvaldsson, Eric *WhAm H*
Thouin, Andre 1747-1824 *DcScB*
Thouron, Henry Joseph 1852- *NatCAB 13*
Thrall, A N *NewYHSD*
Thrall, Homer Loveland 1802-1870 *ApCAB X,*
  NatCAB 8, TwCBDA
Thrash, Jacksie Daniel *WomWWA 14*
Thrasher, Allen Benton 1851-1927 *NatCAB 23,*
  WhAm 1
Thrasher, Frederic Milton 1892-1962 *WhAm 4*
Thrasher, George *NewYHSD*
Thrasher, John Raymond 1881-1962
  NatCAB 50
Thrasher, John Sidney 1817-1879 *ApCAB,*
  DcAmB, WhAm H
Thrasher, Max Bennett 1860-1903 *WhAm 1*
Thrasher, Paul McNeel 1886-1947 *WhAm 2*
Thrasher, Samuel Powers 1858-1925
  NatCAB 20
Threadgill, Frances Falwell *WhAm 5*
Threadgill, John 1847-1915 *NatCAB 34*
Threlkeld, Clyde Hollis 1890-1966 *WhAm 4*
Thresher, Ebenezer 1798-1886 *NatCAB 12*
Thresher, George *NewYHSD*
Thresher, Henry Gilbert 1855-1946 *NatCAB 33*
Thresher, Joseph Brainerd 1836-1920
  NatCAB 19
Throckmorton, Archibald Hall 1876-1938
  WhAm 1
Throckmorton, Charles Beaujoilais 1842-
  NatCAB 11
Throckmorton, Charlotte Edgerton Alvord 1873-
  WhAm 5, WomWWA 14
Throckmorton, Cleon 1897-1965 *WhAm 4*
Throckmorton, Dean Carlysle 1889-1938
  NatCAB 27
Throckmorton, George Kenneth 1884-1953
  WhAm 3
Throckmorton, J W 1825-1894 *BiAUS*
Throckmorton, James Webb 1825-1894 *ApCAB,*
  BiDrAC, NatCAB 9, TwCBDA,
  WhAm H, WhAmP
Throckmorton, John Ariss 1815-1891
  NatCAB 11
Throckmorton, Tom Bentley 1885-1961
  WhAm 4
Throgmorton, William P 1849-1929 *WhAm 1*
Throop, Benjamin F 1837?- *NewYHSD*
Throop, Benjamin Henry 1811-1897
  NatCAB 15
Throop, Daniel Scrope 1800- *NewYHSD*
Throop, Elizabeth Nichols *WomWWA 14*
Throop, Enos Thompson 1784-1874 *ApCAB,*
  BiAUS, BiDrAC, DcAmB, Drake,
  NatCAB 3, TwCBDA, WhAm H
Throop, Frank Dwight 1878-1943 *WhAm 2*
Throop, Mrs. George Addison *NewYHSD*
Throop, George Reeves 1882-1949 *NatCAB 38,*
  WhAm 2

Throop, John Peter VanNess 1794-1861?
  NewYHSD
Throop, Josephine Livingston 1845-
  WomWWA 14
Throop, Montgomery Hunt 1827-1892 *ApCAB,*
  DcAmB, TwCBDA, WhAm H
Throop, Orramel Hinckley 1798- *NewYHSD*
Throop, Susan Everett *WomWWA 14*
Thropp, Joseph Earlston 1847-1927 *BiDrAC,*
  WhAm 5
Thrower, James Gosling 1837-1920 *NatCAB 19*
Thruston, Buckner d1845 *TwCBDA*
Thruston, Buckner 1763?-1845 *ApCAB,*
  BiAUS, NatCAB 3
Thruston, Buckner 1764-1845 *BiDrAC,*
  WhAm H
Thruston, Charles Mynn 1738-1812 *ApCAB*
Thruston, Charles Mynn 1789-1873 *ApCAB,*
  TwCBDA
Thruston, Gates Phillips 1835- *ApCAB,*
  TwCBDA, WhAm 1
Thruston, John Buckner 1763-1845 *Drake*
Thruston, Lucy Meacham 1862- *TwCBDA,*
  WhAm 4, WomWWA 14
Thruston, Rogers Clark Ballard 1858-1946
  NatCAB 16, WhAm 2
Thucydides 460?BC-401?BC *McGEWB*
Thue, Axel 1863-1922 *DcScB*
Thuerk, Hugh Campbell 1896-1955 *NatCAB 46*
Thuku, Harry 1895-1970 *McGEWB*
Thulman, Robert Kelley 1898-1958 *NatCAB 47*
Thulstrup, Bror Thure 1848-1930 *DcAmB*
Thulstrup, Bror Thure *see also* Thure
  DeThulstrup
Thulstrup, Thure De 1848-1930 *WhAm 1*
Thum, Ernest Edgar 1884-1961 *WhAm 4*
Thum, Patty Prather d1926 *WhAm 1,*
  WomWWA 14
Thum, William 1861- *WhAm 4*
Thuman, J Herman 1880-1960 *WhAm 4*
Thumb, Tom 1832-1883 *Drake*
Thumb, Tom 1838-1883 *AmBi, DcAmB,*
  WhAm H
Thumb, Mrs. Tom 1842- *Drake, NotAW*
Thunberg, Carl Peter 1743-1828 *DcScB*
Thunberg, Thorsten Ludvig 1873-1952 *DcScB*
Thurber, Caroline *WhAm 3, WomWWA 14*
Thurber, Charles 1803-1886 *DcAmB,*
  WhAm H
Thurber, Charles Herbert 1864-1938 *TwCBDA,*
  WhAm 1
Thurber, Christopher Carson 1880-1930 *DcAmB*
Thurber, Edward Allen 1869-1930 *NatCAB 24*
Thurber, Edward Gerrish 1836-1913 *WhAm 1*
Thurber, Francis Beattie 1842-1907 *NatCAB 22*
Thurber, Francis Beatty 1842-1907 *WhAm 1*
Thurber, George 1821-1890 *AmBi, DcAmB,*
  EncAAH, WhAm H
Thurber, George W *NewYHSD*
Thurber, Harry Raymond 1895-1967 *WhAm 4A*
Thurber, Howard Ford 1869-1928 *WhAm 1*
Thurber, James Grove 1894-1961 *McGEWB*
Thurber, James Grover 1894-1961 *NatCAB 57,*
  WebAB, WhAm 4
Thurber, Jeannette Meyer 1850-1946
  DcAmB S4, NotAW
Thurber, Lester Freeman 1858-1935
  NatCAB 37
Thurber, Samuel Wood 1867-1926 *NatCAB 48*
Thurber, Sarah Wood 1840- *WomWWA 14*
Thure DeThulstrup 1848-1930 *DcAmB*
Thure DeThulstrup *see also* Thulstrup, Bror Thure
Thuret, Gustave Adolphe 1817-1875 *DcScB*
Thurlo, Frank 1828-1913 *NewYHSD*
Thurlo, Frank 1838-1913 *NatCAB 17*
Thurlow, Helen 1883- *WomWWA 14*
Thurman, Aaron 1897-1974 *WhAm 6*
Thurman, Allen G 1813-1895 *BiAUS,*
  Drake Sup
Thurman, Allen Granberry 1813-1895 *AmBi,*
  BiDrAC, DcAmB, WhAm H, WhAmP
Thurman, Allen Granbery 1813-1895 *ApCAB,*
  NatCAB 3, TwCBDA
Thurman, Allen William 1847- *WhAm 4*
Thurman, Hal C 1841-1952 *WhAm 3*
Thurman, John Richardson 1814-1854 *BiAUS,*
  BiDrAC, WhAm H

Thurman, Samuel Richard 1850-1941
NatCAB 33,   WhAm 4
Thurmon, Francis M 1898-1959 *WhAm 4*
Thurmond, Erasmus Khleber 1875- *WhAm 5*
Thurmond, James Strom 1902- *BiDrAC,*
EncAAH,   WebAB
Thurmond, John William 1862-1934
NatCAB 38,   WhAm 1
Thurnam, John 1810-1873 *DcScB*
Thurnauer, Gustav 1867-1947 *WhAm 2*
Thurneysser, Leonhard 1531-1596 *DcScB*
Thursby, Emma Cecelia 1854- *TwCBDA*
Thursby, Emma Cecelia 1854-1934 *WhAm 2*
Thursby, Emma Cecilia 1845-1931 *DcAmB,*
NatCAB 22,   NotAW
Thursby, Emma Cecilia 1857- *AmWom,*
ApCAB
Thurston, Alfred Henry 1870-1949 *NatCAB 39*
Thurston, Asa 1787-1868 *ApCAB,   Drake*
Thurston, B *NewYHSD*
Thurston, Benjamin Babock 1804-1886 *BiAUS,*
BiDrAC,   WhAm H,   WhAmP
Thurston, Benjamin Franklin 1858-1939
NatCAB 30
Thurston, Charles Baldwin 1832-1899
NatCAB 6
Thurston, Charles Rawson 1860-1929 *WhAm 1*
Thurston, David 1779-1865 *NatCAB 7*
Thurston, Edward Sampson 1876-1948
NatCAB 36,   WhAm 2
Thurston, Elizabeth *NewYHSD*
Thurston, Elizabeth Peabody 1850-
WomWWA 14
Thurston, Elliott Ladd 1895-1975 *WhAm 6*
Thurston, Ernest Lawton 1873-1958 *WhAm 3*
Thurston, Henry Winfred 1861-1946 *WhAm 2*
Thurston, Howard 1869-1936 *DcAmB S2,*
NatCAB 10,   WhAm 1
Thurston, Ida Treadwell d1918 *WhAm 1*
Thurston, Jack L 1919- *IIBEAAW*
Thurston, John Foster 1910-1974 *WhAm 6*
Thurston, John Mellen 1847-1916 *ApCAB,*
BiDrAC,   NatCAB 5,   TwCBDA,
WhAm 1
Thurston, Johnson 1858-1946 *NatCAB 35*
Thurston, Laura M 1812-1842 *ApCAB*
Thurston, Lee Mohrmann 1895-1953 *WhAm 3*
Thurston, Lloyd 1880-1970 *BiDrAC,   WhAm 5,*
WhAmP
Thurston, Lorrin Andrews 1858-1931 *DcAmB,*
WhAm 1
Thurston, Lucy Goodale 1795-1876 *ApCAB*
Thurston, Martha L Poland 1849- *AmWom*
Thurston, Neptune *NewYHSD*
Thurston, Peris G *NewYHSD*
Thurston, Robert Henry 1839-1903 *AmBi,*
ApCAB,   BiDAmEd,   DcAmB,   DcScB,
NatCAB 4,   TwCBDA,   WhAm 1
Thurston, Robert Lawton 1800-1874 *ApCAB,*
DcAmB,   WhAm H
Thurston, Roger Graves 1880- *WhoColR*
Thurston, Samuel Royal 1816-1851 *BiAUS,*
BiDrAC,   WhAm H
Thurston, Theodore Payne d1941 *WhAm 1*
Thurston, Thomas Wellington, Jr. 1866-
WhoColR
Thurston, Walter 1895-1974 *WhAm 6*
Thurston, William Ravenel 1906-1962 *WhAm 4*
Thurstone, Louis Leon 1887-1955 *BiDAmEd,*
DcAmB S5,   McGEWB,   WhAm 3
Thurwanger, Charles *NewYHSD*
Thurwanger, John *NewYHSD*
Thurwanger, Joseph *NewYHSD*
Thurwanger, Veneria 1813?- *NewYHSD*
Thurwanger, Verena 1813?- *NewYHSD*
Thurwanger, Martin T d1890 *NewYHSD*
Thury, Pierre 1650?-1699 *ApCAB*
Thutmose III 1504BC-1450BC *McGEWB*
Thwaite, Charles Edward, Jr. 1912-1964
WhAm 4
Thwaites, Reuben Gold 1853-1913 *AmBi,*
ApCAB,   DcAmB,   DcAmLiB,   NatCAB 10,
REnAW,   TwCBDA,   WebAB,   WhAm 1
Thwaites, William H *NewYHSD*
Thwaits *IIBEAAW*
Thwaits, Frederick Charles 1871-1944
NatCAB 33
Thweatt, Hiram Harold 1864- *WhoColR*

Thwing, Charles Burton 1860- *WhAm 4*
Thwing, Charles Franklin 1853-1937 *AmBi,*
ApCAB,   BiDAmEd,   DcAmB S2,
NatCAB 7,   NatCAB 27,   TwCBDA,
WhAm 1
Thwing, Edward Waite 1868- *WhAm 4*
Thwing, Eugene 1866-1936 *AmBi,   WhAm 1*
Thwing, Lucy Blakeslee 1869- *WomWWA 14*
Thwing, Mary Gardiner Dunning
WomWWA 14
Thye, Edward John 1896-1969 *BiDrAC,*
NatCAB 55,   WhAm 5
Thymaridas *DcScB*
Thyssens, Francis *NewYHSD*
Tibbals, C Austin, Jr. 1881-1948 *WhAm 2*
Tibbals, Frank Burr 1864-1931 *NatCAB 22*
Tibbals, Kate Watkins 1877- *WomWWA 14*
Tibbals, Miriam Reed 1878- *WomWWA 14*
Tibbals, Seymour Selden 1869-1949 *WhAm 3*
Tibbals, William Huntington 1848- *WhAm 4*
Tibbatts, John Wooleston 1802-1852 *BiAUS,*
BiDrAC,   WhAm H
Tibbets, Addison S 1850- *WhAm 4*
Tibbets, George W 1830?- *NewYHSD*
Tibbets, Paul 1915- *WhWW-II*
Tibbett, Lawrence Mervil 1896-1960 *WhAm 4*
Tibbetts, Delbert Marcus 1878-1952
NatCAB 49
Tibbetts, Frederick Horace 1882-1938 *WhAm 1*
Tibbetts, George *BiAUS*
Tibbetts, George W 1830?- *NewYHSD*
Tibbetts, Lawrence Mervil 1896-1960
NatCAB 48
Tibbetts, Raymond Richard 1873-1957
NatCAB 48
Tibbits, Charles Edward Dudley 1834-1924
WhAm 1
Tibbits, George 1763-1849 *ApCAB,   BiDrAC,*
NatCAB 11,   WhAm H
Tibbits, William Badger 1837-1880 *ApCAB,*
TwCBDA
Tibbles, Susette LaFlesche 1854-1903 *AmBi,*
DcAmB,   NotAW
Tibbles, Thomas Henry 1838-1928 *DcAmB,*
NatCAB 21,   WhAm 1
Tibbles, Yosette LaFlesche 1854-1903
IIBEAAW
Tibbon, Jacob Ben Machir, Ibn 1236?-1305
DcScB
Tibbon, Moses Ben Samuel, Ibn *DcScB*
Tibbott, Harve 1885-1969 *BiDrAC*
Tibbs, William Henry 1816-1906 *BiDConf*
Tibby, James Sloane 1865-1949 *NatCAB 38*
Tiberius 042BC-037AD *McGEWB*
Tibolt, Robert Price 1898-1971 *NatCAB 56,*
WhAm 5
Tibor, Lee Anthony 1893-1962 *WhAm 4*
Tice, Charles Winfield 1810-1870 *NewYHSD*
Tice, Frederick 1871-1953 *NatCAB 41,*
WhAm 3
Tichborne, Josephine Caroline Sawyer 1878-1924
WhAm 1,   WomWWA 14
Tichenor, Alfred Benton 1903-1969 *WhAm 5*
Tichenor, Austin Kent 1872- *WhAm 5*
Tichenor, Carl Martin 1887-1946 *NatCAB 35*
Tichenor, Francis Herbert 1857-1940
NatCAB 31
Tichenor, Henry McDaniel 1900-1965
NatCAB 51
Tichenor, Henry Mulford 1858-1922
NatCAB 20
Tichenor, Isaac 1754-1838 *ApCAB,   BiAUS,*
BiDrAC,   DcAmB,   Drake,   NatCAB 8,
TwCBDA,   WhAm H,   WhAmP
Tichenor, Isaac Taylor 1825-1902 *DcAmB,*
WhAm H
Ticknor, Caleb B 1805-1840 *ApCAB,   Drake*
Ticknor, Caroline d1937 *TwCBDA,   WhAm 1,*
WomWWA 14
Ticknor, Elisha 1757-1821 *ApCAB,   DcAmB,*
WhAm H
Ticknor, Francis Orray 1822-1874 *DcAmB,*
WhAm H
Ticknor, Francis Orrery 1822-1874 *NatCAB 11*
Ticknor, George 1791-1871 *AmBi,   ApCAB,*
BiDAmEd,   DcAmB,   DcAmLiB,   Drake,
NatCAB 6,   NewYHSD,   TwCBDA,
WebAB,   WhAm H

Ticknor, George 1822-1866 *ApCAB,   Drake*
Ticknor, Howard Malcom 1836-1905
NatCAB 15,   WhAm 1
Ticknor, Willard Harry 1853-1934 *NatCAB 25*
Ticknor, William Davis 1810-1864 *AmBi,*
ApCAB,   DcAmB,   Drake,   NatCAB 5,
TwCBDA,   WhAm H
Tidball, Charles Caldwell 1825- *TwCBDA*
Tidball, John Caldwell 1825-1906 *ApCAB,*
DcAmB,   Drake,   IIBEAAW,   NewYHSD,
WhAm 1
Tidball, Thomas Allen 1847- *WhAm 4*
Tidball, Volney Jean 1883-1949 *NatCAB 41*
Tidd, Marshall M *NewYHSD*
Tidemann, Karl 1878- *WhAm 6*
Tidmore, Thomas Lee 1900-1956 *NatCAB 50*
Tidoldi, John C *NewYHSD*
Tidwell, Josiah Blake 1870-1946 *WhAm 2*
Tiebout, Mademoiselle *NewYHSD*
Tiebout, Cornelius 1773?-1832 *NewYHSD*
Tiebout, Cornelius 1777-1830? *ApCAB*
Tiebout, Cornelius 1777-1832? *DcAmB,*
WhAm H
Tiebout, Cornelius Henry 1876-1951
NatCAB 38
Tiebout, Harry Morgan 1896-1966 *WhAm 4*
Tieck, Ludwig 1773-1853 *McGEWB*
Tiedeman, Christopher Gustavus 1857-1903
DcAmB,   TwCBDA,   WhAm 1
Tiedemann, Friedrich 1781-1861 *DcScB*
Tiedemann, Tudor H A 1889-1956 *WhAm 3*
Tiedjens, Victor Alphons 1895-1975 *WhAm 6*
Tiedtke, Ernest 1872-1950 *NatCAB 38*
Tief, Francis Joseph 1881-1965 *WhAm 4*
Tieghem, Philippe, Van 1839-1914 *DcScB*
Tieken, Robert 1903-1973 *WhAm 6*
Tieken, Theodore 1866-1932 *WhAm 1*
Tiemann, Daniel Fawcett 1805-1899
ApCAB Sup,   NatCAB 10,   WhAm 1
Tiemann, Johann Carl Wilhelm Ferdinand
1848-1899 *DcScB*
Tiemann, Susie Cresswell *WomWWA 14*
Tiepolo, Giovanni Battista 1696-1770 *McGEWB*
Tierman, Frances Christine 1846-1920 *TwCBDA*
Tiernan, Charles Bernard 1840- *WhAm 1*
Tiernan, Frances Christine Fisher 1846-1920
DcAmB,   NatCAB 20,   NotAW,
WomWWA 14
Tiernan, Luke 1757-1839 *ApCAB,   NatCAB 11*
Tiernan, Martin Farnan 1882-1968 *NatCAB 56*
Tiernan, Michael *NewYHSD*
Tiernan, Robert Owens 1929- *BiDrAC*
Tierney, Edward Martin 1858-1927 *NatCAB 46*
Tierney, Harry Austin 1890-1965 *WhAm 4*
Tierney, John M 1860- *WhAm 4*
Tierney, John Thomas 1882-1944 *WhAm 2*
Tierney, Laurence Edward, Jr. 1906-1972
NatCAB 57
Tierney, Leo Francis 1894-1973 *WhAm 5*
Tierney, Michael 1839-1908 *NatCAB 10,*
TwCBDA,   WhAm 1
Tierney, Richard Henry 1870-1928 *DcAmB,*
WhAm 1
Tierney, William Laurence 1876-1958 *BiDrAC,*
WhAm 3
Tiernon, John Luke 1841-1910 *WhAm 1*
Tierny, Harry Austin 1890-1965 *NatCAB 53*
Tiers, Montgomery C *NewYHSD*
Tietjens, Eunice 1884-1944 *NotAW,   WhAm 2*
Tietjens, Paul 1877- *WhAm 5*
Tietsort, Francis Judson 1877- *WhAm 5*
Tietz, J D *DcScB*
Tifashi, Shihab Al-Din Abul-Abbas, Al-
1184-1254? *DcScB*
Tiffan, William H 1820?- *NewYHSD*
Tiffany, Alexander Ralston 1796-1868 *ApCAB,*
NatCAB 10,   WhAm H
Tiffany, Belle Louise *WomWWA 14*
Tiffany, Charles Comfort 1829-1907 *TwCBDA,*
WhAm 1
Tiffany, Charles Lewis 1812-1902 *AmBi,*
DcAmB,   NatCAB 2,   TwCBDA,   WebAB,
WhAm 1
Tiffany, Charles Lewis 1878-1947 *WhAm 2*
Tiffany, Charles Louis 1812-1902 *ApCAB*
Tiffany, Flavel Benjamin 1846-1918 *WhAm 1*
Tiffany, Francis 1827-1908 *WhAm 1*
Tiffany, Francis Buchanan 1855-1936 *WhAm 3*

Tiffany, Hanford 1894-1965 *NatCAB 52,*
WhAm 4
Tiffany, Henry Dyer 1841-1917 *NatCAB 29*
Tiffany, Herbert Thorndike 1861-1944 *WhAm 2*
Tiffany, J Raymond 1888-1956 *WhAm 3*
Tiffany, Katrina Brandes Ely 1875-1927 *DcAmB,*
WomWWA 14
Tiffany, Louis Comfort 1848-1933 *AmBi,*
ApCAB, BnEnAmA, DcAmB, EncAB,
McGEWB, NatCAB 7, NatCAB 36,
TwCBDA, WebAB, WhAm 1
Tiffany, Louis McLane 1844-1916 *DcAmB,*
NatCAB 12, NatCAB 24, WhAm 1
Tiffany, Nina Moore d1958 *WhAm 3,*
WomWWA 14
Tiffany, Orrin Edward 1868-1950 *WhAm 4*
Tiffany, Osmond 1823- *ApCAB, Drake*
Tiffany, Ross Kerr 1879-1939 *WhAm 1*
Tiffany, Walter Checkley 1857- *WhAm 4*
Tiffany, William Shaw 1824-1907 *NewYHSD*
Tiffin, Edward 1766-1829 *AmBi, ApCAB,*
BiAUS, BiDrAC, DcAmB, Drake,
NatCAB 3, TwCBDA, WhAm H,
WhAmP
Tifft, Henry Neville 1854-1925 *WhAm 1*
Tift, Henry Harding 1841-1922 *NatCAB 27*
Tift, Nelson 1810-1891 *BiAUS, BiDConf,*
BiDrAC, WhAm H
Tigert, John James 1856-1906 *ApCAB Sup,*
DcAmB, TwCBDA, WhAm 1
Tigert, John James 1882-1965 *BiDAmEd,*
NatCAB 52, WhAm 2, WhAm 4
Tigh, William Frederick 1911-1964 *WhAm 4*
Tighe, Ambrose 1859-1928 *WhAm 1*
Tighe, Laurence Gotzian 1894-1954 *WhAm 3*
Tighe, Thomas 1897-1964 *NatCAB 50*
Tight, William George 1865-1910 *WhAm 1*
Tiglath-Pileser III *McGEWB*
Tigre, Lawrence Giblin 1886- *WhAm 2*
Tihen, John Henry 1861-1940 *NatCAB 16,*
WhAm 1
Tijerina, Reies 1926- *REnAW*
Tikamthi 1768?-1813 *AmBi, DcAmB*
Tikhov, Gavriil Adrianovich 1875-1960 *DcScB*
Tilander, Artur Gunnar 1894-1973 *WhAm 6*
Tilas, Daniel 1712-1772 *DcScB*
Tilden 1686-1766? *ApCAB*
Tilden, Bert Olin 1867-1953 *NatCAB 57*
Tilden, Charles Joseph 1873-1959 *WhAm 3*
Tilden, Charles Lee 1857-1950 *NatCAB 40*
Tilden, Daniel Rose 1804-1890 *BiAUS,*
BiDrAC, WhAm H
Tilden, Douglas 1860-1935 *AmBi, ApCAB X,*
NatCAB 26, TwCBDA, WhAm 1
Tilden, Edward 1858-1915 *ApCAB X,*
WhAm 1
Tilden, Francis Calvin 1872-1958 *WhAm 4*
Tilden, George Thomas 1845-1919 *WhAm 1*
Tilden, John Henry 1851- *WhAm 4*
Tilden, Joseph Mayo 1873-1928 *WhAm 1*
Tilden, Josephine Elizabeth *WhAm 3*
Tilden, Louis Edward 1900-1970 *WhAm 5*
Tilden, Samuel Jones 1814-1886 *AmBi,*
ApCAB, BiAUS, DcAmB, Drake,
EncAAH, EncAB, McGEWB, NatCAB 3,
TwCBDA, WebAB, WhAm H, WhAmP
Tilden, William A 1861- *ApCAB X*
Tilden, Sir William Augustus 1842-1926 *DcScB*
Tilden, William Tatem 1855-1915 *WhAm 1*
Tilden, William Tatem 1893-1953 *DcAmB S5,*
WebAB, WhAm HA, WhAm 4
Tildon, Frederick Douglas 1867- *WhoColR*
Tildsley, John Lee 1867-1948 *WhAm 2*
Tildy, Zoltan 1889-1961 *WhAm 4*
Tilesius VonTilenau, Wilhelm Gottlief 1769-1857
NewYHSD
Tileston, Mary Wilder 1843-1934 *TwCBDA,*
WhAm 1, WomWWA 14
Tileston, Thomas 1793-1864 *DcAmB,*
NatCAB 2, WhAm H
Tileston, Wilder 1875- *WhAm 5*
Tilford, Frank 1852-1924 *NatCAB 5,*
WhAm 1
Tilford, Henry Johnson 1880-1968 *WhAm 5*
Tilford, Henry Morgan 1856-1919 *NatCAB 18*
Tilford, Joseph Green 1829-1911 *WhAm 1*
Tilghman, Benjamin Chew 1821-1901
NatCAB 15

Tilghman, Benjamin Chew 1822-1901 *TwCBDA*
Tilghman, Edward 1750-1815 *ApCAB, BiAUS,*
DcAmB, Drake, NatCAB 2
Tilghman, Edward 1751-1815 *WhAm H*
Tilghman, Horace Lee 1874-1937 *NatCAB 37*
Tilghman, James 1716-1793 *ApCAB,*
NatCAB 1, TwCBDA
Tilghman, Lloyd 1816-1863 *ApCAB, Drake,*
NatCAB 13, TwCBDA
Tilghman, Matthew 1718-1790 *AmBi, ApCAB,*
BiAUS, BiDrAC, DcAmB, NatCAB 1,
TwCBDA, WhAm H, WhAmP
Tilghman, Richard Albert 1824-1899 *DcAmB,*
WhAm H
Tilghman, Richard Lloyd 1810-1867 *ApCAB,*
NatCAB 4
Tilghman, Tench 1744-1786 *AmBi, ApCAB,*
BiAUS, DcAmB, Drake, NatCAB 4,
TwCBDA, WebAMB, WhAm H
Tilghman, Tench 1810-1874 *ApCAB,*
NatCAB 4, TwCBDA
Tilghman, William 1756-1827 *AmBi, ApCAB,*
BiAUS, DcAmB, Drake, NatCAB 6,
TwCBDA, WhAm H
Tilghman, William Matthew 1854-1924 *DcAmB,*
REnAW, WhAm HA, WhAm 4
Till, William 1697-1766 *NatCAB 16*
Tillar, Benjamin Johnston 1866-1926
NatCAB 18, NatCAB 28
Tillar, Benjamin Johnston 1867-1926 *ApCAB X*
Tillar, Joshua Thomas Westbrook 1833-1908
NatCAB 18
Tillary, James d1818 *Drake*
Tiller, Frederick *NewYHSD*
Tiller, Robert *NewYHSD*
Tiller, Robert, Jr. *NewYHSD*
Tiller, Theodore Hance 1881- *WhAm 3*
Tillery, Lee 1902-1964 *WhAm 4*
Tilles, Roy E 1887-1961 *WhAm 4*
Tillet, Mathieu 1714-1791 *DcScB*
Tillett, Charles Walter 1857-1936 *WhAm 1*
Tillett, Charles Walter 1888-1952 *NatCAB 42,*
WhAm 3
Tillett, Wilbur Fisk 1854-1936 *WhAm 1*
Tillett, William S 1892-1974 *WhAm 6*
Tilley, Benjamin Franklin 1848-1907 *WhAm 1*
Tilley, Cecil Edgar 1894-1973 *WhAm 6*
Tilley, Jean LeGardeur 1740-1792? *ApCAB*
Tilley, Laura Etta Sawin *WomWWA 14*
Tilley, LeGardeur De *Drake*
Tilley, Lucy Evangeline 1859-1890 *NatCAB 4*
Tilley, Morris Palmer 1876-1947 *NatCAB 36,*
WhAm 2
Tilley, Norman Nevil 1892-1962 *NatCAB 49*
Tilley, Sir Samuel Leonard 1818-1896 *ApCAB,*
Drake, McGEWB
Tillich, Paul Johannes 1886-1965 *DcAmReB,*
EncAB, McGEWB, WebAB, WhAm 4
Tillinghast, A Roy 1883-1939 *NatCAB 30*
Tillinghast, Albert Harris 1843-1922
NatCAB 20
Tillinghast, Anna Churchill Moulton 1874-1951
NatCAB 46, WomWWA 14
Tillinghast, Benjamin Franklin 1849-1937
WhAm 1, WhAm 3
Tillinghast, Caleb Benjamin 1843-1909
ApCAB Sup, WhAm 1
Tillinghast, Charles Carpenter 1884-1962
WhAm 4
Tillinghast, Charles Foster 1871-1948
NatCAB 37
Tillinghast, Elizabeth Sheldon 1866-
WomWWA 14
Tillinghast, Francis 1743-1821 *Drake*
Tillinghast, Harold Morton 1884-1958
NatCAB 46, WhAm 3
Tillinghast, James 1822-1898 *NatCAB 8*
Tillinghast, James Alexander 1889-1957
NatCAB 46
Tillinghast, Joseph Leonard 1790-1844 *ApCAB,*
TwCBDA
Tillinghast, Joseph Leonard 1791-1844 *BiAUS,*
BiDrAC, Drake, WhAm H, WhAmP
Tillinghast, Mary Elizabeth 1845-1912
NatCAB 19, WhAm 1
Tillinghast, Mary Isabel Nelson *WomWWA 14*
Tillinghast, Nicholas 1804-1856 *ApCAB*
Tillinghast, Pardon 1622-1718 *ApCAB, Drake*

Tillinghast, Pardon Elisha 1836-1905
NatCAB 13, WhAm 1
Tillinghast, Thomas 1742-1821 *ApCAB,*
BiAUS, BiDrAC, NatCAB 2, WhAm H,
WhAmP
Tillman, Abram Martin 1863- *WhAm 2*
Tillman, Albert Gallatin, III 1921-1972
WhAm 6
Tillman, Benjamin Ryan 1847-1918 *AmBi,*
ApCAB Sup, BiDrAC, DcAmB, EncAAH,
EncAB, McGEWB, NatCAB 1,
NatCAB 12, TwCBDA, WebAB,
WhAm 1, WhAmP
Tillman, Frederick 1860-1942 *NatCAB 31*
Tillman, George D 1826-1901 *TwCBDA*
Tillman, George Dionysius 1826-1902 *BiDrAC,*
WhAmP
Tillman, George Newton 1851-1923 *NatCAB 8,*
WhAm 1
Tillman, James Davidson 1841- *NatCAB 12,*
WhAm 4
Tillman, John Newton 1859-1929 *BiDrAC,*
NatCAB 26, WhAm 1, WhAmP
Tillman, John Plummer 1849-1923 *WhAm 1*
Tillman, Lewis 1816-1886 *BiAUS, BiDrAC,*
WhAm H
Tillman, Nathaniel Patrick 1898-1965 *WhAm 4*
Tillman, Paul Edward 1899-1975 *WhAm 6*
Tillman, Samuel Dyer 1815-1875 *ApCAB*
Tillman, Samuel Escue 1847-1942 *WhAm 2*
Tillo, Aleksey Andreevich 1839-1900 *DcScB*
Tilloch, Alexander 1759-1825 *DcScB*
Tillotson, Edwin Ward 1884-1965 *WhAm 4*
Tillotson, Loyal Garis 1889-1961 *WhAm 4*
Tillotson, Thomas 1750-1832 *BiDrAC,*
WhAm H
Tillou, Elizabeth *NewYHSD*
Tillson, Davis 1830- *ApCAB*
Tillson, George William 1852-1940 *WhAm 1*
Tillson, John Charles Fremont 1856-1941
WhAm 1, WhAm 2
Tillstrom, Burr 1917- *WebAB*
Tilly, David L 1887-1949 *WhAm 2*
Tilly, Johann Tserclaes, Graf Von 1559-1632
WhoMilH
Tilly, Joseph-Marie De 1837-1906 *DcScB*
Tilmidh, Amin Al-Dawla Abu'l-H, Ibn Al-
1073?-1165 *DcScB*
Tilney, Albert Arthur 1868-1937 *WhAm 1*
Tilney, Frederick 1875-1938 *DcAmB S2,*
WhAm 1
Tilney, Frederick 1876-1938 *NatCAB 36*
Tilney, John Stringer 1836-1928 *ApCAB X,*
NatCAB 22
Tilroe, William Edwin 1861-1940 *WhAm 1*
Tilson, Ann Coe 1904-1968 *WhAm 5*
Tilson, John Quillin 1866-1958 *BiDrAC,*
NatCAB 49, WhAm 3, WhAmP
Tilson, Julia Romare 1879- *WomWWA 14*
Tilson, William J 1871-1949 *WhAm 2*
Tilt, Albert 1841-1900 *NatCAB 11*
Tilt, Charles Arthur 1877-1956 *NatCAB 47,*
WhAm 3
Tilton, Annie Eugenia *WomWWA 14*
Tilton, Benjamin Trowbridge 1868-1945
NatCAB 34
Tilton, Benjamin W *NewYHSD*
Tilton, Daniel *BiAUS*
Tilton, Dwight *WhAm 1*
Tilton, Edward Lippincott 1861-1933 *DcAmB,*
DcAmLiB, NatCAB 10, NatCAB 11,
WhAm 1
Tilton, Elizabeth 1869- *WhAm 5*
Tilton, Frederic Arthur 1876-1942 *WhAm 2*
Tilton, Frederic William 1839- *NatCAB 10*
Tilton, George Henry 1845-1926 *WhAm 1*
Tilton, Howard Winslow 1849-1902 *WhAm 1*
Tilton, James 1745-1822 *AmBi, ApCAB,*
BiDrAC, BiHiMed, DcAmB, Drake,
NatCAB 3, WebAMB, WhAm H
Tilton, James 1751-1822 *BiAUS*
Tilton, John Philip 1900-1959 *WhAm 3*
Tilton, John Rollin 1828-1888 *DcAmB,*
NewYHSD, WhAm H
Tilton, John Rollin 1833-1888 *ApCAB*
Tilton, L Deming 1890-1949 *NatCAB 38*
Tilton, Lydia H 1839- *AmWom*
Tilton, McLane, Jr. 1874-1937 *WhAm 1*

Tilton, Ralph 1869-1907 *WhAm 1*
Tilton, Theodore 1835-1907 *AmBi, ApCAB, DcAmB, Drake, NatCAB 8, WhAm 1*
Tily, Herbert James 1866-1948 *WhAm 2*
Tilyard, Philip Thomas Coke 1785-1830 *NewYHSD*
Tilyou, George Cornelius 1862-1914 *DcAmB, NatCAB 16, WebAB, WhAm HA, WhAm 4*
Tilzer, Harry Von 1872-1946 *DcAmB S4*
Timasheff, Nicholas Sergeevitch 1886-1970 *NatCAB 54*
Timberlake, Charles Bateman 1854-1941 *BiDrAC, WhAm 1, WhAmP*
Timberlake, Gideon 1876-1951 *DcAmB S5, NatCAB 40, WhAm 3*
Timberlake, Henry 1730-1765 *DcAmB, WhAm H*
Timberlake, John Jay 1912-1973 *NatCAB 57*
Timberlake, John Romulus 1833-1902 *NatCAB 12*
Timberman, Andrew 1864-1946 *WhAm 2*
Timblin, Louis M 1899-1955 *WhAm 3*
Timblin, William Stanley 1889-1956 *NatCAB 45*
Timby, Theodore Ruggles 1819-1909 *WhAm 1*
Timby, Theodore Ruggles 1822-1909 *AmBi, ApCAB, DcAmB, NatCAB 9, TwCBDA*
Timeche, Bruce 1923- *IlBEAAW*
Timiryazev, Kliment Arkadievich 1843-1920 *DcScB*
Timken, Henry 1831-1909 *DcAmB, WhAm HA, WhAm 4*
Timken, Henry H 1868-1940 *NatCAB 30*
Timken, Henry H, Jr. 1906-1968 *NatCAB 54, WhAm 4A*
Timlin, William Henry 1852-1916 *WhAm 1*
Timlow, Elizabeth Weston 1861-1931 *WhAm 1, WomWWA 14*
Timm, Henry Christian 1811-1892 *ApCAB, DcAmB, WhAm H*
Timm, John Arrend 1898-1969 *NatCAB 55, WhAm 5*
Timme, E A *NewYHSD*
Timme, Ernst G 1843- *WhAm 4*
Timme, Walter 1874-1956 *WhAm 3*
Timmerman, Arthur Henry 1871- *WhAm 5*
Timmerman, George Bell 1881-1966 *WhAm 4, WhAm 5*
Timmermann, Gerard John 1887-1957 *NatCAB 43*
Timmins, Jules Robert 1888-1971 *WhAm 5*
Timmons, Dever 1898-1960 *WhAm 4*
Timmons, Edward J Finley 1882-1960 *WhAm 4*
Timmons, Henry Davis 1848-1915 *NatCAB 18*
Timmons, Wofford Colquitt 1888-1957 *WhAm 3*
Timon, John 1795-1867 *Drake*
Timon, John 1797-1867 *ApCAB, DcAmB, NatCAB 12, TwCBDA, WhAm H*
Timonte, Alphonse *NewYHSD*
Timoshenko, Semen Konstantinovich 1895-1970 *WhoMilH*
Timoshenko, Semyon 1895-1970 *WhWW-II*
Timoshenko, Stephen Prokofievitch 1878-1972 *NatCAB 57, WhAm 5*
Timothy, Ann 1727?-1792 *NotAW*
Timothy, Elizabeth d1757 *NotAW*
Timothy, Lewis d1738 *DcAmB, WhAm H*
Timpson, Jeanie Stone 1846- *WomWWA 14*
Timpy, Jack J 1897-1960 *WhAm 3*
Timpy, John Joseph 1897-1960 *NatCAB 48*
Timrod, Henry 1828-1867 *AmBi, DcAmB, WebAB, WhAm H*
Timrod, Henry 1829-1867 *ApCAB, NatCAB 7, TwCBDA*
Tims, John Chapel 1870-1933 *WhAm 1*
Tims, John Francis 1892-1969 *WhAm 5*
Tims, Thomas Dillon 1825- *ApCAB*
Tinbergen, Jan 1903- *McGEWB*
Tincher, J N 1878-1951 *WhAm 3*
Tincher, Jasper Napoleon 1878-1951 *BiDrAC, WhAmP*
Tincker, Mary Agnes d1907 *WhAm 1*
Tincker, Mary Agnes 1831-1907 *DcAmB*
Tincker, Mary Agnes 1833-1907 *ApCAB, TwCBDA*
Tincker, Mary Agnes 1837-1907 *NatCAB 8*

Tindall, Glenn Means 1894-1972 *WhAm 5*
Tindall, N *IlBEAAW*
Tingelstad, Oscar Adolf 1882-1953 *WhAm 3*
Tingey, Thomas 1750-1829 *ApCAB, DcAmB, Drake, TwCBDA, WhAm H*
Tingle, John Bishop 1866-1918 *WhAm 3*
Tingle, Leonard 1894-1963 *WhAm 4*
Tingley, Charles Love Scott 1865- *WhAm 4*
Tingley, Claude Fernando 1878-1948 *NatCAB 36*
Tingley, Clyde 1883-1960 *WhAm 4*
Tingley, Ella May 1871- *WomWWA 14*
Tingley, Josephine Rice 1875- *WomWWA 14*
Tingley, Katherine Augusta Westcott 1847-1929 *DcAmB, NotAW*
Tingley, Katherine Augusta Westcott 1852-1929 *NatCAB 15, WhAm 1, WomWWA 14*
Tingley, Louisa Paine 1869-1952 *WhAm 3, WomWWA 14*
Tingley, Lutie Ogden *WomWWA 14*
Tingley, Marie Cesarine Secorre Quetil 1857- *WomWWA 14*
Tingley, Richard Hoadley 1856-1935 *WhAm 1*
Tingue, William James 1878-1948 *NatCAB 38*
Tinker, Charles Almerin 1838-1917 *NatCAB 2*
Tinker, Chauncey Brewster 1876-1963 *WhAm 4*
Tinker, Clarence L 1887-1942 *WhAm 2*
Tinker, Earl Warren 1890-1957 *WhAm 3*
Tinker, Edward Larocque 1881-1968 *WhAm 5*
Tinker, Edward Richmond 1822-1915 *ApCAB X*
Tinker, Edward Richmond 1878-1959 *ApCAB X, WhAm 3*
Tinker, Giles Knight 1856- *ApCAB X*
Tinker, Martin Buel 1869-1954 *WhAm 3*
Tinker, Reuben 1799-1854 *ApCAB*
Tinker, Robert Hall 1836-1924 *NatCAB 6*
Tinkham, Ernest Winfield 1857-1940 *NatCAB 30*
Tinkham, Foster *NewYHSD*
Tinkham, George Holden 1870-1956 *BiDrAC, NatCAB 46, WhAmP*
Tinkham, Henry Crain 1856-1925 *WhAm 1*
Tinkham, Herbert Linwood 1869-1941 *WhAm 1*
Tinkham, Richard Parsons 1902-1973 *WhAm 5*
Tinkham, William 1823-1914 *NatCAB 27*
Tinkler, Loyal George 1893-1959 *NatCAB 45*
Tinkman, George Holden 1870-1956 *WhAm 3*
Tinley, Mat 1876-1956 *NatCAB 45*
Tinley, Mathew Adrian 1876-1956 *WhAm 3*
Tinnerman, Albert H 1879-1961 *NatCAB 52*
Tinney, Eric 1907-1971 *NatCAB 56*
Tinney, Frank 1878-1940 *WhAm 1*
Tinnon, Robert McCracken 1840-1917 *WhAm 1*
Tinnon, Thomas B 1915-1973 *WhAm 6*
Tinseau D'Amondans, Charles De 1748-1822 *DcScB*
Tinsley, Charles *NewYHSD*
Tinsley, Gladney Jack 1896-1951 *WhAm 3*
Tinsley, Henry Clay 1869- *WhoColR*
Tinsley, John Francis 1880-1950 *WhAm 3*
Tinsley, Richard Parran 1867-1936 *WhAm 1*
Tinsley, William *NewYHSD*
Tinsman, Homer E d1937 *WhAm 2*
Tintoretto 1518-1594 *McGEWB*
Tiomkin, Dimitri 1899- *WebAB*
Tippet, Charles Frederick Basil 1896-1959 *WhAm 4*
Tippets, Joseph Henderson 1913-1968 *WhAm 5*
Tippett, James Sterling 1885-1958 *BiDAmEd, NatCAB 48*
Tippett, Sir Michael Kemp 1905- *McGEWB*
Tippett, Richard Beauregard 1862-1942 *NatCAB 34*
Tippetts, Charles Sanford 1893-1967 *WhAm 5*
Tippetts, Charles Sanford 1893-1968 *NatCAB 55*
Tippie, Frank Emerson 1917-1967 *NatCAB 54*
Tipple, Bertrand Martin 1868- *WhAm 5*
Tipple, Ezra Squier 1861-1936 *NatCAB 15, WhAm 1*
Tippu Sultan 1749-1799 *WhoMilH*
Tippu Sultan *see also* Tipu Sultan
Tippu Tip 1840?-1905 *McGEWB*
Tippy, William Bruce 1908-1973 *WhAm 6*
Tippy, Worth Marion 1866-1961 *WhAm 4*
Tipton, Ernest Moss 1889-1955 *WhAm 3*
Tipton, John 1730-1813 *DcAmB, WhAm H*

Tipton, John 1785-1839 *BiAUS*
Tipton, John 1786-1830 *ApCAB*
Tipton, John 1786-1839 *BiDrAC, DcAmB, NatCAB 11, TwCBDA, WhAm H*
Tipton, Laurence B 1910-1957 *WhAm 3*
Tipton, Royce Jay 1893-1967 *WhAm 4A, WhAm 5*
Tipton, Thomas Foster 1833-1904 *BiDrAC*
Tipton, Thomas W 1817-1899 *ApCAB, BiAUS, NatCAB 12*
Tipton, Thomas Warren 1817-1899 *TwCBDA*
Tipton, Thomas Weston 1817-1899 *BiDrAC, WhAmP*
Tipu Sultan 1750-1799 *McGEWB*
Tipu Sultan *see also* Tippu Sultan
Tiradentes 1748-1792 *McGEWB*
Tirey, Ralph Noble 1882-1964 *NatCAB 52, WhAm 4*
Tirindelli, Pier Adolfo 1858- *WhAm 4*
Tirpitz, Alfred 1849-1930 *WhoMilH*
Tirrell, Charles Quincy 1844-1910 *BiDrAC, NatCAB 16, WhAm 1, WhAmP*
Tirrell, Chester Malcolm 1902-1962 *NatCAB 51*
Tirrell, Frank A, Jr. *WhAm 3*
Tirrell, Henry Archelaus 1873- *WhAm 5*
Tirrell, John *NewYHSD*
Tirso De Molina 1584-1648 *McGEWB*
Tisch, Alfred Francis 1908-1968 *WhAm 5*
Tischenkel, Jacob 1899-1955 *NatCAB 44*
Tiscornia, James Walter 1885-1960 *NatCAB 49*
Tiscornia, Waldo Vincent 1892-1968 *NatCAB 54*
Tisdale, Alfred Dent 1893-1959 *NatCAB 49*
Tisdale, Elkanah 1771- *NewYHSD*
Tisdale, George Augustine 1821-1893 *NatCAB 18*
Tisdale, John B 1822?- *NewYHSD*
Tisdall, FitzGerald 1840-1915 *WhAm 1*
Tisdel, Frederick Monroe 1869- *WhAm 5*
Tiselius, Arne Wilhelm Kaurin 1902-1971 *AsBiEn, DcScB, McGEWB, WhAm 5*
Tisher, Paul Winslow 1909-1974 *WhAm 6*
Tisinger, Benjamin Louis 1866-1925 *WhAm 1*
Tiso, Joseph 1887-1946 *WhWW-II*
Tison, Alexander 1857-1938 *WhAm 1*
Tisquantum *AmBi, DcAmB, WebAB, WhAm H*
Tisserand, Francois Felix 1845-1896 *DcScB*
Tisserant, H E Cardinal Eugene 1884-1972 *WhAm 5*
Tissot, Simon-Andre-David 1728-1797 *BiHiMed*
Titchener, Edward Bradford 1867-1927 *AmBi, BiDAmEd, DcAmB, McGEWB, NatCAB 22, WebAB, WhAm 1*
Titchener, John Bradford 1898-1972 *WhAm 5*
Titchener, Paul Frederick 1891-1963 *NatCAB 50*
Titchmarsh, Edward Charles 1899-1963 *DcScB*
Titcomb, Harold Abbot 1874-1953 *NatCAB 41*
Titcomb, Harvey Burgess 1871- *WhAm 5*
Titcomb, John Wheelock 1860-1932 *DcAmB, WhAm 1*
Titcomb, Jonathan 1728-1817 *ApCAB, BiAUS, Drake*
Titcomb, Martha Ross 1862- *WomWWA 14*
Titcomb, Mary Lemist 1857-1932 *DcAmLiB, WhAm 1, WomWWA 14*
Titcomb, Miriam 1879- *WhAm 6*
Titcomb, Moses d1755 *Drake*
Titcomb, Timothy *AmBi, WebAB*
Titcomb, Virginia Chandler *WhAm 5*
Titcomb, William H 1824-1888 *NewYHSD*
Titherington, Richard Handfield 1861-1935 *WhAm 1*
Titian 1488?-1576 *McGEWB*
Titius, Johann Daniel 1729-1796 *DcScB*
Tito, Marshal 1892- *McGEWB*
Tito, Josip Broz 1892- *WhWW-II, WhoMilH*
Titsworth, Alfred Alexander 1852-1936 *WhAm 1*
Titsworth, Clarence E 1872- *WhAm 5*
Titsworth, Grant 1908-1960 *WhAm 4*
Titsworth, Judson 1845-1919 *WhAm 1*
Titsworth, Paul Emerson 1881-1933 *WhAm 1*
Titterington, Miles Bronson 1870-1923 *NatCAB 20*

Titterington, Morris Maxey 1891-1928
NatCAB 21
Titterington, Paul Francis 1895-1969
NatCAB 55
Titterington, Sophie Bronson 1846- *WhAm 4*
Tittle, Elmer Anthony 1903-1972 *WhAm 5*
Tittle, Ernest Fremont 1885-1949 *DcAmB S4,*
DcAmReB, WhAm 2
Tittle, Horatio Seymour 1868-1933 *NatCAB 38*
Tittle, Walter 1883-1966 *WhAm 4*
Tittmann, Charles Trowbridge 1883-1964
WhAm 4
Tittmann, Otto Hilgard 1850-1938 *NatCAB 13,*
TwCBDA, WhAm 1
Titulescu, Nicolae 1882-1941 *McGEWB*
Titus Flavius Vespasianus 039-081 *McGEWB*
Titus, Andrew Phillips 1875- *WhAm 5*
Titus, Bennett Eaton 1859-1913 *WhAm 1*
Titus, Edward Coddington 1863- *WhAm 5*
Titus, Ellwood Valentine 1853-1944 *WhAm 2*
Titus, Francis 1829?- *NewYHSD*
Titus, Franz M 1829?- *NewYHSD*
Titus, Gottfried *NewYHSD*
Titus, Harry L 1858-1917 *NatCAB 18*
Titus, John *BiAUS*
Titus, Louis 1872- *WhAm 5*
Titus, Norman Edwin 1889-1965 *NatCAB 51*
Titus, Obadiah 1789-1854 *BiAUS, BiDrAC,*
WhAm H
Titus, Paul 1885-1951 *NatCAB 40, WhAm 3*
Titus, Paul 1905- *WhAm 5*
Titus, Robert Cyrus 1839-1918 *NatCAB 7,*
WhAm 1
Titus, Robert Richard 1894-1967 *NatCAB 54*
Titus, Rolla Williams 1884-1956 *NatCAB 45*
Tivnan, Edward Patrick 1882-1937 *NatCAB 30,*
WhAm 1
Tiyanoga *AmBi, WhAm H*
Tizard, Sir Henry 1885-1959 *WhWW-II*
Tizoc d1482 *ApCAB*
Tjader, Charles Richard 1869-1916 *NatCAB 17*
Tjader, Richard 1869-1916 *WhAm 1*
Tl'ah Hastiin 1867-1937 *REnAW*
Tlalhuicole d1518 *ApCAB*
Tlaxpanquizqui *ApCAB*
To-Mo-Chi-Chi 1642?-1739 *ApCAB*
Toaspern, Otto 1863- *WhAm 4*
Toba, Sojo 1053-1140 *McGEWB*
Tobani, Theodore Moses 1855-1933 *DcAmB*
Tobar, Juan 1543-1623 *ApCAB*
Tobenkin, Elias 1882-1963 *WhAm 4*
Tobey, Charles William 1880-1953 *BiDrAC,*
DcAmB S5, WhAm 3, WhAmP
Tobey, Edward Silas 1813-1891 *DcAmB,*
NatCAB 13, WhAm H
Tobey, Frank Bassett 1833- *NatCAB 1*
Tobey, Frank Ross 1847- *NatCAB 10*
Tobey, Frank Thrall 1890-1955 *NatCAB 43*
Tobey, Mark 1890- *BnEnAmA, WebAB*
Tobey, Samuel *NewYHSD*
Tobias, Channing Heggie 1882-1961 *WhAm 4*
Tobias, Channing Higgie 1882-1961 *WhoColR*
Tobias, Norman 1898-1974 *WhAm 6*
Tobias, Phil William 1898-1962 *NatCAB 49*
Tobias, Sarah 1844- *WomWWA 14*
Tobin, Arthur Collson 1879-1940 *NatCAB 33*
Tobin, Benjamin Franklin 1865-1920
NatCAB 19
Tobin, Charles Milton 1871- *WhAm 5*
Tobin, Daniel Aloysius 1883-1942 *WhAm 2*
Tobin, Daniel Joseph 1875-1955 *DcAmB S5,*
NatCAB 42, WhAm 3
Tobin, Edmund Paul 1904-1969 *WhAm 5*
Tobin, Emma Linburg 1874- *WomWWA 14*
Tobin, Flora Lewis 1882- *WomWWA 14*
Tobin, Frederick *NewYHSD*
Tobin, George Timothy 1864- *WhAm 4*
Tobin, James Edward 1905-1968 *WhAm 5*
Tobin, James F 1912-1975 *WhAm 6*
Tobin, John Charles 1886-1956 *WhAm 3*
Tobin, John W 1834?-1888 *REnAW*
Tobin, Maurice Joseph 1901-1953 *BiDrUSE,*
DcAmB S5, WhAm 3
Tobin, Ralph C 1890-1957 *WhAm 3*
Tobin, Richard Montgomery 1866-1952
NatCAB 41, WhAm 3
Tobin, Robert Gibson 1894- *WhAm 3*
Tobin, Robert James 1897-1966 *NatCAB 51,*

WhAm 5
Tobitt, Edith 1868-1939 *WhAm 3*
Tobolsky, Arthur Victor 1919-1972 *WhAm 5*
Toby, Edward 1858- *WhAm 4*
Toch, Ernst 1887-1964 *WhAm 4*
Toch, Maximilian 1864-1946 *WhAm 2*
Tocornal Y Grez, Manuel Antonio 1817-1867
ApCAB
Tocqueville, Alexis Charles H Clerel De
1805-1859 *AmBi, ApCAB, Drake,*
McGEWB, REnAW
Tocqueville, Alexis Henri M Clerel De 1805-1859
WhAm H
Tod, David 1805-1868 *ApCAB, BiAUS,*
DcAmB, Drake, NatCAB 3, TwCBDA,
WhAm H
Tod, George 1773-1841 *ApCAB, BiAUS,*
DcAmB, Drake, WhAm H
Tod, J Kennedy 1852-1925 *WhAm 1*
Tod, John 1779-1830 *BiAUS, BiDrAC,*
DcAmB, NatCAB 16, WhAm H
Tod, John 1870-1953 *WhAm 3*
Tod, Robert Elliot 1867-1944 *ApCAB X,*
NatCAB 33
Todaro, Vincent Settimo 1891-1972 *WhAm 6*
Todd *NewYHSD*
Todd, A *NewYHSD*
Todd, Adah J *AmWom*
Todd, Albert May 1850-1931 *BiDrAC,*
NatCAB 45, WhAm 1, WhAm 1C
Todd, Albert W 1884-1949 *WhAm 2*
Todd, Lord Alexander Robertus 1907- *AsBiEn*
Todd, Alfred 1821-1874 *ApCAB*
Todd, Alpheus 1821-1884 *ApCAB*
Todd, Ambrose Giddings 1863-1947 *WhAm 2*
Todd, Arthur James 1878-1948 *WhAm 2*
Todd, Casey 1873- *WhAm 5*
Todd, Chapman Coleman 1848-1929 *WhAm 1*
Todd, Charles Burr 1849- *ApCAB, TwCBDA,*
WhAm 4
Todd, Charles S 1791-1871 *BiAUS*
Todd, Charles Scott 1791-1871 *ApCAB, Drake,*
NatCAB 1
Todd, Charles Smith 1851-1924 *NatCAB 6*
Todd, Charles Stewart 1791-1871 *DcAmB,*
WhAm H
Todd, Clare Chrisman 1880-1954 *WhAm 3*
Todd, Daniel Malcolm 1871-1942 *NatCAB 45*
Todd, David Peck 1855-1939 *ApCAB,*
NatCAB 7, NatCAB 28, TwCBDA,
WhAm 1
Todd, Dorothy Payne 1768-1849 *AmBi*
Todd, Earle Marion 1863-1940 *WhAm 1*
Todd, Edward 1826-1898 *NatCAB 2*
Todd, Edward Howard 1863- *WhAm 5*
Todd, Eli 1769-1833 *ApCAB, DcAmB, Drake,*
WhAm H
Todd, Elmer Ely 1873-1962 *WhAm 4*
Todd, Elmer Kenneth 1894-1969 *WhAm 5*
Todd, Ethel Hastings 1876- *WomWWA 14*
Todd, Eugene, Jr. 1916-1970 *WhAm 5*
Todd, Fannie Burgess d1970 *WhAm 5*
Todd, Forde Anderson 1881-1971 *WhAm 5*
Todd, Frank Chisholm 1869-1918 *NatCAB 18,*
WhAm 1
Todd, Frank Morton 1871-1940 *NatCAB 30*
Todd, G Carroll 1879-1947 *WhAm 2*
Todd, George *NewYHSD*
Todd, George Davidson 1856- *NatCAB 10,*
WhAm 4
Todd, George Walter 1860-1938 *NatCAB 42,*
WhAm 1
Todd, Gordon Livingston 1914-1964
NatCAB 51
Todd, Harold Arthur 1893-1967 *WhAm 4A*
Todd, Harry L 1868-1938 *WhAm 1*
Todd, Helen McGregor *WomWWA 14*
Todd, Henry Alfred 1854-1925 *AmBi, DcAmB,*
NatCAB 14, NatCAB 24, WhAm 1
Todd, Henry Davis 1838-1907 *NatCAB 13,*
NatCAB 19, TwCBDA, WhAm 1
Todd, Henry Davis, Jr. 1866-1964 *NatCAB 51*
Todd, Henry Stanley 1871-1941 *WhAm 1*
Todd, Hiram Charles 1876-1965 *WhAm 4*
Todd, Hiram Eugene 1874-1946 *WhAm 2*
Todd, James Edward 1846-1922 *NatCAB 10,*
WhAm 1
Todd, James Marcus 1858-1939 *NatCAB 29*

Todd, John d1830 *BiAUS*
Todd, John 1750-1782 *ApCAB, Drake*
Todd, John 1800-1873 *ApCAB, DcAmB,*
Drake, NatCAB 8, WhAm H
Todd, John Blair Smith 1814-1872 *ApCAB,*
BiAUS, BiDrAC, NatCAB 4, TwCBDA,
WhAm H
Todd, John Blair Smith 1814-1884 *REnAW*
Todd, John Reynard 1867-1945 *ApCAB X,*
NatCAB 35, WhAm 2
Todd, Joseph Clinton 1879-1962 *WhAm 4*
Todd, Jouett Ross 1903-1967 *WhAm 4*
Todd, Laurence 1882-1957 *WhAm 3*
Todd, Lawrie *WhAm H*
Todd, Lemuel 1817-1891 *BiAUS, BiDrAC,*
WhAm H
Todd, Leslie Jay 1900-1972 *NatCAB 57*
Todd, Letitia Willey 1835- *AmWom*
Todd, Libanus McLouth 1862-1933 *NatCAB 26*
Todd, Lois Pendleton 1894-1968 *NatCAB 54*
Todd, Luther Edward 1874-1937 *WhAm 1*
Todd, Mabel Loomis d1932 *WhAm 1,*
WomWWA 14
Todd, Mabel Loomis 1856-1932 *DcAmB,*
NatCAB 28, NatCAB 41, NotAW
Todd, Mabel Loomis 1858-1932 *AmBi,*
AmWom, NatCAB 9, TwCBDA
Todd, Marguerite Raiguel 1879-
WomWWA 14
Todd, Marion Marsh 1841-1913 *AmWom,*
NotAW, WhAm 4, WomWWA 14
Todd, Michael 1909-1958 *WhAm 3*
Todd, Millicent *WomWWA 14*
Todd, Milo Eugene 1884-1967 *NatCAB 54*
Todd, Minnie J Terrell 1844- *AmWom*
Todd, Moses Hampton 1845- *WhAm 4*
Todd, Pamela *NewYHSD*
Todd, Paul Harold 1887-1969 *WhAm 5*
Todd, Paul Harold, Jr. 1921- *BiDrAC*
Todd, Percy R 1859-1935 *WhAm 1*
Todd, Robert Henry 1862- *WhAm 4*
Todd, Robert Isaac 1869-1928 *NatCAB 22,*
WhAm 1
Todd, Robert Nathaniel 1827-1883 *NatCAB 11*
Todd, Roscoe Johnson 1895-1972 *WhAm 6*
Todd, Sereno Edwards 1820-1898 *DcAmB,*
NatCAB 9, WhAm H
Todd, Theodore Wallace 1825-1905 *NatCAB 5*
Todd, Thomas 1765-1826 *AmBi, ApCAB,*
BiAUS, DcAmB, Drake, NatCAB 2,
TwCBDA, WebAB, WhAm H
Todd, Thomas 1878-1956 *WhAm 3*
Todd, Thomas Wingate 1885-1938 *DcAmB S2,*
NatCAB 38, WhAm 1
Todd, Walter Edmond Clyde 1874-1967
WhAm 5
Todd, Walter Ledyard 1886- *WhAm 5*
Todd, William *NewYHSD*
Todd, William Cleaves 1823- *NatCAB 9*
Todd, William Henry 1864-1932 *NatCAB 25*
Todd, William Henry 1867-1932 *WhAm 1*
Todd, William T, Jr. 1893-1957 *WhAm 3*
Toddy, Jimmy *IlBEAAW*
Tode, Arthur Monroe 1894-1966 *NatCAB 52*
Todhunter, Isaac 1820-1884 *DcScB*
Todhunter, Richard Thomas 1876-1967
NatCAB 55
Todleben, Franz Eduard Ivanovich 1814-1884
WhoMilH
Toebaas, Oscar Theodore 1888-1959
NatCAB 48
Toebbe, Augustus Marie 1829-1884 *WhAm H*
Toebbe, Augustus Mary 1829-1884 *ApCAB,*
NatCAB 12, TwCBDA
Toenjes, David Burdette 1894-1966 *NatCAB 53*
Toensfeldt, Hans Carl Thomas 1879-1960
NatCAB 51
Toeplitz, Otto 1881-1940 *DcScB*
Toffenetti, Dario Louis 1889-1962 *NatCAB 53,*
WhAm 4
Toffteen, Olof Alfred 1863- *WhAm 4*
Toft, Peter Petersen 1825-1901 *IlBEAAW*
Toftoy, Holger Nelson 1902-1967 *WhAm 4*
Togliatti, Palmiro d1964 *WhAm 4*
Tognazzini, Roland 1903-1970 *NatCAB 54*
Tognazzini, Roland 1903-1971 *WhAm 5*
Togo, Heihachiro 1849-1934 *WhoMilH*
Togo, Shigenori 1882-1950 *WhWW-II*

Toict, Nicolas 1611-1680 *ApCAB*
Toiry, P *NewYHSD*
Tojo, Hideki 1884-1948 *McGEWB, WhWW-II, WhoMilH*
Tokugawa, Ieyasu 1542-1616 *McGEWB*
Tokugawa, Yoshimune 1684-1751 *McGEWB*
Tokyo Rose 1916- *WhWW-II*
Tolan, Edwin Kirkman 1921-1976 *WhAm 6*
Tolan, John Harvey 1877-1947 *BiDrAC, WhAm 2, WhAmP*
Toland, Clarence G 1875- *WhAm 5*
Toland, Edmund M 1898-1942 *WhAm 2*
Toland, George Washington 1796-1869 *BiAUS, BiDrAC*
Toland, Hugh Huger 1806-1880 *BiDAmEd, DcAmB, WhAm H*
Toland, John 1670-1722 *McGEWB*
Toland, P *NewYHSD*
Tolansky, Samuel 1907-1973 *WhAm 6*
Tolbert, Benjamin Arthur 1882-1937 *WhAm 1*
Tolbert, Joseph W 1870- *WhAm 5*
Tolbert, Raymond Augustine 1890-1960 *NatCAB 50, WhAm 4*
Tolbert, Ward VanDerHoof 1877-1946 *NatCAB 34, WhAm 2*
Tolbukhin, Fyodor 1894-1949 *WhWW-II*
Toledano, Rachel *WomWWA 14*
Toledano, Vicente Lombardo 1894-1968 *McGEWB*
Toledo, Antonio Sebastian De *ApCAB*
Toledo, Fernando Alvarez De *ApCAB*
Toledo, Francisco De 1515-1584 *McGEWB*
Toledo, Francisco De 1520?-1583? *ApCAB*
Toledo, Garcia De 1510?-1583? *ApCAB*
Toledo, Jose Rey 1915- *IIBEAAW*
Toledo-Herrarte, Luis 1871- *WhAm 5*
Toler, Enoch McLain 1874-1954 *NatCAB 44*
Toler, Fred W 1926- *WhAm 5*
Toler, Richard H d1848 *Drake*
Tolfree, Aline Gorren *WomWWA 14*
Tolfree, Edward Rogers 1873-1954 *NatCAB 41*
Tolfree, James Edward 1837-1920 *TwCBDA, WhAm 1*
Tolin, Ernest Allen 1904-1961 *NatCAB 47, · NatCAB 49, WhAm 4*
Tolischus, Otto David 1890-1967 *WhAm 4*
Toliver, William Robert 1880- *WhoColR*
Tolkien, John Ronald Reuel 1892- *WhAm 6*
Toll, Charles Hansen 1850-1901 *NatCAB 31*
Toll, Henry Wolcott d1975 *WhAm 6*
Toll, Herman 1907-1967 *BiDrAC*
Toll, Philip Riley 1863-1929 *NatCAB 34*
Toll, Roger Wolcott 1883-1936 *WhAm 1*
Toll, William Edward 1843-1915 *NatCAB 25, WhAm 1*
Tolle, Augustus *NewYHSD*
Tollefson, Martin 1894-1963 *WhAm 4*
Tollefson, Thor Carl 1901- *BiDrAC*
Tollen, William B 1910-1966 *NatCAB 54*
Toller, Ernst 1893-1939 *McGEWB, WhAm HA, WhAm 4*
Tolles, Frederick Barnes 1915-1975 *WhAm 6*
Tolles, Jason Elbridge 1852-1921 *NatCAB 20*
Tolles, Marian Donahue 1902-1969 *WhAm 5*
Tolles, Newman Arnold 1903-1973 *WhAm 5*
Tolles, Robert B 1825?-1883 *NatCAB 13*
Tolles, Sheldon Hitchcock 1858-1926 *WhAm 1*
Tolleson, William N 1886-1946 *WhAm 2*
Tollett, Raymond Lee 1907-1969 *NatCAB 56, WhAm 5*
Tolley, Augustus *NewYHSD*
Tolley, Harold Sumner 1894-1956 *BiDrAC, WhAm 3*
Tolley, Howard Ross 1889-1958 *EncAAH, NatCAB 43, WhAm 3*
Tollmien, Walter Gustav 1900-1968 *WhAm 5*
Tolman, Albert Harris 1856-1928 *WhAm 1*
Tolman, Albert Walter 1866- *WhAm 5*
Tolman, Anna C 1859- *WomWWA 14*
Tolman, Charles Prescott d1961 *WhAm 4*
Tolman, Cyrus Fisher, Jr. 1873-1942 *WhAm 2*
Tolman, Edgar Bronson 1859-1947 *WhAm 2*
Tolman, Edward Chace 1886-1959 *McGEWB, WhAm 4*
Tolman, Frank Leland 1876-1957 *WhAm 4*
Tolman, Henry, Jr. 1879-1954 *NatCAB 41*
Tolman, Herbert Cushing 1865-1923 *DcAmB, NatCAB 9, NatCAB 26, WhAm 1*

Tolman, James 1819- *NatCAB 4*
Tolman, John, Jr. *NewYHSD*
Tolman, Judson Allen 1879-1949 *WhAm 2*
Tolman, Julia *WomWWA 14*
Tolman, L A *NewYHSD*
Tolman, Richard Chace 1881-1948 *DcAmB S4, DcScB, WhAm 2*
Tolman, Ruth S 1893-1957 *WhAm 3*
Tolman, Warren Winfield 1861-1940 *NatCAB 29, WhAm 1*
Tolman, William Howe 1861- *NatCAB 9, NatCAB 14, WhAm 3*
Tolmie, William Fraser *WhAm H*
Tolon, Miguel Teurbe 1820-1858 *ApCAB*
Tolsa, Manuel 1750?-1810? *ApCAB*
Tolson, Clyde Anderson 1900-1975 *WhAm 6*
Tolson, George Tolover 1876-1965 *WhAm 4*
Tolson, Theodore Elliott 1879-1944 *NatCAB 34*
Tolstoy, Count Alexei Nikolaevich 1883-1945 *WhAm 4*
Tolstoy, Leo 1828-1910 *McGEWB*
Tolti, John 1822?- *NewYHSD*
Toltz, Max 1857-1932 *WhAm 1*
Tom 1838?- *Drake*
Tom 1849- *ApCAB*
Tom 1850?- *NatCAB 10*
Tom Thumb *AmBi*
Tom, Howard 1902-1962 *WhAm 4*
Tomaiuoli, Michael Francis 1899-1962 *NatCAB 49*
Tomajan, John S 1892-1972 *WhAm 5*
Tomb, George 1791-1870 *NatCAB 8*
Tomb, Robert *NewYHSD*
Tombalbaye, Francois 1918-1975 *WhAm 6*
Tombaugh, Clyde William 1906- *AsBiEn*
Tomber, Max L 1898-1968 *WhAm 5*
Tome, Jacob 1810-1898 *ApCAB Sup, DcAmB, NatCAB 28, TwCBDA, WhAm H*
Tomei, Peter Andrew 1934-1971 *WhAm 5*
Tomes, Robert 1816-1882 *Drake*
Tomes, Robert 1817-1882 *ApCAB, NatCAB 18*
Tomkies, Amanda Allison 1872- *WomWWA 14*
Tomkins, Caleb *BiAUS*
Tomkins, Calvin 1858-1921 *WhAm 1*
Tomkins, Christopher d1845 *BiAUS*
Tomkins, Cydnor B 1810- *BiAUS*
Tomkins, Daniel D 1774-1825 *BiAUS*
Tomkins, Floyd Williams 1850-1932 *DcAmB, WhAm 1*
Tomkins, Gordon Mayer 1926-1975 *WhAm 6*
Tomkins, Lewis *NewYHSD*
Tomlin, Bradley Walker 1899-1953 *BnEnAmA, DcAmB S5, WhAm 3*
Tomlin, James Harvey 1856- *WhAm 4*
Tomlins, William Lawrence 1844-1930 *BiDAmEd, DcAmB, WhAm 4*
Tomlinson, Allen U 1875-1956 *WhAm 3*
Tomlinson, Ambrose Jessup 1865-1943 *DcAmReB*
Tomlinson, Arthur Hibbs 1856-1920 *WhAm 1*
Tomlinson, Carl Perkins 1886-1967 *NatCAB 54*
Tomlinson, Charles Creighton 1884-1955 *NatCAB 43, WhAm 3*
Tomlinson, Charles Fawcett 1871-1943 *NatCAB 33, WhAm 2*
Tomlinson, Daniel Webb 1849-1917 *NatCAB 17*
Tomlinson, Douglas 1888-1971 *WhAm 6*
Tomlinson, Edward 1892-1974 *WhAm 6*
Tomlinson, Ella Merrick 1863- *WomWWA 14*
Tomlinson, Everett Titsworth 1859-1931 *DcAmB, NatCAB 25, TwCBDA, WhAm 1*
Tomlinson, Frank *NewYHSD*
Tomlinson, George Ashley 1866-1942 *NatCAB 31*
Tomlinson, George Ashley 1869-1942 *REnAW, WhAm 1*
Tomlinson, Gideon 1780-1854 *ApCAB, BiAUS, BiDrAC, Drake, NatCAB 10, TwCBDA, WhAm H, WhAmP*
Tomlinson, H M 1873-1958 *WhAm 3*
Tomlinson, Homer Aubrey 1892-1968 *WhAm 5*
Tomlinson, Roy Everett 1877-1968 *ApCAB X, WhAm 5*
Tomlinson, Sidney Halstead 1876-1949 *NatCAB 37*
Tomlinson, Thomas Ash 1802-1872 *BiAUS,*

BiDrAC, WhAm H
Tomlinson, Thomas Henry 1836-1919 *NatCAB 17*
Tomlinson, Vincent Eaton 1862-1938 *NatCAB 28, WhAm 1*
Tomlinson, William *NewYHSD*
Tomlinson, William A *NewYHSD*
Tomlinson, William Gosnell 1897-1972 *WhAm 5*
Tommey, Bob *IIBEAAW*
Tomo-Chi-Chi d1739 *Drake*
Tomochichi 1650?-1739 *DcAmB, WhAm H*
Tomonaga, Sin-Itiro 1906- *AsBiEn, McGEWB*
Tompers, George Urban 1877-1936 *NatCAB 29, WhAm 1*
Tompers, Lucie Margaret 1874-1938 *NatCAB 29*
Tompert, Russell Howard 1892-1934 *WhAm 1*
Tompkins, Arnold 1849-1905 *BiDAmEd, DcAmB, WhAm 1*
Tompkins, Arthur Sidney 1865-1938 *BiDrAC, WhAm 1*
Tompkins, Boylston Adams 1891-1972 *WhAm 5*
Tompkins, Caleb 1759-1846 *BiDrAC, WhAm H, WhAmP*
Tompkins, Charles Henry 1830-1915 *ApCAB, NatCAB 34, WhAm 1*
Tompkins, Charles Hook 1883-1956 *WhAm 3*
Tompkins, Christopher 1780-1858 *BiDrAC, WhAm H*
Tompkins, Christopher 1847- *WhAm 4*
Tompkins, Cydnor Bailey 1810-1862 *BiDrAC, WhAm H*
Tompkins, Daniel A 1852-1914 *WhAm 1*
Tompkins, Daniel Augustus 1851-1914 *DcAmB*
Tompkins, Daniel D 1774-1825 *AmBi, ApCAB, BiDrAC, BiDrUSE, DcAmB, Drake, TwCBDA, WebAB, WhAm H, WhAmP*
Tompkins, Daniel D 1774-1835 *NatCAB 6*
Tompkins, Daniel D 1799-1863 *ApCAB, Drake*
Tompkins, DeLoss Monroe 1849- *WhAm 4*
Tompkins, Elizabeth Knight 1865- *WhAm 4*
Tompkins, Emmett 1853-1917 *BiDrAC*
Tompkins, Frank Hector 1847-1922 *WhAm 1*
Tompkins, George 1780-1846 *BiAUS, Drake, NatCAB 3*
Tompkins, George Ricks 1881- *WhoColR*
Tompkins, George Washington 1855-1939 *NatCAB 30*
Tompkins, H D 1893-1960 *WhAm 3A*
Tompkins, Hamilton Bullock 1843- *NatCAB 11*
Tompkins, Henry Clay 1845- *NatCAB 7*
Tompkins, Juliet Wilbor 1871-1956 *WhAm 3*
Tompkins, Leslie Jay 1867- *WhAm 3*
Tompkins, Leslie Jay 1868- *NatCAB 14*
Tompkins, Lucius Douglas 1889-1971 *WhAm 5*
Tompkins, Miriam Downing 1892-1954 *DcAmLiB*
Tompkins, Nathaniel 1879-1949 *WhAm 3*
Tompkins, Patrick Watson 1804-1853 *BiAUS, BiDrAC, WhAm H*
Tompkins, Sally Louisa 1833-1916 *BiDConf, DcAmB, NotAW, WebAB, WebAMB*
Tompson, Benjamin 1642-1714 *ApCAB, DcAmB, Drake, NatCAB 8, WhAm H*
Tompson, Edward 1665-1705 *ApCAB, Drake*
Tompson, George Morris 1852-1949 *NatCAB 38*
Tompson, William 1598-1666 *ApCAB*
Tompson, William M *NewYHSD*
Toms, Robert Morrell 1886-1960 *WhAm 3*
Toms, Zach 1901-1964 *WhAm 4*
Tomson, John 1849-1918 *NatCAB 18*
Ton, Cornelius John 1876-1915 *NatCAB 18*
Tondorf, Francis Anthony 1870-1929 *DcAmB, NatCAB 21, WhAm 1*
Tone, Franchot 1905-1968 *WhAm 5*
Tone, Frank Jerome 1868-1944 *WhAm 2*
Tone, William Theobald Wolfe 1791-1828 *ApCAB*
Toner, Edward C 1871-1927 *WhAm 1*
Toner, James Vincent 1888-1951 *WhAm 3*
Toner, Joseph Meredith 1825-1896 *ApCAB, DcAmB, NatCAB 7, WhAm H*
Toner, Royal 1894-1959 *NatCAB 47*
Tong, Hollington K 1887-1971 *WhAm 5*
Tongue, Thomas H 1844-1903 *BiDrAC, WhAm 1, WhAmP*

Toniere, Gaetano *NewYHSD*
Tonjes, Helena Secor 1867- *WomWWA 14*
Tonk, Ernest 1889- *IIBEAAW*
Tonks, Oliver Samuel 1873-1953 *NatCAB 42,*
WhAm 3
Tonne, Herbert Arthur 1904- *BiDAmEd*
Tonnellier, Francois *NewYHSD*
Tonner, John Andrew 1868- *WhAm 4*
Tonnies, Ferdinand 1855-1936 *McGEWB*
Tonry, Richard Joseph 1893-1971 *BiDrAC*
Tonti, Henri De 1650?-1704 *AmBi,* *REnAW*
Tonty, Henri De 1650?-1704 *AmBi,* *WebAB*
Tonty, Henry De 1650?-1704 *ApCAB,* *DcAmB,*
WhAm H
Tonyn, Patrick 1725-1804 *ApCAB,* *Drake*
Toohey, John Peter d1946 *WhAm 2*
Tooke, John Horne 1736-1812 *ApCAB*
Tooker, Clyde 1896-1971 *NatCAB 57*
Tooker, Edward B *NewYHSD*
Tooker, Frederick Jagger 1871-1952
NatCAB 42
Tooker, George 1920- *BnEnAmA*
Tooker, Lewis Frank 1854-1925 *NatCAB 20*
Tooker, Lewis Frank 1855-1925 *WhAm 1*
Tooker, Norman Brown 1884-1967 *WhAm 4*
Tooker, Sterling Twiss 1913-1969 *NatCAB 53,*
WhAm 5
Tookey, Clarence Hall 1896-1967 *NatCAB 54,*
WhAm 5
Toole, Edwin Warren 1839-1905 *DcAmB*
Toole, Joseph Kemp 1851-1929 *BiDrAC,*
DcAmB, *NatCAB 1,* *NatCAB 11,*
TwCBDA, *WhAm 1,* *WhAmP*
Toole, K Ross 1920- *REnAW*
Toole, S Westcott 1900-1969 *WhAm 5*
Tooley, James, Jr. 1816-1844 *NewYHSD*
Tooley, William Lander 1906-1966 *NatCAB 53*
Toolin, John Martin 1891-1971 *WhAm 5*
Toombs, Henry Johnston 1896-1967 *WhAm 5*
Toombs, Percy Walthall 1880-1933 *WhAm 1*
Toombs, Robert Augustus 1810-1885 *AmBi,*
ApCAB, *BiAUS,* *BiDConf,* *BiDrAC,*
DcAmB, *Drake,* *McGEWB,* *NatCAB 4,*
TwCBDA, *WebAB,* *WhAm H,* *WhAmP*
Toomer, John DeRossett 1784-1856 *BiAUS,*
NatCAB 7
Toomey, DeLally Prescott 1868-1918 *WhAm 1*
Toomey, Edmond Galbraith 1892-1960
NatCAB 49
Toomey, Floyd F 1894-1975 *WhAm 6*
Toomey, Mary Isabelle Vogt 1859-
WomWWA 14
Toompas, Charles Arthur 1911-1964
NatCAB 50
Toon, Thomas Fentress 1840-1902 *WhAm 1*
Toops, Herbert Anderson 1895-1972 *WhAm 6*
Toor, Nishan 1888-1966 *NatCAB 54*
Tootell, Robert Ballard 1904-1971 *WhAm 5*
Toothaker, Charles Robinson 1873-1952
WhAm 3
Toothe, William 1831- *NatCAB 4*
Tootle, Milton, Jr. 1872-1946 *WhAm 2*
Topakyan, Haigazoun Hohannes 1864-1926
WhAm 1
Tope, Homer W 1859-1936 *WhAm 1*
Topete, Juan Bautista 1821- *ApCAB*
Toph, Ollah Perkins 1862- *WomWWA 14*
Topliff, Samuel 1789-1864 *DcAmB,* *WhAm H*
Toplitzky, Joe 1888-1935 *WhAm 1*
Topp, Alexander 1815-1879 *ApCAB*
Toppan, Charles 1796-1874 *NewYHSD,*
WhAm H
Toppan, Charles, Jr. 1826?- *NewYHSD*
Toppan, Harriet 1834?- *NewYHSD*
Toppan, Robert Noxon 1836-1901 *ApCAB,*
WhAm 1
Toppan, Roland Worthington 1841-
NatCAB 11
Topper, Raymond Frederick 1885-1954
NatCAB 44
Toppin, Harry Pattinson 1898-1971 *WhAm 5*
Topping, Daniel Reid 1912-1974 *WhAm 6*
Topping, John Alexander 1860-1934 *ApCAB X,*
WhAm 1
Topping, Leila Lyons *WomWWA 14*
Toral, Francisco De 1502-1571 *ApCAB*
Torbert, Alfred Thomas Archimedes 1833-1880
AmBi, *ApCAB,* *DcAmB,* *Drake,*

NatCAB 4, *TwCBDA,* *WebAMB,*
WhAm H
Torbert, John Bryant 1867- *WhAm 1*
Torbert, William Sydenham 1872- *WhAm 5*
Torbet, David 1844-1916 *NatCAB 18*
Torbett, Charles W *NewYHSD*
Torbett, Joe Hall 1899-1954 *WhAm 3*
Torbett, John Walter 1871-1949 *NatCAB 38*
Torchiana, Henry Albert VanCoenen 1867-1940
WhAm 1
Torchio, Philip 1868-1942 *NatCAB 31,*
WhAm 1
Torchio, Phillip, Jr. 1908-1953 *WhAm 3*
Torek, Franz 1861-1938 *WhAm 1*
Torelle, Ellen *WomWWA 14*
Torgersen, Harold 1910-1961 *WhAm 4*
Torgerson, Reinert Martin 1908-1962
NatCAB 49
Torian, Oscar Noel 1875-1971 *NatCAB 57,*
WhAm 5
Toribio, Saint 1538-1606 *ApCAB*
Torices, Manuel Rodriguez 1788-1816 *ApCAB*
Torkelson, Martin Wilhelm 1878-1963 *WhAm 4*
Torlinski, Michael John 1885-1954 *NatCAB 43*
Tormoen, Clarence Oliver 1903-1956
NatCAB 46
Tornatore, Maximo J 1905-1957 *NatCAB 48*
Torneman, Axel *IIBEAAW*
Torney, George Henry 1850-1913 *WhAm 1*
Torney, George Henry 1872-1948 *NatCAB 41*
Torngren, Ralf 1899-1961 *WhAm 4*
Tornos, Alberto De 1821-1887 *ApCAB*
Tornos, Manuel Alberto 1862- *ApCAB*
Toro, Emilio Del 1876-1955 *WhAm 4*
Toro, Fermin 1807-1865 *ApCAB*
Toro Zambrano, Mateo De 1724-1811 *ApCAB*
Torpe, August 1875-1957 *NatCAB 45*
Torquemada, Juan De 1550?-1625? *ApCAB,*
Drake
Torrance, David 1840-1906 *NatCAB 12,*
WhAm 1
Torrance, Eli 1844- *WhAm 4*
Torrance, Ell 1844- *NatCAB 12*
Torrance, Francis 1816-1886 *ApCAB X*
Torrance, Francis John 1859-1919 *ApCAB X,*
NatCAB 11, *NatCAB 22,* *WhAm 1*
Torrance, Frederick William 1823- *ApCAB*
Torrance, George 1847- *NatCAB 11*
Torrance, Henry 1870- *WhAm 5*
Torrance, Jared Sidney 1852-1921 *NatCAB 19*
Torrance, Jessie Archer Groves *WomWWA 14*
Torrance, Lewis Curtiss 1855- *ApCAB X*
Torrance, Stiles Albert 1872-1953 *WhAm 3*
Torrance, Theodora McGill 1880-
WomWWA 14
Torrans, Rosella *NewYHSD*
Torre, Carlos DeLa 1858- *WhAm 5*
Torre, Jose Maria DeLa 1815-1873 *ApCAB*
Torre, Marcantonio Della 1481-1511 *DcScB*
Torre, Tomas DeLa 1510?-1567 *ApCAB*
Torre-Tagle, Jose Bernardo, Marquis De
1779-1825 *ApCAB*
Torrence, Frederick Ridgely 1874-1950
DcAmB S4
Torrence, George Paull 1887-1965 *NatCAB 54,*
WhAm 4
Torrence, Joseph Thatcher 1843-1896
ApCAB Sup, *DcAmB,* *NatCAB 2,*
WhAm H
Torrence, Olivia Howard Dunbar *WhAm 5*
Torrence, Ridgely d1950 *WhAm 3*
Torrence, William G 1880- *WhoColR*
Torrens, D T 1873- *WhAm 5*
Torrens, James H 1874-1952 *BiDrAC*
Torrens, Rosalba *NewYHSD*
Torrens, William Erskine 1870-1914 *WhAm 1*
Torres, Camilo 1766-1816 *ApCAB*
Torres, Diego De 1551-1638 *ApCAB*
Torres Caicedo, Jose Maria 1830- *ApCAB*
Torres Quevedo, Leonardo 1852-1936 *DcScB*
Torres Rubio, Diego De 1547-1638 *ApCAB*
Torres Y Ayala, Laureano 1645-1722 *ApCAB*
Torres Y Rueda, Marcos De 1591-1649 *ApCAB*
Torrey, Bradford 1843-1912 *AmBi,* *ApCAB,*
DcAmB, *NatCAB 10,* *TwCBDA,*
WhAm 1
Torrey, Charles Cutler 1799-1827 *NewYHSD*
Torrey, Charles Cutler 1863-1956 *NatCAB 42,*

WhAm 5
Torrey, Charles Turner 1813-1846 *AmBi,*
ApCAB, *DcAmB,* *Drake,* *NatCAB 6,*
WhAm H
Torrey, Clarence Ezra, Jr. 1913-1973 *WhAm 6*
Torrey, Elbridge 1837-1914 *WhAm 1*
Torrey, Elliot 1867-1949 *WhAm 2*
Torrey, Franklin 1830-1912 *ApCAB X,*
NewYHSD
Torrey, George Burroughs 1863-1942
NatCAB 36, *WhAm 2*
Torrey, Henry Norton 1880-1945 *NatCAB 39*
Torrey, Herbert Gray 1841-1915 *WhAm 1*
Torrey, Hiram Dwight 1820-1900 *NewYHSD*
Torrey, John 1796-1873 *AmBi,* *ApCAB,*
DcAmB, *DcScB,* *EncAAH,* *NatCAB 6,*
TwCBDA, *WebAB,* *WhAm H*
Torrey, John 1798-1873 *Drake*
Torrey, Joseph 1797-1867 *ApCAB,* *Drake,*
NatCAB 2, *TwCBDA,* *WhAm H*
Torrey, Joseph William 1828-1884 *AmBi,*
ApCAB
Torrey, Juliette E *NewYHSD*
Torrey, Manasseh Cutler 1807-1837 *NewYHSD*
Torrey, Marian Marsh 1893-1971 *WhAm 5*
Torrey, Mary Cutler 1831- *ApCAB*
Torrey, Ralph Martin 1888-1962 *NatCAB 48*
Torrey, Raymond Hezekiah 1880-1938
WhAm 1, *WhAm 1C*
Torrey, Reuben Archer 1856-1928 *DcAmReB,*
NatCAB 21, *WhAm 1*
Torrey, Samuel 1631-1707 *ApCAB*
Torrey, William 1590-1675? *ApCAB,* *Drake*
Torrey, William Ford 1911-1957 *NatCAB 47*
Torreyson, Burr Walter 1855-1932 *WhAm 1*
Torricelli, Evangelista 1608-1647 *AsBiEn,*
DcScB, *McGEWB*
Torrington, Arthur Herbert, Earl Of 1647-1716
WhoMilH
Torrington, Rosaline Rebecca *WomWWA 14*
Torrison, John William 1908-1966 *NatCAB 54,*
WhAm 4
Torrison, Oscar M 1861-1931 *WhAm 1*
Torrubia, Jose d1768 *ApCAB*
Torsch, John W *NewYHSD*
Torstensson, Lennart 1603-1651 *WhoMilH*
Tory, John Stewart Donald 1903-1965 *WhAm 4*
Toscanelli, Paolo 1397-1482 *AsBiEn*
Toscanelli DalPozzo, Paolo 1397-1482 *DcScB*
Toscanini, Arturo 1867-1957 *McGEWB,*
WebAB, *WhAm 3*
Toschik, Larry 1925- *IIBEAAW*
Toshach, Clarence Eneas 1894-1966
NatCAB 53
Totepehu d927 *ApCAB*
Toth, William 1905-1963 *WhAm 4*
Totiri, Stephen *ApCAB*
Totleben *WhoMilH*
Totoquiyauhtzin d1469 *ApCAB*
Totten, Benjamin J 1806-1877 *ApCAB*
Totten, Charles Adiel Lewis 1851-1908 *ApCAB,*
NatCAB 10, *WhAm 1*
Totten, George Muirson 1809-1884 *ApCAB,*
DcAmB, *Drake,* *NatCAB 18,* *WhAm H*
Totten, George Oakley, Jr. 1866-1939
NatCAB 41, *WhAm 1*
Totten, James 1818-1871 *ApCAB*
Totten, Joe Byron 1875-1946 *WhAm 2*
Totten, Joseph Gilbert 1788-1864 *AmBi,*
ApCAB, *DcAmB,* *Drake,* *NatCAB 4,*
TwCBDA, *WebAMB,* *WhAm H*
Totten, Ralph James 1877-1949 *WhAm 2*
Totten, Silas 1804-1873 *ApCAB,* *NatCAB 3,*
TwCBDA, *WhAm H*
Totton, Frank Mortimer 1890-1954 *WhAm 3*
Totty, S V 1914-1957 *WhAm 4*
Tou, Erik Hansen 1857-1917 *DcAmB*
Tou Velle, William Ellsworth 1862-1951
BiDrAC
Toubat, Francis Joseph 1802-1868 *Drake*
Toucey, Isaac 1792-1869 *AmBi,* *DcAmB*
Toucey, Isaac 1796-1869 *ApCAB,* *BiAUS,*
BiDrAC, *BiDrUSE,* *Drake,* *NatCAB 5,*
TwCBDA, *WhAm H,* *WhAmP*
Touchard, Louis Charles 1741-1782 *ApCAB*
Touchimbert, Eloi A P Sansac, Marquis De
1786-1839 *ApCAB*
Toulmin, George Hoggart 1754-1817 *DcScB*

Toulmin, Harry 1766-1823 *DcAmB, WhAm H*
Toulmin, Harry 1767-1823 *BiAUS, Drake, NatCAB 4*
Toulmin, Harry Aubrey, Jr. 1890-1965 *WhAm 4*
Toulmin, Harry Theophilus 1838-1916 *DcAmB, WhAm H*
Toulmin, Henry 1767-1823 *ApCAB, TwCBDA*
Toulmin, John Edwin 1902-1968 *WhAm 5*
Toulmin, Priestley, Jr. 1893-1969 *NatCAB 54*
Toulouse-Lautrec, Henri De 1864-1901 *McGEWB*
Toumey, James William 1865-1932 *DcAmB, WhAm 1*
Toupin, Marie *NotAW*
Toups, Roland Leon 1911-1969 *WhAm 5*
Tour, Charles Amador DeSt. Etienne d1665? *ApCAB*
Tour, Charles T DeSt. E, Sieur DeLa d1635? *ApCAB*
Tour, LeBlond DeLa d1725? *ApCAB*
Tour, Reuben S 1889-1952 *WhAm 3*
Toure, Samory 1830-1900 *McGEWB*
Toure, Sekou 1922- *McGEWB*
Tourel, Jennie d1973 *WhAm 6*
Touret, Frank Hale 1875-1945 *WhAm 2*
Tourgee, Albion Winegar 1838-1905 *AmBi, ApCAB, DcAmB, McGEWB, NatCAB 7, TwCBDA, WhAm 1*
Tourgee, Eben 1834- *ApCAB*
Tourgee, Eben 1834-1890 *TwCBDA*
Tourjee, Eben 1834-1891 *BiDAmEd, DcAmB, NatCAB 7, WhAm H*
Tournefort, Joseph Pitton De 1656-1708 *DcScB*
Touro, Judah 1775-1854 *ApCAB, Drake, NatCAB 6*
Touroff, Arthur Sigmund Wood 1900-1973 *NatCAB 57*
Touroff, Eleanor *WebAB*
Tourscher, Francis Edward 1870-1939 *WhAm 1*
Tourtellot, George P 1895-1946 *WhAm 2*
Tourtellotte, Edward Everett 1893- *WhAm 1*
Tourtillotte, Lillian Adele 1870- *AmWom*
Tourville, Anne Hilarion DeC, Comte De 1642-1701 *WhoMilH*
Tousant, Emma Sanborn 1890-1970 *WhAm 5*
Tousard, Anne Louis De 1749-1817 *DcAmB*
Tousey, Sinclair 1815-1887 *DcAmB, WhAm H*
Tousey, Sinclair 1818-1887 *ApCAB*
Tousey, Sinclair 1864-1937 *NatCAB 27*
Tousey, T Sanford *IIBEAAW*
Tousey, William George 1842- *WhAm 1*
Toussaint 1743-1803 *WhoMilH*
Toussaint, Dieudonne Gabriel 1717-1799 *ApCAB*
Toussaint, Dominique Francois 1743-1803 *ApCAB*
Toussaint, Emma 1862- *AmWom*
Toussaint L'Ouverture, Francois D 1743-1803 *Drake, McGEWB*
Toussaint L'Ouverture, Pierre F D 1743-1803 *WhAm H*
Toussard, Louis 1749-1820? *Drake*
Toussard, Louis 1749-1821 *ApCAB*
Touton, Frank Charles 1880-1936 *WhAm 1*
Touvelle, William E 1861- *WhAm 4*
Touzjian, Yacoub 1884-1963 *NatCAB 49*
Tovell, Ralph Moore 1901-1967 *NatCAB 53*
Toven, Joseph Richard 1901-1973 *WhAm 5*
Tovey, Sir John Cronyn 1885-1971 *WhWW-II, WhoMilH*
Towar, Albert Selah 1845- *WhAm 4*
Towart, William G 1880-1949 *WhAm 2*
Towe, Harry Lancaster 1898- *BiDrAC*
Tower, Carl Vernon 1869- *WhAm 5*
Tower, Charlemagne 1809-1889 *NatCAB 5*
Tower, Charlemagne 1848-1923 *AmBi, DcAmB, NatCAB 5, NatCAB 26, TwCBDA, WhAm 1*
Tower, Edwin Briggs Hale, Jr. 1879-1948 *NatCAB 39, WhAm 2C, WhAm 3*
Tower, F B 1817-1857 *NewYHSD*
Tower, Fayette Bartholomew 1817-1857 *ApCAB*
Tower, George Edward 1836-1914 *WhAm 1*
Tower, George Warren 1900-1968 *NatCAB 54*
Tower, George Warren, Jr. 1871-1939 *WhAm 1*
Tower, James Eaton 1863-1947 *WhAm 2*
Tower, John 1758-1831 *WhAm H*
Tower, John Benjamin 1877-1928 *NatCAB 22*

Tower, John Goodwin 1925- *BiDrAC*
Tower, Olin Freeman 1872-1945 *WhAm 2*
Tower, Ralph Winfred 1870-1926 *WhAm 1*
Tower, Ray Jay 1859-1927 *NatCAB 23*
Tower, Walter Sheldon 1881-1969 *WhAm 5*
Tower, William A 1825-1904 *NatCAB 15*
Tower, William Lawrence 1872- *NatCAB 15, WhAm 5*
Tower, Zealous Bates 1819-1900 *AmBi, ApCAB, DcAmB, Drake, NatCAB 4, TwCBDA*
Tower, Zealous Bates *see also* Towner, Zealous Bates
Towers, Albert Garey 1873- *WhAm 5*
Towers, Charles Daughtry 1894-1969 *NatCAB 54*
Towers, J *NewYHSD*
Towers, James Fullton 1881-1970 *NatCAB 55*
Towers, John Alden 1894-1956 *WhAm 3*
Towers, John Henry 1885-1955 *DcAmB S5, NatCAB 41, WebAMB, WhAm 3*
Towers, Walter Kellogg 1888-1931 *WhAm 1*
Towey, Frank William, Jr. 1895- *BiDrAC*
Towl, Forrest Milton 1863-1946 *WhAm 2*
Towle, Carroll Sherburne 1901-1962 *NatCAB 50, WhAm 4*
Towle, Charles Brother 1875-1951 *WhAm 3*
Towle, Charlotte 1896-1966 *WhAm 4*
Towle, Edwin Herman 1869-1963 *NatCAB 51*
Towle, Elizabeth Williams 1876- *WomWWA 14*
Towle, Eunice Makepeace *NewYHSD*
Towle, George Makepeace 1841-1893 *AmBi, ApCAB, DcAmB, NatCAB 8, TwCBDA, WhAm H*
Towle, Harry Freeman 1852-1912 *NatCAB 15*
Towle, J Norman 1864-1932 *WhAm 3*
Towle, J Norman 1864-1934 *NatCAB 38*
Towle, Jeremiah 1800-1880 *NatCAB 11*
Towle, Joseph Henry 1889-1951 *NatCAB 40*
Towle, Katherine Amelia 1898- *WebAMB*
Towle, Lawrence William 1902-1974 *WhAm 6*
Towle, Loren Delbert 1874- *NatCAB 16*
Towle, Mary Rutter 1876- *WomWWA 14*
Towle, Norman Lincoln 1895-1963 *WhAm 4*
Towle, Stevenson 1837- *NatCAB 11*
Towle, William Mason 1851-1930 *NatCAB 24*
Towler, John 1811-1889 *ApCAB, DcAmB, WhAm H*
Towler, Thomas Willard 1891-1972 *WhAm 5*
Towles, Catherine Webb 1823- *ApCAB*
Towles, Thomas *BiAUS*
Town, Arno Emerson 1901-1967 *NatCAB 54*
Town, David Edward 1871-1933 *WhAm 1*
Town, Ithiel 1784-1844 *AmBi, ApCAB, BnEnAmA, DcAmB, Drake, WebAB, WhAm H*
Town, Salem 1779-1864 *ApCAB, BiDAmEd*
Towndrow, Thomas 1810-1898 *ApCAB Sup, NatCAB 9*
Towne, Ann Sophia *NewYHSD*
Towne, Arthur Whittlesey 1878-1954 *WhAm 3*
Towne, Belle Kellogg 1844- *AmWom*
Towne, Benjamin d1793 *DcAmB, WhAm H*
Towne, Charles Arnette 1858-1928 *BiDrAC, DcAmB, NatCAB 12, TwCBDA, WhAm 1*
Towne, Charles Hanson 1877-1949 *DcAmB S4, WhAm 2*
Towne, Charles Wayland 1875- *WhAm 6*
Towne, Edward Owings 1859- *WhAm 1*
Towne, Elizabeth 1865- *BiCAW, WomWWA 14*
Towne, Elizabeth 1865-1961 *WhAm 4*
Towne, Elizabeth Lois 1865-1960 *NatCAB 46*
Towne, Ezra Thayer 1873-1952 *WhAm 4*
Towne, Frank Beckwith 1865-1946 *NatCAB 34*
Towne, George Lewis 1873-1961 *WhAm 4*
Towne, Henry Robinson 1844-1924 *ApCAB X, DcAmB, NatCAB 12, NatCAB 21, WhAm 1*
Towne, John Gerald 1877-1954 *NatCAB 42*
Towne, John Henry 1818-1875 *DcAmB, NatCAB 24, WhAm H*
Towne, John Henry 1869-1942 *NatCAB 32, WhAm 2*
Towne, Joseph Minott 1875-1958 *NatCAB 44*
Towne, Laura Matilda 1825-1901 *NotAW*

Towne, Percy Edgar 1875-1941 *NatCAB 30*
Towne, Robert Duke 1866-1952 *NatCAB 39, WhAm 3*
Towne, Rosalba M 1827- *NewYHSD*
Towne, Salem 1779-1864 *Drake*
Towne, Salem B 1847-1933 *WhAm 1*
Towne, Walter James 1867-1930 *WhAm 1*
Towne, William Elmer 1874- *WhAm 5*
Towneley, Richard 1629-1707 *DcScB*
Towner, Daniel Brink 1850-1919 *WhAm 1*
Towner, Harriet C 1869- *WomWWA 14*
Towner, Horace Mann 1855-1937 *AmBi, BiDrAC, WhAm 1, WhAmP*
Towner, Neile Fassett 1875-1962 *NatCAB 49, WhAm 4*
Towner, Rutherford Hamilton 1870-1950 *WhAm 2*
Towner, Zealous Bates 1819-1900 *WhAm H*
Towner, Zealous Bates *see also* Tower, Zealous Bates
Townes, Charles Dwight 1899-1972 *NatCAB 57*
Townes, Charles Hard 1915- *AsBiEn, WebAB*
Townes, Edgar Eggleston 1878-1962 *WhAm 4*
Townes, John Charles 1852-1923 *NatCAB 32, WhAm 1*
Townley, Alfred Hudson 1876-1954 *NatCAB 48*
Townley, Alice Ashworth 1870- *WomWWA 14*
Townley, Arthur Charles 1880-1959 *EncAAH, REnAW*
Townley, Calvert 1864-1933 *NatCAB 24, WhAm 1, WhAm 1C*
Townley, Frank Maxwell 1870-1940 *NatCAB 30*
Townley, Ruth Francis 1886- *WomWWA 14*
Townley, Sidney Dean 1867-1946 *NatCAB 42, WhAm 2*
Towns, Charles B 1862-1947 *WhAm 2*
Towns, George Alexander 1870- *WhoColR*
Towns, George Washington Bonaparte 1801-1854 *ApCAB, BiDrAC, DcAmB, Drake, TwCBDA, WhAm H*
Towns, George Washington Bonaparte 1802-1854 *BiAUS, NatCAB 1*
Townsend, Alexander 1784-1835 *ApCAB*
Townsend, Alice Greenough 1872- *WomWWA 14*
Townsend, Amos 1821-1895 *BiDrAC, WhAm H*
Townsend, Amos 1831-1895 *NatCAB 2*
Townsend, Arthur Melvin 1875- *WhoColR*
Townsend, Charles 1836-1894 *NewYHSD*
Townsend, Charles Champlain 1841-1910 *BiDrAC*
Townsend, Charles Champlin 1841-1910 *NatCAB 7*
Townsend, Charles E *NewYHSD*
Townsend, Charles Elroy 1856-1924 *BiDrAC, NatCAB 15, WhAm 1, WhAmP*
Townsend, Charles H T 1863-1944 *WhAm 2*
Townsend, Charles Haskell *WhAm H*
Townsend, Charles Haskins 1859-1944 *NatCAB 32, WhAm 2*
Townsend, Charles Orrin 1863-1937 *WhAm 1*
Townsend, Charles Wendell 1859-1934 *WhAm 1*
Townsend, Charlotte *NewYHSD*
Townsend, Christopher 1807-1881 *NatCAB 8*
Townsend, Clarence Ellsworth 1882-1967 *NatCAB 53*
Townsend, Claudius Barringer 1851-1940 *NatCAB 31*
Townsend, Curtis McDonald 1856-1941 *WhAm 1*
Townsend, Dallas Selwyn 1888-1966 *WhAm 4*
Townsend, David 1856-1918 *NatCAB 26*
Townsend, David 1873-1950 *NatCAB 39*
Townsend, Dwight 1826-1899 *BiAUS, BiDrAC*
Townsend, Edgar Jerome 1864-1955 *NatCAB 44, WhAm 3*
Townsend, Edward Davis 1817-1893 *ApCAB, DcAmB, Drake, NatCAB 11, TwCBDA, WhAm H*
Townsend, Edward Perry 1881-1962 *NatCAB 50*
Townsend, Edward Waterman 1855-1942 *BiDrAC, NatCAB 14, WhAm 2*
Townsend, Edward Y 1824-1891 *NatCAB 3*
Townsend, Edwin Franklin 1833-1909 *WhAm 1*

Townsend, Eliza 1789-1854 *ApCAB, Drake*
Townsend, Elli Moore 1861- *WomWWA 14*
Townsend, Emily Allison *WomWWA 14*
Townsend, Ernest Nathaniel 1893-1945 *WhAm 2*
Townsend, Ferdinand Charles 1869-1958 *NatCAB 43*
Townsend, Frances Hodgson *TwCBDA*
Townsend, Francis Everett 1867-1960 *WebAB, WhAm 4*
Townsend, Francis Everitt 1867-1960 *McGEWB*
Townsend, Frederic Martin 1860- *WhAm 4*
Townsend, Frederick 1825-1898 *ApCAB, NatCAB 4, TwCBDA*
Townsend, Frederick 1871-1949 *NatCAB 38, WhAm 2*
Townsend, George *NewYHSD*
Townsend, George 1769-1844 *BiAUS, BiDrAC, WhAm H*
Townsend, George Alfred 1841-1914 *AmBi, ApCAB, DcAmB, NatCAB 1, TwCBDA, WhAm 1*
Townsend, George Lybrand 1841-1917 *NatCAB 31*
Townsend, George Washington 1839-1905 *WhAm 1*
Townsend, Grace Beach 1872- *WomWWA 14*
Townsend, Harry Pond 1875-1942 *NatCAB 32*
Townsend, Harvey Gates 1885-1948 *WhAm 2*
Townsend, Henry C 1849- *WhAm 1*
Townsend, Henry L L *NewYHSD*
Townsend, Horace 1859-1922 *WhAm 1*
Townsend, Hosea 1840-1909 *BiDrAC, WhAm 1*
Townsend, Howard 1823-1867 *ApCAB*
Townsend, Howard 1858-1935 *NatCAB 31*
Townsend, James d1791 *BiAUS*
Townsend, James 1882-1948 *NatCAB 37*
Townsend, James Bliss 1855-1921 *WhAm 1*
Townsend, James Mulford 1825-1901 *NatCAB 4, WhAm 1*
Townsend, James Mulford 1852-1913 *NatCAB 14, WhAm 1*
Townsend, James Robert 1858- *ApCAB X*
Townsend, Mrs. John F *NewYHSD*
Townsend, John Ferrars 1880-1962 *NatCAB 49*
Townsend, John Gillis, Jr. 1871-1964 *BiDrAC, WhAm 4, WhAmP*
Townsend, John Kirk 1809-1851 *ApCAB, DcAmB, TwCBDA, WhAm H*
Townsend, John Kirk 1809-1861 *Drake*
Townsend, John MacMillan 1906-1962 *NatCAB 50*
Townsend, John Pomeroy 1832-1898 *ApCAB Sup*
Townsend, John Sealy Edward 1868-1957 *DcScB*
Townsend, John Wilson 1885-1968 *WhAm 4A*
Townsend, Joseph 1739-1816 *DcScB*
Townsend, Joseph Hendley 1862-1916 *WhAm 1*
Townsend, Joseph Winter 1899-1963 *NatCAB 50*
Townsend, Julius Curtis 1881-1939 *NatCAB 42, WhAm 1*
Townsend, Katherine Crawford Poage *WomWWA 14*
Townsend, Lawrence 1860-1954 *NatCAB 12, TwCBDA, WhAm 3*
Townsend, Levi Scott 1867-1918 *NatCAB 17*
Townsend, Luther Tracy 1838-1922 *ApCAB, DcAmB, NatCAB 10, TwCBDA, WhAm 1*
Townsend, M Clifford 1884-1954 *NatCAB 46, WhAm 3*
Townsend, Marion Ernest 1889-1939 *NatCAB 29, WhAm 1*
Townsend, Martin Ingham 1810-1903 *ApCAB, BiAUS, BiDrAC, NatCAB 4, TwCBDA, WhAm 1*
Townsend, Mary Ashley 1832-1901 *DcAmB, NatCAB 1*
Townsend, Mary Ashley 1836?-1901 *AmWom, ApCAB, TwCBDA, WhAm 1*
Townsend, Mary Evelyn 1884-1954 *WhAm 3*
Townsend, Mary Louise 1870- *WomWWA 14*
Townsend, Mira Sharpless 1798-1859 *DcAmB, WhAm H*
Townsend, N S *BiAUS*
Townsend, Oliver Henry 1917-1969 *NatCAB 55,*

WhAm 5
Townsend, Oscar 1874- *WhAm 5*
Townsend, Penn 1651-1727 *ApCAB, Drake*
Townsend, Peter 1730?-1790 *NatCAB 8*
Townsend, Prescott Winson 1893-1961 *WhAm 4*
Townsend, Randolph Wanton 1812- *ApCAB, WhAm 1*
Townsend, Robert 1819-1866 *ApCAB, DcAmB, Drake, WhAm H*
Townsend, Robert Donaldson 1854-1933 *WhAm 1*
Townsend, Smith DeLancey 1860-1944 *WhAm 2*
Townsend, Stephen Sumner 1865-1941 *NatCAB 30*
Townsend, Sylvester Deputy 1870-1947 *NatCAB 37, WhAm 2*
Townsend, Theodore Irving 1869-1932 *WhAm 1*
Townsend, Thomas Chesteen 1877-1949 *NatCAB 45*
Townsend, Thomas Seaman 1829-1908 *ApCAB*
Townsend, Thomas Seaman 1830-1908 *AmBi*
Townsend, Virginia Frances d1920 *Drake*
Townsend, Virginia Frances 1830-1920 *WhAm 4*
Townsend, Virginia Frances 1836-1920 *ApCAB, DcAmB, NatCAB 13, TwCBDA, WomWWA 14*
Townsend, Washington 1813-1894 *BiAUS, BiDrAC, NatCAB 3, WhAm H*
Townsend, Wayne LaSalle 1896-1969 *WhAm 5*
Townsend, Willa A 1880- *WhoColR*
Townsend, Willard Saxby 1895-1957 *WhAm 3*
Townsend, William Bolden *WhoColR*
Townsend, William H *NewYHSD*
Townsend, William Hay 1868-1934 *NatCAB 29, WhAm 1*
Townsend, William Henry 1890-1964 *NatCAB 51, WhAm 4*
Townsend, William Kneeland 1849-1907 *AmBi, NatCAB 19, NatCAB 20, WhAm 1*
Townsend, William Penn 1817-1894 *NatCAB 6*
Townsend, William Warren 1870-1928 *WhAm 1*
Townsend, Wisner Robinson 1856-1916 *NatCAB 20*
Townsend, Wisner Robinson 1857-1916 *WhAm 1*
Townshend, Charles 1725-1767 *ApCAB, Drake, WhAm H*
Townshend, Charles Hervey 1833-1904 *NatCAB 29*
Townshend, Sir Charles Vere Ferrers 1861-1924 *WhoMilH*
Townshend, George 1724-1807 *ApCAB, Drake*
Townshend, Hannah Draper Osgood 1882- *BiCAW*
Townshend, Norton Strange 1815-1895 *ApCAB, BiDrAC, NatCAB 7, TwCBDA, WhAm H*
Townshend, Raynham 1878-1940 *NatCAB 29*
Townshend, Richard Wellington 1840-1889 *ApCAB, BiDrAC, TwCBDA, WhAm H, WhAmP*
Townshend, Roger 1730?-1759 *ApCAB*
Townsley, Clarence Page 1855-1926 *NatCAB 18, WhAm 1*
Townsley, Frances Eleanor 1850- *AmWom*
Townsley, Louis 1877- *WhAm 5*
Townson, Andrew Johnston 1856-1920 *NatCAB 19*
Townson, Marie Antoinette Castle *WomWWA 14*
Towse, J Ranken 1845-1933 *WhAm 1*
Towson, Morris Sherman 1865-1942 *NatCAB 32*
Towson, Nathan 1784-1854 *ApCAB, Drake, NatCAB 7*
Towson, Sheldon Kerruish 1902-1958 *NatCAB 46*
Toy, Crawford Howell 1836-1919 *AmBi, ApCAB, DcAmB, DcAmReB, NatCAB 6, TwCBDA, WhAm 1*
Toy, Harry Stanley 1892-1955 *WhAm 3*
Toy, James Frederick 1867-1937 *NatCAB 28*
Toy, Walter Dallam 1854- *WhAm 4*
Toy, Walter Ludman 1889-1940 *NatCAB 38*
Toye, John Ernest 1876-1943 *NatCAB 33*
Toynbee, Arnold Joseph 1889-1975 *McGEWB,*

WhAm 6
Toyoda, Soemu 1885- *WhWW-II*
Toyotomi, Hideyoshi 1536-1598 *McGEWB*
Tozere, Frederic 1901-1972 *WhAm 5*
Tozier, Josephine 1861- *WhAm 4*
Tozier, Kathleen B *WomWWA 14*
Tozzer, Alfred Marston 1877-1954 *WhAm 3*
Tozzer, Arthur Clarence 1879-1942 *WhAm 2*
Tozzi, Don Bruno 1656-1743 *DcScB*
Trabert, George Henry 1843- *WhAm 4*
Trabue, Charles Clay 1872-1942 *WhAm 2*
Trabue, Edmund Francis 1855-1936 *WhAm 1*
Trabue, Isaac Hodgen 1829-1907 *WhAm 1*
Trabue, Marion Rex 1890-1972 *BiDAmEd, WhAm 5*
Tracewell, Robert John 1852-1922 *BiDrAC, WhAm 1*
Tracey, Albert Haller 1793-1859 *BiAUS*
Tracey, Charles 1847-1905 *BiDrAC, NatCAB 12, WhAm 1*
Tracey, James Francis 1854-1925 *WhAm 1*
Tracey, John Plank 1836-1910 *BiDrAC*
Tracht, Frederick Homer 1875-1952 *NatCAB 39*
Tracht, Robert Russell 1899-1956 *NatCAB 45*
Trachtman, Joseph 1901-1975 *WhAm 6*
Tracy, Albert Haller 1793-1859 *ApCAB, BiDrAC, TwCBDA, WhAm H*
Tracy, Alexander DeProuville De 1603-1670 *Drake*
Tracy, Alexandre DeProuville De 1603-1670 *ApCAB*
Tracy, Andrew 1797-1868 *BiAUS, BiDrAC, WhAm H*
Tracy, Benjamin Franklin 1830-1915 *AmBi, ApCAB Sup, ApCAB X, BiDrUSE, DcAmB, NatCAB 1, TwCBDA, WhAm 1*
Tracy, Charles 1810-1885 *ApCAB, NatCAB 12*
Tracy, Charles Chapin 1838-1917 *ApCAB, NatCAB 11, TwCBDA, WhAm 1*
Tracy, Charles Edward 1845-1896 *NatCAB 31*
Tracy, Clarissa Tucker 1818-1905 *WhAm 1*
Tracy, Daniel William 1886-1955 *WhAm 3*
Tracy, Ebenezer Carter 1796-1862 *ApCAB, Drake*
Tracy, Edward Huntington 1817-1875 *NatCAB 9*
Tracy, Elizabeth Blakeslee 1869- *WomWWA 14*
Tracy, Elizabeth Strong 1838- *WomWWA 14*
Tracy, Ernest Bell 1884-1948 *NatCAB 36, WhAm 2*
Tracy, Evarts 1868-1922 *WhAm 1*
Tracy, Frank Basil 1866-1912 *WhAm 1*
Tracy, Frank W 1833-1903 *WhAm 1*
Tracy, G P *NewYHSD*
Tracy, George Allison 1907-1971 *WhAm 5*
Tracy, George Lowell 1855-1921 *NatCAB 8*
Tracy, H W 1807-1886 *BiAUS*
Tracy, Hannah Maria Conant *NotAW*
Tracy, Henry Chester 1876-1958 *WhAm 3*
Tracy, Henry Wells 1807-1886 *BiDrAC, WhAm H*
Tracy, Howard 1856-1922 *NatCAB 17*
Tracy, Howard Crosby 1866- *NatCAB 15*
Tracy, Howard VanSinderen 1887-1945 *NatCAB 18, WhAm 2*
Tracy, Ira 1806-1875 *ApCAB*
Tracy, James Grant 1873-1943 *WhAm 2*
Tracy, James Madison 1837-1928 *WhAm 1*
Tracy, Jeremiah Evarts 1835-1923 *NatCAB 9, NatCAB 21*
Tracy, John Cadman 1884-1937 *NatCAB 28*
Tracy, John Clayton 1869-1955 *WhAm 3*
Tracy, John Evarts 1880-1959 *WhAm 3*
Tracy, Joseph 1793-1874 *DcAmB, WhAm H*
Tracy, Joseph 1794-1874 *ApCAB, Drake, NatCAB 13*
Tracy, Joseph Powell 1874-1950 *WhAm 3*
Tracy, Lee 1898-1968 *WhAm 5*
Tracy, Leo James 1890-1960 *WhAm 4*
Tracy, Lyall 1893-1959 *WhAm 3*
Tracy, Marguerite 1875- *WomWWA 14*
Tracy, Martha 1876-1942 *NatCAB 31, NotAW, WhAm 2, WomWWA 14*
Tracy, Mary Clemmer 1871- *WomWWA 14*

Tracy, Merle Elliott 1879-1945 *NatCAB 33,
WhAm 2*
Tracy, Nathaniel 1751-1796 *DcAmB,
WhAm H*
Tracy, Olin Hobbs 1857-1944 *NatCAB 34*
Tracy, Phineas Lyman 1786-1876 *ApCAB,
BiAUS, BiDrAC, WhAm H*
Tracy, R D d1863 *Drake*
Tracy, Roger Sherman 1841-1926 *ApCAB,
WhAm 1*
Tracy, Roger Walker 1903-1964 *WhAm 4*
Tracy, Russel Lord 1860-1945 *WhAm 2*
Tracy, S *NewYHSD*
Tracy, Samuel Mills 1847-1920 *NatCAB 18,
WhAm 1*
Tracy, Spencer 1900-1967 *WebAB, WhAm 4*
Tracy, Thomas Henry 1859- *WhAm 4*
Tracy, Uri 1764-1813 *BiAUS*
Tracy, Uri 1764-1838 *BiDrAC, WhAm H*
Tracy, Uriah 1735-1807 *WhAm H*
Tracy, Uriah 1755-1807 *ApCAB, BiAUS,
BiDrAC, DcAmB, Drake, NatCAB 2,
TwCBDA, WhAmP*
Tracy, William Dwight 1873-1937 *NatCAB 27*
Tracy, William Edward 1896-1958 *NatCAB 43*
Tracy, William W 1845-1932 *WhAm 1*
Trader, Ella King Newsom 1838-1919 *NotAW*
Trader, Florence Bishop *WomWWA 14*
Trader, Georgia Duckworth *WomWWA 14*
Tradescant, John 1570?-1638 *DcScB*
Tradescant, John 1608-1662 *DcScB*
Traeger, Cornelius Horace 1896-1968
NatCAB 54, WhAm 5
Traeger, William Isham 1880-1935 *BiDrAC,
WhAm 1*
Traer, Charles Solberg 1890-1949 *WhAm 2*
Traer, Glenn Wood 1889-1962 *NatCAB 49*
Traetta, Filippo 1776?-1854 *DcAmB*
Trafford, Bernard Walton 1871-1941 *WhAm 2*
Trafton, Adeline 1845?- *ApCAB*
Trafton, Gilbert Haven 1874-1943 *WhAm 2*
Trafton, Mark 1810-1901 *AmBi, ApCAB,
BiAUS, BiDrAC, WhAm 1*
Trafton, William Henry 1857-1926 *WhAm 1*
Tragethon, Herbert Norman 1898-1963
NatCAB 49
Tragus, Hieronymus *DcScB*
Trail, Florence 1854- *AmWom, ApCAB Sup*
Traill, Catherine Parr Strickland 1802-1899
ApCAB, McGEWB
Traill, Catherine Parr Strickland 1805?-1899
Drake
Train, Arthur Cheney 1875-1945 *DcAmB S3,
NatCAB 14, WhAm 2*
Train, Arthur Savage 1812-1872 *ApCAB*
Train, Charles 1783-1849 *ApCAB*
Train, Charles Jackson 1845-1906 *NatCAB 21,
WhAm 1*
Train, Charles Russell 1817-1885 *ApCAB,
BiAUS, BiDrAC, Drake, WhAm H*
Train, Charles Russell 1879-1967 *NatCAB 53,
WhAm 4A*
Train, Daniel N *NewYHSD*
Train, Elizabeth Phipps 1856- *TwCBDA,
WhAm 4, WomWWA 14*
Train, Enoch 1801-1868 *DcAmB*
Train, Enoch 1801-1869 *WhAm H*
Train, Ethel Kissam 1875-1923 *WhAm 1*
Train, George Frances 1829-1904 *WebAB*
Train, George Francis 1829-1904 *AmBi,
ApCAB, DcAmB, NatCAB 9, TwCBDA,
WhAm 1*
Train, George Francis 1830-1904 *Drake*
Train, Harold Cecil 1887-1968 *NatCAB 55,
WhAm 5*
Train, John Kirk 1880-1955 *NatCAB 46*
Train, John Lambert 1883-1958 *WhAm 3*
Trainer, David Woolsey, Jr. 1899-1965 *WhAm 4*
Trainer, Maurice Newlin 1889-1969
NatCAB 56, WhAm 5
Trainor, Raymond John 1876-1949 *NatCAB 38*
Traisman, Alfred Stanley 1896-1974 *WhAm 6*
Trajan 053?-117 *McGEWB*
Trajetta, Philip 1776?-1854 *DcAmB,
WhAm H*
Trall, Russell Thacher 1812-1877 *ApCAB,
Drake*
Tralle, Henry Edward 1867-1942 *WhAm 2*

Tramburg, John William 1913-1963 *WhAm 4*
Trammell, Leander Newton 1830-1900
NatCAB 3, WhAm 1
Trammell, Niles 1894-1973 *WhAm 5*
Trammell, Park 1876-1936 *ApCAB X,
BiDrAC, NatCAB 32, WhAm 1,
WhAmP*
Tramwell, Paul Barclay 1878-1936 *WhAm 4*
Tranchepain DeSaint Augustine, Marie De d1733
ApCAB
Trane, Reuben Nicholas 1886-1954 *NatCAB 46,
WhAm 3*
Traner, Fredrick W 1886-1963 *WhAm 4,
WhAm 5*
Trangmar, Earl R 1890-1961 *NatCAB 49*
Transeau, Edgar Nelson 1875- *WhAm 5*
Transeau, Gertrude Hastings 1878-
WomWWA 14
Translot, Mrs. Eugene *NewYHSD*
Transue, Andrew Jackson 1903- *BiDrAC*
Trant, James Buchanan 1890-1970 *WhAm 5*
Tranter, Henry 1865-1940 *NatCAB 49*
Trantham, Betsey d1834 *Drake*
Trantham, Henry 1882-1962 *WhAm 4*
Trap, William Martin 1887-1958 *WhAm 3*
Traphagen, Ethel 1882-1963 *NatCAB 54*
Traphagen, Frank Weiss 1861-1941 *WhAm 1*
Traphagen, William Conselyea 1837-1894
NatCAB 25
Trapier, Paul 1749-1778 *BiAUS, BiDrAC,
WhAm H*
Trapnell, Frederick Mackay 1902-1975
WhAm 6
Trapnell, William Colston 1906-1974 *WhAm 6*
Trapnell, William Holmes 1905-1973 *WhAm 6*
Trapp, August *NewYHSD*
Trapp, Harry Edwin, Jr. 1918-1971 *NatCAB 57*
Trapp, Martin Edwin 1877-1951 *WhAm 3*
Trapper, Emma Louise *WomWWA 14*
Traquair, James 1756-1811 *NewYHSD*
Trask, George 1798-1875 *ApCAB*
Trask, James Dowling 1890-1942 *DcAmB S3,
NatCAB 31*
Trask, James Elisha 1855- *NatCAB 16*
Trask, John Ellingwood Donnell 1871-1926
WhAm 1
Trask, John William 1877-1951 *NatCAB 38,
WhAm 3*
Trask, Kate Nichols 1853-1922 *NotAW,
WhAm 1, WomWWA 14*
Trask, Katrina 1853-1922 *NatCAB 11,
NotAW*
Trask, Spencer 1844-1909 *NatCAB 11,
WhAm 1*
Trask, Verne Alva 1896-1971 *NatCAB 56*
Trask, Walter Jones 1862-1911 *NatCAB 16*
Trask, Warren Dudley 1886-1958 *NatCAB 47*
Trask, William Blake 1812-1906 *ApCAB,
Drake, WhAm 1*
Tratman, Edward Ernest Russell *WhAm 5*
Trattner, Ernest Robert 1898-1963 *WhAm 4*
Trattner, Sidney 1892-1957 *NatCAB 45*
Traub, Frank Milton 1873-1923 *NatCAB 6*
Traub, Martin 1900-1967 *NatCAB 53*
Traub, Peter Edward 1864-1956 *WhAm 3*
Traube, Ludwig 1818-1876 *BiHiMed*
Traube, Moritz 1826-1894 *DcScB*
Traubel, Helen d1972 *WhAm 5*
Traubel, Horace L 1858-1919 *DcAmB,
WhAm 1*
Traubel, M 1820-1897 *NewYHSD*
Traudt, Bernard G 1876- *WhAm 5*
Traugott, Albert Maser 1882-1954 *WhAm 3*
Traut, George Washington 1869-1927
NatCAB 33
Trautman, George M 1890-1963 *WhAm 4*
Trautmann, William Emil 1872- *WhAm 5*
Trautwein, Alfred Philip 1857-1914 *NatCAB 18*
Trautwine, John Cresson 1810-1883 *ApCAB,
DcAmB, NatCAB 5, NewYHSD,
WhAm H*
Trautwine, John Cresson, Jr. 1850-1924
WhAm 1
Travell, Janet Davidson 1870- *WomWWA 14*
Travell, Willard 1869-1961 *NatCAB 52*
Traven, B d1969 *WhAm 5*
Traver, Harry Guy 1877-1961 *NatCAB 49*
Traver, Hope *WomWWA 14*

Traver, John Gideon 1863-1941 *WhAm 2*
Travers, Benjamin 1783-1858 *BiHiMed*
Travers, Edward Schofield 1874-1942 *WhAm 2*
Travers, James Wadsworth 1865-1949
NatCAB 42
Travers, Jerome Dunstan 1887-1951 *DcAmB S5*
Travers, Morris William 1872-1961 *DcScB*
Travers, Philip Lee 1878-1961 *NatCAB 51*
Travers, Robert Morris William 1913-
BiDAmEd
Travers, William Riggin 1819-1887 *NatCAB 8*
Travis, Charles Mabbett 1885-1948 *NatCAB 37,
WhAm 2*
Travis, Emma Helen Begg 1881-
WomWWA 14
Travis, Eugene Mabbett 1863-1940 *NatCAB 49*
Travis, Everett Hustis 1867-1941 *NatCAB 31*
Travis, Homer Lee 1908-1962 *WhAm 4*
Travis, Ira Dudley 1858-1939 *NatCAB 29,
WhAm 5*
Travis, Joseph 1786-1858 *ApCAB*
Travis, Judson Cooper 1902-1973 *WhAm 6*
Travis, Julius Curtis 1868-1961 *WhAm 4*
Travis, Olin Herman 1888- *IIBEAAW*
Travis, Philip H 1865-1942 *WhAm 2*
Travis, Robert Falligant 1904-1950 *WhAm 3*
Travis, Simeon Ezekiel 1866-1952 *WhAm 3*
Travis, Walter John 1862-1927 *DcAmB,
WhAm HA, WhAm 4*
Travis, Wesley Elgin 1870- *WhAm 5*
Travis, William B 1811-1836 *Drake*
Travis, William Barret 1809-1836 *AmBi,
DcAmB, EncAAH, McGEWB, WebAB,
WebAMB, WhAm H*
Travis, William Barrett 1805-1836 *NatCAB 4*
Travis, William Barrett 1811-1836 *ApCAB*
Travis, William DeLaney Trimble 1839-1916
NatCAB 17, NewYHSD
Traweek, Albert Carroll 1875-1959 *NatCAB 47*
Trawick, Arcadius McSwain 1869- *WhAm 5*
Trawick, Henry 1868-1913 *WhAm 1*
Trawick, Leonard M 1904-1964 *WhAm 4*
Traxler, Arthur Edwin 1900- *BiDAmEd*
Traylor, John H 1839- *WhAm 4*
Traylor, Melvin Alvah 1878-1934 *DcAmB,
NatCAB 17, NatCAB 25, WhAm 1*
Traylor, Robert Lee 1864- *WhAm 4*
Traylor, Samuel William 1869-1947
NatCAB 38
Traylor, Thomas Regis 1886- *WhoColR*
Traynor, Philip Andrew 1874-1962 *BiDrAC,
WhAm 5*
Traynor, William Bernard 1886-1968
WhAm 4A
Traynor, William James Henry 1845- *WhAm 4*
Trayser, Lewis William 1895-1964 *NatCAB 52,
WhAm 4*
Treacy, John P 1890-1964 *WhAm 4*
Treadway, Allen Towner 1867-1947 *BiDrAC,
NatCAB 35, WhAm 2, WhAmP*
Treadway, Charles Terry 1877-1958
NatCAB 50, WhAm 3
Treadway, Esther *WomWWA 14*
Treadway, Walter Lewis 1886-1973 *WhAm 6*
Treadwell, Aaron Louis 1866-1947 *WhAm 2*
Treadwell, Alliene Wetmore 1869-1950
NatCAB 40
Treadwell, Daniel 1791-1872 *AmBi, ApCAB,
DcAmB, Drake, NatCAB 10, WhAm H*
Treadwell, Edward Francis 1875-1955
NatCAB 43, WhAm 5
Treadwell, George A *WhAm 5*
Treadwell, John 1745-1823 *ApCAB, BiAUS,
BiDrAC, Drake, NatCAB 10, TwCBDA,
WhAm H*
Treadwell, John Goodhue 1805-1856 *ApCAB,
Drake*
Treadwell, Jona *NewYHSD*
Treadwell, Nancy Claar 1924-1970 *WhAm 5*
Treadwell, Seymour Boughton 1795-1867
ApCAB, Drake
Treadwell, Thomas 1743-1832 *NatCAB 3*
Treaga, Genoza *NewYHSD*
Treaga, Santonio *NewYHSD*
Treanor, Arthur Ryan 1883-1956 *WhAm 3*
Treanor, James Aloysius, Jr. 1904-1964
WhAm 4
Treanor, John 1883-1936 *WhAm 1*

Treanor, Joseph Holland 1902-1961 *WhAm 4*
Treanor, Tom 1908-1944 *NatCAB 42*
Treanor, Walter Emanuel 1883-1941 *WhAm 1*
Treat, Anna Elizabeth 1843- *AmWom*
Treat, Archibald Jennings 1864-1949
NatCAB 39
Treat, Charles Gould 1859-1941 *NatCAB 42,*
WhAm 1
Treat, Charles Henry 1841-1910 *WhAm 1*
Treat, Charles Payson 1847-1926 *WhAm 1*
Treat, Charles Watson 1860- *WhAm 4*
Treat, Ellis Milo 1872-1933 *NatCAB 24*
Treat, Gail *BiCAW*
Treat, George 1819-1907 *NatCAB 25*
Treat, George Winfield 1875-1952 *NatCAB 45,*
WhAm 3
Treat, Guy Bradford 1888-1963 *NatCAB 51*
Treat, Jay Porter 1851- *WhAm 4*
Treat, John Harvey 1839-1908 *ApCAB,*
WhAm 1
Treat, Joseph 1775-1853 *ApCAB*
Treat, Joseph Bradford 1836- *WhAm 4*
Treat, Mary 1830- *WhAm 1*
Treat, Milo Clinton 1841-1925 *NatCAB 24*
Treat, Payson Jackson 1879-1972 *WhAm 5*
Treat, Robert 1622-1710 *AmBi, ApCAB,*
DcAmB, Drake, NatCAB 10, TwCBDA,
WhAm H
Treat, Robert Byron 1868-1926 *WhAm 1*
Treat, Samuel d1887 *BiAUS*
Treat, Samuel 1648-1717 *ApCAB, Drake*
Treat, Samuel 1815-1902 *ApCAB, DcAmB,*
WhAm H
Treat, Samuel Hubbel 1811-1887 *ApCAB,*
DcAmB, NatCAB 12, WhAm H
Treat, Samuel Hubbel 1812-1887 *BiAUS*
Treble, Lillian Massey *WomWWA 14*
Trebra, Friedrich Wilhelm Heinrich Von
1740-1819 *DcScB*
Trecker, Joseph Leonard 1902-1947 *WhAm 2*
Trecker, Theodore 1868-1955 *WhAm 3*
Tredell, Harvey 1856-1944 *NatCAB 34*
Treder, Oscar Frederick Rudolph 1877-1952
NatCAB 40, WhAm 3
Tredick, Helen Folsom *WomWWA 14*
Tredtin, Walter C 1881- *WhAm 6*
Tredway, William Marshall 1807-1891 *BiAUS,*
BiDrAC, WhAm H
Tredwell, Daniel M 1826-1921 *WhAm 1*
Tredwell, Thomas 1742-1832 *ApCAB, BiAUS,*
Drake
Tredwell, Thomas 1743-1831 *BiDrAC,*
WhAm H
Tredwell, Winifred VanSchaick 1884-
WomWWA 14
Tree, Herbert Beerbohm 1853-1917 *WhAm 1*
Tree, Lambert 1832-1910 *ApCAB Sup,*
DcAmB, NatCAB 6, TwCBDA,
WhAm 1
Treece, Elbert Lee 1892-1961 *WhAm 4*
Trees, Clyde 1885-1960 *WhAm 4*
Trees, Harry A 1903-1967 *WhAm 4*
Trees, Joe Clifton 1869-1943 *NatCAB 32,*
WhAm 2
Trees, Merle Jay 1883-1954 *NatCAB 44,*
WhAm 3
Trefethen, Jessie Bryan 1882- *WomWWA 14*
Trefzger, Emli Anton 1888-1961 *WhAm 4*
Tregaskis, Richard William 1916-1973
WebAMB, WhAm 6
Tregellas, Samuel Rogers 1855- *NatCAB 2*
Trego, Alfred Henry 1838-1915 *NatCAB 17*
Trego, Edward Francis 1876-1943 *NatCAB 33*
Trego, Jonathan K 1817-1868? *NewYHSD*
Trego, Thomas Markley 1847- *NatCAB 3*
Trego, William Henry 1837- *ApCAB*
Tregoe, James Harry 1865-1935 *WhAm 1*
Treitschke, Heinrich Von 1834-1896 *McGEWB*
Trejo, Hernando De 1510?-1555 *ApCAB*
Trejo, Hernando DeTrejo Y Sanabria 1553-1614
ApCAB
Trejo, Rafael De d1540? *ApCAB*
Trelawney, Harry d1800 *Drake*
Trelease, Richard Mitchell 1886-1963 *WhAm 4*
Trelease, Sam Farlow 1892-1958 *WhAm 3,*
WhAm 4
Trelease, William 1857-1945 *DcAmB S3,*
DcScB, NatCAB 11, TwCBDA, WhAm 2

Treloar, William Mitchellson 1850-1935
BiDrAC
Tremain, Albert Wright 1872- *WhAm 5*
Tremain, Eloise Ruthven d1946 *WhAm 2*
Tremain, George Lee 1874- *WhAm 5*
Tremain, Henry Edwin 1840-1910 *ApCAB,*
DcAmB, NatCAB 10, WhAm 1
Tremain, Lyman 1819-1878 *ApCAB, BiAUS,*
BiDrAC, NatCAB 11, WhAm H
Tremain, Lyman 1843-1865 *ApCAB*
Tremaine, Burton Gad 1863-1948 *WhAm 2*
Tremaine, Charles Milton 1870- *WhAm 5*
Tremaine, Frederick Orlin 1899-1956 *WhAm 3*
Tremaine, H Alan 1905-1946 *NatCAB 35*
Tremaine, Henry Barnes 1866-1932 *DcAmB,*
NatCAB 18, WhAm 1
Treman, Charles Edward 1868-1930
NatCAB 22, WhAm 1
Treman, Robert Elias 1888-1953 *NatCAB 42*
Treman, Robert Henry 1858-1937 *NatCAB 28,*
WhAm 1
Tremblay, Rene 1923-1968 *WhAm 4A*
Trembley, Abraham 1710-1784 *DcScB*
Trembley, Ralph 1817?- *NewYHSD*
Trenary, James Marshall 1903-1961 *WhAm 4*
Trench, William Washington 1892-1954
WhAm 3
Trenchard, Edward 1850- *ApCAB,*
NatCAB 10
Trenchard, Edward C 1777?-1824 *NewYHSD,*
WhAm H
Trenchard, Edward C 1784-1824 *ApCAB,*
Drake, NatCAB 10
Trenchard, Hugh Montague 1873-1956
WhAm 3, WhoMilH
Trenchard, James 1747- *NewYHSD*
Trenchard, Stephen Decatur 1817-1883 *Drake*
Trenchard, Stephen Decatur 1818-1883 *AmBi,*
ApCAB, DcAmB, NatCAB 10, TwCBDA,
WhAm H
Trenchard, Thomas Whitaker 1863-1911
WhAm 1
Trendelenburg, Friedrich 1844-1924 *BiHiMed*
Trendle, George Washington 1884-1972
WhAm 5
Treneer, Joseph Maurice 1881-1968
NatCAB 54
Trenery, Matthew John 1870- *WhAm 5*
Trenholm, George A 1806-1876 *AmBi, ApCAB,*
NatCAB 4, TwCBDA
Trenholm, George Alfred 1807-1876 *BiDConf,*
DcAmB S1, WhAm H
Trenholm, Portia Ashe 1812?-1892 *NewYHSD*
Trenholm, William Lee 1836-1901 *NatCAB 28,*
WhAm 1
Trenholme, Norman Maclaren 1874-1925
NatCAB 20, WhAm 1
Trent, Josiah Charles 1914-1948 *NatCAB 36*
Trent, Richard Henderson 1867-1939 *WhAm 1*
Trent, William 1655?-1724 *ApCAB Sup,*
NatCAB 12
Trent, William 1715-1787 *ApCAB Sup,*
DcAmB, WhAm H
Trent, William Johnson 1873-1963 *WhAm 4*
Trent, William Leftridge 1855- *NatCAB 10*
Trent, William Peterfield 1862-1939
ApCAB Sup, BiDAmEd, DcAmB S2,
TwCBDA, WhAm 1
Trepper, Leopold 1904- *WhWW-II*
Tresca, Carlo 1879-1943 *DcAmB S3*
Trescot, William Henry 1822-1898 *AmBi,*
ApCAB, DcAmB, NatCAB 13, TwCBDA,
WhAm H
Trescott, Mary Luella *WomWWA 14*
Trescott, Paul Henry 1898-1974 *WhAm 6*
Trescott, William Henry 1822- *BiAUS, Drake*
Tresidder, Donald Bertrand 1894-1948
NatCAB 38, WhAm 2
Treskow, Henning Von 1901-1944 *WhWW-II*
Tresolini, Rocco John 1920-1967 *WhAm 5*
Tressan, Philippe F DeLaRenaudiere De
1781-1845 *ApCAB*
Tressler, Albert Willis 1866-1950 *NatCAB 38*
Tressler, David Loy 1839-1880 *ApCAB,*
TwCBDA
Tressler, Irving Dart 1908-1944 *WhAm 2*
Tressler, Jacob Cloyd 1882-1956 *WhAm 3*

Tressler, Victor George Augustine 1865-1923
WhAm 1
Trested, Richard *NewYHSD*
Trettien, Augustus William 1867-1936
NatCAB 26, WhAm 1
Treub, Melchior 1851-1910 *DcScB*
Treudley, Frederick 1852- *WhAm 4*
Treutlen, John Adam *NatCAB 1, TwCBDA*
Trevellick, Richard F 1830-1895 *DcAmB,*
WebAB, WhAm H
Trevelyan, George Macaulay 1876-1962
McGEWB, WhAm 4
Trever, Albert Augustus 1874-1940 *WhAm 1*
Trever, George Henry 1856- *WhAm 1*
Treves, Norman 1894-1964 *NatCAB 50,*
WhAm 4
Trevett, John d1823 *Drake*
Trevett, John 1747-1823 *ApCAB*
Trevett, John 1757-1833 *NatCAB 8*
Trevett, Russell 1817-1865 *ApCAB*
Trevett, Samuel Russell 1751-1832 *ApCAB,*
Drake
Trevett, Samuel Russell 1783-1822 *ApCAB*
Treville, Abigail *NotAW*
Trevino, Lee 1939- *WebAB*
Treviranus, Gottfried Reinhold 1776-1837
DcScB
Treviranus, Ludolph Christian 1779-1864 *DcScB*
Trevisan, Vittorio 1868- *WhAm 4*
Trevisanus *DcScB*
Trevithick, Richard 1771-1833 *AsBiEn*
Trevor, John Bond 1822-1890 *NatCAB 32*
Trevor, John Bond 1878-1956 *WhAm 3*
Trevor, Joseph Ellis 1864-1941 *WhAm 1*
Trevorrow, Robert Johns 1877-1943 *WhAm 2*
Trevoy, William Vivian 1880-1938 *WhAm 1*
Trewin, James Henry 1858-1927 *WhAm 1*
Trexler, Frank M 1861-1947 *WhAm 2*
Trexler, Harry Clay 1854-1933 *NatCAB 39,*
WhAm 1
Trexler, Jacob Amos 1873-1956 *NatCAB 46*
Trexler, Samuel Geiss 1877-1949 *NatCAB 37,*
WhAm 2
Treynor, Jack Vernon 1897-1966 *NatCAB 51*
Trezevant, John Timothy 1814-1887
NatCAB 34
Trezevant, Marye Beattie 1846-1915
NatCAB 34
Trezevant, Marye Beattie 1872-1930
NatCAB 34
Trezevant, Peter John 1844- *NatCAB 10*
Trezvant, James d1838 *BiAUS*
Trezvant, James d1841 *BiDrAC, WhAm H*
Triana, Jose Geronimo 1826-1890 *DcScB*
Tribble, Lewis Herndon 1891-1963 *WhAm 4*
Tribble, Samuel Joel 1868-1916 *WhAm 1*
Tribble, Samuel Joelah 1869-1916 *BiDrAC,*
NatCAB 18
Trible, George Barnett 1883-1964 *NatCAB 51*
Trible, John Metcalf 1884-1947 *NatCAB 41*
Tribus, Louis Lincoln 1865-1930 *WhAm 1*
Trichon *NewYHSD*
Trickett, William 1840-1928 *WhAm 1*
Triebel, Frederick Ernst 1865- *WhAm 4*
Trieber, Jacob 1853-1927 *ApCAB X,*
NatCAB 8, WhAm 1
Trier, Charles Augustus 1863-1949 *NatCAB 38*
Trifari, Gustavo 1883-1952 *NatCAB 41*
Trigand, Jacques Nicolas Bellin De 1703-1772
ApCAB
Trigg, Abram 1750- *BiAUS, BiDrAC,*
WhAm H, WhAmP
Trigg, Connally Findlay 1847-1907 *BiAUS,*
BiDrAC
Trigg, Ernest T 1877-1957 *WhAm 3*
Trigg, John Johns 1748-1804 *BiAUS, BiDrAC,*
WhAm H, WhAmP
Trigg, Stephen d1782 *Drake*
Trigg, William d1837 *Drake*
Triggs, Flloyd Willding 1879-1919 *WhAm 1*
Triggs, James Martin 1924- *IlBEAAW*
Triggs, Oscar Lovell 1865- *NatCAB 12,*
WhAm 4
Trigpen, Timothy S 1878- *WhoColR*
Trilia, Bernard Of *DcScB*
Trilley, Joseph 1838-1911 *TwCBDA, WhAm 1*
Trilling, Lionel 1905-1975 *WebAB, WhAm 6*
Trim, Gordon Mariner 1903-1961 *WhAm 4*

Trimadeuc, Gui Plouvencal, Baron De 1720-1784
ApCAB
Trimble, Allen 1783-1870 *ApCAB, BiAUS,
DcAmB, Drake, NatCAB 3, TwCBDA,
WhAm H*
Trimble, Carey Allen 1813-1887 *BiDrAC,
WhAm H*
Trimble, Cary A 1813-1887 *BiAUS*
Trimble, David 1782-1842 *ApCAB, BiAUS,
BiDrAC, TwCBDA, WhAm H, WhAmP*
Trimble, Ernest Greene 1897-1972 *WhAm 5*
Trimble, Harvey Marion 1842-1918 *WhAm 1*
Trimble, Henry 1853- *NatCAB 5*
Trimble, Henry Weeks 1886-1964 *NatCAB 51*
Trimble, Isaac Ridgeway 1800?-1888 *Drake*
Trimble, Isaac Ridgeway 1802-1888 *ApCAB,
BiDConf, DcAmB, NatCAB 4, TwCBDA,
WhAm H*
Trimble, James Guinne *WhoColR A*
Trimble, James William 1894-1972 *BiDrAC,
WhAm 5, WhAmP*
Trimble, Jeanette Huntington Hooker
WomWWA 14
Trimble, John 1812-1884 *BiAUS, BiDrAC,
NatCAB 3, WhAm H*
Trimble, John Harrison 1783-1852 *ApCAB,
BiAUS*
Trimble, Lawrence Strother 1825-1904 *BiAUS,
BiDrAC*
Trimble, Richard 1858-1924 *WhAm 1*
Trimble, Robert 1776-1828 *BiAUS, NatCAB 2*
Trimble, Robert 1777-1828 *ApCAB, DcAmB,
Drake, TwCBDA, WebAB, WhAm H*
Trimble, Robert Maurice 1871-1966 *WhAm 4*
Trimble, Selden Y 1867- *WhAm 4*
Trimble, South 1864-1946 *BiDrAC, WhAm 2,
WhAmP*
Trimble, South, Jr. 1896-1973 *WhAm 6*
Trimble, William Allen 1786-1821 *ApCAB,
BiAUS, Drake, NatCAB 10,
TwCBDA, WhAm H*
Trimble, William Burwell 1870-1925
NatCAB 26
Trimble, William Kirk 1873-1952 *NatCAB 41*
Trimble, William Pitt 1863-1943 *ApCAB X,
WhAm 2*
Trinchard, J B *NewYHSD*
Trine, Charles Clarke 1866- *WhAm 4*
Trine, Ralph Waldo 1866-1958 *DcAmReB,
WhAm 5*
Trinkle, Elbert Lee 1876-1939 *NatCAB 33,
WhAm 1*
Trinks, Willibald 1874- *WhAm 5*
Triolo, Antony 1902-1955 *NatCAB 48*
Tripler, Charles Eastman 1849-1905
NatCAB 11, WhAm 4
Triplett, Arthur Fairfax 1891-1958 *WhAm 3*
Triplett, Clarence Patton 1872-1948
NatCAB 37
Triplett, Elijah Henry 1857- *WhAm 4*
Triplett, George W 1809-1894 *BiDConf*
Triplett, John Edwin 1809-1943 *WhAm 2*
Triplett, Norman 1861-1934 *WhAm 1*
Triplett, Philip 1799-1852 *BiAUS, BiDrAC,
WhAm H*
Tripoli, Carlo Joseph 1905-1962 *NatCAB 57*
Tripp, B Ashburton 1887-1955 *NatCAB 44*
Tripp, Bartlett 1842-1911 *DcAmB, NatCAB 8,
TwCBDA, WhAm 1*
Tripp, Edward Sequist 1919-1966 *NatCAB 52*
Tripp, Frank Elihu 1882-1964 *WhAm 4*
Tripp, Guy Eastman 1865-1927 *DcAmB,
NatCAB 20, WhAm 1*
Tripp, James Gregory 1888-1971 *NatCAB 57*
Tripp, Lena Elvina Flack 1899- *WhAm 6*
Tripp, Louis H 1884-1963 *WhAm 4*
Tripp, Robert P 1819-1900 *BiAUS*
Tripp, Thomas Bush 1838-1912 *ApCAB X*
Tripp, William Henry, Jr. 1919-1971 *WhAm 5*
Trippe, Alvin Chamberlaine 1898-1951
NatCAB 41
Trippe, Andrew Cross 1839-1918 *WhAm 1*
Trippe, James McConky 1874-1936 *WhAm 1*
Trippe, John 1785-1810 *ApCAB, DcAmB,
Drake, WhAm H*
Trippe, Robert Pleasant 1819-1900 *BiDConf,
BiDrAC*

Trippet, Oscar A 1856-1923 *NatCAB 20,
WhAm 1*
Trippet, Oscar A 1905-1967 *NatCAB 52*
Triscott, Samuel Peter Rolt 1846-1925 *WhAm 1*
Trismegistus *DcScB*
Trissal, John Meredith 1903-1975 *WhAm 6*
Trist, Nicholas Philip 1800-1874 *AmBi,
ApCAB, DcAmB, Drake, EncAB,
McGEWB, NatCAB 7, WebAB,
WhAm H*
Trist, T J *NewYHSD*
Tritle, Eleanor Hoblitzelle *WomWWA 14*
Tritle, Frederick A 1833- *NatCAB 3,
NatCAB 11*
Tritle, John Stewart 1871-1947 *NatCAB 36*
Tritle, John Stewart 1872-1947 *WhAm 2*
Tritsch, John Edgar 1895-1956 *NatCAB 47*
Trivelli, Albert F 1863- *WhAm 4*
Trix, Harriet Phelps 1850- *NatCAB 18*
Troast, Paul Lyman 1894-1972 *NatCAB 57*
Trobec, James 1838- *ApCAB Sup,
NatCAB 12, TwCBDA, WhAm 4*
Troche, Ernst Gunter 1909-1971 *WhAm 5*
Trochu, Louis Jules 1815-1896 *WhoMilH*
Troeger, John Winthrop 1849-1936 *WhAm 1*
Troeltsch, Ernst 1865-1923 *McGEWB*
Troendle *NewYHSD*
Troendle, Joseph F *NewYHSD*
Trogdon, Ray Lando 1901-1972 *NatCAB 57*
Troger, Henry Herman 1904-1950 *NatCAB 40*
Troger, Paul 1698-1762 *McGEWB*
Troja, Michele 1747-1827 *DcScB*
Troland, Leonard Thompson 1889-1932 *DcAmB,
WhAm 1*
Troll, Irving Russell 1894-1970 *NatCAB 54*
Trollope, Anthony 1815-1882 *McGEWB*
Trollope, Frances 1790-1863 *Drake*
Trollope, Frances Milton 1780?-1863 *ApCAB*
Trollope, Sir Henry 1756-1839 *ApCAB, Drake*
Trommsdorff, Johann Bartholomaus 1770-1837
DcScB
Tromp, Sir Cornelis Van 1629-1691 *WhoMilH*
Tromp, Sir Maarten Van 1598-1653 *WhoMilH*
Trondle *NewYHSD*
Troop, J G Carter 1869-1930 *WhAm 1,
WhAm 1C*
Troost, George Wilbur 1902-1956 *WhAm 3*
Troost, Gerard 1776-1850 *ApCAB, DcAmB,
DcScB, Drake, NatCAB 7, TwCBDA,
WhAm H*
Troost, Louis Joseph 1825-1911 *DcScB*
Troostwijk, Adriaan Paets Van 1752-1837
DcScB
Troper, Morris C 1892-1962 *WhAm 4*
Tropfke, Johannes 1866-1939 *DcScB*
Trosdal, Einar Storm 1880-1932 *NatCAB 25*
Trostel, Gustav John August 1864-1936
NatCAB 28
Troth, Henry 1794-1842 *TwCBDA*
Trotsky, Leon 1879-1940 *McGEWB*
Trotsky, Lev Davidovich 1879-1940 *WhoMilH*
Trott, Alfred Blake 1877-1944 *NatCAB 33*
Trott, Benjamin 1770?-1841? *DcAmB,
WhAm H*
Trott, Benjamin 1770?-1843 *NewYHSD*
Trott, Clement Augustus 1877- *WhAm 5*
Trott, Eli 1832-1920 *NatCAB 19*
Trott, Lois E *AmWom*
Trott, Nicholas 1662?-1739? *DcAmB*
Trott, Nicholas 1663-1740 *ApCAB, Drake,
NatCAB 12, WhAm H*
Trott, Norman Liebman 1901-1975 *WhAm 6*
Trott, Novella Jewell 1846- *AmWom*
Trott, Stanley B 1896-1959 *WhAm 3*
Trotter, Alfred Williams 1856-1928 *WhAm 1,
WhAm 1C*
Trotter, F James *BiAUS*
Trotter, Frank Butler 1863-1940 *WhAm 1*
Trotter, George 1779-1815 *ApCAB, Drake*
Trotter, James Fisher 1802-1866 *ApCAB,
BiDrAC, NatCAB 12, TwCBDA,
WhAm H*
Trotter, Melvin E 1870-1940 *WhAm 1*
Trotter, Newbold Hough 1827-1898 *ApCAB,
IlBEAAW, NewYHSD, WhAm H*
Trotter, Spencer 1860-1931 *WhAm 1*
Trotter, William Henry 1869-1933 *NatCAB 25*
Trotter, William Monroe 1872-1934 *EncAB,*

WhoColR
Trotti, Lamar 1900-1952 *WhAm 3*
Trotti, Samuel Wilds 1810-1856 *BiDrAC,
WhAm H*
Trottman, James Franklin 1860- *WhAm 4*
Trotz, J O Emmaneul 1860-1925 *WhAm 1*
Trouard *NewYHSD*
Troubat, Francis Joseph 1802-1868 *ApCAB*
Troubetzkoy, Princess Amelie Rives 1863-1945
NotAW, TwCBDA, WhAm 2
Troubetzkoy, Princess Pierre *WomWWA 14*
Troubetzkoy, Prince Pierre 1864-1936 *WhAm 1*
Trouche, Auguste Paul d1846 *NewYHSD*
Troude, Aimable Gilles 1762-1824 *ApCAB*
Troughton, Edward 1753-1836 *DcScB*
Troup, Alexander 1840-1908 *NatCAB 17,
WhAm 1*
Troup, Augusta Lewis 1848?-1920 *NotAW*
Troup, George M 1780-1856 *BiAUS*
Troup, George McIntosh 1780-1856 *ApCAB,
Drake, TwCBDA*
Troup, George Michael 1780-1856 *AmBi,
BiDrAC, DcAmB, NatCAB 1, WhAm H,
WhAmP*
Troup, Robert 1757-1822 *BiAUS*
Troup, Robert 1757-1832 *ApCAB, DcAmB,
Drake, WhAm H*
Trousdale, Leonidas 1823-1897 *NatCAB 8*
Trousdale, William 1790-1872 *ApCAB, BiAUS,
Drake, NatCAB 7, TwCBDA*
Trousseau, Armand 1801-1867 *BiHiMed*
Trout, Charles Eliphalet 1871-1959 *NatCAB 48*
Trout, Clement E 1891-1960 *WhAm 4*
Trout, David McCamel 1891-1954 *WhAm 3*
Trout, Ethel Wendell 1878-1935 *WhAm 1*
Trout, Grace Wilbur d1955 *BiCAW, WhAm 3,
WomWWA 14*
Trout, Hugh Henry, Sr. 1878-1950 *WhAm 2A*
Trout, Jenny Kidd *WomWWA 14*
Trout, Michael Carver 1810-1873 *BiAUS,
BiDrAC, WhAm H*
Troutman, Carl Frederick 1896-1956
NatCAB 47
Troutman, Greyson Prevost 1880-1943
NatCAB 32
Troutman, William Irvin 1905- *BiDrAC*
Trouton, Frederick Thomas 1863-1922 *DcScB*
Trouve, Claude 1642- *ApCAB*
Trouvelot, Etienne Leopold 1827-1895 *DcScB*
Trouvelot, L *NewYHSD*
Trouyet, Carlos 1904-1971 *WhAm 5*
Trova, Ernest 1927- *BnEnAmA*
Trovillion, Howard Waters 1899-1956
NatCAB 44
Trow, Cora Welles *WomWWA 14*
Trow, James 1827- *ApCAB*
Trow, John Fowler 1810-1886 *ApCAB,
DcAmB, WhAm H*
Trowbridge, Alexander Buel 1868-1950
NatCAB 40, WhAm 4
Trowbridge, Alexander Buel 1929- *BiDrUSE*
Trowbridge, Alvah 1835-1907 *NatCAB 12,
WhAm 1*
Trowbridge, Arthur Carleton 1885-1971
WhAm 5
Trowbridge, Augustus 1870-1934 *AmBi,
DcAmB, WhAm 1*
Trowbridge, Carl Hoyt 1874- *WhAm 5*
Trowbridge, Charles Arthur 1886-1956
NatCAB 43
Trowbridge, Charles Christopher 1870-1918
NatCAB 18, WhAm 1
Trowbridge, Cornelia Rogers *WomWWA 14*
Trowbridge, Edmund 1709-1792 *ApCAB*
Trowbridge, Edmund 1709-1793 *AmBi,
DcAmB, Drake, WhAm H*
Trowbridge, Edward Dwight 1870-1929
WhAm 1
Trowbridge, Edward Henry 1856-1937
NatCAB 27
Trowbridge, John 1843-1923 *AmBi, ApCAB,
BiDAmEd, DcAmB, DcScB, NatCAB 23,
TwCBDA, WhAm 1*
Trowbridge, John Eliot 1845- *NatCAB 7*
Trowbridge, John Townsend 1827-1916 *AmBi,
ApCAB, DcAmB, Drake, NatCAB 3,
TwCBDA, WhAm 1*

Trowbridge, Mary Elizabeth Day d1918
WhAm 1, WomWWA 14
Trowbridge, N C *NewYHSD*
Trowbridge, Perry Fox 1866-1937 *WhAm 1*
Trowbridge, Rowland Ebenezer 1821-1881
BiAUS, BiDrAC, WhAm H
Trowbridge, Samuel Breck Parkman 1862-1925
NatCAB 14, WhAm 1
Trowbridge, Thomas Rutherford 1810-1887
NatCAB 28
Trowbridge, Thomas Rutherford 1839-1898
NatCAB 28
Trowbridge, Vaughan 1869- *WhAm 5*
Trowbridge, William Petit 1828-1892 *AmBi,*
ApCAB, DcAmB
Trowbridge, William Pettit 1828-1892
NatCAB 4, WhAm H
Troxel, David Shaum 1864-1925 *NatCAB 20*
Troxell, Edgar Rudolphus 1850-1928
NatCAB 22
Troxell, Edward Leffingwell 1884-1972
NatCAB 57, WhAm 5
Troxell, Millard Francis 1857- *WhAm 4*
Troxell, Thomas Franklin 1895-1971 *WhAm 5*
Troxell, Thomas Nugent 1880-1962 *NatCAB 50*
Troy, Alexander 1853- *WhAm 1*
Troy, Mrs. Edward Henry Gray 1866-
WomWWA 14
Troy, George Francis 1876- *WhAm 5*
Troy, Ida L 1861- *WomWWA 14*
Troy, John Henry 1856-1931 *WhAm 3*
Troy, John Weir 1868-1942 *WhAm 2*
Troy, Matthew Orpheus 1872-1944 *NatCAB 33*
Troy, Peter Henry 1868-1958 *WhAm 3*
Troy, Thomas Francis 1905-1965 *WhAm 4*
Troy, William Eugene 1903-1961 *NatCAB 46*
Troye, Edward 1808-1874 *DcAmB, NewYHSD,*
WhAm H
Troyes, Pierre De d1687 *ApCAB*
Truair, George Galitzin 1842-1888 *NatCAB 7*
Truant, Aldo Peter 1920-1973 *WhAm 6*
Truax, Arthur Harold 1889-1963 *WhAm 4*
Truax, Charles Henry 1846-1910 *ApCAB Sup,*
NatCAB 12, WhAm 1
Truax, Charles Vilas 1887-1935 *BiDrAC,*
WhAm 1
Truax, Chauncey Shaffer 1854- *ApCAB Sup,*
WhAm 1
Trubek, Moses 1868-1935 *NatCAB 36*
Truby, Albert Ernest 1871-1954 *NatCAB 40,*
WhAm 5
Trucco, Manuel 1875- *WhAm 5*
Trude, Alfred Samuel 1846-1933 *NatCAB 14*
Trude, Alfred Samuel 1847-1933 *DcAmB,*
WhAm 1
Trudeau, Edward Livingston 1848-1915 *AmBi,*
DcAmB, NatCAB 13, WhAm 1
Trudeau, Henry Livingston 1848-1915
ApCAB X
Trudeau, Justinian 1827?- *NewYHSD*
Trudel, Francois-Xavier Anselme 1838-1890
ApCAB
Trudgian, Andrew B 1895-1974 *WhAm 6*
True, Alfred Charles 1853-1929 *AmBi,*
BiDAmEd, DcAmB, WhAm 1
True, Allen Tupper 1881-1955 *IIBEAAW,*
WhAm 3
True, Benjamin C *NewYHSD*
True, Charles Kittredge 1809-1878 *AmBi*
True, Charles Kittridge 1809-1878 *ApCAB*
True, Daniel *NewYHSD*
True, Edward Russell 1839-1928 *NatCAB 22*
True, Frank Daniel 1868-1928 *NatCAB 39*
True, Frederick William 1858-1914 *DcAmB,*
NatCAB 19, WhAm 1
True, Gordon Haines 1868-1928 *WhAm 1*
True, Henry Oscar 1857-1927 *NatCAB 21*
True, Hiram L 1845- *WhAm 4*
True, John Preston 1859-1933 *NatCAB 27,*
WhAm 1
True, Lilian Crawford *WhAm 5*
True, Lillian Sarah Crawford *WomWWA 14*
True, Margaret T 1858- *WomWWA 14*
True, Rodney Howard 1866-1940 *EncAAH,*
WhAm 1
True, Theodore Edmond 1842-1925 *ApCAB X,*
WhAm 1

Trueblood, Benjamin Franklin 1847-1916
DcAmB, NatCAB 18, WhAm 1
Trueblood, Dennis Lee 1925-1964 *WhAm 4*
Trueblood, Mary Esther 1872- *WomWWA 14*
Trueblood, Ralph Waldo 1885-1954 *NatCAB 44,*
WhAm 3
Trueblood, Robert Martin 1916-1974 *WhAm 6*
Trueblood, Thomas Clarkson 1856-1951
BiDAmEd, NatCAB 42, WhAm 3
Truell, Rohn 1913-1968 *WhAm 5*
Truelsen, Henry 1844- *WhAm 4*
Trueman, Walter Harley 1870- *WhAm 5*
Trueman, William H 1904-1970 *WhAm 5*
Truesdale, Harry Alfred 1863-1958 *NatCAB 44*
Truesdale, Hiram Clark 1860-1897 *ApCAB Sup*
Truesdale, Philemon Edwards 1874-1945
NatCAB 40, WhAm 2
Truesdale, William Haynes 1851-1935
NatCAB 14, WhAm 1
Truesdall, Elizabeth West 1867- *WomWWA 14*
Truesdell, Hobart George 1882-1924 *WhAm 1*
Truesdell, Janette C Cook 1841- *WomWWA 14*
Truesdell, Karl 1882-1955 *WhAm 3*
Truett, George d1818 *BiAUS, Drake*
Truett, George Washington 1867-1944
DcAmB S3, DcAmReB, WhAm 2
Truette, Everett Ellsworth 1861-1933
NatCAB 25, WhAm 1
Trufant, Mabel Hodnett 1882- *WomWWA 14*
Truffaut, Francois 1932- *McGEWB*
Truguet, Laurent Jean Francois 1752-1839
ApCAB
Truist, Sigmund *NewYHSD*
Truitt, Anna Augusta 1837- *AmWom*
Truitt, Anne 1921- *BnEnAmA*
Truitt, George 1756-1818 *NatCAB 11,*
TwCBDA
Truitt, James Joshua 1893-1955 *NatCAB 47*
Truitt, James Steele 1868- *WhAm 5*
Truitt, Max O'Rell 1904-1956 *WhAm 3*
Truitt, Ralph Purnell 1885-1966 *WhAm 5*
Truitt, Mrs. Warren *WomWWA 14*
Truitt, William d1935 *WhAm 1*
Truitt, William Jennings Bryan 1896-1956
NatCAB 43
Trujillo Molina, Rafael Leonidas 1891-1961
McGEWB, WhAm 4
Trull, J Frank 1868-1922 *NatCAB 6*
Trull, Jane Crombie 1871- *WomWWA 14*
Trulli, Giovanni 1598-1661 *DcScB*
Trullinger, R W 1889-1955 *WhAm 3*
Truly, Jefferson 1861- *WhAm 4*
Truman, Benjamin Cummings 1835-1916
ApCAB, DcAmB, WhAm 1
Truman, Edward *NewYHSD*
Truman, Harry S 1884-1972 *BiDrAC,*
BiDrUSE, EncAAH, EncAB, McGEWB,
NatCAB 57, WebAB, WhAm 5, WhAmP,
WhWW-II
Truman, Irwin Joseph 1840-1918 *NatCAB 17*
Truman, James 1826-1914 *NatCAB 25,*
WhAm 1
Truman, Ralph Emerson 1880-1962 *WhAm 4*
Trumbauer, Frank 1900-1956 *WhAm 4*
Trumbauer, Horace 1868-1938 *BnEnAmA,*
DcAmB S2, NatCAB 28, WhAm HA,
WhAm 4
Trumbo, Andrew 1797-1871 *BiDrAC,*
WhAm H
Trumbo, Andrew 1799-1871 *BiAUS*
Trumbo, Arthur Cook 1866-1954 *WhAm 3*
Trumbo, Eunice Belle 1871- *WomWWA 14*
Trumbull, Annie Eliot d1949 *WhAm 2,*
WomWWA 14
Trumbull, Benjamin 1735-1820 *ApCAB,*
DcAmB, Drake, NatCAB 11, TwCBDA,
WhAm H
Trumbull, Charles Gallaudet 1872-1941
WhAm 1
Trumbull, Donald Shurtleff 1875-1951
NatCAB 38
Trumbull, Frank 1858-1920 *WhAm 1*
Trumbull, Gurdon 1841-1903 *ApCAB,*
WhAm 1
Trumbull, Henry Clay 1830-1903 *DcAmB,*
NatCAB 9, TwCBDA, WhAm 1
Trumbull, Henry Clay 1831-1903 *ApCAB*
Trumbull, James Hammond 1821-1897 *AmBi,*

ApCAB, DcAmB, Drake, NatCAB 9,
TwCBDA, WhAm H
Trumbull, John 1750-1831 *AmBi, ApCAB,*
BiAUS, DcAmB, Drake, NatCAB 7,
WebAB, WhAm H
Trumbull, John 1750-1835 *TwCBDA*
Trumbull, John 1756-1843 *AmBi, ApCAB,*
BiAUS, BnEnAmA, DcAmB, Drake,
EncAB, McGEWB, NatCAB 3,
NewYHSD, TwCBDA, WebAB,
WhAm H
Trumbull, Mrs. John 1774-1824 *NewYHSD*
Trumbull, John H 1873-1961 *ApCAB X,*
WhAm 4
Trumbull, Jonathan 1710-1785 *AmBi, ApCAB,*
BiAUS, DcAmB, Drake, NatCAB 10,
TwCBDA, WebAB, WhAm H
Trumbull, Jonathan 1740-1809 *AmBi, ApCAB,*
BiAUS, BiDrAC, DcAmB, Drake,
NatCAB 10, TwCBDA, WebAB,
WhAm H, WhAmP
Trumbull, Jonathan 1844-1919 *WhAm 1*
Trumbull, Joseph 1737-1778 *ApCAB, BiAUS,*
BiDrAC, DcAmB, Drake, TwCBDA,
WebAMB, WhAm H, WhAmP
Trumbull, Joseph 1782-1861 *ApCAB, BiDrAC,*
Drake, NatCAB 10, TwCBDA, WhAm H,
WhAmP
Trumbull, Joseph 1783-1861 *BiAUS*
Trumbull, Levi R 1834- *WhAm 4*
Trumbull, Lyman 1813-1896 *AmBi, ApCAB,*
BiAUS, BiDrAC, DcAmB, Drake,
McGEWB, NatCAB 12, TwCBDA,
WhAm H, WhAmP
Trumbull, Matthew Moore 1826- *ApCAB Sup*
Trumbull, Millie Reid 1866- *WomWWA 14*
Trump, Edward Needles 1857- *WhAm 4*
Trumper, Jessie Smith *WomWWA 14*
Trumpler, Robert Julius 1886-1956 *AsBiEn,*
DcScB, NatCAB 54, WhAm 3
Trundle, George Thomas 1884-1954
NatCAB 43
Trung, F *NewYHSD*
Truong, Chinh 1909- *McGEWB*
Truscott, Frederick Wilson 1870-1937 *WhAm 1*
Truscott, Lucian King, Jr. 1895-1965 *WebAMB,*
WhAm 4
Truscott, Sarah L *WomWWA 14*
Trusdell, Charles Gregory 1826-1903 *ApCAB,*
WhAm 1
Trusler, William Ernest 1888-1970 *NatCAB 55*
Truslow, Francis Adams 1906-1951 *NatCAB 39,*
WhAm 3
Trussell, C P 1892-1968 *WhAm 5*
Trusta, H 1815-1852 *AmBi*
Trusty, S David 1913-1968 *WhAm 5*
Trutch, Joseph William 1826- *ApCAB*
Truteau, Jean Baptiste 1748-1827 *DcAmB,*
WhAm H
Truth, Sojourner 1797?-1883 *AmBi, DcAmReB,*
EncAB, McGEWB, NotAW, WebAB
Truth, Soujourner 1797?-1883 *WhAmP*
Truxal, Andrew Gehr 1900-1971 *WhAm 5*
Truxton, Thomas 1755-1822 *Drake*
Truxton, William Talbot 1824-1887
NatCAB 11
Truxtun, Thomas 1755-1822 *AmBi, ApCAB,*
DcAmB, NatCAB 2, TwCBDA, WebAB,
WebAMB, WhAm H
Truxtun, William Talbot 1824-1887 *ApCAB,*
DcAmB, TwCBDA, WhAm H
Tryon, Benjamin F 1824-1896 *NewYHSD*
Tryon, Mrs. Brown *NewYHSD*
Tryon, Clarence Archer, Jr. 1911-1973 *WhAm 6*
Tryon, Dwight William 1849-1925 *AmBi,*
ApCAB, BnEnAmA, DcAmB, NatCAB 8,
TwCBDA, WhAm 1
Tryon, Mrs. E A *NewYHSD*
Tryon, Frederick Gale 1892-1940 *WhAm 1*
Tryon, Geneva 1873- *WomWWA 14*
Tryon, George Washington 1838-1888 *ApCAB,*
DcAmB, TwCBDA, WhAm H
Tryon, Horatio L 1826?- *NewYHSD*
Tryon, James Libby 1864-1958 *WhAm 3*
Tryon, James Rufus 1837-1912 *WhAm 1*
Tryon, John 1801?- *NewYHSD*
Tryon, Kate Allen 1865- *AmWom,*
WomWWA 14

Tryon, Lillian Hart 1870- *WhAm 5*
Tryon, Margaret B *NewYHSD*
Tryon, Moses d1818 *Drake*
Tryon, Rolla Milton 1875-1954 *WhAm 3*
Tryon, Rufus James 1837-1912 *NatCAB 28*
Tryon, William d1788 *Drake*
Tryon, William 1725?-1788 *ApCAB,*
NatCAB 7, TwCBDA
Tryon, William 1729-1788 *AmBi, DcAmB,*
EncAAH, McGEWB, WhAm H
Tryon, Winthrop Pitt 1869- *WhAm 5*
Trythall, Sylvester Wayne 1901-1970
NatCAB 56
Tsai, Lun 050?-118? *AsBiEn*
Ts'ai, Yuan-P'ei 1867-1940 *McGEWB*
Tsaldaris, Constantin d1970 *WhAm 5*
Tsaltas, Theodore Theodosios 1923-1970
NatCAB 54
Ts'ao, Ts'ao 155-220 *McGEWB*
Tsatoke, Monroe 1904-1937 *IIBEAAW*
Tschappat, William H 1874- *WhAm 5*
Tschermak, Gustav 1836-1927 *DcScB*
Tschermak VonSeysenegg, Erich 1871-1962
DcScB
Tschernichowsky, Saul 1875-1943 *McGEWB*
Tschirky, Oscar 1866-1950 *WhAm 3*
Tschirnhaus, Ehrenfried Walther 1651-1708
DcScB
Tschopik, Harry, Jr. 1915-1956 *NatCAB 45*
Tschudi, Johann Jakob Von 1818- *ApCAB*
Tschudi, Rudolf 1855-1923 *IIBEAAW*
Tschudy, Arnold Nord 1902-1955 *WhAm 3*
Tschudy, Herbert Bolivar 1874-1946 *WhAm 2*
Tseng, Kuo-Fan 1811-1872 *McGEWB*
Tserasky, Vitold Karlovich 1849-1925 *DcScB*
Tshombe, Moise Kapenda 1919-1969 *McGEWB*
Tsiang, Tingfu F 1895-1965 *WhAm 4*
Tsinajinie, Andrew Van 1918- *IIBEAAW*
Tsiolkovsky, Konstantin Eduardovich 1857-1935
AsBiEn, DcScB, McGEWB
Tso, Tsung-T'ang 1812-1885 *McGEWB*
Tsondatsaa, Charles *ApCAB*
Tsou, Yen *McGEWB*
Tsu, Ch'ung-Chih 429?-500? *DcScB*
Tsukiyama, Wilfred C 1897-1965 *WhAm 4*
Tsvet, Mikhail Semenovich 1872-1919 *DcScB*
Tsvett, Mikhail Semenovich 1872-1920 *AsBiEn*
Tu, Fu 712-770 *McGEWB*
Tubb, James Richardson, Jr. 1894-1951
NatCAB 40
Tubbs, Arthur Lewis 1867-1946 *WhAm 2*
Tubbs, Edward 1900- *WhAm 3*
Tubbs, Eston Valentine 1883-1947 *WhAm 2*
Tubbs, Frank Dean 1864-1939 *WhAm 1*
Tubby, Joseph 1821-1896 *NewYHSD*
Tubby, Mary Peckham *WomWWA 14*
Tubby, William Bunker 1858-1944 *NatCAB 33,*
WhAm 2
Tuberman, Walter H 1879-1960 *WhAm 3*
Tubesing, Henry *NewYHSD*
Tubman, Harriet d1913 *WhAm 4*
Tubman, Harriet 1820?-1913 *McGEWB,*
NotAW, WebAB, WhAm HA
Tubman, Harriet 1821?-1913 *AmBi, ApCAB,*
DcAmB, EncAAH, EncAB, WhAmP
Tubman, William Vacanarat Shadrach
1895-1971 *McGEWB, WhAm 5*
Tuck, Amos 1810-1879 *BiAUS, BiDrAC,*
DcAmB, NatCAB 13, WhAm H
Tuck, Clyde Edwin 1880- *WhAm 6*
Tuck, Edward 1842-1938 *NatCAB 16,*
NatCAB 31, WhAm 4
Tuck, Gaillard Osterlony 1875- *NatCAB 18*
Tuck, Henry 1842-1904 *WhAm 1*
Tuck, Joseph Henry 1812-1875 *ApCAB, Drake,*
NatCAB 8
Tuck, Somerville Pinckney 1891-1967 *WhAm 4*
Tuck, Somerville Pinkney 1848-1923
NatCAB 12, WhAm 1
Tuck, William Hallam 1890-1966 *NatCAB 52,*
WhAm 4
Tuck, William Munford 1896- *BiDrAC*
Tucker, Alice *NewYHSD*
Tucker, Allen 1866-1939 *DcAmB S2,*
IIBEAAW
Tucker, Anna Lynn 1883- *WomWWA 14*
Tucker, B Fain d1970 *WhAm 5*
Tucker, Benjamin 1768- *NewYHSD*

Tucker, Benjamin Ferree 1870- *WhAm 5*
Tucker, Benjamin Ricketson 1854-1939
DcAmB S2, NatCAB 13, WebAB,
WhAm HA, WhAm 4
Tucker, Beverley 1784-1851 *WhAm H*
Tucker, Beverley Dandridge 1846-1930
NatCAB 39, WhAm 1
Tucker, Beverley Dandridge 1882-1969
WhAm 5
Tucker, Beverley Randolph 1874-1945 *WhAm 2*
Tucker, Beverley Randolph, Jr. 1916-1973
NatCAB 57
Tucker, Beverly *BiAUS*
Tucker, Beverly Randolph 1874-1945
NatCAB 34
Tucker, C M 1897-1954 *WhAm 3*
Tucker, Carll 1881-1956 *NatCAB 54*
Tucker, Carll 1921-1968 *NatCAB 54*
Tucker, Carlton Everett 1896-1966 *WhAm 4*
Tucker, Caroline Kimball 1846- *WomWWA 14*
Tucker, Charles Cowles 1869- *WhAm 5*
Tucker, Charlotte Barrell Cheever 1858-
WomWWA 14
Tucker, Chester Everett 1897-1975 *WhAm 6*
Tucker, Clarence R 1897- *WhAm 5*
Tucker, DeWitt Clinton 1877- *WomWWA 14*
Tucker, Ebenezer 1758-1845 *BiAUS, BiDrAC,*
WhAm H
Tucker, Eva Sophie Forte 1879- *WomWWA 14*
Tucker, Frank 1861-1946 *WhAm 2*
Tucker, Gardiner Chylson 1851-1941 *WhAm 1*
Tucker, Garland Scott 1869-1949 *NatCAB 39*
Tucker, George 1775-1861 *ApCAB, BiAUS,*
BiDAmEd, BiDrAC, DcAmB, Drake,
McGEWB, NatCAB 7, TwCBDA,
WhAm H, WhAmP
Tucker, George Fox 1852-1929 *NatCAB 11,*
WhAm 1
Tucker, Gilbert Milligan 1847-1932 *DcAmB,*
WhAm 1
Tucker, Gregory 1908-1971 *NatCAB 57*
Tucker, Harold Walton 1915-1973 *DcAmLiB*
Tucker, Harry 1890-1942 *NatCAB 38,*
WhAm 2
Tucker, Helen Augusta *WomWWA 14*
Tucker, Henry Holcombe 1819-1889 *ApCAB,*
DcAmB, Drake, NatCAB 6, NatCAB 9,
TwCBDA, WhAm H
Tucker, Henry St. George 1779-1848 *BiAUS*
Tucker, Henry St. George 1780-1848 *ApCAB,*
BiDrAC, DcAmB, NatCAB 7, TwCBDA,
WhAm H, WhAmP
Tucker, Henry St. George 1781-1848 *Drake*
Tucker, Henry St. George 1853-1932 *BiDrAC,*
DcAmB, NatCAB 7, TwCBDA,
WhAm 1, WhAmP
Tucker, Henry St. George 1874-1959
NatCAB 43, WhAm 3
Tucker, Herman Franklin 1878-1955
NatCAB 44
Tucker, Hiram G 1851- *WhAm 4*
Tucker, Hugh Clarence 1857- *WhAm 5*
Tucker, Irvin B 1878-1943 *WhAm 2*
Tucker, J R 1823-1897 *BiAUS*
Tucker, John *BiAUS*
Tucker, John 1719-1792 *ApCAB*
Tucker, John Francis 1871-1921 *WhAm 1,*
WhAm 5
Tucker, John J *NewYHSD*
Tucker, John Randolph 1812-1883 *AmBi,*
ApCAB, BiDConf, DcAmB, NatCAB 4,
TwCBDA, WebAMB, WhAm H
Tucker, John Randolph 1823-1897 *ApCAB,*
BiDrAC, DcAmB, NatCAB 7, TwCBDA,
WhAm H, WhAmP
Tucker, Joshua Thomas 1812- *ApCAB*
Tucker, Josiah 1711-1799 *ApCAB, Drake*
Tucker, Katharine Dickinson 1873-1957
WhAm 3
Tucker, Louise Emery 1877- *WomWWA 14*
Tucker, Luther 1802-1873 *ApCAB, DcAmB,*
Drake, EncAAH, NatCAB 24, TwCBDA,
WhAm H
Tucker, Luther Henry 1834-1897 *NatCAB 24*
Tucker, Mary B *NewYHSD*
Tucker, Mary Eliza 1838- *ApCAB*
Tucker, Mary Frances 1837- *AmWom*
Tucker, Mona House 1882- *WomWWA 14*

Tucker, N Beverley 1867- *WhAm 4*
Tucker, Nathaniel Beverley 1784-1851 *AmBi,*
ApCAB, DcAmB, Drake, NatCAB 7,
TwCBDA
Tucker, Nathaniel Beverley 1820-1890 *ApCAB,*
DcAmB, NatCAB 7, WhAm H
Tucker, Nion Robert 1885-1950 *NatCAB 39*
Tucker, Pomeroy 1802-1870 *ApCAB*
Tucker, Preston Thomas 1903-1957 *WhAm 3*
Tucker, Raymond R 1896-1970 *WhAm 5*
Tucker, Richard d1975 *WhAm 6*
Tucker, Richard Blackburn 1886-1959
NatCAB 46, WhAm 3
Tucker, Richard Hawley 1859-1952 *NatCAB 18,*
NatCAB 41, WhAm 3
Tucker, Robert Gilbert 1873-1941 *NatCAB 30*
Tucker, Robert Henry 1875- *WhAm 6*
Tucker, Robert Oliver 1863-1945 *NatCAB 37*
Tucker, Rosa Lee 1868- *AmWom*
Tucker, Samuel 1747-1833 *AmBi, ApCAB,*
DcAmB, Drake, NatCAB 12, TwCBDA,
WebAMB, WhAm H
Tucker, Samuel Marion 1876-1962 *NatCAB 49,*
WhAm 4
Tucker, Sarah 1779-1840 *ApCAB, Drake*
Tucker, Sophie 1884-1966 *WebAB, WhAm 4*
Tucker, St. George 1752- *BiAUS*
Tucker, St. George 1752-1827 *DcAmB, Drake,*
NatCAB 7, TwCBDA, WhAm H
Tucker, St. George 1752-1828 *ApCAB*
Tucker, Starling 1770-1834 *BiAUS, BiDrAC,*
WhAm H, WhAmP
Tucker, Stephen Davis 1818-1902 *DcAmB*
Tucker, Thomas Tudor 1745-1828 *ApCAB,*
BiAUS, BiDrAC, Drake, TwCBDA,
WhAm H, WhAmP
Tucker, Tilghman Mayfield 1802-1859 *ApCAB,*
BiAUS, BiDrAC, Drake, NatCAB 13,
TwCBDA, WhAm H
Tucker, W Leon 1871-1934 *WhAm 1*
Tucker, William Austin 1850-1931 *NatCAB 18,*
NatCAB 26
Tucker, William Clifford 1898-1961 *WhAm 4*
Tucker, William Conquest 1863- *WhAm 4*
Tucker, William E 1801-1857 *NewYHSD*
Tucker, William Jewett 1839-1926 *AmBi,*
ApCAB, BiDAmEd, DcAmB, DcAmReB,
NatCAB 9, NatCAB 18, NatCAB 24,
TwCBDA, WhAm 1
Tucker, Willis Gaylord 1849-1922 *ApCAB,*
NatCAB 28, TwCBDA, WhAm 1
Tucker, Winston Harris 1901-1958 *NatCAB 47*
Tuckerman, Alfred 1848-1925 *WhAm 1*
Tuckerman, Arthur 1896-1955 *WhAm 3*
Tuckerman, Arthur Lyman 1861- *ApCAB*
Tuckerman, Bayard 1855-1923 *ApCAB,*
DcAmB, TwCBDA, WhAm 1
Tuckerman, Charles Keating 1821-1896 *ApCAB,*
TwCBDA
Tuckerman, Charles Keating 1827-1896
NatCAB 14
Tuckerman, Charles T *BiAUS*
Tuckerman, Edward 1817-1886 *AmBi, ApCAB,*
DcAmB, Drake, NatCAB 5, TwCBDA,
WhAm H
Tuckerman, Frederick 1857-1929 *DcAmB,*
WhAm 1
Tuckerman, Frederick Goddard 1821-1873
DcAmB, WhAm H
Tuckerman, Frederick Goddard 1821-1877
ApCAB
Tuckerman, Henry Theodore 1813-1871 *AmBi,*
ApCAB, BnEnAmA, DcAmB, Drake,
NatCAB 7, TwCBDA, WhAm H
Tuckerman, Jacob Edward 1876- *WhAm 6*
Tuckerman, Joseph 1778-1840 *AmBi, ApCAB,*
DcAmB, DcAmReB, Drake, NatCAB 6,
TwCBDA, WhAm H
Tuckerman, Lilia McCauley 1882- *IIBEAAW*
Tuckerman, Louis Bryant 1879-1962
NatCAB 50, WhAm 4
Tuckerman, Samuel Parkman 1819- *ApCAB,*
Drake
Tuckerman, Samuel Parkman 1819-1880
WhAm H
Tuckerman, Samuel Parkman 1819-1891
NatCAB 12

Tuckerman, Stephen Salisbury 1830-1904 *ApCAB, NewYHSD*
Tuckey, William 1708?-1781 *DcAmB, WhAm H*
Tuckey, William Dyson 1866-1930 *NatCAB 22*
Tudor, Charles William 1903-1970 *WhAm 5*
Tudor, Frederic 1783-1864 *DcAmB, NatCAB 6, WhAm H*
Tudor, Frederic 1845-1902 *NatCAB 32*
Tudor, John William 1876-1936 *NatCAB 28*
Tudor, Ralph Arnold 1902-1963 *WhAm 4*
Tudor, Robert M *NewYHSD*
Tudor, Rosamond *WomWWA 14*
Tudor, William 1750-1819 *ApCAB, BiAUS, Drake, NatCAB 7*
Tudor, William 1779-1830 *AmBi, ApCAB, BiAUS, DcAmB, Drake, NatCAB 8, TwCBDA, WhAm H*
Tuechter, August Herman 1869-1947 *WhAm 2*
Tuell, Samuel Bennett 1881-1942 *NatCAB 31*
Tuerk, John 1892-1951 *NatCAB 39*
Tufayl, Abu Bakr Muhammad, Ibn 1110?-1185 *DcScB*
Tufts, Bowen 1884-1935 *NatCAB 25, WhAm 1*
Tufts, Charles 1781-1876 *ApCAB, DcAmB, WhAm H*
Tufts, Cotton 1732-1815 *DcAmB, WhAm H*
Tufts, Cotton 1734-1815 *ApCAB, Drake*
Tufts, Edgar 1869- *WhAm 5*
Tufts, James Arthur 1855-1938 *NatCAB 10, WhAm 1*
Tufts, James Hayden 1858?- *NatCAB 11*
Tufts, James Hayden 1862-1942 *DcAmB S3, WhAm 2*
Tufts, John 1689-1750 *ApCAB, Drake*
Tufts, John 1689-1752 *DcAmB, WhAm H*
Tufts, John Quincy 1840-1908 *BiAUS, BiDrAC*
Tufts, Quincy 1791-1872 *ApCAB*
Tufts, Walter 1860-1924 *NatCAB 26*
Tufty, Herbert Iver 1903-1973 *WhAm 5*
Tuggle, Carrie A 1859- *WhoColR*
Tuggle, Charles Summey 1899-1972 *WhAm 6*
Tugman, William Masten 1893-1960 *WhAm 4*
Tugwell, Rexford Guy 1891- *EncAAH, EncAB, WebAB*
Tuholske, Herman 1848-1922 *NatCAB 5, WhAm 1*
Tuigg, John 1820-1889 *ApCAB, NatCAB 6, TwCBDA*
Tuigg, John 1821-1889 *WhAm H*
Tukey, Harold Bradford 1896-1971 *WhAm 5*
Tukhachevsky, Mikhail Nicolaevich 1893-1937 *WhoMilH*
Tulane, Paul 1801-1887 *AmBi, ApCAB, DcAmB, NatCAB 9, TwCBDA, WhAm H*
Tulasne, Louis-Rene 1815-1885 *DcScB*
Tuley, Henry Enos 1870-1923 *NatCAB 16, WhAm 1*
Tuley, Murray F 1827-1905 *WhAm 1*
Tuley, Philip Speed 1868-1943 *WhAm 2*
Tull, Jethro 1674-1740 *EncAAH*
Tuller, Edward Pratt 1859- *WhAm 5*
Tuller, John Jay 1861- *WhAm 4*
Tuller, Walter Kilbourne 1886-1939 *NatCAB 29*
Tulley, David Henry 1904-1975 *WhAm 6*
Tullidge, John 1836-1899 *IlBEAAW*
Tullis, Garner Hugh 1893-1966 *NatCAB 51*
Tullis, H H 1901-1958 *WhAm 3*
Tullis, Robert Lee 1864- *WhAm 5*
Tulloch, Earl Franklin 1894-1952 *NatCAB 40*
Tulloss, Rees Edgar 1881-1959 *NatCAB 46, WhAm 3*
Tully, Christopher *NewYHSD*
Tully, Jim 1891-1947 *WhAm 2*
Tully, John 1638-1701 *ApCAB, Drake*
Tully, Joseph Merit 1893-1963 *WhAm 4*
Tully, Pleasant Britton 1829-1897 *BiDrAC, WhAm H*
Tully, Richard Walton 1877-1945 *NatCAB 16, WhAm 2*
Tully, William 1785-1859 *ApCAB, DcAmB, Drake, WhAm H*
Tully, William John 1870-1930 *WhAm 1, WhAm 1C*
Tulp, Arnold 1910-1973 *WhAm 6*

Tulp, Nicolaas 1593-1674 *BiHiMed, DcScB*
Tumilty, Howard T 1898-1969 *WhAm 5*
Tumpeer, I Harrison 1893-1939 *NatCAB 30*
Tumulty, Joseph Patrick 1879-1954 *DcAmB S5, WhAm 3*
Tumulty, Thomas James 1913- *BiDrAC*
Tung, Ch'i-Ch'ang 1555-1636 *McGEWB*
Tung, Chung-Shu 179?BC-104BC *McGEWB*
Tung, Pi-Wu 1886-1975 *WhAm 6*
Tunison, Abram Vorhis 1909-1971 *WhAm 5*
Tunison, George McGregor 1882-1954 *WhAm 3*
Tunison, Joseph Salathiel 1849- *WhAm 4*
Tunks, Walter F 1886-1958 *WhAm 3*
Tunnell, Ebe Walter 1844-1917 *NatCAB 11, TwCBDA, WhAm 1*
Tunnell, James Miller 1879-1957 *BiDrAC, NatCAB 46*
Tunney, Gene 1898- *WebAB*
Tunney, James Joseph *WebAB*
Tunney, John Varick 1934- *BiDrAC*
Tunnicliff, Damon George 1829-1901 *NatCAB 18*
Tunnicliff, Nelson 1867-1938 *NatCAB 28*
Tunnicliff, Ruth 1876- *WomWWA 14*
Tunnicliff, Sarah Bacon 1872- *WomWWA 14*
Tunstall, Mrs. A M 1879- *WhAm 6*
Tunstall, Cuthbert 1474-1559 *DcScB*
Tunstall, John *REnAW*
Tunstall, Richard Baylor 1848-1919 *WhAm 1*
Tunstall, Robert Baylor 1880-1956 *NatCAB 44, WhAm 3*
Tunstall, Robert Williamson 1851-1917 *WhAm 1*
Tunstill, Clover Dell Hill 1909-1972 *WhAm 6*
Tuohy, Edward Boyce 1908-1959 *WhAm 3*
Tuohy, Walter Joseph 1901-1966 *WhAm 4*
Tuomey, Michael 1805-1857 *TwCBDA*
Tuomey, Michael 1808-1857 *ApCAB, NatCAB 13, WhAm H*
Tuomioja, Sakari Severi 1911-1964 *WhAm 4*
Tupac-Amaru 1540-1573 *ApCAB*
Tupac Amaru, Jose Gabriel 1742-1781 *McGEWB*
Tupac Inca Yupanqui 1420?-1483 *ApCAB*
Tupman, Eva Smillie *WomWWA 14*
Tupolev, Andrei Nikolaevich 1888-1972 *McGEWB, WhAm 5*
Tupolev, Andrey Nikolaevich 1888-1972 *DcScB, WhWW-II*
Tupper, Benjamin 1738-1792 *ApCAB, DcAmB, Drake, TwCBDA, WhAm H*
Tupper, Charles 1794-1881 *ApCAB*
Tupper, Sir Charles 1821-1915 *ApCAB, McGEWB*
Tupper, Charles Hibbert 1855- *ApCAB*
Tupper, Clarence Edgar 1871-1964 *NatCAB 51*
Tupper, Claude A 1877-1937 *WhAm 1*
Tupper, Elias Doar 1878-1949 *NatCAB 38*
Tupper, Ellen Smith 1822-1888 *AmWom*
Tupper, Frederick 1871-1950 *WhAm 4*
Tupper, Henry Allen 1828-1902 *ApCAB, DcAmB, NatCAB 1, WhAm 1*
Tupper, Henry Allen 1856- *WhAm 1*
Tupper, Henry Martin 1831-1893 *NatCAB 1, TwCBDA*
Tupper, Henry Marty 1831-1893 *ApCAB Sup*
Tupper, James Waddell 1870- *WhAm 5*
Tupper, Kerr Boyce 1854- *NatCAB 8, WhAm 1*
Tupper, Mila Frances 1864- *AmWom*
Tupper, Samuel Y 1817-1891 *NatCAB 1*
Tupper, Stanley Roger 1921- *BiDrAC*
Tupper, Virgil Langstaff 1869-1951 *NatCAB 41*
Tuqua, Edward *NewYHSD*
Tura, Cosimo 1430-1495 *McGEWB*
Turchin, John Basil 1822-1901 *ApCAB, NatCAB 12, WhAm 1*
Turck, Fenton Benedict 1857-1932 *ApCAB X, NatCAB 25, WhAm 1*
Turck, Fenton Benedict 1902-1970 *NatCAB 56, WhAm 6*
Turck, Ludwig 1810-1868 *DcScB*
Turck, Raymond Custer 1874- *WhAm 6*
Turcotte, Edmond 1898-1960 *WhAm 4*
Turcotte, Henry Rene Arthur 1846- *ApCAB*
Turcotte, Joseph Edouard 1808-1864 *ApCAB*
Tureaud, Alexander Pierre 1899-1972 *NatCAB 57*

Turell, Charles 1786-1863 *ApCAB Sup*
Turell, Ebenezer 1702-1778 *ApCAB, Drake, NatCAB 8*
Turell, Jane 1708-1735 *ApCAB, DcAmB, Drake, NatCAB 7, NotAW*
Turenne, Henri D'Auvergne, Vicomte De 1611-1675 *WhoMilH*
Turgenev, Ivan Sergeyevich 1818-1883 *McGEWB*
Turgeon, Pierre Flavian 1787-1867 *ApCAB, Drake*
Turgot, A R J, Baron DeL'Aulne 1721-1781 *McGEWB*
Turgot, Anne-Robert-Jacques 1727-1781 *DcScB*
Turgot, Anne Robert Joseph 1727-1781 *ApCAB*
Turgot, Etienne-Francois 1721-1788 *DcScB*
Turgot, Etienne Francois 1721-1789 *ApCAB*
Turin, John Joseph 1913-1973 *WhAm 6*
Turing, Alan Mathison 1912-1954 *DcScB*
Turini, Giovanni 1841-1899 *ApCAB, WhAm 1*
Turk, Francis H *NewYHSD*
Turk, Karl 1883-1954 *NatCAB 45*
Turk, Milton Haight 1866-1949 *WhAm 2*
Turk, Morris Howland 1867-1939 *WhAm 1*
Turk, Richard Henry 1904-1968 *NatCAB 55*
Turkevich, Leonty 1865-1965 *WhAm 4*
Turkington, Grace Alice 1871- *WomWWA 14*
Turkington, Grace Alice 1879- *WhAm 6*
Turkle, Alonzo John 1859-1937 *WhAm 1*
Turley, Clarence Milton 1893-1970 *WhAm 5*
Turley, Henry Clay 1897- *WhAm 4*
Turley, Jay 1877-1942 *WhAm 2*
Turley, Thomas Battle 1845-1910 *ApCAB Sup, BiDrAC, NatCAB 12, TwCBDA, WhAm 1*
Turlington, Edgar 1891-1959 *WhAm 3*
Turman, Moe 1896-1957 *NatCAB 43*
Turnage, Allen Hal 1891-1971 *WhAm 5*
Turnage, Needham Coy 1888-1949 *NatCAB 38*
Turnbow, Grover Dean 1892-1971 *NatCAB 57*
Turnbull, Andrew 1718?-1792 *DcAmB, WhAm H*
Turnbull, Andrew Blair 1884-1960 *WhAm 4*
Turnbull, Andrew Winchester 1921-1970 *NatCAB 55, WhAm 5*
Turnbull, Barton P d1948 *WhAm 2*
Turnbull, Charles Nesbit 1832-1874 *ApCAB*
Turnbull, Charles Smith 1847-1918 *ApCAB, NatCAB 8, WhAm 1*
Turnbull, Edwin Litchfield 1872-1927 *NatCAB 21, WhAm 1*
Turnbull, Frances Hubbard Litchfield d1927 *WomWWA 14*
Turnbull, Francese Hubbard Litchfield d1927 *WhAm 1*
Turnbull, George d1810 *Drake*
Turnbull, Henry Rutherford 1905-1976 *WhAm 6*
Turnbull, J Gordon 1891-1953 *NatCAB 41, WhAm 3*
Turnbull, Julia Anna 1822-1887 *NotAW*
Turnbull, Laurence 1821-1900 *ApCAB, WhAm 1*
Turnbull, Margaret d1942 *WhAm 2*
Turnbull, Martin Ryerson 1886-1949 *WhAm 2*
Turnbull, Phillips Roome 1921-1974 *WhAm 6*
Turnbull, Robert 1809-1877 *ApCAB, Drake, NatCAB 10, WhAm H*
Turnbull, Robert 1850-1920 *BiDrAC, WhAm 4*
Turnbull, Robert James 1775-1833 *AmBi, ApCAB, DcAmB, Drake, TwCBDA, WhAm H*
Turnbull, Walter Mason 1881-1930 *WhAm 1*
Turnbull, William 1800-1857 *AmBi, ApCAB, DcAmB, NatCAB 12, WhAm H*
Turnbull, William Paterson 1830-1871 *ApCAB*
Turneaure, Frederick Eugene 1866-1951 *NatCAB 39, WhAm 3*
Turner, Abe W 1893-1947 *WhAm 2*
Turner, Albert Edward 1865-1920 *NatCAB 19*
Turner, Alexander 1867-1945 *NatCAB 37*
Turner, Alice Bellvadore Sams 1859- *AmWom*
Turner, Archelaus Ewing 1861-1938 *TwCBDA, WhAm 1*
Turner, Arthur Henry 1873-1938 *WhAm 1*
Turner, Asa 1799-1885 *DcAmB, WhAm H*
Turner, August 1865- *NatCAB 17*

Turrell, Jane 1709-1735 *WhAm H*
Turrell, Joel 1794-1859 *BiAUS*
Turrell, Orlando Beach 1834-1917 *NatCAB 17*
Turrentine, Samuel Bryant 1861-1949 *WhAm 3*
Turrill, Charles Beebe 1854-1927 *WhAm 1*
Turrill, Joel 1794-1859 *BiDrAC, WhAm H*
Turrish, Henry 1864-1934 *NatCAB 31*
Turtaz, Lewis *NewYHSD*
Turton, Franklin E 1891-1952 *WhAm 3*
Turville, George Albert 1873- *ApCAB X*
Tusi, Muhammad Ibn Muhammad Ibn, Al-
  1201-1274 *DcScB*
Tusi, Sharaf Al-Din Al-Muzaffar Ibn, Al-
  d1213? *DcScB*
Tuska, Gustave Robisher 1869-1931
  NatCAB 24, WhAm 1
Tusten, Benjamin *Drake*
Tustin, Ernest Leigh 1862-1921 *WhAm 1*
Tutankhamen *McGEWB*
Tuten, James Russell 1911-1968 *BiDrAC,
  WhAm 5*
Tutherly, Herbert Everett 1848- *NatCAB 4*
Tuthill, A G D 1776-1843 *Drake*
Tuthill, Abraham G D 1776-1843 *NewYHSD*
Tuthill, Alexander Mackenzie 1871-1958
  WhAm 5
Tuthill, Alexander McKenzie 1871-1958
  NatCAB 44
Tuthill, Cornelia 1820-1870 *ApCAB*
Tuthill, Daniel *NewYHSD*
Tuthill, Frank 1822-1865 *Drake*
Tuthill, Horace Stephen 1871-1942 *NatCAB 31*
Tuthill, Horace Sweezy 1844-1919 *NatCAB 31*
Tuthill, Jeremiah Goldsmith 1861-1944
  NatCAB 33
Tuthill, Job 1855-1928 *NatCAB 22*
Tuthill, Joseph Hasbrouck 1811-1877 *BiAUS,
  BiDrAC, WhAm H*
Tuthill, Louisa Caroline 1800?-1879 *Drake*
Tuthill, Louisa Caroline Huggins 1799-1879
  NotAW
Tuthill, Louisa Cornelia 1798-1879 *ApCAB*
Tuthill, Richard Stanley 1841-1920 *WhAm 1*
Tuthill, Selah 1771-1821 *BiAUS, BiDrAC,
  WhAm H*
Tuthill, Theodore Robinson 1868-1922
  NatCAB 6, WhAm 1
Tuthill, William Burnet 1855-1929 *DcAmB,
  WhAm HA, WhAm 4*
Tuthill, William H *NewYHSD*
Tuthill, William H 1808- *Drake*
Tutt, Charles Leaming 1889-1961 *WhAm 4*
Tutt, John Calhoun 1851-1917 *WhAm 1*
Tuttle, Affa Miner 1859- *WomWWA 14*
Tuttle, Albert Henry 1844- *ApCAB, WhAm 1*
Tuttle, Alexander Harrison 1844-1932 *WhAm 1*
Tuttle, Allison Orang 1869-1927 *NatCAB 22*
Tuttle, Anna Stockbridge 1859- *WomWWA 14*
Tuttle, Arthur J 1868-1944 *NatCAB 34,
  WhAm 2*
Tuttle, Arthur Lemuel 1870-1958 *WhAm 3*
Tuttle, Arthur Smith 1865-1949 *NatCAB 40,
  WhAm 2*
Tuttle, Bloodgood 1889- *WhAm 1*
Tuttle, Charles Augustus d1935 *WhAm 1*
Tuttle, Charles Henry 1879-1971 *NatCAB 57,
  WhAm 5*
Tuttle, Charles Wesley 1829-1881 *ApCAB,
  DcAmB, Drake, WhAm H*
Tuttle, Clarence Ewing 1884-1962 *NatCAB 50,
  WhAm 4*
Tuttle, Daniel Sylvester 1837-1923 *ApCAB,
  DcAmB, DcAmReB, NatCAB 6,
  TwCBDA, WhAm 1*
Tuttle, David H *NewYHSD*
Tuttle, David Kitchell 1835-1915 *WhAm 1*
Tuttle, Edwin Frank 1875- *WhAm 5*
Tuttle, Ella Maria 1856- *WomWWA 14*
Tuttle, Emerson 1890-1946 *WhAm 2*
Tuttle, Emma Rood 1837- *WomWWA 14*
Tuttle, Emma Rood 1839- *AmWom, ApCAB,
  WhAm 4*
Tuttle, Ezra Benjamin 1834- *NatCAB 14*
Tuttle, Fordyce Eddy 1903-1969 *NatCAB 54*
Tuttle, Frank Day 1864-1926 *NatCAB 30*
Tuttle, Frank Jefferson 1855-1920 *NatCAB 6*
Tuttle, George Albert 1859-1942 *WhAm 2*
Tuttle, George Fuller 1852-1926 *NatCAB 20*

Tuttle, George Marvine 1866-1926 *WhAm 1*
Tuttle, George Montgomery 1856-1912
  WhAm 1
Tuttle, George Reid 1901-1957 *NatCAB 47*
Tuttle, George Thomas 1850-1927 *ApCAB X,
  NatCAB 20, WhAm 1*
Tuttle, George W *NewYHSD*
Tuttle, George Webster 1866-1929 *NatCAB 24*
Tuttle, Harry A 1846-1919 *NatCAB 17*
Tuttle, Henry 1897-1959 *WhAm 3*
Tuttle, Henry William 1861- *WhAm 4*
Tuttle, Herbert 1846-1894 *AmBi, ApCAB,
  DcAmB, NatCAB 10, TwCBDA,
  WhAm H*
Tuttle, Hiram Americus 1837-1911 *NatCAB 11,
  TwCBDA, WhAm 1*
Tuttle, Horace Parnell 1839- *ApCAB*
Tuttle, Hudson *NewYHSD*
Tuttle, Hudson 1836-1910 *ApCAB, WhAm 1*
Tuttle, Isidora Barker Cheney 1833-
  WomWWA 14
Tuttle, James Madison 1823-1892 *ApCAB*
Tuttle, James Madison 1832-1892 *NatCAB 5,
  TwCBDA*
Tuttle, James Patterson 1856-1935 *WhAm 1*
Tuttle, Joseph Farrand 1818-1901 *ApCAB,
  NatCAB 28, TwCBDA, WhAm 1*
Tuttle, Joseph W *NewYHSD*
Tuttle, Julius Herbert 1857-1945 *WhAm 2*
Tuttle, Kate Austin Seeley 1849-
  WomWWA 14
Tuttle, Lucius 1846-1914 *NatCAB 33,
  WhAm 1*
Tuttle, Mabel Chauvenet Holden 1873- *BiCAW,
  WomWWA 14*
Tuttle, Margaretta Muhlenberg 1880-
  WomWWA 14
Tuttle, Mary McArthur Thompson 1849-1916
  NatCAB 10, WhAm 1, WomWWA 14
Tuttle, Morton Chase 1875-1957 *WhAm 3*
Tuttle, Otis P *NewYHSD*
Tuttle, Penelope T Sturgis Cook *WomWWA 14*
Tuttle, Thomas Dyer 1869- *WhAm 5*
Tuttle, W B 1874- *WhAm 5*
Tuttle, Will Rockwell 1887-1954 *NatCAB 40*
Tuttle, William Edgar, Jr. 1870-1923 *BiDrAC,
  WhAm 1*
Tuttle, William Stearns 1874-1955 *NatCAB 42*
Tutton, Alfred Edwin Howard 1864-1938 *DcScB*
Tutuola, Amos 1920- *McGEWB*
Tutwiler, Carrington Cabell 1874-1956
  NatCAB 46
Tutwiler, Edward Magruder 1846-1925
  NatCAB 38
Tutwiler, Henry 1807-1884 *ApCAB, BiDAmEd,
  DcAmB, WhAm H*
Tutwiler, Herbert 1882-1945 *NatCAB 37*
Tutwiler, Julia Strudwick d1916 *AmWom,
  WhAm 1*
Tutwiler, Julia Strudwick 1835-1916
  NatCAB 15
Tutwiler, Julia Strudwick 1841-1916 *AmBi,
  BiDAmEd, DcAmB, NotAW*
Tutwiler, Temple William 1879-1950
  NatCAB 38
Tutwiler, Temple Wilson 1879-1950 *WhAm 3*
Tutwiler, Thomas Henry 1866-1938 *WhAm 1*
Tuve, Anthony G 1864- *WhAm 4*
Tuve, Rosemond 1903-1964 *WhAm 4*
Tuxbury, Helen *WomWWA 14*
Tvardovsky, Alexandr Trifonovich 1910-1971
  WhAm 5
Twachtman, John Henry 1853-1902 *AmBi,
  ApCAB, BnEnAmA, DcAmB, IlBEAAW,
  McGEWB, NatCAB 13*
Twaddell, William Powell 1879-1949 *WhAm 3*
Twaddle, Harry Lewis 1888-1954 *NatCAB 43*
Twain, Mark 1835-1910 *AmBi, DcAmB,
  EncAAH, EncAB, McGEWB, REnAW,
  WebAB*
Twaits, William 1781-1814 *Drake*
Twatchman, John Henry 1853-1902 *WhAm 1*
Tweddle, Herbert W C 1832- *NatCAB 12*
Tweed, Blanche Oelrichs Thomas Barrymore
  1890-1950 *NotAW*
Tweed, Charles A *BiAUS*
Tweed, Charles Harrison 1844-1917
  NatCAB 17, WhAm 1

Tweed, George P 1871-1946 *WhAm 2*
Tweed, Harrison 1885-1969 *NatCAB 55,
  WhAm 5*
Tweed, John Hancock 1895-1961 *NatCAB 52*
Tweed, William Marcy 1823-1878 *AmBi,
  ApCAB, BiAUS, BiDrAC, DcAmB,
  EncAB, McGEWB, NatCAB 3, WebAB,
  WhAm H, WhAmP*
Tweedale, William 1823- *ApCAB*
Tweedall, Daniel Greenwood 1881-1957
  NatCAB 46
Tweeddale, William 1823- *NatCAB 5*
Tweedell, Edward Davis 1879-1928 *WhAm 1*
Tweedell, James Collier 1900-1966 *WhAm 4*
Tweedie, Douglas Herbert 1890-1954
  NatCAB 42
Tweedy, Arthur Edward 1865-1955 *NatCAB 43*
Tweedy, Donald Nichols 1890-1948 *NatCAB 37*
Tweedy, Frank 1854-1937 *WhAm 1*
Tweedy, Henry Hallam 1868-1953 *NatCAB 44,
  WhAm 3*
Tweedy, John Hubbard 1814-1891 *BiAUS,
  BiDrAC, NatCAB 16, WhAm H*
Tweedy, Lawrence Leslie 1882-1943
  NatCAB 41
Tweedy, Samuel 1776-1868 *BiAUS, BiDrAC,
  WhAm H*
Twells, Robert 1895-1966 *WhAm 4*
Twenhofel, William Henry 1875-1957 *DcScB,
  NatCAB 45, WhAm 3*
Twente, George Edward 1911-1971 *NatCAB 57*
Twibill, George W 1806?-1836 *ApCAB,
  NewYHSD*
Twichell, David Cushman 1874-1924
  NatCAB 37
Twichell, Ginery 1811-1883 *ApCAB, BiDrAC,
  WhAm H*
Twichell, James Ashburne 1855-1929
  NatCAB 21
Twichell, Jerome 1844- *NatCAB 16*
Twichell, Joseph Hopkins 1838-1918 *DcAmB,
  NatCAB 29, WhAm 1*
Twigg, Mrs. William Albert *NewYHSD*
Twiggs, David Emanuel 1790-1862 *AmBi,
  ApCAB, DcAmB, Drake, NatCAB 4,
  TwCBDA, WebAMB, WhAm H*
Twiggs, Hansford Dade Duncan 1839-
  NatCAB 2
Twiggs, Levi 1793-1847 *ApCAB*
Twiggs, Sarah Lowe 1839- *AmWom,
  WomWWA 14*
Twine, William Henry 1862- *WhoColR*
Twing, Alvin Tabor 1811-1882 *ApCAB*
Twing, Martin Walter 1857- *WhAm 4*
Twining, Alexander Catlin 1801-1884 *ApCAB,
  DcAmB, NatCAB 19, WhAm H*
Twining, Frank Barton 1856-1945 *NatCAB 34,
  WhAm 2*
Twining, Kingsley 1823-1901 *ApCAB*
Twining, Kinsley 1832-1901 *NatCAB 13,
  WhAm 1*
Twining, Nathan Crook 1869-1924 *WhAm 1*
Twining, Nathan Farragut 1897- *WebAMB,
  WhWW-II*
Twining, William Stanton 1865-1937
  NatCAB 27
Twiss, George Ransom 1863-1944 *WhAm 2*
Twitchel, Thomas *NewYHSD*
Twitchell, Amos 1781-1850 *DcAmB, WhAm H*
Twitchell, Asa Weston 1820-1904 *NewYHSD*
Twitchell, Ginery 1811-1883 *BiAUS,
  NatCAB 5*
Twitchell, Hannah *WhAm 5*
Twitchell, Herbert Kenaston 1865-1928
  WhAm 1
Twitchell, LaFayette 1859-1936 *WhAm 1*
Twitchell, Pierrepont Edwards 1894-1962
  WhAm 4
Twitchell, Ralph Emerson 1859-1925 *REnAW,
  WhAm 1*
Twitchell, Theodore Andow 1902-1955
  NatCAB 43
Twitmyer, Edwin Burket 1873-1943 *NatCAB 33,
  WhAm 2*
Twitty, Joseph Jones 1894-1959 *WhAm 4*
Twitty, Victor Chandler 1901-1967 *WhAm 4*
Twohig, John Elmer 1887-1953 *NatCAB 43*
Twohy, Daniel W 1864- *WhAm 5*

Twohy, Edmund Paul 1885-1944 *NatCAB 34*

Twombly, Alexander Stevenson 1832-1907 *WhAm 1*

Twombly, Clifford Gray 1869-1942 *WhAm 2*

Twombly, Edward Bancroft 1891-1969 *NatCAB 54*, *WhAm 5*

Twombly, Miss H M *NewYHSD*

Twombly, Hamilton McKown 1849-1910 *NatCAB 30*, *WhAm 1*

Twombly, Henry Bancroft 1862-1955 *NatCAB 43*, *WhAm 3*

Twombly, John Hanson 1814-1893 *NatCAB 12*

Twombly, Minnie S 1880- *WomWWA 14*

Twomey, M Joseph 1871-1948 *WhAm 2*

Twomy, Dennis *NewYHSD*

Tworkov, Jack 1900- *BnEnAmA*

Twort, Frederick William 1877-1950 *AsBiEn*, *DcScB*

Twyman, Robert Joseph 1897- *BiDrAC*

Tybout, Ella Middleton *WomWWA 14*

Tydings, Joseph Davies 1928- *BiDrAC*

Tydings, Millard Evelyn 1890-1961 *BiDrAC*, *WhAm 4*, *WhAmP*

Tydings, Richard 1783-1865 *ApCAB*

Tye, Hiram H 1868-1948 *WhAm 2*

Tye, John L 1859-1935 *WhAm 1*

Tyler, Adeline Blanchard 1805-1875 *NotAW*

Tyler, Albert Clinton 1872-1945 *NatCAB 35*

Tyler, Albert Franklin 1881-1944 *NatCAB 35*

Tyler, Alice Sarah 1859-1944 *DcAmLiB*, *NatCAB 33*, *NotAW*, *WhAm 5*

Tyler, Ansel Augustus 1869- *WhAm 5*

Tyler, Asher 1798-1875 *BiAUS*, *BiDrAC*, *WhAm H*

Tyler, Bayard Henry 1855-1931 *WhAm 1*

Tyler, Benjamin Bushrod 1840- *WhAm 4*

Tyler, Benjamin Owen *NewYHSD*

Tyler, Bennet 1783-1858 *ApCAB*, *DcAmReB*, *Drake*, *WhAm H*

Tyler, Bennett 1783-1858 *NatCAB 9*, *TwCBDA*

Tyler, Carl Hamilton 1896-1973 *WhAm 6*

Tyler, Charles A 1877-1952 *WhAm 3*

Tyler, Charles Humphrey 1826-1865 *ApCAB*, *Drake*

Tyler, Charles Mellen 1832-1918 *DcAmB*, *WhAm 1*

Tyler, Comfort 1764-1827 *NatCAB 2*

Tyler, Cornelius Boardman 1875-1955 *NatCAB 47*, *WhAm 3*

Tyler, Daniel 1799-1882 *ApCAB*, *DcAmB*, *Drake*, *NatCAB 4*, *TwCBDA*, *WhAm H*

Tyler, Daniel, Jr. 1899-1967 *NatCAB 53*

Tyler, David Gardiner 1846-1927 *BiDrAC*, *TwCBDA*, *WhAm 1*, *WhAmP*

Tyler, Earl Cottler 1910-1973 *WhAm 6*

Tyler, Edgar Babcock 1865-1922 *NatCAB 17*

Tyler, Edna Ione Smith 1861- *WomWWA 14*

Tyler, Edward *NewYHSD*

Tyler, Edward Royall 1800-1848 *ApCAB*

Tyler, Eliphalet Williams 1846-1929 *NatCAB 25*

Tyler, Emma Farrand 1850- *WomWWA 14*

Tyler, Erastus Barnard 1822-1891 *ApCAB*, *TwCBDA*

Tyler, Frances Maria *WomWWA 14*

Tyler, Frank Edwards d1964 *WhAm 4*

Tyler, Frank Johnson 1863-1914 *NatCAB 17*

Tyler, George Crouse 1867-1946 *DcAmB S4*, *WhAm 2*

Tyler, George Washington 1803?-1833 *NewYHSD*

Tyler, Gerald Hall 1897- *IlBEAAW*

Tyler, Hal Clement 1878-1941 *NatCAB 41*

Tyler, Harry Walter 1863-1938 *WhAm 1*

Tyler, Henry Mather 1843-1931 *WhAm 1*

Tyler, Ivan Louis 1898-1967 *NatCAB 56*

Tyler, James Gale 1855-1931 *AmBi*, *WhAm 1*

Tyler, James Hoge 1846-1925 *NatCAB 13*, *NatCAB 27*, *TwCBDA*, *WhAm 1*

Tyler, James Manning 1835-1926 *BiDrAC*, *WhAm 1*

Tyler, John d1813 *BiAUS*

Tyler, John 1747-1813 *DcAmB*, *NatCAB 5*, *TwCBDA*, *WhAm H*, *WhAmP*

Tyler, John 1748-1813 *Drake*

Tyler, John 1790-1862 *AmBi*, *ApCAB*, *BiAUS*, *BiDConf*, *BiDrAC*, *BiDrUSE*, *DcAmB*, *Drake*, *EncAAH*, *EncAB*, *McGEWB*, *NatCAB 6*, *TwCBDA*, *WebAB*, *WhAm H*, *WhAmP*

Tyler, John J 1852-1930 *NatCAB 22*

Tyler, John Mason 1851-1929 *NatCAB 21*, *WhAm 1*

Tyler, John Poyntz 1862-1931 *NatCAB 24*, *WhAm 1*

Tyler, John W 1917-1968 *WhAm 4A*

Tyler, Joseph 1749-1823 *Drake*

Tyler, Joseph Beck 1876-1948 *NatCAB 37*

Tyler, Julia Gardiner 1820-1889 *AmWom*, *ApCAB*, *NatCAB 6*, *NotAW*

Tyler, Letitia Christian 1790-1842 *ApCAB*, *NotAW*

Tyler, Lyon Gardiner 1853-1935 *AmBi*, *ApCAB*, *DcAmB S1*, *NatCAB 3*, *TwCBDA*, *WhAm 1*

Tyler, Mason Whiting 1840-1907 *ApCAB Sup*, *NatCAB 10*, *WhAm 1*

Tyler, Morris Franklin 1848-1907 *NatCAB 33*, *WhAm 1*

Tyler, Moses Coit 1835-1900 *AmBi*, *ApCAB*, *BiDAmEd*, *DcAmB*, *Drake*, *McGEWB*, *NatCAB 4*, *TwCBDA*, *WebAB*, *WhAm 1*

Tyler, Odette 1869-1936 *WhAm 2*

Tyler, Odette 1872-1936 *WomWWA 14*

Tyler, Priscilla Cooper 1816-1889 *NotAW*

Tyler, Ralph *NewYHSD*

Tyler, Ralph W *WhoColR*

Tyler, Ralph Winfred 1902- *BiDAmEd*

Tyler, Ransom Hebbard 1813-1881 *ApCAB*, *NatCAB 10*

Tyler, Ransom Hubert 1815-1881 *DcAmB*, *WhAm H*

Tyler, Robert 1816-1877 *DcAmB*, *WhAm H*

Tyler, Robert 1818-1877 *ApCAB*, *NatCAB 10*

Tyler, Robert C d1865 *TwCBDA*

Tyler, Robert Ogden 1831-1874 *ApCAB*, *DcAmB*, *Drake*, *NatCAB 4*, *TwCBDA*, *WhAm H*

Tyler, Rollin Usher 1864-1948 *NatCAB 37*

Tyler, Rosa Barton 1841- *WomWWA 14*

Tyler, Royall 1757-1826 *AmBi*, *ApCAB*, *BiAUS*, *DcAmB*, *Drake*, *McGEWB*, *NatCAB 7*, *TwCBDA*, *WebAB*, *WhAm H*

Tyler, Royall 1884-1953 *DcAmB S5*

Tyler, Samuel 1766-1812 *TwCBDA*

Tyler, Samuel 1776?-1812 *NatCAB 5*

Tyler, Samuel 1809- *Drake*

Tyler, Samuel 1809-1877 *DcAmB*, *WhAm H*

Tyler, Samuel 1809-1878 *ApCAB*, *TwCBDA*

Tyler, Sidney Frederick 1850-1935 *NatCAB 25*

Tyler, Stanley A 1906-1963 *WhAm 4*

Tyler, Stephen Leslie 1889-1966 *WhAm 4*

Tyler, Therese Pauline 1884- *WomWWA 14*

Tyler, Thomas *NewYHSD*

Tyler, Victor Morris 1875-1959 *NatCAB 48*

Tyler, Wilfred Charles 1901-1965 *WhAm 4*

Tyler, William 1806-1849 *ApCAB*, *DcAmB*, *Drake*, *NatCAB 10*, *TwCBDA*, *WhAm H*

Tyler, William H *NewYHSD*

Tyler, William Seymour 1810-1897 *ApCAB*, *BiDAmEd*, *DcAmB*, *Drake*, *NatCAB 10*, *WhAm H*

Tyler, William Trevor 1871-1924 *WhAm 1*

Tyler, Willis Oliver 1880- *WhoColR*

Tylor, Sir Edward Burnett 1832-1917 *McGEWB*

Tynan, Joseph James 1871-1933 *WhAm 1*

Tynan, Thomas J 1874- *WhAm 5*

Tyndale, Hector 1821-1880 *ApCAB*, *DcAmB*, *NatCAB 4*, *TwCBDA*, *WhAm H*

Tyndale, William 1495?-1536 *McGEWB*

Tyndale, William Robert 1873-1950 *NatCAB 39*

Tyndall, Charles Herbert 1857-1935 *WhAm 1*

Tyndall, Henry Myron 1885-1943 *WhAm 2*

Tyndall, John 1820-1893 *AsBiEn*, *BiHiMed*, *DcScB*, *McGEWB*

Tyndall, Robert H 1877-1947 *WhAm 2*

Tyndall, William Thomas 1862-1928 *BiDrAC*, *WhAm 4*

Tyndell, Charles Noyes 1876- *WhAm 5*

Tyne, Thomas James 1868-1936 *WhAm 1*

Tyner, Carl Vann 1890-1969 *NatCAB 55*

Tyner, Charles L d1939 *WhAm 1*

Tyner, George Parker 1876- *WhAm 5*

Tyner, James Noble 1826-1904 *ApCAB*, *BiAUS*, *BiDrAC*, *BiDrUSE*, *NatCAB 4*, *TwCBDA*, *WhAm 1*

Tyner, Mary L 1871- *WomWWA 14*

Tynes, William Doric 1863-1933 *NatCAB 25*

Tyng, Dudley Atkins 1760-1829 *ApCAB*, *Drake*

Tyng, Dudley Atkins 1825-1858 *ApCAB*, *Drake*

Tyng, Edward 1683-1755 *ApCAB*, *DcAmB*, *Drake*, *WhAm H*

Tyng, Lucien Hamilton 1873- *ApCAB X*

Tyng, Sewell Tappan 1895-1946 *WhAm 2*

Tyng, Stephen Higginson 1800-1885 *ApCAB*, *DcAmB*, *Drake*, *NatCAB 2*, *TwCBDA*, *WhAm H*

Tyng, Stephen Higginson 1839-1898 *ApCAB*, *Drake*, *NatCAB 2*, *TwCBDA*

Tyng, Theodosius Stevens 1849- *WhAm 4*

Typhoid Mary *WebAB*

Tyrconnell, Richard Talbot, Earl Of 1630-1691 *WhoMilH*

Tyree, Evans 1854- *WhAm 4*, *WhoColR*

Tyree, Lewis 1892-1957 *WhAm 3*

Tyrell, Bernard 1859- *WhoColR*

Tyrker *ApCAB*

Tyrone, Hugh O'Neill, Earl Of 1540-1616 *WhoMilH*

Tyrrell, Frank Gill 1865- *NatCAB 5*, *WhAm 4*

Tyrrell, Henry 1865-1933 *WhAm 1*

Tyrrell, Henry Grattan d1948 *WhAm 2*

Tyrrell, Joseph Burr 1858-1957 *DcScB*

Tyrrell, Peter Aloysius 1896-1973 *NatCAB 57*

Tyrrell, W Bradley 1883-1964 *WhAm 4*

Tyrrell, William Casper 1847-1924 *NatCAB 20*

Tysen, John Colquhoun 1913-1972 *WhAm 5*

Tyson, Bettie Humes 1865- *WomWWA 14*

Tyson, Carroll Sargent, Jr. 1877-1956 *NatCAB 47*, *WhAm 3*

Tyson, Charles McGhee 1889-1918 *ApCAB X*

Tyson, Edward 1650?-1708 *DcScB*

Tyson, Elisha 1749-1824 *ApCAB*

Tyson, Forrest Clark 1881-1953 *NatCAB 42*

Tyson, Francis Doughton 1888-1961 *NatCAB 47*, *WhAm 4*

Tyson, George Emory 1829-1906 *DcAmB*

Tyson, J W *BiAUS*

Tyson, Jacob 1773-1848 *BiAUS*, *BiDrAC*, *WhAm H*

Tyson, James 1841-1919 *ApCAB*, *ApCAB X*, *DcAmB*, *NatCAB 9*, *TwCBDA*, *WhAm 1*

Tyson, Job Roberts 1803-1858 *ApCAB*, *BiDrAC*, *DcAmB*

Tyson, Job Roberts 1804-1858 *BiAUS*, *Drake*, *WhAm H*

Tyson, John Ambrose 1873-1971 *NatCAB 57*, *WhAm 5*

Tyson, John D 1899-1965 *WhAm 4*

Tyson, John Russell 1856-1923 *BiDrAC*, *NatCAB 12*, *WhAm 1*

Tyson, Lawrence Davis 1861-1929 *ApCAB X*, *BiDrAC*, *DcAmB*, *NatCAB 10*, *NatCAB 21*, *WhAm 1*

Tyson, Levering 1889-1966 *WhAm 4*

Tyson, McGhee 1889-1918 *NatCAB 46*

Tyson, Philip Thomas 1799-1877 *ApCAB*, *NatCAB 13*

Tyson, Ralph Maguire 1888-1962 *WhAm 4*

Tyson, Robert Carroll 1905-1974 *WhAm 6*

Tyson, Robert Stafford 1877-1951 *NatCAB 47*

Tyson, Stuart Lawrence 1873-1932 *DcAmB*, *WhAm 1*

Tyssowski, John 1887-1960 *NatCAB 49*, *WhAm 4*

Tytler, James 1747-1804 *Drake*

Tytler, James 1747-1805 *ApCAB*

Tytler, James Edwin 1880-1950 *NatCAB 39*

Tytus, John Butler 1875-1944 *DcAmB S3*

Tytus, Robb DePeyster 1876-1913 *NatCAB 47*

Tyulenev, Ivan 1892- *WhWW-II*

Tzschumansky *NewYHSD*

Tzschumansky, Stanislas *NewYHSD*

Tz'u-Hsi 1835-1908 *McGEWB*

U

Uanna, William Lewis 1909-1961 *WhAm 4*
Ubaldo, Guido *DcScB*
Ubico, Jorge 1878-1946 *WhAm 2*
Ubilla, Andres 1540?-1601 *ApCAB*
Uccello, Paolo 1397-1475 *McGEWB*
Uchida, Baron Yasuya 1865- *WhAm 4*
Udall, David King 1851-1938 *REnAW*
Udall, Denny Hammond 1874-1955 *NatCAB 46,*
 WhAm 3
Udall, Levi Stewart 1891-1958 *REnAW*
Udall, Levi Stewart 1891-1960 *WhAm 4*
Udall, Morris King 1922- *BiDrAC, REnAW*
Udall, Stewart Lee 1920- *BiDrAC, BiDrUSE,*
 EncAAH, REnAW
Udden, Johan August 1859-1932 *DcAmB,*
 WhAm 1
Udell, Alonzo E 1890-1960 *WhAm 4*
Udet, Ernst 1896-1941 *WhWW-II, WhoMilH*
Udree, Daniel 1751-1828 *BiAUS, BiDrAC,*
 WhAm H, WhAmP
Udy, Murray Cowley 1916-1965 *NatCAB 52*
Uebelacker, Charles Frederick 1868-1940
 NatCAB 35
Uebelacker, David Adams 1889-1964
 NatCAB 51
Uebelacker, David Adams 1899-1964 *WhAm 4*
Uehling, Edward A 1849-1952 *WhAm 3*
Ueland, Andreas 1853-1933 *WhAm 1*
Ueland, Clara Hampson 1860-1927 *BiCAW,*
 NotAW, WomWWA 14
Uelsmann, Jerry N 1934- *BnEnAmA*
Uexkull, Jakob Johann Von 1864-1944
 DcScB Sup
Ufer, Walter 1876-1936 *IlBEAAW, WhAm 1*
Uffenbach, Bernard Von 1691-1759 *ApCAB*
Uffert, John Frederick 1881-1959 *NatCAB 48*
Ufford, Bertha Hazard Tierney 1871-
 WomWWA 14
Ufford, Mabelle Morris *WomWWA 14*
Ufford, Walter Shepard 1859-1940 *NatCAB 29,*
 WhAm 1
Ugarte, Juan 1662-1730 *ApCAB*
Ugarte, Manuel 1878-1967 *WhAm 4*
Ugarte, Salvador 1880-1962 *WhAm 4*
Ughetta, Henry Leopold 1898-1967 *WhAm 4A*
Uhde, Hermann 1914-1965 *WhAm 4*
Uhl, Adolph 1870-1951 *NatCAB 41*
Uhl, Charles F 1871-1951 *WhAm 4*
Uhl, Edward Henry 1870-1940 *NatCAB 30*
Uhl, Edwin Fuller 1841-1901 *NatCAB 12,*
 NatCAB 15, TwCBDA
Uhl, John Hamilton 1890-1958 *NatCAB 52*
Uhl, William *NewYHSD*
Uhl, William Frank 1880-1963 *NatCAB 50*
Uhl, Willis Lemon 1885-1940 *WhAm 1*
Uhland, Maximilian 1475?-1538 *ApCAB*
Uhle, Albrecht Bernhard 1847- *ApCAB,*
 WhAm 4
Uhle, Bernard *NewYHSD*
Uhle, Friedrich Max 1856- *WhAm 4*
Uhle, G Anton *NewYHSD*
Uhlenbeck, George Eugene 1900- *AsBiEn*
Uhler, Horace Scudder 1872-1956 *WhAm 3*
Uhler, Jacob P 1854- *WhAm 4*
Uhler, Joseph Michael 1881-1947 *WhAm 2*
Uhler, Philip Reese 1835-1913 *ApCAB,*
 DcAmB, NatCAB 8, TwCBDA,
 WhAm 1
Uhler, Stewart Mann 1879-1952 *NatCAB 39*
Uhlig, Johannes Konrad 1875-1950 *NatCAB 39*
Uhlig, Richard William 1859-1937 *NatCAB 13,*
 NatCAB 28
Uhlmann, Erich Myron 1901-1964 *WhAm 4*
Uhlmann, Fred 1864-1938 *WhAm 1*

Uihlein, Edgar John 1877-1956 *WhAm 3*
Uihlein, Edward Gustav 1845-1921 *NatCAB 23*
Uihlein, Erwin Charles 1886-1968 *NatCAB 54,*
 WhAm 5
Uihlein, George Edward 1880-1950 *NatCAB 45*
Uihlein, Joseph Edgar 1875-1968 *NatCAB 54*
Uihlein, Robert A 1888-1960 *WhAm 3*
Uihlein, Robert August 1883-1959 *NatCAB 49,*
 WhAm 3
Uihlein, William Benedict 1880-1953
 NatCAB 46
Ukers, William Harrison 1873-1954 *WhAm 3*
Ukhtomsky, Alexei Alexeivich 1875-1942 *DcScB*
Ulate, Otilio 1896-1973 *WhAm 6*
Ulberti, Joseph *NewYHSD*
Ulbricht, Walter 1893-1973 *McGEWB,*
 WhAm 5
Ule, Guy Maxwell 1907-1971 *WhAm 5*
Ulen, Henry Charles 1871-1963 *NatCAB 53*
Ulfilas 311?-382? *McGEWB*
Ulich, Robert 1890-1977 *BiDAmEd*
Ulinski, Bronislaus Ignatius 1902-1973
 WhAm 6
Ulio, James Alexander 1882-1958 *WhAm 3*
Ulke, Henry 1821-1910 *ApCAB Sup,*
 NewYHSD, WhAm 1
Ullman, Adolph 1885-1957 *NatCAB 42*
Ullman, Albert Conrad 1914- *BiDrAC*
Ullman, Alice Woods *WomWWA 14*
Ullman, Berthold Louis 1882-1965 *WhAm 4*
Ullman, David Louis 1895-1972 *NatCAB 57*
Ullman, Frederic, Jr. 1903-1948 *WhAm 2*
Ullman, James Ramsey 1907-1971 *NatCAB 56,*
 WhAm 5
Ullman, Sigmund 1841-1918 *NatCAB 38*
Ullmann, Daniel 1810-1892 *ApCAB, TwCBDA*
Ullmann, Harry Maas 1868- *WhAm 5*
Ullmann, Siegfried 1894-1965 *WhAm 4*
Ulloa, Antonio De 1716-1795 *AmBi, ApCAB,*
 DcAmB, Drake, REnAW, WhAm H
Ulloa, Francisco De d1540 *ApCAB, Drake,*
 WhAm H
Ulloa, Francisco De 1498?-1574 *ApCAB*
Ulloa Y DeLaTorre Giral, Antonio De 1716-1795
 DcScB
Ulman, Douglas *WebAB*
Ulman, Joseph N 1878-1943 *WhAm 2*
Ulman, William Alban 1867- *WhAm 4*
Ulmann, Albert 1861-1948 *WhAm 2*
Ulmann, Doris d1934 *WhAm 1*
Ulmar, Geraldine *AmWom*
Ulmer, Anderson Glasco 1892-1948 *NatCAB 36*
Ulphilas, Herman 1702-1761 *ApCAB*
Ulpian, Domitius d228 *McGEWB*
Ulreich, Eduard Buk 1889- *IlBEAAW*
Ulrey, Albert Brennus 1860-1932 *WhAm 3*
Ulrich Of Strasbourg d1278? *DcScB*
Ulrich, Barry Stribling 1888-1936 *WhAm 1,*
 WhAm 2
Ulrich, Bartow Adolphus 1840- *NatCAB 16*
Ulrich, Carl T 1885-1960 *NatCAB 48*
Ulrich, Charles Frederic 1858-1908 *NatCAB 1,*
 WhAm 1
Ulrich, Charles Frederick 1858-1908 *AmBi,*
 ApCAB
Ulrich, Edward Oscar 185-?-1944 *WhAm 2*
Ulrich, Edward Oscar 1851-1944 *ApCAB Sup*
Ulrich, Edward Oscar 1857-1944 *DcAmB S3,*
 DcScB, NatCAB 33
Ulrich, Henry Ludwig 1876-1963 *NatCAB 50*
Ulrich, Leslie Robert 1905-1966 *NatCAB 51,*
 WhAm 4
Ulrich, Mabel Simis 1897- *WomWWA 14*
Ulshoeffer, Michael 1793-1881 *ApCAB Sup*

Ulstad, Philipp *DcScB*
Ulugh Beg 1393-1449 *AsBiEn*
Ulugh Beg 1394-1449 *DcScB*
Ulyanov, Vladimir Ilyich *DcScB*
Umar Al-Khayyami *DcScB*
Umar Ibn Al-Farrukhan Al-Tabari *DcScB*
Umawi, Abu Abdallah Yaish Ibn I, Al- *DcScB*
Umbeck, Sharvy Greiner 1912-1973 *WhAm 5*
Umbel, Robert Emory 1863-1945 *WhAm 2*
Umberger, Harry John Charles 1881-1951
 WhAm 3
Umbreit, Samuel John 1871- *WhAm 5*
Umbscheiden, Franz 1821-1874 *ApCAB*
Umbstaetter, Herman Daniel 1851-1913
 WhAm 1
Umezu, Yoshijiro 1880-1949 *WhWW-II*
Umlauf, Susanne Cooper 1873- *WomWWA 14*
Umphrey, Harry E 1894- *WhAm 4*
Umpleby, Joseph B 1883-1967 *WhAm 4*
Umstattd, William Earle 1894-1973 *WhAm 6*
Umstead, William Bradley 1895-1954 *BiDrAC,*
 NatCAB 42, WhAm 3, WhAmP
Unamuno Y Jugo, Miguel De 1864-1936
 McGEWB
Unander, Eric d1759? *ApCAB*
Unangst, Elias 1824-1903 *ApCAB*
Unangst, Erias 1824-1903 *DcAmB*
Unanue, Jose Hipolito 1755-1833 *DcScB,*
 McGEWB
Unanue, Jose Hipolito 1758-1833 *ApCAB*
Uncas 1588?-1682 *ApCAB, NatCAB 12*
Uncas 1588?-1683? *AmBi, DcAmB, Drake,*
 WhAm H
Uncle Sam *WebAB, WhAm H*
Uncles, Charles Randolph *WhoColR*
Uncles, John Francis 1898-1967 *NatCAB 51,*
 WhAm 4
Unden, Bo Osten 1886-1974 *WhAm 6*
Underdoow, E Marvin 1877-1960 *WhAm 4*
Underhill, Adelaide *WomWWA 14*
Underhill, Charles Lee 1867-1946 *BiDrAC,*
 WhAm 2, WhAmP
Underhill, Charles Reginald 1874-1950
 NatCAB 39, WhAm 3
Underhill, Daniel 1874-1951 *NatCAB 40*
Underhill, Edward Fitch 1830- *ApCAB*
Underhill, Edwin Stewart 1861-1929 *BiDrAC,*
 WhAm 1
Underhill, Frank Pell 1877-1932 *DcAmB,*
 NatCAB 25, WhAm 1
Underhill, James 1871-1954 *WhAm 3*
Underhill, John 1597?-1672 *AmBi, ApCAB,*
 DcAmB, Drake, McGEWB, NatCAB 1,
 WebAB, WebAMB, WhAm H
Underhill, John Garrett 1876-1946 *WhAm 2*
Underhill, John Quincy 1848-1907 *BiDrAC,*
 WhAm 1
Underhill, Orra Ervin 1898-1943 *NatCAB 32*
Underhill, Walter 1795-1866 *BiAUS, BiDrAC,*
 WhAm H
Underwood, Adin Ballou 1828-1888 *ApCAB,*
 Drake, NatCAB 4
Underwood, Benjamin Franklin 1839-1914
 ApCAB Sup, DcAmB, WhAm 1
Underwood, Bert Elias 1862-1943 *WhAm 2*
Underwood, Clarence F 1871-1929 *WhAm 1*
Underwood, E Victor 1889- *WhAm 6*
Underwood, Edna Worthley 1873- *ApCAB X*
Underwood, Edward Ellsworth 1864- *WhoColR*
Underwood, Elmer Judson 1859-1947
 NatCAB 35
Underwood, Fannie Rust 1873- *WomWWA 14*
Underwood, Felix Joel 1882-1959 *WhAm 3*
Underwood, Francis Henry 1825-1894 *ApCAB,*

DcAmB, NatCAB 5, TwCBDA, WhAm H

Underwood, Frederick Douglas 1849-1942 *DcAmB S3*

Underwood, Frederick Douglas 1852-1942 *NatCAB 14*

Underwood, Frederick Douglass d1942 *WhAm 2*

Underwood, George Arthur 1882-1944 *WhAm 2*

Underwood, Harry L 1883-1956 *NatCAB 46*

Underwood, Henry Oliver 1858-1921 *NatCAB 20*

Underwood, Herbert Shapleigh 1861- *WhAm 4*

Underwood, Horace Grant 1859-1916 *DcAmB, NatCAB 31, WhAm 1*

Underwood, Ira Julian 1891-1947 *WhAm 2*

Underwood, J A *NewYHSD*

Underwood, John Cox 1840-1913 *ApCAB, TwCBDA, WhAm 1*

Underwood, John Curtiss 1808-1873 *ApCAB, BiAUS*

Underwood, John Curtiss 1809-1873 *DcAmB, WhAm H*

Underwood, John Thomas 1857-1937 *DcAmB S2, NatCAB 29, WhAm HA, WhAm 4*

Underwood, John W H 1816-1888 *BiAUS*

Underwood, John William Henderson 1816-1888 *BiDrAC, WhAm H*

Underwood, John William Henry 1816-1888 *ApCAB*

Underwood, Jonathan Platt 1849-1927 *NatCAB 21*

Underwood, Joseph Merritt 1844- *WhAm 3*

Underwood, Joseph Rogers 1791-1876 *ApCAB, BiAUS, BiDrAC, DcAmB, Drake, NatCAB 3, TwCBDA, WhAm H, WhAmP*

Underwood, Julius Gay 1915-1975 *WhAm 6*

Underwood, Kennard 1886-1966 *NatCAB 51*

Underwood, Lillias Stirling Horton 1851-1921 *NotAW, WhAm 4*

Underwood, Lineas Dott 1872-1933 *WhAm 1*

Underwood, Loring 1874-1930 *ApCAB X, DcAmB, WhAm 1, WhAm 1C*

Underwood, Lucien Marcus 1853-1907 *AmBi, ApCAB Sup, DcAmB, NatCAB 12, TwCBDA, WhAm 1*

Underwood, Lucius Marcus 1853-1907 *ApCAB*

Underwood, Mell Gilbert 1892-1972 *BiDrAC, WhAm 5*

Underwood, Oscar Wilder 1862-1929 *AmBi, ApCAB X, BiDrAC, DcAmB, EncAAH, EncAB, NatCAB 12, NatCAB 21, TwCBDA, WebAB, WhAm 1, WhAmP*

Underwood, Oscar Wilder, Jr. 1890-1962 *WhAm 4*

Underwood, Paul Halladay 1881- *WhAm 6*

Underwood, Sara A 1838-1911 *WhAm 1*

Underwood, Thomas 1795-1849 *NewYHSD*

Underwood, Thomas Ingle 1898-1957 *WhAm 3*

Underwood, Thomas Rust 1898-1956 *BiDrAC, NatCAB 42, WhAm 3, WhAmP*

Underwood, Warner Lewis 1808-1872 *ApCAB, BiAUS, BiDrAC, TwCBDA, WhAm H, WhAmP*

Underwood, William 1787-1864 *NatCAB 25*

Underwood, William Henderson 1779-1859 *ApCAB, NatCAB 5*

Underwood, William Jackson 1852-1917 *WhAm 1*

Underwood, William Lawrence 1858-1919 *ApCAB X*

Underwood, William Lyman 1864-1929 *ApCAB X, NatCAB 23, WhAm 1*

Undset, Sigrid 1882-1949 *McGEWB, WhAm 2*

Ungar, Arthur Arnold 1884-1969 *WhAm 5*

Ungaretti, Giuseppe 1888-1970 *McGEWB*

Unger *NewYHSD*

Unger, Edward Frank 1890-1962 *NatCAB 47*

Unger, Franz 1800-1870 *DcScB*

Unger, Frederic William 1875- *WhAm 5*

Unger, Harry 1887-1938 *NatCAB 29*

Unger, Irwin 1927- *EncAAH*

Unger, William Hudson Roosevelt 1905-1951 *NatCAB 41*

Ungerer, Heiby Wetling 1889-1947 *NatCAB 41*

Ungerleider, Samuel, Jr. 1917-1973 *WhAm 5*

Ungraham, Duncan Nathaniel 1802-1891 *WebAMB*

Unitas, John 1933- *WebAB*

Unkart, Mrs. E *NewYHSD*

Unke, Herman Albert 1886-1948 *NatCAB 37*

Unna, Paul Gerson 1850-1929 *BiHiMed*

Unness, George 1825-1894 *EncAAH*

Unnever, John Gerhard 1822-1893 *ApCAB Sup*

Unseld, Benjamin Carl 1843- *WhAm 1*

Unsell, Eve *ApCAB X*

Untenreith, L *NewYHSD*

Untermyer, Henry 1849-1913 *NatCAB 18*

Untermeyer, Jean Starr 1886-1970 *WhAm 5*

Untermeyer, Louis 1885- *ApCAB X*

Untermyer, Alvin 1882-1963 *NatCAB 50, WhAm 4*

Untermyer, Samuel 1858-1940 *AmBi, ApCAB X, DcAmB S2, NatCAB 1, NatCAB 17, WebAB, WhAm 1*

Unthank, James Bryant 1849- *WhAm 4*

Unthank, William S 1813-1892 *NewYHSD*

Unwin, Sir Stanley 1884-1968 *WhAm 5*

Unzaga, Luis De 1720?-1790? *ApCAB*

Unzer, Johann August 1727-1799 *DcScB*

Upchurch, John Jordan 1820-1887 *DcAmB, WhAm H*

Upchurch, John Jorden 1822-1887 *ApCAB*

Upchurch, Roy Wakefield 1902-1964 *NatCAB 51*

Upchurch, Vernon Hill 1918-1975 *WhAm 6*

Updegraff, Allan 1883-1965 *WhAm 4*

Updegraff, David Brainard 1830-1894 *DcAmB, WhAm H*

Updegraff, Harlan 1874-1953 *WhAm 3*

Updegraff, Jonathan Taylor 1822-1882 *BiDrAC*

Updegraff, Milton 1861-1938 *NatCAB 15, WhAm 1*

Updegraff, Paul Walter 1906-1959 *WhAm 3*

Updegraff, Thomas 1834-1910 *BiDrAC, TwCBDA, WhAm 1, WhAmP*

Updegrave, William Marsh 1867-1942 *NatCAB 32*

Updegrove, Harvey Claude 1886-1962 *NatCAB 50*

Updike, Daniel 1680?-1757 *NatCAB 8*

Updike, Daniel 1693?-1757 *DcAmB, WhAm H*

Updike, Daniel Berkeley 1860-1941 *DcAmB S3, WhAm 2*

Updike, Edward Lafayette 1899-1953 *WhAm 3*

Updike, Eugene Grover 1850- *WhAm 4*

Updike, Godfrey Ernest 1896-1966 *WhAm 4*

Updike, John Hoyer 1932- *EncAB, WebAB*

Updike, Ralph Eugene, Sr. 1894-1953 *BiDrAC, WhAm 3*

Updike, Wilkins 1784-1867 *ApCAB, Drake, NatCAB 8*

Updyke, Frank Arthur 1866-1918 *WhAm 1*

Upfold, George 1796-1872 *ApCAB, Drake, NatCAB 3, TwCBDA*

Upham, Albert Gookin 1819-1847 *ApCAB*

Upham, Alfred Horatio 1877-1945 *NatCAB 42, WhAm 2*

Upham, Charles Carroll 1854-1931 *NatCAB 24*

Upham, Charles Melville 1886-1966 *WhAm 4*

Upham, Charles Wentworth 1802-1875 *ApCAB, BiAUS, BiDrAC, DcAmB, Drake, NatCAB 8, WhAm H, WhAmP*

Upham, Don Alonzo Joshua 1809-1877 *NatCAB 10*

Upham, Elizabeth Greene *BiCAW*

Upham, Francis B, Jr. 1894-1962 *WhAm 4*

Upham, Francis Bourne 1862-1941 *NatCAB 30, WhAm 1*

Upham, Francis William 1817- *ApCAB*

Upham, Frank Brooks 1872-1939 *WhAm 1*

Upham, Frederic William 1861-1925 *WhAm 1*

Upham, George Baxter 1768-1848 *BiAUS, BiDrAC, WhAm H, WhAmP*

Upham, Hervey *NewYHSD*

Upham, Horace Alonzo Jaques 1853-1919 *NatCAB 10, NatCAB 29*

Upham, J Duncan 1853-1948 *NatCAB 37*

Upham, Jabez 1764-1811 *BiAUS, BiDrAC, WhAm H, WhAmP*

Upham, James 1815- *ApCAB*

Upham, John Howell Janeway 1871- *WhAm 5*

Upham, John Jaques 1837-1898 *NatCAB 10*

Upham, Joshua 1741-1808 *ApCAB, NatCAB 5*

Upham, Mary Cornelia Kelley 1843-1912 *BiCAW*

Upham, Nathaniel 1774-1829 *BiAUS, BiDrAC, WhAm H, WhAmP*

Upham, Nathaniel Gookin 1801-1869 *ApCAB, Drake, NatCAB 5*

Upham, Nathaniel Lookin 1801-1869 *BiAUS*

Upham, Robert Wayland 1893-1970 *NatCAB 55*

Upham, Roy 1879-1956 *WhAm 3*

Upham, Samuel Foster 1834-1904 *DcAmB, WhAm 1*

Upham, Thomas Cogswell 1799-1872 *ApCAB, DcAmB, Drake, NatCAB 13, WhAm H*

Upham, Timothy 1783-1855 *ApCAB, Drake, NatCAB 4*

Upham, Warren 1850-1934 *AmBi, DcAmB, NatCAB 7, TwCBDA, WhAm 1*

Upham, William 1792-1853 *ApCAB, BiAUS, BiDrAC, NatCAB 6, WhAm H, WhAmP*

Upham, William Henry 1841-1924 *NatCAB 12, TwCBDA, WhAm 1*

Upjohn, Hobart Brown 1876-1949 *WhAm 2*

Upjohn, Hubert S 1881- *WhAm 6*

Upjohn, Lawrence Northcote 1873-1967 *NatCAB 53*

Upjohn, Richard 1802-1878 *AmBi, ApCAB, BnEnAmA, DcAmB, McGEWB, NatCAB 2, NewYHSD, TwCBDA, WebAB, WhAm H*

Upjohn, Richard Michell 1828-1903 *ApCAB, BnEnAmA, DcAmB, NatCAB 2*

Upjohn, Richard Mitchell 1828-1903 *TwCBDA, WhAm H*

Upjohn, William Erastus 1853-1932 *NatCAB 24*

Upleger, Arthur C 1883-1969 *WhAm 5*

Upp, Charles W 1898-1964 *WhAm 4*

Uppercu, Inglis Moore 1875-1944 *NatCAB 36*

Uppvall, Axel Johan 1872-1960 *WhAm 4*

Upshaw, William David 1866-1952 *BiDrAC, DcAmB S5, NatCAB 41, WhAm 3, WhAmP*

Upshur, Abel Parker 1790-1844 *ApCAB, BiAUS, BiDrUSE, Drake, NatCAB 6, TwCBDA, WhAm H*

Upshur, Abel Parker 1791-1844 *AmBi, DcAmB*

Upshur, Alfred Parker 1885-1964 *NatCAB 52*

Upshur, George Parker 1799-1852 *ApCAB, NatCAB 4*

Upshur, John Henry 1823-1917 *ApCAB, DcAmB, NatCAB 4, TwCBDA, WhAm 1*

Upshur, John Nottingham 1848-1924 *NatCAB 29, WhAm 1*

Upshur, Mary Jane Stith 1828- *ApCAB*

Upshur, William Peterkin 1881-1943 *WhAm 2*

Upson, Andrew Seth 1835-1911 *NatCAB 10, WhAm 1*

Upson, Ansel Judd 1823-1902 *ApCAB*

Upson, Anson Judd 1823-1902 *NatCAB 4, TwCBDA, WhAm 1*

Upson, Arthur 1877- *WhAm 5*

Upson, Charles 1821-1885 *BiAUS, BiDrAC, WhAm H, WhAmP*

Upson, Charles Ayrault 1875-1969 *WhAm 5*

Upson, Christopher Columbus 1829-1902 *BiDrAC*

Upson, Fred Wilbert 1883-1942 *WhAm 2*

Upson, Jefferson T *NewYHSD*

Upson, Lent Dayton 1886-1949 *WhAm 2*

Upson, Maxwell Mayhew 1876-1969 *WhAm 5*

Upson, Oliver Welton 1875-1941 *NatCAB 31*

Upson, Ralph Hazlett 1888-1968 *NatCAB 54, WhAm 5*

Upson, W Harrison 1881-1960 *NatCAB 48*

Upson, Walter Lyman 1877- *WhAm 5*

Upson, William Hanford 1823-1910 *BiAUS, BiDrAC*

Upson, William Hazlett 1891-1975 *WhAm 6*

Upston, John Edwin 1890-1952 *NatCAB 42, WhAm 3*

Upthegrove, Fay R 1905-1946 *WhAm 2*

Upton, Abraham Lincoln 1865-1923 *NatCAB 39*

Upton, Charles Horace 1812-1877 *ApCAB, BiDrAC, WhAm H*

Upton, Clifford Brewster 1877-1957 *WhAm 3,*

WhAm 4
Upton, Daniel 1864-1919 *WhAm 1*
Upton, Edward Peirce 1816- *ApCAB*
Upton, Emory 1839-1881 *AmBi, ApCAB, DcAmB, Drake, NatCAB 4, TwCBDA, WebAMB, WhAm H*
Upton, Francis Henry 1814-1876 *ApCAB*
Upton, George Bruce 1804-1874 *ApCAB, DcAmB, WhAm H*
Upton, George Burr 1882-1942 *NatCAB 33, WhAm 2*
Upton, George Putnam 1834-1919 *ApCAB, DcAmB, NatCAB 18, TwCBDA, WhAm 1*
Upton, Harriet Taylor 1853-1945 *NotAW, WhAm 2*
Upton, Hiram Eugene 1902-1964 *NatCAB 50*
Upton, Jacob Kendrick 1837-1902 *ApCAB, WhAm 1*
Upton, James 1813-1879 *ApCAB*
Upton, LaRoy Sunderland 1869-1927 *WhAm 1*
Upton, Louis Cassius 1886-1952 *NatCAB 42, WhAm 3*
Upton, Marian Burton 1850- *WomWWA 14*
Upton, Robert *WhAm H*
Upton, Robert William 1884-1972 *BiDrAC, WhAm 5*
Upton, Samuel 1784-1842 *ApCAB*
Upton, Sara Carr 1843- *ApCAB*
Upton, Wheelock Samuel 1811-1860 *ApCAB*
Upton, William Treat 1870- *WhAm 5*
Upton, William W 1817-1896 *ApCAB, NatCAB 12*
Upton, Winslow 1853-1914 *ApCAB, ApCAB Sup, DcAmB, NatCAB 12, TwCBDA, WhAm 1*
Uqlidisi, Abu'l-Hasan Ahmad Ibn I, Al- *DcScB*
Urann, Marcus Libby 1873-1963 *WhAm 4*
Urbach, Erich 1893-1946 *BiHiMed*
Urbain, Georges 1872-1938 *AsBiEn, DcScB*
Urban II 1042-1099 *McGEWB*
Urban VI 1318-1389 *McGEWB*
Urban, George 1820-1887 *NatCAB 21*
Urban, George, Jr. 1850-1928 *NatCAB 21*
Urban, Joseph 1872-1933 *AmBi, DcAmB, NatCAB 25, WebAB, WhAm 1*
Urban, Percy Linwood 1886-1974 *WhAm 6*
Urban, Wilbur Marshall 1873- *WhAm 5*
Urbani, F *NewYHSD*
Urchs, Ernest 1864-1928 *ApCAB X*
Urdaneta, Andres 1499-1568 *ApCAB*
Urdaneta, Francisco 1791-1861 *ApCAB*
Urdaneta, Rafael 1789-1845 *ApCAB*
Urdang, George 1882-1960 *NatCAB 45, WhAm 4*
Ure, Andrew 1778-1857 *DcScB*
Ure, Mary 1933-1975 *WhAm 6*
Ure, Robert 1823- *ApCAB*
Ure, William Andrew 1839-1896 *NatCAB 6*
Urell, M Emmet 1844- *WhAm 4*
Uren, Lester Charles 1888-1960 *WhAm 4*
U'Ren, William Simon 1859-1949 *DcAmB S4, WebAB, WhAm 4*
Uretz, Lester Robert 1922-1972 *WhAm 5*
Urey, Harold Clayton 1893- *AsBiEn, EncAB, McGEWB, WebAB*
Urfe, Gabriel Jules 1795-1833 *ApCAB*
Urfe, Louis Edouard D' 1699-1762 *ApCAB*
Urice, Jay Adams 1891-1957 *WhAm 3*
Urich, Walter K 1902-1952 *WhAm 3*
Uricochea, Ezequiel 1834- *ApCAB*
Uriell, Frank Harold 1899- *WhAm 5*
Uring, Nathaniel *Drake*
Urion, Henry Kimball 1889-1962 *WhAm 4*
Uris, Leon Marcus 1924- *WebAB*
Uris, Percy 1899-1971 *WhAm 5*
Urmy, Clarence 1858- *WhAm 1*
Urner, Hammond 1868-1942 *WhAm 2*
Urner, Mabel Herbert 1881-1957 *WhAm 3, WomWWA 14*
Urner, Milton George 1839-1926 *BiDrAC*
Urquhart, Georgina Lily *WomWWA 14*
Urquhart, Leonard Church 1886-1960 *WhAm 3*
Urquhart, Norman Currie 1893-1966 *WhAm 5*
Urquiza, Juste Jose De 1800-1870 *Drake*
Urquiza, Justo Jose De 1801-1870 *McGEWB*
Urquiza, Justo Jose De 1800-1870 *ApCAB*
Urriolagoitia, H Mamerto 1895-1974 *WhAm 6*

Urrutia, Ignacio J De 1730-1798 *ApCAB*
Urso, Camilla 1842-1902 *AmBi, DcAmB, NotAW, WhAm H*
Urtiaga, Pedro 1650?-1720? *ApCAB*
Uruguay, Paulino J Soares E Souza 1807-1866 *ApCAB*
Urwiler, Benjamin *NewYHSD*
Ury, Ralph Jay 1890-1971 *WhAm 5*
Uryson, Pavel Samuilovich 1898-1924 *DcScB*
Usher, Abbott Payson 1883-1965 *NatCAB 52, WhAm 4*
Usher, Edward Preston 1851-1923 *NatCAB 20, WhAm 1*
Usher, Florence Wyman Richardson 1889- *WomWWA 14*
Usher, Hezekiah 1615?-1676 *ApCAB*
Usher, Hezekiah 1639-1679 *ApCAB*
Usher, John 1648-1726 *ApCAB, Drake, NatCAB 13*
Usher, John Palmer 1816-1889 *ApCAB, BiAUS, BiDrUSE, DcAmB, Drake, NatCAB 2, WhAm H*
Usher, Leila *BiCAW, WomWWA 14*
Usher, Nathaniel Reilly 1855-1931 *DcAmB, NatCAB 25, WebAMB, WhAm 1*
Usher, Noble Luke d1815 *WhAm H*
Usher, Rebecca R 1821-1912 *BiCAW*
Usher, Robert James 1880-1944 *WhAm 2*
Usher, Roland Greene 1880- *WhAm 6*
Ushijima, Mitsuru *WhWW-II*
Usinger, Robert L 1912-1968 *WhAm 5*
Ussher, Brandram Boileau 1845-1925 *ApCAB, ApCAB Sup, NatCAB 4, WhAm 1*
Ussher, Neville Thompson 1901-1963 *NatCAB 54*
Ussieux, Jacques Gerard Des 1719-1781 *ApCAB*
Utamaro, Kitagawa 1753-1806 *McGEWB*
Utassy, George D' 1870- *WhAm 3*
Uterhart, Henry Ayres 1875-1946 *WhAm 2*
Uthman Don Fodio 1755-1816 *McGEWB*
Utley, Edward Huntington 1850-1924 *NatCAB 22*
Utley, Francis Lee 1907-1974 *WhAm 6*
Utley, George Burwell 1876-1946 *DcAmB S4, DcAmLiB, NatCAB 33, WhAm 2*
Utley, Henry Munson 1836-1917 *DcAmLiB, NatCAB 12, NatCAB 17, WhAm 1*
Utley, Joseph Simeon 1876-1943 *WhAm 2*
Utley, Robert M 1929- *REnAW*
Utley, Samuel 1843-1930 *WhAm 1, WhAm 1C*
Utley, Stuart Wells 1879-1946 *WhAm 2*
Utley, William L *NewYHSD*
Utne, John Arndt 1890-1970 *WhAm 5*
Utt, James Boyd 1899-1970 *BiDrAC, WhAm 5*
Utter, David 1844- *WhAm 4*
Utter, George Benjamin 1881-1955 *NatCAB 46, WhAm 3*
Utter, George Herbert 1854-1912 *BiDrAC, NatCAB 13, WhAm 1, WhAmP*
Utter, Rebecca Palfrey 1844-1905 *WhAm 1*
Utter, Robert Palfrey 1875-1936 *WhAm 1*
Utterback, Hubert 1880-1942 *BiDrAC, WhAm 2*
Utterback, John Gregg 1872-1955 *BiDrAC, NatCAB 47, WhAm 5*
Utterback, William Elbert 1874-1950 *NatCAB 38*
Uttley, Clinton B 1887-1953 *WhAm 3*
Uttmark, Fritz Emmerick Nilson 1871- *NatCAB 17*
Utudjian, Edouard 1905-1975 *WhAm 6*
Utz, Henry Jacob 1850-1926 *NatCAB 22*
Utz, William David 1892-1968 *NatCAB 57*
Uzzell, Edward Foy 1892-1956 *NatCAB 47, NatCAB 48*
Uzzell, George Randolph 1903-1967 *NatCAB 54*
Uzzell, Mary Blaine 1877- *WomWWA 14*
Uzzell, Rudyard Stephen 1874-1962 *NatCAB 52*

V

Vaca, Alvar Nunez Cabeza De 1490?-1557? *AmBi, DcAmB*

Vaccaro, Leopold Saverio 1887-1963 *NatCAB 49*

Vachon, Achille *NewYHSD*

Vachon, Alexandre 1885-1953 *WhAm 3*

Vachon, Joseph Peter 1887-1961 *WhAm 4*

Vachon, Louis A, Jr. 1905-1968 *WhAm 5*

Vaden, Robert Carrington 1882-1954 *NatCAB 42*

Vagis, Polygnotos G 1894- *WhAm 5*

Vagner, Egor Egorovich 1849-1903 *DcScB*

Vagtborg, Harold 1904-1976 *WhAm 6*

Vahey, James Henry 1871- *NatCAB 14*

Vahey, James Henry 1900-1949 *WhAm 2*

Vahlsing, Frederick Henry 1891-1969 *NatCAB 56*

Vail, Aaron 1796-1878 *BiAUS, DcAmB, NatCAB 5, WhAm H*

Vail, Albert Adlasca 1905-1971 *NatCAB 56*

Vail, Albert Ross 1880- *WhAm 6*

Vail, Alfred Lewis 1807-1859 *AmBi, ApCAB, DcAmB, NatCAB 4, TwCBDA, WebAB, WhAm H*

Vail, Aramenta Dianthe *NewYHSD*

Vail, Charles Davis 1868-1945 *WhAm 2*

Vail, Charles Delamater 1837-1921 *WhAm 1*

Vail, Charles Henry 1866-1924 *NatCAB 11, WhAm 1*

Vail, Curtis Churchill Doughty 1903-1957 *WhAm 3*

Vail, David Jameson 1926-1971 *WhAm 6*

Vail, Derrick T, Sr. 1864-1930 *WhAm 1*

Vail, Derrick Tilton 1898-1973 *WhAm 5*

Vail, Eugene 1856- *WhAm 4*

Vail, George 1803-1875 *BiAUS*

Vail, George 1809-1875 *ApCAB, BiDrAC, WhAm H*

Vail, Harry Lorenzo 1859-1935 *NatCAB 27*

Vail, Henry 1782-1833 *BiAUS*

Vail, Henry 1782-1853 *BiDrAC, WhAm H*

Vail, Henry Hobart 1839-1925 *WhAm 1*

Vail, James Garrett 1886-1951 *NatCAB 44*

Vail, Jesse Aaron 1856-1926 *NatCAB 20*

Vail, Joseph *NewYHSD*

Vail, Mary Beals 1860- *WomWWA 14*

Vail, May Belle Sherriff 1861- *WomWWA 14*

Vail, Richard Bernard 1895-1955 *BiDrAC, WhAm 3*

Vail, Robert William Glenroie 1890-1966 *DcAmLiB*

Vail, Robert William Glenrole 1890-1966 *WhAm 4*

Vail, Stephen 1780-1864 *ApCAB, NatCAB 12*

Vail, Stephen Montford 1818-1880 *ApCAB*

Vail, Stephen Montfort 1816-1880 *DcAmB, WhAm H*

Vail, Theodore Newton 1845-1920 *AmBi, ApCAB X, DcAmB, EncAB, NatCAB 28, WebAB, WhAm 1*

Vail, Thomas 1860-1925 *NatCAB 46*

Vail, Thomas Hubbard 1812-1889 *ApCAB, NatCAB 12, TwCBDA, WhAm H*

Vail, William Berrian 1823- *ApCAB*

Vailati, Giovanni 1863-1909 *DcScB*

Vaile, Anna Louise Wolcott 1868-1928 *WhAm 1*

Vaile, Edwin Orlando 1843-1922 *BiDAmEd, NatCAB 20*

Vaile, Joel Frederick 1848-1916 *NatCAB 17, WhAm 1*

Vaile, Rawson 1888-1954 *WhAm 3*

Vaile, William Newell 1876-1927 *BiDrAC, WhAm 1, WhAmP*

Vaill, Joseph 1750-1838 *ApCAB, Drake, NatCAB 4*

Vaill, Joseph 1790-1869 *ApCAB*

Vaillancourt, Cyrille 1892-1969 *WhAm 5*

Vaillant, Madame *NewYHSD*

Vaillant, Abby Augusta 1872- *WomWWA 14*

Vaillant, Auguste Nicolas 1793-1858 *ApCAB*

Vaillant, Francois Le 1753-1824 *ApCAB*

Vaillant, George Clapp 1901-1945 *DcAmB S3, NatCAB 34, WhAm 2*

Vaillant, Leon-Louis 1834-1914 *DcScB*

Vaillant, Louis David 1875-1944 *WhAm 2*

Vaillant, Sebastien 1669-1722 *DcScB*

Vaillant DeGueslis, Francois 1646-1718 *WhAm H*

Vajda, Ernest 1886-1954 *NatCAB 43*

Vajna, George 1889-1968 *WhAm 5*

Vakil, Nusservanji Kavasji 1908-1974 *WhAm 6*

Vakil, Rustom Jal 1911-1974 *WhAm 6*

Valades, Diego 1520?-1590? *ApCAB*

Valaperta, Giuseppe d1817? *NewYHSD*

Valasek, Otakar 1884-1950 *WhAm 3*

Valaske, M Thomas 1911-1958 *NatCAB 44*

Valden, Pavel Ivanovich *DcScB*

Valdenuit, Thomas Bluget De 1763-1846 *NewYHSD*

Valdes, Antonio Jose 1770-1824 *ApCAB*

Valdes, Gabriel DeLaConcepcion 1809-1844 *ApCAB*

Valdes, Geronimo 1784-1857 *ApCAB*

Valdes, Jose Manuel 1780?-1840 *ApCAB*

Valdes Y Sierra, Geronimo 1646-1729 *ApCAB*

Valdevieira, Miguel 1480?-1540 *ApCAB*

Valdivia, Luis De 1561-1642 *ApCAB*

Valdivia, Pedro De 1490?-1554 *ApCAB*

Valdivia, Pedro De 1502?-1553 *McGEWB*

Valdivia, Pedro De 1510?-1559 *Drake*

Valdivieso, Antonio De d1535? *ApCAB*

Valdivieso Y Zanartu, Rafael Valentin 1804-1878 *ApCAB*

Valdurezo, Ignacio De *ApCAB*

Vale, Clair Fremont 1887-1966 *NatCAB 54*

Vale, Euphemia Vale Blake 1824- *ApCAB*

Vale, Gilbert 1788-1866 *ApCAB*

Vale, Roy Ewing 1885-1959 *NatCAB 54, WhAm 3*

Valencia, Guillermo Leon 1909-1971 *WhAm 5*

Valencia, Manuel 1856-1935 *IIBEAAW*

Valencia, Martin De 1466?-1533 *ApCAB*

Valenciennes, Achille 1794-1865 *DcScB*

Valencin, Signor *NewYHSD*

Valenta, Frank Louis 1906-1957 *WhAm 3*

Valente, Francis Louis 1905-1966 *WhAm 4*

Valente, Frank Aloysius 1883-1957 *NatCAB 49*

Valentien, Anna Marie 1862- *WhAm 4*

Valentin, Gabriel Gustav 1810-1883 *BiHiMed, DcScB*

Valentin, Louis 1758-1829 *ApCAB*

Valentine, Albertine Whitney Flershem *WomWWA 14*

Valentine, Basil *DcScB*

Valentine, Byron Warren 1866- *WhAm 4*

Valentine, C Braxton 1897-1970 *NatCAB 56*

Valentine, Caro Syron 1855- *WhAm 4, WomWWA 14*

Valentine, Charles Augustus 1880-1932 *NatCAB 35*

Valentine, Charles M *NewYHSD*

Valentine, Charles Post 1871-1928 *NatCAB 23*

Valentine, Daniel Mulford 1830- *NatCAB 5*

Valentine, David Thomas 1801-1869 *ApCAB, DcAmB, Drake, NatCAB 10, WhAm H*

Valentine, Edward Abram Uffington 1870- *WhAm 5*

Valentine, Edward Kimble 1843-1916 *BiDrAC, WhAmP*

Valentine, Edward Robinson 1908-1968 *WhAm 5*

Valentine, Edward Virginius 1838-1930 *AmBi, ApCAB, DcAmB, NatCAB 10, NewYHSD, TwCBDA, WhAm 1*

Valentine, Elias *NewYHSD*

Valentine, Frederick Stuart 1866-1940 *NatCAB 29*

Valentine, Granville Gray 1860-1943 *NatCAB 48*

Valentine, James Andrew 1887-1952 *NatCAB 43*

Valentine, Jane Burnette 1879- *WomWWA 14*

Valentine, John *NewYHSD*

Valentine, John J 1840-1901 *NatCAB 3, WhAm 1*

Valentine, John King 1827-1898 *NatCAB 18*

Valentine, John W 1906-1969 *WhAm 5*

Valentine, Julius *NewYHSD*

Valentine, Lewis Joseph 1882-1946 *WhAm 2*

Valentine, Lila Hardaway Meade 1865-1921 *NotAW, WhAm 1, WomWWA 14*

Valentine, Milton 1825-1906 *ApCAB, BiDAmEd, DcAmB, NatCAB 10, TwCBDA, WhAm 1*

Valentine, Milton Henry 1864- *WhAm 4*

Valentine, Patrick Anderson 1861-1916 *WhAm 1*

Valentine, Richard Henry 1888-1971 *NatCAB 57*

Valentine, Robert Grosvenor 1872-1916 *DcAmB, NatCAB 17, WhAm 1*

Valentine, Samuel *NewYHSD*

Valentine, Thomas Weston 1818-1879 *BiDAmEd*

Valentine, Washington Samuel 1859-1920 *NatCAB 18*

Valentine, Willard Lee 1904-1947 *WhAm 2*

Valentine, William Lucas 1870-1942 *NatCAB 32*

Valentine, William Robert 1879- *WhoColR*

Valentine, William Winston *NewYHSD*

Valentiner, William Reinhold 1880-1958 *NatCAB 48, WhAm 3*

Valentino, Rudolph 1895-1926 *AmBi, WebAB, WhAm 1*

Valenzuela, Crisanto 1777-1816 *ApCAB*

Valenzuela, Pedro Fernandez *ApCAB*

Valera Y Alcala Galiano, Juan 1824-1905 *McGEWB*

Valerian 200?-260? *McGEWB*

Valeriano, Antonio 1525?-1605 *ApCAB*

Valerianos, Apostolos 1531-1602 *ApCAB*

Valerianus, Magnus *DcScB*

Valerio, Luca 1552-1618 *DcScB*

Valery, Paul Ambroise 1871-1945 *McGEWB, WhAm 4*

Valesh, Eva MacDonald 1871- *WomWWA 14*

Valesh, Eva McDonald 1866- *AmWom*

Valette *NewYHSD*

Valeur, Robert 1903-1973 *WhAm 5*

Valframbert, Mademoiselle *NewYHSD*

Valiniere, Pierre Huet DeLa 1732-1806 *ApCAB*

Valk, Francis 1845- *NatCAB 1, NatCAB 2*

Valk, Joseph Elihu 1915-1967 *WhAm 5*

Valk, William Weightman 1806-1879 *BiAUS, BiDrAC, WhAm H*

Valla, Lorenzo 1407?-1457 *McGEWB*

Valladolid, Bernardino De 1617-1652 *ApCAB*

Vallance, Harvard Forrest 1879-1956 *WhAm 3*

Vallance, John 1770?-1823 *NewYHSD*

Vallance, William Roy 1887-1967 *WhAm 4*

Vallandigham, Clement C 1822-1871 *Drake*

Vallandigham, Clement L 1822-1871 *BiAUS*

Vallandigham, Clement Laird 1820-1871 *AmBi, ApCAB, BiDrAC, DcAmB, EncAB, McGEWB, NatCAB 3, TwCBDA, WebAB, WhAm H, WhAmP*

Vallandigham, James Laird 1812- *TwCBDA*

Valle, Jules Felix 1859- *NatCAB 5*

Valle, Leandro Del 1833-1861 *ApCAB*

Valle, Lincoln Charles 1863- *WhoColR*

Valle Inclan, Ramon Maria Del 1866?-1936 *McGEWB*

Vallee, Jean Francois De *NewYHSD*

Vallee, P R *NewYHSD*

Vallee, Rudy 1901- *WebAB*

Vallee-Poussin, Charles-J-G-N DeLa 1866-1962 *DcScB*

Vallejo, Cesar Abraham 1892-1938 *McGEWB*

Vallejo, Mariano Guadalupe 1808-1890 *DcAmB, WebAB, WebAMB, WhAm H*

Vallentine, Benjamin Bennaton 1843-1926 *DcAmB, WhAm 2*

Vallentine, Benjamin Benton 1843-1926 *WhAm 1*

Valleria, Alvina 1848- *NatCAB 1*

Valletta, Vittorio 1883-1967 *WhAm 4*

Vallette, Edwin F 1829?- *NewYHSD*

Vallette, James *NewYHSD*

Valliant, Leroy Branch 1838-1913 *DcAmB, WhAm 1*

Vallisnieri, Antonio 1661-1730 *DcScB*

Valmont DeBomare, Jacques-Christophe 1731-1807 *DcScB*

Valois, Edward *NewYHSD*

Valsalva, Anton Maria 1666-1723 *DcScB*

Valsalva, Antonio Maria 1666-1723 *BiHiMed*

Valturio, Roberto 1405-1475 *DcScB*

Value, Miss *NewYHSD*

Value, Beverly Reid 1863-1920 *NatCAB 15, WhAm 1*

Valverde, Juan De 1520?-1588? *DcScB*

Valverde, Vicente 1490?-1543 *ApCAB*

Valyi, Peter 1919-1973 *WhAm 6*

Van, Billy B 1870-1950 *WhAm 3*

Van-Allen, John W 1876-1958 *WhAm 3*

VanAarsdale, Elias d1846 *Drake*

VanAcker, Achille H 1898- *WhAm 6*

VanAernam, Henry 1819-1894 *BiAUS, BiDrAC, NatCAB 5, WhAm H, WhAmP*

VanAlen, James Isaac 1776-1870 *BiDrAC, WhAm H, WhAmP*

VanAlen, James Laurens 1878-1927 *ApCAB X*

VanAlen, John Evert 1749-1807 *BiDrAC, WhAm H*

VanAlen, William 1882-1954 *WhAm 3*

VanAllen, Daniel D 1834-1913 *WhAm 1*

VanAllen, Frank 1860-1923 *DcAmB*

VanAllen, Frederick Holmes 1878-1953 *NatCAB 42*

VanAllen, Garret Adam 1835- *NatCAB 2*

VanAllen, Harvey Ward 1869-1938 *NatCAB 29*

VanAllen, James Alfred 1914- *AsBiEn, WebAB*

VanAllen, James Q *BiAUS*

VanAllen, John E *BiAUS*

VanAllen, John T *BiAUS*

VanAllen, William Harman 1870- *WhAm 5*

VanAllstyne, Frances Jane 1820- *TwCBDA*

VanAlstyne, Archibald C *NewYHSD*

VanAlstyne, Eleanor VanNess 1881-1942 *WhAm 2*

VanAlstyne, Fanny Crosby 1820-1915 *AmBi, DcAmB*

VanAlstyne, Frances Jane Crosby 1820-1915 *NatCAB 7, NotAW, WomWWA 14*

VanAlstyne, George Washington 1854-1935 *NatCAB 26*

VanAlstyne, Henry Arthur 1869-1947 *NatCAB 35, WhAm 5*

VanAlstyne, J H d1944 *WhAm 2*

VanAlstyne, Mary *NewYHSD*

VanAlstyne, Thomas Jefferson 1827-1903 *BiDrAC, NatCAB 9, WhAm 1*

VanAmburgh, Fred DeWitt 1866-1934 *NatCAB 25, WhAm 1*

Vanamee, Grace Davis 1876-1946 *WhAm 2*

Vanamee, William 1847-1914 *NatCAB 16*

VanAmringe, Guy 1868-1936 *NatCAB 29*

VanAmringe, John Howard 1835-1915 *DcAmB,*

WhAm 1

VanAmringe, John Howard 1836-1915 *NatCAB 13, NatCAB 29*

VanAnda, Carr Vattel 1864-1945 *DcAmB S3, WhAm 4*

VanAnden, Isaac 1812-1875 *NatCAB 27*

VanAntwerp, Eugene Ignatius 1889-1962 *WhAm 4*

VanAntwerp, William Clarkson 1867-1938 *WhAm 1*

Vanarden, George *NewYHSD*

VanArsdale, John 1756-1836 *ApCAB*

VanArsdale, Nathaniel H 1838- *WhAm 4*

VanArsdall, Condit Brewer 1875-1958 *NatCAB 44*

VanArsdall, Harold Poston 1888-1950 *NatCAB 41*

Vanartsdalen, James 1811?- *NewYHSD*

Vanasse Vertefeuille, Fabien 1849- *ApCAB*

VanAtta, Robert S d1966 *WhAm 5*

VanAtten, William Teunis 1892-1968 *WhAm 5*

Vanauchi *NewYHSD*

VanAuken, Charles S 1888-1968 *WhAm 5*

VanAuken, Daniel Myers 1826-1908 *BiDrAC*

VanAuken, Dennis M 1826- *BiAUS*

VanAuken, Glenn 1883-1943 *NatCAB 32*

VanAuken, Howell 1888-1966 *NatCAB 53*

VanAuken, Wilbur Rice 1882-1953 *WhAm 3*

VanBarneveld, Charles Edwin 1874-1942 *WhAm 2*

VanBarneveld, Charles Edwyn 1874-1942 *NatCAB 39*

VanBaun, William Weed 1858-1930 *NatCAB 3, WhAm 1*

VanBeest *NewYHSD*

VanBeinum, Eduard 1900-1959 *WhAm 3*

VanBenschoten, Anna Lavinia 1866- *WomWWA 14*

VanBenschoten, James Cooke 1827-1902 *WhAm 1*

VanBenschoten, Mary Crowell *AmWom*

VanBenschoten, William Henry 1872-1928 *ApCAB X, NatCAB 32, WhAm 1*

VanBerckel, Peter I d1800 *Drake*

VanBeuren, Amedee J 1880-1938 *WhAm 1*

VanBeuren, Archibold 1905-1974 *WhAm 6*

VanBeuren, Frederick Theodore, Jr. 1876-1943 *NatCAB 34, WhAm 2*

VanBeuren, Johannes 1680?-1755 *DcAmB, WhAm H*

VanBeuren, Michael Murray 1872-1951 *NatCAB 39*

VanBiema, Adolf 1910-1964 *NatCAB 50*

VanBiesbroeck, George 1880-1974 *WhAm 6*

VanBlarcom, Clifford Winters 1907-1965 *NatCAB 52*

VanBlarcom, Conant 1887-1955 *NatCAB 43*

VanBlarcom, Jacob Craig 1849-1908 *NatCAB 12, NatCAB 16*

VanBokkelen, Libertus 1815-1889 *BiDAmEd, NatCAB 3*

VanBomel, Howard Slawson 1889-1953 *NatCAB 42*

VanBomel, Isaac Allison 1856-1928 *NatCAB 25*

VanBomel, Leroy Allison 1885-1966 *NatCAB 53, WhAm 4*

VanBoskerck, Robert Ward 1855-1932 *TwCBDA, WhAm 1*

VanBriggle, Artus 1869-1904 *NatCAB 14*

Vanbrugh, Sir John 1664-1726 *McGEWB*

VanBrunt, Allison James 1862-1932 *NatCAB 23*

VanBrunt, Charles H 1835-1905 *WhAm 1*

VanBrunt, Charles H 1836-1905 *NatCAB 10*

VanBrunt, Gershom Jaques 1798-1863 *ApCAB*

VanBrunt, Gershom Jaques 1800-1863 *Drake*

VanBrunt, Henry 1832-1903 *AmBi, BnEnAmA, DcAmB, NatCAB 11, WhAm 1*

VanBrunt, Jeremiah Rutger 1867-1950 *WhAm 2*

VanBunschooten, Elias 1738-1815 *ApCAB*

VanBuren, Abby *WebAB*

VanBuren, Abraham 1807-1873 *ApCAB*

VanBuren, Albert Alexander 1852-1910 *WhAm 1*

VanBuren, Albert William 1878- *WhAm 6*

VanBuren, Alfred Deyo McKinstry 1884-1947 *NatCAB 35*

VanBuren, Alicia Keisker 1860-1922 *WhAm 1*

VanBuren, Angelica Singleton 1820?-1878 *AmWom, ApCAB, NatCAB 6*

VanBuren, Charles Henry 1861-1941 *NatCAB 30*

VanBuren, Daniel Tompkins 1824-1890 *ApCAB Sup*

VanBuren, Hannah Hoes 1782-1819 *ApCAB*

VanBuren, Hannah Hoes 1783-1819 *NotAW*

VanBuren, James Heartt 1850-1917 *NatCAB 1, TwCBDA, WhAm 1*

VanBuren, James Lyman 1837-1866 *ApCAB*

VanBuren, John 1799-1855 *BiAUS, BiDrAC, WhAm H*

VanBuren, John 1810-1866 *ApCAB, DcAmB, Drake, NatCAB 3, WhAm H*

VanBuren, John Dash 1811-1885 *ApCAB, NatCAB 10*

VanBuren, John Dash 1838-1918 *ApCAB, NatCAB 10, NatCAB 33, WhAm 4*

VanBuren, Lawrence 1783-1868 *ApCAB*

VanBuren, Martin 1782-1862 *AmBi, ApCAB, BiAUS, BiDrAC, BiDrUSE, DcAmB, Drake, EncAAH, EncAB, McGEWB, NatCAB 6, TwCBDA, WebAB, WhAm H, WhAmP*

VanBuren, Maud 1869-1959 *WhAm 3, WomWWA 14*

VanBuren, Raeburn *WebAB*

VanBuren, Robert 1843-1919 *NatCAB 10, WhAm 3*

VanBuren, William Holme 1819-1883 *AmBi, ApCAB, DcAmB, NatCAB 10, WhAm H*

VanBuskirk, Arthur B 1896-1972 *WhAm 5*

VanBuskirk, Edmund Michael 1875-1950 *NatCAB 38*

VanBuskirk, Marion Flahart 1862-1915 *NatCAB 16*

VanCamp, Cortland 1852-1923 *NatCAB 30*

VanCamp, Frank 1863-1937 *NatCAB 28*

VanCamp, George 1861-1926 *NatCAB 32*

VanCamp, Gilbert C 1817-1900 *NatCAB 28*

VanCampen, Helen Green 1883- *WomWWA 14*

Vance, Ap Morgan 1854-1915 *DcAmB*

Vance, Arthur Turner 1872-1930 *WhAm 1*

Vance, Burton 1856- *WhAm 4*

Vance, Clara *NotAW*

Vance, Estil 1906-1959 *WhAm 3*

Vance, Frank Leslie 1847-1908 *NatCAB 16*

Vance, Harold Sines 1890-1959 *NatCAB 47, WhAm 3*

Vance, Harrell Taylor, Jr. 1919-1964 *WhAm 4*

Vance, Henry T 1906-1972 *WhAm 5*

Vance, Hiram Albert 1860-1906 *WhAm 1*

Vance, J Madison *WhoColR*

Vance, J Milton 1875-1948 *WhAm 2*

Vance, James Isaac 1862-1939 *NatCAB 8, WhAm 1*

Vance, James Nelson 1828-1913 *NatCAB 15, NatCAB 29*

Vance, Jessica Smith d1939 *WhAm 1*

Vance, John Edward 1905-1975 *WhAm 6*

Vance, John Luther 1839-1921 *BiAUS, BiDrAC*

Vance, John Thomas 1884-1943 *NatCAB 33, WhAm 2*

Vance, Johnstone 1890-1951 *WhAm 3*

Vance, Joseph 1781-1852 *TwCBDA*

Vance, Joseph 1786-1851 *BiAUS*

Vance, Joseph 1786-1852 *ApCAB, BiDrAC, Drake, NatCAB 3, WhAm H, WhAmP*

Vance, Joseph Anderson 1864-1951 *NatCAB 41, WhAm 3*

Vance, Louis Joseph 1879-1933 *AmBi, DcAmB S1, WhAm 1*

Vance, Robert Brank 1793-1827 *BiAUS, BiDrAC, WhAm H, WhAmP*

Vance, Robert Brank 1828-1899 *BiAUS, BiDrAC, TwCBDA, WhAmP*

Vance, Robert Cummings 1894-1959 *WhAm 3*

Vance, Robert Johnstone 1854-1902 *BiDrAC*

Vance, Rupert Bayless 1899-1975 *WhAm 6*

Vance, Selby Frame 1864-1937 *WhAm 1*

Vance, William Ford 1909-1972 *WhAm 6*

Vance, William Reynolds 1870-1940 *WhAm 1*

Vance, Wilson 1845- *WhAm 1*

Vance, Zebulon Baird 1830-1894 *AmBi, ApCAB, BiAUS, BiDConf, BiDrAC,*

VanDerStucken, Frank Valentine 1858-1929
 NatCAB 11

Vanderveer, Abraham 1781-1839 *BiAUS,*
 BiDrAC, WhAm H

VanderVeer, Albert 1841-1929 *ApCAB,*
 DcAmB, NatCAB 3, NatCAB 16,
 WhAm 1

VanderVeer, Albert 1879-1959 *NatCAB 47*

VanDerveer, Ferdinand 1823- *ApCAB, Drake*

VanDerveer, Joe 1914-1963 *NatCAB 52*

Vanderveer, Miss M H *IIBEAAW*

VanDerVeer, Mary *WomWWA 14*

VanDerVeer, McClellan 1895-1961 *WhAm 4*

VanderVeer, Milton T 1901-1973 *WhAm 6*

Vandervelde, Bert 1885-1948 *NatCAB 40*

Vandervelde, Conrad 1879- *WhAm 6*

VanderVelde, Lewis George 1890-1975
 WhAm 6

VanDervoort, Ed 1900-1952 *NatCAB 41*

Vandervoort, James W 1855- *WhAm 4*

VanDerVoort, Paul 1846- *NatCAB 4*

VanDervoort, William H 1869-1921 *WhAm 1*

VanderVries, John Nicholas 1876-1936
 WhAm 1

VanDerWaals, Johannes Diderik 1837-1923
 AsBiEn, DcScB

Vanderwarker, Richard Dean 1911-1971
 WhAm 5

VanderWee, John Baptist 1824-1900 *DcAmB,*
 WhAm H

VanDerWeyden, Harry 1868- *WhAm 4*

VanderZee, Abram 1893-1967 *NatCAB 53,*
 WhAm 4

VanDerzee, Anna Wood Blackmer 1872-
 WomWWA 14

VanDeusen, Clarence Elmer 1878-1962
 NatCAB 49

VanDeusen, Donald Earl 1896-1957 *NatCAB 46*

VanDeusen, Edwin H 1828- *WhAm 4*

VanDeusen, George William 1859- *WhAm 4*

VanDeusen, Glyndon Garlock 1897- *EncAAH*

VanDeusen, Henry Reed 1872- *WhAm 5*

VanDeusen, Mary Westbrook 1829- *AmWom*

VanDeusen, Robert Hicks 1891-1971 *WhAm 5*

VanDevanter, Willis 1859-1941 *DcAmB S3,*
 NatCAB 12, REnAW, WebAB, WhAm 1

VanDeVelde, James Oliver 1792-1855 *Drake*

VanDeVelde, James Oliver 1793-1855
 NatCAB 9

VanDeVelde, James Oliver 1795-1855 *ApCAB,*
 DcAmB, TwCBDA, WhAm H

Vandevelde, Petro *NewYHSD*

VanDeVen, Cornelius 1865-1932 *NatCAB 5,*
 WhAm 1

Vandeventer, Braden 1878-1943 *WhAm 2*

VanDeventer, Harry Brown 1881-1945
 NatCAB 33

VanDeventer, Horace 1867-1951 *NatCAB 38*

VanDeventer, John Herbert 1881-1956 *WhAm 3*

Vandeventer, William Luther 1889-1953
 NatCAB 42, WhAm 3

Vandever, William 1817-1893 *BiAUS, BiDrAC,*
 NatCAB 4, TwCBDA, WhAm H,
 WhAmP

VanDeVyver, Augustine 1844-1911 *TwCBDA,*
 WhAm 1

VanDeWall, Willem 1887-1953 *NatCAB 43*

VanDeWarker, Edward Ely 1841-1910 *DcAmB,*
 NatCAB 12

Vandewater, Edwin 1880-1953 *NatCAB 43*

VanDeWater, Frederic F 1890-1968 *WhAm 5*

Vandewater, George Roe 1854-1925 *ApCAB,*
 WhAm 1

VanDeWater, Virginia Terhune d1945
 WhAm 2, WomWWA 14

Vandewater, William Collins 1886-1942
 NatCAB 33

VanDiemen, Anthony Meuza 1593-1645
 McGEWB

VanDiest, Edmond Cornelis 1865-1950
 NatCAB 40, WhAm 3

VanDine, S S 1888-1939 *DcAmB S2,*
 WhAm 1

VanDissel, E F Cartier 1863- *WhAm 4*

Vandiver, Almuth Cunningham 1879-1931
 WhAm 1

Vandiver, Harry Shultz 1882-1973 *WhAm 5*

Vandiver, J S d1950 *WhAm 3*

Vandiver, Marie Louise Ayer *WomWWA 14*

Vandiver, Willard Duncan 1854-1932 *BiDrAC,*
 WhAm 1, WhAmP

VanDongen, Cornelius Theodore Marie 1877-
 WhAm 6

VanDoorn, William 1872-1944 *WhAm 2*

VanDoort, M *NewYHSD*

VanDoren, Carl Clinton 1884-1950 *DcAmB S4*

VanDoren, Carl Clinton 1885-1950 *NatCAB 39,*
 WebAB, WhAm 3

VanDoren, Harold Livingston 1895-1957
 WhAm 3

VanDoren, Irita 1891-1966 *WhAm 4*

VanDoren, Mark 1894-1972 *BiDAmEd,*
 WebAB, WhAm 5

VanDoren, Mary A 1869- *WomWWA 14*

VanDoren, Ray Newton 1878-1933 *WhAm 1*

VanDorn, Earl 1820-1863 *AmBi, ApCAB,*
 BiDConf, DcAmB, NatCAB 4, TwCBDA,
 WebAMB, WhAm H

VanDorn, Earl 1821-1863 *Drake*

VanDorn, James Peter 1876-1947 *NatCAB 35*

VanDresser, Jasmine Stone 1878- *WhAm 6*

VanDresser, Marcia d1937 *WhAm 1*

VanDruten, John William 1901-1957 *WhAm 3*

VanDuke, Carl Chester 1881-1919 *WhAmP*

VanDusen, Arthur 1886-1949 *NatCAB 50*

VanDusen, Charles B 1871-1958 *WhAm 3*

VanDusen, Henry Pitney 1897-1975 *BiDAmEd,*
 DcAmReB, WhAm 6

VanDuyn, Edward Seguin 1872-1955
 NatCAB 47, WhAm 5

VanDuzee, Arthur Henry 1852-1928
 NatCAB 21

Vanduzee, Benjamin C *NewYHSD*

VanDuzer, Clarence Dunn 1866-1947 *BiDrAC,*
 WhAmP

VanDuzer, Edna Slocum 1859- *WomWWA 14*

VanDuzer, Henry Brooks 1874-1951
 NatCAB 40

VanDuzer, Henry Sayre 1853-1928 *WhAm 1*

VanDuzer, Lewis Sayre 1861-1936 *NatCAB 27,*
 WhAm 1

VanDyck, Anthony 1599-1641 *McGEWB*

VanDyck, Cornelius VanAlen 1818-1895 *AmBi,*
 DcAmB, NatCAB 5, WhAm H

VanDyck, Ernest-Marie Hubert 1861-1923
 WhAm 3

VanDyck, Francis Cuyler 1844-1927 *WhAm 1*

VanDyck, Henry Herbert 1809-1888
 NatCAB 23

VanDyck, James *NewYHSD*

VanDyck, Laird Sumner 1893-1944 *NatCAB 33*

VanDyck, Peter 1684-1750 *BnEnAmA*

VanDyck, Vedder 1889-1960 *WhAm 4*

VanDyke, Carl Chester 1881-1919 *BiDrAC,*
 WhAm 1

VanDyke, Cornelius VanAllen 1818- *ApCAB*

VanDyke, Douglass 1881-1958 *NatCAB 49*

VanDyke, Edward Burton 1860- *WhoColR*

VanDyke, Edwin Cooper 1869- *WhAm 5*

VanDyke, Harry Benjamin 1895-1971
 NatCAB 56, WhAm 5

VanDyke, Hendrick 1599?-1688 *ApCAB*

VanDyke, Henry 1852-1933 *AmBi, ApCAB,*
 ApCAB X, DcAmB, DcAmReB,
 NatCAB 7, NatCAB 25, TwCBDA,
 WhAm 1

VanDyke, Henry Herbert 1809-1888 *ApCAB*

VanDyke, Henry Jackson 1822-1891 *ApCAB,*
 NatCAB 7, TwCBDA, WhAm H

VanDyke, J W 1849-1939 *WhAm 1*

VanDyke, John 1807-1878 *ApCAB, BiAUS,*
 BiDrAC, TwCBDA, WhAm H

VanDyke, John Charles 1856-1932 *AmBi,*
 ApCAB, BiDAmEd, DcAmB, TwCBDA,
 WhAm 1

VanDyke, John Wesley 1849-1939 *DcAmB S2*

VanDyke, Joseph Smith 1832-1915 *ApCAB,*
 WhAm 1

VanDyke, Karl Skillman 1892-1966 *WhAm 4*

VanDyke, Nicholas d1826 *WhAm H*

VanDyke, Nicholas 1738-1789 *ApCAB, BiAUS,*
 BiDrAC, DcAmB, Drake, NatCAB 4,
 TwCBDA, WhAm H, WhAmP

VanDyke, Nicholas 1769-1826 *ApCAB,*
 BiDrAC, TwCBDA, WhAm H, WhAmP

VanDyke, Nicholas 1770-1826 *DcAmB,*

 NatCAB 4

VanDyke, Paul 1859-1933 *AmBi, DcAmB,*
 WhAm 1

VanDyke, Tertius 1886-1958 *NatCAB 46,*
 WhAm 3

VanDyke, Theodore Strong 1842- *ApCAB,*
 TwCBDA, WhAm 4

VanDyke, Walter 1823-1905 *NatCAB 8,*
 WhAm 1

VanDyke, William Duncan 1856-1932
 NatCAB 23, WhAm 1

VanDyke, William Duncan, Jr. 1893-1959
 WhAm 3

VanDyne, Edith *WebAB*

VanDyne, Frederick 1861-1915 *WhAm 1*

Vane, Sir Henry 1612-1662 *ApCAB, Drake,*
 NatCAB 7, TwCBDA

Vane, Sir Henry 1613-1662 *AmBi, DcAmB,*
 McGEWB, TwCBDA, WhAm H

VanEaton, Henry Smith 1826-1898 *BiDrAC*

VanElten, Hendrick Dirk Kruseman 1829-
 ApCAB

VanElten, Hendrik Dirk Kruseman 1829-
 NatCAB 7

VanElten, Kruseman 1829-1904 *TwCBDA,*
 WhAm 1

VanEpps, Clarence 1875- *WhAm 5*

VanEpps, Eugene Francis 1912-1970 *WhAm 5*

VanEpps, Howard 1847- *NatCAB 10*

VanEpps, Percy Myers 1859- *WhAm 4*

VanEps, Frank Stanley 1859-1921 *WhAm 1*

VanEs, Leunis 1868-1956 *WhAm 3*

VanEtten, Edgar 1843- *WhAm 4*

VanEtten, Nathan Bristol 1866-1954
 NatCAB 40, WhAm 3

VanEttisch, Raymond Treder 1886-1951
 WhAm 3

VanEvera, Benjamin Douglass 1901-1970
 WhAm 5

VanEveren, Alice B 1869- *WomWWA 14*

VanEvery, Dale 1896- *REnAW*

VanEvery, John Brock 1839- *NatCAB 14*

VanEvery, William Stanley 1892-1972 *WhAm 6*

VanFavoren, J H *NewYHSD*

VanFleet, Dick Scott 1912-1975 *WhAm 6*

VanFleet, Ellen Oliver 1842- *AmWom*

VanFleet, Frederick Alvin 1874-1952 *WhAm 3*

VanFleet, James Alward 1892- *WebAMB*

VanFleet, John Ricard 1881-1947 *NatCAB 36*

VanFleet, Vernon Wick 1866-1932 *NatCAB 24,*
 WhAm 1, WhAm 1C

VanFleet, Walter 1857-1922 *DcAmB,*
 WhAm 1

VanFleet, William Cary 1852-1923 *WhAm 1*

VanGaasbeck, Peter 1754-1797 *BiAUS,*
 BiDrAC, WhAm H

VanGelder, Robert 1904-1952 *WhAm 3*

Vangelderin, George *NewYHSD*

VanGogh, Vincent 1853-1890 *McGEWB*

VanGorder, Albert Hapgood 1852-1941
 NatCAB 31

VanGordon, Cyrena d1964 *WhAm 4*

VanGuysling, George Edmund 1865- *ApCAB X*

VanHaersolte, Wiliem 1909-1974 *WhAm 6*

VanHagan, Leslie Flanders 1878-1967
 WhAm 4A

VanHagen, George Ely 1873-1946 *NatCAB 44*

VanHagen, Leslie Flanders 1878-1967 *WhAm 6*

VanHagen, Peter Albrecht *WhAm H*

VanHaitsma, John Peter 1884-1965 *NatCAB 51*

VanHamm, Caleb Marsh 1861-1919 *WhAm 1*

Vanhanswyk, Louis John 1905-1971 *WhAm 5*

VanHarlingen, Arthur 1845-1936 *WhAm 1*

VanHase, David *NewYHSD*

VanHazel, Willard 1896-1961 *WhAm 4*

VanHecke, Maurice Taylor 1892-1963 *WhAm 4*

VanHelmont, Jean Baptiste 1577-1644 *BiHiMed*

VanHeusen, John Manning 1869-1931
 NatCAB 24

VanHise, Charles Richard 1857-1918
 ApCAB Sup, BiDAmEd, DcAmB, DcScB,
 EncAB, NatCAB 10, NatCAB 19,
 TwCBDA, WebAB, WhAm 1

VanHoesen, Henry Bartlett 1885-1965
 DcAmLiB, WhAm 4

VanHoogstraten, Willem 1884-1965 *WhAm 4*

VanHook, LaRue 1877-1951 *WhAm 3*

VanHook, Loretta C 1852- *AmWom*

VanHook, Weller 1862-1933 *DcAmB, WhAm 1*
VanHoose, Azor Warner 1860-1921 *NatCAB 19, WhAm 1*
VanHoosen, Bertha 1863-1952 *WhAm 3*
VanHorn, Burt 1823-1896 *BiAUS, BiDrAC, WhAm H*
VanHorn, Charles William 1879-1965 *WhAm 4*
VanHorn, Francis Joseph 1865-1949 *ApCAB X, WhAm 3*
VanHorn, Frank Robertson 1872-1933 *NatCAB 24, WhAm 1*
VanHorn, George 1850-1904 *BiDrAC*
VanHorn, Peter Harry 1893-1936 *WhAm 1*
VanHorn, Robert Bowman 1893-1972 *WhAm 5*
VanHorn, Robert Osborn 1876-1941 *WhAm 1*
VanHorn, Robert Thompson 1824-1916 *BiAUS, BiDrAC, DcAmB, NatCAB 3, TwCBDA, WhAm 1, WhAmP*
VanHorne, Archibald 1798-1817 *BiAUS, BiDrAC, WhAm H*
VanHorne, David 1837-1930 *WhAm 1*
VanHorne, Espy 1795-1829 *BiAUS, BiDrAC, WhAm H*
VanHorne, Isaac 1754-1834 *BiAUS, BiDrAC, WhAm H*
VanHorne, John 1889-1959 *WhAm 3*
VanHorne, Thomas Calvin 1875-1958 *NatCAB 47*
VanHorne, Sir William Cornelius 1843-1915 *ApCAB, DcAmB, McGEWB, WhAm 1*
VanHorne, William Grant 1855- *WhAm 4*
VanHorne, William McCadden 1842-1923 *WhAm 1*
VanHouteano *NewYHSD*
VanHouten, Isaac B 1776-1850 *BiDrAC, WhAm H*
VanHouten, Jan d1949 *WhAm 3*
VanHouton, Isaac B 1776-1850 *BiAUS*
VanHummell, Henry 1868-1944 *NatCAB 33*
VanHusen, John *NewYHSD*
VanIderstine, Robert 1873-1933 *WhAm 1*
Vanier, Georges Philias 1888-1967 *WhAm 4*
Vanik, Charles Albert 1913- *BiDrAC*
VanIlpendam, Jan Jansen 1595?-1647 *DcAmB, WhAm H*
Vaniman, Roy Lawrence 1889-1956 *NatCAB 43, WhAm 3*
VanIngen, Gilbert 1869-1925 *NatCAB 22, WhAm 1*
VanIngen, Hendrik 1871-1923 *NatCAB 21*
VanIngen, Henry A 1833-1899 *NewYHSD*
VanIngen, Philip 1875-1953 *WhAm 3*
VanIngen, W B 1858-1955 *WhAm 3*
VanIngen, William H 1831?- *NewYHSD*
Vanini, Giulio Cesare 1585?-1619 *DcScB*
VanKaathoven, Jean Jacques Abram 1877-1928 *NatCAB 23*
VanKeuren, Alexander Hamilton 1881-1966 *WhAm 4*
VanKeuren, Floyd 1880- *WhAm 6*
VanKeuren, Philip 1882-1942 *NatCAB 31*
VanKirk, Charles Clark 1862-1937 *NatCAB 27, WhAm 1*
VanKirk, Jay Calvin 1896-1963 *WhAm 4*
VanKirk, Lawrence E 1895-1953 *WhAm 3*
VanKirk, Walter William 1891-1956 *WhAm 3*
VanKleeck, Edwin Robert 1906-1965 *WhAm 4*
VanKleeck, Louis Ashley 1887-1957 *NatCAB 43*
VanKleeck, Marie Tallmadge *WomWWA 14*
VanKleeck, Mary 1883-1972 *WhAm 5*
VanKoughnet, Philip 1789-1873 *ApCAB*
VanKoughnet, Philip Michael Scott 1823-1869 *ApCAB*
VanLaer, Alexander Theabald 1857-1920 *TwCBDA, WhAm 1*
VanLaer, Arnold Johan Ferdinand 1869-1955 *WhAm 3*
VanLahr, Leo J d1946 *WhAm 2*
VanLare, Stanley Everett 1908-1969 *WhAm 5*
VanLear, J Findlay 1873-1942 *NatCAB 30*
VanLeer, Blake Ragsdale 1893-1956 *WhAm 3*
VanLeer, Carlos Clark 1865- *WhAm 5*
VanLeeuwenhoek, Antony 1632-1723 *BiHiMed*
VanLennep, Henry John 1815-1889 *ApCAB, DcAmB, WhAm H*
VanLennep, Mary Elizabeth 1821-1844 *ApCAB*

VanLennep, William Bird 1853-1919 *DcAmB, NatCAB 3, WhAm 1*
VanLew, Elizabeth L 1818-1900 *NotAW, WebAMB*
VanLiew, Charles Cecil 1862- *WhAm 4*
VanLoan, Charles Emmet 1876-1919 *WhAm 1*
VanLoben Sols, Ernst Diederick 1879-1965 *WhAm 4*
VanLone, Earl Moses 1890-1967 *NatCAB 54*
VanLoo, Pierre 1837-1858 *NewYHSD*
VanLoon, Hendrik Willem 1882-1944 *DcAmB S3, NatCAB 33, WhAm 2*
VanMaanen, Adriaan 1884-1946 *WhAm 2*
VanMarter, Martha 1839- *WhAm 4*
VanMeter, John Blackford 1842-1930 *DcAmB, NatCAB 26, WhAm 1*
Vanmeter, John Inskeep 1798-1875 *BiDrAC, WhAm H*
VanMeter, Ralph Albert 1893-1958 *WhAm 3*
VanMetre, John J *BiAUS*
VanMetre, Thurman William 1884-1961 *WhAm 4*
Vann, Henry 1892-1964 *NatCAB 53*
Vann, Homer King 1902-1969 *NatCAB 54*
Vann, Irving Goodwin 1842-1921 *NatCAB 6, TwCBDA, WhAm 1*
Vann, Richard Tilman 1851-1941 *NatCAB 35; WhAm 2*
Vann, Samuel Cannady 1852-1924 *NatCAB 43*
Vannah, Kate 1855-1943 *WhAm 2, WhAm 4*
VanName, Addison 1835-1922 *DcAmB, DcAmLiB, NatCAB 19, WhAm 1*
VanName, Elmer Garfield 1888-1971 *NatCAB 56, WhAm 5*
VanName, F W, Jr. 1920-1967 *WhAm 4A*
VanName, George W *NewYHSD*
VanName, Ralph Gibbs 1877-1961 *NatCAB 49*
VanNamee, George Rivet 1877-1949 *WhAm 2*
Vannasse, Edward Theophile 1905-1971 *WhAm 6*
VanNatta, John Wilson 1880-1963 *WhAm 4*
Vanneck, John 1906-1974 *WhAm 6*
VanNess, Abraham Rynier 1823-1839 *TwCBDA*
VanNess, Cornelius 1803-1842 *NatCAB 6*
VanNess, Cornelius Peter 1782-1852 *ApCAB, BiAUS, Drake, NatCAB 8, TwCBDA*
VanNess, Isaac J 1860-1947 *WhAm 2*
VanNess, John Peter 1770-1846 *BiAUS, BiDrAC, WhAm H*
VanNess, John Peter 1770-1847 *ApCAB, NatCAB 6*
VanNess, Joseph 1849-1901 *NatCAB 18*
VanNess, Marcia Burns 1782-1832 *ApCAB*
VanNess, Sarah Bowman 1859- *BiCAW, WomWWA 14*
VanNess, Thomas 1859-1931 *WhAm 1*
VanNess, William Peter 1778-1826 *ApCAB, BiAUS, DcAmB, NatCAB 3, TwCBDA, WhAm H*
VanNess, William W 1776-1823 *ApCAB, BiAUS, Drake*
VanNest, Abraham Rynier 1823-1892 *ApCAB, DcAmB, WhAm H*
Vannest, Charles Garrett 1880-1947 *WhAm 2*
VanNest, G Willett 1852- *WhAm 4*
VanNest, Rynier 1739-1776 *ApCAB*
VanNice, Errett 1908-1970 *WhAm 5*
VanNieuwenhuysen, Wilhelmus 1645?-1681 *ApCAB, NatCAB 12*
VanNoppen, Ina Woestemeyer 1906- *EncAAH*
VanNoppen, Leonard Charles 1868-1935 *NatCAB 26, WhAm 1*
VanNorden, Charles 1843-1913 *WhAm 1*
VanNorden, Cora Langdon *WomWWA 14*
VanNorden, Grace Talcott *WomWWA 14*
VanNorden, John H *NewYHSD*
VanNorden, Rudolph Warner *WhAm 5*
VanNorden, Warner 1841-1914 *WhAm 1*
VanNorden, Warner Montagnie 1873-1959 *WhAm 3*
VanNorman, Amelie R Veiller d1920 *NatCAB 1, WhAm 1, WomWWA 14*
VanNorman, Charles Edward 1859-1946 *NatCAB 35*
VanNorman, Mrs. D C *NewYHSD*
VanNorman, Daniel Cummings 1815-1886 *ApCAB, NatCAB 1*
VanNorman, Frederick Dewey 1862- *WhAm 5*

VanNorman, Hubert Everett 1872-1938 *WhAm 1*
VanNorman, Louis Edwin 1869-1956 *WhAm 3*
VanNorstrand, David 1811-1886 *WhAm H*
VanNostrand, David 1811-1886 *ApCAB, DcAmB, NatCAB 9*
VanNostrand, Henry *NewYHSD*
VanNostrand, John James 1844- *NatCAB 18*
Vannuchi, F 1800?- *NewYHSD*
Vannuchi, S 1800?- *NewYHSD*
VanNuys, Ezra Allen 1877-1947 *WhAm 2*
VanNuys, Frederick 1874-1944 *BiDrAC, NatCAB 44, WhAm 2, WhAmP*
VanNuys, James Benton 1883-1962 *WhAm 4*
VanOosten, John 1891-1966 *NatCAB 51*
VanOrden, George Owen 1906-1967 *NatCAB 53*
VanOrman, F Harold 1884-1958 *WhAm 3*
VanOrnum, John Lane 1864-1943 *WhAm 2*
VanOrsdall, Carrie 1864- *WomWWA 14*
VanOrsdel, Josiah Alexander 1860-1937 *NatCAB 29, WhAm 1*
VanOrsdell, John Calvin 1847-1914 *NatCAB 18*
VanOrstrand, Charles Edwin 1870-1959 *NatCAB 49*
VanOsdel, John Mills 1811-1891 *DcAmB, WhAm H*
VanOsdol, Harry Allen 1880-1957 *NatCAB 45*
Vanosten, Joseph *NewYHSD*
VanPaassen, Pierre 1895-1968 *WhAm 4A*
VanPatten, Nathan 1887-1956 *DcAmLiB, WhAm 3*
VanPatten, William James d1920 *WhAm 1*
VanPelt, Betsey Southworth 1873- *WomWWA 14*
VanPelt, Clayton Forrest d1966 *WhAm 4*
VanPelt, Gertrude Wyckoff 1856- *WomWWA 14*
VanPelt, John Robert 1862-1962 *WhAm 4*
VanPelt, John Vredenburgh 1874-1962 *WhAm 4*
VanPelt, William Kaiser 1905- *BiDrAC, WhAmP*
VanPetten, Edward Cyrus 1873- *WhAm 5*
VanPetten, John B 1827-1908 *WhAm 1*
VanPoole, Chalmer Melanchton 1854-1933 *WhAm 3*
VanPraag, Henry L d1946 *WhAm 2*
VanQuickenborne, Charles Felix 1788-1837 *DcAmB, WhAm H*
VanRaalte, Albertus Christiaan 1811-1876 *DcAmB, WhAm H*
VanRensselaer, Caroline Elizabeth *WomWWA 14*
VanRensselaer, Cortland 1808-1860 *Drake, WhAm H*
VanRensselaer, Cortlandt 1808-1860 *ApCAB, DcAmB, NatCAB 7*
VanRensselaer, Cortlandt Schuyler 1859-1927 *NatCAB 23*
VanRensselaer, Hendrick 1667?-1740 *ApCAB, NatCAB 7*
VanRensselaer, Henry Bell 1810-1864 *ApCAB, BiDrAC, Drake, WhAm H, WhAmP*
VanRensselaer, Henry Bell 1811-1864 *BiAUS*
VanRensselaer, Henry Killian 1744-1816 *ApCAB, Drake, NatCAB 7*
VanRensselaer, Howard 1858-1925 *NatCAB 3, WhAm 1*
VanRensselaer, Jeremiah 1738-1810 *BiDrAC, WhAm H, WhAmP*
VanRensselaer, Jeremiah 1741-1810 *ApCAB, Drake*
VanRensselaer, Jeremiah 1741-1820 *BiAUS*
VanRensselaer, Jeremiah 1793-1871 *NatCAB 7*
VanRensselaer, Jeremias 1632?-1674 *ApCAB, NatCAB 2*
VanRensselaer, Kiliaen 1580?-1643 *McGEWB*
VanRensselaer, Killian 1595-1644 *ApCAB*
VanRensselaer, Killian 1662-1719 *ApCAB*
VanRensselaer, Killian Killian 1763-1845 *ApCAB, BiAUS, BiDrAC, NatCAB 2, WhAm H, WhAmP*
VanRensselaer, Louisa *WomWWA 14*
VanRensselaer, M King 1848-1925 *WhAm 1, WomWWA 14*
VanRensselaer, Maria VanCortlandt 1645-1688? *NotAW*

VanRensselaer, Mariana Griswold d1934
WhAm 1, WomWWA 14
VanRensselaer, Mariana Griswold 1851-1934
ApCAB, DcAmB, NotAW
VanRensselaer, Mariana Griswold 1853?-1934
ApCAB Sup
VanRensselaer, Marianna 1851-1934
NatCAB 14
VanRensselaer, Martha 1864-1932 *AmBi,*
BiDAmEd, DcAmB, NatCAB 23,
NotAW, WhAm 1, WomWWA 14
VanRensselaer, Maunsell 1819-1900 *ApCAB,*
ApCAB Sup, NatCAB 2, WhAm 1
VanRensselaer, Nicholas 1636-1678 *DcAmB,*
WhAm H
VanRensselaer, Nicholas 1638?-1678 *ApCAB,*
NatCAB 7
VanRensselaer, Nicholas 1754-1848 *ApCAB,*
NatCAB 7
VanRensselaer, Philip 1747-1798 *NatCAB 7*
VanRensselaer, Philip S 1767-1824 *ApCAB,*
NatCAB 7
VanRensselaer, Robert 1741-1802 *ApCAB*
VanRensselaer, Mrs. Schuyler *NotAW*
VanRensselaer, Solomon VanVechten 1774-1852
ApCAB, BiAUS, BiDrAC, DcAmB, Drake,
NatCAB 11, WhAm H, WhAmP
VanRensselaer, Stephen 1764-1839 *AmBi,*
BiAUS, BiDrAC, DcAmB, Drake,
EncAAH, NatCAB 2, WebAB, WebAMB,
WhAm H, WhAmP
VanRensselaer, Stephen 1765-1839 *ApCAB*
VanRensselaer, Stephen 1789-1868 *ApCAB,*
NatCAB 2, TwCBDA
VanReypen, William Knickerbocker 1840-1924
ApCAB Sup, NatCAB 13, WhAm 1
VanRiper, Carl 1879-1950 *NatCAB 38*
VanRiper, Cornelius S 1837-1919 *NatCAB 18*
VanRiper, John Crowell 1863-1926 *WhAm 1*
VanRiper, Walter David 1895-1973 *NatCAB 57,*
WhAm 5
VanRoosbroeck, Gustave Leopold 1888-1936
WhAm 1
VanRoyen, Jan Herman 1871-1933 *WhAm 1*
VanRoyen, William 1900-1973 *WhAm 6*
VanRyder, Jack 1898-1968 *IIBEAAW*
VanRyn VanAlkemaude, Marius Anne 1902-1974
WhAm 6
VanSandt, Max Morton 1904-1961 *NatCAB 51*
VanSant, Edgar Sands 1874-1944 *NatCAB 34*
VanSant, Joshua 1803-1884 *BiAUS, BiDrAC,*
WhAm H
VanSant, Samuel Rinnah 1844-1936
NatCAB 13, TwCBDA, WhAm 1
VanSant, Wilbur 1890-1970 *WhAm 5*
VanSantvoord, Abraham 1784-1858
NatCAB 24
VanSantvoord, Alfred 1819-1901 *NatCAB 22,*
WhAm 1
VanSantvoord, Cornelius 1637-1752 *ApCAB*
VanSantvoord, Cornelius 1816- *ApCAB*
VanSantvoord, George 1819-1863 *ApCAB,*
DcAmB, Drake, TwCBDA, WhAm H
VanSantvoord, Seymour 1858-1938 *NatCAB 29,*
WhAm 1
VanSantvoord, Staats 1790-1882 *ApCAB*
VanSatlee, Antony Jansen 1600?-1670 *ApCAB*
Vansaun, Peter D *NewYHSD*
VanSaun, Walter 1889-1950 *WhAm 3*
VanSchaack, Henry Cruger 1802-1887 *ApCAB,*
DcAmB, WhAm H
VanSchaack, Henry Cruger 1887-1963
WhAm 4
VanSchaack, Peter 1747-1832 *ApCAB,*
DcAmB, Drake, WhAm H
VanSchaick, Clarence Llewellyn 1904-1971
WhAm 5
VanSchaick, Goose 1736-1789 *AmBi, DcAmB*
VanSchaick, Gosen 1736-1789 *WhAm H*
VanSchaick, Gosen 1737-1787 *NatCAB 1*
VanSchaick, Gozen 1736-1789 *TwCBDA*
VanSchaick, Gozen 1737-1787 *ApCAB*
VanSchaick, Gozen 1737-1789 *Drake*
VanSchaick, Guy 1876- *NatCAB 18*
VanSchaick, Isaac Whitbeck 1817-1901 *BiDrAC*
VanSchaick, John, Jr. 1873-1949 *NatCAB 38*
VanSchoick, J A *NewYHSD*

VanSciver, George Dobbins 1862-1942
NatCAB 31
VanSciver, J Howard 1888-1953 *NatCAB 42*
VanSciver, Joseph Bishop 1861-1943
NatCAB 32
VanSciver, Lloyd 1896-1954 *NatCAB 47*
VanScoy, Thomas 1848-1901 *WhAm 1*
VanScoyoc, Leland Stanford 1900-1972
WhAm 5
VanSickle, Adolphus 1835- *NewYHSD*
VanSickle, Ellis 1894-1962 *NatCAB 50*
VanSickle, Frederick Levi 1862-1938 *WhAm 1*
VanSickle, J N *NewYHSD*
VanSickle, James Hixon 1852-1926 *NatCAB 21,*
WhAm 1
VanSickle, Kenneth Ardean 1911-1960
WhAm 3
VanSickle, Selah 1812- *NewYHSD, WhAm H*
VanSiclen, James Cornell 1869-1963
NatCAB 49
VanSiclen, Matthew 1880-1941 *WhAm 1*
VanSinderen, Adrian 1887-1963 *NatCAB 50,*
WhAm 4
VanSinderen, Henry Brinsmade 1889-1968
WhAm 4A
Vansittart, Henry 1779-1844 *ApCAB*
Vansittart, Robert G, Baron Of Denham
1881-1957 *WhAm 3*
VanSlingerland, Nellie Bingham 1850-
WhAm 4, WomWWA 14
VanSlyke, Clarence Allan 1880-1932 *WhAm 1*
VanSlyke, Donald Dexter 1883-1971 *DcScB,*
NatCAB 56, WhAm 5
VanSlyke, Elizabeth Johnson *WomWWA 14*
VanSlyke, George Martin 1881-1961 *WhAm 4*
VanSlyke, Lucille Baldwin 1880- *WhAm 6*
VanSlyke, Lucius Lincoln 1859-1931 *DcAmB,*
WhAm 1
VanSoelen, Theodore 1890-1964 *IIBEAAW,*
WhAm 4
VanSplunter, John Marcus 1881-1957 *WhAm 3*
VanStarkenborgh *NewYHSD*
VanStavoren *NewYHSD*
VanSteenderen, Frederick C Leonard 1864-
WhAm 5
VanSteenwyk, Elmer Arnold 1905-1962
NatCAB 50, WhAm 4
VanSteenwyk, Gysbert 1876-1967 *NatCAB 54*
Vanston, W Justus K 1881-1957 *WhAm 3*
VanStone, Nathan Edward 1890-1971
NatCAB 57, WhAm 5
Vanstrydonck, Charles *NewYHSD*
VanSwearingen, John Quincy 1866-1925
NatCAB 21
VanSwearingen, Thomas 1784-1822 *BiDrAC,*
WhAm H
VanSweringen, Mantis James 1881-1935 *AmBi,*
DcAmB, WhAm 1
VanSweringen, Oris Paxton 1879-1936 *AmBi,*
WebAB, WhAm 1
VanSwieten, Gerhard 1700-1772 *BiHiMed*
VanSyckel, Bennet 1830-1921 *NatCAB 20,*
WhAm 1
VanSyckle, Raymond Elmoine 1868-
NatCAB 16
VanSyoc, Auburn Gerald 1902-1970
NatCAB 50
Vant, Irving Artemus 1871-1934 *WhAm 1*
Van't Hoff, Jacobus Hendricus 1852-1911
McGEWB
Van't Hoff, Jacobus Henricus 1852-1911 *AsBiEn,*
DcScB
VanTassel, Anna Belle Aldridge 1873-
WomWWA 14
VanTassell, Mary Ann Deach *WomWWA 14*
VanTil, William 1911- *BiDAmEd*
VanTrump, Philadelph 1810-1874 *BiAUS,*
BiDrAC, WhAm H
VanTuyl, George Casey, Jr. 1872-1938 *WhAm 1*
VanTwiller, Walter 1580?-1646? *NatCAB 13*
VanTwiller, Walter 1580?-1647? *TwCBDA*
VanTwiller, Wouter 1580?-1646? *ApCAB,*
NatCAB 13
VanTwiller, Wouter 1580?-1656? *DcAmB,*
WhAm H
VanTyne, Claude Halstead 1869-1930 *DcAmB,*
NatCAB 26, WhAm 1
Vanuchi *NewYHSD*

Vanuranken, John *NewYHSD*
Vanuxem, Lardner 1792-1848 *AmBi, ApCAB,*
DcAmB, DcScB, NatCAB 8, TwCBDA,
WhAm H
VanValkenburg, Edward Schuyler 1872-1954
NatCAB 45
VanValkenburg, Edwin Augustus 1869-1932
NatCAB 41
VanValkenburg, Hermon Leach 1874-1962
WhAm 4, WhAm 5
VanValkenburg, Robert Bruce 1821-1888
ApCAB, NatCAB 7, TwCBDA
VanValkenburgh, Arba Seymour 1862-1944
NatCAB 33, WhAm 2
VanValkenburgh, Charles M 1854-1931
WhAm 1
VanValkenburgh, Robert Bruce 1821-1888
BiAUS, BiDrAC, WhAm H
VanValzah, Eudora Blair 1862- *WomWWA 14*
VanValzah, Robert 1882-1946 *NatCAB 36,*
WhAm 2
VanVechten, Abraham 1762-1837 *ApCAB,*
DcAmB, NatCAB 9, TwCBDA,
WhAm H
VanVechten, Abraham VanWyck 1828-1906
NatCAB 25
VanVechten, Carl 1880-1964 *WhAm 4*
VanVechten, Jacob 1788-1871 *ApCAB*
VanVechten, Ralph 1862-1927 *NatCAB 31,*
WhAm 1
VanVleck, Durbin *NewYHSD*
VanVleck, Edward Burr 1863-1943 *DcAmB S3,*
WhAm 2
VanVleck, Ernest Alan 1875-1956 *NatCAB 43*
VanVleck, Henry Jacob 1822- *ApCAB*
VanVleck, Jacob 1751-1831 *ApCAB*
VanVleck, John Monroe 1833-1912 *ApCAB,*
WhAm 1
VanVleck, Joseph 1875-1948 *NatCAB 40*
VanVleck, Natalie Dalton Johnson 1893-1950
NatCAB 39
VanVleck, Will George 1857- *WhAm 4*
VanVleck, William Cabell 1885-1956 *WhAm 3*
VanVleck, William Henry 1790-1853 *ApCAB,*
NatCAB 5
VanVliet, Robert Campbell 1857-1943 *WhAm 2*
VanVliet, Stewart 1815-1901 *ApCAB,*
TwCBDA
VanVoast, James 1827-1915 *WhAm 1*
VanVoast, Phoebe M 1879- *WomWWA 14*
VanVolkenburg, Jack Lamont 1903-1963
WhAm 4
VanVoorhes, Nelson H 1822- *BiAUS,*
NatCAB 3
VanVoorhis, Daniel 1878-1956 *NatCAB 44,*
WhAm 3
VanVoorhis, Eugene 1864-1943 *NatCAB 43*
VanVoorhis, Henry Clay 1852-1927 *BiDrAC,*
WhAm 2, WhAmP
VanVoorhis, J Fulton 1882-1966 *NatCAB 56*
VanVoorhis, John 1826-1905 *BiDrAC,*
WhAm 1
VanVoorhis, Robert Henry 1917-1962 *WhAm 4*
VanVorhes, Nelson Holmes 1822-1882 *BiDrAC,*
WhAm H
VanVorhis, Flavius Josephus 1840- *NatCAB 10,*
WhAm 1
VanVorst, Bessie 1872-1928 *WomWWA 14*
VanVorst, Bessie 1873-1928 *WhAm 1*
VanVorst, Hooper C 1817-1888 *NatCAB 13*
VanVorst, Marie Louise 1867-1936 *NotAW,*
WhAm 1, WomWWA 14
VanWagenen, Anna Romeyn 1849-
WomWWA 14
VanWagenen, Anthony 1852-1937 *WhAm 1*
VanWagenen, Isabella *EncAB*
VanWagenen, James Hubert 1881-1935
WhAm 1
VanWagener, Isabella *NotAW, WebAB*
VanWagenin, Kathrina Holland *WomWWA 14*
VanWart, Ames d1927? *IIBEAAW*
VanWart, Isaac 1746-1828 *Drake*
VanWart, Isaac 1760-1828 *ApCAB*
VanWart, Walter Bright 1900-1967 *WhAm 5*
VanWaters, Miriam 1887-1974 *WhAm 6*
VanWerden, Helen R DeKalb 1869-
WomWWA 14
VanWert, Susan Evens 1875- *WomWWA 14*

VanWesep, Alleda 1891-1962 *WhAm 4*
VanWestrum, Adriaan Schade 1865-1917
WhAm 1
VanWickel, Jesse Frederick 1890-1958
WhAm 3
VanWickle, Augustus Stout 1856- *NatCAB 5*
VanWillis *NewYHSD*
VanWinkle, Benjamin Armstead 1853-1933
NatCAB 32
VanWinkle, Charles Arthur 1880-1967
NatCAB 56
VanWinkle, Mrs. Charles D 1866-
WomWWA 14
VanWinkle, Edgar Beach 1842-1920
NatCAB 23, *WhAm 1*
VanWinkle, Edgar Simeon 1810-1882
NatCAB 23
VanWinkle, Isaac Homer 1870-1943 *WhAm 2*
VanWinkle, Marshall 1869-1957 *BiDrAC*,
WhAm 5
VanWinkle, Peter Godwin 1808-1872 *ApCAB*,
BiAUS, *BiDrAC*, *DcAmB*, *NatCAB 4*,
TwCBDA, *WhAm H*, *WhAmP*
VanWinkle, Walling Wallenson 1845-1921
WhAm 1
VanWinkle, William Mitchell 1885-1965
NatCAB 51
VanWinkle, Winant 1879-1943 *NatCAB 36*
VanWormer, John Rufus 1849- *NatCAB 4*
VanWyck, Augustus 1846-1922 *ApCAB Sup*
VanWyck, Augustus 1850-1922 *WhAm 1*
VanWyck, Charles Henry 1824-1895 *ApCAB*,
BiAUS, *BiDrAC*, *DcAmB*, *NatCAB 5*,
TwCBDA, *WhAm H*, *WhAmP*
VanWyck, Robert Anderson 1849-1918
ApCAB Sup, *TwCBDA*, *WhAm 1*
VanWyck, Robert Anderson 1851-1918
NatCAB 13
VanWyck, Sallie Floyd *WomWWA 14*
VanWyck, Samuel 1824- *NatCAB 1*
VanWyck, Sidney McMechen 1868-1931
NatCAB 23
VanWyck, William 1883-1956 *WhAm 3*
VanWyck, William William 1777-1840 *BiAUS*,
BiDrAC, *WhAm H*
VanWyk, William P 1874-1943 *WhAm 2*
VanZandt, Charles Collins 1830-1894
NatCAB 9, *TwCBDA*, *WhAm H*
VanZandt, Clarence Duncan 1853-1926
WhAm 1
VanZandt, Clarence Elmer 1861-1936 *WhAm 1*
VanZandt, James Edward 1898- *BiDrAC*,
WhAmP
VanZandt, Khleber Miller 1836-1930 *WhAm 1*
VanZandt, Marie 1858-1918 *WhAm 1*
VanZandt, Marie 1858-1919 *NotAW*
VanZandt, Marie 1861- *AmWom*, *ApCAB*
VanZandt, Richard Lipscomb 1871-1940
WhAm 1
VanZandt, Thomas K *NewYHSD*
VanZandt, W Thompson *NewYHSD*
VanZelm, L Franklin 1895-1961 *NatCAB 50*
Vanzetti, Bartolomeo 1888-1927 *AmBi*,
DcAmB, *WebAB*, *WhAm 4*
VanZile, Edward Sims 1863-1931 *NatCAB 10*,
NatCAB 25, *WhAm 1*
VanZile, Mary Bulkeley *WomWWA 14*
VanZile, Philip Taylor 1843-1917 *WhAm 1*
VanZwalenburg, Cornelius 1862-1935
NatCAB 26
Vanzwoll, Henry Benjamin 1870-1959
NatCAB 47
Vaquez, Louis Henri 1860-1936 *BiHiMed*
Varahamihira *DcScB*
Vardaman, James Kimber 1861-1930
NatCAB 13
Vardaman, James Kimble 1861-1930 *BiDrAC*,
DcAmB, *EncAAH*, *WhAm 1*, *WhAmP*
Vardell, Charles Gildersleeve 1893-1962
WhAm 4
Vardell, Charles Graves 1860-1958 *WhAm 3*
Varden, George d1917 *WhAm 3*
Vardhamana Mahavira 540?BC-470BC
McGEWB
Vardill, John 1749-1811 *DcAmB*, *WhAm H*
Vare, William Scott 1867-1934 *AmBi*, *BiDrAC*,
DcAmB, *NatCAB 27*, *WhAm 1*, *WhAmP*
Varela, Florencio 1807-1848 *ApCAB*

Varela, Hector Florencio 1832- *ApCAB*
Varela, Jacobo 1876- *WhAm 5*
Varela, Juan Cruz 1794-1839 *ApCAB*
Varela, Juan Cruz 1843- *ApCAB*
Varela, Luis Vicente 1845- *ApCAB*
Varela, Mariano 1834- *ApCAB*
Varela, Pedro 1834- *ApCAB*
Varela, Rufino 1801-1840 *ApCAB*
Varela Y Morales, Felix 1788-1853 *ApCAB*
Varela Y Morales, Felix DeLaConcepcion
1788-1853 *WhAm H*
Varela Y Morales, Felix Francisco Jose
1788-1853 *DcAmB*
Varela Y Ulloa, Jose 1748-1794 *ApCAB*
Varenius, Bernhardus 1622-1650 *DcScB*
Varennes, Pierre Gaultier De *REnAW*
Varese, Edgard 1883-1965 *McGEWB*, *WebAB*,
WhAm 4
Vargas, Diego De 1643-1704 *REnAW*
Vargas, Getulio Dornelles 1882-1954 *WhAm 3*
Vargas, Getulio Dornelles 1883-1954 *McGEWB*,
WhWW-II
Vargas, Jose Maria 1786-1854 *ApCAB*, *Drake*
Vargas-Machuca, Bernardo 1550?-1620?
ApCAB
Vargas Y Ponce, Juan Jose 1755-1821 *ApCAB*
Varian, Bertram Stetson 1872- *WhAm 5*
Varian, Charles Stetson 1846-1922 *WhAm 1*
Varian, Donald Cord 1902-1969 *WhAm 5*
Varian, George Edmund 1865-1923 *IlBEAAW*,
WhAm 1
Varian, Russell Harrison 1898-1959
NatCAB 49, *WhAm 3*
Varian, Sigurd Furgus 1901-1961 *NatCAB 49*
Varick, James 1750?-1827 *DcAmReB*
Varick, James 1750?-1828 *DcAmB*, *WhAm H*
Varick, Richard 1753-1831 *ApCAB*, *DcAmB*,
Drake, *NatCAB 1*, *NatCAB 13*,
TwCBDA, *WhAm H*
Varick, Theodore Romeyn 1825-1887 *ApCAB*
Variell, Arthur Davis 1868-1940 *NatCAB 30*,
WhAm 1
Varignon, Pierre 1654-1722 *DcScB*
Varlet, Domingue Marie 1678-1742 *ApCAB*
Varley, Frederick Horsman 1881-1969
IlBEAAW
Varley, John *NewYHSD*
Varley, John Philip 1862-1935 *AmBi*, *WhAm 1*
Varnau, Bernard Henry 1872-1955 *NatCAB 48*
Varney, Alice Lucy 1836- *WomWWA 14*
Varney, Charles Edward 1867- *WhAm 4*
Varney, William Frederick 1884-1960
NatCAB 49, *WhAm 4*
Varney, William Henry 1838- *WhAm 4*
Varney, William Wesley 1864-1943 *WhAm 2*
Varnhagen, Francisco Adolfo De 1816-1878
McGEWB
Varnhagen, Francisco Adolpho De 1816-1878
ApCAB
Varnum, James Mitchel 1748-1789 *ApCAB*
Varnum, James Mitchell 1748-1789 *BiDrAC*,
DcAmB, *TwCBDA*, *WebAMB*, *WhAm H*,
WhAmP
Varnum, James Mitchell 1749-1789 *Drake*,
NatCAB 6
Varnum, James Mitchell 1749-1790 *BiAUS*
Varnum, James Mitchell 1848-1907 *NatCAB 31*,
WhAm 1
Varnum, John d1846 *BiAUS*
Varnum, John 1778-1836 *BiDrAC*, *WhAm H*,
WhAmP
Varnum, Joseph Bradley 1750-1821 *AmBi*,
ApCAB, *BiDrAC*, *DcAmB*, *Drake*,
NatCAB 1, *TwCBDA*, *WhAm H*,
WhAmP
Varnum, Joseph Bradley 1751-1821 *WebAB*
Varnum, Joseph Bradley 1759-1821 *BiAUS*
Varnum, Joseph Bradley 1818-1874 *ApCAB*
Varnum, Robert Taylor 1865-1953 *NatCAB 42*
Varnum, William Harrison 1878-1946 *WhAm 2*
Varolio, Costanzo 1543-1575 *DcScB*
Varona, Enrique Jose 1849- *ApCAB*
Varrell, Harry Maxwell 1878-1940 *NatCAB 29*
Varrick, James 1760?-1836 *ApCAB*
Varro, Marcus Terentius 116BC-027BC *DcScB*,
McGEWB
Varser, Lycurgus Rayner 1878-1959 *WhAm 4*
Varthema, Ludovico Di 1470?-1517? *McGEWB*

Vasari, Giorgio 1511-1570 *McGEWB*
Vasche, Joseph Burton 1910-1962 *WhAm 4*
Vasconcellos, Andres De *ApCAB*
Vasconcellos, Simon 1599-1670 *ApCAB*
Vasconcelos, Jose 1882-1959 *McGEWB*
Vasey, Frank Thomas 1876-1936 *WhAm 1*
Vasey, George 1822-1893 *AmBi*, *ApCAB*,
DcAmB, *WhAm H*
Vasilevsky, Aleksander Mikhailovich 1895-1977
WhoMilH
Vasilieff, Nicholas Loanovich 1892-1970
WhAm 5
Vasiliev, Alexander Alexandrovich 1867-1953
DcAmB S5, *WhAm 5*
Vasilievsky, Alexander 1895-1977 *WhWW-II*
Vasquez, Francisco 1600?-1660? *ApCAB*
Vasquez, Francisco Leonte 1858- *WhAm 4*
Vasquez, Francisco Pablo 1769-1847 *ApCAB*
Vasquez, Horacio 1860-1936 *McGEWB*
Vasquez, Louis 1798-1868 *REnAW*
Vasquez, Tiburcio 1835-1875 *REnAW*
Vass, Alonzo Frederick 1888-1960 *WhAm 4*
Vass, Samuel N 1866- *WhoColR*
Vass, William Worrell 1872-1941 *NatCAB 31*
Vassale, Giulio 1862-1913 *DcScB*
Vassalio, Edward Andrew 1916-1974 *WhAm 6*
Vassall, John 1625-1688 *DcAmB*, *WhAm H*
Vasser, John Ellison 1813-1878 *ApCAB*,
NatCAB 5
Vassar, John Guy 1811-1888 *ApCAB*,
NatCAB 5, *TwCBDA*
Vassar, Mathew 1792-1868 *Drake*
Vassar, Matthew 1792-1864 *AmBi*
Vassar, Matthew 1792-1868 *ApCAB*, *DcAmB*,
NatCAB 5, *TwCBDA*, *WebAB*,
WhAm H
Vassar, Matthew 1809-1881 *ApCAB*,
NatCAB 5, *TwCBDA*
Vassar, Thomas Edwin 1834-1918 *ApCAB*,
NatCAB 6
Vasseur, Hermann *NewYHSD*
Vastarini-Cresi, Giovanni 1870-1924 *DcScB*
Vatel, John *NewYHSD*
Vatesvara 880- *DcScB*
Vatry, Marc Antoine Bourdon, Baron De
1761-1828 *ApCAB*
Vattemare, Alexandre 1796-1864 *ApCAB*
Vattemare, Nicolas Marie Alexandre 1796-1864
DcAmB, *DcAmLiB*, *WhAm H*
Vatterott, Charles Francis, Jr. 1902-1971
NatCAB 56
Vatutin, Nikolay 1901-1944 *WhWW-II*
Vauban, Sebastien LePrestre De 1633-1707
DcScB, *WhoMilH*
Vaublanc, Vincent Marie Vienot, Count De
1756-1845 *ApCAB*
Vaucher, Jean Pierre Etienne 1763-1841 *DcScB*
Vauclain, Samuel Matthew 1856-1940
NatCAB 33
Vauclain, Samuel Matthews 1856-1940
ApCAB X, *DcAmB S2*, *WhAm 1*
Vaudechamp, Jean Joseph 1790-1866
NewYHSD
Vaudreuil, Jean F DeR DeP, Count De 1740-1817
ApCAB
Vaudreuil, Jean Louis DeR, Count De 1762-1816
ApCAB
Vaudreuil, Louis P DeR, Marquis De 1691-1763
ApCAB
Vaudreuil, Louis P DeR, Marquis De 1724-1802
ApCAB
Vaudreuil, Philippe DeR, Marquis De 1640-1725
ApCAB, *Drake*
Vaudreuil, Pierre F, Marquis De 1698-1765
ApCAB
Vaudreuil, Pierre F DeR, Marquis De 1704-1772
ApCAB
Vaudreuil, Pierre F Rigaud, Marquis De 1704-
Drake
Vaudreuil-Cavagnal, Pierre, Marquis De
1704-1778 *DcAmB*, *WhAm H*
Vaudreuil-Cavagnal, Pierre F, Marquis De
1698-1778 *McGEWB*
Vaudricourt, A De *NewYHSD*
Vaudry, Mary Olive *WomWWA 14*
Vaugh, Albert Clinton, Sr. 1894-1951
NatCAB 41

Vaughan, Alfred Jefferson 1830-1899
ApCAB Sup, NatCAB 6, WhAm 1
Vaughan, Arthur Winn 1882-1948 WhAm 2
Vaughan, Barrett Daniel 1860-1915 NatCAB 17
Vaughan, Benjamin 1751-1835 ApCAB,
DcAmB, Drake, WhAm H
Vaughan, Cecil Calvert, III 1895-1960
NatCAB 48
Vaughan, Charles 1759-1839 ApCAB, DcAmB,
Drake, WhAm H
Vaughan, Charles A NewYHSD
Vaughan, Charles Parker 1867-1936 WhAm 1
Vaughan, Daniel 1818?-1879 DcAmB,
WhAm H
Vaughan, Daniel 1821?-1879 ApCAB,
NatCAB 13
Vaughan, David Davies 1876- WhAm 5
Vaughan, Elbert Hunter 1849- NatCAB 9
Vaughan, Elmer E 1865-1926 WhAm 1
Vaughan, Ernest Howe 1858-1937 NatCAB 28
Vaughan, Floyd Lamar 1891-1955 WhAm 3
Vaughan, George 1873-1945 WhAm 2
Vaughan, George Curtis 1858-1940 NatCAB 29
Vaughan, George Tully 1859-1948 NatCAB 18,
NatCAB 38, WhAm 2
Vaughan, George William 1918-1963
NatCAB 50, WhAm 4
Vaughan, Guy Warner 1884-1966 ApCAB X,
NatCAB 53, WhAm 4
Vaughan, Harold Stearns 1876- WhAm 5
Vaughan, Harry Briggs, Jr. 1888-1964 WhAm 4
Vaughan, Hattie Buckley 1853- WomWWA 14
Vaughan, Hector W NewYHSD
Vaughan, Hendrix 1898-1959 NatCAB 48
Vaughan, Henry 1621?-1695 McGEWB
Vaughan, Herbert Hunter 1884-1948 WhAm 2
Vaughan, Horace Worth 1867-1922 BiDrAC,
WhAm 1
Vaughan, James Albert 1882-1941 NatCAB 34
Vaughan, James W NewYHSD
Vaughan, Sir John 1738-1795 ApCAB, Drake
Vaughan, John 1775-1807 ApCAB
Vaughan, John Apthorp 1795-1865 ApCAB
Vaughan, John Colin 1871-1940 WhAm 1
Vaughan, John Fairfield 1872-1953 NatCAB 40
Vaughan, John Gaines 1858-1921 WhAm 1
Vaughan, John George 1878-1948 NatCAB 37,
WhAm 2
Vaughan, John Henry 1880- WhAm 1
Vaughan, John Russell 1888-1952 WhAm 3
Vaughan, John Samuel 1885-1951 WhAm 3
Vaughan, John Walter 1880-1949 WhAm 2
Vaughan, Lawrence J 1864-1909 WhAm 1
Vaughan, Mary Drew 1872- WomWWA 14
Vaughan, Myra McAlmont WomWWA 14
Vaughan, N J NewYHSD
Vaughan, Raymond Coleman 1887-1964
NatCAB 51
Vaughan, Richard Miner 1870-1954 WhAm 3
Vaughan, Robert Ferguson 1887-1949
NatCAB 40
Vaughan, Sue Landon 1835- NatCAB 14
Vaughan, Thomas Wayland 1870-1952
DcAmB S5, NatCAB 38, NatCAB 47,
WhAm 3
Vaughan, Victor Clarence 1851-1929 AmBi,
ApCAB X, DcAmB, NatCAB 12,
NatCAB 29, WhAm 1
Vaughan, Warren Taylor 1893-1944
NatCAB 33, WhAm 2
Vaughan, Wayland Farries 1901-1961 WhAm 4
Vaughan, Sir William 1577-1640? ApCAB,
Drake
Vaughan, William 1703-1746 ApCAB, Drake
Vaughan, William Hutchinson 1899-1972
WhAm 5
Vaughan, William Wirt 1831-1878 BiAUS,
BiDrAC, WhAm H
Vaughan Williams, Ralph 1872-1958 McGEWB,
WhAm 3
Vaughn, Albert Clinton, Sr. 1894-1951 BiDrAC
Vaughn, Earnest VanCourt 1877- WhAm 5
Vaughn, Francis Arthur 1871-1934 WhAm 1
Vaughn, Howard 1890-1953 NatCAB 41
Vaughn, James 1898-1957 NatCAB 43
Vaughn, Mrs. Marion WomWWA 14
Vaughn, Robert 1836- ApCAB X
Vaughn, Robert Gallaway 1868- WhAm 3

Vaughn, Samuel Jesse 1877- WhAm 5
Vaughn, William James 1834- WhAm 1
Vaught, Edgar Sullins 1873-1959 WhAm 3
Vaugiraud, Pierre Rene Marie, Comte De
1741-1819 ApCAB
Vauquelin 1726-1763 ApCAB
Vauquelin, Louis Nicolas 1763-1829 AsBiEn
Vauquelin, Nicolas Louis 1763-1829 DcScB
Vauthier, Lucy Mary Woodward 1877-
WomWWA 14
Vautin, N NewYHSD
Vautrin, Minnie 1886-1941 NotAW
Vaux, Calvert 1824-1895 AmBi, ApCAB,
DcAmB, NatCAB 9, TwCBDA,
WhAm H
Vaux, George, Jr. 1863-1927 WhAm 1
Vaux, Richard 1816-1895 ApCAB, BiDrAC,
DcAmB, NatCAB 3, TwCBDA,
WhAm H
Vaux, Richard 1817-1895 Drake
Vaux, Roberts 1786-1836 ApCAB, BiAUS,
DcAmB, Drake, NatCAB 15, WhAm H
Vaux, William Sansom 1811-1882 ApCAB
Vaux-Royer, Rose M De 1861- WomWWA 14
Vavilov, Nikolai Ivanovich 1887-1943 McGEWB
Vavilov, Nikolay Ivanovich 1887-1943
DcScB Sup
Vavilov, Sergey Ivanovich 1891-1951 DcScB
Vavra, A Stephan 1869-1947 NatCAB 36
Vavra, Frank Joseph 1898-1967 IIBEAAW
Vavruska, Frank d1974 WhAm 6
Vawter, Charles Erastus 1841-1905 BiDAmEd,
DcAmB, WhAm 1
Vawter, Edwin James 1848-1914 NatCAB 32
Vawter, Edwin James, Jr. 1871-1926
NatCAB 20
Vawter, Jamison 1889-1959 NatCAB 50
Vawter, John 1782-1862 ApCAB
Vawter, John William 1871-1941 WhAm 1
Vawter, Keith 1872-1937 WhAm 1
Vawter, William Arthur 1858-1921 NatCAB 19
Vayhinger, Culla Johnson 1867- WomWWA 14
Vayhinger, Monroe 1855-1938 WhAm 1
Veach, Robert Wells 1871- WhAm 5
Veal, Frank Richard 1913-1969 WhAm 5
Veale, Moses 1832- NatCAB 1
Veasey, Clarence Archibald 1869-1957
NatCAB 47, WhAm 3
Veasey, Clarence Archibald, Jr. 1895-1960
NatCAB 50
Veasey, Thomas NewYHSD
Veatch, Arthur Clifford 1876-1938 NatCAB 29
Veatch, Arthur Clifford 1878-1938 DcAmB S2,
WhAm 1
Veatch, Byron Elbert 1858-1930 WhAm 1
Veatch, George Lovett 1871- ApCAB X
Veatch, James Clifford 1819-1895 ApCAB,
TwCBDA
Veatch, Nathan Thomas 1886-1975 WhAm 6
Veazey, I Parker 1882-1963 WhAm 4
Veazey, Thomas Ward 1774-1842 DcAmB,
Drake, WhAm H
Veazey, Thomas Ward 1774-1848 BiAUS,
NatCAB 9, TwCBDA
Veazey, Wheelock Graves 1835-1898
ApCAB Sup, NatCAB 4, TwCBDA
Veazey, William Reed 1883-1958 NatCAB 47
Veazie, George Augustus 1835-1915 WhAm 1
Veazie, Jesse Clarence 1871-1952 NatCAB 41
Vebell, Edward T 1921- IIBEAAW
Veblen, Andrew Anderson 1848-1932 WhAm 1
Veblen, Oswald 1880-1960 BiDAmEd, DcScB,
WebAB, WhAm 4
Veblen, Thorstein Bunde 1857-1929 AmBi,
DcAmB, EncAAH, EncAB, McGEWB,
NatCAB 21, WebAB, WhAm 1
Vecki, Victor G 1857-1938 WhAm 1
Vedder, Beverly Blair 1877-1955 WhAm 3
Vedder, Charles Stuart 1826-1917 NatCAB 9,
WhAm 1
Vedder, Commodore Perry 1838-1910
NatCAB 2, WhAm 1
Vedder, Edward Bright 1878-1952 DcAmB S5,
NatCAB 41, WhAm 3
Vedder, Elihu 1836-1923 AmBi, ApCAB,
ApCAB X, BnEnAmA, DcAmB, Drake,
NatCAB 6, NewYHSD, TwCBDA,
WhAm 1

Vedder, Henry Clay 1853-1935 DcAmB S1,
WhAm 1
Vedder, Neil Davis 1880-1957 NatCAB 46
Veditz, Charles William Augustus 1872-1926
NatCAB 23, WhAm 1
Veeck, William Louis, Jr. 1914- WebAB
Veeder, Albert Henry 1844-1914 ApCAB X,
NatCAB 16, WhAm 1, WhAm 1C
Veeder, Curtis Hussey 1862-1943 NatCAB 15,
NatCAB 35, WhAm 2
Veeder, Emily Elizabeth AmWom
Veeder, Henry 1867-1942 ApCAB X,
WhAm 2
Veeder, Major Albert 1848-1915 WhAm 1
Veeder, VanVechten 1867-1942 WhAm 2
Veeder, William Davis 1835-1910 BiDrAC
Veeneman, William H d1968 WhAm 5
Vega, Feliciano De 1580-1640 ApCAB
Vega, Ventura DeLa 1807-1865 ApCAB
Vehslage, John Herman George 1842-1904
BiDrAC
Veigl, Franz Xavier 1723-1798 ApCAB
Veiler, Joseph NewYHSD
Veiller, Bayard 1869-1943 NatCAB 33
Veintimilla, Ignacio De 1830?- ApCAB
Veitch, Fletcher Pearre 1868-1943 WhAm 2
Vejdovsky, Frantisek 1849-1939 DcScB,
DcScB Sup
Veksler, Vladimir Iosifovich 1907-1966 AsBiEn,
DcScB
Veksler, Vladimir Iosifovich 1908-1966
WhAm 4
Velarde, Hernan 1863-1935 WhAm 1
Velarde, Publita 1918- IIBEAAW
Velasco, Jose Maria 1840-1912 McGEWB
Velasco, Jose Miguel De 1790?-1859 ApCAB
Velasco, Juan De 1727-1819 ApCAB
Velasco, Luis 1535-1614 ApCAB
Velasco, Luis De 1500?-1564 ApCAB
Velasco, Luis De 1511-1564 McGEWB
Velasco, Luis Vicente 1710?-1762 ApCAB
Velasco, Pedro De 1581-1649 ApCAB
Velasco Ibarra, Jose Maria 1893- McGEWB
Velasquez, Diego d1523 Drake
Velazquez, Diego De 1460?-1532 ApCAB
Velazquez, Diego Rodriguez DeSilva Y
1599-1660 McGEWB
Velazquez, Hector 1865- WhAm 4
Velazquez Cardenas DeLeon, Joaquin 1732-1786
ApCAB
Velazquez DeCuellar, Diego 1465?-1523
McGEWB
Velazquez DeLaCadena, Mariano 1778-1860
ApCAB
Velde, Harold Himmel 1910- BiDrAC
Velde, Henry VanDe 1863-1957 McGEWB
Velez-Herrera, Ramon 1808-1887 ApCAB
Vellosino, Jayme Andrada 1639-1712 ApCAB
Velloso, Jose Mariano DaConceicao 1742-1811
ApCAB
Vellozo, Jose Mariano DaConceicao 1742-1811
DcScB
Velluto NewYHSD
Velpeau, Alfred 1795-1867 BiHiMed
Veltin, Louise DeLaunay d1934 WhAm 1,
WomWWA 14
Velvin, Ellen WhAm 1
Venable, Abraham B d1811 BiAUS, Drake
Venable, Abraham B 1760-1811 ApCAB,
NatCAB 11, TwCBDA
Venable, Abraham Bedford 1758-1811 BiDrAC,
WhAm H, WhAmP
Venable, Abraham W 1799-1876 BiAUS,
BiAUS Sup
Venable, Abraham Watkins 1799-1876 BiDConf,
BiDrAC, WhAm H, WhAmP
Venable, Abraham Woodson 1799-1876 ApCAB,
NatCAB 13
Venable, Charles Scott 1827-1900 ApCAB,
DcAmB, NatCAB 10, WhAm 1
Venable, Edward Carrington 1853-1908 BiDrAC
Venable, Emerson 1875- WhAm 6
Venable, Francis Preston 1856-1934 DcAmB,
NatCAB 13, NatCAB 28, TwCBDA,
WhAm 1
Venable, Frank Preston 1856-1934 ApCAB,
NatCAB 10
Venable, Joseph Glass 1877-1928 WhAm 1

Venable, Richard Morton 1839-1910 *WhAm 1*
Venable, Samuel Hoyt 1856- *ApCAB X*
Venable, William Edward 1804-1857 *BiAUS, NatCAB 13*
Venable, William Henry 1836-1920 *ApCAB, BiDAmEd, DcAmB, NatCAB 7, NatCAB 19, TwCBDA, WhAm 1*
Venable, William Mayo 1871-1955 *WhAm 3*
Venable, William Webb 1880-1948 *BiDrAC, WhAm 6*
Venant, Jean Barre De 1737-1810 *ApCAB*
Vendome, Louis Joseph, Duc De 1654-1712 *WhoMilH*
Venegas, Francisco Javier De 1760?-1820? *ApCAB*
Venegas, Miguel 1680-1764 *ApCAB*
Venel, Gabriel Francois 1723-1775 *DcScB*
Venemann, H Gerald 1884-1954 *WhAm 3*
Venetz, Ignatz 1788-1859 *DcScB*
Veniaminov, Ioann 1797-1879 *REnAW*
Vening Meinesz, Felix Andries 1887-1966 *DcScB, McGEWB*
Vening Meinisz, Felix 1887-1966 *WhAm 4*
Venino, Francis *NewYHSD*
Venizelos, Eleutherios 1864-1936 *McGEWB*
Venn, John 1834-1923 *DcScB*
Venne, Jus *NewYHSD*
Vennema, Ame 1857-1925 *WhAm 1*
Vennema, John 1871-1960 *WhAm 3A*
Vennor, Henry George 1840-1884 *ApCAB*
Ventadour, Henry DeL-LaVoute, Duke De 1595-1651 *ApCAB*
Venth, Carl 1860-1938 *NatCAB 12, NatCAB 18, WhAm 1*
Venting, Albert 1883-1965 *WhAm 4*
Ventres, Adelaide Brainerd *WomWWA 14*
Ventres, M P *IlBEAAW*
Ventris, Michael George Francis 1922-1956 *WhAm 4*
Venturi, Robert 1925- *BnEnAmA*
Venzke, Harry 1889-1949 *NatCAB 39*
Vera-Cruz, Alonso DeLa 1504-1584 *ApCAB*
Verandrye, Pierre Gautier DeV DeLa 1685-1749 *ApCAB*
Verantius, Faustus 1551-1617 *DcScB*
Verazzani, Jean d1525 *Drake*
Verbeck, Guido Fridolin 1887-1940 *WhAm 1*
Verbeck, Guido Herman Fridolin 1830-1898 *AmBi, ApCAB, DcAmB, WhAm H*
VerBeck, Hanna *WhAm 1*
Verbeck, William 1861-1930 *DcAmB, NatCAB 27, WhAm 1*
VerBeck, William Francis 1858-1933 *AmBi, WhAm 1, WhAm 4*
Verbeek, Gustave 1867- *WhAm 4*
Verbeke, Alexis O 1902-1964 *WhAm 4*
Verbrick, Richard *NewYHSD*
Verbrugghen, Henri 1873-1934 *DcAmB, WhAm 1*
VerBryck, Cornelius 1813-1844 *ApCAB, Drake, NewYHSD*
Verbryck, George Garrison 1895-1966 *NatCAB 53*
VerBryck, William 1823-1899 *NewYHSD*
Verbrycke, J Russell, Jr. 1885-1957 *NatCAB 43*
Vercheres, Mary Madeleine De 1678-1700 *ApCAB*
Verdaguer, Peter 1835-1911 *NatCAB 16, WhAm 1*
Verdelin, Henry 1899-1961 *NatCAB 50, WhAm 4*
Verden, Karl Von 1620?-1697 *ApCAB*
Verdery, Marion Jackson 1850-1924 *ApCAB X*
Verdet, Marcel Emile 1824-1866 *DcScB*
Verdi, Claudius *NewYHSD*
Verdi, Giuseppe Fortunino Francesco 1813-1901 *McGEWB*
Verdi, Tullio Suzzara 1829- *ApCAB*
Verdi, William Francis 1873- *WhAm 5*
Verdugo, Vicente 1690?-1775 *ApCAB*
Verdy DuVernois, Julius Von 1832-1910 *WhoMilH*
Vere, Maximilian 1820- *ApCAB*
VerEecke, Paul 1867-1959 *DcScB*
Vereen, Eugene Michael 1893-1969 *NatCAB 57*
Vereen, William Jerome 1885-1952 *WhAm 3*
Verelst, Francis *NewYHSD*
Verelst, John 1648-1719 *IlBEAAW*

Verendrye, Pierre G DeV, Sieur DeLa 1685-1749 *AmBi, DcAmB, Drake, WhAm H*
Vergara Y Zamoral, Diego Hernandez De 1526-1593 *ApCAB*
Vergennes, Comte De *WhAm H*
Vergennes, Charles Gravier, Count De 1717-1787 *ApCAB, Drake*
Verger, Peter C *NewYHSD*
Vergries, M *NewYHSD*
Verhaegen, Louis *NewYHSD*
Verhaegen, Peter Joseph 1800-1868 *DcAmB, WhAm H*
Verhagen, Aloysius Alphonsus 1869-1938 *WhAm 1*
Verhoeff, Frederick Herman 1874-1968 *NatCAB 55, WhAm 5*
Verhoeff, Herman 1827-1893 *NatCAB 30*
Verhuen, Jacobus 1709-1777 *ApCAB*
Verhulst, Pierre-Francois 1804-1849 *DcScB*
Verity, George Matthew 1865- *ApCAB X*
Verity, George Matthew 1865-1941 *WhAm 2*
Verity, George Matthew 1865-1942 *DcAmB S3*
Verity, Jonathan 1836-1917 *NatCAB 19*
Verkuyl, Gerrit 1872- *WhAm 5*
Verlaine, Paul Marie 1844-1896 *McGEWB*
Verleger, Charles Frederick *NewYHSD*
Verlenden, Jacob Serrill 1879- *WhAm 6*
Verliger, Charles Frederick *NewYHSD*
VerLinden, Edward 1869-1941 *NatCAB 36*
Vermeer, Jan 1632-1675 *McGEWB*
Vermeule, Cornelius Clarkson 1858-1950 *NatCAB 14, WhAm 2*
Vermeule, John Davis 1822-1915 *NatCAB 8*
Vermilion, Charles William 1866-1927 *WhAm 1*
Vermilya, Charles E 1872- *WhAm 5*
Vermilye, Ashbel Green 1822- *ApCAB*
Vermilye, Elizabeth B 1858- *WomWWA 14*
Vermilye, Herbert 1887-1950 *NatCAB 38*
Vermilye, Kate Jordan d1926 *WhAm 1, WomWWA 14*
Vermilye, Kate Jordan 1862-1926 *DcAmB*
Vermilye, Kate Jordan 1871-1926 *NatCAB 20*
Vermilye, Robert George 1813-1875 *ApCAB*
Vermilye, Thomas Edward 1803-1893 *ApCAB, NatCAB 10*
Vermilye, William Moorhead 1880-1944 *NatCAB 33, WhAm 2*
Vermonnet *NewYHSD*
Vermont, Eloi Lemercier B, Marquis De 1762-1832 *ApCAB*
Vernadsky, George 1887-1973 *WhAm 6*
Vernadsky, Vladimir Ivanovich 1863-1945 *DcScB*
Vernam, Almeda *WomWWA 14*
Verne, Jules 1828-1905 *McGEWB*
Vernelle, Bernard *NewYHSD*
Verner, Frederick Arthur 1836-1928 *IlBEAAW*
Verner, James 1818-1901 *NatCAB 12*
Verner, Murry A 1852- *NatCAB 12*
Verner, Samuel Phillips 1873- *WhAm 5*
Vernert, Leon Job *NewYHSD*
Vernet, Charles *NewYHSD*
Verneuil, Philippe Edouard Poulletier De 1805-1873 *DcScB*
Vernier, Chester Garfield 1881-1949 *NatCAB 37, WhAm 2*
Vernier, Pierre 1584-1638 *DcScB*
Vernier, Wesley *NewYHSD*
Vernlund, Carl Frithiof 1885-1973 *NatCAB 57*
Vernon, Ambrose White 1870- *WhAm 5*
Vernon, Clarence Clark 1896-1948 *WhAm 2*
Vernon, Edward 1684-1757 *ApCAB, Drake*
Vernon, Howard Wills 1867-1942 *NatCAB 31*
Vernon, James William 1886-1955 *WhAm 3*
Vernon, Jane Marchant Fisher 1796-1869 *ApCAB, Drake, NatCAB 10*
Vernon, Leroy Monroe 1838-1896 *NatCAB 2*
Vernon, Leroy Tudor 1878-1938 *NatCAB 28, WhAm 1*
Vernon, Paul Egbert 1869-1957 *NatCAB 44*
Vernon, Robert Orion 1912-1974 *WhAm 6*
Vernon, S Geraldine *WomWWA 14*
Vernon, Samuel 1683-1737 *DcAmB, WhAm H*
Vernon, Samuel Milton 1841-1920 *WhAm 1*
Vernon, Thomas 1824?-1872 *NewYHSD*
Vernon, William 1719-1806 *DcAmB, NatCAB 8, WhAm H*
Vernon, William Tecumseh 1871- *WhAm 5,*

WhoColR
Vernor, James 1843-1927 *NatCAB 22*
Vernor, Richard Edward 1890-1958 *WhAm 3*
Vernoy, William Broadbent 1883-1959 *NatCAB 47*
Veronda, Maurice 1892-1961 *WhAm 4*
Veronese, Giuseppe 1854-1917 *DcScB*
Veronese, Paolo 1528-1588 *McGEWB*
Verot, Augustin 1804-1876 *NatCAB 12*
Verot, Augustine 1804-1876 *ApCAB*
Verot, Jean Marcel Pierre Auguste 1805-1876 *DcAmB, WhAm H*
Verot, Jean Marcellus Pierre Auguste 1805-1876 *TwCBDA*
Verot, Jean Pierre Augustin Marcellin 1805-1876 *BiDConf, DcAmReB*
Verplanck, Daniel Crommelin 1761-1834 *ApCAB, BiAUS*
Verplanck, Daniel Crommelin 1762-1834 *BiDrAC, WhAm H, WhAmP*
Verplanck, Gulian 1751-1799 *NatCAB 11*
Verplanck, Gulian Crommelin 1786-1870 *AmBi, ApCAB, BiAUS, BiDrAC, DcAmB, Drake, NatCAB 5, TwCBDA, WhAm H*
Verplanck, Gullian Crommelin 1786-1870 *WhAmP*
Verplanck, Isaac A 1812-1873 *ApCAB*
Verplanck, Katharine Rankin Wolcott 1855- *WomWWA 14*
VerPlanck, William Gordon 1861-1931 *NatCAB 24*
Verplank, Grover Lawrence 1887-1965 *NatCAB 50*
Verrall, Richard P 1868-1952 *WhAm 3*
Verrazano, Giovanni Da 1480?-1527? *AmBi, WhAm H*
Verrazano, Giovanni Da 1485?-1528? *McGEWB*
Verrazano, Giovanni De 1470-1527 *ApCAB*
Verreau, Hospice-Anthelme Jean Baptiste 1828- *ApCAB*
Verree, John Paul 1817-1889 *BiDrAC, WhAm H*
Verree, John Paul 1819-1889 *BiAUS*
Verren, Antoine 1801-1874 *ApCAB*
Verrick, William *NewYHSD*
Verrill, Addison Emery 1839-1926 *DcAmB, DcScB, NatCAB 21, WhAm 1*
Verrill, Addison Emory 1830-1926 *NatCAB 3*
Verrill, Addison Emory 1839-1926 *AmBi, ApCAB, TwCBDA*
Verrill, Alpheus Hyatt 1871-1954 *DcAmB S5, WhAm 3*
Verrill, Charles Henry 1866-1928 *WhAm 1*
Verrill, Elmer Russell 1881- *WhAm 6*
Verrill, Harry Mighels 1868-1964 *NatCAB 52, WhAm 5*
Verrill, Robinson 1896-1970 *WhAm 5*
Verrocchio, Andrea Del 1435-1488 *McGEWB*
Verschoor, Julius Wilhelm Van 1575-1640 *ApCAB*
Versfelt, William H 1898-1956 *WhAm 3*
Verson, David C 1894-1969 *WhAm 5*
Verson, John 1895-1960 *NatCAB 47*
VerSteeg, Karl 1891-1952 *WhAm 3*
Verstille, William 1755?-1803 *NewYHSD*
Vertes, Marcel 1895-1961 *WhAm 4*
Vertin, John 1844-1899 *ApCAB, NatCAB 12, TwCBDA*
Verulam, Baron *DcScB*
Vervoort, V *NewYHSD*
Verwoerd, Hendrik Frensch 1901-1966 *McGEWB, WhAm 4*
Verworn, Max 1863-1921? *DcScB*
Verwyst, Chrysostom Adrian 1841-1925 *DcAmB*
Very, Frank Washington 1852-1927 *NatCAB 12, WhAm 1*
Very, Jones 1813-1880 *AmBi, ApCAB, DcAmB, Drake, NatCAB 6, WebAB, WhAm H*
Very, Lydia Louisa Ann 1823-1901 *DcAmB*
Very, Lydia Louisa Anna 1823-1901 *AmWom, ApCAB, NatCAB 6, WhAm 1*
Very, Samuel Williams 1846-1919 *TwCBDA, WhAm 1*
Vesalius, Andreas 1514-1564 *AsBiEn, BiHiMed, DcScB, McGEWB*
Vesey, Denmark 1767?-1822 *AmBi, ApCAB,*

DcAmB, EncAAH, EncAB, McGEWB,
WebAB, WhAm H
Vesey, Telemaque 1767?-1822 *DcAmB*
Vesey, Thomas *NewYHSD*
Vesey, William 1674-1746 *ApCAB, DcAmB,*
NatCAB 1, TwCBDA, WhAm H
Vesling, Johann 1598-1649 *DcScB*
Vespasian 009-079 *McGEWB*
Vesper, Frederick William August 1873-1946
NatCAB 36
Vespucci, Amerigo 1451-1512 *Drake,*
WhAm H
Vespucci, Amerigo 1452-1512 *TwCBDA*
Vespucci, Amerigo 1454-1512 *McGEWB,*
WebAB
Vespucius, Americus 1451-1512 *NatCAB 3*
Vessella, Oreste 1877- *WhAm 5*
Vessey, Robert Scadden 1858- *NatCAB 14,*
WhAm 4
Vessiot, Ernest 1865-1952 *DcScB*
Vest, George Graham 1830-1904 *ApCAB,*
BiDConf, BiDrAC, DcAmB, NatCAB 2,
TwCBDA, WhAm 1, WhAmP
Vest, H Grant 1908-1972 *WhAm 5*
Vest, Samuel Alexander, Jr. 1905-1958
WhAm 3
Vest, Walter Edward 1882-1962 *WhAm 4*
Vestal, Albert Henry 1875-1932 *BiDrAC,*
WhAm 1, WhAmP
Vestal, Edward McMillan 1881-1946
NatCAB 35
Vestal, Mrs. P E *WomWWA 14*
Vestal, Samuel Curtis 1873-1958 *WhAm 3*
Vestal, Stanley 1887-1957 *REnAW*
Vestin, John 1844-1889 *WhAm 1*
Vestine, Ernest Harry 1906-1968 *WhAm 5*
Vestling, Axel Ebenezer 1879-1944 *WhAm 2*
Vesugar, Jamshed 1894-1971 *NatCAB 56*
Vetch, James 1789-1869 *ApCAB*
Vetch, Samuel 1668-1732 *ApCAB, DcAmB,*
Drake, WhAm H
Veth, Martin 1874- *WhAm 5*
Vethake, Adriana *NewYHSD*
Vethake, Henry 1792-1866 *ApCAB, DcAmB,*
Drake, NatCAB 1, NatCAB 3, TwCBDA,
WhAm H
Vetromile, Eugene 1819-1880 *ApCAB*
Veuducourt *NewYHSD*
Veuillot, Desire 1653-1732 *ApCAB*
Veyra, Mrs. Jaime C De 1876- *WhAm 5*
Veyra, Jaime Carlos De 1873- *WhAm 5*
Veyrier, Joseph *NewYHSD*
Veytia, Mariano 1718-1779 *ApCAB*
Vezin, Charles 1858-1942 *WhAm 2*
Vezin, Herman 1829-1910 *NatCAB 5*
Vezin, Hermann 1829-1910 *ApCAB, DcAmB*
Via, Lemuel R 1873- *WhAm 5*
Vial, George McNaughten 1850-1915
ApCAB X, NatCAB 16
Vial, Pedro 1746?-1814 *REnAW*
Viale, Agostinho 1620?-1667 *ApCAB*
Viall, Ethan 1873-1949 *WhAm 3*
Viall, Richmond 1896-1973 *WhAm 6*
Vian, Sir Philip 1894-1968 *WhWW-II*
Viana, Francisco De 1530?-1609 *ApCAB*
Viana, Miguel Pereira, Viscount De 1779-1838
ApCAB
Vianden, Heinrich 1814-1899 *NewYHSD*
Vianney, Jean Baptiste, Saint 1786-1859
McGEWB
Viaut, Andre Jules Armand 1899-1973 *WhAm 6*
Vibbard, Chauncey 1811-1891 *BiDrAC,*
DcAmB, WhAm H
Vibbard, Chauncy 1811-1891 *BiAUS*
Vibbert, William H 1839-1918 *WhAm 1*
Vicary, Arthur Charles 1882-1963 *NatCAB 51*
Vicente, Esteban 1906- *BnEnAmA*
Vicente, Gil 1465?-1536? *McGEWB*
Vicente Y Bennazar, Andres *ApCAB*
Vichert, John Frederick 1874-1948 *WhAm 2*
Vick, James 1818-1882 *ApCAB, DcAmB,*
NatCAB 4, TwCBDA, WebAB,
WhAm H
Vick, Robert Ellsworth 1914-1967 *WhAm 5*
Vick, Walker Whiting 1878-1926 *WhAm 1*
Vickers, Alonzo Knox 1853-1915 *WhAm 4*
Vickers, Enoch Howard 1869- *WhAm 5*
Vickers, George 1801-1879 *ApCAB, BiAUS,*

BiDrAC, NatCAB 7, TwCBDA,
WhAm H
Vickers, George Morley 1841- *NatCAB 4,*
WhAm 4
Vickers, James Cator 1877- *WhAm 5*
Vickers, Thomas 1835-1917 *NatCAB 28*
Vickery, Herman Frank 1856-1940 *WhAm 1*
Vickery, Howard Leroy 1892-1946 *DcAmB S4,*
NatCAB 40, WebAMB, WhAm 2
Vickery, J Allen 1905-1957 *NatCAB 47*
Vickner, Edwin Johan 1878-1958 *NatCAB 48*
Vickrey, Charles Vernon 1876-1966 *WhAm 4*
Vickrey, Fanny Randolph 1865- *WomWWA 14*
Vico, Domingo De 1485-1555 *ApCAB*
Vico, Giambattista 1668-1744 *McGEWB*
Vicq D'Azyr, Felix 1748-1794 *DcScB*
Victor Amadeus II 1666-1732 *McGEWB,*
WhoMilH
Victor Emmanuel II 1820-1878 *McGEWB*
Victor Emmanuel III 1869-1947 *McGEWB,*
WhWW-II
Victor, Alexander F 1878-1961 *WhAm 4*
Victor, Claude-Victor Perrin 1766-1841
WhoMilH
Victor, Frances Auretta Fuller 1826-1902
AmWom, ApCAB, DcAmB, NatCAB 13,
NotAW, REnAW, TwCBDA, WhAm H
Victor, John Harvey d1957 *WhAm 3*
Victor, Metta Victoria Fuller 1831- *Drake*
Victor, Metta Victoria Fuller 1831-1885
AmWom, NotAW
Victor, Metta Victoria Fuller 1831-1886 *ApCAB,*
NatCAB 4, TwCBDA, WhAm H
Victor, Michael *NewYHSD*
Victor, Orville James 1827-1910 *ApCAB,*
DcAmB, Drake, NatCAB 10,
NatCAB 11, TwCBDA, WhAm 1
Victoria 1819-1901 *McGEWB*
Victoria, Guadalupe 1789-1843 *ApCAB*
Victoria, Pedro De *ApCAB*
Victoria, Tomas d1600? *ApCAB*
Victoria, Tomas Luis De 1548?-1611 *McGEWB*
Victorio 1809?-1880 *REnAW*
Victory, John Patrick 1837- *WhAm 4*
Vicuna, Benjamin Vicuna-Mackenna 1831-1886
ApCAB
Vicuna, Manuel 1778-1843 *ApCAB*
Vicuna, Pedro Felix 1806-1874 *ApCAB*
Vidal, Alexander 1819- *ApCAB*
Vidal, Eugene Luther 1895-1969 *WhAm 5*
Vidal, Francisco Antonio 1827- *Drake*
Vidal, Gore 1925- *WebAB*
Vidal, J-B Emile 1825-1893 *BiHiMed*
Vidal, Michel 1824- *BiDrAC, WhAm H*
Vidal DeLaBlache, Paul 1845-1918 *McGEWB*
Vidaurre, Manuel Lorenzo De 1773-1841
ApCAB
Vidaurri, Santiago 1803?-1867 *ApCAB, Drake*
Vidaver, Sidney Joseph 1910-1969 *WhAm 5*
Videl, Michel *BiAUS*
Vidmer, George 1871-1952 *NatCAB 46,*
WhAm 5
Vidus Vidius *DcScB*
Viebahn, Charles Frederick 1842-1915
NatCAB 17
Vieder, Alfred *NewYHSD*
Viehoever, Arno 1885-1969 *NatCAB 55,*
WhAm 5
Vieira, Antonio 1608-1697 *ApCAB, McGEWB*
Vieira, Joao Fernandes 1600?-1660? *ApCAB*
Viel, Etienne Bernard Alexandre 1736-1821
ApCAB, WhAm H
Viel, Francois Etienne Bernard Alexandre
1736-1821 *DcAmB*
Viele, Aernout Cornelissen 1640-1704? *DcAmB*
Viele, Aernout Cornellissen 1640-1704
WhAm H
Viele, Arnaud Cornelius 1620?-1700? *ApCAB*
Viele, Charles Delavan 1841-1916 *WhAm 1*
Viele, Egbert L 1825-1902 *Drake*
Viele, Egbert Lodovikus 1825-1902 *TwCBDA*
Viele, Egbert Ludovicus 1825-1902 *BiDrAC*
Viele, Egbert Ludovecus 1825-1902 *NatCAB 2*
Viele, Egbert Ludovickus 1825-1902 *ApCAB,*
WhAm 1
Viele, Egbert Ludovicus 1825-1902 *AmBi,*
DcAmB
Viele, Egbert Ludovicus 1863-1937 *WhAm 1*

Viele, Herman Knickerbocker 1856-1908
NatCAB 14, WhAm 1
Viele, John Ludovickus 1788-1832 *ApCAB*
Viele, Kathlyne Knickerbacker 1853-
WomWWA 14
Vielleret, Pierre *NewYHSD*
Viener, Hyman 1882-1969 *NatCAB 54*
Vier, August Peter 1842-1910 *ApCAB X*
Vier, Edmund Aloysius 1881- *ApCAB X*
Viereck, George Sylvester 1884-1962 *WhAm 4*
Viereck, Louis C 1911-1969 *WhAm 5*
Vierheller, Irvin Theodore 1888-1961
NatCAB 50
Vierra, Carlos 1876-1937 *IIBEAAW*
Viesselman, Percival William 1890-1946
WhAm 2
Vieta, Franciscus 1540-1603 *AsBiEn*
Viete, Francois 1540-1603 *DcScB*
Vieth, Henry Alvin 1870- *WhAm 5*
Vietor, Agnes C *WomWWA 14*
Vietor, Frederick Albert 1891-1941 *NatCAB 30*
Vietor, George Frederick 1839-1910 *WhAm 1*
Vietor, John Adolf 1884-1944 *NatCAB 33*
Vietor, Karl 1892-1951 *WhAm 3*
Viett, George Frederic 1868- *WhAm 3*
Vieussens, Raymond 1635?-1715 *DcScB*
Vieussens, Raymond De 1641-1715 *BiHiMed*
Vieweg, Frederic d1947 *WhAm 2*
Vigani, John Francis 1650?-1713 *DcScB*
Viger, Denis Benjamin 1774-1861 *ApCAB*
Viger, James 1787-1858 *ApCAB, Drake*
Vigier, George 1710?-1779 *ApCAB*
Vignan, Nicolas 1587?-1630? *ApCAB*
Vignaud, Henry 1830-1922 *DcAmB, WhAm 1*
Vignaud, Jean Henry 1830-1922 *AmBi,*
ApCAB
Vigne, Charles DeLa 1530?-1565 *ApCAB*
Vignec, Alfred J 1905-1962 *WhAm 4*
Vignes, Jean Paul 1779-1862 *EncAAH*
Vigness, Lauritz Andreas 1864-1947 *WhAm 2*
Vignier, A *NewYHSD*
Vignola, Giacomo Da 1507-1573 *McGEWB*
Vignoles, Charles Blacker 1793-1875
NewYHSD
Vignos, Blanche 1870- *WomWWA 14*
Vigny, Alfred Victor, Comte De 1797-1863
McGEWB
Vigo, Francis 1747-1835 *ApCAB*
Vigo, Giovanni Da 1450-1525 *DcScB*
Vigo, Joseph Maria Francesco 1747-1836
DcAmB, WhAm H
Vigorito, Joseph Phillip 1918- *BiDrAC*
Vigran, Nathan 1893-1972 *WhAm 5*
Viguers, Richard Thomson 1911-1969
NatCAB 57, WhAm 5
Viguers, Ruth Hill 1903-1971 *BiDAmEd,*
WhAm 5
Vijayananda *DcScB*
Vijitavongs, Phya 1877- *WhAm 5*
Viko, Eindred 1863-1921 *NatCAB 6*
Viko, Louis Eindred 1896-1968 *NatCAB 54*
Vilas, Charles Harrison 1846-1920 *WhAm 1*
Vilas, Charles Nathaniel 1852-1931 *NatCAB 24*
Vilas, George Byron 1868- *WhAm 5*
Vilas, George Hooker 1835-1907 *ApCAB X*
Vilas, Malcolm Gorham 1857- *ApCAB X*
Vilas, William Freeman 1840-1908 *AmBi,*
ApCAB, ApCAB X, BiDrAC, BiDrUSE,
DcAmB, NatCAB 2, TwCBDA,
WhAm 1, WhAmP
Vilatte, Joseph Rene 1854- *WhAm 4*
Vilbrandt, Frank Carl 1893-1960 *NatCAB 49,*
WhAm 4
Viles, Blaine Spooner 1879-1943 *WhAm 2*
Viles, Jonas 1875-1948 *WhAm 2*
Viljoen, Benjamin Johannis 1868- *WhAm 4*
Villa, Francisco 1878-1923 *McGEWB,*
WhAm HA, WhAm 4
Villa, Hernando Gonzalo 1881-1952 *IIBEAAW*
Villa-Lobos, Heitor 1884-1959 *WhAm 3*
Villa-Lobos, Heitor 1887-1959 *McGEWB*
Villa-Real, Antonio 1880- *WhAm 6*
Villadarias, Manoel D C Centenera De
1690-1759 *ApCAB*
Villafane, Angel De d1548 *ApCAB*
Villagra, Gaspar De 1550?-1620? *ApCAB*
Villagra, Gaspar Perez De d1620? *WhAm H*
Villagra, Gaspar Perez De 1555?-1620? *DcAmB*

Villagutierrez Y Sotomayor, Juan De *ApCAB*
Villalobos, Ruy Lopez De 1500?-1544 *ApCAB*
Villalpando, Juan Bautist 1552-1608 *DcScB*
Villalpando, Luis De 1480?-1560? *ApCAB*
Villamor, Ignacio 1863-1933 *WhAm 1*
Villani, Giovanni 1270?-1348 *McGEWB*
Villani, Ralph A 1901-1974 *WhAm 6*
Villano, Anthony Guy 1896-1970 *NatCAB 55*
Villanova *DcScB*
Villard DeHonnecourt 1190?- *DcScB*
Villard, Fanny Garrison 1844-1928 *DcAmB, NotAW*
Villard, Helen Frances Garrison 1844-1928 *DcAmB*
Villard, Henry 1835-1900 *AmBi, ApCAB, DcAmB, EncAB, NatCAB 3, REnAW, TwCBDA, WebAB, WhAm H*
Villard, Oswald Garrison 1872-1949 *DcAmB S4, EncAB, McGEWB, WebAB, WhAm 2*
Villard, Paul Ulrich 1860-1934 *AsBiEn, DcScB*
Villaret DeJoyeuse, Count Louis Thomas 1750-1812 *ApCAB*
Villari, Emilio 1836-1904 *DcScB*
Villaroel, Gaspar De 1587-1671 *ApCAB*
Villaroel, Gualberto 1907-1946 *WhAm 2*
Villars, Charles 1760?-1814 *ApCAB*
Villars, Claude Louis Hector, Duc De 1653-1734 *WhoMilH*
Villasenor Y Sanchez, Jose Antonio 1700?-1760? *ApCAB*
Villaume, Walter Francois 1902-1960 *NatCAB 48*
Villaverde, Cirilo 1812- *ApCAB*
Villeda-Morales, Ramon 1909-1971 *WhAm 5*
Villefranche *DcScB*
Villefranche, Charles Pierre De 1756-1809 *ApCAB*
Villegaignon, Nicolas Durand 1510-1571 *ApCAB*
Villegas Coras, Jose Antonio 1713-1785 *ApCAB*
Villehardouin, Geffroi De 1150?-1213 *McGEWB*
Villeneuve, Alexandre Louis Ducrest De 1777-1852 *ApCAB*
Villeneuve, J M Rodrigue 1883-1947 *WhAm 2*
Villeneuve, Jules Edmond Francois De 1804-1863 *ApCAB*
Villeneuve, Pierre Charles J Baptiste De 1763-1806 *ApCAB, WhoMilH*
Villepigue, John Bordenave 1830-1862 *ApCAB*
Villeraye, Charles S, Viscount De 1820?-1854 *ApCAB*
Villere, Charles J 1830-1899 *BiDConf*
Villere, Gabriel 1785-1852 *ApCAB, Drake*
Villere, Jacques 1761-1831 *ApCAB*
Villere, Jacques Philippe 1760-1830 *NatCAB 10*
Villere, Jacques Philippe 1761-1830 *DcAmB, WhAm H*
Villere, James Philip 1760-1830 *TwCBDA*
Villere, Jaquez *BiAUS, Drake*
Villere, Joseph Philippe Roy De d1769 *ApCAB*
Villere, Omer 1855-1911 *NatCAB 18*
Villere, Walter Peter 1885-1966 *NatCAB 54*
Villermet, Jules Guillaume Ferdinand De 1802-1859 *ApCAB*
Villers, Thomas Jefferson 1861- *WhAm 1*
Villiers, Frederick 1852-1922 *IlBEAAW*
Villiers, Jean Pierre d1672 *ApCAB*
Villon, Francois 1431-1463? *McGEWB*
Villon, Jacques 1875-1963 *WhAm 4*
Vilmer, Colby *NewYHSD*
Vilmorin, Pierre Louis F Leveque De 1816-1860 *DcScB*
Vilmot, Charles Stanislas 1749-1794 *ApCAB*
Vilter, Emil 1871-1940 *NatCAB 30*
Vimeur, Jean Baptiste Donatien De 1725-1807 *WhAm H*
Vin, Moyse Van 1627?-1678 *ApCAB*
Vinal, Harold 1891-1965 *WhAm 4*
Vinal, William Gould 1881- *WhAm 6*
Vinaver, Chemjo 1900-1973 *WhAm 6*
Vincennes, Sieur De *WhAm H*
Vincennes, Bissot M De d1736 *Drake*
Vincennes, Francois M Bissot, Sieur De 1700-1736 *AmBi, DcAmB*
Vincennes, J Baptiste Bissot, Sieur De 1668-1719 *AmBi, DcAmB*
Vincennes, Jean Baptiste Bissot 1688-1736 *ApCAB*

Vincent De Paul, Saint 1581-1660 *McGEWB*
Vincent Of Beauvais 1190?-1264? *DcScB*
Vincent, Albert Oliver 1842-1882 *ApCAB*
Vincent, Andrew Brown 1858- *WhoColR*
Vincent, Beverly Mills 1890- *BiDrAC*
Vincent, Bird J 1880-1931 *BiDrAC, WhAm 1, WhAm*
Vincent, Boyd 1845-1935 *ApCAB, NatCAB 13, TwCBDA, WhAm 1*
Vincent, Charles 1739-1794 *ApCAB*
Vincent, Clarence Augustus 1859-1943 *WhAm 2*
Vincent, Clarence Cornelius 1884-1934 *WhAm 1*
Vincent, Clinton Dermott 1914-1955 *WhAm 3*
Vincent, Clive Belden 1863-1936 *WhAm 1*
Vincent, Dean 1881-1963 *NatCAB 54*
Vincent, Earl Wright 1886-1953 *BiDrAC, NatCAB 47, WhAm 3*
Vincent, Edgar LaVerne 1851- *WhAm 4*
Vincent, Francis 1822-1884 *ApCAB*
Vincent, Frank 1848-1916 *AmBi, ApCAB, DcAmB, TwCBDA, WhAm 1*
Vincent, George Carothers 1813-1889 *NatCAB 13*
Vincent, George Edgar 1864-1941 *DcAmB S3, NatCAB 15, WhAm 1*
Vincent, Harold S 1900-1968 *WhAm 5*
Vincent, Harry Aiken 1864-1931 *WhAm 1*
Vincent, Henry Bethuel d1941 *WhAm 1*
Vincent, Mrs. James R *NotAW*
Vincent, Jesse Gurney 1880-1962 *NatCAB 52, WhAm 4*
Vincent, John 1765-1848 *ApCAB*
Vincent, John Carter 1900-1972 *WhAm 5*
Vincent, John Heyl 1832-1920 *AmBi, ApCAB, ApCAB X, BiDAmEd, DcAmB, EncAAH, McGEWB, NatCAB 9, NatCAB 24, TwCBDA, WebAB, WhAm 1*
Vincent, John Martin 1857-1939 *NatCAB 13, WhAm 1*
Vincent, Leon Henry 1859-1941 *WhAm 1*
Vincent, M Ella 1835- *WomWWA 14*
Vincent, Marvin Richardson 1834-1922 *AmBi, ApCAB, DcAmB, NatCAB 9, TwCBDA, WhAm 1*
Vincent, Mary Ann Farlow 1818-1887 *DcAmB, NatCAB 10, NotAW, WhAm H*
Vincent, Mary Anne Farlow 1818-1887 *AmBi, ApCAB*
Vincent, Mary Berta 1880- *WhoColR*
Vincent, Philip 1600-1638? *ApCAB, Drake*
Vincent, Sidney Coombe 1883-1944 *NatCAB 34*
Vincent, Strong 1837-1863 *ApCAB, Drake, NatCAB 7*
Vincent, Thomas MacCurdy 1832-1909 *WhAm 1*
Vincent, Thomas McCurdy 1832-1909 *ApCAB*
Vincent, Walter B 1845-1931 *WhAm 1*
Vincent, Wilber Ddwain 1876- *WhAm 5*
Vincent, William David 1866-1935 *WhAm 1*
Vincent, William Davis 1852-1922 *BiDrAC*
Vincent, William Henry 1859-1919 *NatCAB 18*
Vincenti, Francis *NewYHSD*
Vinci, Henry d1971 *WhAm 5*
Vinci, Leonardo Da *DcScB*
Vinckleback, William *NewYHSD*
Viner, Jacob 1892-1970 *WhAm 5*
Vines, Fred Daniel 1902-1965 *WhAm 4*
Vines, John Finley 1873- *WhAm 5*
Vines, Richard 1585?-1651 *ApCAB*
Vines, William Madison 1867- *WhAm 5*
Viney, Alvin Galt 1905-1962 *NatCAB 52*
Vingut, Francisco Javier 1823- *ApCAB*
Vingut, Gertrude 1830?- *ApCAB*
Vining, Edward Payson 1847-1920 *WhAm 1*
Vining, John 1758-1802 *ApCAB, BiAUS, BiDrAC, Drake, NatCAB 2, TwCBDA, WhAm H, WhAmP*
Vinje, Aad John 1857-1929 *WhAm 1*
Vinnedge, Sydney Dryden 1882-1946 *NatCAB 35*
Vinogradoff, Sir Paul Gavrilovitch 1854-1925 *McGEWB*
Vinogradsky, Sergey Nikolaevich 1856-1953 *DcScB*
Vinson, Albert Earl 1873- *WhAm 5*
Vinson, Arthur Ferle 1907-1963 *WhAm 4*

Vinson, Carl 1883- *BiDrAC, WhAmP*
Vinson, Fred Moore 1890-1953 *DcAmB S5, NatCAB 41*
Vinson, Frederic Moore 1890-1953 *WhAm 3*
Vinson, Frederick Moore 1890-1953 *BiDrAC, BiDrUSE, WebAB, WhAmP*
Vinson, Porter Paisley 1890-1959 *NatCAB 47*
Vinson, Robert Ernest 1876-1945 *WhAm 2*
Vinson, Taylor 1857-1929 *WhAm 1*
Vinson, William Ashton 1874-1951 *NatCAB 40, WhAm 3*
Vinsonhaler, Frank 1864-1942 *WhAm 2*
Vinton, Alexander Hamilton 1807-1881 *ApCAB, DcAmB, Drake, NatCAB 4, TwCBDA, WhAm H*
Vinton, Alexander Hamilton 1852-1911 *TwCBDA, WhAm 1*
Vinton, Arthur Dudley 1852-1906 *ApCAB, TwCBDA, WhAm 1*
Vinton, Calesta Holman 1809-1864 *ApCAB*
Vinton, David Hammond 1803-1873 *ApCAB, NatCAB 4*
Vinton, E P *NewYHSD*
Vinton, Ellen Amelia 1857- *WomWWA 14*
Vinton, Francis 1809-1872 *ApCAB, DcAmB, Drake, NatCAB 7, TwCBDA, WhAm H*
Vinton, Francis Laurens 1835-1879 *ApCAB, DcAmB, Drake, NatCAB 7, WhAm H*
Vinton, Frederic 1817-1890 *ApCAB, DcAmB, DcAmLiB, NatCAB 6, WhAm H*
Vinton, Frederic Porter 1846-1911 *AmBi, ApCAB Sup, DcAmB, NatCAB 5, TwCBDA, WhAm 1*
Vinton, Frederick 1817-1890 *TwCBDA*
Vinton, Frederick Porter 1846-1911 *ApCAB*
Vinton, John Adams 1801-1877 *ApCAB, Drake, NatCAB 5, TwCBDA, WhAm H*
Vinton, John Rogers 1801-1847 *ApCAB, Drake, NatCAB 9*
Vinton, Justus Hatch 1806-1858 *ApCAB*
Vinton, Maria Mitchell 1862- *WomWWA 14*
Vinton, Samuel Finley 1792-1862 *ApCAB, BiAUS, BiDrAC, DcAmB, TwCBDA, WhAm H, WhAmP*
Vinton, Warren Jay 1889-1969 *WhAm 5*
Vinton, William Bartleff 1862-1918 *NatCAB 6*
Vintschger, Edward John 1875-1955 *NatCAB 49*
Vintschger, Gustav 1847-1930 *NatCAB 26*
Vioget, Jean Jacques 1799-1855 *IlBEAAW, NewYHSD*
Viol, Charles Herman 1886-1928 *ApCAB X, NatCAB 35*
Violette, Ebal E 1880- *WhAm 6*
Violette, Willis Gordon *WhAm 4*
Violle, Jules Louis Gabriel 1841-1923 *DcScB*
Viollet-Le-Duc, Eugene Emmanuel 1814-1879 *McGEWB*
Viomenil, Antoine C DuHoux, Baron De 1728-1792 *ApCAB, Drake*
Viomenil, Antoine Louis DuHoux 1745-1788 *ApCAB*
Viomenil, Charles J Hyacinthe DuHoux De 1734-1827 *ApCAB, Drake*
Vipond, Jonathan d1954 *WhAm 3*
Vipond, Kenneth C 1880- *WhAm 6*
Virchow, Rudolf Ludwig Carl 1821-1902 *DcScB, McGEWB*
Virchow, Rudolph 1821-1902 *AsBiEn, BiHiMed*
VirDen, Ray 1895-1955 *WhAm 3*
Virey, Julien-Joseph 1775-1846 *DcScB*
Virgil 070BC-019BC *McGEWB*
Virgil, Almon Kincaid 1842- *WhAm 4*
Virgil, Antha Minerva d1939 *WhAm 1, WomWWA 14*
Virgil, Ebenezer Henry 1808-1892 *NatCAB 2*
Virgin, Edward Harmon 1876- *WhAm 5*
Virgin, Herbert Whiting 1872- *WhAm 5*
Virgin, Samuel Henderson 1842- *NatCAB 11*
Virkus, Frederick Adams d1955 *WhAm 3*
Virot, Claude Francis 1721-1759 *ApCAB*
Virtanen, Artturi Ilmari 1895-1973 *AsBiEn, DcScB, WhAm 6*
Virtue, Charles Franklin 1901-1971 *WhAm 5*
Virtue, George Olien 1861- *WhAm 5*
Vis, William Ryerson 1886-1969 *NatCAB 54*

Visanska, Sarah Bentschner 1870-
  WomWWA 14
Viscaino, Sebastian *Drake*
Vischer, Carl V 1866- *NatCAB 3*
Vischer, Carl Victor, Jr. 1896-1932 *NatCAB 25*
Vischer, Edward 1809-1879 *IIBEAAW,*
  NewYHSD
Visconti, Gian Galeazzo 1351-1402 *McGEWB*
Visconti, Luchino 1906-1976 *WhAm 6*
Visher, Stephen Sargent 1887-1967 *NatCAB 53,*
  WhAm 4A, WhAm 5
Vishinsky, Andrey 1885-1955 *WhWW-II*
Vishniac, Wolf Vladimir 1922-1973 *WhAm 6*
Visscher, J Paul 1895-1950 *WhAm 3*
Visscher, Max *NewYHSD*
Visscher, William Lightfoot 1842-1924 *DcAmB,*
  WhAm 1
Vitale, Ferruccio 1875-1933 *DcAmB,*
  NatCAB 31, WhAm 1
Vitali, Giuseppe 1875-1932 *DcScB*
Vitelo *DcScB*
Vitettl, Leonardo 1894-1973 *WhAm 6*
Vitoria, Francisco De 1483?-1546 *McGEWB*
Vitruvius 070?BC-025?BC *AsBiEn*
Vitruvius Pollio 070?BC-025?BC *DcScB Sup*
Vitry, Philippe De 1291-1360 *McGEWB*
Vits, George 1878-1933 *WhAm 1*
Vits, Henry 1842-1921 *NatCAB 39*
Vitt, Bruno Ceaser 1894-1966 *WhAm 4*
Vittorini, Elio 1908-1966 *McGEWB*
Vittorino Da Feltre 1378-1446 *McGEWB*
Vittum, Edmund March 1855-1938 *WhAm 1,*
  WhAm 2
Vittum, Harriet E 1872-1953 *WhAm 3*
Vivaldi, Antonio 1678-1741 *McGEWB*
Vivanco, Manuel Ignacio De 1806-1873 *ApCAB*
Vivekananda 1863-1902 *DcAmReB, McGEWB*
Vives, Juan Luis 1492-1540 *DcScB*
Vivian, Alfred 1867- *WhAm 4*
Vivian, Calthea Campbell 1870?- *IIBEAAW*
Vivian, Harold Acton 1877-1929 *WhAm 1*
Vivian, John Charles 1887-1964 *WhAm 4*
Vivian, John Frederick 1864-1954 *WhAm 3*
Vivian, Leslie Langdon 1891-1943 *NatCAB 33*
Vivian, Roxana Hayward 1871- *WomWWA 14*
Vivian, Thomas Jondrie 1858-1925 *WhAm 1*
Vivian, Weston Edward 1924- *BiDrAC*
Viviani, Vincenzo 1622-1703 *AsBiEn, DcScB*
Vivier, Jacques Du 1720-1793 *ApCAB*
Vizcaino, Sebastian 1550?-1615 *ApCAB*
Vizcaino, Sebastian 1550?-1628? *AmBi,*
  DcAmB, WhAm H
Vize, Vladimir Yulevich 1886-1954 *DcScB*
Vizetelly, Frank Horace 1864-1938 *AmBi,*
  DcAmB S2, NatCAB 30, WhAm 1
Vlacq, Adriaan 1600-1667? *DcScB*
Vladeck, Baruch Charney 1886-1938
  DcAmB S2
Vladimir I d1015 *McGEWB*
Vladimiroff, Pierre 1893-1970 *NatCAB 54*
Vlaminck, Maurice 1876-1958 *McGEWB*
Vlasov, Andrey 1900-1945 *WhWW-II*
Vocke, William 1839- *NatCAB 11*
Voegele, William Frederick 1876-1949
  NatCAB 42
Voegeli, Henry Edward 1876-1943 *WhAm 2*
Voegtlin, Carl 1879- *WhAm 4*
Voehringer, John Kasper, Jr. 1897-1967
  WhAm 5
Voelbel, Gordon William 1909-1965
  NatCAB 55
Voelker, Paul Frederick 1875- *WhAm 5*
Voetter, Thomas Wilson 1869- *WhAm 5*
Voeykov, Aleksandr Ivanovich 1842-1916 *DcScB*
Vogdes, Anthony Wayne 1843- *WhAm 4*
Vogdes, Israel 1816-1889 *ApCAB, Drake,*
  TwCBDA
Vogdes, Joseph *NewYHSD*
Vogdes, William 1802-1886 *ApCAB, Drake*
Voge, Richard George 1904-1948 *NatCAB 38*
Vogel, Augustus Hugo 1862-1930 *WhAm 1*
Vogel, Bertram 1918-1967 *NatCAB 54*
Vogel, Charles Pfister 1895-1959 *NatCAB 48,*
  WhAm 4
Vogel, Charles W 1870-1950 *WhAm 3*
Vogel, Clayton Barney 1882-1964 *WhAm 4*
Vogel, Edwin Chester 1883-1973 *WhAm 6*
Vogel, Emil *NewYHSD*

Vogel, Frank 1863-1932 *WhAm 1*
Vogel, Fred, Jr. d1936 *WhAm 1*
Vogel, Hermann Carl 1841-1907 *DcScB*
Vogel, Hermann Carl 1842-1907 *AsBiEn*
Vogel, Hyman Allen 1901-1958 *NatCAB 53*
Vogel, Joseph Richard 1895-1969 *WhAm 5*
Vogel, Joshua Holmes 1889-1970 *WhAm 5*
Vogel, Sir Julius 1835-1899 *McGEWB*
Vogel, Leo E 1863- *WhAm 4*
Vogel, Ralph Harold 1913-1969 *NatCAB 54*
Vogel, Robert Willis 1914-1971 *WhAm 5*
Vogel, Rudolph Emerson 1900-1971 *WhAm 5*
Vogelbach, Oscar 1897-1959 *NatCAB 48*
Vogelback, William Edward 1893-1960
  WhAm 3A
Vogeler, Rudolf Frederick 1902-1974 *WhAm 6*
Vogelgesang, Carl Theodore 1869-1927
  WhAm 1
Vogelgesang, Shepard 1901-1969 *WhAm 5*
Vogelsang, Alexander Theodore 1861-1930
  WhAm 1
Vogelstein, Hans Alfred 1904-1960 *WhAm 4*
Vogelstein, Ludwig 1871-1934 *NatCAB 27*
Vogeltanz, Edward Louis 1895-1968 *WhAm 5*
Vogler, E A *NewYHSD*
Vogler, John 1783-1881 *NewYHSD*
Vogler, William L 1898-1969 *WhAm 5*
Vogrich, Max Wilhelm Karl 1852-1916 *DcAmB*
Vogrich, Max William Charles 1852-1916
  NatCAB 8
Vogt, Carl 1817-1895 *DcScB*
Vogt, Carl James 1899-1965 *NatCAB 51*
Vogt, Ferdinand August 1896-1954 *NatCAB 43*
Vogt, Frederick Augustus 1859-1919
  NatCAB 23
Vogt, Harry Frederick 1883-1951 *NatCAB 39*
Vogt, Henry F 1879- *WhAm 6*
Vogt, Johan Hermann Lie 1858-1932 *DcScB*
Vogt, Paul Leroy 1878- *WhAm 6*
Vogt, Thorolf 1888-1958 *DcScB*
Vogt, V Ogden 1879-1964 *WhAm 4*
Vogt, William 1902-1968 *WhAm 5*
Vogue, Jean Pierre De 1570-1930 *ApCAB*
Voight, Lewis Towson *NewYHSD*
Voight, Walter Wilhelm 1879-1941 *NatCAB 31*
Voigt, Andrew 1867-1939 *REnAW*
Voigt, Andrew George 1859-1933 *WhAm 1*
Voigt, Charles 1876-1958 *NatCAB 48*
Voigt, Edward 1873-1934 *BiDrAC, WhAm 1,*
  WhAmP
Voigt, Elmer Gardner 1885-1962 *NatCAB 50*
Voigt, Irma Elizabeth 1882-1953 *WhAm 3*
Voigt, Johann Carl Wilhelm 1752-1821 *DcScB*
Voigt, Woldemar 1850-1919 *DcScB*
Voisin, Charles Antoine 1698-1764 *ApCAB*
Voisin, Pierre Joseph 1759-1821 *ApCAB*
Voislawsky, Antonie Phineas 1872-1939
  WhAm 1
Voit, Carl Von 1831-1908 *DcScB*
Voit, Karl Von 1831-1908 *AsBiEn*
Voit, William Julius 1880-1946 *NatCAB 35*
Voiture, Nicolas Auguste 1764?-1821 *ApCAB*
Volck, Adalbert John 1828-1912 *DcAmB,*
  NewYHSD
Volck, Frederick 1833-1891 *NewYHSD*
Vold, George Bryan 1896-1967 *NatCAB 54,*
  WhAm 4
Voldeng, Mathew Nelson 1863-1934 *WhAm 1*
Voldeng, Sadie Rosemond 1874- *WomWWA 14*
Volini, Italo Frederick 1893-1950 *WhAm 3*
Voliva, Wilbur Glenn 1870-1942 *NatCAB 32,*
  WhAm 2
Volk, Douglas 1856-1935 *AmBi, WhAm 1*
Volk, Harriet E Town *WomWWA 14*
Volk, Leonard Wells 1828-1895 *AmBi, ApCAB,*
  BnEnAmA, DcAmB, NatCAB 7,
  NewYHSD, TwCBDA, WhAm H
Volk, Lester David 1884-1962 *BiDrAC*
Volk, Stephen Arnold Douglas 1856-1935
  ApCAB, IIBEAAW, NatCAB 7, TwCBDA
Volker, William 1859-1947 *NatCAB 35,*
  WhAm 2
Volkert, Edward Charles 1871-1935 *WhAm 1*
Volkmann, Louise C A 1845- *WomWWA 14*
Volkmann, Paul Oskar Eduard 1856-1938 *DcScB*
Volkmar, Charles 1809?- *NewYHSD*
Volkov, Vladislav N 1935-1971 *WhAm 5*
Volland, Roscoe Henry 1877- *WhAm 5*

Vollbrecht, Justus Thomas 1900-1964
  NatCAB 52
Volleen, Frank *NewYHSD*
Vollintine, Minnie E G 1865- *WomWWA 14*
Vollmer, August 1876-1955 *WhAm 3*
Vollmer, Henry 1867-1930 *BiDrAC*
Vollmer, Hermann 1896-1959 *NatCAB 43*
Vollmer, John Phillip 1847-1917 *WhAm 1*
Vollmer, Karl 1869-1948 *NatCAB 36*
Vollmer, Lula d1955 *WhAm 3*
Vollmer, Philip 1860-1929 *NatCAB 22,*
  WhAm 1
Vollmer, Susan Homans 1869- *WomWWA 14*
Vollmer, William Auerbach 1886-1944
  NatCAB 40
Vollmering, Joseph 1810-1887 *ApCAB,*
  NewYHSD
Vollrath, Edward 1858-1931 *WhAm 1*
Vollrath, Edwin 1880-1944 *NatCAB 33*
Vollum, Edward P *NewYHSD*
Volney, Constantin-Francois C, Comte De
  1757-1820 *ApCAB, DcScB*
Volney, Constantine F C, Count De 1757-1820
  Drake
Volozan, Denis A *NewYHSD*
Volpe, Arnold 1869-1940 *WhAm 1*
Volpe, Arnold David 1870-1940 *NatCAB 29*
Volpe, John Anthony 1908- *BiDrUSE*
Volpe, Paul Anthony 1915-1968 *WhAm 5*
Volstead, Andrew J 1859-1947 *WhAm 2*
Volstead, Andrew John 1860-1947 *BiDrAC,*
  DcAmB S4, WhAmP
Volstead, Andrew Joseph 1859-1947
  NatCAB 41
Volta, Alessandro Giuseppe A Anastasio
  1745-1827 *AsBiEn, DcScB, McGEWB*
Voltaire 1694-1778 *AsBiEn, McGEWB*
Voltaire, Francois Marie Arouet De 1694-1778
  DcScB
Volterra, Vito 1860-1940 *DcScB*
Voltz, Philippe Louis 1785-1840 *DcScB*
Volwiler, Albert Tangeman 1888-1957
  NatCAB 47, WhAm 3
Volz, Charles Reginald 1905-1956 *NatCAB 43*
Volz, Edward J 1879- *WhAm 6*
VonBaer, Karl Ernst 1792-1876 *BiHiMed*
VonBeckh, H V A *IIBEAAW, NewYHSD*
VonBehring, Emil Adolf 1854-1917 *BiHiMed*
VonBekesy, Georg 1899-1972 *WhAm 5*
VonBerg, Charles L 1835-1918 *IIBEAAW*
VonBertalanffy, Ludwig 1901-1972 *WhAm 5*
VonBonnewitz, Orlando R 1868- *WhAm 5*
VonBrandes, W F *NewYHSD*
VonBraun *WebAMB*
VonBraun, Wernher 1912- *McGEWB, WebAB*
VonBrentano, Heinrich 1904-1964 *WhAm 4*
VonBriesen, Arthur 1843- *NatCAB 13*
Voncanon, Charles Banner 1872-1922
  NatCAB 19
VonCholtitz, Dietrich 1894-1966 *WhAm 4*
Vondel, Joost VanDen 1587-1679 *McGEWB*
VonderHaar, Edward P 1908-1973 *WhAm 6*
VonDerHeyde, Matthew Jennings 1906-1974
  WhAm 6
VonDerLauritz, Robert Eberhard Schmidt
  1806-1870 *WhAm H*
Vonderlehr, Raymond Aloysius 1897-1973
  WhAm 5
VonDerPalen-Klar, Adolphe J 1870- *ApCAB X*
VonDewall, Hans Werner 1901-1974 *WhAm 6*
VonDohlen, James Albert 1880-1945
  NatCAB 33
VonEgloffstein, F W 1824-1898 *IIBEAAW*
VonEgloffstein, Frederick W 1824-1885
  WhAm H
VonElm, Henry C 1887-1969 *NatCAB 55,*
  WhAm 5
VonEnde, Carl Leopold 1870-1934 *WhAm 1*
VonEngelken, Friedrich Johannes Hugo 1881-
  WhAm 4
VonEngeln, Oskar Deitrich 1880-1965 *WhAm 6*
VonEngeln, Oskar Dietrich 1880-1965
  NatCAB 54
VonEsmarch, Friedrich 1823-1908 *BiHiMed*
VonEuler-Chelpin, Hans 1873-1964 *WhAm 4*
VonFaber DuFaur, Curt 1890-1966 *WhAm 4*
VonFersen, Count *WhAm H*
VonFielitz, Alexander 1860- *WhAm 4*

VonFrantzius, Fritz 1865- *NatCAB 15*
VonFremd, Charles Spencer 1925-1966
WhAm 4
VonFrerichs, Friedrich Theodor 1819-1885
BiHiMed
VonGottschalck, Oscar Hunt 1865- *WhAm 4*
VonGraefe, F W E Albrecht 1828-1870 *BiHiMed*
VonGrave-Jonas, Elsa 1875- *WhAm 5*
VonGrunebaum, Gustave E 1909-1972 *WhAm 5*
VonGuttenberg, Karl Theodore 1921-1972
WhAm 5
VonHagen, Hugo Joseph 1866-1939 *NatCAB 38*
VonHaller, Albrecht 1708-1777 *BiHiMed*
VonHebra, Ferdinand 1816-1880 *BiHiMed*
VonHelmholtz, Hermann 1821-1894 *BiHiMed*
VonHoffmann, Bernard 1900-1947 *NatCAB 36,*
WhAm 2
VonHolst, Hermann Eduard 1841-1904 *AmBi,*
DcAmB, WhAm 1
VonHutten, Baroness Bettina 1874-1957
WhAm 3
VonHutten, Ulrich 1488-1523 *BiHiMed*
VonIwonski *NewYHSD*
VonIwonski, Carl G 1830-1922 *IIBEAAW*
VonJagemann, Hans Carl Gunther 1859-1926
NatCAB 20
VonKahler, Erich Gabriel 1885-1970 *WhAm 5*
VonKaltenborn, Hans *WebAB*
VonKarman *WebAMB*
VonKarman, Theodore 1881-1963 *WebAB,*
WhAm 4
VonKeler, Theodore M R 1877- *WhAm 1*
VonKleinsmid, Rufus Bernhard 1875-1964
NatCAB 52
VonKleinwaechter, Ludwig Paul Viktor
1882-1973 *WhAm 5*
VonKlenze, Camillo 1865-1943 *WhAm 2*
VonKlenze, Henrietta 1871- *WomWWA 14*
VonKocherthal, Josua 1669?-1719 *WhAm H*
VonKohorn, Oscar 1882-1963 *NatCAB 48*
VonKolliker, Albert 1817-1905 *BiHiMed*
VonLackum, John Peter 1894-1964 *WhAm 4*
VonLackum, William Harrison 1893-1969
NatCAB 55
VonLangenbeck, Bernhard 1810-1887 *BiHiMed*
VonLangsdorff, Georg Heinrich 1773-
IIBEAAW
VonLaue, Max 1879-1960 *WhAm 4*
VonLeyden, Ernst 1832-1910 *BiHiMed*
VonLiebig, Justus 1803-1873 *BiHiMed*
VonMach, Edmund 1870-1927 *WhAm 1*
VonMering, Josef 1849-1908 *BiHiMed*
VonMering, Otto Oswald Hermann Hubert
1888-1963 *NatCAB 52*
VonMikulicz, Johann 1850-1905 *BiHiMed*
VonMinden, William John 1901-1973 *WhAm 6*
VonMises, Ludwig Edler 1881-1973 *WhAm 6*
VonMises, Richard 1883-1953 *WhAm 3*
VonMonakow, Constantin 1853-1930 *BiHiMed*
VonMoschzisker, Robert 1870-1939 *DcAmB S2,*
WhAm 1
VonNardroff, Robert 1895-1966 *NatCAB 52*
Vonnegut, Bernard 1914- *AsBiEn*
Vonnegut, Kurt, Jr. 1922- *EncAB, WebAB*
VonNeumann, Johann 1903-1957 *DcScB*
VonNeumann, John 1903-1957 *EncAB,*
McGEWB, NatCAB 46, WebAB,
WhAm 3
VonNiessen-Stone, Marja 1870- *NatCAB 14*
Vonnoh, Bessie Potter 1872-1955 *BnEnAmA,*
NatCAB 11, WhAm 3, WomWWA 14
Vonnoh, Robert William 1858-1933 *AmBi,*
ApCAB X, BnEnAmA, DcAmB,
NatCAB 7, TwCBDA, WhAm 1
VonNoorden, Carl 1858-1944 *BiHiMed*
VonPagenhardt, Maximilian Hugo 1884-1943
WhAm 2
VonPerbandt, Carl Adolf Rudolf Julius
1832-1911 *IIBEAAW*
VonPettenkofer, Max 1818-1901 *BiHiMed*
VonPhul, Anna Maria 1786-1823 *NewYHSD,*
WhAm H
VonPhul, William 1871-1949 *NatCAB 36,*
WhAm 2
VonPrittwitz Und Gaffron, Friedrich W
1884-1955 *WhAm 3*
VonRecklinghausen, Friedrich 1833-1910
BiHiMed

VonRosenstein, Nils Rosen 1706-1773 *BiHiMed*
VonRuck, Karl 1849-1922 *DcAmB,*
NatCAB 20, WhAm 1
VonRuck, Silvio Henry 1875-1918 *NatCAB 18*
VonSallmann, Ludwig 1892-1975 *WhAm 6*
VonSaltza, Charles Frederick 1858-1905
WhAm 1
VonSchierbrand, Wolf 1851- *WhAm 4*
VonSchiller, Norma 1889- *WomWWA 14*
VonSchlieder, Albert 1869- *WhAm 5*
VonSchmidt, Harold 1893- *IIBEAAW*
VonSchon, Hans August Evald Conrad 1851-
WhAm 4
VonSchrader, Alexander 1821?-1867 *ApCAB*
VonSchrader, Irene Bond 1885- *WomWWA 14*
VonSchrenk, Hermann 1873-1953 *WhAm 3*
VonSchweinitz, Lewis David 1780-1834
WhAm H
VonSmith, Augustus A *NewYHSD*
VonSteuben *WebAMB*
VonSteuben, Friedrich Wilhelm L G A 1730-1794
WhAm H
VonStiegel, Baron *WhAm H*
VonStroheim, Erich 1885-1957 *WebAB,*
WhAm 3
VonStrumpell, Adolph 1853-1925 *BiHiMed*
VonStruve, Henry Clay 1874-1933 *WhAm 1*
VonTempski, Armine 1899-1943 *WhAm 2*
VonTeuffel, Blanche Willis Howard 1847-1898
DcAmB
VonTeuffel, Blanche Willis Howard 1851-1898
AmWom
VonTilenau *NewYHSD*
VonTresckow, Egmont Charles 1872- *WhAm 5*
VonTresckow, Walter 1897-1958 *NatCAB 47*
VonTungeln, George Henry 1883- *WhAm 3*
VonUnschuld, Marie 1881- *WomWWA 14*
VonVoit, Carl 1831-1908 *BiHiMed*
VonVolkmann, Richard 1830-1889 *BiHiMed*
VonWalther, Eckert 1867- *WhAm 4*
VonWassermann, August 1866-1925 *BiHiMed*
VonWebber *NewYHSD*
VonWedel, Curt Otto 1885-1963 *NatCAB 50*
VonWedel, Hassow Otto 1886-1943 *NatCAB 32*
VonWening, Anthony 1897-1971 *WhAm 5*
VonWicht, John 1888-1970 *WhAm 5*
VonWiller, Harry Walter 1896-1971 *WhAm 5*
VonWindegger, Marie Therese Peugnet
WomWWA 14
VonWittkamp, Andrew L *NewYHSD*
Voorhees, Boynton Stephen 1886-1973 *WhAm 6*
Voorhees, Charles Stewart 1853-1909 *BiDrAC,*
NatCAB 5, WhAmP
Voorhees, Clark Greenwood 1871-1938
WhAm 1
Voorhees, Clifford Irving 1884-1961
NatCAB 50
Voorhees, Cornelia Estelle 1877-
WomWWA 14
Voorhees, Daniel Wolsey 1827-1897 *AmBi,*
ApCAB, BiDrAC, DcAmB, NatCAB 2,
TwCBDA, WhAm H, WhAmP
Voorhees, Daniel Wolsey 1828-1897 *BiAUS,*
Drake
Voorhees, Edward Burnett 1856-1911 *DcAmB,*
EncAAH, NatCAB 13, WhAm 1
Voorhees, Florence Edgar 1879-1946
NatCAB 36
Voorhees, Foster MacGowan 1856-1927
ApCAB Sup, NatCAB 14, TwCBDA,
WhAm 1
Voorhees, Henriette Aimee LePrince 1874-1951
NatCAB 39
Voorhees, Henry Belin 1876-1966 *WhAm 4*
Voorhees, Herbert Weart 1901-1959
NatCAB 47
Voorhees, James Ditmars 1869-1929
NatCAB 31, WhAm 5
Voorhees, John Howard 1867-1946 *WhAm 2*
Voorhees, Louis A 1865-1945 *WhAm 2*
Voorhees, Melvin Harold 1880- *WhAm 6*
Voorhees, Oscar McMurtrie 1864-1947
WhAm 2
Voorhees, Philip Falkerson 1792-1862 *ApCAB,*
DcAmB, Drake, WebAMB, WhAm H
Voorhees, Samuel Stockton 1867-1921
NatCAB 19, WhAm 1

Voorhees, Stephen Francis 1878-1965
NatCAB 51, WhAm 4
Voorhees, Stephen Hegeman 1864-1940
ApCAB X, NatCAB 37, WhAm 1
Voorhees, Theodore 1847-1916 *NatCAB 17,*
WhAm 1
Voorhees, Tracy S 1890-1974 *WhAm 6*
Voorhees, Willard Penfield 1851-1914 *WhAm 1*
Voorheis, George Philemon 1847-1912
NatCAB 38
Voorhies, Annie Bailey 1845- *WomWWA 14*
Voorhies, Frank Corey 1877- *WhAm 5*
Voorhies, John Stevens 1809-1865 *ApCAB*
Voorhies, Paul Warren 1875-1952 *WhAm 3*
Voorhis, Charles Brown 1870- *WhAm 5*
Voorhis, Charles Henry 1833-1896 *BiDrAC,*
WhAm H
Voorhis, Horace Jerry 1901- *BiDrAC,*
WhAmP
Voorhis, Warren Rollin 1873-1953 *WhAm 3*
Voorsanger, Jacob 1852-1908 *DcAmB,*
WhAm 1
Vopicka, Charles Joseph 1857-1935 *DcAmB S1,*
NatCAB 25, WhAm 1
Vorberg, Martin Philip 1901-1973 *WhAm 6*
Vorenberg, Felix 1868-1943 *NatCAB 32,*
WhAm 2
Vorhauer, John Cook 1890-1964 *WhAm 4*
Vorhies, Charles Taylor 1879-1949 *NatCAB 39,*
WhAm 2
Voris, John Ralph 1880-1968 *WhAm 4A*
Voronin, Mikhail Stepanovich 1838-1903 *DcScB*
Voronoff, Evelyn Bostwick 1872-1921 *BiCAW*
Voronov, Nikolay N 1899- *WhWW-II*
Voronoy, Georgy Fedoseevich 1868-1908 *DcScB*
Vorontsov, Mikhail Semenovich 1782-1856
WhoMilH
Voroshilov, Kliment 1881-1969 *WhWW-II*
Voroshilov, Kliment Efremovich 1881-1969
WhoMilH
Voroshilov, Mazshal Kliment Yefremovich
1881-1969 *WhAm 5*
Vorse, Albert White 1866-1910 *WhAm 1*
Vorse, Mary Heaton d1966 *WhAm 4,*
WomWWA 14
Vorster, Balthazar Johannes 1915- *McGEWB*
Vorwald, Arthur John 1904-1974 *WhAm 6*
Vorys, Arthur Isaiah 1856-1933 *WhAm 1*
Vorys, John Martin 1896-1968 *BiDrAC,*
WhAm 5, WhAmP
Vorys, Webb Isaiah 1892-1972 *WhAm 5*
Vos, Bert John 1867-1945 *WhAm 2*
Vos, Hubert 1855-1935 *NatCAB 25*
Vosburgh, Emma 1866- *WomWWA 14*
Vosburgh, George Bedell 1849-1940 *WhAm 1*
Vosburgh, George Bedell 1850-1940
NatCAB 14
Vosburgh, Maude Batchelder *WomWWA 14*
Vosburgh, William Wallace, Jr. 1900-1962
NatCAB 49, WhAm 4
Vose, Alice Owsley 1883- *WomWWA 14*
Vose, Edward Neville 1870-1949 *WhAm 2*
Vose, Frederic Perry 1870-1952 *NatCAB 41*
Vose, George Leonard 1831-1910 *AmBi,*
ApCAB, DcAmB
Vose, Henry 1817-1869 *BiAUS*
Vose, James Wilson 1881- *WhAm 6*
Vose, Joseph 1738-1816 *ApCAB, Drake*
Vose, Robert Churchill 1873-1964 *NatCAB 53,*
WhAm 4
Vose, Roger 1763-1841 *BiDrAC, WhAm H*
Vose, Roger 1763-1842 *BiAUS*
Vose, William Preston 1839-1906 *WhAm 1*
VosGeerhardus, 1862-1949 *WhAm 3*
Voshell, Allen Fiske 1893-1973 *WhAm 6*
Voss, Carl August 1876-1943 *WhAm 2*
Voss, Ernst Karl Johann Heinrich 1860-1937
WhAm 1
Voss, Fred James 1905-1961 *WhAm 4*
Voss, Johann Heinrich Hermann 1882-1946
NatCAB 34
Voss, Tarquinia Losa 1858- *WomWWA 14*
Vosseller, William Fisher 1876-1945
NatCAB 34
Vostey, Gabriel Henry, Count De 1768?-1831
ApCAB
Votan *ApCAB*
Votaw, Albert Hiatt 1850-1931 *WhAm 1*

Votaw, Clyde Weber 1864-1946 *NatCAB 37,*
WhAm 4
Votaw, Heber Herbert 1881-1962 *WhAm 4*
Votaw, Lillian Ford 1878- *WomWWA 14*
Voter, Perley Conant 1889-1953 *WhAm 3*
Votey, Charles A *NewYHSD*
Votey, Edwin Scott 1856-1931 *WhAm 1,*
WhAm 1C
Votey, Josiah William 1860-1931 *WhAm 1*
Votipka, Thelma 1898-1972 *WhAm 5*
Vought, Chance Milton 1890-1930 *DcAmB,*
WebAB, WhAm HA, WhAm 4
Vought, John Henry 1870-1943 *NatCAB 33*
Vought, Sabra Wilbur 1877- *WomWWA 14*
Voulkos, Peter 1924- *BnEnAmA*
Vox, Herman H 1911-1971 *WhAm 5*
Voyer, Jane *NewYHSD*
Voyles, Charles Franklin 1872-1961
NatCAB 49
Vredenburgh, Peter 1805-1873 *ApCAB*
Vredenburgh, William Henry 1840-1920
NatCAB 33, WhAm 4
Vreeland, Albert Lincoln 1901-1975 *BiDrAC,*
WhAm 6
Vreeland, Edward Butterfield 1856-1936
BiDrAC, WhAmP
Vreeland, Edward Butterfield 1857-1936
WhAm 1
Vreeland, Frederick King 1874-1964
NatCAB 51
Vreeland, Hamilton, Jr. 1892-1969 *WhAm 5*
Vreeland, Herbert Harold 1856-1945
NatCAB 44, WhAm 2
Vreeland, John Beam 1852- *NatCAB 9*
Vreeland, T Reed 1899-1966 *WhAm 4*
Vreeland, Walter J 1880-1939 *WhAm 1*
Vreeland, Williamson Updike 1870-1942
WhAm 2
Vries, Hugo De 1848-1935 *DcScB, McGEWB*
Vrionides, Christos Peter 1894-1961
NatCAB 50
Vroom, Garret Dorset Wall 1843-1914 *ApCAB,*
TwCBDA, WhAm 1
Vroom, Garrett Dorsett Wall 1843-1914
NatCAB 14
Vroom, Mary 1865- *WomWWA 14*
Vroom, Peter Dumont 1791-1873 *ApCAB,*
BiAUS, BiDrAC, DcAmB, Drake,
NatCAB 5, TwCBDA, WhAm H,
WhAmP
Vroom, Peter Dumont 1842-1926 *ApCAB,*
WhAm 1
Vroom, Robert Allyn 1898-1962 *WhAm 4*
Vrooman, Carl 1872-1966 *WhAm 4*
Vrooman, Clare Martin 1892-1944 *WhAm 2*
Vrooman, Earle Morey 1877-1955 *NatCAB 44*
Vrooman, John Wright 1844-1929 *NatCAB 1,*
WhAm 1
Vu-Van-Mau 1914-1963 *WhAm 4*
Vucassovich, Michel Pierre 1881-1962
NatCAB 49
Vuillard, Jean Edouard 1868-1940 *McGEWB*
Vuilleumier, Ernest Albert 1894-1958 *WhAm 3*
Vulf, Yuri Viktorovich *DcScB*
Vultee, Frederick L *NewYHSD*
Vultee, Howard Fleming 1905-1973 *WhAm 5*
Vursell, Charles Wesley 1881-1974 *BiDrAC,*
WhAm 6, WhAmP
Vvedensky, Nikolay Evgenievich 1852-1922
DcScB
Vyshinsky, Andrei Yanuarievich 1883-1954
WhAm 3
Vyshnegradsky, Ivan Alekseevich 1831-1895
DcScB
Vysotsky, Georgy Nikolaevich 1865-1940 *DcScB*

W

Waage, Peter 1833-1900 *AsBiEn, DcScB*
Waagen, Mary Elizabeth Hickson 1884- *WomWWA 14*
Waalkes, Wallace 1911-1966 *NatCAB 53*
Waals, Johannes Diderik VanDer 1837-1923 *DcScB, McGEWB*
Waano-Gano, Joe T N 1906- *IIBEAAW*
Wabasha 1773?-1855? *DcAmB, WhAm H*
Wach, Joachim 1898-1955 *WhAm 3*
Wachenfeld, William A 1889-1969 *WhAm 5*
Wachenheimer, J d1934 *WhAm 1*
Wachob, Frank Alonzo 1889-1955 *NatCAB 43*
Wachowitz, Walter John 1893-1955 *NatCAB 45*
Wachsmuth, Charles 1829-1896 *AmBi, DcAmB, NatCAB 7, WhAm H*
Wachstein, Max 1905-1965 *NatCAB 51*
Wachtel, Elmer 1864-1929 *IIBEAAW*
Wachtel, Marion Kavanagh 1875?-1954 *IIBEAAW*
Wachtell, Samuel Robert 1886-1943 *NatCAB 32*
Wachter, Frank Charles 1861-1910 *BiDrAC, WhAm 1, WhAmP*
Wachter, Mileus *NewYHSD*
Wack, Henry Wellington 1867-1954 *NatCAB 54, WhAm 3*
Wack, Otis 1880-1951 *WhAm 3*
Wackenroder, Heinrich Wilhelm Ferdinand 1798-1854 *DcScB*
Wacker, Charles Henry 1856-1929 *DcAmB, NatCAB 24, WhAm 1*
Wacker, George Frederick 1885-1950 *NatCAB 38*
Wackerbarth, Fred 1891-1955 *NatCAB 42*
Wackerhagen, Augustus 1774-1865 *ApCAB*
Wackernagel, William 1838-1926 *WhAm 1*
Wackernister, William 1880- *WhAm 6*
Wackman, Kenneth B 1912-1974 *WhAm 6*
Waddel see also Waddell
Waddel, Isaac Watts 1849- *TwCBDA*
Waddel, James 1739-1805 *ApCAB, DcAmB, NatCAB 2, TwCBDA, WhAm H*
Waddel, John Newton 1812-1895 *BiDAmEd, DcAmB, NatCAB 13, TwCBDA*
Waddel, Louise Forsslund 1873-1910 *WhAm 1*
Waddel, Moses 1770-1840 *BiDAmEd, DcAmB, TwCBDA, WebAB, WhAm H*
Waddell see also Waddel
Waddell, Alfred Moore 1834-1912 *ApCAB, BiAUS, BiDrAC, DcAmB, NatCAB 8, TwCBDA, WhAm 1, WhAmP*
Waddell, Charles Carey 1868-1930 *WhAm 1, WhAm 1C*
Waddell, Charles Edward 1877-1945 *WhAm 2*
Waddell, Charles Wilkin 1875- *WhAm 5*
Waddell, Hugh 1734?-1773 *ApCAB, DcAmB, NatCAB 9, TwCBDA, WebAMB, WhAm H*
Waddell, Hugh 1799-1878 *ApCAB*
Waddell, James 1739-1805 *Drake*
Waddell, James Iredell 1824-1886 *AmBi, ApCAB, DcAmB, NatCAB 5, TwCBDA, WebAB, WebAMB, WhAm H*
Waddell, James Pleasants 1801-1867 *ApCAB*
Waddell, Jessie V Mann 1887- *WomWWA 14*
Waddell, John Alexander Low 1854-1938 *ApCAB X, DcAmB S2, NatCAB 12, NatCAB 27, WhAm 1*
Waddell, John Newton 1812-1895 *ApCAB, WhAm H*
Waddell, Joseph Addison 1823-1914 *WhAm 1*
Waddell, Joseph Addison 1825-1914 *NatCAB 19*

Waddell, Joseph Addison, II 1877-1934 *NatCAB 25*
Waddell, Montgomery 1862-1951 *NatCAB 42*
Waddell, Moses 1770-1840 *ApCAB, Drake, NatCAB 9*
Waddell, Nina T 1855- *WomWWA 14*
Waddell, William Bradford 1807-1872 *REnAW*
Waddell, William Henry 1834-1878 *NatCAB 9*
Waddill, Edmund, Jr. 1855-1931 *BiDrAC, NatCAB 27, TwCBDA, WhAm 1*
Waddill, James Richard 1842-1917 *BiDrAC*
Waddington, Benjamin Archer 1841-1917 *NatCAB 18*
Waddington, Conrad Hal 1905-1975 *WhAm 6*
Waddington, Jennie Fonda 1865- *WomWWA 14*
Waddington, Ralph Henry 1900-1967 *WhAm 5*
Waddington, William Holt 1885-1948 *NatCAB 39*
Wade, Benjamin Franklin 1800-1878 *AmBi, ApCAB, BiAUS, BiDrAC, DcAmB, Drake, EncAB, McGEWB, NatCAB 2, TwCBDA, WebAB, WhAm H, WhAmP*
Wade, Blanche Elizabeth *WomWWA 14*
Wade, Claude Melnotte 1863- *WhoColR*
Wade, Cyrus U 1849- *WhAm 4*
Wade, Decius Spear 1835-1905 *BiAUS, DcAmB, NatCAB 12*
Wade, Edward 1802-1866 *BiDrAC, WhAm H, WhAmP*
Wade, Edward 1803-1862 *TwCBDA*
Wade, Edward 1803-1866 *BiAUS*
Wade, Ethel Marion 1883- *WomWWA 14*
Wade, Festus J 1860- *NatCAB 12*
Wade, Festus John 1859-1927 *NatCAB 33, WhAm 1*
Wade, Frank Bertram 1875-1950 *WhAm 3*
Wade, Frank Charles 1878-1945 *NatCAB 35*
Wade, Frank Edward 1862-1919 *NatCAB 18*
Wade, Frank Edward 1873-1930 *WhAm 1*
Wade, George Garretson 1882-1957 *WhAm 3*
Wade, H *NewYHSD*
Wade, Hannah C *NewYHSD*
Wade, Harry Vincent 1894-1973 *WhAm 6*
Wade, Herbert Treadwell 1872-1955 *WhAm 3*
Wade, James Francis 1896-1962 *WhAm 4*
Wade, James Franklin 1843-1921 *TwCBDA, WhAm 1*
Wade, Jason Lloyd 1901-1968 *WhAm 5*
Wade, Jephtha Homer 1811-1890 *NatCAB 1*
Wade, Jeptha Homer 1811-1890 *DcAmB, WhAm H*
Wade, Jeptha Homer 1857-1926 *DcAmB S1*
Wade, John C 1827?- *NewYHSD*
Wade, John Donald 1892-1963 *WhAm 4*
Wade, John E 1877- *WhAm 5*
Wade, John William 1877-1926 *NatCAB 21*
Wade, Joseph Sanford 1880-1961 *NatCAB 49, WhAm 4*
Wade, Lester A 1889-1966 *WhAm 4*
Wade, Levi Clifford 1843-1891 *NatCAB 15*
Wade, Margaret *WomWWA 14*
Wade, Margaret Burnet Silsbee 1877- *WomWWA 14*
Wade, Martin Joseph 1861-1931 *BiDrAC, DcAmB, WhAm 1*
Wade, Mary Hazelton 1860-1936 *WhAm 1, WomWWA 14*
Wade, Mary L Hill 1855- *WhAm 4*
Wade, Mary Virginia 1843- *NatCAB 2*
Wade, Melancthon Smith 1802-1868 *ApCAB*
Wade, Neill Gillespie 1850-1938 *NatCAB 31*
Wade, Nellie 1867- *WomWWA 14*

Wade, Richard C 1922- *EncAAH*
Wade, Samuel 1820?- *NewYHSD*
Wade, Sherman Mac 1910-1965 *NatCAB 51*
Wade, William *NewYHSD*
Wade, William Henry 1835-1911 *BiDrAC, WhAmP*
Wade, William Ligon 1906-1968 *WhAm 5*
Wade, Winthrop Howland 1860-1952 *NatCAB 38*
Wademan, Lloyd Charles 1899-1959 *NatCAB 48*
Wadewitz, Edward Henry 1878-1955 *NatCAB 47*
Wadham, Harvey Nash 1871-1957 *NatCAB 47*
Wadhams, Albion Varette 1847-1927 *WhAm 1*
Wadhams, Edgar Philip 1817-1891 *ApCAB, NatCAB 12, TwCBDA, WhAm H*
Wadhams, Frederick Eugene 1848-1926 *NatCAB 24, WhAm 1*
Wadhams, Robert Pelton 1879-1940 *WhAm 1*
Wadhams, Sanford Hosea 1874-1959 *NatCAB 46*
Wadhams, William Henderson 1873- *WhAm 5*
Wadleigh, Bainbridge 1831-1891 *ApCAB, BiAUS, BiDrAC, NatCAB 7, NatCAB 24, TwCBDA, WhAm H, WhAmP*
Wadleigh, Francis Rawle 1864- *WhAm 4*
Wadleigh, George Henry 1842-1927 *ApCAB Sup, TwCBDA, WhAm 1*
Wadley, David Richard 1819-1883 *NatCAB 2*
Wadley, Dole 1824- *NatCAB 1*
Wadley, Moses 1822-1887 *NatCAB 3*
Wadley, William Morrill 1812-1882 *BiDConf*
Wadley, William Morrill 1813-1882 *NatCAB 1*
Wadlin, Horace Greeley 1851-1925 *NatCAB 16, WhAm 1*
Wadsted, Otto 1881- *WhAm 6*
Wadsworth, Alexander Scammell 1790-1851 *ApCAB, Drake, TwCBDA*
Wadsworth, Alfred Powell 1891-1956 *WhAm 3*
Wadsworth, Alice Hay 1880- *BiCAW, WhAm 6, WomWWA 14*
Wadsworth, Arthur Littleford 1910-1970 *WhAm 5*
Wadsworth, Augustus Baldwin 1872-1954 *WhAm 3A*
Wadsworth, Benjamin 1669-1737 *ApCAB, Drake, NatCAB 6, TwCBDA*
Wadsworth, Charles 1814-1882 *ApCAB*
Wadsworth, Charles, Jr. 1860-1925 *NatCAB 21, WhAm 1*
Wadsworth, Charles Curtiss 1849- *WhAm 4*
Wadsworth, Craig Wharton 1872-1960 *WhAm 4, WhAm 5*
Wadsworth, Daniel 1771-1848 *NewYHSD, WhAm H*
Wadsworth, Eliot 1876-1959 *ApCAB X, WhAm 3*
Wadsworth, Emily Otis Marshall 1836- *WomWWA 14*
Wadsworth, Frank Herbert 1870-1927 *NatCAB 20*
Wadsworth, Frank Lawton Olcott 1866-1936 *NatCAB 26*
Wadsworth, Frank Lawton Olcott 1867-1936 *AmBi, NatCAB 13, WhAm 1*
Wadsworth, George 1893-1958 *WhAm 3*
Wadsworth, Guy Woodbridge 1861- *WhAm 4*
Wadsworth, Harrison Lowell 1842- *WhAm 4*
Wadsworth, Harry Hinman 1857-1915 *NatCAB 18*
Wadsworth, Henry 1783?-1804 *ApCAB*

Wadsworth, Hiram Warren 1862-1939
WhAm 1
Wadsworth, James 1730-1817 *ApCAB, BiAUS,
BiDrAC, Drake, NatCAB 1, TwCBDA,
WhAm H*
Wadsworth, James 1768-1844 *ApCAB,
BiDAmEd, DcAmB, Drake, TwCBDA,
WhAm H*
Wadsworth, James Samuel 1807-1864 *AmBi,
ApCAB, DcAmB, Drake, NatCAB 5,
TwCBDA*
Wadsworth, James Wolcott 1846-1926
*ApCAB Sup, BiDrAC, NatCAB 34,
TwCBDA, WhAm 1, WhAmP*
Wadsworth, James Wolcott, Jr. 1877-1952
*ApCAB X, BiDrAC, DcAmB S5,
NatCAB 15, NatCAB 45, WhAm 4,
WhAmP*
Wadsworth, Jeremiah 1743-1804 *ApCAB,
BiAUS, BiDrAC, DcAmB, Drake,
EncAAH, NatCAB 1, TwCBDA,
WhAm H, WhAmP*
Wadsworth, John Baker 1898-1966 *NatCAB 52*
Wadsworth, Lue Stuart *WomWWA 14*
Wadsworth, Marshman Edward 1847-1921
*ApCAB, NatCAB 13, TwCBDA,
WhAm 1*
Wadsworth, Oliver Fairfield 1838-1911
NatCAB 20, WhAm 1
Wadsworth, Peleg 1748-1829 *ApCAB, BiAUS,
BiDrAC, DcAmB, Drake, NatCAB 1,
NatCAB 2, TwCBDA, WebAMB,
WhAm H, WhAmP*
Wadsworth, W *NewYHSD*
Wadsworth, William *NewYHSD*
Wadsworth, William 1732-1833 *ApCAB,
Drake*
Wadsworth, William Austin 1847-1918
WhAm 1
Wadsworth, William Henry 1821-1893 *BiAUS,
BiDrAC, TwCBDA, WhAm H, WhAmP*
Wady, Clifton Sanford 1860-1936 *WhAm 3*
Waer, Oscar Edward 1883-1965 *NatCAB 51*
Waesche, Metta Henrietta 1806-1900
NewYHSD
Waesche, Russell Randolph 1886-1946
*DcAmB S4, NatCAB 38, WebAMB,
WhAm 2*
Wafer, Lionel 1640?-1705? *ApCAB, Drake*
Waffle, Albert Edward 1846- *WhAm 4*
Waffle, Jonas 1880-1943 *NatCAB 34*
Wafid, Abu Al-Mutarrif Abd Al-R, Ibn *DcScB*
Waganer, Anthony *NewYHSD*
Wageman, Michael *NewYHSD*
Wagenaar, Bernard 1894-1971 *WhAm 5*
Wagener, Anthony Pelzer 1887-1972 *WhAm 5*
Wagener, David Douglas 1792-1860 *BiAUS,
BiDrAC, TwCBDA, WhAm H, WhAmP*
Wagener, Johann Andreas 1816-1876
NatCAB 11
Wagener, John Andreas 1816-1876 *DcAmB S1*
Wagenheim, Michael Benjamin 1900-1972
WhAm 5
Wager, Alan Turner 1904-1966 *NatCAB 53,
WhAm 4*
Wager, Charles Henry Adams 1869-1939
WhAm 1
Wager, Ralph Edmond 1881- *WhAm 6*
Wager-Smith, E 1872-1920 *NatCAB 19*
Waggaman, George Augustus 1790-1843
BiDrAC, WhAm H
Waggaman, Mary Teresa McKee 1846-1931
DcAmB
Waggamann, George Augustus 1782-1843
ApCAB, BiAUS, NatCAB 11, TwCBDA
Waggener, Balie Peyton 1847-1918 *NatCAB 7,
NatCAB 17, WhAm 1*
Waggener, Isaac Denton 1866-1918 *NatCAB 20*
Waggener, Leslie 1841-1896 *NatCAB 5*
Waggener, Leslie 1876-1951 *NatCAB 41,
WhAm 3*
Waggener, William Peyton 1870-1943 *WhAm 2*
Waggoner, Alvin 1879-1939 *NatCAB 36,
WhAm 1*
Waggoner, Clark 1820-1903 *NatCAB 14*
Waggoner, D Easley 1892-1956 *NatCAB 48*
Waggoner, Daniel 1828-1902 *REnAW*
Waggoner, David E 1867-1948 *WhAm 2*

Waggoner, Norman Lee 1887-1952 *NatCAB 41*
Waggoner, William Henry 1839-1921
NatCAB 19
Waggoner, William Thomas 1852-1934
NatCAB 32
Waggoner, William W *NewYHSD*
Waggonner, Joseph David, Jr. 1918- *BiDrAC*
Wagman, George Aloysious 1881-1952
NatCAB 41
Wagnalls, Adam Willis 1843-1924 *NatCAB 23,
WhAm 1*
Wagnalls, Mabel 1871- *TwCBDA,
WomWWA 14*
Wagner *NewYHSD*
Wagner, Andrew *NewYHSD*
Wagner, Arnold Henry 1878-1949 *NatCAB 37*
Wagner, Arthur Lockwood 1853-1905 *WebAMB,
WhAm 1*
Wagner, Carl Washington 1863-1921
NatCAB 19
Wagner, Charles 1837-1912 *NatCAB 15*
Wagner, Charles Conroy 1893-1946
NatCAB 35
Wagner, Charles Gray 1856-1923 *WhAm 1*
Wagner, Charles Gray 1858-1923 *NatCAB 24*
Wagner, Charles L d1956 *WhAm 3*
Wagner, Charles Philip 1876-1964 *NatCAB 50,
WhAm 4*
Wagner, Clarence 1905-1964 *NatCAB 52*
Wagner, Clinton 1837-1914 *DcAmB,
NatCAB 1*
Wagner, Daniel 1802-1888 *NewYHSD,
WhAm H*
Wagner, Daniel Christian 1501?-1552 *ApCAB*
Wagner, Daniel Eugene 1882-1972 *NatCAB 56*
Wagner, David 1826-1902 *NatCAB 12*
Wagner, Dwight Homans 1874-1958
NatCAB 47
Wagner, E *NewYHSD*
Wagner, E W 1864- *ApCAB X*
Wagner, Earl Thomas 1908- *BiDrAC*
Wagner, Edward Richard 1873-1956
NatCAB 48
Wagner, Ethel Putnam 1876- *WomWWA 14*
Wagner, Frank Caspar 1864-1928 *WhAm 1*
Wagner, Frederick Runyon 1873-1953 *WhAm 3*
Wagner, George 1904-1964 *WhAm 4*
Wagner, George Raymond *WebAB*
Wagner, George Washington 1861-1923
NatCAB 20
Wagner, H Hughes 1903-1973 *WhAm 6*
Wagner, Harr 1857-1936 *WhAm 1*
Wagner, Harry Samuel 1877-1935 *NatCAB 26*
Wagner, Hattie B 1870- *WomWWA 14*
Wagner, Helena Corinne 1875- *WomWWA 14*
Wagner, Henry Franklin 1874-1943 *WhAm 2*
Wagner, Henry Raup 1862-1957 *NatCAB 45,
REnAW, WhAm 3*
Wagner, Henry S *NewYHSD*
Wagner, Herbert Appleton 1867-1947 *WhAm 2*
Wagner, Herman Alexander 1864-1960
WhAm 4
Wagner, Honus 1874-1955 *WebAB*
Wagner, Hugh Kiernan 1870- *NatCAB 17,
WhAm 1*
Wagner, J F *NewYHSD*
Wagner, J Fred 1879-1946 *NatCAB 35*
Wagner, James Elvin 1873- *WhAm 5*
Wagner, James Haag 1861-1943 *NatCAB 37*
Wagner, Janette Burwell Yates *WomWWA 14*
Wagner, John 1791-1841 *ApCAB*
Wagner, John 1892-1956 *NatCAB 47*
Wagner, John George 1859-1926 *NatCAB 23*
Wagner, John Henry 1874-1955 *WhAm HA,
WhAm 4*
Wagner, John Peter 1874-1955 *DcAmB S5,
WebAB*
Wagner, Jonathan Howard 1873-1953
BiDAmEd, WhAm 5
Wagner, Kenneth Hall 1901-1966 *WhAm 4*
Wagner, Kip Lowell 1905-1972 *WhAm 6*
Wagner, Laura Virginia *WomWWA 14*
Wagner, Louis 1838-1914 *NatCAB 4,
WhAm 1*
Wagner, Madge Morris 1862- *ApCAB Sup*
Wagner, Maria Louisa *NewYHSD*
Wagner, Martin 1885-1957 *WhAm 3*
Wagner, Moritz Friedrich 1813- *ApCAB*

Wagner, Myron Leroy 1923-1975 *WhAm 6*
Wagner, Myrtie Hudson *WomWWA 14*
Wagner, Oscar 1893-1971 *WhAm 5*
Wagner, Peter Joseph 1795-1884 *BiAUS,
BiDrAC, WhAm H*
Wagner, Philip 1811?- *NewYHSD*
Wagner, Richard 1813-1883 *McGEWB*
Wagner, Rob 1872-1942 *WhAm 2*
Wagner, Robert Ferdinand 1877-1953 *BiDrAC,
DcAmB S5, EncAB, McGEWB,
NatCAB 48, WebAB, WhAm 3, WhAmP*
Wagner, Rudolph *NewYHSD*
Wagner, Rudolph 1805-1864 *DcScB*
Wagner, Russell Halderman 1894-1952
WhAm 3
Wagner, Samuel 1842-1937 *WhAm 1*
Wagner, Samuel, Jr. 1895-1939 *NatCAB 29*
Wagner, Samuel Tobias 1861-1931 *NatCAB 44,
WhAm 1*
Wagner, Steward 1886-1958 *WhAm 3*
Wagner, Theodore Brentano 1869-1936
NatCAB 27
Wagner, Thomas S *NewYHSD*
Wagner, W A *NewYHSD*
Wagner, Webster 1817-1882 *ApCAB, DcAmB,
NatCAB 9, TwCBDA, WhAm H*
Wagner, Wieland 1917-1966 *WhAm 4*
Wagner, William *NewYHSD*
Wagner, William 1796-1885 *ApCAB, DcAmB,
NatCAB 6, TwCBDA, WhAm H*
Wagner, William George 1858-1928 *ApCAB X*
Wagner, William Huff 1888-1953 *NatCAB 41*
Wagner, William W 1817?- *NewYHSD*
Wagner, Wilmer Gouger 1866- *WhAm 4*
Wagner VonJauregg, Julius 1857-1940 *DcScB*
Wagoner, Charles *NewYHSD*
Wagoner, George 1896-1957 *NatCAB 45*
Wagoner, George Chester Robinson 1863-1946
BiDrAC
Wagoner, George Washington 1856-
NatCAB 14
Wagoner, Harry B 1889-1950 *IIBEAAW*
Wagoner, Philip Dakin 1876-1962 *WhAm 4*
Wagoner, Robert 1928- *IIBEAAW*
Wagoner, Winfred Ethestal 1889-1948
NatCAB 39, WhAm 2
Wagstaff, Alfred 1844-1921 *WhAm 1*
Wagstaff, Bertha Scram 1858- *WomWWA 14*
Wagstaff, Blanche Shoemaker 1888- *BiCAW*
Wagstaff, Charles Edward 1808- *NewYHSD*
Wagstaff, David 1882-1951 *NatCAB 46*
Wagstaff, Henry McGilbert 1876- *WhAm 5*
Wagstaff, John C *NewYHSD*
Wagstaff, Robert McAlpine 1892-1973
WhAm 6
Wahl, Christian 1829-1901 *NatCAB 27*
Wahl, George Moritz 1851-1923 *NatCAB 20,
WhAm 1*
Wahl, H Roswell 1886-1956 *NatCAB 45*
Wahl, John Conrades 1876- *ApCAB X*
Wahl, Lutz 1869-1928 *WhAm 1*
Wahl, Robert 1858-1937 *NatCAB 27*
Wahl, William Henry 1848-1909 *DcAmB,
NatCAB 21, WhAm 1*
Wahlenberg, Goran 1780-1851 *DcScB*
Wahlmann, Frederick *NewYHSD*
Wahlquist, John Thomas 1899- *BiDAmEd*
Wahlstrom, Matthias 1851- *TwCBDA,
WhAm 4*
Wahrhaftig, Felix Solomon 1909-1969 *WhAm 5*
Wahshiyya, Abu Bakr Ahmad Ibn Sali, Ibn
860?-935? *DcScB*
Wahunsonacock *WebAB*
Waid, Dan Everett 1864-1939 *NatCAB 29,
WhAm 1*
Waid, Eva Clark *WomWWA 14*
Waid, George S 1863- *WhAm 4*
Waidner, Charles William 1873-1922 *DcAmB,
WhAm 1*
Wailes, Benjamin Leonard Covington 1797-1862
DcAmB, WhAm H
Wailes, Edward Thompson 1903-1969 *WhAm 5*
Wailes, George Handy 1866-1967 *WhAm 4,
WhAm 5*
Wailly, Jacques Warnier De 1903-1971
WhAm 6
Waindle, Roger F 1909-1973 *WhAm 5*
Wainwright, Dallas Bache 1852- *WhAm 4*

Wainwright, Guy Alwyn 1889-1956 *NatCAB 45, WhAm 3*
Wainwright, John 1839- *WhAm 4*
Wainwright, Jonathan Mayhew 1792-1854 *DcAmB, NatCAB 1, TwCBDA*
Wainwright, Jonathan Mayhew 1793-1854 *ApCAB, Drake*
Wainwright, Jonathan Mayhew 1821-1863 *ApCAB, DcAmB, Drake, NatCAB 4, TwCBDA, WhAm H*
Wainwright, Jonathan Mayhew 1849-1870 *ApCAB, NatCAB 4*
Wainwright, Jonathan Mayhew 1864-1945 *BiDrAC, NatCAB 47, WhAm 2, WhAmP*
Wainwright, Jonathan Mayhew 1883-1953 *DcAmB S5, McGEWB, NatCAB 44, WebAMB, WhAm 3, WhWW-II*
Wainwright, Lucius Morton 1860-1931 *NatCAB 36*
Wainwright, Marie Page 1860-1923 *WhAm 1, WomWWA 14*
Wainwright, Richard 1817-1862 *ApCAB, DcAmB, NatCAB 5, TwCBDA, WhAm H*
Wainwright, Richard 1849-1926 *AmBi, ApCAB Sup, DcAmB, NatCAB 9, TwCBDA, WebAMB, WhAm 1*
Wainwright, Samuel Hayman 1863-1950 *WhAm 3*
Wainwright, Stuyvesant, II 1921- *BiDrAC*
Wainwright, William Alonzo 1832-1905 *NatCAB 36*
Wait, Aaron E 1813- *NatCAB 5*
Wait, Anna C 1837- *AmWom*
Wait, Benjamin 1813- *ApCAB*
Wait, Carrie Stow 1852- *WomWWA 14*
Wait, Charles Edmund 1849-1923 *WhAm 1*
Wait, George Ray 1886-1953 *NatCAB 42*
Wait, Henry Heileman 1869-1931 *AmBi, NatCAB 31, WhAm 1*
Wait, Horatio Loomis 1836-1916 *NatCAB 16, WhAm 1*
Wait, John Cassan 1860-1936 *NatCAB 13, NatCAB 29, WhAm 1*
Wait, John Turner 1811-1899 *BiDrAC, TwCBDA, WhAmP*
Wait, Lizzie Frances *WomWWA 14*
Wait, Lucien Augustus 1846-1913 *WhAm 1*
Wait, Oren J 1810-1894 *NatCAB 12*
Wait, Phebe Jane Babcock 1838-1904 *NatCAB 2*
Wait, Phoebe Jane Babcock 1838-1904 *AmWom*
Wait, Robert T P 1846-1898 *WhAm H*
Wait, Samuel 1789-1867 *ApCAB, BiDAmEd, DcAmB, NatCAB 21, TwCBDA, WhAm H*
Wait, Wesley 1861-1949 *NatCAB 38*
Wait, William 1821-1880 *ApCAB, DcAmB, WhAm H*
Wait, William Bell 1839-1916 *BiDAmEd, DcAmB, NatCAB 2, WhAm 1*
Wait, William Cushing 1860-1935 *AmBi, WhAm 1*
Wait, William Henry 1854-1939 *WhAm 1*
Waite, Alice Vinton 1864-1943 *WhAm 2*
Waite, Benjamin Franklin 1817- *NewYHSD*
Waite, Byron Sylvester 1852-1930 *WhAm 1*
Waite, Carlos Adolphus 1800-1866 *ApCAB, Drake*
Waite, Catharine VanValkenburg 1829-1913 *ApCAB, NotAW, WhAm 4*
Waite, Catherine VanValkenburg 1829-1913 *AmWom*
Waite, Charles Burlingame 1824-1909 *ApCAB, BiAUS, WhAm 1*
Waite, Clark Francis 1877-1958 *WhAm 3*
Waite, David Simmons 1846-1917 *NatCAB 18*
Waite, Davis Hanson 1825-1901 *NatCAB 6, REnAW, TwCBDA, WhAm 1*
Waite, Edward Foote 1860-1958 *NatCAB 17, WhAm 3*
Waite, Elizabeth Richardson *WomWWA 14*
Waite, Ella Raymond *WomWWA 14*
Waite, Frederick Clayton 1870-1956 *NatCAB 44, WhAm 3*
Waite, George Thomas 1883- *WhAm 1*
Waite, Harvey Rice 1876- *WhAm 5*
Waite, Henry Matson 1787-1869 *ApCAB,*

BiAUS, Drake, NatCAB 30, TwCBDA
Waite, Henry Matson 1869-1944 *DcAmB S3, NatCAB 34, WhAm 2*
Waite, Henry Randall 1845-1909 *ApCAB*
Waite, Henry Randall 1846-1909 *WhAm 1*
Waite, Herbert Harold 1868-1931 *WhAm 1, WhAm 1C*
Waite, J Herbert 1889-1957 *WhAm 3*
Waite, John Barker 1882-1967 *NatCAB 54*
Waite, John David 1858- *WhAm 4*
Waite, John Leman 1840-1924 *ApCAB X, NatCAB 16, WhAm 1*
Waite, Kate Robinson 1861- *WomWWA 14*
Waite, Lucretia Ann *NewYHSD*
Waite, Merton Benway 1865-1945 *WhAm 2*
Waite, Morison Remich 1866-1962 *WhAm 4*
Waite, Morrison Remick 1816-1888 *AmBi, ApCAB, BiAUS, DcAmB, EncAB, McGEWB, NatCAB 1, NatCAB 26, TwCBDA, WebAB, WhAm H*
Waite, Stand 1810-1867 *ApCAB Sup*
Waite, Sumner 1888-1952 *WhAm 3*
Waite, Warren C 1896-1950 *WhAm 3*
Waites, Edward P *NewYHSD*
Waitie, Stand 1795?-1877 *TwCBDA*
Waits, Edward McShane 1871-1949 *NatCAB 38, WhAm 2*
Waitt, Benjamin Franklin 1817- *NewYHSD*
Waitt, Ernest Linden 1872- *WhAm 5*
Wakasugi, Sueyuki 1903-1973 *WhAm 6*
Wake, Charles Staniland 1835-1910 *WhAm 1*
Wakefield, Mrs. A C d1870 *Drake*
Wakefield, Arthur Paul 1878-1942 *WhAm 2*
Wakefield, Cyrus 1811-1873 *ApCAB, Drake Sup, NatCAB 12, WhAm H*
Wakefield, Edmund Burritt 1846-1921 *WhAm 1*
Wakefield, Edward Gibbon 1796-1862 *McGEWB*
Wakefield, Emily Watkins *AmWom*
Wakefield, Ernest Alonzo 1868- *WhAm 4*
Wakefield, Eva Ingersoll 1891-1970 *WhAm 5*
Wakefield, Henriette d1974 *WhAm 6*
Wakefield, James Beach 1825-1910 *BiDrAC, WhAmP*
Wakefield, Lyman E 1880-1945 *WhAm 2*
Wakefield, Mary Wiley Cameron *WomWWA 14*
Wakefield, Milton C 1917-1974 *WhAm 6*
Wakefield, Nancy Amelia Woodbury Priest 1836-1870 *ApCAB*
Wakefield, Paul M 1905-1967 *WhAm 5*
Wakefield, Ralph 1876- *WhAm 5*
Wakefield, Ray Bruchman 1910-1963 *WhAm 4*
Wakefield, Ray Cecil 1895-1949 *WhAm 2*
Wakefield, Sherman Day 1894-1971 *WhAm 5*
Wakefield, William J C 1862- *ApCAB X*
Wakehurst, Lord 1895-1970 *WhAm 5*
Wakeland, Charles Richard 1870- *WhAm 5*
Wakelaw, Frederick *NewYHSD*
Wakelaw, William J *NewYHSD*
Wakelee, Edmund Waring 1869-1945 *WhAm 2*
Wakeley, Arthur Cooper 1855-1928 *WhAm 1*
Wakeley, Joseph B 1804-1876 *ApCAB*
Wakeley, Joseph Burton 1809-1875 *DcAmB, WhAm H*
Wakeley, Thompson Morris 1897-1972 *WhAm 5*
Wakelin, James Henry 1876-1941 *NatCAB 34*
Wakely, Ebenezer *BiAUS*
Wakeman, A Maurice 1897-1929 *NatCAB 25*
Wakeman, Abraham 1824-1889 *BiAUS*
Wakeman, Abram 1824-1889 *ApCAB Sup, BiDrAC, WhAm H*
Wakeman, Antoinette VanHoesen 1856- *AmWom, WhAm 4*
Wakeman, Antoinette VanHosan 1856- *WomWWA 14*
Wakeman, Don Conklin 1905-1966 *NatCAB 53*
Wakeman, Earl Seeley 1881- *WhAm 6*
Wakeman, George 1841-1870 *Drake*
Wakeman, Helen Edith Ainsworth *WomWWA 14*
Wakeman, James Meanley 1865-1932 *NatCAB 24*
Wakeman, Keith 1874-1933 *WhAm 1, WomWWA 14*
Wakeman, Nellie Antoinette *WomWWA 14*
Wakeman, S Wiley 1876-1940 *NatCAB 31*

Wakeman, Seth 1811-1880 *BiDrAC, WhAm H*
Wakeman, Seth 1893-1968 *WhAm 5*
Wakeman, Sophie Susan Reynolds 1875- *WomWWA 14*
Wakeman, Thaddeus Burr 1834-1913 *ApCAB Sup, WhAm 1*
Wakeman, Thomas 1812-1878 *NewYHSD*
Wakeman, Wilbur Fisk 1857-1931 *WhAm 1*
Wakley, Thomas 1795-1862 *BiHiMed*
Waksman, Selman Abraham 1888-1973 *AsBiEn, EncAAH, McGEWB, WebAB*
Waksmen, Selman Abraham 1888-1973 *WhAm 6*
Walb, Clyde Allison 1878-1945 *NatCAB 35*
Walbach, John Baptiste DeBarth 1766-1857 *ApCAB*
Walbach, John DeBarth 1764-1857 *Drake*
Walbridge, Arthur Dewey 1843-1872 *ApCAB*
Walbridge, Charles Eliphalet 1841-1913 *NatCAB 28*
Walbridge, Cyrus Packard 1849-1921 *NatCAB 12, WhAm 1*
Walbridge, David Safford 1802-1868 *BiAUS, BiDrAC, WhAm H*
Walbridge, Earle F 1896-1962 *WhAm 4*
Walbridge, Edward Langdon 1887-1938 *NatCAB 28*
Walbridge, George Hicks 1869-1936 *WhAm 1*
Walbridge, Henry Sanford 1801-1869 *BiAUS, BiDrAC, WhAm H*
Walbridge, Hiram 1821-1870 *ApCAB, BiAUS, BiDrAC, Drake, WhAm H*
Walbridge, Nelson Lee 1902-1973 *WhAm 5*
Walbridge, William Spooner 1854-1935 *NatCAB 31*
Walch, Johann Ernst Immanuel 1725-1778 *DcScB*
Walchli, Otto William 1895-1968 *NatCAB 55*
Walcot, Charles Melton 1815-1868 *ApCAB, NatCAB 11, TwCBDA*
Walcot, Charles Melton 1816?-1868 *DcAmB, Drake, WhAm H*
Walcot, Charles Melton 1840-1921 *ApCAB, DcAmB, Drake, NatCAB 11, TwCBDA*
Walcott, Anabel Havens *WomWWA 14*
Walcott, C P *BiAUS*
Walcott, Charles Carroll 1838-1898 *ApCAB Sup*
Walcott, Charles Doolittle 1850-1927 *AmBi, ApCAB, ApCAB X, DcAmB, DcScB, NatCAB 10, NatCAB 22, TwCBDA, WebAB, WhAm 1*
Walcott, Chester Howe 1883-1947 *WhAm 2*
Walcott, Earle Ashley 1859-1931 *ApCAB X, WhAm 1*
Walcott, Frederic Collin 1869-1949 *BiDrAC, NatCAB 17, NatCAB 42, WhAm 3*
Walcott, Gregory Dexter 1869-1959 *NatCAB 43, WhAm 3, WhAm 4*
Walcott, Harry Mills 1870-1944 *WhAm 2*
Walcott, Henry Pickering 1838-1932 *DcAmB, NatCAB 12, WhAm 1, WhAm 1C*
Walcott, Mary Morris Vaux 1860-1940 *NotAW*
Walcott, Robert 1874-1956 *WhAm 3*
Walcott, William Stuart 1843-1905 *NatCAB 41*
Walcutt, Charles C, Jr. 1861-1925 *WhAm 1*
Walcutt, Charles Carroll 1838-1898 *NatCAB 6, TwCBDA*
Walcutt, David Broderick 1825- *NewYHSD*
Walcutt, George 1825- *NewYHSD*
Walcutt, William 1819- *NatCAB 13*
Walcutt, William 1819-1882? *WhAm H*
Walcutt, William 1819-1895? *NewYHSD*
Wald, Abraham 1902-1950 *DcScB, WhAm 3*
Wald, Frantisek 1861-1930 *DcScB*
Wald, George 1906- *AsBiEn, WebAB*
Wald, Gustavus Henry 1853-1902 *WhAm 1*
Wald, Jerry 1912-1962 *WhAm 4*
Wald, Lillian D 1867-1940 *BiDAmEd, DcAmB S2, EncAB, McGEWB, NatCAB 29, NotAW, WebAB, WhAm 1, WomWWA 14*
Wald, Solomon Abraham 1886-1970 *NatCAB 54*
Waldbauer, Louis Julius 1896-1959 *NatCAB 47*
Waldeck, Carl Gustav 1866-1931 *NatCAB 13, WhAm 1*
Waldeck, Edward Alvin 1897-1963 *NatCAB 50*

Waldeck, Herman 1871-1960 *WhAm 3*
Waldeck, Jean Frederic De 1766-1875 *ApCAB*
Waldeisen, William Robert 1892-1967
NatCAB 54
Waldemar, Gertrude Bucklin 1870-
WomWWA 14
Walden, Anne Brevoort Eddy *WomWWA 14*
Walden, Austin Thomas 1885-1965 *WhAm 4*
Walden, Franklin 1847-1927 *NatCAB 22*
Walden, Freeman 1839- *WhAm 1*
Walden, Hiram 1800-1880 *BiAUS, BiDrAC,
WhAm H*
Walden, Jacob Treadwell 1830-1918 *DcAmB*
Walden, James Henry 1854-1942 *NatCAB 32*
Walden, John Morgan 1831-1914 *ApCAB,
DcAmB, NatCAB 12, TwCBDA,
WhAm 1*
Walden, Lionel 1861-1933 *WhAm 1*
Walden, Madison Miner 1836-1891 *BiAUS,
BiDrAC, WhAm H*
Walden, Paul 1863-1957 *AsBiEn, DcScB*
Walden, Percy Talbot 1869-1943 *NatCAB 31,
WhAm 2*
Walden, Sarah S W 1872- *WomWWA 14*
Walden, Treadwell 1830-1918 *WhAm 1*
Walden, Walter 1870- *WhAm 5*
Walder, Pauline J 1842- *WomWWA 14*
Walder, William Alfred 1898-1949 *NatCAB 38*
Walderne, Richard 1615?-1689 *DcAmB,
WhAm H*
Waldersee, Alfred Graf Von 1832-1904
WhoMilH
Waldersee, Mary, Countess Von 1837- *ApCAB*
Waldeyer, Heinrich Wilhelm Gottfried Von
1836-1921 *AsBiEn*
Waldeyer-Hartz, Wilhelm Von 1836-1921
DcScB
Waldie, Jerome Russell 1925- *BiDrAC*
Waldo, Albigence 1750-1794 *ApCAB*
Waldo, Charles Gilbert 1857- *WhAm 4*
Waldo, Charles Merrel 1906-1953 *NatCAB 42*
Waldo, Clarence Abiathar 1852-1926
NatCAB 23, WhAm 1
Waldo, Daniel 1762-1864 *ApCAB, Drake*
Waldo, David 1802-1878 *DcAmB, WhAm H*
Waldo, Dwight Bryant 1864-1939 *NatCAB 41,
WhAm 1*
Waldo, Edward Hardenbergh 1866-1950
NatCAB 39
Waldo, Frances Hall 1869- *WomWWA 14*
Waldo, Francis 1723-1784 *ApCAB*
Waldo, Frank 1857-1920 *WhAm 1*
Waldo, Fullerton Leonard 1877- *WhAm 5*
Waldo, George C 1888-1956 *WhAm 3*
Waldo, George Curtis 1837-1921 *NatCAB 29*
Waldo, George Ernest 1851- *NatCAB 18*
Waldo, George Ernest 1851-1942 *BiDrAC*
Waldo, George Ernest 1851-1943 *WhAm 2*
Waldo, H L *BiAUS*
Waldo, John Breckenridge 1844- *NatCAB 5*
Waldo, Leonard 1853-1929 *ApCAB, WhAm 1*
Waldo, Lillian McLean 1873- *WhAm 5*
Waldo, Loren Pinckney 1802-1881 *BiDrAC,
WhAm H*
Waldo, Lorin P 1802-1881 *BiAUS*
Waldo, Peter *McGEWB*
Waldo, Rhinelander 1877-1927 *WhAm 1*
Waldo, Richard Harold 1878-1943 *NatCAB 32,
WhAm 2*
Waldo, Samuel 1695-1759 *DcAmB, WhAm H*
Waldo, Samuel 1696-1759 *ApCAB, Drake*
Waldo, Samuel 1721-1770 *ApCAB*
Waldo, Samuel Lovett 1783-1861 *AmBi,
ApCAB, BnEnAmA, DcAmB, Drake,
NatCAB 14, NewYHSD, WhAm H*
Waldo, Samuel Putnam d1826 *Drake,
WhAm H*
Waldo, Samuel Putnam 1779-1826 *DcAmB*
Waldo, Samuel Putnam 1780-1826 *ApCAB*
Waldo, Selden Fennell 1915-1950 *WhAm 3*
Waldo, William Earl 1885-1962 *WhAm 4*
Waldon, Sidney Dunn 1873-1945 *WhAm 2*
Waldorf, Ernest Lynn 1876-1943 *NatCAB 33,
WhAm 2*
Waldorf, Wilella Louise 1899-1945 *WhAm 2*
Waldow, William F 1872-1930 *WhAm 1*
Waldow, William Frederick 1882-1930 *BiDrAC*
Waldrip, Marion Nelson 1873- *WhAm 5*

Waldron, Adelia *NewYHSD*
Waldron, Alfred Marpole 1865-1952 *BiDrAC,
WhAm 4*
Waldron, Arthur Maxson 1884-1959 *WhAm 3*
Waldron, Clare Bailey 1865-1947 *WhAm 2*
Waldron, Edmund Quincy Sheafe 1812-1888
ApCAB
Waldron, Edward Mathew 1864- *ApCAB X*
Waldron, Henry 1819-1880 *BiAUS, BiDrAC,
WhAm H, WhAmP*
Waldron, James Albert 1852-1931 *WhAm 1*
Waldron, Jeremy Richard 1889-1949 *WhAm 3*
Waldron, John J d1971 *WhAm 5*
Waldron, John Milton 1863- *WhoColR*
Waldron, John William 1873-1935 *WhAm 1*
Waldron, Martha M 1850- *WomWWA 14*
Waldron, Richard 1615-1689 *ApCAB, DcAmB,
Drake, NatCAB 13*
Waldron, Richard 1650-1730 *ApCAB*
Waldron, Richard 1694-1753 *ApCAB*
Waldron, Webb 1882-1945 *NatCAB 34,
WhAm 2*
Waldron, William Henry 1877-1947 *WhAm 2*
Waldrop, R Walter 1872-1948 *WhAm 2*
Waldrop, Mrs. Robert Ross *WomWWA 14*
Waldseemuller, Martin 1470?-1518? *DcScB,
McGEWB*
Waldseemuller, Martin 1470?-1522? *ApCAB,
Drake, WhAm H*
Waldstein, Charles 1856- *ApCAB,
NatCAB 11, TwCBDA*
Waldstein, Louis 1853-1915 *WhAm 1*
Waldstein, Martin E 1854- *WhAm 4*
Wale, T *NewYHSD*
Wales, Charles Marshall 1862-1930
NatCAB 23
Wales, Edward Howe 1856-1922 *NatCAB 32*
Wales, Ernest DeWolfe 1873-1950 *NatCAB 39*
Wales, George C 1868-1940 *WhAm 1*
Wales, George Edward 1792-1860 *BiAUS,
BiDrAC, WhAm H*
Wales, George Russell 1862-1933 *WhAm 1*
Wales, Henry 1888-1960 *WhAm 3A*
Wales, James Albert 1852-1886 *ApCAB,
DcAmB, WhAm H*
Wales, James Albert 1879-1970 *WhAm 5*
Wales, John 1783-1863 *ApCAB, BiAUS,
BiDrAC, NatCAB 11, TwCBDA,
WhAm H*
Wales, John Patten 1831-1912 *NatCAB 33*
Wales, Julia Grace 1881- *WhAm 6*
Wales, Leonard Eugene 1823-1897 *ApCAB Sup,
DcAmB, NatCAB 11, WhAm H*
Wales, Leonard Eugene 1870-1943 *NatCAB 33*
Wales, N F *NewYHSD*
Wales, Philip Skinner 1837-1906 *ApCAB,
NatCAB 11, WhAm 1*
Wales, Royal Linfield 1878- *WhAm 6*
Wales, Salem Howe 1825-1902 *ApCAB,
NatCAB 3, WhAm 1*
Wales, Samuel 1748-1794 *ApCAB, Drake*
Wales, Thomas Beale 1839-1922 *ApCAB X*
Wales, Thomas Crane 1805-1880 *NatCAB 10*
Wales, Wellington 1917-1966 *WhAm 4*
Wales, William 1734?-1798 *ApCAB*
Walet, Eugene Henry, Jr. 1901-1968 *WhAm 5*
Walgreen, Charles Rudolph 1873-1939
*DcAmB S2, NatCAB 29, WebAB,
WhAm 1*
Walk, Arthur Richard 1895-1953 *NatCAB 42*
Walk, Carl Ferdinand 1870-1963 *NatCAB 52*
Walk, Charles Edmonds 1875- *WhAm 5*
Walk, George Everett 1876-1962 *WhAm 4*
Walk, James Wilson 1853-1918 *WhAm 1*
Walk-In-The-Water d1817? *ApCAB*
Walkara 1808?-1855 *REnAW*
Walke, Frank Hicks 1886-1939 *WhAm 1*
Walke, Henry 1808-1896 *AmBi, ApCAB,
DcAmB, NatCAB 6, NewYHSD,
TwCBDA, WebAMB, WhAm H*
Walke, Henry 1809-1896 *Drake*
Walke, Willoughby 1859-1928 *WhAm 1*
Walkem, George Anthony 1834- *ApCAB*
Walkem, Richard Thomas 1840- *ApCAB*
Walker *NewYHSD*
Walker, Miss A M *NewYHSD*
Walker, A W *NewYHSD*
Walker, Aaron Thibaud 1909-1975 *WhAm 6*

Walker, Abbie Phillips 1867-1943 *WhAm 2*
Walker, Abraham Joseph 1818-1872 *ApCAB*
Walker, Abraham Joseph 1819-1872 *NatCAB
TwCBDA*
Walker, Albert Henry 1844-1915 *NatCAB 1,
NatCAB 17, WhAm 1*
Walker, Albert Perry 1862-1911 *WhAm 1*
Walker, Aldace Freeman 1842-1901
NatCAB 10, WhAm 1
Walker, Alexander 1779-1852 *DcScB*
Walker, Alexander 1818-1893 *DcAmB,
WhAm H*
Walker, Alexander 1819-1893 *ApCAB*
Walker, Alexander 1852-1934 *NatCAB 25*
Walker, Alexander Edward 1887-1960
NatCAB 48
Walker, Alexander Edward 1887-1961 *WhAm*
Walker, Alexander Stewart 1876-1952
NatCAB 41, WhAm 3
Walker, Alfred 1876-1948 *WhAm 2*
Walker, Alice Johnstone 1871- *WhAm 5*
Walker, Alice Mather 1862- *WomWWA 14*
Walker, Amasa 1799-1875 *AmBi, ApCAB,
BiAUS, BiDrAC, DcAmB, Drake,
NatCAB 11, TwCBDA, WebAB,
WhAm H*
Walker, Amelia Himes *WomWWA 14*
Walker, Anna Williams 1865- *WomWWA 14*
Walker, Annie Kendrick 1876- *WhAm 5*
Walker, Arthur John 1886-1953 *NatCAB 43*
Walker, Arthur Lucian 1863-1952 *WhAm 3*
Walker, Arthur Tappan 1867-1948 *WhAm 2*
Walker, Arthur Wellington 1874-1955
NatCAB 44
Walker, Asa 1845-1916 *DcAmB, WhAm 1*
Walker, Audiss Moore 1886-1957 *NatCAB 44*
Walker, Mrs. Barbour 1866-1950 *WhAm 2*
Walker, Mrs. Barbour see also Walker, Mary
Adelaide
Walker, Belle Maude *WomWWA 14*
Walker, Benjamin 1753-1818 *ApCAB, BiAUS,
BiDrAC, Drake, NatCAB 5, WhAm H*
Walker, Bertha Elizabeth 1867- *WomWWA 14*
Walker, Bradford Hastings 1884-1949 *WhAm 2*
Walker, Bradley 1877-1951 *NatCAB 40*
Walker, Bryant 1856-1936 *WhAm 1*
Walker, Buz M 1863-1949 *WhAm 2*
Walker, C C B 1824-1888 *BiAUS*
Walker, C C B see also Walker, Charles
Christopher Brainerd
Walker, C Irvine 1842- *WhAm 4*
Walker, C J 1867- *WhoColR*
Walker, C J, Madame *DcAmB, NotAW*
Walker, C S *NewYHSD*
Walker, C W *NewYHSD*
Walker, Caroline Burnite 1875-1936 *DcAmLiB*
Walker, Chapman Johnston 1909-1971
WhAm 6
Walker, Charles 1802-1868 *NatCAB 20*
Walker, Charles Abbot 1868-1930 *WhAm 1*
Walker, Charles Bertram 1875- *WhAm 5*
Walker, Charles Christopher Brainerd 1824-1888
BiDrAC, WhAm H
Walker, Charles Christopher Brainerd see also
Walker, C C B
Walker, Charles Clement 1877- *WhAm 5*
Walker, Charles Howard 1857-1936 *AmBi,
NatCAB 14, WhAm 1*
Walker, Charles Irish 1814-1895 *TwCBDA*
Walker, Charles Jabez 1869-1938 *NatCAB 28,
WhAm 1*
Walker, Charles Manning 1834- *ApCAB,
BiAUS, WhAm 4*
Walker, Charles Monson 1857-1947
NatCAB 36
Walker, Charles Morehead 1859-1920
NatCAB 29
Walker, Charles Rumford 1893-1974 *WhAm 6*
Walker, Charles Swan 1846- *WhAm 4*
Walker, Charles Thomas 1858-1921
NatCAB 13, WhAm 1
Walker, Charles Wellington 1889-1967
NatCAB 53, WhAm 5
Walker, Charles Wheeler 1879-1964
NatCAB 51
Walker, Charlotte Abell 1863- *WhAm 4*
Walker, Cinderella Dalrymple *WomWWA 14*

Walker, Clement Adams 1820-1883
NatCAB 30
Walker, Clifford Black 1884-1943 *NatCAB 40*
Walker, Clifford Mitchell 1877-1954 *WhAm 3*
Walker, Clyde S 1883-1952 *NatCAB 43*
Walker, Cornelius 1819-1907 *ApCAB,*
TwCBDA, WhAm 1
Walker, Curtis Howe 1877-1956 *WhAm 3*
Walker, Cyrus 1827-1913 *NatCAB 32*
Walker, Daniel *NewYHSD*
Walker, Danton MacIntyre 1899-1960 *WhAm 4*
Walker, Darrell E 1920-1973 *WhAm 6*
Walker, David d1820 *BiAUS, BiDrAC,*
WhAm H, WhAmP
Walker, David 1785-1830 *DcAmB, McGEWB,*
NatCAB 14, WebAB, WhAm H
Walker, David 1806-1879 *DcAmB,*
NatCAB 13, TwCBDA, WhAm H
Walker, David 1837-1917 *NatCAB 17*
Walker, David Harold 1873-1963 *NatCAB 50,*
WhAm 4
Walker, David Shelby 1815-1891 *BiAUS,*
BiDAmEd, DcAmB, NatCAB 11,
TwCBDA, WhAm H
Walker, Dean H 1889-1953 *NatCAB 41*
Walker, Dougal Ormonde Beaconsfield
1890-1955 *WhAm 3*
Walker, Dow Vernon 1885-1947 *WhAm 2*
Walker, Dugald Stewart d1937 *WhAm 1*
Walker, Miss E *NewYHSD*
Walker, E L *NewYHSD*
Walker, E S Johnny 1911- *BiDrAC*
Walker, Edward Allan 1869-1951 *NatCAB 39*
Walker, Edward Dwight 1858-1890 *NatCAB 6,*
WhAm H
Walker, Edward Franklin 1852-1918
NatCAB 17
Walker, Edward Valentine 1894-1964
NatCAB 54
Walker, Edward Wood 1853-1925 *NatCAB 27*
Walker, Edwin 1830- *NatCAB 10*
Walker, Edwin 1832-1910 *ApCAB Sup,*
WhAm 1
Walker, Edwin Robert 1862-1932 *WhAm 1*
Walker, Edwin Ruthven 1906-1974 *WhAm 6*
Walker, Edyth 1867-1950 *NotAW*
Walker, Elisha 1879-1950 *NatCAB 50,*
WhAm 3
Walker, Elizabeth Harrison 1897- *BiCAW*
Walker, Elizabeth L *NewYHSD*
Walker, Elmer Theophilus 1867-1955
NatCAB 48
Walker, Elmer Warren 1863- *NatCAB 16*
Walker, Elmer Woodbury 1848-1922
NatCAB 19
Walker, Emily Talbot *WomWWA 14*
Walker, Emma Elizabeth *WomWWA 14*
Walker, Emory Judson 1844-1918 *WhAm 1*
Walker, Ernest George 1869-1944 *WhAm 2*
Walker, Ethel Hornick *WomWWA 14*
Walker, Eveline *NewYHSD*
Walker, Evelyn *WomWWA 14*
Walker, Faye 1848-1903 *TwCBDA, WhAm 1*
Walker, Felix 1753-1828 *BiDrAC, NatCAB 7,*
WhAm H, WhAmP
Walker, Felix 1753-1830? *BiAUS, TwCBDA*
Walker, Ferdinand Graham 1859-1927
WhAm 1
Walker, Francis 1764-1806 *BiAUS, BiDrAC,*
WhAm H
Walker, Francis 1870-1950 *NatCAB 40,*
WhAm 2
Walker, Francis Amasa 1840-1897 *AmBi,*
ApCAB, BiAUS, BiDAmEd, DcAmB,
Drake, EncAB, NatCAB 5, TwCBDA,
WebAB, WhAm H
Walker, Francis John Harwell 1881- *WhAm 6*
Walker, Francis Stoughton 1909-1952
NatCAB 40
Walker, Frank Banghart 1867-1927 *NatCAB 16,*
WhAm 1
Walker, Frank Buckley 1889-1963 *WhAm 4*
Walker, Frank Comerford 1886-1959 *BiDrUSE,*
NatCAB 47, WhAm 3
Walker, Frank Ray 1877-1949 *WhAm 2*
Walker, Frank Robinson 1855- *WhAm 4*
Walker, Fred Allan 1867-1947 *WhAm 2*
Walker, Fred Livingood 1887-1969 *WhAm 5*

Walker, Frederick 1907-1962 *WhAm 4*
Walker, Freeman 1780-1827 *ApCAB, BiAUS,*
BiDrAC, NatCAB 11, TwCBDA,
WhAm H
Walker, Gale Havard 1906-1958 *NatCAB 48*
Walker, Gayle Courtney 1903-1941 *WhAm 1*
Walker, George d1819 *BiAUS*
Walker, George 1763-1819 *BiDrAC, WhAm H,*
WhAmP
Walker, George 1768-1819 *ApCAB,*
NatCAB 12, TwCBDA
Walker, George 1824-1888 *ApCAB, TwCBDA*
Walker, George 1869-1937 *WhAm 1*
Walker, George Abram 1879-1959 *WhAm 3*
Walker, George Clarke 1835-1905 *NatCAB 20*
Walker, George Henry 1914-1969 *NatCAB 55,*
WhAm 5
Walker, George Leon 1830-1900 *WhAm 1*
Walker, George Levi 1867- *WhAm 4*
Walker, George Richard 1857- *WhAm 4*
Walker, George Rowland 1879- *WhAm 6*
Walker, George Winfield 1861-1943 *WhAm 2*
Walker, Gilbert Carlton 1832-1885 *ApCAB,*
BiAUS, DcAmB, NatCAB 5
Walker, Gilbert Carlton 1833-1885 *BiDrAC,*
TwCBDA, WhAm H
Walker, Gilbert M 1927- *IlBEAAW*
Walker, Gilbert Marshal 1864-1928
NatCAB 33
Walker, Grant 1852-1920 *ApCAB X*
Walker, Guy Morrison 1870- *ApCAB X,*
WhAm 5
Walker, Harold 1876-1938 *NatCAB 28*
Walker, Harriet Granger Hulet 1841-1917
AmWom, BiCAW, NatCAB 6,
WomWWA 14
Walker, Harry 1900-1968 *WhAm 5*
Walker, Harry Bruce 1884-1957 *NatCAB 47,*
WhAm 3
Walker, Harry L 1875- *WhoColR*
Walker, Harry Leslie 1877-1954 *NatCAB 42,*
WhAm 3
Walker, Harry Lewis 1863-1957 *NatCAB 48*
Walker, Harry Wilson 1859-1926 *NatCAB 20,*
WhAm 1
Walker, Harvey 1900-1971 *WhAm 5*
Walker, Henderson 1660-1704 *ApCAB, BiAUS,*
Drake
Walker, Henry Clay, Jr. 1885-1963 *WhAm 4*
Walker, Henry Hammersley 1871-1927
WhAm 1
Walker, Henry Harrison d1917 *NatCAB 18*
Walker, Henry Lee 1905-1964 *NatCAB 52,*
WhAm 4
Walker, Henry Oliver 1843-1929 *AmBi,*
DcAmB, NatCAB 9, NatCAB 13,
NatCAB 22, TwCBDA, WhAm 1
Walker, Henry Yonge 1879-1955 *WhAm 3*
Walker, Herbert William 1895-1967 *WhAm 4*
Walker, Herman 1850-1913 *NatCAB 8*
Walker, Horatio 1858-1938 *AmBi, BnEnAmA,*
WhAm 1
Walker, Sir Hoveden 1660?-1726 *Drake*
Walker, Sir Hovenden 1660?-1726 *ApCAB*
Walker, Hubert Millar 1887-1943 *NatCAB 32*
Walker, Hugh Kelso 1861-1949 *NatCAB 13,*
WhAm 2
Walker, Irving Miller 1885-1969 *WhAm 5*
Walker, Irwin Nolan d1973 *WhAm 6*
Walker, Isaac Chandler 1883-1950 *NatCAB 43*
Walker, Isaac Pigeon d1872 *BiAUS*
Walker, Isaac Pigeon 1813-1872 *ApCAB,*
NatCAB 3, TwCBDA
Walker, Isaac Pigeon 1815-1872 *BiDrAC,*
WhAm H
Walker, Ivan 1892-1957 *NatCAB 47*
Walker, Ivan N 1839-1905 *NatCAB 12,*
WhAm 1
Walker, J Frederic 1903-1969 *WhAm 5*
Walker, J Herbert 1890-1947 *WhAm 2*
Walker, Jacob Garrett 1840-1915 *WhAm 1*
Walker, James *NewYHSD*
Walker, James 1794-1874 *AmBi, ApCAB,*
DcAmB, Drake, NatCAB 6, TwCBDA,
WhAm H
Walker, James 1819-1889 *BiAUS, IlBEAAW,*
NewYHSD, REnAW, WhAm H

Walker, James Alexander 1832-1901
ApCAB Sup, BiDConf, BiDrAC,
NatCAB 9, TwCBDA, WhAm 1
Walker, James Barr 1805-1887 *ApCAB,*
DcAmB, Drake, WhAm H
Walker, James Baynes 1846-1910 *WhAm 1*
Walker, James Bradford Richmond 1821-
ApCAB
Walker, James Daniel 1830-1906 *ApCAB,*
NatCAB 12, TwCBDA
Walker, James David 1830-1906 *BiDrAC,*
WhAmP
Walker, James E *NewYHSD*
Walker, James Everett 1854- *WhAm 4*
Walker, James Hume 1872-1939 *NatCAB 30*
Walker, James John 1846-1946 *DcAmB S4,*
NatCAB 34, WebAB, WhAm 2
Walker, James L *NewYHSD*
Walker, James Monroe 1820-1881 *NatCAB 15*
Walker, James Murdock 1813-1854 *ApCAB*
Walker, James Perkins 1829-1868 *ApCAB*
Walker, James Peter 1851-1890 *BiDrAC,*
WhAm H
Walker, James V 1859- *WhAm 4*
Walker, James Wilson Grimes 1868-1950
WhAm 3
Walker, Jay P d1966 *WhAm 4*
Walker, Jesse 1760?-1835 *ApCAB*
Walker, John 1731-1803 *DcScB*
Walker, John 1744-1809 *ApCAB, BiAUS,*
BiDrAC, NatCAB 11, TwCBDA,
WhAm H
Walker, John 1832- *ApCAB*
Walker, John 1858-1928 *NatCAB 48*
Walker, John A 1837-1907 *NatCAB 8*
Walker, John Baldwin 1860-1942 *ApCAB X,*
NatCAB 15, WhAm 2
Walker, John Brisben 1847-1931 *ApCAB Sup,*
DcAmB, NatCAB 9, WhAm 1
Walker, John Charles 1893-1960 *NatCAB 48*
Walker, John Earl 1886-1955 *WhAm 3*
Walker, John Franklin 1873-1953 *NatCAB 44*
Walker, John Franklin 1925-1973 *WhAm 6*
Walker, John George 1822-1893 *ApCAB Sup,*
BiDConf, TwCBDA
Walker, John Grimes 1835-1907 *AmBi,*
ApCAB, ApCAB X, DcAmB,
NatCAB 11, TwCBDA, WebAMB,
WhAm 1
Walker, John H *BiAUS*
Walker, John Leonard 1909- *WhAm 5*
Walker, John Marshall 1838-1919 *NatCAB 18*
Walker, John Moore 1888-1951 *NatCAB 38,*
WhAm 3
Walker, John Randall 1874- *BiDrAC,*
WhAm 5, WhAmP
Walker, John Williams d1823 *BiAUS*
Walker, John Williams 1783-1823 *BiDrAC,*
WhAm H
Walker, John Williams 1789-1823 *ApCAB,*
NatCAB 11, TwCBDA
Walker, John Yates Gholson 1871-1940
WhAm 1
Walker, Jonathan 1799-1878 *ApCAB*
Walker, Jonathan Hoge 1754-1824 *DcAmB,*
WhAm H
Walker, Joseph *BiAUS*
Walker, Joseph 1865-1941 *NatCAB 31,*
WhAm 2
Walker, Joseph Albert 1921-1966 *WhAm 4*
Walker, Joseph Burbeen 1822- *ApCAB*
Walker, Joseph Edison 1880-1958 *NatCAB 50*
Walker, Joseph Henry 1829-1907 *BiDrAC,*
NatCAB 10, TwCBDA, WhAm 1,
WhAmP
Walker, Joseph Henry 1865-1933 *NatCAB 25*
Walker, Joseph Marshall 1780?-1856
NatCAB 10, TwCBDA
Walker, Joseph Reddeford 1798-1876 *ApCAB,*
DcAmB, NatCAB 5, REnAW, WebAB,
WhAm H
Walker, Joseph Robinson 1863-1944
NatCAB 39
Walker, Katherine Kent Child 1840?- *ApCAB*
Walker, Kenneth N 1898-1945 *WhAm 3*
Walker, Kenzie Wallace 1870-1958 *WhAm 3*
Walker, Lapsley Greene 1854-1939 *WhAm 1*
Walker, Leroy Pope 1817-1884 *AmBi, ApCAB,*

Walker, ApCAB Sup, BiDConf, DcAmB, NatCAB 5, TwCBDA, WhAm H
Walker, Lewis 1855-1938 NatCAB 27, NatCAB 28
Walker, Lewis, III 1913-1973 WhAm 5
Walker, Lewis B 1890-1962 WhAm 4
Walker, Lewis Carter 1875-1947 WhAm 2
Walker, Lewis Leavell 1873-1944 BiDrAC
Walker, Lewis M 1892-1960 NatCAB 48
Walker, Lewis Marshall 1867-1939 NatCAB 29
Walker, Louis Carlisle 1875-1963 NatCAB 50, WhAm 4
Walker, Lucius Marsh 1829-1863 TwCBDA
Walker, M NewYHSD
Walker, Maggie Lena 1867-1934 NotAW
Walker, Margaret Burt Gardner 1860- WomWWA 14
Walker, Margaret Coulson WomWWA 14
Walker, Mary 1811- WhAm H
Walker, Mary Adelaide 1866-1950 WomWWA 14
Walker, Mary Adelaide see also Walker, Mrs. Barbour
Walker, Mary Cynthia 1861- WomWWA 14
Walker, Mary Edwards 1832-1919 AmBi, AmWom, DcAmB, NatCAB 13, WebAMB, WhAm 1
Walker, Matthew Henry 1845- NatCAB 7, NatCAB 15
Walker, Meriwether Lewis 1869-1947 NatCAB 40, WhAm 2
Walker, Minerva 1853- AmWom
Walker, Minnie Lulu Royse 1869- WomWWA 14
Walker, Myron Hamilton 1855-1928 WhAm 1
Walker, Nat Gaillard 1886-1946 WhAm 2
Walker, Nathan Wilson 1875-1936 WhAm 1
Walker, Nathaniel Daniel 1886- WhoColR
Walker, Nellie Verne 1874- WhAm 5, WomWWA 14
Walker, Nelson Macy 1891-1944 WhAm 2
Walker, Newton Farmer 1845-1927 WhAm 4
Walker, Norman McFarlane 1853- WhAm 4
Walker, Oliver David 1860-1954 NatCAB 43
Walker, Paul Atlee 1881-1965 WhAm 4
Walker, Percival John 1875-1938 NatCAB 41
Walker, Percy 1812-1880 BiAUS, BiDrAC, WhAm H
Walker, Perley F 1875-1927 WhAm 1
Walker, Pinkney Houston 1815-1885 DcAmB, NatCAB 5, WhAm H
Walker, Platt Dickinson 1849-1923 WhAm 1
Walker, Prentiss Lafayette 1917- BiDrAC
Walker, Ralf Marc 1873-1935 NatCAB 41
Walker, Ralph Curry 1892-1962 WhAm 4
Walker, Ralph Merritt 1881-1941 NatCAB 38
Walker, Ralph Thomas 1889-1973 WhAm 5
Walker, Ramsay M 1867-1959 WhAm 3
Walker, Reuben Eugene 1851-1922 WhAm 1
Walker, Reuben Lindsay 1827-1890 ApCAB Sup, BiDConf, DcAmB, TwCBDA, WhAm H
Walker, Richard Earl 1884-1935 NatCAB 26
Walker, Richard Wilde 1823-1874 BiDConf
Walker, Richard Wilde 1857-1936 NatCAB 28, WhAm 1
Walker, Robert d1772 Drake
Walker, Robert d1951 WhAm 3
Walker, Robert Barney 1913-1973 WhAm 5
Walker, Robert Coleman 1889-1954 NatCAB 44, WhAm 3
Walker, Robert D W NewYHSD
Walker, Robert E 1906-1958 WhAm 3
Walker, Robert Franklin 1850-1930 DcAmB, NatCAB 26, WhAm 1, WhAm 1C
Walker, Robert J 1801-1869 BiAUS
Walker, Robert J 1844- NatCAB 3
Walker, Robert James 1801-1869 BiDrAC, BiDrUSE, Drake, WhAm H, WhAmP
Walker, Robert Jarvis Cochran 1838-1903 BiDrAC
Walker, Robert John 1801-1869 AmBi, ApCAB, DcAmB, EncAB, McGEWB, NatCAB 6, REnAW, TwCBDA, WebAB, WhAm H
Walker, Robert Murdoch 1864-1920 NatCAB 18
Walker, Robert Sparks 1878- WhAm 6

Walker, Robert Tunstall 1879-1957 NatCAB 44
Walker, Roberts 1874-1926 WhAm 1
Walker, Roger A P 1879-1955 WhAm 3
Walker, Roger Venning 1895-1961 NatCAB 48
Walker, Rollin Hough 1865-1955 WhAm 3
Walker, Rome Haward 1888-1942 NatCAB 33
Walker, Rose Kershaw 1847- AmWom
Walker, Ross Graham 1891-1970 NatCAB 56
Walker, Ross H 1894-1972 WhAm 5
Walker, Roy 1889-1939 NatCAB 30
Walker, Ruth Irene 1896-1962 WhAm 4
Walker, Ryan 1870-1932 WhAm 1
Walker, Samuel NewYHSD
Walker, Samuel DeBow 1893-1952 NatCAB 42
Walker, Samuel J 1895-1964 WhAm 4
Walker, Samuel Swan 1806-1848 NewYHSD
Walker, Sarah Breedlove 1867-1919 DcAmB, NotAW, WebAB
Walker, Scott Wells 1909-1965 WhAm 4
Walker, Sears Cook 1805-1853 AmBi, ApCAB, DcAmB, Drake, NatCAB 8, WhAm H
Walker, Simeon NewYHSD
Walker, Stanley 1898-1962 WhAm 4
Walker, Stanton 1894-1971 WhAm 5
Walker, Stewart McCulloch 1903-1966 WhAm 4
Walker, Stuart Armstrong 1880-1941 DcAmB S3, NatCAB 38, WhAm 1
Walker, Stuart Wilson 1862-1923 WhAm 1
Walker, Susan Baldwin 1860- WomWWA 14
Walker, Talbot Cyrus 1886-1956 NatCAB 46
Walker, Theodore C 1839- WhAm 4
Walker, Theodore Penfield 1886-1951 WhAm 3
Walker, Thomas NewYHSD
Walker, Thomas 1715-1794 ApCAB, DcAmB, EncAAH, WebAB, WhAm H
Walker, Thomas Barlow 1840-1928 ApCAB X, DcAmB, NatCAB 6, WhAm 1
Walker, Thomas Hamilton Beb 1873- WhoColR
Walker, Thomas Joseph 1877-1945 WhAm 2
Walker, Thomas Woodruff 1833-1890 NatCAB 18
Walker, Tillie 1929- REnAW
Walker, Timothy 1705-1782 ApCAB, DcAmB, WhAm H
Walker, Timothy 1737-1822 ApCAB, BiAUS, Drake
Walker, Timothy 1802-1856 AmBi, DcAmB, Drake, NatCAB 5, WhAm H
Walker, Timothy 1806-1856 ApCAB
Walker, Tom P 1891-1961 WhAm 4
Walker, W Harrison 1874-1951 NatCAB 40
Walker, Wallace Delamater 1887-1939 NatCAB 28
Walker, Walter 1883-1956 BiDrAC, WhAm 3, WhAm 4
Walker, Walton Harris 1889-1950 DcAmB S4, WebAMB, WhAm 3
Walker, William NewYHSD
Walker, William 1793-1863 ApCAB
Walker, William 1800-1874 REnAW
Walker, William 1824-1860 AmBi, ApCAB, DcAmB, Drake, McGEWB, NatCAB 11, WebAB, WhAm H
Walker, William Adams 1805-1861 BiAUS, BiDrAC, WhAm H
Walker, William Aiken 1838?-1921 NewYHSD
Walker, William Alexander 1894-1975 WhAm 6
Walker, William Baker 1867- NatCAB 15
Walker, William Bradley 1873-1934 NatCAB 26
Walker, William David 1839-1917 ApCAB, NatCAB 12, TwCBDA, WhAm 1
Walker, William F NewYHSD
Walker, William G 1890-1974 WhAm 6
Walker, William H T 1816-1864 ApCAB
Walker, William H T 1817-1864 Drake
Walker, William Henry 1826-1903 NatCAB 6
Walker, William Henry 1871-1938 WhAm 1
Walker, William Henry Talbot 1816-1864 BiDConf, DcAmB, TwCBDA, WebAMB, WhAm H
Walker, William Henry Thomas 1816-1864 NatCAB 13
Walker, William Hultz 1869-1934 AmBi, ApCAB X, WhAm 1
Walker, William Johnson 1790-1865 ApCAB,

DcAmB, Drake, WhAm H
Walker, William Kemble 1867-1937 WhAm 1
Walker, William Lester 1872-1917 NatCAB 18
Walker, William Lippitt 1884-1966 NatCAB 5
Walker, William May 1905-1974 WhAm 6
Walker, William McCreary 1813-1866 ApCAB Drake
Walker, William Pomp 1868-1930 NatCAB 24
Walker, William Russell 1884-1936 NatCAB 2
Walker, William S 1793-1863 ApCAB
Walker, William S 1889-1955 WhAm 3
Walker, Willis J 1873-1943 WhAm 2
Walker, Williston 1860-1922 DcAmB, DcAmReB, NatCAB 19, WhAm 1
Walker-Martinez, Carlos 1842- ApCAB
Walkinshaw, Robert Boyd 1884-1963 NatCAB 52, WhAm 4
Walkley, Raymond Lowrey 1888-1962 WhAm
Walkowitz, Abraham 1880?-1965 BnEnAmA, WhAm 4
Walkup, Liberty 1844- NatCAB 4
Wall, Albert Chandler 1866-1945 WhAm 2
Wall, Alexander James 1884-1944 WhAm 2
Wall, Alfred S 1809-1896 NewYHSD
Wall, Annie Carpenter 1859- AmWom, NatCAB 5
Wall, Bernhardt T 1872- IlBEAAW
Wall, Edward Clarence 1843-1915 WhAm 1
Wall, Edward Everett 1860-1944 WhAm 2
Wall, Edward John 1860-1928 WhAm 1
Wall, Enos Andrew 1839-1920 NatCAB 20
Wall, Francis Lowry 1885-1964 WhAm 4
Wall, Frank Jerome 1886-1947 WhAm 2
Wall, Garret Dorset 1783-1850 ApCAB, BiAUS, BiDrAC, Drake, NatCAB 5, TwCBDA, WhAm H
Wall, Garrett Buckner 1870-1928 WhAm 1
Wall, George Willard 1839- WhAm 4
Wall, Harry Rutherford 1909-1973 WhAm 6
Wall, Hubert Stanley 1902-1971 WhAm 5
Wall, James Walter 1820-1872 ApCAB, BiAUS, BiDrAC, Drake, NatCAB 10, WhAm H
Wall, John Perry 1836-1895 NatCAB 4
Wall, Joseph Baisden 1847- NatCAB 6
Wall, Leo Aloysius 1918-1972 NatCAB 56
Wall, Louise Herrick 1866- WomWWA 14
Wall, Stuart Sipley 1891-1963 NatCAB 50, WhAm 4
Wall, William 1800-1872 BiDrAC, WhAm H
Wall, William Allen 1801-1885 BiAUS, NewYHSD
Wall, William Archibald 1828-1875? NewYHSD
Wall, William Coventry 1810-1886 NewYHSD
Wall, William Guy 1792-1864? NewYHSD, WhAm H
Wall, William Guy 1876-1941 WhAm 1
Wallace NewYHSD
Wallace, A H NewYHSD
Wallace, Addison Alexander 1862-1954 WhAm 3
Wallace, Adelle Lackey 1870- WomWWA 14
Wallace, Alexander Gilfillan 1829-1913 WhAm 1
Wallace, Alexander Stuart 1810-1893 BiAUS, BiDrAC, WhAm H
Wallace, Alfred Russel 1822-1913 ApCAB
Wallace, Alfred Russel 1823-1913 AsBiEn, DcScB, McGEWB
Wallace, Austin Edward 1879-1936 WhAm 1
Wallace, Benjamin A NewYHSD
Wallace, Benjamin Bruce 1882-1947 WhAm 2
Wallace, Bruce Hinds 1890-1961 WhAm 4
Wallace, Campbell 1806-1895 NatCAB 2
Wallace, Carleton Lyman 1865-1919 NatCAB 17
Wallace, Charles Frederick 1885-1964 NatCAB 51, WhAm 4
Wallace, Charles Hodge 1858-1946 NatCAB 13 WhAm 2
Wallace, Charles William 1865-1932 AmBi, DcAmB, NatCAB 15, NatCAB 23, WhAm 1
Wallace, Charlton 1872-1946 WhAm 2
Wallace, Cyrus Washington 1805-1889 NatCAB 5
Wallace, Daniel 1801-1859 BiAUS, BiDrAC,

WhAm H

Wallace, Daniel Alden 1878-1954 *WhAm 3*

Wallace, David 1799-1859 *ApCAB, BiAUS, BiDrAC, DcAmB, Drake, NatCAB 13, TwCBDA, WhAm H*

Wallace, David A 1888-1970 *WhAm 5*

Wallace, David Alexander 1826-1883 *NatCAB 13*

Wallace, David Duncan 1874-1951 *NatCAB 5, WhAm 3*

Wallace, Dewitt 1889- *EncAB, WebAB*

Wallace, Dillon 1863-1939 *NatCAB 34, WhAm 1*

Wallace, Donald H 1903-1953 *WhAm 3*

Wallace, Edwin Sherman 1864- *WhAm 4*

Wallace, Elizabeth 1865-1960 *WhAm 3A*

Wallace, Elizabeth 1866-1960 *BiCAW, WomWWA 14*

Wallace, Ellen Alfleda 1853- *WomWWA 14*

Wallace, Fannie Seymour Ware 1852- *WomWWA 14*

Wallace, Frank 1911-1962 *NatCAB 49*

Wallace, Frederick Ellwood 1893-1958 *NatCAB 44*

Wallace, G Frank 1887-1964 *NatCAB 50*

Wallace, George Barclay 1874-1948 *NatCAB 36, WhAm 2*

Wallace, George Corley 1919- *EncAAH, EncAB, McGEWB, WebAB*

Wallace, George Loney 1872-1930 *NatCAB 26*

Wallace, George Macdonald 1885-1956 *NatCAB 52*

Wallace, George Macdonald 1885-1957 *WhAm 3*

Wallace, George Riddle 1865-1929 *NatCAB 29*

Wallace, George Rodney 1859-1931 *NatCAB 32*

Wallace, George Selden 1871- *WhAm 6*

Wallace, George VanNess 1897-1961 *NatCAB 49*

Wallace, Grace Seccomb *WomWWA 14*

Wallace, Grant 1868- *WhAm 4*

Wallace, Harold Ayer 1902-1958 *WhAm 3*

Wallace, Harry Brookings 1877-1955 *WhAm 3*

Wallace, Helen Peters 1875- *WomWWA 14*

Wallace, Henry 1836-1916 *AmBi, DcAmB, EncAAH, McGEWB, WhAm 1, WhAm 1C*

Wallace, Henry Agard 1888-1965 *BiDrAC, BiDrUSE, EncAAH, EncAB, McGEWB, NatCAB 53, REnAW, WebAB, WhAm 4, WhAmP*

Wallace, Henry Cantwell 1866-1924 *AmBi, BiDrUSE, DcAmB, EncAAH, NatCAB 19, REnAW, WhAm 1*

Wallace, Herbert Meade 1885-1942 *NatCAB 32*

Wallace, Horace Binney 1817-1852 *DcAmB, Drake, NatCAB 6, WhAm H*

Wallace, Horace Binney 1817-1856 *AmBi, ApCAB*

Wallace, Howard T 1856- *WhAm 4*

Wallace, Hugh 1728?-1788 *NatCAB 1*

Wallace, Hugh 1862-1931 *NatCAB 17*

Wallace, Hugh Campbell 1863-1931 *DcAmB, NatCAB 43, WhAm 1*

Wallace, Hugh D 1892-1953 *WhAm 3*

Wallace, Ira 1898-1964 *WhAm 4*

Wallace, James *NewYHSD*

Wallace, Sir James d1803 *ApCAB, Drake*

Wallace, James d1851 *Drake*

Wallace, James 1849-1939 *WhAm 1*

Wallace, James Hope 1807-1854 *ApCAB*

Wallace, James M 1750-1823 *BiAUS, BiDrAC, WhAm H, WhAmP*

Wallace, John Bradford 1778-1837 *ApCAB, Drake*

Wallace, John Findley 1852-1921 *ApCAB X, DcAmB, NatCAB 10, WhAm 1*

Wallace, John Hankins 1822-1903 *DcAmB*

Wallace, John J 1857-1933 *WhAm 1*

Wallace, John Sherman 1877-1934 *WhAm 1*

Wallace, John William 1815-1884 *AmBi, ApCAB, BiAUS, DcAmB, Drake, WhAm H*

Wallace, John Winfield 1818-1889 *BiAUS, BiDrAC, WhAm H*

Wallace, Jonathan Hasson 1824-1892 *BiDrAC, WhAm H*

Wallace, Joseph 1834-1904 *WhAm 1*

Wallace, Karl Richards 1905-1973 *WhAm 6*

Wallace, Lawrence Wilkerson 1881-1973 *WhAm 6*

Wallace, Lew 1827-1905 *AmBi, ApCAB X*

Wallace, Lewis 1827-1905 *AmBi, ApCAB, DcAmB, EncAB, IlBEAAW, McGEWB, NatCAB 4, NewYHSD, TwCBDA, WebAB, WebAMB, WhAm 1*

Wallace, Lewis 1828-1905 *Drake*

Wallace, Lila Bell Acheson *WebAB*

Wallace, Louis Osgood Sanborn 1887-1958 *NatCAB 49*

Wallace, Louise Baird 1867- *WomWWA 14*

Wallace, Lulu Norvell 1866- *WomWWA 14*

Wallace, Lurleen Burns 1926-1968 *WhAm 5*

Wallace, Mrs. M R M 1841- *AmWom*

Wallace, Margaret Adair 1900-1969 *WhAm 5*

Wallace, Margaret Stirling 1869- *WomWWA 14*

Wallace, Mary Kent d1948 *WhAm 6*

Wallace, Nathaniel Dick 1845-1894 *BiDrAC, WhAm H*

Wallace, Neil Robinson 1869- *WomWWA 14*

Wallace, Nina Eggleston 1874- *WomWWA 14*

Wallace, Oates Charles Symonds 1856-1947 *NatCAB 36, WhAm 2*

Wallace, Oscar J *NewYHSD*

Wallace, Robert A 1856-1932 *NatCAB 30*

Wallace, Robert Charles 1881-1955 *WhAm 3*

Wallace, Robert Dwight 1907-1962 *WhAm 4*

Wallace, Robert James 1868-1945 *NatCAB 35, WhAm 4*

Wallace, Robert Minor 1856-1942 *BiDrAC, NatCAB 49, WhAmP*

Wallace, Robert Minor 1857-1942 *WhAm 3*

Wallace, Robert Moore 1847-1913 *WhAm 1*

Wallace, Rodney 1823-1903 *BiDrAC, NatCAB 47*

Wallace, Rothvin 1882- *WhAm 1*

Wallace, Rush Richard 1835-1914 *WhAm 1*

Wallace, S Mayner 1886-1975 *WhAm 6*

Wallace, Schuyler Crawford 1898-1969 *WhAm 5*

Wallace, Sebon Rains 1913-1973 *WhAm 6*

Wallace, Stuart Allen 1898-1965 *WhAm 4*

Wallace, Susan Arnold Elston 1830-1907 *AmWom, ApCAB, NatCAB 10, TwCBDA, WhAm 1*

Wallace, Theodoric Boulware 1860-1949 *NatCAB 38*

Wallace, Thomas 1797-1875 *NatCAB 40*

Wallace, Thomas 1826-1916 *NatCAB 40*

Wallace, Thomas F 1871- *WhAm 5*

Wallace, Thomas J *NewYHSD*

Wallace, Thomas Ross 1848-1929 *WhAm 3*

Wallace, Thomas Walker 1879- *WhoColR*

Wallace, Tom 1874-1961 *WhAm 4*

Wallace, Walter Richard 1879-1937 *NatCAB 28*

Wallace, Warrack 1894-1969 *NatCAB 55*

Wallace, Sir William 1270?-1305 *McGEWB*

Wallace, William 1768-1843 *DcScB*

Wallace, William 1820- *ApCAB*

Wallace, William 1825-1904 *DcAmB*

Wallace, William, Jr. 1864-1939 *WhAm 1*

Wallace, William Alexander Anderson 1817-1899 *DcAmB, WhAm H*

Wallace, William Andrew 1827-1896 *ApCAB, BiAUS, BiDrAC, TwCBDA, WhAm H*

Wallace, William Andrew 1828-1896 *NatCAB 10*

Wallace, William Charles 1875-1934 *NatCAB 24, WhAm 5*

Wallace, William Copeland 1856-1901 *BiDrAC*

Wallace, William H *NewYHSD*

Wallace, William Harvey Lamb 1821-1862 *ApCAB, Drake, NatCAB 6, TwCBDA*

Wallace, William Henry 1861-1933 *NatCAB 24, WhAm 1*

Wallace, William Henry 1887-1951 *WhAm 3*

Wallace, William Henson 1811-1879 *BiAUS, BiDrAC, WhAm H, WhAmP*

Wallace, William James 1839-1917 *BiAUS, DcAmB, NatCAB 17, TwCBDA, WhAm 1*

Wallace, William James 1839-1917 *ApCAB*

Wallace, William McLean 1912-1968 *WhAm 5*

Wallace, William Miller 1844-1924 *WhAm 1*

Wallace, William R *NewYHSD*

Wallace, William Robert 1886-1960 *WhAm 4*

Wallace, William Ross 1819-1881 *ApCAB, DcAmB, Drake, NatCAB 8, TwCBDA, WhAm H*

Wallace, William T 1828- *NatCAB 13*

Wallace, William Vincent 1814-1865 *ApCAB, NatCAB 5*

Wallace, Wilton Harris 1898-1959 *NatCAB 47*

Wallace, Zerelda Gray Sanders 1817-1901 *AmWom, NatCAB 5, NotAW*

Wallace-Johnson, Isaac Theophilus Akunna 1895-1965 *McGEWB*

Wallach, Antony 1834- *NatCAB 1*

Wallach, Otto 1847-1931 *AsBiEn, DcScB*

Wallach, Roger Nestor 1882-1941 *NatCAB 31*

Wallack, Henry John 1790-1870 *DcAmB, WhAm H*

Wallack, James W, Jr. *Drake*

Wallack, James William 1794-1864 *ApCAB*

Wallack, James William 1795-1864 *AmBi, DcAmB, Drake, NatCAB 4, TwCBDA, WebAB, WhAm H*

Wallack, James William 1818-1873 *DcAmB, WhAm H*

Wallack, John Johnstone Lester 1820-1888 *TwCBDA, WebAB, WhAm H*

Wallack, John Lester 1819-1888 *Drake*

Wallack, John Lester 1820-1888 *ApCAB, NatCAB 4*

Wallack, Lester 1820-1888 *AmBi, DcAmB, WebAB*

Wallas, Graham 1858-1932 *McGEWB*

Wallau, Herman L 1877- *WhAm 5*

Wallbridge, Lewis 1816- *ApCAB*

Wallen, Henry Davies 1819-1886 *ApCAB*

Wallen, Saul 1910-1969 *NatCAB 55, WhAm 5*

Wallen, Theodore Clifford 1894-1936 *WhAm 1*

Wallenberg, Axel Fingal 1874- *WhAm 5*

Wallenberg, Marc, Jr. 1924-1971 *WhAm 5*

Wallenius, Carl Gideon 1865-1947 *WhAm 2*

Wallenstein, Albrecht E Wenzel Von 1583-1634 *WhoMilH*

Wallenstein, Albrecht Wenzel E Von 1583-1634 *McGEWB*

Wallenstein, Merrill Bernard 1920-1968 *WhAm 5*

Waller, Absalom 1860-1937 *NatCAB 33*

Waller, Alexander Arthur 1872- *WhoColR*

Waller, Allen George 1892-1964 *WhAm 4*

Waller, Augustus Desire 1856-1922 *BiHiMed*

Waller, Augustus Volney 1816-1870 *BiHiMed, DcScB*

Waller, Calvin Hoffman 1880- *WhoColR*

Waller, Cecile Howell 1893-1953 *WhAm 3*

Waller, Charles Buckalew 1890-1970 *NatCAB 56*

Waller, Claude 1864-1918 *WhAm 1*

Waller, Curtis Longino 1887-1950 *NatCAB 40, WhAm 3*

Waller, David Jewett, Jr. 1846-1941 *NatCAB 34, TwCBDA, WhAm 1*

Waller, Edward Carson 1845-1931 *NatCAB 37*

Waller, Edward L *NewYHSD*

Waller, Edwin James 1925-1975 *WhAm 6*

Waller, Elwyn 1846-1919 *ApCAB, NatCAB 13, TwCBDA, WhAm 1*

Waller, Emma 1820-1899 *DcAmB, NatCAB 11, WhAm H*

Waller, Fats *DcAmB S3*

Waller, Frank 1842-1923 *AmBi, ApCAB, NatCAB 23, TwCBDA, WhAm 1*

Waller, Frederic 1886-1954 *DcAmB S5*

Waller, George Platt 1889-1962 *NatCAB 50, WhAm 4*

Waller, Gilbert Johnson 1859- *NatCAB 16, WhAm 4*

Waller, Helen Hiett 1913-1961 *WhAm 4*

Waller, Henry 1864- *WhAm 4*

Waller, Henry Davey 1852-1925 *ApCAB X*

Waller, John *NewYHSD*

Waller, John 1741-1802 *ApCAB*

Waller, John Lightfoot 1809-1854 *ApCAB, DcAmB, NatCAB 5, WhAm H*

Waller, John Robert 1883-1961 *WhAm 4*
Waller, Lewis 1860- *WhAm 1*
Waller, Littleton W T 1886-1967 *WhAm 4*
Waller, Littleton Waller Tazewell 1856-1926 *WebAMB, WhAm 1*
Waller, Mary Ella d1938 *WhAm 1*
Waller, Osmar Lysander 1857-1935 *NatCAB 26, WhAm 1*
Waller, Peter August 1868-1932 *WhAm 1*
Waller, Rose d1941 *WhAm 1*
Waller, Thomas Macdonald 1839-1924 *NatCAB 10*
Waller, Thomas Macdonald 1840?-1924 *DcAmB*
Waller, Thomas McDonald 1840?-1924 *ApCAB, TwCBDA, WhAm 1*
Waller, Thomas Wright 1904-1943 *DcAmB S3, WhAm 4*
Waller, Willard Walter 1899-1945 *DcAmB S3, WhAm 2*
Waller, Sir William 1597-1668 *WhoMilH*
Waller, Wilmer Joyce 1889-1969 *WhAm 5*
Wallerius, Johan Gottschalk 1709-1785 *DcScB*
Wallerstein, Edward 1891-1970 *NatCAB 55, WhAm 5*
Wallerton, Charles Louis Auguste 1721-1788 *ApCAB*
Wallestein, Julius *NewYHSD*
Walley, John 1644-1712 *ApCAB, Drake*
Walley, Samuel Hurd 1805-1877 *BiAUS, BiDrAC, NatCAB 11, WhAm H*
Wallgren, Monrad Charles 1891-1961 *BiDrAC, WhAm 4, WhAmP*
Wallhauser, George Marvin 1900- *BiDrAC, WhAmP*
Wallich, George Charles 1815-1899 *DcScB*
Wallichs, Glenn Everett 1910-1971 *WhAm 5*
Wallihan, Allen Grant 1859- *WhAm 4*
Wallin, Alfred 1836-1923 *NatCAB 5, WhAm 1*
Wallin, John Edward Wallace 1876-1969 *BiDAmEd, WhAm 5*
Wallin, Mathilda K 1858- *BiCAW, WomWWA 14*
Wallin, Samuel *NewYHSD*
Wallin, Samuel 1856-1917 *BiDrAC, NatCAB 17, WhAm 4*
Wallin, Samuel, Jr. *NewYHSD*
Wallin, Van Arthur 1866-1942 *WhAm 2*
Wallin, William John 1879-1963 *WhAm 4*
Walling, Anna Strunsky 1879-1964 *WhAm 4*
Walling, Ansel Tracy 1824-1896 *BiAUS, BiDrAC, WhAm H*
Walling, Clarence Dallas 1890-1969 *NatCAB 56*
Walling, Emory A 1854-1931 *WhAm 1*
Walling, Everett Lewis 1875-1957 *NatCAB 47*
Walling, Henry Francis 1825-1888 *ApCAB, NewYHSD*
Walling, Mary Cole 1838- *AmWom*
Walling, William English 1877-1936 *AmBi, DcAmB S2, WhAm 1*
Walling, William Henry 1895-1973 *WhAm 5*
Walling, Willoughby 1848-1916 *NatCAB 18*
Walling, Willoughby George 1878-1938 *NatCAB 29, WhAm 1*
Wallingford *DcScB*
Wallingford, John Duvall 1869-1924 *WhAm 1*
Wallingford, Vere Olney 1876-1945 *NatCAB 34*
Wallington, Nellie Urner 1847- *WhAm 4, WomWWA 14*
Wallis, Sir Barnes 1887- *WhWW-II*
Wallis, Ella May 1869- *WomWWA 14*
Wallis, Everett Stanley 1899-1965 *NatCAB 52, WhAm 4*
Wallis, Frank E 1862-1929 *NatCAB 22*
Wallis, Frederick Alfred 1869-1951 *NatCAB 41, WhAm 3*
Wallis, Frederick I *NewYHSD*
Wallis, George Edward 1886-1971 *WhAm 5*
Wallis, Gustav 1830-1878 *ApCAB*
Wallis, Hal Brent 1899- *WebAB*
Wallis, Jenny *WhAm 1*
Wallis, John 1616-1703 *AsBiEn, DcScB*
Wallis, Katherine Elizabeth 1861- *WomWWA 14*
Wallis, Nathaniel Thomas 1885- *WhoColR*
Wallis, Philip 1899-1960 *WhAm 4*
Wallis, Samuel 1720-1795 *ApCAB*

Wallis, Severn Teackle 1816-1894 *AmBi, ApCAB, DcAmB, NatCAB 9, WhAm H*
Wallis, William Fisher 1874- *WhAm 5*
Wallon, Louis Florentin 1670?-1725 *ApCAB*
Walls, David Crawford 1882-1958 *WhAm 3*
Walls, Frank Xavier 1869- *WhAm 5*
Walls, Josiah Thomas 1842-1905 *BiAUS, BiDrAC, WhAmP*
Walls, Stanley King *IlBEAAW*
Walls, William Jacob 1885-1975 *WhAm 6*
Walls, William L 1868-1935 *WhAm 1*
Wallstein, Leonard Michael 1884-1968 *ApCAB X, NatCAB 54*
Walmer, Charles Richard 1911-1972 *NatCAB 57*
Walmsley, Robert Miller 1833- *NatCAB 10*
Walmsley, Walter Newbold, Jr. 1904-1973 *WhAm 5*
Waln, Nicholas 1742-1813 *DcAmB, WhAm H*
Waln, Nora 1895-1964 *WhAm 4*
Waln, Robert 1765-1836 *ApCAB, BiAUS, BiDrAC, DcAmB, Drake, NatCAB 10, WhAm H*
Waln, Robert 1794-1825 *ApCAB, DcAmB, Drake, WhAm H*
Walpole, Robert 1676-1745 *McGEWB*
Walras, Marie Esprit Leon 1834-1910 *McGEWB*
Walrath, Florence Dahl 1877-1958 *WhAm 3*
Walrath, Herbert Raymond 1883-1943 *NatCAB 33*
Walrath, John Henry 1866- *WhAm 4*
Walser, Eleanor E 1853- *WomWWA 14*
Walser, Henry 1875-1957 *NatCAB 43*
Walser, Jacob Joseph 1848-1914 *NatCAB 18*
Walser, William Charles 1851-1917 *NatCAB 17*
Walser, Zeb Vance 1863- *TwCBDA*
Walsh, Alice M Durkin 1880- *WomWWA 14*
Walsh, Allan Bartholomew 1874-1953 *BiDrAC, WhAm 5*
Walsh, Arthur 1896-1947 *BiDrAC, NatCAB 36, WhAm 2*
Walsh, Basil Sylvester 1878-1943 *WhAm 2*
Walsh, Benjamin Dann 1808-1869 *ApCAB, DcAmB, WhAm H*
Walsh, Blanche 1873-1915 *DcAmB, NatCAB 12, WhAm 1, WomWWA 14*
Walsh, Carrie Belle Reed d1932 *NatCAB 26*
Walsh, Catherine Shellew 1882-1944 *WhAm 2*
Walsh, Charles Clinton 1867-1943 *WhAm 2*
Walsh, Correa Moylan 1862- *WhAm 3*
Walsh, Sir Cyril Ambrose 1909-1973 *WhAm 6*
Walsh, David *NewYHSD*
Walsh, David Ignatius 1872-1947 *ApCAB X, BiDrAC, DcAmB S4, NatCAB 15, NatCAB 38, WhAm 2, WhAmP*
Walsh, Edmund 1885-1956 *NatCAB 47, WhAm 3*
Walsh, Edward *NewYHSD*
Walsh, Edward Anthony 1900-1973 *WhAm 6*
Walsh, Edward J 1877-1947 *WhAm 2*
Walsh, Emmet M 1892-1968 *WhAm 4A*
Walsh, Sister Frances Marie 1893-1968 *WhAm 5*
Walsh, Francis *NewYHSD*
Walsh, Francis Patrick 1864-1939 *DcAmB S2*
Walsh, Francis Patrick 1912-1964 *NatCAB 51*
Walsh, Frank P 1864-1939 *WhAm 1*
Walsh, Frederick Harper 1884-1964 *WhAm 4*
Walsh, George Ethelbert 1865-1941 *WhAm 1*
Walsh, Gerald Groveland 1892-1951 *WhAm 3*
Walsh, Gerald Powers 1910-1960 *WhAm 4*
Walsh, Groesbeck Francis 1878-1944 *NatCAB 34*
Walsh, Harriet *WomWWA 14*
Walsh, Henry Collins 1863-1927 *DcAmB, WhAm 1*
Walsh, Honor *WomWWA 14*
Walsh, J Hartt 1902-1975 *WhAm 6*
Walsh, James *NewYHSD*
Walsh, James A d1963 *WhAm 4*
Walsh, James Anthony 1867-1936 *DcAmB S2, NatCAB 26, WhAm 1*
Walsh, James Joseph 1858-1909 *BiDrAC*
Walsh, James Joseph 1865-1942 *NatCAB 46, WhAm 2*
Walsh, James Lawrence 1886-1952 *WhAm 3*

Walsh, James William 1868-1932 *NatCAB 25*
Walsh, Jeremiah *NewYHSD*
Walsh, Jessie Chambers McBride 1877- *WomWWA 14*
Walsh, John 1830- *ApCAB*
Walsh, John 1872-1941 *WhAm 2*
Walsh, John Edward 1919-1972 *WhAm 5*
Walsh, John Gaynor 1891-1953 *WhAm 3*
Walsh, John Henry 1853-1924 *WhAm 1*
Walsh, John Henry 1879-1962 *NatCAB 48*
Walsh, John Johnson 1820-1884 *ApCAB*
Walsh, John Klaerr 1887-1964 *WhAm 4*
Walsh, John Richard 1913- *BiDrAC*
Walsh, Joseph 1870-1946 *NatCAB 34*
Walsh, Joseph 1875-1946 *BiDrAC, WhAm 2, WhAmP*
Walsh, Joseph Leonard 1895-1973 *WhAm 6*
Walsh, Joseph Patrick 1902-1971 *WhAm 5*
Walsh, Joseph W 1828?- *NewYHSD*
Walsh, Julius Sylvester 1842-1923 *NatCAB 12, WhAm 1*
Walsh, Lawrence Aloysius 1896-1968 *WhAm 5*
Walsh, Louis Sebastian 1858-1924 *NatCAB 15, WhAm 1*
Walsh, Lucy Pierce Bartlett 1873- *WomWWA 14*
Walsh, M Robert *BiAUS*
Walsh, Matthew James 1882-1963 *WhAm 4*
Walsh, Michael 1763-1840 *ApCAB, Drake*
Walsh, Michael 1810-1859 *ApCAB, BiDrAC, Drake*
Walsh, Michael 1815?-1859 *DcAmB, WhAm H*
Walsh, Michael Francis 1894-1956 *NatCAB 42*
Walsh, Mike d1859 *BiAUS*
Walsh, Patrick 1840-1899 *BiDrAC, NatCAB 2, TwCBDA*
Walsh, Philip F d1973 *WhAm 6*
Walsh, Raycroft 1888-1952 *WhAm 3*
Walsh, Raymond Arnold 1889-1939 *WhAm 1*
Walsh, Raymond James 1917-1960 *WhAm 4*
Walsh, Richard John 1886-1960 *WhAm 4*
Walsh, Robert 1784-1859 *AmBi, ApCAB, DcAmB, Drake, NatCAB 5, WhAm H*
Walsh, Robert Douglas 1928 *WhAm 1*
Walsh, Roy Edward 1920-1968 *WhAm 5*
Walsh, Theodore Edwin 1900-1971 *WhAm 5*
Walsh, Thomas d1928 *WhAm 1C*
Walsh, Thomas 1871-1928 *DcAmB*
Walsh, Thomas 1875-1928 *WhAm 1*
Walsh, Thomas F 1866- *NatCAB 12*
Walsh, Thomas Francis 1851-1910 *NatCAB 15, WhAm 1*
Walsh, Thomas James 1859-1933 *AmBi, ApCAB X, BiDrAC, DcAmB, EncAAH, EncAB, McGEWB, NatCAB 15, NatCAB 24, WebAB, WhAm 1, WhAmP*
Walsh, Thomas Joseph 1873-1952 *DcAmB S5, NatCAB 38, WhAm 3*
Walsh, Thomas Joseph 1882- *ApCAB X*
Walsh, Thomas W 1826-1890 *WhAm H*
Walsh, Thomas Yates 1809-1865 *BiAUS, BiDrAC, NatCAB 10, WhAm H*
Walsh, Timothy Francis 1868-1934 *NatCAB 33*
Walsh, William 1804-1858 *ApCAB*
Walsh, William 1828-1892 *BiAUS, BiDrAC, WhAm H*
Walsh, William Concannon 1890-1975 *WhAm 6*
Walsh, William Edwin 1903-1975 *WhAm 6*
Walsh, William Francis 1875-1946 *WhAm 2*
Walsh, William Henry 1882-1941 *WhAm 1*
Walsh, William Shepard 1854- *ApCAB*
Walsh, William Thomas 1891-1949 *NatCAB 35, WhAm 2*
Walshe, Leo Augustus 1902-1964 *NatCAB 50*
Walson, Charles Moore 1883-1959 *NatCAB 48, WhAm 3*
Walster, Harlow Leslie 1883-1957 *NatCAB 43, WhAm 3*
Walston, Charles 1856-1927 *WhAm 1*
Walston, Vernon C 1906-1964 *WhAm 4*
Walsworth, James Edwin 1889-1961 *NatCAB 49*
Walsworth, Minnie Gow 1859- *AmWom*
Walter Burley *DcScB*
Walter Of Evesham *DcScB*
Walter Of Odington *DcScB*

Walter, Adam B 1820-1875 *NewYHSD*
Walter, Albert G 1811-1876 *DcAmB,*
WhAm H
Walter, Alfred 1851-1907 *WhAm 1*
Walter, Allan Wylie 1903-1961 *WhAm 4*
Walter, Anna 1865- *WomWWA 14*
Walter, Arthur Henry 1899-1962 *WhAm 4*
Walter, Bruno 1876-1962 *NatCAB 52,*
WebAB, WhAm 4
Walter, Caroline Packer Sargent 1873-
WomWWA 14
Walter, Carrie Stevens 1846- *AmWom*
Walter, Charles Albert 1876-1943 *NatCAB 40*
Walter, Cornelia Wells 1813?-1898 *NotAW*
Walter, Ellery 1905-1935 *NatCAB 26*
Walter, Ellery 1906-1935 *WhAm 1*
Walter, Elliot Vincent d1971 *WhAm 5*
Walter, Eugene 1874-1941 *DcAmB S3,*
WhAm H
Walter, Francis Eugene 1894-1963 *BiDrAC,*
WhAm 4, WhAmP
Walter, Frank J 1900-1965 *WhAm 4*
Walter, Frank Keller 1874-1945 *DcAmLiB,*
NatCAB 39, WhAm 2
Walter, George William 1851- *ApCAB,*
WhAm 1
Walter, Harold John 1900-1962 *NatCAB 46*
Walter, Harvey Washington 1819-1878
NatCAB 24
Walter, Herbert Eugene 1867-1945 *WhAm 2*
Walter, Howard Arnold 1883-1918 *WhAm 1*
Walter, Israel David 1815-1866 *NatCAB 3*
Walter, Johann 1496-1570 *McGEWB*
Walter, John *NewYHSD*
Walter, Joseph 1783-1856 *NewYHSD*
Walter, Joseph Saunders *NewYHSD*
Walter, Josephine *WomWWA 14*
Walter, Kent Elno 1892-1964 *NatCAB 50*
Walter, Luther Mason 1877-1947 *WhAm 2*
Walter, Lynde Minshall 1799-1842 *Drake*
Walter, Martin Emmet 1892-1966 *NatCAB 52,*
WhAm 4
Walter, Nehemiah 1663-1750 *ApCAB, Drake*
Walter, Paul Alfred Francis, Jr. 1901-1973
WhAm 6
Walter, Philip 1843- *NatCAB 5*
Walter, Philippe 1810-1847 *DcScB*
Walter, Raymond F 1873-1940 *WhAm 1*
Walter, Robert 1841-1921 *WhAm 1*
Walter, Thomas 1696-1725 *ApCAB, DcAmB,*
Drake
Walter, Thomas 1740?-1789 *DcAmB,*
WhAm H
Walter, Thomas 1745?-1800? *ApCAB, Drake*
Walter, Thomas Ustick 1804-1887 *AmBi,*
ApCAB, BiAUS, BnEnAmA, DcAmB,
Drake, NatCAB 9, NewYHSD,
WhAm H
Walter, William 1737-1800 *ApCAB*
Walter, William Bicker 1796-1822 *ApCAB,*
Drake
Walter, William Emley 1870- *WhAm 5*
Walter, William Grey 1910- *AsBiEn*
Walter, William Henry 1825-1870? *ApCAB,*
WhAm H
Walter, William Joseph d1846 *ApCAB*
Walters, Alexander 1858-1917 *DcAmB,*
WhAm 1, WhoColR
Walters, Anderson Howel 1862-1927 *WhAm 1*
Walters, Anderson Howell 1862-1927 *BiDrAC,*
WhAmP
Walters, Arthur Leonard 1879-1966
NatCAB 53
Walters, Arthur Louis 1884-1961 *NatCAB 49*
Walters, Basil L 1896-1975 *WhAm 6*
Walters, Carl 1883-1955 *WhAm 3*
Walters, Charles Sylvanus 1871-1959
NatCAB 47, WhAm 3
Walters, Emil 1893- *IIBEAAW*
Walters, Francis Marion, Jr. 1888-1953
WhAm 3
Walters, Frank 1864- *WhAm 4*
Walters, Frederick Valentine 1878- *ApCAB X*
Walters, George Alexander 1872-1960 *WhAm 3*
Walters, Gus Washington 1857-1942 *WhAm 2*
Walters, Henry 1848-1931 *DcAmB,*
NatCAB 37, WhAm 1
Walters, Henry C 1870-1931 *WhAm 1*

Walters, Herald Everett 1898-1956 *NatCAB 49*
Walters, Herbert Sanford 1891-1973 *BiDrAC,*
WhAm 6
Walters, J Henry 1874-1952 *NatCAB 40*
Walters, Jack Edward 1896-1967 *WhAm 4*
Walters, James L *NewYHSD*
Walters, John *NewYHSD*
Walters, Josephine *NewYHSD*
Walters, Leon L 1888-1956 *WhAm 3*
Walters, Orville Selkirk 1903-1975 *WhAm 6*
Walters, R G 1888-1952 *WhAm 3*
Walters, Raymond 1885-1970 *WhAm 5*
Walters, Rolland J D 1878-1944 *WhAm 2*
Walters, Susane *NewYHSD*
Walters, Theodore Augustus 1876-1937
WhAm 1
Walters, William H 1925-1970 *WhAm 5*
Walters, William Thompson 1820-1894 *ApCAB,*
DcAmB, NatCAB 1, TwCBDA,
WhAm H
Walthall, Edward Cary 1831-1898 *ApCAB,*
BiDConf, BiDrAC, DcAmB, NatCAB 1,
TwCBDA, WebAMB, WhAm H,
WhAmP
Walthall, Henry Brazeal 1878-1936 *DcAmB S2*
Walther VonDerVogelweide 1170?-1229
McGEWB
Walther, Carl Ferdinand Wilhelm 1811-1887
ApCAB, DcAmB, DcAmReB, NatCAB 26,
WebAB, WhAm H
Walther, Frederick Peter 1882-1950
NatCAB 39
Walther, Henry *NewYHSD*
Walther, Henry Wellman Emile 1888-1945
WhAm 2
Walther, Henry Wellman Emile 1888-1946
NatCAB 35
Walthers, William Kearney 1893-1967
NatCAB 54
Walthour, John Buckman 1904-1952
NatCAB 42
Waltman, Harry Franklin 1871-1951 *WhAm 3*
Waltman, William DeWitt 1875-1955
NatCAB 42, WhAm 3
Walton, Abigail Woodworth 1866-
WomWWA 14
Walton, Albert Douglass 1886-1951 *WhAm 3*
Walton, Alfred Grant 1887-1970 *WhAm 5*
Walton, Alice *WomWWA 14*
Walton, Arthur Calvin 1892-1967 *WhAm 5*
Walton, Arthur Keith 1909-1972 *WhAm 5*
Walton, Charles Edgar 1849-1926 *WhAm 1*
Walton, Charles Milton, Jr. 1891-1968
NatCAB 54, WhAm 5
Walton, Charles Spittall, Jr. 1893-1973
WhAm 6
Walton, Charles Wesley 1819-1900 *BiAUS,*
BiDrAC
Walton, Clara Louise *WomWWA 14*
Walton, Clifford Stevens 1861-1912
NatCAB 15, WhAm 1
Walton, Clyde 1876-1959 *NatCAB 49*
Walton, David Henry 1874-1927 *ApCAB X*
Walton, Duane Edward 1915-1973 *WhAm 6*
Walton, E P 1812-1890 *BiAUS*
Walton, Eleanor Going *WhAm 5*
Walton, Electa Noble Lincoln 1824- *AmWom*
Walton, Eliakim Persons 1812-1890 *BiDrAC,*
NatCAB 20, WhAm H, WhAmP
Walton, Ernest Thomas Sinton 1903- *AsBiEn*
Walton, Ezekiel Parker 1789-1855 *NatCAB 16*
Walton, Florence Louise *WomWWA 14*
Walton, Frank Richmond 1886-1956 *WhAm 3*
Walton, George 1740-1804 *AmBi, ApCAB,*
BiAUS, Drake, NatCAB 1
Walton, George 1741-1804 *DcAmB, WhAm H*
Walton, George 1749-1804 *TwCBDA*
Walton, George 1750-1804 *BiDrAC, WhAmP*
Walton, George Augustus 1822-1908 *WhAm 1*
Walton, George Edward 1839- *ApCAB*
Walton, George Lincoln 1854-1941 *NatCAB 30,*
WhAm 1
Walton, Henry 1804?-1865? *IIBEAAW,*
NewYHSD
Walton, Howard Charles 1897-1966 *WhAm 4,*
WhAm 5
Walton, Izaak 1593-1683 *DcScB, McGEWB*
Walton, James Henry 1878-1947 *WhAm 2*

Walton, James Tart 1875- *WhoColR*
Walton, John 1738-1783 *BiDrAC, WhAmP*
Walton, John Fawcett, Jr. 1893-1974 *WhAm 6*
Walton, John James 1846-1927 *ApCAB X*
Walton, John Whittlesey 1845-1926
NatCAB 22
Walton, Joseph 1826-1892 *NatCAB 12*
Walton, Katharine Kent *WomWWA 14*
Walton, Lee Barker 1871-1937 *WhAm 1*
Walton, Leslie Harvey 1875-1940 *NatCAB 30*
Walton, Lester Aglar 1881?-1965 *WhoColR*
Walton, Lester Aglar 1882-1965 *WhAm 4*
Walton, Lucius Leedom 1865-1935 *WhAm 1*
Walton, Mason Augustus 1838-1917 *WhAm 1*
Walton, Matthew d1819 *BiAUS, BiDrAC,*
WhAm H, WhAmP
Walton, N *NewYHSD*
Walton, Norman Burdett 1884-1950 *WhAm 2*
Walton, Norton Hall 1910-1969 *WhAm 5*
Walton, Octavia *NotAW*
Walton, Sarah Stokes 1844- *AmWom*
Walton, Sophie Porter Todd 1858-
WomWWA 14
Walton, Sydney Grant 1901-1960 *WhAm 4*
Walton, Thomas Cameron 1838-1909 *WhAm 1*
Walton, Thomas Otto 1884-1961 *NatCAB 48,*
WhAm 4
Walton, William 1725?-1796 *NatCAB 1*
Walton, William 1784-1857 *ApCAB*
Walton, William 1843-1915 *WhAm 1*
Walton, William Bell 1871-1939 *BiDrAC,*
WhAm 1, WhAmP
Walton, William Claiborne 1793-1834 *ApCAB*
Walton, William E 1824?- *NewYHSD*
Walton, William Randolph 1873-1952
NatCAB 45, WhAm 3
Walton, Sir William Turner 1902- *McGEWB*
Waltz, Arthur David 1884-1974 *WhAm 6*
Waltz, Elizabeth Cherry 1866-1903 *WhAm 1*
Waltz, Merle Bowman 1873-1956 *NatCAB 42*
Waltz, Millard Fillmore 1857- *WhAm 4*
Waltzinger, Fredrick John 1899-1957
NatCAB 46
Walworth, Clarence Alfonsus 1820-1900
NatCAB 3, TwCBDA
Walworth, Clarence Alphonsus 1820-1900
ApCAB, WhAm 1
Walworth, Clarence Augustus 1820-1900
DcAmB
Walworth, Ellen Hardin 1832-1915 *AmWom,*
ApCAB, NotAW, TwCBDA, WhAm 1,
WomWWA 14
Walworth, Ellen Hardin 1858- *ApCAB*
Walworth, James Jones 1808-1896 *NatCAB 18*
Walworth, Jeannette Ritchie Haderman
1837-1918 *WhAm 4*
Walworth, Jeannette Ritchie Hadermann
1835-1918 *AmWom*
Walworth, Jeannette Ritchie Hadermann
1837-1918 *ApCAB, DcAmB, NatCAB 8*
Walworth, John 1765-1812 *ApCAB*
Walworth, Julianna Morgan 1769-1853 *ApCAB*
Walworth, Mansfield Tracy 1830-1873 *ApCAB,*
NatCAB 5, WhAm H
Walworth, Reuben Hyde 1788-1867 *ApCAB,*
BiDrAC, DcAmB, TwCBDA, WhAm H,
WhAmP
Walworth, Reuben Hyde 1789-1867 *BiAUS,*
Drake, NatCAB 3
Walworth, Reubena Hyde 1867- *ApCAB*
Walz, Edgar Alfred 1859-1935 *NatCAB 28*
Walz, John Albrecht 1871-1954 *WhAm 3*
Walz, William Emanuel 1860- *WhAm 4*
Walzer, Elmer C d1974 *WhAm 6*
Wambaugh, Eugene 1856-1940 *WhAm 1*
Wambaugh, Sarah 1882-1955 *DcAmB S5,*
WhAm 3
Wamboldt, Lucy E 1855- *WomWWA 14*
Wampler, Cloud 1895-1973 *WhAm 6*
Wampler, Fred 1909- *BiDrAC*
Wampler, William Creed 1926- *BiDrAC*
Wanamaker, Allison Temple 1881-1944
NatCAB 33, WhAm 2
Wanamaker, John 1837-1922 *ApCAB X,*
NatCAB 1
Wanamaker, John 1838-1922 *AmBi, ApCAB,*
BiDrUSE, DcAmB, EncAB, TwCBDA,
WebAB, WhAm 1

Ward, Mrs. H O *NotAW*

Ward, Hallett Sydney 1870-1956 *BiDrAC, WhAm 5*

Ward, Hamilton 1829-1898 *ApCAB Sup, BiAUS, BiDrAC, TwCBDA*

Ward, Hamilton 1871-1932 *WhAm 1*

Ward, Harry Edwin 1879-1960 *WhAm 4*

Ward, Harry Frederick 1873-1966 *WhAm 4*

Ward, Henry 1732-1797 *ApCAB, BiAUS, Drake, NatCAB 11*

Ward, Henry Augustus 1834-1906 *ApCAB, DcAmB, NatCAB 3, NatCAB 28, TwCBDA, WhAm 1*

Ward, Henry Baldwin 1865-1945 *DcAmB S3, NatCAB 13, NatCAB 35, WhAm 2*

Ward, Henry Clay 1843-1925 *WhAm 1*

Ward, Henry Dana 1797-1884 *DcAmB, NatCAB 23, WhAm H*

Ward, Henry Galbraith 1851-1933 *ApCAB X, NatCAB 23, WhAm 1*

Ward, Sir Henry George 1796?-1860 *ApCAB*

Ward, Henry Heber 1871- *WhAm 5*

Ward, Henry Levi 1863-1943 *WhAm 2*

Ward, Henry Levy 1888-1970 *NatCAB 56*

Ward, Henry Tibbels 1897-1960 *WhAm 4*

Ward, Henry Winfield 1861- *WhAm 4*

Ward, Henshaw 1872-1935 *WhAm 1*

Ward, Herbert Dickinson 1861-1932 *DcAmB, TwCBDA, WhAm 1*

Ward, Herbert Hamilton 1856-1927 *NatCAB 22*

Ward, Herbert Shaeffer 1882-1962 *WhAm 4*

Ward, Herbert William 1894-1967 *WhAm 4A*

Ward, Hiram Owen 1842-1914 *NatCAB 16*

Ward, Holcombe 1878- *WhAm 6*

Ward, Horatio 1810?-1868 *ApCAB*

Ward, Hortense Sparks Malsch 1872-1944 *NotAW, WomWWA 14*

Ward, Irving 1866-1924 *NatCAB 20*

Ward, J H d1958 *WhAm 3*

Ward, J Q A 1832?-1910 *Drake*

Ward, Jacob C 1809-1891 *NewYHSD, WhAm H*

Ward, James Alto 1892-1943 *NatCAB 34*

Ward, James C *NewYHSD*

Ward, James Edward 1836-1894 *DcAmB, NatCAB 6, WhAm H*

Ward, James Harman 1806-1861 *ApCAB, Drake, TwCBDA*

Ward, James Harmon 1806-1861 *DcAmB, WebAMB, WhAm H*

Ward, James Hugh 1853-1916 *BiDrAC*

Ward, James Thomas 1820-1897 *NatCAB 1, TwCBDA*

Ward, James Warner 1816-1897 *DcAmB, NatCAB 10, WhAm H*

Ward, James Warner 1817-1897 *ApCAB*

Ward, James Warner 1818-1897 *Drake*

Ward, James Washington 1879-1956 *NatCAB 47*

Ward, James William 1861-1939 *NatCAB 7, WhAm 1*

Ward, Jasper Delos 1829-1902 *BiAUS, BiDrAC*

Ward, John 1606-1693 *ApCAB, NatCAB 12*

Ward, John 1838- *ApCAB*

Ward, John Chamberlain 1873-1929 *WhAm 1*

Ward, John Chamberlain 1873-1949 *WhAm 2*

Ward, John E 1814-1902 *BiAUS*

Ward, John Elliot 1814-1902 *TwCBDA*

Ward, John Elliott 1814-1902 *ApCAB, DcAmB, NatCAB 1, WhAm 1*

Ward, John F *NewYHSD*

Ward, John Harris 1908-1974 *WhAm 6*

Ward, John Henry Hobart 1823-1903 *ApCAB, NatCAB 4, TwCBDA, WhAm 1*

Ward, John Quincy Adams 1830-1910 *AmBi, ApCAB, BnEnAmA, DcAmB, IlBEAAW, NatCAB 2, NewYHSD, TwCBDA, WebAB, WhAm 1*

Ward, John Wesley 1840-1916 *WhAm 1*

Ward, John William George d1945 *WhAm 2*

Ward, Jonathan 1768-1842 *BiAUS, BiDrAC, WhAm H*

Ward, Joseph *NewYHSD*

Ward, Joseph 1838-1889 *BiDAmEd, DcAmB, NatCAB 23, WhAm H*

Ward, Joseph Frederick 1843-1923 *ApCAB X*

Ward, Joseph Henry 1850-1917 *NatCAB 17*

Ward, Josephine Clark 1874- *WomWWA 14*

Ward, Joshua 1894-1970 *WhAm 5*

Ward, Julia Elizabeth 1832-1921 *WhAm 1, WomWWA 14*

Ward, Julia Rush 1796-1824 *ApCAB*

Ward, Julius Hammond 1837- *ApCAB*

Ward, Justina Bayard 1879- *WomWWA 14*

Ward, Kate Morgan 1869- *WomWWA 14*

Ward, Kenneth William 1909-1972 *WhAm 5*

Ward, Lauriston 1882-1930 *NatCAB 48*

Ward, Lebbeus Baldwin 1801-1885 *NatCAB 1*

Ward, Leo L 1898-1953 *WhAm 3*

Ward, Leslie Dodd 1845-1909 *NatCAB 25*

Ward, Leslie Dodd 1845-1910 *WhAm 1*

Ward, Lester Frank 1841-1913 *AmBi, ApCAB, BiDAmEd, DcAmB, EncAB, McGEWB, NatCAB 13, TwCBDA, WebAB, WhAm HA, WhAm 1, WhAm 4A*

Ward, Levi 1771-1861 *ApCAB*

Ward, Louis Henry 1876-1950 *NatCAB 39*

Ward, Lydia Arms Avery Coonley 1845-1924 *DcAmB, NatCAB 34, WhAm 1*

Ward, Lydia Arms Avery Coonly 1845-1924 *WomWWA 14*

Ward, Lyman 1868-1948 *NatCAB 50, WhAm 2*

Ward, Marcus Lawrence 1812-1884 *ApCAB, BiAUS, BiDrAC, DcAmB, NatCAB 5, TwCBDA, WhAm H, WhAmP*

Ward, Marcus Llewellyn 1875-1963 *WhAm 4*

Ward, Mary E 1843- *AmWom*

Ward, Mary Holyoke 1800-1880 *NewYHSD*

Ward, Matt Flournoy 1826-1862 *ApCAB*

Ward, Matthias 1800?-1861 *ApCAB, BiAUS, NatCAB 4, TwCBDA*

Ward, Matthias 1805-1861 *BiDrAC, WhAm H, WhAmP*

Ward, May Alden 1853-1918 *AmWom, BiCAW, TwCBDA, WhAm 1, WomWWA 14*

Ward, Milan Lester 1829- *WhAm 4*

Ward, Minnie Marks 1860- *WomWWA 14*

Ward, Montgomery 1843-1913 *DcAmB, WebAB*

Ward, Montgomery 1844-1913 *WhAm 1*

Ward, Nancy d1822 *DcAmB*

Ward, Nancy 1738?-1822 *NotAW*

Ward, Nancy 1740?-1822 *ApCAB, WhAm H*

Ward, Nathaniel 1578?-1652 *AmBi, ApCAB, DcAmB, Drake, WebAB, WhAm H*

Ward, Nathaniel 1580?-1653 *NatCAB 7*

Ward, Orlando 1891-1972 *WhAm 5*

Ward, Ossian Peay 1875-1966 *WhAm 5*

Ward, Peirce Colton 1885-1970 *WhAm 5*

Ward, Perley Erik 1880-1939 *WhAm 1*

Ward, Ralph Ansel 1882-1958 *WhAm 3*

Ward, Reginald Henshaw 1862-1925 *WhAm 1*

Ward, Richard 1689-1763 *ApCAB, DcAmB, NatCAB 10, WhAm H*

Ward, Richard Halsted 1837-1917 *ApCAB, DcAmB, NatCAB 13, TwCBDA, WhAm 1*

Ward, Robert Boyd 1852-1915 *ApCAB X, NatCAB 36*

Ward, Robert DeCourcy 1867-1931 *AmBi, DcAmB, NatCAB 24, WhAm 1*

Ward, Robert Stafford 1906-1975 *WhAm 6*

Ward, Robert W 1891-1969 *WhAm 5*

Ward, Robert William 1905-1960 *WhAm 3*

Ward, Rodney C 1837-1889 *NatCAB 5*

Ward, Samuel 1725-1776 *ApCAB, BiAUS, BiDrAC, DcAmB, Drake, NatCAB 5, NatCAB 10, TwCBDA, WhAm H, WhAmP*

Ward, Samuel 1756-1832 *ApCAB, DcAmB, Drake, NatCAB 5, WhAm H*

Ward, Samuel 1786-1839 *AmBi, ApCAB, DcAmB, NatCAB 4, WhAm H*

Ward, Samuel 1814-1884 *ApCAB, DcAmB, TwCBDA, WhAm H*

Ward, Samuel 1845- *WhAm 4*

Ward, Samuel Baldwin 1842-1915 *NatCAB 1, WhAm 1*

Ward, Samuel Ringgold 1817-1866? *DcAmB, WhAm H*

Ward, Seth 1617-1689 *DcScB*

Ward, Seth 1858-1909 *NatCAB 26, WhAm 1*

Ward, Shirley Christopher 1861-1929 *NatCAB 42*

Ward, Stevenson E 1879-1950 *WhAm 3*

Ward, Susan Hayes 1838- *WhAm 4, WomWWA 14*

Ward, Thomas 1641-1689 *NatCAB 5*

Ward, Thomas 1759?-1842 *BiAUS, BiDrAC, WhAm H*

Ward, Thomas 1807-1873 *ApCAB, DcAmB, Drake, NatCAB 10, WhAm H*

Ward, Thomas 1823- *ApCAB*

Ward, Thomas 1839-1926 *WhAm 1*

Ward, Thomas Bayless 1835-1892 *BiDrAC, WhAm H, WhAmP*

Ward, Thomas Johnson 1886-1966 *WhAm 4*

Ward, Thomas Robinson 1870-1956 *NatCAB 43*

Ward, Thomas Walter 1758-1835 *NatCAB 23*

Ward, Thomas Wren 1786-1858 *DcAmB, WhAm H*

Ward, W Douglas 1874-1936 *NatCAB 28*

Ward, Wilbert 1888-1959 *WhAm 3*

Ward, Wilbur 1879-1954 *NatCAB 43, WhAm 3*

Ward, Willard Parker 1845-1928 *WhAm 1*

Ward, William *NewYHSD*

Ward, William 1827-1895 *WhAm H*

Ward, William 1837-1895 *BiDrAC*

Ward, William Allen 1893-1959 *WhAm 4*

Ward, William Breining 1884-1929 *ApCAB X, WhAm 1*

Ward, William Edgar 1874- *WhAm 5*

Ward, William Evans 1912-1973 *WhAm 4*

Ward, William Godman 1848-1923 *TwCBDA, WhAm 1*

Ward, William Greene 1832- *ApCAB*

Ward, William Hayes 1835-1916 *AmBi, ApCAB, DcAmB, NatCAB 8, WhAm 1*

Ward, William Hilles 1892-1961 *WhAm 4*

Ward, William I 1857-1956 *WhAm 3*

Ward, William Lukens 1856-1933 *BiDrAC*

Ward, William Rankin 1870-1955 *WhAm 3*

Ward, William Thomas 1808-1878 *ApCAB, BiAUS, BiDrAC, TwCBDA, WhAm H*

Wardall, Ruth Aimee d1936 *WhAm 1*

Wardall, William Jed 1885-1972 *WhAm 5*

Warde, Frances 1810-1884 *DcAmReB*

Warde, Frederick Barkham 1851-1935 *AmBi, DcAmB S1, NatCAB 11, WhAm 1*

Warde, Margaret *WomWWA 14*

Warde, Mary Francis Xavier 1810-1884 *WhAm H*

Wardell, Daniel 1791- *BiAUS*

Wardell, Justus S 1872-1945 *WhAm 2*

Wardell, Morris L 1889-1957 *WhAm 3*

Wardell, S R *NewYHSD*

Warden, Miss C A *NewYHSD*

Warden, David Bailie 1772-1845 *DcAmB, WhAm H*

Warden, David Bailie 1778-1845 *ApCAB, Drake*

Warden, James 1907-1973 *WhAm 6*

Warden, Oliver Sherman 1865-1951 *WhAm 3*

Warden, Robert Bruce 1824- *ApCAB*

Warden, Robert Bruce 1824-1883 *WhAm H*

Warden, Robert Bruce 1824-1883 *DcAmB*

Warden, William Franklin 1874-1921 *NatCAB 19*

Wardenburg, F A 1881-1966 *WhAm 4*

Warder, George Woodward 1848- *WhAm 1*

Warder, John Aston 1812-1883 *ApCAB, DcAmB, EncAAH, NatCAB 4, WhAm H*

Warder, John Aston 1813-1883 *Drake*

Warder, John Haines 1846-1915 *WhAm 1*

Warder, Robert Bowne 1848-1905 *ApCAB, NatCAB 13, WhAm 1*

Warder, Walter 1851- *WhAm 4*

Wardlaw, James Langdon 1913-1965 *NatCAB 51*

Wardlaw, Joseph Coachman 1876-1947 *WhAm 2*

Wardlaw, Patterson 1859-1948 *WhAm 2*

Wardlaw, William Clarke 1874-1948 *NatCAB 37*

Wardle, Harriet Newell *WomWWA 14*

Wardle, Henry 1885-1959 *NatCAB 47*

Wardle, Richard C *NewYHSD*

Wardle, Robert, Jr. 1911-1969 *WhAm 5*
Wardley, Russell George 1909-1968 *WhAm 5*
Wardman, Ervin 1865-1923 *DcAmB, WhAm 1*
Wardner, G Philip 1867-1963 *NatCAB 49*
Wardner, Mary Rankin 1870- *WomWWA 14*
Wardrop, Robert 1850-1937 *WhAm 1*
Wardrope, William S *NewYHSD*
Wardwell, Allen 1873-1953 *WhAm 3*
Wardwell, Daniel 1791-1878 *BiDrAC, WhAm H*
Wardwell, Frank Carlton 1887-1968 *WhAm 5*
Wardwell, George Smith 1829-1895 *NatCAB 19*
Wardwell, Harold Fletcher 1883-1962 *WhAm 4*
Wardwell, Henry 1840-1922 *ApCAB X*
Wardwell, Henry Fitch 1876-1960 *NatCAB 48*
Wardwell, J Otis 1857-1940 *NatCAB 33*
Wardwell, Linda B 1865- *WomWWA 14*
Wardwell, Mary Margaretta 1866- *WomWWA 14*
Wardwell, Sheldon Eaton 1882-1961 *WhAm 4*
Wardwell, William Thomas 1827-1911 *ApCAB X, NatCAB 27, WhAm 1*
Ware, Alice Holdship 1872- *WomWWA 14*
Ware, Allison 1880- *WhAm 6*
Ware, Arthur 1876-1939 *NatCAB 28, WhAm 1*
Ware, Ashur 1782-1873 *ApCAB, BiAUS, DcAmB, Drake, NatCAB 5, WhAm H*
Ware, Catharine Augusta 1797-1843 *Drake*
Ware, Catherine Augusta 1797-1843 *NatCAB 5*
Ware, Charlotte Barrell 1862- *WomWWA 14*
Ware, Darrell 1906-1944 *NatCAB 33*
Ware, Edmund Asa 1837-1885 *BiDAmEd, DcAmB, NatCAB 5, WhAm H*
Ware, Edward Twichell 1874-1927 *NatCAB 22, WhAm 1*
Ware, Eugene F 1841-1911 *NatCAB 9, WhAm 1*
Ware, Florence Ellen 1891-1971 *IlBEAAW*
Ware, Franklin B 1873-1945 *WhAm 2*
Ware, Harriet d1962 *WhAm 4, WomWWA 14*
Ware, Harry Hudnall, Jr. 1898-1973 *WhAm 5*
Ware, Helen 1875-1939 *NatCAB 31*
Ware, Helen 1877-1939 *WhAm 1*
Ware, Henry 1764-1845 *AmBi, ApCAB, DcAmB, Drake, NatCAB 5, TwCBDA, WhAm H*
Ware, Henry 1794-1843 *AmBi, ApCAB, DcAmB, Drake, NatCAB 5, TwCBDA, WhAm H*
Ware, Henry 1871-1956 *NatCAB 46*
Ware, Horace 1812-1890 *BiDConf*
Ware, Horace Everett 1845- *WhAm 4*
Ware, Jeannette Philena Huntington *WomWWA 14*
Ware, John 1795-1864 *ApCAB, DcAmB, Drake, WhAm H*
Ware, John Fothergill Waterhouse 1818-1881 *ApCAB, DcAmB, WhAm H*
Ware, John Haines, III 1908- *BiDrAC*
Ware, Joseph 1827- *NewYHSD*
Ware, Katharine Augusta 1797-1843 *ApCAB*
Ware, Lewis Sharpe 1851-1918 *NatCAB 12, WhAm 1*
Ware, Mary 1828- *AmWom*
Ware, Mary Greene Chandler 1818- *ApCAB*
Ware, Mary Lovell Pickard 1798-1849 *ApCAB*
Ware, Mary S 1842-1933 *WhAm 3*
Ware, Nathaniel A d1854 *DcAmB*
Ware, Nathaniel A 1780?-1854 *ApCAB, WhAm H*
Ware, Nathaniel A 1789?-1854 *NatCAB 5*
Ware, Nicholas 1769-1824 *ApCAB, BiAUS, BiDrAC, NatCAB 5, TwCBDA, WhAm H*
Ware, Norman Joseph 1886-1949 *WhAm 2*
Ware, Orie S 1882- *BiDrAC*
Ware, Paul 1904-1969 *WhAm 5*
Ware, Sedley Lynch 1868- *WhAm 5*
Ware, Walter Ellsworth 1861-1951 *WhAm 4*
Ware, William 1797-1852 *AmBi, ApCAB, DcAmB, Drake, NatCAB 5, TwCBDA, WhAm H*
Ware, William Robert 1832-1915 *AmBi, ApCAB, BiDAmEd, DcAmB, NatCAB 8, WhAm 1*
Wareham, Harry P 1883-1951 *WhAm 3*

Wareham, John Hamilton Dee 1881- *WhAm 6*
Wareing, Ernest Clyde 1872-1944 *WhAm 2*
Waren *NewYHSD*
Warfel, Jacob Eshleman 1826-1855 *NewYHSD*
Warfield, Augustus Bennett 1878-1960 *WhAm 4*
Warfield, Benjamin Breckinridge 1851-1921 *ApCAB Sup, DcAmB, DcAmReB, NatCAB 20, TwCBDA, WhAm 1*
Warfield, C Dorsey 1898-1947 *WhAm 2*
Warfield, Catharine Ann 1816-1877 *ApCAB*
Warfield, Catharine Anne 1816-1877 *NatCAB 5*
Warfield, Catharine Anne 1817-1877 *Drake*
Warfield, Catherine Ann Ware 1816-1877 *DcAmB, WhAm H*
Warfield, Catherine Anne 1816-1877 *TwCBDA*
Warfield, David 1866-1951 *ApCAB X, DcAmB S5, NatCAB 14, NatCAB 38, WhAm 3*
Warfield, Edwin 1848-1920 *NatCAB 13, WhAm 1*
Warfield, Eleanor Percy Ware Lee 1820-1849 *ApCAB*
Warfield, Ethelbert 1898-1974 *WhAm 6*
Warfield, Ethelbert Dudley 1861-1936 *ApCAB Sup, NatCAB 11, TwCBDA, WhAm 1*
Warfield, George Alfred 1871-1939 *WhAm 1*
Warfield, Harry Ridgely, Jr. 1904-1969 *WhAm 5*
Warfield, Henry Mactier 1825-1885 *ApCAB X*
Warfield, Henry Mactier 1867-1947 *NatCAB 38, WhAm 4*
Warfield, Henry Ridgely 1774-1839 *BiAUS, BiDrAC, TwCBDA, WhAm H, WhAmP*
Warfield, Nellie Frances Tilton 1864- *WomWWA 14*
Warfield, R Emory 1855-1924 *WhAm 1*
Warfield, Ralph Mervine 1880-1939 *NatCAB 29*
Warfield, Ridgely Brown 1864-1920 *WhAm 1*
Warfield, S Davies 1859-1927 *ApCAB X, NatCAB 20, WhAm 1*
Warfield, Solomon Davies 1859-1927 *DcAmB*
Warfield, Wallis *WebAB*
Warfield, William 1827- *TwCBDA*
Warfield, William 1891-1947 *NatCAB 35, WhAm 2*
Warfield, William A 1866- *WhoColR*
Wargentin, Pehr Wilhelm 1717-1783 *DcScB*
Warham, John d1670 *Drake*
Warheit, Isarel Albert 1912-1973 *WhAm 5*
Warhol, Andy 1930- *BnEnAmA, EncAB, McGEWB, WebAB*
Warin, Joseph *NewYHSD*
Waring, Clarence Henry 1882-1949 *WhAm 3*
Waring, Dwight Stowe 1882-1961 *NatCAB 48*
Waring, Edward 1736?-1798 *DcScB*
Waring, Etta Richardson 1856- *WomWWA 14*
Waring, George Edwin 1833-1898 *AmBi, ApCAB, DcAmB, NatCAB 6, WhAm H*
Waring, J Waties 1880-1968 *WhAm 4A*
Waring, James Henry 1848-1906 *NatCAB 17*
Waring, James Howard 1889-1959 *WhAm 3*
Waring, James Johnston 1883-1962 *NatCAB 50, WhAm 4*
Waring, Jane Leary 1853- *WomWWA 14*
Waring, Malvina Sarah 1842-1930 *WhAm 3, WomWWA 14*
Waring, Martha Gallaudet 1873- *WomWWA 14*
Waring, Mary Kimberley *WomWWA 14*
Waring, Roane 1881-1958 *NatCAB 46, WhAm 3*
Waring, Sophia F Malbone 1787-1823 *NewYHSD*
Waring, Thomas Richard 1871-1935 *WhAm 1*
Waring, Tracy Dickey 1873-1947 *NatCAB 42*
Waring, W George 1847-1935 *NatCAB 30*
Wark, Daniel 1804- *ApCAB Sup*
Wark, George H 1878- *WhAm 6*
Wark, Homer Ethan 1875- *WhAm 5*
Warlick, Hulon Otis, Jr. 1903-1964 *WhAm 4*
Warlimont, Walther 1894- *WhWW-II*
Warman, Cy 1855-1914 *DcAmB, NatCAB 15, TwCBDA, WhAm 1*
Warman, Edward B 1847-1931 *WhAm 1*

Warman, Philip Creveling 1859-1908 *WhAm 1*
Warmcastle, Grace Watson *WomWWA 14*
Warming, Johannes Eugenius Bulow 1841-1924 *DcScB*
Warmoth, Henry Clay 1842- *NatCAB 10, TwCBDA*
Warmoth, Henry Clay 1842-1931 *DcAmB, NatCAB 23*
Warmoth, Henry Clay 1842-1932 *WhAm 1*
Warmouth, Henry C 1842- *BiAUS*
Warnach, Paul Victor 1909-1970 *WhAm 6*
Warndorf, Joseph Henry 1890-1956 *NatCAB 43*
Warne, Francis Wesley 1854-1932 *NatCAB 26, WhAm 1*
Warne, Frank Julian 1874- *WhAm 2*
Warne, Thomas *NewYHSD*
Warnecke, Anna *WomWWA 14*
Warneke, Heinz 1895- *BnEnAmA*
Warnell, Daniel Brooks 1881-1945 *NatCAB 34*
Warner, Adoniram Judson 1834-1910 *ApCAB, BiDrAC, DcAmB, NatCAB 10, TwCBDA, WhAm 1, WhAmP*
Warner, Albert d1967 *WhAm 4A*
Warner, Albert 1883-1967 *NatCAB 54*
Warner, Albert 1884-1967 *WebAB*
Warner, Albert Lyman 1903-1971 *WhAm 5*
Warner, Alfred *NewYHSD*
Warner, Alfred DuPont 1847-1915 *NatCAB 32*
Warner, Alice Perryman 1860- *WomWWA 14*
Warner, Alton G 1858- *WhAm 4*
Warner, Amos Griswold 1861-1900 *DcAmB, NatCAB 13, WhAm 1*
Warner, Andrew Jackson 1850- *WhoColR*
Warner, Anna Bartlett d1915 *Drake, WhAm 1, WomWWA 14*
Warner, Anna Bartlett 1820-1915 *AmBi, ApCAB, NatCAB 4*
Warner, Anna Bartlett 1827-1915 *DcAmB, NotAW*
Warner, Anne Richmond 1869-1913 *DcAmB, WhAm 1*
Warner, Anthony Kimmel 1863- *NatCAB 18*
Warner, Arthur Pratt 1870-1957 *NatCAB 44*
Warner, Bessie Sarah 1874- *WomWWA 14*
Warner, Beverley Ellison 1855-1910 *WhAm 1*
Warner, Bradford Greenman 1901-1963 *NatCAB 51*
Warner, Bradford Newman 1924-1971 *WhAm 6*
Warner, Brainard Henry 1847-1916 *NatCAB 25, WhAm 1*
Warner, C A 1894-1968 *WhAm 5*
Warner, C J *NewYHSD*
Warner, Catherine Townsend *NewYHSD*
Warner, Charles *NewYHSD*
Warner, Charles 1877-1956 *NatCAB 45, WhAm 3*
Warner, Charles Dudley 1829-1900 *AmBi, ApCAB, DcAmB, NatCAB 2, TwCBDA, WebAB, WhAm 1*
Warner, Charles Guille 1844- *NatCAB 12*
Warner, Charles Henry 1872-1944 *NatCAB 33*
Warner, Charles Mortimer 1845-1923 *NatCAB 5*
Warner, Charles Mortimer 1846-1923 *WhAm 1*
Warner, Cornelia Blakemore 1859- *WomWWA 14*
Warner, David Ashley 1883-1966 *NatCAB 53, WhAm 4*
Warner, DeVer Howard 1868-1934 *WhAm 1*
Warner, Donald Franklin 1898-1952 *NatCAB 39*
Warner, Donald Ticknor 1850-1929 *WhAm 1*
Warner, Edward 1894-1958 *WhAm 3*
Warner, Ellsworth C 1864-1942 *WhAm 2*
Warner, Eltinge Fowler 1879-1965 *NatCAB 53*
Warner, Eltinge Fowler 1880-1965 *WhAm 4*
Warner, Ernest Noble 1868-1930 *WhAm 1*
Warner, Everett Longley 1877-1963 *NatCAB 50, WhAm 4*
Warner, Ezra Joseph 1841-1910 *NatCAB 15, WhAm 1*
Warner, Ezra Joseph 1877-1933 *WhAm 1*
Warner, Frank 1855-1943 *NatCAB 34, WhAm 2*
Warner, Fred Maltby 1865-1923 *DcAmB, NatCAB 13, WhAm 1*
Warner, George D *NewYHSD*

Warner, George Russell 1872-1957 *NatCAB 48*
Warner, Gertrude Bass 1863- *WhAm 3*
Warner, Glen Wones 1883-1968 *NatCAB 55*
Warner, Glenn Scobey 1871-1954 *DcAmB S5, WebAB, WhAm 3*
Warner, Hannah *WhAm 4*
Warner, Harold d1948 *WhAm 2*
Warner, Harry Jackson 1880-1954 *WhAm 3*
Warner, Harry Mead 1873-1931 *NatCAB 24*
Warner, Harry Morris 1881-1958 *WebAB, WhAm 3*
Warner, Harry O d1950 *WhAm 3*
Warner, Henry Byron 1877- *WhAm 5*
Warner, Henry Chester 1876-1960 *NatCAB 49*
Warner, Henry Edward 1876-1941 *WhAm 2*
Warner, Hiram 1802-1881 *ApCAB, BiAUS, BiDrAC, DcAmB, NatCAB 7, TwCBDA, WhAm H*
Warner, Horace Emory 1855- *WhAm 4*
Warner, Horace Everett 1839-1930 *WhAm 1*
Warner, Horatio Gates 1801-1876 *NatCAB 2*
Warner, Ira David 1886-1964 *WhAm 4*
Warner, J Foster 1859-1937 *WhAm 1*
Warner, J H *NewYHSD*
Warner, Jack *WebAB*
Warner, Jack F 1912-1967 *WhAm 6*
Warner, James Cartwright 1830-1895 *DcAmB, WhAm H*
Warner, James Edward 1905-1975 *WhAm 6*
Warner, James Meech 1836-1897 *ApCAB Sup, TwCBDA*
Warner, John DeWitt 1851-1925 *BiDrAC, NatCAB 9, WhAm 1*
Warner, John F 1899-1962 *WhAm 4*
Warner, John Russell 1887-1953 *NatCAB 43*
Warner, Jonathan 1865- *WhAm 4*
Warner, Jonathan Trumbull 1807-1895 *DcAmB, WhAm H*
Warner, Joseph Bangs 1848-1923 *WhAm 1*
Warner, Joseph Everett 1884-1958 *NatCAB 44, WhAm 3*
Warner, Juan Jose 1807-1895 *DcAmB*
Warner, Kenneth Bryant 1894-1948 *NatCAB 37*
Warner, Keren Osborne 1849- *WomWWA 14*
Warner, Langdon 1881-1955 *DcAmB S5, WhAm 3*
Warner, Lena A 1868- *WomWWA 14*
Warner, Leon *NewYHSD*
Warner, Levi 1831-1911 *BiDrAC*
Warner, Lillian Dale Baker *WomWWA 14*
Warner, Lillian Houghton *WomWWA 14*
Warner, Lucien Calvin 1841-1925 *ApCAB X, WhAm 1*
Warner, Lucien Thompson 1877-1950 *WhAm 3*
Warner, Lucy Hunt *WomWWA 14*
Warner, Marion E Knowlton 1839- *AmWom*
Warner, Mary Belle 1864- *WomWWA 14*
Warner, Millard Fillmore 1848- *TwCBDA*
Warner, Milo Joseph 1891-1968 *NatCAB 54, WhAm 4A*
Warner, Milton Jones 1873-1952 *NatCAB 42, WhAm 3*
Warner, Olin Levi 1844-1896 *AmBi, ApCAB, ApCAB X, BnEnAmA, DcAmB, IIBEAAW, NatCAB 8, TwCBDA*
Warner, Paul McC 1891-1964 *WhAm 4*
Warner, Ralph N *NewYHSD*
Warner, Rawleigh 1891-1971 *WhAm 5*
Warner, Raymond Yardley 1873- *NatCAB 16*
Warner, Richard 1835-1915 *BiDrAC*
Warner, Richard Ambrose 1878-1955 *WhAm 3*
Warner, Robert Foresman 1909-1973 *WhAm 6*
Warner, Robert Wilberforce 1889-1961 *WhAm 4*
Warner, Samuel L 1829-1893 *BiAUS, NatCAB 3*
Warner, Samuel Larkin 1828-1893 *BiDrAC, WhAm H*
Warner, Samuel Louis 1887-1927 *NatCAB 21*
Warner, Seth 1743-1784 *AmBi, ApCAB, DcAmB, Drake, NatCAB 1, TwCBDA, WebAMB, WhAm H*
Warner, Southard Parker 1881-1914 *WhAm 1*
Warner, Susan Bogert 1818-1885 *Drake*
Warner, Susan Bogert 1819-1885 *AmBi, ApCAB, DcAmB, NatCAB 5, NotAW,*

TwCBDA, WhAm H
Warner, Theodore Blanchard 1887-1928 *ApCAB X*
Warner, Thomas Leroy 1892-1953 *NatCAB 43*
Warner, Thomas William 1874-1947 *NatCAB 36*
Warner, Thor 1883-1956 *WhAm 3*
Warner, Vespasian 1842-1925 *BiDrAC, NatCAB 13, NatCAB 21, TwCBDA, WhAm 1, WhAmP*
Warner, W Lloyd 1898-1970 *WhAm 6*
Warner, Willard 1826-1906 *ApCAB, BiAUS, BiDrAC, NatCAB 10, TwCBDA, WhAm 1*
Warner, William 1839-1916 *NatCAB 20*
Warner, William 1840-1916 *ApCAB, BiDrAC, DcAmB, NatCAB 13, WhAm 1, WhAmP*
Warner, William 1841-1916 *TwCBDA*
Warner, William, Jr. 1813?-1848 *NewYHSD*
Warner, William Bishop 1874-1946 *WhAm 2*
Warner, William Desire 1912-1968 *NatCAB 57*
Warner, William Everett 1897-1971 *BiDAmEd, WhAm 5*
Warner, William Henry 1849- *ApCAB X*
Warner, William Houston 1869-1927 *NatCAB 21*
Warner, William Richard 1836-1901 *NatCAB 2*
Warner, Worcester Reed 1846-1929 *DcAmB, NatCAB 13, NatCAB 21, WhAm 1*
Warner, Wyllys 1800-1869 *ApCAB Sup*
Warner, Zebedee 1833- *ApCAB*
Warner Brothers *WebAB*
Warnick, John G d1818 *NewYHSD*
Warnick, Spencer K 1874- *WhAm 5*
Warnicke, John G d1818 *NewYHSD*
Warnock, Amelia Beers *WomWWA 14*
Warnock, Arthur Ray 1883-1951 *WhAm 3*
Warnock, Ernest Henry 1903-1974 *WhAm 6*
Warnock, John Barr 1871-1949 *NatCAB 38*
Warnock, William Robert 1838-1918 *BiDrAC, WhAm 4*
Warnow, Mark 1902-1949 *WhAm 2A*
Warnshuis, Abbe Livingston 1877-1958 *WhAm 3*
Warr, John 1798?- *NewYHSD*
Warr, William 1828?- *NewYHSD*
Warrall, John *NewYHSD*
Warre, Sir Henry James 1819-1898 *IIBEAAW, NewYHSD, REnAW*
Warrell, James 1780?-1854? *NewYHSD, WhAm H*
Warren, Aldred Kennedy 1866-1948 *NatCAB 37*
Warren, Alice Edith 1863- *ApCAB X*
Warren, Althea Hester 1886-1958 *DcAmLiB, WhAm 3A*
Warren, Andrew W d1873 *NewYHSD*
Warren, Ann Brunton 1770-1808 *NotAW*
Warren, Anne Brunton 1770-1808 *Drake*
Warren, Arletta L 1867- *WomWWA 14*
Warren, Arthur 1860-1924 *WhAm 1*
Warren, Arthur Fiske 1875- *WhAm 5*
Warren, Asa *NewYHSD*
Warren, Asa Coolidge 1819-1904 *NewYHSD*
Warren, Avra Milvin 1893-1957 *NatCAB 44, WhAm 3*
Warren, Benjamin Franklin 1845-1914 *NatCAB 16*
Warren, Benjamin S 1871-1935 *WhAm 1*
Warren, Benjamin Streeter 1865-1930 *NatCAB 32*
Warren, Bentley Wirt 1864-1947 *NatCAB 34, WhAm 2*
Warren, Burtt Ellmore 1874-1950 *NatCAB 40*
Warren, Casper Carl 1896-1973 *WhAm 6*
Warren, Catherine Carter 1874- *WomWWA 14*
Warren, Charles 1868-1954 *ApCAB X, DcAmB S5, WhAm 3*
Warren, Charles Beecher 1870-1936 *ApCAB X, NatCAB 26, WhAm 1*
Warren, Charles Elliott 1864-1945 *WhAm 2*
Warren, Charles Howard 1856-1935 *WhAm 1*
Warren, Charles Hyde 1876-1950 *WhAm 3*
Warren, Charles Kirk 1871-1932 *NatCAB 24*
Warren, Clara Sizer Davock *WomWWA 14*
Warren, Constance 1880-1971 *WhAm 5*
Warren, Constance M 1877- *WomWWA 14*

Warren, Constance Whitney 1888-1948 *IIBEAAW*
Warren, Cornelia 1857- *WhAm 5, WomWWA 14*
Warren, Cornelius 1790-1849 *BiAUS, BiDrAC, WhAm H*
Warren, Cyrus Moors 1824-1891 *DcAmB, NatCAB 10*
Warren, Cyrus More 1824-1891 *ApCAB*
Warren, Earl 1891-1974 *EncAB, McGEWB, WebAB, WhAm 6*
Warren, Edward 1804- *ApCAB*
Warren, Edward 1828-1893 *BiDConf, NatCAB 33*
Warren, Edward Allen 1818-1875 *BiAUS, BiDrAC, WhAm H, WhAmP*
Warren, Edward Henry 1873-1945 *WhAm 2*
Warren, Edward Kirk 1847-1919 *ApCAB X, NatCAB 17, WhAm 1*
Warren, Edward Leroy 1852-1931 *WhAm 1*
Warren, Edward Perry 1860-1928 *NatCAB 21*
Warren, Edward Royal 1860-1942 *WhAm 2*
Warren, Edward Walpole 1839-1903 *ApCAB Sup, NatCAB 10*
Warren, Edwin Walpole 1839-1903 *WhAm 1*
Warren, Ernest Ross 1888-1958 *NatCAB 46*
Warren, Fiske 1862-1938 *NatCAB 41, WhAm 1*
Warren, Fitz Henry 1816-1878 *ApCAB, BiAUS, NatCAB 12*
Warren, Francis E 1844-1929 *REnAW*
Warren, Francis Emory 1844-1929 *TwCBDA*
Warren, Francis Emroy 1844-1929 *AmBi, ApCAB Sup, ApCAB X, BiDrAC, DcAmB, EncAAH, NatCAB 11, NatCAB 23, WhAm 1, WhAmP*
Warren, Francis Herbert 1864- *WhoColR*
Warren, Frank Edward 1919-1972 *WhAm 5*
Warren, Frank Furniss 1899-1963 *NatCAB 52, WhAm 4*
Warren, Frank Lincoln 1875- *WhAm 5*
Warren, Fred D 1872-1959 *WhAm 3*
Warren, Frederick Andrew 1877-1944 *WhAm 2*
Warren, Frederick Emroy 1884-1949 *WhAm 2*
Warren, Frederick Morris 1859-1931 *AmBi, NatCAB 14, WhAm 1*
Warren, Fuller 1905-1973 *WhAm 6*
Warren, George Earle 1881- *WhAm 6*
Warren, George Eddy 1868-1935 *ApCAB X, NatCAB 29*
Warren, George Frederick 1874-1938 *DcAmB S2, EncAAH, NatCAB 28, WhAm 1*
Warren, George Herbert 1860- *NatCAB 17*
Warren, George Washington 1813-1883 *ApCAB X, NatCAB 5*
Warren, George Washington 1863-1934 *WhAm 1*
Warren, George William 1828-1902 *ApCAB, NatCAB 4, NewYHSD, WhAm 1*
Warren, Gouverneur Kemble 1830-1882 *AmBi, ApCAB, DcAmB, Drake, NatCAB 4, REnAW, TwCBDA, WebAMB, WhAm H*
Warren, Harold Broadfield 1859-1934 *WhAm 1*
Warren, Harry Claude 1881-1949 *NatCAB 37*
Warren, Harry Marsh 1867-1940 *WhAm 1*
Warren, Henry *NewYHSD*
Warren, Henry 1793?- *NewYHSD*
Warren, Henry Clarke 1854-1899 *DcAmB, WhAm H*
Warren, Henry Ellis 1872-1957 *NatCAB 46, WhAm 3*
Warren, Henry Kimball 1858-1938 *NatCAB 29, WhAm 4*
Warren, Henry Pitt 1846-1919 *WhAm 1*
Warren, Henry White 1831-1912 *ApCAB, DcAmB, NatCAB 9, TwCBDA, WhAm 1*
Warren, Herbert Langford 1857-1917 *DcAmB S1, WhAm 1*
Warren, Homer 1855-1926 *NatCAB 25*
Warren, Howard Crosby 1867-1934 *DcAmB, NatCAB 25, WhAm 1*
Warren, Ina Russelle *WomWWA 14*
Warren, Ira 1806-1864 *ApCAB*
Warren, Ira DeForest 1831-1907 *NatCAB 8*
Warren, Irene 1875- *WhAm 5*

Warren, Israel Perkins 1814-1892 *ApCAB,
DcAmB, NatCAB 4, WhAm H*
Warren, J *NewYHSD*
Warren, James 1726-1808 *ApCAB, DcAmB,
Drake, NatCAB 5, TwCBDA, WhAm H*
Warren, James Adolphus 1881-1958
NatCAB 52
Warren, James Carey 1896-1959 *WhAm 3*
Warren, James Dunlap 1823-1886 *NatCAB 27*
Warren, James E 1878-1952 *WhAm 3*
Warren, James Garfield 1862-1949 *NatCAB 36*
Warren, James Goold 1858-1937 *NatCAB 28,
WhAm H*
Warren, James Thomas 1884-1948 *WhAm 2*
Warren, James Walter 1875-1956 *NatCAB 43*
Warren, John 1753-1815 *AmBi, ApCAB,
BiDAmEd, BiHiMed, DcAmB, Drake,
NatCAB 10, WebAB, WhAm H*
Warren, John Brush 1886- *ApCAB X*
Warren, John Collins 1778-1856 *AmBi,
ApCAB, BiDAmEd, BiHiMed, DcAmB,
Drake, NatCAB 6, TwCBDA, WebAB,
WhAm H*
Warren, John Collins 1842-1927 *ApCAB,
DcAmB, NatCAB 13, TwCBDA,
WhAm 1*
Warren, John Davock 1904-1975 *WhAm 6*
Warren, Jonathan Mason 1810-1867 *Drake*
Warren, Jonathan Mason 1811-1867 *ApCAB*
Warren, Joseph 1741-1775 *AmBi, ApCAB,
BiHiMed, DcAmB, Drake, NatCAB 1,
TwCBDA, WebAB, WebAMB, WhAm H*
Warren, Joseph 1829-1876 *ApCAB*
Warren, Joseph 1876-1942 *WhAm 2*
Warren, Joseph Mabbett 1813-1896 *BiAUS,
BiDrAC, NatCAB 4, WhAm H*
Warren, Joseph Weatherhead 1849-1916
WhAm 1
Warren, Josiah 1798-1873 *NatCAB 5*
Warren, Josiah 1798?-1874 *DcAmB,
WhAm H*
Warren, Josiah 1799-1874 *ApCAB*
Warren, Julius Ernest 1888-1962 *WhAm 4*
Warren, Laura Elizabeth 1866- *WhoColR*
Warren, Lavinia *NotAW*
Warren, Leonard 1911-1960 *NatCAB 47,
WhAm 3*
Warren, Lillie Eginton 1859- *WhAm 4*
Warren, Lindsay Carter 1889- *BiDrAC,
WhAmP*
Warren, Lizzie Maude 1882- *WomWWA 14*
Warren, Lott 1797-1861 *ApCAB, BiAUS,
BiDrAC, WhAm H*
Warren, Louis John 1877-1934 *NatCAB 40*
Warren, Louise Bird 1876- *WomWWA 14*
Warren, Lucius Henry 1838-1924 *ApCAB X,
NatCAB 21*
Warren, M, Jr. *NewYHSD*
Warren, M Allen 1876-1942 *NatCAB 33*
Warren, Mary Evalin 1829- *AmWom*
Warren, Mary Whitson *WomWWA 14*
Warren, Maude Lavinia Radford d1934
WhAm 1, WomWWA 14
Warren, Melvin C 1920- *IIBEAAW*
Warren, Mercy Lavinia Bump 1838-1883 *AmBi*
Warren, Mercy Otis 1728-1814 *AmBi, ApCAB,
DcAmB, Drake, EncAB, McGEWB,
NatCAB 7, NotAW, WebAB, WhAm H,
WhAmP*
Warren, Minnie 1849-1878 *ApCAB*
Warren, Minton 1850-1907 *DcAmB,
NatCAB 12, NatCAB 45, TwCBDA,
WhAm 1*
Warren, Minton M 1888-1947 *WhAm 2*
Warren, Nathan Boughton 1805-1898 *ApCAB*
Warren, Nathan Bouton 1805-1898 *NatCAB 3*
Warren, Nellie 1889- *WomWWA 14*
Warren, Orris Hubert 1835- *NatCAB 3*
Warren, Percy Holmes 1906-1965 *WhAm 4*
Warren, Sir Peter 1703-1752 *ApCAB, DcAmB,
Drake, WhAm H*
Warren, Rhoda Adalia 1891- *WhoColR*
Warren, Richard Henry 1859-1933 *DcAmB,
WhAm 1*
Warren, Robert Andrew 1884-1945 *NatCAB 34*
Warren, Robert B 1891-1950 *WhAm 2*
Warren, Robert Fiske 1908-1973 *NatCAB 57*
Warren, Robert Penn 1905- *McGEWB,*

WebAB
Warren, Russell 1783-1860 *BnEnAmA,
DcAmB, WhAm H*
Warren, Ruth Annette *WomWWA 14*
Warren, Salome Machado *WomWWA 14*
Warren, Samuel Dennis 1817-1888 *ApCAB X*
Warren, Samuel Dennis 1852-1910 *WhAm 1*
Warren, Samuel Dennis 1885-1927 *NatCAB 45*
Warren, Samuel Edward 1831-1909 *ApCAB,
BiDAmEd, NatCAB 4, TwCBDA,
WhAm 1*
Warren, Samuel Prowse 1841-1915 *ApCAB,
DcAmB, NatCAB 9, WhAm 1*
Warren, Speed 1870- *WhAm 5*
Warren, Stanley Perkins 1846- *WhAm 4*
Warren, Theodore Edward 1897-1969
NatCAB 57
Warren, Thomas *NewYHSD*
Warren, Thomas Davis 1872- *WhAm 5*
Warren, W L F 1793-1875 *BiAUS*
Warren, W W 1834-1880 *BiAUS*
Warren, W W *see also* Warren, William Wirt
Warren, Walter Phelps 1841-1914 *NatCAB 16*
Warren, Whitney 1864-1943 *NatCAB 34,
WhAm 2*
Warren, Willard Clinton 1866-1928 *WhAm 1*
Warren, William 1767-1832 *ApCAB, DcAmB,
Drake, WhAm H*
Warren, William 1806-1879 *ApCAB*
Warren, William 1812-1888 *AmBi, ApCAB,
DcAmB, Drake, NatCAB 5, TwCBDA,
WhAm H*
Warren, William Candee 1859-1935
NatCAB 27, WhAm 1
Warren, William Candee, Jr. 1892-1965
NatCAB 53
Warren, William Fairfield 1833-1929 *ApCAB,
BiDAmEd, DcAmB, NatCAB 11,
TwCBDA, WhAm 1*
Warren, William Homer 1866- *WhAm 4*
Warren, William Marshall 1865-1953 *WhAm 3*
Warren, William Robinson 1868-1947 *WhAm 2*
Warren, William Tilman 1877-1962
NatCAB 49, WhAm 4
Warren, William Walter 1882-1964 *NatCAB 50*
Warren, William Wirt 1834-1880 *BiDrAC,
WhAm H*
Warren, William Wirt *see also* Warren, W W
Warren, Willis Dow Peck 1882-1954
NatCAB 43
Warren, Winslow 1838-1930 *NatCAB 12,
WhAm 1*
Warrick, Charles Fredricks 1890-1960
NatCAB 49
Warrick, Dupuy Goza 1898-1964 *NatCAB 51,
WhAm 4*
Warrick, Lutie Burton *WomWWA 14*
Warrick, Walter Dempsey 1893-1958
NatCAB 50
Warrick, Woodward Alfred 1893-1956
NatCAB 46
Warriner, Edward Augustus 1829-1908
NatCAB 13, WhAm 1
Warriner, Eugene Clarence 1866-1945 *WhAm 2*
Warriner, Francis 1805-1866 *ApCAB, Drake*
Warriner, Lewis Legrand 1898-1965 *WhAm 4*
Warriner, Reuel Edward 1910-1972 *WhAm 5,
WhAm 6*
Warriner, Samuel Dexter 1867-1942 *WhAm 2*
Warring, Charles Bartlett 1825-1907 *WhAm 1*
Warrington, Albert Powell 1866-1939
DcAmB S2, WhAm 1
Warrington, George Howard 1872-1940
WhAm 1
Warrington, John Wesley 1844-1921
NatCAB 30
Warrington, John Wesley 1846-1921 *WhAm 1*
Warrington, Lewis 1782-1851 *ApCAB, DcAmB,
Drake, NatCAB 6, TwCBDA, WebAMB,
WhAm H*
Warrock, John 1774-1858 *ApCAB*
Warshaw, Jacob 1878-1944 *BiDAmEd,
NatCAB 42, WhAm 2*
Warshawsky, Abel George 1883-1962 *WhAm 4*
Wartenberg, Robert 1887-1956 *WhAm 3*
Warterfield, Floyd Edward 1870-1954
NatCAB 44
Warthen, Richard 1794-1861 *NatCAB 1*

Warthen, William Horace Franklin 1897-1974
WhAm 6
Warthin, Aldred Scott 1866-1931 *DcAmB,
NatCAB 25, WhAm 1*
Warton, Frank Riggs 1889-1959 *WhAm 3*
Wartz, Michael *NewYHSD*
Warvelle, George William 1852- *NatCAB 9,
WhAm 4*
Warwell d1767 *NewYHSD*
Warwell, Maria *NewYHSD*
Warwick, Bishop Billings 1879-1947
NatCAB 40
Warwick, C Laurence 1889-1952 *WhAm 3*
Warwick, Charles Franklin 1852-1913 *WhAm 1*
Warwick, Edward 1881- *WhAm 6*
Warwick, Herbert Sherwood, Jr. 1910-1970
WhAm 5
Warwick, John George 1830-1892 *BiDrAC,
WhAm H*
Warwick, Richard Neville, Earl Of 1428-1471
McGEWB
Warwick, Robert 1878-1964 *NatCAB 52*
Warwick, Walter Winter 1868-1932 *WhAm 1*
Warwick, William Edmund 1862-1936
WhAm 1
Was, Francois John Theodore 1881-1928
NatCAB 22
Wascher, Howard George 1885-1964 *WhAm 4*
Wasdell, Henry 1831?- *NewYHSD*
Wasey, L R 1884-1961 *WhAm 4*
Wash, Carlyle Hilton 1889-1943 *WhAm 2*
Washabaugh, Jacob Edgar 1866-1965 *WhAm 4*
Washabaugh, William Braham 1878-1965
NatCAB 51
Washakie 1804?-1900 *DcAmB, REnAW,
WebAB, WhAm H*
Washburn, Albert Henry 1866-1930 *AmBi,
DcAmB, NatCAB 26, WhAm 1*
Washburn, Alfred Hamlin 1895-1972 *WhAm 5*
Washburn, Benjamin Martin 1887-1966
WhAm 4
Washburn, Cadwalader Colden 1818-1882
BiAUS
Washburn, Cadwalader Colden *see also*
Washburne, Cadwallader C
Washburn, Cadwallader d1965 *WhAm 4*
Washburn, Cadwalader Colden 1818-1882
*AmBi, ApCAB, BiDrAC, DcAmB,
NatCAB 12, TwCBDA, WhAm H,
WhAmP*
Washburn, Charles Ames 1822-1889 *ApCAB,
BiAUS, NatCAB 5, TwCBDA, WhAm H*
Washburn, Charles Grenfill 1857-1928 *BiDrAC,
DcAmB, NatCAB 27, WhAm 1*
Washburn, Claude Carlos 1883-1926 *WhAm 1*
Washburn, Edward Abel 1868-1934 *NatCAB 26*
Washburn, Edward Abiel 1819-1881 *ApCAB,
DcAmB, NatCAB 9, WhAm H*
Washburn, Edward Payson 1831-1860
NewYHSD
Washburn, Edward Roger 1899-1967
NatCAB 55, WhAm 5
Washburn, Edward Wight 1881-1934 *AmBi,
DcAmB, DcScB, WhAm 1*
Washburn, Elihu Benjamin 1816-1887 *AmBi,
ApCAB, DcAmB, TwCBDA*
Washburn, Emory 1800-1877 *AmBi, ApCAB,
BiAUS, DcAmB, Drake, NatCAB 1,
TwCBDA, WhAm H*
Washburn, F S 1895-1963 *WhAm 4*
Washburn, Frances Wilcox *WomWWA 14*
Washburn, Francis 1843-1914 *WhAm 1*
Washburn, Frank Sherman 1860-1922
NatCAB 32, WhAm 1
Washburn, Frederic Augustus 1869-1949
NatCAB 47, WhAm 2
Washburn, Frederic Baldwin 1871-1944
WhAm 2
Washburn, Frederic Leonard 1860-1927
WhAm 1
Washburn, Frederick Augustus 1869-1949
ApCAB X
Washburn, Frederick Leonard 1860-1927
NatCAB 18
Washburn, George 1833-1915 *AmBi, ApCAB,
ApCAB X, DcAmB, NatCAB 10,
NatCAB 26, WhAm 1*
Washburn, George Frederic 1859- *WhAm 4*

Washburn, George Hamlin 1860-1933 *WhAm 1*
Washburn, Harold Edward 1889-1964
  NatCAB 50
Washburn, Henry Bradford 1869-1962
  NatCAB 47, WhAm 4
Washburn, Henry Dana 1832-1871 *BiAUS,
  BiDrAC, WhAm H, WhAmP*
Washburn, Henry Stevenson 1813-1903 *ApCAB,
  WhAm 1*
Washburn, Henry Stevenson 1885-1955
  NatCAB 43
Washburn, Homer Charles 1876-1964 *WhAm 4*
Washburn, Mrs. Horace B *NewYHSD*
Washburn, Ichabod 1798-1868 *DcAmB,
  NatCAB 10, WhAm H*
Washburn, Israel 1813-1883 *ApCAB, BiAUS,
  BiDrAC, DcAmB, Drake, NatCAB 5,
  TwCBDA, WhAm H, WhAmP*
Washburn, Ives 1887-1947 *WhAm 2*
Washburn, Jed L 1856-1931 *WhAm 1*
Washburn, John 1858-1919 *WhAm 1*
Washburn, John Davis 1833-1903 *NatCAB 12*
Washburn, John Henry 1828-1909 *NatCAB 2,
  WhAm 1*
Washburn, John Hosea 1859-1932 *WhAm 1*
Washburn, Louis Cope 1860-1938 *NatCAB 28,
  WhAm 1*
Washburn, Margaret Floy 1871-1939 *BiDAmEd,
  DcAmB S2, NatCAB 30, NotAW,
  WhAm 1, WomWWA 14*
Washburn, Mary Nightingale 1861-
  WomWWA 14
Washburn, Maurice King 1872-1931
  NatCAB 25
Washburn, Nathan 1816-1903 *NatCAB 10*
Washburn, Nathan 1818-1903 *DcAmB*
Washburn, Peter Thacher 1814-1870 *ApCAB,
  BiAUS, Drake, NatCAB 8, TwCBDA,
  WhAm H*
Washburn, Reginald 1871-1955 *WhAm 3*
Washburn, Robert 1868-1946 *WhAm 2*
Washburn, Stanley 1878-1950 *ApCAB X,
  NatCAB 43, WhAm 3*
Washburn, Victor Duke 1882-1966 *WhAm 4*
Washburn, Watson 1894-1973 *WhAm 6*
Washburn, William *NewYHSD*
Washburn, William Barrett 1820-1887 *AmBi,
  ApCAB, BiAUS, BiDrAC, Drake,
  NatCAB 1, TwCBDA, WhAm H,
  WhAmP*
Washburn, William Drew 1831-1912 *ApCAB,
  BiDrAC, DcAmB, NatCAB 3,
  NatCAB 16, TwCBDA, WhAm 1,
  WhAmP*
Washburn, William Ives d1933 *WhAm 1*
Washburn, William Sherman 1860-1923
  WhAm 1
Washburn, William Tucker 1841-1916 *WhAm 1*
Washburne, Cadwallader Colden 1818-1882
  Drake
Washburne, Cadwallader Colden *see also*
  Washburn, Cadwalder C
Washburne, Carleton Wolsey 1889-1968
  BiDAmEd, NatCAB 54
Washburne, Charles Lee 1877-1961 *NatCAB 48*
Washburne, Elihu Benjamin 1816-1887 *AmBi,
  BiAUS Sup, BiDrAC, BiDrUSE, DcAmB,
  Drake, NatCAB 4, WhAm H, WhAmP*
Washburne, Ellihu Benjamin 1816-1887 *BiAUS*
Washburne, George Adrian 1884-1948 *WhAm 2*
Washburne, George Rudy 1860-1923
  NatCAB 40
Washburne, Heluiz Chandler 1892- *WhAm 5*
Washburne, Marion Foster 1863-
  WomWWA 14
Washinger, William Henry 1862-1928 *WhAm 1*
Washington, Benjamin 1873- *WhoColR*
Washington, Booker Taliaferro 1856-1915 *AmBi,
  ApCAB, BiDAmEd, DcAmB, DcAmReB,
  EncAB, McGEWB, WebAB*
Washington, Booker Taliaferro 1858?-1915
  WhoColR
Washington, Booker Taliaferro 1859?-1915
  TwCBDA, WhAm 1
Washington, Booker Taliferro 1856-1915
  EncAAH
Washington, Booker Talliaferro 1857?-1915
  ApCAB X, NatCAB 7

Washington, Bushrod 1762-1829 *AmBi,
  ApCAB, BiAUS, DcAmB, Drake,
  NatCAB 2, TwCBDA, WebAB,
  WhAm H*
Washington, George 1732-1799 *AmBi, ApCAB,
  BiAUS, BiDrAC, BiDrUSE, DcAmB,
  Drake, EncAAH, EncAB, McGEWB,
  REnAW, TwCBDA, WebAB, WebAMB,
  WhAm H, WhAmP, WhoMilH*
Washington, George 1843-1905 *NatCAB 8*
Washington, George Constant Louis 1871-1946
  NatCAB 34
Washington, George Corbin 1789-1854 *ApCAB,
  BiAUS, BiDrAC, WhAm H, WhAmP*
Washington, George Thomas 1908-1971
  WhAm 5
Washington, Henry Stephens 1867-1934 *DcAmB,
  DcScB, WhAm 1*
Washington, Horace Lee 1864-1938
  NatCAB 28, WhAm 4
Washington, James Barroll 1839-1900
  ApCAB X
Washington, John Augustine 1821-1861 *ApCAB,
  NatCAB 21*
Washington, John Macrae 1797-1853 *DcAmB,
  WebAMB, WhAm H*
Washington, John Marshall 1797-1853 *ApCAB*
Washington, Joseph Edwin 1851-1915 *BiDrAC,
  NatCAB 18, WhAmP*
Washington, Lawrence 1854-1920 *WhAm 1*
Washington, Lewis William 1825?-1871 *ApCAB*
Washington, Lucy H 1835- *AmWom*
Washington, Margaret J Murray 1865-
  WhoColR
Washington, Martha Dandridge Custis
  1731-1802 *NotAW*
Washington, Martha Dandridge Custis
  1732-1801 *NatCAB 1*
Washington, Martha Dandridge Custis
  1732-1802 *AmBi, AmWom, ApCAB,
  TwCBDA, WhAm H*
Washington, Mary 1706-1789 *NatCAB 8*
Washington, Mary 1713?-1789 *AmWom*
Washington, Peter G *BiAUS*
Washington, Thomas 1865-1954 *WhAm 3*
Washington, William Augustine 1752-1810
  ApCAB, Drake, NatCAB 2, WebAMB
Washington, William DeHartburn 1834-1870
  NewYHSD
Washington, William Henry 1813-1860 *BiAUS,
  BiDrAC, WhAm H*
Washington, William Lanier 1865-1933
  ApCAB X, WhAm 1
Washken, Edward 1912-1967 *NatCAB 53*
Wasielewski, Thaddeus Francis Boleslaw 1904-
  BiDrAC
Wasinger, Gordon Bernard 1922-1972 *WhAm 5*
Waskey, Frank Hinman 1875-1964 *BiDrAC,
  WhAm 4, WhAm 5, WhAmP*
Wasley, Ruth Ellen 1914-1969 *WhAm 5*
Wason, Charles William 1854-1918 *ApCAB X,
  NatCAB 33, WhAm 1*
Wason, Edward Hills 1865-1941 *BiDrAC,
  WhAm 1, WhAmP*
Wason, Leonard Chase 1868-1937 *WhAm 1*
Wason, Robert Alexander 1874-1955
  NatCAB 44, WhAm 3
Wason, Robert R 1888-1950 *WhAm 3*
Wassam, William J, Jr. 1872-1958 *WhAm 3*
Wassam, Clarence Wyckliffe 1887- *WhAm 3*
Wassell, Bettie McConaughey 1859-
  WomWWA 14
Wasserman, August Von 1866-1925 *AsBiEn*
Wasserman, Earl Reeves 1913-1973 *WhAm 5*
Wasserman, J Edward 1897-1964 *NatCAB 51*
Wasserman, Joseph 1858-1937 *NatCAB 28*
Wassermann, August Paul Von 1866-1925
  DcScB, DcScB Sup
Wassermann, Friedrich 1884-1969 *WhAm 5*
Wassermann, Jakob 1873-1934 *McGEWB*
Wasservogel, Isidor 1875-1962 *WhAm 4*
Wasson, Alfred Washington 1880-1964
  WhAm 4
Wasson, Alonzo 1870- *WhAm 6*
Wasson, David Atwood 1823-1887 *ApCAB,
  NatCAB 9*
Wasson, George Savary 1855-1931 *ApCAB,
  WhAm 3*

Wasson, Henry Grant 1868-1940 *NatCAB 50*
Wasson, Pearl Randall 1878- *WomWWA 14*
Wasson, Theron 1887-1970 *NatCAB 55,
  WhAm 5*
Wasson, Thomas C 1896-1948 *WhAm 2*
Wasson, William Dixon 1871-1962 *NatCAB 50*
Wasson, William Walter 1884-1968 *WhAm 5*
Wasson, William Ward 1888-1948 *NatCAB 36*
Waste, William Harrison 1868-1940 *WhAm 1*
Watchetaker, George Smith 1916- *IIBEAAW*
Watchorn, Robert 1858-1944 *NatCAB 32,
  WhAm 4*
Waterbury, David 1716-1801 *TwCBDA*
Waterbury, David 1722-1801 *ApCAB, Drake,
  WebAMB*
Waterbury, Frank Calvin 1866-1930
  NatCAB 16, WhAm 1
Waterbury, Frederick 1868-1960 *WhAm 4*
Waterbury, Harry Guley 1868-1950
  NatCAB 40
Waterbury, Henry S d1953 *WhAm 3*
Waterbury, Jared Bell 1799-1876 *ApCAB,
  Drake*
Waterbury, John Isaac 1850-1929 *WhAm 1*
Waterbury, Lucy McGill *NotAW*
Waterbury, Nelson Jarvis 1819- *NatCAB 12*
Waterfall, Harry William 1847-1947 *WhAm 2*
Waterfall, Wallace 1900-1974 *WhAm 6*
Waterhouse, Alfred James 1855- *WhAm 4*
Waterhouse, Benjamin 1754-1846 *ApCAB,
  BiHiMed, DcAmB, Drake, EncAAH,
  EncAB, McGEWB, NatCAB 9,
  TwCBDA, WebAB, WhAm H*
Waterhouse, Edson Willey Alden 1873-1919
  NatCAB 19
Waterhouse, Frank 1867-1930 *DcAmB,
  WhAm 1, WhAm 1C*
Waterhouse, George Booker 1883-1952
  WhAm 3
Waterhouse, George Boyd 1863-1923
  NatCAB 6
Waterhouse, George Shadford 1875- *WhAm 5*
Waterhouse, John 1873-1945 *WhAm 2*
Waterhouse, John Fothergill 1791-1817 *Drake*
Waterhouse, Joseph Raymond 1913-1967
  WhAm 4
Waterhouse, Richard Green 1855-1922
  NatCAB 27, WhAm 1
Waterhouse, Sylvester 1830-1902 *DcAmB,
  NatCAB 8, WhAm H*
Waterloo, Stanley 1846-1913 *TwCBDA,
  WhAm 1*
Waterman, Alan Tower 1892-1967 *NatCAB 53,
  WhAm 4A*
Waterman, Annie Louise 1878- *WomWWA 14*
Waterman, Arba Nelson 1836-1917 *WhAm 1*
Waterman, Cameron Beach 1875- *ApCAB X*
Waterman, Charles Dana 1891-1963 *WhAm 4*
Waterman, Charles M 1847-1924 *WhAm 1*
Waterman, Charles Winfield 1861-1932 *BiDrAC,
  NatCAB 24, WhAm 1, WhAm 4,
  WhAmP*
Waterman, Earle Lytton 1885-1951 *WhAm 3*
Waterman, Elijah 1769-1825 *ApCAB*
Waterman, Frank Allan 1865- *WhAm 5*
Waterman, Harrison Lyman 1840-1918
  NatCAB 17
Waterman, Herbert 1903-1947 *WhAm 2*
Waterman, John Robinson 1783-1876
  NatCAB 8
Waterman, Julian Seesel 1891-1943 *WhAm 2*
Waterman, Leroy 1875-1972 *WhAm 5*
Waterman, Lewis Anthony 1871-1923 *WhAm 1*
Waterman, Lewis Edson 1837-1901 *AmBi,
  DcAmB, NatCAB 1, WebAB, WhAm H*
Waterman, Lucius 1851-1923 *WhAm 1*
Waterman, Marcus 1834-1914 *AmBi, ApCAB,
  NewYHSD, TwCBDA, WhAm 4*
Waterman, Nixon 1859-1944 *WhAm 2*
Waterman, Ralph Douglas 1892-1962
  NatCAB 50
Waterman, Richard d1673 *NatCAB 8*
Waterman, Richard Alan 1914-1971
  NatCAB 57
Waterman, Robert H 1808-1884 *DcAmB,
  WhAm H*
Waterman, Robert Whitney 1826-1891 *ApCAB,
  NatCAB 4, TwCBDA*

Waterman, Sara Clifford Brown 1852-
  WomWWA 14
Waterman, Sigismund 1819- *ApCAB,*
  WhAm 4
Waterman, Stephen 1863-1944 *NatCAB 34*
Waterman, Thomas Glasby 1788-1862 *ApCAB*
Waterman, Thomas Tileston 1900-1951
  NatCAB 40
Waterman, Thomas Whitney 1821-1898 *ApCAB,*
  DcAmB, Drake, NatCAB 4, WhAm H
Waterman, Warren Gookin 1872-1952 *WhAm 3*
Waterman, Willoughby Cyrus 1888-1964
  WhAm 4
Watermire, Emily G 1879- *WomWWA 14*
Watermulder, Louis F 1901-1975 *WhAm 6*
Waters, Almira *NewYHSD*
Waters, Beverly Lyon 1875-1949 *NatCAB 42*
Waters, Campbell Easter 1872- *WhAm 5*
Waters, Charles J B *NewYHSD*
Waters, Chester Hill, Jr. 1911-1968 *NatCAB 55*
Waters, Clara Erskine Clement 1834-1916
  AmWom, NotAW, WhAm 1
Waters, D E *NewYHSD*
Waters, Daniel 1731-1816 *DcAmB, WebAMB,*
  WhAm H
Waters, Daniel Howard 1834-1894 *NatCAB 10*
Waters, Dudley E 1862-1931 *WhAm 1*
Waters, E A *NewYHSD*
Waters, Ethel 1900- *WebAB*
Waters, Eugene A 1899-1956 *WhAm 3*
Waters, Francis E 1856-1936 *WhAm 1,*
  WhAm 1C
Waters, Frank 1902- *REnAW*
Waters, George W 1832-1912 *NewYHSD*
Waters, Harriet Bishop *WomWWA 14*
Waters, Henry Fitz-Gilbert 1833- *ApCAB*
Waters, Henry Goodman 1880-1930
  NatCAB 23
Waters, Henry Jackson 1865-1925 *BiDAmEd,*
  NatCAB 24, WhAm 1
Waters, James Stephen 1894-1964 *WhAm 4*
Waters, John H d1933 *WhAm 1*
Waters, John P *NewYHSD*
Waters, John W *NewYHSD*
Waters, Lewis William 1888-1944 *WhAm 2*
Waters, Matthew *NewYHSD*
Waters, Moses H 1837- *WhAm 4*
Waters, N McGee 1866-1916 *WhAm 1*
Waters, Nicholas Baker 1764-1796 *ApCAB*
Waters, Robert 1835-1910 *ApCAB, WhAm 1*
Waters, Russell Judson 1843-1911 *BiDrAC,*
  WhAm 1
Waters, Samuel Blackburn 1866-1935
  NatCAB 27
Waters, Samuel M 1883-1952 *WhAm 3*
Waters, Thomas Franklin 1851-1919 *WhAm 1*
Waters, Vincent S d1974 *WhAm 6*
Waters, William Everett 1856-1924 *DcAmB,*
  TwCBDA, WhAm 1
Waters, William Laurence d1956 *WhAm 3*
Waters, William Otis 1861-1925 *WhAm 1*
Waters, William P 1886-1957 *WhAm 3*
Waters, Yssabella 1862- *WomWWA 14*
Waterson, James R *NewYHSD*
Waterson, Karl William 1876-1961 *WhAm 4*
Waterston, Anne C 1812-1899 *ApCAB Sup*
Waterston, James R *NewYHSD*
Waterston, John James 1811-1883 *DcScB*
Waterston, Robert Cassie 1812-1893 *ApCAB,*
  ApCAB Sup, Drake
Waterton, Charles 1782-1865 *ApCAB, DcScB,*
  Drake
Wathen, John Roach 1872-1935 *WhAm 1*
Watie, Stand 1806-1871 *AmBi, BiDConf,*
  DcAmB, REnAW, WebAMB, WhAm H
Watie, Stand 1815-1877 *ApCAB*
Waties, James Rives 1845- *WhAm 4*
Waties, Julius Pringle *NewYHSD*
Watkeys, Charles W 1877- *WhAm 5*
Watkin, William Ward 1886-1952 *WhAm 3*
Watkins, Aaron Sherman 1863-1941 *WhAm 1*
Watkins, Albert 1848-1923 *WhAm 1*
Watkins, Albert Galiton 1818-1895 *BiAUS,*
  BiDrAC, WhAm H, WhAmP
Watkins, Alexander Farrar 1856-1929 *WhAm 1*
Watkins, Arthur Charles 1873-1953 *WhAm 3*
Watkins, Arthur Vivian 1886-1973 *BiDrAC,*
  WhAm 6, WhAmP

Watkins, Blanche Bowman 1869-
  WomWWA 14
Watkins, Charles D 1886-1962 *WhAm 4*
Watkins, Charles L 1879-1966 *WhAm 4*
Watkins, Charles Law 1886-1945 *ApCAB X,*
  NatCAB 34
Watkins, Charles W d1906 *WhAm 1*
Watkins, Curtis Gardner 1906-1967
  NatCAB 53
Watkins, Dale Baxter 1914-1971 *WhAm 5*
Watkins, David Ogden 1862-1938 *NatCAB 29,*
  WhAm 1
Watkins, Dwight Everett 1878- *WhAm 6*
Watkins, Edgar 1868-1945 *WhAm 2*
Watkins, Edward Goodrich 1865-1942
  NatCAB 32
Watkins, Elsie Gardner 1887- *WomWWA 14*
Watkins, Elton 1881-1956 *BiDrAC,*
  NatCAB 45, WhAm 3
Watkins, Everett Andrew 1882-1963
  NatCAB 51
Watkins, Everett C d1955 *WhAm 3*
Watkins, Ferre C 1893-1966 *WhAm 4*
Watkins, Frances Ellen *NotAW*
Watkins, Frank Thomas 1898- *WhAm 3*
Watkins, Franklin Chenault 1894-1972
  WhAm 5
Watkins, Frederick Mundell 1910-1972
  WhAm 5
Watkins, G Robert 1902-1970 *WhAm 5*
Watkins, George Benson 1895-1966 *NatCAB 53*
Watkins, George Claiborne 1815-1872 *DcAmB,*
  NatCAB 13, WhAm H
Watkins, George Robert 1902-1970 *BiDrAC*
Watkins, Harold Ryburn 1888-1966
  NatCAB 53
Watkins, Harry Evans 1898-1963 *WhAm 4*
Watkins, Harvey Middleton 1894-1962
  NatCAB 50
Watkins, Henrietta Stokes 1875-
  WomWWA 14
Watkins, Henry Hitt 1866- *WhAm 5*
Watkins, Henry Vaughan 1884-1944 *WhAm 2*
Watkins, Irene Wickersham 1856-
  WomWWA 14
Watkins, J Stephen 1892-1967 *WhAm 5*
Watkins, Jabez Bunting 1845-1921 *NatCAB 19,*
  WhAm 1
Watkins, James 1887-1970 *WhAm 5*
Watkins, James Thomas 1871-1934 *NatCAB 24*
Watkins, John Benjamin 1855-1931 *NatCAB 30*
Watkins, John Elfreth d1946 *WhAm 2*
Watkins, John Elfreth 1852-1903 *ApCAB Sup,*
  DcAmB, WhAm 1
Watkins, John Stradley 1879-1962 *NatCAB 50*
Watkins, John Thomas 1854-1925 *BiDrAC,*
  WhAm 1, WhAmP
Watkins, Joseph Conrad 1873- *WhAm 5*
Watkins, Louis Douglas 1835?-1868 *ApCAB*
Watkins, Macy Everson 1884-1963 *NatCAB 50*
Watkins, Mark Hanna 1903-1976 *WhAm 6*
Watkins, Miles Abernathy 1884-1949
  NatCAB 38
Watkins, Paul Ferguson 1895-1951 *NatCAB 42*
Watkins, Raymond Edward 1882-1945
  WhAm 2
Watkins, Robert Henry 1857- *WhAm 4*
Watkins, Robert Malcolm 1901-1954
  NatCAB 44
Watkins, Samuel 1794-1880 *ApCAB*
Watkins, Samuel Asbury Thompson 1869-
  WhoColR
Watkins, Samuel C G 1853- *NatCAB 1*
Watkins, Susan *WomWWA 14*
Watkins, Thomas David 1870-1912 *NatCAB 18*
Watkins, Thomas Franklin 1881-1973 *WhAm 6*
Watkins, Thomas Henry 1872-1949 *NatCAB 40*
Watkins, Thomas Horace 1860- *ApCAB X,*
  WhAm 4
Watkins, Thomas James 1863-1925 *NatCAB 28,*
  WhAm 1
Watkins, Thomas Richard 1885-1954
  NatCAB 43
Watkins, Tobias 1780-1855 *ApCAB, BiAUS,*
  Drake
Watkins, Vernon Phillips 1906-1967 *WhAm 5*
Watkins, Virginia Stephenson 1875-
  WomWWA 14

Watkins, Walter Kendall 1855- *WhAm 4*
Watkins, William *NewYHSD*
Watkins, William Brown 1834- *ApCAB*
Watkins, William Clarence 1879-1941
  NatCAB 30
Watkins, William Turner 1895-1961 *WhAm 4*
Watkins, William Wirt 1826-1898 *BiDConf*
Watkins, William Woodbury 1846-1900
  WhAm 1
Watkinson, David 1778-1857 *ApCAB*
Watling, John Wright 1883-1951 *WhAm 3*
Watmough, E C *NewYHSD*
Watmough, James Horatio 1822-1917 *ApCAB,*
  NatCAB 11, WhAm 1
Watmough, John Goddard 1793-1861 *ApCAB,*
  BiAUS, BiDrAC, Drake, NatCAB 11,
  WhAm H
Watmough, Pendleton Gaines 1828- *ApCAB,*
  NatCAB 11
Watner, Abraham 1891- *WhAm 4*
Watres, Laurence Hawley 1882-1964 *BiDrAC,*
  WhAmP
Watres, Louis Arthur 1851-1937 *NatCAB 8,*
  NatCAB 28, WhAm 1
Watrin, T T *NewYHSD*
Watrous, Charles Leach 1837-1916 *WhAm 1*
Watrous, Elizabeth Snowden Nichols 1858-1921
  WhAm 1, WomWWA 14
Watrous, George Ansel 1872- *WhAm 1*
Watrous, George Dutton 1858-1940
  NatCAB 30, WhAm 1
Watrous, George Henry 1829-1889 *NatCAB 24*
Watrous, Grace Greenwood 1876-
  WomWWA 14
Watrous, Harry Willson 1857-1940 *NatCAB 13,*
  TwCBDA
Watrous, Harry Wilson 1857-1940 *WhAm 1*
Watrous, Jerome A 1840- *NatCAB 3*
Watrous, John C 1806-1874 *BiAUS,*
  NatCAB 3
Watrous, Richard Benedict 1869- *WhAm 3*
Watrous, Robert Morgan 1908-1963
  NatCAB 51
Watrous, William Henry 1841- *NatCAB 5*
Watry, Joseph 1860-1942 *NatCAB 31*
Watson, Adolphus Eugene 1878-1949 *WhAm 2*
Watson, Albert 1857-1944 *NatCAB 35,*
  WhAm 3
Watson, Albert William 1922- *BiDrAC*
Watson, Alfred Augustin 1818-1905 *ApCAB,*
  NatCAB 5, TwCBDA, WhAm 1
Watson, Alonzo Richard 1900-1967 *WhAm 4*
Watson, Amelia Montague 1856-1934 *WhAm 1,*
  WomWWA 14
Watson, Andrew 1834-1916 *DcAmB, WhAm 1*
Watson, Annah Walker Robinson *AmWom,*
  WomWWA 14
Watson, Archibald Robinson d1957 *WhAm 3*
Watson, Arthur Clinton 1878- *WhAm 6*
Watson, Arthur Comstock 1881-1940
  NatCAB 30
Watson, Arthur Kittredge 1919-1974 *WhAm 6*
Watson, Arthur Wellesley 1851-1924 *ApCAB X*
Watson, Benjamin Frank 1826-1905 *ApCAB,*
  WhAm 1
Watson, Benjamin Philip 1880- *WhAm 6*
Watson, Beriah Andre 1836- *ApCAB*
Watson, Sir Brook 1735-1807 *ApCAB, Drake*
Watson, Bruce Mervellon 1860-1943 *WhAm 2*
Watson, Burl Stevens 1893-1975 *WhAm 6*
Watson, Byron S 1876-1947 *WhAm 2*
Watson, C A *NewYHSD*
Watson, C Hoyt 1888-1969 *NatCAB 55*
Watson, Charles G 1891- *WhAm 5*
Watson, Charles Henry 1847-1931 *WhAm 1*
Watson, Charles Masena 1873-1949
  NatCAB 40
Watson, Charles Roger 1873-1948 *DcAmB S4,*
  WhAm 2
Watson, Clarence Wayland 1864-1940 *BiDrAC,*
  NatCAB 31, WhAm 1
Watson, Cooper Kinderdine 1810-1880 *BiAUS,*
  BiDrAC, WhAm H
Watson, Cornelius Bushnell 1887-1950
  NatCAB 40
Watson, Daniel 1801-1871 *NatCAB 8*
Watson, David Emmett 1870- *WhAm 1*
Watson, David Kemper 1849-1918 *BiDrAC,*

WhAm 4
Watson, David Robert 1902-1968 *WhAm 5*
Watson, David Thompson 1844-1916 *DcAmB, WhAm 1*
Watson, Dawson *IIBEAAW*
Watson, Donald Reed 1901-1963 *NatCAB 51*
Watson, Drake 1885-1951 *WhAm 3*
Watson, Dudley Crafts 1885-1972 *WhAm 5*
Watson, Earnest Charles 1892-1970 *WhAm 5*
Watson, Earnest William 1884-1969 *WhAm 5*
Watson, Ebbie Julian 1869-1917 *WhAm 1*
Watson, Ebenezer 1744-1777 *ApCAB*
Watson, Edith Sarah 1861- *WhAm 3*
Watson, Edward Fisk 1892-1959 *NatCAB 47*
Watson, Edward Hann 1902-1975 *WhAm 6*
Watson, Edward Minor 1874-1938 *WhAm 1, WhAm 2*
Watson, Edward Willard 1843-1925 *WhAm 1*
Watson, Edwin Martin 1883-1945 *WhAm 2*
Watson, Elizabeth Lowe 1842- *AmWom, WomWWA 14*
Watson, Elizabeth Lowe 1843- *WhAm 4*
Watson, Elizabeth Vila Taylor *WomWWA 14*
Watson, Elkanah 1758-1842 *ApCAB, DcAmB, Drake, EncAAH, McGEWB, NatCAB 5, WebAB, WhAm H*
Watson, Ella *REnAW*
Watson, Ellen Maria 1842- *AmWom*
Watson, Emile Emdon 1885-1958 *WhAm 3*
Watson, Emory Olin 1865-1935 *WhAm 1*
Watson, Ernest Milton 1884-1948 *NatCAB 40*
Watson, Ernest William 1884-1969 *NatCAB 54*
Watson, Esther Josephine 1859- *WomWWA 14*
Watson, Eugene Alexander 1870- *WhoColR*
Watson, Eugene Payne 1911-1964 *WhAm 4*
Watson, Eugene Winslow 1843-1914 *WhAm 1*
Watson, F B 1870-1955 *WhAm 3*
Watson, Fletcher Guard 1912- *BiDAmEd*
Watson, Floyd Rowe 1872- *WhAm 5*
Watson, Francis Sedgwick 1853-1942 *NatCAB 32*
Watson, Frank Dekker 1883-1959 *NatCAB 43, WhAm 3*
Watson, Frank Rushmore 1859-1940 *WhAm 1*
Watson, Frederica King Davis 1869- *WomWWA 14*
Watson, G Clarke 1907-1966 *WhAm 4*
Watson, George Chapin 1880-1948 *NatCAB 45*
Watson, George D 1845- *WhAm 1*
Watson, George Henry 1883-1952 *WhAm 3*
Watson, George Neville 1886-1965 *DcScB*
Watson, Harley Albro 1890-1967 *NatCAB 53*
Watson, Harold Dollner 1874-1965 *NatCAB 50*
Watson, Harry Legare 1876-1956 *WhAm 3*
Watson, Hattie Rutherford 1884- *WhoColR*
Watson, Helen 1884- *WomWWA 14*
Watson, Henry Chapman 1870-1909 *WhAm 1*
Watson, Henry Clay 1831-1867 *DcAmB, WhAm H*
Watson, Henry Clay 1831-1869 *ApCAB, Drake*
Watson, Henry Cood 1816-1875 *ApCAB, NatCAB 5*
Watson, Henry Cood 1818-1875 *DcAmB, WhAm H*
Watson, Henry David 1846- *WhAm 1*
Watson, Henry Sumner 1868-1933 *WhAm 1*
Watson, Henry Winfield 1856-1933 *BiDrAC, WhAm 1, WhAmP*
Watson, Hewett Cottrell 1804-1881 *DcScB*
Watson, Hugh Hammond 1885-1947 *WhAm 2*
Watson, Irving Allison 1849-1918 *NatCAB 19, WhAm 1*
Watson, J R *NewYHSD*
Watson, James 1750-1806 *ApCAB, BiAUS, BiDrAC, NatCAB 2, TwCBDA, WhAm H*
Watson, James 1845- *WhAm 1*
Watson, James Craig 1838-1880 *AmBi, ApCAB, DcAmB, Drake, NatCAB 7, TwCBDA, WhAm H*
Watson, James D 1870-1932 *WhAm 1*
Watson, James Dewey 1928- *AsBiEn, EncAB, McGEWB, WebAB*
Watson, James Eli 1863-1948 *BiDrAC, WhAm 2, WhAmP*
Watson, James Eli 1864-1948 *DcAmB S4, NatCAB 40*
Watson, James Fraughtman 1879- *WhAm 6*

Watson, James Gray 1886-1956 *WhAm 3*
Watson, James Madison 1827-1900 *ApCAB, BiDAmEd, DcAmB, NatCAB 10, WhAm 1*
Watson, James Muir 1808-1873 *ApCAB*
Watson, James Samuel 1882-1952 *NatCAB 40, WhoColR*
Watson, James Sibley 1860-1951 *WhAm 3*
Watson, James V 1814-1856 *ApCAB, NatCAB 5*
Watson, James Webster 1879-1951 *WhAm 3*
Watson, Jeannette Kittredge 1883-1966 *NatCAB 51*
Watson, John *NewYHSD*
Watson, John 1685-1768 *BnEnAmA, NewYHSD*
Watson, John 1807-1863 *ApCAB, Drake*
Watson, John Broadus 1878-1958 *ApCAB X, AsBiEn, BiDAmEd, EncAB, McGEWB, NatCAB 48, WebAB, WhAm 3*
Watson, John Brown 1872-1942 *WhAm 2, WhoColR*
Watson, John Crittenden 1842-1923 *AmBi, ApCAB Sup, DcAmB, NatCAB 9, TwCBDA, WhAm 1*
Watson, John Fanning 1779-1860 *DcAmB, Drake, NatCAB 7, WhAm H*
Watson, John Frampton *NewYHSD*
Watson, John Franklin 1871- *WhAm 5*
Watson, John H, Jr. 1883-1962 *WhAm 4*
Watson, John Henry 1851-1929 *NatCAB 21, WhAm 1*
Watson, John Jay 1841-1912 *NatCAB 29*
Watson, John Jay, Jr. 1874-1939 *ApCAB X, WhAm 1*
Watson, John Jordan Crittenden 1878-1932 *WhAm 1*
Watson, John Tadwell 1748-1826 *ApCAB*
Watson, John Thomas 1885-1954 *WhAm 3*
Watson, John W *NewYHSD*
Watson, John Watson Tadwell 1748-1826 *Drake*
Watson, John Whitaker 1824-1890 *ApCAB*
Watson, John William Clark 1808-1890 *BiDConf, DcAmB, WhAm H*
Watson, Joseph Franklin 1849-1922 *WhAm 1*
Watson, Joseph Jenkins 1872-1924 *NatCAB 20*
Watson, Joseph McCord 1873-1954 *NatCAB 46*
Watson, Kenneth Nicoll 1907-1970 *WhAm 5*
Watson, Leroy Hugh 1893-1975 *WhAm 6*
Watson, Lewis Findlay 1819-1890 *BiDrAC, WhAm H*
Watson, Lucy Carlile 1855- *WomWWA 14*
Watson, Luke L 1879-1956 *NatCAB 42*
Watson, Mark Skinner 1887-1966 *WhAm 4*
Watson, Mark Walton 1828-1909 *NatCAB 29*
Watson, Mary Devereaux *WomWWA 14*
Watson, Mary Eunice 1861- *WomWWA 14*
Watson, Mary J 1840- *WomWWA 14*
Watson, Mary Maud Carr 1865- *WomWWA 14*
Watson, Milton Tate 1872-1933 *NatCAB 16, NatCAB 25*
Watson, P H *BiAUS*
Watson, Paul Barron 1861-1948 *ApCAB, WhAm 2*
Watson, Philip Jay, Jr. 1886-1946 *NatCAB 36*
Watson, Ralph Hopkins 1878-1961 *NatCAB 49, WhAm 4*
Watson, Richard *NewYHSD*
Watson, Richard 1737-1816 *DcScB*
Watson, Robert 1865-1936 *WhAm 1*
Watson, Robert 1882-1948 *WhAm 2*
Watson, Robert Walker 1894-1944 *WhAm 2*
Watson, Rom Purefoy 1869-1932 *NatCAB 38*
Watson, Roy Seymour 1881-1935 *NatCAB 37*
Watson, Russell Ellsworth 1885-1970 *WhAm 5*
Watson, Samuel Humes 1877-1948 *NatCAB 37*
Watson, Samuel Newell 1861-1942 *WhAm 2*
Watson, Sereno 1826-1892 *ApCAB, DcAmB, DcScB, NatCAB 6, WhAm H*
Watson, Stewart *NewYHSD*
Watson, Thomas Augustus 1854-1934 *ApCAB X, DcAmB, NatCAB 27, WebAB, WhAm 1*
Watson, Thomas E 1856-1922 *WhAm 1*
Watson, Thomas Edward 1856-1922 *AmBi, BiDrAC, DcAmB, EncAAH, EncAB, McGEWB, NatCAB 3, TwCBDA,*

WebAB
Watson, Thomas Eugene 1892-1966 *NatCAB 52*
Watson, Thomas Evans 1856-1922 *ApCAB Sup*
Watson, Thomas John 1874-1956 *EncAB, McGEWB, NatCAB 47, WebAB, WhAm 3*
Watson, Thomas Leonard 1871-1924 *WhAm 1*
Watson, Tolbert 1879-1959 *NatCAB 47*
Watson, Walter 1851-1922 *NatCAB 19*
Watson, Walter Allen 1867-1919 *BiDrAC, WhAm 1, WhAmP*
Watson, Walter Lyndall 1870-1923 *NatCAB 35*
Watson, Willard Oliphint 1902- *WhAm 5*
Watson, William 1715-1787 *DcScB*
Watson, William 1834-1915 *ApCAB, DcAmB, NatCAB 12, TwCBDA, WhAm 1*
Watson, William Franklin 1861-1953 *WhAm 3*
Watson, William Gorrell 1907-1962 *WhAm 4*
Watson, William Henry 1829-1913 *ApCAB, NatCAB 4, NatCAB 7, WhAm 1*
Watson, William James 1872-1940 *NatCAB 30*
Watson, William Marvin, Jr. 1924- *BiDrUSE*
Watson, William Perry 1854-1925 *NatCAB 19*
Watson, William Richard 1867-1926 *WhAm 1*
Watson, William Robinson 1799-1864 *ApCAB, NatCAB 8*
Watson, William Tharp 1849- *TwCBDA*
Watson, Winslow Cossoul 1803- *ApCAB, Drake*
Watson-Watt, Sir Robert 1892-1973 *WhAm 6*
Watson-Watt, Sir Robert 1892-1974 *WhWW-II*
Watson-Watt, Sir Robert Alexander 1892- *AsBiEn, McGEWB*
Watt, Barbara Hall 1912-1970 *WhAm 5*
Watt, Ben H 1889-1961 *WhAm 4*
Watt, Charles Hansell 1886-1958 *NatCAB 45*
Watt, David Alexander 1865- *WhAm 4*
Watt, George Frederick 1867-1917 *NatCAB 17*
Watt, Gertrude B *WomWWA 14*
Watt, Homer Andrew 1884-1948 *WhAm 2*
Watt, James 1736-1819 *AsBiEn, DcScB, McGEWB*
Watt, James Robert 1869-1941 *WhAm 1*
Watt, Madge Robertson *WomWWA 14*
Watt, Richard Morgan 1872-1938 *NatCAB 28, WhAm 1*
Watt, Robert 1832-1907 *NatCAB 33*
Watt, Robert E 1774-1819 *BiHiMed*
Watt, Robert J 1894-1947 *WhAm 2*
Watt, Robert McDowell 1888-1963 *WhAm 4*
Watt, Rolla Vernon 1857-1926 *WhAm 1*
Watteau, Antoine 1684-1721 *McGEWB*
Watteau, Boudoin Louis 1570-1627 *ApCAB*
Watters, Henry Eugene 1876-1938 *WhAm 1*
Watters, John 1831-1874 *ApCAB*
Watters, Philip Melancthon 1860-1926 *WhAm 1*
Watters, Philip Sidney 1890-1972 *WhAm 5*
Watters, Thomas 1860-1940 *WhAm 1*
Watters, W Oral 1875-1948 *NatCAB 38*
Watters, William 1751-1829 *ApCAB*
Watters, William Henry 1876-1949 *WhAm 3*
Watterson, Alfred Valentine Demetrius 1855- *NatCAB 12*
Watterson, George 1783-1854 *TwCBDA*
Watterson, Harvey M 1811-1891 *BiAUS*
Watterson, Harvey Magee 1811-1891 *BiDrAC, DcAmB, NatCAB 1, TwCBDA, WhAm H, WhAmP*
Watterson, Harvey McGee 1811-1891 *ApCAB*
Watterson, Henry 1840-1921 *AmBi, ApCAB, ApCAB X, BiDConf, BiDrAC, DcAmB, EncAAH, NatCAB 1, TwCBDA, WebAB, WhAm 1, WhAmP*
Watterson, John Ambrose 1844-1899 *ApCAB, NatCAB 9, TwCBDA*
Watterson, Joseph 1900-1971 *WhAm 6*
Watterston, George 1783-1854 *ApCAB, BiAUS, DcAmB, DcAmLiB, Drake, NatCAB 7, WhAm H*
Watteville, Henrietta Benigna J VonZ 1725-1789 *BiDAmEd*
Watteville, Henrietta Benigna J Z Von 1725-1789 *NotAW*
Watteville, John, Baron De 1718-1788 *NatCAB 3*
Wattie, James 1902-1974 *WhAm 6*

Wattis, Edmund Orson 1855-1934 *NatCAB 25,*
WhAm 1
Wattles, Andrew D *NewYHSD*
Wattles, Gurdon Wallace 1855-1932 *ApCAB X,*
NatCAB 12, WhAm 1
Wattles, J Henry *NewYHSD*
Wattles, James L *NewYHSD*
Wattles, W *NewYHSD*
Wattles, Willard Austin 1888-1950 *NatCAB 39,*
WhAm 3
Watts, Alan Wilson 1915-1973 *WhAm 6*
Watts, Alan Witson 1915-1973 *WebAB*
Watts, Albert Edward 1881-1969 *NatCAB 54,*
WhAm 5
Watts, Arthur Simeon 1876-1963 *NatCAB 49,*
WhAm 5
Watts, Arthur Thomas 1837-1921 *NatCAB 20,*
WhAm 4
Watts, Beaufort T *BiAUS*
Watts, Charles Henry 1881-1955 *WhAm 3*
Watts, Charles Wellington 1867-1934
NatCAB 33
Watts, Charles Wesley 1875-1952 *NatCAB 40*
Watts, Chester Burleigh 1889-1971 *NatCAB 57*
Watts, David 1764-1819 *ApCAB*
Watts, Edward Seabrook 1882-1916 *WhAm 1*
Watts, Ethelbert 1845-1919 *NatCAB 30,*
WhAm 1
Watts, Frank Overton 1867-1946 *NatCAB 33,*
WhAm 2
Watts, Frederick 1719-1795 *ApCAB*
Watts, Frederick 1801-1889 *ApCAB, BiAUS,*
DcAmB, EncAAH, WhAm H
Watts, Frederick William 1886-1957
NatCAB 43
Watts, George Washington 1851-1921
NatCAB 19, WhAm 1
Watts, H Bascom 1890-1959 *WhAm 3*
Watts, Harry Dorsey 1885-1952 *WhAm 3*
Watts, Harvey Maitland 1864- *WhAm 4*
Watts, Henry Miller 1805-1890 *ApCAB,*
BiAUS, NatCAB 4
Watts, Herbert Charles 1874- *WhAm 5*
Watts, J Murray 1879-1951 *NatCAB 39*
Watts, James W d1895 *NewYHSD*
Watts, John 1715-1789 *ApCAB, Drake*
Watts, John 1749-1836 *ApCAB, BiAUS,*
BiDrAC, TwCBDA, WhAm H
Watts, John Clarence 1902-1971 *BiDrAC,*
WhAm 5
Watts, John Dennis 1895-1966 *NatCAB 52*
Watts, John Sebrie 1816-1876 *BiAUS, BiDrAC,*
WhAm H, WhAmP
Watts, Joseph Thomas 1874-1957 *WhAm 3*
Watts, Legh Richmond 1843-1920 *WhAm 1*
Watts, Lyle Ford 1890-1962 *WhAm 4*
Watts, Margaret Anderson 1832- *AmWom*
Watts, Mary Jennings Orton 1868-
WomWWA 14
Watts, Mary Stanbery 1868- *WhAm 4,*
WomWWA 14
Watts, May Petrea Theilgaard 1893-1975
WhAm 6
Watts, Ralph L 1869-1949 *WhAm 2*
Watts, Richard Cannon 1853-1930 *NatCAB 39,*
WhAm 1
Watts, Ridley 1872-1937 *WhAm 1*
Watts, Ridley 1901-1975 *WhAm 6*
Watts, Robert 1812-1867 *ApCAB, Drake*
Watts, Robert 1820- *ApCAB*
Watts, Robert Crenshaw 1883-1951
NatCAB 40
Watts, Roderick John 1904-1959 *WhAm 3*
Watts, Stanley Saul 1922-1972 *WhAm 5*
Watts, Stephen 1743?-1788 *ApCAB*
Watts, Stephen Hurt 1877-1953 *NatCAB 46*
Watts, T Ashby, Jr. 1906-1959 *NatCAB 45*
Watts, Thomas Hill 1819-1892 *ApCAB,*
BiAUS, BiDConf, DcAmB, NatCAB 10,
TwCBDA, WhAm H
Watts, Thomas Joseph 1874-1948 *WhAm 3*
Watts, William Bowers 1892-1945 *NatCAB 39*
Watts, William Bragg 1851-1925 *ApCAB X*
Watts, William Carleton 1880-1956
NatCAB 44, WhAm 3
Watts, William Lord 1850- *WhAm 4*
Wattson, Lewis Thomas 1863-1940 *DcAmB S2*

Wauchope, George Armstrong 1862-1943
WhAm 2
Wauchope, John Andrew 1904-1968
NatCAB 54
Waud, Alfred R 1828-1891 *IIBEAAW,*
NewYHSD, TwCBDA
Waud, William d1878 *IIBEAAW, NewYHSD*
Waugh, Alfred S 1810?-1856 *IIBEAAW,*
NewYHSD, WhAm H
Waugh, Benjamin Adair 1872-1953 *NatCAB 41*
Waugh, Beverly 1789-1858 *ApCAB, DcAmB,*
NatCAB 11, TwCBDA, WhAm H
Waugh, Coulton 1896-1973 *WhAm 6*
Waugh, Daniel Webster 1842-1921 *BiDrAC*
Waugh, Edward Walter 1913-1966 *NatCAB 52*
Waugh, Evelyn Arthur St. John 1903-1966
McGEWB, WhAm 4
Waugh, Frank Albert 1869-1943 *NatCAB 33,*
WhAm 2
Waugh, Frederick Judd 1861-1940 *BnEnAmA,*
DcAmB S2, WhAm 1
Waugh, Henry W *NewYHSD*
Waugh, Ida d1919 *WhAm 1, WomWWA 14*
Waugh, John McMaster 1905-1962 *NatCAB 50,*
WhAm 4
Waugh, Karl Tinsley 1879-1971 *NatCAB 57,*
WhAm 5
Waugh, Lura Lee 1867- *WomWWA 14*
Waugh, Mary Eliza *NewYHSD*
Waugh, Samuel Bell 1814-1855 *WhAm H*
Waugh, Samuel Bell 1814-1885 *NewYHSD*
Waugh, Samuel Clark 1890-1970 *NatCAB 56,*
WhAm 5
Waugh, Sidney 1904-1963 *IIBEAAW,*
NatCAB 47, WhAm 4
Waugh, William *NewYHSD*
Waugh, William Francis 1849-1918 *WhAm 1*
Waugh, William Hammond 1875- *WhAm 5*
Waugh, William Jasper 1913-1972 *WhAm 5*
Waughop, John Wesley 1839-1903 *NatCAB 17*
Waul, Thomas Neville 1813-1903 *BiDConf,*
WhAm 1
Waul, Thomas Neville 1815-1903 *ApCAB*
Wavell, Archibald Percival 1883-1950
McGEWB, WhAm 3, WhWW-II,
WhoMilH
Waverley, Viscount 1882-1958 *WhAm 3*
Waxman, Franz d1967 *WhAm 4*
Waxman, Percy d1948 *WhAm 2*
Way, Albert Pratt 1868-1962 *NatCAB 53*
Way, Amanda M 1828-1914 *NotAW*
Way, Andrew John Henry 1826-1888 *ApCAB,*
NewYHSD
Way, Bayard Chandler 1869-1950 *NatCAB 38*
Way, Cassius 1881-1948 *NatCAB 37,*
WhAm 2
Way, David Leroy 1838- *NatCAB 4*
Way, George Brevitt 1854- *ApCAB, WhAm 4*
Way, Gordon L 1913-1974 *WhAm 6*
Way, Harold David 1883-1959 *NatCAB 45*
Way, Henry Truman 1896-1957 *NatCAB 47*
Way, John 1871-1929 *WhAm 1*
Way, Joseph Howell 1865- *WhAm 1*
Way, Luther B d1942 *WhAm 2*
Way, Marie Wagener 1876- *WomWWA 14*
Way, Mary *NewYHSD*
Way, Royal Brunson 1873-1937 *WhAm 1*
Way, Sylvester Bedell 1874-1946 *NatCAB 37,*
WhAm 2
Way, Warren Wade 1869-1943 *WhAm 2*
Way, William *NewYHSD*
Way, William 1877- *WhAm 5*
Way, William Addison 1867-1948 *NatCAB 38*
Wayburn, Ned 1874-1942 *WhAm 2*
Waygood, James Jamison 1893-1965
NatCAB 54
Wayjan Ibn Rustam *DcScB*
Wayland, Frances Mary Green 1840-
WomWWA 14
Wayland, Francis 1796-1865 *AmBi, ApCAB,*
BiDAmEd, DcAmB, DcAmReB, Drake,
McGEWB, NatCAB 1, NatCAB 8,
TwCBDA, WebAB, WhAm H
Wayland, Francis 1826-1904 *ApCAB, DcAmB,*
NatCAB 12, TwCBDA, WhAm 1
Wayland, Heman Lincoln 1830-1898 *ApCAB,*
NatCAB 10, TwCBDA
Wayland, John Walter 1872-1962 *BiDAmEd*

Wayland, Julius Augustus 1854-1912 *WhAm 1*
Wayland, Raymond Theodore 1890-1957
NatCAB 46
Wayland-Smith, Robert 1905-1961 *WhAm 4*
Waymack, William Wesley 1888-1960 *WhAm 4*
Wayman, Alexander Walker 1821-1895 *DcAmB,*
WhAm H
Wayman, Alexander Walter 1821-1895
NatCAB 4
Wayman, Alexander Washington 1821-1895
ApCAB
Wayman, Dorothy C 1893-1975 *WhAm 6*
Wayman, Harry Clifford 1881- *WhAm 6*
Waymouth, George d1612? *DcAmB,*
WhAm H
Wayne, Anthony 1745-1796 *AmBi, ApCAB,*
BiDrAC, DcAmB, Drake, EncAAH,
EncAB, McGEWB, NatCAB 1, REnAW,
TwCBDA, WebAB, WebAMB, WhAm H,
WhAmP
Wayne, Anthony 1746-1796 *BiAUS*
Wayne, Arthur Trezevant 1863-1930 *DcAmB,*
WhAm 4
Wayne, Charles Stokes 1858- *WhAm 4*
Wayne, Henry Constantine 1815-1883 *ApCAB,*
TwCBDA
Wayne, Isaac d1852 *BiAUS*
Wayne, Isaac 1770-1852 *ApCAB*
Wayne, Isaac 1772-1852 *BiDrAC, WhAm H,*
WhAmP
Wayne, James Moore 1790-1867 *ApCAB,*
BiAUS, BiDrAC, DcAmB, Drake,
NatCAB 2, TwCBDA, WebAB,
WhAm H, WhAmP
Wayne, John 1907- *WebAB*
Wayne, Joseph, Jr. 1873-1942 *NatCAB 54,*
WhAm 2
Wayne, June 1918- *BnEnAmA*
Wayne, William 1828- *ApCAB, NatCAB 4*
Wayson, James Thomas 1870-1945 *NatCAB 36,*
WhAm 6
Wayson, Newton Edward 1883-1962
NatCAB 50
Wazzan Al-Zayyati Al-Gharnati, Al-H, Al-
DcScB
Wead, Charles Kasson 1848-1925 *ApCAB,*
WhAm 1
Wead, Eunice 1881- *WhAm 6*
Weadock, Bernard Francis 1884-1947 *WhAm 4*
Weadock, Edward E 1901-1966 *WhAm 4*
Weadock, John C 1860-1950 *WhAm 3*
Weadock, Paul 1886-1947 *NatCAB 50*
Weadock, Thomas Addis Emmet 1850-1938
BiDrAC, NatCAB 39, WhAm 1, WhAmP
Weagant, Roy Alexander 1881-1942 *ApCAB X,*
WhAm 2
Weagly, Mrs. Roy C F 1886-1957 *WhAm 3*
Weakley, Charles Enright 1906-1972 *WhAm 5*
Weakley, Robert 1764-1845 *ApCAB, BiAUS,*
BiDrAC, WhAm H
Weakley, Samuel Davies 1860-1921
NatCAB 19, WhAm 1
Wean, Frank Lincoln 1860- *ApCAB X*
Wear, D Walker 1879-1960 *WhAm 4*
Wear, Frank Lucian 1873- *WhAm 5*
Wear, Joseph W 1876-1941 *WhAm 1*
Wear, Samuel McConnell 1880- *WhAm 6*
Weare, Meshech 1713-1786 *AmBi, ApCAB,*
DcAmB, NatCAB 13, TwCBDA,
WhAm H
Weare, Mesheck 1713-1786 *Drake*
Weare, Portus Baxter 1842- *NatCAB 10*
Wearin, Otha Donner 1903- *BiDrAC*
Wearing, Thomas 1881-1961 *WhAm 4*
Wearn, Joseph Henry 1861-1936 *NatCAB 37*
Weart, Douglas Lafayette 1891-1975 *WhAm 6*
Weatherbe, Robert Linton 1836- *ApCAB Sup*
Weatherbee, Edwin Henry 1852-1912
NatCAB 16
Weatherby, Charles Alfred 1875-1949
NatCAB 38, WhAm 2
Weatherby, Delia L 1843- *AmWom*
Weatherby, J A *NewYHSD*
Weatherby, LeRoy Samuel 1880-1946 *WhAm 2*
Weathered, Roy Bishop 1911-1972 *WhAm 6*
Weatherford, Mark Vern 1886-1962
NatCAB 51
Weatherford, William 1765-1824 *NatCAB 18*

Weatherford, William 1780?-1824 *AmBi,*
DcAmB, WebAMB, WhAm H
Weatherford, Willis Duke 1875-1970 *WhAm 5*
Weatherford, Zadoc Lorenzo 1888- *BiDrAC*
Weatherhead, Albert J, Jr. 1892-1966 *WhAm 4*
Weatherly, James Meriwether 1856- *WhAm 4*
Weatherly, Josephine *WomWWA 14*
Weatherly, Ulysses Grant 1865-1940
NatCAB 30, WhAm 1
Weatherly, W H 1864- *WhAm 5*
Weatherred, Preston Alonzo 1884-1967
WhAm 5
Weathers, Brantley Alexander, Jr. 1890-1953
NatCAB 42
Weathers, Lee Beam 1886-1958 *NatCAB 48*
Weathersby, Eliza 1849-1887 *NatCAB 5*
Weathersford, William d1824 *Drake*
Weathersford, William 1770?-1824 *ApCAB*
Weatherspoon, W Herbert 1884-1972
NatCAB 57
Weatherwax, Hazelett Paul 1907-1967
WhAm 5
Weatherwax, James Lloyd 1884-1965
NatCAB 51
Weaver *NewYHSD*
Weaver, Aaron Ward 1832-1919 *ApCAB,*
DcAmB, NatCAB 13, TwCBDA,
WhAm 1
Weaver, Alexander Hamilton Stephens
1899-1959 *NatCAB 50*
Weaver, Andrew Thomas 1890-1965 *WhAm 4*
Weaver, Anna M Sewell 1866- *WomWWA 14*
Weaver, Archibald Jerard 1844-1887 *BiDrAC,*
WhAm H
Weaver, Arthur J 1873-1945 *WhAm 2*
Weaver, Arthur J 1873-1954 *NatCAB 40*
Weaver, Aubrey Gardner 1882-1944
NatCAB 40
Weaver, Bennett 1892-1970 *WhAm 5*
Weaver, Bessie May 1882- *WhoColR*
Weaver, Charles Blanchard 1903-1967
NatCAB 53, WhAm 4
Weaver, Charles Clinton 1875-1946 *NatCAB 38,*
WhAm 2
Weaver, Charles Parsons 1851- *WhAm 4*
Weaver, Clarence Eugene 1877-1938 *WhAm 1*
Weaver, Claude 1867-1954 *BiDrAC, WhAm 3*
Weaver, Dempsey 1815-1880 *NatCAB 8*
Weaver, Dempsey 1875-1938 *NatCAB 31*
Weaver, Dempsey, Jr. 1914-1969 *NatCAB 54*
Weaver, Edgar 1852-1914 *NatCAB 16*
Weaver, Edward Ebenezer 1864-1931 *WhAm 1*
Weaver, Emily Poynton 1865- *WomWWA 14*
Weaver, Erasmus Morgan 1854-1920 *WhAm 1*
Weaver, Fortune J 1874- *WhoColR*
Weaver, Francis Heyer 1844-1928 *NatCAB 21*
Weaver, Frank Harvey 1889- *WhoColR*
Weaver, Fred H 1915-1972 *WhAm 5*
Weaver, Gailard Evert 1883-1942 *NatCAB 31*
Weaver, George Calvin 1905-1960 *WhAm 3*
Weaver, George Howitt 1866-1947 *WhAm 2*
Weaver, George M *NewYHSD*
Weaver, George Sumner 1818- *ApCAB*
Weaver, Gilbert Grimes 1889-1968 *WhAm 5*
Weaver, Harry Leroy 1893-1971 *NatCAB 57*
Weaver, Harry Otis 1866-1933 *WhAm 1*
Weaver, Harry Sands 1868-1938 *WhAm 1*
Weaver, Henry Grady 1889-1949 *NatCAB 37,*
WhAm 5
Weaver, Ira Adalbert 1871-1965 *NatCAB 52*
Weaver, Isaac Hoover 1864-1920 *NatCAB 18*
Weaver, James Baird 1833-1912 *AmBi,*
ApCAB, BiDrAC, DcAmB, EncAAH,
EncAB, McGEWB, NatCAB 11,
NatCAB 16, REnAW, TwCBDA,
WebAB, WhAm 1, WhAmP
Weaver, James Bellamy 1861-1940 *NatCAB 46,*
WhAm 1
Weaver, James Dorman 1920- *BiDrAC*
Weaver, James Harvey 1903-1970 *WhAm 5*
Weaver, Jerrie Arjyra *WomWWA 14*
Weaver, John 1861-1928 *WhAm 1*
Weaver, John G 1812- *NatCAB 3*
Weaver, John Heisley 1860-1934 *NatCAB 25*
Weaver, John VanAlstyn 1893-1938 *AmBi,*
NatCAB 29, WhAm 1
Weaver, Jonathan 1824-1901 *ApCAB,*
NatCAB 11, WhAm 1

Weaver, Joseph B 1880- *WhAm 6*
Weaver, Junius Vaden 1927-1972 *WhAm 6*
Weaver, Lewis *NewYHSD*
Weaver, Lucile Anne Porter *WomWWA 14*
Weaver, Martha Collins 1865- *WhAm 4*
Weaver, Mima J 1877- *WomWWA 14*
Weaver, Myron McDonald 1901-1963 *WhAm 4*
Weaver, Paul John 1889-1946 *WhAm 2*
Weaver, Paul Leicester Ford 1902-1957
NatCAB 46
Weaver, Philip 1791-1861 *DcAmB, WhAm H*
Weaver, Philip Johnson 1913-1969 *WhAm 5*
Weaver, Philip Tennant 1922-1973 *WhAm 6*
Weaver, Phillip Hart 1919- *BiDrAC, WhAmP*
Weaver, Powell 1890-1951 *WhAm 3*
Weaver, R C d1968 *WhAm 5*
Weaver, R H 1903-1973 *WhAm 6*
Weaver, Richard L 1911-1964 *NatCAB 52*
Weaver, Robert Clifton 1907- *BiDrUSE,*
EncAB, WebAB
Weaver, Rudolph 1880-1944 *NatCAB 36,*
WhAm 2
Weaver, Rufus B 1841-1936 *NatCAB 3,*
WhAm 1
Weaver, Rufus Washington 1870-1947
NatCAB 35, WhAm 2
Weaver, Samuel Pool 1882-1963 *WhAm 4*
Weaver, Silas Matteson 1843-1923 *NatCAB 22*
Weaver, Silas Matteson 1845-1923 *WhAm 1*
Weaver, Spencer Fullerton 1879-1939
NatCAB 33
Weaver, Stephen Jacob 1844-1933 *NatCAB 25*
Weaver, T Walker 1885-1962 *NatCAB 49*
Weaver, W H *IIBEAAW*
Weaver, Walter Lowrie 1851-1909 *BiDrAC,*
WhAm 1
Weaver, Walter Reed 1885-1944 *NatCAB 39,*
WhAm 2
Weaver, William Augustus 1797-1846 *ApCAB*
Weaver, William Dixon 1857-1919 *DcAmB,*
WhAm 1
Weaver, William Trotter 1858-1916
NatCAB 36
Weaver, Zebulon 1872-1948 *BiDrAC,*
WhAm 2, WhAmP
Webb, Alexander Stewart 1834?-1911 *Drake*
Webb, Alexander Stewart 1835-1911 *AmBi,*
ApCAB, DcAmB, NatCAB 3,
NatCAB 34, TwCBDA, WebAMB,
WhAm 1
Webb, Alexander Stewart 1870-1948
NatCAB 34, WhAm 2
Webb, Atticus 1869- *WhAm 5*
Webb, Beatrice Potter 1858-1943 *McGEWB*
Webb, Bertha *AmWom*
Webb, Carl N 1900-1951 *WhAm 3*
Webb, Charles 1724-1782? *Drake*
Webb, Charles 1724-1794? *ApCAB*
Webb, Charles Aurelius 1866- *WhAm 2*
Webb, Charles Henry 1834-1905 *AmBi,*
ApCAB, DcAmB, Drake, NatCAB 10,
TwCBDA, WhAm 1
Webb, Charles James 1858-1930 *NatCAB 54*
Webb, Charles M *WhAm 5*
Webb, Charles Wallace 1878-1949 *NatCAB 38,*
WhAm 2
Webb, Clarence Otto 1888-1948 *NatCAB 36*
Webb, Sir Clifton 1889- *WhAm 4*
Webb, Clifton 1889-1966 *WhAm 4*
Webb, Daniel 1700?-1773 *DcAmB, WhAm H*
Webb, Daniel Clary 1881-1954 *WhAm 3*
Webb, Del E 1899-1974 *WhAm 6*
Webb, Earle Wayne 1883-1965 *NatCAB 52,*
WhAm 4
Webb, Ebenezer R *NewYHSD*
Webb, Edward Fleming 1875-1928 *WhAm 1*
Webb, Edward J *NewYHSD*
Webb, Edwin Douglas 1873- *WhAm 5*
Webb, Edwin Yates 1872-1955 *BiDrAC,*
NatCAB 46, WhAm 3, WhAmP
Webb, Ella Sturtevant 1856- *AmWom*
Webb, Ernest Clay 1887-1952 *WhAm 3*
Webb, Frank Carlos 1860-1926 *NatCAB 20*
Webb, Frank Elbridge 1869-1949 *WhAm 2*
Webb, Frank Rush 1851-1934, *WhAm 1*
Webb, George Creighton 1854- *NatCAB 12*
Webb, George H 1860-1921 *WhAm 1*
Webb, George Heber 1867-1926 *NatCAB 20*

Webb, George James 1803-1887 *ApCAB,*
DcAmB, Drake, WhAm H
Webb, George Thomas 1866- *WhAm 4*
Webb, Gerald Bertram 1871-1948 *NatCAB 36,*
WhAm 2
Webb, H T *NewYHSD*
Webb, Hanor A 1888-1965 *WhAm 4*
Webb, Harold George 1888-1946 *NatCAB 36*
Webb, Harry Howard 1853-1939 *DcAmB S2*
Webb, Henry Livingston 1795-1876 *ApCAB*
Webb, Henry Walter 1852-1900 *WhAm 1*
Webb, Herbert Keen 1891-1966 *NatCAB 54*
Webb, J Griswold 1890-1934 *NatCAB 25*
Webb, James *NewYHSD*
Webb, James 1792-1856 *ApCAB, BiAUS,*
Drake, NatCAB 25
Webb, James Avery 1868-1953 *NatCAB 39,*
WhAm 3
Webb, James Duncan 1908-1960 *WhAm 4*
Webb, James Henry 1854-1924 *WhAm 1*
Webb, James Morris 1874- *WhoColR*
Webb, James Ruffin 1909-1974 *WhAm 6*
Webb, James Watson 1802-1884 *AmBi,*
ApCAB, BiAUS, DcAmB, Drake,
NatCAB 3, TwCBDA, WhAm H
Webb, John Burkitt 1841-1912 *DcAmB,*
WhAm 4
Webb, John Maurice 1847-1916 *WhAm 1*
Webb, John Russell 1824-1887 *ApCAB*
Webb, John William Saunderson 1852-1928
NatCAB 21
Webb, Joseph d1787 *Drake*
Webb, Joseph James 1878-1958 *WhAm 3*
Webb, Kenneth Seymour 1885-1966 *WhAm 4*
Webb, Nathan 1825-1902 *WhAm 1*
Webb, Richard L 1902-1961 *WhAm 4*
Webb, Robert Alexander 1856-1919 *WhAm 1*
Webb, Robert Henning 1882-1952 *NatCAB 42,*
WhAm 3
Webb, Robert Thomas 1866-1940 *WhAm 1*
Webb, Robert Williams 1869-1948 *WhAm 2*
Webb, Rollin Edward 1875-1953 *NatCAB 45*
Webb, Samuel Blatchley 1753-1807 *AmBi,*
ApCAB, Drake, NatCAB 3, TwCBDA
Webb, Sidney James 1859-1947 *McGEWB*
Webb, St. Clair 1894-1955 *NatCAB 46*
Webb, Stuart Weston 1883-1968 *WhAm 5*
Webb, T Dwight 1867- *WhAm 5*
Webb, Thomas 1724?-1796 *AmBi, ApCAB,*
DcAmB, WhAm H
Webb, Thomas Smith 1771-1819 *ApCAB,*
DcAmB, Drake, WhAm H
Webb, Thomas T 1806?-1853 *ApCAB*
Webb, Thompson 1887-1975 *WhAm 6*
Webb, Ulys Robert 1874- *WhAm 3*
Webb, Ulysses Sigel 1864-1947 *NatCAB 37,*
WhAm 2
Webb, Vanderbilt 1891-1956 *NatCAB 42,*
WhAm 3
Webb, Vivian Howell 1894-1971 *WhAm 5*
Webb, Vonna Owings 1876-1964 *IIBEAAW*
Webb, Walter Loring 1863-1941 *WhAm 1*
Webb, Walter Prescott 1888-1963 *NatCAB 51,*
REnAW, WhAm 4
Webb, Walter Prescott 1889-1963 *EncAAH*
Webb, Walter Whayne 1906-1965 *NatCAB 51*
Webb, Willard Isaac, Jr. 1902-1972 *WhAm 5*
Webb, William Alexander 1867-1919 *WhAm 1*
Webb, William Alfred 1878-1936 *NatCAB 27,*
WhAm 2
Webb, William Benning 1825-1896 *ApCAB,*
NatCAB 2
Webb, William Edward 1844-1915 *NatCAB 16*
Webb, William Henry 1816-1899 *ApCAB,*
DcAmB, Drake, NatCAB 2, WhAm 1
Webb, William N *NewYHSD*
Webb, William Robert 1842-1926 *BiDAmEd,*
BiDrAC, DcAmB, NatCAB 37, WhAm 1,
WhAmP
Webb, William Seward 1851-1926 *ApCAB Sup,*
NatCAB 1, TwCBDA, WhAm 1
Webb, William Snyder 1882-1964 *WhAm 4*
Webb, William Walter 1857-1933 *NatCAB 16,*
WhAm 1
Webber, Mrs. *NewYHSD*
Webber, Amos Richard 1852-1948 *BiDrAC,*
WhAm 2

Webber, Charles Christopher 1859-1944
NatCAB 33
Webber, Charles T 1825-1911 *IlBEAAW,*
NewYHSD
Webber, Charles Wilkins 1819-1856 *ApCAB,*
DcAmB, Drake, NatCAB 4, WhAm H
Webber, Frederick Sanford 1863-1952
NatCAB 42
Webber, George Harris 1882-1934 *WhAm 1*
Webber, George Washington 1825-1900 *BiDrAC*
Webber, Henry William 1869-1935 *WhAm 1*
Webber, Herbert John 1865-1946 *DcAmB S4,*
NatCAB 17, WhAm 2
Webber, James Benson, Jr. 1911-1956 *WhAm 3*
Webber, John 1750?-1793 *IlBEAAW,*
NewYHSD
Webber, Lane Davis 1885-1953 *NatCAB 41*
Webber, LeRoy 1891-1935 *WhAm 1*
Webber, Oscar 1889-1967 *WhAm 4*
Webber, Richard Hudson 1879-1967
NatCAB 53, WhAm 4
Webber, Samuel 1759-1810 *ApCAB,*
NatCAB 6, TwCBDA, WhAm H
Webber, Samuel 1760-1810 *Drake*
Webber, Samuel 1797-1880 *ApCAB*
Webber, Samuel Gilbert 1838- *WhAm 4*
Webbink, Paul 1903-1973 *WhAm 5*
Webel, Janet Darling 1913-1966 *NatCAB 54*
Weber, Adna Ferrin 1870- *WhAm 5*
Weber, Albert 1828-1879 *DcAmB, WhAm H*
Weber, Albert J 1859- *WhAm 4*
Weber, Alfred 1868-1958 *WhAm 3*
Weber, Andrew Raymond 1895-1971
NatCAB 56
Weber, Arthur William 1910-1968 *WhAm 5*
Weber, Carl Jefferson 1894-1966 *WhAm 4*
Weber, Carl Maria Friedrich Ernst Von
1786-1826 *McGEWB*
Weber, Caroline *NewYHSD*
Weber, Charles Marie 1814-1881 *NatCAB 7*
Weber, Don Andrew 1895-1966 *NatCAB 54*
Weber, Edouard 1901-1970 *WhAm 5*
Weber, Edward *NewYHSD*
Weber, Ernst Heinrich 1795-1878 *AsBiEn,*
BiHiMed, DcScB
Weber, Frank Joseph 1849-1943 *NatCAB 36*
Weber, Frederick Clarence 1878- *WhAm 6*
Weber, Frederick Theodore 1883-1956 *WhAm 3*
Weber, Gustav Carl Erich 1828-1912 *ApCAB,*
DcAmB, WhAm H
Weber, Gustave Frederick 1910-1971 *WhAm 6*
Weber, Gustavus Adolphus 1863-1942
NatCAB 16, WhAm 2
Weber, Hanns Paul 1890-1946 *NatCAB 35*
Weber, Harry Mathew 1899-1958 *NatCAB 45,*
WhAm 3
Weber, Heinrich 1842-1913 *DcScB*
Weber, Henri Carleton 1860-1930 *WhAm 1*
Weber, Henry Adam 1845-1912 *DcAmB,*
NatCAB 19, WhAm 4
Weber, Henry Charles 1887-1958 *NatCAB 49*
Weber, Herman Carl 1873-1939 *NatCAB 38,*
WhAm 1
Weber, Herman Gustav 1878-1943 *NatCAB 33*
Weber, Jessie Palmer 1863-1926 *ApCAB X,*
WhAm 1
Weber, Joe Nicholas 1866- *WhAm 5*
Weber, John 1885-1966 *WhAm 4*
Weber, John Baptiste 1842-1926 *BiDrAC,*
NatCAB 24, WhAm 1
Weber, John H 1799-1859 *REnAW*
Weber, John Langdon 1862-1923 *WhAm 1*
Weber, John S *NewYHSD*
Weber, John William 1857-1933 *NatCAB 25*
Weber, Joseph Morris 1867-1942 *DcAmB S3,*
WhAm 2
Weber, Kem 1889-1963 *BnEnAmA*
Weber, Lila Long 1880- *WomWWA 14*
Weber, Lois 1881-1939 *NotAW, WhAm 1*
Weber, Max 1824-1901 *ApCAB, NatCAB 12,*
TwCBDA, WhAm 1
Weber, Max 1864-1920 *McGEWB*
Weber, Max 1881-1961 *BnEnAmA, McGEWB,*
WebAB, WhAm 4
Weber, Max Wilhelm Carl 1852-1937 *DcScB*
Weber, Oliver Arkenbrugh 1880-1951
NatCAB 42

Weber, Orlando Franklin 1879-1945
NatCAB 36
Weber, Paul 1823?-1916 *ApCAB, NewYHSD*
Weber, Paul 1884-1954 *WhAm 3*
Weber, Pearl Louise Hunter 1878-
WomWWA 14
Weber, Randolph Henry 1909-1961 *NatCAB 55,*
WhAm 4
Weber, Samuel Adam 1838- *NatCAB 10*
Weber, Samuel Edwin 1875- *WhAm 5*
Weber, Wilhelm Eduard 1804-1891 *AsBiEn,*
DcScB
Weber, William A 1880- *WhAm 6*
Weber, William Lander 1866-1910 *WhAm 1*
Webern, Anton 1883-1945 *McGEWB,*
WhAm 4
Webner, Frank Erastus 1865- *WhAm 4*
Webre, Edward Charles 1872-1917 *NatCAB 17*
Webster, Albert Falvey 1848-1876 *ApCAB*
Webster, Albert Lowry 1859-1930 *NatCAB 35*
Webster, Alice Jane Chandler 1876-1916
DcAmB
Webster, Anna Jenkins 1867- *WomWWA 14*
Webster, Arthur Gordon 1863-1923 *DcAmB,*
NatCAB 13, WhAm 1
Webster, Benjamin Francis 1909-1973 *WhAm 6*
Webster, Bradford 1881- *NatCAB 17*
Webster, Bruce Peck 1901-1976 *WhAm 6*
Webster, Clyde Irvin 1877- *WhAm 5*
Webster, Cornelius Crosby 1886-1947 *WhAm 2*
Webster, Daniel 1782-1852 *AmBi, ApCAB,*
BiAUS, BiDrAC, BiDrUSE, DcAmB,
Drake, EncAAH, EncAB, McGEWB,
NatCAB 3, TwCBDA, WebAB,
WhAm H, WhAmP
Webster, Daniel C *NewYHSD*
Webster, Daniel Thomas 1877-1939
NatCAB 29
Webster, David 1842-1923 *WhAm 1*
Webster, David Henry 1885-1967 *NatCAB 55*
Webster, Dean Kingman 1870-1951 *NatCAB 38*
Webster, Ebenezer 1739-1806 *ApCAB,*
NatCAB 10
Webster, Edward d1847 *Drake*
Webster, Edward Harlan 1876-1937 *WhAm 1*
Webster, Edward Jerome 1881- *WhAm 6*
Webster, Edwin Hanson 1829-1893 *BiAUS,*
BiDrAC, WhAm H, WhAmP
Webster, Edwin Harrison 1871- *WhAm 5*
Webster, Edwin Sibley 1867-1950 *DcAmB S3,*
NatCAB 38, WhAm 3
Webster, Edwin Sibley, Jr. 1899-1957
NatCAB 47, WhAm 3
Webster, Elizabeth Rogers Fox *WomWWA 14*
Webster, Ephraim 1752-1825 *NatCAB 4*
Webster, Eugene Carroll 1864-1939
NatCAB 30, WhAm 1
Webster, Euphania M C 1859- *WomWWA 14*
Webster, Ezekiel 1780-1829 *ApCAB*
Webster, Fletcher 1813-1862 *ApCAB, Drake,*
NatCAB 13
Webster, Francis Marion 1849-1916
NatCAB 13, WhAm 1
Webster, Frank Daniel 1866-1932 *WhAm 1*
Webster, Frank G 1841-1930 *WhAm 1*
Webster, Frederic Smith 1849- *WhAm 4*
Webster, Frederick William 1884-1948
NatCAB 37
Webster, George Sidney 1853-1937 *WhAm 1*
Webster, George Smedley 1855-1931
NatCAB 25, WhAm 1
Webster, George VanO'Linda 1880- *WhAm 1*
Webster, George Washington 1857-1931
WhAm 1
Webster, Harold Edward 1885-1966
NatCAB 53, WhAm 4
Webster, Harold Tucker 1885-1952 *DcAmB S5,*
WhAm 3
Webster, Harrie 1843-1921 *WhAm 1*
Webster, Harrison Edwin 1841- *NatCAB 7*
Webster, Harrison Edwin 1842- *ApCAB*
Webster, Helen Livermore 1853-1928 *AmWom,*
WhAm 1, WomWWA 14
Webster, Henry Kingman 1835-1920
NatCAB 29
Webster, Henry Kitchell 1875-1932 *AmBi,*
WhAm 1
Webster, Homer Harris 1870-1955 *NatCAB 44*

Webster, Horace 1794-1871 *ApCAB,*
BiDAmEd, NatCAB 19, TwCBDA
Webster, Horace 1795-1871 *Drake*
Webster, Howard Jeffries 1875-1942
NatCAB 32
Webster, Hutton 1875-1955 *WhAm 3*
Webster, Hutton, Jr. 1910-1956 *WhAm 3*
Webster, Ira *NewYHSD*
Webster, James 1743?-1781 *ApCAB, Drake*
Webster, James Randolph 1906-1958
NatCAB 44, WhAm 3
Webster, Jean 1876-1916 *DcAmB, NotAW,*
WhAm 1, WomWWA 14
Webster, Jennie Josephine *WomWWA 14*
Webster, Jerome Pierce 1888-1974 *WhAm 6*
Webster, John d1661 *Drake, NatCAB 10*
Webster, John 1580?-1634? *McGEWB*
Webster, John 1610-1682 *DcScB*
Webster, John Adams 1785-1876 *ApCAB*
Webster, John Adams 1823-1875 *ApCAB*
Webster, John Clarence 1863-1950 *NatCAB 17,*
WhAm 2
Webster, John Hunter 1862-1933 *WhAm 1*
Webster, John Lee 1847- *NatCAB 12,*
WhAm 1
Webster, John Stanley 1877-1962 *BiDrAC,*
WhAm 4, WhAmP
Webster, John Taylor 1872-1946 *NatCAB 37*
Webster, John White 1793-1850 *ApCAB,*
DcAmB, Drake, TwCBDA, WhAm H
Webster, Joseph Dana 1811-1876 *ApCAB,*
DcAmB, Drake, TwCBDA, WhAm H
Webster, Joseph Philbrick 1819-1875
NatCAB 19
Webster, Joseph Philbrick 1820-1875 *ApCAB*
Webster, Leslie Tillotson 1894-1943
NatCAB 32, WhAm 2
Webster, Lorin 1857-1923 *NatCAB 26,*
WhAm 1
Webster, Margaret 1905-1972 *WhAm 5*
Webster, Marjorie Fraser 1896-1963 *WhAm 4*
Webster, Martha Farnham 1846-
WomWWA 14
Webster, Merton Wells 1884-1956 *NatCAB 45*
Webster, Montgomery 1876-1963 *NatCAB 50*
Webster, Nathan Burnham 1821-1900 *ApCAB,*
TwCBDA, WhAm 1
Webster, Noah 1758-1843 *AmBi, ApCAB,*
BiDAmEd, DcAmB, Drake, EncAB,
McGEWB, NatCAB 2, TwCBDA,
WebAB, WhAm H
Webster, Paul Kimball 1905-1957 *WhAm 3*
Webster, Paul Reichard 1897-1949 *NatCAB 38*
Webster, Pelatiah 1725-1795 *AmBi, ApCAB,*
Drake, NatCAB 7, TwCBDA
Webster, Pelatiah 1726-1795 *DcAmB,*
WhAm H
Webster, Ralph Waldo 1873-1930 *WhAm 1*
Webster, Reginald H 1857- *WhAm 4*
Webster, Richard 1811-1856 *ApCAB, Drake*
Webster, Richard Montgomery 1869-1953
NatCAB 41
Webster, Robert Morris 1892-1972 *WhAm 5*
Webster, Sidney 1828-1910 *ApCAB X,*
WhAm 1
Webster, Taylor 1800-1876 *BiAUS, BiDrAC,*
WhAm H, WhAmP
Webster, Thomas 1773-1844 *DcScB*
Webster, Walter *NewYHSD*
Webster, Warren 1835- *ApCAB*
Webster, Warren 1863-1938 *NatCAB 35,*
WhAm 1
Webster, William 1900-1972 *WhAm 5*
Webster, William Clarence 1866- *WhAm 5*
Webster, William Franklin 1862- *WhAm 4*
Webster, William Grant 1866- *WhAm 4*
Webster, William Reuben 1868-1945
NatCAB 34, WhAm 2
Webster-Powell, Alma 1874-1930 *DcAmB,*
NatCAB 14
Wechsler, Israel Spanier 1886-1962 *NatCAB 47,*
WhAm 4
Weckler, Herman Ludwig 1888-1970
NatCAB 55, WhAm 5
Weckstein, Isidore 1896-1956 *NatCAB 45*
Wecter, Dixon 1906-1950 *WhAm 3*
Wedd, Alfred Matthew 1887-1967 *NatCAB 53*

Weddell, Alexander Wilbourne 1876-1948
  DcAmB S4, NatCAB 35, WhAm 2
Weddell, Donald J 1903-1956 *WhAm 3*
Wedderburn, Alexander *NewYHSD*
Wedderburn, Alexander 1733-1805 *ApCAB*
Wedderburn, Joseph Henry Maclagan 1882-1948
  DcScB, WhAm 2
Wedderburne, Alexander 1733-1805 *Drake*
Wedderspoon, William Rhind d1939 *WhAm 1*
Weddington, Frank Ruel 1901-1959 *NatCAB 47,*
  WhAm 4
Wedekind, Frank 1864-1918 *McGEWB*
Wedel, Georg Wolfgang 1645-1721 *DcScB*
Wedel, Paul John 1896-1971 *WhAm 5*
Wedel, Theodore Otto 1892-1970 *NatCAB 56,*
  WhAm 5
Wedemeyer, Albert Coady 1897- *WebAMB,*
  WhWW-II
Wedemeyer, William Walter 1873-1913 *BiDrAC,*
  WhAm 1
Wedgwood, Edgar A 1856-1920 *NatCAB 19*
Wedgwood, Josiah 1730-1795 *DcScB,*
  McGEWB
Wedgwood, Kennard Laurence 1873-1950
  NatCAB 38
Wee, Mons O 1871-1942 *WhAm 2*
Weed, Alonzo Rogers 1867-1936 *NatCAB 29*
Weed, Alonzo Rogers 1867-1937 *WhAm 1*
Weed, Charles Frederick 1874-1940 *WhAm 1*
Weed, Chester Alberti 1917-1972 *NatCAB 57*
Weed, Clarence Moores 1864-1947 *NatCAB 41,*
  WhAm 2
Weed, Clive 1884-1936 *NatCAB 27, WhAm 1*
Weed, Clyde E 1890-1973 *WhAm 6*
Weed, Edwin A 1828?- *NewYHSD*
Weed, Edwin Gardner 1837-1924 *ApCAB,*
  WhAm 1
Weed, Edwin Gardner 1847-1924 *NatCAB 9,*
  TwCBDA
Weed, Ella 1853-1894 *BiDAmEd, NotAW*
Weed, Frank Jones 1845-1891 *NatCAB 3*
Weed, Frank Watkins 1881-1945 *WhAm 2*
Weed, George Ludington 1828-1904 *WhAm 1*
Weed, Helena Charlotte Hill 1875-
  WomWWA 14
Weed, Hugh Hourston Craigie 1883-1957
  WhAm 3
Weed, Ida Belle Rosbrook 1885- *WomWWA 14*
Weed, J Spencer 1879-1969 *WhAm 5*
Weed, Jefferson 1907-1963 *WhAm 4*
Weed, LeRoy Jefferson 1878-1961 *WhAm 4*
Weed, Lewis Hill 1886-1952 *DcAmB S5,*
  WhAm 3
Weed, Nellie S Jones *WomWWA 14*
Weed, Ruth Sarissa 1885- *WomWWA 14*
Weed, Samuel Henry 1843-1927 *NatCAB 22*
Weed, Samuel Richards 1837- *WhAm 1*
Weed, Smith Mead 1833-1920 *NatCAB 2,*
  WhAm 1
Weed, Stephen Hinsdale 1834-1863 *ApCAB,*
  Drake, TwCBDA
Weed, Theodore Linus 1876- *WhAm 5*
Weed, Thurlow 1797- *Drake*
Weed, Thurlow 1797-1882 *AmBi, ApCAB,*
  DcAmB, EncAB, McGEWB, TwCBDA,
  WebAB, WhAm H
Weed, Thurlow 1797-1884 *NatCAB 3*
Weed, Walter Harvey 1862-1944 *ApCAB X,*
  NatCAB 13, WhAm 2
Weeden, Anne Tillinghast 1863- *WomWWA 14*
Weeden, Charles Foster 1856-1928 *NatCAB 21*
Weeden, William Babcock 1834-1912 *AmBi,*
  DcAmB, NatCAB 17, WhAm 1
Weeding, Nathaniel *NewYHSD*
Weedn, Alton James 1907-1956 *NatCAB 46*
Weedon, George 1730?-1790? *ApCAB, Drake,*
  NatCAB 12
Weedon, Leslie Washington 1860-1937
  NatCAB 28
Weedon, Leslie Washington 1860-1938
  WhAm 1
Weekes, H Hobart 1867-1950 *NatCAB 39*
Weekes, Stephen *NewYHSD*
Weekley, William Marion 1851-1926 *WhAm 1*
Weeks, Alanson 1877-1947 *WhAm 2*
Weeks, Andrew Jackson 1869-1939 *WhAm 1*
Weeks, Arland Deyett 1871-1936 *WhAm 1*
Weeks, Arthur John 1847-1921 *NatCAB 19*

Weeks, Bartow Sumter 1861-1922 *NatCAB 2,*
  WhAm 1
Weeks, Benjamin D 1881-1950 *WhAm 3*
Weeks, Carl 1876-1962 *WhAm 4*
Weeks, Charles Peter 1870-1928 *NatCAB 21,*
  WhAm 1, WhAm 1C
Weeks, Charles Rapelyea 1876-1948
  NatCAB 37
Weeks, David Fairchild 1874-1929 *WhAm 1*
Weeks, Edgar 1839-1904 *BiDrAC, WhAm 1,*
  WhAmP
Weeks, Edward Henry 1871-1962 *NatCAB 53*
Weeks, Edward Mitchell 1866-1959
  NatCAB 46
Weeks, Edwin Lord 1849-1903 *AmBi, ApCAB,*
  DcAmB, IIBEAAW, NatCAB 12,
  TwCBDA, WhAm 1
Weeks, Edwin Ruthven 1855-1938 *WhAm 1*
Weeks, Francis Darling 1896-1962 *WhAm 4*
Weeks, Frank Bentley 1854-1935 *WhAm 1*
Weeks, George H 1834-1905 *WhAm 1*
Weeks, George Keith 1877-1953 *NatCAB 45*
Weeks, Grenville Mellen 1837-1919 *WhAm 1*
Weeks, H Hobart 1867-1950 *WhAm 3*
Weeks, Harry Curtis 1890-1973 *WhAm 6*
Weeks, Harvey 1888-1958 *NatCAB 43*
Weeks, Helen C *NotAW*
Weeks, Henry Astor 1822-1891 *NatCAB 2*
Weeks, Herma Letts 1888- *WomWWA 14*
Weeks, Ila Delbert 1901- *BiDAmEd*
Weeks, Imogene 1871- *WomWWA 14*
Weeks, John A 1899-1968 *WhAm 5*
Weeks, John Eliakim 1853-1949 *BiDrAC,*
  NatCAB 38, WhAm 2, WhAmP
Weeks, John Elmer 1853-1949 *DcAmB S4,*
  NatCAB 38, WhAm 2
Weeks, John L 1882-1951 *WhAm 3*
Weeks, John M 1788-1858 *ApCAB, Drake*
Weeks, John Wingate 1781-1853 *BiAUS,*
  BiDrAC, WhAm H, WhAmP
Weeks, John Wingate 1860-1926 *AmBi,*
  ApCAB X, BiDrAC, BiDrUSE, DcAmB,
  NatCAB 15, NatCAB 20, WhAm 1,
  WhAmP
Weeks, Joseph 1773-1845 *BiAUS, BiDrAC,*
  WhAm H, WhAmP
Weeks, Joseph Dame 1840-1896 *DcAmB,*
  NatCAB 13, WhAm H
Weeks, Lawrence Babbitt 1888-1959
  NatCAB 53
Weeks, Mary Harmon 1851-1940 *WhAm 1,*
  WomWWA 14
Weeks, Ralph Emerson 1878-1950 *NatCAB 39,*
  WhAm 3
Weeks, Raymond 1863-1954 *NatCAB 18,*
  WhAm 3
Weeks, Robert Kelley 1840-1876 *ApCAB,*
  NatCAB 8, WhAm H
Weeks, Rufus Wells 1846-1930 *NatCAB 14,*
  WhAm 1
Weeks, Ruth Mary 1886- *WomWWA 14*
Weeks, Sinclair 1893-1972 *BiDrAC, BiDrUSE,*
  WhAm 5, WhAmP
Weeks, Stephen *NewYHSD*
Weeks, Stephen Beauregard 1865-1918 *DcAmB,*
  NatCAB 10, TwCBDA, WhAm 1
Weeks, Stephen Holmes 1835-1909 *WhAm 1*
Weeks, Thomas Edwin 1853-1938 *BiDAmEd,*
  NatCAB 6
Weeks, Walter Scott 1882-1946 *NatCAB 37,*
  WhAm 2
Weeks, Webb William 1886-1940 *NatCAB 32*
Weeks, William 1813-1900 *NewYHSD*
Weeks, William Raymond 1783-1848 *ApCAB*
Weeks, William Raymond 1848- *NatCAB 10,*
  WhAm 4
Weems, Capell Lain 1860-1913 *WhAm 4*
Weems, Capell Lane 1860-1913 *BiDrAC*
Weems, Daisy Williams 1869- *WomWWA 14*
Weems, Elizabeth W *WomWWA 14*
Weems, John Crompton 1778-1862 *BiAUS,*
  BiDrAC, WhAm H
Weems, Julius Buel 1865-1930 *WhAm 1*
Weems, Mason Locke d1825 *Drake*
Weems, Mason Locke 1759-1825 *DcAmB,*
  McGEWB, WebAB, WhAm H
Weems, Mason Locke 1760?-1825 *AmBi,*
  ApCAB, NatCAB 5, TwCBDA

Weems, Wharton Ewell 1889-1961 *WhAm 4*
Weer, John Henry 1873-1942 *WhAm 2*
Weer, Paul Wiley 1886-1956 *NatCAB 45*
Weese, A O 1885- *WhAm 3*
Weese, Harry 1915- *BnEnAmA*
Weesner, Edwin Lenox 1867-1936 *NatCAB 32*
Weet, Herbert Seeley 1871- *WhAm 5*
Weeter, Harry Montgomery 1887-1951
  NatCAB 41
Wefald, Knud 1869-1936 *BiDrAC, WhAm 1,*
  WhAmP
Wefel, Walther John 1889-1946 *NatCAB 36*
Wege, Peter Martin 1870-1947 *NatCAB 34*
Wegeforth, Harry Milton 1882-1941
  NatCAB 42
Wegelin, Oscar 1876-1970 *NatCAB 55*
Wegemann, Carroll Harvey 1879- *WhAm 6*
Wegener, Alfred Lothar 1880-1930 *AsBiEn,*
  DcScB, McGEWB
Wegener, James Hugo 1899-1960 *NatCAB 50*
Wegener, Theodore H 1892-1958 *WhAm 3*
Weger, George Stephen 1874-1935 *WhAm 1*
Wegg, David Spencer 1847-1919 *NatCAB 18,*
  WhAm 1
Weggeland, Danquart Anthon 1827-1918
  IIBEAAW
Weglein, David Emrich 1875-1950 *NatCAB 39*
Weglein, David Emrich 1876-1950 *WhAm 5*
Wegmann, Edward 1850-1935 *DcAmB S1,*
  NatCAB 10, NatCAB 25, WhAm 1
Wegmann, Sarah J Boland 1905-
  WomWWA 14
Wehe, Frank Rumrill 1855- *WhAm 4*
Wehle, Louis Brandeis 1880-1959 *NatCAB 49,*
  WhAm 3
Wehler, Charles Emanuel 1864- *WhAm 3*
Wehling, Louis Albert 1910-1974 *WhAm 6*
Wehmeyer, Lewis Edgar 1897-1971 *NatCAB 57,*
  WhAm 5
Wehmiller, Fred 1873-1927 *NatCAB 24*
Wehnelt, Arthur Rudolph Berthold 1871-1944
  DcScB
Wehnere, Edward *NewYHSD*
Wehrhan, Nelson W 1878- *WhAm 6*
Wehrle, Henry Bernard 1898-1967 *NatCAB 54*
Wehrle, Lawrence Paul 1887-1950 *NatCAB 39*
Wehrle, Vincent 1855-1941 *NatCAB 15,*
  WhAm 2
Wehrle, William Otto Joseph 1896-1959
  WhAm 3
Wehrmann, Henry 1871- *WhAm 5*
Wehrwein, George Simon 1883-1945 *WhAm 2*
Wei, Hsiao-Wen-Ti 467-499 *McGEWB*
Wei, Yuan 1794-1856 *McGEWB*
Weibel, E Edwin 1896-1961 *NatCAB 50*
Weible, Ralph Emerson 1878-1942 *NatCAB 38*
Weible, Rillmond Fernando 1912-1970
  WhAm 5
Weiby, Maxwell Oliver 1904-1967 *WhAm 4A*
Weichel, Alvin Ferdinand 1891-1956 *BiDrAC,*
  NatCAB 43, WhAm 4, WhAmP
Weicher, John 1904-1969 *WhAm 5*
Weichs, Maximilian Freiherr Von 1881-1954
  WhoMilH
Weichsel, Christian C 1870- *WhAm 5*
Weichselbaum, Anton 1845-1920 *DcScB*
Weicker, Lowell Palmer, Jr. 1931- *BiDrAC*
Weicker, Robert Valentine 1864-1949
  NatCAB 38
Weicker, Theodore 1861-1940 *NatCAB 29,*
  WhAm 1
Weicker, Theodore 1902-1968 *NatCAB 55,*
  WhAm 5
Weicksel, Amelia 1861- *WomWWA 14*
Weideman, Carl May 1898- *BiDrAC*
Weidemeyer, John William 1819- *ApCAB,*
  NatCAB 12
Weidenbach, Augustus *NewYHSD*
Weidenmann, Jacob 1829-1893 *DcAmB,*
  WhAm H
Weidenreich, Franz 1873-1948 *DcAmB S4,*
  McGEWB
Weidensall, Clara Jean *WomWWA 14*
Weidig, Adolf 1867-1931 *DcAmB, WhAm 1*
Weidlein, Ivan Ford 1898-1955 *NatCAB 43*
Weidler, Albert Greer 1882-1957 *WhAm 3*
Weidler, Deleth Eber 1885-1963 *WhAm 4*

Weidler, George Washington 1837-1908
NatCAB 16
Weidler, Victor Otterbein 1887-1950 *WhAm 3*
Weidman, Adda Josephine 1876-
WomWWA 14
Weidman, Charles 1901-1975 *WhAm 6*
Weidman, Frederick Deforest 1881-1956
WhAm 3
Weidman, Samuel 1870-1945 *NatCAB 13,*
WhAm 2
Weidman, W Murray 1835-1902 *NatCAB 27*
Weidmann, Jacob 1845- *NatCAB 4*
Weidner, Carl A 1865-1906 *WhAm 1*
Weidner, Revere Franklin 1851-1915 *ApCAB,*
DcAmB, NatCAB 21, WhAm 1
Weierstrass, Karl Theodor Wilhelm 1815-1897
DcScB
Weigel, Albert Charles 1887-1964 *WhAm 4*
Weigel, Christian Ehrenfried 1748-1831 *DcScB*
Weigel, Eugene John 1894-1973 *WhAm 6*
Weigel, George Kibler 1915-1972 *WhAm 5*
Weigel, Gustave 1906-1964 *DcAmReB*
Weigel, Valentin 1533-1588 *DcScB*
Weigel, William 1863-1936 *NatCAB 26,*
WhAm 1
Weigert, Carl 1845-1904 *BiHiMed, DcScB*
Weightman, Richard Coxe 1844-1914
NatCAB 16
Weightman, Richard Coxe 1845-1914 *WhAm 1*
Weightman, Richard Hanson d1861 *BiAUS,*
Drake
Weightman, Richard Hanson 1816-1861
BiDrAC, WhAm H, WhAmP
Weightman, Richard Hanson 1818-1861 *ApCAB*
Weightman, Roger C 1786-1876 *ApCAB,*
BiAUS
Weightman, William 1813-1904 *DcAmB,*
NatCAB 14
Weigl, Karl 1881-1949 *NatCAB 42*
Weigle, Luther Allan 1880-1976 *BiDAmEd*
Weigle, Luther Allen 1880-1976 *WhAm 6*
Weigold, George 1871-1951 *NatCAB 41*
Weihl, Archibald Peter 1904-1962 *NatCAB 47*
Weik, Jesse William 1857-1930 *ApCAB Sup,*
WhAm 3
Weikel, Anna Hamlin *WhAm 5*
Weikel, Charles Henry Harrison 1894-1968
WhAm 5
Weil, A Leo 1858-1938 *ApCAB X, WhAm 1*
Weil, Adele Kahn 1873- *WomWWA 14*
Weil, Adolph Leopold 1876-1952 *NatCAB 53,*
WhAm 3
Weil, Alexander 1818?- *NewYHSD*
Weil, Ann Yezner 1908-1969 *WhAm 5*
Weil, Aron 1862-1915 *NatCAB 17*
Weil, Benjamin M 1850- *NatCAB 2*
Weil, Carl 1882-1934 *WhAm 1*
Weil, Charles Lewis 1866-1921 *NatCAB 19*
Weil, David *NewYHSD*
Weil, Frank L 1894-1957 *WhAm 3*
Weil, Fred Alban 1874-1933 *WhAm 1*
Weil, Irving 1878-1933 *WhAm 1*
Weil, John *NewYHSD*
Weil, Lee Herman 1875- *WhAm 5*
Weil, Louis A 1878-1959 *WhAm 3*
Weil, Mamie Greil 1875- *WomWWA 14*
Weil, Mathilde 1871- *WomWWA 14*
Weil, Oscar 1840- *NewYHSD*
Weil, Richard 1876-1917 *ApCAB X, DcAmB*
Weil, Richard, Jr. 1907-1958 *NatCAB 44,*
WhAm 3
Weil, Robert T, Jr. d1974 *WhAm 6*
Weil, Sarah 1858- *WomWWA 14*
Weiland, Christian Frederick VanLeeuwen
1887-1953 *WhAm 3*
Weilepp, Carl Nogle 1886-1955 *NatCAB 47*
Weiler, Fred Wilson 1902-1951 *NatCAB 42*
Weiler, Royal William 1880-1948 *WhAm 2*
Weill, Kurt 1900-1950 *DcAmB S4, McGEWB,*
WebAB
Weill, Milton 1891-1975 *WhAm 6*
Weiman, Rita d1954 *WhAm 3*
Weimar, George Martin 1882-1948 *NatCAB 36*
Weimer, Albert Barnes 1857-1938 *WhAm 1*
Weimer, Bernal Robinson 1894-1970 *WhAm 5*
Weimer, Claud F 1902-1955 *WhAm 3*
Weimer, David Palmer 1873-1949 *NatCAB 39*
Weimer, Dean Herbert 1892-1947 *NatCAB 35*

Wein, Wilhelm 1864-1928 *AsBiEn*
Weinand, John Nicholas 1864-1928 *NatCAB 22*
Weinberg, Benjamin Franklin 1892-1970
WhAm 5
Weinberg, Bernard 1909-1973 *WhAm 5*
Weinberg, Robert Charles 1901-1974 *WhAm 6*
Weinberg, Sidney James 1891-1969 *WhAm 5*
Weinberg, Tobias 1910-1969 *WhAm 5*
Weinberg, Wilhelm 1862-1937 *DcScB*
Weinberger, Jacob 1882-1974 *WhAm 6*
Weindrug, Albert Leo 1873-1923 *NatCAB 6*
Weinedel, Carl 1795-1845 *NewYHSD*
Weiner, Joseph Lee 1902-1976 *WhAm 6*
Weinerman, Edwin Richard 1917-1970
NatCAB 55, WhAm 5
Weinert, Albert 1863-1947 *NatCAB 10,*
WhAm 2
Weingaertner, Adam *NewYHSD*
Weingarten, David 1855-1919 *NatCAB 18*
Weingarten, Edward Adolph 1898-1963
NatCAB 50
Weingarten, Joe 1884-1967 *NatCAB 55,*
WhAm 4
Weingarten, Julius 1836-1910 *DcScB*
Weingarten, Lawrence A d1975 *WhAm 6*
Weinhandl, Ferdinand 1896- *WhAm 6*
Weinhardt, Emma Kantmann *WomWWA 14*
Weinig, Arthur John 1883-1966 *WhAm 4*
Weinman, Adolph Alexander 1870-1952
IIBEAAW, WhAm 3
Weinman, William John 1872-1966 *NatCAB 56*
Weinmann, Joseph Peter 1896-1960 *WhAm 4*
Weinmann, R *NewYHSD*
Weinreich, Uriel 1926-1967 *WhAm 4*
Weinstein, Alexander 1891-1947 *WhAm 2*
Weinstein, Isidor 1872-1943 *NatCAB 32*
Weinstein, Jacob Joseph 1902-1974 *WhAm 6*
Weinstein, Joe 1894-1963 *WhAm 4*
Weinstein, Nathan Wallenstein *WebAB*
Weinstock, Harris 1854-1922 *NatCAB 19,*
WhAm 1
Weinstock, Herbert 1905-1971 *WhAm 5*
Weintal, Edward 1901-1973 *WhAm 5*
Weintraub, Abraham Allen 1917-1974 *WhAm 6*
Weinzirl, Adolph 1900-1967 *WhAm 4*
Weir, Charles E 1823?-1845 *NewYHSD*
Weir, Ernest Tener 1875-1957 *WhAm 3*
Weir, Florence Roney 1861-1932 *WhAm 1,*
WomWWA 14
Weir, Henry Cary 1839-1927 *NatCAB 34*
Weir, Hugh C 1884-1934 *WhAm 1*
Weir, Irene 1862-1944 *BiCAW, BiDAmEd,*
NotAW, WhAm 2
Weir, James 1821- *Drake*
Weir, James, Jr. 1856-1906 *WhAm 1*
Weir, John Ferguson 1841-1926 *AmBi, ApCAB,*
BnEnAmA, DcAmB, NatCAB 6,
TwCBDA, WhAm 1
Weir, John M 1891-1948 *WhAm 2*
Weir, Julian Alden 1852-1919 *AmBi, ApCAB,*
BnEnAmA, DcAmB, NatCAB 11,
NatCAB 22, TwCBDA, WhAm 1
Weir, Levi Candee d1910 *WhAm 1*
Weir, Minnie Lorena *WomWWA 14*
Weir, Paul 1894-1972 *WhAm 5*
Weir, Robert Fulton 1838-1927 *DcAmB,*
NatCAB 12, WhAm 1
Weir, Robert Walter 1803-1889 *AmBi, ApCAB,*
BiAUS, BnEnAmA, DcAmB, Drake,
IIBEAAW, NatCAB 11, NewYHSD,
TwCBDA, WhAm H
Weir, Samuel 1860-1943 *WhAm 2*
Weir, W Victor 1902-1959 *WhAm 4*
Weir, William Clarence 1874- *WhAm 5*
Weir, William Figley 1861-1949 *WhAm 3*
Weir, William Hawksley 1876-1964
NatCAB 50
Weir, William R *WhoColR*
Weis, Mrs. Charles William, Jr. 1901-1963
WhAm 4
Weis, George *NewYHSD*
Weis, Howard Archibald 1895-1961
NatCAB 49
Weis, Isaac Mayer *WebAB*
Weis, Jessica McCullough 1901-1963 *BiDrAC*
Weis, John Peter Carl 1866-1945 *NatCAB 46*
Weis, Joseph Francis 1894-1964 *NatCAB 51*
Weisbach, Julius Ludwig 1806-1871 *DcScB*

Weisberg, Harold Charles 1925-1970
NatCAB 56, WhAm 5
Weisberg, Mark 1890-1963 *NatCAB 51*
Weisberger, Austin Stanley 1913-1970
NatCAB 56
Weisberger, David 1904-1966 *NatCAB 52,*
WhAm 4
Weise, Arthur James 1838- *ApCAB Sup,*
WhAm 4
Weisel, William Francis 1882-1956 *NatCAB 46*
Weisenburg, Theodore Herman 1876-1934
DcAmB, WhAm 1
Weisenburger, Walter Bertheau 1888-1947
WhAm 2
Weiser, Conrad 1696-1760 *NatCAB 14,*
REnAW, WebAB
Weiser, Emilius James 1867-1937 *WhAm 1*
Weiser, Harry Boyer 1887-1950 *NatCAB 39,*
WhAm 3
Weiser, Johann Conrad 1696-1760 *AmBi,*
DcAmB, WhAm H
Weiser, Walter R 1870-1937 *WhAm 1*
Weisgerber, William Edwin 1881-1953
WhAm 3
Weisiger, Kendall 1880- *WhAm 6*
Weiskotten, Samuel George 1863-1924
NatCAB 20
Weisl, Edwin Louis 1897-1972 *WhAm 5*
Weisman, Joseph *NewYHSD*
Weisman, Russell 1890-1949 *WhAm 2*
Weismann, August Freidrich Leopold 1834-1914
McGEWB
Weismann, August Friedrich Leopold 1834-1914
AsBiEn, DcScB
Weismann, Walter W 1891-1969 *WhAm 5*
Weiss, Adolph A 1891-1971 *WhAm 5*
Weiss, Albert Paul 1879-1931 *WhAm 1*
Weiss, Anton Charles 1862-1938 *NatCAB 16*
Weiss, Anton Charles 1863-1938 *WhAm 1*
Weiss, Christian Samuel 1780-1856 *DcScB*
Weiss, Edmund 1837-1917 *DcScB*
Weiss, Ehrich *DcAmB, WebAB*
Weiss, Franz Karl 1895-1973 *NatCAB 57*
Weiss, George Martin 1895-1972 *NatCAB 57,*
WhAm 5
Weiss, George Michael 1697-1762 *ApCAB*
Weiss, Jacob *NewYHSD*
Weiss, John 1818-1879 *ApCAB, DcAmB,*
Drake, NatCAB 10, WhAm H
Weiss, John E *NewYHSD*
Weiss, John Fox 1873-1947 *NatCAB 39*
Weiss, John Morris 1885-1963 *WhAm 4*
Weiss, Lewis 1717-1796 *ApCAB*
Weiss, Lewis Allen 1893-1953 *NatCAB 41,*
WhAm 3
Weiss, Louis Stix 1894-1950 *WhAm 3*
Weiss, M Herbert 1882-1944 *NatCAB 34*
Weiss, Morris M 1901-1963 *NatCAB 50*
Weiss, Nina McCarthy 1873- *WomWWA 14*
Weiss, Pierre 1865-1940 *DcScB*
Weiss, Richard Alexander 1910-1974 *WhAm 6*
Weiss, Rudolph 1826?- *NewYHSD*
Weiss, S Paul, Jr. 1913-1960 *NatCAB 47*
Weiss, Samuel 1885-1966 *WhAm 4*
Weiss, Samuel 1892-1956 *WhAm 3*
Weiss, Samuel Arthur 1902- *BiDrAC*
Weiss, Seymour 1896-1969 *NatCAB 57,*
WhAm 5
Weiss, Soma 1899-1942 *DcAmB S3*
Weiss, Susan Archer Talley 1835- *AmWom,*
ApCAB
Weiss, William 1887-1958 *WhAm 3*
Weiss, William Casper 1882-1934 *WhAm 1*
Weiss, William Erhard 1877-1942 *NatCAB 32*
Weiss, William Erhard 1879-1942 *WhAm 2*
Weisse, Charles Herman 1866-1919 *BiDrAC,*
NatCAB 19, WhAm 1, WhAmP
Weisse, Faneuil Dunkin 1842-1915 *NatCAB 5,*
WhAm 1
Weisse, John Adam 1810-1888 *ApCAB*
Weisse, Mary Churchill Ripley 1849-
WomWWA 14
Weissenborn, G *NewYHSD*
Weissenfels, Frederick H, Baron De 1738-1806
ApCAB
Weissenfels, Frederick H, Baron De 1739-1806
Drake
Weissert, Augustus Gordon 1843- *NatCAB 4,*

Welles, Henry Titus 1821-1898 *NatCAB 21*
Welles, Kenneth Brakeley 1886-1953 *WhAm 3*
Welles, Lemuel Aiken 1870-1953 *NatCAB 41*
Welles, Martin 1859-1943 *NatCAB 35*
Welles, Mary Crowell 1860- *BiCAW,*
WomWWA 14
Welles, Noah 1718-1776 *ApCAB, DcAmB,*
WhAm H
Welles, Orson 1915- *EncAB, WebAB*
Welles, Paul 1884-1950 *NatCAB 39*
Welles, Paul Gould 1901-1959 *NatCAB 48*
Welles, Roger 1862-1932 *DcAmB, NatCAB 23,*
WhAm 1
Welles, Sumner 1892-1961 *EncAB, McGEWB,*
WhAm 4
Welles, Thomas 1598?-1660 *ApCAB,*
NatCAB 10
Wellesley, Richard Colley, Marquess 1760-1842
McGEWB
Wellesz, Egon Joseph 1885-1974 *WhAm 6*
Wellford, Beverly R 1797-1870 *NatCAB 12*
Wellford, Edwin Taliaferro 1870-1956 *WhAm 3*
Wellhouse, Frederick 1828-1911 *NatCAB 15,*
WhAm 1
Welling, James 1825-1894 *Drake*
Welling, James Clark 1825-1894 *NatCAB 1,*
TwCBDA
Welling, James Clarke 1825-1894 *ApCAB,*
BiDAmEd, DcAmB, WhAm H
Welling, John C 1840- *WhAm 4*
Welling, Milton Holmes 1876-1947 *BiDrAC,*
WhAm 5, WhAmP
Welling, Richard Ward Greene 1858-1946
DcAmB S4, NatCAB 12, NatCAB 36,
WhAm 2
Welling, William *NewYHSD*
Wellington, Arthur Mellen 1847-1895 *ApCAB,*
DcAmB, NatCAB 11, WhAm H
Wellington, Arthur Wellesley, Duke Of
1769-1851 *WhoMilH*
Wellington, Arthur Wellesley, Duke Of
1769-1852 *McGEWB*
Wellington, Arthur Wight 1869-1938
NatCAB 45
Wellington, Austin Clark 1840-1888 *ApCAB X*
Wellington, Charles 1853-1926 *WhAm 1*
Wellington, Charles Henry 1840-1920
NatCAB 19
Wellington, Charles Oliver 1886-1959 *WhAm 3*
Wellington, Clarence George 1890-1959
WhAm 3A
Wellington, Clarence George 1890-1960
NatCAB 48
Wellington, George Brainerd 1856-1921
WhAm 1
Wellington, George Louis 1852-1927
ApCAB Sup, BiDrAC, NatCAB 12,
NatCAB 13, TwCBDA, WhAm 1,
WhAmP
Wellington, Herbert Galbraith 1891-1965
WhAm 4
Wellington, Hiram Bartlett 1840-1919
ApCAB X
Wellington, Marcellus Burr 1882-1953
NatCAB 43
Wellington, Richard 1884-1975 *WhAm 6*
Wellington, Sarah Cordelia Fisher 1841-
ApCAB X
Wellington, Stanwood Gray 1879-1921
NatCAB 19
Wellington, Violet Irene *NatCAB 19*
Wellington, William H 1849-1925 *WhAm 1*
Welliver, Judson Churchill 1870-1943 *WhAm 2*
Welliver, Les 1920?- *IIBEAAW*
Welliver, Lester Allen 1896-1973 *WhAm 6*
Wellman, Arthur Holbrook 1855-1948
NatCAB 14, WhAm 2
Wellman, Arthur Willis 1856-1937 *NatCAB 27*
Wellman, Beth Lucy 1895-1952 *WhAm 3*
Wellman, Betsy *NewYHSD*
Wellman, Charles Aaron 1915-1970 *WhAm 5*
Wellman, Charles Henry 1865-1905
NatCAB 32
Wellman, Creighton 1873- *WhAm 5*
Wellman, Mrs. Francis L *WomWWA 14*
Wellman, Francis Lewis 1854-1942 *NatCAB 37,*
WhAm 1
Wellman, Guy 1876-1941 *NatCAB 31,*

WhAm 1
Wellman, Hiller Crowell 1871-1956 *DcAmLiB,*
NatCAB 44, WhAm 3
Wellman, Holley Garfield 1881- *WhAm 6*
Wellman, Joshua Wyman 1821- *NatCAB 14*
Wellman, Mabel Thacher 1872- *WhAm 5,*
WomWWA 14
Wellman, Paul Iselin 1898-1966 *REnAW,*
WhAm 4
Wellman, Samuel Knowlton 1892-1969
NatCAB 57
Wellman, Samuel Thomas 1847-1919 *DcAmB,*
NatCAB 13, WhAm 1
Wellman, Sargent Holbrook 1892-1961
NatCAB 50, WhAm 4
Wellman, Victor Elliott 1903-1964 *NatCAB 51*
Wellman, Walter 1858-1934 *AmBi, ApCAB X,*
DcAmB, TwCBDA, WebAB, WhAm 1
Wellman, Walter 1860?-1934 *ApCAB Sup*
Wellman, William Augustus 1896-1975
WhAm 6
Wellmore, Edward *NewYHSD*
Wellons, William Brock 1821-1877 *DcAmB,*
WhAm H
Wells, Addison E 1856-1933 *WhAm 1*
Wells, Agnes Ermina 1876-1959 *WhAm 3*
Wells, Alexander 1815?-1854 *BiAUS*
Wells, Alfred 1814-1857 *BiAUS*
Wells, Alfred 1814-1867 *BiDrAC, WhAm H*
Wells, Alice Stebbins 1873- *WomWWA 14*
Wells, Almond Brown 1842-1912 *WhAm 1*
Wells, Amos Russel 1862-1933 *NatCAB 25,*
WhAm 1
Wells, Anna Holmes 1879- *WomWWA 14*
Wells, Arthur Edward 1884-1939 *NatCAB 42*
Wells, Arthur George 1861-1932 *WhAm 1*
Wells, Arthur Register 1873-1955 *NatCAB 43,*
WhAm 3
Wells, Benjamin Willis 1856-1923 *WhAm 1*
Wells, Brooks Hughes 1859-1917 *WhAm 1*
Wells, Bulkeley 1872-1931 *WhAm 1*
Wells, Cady 1904-1954 *IIBEAAW*
Wells, Calvin 1827-1909 *NatCAB 7, WhAm 1*
Wells, Carolyn d1942 *TwCBDA, WhAm 2,*
WomWWA 14
Wells, Carolyn 1862-1942 *NotAW*
Wells, Carolyn 1869-1942 *NatCAB 13*
Wells, Carveth 1887-1957 *WhAm 3*
Wells, Cate Gilbert 1863- *WomWWA 14*
Wells, Catharine Boott 1838-1911 *TwCBDA*
Wells, Catherine Boott 1838-1911 *WhAm 1*
Wells, Channing McGregory 1870- *WhAm 5*
Wells, Charles Edwin 1858-1940 *NatCAB 30,*
WhAm 1
Wells, Charles J 1881- *WhAm 6*
Wells, Charles Luke 1858-1938 *WhAm 1*
Wells, Charles R *NewYHSD*
Wells, Charles Raymond 1895-1966 *WhAm 4*
Wells, Charlotte Fowler 1814-1901 *AmWom,*
ApCAB, NotAW
Wells, Chester 1870-1948 *WhAm 2*
Wells, Clark Henry 1822-1888 *ApCAB,*
TwCBDA
Wells, Cora Agnew 1866- *WomWWA 14*
Wells, Cyrus Campbell 1870-1932 *NatCAB 25*
Wells, Daniel, Jr. 1808-1902 *BiAUS, BiDrAC*
Wells, Daniel Halsey 1845-1929 *NatCAB 14,*
WhAm 1
Wells, Daniel Hanmer 1814-1891 *NatCAB 16*
Wells, Darius 1800-1875 *ApCAB, NewYHSD*
Wells, David Ames 1828-1898 *AmBi, ApCAB,*
BiAUS, DcAmB, Drake, EncAB,
NatCAB 10, TwCBDA, WebAB,
WhAm H
Wells, David Collin 1858-1911 *NatCAB 9,*
WhAm 1
Wells, David Dwight 1868-1900 *WhAm 1*
Wells, Delphine B 1847- *WomWWA 14*
Wells, Donald A 1920-1971 *WhAm 5*
Wells, Ebenezer Tracy 1835- *WhAm 4*
Wells, Edgar Herbert 1887-1939 *WhAm 1,*
WhAm 1C
Wells, Edgar Huldekoper 1875-1938 *WhAm 1*
Wells, Edward 1835-1907 *NatCAB 16*
Wells, Edward D 1916-1962 *WhAm 4*
Wells, Edward Hubbard 1859-1927 *WhAm 1*
Wells, Edward L 1839- *WhAm 4*
Wells, Edward P 1847-1936 *WhAm 1*

Wells, Eloise Stebbins 1870- *WomWWA 14*
Wells, Emilie Louise *WomWWA 14*
Wells, Emmeline Blanche Woodward 1828-1921
NotAW
Wells, Erastus 1822-1893 *NatCAB 5*
Wells, Erastus 1823-1893 *ApCAB, BiAUS,*
BiDrAC, DcAmB, WhAm H, WhAmP
Wells, Evenezer Tracy 1835- *BiAUS*
Wells, Everett Franklin 1905-1972 *NatCAB 56,*
WhAm 5
Wells, Frances Gibson 1876- *WomWWA 14*
Wells, Frank Oren 1855-1935 *WhAm 1*
Wells, Fred Lloyd 1868-1953 *NatCAB 43*
Wells, Frederic DeWitt 1874- *WhAm 1*
Wells, Frederic Lyman 1884-1964 *NatCAB 51,*
WhAm 4
Wells, Frederick Brown 1873-1953 *NatCAB 44,*
WhAm 3
Wells, Gabriel 1862-1946 *NatCAB 35*
Wells, George Burnham 1902-1967 *NatCAB 53,*
WhAm 4
Wells, George Fitch 1872-1933 *WhAm 1*
Wells, George Harlan 1880- *WhAm 6*
Wells, George Miller 1879-1957 *NatCAB 44,*
WhAm 3
Wells, George Ross Maurice 1884-1962
NatCAB 51
Wells, George Washington 1846-1912 *WhAm 1*
Wells, Georgina Betts 1868- *WomWWA 14*
Wells, Granville 1874-1948 *NatCAB 39*
Wells, Guilford Wiley 1840-1909 *BiAUS,*
BiDrAC
Wells, Guy William 1891-1948 *NatCAB 39*
Wells, H Edward 1874-1947 *WhAm 2*
Wells, H H 1823- *BiAUS*
Wells, Haidee Elder 1872- *WomWWA 14*
Wells, Harry Gideon 1875-1943 *DcAmB S3,*
DcScB, NatCAB 37, WhAm 2
Wells, Harry Lord 1880-1954 *NatCAB 45*
Wells, Harry Lumm 1889-1976 *WhAm 6*
Wells, Heber Manning 1859-1938 *AmBi,*
NatCAB 7, NatCAB 32, TwCBDA,
WhAm 1
Wells, Helen Butler 1862- *WomWWA 14*
Wells, Henry *NewYHSD*
Wells, Henry 1805-1878 *AmBi, ApCAB,*
DcAmB, EncAAH, NatCAB 39, REnAW,
TwCBDA, WebAB, WhAm H
Wells, Henry Horatio 1823- *ApCAB, BiAUS,*
NatCAB 5
Wells, Henry Parkhurst 1842-1904 *WhAm 1*
Wells, Herbert George 1866-1946 *McGEWB,*
WhAm 2
Wells, Herbert Johnson 1850-1933 *WhAm 1*
Wells, Herman B 1902- *BiDAmEd*
Wells, Hermon J 1891-1950 *WhAm 3*
Wells, Hezekiah G 1812- *BiAUS*
Wells, Horace 1815-1848 *AmBi, ApCAB,*
DcAmB, Drake, McGEWB, NatCAB 6,
TwCBDA, WebAB, WhAm H
Wells, Horace Lemuel 1855-1924 *WhAm 1*
Wells, Ida Bell 1862-1931 *WebAB*
Wells, Ira Kent 1871-1934 *WhAm 1,*
WhAm 1C
Wells, J Brent 1901-1962 *WhAm 4*
Wells, J W *NewYHSD*
Wells, Jacob *NewYHSD*
Wells, James Earl 1895-1967 *WhAm 4A*
Wells, James Lee 1843- *NatCAB 8*
Wells, James Madison 1808-1899 *BiAUS,*
DcAmB, NatCAB 10, TwCBDA,
WhAm H
Wells, James Simpson Chester 1851-1931
WhAm 1
Wells, Joel Cheney 1874-1960 *WhAm 3,*
WhAm 3A
Wells, Joel Reaves 1903-1969 *WhAm 5*
Wells, John *NewYHSD*
Wells, John 1770?-1823 *ApCAB, DcAmB,*
TwCBDA, WhAm H
Wells, John 1817-1877 *BiAUS, BiDrAC,*
WhAm H
Wells, John 1819-1875 *NatCAB 13*
Wells, John Barnes 1880-1935 *WhAm 1*
Wells, John Daniel 1878-1932 *WhAm 1*
Wells, John Edwin 1875-1943 *WhAm 2*
Wells, John Mason 1877- *WhAm 5*
Wells, John Miller 1870-1947 *NatCAB 42,*

WhAm 2

Wells, John Sullivan 1803-1860 *ApCAB,
BiAUS, BiDrAC, NatCAB 3, TwCBDA,
WhAm H*
Wells, John Walter 1848-1921 *WhAm 1*
Wells, Joseph R *NewYHSD*
Wells, Kate Gannett 1838-1911 *NotAW*
Wells, Kenneth Robert 1904-1958 *WhAm 3*
Wells, Lemuel Henry 1841-1936 *NatCAB 12,
TwCBDA, WhAm 1*
Wells, Lewis I B *NewYHSD*
Wells, Linton 1893-1976 *WhAm 6*
Wells, Marguerite Jo VanDalsem 1904-1970
WhAm 5
Wells, Marquerite Milton 1872-1958 *WhAm 4*
Wells, Mary Evelyn 1818- *WhAm 6*
Wells, Mary Fletcher *AmWom*
Wells, Mary Jane 1854- *WomWWA 14*
Wells, Merle W 1918- *REnAW*
Wells, Merrill 1889-1966 *NatCAB 52*
Wells, Morris *NewYHSD*
Wells, Newell Woolsey 1851- *WhAm 4*
Wells, Newton Alonzo 1852- *WhAm 1*
Wells, Orlando William 1878-1956 *WhAm 3*
Wells, Oscar 1875-1953 *WhAm 3*
Wells, Owen Augustine 1844-1935 *BiDrAC*
Wells, Philip Patterson 1868- *WhAm 1*
Wells, Rachel *NewYHSD*
Wells, Ralph Gent 1879-1958 *NatCAB 47,
WhAm 6*
Wells, Ralph Olney 1879-1946 *WhAm 2*
Wells, Ralph Ray 1889-1962 *NatCAB 50*
Wells, Richard Harris 1896-1947 *WhAm 2*
Wells, Robert 1728-1794 *ApCAB*
Wells, Robert William 1795-1864 *BiAUS,
DcAmB, WhAm H*
Wells, Roger Clark 1877-1944 *WhAm 2*
Wells, Rolla 1856-1944 *NatCAB 12, WhAm 2*
Wells, Samuel 1801-1868 *ApCAB, NatCAB 6,
TwCBDA*
Wells, Samuel 1805?-1868 *BiAUS, Drake*
Wells, Samuel Calvin 1849- *WhAm 4*
Wells, Samuel Roberts 1820-1875 *ApCAB,
DcAmB, WhAm H*
Wells, Stuart Wilder 1876- *WhAm 5*
Wells, Theodore D 1875- *WhAm 5*
Wells, Thomas Bucklin 1875-1941 *WhAm 2*
Wells, Thomas Tileston 1865-1946 *WhAm 2*
Wells, Vina Guyer *WomWWA 14*
Wells, W Frank 1884-1947 *NatCAB 36*
Wells, Walter 1830-1881 *ApCAB*
Wells, Walter Farrington 1870-1958 *WhAm 3*
Wells, Walter Todd 1886-1964 *NatCAB 54*
Wells, Webster 1851-1916 *BiDAmEd,
NatCAB 17, WhAm 1*
Wells, Wellington 1868- *ApCAB X*
Wells, William 1770?-1812 *ApCAB*
Wells, William 1837-1892 *ApCAB, NatCAB 5,
TwCBDA*
Wells, William Barton 1847- *NatCAB 12*
Wells, William Calvin 1878-1957 *NatCAB 46,
WhAm 3*
Wells, William Charles 1757-1817 *AmBi,
ApCAB, BiHiMed, DcAmB, DcScB,
Drake, NatCAB 12, WhAm H*
Wells, William Charles 1860- *WhAm 1*
Wells, William Edwin 1863-1931 *WhAm 1*
Wells, William Harvey 1812-1885 *ApCAB,
BiDAmEd, DcAmB, Drake, WhAm H*
Wells, William Hill d1829 *BiAUS*
Wells, William Hill 1760?-1829 *ApCAB,
NatCAB 2, TwCBDA*
Wells, William Hill 1769-1829 *BiDrAC,
WhAm H, WhAmP*
Wells, William Hughes 1859-1919 *WhAm 1*
Wells, William Leonidas 1848-1929 *IIBEAAW,
NatCAB 22*
Wells, William Vincent 1826-1876 *ApCAB,
DcAmB, Drake, NatCAB 18, WhAm H*
Wells, William Widney 1910-1967 *WhAm 5*
Wells-Barnett, Ida Bell 1862-1931 *EncAB,
NotAW*
Wellstood, James 1855-1880 *ApCAB*
Wellstood, John Geikie 1813-1893 *ApCAB,
NewYHSD*
Wellstood, William 1819-1900 *ApCAB,
NewYHSD, WhAm 1*
Welmore *NewYHSD*

Welmore, J *NewYHSD*
Welpton, John Walter 1859-1918 *NatCAB 17*
Wels, Charles 1825- *NatCAB 7*
Welsch *NewYHSD*
Welsch, Theodore *NewYHSD*
Welsch, Thomas C *NewYHSD*
Welser, Prince Bartholomeus 1475?-1559
ApCAB
Welsh *NewYHSD*
Welsh, Alfred Hix 1850- *ApCAB*
Welsh, Ashton Leroy 1906-1963 *NatCAB 52,
WhAm 4*
Welsh, Charles *NewYHSD*
Welsh, Charles 1850-1914 *WhAm 1*
Welsh, Edward *NewYHSD*
Welsh, George Austin 1878-1970 *BiDrAC,
WhAm 5, WhAm 6*
Welsh, George Wilson 1883-1974 *WhAm 6*
Welsh, Herbert 1851-1941 *ApCAB Sup,
NatCAB 3, REnAW, WhAm 1*
Welsh, Isaac *NewYHSD*
Welsh, Israel 1822-1869 *BiDConf*
Welsh, James Breath 1855-1926 *NatCAB 23*
Welsh, James Wilson 1888-1949 *NatCAB 37*
Welsh, John 1805-1886 *ApCAB, DcAmB,
NatCAB 3, TwCBDA, WhAm H*
Welsh, John Rushing, III 1916-1974 *WhAm 6*
Welsh, Judson Perry 1857- *WhAm 4*
Welsh, Lilian 1858-1938 *NotAW, WhAm 4*
Welsh, Lillian 1858-1938 *WomWWA 14*
Welsh, Robert James 1903-1968 *WhAm 5*
Welsh, Robert Kaye 1862-1942 *WhAm 2*
Welsh, Thomas 1824-1863 *ApCAB, TwCBDA*
Welsh, Vernon M 1891-1969 *WhAm 5*
Welsh, Willard 1865-1950 *NatCAB 38*
Welsh, William 1810?-1878 *ApCAB*
Welshimer, Helen Louise d1954 *WhAm 3*
Welshimer, Pearl H 1873-1957 *WhAm 3*
Welt, Ida *WomWWA 14*
Welte, Carl Michael 1872-1955 *WhAm 3*
Weltman, Sol Walter 1896-1965 *NatCAB 52*
Weltmer, Ernest 1880- *WhAm 6*
Weltmer, Sidney Abram 1858-1930 *WhAm 1*
Weltner, Charles Longstreet 1927- *BiDrAC*
Welton, Gertrude Webster 1881-
WomWWA 14
Welton, Richard 1675?-1726 *ApCAB*
Welty, Benjamin Franklin 1870-1962 *BiDrAC,
WhAm 5*
Welty, Eudora 1909- *WebAB*
Welty, Genevieve Leinhart 1870-
WomWWA 14
Welty, Grace DeWitte 1868- *WomWWA 14*
Welty, John Cullen 1852-1922 *ApCAB X*
Wemmel, Charles W 1839?-1916 *NewYHSD*
Wemmer, N J *NewYHSD*
Wemmer, William Henry 1903-1949
NatCAB 37
Wemple, Edward 1843-1920 *BiDrAC*
Wemple, William Lester 1877- *WhAm 5*
Wemple, William Yates 1859-1933 *WhAm 1*
Wemyss, Francis Courtney 1797-1859 *ApCAB,
DcAmB, Drake, WhAm H*
Wemyss, James Strembeck 1878-1946
NatCAB 34
Wemyss, William Hatch 1879-1973 *WhAm 5*
Wen, T'ien-Hsiang 1236-1283 *McGEWB*
Wen-Hsiang 1818-1876 *McGEWB*
Wencel, Allen Arthur 1895-1965 *NatCAB 51*
Wenceslaus 1361-1419 *McGEWB*
Wenchel, John Philip 1886-1962 *WhAm 4*
Wenck, Paul 1892- *IIBEAAW*
Wencke, Carl George 1889-1967 *NatCAB 54*
Wenckebach, Anna Doris Amalie C Carla
1853-1902 *NatCAB 10*
Wenckebach, Carla 1853-1902 *WhAm 1*
Wende, Ernest 1853-1910 *DcAmB, NatCAB 4,
WhAm 1*
Wende, Grover William 1867-1926 *DcAmB*
Wendel, Harold Fox 1892-1967 *NatCAB 54*
Wendel, Hugo Christian Martin 1884-1949
WhAm 2
Wendel, Jacob Sterling 1884-1961 *NatCAB 50*
Wendel, John Gottlieb 1835-1914 *NatCAB 16*
Wendel, Rudolf Pierre 1902-1955 *NatCAB 41*
Wendelin, Godfroy 1580-1667 *AsBiEn*
Wendelin, Gottfried 1580-1667 *DcScB*
Wendell, Arthur Rindge 1876-1952 *WhAm 3*

Wendell, Barrett 1855-1921 *AmBi,
ApCAB Sup, BiDAmEd, DcAmB,
NatCAB 9, TwCBDA, WhAm 1*
Wendell, Barrett 1859-1921 *ApCAB X*
Wendell, Barrett 1881-1973 *NatCAB 57*
Wendell, Cornelius *BiAUS*
Wendell, Edith Greenough 1859-1938 *BiCAW,
WhAm 1*
Wendell, Evert Jansen 1860-1917 *NatCAB 20*
Wendell, Frank Thaxter 1852-1906 *NatCAB 23*
Wendell, George Vincent 1871-1922 *WhAm 1*
Wendell, James Isaac 1890-1958 *WhAm 3*
Wendell, John Lansing 1784-1861 *Drake*
Wendell, John Lansing 1785-1861 *ApCAB*
Wendell, May Dwight Foote 1868-
WomWWA 14
Wendell, Oliver Clinton 1845-1912 *WhAm 1*
Wender, Louis 1890-1966 *NatCAB 56*
Wender, Max 1886-1956 *NatCAB 43*
Wenderoth, August 1825- *NewYHSD*
Wenderoth, Fannie Belle 1863- *WomWWA 14*
Wenderoth, Frederick A *NewYHSD*
Wenderoth, Oscar 1871- *WhAm 5*
Wendling, George Reuben 1845-1915 *WhAm 1*
Wendover, Peter Hercules 1768-1834 *BiAUS,
BiDrAC, WhAm H*
Wendt, Edwin Frederick 1869-1952 *WhAm 3*
Wendt, Gerald 1891-1973 *WhAm 6*
Wendt, Henry W 1891-1966 *WhAm 4*
Wendt, Julia Bracken 1871-1942 *WhAm 2,
WomWWA 14*
Wendt, William 1865-1946 *IIBEAAW,
WhAm 2*
Wendte, Charles William 1844-1931 *DcAmB,
NatCAB 14, WhAm 1*
Wene, Elmer H 1892-1957 *BiDrAC, WhAm 3*
Wenger, Christian Showalter 1914-1966
NatCAB 51
Wenger, Joseph Numa 1901-1970 *NatCAB 56,
WhAm 5*
Wenger, Oliver Clarence 1884-1958 *WhAm 3*
Wengert, Egbert Semmann 1912-1964 *WhAm 4*
Wengler, John B *NewYHSD*
Wenham, Frederick L 1916-1965 *NatCAB 52*
Wenige, G *NewYHSD*
Weniger, Willibald 1884-1959 *WhAm 3*
Wenke, Adolph E 1898-1961 *NatCAB 52,
WhAm 4*
Wenley, Archibald Gibson 1898-1962
NatCAB 46, WhAm 4
Wenley, Robert Mark 1861-1929 *AmBi,
DcAmB, WhAm 1*
Wennagel, Leonard Alvin 1911-1975 *WhAm 6*
Wenneker, Charles Frederick 1853-
NatCAB 12
Wenner, Frank 1873-1954 *WhAm 3*
Wenner, George Unangst 1844-1934 *DcAmB,
WhAm 1*
Wenner, Howard Theodore 1909-1968 *WhAm 5*
Wenner, William E *NewYHSD*
Wenner, William Ervin 1872-1949 *WhAm 2*
Wenning, T H 1903-1962 *WhAm 4*
Wenninger, Francis Joseph 1888-1940 *WhAm 1*
Wenrich, Calvin Naftzinger 1873- *WhAm 5*
Wensley, Richard 1872-1948 *NatCAB 34*
Wensley, Roger Lytle 1894-1967 *WhAm 4*
Went, Friedrich August F Christian 1863-1935
DcScB
Wente, Carl Frederick 1889-1971 *WhAm 5*
Wente, Edward Christopher 1889-1972
NatCAB 56, WhAm 5
Wente, Herman Louis 1892-1961 *NatCAB 54*
Wente, William 1848-1915 *NatCAB 17*
Wenter, Frank 1854-1929 *NatCAB 24*
Wentworth, Benning 1696-1770 *AmBi, ApCAB,
DcAmB, Drake, NatCAB 6, TwCBDA,
WhAm H*
Wentworth, Caroline Young 1864-
WomWWA 14
Wentworth, Catherine Denkman d1948
WhAm 2
Wentworth, Cecile De d1933 *DcAmB,
WhAm 1*
Wentworth, Sir Charles Mary d1844 *Drake*
Wentworth, Claude *NewYHSD*
Wentworth, Edward Norris 1878-1959 *EncAAH*
Wentworth, Edward Norris 1887-1959
NatCAB 47, WhAm 3

West, Charles 1872- *WhAm 5*
West, Charles Cameron 1877-1957 *WhAm 3*
West, Charles Edwin 1809-1900 *BiDAmEd,*
NatCAB 8, WhAm 1
West, Charles Franklin 1895-1955 *BiDrAC,*
NatCAB 42
West, Charles H 1858-1933 *WhAm 1*
West, Charles Howard 1865-1943 *NatCAB 34*
West, Charles W 1810-1884 *ApCAB*
West, Christopher 1915- *WhAm 6*
West, Clifford Hardy 1846-1911 *WhAm 1*
West, Cora Smith 1866- *WomWWA 14*
West, Dandridge Payne 1886-1962 *NatCAB 50*
West, Davenport 1882-1960 *NatCAB 49*
West, DuVal 1861- *WhAm 3*
West, E Lovette 1875-1944 *NatCAB 32,*
WhAm 2
West, Edith Brake 1884- *WomWWA 14*
West, Edmund Swem 1879-1950 *NatCAB 42*
West, Edward Augustus 1882-1955 *WhAm 3*
West, Egbert Watson 1863-1944 *NatCAB 49,*
WhAm 2
West, Elizabeth Howard 1873-1948 *WhAm 2*
West, Erdman 1894-1965 *WhAm 4*
West, Ernest Holley 1874- *WhAm 5*
West, Francis 1586-1634 *DcAmB, NatCAB 10,*
NatCAB 13, WhAm H
West, Fred Columbus 1870- *WhoColR*
West, Frederic Beall 1869-1949 *NatCAB 38*
West, Frederick *NewYHSD*
West, G *NewYHSD*
West, George 1823-1901 *ApCAB, BiDrAC,*
DcAmB, NatCAB 7, WhAm H
West, George Henry 1893- *WhAm 2*
West, George N 1847- *WhAm 1*
West, George R *NewYHSD*
West, George V 1919-1974 *WhAm 6*
West, George William 1770-1795 *NewYHSD*
West, Hamilton Atchison 1849-1903 *WhAm 1*
West, Harold Edward 1902- *IIBEAAW*
West, Helen 1926- *IIBEAAW*
West, Helen Andrews Stevens 1889-
WomWWA 14
West, Helen Hunt 1892-1964 *WhAm 4*
West, Henry Litchfield 1859- *WhAm 4*
West, Henry Sergeant 1827-1876 *DcAmB,*
WhAm H
West, Henry Skinner 1870- *WhAm 5*
West, Herbert Faulkner 1898-1974 *WhAm 6*
West, Howard H 1903-1971 *WhAm 5*
West, J R 1822-1898 *BiAUS*
West, J R *see also* West, Joseph Rodman
West, James Edward 1876-1948 *DcAmB S4,*
NatCAB 34, WhAm 2
West, James Harcourt 1856- *WhAm 4*
West, James Hartwell 1897-1966 *WhAm 4*
West, James Samuel 1875- *WhAm 5*
West, Jennie 1854- *WomWWA 14*
West, Jesse Felix 1862-1929 *WhAm 1*
West, John 1590-1659? *NatCAB 13*
West, John B *NewYHSD*
West, John Briggs 1852-1922 *NatCAB 27*
West, John Chester 1885-1961 *WhAm 4*
West, John Walter 1853-1915 *NatCAB 17*
West, Jonathan Burns 1833- *NatCAB 10*
West, Joseph *NatCAB 12*
West, Joseph d1691? *DcAmB*
West, Joseph d1692 *WhAm H*
West, Joseph Rodman 1822-1898 *ApCAB,*
BiDrAC, NatCAB 9, TwCBDA
West, Joseph Roman *see also* West, J R
West, Judson S 1855- *WhAm 3*
West, Julia E Houston 1832- *AmWom*
West, Junius Edgar 1866-1947 *WhAm 2*
West, Kenyon 1855- *WhAm 4,*
WomWWA 14
West, Levon 1900-1968 *IIBEAAW, WhAm 5*
West, Lillian Clarkson 1869- *WomWWA 14*
West, Lillie *NotAW*
West, Lionel Sackville Sackville 1827- *ApCAB*
West, Lowren 1923- *IIBEAAW*
West, Mae 1892- *WebAB*
West, Mary Allen 1837-1892 *AmWom,*
ApCAB
West, Mary Brodie Crump 1865- *WhAm 4*
West, Mary Mills 1868- *WomWWA 14*
West, Max 1870-1909 *WhAm 1*
West, Millard F 1877-1938 *WhAm 1*

West, Milton Horace 1888-1948 *BiDrAC,*
WhAm 2, WhAmP
West, Nathanael 1902-1940 *WhAm HA,*
WhAm 4
West, Nathanael 1903-1940 *McGEWB,*
WebAB
West, Nathaniel 1794-1864 *ApCAB*
West, Olin 1874-1952 *NatCAB 41, WhAm 3*
West, Oswald 1873-1960 *NatCAB 16,*
REnAW, WhAm 5
West, Paul 1871-1918 *WhAm 1*
West, Paul Brown 1892-1960 *WhAm 4*
West, Preston C 1868- *WhAm 5*
West, R C *NewYHSD*
West, Raphael Lamarr 1769-1850 *NewYHSD*
West, Raymond M 1862-1933 *WhAm 1*
West, Robert Henry 1847-1929 *NatCAB 26*
West, Robert Henry 1875-1942 *NatCAB 32*
West, Robert Rout 1893-1962 *WhAm 4*
West, Roy Owen 1868-1958 *BiDrUSE,*
NatCAB 45, WhAm 3
West, Samuel 1730-1807 *ApCAB, DcAmB,*
Drake
West, Samuel 1731-1807 *WhAm H*
West, Samuel H 1872-1938 *WhAm 1*
West, Samuel S *NewYHSD*
West, Samuel Wallens 1899-1969 *NatCAB 54,*
WhAm 5
West, Sophie 1825-1914 *NewYHSD*
West, Stephen 1735-1819 *ApCAB, Drake*
West, Thomas, Baron DeLaWarr 1577-1618
AmBi, NatCAB 13, WebAB, WhAm H
West, Thomas Dyson 1851-1915 *WhAm 1*
West, Thomas Franklin 1874-1931 *NatCAB 23,*
WhAm 1
West, Thomas Hector 1905-1973 *WhAm 6*
West, Thomas Henry 1846-1926 *WhAm 1*
West, Thomas Henry 1888-1963 *WhAm 4*
West, Thomas Henry, Jr. 1875-1936 *WhAm 1*
West, Thomas Poindexter 1874-1949
NatCAB 40
West, Victor J 1880-1927 *WhAm 1*
West, W Nelson L 1871-1954 *NatCAB 43*
West, W R *NewYHSD*
West, Walter Richard 1912- *IIBEAAW,*
REnAW
West, William *NewYHSD*
West, William 1739-1791 *ApCAB*
West, William Edward 1788-1857 *ApCAB,*
DcAmB, Drake, NewYHSD, WhAm H
West, William Henry 1824-1911 *WhAm 1*
West, William Russell 1857-1932 *NatCAB 30*
West, William Stanley 1849-1914 *BiDrAC,*
NatCAB 18, WhAm 1
West, Willis Kelly 1890-1962 *NatCAB 50*
West, Willis Mason 1857-1931 *BiDAmEd,*
NatCAB 5, WhAm 1
Westberg, Mary Barbara Christine 1872-
WomWWA 14
Westberg, Lieutenant *NewYHSD*
Westbrook, Albert Ernest 1840-1926 *NatCAB 6*
Westbrook, Arthur E 1887-1961 *WhAm 4*
Westbrook, Clifton Minniece 1897-1947
NatCAB 35
Westbrook, Elroy Herman 1887-1939 *WhAm 1*
Westbrook, John 1789-1852 *BiAUS, BiDrAC,*
WhAm H
Westbrook, Joseph Henry Parson 1878-
WhoColR
Westbrook, Lawrence 1889-1964 *NatCAB 52,*
WhAm 4
Westbrook, Richard Ward 1864-1932
NatCAB 23
Westbrook, Theodoric Romeyn 1821-1885
BiAUS, BiDrAC, WhAm H
Westbrook, Titus Carr 1842-1893 *NatCAB 8*
Westbrooks, Richard Edward 1886-
WhoColR A
Westcott, Ada L 1855- *WomWWA 14*
Westcott, Allan Ferguson 1882-1953 *WhAm 3*
Westcott, Charles Drake 1871- *WhAm 5*
Westcott, Edward Noyes 1846-1898 *AmBi,*
ApCAB X, DcAmB, WebAB, WhAm H
Westcott, Edward Noyes 1847-1898
ApCAB Sup, NatCAB 27
Westcott, Frank Nash 1858-1915 *WhAm 1*
Westcott, Frederick Russell 1899-1965
NatCAB 52

Westcott, Harry R 1881- *WhAm 6*
Westcott, James Diament 1802-1880 *ApCAB,*
BiAUS, BiDrAC, NatCAB 12, TwCBDA,
WhAm H
Westcott, James Diament 1839- *ApCAB*
Westcott, John Howell 1858-1942 *NatCAB 13,*
WhAm 2
Westcott, Richard Nutter 1918-1973 *WhAm 6*
Westcott, Thompson 1820-1888 *ApCAB,*
DcAmB, Drake, WhAm H
Westcott, Thompson Seiser 1862-1933 *WhAm 3*
Westengard, Jens Iverson 1871-1918
NatCAB 18, WhAm 1
Westenhaver, David C 1865-1928 *ApCAB X,*
WhAm 1
Westerberg, George Edward 1888-1962
NatCAB 50
Westerfield, Ray Bert 1884-1961 *WhAm 4*
Westerfield, Samuel Zaza, Jr. 1919-1972
WhAm 5
Westergaard, Harald Malcolm 1888-1950
DcAmB S4, NatCAB 42, WhAm 3
Westerl, Robert *NewYHSD*
Westerlind, Knute Enock 1889-1960
NatCAB 51
Westerlo, Eilardus 1738-1790 *ApCAB*
Westerlo, Rensselaer d1851 *BiAUS*
Westerlo, Rensselaer 1775-1851 *ApCAB*
Westerlo, Rensselaer 1776-1851 *BiDrAC,*
WhAm H
Westerman, Hans 1660-1721 *ApCAB*
Westerman, Harry James 1876-1945 *WhAm 2*
Westermann, H C, Jr. 1922- *BnEnAmA*
Westermann, Julius Tyndale 1871-1935
NatCAB 26
Westermann, William Linn 1873-1954
DcAmB S5, WhAm 3
Westermeier, Clifford P 1910- *REnAW*
Westermeyer, H E 1896-1974 *WhAm 6*
Western, A S *NewYHSD*
Western, Forrest 1902-1972 *WhAm 5*
Western, Lucille 1843-1877 *DcAmB,*
WhAm H
Western, Pauline Lucille 1843-1877 *ApCAB*
Western, Theodore B *NewYHSD*
Westervelt, Emery Emmanuel 1863- *WhAm 4*
Westervelt, Esther Julia Manning d1975
WhAm 6
Westervelt, George Conrad 1879-1956
NatCAB 43
Westervelt, Jacob Aaron 1800-1879 *DcAmB,*
WhAm H
Westervelt, Leonidas Doty 1875-1952
NatCAB 38
Westervelt, Marvin Zabriskie 1876-1929
WhAm 1
Westervelt, William Irving 1876-1960 *WhAm 3*
Westervelt, William Young 1872-1958 *WhAm 3*
Westfall, Alfred R 1889-1953 *WhAm 3*
Westfall, Byron Lee 1903-1972 *WhAm 5*
Westfall, John VanEtten 1872-1944 *ApCAB X,*
NatCAB 33
Westfall, Katherine Storey 1863- *WhAm 1*
Westfall, Othel D 1908-1964 *WhAm 4*
Westfall, W D A 1879-1951 *WhAm 3*
Westfeldt, George G 1880- *WhAm 6*
Westgate, John Minton 1878-1937 *WhAm 1*
Westgate, Lewis Gardner 1868-1948 *WhAm 2*
Westhafer, William Rader 1879-1945 *WhAm 2*
Westhues, Henry John 1888-1969 *NatCAB 54,*
WhAm 5
Westinghouse, George 1846-1914 *AmBi,*
ApCAB X, AsBiEn, DcAmB, EncAB,
McGEWB, NatCAB 11, NatCAB 15,
TwCBDA, WebAB, WhAm 1
Westinghouse, Henry Herman 1853-1933 *AmBi,*
WhAm 1
Westinghouse, Marguerite Erskine Walker
1842-1914 *ApCAB X, NatCAB 15,*
WhAm 1, WomWWA 14
Westlake, Emory H d1967 *WhAm 4*
Westlake, J Willis 1830-1912 *WhAm 1*
Westlake, Kate Eva *AmWom*
Westlake, William 1831- *NatCAB 2*
Westland, Alfred John 1904- *BiDrAC,*
WhAmP
Westland, Ella Lydia 1867- *WomWWA 14*
Westlaver *NewYHSD*

Westley, George Hembert 1865-1936 *WhAm 1, WhAm 1C*
Westley, Helen 1875-1942 *DcAmB S3, NotAW*
Westmore, George Bud 1918-1973 *WhAm 6*
Westmoreland, William Childs 1914- *EncAB, McGEWB, WebAB, WebAMB*
Weston, Charles Sidney 1860-1947 *WhAm 2*
Weston, Charles Valentine 1857-1933 *NatCAB 25, WhAm 1*
Weston, Claude LaVerne 1896-1971 *NatCAB 57*
Weston, Edmund Brownell 1850-1916 *WhAm 1*
Weston, Edward 1850-1936 *AmBi, ApCAB, DcAmB S2, NatCAB 5, WhAm 1*
Weston, Edward 1866-1958 *WebAB*
Weston, Edward 1886-1957 *WhAm 3*
Weston, Edward 1886-1958 *BnEnAmA*
Weston, Edward F 1878-1971 *WhAm 5*
Weston, Edward Paycon 1839-1929 *WebAB*
Weston, Edward Payson 1839-1929 *AmBi, DcAmB, WhAm 1*
Weston, Elizabeth Stewart d1973 *WhAm 6*
Weston, Eugene, Jr. 1896-1969 *WhAm 5*
Weston, Francis Hopkins 1866- *WhAm 4*
Weston, Frank Morey 1873- *WhAm 5*
Weston, Franklin 1866-1920 *NatCAB 19*
Weston, George d1965 *WhAm 4*
Weston, George 1861-1920 *ApCAB X*
Weston, Grace 1870- *WomWWA 14*
Weston, H *NewYHSD*
Weston, Harold 1894-1972 *WhAm 5*
Weston, Harry Elisha 1897- *WhAm 5*
Weston, Henry Griggs 1820-1909 *ApCAB, NatCAB 12, TwCBDA, WhAm 1*
Weston, Henry W *NewYHSD*
Weston, J G *NewYHSD*
Weston, James *NewYHSD*
Weston, James A *BiAUS*
Weston, James Adams 1827-1895 *BiAUS, NatCAB 11*
Weston, James Augustus 1838-1905 *WhAm 1*
Weston, James Francis 1868-1950 *WhAm 3*
Weston, James Partelow 1815-1888 *TwCBDA*
Weston, John Burns 1821-1912 *NatCAB 6, WhAm 1*
Weston, John Francis 1845-1917 *WhAm 1*
Weston, Karl Ephraim 1874-1956 *NatCAB 45, WhAm 3*
Weston, Mary Catharine North 1822-1882 *ApCAB*
Weston, Mary Josephine 1878- *WomWWA 14*
Weston, Mary Pillsbury 1817-1894 *NewYHSD*
Weston, May 1867- *WomWWA 14*
Weston, Nathan 1782-1859 *NatCAB 7*
Weston, Nathan Austin 1868-1933 *DcAmB, WhAm 1*
Weston, Paul Garfield 1881-1939 *NatCAB 30*
Weston, Robert Spurr 1869-1943 *WhAm 2*
Weston, S Burns 1855-1936 *NatCAB 27, WhAm 1*
Weston, Sidney Adams 1877- *WhAm 5*
Weston, Stephen Francis 1855-1935 *WhAm 1*
Weston, Sullivan Hardy 1816-1887 *ApCAB, NatCAB 9*
Weston, Theodore 1832-1919 *ApCAB X, WhAm 1*
Weston, Thomas 1575?-1624? *ApCAB*
Weston, Thomas 1575?-1644? *DcAmB, WhAm H*
Weston, Will Bunker 1884-1972 *NatCAB 57*
Weston, William 1752?-1833 *DcAmB, WhAm H*
Weston, William 1874- *WhAm 5*
Weston, William Percy 1879-1967 *IIBEAAW*
Westover, Cynthia M 1858- *AmWom*
Westover, Frederick Carl 1877-1940 *NatCAB 36*
Westover, Myron F 1860-1933 *WhAm 1*
Westover, Oscar 1883-1938 *NatCAB 32, WebAMB, WhAm 1*
Westover, Russell Channing 1886-1966 *WhAm 4*
Westover, Wendell 1895-1960 *NatCAB 49, WhAm 4*
Westphal, William Alfred 1922-1970 *NatCAB 55*

Westropp, Clara Elizabeth 1886-1965 *NatCAB 51*
Westwood, Horace 1884-1956 *WhAm 3*
Westwood, Richard W 1896-1961 *WhAm 4*
Wetherald, Agnes Ethelwyn 1857- *AmWom, WomWWA 14*
Wetherald, Charles E 1884-1969 *WhAm 5*
Wetherald, Samuel B *NewYHSD*
Wetherall, Sir George Augustus 1788-1868 *ApCAB*
Wetherall, Samuel H *NewYHSD*
Wetherbee, Emily Greene 1845- *AmWom*
Wetherbee, Frank Irving 1869- *WhAm 5*
Wetherbee, George 1851- *WhAm 4*
Wetherbee, Henry 1827-1892 *NatCAB 17*
Wetherby, Benedict Jones 1859-1915 *NatCAB 16*
Wetherby, Isaac Augustus 1819-1904 *NewYHSD*
Wetherby, Jeremiah Wood 1780- *NewYHSD*
Wethered, John 1809-1888 *BiAUS, BiDrAC, WhAm H*
Wetherell, Elizabeth *AmBi, NotAW, WhAm H*
Wetherell, Emma Abbott 1849-1891 *NatCAB 3*
Wetherell, Emma Abbott 1850-1891 *NotAW*
Wetherill, Charles Mayer 1825-1871 *ApCAB, DcAmB, NatCAB 13, WhAm H*
Wetherill, Henry Emerson 1871-1946 *NatCAB 35*
Wetherill, Horace Greeley 1856- *WhAm 4*
Wetherill, John Price 1824-1888 *ApCAB*
Wetherill, John Price 1844-1906 *NatCAB 27*
Wetherill, Richard 1850- *NatCAB 4*
Wetherill, Robert 1847- *NatCAB 4*
Wetherill, Samuel 1736-1816 *ApCAB, DcAmB, Drake, WhAm H*
Wetherill, Samuel 1821-1890 *ApCAB, DcAmB, NatCAB 7, WhAm H*
Wetherill, Samuel Price 1846-1926 *NatCAB 20*
Wetjen, Albert Richard 1900-1948 *WhAm 2*
Wetmore, Alphonso d1849 *Drake*
Wetmore, C F *NewYHSD*
Wetmore, C G *NewYHSD*
Wetmore, Charles Delevan 1866-1941 *NatCAB 42*
Wetmore, Charles Whitman 1854-1919 *NatCAB 18*
Wetmore, Claude Hazeltine 1863- *WhAm 4*
Wetmore, Edmund 1838-1918 *NatCAB 13, WhAm 1*
Wetmore, Edward Ditmars 1861-1946 *NatCAB 43, WhAm 2*
Wetmore, Elizabeth Bisland 1861-1929 *AmWom, WhAm 1, WomWWA 14*
Wetmore, Frank O 1867-1930 *WhAm 1*
Wetmore, George Melancthon 1858-1923 *NatCAB 40*
Wetmore, George Peabody 1846-1921 *ApCAB Sup, BiDrAC, NatCAB 9, NatCAB 35, TwCBDA, WhAm 1, WhAmP*
Wetmore, James 1695-1760 *ApCAB*
Wetmore, James Alphonso 1863-1940 *WhAm 1*
Wetmore, Leonidas d1849 *Drake*
Wetmore, Louise Southworth 1874- *WomWWA 14*
Wetmore, Mary Minerva *WomWWA 14*
Wetmore, Maude A K 1873-1951 *WhAm 3*
Wetmore, Monroe Nichols 1863-1954 *NatCAB 47, WhAm 3*
Wetmore, Prosper Montgomery 1798-1876 *ApCAB, Drake*
Wetmore, Sara T 1871- *ApCAB X*
Wetmore, Sarah Adeline Pollard 1842- *WomWWA 14*
Wettach, Robert Hasley 1891-1964 *WhAm 4*
Wetten, Albert Hayes 1869-1953 *WhAm 3*
Wetten, Emil C d1947 *WhAm 2*
Wetterau, Oliver George 1908-1973 *WhAm 6*
Wetterau, Theodore Carl, Jr. 1927-1971 *WhAm 5*
Wettling, Louis Eugene 1863-1938 *WhAm 1*
Wettstein, John Rudolph 1867- *ApCAB X*
Wetzel, Charles *NewYHSD*
Wetzel, Harry H 1888-1938 *WhAm 1*
Wetzel, John Wesley 1871-1945 *WhAm 2*
Wetzel, Lewis 1764-1808? *DcAmB, WebAB,*

WhAm H
Wetzel, Richard Clay 1888-1968 *NatCAB 55*
Wetzler, Ernest *NewYHSD*
Wetzler, Joseph 1863-1911 *WhAm 1*
Wever, Adolph *NewYHSD*
Wever, John Madison 1847-1914 *BiDrAC*
Wevil, George, Jr. *NewYHSD*
Wevill, George, Jr. *NewYHSD*
Wexler, Harry 1911-1962 *NatCAB 53, WhAm 4*
Wexler, Irving 1888-1952 *DcAmB S5*
Wexler, Jacob 1904-1972 *WhAm 6*
Wexler, Solomon 1867- *WhAm 1*
Wey, Frances Christina *WomWWA 14*
Weyand, Frederick Carlton 1916- *WebAMB*
Weyandt, Carl Stanley 1892-1964 *WhAm 4*
Weybrecht, Charles Christopher 1868-1919 *NatCAB 18*
Weyburn, Lyon 1882-1963 *WhAm 4*
Weyden, Rogier VanDer 1399?-1464 *McGEWB*
Weyer, Edward Moffat 1872- *WhAm 5*
Weyerhaeuser, Charles Augustus 1866-1930 *NatCAB 34, WhAm 1*
Weyerhaeuser, Frederick 1834-1914 *ApCAB X, NatCAB 14, WebAB, WhAm 1*
Weyerhaeuser, Frederick 1906-1961 *NatCAB 50*
Weyerhaeuser, Frederick Edward 1872-1945 *DcAmB S3, NatCAB 37, WhAm 2*
Weyerhaeuser, John Philip 1858-1935 *NatCAB 42, WhAm 1*
Weyerhaeuser, John Philip, Jr. 1899-1956 *WhAm 3*
Weyerhaeuser, Rudolph Michael 1868-1946 *WhAm 2*
Weygand, Maxime 1867-1965 *WhWW-II, WhoMilH*
Weygandt, Carl Victor 1888-1964 *WhAm 4*
Weygandt, Cornelius 1871-1957 *WhAm 3*
Weygold, Frederick P 1870-1941 *IIBEAAW*
Weyhe, Erhard 1882-1972 *WhAm 5*
Weyl, Charles 1896-1967 *WhAm 5*
Weyl, Hermann 1885-1955 *DcAmB S5, DcScB, WhAm 3*
Weyl, Maurice Nathan 1869-1936 *NatCAB 49*
Weyl, Max 1837-1914 *NewYHSD, WhAm 1*
Weyl, Walter Edward 1873-1919 *WhAm 1*
Weyl, Woldemar Anatol 1901-1975 *WhAm 6*
Weyland, Grover Cleveland 1885-1953 *NatCAB 48*
Weyler, George Lester 1886-1971 *WhAm 5*
Weyler, Valeriano Y Nicolau 1840- *ApCAB Sup*
Weyman, Miss *NewYHSD*
Weyman, Wesley 1877-1931 *NatCAB 23*
Weymann, Henry 1846-1929 *NatCAB 24*
Weymouth, Aubrey 1872-1939 *WhAm 1*
Weymouth, Clarence Raymond 1876-1949 *WhAm 2*
Weymouth, Frank Elwin 1874-1941 *DcAmB S3, WhAm 1*
Weymouth, George Warren 1850-1910 *BiDrAC, WhAm 1*
Weymouth, Thomas Rote 1876-1958 *WhAm 3*
Weyrauch, Martin Henry 1885-1958 *WhAm 3*
Weyss, John E 1820?-1903 *IIBEAAW*
Weysse, Arthur Wisswald 1867- *WhAm 5*
Whaites, Edward P *NewYHSD*
Whaites, John A *NewYHSD*
Whaites, John L *NewYHSD*
Whaites, William *NewYHSD*
Whaites, William N *NewYHSD*
Whalen, Charles William, Jr. 1920- *BiDrAC*
Whalen, Grover A 1886-1962 *WhAm 4*
Whalen, John d1926 *WhAm 1*
Whalen, Joseph D A 1884-1971 *NatCAB 56*
Whalen, Robert E 1874-1951 *WhAm 3*
Whaley, A R 1862- *WhAm 4*
Whaley, Arthur Maunder 1872-1954 *NatCAB 41*
Whaley, George P 1870-1949 *WhAm 2*
Whaley, James V 1903-1960 *WhAm 4*
Whaley, Kellian VanRensalear 1821-1876 *BiAUS, BiDrAC, NatCAB 3, WhAm H*
Whaley, Marcellus Seabrook 1885-1961 *NatCAB 50*
Whaley, Percival Huntington 1880-1963 *WhAm 4*

Whaley, Richard Smith 1874-1951 *BiDrAC,*
NatCAB 41, WhAm 3, WhAmP
Whaley, Robert Jerome 1840-1922 *NatCAB 6*
Whaling, Horace Morland, Jr. 1881- *WhAm 6*
Whaling, Thornton 1858- *WhAm 4*
Whalley, Edward d1674? *DcAmB,*
NatCAB 11
Whalley, Edward 1615?-1675? *AmBi*
Whalley, Edward 1620?-1674? *WhAm H*
Whalley, Edward 1620?-1678? *ApCAB*
Whalley, John Irving 1902- *BiDrAC*
Whallon, Edward Payson 1849-1939 *WhAm 1*
Whallon, Reuben 1776-1843 *BiAUS, BiDrAC,*
WhAm H
Whallon, Walter Lowrie 1878- *WhAm 6*
Whalter, R *NewYHSD*
Wham, Benjamin 1891-1969 *NatCAB 55,*
WhAm 5
Wham, Fred Louis 1884-1967 *NatCAB 54*
Whaples, Meigs H 1845-1928 *WhAm 1*
Wharey, James 1789-1842 *ApCAB*
Wharey, James Blanton 1872-1946 *WhAm 2*
Wharton, Anne Hollingsworth 1845-1928 *AmBi,*
ApCAB, ApCAB Sup, DcAmB,
NatCAB 13, TwCBDA, WhAm 1,
WomWWA 14
Wharton, Arthur Orlando 1873- *WhAm 5*
Wharton, Carol Forbes 1907-1958 *WhAm 3*
Wharton, Charles Henry 1748-1833 *ApCAB,*
DcAmB, Drake, NatCAB 20, TwCBDA,
WhAm H
Wharton, Charles Stuart 1875-1939 *BiDrAC,*
WhAm 5
Wharton, Edith 1861-1937 *McGEWB*
Wharton, Edith 1862-1937 *AmBi, ApCAB X,*
DcAmB S2, EncAB, NatCAB 14,
NotAW, TwCBDA, WebAB, WhAm 1,
WomWWA 14
Wharton, Francis 1820-1889 *AmBi, ApCAB,*
DcAmB, Drake, NatCAB 11, TwCBDA,
WhAm H
Wharton, Franklin 1767-1818 *ApCAB,*
WebAMB
Wharton, Gabriel Caldwell 1839-1887 *ApCAB,*
NatCAB 5
Wharton, Gabriel Colvin 1824- *TwCBDA*
Wharton, George 1617-1681 *DcScB*
Wharton, Greene Lawrence 1847-1906 *DcAmB*
Wharton, Henry 1827-1880 *ApCAB*
Wharton, Henry Marvin 1848-1928 *WhAm 1*
Wharton, Henry Redwood 1853-1925 *WhAm 1*
Wharton, James E 1894-1944 *WhAm 2*
Wharton, James Ernest 1899- *BiDrAC,*
WhAmP
Wharton, James Pearce 1893-1963 *WhAm 4*
Wharton, Jesse d1833 *BiAUS*
Wharton, Jesse 1760?-1833 *ApCAB,*
NatCAB 4
Wharton, Jesse 1782-1833 *BiDrAC, WhAm H*
Wharton, John *ApCAB*
Wharton, John A d1838 *NatCAB 4*
Wharton, John Austin 1828-1865 *BiDConf*
Wharton, John Austin 1829-1865 *NatCAB 15*
Wharton, John Austin 1831-1865 *ApCAB Sup,*
TwCBDA
Wharton, Joseph *NewYHSD*
Wharton, Joseph 1707-1776 *ApCAB*
Wharton, Joseph 1733-1816 *ApCAB*
Wharton, Joseph 1826-1909 *ApCAB, DcAmB,*
NatCAB 13, TwCBDA, WhAm 1
Wharton, R, Lang 1880-1949 *WhAm 2*
Wharton, Moore 1875-1961 *NatCAB 49*
Wharton, Morton Bryan 1839-1908 *WhAm 1*
Wharton, Philip Fishbourne 1841-1880 *ApCAB*
Wharton, Richard d1689 *DcAmB, WhAm H*
Wharton, Robert 1757-1834 *ApCAB, DcAmB,*
TwCBDA, WhAm H
Wharton, Rosa Neilson 1876- *WomWWA 14*
Wharton, Samuel 1732-1800 *ApCAB, BiDrAC,*
DcAmB, TwCBDA, WhAm H
Wharton, Samuel 1732-1810 *BiAUS*
Wharton, Theodore Finley 1870-1943 *WhAm 2*
Wharton, Thomas 1614-1673 *DcScB*
Wharton, Thomas 1735-1778 *AmBi, ApCAB,*
DcAmB, NatCAB 2, TwCBDA,
WhAm H
Wharton, Thomas Isaac 1791-1856 *ApCAB,*
DcAmB, Drake, TwCBDA, WhAm H

Wharton, Thomas Isaac 1859- *ApCAB*
Wharton, Thomas Kelah 1814-1862 *NewYHSD,*
WhAm H
Wharton, Turner Ashby 1862-1935 *WhAm 1*
Wharton, Vernon Lane 1907-1964 *WhAm 4*
Wharton, William Fisher 1847-1919 *WhAm 1*
Wharton, William H 1802-1839 *DcAmB,*
NatCAB 4, WhAm H
Wharton, William P 1880- *WhAm 6*
Whatcoat, Richard 1736-1806 *ApCAB,*
DcAmB, NatCAB 13, WhAm H
Whateley, H *NewYHSD*
Whately, Richard 1787-1863 *DcScB*
Whatmough, Joshua 1897-1964 *WhAm 4*
Wheat, Alfred Adams 1867-1943 *NatCAB 33,*
WhAm 2
Wheat, Benjamin Patterson 1871-1933
NatCAB 25
Wheat, Carl Irving 1892-1966 *WhAm 4*
Wheat, Chatham Roberdeau 1826-1862
NatCAB 9
Wheat, George Seay 1886-1937 *WhAm 1*
Wheat, Harry G 1890-1975 *WhAm 6*
Wheat, John Thomas 1800-1888 *ApCAB*
Wheat, Renville 1893-1968 *NatCAB 54,*
WhAm 5
Wheat, Silas Carmi 1852-1922 *NatCAB 19*
Wheat, William Howard 1879-1944 *BiDrAC,*
WhAm 2
Wheat, Zachariah 1806- *NatCAB 12*
Wheatland, Henry 1812- *Drake*
Wheatland, Marcus Fitzherbert 1868-1934
WhAm 1, WhoColR
Wheatleigh, Charles 1823-1895 *ApCAB Sup*
Wheatley, Charles Moore 1822-1882 *ApCAB*
Wheatley, Elizabeth Starr 1866-
WomWWA 14
Wheatley, Florence Bacon 1882-
WomWWA 14
Wheatley, Louis Frederick 1876-1964
NatCAB 51
Wheatley, Noah M 1878-1955 *NatCAB 46*
Wheatley, Phillis 1751-1784 *NatCAB 1*
Wheatley, Phillis 1753?-1784 *ApCAB, DcAmB,*
Drake, McGEWB, NotAW, WebAB,
WhAm H
Wheatley, Phillis 1754?-1784 *AmBi*
Wheatley, Richard 1831- *WhAm 4*
Wheatley, Sarah Ross 1790-1854 *ApCAB,*
NatCAB 1
Wheatley, William 1816-1876 *ApCAB,*
DcAmB, NatCAB 1, WhAm H
Wheatley, William Alonzo 1869-1955 *BiDAmEd,*
WhAm 5
Wheaton, Charles 1834-1886 *NatCAB 33*
Wheaton, Charles Augustus 1853- *NatCAB 6*
Wheaton, Daniel *NewYHSD*
Wheaton, Edgar Mason 1851-1920 *NatCAB 18*
Wheaton, Frank 1833-1903 *AmBi, ApCAB,*
DcAmB, Drake, NatCAB 4, NatCAB 28,
TwCBDA, WebAMB, WhAm 1
Wheaton, Henry 1785-1848 *AmBi, ApCAB,*
BiAUS, DcAmB, Drake, NatCAB 1,
TwCBDA, WebAB, WhAm H
Wheaton, Henry Steward 1820?-1862
NatCAB 18
Wheaton, Horace 1803-1882 *BiAUS, BiDrAC,*
WhAm H
Wheaton, J Frank 1866- *WhoColR*
Wheaton, John Francis 1822-1898 *ApCAB Sup*
Wheaton, Laban 1754-1846 *BiAUS, BiDrAC,*
TwCBDA, WhAm H, WhAmP
Wheaton, Loyd 1838-1918 *ApCAB Sup,*
TwCBDA, WebAMB, WhAm 1
Wheaton, Miles K *NewYHSD*
Wheaton, Milton Alvord 1830- *NatCAB 7*
Wheaton, Nathaniel Sheldon 1792-1862 *ApCAB,*
DcAmB, Drake, NatCAB 3, TwCBDA,
WhAm H
Wheaton, Robert 1826-1851 *ApCAB, Drake*
Wheatstone, Sir Charles 1802-1875 *AsBiEn,*
DcScB
Whedon, Burt Denison 1878-1947 *NatCAB 37*
Whedon, Daniel Denison 1808-1885 *ApCAB,*
DcAmB, Drake, NatCAB 8, WhAm H
Whedon, John Fielding 1899-1969 *WhAm 5*
Whedon, Mary Allen 1862- *WomWWA 14*

Wheelan, Albertine Randall 1863-
WomWWA 14
Wheelan, Fairfax Henry 1856-1915 *WhAm 1*
Wheelan, James Nicholas 1837-1922 *WhAm 1*
Wheeler, Adele Maria Graves 1871-
WomWWA 14
Wheeler, Albert Gallatin 1854-1917
NatCAB 14, WhAm 1
Wheeler, Albert Harry 1873- *WhAm 5*
Wheeler, Alice Clara 1868- *WomWWA 14*
Wheeler, Alonzo Clifford 1880-1960
NatCAB 49
Wheeler, Alton Chapman 1877-1942
NatCAB 31
Wheeler, Alvin Sawyer 1866-1940 *WhAm 1*
Wheeler, Amey Webb *WomWWA 14*
Wheeler, Andrew Carpenter 1832-1903
NatCAB 25
Wheeler, Andrew Carpenter 1835-1903 *AmBi,*
ApCAB, DcAmB, WhAm 1
Wheeler, Anna Johnson Pell 1883-1966
BiDAmEd
Wheeler, Arthur Dana 1861-1912 *WhAm 1*
Wheeler, Arthur Leslie 1871-1932 *WhAm 1*
Wheeler, Arthur Leslie 1872-1932 *DcAmB S1*
Wheeler, Arthur Loring 1883-1942 *NatCAB 37*
Wheeler, Arthur Martin 1836-1918 *WhAm 1*
Wheeler, Asa H *NewYHSD*
Wheeler, Benjamin Ide 1854-1927 *AmBi,*
ApCAB Sup, BiDAmEd, DcAmB,
NatCAB 4, TwCBDA, WhAm 1
Wheeler, Burr 1884-1964 *WhAm 4*
Wheeler, Burton Kendall 1882-1975 *ApCAB X,*
BiDrAC, EncAAH, WhAm 6, WhAmP
Wheeler, Candace Thurber d1923 *WhAm 1,*
WhAm 2, WomWWA 14
Wheeler, Candace Thurber 1827-1923 *BiCAW,*
NotAW
Wheeler, Candace Thurber 1828-1923
NewYHSD
Wheeler, Charles Barker 1851-1935 *NatCAB 12,*
WhAm 1
Wheeler, Charles Brewster 1865-1946 *WhAm 2*
Wheeler, Charles Francis 1906-1974 *WhAm 6*
Wheeler, Charles Gardner 1855-1946 *WhAm 3*
Wheeler, Charles Gilbert 1836-1912 *WhAm 1*
Wheeler, Charles Kennedy 1863-1933 *BiDrAC,*
WhAm 4, WhAmP
Wheeler, Charles Reginald 1904-1975 *WhAm 6*
Wheeler, Charles Rollin 1841-1917 *NatCAB 18*
Wheeler, Charles Stearns 1816-1843 *ApCAB,*
Drake
Wheeler, Charles Stetson 1863-1923 *WhAm 1*
Wheeler, Charles Yandes 1843-1899
NatCAB 18
Wheeler, Clara Marian 1861- *WomWWA 14*
Wheeler, Clayton Eugene 1885- *ApCAB X*
Wheeler, Cora Stuart 1852-1897 *AmWom*
Wheeler, Cyrenus 1817-1899 *NatCAB 12*
Wheeler, Daniel Davis 1841-1916 *WhAm 1*
Wheeler, Daniel Edwin 1880- *WhAm 6*
Wheeler, Daniel Merrick 1846-1943
NatCAB 33
Wheeler, David Hilton 1829-1902 *ApCAB,*
NatCAB 4, NatCAB 25, TwCBDA,
WhAm 1
Wheeler, Dewitt Clinton 1838-1916 *NatCAB 17*
Wheeler, Dexter 1777-1835 *NatCAB 12*
Wheeler, Dora 1858- *AmWom, ApCAB*
Wheeler, Dora 1860- *NatCAB 1*
Wheeler, Earle Gilmore 1908-1975 *WebAMB,*
WhAm 6
Wheeler, Ebenezer Smith 1839-1913 *WhAm 1*
Wheeler, Edward Jewitt 1859-1922 *NatCAB 15,*
NatCAB 18, TwCBDA, WhAm 1
Wheeler, Edward Warren 1876-1963
NatCAB 50, WhAm 4
Wheeler, Edwin Bent 1877-1944 *NatCAB 34*
Wheeler, Ella *NotAW*
Wheeler, Emily Frances *WomWWA 14*
Wheeler, Emma Grimwood 1856-
WomWWA 14
Wheeler, Esther Willard 1898-1959 *WhAm 3*
Wheeler, Everett Pepperrell 1840-1925 *DcAmB,*
NatCAB 12, WhAm 1
Wheeler, Ezra 1820-1871 *BiAUS, BiDrAC,*
WhAm H
Wheeler, Florence Evelyn 1851- *WomWWA 14*

Wheeler, Florence Lillie *WomWWA 14*
Wheeler, Francis Brown 1818- *NatCAB 1*
Wheeler, Frank Willis 1853-1921 *BiDrAC*
Wheeler, Franklin Carroll 1893-1961 *WhAm 4*
Wheeler, Frederick Freeman 1859-1917
  WhAm 1
Wheeler, Frederick Seymour 1861-1936
  NatCAB 31, WhAm 1
Wheeler, Fredrick Freeman 1859-1917
  NatCAB 17
Wheeler, Genevra Leslie 1849- *WomWWA 14*
Wheeler, George Bourne 1853-1943 *NatCAB 16,
  WhAm 2*
Wheeler, George Carpenter 1872-1934 *WhAm 1*
Wheeler, George Montague 1842-1905 *ApCAB,
  DcAmB, REnAW, WebAMB, WhAm 4*
Wheeler, George Wakeman 1860-1932 *DcAmB,
  NatCAB 24, WhAm 1*
Wheeler, Gervase *NewYHSD*
Wheeler, Grace Denison 1858- *WomWWA 14*
Wheeler, Grattan Henry 1783-1852 *BiAUS,
  BiDrAC, WhAm H*
Wheeler, Hallie Erminie Rives 1878-
  WomWWA 14
Wheeler, Hamilton Kinkaid 1848-1918 *BiDrAC*
Wheeler, Harold Francis 1888-1956 *WhAm 3*
Wheeler, Harris Ansel 1850- *NatCAB 10,
  WhAm 4*
Wheeler, Harrison H 1829-1896 *WhAm H*
Wheeler, Harrison H 1839-1896 *BiDrAC*
Wheeler, Harry A 1866-1960 *WhAm 3A*
Wheeler, Hayden Willard 1827- *NatCAB 12*
Wheeler, Henry 1835-1925 *WhAm 1*
Wheeler, Henry Lord 1867-1914 *WhAm 1*
Wheeler, Henry Nathan 1850-1905 *WhAm 1*
Wheeler, Herbert Allen 1859-1950 *NatCAB 38*
Wheeler, Herbert Locke 1869-1929 *WhAm 1*
Wheeler, Hetty Shepard *WomWWA 14*
Wheeler, Hiram C 1835- *NatCAB 1,
  WhAm 4*
Wheeler, Hiram Nicholas 1844-1916 *WhAm 1*
Wheeler, Homer Jay 1861-1945 *ApCAB X,
  WhAm 2*
Wheeler, Homer Webster 1848- *WhAm 1*
Wheeler, Howard 1873-1931 *NatCAB 23*
Wheeler, Howard Duryce 1880-1958 *WhAm 3*
Wheeler, Howard Victor 1874-1951 *NatCAB 41,
  WhAm 3*
Wheeler, Hoyt Henry 1833-1906 *TwCBDA,
  WhAm 1*
Wheeler, Hughlette Tex 1900?-1955 *IlBEAAW*
Wheeler, James Cooper 1849- *WhAm 1*
Wheeler, James Everett 1870-1954 *NatCAB 43,
  WhAm 3*
Wheeler, James Hartwick 1891-1959
  NatCAB 47
Wheeler, James Rignall 1859-1918 *DcAmB,
  WhAm 1*
Wheeler, Janet d1945 *WhAm 2,
  WomWWA 14*
Wheeler, Jean Huleatt 1927-1969 *WhAm 5*
Wheeler, Jennie Pearl Mowbray *WomWWA 14*
Wheeler, Jerome Byron 1841-1918 *WhAm 1*
Wheeler, Jessie F *WomWWA 14*
Wheeler, John 1798-1862 *ApCAB Sup, Drake,
  NatCAB 2, TwCBDA*
Wheeler, John 1823-1906 *BiAUS, BiDrAC*
Wheeler, John Brooks 1853-1942 *NatCAB 34,
  WhAm 2*
Wheeler, John DeBerry 1888-1969 *WhAm 5*
Wheeler, John Egbert 1879-1943 *NatCAB 37,
  WhAm 2*
Wheeler, Mrs. John Hill *NewYHSD*
Wheeler, John Hill 1806-1882 *ApCAB, BiAUS,
  DcAmB, Drake Sup, NatCAB 6,
  TwCBDA, WhAm H*
Wheeler, John Martin 1879-1938 *DcAmB S2,
  NatCAB 47, WhAm 1*
Wheeler, John Neville 1886-1973 *NatCAB 57,
  WhAm 6*
Wheeler, John Samuel 1904-1968 *WhAm 5*
Wheeler, John Taylor 1886-1950 *WhAm 3*
Wheeler, John Tipton 1867-1951 *NatCAB 40*
Wheeler, John Wilson 1832- *NatCAB 3,
  WhAm 1*
Wheeler, Joseph 1836-1906 *AmBi, ApCAB,
  BiDConf, BiDrAC, DcAmB, NatCAB 9,
  TwCBDA, WebAB, WebAMB, WhAm 1,*

Wheeler, Joseph C 1912-1970 *WhAm 5*
Wheeler, Joseph Lewis 1884-1970 *DcAmLiB*
Wheeler, Joseph Porter 1891-1970 *NatCAB 56*
Wheeler, Joseph Trank 1868-1919 *WhAm 1*
Wheeler, Josepha Virginia 1868-
  WomWWA 14
Wheeler, Junius Brutus 1830-1886 *ApCAB*
Wheeler, Lawrence Raymond 1888-1938
  NatCAB 35
Wheeler, Leonard 1845-1935 *NatCAB 27*
Wheeler, Leslie Allen 1899-1968 *WhAm 5*
Wheeler, Loren Edgar 1862-1932 *BiDrAC,
  WhAm 1, WhAmP*
Wheeler, Mabel Blanche *WomWWA 14*
Wheeler, Mabel Gregg 1866- *WomWWA 14*
Wheeler, Marcellus Edgar 1850-1927
  NatCAB 27
Wheeler, Marianna 1856- *WhAm 4*
Wheeler, Mary Curtis 1869- *WhAm 5*
Wheeler, Mary Sparkes 1835-1919 *AmWom,
  WhAm 1, WomWWA 14*
Wheeler, Maxwell Stevenson 1874-1956
  WhAm 3
Wheeler, N *NewYHSD*
Wheeler, Nathan W *NewYHSD*
Wheeler, Nathaniel 1820-1893 *ApCAB,
  DcAmB, NatCAB 9, WhAm H*
Wheeler, Nelson Platt 1841-1920 *BiDrAC,
  NatCAB 35, WhAm 4*
Wheeler, Olin Dunbar 1852- *WhAm 4*
Wheeler, Orlando Belina 1835- *ApCAB*
Wheeler, Post 1869-1956 *NatCAB 42,
  WhAm 3*
Wheeler, Raymond Albert 1885-1974 *WhAm 6*
Wheeler, Raymond Holder 1892-1961
  BiDAmEd, WhAm 4
Wheeler, Richard Smith 1909-1972 *WhAm 5*
Wheeler, Rollo Clark d1962 *WhAm 4*
Wheeler, Royal T 1810-1864 *NatCAB 7*
Wheeler, Royall Tyler 1810-1864 *DcAmB,
  WhAm H*
Wheeler, Ruth 1877-1948 *NotAW, WhAm 2,
  WomWWA 14*
Wheeler, Samuel 1742-1820 *ApCAB*
Wheeler, Schuyler Skaats 1860-1923 *AmBi,
  DcAmB, NatCAB 10, NatCAB 41,
  WhAm 1*
Wheeler, Scott 1870- *WhAm 5*
Wheeler, Stephen Morse 1900-1967 *WhAm 4A*
Wheeler, Sylvia A *NewYHSD*
Wheeler, Thomas 1620?-1686 *ApCAB, Drake,
  NatCAB 8*
Wheeler, Thomas Benton 1840-1913
  NatCAB 15
Wheeler, Walter Heber, Jr. 1897-1974 *WhAm 6*
Wheeler, Walton M, Jr. 1908-1960 *WhAm 4*
Wheeler, Warren Gregg 1897-1963 *NatCAB 50*
Wheeler, Wayne Bidwell 1869-1927 *AmBi,
  DcAmB, DcAmReB, NatCAB 20,
  WebAB, WhAm 1*
Wheeler, William 1851-1932 *DcAmB*
Wheeler, William A 1820-1887 *BiAUS*
Wheeler, William Adolphus 1833-1874 *AmBi,
  ApCAB, DcAmB, Drake, NatCAB 1,
  WhAm H*
Wheeler, William Alman 1819-1887 *WhAm H*
Wheeler, William Almon 1819-1887 *AmBi,
  ApCAB, BiDrAC, BiDrUSE, DcAmB,
  NatCAB 3, TwCBDA, WebAB, WhAmP*
Wheeler, William Archie 1876- *WhAm 5*
Wheeler, William Egbert 1843-1911
  NatCAB 29
Wheeler, William French 1811-1892
  NatCAB 17
Wheeler, William Henry 1887-1960 *NatCAB 45*
Wheeler, William McDonald 1915- *BiDrAC*
Wheeler, William Morton 1865-1937 *AmBi,
  DcAmB S2, DcScB, NatCAB 27,
  WhAm 1*
Wheeler, William R 1832-1894? *NewYHSD*
Wheeler, William Reginald 1889-1963
  NatCAB 49, WhAm 4
Wheeler, William Riley 1860-1935 *WhAm 1*
Wheeler, William Webb 1845-1925 *NatCAB 18,
  WhAm 1*
Wheeler, Wilmot Fitch 1882-1963 *NatCAB 52,
  WhAm 4*

Wheelock, Arthur 1851-1927 *NatCAB 32*
Wheelock, Charles 1812-1865 *ApCAB*
Wheelock, Charles Delorma 1897- *WhAm 4*
Wheelock, Dora V 1847- *AmWom*
Wheelock, Edward 1863-1917 *WhAm 1*
Wheelock, Edwin Dwight 1853- *WhAm 4*
Wheelock, Eleazar 1711-1779 *AmBi, ApCAB,
  BiDAmEd, DcAmB, DcAmReB,
  McGEWB, TwCBDA, WebAB,
  WhAm H*
Wheelock, Eleazer 1711-1779 *Drake,
  NatCAB 9*
Wheelock, Harry Bergen 1861-1934 *WhAm 1*
Wheelock, Irene Grosvenor 1867-1927 *WhAm 1*
Wheelock, John 1754-1817 *AmBi, ApCAB,
  BiDAmEd, DcAmB, Drake, NatCAB 9,
  TwCBDA, WebAB, WhAm H*
Wheelock, Joseph Albert 1831-1906 *ApCAB,
  DcAmB, NatCAB 13, WhAm 1*
Wheelock, Julia Susan 1833- *ApCAB*
Wheelock, Lucy 1857- *AmWom*
Wheelock, Lucy 1857-1946 *BiDAmEd,
  DcAmB S4, NotAW*
Wheelock, Lucy 1857-1947 *NatCAB 39*
Wheelock, Lucy 1859-1946 *WhAm 2*
Wheelock, Merrill G 1822-1866 *NewYHSD*
Wheelock, Walter W *NewYHSD*
Wheelock, Ward 1896-1955 *WhAm 3*
Wheelock, Webster 1870- *NatCAB 13*
Wheelock, William Almy 1825-1905 *WhAm 1*
Wheelock, William Hawxhurst 1876-1942
  NatCAB 35, WhAm 2
Wheelwright, Edmund March 1854-1912
  DcAmB, WhAm 1
Wheelwright, Edward 1824-1900 *NewYHSD*
Wheelwright, John 1592?-1679 *AmBi, ApCAB,
  DcAmB, Drake, WhAm H*
Wheelwright, John 1594-1679 *NatCAB 1*
Wheelwright, John Tyler 1856-1925 *ApCAB,
  WhAm 1*
Wheelwright, Mary Cabot 1878- *WhAm 6*
Wheelwright, Philip Ellis 1901-1970 *WhAm 5*
Wheelwright, Robert 1884-1965 *WhAm 4*
Wheelwright, Thomas Stewart 1866-1936
  NatCAB 27, WhAm 1
Wheelwright, William 1798-1873 *AmBi,
  ApCAB, DcAmB, McGEWB, WhAm H*
Wheelwright, William Dana 1849-1926
  NatCAB 16, NatCAB 26, WhAm 1
Wheildon, William Willder 1805- *ApCAB*
Whelan, Charles 1745?-1809 *ApCAB*
Whelan, Charles A 1863-1941 *WhAm 2*
Whelan, Charles Elbert 1862-1928 *WhAm 1*
Whelan, Edward J 1887-1971 *WhAm 5*
Whelan, James 1822-1878 *WhAm H*
Whelan, James 1823-1878 *ApCAB,
  NatCAB 12, TwCBDA*
Whelan, Peter 1800-1871 *ApCAB*
Whelan, Ralph 1852-1942 *WhAm 2*
Whelan, Richard Vincent 1809-1874 *ApCAB,
  NatCAB 10, TwCBDA, WhAm H*
Whelan, Roderick Joseph 1891-1961
  NatCAB 52
Wheland, Edward F 1878-1959 *WhAm 3*
Wheland, Zenas Windsor 1873-1957 *WhAm 3*
Whelchel, B Frank 1895-1954 *WhAm 3*
Whelchel, Benjamin Frank 1895-1954 *BiDrAC,
  WhAmP*
Whelchel, Clarence Anthony 1899-1972
  WhAm 6
Whelchel, Frederic Cooper 1891-1955
  NatCAB 45
Whelchel, John Esten 1898-1973 *WhAm 6*
Whelen, Thomas Duncan 1879-1931
  NatCAB 24
Whelen, Townsend 1877-1961 *WhAm 4*
Wheless, Joseph 1868-1950 *NatCAB 39,
  WhAm 5*
Whelpley, Benjamin Lincoln 1864- *WhAm 4*
Whelpley, Henry Milton 1861-1926 *DcAmB,
  NatCAB 20, WhAm 1*
Whelpley, James Davenport 1817-1872 *ApCAB*
Whelpley, James Davenport 1863- *WhAm 4*
Whelpley, Medley Gordon Brittain 1893-1968
  WhAm 5
Whelpley, Philip M *NewYHSD*
Whelpley, Philip Melancthon 1792-1824 *ApCAB,
  Drake*

Whelpley, Samuel 1766-1817 *ApCAB, Drake*
Whelpley, Thomas *NewYHSD*
Whelpton, Pascal Kidder 1893-1964 *WhAm 4*
Wherrett, Harry Scott 1876-1944 *NatCAB 34, WhAm 2*
Wherritt, Frank Dorsey 1889-1948 *NatCAB 37*
Wherry, Arthur Cornelius 1880-1944 *NatCAB 37, WhAm 2*
Wherry, Elwood Morris 1843-1927 *DcAmB, WhAm 1*
Wherry, Frank Gilbert 1922-1974 *WhAm 6*
Wherry, John 1837-1919 *WhAm 1*
Wherry, Kenneth Spicer 1892-1951 *BiDrAC, DcAmB S5, NatCAB 40, REnAW, WhAm 3, WhAmP*
Wherry, William Buchanan 1875-1936 *WhAm 1*
Wherry, William Mackey 1836-1918 *NatCAB 38, TwCBDA, WhAm 1*
Wherry, William Mackey, Jr. 1878-1960 *WhAm 4*
Whetstone, John S *NewYHSD*
Whetstone, Mary Snoddy *WomWWA 14*
Whetstone, Walter 1876-1940 *WhAm 1*
Whetting, John *NewYHSD*
Whetzel, Herbert Hice 1877-1944 *DcAmB S3, WhAm 2*
Whewell, William 1794-1866 *DcScB*
Whicher, George Frisbie 1889-1954 *WhAm 3*
Whicher, George Meason 1860-1937 *WhAm 1*
Whidden, Benjamin F *BiAUS*
Whidden, Bruce 1909-1972 *WhAm 5*
Whidden, Ray Allen 1878- *WhAm 6*
Whiddon, Rufus Carroll 1887-1950 *NatCAB 38*
Whiffen, Blanche Galton 1845-1936 *NotAW*
Whiffen, Lawrence Charles 1901-1960 *NatCAB 47*
Whiffen, Mrs. Thomas 1845-1936 *WhAm HA, WhAm 4*
Whigham, Henry James 1869-1954 *NatCAB 47, WhAm 3*
Whiley, Charles Whipple 1848- *WhAm 1*
Whinery, Joseph Burgess 1866-1957 *NatCAB 49*
Whinery, Samuel 1845-1925 *NatCAB 10, WhAm 1*
Whinnery, Abbie *WomWWA 14*
Whipple *NewYHSD*
Whipple, Abraham 1733-1819 *AmBi, ApCAB, DcAmB, Drake, NatCAB 2, TwCBDA, WebAMB, WhAm H*
Whipple, Allen Oldfather 1881-1963 *NatCAB 51, WhAm 4*
Whipple, Amiel Weeks 1816-1863 *DcAmB, WebAMB, WhAm H*
Whipple, Amiel Weeks 1817-1863 *Drake*
Whipple, Amiel Weeks 1818-1863 *ApCAB, NatCAB 10, TwCBDA*
Whipple, Carolyn Shipman *WomWWA 14*
Whipple, Charles Henry 1849-1932 *NatCAB 25, WhAm 1*
Whipple, Charles John 1885-1958 *NatCAB 49, WhAm 3*
Whipple, Charles Wiley 1805-1856 *BiAUS, NatCAB 5*
Whipple, Charles William 1846-1916 *NatCAB 17*
Whipple, Earle Rogers 1882-1939 *NatCAB 31*
Whipple, Edwin Percy 1819-1886 *AmBi, ApCAB, DcAmB, Drake, NatCAB 1, TwCBDA, WhAm H*
Whipple, Florence Brandenburg 1877- *WomWWA 14*
Whipple, Frances Harriet 1805-1878 *DcAmB*
Whipple, Frank E 1874- *NatCAB 17*
Whipple, Fred Lawrence 1906- *AsBiEn*
Whipple, George Chandler 1866-1924 *NatCAB 24, WhAm 1*
Whipple, George Hoyt 1878-1976 *AsBiEn, McGEWB, WebAB, WhAm 6*
Whipple, Gertrude Kimball 1867- *WomWWA 14*
Whipple, Guy Montrose 1876-1941 *BiDAmEd, NatCAB 31, WhAm 1*
Whipple, Harvey 1884-1952 *WhAm 3*
Whipple, Henry Benjamin 1822-1901 *AmBi, ApCAB, DcAmB, EncAAH, NatCAB 4, TwCBDA, WebAB*

Whipple, Henry Benjamin 1823-1901 *WhAm 1*
Whipple, Howard Gregory 1881-1959 *NatCAB 50, WhAm 6*
Whipple, Jay Northam 1897-1973 *WhAm 6*
Whipple, John Adams 1822- *ApCAB, NatCAB 7*
Whipple, Joseph Reed 1842- *NatCAB 4*
Whipple, Leonidas Rutledge 1882-1964 *WhAm 4*
Whipple, Lewis Erwin 1882-1959 *NatCAB 48*
Whipple, Lucius Albert 1887-1952 *NatCAB 41, WhAm 3*
Whipple, M Ella 1851- *AmWom*
Whipple, Oliver Mayhew 1901-1959 *WhAm 3*
Whipple, Ralph W 1890-1954 *WhAm 3*
Whipple, Sherman Leland 1862-1930 *DcAmB, NatCAB 26, WhAm 1*
Whipple, Squire 1804-1888 *AmBi, ApCAB, DcAmB, NatCAB 9, WhAm H*
Whipple, Thomas, Jr. 1787-1835 *BiAUS, BiDrAC, WhAm H, WhAmP*
Whipple, Wayne 1856-1942 *NatCAB 34, WhAm 2*
Whipple, William 1730-1785 *AmBi, ApCAB, BiAUS, BiDrAC, DcAmB, Drake, NatCAB 4, TwCBDA, WhAm H, WhAmP*
Whipple, William Denison 1826-1902 *ApCAB, NatCAB 4, TwCBDA, WhAm 1*
Whipple, William Denison 1830?-1902 *Drake*
Whipple, William G *WhAm 5*
Whisenand, James Franklin 1911-1967 *WhAm 4*
Whisnant, Albert Miller 1867-1963 *NatCAB 50*
Whistler, Daniel 1619-1684 *BiHiMed*
Whistler, George Washington 1800-1848 *WhAm H*
Whistler, George Washington 1800-1849 *ApCAB, DcAmB, Drake, NatCAB 1, NatCAB 9, NewYHSD, TwCBDA*
Whistler, George William 1822-1869 *ApCAB, NatCAB 9*
Whistler, James Abbott McNeill 1834-1903 *AmBi, ApCAB, BnEnAmA, DcAmB, EncAB, McGEWB, NatCAB 9, NewYHSD, TwCBDA, WebAB, WhAm H*
Whistler, John 1756?-1829 *ApCAB, NatCAB 9*
Whistler, Joseph Nelson Garland 1822-1899 *ApCAB, NatCAB 9, WhAm 1*
Whistler, William 1780-1863 *ApCAB, Drake*
Whiston, Frank Michael 1894-1970 *NatCAB 55, WhAm 5*
Whiston, William 1667-1752 *DcScB*
Whitacre, Frank Edward 1897-1971 *NatCAB 56, WhAm 5*
Whitacre, Horace J 1869-1944 *WhAm 2*
Whitacre, John Jefferson 1860-1938 *BiDrAC, WhAm 4*
Whitacre, Marion 1871-1938 *NatCAB 29*
Whitaker, Albert Conser 1877- *WhAm 5*
Whitaker, Alexander 1585- *Drake*
Whitaker, Alexander 1585-1613? *ApCAB*
Whitaker, Alexander 1585-1614? *NatCAB 7*
Whitaker, Alexander 1585-1616? *DcAmB, WhAm H*
Whitaker, Alice E 1851- *WomWWA 14*
Whitaker, Alma d1956 *WhAm 3*
Whitaker, Benjamin Palmer 1899-1974 *WhAm 6*
Whitaker, Charles *NewYHSD*
Whitaker, Charles Harris 1872-1938 *DcAmB S2, WhAm 1*
Whitaker, Charles Henry 1846-1926 *NatCAB 20*
Whitaker, Clem 1899-1961 *WhAm 4*
Whitaker, Daniel Kimball 1801-1881 *ApCAB, DcAmB, NatCAB 1, TwCBDA, WhAm H*
Whitaker, Douglas 1904-1973 *WhAm 6*
Whitaker, Edward Gascoigne 1853-1931 *WhAm 1*
Whitaker, Edward H 1808?- *NewYHSD*
Whitaker, Edwards 1848- *NatCAB 12, WhAm 4*
Whitaker, Eileen 1911- *IIBEAAW*
Whitaker, Elbert Coleman 1919-1971 *WhAm 6*
Whitaker, Epher 1820-1916 *ApCAB,*

NatCAB 17, *WhAm 1*
Whitaker, Frank M 1867-1939 *WhAm 1*
Whitaker, Frederic 1891- *IIBEAAW*
Whitaker, George 1836-1917 *WhAm 1*
Whitaker, George 1863-1925 *NatCAB 6*
Whitaker, Harriet Catherine Reed 1869-1967 *WhAm 4, WhAm 5*
Whitaker, Herbert Coleman 1862-1921 *WhAm 1*
Whitaker, Herman 1867-1919 *WhAm 1*
Whitaker, Herschel 1847-1900 *NatCAB 5*
Whitaker, Hervey Williams 1857-1937 *WhAm 1*
Whitaker, John Albert 1901-1951 *BiDrAC, NatCAB 41, WhAm 3, WhAmP*
Whitaker, John Thompson 1906-1946 *WhAm 2*
Whitaker, Lewis Alfred 1881- *WhAm 6*
Whitaker, Lily C 1850?- *ApCAB*
Whitaker, Lorenzo Robert 1899-1961 *NatCAB 49*
Whitaker, Martin D 1902-1960 *WhAm 4*
Whitaker, Mary Scrimgeour 1820- *NatCAB 1*
Whitaker, Mary Scrimzeour 1820- *ApCAB, WhAm 4*
Whitaker, Milton C 1870-1963 *NatCAB 50, WhAm 4*
Whitaker, Nathaniel 1730-1795 *DcAmB, WhAm H*
Whitaker, Nathaniel 1732-1795 *ApCAB, NatCAB 9, TwCBDA*
Whitaker, Nelson L 1878-1958 *WhAm 3*
Whitaker, Nelson Price 1874-1922 *NatCAB 22*
Whitaker, Nicholas Tillinghast 1840-1923 *WhAm 1*
Whitaker, Orvil R 1875- *WhAm 5*
Whitaker, Ozi William 1830-1911 *ApCAB, BiDAmEd, NatCAB 3, TwCBDA, WhAm 1*
Whitaker, Robert 1863-1944 *WhAm 2*
Whitaker, Samuel Adams 1876-1923 *NatCAB 26*
Whitaker, Samuel Estill 1886-1967 *WhAm 4*
Whitaker, Thomas Drake 1860-1896 *NatCAB 16*
Whitaker, U A 1900-1975 *WhAm 6*
Whitaker, Walter C 1823-1887 *ApCAB, TwCBDA*
Whitaker, Walter Claiborne 1867-1938 *WhAm 1*
Whitaker, Wayne Lewis 1904-1957 *NatCAB 49*
Whitaker, William Force 1853-1916 *NatCAB 17, WhAm 1*
Whitall, Samuel Rucker 1844-1919 *WhAm 1*
Whitbeck, R H 1871-1939 *WhAm 1*
Whitbeck, Sherwood Volkert 1879-1953 *NatCAB 42*
Whitby, Abraham Baxter 1868- *WhoColR*
Whitcher, Frances Miriam Berry 1811-1852 *ApCAB, NatCAB 6, NotAW, TwCBDA*
Whitcher, Frances Miriam Berry 1814-1852 *DcAmB, WhAm H*
Whitcher, Frank Weston 1855-1940 *WhAm 1*
Whitcher, Mary d1797 *WhAm H*
Whitchurch, Irl Goldwin 1889-1969 *WhAm 5*
Whitcomb, David 1879- *WhAm 6*
Whitcomb, David Twining 1928-1968 *WhAm 6*
Whitcomb, G Henry 1842-1916 *WhAm 1*
Whitcomb, George Herbert 1858-1933 *NatCAB 42*
Whitcomb, Ida Prentice d1931 *WhAm 1, WomWWA 14*
Whitcomb, James 1791-1852 *Drake*
Whitcomb, James 1795-1852 *ApCAB, BiAUS, BiDrAC, DcAmB, NatCAB 13, WhAm H, WhAmP*
Whitcomb, James Arthur 1854- *ApCAB X*
Whitcomb, James Scripps 1892-1963 *NatCAB 51*
Whitcomb, Jessie E Wright 1864- *WomWWA 14*
Whitcomb, John d1812 *Drake*
Whitcomb, John 1713-1785 *ApCAB*
Whitcomb, Merrick 1859- *WhAm 4*
Whitcomb, Selden Lincoln 1866-1930 *DcAmB, WhAm 1, WhAm 1C*
Whitcomb, Susan *NewYHSD*
Whitcomb, William Arthur 1873-1946 *WhAm 2*

Whitcomb, William Henry 1880-1956
NatCAB 44
White, Aaron Pancoast 1882-1945 *WhAm 2*
White, Addison 1824-1909 *BiAUS, BiDrAC,
WhAmP*
White, Albert Beebe 1871-1952 *WhAm 3*
White, Albert Blakeslee 1856-1941 *NatCAB 12,
TwCBDA, WhAm 1*
White, Albert Easton 1884-1956 *NatCAB 45,
WhAm 4*
White, Albert Smith 1803-1864 *ApCAB,
BiAUS, BiDrAC, DcAmB, NatCAB 3,
TwCBDA, WhAm H, WhAmP*
White, Alexander 1738-1804 *ApCAB, BiAUS,
BiDrAC, DcAmB, Drake, NatCAB 3,
TwCBDA, WhAm H, WhAmP*
White, Alexander 1814-1872 *ApCAB, DcAmB,
WhAm H*
White, Alexander 1816-1893 *ApCAB, BiAUS,
BiDrAC, WhAm H*
White, Mrs. Alexander B *WhAm 5*
White, Alexander Colwell 1833-1906 *BiDrAC*
White, Alexander Moss 1904-1968 *NatCAB 54,
WhAm 5*
White, Alfred Holmes 1873-1953 *NatCAB 49,
WhAm 3*
White, Alfred Ludlow 1850- *WhAm 4*
White, Alfred Tredway 1846-1921 *DcAmB,
EncAB, NatCAB 23, WhAm 1*
White, Allison 1816-1886 *BiAUS, BiDrAC,
WhAm H*
White, Alma Bridwell 1862-1946 *DcAmB S4,
DcAmReB, NatCAB 35, NotAW,
WhAm 2*
White, Alvan Newton 1869- *WhAm 2*
White, Amelia Elizabeth *WomWWA 14*
White, Amos *NewYHSD*
White, Andrew 1579-1656 *ApCAB, DcAmB,
DcAmReB, WhAm H*
White, Andrew Dickson 1832-1918 *AmBi,
ApCAB, ApCAB X, BiDAmEd, DcAmB,
Drake, EncAB, McGEWB, NatCAB 4,
TwCBDA, WebAB, WhAm 1*
White, Andrew John, Jr. 1901-1970 *WhAm 5*
White, Andrew Strong 1867-1952 *NatCAB 44*
White, Anna 1831-1910 *NotAW*
White, Anna Beatrice Goldstine *WomWWA 14*
White, Anthony Walton 1750-1803 *ApCAB,
NatCAB 1*
White, Anthony Walton 1751-1803 *Drake*
White, Arthur Cleveland 1891-1961 *WhAm 4*
White, Arthur Fairchild 1895-1940 *WhAm 1*
White, Arthur Weaver 1877-1945 *NatCAB 38*
White, Aubrey Lee 1869-1949 *WhAm 3*
White, Austin John 1892-1949 *NatCAB 38,
WhAm 2*
White, Bartow W 1776-1862 *BiAUS, BiDrAC,
WhAm H*
White, Beaver 1874- *WhAm 5*
White, Benjamin 1790-1860 *BiAUS, BiDrAC,
WhAm H*
White, Benjamin 1828?- *NewYHSD*
White, Benjamin Dey 1868-1946 *NatCAB 35*
White, Benjamin Franklin 1838- *NatCAB 11,
WhAm 4*
White, Bessie Bruce 1876- *WhAm 5*
White, Bouck 1874- *WhAm 5*
White, Byron Raymond 1917- *WebAB*
White, C Paul 1890-1966 *NatCAB 53*
White, Campbell Patrick 1787-1859 *BiAUS,
BiDrAC, WhAm H, WhAmP*
White, Canvass 1790-1834 *DcAmB,
NatCAB 12, WebAB, WhAm H*
White, Carlton 1860- *ApCAB X*
White, Caroline Earle 1833-1916 *WhAm 1*
White, Carolyn Hall 1854- *WomWWA 14*
White, Carrie Harper 1875- *WomWWA 14*
White, Cecil Fielding 1900- *BiDrAC*
White, Charles 1728-1813 *DcScB*
White, Charles 1795-1861 *ApCAB, Drake,
TwCBDA*
White, Charles Abiathar 1826-1910 *AmBi,
ApCAB, DcAmB, NatCAB 6, TwCBDA,
WhAm 1*
White, Charles Alexander 1899-1975 *WhAm 6*
White, Charles Braman 1826-1882 *NatCAB 13*
White, Charles Daniel 1879-1955 *WhAm 3*
White, Charles David 1862-1935 *DcScB*

White, Charles Davis 1860-1947 *NatCAB 35*
White, Charles Edgar 1868- *WhAm 4*
White, Charles Elliot 1864-1946 *NatCAB 34*
White, Charles Elmer, Jr. 1876-1936 *WhAm 1*
White, Charles Harrison 1888- *WhAm 2*
White, Charles Henry 1838-1914 *WhAm 1*
White, Charles Henry 1865-1952 *WhAm 3*
White, Charles Ignatius 1807-1877 *ApCAB*
White, Charles Ignatius 1807-1878 *DcAmB,
WhAm H*
White, Charles James 1868-1964 *NatCAB 53,
WhAm 4*
White, Charles Joyce 1839-1917 *WhAm 1*
White, Charles Lincoln 1863-1941 *NatCAB 13,
NatCAB 32, WhAm 1*
White, Charles Stanley 1877-1969 *WhAm 5*
White, Charles Thomas 1863-1954 *WhAm 3*
White, Chester Field 1852-1917 *NatCAB 17*
White, Chilton Allen 1826-1900 *BiAUS,
BiDrAC*
White, Clarence Bailey 1885-1950 *NatCAB 39*
White, Clarence Cameron 1879-1960 *WhoColR*
White, Clarence Cameron 1880-1960 *WhAm 4*
White, Clarence H 1874-1945 *NatCAB 35,
WhAm 2*
White, Clarence Henry 1848-1927 *NatCAB 29*
White, Clarence Hudson 1871-1925 *WhAm 1*
White, Clarence Hunt 1906-1964 *NatCAB 51*
White, Compton Ignatius 1877-1956 *BiDrAC,
WhAm 3, WhAmP*
White, Compton Ignatius, Jr. 1920- *BiDrAC*
White, Courtland Yardley, Jr. 1873-1938
WhAm 1
White, Daniel Appleton 1776-1861 *ApCAB,
TwCBDA*
White, Daniel Price 1814-1890 *BiDConf*
White, David 1785-1834 *BiDrAC, WhAm H*
White, David 1785-1835 *BiAUS*
White, David 1862-1935 *DcAmB S1,
NatCAB 18, WebAB, WhAm 1*
White, David Nye 1805-1888 *ApCAB*
White, David Stuart 1869-1944 *WhAm 2*
White, D'Orsay McCall 1880-1950 *NatCAB 17,
NatCAB 39*
White, Dudley Allen 1901-1957 *BiDrAC,
WhAm 3*
White, Duke *NewYHSD*
White, E Laurence 1884-1968 *WhAm 5*
White, Ebenezer Baker 1806-1888 *NewYHSD*
White, Edmund Valentine 1879-1955 *WhAm 3*
White, Edward Albert 1872-1943 *WhAm 2*
White, Edward B *NewYHSD*
White, Edward Brickell 1806-1882 *ApCAB,
WhAm H*
White, Edward D 1795-1847 *BiAUS, Drake*
White, Edward Douglas 1795-1847 *ApCAB,
NatCAB 10*
White, Edward Douglas 1845-1921 *ApCAB,
NatCAB 11, NatCAB 21*
White, Edward Douglass 1795-1847 *BiDrAC,
DcAmB, TwCBDA, WhAm H*
White, Edward Douglass 1845-1921 *AmBi,
BiDrAC, DcAmB, EncAB, McGEWB,
TwCBDA, WebAB, WhAm 1, WhAmP*
White, Edward Franklin 1858-1932 *WhAm 1*
White, Edward Higgins, II 1930-1967 *WhAm 4*
White, Edward Hollingsworth 1855-1899
NatCAB 13
White, Edward Joseph 1869-1935 *NatCAB 30,
WhAm 1*
White, Edward Joseph 1891-1959 *NatCAB 52*
White, Edward Lane 1857-1922 *ApCAB X*
White, Edward Lucas 1866-1934 *NatCAB 18,
WhAm 1*
White, Edwin 1817-1877 *AmBi, ApCAB,
NatCAB 14, NewYHSD, TwCBDA*
White, Edwin 1842-1903 *TwCBDA*
White, Edwin 1843-1903 *WhAm 1*
White, Edwin 1882-1951 *NatCAB 40,
WhAm 3*
White, Edwin Augustine 1854-1925 *WhAm 1*
White, Egbert 1894-1976 *WhAm 6*
White, Elijah B 1864-1926 *WhAm 1*
White, Eliza Matilda Chandler 1831-1907
BiCAW
White, Eliza Orne 1856-1947 *NatCAB 13,
NotAW, TwCBDA, WhAm 2,
WomWWA 14*

White, Ellen Gould Harmon 1827-1915 *DcAmB,
DcAmReB, NotAW, WhAm HA,
WhAm 4*
White, Ellen Pawling Corson *WomWWA 14*
White, Elsie Hadley 1864- *WomWWA 14*
White, Elwyn Brooks 1899- *WebAB*
White, Emerson Elbridge 1829-1902 *ApCAB,
BiDAmEd, DcAmB, NatCAB 13,
TwCBDA, WhAm 1*
White, Emily Thorn Vanderbilt Sloane
1852-1946 *NatCAB 35*
White, Emma Eaton 1868- *WhAm 5*
White, Emma Ruth 1884- *WomWWA 14*
White, Emma Siggins *WomWWA 14*
White, Emory Calvin 1857- *TwCBDA*
White, Emory Calvin 1858- *ApCAB*
White, Ernest Ingersol 1869-1957 *NatCAB 47*
White, Erskine Norman 1833-1911 *WhAm 1*
White, Esther Griffin *WomWWA 14*
White, Eugene Leslie 1891-1951 *NatCAB 45*
White, Ferdinand Roebling 1907-1971
NatCAB 57
White, Florence Donnell 1882-1950 *WhAm 3*
White, Florence Smith 1861- *WomWWA 14*
White, Floyd Garrison 1879-1945 *NatCAB 33*
White, Fortune C 1787-1866 *BiAUS*
White, Frances Hodges 1866- *WhAm 4,
WomWWA 14*
White, Francis d1826 *BiAUS, BiDrAC,
WhAm H*
White, Francis 1825-1904 *ApCAB X*
White, Francis 1892-1961 *WhAm 4*
White, Francis J 1842-1875 *ApCAB*
White, Francis Johnstone 1870- *WhAm 5*
White, Francis Samuel 1868-1934 *WhAm 1*
White, Francis Shelley 1847-1922 *BiDrAC*
White, Francis W 1893-1957 *WhAm 3*
White, Frank 1856-1940 *NatCAB 13,
TwCBDA, WhAm 1*
White, Frank 1858-1927 *WhAm 1*
White, Frank Edson 1873-1931 *WhAm 1*
White, Frank Edson 1873-1932 *NatCAB 23*
White, Frank J 1842-1875 *NatCAB 4*
White, Frank Marshall 1861- *WhAm 4*
White, Frank Newhall 1858-1926 *WhAm 1*
White, Frank Russell 1875-1913 *WhAm 1*
White, Frank Shelley 1847-1922 *NatCAB 29,
WhAm 1*
White, Frank Thomas Matthews 1909-1971
WhAm 6
White, Franklin *NewYHSD*
White, Fred Rollin 1872-1936 *NatCAB 27*
White, Frederic Charles 1867-1948 *NatCAB 37*
White, Frederick Edward 1844-1920 *BiDrAC*
White, Frederick W 1863-1937 *WhAm 1*
White, Fritz *IlBEAAW*
White, G Derby 1870-1939 *NatCAB 27*
White, Gaylord Starin 1864-1931 *WhAm 1*
White, George *NewYHSD*
White, George 1802-1887 *DcAmB, WhAm H*
White, George 1872-1953 *BiDrAC,
NatCAB 41, WhAm 3, WhAmP*
White, George Ared 1881- *WhAm 2*
White, George Avery 1896-1951 *WhAm 3*
White, George Edward 1861-1946 *WhAm 2*
White, George Elon 1848-1935 *BiDrAC*
White, George Frederic 1885-1929 *WhAm 1*
White, George Gorgas 1835?-1898 *IlBEAAW,
NewYHSD*
White, George Harlow 1817-1888 *IlBEAAW*
White, George Harvey 1872-1936 *NatCAB 27*
White, George Henry 1852-1918 *BiDrAC,
WhAmP, WhoColR*
White, George Irwine *NewYHSD*
White, George Leonard 1838-1895 *ApCAB,
DcAmB, WebAB, WhAm H*
White, George Loring 1872- *WhAm 5*
White, George R 1811?- *NewYHSD*
White, George Robert 1847-1922 *ApCAB X,
NatCAB 32*
White, George Savage 1784-1850 *ApCAB,
NatCAB 4*
White, George Starr 1866- *WhAm 4*
White, George T *NewYHSD*
White, George W *NewYHSD*
White, George W 1826-1890 *NewYHSD,
WhAm H*
White, George Walker 1883-1965 *NatCAB 53*

White, George Washington 1858-1940 *WhAm 1*
White, George Whitney 1870-1938 *NatCAB 29,*
WhAm 1
White, Georgia Laura 1872-1949 *WhAm 3,*
WomWWA 14
White, Gilbert 1720-1793 *DcScB*
White, Gilbert 1877-1939 *AmBi, WhAm 1*
White, Grace Peckham Baldwin 1874-
WomWWA 14
White, Greenough 1863-1901 *NatCAB 11,*
WhAm 1
White, H Lee 1912-1971 *WhAm 5*
White, Hamilton Salisbury 1853-1899
NatCAB 33
White, Harold Tredway 1875-1960 *WhAm 4*
White, Harrie Clinton 1876-1954 *NatCAB 44*
White, Harry 1834-1920 *ApCAB, BiDrAC*
White, Harry 1878-1955 *WhAm 3*
White, Harry A 1883-1949 *NatCAB 39*
White, Harry Dexter 1892-1948 *WhAm HA,*
WhAm 2, WhAm 4A
White, Hays Baxter 1855-1930 *BiDrAC,*
WhAm 1, WhAmP
White, Helen Constance 1896-1967 *NatCAB 53,*
WhAm 4
White, Helen Magill 1853-1944 *NotAW,*
WomWWA 14
White, Helene Maynard *WomWWA 14*
White, Henry 1720?-1786 *NatCAB 1*
White, Henry 1732-1786 *DcAmB, WhAm H*
White, Henry 1790-1858 *ApCAB*
White, Henry 1800-1850 *NatCAB 7,*
WhAm H
White, Henry 1850-1927 *AmBi, ApCAB X,*
DcAmB, NatCAB 14, WhAm 1
White, Henry Adelbert 1880-1951 *WhAm 3*
White, Henry Alexander 1861-1926 *WhAm 1*
White, Henry Clay 1838-1905 *NatCAB 17,*
WhAm 1
White, Henry Clay 1848-1927 *DcAmB,*
WhAm 1
White, Henry Clay 1850-1927 *ApCAB,*
NatCAB 9, TwCBDA
White, Henry Cooke 1861-1952 *NatCAB 48*
White, Henry Dale 1869- *WhAm 5*
White, Henry F *NewYHSD*
White, Henry Ford d1966 *WhAm 4*
White, Henry Middleton 1874-1950 *WhAm 3*
White, Henry Schroeder Taylor 1903-1944
NatCAB 33
White, Henry Seely 1861-1943 *NatCAB 14,*
NatCAB 33, WhAm 2
White, Herbert Humphrey 1858-1934 *WhAm 1*
White, Herbert Judson 1864-1945 *WhAm 2*
White, Hervey 1866- *WhAm 4*
White, Horace 1834-1916 *AmBi, ApCAB,*
DcAmB, NatCAB 10, TwCBDA,
WhAm 1
White, Horace 1865-1943 *NatCAB 16,*
WhAm 2
White, Horace Glenn 1886-1965 *NatCAB 51*
White, Horace Greeley 1873-1934 *WhAm 1*
White, Horace Henry 1864-1946 *WhAm 2*
White, Horatio Stevens 1852-1934 *AmBi,*
NatCAB 4, WhAm 1
White, Howard Ganson 1856- *NatCAB 5,*
WhAm 4
White, Howard Judson 1870-1936 *NatCAB 26,*
WhAm 1
White, Howard Julian 1884-1963 *NatCAB 50*
White, Hugh 1737-1822 *ApCAB*
White, Hugh 1798-1870 *BiDrAC, WhAm H*
White, Hugh 1799-1870 *BiAUS*
White, Hugh 1876-1936 *ApCAB X, WhAm 1*
White, Hugh Lawson 1773-1840 *AmBi,*
ApCAB, BiAUS, BiDrAC, DcAmB,
Drake, NatCAB 11, TwCBDA, WhAm H,
WhAmP
White, Hugh Lawson 1881-1965 *WhAm 4*
White, Hutchins Mark 1879- *WhAm 6*
White, Ike D 1867- *WhAm 5*
White, Isaac Deforest 1864- *WhAm 4*
White, Israel Charles 1848-1927 *AmBi,*
ApCAB, DcAmB, DcScB, NatCAB 13,
NatCAB 18, WhAm 1
White, J *NewYHSD*
White, J Harrison 1840- *WhAm 4*
White, J Harry 1889-1966 *NatCAB 53*

White, J Harvey 1875-1946 *NatCAB 34*
White, J Russell 1892-1948 *NatCAB 37*
White, Jacob Lee 1862-1948 *WhAm 2*
White, James *BiAUS*
White, James 1737-1815 *ApCAB, NatCAB 11,*
TwCBDA
White, James 1747-1821 *DcAmB, WhAm H*
White, James 1749-1809 *BiDrAC, REnAW,*
WhAm H, WhAmP
White, James Alexander 1872-1949 *NatCAB 41,*
WhAm 2
White, James Andrew 1859-1932 *WhAm 1*
White, James Bain 1835-1897 *BiDrAC,*
WhAm H
White, James Bamford 1842-1931 *BiDrAC*
White, James Barlow 1897-1964 *WhAm 4*
White, James Charles 1889-1973 *WhAm 5*
White, James Clarke 1833-1915 *NatCAB 19*
White, James Clarke 1833-1916 *DcAmB,*
WhAm 1
White, James Dempsey 1831- *WhAm 4*
White, James Garrard 1846-1913 *NatCAB 15*
White, James Gilbert 1861-1942 *NatCAB 15,*
WhAm 2
White, James Halley 1906-1967 *WhAm 5*
White, James McLaren 1867-1933 *NatCAB 24,*
WhAm 1
White, James Penfield 1844-1894 *NatCAB 7*
White, James Platt 1811-1881 *NatCAB 7*
White, James Randall *WhoColR A*
White, James Terry 1845-1920 *NatCAB 19,*
WhAm 1
White, James W 1807-1867 *BiAUS*
White, James Watson 1876-1946 *WhAm 2*
White, James William 1850-1916 *DcAmB,*
NatCAB 17, WhAm 1
White, Jasper Newton 1866-1949 *NatCAB 38*
White, Jay 1869-1918 *WhAm 1*
White, Jay Henry 1875-1959 *NatCAB 49*
White, Jesse Hayes 1877-1969 *NatCAB 54,*
WhAm 5
White, Jessie Carter 1865- *WomWWA 14*
White, Joan Fulton 1923-1973 *WhAm 6*
White, Joel 1808- *NatCAB 7*
White, Joel Jesse 1890-1966 *NatCAB 53*
White, John d1780? *ApCAB, Drake*
White, John 1550?-1593? *BnEnAmA, DcAmB,*
IIBEAAW, NewYHSD, WebAB,
WhAm H
White, John 1574-1648 *Drake*
White, John 1575-1648 *ApCAB, NatCAB 5,*
WhAm H
White, John 1590-1645 *ApCAB*
White, John 1677-1760 *ApCAB*
White, John 1802-1845 *BiDrAC, NatCAB 13,*
WhAm H, WhAmP
White, John 1805-1845 *ApCAB, BiAUS,*
Drake, NatCAB 12, TwCBDA
White, John Baker 1868- *WhAm 4*
White, John Barber 1847-1923 *NatCAB 15,*
WhAm 1
White, John Barker 1847-1923 *ApCAB X*
White, John Blake 1781-1857 *NatCAB 3*
White, John Blake 1781-1859 *AmBi, ApCAB,*
DcAmB, Drake, NewYHSD, TwCBDA,
WhAm H
White, John Blake 1850- *NatCAB 3,*
WhAm 4
White, John Campbell 1870-1962 *NatCAB 47,*
WhAm 4
White, John Campbell 1884-1967 *NatCAB 54,*
WhAm 4
White, John Chanler 1867-1956 *NatCAB 43,*
WhAm 3
White, John Daugherty 1849-1920 *BiDrAC,*
WhAmP
White, John DeHaven 1815-1895 *DcAmB,*
WhAm H
White, John Ellington 1868-1931 *WhAm 1*
White, John Franklin 1853-1945 *NatCAB 34*
White, John Griswold 1845-1928 *NatCAB 22,*
WhAm 1
White, John Hazen 1849-1925 *ApCAB Sup,*
NatCAB 13, NatCAB 26, TwCBDA,
WhAm 1
White, John Josiah 1863-1930 *ApCAB X*
White, John P 1915-1969 *WhAm 5*
White, John Phillip 1870- *WhAm 5*

White, John Roberts 1879-1961 *WhAm 4*
White, John Silas 1847-1922 *ApCAB*
White, John Stuart 1847-1922 *BiDAmEd,*
NatCAB 2, WhAm 1
White, John Turner 1854- *WhAm 2*
White, John W 1889-1951 *WhAm 3*
White, John Williams 1849-1917 *ApCAB,*
DcAmB, NatCAB 12, WhAm 1
White, John Z 1854- *WhAm 4*
White, Joseph *NewYHSD*
White, Joseph Augustus 1848-1941 *NatCAB 32,*
WhAm 4
White, Joseph Hill 1859-1953 *NatCAB 40,*
WhAm 5
White, Joseph Huntington 1824-1915
NatCAB 17
White, Joseph Josiah 1846-1924 *NatCAB 22*
White, Joseph Livingston d1861 *BiAUS,*
BiDrAC, WhAm H
White, Joseph M 1781-1839 *ApCAB, BiAUS,*
BiDrAC, Drake, WhAm H, WhAmP
White, Joseph Warren 1892-1959 *WhAm 4*
White, Joseph Worthington 1822-1892 *BiAUS,*
BiDrAC, WhAm H
White, Josh 1908- *WhAm 5*
White, Joshua Warren 1875-1953 *WhAm 3*
White, Josiah *NewYHSD*
White, Josiah 1841-1914 *ApCAB X,*
NatCAB 31
White, Julius 1816- *BiAUS*
White, Julius 1816-1890 *ApCAB*
White, Julius 1816-1893 *NatCAB 4*
White, Justin DuPratt 1869-1939 *WhAm 1*
White, Kathleen Merell 1889-1973 *WhAm 6*
White, Kemble 1873- *WhAm 5*
White, Ken Ray 1919-1963 *NatCAB 50*
White, Kent 1860-1940 *NatCAB 35*
White, Laura Rogers 1852- *WomWWA 14*
White, Laura Rosamond *AmWom*
White, Lawrence Grant 1887-1956 *WhAm 3*
White, Lazarus 1874-1953 *NatCAB 47,*
WhAm 3
White, Lee A 1886-1971 *WhAm 5*
White, Lemuel *NewYHSD*
White, Leonard 1767-1849 *BiAUS, BiDrAC,*
WhAm H
White, Leonard Dalton 1833- *NatCAB 3*
White, Leonard Dalton 1867-1963 *NatCAB 50*
White, Leonard Dupee 1891-1958 *BiDAmEd,*
NatCAB 44, WhAm 3
White, Leslie Alvin 1900-1975 *WhAm 6*
White, Lewis Charles 1915-1973 *WhAm 6*
White, Llewellyn Brooke 1899-1959 *WhAm 3*
White, Lorenzo d1834 *NewYHSD*
White, Louise Lyman Peck 1881-
WomWWA 14
White, Lucien 1914-1975 *WhAm 6*
White, Lucy Elizabeth 1871- *WomWWA 14*
White, Luke Matthews 1877-1955 *WhAm 3*
White, Luther 1841-1914 *NatCAB 16*
White, Luther Clark 1867-1926 *NatCAB 21*
White, Lynn Townsend 1876-1953 *WhAm 3*
White, Lynne Loraine 1889-1964 *WhAm 4*
White, M *NewYHSD*
White, Mabel Reynolds 1872- *WomWWA 14*
White, Mabel Townley *WomWWA 14*
White, Marcus 1861-1930 *WhAm 1*
White, Margaret *WebAB*
White, Marian Ainsworth *WhAm 5*
White, Martha Evelyn Davis 1863- *BiCAW,*
WomWWA 14
White, Martha Root *WomWWA 14*
White, Mary Houghton 1856- *WomWWA 14*
White, Matthew, Jr. 1857-1940 *WhAm 1*
White, Melvin Johnson 1877-1931 *NatCAB 23*
White, Michael Alfred Edwin 1866- *WhAm 4*
White, Michael Doherty 1827-1917 *BiDrAC*
White, Michael Edward 1861-1942 *NatCAB 41*
White, Milo 1830-1913 *BiDrAC*
White, Minor 1908- *BnEnAmA*
White, Mordecai Morris 1830-1913 *NatCAB 12,*
NatCAB 22
White, Morris 1888-1962 *NatCAB 48*
White, Nathan F *NewYHSD*
White, Nathaniel 1811-1880 *NatCAB 2*
White, Nehemiah 1835- *WhAm 1*
White, Nelia Gardner 1894-1957 *NatCAB 44,*
WhAm 3

White, Nettie L *AmWom*

White, Newman Ivey 1892-1948 *NatCAB 37,*
WhAm 2

White, Octavius Augustus 1826-1903 *ApCAB,*
NatCAB 3, WhAm 1

White, Oliver Wilson 1876- *NatCAB 16*

White, Orrin Augustine 1883-1969 *IlBEAAW*

White, Otis Converse 1874-1957 *NatCAB 46*

White, Patrick Victor Martindale 1912-
McGEWB

White, Paul Amos 1884-1955 *NatCAB 47*

White, Paul Dudley 1886-1973 *WhAm 6*

White, Paul Lambert 1890-1922 *NatCAB 6*

White, Paul W 1902-1955 *WhAm 3*

White, Pearl 1889-1938 *DcAmB S2, NotAW,*
WhAm HA, WhAm 4

White, Percival 1887-1970 *WhAm 5*

White, Peregrine 1620-1704 *ApCAB, Drake*

White, Peregrine 1620-1724 *AmBi*

White, Peter 1830-1908 *WhAm 1*

White, Peter 1831-1908 *REnAW*

White, Philip 1901-1968 *WhAm 5*

White, Phillips d1811 *BiAUS*

White, Phillips 1729-1811 *BiDrAC, TwCBDA,*
WhAm H

White, Phillips 1730?-1811 *ApCAB*

White, Philo 1796-1874 *BiAUS, NatCAB 5*

White, Phineas 1770-1847 *BiAUS, BiDrAC,*
WhAm H

White, Pliny Holton 1822-1869 *ApCAB, Drake*

White, Raleigh Richardson 1872-1917
NatCAB 36

White, Ralph Huntington 1841-1917
NatCAB 18

White, Ralston Lovell 1877-1943 *NatCAB 36*

White, Rassie Hoskins *WomWWA 14*

White, Ray Bridwell 1892-1946 *NatCAB 35,*
WhAm 2

White, Rhoda M *WomWWA 14*

White, Richard 1834- *ApCAB*

White, Richard Crawford 1923- *BiDrAC*

White, Richard Grant 1821-1885 *AmBi,*
ApCAB, DcAmB, TwCBDA, WhAm H

White, Richard Grant 1822-1885 *Drake,*
NatCAB 1

White, Richard Janney 1867-1929 *NatCAB 21*

White, Robe Carl 1869-1951 *WhAm 3*

White, Robert 1833-1916 *WhAm 1*

White, Robert Charles 1884-1965 *NatCAB 51*

White, Robert Gray 1807-1878 *ApCAB*

White, Robert Vose 1886-1960 *WhAm 4*

White, Rodney Douglas 1883-1964 *WhAm 4*

White, Rollin Charles 1837-1920 *NatCAB 24*

White, Rollin Henry 1872-1962 *NatCAB 52,*
WhAm 4

White, Rosalie Raymond 1857- *WomWWA 14*

White, Roswell N *NewYHSD*

White, Roy Barton 1883-1961 *WhAm 4*

White, Rufus Austin d1937 *WhAm 1*

White, S Etelka d1973 *WhAm 6*

White, S Marx 1873-1966 *WhAm 4*

White, Sallie Joy d1909 *WhAm 1*

White, Samuel d1809 *BiAUS*

White, Samuel 1762-1809 *TwCBDA*

White, Samuel 1770-1809 *ApCAB, BiDrAC,*
DcAmB, NatCAB 13, WhAm H

White, Samuel Holmes 1830-1882 *BiDAmEd,*
NatCAB 13

White, Samuel Stockton 1822-1879 *DcAmB,*
WhAm H

White, Sebastian Harrison 1864-1945 *BiDrAC,*
NatCAB 39, NatCAB 47, WhAm 2,
WhAmP

White, Stanford 1853-1906 *AmBi, ApCAB,*
BnEnAmA, DcAmB, EncAB, McGEWB,
NatCAB 11, NatCAB 23, TwCBDA,
WebAB, WhAm 1

White, Stanley 1862-1930 *WhAm 1*

White, Stephen Mallory 1853-1901 *ApCAB Sup,*
BiDrAC, DcAmB, EncAAH, NatCAB 12,
TwCBDA, WhAm 1

White, Stephen VanCulen 1831- *ApCAB*

White, Stephen VanCulen 1831-1912 *WhAm 1*

White, Stephen VanCulen 1831-1913 *BiDrAC,*
DcAmB

White, Stephen VanCullen 1831- *NatCAB 5*

White, Stewart Edward 1873-1946 *DcAmB S4,*
NatCAB 13, REnAW, TwCBDA,

WhAm 2

White, Sue Shelton 1887-1943 *NotAW*

White, Terence Hanbury 1906-1964 *WhAm 4*

White, Theodore Albert 1892-1966 *NatCAB 53*

White, Theophilus 1876-1950 *NatCAB 39*

White, Theresa Bryant 1867- *WomWWA 14*

White, Thomas d1866 *BiAUS*

White, Thomas 1593-1676 *DcScB*

White, Thomas 1804-1896 *ApCAB X*

White, Thomas 1830-1888 *ApCAB*

White, Thomas Dresser 1901-1965 *WebAMB,*
WhAm 4

White, Thomas Gilbert 1877-1939 *AmBi,*
IlBEAAW

White, Thomas Henry 1869- *WhoColR*

White, Thomas Holden 1894-1951 *WhAm 3*

White, Thomas Howard 1836-1914 *NatCAB 21*

White, Thomas Jefferson 1890-1958
NatCAB 45

White, Thomas Justin 1884-1948 *WhAm 2*

White, Thomas Raeburn 1875-1959 *WhAm 3A*

White, Thomas Riddick 1893-1970 *NatCAB 54*

White, Thomas Willis 1788-1843 *DcAmB,*
WhAm H

White, Trentwell Mason 1901-1959 *NatCAB 48,*
WhAm 3

White, Trueman Clark 1840-1912 *WhAm 1*

White, Trumbull 1868-1941 *WhAm 1,*
WhAm 2

White, Verner Moore 1863-1923 *NatCAB 20*

White, W Culver 1907-1948 *NatCAB 37*

White, W King 1901-1947 *WhAm 2*

White, Wallace Humphrey, Jr. 1877-1952
BiDrAC, NatCAB 39, WhAm 3, WhAmP

White, Walter Charles 1876-1929 *NatCAB 21,*
WhAm 1

White, Walter Francis 1893-1955 *DcAmB S5,*
EncAB, NatCAB 40, WebAB, WhAm 3

White, Walter Louis d1963 *WhAm 4*

White, Walter Porter 1867-1946 *NatCAB 33,*
WhAm 2

White, Walter William 1900-1969 *NatCAB 55,*
WhAm 5

White, Weldon Bailey 1907-1967 *WhAm 4*

White, Wendelyn Florence Wheeler 1939-1973
WhAm 6

White, Wilbert Webster 1863-1944 *WhAm 2*

White, Wilbur McKee 1890- *BiDrAC*

White, Wilbur Wallace 1903-1950 *WhAm 3*

White, William *NewYHSD*

White, William 1748-1836 *AmBi, ApCAB,*
DcAmB, DcAmReB, Drake, NatCAB 3,
WebAB, WhAm H

White, William 1822-1883 *NatCAB 4*

White, William 1830- *ApCAB*

White, William 1897-1967 *WhAm 4*

White, William Alanson 1870-1937 *AmBi,*
DcAmB S2, McGEWB, NatCAB 38,
WhAm 1

White, William Alfred 1876- *WhAm 5*

White, William Allen 1868-1944 *ApCAB X,*
DcAmB S3, EncAAH, EncAB, McGEWB,
NatCAB 11, REnAW, WebAB, WhAm 2

White, William Augustus 1843-1927
NatCAB 34

White, William Braid 1878-1959 *NatCAB 44*

White, William Chapman 1903-1955 *WhAm 3*

White, William Charles 1777-1818 *ApCAB,*
Drake

White, William Charles 1874-1947 *WhAm 2*

White, William Comings 1890-1965
NatCAB 51

White, William Crawford 1886-1962 *WhAm 4*

White, William Dwight 1849-1921 *NatCAB 20*

White, William E 1861-1935 *WhAm 1*

White, William Francis 1890-1959 *NatCAB 48*

White, William Fullerton 1867- *ApCAB X*

White, William G *NewYHSD*

White, William Henry 1823-1880 *NatCAB 5*

White, William Henry 1847-1920 *WhAm 1*

White, William Henry, Jr. 1881- *WhAm 6*

White, William Jacob Peter 1872-1936
NatCAB 28

White, William James *NewYHSD*

White, William John 1850-1923 *BiDrAC,*
NatCAB 2

White, William Lawrence 1908-1952 *WhAm 3*

White, William Lindsay 1900-1973 *WhAm 5,*

WhAm 6

White, William Mathews 1911-1966
NatCAB 53, WhAm 4

White, William Monroe 1871-1949 *NatCAB 51,*
WhAm 2

White, William Nathaniel 1819-1867 *ApCAB,*
DcAmB, WhAm H

White, William Parker 1865- *WhAm 2*

White, William Pierrepont 1867-1938 *WhAm 1*

White, William Plunkett 1885-1973 *NatCAB 57*

White, William Porter 1859-1926 *NatCAB 21*

White, William Prescott 1840- *WhAm 4*

White, William Townsend 1878-1957
NatCAB 42

White, William Wallace 1862-1944 *NatCAB 33,*
WhAm 2

White, William Wilson 1906-1964 *WhAm 4*

White, William Wurts 1909-1969 *WhAm 5*

White, Wilson Henry Stout 1881- *WhAm 6*

White, Windsor T 1866-1958 *WhAm 3*

White Bear 1869- *IlBEAAW*

White Bear 1906- *IlBEAAW*

White Eyes d1778 *DcAmB, WhAm H*

Whiteaker, John 1820-1902 *BiDrAC,*
NatCAB 8, WhAmP

Whiteaker, Robert O 1882-1959 *WhAm 3*

Whiteaves, Joseph Frederick 1835- *ApCAB*

Whitebrook, Lloyd George 1919-1962 *WhAm 4*

Whitechurch, Robert 1814-1880? *NewYHSD*

Whitefield, Charles T *WebAB*

Whitefield, Edwin 1816-1892 *IlBEAAW,*
NewYHSD, WhAm H

Whitefield, George 1714-1770 *AmBi, ApCAB,*
DcAmB, DcAmReB, Drake, EncAB,
McGEWB, NatCAB 5, TwCBDA

Whitefield, George 1715-1770 *EncAAH,*
WhAm H

Whitefield, J W 1818-1879 *BiAUS*

Whitefield, J W *see also* Whitfield John Wilkins

Whitefield, James d1875 *BiAUS*

Whitefield, James 1770-1834 *Drake*

Whitefield, James *see also* Whitfield, James

Whiteford, G H 1876-1947 *WhAm 2*

Whiteford, Robert Naylor 1870-1959
NatCAB 48

Whiteford, Robert Naylor *see also* Whitford,
Robert Naylor

Whiteford, Roger J 1886-1965 *WhAm 4*

Whiteford, William Kepler 1900-1968
NatCAB 56, WhAm 5

Whitehair, Charles Wesley 1887-1933 *WhAm 1*

Whitehead, Alfred North 1861-1947 *AsBiEn,*
DcAmB S4, DcScB, EncAB, McGEWB,
NatCAB 37, WebAB, WhAm 2

Whitehead, Asa Carter 1904-1976 *WhAm 6*

Whitehead, Cabell 1863-1908 *WhAm 1*

Whitehead, Charles Nelson 1878-1926
NatCAB 24, WhAm 1

Whitehead, Cortlandt 1842-1922 *ApCAB,*
NatCAB 3, TwCBDA, WhAm 1

Whitehead, Donald Strehle 1888-1957 *WhAm 3*

Whitehead, Edwin Kirby 1861- *WhAm 4*

Whitehead, Ennis Clement 1895-1964 *WhAm 4*

Whitehead, Harold 1880- *WhAm 6*

Whitehead, Henry C 1873- *WhAm 5*

Whitehead, Ira C 1798-1867 *BiAUS*

Whitehead, James Thomas 1864-1930 *WhAm 1*

Whitehead, John 1819-1905 *NatCAB 6*

Whitehead, John 1850-1930 *WhAm 1*

Whitehead, John Boswell 1872-1954
NatCAB 46, WhAm 3

Whitehead, John Henry Constantine 1904-1960
DcScB

Whitehead, John Meek 1852-1924 *NatCAB 36,*
WhAm 1

Whitehead, Joseph 1867-1938 *BiDrAC,*
NatCAB 29, WhAm 4

Whitehead, Laura Wadsworth 1871-
WomWWA 14

Whitehead, Lewis Emory 1890-1936
NatCAB 33

Whitehead, Ralph Radcliffe 1854-1929
WhAm 1

Whitehead, Reah Mary *BiCAW*

Whitehead, Richard Henry 1865-1916 *WhAm 1*

Whitehead, Robert Frederick 1869-1951
NatCAB 38, NatCAB 47, WhAm 5

Whitehead, T North 1891-1969 *WhAm 5*

Whitehead, Thomas 1825-1901 *BiAUS, BiDrAC*

Whitehead, Wilbur Cherrier 1866-1931 *DcAmB, WhAm HA, WhAm 4*

Whitehead, William Adee 1810-1884 *ApCAB, DcAmB, Drake, WhAm H*

Whitehead, William Riddick 1831- *NatCAB 10*

Whitehill, Clarence Eugene 1871-1932 *AmBi, DcAmB, NatCAB 14, WhAm 1*

Whitehill, Clyde Emerson 1879-1952 *NatCAB 40*

Whitehill, Howard Joseph 1894-1963 *WhAm 4*

Whitehill, James 1762-1822 *BiAUS, BiDrAC, WhAm H, WhAmP*

Whitehill, James Lorrin 1897-1955 *NatCAB 47*

Whitehill, John 1729-1815 *BiAUS, BiDrAC, WhAm H, WhAmP*

Whitehill, Robert 1738-1813 *ApCAB, BiAUS, BiDrAC, DcAmB, WhAm H, WhAmP*

Whitehorne, Earl 1881-1941 *WhAm 1*

Whitehorne, James A 1803-1888 *ApCAB, NewYHSD*

Whitehouse, Brooks 1904-1969 *NatCAB 55, WhAm 5*

Whitehouse, Fitz Hugh 1842-1909 *NatCAB 43*

Whitehouse, Florence Brooks *WhAm 5, WomWWA 14*

Whitehouse, Francis Meredyth 1848-1938 *NatCAB 28*

Whitehouse, Frederic Cope 1842-1911 *DcAmB, WhAm 1*

Whitehouse, Henry Howard 1864-1938 *NatCAB 37*

Whitehouse, Henry John 1803-1874 *ApCAB, Drake, NatCAB 11, TwCBDA*

Whitehouse, Henry Remsen 1857-1935 *NatCAB 26, WhAm 4*

Whitehouse, Horace 1881-1958 *WhAm 3*

Whitehouse, James Horton 1833-1902 *ApCAB, NatCAB 4, NewYHSD, WhAm 1*

Whitehouse, John Osborne 1817-1881 *BiAUS, BiDrAC, WhAm H*

Whitehouse, Morris Homans 1878-1944 *NatCAB 43*

Whitehouse, Robert Treat 1869-1924 *NatCAB 20*

Whitehouse, Robert Treat 1870-1924 *WhAm 5*

Whitehouse, Sheldon 1883-1965 *WhAm 4*

Whitehouse, Vira Boarman 1875- *WhAm 5*

Whitehouse, William FitzHugh 1877-1909 *WhAm 1*

Whitehouse, William Penn 1842-1922 *NatCAB 10, WhAm 1*

Whitehurst, Camelia d1936 *WhAm 1*

Whitehurst, George William 1925- *BiDrAC*

Whitehurst, John 1713-1788 *DcScB*

Whitehurst, John Leyburn d1966 *WhAm 4*

Whiteis, William Robert 1869- *WhAm 5*

Whitelaw, James 1748-1829 *NatCAB 16*

Whitelaw, John Bertram 1905-1968 *WhAm 5*

Whitelaw, Robert Henry 1854-1937 *BiDrAC*

Whiteley, Emily Stone d1939 *WhAm 1*

Whiteley, Harry Huntington 1882-1957 *NatCAB 44*

Whiteley, Isabel Nixon *WhAm 5*

Whiteley, James Gustavus 1866-1947 *NatCAB 39, WhAm 5*

Whiteley, Richard Henry 1830-1890 *ApCAB, BiAUS, BiDrAC, WhAm H*

Whiteley, Robert Henry Kirkwood 1809- *ApCAB*

Whiteley, Robert Henry Kirkwood 1866-1923 *NatCAB 20*

Whiteley, William Gustavus 1819-1886 *BiAUS, BiDrAC, WhAm H*

Whitelock, George 1854-1920 *WhAm 1*

Whitelock, Louise Clarkson 1865-1928 *WhAm 1, WhAm 4, WomWWA 14*

Whitelock, Samuel West *NewYHSD*

Whitelock, William 1815-1893 *NatCAB 25*

Whitelock, William Wallace 1869-1940 *NatCAB 37, WhAm H*

Whitelocke, John 1757?-1808? *ApCAB*

Whiteman, Daniel Swab 1893-1952 *NatCAB 43*

Whiteman, Jacob Harvey 1863-1928 *NatCAB 23*

Whiteman, Paul 1890-1967 *NatCAB 56*

Whiteman, Paul 1891-1967 *WebAB,*

WhAm 4A

Whiteman, Samuel Dickey 1900-1972 *WhAm 5*

Whiteman, Theodore Carmichael 1876-1954 *NatCAB 48*

Whitener, Basil Lee 1915- *BiDrAC, WhAmP*

Whitener, Catherine Evans 1880-1964 *NatCAB 51*

Whitener, Daniel Jay 1898-1964 *WhAm 4*

Whitener, Paul A W 1911-1959 *WhAm 3*

Whitenton, William Maynard 1869-1929 *WhAm 1*

Whiter, Edward Tait 1864- *WhAm 4*

Whitesell, William M 1888-1962 *WhAm 4*

Whiteside *NewYHSD*

Whiteside, Alexander 1874-1966 *NatCAB 51*

Whiteside, Arthur Dare 1882-1960 *WhAm 4*

Whiteside, Frank Reed 1866?-1929 *IlBEAAW, WhAm 1*

Whiteside, Fred William 1875-1961 *NatCAB 50*

Whiteside, George Morris, II 1884-1963 *WhAm 4*

Whiteside, George Walter 1880-1962 *WhAm 4*

Whiteside, Horace Eugene 1891-1956 *WhAm 3*

Whiteside, James Leonard 1864-1928 *WhAm 1*

Whiteside, Jenkin 1772-1822 *BiDrAC, WhAm H*

Whiteside, Jenkin 1782-1822 *ApCAB*

Whiteside, Jenkins d1822 *BiAUS*

Whiteside, Jenkins 1782-1822 *NatCAB 11*

Whiteside, John 1773-1830 *BiAUS, BiDrAC, WhAm H*

Whiteside, Peter 1752-1828 *ApCAB*

Whiteside, Walker 1869-1942 *NatCAB 33, WhAm 2*

Whitesides, Virgil Stuart 1890-1957 *NatCAB 47*

Whiteway, Sir William Vallance 1828- *ApCAB Sup*

Whitfield, Albert Hall 1849- *NatCAB 13, TwCBDA, WhAm 4*

Whitfield, Amelia Atkins 1857- *WomWWA 14*

Whitfield, Augustus Foscue 1861-1947 *NatCAB 36*

Whitfield, E *NewYHSD*

Whitfield, Emma Morehead 1874- *WomWWA 14*

Whitfield, Harold Barnard 1895-1965 *NatCAB 51*

Whitfield, Henry 1597-1651? *ApCAB, Drake*

Whitfield, Henry 1597-1657? *DcAmB, WhAm H*

Whitfield, Henry Lewis 1868-1927 *BiDAmEd, NatCAB 21, WhAm 1*

Whitfield, Inez Harrington 1867- *WomWWA 14*

Whitfield, J Edward 1859-1930 *WhAm 1*

Whitfield, J Vivian 1894-1968 *NatCAB 55*

Whitfield, James 1770-1834 *ApCAB, NatCAB 1, TwCBDA, WhAm H*

Whitfield, James 1791-1875 *BiAUS, NatCAB 13*

Whitfield, James *see also* Whitefield, James

Whitfield, James Bryan 1860-1948 *NatCAB 18, WhAm 2*

Whitfield, John S *NewYHSD*

Whitfield, John Wilkins 1818-1879 *BiDrAC, WhAm H*

Whitfield, John Wilkins *see also* Whitefield, J W

Whitfield, Robert Henry 1814-1868 *BiDConf*

Whitfield, Robert Parr 1828-1910 *ApCAB, DcAmB, DcScB, NatCAB 5, TwCBDA, WhAm 1*

Whitfield, William Kinney, Jr. 1902-1963 *NatCAB 50*

Whitford, Alfred E 1875- *WhAm 5*

Whitford, Edward Everett 1865-1946 *WhAm 3*

Whitford, Gertrude Edith Leonard 1876- *WomWWA 14*

Whitford, Greeley Webster 1856- *WhAm 1*

Whitford, O'Dillon Barret 1834- *NatCAB 16*

Whitford, Oscar F 1833- *WhAm 1*

Whitford, Robert Naylor 1870-1959 *WhAm 3A*

Whitford, Robert Naylor *see also* Whiteford, Robert Naylor

Whitford, William Calvin 1865-1925 *WhAm 1*

Whitford, William Clarke 1828-1902 *BiDAmEd, NatCAB 6, WhAm 1*

Whitham, Jay Manuel 1858-1951 *NatCAB 38*

Whithorne, Emerson 1884-1958 *WhAm 3*

Whitin, Ernest Stagg 1881- *WhAm 2*

Whitin, George Marston 1856-1920 *NatCAB 32*

Whiting, Almon Clark 1878- *WhAm 6*

Whiting, Arthur Battelle 1861-1936 *AmBi, ApCAB X, DcAmB S2, NatCAB 27, WhAm 1*

Whiting, Borden Durfee 1876-1961 *WhAm 4*

Whiting, Charles Goodrich 1842-1922 *DcAmB, NatCAB 9, WhAm 1*

Whiting, Charles Sumner 1863-1922 *NatCAB 17, WhAm 1*

Whiting, D W *NewYHSD*

Whiting, Daniel Powers 1808- *ApCAB, Drake, NewYHSD*

Whiting, Earl Bernard 1896-1965 *NatCAB 51*

Whiting, Edward Clark 1881-1962 *NatCAB 51, WhAm 6*

Whiting, Edward Elwell 1875-1956 *WhAm 3*

Whiting, F H *NewYHSD*

Whiting, Fabius 1792-1842 *NewYHSD*

Whiting, Frank Brockway 1885-1952 *NatCAB 42*

Whiting, Fred 1915-1969 *WhAm 5*

Whiting, Fred T 1890-1953 *WhAm 3*

Whiting, Frederic Allen 1873-1959 *NatCAB 43, WhAm 5*

Whiting, George C 1816-1867 *BiAUS*

Whiting, George Elbridge 1840-1923 *DcAmB*

Whiting, George Elbridge 1842-1923 *ApCAB, WhAm 1*

Whiting, George Elbridge 1843-1923 *NatCAB 8*

Whiting, Gertrude d1951 *WhAm 3*

Whiting, Giles 1873-1937 *NatCAB 29*

Whiting, Harry Hayes 1877-1936 *WhAm 1*

Whiting, Henry d1851 *Drake*

Whiting, Henry 1788-1851 *NatCAB 10, WhAm H*

Whiting, Henry 1790?-1851 *ApCAB, TwCBDA*

Whiting, Henry Hyer 1875-1939 *WhAm 1*

Whiting, John 1706-1786 *ApCAB*

Whiting, John Talman 1887-1965 *NatCAB 53, WhAm 4*

Whiting, Justin Rice 1847-1903 *BiDrAC, WhAm 1, WhAmP*

Whiting, Justin Rice 1886-1965 *WhAm 4*

Whiting, Katharine A 1877- *WomWWA 14*

Whiting, Lawrence Harley 1890-1974 *WhAm 6*

Whiting, Leonard Clarke 1888-1954 *NatCAB 44*

Whiting, Lilian d1942 *AmWom*

Whiting, Lilian 1847-1942 *NotAW*

Whiting, Lilian 1855-1942 *NatCAB 9*

Whiting, Lilian 1859-1942 *WhAm 2, WomWWA 14*

Whiting, Mary A Cosad 1869- *WomWWA 14*

Whiting, Mary Collins 1835- *AmWom*

Whiting, Mary Gray d1964 *WhAm 4*

Whiting, Nathan 1724-1771 *ApCAB*

Whiting, Nathaniel 1724-1771 *Drake*

Whiting, Percy Hollister 1880- *WhAm 6*

Whiting, Richard Armstrong 1891-1938 *NatCAB 28*

Whiting, Richard Henry 1826-1888 *BiAUS, BiDrAC, WhAm H*

Whiting, Robert Rudd 1877-1918 *WhAm 1*

Whiting, Samuel 1597-1679 *ApCAB, Drake, NatCAB 10, WhAm H*

Whiting, Samuel Raynor 1867-1933 *NatCAB 32*

Whiting, Sarah Frances 1847-1927 *NotAW, WhAm 1, WomWWA 14*

Whiting, Stephen Betts 1834-1915 *NatCAB 17*

Whiting, Walter Rogers 1875- *WhAm 5*

Whiting, William 1813-1873 *ApCAB, BiDrAC, DcAmB S1, Drake, NatCAB 10, WhAm H*

Whiting, William 1841-1911 *BiDrAC, NatCAB 14, WhAm 1, WhAmP*

Whiting, William Alonzo 1890-1957 *WhAm 3*

Whiting, William B 1813-1883 *ApCAB*

Whiting, William Danforth 1823-1894 *ApCAB, TwCBDA*

Whiting, William Fairfield 1864-1936 *BiDrUSE, WhAm 1*

Whiting, William H *NewYHSD*

Whiting, William Henry 1843-1925 *TwCBDA,*

WhAm 1

Whiting, William Henry, Jr. 1862-1949
WhAm 2

Whiting, William Henry Chase 1824-1865
BiDConf, DcAmB, WebAMB, WhAm H

Whiting, William Henry Chase 1825-1865 *AmBi,
ApCAB, Drake, NatCAB 4, TwCBDA*

Whitley, Cora Call 1862-1937 *WhAm 1*

Whitley, Erminia Minerva *WomWWA 14*

Whitley, George Washington 1865- *WhoColR*

Whitley, Hobart Johnston 1868- *ApCAB X*

Whitley, James Lucius 1872-1959 *BiDrAC,
WhAm 5, WhAmP*

Whitley, Johnson Decosta 1910-1968 *WhAm 5*

Whitley, Mary Theodora 1878- *WhAm 6*

Whitley, Samuel Henry 1878-1946 *WhAm 2*

Whitley, Thomas W *NewYHSD*

Whitlock, Brand 1869-1934 *AmBi, ApCAB X,
DcAmB, NatCAB 14, WebAB, WhAm 1*

Whitlock, Douglas 1904-1973 *NatCAB 57,
WhAm 6*

Whitlock, Eliza Kemble 1762-1836 *WhAm H*

Whitlock, Elliott Howland 1867- *WhAm 5*

Whitlock, Herbert Percy 1868-1948 *NatCAB 36,
WhAm 2*

Whitlock, Paul Cameron 1878- *WhAm 6*

Whitlock, Philip 1838-1919 *NatCAB 19*

Whitlock, Sturges 1844-1914 *NatCAB 30*

Whitlock, William Francis 1833-1909 *WhAm 1*

Whitman, Albery Allson 1851-1901 *DcAmB*

Whitman, Alfred Freeman 1882-1951 *WhAm 3*

Whitman, Alvah F 1831-1913 *NatCAB 15*

Whitman, Armitage 1887-1962 *NatCAB 49,
WhAm 4*

Whitman, Arthur Dudley 1884-1957
NatCAB 44, WhAm 3

Whitman, Benaiah Longley 1862-1911
NatCAB 8, TwCBDA, WhAm 1

Whitman, Bernard 1796-1834 *ApCAB*

Whitman, Bernard Crosby 1827-1885
NatCAB 12

Whitman, Charles Huntington 1873-1937
WhAm 1

Whitman, Charles Otis 1842-1910 *AmBi,
DcAmB, DcScB, NatCAB 11, WhAm 1*

Whitman, Charles Seymour 1868-1947
*DcAmB S4, NatCAB 15, NatCAB 33,
WhAm 2*

Whitman, Edith Moore 1883- *WomWWA 14*

Whitman, Edmund Allen 1860- *WhAm 5*

Whitman, Edward A d1947 *WhAm 2*

Whitman, Eugene Winfield 1907-1966 *WhAm 4*

Whitman, Ezekiel 1776-1866 *ApCAB, BiAUS,
BiDrAC, DcAmB, Drake, NatCAB 11,
TwCBDA, WhAm H*

Whitman, Ezra Bailey 1880-1966 *WhAm 4*

Whitman, Florence Lee 1862- *WomWWA 14*

Whitman, Frank Ellsworth 1862-1946
NatCAB 34

Whitman, Frank Perkins 1853-1919 *WhAm 1*

Whitman, Frank S 1849-1939 *WhAm 1*

Whitman, Harold Cutler 1883-1966 *NatCAB 53*

Whitman, Hendricks Hallett 1884-1950
WhAm 3

Whitman, Henry Harold 1897-1963 *WhAm 4*

Whitman, Howard 1914-1975 *WhAm 6*

Whitman, Jacob d1798 *NewYHSD*

Whitman, Jason 1799-1848 *ApCAB*

Whitman, John Lorin 1862-1926 *NatCAB 15,
WhAm 1*

Whitman, John Munro 1837-1912 *NatCAB 10,
WhAm 1*

Whitman, Lemuel 1780-1841 *BiAUS, BiDrAC,
WhAm H*

Whitman, LeRoy 1902-1968 *WhAm 5*

Whitman, Lloyd Charles 1875-1952 *NatCAB 42*

Whitman, Mabel 1871- *WomWWA 14*

Whitman, Malcolm Douglass d1932 *WhAm 1*

Whitman, Marcus 1802-1847 *AmBi, ApCAB,
DcAmB, DcAmReB, EncAAH, McGEWB,
NatCAB 11, REnAW, TwCBDA,
WebAB, WhAm H*

Whitman, Narcissa Prentiss 1808-1847
DcAmReB, NotAW, WhAm H

Whitman, Olive Hitchcock 1880-
WomWWA 14

Whitman, Olive Hitchcock 1882- *BiCAW*

Whitman, Ralph 1880-1946 *WhAm 2*

Whitman, Robert 1935- *BnEnAmA*

Whitman, Roger B 1875-1942 *WhAm 2*

Whitman, Roscoe Leighton 1869-1955
NatCAB 44

Whitman, Roswell Hartson 1908-1962 *WhAm 4*

Whitman, Royal 1857-1946 *DcAmB S4,
REnAW, WhAm 2*

Whitman, Russell 1861-1949 *WhAm 2*

Whitman, Russell Ripley 1868-1939 *WhAm 1*

Whitman, Ruth Loring 1877- *WomWWA 14*

Whitman, Sallie Shaw Bishop 1861-
WomWWA 14

Whitman, Sarah Helen Power 1803-1878 *AmBi,
AmWom, ApCAB, DcAmB, NatCAB 8,
NotAW, WhAm H*

Whitman, Sarah Helen Power 1813-1878 *Drake*

Whitman, Stephen F 1880- *WhAm 6*

Whitman, Walt 1819-1892 *AmBi, ApCAB,
DcAmB, EncAAH, EncAB, McGEWB,
WebAB*

Whitman, Walter 1819-1892 *ApCAB X, Drake,
NatCAB 1, TwCBDA, WhAm H*

Whitman, Walter Gordon 1895-1974 *WhAm 6*

Whitman, William 1842-1928 *ApCAB X,
NatCAB 14, WhAm 1*

Whitman, William Edward Seaver 1832-1901
NatCAB 5, WhAm 1

Whitman, William Francis 1859-1936
NatCAB 27

Whitman, William R 1876- *WhAm 6*

Whitmar, Julia *NewYHSD*

Whitmarsh, Caroline Snowden 1827- *ApCAB*

Whitmarsh, Francis Leggett 1893-1969
WhAm 5

Whitmarsh, Henry Allen 1854-1939
NatCAB 30, WhAm 1

Whitmarsh, Hubert Phelps 1863- *WhAm 4*

Whitmarsh, Theodore Francis 1869-1936
ApCAB X, WhAm 1

Whitmer, David 1805-1888 *ApCAB, DcAmB,
WhAm H*

Whitmer, LeRoy Grove 1871-1946 *NatCAB 36*

Whitmer, Robert Forster 1864- *WhAm 4*

Whitmore, Adah 1886- *WomWWA 14*

Whitmore, Annie Goodell 1855- *WhAm 4,
WomWWA 14*

Whitmore, Brewer Goddard 1886-1943
NatCAB 33

Whitmore, Carl 1884-1958 *WhAm 3*

Whitmore, Clara Helen 1865- *WomWWA 14*

Whitmore, Daniel Webster 1853-1932
NatCAB 24

Whitmore, Edward 1691-1761 *ApCAB, Drake*

Whitmore, Elias 1772-1853 *BiDrAC,
WhAm H*

Whitmore, Eugene R 1874- *WhAm 5*

Whitmore, Frank Clifford 1887-1947
DcAmB S4, NatCAB 39, WhAm 2

Whitmore, George Washington 1824-1876
BiAUS, BiDrAC, WhAm H

Whitmore, Ida Jane Knowlton 1858-
WomWWA 14

Whitmore, J *NewYHSD*

Whitmore, Samuel Jackson 1865-1952
NatCAB 43

Whitmore, Willet Francis 1894-1950
NatCAB 39

Whitmore, William Henry 1836-1900 *ApCAB,
DcAmB, Drake, WhAm 1*

Whitmore, William Wallace 1870-1943
NatCAB 33

Whitmyer, Edward Charles 1861-1933 *WhAm 1*

Whitnall, Harold Orville 1877-1945 *WhAm 2*

Whitney, Adeline Dutton Train 1824-1906
*AmWom, ApCAB, DcAmB, Drake,
NatCAB 2, NotAW, TwCBDA,
WhAm 1*

Whitney, Alexander Fell 1873-1949 *DcAmB S4,
WhAm 2*

Whitney, Alfred Rutgers 1868-1946 *WhAm 2*

Whitney, Allen Banks 1877-1958 *NatCAB 48,
WhAm 5*

Whitney, Allen Sisson 1857-1944 *WhAm 3*

Whitney, Amos 1832-1920 *NatCAB 15,
NatCAB 32*

Whitney, Amy Isabel 1878- *WomWWA 14*

Whitney, Andrew 1826-1912 *NatCAB 15*

Whitney, Anne 1821-1915 *AmWom, ApCAB,*

*BnEnAmA, DcAmB, NatCAB 7,
NewYHSD, NotAW, WhAm H*

Whitney, Arthur Herbert 1859-1927 *ApCAB X*

Whitney, Asa 1791-1874 *AmBi, ApCAB,
DcAmB, TwCBDA, WebAB, WhAm H*

Whitney, Asa 1797-1872 *AmBi, ApCAB,
DcAmB, REnAW*

Whitney, Asa 1797-1877 *WhAm H*

Whitney, Belle Armstrong *WomWWA 14*

Whitney, Carl Everett 1876-1940 *WhAm 1*

Whitney, Carrie Westlake *WhAm 5,
WomWWA 14*

Whitney, Caspar 1861-1929 *DcAmB S1,
NatCAB 25*

Whitney, Caspar 1862-1929 *AmBi*

Whitney, Caspar 1864-1929 *WhAm 1*

Whitney, Charles Pratt 1866-1932 *NatCAB 34*

Whitney, Charles Smith 1892-1959 *WhAm 3*

Whitney, Charlotte Anita 1867-1955
DcAmB S5, WomWWA 14

Whitney, Courtney d1969 *WhAm 5*

Whitney, David Charles 1867-1942 *NatCAB 33*

Whitney, David Day 1878- *WhAm 6*

Whitney, David Rice 1828-1914 *WhAm 1*

Whitney, Edward Baldwin 1857-1911 *WhAm 1*

Whitney, Edward Samuel 1867-1951
NatCAB 40

Whitney, Edwin Morse 1877-1957 *WhAm 3*

Whitney, Eli 1765-1825 *AmBi, ApCAB,
AsBiEn, DcAmB, Drake, EncAAH,
EncAB, McGEWB, NatCAB 4,
TwCBDA, WebAB, WhAm H*

Whitney, Eli 1847-1924 *ApCAB X,
NatCAB 10, WhAm 1*

Whitney, Elias James 1827- *NewYHSD*

Whitney, Emily Henrietta 1864- *WhAm 4,
WomWWA 14*

Whitney, Erval McIlvaine 1870- *WomWWA 14*

Whitney, Eugene 1838-1889 *NatCAB 1*

Whitney, Frank I *WhAm 5*

Whitney, Fred Brown 1874-1954 *NatCAB 43*

Whitney, Frederic Augustus 1812-1880 *ApCAB*

Whitney, Frederick Augustus 1812-1880 *Drake*

Whitney, George 1804-1842 *ApCAB*

Whitney, George 1885-1963 *NatCAB 50,
WhAm 4*

Whitney, George Ellis 1864-1944 *NatCAB 39*

Whitney, George Herbert 1863-1928
NatCAB 21

Whitney, George J 1819-1878 *NatCAB 5*

Whitney, George Tapley 1871-1938 *NatCAB 31*

Whitney, Gertrude Capen 1861-1941 *WhAm 1,
WomWWA 14*

Whitney, Gertrude Holbrook Churchill
WomWWA 14

Whitney, Gertrude Vanderbilt 1875-1942
*ApCAB X, BiCAW, DcAmB S3,
NatCAB 17, NotAW, WhAm 2*

Whitney, Guilford Harrison 1888-1968
WhAm 5

Whitney, Gwin Allison 1893-1939 *WhAm 1*

Whitney, Harry 1873-1936 *WhAm 1*

Whitney, Harry Edward 1851-1926 *WhAm 1*

Whitney, Harry Payne 1872-1930 *DcAmB,
NatCAB 21, WhAm 1*

Whitney, Helen Hay 1876-1944 *NatCAB 33,
WomWWA 14*

Whitney, Henry Clay 1831- *WhAm 4*

Whitney, Henry Howard 1866-1949 *WhAm 2*

Whitney, Henry Melville 1839-1923
NatCAB 10, WhAm 1

Whitney, Henry Mitchell 1843-1911 *TwCBDA,
WhAm 1*

Whitney, Herbert Baker 1856- *WhAm 4*

Whitney, Herbert Porter 1877-1957 *NatCAB 45*

Whitney, J D *NewYHSD*

Whitney, James Amaziah 1839- *ApCAB,
WhAm 1*

Whitney, James Goodrich 1916-1966
NatCAB 53

Whitney, James Lyman 1835-1910 *DcAmB,
TwCBDA, WhAm 1*

Whitney, James Scollay 1811-1878 *NatCAB 10*

Whitney, Jason F 1878- *WhAm 6*

Whitney, Jessamine S 1880- *WomWWA 14*

Whitney, John d1673 *NatCAB 10*

Whitney, John Dunning 1898- *WhAm 4*

Whitney, John Henry Ellsworth 1840-1891
NewYHSD
Whitney, John P *NewYHSD*
Whitney, Joseph Lafeton 1894-1966 *WhAm 4*
Whitney, Josepha 1871- *WomWWA 14*
Whitney, Josiah 1731-1806 *NatCAB 10*
Whitney, Josiah Dwight 1819-1896 *AmBi,*
ApCAB, DcAmB, DcScB, Drake,
McGEWB, NatCAB 9, TwCBDA,
WebAB, WhAm H
Whitney, Josiah Dwight 1878-1926 *NatCAB 21*
Whitney, Leon Fradley 1894-1973 *WhAm 6*
Whitney, Loren Harper 1834-1912 *WhAm 1*
Whitney, Louisa Goddard 1819-1882 *ApCAB*
Whitney, Marian Parker 1861-1946 *WhAm 2,*
WomWWA 14
Whitney, Mary Traffarn 1852- *AmWom*
Whitney, Mary Watson 1847-1921 *DcAmB,*
NotAW, WhAm 1, WomWWA 14
Whitney, Milton 1860-1927 *WhAm 1*
Whitney, Myron William 1835-1910 *WhAm 1*
Whitney, Myron William 1836-1910 *ApCAB,*
DcAmB, NatCAB 2
Whitney, Nathaniel Ruggles 1882-1964
WhAm 4
Whitney, Nelson Oliver 1858-1901 *WhAm 1*
Whitney, Paul Clinton 1882-1954 *WhAm 3*
Whitney, Payne 1876-1927 *NatCAB 21,*
WhAm 1
Whitney, Peter 1744-1816 *ApCAB, Drake*
Whitney, Richard 1888-1974 *WhAm 6*
Whitney, Robert Bacon 1916-1952 *WhAm 3*
Whitney, Samuel Brenton 1842-1913 *NatCAB 9,*
WhAm 1
Whitney, Thomas Richard 1804-1858 *ApCAB,*
BiAUS, Drake
Whitney, Thomas Richard 1807-1858 *BiDrAC,*
NewYHSD, WhAm H
Whitney, Walter Langdon 1895-1958
NatCAB 43
Whitney, Warren Appleton 1883-1944
NatCAB 33
Whitney, Wheelock 1894-1957 *NatCAB 53,*
WhAm 3
Whitney, William Belcher 1866-1936
NatCAB 27
Whitney, William Channing 1851-1945
WhAm 2
Whitney, William Collins 1841- *ApCAB,*
TwCBDA
Whitney, William Collins 1841-1902 *BiDrUSE*
Whitney, William Collins 1841-1904 *AmBi,*
DcAmB, EncAB, NatCAB 2, WebAB,
WhAm 1
Whitney, William Dwight 1827-1894 *AmBi,*
ApCAB, DcAmB, Drake, NatCAB 2,
TwCBDA, WebAB, WhAm H
Whitney, William Fiske 1850-1921 *WhAm 1*
Whitney, William K *NewYHSD*
Whitney, William Locke 1876-1920 *WhAm 1*
Whitney, Willis Rodney 1868-1958 *NatCAB 15,*
NatCAB 46, WhAm 3
Whiton, Augustus Sherrill 1820- *NatCAB 1*
Whiton, Edward Vernon 1805-1859 *NatCAB 12*
Whiton, Ella C R *WomWWA 14*
Whiton, Francis Henry 1846-1922 *NatCAB 19*
Whiton, Helen Isabel 1874- *WomWWA 14*
Whiton, Henry Devereux 1871-1930
NatCAB 24
Whiton, Herman Frasch 1904-1967 *WhAm 4A*
Whiton, James Morris 1833-1920 *ApCAB,*
DcAmB, NatCAB 8, TwCBDA,
WhAm 1
Whiton, John Milton 1785-1856 *ApCAB,*
Drake
Whiton, John Milton 1845-1927 *NatCAB 20*
Whiton, Mary Bartlett 1857- *ApCAB,*
WomWWA 14
Whiton, Sylvester Gilbert 1846-1910
NatCAB 15
Whitridge, Frederick Wallingford 1852-1916
NatCAB 15, NatCAB 27, WhAm 1
Whitridge, John Clifford 1872-1936 *NatCAB 26*
Whitridge, Morris 1865-1935 *WhAm 1*
Whitsett, William Thornton 1866-1934
WhAm 1
Whitside, Samuel Marmaduke 1839-1904
WhAm 1

Whitsitt, James McFarland 1884-1958
NatCAB 51
Whitsitt, William Heth 1841-1911 *ApCAB,*
DcAmB, NatCAB 10, WhAm 1
Whitson, Andrew Robeson 1870- *WhAm 5*
Whitson, Edward 1852-1910 *WhAm 1*
Whitson, John Harvey 1854-1936 *WhAm 1*
Whitson, W C d1875 *BiAUS*
Whitt, Hugh 1888-1955 *WhAm 3*
Whittaker, Alexander Relyea 1869-1928
ApCAB X
Whittaker, Charles Evans 1901-1973 *WebAB,*
WhAm 6
Whittaker, Edmund Boyd 1902-1958 *WhAm 3*
Whittaker, Edmund Taylor 1873-1956 *DcScB*
Whittaker, Elizabeth Leigh *WomWWA 14*
Whittaker, Frederick 1838- *ApCAB*
Whittaker, Henry 1808-1881 *ApCAB*
Whittaker, James 1751-1787 *ApCAB*
Whittaker, James 1891-1964 *WhAm 4*
Whittaker, James Thomas 1843-1900 *WhAm 1*
Whittaker, John *BiAUS*
Whittaker, John Bernard 1836- *NewYHSD*
Whittaker, Miller F 1892-1949 *WhAm 3*
Whittaker, William Henry 1853-1915
NatCAB 17
Whitted, Elmer Ellsworth 1861- *WhAm 4*
Whitteker, John Edwin 1851-1925 *WhAm 1*
Whittelsey, Abigail Goodrich 1788-1858 *DcAmB,*
NotAW, WhAm H
Whittelsey, Delia Maria Taylor 1861-
WomWWA 14
Whittelsey, Henry Newton 1872-1945
NatCAB 34
Whittemore, Albert Gallatin 1844-1922
NatCAB 6
Whittemore, Almeda G 1867- *WomWWA 14*
Whittemore, Amos 1759-1828 *ApCAB,*
DcAmB, Drake, NatCAB 7, WhAm H
Whittemore, Arthur Easterbrook 1896-1969
WhAm 5
Whittemore, Arthur Gilman 1856-1931
NatCAB 34
Whittemore, Benjamin Franklin 1824-1894
BiAUS, BiDrAC, WhAm H
Whittemore, Charles Otto 1862-1920
NatCAB 19, WhAm 4
Whittemore, Clark McKinley 1876-1953
WhAm 3
Whittemore, Don Juan 1830-1916 *ApCAB,*
NatCAB 13, WhAm 1
Whittemore, Edward Loder 1861-1930
NatCAB 22, WhAm 1
Whittemore, Elias *BiAUS*
Whittemore, Eugene Beede 1902-1962 *WhAm 4*
Whittemore, Frank Hamilton 1854-1920
NatCAB 19
Whittemore, Harris 1864-1927 *NatCAB 21,*
WhAm 1
Whittemore, Henry 1843- *WhAm 4*
Whittemore, Herbert Lucius 1876-1954
WhAm 3
Whittemore, Horace Alan 1863-1930 *ApCAB X*
Whittemore, Ira Matthews 1869-1944
NatCAB 34
Whittemore, James 1860-1941 *NatCAB 31*
Whittemore, James Madison 1836-1916
WhAm 1
Whittemore, John Howard 1837-1910
NatCAB 15
Whittemore, John Weed 1897-1963 *WhAm 4*
Whittemore, Laurence Frederick 1894-1960
WhAm 4
Whittemore, Lewis Bliss 1885-1965 *NatCAB 52*
Whittemore, Luther Denny 1858- *WhAm 4*
Whittemore, Manvel 1890-1961 *NatCAB 46*
Whittemore, Mary B Eastman 1872-
WomWWA 14
Whittemore, Norman Clark 1870-1952
NatCAB 40
Whittemore, Thomas 1800-1861 *ApCAB,*
DcAmB, Drake, NatCAB 1, WhAm H
Whittemore, Thomas 1871-1950 *DcAmB S4,*
WhAm 3
Whittemore, William John 1860-1955
NatCAB 14, NatCAB 44, WhAm 3
Whittemore, Wyman 1879-1957 *WhAm 3A*
Whitten, Benjamin Otis 1886-1970 *NatCAB 57*

Whitten, Jamie Lloyd 1910- *BiDrAC*
Whitten, John Charles 1866-1922 *WhAm 1*
Whitten, Martha Elizabeth Hotchkiss 1842-
AmWom
Whitten, Mary Seys 1867- *WomWWA 14*
Whitten, Robert 1873-1936 *WhAm 1*
Whitthorne, Washington Curran 1825-1891
ApCAB, BiAUS, BiDrAC, NatCAB 10,
TwCBDA, WhAm H, WhAmP
Whittier, Albert Rufus 1840-1922 *ApCAB X*
Whittier, Charles Comfort 1876-1950
NatCAB 40, WhAm 5
Whittier, Charles Franklin 1843-1909 *WhAm 1*
Whittier, Charles Robert 1857-1945
NatCAB 32
Whittier, Clarke Butler 1872-1943 *WhAm 2*
Whittier, Cordelia Melvina 1872-
WomWWA 14
Whittier, Elizabeth Hussey 1815-1864 *ApCAB,*
Drake, NatCAB 8
Whittier, Frank Nathaniel 1861-1924
NatCAB 38
Whittier, Helen Augusta 1846- *WomWWA 14*
Whittier, John Greenleaf 1807-1892 *AmBi,*
ApCAB, DcAmB, Drake, EncAAH,
EncAB, McGEWB, NatCAB 1,
TwCBDA, WebAB, WhAm H
Whittier, William *NewYHSD*
Whittier, William Frank 1832-1917 *WhAm 1*
Whittier, William Franklin 1832-1917
NatCAB 17
Whittingham, William Rollinson 1805-1879
AmBi, ApCAB, DcAmB, Drake,
NatCAB 6, TwCBDA, WhAm H
Whittinghill, Dexter Gooch 1866- *WhAm 5*
Whittington, Anna Ward Aven *WomWWA 14*
Whittington, William Madison 1878-1962
BiDrAC, WhAm 4, WhAmP
Whittington, William Penrose 1887-1948
NatCAB 37
Whittle, B *NewYHSD*
Whittle, Francis McNeece 1823-1902 *ApCAB,*
NatCAB 7, TwCBDA, WhAm 1
Whittle, Sir Frank 1907- *McGEWB*
Whittle, Gilberta Sinclair *WomWWA 14*
Whittle, Kennon Caithness 1891-1967
NatCAB 53
Whittle, Stafford Gorman 1849-1931 *WhAm 1*
Whittles, Thomas Davis 1873- *WhAm 5*
Whittlesey, Abigail Goodrich 1788-1858 *ApCAB*
Whittlesey, Charles 1808-1886 *ApCAB, Drake*
Whittlesey, Charles Boardman 1871-1932
NatCAB 29
Whittlesey, Charles White 1884-1921
NatCAB 20, WebAMB
Whittlesey, Charles Wilcoxson 1860-1941
NatCAB 30
Whittlesey, Derwent Stainthorpe 1890-1956
NatCAB 42, WhAm 3
Whittlesey, Eliphalet 1821-1909 *WhAm 1*
Whittlesey, Elisha 1783-1863 *ApCAB, BiAUS,*
BiDrAC, NatCAB 14, WhAm H,
WhAmP
Whittlesey, Frederick 1799-1851 *ApCAB,*
BiAUS, BiDrAC, Drake, NatCAB 3,
TwCBDA, WhAm H, WhAmP
Whittlesey, Henry DeWitt, Sr. 1872-1961
WhAm 4
Whittlesey, Joseph H 1821-1886 *ApCAB*
Whittlesey, Mary Reed Eastman 1870-
WomWWA 14
Whittlesey, Sarah Johnson Cogswell 1825?-
ApCAB
Whittlesey, Thomas Tucker 1798-1868 *BiAUS,*
BiDrAC, WhAm H, WhAmP
Whittlesey, William Augustus 1796-1866
BiAUS, BiDrAC, WhAm H, WhAmP
Whittlesley, Derwent Stainthorpe 1890-1956
BiDAmEd
Whitton, Charlotte Elizabeth 1896-1975 *BiCAW,*
WhAm 6
Whittredge, Euphemia 1874- *WomWWA 14*
Whittredge, Thomas Worthington 1820-1910
IlBEAAW, NewYHSD
Whittredge, Worthington 1820-1910 *AmBi,*
ApCAB, BnEnAmA, DcAmB, Drake,
NatCAB 7, TwCBDA, WhAm 1
Whitty, James Howard 1859-1937 *WhAm 1*

Whitty, May d1948 *WhAm 2*
Whitwell, Frederick Silsbee 1862-1941 *WhAm 1*
Whitwell, Gertrude Howard *BiCAW*
Whitworth, George Frederic 1816-1907
BiDAmEd, DcAmB, NatCAB 2
Whitworth, George Gillatt 1850-1925 *WhAm 1*
Whitworth, John Ewing 1904-1970 *NatCAB 55*
Whitworth, Pegram 1871- *WhAm 5*
Wholberg, Gerald Walter 1939-1973 *WhAm 6*
Whorf, Benjamin Lee 1897-1941 *DcAmB S3,
NatCAB 30*
Whorf, John 1903-1959 *WhAm 3*
Whorf, Richard 1906-1966 *WhAm 4*
Whorton, John Lacy 1888-1941 *WhAm 1*
Whyburn, Gordon Thomas 1904-1969 *WhAm 5*
Whyburn, William Marvin 1901-1972
NatCAB 56, WhAm 5
Whyland, Calvin Arthur 1858- *NatCAB 11*
Whyte, Carl Barzellous 1902-1967 *WhAm 4*
Whyte, Frederick William Carrick 1863-1949
WhAm 3
Whyte, James Primrose 1868-1937 *NatCAB 27,
WhAm 1*
Whyte, Jessel Stuart 1890-1952 *WhAm 3*
Whyte, John 1887-1952 *WhAm 3*
Whyte, Malcolm Kenneth 1891-1967
NatCAB 53, WhAm 4A
Whyte, William Pinckney 1824-1908 *WhAm 1*
Whyte, William Pinkney 1824-1908 *ApCAB,
BiAUS, BiDrAC, DcAmB, NatCAB 9,
TwCBDA, WhAmP*
Whytlaw-Gray, Robert 1877-1958 *DcScB*
Whytt, Robert 1714-1766 *BiHiMed, DcScB*
Wiant, Thoburn Hughes 1911-1963 *NatCAB 50*
Wiard, Harry 1839-1914 *NatCAB 22*
Wiarda, Roy John, Jr. 1922-1965 *NatCAB 52*
Wiberg, Andreas 1816-1887 *ApCAB*
Wiberg, Peter Eric 1858-1954 *NatCAB 46*
Wibird, Richard 1702-1765 *NatCAB 5*
Wiboltt, Aage Christian 1894- *IIBEAAW*
Wiborg, Adeline M Sherman *WomWWA 14*
Wiborg, Frank Bestow 1855-1930 *ApCAB X,
WhAm 1*
Wicher, Edward Arthur 1872- *WhAm 3*
Wick, Charles J 1911-1966 *WhAm 4*
Wick, Frances Gertrude 1875-1941 *NatCAB 34,
WomWWA 14*
Wick, George Dennick 1854-1912 *NatCAB 18*
Wick, Hugh Bryson 1870-1933 *NatCAB 36*
Wick, James Lester 1897-1964 *NatCAB 51,
WhAm 4*
Wick, John Cooke 1836-1919 *NatCAB 17*
Wick, Kenneth Bryant 1888-1960 *NatCAB 48*
Wick, Myron Converse, Jr. 1892-1930
NatCAB 24
Wick, Philip 1886-1935 *NatCAB 27*
Wick, Samuel 1906- *WhAm 5*
Wick, William Watson 1796-1868 *BiAUS,
BiDrAC, NatCAB 3, WhAm H*
Wickard, Claude Raymond 1893-1967 *BiDrUSE,
EncAAH, WhAm 4*
Wickenden, Arthur Consaul 1893-1967
WhAm 4
Wickenden, William Elgin 1882-1947
NatCAB 36, WhAm 2
Wickens, Margaret R 1843- *AmWom*
Wicker, August *NewYHSD*
Wicker, Cassius Milton 1846-1913 *NatCAB 12,
WhAm 1*
Wicker, George Ray 1870-1917 *NatCAB 18,
WhAm 1*
Wicker, John Jordan d1958 *WhAm 3*
Wickersham, Cornelius Wendell 1884-1968
WhAm 4A
Wickersham, Cornelius Wendell, Jr. 1910-1966
WhAm 4
Wickersham, Edward Dean 1927-1966 *WhAm 4*
Wickersham, George Woodward 1858-1936
*AmBi, BiDrUSE, DcAmB S2, NatCAB 14,
WebAB, WhAm 1*
Wickersham, James 1857-1939 *BiDrAC,
WhAm 1, WhAmP*
Wickersham, James Pyle 1825-1891 *AmBi,
ApCAB, BiDAmEd, DcAmB,
NatCAB 12, WhAm H*
Wickersham, Morris Dickenson 1839-1903
NatCAB 8
Wickersham, Thomas *NewYHSD*

Wickersham, Victor Eugene 1906- *BiDrAC*
Wickersheimer, Ernest 1880-1965 *DcScB*
Wickes, Edward Allen 1843-1918 *NatCAB 22*
Wickes, Eliphalet 1769-1850 *BiAUS, BiDrAC,
WhAm H*
Wickes, Forsyth 1876-1964 *WhAm 4*
Wickes, Harvey Randall 1889-1974 *WhAm 6*
Wickes, Joseph Augustus 1826-1915
NatCAB 33
Wickes, Lambert 1735?-1777 *DcAmB,
WebAMB, WhAm H*
Wickes, Lambert 1735?-1778 *ApCAB,
NatCAB 2*
Wickes, Stephen 1813-1889 *ApCAB, DcAmB,
WhAm H*
Wickes, Thomas 1814-1870 *ApCAB*
Wickes, Thomas H 1846-1905 *WhAm 1*
Wickett, Frederick Henry 1868-1929
NatCAB 21, WhAm 1
Wickey, Andrew 1845-1927 *NatCAB 41*
Wickham, Charles Preston 1836-1925 *BiDrAC,
NatCAB 2*
Wickham, Clarence Horace 1860-1945
NatCAB 34
Wickham, Delos Olcott 1840-1914 *NatCAB 25*
Wickham, Gertrude VanRensselaer 1844-
WomWWA 14
Wickham, Henry Frederick 1866-1933 *WhAm 1*
Wickham, Henry Taylor 1849-1943 *NatCAB 13,
NatCAB 36, WhAm 3*
Wickham, Horace John 1836-1914 *NatCAB 26*
Wickham, John 1763-1839 *ApCAB, DcAmB,
Drake, WhAm H*
Wickham, Thomas Youngs 1873-1956
NatCAB 46
Wickham, William Hull 1846- *NatCAB 3*
Wickham, Williams Carter 1820-1888 *ApCAB,
BiDConf, NatCAB 13, TwCBDA*
Wickhem, John Dunne 1888-1949 *WhAm 2*
Wickler, Gerhard Siegfried 1905-1954
NatCAB 42
Wickliffe, Charles Anderson 1788-1869 *ApCAB,
BiAUS, BiDrAC, BiDrUSE, DcAmB,
Drake, NatCAB 6, TwCBDA, WhAm H,
WhAmP*
Wickliffe, Robert, Jr. d1850 *BiAUS*
Wickliffe, Robert Charles d1895 *BiAUS*
Wickliffe, Robert Charles 1819-1895 *DcAmB,
WhAm H, WhAmP*
Wickliffe, Robert Charles 1820-1895
ApCAB Sup, NatCAB 10
Wickliffe, Robert Charles, Jr. 1874-1912
BiDrAC, WhAm 1, WhAmP
Wicklow, Norman Louis 1906-1973 *WhAm 6*
Wickman, Carl Eric 1887-1954 *NatCAB 44,
WhAm 3*
Wicks, Frank Scott Corey 1868-1952
NatCAB 40, WhAm 3
Wicks, John Oliver 1880-1947 *NatCAB 35*
Wicks, Lillian Mae 1879- *WomWWA 14*
Wicks, Olivia Lula 1871- *WomWWA 14*
Wicks, Robert Russell 1882-1963 *WhAm 4*
Wicks, Ruth Egert 1884- *WomWWA 14*
Wickser, John George 1856-1928 *NatCAB 22*
Wickser, Philip John 1887-1949 *NatCAB 38,
WhAm 2*
Wickson, Edward James 1848-1923 *DcAmB,
EncAAH, NatCAB 18, WhAm 1*
Wicksteed, Gustavus William 1799- *ApCAB*
Wickware, Francis Graham 1883-1940
WhAm 1
Wickwire, Chester Franklin 1843-1910
NatCAB 19
Wickwire, Josephine Reeser 1864-
WomWWA 14
Wickwire, Theodore Harry, Jr. 1879- *WhAm 6*
Wickwire, Ward Alington 1885-1952
NatCAB 41
Wicoff, John VanBuren 1878-1952 *WhAm 3*
Widal, Fernand 1862-1929 *BiHiMed*
Widdemer, Mabel Cleland d1964 *WhAm 4*
Widdifield, Albert Edward 1906-1956
NatCAB 42
Widdifield, John Henry 1812- *ApCAB*
Wideman, Francis James 1891-1952 *WhAm 3*
Widener, George Dunton 1861-1912 *ApCAB X,
NatCAB 15*

Widener, George Dunton 1889-1971
NatCAB 57, WhAm 5
Widener, Harry Elkins 1885-1912 *AmBi,
ApCAB X, DcAmB, NatCAB 15*
Widener, Joseph Early 1872-1943 *WhAm HA,
WhAm 2, WhAm 4A*
Widener, Peter Arrell Brown 1834-1915 *AmBi,
DcAmB, NatCAB 15, WhAm 1*
Widener, Peter Arrell Brown 1895-1948
NatCAB 36
Wider, Charles *NewYHSD*
Wideveld *NewYHSD*
Widforss, Gunnar Mauritz 1879-1934 *DcAmB,
IIBEAAW*
Widgeon, John William 1850- *WhoColR*
Widgery, William 1753?-1822 *BiAUS, BiDrAC,
WhAm H*
Widman, Johannes 1462?-1498? *DcScB*
Widmann, Bernard Pierre 1890-1971 *WhAm 5*
Widmann, Frederick 1859-1925 *NatCAB 21*
Widmannstatten, Aloys Joseph Beck E Von
1754-1849 *DcScB*
Widmer, Christopher 1780-1858 *ApCAB*
Widmer, Kate Webb 1864- *WomWWA 14*
Widnall, William Beck 1906- *BiDrAC*
Widney, Joseph Pomeroy 1841-1938 *DcAmB S2*
Widtmann, Arthur Albert 1917-1974 *WhAm 6*
Widtsoe, John Andreas 1872-1952 *NatCAB 52,
WhAm 3*
Widtsoe, Leah Eudora Dunford 1874- *WhAm 5,
WomWWA 14*
Wieand, Albert Cassel 1871-1954 *WhAm 3*
Wieboldt, Elmer F d1972 *WhAm 5*
Wieboldt, Raymond Carl 1886-1968 *WhAm 5*
Wieboldt, Werner A 1884-1973 *WhAm 6*
Wieboldt, William A 1857-1954 *WhAm 3*
Wiechert, Emil 1861-1928 *DcScB*
Wiechmann, Ferdinand Gerhard 1858-1919
DcAmB, NatCAB 14, WhAm 1
Wieck, Fred Dernburg 1910-1973 *WhAm 6*
Wieczorek, Max 1863-1955 *WhAm 3*
Wied, Maximilian Zu 1782-1867 *DcScB*
Wiedemann, Gustav Heinrich 1826-1899 *DcScB*
Wiedemann, Joseph John 1908-1965
NatCAB 51
Wiedersheim, Robert 1848-1923 *DcScB*
Wiedersheim, Theodore Edward 1846-1916
NatCAB 17
Wiedhopf, Jacob Seerman 1889-1971
NatCAB 56
Wiedmaier, Charles Franklin 1859-1918
NatCAB 18
Wiedmann, Francis Edward 1925-1970
WhAm 6
Wiegand, Charles Dudley 1906-1972 *WhAm 5*
Wiegand, Ernest Herman 1886-1973 *WhAm 6*
Wiegand, Gustave Adolph 1870-1957 *WhAm 3*
Wiegand, Karl McKay 1873-1942 *NatCAB 42,
WhAm 2*
Wiegand, Maude Cipperly 1879-
WomWWA 14
Wieghorst, Olaf 1899- *IIBEAAW*
Wiegleb, Johann Christian 1732-1800 *DcScB*
Wiegman, Fred Conrad 1899-1957 *WhAm 3*
Wiehe, Theodore Charles 1880-1973 *WhAm 5*
Wiel, Eli Hecht 1873-1951 *NatCAB 38*
Wieland, Arthur J 1895-1957 *WhAm 3*
Wieland, Christoph Martin 1733-1813
McGEWB
Wieland, George Reber 1865-1953 *DcAmB S5,
NatCAB 39, WhAm 3*
Wieland, Heinrich Otto 1877-1957 *AsBiEn,
DcScB, WhAm 3*
Wieland, Melchior 1520?-1589 *DcScB*
Wieleitner, Heinrich 1874-1931 *DcScB*
Wieman, Elton Ewart 1896-1971 *WhAm 5*
Wieman, Henry Nelson 1884-1975 *DcAmReB,
WhAm 6*
Wien, Wilhelm Carl Werner O Fritz Franz
1864-1928 *DcScB*
Wiener, Isidor 1886-1970 *BnEnAmA*
Wiener, Leo 1862-1939 *BiDAmEd, DcAmB S2,
WhAm 1*
Wiener, Ludwig Christian 1826-1896 *DcScB*
Wiener, Meyer 1876- *WhAm 5*
Wiener, Norbert 1894-1964 *AsBiEn, DcScB,
EncAB, McGEWB, WebAB, WhAm 4*
Wiener, Otto 1862-1927 *DcScB*

Wiener, Paul Lester 1895-1967 *WhAm 4A*
Wiens, Henry Warkentin 1911-1968 *WhAm 5*
Wier, Eva Amelia 1868- *WomWWA 14*
Wier, Jeanne Elizabeth 1870-1950 *BiDAmEd,
NatCAB 51, REnAW, WhAm 3*
Wier, John 1852- *WhAm 4*
Wier, Robert Withrow 1873- *WhAm 5*
Wier, Roy William 1888-1963 *BiDrAC,
NatCAB 51, WhAm 4, WhAmP*
Wiers, Edgar Swan 1873-1931 *NatCAB 23,
WhAm 1*
Wierzbicki, Felix Paul d1861 *ApCAB*
Wiese, Otis Lee 1905-1972 *NatCAB 56,
WhAm 5*
Wiesenberger, Arthur 1896-1970 *WhAm 5*
Wiesenfeld, Paul Cholmar 1914-1958
NatCAB 43
Wiesner, Julius Von 1838-1916 *DcScB*
Wiess, Harry Carothers 1887-1948 *NatCAB 35,
WhAm 2*
Wiest, Don 1920?- *IIBEAAW*
Wiest, Edward 1878- *WhAm 6*
Wiest, Howard 1864-1945 *WhAm 2*
Wiestling, Helen Merwin 1889-1969 *WhAm 6*
Wieting, John Manchester 1817-1888
NatCAB 2
Wigand, Adeline Albright *WomWWA 14*
Wigand, Albert Julius Wilhelm 1821-1886
DcScB
Wigby, Bart Delmar 1907-1962 *NatCAB 49*
Wigen, Joris Odin 1883-1958 *NatCAB 51*
Wigfall, Lewis T 1816-1874 *BiAUS*
Wigfall, Louis Tresevant 1816-1874 *WhAm H*
Wigfall, Louis Tresvant 1816-1874 *BiDrAC*
Wigfall, Louis Trezevant 1816-1874 *AmBi,
ApCAB, BiDConf, DcAmB, NatCAB 5,
TwCBDA*
Wiggam, Albert Edward 1871-1957 *NatCAB 44,
WhAm 3*
Wiggans, Cleo Claude 1889-1967 *WhAm 5*
Wigger, Winand Michael 1841-1901 *ApCAB,
DcAmB, NatCAB 12, TwCBDA,
WhAm 1*
Wiggers, Carl John 1883-1963 *NatCAB 50,
WhAm 4*
Wiggers, Herbert August 1907-1953
NatCAB 40
Wiggin, Albert Henry 1868-1951 *ApCAB X,
DcAmB S5, NewYHSD, WhAm 3*
Wiggin, Alfred J *NewYHSD*
Wiggin, Frank H 1851-1920 *WhAm 1*
Wiggin, Frederick Alonzo 1858-1940 *WhAm 1*
Wiggin, Frederick Holme 1853-1910
NatCAB 12, WhAm 1
Wiggin, Frederick Holme 1882-1963 *WhAm 4*
Wiggin, Henry Dwight 1879-1957 *NatCAB 46*
Wiggin, James Henry 1836-1900 *DcAmB*
Wiggin, Joseph 1871-1948 *NatCAB 37*
Wiggin, Kate Douglas d1923 *AmWom,
TwCBDA*
Wiggin, Kate Douglas 1856-1923 *AmBi,
BiDAmEd, DcAmB, NatCAB 6, NotAW,
WebAB*
Wiggin, Kate Douglas 1859-1923 *ApCAB X,
WhAm 1, WomWWA 14*
Wiggin, Parry Cate 1861-1949 *NatCAB 38*
Wiggin, Samuel Adams 1832- *NatCAB 3*
Wiggin, Twing Brooks 1865- *WhAm 4*
Wiggin, William Harrison 1867-1951
NatCAB 40
Wiggin, William Irving 1879-1945 *NatCAB 34*
Wiggins, Benjamin Lawton 1861-1909
NatCAB 13, WhAm 1
Wiggins, Carleton 1848-1932 *AmBi,
ApCAB X, DcAmB, NatCAB 50,
TwCBDA, WhAm 1*
Wiggins, Charles 1885-1943 *NatCAB 34,
WhAm 2*
Wiggins, Charles Edward 1927- *BiDrAC*
Wiggins, Ezekiel Stone 1839- *ApCAB*
Wiggins, Frank 1849-1924 *ApCAB X,
WhAm 1*
Wiggins, Guy 1883-1962 *WhAm 4*
Wiggins, Horace Leland 1871-1933 *WhAm 1*
Wiggins, Inez Louise 1877- *WomWWA 14*
Wiggins, John Carleton 1848- *NatCAB 11*
Wiggins, Myra Albert 1869-1956 *IIBEAAW*
Wiggins, Samuel A *NewYHSD*

Wiggins, Sterling Pitts 1874-1945 *WhAm 2*
Wiggins, Susan Anna Gunhilda 1846- *ApCAB*
Wiggins, William D 1873-1949 *WhAm 3*
Wigginton, George Peter 1875- *WhAm 1*
Wigginton, P D 1839-1890 *BiAUS*
Wigginton, Peter Dinwiddie 1839-1890 *BiDrAC,
WhAm H*
Wigginton, Thomas Albert 1863- *WhAm 4*
Wigglesworth, Albert Wesley 1872-1950
NatCAB 40
Wigglesworth, Edward 1692?-1765 *TwCBDA*
Wigglesworth, Edward 1693?-1765 *ApCAB,
BiDAmEd, DcAmB, NatCAB 9*
Wigglesworth, Edward 1732-1794 *ApCAB,
DcAmB, Drake, WhAm H*
Wigglesworth, Edward 1742-1826 *ApCAB,
Drake, TwCBDA*
Wigglesworth, Edward 1804-1876 *ApCAB*
Wigglesworth, Edward 1840-1896 *DcAmB,
WhAm H*
Wigglesworth, Edward 1885-1945 *WhAm 2*
Wigglesworth, George 1853-1930 *WhAm 1*
Wigglesworth, Michael 1631-1705 *AmBi,
ApCAB, DcAmB, Drake, McGEWB,
NatCAB 8, WebAB, WhAm H*
Wigglesworth, Richard Bowditch 1891-1960
BiDrAC, WhAm 4, WhAmP
Wigglesworth, Samuel 1689-1768 *ApCAB*
Wight, Charles Albert 1899-1972 *WhAm 5*
Wight, E VanDyke 1869-1957 *WhAm 3*
Wight, Emma Howard *AmWom*
Wight, Francis Asa 1854-1942 *WhAm 2*
Wight, Frank Clinton 1882-1927 *WhAm 1*
Wight, Frederick Coit 1859-1933 *DcAmB*
Wight, Hariott Barrington 1856-
WomWWA 14
Wight, John Fitch 1928-1970 *WhAm 5*
Wight, John Green 1842-1913 *WhAm 1*
Wight, Moses 1827-1895 *AmBi, ApCAB,
Drake, NatCAB 12, NewYHSD*
Wight, Orlando Williams 1824-1888 *ApCAB,
Drake, NatCAB 7, WhAm H*
Wight, Pearl 1844-1920 *WhAm 1*
Wight, Peter Bonnett 1838-1925 *ApCAB,
DcAmB, NatCAB 21, TwCBDA,
WhAm 4*
Wight, Sedgwick North 1879-1968 *NatCAB 54*
Wight, Thomas 1874- *WhAm 5*
Wight, W *NewYHSD*
Wight, William Drewin 1882-1947 *WhAm 2*
Wight, William Ward 1849-1931 *NatCAB 3,
WhAm 1*
Wightman, George D *NewYHSD*
Wightman, N *NewYHSD*
Wightman, Orrin Sage 1873-1965 *NatCAB 51*
Wightman, Thomas *NewYHSD*
Wightman, Thomas 1811-1888 *NewYHSD*
Wightman, Valentine 1681-1747 *ApCAB*
Wightman, William May 1808-1882 *ApCAB,
TwCBDA*
Wigman, John Henry Mary 1835-1920
NatCAB 19
Wigmore, Francis Marion 1872-1952
NatCAB 44
Wigmore, John Henry 1863-1943 *DcAmB S3,
WebAB, WhAm 2*
Wignell, Ann Brunton *NotAW*
Wignell, Thomas 1753?-1803 *DcAmB, Drake,
WhAm H*
Wigner, Eugene Paul 1902- *AsBiEn,
McGEWB, WebAB*
Wigton, C Benson 1885-1961 *NatCAB 50*
Wiht, Thomas 1874-1949 *WhAm 3*
Wik, Reynold Millard 1910- *EncAAH*
Wike, Scott 1824-1901 *BiAUS*
Wike, Scott 1834-1901 *BiDrAC, WhAmP*
Wikoff, Charles Augustus 1837-1898
ApCAB Sup, TwCBDA
Wikoff, Frank J 1867- *WhAm 4*
Wikoff, Henry d1844 *Drake*
Wikoff, Henry 1810?-1884 *NatCAB 1*
Wikoff, Henry 1813?-1884 *ApCAB, DcAmB,
WhAm H*
Wilbar, Alexander Perry 1860-1948 *NatCAB 37*
Wilbar, Charles Luther, Jr. 1907-1969 *WhAm 5*
Wilber, David 1820-1890 *BiAUS, BiDrAC,
WhAm H, WhAmP*
Wilber, David Forrest 1859-1928 *BiDrAC,*

WhAm 1, WhAmP
Wilber, Edward Bacon 1902-1956 *WhAm 3*
Wilber, Francis Allen 1855- *WhAm 4*
Wilber, George M 1862-1939 *WhAm 1*
Wilber, Herbert Wray 1888-1963 *WhAm 4*
Wilber, Sarah S *WomWWA 14*
Wilberforce, William 1759-1833 *McGEWB*
Wilbern, Edward Valentine 1869-1950
NatCAB 39
Wilbor, Leon Mitchell 1888-1945 *NatCAB 40*
Wilbor, William Chambers 1852- *WhAm 4*
Wilbour, Charles Edwin 1833- *ApCAB*
Wilbour, Charlotte Beebee 1830- *ApCAB*
Wilbour, Charlotte Beebee 1833- *NatCAB 13*
Wilbour, Isaac 1763-1837 *BiDrAC, WhAm H*
Wilbour, Isaac 1783-1837 *NatCAB 9*
Wilbour, Linda Olney Hathaway 1844-
WomWWA 14
Wilbrand, Johann Bernhard 1779-1846 *DcScB*
Wilbur, Anne Toppan 1817-1864 *ApCAB,
Drake*
Wilbur, Charles Edgar 1853-1931 *WhAm 1*
Wilbur, Charles Toppan 1835-1909 *ApCAB,
NatCAB 10, WhAm 1*
Wilbur, Cressy Livingston 1865-1928 *DcAmB,
WhAm 1*
Wilbur, Curtis Dwight 1867-1954 *ApCAB X,
BiDrUSE, DcAmB S5, WhAm 3*
Wilbur, Earl Morse 1866-1956 *NatCAB 42*
Wilbur, Elisha Packer 1833-1910 *WhAm 1*
Wilbur, Frances M *WomWWA 14*
Wilbur, Henry W 1851-1914 *WhAm 1*
Wilbur, Hervey 1786-1852 *NatCAB 10,
WhAm H*
Wilbur, Hervey 1787-1852 *ApCAB*
Wilbur, Hervey Backus 1820-1883 *ApCAB,
BiDAmEd, DcAmB, NatCAB 10,
WhAm H*
Wilbur, Isaac *BiAUS*
Wilbur, Isaac E *NewYHSD*
Wilbur, James Benjamin 1856-1929 *WhAm 1*
Wilbur, John 1774-1856 *AmBi, ApCAB,
DcAmB, Drake, NatCAB 10, WhAm H*
Wilbur, John Milnor 1870- *WhAm 5*
Wilbur, Myron Thomas 1847- *NatCAB 14*
Wilbur, Ralph William 1869-1952 *NatCAB 42*
Wilbur, Ray Lyman 1875-1949 *BiDAmEd,
BiDrUSE, BiHiMed, DcAmB S4,
NatCAB 15, NatCAB 54, WhAm 2*
Wilbur, Rollin Henry 1863-1938 *WhAm 1*
Wilbur, S *NewYHSD*
Wilbur, Samuel 1585?-1656 *DcAmB,
NatCAB 12, WhAm H*
Wilbur, Sibyl 1871-1946 *WhAm 2*
Wilbur, VanRensselaer Gideon 1888-1962
NatCAB 49
Wilbur, William Allen 1864-1945 *NatCAB 33,
WhAm 2*
Wilbur, William Nelson 1860-1916 *NatCAB 17*
Wilby, Arthur Clyde 1885-1963 *WhAm 4*
Wilby, Ernest 1868-1957 *WhAm 3*
Wilby, Francis Bowditch 1883-1965 *WhAm 4*
Wilcke, Johan Carl 1732-1796 *DcScB*
Wilcocks, Alexander 1817- *Drake*
Wilcocks, Albert Spencer 1844-1919 *NatCAB 40*
Wilcox, Alexander Martin 1849-1929 *WhAm 1*
Wilcox, Alice Blythe Tucker *WomWWA 14*
Wilcox, Alice Hurd 1863- *WomWWA 14*
Wilcox, Alice Wilson 1871- *WomWWA 14*
Wilcox, Ansley 1856-1930 *NatCAB 12,
NatCAB 21, WhAm 1*
Wilcox, Armor David 1868- *WhAm 1*
Wilcox, Arthur Noble 1898-1963 *NatCAB 50*
Wilcox, Cadmus Marcellus 1824-1890 *BiDConf,
DcAmB, WebAMB, WhAm H*
Wilcox, Cadmus Marcellus 1825?-1890 *Drake,
NatCAB 11*
Wilcox, Cadmus Marcellus 1826-1890 *AmBi,
ApCAB, TwCBDA*
Wilcox, Carl C 1880- *WhAm 6*
Wilcox, Carlos 1794-1827 *ApCAB, Drake,
NatCAB 1*
Wilcox, Charles Bowser 1851-1940 *NatCAB 8,
WhAm 1*
Wilcox, Clair 1898-1970 *WhAm 5*
Wilcox, Clarence E 1880-1958 *WhAm 3*
Wilcox, Clarence Rothwell 1888-1960 *WhAm 4*
Wilcox, Delos Franklin 1873-1928 *DcAmB,*

WhAm 1
Wilcox, DeWitt Gilbert 1858-1951 *NatCAB 38,*
WhAm 5
Wilcox, Edward Byers 1893-1972 *WhAm 5*
Wilcox, Edwin Mead 1876-1931 *WhAm 1*
Wilcox, Elgin Roscoe 1892-1974 *WhAm 6*
Wilcox, Elias Bunn 1869-1942 *WhAm 5*
Wilcox, Elias Burn 1869-1942 *NatCAB 34*
Wilcox, Ella Wheeler 1845?-1919 *ApCAB*
Wilcox, Ella Wheeler 1850-1919 *AmBi,*
DcAmB, NotAW, WebAB
Wilcox, Ella Wheeler 1853-1919 *AmWom,*
NatCAB 11
Wilcox, Ella Wheeler 1855-1919 *WhAm 1,*
WomWWA 14
Wilcox, Elmer Almy 1867-1929 *WhAm 1*
Wilcox, Elsie Hart 1879-1954 *NatCAB 48*
Wilcox, Floyd Cleveland 1886-1958 *NatCAB 45*
Wilcox, Frances Gertrude Scott 1877-
WomWWA 14
Wilcox, Frank Langdon 1859-1963 *WhAm 4*
Wilcox, Frank Nelson 1887- *IIBEAAW*
Wilcox, Frank Stuart 1868-1942 *NatCAB 32*
Wilcox, Frank Z 1851- *NatCAB 13*
Wilcox, Frederick Bernon 1879-1965 *WhAm 4*
Wilcox, George Ansley 1849-1915 *NatCAB 16*
Wilcox, George Augustus 1830-1928
NatCAB 21
Wilcox, George Horace 1856-1940 *WhAm 1*
Wilcox, George Milo 1890-1965 *WhAm 4*
Wilcox, George Norton 1839-1933 *NatCAB 40*
Wilcox, Grace Rumsey *WomWWA 14*
Wilcox, Grafton Stiles 1879- *WhAm 6*
Wilcox, Hannah Tyler 1838- *AmWom*
Wilcox, Henry Buckley 1864-1931 *WhAm 1*
Wilcox, Herbert Budington 1874-1955
NatCAB 43, WhAm 3
Wilcox, Homer Bowen 1877-1950 *NatCAB 39*
Wilcox, Horace Cornwall 1824-1890 *NatCAB 9*
Wilcox, James Mark 1890-1956 *BiDrAC,*
WhAm 3, WhAmP
Wilcox, Jeduthun 1768-1838 *BiDrAC,*
WhAm H
Wilcox, Jeduthun 1769-1838 *BiAUS*
Wilcox, Jerome K 1902-1961 *WhAm 4*
Wilcox, John Alexander 1819-1864 *BiAUS,*
BiDConf, BiDrAC, WhAm H
Wilcox, John Angel James 1835- *NewYHSD*
Wilcox, John C 1870-1947 *WhAm 2*
Wilcox, John Walter, Jr. 1882-1942 *WhAm 2*
Wilcox, Joseph P *NewYHSD*
Wilcox, Leonard 1799-1850 *ApCAB, BiAUS,*
BiDrAC, NatCAB 11, TwCBDA,
WhAm H
Wilcox, LeRoy T 1876- *WhAm 3*
Wilcox, Lucius Merle 1858- *WhAm 4*
Wilcox, Marion Lawall 1872- *WomWWA 14*
Wilcox, Marrion 1858-1926 *WhAm 1*
Wilcox, Mary DeVol 1866- *WomWWA 14*
Wilcox, Mary Maul 1862- *WomWWA 14*
Wilcox, Nelson James 1875-1949 *WhAm 2*
Wilcox, Owen Nelson 1880-1950 *NatCAB 39*
Wilcox, Paul 1858-1912 *ApCAB X*
Wilcox, Perley Smith 1874-1953 *NatCAB 49,*
WhAm 3
Wilcox, Phineas Bacon 1795-1863 *Drake*
Wilcox, Phineas Bacon 1798-1863 *ApCAB*
Wilcox, Reynold Webb 1856-1931 *DcAmB,*
NatCAB 23, WhAm 1
Wilcox, Robert William 1855-1903 *BiDrAC,*
WhAm 1, WhAmP
Wilcox, Roy C 1891-1975 *WhAm 6*
Wilcox, Roy Porter 1873-1946 *WhAm 2*
Wilcox, Samuel Whitney 1847-1929
NatCAB 48
Wilcox, Sheldon E 1850- *WhAm 4*
Wilcox, Sidney Freeman 1855- *WhAm 1*
Wilcox, Stephen 1830-1893 *DcAmB,*
WhAm H
Wilcox, Theodore Burney 1856-1918
NatCAB 34
Wilcox, Timothy Erastus 1840-1932 *WhAm 1*
Wilcox, Urquhart 1874-1941 *NatCAB 53*
Wilcox, W H *NewYHSD*
Wilcox, Walter Dwight 1869- *WhAm 3*
Wilcox, Wayne Ayres 1932-1974 *WhAm 6*
Wilcox, William Craig 1867-1916 *WhAm 1*
Wilcox, William H 1831?- *NewYHSD*

Wilcox, William Walter 1862-1941 *NatCAB 30,*
WhAm 2
Wilcox, William Walter 1901-1940 *NatCAB 30*
Wilcox, William Walter, II 1825-1903
NatCAB 26
Wilczynski, Ernest Julius 1876-1932 *DcAmB,*
DcScB, WhAm 1
Wild, A Clement 1875-1950 *NatCAB 41*
Wild, Alexander *NewYHSD*
Wild, Edward Augustus 1825-1891 *ApCAB,*
NatCAB 5
Wild, Fred 1859- *WhAm 4*
Wild, Hamilton Gibbs 1827-1884 *NewYHSD*
Wild, Harrison Major 1861-1929 *WhAm 1*
Wild, Heinrich 1833-1902 *DcScB*
Wild, Henry Daniel 1866- *WhAm 4*
Wild, John Bannister 1839-1917 *NatCAB 17*
Wild, John Caspar 1804?-1846 *NewYHSD,*
WhAm H
Wild, John Caspar 1806?-1846 *IIBEAAW*
Wild, John Daniel 1902-1972 *WhAm 5*
Wild, Joseph 1834- *ApCAB*
Wild, Laura Hulda 1870- *WhAm 5*
Wild, Norman Russell 1921-1971 *WhAm 6*
Wild Bunch *REnAW*
Wilde, Arthur Herbert 1865-1944 *WhAm 2*
Wilde, Carl John 1888-1947 *NatCAB 37*
Wilde, David *NewYHSD*
Wilde, George Francis Faxon 1845-1911 *DcAmB,*
TwCBDA, WhAm 1
Wilde, Hamilton Gibbs 1827-1884 *NewYHSD*
Wilde, Laura Huldah *WomWWA 14*
Wilde, Norman 1867-1936 *NatCAB 42,*
WhAm 1
Wilde, Oscar Fingall O'Flahertie Wills
1854-1900 *McGEWB*
Wilde, Percival 1887-1953 *WhAm 3*
Wilde, Richard Henry 1789-1847 *ApCAB,*
BiAUS, BiDrAC, DcAmB, Drake,
NatCAB 1, TwCBDA, WhAm H,
WhAmP
Wilde, Samuel 1831-1890 *NatCAB 2*
Wilde, Samuel Sumner 1771-1855 *ApCAB,*
BiAUS, Drake
Wilde, William Allan 1827-1902 *NatCAB 15*
Wildenhain, Marguerite 1896- *BnEnAmA*
Wildenstein, Lazare Georges 1892-1963
WhAm 4
Wildenthal, Bryan 1904-1965 *WhAm 4*
Wilder, A Carter 1828-1875 *BiAUS*
Wilder, Abel Carter 1828-1875 *BiDrAC,*
WhAm H, WhAmP
Wilder, Alexander 1823-1908 *ApCAB, DcAmB,*
NatCAB 9, WhAm 1
Wilder, Amos Parker 1862-1936 *NatCAB 45,*
WhAm 1
Wilder, Arthur Ashford 1873- *WhAm 1*
Wilder, Burt Green 1841-1925 *ApCAB,*
NatCAB 4, WebAB, WhAm 1
Wilder, Charles Edward 1889-1950 *NatCAB 41*
Wilder, Charles Wesley 1877- *WhAm 5*
Wilder, Charlotte Frances d1916 *WhAm 1,*
WomWWA 14
Wilder, Daniel Webster 1832-1911 *ApCAB,*
NatCAB 11, WhAm 1
Wilder, David Robert d1932 *NatCAB 24*
Wilder, Edward 1843- *NatCAB 11*
Wilder, Ella Caroline Abbot *WomWWA 14*
Wilder, Emil *NewYHSD*
Wilder, F H *NewYHSD*
Wilder, George Warren 1866-1931 *NatCAB 13,*
NatCAB 22, WhAm 1
Wilder, Gerald Gardner 1879-1944 *WhAm 2*
Wilder, Gerrit Parmile 1863-1935 *WhAm 1*
Wilder, Harris Hawthorne 1864-1928 *AmBi,*
DcAmB, WhAm 1
Wilder, Harry C 1891-1965 *NatCAB 52*
Wilder, Herbert Augustus 1837-1922 *WhAm 1*
Wilder, Herbert Merrill 1864- *WhAm 1*
Wilder, Inez Whipple 1871-1929 *WhAm 1,*
WomWWA 14
Wilder, James Austin 1868-1934 *NatCAB 37*
Wilder, John Emery 1861-1932 *WhAm 1*
Wilder, John Francis 1864-1918 *NatCAB 17*
Wilder, John Thomas 1830-1917 *DcAmB,*
NatCAB 22, WhAm 2
Wilder, Jones Warren 1832-1894 *NatCAB 13*
Wilder, Kate Selby 1876- *WomWWA 14*

Wilder, Laura Ingalls 1867-1957 *REnAW,*
WhAm 3
Wilder, Laurence Russell 1887-1937 *WhAm 1*
Wilder, Louise Beebe 1878-1938 *WhAm 1*
Wilder, Marshall Pinckney 1798-1886 *AmBi,*
ApCAB, DcAmB, Drake, NatCAB 1,
TwCBDA, WhAm H
Wilder, Marshall Pinckney 1859- *ApCAB Sup*
Wilder, Marshall Pinckney 1859-1914
NatCAB 6
Wilder, Marshall Pinckney 1859-1915 *WhAm 1*
Wilder, Mary Field 1852- *WomWWA 14*
Wilder, Matilda *NewYHSD*
Wilder, Milton Jay 1915-1967 *NatCAB 53*
Wilder, Ralph Everett 1875-1924 *WhAm 1*
Wilder, Robert Ingersoll 1901-1974 *WhAm 6*
Wilder, Robert Parmalee 1863-1938 *DcAmReB*
Wilder, Robert Parmelee 1863-1938 *WhAm 1*
Wilder, Russell Morse 1885-1959 *NatCAB 45,*
WhAm 3A
Wilder, S Fannie Gerry 1850- *AmWom,*
WomWWA 14
Wilder, Salmon Willoughby 1870- *ApCAB X,*
WhAm 5
Wilder, Sampson Uryling Stoddard 1780-1865
WhAm H
Wilder, Sampson Vryling Stoddard 1780-1865
NatCAB 7
Wilder, Samson Vryling Stoddard 1780-1865
ApCAB
Wilder, T Edward 1855-1919 *WhAm 1*
Wilder, Thornton Niven 1897-1975 *EncAB,*
McGEWB, WebAB, WhAm 6
Wilder, Wilbur Elliott 1856-1952 *WhAm 3*
Wilder, William Hamlin 1860-1935 *WhAm 1*
Wilder, William Henry 1849-1920 *NatCAB 24,*
WhAm 1
Wilder, William Henry 1855-1913 *BiDrAC,*
WhAm 1
Wildermuth, Joe Henry 1897-1972 *WhAm 6*
Wildermuth, Ora Leonard 1882-1964 *WhAm 4*
Wildes, Frank 1843-1903 *ApCAB Sup,*
TwCBDA, WhAm 1
Wildes, George Dudley 1819- *ApCAB*
Wildes, Mary 1876- *WomWWA 14*
Wildey, Thomas 1782-1861 *NatCAB 11*
Wildey, Thomas 1783-1861 *ApCAB, Drake*
Wildi, John 1853-1910 *NatCAB 33*
Wildman, Clyde Everett 1889-1955 *NatCAB 43,*
WhAm 3
Wildman, Edwin 1863-1932 *AmBi*
Wildman, Edwin 1867-1932 *WhAm 1*
Wildman, Frank Black 1856-1947 *NatCAB 39*
Wildman, Jennie Gray *WomWWA 14*
Wildman, Marian Warner 1876- *WhAm 5,*
WomWWA 14
Wildman, Murray Shipley 1868-1930 *DcAmB,*
NatCAB 25, WhAm 1
Wildman, Rounseville 1864- *ApCAB Sup*
Wildman, Zalmon 1775-1835 *BiAUS, BiDrAC,*
WhAm H
Wildner, Harry Charles 1893-1966 *WhAm 4*
Wildrick, Isaac 1803-1892 *BiAUS, BiDrAC,*
WhAm H
Wilds, Elmer Harrison 1888-1960 *NatCAB 50*
Wilds, George James, Jr. 1889-1951
NatCAB 40, WhAm 3
Wilds, Robert Henry 1883-1949 *NatCAB 38*
Wilds, William Naylor 1879-1951 *WhAm 3*
Wildt, Rupert 1905-1976 *AsBiEn, WhAm 6*
Wile, Frank Sloan 1925-1974 *WhAm 6*
Wile, Frederic William 1873-1941 *WhAm 1*
Wile, Frederic William, Jr. 1908-1961 *WhAm 4*
Wile, Ira Solomon 1877-1943 *NatCAB 35,*
WhAm 2
Wile, Udo Julius 1882-1965 *WhAm 4*
Wile, William Conrad 1847-1913 *WhAm 1*
Wilenchik, Israel William 1894-1961
NatCAB 49
Wiles, Charles Peter 1870-1944 *WhAm 2*
Wiles, Cora Young 1864-1950 *NatCAB 39,*
WomWWA 14
Wiles, Irving Ramsay 1861-1948 *ApCAB,*
ApCAB X, NatCAB 6, TwCBDA,
WhAm 2
Wiles, John Henry 1861-1941 *WhAm 1*
Wiles, Kimball 1913-1968 *BiDAmEd,*
WhAm 5

Wiles, Lemuel Maynard 1826-1905 *AmBi,
ApCAB, IIBEAAW, NatCAB 12,
NewYHSD, TwCBDA, WhAm 1*
Wiles, V McKinley 1906-1970 *NatCAB 55*
Wiles, William *NewYHSD*
Wiley, Alexander 1884-1967 *BiDrAC,
NatCAB 53, WhAm 4A, WhAmP*
Wiley, Andrew Jackson 1862-1931 *DcAmB,
WhAm 1*
Wiley, Anna Kelton 1877- *WomWWA 14*
Wiley, Ariosto Appling d1908 *WhAm 1*
Wiley, Ariosto Appling 1848-1908 *BiDrAC,
WhAmP*
Wiley, Ariosto Appling 1849-1908 *NatCAB 8*
Wiley, Calvin Henderson 1819-1887 *ApCAB,
BiDAmEd, DcAmB, Drake, WhAm H*
Wiley, David d1813? *DcAmB*
Wiley, David 1758?-1815? *EncAAH*
Wiley, David 1768?-1813 *WhAm H*
Wiley, Edwin 1872-1924 *NatCAB 19,
WhAm 1*
Wiley, Edwin Hardin 1877-1951 *NatCAB 40*
Wiley, Ephraim Emerson 1814-1893 *DcAmB,
WhAm H*
Wiley, Forbes Bagley 1880-1956 *NatCAB 45*
Wiley, Franklin Baldwin 1861-1930 *WhAm 1*
Wiley, H Orton 1877- *WhAm 5*
Wiley, Harvey Washington 1844-1930 *AmBi,
ApCAB, ApCAB X, DcAmB, DcScB,
EncAAH, EncAB, McGEWB, NatCAB 9,
NatCAB 21, TwCBDA, WebAB,
WhAm 1*
Wiley, Henry Ariosto 1867-1943 *NatCAB 33,
WhAm 2*
Wiley, Herbert Victor 1891-1954 *NatCAB 45,
WhAm 3*
Wiley, Hugh 1884-1969 *WhAm 5*
Wiley, Isaac William 1825-1884 *ApCAB,
NatCAB 5, TwCBDA, WhAm H*
Wiley, James Sullivan 1808-1891 *BiAUS,
BiDrAC, WhAm H*
Wiley, John 1808-1891 *ApCAB Sup*
Wiley, John Adams 1825-1905 *NatCAB 17*
Wiley, John Alexander 1843-1909 *ApCAB Sup,
WhAm 1*
Wiley, John Cooper 1893-1967 *NatCAB 53,
WhAm 4*
Wiley, John McClure 1846-1912 *BiDrAC*
Wiley, Josephus Lee 1873- *WhoColR*
Wiley, Louis 1869-1935 *WhAm 1*
Wiley, Mary Marshall 1859- *WomWWA 14*
Wiley, Merlin 1875-1963 *NatCAB 50*
Wiley, Oliver Cicero 1851-1917 *BiDrAC,
WhAmP*
Wiley, Reeley B 1896-1942 *NatCAB 33*
Wiley, Robert Hopkins 1886-1952 *WhAm 3*
Wiley, Samuel Ernest 1904-1968 *WhAm 5*
Wiley, Samuel Whitsitt 1851-1923 *NatCAB 20*
Wiley, Samuel William 1878-1932 *NatCAB 23*
Wiley, Walter H 1862-1931 *WhAm 1*
Wiley, William Foust d1944 *WhAm 2*
Wiley, William Halsted 1842-1925 *BiDrAC,
NatCAB 12, WhAm 1*
Wiley, William Ogden 1862-1958 *WhAm 3*
Wilfley, Arthur Redman 1860-1927 *NatCAB 21*
Wilfley, Earle 1867-1936 *NatCAB 27*
Wilfley, Lebbeus Redman 1866-1926 *WhAm 1*
Wilfley, Lebbeus Redman 1867-1926
NatCAB 41
Wilfley, Xenophon Pierce 1871-1931 *BiDrAC,
NatCAB 25, WhAm 1*
Wilford, James William 1878-1941 *NatCAB 30*
Wilford, Loran Frederick 1893-1972 *WhAm 5*
Wilfred, Thomas 1889-1968 *NatCAB 55*
Wilgress, L Dana 1892-1969 *WhAm 5*
Wilgus, Horace LaFayette 1859-1935 *WhAm 1*
Wilgus, Sidney Dean 1872-1940 *NatCAB 42,
WhAm 1*
Wilgus, William John 1819-1853 *IIBEAAW,
NewYHSD*
Wilgus, William John 1865-1949 *NatCAB 11,
WhAm 2*
Wilhelm IV, Landgrave Of Hesse 1532-1592
DcScB
Wilhelm, August *NewYHSD*
Wilhelm, Charles Marcus 1858-1947
NatCAB 51
Wilhelm, Donald 1887-1945 *WhAm 2*

Wilhelm, Richard 1868-1940 *NatCAB 33*
Wilhelm, Richard Herman 1909-1968
NatCAB 54, WhAm 5
Wilhelm, Stephen Roger 1905-1967 *NatCAB 53,
WhAm 4*
Wilhelmina, Queen 1880-1962 *McGEWB,
WhWW-II*
Wilhelmina, Helena Pauline Maria 1880-1962
WhAm 4
Wilhelmj, Charles Martel 1896-1963 *WhAm 4*
Wilhelmsen, Karl John 1894-1964 *WhAm 4*
Wilhelmy, Ludwig Ferdinand 1812-1864 *DcScB*
Wilhite, Mary Holloway 1831-1892 *AmWom*
Wilhoit, Edward Morton 1864-1929
NatCAB 23
Wilhoit, Eugene Lovell d1961 *WhAm 4*
Wilhorst, Cora De 1835- *ApCAB*
Wilke, Hubert 1855-1940 *NatCAB 29*
Wilke, Otto John 1874- *WhAm 5*
Wilke, William 1855-1930 *NatCAB 29*
Wilkening, Frederic Wilhelm 1881-1954
NatCAB 46
Wilkens, Henry A J 1868- *NatCAB 15*
Wilker, Arthur V 1888-1960 *WhAm 3*
Wilkerson, Albert Wadsworth 1870-1941
WhAm 1
Wilkerson, James Herbert 1869-1948 *WhAm 2*
Wilkerson, Marcus Manley 1896-1953 *WhAm 3*
Wilkerson, Thomas Jefferson 1868-1949
NatCAB 38
Wilkerson, William Wesley, Jr. 1897-1961
NatCAB 48, WhAm 4
Wilkes, Charles 1798-1877 *AmBi, ApCAB,
DcAmB, McGEWB, NatCAB 2,
NewYHSD, TwCBDA, WebAB,
WebAMB, WhAm H*
Wilkes, Charles 1801- *BiAUS, Drake*
Wilkes, Charles S 1920- *WhAm 6*
Wilkes, Edmund, Jr. 1885-1962 *NatCAB 50*
Wilkes, Eliza Tupper 1844- *AmWom,
WhAm 4*
Wilkes, Frances Willamen *WomWWA 14*
Wilkes, George d1885 *Drake*
Wilkes, George 1817-1885 *DcAmB, WhAm H*
Wilkes, George 1820-1885 *ApCAB*
Wilkes, George Henry 1866-1950 *NatCAB 39*
Wilkes, Henry 1805-1886 *ApCAB*
Wilkes, Jack Stauffer 1917-1969 *WhAm 5*
Wilkes, James Claiborne, Sr. 1899-1968
WhAm 5
Wilkes, John 1725-1797 *McGEWB*
Wilkes, John 1827-1900? *BiDConf*
Wilkes, John 1895-1957 *WhAm 3*
Wilkes, John Summerfield 1841-1908 *WhAm 1*
Wilkes, Peter Singleton 1827-1900 *BiDConf*
Wilkeson, Bayard 1844-1863 *ApCAB*
Wilkeson, Frank 1845- *ApCAB*
Wilkeson, Frank 1848- *WhAm 4*
Wilkeson, Mary Juana 1879- *WomWWA 14*
Wilkeson, Samuel 1781-1848 *ApCAB, DcAmB,
NatCAB 4, REnAW, WhAm H*
Wilkeson, Samuel 1817- *ApCAB*
Wilkie, Franc B 1830-1892 *NatCAB 1*
Wilkie, Franc Bangs 1832-1892 *DcAmB,
WhAm H*
Wilkie, Francis Bangs 1832-1892 *ApCAB*
Wilkie, Harold McLean 1890-1950 *WhAm 3*
Wilkie, Janet Ormsbee 1862- *WomWWA 14*
Wilkie, John *NewYHSD*
Wilkie, John Elbert 1860-1934 *WhAm 1*
Wilkie, Robert D 1828-1903 *NewYHSD*
Wilkie, Thomas *NewYHSD*
Wilkin, Herbert Rae 1891-1938 *NatCAB 29*
Wilkin, Jacob Wilson 1837-1907 *NatCAB 13,
WhAm 1*
Wilkin, James Foster 1853-1914 *NatCAB 16*
Wilkin, James Whitney 1762-1845 *BiAUS,
BiDrAC, WhAm H*
Wilkin, Matilda Jane Campbell 1846-
WomWWA 14
Wilkin, Samuel Jones 1793-1866 *BiAUS,
BiDrAC, WhAm H*
Wilkins, Beriah 1846-1905 *BiDrAC,
NatCAB 6, WhAm 1, WhAmP*
Wilkins, Charles Trowbridge 1861-1921
NatCAB 18
Wilkins, Ernest Hatch 1880-1966 *NatCAB 53,
WhAm 4*

Wilkins, Frank Lemoyne 1851-1926 *WhAm 1*
Wilkins, Sir George Hubert 1888-1958
McGEWB
Wilkins, George W *NewYHSD*
Wilkins, H Blakiston 1871-1940 *NatCAB 42*
Wilkins, Harold Tom 1891-1960 *WhAm 4*
Wilkins, Horace M 1885-1953 *WhAm 3*
Wilkins, Sir Hubert 1888-1958 *WhAm 3*
Wilkins, Isaac 1742-1830 *ApCAB*
Wilkins, J Ernest 1894-1959 *WhAm 3*
Wilkins, James F 1808-1888 *IIBEAAW,
NewYHSD*
Wilkins, John 1614-1672 *DcScB*
Wilkins, John 1733-1809 *ApCAB*
Wilkins, John A 1843- *WhAm 3*
Wilkins, John Howard, Jr. 1901-1967
NatCAB 53
Wilkins, John Julian 1866-1940 *NatCAB 43*
Wilkins, John Julian, Jr. 1899-1954 *NatCAB 43*
Wilkins, Lawrence Augustus 1878-1945
WhAm 2
Wilkins, Lawson 1894-1963 *NatCAB 53,
WhAm 4*
Wilkins, Lewanna 1869- *WomWWA 14*
Wilkins, Lewis Morris 1801-1885 *ApCAB*
Wilkins, Lydia K 1873- *WomWWA 14*
Wilkins, Mary Eleanor d1930 *NotAW,
WebAB*
Wilkins, Mary Eleanor 1852-1930 *AmBi*
Wilkins, Mary Eleanor 1862-1930 *AmWom,
NatCAB 9*
Wilkins, Maurice Hugh Frederick 1916- *AsBiEn*
Wilkins, Milan William 1856- *WhAm 1*
Wilkins, Ralph Whorton 1901-1966 *NatCAB 52*
Wilkins, Raymond Sanger 1891-1971 *WhAm 5*
Wilkins, Robert Bruce 1884-1968 *NatCAB 55*
Wilkins, Robert Wallace 1906- *AsBiEn*
Wilkins, Ross 1799-1872 *BiAUS, DcAmB,
NatCAB 18, WhAm H*
Wilkins, Roy 1901- *EncAB, McGEWB,
WebAB*
Wilkins, Sarah *NewYHSD*
Wilkins, Thomas Russell 1891-1940 *WhAm 1,
WhAm 2*
Wilkins, Vaughan 1890-1959 *WhAm 3*
Wilkins, Walter 1908-1953 *WhAm 4*
Wilkins, William 1779-1865 *ApCAB, BiAUS,
BiDrAC, BiDrUSE, DcAmB, Drake,
NatCAB 6, TwCBDA, WhAm H,
WhAmP*
Wilkins, William 1825- *NatCAB 1*
Wilkins, William Duncan 1826-1882
NatCAB 18
Wilkins, William Glyde 1854-1921 *WhAm 1*
Wilkins, William James 1898-1950 *NatCAB 39,
WhAm 3*
Wilkins-Freeman, Mary Eleanor *TwCBDA*
Wilkinson *NewYHSD*
Wilkinson, Albert Edmund 1879- *WhAm 6*
Wilkinson, Alfred Dickinson 1907-1970
WhAm 5
Wilkinson, Alfred Ernest 1846-1932 *WhAm 1*
Wilkinson, Andrew d1921 *WhAm 1*
Wilkinson, Annie Carter *WomWWA 14*
Wilkinson, Cecil J 1894-1961 *WhAm 4*
Wilkinson, Charles Edward 1869-1952
NatCAB 41
Wilkinson, Charles Fore, Jr. 1912-1959
WhAm 3
Wilkinson, Clarence 1882-1954 *NatCAB 41*
Wilkinson, David 1771-1852 *DcAmB,
NatCAB 8, WhAm H*
Wilkinson, Drusilla Dallman *WomWWA 14*
Wilkinson, Edith *WomWWA 14*
Wilkinson, Edwin 1875-1919 *NatCAB 19*
Wilkinson, Elizabeth Hays 1880- *WhAm 6*
Wilkinson, Florence *WomWWA 14*
Wilkinson, Ford Lee, Jr. 1895-1958 *NatCAB 49,
WhAm 3*
Wilkinson, Garnet Crummel 1879- *WhoColR*
Wilkinson, George Lawrence 1868-1958
WhAm 3
Wilkinson, George Richard 1891-1964
NatCAB 53
Wilkinson, George William 1831-1924
NatCAB 6
Wilkinson, Gwendolen Overton 1874-
WomWWA 14

Wilkinson, Horace Simpson 1867-1937
NatCAB 40
Wilkinson, Horace Simpson 1868-1937
WhAm 1
Wilkinson, Howard Sargent d1948 *WhAm 2*
Wilkinson, Ignatius Martin 1887-1953
NatCAB 42, WhAm 3
Wilkinson, Mrs. J *NewYHSD*
Wilkinson, James 1757-1825 *AmBi, ApCAB,
BiAUS, DcAmB, Drake, EncAB,
McGEWB, NatCAB 1, REnAW,
TwCBDA, WebAB, WebAMB, WhAm H*
Wilkinson, James Cuthbert 1880- *WhAm 6*
Wilkinson, Jasper Newton 1851- *WhAm 4*
Wilkinson, Jemima 1752-1819 *DcAmB,
DcAmReB, EncAAH, NatCAB 8,
NotAW, WhAm H*
Wilkinson, Jemima 1753?-1819 *ApCAB, Drake,
NatCAB 1*
Wilkinson, Jeremiah 1741-1831 *DcAmB,
NatCAB 8, WhAm H*
Wilkinson, Jesse 1790?-1861 *ApCAB*
Wilkinson, John *NewYHSD*
Wilkinson, John 1821-1891 *ApCAB, BiDConf,
DcAmB, TwCBDA, WebAMB, WhAm H*
Wilkinson, John 1840-1919 *NatCAB 2*
Wilkinson, John 1913-1974 *WhAm 6*
Wilkinson, Joseph A 1851-1930 *WhAm 3*
Wilkinson, Joseph Biddle 1845- *WhAm 4*
Wilkinson, Joseph Green 1857-1933 *WhAm 1*
Wilkinson, Mai Scott 1872- *WomWWA 14*
Wilkinson, Marguerite Ogden Bigelow 1883-1928
NatCAB 21, WhAm 1
Wilkinson, Melville LeVaunt 1865-1925
WhAm 1
Wilkinson, Morton Smith 1819-1894 *ApCAB,
BiAUS, BiDrAC, NatCAB 12, TwCBDA,
WhAm H, WhAmP*
Wilkinson, Oscar 1870-1950 *NatCAB 39*
Wilkinson, Oziel 1744-1815 *NatCAB 8*
Wilkinson, Paul Judson 1893-1967 *NatCAB 53*
Wilkinson, Robert Johnson 1888-1953 *WhAm 3*
Wilkinson, Robert Shaw 1865-1932 *AmBi,
BiDAmEd, DcAmB, EncAAH, WhAm 1,
WhoColR*
Wilkinson, Theodore Stark 1847-1921 *BiDrAC,
NatCAB 14*
Wilkinson, Theodore Stark 1888-1946
DcAmB S4, WebAMB, WhAm 2
Wilkinson, Warring 1834-1918 *NatCAB 18,
WhAm 1*
Wilkinson, William 1760-1852 *NatCAB 10*
Wilkinson, William Albert 1873- *WhAm 5*
Wilkinson, William Cleaver 1833-1920 *ApCAB,
NatCAB 11, WhAm 1*
Wilkinson, William Cook 1866-1930 *WhAm 1*
Wilkinson, William Donald 1901-1969 *WhAm 5*
Wilkinson, William John 1874-1950 *WhAm 3*
Wilkof, Morris 1890-1968 *NatCAB 57*
Wilks, Katherine L *WomWWA 14*
Wilks, Sir Samuel 1824-1911 *BiHiMed*
Wilks, Samuel Stanley 1906-1964 *DcScB,
WhAm 4*
Will, Allen Sinclair 1868-1934 *DcAmB,
WhAm 1*
Will, Arthur A 1871-1940 *WhAm 2*
Will, Arthur Percival 1868-1950 *WhAm 3*
Will, George Francis 1884-1955 *NatCAB 49*
Will, Harold Henry 1889-1963 *NatCAB 55*
Will, Howard Chester 1892-1962 *NatCAB 54*
Will, John M August 1834-1910 *NewYHSD*
Will, Louis 1857-1932 *WhAm 1*
Will, Theodore St. Clair 1886-1944 *WhAm 2*
Will, Thomas Elmer 1861- *WhAm 4*
Willaert, Adrian 1480?-1562 *McGEWB*
Willan, Robert 1757- *BiHiMed*
Willard, Abijah 1722-1789 *ApCAB, Drake*
Willard, Allie C 1860- *AmWom*
Willard, Archibald MacNeal 1836-1918
*NatCAB 24, NewYHSD, WhAm HA,
WhAm 4*
Willard, Arthur Cutts 1878-1960 *NatCAB 49,
WhAm 4*
Willard, Arthur Lee 1870-1935 *WhAm 1*
Willard, Asaph 1786-1880 *NewYHSD*
Willard, Ashbel P 1820-1861 *BiAUS*
Willard, Ashbel Parsons 1820-1860 *NatCAB 13,
TwCBDA*

Willard, Ashton Rollins 1858-1918 *WhAm 1*
Willard, Calla Scott *WomWWA 14*
Willard, Charles Andrew 1857-1914 *WhAm 1*
Willard, Charles J 1889-1974 *WhAm 6*
Willard, Charles Wesley 1827-1880 *BiAUS,
BiDrAC, WhAm H, WhAmP*
Willard, Charlotte Richards *WomWWA 14*
Willard, Chester Ezra 1886-1961 *WhAm 4*
Willard, Clarence George 1886-1956
NatCAB 43
Willard, Cordelia Young 1822- *AmWom*
Willard, Daniel 1861-1942 *DcAmB S3,
NatCAB 18, NatCAB 30, WhAm 2*
Willard, Daniel, Jr. 1894-1940 *NatCAB 29*
Willard, Daniel Everett 1862- *NatCAB 13,
WhAm 4*
Willard, DeForest 1846-1910 *DcAmB,
NatCAB 12, NatCAB 15, WhAm 1*
Willard, DeForest Porter 1884-1957
NatCAB 47, WhAm 3
Willard, Edward Lawrence 1904-1973 *WhAm 6*
Willard, Edward Newell 1835-1910 *NatCAB 8*
Willard, Edward Smith 1853-1915 *WhAm 1*
Willard, Eleanor Withey 1858- *WhAm 4,
WomWWA 14*
Willard, Emma Hart 1787-1870 *AmBi,
AmWom, ApCAB, BiDAmEd, DcAmB,
Drake, EncAB, McGEWB, NotAW,
TwCBDA, WebAB, WhAm H*
Willard, Emma Hart 1787-1876 *NatCAB 1*
Willard, Ernest Russell 1856-1937 *NatCAB 28,
WhAm 4*
Willard, F W *NewYHSD*
Willard, Frances Elizabeth Caroline 1839-1898
*AmBi, AmWom, ApCAB, BiDAmEd,
DcAmB, DcAmReB, Drake, EncAB,
McGEWB, NatCAB 1, NotAW,
TwCBDA, WebAB, WhAm H, WhAmP*
Willard, Frank Harvey 1865-1937 *NatCAB 27*
Willard, Frank Henry 1893-1958 *NatCAB 46,
WhAm 3, WhAm 4*
Willard, Frederic Wilson 1881-1947 *WhAm 2*
Willard, George 1824-1901 *BiAUS, BiDrAC,
WhAmP*
Willard, Harley Richard 1875-1946 *NatCAB 37*
Willard, Henry 1802-1855 *NewYHSD*
Willard, Henry Augustus 1822-1909
NatCAB 22, WhAm 1
Willard, Henry Kellogg 1856-1926 *NatCAB 22*
Willard, Hobart Hurd 1881-1974 *WhAm 6*
Willard, Horace Mann 1842-1907 *NatCAB 15,
WhAm 1*
Willard, Hudson Elliott 1860-1948 *NatCAB 37*
Willard, Ira Farnum 1911-1965 *WhAm 4*
Willard, James Daniel 1817- *NewYHSD*
Willard, James Field 1876-1935 *DcAmB S1,
WhAm 1*
Willard, James Orville 1814-1855 *NatCAB 15*
Willard, John 1792-1862 *ApCAB, BiAUS,
NatCAB 4, WhAm H*
Willard, John 1826-1913 *NatCAB 16*
Willard, John Artemas 1887-1963 *WhAm 4*
Willard, John Dayton 1885-1931 *NatCAB 23*
Willard, John Dwight 1799-1864 *ApCAB,
BiAUS, Drake, NatCAB 5*
Willard, Joseh Edward 1865-1924 *WhAm 1*
Willard, Joseph 1738-1804 *AmBi, ApCAB,
DcAmB, Drake, NatCAB 6, TwCBDA,
WhAm H*
Willard, Joseph 1798-1865 *ApCAB, DcAmB,
Drake, NatCAB 4, WhAm H*
Willard, Joseph Augustus 1816- *WhAm 4*
Willard, Joseph Edward 1863-1924 *NatCAB 20*
Willard, Joseph Edward 1865-1924 *DcAmB*
Willard, Josiah 1681-1756 *ApCAB, NatCAB 4*
Willard, Josiah Flint 1869-1907 *DcAmB S1*
Willard, Josiah Flynt 1869-1907 *AmBi,
NatCAB 13, WhAm 1*
Willard, Julia Reid 1871- *WomWWA 14*
Willard, Julius Terrass 1862-1950 *WhAm 3*
Willard, Katherine 1866- *AmWom*
Willard, Leigh 1880-1951 *WhAm 3*
Willard, Leroy Randall 1864-1917 *NatCAB 18*
Willard, Lillian Winifred 1876- *WhAm 5*
Willard, Luvia Margaret 1882- *BiCAW,
WomWWA 14*
Willard, Mary Bannister 1841- *AmWom*

Willard, Mary Ella Stoner 1876-
WomWWA 14
Willard, Mary Frances *WomWWA 14*
Willard, Mary Hatch 1855-1926 *WomWWA 14*
Willard, Mary Hatch 1856-1926 *DcAmB*
Willard, Mary Thompson Hill 1805-1892
AmWom
Willard, Monroe Livingstone 1853- *WhAm 4*
Willard, Roy H 1902-1968 *WhAm 5*
Willard, Samuel 1639?-1707 *DcAmB*
Willard, Samuel 1640-1707 *AmBi, ApCAB,
DcAmReB, Drake, NatCAB 6, TwCBDA,
WhAm H*
Willard, Samuel 1705-1741 *ApCAB*
Willard, Samuel 1775-1859 *ApCAB, DcAmB,
WhAm H*
Willard, Samuel 1776-1859 *Drake*
Willard, Sidney 1780-1856 *ApCAB, DcAmB,
Drake, NatCAB 4, WhAm H*
Willard, Sidney 1831-1862 *ApCAB,
NatCAB 4*
Willard, Simon 1605-1676 *ApCAB, DcAmB,
Drake, NatCAB 4, WhAm H*
Willard, Simon 1753-1848 *DcAmB, WhAm H*
Willard, Simon 1795-1874 *ApCAB*
Willard, Solomon 1783-1861 *DcAmB,
NewYHSD, WhAm H*
Willard, Solomon 1783-1862 *ApCAB,
NatCAB 1, NatCAB 4*
Willard, Sylvester David 1825-1865 *ApCAB,
NatCAB 7, NatCAB 4*
Willard, Theodore Arthur 1862-1943
NatCAB 31, WhAm 2
Willard, Thomas Rigney 1844-1929 *WhAm 1*
Willard, William 1819-1904 *Drake, NewYHSD*
Willard, William A 1873- *WhAm 5*
Willard, William Charles 1872-1930 *WhAm 1*
Willard, William Dodsworth 1867-1952
NatCAB 46
Willauer, Arthur Ebbs 1876-1912 *NatCAB 37*
Willauer, Katherine Whiting 1880-
WomWWA 14
Willauer, Whiting 1906-1962 *WhAm 4*
Willaumetz, Jean-Baptiste Philibert 1763-1845
ApCAB
Willcox, Albert Oliver 1810- *ApCAB*
Willcox, Charles Henry 1839-1909 *NatCAB 19*
Willcox, Cornelis DeWitt 1861-1938 *WhAm 1*
Willcox, David 1849-1907 *WhAm 1*
Willcox, Ella Goodenow 1854- *WomWWA 14*
Willcox, James M 1861-1935 *WhAm 1*
Willcox, Julius Abner d1932 *WhAm 1,
WhAm 1C*
Willcox, Louise Collier 1865-1929 *DcAmB,
WhAm 1, WomWWA 14*
Willcox, Mary Alice 1856- *WhAm 3,
WomWWA 14*
Willcox, Orlando Boialvr 1823-1907 *NatCAB 4*
Willcox, Orlando Bolivar 1823-1907 *AmBi,
ApCAB, DcAmB, Drake, TwCBDA,
WhAm 1*
Willcox, Walter Francis 1861-1964 *WhAm 4,
WhAm 6*
Willcox, Walter Ross Baumes d1947 *WhAm 2*
Willcox, Washington Frederick 1834-1909
BiDrAC
Willcox, Westmore 1894-1971 *WhAm 5*
Willcox, William G 1859-1923 *WhAm 1*
Willcox, William H 1831?- *NewYHSD*
Willcox, William Henry 1821-1904 *WhAm 1*
Willcox, William Russell 1863-1940
NatCAB 14, WhAm 1
Willcutt, Clarence Elvin 1884-1958 *NatCAB 47*
Willdenow, Karl Ludwig 1765-1812 *DcScB*
Willebrandt, Mabel Walker 1889-1963
ApCAB X, WhAm 4
Wilekens, Jacobus 1571-1633 *ApCAB*
Willen, Pearl Larner 1904- *WhAm 5*
Willet, Anne Lee 1866-1943 *NatCAB 34,
WhAm 2*
Willet, Joseph Edgerton 1826- *ApCAB*
Willet, William 1867-1921 *DcAmB*
Willets, David Gifford 1873- *WhAm 5*
Willets, Elmore Abram 1861-1949 *NatCAB 38*
Willets, Gilson 1869- *WhAm 5*
Willets, Samuel 1795-1883 *NatCAB 8*
Willett, Francis 1693-1776 *NatCAB 4*
Willett, George F 1870- *WhAm 5*

Willett, Herbert Lockwood 1864-1944
DcAmB S3, DcAmReB, WhAm 2
Willett, Howard Levanselaer, Sr. 1884-1965
WhAm 4
Willett, Howard Levansellar 1884-1963
NatCAB 53
Willett, Mabel Hind 1874- *WomWWA 14*
Willett, Marinus 1740-1830 *AmBi, ApCAB,
DcAmB, Drake, NatCAB 1, NatCAB 3,
TwCBDA, WhAm H*
Willett, Oscar Louis 1881-1945 *WhAm 2*
Willett, Raymond Clair 1877-1950 *NatCAB 42*
Willett, Thomas 1611?-1674 *ApCAB,
NatCAB 8*
Willett, Thomas 1646- *ApCAB*
Willett, William Forte, Jr. 1869-1938 *BiDrAC,
WhAm 5*
Willett, William Marinus 1803-1895 *ApCAB,
TwCBDA*
Willetts, Deborah 1789-1880 *ApCAB*
Willetts, Ernest Ward 1879- *WhAm 6*
Willetts, Herbert 1899-1968 *WhAm 5*
Willetts, Jacob 1785-1860 *ApCAB*
Willetts, William Prentice 1890-1964 *WhAm 4*
Willever, John Calvin 1865- *WhAm 5*
Willey, Austin 1806- *ApCAB*
Willey, Benjamin Glazier 1796-1867 *ApCAB*
Willey, Calvin 1776-1838 *TwCBDA*
Willey, Calvin 1776-1858 *ApCAB, BiAUS,
BiDrAC, NatCAB 11, WhAm H*
Willey, Charles Herbert 1898-1969 *WhAm 5*
Willey, D Allen 1860-1917 *WhAm 1*
Willey, Earle Dukes 1889-1950 *BiDrAC,
NatCAB 39, WhAm 2*
Willey, Fay Henry 1894-1950 *NatCAB 52*
Willey, Henry 1824- *ApCAB, NatCAB 10,
WhAm 1*
Willey, John Heston 1854-1942 *NatCAB 3,
WhAm 2*
Willey, Malcolm Macdonald 1897-1974
WhAm 6
Willey, Norman Bushnell 1838- *NatCAB 1,
NatCAB 12, WhAm 4*
Willey, Norman LeRoy 1882-1959 *WhAm 4*
Willey, Samuel Hopkins 1821-1914 *DcAmB,
WhAm 4*
Willey, Stansbury Jacobs 1845- *NatCAB 2*
Willey, Waitman Thomas 1811- *ApCAB,
BiAUS*
Willey, Waitman Thomas 1811-1900 *BiDrAC,
DcAmB, TwCBDA, WhAmP*
Willey, Waitman Thomas 1811-1901
NatCAB 12
Willford, Albert Clinton 1877-1937 *BiDrAC,
WhAm 3*
Willging, Eugene P 1909-1965 *WhAm 4*
Willging, Joseph C 1884-1959 *WhAm 3*
Willhite, Frank Vanatta 1878-1944 *WhAm 2*
Willi, Albert B 1895-1968 *WhAm 5*
William I 1027?-1087 *McGEWB*
William I 1772-1843 *McGEWB*
William I 1797-1888 *McGEWB*
William II 1058?-1100 *McGEWB*
William II 1859-1941 *McGEWB*
William III 1650-1702 *McGEWB, WhAm H*
William IV 1765-1837 *McGEWB*
William Heytesbury *DcScB*
William Of Auvergne 1180?-1249 *DcScB*
William Of Malmesbury 1090?-1142? *McGEWB*
William Of Moerbeke *DcScB*
William Of Ockham 1284?-1347 *DcScB,
McGEWB*
William Of Saint-Cloud *DcScB*
William Of Sherwood *DcScB*
William Of Tyre 1130?-1185? *McGEWB*
William The Englishman *DcScB*
William The Silent 1533-1584 *McGEWB,
WhoMilH*
William, Maurice 1881-1973 *WhAm 6*
Williams *NewYHSD*
Williams, A *NewYHSD*
Williams, A J 1898-1956 *WhAm 3*
Williams, A Wilberforce 1865- *WhoColR*
Williams, Abigail Osgood 1823-1913 *NewYHSD*
Williams, Abraham Pease 1832-1911 *WhAm 1*
Williams, Abram Pease 1832-1911 *ApCAB,
BiDrAC, NatCAB 13, TwCBDA*
Williams, Adele 1868- *AmWom*

Williams, Adolph Dill 1871-1952 *NatCAB 46*
Williams, Alan Meredith 1909-1972 *WhAm 6*
Williams, Albert Frank 1876-1958 *WhAm 3*
Williams, Albert Nathaniel 1888-1961 *WhAm 4*
Williams, Albert Rhys 1883-1962 *WhAm 4*
Williams, Alexander Elliot 1875-1948 *WhAm 3*
Williams, Alexander John 1790-1814 *ApCAB*
Williams, Alexander Scott 1867- *WhAm 4*
Williams, Alford Joseph, Jr. 1896-1958
WhAm 3
Williams, Alfred Brockenbrough 1856-1930
WhAm 1
Williams, Alfred Hector 1893-1974 *WhAm 6*
Williams, Alfred Hicks 1912-1972 *WhAm 5*
Williams, Alfred Mason 1840-1896 *NatCAB 4,
WhAm H*
Williams, Alfred Melvin 1874- *WhAm 5*
Williams, Alice 1853- *AmWom*
Williams, Alice Charlotte 1878- *WomWWA 14*
Williams, Alice Laidlaw *WomWWA 14*
Williams, Allen *NewYHSD*
Williams, Allen Burnett 1890-1958 *NatCAB 45*
Williams, Almeron Newberry 1862-1929
NatCAB 26
Williams, Alonzo Roger 1877-1948 *NatCAB 37*
Williams, Alpheus Americus 1870- *WhAm 5*
Williams, Alpheus Starkey 1810-1878 *AmBi,
ApCAB, BiAUS, BiDrAC, DcAmB,
Drake, NatCAB 4, TwCBDA, WhAm H*
Williams, Amelia Worthington 1876-1958
NatCAB 44
Williams, Andrew 1828-1907 *BiAUS, BiDrAC*
Williams, Anna Bolles 1840- *WhAm 4,
WomWWA 14*
Williams, Anna L Osborne 1833-
WomWWA 14
Williams, Anna Vernon Dorsey *WomWWA 14*
Williams, Anna Wessels 1863- *WhAm 5*
Williams, Annie Frances Day 1853-1931
NatCAB 31, WomWWA 14
Williams, Archibald Hunter Arrington
1842-1895 *BiAUS, BiDrAC, WhAm H*
Williams, Arthur 1868-1937 *ApCAB X,
NatCAB 30, WhAm 1*
Williams, Arthur Bruce 1872-1925 *BiDrAC,
WhAm 1*
Williams, Arthur Llewellyn 1853-1919
ApCAB Sup
Williams, Arthur Llewellyn 1856-1919
NatCAB 12, TwCBDA, WhAm 1
Williams, Arthur Trefusis Heneage 1837-1885
ApCAB
Williams, Ashton Hilliard 1891-1962 *WhAm 4*
Williams, Aubrey Willis 1890-1965 *WhAm 4*
Williams, Augustus Lewis 1873- *WhoColR*
Williams, B Y d1951 *WhAm 3*
Williams, Barney 1823-1876 *ApCAB, DcAmB,
WhAm H*
Williams, Barney 1824-1876 *NatCAB 5*
Williams, Beatty Bricker 1876- *WhAm 6*
Williams, Ben Ames 1889-1953 *DcAmB S5,
WhAm 3*
Williams, Ben J 1891-1956 *WhAm 3*
Williams, Benezette 1844-1914 *NatCAB 16*
Williams, Benjamin d1814 *BiAUS*
Williams, Benjamin 1751-1814 *BiDrAC,
WhAm H*
Williams, Benjamin 1754-1814 *ApCAB, Drake,
NatCAB 4, TwCBDA*
Williams, Benjamin Franklin 1876-1958
NatCAB 48
Williams, Benjamin Harrison 1889-1974
WhAm 6
Williams, Berkeley 1878-1954 *WhAm 3*
Williams, Bert 1876?-1922 *DcAmB, WebAB,
WhAm 4, WhoColR*
Williams, Bert C 1909-1954 *WhAm 3*
Williams, Bertha Gardner 1870- *WomWWA 14*
Williams, Betsey 1789-1871 *ApCAB*
Williams, Blanche Colton 1879-1944 *WhAm 2*
Williams, Blanche Emily 1870- *WomWWA 14*
Williams, Bradford 1897-1960 *WhAm 4*
Williams, C Arthur 1876-1908 *WhAm 1*
Williams, Carl 1878-1953 *WhAm 3*
Williams, Carlos Grant 1863-1946 *WhAm 2*
Williams, Caroline Kitchell Wythe 1856-
WomWWA 14
Williams, Catharine R 1790-1872 *Drake*

Williams, Catharine Read Arnold 1787-1872
DcAmB, WhAm H
Williams, Catherine Read Arnold 1787-1872
ApCAB
Williams, Cecil Brown 1901-1966 *WhAm 4*
Williams, Channing Moore 1829-1910 *ApCAB,
DcAmB, NatCAB 5, TwCBDA,
WhAm 1*
Williams, Charles *NewYHSD*
Williams, Charles Andrew 1852-1926
NatCAB 20
Williams, Charles Bray 1869-1952 *WhAm 3*
Williams, Charles Burgess 1871-1947 *WhAm 2*
Williams, Charles David 1860-1923 *DcAmB,
NatCAB 19, WhAm 1*
Williams, Charles Finn 1873-1952 *NatCAB 41,
WhAm 3*
Williams, Charles Frank 1859-1914 *NatCAB 17*
Williams, Charles Frederick 1842-1895
ApCAB Sup
Williams, Charles Grandison 1829-1892 *BiAUS,
BiDrAC, WhAm H, WhAmP*
Williams, Charles Grant 1863- *WhoColR*
Williams, Charles Hamilton 1880- *WhAm 6*
Williams, Charles Ira 1900- *WhAm 6*
Williams, Charles Kaufman 1862-1944
NatCAB 33
Williams, Charles Kilborn 1782-1853
NatCAB 8
Williams, Charles Kilbourne 1782-1853 *ApCAB,
BiAUS, Drake*
Williams, Charles Langdon 1821-1861 *ApCAB,
Drake*
Williams, Charles LeRoy 1888-1954
NatCAB 41
Williams, Charles Luther 1851-1933 *WhAm 1*
Williams, Charles Mallory 1872-1951
NatCAB 42, WhAm 3
Williams, Charles McCay 1853- *WhAm 4*
Williams, Charles Page 1866-1955 *NatCAB 45,
WhAm 3*
Williams, Charles Parker 1872-1951 *WhAm 3*
Williams, Charles Richard 1853-1927 *DcAmB,
NatCAB 21, WhAm 1*
Williams, Charles Richard 1907-1975 *WhAm 6*
Williams, Charles Sneed 1882-1964 *WhAm 4*
Williams, Charles Sumner 1856-1936 *WhAm 1*
Williams, Charles Sumner 1889-1952
NatCAB 46
Williams, Charles Thomas 1910-1965
NatCAB 51, WhAm 4
Williams, Charles Turner 1874-1933 *AmBi,
WhAm 1*
Williams, Charles Urban 1867-1953
NatCAB 42
Williams, Charles Urquhart 1840-1910
WhAm 1
Williams, Charles Wesley 1911-1960 *WhAm 4*
Williams, Charles Weston 1899-1961 *WhAm 4*
Williams, Chauncey Lawrence 1895-1964
NatCAB 51
Williams, Chauncey Pratt 1817-1894 *NatCAB 2,
NatCAB 28*
Williams, Christopher Harris 1798-1857 *BiAUS,
BiDrAC, TwCBDA, WhAm H, WhAmP*
Williams, Churchill 1869-1945 *NatCAB 38*
Williams, Clarence Edwin 1851-1892
NatCAB 26
Williams, Clarence Russell 1870-1949 *WhAm 2*
Williams, Clarence Stewart 1863-1951
NatCAB 40, WhAm 3
Williams, Clarissa Smith 1859- *WhAm 1*
Williams, Clark 1870-1946 *WhAm 2*
Williams, Claude Allen 1904-1957 *WhAm 3*
Williams, Clayton Epes 1890-1968 *WhAm 5*
Williams, Clement Clarence 1882-1947
NatCAB 33, WhAm 2
Williams, Clifford Leland 1901-1967
NatCAB 53, WhAm 5
Williams, Clifton Curtis, Jr. 1932-1967
WhAm 4A, WhAm 5
Williams, Clyde 1873-1954 *BiDrAC, WhAm 3,
WhAmP*
Williams, Cohen Ewing 1883-1969 *NatCAB 55*
Williams, Constant 1843-1922 *WhAm 1*
Williams, Cora Lenore 1865-1937 *WhAm 1*
Williams, Curtis Chandler 1861-1942
NatCAB 31, WhAm 2

Williams, Cyril 1907-1970 *WhAm 5*
Williams, Cyrus Vance 1879-1944 *WhAm 2*
Williams, D B 1910-1969 *WhAm 5*
Williams, Dana Scott 1878-1940 *NatCAB 32,*
 WhAm 1
Williams, Daniel Albert 1914-1968 *WhAm 5*
Williams, Daniel Day 1910-1973 *WhAm 6*
Williams, Daniel Hale 1856-1931 *McGEWB*
Williams, Daniel Hale 1858-1931 *DcAmB,*
 WebAB, WhAm 1, WhoColR
Williams, Daniel Roderick 1871- *WhAm 5*
Williams, David 1754-1831 *ApCAB*
Williams, David 1841-1927 *NatCAB 29,*
 WhAm 1
Williams, David 1843-1902 *WhAm 1*
Williams, David Benjamin 1890- *WhoColR*
Williams, David Evans 1889-1961 *NatCAB 49,*
 WhAm 4
Williams, David P, Jr. 1908-1971 *WhAm 5*
Williams, David Percy 1875-1950 *NatCAB 39*
Williams, David Reichard 1890-1962 *WhAm 4*
Williams, David Rogerson 1776-1830 *ApCAB,*
 BiDrAC, DcAmB, Drake,
 NatCAB 12, WhAm H, WhAmP
Williams, David Rogerson 1885-1969
 NatCAB 56
Williams, David Willard 1853-1909 *NatCAB 30*
Williams, Dean 1891-1955 *WhAm 3*
Williams, Delia Lathrop 1836- *WomWWA 14*
Williams, Delon Acree 1891-1962 *NatCAB 50*
Williams, Dion 1869- *WhAm 5*
Williams, Dora 1859- *WomWWA 14*
Williams, Dwight 1856-1932 *WhAm 1*
Williams, E *NewYHSD*
Williams, E F *NewYHSD*
Williams, Edgar Irving 1884-1974 *WhAm 6*
Williams, Edmund Randolph 1871-1952
 WhAm 3
Williams, Ednyfed H 1882-1958 *WhAm 3*
Williams, Edward *ApCAB*
Williams, Edward Bennett 1920- *WebAB*
Williams, Edward Christopher 1871-1929
 DcAmLiB
Williams, Edward Franklin 1832-1919 *WhAm 1*
Williams, Edward Higginson, Jr. 1849-1933
 NatCAB 24, WhAm 1
Williams, Edward Huntington 1868-1944
 WhAm 2
Williams, Edward Locke 1891-1957 *NatCAB 48*
Williams, Edward Mason 1871-1936
 NatCAB 35
Williams, Edward P 1833-1870 *ApCAB*
Williams, Edward Porter 1843-1903
 NatCAB 21
Williams, Edward Russell 1872-1951
 NatCAB 40
Williams, Edward Thomas 1854-1944
 DcAmB S3, NatCAB 18, WhAm 2
Williams, Edward Thomas Towson 1896-1968
 WhAm 4A
Williams, Edwin 1797-1854 *ApCAB, DcAmB,*
 Drake, WhAm H
Williams, Edwin Bucher 1891-1975 *WhAm 6*
Williams, Egbert Austin 1876-1922 *DcAmB,*
 WebAB
Williams, Egerton Ryerson, Jr. 1873- *WhAm 5*
Williams, Eleazar 1787?-1858 *AmBi*
Williams, Eleazar 1789?-1858 *DcAmB,*
 WebAB, WhAm H
Williams, Eleazer d1858 *Drake*
Williams, Eleazer 1688-1742 *ApCAB*
Williams, Eleazer 1787?-1858 *ApCAB,*
 NatCAB 1
Williams, Elihu Stephen 1835-1903 *BiDrAC,*
 NatCAB 1, WhAm 1
Williams, Eliphalet 1727-1803 *ApCAB,*
 NatCAB 4
Williams, Eliphalet Scott 1757-1845 *ApCAB,*
 NatCAB 4
Williams, Elisha 1694-1755 *AmBi, ApCAB,*
 DcAmB, Drake, NatCAB 1, WhAm H
Williams, Elisha 1773-1833 *ApCAB, DcAmB,*
 WhAm H
Williams, Elizabeth Giddings 1855-
 WomWWA 14
Williams, Elizabeth Sprague 1869-1922 *NotAW,*
 WhAm 1, WomWWA 14
Williams, Elkanah 1822-1888 *ApCAB, DcAmB,*

Williams, *NatCAB 3, WhAm H*
Williams, Ellen Poultney 1874- *WomWWA 14*
Williams, Emerson Milton 1862- *WhAm 4*
Williams, Emma Elizabeth Thomas d1969
 WhAm 5
Williams, Emmons Levi 1854- *WhAm 3*
Williams, Ennion Gifford 1874-1931 *WhAm 1*
Williams, Ennion Skelton 1906-1965 *WhAm 4*
Williams, Ephraim 1714-1755 *AmBi, DcAmB,*
 WebAMB, WhAm H
Williams, Ephraim 1715-1755 *ApCAB, Drake,*
 NatCAB 6, TwCBDA
Williams, Erastus Appleman 1850- *WhAm 4*
Williams, Ernest 1862-1929 *WhAm 1*
Williams, Ernest 1892-1961 *NatCAB 49*
Williams, Ernest Bland, Jr. 1899- *WhAm 5*
Williams, Ernest S 1881-1947 *WhAm 2*
Williams, Espy 1852-1908 *WhAm 1*
Williams, Eugene E 1913-1975 *WhAm 6*
Williams, Eunice 1696-1786 *ApCAB*
Williams, Eustace Leroy 1874- *WhAm 5*
Williams, Everard Mott 1915-1972 *NatCAB 57,*
 WhAm 5
Williams, F *NewYHSD*
Williams, Faith Moors 1893-1958 *NatCAB 49*
Williams, Fannie Barrier 1855-1944 *DcAmB S3,*
 NotAW
Williams, Fannie Ransom 1856-1927
 NatCAB 21
Williams, Florence B 1865- *AmWom*
Williams, Florence L *WomWWA 14*
Williams, Frances Scudder *WomWWA 14*
Williams, Francis Bennett 1849-1929
 NatCAB 14, NatCAB 26
Williams, Francis Bennett 1853-1929 *WhAm 1*
Williams, Francis Churchill 1869-1945
 NatCAB 13, WhAm 2
Williams, Francis Henry 1852-1926 *WhAm 1*
Williams, Francis Henry 1852-1936 *AmBi,*
 DcAmB S2, NatCAB 32
Williams, Francis Howard 1844-1922
 NatCAB 10, WhAm 1
Williams, Frank Alvan 1851- *WhAm 4*
Williams, Frank B 1871-1933 *WhAm 1*
Williams, Frank Backus 1864-1954 *WhAm 3*
Williams, Frank Ernest 1877-1960 *NatCAB 49*
Williams, Frank Eugene 1892-1957 *WhAm 3*
Williams, Frank French 1855-1936 *WhAm 1*
Williams, Frank L 1866-1943 *WhAm 2*
Williams, Frank Leslie 1855-1916 *NatCAB 17*
Williams, Frank Martin 1873-1930 *DcAmB,*
 WhAm 1
Williams, Frank Purdy 1848- *NatCAB 8*
Williams, Franklin Grandey 1893-1963
 NatCAB 50, WhAm 4
Williams, Frankwood Earl 1883-1936 *AmBi,*
 WhAm 1
Williams, Frankwood Earle 1883-1936
 NatCAB 33
Williams, Fred Lincoln 1879-1949 *WhAm 3*
Williams, Frederic Arlington 1883-1953
 WhAm 3
Williams, Frederic M 1862-1934 *WhAm 1*
Williams, Frederick 1885-1958 *NatCAB 47*
Williams, Frederick Ballard 1871-1956
 IIBEAAW, NatCAB 17, NatCAB 46,
 WhAm 3, WhAm 5
Williams, Frederick Crawford 1890-1957
 WhAm 3
Williams, Frederick Dickinson 1828-1915 *Drake*
Williams, Frederick Dickinson 1829-1915
 NewYHSD
Williams, Frederick Wells 1857-1928 *DcAmB,*
 WhAm 1
Williams, G Alvin 1890-1943 *NatCAB 33*
Williams, Gaar Campbell 1880-1935
 DcAmB S1
Williams, Gardner Fred 1842-1922 *DcAmB,*
 WhAm 1
Williams, Gardner Stewart 1866-1931
 NatCAB 27, NatCAB 54, WhAm 1
Williams, George *NewYHSD*
Williams, George 1873-1951 *WhAm 3*
Williams, George Alfred 1875-1932 *WhAm 1*
Williams, George Bassett 1878-1946 *WhAm 2*
Williams, George Burchell 1841-1912 *ApCAB*
Williams, George Burchell 1842-1912
 NatCAB 11, WhAm 1

Williams, George C 1874-1971 *WhAm 5*
Williams, George Clinton Fairchild 1857-1933
 NatCAB 24, WhAm 1
Williams, George Forrester 1837-1920 *WhAm 1*
Williams, George Fred 1852-1932 *BiDrAC,*
 NatCAB 30, WhAm 1
Williams, George Gilbert 1826-1903 *NatCAB 1,*
 WhAm 1
Williams, George Grant 1868- *WhoColR*
Williams, George Henry 1820-1910 *AmBi,*
 DcAmB
Williams, George Henry 1823-1910 *ApCAB,*
 ApCAB X, BiAUS, BiDrAC, BiDrUSE,
 Drake, NatCAB 4, TwCBDA, WhAm 1,
 WhAmP
Williams, George Howard 1871-1963 *BiDrAC,*
 NatCAB 56, WhAm 5
Williams, George Huntington 1856-1894
 ApCAB Sup, ApCAB X, DcAmB,
 NatCAB 42, TwCBDA, WhAm H
Williams, George Orchard 1890-1952 *WhAm 3*
Williams, George Philip 1859-1940 *WhAm 1*
Williams, George S 1882-1953 *WhAm 3*
Williams, George Short 1877-1961 *BiDrAC,*
 WhAmP
Williams, George St. John 1888-1922
 NatCAB 20
Williams, George VanSiclen 1869-1942
 WhAm 2
Williams, George Walton 1820-1903 *NatCAB 6,*
 WhAm 1
Williams, George Walton 1860-1923
 NatCAB 36
Williams, George Washington 1849-1891
 ApCAB, DcAmB, NatCAB 10, WhAm H
Williams, George Washington 1869-1925
 WhAm 1
Williams, George Woodruff 1892-1943
 NatCAB 33
Williams, Gerard Robert 1895-1958
 NatCAB 47
Williams, Gershom Mott 1857-1923
 NatCAB 12, TwCBDA, WhAm 1
Williams, Gladstone 1898-1968 *WhAm 5*
Williams, Gorham Deane 1842- *WhAm 1*
Williams, Griff 1908-1959 *WhAm 3*
Williams, Gross Taylor 1889-1944 *NatCAB 33*
Williams, Guinn 1871-1948 *BiDrAC,*
 NatCAB 55, WhAm 2, WhAmP
Williams, Guy Ellsworth 1891-1965 *NatCAB 53*
Williams, Guy Harrison 1868-1968 *NatCAB 56*
Williams, Guy Rulon 1872-1940 *NatCAB 33*
Williams, Guy Yandall 1881- *WhAm 6*
Williams, H Evan 1867-1918 *WhAm 1*
Williams, Hank 1923-1953 *DcAmB S5*
Williams, Harold 1853-1926 *WhAm 1*
Williams, Harold E 1877-1972 *WhAm 5*
Williams, Harold E 1892-1955 *WhAm 3*
Williams, Harold Putnam 1882-1965 *WhAm 4*
Williams, Harold Wesley 1904- *WhAm 6*
Williams, Harris Folden 1869-1944 *NatCAB 33*
Williams, Harrison Arlington, Jr. 1919- *BiDrAC*
Williams, Harrison Charles 1873-1953
 ApCAB X, DcAmB S5, WhAm 3
Williams, Harry 1869-1948 *NatCAB 38*
Williams, Harry Edward 1871-1933
 NatCAB 27
Williams, Harry Palmerston 1889-1936
 NatCAB 27
Williams, Helen Burton 1877- *WhAm 5*
Williams, Helen Fallows *WomWWA 14*
Williams, Henry 1787-1830 *NewYHSD*
Williams, Henry 1804-1887 *BiAUS*
Williams, Henry 1805-1887 *BiDrAC,*
 WhAm H
Williams, Henry 1840-1916 *NatCAB 36*
Williams, Henry 1877-1973 *WhAm 6*
Williams, Henry A 1895-1958 *WhAm 3*
Williams, Henry Davison 1863- *WhAm 2*
Williams, Henry Edison 1886-1946 *WhAm 2*
Williams, Henry Eugene 1844-1930 *WhAm 1*
Williams, Henry Francis 1847-1933 *WhAm 1*
Williams, Henry Horace 1858-1940 *WhAm 1*
Williams, Henry Knapp Skelding 1859-1944
 NatCAB 32
Williams, Henry Lane 1869-1931 *NatCAB 22*
Williams, Henry Morland 1862- *WhAm 2*
Williams, Henry Robert 1849-1921 *NatCAB 19,*

WhAm 1
Williams, Henry Shaler 1847-1918 *AmBi,
ApCAB, DcAmB, DcScB, NatCAB 21,
WhAm 1*
Williams, Henry Smith 1863-1943 *WhAm 2*
Williams, Henry Sylvester 1869-1911 *McGEWB*
Williams, Henry Wilber 1875-1940 *NatCAB 30*
Williams, Henry Willard 1821-1895 *ApCAB,
DcAmB, Drake, NatCAB 3, WhAm H*
Williams, Henry Winslow 1864-1927
NatCAB 21, WhAm 1
Williams, Herbert Oswald 1873-1939 *WhAm 1*
Williams, Herbert Owen 1866-1936 *WhAm 1*
Williams, Herbert Pelham 1871- *WhAm 5*
Williams, Herbert Upham 1866-1938 *WhAm 1*
Williams, Hermann Warner, Jr. 1908-1974
WhAm 6
Williams, Herschel d1935 *WhAm 1*
Williams, Hezekiah 1798-1856 *BiAUS,
BiDrAC, WhAm H, WhAmP*
Williams, Homer B 1865- *WhAm 4*
Williams, Homer David 1863-1937 *NatCAB 29,
WhAm 1*
Williams, Horatio Burt 1877-1955 *NatCAB 43,
WhAm 3*
Williams, Howard James 1858-1918
NatCAB 18
Williams, Howard Joseph 1883-1956
NatCAB 46
Williams, Howard Rees 1881- *WhAm 6*
Williams, Hugh 1872-1945 *WhAm 2*
Williams, Hugh Spencer 1841-1913 *NatCAB 16*
Williams, Ira Jewell 1873- *WhAm 5*
Williams, Irving 1873-1957 *WhAm 3*
Williams, Isaac *REnAW*
Williams, Isaac, Jr. 1777-1860 *BiAUS, BiDrAC,
WhAm H*
Williams, Isaac L 1817-1895 *NewYHSD*
Williams, Israel 1709-1788 *DcAmB, WhAm H*
Williams, J *NewYHSD*
Williams, J C *NewYHSD*
Williams, J Harvey 1882-1942 *NatCAB 40*
Williams, J Ross 1887-1966 *WhAm 4*
Williams, Jack 1879-1957 *WhAm 3*
Williams, James 1740-1780 *ApCAB, Drake*
Williams, James 1796-1869 *BiDConf, DcAmB,
WhAm H*
Williams, James 1825-1899 *BiAUS, BiDrAC,
WhAmP*
Williams, James Baker 1818-1907 *NatCAB 6*
Williams, James Cranston 1869-1936 *WhAm 1*
Williams, James Douglas 1808-1880 *AmBi,
ApCAB, BiAUS, BiDrAC, DcAmB,
NatCAB 13, TwCBDA, WhAm H,
WhAmP*
Williams, James Leon 1852-1932 *NatCAB 24,
WhAm 4*
Williams, James Mickel 1876-1973 *WhAm 6*
Williams, James Monroe 1833-1907 *WhAm 1*
Williams, James Nelson 1894-1962 *WhAm 4*
Williams, James Oscar 1868- *ApCAB X*
Williams, James Peter, Jr. 1884-1964 *WhAm 4*
Williams, James Robert 1850-1923 *BiDrAC,
WhAm 1, WhAmP*
Williams, James Robert 1888-1957 *IIBEAAW,
NatCAB 47, WhAm 3*
Williams, James S 1871- *WhoColR*
Williams, James Steele 1896-1957 *NatCAB 46*
Williams, James Stoddard 1859-1936
NatCAB 28
Williams, James Thomas, Jr. 1881-1969
WhAm 5
Williams, James W *NewYHSD*
Williams, James W 1787?- *NewYHSD*
Williams, James Watson 1810-1873 *NatCAB 7*
Williams, James William 1825- *ApCAB*
Williams, James Wray 1792-1842 *BiDrAC,
WhAm H*
Williams, James Wray 1792-1843? *BiAUS*
Williams, Jared 1766-1831 *BiAUS, BiDrAC,
WhAm H*
Williams, Jared Warner 1796-1864 *ApCAB,
BiAUS, BiDrAC, Drake, NatCAB 11,
TwCBDA, WhAm H, WhAmP*
Williams, Jean Stuart Brown *WomWWA 14*
Williams, Jeremiah Norman 1829-1915 *BiAUS,
BiDrAC*
Williams, Jerome Oscar 1885-1953 *WhAm 3*

Williams, Jesse Feiring 1886-1966 *BiDAmEd,
WhAm 4*
Williams, Jesse Lynch 1807-1886 *ApCAB,
DcAmB, WhAm H*
Williams, Jesse Lynch 1871-1929 *AmBi,
ApCAB X, DcAmB, NatCAB 21,
TwCBDA, WhAm 1*
Williams, Jesse Raymond 1878- *WhAm 6*
Williams, Job 1842-1914 *NatCAB 16,
WhAm 1*
Williams, John *NewYHSD*
Williams, John d1799 *ApCAB, BiAUS, Drake*
Williams, John d1818 *Drake*
Williams, John 1644-1729 *ApCAB*
Williams, John 1664-1729 *AmBi, DcAmB,
Drake, NatCAB 1, WhAm H*
Williams, John 1731-1799 *BiDrAC, WhAm H*
Williams, John 1740?-1799 *NatCAB 1*
Williams, John 1752-1806 *BiAUS, BiDrAC,
WhAm H, WhAmP*
Williams, John 1757?-1818 *NatCAB 1*
Williams, John 1761-1818 *DcAmB, WhAm H*
Williams, John 1765?-1818 *ApCAB*
Williams, John 1778-1837 *ApCAB, BiAUS,
BiDrAC, DcAmB, Drake, NatCAB 1,
TwCBDA, WhAm H, WhAmP*
Williams, John 1807-1875 *BiAUS, BiDrAC,
WhAm H*
Williams, John 1817-1899 *AmBi, ApCAB,
DcAmB, Drake, NatCAB 3, TwCBDA,
WhAm H*
Williams, John 1835- *WhAm 4*
Williams, John Adam 1883- *NatCAB 18*
Williams, John Aethurhuld 1817- *ApCAB*
Williams, John Alonzo 1869-1951 *WhAm 3*
Williams, John Augustus 1824-1903
NatCAB 26
Williams, John Bell 1918- *BiDrAC*
Williams, John C *NewYHSD*
Williams, John Castree 1903-1960 *WhAm 3*
Williams, John Charles 1876-1936 *NatCAB 27*
Williams, John Clark 1877-1947 *WhAm 2*
Williams, John Edward 1867-1943 *WhAm 2*
Williams, John Elias 1853-1919 *DcAmB,
WhAm 1*
Williams, John Elias 1871-1927 *DcAmB,
NatCAB 21*
Williams, John Fletcher 1834-1895 *ApCAB Sup,
DcAmB, NatCAB 4, WhAm H*
Williams, John Foster 1743-1814 *ApCAB,
DcAmB, Drake, NatCAB 4, WebAMB,
WhAm H*
Williams, John H 1908-1966 *WhAm 4*
Williams, John Harvey 1864- *WhAm 4*
Williams, John Healy 1843-1924 *NatCAB 31,
WhAm 4*
Williams, John Howard 1894-1958 *WhAm 3*
Williams, John Insco 1813-1873 *NewYHSD,
WhAm H*
Williams, Mrs. John Insco 1833?- *NewYHSD*
Williams, John Irving 1824-1907 *NatCAB 11*
Williams, John James 1904- *BiDrAC*
Williams, John Joseph 1822-1907 *ApCAB,
DcAmB, NatCAB 4, TwCBDA,
WhAm 1*
Williams, John Joseph 1852- *NatCAB 9*
Williams, John Joseph, Jr. 1886-1968
NatCAB 54, WhAm 5
Williams, John L *NewYHSD*
Williams, John Langbourne 1831-1915
WhAm 1
Williams, John Lee 1775?-1856 *ApCAB Sup*
Williams, John Mason 1780-1868 *ApCAB*
Williams, John McKeown Snow 1818-1886
BiAUS, BiDrAC, WhAm H
Williams, John Paul 1900-1973 *WhAm 5*
Williams, John Powell 1894-1954 *NatCAB 45,
WhAm 3*
Williams, John Ralston 1874-1965 *WhAm 4*
Williams, John S 1825- *ApCAB, NatCAB 11*
Williams, John Scott d1975 *WhAm 6*
Williams, John Sharp 1854-1932 *BiDrAC,
DcAmB, NatCAB 13, NatCAB 37,
TwCBDA, WhAm 1, WhAmP*
Williams, John Sharp 1886-1949 *NatCAB 43*
Williams, John Skelton 1865-1926 *DcAmB,
NatCAB 29, WhAm 1*
Williams, John Stuart 1818-1898 *BiDConf,

BiDrAC
Williams, John Stuart 1820-1898 *AmBi,
ApCAB, NatCAB 12, TwCBDA*
Williams, John Taylor 1904-1971 *WhAm 5*
Williams, John Thomas 1882-1955 *NatCAB 45*
Williams, John Townsend 1852- *WhAm 4*
Williams, John Whitridge 1866-1931 *AmBi,
DcAmB, NatCAB 25, WhAm 1*
Williams, John Wilson Montgomery 1820-1894
ApCAB, NatCAB 5
Williams, Jonathan 1750-1815 *AmBi, ApCAB,
BiDrAC, DcAmB, NatCAB 3, TwCBDA,
WebAMB, WhAm H*
Williams, Jonathan 1752-1815 *BiAUS, Drake*
Williams, Joseph *BiAUS*
Williams, Joseph 1801-1871 *NatCAB 12*
Williams, Joseph Hartwell 1814-1896 *ApCAB,
BiAUS, NatCAB 6*
Williams, Joseph John 1875-1940 *WhAm 1*
Williams, Joseph Judson, Jr. 1905-1968
WhAm 5
Williams, Joseph Lanier d1865 *BiAUS*
Williams, Joseph Lanier 1800?-1865 *ApCAB*
Williams, Joseph Lanier 1807-1865 *TwCBDA*
Williams, Joseph Lanier 1810-1865 *BiDrAC,
WhAm H, WhAmP*
Williams, Joseph Peter 1890-1972 *NatCAB 56*
Williams, Joseph Thomson 1838-1906
NatCAB 33
Williams, Joseph Tuttle 1878- *WhAm 6*
Williams, Joseph Vincent 1872-1947 *WhAm 2*
Williams, Joseph White 1879-1941 *WhAm 1*
Williams, Josiah Butler 1810-1883 *NatCAB 34*
Williams, Judith Blow 1890-1956 *WhAm 3*
Williams, Kathleen Mary d1974 *WhAm 6*
Williams, Keith Shaw 1905-1951 *NatCAB 38,
WhAm 3*
Williams, Kenneth Powers 1887-1958 *WhAm 3*
Williams, L Judson 1856-1921 *WhAm 1*
Williams, Lacey Kirk d1940 *WhAm 2*
Williams, Langbourne M 1872-1931 *WhAm 1*
Williams, Laurens 1906-1975 *WhAm 6*
Williams, Lawrence 1859-1920 *NatCAB 19*
Williams, Lawrence Gordon 1913- *BiDrAC*
Williams, Ledru A 1893-1964 *WhAm 4*
Williams, Lemuel d1827 *BiAUS*
Williams, Lemuel 1747-1828 *BiDrAC,
WhAm H*
Williams, Leonard Franklin 1901-1964
NatCAB 50
Williams, Leroy Blanchard 1867-1945 *WhAm 2*
Williams, Leslie 1904-1971 *NatCAB 56*
Williams, Leslie Benjamin 1914-1974 *WhAm 6*
Williams, Lester Alonzo 1880-1960 *NatCAB 49,
WhAm 6*
Williams, Lester James 1880-1951 *NatCAB 40*
Williams, Lewis d1842 *BiAUS*
Williams, Lewis 1782-1842 *BiDrAC,
NatCAB 3, WhAmP*
Williams, Lewis 1786-1842 *ApCAB, TwCBDA,
WhAm H*
Williams, Lewis Blair 1880-1966 *WhAm 4*
Williams, Lewis Kemper 1887-1971 *WhAm 5*
Williams, Linsly Rudd 1875-1934 *DcAmB,
WhAm 1*
Williams, Lizzie Annie 1852- *WomWWA 14*
Williams, Lloyd Thomas 1874- *WhAm 6*
Williams, Louis Coleman 1892-1955 *WhAm 3*
Williams, Louis Laval 1859- *WhAm 3*
Williams, Louis Laval, Jr. 1889-1967
NatCAB 53
Williams, Louis Sheppard 1865- *WhAm 4*
Williams, Louisa Brewster 1832- *AmWom*
Williams, Lucy White 1858- *WomWWA 14*
Williams, Lydia Adams *WomWWA 14*
Williams, Lynn Alfred 1878-1944 *NatCAB 33*
Williams, Maria Pray 1828- *ApCAB*
Williams, Marmaduke 1772-1850 *ApCAB,
BiAUS, WhAm H*
Williams, Marmaduke 1774-1850 *BiDrAC,
TwCBDA, WhAmP*
Williams, Marshall Jay 1837-1902 *DcAmB,
NatCAB 12, WhAm 1*
Williams, Martha 1858- *WomWWA 14*
Williams, Martha McCulloch *WhAm 5,
WomWWA 14*
Williams, Mary *NewYHSD*
Williams, Mary A W 1853- *WomWWA 14*

Williams, Mary Ann 1822-1874 *NatCAB 7*
Williams, Mary Bushnell 1826- *ApCAB*
Williams, Mary Edith 1883-1956 *NatCAB 44*
Williams, Mary Elizabeth 1825-1902
NewYHSD
Williams, Mary Gilmore 1863- *WomWWA 14*
Williams, Mary Mayne 1864- *WomWWA 14*
Williams, Mary Mildred Fancher 1855-
WomWWA 14
Williams, Mary Wheeler *WomWWA 14*
Williams, Mary Wilhelmine 1878-1944 *NotAW,*
WhAm 2
Williams, Mayes Bell 1890-1966 *NatCAB 55*
Williams, Maynard Owen 1888-1963
NatCAB 52, WhAm 4
Williams, Micah *BnEnAmA, NewYHSD*
Williams, Michael *NewYHSD*
Williams, Michael 1877-1950 *WhAm 3*
Williams, Miles Evans 1836- *WhAm 4*
Williams, Milton Mathias 1848-1926 *WhAm 1*
Williams, Morgan B 1831-1903 *BiDrAC*
Williams, Mornay 1856-1926 *NatCAB 21,*
WhAm 1
Williams, Moseley Hooker 1839-1917 *WhAm 1*
Williams, Moses *NewYHSD*
Williams, Moses 1846-1919 *WhAm 1*
Williams, Moses 1869-1940 *WhAm 1*
Williams, Nathan 1773-1835 *BiAUS, BiDrAC,*
WhAm H
Williams, Nathan Boone 1873- *WhAm 5*
Williams, Nathan Winslow 1860-1924
NatCAB 22
Williams, Nathan Winslow 1860-1925 *WhAm 1*
Williams, Nathanael 1675-1737? *DcAmB*
Williams, Nathaniel 1675-1737? *WhAm H*
Williams, Nathaniel 1741-1805 *TwCBDA*
Williams, Nathaniel John 1857-1943
NatCAB 33
Williams, Neil 1934- *BnEnAmA*
Williams, Neil Hooker 1870-1956 *WhAm 3*
Williams, Nelson Grosvenor 1823- *ApCAB*
Williams, Norman Charles 1917-1968
NatCAB 54
Williams, O B 1895-1959 *WhAm 3*
Williams, Ora 1862- *WhAm 5*
Williams, Orva Gilson 1865-1930 *WhAm 1*
Williams, Oscar Fitzalan 1843-1909 *WhAm 1*
Williams, Othneil Glanville 1900-1960
WhAm 3A
Williams, Othniel S 1813-1880 *NatCAB 7*
Williams, Otho Holland 1747-1794 *WhAm H*
Williams, Otho Holland 1749-1794 *AmBi,*
DcAmB, Drake, NatCAB 1, TwCBDA,
WebAMB
Williams, Otho Holland 1749-1800? *ApCAB*
Williams, Pardon Clarence 1842-1925
NatCAB 40, WhAm 1
Williams, Parley Lycurgus 1842-1936 *WhAm 1*
Williams, Pendleton Long 1880-1947
NatCAB 36
Williams, Peter 1780?-1840 *ApCAB,*
NatCAB 10
Williams, Phil Thomas 1895-1945 *NatCAB 35*
Williams, Philip Francis 1884-1950 *WhAm 5*
Williams, Prentice Washington 1892-1964
NatCAB 51
Williams, R Reche 1881- *WhoColR*
Williams, Ralph Brown 1881-1948 *NatCAB 39*
Williams, Ralph Coplestone 1887-1967
NatCAB 53
Williams, Ralph E 1870-1940 *WhAm 1*
Williams, Ralph Edward 1869-1940 *NatCAB 45*
Williams, Ralph Olmsted 1838-1908 *WhAm 1*
Williams, Ransome Judson 1892-1970 *WhAm 5*
Williams, Reginald Victor 1894-1967
NatCAB 54
Williams, Reid 1899-1961 *NatCAB 49*
Williams, Reuel 1783-1862 *ApCAB, BiAUS,*
BiDrAC, DcAmB, Drake, NatCAB 10,
TwCBDA, WhAm H
Williams, Richard 1836-1914 *BiDrAC*
Williams, Richard Lloyd 1880-1961 *NatCAB 54*
Williams, Richard Peters 1879-1950 *WhAm 2*
Williams, Richard Richardson 1843-1915
WhAm 1
Williams, Robert 1745?-1775 *ApCAB, DcAmB,*
WhAm H
Williams, Robert 1765?- *ApCAB, NatCAB 13*

Williams, Robert 1765-1820? *NatCAB 2*
Williams, Robert 1768-1836 *TwCBDA*
Williams, Robert 1773-1820? *ApCAB,*
TwCBDA
Williams, Robert 1773-1836 *BiAUS, BiDrAC,*
WhAm H, WhAmP
Williams, Robert 1829-1901 *ApCAB,*
NatCAB 12, WhAm 1
Williams, Robert 1860-1923 *WhAm 1*
Williams, Robert 1884-1944 *WhAm 2*
Williams, Robert 1892-1953 *WhAm 3*
Williams, Robert Campbell 1891-1966 *WhAm 4*
Williams, Robert Carlton 1893-1956 *WhAm 3*
Williams, Robert Day 1881-1930 *NatCAB 22,*
WhAm 1
Williams, Robert E 1912-1959 *WhAm 3*
Williams, Robert Einion 1856-1940 *WhAm 1*
Williams, Robert Gray 1878-1946 *NatCAB 37,*
WhAm 2
Williams, Robert Lancaster 1869-1935
WhAm 1
Williams, Robert Lee 1868-1948 *NatCAB 14,*
WhAm 2
Williams, Robert Maurice 1898-1960 *WhAm 4*
Williams, Robert Parvin 1891-1967 *WhAm 5*
Williams, Robert Purcell, Jr. 1908-1958
WhAm 3
Williams, Robert Runnels 1886-1965 *AsBiEn,*
DcScB, WhAm 4
Williams, Robert Seaton 1880- *WhAm 6*
Williams, Robert Simeon 1858- *WhoColR*
Williams, Robert Stanton 1828-1899
NatCAB 19
Williams, Robert White 1877-1940 *WhAm 2*
Williams, Robert Willoughby 1845- *WhAm 4*
Williams, Robley 1908- *AsBiEn*
Williams, Roger 1599-1683 *ApCAB, Drake,*
TwCBDA
Williams, Roger 1603?-1682? *DcAmB*
Williams, Roger 1603?-1683? *AmBi,*
DcAmReB, EncAAH, EncAB, McGEWB,
WebAB, WhAm H
Williams, Roger 1603?-1684 *WhAmP*
Williams, Roger 1604?-1683 *NatCAB 10*
Williams, Roger 1879-1959 *WhAm 3A,*
WhAm 4
Williams, Roger Butler 1848-1933 *NatCAB 36,*
WhAm 1
Williams, Roger D 1856-1925 *WhAm 1*
Williams, Roger Henry 1874-1950 *WhAm 3*
Williams, Roswell Carter, Jr. 1869-1946
NatCAB 42, WhAm 5
Williams, Roy Hughes 1874-1946 *NatCAB 36,*
WhAm 2
Williams, Roy T d1946 *WhAm 2*
Williams, Rufus K *NatCAB 12*
Williams, Rufus Phillips 1851-1911 *WhAm 1*
Williams, Russel Stanley 1898-1956
NatCAB 43
Williams, Russell Raymond, Jr. 1920-1961
WhAm 4
Williams, Ruth Churchyard 1856-
WomWWA 14
Williams, S *NewYHSD*
Williams, Samuel 1743-1817 *ApCAB, Drake,*
NatCAB 1
Williams, Samuel 1786-1859 *ApCAB,*
NatCAB 1
Williams, Samuel Clay 1884-1949 *NatCAB 38,*
WhAm 2
Williams, Samuel Cole 1864-1947 *NatCAB 42,*
WhAm 2
Williams, Samuel Gardner 1827-1900
NatCAB 8
Williams, Samuel Hubbard 1864-1951
NatCAB 48, WhAm 3
Williams, Samuel Laing 1863- *WhoColR*
Williams, Samuel Leonard 1905-1968 *WhAm 5*
Williams, Samuel May 1795-1858 *DcAmB,*
WhAm H
Williams, Samuel Porter 1779-1826 *ApCAB,*
NatCAB 1
Williams, Samuel Robinson 1879-1955
NatCAB 43, WhAm 6
Williams, Samuel Wardell 1851-1913
NatCAB 20
Williams, Samuel Wells 1812-1884 *AmBi,*
ApCAB, BiAUS, DcAmB, Drake,

NatCAB 1, TwCBDA, WhAm H
Williams, Samuel Wright 1828- *NatCAB 7*
Williams, Sarah 1857- *WhAm 4*
Williams, Seth 1822-1866 *AmBi, ApCAB,*
Drake, NatCAB 10, TwCBDA
Williams, Seth 1880-1963 *WhAm 4*
Williams, Seward Henry 1870-1922 *BiDrAC,*
WhAm 5
Williams, Sherman 1846-1923 *WhAm 1*
Williams, Sherrod 1804- *BiAUS, BiDrAC,*
WhAm H, WhAmP
Williams, Sidney Clark 1878-1949 *NatCAB 37,*
WhAm 3
Williams, Sidney James 1886-1956 *WhAm 3*
Williams, Silas 1888-1944 *NatCAB 34*
Williams, Solomon 1700-1776 *ApCAB,*
NatCAB 1
Williams, Stanley Thomas 1888-1956
NatCAB 46, WhAm 3
Williams, Stephen 1693-1782 *ApCAB,*
NatCAB 1
Williams, Stephen Ellsworth 1878-1954
NatCAB 47
Williams, Stephen Miller, Jr. 1887-1961
NatCAB 49
Williams, Stephen Riggs 1870- *WhAm 5*
Williams, Stephen West 1790-1855 *ApCAB,*
DcAmB, Drake, NatCAB 1, WhAm H
Williams, T *NewYHSD*
Williams, Talcott 1849-1928 *DcAmB,*
NatCAB 15, WhAm 1
Williams, Ted 1918- *WebAB*
Williams, Tennessee 1911- *EncAB, WebAB*
Williams, Tennessee 1914- *McGEWB*
Williams, Theodore Chickering 1855-1915
ApCAB X, WhAm 1
Williams, Theodore Samuel *WebAB*
Williams, Theresa Amelia 1853- *WhAm 4*
Williams, Theresa Olive Foster *WomWWA 14*
Williams, Thomas *NewYHSD*
Williams, Thomas 1718-1775 *ApCAB,*
NatCAB 1
Williams, Thomas 1779-1876 *ApCAB,*
NatCAB 1
Williams, Thomas 1806-1872 *ApCAB, BiAUS,*
BiDrAC, NatCAB 3, NatCAB 15,
TwCBDA, WhAm H
Williams, Thomas 1815-1862 *ApCAB, Drake,*
NatCAB 1, TwCBDA
Williams, Thomas 1825-1903 *BiDrAC,*
WhAmP
Williams, Thomas 1856-1935 *WhAm 1*
Williams, Thomas Calvin 1875- *WhoColR*
Williams, Thomas Frederick 1876- *WhAm 2*
Williams, Thomas H 1795?- *ApCAB*
Williams, Thomas Henry 1822-1904 *BiDConf*
Williams, Thomas Hickman 1801-1851 *BiAUS,*
BiDrAC, WhAm H
Williams, Thomas Hill 1780?-1840? *ApCAB,*
BiAUS, BiDrAC, NatCAB 11, WhAm H
Williams, Thomas Jefferson 1893-1966
WhAm 4
Williams, Thomas Lanier *WebAB*
Williams, Thomas Lanier 1786-1856 *ApCAB,*
TwCBDA
Williams, Thomas R 1881- *WhAm 6*
Williams, Thomas Reynolds 1878-1937
WhAm 1
Williams, Thomas Scott 1777-1861 *ApCAB,*
BiAUS, BiDrAC, DcAmB, Drake,
NatCAB 4, WhAm H
Williams, Thomas Sutler 1872-1940 *BiDrAC,*
NatCAB 30, WhAm 1, WhAmP
Williams, Thomas Wheeler 1789-1874 *BiAUS,*
BiDrAC, WhAm H
Williams, Timothy Shaler 1862-1930
NatCAB 22, WhAm 1
Williams, Travis 1876- *WhAm 5*
Williams, Tyrrell 1875-1947 *NatCAB 36,*
WhAm 2
Williams, VanZandt 1916-1966 *WhAm 4*
Williams, Velma Curtis *WomWWA 14*
Williams, Vernon 1896-1955 *NatCAB 44*
Williams, Virgil 1830-1886 *IlBEAAW,*
NewYHSD
Williams, W L 1856-1945 *WhAm 2*
Williams, Wallace Alfred 1875-1953
NatCAB 41

Williams, Walter 1864-1935 *AmBi, BiDAmEd, DcAmB S1, NatCAB 28, WhAm 1*
Williams, Walter Erskine 1860-1938 *WhAm 1*
Williams, Walter McAdoo 1891-1959 *NatCAB 49*
Williams, Walter Winslow 1873-1953 *NatCAB 45*
Williams, Warham Howard 1853-1914 *NatCAB 17*
Williams, Wayland Wells 1888-1945 *WhAm 2*
Williams, Wayne Cullen 1878-1953 *NatCAB 44, WhAm 3*
Williams, Wellington *NewYHSD*
Williams, Wheeler 1897-1972 *NatCAB 57, WhAm 5*
Williams, Whiting 1878-1975 *WhAm 6*
Williams, William *NewYHSD*
Williams, William 1665-1741 *ApCAB, Drake*
Williams, William 1727-1791 *BnEnAmA*
Williams, William 1731-1811 *AmBi, ApCAB, BiAUS, BiDrAC, DcAmB, Drake, NatCAB 10, TwCBDA, WhAm H, WhAmP*
Williams, Sir William 1776?-1832 *ApCAB*
Williams, William 1787-1850 *ApCAB, DcAmB, NewYHSD, WhAm H*
Williams, William 1796-1874 *NatCAB 12, NewYHSD, WhAm H*
Williams, William 1815-1876 *BiAUS, BiDrAC, WhAm H*
Williams, William 1821-1896 *BiAUS, BiDrAC, NatCAB 12, WhAm H, WhAmP*
Williams, William 1862-1947 *NatCAB 14, NatCAB 35, WhAm 2*
Williams, William Alfred 1880- *WhAm 6*
Williams, William Asbury 1854- *WhAm 4*
Williams, William Brewster 1826-1905 *BiAUS, BiDrAC*
Williams, William Carlos 1883-1963 *McGEWB, WebAB, WhAm 4*
Williams, William Clayton, Jr. 1884-1945 *NatCAB 34, WhAm 2*
Williams, William Crow 1925- *WhAm 5*
Williams, William E 1906-1967 *WhAm 4*
Williams, William Elza 1857-1921 *BiDrAC, WhAm 1*
Williams, Sir William Fenwick 1800-1883 *ApCAB*
Williams, William Frank 1878- *WhoColR*
Williams, William George 1801-1846 *ApCAB, NewYHSD*
Williams, William George 1822-1902 *WhAm 1*
Williams, William Henry 1874-1931 *NatCAB 25, WhAm 1*
Williams, William Horace 1882-1957 *NatCAB 48, WhAm 3*
Williams, William John 1858-1930 *NatCAB 24*
Williams, William Martin 1877-1932 *NatCAB 30, WhAm 1*
Williams, William McKinley 1897-1971 *NatCAB 56*
Williams, William Muir 1850-1916 *WhAm 1*
Williams, William Nugent 1851-1927 *NatCAB 21*
Williams, William Porter 1855-1919 *NatCAB 18*
Williams, William R d1972 *WhAm 5*
Williams, William R 1804-1885 *ApCAB, DcAmB, Drake, NatCAB 10, WhAm H*
Williams, William Reid 1866-1931 *WhAm 1*
Williams, William Robert 1867-1940 *WhAm 1*
Williams, William Robert 1884- *BiDrAC, WhAmP*
Williams, William Sherley 1787-1849 *DcAmB, REnAW, WhAm H*
Williams, William Taylor Burwell 1866-1941 *WhAm 1*
Williams, Wilson 1893-1950 *WhAm 3*
Williams, Wynant James 1884-1950 *WhAm 3*
Williams, Wythe 1881-1956 *WhAm 3*
Williams, Yancey Sullivan 1876-1938 *NatCAB 29, WhAm 1*
Williams, Zachariah Mitchell 1855- *WhAm 4*
Williams-Rebolledo, Juan 1826- *ApCAB*
Williams-Taylor, Jane Fayrer *WomWWA 14*
Williamson *NewYHSD*

Williamson, Alexander William 1824-1904 *AsBiEn, DcScB*
Williamson, Allen Thurman 1876-1949 *NatCAB 38*
Williamson, Andrew 1730?-1786 *DcAmB, WhAm H*
Williamson, Ben Mitchell 1864-1941 *BiDrAC, WhAm 1*
Williamson, Benjamin 1808-1892 *ApCAB Sup, NatCAB 12, TwCBDA*
Williamson, Bernardine Francis 1862- *NatCAB 12*
Williamson, Bright 1861-1927 *NatCAB 21*
Williamson, Charles *NewYHSD*
Williamson, Charles 1757-1808 *DcAmB, WhAm H*
Williamson, Charles Clarence 1877-1965 *BiDAmEd, DcAmLiB, WhAm 4*
Williamson, Charles Frederick 1880- *WhoColR*
Williamson, Charles Penrose 1912-1972 *NatCAB 57*
Williamson, Charles Spencer 1872-1933 *WhAm 1*
Williamson, Clifton P 1876-1968 *WhAm 5*
Williamson, Earl Willbre 1885-1948 *NatCAB 37*
Williamson, Edmund Griffith 1900- *BiDAmEd*
Williamson, Edwin Moore 1910-1972 *WhAm 6*
Williamson, Francis Torrance 1907-1964 *NatCAB 50, WhAm 4*
Williamson, Frederic Ely 1876-1944 *NatCAB 33*
Williamson, Frederick Ely 1876-1944 *WhAm 2*
Williamson, Frederick Warren 1897-1942 *WhAm 2*
Williamson, George 1883-1941 *WhAm 2*
Williamson, George 1898-1968 *WhAm 5*
Williamson, George Emery 1878-1951 *WhAm 3*
Williamson, George McWillie 1829- *BiAUS, NatCAB 12*
Williamson, Henry Albro 1875- *WhoColR*
Williamson, Hiram Louis 1878-1964 *WhAm 4*
Williamson, Hugh 1735-1819 *AmBi, ApCAB, BiAUS, BiDrAC, DcAmB, Drake, NatCAB 2, TwCBDA, WhAm H, WhAmP*
Williamson, Isaac 1769-1844 *Drake*
Williamson, Isaac Dowd 1807-1876 *ApCAB*
Williamson, Isaac H 1769-1844 *BiAUS*
Williamson, Isaac Halstead 1767-1844 *WhAm H*
Williamson, Isaac Halsted 1767-1844 *DcAmB, NatCAB 5*
Williamson, Isaac Halsted 1768-1844 *TwCBDA*
Williamson, Isaac Halsted 1769-1844 *ApCAB*
Williamson, Isaiah Vansant 1803-1889 *ApCAB Sup, NatCAB 5*
Williamson, James 1806- *ApCAB*
Williamson, James 1826- *Drake*
Williamson, James Alexander 1829-1902 *ApCAB, NatCAB 12, WhAm 1*
Williamson, James DeLong 1849-1935 *NatCAB 33, WhAm 1*
Williamson, James Franklin 1853-1934 *NatCAB 33*
Williamson, James Nathaniel 1842-1921 *NatCAB 19*
Williamson, James Nathaniel, Jr. 1872-1945 *NatCAB 33, WhAm 1*
Williamson, James Preston 1898-1964 *WhAm 4*
Williamson, Jessie d1948 *WhAm 2*
Williamson, John 1826-1885 *ApCAB, IlBEAAW, NewYHSD*
Williamson, John Albert 1897-1955 *NatCAB 42*
Williamson, John Ernest 1881-1966 *WhAm 4*
Williamson, John Finley 1887-1964 *WhAm 4*
Williamson, John G A d1840 *BiAUS*
Williamson, John I 1867-1932 *WhAm 1*
Williamson, John Newton 1855-1943 *BiDrAC, WhAm 4, WhAmP*
Williamson, John Pogue 1835-1917 *WhAm 1*
Williamson, Joseph 1828-1902 *ApCAB Sup, NatCAB 8, WhAm 1*
Williamson, Josephine Gillette 1868- *WomWWA 14*
Williamson, Julia May 1859-1909 *WhAm 1*
Williamson, Katherine Marie *WomWWA 14*
Williamson, Lynn Banks d1940 *NatCAB 31*

Williamson, Mary Jane Robinson 1867- *WomWWA 14*
Williamson, Mary Lynn 1850-1923 *WhAm 3, WomWWA 14*
Williamson, Mary Robinson *WhAm 5*
Williamson, Oliver Robison 1871- *WhAm 5*
Williamson, Pauline Brooks 1887-1972 *NatCAB 56, WhAm 6*
Williamson, Percy Eugene 1903-1961 *NatCAB 49*
Williamson, Peter d1799 *ApCAB, Drake*
Williamson, Ralph Bertram 1879-1932 *NatCAB 25*
Williamson, Robert Stockton 1824-1882 *ApCAB*
Williamson, Roy Elisha 1890-1944 *WhAm 2*
Williamson, Samuel 1808-1884 *NatCAB 24*
Williamson, Samuel Eladsit 1844-1903 *NatCAB 12, NatCAB 41, WhAm 1*
Williamson, Sydney Bacon 1865-1938 *AmBi, ApCAB X*
Williamson, Sydney Bacon 1865-1939 *NatCAB 30, WhAm 1*
Williamson, Thom 1833-1918 *WhAm 1*
Williamson, Thomas 1867-1956 *WhAm 3*
Williamson, Walter 1811-1870 *ApCAB, NatCAB 3*
Williamson, Warren Pyatt 1858-1946 *NatCAB 33*
Williamson, William *NewYHSD*
Williamson, William 1875-1972 *BiDrAC, WhAm 5, WhAmP*
Williamson, William Collins 1842-1935 *WhAm 1*
Williamson, William Crawford 1816-1895 *DcScB*
Williamson, William Durkee 1779-1846 *ApCAB, BiAUS, BiDrAC, DcAmB, Drake, NatCAB 6, WhAm H, WhAmP*
Williamson, William F 1904-1965 *NatCAB 52, WhAm 4*
Williamson, William James 1869-1918 *WhAm 1*
Williamson, William Thomas 1871-1939 *WhAm 1*
Williamson, William Wayne 1854- *ApCAB X, NatCAB 16*
Williard, George Washington 1818-1900 *NatCAB 11*
Williard, George Washington 1874-1951 *NatCAB 41*
Williard, Hervie Nicola 1896-1959 *NatCAB 49*
Willibrand, William Anthony 1892-1973 *WhAm 6*
Willich, August 1810-1878 *ApCAB, NatCAB 13*
Willie, Asa H 1829-1899 *BiAUS*
Willie, Asa Hoxey 1829-1899 *NatCAB 11*
Willie, Asa Hoxie 1829-1899 *BiDrAC, DcAmB, WhAm H, WhAmP*
Willien, Leon John 1840-1919 *NatCAB 18*
Williford, Forrest Estey 1882-1955 *WhAm 3*
Willig, Lawrence Henry 1891-1948 *NatCAB 35*
Willing, Charles 1884-1963 *NatCAB 50*
Willing, Jennie Fowler 1834-1916 *AmWom, NotAW*
Willing, John Thomson 1860- *WhAm 4*
Willing, Thomas 1731-1821 *AmBi, ApCAB, BiAUS, BiDrAC, DcAmB, Drake, NatCAB 10, TwCBDA, WhAm H, WhAmP*
Willinger, Aloysius J 1886-1973 *WhAm 6*
Willingham, Broadus Estes 1862-1937 *NatCAB 28*
Willingham, Edward Bacon 1899-1972 *WhAm 5*
Willingham, Edward George 1865-1940 *NatCAB 30*
Willingham, Henry J 1868-1948 *WhAm 2*
Willingham, Robert Josiah 1854-1914 *DcAmB, WhAm 1*
Willingham, William A d1945 *WhAm 2*
Willingham, Wright 1876- *NatCAB 18*
Willings, George Clarke 1888- *WhAm 3*
Willis, Albert S 1843-1897 *NatCAB 12*
Willis, Albert Shelby 1843-1897 *BiDrAC, DcAmB, WhAm H, WhAmP*
Willis, Albert Sydney 1843-1897 *ApCAB Sup*
Willis, Alfred 1872- *WhAm 4*
Willis, Anson 1802-1874 *ApCAB*
Willis, Bailey 1857-1949 *DcAmB S4, DcScB,*

NatCAB 37, TwCBDA, WhAm 2
Willis, Benjamin Albertson 1840-1886 BiAUS,
BiDrAC, WhAm H
Willis, Benjamin Johnson 1893-1965
NatCAB 52
Willis, Charles Francis 1885-1968 WhAm 5
Willis, Clodius Harris 1893-1964 WhAm 4
Willis, Eben Marston 1871-1919 NatCAB 18
Willis, Edmund Aylburton 1808-1899
NatCAB 11, NewYHSD
Willis, Edward Simmons 1881-1936
NatCAB 28
Willis, Edwin Caldwell 1906-1953 WhAm 3
Willis, Edwin Edward 1904-1972 BiDrAC,
WhAm 5, WhAmP
Willis, Eola WomWWA 14
Willis, Francis 1725-1829 BiAUS
Willis, Francis 1745-1829 BiDrAC, WhAm H
Willis, Frank Bartlett 1871-1928 ApCAB X,
BiDrAC, NatCAB 21, WhAmP
Willis, Frank Bartlette 1871-1928 WhAm 1
Willis, Frederick NewYHSD
Willis, George Francis 1879-1932 WhAm 1
Willis, George Roberts 1851- NatCAB 16
Willis, Gwendolen Brown WomWWA 14
Willis, Harold Buckley 1890-1962 WhAm 4
Willis, Henry 1852- WhAm 4
Willis, Henry Parker 1874-1937 AmBi,
DcAmB S2, NatCAB 28, WhAm 1
Willis, Herman Allen 1905-1971 WhAm 5
Willis, Horace Harold 1891-1970 WhAm 5
Willis, Jack Macy 1885-1961 WhAm 4
Willis, John NewYHSD
Willis, John Buckley 1852-1927 ApCAB X
Willis, Jonathan Spencer 1830-1903 BiDrAC
Willis, Louise Hammond 1870- AmWom
Willis, Lucas B 1874- WhoColR
Willis, Mary Jasper WomWWA 14
Willis, Michael 1799-1879 ApCAB
Willis, Nathaniel, Jr. 1780-1870 DcAmB,
NatCAB 14, WhAm H
Willis, Nathaniel Parker 1806-1867 AmBi,
ApCAB, DcAmB, NatCAB 3, TwCBDA,
WebAB, WhAm H
Willis, Nathaniel Parker 1807-1867 Drake
Willis, Olympia Brown 1835-1926 AmBi,
DcAmB, NotAW, WhAm 1
Willis, Park Weed 1867- WhAm 5
Willis, Paul 1863-1935 WhAm 1
Willis, Raymond Eugene 1875-1956 BiDrAC,
WhAm 3
Willis, Richard Lee 1893-1961 NatCAB 49
Willis, Richard Storrs 1819- ApCAB, Drake
Willis, Robert 1800-1875 DcScB
Willis, Robert Ervin 1891-1949 NatCAB 38
Willis, Sara Payson NotAW
Willis, Simeon S 1879-1965 WhAm 4
Willis, Stanley Dutton 1888-1944 NatCAB 33
Willis, Thomas 1621-1675 BiHiMed, DcScB
Willis, William 1794-1870 ApCAB, DcAmB,
Drake, WhAm H
Willis, William Andrew 1875- WhoColR
Willis, William Darrell 1907-1973 WhAm 6
Willis, William H NewYHSD
Willis, William R NewYHSD
Willison, George F 1896-1972 WhAm 5
Williston, Arthur Lyman 1868-1956 BiDAmEd,
NatCAB 46, WhAm 5
Williston, Benjamin Franklin 1853-1925
NatCAB 20
Williston, Constance Bigelow 1873-
WomWWA 14
Williston, Ebenezer Bancroft 1801-1837 ApCAB,
Drake
Williston, Edward Bancroft 1837-1920 WhAm 1
Williston, Harry Stoddard 1872-1942
NatCAB 31
Williston, James Richards 1859-1931
NatCAB 14, NatCAB 23
Williston, Payson 1763-1856 NatCAB 2
Williston, Samuel 1795-1874 AmBi, ApCAB,
DcAmB, Drake, NatCAB 5, WhAm H
Williston, Samuel 1861-1963 NatCAB 51,
WhAm 4
Williston, Samuel Wendell 1851-1918 DcScB,
NatCAB 30
Williston, Samuel Wendell 1852-1918 AmBi,
DcAmB, WhAm 1

Williston, Seth 1770-1851 ApCAB, DcAmB,
WhAm H
Willits, Albert Bower 1851-1926 WhAm 1
Willits, Edwin 1830-1896 BiDrAC, NatCAB 2,
WhAm H, WhAmP
Willits, George Sidney 1853-1917 WhAm 1
Willits, Mary 1863- WomWWA 14
Willits, Merritt Noxon 1874-1930 NatCAB 23
Willits, Oliver Gaston 1892-1971 WhAm 5
Willitts, S C NewYHSD
Willius, Frederick Arthur 1888-1972 WhAm 6
Willkie, E E 1896-1956 WhAm 3
Willkie, Herman Frederick 1890-1959
NatCAB 45, WhAm 3
Willkie, Philip Herman 1919-1974 WhAm 6
Willkie, Wendell Lewis 1892-1944 DcAmB S3,
EncAB, NatCAB 32, WebAB, WhAm 2,
WhAmP, WhWW-II
Willman, Leon Kurtz 1873- WhAm 5
Willmarth, James Willard 1835-1911 WhAm 1
Willmering, Henry 1889-1965 WhAm 4
Willmore, Edward NewYHSD
Willmore, Edward C NewYHSD
Willnus, Harry G 1897-1969 WhAm 5
Willoston, Lorenzo P BiAUS
Willoughby, Barrett d1959 WhAm 3
Willoughby, Benjamin Milton 1855-1940
NatCAB 29, WhAm 1
Willoughby, Charles A 1892-1972 WhAm 5
Willoughby, Charles Clark 1857-1943 WhAm 2
Willoughby, Charles Grant 1866-1951 WhAm 3
Willoughby, Edward C H NewYHSD
Willoughby, Edwin Eliott 1899-1959
NatCAB 56, WhAm 3
Willoughby, Edythe Fuller 1883-
WomWWA 14
Willoughby, Harold Rideout 1890-1962
NatCAB 57, WhAm 4
Willoughby, Hugh DeLaussat 1856-
NatCAB 17
Willoughby, Hugh Laussat 1856- WhAm 4
Willoughby, John Edmund 1861-1929 WhAm 1
Willoughby, John Wallace Cunningham 1845-
NatCAB 7
Willoughby, Julius Edgar 1871-1944
NatCAB 35, WhAm 2
Willoughby, Raymond Royce 1896-1944
NatCAB 33
Willoughby, Westel, Jr. 1769-1844 BiAUS,
BiDrAC, WhAm H
Willoughby, Westel Woodbury 1867-1945
DcAmB S3, NatCAB 13, WhAm 2
Willoughby, William Charles 1857- WhAm 4
Willoughby, William Franklin 1867-1960
ApCAB X, WhAm 4
Willoughby, Woodbury 1904-1964 WhAm 4
Wills, Albert Potter 1873-1937 NatCAB 27,
WhAm 1
Wills, Bob 1905-1975 WhAm 6
Wills, Charles Sinclair 1880-1959 NatCAB 51
Wills, Charles Tomlinson 1851-1915
NatCAB 24, WhAm 1
Wills, Childe Harold 1878-1940 DcAmB S2,
NatCAB 30
Wills, David 1825- WhAm 4
Wills, David Crawford 1872-1925 ApCAB X,
WhAm 1
Wills, Doris Margaret Wood 1902-1963
NatCAB 53
Wills, F Reed 1896-1966 WhAm 4
Wills, Frank Andrew 1864-1941 NatCAB 30
Wills, George Stockton 1866-1956 NatCAB 18,
NatCAB 45, WhAm 3
Wills, Helen Newington 1905- WebAB
Wills, Irving 1894-1967 NatCAB 54
Wills, J R NewYHSD
Wills, James 1760?-1830? ApCAB
Wills, James 1845- NatCAB 14
Wills, Robert REnAW
Wills, Royal Barry 1895-1962 NatCAB 52,
WhAm 4
Wills, William Henry 1882-1946 NatCAB 33,
WhAm 2
Willson, Almyra Henderson WomWWA 14
Willson, Augustus Everett 1846-1931 DcAmB,
NatCAB 14, WhAm 4
Willson, Charles Albert 1878-1936 WhAm 1
Willson, David Burt 1842-1919 ApCAB,

NatCAB 18, WhAm 1
Willson, Elbert Lane 1879-1949 NatCAB 39
Willson, Elizabeth Conwell 1842-1864 ApCAB
Willson, Forceythe 1837-1867 ApCAB,
NatCAB 7, WhAm H
Willson, Frederick Newton 1855-1939 WhAm 1
Willson, George Crapo 1871-1938 NatCAB 36
Willson, George Hayward 1858- WhAm 4
Willson, Harry Leigh 1889-1958 NatCAB 49
Willson, James C 1833-1912 NatCAB 50
Willson, James McCrorry 1887-1972 WhAm 6
Willson, James McLeod 1809-1866 ApCAB
Willson, James Renwick 1780-1853 ApCAB
Willson, James William 1872- WhAm 1
Willson, John Owens 1845-1923 NatCAB 22,
WhAm 1
Willson, Joseph 1825-1857 NewYHSD
Willson, Lester Sebastian 1839-1919 WhAm 1
Willson, Marcius 1813-1905 ApCAB, Drake,
NatCAB 10, WhAm 1
Willson, Mary Ann NewYHSD
Willson, Mary Elizabeth 1842- AmWom
Willson, Nathan Mark 1870-1958 NatCAB 50
Willson, Robert Newton 1839-1922 NatCAB 29
Willson, Robert Newton 1873-1916 WhAm 1
Willson, Robert Wheeler 1853-1922 WhAm 1
Willson, Russell 1883-1948 NatCAB 40,
NatCAB 47, WhAm 2
Willson, Sidney Louis 1867-1944 WhAm 2
Willstatter, Richard 1872-1942 AsBiEn, DcScB
Willughby, Francis 1635-1672 DcScB
Willys, John North 1873-1935 ApCAB X,
DcAmB S1, NatCAB 28, WebAB,
WhAm 1
Wilm, Emil Carl 1877-1932 WhAm 1
Wilm, Grace Gridley 1877- WhAm 5
Wilmarth, Chris 1943- BnEnAmA
Wilmarth, Lemuel Everett 1835-1918 ApCAB,
DcAmB, NatCAB 8, NewYHSD,
TwCBDA, WhAm 1
Wilmarth, Mary Jane Hawes 1837-1919 BiCAW
NotAW, WomWWA 14
Wilmarth, Oscar Rawson 1832-1914
NatCAB 34
Wilmarth, Seth 1810-1886 ApCAB
Wilmer, Cary Breckinridge 1859-1958 WhAm 3
Wilmer, Frank J 1860-1947 WhAm 2
Wilmer, Harry Bond 1884-1943 NatCAB 31
Wilmer, James Jones 1749?-1814 DcAmB
Wilmer, James Jones 1750-1814 WhAm H
Wilmer, Joseph Pere Bell 1812-1878 ApCAB,
DcAmB, NatCAB 11, TwCBDA,
WhAm H
Wilmer, Lambert A 1805?-1863 ApCAB,
Drake
Wilmer, Margaret Elizabeth WomWWA 14
Wilmer, Richard Hooker 1816-1900 ApCAB,
DcAmB, NatCAB 3, TwCBDA,
WhAm H
Wilmer, Richard Hooker 1892-1976 WhAm 6
Wilmer, Simon NatCAB 11
Wilmer, William A d1855 NewYHSD
Wilmer, William Holland 1782-1827 ApCAB,
DcAmB, Drake, NatCAB 3, WhAm H
Wilmer, William Holland 1863-1936 ApCAB X,
DcAmB S2, NatCAB 32, WhAm 1
Wilmerding, Georgiana L WomWWA 14
Wilmerding, Lucius 1879-1949 NatCAB 39
Wilmerding, Lucius Kellogg 1848-1922
WhAm 1
Wilmeroth, Charles William 1860-1943
NatCAB 33
Wilmeth, Frank Lincoln 1862- WhAm 1
Wilmeth, James Lillard 1870-1959 WhAm 3
Wilmore, Augustus Cleland 1849-1933
WhAm 1
Wilmore, Edward NewYHSD
Wilmore, John Jenkins 1864-1943 NatCAB 36,
WhAm 2
Wilmot, Alta E WomWWA 14
Wilmot, David 1814-1868 AmBi, ApCAB,
BiAUS, BiDrAC, DcAmB, Drake,
EncAAH, EncAB, McGEWB, NatCAB 3,
TwCBDA, WebAB, WhAm H, WhAmP
Wilmot, Frank Moore 1872-1930 WhAm 1
Wilmot, George Washington 1867-1936
NatCAB 27, WhAm 1
Wilmot, Lemuel Allan 1809-1878 ApCAB

Wilmot, Nellie Maroa 1868- *WhAm 4*
Wilmot, R J 1898-1950 *WhAm 3*
Wilmot, Robert Duncan 1809- *ApCAB, Drake*
Wilmot, Samuel 1822- *ApCAB*
Wilms, John Henry 1879-1938 *WhAm 1*
Wilmshurst, Zavarr 1824-1887 *ApCAB*
Wilner, Robert Franklin 1889-1960 *WhAm 3*
Wilsey, Edwin Shuey 1880-1952 *NatCAB 41*
Wilsey, Frank Dane 1856-1941 *NatCAB 31*
Wilshire, Gaylord 1861-1927 *NatCAB 42,
WhAm 1*
Wilshire, Joseph 1879-1951 *WhAm 3*
Wilshire, Mary 1880- *WomWWA 14*
Wilshire, William Wallace 1830-1888 *BiAUS,
BiDrAC, NatCAB 13, WhAm H*
Wilshire, William Wallace 1859-1944
NatCAB 33
Wilsing, Johannes 1856-1943 *DcScB*
Wilson *NewYHSD*
Wilson, Mrs. *NewYHSD*
Wilson, Adair 1841- *WhAm 4*
Wilson, Sir Adam 1814- *ApCAB*
Wilson, Albert 1828-1893 *NewYHSD*
Wilson, Albert Dwight 1877-1951 *WhAm 3*
Wilson, Albert Frederick 1883-1940 *WhAm 1*
Wilson, Alda Heaton 1873- *WomWWA 14*
Wilson, Alexander *BiAUS, BiDrAC,
WhAm H*
Wilson, Alexander 1714-1786 *DcScB*
Wilson, Alexander 1766-1813 *AmBi, ApCAB,
DcAmB, DcScB, Drake, McGEWB,
NatCAB 7, NewYHSD, TwCBDA,
WebAB, WhAm H*
Wilson, Alexander 1886-1952 *WhAm 3*
Wilson, Alexander Massey 1876-1944 *WhAm 2*
Wilson, Alfred F *NewYHSD*
Wilson, Alfred Gaston 1883-1962 *NatCAB 50*
Wilson, Mrs. Alfred Gaston 1883-1967
WhAm 5
Wilson, Allen Benjamin 1824-1888 *AmBi,
ApCAB, DcAmB, Drake, NatCAB 9,
WhAm H*
Wilson, Alonzo Edes 1868-1949 *WhAm 2*
Wilson, Alonzo Leon 1890-1961 *NatCAB 51*
Wilson, Alpheus Waters 1834-1916 *ApCAB,
WhAm 1*
Wilson, Andrew 1865-1949 *NatCAB 37*
Wilson, Andrew 1892-1965 *WhAm 4*
Wilson, Andrew Chalmers 1872-1952
NatCAB 39
Wilson, Andrew Gordon 1861- *WhAm 4*
Wilson, Andrew Wilkins, Jr. 1863-1930
WhAm 1
Wilson, Arthur Orville 1869-1942 *WhAm 2*
Wilson, Arthur Riehl 1894-1956 *WhAm 3*
Wilson, Atwood Sylvester 1895-1967 *BiDAmEd*
Wilson, Augusta C Evans 1836- *AmWom*
Wilson, Augusta Jane Evans 1835-1909 *DcAmB,
NatCAB 4, NotAW, TwCBDA,
WhAm 1*
Wilson, Mrs. Augustus *AmWom*
Wilson, Benjamin 1721-1788 *DcScB*
Wilson, Benjamin 1825-1901 *BiAUS, BiDrAC,
WhAmP*
Wilson, Benjamin Frank 1862- *NatCAB 6,
WhAm 3*
Wilson, Benjamin James 1895-1964 *NatCAB 53*
Wilson, Benjamin Lee 1867-1911 *WhAm 1*
Wilson, Bert 1877- *WhAm 5*
Wilson, Bird 1777-1859 *ApCAB, DcAmB,
Drake, NatCAB 2, WhAm H*
Wilson, Bird M 1874- *WomWWA 14*
Wilson, Bluford 1841-1924 *BiAUS Sup,
NatCAB 33*
Wilson, Broadus 1895-1956 *NatCAB 46*
Wilson, Burwell L 1861-1936 *WhAm 3*
Wilson, Byron 1837-1893 *NatCAB 13*
Wilson, Byron Henry 1871-1932 *WhAm 1*
Wilson, Cairine Reay M 1885-1962 *WhAm 4*
Wilson, Calvin Dill 1857-1946 *WhAm 2*
Wilson, Carey 1889-1962 *WhAm 4*
Wilson, Caroline Hardy 1867- *WomWWA 14*
Wilson, Carrington *NewYHSD*
Wilson, Carroll Atwood 1886-1947 *NatCAB 37,
WhAm 2*
Wilson, Carroll Louis 1900-1947 *WhAm 2*
Wilson, Carroll Louis 1900-1958 *WhAm 3*
Wilson, Charles *WhAm HA, WhAm 4*

Wilson, Charles A *WhAm 5*
Wilson, Charles Alfred 1855-1935 *NatCAB 32,
WhAm 4*
Wilson, Charles Banks 1918- *IIBEAAW*
Wilson, Charles Branch 1861-1941 *NatCAB 30,
WhAm 1*
Wilson, Charles Bundy 1861-1938 *NatCAB 13,
WhAm 1*
Wilson, Charles Coker 1864-1933 *NatCAB 33*
Wilson, Charles Edward 1886-1972 *NatCAB 56,
WhAm 5*
Wilson, Charles Erwin 1890-1961 *BiDrUSE,
NatCAB 57, WebAB, WhAm 4*
Wilson, Charles Gustavas 1868-1966 *WhAm 4*
Wilson, Charles Gustavus 1868-1966
NatCAB 55
Wilson, Charles Henry *WhAm 5*
Wilson, Charles Henry 1908-1974 *WhAm 6*
Wilson, Charles Herbert 1917- *BiDrAC*
Wilson, Charles Irving 1837-1913 *WhAm 1*
Wilson, Charles Moseman 1858-1917
NatCAB 18
Wilson, Charles Robert 1863-1951 *NatCAB 44*
Wilson, Charles Scoon 1879-1954 *WhAm 3*
Wilson, Charles Stuart 1884-1972 *WhAm 6*
Wilson, Charles Thomson Rees 1869-1959
AsBiEn, DcScB, McGEWB
Wilson, Charlotte Chaffee 1876-
WomWWA 14
Wilson, Christopher Columbus 1859- *WhoColR*
Wilson, Clarence Hall 1863-1952 *NatCAB 41,
WhAm 5*
Wilson, Clarence Rich 1874-1923 *NatCAB 25,
WhAm 1*
Wilson, Clarence True 1872-1939 *AmBi,
DcAmB S2, NatCAB 7, NatCAB 38,
WhAm 1*
Wilson, Clifford Brittin 1879-1943 *NatCAB 33,
WhAm 2*
Wilson, Clyde 1884-1960 *NatCAB 49*
Wilson, D W *NewYHSD*
Wilson, Sir Daniel 1816- *ApCAB, Drake*
Wilson, Daniel Munro 1848- *WhAm 4*
Wilson, David 1818-1887 *ApCAB*
Wilson, David Arthur 1881-1966 *NatCAB 52*
Wilson, David Cooper 1882-1958 *WhAm 3*
Wilson, David Gilbert, Jr. 1910-1967 *WhAm 4*
Wilson, David Mathias 1896-1961 *WhAm 4*
Wilson, David Roger 1874-1949 *NatCAB 37,
WhAm 2*
Wilson, David West 1799?-1827 *NewYHSD*
Wilson, David Wright 1889-1965 *WhAm 4*
Wilson, Davies 1830-1905 *NatCAB 19*
Wilson, Dunning Steele 1876-1927 *NatCAB 22,
WhAm 1*
Wilson, E *NewYHSD*
Wilson, Miss E *NewYHSD*
Wilson, E H *NewYHSD*
Wilson, E K 1771-1834 *BiAUS*
Wilson, E K *see also* Wilson, Ephraim King
Wilson, Earl 1906- *BiDrAC, WhAmP*
Wilson, Earl B 1891-1973 *WhAm 6*
Wilson, Edgar 1861-1915 *BiDrAC, WhAm 1,
WhAmP*
Wilson, Edgar Bright 1874-1953 *WhAm 3*
Wilson, Edgar Campbell 1800-1860 *BiAUS,
BiDrAC, WhAm H, WhAmP*
Wilson, Edmund 1863- *WhAm 4*
Wilson, Edmund 1895-1972 *EncAB, McGEWB,
WebAB, WhAm 5*
Wilson, Edmund Beecher 1856-1939 *AmBi,
DcAmB S2, DcScB, NatCAB 13,
WhAm 1*
Wilson, Edmund Graham 1884-1963 *WhAm 4*
Wilson, Edward Arthur 1886-1970 *WhAm 5*
Wilson, Edward Clarkson 1870-1944 *WhAm 2*
Wilson, Edward Harlan 1891-1952 *NatCAB 42,
WhAm 4*
Wilson, Edward James 1855-1935 *NatCAB 36*
Wilson, Edward Latimer 1909-1971 *WhAm 5*
Wilson, Edward Livingston 1838-1903 *WhAm 1*
Wilson, Edward Preble 1838- *WhAm 4*
Wilson, Edward Stansbury 1841-1919 *WhAm 1*
Wilson, Edward Taylor 1869-1957 *ApCAB X,
WhAm 3*
Wilson, Edward William 1899-1973 *WhAm 5*
Wilson, Edwin Barnes 1878-1947 *NatCAB 39*
Wilson, Edwin Bidwell 1879-1964 *DcScB,*

NatCAB 54, WhAm 4
Wilson, Edwin Carleton 1893-1972 *WhAm 5*
Wilson, Edwin Mood 1872- *WhAm 5*
Wilson, Edwin Walter 1848-1920 *WhAm 1*
Wilson, Elihu Clement 1870-1950 *NatCAB 42*
Wilson, Elisha Arlington 1876- *WhoColR*
Wilson, Eliza 1845- *WhoColR*
Wilson, Ella Calista 1851- *WhAm 4*
Wilson, Ella Calister 1851- *WomWWA 14*
Wilson, Ellen Louise Axson 1860-1914
*NatCAB 19, NotAW, WhAm 1,
WomWWA 14*
Wilson, Elmina 1870- *WomWWA 14*
Wilson, Elmo C 1906-1968 *WhAm 4A*
Wilson, Emanuel Willis 1844- *NatCAB 12*
Wilson, Emily Rambo Anderson 1863-
WomWWA 14
Wilson, Emmett 1882-1918 *BiDrAC, WhAmP*
Wilson, Ephraim King 1771-1834 *BiDrAC,
WhAm H, WhAmP*
Wilson, Ephraim King 1821-1891 *ApCAB,
BiAUS, BiDrAC, NatCAB 1, TwCBDA,
WhAm H, WhAmP*
Wilson, Ephraim King *see also* Wilson, E K
Wilson, Erasmus 1842-1922 *WhAm 1*
Wilson, Ernest Dana 1890-1958 *NatCAB 46,
WhAm 3*
Wilson, Ernest Henry 1876-1930 *AmBi,
DcAmB, WhAm 1, WhAm 1C*
Wilson, Ernest Theodore 1908-1973 *WhAm 6*
Wilson, Ethel Brown 1879- *WomWWA 14*
Wilson, Eugene Benjamin 1857-1929 *WhAm 1*
Wilson, Eugene Edward 1897-1974 *WhAm 6*
Wilson, Eugene McLanahan 1833-1890 *BiAUS,
BiDrAC, WhAm H, WhAmP*
Wilson, Eugene Smith 1879-1937 *NatCAB 28,
WhAm 1*
Wilson, Eugene Tallmadge 1852-1923
NatCAB 20
Wilson, F M Huntington 1875-1946
NatCAB 38
Wilson, Felix Zollicoffer 1866- *WhAm 4*
Wilson, Fletcher Aloysius 1836-1907 *WhAm 1*
Wilson, Flora 1877- *WomWWA 14*
Wilson, Floyd Baker 1845-1934 *NatCAB 4,
NatCAB 25, WhAm 4*
Wilson, Floyd M 1878-1958 *WhAm 4*
Wilson, Francis 1854-1935 *AmBi, ApCAB Sup,
ApCAB X, DcAmB S1, NatCAB 2,
TwCBDA, WhAm 1*
Wilson, Francis Cushman 1876-1952
NatCAB 38, WhAm 3
Wilson, Francis Henry 1844-1910 *BiDrAC,
WhAmP*
Wilson, Francis Mairs Huntington 1875-1946
WhAm 2
Wilson, Francis Murray 1867-1932 *NatCAB 24,
WhAm 1*
Wilson, Francis Servis 1872-1951 *NatCAB 39,
WhAm 3*
Wilson, Frank Elmer 1885-1944 *WhAm 2*
Wilson, Frank Eugene 1857-1935 *BiDrAC,
WhAmP*
Wilson, Frank John 1887-1970 *WhAm 5*
Wilson, Frank Lyndall 1902-1964 *NatCAB 56*
Wilson, Frank N 1890-1952 *WhAm 3*
Wilson, Frank Palmer 1878-1950 *NatCAB 38*
Wilson, Frank Robert 1881- *WhAm 6*
Wilson, Franklin 1822- *ApCAB*
Wilson, Franklin Augustus 1832-1911 *WhAm 1*
Wilson, Fred Eagle 1889-1966 *NatCAB 54*
Wilson, Fred Stewart 1870-1947 *NatCAB 34*
Wilson, Frederick Morse 1850-1917
NatCAB 34
Wilson, Genevieve *WomWWA 14*
Wilson, George 1839-1908 *NatCAB 1,
WhAm 1*
Wilson, George 1842-1906 *WhAm 1*
Wilson, George Allison 1884-1953 *BiDrAC,
NatCAB 44, WhAm 3, WhAmP*
Wilson, George Arthur 1864-1941 *NatCAB 30,
WhAm 4*
Wilson, George Arthur 1895-1967 *WhAm 5*
Wilson, George Barry 1892-1949 *NatCAB 38,
WhAm 2*
Wilson, George Cunningham, Jr. 1908-1951
NatCAB 39
Wilson, George Francis 1818-1883 *ApCAB,*

Wilson, *DcAmB, WhAm H*

Wilson, George Grafton 1863-1951 *DcAmB S5, NatCAB 47, WhAm 3*

Wilson, George Henry 1854- *ApCAB*

Wilson, George Henry 1855-1922 *WhAm 1*

Wilson, George Henry 1866-1949 *WhAm 2*

Wilson, George Howard 1905- *BiDrAC*

Wilson, George Lloyd 1896-1956 *WhAm 3*

Wilson, George P 1888-1972 *WhAm 5*

Wilson, George Smith 1869-1934 *WhAm 1*

Wilson, George W *NewYHSD*

Wilson, George W d1945 *WhAm 2*

Wilson, George W 1890-1947 *WhAm 2*

Wilson, George Washington 1840-1909 *BiDrAC*

Wilson, George West 1859-1908 *NatCAB 8, WhAm 1*

Wilson, Gilbert 1867- *WhAm 4*

Wilson, Gill Robb 1893-1966 *WhAm 4*

Wilson, Grace Margaret 1875- *WomWWA 14*

Wilson, Grafton Lee 1894-1968 *NatCAB 55, WhAm 5*

Wilson, Grenville Dean 1833-1897 *NatCAB 8, WhAm H*

Wilson, Grove 1883-1954 *WhAm 3*

Wilson, Guy Mitchell 1876-1965 *BiDAmEd, NatCAB 51, WhAm 4*

Wilson, H *NewYHSD*

Wilson, H Augustus 1853-1919 *NatCAB 32, WhAm 1*

Wilson, Halsey William 1868-1954 *DcAmB S5, DcAmLiB, WhAm 3*

Wilson, Harley Peyton 1873-1934 *WhAm 1*

Wilson, Harold 1916- *McGEWB*

Wilson, Harold Albert 1874-1964 *WhAm 4*

Wilson, Harold Edward 1901-1964 *WhAm 4*

Wilson, Harold J 1879- *WhAm 6*

Wilson, Harold Kirby 1900-1958 *WhAm 3*

Wilson, Harris Reid Cooley 1881-1941 *NatCAB 33*

Wilson, Harry Bruce 1874-1932 *WhAm 1*

Wilson, Harry Franklin 1904-1958 *NatCAB 47*

Wilson, Harry Langford 1867-1913 *NatCAB 31, WhAm 1*

Wilson, Harry Leon 1867-1939 *AmBi, DcAmB S2, WebAB, WhAm 1*

Wilson, Harry Robert 1901-1968 *NatCAB 56, WhAm 5*

Wilson, Helen Hopekirk *NotAW, WomWWA 14*

Wilson, Henry *NewYHSD*

Wilson, Henry 1778-1826 *BiAUS, BiDrAC, WhAm H*

Wilson, Henry 1812-1875 *AmBi, ApCAB, BiAUS, BiDrAC, BiDrUSE, DcAmB, Drake, EncAAH, McGEWB, NatCAB 4, TwCBDA, WebAB, WhAm H, WhAmP*

Wilson, Henry Braid 1861-1954 *WebAMB, WhAm 3*

Wilson, Henry Dalzell 1879-1946 *NatCAB 35*

Wilson, Henry H 1854-1941 *NatCAB 18, WhAm 1*

Wilson, Henry Harrison 1882-1933 *NatCAB 25, WhAm 1*

Wilson, Sir Henry Hughes 1864-1922 *WhoMilH*

Wilson, Henry Lane 1856-1932 *WhAm 1*

Wilson, Henry Lane 1857-1932 *AmBi, DcAmB, NatCAB 12*

Wilson, Sir Henry Maitland 1881-1964 *WhWW-II, WhoMilH*

Wilson, Henry Parke Custis 1827-1897 *ApCAB, DcAmB, NatCAB 6, WhAm H*

Wilson, Henry VanPeters 1863-1939 *NatCAB 28, WhAm 1*

Wilson, Herbert Couper 1858-1940 *WhAm 1*

Wilson, Herbert Michael 1860-1920 *WhAm 1*

Wilson, Herbert Taylor Chester 1892-1948 *NatCAB 37*

Wilson, Hiram Roy 1874- *WhAm 5*

Wilson, Hiram V d1866 *BiAUS*

Wilson, Howard Eugene 1901-1966 *BiDAmEd, · WhAm 4*

Wilson, Howard Stebbins 1894-1958 *WhAm 3*

Wilson, Hugh Robert 1885-1946 *DcAmB S4, NatCAB 36, WhAm 2*

Wilson, Hyland Emilio Slatre 1879- *WhoColR*

Wilson, I H d1953 *WhAm 3*

Wilson, Ida Lewis 1841-1911 *NotAW, WhAm 1*

Wilson, Irving Livingstone 1866-1946 *WhAm 2*

Wilson, Isaac 1780-1848 *BiAUS, BiDrAC, WhAm H*

Wilson, J *NewYHSD*

Wilson, J B *NewYHSD*

Wilson, J Christy 1891-1973 *WhAm 6*

Wilson, J Cooke 1879-1944 *NatCAB 33*

Wilson, J Finley 1881-1952 *DcAmB S5*

Wilson, J Frank 1894-1962 *NatCAB 51*

Wilson, J Frank 1897-1972 *WhAm 5*

Wilson, J G *NewYHSD*

Wilson, J Howard 1871-1936 *NatCAB 28*

Wilson, J Stitt 1868-1942 *WhAm 2*

Wilson, Jack *REnAW, WebAB*

Wilson, Jacob 1831-1914 *NatCAB 16*

Wilson, James *NewYHSD*

Wilson, James 1742-1798 *AmBi, ApCAB, BiAUS, BiDrAC, DcAmB, Drake, EncAB, McGEWB, NatCAB 1, TwCBDA, WebAB, WhAm H, WhAmP*

Wilson, James 1757-1839 *BiAUS*

Wilson, James 1763-1855 *NatCAB 17*

Wilson, James 1766-1839 *BiDrAC, WhAm H, WhAmP*

Wilson, James 1779-1868 *BiAUS, BiDrAC, WhAm H*

Wilson, James 1797-1881 *BiAUS, BiDrAC, WhAm H, WhAmP*

Wilson, James 1822-1867 *BiAUS, NatCAB 12*

Wilson, James 1825-1867 *BiDrAC, WhAm H, WhAmP*

Wilson, James 1835- *ApCAB Sup, BiAUS, NatCAB 11, NatCAB 14, TwCBDA*

Wilson, James 1835-1920 *BiDrAC, BiDrUSE, EncAAH, REnAW, WhAm 1, WhAmP*

Wilson, James 1835-1930 *AmBi*

Wilson, James 1836-1920 *DcAmB*

Wilson, James 1848-1927 *WhAm 1*

Wilson, James Adair 1876-1945 *NatCAB 33, WhAm 2*

Wilson, James Claudius *NewYHSD*

Wilson, James Clifton 1874-1951 *BiDrAC*

Wilson, James Cornelius 1847-1934 *AmBi, ApCAB X, NatCAB 12, NatCAB 25, WhAm 1*

Wilson, James Cunningham 1840-1909 *WhAm 1*

Wilson, James Edgar 1860-1940 *WhAm 1*

Wilson, James Edward 1881-1964 *NatCAB 51*

Wilson, James Falconer 1828-1895 *ApCAB, BiAUS, BiDrAC, DcAmB, NatCAB 1, TwCBDA, WhAm H, WhAmP*

Wilson, James Grant 1832-1914 *AmBi, ApCAB, DcAmB, Drake, NatCAB 11, TwCBDA, WhAm 1*

Wilson, James Harrison 1837-1925 *AmBi, ApCAB, DcAmB, NatCAB 2, TwCBDA, WebAMB, WhAm 1*

Wilson, James Harrison 1838?-1925 *Drake*

Wilson, James Jefferson 1775-1824 *ApCAB, BiAUS, BiDrAC, NatCAB 3, TwCBDA, WhAm H*

Wilson, James Knox 1828-1894 *WhAm H*

Wilson, James Ormond 1825-1911 *NatCAB 13, WhAm 1*

Wilson, James Patriot 1769-1830 *ApCAB, Drake*

Wilson, James Reid 1888-1946 *NatCAB 35*

Wilson, James Southall 1880-1963 *NatCAB 51*

Wilson, James Walter 1896-1969 *NatCAB 54, WhAm 5*

Wilson, James Warner 1825-1893 *NewYHSD*

Wilson, James Wilbur 1871- *WhAm 5*

Wilson, Jane Delaplaine 1830- *AmWom*

Wilson, Jeremiah 1825?- *IlBEAAW*

Wilson, Jeremiah Morrow 1828-1901 *BiAUS, BiDrAC*

Wilson, Jeremy *NewYHSD*

Wilson, Jesse Birch 1902-1950 *NatCAB 40*

Wilson, Jesse Everett 1867-1945 *WhAm 2*

Wilson, Joel 1839- *WhAm 4*

Wilson, John *NewYHSD*

Wilson, John d1876 *BiAUS*

Wilson, John 1588-1667 *ApCAB, Drake, NatCAB 20*

Wilson, John 1591?-1667 *AmBi, DcAmB, WhAm H*

Wilson, John 1741-1793 *DcScB*

Wilson, John 1763-1810 *NatCAB 3*

Wilson, John 1773-1828 *BiAUS, BiDrAC, WhAm H*

Wilson, John 1777-1848 *BiAUS, BiDrAC, WhAm H*

Wilson, John 1802-1868 *ApCAB, Drake, NatCAB 9*

Wilson, John 1841-1921 *WhAm 1*

Wilson, John Alfred Baynum 1848- *NatCAB 7*

Wilson, John Allen 1877- *WhoColR*

Wilson, John Allston 1837- *ApCAB*

Wilson, John Appleton 1851-1927 *NatCAB 25*

Wilson, John Arthur 1890-1942 *WhAm 2*

Wilson, John C 1883-1965 *WhAm 4*

Wilson, John Cree 1888-1957 *NatCAB 47*

Wilson, John David 1912-1970 *WhAm 5*

Wilson, John Eldredge 1836-1890 *NatCAB 30*

Wilson, John Fleming 1877-1922 *DcAmB, WhAm 1*

Wilson, John Frank 1846-1911 *BiDrAC, WhAmP*

Wilson, John Franklin 1846-1911 *WhAm 4*

Wilson, John Fry 1869-1930 *WhAm 1*

Wilson, John G 1900-1950 *WhAm 3*

Wilson, John Gordon 1864- *NatCAB 17*

Wilson, John Gordon 1866-1948 *WhAm 2*

Wilson, John Grover 1810-1885 *ApCAB*

Wilson, John Haden 1867-1946 *BiDrAC, WhAm 5*

Wilson, John Henry 1833- *ApCAB*

Wilson, John Henry 1846-1923 *BiDrAC*

Wilson, John Henry 1871-1956 *WhAm 3*

Wilson, John L 1850-1906 *WhAm 1*

Wilson, John Laird 1832- *ApCAB*

Wilson, John Leighton 1809-1886 *ApCAB, DcAmB, NatCAB 21, WhAm H*

Wilson, John Lockwood 1850-1912 *ApCAB Sup, BiDrAC, DcAmB, NatCAB 12, WhAmP*

Wilson, John Lockwood 1851-1912 *NatCAB 27*

Wilson, John Lyde 1784-1849 *ApCAB, BiAUS, NatCAB 12, TwCBDA*

Wilson, John Madison 1931-1969 *WhAm 5*

Wilson, John McCalmont 1876-1940 *NatCAB 34, WhAm 1*

Wilson, John McMillan 1901-1961 *WhAm 4*

Wilson, John Moulder 1837-1909 *NatCAB 4*

Wilson, John Moulder 1837-1919 *ApCAB Sup, WhAm 1*

Wilson, John P 1844-1922 *ApCAB X, NatCAB 23, WhAm 1*

Wilson, John P 1877-1959 *NatCAB 51, WhAm 3*

Wilson, John Reid 1874-1946 *WhAm 2*

Wilson, John Robert 1880-1938 *NatCAB 29*

Wilson, John Smith 1865-1946 *NatCAB 35*

Wilson, John Stewart 1904-1960 *NatCAB 48*

Wilson, John T *NewYHSD*

Wilson, John Thomas 1811-1891 *BiAUS, BiDrAC, WhAm H*

Wilson, John Thomas 1870-1935 *NatCAB 47*

Wilson, John Thompson 1824-1896 *NatCAB 7*

Wilson, John Timothy 1861-1908 *WhAm 1*

Wilson, John Warren 1901-1956 *NatCAB 47*

Wilson, Joseph *NewYHSD*

Wilson, Joseph 1779-1857 *NewYHSD, WhAm H*

Wilson, Joseph C *NewYHSD*

Wilson, Joseph C 1909-1971 *WhAm 5*

Wilson, Joseph Chamberlain 1851-1930 *NatCAB 47, WhAm 1*

Wilson, Joseph Dawson 1840-1925 *WhAm 1*

Wilson, Joseph Franklin 1901-1968 *BiDrAC*

Wilson, Joseph G 1874-1957 *WhAm 3*

Wilson, Joseph Gardner 1826-1873 *BiDrAC, WhAm H*

Wilson, Joseph Miller 1838-1902 *ApCAB, DcAmB, NatCAB 7, WhAm 1*

Wilson, Joseph Robert 1866-1957 *NatCAB 16, NatCAB 44, WhAm 4*

Wilson, Joseph Robert 1882-1962 *NatCAB 52, WhAm 4*

Wilson, Joseph Rogers 1847-1929 *WhAm 1*

Wilson, Joseph S *BiAUS*

Wilson, Joshua Lacy 1774-1846 *DcAmB, NatCAB 12, WhAm H*

Wilson, Juanita Raddant 1881- *WomWWA 14*

Wilson, Julian Alexander 1909-1969 *WhAm 5*

Wilson, Julian DuBois 1896-1958 *WhAm 3*

Wilson, Julian Morris 1866-1931 *WhAm 1*
Wilson, Kate DeNormandie *WomWWA 14*
Wilson, Katharine S J *WomWWA 14*
Wilson, Kenneth Eldredge 1906-1965
NatCAB 52
Wilson, Kirke Ronald 1889-1948 *NatCAB 45*
Wilson, L B 1891-1954 *WhAm 3*
Wilson, L D *NewYHSD*
Wilson, Lawrence Glass 1890-1954 *WhAm 3*
Wilson, Lazarus Brown 1795-1875 *NatCAB 8*
Wilson, Leonard 1869- *WhAm 5*
Wilson, Leonard Seltzer 1909-1970 *WhAm 5*
Wilson, Leroy A 1901-1951 *WhAm 3*
Wilson, Leroy Oliver 1871- *WhoColR*
Wilson, Leslie MacLean 1860-1929 *NatCAB 43*
Wilson, Lester MacLean 1885-1937 *WhAm 1*
Wilson, Lettie Luella Melissa 1841-
NatCAB 10
Wilson, Lewis Albert 1886-1969 *WhAm 5*
Wilson, Lewis Dicken 1789-1847 *NatCAB 7*
Wilson, Lewis Eugene 1900-1957 *NatCAB 45*
Wilson, Lewis Ghriskey 1880-1951 *NatCAB 39*
Wilson, Lewis Gilbert 1858- *WhAm 4*
Wilson, Lloyd Tilghman 1866-1933 *WhAm 1*
Wilson, Lorenzo Arthur 1864-1936 *WhAm 1*
Wilson, Louis Blanchard 1866-1943 *DcAmB S3,*
NatCAB 40, WhAm 2
Wilson, Louis Hugh 1920- *WebAMB*
Wilson, Louis N 1857-1937 *WhAm 1*
Wilson, Louis Round 1876- *BiDAmEd,*
WhAm 5
Wilson, Lucius Edward 1878-1944 *WhAm 2*
Wilson, Lucy James 1880- *WomWWA 14*
Wilson, Lucy Langdon Williams 1864-1937
BiDAmEd, NatCAB 29, WhAm 1,
WomWWA 14
Wilson, Luke Ingals 1872-1937 *NatCAB 32*
Wilson, Luther Barton 1856-1928 *NatCAB 13,*
WhAm 1
Wilson, Lyle Campbell 1899-1967 *WhAm 4*
Wilson, Lyman Perl 1883-1951 *WhAm 3*
Wilson, M Orme 1860-1926 *NatCAB 36*
Wilson, Mardon Dewees 1851- *WhAm 4*
Wilson, Margaret Adelaide *WomWWA 14*
Wilson, Margaret Barclay 1863-1945
NatCAB 34, WhAm 2
Wilson, Margaret O'Connor *WomWWA 14*
Wilson, Margaret Whitelaw 1878-
WomWWA 14
Wilson, Margaret Woodrow 1886-1944
WhAm 2
Wilson, Marion Childress 1886-1958
NatCAB 48
Wilson, Martha Eleanor Loftin 1834- *AmWom*
Wilson, Mary Ann *NewYHSD*
Wilson, Mary Driver Holcomb *WomWWA 14*
Wilson, Mary Elizabeth 1869-1949 *WhAm 3,*
WomWWA 14
Wilson, Mary Isabel *WomWWA 14*
Wilson, Mary Priscilla *NewYHSD*
Wilson, Mary R *NewYHSD*
Wilson, Mary W 1849- *WomWWA 14*
Wilson, Matthew *NewYHSD*
Wilson, Matthew 1731-1790 *ApCAB*
Wilson, Matthew 1814-1892 *ApCAB,*
NewYHSD, WhAm H
Wilson, Maude Stuart Fillmore 1869-
WomWWA 14
Wilson, Maurice Emery 1855-1936 *WhAm 1*
Wilson, Milburn Lincoln 1885-1969 *EncAAH,*
NatCAB 55, WhAm 5
Wilson, Millard Thomas 1902-1960 *WhAm 4*
Wilson, Mira Bigelow 1893-1953 *WhAm 3*
Wilson, Morris Watson 1883-1946 *WhAm 2*
Wilson, Mortimer 1876-1932 *AmBi, DcAmB,*
NatCAB 23, WhAm 1
Wilson, Moses Fleming 1839- *WhAm 4*
Wilson, Murray Alderson 1894-1969 *WhAm 5*
Wilson, Myron Henry 1858-1951 *NatCAB 43*
Wilson, Myron Henry, Jr. 1887-1962
NatCAB 48, WhAm 4
Wilson, Nathan d1834 *BiAUS*
Wilson, Nathan 1758-1834 *BiDrAC*
Wilson, Nathan 1759-1834 *WhAm H*
Wilson, Nathaniel 1836-1922 *NatCAB 12,*
WhAm 1
Wilson, O *NewYHSD*
Wilson, Obed J 1826-1914 *NatCAB 16*

Wilson, Odbert Patton 1888-1958 *NatCAB 48*
Wilson, Oliver *NewYHSD*
Wilson, Oliver Morris 1836-1907 *ApCAB,*
NatCAB 19
Wilson, Oren Elbridge 1844-1917 *NatCAB 17*
Wilson, Orlando Winfield 1900-1972 *WhAm 5*
Wilson, Orme 1885-1966 *WhAm 4*
Wilson, Otis Guy 1877- *WhAm 5*
Wilson, Paul Oran 1894-1969 *WhAm 5*
Wilson, Percival Clark 1830-1920 *NatCAB 18*
Wilson, Percy 1890-1950 *WhAm 2*
Wilson, Perry Morton 1885-1942 *NatCAB 31*
Wilson, Peter 1746-1825 *ApCAB, BiDAmEd,*
DcAmB, Drake, NatCAB 6, WhAm H
Wilson, Philip Danforth 1888-1971 *NatCAB 56*
Wilson, Philip Duncan 1886-1969 *NatCAB 55,*
WhAm 5
Wilson, Philip Sheridan 1869-1926 *WhAm 1*
Wilson, Philip St. Julien 1867-1936 *WhAm 1*
Wilson, Philip Whitwell 1875-1956 *WhAm 3*
Wilson, Pliny Jewel 1890-1960 *NatCAB 48*
Wilson, Ramon Ernesto 1852-1893 *NatCAB 26*
Wilson, Respess S 1886-1954 *WhAm 3*
Wilson, Richard 1713?-1782 *McGEWB*
Wilson, Richard Dudley 1921-1972 *NatCAB 57*
Wilson, Richard Henry 1870- *WhAm 5*
Wilson, Richard Hulbert 1853- *WhAm 4*
Wilson, Richard Thornton 1867-1929
NatCAB 23
Wilson, Riley Joseph 1871-1946 *BiDrAC,*
WhAmP
Wilson, Riley Joseph 1871-1947 *WhAm 2*
Wilson, Ripley 1887-1917 *NatCAB 17*
Wilson, Robert d1870 *BiAUS*
Wilson, Robert 1800-1870 *NatCAB 12*
Wilson, Robert 1803-1870 *BiDrAC, WhAm H*
Wilson, Robert 1867-1946 *WhAm 2*
Wilson, Robert Anderson 1803-1872
NatCAB 18
Wilson, Robert Anderson 1812- *Drake*
Wilson, Robert Burns 1850-1916 *DcAmB,*
NatCAB 1, WhAm 1
Wilson, Robert Cade 1870-1954 *NatCAB 41,*
WhAm 3
Wilson, Robert Carlton 1916- *BiDrAC*
Wilson, Robert Christian 1896-1973 *WhAm 6*
Wilson, Robert Clifford 1883-1958 *NatCAB 43*
Wilson, Robert Dick 1856- *WhAm 4*
Wilson, Robert Edward Lee 1865-1933
NatCAB 25, WhAm 1
Wilson, Robert Erastus 1893-1964 *NatCAB 52,*
WhAm 4
Wilson, Robert Forrest 1883-1942 *WhAm 2*
Wilson, Robert G 1768-1851 *NatCAB 4*
Wilson, Robert James 1848-1925 *NatCAB 22*
Wilson, Robert Lee 1871-1957 *WhAm 3*
Wilson, Robert North 1875- *WhAm 5*
Wilson, Robert Patterson Clark 1834-1916
BiDrAC
Wilson, Robert Perry 1912-1969 *WhAm 5*
Wilson, Robert Wilbar 1893-1975 *WhAm 6*
Wilson, Ross Bynum 1898-1964 *NatCAB 51*
Wilson, Roy William 1894-1954 *WhAm 3*
Wilson, Rufus Rockwell 1865-1949 *WhAm 2,*
WhAm 3
Wilson, Rush 1870-1956 *NatCAB 46*
Wilson, Russell 1876-1946 *WhAm 2*
Wilson, Russell H 1908- *WhAm 5*
Wilson, Ruth Danenhower 1887-1974 *WhAm 6*
Wilson, S A Kinnier 1878-1937 *BiHiMed*
Wilson, S Davis d1939 *WhAm 1*
Wilson, S Taylor 1868-1944 *NatCAB 33*
Wilson, Sam Emmett, Jr. 1898-1957
NatCAB 45
Wilson, Samuel *NewYHSD*
Wilson, Samuel 1766-1854 *DcAmB, WebAB,*
WhAm H
Wilson, Samuel B 1782?-1869 *NatCAB 2*
Wilson, Samuel Bailey 1873-1954 *NatCAB 49,*
WhAm 3
Wilson, Samuel Farmer 1805-1870 *ApCAB,*
Drake
Wilson, Samuel Franklin 1845- *NatCAB 12*
Wilson, Samuel Graham 1858-1916 *DcAmB,*
WhAm 4
Wilson, Samuel Kirkbride 1829- *NatCAB 4*
Wilson, Samuel Knox 1882-1959 *NatCAB 45,*
WhAm 3

Wilson, Samuel Mackay 1871-1946 *NatCAB 36,*
WhAm 2
Wilson, Samuel Mountford 1823-1892 *DcAmB,*
NatCAB 7, WhAm H
Wilson, Samuel Ramsay 1818-1886 *DcAmB,*
NatCAB 12, WhAm H
Wilson, Samuel Thomas 1761-1824 *DcAmB,*
WhAm H
Wilson, Samuel Tyndale 1858- *WhAm 4*
Wilson, Sarah 1750- *NotAW*
Wilson, Scott 1870-1942 *NatCAB 32,*
WhAm 1
Wilson, Sidney Smart 1865-1950 *NatCAB 39*
Wilson, Sol 1896-1974 *WhAm 6*
Wilson, Stanley Albert 1897-1955 *NatCAB 45*
Wilson, Stanley Calef 1879-1967 *WhAm 4A*
Wilson, Stanley Kidder 1879- *WhAm 6*
Wilson, Stanyarne 1860-1928 *BiDrAC,*
WhAm 4
Wilson, Stephen 1904-1963 *WhAm 4*
Wilson, Stephen Bayard 1796-1863 *ApCAB*
Wilson, Stephen D 1825?- *NewYHSD*
Wilson, Stephen Fowler 1821-1897 *BiAUS,*
BiDrAC, WhAm H
Wilson, T Bert 1877-1957 *NatCAB 46,*
WhAm 3
Wilson, Theodore Delavan 1840-1896 *ApCAB,*
DcAmB, NatCAB 7, WhAm H
Wilson, Thomas *NewYHSD*
Wilson, Thomas 1761-1824 *ApCAB*
Wilson, Thomas 1765-1826 *BiAUS, BiDrAC,*
WhAm H, WhAmP
Wilson, Thomas 1768?-1828? *ApCAB*
Wilson, Thomas 1772-1824 *BiAUS, BiDrAC,*
WhAm H
Wilson, Thomas 1789-1879 *ApCAB*
Wilson, Thomas 1827-1910 *ApCAB, BiDrAC,*
NatCAB 1, WhAm 1
Wilson, Thomas 1832-1902 *NatCAB 11,*
WhAm 1
Wilson, Thomas Albert 1888-1972 *NatCAB 57,*
WhAm 5
Wilson, Thomas Alexander 1915-1972
NatCAB 57
Wilson, Thomas Aquilla 1900-1943 *NatCAB 38*
Wilson, Thomas Bayne 1892-1963 *WhAm 4*
Wilson, Thomas Bellerby 1807-1865 *ApCAB,*
Drake, NatCAB 13
Wilson, Thomas Edward 1868-1958 *WhAm 3*
Wilson, Thomas Emmet 1847- *NatCAB 5*
Wilson, Thomas Harrington *IIBEAAW*
Wilson, Thomas Henry 1899-1967 *WhAm 4*
Wilson, Thomas James 1902-1969 *WhAm 5*
Wilson, Thomas Murray 1881-1967 *WhAm 4*
Wilson, Thomas R 1897-1970 *WhAm 6*
Wilson, Thomas S *BiAUS*
Wilson, Thomas Webber 1893-1948 *BiDrAC,*
WhAm 2
Wilson, Thomas William 1872-1948
NatCAB 36, WhAm 2
Wilson, Thomas Woodrow 1856-1924 *AmBi,*
BiDAmEd, BiDrAC, EncAAH, EncAB,
McGEWB, WebAB, WhAmP
Wilson, Val Haining 1915-1964 *WhAm 4*
Wilson, Victor Peters 1902-1968 *NatCAB 55*
Wilson, Vincent Edward 1920-1974 *WhAm 6*
Wilson, W Walter 1884-1966 *NatCAB 52*
Wilson, Walter King 1880-1954 *NatCAB 44,*
WhAm 3
Wilson, Walter Lewis 1881- *WhAm 6*
Wilson, Walter Sibbald 1844- *WhAm 4*
Wilson, Warren Hugh 1867-1937 *DcAmB S2,*
WhAm 1
Wilson, Wayne Thomas 1872-1940 *NatCAB 36*
Wilson, Webster Hill 1913-1974 *NatCAB 57,*
WhAm 6
Wilson, Wilbur M 1881-1958 *WhAm 3*
Wilson, Wilford Murry 1860- *WhAm 4*
Wilson, Willard 1904-1974 *WhAm 6*
Wilson, William *BiAUS, BiDrAC,*
NewYHSD, WhAm H
Wilson, William d1850 *NewYHSD*
Wilson, William 1755-1828 *ApCAB*
Wilson, William 1773-1827 *BiAUS, BiDrAC,*
WhAmP
Wilson, William 1773-1853 *WhAm H*
Wilson, William 1794-1856 *Drake*
Wilson, William 1794-1857 *DcAmB,*

NatCAB 5, WhAm H

Wilson, William 1801-1860 ApCAB, DcAmB, Drake, WhAm H

Wilson, William 1855-1937 WhAm 1

Wilson, William 1884-1959 WhAm 3A

Wilson, William Arnott 1867-1915 NatCAB 16

Wilson, William B 1866-1946 WhAm 2

Wilson, William Bauchop 1862-1934 AmBi, ApCAB X, BiDrAC, BiDrUSE, DcAmB, NatCAB 16, WebAB, WhAm 1, WhAmP

Wilson, William Carr 1866-1943 NatCAB 32

Wilson, William Dexter 1816-1900 ApCAB, BiDAmEd, DcAmB, Drake, NatCAB 12

Wilson, William Earl 1896-1971 WhAm 5

Wilson, William Edward 1847- NatCAB 11, WhAm 4

Wilson, William Edward 1870-1948 BiDrAC, WhAm 5

Wilson, William F NewYHSD

Wilson, William Frank 1875-1945 NatCAB 34

Wilson, William Garrick 1871-1935 ApCAB X, NatCAB 26

Wilson, William H 1879- WhoColR

Wilson, William Hasell 1811-1902 DcAmB, WhAm 1

Wilson, William Hassell 1811-1902 NatCAB 14

Wilson, William Henry 1877-1937 BiDrAC, NatCAB 29, WhAm 1

Wilson, William Henry 1877-1960 NatCAB 49

Wilson, William Huntington 1870- WhAm 5

Wilson, William James WhAm 5

Wilson, William Joseph 1909-1974 WhAm 6

Wilson, William Kumbel 1848-1935 NatCAB 25

Wilson, William Lyne 1843-1900 AmBi, ApCAB, ApCAB X, BiDrAC, BiDrUSE, DcAmB, EncAAH, NatCAB 8, TwCBDA, WhAm H, WhAm 2, WhAmP

Wilson, William Oliver 1884-1955 WhAm 3

Wilson, William Otis 1870-1948 WhAm 2

Wilson, William Pannell 1872-1959 NatCAB 46

Wilson, William Powell 1844-1927 ApCAB Sup, WhAm 1

Wilson, William Ralph 1924-1975 WhAm 6

Wilson, William Riley 1860- WhAm 5

Wilson, William Robert Anthony 1870-1911 NatCAB 16, WhAm 1

Wilson, William Sidney 1816-1862 BiDConf

Wilson, William W NewYHSD

Wilson, William Warfield 1868-1942 BiDrAC, NatCAB 43, WhAm 4, WhAmP

Wilson, Winfred 1879-1944 NatCAB 36

Wilson, Winifred Warren 1870- WomWWA 14

Wilson, Wirt Bunten 1881-1955 NatCAB 47

Wilson, Woodrow 1856-1924 AmBi, ApCAB, ApCAB X, BiDrUSE, DcAmB, NatCAB 19, TwCBDA, WebAB, WhAm HA, WhAm 1, WhAm 4A, WhAmP

Wilson, Mrs. Woodrow 1860-1914 WhAm 1

Wilson, York Lowry 1893-1962 NatCAB 50

Wilson, Zara A 1840- AmWom

Wilson, Zillah E WomWWA 14

Wilstach, Frank Jenners 1865-1933 WhAm 1

Wilstach, John Augustine 1824- ApCAB

Wilstach, Joseph Walter 1857- ApCAB

Wilstach, Paul 1870-1952 WhAm 3

Wilt, Napier 1896-1975 WhAm 6

Wiltbank, William White 1840- WhAm 1

Wiltberger, Andrew NewYHSD

Wiltberger, Mary Elizabeth 1858- WomWWA 14

Wilton, Bernard NewYHSD

Wilton, H Leonard 1862-1927 NatCAB 26

Wiltse, Sara Eliza 1849- WhAm 4, WomWWA 14

Wiltsee, Ernest 1863- NatCAB 14

Wiltsee, William Pharo 1878-1958 WhAm 3

Wiltsie, Charles Hastings 1859-1935 NatCAB 25, WhAm 1

Wiltz, Arnold 1889-1937 NatCAB 28

Wiltz, Emile NewYHSD

Wiltz, Leonard, Jr. NewYHSD

Wiltz, Louis Alfred 1843-1881 DcAmB, NatCAB 10, WhAm H*

Wilwerding, Walter Joseph 1891-1966 IlBEAAW, WhAm 4

Wiman, Charles Deere 1892-1955 WhAm 3

Wiman, Erastus 1834-1904 ApCAB, WhAm 1

Wimar, Carl Ferdinand 1828-1862 DcAmB, REnAW, WhAm H

Wimar, Charles 1828-1862 IlBEAAW, NewYHSD, REnAW

Wimar, Karl Ferdinand 1828-1862 BnEnAmA, NewYHSD

Wimberly, Carl Everett 1887-1960 NatCAB 51

Wimberly, Charles Franklin 1866-1946 WhAm 2

Wimberly, Lowry Charles 1890-1959 WhAm 3

Wimmer, Boniface 1809-1887 ApCAB, DcAmB, WhAm H

Wimmer, Sebastian 1831- NatCAB 12

Wimpffen-Berneburg, Alexander Stanislaus 1748-1819 ApCAB

Wimsatt, William Kurtz 1907-1975 WhAm 6

Winans, Charles Sumner 1863-1935 WhAm 1

Winans, Edwin Baruch 1826-1894 BiDrAC, NatCAB 2, TwCBDA, WhAm H, WhAmP

Winans, Edwin Baruch 1869-1947 WhAm 2

Winans, Elizabeth Sweet 1874- WomWWA 14

Winans, Henry Morgan 1893-1965 WhAm 4

Winans, James Albert 1872- WhAm 5

Winans, James January 1818-1879 BiAUS, BiDrAC, NatCAB 3, WhAm H

Winans, John 1831-1907 BiDrAC

Winans, Ross 1796-1877 ApCAB, ApCAB X, DcAmB, NatCAB 11, WhAm H

Winans, Samuel Ross 1855-1910 WhAm 1

Winans, Thomas DeKay 1820-1878 ApCAB, DcAmB, NatCAB 1, WhAm H

Winans, Walter 1852-1920 IlBEAAW

Winans, Wilfred Hughes 1889-1975 WhAm 6

Winans, William 1788-1857 ApCAB, DcAmB, NatCAB 1, WhAm H

Winans, William O 1830?- NewYHSD

Winans, William Parkhurst 1836- ApCAB X

Winant, John Gilbert 1889-1947 DcAmB S4, NatCAB 38, WhAm 2, WhWW-II

Winbigler, Charles Fremont 1857-1925 ApCAB X, WhAm 1

Winborne, John Wallace 1884-1967 WhAm 5

Winborne, Stanley 1886-1966 NatCAB 53

Winbourn, Robert Emmet 1882-1930 WhAm 1

Winburn, Hardy Lathan 1877-1937 WhAm 1

Winch, Horace Carlton 1901-1971 WhAm 5

Winch, Louis Harvey 1862-1927 ApCAB X

Winchell, Alexander 1824-1891 AmBi, ApCAB, BiDAmEd, DcAmB, DcScB, Drake, NatCAB 6, NatCAB 16, TwCBDA, WhAm H

Winchell, Alexander Newton 1874-1958 DcScB, NatCAB 46, WhAm 3

Winchell, Benjamin LaFon 1858-1942 NatCAB 31, WhAm 2

Winchell, F Mabel WomWWA 14

Winchell, Harold Brooks 1894-1929 NatCAB 22

Winchell, Horace Vaughn 1865-1923 DcAmB, DcScB, NatCAB 20, WhAm 1

Winchell, James Manning 1791-1820 ApCAB

Winchell, John H 1892-1970 WhAm 5

Winchell, Newton Horace 1839-1914 AmBi, ApCAB, DcAmB, DcScB, NatCAB 7, NatCAB 31, TwCBDA, WhAm 1

Winchell, Samuel Robertson 1843- WhAm 4

Winchell, Walter 1897-1972 WebAB, WhAm 5

Winchell Family DcScB

Winchester, Benjamin Severance 1868-1955 NatCAB 44, WhAm 3

Winchester, Boyd 1836-1923 BiAUS, BiDrAC, NatCAB 13

Winchester, Caleb Thomas 1847-1920 DcAmB, NatCAB 19, WhAm 1

Winchester, Charles Wesley 1843- WhAm 1

Winchester, Elhanan 1751-1797 ApCAB, DcAmB, DcAmReB, Drake, WhAm H

Winchester, Fanny Ramsay Wilder WomWWA 14

Winchester, James 1752-1826 AmBi, ApCAB, DcAmB, NatCAB 4, TwCBDA, WebAMB, WhAm H

Winchester, James 1756-1826 BiAUS, Drake

Winchester, James Price d1943 WhAm 2

Winchester, James Ridout 1852-1941 NatCAB 30, WhAm 1

Winchester, John Frost 1855-1920 NatCAB 18

Winchester, Maud Tarleton 1869- WomWWA 14

Winchester, Millard E 1893-1960 WhAm 4

Winchester, Oliver Fisher 1810-1880 AmBi, ApCAB, DcAmB, EncAAH, NatCAB 11, WebAB, WhAm H

Winchester, Pearl Adair Gunn 1874- WomWWA 14

Winchester, Samuel Gover 1805-1841 ApCAB, Drake

Winchester, Walter Henry 1875-1963 NatCAB 51

Winchester, William Eugene 1877-1943 WhAm 2

Winchevsky, Morris 1856-1932 DcAmB

Winckelmann, Johann Joachim 1717-1768 McGEWB

Wind, Edgar 1900-1971 WhAm 5

Windaus, Adolf Otto Reinhold 1876-1959 AsBiEn, DcScB

Windeat, William NewYHSD

Windels, Paul 1885-1967 NatCAB 54, WhAm 4A, WhAm 5

Winder, Adam Heber 1882-1940 WhAm 1

Winder, Charles Sidney 1829-1862 ApCAB Sup, NatCAB 5

Winder, Corinne Pope WomWWA 14

Winder, G Norman 1897-1961 NatCAB 53, WhAm 4

Winder, John Henry 1800-1865 ApCAB, BiDConf, DcAmB, Drake, WebAMB, WhAm H

Winder, John Rex 1821-1910 NatCAB 16

Winder, Levin d1819 BiAUS, Drake

Winder, Levin 1756-1819 ApCAB

Winder, Levin 1757-1819 DcAmB, NatCAB 9, TwCBDA, WhAm H

Winder, William BiAUS

Winder, William Henry 1775-1824 AmBi, ApCAB, DcAmB, Drake, NatCAB 10, WebAMB, WhAm H

Windes, Thomas Guilford 1848-1923 NatCAB 17, WhAm 1

Windet, Victor 1867-1945 WhAm 2

Windgassen, Wolfgang Friedrich Hermann 1914- WhAm 6

Windholz, Louis H 1878-1942 WhAm 2

Windingstad, Ole 1886-1959 WhAm 3

Windisch, Charles Frederick 1864-1939 NatCAB 33

Windisch, Conrad 1825-1887 NatCAB 45

Windisch-Graetz, Alfred C F Furst Zu 1787-1862 WhoMilH

Windmueller, Louis 1836-1913 NatCAB 4

Windmuller, Louis 1835-1913 NatCAB 31, WhAm 1

Windom, William 1827-1891 AmBi, ApCAB, BiAUS, BiDrAC, BiDrUSE, DcAmB, EncAAH, NatCAB 1, TwCBDA, WhAm H, WhAmP

Windrim, James Hamilton 1840-1919 NatCAB 3, WhAm 1

Windrim, John Torrey 1866-1934 WhAm HA, WhAm 4

Winds, William 1727?-1789 ApCAB, Drake

Windship, George Barker 1834-1876 ApCAB

Windsor, Duke Of 1894-1972 WhAm 5

Windsor, Helen Howell 1880-1926 NatCAB 20

Windsor, Henry Haven 1859-1924 NatCAB 15, WhAm 1

Windsor, Henry Haven, Jr. 1900-1965 WhAm 4

Windsor, James Harvey 1904-1971 NatCAB 55, WhAm 5

Windsor, Margaret Fursman Boynton 1872- WomWWA 14

Windsor, Phineas Lawrence 1871-1965 DcAmLiB, WhAm 5

Windsor, Wallis Warfield, Duchess Of 1896- WebAB

Windsor, Wilbur Cunningham 1906?-1958 WhAm 3

Windsor, William Augustus 1842-1907 WhAm 1

Wine, Jacob Good 1861-1951 NatCAB 40

Wine, William Edward 1881-1955 NatCAB 46, WhAm 3

Winebrenner, David Charles 1897-1940
NatCAB 30
Winebrenner, John 1797-1860 *AmBi, ApCAB,
DcAmB, Drake, NatCAB 1, WhAm H*
Wineman, Henry 1878- *WhAm 6*
Wineman, Mode 1865-1933 *WhAm 1*
Wines, Enoch Cobb 1806-1879 *AmBi, ApCAB,
DcAmB, Drake, NatCAB 1, TwCBDA,
WhAm H*
Wines, Frederick Howard 1838-1912 *AmBi,
ApCAB, DcAmB, NatCAB 21, WhAm 1*
Winfield, Arthur M *WebAB, WhAm H*
Winfield, Charles Hardenburg 1829-1898
ApCAB Sup
Winfield, Charles Henry 1822-1888 *BiAUS,
BiDrAC, WhAm H*
Winfield, George Freeman 1879-1943 *WhAm 2*
Winfield, James Macfarlane 1859-1923
WhAm 1
Winfield, James Macfarlane 1901- *WhAm 4*
Winfrey, Elisha William 1858-1931 *WhAm 1*
Wing, Amelia Kempshall 1837- *AmWom*
Wing, Asa Shove 1859-1931 *WhAm 1*
Wing, Austin Eli 1792-1849 *BiAUS, BiDrAC,
WhAm H, WhAmP*
Wing, Charles Baldwin 1853- *NatCAB 14*
Wing, Charles Benjamin 1864-1945 *NatCAB 35,
WhAm 2*
Wing, Charles Hallet 1836-1915 *WhAm 1*
Wing, Conway Phelps 1809-1889 *ApCAB*
Wing, Daniel Gould 1868-1936 *NatCAB 15,
NatCAB 38, WhAm 1*
Wing, Donald Goddard 1904-1972 *DcAmLiB,
NatCAB 57*
Wing, E Rumsey 1845-1874 *BiAUS*
Wing, Edward Rumsey 1845-1874 *NatCAB 5*
Wing, Francis Joseph 1850- *WhAm 1*
Wing, Frank 1873- *WhAm 5*
Wing, Frank Everett 1876-1963 *NatCAB 49*
Wing, George Curtis, Jr. 1878-1951 *NatCAB 39*
Wing, George Fox, III 1913-1963 *NatCAB 50*
Wing, George Washington 1843-1925
NatCAB 17
Wing, Grace A *WomWWA 14*
Wing, H McKie 1847-1933 *NatCAB 27*
Wing, Henry Hiram 1859-1936 *NatCAB 37,
WhAm 1*
Wing, John Durham 1882-1960 *WhAm 3*
Wing, Joseph Elwyn 1861-1915 *AmBi, DcAmB,
EncAAH*
Wing, Leonard Fish 1893-1945 *NatCAB 35,
WhAm 2*
Wing, Lucy Madeira 1873-1960 *WhAm 4*
Wing, Orion N 1891-1957 *WhAm 3*
Wing, Russell Merritt 1850-1919 *WhAm 1*
Wing, Vincent 1619-1668 *DcScB*
Wing, Wilson Gordon 1881-1944 *NatCAB 34,
WhAm 2*
Wing, Wilson Munford 1908-1971 *WhAm 5*
Wingard, Robert Frederick 1880-1951
NatCAB 42
Wingate, Charles Edgar Lewis 1861-1944
NatCAB 33, WhAm 2
Wingate, Charles Frederick 1847-1909 *ApCAB*
Wingate, Charles Frederick 1848-1909 *WhAm 1*
Wingate, Curtis 1926- *IIBEAAW*
Wingate, George Wood 1840-1928 *ApCAB,
WhAm 1*
Wingate, Joseph Ferdinand 1786- *BiAUS,
BiDrAC, WhAm H*
Wingate, Orde Charles 1903-1944 *WhWW-II,
WhoMilH*
Wingate, Paine 1739-1838 *ApCAB, BiAUS,
BiDrAC, DcAmB, Drake, NatCAB 3,
NatCAB 12, TwCBDA, WhAm H,
WhAmP*
Wingate, Uranus Owen Brackett 1848-1911
NatCAB 1, NatCAB 23, WhAm 1
Winge, Ojvind 1886-1964 *WhAm 4*
Winger, Albert E 1883-1971 *WhAm 5*
Winger, Maurice Homer 1875-1949 *WhAm 3*
Winger, Otho 1877-1946 *WhAm 2*
Wingert, Emmet Laurson 1899-1971 *WhAm 5*
Winget, Arthur Knox 1882-1971 *WhAm 5*
Winget, Benjamin 1845- *WhAm 4*
Wingfield, Edward Maria *DcAmB, WhAm H*
Wingfield, Edward Maria 1560?- *NatCAB 13*
Wingfield, Edwin Maria *Drake*

Wingfield, Edwin Maria 1570?- *ApCAB*
Wingfield, George 1876-1959 *REnAW*
Wingfield, George 1876-1960 *WhAm 4*
Wingfield, John Henry Ducachet 1833-1898
ApCAB, NatCAB 3, TwCBDA
Wingfield, Marshall 1893-1961 *WhAm 4*
Wingo, Effiegene Locke 1883-1962 *BiDrAC,
WhAmP*
Wingo, Estelle Bradley 1878- *WhoColR*
Wingo, Otis Theodore 1877-1930 *BiDrAC,
NatCAB 22, WhAm 1, WhAmP*
Winick, Ben R 1897-1964 *NatCAB 51*
Winick, Nathan Max 1914-1971 *NatCAB 56*
Winkelman, Nathaniel William 1891-1956
NatCAB 43, WhAm 3
Winkelmann, Christian H 1883-1946 *WhAm 2*
Winkenwerder, Hugo August 1878- *WhAm 6*
Winking, Cyril H d1968 *WhAm 5*
Winkler, Alexander Woodward 1908-1947
NatCAB 35
Winkler, Angelina Virginia 1842- *AmWom*
Winkler, Clemens Alexander 1838-1904 *AsBiEn,
DcScB*
Winkler, Edwin Theodore 1823-1883 *ApCAB,
DcAmB, WhAm H*
Winkler, Ernest William 1875-1960 *WhAm 4*
Winkler, Franz Emil 1907-1971 *NatCAB 57*
Winkler, Georgia Gertrude 1883-
WomWWA 14
Winkler, Harry 1895-1963 *NatCAB 50*
Winkler, John K 1891-1958 *WhAm 3*
Winkler, L E 1891-1970 *NatCAB 56*
Winkler, Lajos Wilhelm 1863-1939 *DcScB*
Winkler, Max 1866-1930 *WhAm 1*
Winkler, Max 1888-1965 *NatCAB 51*
Winkley, Henry 1803-1888 *ApCAB*
Winkworth, Edwin David 1877-1955 *WhAm 3*
Winlock, Herbert Eustis 1884-1950 *DcAmB S4,
NatCAB 37, WhAm 2*
Winlock, Joseph 1826-1875 *ApCAB, BiAUS,
DcAmB, DcScB, NatCAB 9, WhAm H*
Winlock, William Crawford 1859-1896
NatCAB 9
Winlow, Clara Vostrovsky 1871- *WhAm 5*
Winmill, Robert Campbell 1883-1957
NatCAB 47
Winn, A G *WhoColR*
Winn, Alfred *NewYHSD*
Winn, Alice Laura Bond 1864- *WomWWA 14*
Winn, Charles Andrew 1834- *NatCAB 16*
Winn, Charles V 1881- *WhAm 2*
Winn, Edith Lynwood 1867- *WomWWA 14*
Winn, Frank Long 1864-1941 *WhAm 1*
Winn, James Herbert 1866- *WhAm 4*
Winn, Jane Frances d1927 *WhAm 1*
Winn, John F 1852- *WhAm 4*
Winn, John Harvey 1888-1951 *NatCAB 47*
Winn, John Sheridan 1863-1940 *WhAm 1*
Winn, Larry, Jr. 1919- *BiDrAC*
Winn, Lizzie M Turney 1880- *WomWWA 14*
Winn, Milton 1895-1966 *NatCAB 50,
WhAm 4*
Winn, Richard 1750-1818 *BiDrAC, DcAmB,
WhAm H, WhAmP*
Winn, Robert Hiner 1871-1946 *WhAm 2*
Winn, Thomas Clay 1851- *WhAm 4*
Winn, Thomas Elisha 1839-1925 *BiDrAC,
NatCAB 2*
Winn, William Alma 1903-1967 *WhAm 5*
Winne, Alfred *NewYHSD*
Winne, Arthur Lawrence Ingram 1882-1950
NatCAB 38
Winnemucca, Sarah 1844?-1891 *DcAmB,
NotAW, WhAm H*
Winner, Charles Henry 1885-1956 *NatCAB 43*
Winner, Clifford 1894-1961 *WhAm 4*
Winner, H Merrill 1888-1968 *NatCAB 54*
Winner, Percy 1899-1974 *WhAm 6*
Winner, Septimius 1827-1902 *NatCAB 1*
Winner, Septimus 1827-1902 *AmBi, WhAm 1*
Winner, William E 1815?-1883 *NewYHSD*
Winnett, Percy Glen 1881-1968 *NatCAB 54,
WhAm 6*
Winogrand, Garry 1928- *BnEnAmA*
Winrod, Gerald Burton 1899?-1957 *DcAmReB*
Winsborough, Hallie Paxson 1865-1940
WhAm 1
Winser, Beatrice 1869-1947 *DcAmLiB,*

NotAW, WhAm 2
Winser, Henry Jacob 1823-1896 *NatCAB 10,
WhAm H*
Winser, Henry Jacob 1833-1896 *ApCAB*
Winsey, A Reid 1905- *WhAm 5*
Winship, Albert Edward 1845-1933 *AmBi,
BiDAmEd, DcAmB, NatCAB 2,
WhAm 1*
Winship, Blanton 1869-1947 *DcAmB S4,
NatCAB 37, WebAMB, WhAm 2*
Winship, Charles Newell 1863- *NatCAB 15*
Winship, George 1835-1916 *NatCAB 1,
NatCAB 17*
Winship, George Parker 1871-1952 *DcAmB S5,
DcAmLiB*
Winship, Laurence Leathe 1890-1975 *WhAm 6*
Winship, Louis Clarence 1879-1933 *NatCAB 25*
Winship, North 1885-1968 *NatCAB 54*
Winship, W W 1834?- *NewYHSD*
Winship, Walter Edwin 1872- *WhAm 5*
Winslow, Alfred Augustus 1854-1929 *WhAm 1*
Winslow, Anna Green 1759-1779 *ApCAB*
Winslow, Arthur 1860-1938 *NatCAB 13,
WhAm 1*
Winslow, Arthur Ellsworth 1877-1950 *WhAm 3*
Winslow, Benjamin Davis 1815-1839 *ApCAB*
Winslow, Benjamin Emanuel 1867- *WhAm 4*
Winslow, C *NewYHSD*
Winslow, Cameron McRae 1854-1932 *AmBi,
DcAmB, NatCAB 30, WhAm 1*
Winslow, Carleton Monroe 1876-1946 *WhAm 2*
Winslow, Carlile Patterson 1884-1960
NatCAB 48
Winslow, Caroline B 1822- *AmWom*
Winslow, Carroll Dana 1889-1932 *WhAm 3*
Winslow, Catherine Mary Reignolds 1836-1911
NatCAB 23, NotAW, WhAm 1
Winslow, Catherine Waterbury Carman
1799-1837 *ApCAB*
Winslow, Celeste M A 1837- *AmWom*
Winslow, Charles-Edward Amory 1877-1957
BiDAmEd, WhAm 3
Winslow, Charles Frederick 1811- *ApCAB,
Drake*
Winslow, Charles Gardner 1871-1944
NatCAB 33
Winslow, Charles Lathrop 1821-1832 *ApCAB*
Winslow, Clara Austin 1874- *WomWWA 14*
Winslow, Cleveland 1836-1864 *ApCAB*
Winslow, Earle 1896-1966 *NatCAB 53*
Winslow, Eben Eveleth 1866-1928 *NatCAB 21,
WhAm 1*
Winslow, Edward 1595-1655 *AmBi, ApCAB,
DcAmB, Drake, McGEWB, NatCAB 1,
NatCAB 7, TwCBDA, WebAB,
WhAm H*
Winslow, Edward 1669-1753 *BnEnAmA,
DcAmB, WhAm H*
Winslow, Edward 1714-1784 *ApCAB,
NatCAB 1*
Winslow, Edward 1746-1815 *ApCAB,
NatCAB 1*
Winslow, Edward Delbert 1858-1941
NatCAB 30, WhAm 1
Winslow, Edward Francis 1837-1914 *ApCAB,
DcAmB*
Winslow, Ellen Augusta 1860- *WomWWA 14*
Winslow, Erving 1839-1922 *NatCAB 25,
WhAm 1*
Winslow, Francis Asbury 1866-1932 *WhAm 1*
Winslow, Frederic I 1863-1924 *WhAm 1*
Winslow, George Frederick 1842-1928 *WhAm 1*
Winslow, Gordon 1803-1864 *ApCAB,
NatCAB 1*
Winslow, Guy Monroe 1872-1957 *WhAm 3*
Winslow, Harriet Lathrop 1796-1833 *ApCAB*
Winslow, Helen Maria 1851-1938 *AmWom,
WhAm 1, WomWWA 14*
Winslow, Henry J *NewYHSD*
Winslow, Herbert 1848-1914 *WhAm 1*
Winslow, Hubbard 1799-1864 *ApCAB,
DcAmB, Drake, NatCAB 1, WhAm H*
Winslow, Isaac d1819 *Drake*
Winslow, Isaac 1670-1738 *ApCAB*
Winslow, Jacob 1669-1760 *DcScB*
Winslow, James 1814-1874 *NatCAB 1*
Winslow, James 1816-1874 *ApCAB*
Winslow, Jens Olaus 1739-1794 *ApCAB*

Winslow, John 1702-1774 *ApCAB, Drake, NatCAB 1*
Winslow, John 1703-1774 *AmBi, DcAmB, WhAm H*
Winslow, John 1753-1819 *ApCAB, NatCAB 1*
Winslow, John Ancrum 1810-1873 *Drake*
Winslow, John Ancrum 1811-1873 *AmBi, ApCAB, DcAmB, NatCAB 2, TwCBDA, WebAMB, WhAm H*
Winslow, John Bradley 1851-1920 *ApCAB X, DcAmB, NatCAB 14, WhAm 1*
Winslow, John Flack 1810-1892 *ApCAB, DcAmB, NatCAB 4, WhAm H*
Winslow, John Randolph 1866-1937 *NatCAB 28, WhAm 4*
Winslow, Joshua 1727-1801 *ApCAB*
Winslow, Josiah 1629?-1680 *AmBi, ApCAB, DcAmB, Drake, NatCAB 5, TwCBDA, WebAB, WebAMB, WhAm H*
Winslow, Kate Reignolds 1814- *NatCAB 1, WhAm H*
Winslow, Leon Loyal 1886-1965 *WhAm 4*
Winslow, Marlon Hamblen 1864-1926 *NatCAB 20*
Winslow, Miron 1789-1864 *AmBi, ApCAB, DcAmB, Drake, NatCAB 1, WhAm H*
Winslow, Nathan 1878-1937 *NatCAB 28*
Winslow, Paul Virgil 1884-1943 *NatCAB 32*
Winslow, Penelope d1703 *Drake*
Winslow, Randolph 1852-1937 *NatCAB 28, WhAm 4*
Winslow, Rex 1901-1968 *WhAm 5*
Winslow, Robert Lane, Jr. 1917- *WhAm 5*
Winslow, Samuel Ellsworth 1862-1940 *BiDrAC, NatCAB 29, WhAm 4, WhAmP*
Winslow, Sherburn Josiah 1834-1919 *NatCAB 23*
Winslow, Sidney Wilmot 1854-1917 *ApCAB X, DcAmB, NatCAB 15, WhAm 1*
Winslow, Sidney Wilmot, Jr. 1880-1963 *NatCAB 51, WhAm 4*
Winslow, Stephen Noyes 1826- *ApCAB*
Winslow, Thacher 1907-1955 *WhAm 3*
Winslow, Thyra Samter 1903-1961 *WhAm 4*
Winslow, Warren 1810-1862 *ApCAB, BiDrAC, NatCAB 3, WhAm H*
Winslow, Warren 1810-1863 *BiAUS*
Winslow, William Copley 1840-1925 *AmBi, ApCAB, DcAmB, NatCAB 4, TwCBDA, WhAm 1*
Winslow, William Herman 1857-1934 *NatCAB 26*
Winsor, Bessie L *WomWWA 14*
Winsor, Frank Edward 1870-1939 *WhAm 1*
Winsor, Frank Lester 1870-1944 *NatCAB 39*
Winsor, Frederick 1872-1940 *WhAm 1*
Winsor, James Davis, Jr. 1876-1957 *WhAm 3*
Winsor, Justin 1831-1897 *AmBi, ApCAB, DcAmB, DcAmLiB, Drake, NatCAB 1, TwCBDA, WebAB, WhAm H*
Winsor, Mulford 1874-1956 *WhAm 3*
Winsor, Paul 1863-1936 *NatCAB 30, WhAm 4*
Winsor, Robert 1858-1930 *NatCAB 49, WhAm 1*
Winstanley, William *NewYHSD*
Winstead, William Arthur 1904- *BiDrAC, WhAmP*
Winstein, S 1912-1969 *WhAm 5*
Winston, Annie Steger d1927 *WhAm 1, WomWWA 14*
Winston, Charles Henry 1831- *WhAm 4*
Winston, Fendall Gregory 1849-1928 *NatCAB 36*
Winston, Francis Donnell 1857-1941 *WhAm 2*
Winston, Frederick Hampden 1830-1904 *NatCAB 4, WhAm 1*
Winston, Frederick Schaefer 1892-1964 *NatCAB 50*
Winston, Frederick Seymour 1806-1885 *NatCAB 12*
Winston, Frederick Seymour 1856-1909 *WhAm 1*
Winston, Garrard Bigelow 1882-1955 *WhAm 3*
Winston, George Tayloe 1852- *NatCAB 13, TwCBDA, WhAm 4*
Winston, Gilmer d1939 *WhAm 2*
Winston, Isaac 1853-1923 *WhAm 1*

Winston, James Horner 1884-1968 *NatCAB 55*
Winston, James Overton 1864-1947 *NatCAB 38*
Winston, John Anthony 1812-1871 *ApCAB, BiAUS, DcAmB, NatCAB 10, TwCBDA, WhAm H*
Winston, John Clark 1856-1920 *NatCAB 19, WhAm 1*
Winston, Joseph d1840 *Drake*
Winston, Joseph 1746- *BiAUS*
Winston, Joseph 1746-1814 *Drake*
Winston, Joseph 1746-1815 *ApCAB, BiDrAC, DcAmB, NatCAB 6, WebAMB, WhAm H*
Winston, Louise Elenor 1889- *WhoColR*
Winston, Patrick Henry 1881- *WhAm 6*
Winston, Philip Bickerton 1845-1901 *NatCAB 30*
Winston, Robert Watson 1860-1944 *NatCAB 45, WhAm 2*
Winston, Sanford Richard 1897-1969 *NatCAB 55, WhAm 5*
Wint, Theodore Jonathan 1845-1907 *WhAm 1*
Winter, Alice Beach 1877- *WhAm 5, WomWWA 14*
Winter, Alice Vivian Ames 1865-1944 *BiCAW, NotAW, WhAm 2, WomWWA 14*
Winter, Andrew 1892-1958 *NatCAB 47, WhAm 3*
Winter, C *NewYHSD*
Winter, Charles *NewYHSD*
Winter, Charles Allan 1869-1942 *WhAm 2*
Winter, Charles Edwin 1870-1948 *BiDrAC, WhAm 2, WhAmP*
Winter, Elisha I 1781-1849 *BiDrAC, WhAm H*
Winter, Elisha J *BiAUS*
Winter, Elizabeth Campbell 1841-1922 *WhAm 1, WomWWA 14*
Winter, Emil d1941 *WhAm 1*
Winter, Ezra Augustus 1886-1949 *WhAm 2*
Winter, Ferdinand 1843-1935 *WhAm 1*
Winter, Francis Anderson 1867-1931 *NatCAB 28, WhAm 1*
Winter, Frank Cook 1882-1962 *NatCAB 50*
Winter, Frederick Charles 1913-1966 *NatCAB 53*
Winter, George 1810-1876 *IIBEAAW, NewYHSD, WhAm H*
Winter, George Ben Wade 1878-1940 *NatCAB 29, WhAm 1*
Winter, Herman 1884- *WhAm 3A*
Winter, Horace Greeley 1873-1947 *NatCAB 34*
Winter, Irvah Lester 1857-1934 *NatCAB 26, WhAm 1*
Winter, J A *NewYHSD*
Winter, Sir James Spearman 1845- *ApCAB Sup*
Winter, John *NewYHSD*
Winter, John Garrett 1881-1956 *WhAm 3*
Winter, Nevin Otto 1869-1936 *NatCAB 18, WhAm 1*
Winter, R *NewYHSD*
Winter, Robert *NewYHSD*
Winter, Rosetta Lewis Helms 1833- *WomWWA 14*
Winter, S Elizabeth *WomWWA 14*
Winter, T *NewYHSD*
Winter, Thomas Daniel 1896-1951 *BiDrAC, WhAm 3, WhAmP*
Winter, Thomas Gerald 1863-1934 *WhAm 1*
Winter, William *NewYHSD*
Winter, William 1836-1917 *AmBi, ApCAB, DcAmB, Drake, NatCAB 4, TwCBDA, WhAm 1*
Winter, William D d1955 *WhAm 3*
Winterbotham, Joseph 1878-1954 *NatCAB 42, WhAm 3*
Winterbotham, Lydia Sharp 1845- *WomWWA 14*
Winterbotham, William *Drake*
Winterbottom, Thomas M 1766-1859 *BiHiMed*
Winterburn, Florence Hull 1858- *WhAm 5, WomWWA 14*
Winterburn, George William 1845-1911 *WhAm 1*
Winterhalder, J *NewYHSD*
Winterhalter, Albert Gustavus 1856-1920 *WhAm 1*
Winterich, John Tracy 1891-1970 *NatCAB 55*

Wintermute, George Preston 1871-1938 *NatCAB 36*
Wintermute, Martha 1842- *AmWom*
Winternitz, David Henry 1891-1952 *NatCAB 42*
Winternitz, Milton Charles 1885-1959 *WhAm 3*
Winters, Allen Charles 1907-1974 *WhAm 6*
Winters, Byram Lee 1862- *NatCAB 10*
Winters, Harry S 1871- *WhAm 5*
Winters, Helen Clegg 1869- *WomWWA 14*
Winters, Henry H 1860- *WhoColR*
Winters, Joseph Edcil 1850- *NatCAB 2*
Winters, Matthew 1890-1958 *NatCAB 46*
Winters, Robert 1910-1969 *WhAm 5*
Winters, William Huffman 1848- *NatCAB 11*
Winters, Yvor 1900-1968 *WhAm 4A*
Wintersteiner, Oskar Paul 1898-1971 *WhAm 5*
Winther, Arno S 1882-1949 *NatCAB 38*
Winther, Oscar Osborn 1903-1970 *REnAW*
Winther, Oscar Osburn 1903-1969 *EncAAH*
Winther, Oscar Osburn 1903-1970 *WhAm 5*
Winthrop, Beekman 1874-1940 *NatCAB 35, WhAm 1*
Winthrop, Bronson 1863-1944 *NatCAB 33, WhAm 2*
Winthrop, Egerton Leigh 1839-1916 *NatCAB 33*
Winthrop, Egerton Leigh 1862-1926 *NatCAB 38*
Winthrop, Fitz-John 1638-1707 *AmBi, DcAmB, Drake*
Winthrop, Frederick 1839-1865 *ApCAB*
Winthrop, Henry Rogers 1876-1958 *WhAm 3*
Winthrop, James 1752-1821 *DcAmB, WhAm H*
Winthrop, John 1587?-1649 *DcAmB, EncAAH*
Winthrop, John 1588-1649 *AmBi, ApCAB, DcAmReB, Drake, EncAB, McGEWB, NatCAB 6, TwCBDA, WebAB, WhAm H*
Winthrop, John 1605?-1676 *DcAmB*
Winthrop, John 1606-1676 *AmBi, DcScB, Drake, McGEWB, NatCAB 10, WhAm H*
Winthrop, John 1638-1707 *AmBi, DcAmB*
Winthrop, John 1639-1707 *ApCAB, NatCAB 10, WhAm H*
Winthrop, John 1714-1779 *AmBi, ApCAB, BiDAmEd, DcAmB, DcScB, Drake, McGEWB, NatCAB 7, WebAB, WhAm H*
Winthrop, Margaret 1591?-1647 *NotAW*
Winthrop, Robert Charles 1809-1894 *AmBi, BiAUS, BiDrAC, DcAmB, Drake, NatCAB 6, TwCBDA, WebAB, WhAm H, WhAmP*
Winthrop, Theodore 1828-1861 *AmBi, DcAmB, Drake, NatCAB H, WhAm H*
Winthrop, Thomas Lindall 1760-1841 *NatCAB 7*
Winthrop, Wait-Still 1642-1717 *NatCAB 4*
Winthrop, Wait Still 1643-1717 *ApCAB*
Winthrop, Waitstill 1642-1717 *Drake*
Wintner, Aurel 1903-1958 *DcScB, WhAm 3*
Winton, Alexander 1860-1932 *DcAmB, NatCAB 12, WebAB, WhAm 1*
Winton, Andrew Lincoln 1864-1946 *NatCAB 35, WhAm 2*
Winton, Charles Joel 1862-1934 *NatCAB 33*
Winton, George Beverly 1861-1938 *WhAm 1*
Winton, George Peterson 1892-1953 *NatCAB 42*
Winton, Jenevehah Maria 1837- *AmWom*
Winton, William *NewYHSD*
Wintsch, Carl Herman 1871-1954 *NatCAB 46*
Winzler, Richard John 1914-1972 *WhAm 5*
Wire, C Raymond 1901-1963 *NatCAB 51*
Wire, G E 1859-1936 *WhAm 3*
Wire, George Edwin 1859-1936 *DcAmLiB*
Wirebaugh, Evelyn Burbank 1907-1969 *WhAm 5*
Wirgman, Menefee 1878-1958 *NatCAB 44*
Wirjopranoto, Sukardjo 1903-1962 *WhAm 4*
Wirka, Herman Wenzel 1903-1974 *WhAm 6*
Wirt, Benjamin Franklin 1852- *ApCAB X*
Wirt, Elizabeth Washington 1784-1857 *ApCAB, Drake*
Wirt, Loyal Lincoln 1863- *WhAm 5*

Wirt, William 1772-1834 *AmBi, ApCAB, BiAUS, BiDrUSE, DcAmB, Drake, NatCAB 6, TwCBDA, WebAB, WhAm H*
Wirt, William Albert 1874-1938 *BiDAmEd, DcAmB S2, WhAm 1*
Wirth, Colvert *NewYHSD*
Wirth, Fremont Philip 1890-1960 *WhAm 4*
Wirth, Louis 1897-1952 *NatCAB 42, WhAm 3*
Wirth, Robert *NewYHSD*
Wirth, Russell D L 1905-1968 *WhAm 5*
Wirth, William Joseph 1908-1973 *WhAm 6*
Wirthlin, Joseph L 1893-1963 *WhAm 4*
Wirthlin, LeRoy Alvin 1902-1971 *NatCAB 56*
Wirtschafter, Zolton Tillson 1899-1967 *WhAm 4*
Wirtz, Alvin Jacob 1888-1951 *NatCAB 41, WhAm 3*
Wirtz, William Willard 1912- *BiDrUSE*
Wirz, Henry d1865 *WhAm H*
Wischnewetzky, Florence Kelley *NotAW*
Wiscott, William Joseph 1898-1969 *WhAm 5*
Wisdom, Ray Meriwether 1890-1954 *NatCAB 44*
Wise, Aaron 1844-1896 *DcAmB, WhAm H*
Wise, Arthur Chamberlin 1876-1952 *WhAm 3*
Wise, Boyd Ashby 1874- *WhAm 5*
Wise, Byrd Douglas 1886-1969 *WhAm 5*
Wise, C *NewYHSD*
Wise, Claude Merton 1887-1966 *NatCAB 53, WhAm 4*
Wise, Daniel 1813-1898 *ApCAB, DcAmB, NatCAB 13, WhAm H*
Wise, Edmond Eli 1865-1932 *NatCAB 24, WhAm 1*
Wise, Edward 1870-1939 *NatCAB 14, WhAm 1*
Wise, Fred 1881-1950 *NatCAB 38, NatCAB 47*
Wise, George *NewYHSD*
Wise, George Douglas 1831-1898 *ApCAB, BiDrAC, WhAmP*
Wise, Harold A 1896-1954 *WhAm 3*
Wise, Harold Edward 1902-1964 *WhAm 4*
Wise, Henry Alexander 1806-1876 *AmBi, ApCAB, BiAUS, BiDConf, BiDrAC, DcAmB, Drake, NatCAB 5, TwCBDA, WhAm H, WhAmP*
Wise, Henry Augustus 1819-1869 *AmBi, ApCAB, DcAmB, Drake, NatCAB 13, WhAm H*
Wise, Henry Morris 1880-1965 *WhAm 4*
Wise, Isaac Mayer 1819-1900 *AmBi, ApCAB, BiDAmEd, DcAmB, DcAmReB, EncAB, McGEWB, NatCAB 10, WebAB, WhAm H*
Wise, James *NewYHSD*
Wise, James 1875-1939 *NatCAB 29, WhAm 1*
Wise, James Black 1856-1916 *NatCAB 29*
Wise, James Walter 1868-1925 *BiDrAC, WhAm 1, WhAmP*
Wise, Jennings Cropper 1881- *WhAm 6*
Wise, John 1652-1725 *AmBi, ApCAB, DcAmB, DcAmReB, Drake, McGEWB, NatCAB 1, WebAB, WhAm H*
Wise, John 1808-1879 *ApCAB, DcAmB, NatCAB 1, WhAm H*
Wise, John Sergeant 1846-1913 *ApCAB, BiDrAC, DcAmB, NatCAB 11, WhAm 1, WhAmP*
Wise, Jonah Bondi 1881-1959 *WhAm 3*
Wise, Leo Henry 1862-1934 *WhAm 1*
Wise, Louise Waterman 1874-1947 *NotAW, WhAm 2*
Wise, Marion Johnson 1883-1950 *WhAm 3*
Wise, Morgan Ringland 1825-1903 *BiDrAC*
Wise, Otto Irving 1871- *WhAm 1*
Wise, Peter Manuel 1851-1907 *WhAm 1*
Wise, Richard Alsop 1843-1900 *BiDrAC, WhAmP*
Wise, Russell Vincent 1904-1972 *WhAm 5*
Wise, Samuel C *NewYHSD*
Wise, Stephen Samuel 1874-1949 *DcAmB S4, DcAmReB, EncAB, McGEWB, NatCAB 41, WebAB, WhAm 2*
Wise, Thomas Alfred 1865-1928 *DcAmB, WhAm 1*

Wise, Tully R *BiAUS*
Wise, William Clinton 1842-1923 *TwCBDA, WhAm 1*
Wise, William Frederic 1895-1958 *WhAm 3*
Wiseman, Bruce Kenneth 1897-1960 *WhAm 3*
Wiseman, Eugene Gilbert 1885-1967 *NatCAB 54*
Wiseman, Joseph R 1881- *WhAm 6*
Wiseman, Richard 1621?-1676 *BiHiMed*
Wiseman, Sir William 1885-1962 *WhAm 4*
Wisener, Guthrie Howard 1885-1960 *NatCAB 50*
Wiser, Angelo 1841?- *NewYHSD*
Wiser, John 1815?- *NewYHSD*
Wish, Harvey 1909-1968 *WhAm 5*
Wishard, Albert Willard 1854-1917 *NatCAB 33*
Wishard, Fred Bryan 1894-1948 *NatCAB 37*
Wishard, John G 1863-1940 *WhAm 1*
Wishard, Luther DeLoraine 1854-1925 *DcAmReB, WhAm 2*
Wishard, Samuel Ellis 1825-1915 *WhAm 1*
Wishard, William Henry 1816-1913 *NatCAB 33*
Wishard, William Niles 1851-1941 *NatCAB 30, WhAm 1*
Wishard, William Niles, Jr. 1898-1973 *WhAm 6*
Wishart, Alfred Wesley 1865-1933 *WhAm 1*
Wishart, Charles Frederick 1870-1960 *WhAm 3A*
Wishart, Charles Henry 1882-1956 *NatCAB 47*
Wishart, John Elliott 1866-1940 *WhAm 1*
Wishart, William C 1871-1965 *WhAm 4*
Wishek, John Henry 1855-1932 *NatCAB 46*
Wishon, A Emory 1882-1948 *NatCAB 37, WhAm 2*
Wishon, Albert Graves 1858-1936 *WhAm 1*
Wislicenus, Johannes 1835-1902 *AsBiEn, DcScB*
Wislizenus, Frederick Adolph 1810-1889 *DcAmB, WhAm H*
Wislocki, George Bernays 1892-1956 *NatCAB 45, WhAm 3*
Wisman, James Martin 1855- *NatCAB 7*
Wismer, Harry 1913-1967 *WhAm 4A*
Wisner, Benjamin Blydenburg 1794-1835 *ApCAB, Drake, NatCAB 1*
Wisner, Edward 1860-1915 *NatCAB 15*
Wisner, Frank George 1873-1938 *NatCAB 28, WhAm 1*
Wisner, George Monroe 1870-1932 *WhAm 1*
Wisner, George Y 1841-1906 *WhAm 1*
Wisner, Harry J 1875-1962 *NatCAB 50*
Wisner, Henry d1790 *BiAUS*
Wisner, Henry 1720?-1790 *BiDrAC, DcAmB, WhAm H, WhAmP*
Wisner, Henry 1725?-1790 *ApCAB, NatCAB 5, TwCBDA*
Wisner, Moses 1815-1863 *NatCAB 5*
Wisner, Moses 1818-1863 *ApCAB, BiAUS, Drake*
Wisner, Oscar Francis 1858-1947 *WhAm 2*
Wisner, William 1782-1871 *ApCAB*
Wisner, William Carpenter 1808-1880 *ApCAB*
Wisnioski, Stanley Walter 1897-1961 *NatCAB 49*
Wisong, W A *NewYHSD*
Wiss, Aaron 1912-1970 *NatCAB 55*
Wiss, Jerome Baker 1895-1960 *NatCAB 53*
Wisser, Edward Hollister 1895-1970 *NatCAB 56*
Wisser, John Philip 1852-1927 *ApCAB, ApCAB X, NatCAB 10, NatCAB 26, WhAm 1*
Wissler, Clark 1870-1947 *DcAmB S4, NatCAB 33, REnAW, WhAm 2*
Wissler, Jacques 1803-1887 *ApCAB, NewYHSD, WhAm H*
Wist, Benjamin Othello 1889-1951 *BiDAmEd, WhAm 3*
Wistar, Caspar 1696-1752 *BnEnAmA, DcAmB, WhAm H*
Wistar, Caspar 1761-1818 *AmBi, ApCAB, BiHiMed, DcAmB S2, DcScB, Drake, NatCAB 1, TwCBDA, WhAm H*
Wistar, Isaac Jones 1827-1905 *ApCAB, NatCAB 12, TwCBDA, WhAm 1*
Wistar, Owen 1860- *TwCBDA*
Wistar, Richard 1756-1821 *ApCAB*

Wister, Annis Lee 1830-1908 *ApCAB, WhAm 1*
Wister, James Wilson 1874-1955 *NatCAB 45*
Wister, John 1829-1900 *NatCAB 34*
Wister, Owen 1860-1938 *AmBi, ApCAB Sup, DcAmB, EncAAH, EncAB, NatCAB 13, REnAW, WebAB, WhAm 1*
Wister, Sally 1761-1804 *WhAm H*
Wister, Sarah 1761-1804 *AmBi, ApCAB Sup, DcAmB*
Wistrand, Karl Knutsson 1889-1974 *WhAm 6*
Wiswall, Frank Lawrence 1895-1972 *WhAm 5*
Wiswall, Ichabod 1638-1700 *ApCAB, Drake*
Wiswall, Richard H 1886-1955 *WhAm 3*
Wiswell, Andrew Peters 1852-1906 *NatCAB 13, WhAm 1*
Wiswell, George Nelson 1852- *WhAm 4*
Wiswell, Robert Ireland 1876-1951 *NatCAB 40*
Witbeck, Benjamin Franklin 1885-1942 *NatCAB 31*
Witcher, John Seashoal 1839-1906 *BiAUS, BiDrAC*
Witebsky, Ernest 1901-1969 *NatCAB 56, WhAm 5*
Witelo 1230?-1275? *DcScB*
Witham, Ernest C 1880-1958 *WhAm 3*
Witham, Henry 1779-1844 *DcScB*
Witham, Henry Bryan 1894-1973 *WhAm 6*
Witham, Robert Bruce 1893-1948 *NatCAB 43*
Witham, Rose Adelaide 1873- *WomWWA 14*
Witherbee, Frank Spencer 1852-1917 *WhAm 1*
Witherbee, Mary Rhinelander Stewart 1859- *WomWWA 14*
Witherell, Benjamin Franklin Hawkins 1797-1867 *ApCAB*
Witherell, James 1759-1838 *ApCAB, BiAUS, BiDrAC, WhAm H*
Withering, William 1741-1799 *BiHiMed, DcScB*
Witherow, William 1843-1914 *NatCAB 14, NatCAB 26*
Witherow, William Porter 1888-1960 *WhAm 3A*
Withers, Caroline *NewYHSD*
Withers, Ebenezer *NewYHSD*
Withers, Frederick Clarke 1828-1901 *ApCAB, BnEnAmA, DcAmB, NatCAB 2, WhAm H*
Withers, Garrett Lee 1884-1953 *BiDrAC, NatCAB 39, WhAmP*
Withers, Garrett Lee 1885-1953 *WhAm 3*
Withers, Harry Clay 1880- *WhAm 3*
Withers, Jennie B Barnes 1863- *WomWWA 14*
Withers, John Thomas 1872- *WhAm 5*
Withers, John William 1868-1961 *WhAm 4*
Withers, Jones Mitchell 1814-1890 *ApCAB, BiDConf, Drake, NatCAB 11, TwCBDA*
Withers, Robert Edwin 1865-1952 *NatCAB 18, NatCAB 41, WhAm 3*
Withers, Robert Enoch 1821-1907 *ApCAB, BiAUS, BiDrAC, NatCAB 12, NatCAB 48, TwCBDA, WhAm 1, WhAmP*
Withers, T I d1865 *BiAUS*
Withers, Thomas Jefferson 1804-1865 *BiDConf*
Withers, William Alphonso 1864-1924 *WhAm 1*
Withers, William Jerome 1878-1951 *NatCAB 41*
Withers, William Temple 1825-1889 *NatCAB 6*
Witherspoon, Archibald William 1876-1958 *WhAm 3*
Witherspoon, Herbert 1873-1935 *AmBi, DcAmB S1, NatCAB 29, WhAm 1*
Witherspoon, James Hervey 1810-1865 *BiDConf*
Witherspoon, John 1722-1794 *ApCAB, BiAUS, BiDAmEd, Drake, NatCAB 5, TwCBDA*
Witherspoon, John 1723-1794 *AmBi, BiDrAC, DcAmB, DcAmReB, McGEWB, WebAB, WhAm H, WhAmP*
Witherspoon, John Alexander 1864-1929 *BiDAmEd, DcAmB, WhAm 1*
Witherspoon, Pauline F *WomWWA 14*
Witherspoon, Robert 1767-1837 *BiAUS, BiDrAC, WhAm H*
Witherspoon, Ruth Helene Miles *WomWWA 14*
Witherspoon, Samuel Andrew 1855-1915 *BiDrAC, WhAm 1*

Witherspoon, Thomas Casey 1868-1957
WhAm 3
Witherspoon, Thomas Dwight 1836- *ApCAB*
Witherspoon, William Wallace 1905-1972
WhAm 5
Witherstine, Christopher Sumner 1854-1933
WhAm 1
Withey, Henry Franklin 1880- *WhAm 6*
Withey, Morton Owen 1882-1961 *NatCAB 49,*
WhAm 4
Withey, Solomon L 1820- *BiAUS*
Withington, Alfreda Bosworth 1860-
WomWWA 14
Withington, Charles Francis 1852-1917
WhAm 1
Withington, David Little 1854-1919 *NatCAB 42,*
WhAm 1
Withington, Irving Platt 1858- *WhAm 4*
Withington, Leonard 1789-1885 *ApCAB,*
Drake, NatCAB 5, WhAm H
Withington, Lothrop 1889-1967 *NatCAB 57*
Withington, Philip Herbert 1871-1927
NatCAB 23
Withington, Robert 1884-1957 *NatCAB 44,*
WhAm 3
Withington, William Herbert 1835-1903
NatCAB 17
Withington, Winthrop 1878-1953 *WhAm 3*
Withrow, Eva Almond 1858-1928 *IlBEAAW*
Withrow, Gardner Robert 1892-1964 *BiDrAC,*
NatCAB 54, WhAm 4, WhAmP
Withrow, James Renwick 1878-1953
NatCAB 42, WhAm 6
Withrow, John Lindsay 1837-1909 *WhAm 1*
Withrow, Joseph Edmund 1885-1966
NatCAB 53
Withrow, Robert Bruce 1904-1958 *NatCAB 47*
Withrow, William Henry 1839- *ApCAB*
Withrow, Winifred Warren 1876-
WomWWA 14
Withycombe, James 1854-1919 *NatCAB 20,*
WhAm 1
Witman *NewYHSD*
Witmark, Isidore 1869-1941 *DcAmB S3*
Witmer, Abram Harman 1845-1900
NatCAB 21
Witmer, Charles B 1862-1925 *WhAm 1*
Witmer, David Julius 1888-1973 *WhAm 6*
Witmer, Francis Potts 1873- *WhAm 5*
Witmer, Lightner 1867-1956 *WhAm 3*
Witmer, R B 1900-1972 *WhAm 5*
Witschey, Robert E 1908-1967 *WhAm 4*
Witschi, Emil 1890-1971 *WhAm 5*
Witschief, Graham 1875-1945 *NatCAB 37*
Witsell, Edward Fuller 1891-1969 *WhAm 5*
Witsell, William Postell 1874-1959 *WhAm 4*
Witsen, Willem Jacobus 1739-1808 *ApCAB*
Witt, Christopher 1675-1765 *NewYHSD*
Witt, Edgar E 1879- *WhAm 6*
Witt, Jan De 1625-1672 *DcScB*
Witt, Johan De 1625-1672 *McGEWB,*
WhoMilH
Witt, John Henry 1840-1901 *NewYHSD,*
WhAm H
Witt, Joshua Chitwood 1884-1971 *NatCAB 57,*
WhAm 5
Witt, Max Siegfried 1871-1914 *WhAm 1*
Witte, Edwin Emil 1887-1960 *NatCAB 45,*
WhAm 4
Witte, Fred C 1898-1972 *WhAm 5*
Witte, John Wilbert 1890-1967 *NatCAB 53*
Witte, Kinney 1882-1954 *NatCAB 42*
Witte, Max Ernest 1859-1933 *WhAm 1*
Witte, Nicolas 1505?-1565 *ApCAB*
Witte, Count Sergei Yulyevich 1849-1915
McGEWB
Witte, William Henry 1817-1876 *BiAUS,*
BiDrAC, WhAm H
Wittemann, Charles Rudolph 1884-1967
NatCAB 54
Witten, Harold Bryan d1969 *WhAm 5*
Wittenberg, Theodore C *NewYHSD*
Wittenmyer, Annie Turner 1827-1900 *AmWom,*
NatCAB 12, NotAW
Wittenmyer, Clara K *WomWWA 14*
Wittenmyer, Edmund 1862-1937 *WhAm 1*
Witter, Dean 1887-1969 *WhAm 5*
Witter, Ellen Colfax 1868- *WomWWA 14*

Witter, Frank Clarence 1879-1954 *NatCAB 41*
Witter, Jean Carter 1892-1972 *WhAm 5*
Wittgenstein, Ludwig Josef Johann 1889-1951
DcScB, McGEWB, WhAm 4
Wittgenstein, Prinz Ludwig Adolf Peter
1769-1843 *WhoMilH*
Witthaus, Rudolph August 1846-1915 *AmBi,*
DcAmB, NatCAB 11, WhAm 1
Wittich, Fred William 1885-1965 *WhAm 4*
Wittich, Frederick William 1885-1965
NatCAB 51
Wittich, Paul 1555?-1587 *DcScB*
Wittig, Gustav Frederick 1876-1950 *WhAm 3*
Wittke, Carl Frederick 1892-1971 *WhAm 5*
Wittkower, Rudolf 1901-1971 *BiDAmEd,*
WhAm 5
Wittmack, Edgar Franklin 1894-1956 *IlBEAAW*
Wittman, Frank 1912-1967 *NatCAB 53*
Wittmer, John L 1895-1951 *WhAm 3*
Wittner, Fred 1909-1972 *WhAm 5*
Wittpenn, Caroline Bayard Stevens 1859-1932
NotAW
Wittwer, Eldon E 1899-1961 *WhAm 4*
Witty, Paul Andrew 1898-1976 *BiDAmEd,*
WhAm 6
Witty, William Henry 1872- *WhAm 5*
Witwer, Eldwin Roy 1890-1948 *NatCAB 36*
Witwer, Harry Charles 1890-1929 *NatCAB 21,*
WhAm 1
Witz, Konrad 1410?-1446 *McGEWB*
Witzemann, Edgar John 1884-1947 *WhAm 2*
Witzig, Lieutenant *WhWW-II*
Witzleben, Erwin Von 1881-1944 *WhWW-II,*
WhoMilH
Wixom, Emma 1862- *NatCAB 1, NotAW*
Wixom, Henrietta S 1878- *WomWWA 14*
Wixom, Isaac 1803- *NatCAB 1*
Wixon, Susan Helen *AmWom*
Wixson, Franklin Galbraith 1856- *WhAm 4*
Wixson, Helen Marsh d1925 *WhAm 1,*
WomWWA 14
Wizar *NewYHSD*
Wizar, Angelo 1841?- *NewYHSD*
Wo-Jen 1804-1871 *McGEWB*
Wobber, Herman 1879-1965 *WhAm 4*
Woboril, Lawrence Frank 1907-1962
NatCAB 50
Wodehouse, Pelham Grenville 1881-1975
WhAm 6
Wodraska, Tibor W 1912-1960 *NatCAB 49*
Woedtke, De 1740?-1776 *Drake*
Woedtke, Frederick William 1740?-1776
ApCAB
Woehlke, Walter Victor 1881-1954 *WhAm 3*
Woelfel, Albert 1871-1920 *NatCAB 19*
Woelfkin, Cornelius 1859-1928 *NatCAB 13,*
NatCAB 28, WhAm 1
Woelfle, Arthur W 1873-1936 *WhAm 1*
Woelk, Edward August 1845-1914 *NatCAB 51*
Woelk, Norma Marie d1972 *WhAm 6*
Woelper, Benjamin Franklin, Jr. 1869-1932
WhAm 1
Woepcke, Franz 1826-1864 *DcScB*
Woerheide, Arthur Albert Bernhard 1864-
NatCAB 12
Woerishoffer, Emma Carola 1885-1911 *NotAW*
Woermann, Frederick Christian 1877-1957
NatCAB 46
Woermann, John William 1868-1942 *WhAm 2*
Woerner, Emma Josephine 1884-
WomWWA 14
Woerner, John Gabriel 1826-1900 *DcAmB,*
NatCAB 5
Woerner, Kurt 1902-1957 *NatCAB 46*
Woerner, William F 1864-1932 *WhAm 1*
Woert, Jan Jacobus Sebald 1550?-1612?
ApCAB
Woertendyke, James H 1869- *WhAm 5*
Wofford, Kate Vixon d1954 *WhAm 3*
Wofford, Thomas Albert 1908- *BiDrAC*
Wofford, William Tatum 1823-1884 *DcAmB,*
WhAm H
Wofford, William Tatum 1824-1884 *BiDConf*
Wofsey, Michael 1902-1951 *NatCAB 40*
Wogan, John B 1890-1968 *WhAm 5*
Woglom, William Henry 1879-1953 *WhAm 4*
Wogram, Frederick *NewYHSD*
Wohinc, Louie 1888-1950 *NatCAB 40*

Wohl, David Philip 1886-1960 *WhAm 3*
Wohl, Kurt Adolf Ernst 1896-1962 *NatCAB 49*
Wohlenberg, Ernest T F 1889-1963 *WhAm 4*
Wohlenberg, Walter Jacob 1888-1956 *WhAm 3*
Wohler, August 1819-1914 *DcScB*
Wohler, Friedrich 1800-1882 *AsBiEn, DcScB*
Wohlford, Alvin Webster 1858-1924
NatCAB 49
Wohlleben, William Joseph 1876-1964 *WhAm 4*
Wohlsen, Ralph J 1897- *WhAm 5*
Woiseri *NewYHSD*
Wojdyla, Henry Edward 1918-1971 *WhAm 5*
Wolbach, Edwin J 1877-1959 *WhAm 3*
Wolbach, Simeon Burt 1880-1954 *NatCAB 46,*
WhAm 3
Wolbarst, Abraham Leo 1872- *WhAm 5*
Wolcott, Anna Louise 1863- *WomWWA 14*
Wolcott, Daniel Fooks 1910-1973 *WhAm 6*
Wolcott, Edward Oliver 1848-1905 *AmBi,*
ApCAB Sup, BiDrAC, DcAmB,
NatCAB 8, WhAm 1, WhAmP
Wolcott, Erastus 1722-1793 *ApCAB*
Wolcott, Erastus Bradley 1804-1880
NatCAB 16
Wolcott, Frank Bliss, Jr. 1907-1964 *NatCAB 53,*
WhAm 4
Wolcott, George Norton 1889-1965 *NatCAB 55*
Wolcott, Grace 1858- *WomWWA 14*
Wolcott, Henry Merrill 1879- *WhAm 6*
Wolcott, Henry Roger 1846-1921 *ApCAB X,*
NatCAB 6, WhAm 1
Wolcott, James L 1842-1898 *NatCAB 12*
Wolcott, Jesse Paine 1893-1969 *BiDrAC,*
WhAm 5, WhAmP
Wolcott, John Dorsey 1871-1945 *WhAm 2*
Wolcott, Josiah *NewYHSD*
Wolcott, Josiah Oliver 1877-1938 *BiDrAC,*
NatCAB 28, WhAm 1
Wolcott, L W 1872- *WhAm 5*
Wolcott, Lucy Elizabeth *WomWWA 14*
Wolcott, Mary Mills *WomWWA 14*
Wolcott, Oliver 1726-1797 *AmBi, ApCAB,*
BiDrAC, BiDrAC, DcAmB, Drake,
NatCAB 10, TwCBDA, WebAB,
WhAmP
Wolcott, Oliver 1760-1833 *AmBi, ApCAB,*
BiDrUSE, DcAmB, Drake, NatCAB 10,
TwCBDA, WebAB, WhAm H, WhAmP
Wolcott, Robert Henry 1868-1934 *WhAm 1*
Wolcott, Roger 1679-1767 *AmBi, ApCAB,*
DcAmB, Drake, NatCAB 10, TwCBDA,
WebAB, WhAm H, WhAmP
Wolcott, Roger 1847-1900 *ApCAB Sup,*
TwCBDA
Wolcott, Roger 1877- *WhAm 5*
Wolcott, Roger Henry 1885-1948 *WhAm 2*
Wolcott, Samuel 1813-1886 *NatCAB 8*
Wolcott, Samuel Huntington 1881-1965
WhAm 4
Wolcott, W Eugene 1885-1952 *NatCAB 42*
Wold, Emma 1871-1950 *NatCAB 38*
Wold, John Schiller 1916- *BiDrAC*
Wold, Peter Irving 1881-1945 *NatCAB 34,*
WhAm 2
Wold, Theodore 1868- *WhAm 2*
Woldenberg, S Charles 1893-1953 *NatCAB 41*
Woldman, Albert Alexander 1897-1971
NatCAB 56, WhAm 5
Woldman, Norman E 1899-1969 *NatCAB 55*
Wolf, Adolph Grant 1869-1947 *WhAm 2*
Wolf, Arnold Veryl 1916-1975 *WhAm 6*
Wolf, August Stephen 1900- *WhAm 5*
Wolf, Charles George Lewis 1872- *WhAm 5*
Wolf, Charles Joseph Etienne 1827-1918 *DcScB*
Wolf, Edmund Jacob 1840-1905 *WhAm 1*
Wolf, Edwin 1855-1934 *NatCAB 33*
Wolf, Emma 1865- *WhAm 4, WomWWA 14*
Wolf, Eugene Everett 1884-1944 *NatCAB 33*
Wolf, Ezekiel 1895-1958 *NatCAB 44*
Wolf, Frank 1867-1948 *WhAm 2*
Wolf, Friedrich August 1759-1824 *McGEWB*
Wolf, George 1777-1840 *ApCAB, BiAUS,*
BiDrAC, DcAmB, Drake, NatCAB 2,
TwCBDA, WhAm H, WhAmP
Wolf, George 1855-1918 *NatCAB 17*
Wolf, George Wheeler 1892-1962 *NatCAB 48,*
WhAm 4
Wolf, H Carl 1891-1955 *WhAm 3*

Wolf, H D 1895-1960 *WhAm 4*
Wolf, Harry Benjamin 1880-1944 *BiDrAC*
Wolf, Harry Florian 1907-1966 *NatCAB 53*
Wolf, Heinrich Franz 1872-1959 *NatCAB 48*
Wolf, Henry 1852-1916 *DcAmB, NatCAB 10, WhAm 1*
Wolf, Henry 1855-1927 *NatCAB 20*
Wolf, Henry J 1861-1937 *NatCAB 27*
Wolf, Henry John 1881- *WhAm 6*
Wolf, Henry Milton 1860-1935 *WhAm 1*
Wolf, Horace Joseph 1885-1927 *NatCAB 20*
Wolf, Innocent William 1843-1922 *DcAmB*
Wolf, Irwin Damasius 1894-1956 *WhAm 3*
Wolf, Isaac, Jr. 1859- *WhAm 4*
Wolf, Johann Rudolf 1816-1893 *DcScB*
Wolf, Joseph 1820-1899 *IIBEAAW*
Wolf, Joseph 1874-1948 *WhAm 3*
Wolf, Leonard George 1925-1970 *BiDrAC, WhAm 5*
Wolf, Leonard Lauritzen 1908-1962 *NatCAB 50*
Wolf, Luther Benaiah 1857-1939 *WhAm 1*
Wolf, Maximilian Franz Joseph Cornelius 1863-1932 *AsBiEn, DcScB*
Wolf, Orrin E 1895-1966 *WhAm 4*
Wolf, Paul Alexander 1868-1954 *WhAm 3*
Wolf, Pegot *IIBEAAW*
Wolf, Rennold 1872-1922 *NatCAB 19, WhAm 1*
Wolf, Robert Bunsen 1877-1954 *WhAm 3*
Wolf, Rudolf 1892-1948 *NatCAB 36*
Wolf, Samuel 1868-1960 *NatCAB 47*
Wolf, Simon 1836-1923 *ApCAB, DcAmB, WhAm 1*
Wolf, William A d1965 *WhAm 4*
Wolf, William John 1877-1966 *NatCAB 53*
Wolf, William Penn 1833-1896 *BiAUS, BiDrAC, WhAm H*
Wolfe, Albert 1887-1944 *NatCAB 33*
Wolfe, Albert Benedict 1876-1967 *NatCAB 52, WhAm 5*
Wolfe, Albertus Cassius 1858- *NatCAB 17*
Wolfe, Arthur Lester 1866-1931 *WhAm 1*
Wolfe, Byron B 1904-1973 *IIBEAAW*
Wolfe, Catharine Lorillard 1828-1887 *ApCAB, DcAmB, NatCAB 10, NotAW, WhAm H*
Wolfe, Catherine Lorillard 1828-1887 *AmWom*
Wolfe, Charles Spyker 1845- *NatCAB 2*
Wolfe, Clara Snell 1874- *WomWWA 14*
Wolfe, Clayton A 1893-1953 *WhAm 3*
Wolfe, Edgar Thurston d1957 *WhAm 3*
Wolfe, Edwin Philip 1871-1946 *NatCAB 37*
Wolfe, Florence Rockafellar 1862- *WomWWA 14*
Wolfe, Harry Deane 1901-1975 *WhAm 6*
Wolfe, Harry Kirke 1858-1918 *BiDAmEd, DcAmB, NatCAB 18, WhAm 1*
Wolfe, Harry Preston 1872-1946 *NatCAB 35, WhAm 2*
Wolfe, Hugh Claibourne 1892-1957 *NatCAB 47*
Wolfe, J Theodore 1908-1963 *WhAm 4*
Wolfe, James 1726-1759 *Drake*
Wolfe, James 1727-1759 *ApCAB, McGEWB, NatCAB 1, WhAm H, WhoMilH*
Wolfe, James Edward 1902-1971 *WhAm 5*
Wolfe, James H 1884-1958 *WhAm 3*
Wolfe, James Jacob 1875-1920 *WhAm 1*
Wolfe, John C *NewYHSD*
Wolfe, John David 1792-1872 *ApCAB, DcAmB, WhAm H*
Wolfe, John K 1835?- *NewYHSD*
Wolfe, John Marcus 1881- *WhAm 6*
Wolfe, Kenneth B 1896-1971 *WhAm 5*
Wolfe, Lawrence 1890-1953 *WhAm 3*
Wolfe, Manson Horatio 1866- *WhAm 4*
Wolfe, Mary Moore 1874- *WomWWA 14*
Wolfe, Oscar 1889-1963 *NatCAB 50*
Wolfe, Paul Austin 1898-1964 *WhAm 4*
Wolfe, Richard Russell 1907-1970 *NatCAB 55, WhAm 5*
Wolfe, Robert Frederick 1860-1927 *NatCAB 22*
Wolfe, Robert Frederick 1863-1927 *WhAm 1*
Wolfe, Rowland Daniel 1885-1944 *NatCAB 37*
Wolfe, S Herbert 1874-1927 *WhAm 1*
Wolfe, Simeon Kalfius 1824-1888 *BiAUS, BiDrAC, WhAm H, WhAmP*

Wolfe, Theodore Frelinghuysen 1847-1915 *WhAm 1*
Wolfe, Theodore Freylinghuysen 1843-1915 *NatCAB 8, NatCAB 16*
Wolfe, Thomas Clayton 1900-1938 *AmBi, DcAmB S2, EncAB, McGEWB, WebAB, WhAm 1*
Wolfe, Thomas Kennerly 1892-1972 *WhAm 5*
Wolfe, William Henry 1879-1956 *NatCAB 45, WhAm 6*
Wolfel, Paul Ludwig 1862- *WhAm 4*
Wolfenbarger, Andrew G 1856- *WhAm 4*
Wolfenden, James 1889-1949 *BiDrAC, WhAm 2, WhAmP*
Wolfer, John Adam 1880-1955 *NatCAB 47, WhAm 3*
Wolferman, Fred 1870-1955 *WhAm 3*
Wolfers, Arnold Oscar 1892-1968 *WhAm 5*
Wolff *NewYHSD*
Wolff, Bernard Crouse 1794-1870 *ApCAB*
Wolff, Bertram 1898-1963 *NatCAB 49*
Wolff, Caspar Friedrich 1734-1794 *DcScB, DcScB Sup*
Wolff, Christian Von 1679-1754 *DcScB, McGEWB*
Wolff, Frank Alfred 1871- *WhAm 5*
Wolff, George Dering 1822-1894 *WhAm H*
Wolff, Harold G 1898-1962 *WhAm 4*
Wolff, John Eliot 1857-1940 *WhAm 1*
Wolff, Joseph Scott 1878-1958 *BiDrAC*
Wolff, Julius 1836-1902 *BiHiMed*
Wolff, Karl 1900- *WhWW-II*
Wolff, Kaspar Friedrich 1733-1794 *AsBiEn, BiHiMed*
Wolff, Lester Lionel 1919- *BiDrAC*
Wolff, Mary Evaline *BiDAmEd*
Wolff, Samuel 1888-1969 *NatCAB 56*
Wolff, Samuel Udel 1898-1968 *NatCAB 55*
Wolff, William Almon 1885-1933 *WhAm 1*
Wolffe, Joseph Barnett 1896-1966 *NatCAB 53*
Wolfiers, Arnold Oscar 1892-1968 *NatCAB 54*
Wolfit, Donald 1902-1968 *WhAm 4A, WhAm 5*
Wolfkill, Guy Fontelle 1881- *WhAm 6*
Wolfman, Augustus 1908-1974 *WhAm 6*
Wolfner, Henry Lincoln 1860-1935 *NatCAB 26*
Wolford, Charles 1811?- *NewYHSD*
Wolford, Frank Lane 1817-1895 *BiDrAC, WhAm H*
Wolford, Leo Thorp 1890-1971 *WhAm 5*
Wolfram VonEschenbach 1170?-1230? *McGEWB*
Wolfram, Jack Frederick 1899-1971 *NatCAB 57*
Wolfrom, Melville L 1900-1969 *WhAm 5*
Wolfskill, William 1798-1866 *DcAmB, REnAW, WhAm H*
Wolfsohn, Carl 1834-1907 *DcAmB*
Wolfsohn, Joel David 1900-1961 *WhAm 4*
Wolfsohn, Julian Mast 1883-1943 *NatCAB 32*
Wolfson, Erwin Service 1902-1962 *NatCAB 48, WhAm 4*
Wolfson, Harry Austryn 1887-1974 *McGEWB, WhAm 6*
Wolfson, Howard E 1898-1970 *WhAm 5*
Wolfson, Kurt 1898-1969 *WhAm 5*
Wolfson, Leo 1906-1962 *NatCAB 51*
Wolfstein, David I 1862-1944 *WhAm 2*
Wolgamuth, H *NewYHSD*
Wolhaupter, Benjamin 1859-1949 *NatCAB 38*
Wolheim, Louis Robert 1881-1931 *DcAmB S1*
Woljeska-Tindolph, Helen 1875- *WomWWA 14*
Woll, Fritz Wilhelm 1865- *WhAm 1*
Woll, Matthew 1880-1956 *NatCAB 42, WhAm 3*
Wollaston, Francis 1731-1815 *DcScB*
Wollaston, John *BnEnAmA, NewYHSD*
Wollaston, William Hyde 1766-1828 *AsBiEn, DcScB*
Wolle, Francis 1817- *ApCAB, NatCAB 1*
Wolle, John Frederick 1863-1933 *AmBi, DcAmB, NatCAB 14, WhAm 1*
Wolle, Muriel Sibell 1898- *IIBEAAW*
Wolle, Peter 1792-1871 *ApCAB, NatCAB 1*
Wolle, Sylvester 1816-1873 *NatCAB 2*
Wollenhaupt, Hermann Adolf 1827-1863 *WhAm H*

Wollenhaupt, Hermann Adolph 1827-1863 *NatCAB 1*
Wollenweber, Louis August 1807-1888 *ApCAB*
Wollenweber, Ludwig August 1807-1888 *NatCAB 11, WhAm H*
Wollerton, Frederick William 1854-1942 *NatCAB 33*
Wolley, Charles 1652?- *ApCAB, NatCAB 8*
Wollstein, Martha 1868-1939 *NotAW*
Wolman, Leo 1890-1961 *WhAm 4*
Wolpe, Stefan 1902-1972 *WhAm 5*
Wolpers, John Henry 1880-1951 *NatCAB 44*
Wolrich, Irving 1890-1957 *NatCAB 49*
Wolseley, Garnet Joseph 1833-1913 *ApCAB, WhoMilH*
Wolsey, Louis 1877-1953 *WhAm 3*
Wolsey, Thomas 1475?-1530 *McGEWB*
Wolters, Larry 1899-1969 *WhAm 5*
Woltersdorf, Arthur Fred 1870-1948 *WhAm 2*
Woltman, Frederick Enos 1905-1970 *WhAm 5*
Woltman, Henry 1889-1964 *WhAm 4*
Woltman, Reinhard 1757-1837 *DcScB*
Wolverton, Charles Anderson 1880-1969 *BiDrAC, NatCAB 56, WhAm 5, WhAmP*
Wolverton, Charles Edwin 1851-1926 *NatCAB 13, WhAm 1*
Wolverton, John Marshall 1872-1944 *BiDrAC, WhAm 5*
Wolverton, Orlando Price 1872-1950 *NatCAB 39*
Wolverton, Simon Peter 1837-1910 *BiDrAC, NatCAB 7*
Wolvin, Augustus B 1857-1932 *WhAm 1*
Womack, Ennis Bryan 1899-1974 *WhAm 6*
Womack, Joseph Pitts 1871- *WhAm 5*
Womack, Nathan Anthony 1901-1975 *WhAm 6*
Womble, John Philip, Jr. 1900-1956 *WhAm 3*
Womeldorph, Stuart Early 1890-1961 *WhAm 4*
Womer, Parley Paul 1870-1957 *WhAm 3*
Wonderley, Anthony Wayne 1913-1975 *WhAm 6*
Wonnacott, Norman 1903-1974 *WhAm 6*
Wonning, Harvey Henry 1890-1968 *NatCAB 54*
Wonson, Roy Warren 1883-1942 *WhAm 2*
Wood, Abiel 1772-1834 *BiAUS, BiDrAC, WhAm H*
Wood, Abraham 1608?-1680? *DcAmB, REnAW, WhAm H*
Wood, Alan, III 1875-1955 *NatCAB 46*
Wood, Alan, Jr. 1834-1902 *BiAUS, BiDrAC*
Wood, Alexander Cooper 1841-1919 *NatCAB 34, WhAm 4*
Wood, Alexander Thomas 1903-1960 *WhAm 4*
Wood, Alice Holabird 1871-1923 *WhAm 1*
Wood, Alphonso 1810-1881 *ApCAB, Drake, NatCAB 34*
Wood, Amos Eastman 1810-1850 *BiAUS, BiDrAC, WhAm H*
Wood, Andrew Chapman 1852- *NatCAB 16*
Wood, Andrew Hollister 1870-1941 *WhAm 1*
Wood, Ann Toppan 1817-1864 *NatCAB 10*
Wood, Ann VanCleef 1902-1973 *WhAm 6*
Wood, Anna May 1865- *WomWWA 14*
Wood, Arch K 1880-1964 *NatCAB 50*
Wood, Arthur B 1870-1952 *WhAm 3*
Wood, Arthur D 1876-1958 *WhAm 3*
Wood, Arthur Edward 1860-1926 *NatCAB 20*
Wood, Arthur Evans 1881-1960 *NatCAB 47, WhAm 6*
Wood, Arthur Hubbard 1870-1945 *NatCAB 37*
Wood, Arthur Julius 1874-1931 *NatCAB 23, WhAm 1*
Wood, Asa Butler 1865-1945 *WhAm 2*
Wood, Austin Voorhees 1893-1973 *WhAm 6*
Wood, Barry d1970 *WhAm 5*
Wood, Benjamin 1820-1900 *ApCAB, BiAUS, BiDrAC, NatCAB 1, WhAm H, WhAmP*
Wood, Benjamin 1865- *WhAm 4*
Wood, Benjamin 1871- *NatCAB 16*
Wood, Benson 1839-1915 *BiDrAC, WhAm 1*
Wood, Bernard Augustine 1867- *WhAm 4*
Wood, Bradford Ripley 1800-1889 *BiAUS, BiDrAC, NatCAB 12, WhAm H*
Wood, Carl Bruce 1899-1960 *WhAm 4*
Wood, Carolena Morris 1871- *WomWWA 14*
Wood, Carroll David 1857-1941 *WhAm 1*
Wood, Casey Albert 1856-1942 *DcAmB S3, NatCAB 10, WhAm 2*

Wood, Chalmers 1883-1952 *NatCAB 44*
Wood, Chandler Mason 1881-1938 *WhAm 1*
Wood, Charles *NewYHSD*
Wood, Charles 1851-1936 *ApCAB,*
NatCAB 12, NatCAB 27, WhAm 2
Wood, Charles Bryant Drake 1884-1939
NatCAB 38
Wood, Charles C *NewYHSD*
Wood, Charles Erskine Scott 1852-1944
DcAmB S3, NatCAB 36, REnAW,
WhAm 2
Wood, Charles Lincoln 1867-1961 *NatCAB 48*
Wood, Charles Milton 1861-1935 *WhAm 1*
Wood, Charles Morgan 1870-1927 *NatCAB 31*
Wood, Charles Parkinson 1883-1968
NatCAB 56, WhAm 5
Wood, Charles S 1825-1890 *NatCAB 1*
Wood, Charles Seely 1845-1912 *NatCAB 13,*
WhAm 1
Wood, Charlotte Matilda 1836- *ApCAB*
Wood, Chester Corbin 1891-1951 *NatCAB 39*
Wood, Clark Verner 1863- *WhAm 4*
Wood, Clement 1888-1950 *WhAm 3*
Wood, Clinton Tyler 1869-1932 *WhAm 4*
Wood, Corydon L 1852- *WhAm 1*
Wood, Daniel *NewYHSD*
Wood, Daniel Phelps 1819-1891 *NatCAB 2*
Wood, David Duffie 1838-1910 *DcAmB,*
WhAm 1
Wood, David Muir 1892-1960 *WhAm 3*
Wood, Dennistoun 1905-1956 *NatCAB 47*
Wood, DeVolson 1832-1897 *AmBi, ApCAB,*
BiDAmEd, NatCAB 13, WhAm H
Wood, Douglas Fox 1874-1935 *NatCAB 29*
Wood, Eben Albert 1875-1955 *NatCAB 42*
Wood, Edgar Liberty 1869-1958 *WhAm 3*
Wood, Edith Elmer 1871-1945 *DcAmB S3,*
NotAW, WhAm 2, WomWWA 14
Wood, Edmund Burke 1820-1882 *ApCAB*
Wood, Edmund Palmer 1899-1968 *WhAm 5*
Wood, Edward Edgar 1846-1924 *WhAm 1*
Wood, Edward Jenner 1878-1928 *WhAm 1*
Wood, Edward Parker 1848-1899 *ApCAB Sup*
Wood, Edward Randolph 1840-1932
NatCAB 24
Wood, Edward Sharpless 1868-1943
NatCAB 34
Wood, Edward Stickney 1846-1905 *DcAmB,*
WhAm 1
Wood, Edwin Ellsworth 1863-1940 *WhAm 1*
Wood, Edwin Orin 1861-1918 *WhAm 1*
Wood, Edwina 1876- *WomWWA 14*
Wood, Eleazer Derby 1783-1814 *ApCAB,*
Drake
Wood, Elizabeth Ogden Brower 1873- *BiCAW*
Wood, Ella Florence Eames 1861-
WomWWA 14
Wood, Eric Fisher 1889-1962 *NatCAB 52,*
WhAm 4
Wood, Ernest Edward 1875-1952 *BiDrAC,*
WhAm 5
Wood, Ethel 1879- *WomWWA 14*
Wood, Ethel Bryant Harmon 1879-
WomWWA 14
Wood, Eugene 1860-1923 *WhAm 1*
Wood, Ezra 1798-1841 *NewYHSD*
Wood, Fernando 1812-1881 *AmBi, ApCAB,*
BiAUS, BiDrAC, DcAmB, Drake,
McGEWB, NatCAB 3, WebAB,
WhAm H, WhAmP
Wood, Florence *WomWWA 14*
Wood, Floyd Bernard 1900-1956 *WhAm 3*
Wood, Frances Ann 1840- *WomWWA 14*
Wood, Frances Fisher *AmWom,*
WomWWA 14
Wood, Frances Gilchrist 1859-1944 *WhAm 2*
Wood, Francis Asbury 1859-1948 *WhAm 2*
Wood, Francis Carter 1869-1951 *NatCAB 18,*
WhAm 3
Wood, Frank 1858-1926 *NatCAB 38*
Wood, Frank Elmer 1859-1945 *NatCAB 34*
Wood, Frank Hoyt 1864-1930 *WhAm 1*
Wood, Frank Montgomery 1871-1946
NatCAB 36
Wood, Frederic Taylor 1874-1955 *ApCAB X,*
WhAm 3
Wood, Frederick Bertram 1888-1961
NatCAB 48

Wood, Frederick Eugene 1854- *NatCAB 12*
Wood, Frederick Hill 1877-1943 *DcAmB S3,*
WhAm 2
Wood, Frederick Spaulding 1901-1967
NatCAB 54
Wood, Frederick William 1857-1943
NatCAB 33, WhAm 2
Wood, George 1789-1860 *ApCAB, DcAmB,*
WhAm H
Wood, George 1798-1870 *NatCAB 8*
Wood, George 1799-1870 *ApCAB, Drake,*
WhAm H
Wood, George 1842-1926 *WhAm 1*
Wood, George Arthur 1878- *WhAm 1*
Wood, George Bacon 1797-1879 *AmBi,*
ApCAB, BiDAmEd, DcAmB, Drake,
NatCAB 1, NatCAB 5, WhAm H
Wood, George Bacon 1871-1954 *NatCAB 41*
Wood, George Bacon, Jr. 1832-1910 *NewYHSD*
Wood, George Henry 1867- *WhAm 2*
Wood, George McLane 1850-1930 *WhAm 1*
Wood, George T d1856 *NatCAB 9*
Wood, George T d1858 *BiAUS, Drake*
Wood, George Washington 1879-1947
NatCAB 34
Wood, George Willard 1854-1945 *WhAm 2*
Wood, Glen Eyre 1889-1956 *NatCAB 46*
Wood, Grant 1891-1942 *McGEWB*
Wood, Grant 1892-1941 *BnEnAmA*
Wood, Grant 1892-1942 *DcAmB S3, EncAAH,*
NatCAB 35, WebAB, WhAm 1
Wood, Guy Bussey 1878- *WhAm 3*
Wood, Harold Bacon 1878-1958 *NatCAB 48*
Wood, Harold E 1897-1961 *WhAm 4*
Wood, Harriet Ann 1871- *WomWWA 14*
Wood, Harriette M Johnston *WomWWA 14*
Wood, Harry Gardner 1882-1957 *NatCAB 44*
Wood, Harry Parker 1877- *WhAm 1*
Wood, Hart 1880-1957 *WhAm 3*
Wood, Helen Foss 1872- *WomWWA 14*
Wood, Henry 1834-1909 *NatCAB 19,*
WhAm 1
Wood, Henry 1849-1925 *NatCAB 13,*
WhAm 1
Wood, Henry 1878-1946 *WhAm 2*
Wood, Henry Alexander Wise 1866-1939
DcAmB S2, NatCAB 14, NatCAB 41,
WhAm 1
Wood, Henry Billings *NewYHSD*
Wood, Henry Clay 1832-1918 *WhAm 1*
Wood, Henry Wise 1861-1941 *EncAAH*
Wood, Hilliard 1865-1933 *NatCAB 25*
Wood, Hiram Remsen 1867-1920 *NatCAB 19*
Wood, Horatio Charles 1841-1920 *ApCAB,*
DcAmB, DcScB, NatCAB 13, WhAm 1
Wood, Horatio Charles 1874-1920 *WhAm 1*
Wood, Horatio Charles, Jr. 1874-1958 *WhAm 3*
Wood, Horatio Dan 1841-1905 *NatCAB 16,*
WhAm 1
Wood, Horatio Nelson 1839-1931 *ApCAB X,*
NatCAB 24
Wood, Howland 1877-1938 *WhAm 1*
Wood, Hudson A 1841- *WhAm 4*
Wood, Ira Wells 1856-1930 *NatCAB 22,*
WhAm 1
Wood, Ira Wells 1856-1931 *BiDrAC, WhAmP*
Wood, Irving Francis 1861-1934 *AmBi,*
WhAm 1
Wood, Isaac 1793-1868 *ApCAB, Drake,*
NatCAB 20
Wood, Isaac 1815-1889 *NatCAB 4*
Wood, Isaac Lemuel 1860- *WhAm 4*
Wood, Isabel Warwick 1874- *WhAm 5*
Wood, J *NewYHSD*
Wood, Mrs. J G *NewYHSD*
Wood, J K Williams 1890-1961 *NatCAB 50*
Wood, James *NewYHSD*
Wood, James d1813 *BiAUS, Drake*
Wood, James 1747-1813 *NatCAB 5, TwCBDA*
Wood, James 1750-1813 *ApCAB*
Wood, James 1799-1867 *ApCAB, DcAmB,*
NatCAB 2, WhAm H
Wood, James 1803-1867 *NewYHSD*
Wood, James 1839-1925 *DcAmB, NatCAB 25,*
WhAm 1
Wood, James Anderson 1870-1947 *WhAm 2*
Wood, James Craven 1858-1948 *WhAm 2*
Wood, James Earl 1906-1965 *NatCAB 52*

Wood, James F 1813-1883 *Drake Sup*
Wood, James Frederic 1813-1883 *ApCAB,*
NatCAB 7, TwCBDA
Wood, James Frederick 1813-1883 *DcAmB,*
WhAm H
Wood, James J 1856-1928 *DcAmB, WhAm 1*
Wood, James Madison 1875-1958 *NatCAB 46,*
WhAm 3
Wood, James Perry 1854- *WhAm 4*
Wood, James R 1833?-1887 *NewYHSD*
Wood, James R 1843-1917 *WhAm 1*
Wood, James Rushmore 1813-1882 *AmBi,*
DcAmB, WebAB
Wood, James Rushmore 1816-1882 *ApCAB,*
NatCAB 9, WhAm H
Wood, Jay Pendleton 1889-1965 *NatCAB 53*
Wood, Jean Moncure 1754-1823 *ApCAB,*
NatCAB 5
Wood, Jessie Porter *WomWWA 14*
Wood, Jethro 1774-1834 *ApCAB X, DcAmB,*
EncAAH, WhAm H
Wood, Jethro 1774-1840? *NatCAB 11*
Wood, Joanna E *WomWWA 14*
Wood, John 1775-1822 *ApCAB, DcAmB,*
Drake, NewYHSD, WhAm H
Wood, John 1798-1880 *ApCAB, NatCAB 11,*
WhAm H
Wood, John 1816-1898 *BiAUS, BiDrAC*
Wood, Mrs. John 1831-1915 *Drake, NotAW*
Wood, John Anderson 1865-1926 *WhAm 1*
Wood, John Archart 1831- *NatCAB 12*
Wood, John C 1901-1969 *WhAm 5*
Wood, John Dockstader 1904-1968 *NatCAB 56*
Wood, John Enos 1892-1964 *WhAm 4*
Wood, John Hepler 1869-1938 *WhAm 1*
Wood, John Jacob 1784-1874 *BiAUS, BiDrAC,*
WhAm H
Wood, John M 1813-1864 *BiAUS, BiDrAC,*
WhAm H, WhAmP
Wood, John McKee 1854-1926 *NatCAB 21*
Wood, John Perry 1879-1959 *NatCAB 49,*
WhAm 6
Wood, John Quinby 1867- *WhAm 4*
Wood, John S 1888-1966 *WhAm 4*
Wood, John Scott 1872-1957 *WhAm 3*
Wood, John Seymour 1853- *NatCAB 11,*
WhAm 1
Wood, John Stephens 1885-1968 *BiDrAC,*
WhAm 5, WhAmP
Wood, John Taylor 1830-1904 *AmBi, BiDConf,*
DcAmB, NatCAB 12, WebAMB
Wood, John Travers 1878-1954 *BiDrAC,*
WhAm 3, WhAmP
Wood, John Walter 1900-1958 *WhAm 3*
Wood, John Wesley 1865- *WhoColR*
Wood, John Wilson 1866-1947 *WhAm 2*
Wood, Joseph 1712-1789 *ApCAB, BiAUS,*
Drake, TwCBDA
Wood, Joseph 1712-1791 *BiDrAC, WhAm H*
Wood, Joseph 1778?-1830 *NewYHSD*
Wood, Joseph 1778?-1832? *DcAmB,*
WhAm H
Wood, Joseph 1846-1922 *WhAm 1*
Wood, Julia A A 1826-1903 *AmWom*
Wood, Julia Amanda Sargent 1825-1903
NotAW
Wood, Juliana Westray d1836 *ApCAB, Drake*
Wood, Kenneth Axford 1894-1967 *NatCAB 54*
Wood, Kenneth Foster 1873-1925 *NatCAB 21,*
WhAm 1
Wood, Sir Kingsley 1881-1943 *WhWW-II*
Wood, Laurence Irven 1914-1973 *WhAm 6*
Wood, Ledger 1901-1970 *WhAm 5*
Wood, Leland Nelson 1868-1946 *NatCAB 36*
Wood, Leonard 1860-1927 *AmBi, ApCAB Sup,*
ApCAB X, DcAmB, EncAAH, McGEWB,
NatCAB 9, NatCAB 28, REnAW,
TwCBDA, WebAB, WebAMB, WhAm 1
Wood, Leonard Earle 1881- *WhAm 6*
Wood, Leonidas Arnold 1888-1969 *NatCAB 56*
Wood, Lester Gravatt 1893-1969 *NatCAB 54*
Wood, Lewis 1880-1953 *WhAm 3*
Wood, Lloyd Fuller 1918-1968 *WhAm 4*
Wood, Loren Newton 1877-1960 *WhAm 4*
Wood, Lorenzo 1906-1968 *NatCAB 55*
Wood, Lucie Poucher 1880- *WomWWA 14*
Wood, Ludia Collins 1845- *WhAm 4*
Wood, Lydia Cope 1845- *WomWWA 14*

Wood, Lydia Jefferies 1862- *WomWWA 14*
Wood, Lyman Wentch 1899-1966 *NatCAB 53*
Wood, Mabel Janette 1883- *WomWWA 14*
Wood, Marquis Lafayette 1829- *NatCAB 3*
Wood, Marshall William 1846-1933
 NatCAB 16, NatCAB 24, WhAm 4
Wood, Mary C F *AmWom*
Wood, Mary Craige *WomWWA 14*
Wood, Mary Elizabeth 1861-1931 *DcAmB,*
 NotAW
Wood, Mary I 1866- *WhAm 3,*
 WomWWA 14
Wood, Mary Knight 1857- *WomWWA 14*
Wood, Matilda Charlotte Vining 1831-1915
 NotAW
Wood, Matthew Laurence 1858-1932 *WhAm 1*
Wood, Meredith 1895-1974 *WhAm 6*
Wood, Minot Colburn 1876-1952 *NatCAB 41*
Wood, Montraville 1860-1923 *WhAm 1*
Wood, Moses Lindley 1854-1931 *NatCAB 42,*
 WhAm 4
Wood, Myron Ray 1892-1946 *WhAm 2*
Wood, Nathan Eusebius 1849-1937 *WhAm 1*
Wood, Nathan Robinson 1874- *WhAm 5*
Wood, Oakley 1872-1935 *NatCAB 38*
Wood, Oliver Ellsworth 1844-1910 *WhAm 1*
Wood, Orison 1811-1842 *NewYHSD*
Wood, Palmer Gaylord 1843-1915 *WhAm 1*
Wood, Paul Meyer 1894-1963 *WhAm 4*
Wood, Paul Spencer 1882-1955 *WhAm 3*
Wood, Pierpont Jonathan Edwards 1890-1956
 WhAm 3
Wood, Pliny Williams 1848-1926 *NatCAB 20*
Wood, Ralph 1890-1959 *WhAm 3*
Wood, Ralph Emerson 1878-1951 *NatCAB 39*
Wood, Reuben 1792-1864 *ApCAB, BiAUS,*
 DcAmB, Drake, NatCAB 3, WhAm H
Wood, Reuben Terrell 1884-1955 *BiDrAC,*
 WhAm 3, WhAmP
Wood, Richard 1833-1910 *WhAm 1*
Wood, Richard D 1799-1869 *WhAm H*
Wood, Richard Davis 1877-1948 *NatCAB 54*
Wood, Richard Gilpin 1849-1931 *NatCAB 29*
Wood, Richard Lenox 1869-1960 *NatCAB 49*
Wood, Robert *IIBEAAW*
Wood, Robert Coldwell 1923- *BiDrUSE*
Wood, Robert E 1926- *IIBEAAW*
Wood, Robert Elkington 1879-1969 *McGEWB,*
 NatCAB 55, WebAB, WhAm 5
Wood, Robert Harrison 1887-1956 *NatCAB 44*
Wood, Robert Jarvis 1868-1922 *NatCAB 38*
Wood, Robert Williams 1868-1955 *DcScB,*
 NatCAB 14, NatCAB 46, WhAm 3
Wood, Roswell Lincoln 1865-1920 *ApCAB X*
Wood, Ruth Goulding 1875- *WomWWA 14*
Wood, Sally Sayward Barrell Keating 1759-1855
 NotAW
Wood, Samuel 1760-1844 *DcAmB, WhAm H*
Wood, Samuel Casey 1830- *ApCAB*
Wood, Samuel Grosvenor 1884-1949 *WhAm 2*
Wood, Samuel M *NewYHSD*
Wood, Samuel Newitt 1825-1891 *WhAm H*
Wood, Sarah Sayward Barrell Keating 1759-1855
 DcAmB, WhAm H
Wood, Silas *NewYHSD*
Wood, Silas 1769-1847 *ApCAB, BiAUS,*
 BiDrAC, Drake, NatCAB 3, WhAm H,
 WhAmP
Wood, Sol Alphonso 1857-1943 *NatCAB 32*
Wood, Solomon *NewYHSD*
Wood, Spencer Shepard 1861-1940 *NatCAB 32,*
 WhAm 1
Wood, Stanley 1894- *IIBEAAW*
Wood, Stanley L 1860-194-? *IIBEAAW*
Wood, Stella Louise 1865- *WhAm 3*
Wood, Sterling Alexander 1859-1924 *WhAm 1*
Wood, Sterling Alexander Martin 1823-1891
 NatCAB 18
Wood, Stuart 1853-1914 *WhAm 1*
Wood, Susan D *NewYHSD*
Wood, T Kenneth 1877-1958 *NatCAB 48*
Wood, Theodore Thomas 1905-1963 *WhAm 4*
Wood, Thomas *NewYHSD*
Wood, Thomas 1813-1880 *DcAmB, WhAm H*
Wood, Thomas 1814-1880 *NatCAB 28*
Wood, Thomas Bond 1844-1922 *DcAmB*
Wood, Thomas Brenner 1883-1950 *NatCAB 49*
Wood, Thomas Denison 1865-1951 *BiDAmEd,*

WhAm 3
Wood, Thomas Edward 1897-1961 *NatCAB 49,*
 WhAm 4
Wood, Thomas Fanning 1841-1892 *NatCAB 9*
Wood, Thomas Hosmer 1798-1874 *NewYHSD*
Wood, Thomas Jefferson 1825- *Drake*
Wood, Thomas Jefferson 1844-1908 *BiDrAC*
Wood, Thomas John 1823-1906 *AmBi, ApCAB,*
 DcAmB, NatCAB 4, TwCBDA,
 WhAm 1
Wood, Thomas John 1899-1956 *WhAm 3*
Wood, Thomas Waterman 1823-1903 *AmBi,*
 ApCAB, NatCAB 3, NewYHSD,
 TwCBDA, WhAm 1
Wood, Virgil Oliver 1892-1954 *NatCAB 44*
Wood, W Stuart 1899-1944 *NatCAB 35*
Wood, Waddy Butler 1869-1944 *WhAm 2*
Wood, Walter 1849-1934 *WhAm 1*
Wood, Walter 1897-1960 *WhAm 4*
Wood, Walter Aaron 1877- *WhAm 5*
Wood, Walter Abbott 1815-1892 *ApCAB,*
 BiDrAC, DcAmB, NatCAB 6, WhAm H,
 WhAmP
Wood, Walter Abbott, Jr. 1871-1915
 NatCAB 29
Wood, Walter Childs 1864-1953 *NatCAB 47*
Wood, Walter Dongan, Jr. 1914-1972
 NatCAB 56
Wood, Walter Seal 1874-1949 *NatCAB 41*
Wood, Waters Dewees 1826-1899 *NatCAB 12*
Wood, Will Christopher 1880-1939 *NatCAB 29,*
 WhAm 1
Wood, William 1580?-1639 *AmBi, ApCAB,*
 DcAmB, Drake, NatCAB 7, WhAm H
Wood, William 1797-1877 *ApCAB*
Wood, William 1807-1883 *NatCAB 4*
Wood, William 1808-1894 *NatCAB 22*
Wood, William Allen 1874- *WhAm 5*
Wood, William Barry, Jr. 1910-1971
 NatCAB 56, WhAm 5
Wood, William Burke 1779-1861 *ApCAB,*
 DcAmB, Drake, NatCAB 6, WhAm H
Wood, William Carleton 1880- *WhAm 6*
Wood, William Christopher 1880-1939
 BiDAmEd
Wood, William Elliott 1887-1957 *NatCAB 49,*
 WhAm 3
Wood, William F *NewYHSD*
Wood, William Hamilton 1874-1953 *WhAm 3*
Wood, William Henry Searing 1840-1907
 NatCAB 24, WhAm 1
Wood, William Madison 1858-1926 *ApCAB X,*
 NatCAB 15, WhAm 1
Wood, William Madison, II 1892-1922
 ApCAB X
Wood, William Madison, II 1892-1923
 NatCAB 20
Wood, William Maxwell 1809-1880 *ApCAB*
Wood, William Maxwell 1850- *ApCAB*
Wood, William Robert 1861-1933 *BiDrAC,*
 DcAmB, WhAm 1, WhAmP
Wood, William Roscoe 1874-1941 *WhAm 2*
Wood, William S *BiAUS*
Wood, William Thomas 1854-1943 *WhAm 2*
Wood, William Willis Wiley 1818-1882 *ApCAB,*
 Drake, NatCAB 12
Wood, Willis Delano 1872-1957 *NatCAB 45,*
 WhAm 5
Wood, Word Harris 1873-1951 *WhAm 3*
Wood-Allen, Mary 1841-1908 *WhAm 1*
Wood-Seys, Roland Alex 1854- *WhAm 4*
Woodard, Charles Augustus 1876- *WhAm 5*
Woodard, David Warren 1904-1968
 NatCAB 55
Woodard, Frederick Augustus 1854-1915
 BiDrAC, WhAm 1
Woodard, G C *WhAm 4*
Woodard, Isaac Evans 1883-1958 *NatCAB 47*
Woodard, James Edward 1882-1947 *WhAm 2*
Woodard, Myron Chester 1875-1946
 NatCAB 38
Woodberry, Ethel Morton 1875- *WomWWA 14*
Woodberry, George Edward 1855-1930 *AmBi,*
 ApCAB, DcAmB, NatCAB 1,
 NatCAB 23, TwCBDA, WebAB,
 WhAm 1 •
Woodberry, Miriam L 1872- *WhAm 5*
Woodberry, Rosa Louise 1869-1932 *AmWom,*

WhAm 1, WomWWA 14
Woodbery, D Hoyt 1892-1973 *NatCAB 56,*
 WhAm 6
Woodbey, George Washington 1854- *WhoColR*
Woodbine, George Edward 1876-1953 *WhAm 3*
Woodbourne, Harry 1889-1962 *NatCAB 49*
Woodbridge, Abby Dwight 1808-1866 *ApCAB*
Woodbridge, Arthur Loomis 1882-1952
 NatCAB 42
Woodbridge, Benjamin 1622-1684 *ApCAB*
Woodbridge, Benjamin 1709-1728 *ApCAB*
Woodbridge, Benjamin 1710- *ApCAB*
Woodbridge, Benjamin Ruggles 1733-1819
 Drake
Woodbridge, Charles Kingsley 1881-1960
 WhAm 4
Woodbridge, Cora Adams 1880- *WomWWA 14*
Woodbridge, Dudley Warner 1896-1969
 NatCAB 55, WhAm 5
Woodbridge, Dwight Edwards 1865-1944
 WhAm 2
Woodbridge, Enoch 1750-1805 *NatCAB 4*
Woodbridge, Frederick Enoch 1818-1888 *BiAUS,*
 BiDrAC, WhAm H, WhAmP
Woodbridge, Frederick Enoch 1819-1888
 ApCAB
Woodbridge, Frederick James 1900-1974
 WhAm 6
Woodbridge, Frederick James Eugene 1867-1940
 BiDAmEd, DcAmB S2, WebAB, WhAm 1
Woodbridge, Helena Belle Adams 1869-
 WomWWA 14
Woodbridge, Homer Edwards 1882-1958
 WhAm 3
Woodbridge, John 1613-1695 *DcAmB,*
 WhAm H
Woodbridge, John 1614-1691 *ApCAB*
Woodbridge, John Arven 1903-1971 *WhAm 5*
Woodbridge, John J *NewYHSD*
Woodbridge, Mary A Brayton d1894 *AmWom*
Woodbridge, Samuel Homer 1848-1926
 WhAm 1
Woodbridge, Samuel Merrill 1819-1905 *ApCAB,*
 DcAmB, NatCAB 12, WhAm 1
Woodbridge, Timothy 1656-1732 *ApCAB*
Woodbridge, Timothy 1784-1862 *ApCAB*
Woodbridge, William 1755-1836 *NatCAB 10*
Woodbridge, William 1780-1861 *AmBi,*
 ApCAB, BiAUS, DcAmB, Drake,
 NatCAB 5, WhAm H, WhAmP
Woodbridge, William Channing 1794-1845
 ApCAB, BiDAmEd, DcAmB, Drake,
 NatCAB 11, WhAm H
Woodbridge, William Reed 1834- *NatCAB 11*
Woodbridge, William W 1780-1861 *BiDrAC*
Woodburn, Benjamin Franklin 1832-1906
 NatCAB 6
Woodburn, Ethelbert Cooke 1875-1958
 WhAm 4
Woodburn, James Albert 1856-1943
 NatCAB 13, WhAm 2
Woodburn, William 1838-1915 *BiAUS,*
 BiDrAC, NatCAB 1, NatCAB 37,
 WhAmP
Woodburn, William 1880- *WhAm 6*
Woodburne, Angus Stewart 1881-1938 *WhAm 1*
Woodbury, Augustus 1825- *ApCAB, Drake*
Woodbury, Benjamin Collins 1882-1948
 NatCAB 36
Woodbury, Charles Herbert 1864-1940
 ApCAB X, WhAm 1
Woodbury, Charles J 1844- *WhAm 4*
Woodbury, Charles Jeptha Hill 1851-1916
 DcAmB, NatCAB 12, WhAm 1
Woodbury, Charles Levi 1820- *ApCAB, Drake*
Woodbury, Daniel Phineas 1812-1864 *AmBi,*
 ApCAB, DcAmB, Drake, NatCAB 1,
 WhAm H
Woodbury, Egburt Erie 1861-1920 *NatCAB 18*
Woodbury, Ellen Carolina DeQuincy d1909
 WhAm 1
Woodbury, Eri Davidson 1837-1928 *NatCAB 21*
Woodbury, Frank Porter 1839- *WhAm 4*
Woodbury, Frederick Elwell 1862-1914
 NatCAB 19
Woodbury, Gordon 1863-1924 *WhAm 1*
Woodbury, Helen Laura Sumner 1876-1933
 AmBi, DcAmB, NotAW, WhAm 1

Woodbury, Ida Sumner Vose 1854-1934
WhAm 1
Woodbury, Isaac Baker 1819-1858 *ApCAB,*
DcAmB, Drake, NatCAB 2, WhAm H
Woodbury, John Charles 1859-1937 *NatCAB 43*
Woodbury, Leander Seth 1838-1918
NatCAB 19
Woodbury, Levi 1789-1851 *AmBi, ApCAB,*
BiAUS, BiDrAC, BiDrUSE, DcAmB,
Drake, NatCAB 2, TwCBDA, WebAB,
WhAm H, WhAmP
Woodbury, Levi 1834-1925 *NatCAB 22*
Woodbury, Louis Augustus 1844-1916
NatCAB 16
Woodbury, M A *NewYHSD*
Woodbury, Mabel Blanche 1869-
WomWWA 14
Woodbury, Malcolm Sumner 1881-1920
WhAm 1
Woodbury, Marcia Oakes 1865-1913 *WhAm 1,*
WomWWA 14
Woodbury, Mary Cerula 1864- *NatCAB 19*
Woodbury, Mildred Fairchild 1894-1975
WhAm 6
Woodbury, Orpheus Lanphear 1885-1958
NatCAB 49
Woodbury, Robert Morse 1889-1970
NatCAB 55, WhAm 5
Woodbury, Roger Williams 1841-1903
NatCAB 6
Woodbury, Ubran Andrain 1838-1915 *TwCBDA*
Woodbury, Urban Andrain 1838-1915
NatCAB 8, WhAm 1
Woodbury, Walter E 1886-1964 *WhAm 4*
Woodbury, Wiley Egan 1880-1936 *NatCAB 30*
Woodbury, William Blanchard 1876-1951
NatCAB 41
Woodbury, William Richardson 1863-1927
NatCAB 21
Woodcock, Amos Walter Wright 1883-1964
WhAm 4
Woodcock, Charles Edward 1854-1940
NatCAB 5, NatCAB 40, WhAm 1
Woodcock, David 1785-1835 *BiAUS, BiDrAC,*
WhAm H
Woodcock, T S *NewYHSD*
Wooddy, Claiborne Alphonso 1856-1918
WhAm 1
Wooden, Walter Banfil 1882-1949 *NatCAB 39*
Woodfield, Albert Wilbur 1902-1946
NatCAB 36
Woodford, Arthur Burnham 1861- *WhAm 4*
Woodford, Ethelbert George 1850-1923
NatCAB 20
Woodford, Frank B 1903-1967 *WhAm 4*
Woodford, Laura Moore 1838- *WomWWA 14*
Woodford, M DeWitt 1838-1907 *WhAm 1*
Woodford, Stewart Lyndon 1835-1913 *AmBi,*
ApCAB, ApCAB X, BiDrAC, DcAmB,
NatCAB 1, NatCAB 9, TwCBDA,
WhAm 1
Woodford, William 1734-1780 *DcAmB,*
WebAMB, WhAm H
Woodford, William 1735-1780 *ApCAB, Drake,*
NatCAB 6
Woodham, Eva Esther Dowling 1890-1962
NatCAB 45
Woodhead, Charles Burton 1845-1935
NatCAB 36
Woodhead, Edwin Arthur 1887-1957
NatCAB 49
Woodhead, Harry 1889-1961 *WhAm 4*
Woodhead, William 1868- *WhAm 4*
Woodhouse, Arthur Sutherland Pigott 1895-1964
WhAm 4
Woodhouse, Charles Williamson 1835-
WhAm 4
Woodhouse, Chase Going *BiDrAC, WhAmP*
Woodhouse, Henry 1884- *NatCAB 15*
Woodhouse, Henry Francis 1847- *WhoColR*
Woodhouse, James 1770-1809 *ApCAB,*
BiDAmEd, DcAmB, Drake, WhAm H
Woodhouse, Robert 1773-1827 *DcScB*
Woodhouse, S Laurence 1875-1946 *NatCAB 37*
Woodhouse, Samuel d1843 *Drake*
Woodhouse, Samuel W *WhAm H*
Woodhull, Agnes Patton 1877- *WomWWA 14*
Woodhull, Alfred Alexander 1837-1921 *DcAmB,*

WhAm 1
Woodhull, Charles Richard 1878-1951
NatCAB 41
Woodhull, Daniel Ellis 1869- *WhAm 5*
Woodhull, Floyd Thompkins 1856-1928
ApCAB X
Woodhull, Jacob 1792-1832 *NatCAB 5*
Woodhull, John 1744-1824 *ApCAB*
Woodhull, John Francis 1857-1941 *WhAm 1*
Woodhull, Marianna *WomWWA 14*
Woodhull, Maxwell 1813-1863 *ApCAB*
Woodhull, Maxwell VanZandt 1843-1921
WhAm 1
Woodhull, Nathaniel 1722-1776 *AmBi, ApCAB,*
DcAmB, Drake, NatCAB 5, TwCBDA,
WhAm H
Woodhull, Richard 1620-1690 *ApCAB*
Woodhull, Ross Arnold 1879-1944 *NatCAB 33*
Woodhull, Tennessee *WebAB*
Woodhull, Victoria Claflin 1838-1927 *AmBi,*
DcAmB, NotAW, WebAB, WhAm HA,
WhAm 4, WhAmP
Woodhull, William 1741-1824 *ApCAB*
Woodhull, Zula Maud *WhAm 5*
Woodhull, Zulu Maud *WomWWA 14*
Woodin, Gertrude Lee *WomWWA 14*
Woodin, J A *NewYHSD*
Woodin, Mary Eastman *WomWWA 14*
Woodin, Thomas *NewYHSD*
Woodin, William Hartman 1868-1934 *AmBi,*
ApCAB X, BiDrUSE, DcAmB,
NatCAB 17, WhAm 1
Woodin, William Hartmann 1868-1934
NatCAB 25
Wooding, Hugh Olliviere Beresford 1904-1974
WhAm 6
Woodings, Emanuel 1873-1946 *NatCAB 35*
Woodley, Kenneth Koch 1892-1972 *NatCAB 56*
Woodley, Oscar Israel 1861-1931 *NatCAB 24,*
WhAm 1
Woodlock, Thomas Francis 1866-1945
NatCAB 36, WhAm 4
Woodman, Abby Johnson 1828- *WhAm 4*
Woodman, Albert Stanton 1866-1931
NatCAB 25, WhAm 1
Woodman, Alice Kezia 1873- *WomWWA 14*
Woodman, Alpheus Grant 1873- *WhAm 5*
Woodman, Charles Walhart 1844-1898 *BiDrAC*
Woodman, Clarence Albert 1858-1926
ApCAB X
Woodman, Clarence Eugene 1852-1924 *ApCAB,*
NatCAB 19, WhAm 1
Woodman, Durand 1859-1907 *WhAm 1*
Woodman, Frederic Thomas 1872-1949
NatCAB 37, WhAm 3
Woodman, Mrs. George *NewYHSD*
Woodman, Harold David 1928- *EncAAH*
Woodman, J Edmund 1873-1939 *WhAm 1*
Woodman, John 1720-1772 *WhAm H*
Woodman, John Smith 1819-1871 *ApCAB*
Woodman, Lawrence Ewalt 1904- *WhAm 5*
Woodman, Marie S Montague *WomWWA 14*
Woodman, Olivia J C *WomWWA 14*
Woodman, Raymond Huntington 1861-1943
NatCAB 41, WhAm 2
Woodmansee, Joseph Emmett 1882-1952
NatCAB 39
Woodring, Edwin Stephen 1872-1957
NatCAB 45
Woodring, Harry Hines 1890-1967 *WhAm 4A*
Woodring, Henry H 1890-1967 *BiDrUSE*
Woodring, Samuel Thomas 1868-1922
NatCAB 22
Woodrow, H R 1887-1940 *WhAm 1*
Woodrow, James 1828-1907 *DcAmB,*
DcAmReB, NatCAB 11, WhAm 1
Woodrow, Jay W 1884- *WhAm 3*
Woodrow, Nancy Mann Waddel 1866?-1935
NotAW, WhAm 1, WomWWA 14
Woodrow, Samuel Hetherington 1862-1943
WhAm 2
Woodrow, Mrs. Wilson *NotAW*
Woodruff, A Allen 1889-1949 *NatCAB 38*
Woodruff, Anna Florence *WomWWA 14*
Woodruff, Anne Helena 1850- *NatCAB 17,*
WhAm 4, WomWWA 14
Woodruff, Carle Augustus 1841-1913 *WhAm 1*

Woodruff, Caroline Salome 1866-1949
BiDAmEd, WhAm 2, WomWWA 14
Woodruff, Charles Albert 1845-1920 *WhAm 1*
Woodruff, Charles Edward 1860-1915 *DcAmB,*
WhAm 1
Woodruff, Clinton Rogers 1868- *WhAm 2*
Woodruff, Edwin Blanchard 1872- *WhAm 5*
Woodruff, Edwin Hamlin 1862-1941 *WhAm 1*
Woodruff, Ellen E Hamilton 1853-
WomWWA 14
Woodruff, Elmer Grant 1872-1952 *WhAm 3*
Woodruff, Ernest 1863- *WhAm 4*
Woodruff, Francis Eben 1844-1914 *WhAm 1*
Woodruff, Frank Edward 1855-1922
NatCAB 20, WhAm 4
Woodruff, Frederick William 1886-1959
NatCAB 49, WhAm 3
Woodruff, George 1807-1887 *ApCAB*
Woodruff, George 1881-1946 *NatCAB 39,*
WhAm 2
Woodruff, George Augustus 1840-1863 *ApCAB*
Woodruff, George Catlin 1805-1885 *BiAUS,*
BiDrAC, WhAm H
Woodruff, George Hobart 1873-1944 *WhAm 2*
Woodruff, George Washington 1864-1934
NatCAB 26, WhAm 1
Woodruff, Harvey T 1875-1937 *WhAm 1*
Woodruff, Helen Smith 1888-1924 *WhAm 1,*
WomWWA 14
Woodruff, Henry Mygatt 1869-1916 *WhAm 1*
Woodruff, Hiram 1817-1867 *ApCAB, Drake*
Woodruff, Isaac Ogden 1881- *WhAm 6*
Woodruff, Israel Carle 1815-1878 *ApCAB*
Woodruff, James Albert 1877-1969 *WhAm 5*
Woodruff, James Gilbert 1842-1918
NatCAB 24
Woodruff, James Parsons 1868-1931
NatCAB 35
Woodruff, Jane Scott *WomWWA 14*
Woodruff, John 1826-1868 *BiAUS, BiDrAC,*
WhAm H
Woodruff, John Grant 1898-1971 *NatCAB 56*
Woodruff, John Irwin 1864-1962 *NatCAB 48*
Woodruff, John Sitcher 1870-1929 *NatCAB 21*
Woodruff, John T 1868-1949 *WhAm 2*
Woodruff, Joseph Talmage Battis 1894-1937
WhAm 1
Woodruff, Julia Louisa Matilda 1833- *WhAm 1*
Woodruff, Lewis Bartholomew 1809-1875
BiAUS, NatCAB 29
Woodruff, Libbie L 1860- *AmWom*
Woodruff, Lorande Loss 1879-1947 *DcAmB S4,*
WhAm 2
Woodruff, Lucy Seymour Benjamin 1877-
WomWWA 14
Woodruff, M *NewYHSD*
Woodruff, Marston True 1905-1973 *WhAm 6*
Woodruff, Nathan H 1913-1967 *WhAm 4*
Woodruff, Olive 1905-1964 *WhAm 4*
Woodruff, Ray Orchard 1876-1953 *WhAmP*
Woodruff, Robert Eastman 1884-1967
WhAm 4A
Woodruff, Robert Thomson 1885-1948
NatCAB 41
Woodruff, Rollin Simmons 1854-1925
NatCAB 14, WhAm 1
Woodruff, Roy Orchard 1876-1953 *BiDrAC,*
NatCAB 39, WhAm 3
Woodruff, S *NewYHSD*
Woodruff, Theodore Tuttle 1811-1892 *DcAmB,*
NatCAB 14, WhAm H
Woodruff, Thomas Adams 1865-1941 *WhAm 1*
Woodruff, Thomas M 1804-1855 *BiAUS,*
BiDrAC, WhAm H
Woodruff, Timothy Lester 1858-1913
ApCAB Sup, DcAmB, NatCAB 14,
WhAm 1
Woodruff, Wilford 1807-1898 *AmBi, ApCAB,*
DcAmB, NatCAB 7, NatCAB 16,
REnAW, WhAm H
Woodruff, William *NewYHSD*
Woodruff, William E A *NewYHSD*
Woodruff, William Edward 1795-1885 *DcAmB,*
NatCAB 8, REnAW, WhAm H
Woodruff, William Edward 1832-1907
NatCAB 8
Woodruff, William Wight 1872- *WhAm 5*

Woodrum, Clifton Alexander 1887-1950
BiDrAC, WhAm 3, WhAmP
Woodry, Norman Lee 1890-1949 *NatCAB 37*
Woods, A Alfred 1876-1956 *NatCAB 47*
Woods, Abel 1765-1850 *ApCAB X*
Woods, Adella B *WomWWA 14*
Woods, Alan Churchill 1889-1963 *NatCAB 50,*
WhAm 4
Woods, Albert Fred 1866-1948 *BiDAmEd,*
WhAm 2
Woods, Albert Frederick 1866-1948
NatCAB 46
Woods, Alfred W 1857-1942 *WhAm 3*
Woods, Alice 1871- *WhAm 5*
Woods, Alva 1794-1887 *ApCAB, ApCAB X,*
DcAmB, Drake, NatCAB 4, NatCAB 12,
WhAm H
Woods, Alvah 1794-1887 *TwCBDA*
Woods, Andrew Henry 1872- *WhAm 5*
Woods, Andrew Salter 1803-1863 *ApCAB,*
BiAUS, Drake, NatCAB 12
Woods, Arthur 1870-1942 *WhAm 2*
Woods, Baldwin Munger 1887-1956 *WhAm 3*
Woods, Bertha Gerneaux d1952 *WhAm 3,*
WomWWA 14
Woods, Bill Milton 1924-1974 *DcAmLiB,*
WhAm 6
Woods, Charles Albert 1852-1925 *WhAm 1*
Woods, Charles Carroll 1838-1927 *WhAm 1*
Woods, Charles Dayton 1856-1925 *WhAm 1*
Woods, Charles Robert 1827-1885 *ApCAB,*
DcAmB, TwCBDA, WhAm H
Woods, Charles Robert 1830?-1885 *Drake*
Woods, Cyrus E 1861-1938 *NatCAB 44,*
WhAm 1
Woods, David Walker, Jr. 1860- *WhAm 4*
Woods, Edgar Hall 1864-1939 *WhAm 3*
Woods, Edgar Lyons 1882-1964 *WhAm 5*
Woods, Edward Augustus 1865-1927 *WhAm 1*
Woods, Edwin Brewster 1850- *NatCAB 10*
Woods, Eleanor Howard Bush 1873-
WomWWA 14
Woods, Emily Louisa 1847- *WomWWA 14*
Woods, Fanny Soutter Sinclair 1878-
WomWWA 14
Woods, Francis Marion 1843- *WhAm 4*
Woods, Frank Emerson 1860- *ApCAB X*
Woods, Frank Henry 1868-1952 *WhAm 3*
Woods, Frank Plowman 1868-1944 *BiDrAC,*
WhAm 4, WhAmP
Woods, Frederic Jordan 1907-1971 *NatCAB 57*
Woods, Frederick Adams 1873-1939
NatCAB 33, WhAm 1
Woods, Frederick Shenstone 1864-1950
WhAm 3
Woods, George 1813-1899 *NatCAB 21*
Woods, George Benjamin 1878-1958
NatCAB 49, WhAm 3
Woods, George Herbert 1878- *WhAm 6*
Woods, George Lemuel 1832-1890 *BiAUS,*
NatCAB 8
Woods, Granville Cecil 1900-1975 *WhAm 6*
Woods, Harriet DeKrafft 1860- *WomWWA 14*
Woods, Harry Irwin 1870- *WhAm 5*
Woods, Henry 1764-1826 *BiAUS, BiDrAC,*
WhAm H
Woods, Henry 1838-1916 *WhAm 1*
Woods, Henry Cochrane 1895-1968 *WhAm 5*
Woods, Henry Ernest 1857-1919 *WhAm 1*
Woods, Hiram 1857-1931 *NatCAB 28,*
WhAm 1
Woods, Homer Boughner 1869-1941 *WhAm 2*
Woods, Ignatius *NewYHSD*
Woods, Isabelle Batchelder *WomWWA 14*
Woods, J Albert 1897-1964 *WhAm 4*
Woods, James 1793-1875 *NatCAB 9*
Woods, James 1867-1940 *NatCAB 29*
Woods, James Haughton 1864-1935 *DcAmB S1,*
WhAm 1
Woods, James Pleasant 1868-1948 *BiDrAC,*
WhAm 2
Woods, Jesse Wayne 1882-1950 *NatCAB 39*
Woods, John 1761-1816 *BiAUS, BiDrAC,*
WhAm H
Woods, John 1794-1855 *BiAUS, BiDrAC,*
NatCAB 3, WhAm H, WhAmP
Woods, John Carter Brown 1851-1930
ApCAB X, WhAm 1

Woods, John Rodes 1815-1885 *ApCAB*
Woods, John William 1875-1933 *NatCAB 25*
Woods, Joseph Jackson 1823-1889 *ApCAB Sup*
Woods, Kate Tannatt 1838-1910 *AmWom,*
WhAm 1
Woods, Katharine Pearson 1853-1923 *NotAW,*
WhAm 1, WomWWA 14
Woods, Lawrence Crane 1869-1925 *NatCAB 33*
Woods, Leonard 1774-1854 *AmBi, ApCAB,*
DcAmB, DcAmReB, Drake, NatCAB 9,
TwCBDA, WhAm H
Woods, Leonard 1807-1878 *AmBi, ApCAB,*
BiDAmEd, DcAmB, Drake, NatCAB 1,
TwCBDA, WhAm H
Woods, Littleton A 1884-1959 *WhAm 4*
Woods, Louis Earnest 1895-1971 *NatCAB 56,*
WhAm 5
Woods, Luther Eugene 1883-1946 *NatCAB 36*
Woods, Margaret B Allen 1860- *WomWWA 14*
Woods, Maria Louisa 1846- *WomWWA 14*
Woods, Mark White 1870- *WhAm 5*
Woods, Marshall 1824-1899 *ApCAB X*
Woods, Matthew 1849-1916 *WhAm 1*
Woods, Micajah 1776-1837 *ApCAB*
Woods, Michael Leonard 1833- *WhAm 4*
Woods, Neander Montgomery 1844- *WhAm 1*
Woods, Robert Archey 1865-1925 *AmBi,*
DcAmB, EncAB, McGEWB, WhAm 1
Woods, Robert Clisson 1882- *WhoColR*
Woods, Robert Patterson 1870-1958 *WhAm 3*
Woods, Robert Stuart 1819- *ApCAB*
Woods, Roma Wheeler 1835- *WomWWA 14*
Woods, Rufus 1878-1950 *REnAW, WhAm 3*
Woods, Sam Edison 1892-1953 *NatCAB 45,*
WhAm 3
Woods, Samuel 1686-1763 *ApCAB X*
Woods, Samuel, II 1722-1808 *ApCAB X*
Woods, Samuel Davis 1845-1915 *BiDrAC,*
NatCAB 16
Woods, Samuel Ellsworth 1871- *WhoColR*
Woods, Samuel VanHorn 1856-1937
NatCAB 31, WhAm 1
Woods, Solomon Adams 1827-1907 *NatCAB 14*
Woods, Thomas Cochrane 1895-1958 *WhAm 3*
Woods, Thomas Francis 1882-1949 *WhAm 2*
Woods, Thomas Hall 1836-1910 *NatCAB 12,*
WhAm 1
Woods, Thomas Leo 1905-1966 *NatCAB 53*
Woods, Thomas Smith 1868- *WhAm 4*
Woods, Tighe Edward 1910-1974 *WhAm 6*
Woods, Virna 1864-1903 *WhAm 1*
Woods, W B 1824-1887 *BiAUS*
Woods, Walter Leslie James 1897-1971
WhAm 5
Woods, Walter Orr 1873-1951 *NatCAB 40,*
WhAm 3
Woods, William 1738-1819 *ApCAB*
Woods, William 1790-1837 *BiAUS, BiDrAC,*
WhAm H
Woods, William Allen 1837-1901 *DcAmB,*
NatCAB 18, WhAm H
Woods, William Burnham 1824-1887 *AmBi,*
ApCAB, DcAmB, NatCAB 2, TwCBDA,
WebAB, WhAm H
Woods, William Daniel 1867- *WhoColR*
Woods, William Francis 1876-1942 *NatCAB 33*
Woods, William George 1904-1970 *WhAm 5*
Woods, William Hervey 1852- *WhAm 4*
Woods, William Seaver 1872-1962 *NatCAB 47,*
WhAm 4
Woods, William Sharpless Derrick 1901-1971
NatCAB 57, WhAm 5
Woods, William Stone 1840-1917 *NatCAB 6,*
WhAm 1
Woods, William Wells 1841-1920 *NatCAB 19,*
WhAm 1
Woods, William Whitfield 1889-1939
NatCAB 29, WhAm 1
Woodside, Abraham 1819-1853 *NewYHSD*
Woodside, John Archibald 1781-1852 *IIBEAAW,*
NewYHSD, WhAm H
Woodside, John Archibald, Jr. *NewYHSD*
Woodside, John Thomas 1864-1946 *WhAm 2*
Woodside, John Thomas 1890-1956 *NatCAB 45,*
WhAm 3
Woodside, John W 1838- *WhAm 4*
Woodside, Jonathan F *BiAUS*
Woodside, Nova Stuart 1868- *WomWWA 14*

Woodside, Robert I 1873-1949 *WhAm 3*
Woodsmall, Hubert Howes 1875-1961
NatCAB 47
Woodsmall, Ruth Frances 1883-1963 *WhAm 4*
Woodson, Archelaus Marius 1854-1925
NatCAB 20, WhAm 1
Woodson, Aytch P 1881-1958 *WhAm 3*
Woodson, Carter Godwin 1875-1950 *BiDAmEd,*
DcAmB S4, EncAB, NatCAB 38,
WebAB, WhAm 3
Woodson, Carter Goodwin 1875-1950 *WhoColR*
Woodson, Frederick Venable 1900-1957
NatCAB 43
Woodson, George Frederick 1861- *WhAm 4*
Woodson, Mary Blake 1886- *WhAm 1*
Woodson, Omer Lee 1895-1951 *WhAm 3*
Woodson, Robert Everard, Jr. 1904-1963
WhAm 4
Woodson, Samuel Hughes 1777-1827 *BiAUS,*
BiDrAC, WhAm H
Woodson, Samuel Hughes 1815-1881 *BiAUS,*
BiDrAC, WhAm H
Woodson, Silas 1819-1896 *BiAUS,*
NatCAB 12
Woodson, Stewart Floyd 1859- *NatCAB 5*
Woodson, Urey 1859-1939 *NatCAB 29,*
WhAm 1
Woodson, Walter Browne 1881-1948 *WhAm 2*
Woodson, Walter Henderson 1875-1964
NatCAB 52
Woodson, Walter Worsham 1876-1937
WhAm 1
Woodsworth, James Shaver 1874-1942
McGEWB
Woodville, Richard Caton 1825?-1855 *ApCAB,*
BnEnAmA, Drake
Woodville, Richard Caton 1825?-1856
NewYHSD
Woodville, Richard Caton, Jr. 1856-1937
IIBEAAW
Woodward, Adele Mortimer *WomWWA 14*
Woodward, Allan Harvey 1876-1950 *WhAm 3*
Woodward, Ashbel 1804-1885 *ApCAB, Drake*
Woodward, Augustus Brevoort d1827 *BiAUS*
Woodward, Augustus Brevoort 1774-1827
DcAmB, WhAm H
Woodward, Augustus Brevoort 1775?-1827
ApCAB
Woodward, Benjamin Duryea 1868-1948
WhAm 2
Woodward, Calvin Milton 1837- *ApCAB,*
NatCAB 9
Woodward, Calvin Milton 1837-1914 *BiDAmEd,*
DcAmB, EncAB
Woodward, Calvin Milton 1837-1915 *WhAm 1*
Woodward, Carl Raymond 1890-1974 *WhAm 6*
Woodward, Caroline M Clark 1840- *AmWom*
Woodward, Caroline Marshall 1828-1890
AmWom
Woodward, Charles Edgar 1876-1942 *WhAm 2*
Woodward, Chester 1876-1940 *WhAm 1*
Woodward, Clark Howell 1877-1967 *WhAm 4*
Woodward, Clement Josiah 1850-1927
NatCAB 22
Woodward, Clifford Dewey 1878-1949
NatCAB 43, WhAm 2
Woodward, Comer McDonald 1874- *WhAm 5*
Woodward, Comer Vann 1908- *EncAAH,*
McGEWB, WebAB
Woodward, Cora Stranahan 1863-
WomWWA 14
Woodward, D Lucile Field 1883-
WomWWA 14
Woodward, David 1856-1931 *NatCAB 23*
Woodward, David Acheson 1823-1909
NewYHSD
Woodward, Donald Bosley 1905-1974 *WhAm 6*
Woodward, Dudley Kezer, Jr. 1881- *WhAm 6*
Woodward, E F *NewYHSD*
Woodward, Edmund Lee 1873-1948 *WhAm 2*
Woodward, Edward Milton 1846-1923
NatCAB 20
Woodward, Eliza Brand 1811-1897 *ApCAB Sup*
Woodward, Elizabeth Ash 1878- *WhAm 6*
Woodward, Ellen Sullivan d1971 *WhAm 5*
Woodward, Ellsworth 1861-1939 *WhAm 1*
Woodward, Elmer Ellsworth 1882-1940
NatCAB 31

Woodward, Emerson Francis 1879-1943
NatCAB 43
Woodward, Ernest 1877-1968 *WhAm 5*
Woodward, Fletcher Drummond 1895-1969
NatCAB 55, WhAm 5
Woodward, Frank Lincoln 1866-1930 *WhAm 1*
Woodward, Franklin Cowles 1849- *NatCAB 1,
NatCAB 11, WhAm 4*
Woodward, Franklin Tuthill 1882-1945
NatCAB 39
Woodward, Frederic 1874-1956 *WhAm 3*
Woodward, George 1863-1952 *WhAm 3*
Woodward, George Abishai 1835-1916
NatCAB 10, WhAm 1
Woodward, George Washington 1809-1875
*ApCAB, BiAUS, BiDrAC, Drake Sup,
NatCAB 11, WhAm H*
Woodward, Gilbert Motier 1835-1913 *BiDrAC*
Woodward, Guy 1889-1964 *NatCAB 53*
Woodward, Harold Christopher 1901-1964
WhAm 4
Woodward, Helen D *WomWWA 14*
Woodward, Helen E Baldwin 1855-
WomWWA 14
Woodward, Henry *NewYHSD*
Woodward, Henry 1646?-1686? *DcAmB,
WhAm H*
Woodward, Henry Lynde 1876-1971
NatCAB 56
Woodward, Howard Spencer 1877-1942
NatCAB 31
Woodward, Hugh Beistle 1885-1968 *WhAm 5*
Woodward, Hugh McCurdy 1881-1940
WhAm 1
Woodward, Jack Edward 1921-1972 *WhAm 6*
Woodward, James Gardner 1845-1923
NatCAB 19
Woodward, James Thomas 1837-1910
NatCAB 15, WhAm 1
Woodward, John 1665-1728 *DcScB*
Woodward, John 1859-1923 *NatCAB 6,
WhAm 1*
Woodward, John Blackburne 1835-1896
NatCAB 15
Woodward, John Butler 1861-1925 *NatCAB 20,
WhAm 1*
Woodward, John Charles 1866-1939 *WhAm 1*
Woodward, John Douglas 1846-1924
NatCAB 20
Woodward, John Douglas 1848-1924 *IIBEAAW*
Woodward, John Franklin 1866-1962
NatCAB 52
Woodward, Joseph Addison 1806-1885 *BiAUS,
BiDrAC, WhAm H, WhAmP*
Woodward, Joseph Hersey 1843-1917
NatCAB 28
Woodward, Joseph Hersey, II 1912-1965
WhAm 4
Woodward, Joseph Hooker 1882-1928 *WhAm 1*
Woodward, Joseph Janvier 1833-1884 *AmBi,
ApCAB, DcAmB, NatCAB 11, TwCBDA,
WhAm H*
Woodward, Julian Laurence 1900-1952
NatCAB 40
Woodward, Julius Hayden 1858-1916 *WhAm 1*
Woodward, Karl Wilson 1881- *WhAm 6*
Woodward, Katharine Shepherd *WomWWA 14*
Woodward, Lee Roy 1885-1958 *NatCAB 48*
Woodward, Lester Armand 1908-1971 *WhAm 5*
Woodward, Lion LaForge 1879-1927
NatCAB 20
Woodward, Sir Llewellyn 1890-1971 *WhAm 5*
Woodward, Luther Ellis 1897-1961 *WhAm 4*
Woodward, Martha Bond 1851- *WomWWA 14*
Woodward, Nellie F *WomWWA 14*
Woodward, P Henry 1833-1917 *NatCAB 25,
WhAm 1*
Woodward, Paul Maxwell 1894-1955
NatCAB 44
Woodward, Rell Madison 1862-1915
NatCAB 34
Woodward, Rignal Thomas 1838-1904
NatCAB 17
Woodward, Robert B 1840-1915 *WhAm 1*
Woodward, Robert Burns 1917- *AsBiEn,
WebAB*
Woodward, Robert Simpson 1849-1924 *AmBi,
ApCAB Sup, DcAmB, DcScB,*

NatCAB 13, WhAm 1
Woodward, Robert Strong 1885-1957 *WhAm 3*
Woodward, Roland Beavan 1873- *WhAm 3*
Woodward, Samuel Bayard 1787-1850 *ApCAB,
DcAmB, Drake, WhAm H*
Woodward, Samuel Bayard 1853-1946 *WhAm 3*
Woodward, Samuel Lippincott 1840-1924
WhAm 1
Woodward, Samuel W 1750-1835 *ApCAB,
Drake*
Woodward, Samuel Walter 1848-1917
NatCAB 14, WhAm 1
Woodward, Sherman Melville 1871-1953
NatCAB 42
Woodward, Stanley 1833- *WhAm 1*
Woodward, Stanley 1886-1963 *WhAm 4*
Woodward, Stanley Wingate 1890-1970
NatCAB 56
Woodward, Thomas Mullen 1884-1975
WhAm 6
Woodward, Walter Carleton 1878-1942
WhAm 2
Woodward, William *BiAUS, BiDrAC,
WhAm H*
Woodward, William 1770-1833 *NatCAB 5*
Woodward, William 1859-1939 *WhAm 1*
Woodward, William 1876-1953 *DcAmB S5,
NatCAB 40*
Woodward, William Creighton 1867-1949
NatCAB 38, WhAm 2
Woodward, William Edward 1874-1950
NatCAB 38, WhAm 3
Woodward, William Finch 1863-1940 *WhAm 1*
Woodward, William Henry 1834- *NatCAB 12*
Woodward-Moore, Annie Aubertine 1841-
ApCAB, NotAW
Woodward-Vauthier, Lucy Mary
WomWWA 14
Woodwell, Bertha Murtland *WomWWA 14*
Woodwell, John 1860-1932 *NatCAB 29*
Woodworth, Adelaide Eliza 1844-
WomWWA 14
Woodworth, Caroline Josephine Rodgers 1878-
WomWWA 14
Woodworth, Chauncey Booth 1819- *NatCAB 5*
Woodworth, Clyde Melvin 1888-1960 *WhAm 4*
Woodworth, Edward Knowlton 1875-1938
WhAm 1
Woodworth, Floyd Horatio 1888-1960
NatCAB 48
Woodworth, Francis C 1812-1859 *ApCAB,
NatCAB 5*
Woodworth, Frank Goodrich 1853-1930
WhAm 1
Woodworth, G Wallace 1902-1969 *WhAm 5*
Woodworth, Harry Clark 1885-1953
NatCAB 42
Woodworth, Herbert Grafton 1860- *WhAm 3*
Woodworth, James Grant 1864- *WhAm 4*
Woodworth, James Hutchinson 1804-1869
BiAUS, BiDrAC, NatCAB 3, WhAm H
Woodworth, Jay Backus 1865-1925 *DcAmB,
NatCAB 20, WhAm 1*
Woodworth, John 1768-1858 *ApCAB, BiAUS,
Drake*
Woodworth, John Dawson Roswell 1875-1950
NatCAB 39
Woodworth, John Maynard 1837-1879 *ApCAB*
Woodworth, Kennard 1905-1956 *WhAm 3*
Woodworth, Laurin Dewey 1837-1897 *BiAUS,
BiDrAC, WhAm H*
Woodworth, Margaret Kennard 1875-
WomWWA 14
Woodworth, Mary Parker *WomWWA 14*
Woodworth, Melvin J 1880- *WhAm 3*
Woodworth, Newell Bertram 1860-1925
WhAm 1
Woodworth, Philip Bell 1865-1937 *WhAm 1*
Woodworth, Robert Sessions 1869-1962
*ApCAB X, BiDAmEd, NatCAB 48,
WhAm 4*
Woodworth, Samuel 1784-1842 *AmBi, DcAmB,
TwCBDA, WhAm H*
Woodworth, Samuel 1785-1842 *ApCAB, Drake,
NatCAB 1*
Woodworth, Selim E 1815-1871 *ApCAB*
Woodworth, Stewart Campbell 1888-1963
WhAm 4

Woodworth, Thomas Bishop 1907-1967
NatCAB 53
Woodworth, William W 1807-1873 *BiAUS,
BiDrAC, WhAm H*
Woody, Clifford 1884-1948 *BiDAmEd,
NatCAB 37, WhAm 2*
Woody, Frank H 1833- *WhAm 4*
Woody, Mary Williams Chawner 1846-
AmWom
Woody, McIver 1886-1970 *WhAm 5*
Woody, Solomon 1828-1901 *NewYHSD*
Woody, Walter Thomas 1891-1960 *WhAm 4*
Woody, Walton L 1891-1954 *WhAm 3*
Woodyard, Harry Chapman 1867-1929 *BiDrAC,
WhAm 1, WhAmP*
Woodyatt, Rollin Turner 1878-1953 *WhAm 3*
Woofter, Thomas Jackson 1862-1938 *WhAm 1*
Wool, John Ellis 1784-1869 *AmBi, ApCAB,
DcAmB, NatCAB 4, REnAW, TwCBDA,
WebAMB, WhAm H*
Wool, John Ellis 1788-1869 *Drake*
Wool, Theodore Jackson 1865-1943 *NatCAB 42*
Woolard, Warden 1897-1965 *WhAm 4*
Woolbert, Charles Henry 1877-1929 *WhAm 1*
Wooldridge, Charles William 1847-1908
WhAm 1
Wooldridge, Edmund Tyler 1897-1968 *WhAm 5*
Wooldridge, William Flournoy 1899-1971
NatCAB 57
Woolever, Harry Earl 1881-1941 *WhAm 1*
Wooley *NewYHSD*
Wooley, Joseph *NewYHSD*
Woolf, Albert Edward 1846-1920 *WhAm 1*
Woolf, Benjamin Edward 1836-1901 *DcAmB,
NatCAB 1, WhAm H*
Woolf, Herbert M 1880- *WhAm 6*
Woolf, Merritt Edgar 1875-1935 *NatCAB 42*
Woolf, Michael Angelo 1837-1899 *NewYHSD*
Woolf, Philip 1848-1903 *WhAm 1*
Woolf, Samuel Johnson 1880-1948 *NatCAB 36,
WhAm 2*
Woolf, Solomon 1841- *ApCAB*
Woolf, Virginia Stephen 1882-1941 *McGEWB*
Woolfolk, William Gordon 1877-1954 *WhAm 3*
Woolford, John Samuel Benjamin 1871-1932
NatCAB 50
Woollard, William Edward 1876-1940
NatCAB 31, WhAm 1
Woollcott, Alexander Humphreys 1887-1943
DcAmB S3, WebAB, WhAm 2
Woollen, Charles Thomas 1878-1938
NatCAB 29
Woollen, Evans 1864-1942 *WhAm 2*
Woollen, Evans, Jr. 1897-1959 *NatCAB 55,
WhAm 3*
Woollett, William *NewYHSD*
Woollett, William 1815-1874 *WhAm H*
Woollett, William M 1850-1880 *WhAm H*
Woolley, Alice Stone d1946 *WhAm 2*
Woolley, Celia Parker 1848-1918 *AmWom,
DcAmB, WhAm 1, WomWWA 14*
Woolley, Charles H 1872-1952 *WhAm 3*
Woolley, Charles Leonard 1880-1960 *DcScB*
Woolley, Clarence Mott 1863-1956 *NatCAB 46,
WhAm 5*
Woolley, D Wayne 1914-1966 *WhAm 4*
Woolley, Edward Mott 1867-1947 *WhAm 2*
Woolley, Edwin Campbell 1878-1916 *WhAm 1*
Woolley, Helen Bradford Thompson 1874-1947
*BiDAmEd, NotAW, WhAm 3,
WomWWA 14*
Woolley, Herbert Codey 1881-1954 *WhAm 3*
Woolley, Jacob Benjamin 1881- *NatCAB 11*
Woolley, John Granville 1850-1922 *DcAmB,
NatCAB 20, TwCBDA, WhAm 1*
Woolley, Lazelle Thayer 1872- *WhAm 5*
Woolley, Mary Emma 1863-1947 *BiDAmEd,
DcAmB S4, NatCAB 13, NatCAB 37,
NotAW, TwCBDA, WhAm 2,
WomWWA 14*
Woolley, Monty 1888-1963 *WhAm 4*
Woolley, Paul Gerhardt 1875-1932 *WhAm 1*
Woolley, Ralph Edwin 1886-1957 *NatCAB 43*
Woolley, Robert Wickliffe 1871-1958 *WhAm 3*
Woolley, Sue Dana 1857- *WomWWA 14*
Woolley, Victor Baynard 1867-1945 *WhAm 2*
Woolley, William *NewYHSD*
Woolman, C E d1966 *WhAm 4, WhAm 6*

Woolman, Edward Wetherill 1838-1924
NatCAB 24
Woolman, Henry Newbold 1875-1953
NatCAB 44, WhAm 3
Woolman, John 1720-1772 *AmBi, ApCAB,
DcAmB, DcAmReB, Drake, EncAB,
McGEWB, NatCAB 1, WebAB,
WhAm H*
Woolman, Mary Raphael Schenck 1860-1940
*BiCAW, BiDAmEd, NotAW, WhAm 4,
WomWWA 14*
Woolner, Adolph 1907-1963 *WhAm 4*
Woolner, Samuel 1845-1911 *ApCAB X*
Woolnoth, T *NewYHSD*
Woolridge, Harold Dale 1890-1963 *NatCAB 55*
Woolridge, J Hayes 1890-1958 *NatCAB 48*
Woolrych, Francis Humphry William 1864-1941
WhAm 2
Woolsey, Abby Howland 1828-1893 *NotAW*
Woolsey, Elliott Hartman 1843- *NatCAB 7*
Woolsey, George 1861-1950 *NatCAB 39,
WhAm 5*
Woolsey, Georgeanna Muirson 1833-1906
NotAW
Woolsey, Ida C 1852- *WomWWA 14*
Woolsey, Jane Stuart 1830-1891 *NotAW*
Woolsey, John Munro 1877-1945 *DcAmB S3,
WhAm HA, WhAm 2, WhAm 4A*
Woolsey, Lester Hood 1877-1961 *WhAm 4*
Woolsey, Melanchton Brooks 1817-1874
ApCAB
Woolsey, Melanchton Taylor 1780-1838
TwCBDA
Woolsey, Melanchton Taylor 1782-1838 *ApCAB*
Woolsey, Melancthon Brooks 1817-1874 *Drake*
Woolsey, Melancthon Taylor 1780-1838 *DcAmB,
WhAm H*
Woolsey, Melancthon Taylor 1782?-1838 *Drake,
NatCAB 8*
Woolsey, Minthorne 1853-1927 *NatCAB 21*
Woolsey, Ray Taliaferro 1891-1957 *NatCAB 49*
Woolsey, Robert Cushman 1881-1960
NatCAB 47
Woolsey, Ross Arlington 1877-1942
NatCAB 32, WhAm 2
Woolsey, Sarah Chauncey 1835-1905 *AmBi,
NotAW*
Woolsey, Sarah Chauncey 1845-1905 *AmWom,
NatCAB 11, WhAm 1*
Woolsey, Sarah Chauncy 1835-1905 *DcAmB*
Woolsey, Theodore Dwight 1801-1889 *AmBi,
ApCAB, BiDAmEd, DcAmB, Drake,
NatCAB 1, TwCBDA, WebAB,
WhAm H*
Woolsey, Theodore Salisbury 1852-1929 *AmBi,
DcAmB, NatCAB 31, WhAm 1*
Woolsey, Theodore Salisbury 1879-1933
NatCAB 26, WhAm 1
Woolsey, Thomasene Harper Rigby 1859-
WomWWA 14
Woolson, Abba Louisa Goold 1838-1921
ApCAB, DcAmB, NotAW, WhAm 3
Woolson, Abba Louise Goold 1838-1921
AmWom
Woolson, Constance Fenimore 1838-1894
TwCBDA
Woolson, Constance Fenimore 1840-1894 *AmBi,
DcAmB, NotAW, WhAm H*
Woolson, Constance Fenimore 1848-1894
AmWom, ApCAB, NatCAB 1
Woolson, Ezra 1824-1845 *NewYHSD*
Woolson, Harry Thurber 1876- *WhAm 5*
Woolson, Ira Harvey 1856-1927 *NatCAB 22,
WhAm 1*
Woolson, L Irving 1904-1966 *NatCAB 53,
WhAm 4*
Woolston, Florence Guy 1881- *WomWWA 14*
Woolston, Howard Brown 1876- *WhAm 5*
Woolston, William Jenks 1908-1964
NatCAB 53
Woolverton, Corinne Kibbe *WomWWA 14*
Woolverton, Samuel 1864-1952 *NatCAB 38*
Woolwine, Thomas Lee 1874-1925 *WhAm 1*
Woolwine, William David 1855-1927 *WhAm 1*
Woolworth, Charles Sumner 1856-1947
NatCAB 38, WhAm 2
Woolworth, Frank Winfield 1852-1919 *AmBi,
DcAmB, EncAB, McGEWB, NatCAB 11,*

NatCAB 23, WebAB, WhAm 1
Woolworth, Frederick Jonathan 1869-1928
NatCAB 22
Woolworth, James Mills 1829-1906 *NatCAB 3,
NatCAB 11, WhAm 1*
Woolworth, Norman Bailey 1901-1962
NatCAB 47
Woolydie, M *NewYHSD*
Woomer, Ephraim Milton 1844-1897 *BiDrAC,
WhAm H*
Woon, Basil d1974 *WhAm 6*
Woosley, John Brooks 1892-1956 *WhAm 3*
Woosley, William Bryant 1904-1972 *WhAm 6*
Wooster, Charles 1843-1922 *NatCAB 20*
Wooster, Charles Whiting 1780-1848 *DcAmB,
WebAMB, WhAm H*
Wooster, Charles Whiting 1785-1848 *ApCAB*
Wooster, David 1710-1777 *ApCAB, Drake,
NatCAB 1, TwCBDA*
Wooster, David 1711-1777 *AmBi, DcAmB,
WebAMB, WhAm H*
Wooster, David 1825- *ApCAB*
Wooster, Lizzie E 1870- *WomWWA 14*
Wooster, Lorraine Elizabeth 1874- *WhAm 5*
Wooster, Lyman Child 1849- *WhAm 4*
Wooster, William Henry Harrison 1840-1919
NatCAB 33
Wootan, James Blythe 1873-1934 *WhAm 1*
Wootan, James K 1911-1971 *WhAm 5*
Wootassite *DcAmB*
Wooten, Benjamin Allen 1891-1947 *NatCAB 36,
WhAm 2*
Wooten, Benjamin Harrison 1894-1971
WhAm 5
Wooten, Dudley Goodall 1860-1929 *BiDrAC*
Wooten, Horace Oliver 1865-1947 *WhAm 2*
Wooten, June Price 1878-1950 *WhAm 3*
Wooten, M Frank 1881-1961 *NatCAB 46*
Wooten, Ralph H 1893-1969 *WhAm 5*
Wooten, William Arthur 1888-1962
NatCAB 50
Wooten, William Preston 1873-1950 *WhAm 3*
Wooton, Paul 1881-1961 *WhAm 4*
Wootten, Richard Kelly 1863-1934 *NatCAB 36*
Wootton, Bailey Peyton 1870-1949 *WhAm 2*
Wootton, Edwin Hartley 1886-1946 *NatCAB 39*
Wootton, Richens Lacy 1816-1893 *AmBi,
DcAmB, REnAW, WhAm H*
Worcester, Alfred 1855-1951 *WhAm 3*
Worcester, Charles Henry 1864-1956 *WhAm 3*
Worcester, David 1907-1947 *NatCAB 35,
WhAm 2*
Worcester, Dean Conant 1866-1924 *AmBi,
ApCAB Sup, NatCAB 20, TwCBDA,
WhAm 1*
Worcester, Edward Strong 1876-1937 *WhAm 1*
Worcester, Edwin Dean 1828-1904 *DcAmB,
NatCAB 3, NatCAB 25, WhAm 1*
Worcester, Edwin Dean 1856-1929 *NatCAB 25*
Worcester, Elwood 1862-1940 *DcAmB S2,
NatCAB 14, NatCAB 30, WhAm 1*
Worcester, Fernando E 1817?- *NewYHSD*
Worcester, Franklin 1845-1917 *WhAm 1*
Worcester, Harry Augustus 1862-1938
NatCAB 29, WhAm 1
Worcester, Henry E 1875- *WhAm 5*
Worcester, John 1834- *ApCAB*
Worcester, John Locke 1873-1947 *NatCAB 36*
Worcester, Joseph Emerson 1784-1865 *AmBi,
ApCAB, BiDAmEd, DcAmB, Drake,
NatCAB 6, TwCBDA, WebAB,
WhAm H*
Worcester, Joseph Ruggles 1860-1943 *WhAm 2*
Worcester, Noah 1758-1837 *AmBi, ApCAB,
DcAmB, Drake, NatCAB 1, TwCBDA,
WhAm H*
Worcester, Noah 1812-1847 *ApCAB,
NatCAB 1*
Worcester, P G 1884-1969 *WhAm 5*
Worcester, Samuel 1770-1821 *ApCAB,
DcAmB, Drake, NatCAB 1, WhAm H*
Worcester, Samuel Austin 1798-1859 *DcAmB,
NatCAB 1, WhAm H*
Worcester, Samuel Melancthon 1801-1866
ApCAB
Worcester, Samuel Thomas 1804-1882 *BiAUS,
BiDrAC, WhAm H*
Worcester, Thomas 1768-1831 *ApCAB,*

NatCAB 1, WhAm H
Worcester, Thomas 1795-1878 *ApCAB,
NatCAB 1*
Worcester, William Loring 1859-1939 *WhAm 1*
Worcester, Willis George 1918-1970 *WhAm 5*
Word, Thomas Jefferson *BiAUS, BiDrAC,
WhAm H*
Worden, Beverly Lyon 1871-1931 *WhAm 1*
Worden, Charles Beatty 1874- *WhAm 5*
Worden, Charles Howard 1859-1930 *WhAm 1*
Worden, Edward Chauncey 1875-1940 *WhAm 1*
Worden, James Avery 1841-1917 *NatCAB 20,
WhAm 1*
Worden, James Lorenzo 1819-1884 *NatCAB 18*
Worden, John Lorimer 1817-1897 *Drake,
NatCAB 4*
Worden, John Lorimer 1818-1897 *AmBi,
ApCAB, DcAmB, TwCBDA, WebAMB,
WhAm H*
Worden, Perry 1866-1945 *WhAm 2*
Worden, Ralph Percy 1899-1949 *NatCAB 38*
Worden, Sarah A 1853- *AmWom*
Wordin, Nathaniel Eugene 1844-1915
NatCAB 16, WhAm 1
Wordsworth, William 1770-1850 *McGEWB*
Wores, Theodore 1860?-1939 *IIBEAAW*
Work, Edgar Whitaker 1862-1934 *WhAm 1*
Work, Frederick Jerome *WhoColR*
Work, Henry Clay 1832-1884 *AmBi, ApCAB,
DcAmB, NatCAB 1, WebAB, WhAm H*
Work, Hubert 1860-1942 *ApCAB X,
BiDrUSE, DcAmB S3, WhAm 2*
Work, James Aiken 1904-1961 *NatCAB 50,
WhAm 4*
Work, James Anderson, Jr. 1883-1965
NatCAB 52
Work, Jeremiah Boston 1855-1929 *WhAm 1*
Work, John 1792?-1861 *REnAW*
Work, John McClelland 1869-1961 *NatCAB 49*
Work, John Wesley 1873- *WhoColR*
Work, John Wesley, III 1901-1967 *NatCAB 55*
Work, Milton Cooper 1864-1934 *AmBi,
DcAmB, WhAm 1*
Work, Monroe Nathan 1866-1945 *WhAm 2,
WhoColR*
Work, William Roth 1881-1948 *NatCAB 37,
WhAm 2*
Working, Daniel Webster 1862-1944 *WhAm 2*
Working, Elmer Joseph 1900-1968 *NatCAB 54*
Workman, Boyle 1868-1942 *NatCAB 31*
Workman, Fanny Bullock 1859-1925 *AmBi,
DcAmB, NotAW, WhAm 1,
WomWWA 14*
Workman, James Mims 1867- *WhAm 4*
Workman, Thomas 1813- *ApCAB*
Workman, W Hunter 1847- *WhAm 4*
Workman, William Henry 1874-1951
NatCAB 39
Workman, William Henry 1893-1918
ApCAB X, NatCAB 19
Works, George A 1877-1957 *WhAm 3*
Works, John Downey 1847-1928 *BiDrAC,
NatCAB 13, NatCAB 49, WhAm 1,
WhAmP*
Workum, Julius F 1866-1924 *ApCAB X,
NatCAB 48*
Worlds, Clint 1922- *IIBEAAW*
Worley, Clair L 1912-1963 *WhAm 4*
Worley, Francis Eugene 1908-1974 *BiDrAC,
WhAm 6*
Worley, George *NewYHSD*
Worley, Henry William 1877-1938 *WhAm 1*
Worley, John Stephen 1876-1956 *NatCAB 44,
WhAm 3*
Worley, Laura Davis *AmWom*
Worm, Ole 1588-1654 *DcScB*
Worman, Ben James 1870- *WhAm 5*
Worman, James Henry 1835-1930 *ApCAB*
Worman, James Henry 1845-1930 *TwCBDA,
WhAm 1*
Worman, Ludwig 1761-1822 *BiAUS, BiDrAC,
WhAm H*
Wormeley, Ariana Randolph 1835- *ApCAB*
Wormeley, James Preble 1826-1851 *NatCAB 9*
Wormeley, Katharine Prescott 1830-1908
*DcAmB, NatCAB 8, NotAW, TwCBDA,
WhAm 1*

Wormeley, Katharine Prescott 1832-1908
ApCAB
Wormeley, Katherine Prescott 1830-1908
AmWom, Drake
Wormeley, Mary Elizabeth 1822-1904 *ApCAB,*
DcAmB, Drake
Wormington, Frank Lonso 1875-1957
NatCAB 48
Wormley, Edward J 1908- *BnEnAmA*
Wormley, James 1819-1884 *DcAmB,*
WhAm H
Wormley, Roscoe Conklin 1882- *WhoColR*
Wormley, Theodore George 1826-1897 *ApCAB,*
DcAmB, NatCAB 13, WhAm H
Wormser, I Maurice 1887-1955 *WhAm 3*
Wormser, Leo Falk 1884-1934 *NatCAB 17,*
WhAm 1
Wormwood, Kenneth Mendum 1902-1970
NatCAB 56, WhAm 5
Worner, Jno 1888-1957 *WhAm 3*
Worrall, Ambrose Alexander 1899-1973
WhAm 5
Worrall, David Elbridge 1886-1944 *NatCAB 33,*
WhAm 2
Worrall, Henry 1825-1902 *IIBEAAW,*
NewYHSD, REnAW
Worrall, Joseph Howard 1885-1964 *WhAm 4*
Worrell, Charles 1819- *NewYHSD*
Worrell, Grover Cleveland 1885-1952
NatCAB 41
Worrell, Howard George 1887-1954
NatCAB 43
Worrell, James *NewYHSD*
Worrell, John *NewYHSD*
Worrell, Jonathan Pyle 1844-1924 *NatCAB 20*
Worrell, William Hoyt 1879-1953 *WhAm 3*
Worrilow, George Melville 1904-1975 *WhAm 6*
Worrilow, William Henry 1877- *WhAm 6*
Worsaae, Jens Jacob 1821-1885 *DcScB*
Worsham, William A 1878- *WhAm 6*
Worship *NewYHSD*
Worsley, Abinus A 1868- *WhAm 1*
Worsley, Wallace 1878-1944 *NatCAB 33*
Worst, John H 1850-1945 *WhAm 3*
Wortendyke, Jacob Reynier 1818-1868 *BiAUS,*
BiDrAC, WhAm H
Wortendyke, Reynier Jacob 1860-1952
NatCAB 44
Worth, David G *NewYHSD*
Worth, James Huntting 1918-1972 *WhAm 5*
Worth, Jonathan d1869 *Drake*
Worth, Jonathan 1797-1869 *BiAUS*
Worth, Jonathan 1802-1869 *ApCAB, BiDConf,*
DcAmB, NatCAB 4, TwCBDA,
WhAm H
Worth, Nicholas *WebAB*
Worth, Thomas 1834-1917 *ApCAB,*
NewYHSD
Worth, William E *WhAm 3*
Worth, William Jenkins 1794-1849 *AmBi,*
ApCAB, DcAmB, Drake, NatCAB 4,
WebAMB, WhAm H
Worth, William Penn 1856-1923 *NatCAB 33*
Worth, William Scott 1840-1904 *ApCAB Sup,*
WhAm 1
Wortham, James Lemuel 1911-1958 *WhAm 3*
Worthen, Amos Henry 1813-1888 *ApCAB,*
DcAmB, NatCAB 6, WhAm H
Worthen, Augusta Harvey 1823- *AmWom*
Worthen, Edmund Louis 1882-1965 *WhAm 4*
Worthen, George d1958 *WhAm 3*
Worthen, Thacher Washburn 1886-1964
NatCAB 51
Worthen, Thomas Wilson Dorr 1845-1927
NatCAB 27, WhAm 1
Worthen, William Booker 1852-1911 *NatCAB 8*
Worthen, William Ezra 1819-1897 *ApCAB,*
DcAmB, NatCAB 12
Worthing, Archie Garfield 1881-1949
NatCAB 41, WhAm 2
Worthington, Augustus Storrs 1843-1922
WhAm 1
Worthington, Charles Campbell 1854-1944
WhAm 2
Worthington, Edward William 1854-1906
NatCAB 7, WhAm 1
Worthington, Erastus 1779-1842 *ApCAB,*
Drake

Worthington, Frank Corbin 1866-1944
NatCAB 39
Worthington, George 1840-1908 *NatCAB 12,*
TwCBDA, WhAm 1
Worthington, George 1848-1908 *ApCAB*
Worthington, George 1855-1933 *NatCAB 27*
Worthington, George Cushing 1868-1942
NatCAB 32
Worthington, George Heber 1850-1924
WhAm 1
Worthington, H G 1828-1909 *BiAUS,*
NatCAB 12
Worthington, Harriet Elizabeth 1884-
WomWWA 14
Worthington, Henry Gaither 1828-1909 *BiDrAC*
Worthington, Henry Rossiter 1817-1880 *ApCAB,*
DcAmB, NatCAB 6, NatCAB 28,
WhAm H
Worthington, John 1719-1800 *DcAmB,*
NatCAB 5, WhAm H
Worthington, John 1848-1918 *NatCAB 17*
Worthington, John I 1857-1924 *WhAm 1*
Worthington, John Tolley Hood 1788-1849
BiAUS, BiDrAC, WhAm H, WhAmP
Worthington, Laura Katherine Madison 1865-
WomWWA 14
Worthington, Marjorie d1976 *WhAm 6*
Worthington, Nicholas Ellsworth 1836-1916
BiDrAC
Worthington, Thomas 1769?-1827 *BiAUS,*
NatCAB 3
Worthington, Thomas 1773-1827 *ApCAB,*
BiDrAC, DcAmB, Drake, TwCBDA,
WhAm H, WhAmP
Worthington, Thomas C d1827 *BiAUS*
Worthington, Thomas Contee 1782-1847
BiDrAC, WhAm H
Worthington, Walter Fitzhugh 1855-1937
WhAm 1
Worthington, William 1847-1923 *NatCAB 20,*
WhAm 1
Worthington, William Alfred 1872-1945
WhAm 2
Worthy, Edmund Henry 1909-1970 *WhAm 5*
Wortis, S Bernard 1904-1969 *NatCAB 55*
Wortley, David *NewYHSD*
Wortman, Denys 1887-1958 *WhAm 3*
Wortman, Doris Nash 1890-1967 *WhAm 4*
Wortman, Hardy Christian 1859-1934
NatCAB 41
Wose, Alfred Millard 1876-1946 *NatCAB 35*
Wotherspoon, Marion Foster 1863-1944
WhAm 2
Wotherspoon, William Wallace 1821-1888
NewYHSD
Wotherspoon, William Wallace 1850-1921
NatCAB 19, WebAMB, WhAm 1
Wotruba, Fritz 1907-1975 *WhAm 6*
Wotton, Edward 1492-1555 *DcScB*
Wotton, Grigsby Hart 1911-1965 *WhAm 4*
Wottrich, Wilfred 1896-1963 *NatCAB 51,*
WhAm 4
Woughter, Harold Wardell 1907-1961
NatCAB 49
Wouk, Herman 1915- *WebAB*
Woulfe, Henry Francis 1898-1961 *WhAm 4*
Woulfe, Peter 1727?-1803 *DcScB*
Wouwerman, Simon Van 1690-1743 *ApCAB*
Wovoka 1856?-1932 *DcAmB, DcAmReB,*
WhAm HA, WhAm 4
Wovoka 1858?-1932 *WebAB*
Woytinsky, Wladimir S 1885-1960 *WhAm 4*
Wozencraft, Frank Wilson 1892-1966 *WhAm 4*
Wragg, J P *WhoColR A*
Wragg, Samuel Holmes 1882-1959 *WhAm 3*
Wragg, William 1714-1777 *ApCAB, DcAmB,*
Drake, WhAm H
Wraith, William 1872-1956 *NatCAB 46,*
WhAm 5
Wrangel, Charles Magnus Von 1730?-1786
ApCAB
Wrangel, Baron Ferdinand Petrovitch Von
1795-1870 *ApCAB*
Wrangel, Friedrich Heinrich Ernst 1784-1877
WhoMilH
Wrangel, Baron Petr Nikolaevich 1878-1928
WhoMilH

Wrangell, Ferdinand P, Baron Von 1796-1870
ApCAB
Wrape, James Wyre 1903-1970 *WhAm 5*
Wrather, William Embry 1883-1963
NatCAB 52, WhAm 4
Wraxall, Peter d1759 *DcAmB, WhAm H*
Wray, James Bailey 1926-1973 *NatCAB 57,*
WhAm 6
Wray, James Glendenning 1872- *WhAm 5*
Wray, Mary A 1805-1892 *AmWom*
Wray, Newton 1854- *WhAm 4*
Wrede, Karl Phillip 1767-1838 *WhoMilH*
Wreden, Nicholas 1901-1955 *NatCAB 48,*
WhAm 3
Wree, Oliver VanDer d1649 *ApCAB*
Wren, Alphonse Aloysius 1877-1953
NatCAB 42
Wren, Amy 1872- *WomWWA 14*
Wren, Charles Francis 1883-1944 *NatCAB 37*
Wren, Sir Christopher 1632-1723 *AsBiEn,*
BiHiMed, DcScB, McGEWB
Wren, Christopher 1853-1921 *WhAm 1*
Wren, Christopher 1853-1922 *NatCAB 19*
Wren, Frank George 1874-1940 *WhAm 1*
Wren, Thomas 1826-1904 *BiDrAC*
Wren, William Clinton 1891-1956 *NatCAB 45,*
WhAm 3
Wrench, Sir Evelyn 1882-1966 *WhAm 4*
Wrench, Jesse E 1882-1958 *WhAm 4*
Wrench, Polly *NewYHSD*
Wrenn, Charles Gilbert 1902- *BiDAmEd*
Wrenn, Harold Holmes 1887-1967 *NatCAB 54*
Wrenn, Henry S 1907-1958 *WhAm 3*
Wrenn, John H 1841-1911 *ApCAB X*
Wrenn, Manleff Jarrell 1858-1934 *NatCAB 26*
Wrenn, Thomas Franklin 1860-1940
NatCAB 30
Wrenne, Michael Joseph Coleman 1847-1915
NatCAB 17
Wrenne, Thomas William 1851-1925 *NatCAB 8,*
WhAm 1
Wrentmore, Clarence George 1867-1934
NatCAB 31
Wright *NewYHSD*
Wright, Adam Henry 1846- *ApCAB*
Wright, Agnes Foster 1882- *BiCAW*
Wright, Albert 1870-1933 *NatCAB 24*
Wright, Albert Allen 1846-1905 *WhAm 1*
Wright, Albert Hazen 1879- *WhAm 6*
Wright, Albert Jay 1858-1940 *NatCAB 30*
Wright, Alexander 1751- *ApCAB*
Wright, Alfred 1889-1952 *WhAm 3*
Wright, Alma Brockerman 1875-1952
IIBEAAW
Wright, Almira Kidder *NewYHSD*
Wright, Almroth Edward 1861-1947 *DcScB*
Wright, Alonzo 1825- *ApCAB*
Wright, Ambrose *NewYHSD*
Wright, Ambrose Ransom 1826-1872 *ApCAB,*
BiDConf, NatCAB 12, TwCBDA
Wright, Ammi Willard 1822-1912 *ApCAB X,*
NatCAB 18, WhAm 1
Wright, Arnauld Leonard 1908-1970 *WhAm 5*
Wright, Arthur Davis 1885-1947 *BiDAmEd,*
NatCAB 37, WhAm 2
Wright, Arthur Mullin 1879-1948 *WhAm 2*
Wright, Arthur Silas 1858-1928 *WhAm 1*
Wright, Arthur St. Clair 1832-1924 *NatCAB 20*
Wright, Arthur Williams 1836-1915 *AmBi,*
ApCAB, NatCAB 13, WhAm 1
Wright, Asher 1803-1875 *ApCAB*
Wright, Ashley Bascom 1841-1897 *BiDrAC,*
WhAm H, WhAmP
Wright, Augustine Washington 1847-1918
NatCAB 21, WhAm 1
Wright, Augustus 1841- *NatCAB 10*
Wright, Augustus B 1813-1891 *BiAUS*
Wright, Augustus Romaldus 1813-1891
BiDConf, BiDrAC, WhAm H
Wright, Austin Tappan 1883-1931 *WhAm 1*
Wright, Ben D 1866- *WhAm 4*
Wright, Ben F 1867- *WhAm 4*
Wright, Benjamin 1770-1842 *ApCAB, DcAmB,*
NatCAB 1, WhAm H
Wright, Benjamin 1784-1860 *ApCAB,*
NatCAB 1
Wright, Benjamin D d1875 *NatCAB 12*

Wright, Benjamin Franklin 1848-1926
NatCAB 21
Wright, Benjamin Hall 1801-1881 *ApCAB,*
NatCAB 1
Wright, Bernice M d1975 *WhAm 6*
Wright, Boykin 1853-1932 *NatCAB 26*
Wright, Boykin Cabell 1891-1956 *WhAm 3*
Wright, Branson 1898-1961 *NatCAB 49*
Wright, Bruce Simpson 1879-1942 *WhAm 2*
Wright, Burton Harry 1905-1971 *WhAm 6*
Wright, Burton Henry 1859-1933 *WhAm 1*
Wright, C Irving 1876-1932 *NatCAB 27*
Wright, Carrie Douglas 1862- *WhAm 4*
Wright, Carroll 1854-1911 *WhAm 1*
Wright, Carroll Davidson 1840-1909 *AmBi,*
ApCAB, ApCAB X, DcAmB, EncAB,
McGEWB, NatCAB 19, TwCBDA,
WebAB, WhAm 1
Wright, Carroll Maryott 1887-1972 *WhAm 6*
Wright, Cecil Augustus 1904-1967 *WhAm 4,*
WhAm 5
Wright, Charles 1811-1885 *DcAmB, WhAm H*
Wright, Charles, Jr. 1883-1961 *WhAm 4*
Wright, Charles Albert 1860-1944 *NatCAB 37*
Wright, Charles Baker 1859-1942 *WhAm 2*
Wright, Charles Barstow 1822-1898 *ApCAB,*
DcAmB, NatCAB 8, WhAm H
Wright, Charles Cushing 1796-1854 *NewYHSD,*
WhAm H
Wright, Mrs. Charles Cushing 1805-1869
NewYHSD
Wright, Charles Edward 1868- *WhAm 4*
Wright, Charles Frederick 1856-1925 *BiDrAC,*
NatCAB 20, WhAmP
Wright, Charles Henry Conrad 1869-1957
WhAm 2
Wright, Charles Herbert 1857- *WhAm 4*
Wright, Charles Jefferson 1839-1910 *WhAm 1*
Wright, Charles Lovel 1885-1954 *WhAm 3*
Wright, Charles Washington 1824-1869
NewYHSD
Wright, Chauncey 1830-1875 *ApCAB, DcAmB,*
NatCAB 1, WebAB, WhAm H
Wright, Chauncy *NewYHSD*
Wright, Chester Whitney 1879-1966 *WhAm 4*
Wright, Christopher Columbus 1849-
NatCAB 13
Wright, Clifford Ramsey 1889-1963 *WhAm 4*
Wright, Cobina d1970 *WhAm 5*
Wright, Crafts James 1808-1883 *ApCAB*
Wright, Cyrus Mansfield 1842-1911 *WhAm 1*
Wright, Daniel Boone 1812-1887 *BiAUS,*
BiDrAC, WhAm H
Wright, Daniel Edward 1883-1962 *NatCAB 51*
Wright, Daniel Knight 1883-1964 *NatCAB 50*
Wright, Daniel Thew 1864-1943 *NatCAB 32,*
WhAm 4
Wright, David McCord 1909-1968 *WhAm 5*
Wright, Delia Smith *WomWWA 14*
Wright, Donald Rhodes 1895-1967 *NatCAB 54*
Wright, Donald S 1897-1956 *WhAm 3*
Wright, Donald Thomas 1894-1965 *NatCAB 51,*
WhAm 4
Wright, Dudley Hugh Aloysius 1912-1973
WhAm 6
Wright, Ebenezer Kellogg 1837-1895
NatCAB 8
Wright, Edgar Wilson 1863-1930 *NatCAB 22*
Wright, Edmond Fleming 1898-1974 *WhAm 6*
Wright, Edward *NewYHSD*
Wright, Edward 1561-1615 *DcScB*
Wright, Edward 1824-1895 *ApCAB Sup*
Wright, Edward Bingham 1838-1914 *WhAm 1*
Wright, Edward Everett 1856-1921 *WhAm 1*
Wright, Edward Harland *NewYHSD*
Wright, Edward Pulteney 1894-1962 *WhAm 4*
Wright, Edward Reynolds 1877-1956
NatCAB 46, WhAm 3
Wright, Edward Richard 1872-1941 *WhAm 2*
Wright, Edwin Ruthvin Vincent 1812-1871
BiAUS, BiDrAC, NatCAB 8, WhAm H,
WhAmP
Wright, Edwina MaBelle 1891- *WhoColR*
Wright, Eliphalet Nott 1858- *WhAm 4*
Wright, Elizabeth *NewYHSD*
Wright, Elizabeth Washburn *WomWWA 14*
Wright, Elizabeth Washburne *WhAm 5*
Wright, Elizur 1804-1885 *ApCAB, DcAmB,*

Drake, McGEWB, NatCAB 2, TwCBDA,
WebAB, WhAm H
Wright, Ellen C 1845- *WomWWA 14*
Wright, Elva Annis 1868- *WomWWA 14*
Wright, Emma Palmer White 1876-
WomWWA 14
Wright, Ernest Hunter 1882-1968 *WhAm 5*
Wright, Ernest Linwood 1893-1974 *WhAm 6*
Wright, Eugene Ignatius 1872- *WhoColR*
Wright, Ewing Ellsworth 1903-1961
NatCAB 50
Wright, Fanny 1795-1852 *ApCAB, NatCAB 2*
Wright, Fielding Lewis 1895-1956 *WhAm 3*
Wright, Frances 1795-1852 *AmBi, DcAmB,*
Drake, EncAB, McGEWB, NotAW,
WebAB, WhAm H, WhAmP
Wright, Francis Marion 1843-1917 *NatCAB 28*
Wright, Francis Marion 1844-1917 *WhAm 1*
Wright, Frank Ayres 1854-1949 *WhAm 2*
Wright, Frank C 1871-1946 *WhAm 2*
Wright, Frank James 1888-1954 *NatCAB 44,*
WhAm 3
Wright, Frank Lee 1884-1953 *NatCAB 43,*
WhAm 3
Wright, Frank Lloyd 1869-1959 *BnEnAmA,*
EncAAH, EncAB, McGEWB, WebAB,
WhAm 3
Wright, Fred Eugene 1877-1953 *NatCAB 41*
Wright, Frederick Eugene 1877-1953 *DcScB,*
WhAm 3
Wright, G Ernest 1909-1974 *WhAm 6*
Wright, George *NewYHSD*
Wright, George 1803-1865 *ApCAB, Drake*
Wright, George 1847-1937 *DcAmB S2*
Wright, George Bohan 1815-1903 *WhAm 1*
Wright, George C 1820- *BiAUS, NatCAB 3*
Wright, George E 1867-1923 *WhAm 1*
Wright, George Edward 1851- *NatCAB 9*
Wright, George Francis 1892-1967 *NatCAB 53,*
WhAm 4, WhAm 5
Wright, George Frederick 1828-1881
NewYHSD, WhAm H
Wright, George Frederick 1838-1921 *AmBi,*
ApCAB, DcAmB, DcAmReB, DcScB,
NatCAB 7, TwCBDA, WhAm 1
Wright, George Frederick 1881-1938
NatCAB 40
Wright, George Grover 1820-1896 *ApCAB,*
BiDrAC, DcAmB, TwCBDA, WhAm H,
WhAmP
Wright, George H 1817- *BiAUS*
Wright, George Hand 1872-1951 *WhAm 3*
Wright, George Herdman 1858-1930
NatCAB 27
Wright, George Lathrop 1843- *NatCAB 1,*
NatCAB 3
Wright, George Mann 1879-1963 *NatCAB 50,*
WhAm 6
Wright, George Morrison 1844- *NatCAB 12*
Wright, George Murray 1852- *WhAm 4*
Wright, George Spencer 1881-1953 *NatCAB 43*
Wright, George Washington 1816-1885 *BiDrAC,*
WhAm H
Wright, George William 1868- *WhAm 4*
Wright, Gilbert G 1866-1933 *WhAm 1*
Wright, Grace Stevens 1868- *WomWWA 14*
Wright, Graham 1892-1958 *WhAm 3*
Wright, Grant 1865- *WhAm 4*
Wright, Hamilton Kemp 1867-1917 *ApCAB X,*
DcAmB, NatCAB 22, WhAm 1
Wright, Hamilton Mercer 1874-1954
NatCAB 43
Wright, Hamilton Mercer 1875-1954 *WhAm 3*
Wright, Hannah Amelia 1836- *AmWom*
Wright, Harold Abbott 1901-1965 *WhAm 4*
Wright, Harold Bell 1872-1944 *DcAmB S3,*
NatCAB 34, WebAB, WhAm 2
Wright, Harold Edson 1894-1950 *NatCAB 45*
Wright, Harriet Lawson 1866- *WomWWA 14*
Wright, Harriett G R *WomWWA 14*
Wright, Harrison 1850-1885 *ApCAB,*
NatCAB 3
Wright, Harry Garfield 1881-1940 *NatCAB 31*
Wright, Harry Josiah 1872-1959 *NatCAB 52*
Wright, Harry Noble 1881-1969 *WhAm 5*
Wright, Hattie Haw 1866- *WomWWA 14*
Wright, Helen Gertrude 1884- *WomWWA 14*
Wright, Helen R 1891-1969 *WhAm 5*

Wright, Helen Smith 1874- *WhAm 5,*
WomWWA 14
Wright, Hendrick Bradley 1808-1881 *ApCAB,*
BiAUS, BiDrAC, DcAmB, NatCAB 3,
WhAm H, WhAmP
Wright, Henry 1835-1895 *DcAmB, WebAB,*
WhAm H
Wright, Henry 1878-1936 *DcAmB S2,*
NatCAB 27, WebAB
Wright, Henry Burt 1877-1923 *WhAm 1*
Wright, Henry Charles Seppings 1849-1937
IlBEAAW
Wright, Henry Clarke 1797-1870 *ApCAB,*
Drake, NatCAB 2, WhAm H
Wright, Henry Collier 1868-1935 *WhAm 1*
Wright, Henry John 1866-1935 *WhAm 1*
Wright, Henry Parks 1839-1918 *NatCAB 19,*
WhAm 1
Wright, Henry Wilkes 1878- *WhAm 6*
Wright, Herbert E 1872-1943 *WhAm 2*
Wright, Herbert Francis 1892-1945 *NatCAB 34,*
WhAm 2
Wright, Herbert Perry 1865-1945 *WhAm 2*
Wright, Herbert Richard *WhoColR*
Wright, Horace Caldwell 1881-1961 *WhAm 4*
Wright, Horace Melville 1879-1951 *WhAm 3*
Wright, Horatio Gates 1820?- *Drake*
Wright, Horatio Gouverneur 1820-1899 *DcAmB,*
WebAMB
Wright, Horatio Gouverneur 1829-1899 *AmBi*
Wright, Horatio Governeur 1820-1899 *ApCAB,*
NatCAB 4, TwCBDA, WhAm H
Wright, Irene Aloha 1879-1972 *WhAm 5*
Wright, Isaac Miles 1879-1948 *WhAm 2*
Wright, J Hood 1836-1894 *NatCAB 33*
Wright, J Warren 1899-1957 *NatCAB 43*
Wright, J William 1887-1957 *NatCAB 47*
Wright, James *ApCAB, NewYHSD*
Wright, Sir James 1714?-1785 *ApCAB,*
NatCAB 1
Wright, Sir James 1714?-1786 *Drake*
Wright, James Assion 1902-1963 *BiDrAC*
Wright, James Claude, Jr. 1922- *BiDrAC*
Wright, James D *NewYHSD*
Wright, James Elwin 1890-1973 *WhAm 6*
Wright, James Franklin 1862-1940 *WhAm 1*
Wright, James Frederick 1914- *WhAm 6*
Wright, James Harris 1907-1947 *WhAm 2*
Wright, James Henry 1813-1883 *NewYHSD*
Wright, James Homer 1869-1928 *WhAm 1*
Wright, James Lendrew 1816-1893 *DcAmB,*
WhAm H
Wright, James Lloyd 1885-1952 *WhAm 3*
Wright, Jefferson 1798-1846 *NewYHSD*
Wright, Jennie *WomWWA 14*
Wright, Jermyn *ApCAB*
Wright, Jessie 1900-1970 *NatCAB 55,*
WhAm 5
Wright, Joanna Maynard Shaw 1830- *WhAm 4,*
WomWWA 14
Wright, Joel Tombleson 1834- *ApCAB*
Wright, John *NewYHSD*
Wright, John 1836-1919 *NatCAB 12,*
WhAm 1
Wright, John Bittinger 1872- *WhAm 1*
Wright, John Calvin 1876-1955 *BiDAmEd,*
WhAm 5
Wright, John Crafts 1783-1861 *ApCAB,*
BiAUS, BiDrAC, Drake, WhAm H,
WhAmP
Wright, John Crafts 1784-1861 *NatCAB 3*
Wright, John Dutton 1866-1952 *NatCAB 38*
Wright, John Edwards 1860-1924 *NatCAB 20*
Wright, John H 1867-1951 *NatCAB 39*
Wright, John Henry 1852-1908 *DcAmB,*
NatCAB 8, WhAm 1
Wright, John Horning 1881-1956 *NatCAB 46*
Wright, John Howard 1828-1914 *ApCAB X*
Wright, John Kirtland 1891-1969 *WhAm 5*
Wright, John Lloyd 1892-1972 *WhAm 5*
Wright, John Montgomery d1915 *WhAm 1*
Wright, John Pilling 1881-1947 *NatCAB 37,*
WhAm 2
Wright, John Rutherford 1847-1928
NatCAB 21
Wright, John Stephen 1815-1874 *ApCAB,*
DcAmB, WhAm H
Wright, John Vines 1828- *ApCAB, BiAUS,*

TwCBDA

Wright, John Vines 1828-1903 *NatCAB 21*

Wright, John Vines 1828-1908 *BiDConf, BiDrAC, WhAm 1, WhAmP*

Wright, John Wells 1868-1937 *NatCAB 28, WhAm 1*

Wright, John Westley 1842-1935 *WhAm 1, WhAm 2*

Wright, John William 1868-1926 *NatCAB 20*

Wright, John Womack 1876-1952 *WhAm 3*

Wright, Jonathan Jasper 1840-1885 *DcAmB, WhAm H*

Wright, Joseph 1756-1793 *AmBi, ApCAB, BnEnAmA, DcAmB, Drake, NatCAB 20, NewYHSD, WhAm H*

Wright, Joseph Albert 1809-1867 *NatCAB 13*

Wright, Joseph Albert 1810-1867 *ApCAB, BiAUS, BiDrAC, DcAmB, Drake, TwCBDA, WhAm H, WhAmP*

Wright, Joseph Alexander 1877- *WhAm 5*

Wright, Joseph Jefferson Burr 1800-1878 *ApCAB*

Wright, Joseph Jefferson Burr 1801-1878 *DcAmB, WhAm H*

Wright, Joseph Purdon 1884-1967 *WhAm 5*

Wright, Joshua Butler 1877-1939 *NatCAB 30, WhAm 1*

Wright, Joshua G d1811 *BiAUS*

Wright, Julia MacNair 1840-1903 *WhAm 1*

Wright, Julia McNair 1840-1903 *AmWom, ApCAB*

Wright, Julian May 1884-1938 *NatCAB 29, WhAm 1, WhAm 1C*

Wright, Laura M 1840- *AmWom*

Wright, Laura Maria Sheldon 1809-1886 *NotAW*

Wright, Leroy A 1863-1944 *WhAm 2*

Wright, Louis Clinton 1879- *WhAm 6*

Wright, Louis Tompkins 1891-1952 *NatCAB 43, WhAm 3*

Wright, Louisa V 1862- *WomWWA 14*

Wright, Louise Sophie Wigfall 1846- *WhAm 4, WomWWA 14*

Wright, Loyd 1892-1974 *WhAm 6*

Wright, Lucy 1760-1821 *NotAW*

Wright, Luke Edward 1846-1922 *AmBi, BiDrUSE, DcAmB, NatCAB 14, NatCAB 26, WhAm 1*

Wright, Luther 1796-1870 *ApCAB*

Wright, Luther Lamphear 1856- *WhAm 1*

Wright, Mabel Osgood 1859-1934 *AmBi, NatCAB 12, NotAW, WhAm 1*

Wright, Marcellus Eugene 1881-1962 *WhAm 4*

Wright, Marcus Joseph 1831-1922 *ApCAB, BiDConf, DcAmB, NatCAB 4, TwCBDA, WhAm 1*

Wright, Margaret Hardon 1869- *WomWWA 14*

Wright, Marie Robinson d1914 *WhAm 1*

Wright, Marie Robinson 1853-1914 *AmWom*

Wright, Marie Robinson 1867-1914 *WomWWA 14*

Wright, Martha Coffin Pelham 1806-1875 *NotAW*

Wright, Mary Clabaugh 1917-1970 *WhAm 5*

Wright, Mary Courtney Clark 1867- *WomWWA 14*

Wright, Mary Eliza 1854- *WomWWA 14*

Wright, Mary Page *WomWWA 14*

Wright, Mary Tappan 1851- *WhAm 1, WomWWA 14*

Wright, Maurice Lauchlin 1845-1911 *WhAm 1*

Wright, Merle St. Croix 1859- *WhAm 2*

Wright, Milton 1828-1917 *ApCAB, WhAm 1*

Wright, Milton 1887-1941 *NatCAB 31, WhAm 2*

Wright, Moorhead 1872-1945 *NatCAB 35, WhAm 2*

Wright, Moorhead 1906-1962 *NatCAB 50*

Wright, Moses *NewYHSD*

Wright, Muriel Hazel d1975 *WhAm 6*

Wright, Myron Benjamin 1847-1894 *BiDrAC, WhAm H, WhAmP*

Wright, Nathaniel Curwin 1869-1923 *NatCAB 20, WhAm 1*

Wright, Nathaniel H 1787-1824 *Drake*

Wright, Neziah *NewYHSD*

Wright, Norris N 1886-1951 *WhAm 3*

Wright, Ora Campbell 1872- *WhAm 6*

Wright, Orville 1871-1948 *AsBiEn, DcAmB S4, DcScB, EncAB, McGEWB, NatCAB 14, WebAB, WhAm 2*

Wright, Patience 1725-1785 *NatCAB 8*

Wright, Patience Lovell 1725-1786 *AmBi, BnEnAmA, DcAmB, NewYHSD, NotAW, WhAm H*

Wright, Paul 1876-1965 *WhAm 4*

Wright, Peter Clark 1870-1947 *WhAm 2*

Wright, Philip Green 1861-1934 *DcAmB, NatCAB 25*

Wright, Purd B 1860- *WhAm 4*

Wright, Quincy 1890-1970 *WhAm 5*

Wright, Ralph Garrigue 1875-1954 *NatCAB 40*

Wright, Raymond Garfield 1880-1969 *NatCAB 54*

Wright, Rebecca McPherson 1838- *ApCAB*

Wright, Richard 1908-1960 *EncAB, McGEWB, WebAB, WhAm 4*

Wright, Richard Harvey 1851-1929 *NatCAB 22*

Wright, Richard Robert 1853-1947 *BiDAmEd, DcAmB S4*

Wright, Richard Robert 1855-1947 *WhAm 2, WhoColR*

Wright, Richard Robert, Jr. 1878-1967 *WhAm 4A, WhoColR*

Wright, Richardson Little 1887-1961 *WhAm 4*

Wright, Riley Erastus 1839- *NatCAB 16*

Wright, Robert d1826 *BiAUS, Drake*

Wright, Robert 1752-1826 *BiDrAC, DcAmB, WhAm H, WhAmP*

Wright, Robert 1765?-1826 *ApCAB, NatCAB 9*

Wright, Robert Charlton 1873-1947 *WhAm 2*

Wright, Robert Clinton 1869-1924 *WhAm 1*

Wright, Robert Emmet 1810- *ApCAB, Drake*

Wright, Robert Herring 1870-1934 *WhAm 1*

Wright, Robert Jefferson 1842- *NatCAB 2*

Wright, Robert William 1816-1885 *ApCAB, DcAmB, WhAm H*

Wright, Ross Pier 1874-1967 *WhAm 4A*

Wright, Roydon Vincent 1876-1948 *WhAm 2*

Wright, Rufus 1832- *ApCAB, IlBEAAW, NewYHSD, WhAm H*

Wright, Salmon Lusk 1852-1929 *NatCAB 30*

Wright, Samuel Gardiner 1781-1845 *BiDrAC, WhAm H*

Wright, Samuel Gardiner 1787-1845 *BiAUS*

Wright, Samuel John 1851-1926 *NatCAB 31*

Wright, Sara Rowell 1864- *WomWWA 14*

Wright, Silas 1795-1847 *AmBi, ApCAB, BiAUS, BiDrAC, DcAmB, Drake, EncAB, NatCAB 3, WhAm H, WhAmP*

Wright, Silas 1795-1848 *TwCBDA*

Wright, Sophie Bell 1866-1912 *NatCAB 10, NotAW*

Wright, Stanley Willard 1921-1971 *WhAm 5*

Wright, Stephen Mott 1841-1906 *WhAm 1*

Wright, Stephen Pearl 1858-1922 *NatCAB 19*

Wright, Susanna 1697-1784 *NotAW*

Wright, Sydney Longstreth 1896-1970 *NatCAB 55, WhAm 5*

Wright, T Jefferson 1798-1846 *NewYHSD*

Wright, Theodore 1830-1924 *WhAm 1*

Wright, Theodore Francis 1845-1907 *WhAm 1*

Wright, Theodore Lyman 1858-1926 *DcAmB, WhAm 1*

Wright, Theodore Paul 1895-1970 *WhAm 5*

Wright, Thew 1877- *WhAm 5*

Wright, Thomas 1711-1786 *DcScB*

Wright, Thomas Houard 1860-1918 *NatCAB 17*

Wright, Thomas Jefferson 1798-1846 *IlBEAAW*

Wright, Thomas Lee 1825- *ApCAB*

Wright, Thomas Roane Barnes 1842-1914 *NatCAB 19, WhAm 4*

Wright, Turbett 1741-1783 *BiAUS*

Wright, Turbutt 1741-1783 *BiDrAC, WhAm H, WhAmP*

Wright, Walter Henry 1893-1951 *NatCAB 41, WhAm 3*

Wright, Walter King 1858- *WhAm 4*

Wright, Walter Livingston, Jr. 1900-1946 *WhAm 2*

Wright, Warren 1875-1950 *NatCAB 39, WhAm 3*

Wright, Wilbur 1867-1912 *AmBi, ApCAB X,*

AsBiEn, DcAmB, DcScB, McGEWB, NatCAB 14, WebAB, WhAm 1

Wright, Wilbur Seaman 1871-1937 *WhAm 1*

Wright, Wilfred LaSalles 1877-1947 *NatCAB 36, WhAm 2*

Wright, Willard Huntington 1888-1939 *DcAmB S2, WhAm 1*

Wright, William 1790-1866 *BiDrAC, WhAmP*

Wright, William 1794-1866 *ApCAB, BiAUS, DcAmB, Drake, NatCAB 4, TwCBDA*

Wright, William 1824-1866 *ApCAB*

Wright, William 1829-1898 *DcAmB S1, REnAW, WhAm H*

Wright, William Ambrose 1844-1929 *NatCAB 21*

Wright, William Bacon 1830-1895 *BiDConf*

Wright, William Bleecker 1895-1966 *WhAm 4*

Wright, William Bull 1840-1880 *ApCAB, NatCAB 4, WhAm H*

Wright, William Burnet 1838-1924 *NatCAB 21, WhAm 1*

Wright, William Carter 1866-1933 *BiDrAC, WhAm 1, WhAmP*

Wright, William Frederick 1858- *WhAm 4*

Wright, William Hammond 1871-1959 *DcScB, WhAm 3*

Wright, William Henry 1814-1845 *ApCAB*

Wright, William Henry 1858- *NatCAB 10*

Wright, William James 1831- *ApCAB Sup*

Wright, William Janes 1831- *ApCAB, WhAm 1*

Wright, William Kelley 1877-1956 *NatCAB 44, WhAm 3*

Wright, William Mason 1863-1943 *WebAMB, WhAm 2*

Wright, William Ryer 1888-1952 *WhAm 3*

Wright, William Thomas, Jr. 1891-1954 *WhAm 3*

Wright, William Wood 1917-1971 *WhAm 5*

Wright, Wirt 1878- *WhAm 6*

Wright Brothers *WebAB*

Wrightington, Edgar Newcomb 1875-1945 *NatCAB 36*

Wrightsman, Charles John 1870-1959 *WhAm 3*

Wrightson, A *NewYHSD*

Wrightson, George D 1889-1965 *WhAm 4*

Wrigley, Thomas 1882-1970 *WhAm 5*

Wrigley, William, Jr. 1861-1932 *DcAmB S1, NatCAB 23, WebAB, WhAm 1*

Wrigley, William, Jr. 1864-1932 *ApCAB X*

Wrinch, Dorothy d1976 *WhAm 6*

Wrisley, George A 1895-1963 *WhAm 4*

Wriston, Henry Lincoln 1861-1955 *NatCAB 45*

Wriston, Henry Merritt 1889- *BiDAmEd*

Writ, R W *NewYHSD*

Wroblewski, Wladyslaw 1875- *WhAm 5*

Wroblewski, Zygmunt Florenty Von 1845-1888 *DcScB*

Wrock, Arthur Henry 1911-1962 *NatCAB 49, WhAm 4*

Wrong, H Hume 1894-1954 *WhAm 3*

Wronski, Jozef Maria *DcScB*

Wrosetasatow *DcAmB*

Wroth, Edward Pinkney 1889-1946 *WhAm 2*

Wroth, Lawrence Counselman 1884-1970 *DcAmLiB*

Wroth, Peregrine, Jr. 1882-1956 *NatCAB 47*

Wroughton, Oliver Loraine 1881-1960 *NatCAB 48*

Wu, Chao-Chu 1887-1933 *WhAm 1*

Wu, Hsien 1893-1959 *DcScB, NatCAB 44*

Wu, P'An-Chao 1866-1931 *DcAmB*

Wu, P'ei-Fu 1874-1939 *McGEWB*

Wu, San-Kuei 1612-1678 *WhoMilH*

Wu, Tao-Tzu 689?-758? *McGEWB*

Wu, Ting-Fang d1922 *WhAm 2*

Wu, Tse-T'ien 623-705 *McGEWB*

Wu, Wang d1116?BC *McGEWB*

Wuensch, Robert Haws 1908-1964 *NatCAB 51*

Wuerpel, Edmund Henry 1866- *WhAm 5*

Wuerthele, Herman William 1883-1967 *NatCAB 53*

Wueste, Louise Heuser 1803-1875 *IlBEAAW, NewYHSD*

Wulff, Emma Louise Schweickert 1856- *WomWWA 14*

Wulff, Georg 1863-1925 *DcScB*

Wulling, Frederick John 1866-1947 *BiDAmEd,*

WhAm 2

Wullweber, Christian F Wilhelm Jurgen 1833-1877 *BiAUS, NatCAB 5*

Wulp, George Adolph 1896-1956 *NatCAB 46*

Wulsin, Frederick Roelker 1891-1961 *WhAm 4*

Wulsin, Lucien 1845- *NatCAB 12*

Wulsin, Lucien 1889-1964 *WhAm 4, WhAm 5*

Wunder, Adalbert 1827- *NewYHSD*

Wunder, Charles Newman 1884-1960 *WhAm 4*

Wunder, Clarence Edmond 1886-1940 *NatCAB 46, WhAm 1*

Wunderlich, Carl Reinhold August 1815-1877 *AsBiEn*

Wunderlich, Fritz 1930-1966 *WhAm 4*

Wunderlich, George 1826?- *NewYHSD*

Wunderlich, William 1859-1926 *NatCAB 20*

Wundheiler, Alexander Wundt 1902-1957 *WhAm 3*

Wundt, Wilhelm Max 1832-1920 *AsBiEn, DcScB, McGEWB*

Wunsch, Ernest Conrad 1894-1963 *WhAm 4*

Wuorinen, John H 1897-1969 *WhAm 5*

Wuppermann, Adolph Edward 1872-1937 *NatCAB 35*

Wuppermann, Carlos Siegert 1887-1919 *ApCAB X*

Wuppermann, George Diogracia 1838-1915 *ApCAB X, NatCAB 27*

Wuppermann, Josephine Wright Hancox 1851-1936 *BiCAW, NatCAB 27*

Wurdack, John Herman 1888-1954 *NatCAB 44*

Wurdeman, Charles 1871-1961 *NatCAB 50*

Wurdemann, Audrey May 1911-1960 *WhAm 4*

Wurdemann, Harry Vanderbilt 1865-1938 *ApCAB X, WhAm 1*

Wurlitzer, Farny Reginald 1883-1972 *NatCAB 57, WhAm 5*

Wurlitzer, Howard Eugene 1871-1928 *NatCAB 25*

Wurlitzer, Rudolph 1831-1914 *NatCAB 16*

Wurlitzer, Rudolph H 1873-1948 *WhAm 2*

Wurman, Harry Paul 1896-1960 *NatCAB 47, WhAm 4*

Wurms, Gottlieb *NewYHSD*

Wurmser, Dagobert Sigismund 1724-1797 *WhoMilH*

Wurmski, General *NewYHSD*

Wurst, Perry Edward 1878-1943 *NatCAB 32*

Wurster, Catherine Bauer 1905-1964 *NatCAB 51*

Wurster, Oscar Herman 1881-1946 *NatCAB 35*

Wurster, William Wilson 1895-1973 *BnEnAmA, WhAm 6*

Wurtele, Arthur 1877-1946 *NatCAB 35*

Wurtele, Jonathan Saxton Campbell 1828- *ApCAB*

Wurtenberg, William Charles 1863-1957 *NatCAB 48*

Wurts, Alexander Jay 1862-1932 *AmBi, WhAm 1*

Wurts, Elizabeth Wister *WomWWA 14*

Wurts, George Washington 1843- *NatCAB 13*

Wurts, John 1792-1861 *BiDrAC, WhAm H*

Wurts, John 1855- *WhAm 4*

Wurts, John Halsey 1910-1966 *WhAm 4*

Wurts, Pierre Jay 1869-1953 *NatCAB 42*

Wurtsmith, Paul Bernard 1906-1946 *WhAm 2*

Wurttemberg, Friedrich Paul Wilhelm 1797-1860 *WhAm H*

Wurtz, Charles-Adolphe 1817-1884 *DcScB*

Wurtz, Henry 1828?-1910 *ApCAB, DcAmB, NatCAB 7*

Wurtz, John d1861 *BiAUS*

Wurz, John Francis 1885-1965 *WhAm 4*

Wurzbach, Harry McLeary 1874-1931 *BiDrAC, WhAm 1, WhAmP*

Wurzbach, W *NewYHSD*

Wurzburg, Abe 1896-1967 *NatCAB 54*

Wurzburg, Francis Lewis 1877-1954 *WhAm 3*

Wust, Alexander 1837-1876 *NewYHSD*

Wyand, George *NewYHSD*

Wyant, Adam Martin 1869-1935 *BiDrAC, WhAm 1, WhAmP*

Wyant, Alexander Helwig 1836-1892 *AmBi, ApCAB, BnEnAmA, DcAmB, McGEWB, NatCAB 10, NewYHSD, WhAm H*

Wyant, Andrew Robert Elmer 1867-1964 *NatCAB 53*

Wyant, Paul Byron 1905-1958 *WhAm 3*

Wyatt, Bernard Langdon 1883-1961 *WhAm 4*

Wyatt, Edith Franklin 1873-1958 *WhAm 3, WomWWA 14*

Wyatt, Sir Francis d1644 *Drake*

Wyatt, Sir Francis 1575?-1644 *ApCAB, NatCAB 13*

Wyatt, Sir Francis 1588-1644 *AmBi, DcAmB, WhAm H*

Wyatt, Francis Dale 1890-1957 *NatCAB 47*

Wyatt, J B Noel 1847-1926 *WhAm 1*

Wyatt, James Louis, Sr. 1893-1961 *NatCAB 48*

Wyatt, Josephine Ernestine Hughes 1884- *WhoColR*

Wyatt, Landon R 1891-1971 *WhAm 5*

Wyatt, Lee B 1890-1960 *WhAm 3A*

Wyatt, Robert H 1903-1975 *WhAm 6*

Wyatt, Sir Thomas 1503-1542 *McGEWB*

Wyatt, Wendell 1917- *BiDrAC*

Wyatt, William Edward 1789-1864 *ApCAB*

Wyatt, William Johnson 1866-1938 *NatCAB 35*

Wyatt-Brown, Hunter 1884-1952 *WhAm 3*

Wybrant *NewYHSD*

Wyche, Charles Cecil 1885-1966 *NatCAB 51, WhAm 4*

Wyche, James E *BiAUS*

Wyche, Richard Thomas 1867-1930 *NatCAB 24, WhAm 1*

Wycherley, William 1640?-1716 *McGEWB*

Wyckoff, Albert Clarke 1874- *WhAm 5*

Wyckoff, Ambrose Barkley 1848- *WhAm 4*

Wyckoff, Arcalous Welling 1873-1936 *WhAm 1*

Wyckoff, Cecelia G 1888-1966 *WhAm 4, WhAm 5*

Wyckoff, Charles Truman 1861- *WhAm 4*

Wyckoff, DeWitte 1887-1957 *NatCAB 45*

Wyckoff, Edward Guild 1867-1924 *NatCAB 6*

Wyckoff, Frederick Albert 1879-1943 *NatCAB 31*

Wyckoff, Isaac Newton 1792-1869 *ApCAB*

Wyckoff, Isabel Dunham *NewYHSD*

Wyckoff, J Lewis 1864-1931 *NatCAB 33*

Wyckoff, John Henry 1881-1937 *DcAmB S2, WhAm 1*

Wyckoff, Ralph Walter Graystone 1897- *AsBiEn*

Wyckoff, Richard Demille 1873- *WhAm 5*

Wyckoff, Sarah D 1872- *WomWWA 14*

Wyckoff, Stephen Nicholas 1891-1959 *NatCAB 46*

Wyckoff, Walter Augustus 1865-1908 *AmBi, DcAmB, WhAm 1*

Wyckoff, Walter Cornelius 1872-1930 *ApCAB X*

Wyckoff, William Cornelius 1832-1888 *ApCAB*

Wyckoff, William Henry 1807-1877 *ApCAB*

Wyckoff, William Ozmun 1835- *NatCAB 3*

Wyckoff, William Watson 1873-1947 *NatCAB 37*

Wyclif, John 1330?-1384 *McGEWB*

Wyder, Robert 1871-1935 *NatCAB 28*

Wydeveld, Arnoud *NewYHSD*

Wydler, John Waldemar 1924- *BiDrAC*

Wyer, Berenice Crumb 1873- *WomWWA 14*

Wyer, James Ingersoll 1869-1955 *DcAmLiB, WhAm 3*

Wyer, Malcolm Glenn 1877-1965 *DcAmLiB, NatCAB 52, WhAm 4*

Wyer, Samuel S 1879-1955 *WhAm 3*

Wyess, John E 1820?-1903 *NewYHSD*

Wyeth, Andrew 1917- *BnEnAmA, McGEWB*

Wyeth, Andrew Nelson 1917- *EncAAH, WebAB*

Wyeth, Andrew Newell 1917- *EncAB, IIBEAAW*

Wyeth, Francis *NewYHSD*

Wyeth, Henriette Zirngiebel 1907- *IIBEAAW*

Wyeth, John 1770-1858 *DcAmB, WhAm H*

Wyeth, John Allan 1845-1922 *AmBi, ApCAB, DcAmB, NatCAB 6, WhAm 1*

Wyeth, John Allen 1845-1922 *NatCAB 41*

Wyeth, Louis Weiss 1812-1889 *NatCAB 6*

Wyeth, Nathan Corwith 1870-1963 *NatCAB 50, WhAm 4*

Wyeth, Nathaniel Jarvis 1802-1856 *AmBi, DcAmB, NatCAB 6, REnAW, WhAm H*

Wyeth, Newell Convers 1882-1945 *DcAmB S3, IIBEAAW, WebAB, WhAm 2*

Wyeth, Ola M 1882- *WomWWA 14*

Wyeth, P C *NewYHSD*

Wygant, Grace Peirce *WomWWA 14*

Wygant, Theodore 1831-1905 *NatCAB 16*

Wyka, Kazimierz 1910-1975 *WhAm 6*

Wykoff, Leward Cornelius 1892-1966 *WhAm 4*

Wyle, Florence 1881- *IIBEAAW*

Wyle, Florence 1882- *WomWWA 14*

Wylegala, Victor Bernard 1892- *WhAm 4*

Wyles, Tom Russell 1872-1959 *WhAm 3*

Wylie, Andrew 1789-1851 *ApCAB, BiDAmEd, DcAmB, Drake, NatCAB 13, TwCBDA, WhAm H*

Wylie, Andrew 1814-1905 *ApCAB Sup, BiAUS, WhAm 1*

Wylie, Arthur Morton 1873-1926 *NatCAB 23*

Wylie, Barbara Halcrow 1865- *WomWWA 14*

Wylie, Chalmers Pangburn 1920- *BiDrAC*

Wylie, Curtis Monteith 1890-1958 *NatCAB 49*

Wylie, David Gourley 1857-1930 *WhAm 1*

Wylie, David Gray 1898-1966 *NatCAB 52*

Wylie, Douglas M 1865-1914 *WhAm 1*

Wylie, Dwight Witherspoon 1876-1940 *NatCAB 30, WhAm 1*

Wylie, Edna Edwards 1876-1907 *WhAm 1*

Wylie, Elinor Morton Hoyt 1885-1928 *AmBi, DcAmB, NatCAB 21, NotAW, WebAB, WhAm 1*

Wylie, Ella Gertrude Hulbert *WomWWA 14*

Wylie, Emily Ritchie McLean 1888- *WomWWA 14*

Wylie, Herbert George 1867- *WhAm 4*

Wylie, Ida Alexa Ross 1885-1959 *WhAm 3*

Wylie, James Renwick, Jr. 1897-1974 *WhAm 6*

Wylie, James Robinson 1831- *NatCAB 3*

Wylie, John Dunovant 1891-1958 *NatCAB 51*

Wylie, Laura Johnson 1855-1932 *WhAm 1, WomWWA 14*

Wylie, Lollie Belle *AmWom*

Wylie, Martha Rachel 1846- *WomWWA 14*

Wylie, Max d1975 *WhAm 6*

Wylie, Philip Gordon 1902-1971 *WebAB, WhAm 5*

Wylie, Richard Cameron 1846-1928 *WhAm 1*

Wylie, Robert 1839-1877 *AmBi, ApCAB, DcAmB, NewYHSD, WhAm H*

Wylie, Robert Bradford 1870-1959 *NatCAB 50, WhAm 3*

Wylie, Robert H 1899-1962 *WhAm 4*

Wylie, Robert Hawthorne 1863-1933 *NatCAB 26*

Wylie, Samuel Brown 1773-1852 *ApCAB, DcAmB, Drake, NatCAB 1, WhAm H*

Wylie, Samuel Joseph 1918-1974 *WhAm 6*

Wylie, Theodore William John 1818-1898 *ApCAB, Drake, NatCAB 10*

Wylie, Theophilus Adam 1810- *ApCAB*

Wylie, Walker Gill 1848-1923 *ApCAB X, NatCAB 1, NatCAB 37, WhAm 1*

Wylie, William DeKalb 1897-1966 *NatCAB 52*

Wylie, Winfred 1855-1939 *NatCAB 30*

Wyllie, Irvin Gordon 1920-1974 *WhAm 6*

Wyllie, John Cook 1908-1968 *WhAm 5*

Wyllie, Robert Evan 1873- *WhAm 5*

Wylly, William 1757-1828 *ApCAB*

Wyllys, George d1645 *Drake*

Wyllys, George 1570?-1645 *ApCAB*

Wyllys, George 1590-1645 *NatCAB 10*

Wyllys, George 1710-1796 *ApCAB, DcAmB, Drake, WhAm H*

Wyllys, Hezekiah d1741 *Drake*

Wyllys, Samuel 1632-1709 *ApCAB, Drake*

Wyllys, Samuel 1739-1823 *ApCAB, Drake*

Wyman, Alfred Lee 1874-1953 *WhAm 3*

Wyman, Anna Cora Southworth *WomWWA 14*

Wyman, Bruce 1876-1926 *WhAm 1*

Wyman, Charles Alfred 1914-1971 *NatCAB 57, WhAm 5*

Wyman, Eugene Lester 1924-1973 *WhAm 5*

Wyman, Ferdinand Adolphus 1850- *ApCAB X*

Wyman, Frank Theodore 1868-1935 *WhAm 1*

Wyman, Hal C 1852-1908 *WhAm 1*

Wyman, Hans 1885-1960 *NatCAB 46*

Wyman, Henry Augustus 1861-1935 *NatCAB 26, WhAm 1*

Wyman, Henry Lake 1878-1937 *NatCAB 42*

Wyman, Herbert Gardner 1904-1966 *WhAm 4*

Wyman, Horace 1827-1915 *DcAmB,*
NatCAB 13
Wyman, Jefferies 1814-1874 *WhAm H*
Wyman, Jeffries 1814-1874 *AmBi, ApCAB,*
DcAmB, DcScB, Drake, NatCAB 2,
TwCBDA
Wyman, John *NewYHSD*
Wyman, Levi Parker 1873-1950 *WhAm 3*
Wyman, Lillie Buffum Chace 1847-1929
AmWom, WhAm 1
Wyman, Louis Crosby 1917- *BiDrAC*
Wyman, Louis Eliot 1878-1957 *NatCAB 49*
Wyman, Marion Hay 1887-1972 *NatCAB 57*
Wyman, Morrill 1812-1903 *ApCAB, DcAmB,*
NatCAB 28, WhAm H
Wyman, Oliver Cromwell 1837-1923
NatCAB 34
Wyman, Phillips 1895-1955 *WhAm 3*
Wyman, Robert Harris 1822-1882 *ApCAB,*
DcAmB, NatCAB 4, TwCBDA,
WebAMB, WhAm H
Wyman, Seth 1784-1843 *DcAmB, WhAm H*
Wyman, Thomas White 1793-1854 *ApCAB*
Wyman, Walter 1848-1911 *ApCAB Sup,*
NatCAB 12, WhAm 1
Wyman, Walter Forestus 1881-1940 *WhAm 1*
Wyman, Walter Scott 1874-1942 *NatCAB 33,*
WhAm 2
Wyman, Willard Gordon 1898-1969 *WhAm 5*
Wyman, William Dow 1859-1923 *NatCAB 20,*
WhAm 1
Wyman, William Frizzell 1902-1962
NatCAB 53, WhAm 4
Wyman, William Stokes 1830-1915
ApCAB Sup, NatCAB 12, WhAm 1
Wymer, Floyd Pierce 1905-1971 *NatCAB 56*
Wyncoop, Henry *BiAUS*
Wynegar, Howard LaVerne 1884-1957
WhAm 3
Wynekoop, Alice Lois Lindsay *WomWWA 14*
Wynekoop, Charles Ira 1872-1946 *NatCAB 34*
Wynkoop, Asa 1863-1942 *WhAm 2*
Wynkoop, Bernard Martell 1873-1934 *WhAm 1*
Wynkoop, Frederick 1885-1972 *NatCAB 57*
Wynkoop, Gerardus Hilles 1843- *NatCAB 10*
Wynkoop, Gillett 1865-1930 *NatCAB 23*
Wynkoop, Henry 1737-1812 *NatCAB 11*
Wynkoop, Henry 1737-1816 *ApCAB, BiDrAC,*
WhAm H
Wynn, Chestien 1870-1955 *NatCAB 42*
Wynn, Ed 1886-1966 *WebAB, WhAm 4*
Wynn, Francis Barbour 1860-1922 *NatCAB 17*
Wynn, James Oscar 1897-1975 *WhAm 6*
Wynn, Richard 1750?-1813 *ApCAB, BiAUS,*
Drake
Wynn, Thomas d1825 *BiAUS, Drake*
Wynn, William Joseph 1860-1935 *BiDrAC,*
WhAm 4
Wynn, William Thomas 1874-1954 *WhAm 3*
Wynn, William Thomas 1890-1959 *NatCAB 48*
Wynne, Cyril 1890-1939 *WhAm 1*
Wynne, James 1814-1871 *ApCAB, Drake*
Wynne, John Huddlestone 1743-1788 *Drake*
Wynne, Madeline Yale 1847- *WhAm 4,*
WomWWA 14
Wynne, Margaret Welch 1862- *WomWWA 14*
Wynne, Robert John 1851-1922 *BiDrUSE,*
NatCAB 14, WhAm 1
Wynne, Shirley Wilmott 1882-1942 *WhAm 2*
Wynne, Thomas 1630?-1692 *NatCAB 17*
Wynne, Thomas Alfred 1864-1924 *NatCAB 43*
Wynne, Thomas Neil 1890-1953 *WhAm 3*
Wynns, Thomas 1764-1825 *ApCAB, BiDrAC,*
NatCAB 2, WhAm H, WhAmP
Wynter, Bryan Herbert 1915-1975 *WhAm 6*
Wyse, F H *NewYHSD*
Wysor, Rufus Johnston 1885-1967 *NatCAB 54*
Wyszynski, Eustace *NewYHSD*
Wythe, George 1726-1806 *AmBi, ApCAB,*
BiDAmEd, BiDrAC, DcAmB, Drake,
EncAB, McGEWB, NatCAB 3,
TwCBDA, WebAB, WhAm H, WhAmP
Wythe, George 1728-1806 *BiAUS*
Wythe, J *NewYHSD*
Wythe, Joseph Henry 1822-1901 *ApCAB,*
NatCAB 30
Wyttenbach, E *IIBEAAW*
Wyum, Obed Alonzo 1897-1969 *WhAm 5*

Wyvell, Manton M 1878-1935 *WhAm 1*

X

Xantus, Janos 1825-1894 *DcAmB, NewYHSD, WhAm H*

Xceron, Jean 1890-1967 *WhAm 4*

Xenakis, Iannis 1922- *McGEWB*

Xenocrates Of Chalcedon 396?BC-313?BC *DcScB*

Xenophanes 570?BC-480?BC *AsBiEn*

Xenophanes 580?BC-478?BC *DcScB*

Xenophon 430?BC-355?BC *McGEWB*

Xeres, Francois De *Drake*

Xerxes *McGEWB*

Ximenes, Francisco 1600?-1680? *ApCAB*

Ximenes DeQuesada, Gonzalo 1495-1546 *Drake*

Ximenez, Francisco d1537 *ApCAB*

Xiuhtemoc I *ApCAB*

Xiuhtemoc II *ApCAB*

Xiutlaltzin *ApCAB*

Xochitl *ApCAB*

Xolotl *ApCAB*

Xuarez, Pedro *ApCAB*

Y

WhAmP

Yeaman, Malcolm 1841- *WhAm 1*
Yeaman, William Pope 1832-1904 *DcAmB*
Yeamans, Sir John *Drake*
Yeamans, Sir John 1605?-1676? *ApCAB,*
NatCAB 12
Yeamans, Sir John 1610?-1674 *DcAmB,*
NatCAB 12
Yeamans, Sir John 1611?-1675? *WhAm H*
Yeaple, Whitney S K 1894-1962 *WhAm 4*
Yeardley, Sir George d1627 *Drake*
Yeardley, Sir George 1580?-1627 *ApCAB,*
NatCAB 13
Yeardley, Sir George 1587?-1627 *AmBi,*
DcAmB, WhAm H
Yeardon, Richard 1802-1870 *WhAm H*
Yearsley, Joseph *NewYHSD*
Yeasting, William Henry 1874- *WhAm 5*
Yeater, Charles Emmett 1861- *WhAm 4*
Yeater, Laura Jameson *WomWWA 14*
Yeates, Catharine 1783-1866 *ApCAB*
Yeates, Jasper d1720 *ApCAB*
Yeates, Jasper 1745-1817 *ApCAB, BiAUS,*
DcAmB, Drake, WhAm H
Yeates, Jesse Johnson 1829-1892 *BiDrAC,*
NatCAB 13, WhAm H, WhAmP
Yeates, Jesse Johnson *see also* Yates, Jesse J
Yeates, William Smith 1856-1908 *NatCAB 13,*
WhAm 1
Yeatman, James Erwin 1818-1901 *DcAmB,*
DcAmReB, WhAm 1
Yeatman, Pope 1861-1953 *ApCAB X,*
NatCAB 18, WhAm 3
Yeatman, Richard Thompson 1848-1930
WhAm 1
Yeatman, Rudolph Henry 1885-1947
NatCAB 36
Yeaton, Arthur Charles 1871-1955 *WhAm 3*
Yeaton, J Southgate 1850-1911 *NatCAB 35*
Yeaton, Philip Osborne 1892-1956 *NatCAB 45*
Yeats, William Butler 1865-1939 *McGEWB*
Yeazell, Cornelia Sarah Campbell
WomWWA 14
Yechton, Barbara *WhAm 1*
Yegge, Ronald VanKirk 1905-1970 *NatCAB 57*
Yeh-Lu, Ch'u-Ts'ai 1189-1243 *McGEWB*
Yeiser, Henry Craig 1852- *NatCAB 12*
Yeiser, John O 1866-1928 *WhAm 1*
Yeiser, John Otho, III 1923-1974 *WhAm 6*
Yeisley, George Conrad 1849-1929 *WhAm 1*
Yekuno Amlak *McGEWB*
Yell, Archibald 1797-1847 *ApCAB, BiAUS,*
BiDrAC, DcAmB, Drake, NatCAB 10,
REnAW, TwCBDA, WhAm H, WhAmP
Yelland, Raymond Dabb 1848-1900 *ApCAB,*
IIBEAAW
Yellin, Samuel 1885-1940 *DcAmB S2,*
WhAm 1
Yellowley, Edward C 1873- *WhAm 5*
Yen, Fu 1853-1921 *McGEWB*
Yen, Hsi-Shan 1883-1960 *McGEWB*
Yen, Li-Pen d673 *McGEWB*
Yena, Donald *IIBEAAW*
Yendes, Lucy A 1851- *WhAm 4,*
WomWWA 14
Yenney, Robert Clark 1868-1921 *NatCAB 19*
Yenni *NewYHSD*
Yens, Karl 1868-1945 *NatCAB 34, WhAm 2*
Yensen, Trygve Dewey 1884-1950 *NatCAB 39*
Yeo, James 1832- *ApCAB*
Yeo, Sir James Lucas 1782-1819 *ApCAB,*
Drake
Yeo, Mary Emma *WomWWA 14*
Yeo-Thomas, Edward White Rabbit 1902-1964
WhWW-II
Yeomans, Amelia LeSueur *WomWWA 14*
Yeomans, Andrew 1907-1953 *NatCAB 41*
Yeomans, Charles 1877-1959 *WhAm 3*
Yeomans, Donald Henry 1907-1968 *NatCAB 54*
Yeomans, Earl Raymond 1894-1973 *WhAm 5*
Yeomans, Edward Dorr 1829-1868 *ApCAB*
Yeomans, Frank Clark 1871-1969 *WhAm 5*
Yeomans, George *NewYHSD*
Yeomans, George Dallas 1867-1939 *WhAm 1*
Yeomans, Henry Aaron 1877- *WhAm 5*
Yeomans, James D 1845-1906 *WhAm 1*
Yeomans, John William 1800-1863 *ApCAB,*
DcAmB, NatCAB 11, WhAm H

Yeomans, Lilian Barbara 1861- *WomWWA 14*
Yeomans, Mabel Ford 1884- *WomWWA 14*
Yeomans, Robert Dewitte 1912-1973 *WhAm 5*
Yepsen, Lloyd Nicoll 1896-1955 *WhAm 3*
Yerby, Cecilia Kennedy 1874- *WhoColR*
Yerby, Frank Garvin 1916- *WebAB*
Yerby, William James 1867-1950 *WhAm 3*
Yerby, William James 1869-1950 *WhoColR*
Yeremenko, Andrei Ivanovich 1893-1970
WhoMilH
Yeremenko, Andrey 1892-1970 *WhWW-II*
Yerger, George Shall 1801-1860 *ApCAB*
Yerger, William 1816-1872 *DcAmB, WhAm H*
Yergey, Henry Fritz 1852-1922 *NatCAB 6*
Yergin, Howard Vernon 1885-1951 *WhAm 3*
Yerkes, Ada Watterson *WomWWA 14*
Yerkes, Charles Tyson 1837-1905 *AmBi,*
ApCAB Sup, DcAmB, EncAB,
NatCAB 9, WhAm 1
Yerkes, John Watson 1854-1922 *ApCAB Sup,*
NatCAB 27, WhAm 1
Yerkes, Leonard A 1880-1967 *WhAm 4*
Yerkes, Robert Mearns 1876-1956 *ApCAB X,*
DcScB, McGEWB, NatCAB 43, WebAB,
WhAm 3
Yerkes, Royden Keith 1881-1964 *NatCAB 50,*
WhAm 4
Yerrall, William Wood 1896-1972 *NatCAB 57*
Yersin, Alexandre 1863-1943 *DcScB*
Yerushalmy, Jacob 1904-1973 *WhAm 6*
Yesko, Elmer George 1918- *WhAm 6*
Yetman, Laura Blatchford 1872-
WomWWA 14
Yeuell, Gladstone Horace 1892-1966 *WhAm 4*
Yevtushenko, Yevgeny Alexandrovich 1933-
McGEWB
Yewell, George Henry 1830-1923 *ApCAB,*
NewYHSD, TwCBDA, WhAm 1
Yi, Ha-Yun 1906-1974 *WhAm 6*
Yi, Hwang 1501-1570 *McGEWB*
Yi, Song-Gye 1335-1408 *McGEWB*
Yi, Sunsin 1545-1598 *McGEWB*
Ylvisaker, Ivar Daniel 1868-1926 *WhAm 1*
Ylvisaker, Lauritz S 1889-1962 *NatCAB 50,*
WhAm 4
Yntema, Hessel Edward 1891-1966 *NatCAB 52,*
WhAm 4
Yo, Fei 1103-1141 *McGEWB*
Yoakum, Benjamin Franklin 1859-1929 *DcAmB,*
NatCAB 33, WhAm 1
Yoakum, Charles Henderson 1849-1909 *BiDrAC*
Yoakum, Clarence Stone 1879-1945 *NatCAB 34,*
WhAm 2
Yoakum, Henderson 1810-1856 *ApCAB,*
DcAmB, Drake, WhAm H
Yochum, H L 1903-1974 *WhAm 6*
Yocum, Albert Duncan 1869-1936 *ApCAB X,*
WhAm 1
Yocum, May Turner 1872- *WomWWA 14*
Yocum, Seth Hartman 1834-1895 *BiDrAC,*
WhAm H
Yocum, Wilbur Fisk 1840- *WhAm 4*
Yoder, Albert Henry 1866-1940 *WhAm 2*
Yoder, Allen Alfred 1870-1945 *NatCAB 34*
Yoder, Anne Elizabeth 1879- *WhAm 6*
Yoder, Carl Minter 1885-1944 *NatCAB 33*
Yoder, David Carl 1869-1963 *WhAm 4*
Yoder, Jacob 1758-1832 *ApCAB*
Yoder, Jocelyn Paul 1884-1950 *WhAm 3*
Yoder, Lloyd Edward 1903-1967 *WhAm 4A*
Yoder, Monroe Craig 1893-1959 *NatCAB 48*
Yoder, Robert Anderson 1853-1911 *WhAm 1*
Yoder, Robert McAyeal 1907-1959 *WhAm 3*
Yoder, Samuel S 1841-1921 *BiDrAC*
Yoder, Worth Nicholas 1899-1972 *WhAm 5*
Yoelson, Asa *WebAB*
Yoerg, Louis Edward 1874-1950 *NatCAB 39*
Yoerg, Otto William 1886-1965 *NatCAB 51*
Yogananda, Paramhansa 1893-1952 *DcAmReB*
Yohn, Frederick Coffay 1875-1933 *DcAmB,*
IIBEAAW, NatCAB 24, WhAm 1
Yokoyama, Taikan 1868-1958 *WhAm 3*
Yon, Pietro Alessandro 1886-1943 *DcAmB S3,*
WhAm 2
Yon, Thomas *NewYHSD*
Yon, Thomas Alva 1882-1971 *BiDrAC,*
WhAmP
Yonge *NewYHSD*

Yonge, Ena Laura 1895-1971 *DcAmLiB*
Yonge, Julien C 1879- *WhAm 6*
Yonge, Philip Keyes 1850-1934 *WhAm 3*
Yongjo 1694-1776 *McGEWB*
Yonker, Edward George 1879-1939 *NatCAB 31*
Yook, Young-Soo 1925-1974 *WhAm 6*
Yoran, George Francis 1892-1974 *WhAm 6*
Yorck VonWartenburg, Hans David Ludwig
1759-1830 *WhoMilH*
Yore, Clem 1875-1936 *WhAm 1*
York, Alice Margaret Magnon 1857-
WomWWA 14
York, Alvin Cullum 1887-1964 *WebAB,*
WebAMB
York, Amos Chesley 1884-1952 *WhAm 3*
York, Brantley 1805-1891 *NatCAB 3*
York, Edward Howard, Jr. 1890-1966 *WhAm 5*
York, Edward Palmer 1865-1928 *BnEnAmA,*
WhAm 1
York, Francis Lodowick 1861-1955 *WhAm 3*
York, Frank L 1885-1965 *WhAm 4*
York, Harlan Harvey 1875- *WhAm 5*
York, Harry Clinton 1878-1948 *WhAm 3*
York, John Y, Jr. 1890-1971 *NatCAB 56*
York, Miles Frederick 1901-1973 *WhAm 6*
York, Robert 1909-1975 *WhAm 6*
York, Samuel Albert 1868-1931 *WhAm 1*
York, Tyre 1836-1916 *BiDrAC*
York And Albany, Prince Frederick, Duke
1763-1827 *WhoMilH*
York And Sawyer *BnEnAmA*
Yorke, George Marshall 1870-1934 *WhAm 1*
Yorke, John 1745-1825 *Drake*
Yorke, Peter Christopher 1864-1925 *DcAmB,*
WhAm 1
Yorke, Thomas Jones 1801-1882 *BiAUS,*
BiDrAC, WhAm H
Yorty, Samuel William 1909- *BiDrAC*
Yoshida, Shigeru 1878-1967 *McGEWB,*
WhAm 4A
Yoshida, Tomizo 1903-1973 *WhAm 6*
Yost, Bartley Francis 1877- *WhAm 5*
Yost, Casper Enoch 1841-1922 *NatCAB 28*
Yost, Casper Salathiel 1864-1941 *DcAmB S3,*
WhAm 1
Yost, Fielding Harris 1871-1946 *DcAmB S4,*
WhAm 2
Yost, Gaylord 1888-1958 *WhAm 3*
Yost, George Alfred 1878-1950 *NatCAB 39*
Yost, George Washington Newton 1831-
NatCAB 3
Yost, Jacob 1853-1933 *BiDrAC, WhAm 4*
Yost, Jacob Senewell 1801-1872 *BiAUS,*
BiDrAC, WhAm H
Yost, Joseph Warren 1847- *NatCAB 13,*
WhAm 4
Yost, Lenna Lowe 1878- *WhAm 6,*
WomWWA 14
Yost, Mary 1881-1954 *WhAm 3*
Yost, Orin Ross 1906-1955 *NatCAB 44*
Yost, Robert Morris 1856-1916 *NatCAB 16*
You, Dominique 1772?-1830 *DcAmB,*
WhAm H
You, Dominique 1775-1830 *ApCAB*
You, Thomas *NewYHSD*
Youche, Julian Higgins 1884-1938 *NatCAB 30*
Youden, William John 1900-1971 *DcScB,*
NatCAB 56
Youlou, Fulbert 1917-1972 *McGEWB*
Youmans, Edward Livingston 1821-1887 *AmBi,*
ApCAB, BiDAmEd, DcAmB, Drake,
NatCAB 2, TwCBDA, WhAm H
Youmans, Eliza Ann 1826- *ApCAB,*
NatCAB 3
Youmans, Frank Abijah 1860-1932 *NatCAB 28,*
WhAm 1
Youmans, Henry Melville 1832-1920 *BiDrAC*
Youmans, Iva Catherine 1878- *WomWWA 14*
Youmans, Letitia Creighton 1827- *AmWom,*
ApCAB
Youmans, Theodora Winton 1863- *AmWom,*
WomWWA 14
Youmans, Vincent Millie 1898-1946 *DcAmB S4*
Youmans, William Jay 1838-1901 *ApCAB,*
DcAmB, NatCAB 2, TwCBDA,
WhAm H
Young, Miss *NewYHSD*
Young, Reverend *NewYHSD*

Young, Aaron 1819-1898 *DcAmB, WhAm H*
Young, Abram VanEps 1853-1921 *WhAm 1*
Young, Agatha 1898-1974 *WhAm 6*
Young, Agnes VanGieson *WomWWA 14*
Young, Albert Gayland 1898-1970 *NatCAB 55*
Young, Albion Gustavus 1843-1926 *NatCAB 20*
Young, Alden March 1853-1911 *NatCAB 25*
Young, Alexander *NewYHSD*
Young, Alexander 1798-1884 *NatCAB 6*
Young, Alexander 1800-1854 *ApCAB, DcAmB, Drake, TwCBDA, WhAm H*
Young, Alexander 1833-1910 *NatCAB 12, NatCAB 40*
Young, Alexander 1836- *ApCAB*
Young, Alfred 1831-1900 *ApCAB, DcAmB, NatCAB 2, TwCBDA, WhAm H*
Young, Sir Allen William 1830- *ApCAB*
Young, Allyn Abbott 1876-1929 *DcAmB, WhAm 1*
Young, Ammi Burnham 1798-1874 *BnEnAmA, DcAmB S1, WhAm H*
Young, Andrew *NewYHSD*
Young, Andrew Harvey 1852-1926 *NatCAB 2, NatCAB 22, WhAm 1*
Young, Andrew White 1802-1877 *ApCAB, BiDAmEd*
Young, Ann Eliza Webb 1844-1908 *NotAW*
Young, Anna Rand 1873- *WomWWA 14*
Young, Anne Sewell 1871- *WomWWA 14*
Young, Archer Everett 1873-1951 *NatCAB 40, WhAm 5*
Young, Sir Aretas William 1778?-1835 *ApCAB*
Young, Art 1866-1943 *BnEnAmA, DcAmB S3, WhAm 2*
Young, Arthur Howland 1882-1964 *NatCAB 51, WhAm 4*
Young, Arthur J 1904-1966 *WhAm 4*
Young, August 1837-1913 *NewYHSD*
Young, Augustus 1784-1857 *BiDrAC, WhAm H*
Young, Augustus 1785-1857 *ApCAB, BiAUS, NatCAB 3*
Young, B *NewYHSD*
Young, Barnard Abraham 1911-1969 *NatCAB 54*
Young, Benjamin 1868- *WhAm 4*
Young, Benjamin E 1897-1957 *WhAm 3*
Young, Benjamin Loring 1885-1964 *WhAm 4*
Young, Benjamin Percy 1887-1958 *NatCAB 47*
Young, Bennett Henderson 1843-1919 *NatCAB 3, NatCAB 11, WhAm 1*
Young, Bert Edward 1875-1949 *WhAm 2*
Young, Bertha Kedzie *WomWWA 14*
Young, Bessy Colston 1879- *WomWWA 14*
Young, Bicknell d1938 *WhAm 1*
Young, Brigham 1801-1877 *AmBi, ApCAB, BiAUS, DcAmB, DcAmReB, Drake, EncAAH, EncAB, McGEWB, NatCAB 7, NatCAB 16, REnAW, TwCBDA, WebAB, WhAm H*
Young, Bryan Rust 1800-1882 *BiAUS, BiDrAC, WhAm H*
Young, C C 1869-1947 *WhAm 2*
Young, C Griffith 1866- *WhAm 4*
Young, Casey 1832- *BiAUS*
Young, Charles *WhoColR*
Young, Charles 1812- *ApCAB*
Young, Charles 1867- *ApCAB Sup*
Young, Charles Albert 1902-1955 *NatCAB 42*
Young, Charles Augustus 1834-1908 *AmBi, ApCAB, BiDAmEd, DcAmB, DcScB, NatCAB 6, TwCBDA, WhAm 1*
Young, Charles Augustus 1889-1957 *NatCAB 46*
Young, Charles Duncanson 1878-1955 *WhAm 3*
Young, Charles Elisha 1858- *NatCAB 5*
Young, Charles Henry 1876- *WhAm 5*
Young, Charles Jac 1880-1940 *WhAm 1*
Young, Charles Lowell 1865-1937 *NatCAB 27*
Young, Charles Luther 1838-1913 *NatCAB 5, WhAm 1*
Young, Charles Sommers 1873- *WhAm 5*
Young, Charles VanPatten 1876- *WhAm 5*
Young, Charlotte Soutter Murdock *WomWWA 14*
Young, Chic 1901-1973 *WebAB, WhAm 5, WhAm 6*
Young, Claiborne Addison *WhAm 5*

Young, Clara Kimball d1960 *WhAm 4*
Young, Clarence *WebAB*
Young, Clarence Clifton 1922- *BiDrAC*
Young, Clarence Hoffman 1866-1957 *NatCAB 46, WhAm 3*
Young, Clarence Marshall d1973 *WhAm 5*
Young, Clark Montgomery 1856-1908 *BiDAmEd, DcAmB, WhAm 1*
Young, Coulter Dabney 1890-1941 *NatCAB 32*
Young, Courtland H 1876-1930 *WhAm 1*
Young, Cy 1867-1955 *WebAB*
Young, D Philip 1887-1975 *WhAm 6*
Young, Daniel Joseph 1881-1943 *NatCAB 42*
Young, David 1776-1859 *ApCAB*
Young, David 1781-1852 *DcAmB, WhAm H*
Young, David 1849- *NatCAB 7*
Young, David John 1864-1927 *NatCAB 32*
Young, David Redd 1899-1969 *NatCAB 55*
Young, Denton True 1867-1955 *DcAmB S5, WebAB, WhAm HA, WhAm 4*
Young, Dwight Edwin 1884-1967 *WhAm 4*
Young, E Weldon 1869-1940 *NatCAB 41*
Young, Ebenezer 1783-1851 *BiDrAC, WhAm H, WhAmP*
Young, Ebenezer 1784-1851 *BiAUS*
Young, Edmond Stafford 1827-1888 *ApCAB X*
Young, Edward 1818- *NatCAB 2*
Young, Edward Faitoute Condit 1835-1908 *NatCAB 2*
Young, Edward Joseph 1907-1968 *WhAm 5*
Young, Edward Lorraine 1885-1969 *NatCAB 53*
Young, Edward Mark 1866-1932 *NatCAB 24, WhAm 1*
Young, Edward Shreiner 1858-1914 *NatCAB 16*
Young, Edward T 1858- *WhAm 4*
Young, Egerton Ryerson 1840-1909 *NatCAB 14*
Young, Elizabeth Guion 1876- *WhAm 5*
Young, Ella Flagg 1845-1918 *AmBi, BiCAW, BiDAmEd, DcAmB, NatCAB 19, NotAW, WhAm 1, WomWWA 14*
Young, Ernest Charles 1892-1968 *WhAm 5*
Young, Eugenie E 1872- *WomWWA 14*
Young, Evan Erastus 1878-1946 *NatCAB 36, WhAm 2*
Young, Evangeline Wilson *WomWWA 14*
Young, Ewing 1792?-1841 *AmBi, DcAmB, REnAW, WhAm H*
Young, Frances Speed Graham 1881- *WomWWA 14*
Young, Francis Brett 1884-1954 *WhAm 3*
Young, Frank Herman 1888-1964 *WhAm 4*
Young, Frank Levi 1860-1930 *NatCAB 24*
Young, Frank Mobley, Jr. 1903-1964 *WhAm 4*
Young, Franklin Knowles 1857- *WhAm 4*
Young, Frederic George 1858-1929 *NatCAB 21, WhAm 1*
Young, Gavin William, Jr. 1898-1953 *NatCAB 41*
Young, George 1869-1935 *WhoColR*
Young, George 1870-1935 *DcAmB S1*
Young, George 1894-1957 *WhAm 3*
Young, George, Jr. 1892-1956 *WhAm 3*
Young, George A 1917-1964 *WhAm 4*
Young, George Brigham 1867-1940 *WhAm 1*
Young, George Bright 1860-1934 *WhAm 1*
Young, George Brooks 1840-1906 *WhAm 1*
Young, George Edgar 1888-1960 *NatCAB 49*
Young, George Frank 1863-1920 *NatCAB 28*
Young, George Gilray 1876-1950 *WhAm 3*
Young, George Henry 1876- *WhAm 5*
Young, George Husband 1909-1961 *WhAm 4*
Young, George Joseph 1876- *WhAm 5*
Young, George Morley 1870-1932 *BiDrAC, WhAm 1, WhAmP*
Young, George Murray 1802-1878 *ApCAB X*
Young, George Paxton 1818- *ApCAB*
Young, George R *ApCAB*
Young, George Rude 1857-1916 *ApCAB X, WhAm 1*
Young, George Ulysses 1867- *WhAm 4*
Young, George Washington 1864-1926 *WhAm 1*
Young, Gertrude Atena Hubbard 1887- *WomWWA 14*
Young, Gilbert Amos 1872-1943 *WhAm 2*
Young, Gladwin E 1900-1973 *WhAm 6*
Young, Gordon 1886-1948 *WhAm 3*
Young, Gordon Elmo 1907-1969 *WhAm 5*

Young, Gustav *NewYHSD*
Young, H Walter 1890-1942 *NatCAB 39*
Young, Harry Curtis 1888-1970 *NatCAB 56*
Young, Harvey B 1840-1901 *NewYHSD*
Young, Harvey Otis 1840-1901 *IIBEAAW*
Young, Helen Binkerd 1878- *WomWWA 14*
Young, Helen Louise 1877-1942 *WhAm 2, WomWWA 14*
Young, Henry 1871-1944 *NatCAB 33*
Young, Henry Lane 1878-1966 *WhAm 4*
Young, Herbert A 1906-1965 *WhAm 4*
Young, Herbert William 1875-1946 *NatCAB 44*
Young, Herman H 1887-1931 *NatCAB 23*
Young, Hiram 1830- *NatCAB 3*
Young, Hiram Casey 1828-1899 *BiDrAC, WhAmP*
Young, Horace Autrey 1899-1973 *WhAm 6*
Young, Horace Gedney 1854-1933 *WhAm 1*
Young, Horace Olin 1850-1917 *BiDrAC, NatCAB 17, WhAm 1, WhAmP*
Young, Howard Edward 1856-1939 *NatCAB 30*
Young, Howard Isaac 1889-1965 *WhAm 4*
Young, Howard Sloan 1879- *WhAm 6*
Young, Hugh Hampton 1870-1945 *DcAmB S3, NatCAB 38, WhAm 2*
Young, Ida Clarke 1867- *WomWWA 14*
Young, Ira King 1884-1953 *NatCAB 42*
Young, Isaac Daniel 1849-1927 *BiDrAC*
Young, Isaac Wilhelm 1874- *WhoColR*
Young, J H A *NewYHSD*
Young, J Harvey 1830-1918 *Drake*
Young, Jacob 1776-1859 *Drake*
Young, Jacob William Albert 1865-1948 *BiDAmEd, WhAm 2*
Young, James 1835- *ApCAB*
Young, James 1866-1942 *BiDrAC, WhAm 4, WhAmP*
Young, James, Jr. 1872-1952 *NatCAB 40*
Young, James Addison 1866- *WhAm 4*
Young, James Carleton 1856-1918 *NatCAB 17, WhAm 1*
Young, James H *NewYHSD*
Young, James H 1892-1961 *WhAm 4*
Young, James Harvey 1830-1918 *NewYHSD*
Young, James Henry 1866-1919 *WhAm 1*
Young, James Kelly 1862-1923 *NatCAB 20, WhAm 1*
Young, James Nicholas 1885-1959 *WhAm 3*
Young, James Rankin 1847-1924 *ApCAB, BiDrAC, NatCAB 20, TwCBDA, WhAm 1, WhAmP*
Young, James Scott 1848-1914 *WhAm 1*
Young, James Thomas 1873- *WhAm 5*
Young, James Webb 1886-1973 *WhAm 5*
Young, James Wilson 1897-1961 *NatCAB 49*
Young, Jennie *AmWom*
Young, Jennie B 1869- *AmWom*
Young, Jeremiah Simeon 1866-1947 *WhAm 2*
Young, Jesse Bowman 1844-1914 *DcAmB, NatCAB 5, WhAm 1*
Young, John 1755?-1835 *ApCAB*
Young, John 1773-1837 *ApCAB*
Young, John 1802-1852 *ApCAB, BiAUS, BiDrAC, DcAmB, Drake, NatCAB 3, TwCBDA, WhAm H, WhAmP*
Young, Sir John 1807-1876 *ApCAB, Drake*
Young, John 1811-1878 *ApCAB*
Young, John Alexander 1838- *NatCAB 17*
Young, John Andrew 1916- *BiDrAC*
Young, John Clark 1803-1857 *Drake*
Young, John Clarke 1803-1857 *ApCAB, BiDAmEd, DcAmB, TwCBDA, WhAm H*
Young, John Duncan 1823-1910 *BiAUS, BiDrAC*
Young, John Edwin 1855-1926 *WhAm 1*
Young, John Frederick 1865-1947 *NatCAB 36*
Young, John Freeman 1820-1885 *ApCAB, NatCAB 13, TwCBDA*
Young, John J 1830?-1879 *IIBEAAW, NewYHSD*
Young, John L *NewYHSD*
Young, John Paul 1873-1957 *NatCAB 47*
Young, John Philip 1849-1921 *NatCAB 17, WhAm 1*
Young, John Richardson 1782-1804 *DcAmB, DcScB, WhAm H*
Young, John Russell 1840-1899 *AmBi, DcAmB, DcAmLiB, WhAm H*

Young, John Russell 1841-1899 *ApCAB, NatCAB 2, TwCBDA*
Young, John Russell 1882-1967 *WhAm 4*
Young, John Smith 1834-1916 *BiDrAC*
Young, John T 1814?-1842 *NewYHSD*
Young, John Wesley 1879-1932 *AmBi, BiDAmEd, DcAmB, DcScB, NatCAB 23, WhAm 1*
Young, Jonathan 1825-1885 *ApCAB*
Young, Joseph A, Jr. 1886- *WhoColR*
Young, Joseph Franklin 1871- *WhoColR*
Young, Joseph Hardie 1864-1958 *WhAm 3*
Young, Josephine Bowen 1876- *WomWWA 14*
Young, Josue Maria 1808-1866 *DcAmB, WhAm H*
Young, Josue Marie 1808-1866 *ApCAB, Drake, NatCAB 13*
Young, Josue Moody 1808-1866 *TwCBDA*
Young, Julia Evelyn Ditto 1857- *AmWom, WhAm 4*
Young, Karl 1879-1943 *DcAmB S3, NatCAB 42, WhAm 2*
Young, Kate C 1859- *WomWWA 14*
Young, Kenneth Todd 1916-1972 *WhAm 5*
Young, Kimball 1893-1973 *WhAm 6*
Young, Lafayette 1848-1926 *BiDrAC, DcAmB, NatCAB 32, WhAm 1*
Young, Lafayette, Jr. 1877-1930 *WhAm 1*
Young, Laurence W 1877- *WhAm 5*
Young, Leon Decatur 1872-1947 *WhAm 2*
Young, Leonard 1871- *WhAm 5*
Young, Leonard Augustus 1877-1964 *WhAm 4*
Young, Lester Willis d1959 *WhAm 5*
Young, Levi Edgar 1874- *WhAm 5*
Young, Lewis Emanuel 1878-1953 *WhAm 3*
Young, Louise Schafer *WomWWA 14*
Young, Loyal 1806- *ApCAB*
Young, Lucien 1852-1912 *ApCAB Sup, NatCAB 16, WhAm 1*
Young, Mahonri 1877-1957 *BnEnAmA, WhAm 3*
Young, Mahonri Macintosh 1877-1957 *REnAW*
Young, Mahonri Mackintosh 1877-1957 *IIBEAAW*
Young, Margaret Rankin 1871-1930 *WhAm 1, WomWWA 14*
Young, Martha *AmWom, WomWWA 14*
Young, Mary Eliza *NewYHSD*
Young, Mary Elizabeth 1929- *EncAAH*
Young, Mary Stuart 1847- *WomWWA 14*
Young, Mary Vance 1866-1946 *NatCAB 33, WhAm 2, WomWWA 14*
Young, McClintock 1836- *NatCAB 10*
Young, Meichel Harry De 1848- *NatCAB 1*
Young, Milton 1851-1918 *NatCAB 17*
Young, Milton Ruben 1897- *BiDrAC*
Young, Minnie Ella 1858- *WomWWA 14*
Young, Morrison Waite 1860-1932 *WhAm 1*
Young, Murat Bernard 1901-1973 *WebAB*
Young, Nathan Benjamin 1862- *WhoColR*
Young, Nellie Gray 1867- *WomWWA 14*
Young, Newton Clarence 1862-1923 *ApCAB X, NatCAB 5, WhAm 1*
Young, Odus Graham 1858- *WhAm 1*
Young, Otto 1844-1906 *WhAm 1*
Young, Owen D 1874-1962 *ApCAB X, EncAB, McGEWB, WhAm 4*
Young, P M B 1838- *BiAUS*
Young, Percy S 1870-1950 *WhAm 3*
Young, Philip *NewYHSD*
Young, Philip 1874-1953 *WhAm 3*
Young, Philip Endicott 1885-1955 *NatCAB 44, WhAm 3*
Young, Phineas Howe 1847-1868 *IIBEAAW*
Young, Pierce Manning Butler 1836-1896 *BiDConf, BiDrAC, DcAmB, WhAmP*
Young, Pierce Manning Butler 1836-1898 *WhAm H*
Young, Pierce Manning Butler 1839- *ApCAB, NatCAB 2*
Young, Pierce Manning Butler 1839-1896 *TwCBDA*
Young, Plummer Bernard 1884-1962 *NatCAB 49, WhAm 4*
Young, Raymond Milton 1911-1970 *NatCAB 56*
Young, Richard 1846-1935 *BiDrAC, WhAm 5*
Young, Richard Elliott 1904-1969 *NatCAB 56*

Young, Richard Hale 1905-1970 *WhAm 5*
Young, Richard Hart 1904-1953 *NatCAB 45*
Young, Richard Montgomery *BiAUS*
Young, Richard Montgomery 1796-1852? *ApCAB, NatCAB 12, TwCBDA*
Young, Richard Montgomery 1798-1861 *BiDrAC, WhAm H*
Young, Richard Whitehead 1858-1919 *WhAm 1*
Young, Rida Johnson d1926 *WhAm 1*
Young, Robert Anderson 1824-1902 *NatCAB 8, WhAm 1*
Young, Robert Nicholas 1900-1964 *WhAm 4*
Young, Robert Ralph 1897-1958 *NatCAB 50, WhAm 3*
Young, Robert Thompson 1874- *WhAm 5*
Young, Robert Winthrop 1887-1974 *WhAm 6*
Young, Rodney Stuart 1907-1974 *WhAm 6*
Young, Roland 1887-1953 *NatCAB 40, WhAm 3*
Young, Rosalind Watson 1874- *WomWWA 14*
Young, Rose d1941 *WhAm 1, WomWWA 14*
Young, Roy Archibald 1882-1960 *WhAm 4*
Young, Roy Carl 1895-1954 *NatCAB 45*
Young, Roy Odo 1870-1951 *WhAm 3*
Young, Sam Martin 1861-1935 *WhAm 1*
Young, Samuel Baldwin Marks 1840-1924 *ApCAB Sup, NatCAB 13, TwCBDA, WebAMB, WhAm 1*
Young, Samuel Edward 1866-1927 *WhAm 1*
Young, Samuel Hall 1847-1927 *DcAmB, WhAm 2*
Young, Samuel M 1806-1897 *ApCAB X*
Young, Samuel Marsh 1867-1929 *NatCAB 24*
Young, Sanborn 1873- *WhAm 5*
Young, Sarah Graham 1831- *AmWom*
Young, Smith Greshem 1866- *WhAm 4*
Young, Stanley 1906-1975 *WhAm 6*
Young, Stark 1881-1963 *NatCAB 52, WhAm 4*
Young, Stephen Marvin 1889- *BiDrAC*
Young, Stewart Woodford 1869-1930 *WhAm 1*
Young, Sydney 1857-1937 *DcScB*
Young, Thomas *NewYHSD*
Young, Thomas 1731?-1777 *DcAmB*
Young, Thomas 1732-1777 *WhAm H*
Young, Thomas 1773-1829 *AsBiEn, BiHiMed, DcScB, McGEWB*
Young, Thomas 1841- *NatCAB 1*
Young, Thomas A 1837-1913 *NewYHSD*
Young, Thomas Benton 1862-1960 *NatCAB 47*
Young, Thomas Crane 1858-1934 *NatCAB 17, WhAm 1*
Young, Thomas Gorsuch d1953 *WhAm 3*
Young, Thomas John 1803-1852 *ApCAB*
Young, Thomas Kay d1954 *WhAm 3*
Young, Thomas Lowry 1832-1888 *ApCAB, BiDrAC, NatCAB 3, TwCBDA, WhAm H*
Young, Thomas Otto 1893-1968 *NatCAB 54*
Young, Thomas Shields 1863- *WhAm 1*
Young, Thomas White 1908-1967 *WhAm 4A*
Young, Timothy Roberts 1811-1898 *BiAUS, BiDrAC*
Young, Tobias *NewYHSD*
Young, Towne 1883-1966 *NatCAB 55*
Young, Truman Post 1877-1942 *WhAm 2*
Young, Udell Charles 1893-1967 *WhAm 4*
Young, Van B 1836-1892 *NatCAB 4*
Young, Victor 1900-1956 *WhAm 3*
Young, Wallace Jesse 1880-1923 *WhAm 1*
Young, Walter Dickson 1855-1916 *NatCAB 17*
Young, Walter Jorgensen 1883-1940 *WhAm 1*
Young, Walter Stevens 1878-1946 *WhAm 2*
Young, Whitney Moore, Jr. 1921-1971 *EncAB, McGEWB, NatCAB 57, WebAB, WhAm 5*
Young, Sir William 1799-1887 *ApCAB*
Young, William 1809-1888 *ApCAB, Drake*
Young, William 1845-1920 *NatCAB 20*
Young, William 1847-1920 *WhAm 1*
Young, William Albin 1860-1928 *BiDrAC, WhAm 4*
Young, William Bradford 1839-1921 *ApCAB X*
Young, William Brooks 1842- *WhAm 4*
Young, William Brooks 1844- *NatCAB 8*
Young, William Clark 1799-1893 *ApCAB Sup*
Young, William Elmore 1863- *ApCAB X*
Young, William Foster 1867-1935 *NatCAB 18,*

WhAm 1
Young, William H 1860- *ApCAB X*
Young, William Henry 1863-1942 *DcScB*
Young, William Henry Harrison Hutchinson 1819- *ApCAB*
Young, William Hugh 1838-1901 *BiDConf*
Young, William Jackson 1881-1937 *NatCAB 38*
Young, William James 1859- *NatCAB 10*
Young, William John 1897-1948 *NatCAB 37*
Young, William Lesquereux 1889-1972 *WhAm 5*
Young, William Lindsay 1893-1959 *WhAm 3*
Young, William Singleton 1790-1827 *BiAUS, BiDrAC, WhAm H*
Young, William Stewart 1859-1937 *NatCAB 53*
Young, William Wesley 1868- *WhAm 4*
Young Hickory *EncAAH*
Young-Hunter, John 1874-1955 *IIBEAAW, NatCAB 46, WhAm 3*
Young-Man-Afraid-Of-His-Horses 1835-1893 *ApCAB Sup*
Youngberg, Gilbert A 1875- *WhAm 5*
Youngblood, Bonney 1881- *WhAm 6*
Youngblood, Harold Francis 1907- *BiDrAC*
Youngblood, Mary F 1865- *WomWWA 14*
Youngdahl, Benjamin Emanuel 1897-1970 *WhAm 5*
Youngdahl, Oscar Ferdinand 1893-1946 *BiDrAC, WhAm 2, WhAmP*
Youngdahl, Reuben Kenneth Nathaniel 1911-1968 *WhAm 5*
Younger, Cole 1844-1916 *WebAB*
Younger, James 1850-1902 *REnAW*
Younger, Jesse Arthur 1893-1967 *BiDrAC, WhAmP*
Younger, Jesse Authur 1893-1967 *WhAm 4*
Younger, John 1846-1874 *REnAW*
Younger, John 1882-1945 *WhAm 2*
Younger, John Elliott 1892-1958 *WhAm 3*
Younger, Maud 1870-1936 *DcAmB S2, NotAW*
Younger, Paul Clarence 1910-1971 *NatCAB 57*
Younger, Robert 1853-1889 *REnAW*
Younger, Thomas Coleman 1844-1916 *DcAmB, REnAW, WebAB, WhAm HA, WhAm 4*
Younger, William John 1838-1920 *NatCAB 20*
Youngerman, Jack 1926- *BnEnAmA*
Youngert, Sven Gustaf d1939 *WhAm 1*
Younggreen, Charles Clark 1890-1942 *WhAm 2*
Younghusband, Sir Francis Edward 1863-1942 *McGEWB*
Youngken, Heber Wilkinson 1885-1963 *WhAm 4*
Younglieb, Herman 1904-1973 *NatCAB 56*
Younglove, Elbridge G *NewYHSD*
Youngman, Frank Nourse 1893-1968 *WhAm 5*
Youngman, William Sterling 1872-1934 *NatCAB 27*
Youngquist, G Aaron 1885-1959 *WhAm 3*
Youngs, J W T 1910-1970 *WhAm 5*
Youngs, John 1623-1698 *DcAmB, WhAm H*
Youngs, Merle Lealand 1886-1958 *NatCAB 50, WhAm 4*
Youngs, William J 1851-1916 *WhAm 1*
Youngson, Robert George 1917-1974 *NatCAB 57*
Youngson, William Wallace 1869-1955 *NatCAB 43, WhAm 5*
Yount, Barton Kyle 1884-1949 *NatCAB 39, WhAm 2*
Yount, Ella B *WomWWA 14*
Yount, George Concepcion 1794-1865 *DcAmB, WhAm H*
Yount, Herbert Macon 1885-1970 *NatCAB 55*
Yount, Marshall Hill 1870-1948 *NatCAB 36*
Yount, Miles Frank 1880-1933 *WhAm 1*
Yount, Norman Fleming 1917-1972 *WhAm 5*
Youree, Peter 1843- *NatCAB 10*
Yourkevitch, Vladimir 1885-1964 *NatCAB 51*
Youtz, Herbert Alden 1867-1943 *NatCAB 41, WhAm 4*
Youtz, Lewis Addison 1864-1947 *WhAm 3*
Youtz, Philip Newell 1895-1972 *NatCAB 56, WhAm 5*
Yowell, Everett Irving 1870-1959 *NatCAB 47, WhAm 3*
Ysabeau, Alphonse Paul 1811-1848 *ApCAB*
Ysambert, Gustave 1667-1711 *ApCAB*

Ysambert, Jules Henri D' 1739-1795 *ApCAB*
Ysaye, Eugene 1858-1931 *WhAm 1*
Ysoart, Sigismond 1604-1652 *ApCAB*
Yuan, Mei 1716-1798 *McGEWB*
Yuan, Shih-K'ai 1859-1916 *McGEWB*
Yudain, Theodore 1907-1970 *WhAm 5*
Yudkin, Arthur M 1892-1957 *WhAm 3*
Yugov, Anton 1904- *WhAm 4*
Yui, O K 1898-1960 *WhAm 4*
Yuille, Thomas Burks 1869-1934 *NatCAB 33*
Yukawa, Hideki 1907- *AsBiEn, McGEWB*
Yule, George 1824- *ApCAB X*
Yule, George Udny 1871-1951 *DcScB*
Yule, William Head 1883- *NatCAB 16*
Yulee, David Levy 1810-1886 *BiDrAC, DcAmB,*
   REnAW, WhAm H, WhAmP
Yulee, David Levy 1811-1886 *ApCAB, BiAUS,*
   NatCAB 11, TwCBDA
Yun, Sondo 1587-1671 *McGEWB*
Yunck, John Adam 1852-1941 *NatCAB 33*
Yunck, Robert Edmund 1916-1965 *NatCAB 51*
Yuncker, Truman George 1891-1964 *WhAm 4*
Yundt, Michael 1884-1942 *NatCAB 32*
Yung, Julius Rudolph 1878-1952 *NatCAB 38,*
   WhAm 6
Yung, Wing 1828-1912 *ApCAB, DcAmB,*
   WhAm 1
Yung-Lo 1360-1424 *McGEWB*
Yungbluth, Bernard Joseph 1882-1957 *WhAm 3*
Yunkers, Adja 1900- *BnEnAmA*
Yunus, Abul-Hasan Ali Ibn Abd Al-R, Ibn d1009
   DcScB
Yurka, Blanche 1887-1974 *WhAm 6*
Yust, Florence Hosmer French *WomWWA 14*
Yust, Walter 1894-1960 *WhAm 3*
Yust, William Frederick 1869-1947 *WhAm 2*
Yuster, Samuel Terrill 1903-1958 *NatCAB 44*
Yusuf Karamanli *WhAm H*
Yutzy, Henry Clay 1910-1966 *NatCAB 52,*
   WhAm 4
Yutzy, Thomas Daniel 1903-1966 *WhAm 4*
Yver DeChazelles, Jean Pierre 1709-1786
   ApCAB
Yves *IlBEAAW*
Yves D'Evreux, Pierre 1570?-1630? *ApCAB*

Z

Zabarella, Jacopo 1533-1589 *DcScB*
Zabel, Morton Dauwen 1901-1964 *WhAm 4*
Zabinski, Jan Franciszek 1897-1974 *WhAm 6*
Zablocki, Clement John 1912- *BiDrAC*
Zabreski *NewYHSD*
Zabriskie, Abraham Oothout 1807-1873 *ApCAB, NatCAB 3*
Zabriskie, Andrew Christian 1853-1916 *WhAm 1*
Zabriskie, Charles Christian 1883-1964 *NatCAB 50*
Zabriskie, Edward Henry 1892-1951 *NatCAB 40*
Zabriskie, Edwin Garvin 1874-1959 *NatCAB 43, WhAm 3*
Zabriskie, Frederic 1850-1921 *NatCAB 18*
Zabriskie, George 1852-1931 *WhAm 1*
Zabriskie, George Albert 1868-1954 *NatCAB 42, WhAm 3*
Zabriskie, John Banta 1878-1951 *NatCAB 39*
Zabriskie, N Lansing 1838-1926 *NatCAB 25*
Zabriskie, Robert Lansing 1872-1949 *NatCAB 39, WhAm 5*
Zach, Franz Xaver Von 1754-1832 *DcScB*
Zach, Leon 1895-1966 *WhAm 4*
Zach, Max Wilhelm 1864-1921 *DcAmB, WhAm 1*
Zacharias, Ellis Mark 1890-1961 *WhAm 4*
Zacher, Clarence Henry 1908-1974 *WhAm 6*
Zacher, Edmund 1853-1925 *NatCAB 20*
Zacher, Louis Edmund 1878-1945 *WhAm 2*
Zachos, John Celivergas 1820-1898 *WhAm H*
Zachos, John Celivergos 1820-1898 *ApCAB, BiDAmEd, DcAmB*
Zachos, Louis George 1898-1956 *NatCAB 44*
Zachresky *NewYHSD*
Zachry, Caroline Beaumont 1894-1945 *NotAW*
Zackrison, Harry Bertil 1904-1972 *NatCAB 57*
Zacuto, Abraham Bar Samuel Bar Abraham 1450?-1522? *DcScB*
Zadeikis, Povilas 1887-1957 *WhAm 3*
Zadkin, Daniel 1612?-1687 *NatCAB 2*
Zadkine, Ossip Joselyn 1890-1967 *McGEWB, WhAm 4A*
Zaenglein, Paul Carl 1892-1969 *WhAm 5*
Zaff, Fred 1912-1959 *NatCAB 43*
Zagat, Arthur Leo 1896-1949 *NatCAB 37*
Zaghlul Pasha, Saad 1859-1927 *McGEWB*
Zaharias, Babe Didrikson 1912-1956 *WhAm HA*
Zaharias, Mildred Didrikson 1912-1956 *WhAm 4*
Zaharias, Mildred Ella Didrikson 1914-1956 *WebAB*
Zahedi, Fazlollah 1897-1963 *WhAm 4*
Zahm, Albert Francis d1954 *WhAm 3*
Zahm, John Augustine 1851-1921 *DcAmB, DcAmReB, NatCAB 9, TwCBDA, WhAm 1*
Zahn, Edward *NewYHSD*
Zahn, Edward James, Jr. 1921-1962 *WhAm 4*
Zahner, Ralph *NewYHSD*
Zahniser, Arthur DeFrance 1865-1935 *WhAm 1*
Zahniser, Charles Reed 1873- *WhAm 5*
Zahniser, Howard 1906-1964 *NatCAB 50, WhAm 4*
Zahorsky, John 1871-1963 *WhAm 4*
Zahrawi, Abul-Qasim Khalaf Ibn A, Al-936?-1013? *DcScB*
Zain, Rebyl 1909-1973 *WhAm 6*
Zak, Emil Rudolf 1877-1949 *NatCAB 37*
Zakariya Ibn Muhammad Ibn Mahmud *DcScB*
Zakreski, Alexander *NewYHSD*

Zakrzewska, Maria Elizabeth 1829-1902 *AmWom, ApCAB*
Zakrzewska, Marie Elizabeth 1829-1902 *DcAmB, NotAW, WhAm 1*
Zaldivar, Rafael 1830?- *ApCAB*
Zaldivar, Rafael 1865-1922 *WhAm 1*
Zaldivar Mendoza, Vicente 1565-1625? *ApCAB*
Zaleski, Alexander 1906-1975 *WhAm 6*
Zalinski, Agnes DeSchweinitz *WomWWA 14*
Zalinski, Edmund Lewis Gray 1845-1909 *TwCBDA*
Zalinski, Edmund Louis Gray 1849-1909 *AmBi, ApCAB, NatCAB 7, WhAm 1*
Zalinski, Moses Gray 1863-1937 *WhAm 1*
Zaluzansky Ze Zaluzan, Adam 1558?-1613 *DcScB*
Zalvidea, Jose Maria De 1780-1846 *WhAm H*
Zambarano, Ubaldo Edward 1899-1950 *NatCAB 40*
Zambeccari, Giuseppe 1655-1728 *DcScB*
Zambonini, Ferruccio 1880-1932 *DcScB*
Zambrana, Ramon 1817-1866 *ApCAB*
Zamna *ApCAB*
Zamora, Alonso De 1660-1725? *ApCAB*
Zamora, Cristobal De 1500?-1566 *ApCAB*
Zamorano, Agustin Juan Vicente 1798-1842 *DcAmB*
Zamorano, Austin Juan Vincente 1798-1842 *WhAm H*
Zand, Stephen Joseph 1898-1963 *WhAm 4*
Zander, Arnold Scheuer 1901-1975 *WhAm 6*
Zander, Henry George 1869-1937 *WhAm 1*
Zane, Abraham Vanhoy 1850-1919 *WhAm 1*
Zane, Charles Shuster 1831-1915 *ApCAB X, DcAmB, NatCAB 12, WhAm 4*
Zane, Ebenezer 1747-1811 *ApCAB, Drake, NatCAB 11*
Zane, Ebenezer 1747-1812 *AmBi, DcAmB, EncAAH, WhAm H*
Zane, Elizabeth 1759?-1847? *ApCAB*
Zane, Elizabeth 1766?-1831? *NotAW*
Zane, John Maxcy 1863-1937 *ApCAB X, WhAm 1*
Zanetti, Joaquin Enrique 1885-1974 *WhAm 6*
Zang, Adolph Joseph 1856-1916 *NatCAB 17*
Zang, John J *IIBEAAW*
Zangerie, John Adam 1866-1956 *WhAm 5*
Zangerle, John Adam 1866-1956 *NatCAB 45*
Zangwill, Israel 1864-1926 *McGEWB*
Zanotti, Eustachio 1709-1782 *DcScB*
Zantzinger, Clarence Clark 1872-1954 *NatCAB 45, WhAm 3*
Zanuck, Darryl Francis 1902- *WebAB*
Zapata, Emiliano 1879?-1919 *McGEWB*
Zapata, Juan Ortiz De 1620?-1690? *ApCAB*
Zapata-Mendoza, Juan Ventura *ApCAB*
Zapata Y Sandoval, Juan 1545-1630 *ApCAB*
Zapffe, Frederick Carl 1873-1951 *WhAm 3*
Zapiola, Jose 1802-1885 *ApCAB*
Zapotocky, Antonin 1884-1957 *WhAm 3*
Zapp, Carroll Francis 1904-1968 *WhAm 5*
Zaragoza, Ignacio 1829-1862 *ApCAB*
Zarankiewicz, Kazimierz 1902-1959 *DcScB*
Zarate, Agostin De 1493?-1560 *ApCAB, Drake*
Zarate, Geronimo *ApCAB*
Zarate, Miguel d1583 *ApCAB*
Zarate, Pedro Ortiz De 1490?-1545 *ApCAB*
Zarco, Francisco 1829-1869 *ApCAB*
Zarco, Giulio 1490-1549 *ApCAB*
Zardetti, John Joseph Frederic Otto 1847- *TwCBDA*
Zari, Angelo Bartolomeo 1873-1956 *NatCAB 43*
Zaring, Clarence Arthur 1870-1960 *WhAm 4*

Zaring, E Robb 1868- *WhAm 4*
Zariphes, Constantine A Paleologos 1898-1963 *NatCAB 50*
Zarlino, Gioseffo 1517-1590 *McGEWB*
Zaroubin, Georgi N 1900-1958 *WhAm 3*
Zarqali, Abu Ishaq Ibrahim Ibn Y, Al- d1100 *DcScB*
Zartmann, Parley Emmett 1865- *WhAm 5*
Zaugg, Walter Albert 1883-1962 *WhAm 4*
Zavadovsky, Mikhail Mikhaylovich 1891-1957 *DcScB*
Zavala, Lorenzo De 1788-1836 *ApCAB*
Zavala, Lorenzo De 1789-1836 *NatCAB 2*
Zavarzin, Aleksey Alekseevich 1886-1945 *DcScB*
Zavin, William Herman 1912-1955 *NatCAB 45*
Zavitz, Edwin Cornell 1892-1949 *WhAm 2*
Zavytowsky, A *NewYHSD*
Zawadzki, Aleksander 1899-1964 *WhAm 4*
Zawadzki, Edward Stanley 1914-1967 *NatCAB 53*
Zayyati Al-Gharnati, Al-Hasan Ibn, Al- *DcScB*
Zdanowicz, Casimir Douglass 1883-1953 *WhAm 3*
Zea, Francisco Antonio 1770-1822 *ApCAB, Drake*
Zeami, Kanze 1364-1444 *McGEWB*
Zech, Frederick, Jr. 1858-1926 *WhAm 1*
Zecher, Robert Cummings 1904-1942 *NatCAB 31*
Zecher, Walter Edwin 1875-1931 *NatCAB 31*
Zechmeister, Laszlo Karoly Erno 1889-1972 *NatCAB 57, WhAm 5*
Zeckwer, Richard 1850-1922 *WhAm 1*
Zeder, Fred Morrell 1886-1951 *WhAm 3*
Zedler, John 1864-1929 *WhAm 1*
Zeek, Charles Franklin 1862-1920 *NatCAB 20*
Zeeman, Pieter 1865-1943 *AsBiEn, DcScB*
Zehnder, Charles Henry 1856-1927 *ApCAB X, NatCAB 12, NatCAB 24, WhAm 1*
Zehner, Carl Christian 1883-1962 *NatCAB 52*
Zehner, J Alexander 1898-1962 *WhAm 4*
Zehring, Blanche 1867-1950 *WhAm 3, WomWWA 14*
Zehrung, Winfield Scott 1897-1965 *NatCAB 52, WhAm 4*
Zeidler, Carl Frederick 1908-1942 *WhAm 2*
Zeigen, Frederic Herman 1874-1942 *NatCAB 17, NatCAB 31, WhAm 2*
Zeigler, Flora Bamford 1858- *WomWWA 14*
Zeigler, Jesse Reinhart 1877-1920 *NatCAB 19*
Zeigler, Lee Woodward 1868-1952 *WhAm 3*
Zeigler, Marion Eugene 1877-1947 *NatCAB 35*
Zeilin, Jacob 1806-1880 *ApCAB, DcAmB, Drake, NatCAB 11, WebAMB, WhAm H*
Zeiller, Rene Charles 1847-1915 *DcScB*
Zeisberg, Fred Clemens 1888-1938 *NatCAB 33*
Zeisberger, David 1721-1808 *AmBi, ApCAB, BiDAmEd, DcAmB, DcAmReB, Drake, NatCAB 2, WhAm H*
Zeise, William Christopher 1789-1847 *DcScB*
Zeisler, Claire *BnEnAmA*
Zeisler, Fannie Bloomfield d1927 *WomWWA 14*
Zeisler, Fannie Bloomfield 1863-1927 *AmBi, ApCAB X, DcAmB, NotAW, WhAm 1*
Zeisler, Fannie Bloomfield 1865-1927 *NatCAB 14*
Zeisler, Fannie Bloomfield 1866-1927 *AmWom*
Zeisler, Joseph 1858-1919 *WhAm 1*
Zeisler, Sigmund 1860-1931 *DcAmB, WhAm 1*
Zeiss, Carl Henry 1887-1961 *NatCAB 49*

Zeit, F Robert Aenishaenslin 1864-1935
WhAm 1
Zeitler, Emerson Walter 1897-1969 *WhAm 5*
Zeitler, Kurt 1895- *WhWW-II*
Zeitlin, Jacob 1883-1937 *WhAm 1*
Zeitzler, Kurt 1895- *WhoMilH*
Zejszner, Ludwik 1805-1871 *DcScB Sup*
Zekind, Bertha Nelson 1870- *WomWWA 14*
Zelaya, Jose Santos 1853-1919 *McGEWB*
Zelenko, Herbert 1906- *BiDrAC, WhAmP*
Zeleny, Anthony 1870-1947 *WhAm 2*
Zeleny, Charles 1878-1939 *NatCAB 42,
WhAm 1*
Zeleny, John 1872-1951 *NatCAB 40,
WhAm 1*
Zelie, John Sheridan 1866-1942 *WhAm 2*
Zeliff, A E *NewYHSD*
Zelinsky, Nikolay Dmitrievich 1861-1953 *DcScB*
Zell, Bernhard 1715-1779 *ApCAB*
Zell, Christian *NewYHSD*
Zeller, Albert Theodore 1866-1950 *NatCAB 40*
Zeller, Alice Bryant 1871- *WomWWA 14*
Zeller, Edward G 1869-1950 *NatCAB 38*
Zeller, George Anthony 1858-1938 *NatCAB 29,
WhAm 1*
Zeller, Harry A 1871- *WhAm 6*
Zeller, Henry C 1860-1942 *NatCAB 31*
Zeller, Joseph William 1884-1961 *WhAm 4*
Zeller, Julius Christian 1871-1938 *NatCAB 47,
WhAm 1*
Zeller, Robert Carl 1913-1967 *NatCAB 54*
Zeller, Walter George 1912-1968 *WhAm 5*
Zeller, Walter Philip 1890-1957 *WhAm 3*
Zellerbach, Isadore d1941 *WhAm 2*
Zellerbach, James David 1892-1963 *WhAm 4*
Zeltzer, Meyer 1897-1971 *NatCAB 57*
Zemlinsky, Alexander Von 1872-1942
WhAm 4A
Zemmer, Harry Burton 1895-1962 *NatCAB 50*
Zemp, Ernest Russell 1871-1954 *NatCAB 43*
Zemp, W Robin 1877-1964 *NatCAB 50*
Zemplen, Geza 1883-1956 *DcScB*
Zemurray, Samuel 1877-1961 *WhAm 4*
Zendejas, Miguel Geronimo 1724-1816 *ApCAB*
Zender, Austin R d1971 *WhAm 5*
Zender, Joachim Denis Laurent 1805- *ApCAB*
Zenea, Juan Clemente 1834-1871 *ApCAB*
Zenger, John Peter d1746 *Drake*
Zenger, John Peter 1680?-1746 *ApCAB,
TwCBDA*
Zenger, John Peter 1697-1746 *AmBi, DcAmB,
McGEWB, NatCAB 23, WebAB,
WhAm H*
Zenner, Philip McKnight 1897-1960 *WhAm 4*
Zeno 450?BC- *AsBiEn*
Zeno Of Citium 335?BC-263BC *DcScB,
McGEWB*
Zeno Of Elea 490?BC-425?BC *DcScB,
McGEWB*
Zeno Of Sidon 150?BC-070?BC *DcScB*
Zeno, Nicolo 1340?-1391? *ApCAB*
Zenodorus *DcScB*
Zenon, Gora *NewYHSD*
Zenon DeRouvroy, Charles Albert 1698-1759
ApCAB
Zenor, William Taylor 1846-1916 *BiDrAC,
WhAm 4, WhAmP*
Zenos, Andrew C 1855-1942 *WhAm 1*
Zenteno, Carlos DeTapia 1698-1770? *ApCAB*
Zenteno, Jose Ignacio 1785-1847 *ApCAB*
Zentmayer, Joseph 1826-1888 *DcAmB,
NatCAB 13, WhAm H*
Zentmayer, William 1864-1958 *NatCAB 48,
WhAm 5*
Zepeda, Francisco 1525?-1602 *ApCAB*
Zephirin, Antoine 1475?-1530? *ApCAB*
Zeppelin, Ferdinand, Count Von 1838-1917
AsBiEn
Zequeira, Manuel De 1760?-1846 *ApCAB*
Zeran, Franklin Royalton 1906-1974 *WhAm 6*
Zerban, Frederick William 1880-1956 *WhAm 3*
Zerbe, Alvin Sylvester 1847-1935 *WhAm 1*
Zerbe, Farran 1871-1949 *WhAm 2*
Zerbe, James Slough 1849- *WhAm 4*
Zerbe, Karl 1903-1972 *WhAm 5*
Zerbey, Joseph Henry 1858-1933 *NatCAB 39,
WhAm 4*

Zerbey, Joseph Henry, Jr. 1888-1945
NatCAB 34
Zerega DiZerega, Louis Augustus 1864-
WhAm 4
Zermelo, Ernst Friedrich Ferdinand 1871-1953
DcScB
Zernicke, Fritz 1888-1966 *AsBiEn*
Zernike, Frits 1888-1966 *DcScB, WhAm 4*
Zerrahn, Carl 1826-1909 *AmBi, ApCAB,
DcAmB*
Zerrahn, Charles 1826-1909 *NatCAB 1*
Zetterstrand, Ernst Adrian 1863-1911 *WhAm 1*
Zettler, Emil Robert 1878-1946 *WhAm 2*
Zettler, Louis 1832- *NatCAB 9*
Zeuch, Herman J 1867-1937 *WhAm 1*
Zeuner, Charles 1795-1857 *ApCAB, DcAmB,
Drake, NatCAB 1, WhAm H*
Zeuner, Gustav Anton 1828-1907 *DcScB*
Zeuthen, Hieronymus Georg 1839-1920 *DcScB*
Zevallo Y Balboa, Miguel d1595? *ApCAB*
Zevely, Alexander N *BiAUS*
Zevin, Israel Joseph 1872-1926 *DcAmB*
Zhdanov, Andrei Alexandrovich 1896-1948
WhAm 2
Zhdanov, Andrey 1896-1948 *WhWW-II*
Zhukov, Georgi 1896-1974 *WhWW-II*
Zhukov, Georgi Konstantinovich 1895-1974
WhoMilH
Zhukov, Georgi Konstantinovich 1896-1974
McGEWB
Zhukov, Georgi Konstantnovich 1895-1974
WhAm 6
Zhukovsky, Nikolay Egorovich 1847-1921
DcScB
Zieber, Philip Samuel 1861-1940 *NatCAB 30*
Ziegelmeier, Arthur 1877-1945 *NatCAB 33*
Ziegemeier, Henry Joseph 1869-1930 *DcAmB,
WhAm 1*
Ziegenfuss, Henry L 1844- *NatCAB 1*
Ziegenfuss, Samuel Addison 1844-1916
NatCAB 3, WhAm 1
Ziegenhein, William J 1909-1965 *WhAm 4*
Zieget, Julius *WhAm 5*
Ziegfeld, Mrs. Florence *WomWWA 14*
Ziegfeld, Florenz 1869-1932 *AmBi, DcAmB,
EncAB, McGEWB, WebAB, WhAm 1*
Ziegler, Charles Edward 1871- *WhAm 5*
Ziegler, Christian Henry 1881-1957 *NatCAB 46*
Ziegler, David 1748-1811 *DcAmB, WhAm H*
Ziegler, E Matilda Curtis 1841-1932
NatCAB 37
Ziegler, Edward 1870-1947 *WhAm 2*
Ziegler, Edward Danner 1844-1931 *BiDrAC*
Ziegler, Edwin Allen 1880-1967 *WhAm 4A*
Ziegler, Eustace Paul 1881- *IlBEAAW*
Ziegler, George Frederick *NewYHSD*
Ziegler, H *NewYHSD*
Ziegler, Henry 1816- *ApCAB*
Ziegler, Karl 1898-1973 *AsBiEn, WhAm 6*
Ziegler, Lloyd Hiram 1892-1945 *NatCAB 34,
WhAm 2*
Ziegler, Maxine Evelyn Hogue d1968 *WhAm 5*
Ziegler, Paul 1847-1921 *NatCAB 19*
Ziegler, S Lewis 1861-1926 *WhAm 1*
Ziegler, Samuel P 1882-1967 *IlBEAAW*
Ziegler, William 1843-1905 *DcAmB,
NatCAB 16, WhAm 1*
Ziegler, William, Jr. 1891-1958 *NatCAB 45,
WhAm 3*
Ziegler, Winfred Hamlin 1885-1972 *WhAm 5*
Ziehn, Bernard 1845-1912 *DcAmB*
Zielke, George Robert 1911-1973 *WhAm 6*
Zier, Merlin William 1928-1967 *WhAm 5*
Zierden, Alicia M 1874- *WomWWA 14*
Ziesing, August 1858-1942 *WhAm 2*
Ziesing, Richard, Jr. 1895-1968 *WhAm 4A*
Zietlow, John L W 1850- *WhAm 4*
Ziff, Joseph 1898-1954 *NatCAB 41*
Ziff, William Bernard 1898-1953 *DcAmB S5,
WhAm 3*
Zigler, David Howard 1857-1930 *WhAm 1*
Zigler, John *NewYHSD*
Zigler, John Darrel 1906-1966 *WhAm 4*
Zigrosser, Carl 1891-1975 *WhAm 6*
Zihlman, Frederick Nicholas 1879-1935
ApCAB X, BiDrAC, WhAm 1, WhAmP
Zilboorg, Gregory 1890-1959 *NatCAB 43,
WhAm 3*

Zilliox, James 1849-1890 *ApCAB, TwCBDA*
Zimand, Savel 1891-1967 *NatCAB 55,
WhAm 4A*
Zimbalist, Mary Louise Curtis 1876-1970
WhAm 5
Zimbeaux, Frank Ignatius Seraphic 1861-1935
IlBEAAW
Zimm, Bruno Louis 1876-1943 *WhAm 2*
Zimmele, Margaret Scully 1872-
WomWWA 14
Zimmer *NewYHSD*
Zimmer, Bernard Nicolas 1888-1970 *WhAm 5*
Zimmer, Frederick William 1858-1940
NatCAB 30
Zimmer, Grace E 1871- *WomWWA 14*
Zimmer, H Ward 1897-1955 *NatCAB 45,
WhAm 3*
Zimmer, Henry Wenzell 1903-1962 *WhAm 4*
Zimmer, John Todd 1889-1957 *WhAm 3*
Zimmer, Verne A 1886-1946 *WhAm 2*
Zimmer, William Homer 1905-1973
NatCAB 57, WhAm 5
Zimmerer, Charles John 1899-1970 *WhAm 5*
Zimmerley, Howard Henry 1890-1944 *WhAm 2*
Zimmerman, A Wallace 1898-1964 *NatCAB 51*
Zimmerman, Angeline Truesdall 1861-
WomWWA 14
Zimmerman, Charles Ballard 1891-1969
WhAm 5
Zimmerman, Charles Fishburn 1878-1954
WhAm 3
Zimmerman, Edward Americus d1963 *WhAm 4*
Zimmerman, Edward August 1906- *WhAm 6*
Zimmerman, Ethel *WebAB*
Zimmerman, Eugene 1845-1914 *DcAmB,
NatCAB 13*
Zimmerman, Eugene 1862-1935 *DcAmB S1,
WhAm 1*
Zimmerman, Fred 1866-1925 *NatCAB 20*
Zimmerman, Fred Rudolph 1880-1954
NatCAB 40, WhAm 3
Zimmerman, George Frederick 1870-1951
NatCAB 40
Zimmerman, Harvey J 1869- *WhAm 5*
Zimmerman, Henry Martin 1867- *WhAm 3*
Zimmerman, Herbert John 1906-1970 *WhAm 5*
Zimmerman, Hyman Harold 1921- *WhAm 5*
Zimmerman, Ira Melvin 1891-1953 *NatCAB 41*
Zimmerman, James Fulton 1887-1944
NatCAB 40, WhAm 2
Zimmerman, Jeremiah 1848-1937 *WhAm 1*
Zimmerman, John Frederick 1841-1925
NatCAB 20
Zimmerman, Leander M 1860- *WhAm 5*
Zimmerman, Louis Seymour 1876-1954
WhAm 4
Zimmerman, Lulu Ethel Wylie *WomWWA 14*
Zimmerman, M M 1889-1972 *WhAm 5*
Zimmerman, Orville 1880-1948 *BiDrAC,
WhAm 2, WhAmP*
Zimmerman, Percy White 1884-1958 *WhAm 3*
Zimmerman, Robert *WebAB*
Zimmerman, Rufus Eicher 1886-1955 *WhAm 3*
Zimmerman, Thomas C 1838-1914 *WhAm 1*
Zimmerman, Thomas Lawrence 1876-1950
NatCAB 39
Zimmerman, William 1894-1959 *WhAm 4*
Zimmerman, William Carbys 1859-1932
WhAm 1
Zimmermann, Erich Walter 1888-1961
WhAm 4
Zimmermann, Herbert George 1900-1949
WhAm 3
Zimmermann, Herbert P 1880-1962 *WhAm 4*
Zimmermann, Johann Baptist 1680-1758
McGEWB
Zimmermann, John Edward 1874-1943
NatCAB 38, WhAm 2
Zimmermann, Marie *WomWWA 14*
Zimmern, Sir Alfred 1879-1957 *WhAm 3*
Zimpfer, Frederick Paul 1876-1956 *NatCAB 42*
Zingher, Abraham 1885-1927 *NatCAB 26*
Zinin, Nikolay Nikolaevich 1812-1880 *DcScB*
Zink, Harold 1901-1962 *NatCAB 50,
WhAm 4*
Zink, Howard Edward 1897-1957 *NatCAB 47*
Zink, Jack Duane 1916-1966 *NatCAB 51*
Zinke, E Gustav 1846- *WhAm 1*